The Field Day Anthology of Irish Writing

VOLUME I

General Editor: Seamus Deane

Associate Editors: Andrew Carpenter, Jonathan Williams

Derry
Field Day Publications
Distributed by Faber & Faber Limited

First published in 1991
by Field Day Publications, Foyle Arts Centre,
Old Foyle College, Lawrence Hill, Derry,
Northern Ireland BT48 7NJ

Distributed by Faber & Faber Limited
3 Queen Square
London WC1N 3AU

For the Set of Three Volumes ISBN 0 946755 20 5

Typeset in Ireland by Phototype-Set Ltd, Drumcondra, Dublin.
Printed in the United States by Kingsport Press

1 2 3 4 5 6 7 8 9 0

THE FIELD DAY ANTHOLOGY OF IRISH WRITING

Contents

LATIN WRITING IN IRELAND (c.400-c.1200)

CHARLES DOHERTY, *Department of Early and Medieval Irish History, University College, Dublin*

THE LITERATURE OF NORMAN IRELAND

TERENCE DOLAN, *Department of English, University College, Dublin*

Acknowledgments

The editors and the Field Day directors wish to thank the following for their help in the production of the *Anthology*.

FINANCIAL SUPPORT

With special thanks: Dr. Marianne McDonald (California)

Major Funding: Maryon Davies Lewis (San Francisco); American Ireland Fund; Arts Council, Republic of Ireland; European Community; Government of the Republic of Ireland; Irish American Cultural Institute; Institute of New York; Marianne McDonald (California).

Financial assistance was also provided by the Arts Council of Northern Ireland; the National University of Ireland; University College, Dublin; Marks and Spencers; School of Irish Studies.

ORGANIZATIONAL SUPPORT IN RELATION TO FUNDING

Smith and Elizabeth Bagley (Washington D.C.); Kevin Cahill (New York); Anthony Cronin (Dublin); Bill and Mary Doherty (New York); Paul Gillespie (Boston); Ann Graham (Boston); John Hume (Derry); Kevin Mallon (San Francisco); Eoin McKiernan (St Paul); Patricia McManus (New York); His Excellency Ambassador Padraig McKiernan (USA); Maureen Murphy (New York); Paul O'Dwyer (New York); John Scanlon (New York); Elizabeth Shannon (Boston); William Vincent (San Francisco).

Aer Lingus; American-Irish Historical Society; Boston-Eire Society; Boston-Field Day Committee; Charitable Irish Society of Boston; Committee for a New Ireland (USA).

TECHNICAL AND SECRETARIAL SUPPORT

Conall Glynn, National Cash Registers, for the gift of a computer NCR Mate V; Pat O'Connell; Cherry Murphy; Conor Deane; Deirdre Deane; Computer Centre, University College, Dublin, for use of the Kurtzweiler Data Entry Machine (KDEM); Ciaran Deane; Mary Buckley; Vivienne Fogarty; Matthew Williams.

EDITORIAL ASSISTANCE

John Barnes; Charles Benson; Brian Boydell; Mary Brennan; Francis John Byrne; Nicholas Carolan; Dorothy Carpenter; Fr Colm Connellan; Art Cosgrove; Maurice Craig; Clare Craven; Fergus D'Arcy; Emer Deane; Marion Deane; David Dickson; Archibald Elias; Christina Falls; Ronan Fanning; Neville Figgis; Alan Fletcher; Ann Geraghty; Noel Jameson; Norma Jessop; Paul Kelly; Sean Lysaght; Muriel

McCarthy; Donal McCarthy; Eddie McParland; James Maguire; Christopher Morash; Sean Murphy; Proinseas Ní Catháin; Conn Ó Cléirigh; Eamon O'Flaherty; Deirdre O'Grady; Dáithi Ó hÓgain; William O'Sullivan; Eve Patten; Mary Pollard; John Richmond; Andrew Smith; Frank Spiers; Tony Sweeney; Harry White; Matthew Williams; James Woolley.

The editors wish to give special thanks to Phototype-Set Ltd of Drumcondra, Dublin, for the skill and dedication with which they undertook and completed an extremely difficult typesetting assignment; Rory O'Neill, Christy Nolan, Michael Lynam and Noel Murphy.

Thanks are also due to Maureen Loughran, Colette Nelis and Julie Barber of the Field Day office for their help and support.

General Introduction

by

Seamus Deane

One reason for producing an anthology of Irish writing on this scale is, quite simply, that it has never been done before. Of course, anthologies of Irish literature have been published, the most notable being *The Cabinet of Irish Literature*, edited by Charles Read in four volumes in 1879, and its enlarged version co-edited with Katharine Tynan Hinkson in 1903, closely followed in 1911 by Justin McCarthy's ten-volume compilation, alphabetically arranged, *Irish Literature*. Since then, numerous anthologies have concentrated on particular genres — anthologies of poetry and prose, of short stories, of oratory, of speeches from the dock, and so on. But in this anthology we take a much wider time-span, embracing 1,500 years, and we avoid the narrow sense of the word 'literature', extending it to cover various other kinds of writing, especially political speeches, pamphlets and analyses, all of which have played an important part in the story which this anthology has to tell.

There *is* a story here, a meta-narrative, which is, we believe, hospitable to all the micro-narratives that, from time to time, have achieved prominence as the official version of the true history, political and literary, of the island's past and present. It is, for instance, useful to see that Irish writing in English — to take just one important element in the history — is not confined to the late nineteenth and the twentieth centuries. It has a history marked by continuity and discontinuity and it may be that both these features remain puzzlingly present when we speak of a 'tradition' of Irish drama which includes Farquhar, Goldsmith, Sheridan, Shaw and Wilde. The ambivalence is even more pronounced if we posit a connection between Joyce, James Clarence Mangan, the Irish oratorical tradition and Laurence Sterne. It may be that Sterne's connection with Joyce is as frail as, say, that of Congreve with the dramatists just named. By including Sterne and omitting Congreve we emphasize the fictive nature of any tradition that asserts continuity while acknowledging its need to do so. There are obvious repercussions for the canon of English literature if a canon of Irish literature establishes itself by repossessing some of the standard 'English' names — Swift or Sterne, Burke or Wilde. But that is, in fact, a secondary issue. There is no attempt here to establish a canon. Instead, what we show is an example of the way in which canons are established and the degree to which they operate as systems of ratification and authority. Part of the significance of this work for us has been the recognition of the power of the English canonical tradition to absorb a great deal of writing that, from a different point of view, can be reclaimed for the Irish tradition. Such acts of annexation and reclamation are integral to the assertion of cultural authority and confidence, but the assumptions on which they are based are frail indeed. Therefore, we consider ourselves to be engaged in an act of definition rather than in a definitive action.

Because it is a selection from a mass of material, an anthology, no matter how comprehensive it may try to be, implies the existence of a body of writing that could, were it all to be made available to readers at a single moment, truly be coincident with the subject anthologized. This unhappy implication is bound to make an anthologist restless for, once accepted, it has punishing consequences. Among these is the simple sense of an anthology's necessary incompleteness. But, worse than that, there is also the sense that the incompleteness is defined in relation to a specifiable and knowable subject — in this case 'Irish writing' — which another, quite different or heavily modified selection of texts would represent more accurately. I must confess straight away that I am free from the unease created by such considerations. The work of putting together the anthology was itself an exercise in dismantling them, in escaping from their coercive and disheartening power. For all that ever was or may be written which might, by whatever criteria, be included under the rubric 'Irish writing' does not, by virtue of that, become part of the subject of our inquiry. Sheer inclusiveness is not, of itself, a virtue or even an advantage. Selection is not made from a preordained 'tradition'; it is selection which ordains the tradition(s). The subject of our inquiry and selection here is one that has been created and recreated in a variety of ways over the centuries and this anthology is one further act of cultural creation in that mode, one way of envisaging the forces and ideas that have governed the development of the always putative subject 'Irish writing' over 1,500 years. What it does is to re-present texts in relation to one another and to demonstrate, sometimes in detail, sometimes by no more than a general indication, how that constantly changing interrelationship provides for us the nexus of values, assumptions and beliefs in which the idea of Ireland, Irish and writing are grounded.

It is important to do this now because the political crisis in Ireland, precipitated in 1968, but in gestation for many years before that date, has exposed the absence within the island of any system of cultural consent that would effectively legitimize and secure the existing political arrangements. There has rarely been in Ireland any sustained coordination between prevailing cultural and political systems; indeed, when this has existed, its oppressive nature and function has always been visible. The fact that Ireland has been colonized through conquest and invasion several times and in several ways is obviously central to an explanation of this phenomenon. The island was conquered by pre-Christian invaders, Christian missionaries, the Normans, the pre-Reformation English, the Elizabethans, Cromwellians and by the Williamites. It was dominated by imperial England and it remains, to the present day, in thrall to many of the forces, economic and political, that affect the United Kingdom in its troubled post-imperial decline. But other, internal conquests took place as well, deriving from and modifying the supervening realities of colonial rule. Versions of Ireland and its history and culture were created by many groups within the island — colonists and colonized — in attempts to ratify an existing political and economic system or to justify its alteration or its extinction. The failure of these cultural versions to achieve hegemony in alliance with the political system is more remarkable in a European country than it would be in those parts of the world that have been subject to European domination. That is part of the interest of and reason for this project.

The anthology does not propose that we have here an exemplary instance of either a 'national' or a 'colonial' literature or body of writing. It does propose that the interchange between these conceptions of writing, more violently and frequently effected in Ireland than in most European cultures, demonstrates the configurations of power within a society that consistently has refused to accept their force or yield to their allure. What is exemplary, then, is the extent to which, in Irish conditions, canonical forms have not been established and, because of that, how clearly the purpose of such canonical forms is exposed.

Historians of limited philosophical resource still long to answer the question, 'What really happened then?' More modestly, this anthology asks the longer, less abrasive, question: 'How, in the light of what is happening now, can we re-present what was, then and since, believed to have been the significance of what "really" happened?' It also makes a difference *which* 'then' is chosen to be re-presented. Today, medieval Ireland may seem a more innocent, more purely scholarly choice than nineteenth-century Ireland, but it would be odd indeed were we to find that in this century historical scholarship had achieved a degree of political innocence hitherto unknown. It is part of the received wisdom that the Irish past has been (mis)interpreted by historians who had a cause to plead and an axe to grind. It is equally the case that this anthology, like the works it presents to the reader, is at the mercy of the present moment and, also like them, derives its authority (such as it is) from that moment.

A practical consideration in any anthology is the inclusion of material not readily available or widely known. This perforce has been taken into account here, although the consideration raises issues that go the heart of the project. It would be perfectly easy to construct an anthology of Irish literature that would rehearse the achievements of those who have gained world-wide reputations — Swift, Berkeley, Sheridan, Goldsmith, Burke, Wilde, Shaw, Yeats, Joyce and Beckett. These could be interwoven with writers of lesser repute — for example, Francis Hutcheson, Tom Moore, Mangan, George Moore — and, in addition, those whose work is in the Irish language could be included — O Bruadair, O Súilleabháin, O Cadhain, Ó Ríordáin. Such an accumulative procedure has been avoided (although all these writers are indeed to be found here) because it merely reproduces the idea that there is a hierarchy of authors and of texts that is, so to speak, *there*, needing only to be illuminated under one light to show us in what 'Irish literature' or 'Irish writing' truly consists.

Such a procedure fails to deal with the formation of such a hierarchy (for it does, in interestingly varied echelons, exist); it ignores the process by which the categories of 'major' and 'minor' authors are formed and reformed, by which writers are appropriated to different 'traditions', and it fails to acknowledge how such appropriations have a profound impact on their reputations with different audiences. The reputation of Máirtín O Cadhain within the Irish-language tradition is important; within the English-language tradition, it does not exist. Louis MacNeice for long has been an English thirties' poet with an Irish background; today he is being recruited as an Ulster poet. His reputation to a large extent depends on his felt presence for a particular group or generation. Institutional forces play their part too. Most of the 'major' Irish writers have for decades been accommodated within the tradition of English or British literature. Sometimes they are loaned out for exhibitions of International Modernism or are reclaimed for study within the discipline called 'Anglo-Irish Literature'. Large cultural-political investments are involved here, and the publishing industry, both in the United Kingdom and in Ireland, has played and continues to play an important role in producing and reproducing these writers for various audiences and under different banners. This is an inescapable feature of the whole system in which writing and the many categories of judgment and forms of classification are established. What the system disguises — often from itself — are the grounds on which these discriminations are based. Some are clearly commercial; others are more complex and subtle. All have a bearing upon both the work and its reception by a given audience. Writing is a system that produces audiences as well as works of literature.

Before romantic nationalism was born in the late eighteenth century, it was easier than it is now to think of writing as something which included but meant more than 'literature'. 'Polite letters' embraced philosophy, history and many other forms of discursive writing. When literature began to separate itself from other forms of writing, it based its extraordinary claims for itself on two mutually exclusive assertions — not a worrying consideration for literary people, who rather pride themselves, and with reason, on the brilliance with which they can be incoherent about the nature and claims of their chosen avocation. On the one hand, national, vernacular literatures, institutionalized in university departments and courses, were the articulators of the 'national tradition'. If Englishness or Irishness were to be sought, literature would provide it. Yet the greatest national literature, in being essentially English or Irish, also would be universal. It would be a local instance of the 'human spirit' in one of its standard modulations — tragic, comic, heroic, pathetic, and so on. There may be a suspicion of contradiction here, but it can be no more than that since the transition from the written work to the national essence to the human essence is such a mystificatory process that it would be vulgar to make such a commonplace objection. Yet, while claiming this, and, in the twentieth century proclaiming it in evangelical tones (F. R. Leavis in England, Daniel Corkery in Ireland), literature also announces the doctrine of the autonomy of the work of art. The relationship between literature and politics, asserted at one level, is denied at the other. The relationship, of course, is disguised, not broken; but it was (and still is) disguised as broken. In a country like Ireland, where nationalism had to be politically opposed to the prevailing power-systems, there was a serious attempt to create a counter-culture and to define it as authentic to the nation. In doing so, it used historical and archaeological scholarship in a tendentious and polemical fashion. For this, it was rebuked. It distorted the facts of history and reduced literature to propaganda. The rebuke came from groups equally anxious to assert some other position against nationalism — unionism, liberalism, internationalism. The political animus informing all these non-nationalist groups was concealed as much as possible, and the most frequently worn disguise was, in history, the pretence to 'objectivity' and in literature the claim to 'autonomy'. Both words had the magical appeal of not being polemical or political; both were against 'propaganda' which pretended to be either history or art. The modern destruction and deconstruction of author(ity) is not attractive to the cultural-political establishment in Ireland because the defence of authority, understood as the status quo, is such a pressing matter. In this anthology, we do not devote ourselves to the truism that all writing is profoundly political. We are concerned, rather, to show how this is sometimes openly acknowledged and at other times urgently concealed. Consequently, we have adhered to the eighteenth-century convention that many forms of discourse are 'polite' and that literature is one of those forms. The historical achievement, whereby literature attained for itself such a privileged status, is acknowledged and, at times, inspected; but the defence of this status is left to those who have the philosophical resource to show when, where and why a given text can be named as literary and another as not literary. It can be done, of course; but the ground for such naming is political. That does not make it any the less complex.

We are concerned, then, to re-present a series of representations concerning the island of Ireland — its history, geography, political experience, social forms and economy — over a period of 1,500 years. The interrelationship between materials widely separated in time is not always apparent at first glance, but it is part of the organizational structure of the anthology to show how such interrelations run athwart the chronological sequence. The opening excerpt deals with the figure of Cú Chulainn. Much later, we see this figure resurrected by Standish O'Grady and then by Yeats and Pearse. Few would any longer accept those readings as other than enabling versions of the hero-figure, designed to fulfil a specific purpose for those later writers. Yet even in the modern period, we see Ian Adamson, the cultural historian of the Ulster Defence Association, resurrecting Cú Chulainn yet again as a kind of Scottish-Unionist hero. Although it may be the case that our knowledge of the past helps us to exercise power over it, we can hardly dismiss the use of Cú Chulainn by such disparate people as an example of imagination helping out where knowledge failed. The adoption and the dismissal of cult-figures like Cú Chulainn is a telling instance of the relationship between scholarship and politics. There is a current of opinion that holds that we would mythologize less if we knew more. (That itself might be a myth.) But surely what is to be understood here is the felt need for mythologies, heroic lineages, dreams of continuity; in short, the need, expressed by different generations in individual ways, to colonize historical territory and repossess it.

Certain figures have attained an almost symbolic presence in Irish writing. Besides Cú Chulainn, there are Swift, O'Connell and Parnell; in the same way, certain eras are regarded as central to an understanding of the historical process: pagan Ireland, monastic Ireland, eighteenth-century Anglo-Ireland, the Famine, the Literary Revival. At times it seems that there is a link between the impulse to heroicize the past and the consciousness of present political weakness or defeat. Similarly, in those 'revisionist' periods, when the myths are dismantled and the concept of 'objectivity' rules, there is often an anxiety to preserve the status quo, to lower the political temperature and to offer the notion that historical processes are so complex that any attempt to achieve an overview cannot avoid the distortions and dogmatism of simple-minded orthodoxy. This is a powerful antidote against criticism and rebellion. Since rebellion is, of its nature, devoted to a simplified view of a complex situation, its proponents can be accused of indulging in historical fantasy, of intellectual narcosis and uneducated convictions. Yet the same charges could be brought against those who defended the prevailing political-cultural system in Ireland in, say, the 1720s, the 1840s and the 1930s. There is always a reason for reducing or increasing the importance and significance of historical events and sequences. Some events can appear to be very small when they are very far away, but their distance from us is a function of space as well as time. The figure of Cú Chulainn is now very small in the Irish Republic, but in east Belfast he looms larger. The historical space is different for each plea, even though the historical time is the same. Criticism has one advantage over rebellion: it tries to establish the space as well as the time for all groups. It does not reduce everything to one space and one time occupied by all.

It is, therefore, impossible to find an era, a group or an individual in possession of a set of beliefs, ideals or assumptions that scholarly investigation could not show to be flawed or distorted. The English republican ideal of the seventeenth century lived on in the Irish eighteenth century in the writings of Toland, Molyneux, Hutcheson and others, even though the conditions for its survival had long since disappeared in England and had never existed in Ireland. This does not permit us to consign their work to the lumber-room. The republican ideal remained alive in Ireland in their work as an important critique of a society sectarianized by the Williamite confiscations and the Penal Laws. Its promotion by them stands as a corrective to Yeats's remodelling of Anglo-Irish protestant resistance to the inclusion of catholics and dissenters within the political system of the time as a noble and characteristically Irish rejection of modern mass democratic culture. But the Yeatsian version is not thereby cancelled. A different reading of the eighteenth century helps to lay bare the aim and purpose of Yeats's myth, but such an alternative reading is itself subject to the same kind of exposure. The catholic apologists of the eighteenth century, with Charles O'Conor prominent among them, argued for the inclusion of catholics within the political system on the grounds that they belonged to a highly developed civilization and were, therefore, worthy of acceptance. Later, catholic nationalism absorbed this argument, intensified it to the point of saying that the Gaelic civilization was superior to that of the planters and adventurers who came in the train of Cromwell and William and, switching the basis of the argument, claimed admission to political power on the principle of abstract rights. They could have it both ways, even though the much-vaunted Gaelic culture was essentially aristocratic and exclusive and could not have tolerated the doctrines of universal rights and equality.

Nationalism even found a way of converting every past failure and defeat into a proof of the indomitable spirit of the Gael and a warrant of future success. Explanations abound for the failure of political and cultural systems to survive — the evils of colonial rule, the defects of the Irish national character, the malign influence of the protestant garrison or of the catholic church or of the imperial economic system. The variety — by no means infinite — need not be taken to indicate that all are equally suasive or competent accounts. What needs to be reaffirmed is that they are not (although they pretend to be) accounts of the same thing — Ireland. All these explanations *produce* the concept of Ireland, reify it and have it distributed as widely as possible for consumption. It is not one culture or even one place. It can be the Isle of Saints and Scholars, John Bull's Other Island, an intramural example of European colonialism, a laggard remnant of long-exhausted religious wars, a catholic aircraft-carrier off Europe, a neo-colonial culture struggling towards autonomy. The texts included here provide no definitive answer to any question of definition; their role is to demonstrate the genesis of these conceptions and their subsequent distribution and force.

It is in the two languages of Ireland that the history of power and powerlessness is most deeply inscribed. Latin and Norman French have a historical importance, which is recorded here, but it is in Irish and English that the experience of conflict is most memorably registered. The fact that the Irish-language texts are translated into English in this anthology is, in its way, sufficient comment on the relative fortunes of the two languages. It is evident that the wholesale adoption of the English language by the Gaelic-speaking Irish — sometimes voluntary, more often enforced by atrocious pressures — carries with it a psychological heritage, a recriminatory history of scandal, betrayal and shame, the last of these most indelibly associated with poverty and the trauma of the Famine. The subsequent tradition of emigration to the English-speaking centres of economic prosperity in Britain and the United States was sustained for good economic reasons. The Gaelic-speaking Irish surrendered their cultural heritage and thereafter were not able or equipped to adopt an English-speaking heritage that had any comparable presence or meaning for them. Yet it must also be remembered that, since the eighteenth century, the English-speaking Irish have been engaged in a long struggle to possess the Irish language and culture, partly as a means of redefining themselves as other than English, partly as a way of finding in culture a reconciliation of those forces and interests that remained steadfastly opposed in politics.

Charlotte Brooke's attempt in 1789 to promote amity and concord between the languages through translation — accompanied by the original texts in the Gaelic script — is an important moment because it profoundly alters the rationale for colonialism that the Elizabethans and Cromwellians had expounded. By the time Charlotte Brooke wrote, the colonial crusade to conquer, subject and convert the Irish had been transmuted into an internal colonial project. The English-speaking beneficiaries of the 1690 settlement began to consolidate their vision of themselves as playing an interstitial role between the English and Gaelic civilizations, seeing themselves as the only group equipped to modulate the rancorous history of conflict between the two. Cultural reconciliation appeared to be the necessary prelude to political reconciliation. However, a series of catastrophic political developments — the French

Revolution, the rise of the United Irishmen, the 1798 Rebellion and the Act of Union in 1800 — deferred the realization of this ambition. When it re-emerged in the 1830s with Sir Samuel Ferguson, the notion of reconciliation had a new urgency. The catholic political nation had been formed by then, and its accelerating abandonment of the Irish language — encouraged by O'Connell, the national school system and, ultimately, the Famine — left the intellectual leaders of the former protestant ascendancy, now reduced by the Act of Union to a garrison, with the paradoxical task of rescuing into English what their catholic counterparts were abandoning in Irish. The assertion of the existence of a cultural (and largely literary) tradition, embracing both groups, depended to an extraordinary degree on a successful act of translation. Ferguson and Thomas Davis are only the best-known names of those who made the assertion and risked testing it by putting their faith in the possibility of translation as a means of cultural conciliation.

What had to be translated, according to current advanced opinion, was more than individual texts — although these were difficult enough to establish. With them there also had to be translated the spirit that informed them. The English language of translation would have to find some way of embodying the intensity and strangeness of the Irish language. The result would be a language that would retain the most characteristic features of both. As long as this idea of translation survived, Irish nationalism, in alliance with philological scholarship, could give culture precedence over politics, in the belief that the civilizing and ecumenical spirit of the first would soften the harsh and sectarian reality of the second. Thomas Davis and Young Ireland carried this programme a step further by using the influence of the new journalism to start a campaign for the replacement of the British industrial and imperial system with an all-Irish alternative — but in the English language. The fortunes of this project in the nineteenth and twentieth centuries can be followed in this anthology, although the original stream that rose in the eighteenth century and became a river in the nineteenth has now broken into a delta that still has to be mapped.

When colonialism is successful, it reconciles the colonized culture to its own. When it is unsuccessful, it enforces itself by violence — slaughter, confiscation, the demonizing of those who resist it. Nationalism, cultural or political, is no more than an inverted image of the colonialism it seeks to replace. It too is an act of translation or even of retranslation. The assumption it shares with colonialism is the existence of an original condition that must be transmitted, restored, recuperated, and which must replace that fallen condition which at present obtains. It is not necessarily true that something always gets lost in translation. It is necessarily true that translation is founded on the idea of loss and recuperation; it might be understood as an action that takes place in the interval between these alternatives. This conception lies at the heart of much Irish writing, especially in the modern period, and has of course affinities with the modern theories of writing as a practice. The belief in the originary essence, agency or condition and the desire to do something to it or with it — recover it, convert it, adapt it, destroy it — silently patrol the boundaries of both Irish protestant and Irish catholic nationalisms and hold in custody the accompanying visions of literature and politics. The system of thought that turns on the axis of translation is by now so internally coherent that it seems to many that it must also be externally valid. It ain't necessarily so.

One stereotype of Ireland that has remained effective throughout the twentieth century is that of a country where political violence and the literary arts flourish together in ways not emulated (nor sought by) other countries. It is possible to demolish this popular conception, but it is perhaps wiser to wonder at its prevalence and at the elements of reality it contains. If there is an association between violence and writing, how can it be understood? The question is too large for an introduction such as this, but it can be addressed briefly by a glance at the confrontation between the aesthetic and the political realms, which is both important in itself and historically central to much Irish writing, with its obsessional reversions towards translation and the problems that go with it. The aesthetic ideology, which claims autonomy for the work of art, is a political force which pretends not to be so. But within that assertion, this ideology has produced a very powerful form of auto-critique, sometimes known as literary criticism and sometimes not. The ideological appeal is embodied in the claim that a work of art achieves, in Coleridge's famous phrase, 'a reconciliation of opposites'. 'Reconciliation' is a key term in art criticism, in translation theory and in political crisis. In Ireland, the linkages between these fields are so close that there is scarcely a distinction in the vocabularies deployed for each. Art, however, is given priority even in this close-knit family, because it gives the example of how tensions, strains, raw authentic experience and processed moral values can be brought together in a harmonious and triumphant wholeness. The idea that that which is chaotic, disorganized and 'rude' can be converted to order and civilization was shared by English colonial writers and English literary critics, at least until very recent times. It is also shared by those who see a connection between northern Irish violence and the northern Irish literary 'revival'. The literature — autonomous, ordered — stands over against the political system in its savage disorder. The connection here is as interesting as the contrast. Ultimately, any key political term is exchangeable with any key literary term. It is not a new discovery, but an old truth that is, perhaps, worth restating.

In its necessarily unsuccessful, but nevertheless strenuous, attempt to be comprehensive, this anthology includes a great deal of material that has for long been unknown or unacknowledged, usually because it has not been amenable to any of the modern versions of tradition elaborated in the last one hundred years. With that, there is of course a great deal of well-known material, almost all of which has served its purpose in the development of a scheme of Irish history or literature. The appearance of the unfamiliar with the familiar may have a tonic effect on some of our more routine and unexamined reactions and assumptions. But finally, perhaps it might be hoped that the material presented here displays the achievement of Irish people over many centuries in dealing with problems which were in some respects peculiar to themselves and their country but which, in other respects, go beyond the confining circumstances of our own history and find their analogues elsewhere. If we could claim that in every corner of the anthology one could find contained, *in parvo*, the whole scheme and meaning of it, then our ambitions would be fulfilled. But if the scheme of the anthology is not so discovered, we have little doubt that some alternative to it will be revealed, whatever page is opened, whatever work or excerpt is read. It is the endless fecundity of such reading that gives justification to the selections with which we here attempt to define our subject.

PROINSIAS MacCANA, *Editor*

Early and Middle Irish Literature

(c.600–c.1600)

Written literature in Irish can be traced back to the late sixth century, and the orthographic system that made it possible was probably devised about the middle of the century. For several centuries before that there had been a very marginal written form of the vernacular known as Ogham, an arrangement of notches on standing stones, based, like the later system, on the Latin alphabet; but effectively this was restricted to memorial inscriptions containing one or two personal names and had no relevance for the rise of a written literature. Once a serviceable means of writing had been invented, however, literary developments were not long in following, as a result of which Ireland was to produce over the next five or six centuries a literature unparalleled in volume and variety in the rest of western Europe.

Two facts were of special significance in determining the character and evolution of this literature. The first was that the writing of the vernacular was a monastic invention and it remained almost exclusively monastic until the dissolution or displacement of the older native monasteries in the twelfth century. The second was that Ireland had a learned and literary — though not literate — class long before writing, or even Christianity, reached Ireland, and that these traditional savants, who were known as *filidh* and were originally the associates and later the successors of the druids, enjoyed an extraordinary prestige and influence in society at large in matters of politics and ideology as well as of learning and literature. By the end of the sixth century, the church (that is to say the monasteries) and the *filidh* had come to terms and from that time on there is evidence of an ever-increasing practical cooperation and assimilation between them, although the well-organised *filidh* continued to assert the independence and priority of their professional fraternity in matters of social and political concern. From time immemorial the relationship of the individual *fili* to his tribal king and patron had been regarded as crucial to the maintenance of the social order, and much of this relationship survived the establishment of Christianity. Its clearest reflex in the literature is the *fili*'s eulogy of his lord and patron, which had great socio-ideological significance and was therefore crafted with all possible skill and dignity, though, for all its undoubted frequency in practice, it does not occur in any great abundance in the manuscript literature until the post-Norman period. But the repertoire of the *fili* was much wider than eulogy (together with its opposite, satire) and, as keeper and interpreter of tradition, he controlled all that concerned the 'history' of the tribe: genealogies, regnal lists, origin legends, and the wide-ranging miscellany of mythical, heroic and topographical lore that provided the raw material for his 'historical' compositions.

While it is true, therefore, that the monasteries were the cradle of the new written literature, it is inconceivable that this literature could have flowered so rapidly and profusely had there not previously existed a manifold oral tradition and a professional learned class to care for it. In fact, it is a literature with an unwritten dimension, which it would be as unwise to ignore as it is impossible to define. Constantly the written text presupposes a living tradition that is both its source and its continuing referent; this enduring interaction of the oral and the written is a crucial fact of Irish literary history. From the outset the relationship was a complex one. When writing came, it brought not simply a new technique but also new values and to some extent a new concept of literary aesthetics. Where formerly there had been one self-contained culture, there were now two, and the task of creating a fruitful symbiosis of native and Christian culture fell to the scholars of the monasteries, some of whom, in the process, developed new perspectives on vernacular tradition.

EARLY LYRIC VERSE

The change is particularly evident in the early poetry, even in the matter of style and structure. All the evidence suggests that, up until the seventh century, Irish poetry had been mainly accentual and without rhyme, whereas from the seventh to the seventeenth century the poetry of social prestige is almost all syllabic and rhyming; this extension of syllabic prosody has been attributed to the influence of Latin hymn metres mediated by the *literati* of the monasteries. But the change affected the motivation of the verse as well as its form. The monastic poets and their imitators were not subject to the conservatism and other professional constraints of the *filidh*, and they could be innovatory, personal and entertaining in ways that were closed to the learned poets. For one thing, they tended to write more simply in this early period, if only to communicate their Christian message more effectively. For example, when Blathmac, son of Cú Brettan, composed a lengthy sequence to the Virgin Mary and her Son, he employed an artless, uncomplicated style that compels conviction by its very sincerity and lack of pretension, and when other monastic poets began to turn their minds to more subjective kinds of verse, they also favoured a clear, uncluttered diction, very different from the didactic complexity of *fili* poetry. This conscious simplicity of expression became a characteristic of the great body of lyric verse, much of it concerned with the world of nature, which came into being from the seventh or eighth century onwards.

It has often been noted that the Irish poet was not so much concerned with the actual description of nature as with his own emotional response to its endlessly varied phenomena; and it is the peculiarly vivid and imaginative quality of this response that sets these early lyrics apart from more conventional nature poetry. Obviously the genre did not spring forth fully fledged; for example, it probably drew on the seasonal songs of the earlier oral tradition, of which several seem to underlie extant artistic seasonal lyrics of the Old Irish period. There is no sustained description in this verse, and its effect comes from the poet's ability to evoke a succession of vivid images that convey an impression, a subjective perception, rather than a fully drawn picture. This poetry is firmly rooted in the poet's emotional response to his environment, and in that regard it cannot be divorced from the general corpus of personal lyric verse in early Irish.

Some of these lyrics survive on the margins of Latin manuscripts, as if the writer, wearied with transcribing grammatical treatise or biblical exegesis, found release in the vacant spaces of his manuscript, setting down — in the words of the distinguished medievalist Robin Flower — 'personal memoranda, invocations of saints, little fragments of verse, and all the flotsam and jetsam of idle fancy.' Moreover, scribes and lyric poets are often and variously associated with the anchoritic reform movement of the eighth and ninth centuries, and the poet sometimes pictures himself as scribe or anchorite, or both, living in the woodland in intimate contact with nature. Guaire, king of Connacht, questions his half-brother Marbán as to why he has abandoned a life of domestic comfort for the hardship of the wilderness; Marbán's response, the body of the poem, is a eulogy to the beauty and abundance of nature (for, in the evolution of the theme, there is a gradual shift of emphasis, and regard for the traditional diet of the hermit ascetic — water, cress and berries — is gradually transformed into happy contemplation of the rich prodigality of woodland and stream).

This idealization of the retreat from society applies to other typical figures as well as the anchorite. The essential thing they have in common is that they are set apart from the normal concourse and conventions of society, the anchorite by conscious decision, the others by the buffets of fate or misfortune. Deirdre and Naoise, like Tristan and

Iseult after them, have become almost archetypal figures of the lovers separated from king and community by their illicit passion, and Suibhne Geilt (Flann O'Brien's 'Sweeney') is the madman whose lunacy consigns him to the unfettered freedom of nature. Such characters are driven to seek refuge in nature as a haven of primeval innocence and beauty, or to identify with her in an experience compounded of joy and of tragedy, or they may, like Líadan and Cuirithir, carve out their own sphere of loneliness and isolation, regardless of geographical location. It was a theme that often tempted the sensibility of the monastic *littérateurs* of the ninth and tenth centuries, and the result is a numerous miscellany of tales, whose characters express their own experience of life's beauty and sorrow in poems of great imaginative depth and purity.

But the monastic poets were men of wit as well as of feeling, and one could hardly think of a more apt example of this than the well-known poem 'The Scholar and his Cat', furnishing with its cosy domesticity a neat counterbalance to the frequent anecdotes about the hermit's close friendship with the animals of the wilderness. The genial refinement of these verses comes no doubt from the same kind of poet that produced the intensely moving lyrics of 'Líadan and Cuirithir' or 'The Old Woman of Beare' and underlines the creative versatility of these monastic penmen. Many of their lyrics, 'The Scholar and his Cat' for one, were composed as independent poems, but a great many such poems were conceived in relation to a narrative context in prose that may never have been written, or, if it was, may not have survived. Some of these may be mentioned more conveniently in connection with the narrative literature, but no account of early Irish lyric verse, however summary, would be complete without some reference to the splendid poem, 'The Old Woman of Beare'. Originally one of the very many personifications of the goddess of the land and of sovereignty, who passes through endless cycles of youth and age, she is here represented as a withered old nun, contrasting her present condition of hardship and old age with the days of her former glory when she enjoyed the embraces of kings. What confers on the poem its peculiar richness of allusion is the subtlety with which the poet creates a continual interweave of the sacred and the profane with a rich metaphor of colour, raiment and vegetation, implying the identity of the superannuated goddess with the land and its fertility.

THE NARRATIVE CYCLES

Medieval Irish normally told its tales in prose, as did Welsh and presumably the other Celtic literatures, which have long since perished; in this it differs from many of the other major literatures of the world. But prose and verse were frequently combined in Irish storytelling, the prose that carried the narrative being studded with passages of verse used for heightened dialogue or to mark certain moments of tension of emotion. The tales were classified in thematic categories — battles, cattle-raids, births, (violent) deaths, wooings, elopements, and so on — but modern commentators have adopted a broader classification into cycles: the mythological cycle, the king cycle, the Ulster cycle and the Finn cycle. To some extent this is an artificial division, particularly in the case of the mythological tales, for nearly all the traditional literature was coloured by mythic concepts or religious ritual; but what modern writers have in mind generally when they speak of the mythological cycle are those tales whose whole *dramatis personae* are obviously gods and goddesses. The most important of them is 'The Battle of Magh Tuiredh', which features practically the whole Gaelic pantheon. It recounts how the divine people, the Tuatha Dé Danann, vanquished the demonic people known as the Fomhoiri, and how the youthful god Lugh, the paragon of sovereignty, slew the cyclopean Balor of the venomous eye. It is undoubtedly the single most important mythological document in Irish. Indeed its interest is more mythological than literary, and the modern reader is more likely to be moved by the inner dynamic of its subject matter than by the form of its presentation. The same holds true for the *Dindshenchas* (The Lore of Places) and the *Leabhar Gabhála* (The Book of Invasions), two large compilations containing a wealth of mythological tradition.

For a more consciously literary use of this tradition, one must turn elsewhere. 'The Vision of Oengus', for example, is a short lyrical tale on the theme of love-sickness; the victim is Oengus, son of the father-god, the Daghdha. He appears again in *Tochmarc Étaíne* (The Wooing of Étaín), one of the most beautiful of Irish stories, which tells how Midir was parted from Étaín by the jealousy and magic of his first wife and how, after long tribulations, they were finally reunited a thousand years later, following Étaín's rebirth. This gentle, poetic tale is told in the kind of style that is characteristic of the best of early Irish storytelling: a lean, sensitive prose that here conveys subtly the haunting ambivalence of a world that combines the superficial lineaments of the Irish landscape with the quiet timelessness of the supernatural. The idea of an ever-present Otherworld and its relationship to the world of mortal men is one that pervades Irish tradition and seems to have held a strange fascination for the monastic writers. They were particularly preoccupied with the relativities of time and space that characterized the interaction of the two worlds — a topic that crops up, directly or obliquely, in innumerable tales and poems — and with the changing faces and moods that the supernatural realm presents to the finite world of men. Sometimes the Otherworld was seen as a place of menace and hostility, or as a rich and seemingly impregnable stronghold, such as to tempt and challenge the daring of heroes; sometimes it appeared as a land of beauty, abundance and harmony, innocent of sickness and death. Both aspects occur in their numerous variations within the written literature, but naturally there is some difference in their treatment and distribution. On the whole, the darker, more aggressive aspect belongs to the heroic genres, whereas the idea of the Otherworld as a region of happiness and love was admirably attuned to the lyrical cast of much of the monastic literature composed from the seventh century onwards, and the union of the two produced an amount of verse, and indeed some prose, of exceptional lyrical quality.

There is no rigid distinction between the two faces of the Otherworld. One of the intriguing features of *Echtra Nera* (The Adventure of Nera) is the way in which the grim account of the mutual antagonisms of the two worlds is occasionally coloured by the more lyrical view of a land untouched by pain or death, or by rain, storm or snow, as for example when Nera returns briefly to his own people in Cruachain of Connacht at the time of Samhain, or Hallowe'en (when traditionally the barriers between the natural and the supernatural are temporarily lowered), and brings with him the fruits of summer — wild garlic, primrose and golden fern — to prove whence he had come. In keeping with some of the more patently lyrical compositions, the author has deft allusions to the disparity between sacred and profane time and the question of the contingency of historical reality, as when Nera from his supernatural vantage-point witnesses the destruction of Cruachain by the immortal people among whom he now lives (he later learns that this will not take place until next Samhain and is thereby able to reverse history, as it were, by forewarning his kinsmen in Cruachain, who then turn the tables on their Otherworld enemies).

Essentially the same motifs of ambivalence and ambiguity are brought into play in those tales and poems that concentrate on the Otherworld as an Irish Elysium, a 'Land of the Living' where death is unknown, where birds and trees and even the stones make enchanting music, and where love is free and without sin. Sometimes the privileged hero is approached by a beautiful woman who offers to lead him to this land of eternal happiness, as in 'The Adventure of Conle' (*Echtra Conli*) and 'The Voyage of Bran' (*Immram Brain*). In the Conle tale, the main focus is on the conflict set up in the young hero's mind between the mystical and erotic promise of his prospective psychopomp on the one hand, and his sense of loyalty to his father and to his friends on the other, although his eventual departure is inevitable from the outset. Nor does he return, for, as is brought out even more clearly in 'The Voyage of Bran', normally the mortal who ventures into the land of the *sídh* will not or cannot return permanently. In the story of Bran, however, the emphasis shifts to the nature of the Otherworld itself, and the several brief passages of prose that carry the narrative are merely a frame for two long poems spoken by the fairy woman and by the sea-god Manannán mac Lir, both evoking with simple but imaginative imagery the wonder and beauty of 'The Many-Coloured Land'. The poet who composed these two catenas of verse was obviously very conscious of the analogies between this realm of happy innocence and the Christian concept of Paradise, and in later versions of this voyage of discovery — which may have been influenced by legends of historical sea-journeys taken by clerics seeking hermitage or refuge in the wide expanses of the ocean — the pagan Otherworld is increasingly assimilated to the biblical Land of Promise. This development reaches its culmination in the eighth- or ninth-century *Navigatio Brendani*, the legend of St Brendan's quest 'for the land of promise of the saints', which fired the imagination of the whole western world in the later Middle Ages.

It was around this same period — eighth to ninth centuries — that the classical forms of the great heroic tales were redacted. These comprise a vast range of material, since almost all secular narrative was heroic in some degree, but within this great corpus there are certain evident distinctions of theme and function, notably those that mark off the legends of famous rulers from the more specifically heroic cycles. Since the king was the pivot of his tribal kingdom and the embodiment of social order, the tales of the great kings of the past were naturally socially orientated, focussing on the status and functions of the ruler, on the origins of tribes and dynasties and their claim to the lands they occupied, the decisive battles of history, and the exemplary deeds of famous kings and their judgments as lawgivers. The 'justice' or 'truth' of the ruler is the condition for the prosperity of his kingdom and the well-being of his people. The great Cormac mac Airt was pictured as an Irish Solomon, and it was a patently wise decision of his that brought him to the kingship when his predecessor had been deposed for delivering an unjust one. Similarly the fate of Conaire Mór, another model of kingship, hinged upon the scrupulous maintenance of justice. When, through fraternal affection, he exempted his lawless foster-brothers from the full objective rigour of the customary law, his fate was sealed and he was drawn gradually but inexorably towards the violent and bloody extinction of his glorious reign and his life. But not all the king-tales are so closely bound up with social purpose and ideology. For example, *Finghal Rónáin* (Rónán's slaying of his own kin) is an analogue of the classical story of Phaedra and Hippolytus. Whether it is superior to the Greek version of the theme, as the late Frank O'Connor has claimed,[1] is perhaps a matter of personal judgment, but this short, almost terse, version of an old theme is much more skilfully styled and structured than its surface simplicity might suggest, and for those familiar with the values and conventions of early Irish society, the dialogue, always a highly important ingredient within the laconic narrative of early Irish storytelling, is here replete with delicate allusion and nuance.

When we turn from the king-tales to the hero-tales proper, we find that these presuppose more or less the same social *mores*, but that their general orientation, and therefore many of their principal themes, are different. Whereas the subject-matter and its treatment in the king-tales generally reflect the nexus between the rulers and his people, in the genuine hero-tales the main protagonist is essentially a lone wolf, who, even though he is associated with a warlike fraternity within the tribe and is frequently represented as the tribal kingdom's protector, operates primarily on his own initiative, which may on occasion be irrelevant, or even inimical, to the interests of his own tribe. The heroic ethos is competitive — physical prowess secures fame, and fame is more desirable than life itself — but it is generally combined with a conscientious, though not always consistent, adherence to a certain primitive code of chivalry.

Heroic ages tend to take shape around a given tribe or people in a well-defined terrain at a certain point or limited phase in history. In Ireland the focus or theatre of the quintessential heroic age was the kingdom of the Ulaidh or Ulstermen, who in prehistoric times dominated the northern part of Ireland. Their king, Conchobhar mac Nessa, held court at their capital of Emhain Mhacha, a hill-fort some two miles from the later ecclesiastical capital of Armagh. There he presided over a warrior company comprising the various types who reappear in almost all the great historic traditions, and there many of the familiar stories of the cycle have their setting or their *point de départ*. The greatest of these stories — one that generated its own minor cycle of tales — is 'The Cattle Raid of Cuailnge' (*Táin Bó Cúailnge*). The object of the raid into Ulster was to capture the fabulous *Donn Cúailnge*, 'The Brown Bull of Cuailnge', and it was planned and led by the formidable warrior-queen of Connacht, Medhbh, whose name, meaning 'The Intoxicating One', as well as many features of her legend, identify her as the goddess of sovereignty and war, only lightly euhemerized by the monastic redactors. Because of a strange sickness that left the Ulstermen prostrate and unable to confront the armies of Medhbh and her husband Ailill and their allies (and which is provided with its own etiology by two other tales), the task of opposing the Connacht men devolves upon the youthful hero Cú Chulainn, whose unique heroic status is underlined by the fact that he alone is exempt from the temporary weakness of the Ulster warriors.

As Medhbh encourages and incites her armies, the progress of the expedition furnishes the thread

1. In *The Backward Look* (London: Macmillan, 1967), p. 50.

that joins together the various episodes making up the main body of the saga — notably the series of single combats by which Cú Chulainn delays the Connacht advance. In the best tradition of heroic storytelling, the end of the conflict holds few surprises, and the Ulster army, restored once more from its quasi-ritual debility, defeats the Connacht men in a mighty battle. Thus ends the tale on the quasi-historical level; on the mythic level, it closes with the defeat and dismemberment of Medhbh's great 'White-horned Bull' of Connacht by the Brown Bull of Cuailnge, in what has been construed as a Celtic reflex of an Indo-European myth of cosmic creation.

Of the numerous other tales in the Ulster cycle, one can here mention only a few. The longest of them after *Táin Bó Cúailnge* is 'The Feast of Bricriu' (*Fledh Bricrenn*), which is centred on the notorious trickster-figure of Irish literature and on the extraordinary feast he organized as an occasion for sowing dissension among the foremost heroes. It is a boisterously humorous tale that gives its author abundant opportunity to exploit his mastery of all the different stylistic registers of Irish storytelling. Other tales focus on the life and actions of Cú Chulainn: his birth, marriage and death. They cover also such disparate themes as his 'Boyhood Deeds', his adventures in the Otherworld, and his tragic slaying of his own son through an ambiguous combination of mistaken identity and heroic honour or obstinacy.

In general, the longer tales are more loosely structured than the shorter ones and may retain rather more of the forms and diction of oral narrative. Some of the short tales, on the other hand, are so compact in structure and expression that it is difficult to conceive of them otherwise than as tales designed as written texts. A case in point is the story of 'The Exile of the Sons of Uisliu' (later Uisneach), which brought into being one of the great tragedies and, in Deirdre, one of the great heroines of Irish and of all literature. To have created a text of such surface simplicity, yet encompassing so many conflicting social and personal impulses and interweaving such delicate allusions to myth and social usage, is a remarkable achievement, all the more so for being executed with such narrative economy — less than one hundred and fifty lines of printed prose, liberally laced with passages of natural dialogue.

The Deirdre story is set in the geographical context of the Ulster cycle, but in its theme of the rejection of tribal conventions and the escape to the wilderness it comes close to the temper of the other great heroic cycle, that of Finn mac Cumaill and the Fiana, also known as the *Fianaigheacht*. Whereas the Ulster heroes operated within or in relation to tribal boundaries and institutions, the activities of the free-ranging mercenary warriors of the Fiana cut across all such demarcations, not merely those between political kingdoms but also between the natural and the supernatural worlds. This lends the whole cycle a romantic, imaginative and frequently lyrical cast, which is sometimes paralleled, *mutatis mutandis*, in the cognate British cycle of Arthurian romance. But among the Irish *literati*, the very mobility and social ambivalence of the Fiana rendered them suspect, and even though their origins lie deep in mythic prehistory and they seem always to have been popular in oral tradition, it was only in the eleventh and twelfth centuries that they began to be recorded in any considerable volume. The twelfth century saw the rise of the Fian-lay, a genre of story-ballad that was henceforth to be a staple element of *Fianaigheacht*. It also produced the *Agallamh na Seanórach* (The Converse of the Ancients), an anthology of Finn legends in the form of a frame-story comprising over two hundred tales and anecdotes. With its rich miscellany of mythico-historic story, told in an easy, fluent prose interspersed with passages of lyric verse, it is one of the most readable of the longer medieval Irish texts.

The *Agallamh* is only one of a number of large compilatory texts, both 'literary' and didactic, produced in the eleventh and twelfth centuries. They include such major works as the *Leabhar Gabhála* (The Book of Invasions), the great pseudo-history of Ireland, and the *Dindshenchas* or 'Lore of Places', a kind of mythological gazetteer of Ireland, not to mention the major recensions of *Táin Bó Cúailnge* and other tales, and the first of the great collective manuscripts that preserve a mass of material originally written down in the course of the preceding five centuries. Evidently this was a time when the learned poets and *literati* set about compiling, redacting and adapting as much as was feasible of the pre-existing *matière d'Irlande*, both written and oral, almost as if they were deeply apprehensive of what the future might bring.

No doubt there were grounds for such unease, for this was a time heavy with change and with the promise of change. The combined effect of the movement of ecclesiastical reform and the Norman conquest was to undermine the native cultural and social order, and to introduce a wedge of foreign influence that could be expanded whenever the English found the occasion and the resources. The old native monasteries, which had cradled the written literature from its beginnings in the late sixth century, were now displaced by new continental foundations, which had little interest in Irish traditional learning and literature. Partly as a reaction to these developments, a certain cultural regrouping seems to have taken place, and from the gradual assimilation and eventual amalgamation of the native learned poets, the *filidh*, and the scholars of the old monastic schools, a new confederation of learned families came into being, which was to exercise responsibility for the cultivation of traditional learning. Among its remarkable achievements was the establishment of a strict code of metrics and a standard literary language that was adhered to by all learned poets throughout Ireland and Gaelic Scotland from the early thirteenth to the middle of the seventeenth century.

One result of this movement of retrospective consolidation was the restoration of royal praise-poetry to its ancient pre-eminence. The sheer volume of this poetry and the prestige accorded it in post-Norman society tends to dominate and perhaps to distort our view of the literature produced from the twelfth to the seventeenth century; for there is still a substantial body of less pretentious and less conservative verse, much of it, like the Irish derivatives of *amour courtois*, distinguished by a keen sense of style and wit. But the cultivation of all aristocratic verse, whether professional or amateur, depended upon the continuance of the society which maintained it and which, above all, provided the patronage that supported the *filidh* and their schools, and the days of that society were already numbered. The seventeenth century, which began with the native social order still in place, if already seriously undermined, ended with that order broken and discarded. As a result, the aristocratic poetry, which had a written history of one thousand years, came finally to an end.

Prose, as always, had a somewhat different history. The eleventh and twelfth centuries saw the gradual abandonment of the classical concision of Old Irish narrative and the growing popularity of a more prolix style, making greater, and sometimes prodigal, use of devices such as alliteration, repetition and serial synonyms, which most likely derived from the patterns of oral storytelling. Post-Norman prose narrative lacks the precision and careful craftsmanship of the Old Irish tales, yet it is not all as tedious as careless commentators sometimes assume, and there still remains a considerable corpus of varied prose — romantic, heroic, burlesque — that still awaits proper critical assessment. But it must be acknowledged that the prose of the post-Norman period is less distinguished than its poetry; yet this is, in a way, appropriate, for in Irish and Celtic literary tradition, poetry was always considered the senior partner and the most perfect vehicle for the expression of communal identity. In line with this view, readers are provided with Irish texts — as well as with translations — of the verse selected for this section.

Since the texts included in this collection belong to different periods in the history of the Irish language, it is impossible to avoid entirely what appear to be orthographical inconsistencies; for example, an earlier fiana *later becomes* fianna.

from:
TÁIN BÓ CÚAILNGE
(The Cattle Raid of Cuailnge)

[*Táin Bó Cúailnge*, to give it its Irish title, was the centrepiece of Irish heroic literature and, more specifically, of the Ulster Cycle, the great corpus of heroic narrative that told of the deeds and the deaths of the Ulaidh, the people who dominated the whole north of Ireland until their defeat some time in the fifth century. 'The Cattle Raid of Cuailnge' was first written down about the eighth century and continued to be revised and elaborated until the two main extant recensions were recorded in the eleventh and twelfth centuries.

The translation is from Cecile O'Rahilly's edition of

Táin Bó Cúailnge: Recension I (Dublin: Dublin Institute for Advanced Studies, 1976).]

The naming of Cú Chulainn

'Indeed we know that boy', said Conall Cernach, 'and we know him all the better in that he is a fosterling of ours. Not long after the deed which Fergus has just related, he performed another exploit.

'When Culann the smith prepared a feast for Conchobar, he asked Conchobar not to bring a great crowd with him for the feast he had made was not provided by his possession of land or estate but was gained by the work of his hands and his tongs. Then Conchobar set off together with fifty chariot-warriors, the noblest and most illustrious of the heroes.

'Conchobar visited the playing-field then. It was always his custom to pay the boys a fleeting visit to ask a greeting of them. There he saw Cú Chulainn playing ball against thrice fifty boys, and defeating them. When they were engaged in driving the ball into the hole, he would fill the hole with the balls and the boys would not be able to ward him off. When it was they who were throwing at the hole, he by himself would ward them off so that not even a single ball would go into it. When they were wrestling, he alone would throw the thrice fifty boys, yet not all of them together could surround him to throw him. When they were engaged in the game of stripping one another, he would strip them all stark-naked but they could not even take his brooch from his mantle.

'Conchobar marvelled at this. He asked if the boy's deeds would correspond to his present ones when he attained the age of manhood. They all said that they would. Conchobor said to Cú Chulainn:

'"Come with me to the feast to which we are going since you are a guest."

'"I have not yet had my fill of play, master Conchobor," said the boy. "I shall follow you."

'When they had all come to the feast, Culann asked Conchobar:

'"Do you expect anyone to follow you?"

'"No," said Conchobor. He did not remember the arrangement with his fosterling to come after him.

'"I have a blood hound," said Culann. "There are three chains on him and three men holding each chain. He was brought from Spain. Let him be loosed to guard our cattle and our stock and let the fort be shut."

'At that point the boy arrived. The dog made for him. He still kept on with the play; he would throw his ball and then throw his hurley after it so that it struck the ball, neither stroke being greater than the other. And he threw his toy spear after them and caught it before it fell. And though the dog was approaching him, it interfered not with his play. Conchobor and his household were so dismayed by this that they could not move. They thought they would not reach him alive though the fort was open. Now when the hound came towards the boy, he cast aside his ball and his hurley, and he tackled the dog with both hands, that is, he put one hand on the apple of the hound's throat and the other at the back of his head, and dashed him against the pillar-stone that was beside him so that all the hound's limbs sprang apart. According to another version, however, he threw his ball into the hound's mouth and it drove his entrails out through him.

'The Ulstermen rose up to fetch the boy, some leaping over the wall of the court, others going out by the gate. They placed him in Conchobar's arms. A great alarm was raised by them at the thought that the son of the king's sister had almost been killed. At that point Culann entered the house.

'"Welcome, little lad, for your mother's sake. But as for myself, would that I had not prepared a feast! My livelihood is now a livelihood wasted, my husbandry a husbandry lost without my hound. The servant who has been taken from me, that is, my hound, maintained life and honour for me. He was defence and protection for my goods and my cattle. He guarded all my beasts for me in field and in house."

'"That is no great matter," said the boy. "A whelp of the same litter will be reared by me for you, and until such time as that hound grows and is fit for action, I myself shall be a hound to protect your cattle and to protect yourself. And I shall protect all Mag Murthemne; neither flock nor herd shall be taken thence from me without my knowing it."

'"Your name shall be Cú Chulainn (the Hound of Culann) then," said Cathbad.

'"I am glad that it should be my name," said Cú Chulainn.

'It were no cause of wonder that one who had done this when he was seven, should have performed a valiant deed now that he is seventeen years old,' said Conall Cernach.

The death of Nechta Scéne's three sons

'He did still another exploit,' said Fiachu mac Fir Febe.

'Cathbad the druid was with his son Conchobar mac Nessa. There were with him a hundred active men learning the druid's art — that was the number that Cathbad used to instruct. One of his pupils asked him for what that day would be of good omen. Cathbad said that if a warrior took up arms on that day, his name for deeds of valour would be known throughout Ireland and his fame would last for ever.

'Cú Chulainn heard this. He went to Conchobar to ask for arms. Conchobar asked:

'"Who prophesied good fortune for you?"

'"Master Cathbad," said Cú Chulainn.

'"We know him indeed," said Conchobar.

'He gave him a spear and a shield. Cú Chulainn brandished them in the middle of the hall so that not one was left unbroken of the fifteen spare sets of weapons which were kept in Conchobar's household to replace broken weapons or to provide for the taking up of arms by someone. Finally Conchobar's own arms were given to him. They withstood him, and he brandished them and blessed the king whose arms they were, saying: "Happy the people and race over whom reigns the owner of these arms!"

'Then Cathbad came to them and asked:

'"Is the boy taking up arms?"

'"Yes," said Conchobar.

'"That is not lucky for the son of his mother," said he.

'"Why, was it not you who instructed him?"

'"It was not I indeed," said Cathbad.

'"What use is it for you to deceive me so, you sprite?" said Conchobar to Cú Chulainn.

'"O king of the Fían, it is no deceit," said Cú Chulainn. "He prophesied good fortune for his pupils this morning and I heard him from where I was on the south side of Emain, and then I came to you."

'"It is indeed a day of good omen," said Cathbad. "It is certain that he who takes up arms today will be famous and renowned, but he will, however, be short-lived."

'"A mighty thing!" said Cú Chulainn. "Provided I be famous, I am content to be only one day on earth."

'On another day a certain man asked the druids for what that day was a good omen.

'"The name of one who goes for the first time into a chariot on this day," said Cathbad, "will be famed throughout Ireland for ever."

'Then Cú Chulainn heard this, and he came to Conchobar and said to him:

'"Master Conchobar, give me a chariot."

'Conchobar gave him a chariot. Cú Chulainn put his hand between the two shafts and the chariot broke. In the same way he smashed twelve chariots. So finally Conchobar's chariot was given to him and it withstood the test.

'Thereafter he went into the chariot with Conchobar's charioteer. The charioteer, whose name was Ibor, turned the chariot under him.

'"Come out of the chariot now," said the charioteer. "These are fine horses."

'"I am fine too, lad," said Cú Chulainn. "Just go on around Emain and you shall be rewarded for it."

'The charioteer drove off and Cú Chulainn made him go along the road that he might greet the boys, "and so that the boys may wish me well." Then he besought him to go back over the road again. When they had come there Cú Chulainn said to the charioteer:

'"Ply the goad on the horses."

'"In what direction?" asked the charioteer.

'"As far as the road will lead," said Cú Chulainn.

'Thence they came to Slíab Fúait where they found Conall Cernach. It had fallen to Conall to guard the province that day. For each warrior of the Ulstermen spent a day in turn in Slíab Fúait, to protect anyone who came that way with poetry or with challenge to battle, so that there he might be encountered and so that no one should go unnoticed into Emain.

'"I wish you prosperity, victory and triumph!" said Conall.

'"Go to the fort, Conall, and leave me here to watch now," said Cú Chulainn.

'"That will do," said Conall, "if it is merely to undertake the protection of one coming with poetry. However, if it be to fight some one, it is still too soon for you to do that."

'"Perhaps it will not be necessary at all," said Cú Chulainn. "Meanwhile let us go to take a look at the sand-bank of Loch Echtra. There are usually warriors staying there."

'"I am willing," said Conall.

'So they set out. Cú Chulainn threw a stone from his sling and the shaft of Conall Cernach's chariot broke.

'"Why have you thrown the stone, lad?" asked Conall.

'"To test my shooting and the accuracy of my shot," said Cú Chulainn, "And it is the custom with you Ulstermen that you do not drive on in a chariot which is unsafe. Go back to Emain, master Conall, and leave me here to keep watch."

'"I am willing," said Conall.

'Conall Cernach did not go past that spot afterwards.

'Cú Chulainn went on to Loch Echtra but they found no one there. The charioteer told Cú Chulainn that they should go to Emain to be in time for the feasting there.

'"No," said Cú Chulainn. "What mountain is that over there?"

'"Slíab Monduirnd," said the charioteer.

'"Let us go to it," said Cú Chulainn.

'Then they went to it, and when they had reached the mountain, Cú Chulainn asked:

'"What white cairn is that over there on the mountain-top?"

'"Finncharn," said the charioteer.

'"What plain is that yonder?" asked Cú Chulainn.

'"Mag mBreg," said the charioteer.

'So he told him the name of every chief fort between Temair and Cennannas. He named, moreover, their meadowlands and their fords, their renowned places and their dwellings, their forts and their fortified heights. He showed him too the fort of the three sons of Nechta Scéne, to wit, Fóill, Fannall and Túachell.

'"Is it they who say," asked Cú Chulainn, "that there are not more Ulstermen alive than they have killed of them?"

'"It is they indeed," said the charioteer.

'"Let us go to meet them," said Cú Chulainn.

'"It is dangerous for us," said the charioteer.

'"Indeed it is not to avoid danger that we go," said Cú Chulainn.

'Then they set off, and they unyoked their horses at the confluence of a bog and a river, on the south above the fort of the sons of Nechta Scéne. And Cú Chulainn cast the withe[1] that was on the pillar-stone as far as as his arm could throw it out into the river and let it float downstream. This violated a tabu which bound the sons of Nechta Scéne who noticed what had been done and came towards them. But Cú Chulainn, after letting the withe drift with the current, fell asleep at the pillar-stone, having said to the charioteer:

'"Do not wake me for a few, but wake me for several."

'However the charioteer was now sore afraid, and he harnessed the chariot and he tugged at the rugs and skin-coverings that were under Cú Chulainn, though he did not dare to waken him because Cú Chulainn had previously told him not to waken him for a few.

'Then came the sons of Nechta Scéne.

'"Who is here?" said one of them.

'"A little lad who has come on an expedition in a chariot today," answered the charioteer.

'"May his first taking up of arms not bring him prosperity or success. He must not stay in our land and the horses must not graze here any longer," said the warrior.

'"Their reins are ready in my hand," said the charioteer. "You had no reason to show yourself unfriendly to him, and anyway," said Ibor to the warrior, "the lad is asleep."

'"I am no lad indeed," said Cú Chulainn, "but the lad who is here has come to seek battle with a man."

'"That pleases me well," said the warrior.

'"It will please you well now in yonder ford," said Cú Chulainn.

'"This is fitting for you," said the charioteer. "Beware of the man who comes against you. Fóill [Sly] is his name. If you reach him not with the first thrust, you will never reach him."

'"I swear by the god by whom my people swear, he shall not play that trick again on Ulstermen if once the broad spear of my master Conchobar reach him from my hand. It will mean an outlaw's hand, that is, death, for him."

'Then Cú Chulainn cast the spear at Fóill so that his back broke therefrom and he carried off his spoils and his severed head then.

'"Beware of the next man," said the charioteer. "Fannall [Swallow] is his name. He skims over water as lightly as a swan or a swallow."

'"I swear that he will not play that trick on Ulstermen again," said Cú Chulainn. "You have seen how I travel across the pool in Emain."

1. A band or tie of twisted willow branches.

'Then they met in the ford. Cú Chulainn killed that man and carried off his spoils and his head.

'"Beware of the next man who comes to you," said the charioteer. "Túachell [Cunning] is his name, and it is no misnomer for no weapons wound him."

'"Here is the *deil chlis*[2] for him to confound him so that it may riddle him like a sieve," said Cú Chulainn.

'Then he cast the spear at him and knocked him down. He went towards him and cut off his head. He carried off his head and his spoils to his own charioteer.

'Then he heard the cry of their mother, Nechta Scéne, bewailing them. He carried off the spoils and brought the three heads with him in his chariot and said:

'"I will not part from these tokens of my triumph until I reach Emain."

'Thereupon they set forth with their trophies. Cú Chulainn said to the charioteer:

'"You promised us a good drive, and we need it now because of the fight and because of the pursuit behind us."

'They drove on then to Slíab Fúait. So swift was the run they made across Brega after his urging of the charioteer that the chariot-horses used to outstrip the wind and birds in flight, and Cú Chulainn used to catch the stone he had thrown from his sling before it reached the ground.

'On reaching Slíab Fúait they found a herd of deer before them.

'"What are those nimble cattle over there?" asked Cú Chulainn.

'"Wild deer," said the charioteer.

'"Which would the Ulstermen deem best, that I should take them to them alive or dead?"

'"It is more wonderful to take them alive," said the charioteer. "Not every one can do so, but there is not one of them who cannot take them dead. But you cannot carry off any one of them alive," added the charioteer.

'"Indeed I can," said Cú Chulainn. "Ply the goad on the horses and drive them to the bog."

'The charioteer did so, and the horses stuck fast in the bog. Cú Chulainn sprang out of the chariot and caught the deer that was nearest to him and the finest of the herd. He lashed the horses through the bog and subdued the deer immediately and tied it up between the two poles of the chariot.

'Again they saw before them a flock of swans.

'"Which would the Ulstermen deem best," asked Cú Chulainn, "that I should carry them alive to them or carry them dead?"

'"The bravest and most active carry them off alive," said the charioteer.

'Cú Chulainn then threw a small stone at the birds and brought down eight of them. Again he threw a big stone and struck twelve of them. All this was done by his "return-stroke."

'"Collect the birds for me," said Cú Chulainn to his charioteer. "If I go to get them, the wild deer will spring on you."

'"It is not easy for me to go there," said the charioteer. "The horses have become wild so that I cannot go past them. Nor can I go past the iron wheels of the chariot because of their sharpness, and I cannot go past the deer for his antlers have filled all the space between the two poles of the chariot."

'"Step from his antlers then," said Cú Chulainn. "I swear by the god by whom the Ulstermen swear, that I shall so nod at him and so glare at him that he will not move his head towards you and will not dare to stir."

'That was done then. Cú Chulainn fastened the reins and the charioteer collected the birds. Then Cú Chulainn tied the birds to the strings and cords of the chariot. In this wise he went to Emain Macha with a wild deer behind his chariot, a flock of swans fluttering over it and three severed heads in his chariot.

'They reached Emain then.

'"A chariot-warrior is driving towards you!" cried the watchman in Emain Macha. "He will shed the blood of every man in the fort unless heed be taken and naked women go out to meet him."

'Then he turned the left side of his chariot towards Emain which was tabu for it. And Cú Chulainn said:

'"I swear by the god by whom Ulstermen swear that, unless some man is found to fight with me, I shall shed the blood of everyone in the fort."

'"Send forth naked women to meet him!" ordered Conchobor.

'Then the women-folk of Emain came forth to meet him led by Mugain, the wife of Conchobor mac Nessa, and they bared their breasts to him.

"These are the warriors who will encounter you today," said Mugain.

2. One of Cú Chulainn's weapons, a spear or missile.

'He hid his face. Then the warriors of Emain seized him and cast him into a tub of cold water. That tub burst about him. The second tub into which he was plunged boiled hands high .... The third tub into which he went after that he warmed so that its heat and its cold were properly adjusted for him. Then he came out and the queen, Mugain, put on him a blue mantle with a silver brooch therein, and a hooded tunic, and he sat at Conchobor's knee which was his resting-place always after that.

'One who did that in his seventh year,' said Fíachu mac Fir Febe, 'it were no wonder that he should triumph over odds and overcome in fair fight now that his seventeen years are complete today.'

The description of Cú Chulainn

Cú Chulainn came on the morrow to survey the host and to display his gentle and beautiful form to women and girls and maidens, to poets and men of art, for he held not as honourable or dignified the dark magical appearance in which he had appeared to them the previous night. So for that reason he now came on this day to display his beautiful fair appearance.

Beautiful indeed was the youth who thus came to display his form to the hosts, namely, Cú Chulainn mac Súaltaim. He seemed to have three kinds of hair: dark next to his skin, blood-red in the middle and hair like a crown of gold covering them outside. Fair was the arrangement of that hair with three coils in the hollow in the nape of his neck, and like gold thread was each fine hair, loose-flowing, bright-golden, excellent, long-tressed, splendid and of beautiful colour, which fell back over his shoulders. A hundred bright crimson ringlets of flaming red-gold encircled his neck. Around his head a hundred strings interspersed with carbuncle-gems. Four shades in each of his cheeks, a yellow shade and a green, a blue shade and a purple. Seven brilliant gem-like pupils in each of his noble eyes. Seven toes on each of his feet; seven fingers on each of his hands with the grasp of a hawk's claws and the grip of a hedgehog's claws in each separate toe and finger.

So on that day he donned his festive apparel, namely, a fair mantle, well-fitting, bright purple, fringed, five-folded. A white brooch of silver inset with inlaid gold over his white breast as it were a bright lantern that men's eyes could not look at by reason of its brilliance and splendour. Next to his skin he wore a tunic of silky satin reaching to the top of his dark apron, dark-red, soldierly, of royal satin. He carried a dark-red purple shield with five concentric circles of gold and a rim of white bronze. At his girdle hung, ready for action, a golden-hilted, ornamented sword with great knobs of red gold at its end. In the chariot beside him was a long shining-edged spear together with a sharp attacking javelin with rivets of burning gold. In one hand he held nine heads, in the other ten, and these he brandished at the hosts. Those were the trophies of one night's fighting by Cú Chulainn.

Then the women of Connacht climbed up on the hosts and the women of Munster climbed on men's shoulders that they might behold the appearance of Cú Chulainn. But Medb hid her face and dared not show her countenance, but through fear of Cú Chulainn she sheltered under a cover of shields.

The fight of Fer Diad and Cú Chulainn

Then they debated among themselves as to which man would be capable of repelling Cú Chulainn. The four provinces of Ireland named and confirmed and decided whom they should send to the ford to meet Cú Chulainn. They all declared that it was the horn-skinned man from Irrus Domnann, the one whose attack cannot be endured, the battle-stone of doom, Cú Chulainn's own dear foster-brother. Cú Chulainn possessed no feat that Fer Diad had not, except only the feat of the *gáe bulga*.[3] And they thought that Fer Diad could avoid even that and protect himself from it, for he had a horn-skin which weapons and swords could not pierce.

Medb sent messengers for Fer Diad, but he did not come with those messengers. Then Medb sent to fetch him poets and artists and satirists who might satirise him and disgrace him and put him to shame, so that he would find no resting-place in the world until he should come to the tent of Medb and Ailill on the Foray. So for fear that he should be put to shame by them Fer Diad came with those messengers.

Finnabair, the daughter of Medb and Ailill, was placed at his side. It was she who handed Fer Diad every goblet and cup; it was she who gave him three

3. Cú Chulainn's famous spear.

kisses with every one of those cups; it was she who gave him fragrant apples over the bosom of her tunic. She kept saying that Fer Diad was her beloved, her chosen lover from among all the men of the world.

When Fer Diad was sated and cheerful and merry, Medb said:

'Well now, Fer Diad, do you know why you have been summoned to this tent?'

'I know not indeed,' said Fer Diad, 'except that the nobles of the men of Ireland are here, so why should it be less fitting for me to be here than any other nobleman?'

'That is not why, indeed,' said Medb, 'but (you have been summoned for us) to give you a chariot worth thrice seven *cumala*,[4] the equipment of twelve men, the equivalent of Mag Muirthemne in the arable land of Mag nAí, permission to remain at all times in Crúachu with wine poured for you there, and your descendants and your race to be free for ever from tax or tribute, and my leaf-shaped brooch of gold in which there are ten score ounces and ten score half-ounces and ten score crosachs[5] and ten score quarters bestowed on you, and Finnabair, my daughter and Ailill's, as your wedded wife, and my own intimate friendship. And in addition to that, if you require it, you will get the gods as guarantee.'

'Those gifts are great,' said they all.

'That is true,' said Fer Diad. 'They are indeed great. But great though they be, Medb, you will keep them yourself if I am to go and fight with my foster-brother.'

'O my men,' said Medb, intending to stir up strife and dissension and speaking as if she had not heard Fer Diad at all, 'what Cú Chulainn said is true.'

'What did he say, Medb?' asked Fer Diad.

'He said, my friend, that he thought you should fall by his choicest feat of arms in the province to which he would go.'

'It was not right for him to say that for he never found weakness or cowardice in me, day or night. I swear by my people's god that I shall be the first man to come tomorrow morning to the ford of combat.'

'A blessing on you!' said Medb. 'I prefer that rather than finding weakness or cowardice in you. Every man has kindly feeling for his own people. So is it any more fitting for him to work for Ulster's weal since his mother was of Ulster, than for you to seek the good of Connacht, for you are the son of a Connacht king?'

4. A term for a female slave, used as a unit of value.
5. A measure of weight, between a half and a quarter of an ounce.

from:
LONGES MAC N-UISLEANN (The Exile of the Sons of Uisliu)

['The Exile of the Sons of Uisliu' was composed and written down in the ninth, or possibly even in the eighth, century. In the original it is a model of the succinct narrative style of classical Old Irish: concise, controlled and rich in subtle allusion and resonance. It is one of a number of Irish analogues of the medieval romance of *Tristan and Isolde*. A very different telling of the tale, more prolix in style and freer in sentiment, was made in the thirteenth or fourteenth century, and one or other version inspired a number of modern Anglo-Irish writers to attempt their own adaptations of the tragic romance of Deirdre.

The translation is from Vernam Hull's edition of *Longes Mac N-Uisleann: The Exile of the Sons of Uisliu* (New York: The Modern Language Association of America; London: Oxford University Press, 1949.]

Why was the exile of the Sons of Uisliu? It is not hard to relate.

The Ulstermen were drinking in the house of Feidlimid mac Daill, the story-teller of Conchobor. Now the wife of Feidlimid was attending upon the host, standing up and she being pregnant. Drinking horns and portions of food circled around, and they uttered a drunken shout. When they were about to go to bed, the woman came to her bed. While she was going across the middle of the house, the infant in her womb screamed so that it was heard throughout the whole enclosure. At that scream each man within arose from the other so that they were shoulder to shoulder in the house. Then Sencha mac Ailella issued a prohibition:

'Do not stir,' he said. 'Let the woman be brought to us in order that it may be known for what reason is this noise.'

Thereupon the woman was brought to them.

Her consort, namely Feidlimid, then said:

'What is the violent noise that resounds,
That rages throughout your bellowing womb?
The clamor between your sides — strongly it
sounds —

It crushes him who hears with ears.
My heart fears
Much terror that wounds severely.'

Thereupon she rushed to Cathbad, for he was a seer:

'Hear handsome Cathbad of the comely face,
A prince, a diadem great and mighty,
Who is magnified through the wizardries of
druids,
Since I myself have not wise words
With reference to which Feidlimid might
obtain
The illumination of knowledge,
Because a woman does not know
Whatever is wont to be in her womb,
Though it cried out in my womb's receptacle.'

Then Cathbad said:

'In the receptacle of your womb there cried out
A woman of yellow hair with yellow curls,
With comely, grey-blue irised eyes.
Her purplish-pink cheeks are like foxglove;
To the color of snow I compare
The spotless treasure of her set of teeth.
Lustrous are her scarlet-red lips —
A woman for whom there will be many slaughters
Among the chariot-fighters of Ulster.

There screams in your womb which bellows
A woman, fair, tall and long-haired,
Concerning whom champions will contend,
Concerning whom high kings will ask.
They will be in the west with oppressive bodies
of troops,
Supported by the province of Conchobor.
Her scarlet-red lips will be
About her pearly teeth —
Against whom high queens will be jealous,
Against her matchless, faultless form.'

Cathbad thereafter put his hand on the stomach of the woman so that the infant resounded under his hand.

'True it is,' he said, 'that a girl is there, and her name will be Derdriu, and concerning her there will be evil.'

'Let the girl be slain,' said the warriors.

'By no means,' said Conchobor. 'I shall carry off the girl tomorrow,' Conchobor added, 'and she will be reared according to my own will, and she will be the woman who will be in my company.'

And the Ulstermen did not dare to set him right with respect to it. That, moreover, was done. She was reared by Conchobor until she was by far the most beautiful girl who ever had been in Ireland. In a court apart it is that she was brought up in order that no man of the Ulstermen might see her up to the time that she should spend the night with Conchobor, and no person ever was allowed into that court except her foster father and her foster mother and Leborcham; for the last-mentioned one could not be prevented, for she was a female satirist.

Once upon a time, accordingly, the foster father of the maiden was skinning a weaned calf on snow outside in the winter to cook it for her. She saw a raven drinking the blood on the snow. Then she said to Leborcham:

'Beloved would be the one man on whom might be yonder three colors — that is, hair like the raven, and a cheek like blood, and a body like snow.'

'Dignity and fortune to you!' said Leborcham. 'He is not far from you. He is inside near to you, even Noísiu son of Uisliu.'

'I shall, indeed, not be well,' she said, 'until I see him.'

On one occasion, then, the aforementioned Noísiu was alone on the rampart of the earthwork (that is, of Emain) singing in a tenor voice. Melodious, however, was the tenor singing of the Sons of Uisliu. Each cow and each animal that heard it, two thirds of surplus milk always was milked from them. Each person who heard it always had a sufficient peaceful disposition and musical entertainment. Good also were their arms. Although the whole province of the Ulstermen were in one place about them, they might not gain the victory over them on account of the excellence of the parrying and the self-defence, provided that every one of the three of them put his back against the other. As swift as hounds, moreover, they were at hunting. By virtue of their swiftness they used to kill the wild animals.

While, therefore, the aforesaid Noísiu was alone outside, she quickly stole out to him as if to go past him, and he did not recognize her.

'Fair,' he said, 'is the heifer that goes past me.'

'Heifers,' she said, 'are bound to be big where bulls are not wont to be.'

'You have the bull of the province,' he said, 'namely, the king of the Ulstermen.'

'I would choose between the two of you,' she

her, I have no power to give her to you, and you may only see her.'

They came then to the lake. They saw three times fifty grown girls, and the girl herself among them. The girls did not reach above her shoulder. There was a chain of silver between each couple; and a necklet of silver round her own throat, and a chain of refined gold. Then Bodhbh said, 'Do you recognise that girl?' 'I do indeed,' said Oenghus. 'I can do no more for you,' said Bodhbh. 'That is no matter, then,' said Oenghus, 'since it is she that I saw; I cannot take her this time. Who is this girl, Bodhbh?' said Oenghus, 'I know, truly,' said Bodhbh, 'she is Caer Ibhormheith, daughter of Ethal Anbhuail from the fairy hill of Uamhan in the land of Connaught.'

Then Oenghus and his people set off for their own country. Bodhbh went with him, and talked with the Daghdhae and Boann at Bruigh Maic ind Óaig. They told them their news, and told how she seemed, in figure and form, just as they had seen; and they told her name and the name of her father and grandfather. 'We feel it to be discourteous that we cannot content you,' said the Daghdhae. 'What you should do, Daghdhae,' said Bodhbh, 'is to go to Ailill and Medhbh, for they have the girl in their province.'

The Daghdhae went till he reached the lands of Connaught, with three score chariots in his company. The king and queen made them welcome. They spent a full week banqueting round the ale after that. 'What has brought you?' said the king. 'You have a girl in your country,' said the Daghdhae, 'and my son has fallen in love with her, and has become sick. I have come to you to find out whether you would give her to the lad.' 'Who?' said Ailill. 'The daughter of Ethal Anbhuail.' 'We have no power over her,' said Ailill and Medhbh, 'if we had she should be given him.' 'This would be good — let the king of the fairy hill be summoned to you,' said the Daghdhae.

Ailill's steward went to him. 'You have been ordered by Ailill and Medhbh to go to speak with them.' 'I will not go,' said he, 'I will not give my daughter to the son of the Daghdhae.' That is told to Ailill; 'He cannot be made to come, but he knows why he is summoned.' 'No matter,' said Ailill, 'he shall come, and the heads of his warriors shall be brought with him.' At that, Ailill's household troops and the men of the Daghdhae rose up against the fairy hill, and overran the whole hill. They brought out three score heads, and the king, so that he was in captivity at Cruachu.

Then Ailill said to Ethal Anbhuail, 'Give your daughter to the son of the Daghdhae.' 'I cannot,' said he, 'her magic power is greater than mine.' 'What is this great magic power she has?' said Ailill. 'Easily told; she is in the shape of a bird every other year, and in human shape the other years.' 'What year is she in the shape of a bird?' said Ailill. 'It is not for me to betray her,' said her father. 'Off with your head, unless you tell us!' said Ailill. 'I will not hold out any longer,' said he; 'I will tell you,' said he, 'since you are so persistent about her. Next All Hallows she will be at Loch Bél Dragon in the shape of a bird, and wonderful birds will be seen with her there, there will be three times fifty swans around her; and I have made preparations for them.' 'I do not care, then,' said the Daghdhae; 'since you know her nature, do you bring her.'

Then a treaty was made between them, between Ailill and Ethal and the Daghdhae, and Ethal was let go. The Daghdhae bade them farewell and came to his house and told his news to his son. 'Go next All Hallows to Loch Bél Dragon, and call her to you from the lake.' The Mac Óag went to Loch Bél Dragon. He saw three times fifty white birds with their silver chains, and curls of gold about their heads. Oenghus was in human shape on the brink of the lake. He called the girl to him. 'Come to speak to me, Caer!' 'Who calls me?' said Caer. 'Oenghus calls you.' 'I will go, if you will undertake on your honour that I may come back to the lake again.' 'I pledge your protection,' said he.

She went to him. He cast his arms about her. They fell asleep in the form of two swans, and went round the lake three times, so that his promise might not be broken. They went away in the form of two white birds till they came to Bruigh Maic ind Óaig, and sang a choral song so that they put the people to sleep for three days and three nights. The girl stayed with him after that.

from:
AISLINGE MAC CONGLINNE
(The Vision of MacConglinne)

[This exuberant story of the wondrous vision of the wandering scholar Mac Conglinne combines a rollicking satire on Irish monastic life and devotion with the tradition of a Land of Cokaygne and the motif — one well rooted in Irish folklore — of physical possession by an insatiable demon of voracity. It also parodies wickedly many of the themes, genres and stylistic features of the written literature. In its primary form the *Vision* was composed in the eleventh or twelfth century.

The translation is from Kuno Meyer's edition of *Aislinge Meic Conglinne: The Vision of MacConglinne* (London: David Nutt, 1892).]

The four things to be asked of every composition must be asked of this composition, viz., place, and person, and time, and cause of invention.

The place of this composition is great Cork of Munster, and its author is Aniér MacConglinne of the Onaght Glenowra. In the time of Cathal MacFinguine, son of Cúcengairm, or son of Cúcenmáthir, it was made. The cause of its invention was to banish the demon of gluttony that was in the throat of Cathal MacFinguine.

Cathal MacFinguine was a good king, who governed Munster; a great warrior prince was he. A warrior of this sort: with the edge of a hound, he ate like a horse. Satan, viz. a demon of gluttony that was in his throat, used to devour his rations with him. A pig and a cow and a bull-calf of three hands, with three score cakes of pure wheat, and a vat a new ale, and thirty heathpoults'[1] eggs, that was his first dole,[2] besides his other snack, until his great feast was ready for him. As regards the great feast, that passes account or reckoning.

The reason of the demon of gluttony being in the throat of Cathal MacFinguine was, because he had, though he had never seen her, a first love for Lígach, daughter of Maeldúin, king of Ailech; and she sister to Fergal, son of Maeldúin, also king of Ailech, who was then contending for the kingship of Ireland against Cathal MacFinguine, as is plain from the quarrel of the two hags, when they had a duel in quatrains at Freshford:

'He comes from the North, comes from the North,
The son of Maeldúin, over the rocks,
Over Barrow's brink, over Barrow's brink,
Till kine[3] he take he will not stay.'

'He shall stay, shall stay,' said the Southern hag;
'He will be thankful if he escapes.
By my father's hand, by my father's hand,
If Cathal meets him, he'll take no kine.'

1. young grouses'.
2. portion.
3. cattle.

Then kernels and apples and many sweets used to be brought from Lígach, Maeldúin's daughter, to Cathal MacFinguine, for his love and affection. Fergal, son of Maeldúin, heard this, and his sister was called unto him. And he gave her a blessing if she should tell him truth, and a curse if she should deny him it. The sister told him; for great as was her love and affection for Cathal MacFinguine, she feared her brother's curse reaching her. Then she told the true story.

The brother told her to send the apples to himself. And a scholar was summoned unto him, and he promised great rewards to the scholar for putting charms in those numerous sweets, to the destruction of Cathal MacFinguine. And the scholar put charms and heathen spells in those numerous sweets, and they were delivered to Fergal, who despatched messengers to convey them to Cathal. And they entreated him by each of the seven universal things, sun and moon, dew and sea, heaven and earth, day and night . . . that he would eat those apples, since it was out of love and affection for him they were brought from Lígach, daughter of Maeldúin.

Cathal thereupon ate the apples, and little creatures through the poison spells were formed of them in his inside. And those little creatures gathered in the womb of one — in that animal, so that there was formed the demon of gluttony. And this is the cause why the demon of gluttony abode in the throat of Cathal MacFinguine, to the ruin of the men of Munster during three half-years; and it is likely he would have ruined Ireland during another half-year. . . .

Aniér MacConglinne was a famous scholar, with abundance of knowledge. The reason why he was called Aniér was because he would satirise and praise all. No wonder, indeed; for there had not come before him, and came not after him, one whose satire or praise was harder to bear, wherefore he was called Anéra [i.e. Non-refusal], for that there was no refusing him.

A great longing seized the mind of the scholar, to follow poetry, and to abandon his reading. For wretched to him was his life in the shade of his studies. And he searched in his mind whither he would make his first poetical journey. The result of his search was, to go to Cathal MacFinguine, who was then on a royal progress in Iveagh of Munster. The scholar had heard that he would get plenty and enough of all kinds of whitemeats; for greedy and hungry for whitemeats was the scholar.

This came into the mind of the scholar on a Saturday eve exactly, at Roscommon; for there he was pursuing his reading. Then he sold the little stock he possessed for two wheaten cakes and a slice of old bacon with a streak across its middle. These he put in his book-satchel. And on that night two pointed shoes of hide, of seven-folded dun leather, he shaped for himself.

He arose early on the morrow, and tucked up his shirt over the rounds of his fork, and wrapped him in the folds of his white cloak, in the front of which was an iron brooch. He lifted his book-satchel on to the arched slope of his back. In his right hand he grasped his even-poised knotty staff, in which were five hands from one end to the other. Then, going right-hand-wise round the cemetery, he bade farewell to his tutor, who put gospels around him.

He set out on his way and journey, across the lands of Connaught into Aughty, to Limerick, to Carnarry, to Barna-trí-Carbad, into Slieve-Keen, into the country of the Fir-Féni, which is this day called Fermoy, across Moinmore, until he rested a short time before vespers in the guest-house of Cork. On that Saturday he had gone from Roscommon to Cork.

This was the way in which he found the guest-house on his arrival, it was open. That was one of the days of the three things, viz., wind and snow and rain about the door; so that the wind left not a wisp of thatch, nor a speck of ashes that it did not sweep with it through the other door, under the beds and couches and screens of the princely house.

The blanket of the guest-house was rolled, bundled, in the bed, and was full of lice and fleas. No wonder, truly, for it never got its sunning by day, nor its lifting at night; for it was not wont to be empty at its lifting. The bath-tub of the guest-house, with the water of the night before in it, with its stones, was by the side of the door-post.

The scholar found no one who would wash his feet. So he himself took off his shoes and washed his feet in that bath-tub, in which he afterwards dipped his shoes. He hung his book-satchel on the peg in the wall, took up his shoes, and gathered his hands into the blanket, which he tucked about his legs. But, truly, as numerous as the sand of the sea, or sparks of fire, or dew on a May morning, or the stars of heaven, were the lice and fleas nibbling his legs, so that weariness seized him. And no one came to visit him or do reverence to him.

He took down his book-satchel, and brought out his psalter, and began singing his psalms. What the learned and the books of Cork relate is, that the sound of the scholar's voice was heard a thousand paces beyond the city, as he sang his psalms, through spiritual mysteries, in lauds, and stories, and various kinds, in dia-psalms and syn-psalms and sets of ten, with paters and canticles and hymns at the conclusion of each fifty. Now, it seemed to every man in Cork that the sound of the voice was in the house next himself. This came of original sin, and MacConglinne's hereditary sin and his own plain-working bad luck; so that he was detained without drink, without food, without washing, until every man in Cork had gone to his bed....

He remained there until midnight. Then an angel of God came to him on the pillar-stone, and began to manifest the vision unto him. As long as the angel was on the pillar-stone it was too hot for MacConglinne, but when he moved on a ridge away from him, it was comfortable. (Hence the 'Angel's Ridge' in the green of Cork, which was never a morning without dew.) At the end of the night the angel departed from him.

Thereupon he shaped a little rhyme of his own, which would serve to relate what had been manifested to him, and there he remained until morning with the poetical account of his vision ready....

MacConglinne began to recount his vision, and it is said that from here onward is what the angel manifested to him, as he said:

A vision that appeared to me,
An apparition wonderful
  I tell to all:
A lardy coracle all of lard
Within a port of New-milk Loch,
  Up on the World's smooth sea.

We went into the man-of-war,
'Twas warrior-like to take the road
  O'er ocean's heaving waves.
Our oar-strokes then we pulled
Across the level sea,
Throwing the sea's harvest up,
  Like honey, the sea-soil.

The fort we reached was beautiful,
With works of custards thick,
  Beyond the loch.
New butter was the bridge in front,
The rubble dyke was wheaten white,
  Bacon the palisade.

Stately, pleasantly it sat,
A compact house and strong.
  Then I went in:
The door of it was dry meat,
The threshold was bare bread,
  Cheese-curds the sides.

Smooth pillars of old cheese,
And sappy bacon props
  Alternate ranged;
Fine beams of mellow cream,
White rafters — real curds,
  Kept up the house.

Behind was a wine well,
Beer and bragget[4] in streams,
  Each full pool to the taste.
Malt in smooth wavy sea,
Over a lard-spring's brink
  Flowed through the floor.

A loch of pottage fat
Under a cream of oozy lard
  Lay 'tween it and the sea.
Hedges of butter fenced it round,
Under a blossom of white-mantling lard,
  Around the wall outside.

A row of fragrant apple-trees,
An orchard in its pink-tipped bloom,
  Between it and the hill.
A forest tall of real leeks,
Of onions and of carrots, stood
  Behind the house.

Within, a household generous,
A welcome of red, firm-fed men,
  Around the fire.
Seven bead-strings, and necklets seven,
Of cheeses and of bits of tripe,
  Hung from each neck.

4. A drink make of honey and ale.

The Chief in mantle of beefy fat
Beside his noble wife and fair
  I then beheld.
Below the lofty cauldron's spit
Then the Dispenser I beheld,
  His fleshfork on his back.

The good Cathal MacFinguine,
He is a good man to enjoy
  Tales tall and fine.
That is a business for an hour,
And full of delight 'tis to tell
The rowing of the man-of-war
  O'er Loch Milk's sea.

He then narrated his entire vision in the presence of the monks of Cork until he reached its close (but this is not its close), and the virtues of the vision were manifested unto Manchín.

'Excellent, thou wretch,' said Manchín, 'go straight to Cathal MacFinguine, and relate the vision to him; for it was revealed to me last night that this evil which afflicts Cathal would be cured through that vision.'

from: FLEDH BRICRENN (The Feast of Bricriu)

[Bricriu is the great mischief-maker of the heroic cycle of Ulster. The tale of *Fledh Bricrenn* (The Feast of Bricriu), which was first composed in writing probably in the eighth century, tells how he invited the heroes of Ulster and their wives to a great feast with the express intention of setting them at loggerheads with one another. He separately promises the 'champion's portion', the ritual choice portion of the feast, to Cú Chulainn, Lóegaire Buadach and Conall Cernach, and when the ensuing strife is temporarily quelled, he turns his attentions to their wives.

The translation is by the present editor.]

By this time Bricriu and his lady were in his balcony. From his couch he could see the lay-out of the house and all that was going on within it. He pondered in his mind how he might set about inciting the women as he had done with the men. When he had decided how he would go about it, it so happened that at that precise time Fedelm Noíchride came out of the hall with fifty other women in her company, having consumed an immoderate amount of liquor. Bricriu saw her as she passed him. 'Glad am I to see you tonight, wife of Lóegaire Buadach, for Fedelm "of the nine hearts" is no misnomer for you on account of your excellence of form and wisdom and lineage. Conchobor, king of Ulster, is your father and Lóegaire Buadach is your husband, and indeed I should not consider it too great an honour for you that none of the women of Ulster should precede you into the Hall of Mead-circuit, but that instead they should all follow in your train. If you go first tonight into the hall, you will enjoy forever sovereignty over all the women of Ulster.' Fedelm then went off to a distance of three ridges from the house.

Then Lendabair came out, who was the daughter of Eógan mac Derthacht and wife of Conall Cernach. Bricriu spoke to her, saying: 'I am glad to see you, Lendabair, for the name Lendabair is no misnomer for you: you are the darling and the loved one of the men of the whole world for your fame and distinction. By as much as your husband surpasses the warriors of the world in valour and handsomeness, so also do you surpass the women of Ulster.' If he had duped Fedelm greatly, then he duped Lendabair twice as much.

Emer came out then with fifty other women. 'Hail to you,' said Bricriu, 'Emer daughter of Forgoll Manach, and wife of the best man in Ireland. Emer of the Beautiful Hair is no misnomer for you, you for whom the kings and princes of Ireland are in contention. As the sun surpasses the stars of heaven, so do you outshine the women of the whole world in form and shape and lineage, in youth and beauty and dignity, in fame and wisdom and eloquence.' If he had duped the other women, he duped Emer three times as much.

The three companies of women then came to the same place, three ridges length from the hall, and none of them was aware that the others had been incited by Bricriu. Immediately they turned back towards the hall. Even and graceful and stately was their progress over the first ridge; barely did they put one foot before the other. Over the second ridge, however, their gait became more lively and more rapid, and when they came to the ridge nearest the house each of them was striving might and main to pass out the other and they raised their tunics up to their buttocks in their effort to get into the house first, for Bricriu had told each of them unknown to the others that she who would enter first would be queen of the whole province. The noise they made struggling to get there ahead of one another was like the noise of fifty chariots approaching. The whole house shook and the warriors sprang to their arms and sought to kill one another.

'Stop,' said Sencha, 'they are not enemies who have come; it is Bricriu who has made trouble among the women who went outside. I swear by all that my people swear,' he said, 'if the house is not closed against them, our dead will outnumber our living.' With that the doorkeepers closed the door. Emer, daughter of Forgall Manach and wife of Cú Chulainn, came up at full tilt ahead of the other women and put her back to the door, calling on the doorkeeper, before the others arrived. Their husbands inside the house jumped up, each of them making to open the door for his own wife so that she would be the first into the house. 'It's going to be a rough night,' said Conchobor. He struck the silver spike that was in his hand against the bronze pillar of his *imdae*[1] and the hosts sat down again. 'Stop,' he said, 'the battle that will be fought here will be fought not with arms but with words.' Each woman came in under the protection of her husband and it was then they waged the Ulsterwomen's War of Words....

Then, as their warrior's moon arose on hearing the women's talk, the men who were in the house, that is Lóegaire and Conall, broke one of the houseposts of the royal hall facing them, and that was the way their wives came into the house to them. Cú Chulainn on the other hand raised up the house opposite his couch so that the stars of heaven were visible from under the wall, and that was the way his wife entered as well as fifty women accompanying the other two and fifty with his own wife, this in order that she should not stand equal to the other women since he was not equal to the rest. After that Cú Chulainn let the house drop so that seven man-lengths of the wall went into the ground and it shook the whole enclosure, toppling Bricriu's balcony to the ground and letting Bricriu himself and his queen fall into the dung in the middle of the court among the hounds. 'We're done for!', said Bricriu getting up quickly, 'enemies have attacked the fort.' He made a circuit of the royal hall and saw

1. A compartment or cubicle in a large hall, containing a couch or couches for sleeping.

how his house had been tilted so that it lay all askew. He beat his hands and then went into the house and there was not one of the Ulstermen who could have recognized him so filthy was he; it was by his speech they recognized him.

CREATURES GREAT AND SMALL

[A frequent topic in the Lives of the Saints, particularly those especially associated with the ascetic or anchoretic element in the Irish church, is the friendly familiarity of the hermit saint with the creatures of the wild. It often retains much of its primitive sincerity and childlike simplicity and elsewhere it is saved from becoming a mere conceit by a touch of gentle, tongue-in-cheek humour.]

Ciarán of Saigir

[This passage is from an eleventh- or twelfth-century Life which is based on older materials. It appears in Robin Flower, *The Irish Tradition* (Oxford: Clarendon Press, 1947).]

The blessed Ciarán took up his habitation like a hermit in the waste, for all about was a waste and tangled woodland. He began to build his little cell of mean stuff, and that was the beginning of his monastery. Afterwards a settlement grew up by God's gift and the grace of the holy Ciarán. And all these have the one name, Saigir.

Now when he came there he sat down under a tree in the shade of which was a boar of savage aspect. The boar seeing a man for the first time fled in terror, but afterwards, being tamed by God, it returned like a servant to the man of God. And that boar was Ciarán's first disciple and served him like a monk in that place. For the boar immediately fell to before the eyes of the man of God and with his teeth stoutly severed branches and grasses to serve for the building of the cell. For there was none with the holy man of God in that place. For he had fled to the waste from his own disciples. Then came other animals from the lairs of the waste to the holy Ciarán, a fox, a badger, a wolf and a stag. And they abode with him as tame as could be. For they followed the commands of the holy man in all things like monks.

One day the fox, being more subtle and full of guile than the rest, stole the slippers of the abbot, the holy Ciarán, and turning false to his vow carried them off to his old earth in the waste, designing to devour them there. And when the holy Ciarán knew of this, he sent another monk or disciple, the badger, to follow the fox into the waste and to bring his brother back to his obedience. So the badger, who knew the ways of the woods, immediately obeyed the command of his elder and went straight to the earth of brother fox. He found him intent on eating his lord's slippers, so he bit off his ears and his brush and tore out his hairs. And then he constrained him to accompany him to his monastery that there he might do penance for his theft. So the fox, yielding to force, came back with the badger to his own cell to the holy Ciarán, bringing the slippers still uneaten. And the holy man said to the fox: 'Wherefore, brother, hast thou done this evil thing, unworthy of a monk? Behold! our water is sweet and common to all, and our food likewise is distributed in common among us all. And if thou hadst a desire of thy natural craving to eat flesh, the omnipotent God would have made thee flesh of the bark of trees at our prayer.' Then the fox, craving forgiveness, did penance fasting, and ate nothing until the holy man commanded him. Then he abode with the rest in familiar converse.

Afterwards his own disciples and many others from every side gathered about the holy Ciarán in that place; and there a famous monastery was begun. But the tame creatures aforesaid abode there all his life, for the holy elder had pleasure to see them.

St Maelanfaid of Dairinis

[This is taken from the notes added later to the *Martyrology* of *Oengus*, which was compiled *c.* 800. From: Robin Flower, *The Irish Tradition* (Oxford: Clarendon Press, 1947).]

Maelanfaid abbot of Dairinis, a cell of Mochuda's Lismore, placed where Blackwater runs into the sea. This is that Maelanfaid that saw one day a little bird weeping and making moan. 'O my God,' said he, 'what has befallen the creature yonder? Now, I swear,' said he, 'that I will eat no food until it be revealed to me.' So abiding there he beheld an angel coming his way. 'Hail, cleric!' says the angel, 'let the trouble of this vex thee no longer. Molua, Ocha's son, is dead. And for this cause the creatures lament him, for that he never killed any creature, little or big. And not more do men bewail him than the creatures, and among them the tiny bird thou seest.'

St Mochua

[This is taken from Geoffrey Keating's seventeenth-century *History of Ireland* and is later than the rest of the material in this section; but Keating's work was based on older sources. From: Robin Flower, *The Irish Tradition* (Oxford: Clarendon Press, 1947).]

Mochua and Columcille lived at the same time and Mochua, being a hermit in the waste, had no worldly goods but only a cock, a mouse and a fly. And the office of the cock was to keep the hour of matins for him. As for the mouse it would never suffer him to sleep but five hours, day and night, and if he was like to sleep longer, being weary with vigils and prostrations, the mouse would fall to licking his ear till it woke him. And the fly's office was to be walking along each line of his psalter as he read it, and when he was wearied with singing his psalms, the fly would abide upon the line where he left off until he could return again to the saying of the psalms. Now it came to pass that these three precious ones died soon. And upon that Mochua wrote a letter to Columcille in Alba, sorrowing for the death of his flock. Columcille replied to him and this is what he said: 'My brother,' he said, 'marvel not that thy flock should have died, for misfortune ever waits upon wealth.'

from:
TOGAIL BRUIDNE DA DERGA
(The Destruction of the Hall of Da Derga)

[When the legendary king of Ireland, Eochaid Feidlech, was crossing the fair-green of Brí Léith (in modern County Longford) he saw a beautiful woman washing herself at a well. She was, he found, Étaín, daughter of Étar, who had long been in love with him, as he now was with her. Early Irish storytellers set great store by such passages of artistic description, and this feature was taken over and refined by the monastic redactors of the written texts. The following passage is taken from the ninth-century tale of 'The Destruction of the Hall of Da Derga' (*Togail Bruidne Da Derga*).

It appears in Kenneth H. Jackson, *A Celtic Miscellany* (London: Routledge & Kegan Paul, 1951).]

. . . He saw a woman at the edge of the spring, with a bright silver comb ornamented with gold, washing her hair in a silver bowl with four golden birds on it, and little flashing jewels of purple carbuncle on the rims of the bowl. She had a shaggy purple cloak made of fine fleece, and silver brooches of filigree work decorated with handsome gold, in the cloak; a long-hooded tunic on her, stiff and smooth, of green silk with embroidery of red gold. Wonderful ornaments of gold and silver with twining animal designs, in the tunic on her breast and her shoulders and her shoulder-blades on both sides. The sun was shining on her, so that the men could plainly see the glistening of the gold in the sunlight amid the green silk. There were two golden-yellow tresses on her head; each one was braided of four plaits, with a bead at the end of each plait. The colour of her hair seemed to them like the flower of the water-flag in summer, or like red gold that has been polished.

She was loosening her hair to wash it, and her arms were out through the opening at the neck of her dress. Her wrists were as white as the snow of a single night, and they were soft and straight; and her clear and lovely cheeks were as red as the fox-glove of the moor. Her eyebrows were as black as a beetle's wing; her teeth were like a shower of pearls in her head; her eyes were as blue as the bugloss;[1] her lips were as red as vermilion; her shoulders were high and smooth and soft and white; her fingers were pure white and long; her arms were long; her slender long yielding smooth side, soft as wool, was as white as the foam of the wave. Her thighs were warm and glossy, sleek and white. Round and small, firm and white, were her knees. Her shins were short and white and straight. Her heels were fine and straight and lovely from behind. If a ruler were laid against her feet, it would be hard to find any fault in them, unless it should make the flesh or skin swell out on them. The bright blush of the moon was in her noble face; the lifting of pride in her smooth brows; the ray of love in both her royal eyes; a dimple of sport in both her cheeks, in which there came and went flushes of fast purple as red

1. Viper's bugloss or blueweed, a plant whose flowers turn from a bright rose colour to brilliant blue.

as the blood of a calf, and others of the bright whiteness of snow. A gentle womanly dignity in her voice; a steady stately walk, a queenly pace. She was the fairest and loveliest and most perfect of the women of the world that the eyes of men had ever seen; they thought she must be of the fairies ....

from: SERGLIGE CON CULAINN (The Wasting Sickness of Cú Chulainn)

[The tale of 'The Wasting Sickness of Cú Chulainn' (*Serglige Con Culainn*) was originally written about the eighth century. In it, Cú Chulainn is invited to the Otherworld, where he defeats the enemies of Labraid, one of the Otherworld kings. In the section quoted below, he spends a month with Fand, wife of the sea-god Manannán mac Lir, who has fallen in love with him, before returning to Ireland. But before leaving, he makes a tryst to meet Fand a year from then. His wife Emer and fifty of her women friends come at that time armed with knives to kill Fand. The ensuing exchanges between Fand and Emer are marked by a combination of jealousy, sympathy and sad resignation, and in the end Fand returns to her husband Manannán, while Cú Chulainn remains with Emer.

This is the story on which Yeats based *The Only Jealousy of Emer*. The present translation by Myles Dillon, comes from *Scottish Gaelic Studies* VII (1953).]

Cú Chulainn spent the night then with the girl; and he stayed with her for a month. And after a month he bade her farewell, and she said to him: 'Wherever thou tellest me to go to meet thee I shall go.' And then they made a tryst at Ibar Cind Tráchta. He told that to Emer. Knives were made by her to kill the girl. She came with fifty maidens to the tryst. Cú Chulainn and Lóeg were there, playing chess; and they did not notice the women approaching. Then Fand perceived it, and she said to Lóeg: 'Look, Lóeg, at what I see!' 'What is that?' said Lóeg. Lóeg looked, and then the girl said this:

> 'Look behind thee, Lóeg! Fair clever women are listening to thee, with sharp grey knives in their hands and gold on their breasts. Thou shalt see a fine sight, like warriors storming over battle-chariots. It is clear that Emer, daughter of Forgall, has changed her form.'

> 'Do not fear!' said Cú Chulainn, 'and she will never reach thee. Come into the mighty car with the shining seat before me, for thy protection against many women in the four quarters of Ulster. For though Forgall's daughter, surrounded by her companions, threatens a mighty deed, perhaps she will not dare with me.'

Cú Chulainn said further:

> 'I avoid thee, woman, as every man avoids his yoke. I do not strike the hard spear in thy trembling hand, nor thy feeble slender knife, nor thy weak and feeble-hearted anger for it were a great pity to let loose my strength on account of the strength of a woman.'

'But say,' said Emer, 'what caused thee, Cú Chulainn, to dishonour me before the many women of the province and before the many women of Ireland, and before all honourable men? For it is under thy guard I came, and under the might of thy protection; and although the pride of mighty conflict puff thee up, perhaps thou shouldst not find it easy to leave me, lad, if thou shouldst try.'

'But say, Emer,' said Cú Chulainn, 'why shouldst thou not allow me a while of trysting? First as to this woman, she is pure and chaste and clever and fit for a king. Much gifted is this girl from the waves beyond wide seas, endowed with beauty and grace and nobility, with skill in embroidery and handicraft, with sense and wisdom and steadfastness, with many horses and herds of cattle. For there is nothing under heaven that her fellow-wife would wish that she would not do, if thou wouldst join in a bond. Emer,' said he, 'thou shalt not find a hero, handsome, wounding in conflict, triumphant, who is equal to me.'

'Perhaps,' said Emer, 'the woman thou followest is not better than I. However, all that is bright is beautiful, all that is new is pleasing, all that is lacking is delightful, all that is familiar is neglected, till all be known. Lad,' said she, 'thou hadst us once in dignity together, and we should be so again if thou didst desire it.' And she was sad. 'On my word,' said he, 'I desire thee, and I shall desire thee as long as thou livest!'

'Leave me then!' said Fand. 'It were more just to leave me,' said Emer. 'No,' said Fand, 'it is I who shall be abandoned, and it is I who was taken unawares just now.' And she began to be sad and very faint in spirit, for she was ashamed at being abandoned, and to go so soon back to her house. And the great love that she had given to Cú Chulainn troubled her. And thus she was lamenting, and she made this lay:

'I shall go on a journey, though I like our adventure best. Though a famous man should come to me, I would liefer stay.

I would liefer be here — I shall confess it to thee without grudge — than to go — though thou mayest wonder — to the sun-palace of Áed Abrat.

Emer, the man is thine; and mayest thou enjoy him, good woman! I must long for what my hand cannot yet reach.

Many men were wooing me, under the roof and in secret places: I made no tryst with them, for I was faithful.

Unhappy is one who gives love to another, unless it be cherished: it is better to be thrust aside, unless love is given for love.

Thou art come with fifty women, noble Emer of the yellow hair, to overwhelm Fand — it is not well done — and to kill her through suffering.

I have, so long as I live, three times fifty women, beautiful maids, together at my dwelling, who would not abandon me.'

Then that was revealed to Manannán, that Fand, the daughter of Áed Abrat, held unequal conflict against the women of Ulster; and that Cú Chulainn was leaving her. And Manannán came to the girl out of the east, and was before her, and none of them perceived that save Fand alone. And it was then that the girl was seized with regret and faintness of spirit, when she looked upon Manannán and she made a lay:

'See the son of the heroes of the sea from the plains of Éogan Inbir; Manannán, Lord of the world, once he was dear to me.

But today I would weep; my proud spirit does not love him. Love is vain: it vanishes quickly.

When the son of Ler and I were together in the sun-palace of Dún Inbir, we thought always that we should never be separated.

When noble Manannán took me I was a fitting spouse: he could not in his time win an extra game against me at chess.

When noble Manannán brought me home, I was a fitting spouse; I have a gold bracelet that he gave me as the price of my maidenhead.

I had, out over the heath, fifty maidens arrayed in many colours: I gave him fifty men beside the fifty maidens.

Four times fifty without error was the number of the household; a hundred prosperous healthy men, a hundred fair and healthy maidens.

I see coming hither over the sea — the dull-witted do not see him — the horseman of the white-haired sea: he does not use long ships.

None but a fairy sees thy coming hither by us; thy sense perceives each small company, though they be far away.

As for me, it was my desert; for women are foolish. He whom I loved exceedingly has brought me here into distress.

Farewell to thee, fair Cú! I go from thee proudly. I am impatient to be gone. All is well till the moment of parting!

Now it is time for me to go. There is one who finds it hard. It is a great distress, O Lóeg son of Riangabur.

I shall go with my own spouse, for he will not oppose me. Say not that I go secretly. Watch me, if you will.'

The girl set out then after Manannán, and Manannán welcomed her, and he said: 'Well, girl,' said he, 'will you wait upon Cú Chulainn now, or will you come with me?' 'Upon my word,' said she, 'there is one of you whom I would liefer follow than the other. But,' said she, 'I will go with you, and I will not wait upon Cú Chulainn, for he has abandoned me. And there is another reason, good man! Thou hast not a worthy queen already, but Cú Chulainn has.'

When Cú Chulainn saw the girl going away from him to Manannán, he said to Lóeg: 'How is that?' said he. 'Not difficult,' said Lóeg. 'Fand is going away with Manannán son of Ler, because she was not pleasing to thee.' Then Cú Chulainn made three high leaps and three leaps southward to Lúachair, and he was for a long time without drink or food, wandering through the mountains. And he used to sleep every night on Slige Midlúachra.

Emer went to Conchobor at Emain, and told him how Cú Chulainn was. Conchobor sent the poets and learned men and druids of Ulster to seek him so that they might seize him and bring him to Emain. But he tried to kill the learned men. They sang druid spells against him, so that his feet and his hands were bound, until his sense returned for a while. Then he asked them for a drink. The druids gave him a drink of forgetfulness. When he had taken the drink, he did not remember Fand, nor anything that he had done. And drinks of forgetfulness were given to Emer for her jealousy, for she was in no better case. And Manannán shook his cloak between Cú Chulainn and Fand so that they should never meet.

from: TOCHMARC ÉTAÍNE (The Wooing of Étaín)

[*Tochmarc Étaíne* (The Wooing of Étaín) was written probably in the ninth century. It is a trilogy of tales about the love of the god Midir for the beautiful Étaín. It tells how Étaín was transformed into a beautiful insect through the vindictive magic of Midir's first wife, Fuamnach, how she was driven abroad for a thousand years before being reborn in human form to become the wife of Eochaid Airem, king of Ireland, and how Midir finally won her back and carried her with him to the Otherworld. This is one section of the narrative.

The present translation is from Osborn Bergin and R. I. Best (eds), *Tochmarc Étaíne* (Dublin: Hodges Figgis for the Royal Academy, 1938).]

Eochaid Airem took the kingship of Ireland. The five Fifths of Ireland submitted to him, that is a king of each Fifth. These were their kings at that time: Conchobar son of Nesa and Mess Gegra and Tigernach Tébannach and Cú Ruí and Ailill son of Máta Murisc. Eochaid's strongholds were Dún Frémainn in Meath and Dún Frémainn in Tethba. Frémainn in Tethba was the one most dear to him of the strongholds of Ireland.

Eochaid, the year after he became king, commanded the men of Ireland to hold the Festival of Tara, in order to assess their tributes and taxes for five years. The men of Ireland made the same reply to Eochaid, that they would not convene the Festival of Tara for a king that had no queen: for Eochaid had no queen when he took the kingship. Thereupon Eochaid dispatched envoys to every province throughout Ireland to seek out for him the fairest woman in Ireland. For he said that none should be his wife save a woman that none of the men of Ireland had known before him. There was found for him at Inber Cíchmaine, Étaín daughter of Étar, and Eochaid wedded her then, for she was his match in beauty and form and lineage, in splendour and youth and fame.

The three sons of Find son of Findlug, the queen's sons, were Eochaid Feidlech and Eochaid Airem and Ailill Ánguba. Ailill Ánguba came to love Étaín at the Festival of Tara, after she had lain with Eochaid, for it was his wont to gaze at her continually, and such gazing is a token of love. His heart reproached Ailill for the deed that he had wrought, but it availed him in no wise. Desire was stronger than character. Ailill fell into a decline lest his honour should be stained, nor had he spoken of it to the woman herself.

When he expected death, Fachtna, Eochaid's physician, was brought to see him. The physician said to him, 'One of the two pains thou hast that kill man and that no physician can heal, the pain of love and the pain of jealousy.' Ailill did not confess to him, for he was ashamed. Then Ailill was left in Frémainn Tethba dying, and Eochaid went on a circuit of Ireland. And Étaín was left with Ailill that his last rites might be paid by her — that is, his grave dug, his lamentation made, his cattle slain.

Every day Étaín used to come to the house wherein Ailill lay sick to speak with him, and thus his sickness was alleviated, and as long as Étaín remained there he would be gazing at her. Étaín observed this, and pondered the matter. One day as they were together in her house, Étaín asked him what was the cause of his sickness. 'It is from love of thee,' said Ailill. 'Pity that thou hast been so long without telling it,' said she. 'Had we but known, thou shouldst have been healed a while ago.' 'Even this day shall I be whole again if thou be willing.' 'I am willing indeed,' said she.

Every day then she would come to bathe his head and to carve his meat and to pour water on his hands. After thrice nine days Ailill was healed. He said to Étaín: 'And when shall I have from thee what is still lacking to cure me?' 'Thou shall have it tomorrow,' said she; 'but not in the prince's dwelling shall he be put to shame. Come to me tomorrow on the hill above the court.'

Ailill watched throughout the night. But at the hour of his tryst he fell asleep, and did not wake until the third hour on the morrow. Étaín went to meet him, and saw a man awaiting her like unto Ailill in appearance, and he lamented his weakness due to his ailment. The speech that Ailill would have wished that is what he spoke. At the hour of tierce[1] Ailill awoke. He began to be sorrowful for a

1. Nine in the morning — the third hour of the canonical day when the office of the tierce was said.

long while when Étaín came into the house. 'Why art thou sad?' said she. 'That I should have sent thee to a tryst with me and was not there to meet thee. For sleep fell upon me, and I am only now arisen. It is manifest that I have not yet attained my cure.' 'That matters not,' said Étaín, 'one day follows another.' He watched that night with a huge fire in front of him and water by his side for bathing his eyes.

At the hour of her tryst Étaín comes to meet him and saw the same man like unto Ailill. Étaín returned home. Ailill fell to weeping. Three times Étaín came and Ailill did not keep his tryst. She found ever the same man. ''Tis not with thee that I have trysted,' said she. 'Who are thou that hast come to meet me? The man with whom I have made a tryst, 'tis not for sin or hurt that the tryst has been made with him, but that one fit to be king of Ireland might be saved from the sickness that has fallen upon him.' ''Twere more fitting for thee to come to me, for when thou wast Étaín Echraide, daughter of Ailill, 'tis I that was thy husband. I had paid thy huge brideprice in great plains and rivers of Ireland, and had left in place of thee thy weight of gold and silver.' 'Tell me,' said she, 'what is thy name?' 'No hard matter, Midir of Brí Léith,' said he. 'Tell me,' said she, 'what was it that parted us?' 'No hard matter, the sorcery of Fuamnach and the spells of Bresal Etarlám.' Midir said to Étaín, 'Wilt thou go with me?' 'Nay,' said she, 'I will not barter the king of Ireland for a man whose kindred or race I know not.' 'It was I,' said Midir, 'that put love for thee into Ailill's mind, so that his flesh and blood fell away from him. And it was I that took from him all carnal desire, so that thine honour might not suffer therein. But come to my land with me if Eochaid bids thee.' 'Willingly,' said Étaín.

Then she comes to her house. 'We are well met', said Ailill. 'Now am I healed, and yet thine honour has not suffered.' 'It is well thus,' said Étaín. After that Eochaid returned from his circuit, and rejoiced that his brother was alive, and Étaín received thanks for what she had done until he had come again.

FIANAIGHEACHT
(Membership of the Fianna)

[The Fianna was a fraternity of free-lancing warriors whose activities transcended tribal boundaries. By the tenth century, monastic redactors had begun to attach them to the legendary King Cormac mac Airt as his professional warband, but this did not seriously alter their traditional character of a roving mercenary brotherhood whose principal occupations were fighting and hunting. Their leader, Finn mac Cumaill, was originally probably a deity, and the normal habitat of the Fianna was the natural wilderness beyond the borders of organized society, which was also the indeterminate area between the secular and the supernatural worlds. This little text, here translated by Standish H. O'Grady (ed.), *Silva Gadelica ... Translations and Notes* (London: Williams and Norgate, 1892), p. 99f., details some of the qualities required of the aspiring member of the Fianna and the physical tests to which he was subjected.]

This is the enumeration and description of Finn's people: their strength was seven score and ten officers, each man of these having thrice nine warriors, every one bound (as was the way with Cuchullin in the time when he was there) to certain conditions of service, which were: that in satisfaction of their guarantee violated they must not accept material compensation; in the matter of valuables or of meat must not deny any; no single individual of them to fly before nine warriors.

Of such not a man was taken into the Fianna; nor admitted whether to the great Gathering of Usnach, to the Convention of Taillte, or to Tara's Feast; until both his paternal and his maternal correlatives, his peoples and kindreds, had given securities for them to the effect that, though at the present instant they were slain, yet should no claim be urged in lieu of them: and this in order that to none other but to themselves alone they should look to avenge them. On the other hand: in case it were they that inflicted great mischiefs upon others, reprisals not to be made upon their several people.

Of all these again not a man was taken until he were a prime poet versed in the twelve books of poesy. No man was taken till in the ground a large hole had been made (such as to reach the fold of his belt) and he put into it with his shield and a fore-arm's length of a hazel stick. Then must nine warriors, having nine spears, with a ten furrows' width betwixt them and him, assail him and in concert let fly at him. If past that guard of his he were hurt then, he was not received into Fianship.

Not a man of them was taken till his hair had been interwoven into braids on him and he started at a run through Ireland's woods; while they, seeking to wound him, followed in his wake, there having been between him and them but one forest bough by way of interval at first. Should he be overtaken, he was wounded and not received into the Fianna after. If his weapons had quivered in his hand, he was not taken. Should a branch in the wood have disturbed anything of his hair out of its braiding, neither was he taken. If he had cracked a dry stick under his foot as he ran he was not accepted. Unless that at his full speed he had both jumped a stick level with his brow, and stooped to pass under one even with his knee, he was not taken. Also, unless without slackening his pace he could with his nail extract a thorn from his foot, he was not taken into Fianship: but if he performed all this he was of Finn's people.

A good man verily was he that had those Fianna, for he was the seventh king ruling Ireland: that is to say there were five kings of the provinces, and the king of Ireland; he being himself the seventh, conjointly with the king of all Ireland.

from: AGALLAMH NA SEANÓRACH (The Converse of the Ancients)

[Towards the end of the twelfth century, an unknown author made a compilation of tales and poems about the Fianna, cast in the form of a capacious frame-story entitled *Agallamh na Seanórach* (The Converse of the Ancients); in this text, two survivors from the age of the Fiana, Cáilte and Oisín, recount for St Patrick and his companions some of the legends relating to the landmarks and the placenames of the Irish countryside. Of the two passages which follow, the first tells the tragic story of Cael and Créidhe and the second epitomizes the Fianna's predilection for the beauty and variety of the wilderness as against the material wealth and comfort of settled society. They are quoted here in the sonorous translation of Standish H. O'Grady, *Silva Gadelica ... Translation and Notes* (London: Williams and Norgate, 1892), pp. 118-22, 164f.]

Patrick said: 'good now, Caeilte, and wherefore was the name of *fionntulach* [i.e. 'white hill'] given to this eminence on which we stand?' 'I will tell you the truth of it,' answered Caeilte: 'it was hence that we, the three battalions of the Fianna marched to give battle at Ventry. Hither our spears had been brought to us, charmed withies[1] also for our spear-shafts. Finn surveyed the hill round about him, and said: "the hill is white; what better name then could it have than *fionntulach*?"'

'From this spot also it was that, as aforesaid, we marched to fight the battle of Ventry; and as we did so we saw approach us out of another quarter a young man of Finn's people: the valiant and hundred-slaying Cael, grandson of Nemhnann. "Whence art thou come, Cael?" asked Finn. "Out of the dewy palace to the northward." "What sought'st thou there?" "To have speech of Muirenn daughter of Derg, mine own nurse." "What was the motive of that?" "It was because of a fairy sweetheart and of a splendid match propounded to me in a dream: Créidhe, daughter of Cairbre surnamed 'Whiteskin,' king of Ciarraighe Luachra." Finn said: "knowest thou, Cael, that of all Ireland's women she is the arch-she-deceiver? few costly things there are but she has coaxed away to her own mansion and grand dwelling-place." Cael said: "and knowest thou what the condition also is which she requires of all that would woo her?" "I know it," Finn answered: "she will entertain none but him, whosoe'er he be, that of art or poetic skill shall have sufficient to make for her a bardic poem setting forth a full description of her goblets, her horns, her cups, her flagons and all other her fine vessels, together with that of her various vast palaces." "All which I have in readiness: given to me by Derg's daughter Muirenn, mine own nurse."

'Then for that time we renounced the battle, and over regions of hills, of rocks, of mounds, took our way until we came to loch Cuire in the west of Ireland. We reached the door of the *sídh*,[2] and with the shafts of our long and gold-socketted spears there performed the *dórd fiansa*.[3] Girls, yellow-haired, of marriageable age, shewed on the balconies of bowers; and Créidhe, accompanied by three fifties of women, issued forth to speak with us. Said the Fian-chief to her: "to elect and to woo thee we are come." The lady enquired who it might be that sought to court her. "Cael it is, the valiant, the hundred-slayer, grandson of Nemhnann, son of the king of Leinster in the east!" She said: "we have heard his report, albeit we never have seen him. But has he my poem for me?" Cael answered: "I have so," then rose and sang his poem. . . .

1. Flexible branches of willow, used for tying and binding.

2. fairy people.
3. A cry or chant practised by the Fianna.

'Then that couple were bedded, and there they, the Fianna, were for seven days: drinking and in all enjoyment, without lack whether of meat, of liquor, or of any good thing whatsoever, were it not that one other care oppressed Finn: the foreigners' presence at Ventry. Then the woman presented to each one of them individually a special and sufficient battle-dress, and we took leave of each other.

'"Let the woman come with us," Finn said, "that we may learn to which of us either good or ill shall befall in this present business." The woman brought with her vast numbers of cattle to supply their sick and wounded; and she it was that so long as the battle was a-fighting fed them all with lacteal produce, with new milk. In her house too it was that the invalids and sick of the Fianna lay. And even as in lavishing of jewels and of treasure the woman outdid the women of the Fianna, so also in valour and in skill at arms her husband in that battle outstripped the three battalions of the Fianna. Truly a calamity was that which on the last day of the battle was effected: the drowning of Cael namely; and other beings too there were, of the brute kind, which had a life of length equal to his [i.e. that perished at the same time]. He being drowned then, the outside swell washed him in. The women and the nobles of the Fianna came to seek him; by them he was raised and carried to the southern strand (to the southward of Ventry that is to say), so that *Trágh Chaeil* or "Cael's Strand" is that shore's name ever since, and *Fert Chaeil* or "Cael's Grave."

'The woman came and stretched her by his side; she raised a clamorous weeping and greatly wailed: "why should not I," she said, "die of grief for my mate, when even the restless wild creatures die there of sorrowing after him!" Then Créidhe said:

The haven roars,
Over the rushing race of Rinn dá Barc,
The drowning of the warrior of Loch dá Chonn,
That is what the wave impinging on the strand laments....

'Then the young woman stretched herself out by Cael's side and, for grief that he was gone, died. In the one grave they both were buried there; and I myself it was that raised the stone which is over the resting-place, and hence is called "the tomb of Cael and of Créidhe."'

'Success and benediction, Caeilte!' Patrick said: ''tis a good story thou hast told; and where is scribe Brogan?' 'Here am I.' 'By thee be written down all that Caeilte hath uttered.' And written down it was.

Then came Trenbrugaid son of Treon, a rich and powerful hospitaller to the king of Ireland, accompanied with three times fifty men of stature. Every man of them had on a deep blue mantle; beautiful shirts of pure white they wore too, and in their hands they had three times fifty fork-spears distributed. They salute the king of Ireland, and he answers them. 'King,' they said, 'we have a great banquet for thee: nine score vats of mead, and of clear fermented ale ten score, along with their sufficient proportion of diverse and varied meats.' Which provisions and liquor they had brought with them for the king. He enquired of Oisín: 'is it together with the gentles of Ireland that ye, like the rest, will repair to the house of drinking and of pleasure?' Oisín answered: 'be our share of meat and fluid given to us apart; for they of the present are not people of one generation nor of one time with us.' 'How many are ye?' asked the king. Oisín said: 'twice nine men; being nine to me, and to my comrade, to Caeilte, nine.' 'Twenty vats to you, with their sufficiency of meat,' said the king. 'Good now, King,' objected Caeilte: 'neither as regards meat nor in respect of liquor put us on the same footing; for where to me should be given ten vats, thirty vats it were right that Oisín should obtain.' Thus then they spent that night mirthfully and of good cheer, without shortcoming whether of meat or of drink.

On the morrow they all rose, and on a mound the king of Ireland's tent was spread over him: into which tent was admitted none but either chief or chief's heir-apparent; Patrick with his clergy being lodged in the tent's second half, whither in turn were suffered to enter none but bishop, priest, or the specially devoted to the King of Heaven and of Earth. Oisín sat before Patrick; Caeilte before the king of Ireland, who asked: 'which of you is the elder?' 'I am,' Caeilte answered: 'for when Oisín was born I had thirty years completed; for now seventeen years he has shared my bed, and out of my house it was that he got his first command of Fianna and a band of followers.'

Then the king questioned farther: 'what was the number of Ireland's kings by whom lands were granted to the Fianna?' Caeilte (for he knew it) made answer: 'it was a king that attained to rule Ireland, Feradach Fechtnach, and he had two sons:

Tuathal and Fiacha. Feradach died, and his two sons between them divided Ireland: her precious things, her various wealth and her treasures, her kine and cattle-herds, her forts and hill-strengths, to the one; to the other: her cliffs and her estuaries, her mast and her "sea-fruit," her salmon beautiful in their graduated hues, her hunting and her venery.' Dermot asked: 'where made they this partition?' 'At this hill upon which we sit now.' 'That partition was not an equitable one,' said Ireland's good men. Oisín asked: 'which of the portions is that which yourselves would have preferred to the other?' 'Her feasts, her dwelling-houses, and all the rest of her good things,' they said. 'The portion which they contemn,' said Caeilte, 'that is the very one which in our eyes had been the better part.'

CAILLECH BÉRRI
(The Old Woman of Beare)

[This remarkable poem was composed *c.* 800. The *Caillech Bérri* or Old Woman of Beare was one of the most celebrated and certainly the most enduring of the Irish epiphanies of the Celtic goddess of the land and of sovereignty, and she survived as a familiar figure in Gaelic folk tradition in Ireland and Scotland until practically our own day. As a goddess she passed repeatedly through the cycle of youth and age, and in the poem she is pictured as an old woman who, having outlived her friends and lovers, has now donned the nun's veil.

Text and translation are taken from David Greene and Frank O'Connor (eds), *A Golden Treasury of Irish Poetry A.D. 600 to 1200* (London: Macmillan, 1967), with several minor alterations by the present editor.]

Aithbe dam cen bés mora
  sentu fom-dera croan;
toirsi oca cia do-gneo
  sona do-tét a loan.

Is mé Caillech Bérri Buí,
no meilinn léini mbithnuí;
  in-diu táthum dom shéimi
  ná melainn cid aithléini.

It móini
cartar lib, nídat doíni;
  sinni, ind indbaid marsaimme
  batar doíni carsaimme.

Batar inmaini doíni
  ata maige 'ma-ríadam;
ba maith no mmeilmis leo
  ba bec no maitis íaram.

In-diu trá caín-timgarat
  ocus ní mór non aithet;
cíasu bec do-n-indagat
  is mór a mét no maithet.

Carpait lúaith
ocus eich no beirtis búaid,
  rom boí denus tuile díb —
  bennacht for ríg roda úaid.

Tocair mo chorp co n-áigthe
dochum adbae díráichne;
  tan bas mithig la Mac nDé
  do-té do brith a aithne.

Ot é cnámacha coela
  ó do-éctar mo láma —
ba inmain dán do-gnítis,
  bítis im ríga rána.

Ó do-éctar mo láma
  ot é cnámacha coela,
nídat fiu turcbáil, taccu,
  súas tarsna maccu coema.

It fáilti na ingena
  ó thic dóib co Beltaine;
is deithbiriu damsa brón:
  sech am tróg, am sentainne.

Ní feraim coirm maith milis,
  ní marbtar muilt dom banais;
is bec is líath mo thrilis,
  ní líach drochcaille tarais.

Ní olc liumm
cia beith caille finn form chiunn;
  boí mór meither cech datha
  form chiunn oc ól daglatha.

Ním-gaib format fri nach sen
inge na-mmá fri Femen;
  messe, rom miult forbuid sin,
  buide beus barr Femin.

Lie na Ríg i Femun,
Caithir Rónáin i mBregun,
cían ó ros-síachtar sína;
a lleicne nít senchrína.

Is labar tonn mora máir
ros gab in gaim cumgabáil;
fer maith, macc moga, in-diu
ní frescim do chéilidiu.

Is mó láu
nád muir n-oíted imma-ráu;
testa már mblíadne dom chruth
dáig fo-rroimled mo chétluth.

Is mó dé
damsa in-diu cen buith té;
gaibthi m'étach cid fri gréin
do-fil aes dom aithgin féin.

Sam oíted i rrabamur
do-miult cona fhagamur;
gaim aís báides cech nduine
dom-ánaic a fhochmuine.

Ro miult m'oítid ar thuus;
is buide lemm ron gleus,
cid bec no léim dar duae
nípa nuae in bratt beus.

Is álainn in bratt úaini
ro scar mo Rí tar drummain;
is saer in Fer nod lúaidi,
do-rat loí fair íar lummain.

Am minecán, mon-úar dam,
cach derc caín is erchraide,
iar feis fri caindlea sorchai
bíthum dorchae derthaige.

Rom boí denus la ríga
oc ól meda ocus fhína;
in-diu ibim medguisce
eter sentainni crína.

Rop ed mo choirm cóidin meidg
ropo toil Dé cecham-theirb;
oc do guidisiu, a Dé bí,
do-rata cró clí fri feirg.

Ad-cíu form bratt brothrach n-aís;
ro gab mo chíall mo thogaís;
líath a finn ásas trim thoinn
is samlaid crotball senchroinn.

Rucad úaimse mo shúil des
dia reic ar thír mbithdíles;
ocus rucad int shúil chlé
do fhormach a fhoirdílse.

Tonn tuili
ocus ind í aithbi áin;
a ndo-beir tonn tuili dait
beirid tonn aithbi as do láim.

Tonn tuili
ocus ind aile aithbi,
dom-áncatarsa uili
conda éolach a n-aithgni.

Tonn tuili
nícon toracht mo chuili;
cid mór mo dám fo-déine
fo-cress lám forru uili.

Ma ro fiad Macc Maire
co mbeth fo chlí mo chuile,
ceni dernsa gart cenae
ní érburt 'nacc' fri duine.

Tróg n-uile —
doíriu dúilib in duine —
nád ndéccas a n-aithbe-se
feib dorr-éccas a tuile.

Céinmair insi mora máir,
dosn-ic tuile íarna tráig;
os mé, ní frescu dom-í
tuile tar ési n-aithbi.

TRANSLATION

Ebb to me, unlike the sea's; old age makes me yellow. Though I may grieve at it, happily does its tide return.

I am the Nun of Béarra Baoi. I used to wear a shift that was always new. Today I have become so thin that I would not wear out even an old shift.

It is riches you love, not people; when we were alive, it was people we loved.

Dear were the people whose plains we ride about;

well did we fare among them and they made little boast of it thereafter.

Today they ask nicely, and it is not much they will pay back; although they give little, they let us off a lot.

Swift chariots and horses that won the prize, once I had plenty of them — God rest the king who gave them.

My body fearfully seeks its way to the house of judgement; when the Son of God thinks it time, let Him come to take his loans.

Bony and thin are my hands; dear was the trade they practised, they would be around splendid kings.

Bony and thin are my hands; I swear they are not worth raising above pretty boys.

The girls are joyous when May approaches. Sorrow is more fitting for me; I am not only sad, but an old woman.

I pour out no good sweet ale, no wethers[1] are killed for my wedding; my hair is grey and scanty, it is no loss to have a miserable veil over it.

I do not care if there is a white veil on my head; I had coverings of every colour on my head when I drank good ale.

I do not envy anything old except Femen; while I have gone through old age Femen's crown is still yellow.

The King's Stone in Femen, Rónán's fort in Bregon, storms have long since reached them, but their cheeks are not old and withered.

The wave of the great sea is noisy, winter has stirred it up; I do not expect nobleman or slave's son to visit me today.

It is many a day since I sailed on the sea of youth; many years of my beauty have departed because wantonness has spent itself.

It is many a day since I have been warm; I have to take my shawl even in sunlight, for old age sets on one like me.

Youth's summer that I knew I have spent with its autumn, wintry age that smothers everyone has begun to approach me.

I wasted my youth to begin with, and I am glad I decided it thus; even if I had not been venturesome, the cloak would now be new no longer.

Beautiful is the distant cloak which the King has thrown over the hillside; the fuller[2] who has covered its bareness is a craftsman.

1. young rams.
2. Someone who cleanses and thickens cloth.

God help me! I am a poor wretch; each bright eye has decayed. After feasting by bright candles, I am in the darkness of a wooden church.

I have had my time with kings, drinking mead and wine; today I drink whey and water among withered old women.

Let my ale-feast be a cup of whey, let all that vexes me be counted God's will. Praying to you, O God, may my body's blood turn from anger.

I see on myself the shaggy cloak of age — no, I am wrong: grey is the hair that grows through my skin, like the lichen on an old tree.

My right eye has been taken away, alienated for my forfeited estate, and the left eye has been taken to complete its bankruptcy.

The flood wave, and the swift ebb; what the flood brings to you the ebb carries out of your hand.

The flood wave, and the following ebb; both have come to me, so that I am well acquainted with them.

The flood wave has not reached my pantry; though my own visitors be many, a hand has been laid on them all.

Well might the Son of Mary spend the night and be under the roof-tree of my pantry; though I am unable to offer any other hospitality, I have never said 'No' to anybody.

God help anybody — man is the most miserable of creatures — whose ebb was not seen as his flood was seen.

Happy is the island of the great sea, for the flood comes to it after the ebb; as for me, I expect no flood after ebb to come to me.

SEASONAL POEMS

['May-time' has been dated to the seventh century, 'Summer has come' to the ninth, and 'Winter' to the ninth or tenth.

'May-time' and 'Summer has come' are taken from James Carney's edition and translation in *Ériu* 22 (1971), 41-47, and 'Winter' is given in the editor's translation.]

May-time

1. Cétamon
 cáin rée,
 rosaír and
  cucht crann;
 canait luin
 laíd láin
 díambi laí
  gaí gann.

2. Gairid caí
 chrúaid den:
 'Is fo-chen
  sam saír';
 suidigthir
 síne serb
 imme-cherb
  caill craíb.

3. Cerbaid sam
súaill sruth,
saigid graig
lúath linn;
lethaid folt
fota fraích,
for-beir canach
fann finn.

4. Berait beich
(becc a nert)
bert bond,
bochtai bláith;
berid búar
slaibre slíab,
feraid seng
saidbir sáith.

5. Seinim crot
caille céol
con-greinn séol
síd slán;
sétair denn
do cach dinn,
dé do loch
linn lán.

6. Labraid tragna,
trén bard,
canaid ess
n-ard n-úar;
fáilte dó
ó linn té,
tánic lúach
fria lúad

7. Léig lath,
fath fég,
fér tar caín
caí crúaid;
cuirithir
íasc brecc bedc,
is balc gedc,
láith lúaith.

8. Losaid fér,
for-beir óg,
má bód
mBreg mbras;
cain cach caille
caindlech clár,
cain cach mag
már mas.

9. Mell dag rée,
ru-an gáith
garb gam;
gel cach ros,
ruirthech síd,
subach sam.

10. Greit mer fort
imrimm ech
imma-sernar
sreth slúag;
ro-sáerad crann
gel is-tír
co ní di ór
eilestair úad.

11. Ecal fer
fann fet,
il fo-cain
ard ucht;
uisse ús menn
imma-chain:
'Cétamon cain
cíuin cucht.'

TRANSLATION

Lovely season of May! Most noble then is the colour of trees; blackbirds sing a full lay, when the shaft of day is slender.

The vigorous harsh cuckoo calls: 'Welcome to noble Summer'; subdued is the bitter weather that caused the branching wood to dwindle.

Summer causes the tiny stream to dwindle; the speedy horses seek a pool; the long tresses of heather spread out; delicate white bog-cotton flourishes.

Bees of little strength carry a foot-load — flowers were reaped; the mountain-pasture takes the cattle; the ant fetches a rich sufficiency.

The music of the woodland is like the playing of harps; the melody brings perfect peace; a haze rises from every hill-fortress, a mist from the full-pooled lake.

The corncrake utters — powerful bard! The cool high waterfall sings; there is welcome to him (Summer) from the warm pool; reward has come for their praise.

The marsh is beautiful, see the covering: there is grass growing across a fine hard path; the speckled fish jumps, stout is the fly — swift warriors.

Grass abounds, fullness flourishes, Brega is still more excellent; beautiful the luminous expanse of every woodland, lovely every great beautiful plain.

Fine time of delights; the rough wind of winter has ceased; every wood is bright, peace abounds, summer is full of joy.

A wild ardour comes on you for horse-racing where a great crowd is stretched out in a line; the white tree has been ennobled in the land, receiving from him (Summer) something of the gold of flag-iris.

The timid lad of weak whistles (now) sings a paean of triumph with puffed-out breast; fitting are the tidings that he announces clearly: 'Beautiful and quiet is the colour of May'.

Summer has come

1. Tánic sam
slán sóer
díambi clóen
caill chíar
(lingid ag
seng snéid)
díambi réid
rón rían.

2. Canaid cuí
céol mbinn mbláith
díambi súan
sáim séim;
lengait éoin
cíuin crúaich
ocus daim
lúaith léith.

3. Foss n-oss
ro-gab tess,
gáir dess
cass cúan;
tibid trácht,
find fonn
díambi lond
ler lúath.

4. Fúam ngáeth
baeth barr
dairi duib
druin daill;
rethid graig
máel múad
díambi dín
Cúan Caill.

5. Maidid glass
for cach luss,
bilech doss
dairi glaiss;
tánic sam,
ro-fáith gaim,
gonit coin
cuilinn chaiss.

6. Canaid lon
dron dord
díambi orbb
caille cerbb;
súanaid ler
lonn líac,
fo-ling íach
brec bedc.

7. Tibid grían
dar cach tír;
dedlai lím,
fris-sil snom;
gáirit coin,
dáilit daim,
for-berat brain,
tánic sam.

TRANSLATION

Noble and perfect summer has come, that makes the dark wood bend (the swift slender stag leaps), that makes smooth the path of seals.

The cuckoo sings a sweet smooth song that brings easy gentle sleep; the birds leap to the quiet hill, and the swift grey stags make a leap.

Heat has seized the shelter of the deer; there is a fine harmonious cry of dog-packs. The strand smiles, fair land that is wont to anger the swift sea.

There is a subdued rustle in the wild top of the stout dark black oakgrove; sleek well-bred herds of horses run, that are wont to find shelter in Caill Cúan.

Every plant bursts out in green; the bush in the green oakwood is full of leaves; summer has come, winter has gone; twisted hollies wound the hound.

The blackbird, inheritor of the thorny wood, sings a bold song; the fierce cliffed sea sleeps, the speckled salmon leaps.

The sun smiles over every land; the edge will cleave, it will strike the bark. Hounds cry out, stags gather, ravens increase, summer has come.

Winter

1. Scél lem dúib:
doraid dam;
snigid gaim;
ro fáith sam;

2. Gáeth ard úar;
ísel grían;
gair a rrith;
ruirthech rían;

3. Rorúad rath;
ro cleth cruth;
ro gab gnáth
giugrann guth.

4. Ro gab úacht
etti én;
aigre ré;
é mo scél.

I have tidings for you: the stag bells,
Winter pours, summer has gone.

The wind is high and cold, the sun low;
Its course is short, the sea runs high.

The bracken has reddened, its shape hidden;
The wild goose has raised his familiar cry.

Cold has seized the wings of birds;
It is the season of ice — these are my tidings.

THE FLIGHTINESS OF THOUGHT

[Approximately tenth century. From: Gerard Murphy's edition *Early Irish Lyrics: Eighth to Twelfth Century* (Oxford: Clarendon Press, 1956), pp. 38-43.]

Is mebul dom imrádud
a méit élas úaimm:
ad-águr a imgábud
i lló brátha búain.

Tresna salmu sétaigid
for conair nád cóir:
reithid, búaidrid, bétaigid
fíad roscaib Dé móir,

Tre airechtu athlama,
tre buidne ban mbóeth,
tre choillte, tre chathracha —
is lúaithiu ná in góeth,

Tresna séta sochraide
 ind ala fecht dó,
tre dimbithe dochraide
 fecht aile (ní gó).

Œn ethar 'na chlóenchéimmim
 cingid tar cech ler;
lúath linges 'na óenléimmim
 ó thalmain co nem.

Reithid (ní rith rogaíse)
 i n-ocus, i céin;
íar réimmennaib robaíse
 taidlid día thig féin.

Œ thríalltar a chuimrechsom
 nó geimel 'na chois,
ní cunnail, ní cuimnechsom
 co ngabad feidm fois.

Fóebur ná fúaimm flescbuille
 ní tráethat co tailc;
sleimnithir eirr n-escuinge
 oc dul as mo glaicc.

Glas, nó charcar chromdaingen,
 nó chuimrech for bith,
dún, nó ler, nó lomdaingen
 nín-astat día rith.

Táet, a Chríst choím chertgenmnaid
 díanid réil cech rosc,
rath in Spirta sechtdelbaig
 día choimét, día chosc.

Follamnaig mo chridesea,
 a Dé dúilig déin,
corop tú mo dilesea,
 co ndernar do réir.

Rís, a Chríst, do chétchummaid:
 ro bem imma-llé;
níta anbsaid éccunnail,
 ní inonn is mé.

TRANSLATION

Shame to my thoughts how they stray from me! I dread great danger from it on the day of lasting doom.

During the psalms they wander on a path that is not right: they run, they disturb, they misbehave before the eyes of great God,

Through eager assemblies, through companies of foolish women, through woods, through cities — swifter than the wind,

Now along pleasant paths, again (no lie) through wild, untamed places.

Without a ferry in their perverse path they go over every sea; swiftly they leap in one bound from earth to Heaven.

They run (not a course of great wisdom) near, afar; after roamings of great folly they visit their own home.

Though one should set about binding them or putting shackles on their feet, they lack constancy and recollection for undertaking the task of remaining still.

Neither edged weapon nor the sound of whip-blows keeps them down firmly; they are as slippery as an eel's tail gliding out of my grasp.

Neither lock, nor firm vaulted dungeon, nor any bond at all, stronghold, nor sea, nor bleak fastness restrains them from their course.

O beloved truly chaste Christ to whom every eye is clear, may the grace of the sevenfold Spirit come to keep and check them.

Rule this heart of mine, O zealous God of creation, that thou mayst be my love, that I may do thy will.

May I attain perfect companionship with thee, O Christ: may we be together; thou art neither fickle nor inconstant — not as I am.

THE DEAD LOVER

[This remarkable poem dates from *c.* 900. As is told in the prose introduction to it, Fothad Canainne, the leader of a Connacht war-band, made a tryst with the beautiful wife of Ailill Flann Bec, himself a leader of a Munster war-band. Ailill followed his wife with his fighters and, in the ensuing battle, Fothad was slain and beheaded. His severed head — a familiar motif, this, in Irish and Celtic literature — then spoke the poem to Ailill's wife, who had carried his head to its burial place. A number of quatrains describing the treasures that he had promised her are omitted here.

Text and translation are taken from David Greene and Frank O'Connor (eds), *A Golden Treasury of Irish Poetry A.D. 600 to 1200* (London: Macmillan, 1967).]

A ben, nacham shaig-i-lle
ní fritt atá mo menme;
atá mo menme co lléic
isind immairiuc oc Féic.

Atá mo chorpán cruach
i taíb Leitrech dá mBruach;
atá mo chenn cen nigi
eter fíana for garbshligi.

Dochtae do neuch dáiles dáil
fácbáil dála éca fri láim;
in dáil dálta co Clárach
tuarnecht im robánad.

Ro delbad dún, trúag ar fecht,
for Féic do-roirned ar lecht;
immon roírad, bág mo líuin,
tothaim la ócu ainíuil.

Ní mé m'oenur i mmúr thal
do-chúaid fordul i ndáil ban;
ní ar aithbiur cid dit ágh,
is duaig ar ndedendál.

Di chéin do-roacht do dáil,
baí gráin for mo choicni máir;
ma ro-fesmais bid am-ne
ba assa ní tairiste.

Ba ó Fhothad ind othair
beirtis co úair do-rochair;
cid am-ne, níth fri fochaid,
ní cen folad guin Fhothaid.

Ním rumartsa m'amusrad,
fían gormainech goburglas;
a techt i n-úire adbai
dirsan dond éochaill amrai.

Matis ésium batis bí
do-festais a tigernai,
mainbed tairbad báis dímair
lemm nípad fían cen dígail.

Co a tiugdáil batar lúaith
ad-cosnaitis bidbad búaid,
fo-cantais rainn, trom a ngáir,
cinsit di chlainn ruirech ráin.

Ba é fíanlach seng subach
cosin aimsir i rrubad;
arus-foet caill duileglas
ropo coicne uilemnas. . . .

Ná tuinite aidche úath
i lleirg eter lechta cúan;
ní fíu cobra fri fer marb;
fot-ruim dot daim, beir latt m'fhadb.

Atot-fuigéra cech doín
nípu étach nach díchoím,
fúan corcra ocus léine gel,
criss arcait, ní aicde mer.

Mo shleg coícrind, gae co fí,
diamtar menci cétguini,
cóicriuth co mbúaile umae
tarsna toingdis derblugae. . . .

Is dúal deitsi, sét nach lac,
m'fhidchell, ata-rella lat,
bruinnid fuil shoer for a bil,
ní cían di shunn indas-fil.

Is mór colnae cúan rinnech
san chan imma deirginnech,
dosn-eim dos dlúith dairbri rúaid
i taíb ind fhirt aniar-túaid.

Oca cuindchid duit co lléir
ní rop mór no labrathar;
ní tarla celtair talman
tar dúil badid n-amrathar. . . .

Ataat immunn san chan
mór fodb asa forderg bal;
dremun inathor dímar
nodus nig an Morrígan.

Don-árlaid, dobail oígi,
is sí cotan-assoídi;
is mór di fhodbaib niges
dremun in caisgen tibes.

Ro lá a moing tar a ais;
cride im aithrecht noda ais;
cid gar di shunn úann i mbé
ná fubthad úaman do gné.

Mad co se dam fri gábud
ní gaibthi frimm do shnádud;
a banscál, not gaib for dol,
caín bláth fa ro scarsammor!

Scarfat fri doennacht don mud
'sin matain íar m'ócánrud;
eirgg dot daim, sonn ní ainfe,
do-fil deäd na haidche.

Immus-ráidfe nech nach ré
reicni Fothaid Chanainne;
mo chobra fritt ní hinglé
ma imráite mo thimne.

In dul bid coimtig mo lecht
ro sáitter m'ail, menn in fert,
ní escor saítha ad-chí
dot fhochaid íar t'inmuini.

Scarfaid frit céin mo chorp toll
m'anam do phianad la Donn;
serc betho cé is mire
binge adrad Ríg nime.

Is é in lon teimen tibes
imchomarc cáich bes ires;
síabra mo chobra, mo gné,
a ben, nacham aicille.

TRANSLATION

Do not come near to me, woman, my mind is not on you; my mind is still on the battle at Féic.

My bloody body lies beside Leitir Dá mBruach, my unwashed head is among warriors in rude slaughter.

It is arrogance for anybody to make a tryst that sets aside the tryst with death; the tryst that was made for Clara, I have come to it in deathly pallor.

Sad was my journey; it was ordained for me; my grave had been marked out on Féic. My grievous fight, it was destined that I should fall by stranger warriors.

I am not the first who went astray in the blaze of desire, trysting with women. I am not reproaching you, though you caused it — gloomy is our parting tryst.

I came from far away to meet you; it shocked my noble company. If I had known it would have been this way, it would have been easy not to persist.

Until the hour he fell it was as sick men that people were carried away from Fothad; even so, sad as the fight was, Fothad's death will not be without profit.

My war-band of noble-faced, grey-horsed warriors have not betrayed me; sad for the marvellous yew-forest to go into the house of clay!

If they were alive, their lords would be avenged; but for the hindrance of almighty death, there would be no warrior of them that I did not avenge.

They were swift to their final tryst, they strove to overcome their enemies; they sang a song — deep was their voice; they came of noble princely stock.

They were a swift joyous company to the moment they were killed; the green-leafed forest has received them; they were a fierce group....

Do not await the horror of the night on the battle-field among the graves of the hosts. It is not worth while to speak to a dead man; go home and take my spoils.

Everyone will tell you this was not the dress of a tasteless man: a purple cloak and white tunic, a silver belt, no commonplace work of art.

My five-pointed spear, a poisonous dart that so often struck the first blow; a five-circled shield with a bronze boss on which true oaths were sworn....

Yours is my chess-board — no small treasure; take it with you. Noble blood flows over its edge; it is not far away.

Many a body of the hosts of spearmen lies here and there about its frame; a tufted bush of red oak hides it beside the mound to the north-west.

Do not speak much as you search for it; earth never hid an object so marvellous....

Here and there around us are many spoils of bloody appearance; frightful are the great guts the Morrigu is washing.

She has descended on us, a gloomy guest; it is she who hurls us into struggle. Many are the spoils she washes, dreadful the twisted laugh she laughs.

She has thrown her mane over her back, the heart in my former shape hates her; though she is not far from us do not let fear assail you.

Since I am in danger do not ask protection from me. Go on your way, woman; let us part while parting is fair.

Now I shall leave all human things in the morning light after my soldiers. Go home, do not wait here, the end of night is at hand.

Someone will remember my song at all times;

my speech with you will not be obscure if you remember my testimony.

So that people will come to my grave, let my stone be dug in, a conspicuous monument; your labour after your love will be no waste of time for you.

My riddled body will part from you, my soul will be tortured by the death god. Earthly love is madness but for adoration of the King of Heaven.

It is the dark blackbird that laughs a greeting to all Christians. My speech, my face are ghostly. Woman, do not speak to me.

ON THE CRUCIFIXION

[These quatrains on the crucifixion are taken from a long sequence to the Virgin Mary and her son, composed in a simple, uncluttered style by a monastic poet named Blathmac son of Cú Brettan about 750-770.

The quatrains appear in James Carney's edition of *The Poems of Blathmac Son of Cú Brettan* (Dublin: Educational Company of Ireland, for the Irish Texts Society, 1964).]

Ó fu-rócbath a chride,
mac ríg na secht noebnime,
do-rórtad fin fu roenu,
fuil Críst triä geltoebu. . . .

Ar-rócaib guth cain cathach
oc atuch a noebathar:
'Cair rom-léicis, a Dé bí,
dom daíri, dom dochraiti?'

To-celt grian a soillsi sain,
ro-coíni a flaithemain,
luid diantemel tar nem nglas,
búiristir rian trethanbras.

Ba dorchae uile in bith,
talam fu durbae rochrith;
oc Ísu uasail aidid
ro-memdatar márailich.

Hierosalem taithsloic dian
marbu a adnacul érchian;
isind uair hi cés Críst guin
dlochtae fial in Tempuil.

To-fích sruth folo — ró tinn! —
combu derg snob cech oenchruinn;
buí crú for bruinnib betho
i mbarraib cech prímfedo.

Ba deithbir do dúilib Dé
muir mas, nem nglas, talam cé
ce imro-chloítis a ngné
oc coíniud a ngalgaite.

Corp Críst fri rinde rubae
fo-rroelangair cruadgubae,
cia no coíntis cruth bath má
in fer trisa torsata.

Robo ainmnetach in rí
oc crochad a oengeindi,
ol ro-coínset cen dúiri
dia festais a degdúili.

Nád torchair nem ina chenn,
nachad loisc in teine tenn,
nachad báid rian romro lir,
níbtis étroma a n-aithbir.

Nachad sloic in talam trom
cuain truaig do-géni mórglonn,
nambath luaithred popul mbras
im Annae, im Chaïphas.

TRANSLATION

The King of the seven holy heavens, when his heart was pierced, wine was spilled upon the pathways, the blood of Christ flowing through his gleaming sides. . . .

He raises a beautiful protesting voice beseeching his holy Father: 'Why have you abandoned me, living God, to servitude and distress?'

The sun hid its own light; it mourned its lord; a sudden darkness went over the blue heavens, the wild and furious sea roared.

The whole world was dark; the land lay under gloomy trembling; at the death of noble Jesus great rocks burst asunder.

Jerusalem swiftly released the dead from ancient burial; when Christ suffered slaying the veil of the Temple was rent.

A stream of blood gushed forth (severe excess!) so that the bark of every tree was red; there was blood on the breasts of the world, in the tree-tops of every great forest.

It would have been fitting for God's elements, the beautiful sea, the blue heaven, the present earth, that they should change their aspect when keening their hero.

The body of Christ pierced by points warranted severe lamentation; it would be fitting that they should keen in a stronger manner the man by whom they were created.

The King was patient at the crucifixion of his only-begotten, for had his good elements known, they would have keened sweetly.

That the sky did not fall on them, that great fire did not burn them, that the great ocean did not drown them! Their reproaches (i.e. that of the elements) would not have been light.

That the heavy earth did not swallow them, the miserable pack who committed a great crime! That the hasty people led by Annas and Caiphas should not have been turned to ashes!

JESUS AND THE SPARROWS

[This is one of several miraculous incidents from the childhood of Christ that are told with refreshing innocence in the Irish translation of the Apocryphal Gospel of St Thomas, which its editor, James Carney, assigns to around 700 (*Ériu* 18 (1958), 10-13).]

Imbu macán cóic bliadnae
  Ísu mac Dé bí
sénais dá huiscén deäc,
  arros-fí de chrí.

Delbais dá énán deäc,
  passir a n-anmann;
diä Sabait dos-géni
  de chrí cen madmann.

Con-saíd alaile Iudea
  Ísu mac Dé máir;
dochum a aiti Ioseph
  dan-indnacht ar láim.

'Ergair do mac, a Ioseph,
  ní maith a ndo-gní;
dië Sabait dos-rigni,
  delba én de chrí.'

Con-ort Ísu a dí bais,
  a guthán ro-cloth;
fiad a súilib — rígdae rath —
  ind énán, fos-mboth.

Ro-clos guthán caín inmain
  for giun Ísu glain:
'Ar fessid cia-b dergéni
  airciub du for ndaim.'

Fásaig alaile co tuaith,
  ba hamrae a scél:
ro-closa for luämain
  garmann inna n-én.

TRANSLATION

When Jesus, son of the living God, was a small boy, five years of age, he blessed twelve small pools; he had fenced them in with clay.

He fashioned twelve small birds — *passeres*[1] they are called; on the Sabbath day he made them smoothly out of clay.

A certain Jew upbraided Jesus, son of the great God; he escorted him by the hand to his foster-father, Joseph.

'Reprove your son, Joseph, not good is what he does; on the Sabbath day he has made clay-images of birds.'

Jesus clapped his two hands, his little voice was heard; before their eyes — kingly the grace! — he scared the birds away.

A dear beautiful little voice was heard on the lips of pure Jesus: 'So that ye may know who has made you, go ye to your home.'

A certain man announced it to the people; wonderful was the news: the cries of the birds in flight were heard.

1. sparrows.

RANNS AND EPIGRAMS

[The following is a brief selection from the many short pieces, whether free-standing or fragments of longer poems, that are found throughout the literature. Because of their brevity, they are often difficult to date accurately; these examples cover the period from the eighth or ninth centuries to the eleventh.]

The Storm

Ron-bris, ron-bruí, ron-báid,
a Rí ríchid rindglaine,
ron-geilt in gáeth feib geiles
némáed forderg fidnaige.

It has broken us, it has crushed us,
it has drowned us,
O King of the star-bright Heaven,
The wind has consumed us
As twigs are consumed by the glowing fire.

— see Kuno Meyer, *Bruchstücke der älteren Lyrik Irlands* (Berlin: Akademie der Wissenschaften, 1919), p. 67.

Pointless Pilgrimage

Teicht do Róim,
mór saído, becc torbai;
in rí chon-daigi hi foss,
mani-mbera latt, ní fogbai

To go to Rome,
Much labour, little profit;
The King you seek here,
Unless you bring him with you,
you will not find.

— see Whitley Stokes and John Strachan (eds), *Thesaurus Palaeohibernicus* (Cambridge: Cambridge University Press, 1901-03; reprinted Dublin, 1975), II, 296.

The Monk's Choice

Clocán bind
benar i n-aidchi gaíthe,
ba ferr limm dola ina dáil
indás i ndáil mná baíthe

The sweet little bell
That is rung on a windy night,
Rather would I tryst with it
Than tryst with a wanton woman.

— see Kuno Meyer, *A Primer of Irish Metrics* (Dublin: Hodges Figgis, 1909), p. 21.

The Light O' Love

Ní fetar
cía lasa fífea Etan
acht ro-fetar Etan bán
nícon fhífea a hoenarán

I do not know
Who Etan will sleep with,
But I do know that fair Etan
Will not sleep alone.

— see K. Meyer, *A Primer of Irish Metrics*, p. 17.

An Uncouth Patron

Ro-cúala
ní tabair eochu ar dúana;
do-beir aní as dúthaig dó:
bó

I have heard
He does not give horses for praise-poems;
He gives what is natural to him:
A cow.

— see K. Meyer, *Bruchstücke* . . . ., p. 32.

Flatulence

Atá ben istír,
Ní abraim a ainm
maidid essi a deilm
amal chloich a tailm

There's a woman in the land —
I won't mention her name —
And when she breaks wind,
It's like a stone from a sling.

— see K. Meyer, *Bruchstücke* . . . ., p. 34.

A Kiss

Cride hé,
daire cnó,
ócán é,
pócán dó

He's my heart,
My grove of nuts;
He's my lad,
And here's a kiss for him.

— see Whitley Stokes and Ernst Windisch (eds), *Irische Texte*, III, i (Leipzig: Hirzel, 1891), p. 100.

THE POET ON HIS DEAD WIFE

[Irish learned court poetry was conventional in its style and conservative and retrospective in its ideology. In the post-Norman period it was dominated by eulogies and elegies of patron-chiefs, but occasionally one finds poems inspired by personal circumstance, as in this piece by the early thirteenth-century poet, Muireadhach Albanach Ó Dálaigh, in which high technical skill and craftsmanship are combined with deep but restrained emotion.

The edition and translation are by Osborn Bergin, *Irish Bardic Poetry,* compiled and edited by David Greene and Fergus Kelly (Dublin: Institute for Advanced Studies, 1970), pp. 101-03.]

M'anam do sgar riomsa a-raoir,
calann ghlan dob ionnsa i n-uaigh;
rugadh bruinne maordha mín
is aonbhla lín uime uainn.

Do tógbhadh sgath aobhdha fhionn
a-mach ar an bhfaongha bhfann:
laogh mo chridhise do chrom,
craobh throm an tighise thall.

M'aonar a-nocht damhsa, a Dhé,
olc an saoghal camsa ad-chí;
dob álainn trom an taoibh naoi
do bhaoi sonn a-raoir, a Rí.

Truagh leam an leabasa thiar,
mo pheall seadasa dhá snámh;
tárramair corp seada saor
is folt claon, a leaba, id lár.

Do bhí duine go ndreich moill
ina luighe ar leith mo phill;
gan bharamhail acht bláth cuill
don sgáth duinn bhanamhail bhinn.

Maol Mheadha na malach ndonn
mo dhabhach mheadha a-raon rom;
mo chridhe an sgáth do sgar riom,
bláth mhionn arna car do chrom.

Táinig an chlí as ar gcuing,
agus dí ráinig mar roinn:
corp idir dá aisil inn
ar dtocht don fhinn mhaisigh mhoill.

Leath mo throigheadh, leath my thaobh,
a dreach mar an droighean bán,
níor dhísle neach dhí ná dhún,
leath mo shúl í, leath mo lámh.

Leath mo chuirp an choinneal naoi;
's guirt riom do roinneadh, a Rí;
agá labhra is meirtneach mé —
dob é ceirtleath m'anma í.

Mo chéadghrádh a dearc mhall mhór,
déadbhán agus cam a cliabh:
nochar bhean a colann caomh
ná a taobh ré fear romham riamh.

Fiche bliadhna inne ar-aon,
fá binne gach bliadhna ar nglór,
go rug éinleanabh déag dhún,
an ghéag úr mhéirleabhar mhór.

Gé tú, nocha n-oilim ann,
ó do thoirinn ar gcnú chorr;
ar sgaradh dár roghrádh rom,
falamh lom an domhnán donn.

Ón ló do sáidheadh cleath corr
im theach nochar ráidheadh rum —
ní thug aoighe d'ortha ann
dá barr naoidhe dhorcha dhunn.

A dhaoine, ná coisgidh damh;
faoidhe ré cloistin ní col;
táinig luinnchreach lom 'nar dteagh —
an bhruithneach gheal donn ar ndol.

Is é rug uan í 'na ghrúg,
Rí na sluagh is Rí na ród;
beag an cion do chúl na ngéag
a héag ó a fior go húr óg.

Ionmhain lámh bhog do bhí sonn,
a Rí na gclog is na gceall:
ach! an lámh nachar logh mionn,
crádh liom gan a cor fám cheann.

TRANSLATION

My soul parted from me last night; a pure body that was dear is in the grave; a gentle stately bosom has been taken from me with one linen shroud about it.

A white comely blossom has been plucked from the feeble bending stalk; my own heart's darling has drooped, the fruitful branch of yonder house.

I am alone tonight, O God; evil is this crooked world that Thou seest; lovely was the weight of the young body that was here last night, O King.

Sad for me (to behold) yonder couch, my long pallet ...; we have seen a tall noble form with waving tresses upon thee, O couch.

A woman of gentle countenance lay upon one side of my pallet; there was naught save the hazel-blossom like to the dark shadow, womanly and sweet-voiced.

Maol Mheadha of the dark brows, my mead-vessel beside me; my heart the shadow that has parted from me, the flower of jewels after being planted has drooped.

My body has passed from my control, and has fallen to her share; I am a body in two pieces since the lovely bright and gentle one is gone.

She was one of my two feet, one of my sides — her countenance like the white-thorn; none belonged to her more than to me, she was one of my eyes, one of my hands.

She was the half of my body, the fresh torch; harshly have I been treated, O King; I am faint as I tell it — she was the very half of my soul.

Her large gentle eye was my first love, her bosom was curved and white as ivory; her fair body belonged to no man before me.

Twenty years we spent together; sweeter was our converse every year; she bore to me eleven children, the tall fresh lithe-fingered branch.

Though I am alive, I am no more, since my smooth hazel-nut is fallen; since my dear love parted from me, the dark world is empty and bare.

From the day that a smooth post was fixed in my house it has not been told me — no guest laid a spell therein upon her youthful dark brown hair.

O men, check me not; the sound of weeping is not forbidden; bare and cruel ruin has come into my house — the bright brown glowing one is gone.

It is the King of Hosts and the King of Roads who has taken her away in His displeasure; little was the fault of the branching tresses that she should die and leave her husband while fresh and young.

Dear the soft hand that was here, O king of bells and churchyards; alas! the hand that never swore (false) oath, 'tis torment to me that it is not placed under my head.

THE SCHOLAR AND HIS CAT

[This refined little *jeu d'esprit* is found, together with several other Irish poems, in a ninth-century manuscript containing a commentary on Virgil, Latin hymns, Greek paradigms and other miscellaneous matter, conserved in the monastery of St Paul at Unterdrauberg in Carinthia. The cat's name, Pangur, is the early Welsh form of modern *pannwr*, 'a fuller', and it is likely our monastic scholar-poet had come by his companion while stopping in Wales en route for the Continent.

The translation is by the present editor.]

Messe ocus Pangur bán,
cechtar nathar fria saindán:
bíth a menma-sam fri seilgg,
mu menma céin im saincheirdd.

Caraim-se fos, ferr cach clú,
oc mu lebrán, léir ingnu;
ní foirmtech frimm Pangur bán:
caraid cesin a maccdán.

Ó ru biam, scél cen scís,
innar tegdais, ar n-óendís,
táithiunn, díchríchide clius,
ní fris-tarddam ar n-áthius.

Gnáth, húaraib, ar gressaib gal
glenaid luch inna lín-sam;
os mé, du-fuit im lín chéin
dliged ndoraid cu ndronchéill.

Fúachaid-sem fri frega fál
a rosc, a nglése comlán;
fúachimm chéin fri fégi fis
mu rosc réil, cesu imdis.

Fáelid-sem cu ndéne dul
hi nglen luch inna gérchrub;
hi tucu cheist ndoraid ndil
os mé chene am fáelid.

Cia beimmi amin nach ré
ní derban cách a chéle:
maith la cechtar nár a dán;
subaigthius a óenurán.

Hé fesin as choimsid dáu
in muid du-ngní cach óenláu;
du thabairt doraid du glé
for mu mud céin am messe.

TRANSLATION

Myself and White Pangur,
each pursues his own calling,
when I'm engaged on my craft,
he's intent on hunting.

Better to me than all fame
to be with my book in quiet concentration;
White Pangur does not envy me,
he loves his own preoccupation.

It is never tiresome
when we're together in our dwelling;
we both have something — an endless sport —
on which to exercise our quickness.

Sometimes by dint of feats of valour
a mouse is trapped within his net,
while into my net there drops
some knotty rule of abstruse meaning.

He points his clear and flawless eye
against the rampart of a wall;
I point mine, still clear though feeble,
against the subtleties of science.

He exults with flurry of movement
when in his sharp claw a mouse adheres;
I too rejoice when I have mastered
some problem difficult but dearly cherished.

Though we are thus at all times,
neither hinders the other;
each of us likes his own art
and has his pleasure to himself.

While he is master of the work
that he performs every day,
I am equal to my task
of bringing obscurity to light.

from:
IMMRAM BRAIN
(The Voyage of Bran)

[*Immram Brain* (The Voyage of Bran) tells of an overseas voyage to the Otherworld by Bran, son of Febhal, and a group of companions. As reported in the brief prose introduction, a woman from the Otherworld visits Bran, and in the first of two lyric poems that make up the major part of the text, she seeks to entice him to follow her by describing the delights of her homeland. The text may belong to the eighth century. Kuno Meyer's translation, upon which this version is based, is almost a hundred years old, but it is reasonably accurate and its line-for-line prose catches some of the imaginative quality of the original. See Kuno Meyer and Alfred Nutt, *The Voyage of Bran son of Fébal to the Land of the Living* (London: David Nutt, 1897) I, p. 2ff.]

Cróib dind abaill a hEmain
dofed samail do gnáthaib,
gésci findarggait fora,
abrait glano co m-bláthaib.

Fil inis i n-eterchéin
immataitnet gabra réin,
rith find fris' tóibgel tondat,
cetheóir cossa foslongat.

Is lí súla, sreth íar mbúaid,
a mmag forclechtat int slúaig:
consna curach fri carpat
isin maig tess Findarggat.

Cossa findrune fóe,
taitni tré bithu gnǫ́e:
cáin tír tría bithu bátha,
forsnig inna hilblátha.

Fil and bile co mbláthaib
forsngairet eóin do thráthaib:
is tré cocetul is gnáth
congairet uili cech tráth.

Taitnet líga cech datho
trésna maige móithgretho,
is gnáth sube, sreth imm chéul,
isin maig tess Arggatnéul.

Ní gnáth écóiniud na mrath
hi mruig dénta etargnath,
ní bíi nach gargg fri crúais,
acht mad céul mbind frismben clúais.

Cen brón, cen duba, cen bás,
cen nach ngalar cen indgás,
is ed etargne nEmne,
ní comtig a comamre.

Cáine tíre adamri,
ata comgnúsi cadli,
asa rodarc find fia,
ní fríthid bíd a cia.

Má adcetha Aircthech íar tain
forsnig dracoin ocus glain,
dosnig am-muir fri tír toind,
trilsí glano asa moing.

Móini, dússi cach datho
hi Ciúin, cáine étatho,
étsecht fri céul co mbindi,
óol fino óingrindi.

Carpait órdi hi Maig Réin,
taircet la tule don gréin,
carpait arggait i Maig Mon
ocus crédumi cen on.

Graig óir budi and fri srath
graig aile co corcardath,
graig aile ualann tar ais
co ndath nime huleglais.

Dofeith la turcbáil ngréne
fer find forosna réde,
rédid mag find frismbein muir,
mescid fairggi co mbí fuil.

Dofeith in slúag tar muir glan,
don tír donaidbri imram,
imráid íarum dond licc léur
asa comérig cét céul.

Canid airbitiud dont slóg
tré bithu sír, nat bí tróg,
tormaig céul co córib cét,
ní frescet aithbe ná éc.

Emne ildelbach fri rían,
bésu ocus, bésu chían,
i fil ilmíli mbrec mban,
immustimerchel muir glan.

Má ruchúala lúad in chiúil,
esnach énán a hImchiúin,
dofeith banchorén di haa
cusa cluchemag itaa.

Dofeith sóire la sláini
don tír frisferat gáiri,
is i nImchiúin cach ági
dofeith búaine la háni. . . .

TRANSLATION

Once when Bran, son of Febhal, was with his warriors in his royal fort, they suddenly saw a woman in strange raiment upon the floor of the house. No one knew whence she had come or how she had entered, for the ramparts were closed. Then she sang these quatrains to Bran while all the host were listening:

I bring a branch of Emhain's apple-tree,
In shape like those you know:
Twigs of white silver are upon it,
Buds of crystal with blossoms.

There is a distant isle,
Around which sea-horses glisten:
A four course against the white-swelling surge —
Four pedestals uphold it.

A delight of the eyes, a glorious range
Is the plain on which the hosts hold games:
Coracle contends against chariot
In White-silver Plain to the southward.

Pedestals of white bronze underneath
Glittering through ages of beauty:

Fairest land throughout the world,
On which the many blossoms drop.

An ancient tree there is in bloom,
On which birds call to the Hours:
In harmony of song they all are wont
To chant together every Hour.

Colours of every shade glisten
Throughout the gentle-voiced plains:
Joy is known, ranked around music,
In Silver-cloud Plain to the southward.

Unknown is wailing or treachery
In the homely well-tilled land:
There is nothing rough or harsh,
But sweet music striking on the ear.

Without grief, without gloom, without death,
Without any sickness or debility —
That is the sign of Emhain:
Uncommon is an equal marvel.

A beauty of a wondrous land,
Whose aspects are lovely
Whose view is wondrous fair,
Incomparable is its haze.

Then if Silverland is seen,
On which dragon-stones and crystals drop —
The sea washes the wave against the land,
A crystal spray drops from its mane.

Wealth, treasures of every hue
Are in the Quiet Land — a beauty of
 freshness:
There is listening to sweet music,
Drinking of the choicest wine.

Golden chariots on the plain of the sea
Heaving with the tide to the sun:
Chariots of silver on the Plain of Sports,
And of bronze that has no blemish.

Steeds of yellow gold are on the sward there,
Other steeds with crimson colour,
Others again with a coat upon their backs
Of the hue of all-blue heaven.

At sunrise there comes
A fair man illumining level lands:
He rides upon the white sea-washed plain,
He stirs the ocean till it is blood.

A host comes across the clear sea,
They display their rowing to the land:
Then they row to the shining stone
From which arises music a hundredfold.

Through ages long unto the host
It sings a strain which is never sad:
Its music swells with choruses of hundreds —
They look for neither decay nor death.

Many-shaped Emhnae by the sea,
Whether it be near, whether it be far —
In which are thousands of many-hued women,
The clear sea encircles it.

If one has heard the voice of the music,
The chorus of little birds from the
 Quiet Land,
A band of women from a height
Comes to the plain of sport in which he is.

There comes happiness with health
To the land against which laughter peals:
Into the Quiet Land at every season
Comes joy everlasting....

LYRICS

[These poems may belong to the ninth century, with the exception of 'The Blackbird', which may be as late as the eleventh. The translations are by the present editor.]

A Stormy Night

Is aicher in gaíth innocht
fu-fúasna fairrge findfholt;
ní ágor réimm mora mind
dond láechraid lainn ua Lothlind.

Bitter is the wind tonight,
It tosses the sea's white tresses;
I do not fear the fierce warriors of Norway,
Who only travel the quiet seas.

The Scribe Out of Doors

Dom-fharcai fidbaide fál
fom-chain loíd luin, lúad nád cél;
húas mo lebrán ind línech
fom-chain trírech inna n-én

Fomm-chain coí menn, medair mass,
hi mbrot glass de dindgnaib doss.
debrath! nom-Choimmdiu coíma,
caín-scríbaimm fo roída ross

A hedge of trees overlooks me,
A blackbird's lay sings to me;
Above my lined book
The birds chant their song to me.

The cuckoo sings to me lovely and clear
In a grey cloak from the ramparts of bushes.
Well indeed does the Lord look after me
As I write with care in the woodland shade.

The Blackbird

Ach, a luin, is buide duit
cáit sa mhuine a fuil do net,
a díthrebaig nád clinn cloc,
is binn boc síthamail t'fhet

Ah, blackbird, it is well for you
Wherever your nest is in the thicket.
Hermit who rings no bell,
Sweet, soft, peaceful is your call.

The Blackbird at Belfast Lough

Int én bec
ro léic feit
do rind guip
glanbuidi;

fo-ceird faíd
ós Loch Laíg,
lon do chraíb
charnbuidi

The little bird which has whistled from the tip of his bright yellow bill,
The blackbird from its branch heaped up with yellow sends out its call over Belfast Lough.

The Blackbird in the Willow

Int én gaires asin tsail
álainn guilbnén as glan gair:
rinn binn buide fir duib druin,
cas cor cuirther, guth ind luin.

The bird that calls from the willow,
Beautiful his little beak with its clear note:
The sweet yellow bill of the stout black lad;
Lively the tune it plays, the blackbird's song.

LÍADAN AND CUIRITHIR

[This ninth-century poem, spoken by Líadan, relates to the lost tale of her love for Cuirithir. She was an early-seventh-century poet from west Munster who had already become a nun when Cuirithir arrived to marry her. He consequently became a monk, and after quarrelling with Líadan, he went on pilgrimage overseas. In this lament, Líadan speaks of their conflicting desires and their tragic separation.

Text and translation are taken, with minor emendation, from David Greene and Frank O'Connor (eds), *A Golden Treasury of Irish Poetry A.D. 600 to 1200* (London: Macmillan, 1967).]

Cen áinius
in gním hí do-rigénus;
an ro charus ro cráidius.

Ba mire
nád dernad a airersom
mainbed omun Ríg nime.

Níbu amlos
dósom in dál dúthracar,
ascnam sech phéin i Pardos.

Bec mbríge
ro chráidi frimm Cuirithir;
frissium ba mór mo míne.

Mé Líadan;
ro carussa Cuirithir;
is fírithir ad-fíadar.

Gair bása
 i comaiteacht Chuirithir;
frissium ba maith mo gnássa.

Céol caille
 fom-chanad la Cuirithir,
la fogur fairrge flainne.

Do-ménainn
 ní cráidfed frimm Cuirithir
do dálaib cacha dénainn.

Ní chela:
 ba hésium mo chridesherc,
cia no carainn cách cena.

Deilm ndega
 ro thethainn mo chridese;
ro-fess nicon bía cena.

TRANSLATION

Joyless is the thing I have done. I have angered the one I loved.

It would be madness not to do what pleased him were it not for fear of the King of Heaven.

The tryst I desire — to escape beyond Hell into Paradise — was no loss to him.

It was a small thing that angered Cuirithir with me. I was very gentle with him.

I am Líadan; I have loved Cuirithir: it is indeed true what they say.

I was only a short while in Cuirithir's company. I had a good time with him.

The music of the wood sang to me when I was with Cuirithir, and the sound of the blue sea.

I would have thought no tryst I ever made would anger Cuirithir against me.

Do not hide it! He was my heart's love, though I had loved everyone else beside.

A blast of flame has pierced my heart. Most certainly, it will not endure without him.

from: FÉLIRE OENGUSSO (The Martyrology of Oengus)

[In this section of the prologue to his *Martyrology* (*c.* 800), Oengus celebrates the triumph of the Christian church over the old pagan order: the famous centres of pagan kingship lie desolate and deserted, while the Christian monasteries flourish and their founders are exalted.

The translation is taken from David Greene and Frank O'Connor (eds), *A Golden Treasury of Irish Poetry A.D. 600 to 1200* (London: Macmillan, 1967).]

In bith trúag i taam,
 is duthain a ríge;
in rí con-ic aingliu
 is coimmdiu cach tíre.

Ced a tír i taam
 ata saidbre saigthi,
de neurt De, delm sochla
 fil and dún ro praidchi.

At-bath borg tromm Temra
 la tairthim a flathae;
co llín corad sruthe
 maraid Ard mór Machae.

Ro múchad, mór tairbaid,
 míad Loeguire roglaig;
ainm Pátraicc án aurdairc
 atá són for forbairt.

For-forbairt in chretem,
 méraid co dé mbrátha;
gennti bidbaid bertar,
 ni trebtar a rátha.

Ráith Chrúachain ro scáichi
 la hAilill gein mbúada;
cain ordan úas flathib
 fil i cathir Chlúana.

Classa búana binne
 im Chíarán cia at-coïs
la sessilbe mbúada
 Chlúana mór maicc Noïs,

Niptá ní bas dilsiu
 seirc Dé má do-rónaid,
adrad in ríg nélaig
 is de ní bet brónaig.

Borg Ailline úallach
 at-bath lia shlóg mbágach;
is mór Brigit búadach,
 is cain a rrúam dálach.

Dún Emna ro tetha
  acht mairde a clocha;
is rúaim iarthair betha
  Glend dálach Dá Locha.

Lóichet lainnrech lígach
  Ferna fortrén éobail;
ní mair in drong úabair
  Ráith Bécce maicc Éogain.

Cid nád ndéccaid uili
  bretha in ríg cétnai?
Ní mair Bécc mac Éogain,
  mairid Aed macc Sétnai.

Senchathraig na ngennti
  imma rérad rudrad
it fássa cen adrad
  amail láthrach Lugdach.

Ind locáin ro gabtha
  dessaib ocus trírib,
it rúama co ndálaib
  co cétaib, co mílib.

Ro milled in genntlecht
  ciarbo lígdae lethan;
ro lín flaith Dé Athar
  nem, talam la trethan.

Táthunn ní as nessa
  ar ar súil, salm sobail,
de neurt Dé dían medair,
  in-díu deüd domain.

Donnchad dricc rúad rogdae
  nó Bran búadach Berbae,
ní beir dím sním lobrae
  athigid a mmemrae.

Mael Rúain iarna gairi
  grían már des maig Midi
oc a lecht co nglaini
  íchtair cnet cech cridi.

Is comiúr in Coimmdiu
  ce thúirtir a thréta,
bithtrágaid a náimtea,
  bithmáraid a gréta.

In gormríg ro múchtha,
  in Domnaill ro plágtha,
in Chíaráin ro rígtha,
  in Chronáin ro mártha.

Na mórshlébe andaig
  ro tesctha co rinnib;
do-rónta co lléce
  slébe donaib glinnib.

TRANSLATION

The sad world in which we are, its kingdoms are brief; the King who rules the angels is the lord of every country.

Even in the land where we are, where riches are sought out, we have a famous example of God's strength to preach to us.

The great settlement of Tara has died with the loss of its princes; great Armagh lives on with its choirs of scholars.

A great cutting off, the pride of Loiguire has been stifled; Patrick's splendid, revered name is spreading.

The faith has spread and will live to the Day of Judgement; wicked pagans are carried off and their fortresses unoccupied.

The fortress of Cruachan has vanished with Ailill, victory's child; a fair dignity greater than kingdoms is in the city of Clonmacnois;

Though you should tell of sweet eternal choirs about Ciarán with the triumphant clamour of great Clonmacnois —

There is nothing that is more your own than God's love if you can achieve it; you will not grieve for adoration of the King of the Clouds.

The proud settlement of Aillin has died with its boasting hosts; great is victorious Brigit and lovely her thronged sanctuary.

The fort of Emain Machae has melted away, all but its stones; thronged Glendalough is the sanctuary of the western world.

Mighty Ferns of the yew-trees is a shining and lovely light; the proud host of the fort of Bécc mac Éogain lives no longer.

Why do you not all consider the judgements of that king? Bécc mac Éogain is dead but Aed mac Sétna is alive.

Old cities of the pagans to which length of

occupation has been refused are deserts without worship like Lugaid's place.

The little places settled by twos and threes are sanctuaries with throngs, with hundreds, with thousands.

Paganism has been destroyed though it was splendid and far-flung; the kingdom of God the Father has filled heaven and earth and sea.

A holy psalm, we have before our eyes a closer example of God's strength, a stern judgement, now at the world's end.

Choice, angry, bloody Donnchad or victorious Bran from the Barrow do not lift from me the sorrow of weakness when I visit their tombs.

Mael Ruain, the sun south of the plain of Meath, after his short life — by his pure tomb the wound of every heart is healed.

The Lord is just though he separates his flocks; for ever he reduces his enemies, for ever he exalts his champions.

The proud kings have been stifled, the Donals have been plagued, the Cíaráns have been crowned, the Cronáns exalted.

The great hills of evil have been cut down with spear-points, while the glens have been made into hills.

DO MHAC Í DHOMHNUILL (In Praise of Conn, Son of Ó Domhnaill)

[The poem by Tadhg Dall Ó hUiginn (1550-91), of which part is quoted here, is a fairly representative example of the formal eulogy of the schooled poets during the period from the thirteenth to the seventeenth century and of the traditional *topoi* used to praise and to exhort the poet's lord and patron. It employs the familiar mythic theme of the land and sovereignty of Ireland conceived as a woman who becomes radiant and beautiful when married to her rightful king. As the result of this propitious union, the earth is restored to full fertility and the people prosper. The translation quoted here (from Eleanor Knott (ed.), *The Bardic Poems of Tadhg Dall Ó Huiginn (1550-1591)* (London: Simpkin, Marshall, Hamilton, Kent, for the Irish Texts Society, 1922) II, p. 1ff.) is literal and scholarly, rather than literary, and does not attempt to reflect the metrical ornament of the original, but it does perhaps give some idea of the formal dignity of this genre of verse.]

Tógaibh eadrad is Éire,
fada atá ar tí aoinchéile;
ar gclódh aoibhneachta fear bhFáil,
gan fear n-aoinleabtha d'fagháil.

Fada nár féad Inis Bhreagh
tógbháil idir í is éinfear;
olc an bhaintreabhthach bean Floinn,
treabh na n-aitreabhchloch n-áloinn.

Éigin dí dul as a cruth,
nós na mban bhíos gan chumhdach;
tír na sruth mbraontana mbinn —
cruth na haontamha ar Éirinn.

Leannán na ríogh, Ráth Uisnigh,
do cuireadh 'sna crothuibhsin,
learga finnmhíolla a gruadh ngeal
gur tuar imsníomha d'feitheamh.

Do trochlaigheadh ceann i gceann
ardphuirt aireachuis Éireann;
earradh clúimh tiomchal gach tuir,
fionnchladh gach dúin 'na dhíoghuidh.

Do maoladh a cnuic corra,
do treabhadh a tóranna;
Múr Té na gclaichfinnteagh gcuir
nách aithintear é ag eólchuibh.

Ní mhair dhíbh trá acht a dtaise,
tugsad maise ar mhíomhaise;
múir bhratsoilse Banbha Néill —
damhna attoirse iaidséin.

Gidh eadh is usaide linn
an ceó tuirse atá ar Éirinn,
Múr Té do hainmnigheadh d'Art —
gur tairngireadh é d'furtacht.

Atá i ndán dó go dtiocfa
fear fuaslaicthe a airmearta,
budh éigin trá a thocht asteagh
lá éigin ar Ghort nGaoidheal.

Ribhse, a Choinnmheic an Chalbhaigh,
iomdha fáidh rod-fiortharngair —
sibh ar tí a chéile is cubhaidh —
do bhí Éire ag anamhain.

Mairg nách tugann, a thaobh slim,
tallann éigin dá hinntinn
don ráith chuirr ghéigiobhraigh gloin,
céidiomdhaidh Chuinn is Chobhthoigh.

Sill go meinic a gruadh gheal,
claon do dhearc uirre os íseal;
tug th'aghaidh ar a slios slim,
labhair gan fios re hÉirinn.

Dlúthaigh ria, luigh 'na leaba,
a chneas áluinn oighreada;
téigh re cneas chéile Logha,
suil bheas Éire i n-aontomha.

Druid an béal mar bhláth suibhe,
'san déad solus sneachtuidhe,
le póig go báintealaigh mBreagh,
go bhfáilteadhaibh chóig gcóigeadh.

Do-rad Niall mór mhac Eachach,
ór fás tú, a ghruadh gheilleathach,
phóig uaidh a hionnamhla sin
dár fuaigh fionnadhbha nÉibhir.

Tug phóig a haithghin oile
dá dtárraidh Brian Bóroimhe,
gan imriosain, a ghlac geal,
an finnliossoin Mhac Míleadh.

Mar mhná na n-ilgheas oile,
fuasgladh Bhanbha braonuighe
atá ar phóig d'foghbháil aguibh,
a bhonnbháin óig abhraduibh.

Nós na mban bhíos fa gheasaibh,
biaidh Éire an fóid bhailbheasaigh —
clár móireithreach na sriobh seang —
ag fior fóireithneach Éireann. . . .

Ar son nách beitheá, a bharr tiogh,
i gceannas chríche Gaoidheal,
críoch Bhanbha do bhuing a glas
tarla, a Chuinn, ar do chumas.

Urusa dhuit déanaimh cean,
tnúthach gcogaidh Meic Mhíleadh;
beag na faghla, a fir Eithne,
do-bhir Banbha buaidheirthe.

Adhnaidh teach don toigh re a thaoibh;
géabhaidh cách dod chéibh bharrchlaoin,
do rún cagaidh dá gcluintear,
tnúdh is abaidh adhuintear.

Do nós leathnuighthe an luisne,
biaidh feadh an Chláir Chobhthuighse
a foghlaidh féin ar gach fonn,
ót foghlaibh ar féin n-eachtronn.

Budh é a chríoch, a chruth sídhe,
lingfidh lucht gach éintíre,
led ghruaidh mónanda ón mall sriobh,
tóranna Gall is Gaoidhiol.

Eirg ina gceannas, a Chuinn,
tar rompa fós go Fréamhuinn;
a chaithleómhain bhasghloin Bhreagh,
aithbheóghaidh gasraidh Ghaoidheal.

Ná léig dhíot ar Dhún na nGall,
ná ar chuan Easa Dá Éagann,
ná ar seanLoch bhfionúr bhFeabhail,
ríomhúr Teamhrach toireamhain.

Mairg fuair go seachónadh sibh
ar choicéadaibh chuain Sligigh,
nó ar Chruachain ngeiltrealmhaigh ngloin,
sein Teamhraigh Thuathail Teachtmhair.

Briathra fádh is fuighle naomh
dá huaimse dot folt bharrchlaon;
nách leó do tiorchanadh thall
an t-eó a fionnchaladh Fréamhann?

Fáidh do reachta, a rí Bearnais,
séan gcnuais ar chraoibh dhuilleaghlais,
fearg bhuinne ag breith a thoraidh,
cleith tuinne 'na torchoraibh.

Iomad asa ag uathadh cruidh,
iomad cruach ar chionn samhraidh —
lucht fáisdine ón fearr t'aithne —
fáistighe ceall cumhdaighthe.

Tú ar toil cháigh is cách dod thoil,
tú ós cách is cách uasoibh;
tú ar breith gach aoinfir 'sgidh eadh,
Gaoidhil fad bhreith do-beirthear.

Faoilidh ród, a rún faoilidh,
don toisgse atáid fionnGhaoidhil;
do nós mhná re a céile cuil
atá Éire ret óguibh.

TRANSLATION

Raise the veil from Ireland; long hath she sought a spouse, finding no mate for her couch after the happiness of the men of Fál was blasted.

It is long since the Isle of Bregia could discover herself to any; a luckless widow is the wife of Flann — land of splendid stone dwellings.

She could not but lose her beauty, it is thus with uncared for women; Ireland, land of sparkling, melodious streams, hath the complexion of loneliness.

Ushnagh's castle, darling of kings, hath been brought to such a state that it is a sorrowful omen to watch over the fair, modest contours of her bright countenance.

Ireland's capitals have been defiled, one after another; a garment of weeds invests each keep, the white rampart of every castle is become a trench.

Her round hills have been stripped, her boundaries plowed over, so that Té's Rampart,[1] with its firm dwellings of white masonry, is not recognized by the guides.

Nought remains of them save their traces, they have exchanged comeliness for uncomeliness; the brightly tapestried castles of Niall's Banbha[2] — a cause of sorrow are they.

Howbeit, we think the more lightly of this mournful gloom which hangs over Ireland, since for Té's Rampart, which was named of Art, succour hath been foretold.

It is in store for it that a man shall come to dissolve its enchantments; needs must, then, that he shall one day take possession of the Field of the Gaels.

For thee, Conn, son of the Calvach, many a prophet hath truly foretold thee — it is fitting that you should seek one another — Ireland hath been waiting.

Alas, thou graceful of form, for him who does not give some thing of her desire to the smooth, yew-timbered, bright rampart, first couch of Conn and Cobhthach.

Look frequently on her bright countenance, bend thine eye upon her in secret; approach her graceful form, speak covertly with Ireland.

Embrace her, go to her couch, thou beautiful yet icy of flesh; take to thee the spouse of Lugh,[3] lest Ireland be left unwedded.

Press the lips like berry-bloom, and the shining, snow-white teeth, in a kiss to Bregia of the smooth hill, amidst the welcome of the five provinces.

Great Niall, son of Eachaidh, from whom thou art sprung, O bright-cheeked countenance, bestowed just such a kiss, whereby he united under his sway the fair Dwelling of Eber.

Another such kiss gave Brian of Bóroimhe,[4] by which he gained without dispute, thou white of hand, that stately dwelling place of the Sons of Míl.

As with other women in manifold enchantments, thou canst procure with a kiss the release of tearful Banbha, O white-footed, black-lashed youth.

As with women under enchantments, Ireland, land of rippling waterfalls, plain of great fins, of shallow streams, will be the possession of him who rescues her. . . .

Even though thou mayst not be supreme in the Land of the Gaels, thou thick-haired one, it is in thy power, Conn, to free the country of Banbha from its fetters.

It is easy for thee to win triumphs, the Sons of Míl are eager for war; it needs few forays, thou man of the Inny, to stir up Banbha.

A house takes fire from the one beside it; if thy intention of battle be heard, from thy head of wavy tresses the rest will take it; it is a ready desire that is ignited.

Even as the spreading of a flame, throughout this Plain of Cobhthach every territory will have its own reaver, from thy raids upon the foreign soldiery.

And the result, O wondrous form, shall be that the people of every territory, together with thee, O face ruddy as the berry, from which the stream is calm, shall storm the dividing boundaries of Gael and foreigner.

Take command of them, Conn, and lead them to

1. A poetical name for Tara.
2. Niall of the Nine Hostages was ancestor of the Uí Néill dynasty; Banbha was one the mythical names of Ireland.
3. The god of arts and crafts, and the archetype of the kingship in Irish tradition.
4. Famous king of Munster who won control of all Ireland. He died at the battle of Clontarf in 1014.

Frewen; thou bright-handed warrior of Bregia, revivify the soldiery of the Gael.

Forsake not for Donegal, or the bay of Eas Dá Éagann, or ancient Loch Foyle, of the sparkling wines, the royal rampart of Tara in the east.

Alas, if anyone found that for the cocket[5] of Sligo Bay, or for bright Croghan of the fair equipment thou wouldst abandon ancient Tara of Tuathal Teachtmhar.

The words of soothsayers, the utterances of saints, mate her with thee, O wavy tresses; did they not prophesy of yore the salmon from Frewen's fair harbor?

Prophets of thy rule, thou lord of Bearnas, are the promise of fruit on the green-leafed bough, the fury of the stream bearing its produce, the wave concealed beneath the washed-up treasure.

Abundance of milk from a small number of cattle, abundance of corn stacks before summer, and — soothsayers through whom thou art most clearly recognized — the ruined buildings of the churches repaired.

Thou at the service of all, and all submitting to thee; thou above everyone, and everyone above thee; thou at the pleasure of every man, and for all that, the Gaels at thy mercy.

The noble Gaels welcome thee to this enterprise, O cheerful heart; as a woman with her unlawful mate, so is Ireland with thy warriors.

5. A customs certificate or duty.

from:
IMMRAM BRAIN
(The Voyage of Bran)

[Mongán was the son of Fiachna, son of Baetán, king of Dál nAraidi in the north-east of Ireland; he flourished in the first quarter of the seventh century. But in the literature his *persona* has acquired a rich mythological dimension, and already about the eighth century a short anecdote told how the god Manannán persuaded Fiachna's wife to lie with him in return for saving the life of her husband, who was at that time aiding the king of Scottish Dál Riada in their war with the Anglo-Saxons. The account of these events dates from a much later period, the fourteenth or fifteenth centuries, and reflects contemporary fashions in narrative. Many of the motifs are ancient, notably the magic powers that Mongán inherited from his divine father and the trickster element in the personalities of both. The author exploits these with a tongue-in-cheek urbanity that belies the popular wonder-tale style and the surface naiveté of the plot.

The translation appears in Kuno Meyer and Alfred Nutt, *The Voyage of Bran son of Fébal to the Land of the Living* (London: David Nutt, 1897) I, p. 70ff.]

Once upon a time Fiachna Finn, son of Baetán, son of Murchertach, son of Muredach, son of Eogan, son of Niall, went forth from Ireland, until he came to Lochlann, over which Eolgarg Mór, son of Magar, was at that time king. There he found great respect and love and honour. And he was not long there, when a disease seized the king of Lochlann, who asked of his leeches and physicians what would help him. And they told him there was in the world nothing that would help him, save a red-eared shining-white cow, which was to be boiled for him. And the people of Lochlann searched for the cow, and there was found the single cow of Caillech Dub (Black Hag). Another cow was offered to her in its stead, but the hag refused. Then four were offered to her, viz., one cow for every foot, and the hag would not accept any other condition but that Fiachna should become security. Now this was the hour and the time that messengers came for Fiachna Finn, the son of Baetán, and he went with those messengers, and took the kingship of Ulster, and was king for one year.

One day at the end of a year he heard cries of distress in front of the fort, and he told his men to go and see who made those cries, and to let the person that made them into the house. And there was the hag from Lochlann come to demand her security. Fiachna knew her and bade her welcome and asked tidings of her. 'Evil tidings I have,' said the hag. 'The king of Lochlann has deceived me in the matter of the four kine that were promised to me for my cow.' 'I will give thee four kine on his behalf, O hag,' said Fiachna. But the hag said she would not take them. 'I will give twenty kine on his behalf,' said Fiachna. 'I shall not take them,' said the hag. 'I will give four times twenty kine,' said Fiachna, 'twenty kine for each cow.' 'By my word,' said the hag, 'if all the kine of the province of Ulster were given to me, I should not take them, until thou come thyself to make war upon the king of Lochlann. As I have come to thee from the east, so do thou come on a journey with me.'

Then Fiachna assembled the nobles of Ulster until he had ten equally large battalions, and went and announced battle to the men of Lochlann. And they were three days a-gathering unto the battle. And combat was made by the king of Lochlann on the men of Ireland. And three hundred warriors fell by Fiachna in the fight. And venomous sheep were let out of the king of Lochlann's tent against them, and on that day three hundred warriors fell by the sheep, and three hundred warriors fell on the second day, and three hundred on the third day. That was grievous to Fiachna, and he said: 'Sad is the journey on which we have come, for the purpose of having our people killed by the sheep. For if they had fallen in battle or in combat by the host of Lochlann, we should not deem their fall a disgrace, for they would avenge themselves. Give me,' saith he, 'my arms and my dress that I may myself go to fight against the sheep.' 'Do not say that, O King,' said they, 'for it is not meet that thou shouldst go to fight against them.' 'By my word,' said Fiachna, 'no more of the men of Ireland shall fall by them, till I myself go to fight against the sheep; and if I am destined to find death there, I shall find it, for it is impossible to avoid fate; and if not, the sheep will fall by me.'

As they were thus conversing, they saw a single tall warlike man coming towards them. He wore a green cloak of one colour, and a brooch of white silver in the cloak over his breast, and a satin shirt next his white skin. A circlet of gold around his hair, and two sandals of gold under his feet. And the warrior said: 'What reward wouldst thou give to him who would keep the sheep from thee?' 'By my word,' said Fiachna, 'whatever thou ask, provided I have it, I should give it.' 'Thou shalt have it to give,' said the warrior, 'and I will tell thee the reward.' 'Say the sentence,' said Fiachna. 'I shall say it,' said he; 'give me that ring of gold on thy finger as a token for me, when I go to Ireland to thy wife to sleep with her.' 'By my word,' said Fiachna, 'I would not let one man of the men of Ireland fall on account of that condition.' 'It shall be none the worse for thee; for a glorious child shall be begotten by me there, and from thee he shall be named, even Mongán the Fair (Finn), son of Fiachna the Fair. And I shall go there in thy shape, so that thy wife shall not be defiled by it. And I am Manannán, son of Ler, and thou shalt seize the kingship of Lochlann and of the Saxons and Britons.' Then the warrior took a venomous hound out of his cloak, and a chain upon it, and said: 'By my word, not a single sheep shall carry its head from her to the fortress of the king of Lochlann, and she will kill three hundred of the hosts of Lochlann, and thou shalt have what will come of it.' The warrior went to Ireland, and in the shape of Fiachna himself he slept with Fiachna's wife, and in that night she became pregnant. On that day the sheep and three hundred of the nobles of Lochlann fell by the dog, and Fiachna seized the kingship of Lochlann and of the Saxons and Britons.

Now, as to the Cailleach Dubh, Fiachna gave her her due, viz., seven castles with their territory and land, and a hundred of every cattle. And then he went into Ireland and found his wife big-bellied and pregnant, and when her time came, she bore a son. Now Fiachna the Fair had an attendant, whose name was An Damh, and in that same night his wife brought forth a son, and they were christened together, and the son of Fiachna was named Mongán, and the son of the attendant was named Mac an Daimh. And there was another warrior reigning together with Fiachna the Fair, to wit Fiachna the Black, son of Demán, who lay heavily on his rule. And to him in the same night a daughter was born, to whom the name Dubh Lacha (The Dark One of the Lake) White-hand was given, and Mongán and Dubh Lacha were affianced to each other. When Mongán was three nights old, Manannán came for him and took him with him to bring him up in the Land of Promise, and vowed that he would not let him back into Ireland before he were twelve years of age.

Now as to Fiachna the Black, son of Demán, he watched his opportunity, and when he found that Fiachna the Fair, son of Baetán, had with him but a small host and force, he went up to his stronghold, and burnt and destroyed it, and killed Fiachna himself, and seized the kingship of Ulster by force. And all the men of Ulster desired Mongán to be brought to them when he was six years old, but Manannán did not bring him to Ulster till he had completed sixteen years. And then he came to Ulster, and the men of Ulster made peace between themselves and Fiachna the Black, to wit, one-half of Ulster to Mongán, and Dubh Lacha to be his wife and consort in retaliation for his father. And it was done so.

One day while Mongán and his wife were playing *fidchell*,[1] they saw a dark black-tufted little cleric at the door-post, who said: 'This inactivity in which

1. A board game.

thou art, O Mongán, is not an inactivity becoming a king of Ulster, not to go to avenge thy father on Fiachna the Black, son of Demán, though Dubh Lacha may think it wrong to tell thee so. For he has now but a small host and force with him; and come with me thither, and let us burn the fortress, and let us kill Fiachna.' 'There is no knowing what luck there may be on that saying, O cleric,' said Mongán, 'and we shall go with thee.' And thus it was done, for Fiachna the Black was killed by them. Mongán seized the kingship of Ulster, and the little cleric who had done the treason was Manannán the great and mighty.

And the nobles of Ulster were gathered to Mongán, and he said to them: 'I desire to go to seek boons from the provincial kings of Ireland, that I may get gold and silver and wealth to give away.' 'That is a good plan,' said they. And he went forth into the provinces of Ireland, until he came to Leinster. And the king of Leinster at that time was Brandubh mac Echach. And he gave a hearty welcome to the king of Ulster, and they slept that night in the place, and when Mongán awoke on the morrow, he saw the fifty white red-eared kine, and a white calf by the side of each cow, and as soon as he saw them he was in love with them. And the king of Leinster observed him and said to him: 'Thou art in love with the kine, O king,' saith he. 'By my word,' said Mongán, 'save the kingdom of Ulster, I never saw anything that I would rather have than them.' 'By my word,' said the king of Leinster, 'they are a match for Dubh Lacha, for she is the one woman that is most beautiful in Ireland, and those kine are the most beautiful cattle in Ireland, and on no condition in the world would I give them except on our making friendship without refusal.'

They did so, and each bound the other. And Mongán went home and took his thrice fifty white kine with him. And Dubh Lacha asked: 'What are these cattle that are the most beautiful that I ever saw?' And Mongán told her how he had obtained the kine. And they were not long there when they saw hosts approaching the place, and 'tis he that was there, even the king of Leinster. 'What hast thou come to seek?' said Mongán. 'For, by my word, if what thou seekest be in the province of Ulster, thou shalt have it.' 'It is, then,' said the king of Leinster. 'To seek Dubh Lacha have I come.'

Silence fell upon Mongán. And he said: 'I have never heard of any one giving away his wife.' 'Though thou hast not heard of it,' said Dubh Lacha, 'give her, for honour is more lasting than life.' Anger seized Mongán, and he allowed the king of Leinster to take her with him. Dubh Lacha called the king of Leinster aside and said to him: 'Dost thou know, O king of Leinster, that the men and one half of Ulster would fall for my sake, except I had already given love to thee? And by my word! I shall not go with thee until thou grant me the sentence of my own lips.' 'What is the sentence?' said the king of Leinster. 'Thy word to fulfil it!' saith she. The king of Leinster gave his word. 'Then, said Dubh Lacha, 'I desire that until the end of one year we be not brought for one night into the same house, and if in the course of a day thou comest into the same house with me, that thou shouldst not sit in the same chair with me, but sit in a chair over against me, for I fear the exceeding great love which I have bestowed upon thee, that thou mayst hate me, and that I may not again be acceptable to my own husband; for if we are a-courting each other during this coming year, our love will not recede.'

And the king of Leinster granted her that condition, and he took her to his house, and there she was for a while. And for that while Mongán was in a wasting sickness continually. And in the night in which Mongán had taken Dubh Lacha, Mac an Daimh had taken her foster-sister, who was her trusty attendant, and who had gone into Leinster with Dubh Lacha. So one day Mac an Daimh came into the house where Mongán was, and said: 'Things are in a bad way with thee, O Mongán,' saith he, 'and evil was thy journey into the Land of Promise to the house of Manannán, since thou hast learnt nothing there, except consuming food and practising foolish things, and it is hard on me that my wife has been taken into Leinster, since *I* have not made "friendship without refusal" with the king of Leinster's attendant, as thou didst with the king of Leinster, thus being unable to follow thy wife.' 'No one deems that worse than I myself,' said Mongán.

And Mongán said to Mac an Daimh: 'Go,' saith he, 'to the cave of the door, in which we left the fuel-basket, and a sod from Ireland and another from Scotland in it, that I may go with thee on thy back; for the king of Leinster will ask of his wizards news of me, and they will say I am with one foot in Ireland, and with the other in Scotland, and he will say that as long as I am like that he need not fear me.'

And in that way they set out. And that was the hour and time in which the feast of Moy-Liffey was held in Leinster, and they came to the Plain of Cell Chamáin in Leinster, and there beheld the hosts and multitudes and the king of Leinster going past them to the feast, and they recognised him. 'That is sad, O Mac an Daimh,' said Mongán, 'evil is the journey on which we have come.' And they saw the holy cleric going past them, even Tibraide, the priest of Cell Chamáin, with his four gospels in his own hand, and the satchel for the holy utensils upon the back of a cleric by his side, and they reading their offices. And wonder seized Mac an Daimh as to what the cleric said, and he kept asking Mongán: 'What did he say?' Mongán said it was reading, and he asked Mac an Daimh whether he understood a little of it. 'I do not understand,' said Mac an Daimh, 'except that the man at his back says "Amen, amen."'

Thereupon Mongán shaped a large river through the midst of the plain in front of Tibraide, and a large bridge across it. And Tibraide marvelled at that and began to bless himself. ''Tis here,' he said, 'my father was born and my grandfather, and never did I see a river here. But as the river has got there, it is well there is a bridge across it.' They proceeded to the bridge, and when they had reached its middle, it fell under them, and Mongán snatched the gospels out of Tibraide's hand, and sent them down the river. And he asked Mac an Daimh whether he should drown them. 'Certainly, let them be drowned!' said Mac an Daimh. 'We will not do it,' said Mongán. 'We will let them down the river the length of a mile, till we have done our task in the fortress.'

Mongán took on himself the shape of Tibraide, and gave Mac an Daimh the shape of the cleric, with a large tonsure on his head, and the satchel on his back. And they go onward before the king of Leinster, who welcomed Tibraide and gave him a kiss, and ''Tis long that I have not seen thee, O Tibraide,' he said, 'and read the gospel to us and proceed before us to the fortress. And let Ceibhín Cochlach, the attendant of my chariot, go with thee. And the queen, the wife of the king of Ulster, is there and would like to confess to thee.' And while Mongán was reading the gospel, Mac an Daimh would say 'Amen, amen.' The hosts said they had never seen a priest who had but one word except that cleric; for he said nothing but 'amen.'

And Mongán went onward to the front of the fortress in which Dubh Lacha was. And she recognised him. And Mac an Daimh said: 'Leave the house all of ye, so that the queen may make her confession.' And her nurse or foster sister ventured out of boldness to stay there. Mac an Daimh closed his arms around her and put her out, and said that no one should be with the queen except the woman that had come with her. And he closed the bower after them and put the glazen door to it, and opened the window of glass. And he lifted his own wife into bed with him, but no sooner than Mongán had taken Dubh Lacha with him. And Mongán sat down by her shoulder and gave her three kisses, and carried her into bed with him, and had his will and pleasure of her. And when that had been done, the hag who guarded the jewels, who was in the corner, began to speak; for they had not noticed her until then. And Mongán sent a swift magical breath at her, so that what she had seen was no longer clear to her. 'That is sad,' said the hag, 'do not rob me of Heaven, O holy cleric! For the thought that I have uttered is wrong, and accept my repentance, for a lying vision has appeared to me, and I dearly love my foster-child.' 'Come hither to me, hag!' said Mongán, 'and confess to me.' The hag arose, and Mongán shaped a sharp spike in the chair, and the hag fell upon the spike, and found death. 'A blessing on thee, O Mongán,' said the queen, 'it is a good thing for us to have killed the woman, for she would have told what we have done.'

Then they heard a knocking at the door, and 'tis he that was there, even Tibraide, and three times nine men with him. The doorkeepers said: 'We never saw a year in which Tibraides were more plentiful than this year. Ye have a Tibraide within and a Tibraide without.' ''Tis true,' said Mongán. 'Mongán has come in my shape. Come out,' said he, 'and I will reward you, and let yonder clerics be killed, for they are noblemen of Mongán's that have been put into the shape of clerics.' And the men of the household came out and killed the clerics, and twice nine of them fell. And the king of Leinster came to them and asked them what course they were on. 'Mongán,' said they, 'has come in Tibraide's shape, and Tibraide is in the place.' And the king of Leinster charged them, and Tibraide reached the church of Cell Chamáin, and none of the remaining nine escaped without a wound.

And the king of Leinster came to his house, and then Mongán departed. And the king asked: 'Where is Tibraide?' saith he. 'It was not Tibraide that was here,' said the woman, 'but Mongán, since you will hear it.' 'Were you with Mongán, girl?' said he. 'I was,' said she, 'for he has the greatest claim on me.' 'Send for Tibraide,' said the king, 'for through ill luck we have chanced to kill his people.' And Tibraide was brought to them, and Mongán went home and did not come again until the end of a quarter, and during that time he was in a wasting sickness.

And Mac an Daimh came to him and said to him: 'Tis wearisome to me,' said he, 'to be without my wife through a clown like myself, since *I* have not made "friendship without refusal" with the king of Leinster's attendant.' 'Go thou for me,' said Mongán, 'to get news to Ráith Descirt of Bregia, where Dubh Lacha of the White Hand is, for I am not myself able to go.' Thereafter Dubh Lacha said: 'Let Mongán come to me,' said she, 'for the king of Leinster is on a journey around Leinster, and Ceibhín Cochlach, the attendant of the king's chariot, is with me and keeps telling me to escape, and that he himself would come with me. And Mongán behaves in a weak manner,' said she. And Mac an Daimh went to incite Mongán.

Thereupon Mongán set out to Ráith Descirt of Bregia, and he sat down at the shoulder of the girl, and a gilded chessboard was brought to them, and they played. And Dubh Lacha bared her breasts to Mongán, and as he looked upon them, he beheld the great paps, which were soft and white, and the middle small and shining-white. And desire of the girl came upon him. And Dubh Lacha observed it. Just then the king of Leinster with his hosts was drawing near the fortress, and the fortress was opened before him. And the king of Leinster asked of the girl whether Mongán had been in the house. She said he had been. 'I wish to obtain a request of thee, girl,' said the king of Leinster. 'It shall be granted. Except thy being with me till the year is ended, there is nothing that thou mayst ask which I will not grant thee.' 'If that be so,' said the king, 'tell me when thou longest for Mongán son of Fiachna; for when Mongán has gone, thou wilt long for him.'

At the end of a quarter Mongán returned, and he was longing for her; and all the hosts of the place were there at the time. Then the hosts of the place came out, and Mongán turned back from the fortress and went home. And that quarter he was in a wasting sickness. And the nobles of Ulster assembled into one place and offered Mongán to go with him to make battle for the sake of his wife. 'By my word,' said Mongán, 'the woman that has been taken from me through my own folly, no woman's son of the men of Ulster shall fall for her sake in bringing her out, until, through my own craftiness, I myself bring her with me.'

And in that way the year passed by, and Mongán and Mac an Daimh set out to the king of Leinster's house. There were the nobles of Leinster going into the place, and a great feast was being prepared towards the marriage of Dubh Lacha. And the king of Leinster vowed he would marry her. And they came to the green outside. 'O Mongán,' said Mac an Daimh, 'in what shape shall we go?' And as they were there, they see the hag of the mill, to wit, Cuimne. And she was a hag as tall as a weaver's beam, and a large chain-dog with her licking the mill-stones, with a twisted rope around his neck, and Brothar was his name. And they saw a hack mare with an old pack-saddle upon her, carrying corn and flour from the mill.

And when Mongán saw them, he said to Mac an Daimh: 'I have the shape in which we will go,' said he, 'and if I am destined ever to obtain my wife, I shall do so this time.' 'That becomes thee, O noble prince,' said Mac an Daimh. 'And come, O Mac an Daimh, and call Cuimne of the mill out to me to converse with me.' 'It is three score years', said Cuimne, 'since any one has asked me to converse with him.' And she came out, the dog following her, and when Mongán saw them, he laughed and said to her: 'If thou wouldst take my advice, I would put thee into the shape of a young girl, and thou shouldst be as a wife with me or with the King of Leinster.' 'I will do that certainly,' said Cuimne. And with the magic wand he gave a stroke to the dog, which became a sleek white lapdog, the fairest that was in the world, with a silver chain around its neck and a little bell of gold on it, so that it would have fitted into the palm of a man. And he gave a stroke to the hag, who became a young girl, the fairest of form and make of the daughters of the world, to wit, Ibhell of the Shining Cheeks, daughter of the king of Munster. And he himself assumed the shape of Aedh, son of the king of Connaught, and Mac an Daimh he put into the shape of his attendant. And he made a shining-white palfrey[2] with crimson hair, and of the pack-saddle he made a gilded saddle with variegated gold and precious stones. And they mounted two other

2. A light saddle horse, especially ridden by women.

mares in the shape of steeds, and in that way they reached the fortress.

And the door-keepers saw them and told the king of Leinster that it was Aed the Beautiful, son of the king of Connaught, and his attendant, and his wife Ibhell of the Shining Cheeks, daughter of the king of Munster, exiled and banished from Connaught, that had come under the protection of the king of Leinster, and he did not wish to come with a greater host or multitude. And the door-keeper made the announcement, and the king came to meet them, and welcomed them. And the king of Leinster called the son of the king of Connaught to his shoulder. 'That is not the custom with us,' said the son of the king of Connaught, 'but that *he* should sit by the side of the king who is the second best man in the palace, and next to thee I am the second best in the house, and by the side of the king I will be.'

And the drinking-house was put in order. And Mongán put a love-charm into the cheeks of the hag, and from the look which the king of Leinster cast on her he was filled with her love, so that there was not a bone of his of the size of an inch, but was filled with love of the girl. And he called his attendant to him and said to him: 'Go to where the wife of the king of Connaught's son is, and say to her "the king of Leinster has bestowed great love upon thee, and that a king is better than a king's heir."' And Mongán understood the whispering, and said to Cuimne: 'There is an attendant coming from the king of Leinster with a message to thee, and I know the secret message which he brings, and if thou wouldst take my advice, thou wouldst not be with a worse man than myself or the king of Leinster.' 'I have no choice of bridegroom, which-ever of you will be husband to me.' 'If that be so,' said Mongán, 'when he comes to thee, say that by his gifts and precious things thou wilt know him who loves thee, and ask him for the drinking-horn which he brings thee.'

And the king of Leinster's attendant came to converse with her, and said: 'Here is a noble horn brought to thee.' 'We should know him who loves us by gifts and precious things.' And the king of Leinster said to the attendant: 'Give her my horn.' But the king's household said: 'Do not give thy treasures to the wife of the King of Connaught's son.' 'I will give them,' said the king of Leinster, 'for the woman and my treasures will come to me.' And Mac an Daimh takes the horn from her and whatever else she got of treasures till the morning.

And Mongán said to Cuimne: 'Ask the king of Leinster for his girdle.' And the girdle was of such a nature that neither sickness nor trouble would seize the side on which it was. And she demanded the girdle, and the king of Leinster gave it her, and Mac an Daimh forthwith took it from her. 'And now say to the king of Leinster's attendant, if he were to give the whole world to thee, thou wouldst not leave thy own husband for him.' And the attendant told that to the king of Leinster, who said to the 'son of the king of Connaught': 'What have you in mind? You know this woman by my side, to wit, Dubh Lacha of the White Hands, daughter of Fiachna Dubh son of Demán. I took her from him on terms of "friendship without refusal," and if thou like, I would make an exchange with thee.' And great anger and ferocity seized the other, and he said: 'If I had brought steeds and studs with me, it would be right to ask them of me. However, it is not right to refuse a lord; though I am loath it should be so, take her to thee.' And as they made the exchange, Mongán gave three kisses to the girl, and said: 'Every one would say that we did not make the exchange from our hearts, if I did not give these kisses.' And they indulged themselves until they were drunk and hilarious.

And Mac an Daimh arose and said: 'It is a great shame that no one puts drink into the hand of the king of Connaught's son.' And as no one answered him, he took the two best steeds that were in the fortress, and Mongán put swiftness of wind into them. And Mongán placed Dubh Lacha behind him, and Mac an Daimh his own wife, and they set forth. And when on the morrow the household of the king of Leinster arose, they saw the cloak of the hag, and the grey tall hag on the bed of the king of Leinster. And they saw the dog with a twisted halter round his neck, and they saw the hack mare and the pack-saddle.... And the people laughed and awoke the king of Leinster, who saw the hag by his side and said: 'Art thou the grey-backed hag of the mill?' 'I am,' said she. 'Pity that I should have slept with thee, O Cuimne!'

Bibliography

James Carney, *Early Irish Poetry* (Cork: Mercier Press, 1965).

———, *Medieval Irish Lyrics; selected and translated* (Dublin: Dolmen Press, 1967).

James Hamilton Delargy, *The Gaelic Story-teller....* (London: G. Cumberlege, Amen House, 1945).

Myles Dillon, *Early Irish Literature* (Chicago: University of Chicago Press, 1948).
———, *Early Irish Society* (Dublin: Sign of the Three Candles, 1954).
———, *Irish Sagas* (Dublin: Stationery Office, 1959).
Robin Flower, *The Irish Tradition* (Oxford: Clarendon Press, 1948).
Jeffrey Gantz (transl.), *Early Irish Myths and Sagas* (Harmondsworth: Penguin Books, 1981).
David Greene and Frank O'Connor (eds), *A Golden Treasury of Irish Poetry A.D. 600 to 1200* (London: Macmillan, 1967).
Kenneth H. Jackson, *A Celtic Miscellany: Translations from the Celtic Literatures* (London: Routledge & Kegan Paul, 1951; Harmondsworth: Penguin Books, 1971).
Thomas Kinsella (transl.), *The Táin* (Oxford: Oxford University Press, 1969).
Eleanor Knott, *Irish Classical Poetry* (Dublin: Sign of the Three Candles, 1957).
Gerard Murphy, *Saga and Myth in Ancient Ireland* (Dublin: Sign of the Three Candles, 1955, reprinted 1971).
———, *The Ossianic Lore and Romantic Tales of Medieval Ireland* (Dublin: Sign of the Three Candles, 1955).
———, *Early Irish Lyrics: Eighth to Twelfth Century* (Oxford: Clarendon Press, 1956).

CHARLES DOHERTY, *Editor*

Latin Writing in Ireland

(c.400–c.1200)

There are few references to Ireland before the arrival in Britain of the forces of the Roman empire under Julius Caesar in the first century B.C., and those that have survived are of little value. It is only really when the Romans, under Claudius, set in earnest about the conquest of Britain that we begin to get an accurate picture of Ireland; but since the Roman legions never actually invaded Ireland — though Agricola did consider it in the late first century A.D. — the country remained on the margin of the world of Graeco-Roman civilization, an island with its own language and way of life, where Latin was always to be a foreign language.

Irish society, in the early centuries of the Christian era, was barbarian — a variant of the societies of north-west Europe. It was Celtic-speaking, but there was probably a very strong pre-Celtic stratum in the population. Politically the country was a mosaic of small kingdoms interwoven in a series of continually changing alliances. Some kingdoms dominated many others and the most powerful political units were the provinces, such as Leinster and Ulster. The highest political position was that of high king of the country, but only the most exceptional men could ever achieve this office. Between the fifth and the twelfth centuries, only eight or nine kings were strong enough to be inaugurated at Tara.

By the fourth century A.D., the wealth of Roman Britain was attracting the interest of barbarians on its borders — the Picts in Scotland and the Scots of Ireland. The word *Scotti* means something like 'raider' and was a nickname the Romans gave to Irish pirates. On occasion, as in June 367, the Irish and Picts to the west and north and the Saxons from the east joined forces to overrun the province of Britain. In eastern Britain, the Romano-British had invited some Germanic peoples to settle there as border troops against further raids from their own kind. It is very likely that a similar policy had been adopted for the protection of the western shores of Britain during the late fourth century. There is strong evidence for the settlement of Irishmen in Wales, particularly South Wales, at about this time. The most obvious sign of their presence is the distribution of Ogham stones there. These upright stones, the edges of which are incised with strokes representing letters and words, are distinctively Irish and are most common in Ireland in an area stretching from Waterford to Kerry. However, they are also found in South Wales, and it is clear that the Irish had established kingdoms there during the fifth century. It was the Déisi of Waterford who had settled most intensively in Wales, while a people from east Cork, the Uí Liatháin, had established themselves in Cornwall. By the fifth century, therefore, some Irish people were settled in Roman territory and were open to the influences of a more advanced civilization.

The Ogham stones, which probably served a number of functions, from boundary-markers to grave-markers, are of particular significance in the history of writing in early Ireland. The strokes incised on the edge of the stones are a cypher, representing words. It is clear that the cypher was based on the Latin alphabet and was a way of representing Irish names. The inscriptions are formulaic, often simply reading 'X son of Y of the tribe of Z'. Some names are written in Latin characters on the face of the stone. The words represented on Ogham stones give us the earliest surviving form of the Irish language, which, at this time, had case endings rather like Latin. We may look upon these stones as an attempt by the Irish to acquire some of the elements of Roman civilization. Barbarians everywhere strove to imitate the ways of the higher civilization, and the Irish were no exception. We can see this in the way that they adopted technical innovations during this period. It is not surprising, then, to find that the Irish language borrowed many words from Latin as it was used and pronounced in Roman Britain. Linguists have been able to date the borrowing of these words to the fifth and sixth centuries.

It is against this background that we may view the introduction of Christianity into Ireland. Some of the earliest Latin vocabulary borrowed into Irish consists of religious terms. It is clear that some of the Irish had been accepting Christianity in a casual way from the fourth century onwards and that by the first few decades of the fifth century there were communities of Christians in Ireland. There is no evidence of martyrs in the conversion of Ireland, probably because the Irish would have seen Christianity as yet another aspect of the higher civilization and therefore something to be acquired. They were polytheistic and this would have allowed for the easier acceptance of the new religion.

Our first reliable date in the fifth century is a reference in the Chronicle of Prosper of Aquitaine under the year 431, when he records that the pope, Celestine, had ordained the deacon Palladius as bishop and sent him to those of the Irish who believed in Christ. This event must be seen in the light of the background of the Pelagian heresy. Pelagius, a Britain of the late fourth century, denied the existence of original sin and taught that man could be saved by the effort of his own will. This view spread, from the late fourth century on, throughout the western church and, although the teachings of Pelagius had been condemned at a number of early fifth-century councils, they were still influential in Roman Britain. Indeed, at a later period in Ireland, there werc texts that ultimately derived from Pelagian schools, although the Irish did not follow his teachings. There was a fear that this heresy might spread among the new communities of Christians in Ireland, so Palladius and his helpers (who were almost certainly based at Auxerre in France) were sent to organize them along orthodox lines and to link them directly with the papacy. Thus, our earliest official Christian contacts are with the church of Gaul. It is possible to trace the activity of the members of this mission to Leinster and the Irish midlands. It is also possible that the short collection of synodal decisions extracted below is the work of this group, but we cannot be certain.

The two documents that we can be sure are from the fifth century are by a Romano-Briton called Patrick: his *Confession* and his *Letter to the Soldiers of Coroticus*. Patrick's own words, halting and inarticulate, give us a glimpse of the world of Roman Britain that was soon to disappear, and a sense of the Christian spirit that soon was to spread so rapidly throughout Ireland. For Patrick, to be Roman was to be Christian and he saw himself as a roving missionary in the north of Ireland. His most successful foundation was to be Armagh, as we can see in the seventh-century documents. The Irish soon accepted this poorly educated, humble bishop as their apostle. His central text was the Bible, which shadows all his writing. His Latin was poor; yet it was men like Patrick who introduced the Irish to the Latin alphabet and the basic elements of grammar. In particular, Patrick espoused monasticism; he longed to visit the brethren in Gaul. It is surely no coincidence that the earliest manuscript of the 'life' of St Martin of Tours, the father of monasticism in the northwest of Europe, is in the Book of Armagh beside material about Patrick. The earliest churches in Ireland had been episcopal, but it was the monastic church that was to provide the inspiration for Christianity in Ireland during the following centuries.

The early monastic schools of Ireland probably owe a greater debt to the early episcopal schools than is realized or is capable of proof. Many of the early monastic founders were educated in Leinster, in the area where the Gaulish mission would have been most active. Here there would have been books and influence from Romano-Gaulish schools.[1] There was a distinct group in the Irish church in the late sixth and seventh centuries called the Romani. They are brought to our attention through the controversy concerning the correct date on which to celebrate Easter and are associated with some statements in the canon law collection — the *Collectio Canonum Hibernensis*. The Romani seem to

1. cf. J.-M. Picard, 'The Schaffhausen Adomnán — A Unique Witness to Hiberno-Latin', *Peritia* 1 (1982), 220.

have stood for the episcopal church and favoured the church in Ireland developing along administrative and liturgical lines similar to those found in Rome and on the Continent. The other party, the Hibernenses, favoured a more monastic church, which suited conditions in Ireland particularly well. The Romani may be associated with the old *domnach* churches (free independent episcopal churches) mentioned in the *Liber Angeli* and in Tírechán's notes on Patrick. By the seventh century they were anxious to use canonical scriptural texts and to study patristic writings critically.[2] They still retained their prestige, but eventually had to integrate with the major monasteries. It is possible that the Romani give us a link with the oldest ecclesiastical schools in Ireland.

Those parts of Europe that had been romanized spoke Latin. Ireland had never been conquered and so Latin had to be taught as a foreign language. Tírechán, writing in the 680s, mentions alphabet stones erected by the early missionaries. The teaching of grammar would have been essential. It is not surprising that many of the grammars of the late Roman world have come down to us by way of an Irish manuscript tradition;[3] nor is it surprising that the Irish were famous as teachers or that they were in such demand in later centuries.

In the fifth and sixth centuries, the main concern in church schools in Ireland was to provide a basic education in Latin and to make sufficient copies of essential liturgical books. By the second half of the sixth century we can see that the schools are beginning to produce works of biblical exegesis, essential as part of the theological training of the students.[4] By this time Ireland had been Christianized. Christians were no longer isolated communities in a sea of paganism. Paganism was a threat no more, and so ideals and aspects of Irish paganism that were not in direct conflict with Christianity were being harmonized with Christian tradition. Moreover, the Latin alphabet was now used to write in Irish, thus preserving the earliest vernacular literature of early medieval Europe.

The Irish had not the same fear of pagan classical mythology as clerics on the Continent. Not only did they read the classical authors for style, but they were also interested in the content of the works. They were especially fond of Virgil. Columbanus, for instance, had read Virgil, Horace, Martial, Juvenal, Statius, Ausonius and Claudian. He takes clear delight in the pagan classics in his poem to Fidolius written in Adonaic metre.[5] Columbanus was particularly fond of Horace, and in the eighth and ninth centuries the Irish played a leading part in the transmission of the poems of the Roman lyricist.[6] Although it is often said that Columbanus did not have access to this material before he went to the Continent, it is becoming clear that by the sixth century the Irish already had very good libraries.

The seventh century rushes upon us with a flood of literature in Latin and in Irish. This is the result of a very long period of gestation and the fruit is rich and varied. In the monastery of Bangor during the abbacy of Cronán (680x691) a book entitled the *Antiphonary of Bangor* (now in the Ambrosiana Library in Milan) was compiled. In this we find some of our earliest examples of hagiography in the form of hymns. The poetical metre used in Ireland had been short, heavily alliterated, and with a strong stress accent. But, with the introduction of Latin hymns such as the *Hymnum dicat* of St Hilary of Poitiers (in the *Antiphonary*), a new form of metre appeared. This consists of quatrains of seven or eight syllables to the line. At about this time it was adapted by the native poets for verse in the *dán dírech* style.[7]

One of our earliest native Latin hymns is the *Audite Omnes*, attributed to St Secundinus but more likely to date from the very early seventh century. Each quatrain of this hymn begins with a letter of the alphabet. It is in praise of St Patrick, and the hymn refers to him as the Apostle of the

2. P. Ó Néill, 'Romani Influences on Seventh-century Hiberno-Latin Literature', in P. Ní Chatháin and M. Richter (eds), *Ireland and Europe: The Early Church* (Stuttgart: Klett-Cotta, 1984), 280-90.
3. L. Holtz, *Donat et la Tradition de l'Enseignement Grammatical* (Paris: Centre National de la Recherche Scientifique, 1981); L. Holtz, 'Les grammairiens hiberno-latins étaient-ils des Anglo-Saxons?', *Peritia* 2 (1983), 169-84.
4. cf. P. Ní Chatháin and M. Richter (eds), *Ireland and Christendom: The Bible and the Missions* (Stuttgart: Klett-Cotta, 1986) for a collection of essays dealing with this topic over a long period; M. Lapidge and R. Sharpe, *A Bibliography of Celtic-Latin Literature 400-1200*, Royal Irish Academy Dictionary of Medieval Latin from Celtic Sources, Ancillary Publications 1 (Dublin: Royal Irish Academy, 1985) Nos. 759-.84, pp. 204-10.
5. L. Bieler, 'The Classics in Celtic Ireland', in R.R. Bolgar (ed.), *Classical Influences on European Culture, A.D. 500-1500* (Cambridge: Cambridge University Press, 1971), 45-49; F.J. Byrne, 'Latin Poetry in Ireland', in J. Carney (ed.), *Early Irish Poetry* (Cork: Mercier Press, 1965; reprinted 1969), 29-44.
6. Bieler, op. cit., p. 48.
7. cf. F.J. Byrne, op. cit., pp. 29-44.

Irish. The primacy of Peter and papal authority are stressed and this gives the poem a heightened significance in Irish ecclesiastical politics of the period.[8] *Audite Omnes* became the model for other writers. The monks of Bangor also wrote a hymn of this type praising their rule: *Benchuir bona regula,/ recta atque divina,/ stricta, sancta, sedula,/ summa, iusta, ac mira* (The good rule of Bangor,/right and divine,/ strict, holy and careful,/ the best of rules, just and wonderful). The poem uses rhyme and alliteration. Rhyme appears to have been developed in Ireland, and in the eighth-century hymn by Colmán mac Murchon of Moville we see the further use of both internal and final rhyme.[9]

By the mid-seventh century, prose hagiography blossoms in the writings of Cogitosus of Kildare, Adamnán of Iona and Muirchú of Armagh. Cogitosus made use of the *Cursus Paschalis* of Victorius of Aquitaine, the Dialogues of Pope Gregory the Great and possibly also his *Ordines Romani*.[10] Cogitosus, Adamnán and Muirchú had some knowledge of the Attic school of *Kunstprosa* or metrical prose. Adamnán's Latin, in particular, was correct, if ornate, and compares well with continental Latin of the same period; and he may have compiled a commentary, based in part on Junius Philargyrius, of the *Eclogues* and *Georgics* of Virgil.[11]

The division of scholarly activity may not have been as discrete as one might imagine, for the influence of one branch of learning can be seen in another. The study of grammar was important in relation to that of biblical exegesis.[12] In the second half of the seventh century there was an important group of schools engaged in biblical exegesis in the south, probably centred on Clonfert Mo-Lua.[13] The major figures of this group (some of whom are mentioned in a contemporary Commentary on the Catholic Epistles[14]) are Manchéne, abbot of Min Droichet + 652; Laidcenn mac Baíth Bannaig + 661, scholar of ? Clonfert Mo-Lua; Banbán + 686, scholar of Kildare; Breccán; and Bercán mac Aido.

In 655 a scholar calling himself Augustine wrote *De Mirabilia Sacrae Scripturae* (On the Wonders of Holy Scripture) in fine Latin and displaying a good knowledge of patristic literature. He has a long discussion about the tides and gives us our earliest list of wild animals in Ireland. Laidcenn wrote the *Ecloga de moralibus Job*, an abridgment of the commentary on the Book of Job by Gregory the Great. Ailerán of Clonard, who died in 665/66, wrote *Interpretatio Mystica Progenitorum Domini Jesu Christi*, an interpretation of the names appearing in Christ's genealogy as given in the Gospel of Matthew. This used the common allegorical method of exposition, whereas the historical method may have been especially favoured by the Irish.[15]

Another important text of the seventh century was the *De Duodecim Abusivis Saeculi* (Concerning the Twelve Evils of the World).[16] This text was taken to the Continent where it became extremely popular; Sedulius Scottus used it for his own book, *Liber de Rectoribus Christianis*. It was eventually to become important in the development of political theory in the later Middle Ages.

Yet another area of activity was that of the computus. This branch of science was necessary in order to regulate the Christian calendar. It received particular stimulation because of the debate over the correct method for dating Easter. Here again there is evidence that the world of the exegete and the computist overlapped.[17] The computus was important in that it was allied to the study of arithmetic, geometry, astronomy and the keeping of annals.

The discussion above has referred only to the more prominent writings in Latin in the seventh century. As we enter the eighth century, the great compilation known as the *Collectio Canonum Hibernensis*[18] was put together. This systematic

8. Ó Néill, op. cit., p. 285.
9. cf. Byrne, op. cit., p. 32.
10. Ó Néill, op. cit., p. 290.
11. Bieler, op. cit., p. 47.
12. cf. M. McNamara, 'Psalter Text and Psalter Study in the Early Irish Church (A.D. 600-1200), *Proceedings of the Royal Irish Academy,* 73c (1973), 210, 259.
13. A. Breen, 'Some Seventh-century Hiberno-Latin Texts and their Relationships', *Peritia* 3 (1984), 204-14.
14. cf. J.F. Kenney, *The Sources for the Early History of Ireland: I. Ecclesiastical* (New York: Columbia University Press, 1929; reprinted 1966), 277-78.
15. P. Ní Chatháin, 'Beobachtungen zur irischen und lateinischen Literature des 8. Jahrhunderts in Irland', in H. Dopsch und R. Juffinger (eds), *Virgil von Salzburg, Missionar und Gelehrter*, (Salzburg: Amt der Salzburger Landesregicrung-Kulturabteilung, 1985), 132.
16. A. Breen, 'Pseudo-Cyprian *De Duodecim Abusivis Saeculi* and the Bible', in P. Ní Chatháin and M. Richter (eds), *Ireland and Christendom: The Bible and the Missions* (Stuttgart: Klett-Cotta, 1986), 230-45.
17. D. Ó Cróinín, 'A Seventh-century Irish Computus from the Circle of Cummian', *Proceedings of the Royal Irish Academy*, 82c (1982), 405-30.
18. H. Wasserschleben (ed.), *Die irische Kanonensammlung*, (2nd ed. Leipzig, 1885; reprinted Scientia Verlag Aalen, 1966); M.P. Sheehy, 'The Collectio Canonum Hibernensis — a Celtic Phenonemon', in H.

arrangement of canon law was also taken to the Continent and again provided a model for subsequent editions of canon law there.

During the course of the eighth century, Latin studies seem to decline in importance in Ireland. This decline may be more apparent than real, however, for writing in Irish begins to become as important as writing in Latin. In particular, we see the flowering of the native vernacular culture, and indeed this too was influenced by Latin. The church itself had become rich and lax. With laymen, or at least a married clergy, in charge of churches, the secular world entered the monastery and perhaps accelerated the drift towards the vernacular. A reform movement, the *Céli Dé* reform, tried to redress the balance. It was successful in its own way, but only for a period. With the coming of the Norse at the end of the century, the laxity continued.

That Latin studies had not been neglected is seen during the course of the ninth century in the flood of Irish scholars to the cathedral and palace schools of Europe. It would be too simple to regard the Viking attacks as being the main reason for this exodus. Just as important was the attraction of patronage and the intellectual excitement created by the groups of foreign scholars at these courts. The Irish who went there, priests and monks (and, in the case of Ériugena, possibly laymen as well), were not the ascetics of the age of Columbanus. They might be religious, but some also enjoyed the pleasures of this world. These men already had a sound education and this is why they were received so readily in the intellectual circles of the Continent. They undoubtedly came across material that was new to them, but they were able to approach it and make it their own. Some of them — for instance, Clemens Scottus, the grammarian — became masters of the palace school. He was teacher to Lothar, son of Louis the Pious, the monk Reccheo-Modestus of Fulda, and possibly Prudentius, later bishop of Troyes.[19] Later Johannes Scottus, or as he called himself, Ériugena, was probably master in the palace school of Charles the Bald. He was the only original thinker between the time of Boethius (*c.* 470-*c.* 525) and St Anselm (1033-1109). There were many who were not so famous, such as are remembered in the death notices in the Necrology of St Gall, at 12 September 'Dubsalan, Irish monk and priest', and at 3 June 'Faillan the Irishman, a very learned kindly teacher'.[20]

The Irish brought many of their own books to the Continent. A Dungal, 'principal of the Irish', presented twenty-nine books to the library of Bobbio.[21] The St Gall catalogue lists thirty books in the Irish hand and others of Irish origin.[22] Many of the Irish scholars formed far-flung networks and were in touch with one another. We have the interesting Bamberg cryptogram (818x844), which was an inscription presented for solution by a certain Dubthach to Irishmen passing through the court of Merfyn, king of Gwynedd in Wales. The solution was to substitute Greek letters for Latin, according to a fixed table. A letter accompanies this cryptogram addressed to Colgu, teacher of a group of Irishmen who had solved the problem. They send the solution so that 'our simple and unsophisticated brethren as may think of sailing across the British sea ... might not be made to blush in the presence of Merfyn ... if they fail to understand the inscription'.[23] The route from Ireland to continental Europe by way of Anglesey was clearly already well worn by the early ninth century. While Sedulius and Ériugena's colleague, Martin, knew Greek, it was little by comparison with that of Ériugena himself. Elementary Greek was known in Ireland, at least in some schools, but Ériugena went far beyond this when he came in contact with Greek sources at the court of Charles the Bald. The great advances that he made, leading to his great work of philosophy, the *De Divisione Naturae* (The Division of Nature), were not really built upon, and the confusion and warfare of the later Carolingian empire brought this great period of the revival of learning to an end.

Löwe (ed.), *Die Iren und Europa im früheren Mittelalter*, Vol. I (Stuttgart: Klett-Cotta, 1982), 525-35; M. Lapidge and R. Sharpe, *A Bibliography of Celtic-Latin Literature 400-1200*, Royal Irish Academy Dictionary of Medieval Latin from Celtic Sources, Ancillary Publications 1 (Dublin: Royal Irish Academy, 1985) Nos. 612-15, pp. 156-57.

19. H. Spilling, 'Irische Handschriftenüberlieferung in Fulda, Mainz und Würzburg', in H. Löwe (ed.), *Die Iren und Europa im früheren Mittelalter*, Vol. II (Stuttgart: Klett-Cotta, 1982), 877-78, 883; J.F. Kenney, *The Sources for the Early History of Ireland: I. Ecclesiastical* (New York: Columbia University Press, 1929; reprinted 1966), 537-38; M. Lapidge and R. Sharpe, *A Bibliography of Celtic-Latin Literature 400-1200*, Royal Irish Academy Dictionary of Medieval Latin from Celtic Sources, Ancillary Publications 1 (Dublin: Royal Irish Academy, 1985) Nos. 665-66, pp. 175-76.
20. Kenney, op. cit., p. 598.
21. Kenney, op. cit., p. 516; Lapidge and Sharpe, *Bibliography*, p. 173.
22. Kenney, op. cit., p. 599.
23. Kenney, op. cit., p. 556; Lapidge and Sharpe, *Bibliography*, p. 181.

Irish pilgrims continued to go to Rome and the Holy Land in the following centuries but not in such great numbers. In the tenth century, reforming kings and bishops in Frankish and Germanic lands still looked to the monks and clergy of Ireland to man their churches and schools. In 946 the Emperor Otto I granted a charter to the Irish monastery of Waulsort in the Ardennes. Its first abbot was a Máel Callain. He was followed by Cadroe and Forannan. Later Cadroe took charge of the monastery of St Clement at Metz and made important reforms in Lorraine before his death in 978.[24] In 992 Fíngen (+ 1005), abbot of St Clement at Metz, rebuilt the monastery of St Symphorian to house Irish pilgrims. It was granted a charter in that year by Emperor Otto II. The practice of inviting Irish monks to come to monasteries in German lands continued throughout the eleventh century.

The deaths of Irishmen on the Continent are mentioned frequently in the native Irish annals during these centuries. Some, such as the Irish monk Aaron of St Martin's at Cologne (a church assigned to the Irish in 975), found themselves at the furthest ends of Europe. In 1049 he was consecrated archbishop of Cracow. He died in 1060. Others such as Marianus Scottus I (Máel Brigte), who entered Moville in County Down in 1052, went to Cologne in 1056 and moved to Fulda, south of Kassel, in 1058. In the following year he was ordained priest and became an *inclusus* (a hermit) there. He died at Mainz in 1082. Marianus wrote a chronicle of great importance for a history of the Irish in Germany during this period. The text influenced Sigebert of Gembloux, Florence of Worcester and others.[25] Later a namesake, Marianus Scottus II (Muiredach mac Robartaig) from Donegal, settled at Regensburg, where he was granted the church of St Peter in 1075. He was famous as a scribe and died in 1088.[26] Regensburg became the centre of Irish Benedictine houses, maintaining close contacts with churches in the south of Ireland in the twelfth century; it was especially under the patronage of the Mac Carthys.

These monks were also interested in learning. David Scottus was head of the cathedral school of Würzburg and accompanied Emperor Henry V on an expedition to Italy in 1110, writing a pro-imperial account of this journey.[27] In 1148/49 Marcus of Regensburg wrote the *Visio Tnugdali*, a contribution to the vision literature of medieval Europe.[28]

In Ireland itself, we have fewer texts in Latin from the late ninth century onwards, but it is clear that Latin learning was far from dead. It must be remembered that Latin epics were being translated into Irish from the late tenth century onwards.[29] From Armagh we have a text of Gregory the Great's *Moralia in Iob*, dating to the twelfth century and containing marginalia in Irish. The text is written in a fine hand for a Máel Brigte.[30]

Another manuscript (Auct.F.3.15 from the Bodleian library in Oxford) is in four parts, containing texts in Latin with glosses in Irish. The handwriting by a scribe named Salmon is Irish and some evidence suggests that it comes from Glendalough, Co. Wicklow. It dates from the late eleventh or early twelfth century. Part I is a Latin translation of Plato's *Timaeus*, with commentary by Chalcidius. Parts III and IV contain an epitome and long extract of Ériugena's *Periphyseon*, or *De Divisione Naturae*. The volume appears to have had a 'director', perhaps the Tuilecnad named by another scribe and possibly a member of the Ó Maelchonaire family.[31]

From Glendalough also we have two fragments of schoolbooks, one containing part of the grammatical work of Clemens Scottus and the other a text of Gerbert of Aurillac's work on the abacus. This text introduced arabic numerals to the West for the first time.[32] These texts from Armagh and Glendalough show that Irish schools were in contact with contemporary learning in continental Europe.

This was also the period of the reform of the church in Ireland, when the older monasteries gave way to an episcopal organization more in line with

24. Kenney, op. cit., pp. 609-10.
25. Kenney, op. cit., pp. 615-16; Lapidge and Sharpe, *Bibliography*, p. 196.
26. Kenney, op. cit., pp. 616-18; Lapidge and Sharpe, *Bibliography*, p. 196.
27. Kenney, op. cit., pp. 619-20.
28. Kenney, op. cit., pp. 741-42; Lapidge and Sharpe, *Bibliography*, p. 197.
29. W.B. Stanford, *Ireland and the Classical Tradition* (Dublin: Allen Figgis/Totowa, New Jersey: Rowman & Littlefield, 1987), pp. 73-89.
30. F.J. Byrne, *A Thousand Years of Irish Script* (Oxford: Bodleian Library, 1979), pp. 15-16.
31. Kenney, op. cit. pp. 679-80; F.J. Byrne, *A Thousand Years of Irish Script*, pp. 14-15.
32. L. Bieler and B. Bischoff, 'Fragmente zweier frühmittelalterlicher schulbücher aus Glendalough', *Celtica* 3 (1956), 211-20; F.J. Byrne, 'The Trembling Sod: Ireland in 1169', in A. Cosgrove (ed.), *The New History of Ireland*. II. *Medieval Ireland, 1169-1534* (Oxford: Clarendon Press, 1987), p. 40.

that on the Continent. The clergy associated with this reform looked to the practices of the universal church. Their training and education were those of the new schools. Bishop Patrick's work reflects the influence of the cathedral schools of northern France, where there was a revival of classical studies. Some of the older monastic schools in Ireland were attempting to move with the times. We have already seen the interest in more recent continental scholarship in Armagh and Glendalough. And it seems that there was an attempt to establish a cathedral school or a university at Armagh when Ruaidrí Ua Conchobair allocated an annual grant to Armagh for the education of students from Ireland and Scotland in 1169. Already in 1162, at the Synod of Clane, it was decreed that only a graduate of Armagh could hold the office of *fer léigind* (head of school) in any church in Ireland. These events are hardly unconnected with the appointment of Flann Ua Gormáin as head of the school in Armagh in 1154. He had studied in France and England for twenty-one years. At his death on 20 March 1174, the annalist calls him 'arch-lector of Armagh and all Ireland'. These fascinating developments were interrupted by the arrival of the Normans and the subsequent disruption of native life and society.

Because of limited space, it is unfortunately impossible to include the Latin texts in this section. However, the Latin of Adamnán's Vita Columbae *(Life of Columba), a unique example of the type of Latin written in Ireland in the seventh century, has been included. The manuscript from which it is taken (now in the Stadtbibliothek of Schaffhausen, Switzerland) was copied in Iona by Dorbbéne (who died in October 713) from Adamnán's original. The text is also of importance since it indicates how Latin was taught — and possibly pronounced — by the Irish of the time.*

SAINT PATRICK

(died *c.* 492)

from: THE CONFESSION

[This document is a meditation by a sincere, humble, but powerful personality. Now coming to the end of his days, Patrick tries to explain that his motivation throughout his extremely difficult and dangerous missionary career had been based on the message of the Gospels and the hope of eternal salvation. He feels that he is the least of the faithful in the eyes of God. Throughout his life he was constantly aware of his lack of education, for which (among other things) he was despised by senior clergymen. The clumsiness and obscurity of some of his sentences emphasize the pain he experienced in trying to express himself in Latin — a language that he had never learnt very well. His mind calls up ideas and phrases from the Bible, which he knew almost by heart. He refers more to the New Testament than to the Old, and, in particular, finds examples and inspiration in Saint Paul's Epistles to the Corinthians. Patrick, like Paul, was very much an apostle to the Gentiles.

The extracts below from the edition and translation of both *The Confession* and *Letter to the Soldiers of Coroticus* are by Ludwig Bieler, whose magisterial work provided a scientific basis for all subsequent studies of the 'Patrician problem'. Text: L. Bieler, *Libri Epistolarum Sancti Patricii Episcopi* (Dublin: Irish Manuscripts Commission, 1952), 56-102; Translation: L. Bieler, *The Works of St Patrick*, Ancient Christian Writers 17 (Westminster, Maryland: The Newman Press/London: Longmans, Green and Co., 1953), 21-54.

Words in italics, here and in the next extract, indicate phrases or echoes from the Bible. Full references to them may be found in the editions cited.]

THE CONFESSION

§1. I am Patrick, a sinner, most unlearned, the least of all the faithful, and utterly despised by many. My father was Calpornius, a deacon, son of Potitus, a priest, of the village Bannavem Taburniae; he had a country seat nearby, and there I was taken captive.

I was then about sixteen years of age. I did not know the true God. I was taken into captivity to Ireland with many thousands of people — and deservedly so, because we turned away from God, and did not keep His commandments, and did not obey our priests, who used to remind us of our salvation. And the Lord *brought over us the wrath of His anger and scattered us among many nations*, even *unto the utmost part of the earth*, where now my littleness is placed among strangers.

§2. And there *the Lord opened the sense of my unbelief* that I might at last remember my sins and *be converted with all my heart to the Lord my God*, who *had regard for my abjection*, and mercy on my youth and ignorance, and watched over me before I knew Him, and before I was able to distinguish between good and evil, and guarded me, and comforted me as would a father his son....

§23. And again after a few years I was in Britain with my people, who received me as their son, and sincerely besought me that now at last, having suffered so many hardships, I should not leave them and go elsewhere.

And there I saw in the night the vision of a man, whose name was Victoricus, coming as it were from Ireland, with countless letters. And he gave me one of them, and I read the opening words of the letter, which were, 'The voice of the Irish'; and as I read the beginning of the letter I thought that at the same moment I heard their voice — they were those beside the Wood of Voclut, which is near the Western Sea — and thus did they cry out *as with one mouth*: 'We ask thee, boy, come and walk among us once more.'

And I was quite broken in heart, and could read no further, and so I woke up. Thanks be to God, after many years the Lord gave to them according to their cry....

§41. Hence, how did it come to pass in Ireland that those who never had a knowledge of God, but until now always worshipped idols and things impure, have now been made a people of the Lord, and are called sons of God, that the sons and daughters of the kings of the Irish are seen to be monks and virgins of Christ?

§42. Among others, a blessed Irishwoman of noble birth, beautiful, full-grown, whom I had baptised, came to us after some days for a particular reason: she told us that she had received a message from a messenger of God, and he admonished her to be a virgin of Christ and draw near to God. Thanks be to God, on the sixth day after this she most laudably and eagerly chose what all virgins of Christ do. Not that their fathers agree with them; no — they often even suffer persecution and undeserved reproaches from their parents; and yet their number is ever increasing. How many have been reborn there so as to be of our kind, I do not know — not to mention widows and those who practice continence.

But greatest is the suffering of those women who live in slavery. All the time they have to endure terror and threats. But the Lord gave His grace to many of His maidens; for, though they are forbidden to do so, they follow Him bravely.

§43. Wherefore, then, even if I wished to leave them and go to Britain — and how I would have loved to go to my country and my parents, and also to Gaul[1] in order to visit the brethren and to see the face of the saints of my Lord! God knows it that I much desired it; but I am bound by the Spirit, who gives evidence against me if I do this, telling me that I shall be guilty; and I am afraid of losing the labour which I have begun — nay, not I, but Christ the Lord who bade me come here and stay with them for the rest of my life, if the Lord will, and will guard me from every evil way that I may not sin before Him....

§48. You know, and so does God, how I have lived among you from my youth in the true faith and in sincerity of heart. Likewise, as regards the heathen among whom I live, I have been faithful to them, and so I shall be. God knows it, I have overreached none of them, nor would I think of doing so, for the sake of God and His Church, for fear of raising persecution against them and all of us, and for fear that through me the name of the Lord be blasphemed; for it is written: *Woe to the man through whom the name of the Lord is blasphemed.*

§49. *For although I be rude in all things*, nevertheless I have tried somehow to keep myself safe, and that, too, for my Christian brethren, and the virgins of Christ, and the pious women who of their own accord made me gifts and laid on the altar some of their ornaments; and I gave them back to them, and they were offended that I did so. But I did it for the hope of lasting success — in order to preserve myself cautiously in everything so that they might not seize upon me or the ministry of my service, under the pretext of dishonesty, and that I would not even in the smallest matter give the infidels an opportunity to defame or defile.

§50. When I baptised so many thousands of people, did I perhaps expect from any of them as much as half a screpall?[2] *Tell me, and I will restore it*

1. The ancient name for modern France.
2. From the Latin *scripulum* ('a scruple'), a 24th part of an ounce.

to you. Or when the Lord ordained clerics everywhere through my unworthy person and I conferred the ministry upon them free, if I asked any of them as much as the price of my shoes, *speak against me and I will return it to you.*

§51. On the contrary, I spent money for you that they might receive me; and I went to you and everywhere for your sake in many dangers, even to the farthest districts, beyond which there lived nobody and where nobody had ever come to baptise, or to ordain clergy, or to confirm the people. With the grace of the Lord, I did everything lovingly and gladly for your salvation.

§52. All the while I used to give presents to the kings, besides the fees I paid to their sons who travel with me. Even so they laid hands on me and my companions, and on that day they eagerly wished to kill me; but my time had not yet come. And everything they found with us they took away, and me they put in irons; and on the fourteenth day the Lord delivered me from their power, and our belongings were returned to us because of God and our dear friends whom we had seen before.

§53. You know how much I paid to those who administered justice in all those districts to which I came frequently. I think I distributed among them not less than the price of fifteen men,[3] so that you might enjoy me, and I might always enjoy you in God. I am not sorry for it — indeed it is not enough for me; I still spend and shall spend more. God has power to grant me afterwards *that I myself may be spent for your souls....*

§58. Wherefore may God never permit it to happen to me that I should lose His people which He purchased in the utmost parts of the world. I pray to God to give me perseverance and to deign that I be a faithful witness to Him to the end of my life for my God.

§59. And if ever I have done any good for my God whom I love, I beg Him to grant me that I may shed my blood with those exiles and captives for His name, even though I should be denied a grave, or my body be woefully torn to pieces limb by limb by hounds or wild beasts, or the fowls of the air devour it. I am firmly convinced that if this should happen to me, I would have gained my soul together with my body, because on that day without doubt we shall rise in the brightness of the sun, that is, in the glory of Christ Jesus our Redeemer, as sons of the living God and *joint heirs with Christ, to be made conformable to His image*; for *of Him, and by Him, and in Him* we shall reign.

3. In the barbaric society of pagan Ireland, every freeman had a 'body price', which was due to his relatives should he be killed. According to the seventh-century law tracts, this was technically his *éraic* — a fixed value equivalent to seven female slaves.

§60. For this sun which we see rises daily for us because He commands so, but it will never reign, nor will its splendour last; what is more, those wretches who adore it will be miserably punished. Not so we, who believe in, and worship, the true sun — Christ — who will never perish, nor will he *who doeth His will*; but he *will abide for ever as Christ abideth for ever*, who reigns with God the Father Almighty and the Holy Spirit before time, and now, and in all eternity. Amen.

§61. Behold, again and again would I set forth the words of my confession. *I testify* in truth and in joy of heart *before God and His holy angels* that I never had any reason except the Gospel and its promises why I should ever return to the people from whom once before I barely escaped.

§62. I pray those who believe and fear God, whosoever deigns to look at or receive this writing which Patrick, a sinner, unlearned, has composed in Ireland, that no one should ever say that it was my ignorance if I did or showed forth anything however small according to God's good pleasure; but let this be your conclusion and let it so be thought, that — as is the perfect truth — it was the gift of God. This is my confession before I die.

from:
LETTER TO THE SOLDIERS OF COROTICUS

[This is the first letter written in Ireland to have survived. It is a more literary document than *The Confession* and was probably written earlier in Patrick's career. Coroticus was a Romanized Briton, a nominal Christian, and a prince who was carving out a kingdom for himself in the south-west of Scotland and north-west of England — probably in an area not far from Patrick's home because there is a hint of familiarity in the document. He had made a raid on Ireland and captured newly baptized converts, whom he then sold to the Picts and pagan Irish. Patrick had sent a first letter in which he had asked for the return of the captives and some of the booty. It had been treated with scorn. His second letter was meant to be read aloud to the general public. In this document we can see the disintegration of Romanized life in Britain and the emergence of the early medieval kingdoms. Patrick's faith and courage are clearly evident in the midst of the appalling conditions that he and his Christian communities had to endure.]

§1. I, Patrick, a sinner, unlearned, resident in Ireland, declare myself to be a bishop. Most assuredly I believe that what I am I have received from God. And so I live among barbarians, a stranger and exile for the love of God. He is witness that this is so. Not that I wished my mouth to utter anything so hard and harsh; but I am forced by the zeal for God; and the truth of Christ has wrung it from me, out of love for my neighbours and sons for whom I gave up my country and parents and *my life to the point of death*. If I be worthy, I live for my God to teach the heathen, even though some may despise me.

§2. With my own hand I have written and composed these words, to be given, delivered, and sent to the soldiers of Coroticus; I do not say, to my fellow citizens, or to fellow citizens of the holy Romans, but to fellow citizens of the demons, because of their evil works. Like our enemies, they live in death, allies of the Scots and the apostate Picts.[1] Dripping with blood, they welter in the blood of innocent Christians, whom I have begotten into the number for God and confirmed in Christ!

§3. The day after the newly baptised, anointed with chrism,[2] in white garments [had been slain] — the fragrance was still on their foreheads when they were butchered and slaughtered with the sword by the above-mentioned people — I sent a letter with a holy presbyter whom I had taught from his childhood, clerics accompanying him, asking them to let us have some of the booty, and of the baptised they had made captives. They only jeered at them.

§4. Hence I do not know what to lament more: those who have been slain, or those whom they have taken captive, or those whom the devil has mightily ensnared. Together with him they will be slaves in Hell in an eternal punishment; for *who committeth sin is a slave* and will be called *a son of the devil*....

§7. Wherefore, then, I plead with you earnestly, *ye holy and humble of heart*, it is not permissible to court the favour of such people, nor to take food or drink with them, nor even to accept their alms, until they make reparation to God in hardships, through penance, with shedding of tears, and set free the baptised servants of God and handmaids of Christ, for whom He died and was crucified....

§10. Did I come to Ireland without God, or according to the flesh? Who compelled me? I am bound by the Spirit not to see any of my kinsfolk. Is it of my own doing that I have holy mercy on the people who once took me captive and made away with the servants and maids of my father's house? I was freeborn according to the flesh. I am the son of a decurion.[3] But I sold my noble rank — I am neither ashamed nor sorry — for the good of others. Thus I am a servant in Christ to a foreign nation for the unspeakable glory *of life everlasting which is in Christ Jesus our Lord*.

§11. And if my own people do not know me, *a prophet hath no honour in his own country*. Perhaps we are not *of the same fold* and have not *one and the same God as father*, as is written: *He that is not with me, is against me, and he that gathereth not with me, scattereth*. It is not right that *one destroyeth, another buildeth up. I seek not the things that are mine.*

It is not my grace, but God *who has given this solicitude into my heart*, to be one of His hunters or fishers whom God once foretold would come in the last days.

§12. I am hated. What shall I do, Lord? I am most despised. Look, Thy sheep around me are torn to pieces and driven away, and that by those robbers, by the orders of the hostile-minded Coroticus. Far from the love of God is a man who hands over Christians to the Picts and Scots. *Ravening wolves* have devoured the flock of the Lord, which in Ireland was indeed growing splendidly with the greatest care; and the sons and daughters of kings were monks and virgins of Christ — I cannot count their number. Wherefore, *be not pleased with the wrong done to the just*; *even to hell it shall not please*.

§13. Who of the saints would not shudder to be merry with such persons or to enjoy a meal with them? They have filled their houses with the spoils of dead Christians, they live on plunder. They do not know, the wretches, that what they offer their

1. The Scots and Picts were nicknames given by the Romans to the inhabitants of Ireland and Scotland respectively. When the Irish later colonized Scotland, their name eventually became the name of the country.
2. A mixture of olive oil and balsam used for sacramental anointing.

3. A minor ranking military officer, or member of a city council (which is probably what Patrick's father was).

friends and sons as food is deadly poison, just as Eve did not understand that it was death she gave to her husband. So are all that do evil: they work death as their eternal punishment.

§14. This is the custom of the Roman Christians of Gaul: they send holy and able men to the Franks[4] and other heathen with so many thousand *solidi*[5] to ransom baptised captives. You prefer to kill and sell them to a foreign nation that has no knowledge of God. You betray the members of Christ as it were into a brothel. What hope have you in God, or anyone who thinks as you do, or converses with you in words of flattery? God will judge. For Scripture says: *Not only they that do evil are worthy to be condemned, but they also that consent to them.*

§15. I do not know what I should say or speak further about the departed ones of the sons of God, whom the sword has touched all too harshly. For Scripture says: *Weep with them that weep*; and again: *If one member be grieved, let all members grieve with it.* Hence the Church mourns and laments her sons and daughters whom the sword has not yet slain, but who were removed and carried off to faraway lands, where sin abounds openly, grossly, impudently. There people who were freeborn have been sold, Christians made slaves, and that, too, in the service of the abominable, wicked, and apostate Picts! . . . .

§19. Where, then, will Coroticus with his criminals, rebels against Christ, where will they see themselves, they who distribute baptised women as prizes — for a miserable temporal kingdom, which will pass away in a moment? *As a cloud or smoke that is dispersed by the wind,* so *shall the* deceitful *wicked perish at the presence of the Lord; but the just shall feast with great constancy* with Christ, *they shall judge nations,* and rule over wicked kings for ever and ever. Amen.

§20. *I testify before God and His angels* that it will be so as He indicated to my ignorance. It is not my words that I have set forth in Latin, but those of God and the apostles and prophets, who have never lied. *He that believeth shall be saved; but he that believeth not shall be condemned, God hath spoken.*

§21. I ask earnestly that whoever is a willing servant of God be a carrier of this letter, so that on no account it be suppressed or hidden by anyone, but rather be read before all the people, and in the presence of Coroticus himself. May God inspire them sometime to recover their senses for God, repenting, however late, their heinous deeds — murderers of the brethren of the Lord! — and to set free the baptised women whom they took captive, in order that they may deserve to live to God, and be made whole, here and in eternity! Be peace to the Father, and to the Son, and to the Holy Spirit. Amen.

4. One of the barbarian groups that invaded Roman Gaul. They gave their name to modern France.
5. A *solidus* was a gold coin weighing 4.5 grams.

from:
THE BISHOP'S SYNOD

[This is a collection of the earliest canon law to have survived from early Ireland. Although there is much debate about this material, it can be argued that most, if not all, of these canons date from the fifth century. As can be seen, the country is still mainly pagan and Christians are advised to have minimal contact with them. The ransoming of captives (§§1-5) reminds us of Patrick's letter to Coroticus in the extract above. In §6 Christian clergy and their wives are asked to wear Roman dress and hairstyle clearly to mark them off from their uncivilized, barbarian and pagan fellow countrymen. §7 indicates that slavery was not a barrier to holy orders, but that allowances had to be made for people under such constraints. §8 Early Irish law allowed for the pursuit of a debtor even to the point of death — an activity in which a clergyman could hardly be expected to engage.

These canons were attributed to Patrick, Auxilius and Iserninus. Patrick's name was frequently added to documents at a later date to give them greater authenticity. The other two names are associated with Leinster — Auxilius giving his name to Killashee near Naas, Co. Kildare, and Iserninus was associated with Ahade in County Carlow.

The translation is to be found in L. Bieler, *The Irish Penitentials*, Scriptores Latini Hiberniae, Vol. V (Dublin: Dublin Institute for Advanced Studies, 1963), 54-59.]

'FIRST SYNOD OF ST. PATRICK'

HERE BEGINS THE SYNOD OF THE BISHOPS, NAMELY, PATRICK, AUXILIUS, ISERNINUS

We give thanks to God the Father, and the Son, and the Holy Ghost.

To the priests, deacons, and all the clergy — Patrick, Auxilius, Iserninus, the bishops, greetings.

We deem it better to forewarn the negligent rather than to condemn accomplished deeds, as Solomon says: *It is better to reason than to be wroth.*

Copies of our decisions are given below, and begin thus:

§1. If anyone has collected money for captives in his community on his own, and without permission, he has deserved to be excommunicated....

§4. If anyone has obtained permission, and money has been collected, he should not ask for more than is needed.

§5. If anything is left over, he should lay it on the bishop's altar, to be given to some [other] needy person.

§6. Any cleric, from ostiary[1] to priest, that is seen without a tunic and does not cover the shame and nakedness of his body, and whose hair is not shorn after the Roman custom, and whose wife goes about with her head unveiled, shall both likewise be held in contempt by the laity and be removed from the Church.

§7. Any cleric who, when summoned, in neglect of the custom fails to appear at the meetings for matins and vespers shall, except he be held under the yoke of servitude, be considered a stranger.

§8. If a cleric has given surety for a pagan in whatsoever amount, and it so happens — as well it might — that the pagan by some ruse defaults upon the cleric, the cleric must pay the debt from his own means; should he contend with him in arms, let him be reckoned to be outside the Church, as he deserves.

§9. A monk and a virgin, the one from one place, the other from another, shall not take lodging in the same inn, nor travel in the same carriage from village to village, nor carry on prolonged conversations together.

§10. If anyone has made a good beginning as a psalmist, and then quits and lets his hair grow, he is to be excluded from the Church, unless he returns to his former status.

§11. If any cleric has been excommunicated by someone [?] and some other person receives him, both are to perform the same penance.

§12. If a Christian has been excommunicated, not even his alms are to be accepted.

§13. Alms offered by pagans are not to be accepted for the Church.

§14. A Christian who has committed murder, or committed adultery, or sworn before a druid as pagans do, shall do a year's penance for each of these crimes; the year of penance completed, he shall present himself, accompanied by witnesses, and then be freed of his obligation by a priest....

1. A porter or doorkeeper.

from: LIBER ANGELI (Book of the Angel)

[The *Liber Angeli* (Book of the Angel) is a quasi legal document produced in Armagh, probably shortly after 640. It is an example of early medieval propaganda. Armagh was making a powerful, and what was to become a successful, bid for leadership of the Patrician cult. By means of having an angel mediate between Patrick and the Lord, we are presented with a blueprint for the physical development of the site of Armagh and for its claim to jurisdiction over all the churches and tribes of the Irish. The word *suburbana* is of interest; it means the territory immediately surrounding the 'city'. Modelled on the concept found in the Bible, Armagh was a 'city of refuge', a place of sanctuary, and its boundaries were now being expanded. This area was also called a *terminus*, which gives us the Irish word *tearmann* (sanctuary, church land). The placenames mentioned are *Mons Berbicis* (Benwilt Hill, north of Cootehill in County Cavan), Slíab Miss (Slemish, Co. Antrim), Bri Erigi (uncertain, either in County Down or to the north-west of Armagh) and Drummai Breg (hills above Slane in

County Meath). The word *domnach*, which now appears in placenames as *Donagh-*, is a very early borrowing during the missionary period of the Latin *dominicum*, the 'house of the Lord'. By this stage it was recognized as an old word and one that was no longer used to name a church.

The translation appears in L. Bieler, *The Patrician Texts in the Book of Armagh*, Scriptores Latini Hiberniae, Vol. X (Dublin: Dublin Institute for Advanced Studies, 1979), 184-91.]

To the holy bishop Patrick, the supreme priest of the Lord, an angel, taught by God, announced the reverence due to his apostolic see and the due honour of his heir [to be] rendered by all the Irish.

Here begins the Book of the Angel

(1) Once, then, holy Patrick went forth from the city of Armagh to baptize, teach, and heal multitudes of both sexes beside the well [that is] close to the said city in the east. (2) And there, before dawn, he awaited many persons to gather from everywhere for the knowledge of the faith; suddenly, then, sleep befell him because he had been tired out previously by night vigils for Christ. (3) And behold, at once an angel came to him from heaven and raised him gently from sleep; and holy Patrick said: 'Here I am. Have I done any wrong recently in the eyes of the Most High? If this has happened, I ask for pardon from God.' (4) The angel answered: 'No, but the Most High Almighty has sent me to you, that is, for the consolation of your spirit after the conversion of the Irish to the faith in Him by you; [for] you have gained them for Him by very hard work and by your tireless preaching, which through the illuminating grace of the Holy Spirit was fruitful to all people. (5) You also were always toiling on many occasions in many dangers from the heathen, in cold and heat, in hunger and thirst, wandering unwearyingly from tribe to tribe for the benefit of many heathen. (6) The Lord your God knows that your present place which we see before us, placed high on the hill, is narrow and has [only] a small church, and is also hemmed in by some inhabitants of the region, and the surrounding territory [*suburbana*] is not sufficient to give shelter to all. (7) Therefore a vast *termonn* is being established by the Lord for the city of Armagh, which you have loved more than all the lands of the Irish, that is, from the top of *mons Berbicis* to Slíab Miss; from Slíab Miss to Bri Erigi; from Bri Erigi to Drummai Breg: this, certainly, if you wish, will be its extent. (8) And further, the Lord God has given all the tribes of the Irish as a *paruchia*[1] to you and to this city, which in Irish is named Ardd Machae.' (9) Holy Patrick, his face bowed down before the angel, said: 'I give thanks to God my eternal Lord, who has deigned in his clemency to give such great glory to his servant.' (10) Also, the holy man said: 'I foresee, however, my holy Lord, that some elect [men] will arise in this island through the ineffable goodness of your mercy and the labour of preaching you, [men] dear to me as if they were issue of my own body, also friends to you, who will serve you devoutly, who will certainly be in need of some suitable provision for the purpose of necessary maintenance for themselves and their churches and monasteries after me; (11) therefore I ought, perfectly and justly, to share with the perfect religious of Ireland the abundance indisputably given me by God, so that I as well as they enjoy in peace the riches of God's bounty — all those things having been granted to me by God's love.' (12) Also, he said: 'Is it not sufficient for me, whatever Christian men have devoutly vowed and wished to offer me from their land, offerings of their own free choice?' (13) Also: 'Am I not content to be the apostolic teacher and chief leader for all the tribes of the Irish, especially as I retain my own tax rightly to be rendered, and this is given me even by the Most High as a truly fitting due all over the free churches of the provinces, and this right is decreed likewise to all monasteries of cenobites[2] without any doubt in favour of the ruler of Armagh for ever?'....

(21) Further, every free church and city of episcopal rank which is seen to have been founded in the whole island of the Irish, and any place anywhere that is called *domnach* [is], according to the word of the angel, in special union with bishop Patrick and the heir of his see of Armagh, because, as we have said above, God has given him the entire island. (22) Further, we ought to know: any monk of any church, if he returns to Patrick, does not deny his own monastic vow, especially if he devotes

1. Originally coterminous with the 'plebs' or early Irish population group (*túath*) — an area ruled by a bishop. It later came to mean a community of monastic houses ruled by an abbot. The meaning here is probably deliberately ambiguous.
2. Or coenobitae — members of a religious order who follow a communal way of life.

[himself to Patrick] with the consent of his former abbot. (23) Therefore whosoever goes over to [Patrick's] church for the love of him must not be blamed nor excommunicated, because he [Patrick] himself will judge all the Irish on the great day of the terrible judgment in the presence of Christ....

TÍRECHÁN

(*fl.* second half of 7th century)

from: COLLECTANEA CONCERNING ST PATRICK

[Tírechán's work is a short book of notes in poor Latin, unpolished, and lacking in structure. Internal evidence suggests that he was following a well-established hagiographical model in the form of an *itinerarium*, as had his master, Bishop Ultán. He is allegedly giving an account of St Patrick's missionary journeys and the churches that he founded. Of course by Tírechán's time much of this was guesswork and legend. It was primarily a work of propaganda for the church of Armagh as she made a bid for headship of all the churches of the Irish. It is clear from the beginning of the extract that she had enemies. We can see echoes of the *Liber Angeli* (Book of the Angel); the emphasis on swearing is a technical legal device used in the secular law courts of early Ireland (cf. Binchy, pp. 61-64). In this case it was a way of saying that no church could be of higher authority than Armagh.

The second episode is the most coherent part of Tírechán's narrative and appears to be a retelling of a story out of oral tradition. Here he is at his most literary. The scene is in *Cruachu* (Rathcroghan, Co. Roscommon), the capital of Connaught. King Loíguire is the fifth-century high king of Ireland. His daughters ask questions that reflect aspects of early Irish society — for example fosterage. Patrick's answer is in the form of a creed. The reference to the *ferta* is to an Iron Age burial within a circular ditch and mound. Since the *relic* (from Latin *reliquiae* 'relics', giving modern Irish *reilig*, a 'graveyard') is mentioned, it is likely that pagan style burial was still being practised.

The translation appears in L. Bieler, *The Patrician Texts in the Book of Armagh*, Scriptores Latini Hiberniae, Vol. X (Dublin: Dublin Institute for Advanced Studies, 1979), 122-67.]

... 18. (1) You know that all the things I have written from the beginning of this work have taken place in your own regions, except that I have related a few, relevant to my enterprise, which I learnt from many elders and from the said bishop Ultán Moccu Conchubair who fostered me. (2) However, my heart within me is filled with the [sorrowing] love for Patrick, because I see deserters and arch-robbers and war-lords of Ireland hate Patrick's territorial supremacy, because they have taken away from him what was his and are afraid; for if an heir of Patrick were to investigate his supremacy he could vindicate for him almost the whole island as his domain, (3) because i. God gave him the whole island with its people through an angel of the Lord, ii. and he taught them the law of the Lord, iii. and baptized them with God's baptism, iiii. and made known to them the cross of Christ, and preached His resurrection; (4) they, however, do not love his community because i. it is not permitted to swear against him, ii. or overswear him, iii. or swear concerning him, iiii. and it is not permitted to draw lots with him, because all the primitive churches of Ireland are his; on the contrary, he overswears whatever is sworn. (5) All the things that I have written from the beginning of this work are unspecified; all that remains will be more specific....

26. (1) Then holy Patrick came to the well called Clébach, on the slopes of Cruachu to the east, before sunrise, and they sat beside the well, (2) and, behold, the two daughters of king Loíguire, fair-haired Ethne and red-haired Fedelm, came to the well, as women are wont to do, in the morning to wash, and they found the holy assembly of bishops with Patrick beside the well. (3) And they did not know whence they were or of what shape or from what people or from what region, but thought they were men of the other world or earth-gods or a phantom; (4) and the maidens said to them: 'Whence are you and whence have you come?' and

Patrick said to them: 'It would be better for you to profess our true God than to ask questions about our race.' (5) The first maiden said: 'Who is God and where is God and whose God is he and where is his dwelling-place? Has your God sons and daughters, gold and silver? Is he ever-living, is he beautiful, have many fostered his son, are his daughters dear and beautiful in the eyes of the men of the earth? (6) Is he in the sky or in the earth or in the water, in rivers, in mountains, in valleys? (7) Give us an account of him; how shall he be seen, how is he loved, how is he found, is he found in youth, in old age?' (8) Replying, holy Patrick, full of the Holy Spirit, said: 'Our God is the God of all men, the God of heaven and earth, of the sea and the rivers, God of the sun and the moon and all the stars, the God of high mountains and low valleys; (9) God above heaven and in heaven and under heaven, he has his dwelling in heaven and earth and sea and in everything that is in them; he breathes in all things, makes all things live, surpasses all things, supports all things; (10) he illumines the light of the sun, he consolidates the light of the night and the stars, he has made wells in the dry earth and dry islands in the sea and stars for the service of the major lights. (11) He has a son, coeternal with him, similar to him; the Son is not younger than the Father nor is the Father older than the Son, and the Holy Spirit breathes in them; the Father and the Son and the Holy Spirit are not separate. (12) Now I wish to join you to the heavenly king since you are daughters of an earthly king, if you are willing to believe.' (13) And the maidens said as with one voice and one heart: 'Teach us with all diligence how we can believe in the heavenly king, so that we may see him face to face. Tell us, and we will do as you say.' (14) And Patrick said: 'Do you believe that through baptism you cast off the sin of your father and mother?' They answered: 'We believe.' 'Do you believe in penance after sin?' 'We believe.' 'Do you believe in life after death? Do you believe in the resurrection on the day of judgment?' 'We believe.' 'Do you believe in the unity of the Church?' 'We believe.' (15) And they were baptized, with a white garment over their heads. And they demanded to see the face of Christ, and the holy man said to them: 'Unless you taste death you cannot see the face of Christ, and unless you receive the sacrament.' (16) And they answered: 'Give us the sacrament so that we may see the Son, our bridegroom', and they received the eucharist of God and fell asleep in death, and their friends placed them on one bed and covered them with their garments, and made a lament and great keening. (17) And the druid Caplit, who had fostered the one, came and wept, and Patrick preached to him and he believed, and the hair of his head was shorn off. (18) And his brother Máel came and said: 'My brother has believed Patrick; not so I, but I will bring him back to heathendom', and he spoke harsh words to Mathonus and Patrick. (19) And Patrick preached the faith to him and converted him to the penance of God, and the hair of his head was shorn off, that is, the [hair cut in] druidic fashion [which was] seen on his head, *airbacc giunnæ*,[1] as it is called. Hence comes the saying that is the most famous of all Irish sayings, 'Máel is like Caplit', because [both] believed in God. (20) And the days of mourning for the king's daughters came to an end, and they buried them beside the well of Clébach, and they made a round ditch after the manner of a *ferta*, because this is what the heathen Irish used to do, but we call it *relic*, that is, the remains of the maidens. (21) And the *ferta* was made over to Patrick with the bones of the holy virgins, and to his heirs after him for ever, and he made an earthen church in that place....

1. frontal curve of tonsure.

COGITOSUS

(*fl.* mid-7th century)

from:
VITA SANCTAE BRIGITAE
(Life of Saint Brigit)

[The 'Life' of Brigit by Cogitosus is the earliest 'life' of the saint to survive. It is a witness to the ambitions of the church of Kildare in Leinster for headship of the Irish churches. In this way she was challenging her greatest rival of the day — Armagh. Ultimately her jurisdiction was to be confined within the province. The 'life', however, shows us the power of Kildare at its greatest extent.

Kildare enters the historical record in 639 when the annals record the death of her bishop and abbot, Áed Dub mac Colmáin, a member of the Uí Dúnlainge dynasty. His brother, Faelán, had recently gained control of the overkingship of Leinster. Kildare was now the focus of new political patronage, to be seen in the reorganization and rebuilding that was taking place. In line with this 'new broom', Cogitosus used a technique of hagiographical writing that best suited the propaganda needs of Kildare in her new role as royal metropolitan church. As Picard has pointed out: 'while being part of the new generation of Irish hagiographers, as can be gathered from his literary skills, his use of the preface and the aims of his work, Cogitosus represents a stage of transition halfway between the tradition of aretalogy as found in sixth and seventh century Gaulish writers and a renewed classical tradition of hagiography, successfully represented by Muirchú.' It is clear that Cogitosus had little genuine historical information about Brigit. The 'life' is very mythological in character, but it is of outstanding value as a source for social conditions in the seventh century. The extracts below are the story of Brigit hanging her clothes on a sunbeam and the famous description of the church of Kildare.

The translation is reproduced by kind permission of S. Connolly and J.-M. Picard from 'Cogitosus: Life of St Brigit', *Journal of the Royal Society of Antiquaries* 117 (1987), 11-27.]

6. OF THE GARMENT THROWN OVER A SUNBEAM

Here, I think I ought to slip in for your Reverences this other miracle in which the pure mind of the virgin and God's cooperating hand clearly appear to combine. As she was grazing her sheep in the course of her work as a shepherdess on a level grassy plain, she was drenched by a very heavy downpour of rain and returned to the house with her clothes wet. There was a ray of sunshine coming into the house through an opening and, as a result, her eyes were dazzled and she took the sunbeam for a slanting tree growing there. So, she put her rainsoaked clothes on it and the clothes hung on the filmy sunbeam as if it were a big solid tree. And the occupants of the house and the neighbours, dumbfounded by this extraordinary miracle, began to extol this incomparable lady with fitting praise.

32. OF THE CHURCH DOOR

Neither should one pass over in silence the miracle wrought in the repairing of the church in which the glorious bodies of both — namely Archbishop Conleth and our most flourishing virgin Brigit — are laid on the right and left of the ornate altar and rest in tombs adorned with a refined profusion of gold, silver, gems and precious stones with gold and silver chandeliers hanging from above and different images presenting a variety of carvings and colours. Thus, on account of the growing number of the faithful of both sexes, a new reality is born in an age-old setting, that is a church with its spacious site and its awesome height towering upwards. It is adorned with painted pictures and inside there are three chapels which are spacious and divided by board walls under the single roof of the cathedral church. The first of these walls, which is painted with pictures and covered with wall hangings, stretches widthwise in the east part of the church from one wall to the other. In it, there are two doors, one at either end, and through the door situated on the right, one enters the sanctuary to the altar where the archbishop offers the Lord's sacrifice together with his monastic chapter and those appointed to the sacred mysteries. Through the other door, situated on the left side of the aforesaid cross-wall, only the abbess and her nuns and faithful widows enter to partake of the banquet of the body and blood of Jesus Christ. The second of these walls divides the floor of the building into two equal parts and stretches from the west wall to the wall running across the church. This church contains many windows and one finely wrought portal on the right side through which the priests and the faithful of the male sex enter the church, and a second portal on the left side through which the nuns and congregation of women faithful are wont to enter. And so, in the one vast basilica, a large congregation of people of varying status, rank, sex and local origin, with partitions placed between them, prays to the omnipotent master, differing in status, but one in spirit.

Now, when the old door of the left portal through which saint Brigit used to enter the church was hung on its hinges by the tradesmen, it was unable to fill completely the newly erected doorway. A quarter of the doorway was unfilled and an open gap was showing and, had a fourth part been added and joined to the height of the door, then it would have been possible to fill up completely the high reconstructed doorway. And, as the tradesmen were wondering whether to make another new and bigger door which would fill up the entire doorway or to attach a piece of board to the old door so that it would afterwards be big enough, the aforementioned master and leader of all Irish craftsmen offered wise advice: 'This coming night, we must pray to the Lord with faith by saint Brigit's side so that in the morning she may guide us as to our course of action in this task.' And so he passed the night praying by the glorious tomb of Brigit and getting up in the morning after that night, having completed his prayer with faith, he had the old door pushed in and placed on its hinges and it filled the whole doorway. Neither did it lack anything in fullness nor was it in any respect excessive in size. And so Brigit extended the door in height so that the whole doorway was filled by it and no gap appeared in it except when the door was pushed back for people to go into the church. And this miracle of God's power was revealed clearly to the eyes of all who saw the door and the doorway.

And who can express in words the exceeding beauty of this church and the countless wonders of that monastic city we are speaking of, if one may call it a city since it is not encircled by any surrounding wall. And yet, since numberless people assemble within it and since a city gets its name from the fact that many people congregate there, it is a vast and metropolitan city. In its suburbs, which saint Brigit had marked out by a definite boundary, no human foe or enemy attack is feared; on the contrary, together with all its outlying suburbs it is the safest city of refuge in the whole land of the Irish for all fugitives, and the treasures of kings are kept there; moreover, it is looked upon as the most outstanding on account of its illustrious supremacy. And who can count the different crowds and numberless peoples flocking from all the provinces — some for the abundant feasting, others for the healing of their afflictions, others to watch the pageant of the crowds, others with great gifts and offerings — to join in the solemn celebration of the feast of saint Brigit who, freed from care, cast off the burden of the flesh and followed the lamb of God into the heavenly mansions, having fallen asleep on the first day of the month of February.

EPILOGUE

I beg pardon of the brethren and the readers perusing or even emending this. I beg them to pardon me who, compelled in the name of obedience and unsupported by any privilege of knowledge, have skimmed in a tiny bark over the vast ocean of saint Brigit's miracles, which is daunting even to very learned men, by recounting in rustic speech these few among her outstanding and innumerable miracles. Pray for me Cogitosus, the blameworthy descendant of Áed, and I implore you to pardon my boldness and commend me to the Lord with the shield of your prayers and may God hear you who pursue the peace of the Gospel. Amen.

MUIRCHÚ MOCCU MACTHÉNI

(*fl.* second half of 7th century)

from: VITA SANCTI PATRICII (Life of St Patrick)

[Muirchú's biography of St Patrick is not a straightforward account of the life of its subject. It is propaganda based on written documents and oral tradition. Unlike the geographically arranged notes of Tírechán, Muirchú's biography, modelled on the 'Life of Martin', and in the best tradition of European hagiography, is coherent, polished and dramatic. Muirchú, following the example of his 'father' in the genre, Cogitosus, who had written a 'Life' of St Brigit *c.* 650, regarded his work as being part of the new trend in the writing of Latin hagiography. Unlike Cogitosus, Muirchú follows a more traditional and classical model, and his work more nearly approximates to the standard biography. The Patrick of Muirchú is not the humble saint of *The Confession*, but a hero capable of standing alongside those of secular saga, overthrowing the representatives of paganism.

The extract opens with a preface addressed to his patron, Áed, bishop of Sletty. Here Muirchú uses his most elaborate Latin and, following hagiographical convention, decries his talent. In part it is based on the beginning of St Luke's Gospel. In his colourful sea imagery, he makes a play on his own name, which means 'Sea-dog'.

The main part of the extract is the highly dramatic core of Muirchú's work, that is the confrontation between Patrick and the high king, Loíguire, at Tara. Borrowing from the Book of Daniel (3. 2-3; 2.2), he models the drama on the court of Nabuchodonosor and compares Tara with Babylon. The lighting of the Paschal fire at Slane in County Meath was a symbol of the light of Christianity against the darkness of paganism. The setting at Tara heightened the tension for the contemporary audience, since it symbolized the political capital of Ireland; and the choice of Easter reflected a major controversy of the day — the problem of the dating of the feast. The message of Muirchú is clear. Patrick was the bishop of all Ireland, the teacher of the Irish; and, by beginning his missionary campaign from Tara, Armagh was firmly allying with the Uí Néill dynasty, the most powerful in the country in the late seventh century. Finally, by introducing the Leinster poets Dubthach and Fíacc, Muirchú was flattering his patron Áed.

The translation appears in L. Bieler, *The Patrician Texts in the Book of Armagh*, Scriptores Latini Hiberniae, Vol. X (Dublin: Dublin Institute for Advanced Studies, 1979), 62-123.]

[*Preface*] (1) Considering, my Lord Áed, that many have attempted to write this story coherently according to the traditions of their fathers and of those who were ministers of the Word from the beginning, but that the great difficulties which the telling of the story presents, and the conflicting opinions and many doubts voiced by many a person have prevented them from ever arriving at one undisputed sequence of events, (2) I might well say that, like boys making their first appearance in the assembly (to quote a familiar saying of ours), I have taken my little talent — a boy's paddle-boat, as it were — out on this deep and perilous sea of sacred narrative, where waves boldly swell to towering heights among rocky reefs in unknown waters, [a sea] on which so far no boat has ventured except the one of my [spiritual] father Cogitosus. (3) However, far from giving the impression that I want to make something big out of something small, I shall [merely] attempt to set forth, bit by bit and step by step, these few of the numerous deeds of holy Patrick, with little knowledge [of traditional lore], on uncertain authority, from an unreliable memory, feebly and in poor style, but with the pious affection of holy love, in obedience to the command of your sanctity and authority....

I 10 (9). (1) In the days when this took place there was in those parts a great king, a fierce pagan, an emperor of non-Romans, with his royal seat at Tara, which was then the capital of the realm of the Irish, by name Loíguire son of Níall, a scion of the family that held the kingship of almost the entire island. (2) He had around him sages and druids, fortune-tellers and sorcerers, and the inventors of every evil craft, who, according to the custom of paganism and idolatry, were able to know and foresee everything before it happened. (3) There were two of these whom he preferred above all the others, whose names are these: Lothroch, also called Lochru, and Lucet Máel, also called Ronal; (4) and these two by their magical art, prophesied frequently that a foreign way of life was about to come to them, a kingdom, as it were, with an unheard-of and burdensome teaching, brought from afar over the seas, enjoined by few, received by many; it would be honoured by all, would overthrow kingdoms, kill the kings who offered resistance, seduce the crowds, destroy all their gods, banish all the works of their craft, and reign for ever. (5) They also described the man who was to bring this way of life and to win them for it, and they prophesied about him in the following words, in the form, as it were, of a poem which these men often recited, and especially during the two or three years immediately before the coming of Patrick. (6) These are the words of the poem — not very intelligible, owing to the peculiarity of their language:

There shall arrive Shaven-head,
with his stick bent in the head,
from his house with a hole in its head
he will chant impiety
from his table in the front of his house;
all his people will answer 'Be it thus, be it thus.'

(7) In our own language all this can be expressed more clearly. 'When all this happens' (the druids would say) 'our kingdom, which is a pagan one, will fall.' And so it happened afterwards: when Patrick came the worship of idols was abolished and the catholic Christian faith spread over our whole country. Enough of this; let us return to our subject....

I 15 (14). (1) It so happened in that year that a feast of pagan worship was being held, which the pagans used to celebrate with many incantations and magic rites and other superstitious acts of idolatry. (2) There assembled the kings, satraps, leaders, princes, and the nobles of the people; furthermore, the druids, the fortune-tellers, and the inventors and teachers of every craft and every skill were also summoned to king Loíguire at Tara, their Babylon, as they had been summoned at one time to Nabuchodonosor, and they held and celebrated their pagan feast on the same night on which holy Patrick celebrated Easter. (3) They also had a custom, which was announced to all publicly, that whosoever, in any district, whether far or near, should have lit a fire on that night before it was lit in the king's house, that is, in the palace of Tara, would have forfeited his life. (4) Holy Patrick, then, celebrating Holy Easter, kindled the divine fire with its bright light and blessed it, and it shone in the night and was seen by almost all the people who lived in the plain. (5) Thus the fire from his tent happened to be seen at Tara, and as they saw it they all gazed at it and wondered. And the king called together the elders and said to them: 'Who is the man who has dared to do such a wicked thing in my kingdom? He shall die.' They all replied that they did not know who had done it, but the druids answered: 'King, may you live for ever! Unless this fire which we see, and which has been lit on this night before the [fire] was lit in your house, is extinguished on this same night on which it has been lit, it will never be extinguished at all; (6) it will even rise above all the fires of our customs, and he who has kindled it and the kingdom that has been brought upon us by him who has kindled it on this night will overpower us all and you, and will seduce all the people of your kingdom, and all kingdoms will yield to it, and it will spread over the whole country and will reign in all eternity.'

I 16 (15). (1) When the king heard this he was greatly alarmed, as once was Herod, and all Tara [was alarmed] with him. And the king answered and said: 'It will not be so, but we shall go and see what is going on, and restrain and kill those who are doing such a wicked thing against our kingdom.' (2) Loíguire ordered thrice nine chariots to be equipped, according to the tradition which they had received from their gods, took with him the two druids who were most powerful of all in a contest, that is, Lucet Máel and Lochru, and towards the end of that night went out from Tara to the burial place of the men of Fíacc; they turned the faces of the men and horses to the left, as was befitting them. (3) As they went along, the druids said to the king: 'King, do not yourself go to the place where the fire is, lest perhaps you afterwards adore him who lit it, but stay outside, and that man will be summoned to your presence so that he may adore you and you be his lord, and we and that man shall dispute before you, o King, and in this way you will test us.' (4) The king answered and said: 'You have devised sound advice; I shall do as you have said.' And they came to the above-mentioned place and dismounted from their horses; and they did not enter the perimeter of the place that was illumined by the light, but sat down beside it.

I 17 (16). (1) And holy Patrick was summoned to the presence of the king outside the illumined place, and the druids said to their people: 'Let us not rise when he comes, for whosoever rises at his coming will believe afterwards and reverence him.' (2) When Patrick rose and saw the great number of their chariots and horses, he fittingly recited with his lips and his heart the verse of the Psalmist: 'Let others [come] on chariots and on horseback, we shall go our way in the name of the Lord our God', and went to them. (3) They did not rise at his coming; there was only one man who, with the help of the Lord, refused to obey the command of the druids, that is Ercc, son of Daig, whose relics are now worshipped in the city called Slane. He stood up, and Patrick blessed him, and he believed in the eternal God. (4) Then they began their dispute, and one of the druids named Lochru provoked the holy man and dared to revile the catholic faith with haughty words. (5) Holy Patrick looked at him as he uttered such words and, as Peter had said concerning Simon, so with power and with a loud voice he confidently said to the Lord: 'O Lord, who art all-powerful and in whose power is everything, who hast sent me here, may this impious man, who blasphemes thy name, now be cast out and quickly perish.' (6) And at these words the druid was lifted up into the air and fell down again; he hit his brain against a stone, and was smashed to pieces, and died in their presence, and the pagans stood in fear.

I 18 (17). (1) The king with his companions was furious with Patrick over this incident and he tried to kill him and said: 'Lay hands on this fellow who is about to ruin us.' (2) When holy Patrick saw that the pagans were on the point of attacking him he rose and said with a loud voice: 'May God bestir Himself, and may His enemies be routed and His illwishers flee before His face.' (3) And at once darkness set in, and there was a dreadful uproar and the infidels fought among themselves, one rising up against the other, and there was a big earthquake which caused the axles of their chariots to collide with each other, and drove them violently forward so that chariots and horses rushed headlong over the plain until, in the end, a few of them escaped barely alive to *Mons Monduirn*, (4) and by this disaster seven times seven men perished through the curse of Patrick before the eyes of the king as a punishment for his words, until there remained only he himself and three other survivors, that is, he and his queen, and two of the Irish, and they were in great fear. (5) And the queen went to Patrick and said to him: 'O just and powerful man, do not bring death upon the king! For the king will come and bend his knees and adore your lord.' (6) And the king came, impelled by fear, and bent his knees before the holy man, and pretended to do him reverence though he did not mean it; and after they had parted and the king had gone a short distance away, he called holy Patrick with false words, wishing to kill him by any means. (7) Patrick, however, knew the wicked thoughts of the wicked king. He blessed his companions, eight men with a boy, in the name of Jesus Christ, and started on his way to the king, and the king counted them as they went along, and suddenly they disappeared from the king's eyes; (8) instead, the pagans merely saw eight deer with a fawn going, as it were, into the wilds. And king Loíguire, sad, frightened, and in great shame, went back to Tara at dawn with the few who had escaped.

I 19 (18). (1) On the following day, that is Easter Day, when the kings and princes and druids were at table with Loíguire — for this was their greatest feast day — eating and drinking wine in the palace of Tara, some of them talking, and others thinking about the things that had happened, (2) holy Patrick with only five companions entered through closed doors, as we read about Christ, in order to vindicate and to preach the holy faith at Tara before all the nations. (3) As he entered the banquet hall of Tara, none of them all rose in order to welcome him, except one man only, Dubthach maccu Lugir, an excellent poet. With him was then in that place a young poet named Fíacc, who afterwards became a renowned bishop, whose relics are worshipped in Sléibte.[1] (4) This Dubthach, as I have said, alone among the pagans rose in honour of holy Patrick, and the holy man blessed him, and he was the first on that day to believe in God, and it was counted to him for righteousness. (5) When the pagans had perceived Patrick they asked him to eat with them in order to put him to the test as I shall relate. He, however, knowing what was to come, did not refuse to eat.

I 20 (19). (1) Now, while they were all eating, the druid Lucet Máel, who had taken part in the conflict on the previous night, was anxious even on that day, now that his colleague had perished, to fight against holy Patrick, and as a start he put a drop [of poison] from his cup into the goblet of Patrick while the others looked on in order to find out what [Patrick] would do. (2) When holy Patrick saw the kind of test to which he was being subjected, he blessed his goblet in the sight of all and the liquor froze like ice; then he turned his goblet upside down, and only the drop which the druid had added fell out. And he blessed the goblet again: the liquor resumed its natural state, and they

1. Sletty, one mile north of Carlow town.

all were greatly astonished. (3) And after a short while the druid said: 'Let us work miracles in this vast plain,' and Patrick replied, saying: 'What sort of miracles?', and the druid said: 'Let us bring snow over the land,' and Patrick said: 'I do not want to bring about anything against God's will,' and the druid said: 'I shall bring it about in the sight of all.' (4) Then, uttering some spells, he brought snow, reaching up as far as [a man's] belt, over the entire plain, and all saw this and were astonished. And the holy man said: 'All right, we see this. Remove it now.' And [the druid] said: 'Until this hour tomorrow I cannot remove it.' And the holy man said: 'You can do evil and cannot do good. Not so I.' (5) Then he blessed the plain all around, and in no time, without rain or mist or wind, the snow vanished, and the crowds cheered and were greatly astonished and touched in their hearts. (6) And a little later the druid, through the invocation of demons, brought a thick fog over the land as a sign [*i.e.* miracle], and the people muttered angrily. And the holy man said: 'Remove the fog'; but again the other was not able to do so. (7) The holy man, however, prayed, blessed [the place], and the fog was dispelled at once and the sun shone again and all the people cheered and gave thanks. (8) After this contest between the druid and Patrick in the king's presence the king said to them: 'Cast your books into the water, and he whose books remain unharmed, him we shall adore.' Patrick answered: 'I will do so,' and the druid said: 'I do not want to undergo a test of water with him; for water is a god of his.' He had heard, no doubt, that Patrick baptized with water. (9) And the king replied; 'Agree [to ordeal] by fire.' And Patrick said: 'I am ready to do so.' But the druid did not want to and said: 'This man worships every second year in turn now water now fire as his god.' (10) And the holy man said: 'Not so: but you yourself, and one of the boys in my service together with you shall go into a divided and closed house, and you shall wear my garment and my boy shall wear yours, and so you two together shall be set on fire and be judged in the presence of the Highest.' (11) And this plan was accepted, and a house was built for them, half of green wood and half of dry wood, and the druid was placed in the green part of the house and one of holy Patrick's boys, Benineus [= Benignus] by name, wearing the druid's garb, in its dry part; then the house was closed from outside and in the presence of the whole crowd was set on fire. (12) And in that hour it so happened through the prayer of Patrick that the flame of the fire consumed the druid together with the green half of the house, and nothing was left intact except the chasuble of holy Patrick, which the fire did not touch. (13) On the other hand, happy Benineus, and the dry half of the house, experienced what has been said of the three young men: the fire did not even touch him, and brought him neither pain nor discomfort; only the garb of the druid, which he had donned, was burnt in accordance with God's will. (14) And the king's anger was aroused against Patrick because of the death of his druid, and he was on the point of attacking him, wishing to take his life; but God held him back. For at the prayer and the word of Patrick the wrath of God descended upon the impious people, and many of them died. (15) And holy Patrick said to the king: 'If you do not believe now you shall die at once, for the wrath of God has come down upon your head.' And the king was in great fear, his heart trembling, and so was his entire city.

I 21 (20). (1) King Loíguire summoned his elders and his whole council and said to them: 'It is better for me to believe than to die', and having held counsel, acting on the advice of his followers, he believed on that day and became converted to the Lord the eternal God, and many others believed on that occasion. (2) And holy Patrick said to the king: 'Since you have resisted my teaching and been offensive to me, the days of your own reign shall run on, but none of your offspring shall ever be king.'

I 22 (21). Holy Patrick, however, following the command of the Lord Jesus, left Tara, going forth and teaching all peoples and baptizing them in the name of the Father and the Son and the Holy Spirit, and preached everywhere, the Lord working with him and confirming his word by the miracles which followed....

COLMÁN MAC MUIRCHON

(died 736)

HYMNUS S. COLMANI IN LAUDEM S. MICHAELIS (The hymn of Saint Colmán in praise of Saint Michael)

[Since the name Muirchú (genitive Muirchon) is rather unusual, it is very likely that our author was the son of Muirchú who wrote the 'life' of Patrick above. This is strengthened by the fact that he was abbot of Moville on Strangford Lough, Co. Down, an area that Muirchú seems to know at first hand. The fact that many prominent churchmen produced sons at this period did not necessarily mean that they were not religious, although it is clear that standards were dropping. The hymn itself is a fine example of Hiberno-Latin poetry. Trisyllabic rhymes are prominent and one can hear the richness of the alliteration and assonances. This hymn seems later to have been taken to the Continent.

The text appears in J.H. Bernard and R. Atkinson (eds), *The Irish Liber Hymnorum*, Vol. I (London: Henry Bradshaw Society, 1898), 44-45.

The translation is to be found in Rev. J. O'Laverty, *An Historical Account of the Diocese of Down and Connor, Ancient and Modern*, Vol. II (Dublin: Gill, 1880), 17.]

In the Trinity my hope is fixed, not in an omen,
And the Archangel I beseech, Michael by name,

That he meet me, and be sent to me by God, the leader,
At the hour of my exit from this life and this body,

Lest the minister of violence lead me into woe,
He, the prince of darkness, and the foot of pride.

May the assistance of Michael, the Archangel, bring succour
To me at the hour when the just and the angels will rejoice.

Him I beseech, that he dismiss from me the foul face
Of the enemy, and that he lead me where is the repose of the kingdom.

May the Holy Michael assist me by day and night;
That he place me in the fellowship of the good saints.

May the Holy Michael, an approved assistant, intercede
For me, for I am a sinner in act, and frail.

May the Holy Michael defend me always by his strength,
Along with thousands of saints, when the soul is departing.

May the Holy Gabriel, the Holy Raphael, and all the angels,
Along with the Archangels, intercede for me always.

May the eternal halls of the King of the Kingdom be given,
That along with Christ, I may possess the joys of Paradise.

Glory always be to God, the Father and the Son,
At the same time with the Holy Ghost in one council.

COLUMBANUS

(*c.* 543-615)

from:
SANCTI COLUMBANI OPERA: EPISTULA II
(The Works of St Columbanus: Letter II)

[Columbanus left the monastery of Bangor in north-east Ireland in 591, to go into voluntary exile for the sake of Christ. He travelled to France where he went to the Austrasian court at Metz. Invited to stay, he founded a monastery in the ruins of a Roman fort at Annegray in the district of Vosges. As followers increased, he founded a new monastery at Luxeuil, which was to become his most famous foundation in France.

During his stay in France he had many enemies among the bishops, for he was an outspoken critic of those who were simoniacal and immoral. The method used by the Irish for dating Easter differed from that of the Frankish church and this also caused friction. The bishops, led by Arigius, eventually tried to confront him at a council to be held at Chalon on the Saône, the capital of Burgundy, in order to expel him in 603. Columbanus side-stepped the issue by refusing to attend and by writing a public letter addressed to all the bishops.

While congratulating the bishops on summoning the council, Columbanus expresses regret that they do not hold councils more frequently. He plays down the Easter dating problem and highlights the moral laxity of the Frankish church.

The translation appears in G.S.M. Walker (ed.), *Sancti Columbani Opera*, Scriptores Latini Hiberniae, Vol. II (Dublin: Dublin Institute for Advanced Studies, 1957), 12-23.]

LETTER II

1. To the holy Lords and Fathers or Brothers in Christ, the Bishops, Priests, and remaining Orders of holy Church, I, Columba the sinner, forward Greeting in Christ.

2. I render thanks to my God, that for my sake so many holy men have been gathered together to treat of the truth of faith and good works, and, as befits such, to judge of the matters under dispute with a just judgement, through senses sharpened to the discernment of good and evil. Would that you did so more often; and though you have not always leisure to maintain this canonical practice once or twice a year, in view of the stormy discords of this age, yet as speedily as may be, though it be too seldom, you should be imbued with this as your chief study, that all the dilatory might be made afraid and the zealous be encouraged to greater progress. Yes, I say, thanks be to God, that even on my account the occasion of a holy synod has been produced for you over the Easter controversy. May our Lord Jesus Christ, that prince of pastors, vouchsafe that your council be of use to the profit of His church; and may God Himself, Who is wont to stand in the congregation of the gods, with His presence inspire the hearts of His people entirely to obey His will through strength of the commandments, so that you may not only treat of the affair of Easter, which has already been long discussed and long decided in diverse ways by different authorities; but also of all the necessary canonical observances, marred as they have been by many, which is a more serious matter, and while the day of judgement is now nearer than it was, you might embark upon some still severer precept of the evangelical religion and apostolical tradition; for if you carefully consider the commandments of the gospel, I am not surprised that they are found to contain the contrary to some men's characters.

3. But let it be enough to have indicated that each will need to be moulded to the example of his redeemer and the pattern of the true shepherd, Who first preaching humility, and adding seven beatitudes to the first, which is poverty of spirit, taught man so fully to follow His footsteps, that by following after righteousness he might attain to the true circumcision of the eighth day; since the eighth beatitude concludes with martyrdom, for the reason that a man is not only righteous by his acts, but also a martyr by his suffering for righteousness' sake, seeing that he is desirous of the heavenly kingdom, and he is crowned with those who strive alike. Thus when, as it is written, He who says that he believes in Christ, ought also himself to walk even as Christ walked — that is, both poor and humble and ever preaching truth under the persecution of mankind — and again, They that will live

a godly life in Christ, shall suffer persecution, and that Faith without works is dead in itself, and the Lord replies to fools who rely on faith alone, That I have now known you, and to those who believe well and keep saying Lord, Lord, He declared, that they shall not enter into the kingdom of heaven; and when men cannot be His disciples or worthy of Him, who have not abandoned all that they possess, let each examine himself, whether he has firmly fulfilled or borne these duties, lest he should be estranged from the disciples of our Lord Jesus Christ, since the son should not be degenerate, and the disciple should not contradict the master in his preaching; For he that does not enter by the door into the fold of the sheep is a thief and a robber, and he who shuns the toil of chastising and opposing sinful men is a hireling, not a son ever to abide in the church.

4. I have touched these matters briefly for this reason, that if you are willing for us juniors to teach you fathers, you may ever keep in work and word this saying of the true shepherd, which His sheep know — for they do not hear the voice of strangers, but flee from him whose voice they know not, which, unless it be exemplified in practice, does not agree with the voice of the true shepherd. Nor can a discourse proceeding from the mouth of a hireling effectually enter the minds of those whom he instructs, for it bears this token, that he does not himself first hear the word that coming from his mouth is heard not; and what the master begins by slighting in his actions, he cannot with bare speech transmit for an example of obedience.

5. Therefore let us all together, whether clergy or monks, first frankly execute these true and unique rules of our Lord Jesus Christ, and thus thereafter, laying aside the swelling growth of pride, seek to record a unanimous verdict on the rest. If we all choose to be humble and poor for Christ's sake, Who for our sakes became poor though He was rich, then, with our various lusts laid aside and our mortal cares cast out from the sinful clay, by humility and by the willing poverty which the gospel teaches, as it were with the causes of disagreement and difference cut off, all the sons of God shall mutually enjoy between themselves a true peace and entire charity, by the likeness of their characters and the agreement of their single will. For great harm has been done and is done to the church's peace by difference of character and diversity of practice; but yet if, as I have said, we first hasten by the exercise of true humility to heal the poisons of pride and envy and vain glory, through the teaching of our Saviour Who says for our example, Learn of Me for I am meek and lowly of heart, and so on, then let us all, made perfect with no further blemish, with hatred rooted out, as the disciples of our Lord Jesus Christ, love one another with our whole heart. And if there be some variety of traditional practice, as there is over Easter, while the humble cannot strive, nor does the church have such a custom, while those will soon know more truly, who with the same purpose and the same desire of knowing truth seek jointly what they may more rightly follow, when none is vanquished except error, and when none boasts in himself but in the Lord; let us then seek together, I beseech you, my most loving fathers and brethren, and let us see which be the more true tradition — yours, or that of your brethren in the West. For, as I have noted in the book of my reply, which I have now sent you, though it was written three years ago, all the churches of the entire West do not consider that the resurrection should take place before the passion, that is, Easter before the equinox, and they do not wait beyond the twentieth moon, lest they should hold a sacrament of the New Testament without authority of the Old. But this I leave to another time; for the rest, I have informed the holy father in three books of their opinions upon Easter, and in a short pamphlet I have further ventured to write the same to your holy brother Arigius.

6. One thing therefore I request of your holiness, that with peace and charity you bear my ignorance and, as some say, my proud impudence in writing, which has been extorted by necessity, not pride, as my very baseness proves; and since I am not the author of this difference, and it is for the sake of Christ the Saviour, our common Lord and God, that I have entered these lands a pilgrim, I beseech you by our common Lord, and entreat you by Him Who is to judge the quick and the dead, if you deserve His recognition Who shall say to many, Amen I say to you that I never knew you, that I may be allowed with your peace and charity to enjoy the silence of these woods and to live beside the bones of our seventeen dead brethren, even as up till now we have been allowed to live twelve years among you, so that, as up till now we have done, we may pray for you as we ought. Let Gaul, I beg, contain us side by side, whom the kingdom of heaven shall contain, if our deserts are good; for we have one

kingdom promised and one hope of our calling in Christ, with Whom we shall together reign, if indeed we first suffer here with Him, that also together with Him we may be glorified. I know that to many this verbosity of mine will seem excessive; but I judged it better that you too should know what we here discuss and ponder amongst ourselves. For these are our rules, the commands of the Lord and the apostles, in these our confidence is placed; these are our weapons, shield and sword, these are our defence; these brought us from our native land; these here too we seek to maintain, though laxly; in these we pray and hope to continue up till death, as we have seen our predecessors do. But do you, holy fathers, look what you do to your poor veterans and aged pilgrims; as I judge, it will be better for you to comfort them than to confound.

7. I however did not venture to appear before you, lest perhaps when present I might strive contrary to the apostle's precept when he says, Do not strive with words, and again, If any man is quarrelsome, we have no such custom nor has the church of God; but I admit the inmost convictions of my conscience, that I have more confidence in the tradition of my native land in accordance with the teaching and reckoning of eighty-four years and with Anatolius, who was commended by Bishop Eusebius the author of the ecclesiastical history and by Jerome the holy writer of the catalogue, for the celebration of Easter, rather than to do so in accordance with Victorius who writes recently and in a doubtful manner, and without defining anything where it was needed, as he himself bears witness in his prologue, and who, after the age of great Martin and great Jerome and Pope Damasus, under Hilary covered a hundred and three years with his compilation. But do you yourselves choose whom you prefer to follow, and whom you rather trust, in accordance with that saying of the apostle, Prove all things, hold what is good. Far be it then that I should maintain the need to quarrel with you, so that a conflict among us Christians should rejoice our enemies, I mean the Jews or heretics or Gentile heathen — far be it indeed, far be it; for the rest, we may agree in some other way, so that either each should remain before God in the condition in which he was called, if both traditions are good, or else both books should be read over in peace and humility without any argument, and what agrees better with the Old and New Testament should be maintained without ill-will at any. For if it is of God that you should drive me hence from the place of seclusion, which I have sought from overseas for the sake of my Lord Jesus Christ, it will be my part to use that prophetic speech, If on my account this storm is upon you, take me and cast me into the sea, that this tempest may recede from you in calm; yet let it first be your part like those mariners to seek to save the shipwrecked by the bowels of godliness, and to draw the ship to land, as they, though Gentiles, did, according to the scripture, which says, And the men sought to return to land and could not, for the sea ran and the swell increased the more. Finally as my last word I advise, admittedly with presumption, that, since many walking on the roomy and broad roadway of this age hasten towards the narrow crossing, if some few are found, who pass through the strait and narrow gate, that leads to life according to the Lord's command, you should rather help them on to life than hinder them, lest perhaps you also with the Pharisees be smitten by the word of the Lord, saying, Woe unto you, scribes and Pharisees, since you shut the kingdom of heaven before men, and Neither do you enter yourselves, nor do you allow them that are entering to enter.

8. But someone will say: Are we really not entering the kingdom of heaven? Why can you not by the Lord's grace, if you become as little children, that is, humble and chaste, simple-hearted and guileless in evil, yet wise in goodness, easy to be entreated and not retaining anger in your heart? But all these things can very hardly be fulfilled by those who often look at women and who more often quarrel and grow angry over the riches of the world. Thus our party, once renouncing the world, and cutting off sins' causes and strifes' incentives at the start, consider that they may more easily fulfil the Lord's word in nakedness than wealth. For before the acquisition of these four qualities there is no entrance to the kingdom of heaven, as St. Jerome witnesses to three and Basil to the fourth, who expound the character of children in accordance with the tenor of the gospel saying. For a child is humble, does not harbour the remembrance of injury, does not lust after a woman when he looks on her, does not keep one thing on his lips and another in his heart. And these, as I have said, will be better maintained by one who is still and sees that God Himself is Lord, than by one who sees and hears all manner of things. Let none disparage the benefits of silence; for unless they grow lax, the

secluded live better than the social, except for that still stricter life which has the greater reward; for where the battle is more stubborn, there is found a crown of higher glory. But yet, as says St. Gregory, they are not credited with private virtues who do not avoid notorious ills. Therefore knowing this, St. Jerome bade bishops imitate the apostles, but taught monks to follow the fathers who were perfect. For the patterns of clergy and of monks are different, and widely distinct from one another. Let each maintain what he has grasped; but let all maintain the gospel, and both parties, like single harmonious members of one body, follow Christ the head of all by His own commands, which were revealed by Him to be accomplished in charity and peace. And these two cannot be perfectly accomplished, save by truly humble and unitedly spiritual men, who fulfil Christ's commands, as the Lord Himself bears witness, If ye love Me, keep My commandments, this is My commandment, that ye love one another, as I also have loved you, for in this shall all know that ye are My disciples, if ye love one another. Thus unity of minds and peace and charity then can be assured, spread abroad in the bowels of believers by the Holy Ghost, when all alike long to fulfil the divine commands; for the fiction of peace and charity between the imperfect will be such as is the measure of disagreement in their practical pursuits. Therefore, that we may love one another in charity unfeigned, let us carefully ponder the commands of our Lord Jesus Christ, and hasten to fulfil them when understood, that by His teaching the whole church may hasten to the heavenly places with one impulse of unbounded zeal. May His free grace afford us this, that we all may shun the world and love Him only and long for Him with the Father and the Holy Ghost, to Whom is the glory unto ages of ages. Amen.

9. For the rest, fathers, pray for us as we also do for you, wretched though we be, and refuse to consider us estranged from you; for we are all joint members of one body, whether Franks or Britons or Irish or whatever our race be. Thus let all our races rejoice in the comprehension of faith and the apprehension of the Son of God, and let us all hasten to approach to perfect manhood, to the measure of the completed growth of the fullness of Jesus Christ, in Whom let us love one another, praise one another, correct one another, encourage one another, pray for one another, that with Him in one another we may reign and triumph. Pray pardon my verbosity and presumption as I toil beyond my strength, most long-suffering and holy fathers and brethren all.

from: SANCTI COLUMBANI OPERA: INSTRUCTIO VIII (The Works of St Columbanus: Sermon VIII)

[The following sermon is one of thirteen still surviving. It is thought that they were preached by Columbanus while he was staying at Milan in 612 after having crossed the Alps from France.

He was now in the territory of the Lombard duke, Agilulf, and his queen Theudelinda. Theudelinda was a 'Roman' Christian, Agilulf an Arian heretic. This situation was probably the cause of a fresh period of literary activity by Columbanus.

Columbanus changed his style according to circumstances, and the language of his sermons is simple and restrained. His models were the classical writers, Virgil, Ovid, Juvenal, Martial and Sallust. He was also familiar with later writers such as Prudentius, Fortunatus, Iuvencus, Sedulius, Ausonius and Claudian. Cassian and Jerome were the ecclesiastical writers on whose work he most relied.

The sermon opens with a theme that recurs in Columbanus's writings — that human life is like a roadway leading ultimately to the heavenly kingdom.

The text appears in G.S.M. Walker (ed.), *Sancti Columbani Opera*, Scriptores Latini Hiberniae, Vol. II (Dublin: Dublin Institute for Advanced Studies, 1957), 94-97.]

SERMON VIII

1. Now, you see, we must speak of the end of the way; for we have already said that human life is a roadway, and by the likeness of a shadow we have shown how doubtful it is and uncertain, and that it is not what it is; in the same manner, we have said before how incalculable and how blind it is; but concerning the end of our life, by the help of the Holy Spirit, our talk must be continued. It is for travellers to hasten to their homeland, likewise their part is anxiety upon the roadway, and in their

homeland peace. Then let us, who are on the way, hasten home; for our whole life is like the journey of a single day. Our first duty is to love nothing here; but let us place our affections above, our desires above, our wisdom above, and above let us seek our home; for the fatherland is there where our Father is. Thus we have no home on earth, since our Father is in heaven. And indeed, if He is everywhere in virtue of His power and by the greatness of His Godhead, He is deeper than ocean, firmer than earth, broader than the world, clearer than air, higher than heaven, brighter than the sun; yet He dwells openly in the heavens, where He is the bread of angels, who as His retinue inhabit the blessed palace of the highest heaven, and enjoy the sight of God. But since our weaker nature could not bear the pure nature of the invisible God, for that reason God in His goodness, in Whom are all things and beyond Whom is nothing, allotted to the supreme virtues the first region of the knowledge of Himself, which He bounded by the first heaven, and mollified that heaven by the waters that are above; for unless that nature of the first heaven were mollified by the aforesaid waters, it would be set on fire by the virtue of the Most High God, and could by no means be endured by lower natures; and so, while everywhere present to all, God remains invisible. For He is greater than what could be seen entire, and greater than all things, for He created all of nothing; and thus when seen He is imperceptible, since Who He is and how great He is, to Himself alone is known. Yet let us beseech Him, since God the Trinity, though imperceptible and imponderable, is known and present to each one, in proportion to the deserts of our purity. Let us beseech Him, I say, at least here, that there we may more closely approach, or more clearly understand, and singing on our journey let us say, Let us run after Thee towards the odour of Thy perfumes, and, My soul has clung behind Thee, and, Draw me after Thee; that with these songs we may speedily pass through the world, and controlled from above may scorn the things of the present, and ever thinking of heavenly things may shun the things of earth; for unless we long unweariedly with heavenly desires, we needs must be entangled in earthly ones.

2. Then, lest we be concerned with human things, let us concern ourselves with things divine, and as pilgrims ever sigh for and desire our homeland; for the end of the road is ever the object of travellers' hopes and desires, and thus, since we are travellers and pilgrims in the world, let us ever ponder on the end of the road, that is of our life, for the end of our roadway is our home. But there all who journey through this age find various lots according to their merits; and the good travellers have peace in their homeland, but the evil shall perish without; for many lose their true home, because they love rather the road. Let us not love the roadway rather than the homeland, lest we lose our eternal home; for we have such a home that we ought to love it. Therefore let this principle abide with us, that on the road we so live as travellers, as pilgrims, as guests of the world, entangled by no lusts, longing with no earthly desires, but let us fill our minds with heavenly and spiritual impressions, singing with grace and power, When shall I come and appear before the face of my God? For my soul thirsts for the mighty and living God, and, My soul is like a waterless land before Thee, and saying with Paul, I desire to be dissolved and to be with Christ, let us know that though we are strangers from the Lord while we remain in the body, yet we are present to the eyes of God. Hence, spurning all wickedness, and laying aside all sloth, let us strive to please Him Who is everywhere present, that with a good conscience we may happily pass over from the roadway of this age to the blessed and eternal homeland of our eternal Father, from present things to things absent, from mournful things to things of joy, from transitory things to things eternal, from earthly things to heavenly, from the sphere of death to that of the living, where we shall see heavenly things face to face, and the Ruler of rulers, ruling His realms with an upright rule, our Lord Jesus Christ, to Whom is glory unto ages of ages. Amen.

from: SANCTI COLUMBANI OPERA: REGULAE (The Works of St Columbanus: Rules)

[Columbanus's 'rule' is probably derived from that in use in Bangor under St Comgall. The rule was strict, although, as the extracts below show, Columbanus urged moderation in all things.

He made use of the works of Cassian, Jerome and Basil. The rule itself was soon overtaken by that of Benedict, although it did exercise an important influence on later compilations.

The translation appears in G.S.M. Walker (ed.), *Sancti Columbani Opera*, Scriptores Latini Hiberniae, Vol. II (Dublin: Dublin Institute for Advanced Studies, 1957), 134-43.]

VIII. OF DISCRETION

. . . (IX) How necessary discretion is for monks is shown by the mistake of many, and indicated by the downfall of some, who beginning without discretion and passing their time without a sobering knowledge, have been unable to complete a praiseworthy life; since, just as error overtakes those who proceed without a path, so for those who live without discretion intemperance is at hand, and this is always the opposite of virtues which are placed in the mean between each extreme. Its onset is a matter of danger, when beside the straight way of discretion our foes place the stumbling-blocks of wickedness and the offences of various mistakes. (X) Therefore we must pray God continually that He would bestow the light of true discretion to illumine this way, surrounded on every side by the world's thickest darkness, so that His true worshippers may be able to cross this darkness without error to Himself. So discretion has got its name from discerning, for the reason that it discerns in us between good and evil, and also between the moderate and the complete. For from the beginning either class has been divided like light and darkness, that is, good and evil, after evil began through the devil's agency to exist by the corruption of good, but through God's agency Who first illumines and then divides. Thus righteous Abel chose the good, but unrighteous Cain fell upon evil. (XI) God made all things good that He created, but the devil sowed[1] evils over them by cunning craftiness and the sly inducement of a perilous design. What things then are good? Doubtless those which are untouched, and have remained in the undefiled state of their creation; which God alone created and prepared, according to the Apostle, that we should walk in them; which are the good works in which in Christ Jesus we were created, namely goodness, innocence, righteousness, justice, truth, pity, love, saving peace, spiritual joy, together with the fruit of the Spirit — all these with their fruits are good. But to these the evils are opposed, namely wickedness, seduction, unrighteousness, injustice, lying, greed, hatred, discord, bitterness, together with their manifold fruits, things which are born from them. For countless are the things that are produced from the two opposites, that is, from goods and evils. (XII) But what departs from its established goodness and innocence is the first evil, which is the pride of primal wickedness; the opposite of which is the lowly esteem of a righteous goodness that acknowledges and glorifies its Creator, and this is a rational creature's first good. Thus the rest also have gradually grown to a huge forest of names in two sections. Since this is so, the good must be firmly held by those that have God's help, which is ever to be prayed for in prosperity and in adversity, lest either in prosperity we be lifted up to pride, or in adversity be cast down to despair. Thus we must always restrain ourselves from either danger, that is, from all excess by a splendid temperance and true discretion, which cleaves to Christian lowliness and opens the way of perfection to Christ's true soldiers, namely by ever discerning rightly in doubtful cases, and everywhere dividing justly between good and evil, whether between both in external acts, or between flesh and spirit in the inner life, or between good works and character, or between action and contemplation, or between official duty and private devotion. Therefore the evils are to be equally avoided, pride, ill will, lying, seduction, unrighteousness, wicked transgression of morality, gluttony, fornication, avarice, wrath, dejection, inconstancy, vainglory, boasting, slander; the goods of the virtues are also to be followed, lowliness, kindness, purity, obedience, temperance, chastity, liberality, patience, cheerfulness, constancy, zeal, persistence, watchfulness, silence, which through an enduring courage and sobering moderation, as in some weighing balance of discretion, are to be weighed in the performance of our customary work, according to the capacity of our endeavour, if everywhere we seek sufficiency. For it is doubtful to none that the man to whom sufficiency is not enough has overstepped the measure of discretion, and whatever oversteps the very measure is clearly a vice.

(XIII) Thus between the little and the excessive there is a reasonable measure in the midst, which ever recalls us from every superfluity on either side, and in every case posited provides what is universally fixed by human need, and spurns the unreasonable demand of superfluous desire. And this

1. cf. the parable of the wheat and tares, Matthew 13. 24-30.

measure of true discretion, weighing all our actions in the scales of justice, in no wise allows us to err from what is just, or to suffer a mistake, if we ever follow straight behind it as our leader. For while we must always restrain ourselves from either side, according to that saying, Keep yourselves from the right and from the left, we must ever proceed straight forward by discretion, that is, by the light of God, while very often we say and sing the victorious psalmist's verse, My God, enlighten my darkness, since in Thee I am rescued from temptation. For temptation is the life of man on earth.

IX. OF MORTIFICATION

(XIV) The chief part of the monks' rule is mortification, since indeed they are enjoined in Scripture, Do nothing without counsel. Thus if nothing is to be done without counsel, everything must be asked for by counsel. Thus we are enjoined through Moses also, Ask thy father and he will show thee, thy elders and they will tell thee. But though this training seem hard to the hard-hearted, namely that a man should always hang upon the lips of another,[2] yet by those who are fixed in their fear of God it will be found pleasant and safe, if it is kept wholly and not in part, since nothing is pleasanter than safety of conscience and nothing safer than exoneration of the soul, which none can provide for himself by his own efforts, since it properly belongs to the judgement of others. For what the judge's examination has already tried preserves from the fear of censure, and on him is laid the weight of another's burden, and he bears all the peril that he undertakes; for, as it is written, the peril of the judge is greater than that of the accused. So anyone who has always asked, if he follows will never err, since if the other's reply has erred, there will be no error in the faith of him who believes and the toil of him who obeys, nor will they lack the reward of his asking. For if he has considered anything by himself when he ought to have asked, he is proved guilty of error in this very fact that he dared to judge when he ought to have been judged; even though it turn out right, it will be reckoned to him as wrong, since he has departed from the right course in this; for the man to whose duty it belongs only to obey presumes to judge nothing by himself.

Then, since this is so, monks must everywhere beware of a proud independence, and learn true lowliness as they obey without murmuring and hesitation, that according to the Lord's word they may feel the yoke of Christ pleasant and His burden light. Otherwise, while they are learning the lowliness of Christ, they will not feel the pleasure of His yoke and the lightness of His burden. For lowliness of heart is the repose of the soul when wearied with vices and toils, and its only refuge from so many evils, and in so far as it is wholly drawn to the meditation of this from so many errant and empty things without, so far does it enjoy repose and refreshment within, with the result that even bitter things are sweet to it, and things before considered hard and toilsome it feels to be plain and easy, and mortification also, which is unbearable to the proud and hard-hearted, become his comfort who takes pleasure only in what is lowly and mild. But we must know that neither this bliss of martyrdom[3] nor any other benefit that follows can be perfectly fulfilled by any, save him who has given particular attention to this, that he be not found unready. For if, in following this pursuit, he has wished to observe or nourish any of his own desires, at once occupied and wholly confused by concern for these intrusions, he will not always be able to follow thankfully where the commandment leads, nor can the disorderly and unthankful perform as is his duty.

Thus there is a threefold scheme of mortification: not to disagree in mind, not to speak as one pleases with the tongue, not to go anywhere with complete freedom. Its part is ever to say to a senior, however adverse his instructions, Not as I will but as thou wilt, following the example of the Lord and Saviour, Who says, I came down from heaven, not to do My will, but the will of Him Who sent Me, the Father.

X. OF THE MONK'S PERFECTION[4]

Let the monk live in a community under the discipline of one father and in company with many, so that from one he may learn lowliness, from another patience. For one may teach him silence and

2. There was a traditional Irish saying that a person without a confessor is like a body without a head.

3. According to Irish teaching, the ascetic life is reckoned to be a form of martyrdom.

4. This entire chapter is taken almost verbatim from Jerome (Epistula CXXV §15).

another meekness. Let him not do as he wishes, let him eat what he is bidden, keep as much as he has received, complete the tale of his work, be subject to whom he does not like. Let him come weary to his bed and sleep walking, and let him be forced to rise while his sleep is not yet finished. Let him keep silence when he has suffered wrong, let him fear the superior of his community as a lord, love him as a father, believe that whatever he commands is healthful for himself, and let him not pass judgement on the opinion of an elder, to whose duty it belongs to obey and fulfil what he is bidden, as Moses says, Hear, O Israel, and the rest.

END OF THE RULE.

from: THE HISPERICA FAMINA (Western Sayings)

(*c.* mid-7th century)

[The *Hisperica Famina* are essays written in Latin about everyday happenings and objects. They are written in a highly ornate and often obscure language, and use poetical words, or employ words in an unfamiliar way. Words frequently are not given their current meaning but a meaning derived from their etymology. New words are invented out of the Latin and others are adapted from Greek, Hebrew and Irish. In their wordplay and use of language they could be regarded as ancestral to the works of James Joyce. There has been much controversy concerning the place of origin and date of these compositions, but it is now generally felt that they were written in Ireland during the seventh century.

The most likely place of writing would have been a large Irish monastery. At this period the Irish were fascinated by Latin grammar. Since the Romans had never conquered Ireland, the Irish had to learn Latin as a foreign language. They had also to use the Latin alphabet to produce a written form of their own language. Thus, they had a heightened awareness of language in all its forms. These essays, then, may have been produced as set pieces by senior students displaying their learning and virtuosity, or by their teachers to demonstrate difficult vocabulary.

The main source appears to have been the *Etymologiae* of Isidore of Seville (a Spanish bishop who died in 636) together with his *De Natura Rerum* and *De Differentiis Verborum.* Other sources suggested by Michael Herren are: *De Ordine Creaturarum*; possibly a glossary of words contained in Gildas's (an early sixth-century Welsh author) *De Excidio Britanniae*; the works of Virgil, together with comments on them; the Scriptures; Graeco-Latin and Hebrew-Latin glossaries; and the works of Virgilius Maro Grammaticus. As J.F. Kenney suggests: 'In fact, the *Hisperica Famina* must have been the product of a literary society dominated by fancies similar to those in which that Gallic Grammarian [Virgilius Maro, who may himself have been an Irishman] delighted.'

The translation appears in M.W. Herren (ed.), *The Hisperica Famina*: I. *The A-Text* (Toronto: Pontifical Institute of Medieval Studies, 1974), 74-91.]

The Rule of the Day

The Titanian star inflames the ceiling of heaven
and illuminates the sea with its warm exhalation;
it traverses the sky in fiery brilliance
and ascends the vault of the bountiful firmament.
Phoebus' glow extinguishes the white moon,
the fiery flashes of the Pleiades do not dart forth,
the sun's effect dispels the nocturnal dark,
and Phaethon's fire clears the dense clouds;
the dewy moistures evaporate in the heat,
nor does the dark storm cloud enshroud the leafy trees.
The mist departs from the meadows,
the scorching blaze parches the tiny ponds,
and its radiance warms the earth's sphere.
The wingèd court echoes a pleasing melody,
they utter ringing harmonies from their open beaks,
and revive the hollow slopes of the ears with their sweetness.
A flock of birds depart from their leafy lairs,
they pierce the clods of the fields,
and swallow bits of worms with their beaks;
they peck through the smelly mixen,[1]
and glut their hungry innards with succulent food.
A herd of cattle wanders the vast pastureland
and meanders along stretches of sand;
motley groups fill the country estates,
they saturate their innards with blue grass,
and chew their herbal fodder with chomping movements.

1. dunghill.

The innocent sheep leave their folds
and cross the wooden foot-bridges;
the woolly flocks go into the meadows
and pluck clumps of grass with their teeth.
A herd of hairy swine has left its hovel,
they dig in the sandy earth with their snouts,
devour the sturdy fern roots
and savour the juicy herbs.
The horses eager for food leave their wooden stables,
they go to their familiar grooms with a noisy clatter,
and the hostlers remove the iron hobbles from their legs;
with noisy chomping they fill their hollow chests.
A frenzied herd of wild colts
trample their nourishing fodder,
they roll over the rough broom with their prancing,
and gaze skittishly at the people of the region.
Huge dolphins sweep the foamy deep,
they suck in salty particles through open jaws,
and devour scaly fish.
All the rustics busy themselves with their usual work.
Some, trowels in hand, dig earthen ditches,
they make fences thick with prickly thorns
and heap up stone walls of massive rock.
Others drive to pasture varied flocks of cattle,
which utter sonorous cries
and disturb the songs of the fields with their fierce lowing.
Countless throngs approach the leafy pasture along the crowded path
and mark the sacred oaks with their knives;
they wrench off the uprooted kindling with their axes,
split the appointed ash trees with wedges,
and sturdy teams carry off the laden carts.
This noisy clatter incites us to stir from our bedrooms
and gather a heap of clothing about our fleshy bodies.
So wrap the soft robes around your limbs,
gird your white shifts of rough linen with leather belts,
fasten silver brooches to your brown stoles.
Remove your comfortable nightgowns
and put on soft woollen garments.
Assemble the colony of rhetors[2]
and scan your letters;
for a scholar celebrates no triumphs,
if he tears healthy slumber from the depths of his breast,
unless while Phoebus is glowing in the East,
he remove the pleasure of sleep from his eyelids
and put the well-worn garment around his loins
to forge his reading assignment.
Why do you oppress us with a thunderous crash of words
and perturb the inner caverns of our ears with turgid speech?
For we have devoted an entire measure of moonlight to studious wakefulness,
but you have pleasured your limbs with the corruption of sleep;
wherefore a feeling of drowsiness now overcomes us.
Let some representative of this learned assembly approach the foaming liquid,
to pour the smooth flood over our dirty hands
and cleanse away nocturnal scum with fountain water.
Remove the speckled volumes from the curved satchels
and heed your rhetoric assignment.
Loud applause would ring through the air
and a verbal din would resound
if the entire assembly remained in one hall;
wherefore separate this cohort;
let some go to the warm cottages,
let others traverse the leafy underwoods,
let others stay in this ample building.
Phoebus' star crosses the centre of the sky,
and the middle of the day draws nigh;
hence the breast seethes with burning hunger.
Therefore let us visit the domains around us
that they might offer sweet food to the famished.
What guide will lead the splendid throng along the highways?
Frequently have I wandered over these secret passes,
I have penetrated the remote farms of this region,
and I seek out the charming inhabitants
who feed the choirs of wandering scholars.
Crowd the path in close formation,
raise your holy headdress toward the sky,
lest cruel savages macerate[3] our limbs with deadly darts.
For stealthy bands of brigands surround these highways,
and despoil numerous crowds of travellers with

2. professional orators.

3. crush.

their aforesaid darts,
and slaughter armed hosts with their swords.
Therefore let us rush through the dangerous regions in a tight wedge.
We trample over the rough farmland
where parched pillars of rock are heaped
and thorny sorrels grow.
These flowery fields are a-sparkle
and replete with purple flowers;
they have no rocky parts
but contain clusters of blue grass.
The barking of a dog resounds within the woods of the town;
perhaps a foreign band of brigands is clinging to the walls,
or else they hear the din of [our] roving throng.
Two knocks arouse a loud clamour.
How cheerfully an inhabitant directs the wandering cohort to the inn!
Remove the tight latch with the hooked key.
This hollow hall surrounds a clean chamber
which is continually swept with switches of birch,
nor does any kindling pile up there.
[Here] there is a foul-smelling room
that contains hardened grains of dirt,
nor do the leafy brooms sweep the aforesaid chamber.
Fill the steady hand basin with water
and wash your dirty feet with flowing draughts;
wipe clean your muddy soles with the clear liquid.
Hang your white booksacks on the wall,
set your lovely satchels in a straight line,
so that they will be deemed a grand sight by the rustics.
Drape the benches with leather coverings,
stoke the glowing, fiery-hot oven in the [?] courtyard,
pile up tiny chips of dry firewood
that it may belch forth a flame-spewing conflagration,
cast a sensation of warmth
and rout the cold from the hearth.
Who will ask these possessors
to grant us their sweet abundance?
For an Ausonian chain[4] binds me;
hence I do not utter good Irish speech.
But I shall rouse the ferocious watch-dogs with my shillelagh.[5]

4. i.e. a chain of elegant diction. Ausonius was a Gaulish poet of the fourth century.
5. A club or cudgel, made of oak or blackthorn.

The charming townspeople apologize
for having such meagre supplies at hand.
Cleave the victuals given to us with sharp knives,
and set the wooden tables with heaps of food,
wash your hands with clear water
that your palms may appear clean.
Divide the chorus of the learned into four rhythms,
sing out a holy harmony for the abundance of food,
so that wholesome strength may flow into our stomachs.
Heat the dry victuals with rays of fire,
that they may conduct a sweeter flavour to our lips.
Store up bits of leftovers in hollow baskets.
Beseech the bountiful master of the universe
that the townspeople not fall into the fiery pit of Cocytus;[6]
but may they reach the uppermost peak of the seven-fold heaven
for having granted us the heaps of sweet food.
Let some spokesman ask the charming woman
to make the salty draughts of water jump over the coals,
that the curling flames may spew forth bits of salt.
Let us approach the appointed town,
where we have established a close agreement with our companions.
What sweeter victuals have you eaten?
We munched on crusts of bread with toothy movements,
for which there abounded a delicious smearing of Irish oil.
We chomped down joints of meat with compressed teeth;
a draught of milk flowed abundantly,
[and] we thirstily drank our fill of the joy-giving ale.

The Titanian star reddens the Western Sea,
it bends its rosy rays toward the bottom of the sphere.
The moon-star sparkles over the vast universe,
the flashing darts of the Pleiades colour the heaven.
The cloud of night weighs heavy on the grass,
a vapour darkens the white banks,
and black night enshadows the disc of the world.
Innumerable flocks of cattle
wander along sandy paths,
and the kine[7] press into their enclosures.

6. One of the rivers of Hades in Greek mythology.
7. cattle.

Throngs of sheep ascend the square folds,
the hairy swine go to their familiar swineherds,
the hostlers fasten iron hobbles to the horses' legs.
Countless numbers of peasants
cast off the accustomed bond of labour from their limbs
and rest in their comfortable houses of dry covering.
Therefore let us approach the protective walls of the town
to request suitable hospitality from the kind inhabitants.
Rouse the porter with a loud shout
to receive the assembly of the learned into the inn.
Spread the appointed couches with leather coverlets,
stoke the raging furnace with kindling,
light the glowing lamp with fire,
pour a clear draught from the wooden tank
and wash your dirty feet.
Divide the nightly chores among the regular groups:
let some rush with hurried sprint to the woodpile
and bring back firewood in tied bundles;
have others go to the water tank
and bring back a full water jug on their shoulders;
let others cook joints of meat in the bronze pot
and knead the cakes of meal.
Divide your apportioned amounts of victuals with your knives,
load the tables with an abundance of food,
and heap the sweet remainders into neat baskets.
I hope from the deepest recess of my heart
that the inhabitants may enjoy a prolonged and worthy life
who have bestowed on us their honeyed abundance
and have given us mounds of delicious food.
Kindle in the furnace your torches dipped in oil
and scrutinize the reading assignment in your books.
Our eyelids are pressed by the weight of sleep;
therefore spread the enticing couches with leather covers,
put on your coarse nightclothes,
fold soft pillows for your round heads,
cover the lumps of coal in the fire pit,
lest they ignite the kindling nearby,
and it burn with the great heat of a fiery furnace.
Close the square entrance with the tight-fitting door,
lest fierce brigands burst in
and stealthily carry off our hidden treasures.
Let some heed their learned reading with a keen mind;
let others receive the warmth of sleep within their limbs;
let others share the night watch,
until the rosy glow of the rising sun flashes forth.

ADAMNÁN
(*c.*624-704)

from: ADAMNÁN'S LIFE OF COLUMBA (*c.* 700)

[Adamnán, the ninth abbot of Iona, was a man of personal humility, humanity and erudition. He was clearly a great abbot who was involved not merely in renovation and construction work on Iona, but was concerned also with the spiritual well-being of his monks. Adamnán wrote his 'life' of Colum Cille partly as a response to Northumbrian propaganda and that of major churches in Ireland, particularly Armagh. But it was also intended as a spiritual model for the monks of Iona, and to elevate the cult of Colum Cille on the Continent. It was written over a period of years and was completed *c.* 700.

Adamnán's model was the 'life' of Martin. He used this source in a manner rather similar to Cogitosus, arranging the life of his saint, not so much chronologically, but thematically (reflecting the grammarian in him, as Picard has recently suggested). In doing this, he was following an ultimately classical technique, which allowed him to demonstrate how divine power manifested itself in his saint. Picard has also pointed out that if this produced a rather static picture of the saint, it echoed the monastic virtue of *constantia* (perseverance), and the presentation 'corresponded to the hero in Celtic mythology'.

Unlike most 'lives' of the saints from Ireland, in Adamnán's 'life' of Colum Cille we feel that we are encountering the real person of the saint. Nowhere is this more keenly felt than in the extract below, which deals with the days leading up to and following his death.

The text and translation appear in A.O. and M.O. Anderson (eds), *Adomnán's Life of Columba* (London: Thomas Nelson and Sons Ltd., 1961), pp. 517-43.]

De transitu ad dominum sancti nostri patroni Columbae

Annorum supra iiii. memoratorum termino jam appropinquante, post quorum conpletionem finem praesentis vitae veridicus praesagator sibi futurum fore multo ante praesciebat tempore, quadam die mense maio, sicut in priore secundo scripsimus libro, ad visitandos operarios fratres sanctus senex senio fessus plaustro vectus pergit. Ad quos in occidua insulae Iovae laborantes parte síc ea die exorsus est loqui, dicens: 'In pascali sollemnitate nuper apreli peracta mense desiderio desideravi | ad Christum dominum, sicut et mihi ab eo concessum erat si malluissem, emigrare. Sed né vobis laetitiae festivitas in tristitiam verteretur, diem meae de mundo emigrationis paulo diutius protellari mallui'.

Hís ab eo mestís monaci familiares auditís interim dictís valde tristificati sunt; quos in quantum poterat verbís coepit consulatoriis laetificare. Quibus finitís ut erat in vechiculo sedens ad orientem suam convertens faciem insulam cum insulanís benedixit habitatoribus. Ex qua die, ut in supra memorato craxatum est libello, viperarum venina trisulcarum linguarum usque in hodiernum diem nullo modo aut homini aut pecori nocere potuere. Post ejusdem benedictionis verba sanctus ad suum revehitur monasterium.

Tum proinde paucís diebus transactís, dum missarum sollempnia ex more dominica celebrarentur die, subito susum elevatís oculís facies venerabilis viri florido respersa rubore videtur; quia sicut scriptum est, 'Corde letante vultus floret'; eadem namque hora angelum domini supra volitantem solus vidit intra ipsius oratorii parietes; et quia sanctorum angelorum amabilis et tranquillus aspectus gaudium et exultationem electorum pectoribus infundit, haec fuit illius subitae causa laetitiae beato infusa[e] viro.

De qua scilicet causa inspiratae laetationis cum qui inerant ibidem praesentes inquirerent, hoc eís sanctus responsum sursum respiciens dedit: 'Mira et inconparabilis angelicae subtilitas naturae. Ecce enim angelus domini, ad repetendum aliquod deo carum misus depossitum, nos desuper intra eclesiam aspiciens et benedicens rursum per parasticiam eclesiae reversus nulla talis vestigia exitus reliquit'.

Haec sanctus, sed tamen de qualitate illius depositi ad quod misus est angelus requirendum nemo de circumstantibus recognoscere potuit. Noster vero patronus sanctam propriam a deo sibi commendatam animam depositum nuncupavit; quae sicuti inferius narrabitur alia senís intervenientibus continuís diebus dominica nocte ad dominum emigravit.

Vir itaque venerabilis in fine ejusdem ebdomadis, hoc est die sabbati, ipse et ejus pius minister Diormitius ad proximum pergunt benedicendum horreum. Quod intrans sanctus cum benedixisset, et duos in eo frugum sequestratos acervos, hoc intulit verbum cum gratiarum actione, inquiens: 'Valde congratulor meís familiaribus monacís, quia hoc etiam anno, si quoquam a vobís emigrare me oportuerit, annuum sufficientem habebitis [panem]'.

Quo audito verbo Diormitius minister tristificari coepit et síc dicere: 'Hujus anni tempore, pater, sepius nos contristas, quia de tuo transitu crebro commemoras'. Cui sanctus dedit responsum: 'Aliquem arcanum habeo sermusculum, quem si mihi firmiter promiseris nemini ante meum denudare obitum, de meo tibi egressu aliquid manifestius intimare potero'. Quam cum talem minister promisionem juxta voluntatem sancti flexís genibus terminasset, vir venerandus consequenter síc profatur: 'Haec in sacrís voluminibus dies sabbatum nuncupatur, quod interpraetatur requies. Et vere mihi est sabbatum haec hodierna, quia hujus praesentis laboriosae vitae mihi ultima est, in qua post meas laborationum molestias sabatizo. Et hac sequenti media venerabili dominica nocte, secundum eloquia scripturarum, patrum gradiar viam. Jam enim dominus meus Jesus Christus me invitare dignatur; ad quem inquam hac mediante nocte ipso me invitante emigrabo. Síc enim mihi ab ipso domino revelatum est'. Haec mesta minister audiens verba coepit amare flere, quem sanctus in quantum potuit consulari conabatur.

Post haec sanctus horreum egreditur, et ad monasterium revertens media resedet via. In quo loco postea crux molari infixa lapidi hodieque stans in margine cernitur viae. Dumque ibidem sanctus, ut praefatus sum, senio fesus paululum sedens requiesceret, ecce albus occurrit cavallus oboediens servitor, qui scilicet lactaria bocetum inter et monasterium vascula gestare consueverat. Hic ad sanctum accedens mirum dictu caput in sinu ejus ponens, ut credo inspirante deo cui omne animal rerum sapit sensu quo juserit ipse creator, dominum a sé suum mox emigraturum et ipsum ultra non visurum sciens, coepit plangere ubertimque quasi homo lacrimas in gremium sancti fundere, et valde spumans flere. Quod videns minister coepit illum flebilem repellere lamentatorem. Sed sanctus prohibuit eum, dicens: 'Sine hunc, sine nostri amatorem, ut in hunc meum sinum fletus effundat amarissimi plangoris. Ecce tu, homo cum sis et rationalem animam habeas, nullo modo scire de meo exitu potuisti, nisi quod tibi ego ipse nuper manifestavi. Huic vero bruto et inrationali animanti, quoquo modo ipse conditor voluit, egresurum a se domnum manifeste revelavit'. Et haec dicens mestum a sé revertentem equm benedixit ministratorem.

Et inde egrediens, et monticellum monasterio supereminentem ascendens, in vertice ejus paululum stetit; et stans ambas elevans palmas suum benedixit cenubium, inquiens: 'Huic loco quamlibet angusto et vili non tantum Scotorum reges cum populís, sed etiam barbararum et exterarum gentium regnatores cum plebibus sibi subjectís, grandem et non mediocrem conferent honorem. A sanctis quoque, etiam aliarum eclesiarum, non mediocris veneratio conferetur'.

Post haec verba de illo discendens monticellulo et ad monasterium revertens sedebat in tegorio psalterium scribens. Et ad illum xxx. tertii psalmi versiculum perveniens ubi scribitur, 'Inquirentes autem dominum non deficient omni bono': 'Hîc' ait, 'in fine cessandum est paginae. Quae vero sequuntur Baitheneus scribat'. Sancto convenienter congruit decessori novissimus versiculus quem scripserat, cui numquam bona deficient aeterna. Successori vero sequens patri spiritalium doctori filiorum, 'Venite filii audite me; timorem domini docebo vos', congruenter convenit, qui sicut decessor commendavit non solum ei docendo sed etiam scribendo successit.

Post talem superius memoratum terminatae versum perscriptum paginae, sanctus ad vespertinalem dominicae noctis misam ingreditur eclesiam. Qua continuo consummata ad hospitiolum revertens in lectulo resedet pernox ubi pro stramine nudam habebat petram, et pro pulvillo lapidem qui hodieque quasi quidam juxta sepulchrum ejus titulus stat monumenti. Ibidem itaque resedens ultima ad fratres mandata solo audiente ministro commendat, inquiens: 'Haec vobís ó filioli novissima commendo verba, ut inter vos motuam et non fictam habeatis caritatem cum pace. Et si ita juxta sanctorum exempla patrum observaveritis, deus confortator bonorum vobís auxiliabitur, et ego cum ipso manens pro vobís interpellabo; et non tantum praesentis vitae necessaria ab eo sufficienter amministrabuntur, sed etiam aeternalium bonorum proemia divinorum observatoribus [mandatorum] praeparata tribuentur'.

Huc usque extrema venerabilis patroni verba quasi de hac tediali perigrinatione ad caelestem patriam transmeantis brevi textu narrata deducta sunt.

Post quae felici appropinquante novissima paulisper hora sanctus conticuit. Tum proinde media nocte pulsata personante cloca festinus surgens ad eclesiam pergit, citiorque ceterís currens solus introgresus juxta altare flexís in oratione genibus recumbit. Diormitius minister tardius prosequtus eodem momento eminus totam intrinsecus eclesiam angelica luce erga sanctum repleri videt. Quo ad januam appropinquante eadem lux visa ocius recessit; quam etiam alii de fra tribus pauci et ipsi eminus adstantes viderant.

Diormitius ergo eclesiam ingrediens flebili ingeminat voce: 'Ubi es, pater?' Et necdum allatís fratrum lucerní s per tenebras palpans sanctum ante altarium recubantem invenit, quem paululum eregens et juxta sedens sanctum in suo gremio possuit caput. Et inter haec coetus monachorum cum luminaribus adcurrens patre viso moriente coepit plangere. Et ut ab aliquibus qui praesentes inerant didicimus, sanctus necdum egrediente anima apertís susum oculís ad utrumque latus cum mira vultus hilaritate et laetitia circumspiciebat, sanctos scilicet obvios intuens angelos. Diormitius tum sanctam sublevat ad benedicendum sancti monachorum chorum dexteram manum. Sed et ipse venerabilis pater in quantum poterat simul suam movebat manum; ut videlicet quod voce in egresu non valebat animae etiam motu manus fratres videretur benedicere. Et post sanctam benedictionem taliter significatam continuo spiritum exalavit.

Quo tabernaculum corporis egreso facies rubens et mirum in modum angelica visione exhilarita in tantum remansit, ut non quasi mortui sed dormientis videretur viventis. Tota interim personabat mestis plangoribus eclesia. Sed non praetereundum videtur quod eadem hora beatae transitus animae cuidam everniensi sancto revelatum est.

In illo namque monasterio quod scotica nominatur lingua Cloni- finchoil quidam homo erat sanctus senex, Christi miles, qui Lugudius vocitabatur, filius Tailchani, justus et sapiens. Hic itaque primo mane cuidam eque christiano militi, Fergnovo nomine, suam enarravit visionem cum ingenti gemitu dicens: 'Hac praeterita nocte media sanctus Columba multarum columna eclesiarum ad dominum transit. Et in hora beati exitus ejus Iovam insulam, ad quam corpore numquam perveni, totam angelorum claritudine in spiritu vidi inradiatam, totaque spatia aeris, usque ad ethera caelorum, eorundem angelorum claritate inlustrata, qui ad sanctam ipsius animam praeferendam de caelís misi discenderant innumeri. Altisona quoque carminalia et valde suavia audivi angelicorum coetuum cantica, eodem momento egresionis inter angelicos sanctae ipsius animae ascendentes choros'.

Hanc angelicam manifestationem Virgnous, ut praedictum est, qui ab ore sancti illius senis cui revelata erat indubitanter didicerat, hísdem diebus de Scotia remigans Hinba in insula reliquiis diebus vitae suae permanens sancti Columbae monacís sepius enarrabat. Qui videlicet Virgnous, post multos in subjectione inter fratres inreprehensibiliter expletos annos, alios xii. in loco anchoritarum in Muirbulc-mar vitam ducens anchoriticam Christi victor miles explevit.

Hanc praedictam visionem non solum paginís inscriptam repperimus, sed et [ab] aliquibus expertís senioribus quibus ipse Virgnous retulerat sine ullo didicimus cunctamine.

Eadem quoque hora aliam visionem aliter revelatam unus ex eís qui viderant, Christi miles, valde senex, cujus nomen etiam potest dici 'ferreolus', scotice vero Ernene, gente mocu Fir-roide, qui inter aliorum sancti Columbae monacorum reliquias, et ipse sanctus monacus, in dorso Tómme sepultus cum sanctis resurrectionem exspectat, mihi Adomnano illo juveni in tempore cum grandi retulerat testificatione, dicens: 'Illa in nocte qua sanctus Columba de terrís ad caelos felici et beato fine transiit, ego et alii mecum viri laborantes in captura piscium in valle piscosi fluminis Fendæ subito totum aerei inlustratum caeli spatium videmus. Cujus mi raculi subitatione permoti oculos ad orientem elevatos convertimus, et ecce quasi quaedam pergrandis ignea apparuit columna, quae in illa nocte media susum ascendens ita nobis videbatur mundum inlustrare totum sicuti aesteus et meridianus sol. Et postquam illa penetravit columna caelum, quasi post occassum solis tenebrae succedunt. Hujus itaque claritudinem luminosae et praedicabilis columnae non tantum nos qui simul in eodem loco ineramus cum ingenti ammiratione vidimus, sed et alii multi piscatores qui sparsim per diversas fluminales piscinas ejusdem fluminis piscabantur, sicut nobis post retulerant, simili apparatione visa magno pavore sunt perculsi'.

Harum igitur trium miracula visionum eadem transitus hora venerandi apparentium patroni aeternos ei a deo conlatos protestantur honores. Ad propossitum revertamur.

Interea post sanctae egresum animae ymnís matutinalibus terminatís sacrum corpus de eclesia ad hospitium, unde paulo ante vivens venerat, cum canora fratrum reportatur psalmodia. Honestaeque ternís diebus et totidem noctibus honorabiles rite explentur exequiae; quibus in dei sapidís laudibus terminatís, sancti et beati patroni venerabile corpus mundís involutum sindonibus et praeparata possitum in rata busta debeta humatur cum veneratione, in luminosa et aeternali resurrecturum claritudine.

De supra memoratís ergo tribus illís exsequiarum diebus, more peractís eclesiastico, quod nobís ab expertís traditum est hujus prope finem enarrabitur libri.

Quidam namque aliquando unus de fratribus coram venerabili viro sempliciter loquens: 'Ad celebrandas' ait ad sanctum, 'tuas post tuum obitum exequias, ut putatur, totus harum provinciarum populus hanc Iovam remigans replebit insulam'. Quod verbum audiens sanctus consequenter ait: 'Ó mí filiole, non ut loqueris síc res probabit. Nam promiscuum populi vulgus nullo modo ad meas poterit exsequias venire. Mei soli familiares monaci mea sepulchralia conplebunt et exsequialia honestabunt officia'.

Quod verbum ejus profeticum statim post transitum ipsius omnipotentia dei adimpleri fecit. Nam per tris illas exsequiales dies et noctes grandis sine pluia facta est ventosa tempestas; qua fortiter prohibente nullus hinc et inde navicella vectus transfretarc poterat. Et post consummatam beati sepultionem viri continuo tempestate sedata et cessante vento totum tranquillatum est equor.

Perpendat itaque lector quanti et qualis apud deum praedicabilis patronus honoris habeatur, cui aliquando in carne mortali conversanti deo dignante oranti tempestates sedatae sunt et maria tranquillata; et rursus quando necesse habuit, supra memorata occassione, orta flamina ventorum et ventosa cum voluit concita sunt equora; quae subsequenter, ut superius dictum est, expletís ejus sepulturae ministeriis in magnam conversa sunt tranquillitatem.

Hic itaque nostro praedicabili patrono vitae terminus fuit; ista meritorum exordia. Qui, secundum sententias scripturarum, aeterníis comes triumphís patribus additus, apostolís et profetís consertus, numero aggregatus albatorum milium agnino in sanguine suas sanctorum qui laverunt stolas, agnum ductorem comitatur; virgo inmaculatus, ab omni intiger labe, ipso domino nostro Jesu Christo dignante, cui est cum patre honor virtus laus gloria et imperium sempeternum, in unitate spiritus sancti, per omnia saecula saeculorum.

Post horum trinalium lectionem libellorum, quisque dilegens annotet lector quanti et qualis meriti sanctus sepe supra memoratus praesul venerandus, quantae et qualis apud deum honorificantiae, fuerit estimatus; quantae et quales angelicae ad ipsum et luminosae frequentationes fuerint; quanta in eo profetalis gratia; quanta dialium efficientia virtutum; quanta et quam frequens eum divini luminis claritudo in carne mortali adhuc commorantem circumfulserit. Quae etiam post egresum animae de tabernaculo corporis almissimae, sicuti quibusdam electís ostensum habetur conpertum, locum in quo ipsius sancta pausant ossa usque hodie eadem caelestis claritas frequentare non cessat, et sanctorum frequens visitatio angelorum.

Et haec etiam eidem beatae memoriae viro a deo non mediocris est conlata gratia, qua nomen ejus non tantum per totam nostram Scotiam, et omnium totius orbis insularum maximam Brittanniam, clare devulgari promeruit in hac parva et extrema ociani brittannici commoratus insula, sed etiam ad trigonam usque Hispaniam, et Gallias, et ultra Alpes pininas Italiam sitam pervenire, ipsam quoque romanam civitatem, quae caput est omnium civitatum, tantus et talis honor noscibilis eidem sancto inter cetera divinae donationis munera condonatus scitur a deo, qui sé diligentes amat, et eos qui eum sapidís magnificant laudibus magis ac magis glorificans inmensís sublimat honoribus. Qui est benedictus in saecula. Amen.

Obsecro eos quicumque voluerint hos discribere libellos, immo potius adjuro per Christum judicem saeculorum, ut postquam deligenter discripserint conferant et emendent cum omni diligentia ad exemplar unde craxerunt, et hanc quoque adjurationem hoc in loco subscribant.

Quicumque hós virtutum libellos Columbae legerit pro me Dorbbeneo deum deprecetur, ut vitam post mortem aeternam possedeam.

TRANSLATION

[III 23] Concerning the passing to the Lord of our holy patron Columba

When the end was drawing near of the four years above-mentioned, after the completion of which the foreteller of truth had long ago foreknown that his present life would come to a close, one day, in the month of May, as we have written in the preceding second book, the saint went, drawn in a wagon (being an old man, weary with age) to visit the labouring brothers, at work in the western part of the island of Io;[1] and on that day he began to speak to them in this manner, saying: 'At the Easter festival recently held, in the month of April, I desired with desire to depart to Christ the Lord, as had indeed been granted by him to me, if I had so chosen; but I chose rather to put off a little longer the day of my departure from the world, so that the festival of joy should not be turned for you into sorrow.'

Meanwhile the monks of his congregation that heard him speak these sad things became very sorrowful; and he began to cheer them, as well as he could, with comforting words. After which, still sitting in the wagon, he turned his face to the east, and blessed the island, with the islanders its inhabitants. And from then to the present day, as has been written in the above-mentioned book, the poison of three-forked tongues of vipers has not been able to do any injury to either man or beast. After the words of this blessing, the saint was carried back to his monastery.

Then after a few days had passed, while the rites of the Mass were being celebrated on a Lord's-day according to the custom, the venerable man lifted up his eyes, and suddenly his face was seen to flush with a ruddy glow; for, as it is written, 'The countenance glows when the heart is glad'; and in fact at the same moment he alone saw an angel of the Lord hovering above, within the walls of the oratory

1. The island of Iona in the Inner Hebrides off the west coast of Scotland. Columba landed here from Ireland in 563 and founded a monastery that became an important centre of the Irish church.

itself; and because the calm and lovely sight of holy angels fills the hearts of the elect with joy and exultation, this was the cause of the sudden gladness that filled the blessed man.

When those that were present there asked about this, the cause of the gladness inspired in him, the saint, gazing upward, gave them this reply: 'Wonderful and incomparable is the fineness of angelic nature! See, an angel of the Lord, sent to recover a deposit dear to God, looking down upon us within the church and blessing us, has returned through the roof-courses of the church, leaving no trace of that departure.'

This the saint said, but yet none of those standing by could know of what kind that deposit was, to recover which the angel had been sent. Our patron, however, described as a 'deposit' his own holy soul, entrusted to him by God, which, as will be related below, departed to the Lord after an interval of six consecutive days, on the Lord's-night following.

In the end of the same week, that is, on the Sabbath day, the venerable man himself, and his devoted attendant Diormit, went to bless the nearest barn. After entering it, and blessing it and two heaps of grain that were there in store, the saint spoke thus, and rendering thanks said: 'I greatly congratulate my family of monks, because in this year also, if I have to depart from you to any place, you will have enough [bread] for the year.'

When the attendant Diormit heard this, he began to be sorrowful, and to speak in this manner: 'This year, father, you very often sadden us, because you frequently speak of your passing.' The saint gave him this answer: 'I have a few secret words concerning my departure that I shall be able to communicate somewhat more plainly to you, if you will faithfully promise me not to disclose them to any one before my death.' After the attendant had completed that promise on bended knees, according to the saint's desire, the venerable man made a statement to this effect: 'This day is called in the sacred books "Sabbath", which is interpreted "rest". And truly this day is for me a Sabbath, because it is my last day of this present laborious life. In it after my toilsome labours I keep Sabbath; and at midnight of this following venerated Lord's-day, in the language of the Scriptures I shall go the way of the fathers. For now my Lord Jesus Christ deigns to invite me. To him I shall depart, I say, when he invites me, in the middle of this night. For so it has been revealed to me by the Lord himself.' The attendant hearing these sad words began to weep bitterly, and the saint tried to comfort him, as well as he could.

After this, the saint left the barn, and returning towards the monastery sat down midway. In that place a cross that was later fixed in a mill-stone is seen, standing by the roadside, even today. And while the saint sat there, resting for a little while, being (as I have said above) weary with age, behold, a white horse came to him, the obedient servant who was accustomed to carry the milk-vessels between the cow-pasture and the monastery. It went to the saint, and strange to tell put its head in his bosom, inspired, as I believe, by God, before whom every living creature has understanding, with such perception of things as the Creator himself has decreed; and knowing that its master would presently depart from it, and that it should see him no more, it began to mourn, and like a human being to let tears fall freely on the lap of the saint, and foaming much, to weep aloud.

When he saw this, the attendant began to drive away the weeping mourner; but the saint forbade him, saying: 'Let him, let him that loves us, pour out the tears of most bitter grief here in my bosom. See, man though you are, and having a rational soul, you could by no means know anything of my departure except what I myself have even now disclosed to you. But to this brute and unreasoning animal the Creator has, in what way he would, revealed clearly that its master is going to depart from it.' Thus speaking, he blessed his servant the horse, as it turned sadly away from him.

Going from there, he climbed a small hill overlooking the monastery, and stood on its summit for a little while. And as he stood he raised both hands, and blessed his monastery, saying: 'On this place, small and mean though it be, not only the kings of the Irish with their peoples, but also the rulers of barbarous and foreign nations, with their subjects, will bestow great and especial honour; also especial reverence will be bestowed by saints even of other churches.'

After these words, he descended from that little hill, returned to the monastery, and sat in the hut, writing a psalter. And when he came to that verse of the thirty-third Psalm where it is written, 'But they that seek the Lord shall not want for anything that is good', he said: 'Here, at the end of the page, I must stop. Let Baithene write what follows.'

The last verse that he wrote aptly befits the holy

predecessor, who will never lack eternal good things. And the verse that follows, 'Come, my sons, hear me; I will teach you fear of the Lord', is fittingly adapted to the successor, the father of spiritual sons, a teacher, who, as his predecessor enjoined, succeeded him not in teaching only, but in writing also.

After he had written the former verse, at the end of the page, the saint entered the church for the vesper office of the Lord's-night. As soon as that was finished, he returned to his lodging, and reclined on his sleeping-place, where during the night he used to have for bed, the bare rock; and for pillow, a stone, which even today stands beside his grave as a kind of epitaph. So while reclining there, he gave his last commands to the brothers, in the hearing of his attendant alone, and said: 'I commend to you, my children, these latest words, that you shall have among yourselves mutual and unfeigned charity, with peace. If you follow this course after the example of the holy fathers, God, who gives strength to the good, will help you; and I, abiding with him, shall intercede for you. And not only will the necessaries of this life be sufficiently provided by him, but also the rewards of eternal good things will be bestowed, that are prepared for those who follow the divine commandments.'

We have carried down to this point, briefly told, the last words of the venerable patron, when he was, as it were, crossing over to the heavenly country from this weary pilgrimage.

After them the saint was silent for a little, as the happy latest hour drew near. Then, when the beaten bell resounded at midnight, he rose in haste and went to the church and, running, entered in advance of the others, alone; and bowing his knees in prayer he sank down beside the altar. In that moment Diormit, the attendant, following later, saw from a distance the whole church filled inside with angelic light about the saint. As Diormit approached the doorway, the light that he had seen quickly faded. A few more of the brothers also had seen it, when they too were a little way off.

So Diormit entering the church cried in a tearful voice: 'Where are you, where are you, father?' And groping in the darkness, since the lamps of the brothers had not yet been brought, he found the saint lying before the altar. Raising him a little, and sitting down beside him, he placed the holy head upon his lap. Meanwhile the company of monks ran up with lights; and when they saw that their father was dying they began to lament. And as we have learned from some men who were present there, the saint, whose soul had not yet departed, opened his eyes, and looked around on either side, with wonderful joy and gladness of countenance; for he was gazing upon the holy angels that had come to meet him. Then Diormit raised the holy right hand, to bless the saint's company of monks. And the venerable father himself at the same time moved his hand, as much as he was able, in order that he might be seen to bless the brothers even by the movement of his hand, a thing that in the departure of his soul he could not do by voice. And after the holy benediction thus expressed he presently breathed out his spirit.

When that had left the tabernacle of the body, his face continued to be ruddy, and in a wonderful degree gladdened by the vision of angels, so much that it seemed like the face not of a dead man, but of a living sleeper. Meanwhile the whole church resounded with sorrowful lamentations.

And it appears right that this should not be omitted that was revealed to a certain saint in Ireland, in the very hour of the passing of the blessed soul. For in the monastery that in the Irish tongue is called *Cloni-finchoil*,[2] there was an aged holy man, a soldier of Christ, righteous and wise, who was called Luguid, son of Tailchan. In the early morning he related a vision that he had had, to a man who was likewise a Christian soldier, by name Virgno; and said, with great lamentation: 'In the middle of this last night Saint Columba, the pillar of many churches, has passed to the Lord. And in the hour of his blessed departure I saw in the Spirit the whole island of Io (where I have never come in the body) lit up with the brightness of angels; and all the spaces of the air, as far as the ethereal skies, illumined by the shining of those angels, who, sent from heaven, had come down without number, to bear aloft his holy soul. Also I heard, sounding on high, the songs, tuneful and very sweet, of the angelic hosts, at the very moment when his holy soul went forth among the ascending companies of angels.'

In those same days Virgno rowed over from Ireland, and he remained for the rest of his life in

2. Unidentified. Perhaps the river Boyne in County Meath. cf. A.D.S. MacDonald, 'Aspects of the Monastery and Monastic Life in Adamnán's Life of Columba', *Peritia* 3 (1984), 276.

the island of Hinba;[3] and he very often described to the monks of Saint Columba this manifestation of angels of which, as has been said above, he had learned indubitably from the mouth of the holy old man to whom it had been revealed. After completing irreproachably many years in subjection among the brothers, this Virgno completed another twelve years as a victorious soldier of Christ, leading the life of an anchorite, in the place of the anchorites, in Muirbolc-már.[4]

We have not only found the foregoing vision set down in writing, but we have learned it with no uncertainty [from] some elders who knew of it, since Virgno himself had told it to them.

Another vision, differently revealed at the same hour, was told with strong asseveration to me, Adamnán, then a young man, by one of those that had seen it, a very aged soldier of Christ, of the family mocu Fir-roide,[5] whose name, in Irish *Ernene*, can also be rendered 'man of iron'. He (himself a holy monk) lies buried among the remains of other monks of Saint Columba, and awaits the resurrection with the saints, in the ridge of Tóimm.[6] He said: 'In that night when Saint Columba passed, by a happy and blessed end, from earth to heaven, I and other men with me, at work on the catching of fish in the valley of the river Fendea,[7] which abounds in fish, saw the whole space of airy heaven suddenly lit up. Startled by the suddenness of this miracle, we raised our eyes and turned them to the region of the rising sun; and behold, there appeared what seemed like a very great pillar of fire which, rising upwards in that midnight, seemed to us to illumine the whole world like the summer sun at midday. And after that pillar pierced the sky, darkness followed, as after the setting of the sun. Not only was the brightness of this luminous and remarkable pillar seen, with great amazement, by us, who were together in the same place, but many other fishers also, who were fishing here and there among the various pools of the same river, were, as they told us afterwards, struck with great terror, through seeing a similar apparition.'

3. Uncertain. Probably an island in the Hebrides. cf. MacDonald, op. cit., p. 298; A.O. and M.O. Anderson (eds), *Adomnán's Life of Columba* (London: Thomas Nelson and Sons Ltd., 1961), pp. 153-54.
4. A place on the island of Hinba.
5. Possibly preserved in the place-name Corca Roíde (barony of Corcaree, Co. Westmeath).
6. Drumhome parish in County Donegal.
7. River Finn, Co. Donegal.

These three miraculous visions, appearing in the very hour of the passing of the venerable patron, testify to the eternal honours conferred on him by God. Let us return to our theme.

In the meanwhile, after the departure of the holy soul, when the matin hymns were ended, the sacred body was carried back from the church, with the brothers' tuneful psalmody, to the lodging from which, alive, he had come a little while before. And for three days and three nights the funeral ceremonies were duly carried out in a worthy and honourable manner. When these had ended in the savoury praises of God, the venerable body of the holy and blessed patron was wrapped in clean fine cloths, and laid in the appointed burial-place that had been made ready, and was interred with fitting veneration, to rise again in bright and eternal light.

What has been handed down to us on good authority concerning those three days of funeral mentioned above, spent according to the custom of the church, shall be related here, almost at the end of this book.

A certain man, one of the brothers, on one occasion in the company of the venerable man spoke unthinkingly, and said to the saint: 'After your death, it is estimated that the entire population of these provinces will row over for the celebration of your funeral, and fill this island of Io.' Upon hearing this, the saint said: 'My child, the event will not prove to be as you say; for a miscellaneous crowd of people will not be able to come to my funeral. Only my family of monks will fulfil the offices of my burial, and worthily perform my funeral rites.'

The omnipotence of God caused this prophetic saying of his to be fulfilled immediately after his death. For during those three days and nights of the funeral a great storm of wind blew without rain, and forbade any one in a small ship to cross the strait in either direction. And after the burial of the blessed man had been completed, straightway the storm was stilled, the wind ceased, and the whole sea was calmed.

Let the reader consider in how great and high honour with God the memorable patron is held, at whose prayer once while he lived in mortal flesh, God granting it, storms were stilled, and seas were calmed; and again, when he had need, on the occasion mentioned above, at his wish blasts of wind sprang up, and stormy seas were raised; which afterwards, as has been said above, when the services of his burial were complete, were changed into a great calm.

This was the end of our memorable patron's life; these were the beginnings of his rewards. Being, in the language of the scriptures, added to the fathers as a sharer in eternal triumphs, united to apostles and prophets, and joined to the number of the thousands of white-robed saints who have washed their robes in the blood of the Lamb, he attends the Lamb his leader; a virgin unstained, free from every flaw, by the grace of our Lord Jesus Christ himself, who has, with the Father, honour, power, praise, glory, and everlasting dominion, in the unity of the Holy Spirit, through all the ages of the ages.

After the reading of these three books, let every attentive reader observe of how great and high merit, how greatly and highly deserving of honour, our venerable holy superior so often named above was esteemed in the sight of God; how much and in what manner he was visited by shining angels; how great in him was the grace of prophecy, how great the power of divine miracles; how great and how frequent was the brightness of divine light that shone about him, while he still lived in mortal flesh. And even after the departure of his most gentle soul from the tabernacle of the body, this same heavenly brightness, as well as the frequent visits of holy angels, does not cease, down to the present day, to appear at the place in which his holy bones repose; as is established through being revealed to certain elect persons.

And this great favour also was conferred by God on that man of blessed memory, that, although he lived in this small and remote island of the Britannic ocean, he merited that his name should not only be illustriously renowned throughout our Ireland, and throughout Britain, the greatest of all the islands of the whole world; but that it should reach even as far as three-cornered Spain, and Gaul, and Italy situated beyond the Pennine Alps; also the Roman city itself, which is the chief of all cities. So great and high honour of fame is known to have been bestowed upon that saint, among the other gifts of divine granting, by God, who loves those that love him, and, more and more glorifying those that magnify him with savoury praises, elevates them with boundless honours. And He is blessed through the ages. Amen.

I beseech all those that may wish to copy these books, nay more I adjure them through Christ, the judge of the ages, that after carefully copying they compare them with the exemplar from which they have written, and emend them with the utmost care; and also that they append this adjuration in this place.

Whoever may read these books of the miraculous powers of Columba, let him pray to God for me, Dorbbene,[8] that I may possess after death eternal life.

8. Dorbbéne, abbot of Iona for five months. He died on 28 October 713. He copied Adamnán's 'Life' of Columba (his manuscript is now in Schaffhausen, Switzerland) from which the above edition was made.

from:
DE LOCIS SANCTIS
(Concerning the Holy Places)

[Adamnán wrote his description of the Holy Places in Palestine after he had met Arculf, a Gaulish bishop. Arculf had travelled throughout the Near East between approximately 679 and 682. On his return home, he was shipwrecked off the coast of Scotland and, after much hardship, arrived eventually at the monastery of Iona. Adamnán interviewed him about the sites he had seen (writing down the information initially on wax tablets), and then checked the information against the books in the monastic library, before composing the final draft on parchment sometime between 683 and 686.

Adamnán presented a copy of his work to the Northumbrian king, Aldfrith, when on a visit to him, possibly in 686. In this way Adamnán's work became widely known and was, at a later date, the basis of the Venerable Bede's own account of the Holy Places. The text is of enormous value in giving an indication of the extensiveness of the library at Iona. As well as consulting the Bible, Adamnán seems to have had available the commentaries and some of the letters of Jerome, the *Chronicon* of Sulpicius Severus, and the *Historiae* of the so-called Hegesippus. He quotes a line from the *Historia Evangelica* of Iuuencus as well as echoing other words. His work is also of great interest for the way in which he handles the vocabulary of an urban civilization.

The translation and note appears in D. Meehan (ed.), *Adomnán's De Locis Sanctis*, Scriptores Latini Hiberniae, Vol. III (Dublin: Dublin Institute for Advanced Studies, 1958), 35, 40-47, 118-19.]

IN THE NAME OF THE FATHER, SON AND HOLY GHOST, I BEGIN TO WRITE A BOOK CONCERNING THE HOLY PLACES

The holy bishop Arculf, a Gaul by race, versed in divers far-away regions, and a truthful and quite reliable witness, sojourned for nine months in the city of Jerusalem, traversing the holy places in daily visitations. In response to my careful inquiries he dictated to me, Adamnan, this faithful and accurate record of all his experiences which is to be set out below. I first wrote it down on tablets: it will now be written succinctly on parchment.

THE BEGINNING OF THE FIRST BOOK CONCERNING THE HOLY PLACES

1. CONCERNING THE SITE OF JERUSALEM

I now propose to write a little of what the holy Arculf told me concerning the site of Jerusalem, omitting the matter that is contained in the books of others about the position of that city. In the great compass of its walls Arculf counted eighty-four towers and six gates, their order in the circuit of the city being thus. The gate of David at the west side of Mount Sion is the first, the second the gate of the fuller's house, the third the gate of the holy Stephen, the fourth the gate of Benjamin: the fifth is a *portula* (a little gate, that is) from which steps lead down to the valley of Josaphat, and the sixth is the gate of Tecua. That is the order then when you make the circuit from the above-mentioned gate of David, northwards and then eastwards, through the spaces between the various gates and towers. But though the number of gates in the walls is six, nevertheless of these, [three] entrances are in common use, one on the west side, the second on the north, the third on the east. That portion of the walls then, with towers at intervals, which extends from the gate of David described above, over the northern summit of mount Sion (which dominates the city from the south), as far as that side of the mountain where a cliff looks out eastwards, is certainly without gates.

This item too which the holy Arculf related to us concerning the special honour in Christ of this city ought not, it seems, to be passed over. On the twelfth day of the month of September, he says, there is an annual custom whereby a huge concourse of people from various nations everywhere is wont to come together in Jerusalem to do business by mutual buying and selling. Consequently it happens inevitably that crowds of different people are lodged in this hospitable city for some days. Owing to the very great number of their camels, horses, asses, and oxen, all carriers of divers merchandise, filth from their discharges spreads everywhere throughout the city streets, the stench proving no little annoyance to the citizens, and walking being impeded. Wonderful to relate, on the night of the day on which the said bands depart with their various beasts of burden, there is released from the clouds an immense downpour of rain, which descends on the city, and renders it clean of dirt by purging away all the abominable filth from the streets. For the site itself of Jerusalem is so arranged by God, its founder, on a gentle incline, falling away from the northern summit of mount Sion to the low-lying regions at the northern and eastern walls, that this great flood of rain cannot by any means lie stagnant on the streets, but flows like torrents from the higher regions to the low-lying. The flood of heavenly waters, then, pouring through the eastern gates, and bearing all the filth and nuisance with it, enters the valley of Josaphat, swells the torrent of Cedron, and after such a baptism of Jerusalem straightway the copious flood ceases. Thus one should carefully note the magnitude and character of the honour which this chosen and famous city has in the sight of the eternal father, who does not suffer it to remain soiled for long, but quickly cleanses it out of reverence for his only begotten son, who has the honoured places of his holy cross and resurrection within the compass of its walls.

However, in the celebrated place where once the temple (situated towards the east near the wall) arose in its magnificence, the Saracens now have a quadrangular prayer house. They built it roughly by erecting upright boards and great beams on some ruined remains. The building, it is said, can accommodate three thousand people at once.

2. CONCERNING A CHURCH OF ROUND SHAPE THAT IS BUILT OVER THE LORD'S SEPULCHRE, (AND CONCERNING THE SHAPE OF THE SEPULCHRE ITSELF AND OF ITS DOMED STRUCTURE)

Arculf then, when we questioned him about the dwellings of the city itself, said in reply: 'I recall seeing and visiting many buildings in the city, and often studying several great stone mansions built with wondrous skill throughout the whole great city within the surrounding walls.' But I think we must now pass over all these, except for those structures which have been wondrously raised in the holy places, the places that is of the cross and resurrection. We questioned the holy Arculf carefully concerning these, especially concerning the sepulchre of the Lord and the church built over it, the shape of which Arculf himself depicted for me on a waxed tablet.

Well, this extremely large church, all of stone, and shaped to wondrous roundness on every side, rises up from its foundations in three walls. Between each two walls there is a broad passage, and three altars too are in three skilfully constructed places of the centre wall. Twelve stone columns of wondrous magnitude support this round and lofty church, where are the altars mentioned, one looking south, the second north, the third towards the west. There are two fourfold portals ([four] entrances that is), which cut across the three solid walls facing one another with passageways in between. Four of these [exits] face the Vulturnus wind (which is also called Caecias): the other four face Eurus.

Centrally placed in the interior of this round building is a round domed structure, carved out of one and the same rock, in which it is possible for thrice three men to pray standing, and from the top of a fairly tall man's head, when standing, to the roof of the domed structure there is a space measuring a foot and a half. The entrance of this domed structure faces east. Outside, it is completely covered with choice marble, and its summit, adorned on the outside with gold, supports a fairly large golden cross. The sepulchre of the Lord is in the northern part of the domed structure, carved out of one and the same rock, but the floor of the domed covering is lower than the place of the sepulchre. For from its floor to the side-edge of the sepulchre one can perceive a space of about three hands' height. Arculf, who used often to visit the sepulchre of the Lord, and made the measurement, told me this definitely.

At this juncture, one should note the propriety, or rather the discrepancy of nomenclature, as between *monumentum* and *sepulchrum*. That round domed structure that has been often mentioned above, the evangelists call by another name, *monumentum*, to the door of which they state the stone was rolled and rolled away from its door when the Lord arose. The *sepulchrum* properly so called is the place inside the domed structure, in the northern portion of the *monumentum* that is, in which was laid the body of the Lord, wrapped in linen cloths. The length of this, as Arculf measured it with his own hand, made seven feet. The *sepulchrum* then is not, as some people wrongly think, a double structure, with a kind of border cut out of the rock itself to separate and divide the two legs and the two thighs: it is undivided from head to foot, providing a pallet large enough for one man lying on his back. It is in the shape of a cave, with the entrance on the side, directly facing the southern portion of the *monumentum*, and with a low, man-made vault rising above. Now in this *sepulchrum*, according to the number of the twelve holy apostles, twelve burning lamps shine always day and night. Four of them are placed low down at the bottom of the sepulchral bed: the other eight are placed higher up above the margin towards the right-hand side. They are fed with oil and shine brightly.

It seems noteworthy moreover that the mausoleum of the Saviour, the domed structure that has often been mentioned above, might correctly be called a cavern or cave; and doubtless the prophet prophesies concerning the burial of the Lord Jesus Christ in it when he says 'he shall dwell in a high cave of the strongest rock', and shortly afterwards (concerning the resurrection of the same Lord), in order to make the apostles rejoice, he adds: 'you shall see the king with glory'.

This drawing appended indicates the shape of the round church mentioned above, with the round domed structure placed in the centre of it, in the northern portion of which is the Lord's sepulchre. It exhibits also plans of three other churches, of which there will be an account below. We have drawn these plans of the four churches after the model which (as already stated) the holy Arculf sketched for me on a wax surface. Not that it is possible to exhibit their likeness in a drawing, but in order that the *monumentum* of the Lord might be shown, placed as it is in the middle of the round church, albeit in a rough sketch, or that it might be made clear which church is situated near or far away from it....

5. CONCERNING THE IMAGE OF THE HOLY MARY[1]

The oft-mentioned Arculf gave us an accurate rendering also of a true story about an ikon of

1. Both this and the preceding narratives seem to indicate the first rumblings of the Iconoclast controversy, which was to manifest itself with such virulence under Leo the Isaurian (716-41). Opposition (sometimes active) to Christian image-cult of course had been operative in Jewish and Saracen circles for a considerable time.

the holy Mary, mother of the Lord, which he learned from some well-informed witnesses in the city of Constantinople. On the wall of a house in the metropolitan city, he said, a picture of the blessed Mary used to hang, painted on a short wooden tablet. A stupid and hardhearted man asked whose picture it was, and was told by someone that it was a likeness of the holy Mary ever virgin. When he heard this that Jewish unbeliever became very angry and, at the instigation of the devil, seized the picture from the wall and ran to a building near by, where it is customary to dispose of the soil from human bodies by means of openings in long planks whereon people sit. There, in order to dishonour Christ, who was born of Mary, he cast the picture of His mother through the opening on the nuisance lying beneath. Then in his stupid folly he sat above himself and evacuated through the opening, pouring the nuisance of his own person on the ikon of the holy Mary which he had just deposited there. After that disgraceful action the hapless creature went away, and what he did subsequently, how he lived, or what sort of end he had, is unknown. After the scoundrel had gone, one of the Christian community came upon the scene, a fortunate man, zealous for the things of the Lord. Knowing what had happened, he searched for the picture of the holy Mary, found it hidden in the refuse and took it up. He wiped it carefully and cleaned it by washing it in the clearest water, and then set it up in honour by him in his house. Wonderful to relate, there is always an issue of genuine oil from the tablet with the picture of the blessed Mary, which Arculf, as he is wont to tell, saw with his own eyes. This wondrous oil proclaims the honour of Mary, the mother of the Lord Jesus of whom the Father says: 'With my oil I have anointed him.' Likewise the psalmist addresses the Son of God himself when he says: 'God thy God hath anointed thee with the oil of joy beyond thy companions.'

The matter given above concerning the site and foundation of Constantinople, and concerning the round church too in which the salutary wood is stored, and the rest, we diligently learned from the lips of the holy priest Arculf, who stayed in the principal city of the Roman empire from Easter until the Lord's nativity, and subsequently took ship from there for Rome.

DÍCUIL

(*fl. c.*760-*c.*825)

from: DICUILI LIBER DE MENSURA ORBIS TERRAE (Dícuil: The Book on the Measurement of the Earth)

[Dícuil's work is important as the earliest medieval treatise on geography. It was finished in 825, probably at the palace school of Louis the Pious at Aix-la-Chapelle. It is essentially a geography of the world as it was known in the Roman empire. The authors whom he consulted at first hand were Pliny, Solinus, Sedulius, Priscian, and Isidore of Seville (*c.*559-636). Dícuil also used sources deriving ultimately from the map of Agrippa (died 12 B.C.) by way of an anonymous work, the *Divisio Orbis*, compiled on the orders of the Emperor Theodosius II, in 435, and known to Dícuil as the *Missi Theodosii*. He also used the *Cosmographia Caesaris*, dating to 44 B.C. Dícuil quotes nineteen other classical authors, but at second hand.

Dícuil's Latin is straightforward, sometimes terse, and Bieler points out that some of his descriptions are reminiscent of the style of Adamnán.

The extracts below begin with Dícuil's introduction, indicating his attitude towards his sources. The next extract (from Chapter VI) is Fidelis's account of his journey along the Nile. § 12 is a reference to the Nile-canal connecting the river to the Gulf of Arabia at Arsinoe; it was built by the Pharaoh Necho. The canal had a tendency to silt up with sand, and for that reason was occasionally renewed. It was still navigable until at least 500, was cleared by the Arabs in 640, and was later blocked by Caliph Almansor in 767. Did Fidelis travel on it before 767 or was it cleared yet again later? In § 13 the 'barns built by holy Joseph' are the pyramids, probably at Gizeh and Sakkara.

The final extract is from Chapter VII and deals with an area that Dícuil knew personally — the north-west of the

British Isles. Thule (§ 7) is Iceland and Dícuil is referring to Irish monks who had been there. In § 13 Dícuil demonstrates his independence of mind in rejecting the opinions of earlier writers whose calculations referred to conditions at the North Pole and not as far south as Iceland. §§ 14-15 deal with the Faeroes, abandoned by Irish hermits since the occupation by the Vikings. §§ 16-17 are examples of the kind of stories common in Dícuil's sources.

The translation appears in J. J. Tierney (ed.), *Dicuili Liber de Mensura Orbis Terrae,* Scriptores Latini Hiberniae, Vol. VI (Dublin: Dublin Institute for Advanced Studies, 1967).]

1. Having composed my letter on ten questions of the art of grammar, I considered that a book might follow on the measurement of the provinces of the earth, according to the authority of the men whom the holy emperor Theodosius[1] had sent to measure the said provinces; and I desire to indicate their dimensions, supplementing this information on the high authority of Plinius Secundus.[2]

2. But I have two reasons for prefixing the account of the envoys of Theodosius to the words of Plinius Secundus in the order of my writing, as against the chronological order, one that the former, in their last twelve lines, assert that their work has been done more carefully than that of the ancients, and the other, that I saw beforehand that the volumes of the Natural History of Plinius Secundus which I had examined, were very much jumbled up by the scribes of recent times.

3. I shall, indeed, devote my attention to correcting, in so far as I can, the reports of the above-mentioned envoys, as they have been composed with fewer mistakes.

4. But where in the books of Plinius Secundus I find figures which I realize to be undoubtedly corrupt, I shall leave their places vacant for the moment, so that if I do not find trusty copies whoever does find them may emend them. Where I am in doubt as to whether the figures are correct or not, I shall write them down as correct, so that, as I have said, whoever finds the true figures may make the appropriate correction.

5. Discrepancies in the number of miles between Plinius Secundus and the emperor's envoys should occasion no surprise to anyone, since the latter truly testify, as I have said, that they accomplished their work with more care than did the ancients....

VI 12. Although we read in no authority that a branch of the Nile flows into the Red Sea, yet brother Fidelis asserted this and related it, in my presence, to my teacher Suibne (to whom, under God, I owe any progress that I may have made), saying that, for purposes of worship, in the city of Jerusalem, both clerics and laymen ... sailed ... as far as the Nile.

13. Then, after a long sail on the Nile, they saw, like mountains, and admired from a distance, the seven barns built by holy Joseph, according to the number of the years of abundance, four in one place, and three in another.

14. From here they went to the three barns to admire them and found beside them a lion and eight people, men and women, lying dead. The lion had killed them in his strength, and they had killed him with spears and swords; both places in which the seven barns are built are desert.

15. After this he carefully examined the three barns and again was filled with amazement that they were entirely made of stone from their very base to the summit. The barns were square at the base, but rounded at the top; at the very apex they have, as it were, a slender point.

16. Then the brother whom I have mentioned measured one side of one barn, from corner to corner, as four hundred feet.

17. Next, embarking on their boats, they sailed along the Nile as far as the entrance of the Red Sea. From this harbour it is a small distance eastwards to the passage of Moses across the Red Sea. He who measured the side of the barn wished to go as far as the harbour where Moses with his people entered the sea, not only to enter the harbour, but in order to see in it the tracks of the chariots and the ruts of Pharaoh's wheels; but the sailors would not oblige. The width of the sea at that place seemed to him to be about six miles.

18. From thence they made a fast voyage in the western part of the Red Sea, that is, in the gulf which extends far towards the north. That is the sea which prevented the people of Israel, when murmuring in the desert, from being able to return to the land of Egypt.

19. It is not surprising that one river should be divided into various branches, whose width, particularly in Egypt, is compared to a great sea, as Priscian[3] in his thirteenth book has it, making the

1. Theodosius was emperor 408-450.
2. Plinius Secundus (23-79 A.D.), encyclopaedist.

3. Priscian, the grammarian, lived in the late fifth century.

comparison: As though, when looking at the sea, we were to say that the Nile is like that.

20. Today, in the *Cosmography* which was made in the consulate of Julius Caesar and Marcus Antonius, I have found a branch of the Nile described as flowing into the Red Sea beside the town Oliva and the camp of Moses.

21. He who would know the length of the Nile must first know how many miles are reckoned from the western part of Africa as far as the eastern side of Egypt, and from there again as far as the mouth by which its branch flows into the Red Sea near the camp of Moses and the town called Oliva: or, if he wishes a greater length, as far as the Pelusiac mouth, by which a second branch enters the Tyrrhenian sea, or, if he reckons it nearly to the end of its full length, he will stop at the Canopic mouth, but it is farther to the Pelusiac mouth. I have been unable to find out how many miles wide this river is....

VII 6. We do not read of islands being found in the sea west or north of Spain. There are islands around our own island Hibernia, some small and some very small. Near the island Britannia are many islands, some large, some small, and some medium-sized. Some are in the sea to her south and some in the sea to her west, but they abound mostly to the north-west and north. Among those I have lived in some, and have visited others; some I have only glimpsed, while others I have read about.

7. Plinius Secundus in his fourth book informs us that Pytheas of Marseilles states that Thule lies six days' sail to the north of Britain.

8. About the same island, which was always uninhabited, Isidorus[4] says in the same fourteenth book of his *Etymologiae*: Thule is the farthest island of the ocean, lying between north and west beyond Britain, getting its name from the sun, since at it the sun reaches its summer solstice.

9. Priscian speaks about the same island in his *Periegesis* more clearly than Isidorus, saying: Here crossing in boats the open waters of the ocean, and coming to Thule, which shines both by day and by night under the rays of the sun, when he ascends in his chariot to the axes of the zodiac, lighting up the north with his torch.

10. Julius Solinus[5] treats of the same island more clearly and fully than Priscian, and, speaking of Britannia, he writes thus in his *Collectanea*: Farthest Thule, in which, at the summer solstice, there is no night, when the sun passes out of the Crab: and in like manner no day at the winter solstice.

11. It is now thirty years since clerics, who had lived on the island from the first of February to the first of August, told me that not only at the summer solstice, but in the days round about it, the sun setting in the evening hides itself as though behind a small hill in such a way that there was no darkness in that very small space of time, and a man could do whatever he wished as though the sun were there, even remove lice from his shirt, and if they had been on a mountain-top perhaps the sun would never have been hidden from them.

12. In the middle of that moment of time it is midnight at the equator, and thus, on the contrary, I think that at the winter solstice and for a few days about it dawn appears only for the smallest space at Thule, when it is noon at the equator.

13. Therefore those authors are wrong and give wrong information, who have written that the sea will be solid about Thule, and that day without night continues right through from the vernal to the autumnal equinox, and that vice versa night continues uninterrupted from the autumnal to the vernal equinox, since these men voyaged at the natural time of great cold, and entered the island and remaining on it had day and night alternately except for the period of the solstice. But one day's sail north of that they did find the sea frozen over.

14. There are many other islands in the ocean to the north of Britain which can be reached from the northern islands of Britain in a direct voyage of two days and nights with sails filled with a continuously favourable wind. A devout priest told me that in two summer days and the intervening night he sailed in a two-benched boat and entered one of them.

15. There is another set of small islands, nearly all separated by narrow stretches of water; in these for nearly a hundred years hermits sailing from our country, Ireland, have lived. But just as they were always deserted from the beginning of the world, so now because of the Northman pirates they are emptied of anchorites, and filled with countless sheep and very many diverse kinds of sea-birds. I have never found these islands mentioned in the authorities.

16. Julius Solinus in his *Collectanea* says about

4. St Isidore of Seville (*c*.559-636), Spanish churchman and encyclopaedist.
5. Julius Solinus lived in the third century and wrote a geographical compendium.

Germany and its islands: In this region and in all the area of the north there are numerous bisons, which are like wild cattle, with shaggy necks and bristling manes. They can run faster than bulls; when captured they cannot be tamed. There are also wild oxen, popularly called buffaloes, but buffaloes have nearly the appearance of deer and are found in Africa. Those, however, which we call wild oxen have bull's horns of such large dimensions, that because of their great capacity they are removed and used as drinking vessels at royal banquets.

17. There is also the elk which may be likened to the mule, whose upper lip hangs down so much that it can feed only by walking backwards. The island Gravia in the Germanic region produces an animal like the elk, but whose houghs cannot bend; for this reason they cannot lie down to sleep, but a tree supports them while sleeping. This is cut to the point of falling, so that the beast topples over when it leans on its accustomed support. In that way it is captured; otherwise it is difficult to catch it, as despite its stiff houghs it can run so fast that it cannot be overtaken. . . .

JOHANNES SCOTTUS (ÉRIUGENA)

(*c.*810-*c.*877)

LUMINE SIDEREO DIONYSIUS AUXIT ATHENAS

(Athens was exalted with heavenly light by Dionysius)

[Johannes Scottus or Ériugena ('Born in Ireland') was a philosopher whose originality was unmatched between the period of Boethius (*c.* 470-*c.* 525) and St Anselm (1033-1109).

Like Sedulius at Liège, Ériugena was a member of a colony of Irishmen at the court of Charles the Bald at Laon. He was profoundly influenced by the works of Dionysius the Areopagite (called Pseudo-Dionysius). Dionysius was thought to have been the pupil of St Paul, but his works were probably those of a Syrian monk living in the early sixth century. This philosopher applied Christian concepts to Neoplatonism. At the request of Charles the Bald, Ériugena undertook to translate the works of Dionysius from Green into Latin in 860. The poem below is a dedication that prefaces this Latin translation.

The translation appears in Peter Godman (ed.), *Poetry of the Carolingian Renaissance* (London: Duckworth, 1985), poem no. 51, pp. 305-07.]

Dionysius the Areopagite

Athens was exalted with heavenly light
by Dionysius the Areopagite and magnificent sage.
He was first astonished by the moon moving in
front of the sun
at the time when Christ was nailed to the Cross.
As soon as he had been converted by the
wondrous eclipse,
he followed the leadership of Hierotheus.
Taught by him (for he was a renowned teacher),
Dionysius was soon reborn in the font of the
Holy Spirit.
Then, without delay, brilliant in the light of
heavenly wisdom,
he taught the people of Athens, his birthplace.
Indeed they say that Paul who spread Christ's
Word on earth
laid his holy hands upon Dionysius.

Then, a perfect champion, like his teacher,
he vigilantly ruled over the Athenians as high
priest.
Finally, following Saint Paul, he soared on high
above the stars
and saw the three realms of the heavenly
empyrean.
He looked at the first seraphim and holy cherubim
and the heavenly thrones where God sits,
then at the virtues, and the powerful dominions.
The following order gleams in their hallowed
ranks:
the princes and choruses of angels and archangels
gleaming from afar
make up the third class of the heavenly spirits.

These numbers, separated by a thrice three-fold division,
are the subject of the mystical teachings of this father.

HELLINAS TROASQUE SUOS CANTARAT HOMERUS (Homer once sang of his Hellenes and Trojans)

[In this poem, Ériugena, like his contemporaries, condemns Louis the German's invasion of West Francia in 858. He also prays for victory against the fleets of the pagan Norse.

The translation appears in Peter Godman (ed.), *Poetry of the Carolingian Renaissance* (London: Duckworth, 1985), poem no. 50, pp. 301-05.]

My Poetry and My Times

Homer once sang of his Hellenes and Trojans
and Virgil composed verse about the descendants of Romulus;
let *us* sing about the kindly deeds of the king of heaven
whom the world never ceases joyously to praise.
Homer and Virgil took pleasure in speaking about the flames that brought
sudden destruction to Troy and about the struggles of their heroes,
but our delight is to sing of Christ
drenched in blood after vanquishing the prince of this world.
They were both learned in how to compose falsehoods
with an appearance of truth and how to deceive in Arcadian verse;
we prefer to sing hymns of fine praise
to the power of the Father and His true wisdom.
The songs of the Muses, their playful, talkative farces,
were what these peoples were accustomed to applaud;
from our hearts, mouths and faith resound in harmony
the sayings of the prophets with beautiful poetry.
Let us therefore hold the supreme victories of Christ
as brilliant stars in our minds.
Behold, the four corners of the world are clasped by the wooden cross
on which the Lord hung of His own will,
and the Word of the Father deigned to take on flesh
there becoming a fitting sacrifice for our sake.
Gaze upon His hands which are pierced through, His shoulders and feet
and His temples encircled by a cruel garland of thorns.
In the middle of His side the fount of salvation is opened
and His blood, the draught of life, flows forth in a wave.
The wave washes the entire world clean of its ancient sin
and the blood makes us mortals divine.
Consider also the two criminals hanging on the two trees:
their merits were identical, but the grace given to them was not the same.
One of them saw in Christ's company the entrance to paradise,
the other was buried in the depths of hell and brimstone.
There was an eclipse of the sun and as the moon ran back
on unaccustomed course to the East, the planet was shadowed,
the earth's centre quaked, stones trembled and split apart,
the holy vault of heaven was shattered and revealed to the peoples.
Meanwhile Christ alone approached Hell joyously
surrendering His limbs to be buried anew.
Armed and strong He unbarred the confines of deepest Hell
and striking down the foe He took away his goods,
not wishing the human race to die and perish,
He rescued them all from the jaws of Hell.
Christ, who hold[s] sway over the heavens and the earth, we worship You
and all things bend the knee to You alone.
You who grant only what You see has been fairly requested
and are accustomed to refuse what we ask for improperly,

grant that our King Charles[1] may retain the kingdom
which You bestowed upon his nobly-born ancestors.
You are the source from which wealthy kingdoms spring:
what does any creature possess that is not given by You?
The miserable hatred of brothers and their barbarous fury
may You deign to calm by Your gentle control.
But lest wickedness with its turmoil throw us into confusion,
remove the sins of evil from our lives!
Thwart the schemes of our enemies and rout the pagan fleets,
grant peace to the people who follow Your laws.
In thankful poetry we now acclaim Charles's return
and after much groaning our joy lightens.
Those who gladly went adventuring for foreign kingdoms
seize their chance and take to flight.
Powerful fears threw their trembling souls into confusion
and forced them to turn and flee from Charles.
Alas, how terrible is the greed that has confounded our hearts
when Christ is expelled from His own home!
Louis, would that there were peace in the lands
which the ruler of everything has granted to you!
Why do you wish to
conquer your brother? Why do you want to drive him from
his realm? Are you not members of the same noble dynasty?
Why do you attempt in this way to undo God's laws?
Ungrateful for your own possessions, why do you seek what belongs
to others? What does baptism, what does the ceremony of holy mass
with its eternally mysterious power mean to you?
Is it not that you should observe the spirit of brotherhood it preaches
and strive with all your strength to live in piety?
Listen with fear to what the wisdom on high proclaims,
for its truthful teaching deceives no one:

1. Charles the Bald, king of the west Franks 840-77, emperor 875-77.

'If you want no evil to come to you from anywhere,
presume not for your part to do harm to anyone else.'
Christ, bestow upon Your servants the reward of life in heaven
and protect in safety these Christian poets.
The servant repays what is due to his lord when he asks for it,
but may the lord acknowledge the servant's reward.

from: DE DIVISIONE NATURAE (The Division of Nature)

[Ériugena was probably a teacher at the palace school of Charles the Bald from *c.* 851 onwards. It is very likely that he was already a distinguished philosopher before joining the court.

Following his translation of the works of Dionysius, Ériugena went on to translate other Greek theological books, such as the *Ambigua* of Maximus the Confessor, the *De Hominis Opificio* of Gregory of Nyssa, and the *De Fide* of Epiphanius. This work gave him the insight and was the basis for his own great work of philosophy — the *De Divisione Naturae*, in five books. The work is concerned with the idea of the movement from God of all that is created and the eventual return of all creatures to Him. The Wulfad to whom the work is dedicated was a friend of Ériugena. He had been abbot of Montiérendon from 856-858 and then abbot of St Médard at Soission when Ériugena completed his work. He was later archbishop of Bourges. In his fifth book Ériugena provided a summary of this work.

The translation appears in Ludwig Bieler, *Ireland, Harbinger of the Middle Ages* (London: Oxford University Press, 1966), pp. 127-31.]

BOOK V: SUMMARY

We have made a fourfold division of all nature, a term by which we understand God and His creation. Firstly we contemplate and distinguish nature that creates and is not created; secondly nature that is created and creates; thirdly nature that is created and does not create; and lastly nature that neither is created nor creates. The first and fourth kind can be predicated only of God. This is not to say that God's nature, which is simple and more-than-simple, admits of division, but merely that it permits contemplation under two aspects.

For when I contemplate the origin and ultimate cause of all things, then my mind is impressed by the truth that the divine essence or substance, goodness, power, wisdom, and whatever else is predicated of God, is not created by anything, because there is nothing beyond and above divine nature, but everything that is or is not is created by it, through it, in it, and towards it. If, however, I contemplate the same essence as the final goal of all things, and my mind dwells on its being the ultimate limit beyond which nothing can go, for which everything strives and where all natural movement comes to rest, then I realize that it is neither created nor does it create. Nature cannot be created out of anything else, because it is of itself. Neither does it create anything, for seeing that everything that is produced by it in the way of intellectual or sensibly perceptible generation must return into it in a regeneration which is wondrous beyond words and everything will be at rest in it because nothing further proceeds from it by new generation, one is entitled to say that it creates nothing. What, I ask, should it create when it will be everything in everything and nothing will be manifest in it but itself? As regards the two kinds between the extremes, enough has been said about them in the preceding pages. They are clear to anyone who cares to investigate them. The one is seen in the first causes, the other in the effects of these causes. The one that consists in the causes is created by the only-begotten Son of God, in whom and through whom all has been created. This nature, in turn, creates everything that emanates from it, that is to say, all its effects, whether they are purely intelligible or perceptible to the senses. The other kind, which consists in the effects of the (first) causes, is created by its own causes but creates nothing, because there is nothing lower in the nature of things. Therefore it consists mainly in those things which can be perceived by the senses.

This need not exclude the possibility that angels or human beings, whether they are good or evil, should often have created something in this world that was new and unknown to the use of man. These beings do not create anything, but merely form something out of the material creation which has been created by God out of its causes, it being their effect. If men are good, they do this in obedience to the divine laws and commandments; if they are bad, they act under the influence and illusion of the devil's fraudulent cunning. All the same, everything is ordained by the providence of God so that there is no evil as a substance in the nature of things — nothing that could disturb the communion and, as it were, the social order of all things.

Having contemplated the four aspects of all nature in its four kinds — two of which, being origin and end, are found in the divine nature, two others, being causes and effects, belong to created nature — we have felt justified in adding some theories concerning the return of the effects to their causes, that is to say, to their essential causes. This return is understood in a threefold manner: The first one, in a general way, is seen in the transformation of all sensible creation within this world, that is, of all bodies, whether they are actually perceived by the senses or escape sense perception because of their being utterly minute; as a result, not a single body remains in the fabric of corporeal nature, neither a body that is moved, secretly or manifestly, only by the motion of life nor one that has an irrational soul and bodily senses. They all return, through life, to their hidden causes, for nothing can be annihilated in anything that from the cause of all things as its substance has received substantial existence. The second form of contemplation is appropriate to the general return of all human nature saved by Christ to its original state of creation, to the dignity of the image of God, and as it were to Paradise, through the merit of the One, whose blood has been shed for the common salvation of all mankind. Thus no human being will be deprived of those natural goods in whose possession that being has been created, no matter whether in this life he was good or wicked. In this way the indescribable and incomprehensible effusion of divine goodness and mercy over all human nature will be made manifest, if in no human being will that which comes from the supreme good be punished. The third form of contemplation applies to those who shall rise not only to the natural excellency of their substance, but by an overflow of divine grace which is given by Christ and in Christ to His elect transcend their own essence beyond all laws and limits of nature and shall enter into God Himself and become one in Him and with Him. In their return to their origin we can, so to say, discern seven steps. The first is the transformation of the physical body into the motion of life. The second is the transformation of vital motion into sense perception. The third is the transformation of sense perception into reason.

Then follows the transformation of reason into mind, and this is the end and goal of all rational creation. After this integration of the five parts, if I may say so, of our nature, namely body, vital motion, sense perception, reason, and mind, which are then no longer five, but only one, because the lower one is always resolved in the higher one (not in such a way that they are no longer, but in such a way that they all are one), there follow the other three steps of the ascent. One of these is the transition of mind to a knowledge of all things that are less than God. The second is the transition of knowledge to wisdom, that is, an intimate contemplation of truth as far as this is possible for a creature. The third and highest is the supernatural submersion of the purest minds into God Himself, into the darkness, as it were, of the incomprehensible and inaccessible light, in which are hidden the causes of all things; and then the night will shine like the day, that is to say, the most intimate of the divine mysteries will be revealed in an indescribable manner to those blessed and illumined minds. Then the perfection of the number Eight, a supernatural cube, so to speak, will be established for ever, having been foreshadowed by the title of the sixth psalm: 'Psalm of David, for the eighth day'. For the resurrection of Our Lord also took place on the eighth day, in order to intimate mystically that blessed life which after the sevenfold rotation of the seven days of this life will follow upon the end of the world. Similarly, as we have said, human nature returns to its origin by an eightfold ascent: a fivefold one within the limits of its own nature, and a threefold one, transcending its nature and essence, within God Himself. When the Fiveness of created nature has been united to the Threeness of the creator, then there is nothing manifest at any step but God alone, similarly as in the purest air only the light shines.

This, then, is the subject of this work in five books. If anybody finds that in it we have written anything novel or unnecessary, may he attribute this to our lack of discipline and prudence and, in the humility of his pious heart, forgive a human mind which is still burdened by his house of flesh. For in our life here on earth, which is obscured by mists, no human endeavour can, I think, be perfect or free from all error. The just also, who still live in the flesh, are so called not because they are really just, but because they desire to be just and strive for perfect justice in the future they are so called by virtue of their heart's desire.... If, however, a reader finds to his delight anything that is profitable, anything that aids his edification in the Catholic faith, then let him attribute this to God alone, who alone can disperse the cloud of darkness and lead those who seek Him to Himself, free from all illusion and all error.... Without prejudice to those who may take kindly to this our common work, reading it with limpid purity of mind, or, perhaps, turn away from it in ill-will and in their bias condemn it even before they have found out what it is about and how the subject is treated, I offer this work first of all to God..., then to you, my beloved brother in Christ and fellow-searcher for truth, Wulfad, for examination and correction. You have given me the courage to embark on it, and it is your merit if I have completed it as best I could.... Let everyone be guided by his own spirit until the coming of that light which changes the light of the false philosophers to darkness and the darkness of the true knowledge-seekers to light.

from: PERIPHYSEON (DE DIVISIONE NATURAE) (On the Division of Nature)

[Ériugena considers the meaning of *nihilum* (nothing), whether it is non-being or the divine super-essence that is more than being. In seeking an answer, he asserts following the teaching of Dionysius, that 'God Himself is both the Maker of all things and is made in all things.' From this it is but a short step to say 'God is all things and all things God.' Ériugena realizes that he could be accused of Pantheism. His way of avoiding this is to examine the monad (the unit or unity), and there follows a discussion of the theory of numbers. The monad is the beginning, middle and end of all numbers, but how can it have a beginning if it extends to infinity? The nature of numbers is considered and, in particular, the perfection of the number six.

Ériugena's work takes the form of a discussion between Alumnus (A), the student, and Nutritor (N), the teacher.

The translation appears in I.P. Sheldon-Williams (ed.), *Iohannis Scotti Eriugenae* Periphyseon (*De Diuisione Naturae*) Liber III (Dublin: Dublin Institute for Advanced Studies, 1981), pp. 98-119.]

CONCERNING THE SCIENCE OF NUMBERS

N. . . . O God, our salvation and redemption, Who bestowed nature, grant also graces: Send forth Thy light upon those who grope in the shadows of ignorance in search of Thee; Recall us from our errors; Stretch forth Thy right hand to us feeble ones who without Thee cannot reach Thee; Show Thyself to those who seek for nothing but Thee; Shatter the clouds of empty phantasies which prevent the glance of the mind from beholding Thee in the way in which Thou grantest Thine invisible self to be seen by those who desire to look upon Thy face, their resting place, their end beyond which they seek for nothing for there is nothing beyond, their superessential Supreme Good.

But go on to the rest of your opinion.

A. What is left but to declare what particularly worries me, namely, how all things are eternal and made, how those things which are without beginning and end are limited by beginning and end. For these are in mutual conflict, and how they should be reconciled I do not know if you do not tell me; for I thought that only God is ἄναρχος, that is, without beginning — for He is the Beginning and the End which arises out of no beginning and concludes in no end — whereas all other things begin and tend each to its proper end, and therefore are not eternal *but* made. And incomparably more profound and wonderful than all this seems to me the assertion you made on the authority of St. Dionysius the Areopagite, namely, that God Himself is both the Maker of all things and is made in all things; for this was never heard or known before either by me or by many, or by nearly all. For if this is the case, who will not at once break out and exclaim in these words: God is all things and all things God? But this will be considered monstrous even by those who are regarded as wise when the manifold variety of things visible and invisible is considered — for God is one —, and unless you support these arguments by illustrations from things which the mind can comprehend there is no alternative but either *to pass over* subjects which have been merely raised without being discussed — which could not be done without my mind regretting it; for those who, being plunged in thickest darkness, hope for the rising of the light to come are not completely overwhelmed by sorrow; but if the light they hope for is taken away from them they will sit not only in darkness but in great torment, for the good which they had hoped for is taken away from them —, or everything that you have said about these things is to be judged by those of limited understanding to be altogether false, and for them to relapse into their former opinions, which they were already abandoning only with reluctance, as being true, and rejecting these. Therefore the path of reasoning must start from illustrations drawn from nature, which no one [unless] blinded by excessive folly rejects.

N. Are you versed in the art of arithmetic?

A. Unless I deceive myself I am. For I have learnt it from my infancy.

N. Define [it], then, clearly and briefly.

A. Arithmetic is the science of numbers, not of those which we count, but of those by which we count.

N. Cautiously and observantly have you defined arithmetic. For if you simply defined arithmetic as the science of numbers you would include all numbers in general, and so the definition would not stand. For that art does not treat of every sort of numbers but only takes into account those numbers which it knows to be by science alone and by intellect, and by which the other sorts of numbers are counted. *For* the wise say that it is *not* the numbers of animals, fruits, crops, and other bodies or things that belong to the science of arithmetic, but they assign to arithmetic only the intellectual, invisible, incorporeal (numbers) which are constituted in the science alone but reside in no subject [substantially except themselves].

For they are not perceived in the science or by the intellect or by the reason or by the memory or by the senses or by diagrams so as themselves to be one with those things in association with which they are seen. For they possess their proper substance (namely) themselves. For if they were of the same substance, the science and the intellect and the reason would not be judging by them but about them. But the art and the model cannot be the same thing. This can only be said of God the Word, Who is both the model and the art of His Father.

Observantly, then, as I said, did you add: 'Not of those which we count but of those by which we count.' For in no corporeal or incorporeal subject do we see them, but beyond every subject by the intellect alone in wisdom and science are they discerned, separated by the excellence of their divine nature from all the things which are counted by them.

A. This I have often thought about, and have come to see it clearly, as I think.

N. Is that art natural [then]?

A. Yes, [and] nothing could be more natural. For not only does it subsist as the immutable basis and primordial cause and principle of the other three branches of mathematics, namely, geometry, music, astronomy, but also the infinite multitude of all things visible and invisible assumes its substance according to the rules of numbers which arithmetic contemplates, as the supreme philosopher Pythagoras, the first inventor of this art, testifies when he gives good reason for asserting that the intellectual numbers are the substances of all things visible and invisible. Nor does Holy Scripture deny this, for it says that all things have been made in measure and number and weight.

N. If then you seek for natural examples of the aforementioned art, and indeed of the numbers which it contains, look carefully at its nature and its rules so that under the guidance of God you may arrive at the knowledge of those things which seem to you to be in conflict among themselves and to be irreconcilable with one another.

A. I freely accept the examples of arithmetic. For it neither deceives nor is deceived. For although the less intelligent are often deceived in it, that is to be judged not as a fault in the art but as the disposition of those who treat it incautiously.

N. You are not, then, in doubt, as I think, that of the numbers of which arithmetic is the science the Monad is the beginning?

A. No one who doubts that is an arithmetician. For the Monad, [that is] unity, is the beginning and the middle and the end of all numbers, and the whole and the part and every quantity of all terms.

N. Tell me, then: Are all numbers, which the reason can multiply at will, causally and eternally in the Monad?

A. True reason does not teach otherwise. For they are in it causally because it subsists as the beginning of all numbers, and in it all are one and simply indivisible, that is, in a universal and multiple mode, in the reason only, but not in act and operation, nor is the one an aggregate of many, but one deriving from its singularity (which is) both simple and multiple, so that both all numbers are in it all at once and simple, as in their cause, and it itself is understood (to be) in them all multiplied by an ineffable distribution, as their substance. For it is the cause and the substance of all numbers, and while it does not relinquish the stability of its own nature it pours itself out as multiplicity into all; and they subsist in it eternally because their beginning in it is not in time. For there was not (ever) unity without the manifold reasons of all the numbers. For who among men of clear intelligence would say that the Monad had had a beginning when he knows that it extends into infinity? For how can an infinite progression arise out of a finite beginning? For the infinite proceeds from the infinite [but nothing infinite from the finite].

[And if anyone should say, How can this hold good when even among the numbers themselves we see many infinites beginning from finites, for from the dyad, which is a finite number, all doubles derive and extend to infinity; similarly from the finite triad all triples take their origin and know no end to their multiplication, and, to speak briefly, there is no number, limited by its factors or merely by its units, from which some multiple does not flow forth to infinity, he must be answered as follows: All these numbers, finite in their parts, from which the multiples proceed into infinity are infinite in that Monad where all are one. Therefore he will either be denying that all numbers are in the Monad and will be affirming that they are finite in their multiplication from it, or if in the teeth of true reason he will not be able to affirm this he will be forced to profess that all numbers finite in their parts subsist as infinite (and) uniformly eternal in the Monad. For it is not where the source appears that the water begins to be, but it flows from somewhere much further afield through channels that are hidden and indefinable to the senses before it appears at the source, and therefore the place where it first rises to view is wrongly called the source, since for a long time previously it existed in hidden places of earth or ocean where it concealed itself from sight, for it is called 'latex' from the fact that it is latent in the veins of the earth. In the same way too the numbers, whose multiplication or other proportions flow into infinity, take their origin not from these finite numbers which are the first to appear to the mind which contemplates them, but from those eternal and infinite reasons in which they causally subsist. But they are in the Monad; in the Monad, therefore, they are infinite, and from it every infinite progression of numbers proceeds and in it ends.]

And to use a stronger argument, consider carefully those who affirm that unity never had a beginning. If unity, which the Greeks call the Monad, is the beginning and middle and end of all numbers — for from it they proceed, through it they move, towards it they tend, in it they come to an end, and none of the wise doubt that this is so —, it will not be one unity from which the numbers proceed and through which they move and another towards which they tend and in which they come to an end, but one and the same *that is* both beginning and middle and end. Therefore, numbers which proceed from their beginning proceed from nowhere else than their end — for their beginning is not one thing and their end another, but they are one and the same unity—, and therefore it must be concluded that if they extend to an infinite end their extension must begin from an infinite beginning. But the infinite end of all numbers is unity; therefore the infinite beginning of all numbers is the same, and if all numbers eternally and immutably subsist in their beginning, they must necessarily subsist eternally and immutably in their end, and as there will be no end without things coming to an end in it, so there was no beginning without things beginning to proceed from it by act and operation of the intelligence. Therefore all numbers subsist eternally in the Monad and while they flow forth from it they do not cease to be in it since they cannot abandon their natural state. For whether by multiplication or by division they proceed from it and return to it in accordance with the rules of the art which considers their reasons. But if this is so, no one who is not shameless will deny that the numbers eternal in unity subsist in their reasons, and anyone who considers carefully will not doubt but that the reasons themselves are eternal.

N. I see that you are not ignorant of the art of arithmetic. For what has been said by you so far true reason proclaims and confirms that it is thus and not otherwise. But in order to establish on a firmer basis your doctrine of the eternity of the numbers in the Monad, give a brief and clear account of their reasons, which you assert to be eternal and immutable.

A. The first progression of the numbers is from the Monad; and the first multiplication is *Δυάς*, that is, the number two, the second *Τριάς*, the number three, the third thereafter the number four, then all the terms, each established in its own place. And the number two is the source of all parity which falls within (the view of) the intellect, but the number three is the source of all disparity. And from these, I mean from parity and disparity, all kinds of numbers are generated whether simple or composite. [The simple are the even and the odd, the composite those that are made up of both these, the evenly even, the evenly odd, the oddly even.]

Do you see how impossible it is that this order of the progression of the numbers could be otherwise, or could be changed into a different mode? For no other number constituted in the natural order occupies the place of the first procession from unity except the number two, nor the second place except the number three, nor the third except the number four, and every number occupies its natural place which no number save that whose place it is is permitted to take. But in unity itself all numbers are at once together and no number precedes or follows another since all are one. And yet they would not immutably possess their natural order by means of which they are contained in their multiplications if their own eternally immutable cause in unity did not precede. Similarly in the case of doubles, which have the number two at their head, and of triples which the number three precedes, and of quadruples which start from the number four, and of all kinds of multiples, it must be understood that each of those starts from its proper beginning and tends towards infinity. But the double or the triple or the quadruple proportion or any other such proportion is not discerned specifically and distinctly in the unity, for in it all multiples are at once and are one, and are one multiple and simple: simple by nature, multiple by the reasons by which they receive their immutable order in their multiplications. What shall I say of the marvellous and divine constitution and proportion of the superparticulars and the superpartients and of the multiple superparticulars and multiple superpartients, which the species receive individually from the unity? What of the proportionalities which we contemplate in the proportions and differences of the terms, in which the ineffable and divine power is so constant that no one who penetrates the secrets of wisdom contends that they are not eternal? For if that is a right definition of the true which says, the true is that which abides for ever, and if what abides for ever is eternal, the reasons of the numbers are true because they abide for ever and immutably, and therefore they are eternal; and if anyone diligently wishes to know of these things let him carefully read the books of the great Boethius[1] on Mathematics.

Again, on the subject of the eternity of the numbers in their beginning, that is, the Monad, here is a very brief argument: If unity is a unity of numbers, there never was unity without the numbers of which it is the unity. Also, if the numbers flow forth from the Monad as from some inexhaustible source and, however much they are multiplied, come to an end in it, they would surely not be flowing forth from it if before their flowing forth they had not subsisted in it as in their cause; nor would they seek their end in it if they did not know by their natural motion that there were not eternally abiding in it their causes towards which they never desist from returning through the same stages by which they had flowed forth from it by the rules of analysis by which every inequality is recalled to equality. Now the rules of analysis will be found at the beginning of the second treatise on *Mathematics* of the great Boethius by any student who pursues the marvellous investigation of such natures. But if someone should say that both the unity of the numbers and the numbers themselves are inseparably one, since they are suitably reckoned among the things that are inseparably one, this should not be denied, indeed, it should be admitted. But it should not therefore be believed or understood that they are eternal and without beginning. For there are many things which begin simultaneously to be and yet are not for that reason bound to subsist for ever [simultaneously]. For both matter and form, and voice and word begin simultaneously (and) end simultaneously, and yet they are not eternal. For if they were eternal they would neither begin nor cease to be, and much else of that sort.

Let our reply be: The number six is not excluded from the unity and multiplication of the other numbers, especially as, alone among the cardinals, that is, among the first series of numbers from one to ten, it is perfect. For it is perfected by its parts, namely, the sixth and the third and the half. For the sixth is one, the third is two, the half is three, and these added together perfect the quantity of six. For one and two and three make six.

There is another reason which in a wonderful way demonstrates the perfection of the number six according to which it perfects by its parts, when set in order, the first series of numbers. Its sixth part, one, occupies the first place of the numbers, its third, two, the second, its half, three, the third, its half and its sixth, which are three and one, the fourth, its half and its third, which are three and two, the fifth, all its parts added together, which are one two three, complete the sixth, itself that is, its whole and its sixth, that is six and one, the seventh, its whole with its third, that is six and two, the eighth, its whole with its half the ninth, six and three, to which if one be added, in which the end of all numbers is constituted, the quantity of ten will be perfected. If, therefore, that perfect number, namely the number six, is constituted in the unity of the numbers, let him take care who says that it is not eternal, for in it the Creator of all things perfected His works. But here it must be noted that the number six is not perfect because in it God concluded all things which He wished to create, but He created His works in it because by the perfection of the number the perfection of His works should be revealed. Is it, then, credible or likely that this most mighty and divine exemplar in which God made His works had a temporal beginning, when in it not only the things which are in times but also the times themselves and the things which subsist beyond the times were constituted by the Creator of all things? Therefore no man of sound wisdom would have any doubt about the eternity of the numbers if he made use of the argument concerning the number six only, for what is understood about its eternity must similarly be understood of the perenniality of the others. For not of the number six alone but generally of the totality of all the numbers was it said, God made 'all things in measure and number and weight'. But if places and times are counted among all the things which God made, the intellectual numbers subsisting in their science alone necessarily precede the places and times in the perpetuity of their nature and are reckoned among the things which are at the same time eternal and made; they are eternal in the Monad, but made in their multiplications.

N. Of the eternity of the numbers in the Monad enough has been said. But it is necessary to investigate how they are made and where and from what. For by arguing from them we are trying to establish that all things that are from God are at the same time eternal and made.

A. The eternity of the Monad and of all numbers in it I have expounded to the best of my ability. But

1. Anicius Manlius Severinus Boethius (*c.*480-526), outstanding philosopher of the late Roman-early Christian world.

how the intellectual numbers after which all things that can be numbered are numbered are made and where and from what is for you to explain. But I say this in the knowledge that it is easier for their eternity than for their being made to be able to be sought and found and demonstrated.

N. You have a high opinion of me, as I see, since you assign to me the things that are harder to seek and find and demonstrate. However, it is my part to seek, but to find is His alone Who illumines the hidden places of darkness. His also is the demonstration because He [alone] can open the sense of those who seek and the intellect. For of what use is a demonstration from without if there is not illumination within? Therefore what was said by you just now, 'eternal in the Monad but made in their multiplications', provides, I think, a foretaste of this question, and if you understood what you said it is superfluous for you to seek what you understand, but if not, it must be sought for.

A. I fully see that the numbers cannot be made save in their multiplications. For in the Monad they are eternal. But how or where or from what they become I do not yet see, and it is for that reason that I ask you to reveal the knowledge of these things.

N. That all numbers are for ever in the Monad causally, that is, potentially, we do not doubt.

A. To doubt of this [is] the mark of the less intelligent.

N. But you understand, as I think, that the Monad subsists eternally in wisdom and knowledge.

A. If I think otherwise I am a stranger to true knowledge of the Monad itself.

N. You think, as I believe, that the numbers that are constituted potentially in the Monad are not other than those that flow forth actually into the genera and species of the intelligible numbers, but the same.

A. They are not other but the same, though in a different mode.

N. Tell me, pray, how in a different mode?

A. They are in the Monad potentially, but in the genera and forms actually.

N. You have answered correctly. Do you then see that the same numbers are eternal there where they are potentially in their cause, that is, in the Monad, but where they are understood to be actually, there they are made?

A. You go too quickly. The path of reasoning must be trodden step by step lest we arrive at conclusions that are hasty and rash. Thus it must first be asked what is the 'force' and what is the 'power' of the numbers in the Monad and what is their 'act' and what their 'operation' in the genera and forms.

N. 'Force' is, as I think, the substantial virtue by which they subsist eternally and immutably in the Monad, while 'power' is the possibility, innate in them, by which they are able to be multiplied and *become* manifest to intellects by certain terminological distinctions, quantitative diversities, differential intervals, [and] the wonderful equality and indissoluble harmony of proportion and proportionalities. Act is the motion of the mind in contemplating in itself and in them the multiplication of the numbers as they proceed from the Monad into the diverse genera and different species before they reach the phantasies of cogitation, that is, in considering with the eye of the intellect beyond all quantity and quality and places and times the numbers themselves [in] the simplicity of their incorporeal nature which lacks all imagery; and, to give a brief definition: Act is the motion of the mind in regarding without any imagery the numbers under the most pure aspect of their nature. Operation, on the other hand, is the motion of the same mind when the pure numbers which it considers in itself it consigns to the memory, embodied as it were by certain corporeal phantasies, and sets them in order there and deals with their reasons more easily; and conveys them, made significant to the corporeal senses, to the knowledge of others. [And do not think that I mean that the numbers themselves are multiplied (and created) by the intellect or reason and not by the Creator and Multiplicator and Ordainer of all things Himself. For if the numbers suffered their first multiplication at the hands of any created intellect there would not be in them the immutability and harmony of their reasons. Therefore, it is not to be thought that the intellect creates the intellectual numbers because it contemplates them in itself — it is, however, to be believed that by the one Creator of all things they were made in the intellects whether human or angelic, and it is by Him also that they are eternally established in the Monad — but they descend through the intellects into knowledge.] For just as, to give an illustration, some project or some art in nature, while it is contained within the most hidden recesses of the intellectual nature, is all together and a simple unity without parts or divisions, without quantity of quality, without place or time, and altogether free from all accidents and barely known to the intellect alone — for the intellect is not the maker but the discoverer of the arts of nature, [though] it does not discover them outside itself but within itself — but when that art begins to descend by an intelligible progress into the reason from its secret places in which it is all one in the mind in which it is, soon it gradually begins to reveal by evident divisions and differences its hidden structure, though as yet in a most pure form free from all imagery — and this initial process of the art out of that science in which it originally subsists is directed by the act of the intellect itself through the intellect to the reason: for everything which comes forth from the hidden places of nature into the reason comes through the action of the intellect—, but then again, by a second descent, as it were, the same art, descending from the reason into the memory, gradually declares itself more openly in phantasies (and), as it were, more distinct in certain forms; but in a third descent it is poured down upon the corporeal senses, where by sensible signs it exhibits its power by means of genera and species and all its divisions and subdivisions and particulars — so the intellectual numbers stream down from the Monad so that they somehow may shine forth in the mind, then by flowing forth from the mind into the reason they reveal themselves more openly; next, descending from the reason into the memory they receive from the nature of the memory itself phantasmal appearances in which they clearly reveal the powers of their multiple forms to those that inquire into them, [then into the senses, lastly into figures].

Do you then see the three things which you had searched for, the How, and the Where, and the Whence? From the Monad. Where? In the intellect. How? By different stages: first they descend from themselves into the intellect; from the intellect into the reason; from the reason into the memory; from the memory into the corporeal senses; and, if it is required for the benefit of students, by a final stage from the senses into visible figures.

A. Plainly and most clearly do I see. . .

SEDULIUS SCOTTUS

(*fl.* 848-859)

FLAMINA NOS BOREAE NIVEO CANENTIA VULTU

(The gusts of the north wind are blowing and there are signs of snow)

[By the mid-ninth century the number of Irishmen on the Continent had greatly increased. They were to be found as teachers and scholars in palace, cathedral, and monastic school. One of the most outstanding of these was Sedulius Scottus. He had a mastery of the Latin language and wrote excellent poetry, using a range of classical metres. From his eighty or more poems, we learn something of his life and situation. Many were written while he was at the court of Hartgar, bishop of Liège.

The first poem below is addressed to Bishop Hartgar just after Sedulius and two companions arrived at Liège. This was sometime in the 840s. They arrive in wet and stormy winter weather, offer their scholarly services and ask for accommodation.

The translation appears in Peter Godman (ed.), *Poetry of the Carolingian Renaissance* (London: Duckworth, 1985), poem no. 46, p. 287.]

Plea for Patronage

The gusts of the north wind are blowing and there
  are signs of snow;
they terrify us with their sudden threatening
  movements;
the earth itself trembles, stricken by great fear,
the sea murmurs and the hard stones groan, as the
  wind from the north

sweeps on its violent way through the expanses of
heaven
with thunder-claps and terrible rumblings:
the fleecy milk-white clouds are banked in the sky
and the earth withers under its snow-covered
mantle,
from the tops of the woods the leaves suddenly
fall,
all the oak trees are standing at this moment like
reeds.
The sun which had been shining resplendently in
its brilliant array
has now withdrawn its beams and disappeared.
The gusts of the north wind ravage us — a pitiable
sight to see —
learned grammarians and pious priests:
sweeping down from the north, it has no mercy
on anything,
however distinguished; it tears us to pieces with
its cruel beak.
And so, splendid bishop Hartgar, look graciously
on our weariness
and, of your kindness, aid us, your Irish scholars:
may you thereby succeed in climbing to the
temples of heaven,
to heavenly Jerusalem and everlasting Sion.
With imperturbable mercy the excellent bishop
has overcome the winds, subduing their pride as
they deserve.
With kindness and generosity he has succoured
and saved
us three scholars exhausted by the noisy southerly
gusts.
He has clothed and enriched the three of us
handsomely,
and, a delightful shepherd, has made us his own
sheep.

GAUDEANT CAELI, MARE, CUNCTA TERRA (Rejoice ye heavens, sea and all the land)

[One of the reasons for the great movement of Irish scholars to the Continent in the ninth century may have been the disruption brought about by the attacks of the Norsemen. Liège was far inland and still, at this period, relatively safe from Viking attacks. The centres of learning had gradually shifted from the coastal areas of Francia to places like Liège. This poem, in celebration of a victory over the Norse, could have been written in Ireland before Sedulius left. The circle of scholars surrounding Sedulius had a particular devotion to St Brigit, so it is likely that they were Leinstermen. In 845 the Council of Meaux re-established hospices for Irish pilgrims on the Continent and in 846 this was confirmed by Charles the Bald. In the same year as the victory in Leinster, Prudentius of Troyes tells us that the Irish sent emissaries to Charles to speak of their successes. They sent gifts and asked for a passage for the king to Rome. It is possible that Sedulius and his friends came with this embassy.

The translation appears in James Carney, 'Sedulius Scottus', in R. McNally (ed.), *Old Ireland* (Dublin: Gill and Sons, 1965), pp. 242-45.]

A Victory over the Vikings

Rejoice ye heavens, sea and all the land;
ye people too who wax in Christ
see the great deeds of the Lord, the Father,
thundering Godhead.

Most worthy of praises, sole author of good,
great in great deeds, blessed creator,
holding firmament's sceptre and with nod of the brow
all things disposing.

World's holy ruler, its hope and salvation,
levelling mountain, raising the valley,
crushing the wicked, crowning the humble,
omnipotent power.

Christ the True Light he causes to shine
on faithful hearts, on mirror of the mind,
cherishing them with constancy,
sustaining creator.

Ye rich and poor, ye high and humble,
clerics too, his tonsured order,
be ye young or old, mankind or women,
praise him ye all.

The stout strong arm of a powerful father
with sudden fury has now prostrated
foes of the faithful, the rebel Northman;
glory to the Father.

The fight is joined on open plain
and weapons glitter in the limpid air
and warrior cry might seem to shake
the scaffolding of sky.

Opposing lines unleash their spearshafts,
unhappy Northman counts his losses,
a mighty army aims and places
its showers of iron.

Those who have thirsted down through the years
are quaffing the blood of a savage oppressor
and finding sweet savour in nourishing breast
on the slaughter of men.

Those who set snares stand there ensnared,
topples a tower reaching to the sky;
a hostile horde, swelling with pride,
Christ has undone them.

There is there laid low a stout strong people,
a cursed mass has now been crumbled,
an evil issue death's maw has swallowed;
be praised, O Christ.

Now can be reckoned a mighty slaughter;
count not unknown, count not the menials,
on that dread field lay bloody there
three times ten thousand.

The judge is just, lord of the world,
Christ the true glory of Christian people,
magnificent ruler, vanquishing evil
in high jurisdiction.

Great tower is he, and shield of salvation,
undoing in battle the strength of the giants,
whose name is high above all names
and ever blessed.

A faithful people has that great avenger
who unleashed the sea in swelling torrents
on proud Egyptian, overwhelming all,
chariots, horsemen.

Christ wearing purple now reigns over
what high Begetter first created,
blessed scion of the House of David
and our glory.

He to whom we offer incense,
whom we name in act of prayer,
King of stars whom we intone
on pipe of praise.

Now cry ye glory and cry Hosanna,
now sing of Father, Christ begotten
and Holy Spirit; sky, earth and water
praise him ye all.

VESTRI TECTA NITENT LUCE SERENA

(*Your* house gleams with calm light)

[From this poem it is clear that the accommodation provided by Bishop Hartgar was in some need of repair. The reference to Lantbert is to the patron saint of Liège and of those who suffered from maladies of the eyes.

The translation appears in Peter Godman (ed.), *Poetry of the Carolingian Renaissance* (London: Duckworth, 1985), poem no. 47, pp. 289-91.]

My Patron's House and Mine

Your house gleams with calm light,
its ceilings brightly painted in the new fashion,
the many colours gaily reflect at the dome
and several designs gleam in their beauty.
The garden of the Hesperides does not bloom in
this way;
it wilts quickly, suddenly losing its flowers,
but the violets and lovely roses that belong to you
are fastened to the dome, their permanent setting;
and so your shades of bramble-purple and
hyacinth
have no fear of the south wind's bluster or gusts.
My house is black with unending night,
inside there is no gleam of light or good cheer.
It lacks beautiful and elegant tapestries;
no door-key or bar keeps it in order,
nor does the ceiling gleam, adorned with pictures;
soot sticks to the high dome.
If Neptune ever teems down in black showers
it would just increase the thick coating on my
home;

when the east wind bellows wildly
it strikes this old hall and makes it tremble.
Like the foul mansion of Cacus
or the dark Labyrinth
which resembled blackest night
is my home — alas what a monstrous injustice! —
as it stands shuddering, dark, and covered with a black pall,
for even in the light of day an appearance of night
lies heavy on these decrepit buildings.
Believe you me, this is not a fitting home for scholars
who love the boon of bright light;
it is a house suitable for bats,
an ideal property for a pack of moles.
O Lantbert, gather all your sightless and blind men,
I pray, and send them here,
and let this dark house thrive forever and ever
under its proper name of Home For The Blind!
But now, exalted father and splendid shepherd,
help me in these troubles, o dear and honoured one,
kindly speak the word so that this gloomy house,
devoid of daylight, may be redecorated.
Let there be a panelled ceiling, finely painted,
a new door-key and a strong lock;
then let there be blue and green windows,
into which Phoebus can shine his welcome rays,
and with his lovely gleam, famous bishop, illumine
your scholars who love the sunshine.
So too, lord, may you be granted
a beautiful, fine and radiant palace in the heights of heaven,
decorated by the Almighty's hand,
in the happy city of heavenly Jerusalem.

CUM DEUS ALTIPOTENS ANIMALIA CONDIDIT ORBIS
(When God in His lofty power created the animals in the world)

[This poem is a lament in mock-heroics for a gelded ram given to Sedulius by Bishop Hartgar. A thief stole the ram and was pursued by a pack of hounds. The thief escaped, but the pack turned on the ram. Initially successful, the ram proclaims its innocence in a speech, but it is eventually killed by the lead dog. Sedulius uses the themes and language of Latin epic. He has many allusions to the *Aeneid*, but there is also a parallel Christian theme in the poem. Kratz suggests that the 'entire narrative may be an extended allusion to the parable of the Good Samaritan' (Luke 10.29-37). There are other Christian elements. As well as the comparison with the suffering of Aeneas, the ram, now a 'martyr', is also interpreted as the figure of Christ.

All of this gives way to lighthearted mocking comedy in the last verse where Sedulius expresses his 'carnal' desire for the ram as he thinks of the cooking pot.

The translation appears in Peter Godman (ed.), *Poetry of the Carolingian Renaissance* (London: Duckworth, 1985), poem no. 49, pp. 293-301.]

Mock Epyllion[1] on a Gelded Ram

When God in His lofty power created the animals in the world
which live in the sea, earth and sky,
He multiplied wethers[2] with much honour
and made them leaders among the bleating flocks.
The gentle creator covered them with a fleece of wool
and clad their bodies with a robe of fat.
He armed their slanting foreheads with curved horns
so that they might wage grand wars against other horned beasts.
He breathed strength and pride into their pair of nostrils
and increased their number in many a snort.
But meek simplicity was instilled into their hallowed horns
and deadly poisons do no harm to those goodly beasts,
and so my affection for them did grow,
as did my love for their fleece and fat belly.
I swear upon my word that in this I never shall be untrue,
that I long for such creatures, love, and adore them,
nor will the river of Lethe wipe out this holy sentiment:
my mouth declares what my conscience demands.
My little verses praise and salute them —

1. A short epic poem, usually dealing with romantic and mythological themes.
2. A wether is a male sheep, especially a castrated ram.

I speak the absolute truth, as you know, sweet father.
In your kindness you gave me dark sheep to match my dark complexion
and you have often given me snow-white ones.
One of them was more handsome and fat than the others.
Alas! he has passed away and his death was cruel.
He was the finest leader of that excellent flock,
none was his equal or his match.
His stiff horns gave powerful protection
to all the horned creatures and little white flocks.
His snow-white fleece gleamed as did his snow-white eyes;
he used to put up a tough fight and was a prodigious victor.
Aries in the sky loved him with chaste passion
and wished to make him a partner in his kingdom.
Because of his snow-white coat powerful Lucina wanted to place
him as a bright star among those who dwell in high heaven.
For they say that the Moon loved woolly fleeces
and that Pan, the god of Arcadia, deceived her with one.
I burned with love for him — for my heart is not made of horn —
who but a fool would not love him?
And you in your generosity and kindness, which refuses nothing,
decided to present this beauty to me.
But then fortune, always hostile to good things,
snatched Tityros from me, alas, in my misery.
There was a wicked brigand descended from Golaith,
like an Ethiopian, as bad as Cacus in his misdeeds,
terrible in shape, pitch-black, with an evil appearance,
cruel in what he did, cruel too in what he said.
He took hold of the godly wether in his wicked grasp
and dragged the poor creature through many thorns.
You were very mild and very calm,
unhappy wether, as you flew through many a field.
A ravening pack of dogs caught sight of the thief as he ran
and saw the horned, great-hearted hero being borne along.
Soon that pack leaped up in eagerness;
there was a huge din, an uproar and a crash;
ravening, they went after the thief and what he had stolen.
The leafy wood clamoured, the entire glade resounded.
Why should I linger here? Alas, that gentle wether was trapped.
The thief fled into the darkness, swifter than the south wind,
the wether was left alone and put up a strong resistance,
threatening with his horns and inflicting many wounds.
The dogs were astounded at being defeated by a two-horned ram
and thought that the beast before them was like a lion.
The hounds all yelped and barked at him,
but he spoke these excellent and kindly words in brilliant reply:
'What madness has arisen in your hearts?' said he.
'Recognize that I am the servant of bishop Hartgar,
I am not an evil brigand, I am not that little thief,
I am the pious wether, excellent leader of the flock.
If you would like to vanquish a cruel enemy,
that thief flees nearby; let us stop him!
But if in your mad frenzy and raucous barking you wish
to call me to fight a bloody war although I love peace,
I swear by my head, by my horns
and by my proud brow that I shall repay you as you deserve.'
With these words he suddenly soothed the hearts of the wild beasts,
peace gradually arose and the two sides sprang apart.
But one of them was like the yelping Anubis,[3]
his black grandfather was Cerberus, the dog of hell,
who with his treble maw was accustomed to hunt
the fleeing stags and bear-cubs like his forbear.
Seeing that the raging band of dogs had grown calm
he gnashed his jaws and made his shaggy neck bristle.

3. Jackal-headed Egyptian god of the dead.

'Bah, shall this sheep trick you,' he said, 'by falsely referring to peace,
deceiving you like a fox with the treacherous bombast of its words?
Here is the wicked thief and his evil companion —
that is why the two of them are making for the shelter of the woods.
The only cause of this great evil, I insist, is the ram
who speaks words of peace but who threatens us with his brow.'
Then the huge wether shook his horns and struck
that liar's mouth, breaking two of his teeth,
smashing the dog's forehead against his own as well.
He would have been victorious had he not fled the battle —
for he tore swiftly along, leaving the enemy behind, as if he had won,
rushing without caution and taking flight without further ado.
He fell into some thorn bushes and then into cruel brambles,
and that goodly beast was caught — alas — in the wilds.
Then the cursed Cerberus pressed on behind him.
biting with his blood-stained jaws and wounding him cruelly.
The wether fell into a faint (a wondrous sight)
bedewing the thorns with his crimson blood.
The nymphs wept, the woods echoed all the uproar,
the flocks of sheep groaned at the crime,
and the bright two-horned moon grieved as she should
for that snow-white wether, as did Aries in the sky.
Did he deserve this a just, simple wether without malice or deceit?
He never touched wine or drank cider.
Drunkenness did not turn him from the path of righteousness,
nor did the banquets of kings nor the feasts of great men.
His regular food was grass in the fields
and the waters of the Meuse provided his sweet drink.
He did not greedily seek raiment of scarlet and purple,
but was content with his woolly tunic.
He did not ride his horse in pride through the green pleasances
but made his way on his own feet, as he should.
No liar was he, nor empty were his words:
'Báá or béé' — mystical were his utterances.
As the lamp enthroned on high, God's son,
experienced death for sinners.
taking the road of death, torn apart by wicked dogs,
so you perish, pious wether, for that wicked thief.
As the holy ram became a sacrifice for Isaac
so you are a fitting sacrifice for that wretch's sake.
Such is the merciful kindness and generous power of the Lord,
who does not want men to succumb to wicked death!
God's heavenly hand, which once aided another man
on the cross, saved that evil thief.
Give thanks to the Lord, wicked, bad lying thief;
wretch, say these words with the Psalmist:
'The right hand of God in heaven has exalted me:
I shall live, I shall not die, I shall sing of God's deeds!
That sweet chastising power has chastened me.
It has not given me up to death but has saved me from destruction.'

EPITAPH

Farewell to you, good wether, fine leader of the snow-white flock,
alas, for you will no longer live in my garden!
Friend, you might perhaps have had a warm bath
for no other purpose than pure hospitality.
Devoutly I would have ministered waters
to your horny head and heels.
I've longed for you — I declare — and continue to long
for your widowed mother and shall always love your brothers. Farewell.

LIBERA PLEBEM TIBI SERVIENTEM
(Set free Thy people, set free Thy servants)

[The translation appears in Helen Waddell, *Medieval Latin Lyrics* (London: Constable & Co. Ltd, 1930), pp. 124-25.]

Intercession against the Plague

Set free Thy people, set free Thy servants,
Lighten Thine anger, Ruler most holy;
Look on their anguish, bitter their weeping,
Christ, in Thy mercy.

Thou art our Father, Master exalted,
We are Thy servants, Thou the Good Shepherd,
Bearing Thy token of blood and of crimson
Marked on our foreheads.

Deep in Thy hell who then shall confess Thee?
Yea, shall the dead give praise to Thy name?
Judge of our dread, Thy rod is of iron,
Spare us, we pray Thee.

Bring not so near to Thy people, Thy servants,
The cup of Thine anger, Thy merited wrath:
Lighten upon us Thine ancient compassion.
We cry. Do Thou hear!

Loosen, we pray Thee, our load of transgression.
Vouchsafe to keep us, Prince ever blessed.
Vanquish the shadow that darkens our spirits,
Light of the world.

Saint of all saints and king of all kingships,
Visit Thy people with Thy right hand.
Lift up the light of Thy countenance upon us,
Lord, or we perish.

SURREXIT CHRISTUS SOL VERUS VESPERE NOCTIS (Last night did Christ the Sun rise from the dark)

[The translation appears in Helen Waddell, *Medieval Latin Lyrics* (London: Constable & Co. Ltd, 1930), pp. 118-19.]

Easter Sunday

Last night did Christ the Sun rise from the dark,
The mystic harvest of the fields of God,
And now the little wandering tribes of bees
Are brawling in the scarlet flowers abroad.
The winds are soft with birdsong; all night long
Darkling the nightingale her descant told,
And now inside church doors the happy folk
The Alleluia chant a hundredfold.
O father of thy folk, be thine by right
The Easter joy, the threshold of the light.

AUT LEGO VEL SCRIBO, DOCEO SCRUTORVE SOPHIAM (I read and write, teach and study Scripture)

[Sedulius loved food and drink and in many of his poems he chides his patrons for lack of provisions and engages in flattery when they arrive.

The translation appears in Peter Godman (ed.), *Poetry of the Carolingian Renaissance* (London: Duckworth, 1985), poem no. 44, p. 283.]

My Life

I read and write, teach and study Scripture;
day and night I pray to my Creator, enthroned
on high.
I eat and drink with a will, and invoke the
Muses in poetry.
While I sleep, I snore; I pray to God while
awake.
My soul, conscious of its sins, weeps for the
wrongs it commits in life.
Christ and Mary, have mercy on this poor man.

BISHOP PATRICK (GILLA PATRAIC)

(died 1084)

from:
LIBER SANCTI PATRICII EPISCOPI
(The Book of Holy Patrick the Bishop)

[The first text below, *Perge Carina*, consists of prefatory verses addressed by Bishop Patrick to his friend Aldwin. In it he sends greetings to Bishop Wulfstan, who was abbot of Worcester during Patrick's episcopate in Dublin, and to the members of the monastic community there. There had been a revival of the writing of poetry in classical form in eleventh-century Europe, and Patrick's verse may be seen against the background of the work of Marbod of Rennes (1035-1123) and Hildebert of Lavardin, bishop of Mans (1056-1133); his own verse is often found in the collections containing these works. He is influenced by Virgil, and more directly his Adonic verses in this poem are borrowed from the work of St Paulinus of Nola. The result is a warm, personal and lively greeting to old friends.

These verses accompanied a booklet, *Liber de Tribus Habitaculis Animae* (Concerning the Three Dwelling Places of the Soul), dealing with good and evil. It is written in simple, straightforward prose. The style is highly rhetorical, suggesting that probably it was originally a sermon. There is a strong Augustinian influence in it. Bishop Patrick was clearly concerned with the main tenets of Christian doctrine — free will, time and eternity, truth and falsehood, the Trinity, the Creed; and this again reflects the preoccupations of one concerned with reform. He was probably familiar with a scholastic textbook of theology for much of his ideas. Bieler has suggested that the few biblical quotations in the text are characteristic of the Irish Bible text of the eighth and ninth centuries.

This was Bishop Patrick's most popular work (now found in over a hundred manuscripts), particularly among English monastic communities. The English translation, written by an R.S., is also of some interest. The R.S. might have been Richard Stanihurst, or the Jesuit Robert Southwell (martyred on Tyburn Hill, London on 21 February 1595). The least improbable candidate is a Richard Smith, later bishop of Chalcedon, who was a young student in Oxford in 1585. Our author was certainly a catholic recusant of the period, probably living in England.

The translation appears in A. Gwynn (ed.), *The Writings of Bishop Patrick, 1074-1084*, Scriptores Latini Hiberniae, Vol. I (Dublin: Dublin Institute for Advanced Studies, 1955), pp. 102-25.]

ONWARD, MY BARQUE

The invocation of Bishop Patrick

Almighty God, Who dost fill the secret places of Heaven,
Hold back with Thy oar the grey-haired waves of the deep sea!

Here begins the prologue of the book of holy Patrick the bishop.

Onward, my barque,
Through the long sea!
Christ on the water
Be thy steersman,
With sure oar
And a clear sky!
Hasten, my barque,
Through the hollow sea,
And cleave the pale
And horrid waves
Foam-besprayed:
Sailor-like, steered by
A favouring breeze!
Onward, my book,
(Be an angel at thy side)
Through the wide sea:
To visit the dear home
Of Bishop Wulfstan!
Is he well
Who is worthy of honour,
Dear in love?
Drive sadness from him!
Sing forth joy
By day and night
With sweet voice,
Even to the sun,
To the topmost stars!
Hasten, my page,
By the holy strength
Of the high cross!

May thy sails swell
Through the clean waves!
Learn, my barque,
To run in safety
Through the fields of the sea!
Learn to be like unto
The dread monsters
Of the sea, by swimming
Through the bitter waters!
Onward, my book!
Though shalt go in joy
Through wind and wave.
The scale-clad throng
Shall keep thee company,
And the helmsman's cry
With sweet tone
Shall sound strongly
From the depths of the sea.
Hasten, my barque,
In joy through the waters!
May the tops of thy sail
Be swollen full
By the eastern breeze!
Without a cloud
May the breezes serve thee,
[Nor] may any error
O'erwhelm [thee]
Until thou art borne
On a straight course
To the fields of England!
Onward, my page!
In my thought following
I shall be thy companion.
I am drawn by love
To visit the dear
Fosterchildren of peace.
To all Christ's faithful
Of kind Bishop Wulfstan,
To them all equally
Bring, as is fitting,
Thrice ten greetings
In fair order!
Onward, my book,
With halting verse:
And from me, Patrick,
Loyal in memory,
Ask, as is fitting,
For my comrade Aldwin
A thousand crowns of blessed life!

Here ends the prologue.

from:
The Three Dwelling Places of the Soul

Here beginneth the book of Saint Patritius the bishop, entreating of the joys of heaven and of the pains of hell, and of the goodness and evilness of this world.

There be three mansions, habitacles[1] and dwelling places made by the hand and power of Almighty God, that is the highest, the middlest and the lowest: of the which places the highest is called the kingdom of God or the kingdom of heaven, the lowest is called hell, the middlest is called this present world or the whole circle and compass of the earth. Of the which three places the two uttermost, that is hell and heaven, are altogether the one contrary to the other, and hath no fellowship and society the one with the other. For what fellowship or agreement can and may be between light and darkness, and Christ and Belial the devil? But the middle place, that is the world, hath a certain agreement, similitude and likeness to both the extreme and outward places: that is with heaven and hell. Whereupon the world hath both light and darkness, cold and heat, grief, dolour and health, mirth and sorrow, hatred and love, good people and bad, righteous and unrighteous, masters and servants, kings and subjects, famine and plenty, death and life and unnumerable the like things. Of the which things the one part beareth and hath the image and similitude of the kingdom of God, and the other part thereof the likeness and face of hell. For both good and bad are joined together in this world. For in the kingdom of God are no evil persons, but all are good persons. But in hell are no good people, but all are evil: and both these two places, heaven and hell, are filled and replenished forth of the middle place, the earth. For some people of this world are lifted up and ascendeth to heaven, and other some are drawn downward and descendeth into hell. For truly the like are joined and put to the like: that is, good to the good and evil to the evil, righteous people to the righteous angels and wicked people and sinners to the wicked angels, the servants of God to God, the servants of the devil to the devil. The blessed people are called to the kingdom of God, prepared for them from the

1. habitations.

beginning of the world, the cursed people are thrust down and expelled into everlasting fire which is made ready and prepared for the devil and his angels. But no person clothed with the flesh and living therein can declare, conceive, and understand in his thought or mind the good things of the kingdom of heaven as they are in deed: for they are far greater and better than they may be conceived in mind or [understood]. Wherefore it is written in the Holy Scripture that neither eye can see nor ear can hear nor it can come or ascend into the heart of man what good things God hath prepared for them that love Him. For the kingdom of God passeth and exceedeth all the fame and report thereof, and is far better than all the praise that can be spoken thereof, and exceedeth all knowledge and understanding that can be had thereof, and is far more excellent than all the renown and glory that can be imagined thereof by any means. Also the evilness and torments of hell no person is able neither to express them with tongue or to conceive them in his mind as they are in deed: for truly they be far worse than either they are said or thought to be. Also the kingdom of God is full of light, peace, charity, wisdom, glory and honesty, sweetness and delight, melody, mirth, gladness and everlasting blessedness, and of all goodness unspeakable which cannot be expressed with tongue nor conceived in the mind, heart and thought. On the contrary part the deep lake, dungeon and pit of hell is full of all darkness, discord, hatred, foolishness, misery, filthiness, bitterness, offence, grief, stink, burning thirst, hunger, unquenchable fire, heaviness, everlasting revenge and all unspeakable evil and naughtiness; the which no tongue is able to tell or heart to think. The citizens and inhabiters of heaven are the righteous and just people and the holy angels, over whom is God Almighty: on the other side the citizens and inhabiters of hell are the ungodly and unmerciful people, devils and fiends, whose captain and head is the devil. The sight of holy people and of holy angels, and above all the vision of God Himself doth feed, fill and satisfy the righteous and good people there. The sight and vision of the damned people, evil spirits and devils, and above all the beholding of the great devil himself doth vex and torment the unmerciful and wicked people. There shall nothing be desired in the kingdom of God but it shall be had: but on the contrary nothing can be come by or had in hell that is worthy to be desired and wished for, neither anything that good is can there be seen or felt. In the kingdom of God nothing is found but that doth please, delight and satisfy the desire: but on the contrary in the bottomless pit and lake of everlasting misery and wretchedness nothing is seen and felt but that only which displeaseth, offendeth and tormenteth the inhabiters. All goodness doth abound and is plentiful in the kingdom of God, and no evil at all: all evilness and naughtiness doth abound and is plentiful in the presence of the devil, and no goodness at all. No unworthy person is received into the kingdom of God: no worthy and just person is thrust down into hell. But there be two principal kinds and sorts of torments in hell: that is, intolerable cold and heat of the unquenchable fire. Whereof it is read in the Holy Gospel, saying: There shall be weeping and gnashing of teeth. For weep and watering of the eyes cometh of the heat: but the gnashing of the teeth cometh of cold. Hereupon also the blessed man Job speaketh: They shall pass and go, saith he, from the waters of snow unto extreme heat. Of the which two sorts of torments there do come, grow, and hang innumerable sorts and kinds of punishments and pains: as the pain of intolerable thirst, the pain of intolerable hunger and famine, the pain of intolerable stink, the pain of intolerable horror, the pain of intolerable fear, the pain of intolerable straitness and anxiety, the pain of intolerable darkness, the intolerable cruelty and severity of the torments, the intolerable presence of the devils, the intolerable fearsomeness of the foul beasts, the intolerable cruelty and unmercifulness of the ministers, the fiery tears, the miserable sighings and sobs, pain and grief without all remedy, bonds and fetters without release, death everlasting, pain without end, the absence of Christ after He hath been seen: the which only absence passeth all the pains aforesaid, and is more intolerable than all other pains, be they never so many and great. Therefore it is a perpetual woe to all them that deserveth to suffer and abide still all these evils, and that without end, for the pleasant and delicate dream and sleep of onc hour. For all the glory, renown and pleasure of this world is but like and so much as an hour's sleep and dream in comparison of the glory and joy of everlasting life. It had been better for them never to have been born, which thing is spoken by Christ of that unhappy man Judas, than by their desert to suffer and abide all the said plagues and torments of hell for their misdeeds and wickedness. What thing can be more foolish, what thing can be more madly done than with the only shadow and the likeness of true glory, true delectation and pleasure, true beauty and fairness, true comeliness, true honour and renown, as children to be deceived, flattered, overcome, and not to seek and get, no not so much as to desire the very true glory and joy itself? What person is that which doth desire the only image and the likeness of the gold appearing in water, neglecting the very gold itself, and bye and bye is not accounted and thought of all people to be a very fool and mad person? What person is he that doth love and esteem the only circle and the image of the sun being formed, made and appearing in a glass or in any other matter whatsoever far more and above the very sun itself, and is not laughed to scorn and jested at of all people? Verily even so he is to be laughed to scorn, yea to be lamented whatsoever he is that loveth, seeketh, contendeth and striveth for the transitory and frail glory and renown of this world and the unprofitable will and pleasure of the flesh, together setting aside and utterly despising the eternal and true glory, and neglecting the unspeakable joys of the kingdom of heaven, making no account or reckoning thereof. This doing is the very work of unwise and most miserable persons, and such as have no sound mind, understanding or heart, also if the lasting punishment, pains and torments of hell did not follow hereof: which pains cannot be spoken with tongue nor thought with heart. Yet it is double pain and plague to be absent and forth of the kingdom of God, and ever to be in hell, and to be forth of the kingdom of Christ, and to be damned with the devil; to lose the presence and sight of holy angels, and continually forever to suffer and abide the terrible presence and sight of fiends and devils. Therefore it cannot be spoken and expressed by no means how great heed ought to be taken thereabout to eschew the same, and how greatly it ought to be feared and dreaded. What person that is well in his wit and hath any understanding and sense will covet and choose the continual and great pains by the space of a hundred years for to have his pleasure and delights the space but of only one day? And yet notwithstanding all these miserable and wretched persons, following the will and desire of the flesh without all wisdom, do not shun nor flee the intolerable pains and torments, not only of a hundred years nor of a thousand years nor of a thousand thousand years, but of all world without end, for the delights and pleasures of forty years or three score years, yea for a very small and corruptible pleasure and delight. For look, what difference there is between one day and a hundred years, verily there is not only so much difference, but far more between 40 or 50 or 100 years and eternity and time without end, whether it shall be spent in joy or in pain. For there is some proportion between one day and a hundred years, although it is but very small: but truly there is no proportion or comparison at all between a hundred years and time everlasting. As if, for example sake, the hundredth or thousandth part was parcel of the time everlasting, the foresaid space thereof would cease to be eternity and everlasting after a hundred or a thousand years ended: the which thing the property and reason of eternity and time everlasting will not permit and suffer. The which, if it could by any means or in any time be ended, could not be at all a time everlasting and eternity. Therefore we ought manfully and strongly to resist and withstand the carnal and fleshly desires and will, and valiantly to fight and strive against the false, flattering and enticing desires and allurements of this world, and to watch with earnest prayers, fasting and all austerity of life very diligently and with all endeavour against the manifold suggestions and wiliness of Satan, the old enemy to mankind. The broad way to the world must be shunned which leadeth to death, and truly with all the desire of heart and mind to covet the strait way and go therein that leadeth to life everlasting. Truly the narrow way is the way of charity, abstinence, chastity and humility and of all godly religion: the which way Christ Himself hath trodden and gone before us, through the which way He went to His kingdom. Whose steps and example we must tread and follow until we come after Him by the same way unto the heavenly and kingly city wherein He now doth reign: touching the which city whatsoever man is able to speak and tell of is in comparison but as a drop of the sea or a spark of a great fire. In the which city most truly the just persons and good people do shine as the sun, as Our Lord saith: in the which city is great peace, great rest and quietness, no labour, no grief or dolour, no poverty, neither old age nor any death nor any night, no lack of meat, no provocation to thirst: but the only sight and vision of Christ Jesus and the Holy Trinity shall be sufficient meat and drink to all people there, and the contemplation and beholding of His Divine Godhead with the pure and clear eye of the heart and mind, and the continual reading (as I may say) of the Book of Life, truth and high wisdom and the word of God, which is the sight and vision of Jesus Christ. Where everything shall be plain and manifest that now is hid from us: where the cause and reason shall be manifest wherefore this person is elected and chosen, and that person is a reprobate and forsaken of God: and wherefore this person is received into the kingdom of God, and wherefore that person is sent and brought into servitude and bondage of the devil: wherefore one infant dieth in his mother's womb, another in his infancy, another in his youth and another in his old age: wherefore one is poor in this world and another rich: wherefore the child of an adulterer and fornicator is baptized, and sometime the lawful begotten child in wedlock dieth before baptism: wherefore that person that beginneth his life godly sometime endeth his life ungodly, and that person that leadeth the first part of his life wickedly oftentimes liveth the other part thereof very godly, and so endeth. All these things and many and infinite other suchlike things shall appear plain and be fully opened, declared and set down in that holy Book of Life. In the same city the reward of every one shall be according to the charity of all and every one. There in that city the goodness of all shall appear to all: there they all shall know one another's thoughts. There shall no person, be he never so high, be proud thereof: nor none, be he never so low, shall envy or disdain thereat. For how can it be by any means that the person which loveth all as himself can envy or hate any other, seeing no person doth envy or hate himself? In that city no person desireth or wisheth to be better or higher than he is, because to be otherwise than he deserveth will not stand with comeliness and justice: but it will make a great deformity and unseemliness in him there. But no person would be misshapen and deformed: therefore no person will desire or will to be otherwise than he shall there be, because so to be as he shall be it shall be very comely and fair, not only to himself, but also to the universal body of the heavenly company and congregation. For if any member or limb within the body be placed and set by any way either higher or lower than nature hath appointed it, it will make a monstrous and a foul body: even so truly if any person should be placed or ordained either higher or lower in the kingdom of God than the art, work and order and the will of Almighty God the workman doth require, it would make a great turpitude, deformity and unseemliness, not only to himself, but to all the congregation and fellowship in that city: in the which what person soever shall be least, he shall have without all peradventure far greater glory than he should have if he had the whole kingdom of this world, yea although the same worldly kingdom was everlasting. For it is a most vile thing to have the use of the elements and all the most precious things in this world in comparison of the fruition and enjoying of the Lord Himself: and to be delighted with corporal sights of our bodily eyes is nothing to be compared to the delight, pleasure and joy that doth come and grow of invisible and uncorporal sight as of the society and fellowship of holy angels and all just and righteous people, and upon the most certain knowledge and understanding of the divine nature itself, and of the sight and vision of God Himself with face to face. At whose beauty and brightness the holy angels are astonied:[2] by whose commandment the dead persons do arise to life again: whose wisdom is without number: whose kingdom hath no end: whose glory is unspeakable: whose light passeth the light of the sun by far, for that the sun hath no light in comparison of his light: whose sweetness passeth the sweetness of honey, the which being compared with the sweetness of God it is far more bitter than wormwood. Whose face if all people enclosed in the most dark dungeon and foul prison of hell might see, they could feel no pain, no grief, no sorrow, or heaviness: whose presence if it did appear in hell to the dwellers there, hell would straightway be turned and become into a most pleasant paradise. Without whose beck the leaves do not fall from the trees. Whose eyes do penetrate and see into the deep pit of hell, casting forth of it most terrible flames of fire: whose ears do hear the still and privy voice of the heart of man, that is his thought: whose eyes do not less hear than see, whose ears do not less see than hear, because they are not corporal, but are the highest and greatest wisdom and most certain knowledge itself. Whose delights and pleasantness do satiate and satisfy all without tediousness or any manner of weariness thereof: the which delights although the blessed people have found and come by, yet they always more and more covet and desire them, yea and they both make them hunger and thirst for them without any pain: that is, they do delight them continually with a most ardent and

2. i.e. astonished, in wonder.

vehement desire. Whose secret marvels and wonderful things are more marvellous to them continually seeing them, and do no more bring them into the marvelling thereof at the first sight thereof than they do after they have seen them by the space of a thousand years, yea of a thousand thousand years: and although the holy angels since the beginning of the world have used continually to see them, yet they do not less marvel at them now this day than they did the first time they did see them: otherwise by the continual use of seeing them the angels would make no account thereof, now the sight thereof being loathsome and tedious to them. To the knowledge of God all things past and all things to come are not as things past and not to come, but are always present: wherefore He shall not see the day of doom and judgement, and likewise He hath not seen the first day of the world, but doth see them both now at this present time. Whose prescience and foreknowledge maketh or compelleth no person to sin, as very many persons being in a foul error and greatly deceived do affirm and say. For they say: if God did beforehand know that Adam would sin and offend, then Adam would not otherwise do but needs must offend and sin: of whose error doth this conclusion come and rise, that God is the cause of all sin, which thing to think is abominable, and much more unlawful to speak. Nevertheless these persons are taken also in their own words, and bound with the same. For if that thing which is in the foreknowledge of God must of necessity be done, then it followeth that man sinneth through and of his own proper will, and not through or by reason of any necessity at all compelling him thereto .... Therefore if the prescience and foreknowledge of God can by no means be eschewed, escaped or shunned, then man cannot otherwise sin but only by reason of his own will without the compulsion or the force of any other thing: because God did see aforehand that he should so sin through his own wilfulness .... Therefore if he had not sinned wilfully without compulsion, the pain of death he should not have received. But if he be not compelled to sin, he might without doubt well enough not have sinned if so he would. Therefore he deserveth the punishment and pain thereof, because he sinneth not against his will: otherwise he should not have received the pain of death of God, righteously and justly. Whose speech is a privy inspiration, whereby He sheweth and declareth His will and His truth invisibly to their minds: the which will and truth the holy angels seeing, they do obey Him in all things. Whose great praise is a manifold and laudable declaration towards the elect, whereby he setteth forth openly the good things of His elect to all persons: but the continual praise of the elect, wherewith they laud and extol Him, is a perpetual admiration concerning Him. Which after a wonderful sort went and was before both the world and the time, but not in time: for there was not so much space and time as the space of one hour before the world. Therefore if time took his beginning and began to slide and pass on only from the beginning and first making of the world, then it was not made before the world: and therefore in no time, as we said before, God went and was before the times and the world, being of like age to the times, yea somewhat before the time: for through the motion and course of time they began to pass on. For what thing soever is moved and stirreth, proceedeth and goeth before his own moving. For God through His infallible eternity was before all the world, not in time: the which time was not before the world. Whose light did expel and put away the darkness of all ignorance: through a certain small portion thereof all those things whereof we have spoken, we know to be most true and certain. And by the same light we see a great deal better the things to be true than false: and yet we know the evilness that is true or the offence and sin that is true to be far worse than the evilness that is false or the sin that is false: not because the thing is true, but because it is evil or sin of itself in deed. But if because it is evil or sin, it is evil or sin because it is true (for otherwise it could not be evil or sin except it was true that it was evil or sin: for a false evil is no evil as false and counterfeit money is no money), peradventure some persons will say by this means evilness or sin doth rise, grow and come of the truth or is made thereof, and after a certain sort evilness to be the work of truth: the which thing is most false. For all that that is true cometh and riseth of the truth: and every thing that is true, in that respect that it is true it is good and not evil. Therefore it cometh of the truth to be true, that the thing is evil or sin itself. For one thing it is the thing to be the sin and evilness itself, and another thing it is the same evilness and sin to be true. Therefore although the very evilness and sin itself is not good, yet to be true as the thing is is good: for except it was good to be evil and sin, by no means God would suffer it to be done. For truly the Almighty God doth make good things of evil things: as of the adultery committed by man He frameth, formeth and maketh good men. But if through that certain small and little portion of His light shining to us, as if it was through very small crevasses and holes, these and all other true things which we do know we know them to be true, then with what manner and how great a light of knowledge and wisdom shall we be lighted where we shall see the very sun of all truth face to face: that is through a most certain and true knowledge and understanding we shall know them. Whose presence maketh them there present like to Himself. For they which do cleave and are associated to true wisdom, that is to true beauty and fairness and true eternity, shall also be wise and beautiful, fair and comely and everlasting: and so His absence also maketh them altogether unlike to Himself. Whose eternity is without beginning and without end: for if there had been any time when God was not, who should have made Him? For so much as He is only God, and before Him there was no other God nor is nor shall be. Except He peradventure create Himself, seeing nothing can create and make itself. For through what power and might should He make Himself which had no beginning at all? Therefore it must need follow that God is not made at all. Therefore seeing God is by no means made, He must needs be without any beginning, before all other things. For what thing soever is made hath a beginning: and what thing soever hath a beginning, without all doubt is made not of any other than of God Himself, which is not made but maketh all things. Whose knowledge without all variety of thought and without any running or moving hither or thither doth comprehend and understand together, always at one instant, the innumerable variety of all creatures, of angels, of men, of stars, of the sands, of hairs, of words, of thoughts, of all moments of time. Therefore it must need follow that God is the fountain and the beginning of all knowledge and understanding: of whom the more than any person doth drink the more he thirsteth and the more he may. Therefore (as we said before) the kingdom of all the whole world is not to be compared to Him, although it was everlasting as it is not. For it passeth and excelleth the society and fellowship of all angels and saints to be at the present vision and sight of His daylight. In whose sight and vision doth a threefold knowledge rise and come: that is by the same knowledge the man that doth see and behold, and God which is seen, and all other persons and things shall be seen, known and understanded[3] as they are. For as by a looking-glass a threefold sight is ministered to us, whereby we see ourselves and the glass itself, and whatsoever thing is there present: so by the glass of the divine brightness we shall see even the Lord God Himself as He is, so much as is possible for a creature to do, and ourselves and others with most true and certain knowledge shall know. Then by and through the seeing of God we shall see the most hid and secret things of all creatures, yea of very hell itself. Then it shall be manifest and evident after what sort God is invisible, immutable, without beginning and without ending, before all things and after all things: and what difference is between being born, which pertaineth to the Son, and proceeding which pertaineth to the Holy Ghost, saving that the one is born of one and the other proceedeth from two: and after what sort the Father is not before the Son or the Holy Ghost through time, but through the beginning: and after what sort all things of God are but one in God, except that thing that pertaineth to the relation of the three persons. For in the wisdom of God both the truth and eternity are undivided between themselves, but they are one as all other things belonging to God. For the wisdom of God is no greater truth than the wisdom is, than the eternity is, than all other things are pertaining to God: for they are one in God, and not only these things among themselves are the same things in God, but it is no other thing than God Himself. And after what sort the world was in God before it was in itself and made: for then it was not the world, but God. And after what fashion God was in all in every place without place, great without quantity and good without quality: and by what means He doth penetrate all things, both clean and unclean, without pollution or defiling of Himself. For if this visible light doth lighten and view every place, and also doth penetrate dunghills and filthy places without stink and defiling itself, how much more God, which is the invisible and immutable light, may penetrate all things, govern all things, sustain all things, compass and go about all things, view and see all things, without any hurt or pollution: not only the heavenly and celestial things and earthly things, but also the infernal things. Then shall the sight and vision of God be threefold to the elect people: that is corporal,

3. i.e. understood.

whereby the bodies shall be seen, certain whereof shall be as bright as the sun, other some as bright as the moon, and other some as bright as the stars: and they thereby shall behold and see the spiritual likeness and image of the bodies in spirit and not in a false fancy and imagination, the which sight and vision of God also at this present time the spirits and souls of righteous and just people do use and enjoy hereafter their bodies: and the sight of understanding shall enjoy the same wherewith they shall see with the pure and clear eye of the mind the Lord God and their souls and inner virtues and powers and the angelical spirits. Then they will give God double thanks, that is for their delivery from the perpetual damnation and for the reward of unspeakable goodness. Then the common destroyer and enemy of all people, the devil, in the sight of all the elect people of God shall be damned: whose damnation and intolerable pain and punishment shall give to the elect people of God a delightful spectacle and sight. Then with a most fervent and burning love they shall love their Redeemer and Giver of all good things, and without end and weariness shall laud and praise with the cry of their hearts the Almighty Lord God, most benign and merciful: to whom be all honour and glory both now and for ever. Amen.

Here endeth the book of St. Patrike
the bishop translated out of
Latin into English by
R. S.
1585.

from:
MENTIS IN EXCESSU
(In Ecstasy of Mind)

[Bishop Patrick addressed the allegory below to his friend, Aldwin, who became a hermit at Great Malvern, Worcestershire and was later, *c.* 1085, the first prior of a Benedictine house there. This allegory of the church and the Christian people seems to reflect the preoccupations of a monastic bishop who was concerned to bring about reforms in the church and society of his day. Central to it is the idea of the heavenly Jerusalem, the celestial city — a very old theme in Irish monastic writing.

Bishop Patrick's style is influenced by Virgil and St Augustine. He was familiar with Servius's commentary on Virgil's *Aeneid*. He also appears to have used Hiberno-Latin texts of an earlier period. His poetry has a 'Hibernian' flavour and there is a hint of Hisperic Latinity (cf. the *Hisperica Famina* extract above). For all that, his Latin has few peculiarities and his poems are modelled on classical and ancient Christian poetry. The glosses that allow us to interpret this allegory were almost certainly made by Patrick himself. In a way the poem foreshadows the sweeping changes which were to take place in the Irish church during the course of the twelfth century.

The translation appears in A. Gwynn (ed.), *The Writings of Bishop Patrick, 1074-1084*, Scriptores Latini Hiberniae, Vol. I (Dublin: Dublin Institute for Advanced Studies, 1955), pp. 84-101.]

An invocation by the writer of this book, 'Bishop Patrick'

Thou who dost rule heaven, earth, and the deep ocean,
Who dost hold all powers subject to thy will:
Show me now thy favour, O most just guardian of the world,
That I may be able to write verses worthy of thy servant Aldwin.

In ecstasy of mind through pleasant places in a wide countryside[1]
It chanced that I seemed to wander with hasty steps:
Thus gazing at length on wondrous sights and things
I was held captive. Then suddenly appeared to me
A woman uttering a stream of lamentable complaints to the skies:
'Woe is me! who am despised now that my husbands are dead,
And no man deigns to have me as his bride.'
She spoke, and I questioning her raised my voice thus:
'Whence comest thou? What makes thee grieve?
By what name art thou known?'
And she: 'From everywhere: that I am a widow:
I am known to my friends as Egle.
Three sisters have I, slender and shining white:
Of whom the first is Esper, the second Medusa,

1. Bishop Patrick wrote detailed glosses on this text. Without them, it would be very difficult to follow the sense of the allegory. The references below are based on some of the glosses in order to give a general outline of his thought. The countryside represents the Scriptures.

And the youngest of the three sisters is Arethusa.[2]
The child whom Esper bears, whom active
Medusa nourishes:
Then does Arethusa clothe the infant in
snow-white garment.
For she fashions robes that are beauteous with
gold and jewels
And silver, embroidered with many a fair figure.
Shall I snatch these three away from those who
will not have me?
Or shall I suffer them to be without honour and
despised? Shall I leave them without children?
For if I give no order, the offspring shall perish
in neglect
Which Esper bears to them, since Medusa will
rightly scorn them:
For without me, I know it well, Esper herself
must surely fail.
But I to him who deigns to have me as
companion
Shall give in dowry myself and my good sisters,
And we shall bear that man beyond the stars to
the stars.'
Now I: 'Say, what dost thou wish? Whither
away?' And she:
'Seeking shelter, few indeed are the homes
Where I gain entry: so well do they love the
brother of bitter fate.'
'Take me,' I said, 'as thy companion for ever.'
And she with a smile answered: 'From many have
I received
That answer: but straightway they have been
overcome and have gone home.
So too, young man, shalt thou soon cease to love
me.'
Thus she spoke, and bade me view the bright
fields
Where I might see strange sights, worthy of
astonished gaze,
And write concerning them all a few verses to be
read by the learned.

Then, moving onward, I saw two lionesses[3]
Agape and roaring, some distance from us.
Of whom one stood on lofty hills, the other
In low valleys: each harmful to men of differing
kind:
For one clawed those who were bright, the other
those who were dark.
I then, in fear of them who sought to tear all men,
Saw two maidens[4] come dropping from a cloud,
Of whom one can see nought behind, but only
before,
Who (was able) with strong hands to overthrow
these beasts. . . .
. . . I am led away by those bright maidens
Through a gateway[5] by which I was able to pass
between these monsters.
'Without our help, young man,' they said, 'no
living man
Can conquer these beasts.' Thence going farther I
saw
Water[6] that was honey-sweet, that tastes sweet to
all men,
And, when drunk, assuages the thirst of those who
drink greater and lesser draughts:
But the greater draught is often harmful, and the
lesser heals.
Whoso drinks of this water, sees clearly things
hidden and future.
From diverse vessels, some black, some beautiful,
This water is poured forth equally, for the good
and often for the evil-minded.
I myself have drunk deeply of it, by the kindly gift
Of Him who is called *Ya*:[7] who cannot fail to do
all that He wills:
Who makes the lofty sad, and the unhappy
blessed.
Then did I wonder at this water which shines
forth in very darkness.

Then did I see five steeds[8] swiftly through the
countryside
Speeding, who reared and threw their rider
Who alone sat and rode those steeds:
For, to his grief, he held them on no bridle.
Of them one was far swifter than the wind,
And outpassed in speed the birds and fleeting
deer.

2. Egle (Study) has three sisters — Esper (Intelligence), Medusa (Memory) and Arethusa (Eloquence). These names are based on the Greek Hesperidae (taken from Servius's commentary on the *Aeneid*, IV, 484), but there is no apparent reason why Bishop Patrick should use them here except for the effect of the classical allusion.
3. The lionesses stand for 'pride' and 'despair'.
4. The maidens are 'hope' and 'humility'.
5. The middle way between pride and despair.
6. Representing 'knowledge'.
7. Yahweh or God.
8. The five steeds represent the 'five senses'.

Coursing over the sea he seeks no ship from man,
And with one leap he rises from earth to highest heaven.
But I wondered to see the rider move more swiftly than the steeds:
For as each of them bounded forward on its own course,
The speedier its flight, the farther went its lonely rider ahead.

Going thence I saw two harvests[9] in one field:
One was of wheat, the other of bitter weed.
But straightway each crop is changed in wondrous fashion:
Whatsoever comes to the weed is made weed, and straightway
The bad that comes to the good grain is made good grain.
Thus speedily, by quitting its own home, does the ear of corn
Change its nature. Then do I spy seven sisters, all alike:[10]
Of whom four are silent, and the other three ready to talk:
The three give fair utterance to the wisdom of the silent four.
One holds a lute: next to her one holds a rod in her hands:
One holds the sun in her right hand, the moon in her left:
The fourth holds the number eight in her right hand, seven in her left,
And is seen to hold unnumbered numbers in her lap.
Thus stood these silent four, in diverse form.
But one of the three holds in her hands the letters of her speechless
Sisters: the second holds strong chains and a spear:
The third a purple cloak, adorned with gold and gems:
All three I beheld with wonder at their great beauty.
The gifts they gave me I omit to tell.

9. The two harvests are the 'church and the people'.
10. The seven sisters are the seven liberal arts. The silent four are arithmetic, music, geometry and astronomy. The other three are grammar, logic and rhetoric. The rest of the stanza refers to grammar, letters and syllables, syllogisms, metrics (probably a reference to Bishop Patrick's own interest in poetry).

Then the woman (she was the first) taught me songs of melody
On a harp that was wont to sound with six strings:
On it I make melody for the people: often I play for my own pleasure.

Passing these sisters by I ran ever swifter and swifter:
For with strange and sudden rumour there called me
An island[11] which, lying in a neighbouring sea,
Was said to be wondrous. I was eager to hasten at a run.
I am borne thither, and see Archipolis,[12] as that island is called
Which is surrounded by the sea's swelling waves:
Yet it stands unmoved amid the winds and waves.
How many wondrous sights that island holds
No man can tell in song or set forth in any speech.
At its first entrance is found a living fountain,[13]
Which slays[14] and also heals all who enter its waters:
It slays to heal, and heals that it may slay.

Then all around I saw woods bearing goodly fruit,[15]
And by their odour many are sated.
This fruit preserves unending salvation of him who eats:
Many are willing to breathe its odour, but few to eat.
Lo, it is custom for those who dwell in that city
To break the rind with their teeth and swallow the hidden fruit.
For others it is custom to break the rind and give food to their neighbours,
Who sate the hunger of others with the rind which they are eager to take.

This mighty city is surrounded by three high walls,[16]

11. The island is the church.
12. The name given to the Heavenly City. The waves that surround it are the hostile elements of the world.
13. The living fountain is baptism, by which one becomes a member of the church.
14. The slaying of sin.
15. The woods are the holy books and the fruits are the commandments.
16. Representing faith in the Trinity.

And lies open and is entered by twice six
beauteous gates.[17]
Moreover, it has lofty and brightly shining towers
And countless houses and golden temples,[18]
Which are founded on a rock and seem to stand
On twice six pillars, all purple save one:
For of these pillars one shines white without, but
within is purple.
From these countless branches hang in due order.
These temples blaze with thrice ten windows of
glass
Through which the sun ever shines full on them.[19]

Here by six flights of steps[20] men mount to the
high summit,
Where from an altar the smoke of incense rises on
the air.
Here stand noble cups full of good wine,
For many are here fed with choice and varied
dishes,
Since they load their tables with honey and their
cups with wine.
Here also I saw others who were not willing to
feast:
Who wished only to gaze at the tables before
them, but not to touch them.
But some I saw who had their eyes in their heads,
Others in their loins, others in their belly.[21]
Then did I ask why these had eyes in their belly
And in their loins. 'The cause is forgetfulness of
the Word
And the holy fountain' was answer made to me.
And I:
'Can any medicine restore eyes that fall from the
brow?'
'A bitter drink[22] can do so' was said to me.
But I ask further: 'Where abides this blessed
drink?'
Answer was made: 'It lies in the western parts of
the city.
This drink indeed seems bitter in the mouth to
all,
But after sleep it will be sweet and will give them
back health.'

Then saw I others slicing with a sword[23] their
limbs
Or their slothful belly or their manly parts all
away:
And thus they cut away all that remains, their
own or of another:
And the great wonder is that, once cut away,
they bear new limbs.
Thus some women who were pregnant gave
birth from their mouth,
Others from their hands, others from the
fields of child-bearing:
But diverse fortune follows the progeny thus
delivered:
For some are hideous, and others fair to see.

In this city I saw wolves overcome by
sheep,[24]
But the wolves overcame sheep-dogs and
their unhappy masters.
Others, both dead and living, I saw buried
In the dust of earth: the dead often rise again,
But the living seldom. I have told much in
short space.
Moreover the Tree of Life[25] overshadows the
whole city,
And its fruit makes everlasting life of death.
Four fountains spring forth from its roots
Which sate the thirsty soil and water the
fields.
A wild beast rages and strives to tear all who
wish
To take the fruit or touch the aforesaid tree:
But a strong lion seizes and casts down the
dreadful beast.[26]
On the summit of the city shines forth a
cistern of snow-white water
That melts stones and hardens loose clay:
There timber ablaze with fire is extinguished

17. The twelve Apostles.
18. The towers are the fathers of the church and the houses represent the fact that the church is spread throughout the world. The golden temples are monasteries.
19. The rock is Christ and the pillars are the Apostles. Purple represents the blood of the martyrs. The white pillar is John the Evangelist. The branches are the successors of the Apostles. The ten windows represent the volumes of canon law, and the sun is Christ.
20. Representing alms, food, drink, visitation of the sick, and so on.
21. The position of the eyes represents the sins of the body.
22. death.
23. The sword is the word of God. The rest of the verse represents the various ways of sinning.
24. The wolves are devils, the sheep are the just.
25. Christ.
26. The four fountains are the four Gospels. The beast is the devil and the lion, Christ.

And, once extinguished, soon is ablaze again.
This same cistern shines forth in dark night to the devout and friendly
Like the sun, and is called 'El Saracin' in that city.[27]

There was a wondrous mill under the northern corner of the city[28]
Which took in grain of wheat and spewed it forth as weed
To harm the people: for it hurts the wretched who eat it.
It was like to a belly, but alas! in evil fashion.
But opposite to it in the south of the city was another and better
Which took in grain of wheat and spewed it forth the same,
To sate all peoples and heal them as they ate.
It takes weed also, and throws it back as wheat from its mouth....
I liken this to a vessel of glass. Then I saw blind men run
A straight course, and many watched them on their way.
Thereafter I saw also clouds watering with sweet dew
The soil that was accustomed to bear fruit in due season.
Last of all that dew seemed to change a hundred stones
Into the nature of fruit-bearing branches,
And by it cruel wolves are changed into tender lambs.

Thereafter I saw some clad in red garments,
Others in white: many I saw without garment,
But none any longer sees their shameful parts.
Others were seen by all clad in white garments,
But their base members appeared to the eyes of all.[29]

27. The cistern is the grace of God. It softens hardened men and gives strength to those of loose life. Fire represents desire or appetites of the flesh. 'El Saracin' is the fountain of divine grace.
28. The northern mill stands for heresy. The southern mill is catholic teaching.
29. The red garments represent the blood of martyrs. The white represent chastity. Those whose members are uncovered are the hypocrites.

These and many other things, greater by far,
Was it granted me to see: but I pass them by for brevity's sake.
For I have sung the midmost, and pass by unsung the lowest and highest.
Who, who could sing them? Who could mark their numbers,
Even their names? The noble hosts, leaders of the assembly?
Who could sing the hosts of young men and fair maidens?
Who the scribes and learned seniors? Who the thousand servers,
The feasts, the varied dainties, the many banquets?
Who the precious raiments of every kind on all sides,
Purple, snow-white, of varied colour, full of gold
And gems, embroidered with many figures?
Who could sing the silent speech of people who see men's hearts?
Who the endless abiding joy of the mind?
Who the united choirs singing hymns and praises,
And the love that burns in the hearts of each and all?
Who the lyres and every apt form of melody,
Psalter and strange harps or threefold organs?
The golden temples, the market-place, the throne, the seated king,
Kindly, gentle in manner, yet just and mighty,
Fearful, unshaken, ruling his realms in righteousness?
He who gives all, if asked and if what is asked is righteous!
Who could tell how great, how wondrous the good? Who the hidden time
Of the star-bearing blessed summit where all these are to be found,
That like a citadel stands forth far above the aforesaid city?
As slaves are less than their masters, as all men less than the king,
As bronze is likewise less than gold, as the sick to the strong,
As its members to the head, as the slight shadow is less
Than that which casts the shadow, as dreams are less than real things:

So the former city[30] is less than this in beauty and all splendour,
In its many honey-sweet foods, its daily banquets.

As I beheld all this, suddenly that island vanished:
But straightway the first woman came
Whom I told of in my first verses, weeping for her dear husbands:
And she spoke to me: 'Hail, blessed youth, all hail!'
And added: 'Tell now briefly all that thou rememberest.'
And I told in summary fashion all the marvels that I remembered.
And she: 'Kindle a small lamp in the darkness
That I may be seen, and that the aforesaid visions may be seen:
And then receive as my gift three nuts,
Of which each holds and encloses three kernels.'[31]
Then I confessed that I had seen study in the gateway:
Then intellect and memory and eloquence of word
Were seen by me: after these swollen pride of mind
And its opposite despair, that bears men down, were seen soon after.
Then their foes, hope and lowliness of mind.
Then shone before me knowledge, honey-sweet to the taste,
Which the Lord grants to many, like other gifts.
Then the five senses: people of evil ways:
And I saw the church's harvests in the field of the world.
Then, before all, the arts running with swift course
Did I see in a single moment of time.
Lastly the present church, with diverse gifts in order
Arrayed, beauteous within and without in many ways,
Did I sing. But of the future church there sounded but the name
On my lips as I ended. 'Now give me my due'
I said to her. 'After these few words that say so much
Receive now thy due reward', so did she speak.
'Tell me where it is always winter, heat in snow, cold in fire:
Break open these nuts, pry out the covered fruit.'
Soon made I reply: 'Either these are in the valley of giants,[32]
Or in life like to our own, or these are seen
In things that hold opposites by use of unequal force.'
Then did she fly away, taking oath once again to visit
Our doors: but I, coming home weary, seemed to be once more
In my own house, whence I had been borne away to these sights of the mind
In ecstasy of mind.

Whilst my tongue sounds forth these words that are rough with rust,
I have written them down briefly for thee, my dear friend,
That being mindful of me thou mayest love one who ever loves thee.
May the grace of Christ guard thee, teach, nourish, guide and crown thee,
Strengthen thee, build thee up, keep thee ever safe!

30. The present church.
31. The three nuts are three questions; the three kernels are three answers.
32. Hell. Perhaps Bishop Patrick is here referring to the tensions and dilemmas of life.

Biographies/Bibliographies

Saint Patrick

LIFE. Saint Patrick was born into a well-to-do family in Roman Britain. He was captured by Irish raiders at about sixteen years of age. After six years of great hardship, he escaped and later heard the 'voice of the Irish' calling him from the Wood of Foclut near the Western Sea to return and bring the word of God to them.

Despite later legend and a library of modern scholarly comment, we know very little about Patrick. His home may have been in a small town in the vicinity of Carlisle. As a slave he probably worked in the forests and mountains of County Mayo above Killala Bay. The modern village of

Foghill above Lackan Bay may preserve the name of *Silva Focluti*, which he mentions. As a missioner he worked in the northern part of the country. Seventh-century tradition was uncertain whether he was buried at Saul or Downpatrick in County Down. Irish *Saball* is a borrowing from Latin *stabulum*, a 'barn'. It is likely that it was from just such a lowly building that Patrick would have conducted his mission. His church of Armagh had become the centre of his cult by the early seventh century. We have no solid dates for St Patrick, least of all the traditional one of his coming in 432. It is possible that the dates recording his death in the *Annals of Ulster* some time in the 490s are closest to reality.

CHIEF WRITINGS. Editions: L. Bieler, *Libri Epistolarum Sancti Patricii Episcopi*, 2 vols (Dublin: Irish Manuscripts Commission, 1952); R.P.C. Hanson and C. Blanc, *Saint Patrick, Confession et Lettre à Coroticus*, Sources chrétiennes CCXLIX (Paris: Editions du Cerf, 1978); A.B.E. Hood, *St Patrick* (London and Chichester: Phillimore & Co. Ltd, 1978).

BIOGRAPHY AND CRITICISM. M. Lapidge and R. Sharpe, *A Bibliography of Celtic-Latin Literature 400-1200*, Royal Irish Academy Dictionary of Medieval Latin from Celtic Sources, Ancillary Publications 1 (Dublin: Royal Irish Academy, 1985) Nos. 25, 26, pp. 9-11; J.B. Bury, *The Life of St Patrick and his Place in History* (London: Macmillan, 1905); T.F. O'Rahilly, *The Two Patricks* (Dublin: Dublin Institute for Advanced Studies, 1942); L. Bieler, *The Life and Legend of St Patrick: Problems of Modern Scholarship* (Dublin: Clonmore and Reynolds, 1941); Christine Mohrmann, *The Latin of Saint Patrick* (Dublin: Dublin Institute for Advanced Studies, 1961); D.A. Binchy, 'Patrick and his Biographers, Ancient and Modern', *Studia Hibernica* 2 (1962), 7-173; R.P.C. Hanson, *St Patrick, his Origins and Career* (Oxford: Clarendon Press, 1968); E. A. Thompson, *Who Was St. Patrick?* (Woodbridge, Suffolk: Boydell Press, 1985).

The Bishop's Synod

EDITIONS AND CRITICISM. M. Lapidge and R. Sharpe, *A Bibliography of Celtic-Latin Literature 400-1200*, Royal Irish Academy Dictionary of Medieval Latin from Celtic Sources, Ancillary Publications 1 (Dublin: Royal Irish Academy, 1985) No. 599, p. 153; L. Bieler, *The Irish Penitentials*, Scriptores Latini Hiberniae, Vol. V (Dublin: Dublin Institute for Advanced Studies, 1963), 54-59; M.J. Faris, *The Bishops' Synod (The First Synod of St. Patrick)* A Symposium with Text Translation and Commentary (Liverpool: Francis Cairns, School of Classics, University of Liverpool, 1976); P.J. Corish, 'The Christian Mission' in P.J. Corish (ed.), *A History of Irish Catholicism*, Vol. I, Part III (Dublin: Gill and Macmillan, 1972), 1-2.

Liber Angeli

EDITIONS AND CRITICISM. M. Lapidge and R. Sharpe, *A Bibliography of Celtic-Latin Literature 400-1200*, Royal Irish Academy Dictionary of Medieval Latin from Celtic Sources, Ancillary Publications 1 (Dublin: Royal Irish Academy, 1985) No. 360, p. 105; L. Bieler, *The Patrician Texts in the Book of Armagh*, Scriptores Latini Hiberniae, Vol. X (Dublin: Dublin Institute for Advanced Studies, 1979), 184-91; K. Hughes, *The Church in Early Irish Society* (London: Methuen, 1966), 275-81; R. Sharpe, 'Armagh and Rome in the Seventh Century', in P. Ní Chatháin and M. Richter (eds), *Ireland and Europe, The Early Church* (Stuttgart: Klett-Cotta, 1984), 58-72.

Tírechán

LIFE. Tírechán was a bishop who came from the territory of *Tír nAmalgado*, 'Tirawley' in County Mayo. His home was the peninsula between Lackan Bay and Rathfran Bay. He had been a pupil of Bishop Ultán (who died on 4 September 657 or 663) of the church of Ardbraccan in County Meath. We have no record of his own death in the annals. He was a strong supporter of the cult of St Patrick.

CHIEF WRITINGS. Editions: J. Gwynn, *Liber Ardmachanus: The Book of Armagh* (Dublin: Royal Irish Academy, 1913), 17-30; L. Bieler, *The Patrician Texts in the Book of Armagh*, Scriptores Latini Hiberniae, Vol. X (Dublin: Dublin Institute for Advanced Studies, 1979), 122-67.

BIOGRAPHY AND CRITICISM. M. Lapidge and R. Sharpe, *A Bibliography of Celtic-Latin Literature 400-1200*, Royal Irish Academy Dictionary of Medieval Latin from Celtic Sources, Ancillary Publications 1 (Dublin: Royal Irish Academy, 1985) No. 301, pp. 83-84; E. Mac Neill, *Saint Patrick* (Dublin: Clonmore and Reynolds, 1964), 115-57; D.A. Binchy, 'Patrick and his Biographers, Ancient and Modern', *Studia Hibernica* 2 (1962), 58-69; L. de Paor, 'The Aggrandisement of Armagh', *Historical Studies* 8 (1971), 95-110; L. Bieler, 'Tírechán als Erzähler. Ein Beitrag zum literarischen Verständnis der Patrickslegende', *Sitzungsberichte der bayerischen Akademie der Wissenschaften, phil.-hist. Kl.*, 6 (1974), 3-22; J.-M. Picard, 'Structural Patterns in Early Hiberno-Latin Hagiography', *Peritia* 4 (1985), 67-82.

Cogitosus

LIFE. Cogitosus was the name used by the author of our 'life' of Brigit. It appears to be a Latinization of a native Irish name. The Irish were fond of such wordplay and it is often possible to guess at the original which lies behind the Latin form. Here it has proved elusive. He tells us that he was a descendant of Áed. All that may be said is that he was most likely a native Leinsterman and a member of the Kildare community.

CHIEF WRITINGS. Editions: J. Colgan, *Triadis thaumaturgae acta . . .: apud C. Coenestenium* (Louvain, 1647), 518-26; Acta SS Feb. I (1658), 135-41. The translation by S. Connolly and J.-M. Picard is in *Journal of the Royal Society of Antiquaries* 117 (1987), 11-27.

BIOGRAPHY AND CRITICISM. M. Lapidge and R. Sharpe, *A Bibliography of Celtic-Latin Literature 400-1200*, Royal Irish Academy Dictionary of Medieval Latin from Celtic Sources, Ancillary Publications 1 (Dublin: Royal Irish Academy, 1985) No. 302, p. 84; R. Sharpe, '*Vitae S. Brigitae*: The Oldest Texts', *Peritia* 1 (1982), 81-106; K. McCone, 'Brigit in the Seventh Century: A Saint with Three Lives?', *Peritia* 1 (1982), 107-45; J.-M. Picard, 'Structural Patterns in Early Hiberno-Latin Hagiography', *Peritia* 4 (1985), 67-82.

Muirchú moccu Macthéni

LIFE. Muirchú may have come from the obscure tribal territory of Tuath Mochtaine, close to Armagh. He was commissioned by Bishop Áed of Sletty, Co. Laois, to write a 'life' of St Patrick, probably in the 690s when Áed was an anchorite in Armagh. Both Áed and Muirchú attended the Synod of Birr in 697. A Colmán mac Murchon, abbot of Moville in County Down, died in 736. He may have been his son.

CHIEF WRITINGS. Editions: L. Bieler, *The Patrician Texts in the Book of Armagh*, Scriptores Latini Hiberniae, Vol. X (Dublin: Dublin Institute for Advanced Studies, 1979), 62-123.

BIOGRAPHY AND CRITICISM. M. Lapidge and R. Sharpe, *A Bibliography of Celtic-Latin Literature 400-1200*, Royal Irish Academy Dictionary of Medieval Latin from Celtic Sources, Ancillary Publications 1 (Dublin: Royal Irish Academy, 1985) No. 303, pp. 84-85; E. Mac Neill, *Saint Patrick* (Dublin: Clonmore and Reynolds, 1964), 115-57; D.A. Binchy, 'Patrick and his Biographers, Ancient and Modern', *Studia Hibernica* 2 (1962), 38-75; L. Bieler, 'Muirchú's Life of St Patrick as a Work of Literature', *Medium Aevum* 43 (1974), 219-33; J.-M. Picard, 'Structural Patterns in Early Hiberno-Latin Hagiography', *Peritia* 4 (1985), 67-82.

Colmán Mac Muirchon

LIFE. Although it is not certain, it is most likely that Colmán was the son of Muirchú moccu Macthéni whose 'life' of Patrick is excerpted above. The churches around the shores of Strangford Lough were closely associated with Armagh. Colmán was abbot of Moville and his death notice is recorded in the *Annals of Ulster* in 736.

CHIEF WRITINGS. J.H. Bernard and R. Atkinson (eds), *The Irish Liber Hymnorum*, Vol. I (London: Henry Bradshaw Society, 1898), 44-45; Rev. J. O'Laverty, *An Historical Account of the Diocese of Down and Connor Ancient and Modern*, Vol. II (Dublin: Gill, 1880), 17.

BIOGRAPHY AND CRITICISM. M. Lapidge and R. Sharpe, *A Bibliography of Celtic-Latin Literature 400-1200*, Royal Irish Academy Dictionary of Medieval Latin from Celtic Sources, Ancillary Publications 1 (Dublin: Royal Irish Academy, 1985) No. 588, p. 150.

Columbanus

LIFE. Columbanus was born in Leinster *c.* 543. After local education, he went to Cleenish in Lough Erne where he studied under Sinell. At about the age of twenty he moved to Bangor to become a monk. He was later ordained and became head of the monastic school there. In 591 Columbanus left Bangor and went as a pilgrim and missioner to Merovingian France. With him went Gall, his linguist, Domoal, his secretary, and a number of other companions, one of whom, Aidus, was a bishop. He journeyed to the Austrasian court at Metz. There he preached a sermon before Childebert, who invited him to stay and granted him land in the wild and wooded frontier district of the Vosges. Here, among the ruins of a Roman fort at Annegray, he founded his first monastery. The old temple of Diana was consecrated as a chapel and dedicated to St Martin. When numbers increased, a new foundation was established at Luxeuil, eight miles distant, and later again Fontaines was established.

Because of Columbanus's stance on a particular method for the dating of Easter, and because of his outspokenness on the moral laxity of the Frankish church (although not all were so), he was eventually forced into exile. The fact that he had refused to bless the illegitimate sons of Theuderic II of Burgundy did not help matters. He was put on board ship for Ireland at Nantes, but a storm forced its return to land and he then fled. After going first to the court of King Clothair at Neustria, he journeyed to Theudebert's court at Metz, where he met some monks from Luxeuil. They decided to take ship up the Rhine and found a new settlement at Bregenz. Columbanus remained there on the shore of Lake Constance for a year. Political problems eventually forced a decision to cross the Alps on foot in 612. He went to Milan in Italy to the court of the Lombard duke, Agilulf, who was an Arian heretic, and his wife, Theudelinda, who was a catholic. After a period of debate and literary activity, he was granted land on the banks of the stream called Bobbio, where, at a place of the same name, stood a ruined church dedicated to St Peter. This monastery was to become one of the most famous in Europe. It was here that Columbanus died on 23 November 615.

CHIEF WRITINGS. Editions: G.S.M. Walker, *Sancti Columbani Opera*, Scriptores Latini Hiberniae, Vol. II (Dublin: Dublin Institute for Advanced Studies, 1957).

BIOGRAPHY AND CRITICISM. J.F. Kenney, *The Sources for the Early History of Ireland*: I. *Ecclesiastical* (New York: Columbia University Press, 1929; reprinted Dublin, 1966), 186-205; M. Lapidge and R. Sharpe, *A Bibliography of Celtic-Latin Literature 400-1200*, Royal Irish Academy Dictionary of Medieval Latin from Celtic Sources, Ancillary Publications 1 (Dublin: Royal Irish Academy, 1985) Nos. 639-42, pp. 165-68; H.B. Clarke and M. Brennan (eds), *Columbanus and Merovingian Monasticism* (Oxford: British Archaeological Reports. International Series; 113, 1981); K. Schäferdiek, 'Columbans Wirken im Frankenreich (591-612)', in H. Löwe (ed.), *Die Iren und Europa im früheren Mittelalter*, 2 vols (Stuttgart: Klett-Cotta, 1982), I, pp. 171-201; D.A. Bullough, 'Colombano', in *Dizionario biografico degli italiani* 27 (1983), pp. 113-29.

The Hisperica Famina

EDITIONS AND CRITICISM. Editions: F.J.H. Jenkinson (ed.), *The Hisperica Famina* (Cambridge: Cambridge University Press, 1908); M.W. Herren (ed.), *The Hisperica Famina*: I. *The A-Text* (Toronto: Pontifical Institute of Medieval Studies, 1974); M.W. Herren, *The Hisperica Famina*: II. *Related Poems* (Toronto: Pontifical Institute of Medieval Studies, 1987); M. Lapidge and R. Sharpe, *A Bibliography of Celtic-Latin Literature 400-1200*, Royal Irish Academy Dictionary of Medieval Latin from Celtic Sources, Ancillary Publications 1 (Dublin: Royal Irish Academy, 1985) Nos. 325-30, pp. 93-94; J.F. Kenney, *The Sources for the Early History of Ireland*: I. *Ecclesiastical* (New York: Columbia University Press, 1929; reprinted Dublin, 1966), 255-58; M. W. Herren, 'Hisperic Latin: "Luxuriant Culture-Fungus of Decay"', *Traditio* 30 (1974), 411-19; C.E. Roth, 'Some Observations on the Historical Background of the Hisperica Famina', *Ériu* 29 (1978), 112-22.

Adamnán

LIFE. Adamnán was born *c.* 624. He was a descendant of Fergus, son of Conall Gulban, from whom Tyrconnall, or Donegal, takes its name. He was thus of the same dynasty, the Uí Néill, as St Colum Cille. His mother, Ronnat, belonged to another branch of the Uí Néill, the Cénel nEnna, who occupied the area around Raphoe in County Donegal where his own cult was subsequently to become strong. He became abbot of Iona in 679 and ruled until his death in 704. Adamnán was an important diplomat of his day and a man of considerable influence. He showed a great concern for the downtrodden of society and in 687 had negotiated the release of sixty Irish captives from the Northumbrians and had led them home to Ireland. He visited Northumbria again in 689. Adamnán had travelled to Ireland on business on a number of occasions. Perhaps the triumph of his career was the calling together of the Synod held at Birr, Co. Offaly in 697 when he was successful in gaining the promulgation of his *Lex Innocentium*, or 'Law of the Innocents'. This was a measure designed to protect women and children, or non-combatants, in time of war. It was also concerned with respect for ecclesiastical sanctuary. Adamnán died in 704.

CHIEF WRITINGS. Editions: W. Reeves, *The Life of St Columba written by Adomnán* (Dublin: Irish Archaeological and Celtic Society, 1857; reprinted Edinburgh, 1874); J.T. Fowler, *Adamnani Vita S. Columbae*, 2nd ed. (Oxford, 1920); A.O. and M.O. Anderson, *Adomnán's Life of Columba* (London: Thomas Nelson and Sons Ltd, 1961); D. Meehan (ed.), *Adomnán's De Locis Sanctis*, Scriptores Latini Hiberniae, Vol. III (Dublin: Dublin Institute for Advanced Studies, 1958).

BIOGRAPHY AND CRITICISM. M. Lapidge and R. Sharpe, *A Bibliography of Celtic-Latin Literature 400-1200*, Royal Irish Academy Dictionary of Medieval Latin from Celtic Sources, Ancillary Publications 1 (Dublin: Royal Irish Academy, 1985) Nos., 304, 305, pp. 85-86; G. Brünning, 'Adamnans *Vita Columbae* und ihre Ableitungen', *Zeitschrift für celtische Philologie*, 11 (1917), 213-304; J.-M. Picard, 'The Purpose of Adomnán's *Vita Columbae*', *Peritia* 1 (1982), 160-77; J.-M. Picard, 'The Schaffhausen Adomnán: A Unique Witness to Hiberno-Latin', *Peritia* 1 (1982), 216-49; J.-M. Picard, 'Structural Patterns in Early Hiberno-Latin Hagiography', *Peritia* 4 (1985), 67-82.

Dícuil

LIFE. Little is known about the life of Dícuil. He was one of the many Irishmen who thronged to the Continent during the late eighth and ninth centuries. In his own words he tells us that he had lived in some of the islands to the north and west of Ireland and Britain (the Hebrides and Orkneys) and had visited others. Was he originally from this area, or did he come from Ireland? From hints in his work, it is possible to calculate that he was born approximately between 760 and 770. He also tells us that he had a teacher called Suibne to whom he was indebted for progress in his studies. Dícuil was in the presence of Suibne when a fellow monk, Fidelis, gave an account of a journey that he had made to the Holy Land, possibly before 767. There was an abbot of Iona called Suibne, who died in 772. A former abbot, Adamnán, whose work is quoted above, wrote a book on the Holy Places. There would have been a tradition of interest in the Near East at Iona and this strengthens the possibility that Iona had been Dícuil's monastery. If his information on Iceland, which he received from Irish monks who had stayed there in 795, had been given to him before he left for the Continent, then his departure must have been later than this date. J.F. Kenney suggested that it was the massacre of sixty-eight members of the community by the Vikings in 806 that caused Dícuil to move to the Continent. He seems to have been about thirty to forty years old at the time.

We first learn of his activity in a book which he wrote on astronomy, *Liber de Astronomia*. This he intended to present to Louis the Pious, king on the death of his father, Charlemagne (on 28 January 814) at a great assembly of the nobles to be held on 1 August at Aix-la-Chapelle. By this stage, Dícuil appears to have been a teacher in the palace school. Louis was probably too preoccupied at the time to take much notice of the book and Dícuil added a second book in the following year, although there is no evidence that this was noticed either. He added a further two books by 816 and a fifth by 818. In the same year he also wrote the *Epistula Census*, a treatise on weights and measures. At about this time Dícuil edited and produced a summary of the *Partitiones XII Versuum Aeneidos Principalium* (an introduction to Latin literature for Greeks) by the grammarian Priscian. From his own writings again we learn that in 825 he wrote his *De Questionibus Decim Artis Grammatice* (a book dealing with grammar); *De Prima Syllaba* (concerned with metrics); and *Liber De Mensura Orbis Terrae* (on geography). This is the last year that we hear of him.

Dícuil's two interests were grammar and computation — the major areas of science at the time. The science of *Computus* was essential in calculating the date of Easter, but it gave rise to an interest in calculations in a much broader sense, as he shows in his writings. Dícuil displays a wide knowledge of ancient sources, although for the most part indirectly. He clearly had a lively and questioning mind since he sometimes challenges his sources. Dícuil made a worthy contribution to the Carolingian Renaissance.

CHIEF WRITINGS. Editions: G. Parthey, *Dicuili Liber de Mensura Orbis Terrae* (Berlin, 1870); J.J. Tierney (ed.), *Dicuili Liber de Mensura Orbis Terrae*, Scriptores Latini Hiberniae, Vol. VI (Dublin: Dublin Institute for Advanced Studies, 1967).

BIOGRAPHY AND CRITICISM. J.F. Kenney, *The Sources for the Early History of Ireland*: I. *Ecclesiastical* (New York: Columbia University Press, 1929; reprinted Dublin, 1966), 545-48; M. Lapidge and R. Sharpe, *A Bibliography of Celtic-Latin Literature 400-1200*, Royal Irish Academy Dictionary of Medieval Latin from Celtic Sources, Ancillary Publications 1 (Dublin: Royal Irish Academy, 1985) Nos. 660-64, pp. 165-68; L. Bieler, 'The Text Tradition of Dícuil's *Liber de mensura orbis terrae*', *Proceedings of the Royal Irish Academy* 64 (1965), 1-31; M. Esposito, 'Dícuil, an Irish Monk in the Ninth Century', *Dublin Review* 137 (1905), 327-37; M. Esposito, 'An Irish Teacher at the Carolingian Court: Dícuil', *Studies* 3 (1914), 651-76.

Johannes Scottus (Ériugena)

LIFE. Johannes Scottus (John the Irishman), or Ériugena (Irish born) as he called himself in one of his manuscripts, was the outstanding philosopher of the so-called Dark Ages. Like so many Irishmen who went to the Continent, his home in Ireland is unknown. We first hear of him when Bishop Pardulus of Laon refers to him as the well-known Irishman in the king's palace. This was the court of Charles the Bald near Laon. Prudentius of Troyes, consecrated bishop in 847, knew him before that date. He probably arrived in Francia during the 840s and it is possible that he was not in clerical orders.

He was a member of the palace school of Charles the Bald. In 851 Hincmar, archbishop of Rheims, and Pardulus, bishop of Laon, asked him to write a refutation of Godescalc's theory of predestination. Ériugena produced his own work, *De Praedestinatione*, which immediately became as controversial as the work it set out to refute. It was attacked and eventually condemned at the Councils of Valence in 855 and Langres in 859. Ériugena and a fellow Irishman, Martin (819-875), were the two dominant scholars at Laon. Both were Greek scholars and masters in the school. As teachers, they emphasized the position of the arts in Christian education.

Ériugena produced a commentary of Martianus Capella's *De Nuptiis* (859-860) and appears to have reworked the text over a long period of time. He translated the work of Pseudo-Dionysius (860 x 862), the *Ambigua* of Maximus the Confessor (862 x 864), the *De Hominis Opificio* of Gregory of Nyssa (862 x 864), the *Quaestiones ad Thalassium* of Maximus the Confessor (864 x 866). He wrote his own work of philosophy, *Periphyseon* (*De Divisione Naturae*) (864 x 866) and his *Expositiones in Hierarchiam Caelestem Pseudo-Dionysii* (On the Celestial Hierarchy) (865 x 870). As well as these major works, he wrote homilies, biblical commentaries and poetry.

Ériugena's work was copied and excerpted in the ninth and following centuries. There was always an ambiguity that surrounded his writings — whether they were pantheistic or not. When later philosophers pointed to Ériugena as their source, his work was condemned at Paris in 1210 and by Pope Honorius in 1225. Ériugena fades from the sources *c.* 870. His passing also saw the fading away of the Carolingian Renaissance.

CHIEF WRITINGS. Editions: M. Lapidge and R. Sharpe, *A Bibliography of Celtic-Latin Literature 400-1200*, Royal Irish Academy Dictionary of Medieval Latin from Celtic Sources, Ancillary Publications 1 (Dublin: Royal Irish Academy, 1985) Nos. 695-713, pp. 183-92; I.P. Sheldon-Williams and L. Bieler, *Iohannis Scotti Eriugenae Periphyseon I-III*, 3 vols, Scriptores Latini Hiberniae VII, IX, XI (Dublin: Dublin Institute for Advanced Studies, 1968-81); G. Madec, *Iohannis Scotti de Diuina Praedestinatione Liber*, Corpus Christianorum L (Turnhout: Brepols, 1978); J. Barbet, *Iohannis Scotti Eriugenae Expositiones in Ierarchiam Caelestem*, Corpus Christianorum XXXI (Turnhout: Brepols, 1975); E. Jeauneau, *Jean Scot, Homélie sur le prologue de Jean*, Sources chrétiennes, CLI (Paris: Editions du Cerf, 1969); E. Jeauneau, *Jean Scot, Commentaire sur l'évangile de Jean*, Sources chrétiennes, CLXXX (Paris: Editions du Cerf, 1972).

BIOGRAPHY AND CRITICISM. J.F. Kenney, *The Sources for the Early History of Ireland:* I. *Ecclesiastical* (New York: Columbia University Press, 1929; reprinted Dublin, 1966), 569-89; M. Lapidge and R. Sharpe, *A Bibliography of Celtic-Latin Literature 400-1200*, Royal Irish Academy Dictionary of Medieval Latin from Celtic Sources, Ancillary Publications 1 (Dublin: Royal Irish Academy, 1985) Nos. 695-713, pp. 183-92; M. Brennan, 'A Bibliography of Publications in the Field of Eriugenian Studies 1800-1975', *Studi Medievali* 3rd series 18 (1977), 401-47; M. Cappuyns, *Jean Scot Érigène, sa vie, son oeuvre, sa pensée* (Louvain and Paris: Universitas Cattolica Louvainiensis, 1933); H. Bett, *Johannes Scotus Erigena: A Study in Mediaeval Philosophy* (Cambridge: Cambridge University Press, 1925); J.J. O'Meara, *Eriugena* (Cork: Mercier Press, 1969); F. Copleston, *A History of Philosophy* Vol. 2 *Mediaeval Philosophy* Part I (New York: Doubleday, 1962), 129-53; J.J. O'Meara and L. Bieler (eds), *The Mind of Eriugena* (Dublin: Irish University Press, for the Royal Irish Academy, 1973); P. Godman (ed.), *Poetry of the Carolingian Renaissance* (London: Duckworth, 1985), 58-63. John J. Contreni, 'John Scottus, Martin Hibernensis, the Liberal Arts, and Teaching', in M.W. Herren (ed.), *Insular Latin Studies, papers on Latin texts and manuscripts of the British Isles: 550-1066* (Toronto: Pontifical Institute of Medieval Studies, 1981), 23-44; Ludwig Bieler, *Ireland, Harbinger of the Middle Ages* (London: Oxford University Press, 1966), pp. 127-31.

Sedulius Scottus

LIFE. We do not know with certainty when Sedulius went to the Continent. He moved among a circle of scholars like himself: Fergus,

Blandus, Marcus, Beuchell, Dubthach. In the margins of their manuscripts are invocations to saints. St Brigit is mentioned most often and this indicates that they probably came from Leinster. They may have come with an embassy to Charles the Bald in 848 telling him of Irish victories over the Norsemen. From about this time onwards, we follow Sedulius through his own writings.

He was on friendly terms with the bishops of Cologne, Münster and Metz. We know that Bishop Hartgar at Liège was a major patron, providing himself and his companions with a house and provisions. Sedulius wrote eulogies for the sons of Louis the Pious and clearly had an eye to patronage from whatever quarter it might come. Ermingarde (died 851), wife of Lothar, had some of his verses embroidered in silk. Sedulius was much more the scholar courtier than the ascetic monk. As well as being an excellent poet, he was a serious scholar. He was one of the few at the time to know Greek reasonably well. As a grammarian, Sedulius wrote commentaries on the work of Donatus, Eutyches and Priscian. As an exegete, he commented on the Gospel of Matthew, the Eusebian Canons, the work of Jerome, and on other texts as well. He made an interlinear Latin translation of the Greek text of the Epistles of St Paul, and also copied a text called the *Proverbia Grecorum* (Sayings of the Greeks), which he probably had brought with him from Ireland. Sedulius also wrote a book, *Liber De Rectoribus Christianis* (Concerning Christian Rulers), for Lothar II, or possibly for Charles the Bald himself. Cruindmáel, in his *Ars Metrica* (The Art of Poetry), claimed him as his collaborator.

Sedulius disappears from view *c.* 874. He was one of the foremost scholars of the Carolingian Renaissance, whose scholarship has not yet been fully assessed.

CHIEF WRITINGS. Editions: L. Traube (ed.), *Monumenta Germaniae Historica. Poetae Latini Aevi Carolini*, III (1886), 151-237; M. Lapidge and R. Sharpe, *A Bibliography of Celtic-Latin Literature 400-1200*, Royal Irish Academy Dictionary of Medieval Latin from Celtic Sources. Ancillary Publications 1 (Dublin: Royal Irish Academy, 1985) Nos. 672-86, pp. 177-80; P. Godman (ed.), *Poetry of the Carolingian Renaissance* (London: Duckworth, 1982), 282-301.

BIOGRAPHY AND CRITICISM. J.F. Kenney, *The Sources for the Early History of Ireland*: I. *Ecclesiastical*, (New York: Columbia University Press, 1929; reprinted Dublin, 1966), 553-69; M. Lapidge and R. Sharpe, *A Bibliography of Celtic-Latin Literature 400-1200*, Royal Irish Academy Dictionary of Medieval Latin from Celtic Sources, Ancillary Publications 1 (Dublin: Royal Irish Academy, 1985) Nos. 672-86, pp. 177-80; S. Hellmann, *Sedulius Scottus* (Munich, 1906); J. Carney, 'Sedulius Scottus', in R. McNally (ed.), *Old Ireland* (Dublin: Gill and Son, 1965), 228-50; R. Düchting, 'Sedulius Scottus — ein "Heilger Drei König mehr" aus dem Abendland', in H. Löwe (ed.), *Die Iren und Europa im früheren Mittelalter* (Stuttgart: Klett-Cotta, 1982), Vol. II, pp. 866-75; P. Godman (ed.), *Poetry of the Carolingian Renaissance* (London: Duckworth, 1985), 53-57; D.M. Kratz, 'Aeneas or Christ? An Epic Parody by Sedulius Scottus', *The Classical World*, February 1976, pp. 319-23; Helen Waddell, *Medieval Latin Lyrics* (London: Constable & Co. Ltd., 1930).

Bishop Patrick (Gilla Patraic)

LIFE. Bishop Patrick (Gilla Patraic) became bishop of the Norse city of Dublin on the death of Dúnán, the first bishop, in 1074. We do not know of his family background, but the clergy and people of Dublin in a letter addressed to Lanfranc, archbishop of Canterbury, recommending him for consecration as bishop of their city, say that he was of noble blood. The ideals of the Gregorian Reform of the church had by now been felt in Ireland, and the Hiberno-Norse citizens looked to those centres in England that had embraced the reforms, rather than to the old monastic churches of Ireland. They also wished to maintain political independence within Ireland. Their choice for bishop, Patrick, had been sent to Worcester, where he had been trained as a Benedictine monk under St Wulfstan. It was consistent that he should be sent to Lanfranc to be consecrated by him in St Paul's in London. Lanfranc received an oath of profession from him (still preserved in the Canterbury Cathedral archives) and sent him home with letters addressed to Irish kings — one to Godfrey, king of Dublin, and another to Toirdelbach Ua Briain, his overlord.

From his writings it is clear that Bishop Patrick maintained close contacts with Worcester and its community. He was especially devoted to Wulfstan. It is likely that he established a Benedictine community at Christ Church in Dublin, which may have been dispersed by the later bishop, Samuel, some time before 1096. There is also the possibility that he occasioned the writing of a chronicle, the evidence for which may be found in *The Annals of St Mary's Abbey*, Dublin.

The influence of the European schools of theology was strong in Worcester during this time, as was the renewal of the writing of verse in classical form. Patrick, then, was a man in tune with the new reforming ideals. He undoubtedly generated support for reform within Ireland, which was eventually to lead to the first great reforming Synod held at Cashel in 1101 under the auspices of Toirdelbach Ua Briain's son, Muirchertach. Bishop Patrick did not live to see this achievement. With his companions, he was drowned crossing the Irish Sea, probably returning from a trip to Worcester, on 10 October 1084.

CHIEF WRITINGS. Editions: A. Gwynn (ed.), *The Writings of Bishop Patrick, 1074-1084*, Scriptores Latini Hiberniae, Vol. I (Dublin: Institute for Advanced Studies, 1955).

BIOGRAPHY AND CRITICISM. J.F. Kenney, *The Sources for the Early History of Ireland*: I. *Ecclesiastical* (New York: Columbia University Press, 1929; reprinted Dublin, 1966), 757-62; M. Lapidge and R. Sharpe, *A Bibliography of Celtic-Latin Literature 400-1200*, Royal Irish Academy Dictionary of Medieval Latin from Celtic Sources, Ancillary Publications 1 (Dublin: Royal Irish Academy, 1985) Nos. 309, 310, p. 88; M. Esposito, 'Notes on Latin Learning in Medieval Ireland, part II: Pseudopatriciana', *Hermathena* 47 (1932), 253-71; W. Delius, 'Die Verfasserschaft der Schrift *De tribus habitaculis*', *Theologische Studien und Kritiken* 108 (1937-38), 28-39; J.E. Cross, '*De signis et prodigiis* in *Versus S. Patricii episcopi de mirabilibus Hibernie*', *Proceedings of the Royal Irish Academy* 71 (1971), 247-54; J.T. Gilbert (ed.), *Chartularies of St Mary's Abbey, Dublin* (Rolls Series 80 (London: Longmans, 1884)); A. Gwynn, 'Some unpublished texts from the Black Book of Christ Church, Dublin', *Analecta Hibernica* 16 (1946), 313-15, 333-34.

TERENCE DOLAN, *Editor*

The Literature of Norman Ireland

Indirectly, the only Englishman ever to be elected Pope, Nicholas Breakspear, may be held responsible for the arrival of the English language in Ireland. In 1155, as Adrian IV, Breakspear issued the Bull *Laudabiliter* in which he authorized Henry II to conduct an invasion of Ireland in order to revive the morality and religious practices of its people. A decade or so passed before any action was taken on the matter, but in the late 1160s, the first groups of Welsh-Norman and Flemish-Norman knights landed on the south coast of Wexford to be followed in 1170 by their leader, Richard de Clare, earl of Pembroke, known as 'Strongbow'. Within a few months they had moved up the country and had occupied Dublin, and towards the end of the next year, in October 1171, Henry himself arrived in Ireland. By the middle of the next century the Normans had penetrated, but by no means saturated, most of the accessible parts of the country. Less arable parts remained in the possession of the native Irish, most of whom continued to conduct their lives just as they had done before the invasions.

The invasions had an interesting effect on the linguistic situation in Ireland. By the end of the twelfth century, three languages other than Irish, which was spoken by the indigenous population and which is dealt with in another section of this anthology, enjoyed currency at different levels and for different purposes among the rest of the population. Latin was spoken and used by churchmen, Norman-French by the ruling classes (religious and lay), and English by their retainers. French was the mother tongue of the Norman invaders of Ireland. Their counterparts in English, from whose ranks they had come, also spoke French. In England, at the highest level of society, the king and the members of the court did not adopt English as a second language until the reign of Edward I (1272-1307), and indeed it was not until the reign of Henry IV (1399-1413), whose first language was English, that the use of French showed obvious signs of decline.

This decline occurred much earlier in Ireland, where it seems that the ruling class exchanged French for Irish from the beginning of the fourteenth century. In the major towns of Ireland (Dublin, Cork, Waterford, Kilkenny, New Ross) French declined as a living language as the thirteenth century drew to its close and was gradually superseded by Irish in the fourteenth century. In general, then, the Anglo-Norman community in Ireland had substantially acclimatized itself to its adopted country by the beginning of the fourteenth century.

So alarmed were the authorities by the accelerating rate of Gaelicization at the expense of Anglo-French culture that in 1366 a parliament was held at Kilkenny, presided over by Lionel, duke of Clarence, son of Edward III. This parliament enacted legislation, known as the Statutes of Kilkenny, to stem the resurgence of native Irish influence — not just in language, but in all aspects of life, social, domestic and cultural — throughout the land. It is highly significant, and also paradoxical, that this document was written in Norman-French. It must be seen as a revisionist document because it seems to have been deliberately designed to give the misleading impression that there were only two languages and cultures in rivalry in Ireland — Irish and English, with French ignored, as if English had been the common spoken tongue of the invading Normans since the time of these original invasions. The gist of the Statutes was that the English born in Ireland (*'lez Engleis nees en Ireland'*) were expected to live and be treated in the same way as if they had been born and were living in England. In relaying this injunction, the document yields a fascinating variety of details about the practical effects of the Normans' assimilation of Irish manners and customs. What the Statutes forbade is testament to what was happening in Ireland among the descendants of the Norman invaders, who had settled and become naturalized in every sense of the word.

For our purpose, the most important and interesting section is that dealing with the linguistic situation, but it should be seen in the context of a general misapprehension on the part of the authorities in England about the increasing hibernicization of the country. Hence, the Statutes cover practically every aspect of day-to-day living, even sport and entertainment. The 'English' are enjoined to give up the sport of hurling, for instance, and to use bows and lances instead. No Irish minstrel was to be admitted into 'English' company: those settlers who received Irish minstrels were to be fined. At the end of the Statutes there is a stern threat that anyone contravening their terms would be liable for excommunication. Despite such heavy-handed but comprehensive instructions and interdicts, the Statues proved to be a notable failure, particularly in the matter of the use of the Irish language. Here is what the document has to say on this point:

> Item ordine est et estabile que chescun Engleys vse la lang Engleys et soit nome par nome Engleys enterlessant oulterment la manere de nomme use par Irroies et que chescun Engleys vse la lang Engleys et soit nome par nome solonc son estat et si nul Engleys ou Irroies conuersant entre Engleys use la lang Irroies entre cux-memes encontre ceste ordinance et de ceo soit atteint soint sez terres et Tenementz s'il eit seisiz en les maines son seignor immediate tanque qu'il veigne a vn des places nostre seignor le Roy et trove sufficient seurtee de prendre et vser la lang Engleis et adonques eit restitucion de sez ditz terres par bref aissir hors de la dit placee....

> [Also, it is ordained and established, that every Englishman use the English language, and be named by an English name, leaving off entirely the manner of naming used by the Irish; and that every Englishman use the English custom, fashion, mode of riding and apparel, according to his estate; and if any English, or Irish living amongst the English, use the Irish language amongst themselves, contrary to this ordinance, and therof be attaint, that his lands and tenements, if he have any, be seized into the lands of his immediate lord, until he come to one of the Places of our lord the King, and find sufficient surety to adopt and use the English language, and then that he have restitution of his said lands, by writ to issue out of the said Place.]

In spite of the fact that these Statutes were not repealed until the end of the fifteenth century, Irish culture in all its forms continued to reassert and re-establish itself among the Norman enclaves, until the Tudors came to Ireland in the sixteenth century. They devised a much more effective method of containing and confronting Irish influence through the institution of plantations, whereby loyal protestants from England, Scotland, and Wales were allowed to settle on lands that originally had belonged to the native population.

The Statutes covertly imply that the French language was in an advanced state of decline as a spoken medium in Ireland by the end of the fourteenth century, as was indeed the case. Nevertheless, French continued to be used in written form for legislative purposes (as the language of the Statutes demonstrates), and also for municipal and commercial transactions, long after its demise as a living vernacular. Many documents relating to the conduct of business survive from this period in French, which was also the language in which Acts of Parliament were framed as late as 1472. In the few exceptions to the use of French in such official documents, Latin and not English was employed. The picture that emerges, then, is that French died out as a spoken language much earlier than it ceased to be used as the normal medium for official documents.

It is difficult to determine the currency of French after the thirteenth century, but this century saw the production of the only two significant examples of literary French written in Ireland in the Middle Ages. Both are poems. The first is one written between 1200 and 1225, known as *The Song of Dermot and the Earl*, of which some 3,459 lines survive. Its hero is Dermot Mac Murrough, king of Dublin and Leinster, who was banished from his kingdom by the High King, Rory O'Connor, for various misdemeanours (including the abduction of the wife of Tiernan O Rourke). Dermot sought help to restore his kingship from England, in particular from Strongbow, the 'Earl' cited in the title of the poem. The story describes Dermot's trip to Bristol and thence across England to Aquitaine to parley with Henry II. Much of the activity is set in Ireland and includes Dermot's offer of his daughter to the bachelor Strongbow. The poem was written by Morice Regan, secretary to Dermot, and understandably shows a healthy bias towards the cause of the king and his allies. Only one manuscript of the poem, from the last quarter of the thirteenth century, survives. In the seventeenth century it came into the possession of Sir George Carew, whose signature appears on the manuscript with the date 1647. It is now listed as Carew manuscript No. 596 in the archiepiscopal library in Lambeth Palace, London.

The poem is remarkably lively. The narrative moves speedily and the speeches convey a distinctly rhetorical energy. For example, Dermot's address to King Henry, edited below, is framed in such a way as to bring out the injustice of the treatment suffered by the king at the hands of his enemies in Ireland. There are many boisterous moments in the narrative, as for instance in one episode of the campaign, when a renowned warrior called Johan le Deue took his axe and chopped off the thigh of another knight (*'Lui first uoler la quisse al champe*— He chopped the thigh off to the ground').

The only other major medieval French work is a poem containing 220 lines entitled *The Walling of New Ross*, which concerns a wall of stone and mortar (*'un mure de morter e de pere'*) that was put up around this Wexford town in 1265. The author of the poem is unknown, but he may have been a member of the Franciscan order, which had established a community in New Ross by 1256. New Ross was a prosperous port whose citizens decided to put up a wall to protect their territory from attacks resulting from a feud between Walter de Burgh, earl of Ulster, and Maurice Fitzgerald. The walling was carried out by the citizens themselves and the work was shared between them on different days of the week. On Wednesdays, for instance, it was the turn of the leather-workers, tanners and butchers, three hundred of them. The poet is careful to note the numbers of citizens involved in the construction work and, from his calculations, it seems that there were over three thousand members of the local community concerned in the labours. The poem ends with the invocation:

> A Deu la vile je command
> E tous qe dedens sunt habitand.
> Amen. Amen. Amen.
>
> [To God I commend the town
> and all who live within it. Amen. Amen. Amen.]

It also gives us the date of completion: *'Ce fut fet l'an de l'incarnation Nostre Seignur* M.CC.LXV.' [This was made in A.D. 1265]

Moving on now to consider what happened to the English language in medieval Ireland, we find that the terms of the Statutes of Kilkenny give a clear indication of the sinking fortunes of English in Ireland towards the end of the fourteenth century. This trend continued into the next century, where other kinds of evidence become more plentiful. Irish was always the common idiom of the majority of the population outside the towns, but there is evidence to suggest that, in urban areas, it became an acceptable medium of communication even for official purposes. There is, for example, an interesting record in the municipal archives of Waterford (1492-93) which states that Irish could be used in court proceedings where one or other of the litigants in a suit was Irish. In the sixteenth century we find an account in the State Papers of the proclamation of a bill in the parliament of Dublin (1541) officially announcing Henry VIII's assumption of the title of king of Ireland. The parliament was attended by the earl of Ormond and other lords whose families had been settled in Ireland since medieval times. It seems that only Ormond was able to understand the proclamation in English. For the rest of his peers Ormond had to translate 'the effecte of the preposicion and answer' into Irish 'greately to their contentation'.

This situation, of course, was not viewed favourably by the authorities, as evidenced in a report by Lord Chancellor Gerrarde, who stated in 1578 that:

> all English, and the most part with delight, even in Dublin, speak Irish, and greatly are spotted in manners, habit and conditions with Irish stains.

The currency of English was also materially affected by the Reformation. The Irish language became associated with catholicism, and English with protestantism. Both native Irish and the 'Old English' (the name given to people whose families had long been settled in Ireland) embraced the Irish language as the symbol of their religious conviction and choice. A number of commentators complained about the ready use that both the Irish and the 'English Irish' made of the Irish language. Among these writers was a fascinating individual called Richard Stanihurst (1547-1618). For generations his family had been prominent citizens in Dublin society and had the reputation of being loyal supporters of the king. His father, a Dublin merchant, had become speaker in the Dublin parliament that passed the Act of Supremacy in 1536. Stanihurst studied at University College, Oxford, and there became a friend and associate of Edmund Campion. Later in life he became a catholic and subsequently fell out with his famous protestant nephew, his sister's son, James Ussher, the scholar and primate. He died a catholic priest in Brussels, where he is buried. His chief claim to fame was the section on Ireland that he contributed to *The Chronicles of England, Scotland, and Ireland*, compiled by Raphael Holinshed, which appeared in 1578 and which was later used by Shakespeare as a sourcebook. Stanihurst's attitude to the encroachment of Irish influence on the settler-class to which he belonged was exactly the same as that voiced in the Statutes of Kilkenny, as will be seen from the following passage in which he speculates on what would have happened if the inhabitants of the Pale (the name given to that part of Ireland consistently under English control, roughly stretching down the coast from Dundalk to Dalkey and inland from Kells and Athboy down to Naas) had not succumbed to the process of gaelicization:

> As long as those empaled dwellers did sunder themselves as well in land as in language from the Irish, rudeness was day by day in the country supplanted, civility engraffed, good laws observed, rebellion suppressed, and, in fine, the coin of a young England was like to shoot in Ireland.

Much to Stanihurst's consternation, this had not happened. He states that 'all Leinster, Meeth, Ulster, the more parte of Connaght and Mounster, all the ciuities & burroughes in Irelande, haue beene wholly Englished', but, despite this, he asks, 'is it decent, thinke you, that theyr owne auncient natiue tongue shal be shrowded in obliuion, and suffer the enemies language, as it were a tettare, or ring woorme, to herborow it self within the iawes of Englishe conquerours?' He answers this question himself — 'no truely'.

Stanihurst's account was corroborated some years later by Fynes Moryson (1566-1630), an Englishman who came to Ireland as secretary to the lord deputy, Lord Mountjoy. He wrote a famous *Itinerary* (1617-26), which included a passage on the forsaking of English by the settler-class:

> Again, contrary to the said law, the Irish-English altogether used the Irish tongue, forgetting or never learning the English .... But the law to spread the English tongue in Ireland was ever interrupted by rebellions, and much more by ill-affected subjects, so as at this time whereof I write, the mere Irish disdained to learn or speak the English tongue; yea, the English-Irish and the very citizens (excepting those of Dublin where the Lord Deputy resides), though they could speak English as well as we, yet commonly speak Irish among themselves and were hardly induced by our familiar conversation to speak English with us.

This passage provides further proof of the failure of the Statutes of Kilkenny to keep the Irish at bay.

The picture that emerges from our description of the fortunes of the English language in Ireland has two main divisions because the English language was twice introduced into Ireland, firstly by the followers of the Norman magnates, and secondly by the people brought over from England and settled in the plantations by the Tudors and their successors. The two introductions were obviously not totally disconnected. There was always a thread of English in the major towns, but this grew very thin as the Middle Ages drew to their close. Outside the towns there are two celebrated exceptions to the general abandonment of English, both in rural areas. The English language was preserved in an area north of Dublin city known as Fingall, comprising the baronies of Nethercross, Balrothery and Coolock, and also in an area of south-east Wexford comprising two baronies, known as Forth and Bargy. The inhabitants of these five baronies preserved an archaic form of English throughout the medieval period. The main difference between them is that the dialect of Fingall seems to have had a higher proportion of Irish words embedded in it than the Wexford dialect. There is no contemporary record of the Wexford speech, but we can derive a reasonably clear impression of its main characteristics from a famous glossary of the dialect compiled by Joseph Poole (1774-1827), a Quaker farmer, who recorded the vocabulary used by his workers and tenants. His glossary was published by the English poet William Barnes in 1867. As for survivals in the Fingall dialect, a few pieces dating from the seventeenth century have been preserved. These relics and the entries in Poole's glossary corroborate what Stanihurst has to say about the two dialects:

> Howbeit to this day, the dregs of the old auncient Chaucer English, are kept as well there [in Forth and Bargy] as in Fingall.

The two dialects are not purely English because of the traces of Irish influence, stronger in Fingall than in Forth and Bargy, as we have noted, but they furnish important, if anomalous, evidence for the continuing tradition of using English outside the major towns. The Wexford dialect is a singularly interesting phenomenon because it shows the tenacity of English speech outside the Pale, in contrast with the dialect of Fingall, which was always within the Pale.

As regards writings in English produced in Ireland during the Middle Ages, it is likely that a great deal has been lost, but it is difficult to determine how much. Of the surviving material, the most important source for our knowledge of medieval Hiberno-English is a manuscript now in the British Library, classified as MS Harley 913. As well as items in Latin and French, it also contains seventeen pieces in English. Its provenance is indisputably Irish and it also may have a connection with the Franciscan Order since it contains a list of the Franciscan Provinces in Ireland as well as two items in Latin concerned with incidents in the life of St Francis. It is not possible, though, to say how close is the relationship with the Order. From internal references and linguistic evidence, the manuscript is dated to some time around 1330. There is some disagreement as to where it was written, but possibly it was Kildare (the author of one of the English poems names himself 'Friar Michael of Kildare'). The contents of the manuscript are mostly satirical or religious, or both.

The general taste of the selection is very well represented by the most celebrated Hiberno-English poem in the manuscript, known as *The Land of Cokaygne*. The poem is set in a land called Cokaygne, 'far at sea to the west of Spain', which is, of course, Ireland. It is a land that is infinitely more luxurious than the Christian notion of Paradise, and here people live an effortless life of drinking, eating and general debauchery. (This preoccupation with food invites comparison with the twelfth-century Irish poem, *The Vision of MacConglinne*.) After the introductory description of the location of this land, the poet describes an abbey where, in defiance of the conventional concern with abstinence, the monks are surrounded by food. They do not even have to cook their geese, because the birds fly in already roasted, calling 'Geese, all hot, all hot!' When the monks go to mass, the windows of the chapel turn into crystal so as to give more light. Even their recreational habits are well catered for. The young monks go out to play after their meal, much to the delight of the abbot, who calls them home by using the bottom of a young maiden as a drum to summon them. If this were not enough distraction, the young nuns in a neighbouring abbey also seem as ready to please as the geese. They go for a swim naked, after which each young monk 'takes one for himself'. It is not certain if the poet had any specific monastery in mind, but a strong case has been made for the Cistercian monastery of Inislounaght on the river Suir, a reasonable distance from Waterford, New Ross, and Kildare.

Other poems in English in the manuscript are important, too, both for their satirical energy and also for the insight they furnish into the life of medieval Ireland. One of these poems, once thought to be a satire on the people of Kildare, but now believed to be concerned with the citizens of Dublin, contains a series of admonitions. Merchants, for instance, are chastized for ignoring the poor, and brewers for cheating their customers. The same reforming zeal lies behind the so-called 'Hymn' of Friar Michael of Kildare, who is also concerned with the plight of the poor. In one stanza he tells the rich man that he is nothing but a brittle tree ('brotil tre'), less than seven feet tall, which the fiend takes great delight in hewing down. Another poem, entitled 'Piers de Bermingham', describes the implacable hostility that Sir Piers, a historical personage who died in 1308, feels towards his Irish enemies, in particular the O'Connor family. He hunted the Irish foe, we are told, like a hunter chasing the hare, and eventually conquers the O'Connors.

A number of plays were either written or copied in Ireland during the later Middle Ages in a form of English that reflects Irish provenance. Perhaps the most famous of these, and certainly the most important, is a morality play called *The Pride of Life*, the title given it by one James Mills, deputy keeper of the Public Records in Dublin, who published an edition of the play under the auspices of the Royal Society of Antiquaries of Ireland in 1891. The original manuscript, as described by Mills, was probably written during the first half of the fifteenth century and the text has some dialectal affinities with that of MS Harley 913 (discussed above); it survived in the Public Record Office in Dublin until the destruction of the Four Courts, where it was kept, in June 1922. The manuscript was written by two monks, whose work is easily distinguishable one from the other since one seems to have worked from a written original and the other from dictation. The play is incomplete in its extant form. Nevertheless about five hundred lines survive, divided into stanzas. The morality theme centres on a character called the King of Life, who refuses to accept his Queen's salutary advice that no one escapes death. As in the later and more famous play *Everyman*, the chief character is aided in his misguided convictions by various associates, in particular by his two knights, Health and Strength. Before the text breaks off, the King challenges Death and, from what is announced in the Prologue, it appears that he is eventually defeated.

The most significant piece of English prose written in Ireland during the fifteenth century was a translation made by James Yonge (*fl.* 1423) of a work known as the *Secreta Secretorum*, the original Greek version of which was attributed to Aristotle. Yonge was a member of an English family that had settled in the Pale. He himself was in the retinue of James Butler, fourth earl of Ormond, at whose request, probably around the year 1423, he made the translation, which seems to have been based on a French version by Gofroi of Waterford. The work, which goes under the name of *The Gouernaunce of Prynces*, has seventy-two chapters and contains a few additional passages in which Yonge relates events in Irish history, which he seems to have considered relevant to the philosophical import of the work. For instance, he gives a brief account of the exploits of Dermot Mac Murrough, whom we have mentioned above, including his abduction of the wife of a neighbouring king: 'Another myschefe hym befell, O'rooryckes wyfe, kynge of Mythe, by hyr owyn assente, in abscence of hyr lorde, he rauysshed.' Yonge is partial to Dermot's plight. He is particularly anxious to establish the justification of the King of England's right to lordship of Ireland:

> But for-alsmoche, gracious lorde, as I haue now her towchid of the conquest of Irland, I shall now declare yow in Partie as y fynde in croncles written, many titles of oure lege lorde the kynge of Englandes ryght to this land of Irland, agaynes the errourse and haynouse Iryshmenes oppynyones, sayinge that thay haue bettyr ryght.

After this forthright statement comes his chapter entitled 'Of the Kynges titles to the land of Irland, aftyr the Cronyclis', which is edited below. The narrative is presented in clear, uncomplicated syntax, which reflects Yonge's determination to give an unambiguously loyal account of the English right to the lordship of Ireland.

We turn finally to Latin, the third of the languages, other than Irish, that was current in Ireland in the Middle Ages. 'Current' is probably too strong a word to use since Latin was always a special case. It differed from all the mother tongues in Europe in one particularly important aspect: it was essentially a book-based discipline, which had to be learned through deliberate study. Whereas all the other languages moved from the spoken sphere to the written, Latin moved from the written medium to the spoken. The pre-eminent value of Latin was its prestige and universality. Even today, some branches of science, for instance ornithology and botany, exploit its universal intelligibility. In the Middle Ages it functioned as the chief medium of international communication in spoken and written form, between governments, scholars and, of course, senior members of the church. However, its use was not restricted to the ecclesiastical sphere since many positions at court and in government were filled by churchmen who had been seconded from their normal duties. It had a higher prestige than any vernacular language because of its association with the authority of the church and, beyond that, with the authority of Ancient Rome. From this authority derived its wholesale application to the work of documentation and record in the secular sphere, in addition to its formally religious role.

Ireland's contribution to the continuation of Latin scholarship, particularly in the so-called 'Dark Ages', is well-known. Later, there seems to have been a decline in the standard of Latin learning in Ireland as a consequence of the social, administrative and ecclesiastical changes brought about by the Norman invasions. Even so, Irish scholars continued to make an important contribution to the development of European scholarship through the medium of Latin. Treatises on morality, biblical exegesis, canon law, and so forth were produced, as well as chronicles and a very large number of sermons. In the two centuries after the invasions, there was a dearth of major works (at least, so the surviving material suggests); but the fourteenth century was singularly rich in a variety of genres. Outstanding among these is an influential work on the Seven Deadly Sins by the Franciscan scholar Malachy of Armagh (*fl. c.* 1310). Another Franciscan, Symon Simeonis, produced a fascinating *Itinerarium* of a journey that he undertook to the Holy Land. He and his companion Hugo left their friary (probably Clane) and, on 16 March 1322, sailed from Ireland and crossed the Irish Sea. They journeyed to London, thence to France and Italy, across to Egypt, and eventually arrived in the Holy Land, where Symon described the scene of the crucifixion, including even the round hole in which the cross of Christ had been fixed.

Another Franciscan, John Clyn, from the friary of Kilkenny, has left us a moving account of the effects of the Plague on that city under the entry for the year 1348, '*inter mortuos mortem expectans*' (waiting for death among the dead). It seems that he, too, succumbed to the pestilence because, after his last entry under the year 1349, another writer put the touching sentence: '*videtur quod Auctor hic obiit* (It seems that the writer died at this point). Clyn's work is especially valuable for the immediacy of his description of the Plague and its effects in Kilkenny. Indeed, so pessimistic was he about his own chances of survival that he says that he will leave parchment so that anyone who survived the pestilence might continue his work. His *Annales Hiberniae*, as his work is called, commences with a few remarks about the circumstances of Christ's birth in the time of Tiberius and moves with exemplary brevity to the period of the Plague in Ireland.

One of the most controversial and colourful ecclesiastics in medieval Ireland was Richard Ledrede, who was born about 1275 in England, became a Franciscan, and eventually bishop of Ossory in 1316, the post he held until his death in 1360. He was thus a contemporary of John Clyn. Outstanding among his controversial activities was his conduct of the famous trial involving the allegations of witchcraft made against Dame Alice Kyteler of Kilkenny in 1324. Dame Alice fled to England, but one of her entourage, a woman from County Meath called Petronilla, suffered death by burning, the first person to do so in Ireland on grounds of heresy. It is, however, as a poet that Ledrede commands our attention here. Sixty songs (the music of which does not, unfortunately, survive) make up the collection. They are all devotional, and were devised as alternative pieces to be used instead of secular, improper songs. He was particularly fond of writing poems commemorating the Virgin Mary and her maternal relationship with Christ. All his poems are contained in a manuscript preserved in the Palace Library of the bishops of Ossory in Kilkenny, known as the Red Book of Ossory (so called because the binding was originally red, some of which survives on the insides of the cover). Among the many fascinating items in this manuscript is a text of the Statutes of Kilkenny. In the main, the Red Book contains documents relating to significant happenings that occurred during Ledrede's term as bishop and was probably written around the time of his death.

Ledrede's death in 1360 coincided with that of an even more famous and controversial Irish ecclesiastic — Richard FitzRalph, a Dundalk man, who was archbishop of Armagh from 1346 until his death. Unlike the Franciscans Clyn and Ledrede, FitzRalph was a secular cleric, and it is ironical that his main claim to fame was his violent opposition to the friars, in particular the Franciscans. He was educated at Oxford and spent a good deal of his career at the papal court in Avignon. From 1350 onwards he prepared and delivered a trenchant series of sermons and treatises against what he considered to be the main reason for the sorry state of the church in his time: the delinquency of the friars, whose lifestyle, in his view, contradicted and insulted the intentions of their founders, who had based their rules on the proposition that Christ was poor. FitzRalph denied that Christ was voluntarily poor and, consequently, so far as he was concerned, the whole basis of the mendicants' claim to be imitating the life of Christ in all its aspects was false.

An active preacher, FitzRalph travelled extensively in the northern part of the Pale, which came under his jurisdiction, although it seems that, because of problems concerning the indigenous Irish of his diocese, he never set foot in his cathedral at Armagh. He delivered sermons in both English, to lay 'Anglo-Irish' congregations, and Latin, to clerics; only the Latin versions survive and we may presume that he gave the vernacular sermons from notes in Latin. It seems that his antipathy to the friars emerged from his experience of running a diocese that was so poor that he could not afford to lose any offerings from his parishioners. The friars were so successful at preaching and giving easy penances in confession that they attracted money which, in FitzRalph's opinion, should have gone to his own clergy. This deflection of funds seems to have been a major factor in his anti-mendicancy, and he castigated the friars in a series of sermons and formal addresses that culminated in a proposition known as the *Defensio Curatorum* (the Defence of the Secular Clergy) which he delivered before Pope Innocent VI at Avignon on 8 November 1357. In it, he assembled every conceivable argument against the friars in such a way as to show them in the worst possible light. This, he hoped, would encourage the pope to disband them.

In the event, he lost his case, and died in Avignon in November 1360. Ten years later his body was brought home to Dundalk, where it was buried in the church of St. Nicholas. Twice in the *Defensio* he refers to his diocese of Armagh, first near the beginning of the address, where he explains why he had to go to Avignon and describes the structure of his case, and secondly, where he supplies evidence of the spiritual anarchy caused by the friars in his territory. These two passages are edited below from British Library MS Lansdowne 393 (a paper manuscript, dated early fifteenth century), one of sixty-odd manuscripts containing the *Defensio*, which ranks as one of the most important anti-mendicant documents of the Middle Ages and which also, incidentally, helps to explain the tradition of anti-mendicant satire reflected in the writings of Geoffrey Chaucer and William Langland.

* * *

French, English, and Latin were all used at one time or another by at least some members of the population of Ireland during the Middle Ages. Under this linguistic overlay, the Irish language continued as a sort of recoverable palimpsest which maintained a healthy currency despite the lowly status accorded it by the speakers who used one or other of the two imported languages. Latin, as we have seen, was always a special case, because it had already enjoyed a distinguished history of use by churchmen and scholars since long before the Norman invasions. English came into the country as the inferior tongue to Norman-French, which, within a century or so after the coming of the Normans, succumbed to pressure from the native tongue and survived, not as a living speech, but mainly as the medium for specialized written purposes and oral formulae in commerce and law. English effectively had disappeared in most areas outside the major towns (with the exception of the baronies of Fingall, Forth and Bargy), as the Statutes of Kilkenny indicate, and was reintroduced during the time of the plantations. From then on, the native population became more and more aware of the merits of learning it as a means of coping with the increasingly widespread anglicization of the country. From the end of the seventeenth century onwards, English gained a progressively stronger hold on the country. For a long time it was associated in the minds of the indigenous Irish with the protestant faith. This was a negative factor in its progress, which was eventually resolved with the institution of St Patrick's Royal Seminary at Maynooth, County Kildare in 1795, in which catholic priests were trained in an English environment and, later still, with the introduction of a system of primary education in 1831, in which English was the medium of instruction. In the medieval period, however, a small number of interesting works was written in languages other than Irish. The authors came from the settler-class and wrote poetry and prose in French and English for a limited audience; their work sought to symbolize in literary form their apartness from the indigenous population, whose own language was so rich and strong that it posed a continuous threat throughout the period, both as a medium that might eventually have displaced the languages of the settlers (firstly, French, where it succeeded, and secondly, English, where it almost succeeded), and as a constant source of semantic and syntactical contamination (in which it obviously succeeded).

[The editor wishes to acknowledge the help of Art Cosgrove, Charles Doherty and Alan Fletcher.]

Norman-French Texts

THE SONG OF DERMOT AND THE EARL (1200-25)

[The text and translation of these extracts are taken from G. H. Orpen's edition (Oxford: Clarendon Press, 1892).]

Quant dermod,[1] li reis uaillant,[2]
Al rei henri[3] par deuant
Esteit uenus a cele fiez,
Par deuant li rei engleis,
Mult le salue curteisement,
Bien ebel deuant la gent:
'Icil deu ke meint en haut
Reis henri, vus ward e saut,
E vus donge ensement
Quer e curage e talent
Ma hunte uenger e ma peine,
Que fet me hunte le men demeine!
Oiez, gentil reis henriz,
Dunc su nez, de quel pais.
De yrlande su sire ne,
En yrlande rei clame;
Mes atort me unt degete
Ma gent demeine del regne.
A vus me venc clamer, bel sire,
Veans les baruns de tun empire.
Ti liges home deuendrai
Tit iors me que uiuerai,
Par si que mai seez aidant,
Que ne sei de tut perdant:
Tei clamerai sire de seignur
Veant baruns e cuntur.'
Dunc li od le rei pramis
De engletere, le poestifs,
Que uolunters lui aidereit
Al plus tost quil porreit.[4]

[When Dermot, the valiant king, before King Henry had come at this time, before the English king, very courteously he saluted him fairly and finely before his men: 'May God who dwells on high guard and save you, King Henry, and give you also heart and courage and will to avenge my shame and my misfortune that my own people have brought upon me! Hear, noble King Henry, whence I was born, of what country. Of Ireland I was born a lord, in Ireland a king; but wrongfully my own people have cast me out of my kingdom. To you I come to make my plaint, good sire, in the presence of the barons of your empire. Your liege man I shall become henceforth all the days of my life, on condition that you be my helper so that I do not lose at all: you I shall acknowledge as sire and lord, in the presence of your barons and lords.' Then the king promised him, the powerful king of England, that wilfully would he help him as soon as he should be able.]

Li quens al hort iert bacheler.
Femme naueit ne mullier,
Si entent del rei dermot
Que sa fille doner lui uolt
Par si que od lui uenist
E sa terre lui conquist.
Li quens respons od sa gent:
'Riche reis, amei entent.
Ici ta fie lelment
Que a tai uendrai assurement;
Mes conge uodrai en iceis
De mander del rei engleis,
Kar il est li mien seignur
De ma terrien honur;
Pur ceo ne pus de sa terre
Sens conge prendre en tel manere.'[5]
Li reis al cunte asura

1. Diarmait Mac Murchada (Dermot Mac Murrough), king of Leinster since 1226. In 1151 he abducted Dervogilla, wife of Tigernán Ua Ruairc (Tiernan O Rourke), king of Breffni, who agitated for his expulsion, which occurred in 1166. Dermot, accompanied by his daughter Aífe (Eva), then sailed for Bristol and subsequently crossed the channel and met Henry II in Aquitaine.
2. Note the poet's favourable view of Dermot.
3. Henry landed at Waterford with an army of four thousand men on 17 October 1171 and remained in Ireland for about six months.
4. Dermot returned to Wales after his meeting with Henry and there offered his daughter to Richard de Clare, earl of Pembroke, known as 'Strongbow'.
5. Strongbow landed near Waterford on 23 August 1170 with Aífe and a thousand soldiers. King Dermot and his son Donal joined forces with him there and, after capturing Waterford, moved up the country and took Dublin.

Que sa fille a lui durra
Quant il lui uendreit en aie
En yrlande de sa baronie.
Quant fini unt icel pleit,
Le reis uers Gales turnat dreit;
Vnques ne finnat de errer i
De cil quil uint a seint daui.

[The earl at this time was a bachelor. He had neither spouse nor wife. When he hears from King Dermot that he was willing to give him his daughter on condition that he would come with him and subdue his land for him, the earl replies before his men: 'Rich king, hearken unto me. Here I assure you loyally that I shall assuredly come to you. But I should wish in these matters to crave licence of the English king, for he is the lord of my landed estate; wherefore I cannot go from his territory without obtaining licence in this way.' The king assured the earl that he would give him his daughter when he should come to his aid to Ireland with his barons. When they had concluded this accord, the king turned straight towards Wales, and never ceased journeying there until he came to St David's.]

THE WALLING OF NEW ROSS (1265)

[The text and translation of these opening lines are taken from the edition by Hugh Shields in *Long Room* 12-13 (1975-76), 24-33. This extract contains 123 of the 220 lines of the complete poem, the source of which is a volume known to the antiquarian Sir James Ware as 'the book of Rosse or of Waterford' (dated 1608).]

Rithmus facture ville de Rosse

Talent me prent de rimaunceir
S'il vous plet de escoteir,
Kar parole qe n'est oie
Ne vaut pas un aillie.
Pur ce vous prie d'escoter
Si me oiés ben aucer
De une vile en Ireland,
La plus bele de sa grand
Qe je sache en nule tere.
Mes poure avoint de un gerre
Qe fu par entre deus barouns;
Vei ci escrit amdeus lur nuns:
Sire Morice e sire Wauter.[1]

1. Maurice Fitzgerald and Walter de Burgh. Shields (p. 24) notes that 'on 6 December 1264 Maurice had provoked a new outbreak of hostilities by imprisoning Henry III's justiciar, Richard de la Rochelle.'

Le noun de la vile voil nomer:
'Ros' le devez apeler,
C'est le novel pont de Ros.[2]
Ce fu lur poure ke ne furent clos.

A lur conseil un joure alerent
E tot la commune ensemblerent;
Lur conseil prísterent en tele maner:
Qe un mure de morter e de pere
Voilent enture la vile feire,
Qe poure avoint de cel geere.
A la Chandeler[3] commencerent;
De mercher la fosse y alerent;
Coment le mure dut aler
Aleint liz prodoms mercher.

E [qant] avoint le mure merché
Pur overors unt tost mandé;
Cent ou plus chescun jour
I vont overer od grand honur.
Les burgeis entur la fosse alerent,
E gent lowis poi espleiterent.
E a lure conseil realerent
E un purveans purparlerent;
Ke unkes tele purveance
Ne fu en Engleter ne en France.
E l'endemain en firent crier
E tot la commune ensembler;
La purveance fu la mustré
E tot la commune ben paié.
Une prodome sus leva,
La purveans i mustra:
  Ke le lundi tot primers
Irrunt a la fosse le vineters,
Mercers, marchans e drapers
Ensemblement od lez vineters.
De l'oure de prime deke nune sonee
Dussent overer au fossee.
E si si funt eus mult bonement,
I vont overir od bele gent;
Mil e plus, pur voir vous die,
I vont overir chescun lundi
O belcs baners e grantz honurs
E od floites e taburs.
E ausi tost cum noune soune
I vont a l'ostel li prodome;
Lure baners y vont devant.
La jeuene gent haut chantant

2. New Ross, Co. Wexford.
3. The event celebrated in the poem began on 2 February 1265.

Par tot la vile karoler
Ove grant joi vount laborer.
E les prestres, qan ont chanté,
Si vont overir au fossé,
E travellent mut durement:
Plus qe ne funt autre gent,
Kar i sunt jeuenz e envuysés
E grans e forts, ben sojornés.
Le mariners, kant a l'ostel sunt,
En bele maner au fossé vount;
Lure baner en vete devont,
La nef dedens est depoint.
E aprés la baner vont suént
Bien sis cenz de bel gent.
E si fusent tuz a l'outeus,
Tuz le nefs e bateus,
Plus i avereit de unze cens,
Sachez pur veir, de bone gens.
Le mardi prochein suént aprés
I vont taillurs e parmenters,
Tenturers, fulrurs e celers;
Bele gent sunt de lur mesters.
I vont overir, cum dit devant,
Mes ne sunt tant de gent;
Mes bien sunt qatre cens,
Sachez pur veir, de bele gens.
Le mekirdi prochein suant
I vont autre maner de gent:
Cordiwaners, tannors, macecrers,
Mult i a de beus bachelers.
Lur baners en sunt depeint
Si com a lur mester apeint.
Treis cens sunt, si cum je quit,
Qe ove grant e ove petit,
E hautement vont karoler,
Ausi com funt li primer.
Le judi vont li pesturs
E lez regraturs trestuz
Qe ble véndunt e peissuns;
Divers sunt lur gonfanuns.
Bien ye vont en icel jure [?]
Qatre cens od grant honur,
E karolent e chantent haut
Com le primers par devant.
Lez waynpayns i vunt ausi
Meimes en icel judi;
Aprés les autres vont derer
E par devant unt bele baner:
Le esquele e le peissun par dedens
En lur baner en est depeins.
Issi vont eus au fossee;
Trent e deus sunt, pur verité.
Le parturs vont le vendredi;
Bien sunt treis cens e demy.
[L]ur baners en sunt devant
[A] l'orle de fosse en estant.
[Le]z carpenters vont le samadi
[E] févers e masuns autresi.
Mult bele gent sunt, je vous plevi;
Ben sunt treis cens e demy.
E tuz vont overir od bon corage;
Sachez, de ce en funt qe sage.
Le demainge les dames i vont;
Sachez de veires, bon óvere i funt....

[Lines on the construction of the town of Ross

I have a desire to versify in French
if you will be pleased to listen,
for words that are not heard
are not worth a clove of garlic [?].
Therefore I ask you to listen
and hear what I have to tell [?]
about a town in Ireland,
the finest of its size
I know in any country.
But they were fearful of a war
that was [going on] between two barons;
here are their two names in writing:
lord Maurice and lord Walter.
I shall tell you the name of the town:
'Ros' you are to call it,
it is the new bridge of Ross.
What they feared was that they had no town walls.
To their council one day they went
and the whole commons assembled [?].
They made a resolution thus:
that a wall of stone and mortar
they would build round the town,
for that war was causing them concern.
At Candlemas they began;
to mark out the fosse they went;
how the wall was to go,
the chief citizens went to mark it out.

And when [?] they had the wall marked
they summoned labourers directly;
a hundred or more each day
go and work there in fine style.
The townsfolk went round the fosse,
but the hired men got little done.
They sat again in council
and discussed a plan,
such a plan as never
was [put into effect] in England or France.

The next day they had it announced
and the whole commons assembled;
the plan was outlined
and all the commons well pleased with it.
A leading citizen stood up
and outlined the plan to them:
on Monday to begin with
the vintners would go to the fosse,
mercers, merchants and drapers
along with the vintners.
From daybreak till the stroke of three [?]
they were to work at the fosse.
And so they do quite readily,
they go to work there with good men;
a thousand and more, I tell you truly,
go to work there every Monday
with fine banners and insignia
and flutes and tabors.
And as soon as it strikes three [?]
the citizens return home
and their banners go ahead of them.
The young folk singing loudly,
carolling up and down the town,
joyfully go to labour.
And the priests, when they have sung [mass],
go to work at the fosse,
and apply themselves energetically:
more so than other people,
for they are young and eager,
big and strong, ready for the task.
The seamen, when they are at home,
in fine manner go to the fosse;
their banner goes before them,
a ship painted in the middle.
And after the banner follow
Six hundred or more fine men.
And if all were at home,
every vessel and boat,
there would be more than eleven hundred
good men, you may well believe.
On Tuesday then following
go tailors and robe-trimmers,
dyers, fullers and saddlers;
good men they are at their trades.
They go to work there, as I have said,
but they are not so numerous;
even so, they make up a good four hundred
fine men, believe me.
On Wednesday then following
goes another group of people:
leather-workers, tanners, butchers,
there are many young men among them.
Their banners are painted
as befits their trade.
There are three hundred of them, I would say,
great and small,
and they go carolling loudly,
just as the first crowd do.
On Thursday go the bakers
and the small traders all
that sell corn and fish;
their flags are varied.
Taking part that day [?] are a good
four hundred in grand array,
and they carol and sing at the tops of their voices
just like the previous ones.
Their helpers [?] go with them
on the Thursday;
after the others they follow on
and in front of them have a fine banner:
a platter and a fish therein
on their banner is depicted.
Thus they go to the fosse;
they would be thirty-two in number certainly.
The porters [?] go on Friday;
there are a good three hundred and fifty.
Their banners are in front
standing at the edge of the fosse.
The carpenters go on Saturday
and smiths and masons also.
These are fine people, I can tell you;
there are a good three hundred and fifty of them.
And they all go to work with good heart;
I tell you, they show good sense in this.
On Sunday the ladies go;
and in truth they do good work. . . .]

Middle English Texts

THE LAND OF COKAYGNE (early 14th century)

[The text is taken from J. A. W. Bennett and G. V. Smithers (eds), *Early Middle English Verse and Prose*, 2nd edition (Oxford: Clarendon Press, 1968), based on British Library MS Harley 913. The translation is by the present editor, who has modernized the orthography.]

Fur in see bi west Spayngne[1]
Is a lond ihote Cokaygne.[2]
Ther nis lond vnder heuenriche
Of wel, of godnis, hit iliche.
Thogh Paradis be miri and bright,
Cokaygn is of fairir sight.

1. The traditional location of Ireland, according to medieval geography.
2. The derivation of the word remains obscure. Possibly it is ultimately connected with Latin *coquere* 'to cook'. *OED* (s.v. 'Cokaigne') cites the Old French expression *trouver cocaigne*, 'to find the country where good things drop of themselves into the mouth.'

What is ther in Paradis
Bot grasse and flure and grene ris?

Thogh ther be ioi and gret dute,
Ther nis met bote frute;
Ther nis halle, bure, no bench,
Bot watir manis thurst to quench.
Beth ther no men bot two —
Hely and Enok[3] also;
Elinglich mai hi go
What ther wonith men no mo.
In Cokaigne is met and drink
Withvte care, how, and swink;
The met is trie, the drink is clere,
To none,[4] russin,[5] and sopper.
I sigge forsoth, boute were,
Ther nis lond on erthe is pere;
Vnder heuen nis lond, iwisse,
Of so mochil ioi and blisse.
Ther is mani swete sighte;
Al is dai, nis ther no nighte.
Ther nis baret nother strif,
Nis ther no deth, ac euer lif;
Ther nis lac of met no cloth,
Ther nis man no womman wroth,
Ther nis serpent, wolf, no fox,
Hors no capil, kowe no ox,
Ther nis schepe no swine no gote,
No non horwg, la, God it wote,
Nother harace nother stode —
The lond is ful of other gode.
Nis ther flei, fle, no lowse
In cloth, in toune, bed, no house;
Ther nis dunnir, slete, no hawle,
No non vile worme no snawile,
No non storme, rein, no winde.
Ther nis man no womman blinde,
Ok al is game, joi, and gle.
Wel is him that ther mai be!
Ther beth riuers gret and fine
Of oile, melk, honi, and wine;
Watir seruith ther to nothing
Bot to sight and to waiissing.
Ther is mani maner frute —
Al is solas and dedute.

Ther is a wel fair abbei[6]
Of white monkes and of grei.
Ther beth bowris and halles:
Al of pasteiis beth the walles,[7]
Of fleis, of fisse, and rich met,
The likfullist that man mai et.
Fluren cakes beth the schingles alle
Of cherch, cloister, boure, and halle.
The pinnes beth fat podinges —
Rich met to princes and kinges.
Man mai therof et inogh,
Al with right and noght with woh.
Al is commune to yung and old,
To stoute and sterne, mek and bold.
Ther is a cloister, fair and light,
Brod and lang, of sembli sight;
The pilers of that cloister alle
Beth iturned of cristale,
With har bas and capitale
Of grene jaspe and rede corale.
In the praer is a tre[8]
Swithe likful forto se:
The rote is gingeuir and galingale,
The siouns beth al sedwale,
Trie maces beth the flure,
The rind canel of swet odur,
The frute gilofre of gode smakke.
Of cucubes ther nis no lakke.
Ther beth rosis of rede ble
And lilie likful forto se;
Thai faloweth neuer dai no night.
This aght be a swet sight!
Ther beth .iiij. willis in the abbei
Of triacle, and halwei,
Of baum, and ek piement,
Euer ernend to right rent.
Of thai stremis al the molde
Stonis preciuse, and golde.
Ther is saphir and vniune,
Carbuncle and astiune,

3. Elias and Enoch were 'translated' to Paradise so that they should not experience death: see M. M. Lascelles, 'Alexander and the Earthly Paradise in Mediæval English Writings', *Medium Ævum*, V (1936), 31-46, 79-104, 173-88.
4. Literally 'the ninth hour of the day', hence 'noon', hence 'midday meal'.
5. One of several Irish words used in this manuscript (cf. *corrin* in *A Satire on the People of Dublin*, q.v.). The Irish word *roisín* (*raisín*) 'luncheon' may ultimately derive from an English word (see *The English Dialect Dictionary*, s.v. 'Rushing').
6. Identified by P. L. Henry, *Studia Hibernica*, XII (1972), 120-41, as the Cistercian monastery of Inislounaght.
7. cf. Kuno Meyer (ed.), *The Vision of MacConglinne* (London: David Nutt, 1892), p. 37, lines 6-35, for a similar passage in which buildings and natural phenomena are made of food.
8. The following lines comprise a list of attributions traditionally associated with Paradise in medieval writings: see Bennett and Smithers, pp. 338-39.

Smaragde, lugre, and prassiune,
Beril, onix, topasiune,
Ametist and crisolite,
Calcedun and epetite.
Ther beth briddes mani and fale:
Throstil, thruisse, and nightingale,
Chalandre, and wodwale,
And other briddes without tale,
That stinteth neuer bi har might
Miri to sing dai and night.

Yite I do yow mo to witte:
The gees irostid on the spitte
Fleeth to that abbi, God hit wot,
And gredith: 'Gees, al hote, al hot!'
Hi bringeth garlek, gret plente,
The best idight that man mai se.
The leuerokes, that beth cuth,
Lightith adun to manis muth
Idight in stu ful swithe wel,
Pudrid with gilofre and canel.
Nis no spech of no drink,
Ak take inogh withvte swink.
Whan the monkes gooth to masse,
Al the fenestres that beth of glasse
Turneth into cristal bright
To giue monkes more light.
Whan the masses beth iseiid
And the bokes up ileiid,
The cristal turnith into glasse
In state that hit rather wasse.

The yung monkes euch dai
Aftir met goth to plai:
Nis ther hauk no fule so swifte
Bettir fleing bi the lifte
Than the monkes, heigh of mode,
With har sleuis and har hode.
Whan the abbot seeth ham flee,
That he holt for moch glee;
Ak natheles, al theramang,
He biddith ham light to euesang.
The monkes lightith noght adun,
Ac furre fleeth in o randun.
Whan the abbot him iseeth
That is monkes fram him fleeth,
He taketh maidin of the route
And turnith vp hir white toute,
And betith the taburs with is hond
To make is monkes light to lond.
Whan is monkes that iseeth,
To the maid dun hi fleeth
And goth the wench al abute,
And thakketh al hir white toute,
And sith aftir her swinke
Wendith meklich hom to drink,
And goth to har collacione[9]
A wel fair processione.

Another abbei[10] is therbi —
Forsoth, a gret fair nunnerie,
Vp a riuer of swet milke,
Whar is gret plente of silk.
Whan the someris dai is hote,
The yung nunnes takith a bote
And doth ham forth in that riuer,
Bothe with oris and with stere.
Whan hi beth fur fram the abbei,
Hi makith ham nakid forto plei,
And lepith dune into the brimme
And doth ham sleilich forto swimme.
The yung monkes that hi seeth:
Hi doth ham vp and forth hi fleeth,
And commith to the nunnes anon,
And euch monke him taketh on,
And snellich berith forth har prei
To the mochil grei abbei,
And technith the nunnes an oreisun
With iambleue vp and dun.
The monke that wol be stalun gode
And kan set aright is hode,
He schal hab withoute danger
xij. wiues euch yere,
Al throgh right and noght throgh grace,
Forto do himsilf solace,
And thilk monke that slepith best,
And doth his likam al to rest,
Of him is hoppe, God hit wote,
To be sone uadir abbot.
Whose wl com that lond to,
Ful grete penance he mot do:
Seue yere in swineis dritte
He mote wade, wol ye iwitte,
Al anon vp to the chynne —
So he schal the lond winne.

9. The word 'collation' originally referred to the spiritual reading to which monks listened before Compline (the last hour of the Divine office). A light meal was taken at this reading. Later the word became associated with the meal itself and came to mean 'a light meal'.

10. P. L. Henry (op. cit., p. 140) suggests 'the convent of Molough on the Suir near Newcastle in Co. Tipperary, five miles south of the abbey of Inislounaght.'

Lordinges gode and hend,
Mot ye neuer of world wend
Fort ye stond to yure cheance
And fulfille that penance,
That ye mote that lond ise
And neuermore turne aye,
Prey we God so mote hit be!
Amen, pur seint charite.

[Far at sea to the west of Spain is a land called Cokaygne. There is no land under the kingdom of heaven like it in wealth or goodness. Though Paradise is fair and bright, Cokaygne is of fairer sight. What is there in Paradise but grass, flowers, and green branches? Though there is joy and great pleasure (in Paradise), there is no food except fruit; there is no hall, no bower, no bench, except water to quench a man's thirst. There are no men there but two, Elias and Enoch. Sadly may they live where no other men dwell. There is food and drink in Cokaygne, without misery, anxiety, and toil. The food is excellent, the drink is clear at the midday meal, afternoon snack, and supper. I speak the truth, without doubt; there is no land on earth its equal. Under heaven there is no land indeed that has such great joy and happiness. There is many a pleasant sight. It's always day, there is no night. There is no conflict, no dispute. There is no death, but always life. There is no lack of food or clothing. No woman or man is angry. There is no snake, wolf, or fox, horse or nag, cow or ox, sheep, pig, goat, or filth, to be sure, God knows, neither horse-breeding nor stud — the land is full of every good. No fly is there, no flea, or louse in clothing, in town, bed, or house; no thunder, sleet, hail, no repulsive worm, snail, storm, rain, or wind. No man or woman is blind, but all is pleasure, joy, and amusement. Well is he who can be there! There are great, splendid rivers of oil, milk, honey, and wine; the water is there only to look at and wash in. There is every kind of fruit — all is delight and pleasure.

There is a very handsome abbey of white and grey monks. There are bowers and halls: the walls are entirely made of pasties, flesh, fish, and excellent food, the most delightful that one can eat. All the shingles of the church, cloister, bower, and hall are made of flour. The pegs are fat sausages, rich food for princes and kings. One can eat plenty of it, all by right and not wrongfully. Everything belongs to young and old, the proud and the fierce, the meek and the bold. There is a cloister fair and bright, broad and long, a beautiful sight; the pillars of that cloister are all shaped in crystal, with their base and capital of green jasper and red coral. In the meadow is a tree, very delightful to look at: the root is ginger and galingale [an aromatic root], all the shoots are zedoary [an aromatic plant], the flowers are choice mace, the bark sweet-smelling cinnamon, the fruit strong-smelling clove. There is no lack of cubebs [a spicy berry] There are roses red in hue and lilies, a delightful sight; they never wither day or night. This must be a lovely sight! There are four wells in the abbey of healing lotion, health-tonic, balm, and also spicy, sweet wine, ever flowing for proper profit. All the earth is drenched in precious stones and gold. There is sapphire, large pearl, carbuncle, and astrion [a precious stone], emerald, ligure [a precious stone], and prasine [a green precious stone], beryl, onyx, topaz, amethyst, and chrysolite [a green gem], chalcedony [a precious stone], and epetite [a red precious stone]. There are many, many birds: song-thrush, thrush, and nightingale, lark, and woodwall [golden oriole], and other birds without number, which never cease with all their might to sing day and night.

Yet I shall let you know more: the geese, roasted on a spit, fly to that abbey, God knows, and cry: 'Geese, all hot, all hot!' They bring garlic in great supply, the best dressed that you may see. The renowned larks come down to a man's mouth, perfectly prepared in the cauldron, seasoned with clove and cinnamon. There is no talk of lack of drink — but each takes plenty, without toil. When the monks go to mass, all the glass windows turn into bright crystal to give the monks more light. When the masses have been said and the books have been put away, the crystal turns back to glass, to the state in which it was originally. Every day after eating, the young monks go out to play: no hawk or bird is as swift, nor better at flying through the air, than the high-spirited monks with their sleeves and hoods. When the abbot sees them fly, he regards it as a great source of amusement; but, nevertheless, in the midst of it all, he bids them come down to evensong. The monks do not come down, but fly further, headlong. When the abbot sees that his monks are flying away from him, he takes a girl from the company and turns up her white bottom and beats the small drums with his hand, to make the monks come down to earth. When his monks see that, they fly down to the girl and circle her, and all pat her white bottom, and afterwards, after their toil, they wend their way meekly home to drink and go to their evening snack, in a splendid procession.

Another abbey stands nearby — a very fine big nunnery, up a river of sweet milk, where there is silk in great abundance. When the summer's day is hot, the young nuns take a boat and betake themselves to that river, both with oars and rudder. When they are far from the abbey, they strip naked in order to amuse themselves and leap down into the water and skilfully begin to swim. The young monks, when they see them, jump up, fly forth, and come at once to the nuns, and each monk takes one for himself, and quickly bears forth his prey to the great grey abbey, and teaches the nuns a prayer, raising the leg up and down. The monk who wishes to be a good stallion and can put his hood at the right angle, he shall have without difficulty twelve wives each year, all by right and not through grace, in order to give himself pleasure; and the monk who sleeps best and puts his body completely to rest, for him there is hope, God knows, that he will soon be father-abbot. Whoever wants to come to that land must do great penance. Seven years in pig-dung he must wade, if you want to know, all the way up to the chin; thus he will reach that land.

Gracious, good sirs, may you never go from the world until you risk your luck and perform that penance, that you might see that land, and never turn back, let us pray to God that it might be so! In the name of holy charity, Amen.]

A SATIRE ON THE PEOPLE OF DUBLIN (early 14th century)

[The text is taken from W. Heuser's edition (Bonn, 1904, reprinted Darmstadt: Wissenschaftliche Buchgesellschaft, 1965), based on British Library MS Harley 913. The translation is by the present editor, who has modernized the orthography.]

Hail seint Michael[1] with the lange sper!
Fair beth thi winges vp thi scholder,
Thou hast a rede kirtil anon to thi fote,
Thou ert best angle that euer god makid.
This uers is ful wel iwroght,
Hit is of wel furre ybroght.

Hail seint Cristofre[2] with thi lang stake!
Thou ber ur louerd Iesus Crist ouer the brod lake,
Mani grete kunger swimmeth abute thi fete.
Hou mani hering to peni at West Chep in London?
This uers is of holi writte,
Hit com of noble witte.

Seint Mari bastard,[3] the Maudlein is sone,
To be wel iclothid wel was thi wone!
Thou berrist a box on thi hond ipeintid al of golde,
Woned thou wer to be hend, giue us sum of thi spicis.
This uers is imakid wel
Of consonans and wowel.

Hail seint Dominik[4] with thi lang staffe!
Hit is at thi ouir end crokid as a gaffe;
Thou berrist a bok on thi bak, ich wen hit is a bible
Thogh thou be a gode clerk, be thou noght to heigh
Trie rime la, god hit wote;
Soch an othir an erthe i note.

Hail seint Franceis[5] with thi mani foulis,
Kites and crowis, reuenes and oules,
Fure and XX[ti] wildges and a poucok!
Mani bold begger siwith thi route.
This uers is ful wel isette,
Swithe furre hit was ivette.

Hail be ye freris with the white copis![6]
Ye habbith a hus at Drochda,[7] war men makith ropis
Euir ye beth roilend the londis al aboute;
Of the watir daissers ye robbith ye churchis.
Maister he was swithe gode,
That this sentence vnderstode.

Hail be ye gilmins with yur blake gunes!
Ye leuith the wildirnis and fillith the tunis,
Menur with oute and prechur with inne;
Yur abite is of gadering, that is mochil schame.
Sleilich is this uers iseid,
Hit wer harme adun ileiid.

Hail ye holi monkes with yur corrin,[8]
Late and rathe ifillid of ale and wine!
Depe cun ye bouse, that is al yure care,
With seint Benet[9] is scurge lome ye disciplineth.
Taketh hed al to me!
That this is sleche, ye mow wel se.

1. Saint Michael the Archangel, regarded as the champion of the church and its members against the assaults of the devil, as the angel who conducted the souls of the dead, and as the patron of the sick.
2. Saint Christopher, patron of travellers. One of the travellers whom he carried across a river was a small child (i.e. Christ) who caused him to bow beneath its weight.
3. None of the canonical hagiographies refers to a son, bastard or otherwise. This might be an idiomatic accretion to received tradition, possibly with a historical referent in mind. We do not know who this person might be.
4. Saint Dominic (1170-1221), founder of the Order of Preachers, otherwise known as the Black Friars or Dominicans.
5. Saint Francis of Assisi (1181/2-1226), founder of the Order of Friars Minor which, together with the Order of Preachers, formed the largest group of mendicant friars ('beggars', since they subsisted by begging) and attracted a great deal of criticism: see Penn R. Szittya, *The Antifraternal Tradition in Medieval Literature* (Princeton, New Jersey: Princeton University Press, 1986).
6. The Carmelite friars (founded *c.* mid-twelfth century) wore a white mantle (whence 'White Friars') over their tunic, which was brown.
7. Drogheda, Co. Louth, was one of the most important English towns in Ireland during the Middle Ages. Some fragments of the Carmelite friary still survive there.
8. *Cuirin* 'pot, can', one of several Irish words found in MS Harley 913 (cf. *russin* in *The Land of Cokaygne*) that corroborate the Irish provenance of the manuscript.
9. Saint Benedict (480-543) founded the monastery at Monte Cassino in 529 for whose monks he wrote his Rule, which was subsequently adopted by all Western monks.

Hail be ye nonnes of seint Mari house,[10]
Goddes bourmaidnes and his owen spouse!
Ofte mistredith ye yur schone, yur fete beth ful
tendre:
Datheit the sotter that tawith yur lethir!
Swithe wel ye vnderstode,
That makid this ditee so gode.

Hail be ye prestis with yur brode bokes!
Thogth yur crune be ischaue,[11] fair beth yur crokes.
Yow and other lewidmen deleth bot ahouue;
Whan ye delith holibrede, yiue me botte a litil
Sikirlich he was a clerk,
That wrochete this craftilich werke.

Hail be ye marchans with yur gret packes
Of draperie, auoir depeise, and yur wol sackes,
Gold, siluer, stones, riche markes and ek pundes!
Litil yiue ye ther of to wrech pouer.
Sleigh he was and ful of witte,
That this lore put in writte.

Hail be ye tailurs with yur scharpe schores!
To mak wronge hodes, ye kittith lome gores.
Agens midwinter hote beth yur neldes;
Thogh yur semes semith fair, hi lestith litil while.
The clerk that this baston wrowghte,
Wel he woke and slepe righte nowghte.

Hail be ye sutters with your mani lestes,
With your blote hides of selcuth bestis,
And trobles and treisuses, bochevampe and alles.
Blak and lothlich beth yur teth, hori was that route.
Nis this bastun wel ipighte?
Euch word him sitte arighte.

Hail be ye skinners with yure drenche kiue!
Who so smillith therto, wo is him aliue,
Whan that hit thonnerith, ye mote ther in schite.
Datheit yur curteisie, ye stinketh al the strete,
Worth hit wer, that he wer king
That ditid this trie thing.

Hail be ye potters with yur bole ax!
Fair beth yur barmhatres, yolow beth yur fax,
Ye stondith at the schamil, brod ferlich bernes;
Fleiis yow folowithe, ye swolowith ynow.
The best clerk of al this tun
Craftfullich makid this bastun.

Hail be ye bakers with yur louis smale
Of white bred and of balke, ful mani and fale!
Ye pincheth on the right white ayens goddes law,
To the fair pillori, ich rede, ye tak hede.
This uers is iwrowghte so welle,
That no tung iwis mai telle.

Hail be ye brewesters with yur galuns,
Potels and quartes ouer al the tounes.
Yur thowmes berrith moch awai, schame hab the
gyle;
Beth iwar of the coking-stole,[12] the lak is dep and hori.
Sikerlich he was a clerk
That so sleilich wroghte this werk.

Hail be ye hokesters dun bi the lake,
With candles and golokes and the pottes blak,
Tripis and kine fete and schepen heuedes!
With the hori tromcheri hori is yure inne!
He is sori of his lif,
That is fast to such a wif.

Fi a debles, kaites, that kemith the wolle,
Al the schindes of the tronn an heigh opon yur sculle.
Ye makid me soch a goshorne ouer al the wowes;
Ther for ich makid on of you sit opon a hechil.[13]
He was a noble clerk and gode,
That this dep lore vnderstode.

Makith glad, mi frendis, ye sittith to long stille,
Spekith now and gladieth and drinketh al yur fille!
Ye habbeth ihird of men lif that wonith in lond;
Drinkith dep and makith glade, ne hab ye non
other nede
This song is yseid of me,
Euer iblessid mot ye be.

[Hail Saint Michael with the long spear!
Fair are thy wings on thy shoulder,
Thou hast a red tunic down to thy feet.
Thou art the best angel that God ever made.
This verse is very well wrought.
It is brought from very far.

10. Many nunneries, including all Cistercian Houses, were dedicated to the Virgin Mary, and so it is impossible to determine which order the poet had in mind here.

11. The tonsure was prescribed by canon law for all clerics as a sign of the clerical state and symbolizes Christ's crown of thorns.

12. The cucking-stool was an instrument of punishment; it consisted of a chair in which transgressors were ducked in a pond or river.

13. A steel flax-comb.

Hail Saint Christopher with thy long stake!
Thou bearest Our Lord Jesus Christ over the broad lake.
Many great congers swim about thy feet.
How many herrings for a penny at West Cheap in London?
This verse is of Holy Writ.
It comes of noble wit.

Saint Mary's bastard, Magdalen's son!
To be well clothed was thy custom.
Thou bearest a box in thy hand, painted all of gold.
Thou wert wont to be gracious, give us some of thy spices.
This verse is well constructed
Of consonants and vowels.

Hail Saint Dominic with thy long staff!
It is at the top end crooked like a fish-hook.
Thou bearest a book on thy back, I think it is a bible.
Though thou art a good cleric, thou should not be so proud.
Lo, a choice rhyme, God knows!
I know of none such other on earth.

Hail Saint Francis with thy many birds,
Kites and crows, ravens and owls,
Four and twenty wild geese and a peacock!
Many a bold beggar follows thy company.
This verse is well constructed.
From very far it was fetched.

Hail be ye friars with the white copes!
Ye have a house at Drogheda, where ropes are made.
Ever are ye roving all about the lands.
Ye rob the churches of the holy-water sprinklers.
He was a very good master
Who understood the meaning of this.

Hail be ye chatterers with your black gowns!
Ye leave the wilderness and fill the towns,
Minor within, and preacher without;
Your habit is gathering together, that is a great shame.
Cunningly is this verse said.
It would be a shame if it were laid aside.

Hail ye holy monks with your can,
Late and early filled with ale and wine!
Deep can ye booze, that is all your care.
With Saint Benedict's scourge often ye are disciplined.
Take ye all heed of me!
That this is cunningly made, ye may well see.

Hail be ye nuns of Saint Mary's House,
God's bower-maidens and His own spouse!
Often ye tread your shoes crookedly — your feet are very tender:
May misfortune befall the cobbler who tans your leather!
He understood ye very well
Who made this splendid ditty.

Hail be ye priests with your broad books!
Though your crowns are shaven, fair are your crooks.
Ye and other laymen give but a hood;
When ye deal holy bread, give me but a little.
Certainly he was a scholar
Who wrought this skilful work.

Hail be ye merchants with your great packs
Of drapery, avoir-dupois, and your wool-sacks,
Gold, silver, stones, rich marks and also pounds!
Little of it do ye give to the wretched poor.
Cunning he was and full of intelligence
Who set down this precept in writing.

Hail be ye tailors with your sharp shears!
To make bad hoods ye cut many gores.
Against midwinter, hot be your needles;
Though your seams appear fair, they last a short while.
The scholar who wrought this stanza,
Well he stayed awake and did not sleep at all.

Hail be ye cobblers with your many lasts,
With your dried supple hides of various beasts,
And waste leather and worn pieces of leather, patched fronts of boots and awls.
Black and filthy are your teeth, dirty was that company.
Isn't this a well-constructed stanza?
Each word is in its right place.

Hail be ye skinners with your drenching-vat!
Whoever sniffs in it, woe is him as he goes about his daily business.
When it thunders, ye might shit yourself during it.
Woe to your courtesy, ye stink all the street.
It would be a worthy thing if he were a king
Who prepared this choice piece.

Hail be ye butchers with your pole-ax!
Fair be your aprons, yellow is your hair.
Ye stand at the meat-block, thick-set strong fellows.
Flies follow you, ye swallow plenty of them.
The best scholar of all this town
Skilfully made this stanza.

Hail be ye bakers with your small loaves
Of white and black bread, many many of them!
You give short weight, against God's law.
I advise ye to take heed of the fair pillory.
This verse is so well constructed
That certainly no tongue may describe it.

Hail be ye brewers with your gallons,
Pottles and quarts, all over the place.

Your thumbs bear much away, shame on your deceit.
Beware of the cucking-stool, the lake is deep and dirty.
Certainly he was a scholar
Who so cunningly made this work.

Hail be ye hucksters down by the lake,
With candles and tubs and black pots,
Tripe and cows' feet and sheeps' heads!
Your inn is fitting for your foul treachery.
He is sorry of his life
Who is bound to such a wife.

Fie in the devil's name, wretches, who comb the wool,
With all the bits of wool on the top of your heads.
Ye made me such a fool everywhere;
Therefore I made one of you sit on a hackle.
He was a noble, good scholar
Who understood this profound doctrine.

Make merry, my friends, ye are sitting still too long.
Speak now and be glad and drink your fill.
Ye have heard of the life of men who live in this land.
Drink deep and make merry, ye have no other obligation.
I have recited this song,
So that ye may always be blessed.]

THE PRIDE OF LIFE
(first half of 15th century)

[The extract is taken from Norman Davis's edition (in *Non-Cycle Plays and Fragments*, Early English Text Society, Supplementary Text No. 1, 1970), based on earlier printed editions, since the original manuscript was destroyed in the Four Courts building in Dublin in 1922. The orthography has been modernized.]

REX. Al in wel ic am biwent,
May no grisful thing me grou;
Likyng is wyt me bilent,
Alyng is it mi behou.

Strent and Hel, knytis kete,
Douti, derrist in ded,
Lok that for no thing ye let
Smartli to me sped.

Bringit wyt you brit brondis,
Helmis brit and schen;
For ic am lord ofir al londis
And that is uel isen.

PRIMUS MILES, FORTITUDO. Lord,
in truthe thou mit trist
Fethfuli to stond,
Thou mit liu as the list,
For wonschildis thu fond.

Ic am Strent, stif and strong,
Neuar is suc non,
In al this world brod and long,
Imad of blod and bon.

Hau no dout of no thing
That euir may befal;
Ic am Streynt thi derling
Flour of knitis al.

SECUNDUS MILES, SANITAS. King of
Lif, that berist the croun,
As hit is skil and righte,
I am Hele icom to toun,
Thi kinde curteyse knighte.

Thou art lord of lim and life,
And king withouten ende;
Stif and strong and sterne in strif,
In londe qwher thou wende.

Thou nast no nede to sike sore
For no thing on lyue;
Thou schal lyue euermore:
Qwho dar with the striue?

REX. Striue? Nay, to me qwho is so gode?
Hit were bot folye;
Ther is no man that me dur bode
Any vileynye.

Qwherof schuld I drede
Qwhen I am King of Life?
Ful evil schuld he spede
To me that wroght striue.

I schal lyue evermo
And croun ber as kinge;
I ne may neuer wit of wo,
I lyue at my likinge.

REGINA. Sire, thou saist as the liste,
Thou liuist at thi wille;
Bot somthing thou miste,
And therfor hold the stille.

Thinke, thou haddist beginninge
Qwhen thou were ibore;

And bot thou mak god endinge
  Thi sowle is forlore.

Loue God and Holy Chirche,
  And haue of him some eye;
Fonde his werkis for to wirch
  And thinke that thou schal deye.

REX. Douce dam, qwhi seistou so?
  Thou spekis noght as the sleye.
I schal lyue euermo
  For bothe two thin eye.

Woldistou that I were dede
  That thou might haue a new?
Hore, the deuil gird of thi hede
  Bot that worde schal the rewe!

REGINA. Dede, sire? Nay, God wote my wil,
  That ne kepte I noghte;
Hit wolde like me full ille
  Were hit thareto broghte.

Yet thogh thou be kinge
  Nede schalt haue ende;
Deth ouercomith al thinge
  Hou-so-euer we wende.

REX. Ye, dam, thou hast wordis fale,
  Hit comith the of kinde;
This nis bot women tale,
  And that I wol the finde.

I ne schal neuer deye
  For I am King of Life;
Deth is vndir myne eye
  And therfor leue thi strife.

Thou dost bot mak myn hert sore,
  For hit nel noght helpe;
I prey the spek of him no more.
  Qwhat wolte of him yelpe?

REGINA. Yilpe, sire? Ney, so mot I the;
  I sigge hit noght therfore,
Bot kinde techith bothe the and me,
  First qwhen we were bore,

For dowte of Dethis maistri,
  To wepe and make sorowe;
Holy writ and prophecye
  Therof I take to borowe.

Therefor, qwhile ye have mighte
  And the worlde at wille,
I rede ye serue God Almighte
  Bothe loude and stille.

This world is bot fantasye
  And ful of trechurye;
God sire, for youre curteysye
  Take this for no folye.

For, God wot the sothe,
  I ne sey hit for no fabil;
Deth wol smyte to the,
  In feith loke thou be stabil.

REX. Qwhat prechistou of Dethis might
  And of his maistrye?
He ne durst onis with me fight
  For his bothe eye.

Streinth and Hele, qwhat say the,
  My kinde korin knightis?
Schal Deth be lord ouer me
  And reue me of mightis?

I MILES. Mi lord, so brouke I my bronde,
  God that me forbede
That Deth schold do the wronge
  Qwhile I am in thi thede.

I wol withstonde him with strife
  And make his sidis blede,
And tel him that thou art King of Life
  And lorde of londe and lede.

II MILES. May I him onis mete
  With this longe launce,
In felde other in strete,
  I wol him giue mischaunce.

REX. Ye, thes be knightis of curteisye
  And doghti men of dede;
Of Deth ne of his maistrie
  Ne have I no drede.

Qwher is Mirth my messager,
  Swifte so lefe on lynde?
He is a nobil bachelere
  That rennis bi the wynde.

Mirth and solas he can make
  And ren so the ro;

Lightly lepe oure the lake
  Qwher-so-euer he go.

Com and her my talente
  Anone and hy the blyue:
Qwher any man, as thou hast wente,
  Dorst with me to striue?

NUNCIUS. King of Lif and lord of londe,
  As thou sittis on thi se
And florresschist with thi bright bronde,
  To the I sit on kne.

I am Mirth, wel thou wost,
  Thi mery messagere;
That wostou wel, withoute bost
  Ther nas neuer my pere

Doghtely to done a dede
  That ye haue for to done,
Hen to Berewik opon Twede[1]
  And com ogein ful sone;

Ther is nothing the iliche
  In al this worlde wide;
Of gold and siluer and robis riche
  And hei hors on to ryde.

I haue ben bothe fer and nere
  In bataile and in strife;
Ocke ther was neuer thy pere,
  For thou art King of Life.

REX. Aha! Solas, now thou seist so,
  Thou miriest me in my mode;
Thou schal, boy, ar thou hennis go
  Be auaunsyd, bi the rode.

Thou schal haue for thi gode wil
  To thin auauncemente,
The castel of Gailispire on the Hil,[2]
  And the erldom of Kente.

Draw the cord, Sire Streynth,
  Rest I wol now take;
On erth in brede ne leynth
  Ne was nere yet my make.

1. Berwick-on-Tweed, a town on the north-east coast of England in Northumberland.
2. An unidentified location.

[KING: I live in complete prosperity, nothing terrible may frighten me; pleasure has come to me, in every way it is to my benefit.

Strength and Health, brave knights, valiant, fierce in deed, see to it that nothing stops you from hastening quickly to me.

Bring with you bright swords, and shining beautiful helmets, for I am lord over all lands, and that is perfectly clear.

FIRST SOLDIER, STRENGTH: Lord, assuredly you must trust in standing firmly. You may live as you please, for you have found defenders of your dwelling.

I am Strength, firm and strong; never was such a one in all the length and breadth of this world made of blood and bone.

Have no fear of anything that may ever happen. I am Strength your favourite, flower of all knights.

SECOND SOLDIER, HEALTH: King of Life, who bears the crown, as is proper and right, I am Health come to town, your gracious, courteous knight.

You are lord of limb and life, and everlasting king; firm and strong and grim in dispute, wherever you go in the land.

You have no need to sigh sorrowfully for anything in this world. You shall live for ever. Who dares compete with you?

KING: Compete? No, who is as good as me? It would be madness. No man dares threaten me with any insult.

What should I dread, since I am King of Life? Very badly would he succeed who opposed me.

I shall live for ever, and bear the king's crown. I shall never know grief. I live at my pleasure.

QUEEN: Sir, you say as you please. You live as you wish; but something you omit — therefore, keep yourself quiet.

Think, you had a beginning, when you were born and, unless you make a good end, your soul is lost.

Love God and Holy Church, and hold Him in awe; try to do His works, and think that you will die.

KING: Sweet lady, why do you speak thus? You are not speaking like the wise man. I shall live for ever, in spite of both your two eyes.

Would you like me to be dead, so that you could have a new husband? Whore, may the devil strike off your head, unless you regret that word.

QUEEN: 'Dead', sir? No, God knows what I wish. I would not wish that; it would please me very badly if it came to that.

Yet, though you are king, there must of necessity be an end. Death overcomes everything, however we go.

KING: Yes, lady, you speak false. It comes from your nature. This is only women's talk, and I will show you that.

I shall never die, for I am King of Life. Death is in awe of me, and therefore give up your quarrelling.

You make my heart sore, for it will not help. I pray you speak of him no more. Why do you speak favourably of him?

QUEEN: 'Speak favourably of him'? No, so may I thrive. I don't speak for that reason, but Nature teaches both you and me, from the time that we were born,

For fear of Death's power, to weep and grieve. Holy Scripture and Prophecy I call to witness.

Therefore, while you have strength and the world under your control, I advise you to serve Almighty God in all circumstances.

This world is but a delusion, and full of treachery. Good sir, in your courtesy, do not regard this as foolish.

For, God knows the truth; I do not say it to lie. Death will strike at you. See to it that you stand firm in faith.

KING: Why do you preach about Death's strength and his power? He doesn't dare even once fight with me, in spite of his eyes.

Strength and Health, what do you say, my gracious, excellent knights? Shall Death be lord over me and deprive me of my power?

FIRST SOLDIER: My Lord, as I may use my sword, God forbid that Death shall do you wrong while I am in your country.

I will withstand him in conflict and make his sides bleed, and tell him that you are King of Life, and lord of land and people.

SECOND SOLDIER: If I once meet him with this long lance, anywhere, I will defeat him.

KING: Yes, these are courteous knights and men valiant in deed; I have no fear of Death or of his power.

Where is Mirth my messenger, swift as the leaf on the linden tree? He is a noble young knight, who runs like the wind.

He can make mirth and pleasure and run like the roe, lightly leaping over the stream, where he goes.

Come and hear my purpose at once and hurry, and tell me did any man on your travels dare strive with me.

MESSENGER: King of Life and lord of this land, as you sit on your horse and brandish your bright sword, to you I kneel.

I am Mirth, as well you know, your joyous messenger; you know well, without boasting, that there never was my equal

To bravely do a deed that you need to have done, from here to Berwick-on-Tweed, and come back at once.

There is nothing like you in all this wide world. With gold and silver and splendid robes and a noble horse to ride.

I have been both far and near in battle and in strife; but there was never your equal, for you are King of Life.

KING: Ah, Joy, now you say so, you make me happy in my mind. You shall, knave, before you go, be promoted, by the Cross.

You shall have at your disposal, for your promotion, the castle at Gailispire on the Hill, and the Earldom of Kent.

Draw the cord, Sir Strength, I will now take my rest. Throughout the breadth and length of the earth, there never was my match.]

from: THE GOUERNAUNCE OF PRYNCES (*c.*1423)

[This extract forms Chapter 32 of James Yonge's translation, and is taken from Robert Steele's edition (Early English Text Society, Extra Series No. 74, 1898), which is based on MS Rawlinson B 490. In the interests of clarity, Steele's punctuation has been modernized here, and new paragraphing introduced.]

Of the Kynges titles to the land of Irland, aftyr the Cronyclis. Capitulum xxxiij.

Fryste[1] atte the begynnynge, afor[2] the comynge of Iryshemen into the londe, they weryn dwellynge in a syde of Spayne whyche is callid Basco,[3] of the whyche Basco, Bayon[4] is the chefe cite, and Basco a membyr of hit.[5] And atte Yryshmen comynge into Irland, Kynge Gurgonynce,[6] son to the nobil Kynge Belynge, and Kynge of Britane the More, whych now is callid England, was Lorde of Bayon as oure kynge[7] now is. And therfor thay sholde be his men, and Irland his land.

The Seconde Tytle is this: atte the same tyme that Yryshmen came out of Basco in Sixti Shippes exilit,[8] thay mete wyth Kynge Gurgnynce vp[9] the see at the Ile of Orcades,[10] atte his comynge fro Denemarke with grete victorie. Than[11] har[12] Captaynes Hyberus[13] and Herymon[14] wenten to this kynge, and hym tolde[15] the cause of har comynge, and hym prayed with grete instaunce,[16] that he wolde[17] graunt ham that thay myght enhabite some lande in the Weste. Atte the laste the kynge, by avyce of his Consaille,[18] graunted ham[19]

1. first. This section is based on Giraldus Cambrensis, *Topographia Hiberniae*: see J.J. O'Meara (ed.), *The Topography of Ireland* ... (Dundalk, 1951).
2. before.
3. Basclonia (Basque country).
4. Bayonne (on the boundary of Gascony).
5. it.
6. Gurguintius, king of the Britons.
7. Henry VI, king of England 1422-61, 1470-71.
8. exiled.
9. on.
10. Orkney Islands.
11. Then.
12. their.
13. Éber.
14. Éremón.
15. told him.
16. urgency.
17. would.
18. by the advice of his Counsel.
19. them.

Irland to enhabite, and assygned ham gides[20] for the see thedyrwarde.[21] And therfor they sholde ben[22] our kynges men.

The Thyrde Title is, as I haue afor declarid, that Dermot,[23] sumtyme Prynce of Leynestere,[24] in Normandy became lege man[25] to Kynge Henry the Seconde, conqueroure of Irland. Wherthrogh[26] he broght pouer of pepill aforsaydyn[27] into the land, and mariet[28] his eldyst doghtyr Eue at Watyrford to Syr Richard fiz Gilbert, Erle of Sragnylle[29] in Walis, and hym graunted the reuersione[30] of Laynestere wyth Eue his doghtyr. Aftyr that the Erle graunted to his Kynge Henry Deuelyn,[31] wyth two candredes[32] nexte to Deuelyn, and al the havyn tounes[33] of Laynestre, to haue that othyr parte in pees, and the kynges good lordshup.[34] And therfor McMurgh[35] hath leste[36] ryght to haue lordshup of al othyr Irysh Captaynes, and oure kynge in especial haue good ryght to Laynystre. Hitte is to witte,[37] that a 'candrede' in Frensh and in Irysh is a porcion of grovnde that may contene an hundrid villachis.[38] In England suche a 'candrede' is y-callit an hundret othyr a wepyn-tale.[39] A 'wepyntaille' is as myche[40] to say as a takynge of wepen,[41] ffor in olde tyme in England, atte the fryst comynge of a newe lorde into an hundret, the tenantes of the same hundrede sholde delyuer to har lorde har wepyn as for har homage.[42]

The iiij^e[43] Title of ryght that oure kynge hath to Irland is, that sethyn[44] in the yere of Oure Lorde M^l. C. and lx^ti, ij,[45] the forsayd Kynge Henry landed atte Watyrforde, and there came to hym Dermot,[46] Kynge of Corke, and of his owyn propyr wille[47] became liege trybutarie[48] for hym and for his kyngedome, and on this he makyd his serement[49] and yawe[50] his hostagis to the kynge. Than the kynge rode to Casshell,[51] and ther came to hym Doneuald,[52] Kynge of Lymerike, and be-came lyege man as did the Kynge of Corke. Than came to hym Dunewalde,[53] Kynge of Ossori, and McSaghlyn,[54] Kynge of Ofaly, and al the prynces of the Southe of Irland, and be-came lege men as is aforsayd. Than wente Kynge Henry to Dyuelyne,[55] and ther came O'Kernel,[56] Kynge of Vriel, O'Rorike,[57] Kynge of Mythe, and Rothorike,[58] Kynge of al Iryshmen of the londe, and of Connaght,[59] with al the princes and men of value[60] of the lande, wythout-take the pepill of Vllystere,[61] and by-came lyeges and subiectes tributarijs[62] by grete othis for ham and hare kyngedomes and lordshuppes[63] to the forsayd Kynge Henry, and that by hare owyn good wille as hit semyth wel,[64] for the cronycles makyth no mencion of no chyualry ne werre[65] done by the kynge al the tyme that he in Irland was.

20. guides.
21. thither.
22. should be.
23. Diarmait Mac Murchada (Dermot Mac Murrough). For Dermot's journey to seek the help of Henry II, see *The Song of Dermot and the Earl* (p. 149).
24. Leinster, one of the four provinces of Ireland.
25. sworn vassal, faithful follower.
26. by which.
27. the army of men referred to earlier.
28. married. For the betrothal of Aífe (Eva) to Richard fitz Gilbert de Clare ('Strongbow'), earl of Pembroke (lord of Strigoil), see *The Song of Dermot and the Earl.*
29. Strigoil.
30. right of succession.
31. granted Dublin to his King Henry; *Deuelyn* = Dublin.
32. A 'cantred' was a hundred (= a district originally containing a hundred townships: see *OED* s.v. 'Cantred').
33. ports.
34. lordship.
35. Mac Murchada (Mac Murrough).
36. least.
37. it is to be known.
38. contain a hundred villages.
39. called a hundred or a wapentake (= a division of a shire).
40. much.
41. weapons.
42. had to deliver to their lord their weapons as a token of their homage.
43. fourth.
44. since.
45. 1162 (i.e. 1171).
46. Diarmait Mór Mac Carthaig (Mac Carthy), king of Thomond, who was killed by Theobald Walter after 25 April 1185; submitted to Henry in October 1171.
47. by his own volition.
48. vassal paying tribute.
49. oath.
50. gave.
51. Cashel, Co. Tipperary, one of the most important political and ecclesiastical towns in Munster; in medieval times it was the ecclesiastical capital of the province.
52. Domnall Mór Ua Briain (O'Brien), king of Thomond, who submitted to Henry near Cashel in October 1171, and died in 1194.
53. Domnall Mac Gilla Pátraic, king of Osraige, who died in 1185.
54. Probably Máel Sechlainn Mac Fáeláin, king of Uí Fáeláin (north Kildare).
55. Henry went to Dublin on 11 November 1171.
56. Probably should read O'Kerrel: Murchad Ua Cerbaill, king of Airgialla, who died in religious retirement at Mellifont Abbey, Co. Louth, in 1189; submitted to Henry at Dublin on 11 November 1171.
57. Tigernán Ua Ruairc (Tiernan O'Rourke), king of Meath, who submitted to Henry at Dublin on 11 November 1171 and was killed at Tlachta (Hill of Ward), Co. Meath in May 1172.
58. Rothericus, i.e., Ruaidrí Ua Conchobair (Rory O'Connor), king of Ireland, who submitted to Henry at Dublin on 11 November 1171, and died on 2 December 1198.
59. Connaught, one of the four provinces of Ireland.
60. men of rank.
61. except the people of Ulster.
62. vassals and subjects paying tribute.
63. by great oaths for them and their kingdoms and lordships.
64. and they did so of their own free will, as seems clear.
65. knightly engagements or war.

The Ve Title is this: the Pope Adriane,[66] for-asmoche as Irland is an ile, and hit and al othyr iles Cristiens to the ryght of Seynte Petyr and the Churche o Rome appartenyth,[67] he grantid the Lordshupe of Irland to the forsayde Kynge Henry, to encresse therin Crystyn feyth and holynesse, and to sette the pepill of the londe in gouernaunce of good lawes and vertues, vices to enchu.[68] This yfte and graunt of Pope Adriane Pope Alexandyr his successoure confermyd.[69] This Titles of ryght oppynly apperyth by the same popis bullys, the copyes of whych bene ryued ynow.[70] Sethyn[71] came Vyuyen,[72] a legate fro the pope, into Irland and assemblid atte Deuelyne al the clergi of the land atte a consaill, atte the whyche consaill this legate declarid and affermyd to the clergy the kynges ryght to be good to Irlande, and comandid and also denunced[73] al the pepill of Irland, on the payne of cursynge,[74] that no man sholde presume folyche[75] to departe fro the liegeaunce[76] and the fayth of the Kynge of England.

The Sixte Title is, that assemblid atte Ardmagh[77] the clergi of al the land atte the tyme of the conqueste vp[78] the comynge of Englyssh-men, by the same consaill[79] hit was decrewite and demet,[80] that throght[81] the synne of the pepill of the londe, by the sentence of God, the myschefis[82] of the Conquest ham befelle.[83]

The vij^{e}[84] Title is, for atte the fryste comynge and beynge[85] of Kynge Richard the Seconde[86] in Irland atte the Cite of Deuelyne, and othyr places of the londe, there come to hym wyth hare owyn goodwille,[87] O'Nelle,[88] Captayne of Iryshemen of Vluestere, O'Bren of Thomond,[89] O'Conghoure of Connaght,[90] Arthure McMurgh,[91] Captayne of Iryshmen in Laynystere, and al othyr grete capitaynes of Iryshmen of Irland, and be-came liege man to the same Kynge Richard, and to hym did homage liege.[92] And for more grettyr surte[93] thay bounde ham in grete somes by dyvers instrumentes[94] to pay to the Popys Chamer,[95] to trewely kepe and holde hare legeaunce[96] in the fourme[97] aforsayde.

There-for, fro the begynnynge to the end, good is oure kynges ryght to the Lordshupe of Irland. And therfor hold thei ham still for shame, that thereof the contrary sayne.[98]

66. Adrian IV, born Nicholas Breakspear, the only English pope, who authorized Henry II to come to Ireland, in the bull *Laudabiliter* (1155), to rid the land of corruption. The authorizing document has been dismissed as a forgery by some scholars, but see *A New History of Ireland* II (Oxford: Clarendon Press, 1987), pp. 57n-58n.
67. it (i.e., Ireland) and all other Christian islands belong to the dispensation of Saint Peter and the Church of Rome. The Holy See claimed extensive secular powers by right of the so-called 'Donation of Constantine', a forged document (probably eighth-century), which professed to be an act of the Emperor Constantine the Great surrendering his temporal power over the western provinces of the empire to the pope.
68. to submit the people of the land to the control of good laws and virtues, and to avoid vices.
69. This gift and grant of Pope Adrian was confirmed by his successor Pope Alexander (Alexander III, 1159-81).
70. These titles clearly seem to be legitimate from the same pope's bulls, copies of which are badly torn.
71. afterwards.
72. Cardinal Vivian, papal legate, presides over synod (*consaill*) at Dublin.
73. ordered.
74. punishment of excommunication.
75. foolishly.
76. allegiance.
77. Armagh, the leading city of Christian Ireland.
78. upon, with.
79. *synod.*
80. decided and ordained.
81. because of.
82. misfortunes.
83. befell them.
84. seventh.
85. presence.
86. Richard II came twice to Ireland, in 1394 and 1399.
87. of their own good will.
88. Niall Mór Ó Néill (king of Tir Eoghain 1364-97) submitted to Richard at Drogheda on 19-20 January 1395, in the Dominican House.
89. Brian Sreamhach Ó Briain (king of Thomond 1369-1400) submitted to Richard at Dundalk on 6 March 1395.
90. There were two rival kings of Connaught at this time. The person in question was either Toirdhealbhach Ruadh Ó Conchobhair (1384-1425/6) or Toirdhealbhac Óg Ó Conchobhair Donn (1384-1406).
91. Art Mór Mac Murchada (king of Leinster 1375-1417) submitted to the earl of Nottingham at Carlow on 16 February 1395.
92. rendered homage as vassals.
93. as a stronger guarantee.
94. bound themselves with great sums of money by various legal documents.
95. chamber.
96. their allegiance.
97. form.
98. let those who say the opposite about this stay quiet out of shame.

Latin Texts

THE *ITINERARIUM* OF SYMON SIMEONIS (first half of 14th century)

[The extract comprises the last seven sections of the *Itinerarium*, which describe his impressions of the city of Jerusalem. The text and translation are taken from Mario Esposito's edition (Dublin: Dublin Institute for

Advanced Studies, 1960) of the sole surviving manuscript (dated 1335-52), now MS 407 in the library of Corpus Christi College, Cambridge.]

Hic autem est sciendum quod ipsa civitas[1] olim fuit sita pro majori parte in Monte Syon; qui mons, licet non sit magnus, tamen est fortissimus et signanter in parte australi, et supereminens civitati; et circumdatus valle Josaphath pro magna parte, sic quod ubi exspirat vallis ibi fuerunt fossata amplissima et profundissima in rupibus cavata, quorum vestigia usque hodie ibidem apparent et ipsius civitatis firmitatem et fortitudinem luculenter demonstrant. Hic autem mons se extendit in longum ad austrum et ad aquilonem. In cujus parte australi ubi exspirat fortitudo vallis, fuit ad tutamentum et defensionem ipsius edificata illa turris famosissima et imperialissima David, que nunc est reedificata per Saracenos et [est] fortalissimum Soldani, et distat oblique ab ecclesia in qua est Sepulcrum gloriosum Domini fere quantum est unius sagitte tractus.

Ad cujus partem aquilonarem immediate est quedam porta per quam intrantes civitatem, intravimus et venimus ad ecclesiam predictam laudantes et benedicentes Dominum, qui nos ibidem suo pretioso sanguine redemit. Ipsa vero ecclesia magna est et pulcra, cujus navis spherice figure facta [est] ex toto ad instar columbaris, hoc excepto quod est sita super columpnas et habet in circuitu deambulatorium. In cujus centro est quedam capella parva marmorea in qua est Sepulcrum Domini gloriosum, quod habet in longitudine tantum ix palmas[2] et est coopertum in toto lapide albo marmoreo sic quod nullubi potest tangi nec videri nisi per tria foramina parva, que sunt in ipsius parte australi. Exterius autem in parte aquilonari ipsius, que est contigua muro ipsius capelle, est quedam lampas, que semper accenditur per unum calogerum[3] sive monachum Cumanum, qui semper cum uno socio [ibi] moratur. Et ex ipsius opposito, in parte australi, est quedam lampas infra capellam prefatam, que omni sabbato sancto, igne desuper misso, infallibiliter accenditur ad gloriam Christi viventis et resurgentis in secula seculorum, amen. Porte vero ipsius ecclesie in parte australi sunt, quarum orientalior est clausa muro lapideo. Ex quarum opposito extra est locus quadrus pulcherrimus, lapide albo totaliter pavimentatus, circa cujus medium est locus ubi Dominus noster afflictus pro nobis requiescebat dum crux in monte portabatur.

Ex parte orientali ipsarum portarum infra ecclesiam ipsam est Mons Calvarie, ad cujus summitatem ubi est foramen rotundum in quo fuit crux Christi fixa, sunt xviii gradus, et de gradu superiori usque ad ipsum foramen sunt x pedes, ad quod videtur de sanguine Domini per montis fissuras cucurrisse. Ex parte vero australi ipsius foraminis apparet manifestissime qualiter in Christi passione erat fissa a summitate equaliter usque deorsum ubi fuit inventum caput Ade, ut dicitur, et juxta illam fissuram quasi immediate est altare devote consecratum. De pede autem predictorum graduum versus orientem usque ad portam ecclesie subterranee, per quam descenditur ad locum ubi Helena, Constantini mater,[4] invenit lignum crucis, sunt xi passus. Et de porta ipsa usque ad primum gradum sunt vii pedes, et postea sunt xxix gradus per quos descenditur. Ad quorum pedem est ecclesia gratiosa, que fabricata est super quatuor columpnas marmoreas, in qua ad orientem est unum solempne altare, et aliud altare quod est ad aquilonem.

De pede autem predictorum graduum usque ad alios xi gradus [sunt] sex passus, et de pede illorum xi graduum usque ad locum ubi fuit inventa sancta crux sunt v passus magni, et juxta illum locum est altare ex lapidibus devote consecratum. De pede vero illorum graduum, per quos ascenditur usque ad Montem Calvarie, usque ad locum ubi laverunt Nichodemus et Joseph corpus Domini Jesu, qui est recte ex opposito porte ecclesie, sunt quatuor passus. De pede etiam predictorum graduum versus eandem partem usque ad Sepulcrum Domini sunt xxxi passus. De Sepulcro Domini usque ad locum in quo apparuit Magdalene, qui est quasi ad partem aquilonarem Sepulcri, sunt vii passus.

De predicto vero graduum pede transeundo per chorum versus aquilonem usque ad partes columpne, ad quam dicitur Dominum ligatum fuisse et flagellatum sunt xxxvi passus, que jacet sub quodam altari, et satis prope [est] pars magna principalioris columpne, cujus etiam alia pars est

1. Jerusalem.
2. About six feet.
3. 'caloyer', a Greek monk.

4. Constantine the Great (*c.* 274-337), Roman emperor 306-37, was converted to Christianity in 312, before the battle with his rival Maxentius. He converted his mother Helena to Christianity, and she is reputed to have discovered the True Cross, on which Christ was crucified, about the year 318.

Rome. De Sepulcro Domini usque ad locum in quo lamentabatur beata Virgo Maria Filium suum in cruce pendentem, qui est ex opposito ipsius montis, in parte aquilonari ecclesie, sunt xviii passus. Et de Sepulcro versus orientem infra hostium chori usque ad foramen rotundum, in quo posuit Christus digitum suum dicens: 'Hic est medium mundi', sunt xiiii passus. Et de hostio chori usque ad majus altare sunt xv passus.

Predicta autem turris est sita in Monte Syon, ad cujus partem quodammodo australem est monasterium Scismaticorum,[5] quod nunc per eos officiatur. In quorum ecclesia est caput beati Jacobi apostoli, ut dicitur. Et ultra ad eandem partem est ecclesia in qua est lapis ille in loco altaris super iiii columpnas, de quo dicebant mulieres: 'Quis revolvet nobis lapidem'[6] et cetera. Et in eodem monte sunt oratoria multa devota, que nunc quasi totaliter sunt destructa, secundum quod inferius in *Locario*[7] luculentius apparebit.

Item ex opposito predicte turris ad orientem est locus in quo fuit olim castrum, quod tantum distabat quod nulla ratione potuit a sepedicta turre protegi nec defendi, nisi forte cum machinis, cujus oppositum habetur in libro *De Proprietatibus Rerum*.[8] Ubi nunc est ecclesia Saracenorum, que est spherice figure, ad quam nullum Christianum permittunt accedere.

[This city was once situated for the greater part on Mount Sion, a mountain which though not large is nevertheless very strong, especially on the south side, and dominates the city. It is to a large extent surrounded by the valley of Josaphat, and where the valley ends there were once broad and very deep ditches excavated in the rocks, traces of which can be seen even to this day, and they testify most clearly to the solidity and strength of the old city. This mountain extends for a long distance to the south and to the north. On the southern side, where the strength of the valley is less, there was built for the protection and defence of the city that most famous and imperial Tower of David, which has now been rebuilt by the Saracens as a fortress of the Sultan, and is distant obliquely from the Church of the Holy Sepulchre by about the length of a bowshot.

On the northern side of this tower is a gate through which we entered and came to the church just mentioned, praising the Lord who in this place redeemed us by His precious blood. This church is large and beautiful, its nave being spherical and closely resembling a pigeon-house, except that it is built upon columns and has all round it an ambulatory. In the centre there is a small chapel of marble in which is the Sepulchre of our Lord, which is only nine palms in length. It is entirely covered over with a slab of white marble in such a manner that it can nowhere be touched nor be seen except through three small holes which are on its southern side. Outside on the northern side of the tomb, which is contiguous to the wall of the chapel itself, is placed a lamp, which is always lit by a *caloyer* or Cuman monk, who always resides there with a companion. Opposite to it on the south side, within the said chapel, is a lamp which on every Holy Saturday is without fail lit by a flame sent down from heaven to the glory of the risen Christ, who liveth for ever, Amen. The doors of this church are on the south side, of which the most easterly one is closed by a stone wall. Opposite these doors on the outside is a very beautiful quadrangle entirely paved with white marble, towards the centre of which is the spot where our Lord, suffering for us, rested while the cross was being carried up the mountain.

To the east of these doors, within the church itself, is Mount Calvary. Eighteen steps lead to its summit, where there is a round hole in which the cross of Christ was fixed. From the uppermost of these steps to the hole are ten feet, where some of the Lord's blood is seen to have run through the fissures of the mountain. To the south of this hole are the clearest traces of the manner in which the rocks were split equally from the summit downwards on the day of the Passion of Christ; and here is the spot, it is said, where the head of Adam was found. Very near that fissure an altar has been piously consecrated. From the foot of the steps just mentioned, towards the east, as far as the door of the subterranean church which leads down to the spot where Helena, mother of Constantine, discovered the wood of the cross, there are eleven paces, and from that door to the first step are seven feet, whence twenty-nine steps go down. At the foot of these steps there is a beautiful church built upon four columns of marble, in which there is a high altar on the eastern side, and another altar on the northern side.

From the foot of those steps to another flight of eleven steps, are six paces; and from the foot of these eleven steps to the place where the holy cross was found, there are five full paces, and in this place there is a consecrated altar of stone. From the foot of those steps, which lead up to Mount Calvary, as far as the place where Nicodemus and Joseph washed the body of the Lord Jesus, which is right opposite the gate of the church, are four paces; and from the same spot, in the same direction to the Sepulchre of

5. According to Esposito (ed. cit., p. 21n), 'In 1323 this monastery belonged to the schismatic Georgians of the Greek rite. Afterwards it came into the possession of the Armenians.'
6. Mark 16.3.
7. Esposito (ed. cit., p. 21) notes that 'This *Locarius* or *Locarium*, which if it really was compiled has not been preserved in the MS, must have been an index of churches, oratories, and places of note.'
8. *De Proprietatibus Rerum*, the most famous encyclopaedia of the Middle Ages, by Bartholomeus Anglicus (*fl. c.* 1230-50), a minorite friar, otherwise known as Bartholomew de Glanville, professor of theology at Paris. Esposito (ed. cit., p. 21n) gives the reference to this passage: Liber XIV, c. 37 (ed. Nuremberg, 1519).

our Lord, are thirty-one paces. From the Sepulchre to the place where the Lord appeared to Mary Magdalen, which is towards the north of the tomb, there are seven paces.

From the foot of the above-mentioned steps, crossing the choir towards the north, in the direction of the column to which, it is said, our Lord was bound and beaten, are thirty-six paces. This column lies under an altar, and near by is a large fragment of the principal column, the remaining part of which is at Rome. From our Lord's Sepulchre to the spot where the blessed Virgin Mary grieved for her Son hanging upon the cross, which is opposite the Mount, to the north of the church, are eighteen paces. From the Sepulchre eastwards within the door of the choir to the round hole into which Christ placed his finger saying: 'Here is the middle of the world', are fourteen paces, and from the door of the choir to the major altar are fifteen paces.

The tower already mentioned is situated on Mount Sion, towards the southern part of which is the monastery of the Schismatics, which is now served by them. In their church is preserved, as is said, the head of the blessed James the Apostle. Beyond, in the same direction, is a church in which, in place of an altar, is that stone slab, supported on four columns, of which the women said: 'Who shall roll back this stone for us?' On the same Mount are many holy oratories, which are now almost entirely destroyed, as will appear more clearly lower down in the *Locarium*.

Opposite the aforementioned tower, to the east, is the place on which was once the fortress [of David], which was so far distant that it could in no way have been protected or defended by that tower, except perhaps by means of military engines. The opposite view is to be found in the book *De Proprietatibus Rerum*. On this spot there is now a Saracen church, which is of spherical shape, and which they permit no Christian to approach.]

TWO POEMS BY RICHARD LEDREDE (*c.* 1275-1360) (1350s)

[The text and translation are taken from Edmund Colledge's edition (Toronto: Pontifical Institute of Mediaeval Studies, 1974), based on the versions in the Red Book of Ossory (poems No. XLII and No. III in his edition).]

Jhesu bone Jhesu pie
Jhesu fili flos Marie
Circumcisus ista die[1]
  Pro nobis mundi miseris

Nomen tuum salutare
Dat scriptura[2] causam quare
Nam tu venisti nos saluare
  Salus in angustijs

Quem adorant magi reges
Pastores pascentes greges
Testantur scientes leges
  Ex libris propheticis

Que genuisti saluatorem
Ducem nostrum et pastorem
Et a morte redemptorem
  Ade peccati veteris

Per tui nati sanctum ortum
Duc nos ad salutis portum
Quo nil graue nichil tortum
  Sed semper frui superis

Amen

[Good Jesu, loving Jesu, Jesu son and flower of Mary, circumcised on this day for the sake of us, the wretched of this world.

Your name means 'Saviour'. Scripture explains why, for you came to save us, our salvation in our peril.

The wise kings who adore you and the shepherds feeding their flocks bear witness to the laws they know from the prophetic books.

You who bore our saviour, our leader and our shepherd, and our redeemer from the death of Adam's ancient sin.

By the holy birth of your child, lead us to the haven of salvation, where there is nothing burdensome, nothing amiss, but always the delight of heavenly things.

Amen]

1. The Church commemorates Christ's circumcision on 1 January.

2. 'And she shall bring forth a son; and thou shalt call his name Jesus: for he shall save his people from their sins' (Matthew 1.21).

Vale mater Christi   virgo regia   in te mea spes

Menti mee tristi   data venia   solamen tu es
Vale mater Christi   virgo regia   in te mea spes

Deum genuisti   dei filia   cuius mater es
Vale mater Christi   virgo regia   in te mea spes

Mortem sustulisti	diua gracia	deum cum pareres
Vale mater Christi	virgo regia	in te mea spes
Vitam peperisti	vice media	mater cum fieres
Vale mater Christi	virgo regia	in te mea spes
Thronum possedisti	dei dextera	cum quo nunc resides
Vale mater Christi	virgo regia	in te mea spes
A te petunt (isti)	celi gloriam	nobis vt impetres
Vale mater Christi	virgo regia	in te mea spes

Amen

[Greetings, mother of Christ, queenly virgin; my hope is you.
You are the solace of my sorrowful mind when it is given pardon.
You bore God, daughter of the God whose mother you are.
You destroyed death by divine grace when you gave birth to God.
You brought forth life by your mediating part when you were made a mother.
You gained a throne at the right hand of God, with whom now you dwell.
Here on earth men beg you to obtain the glory of heaven for us.]

RICHARD FITZRALPH
(*c.* 1300-60)

from: DEFENSIO CURATORUM (1357)

[The text is edited from British Library MS Lansdowne 393, and the translation is by the present editor.]

folio 248r-v

Ecce, Pater Sanctissime,[1] accedens Londoniam pro mee ecclesie Ardmachane[2] quibusdam negotiis, doctores aliquos satis doctos super mendicitate ac mendicacione Domini Saluatoris ex aduerso repperi deceptantes,[3] et sepius inuitatus ut populo predicarem, septem aut octo sermones[4] illi protuli in vulgari et sub protestacione prescripta in publico nouem conclusiones[5] expressi propter quas et alia que tunc dixi fratres ad istam sanctam sedem, licet friuole, appellarunt.

Prima hec erat quod Dominus Noster Ihesus Christus in conuersacione sua humana semper pauper erat non quia propter se paupertatem dilexit aut voluit.

Secunda fuit quod Dominus Noster Ihesus nunquam spontanee mendicauit.

Tercia erat conclusio quod Christus nunquam docuit spontanee mendicare.

Quarta conclusio erat, siue quartus articulus, quod Dominus Noster Ihesus docuit non debere hominem spontanee mendicare.

Quinta erat conclusio, siue quintus articulus, quod nullus potest prudenter et sancte spontaneam mendicitatem super se asserere perpetuo obseruandam.

Sexta erat conclusio quod non est de Regula Fratrum Minorum[6] mendicitatem spontaneam obseruare.

Septima erat de materia illa conclusio quod Bulla Domini Alexandri Quarti[7] que magistrorum Libellum[8] condempnat, nullam premissarum conclusionum impugnat.

Octaua conclusio, et prima de priuilegiorum materia ista, erat quod pro confessione parochianorum alicuius ecclesie facienda cum exclusione loci alterius eligibilior erat parochialis ecclesia quam fratrum oratorium siue ipsorum ecclesia.

Nona erat conclusio, et secunda in ista materia, quod ad confessionem parochianorum cuiusuis ecclesie vni persone singulariter faciendam eligibilior est persona ordinarii quam fratris persona.

1. The Pope is Innocent VI, who reigned 1352-62.
2. FitzRalph was consecrated archbishop of Armagh on 8 July 1347.
3. The dispute over Christ's mendicancy was a very real one since, if Christ did not beg, the friars, who claimed that He did, would have had no justification for their mendicancy. This new phase of the controversy may have been engendered by FitzRalph's completion and circulation of his treatise *De Pauperie Salvatoris* ('Concerning the Poverty of the Saviour') in 1356.
4. Only four of these London sermons survive.
5. The nine conclusions form the basis of the *Defensio Curatorum*.
6. Saint Francis of Assisi (1181-1226), founder of the Order of Friars Minor, who followed the Rule he devised.
7. Alexander IV (1254-61), formerly cardinal protector of the Franciscans, who obviously favoured the friars.
8. William of St Amour, a secular priest at the University of Paris, compiled and edited the first major polemical work against the friars, entitled the *Tractatus Brevis de Periculis Novissimorum Temporum ex Scripturis Sumptus* (A Short Treatise on the Dangers of the Last Times Compiled from Scripture), which was first issued in 1256. The book became known as the *Magistrum Libellus* ('The Book of Masters', whence the reference here); it was condemned by Alexander IV in a bull of 5 October 1256. For a comprehensive survey of William of St Amour's role in the controversy, see Penn R. Szittya, *The Antifraternal Tradition in Medieval Literature* (Princeton, New Jersey: Princeton University Press, 1986), pp. 11-61.

[Behold, Holy Father, I came to London on certain business for my church in Armagh and found there some learned doctors arguing to and fro about whether or not Our Lord the Saviour begged. I was often invited to preach to the people, and I preached seven or eight sermons in English, and presented in public nine conclusions, in accordance with the written summons, on account of which (and of other conclusions I then stated) the friars have summoned me, notwithstanding that they were doing so in a silly manner, to the Holy See.

The first conclusion was that Our Lord Jesus Christ was always poor during His time on earth, but not because He loved or wanted poverty for its own sake.

The second was that Our Lord Jesus never begged voluntarily.

The third was that Christ never taught voluntary mendicancy.

The fourth conclusion (or the fourth article) was that Our Lord Jesus taught that no one should beg voluntarily.

The fifth conclusion(or the fifth article) was that no one can prudently and conscientiously take on the perpetual observance of a vow of voluntary mendicancy.

The sixth was that the Rule of the Friars Minor does not insist on voluntary mendicancy.

The seventh conclusion concerning that matter was that the Bull of the Lord Alexander IV, which condemns the Book of the Masters, did not call in question any of the preceding conclusions.

The eighth conclusion (and the first which deals with the topic of privileges) was that, so far as the obligation of parishioners to make their confessions in one particular church is concerned, the parish church is more suitable than the oratories or churches of the friars.

The ninth conclusion (and the second dealing with that topic) was that, when parishioners of any church have to confess to one particular person, the person of the bishop is more suitable than the person of a friar.]

folio 248r-v

Ego enim in meo diocesi Ardmachana, ut puto, habeo duo milia[9] subditorum qui singulis annis propter sentencias excommunicacionis latas contra homicidas voluntarios, fures publicos, incendiarios, et istis consimiles, sunt excommunicacionis sentenciis inuoluti, de quibus vix veniunt ad me seu penitenciarios[10] meos xl in anno, et recipiunt sacramenta omnes tales ut ceteri, et absoluti dicuntur; nec per alios quam per fratres. Non dubium, cum nulli alii illos absoluant, absoluti creduntur. Vnde a parochianis potest verisimiliter suspicari quod illi confessores sunt tali sentencia inuoluti, ita quod potestas sacerdotalis est in eis ligata, et ita minus tutum est eis talibus confiteri, ex quo sine peccato mortali non possunt eos absoluere, et si illud credant ipsi confessi consenciunt fratrum peccatis, si absolucionem accipiant. Ait enim Apostolus *ad Rom. i capitulo*: 'Qui talia agunt digni sunt morte, non solum autem qui faciunt ea sed eciam qui consenciunt facientibus.'[11] Et *II Paralipomenon xix capitulo* dicitur quod Iesu propheta dixit ad Iozaphat regem Iuda: 'Impio prebes auxilium, et hijs qui oderunt Dominum amicicia iungeris, et idcirco iram quidem Domini merebaris.'[12] Vnde consequitur quod securior est persona ordinarii quam fratrum persone.

9. This is probably an exaggeration.
10. 'Penitenciaries' were priests empowered to absolve major sins reserved for special hearing.
11. Romans 1.32.
12. II Paralipomenon (Chronicles) 19.2.

[In my diocese of Armagh I think I have two thousand subjects — murderers, thieves, arsonists, and others like them — who, because of sins for which the punishment is excommunication, are every year given sentences of excommunication. Of these, scarcely forty come to me or to my penitenciaries. These all receive the sacraments as other men, and are absolved by the friars. There is no doubt about this: they are obviously absolved by none other than the friars. Hence, parishioners can rightly suspect that those confessors are subject to the same sentences, because the priest's power is bound in them, and so it is less safe to confess to such priests. From this it follows that they cannot absolve them without mortal sin, and if those who have confessed their sins believe that to be so, they are conniving at the sins of the friars, if they accept absolution from them, for the Apostle says (Romans 1.32): 'those who do such things are worthy of death, not only those who do them, but those who consent to those who do them.' And in II Paralipomenon Chronicles 19.2 it is said that Jesus the Prophet said to Josaphat, King of Juda: 'you are offering help to the ungodly, and are joined in friendship to those who hate the Lord, and therefore you did indeed deserve the wrath of the Lord.' Hence, it follows that the person of the bishop is safer (as a confessor) than the person of a friar.]

Historical and Linguistic Background

Two excellent, concise monographs on the history of medieval Ireland are Robin Frame's *Colonial Ireland 1169-1369* (Dublin: Helicon, 1981) and Art Cosgrove's *Late Medieval Ireland 1370-1541* (Dublin: Helicon, 1981). See also Michael Richter, *Medieval Ireland, The Enduring Tradition*

(Dublin: Gill and Macmillan, 1988). The most authoritative work on the period is *A New History of Ireland*, II, *Medieval Ireland 1169-1554*, ed. Art Cosgrove (Oxford: Clarendon Press, 1987). The text and translations of the Statutes of Kilkenny are in *Statutes and Ordinances of the Parliament of Ireland*, I, *King John to Henry V* (Dublin: Thom for HMSO, 1907), pp. 431-69.

For Fynes Moryson's *Itinerary*, see James P. Myers (ed.), *Elizabethan Ireland. A Selection of the Writings by Elizabethan Writers on Ireland*, (Hamden, Connecticut: Archon, 1983), pp. 185-240. See also Colm Lennon, *Richard Stanihurst The Dubliner 1547-1618* (Blackrock, Co. Dublin: Irish Academic Press, 1981).

The two most readable accounts of the linguistic situation in medieval Ireland are Edmund Curtis, 'The Spoken Languages of Medieval Ireland', *Studies*, VIII (1919), 234-54, and E. Cahill, 'Norman French and English Languages in Ireland 1170-1540', *Irish Ecclesiastical Record*, LI (1938), 155-73. Some of the statements made in these articles appear overly simple in the light of modern research and they should be supplemented with Alan Bliss's paper on 'Language and Literature' in James Lydon (ed.), *The English in Medieval Ireland* (Dublin: Royal Irish Academy, 1984), pp. 27-45, and also with the survey of the historical background in Alan Bliss's *Spoken English in Ireland 1600-1740* (Dublin: Cadenus Press and Dolmen Press, 1979), pp. 11-30. For the later part of the period, see also Alan Bliss, 'The English Language in Early Modern Ireland', ch. xxi in *A New History of Ireland*, III, *Early Modern Ireland 1534-1691*, ed. T. W. Moody, F. X. Martin, F. J. Byrne (Oxford: Clarendon Press, 1976).

The two most comprehensive surveys of the literature are St John D. Seymour's *Anglo-Irish Literature 1200-1582* (Cambridge: Cambridge University Press, 1929), which covers literature in English, Latin, and French, and, more recently, Alan Bliss and Joseph Long, 'Literature in Norman French and English to 1534', in *A New History of Ireland*, II, ed. cit., pp. 708-36.

For an abstemiously linguistic account of the dialect, see Angus McIntosh and M. L. Samuels, 'Prolegomena to a Study of Medieval Anglo-Irish', *Medium Ævum*, XXXVII (1968), 1-11.

NOTES ON THE TEXTS

French

The Song of Dermot and the Earl was the title given to the poem by G. H. Orpen in his standard edition and translation (Oxford: Clarendon Press, 1892). On the source of the information contained in the poem, see Joseph Long, 'Dermot and the Earl: Who Wrote "The Song"?', *Proceedings of the Royal Irish Academy* LXXV (1975), section C, 263-72. See also M. T. Flanagan, *Irish Society, Anglo-Norman Settlers, Angevin Kingship* (Oxford: Clarendon Press, 1989).

The Walling of New Ross has been edited and translated by Hugh Shields in 'The Walling of New Ross: A Thirteenth-Century Poem in French', *Long Room* 12-13 (1975-76), 24-33.

English

The standard edition of all the 'Kildare Poems', which include *The Land of Cokaygne* and *A Satire on the People of Dublin*, is that by W. Heuser (repr. Darmstadt: Wissenschaftliche Buchgesellschaft, 1965, first published as *Bonner Beiträge zur Anglistik*, XIV, Bonn, 1904). Note that Heuser's ascription 'Satire [on the people of Kildare]' is more likely to be a 'Satire on the People of Dublin' (see Bliss and Long, art. cit., p. 728). There is also an excellent annotated edition of *The Land of Cokaygne* in J. A. W. Bennett and G. V. Smithers (eds), *Early Middle English Verse and Prose*, 2nd edition (Oxford: Clarendon Press, 1968), pp. 136-44.

The identification of the abbey in the poem has been persuasively argued in P. L. Henry's paper 'The Land of Cokaygne: Cultures in Contact in Medieval Ireland', *Studia Hibernica*, XII (1972), 120-41. See also Éilís Ní Dhuibhne's study: '"The Land of Cokaygne": A Middle English Source for Irish Food Historians', *Ulster Folklife* 34 (1988), 48-53. The concept of 'Cokaygne' as a land of Paradise is described by Dorothee Metlitski in *The Matter of Araby in Medieval England* (New Haven and London: Yale University Press, 1977), pp. 210-19. The genre of parody, to which *The Land of Cokaygne* belongs, is discussed by N. F. Blake in *The English Language in Medieval Literature* (London, Melbourne and Toronto: Dent; Totowa, New Jersey: Rowan and Littlefield, 1977), pp. 116-27.

For a full description of MS Harley 913, which contains the 'Kildare Poems', see E. B. Fitzmaurice and A. G. Little, *Materials for the History of the Franciscan Province of Ireland A.D. 1230-1450* (Manchester: Manchester University Press, 1920), pp. 121-26. See also T. J. Garbáty, 'Studies in the Franciscan *The Land of Cokaygne* in the Kildare ms', *Franziscanische Studien*, XLV (1963), 139-53.

For Old French and Middle Dutch analogues, see V. Väänänen, 'Le "fabliau" de Cocagne', *Neuphilologische Mitteilungen*, XLVIII (1947), 3-36. *The Vision of Mac Conglinne*, a twelfth-century Irish poem which invites comparison with *The Land of Cokaygne*, was edited by Kuno Meyer (London: David Nutt, 1892).

The Pride of Life has been edited by Norman Davis in *Non-Cycle Plays and Fragments*, Early English Text Society, Supplementary Text No. 1 (London, New York, Toronto: Oxford University Press, 1970), pp. 90-105. A description of the language of the play is given by W. Heuser in *Die Kildare-Gedichte*, ed. cit., pp. 66-71.

James Yonge's translation of The *Gouernaunce of Prynces* has been edited by Robert Steele in *Three Prose Versions of the Secreta Secretorum*, I, Text and Glossary, Early English Text Society, Extra Series No. 74 (London: Kegan Paul, Trench, Trübner & Co., 1898), pp. 121-248.

Latin

For a general account of the Irish contribution to Graeco-Latin scholarship, see W. B. Stanford, *Ireland and the Classical Tradition* (Dublin: Allen Figgis; Totowa, New Jersey: Rowan and Littlefield, 1966), especially pp. 12-13. See also Mario Esposito, 'A Bibliography of the Latin Writers of Mediaeval Ireland', *Studies* II (1913), 495-521; and Fergal McGrath, *Education in Ancient and Medieval Ireland* (Dublin: Studies 'Special Publications', 1979), pp. 137-223.

Friar John Clyn's description of the Black Death in Ireland, to which reference is made in the Introduction, is to be found in Richard Butler (ed.), *The Annals of Ireland by Friar John Clyn and Thady Dowling together with the Annals of Ross* (Dublin: Irish Archaeological Society, 1849), pp. 37-38.

For the text and translation of the journey of Symon Simeonis, see *Itinerarium Symonis Semeonis Ab Hybernia Ad Terram Sanctam*, ed. Mario Esposito, *Scriptores Latini Hiberniae*, IV (Dublin: Dublin Institute for Advanced Studies, 1960).

A full account of Richard Ledrede's life and an edition of his poems have been published by Edmund Colledge in *The Latin Poems of Richard Ledrede, O.F.M., Bishop of Ossory, 1317-1360* (Toronto: Pontifical Institute of Mediaeval Studies, 1974).

There is no modern edition of Richard FitzRalph's *Defensio Curatorum*. Several editions of the text were published in the seventeenth century, notably E. Brown's version of it, which he included in his *Fasciculus Rerum Expetendarum et Fugiendarum* (London: 1690), II, 466-86. John Trevisa translated the *Defensio Curatorum* into English in the last decade of the fourteenth century and this version will be found in A. J. Perry's edition for the Early English Text Society, Original Series No. 167 (London: Oxford University Press, 1925), pp. 39-93. The manuscripts of FitzRalph's sermons have been comprehensively described in Aubrey Gwynn's paper 'The Sermon-Diary of Richard FitzRalph, Archbishop of Armagh', *Proceedings of the Royal Irish Academy*, XLIV (1937), Section C, 1-57. The standard account of his life is Katherine Walsh's *A Fourteenth-Century Scholar and Primate: Richard FitzRalph in Oxford, Avignon and Armagh* (Oxford: Clarendon Press, 1981).

NICHOLAS CANNY and ANDREW CARPENTER, *Editors*

The Early Planters: Spenser and his Contemporaries

Edmund Spenser (*c.*1552-99) would feature prominently in any anthology of English writing not only as one of the greatest poets of the English Renaissance but also as one of its finest prose writers. The reasons for his place in this anthology of Irish literature might be less obvious, but they are compelling ones. Spenser spent nearly twenty years of his life in Ireland as an official of the Elizabethan administration and later as a 'planter' in Munster. He set some of the most important passages in his poetry in Ireland and, although he had the typical Renaissance humanist's condescending attitude to native Irish culture, he was genuinely interested in the country and its people. However, Spenser was also a colonial administrator with the attitude of mind necessary for the task, and it is this side of his writing that has probably had the most lasting effect on Irish and Anglo-Irish culture. This section, therefore, is divided into two parts: the first concentrates on the political writings of Spenser and his contemporaries, while the second presents a small selection of his poetry.

I POLITICAL WRITINGS

Spenser's political importance lies in the fact that he was the first of his nation to advance a coherent argument for the systematic colonization of Ireland by English people. In taking this stance, he became the prime apologist for the destruction of the Gaelic and Hiberno-Norman civilizations of Ireland; but he also became the most eloquent advocate of the civilizing reform that was meant to follow upon this destruction. The essential element of the reform scheme advocated by Spenser (and it was, in many respects, the official government position that he reflected) was the introduction of English settler communities to Ireland. The settlers and their descendants were to be made responsible for the erection of the political, economic and social framework that was considered the necessary support of a civil life and the protestant faith. In this respect, Spenser's writings on Ireland are of central importance to his age, for through them he gave the English who served in Ireland a sense of moral purpose. As his views were transmitted to later generations of protestant settlers, Spenser's influence became even greater and his attitude affected the outlook of those who are known to literary historians as the Anglo-Irish and whose ascendancy in Ireland was to last until the end of the eighteenth century.

Because we are, in this section, primarily interested in Spenser as a social reformer, attention has been limited to his prose tract, *A View of the Present State of Ireland* (1596), where he most memorably expanded his central thesis. The reader will immediately recognize that much of Spenser's negative portrayal of Gaelic society was derived from the writings of such medieval commentators on Ireland as Giraldus Cambrensis, but he breaks new ground when he asserts that those who make up the Hiberno-Norman population (which he refers to as the Old English) have degenerated from their original standards of civility to the depraved social conditions of their Gaelic neighbours. This argument is advanced by Spenser in the course of a general discussion on how a people become barbaric and how they can be recovered from this condition. On this second point, Spenser concludes that civil conditions can be advanced among a barbaric population only by forceful methods, and the means that he advocates for the reform of the Gaelic Irish involves their being reduced to the point where they would forget their very ancestry and their historical memory. Only then, he contends, would it be possible to advance the Irish to the condition in which they would engage in husbandry rather than in pastoral farming, in which they would welcome the opportunity to become involved with trade and manufacturing processes rather than with wasteful military pursuits, and in which they would turn to the true protestant religion, rather than adhere to the superstition-ridden catholicism that prevailed almost everywhere in Ireland.

It will be clear from this summary, and even more so from the text, that Spenser's argument depends on the contrast between the civility he would advance and the barbarism he depicts as existing in Ireland. This approach was also employed by many of his contemporaries, and it eventually became one of the axioms of Anglo-Irish life that protestantism was symbolized by a tamed and domesticated environment, while catholicism was associated with wild forests and marshy places. Spenser's beliefs, in fact, as much as his methods of argument, were shared by several of his English-born contemporaries in Ireland. The bitter hostility towards the Old English population in Ireland, and especially towards those of the Old English who served in an official capacity, had already been expressed vigorously and repeatedly by Barnabe (or Barnaby) Rich (*c.*1540-1617).[1] Rich opposed them specifically because they had remained catholic and were therefore of questionable loyalty to the protestant crown. Andrew Trollope, who spent the years 1585-87 in Ireland, had carried the argument a stage further by suggesting that the Old English (including those in the towns) had lapsed from the civility of their predecessors.[2] It was this idea that Spenser seized upon, weaving it into his intricate argument concerning the tension between barbarism and civility.

Even in this, however, Spenser was not original. Richard Beacon (a planter and administrator in Ireland, 1586-91 and Spenser's colleague on the provincial council in Munster) had anticipated him in considering how commonwealths undergo decline; he had concluded, as Spenser was later to do, that a truly corrupt society could be brought to civility only by severe military action, followed by a comprehensive scheme of colonization. Beacon, like Spenser, stressed the need for the crown to support those governors who were given responsibility for promoting reform, and they both cited Lord Gray (1536-93) and Sir Richard Byngham or Bingham (1528-99) as exemplary rulers deserving such support. Both were also of one mind that only English-born protestants should participate in the government of Ireland, once this task of reform was underway, for only they could be relied upon to support the government's objectives. In this, too, they were being guided by the advice of men such as Rich and Trollope, although Beacon, through his skilful use of classical parallels, could put his case more delicately than they, invoking, by implication, the authority of antiquity for his proposition. 'If the Lacedamonians', Beacon asserted, '... held it convenient and necessary that the towns and cities of Greece which were not of the league of the Graecians should be removed from the place of a councillor then much more those who are not only parties with the Graecians but of league with the barbarous people, yea their seed and sworn servant, are to be dismissed by the council of Amphictyons.'

To trace such parallels between the texts of Spenser and Beacon is not to suggest that one was a carbon copy of the other. Beacon, for example, seems more optimistic than his colleague that reform would follow quickly upon the success of colonization, but both recognize the possibility that decline would again set in unless the endeavour was

1. See Barnaby Rich to Lord Burghly, 20 May 1591, Public Record Office, London, S.P. 63, vol. 158, no. 12.

2. See Andrew Trollope to Sir Francis Walsingham, 12 September 1585, Public Record Office, London, S.P. 63, vol. 85, no. 39.

carefully monitored by the state. This distrust of the motives of those Englishmen likely to be attracted by service in Ireland, whether in a civil or an ecclesiastical capacity, was widely shared by many of Spenser's contemporaries (including Barnaby Rich), which explains why so many writers give prominence to the qualities that the principal governor should possess.

Fynes Moryson (1566-1630), another important commentator on Ireland, also concentrated on the pivotal role of the principal governor. He believed that the ideal governor had already been found in Charles Blount, lord Mountjoy (1563-1606), who executed a military conquest of Ireland such as Spenser had called for. Moryson served as personal secretary to Mountjoy (as Spenser had done to Lord Gray during the 1580s) and, as he chronicled his master's every action, he also provided a critical appraisal of the society that he was witnessing at close hand, as the English army slowly penetrated the province of Ulster in the wake of Mountjoy's decisive military victory over the rebellious Irish lords and their Spanish allies at Kinsale in December 1601. There is nothing in the writings of his English contemporaries to match the detail on life in Gaelic Ulster that Moryson was able to supply in the relevant passages of his multi-volume *Itinerary* (first published in 1617), but his critical analysis of Irish society followed closely upon that provided in Spenser's *View*, even in matters of word and phrase. Furthermore Moryson, like Spenser, was willing to countenance the atrocities of war that both of them witnessed at first hand; he too believed that the military endeavour would be immediately followed by a concerted effort at social amelioration and religious reform. It came as something of a shock to Moryson, when he revisited Ireland in 1613, to discover that this reform had been partially neglected. This would have been one of the factors that prompted him to compose 'Of the Commonwealth of Ireland', and more especially the extract published here, which reminded his readers of the beneficial end that would have justified the terrible means necessary to achieve the conquest of Ireland.

It will be clear from the foregoing that works such as these served a particular purpose for those engaged upon the conquest of Ireland. The writers identified political targets which, it was hoped, the English government could be persuaded to aim for, and their works served to legitimize both the actions that were necessary for the attainment of those targets and the economic and social advancement that came within the reach of English servitors in Ireland once the policies were pursued. This is not to suggest that all English officials in Ireland were of one mind on how the conquest of Ireland should be achieved or even that any one individual clung rigidly to a single set of principles throughout his career. Nonetheless, a general acceptance emerged among minor English-born officials who had made a career in Ireland that a military conquest of the country was a desirable objective and that this would pave the way for a general reform effort, which would include colonization as a necessary ingredient. The few who dissented from this consensus were those officials recently arrived in Ireland from the English court. These immediately recognized the revolutionary import of what was being recommended and feared that its very mention would either provoke rebellion in Ireland, for which they would be held personally responsible, or else would weaken their personal standing with Queen Elizabeth I, who was certain to be shocked by it. Circumstances favoured the radicals, however, and even the queen was persuaded to seek a new political order in Ireland once her authority there had been repeatedly defied by Hugh O'Neill (*c.*1540-1616), whom she had created earl of Tyrone. It can be said, therefore, that texts such as those presented here were of considerable political and social importance because they provided those engaged upon the military conquest of Ireland with a sense of purpose and mission, which in turn made them conscious of being members of a particular community, despite the differences in their individual ranks and positions.

Besides serving these immediate purposes for the generation in which they were written, these texts continued to enjoy popularity among subsequent generations of protestant settlers in Ireland, especially during the first half of the seventeenth century. Several of those who directed the course of political events in the decades after the Elizabethan conquest are known to have had manuscript copies of Spenser's *View*, and others reveal familiarity with the arguments of the Elizabethan apologists in their own writings. Some, most notably Sir John Davies (1569-1626) in his *A Discovery of the True Causes why Ireland was Never Entirely Subdued* (1612), were drawn to these writings because they could demonstrate how they, in their own generation, had managed to break loose from the inevitability of decline that had confronted all previous generations in Ireland. Others, including Fynes Moryson, were not impressed by such protestations of progress and self-righteousness, and tended to look for evidence of the onset of degeneracy among the settlers themselves as a means of stimulating them to greater effort to achieve the reform of Ireland. A classic example of such a jeremiad is 'A Survey of the State of Ireland, Anno 1615', the anonymous author of which made his purpose clearer by assuming the initials of Edmund Spenser while imitating the title of his text.[3] But even an optimist such as Sir William Parsons (*c.*1570-1650), lord justice of Ireland, had to admit that the social reform of Ireland was far from complete and that the religious reform of the country had hardly begun.[4] Others, and Sir John Davies was among their number, were convinced that the opportunity for religious reform had been missed in the immediate aftermath of the war, and feared the consequences for themselves of the arrival in Ireland of large numbers of priests who had been trained on the Continent and were bent upon the frustration of their efforts.

This identification of Jesuits and seminary priests as the implacable opponents of social and religious reform became a commonplace among Irish protestants, and Sir John Temple (1600-77) encountered little difficulty in explaining the insurrection against the settler interest (which occurred in Ulster in October 1641) in terms of a conspiracy that had been fomented by Jesuits and seminary priests, together with their Old English allies within the English Pale. But while Temple could blame the rising of 1641 on segments of what had apparently been a civilized population among the Irish catholic community, he was more centrally concerned to portray the struggle itself as an onslaught of the forces of evil against good; nothing symbolized these forces more clearly for him than the apparently wanton destruction of the improvements that had been introduced to Ireland by the settler community. By stressing this destruction, Temple reminded the Irish protestant community who they were and what their purpose in Ireland really was. This reminder (which was renewed with printings of Temple's *The Irish Rebellion* through the seventeenth and eighteenth centuries) was an essential ingredient in the making of an Anglo-Irish community.

Thus Spenser and his Anglo-Irish contemporaries are best seen as apologists for English rule in Ireland. The balanced, civilized form of their works (dialogues between temperate philosophers or detailed catalogues of attacks against law and order), as well as their theme of civilization itself, encouraged their readers into a feeling of self-righteousness which, when pushed to excess, could justify all manner of atrocities. In its most benign manifestations, such self-righteousness enabled the English and the protestant Anglo-Irish to feel justified in their possession of Irish land and in their attempts to improve the country. At either end of the scale, however, it served to drive a wedge between the native Irish and those who came to the country from England and Scotland. Spenser may not, even to this day, be remembered with much affection in Munster, but his work had a lasting influence on successive generations of Irish protestant writers and politicians: he provided them with a ready-made sense of purpose and well-being.

3. See the anonymous manuscript signed 'E.S.' entitled 'A Survey of the Present State of Ireland, anno 1615. ...', Huntington Library, San Marino, California, Ellesmere MS. 1746.
4. See William Parsons, 'Reasons for the plantations in Ireland, 16 May 1622', British Library, Harley MS. 3292.

EDMUND SPENSER

(*c.* 1552-99)

from:

A VIEW OF THE PRESENT STATE OF IRELAND (1596)

[Although written in 1596, Spenser's *View* was not printed until 1633 when Sir James Ware included a heavily edited version of the text in his *Ancient Irish Histories.* (For the details of Ware's editorial activity, see Rudolf Gottfried (ed.), *Spenser's Prose Works,* Vol. IX of the variorum edition of Spenser's work (Baltimore: Johns Hopkins University Press, 1949), Appendix III, pp. 516-24.) The delay in publication is explained by the outspoken nature of the text and this is probably why Ware saw the need to truncate the original. Yet although it was not published until 1633, several manuscript copies were in circulation before that date and they appear to have come into the hands of many who had responsibility for governing Ireland. Thereafter, the Ware text held sway until 1934 and the publication by Oxford University Press of a modernized edition prepared by W. L. Renwick; this was followed by the variorum text in 1949. The work is cast in the form of a dialogue between Eudoxus ('of good repute', 'learned') and Irenius, an Englishman who has spent some time in Ireland.]

EUDOXUS: But if that country of Ireland whence you lately came be so goodly and commodious a soil as you report, I wonder that no course is taken for the turning thereof to good uses, and reducing that savage nation to better government and civility.

IRENIUS: Marry, so there have been diverse good plots devised and wise counsels cast already about reformation of that realm, but they say it is the fatal destiny of that land, that no purposes whatsoever are meant for her good will prosper or take good effect; which whether it proceed from the very genius of the soil, or influence of the stars, or that Almighty God hath not yet appointed the time of her reformation, or that He reserveth her in this unquiet state still, for some secret scourge which shall by her come unto England, it is hard to be known but yet much to be feared.

EUDOXUS: Surely I suppose this but a vain conceit of simple men, which judge things by their effects and not by their causes. For I would rather think the cause of this evil, which hangeth upon that country, to proceed rather of the unsoundness of the counsels and plots which you say have been ofttimes laid for her reformation, or of faintness in following and effecting the same, then of[1] any such fatal course or appointment of God as you misdeem,[2] but it is the manner of men that when they are fallen into any absurdity, or their actions succeed not as they would, they are ready always to impute the blame thereof unto the heavens, so to excuse their own follies and imperfections. So have I also heard it often wished (even of some whose great wisdom in opinion should seem to judge more soundly of so weighty a consideration) that all that land were a sea pool; which kind of speech is the manner rather of desperate men far driven, to wish the utter ruin of that which they cannot redress, than of grave counsellors which ought to think nothing so hard but that through wisdom may be mastered and subdued, since the poet says that the wise man shall rule even over the stars, much more over the earth.[3] For were it not the part of a desperate physician to wish his diseased patient dead rather than to apply the best endeavours of his skill for his recovery? But since we are so far entered, let us, I pray you, a little devise of[4] those evils by which that country is held in this wretched case, that it cannot as you say be recured.[5] And if it be not painful to you, tell us what things during your late continuance there, you observed to be most offensive and impeachful[6] unto the good rule and government thereof.

IRENIUS: Surely, Eudoxus, the evils which you desire to be recounted are very many and almost countable with those which were hidden in the basket of Pandora:[7] but since you so please I will out of that infinite number reckon but some that are most capital,[8] and commonly occurent both in the

1. than of.
2. you mistakenly suppose.
3. The author being referred to is Ptolemy, if we are to judge from the same sentiment attributed to Spenser in Lodowick Bryskett, *A Discourse of Civil Life* (London, 1606), p. 172.
4. talk of.
5. restored to health.
6. impeachable.
7. The reference is to Pandora's box. According to Greek mythology, Pandora allowed all the ills of the world to escape from a box that she had been instructed to keep sealed; only Hope remained.
8. most important.

life and conditions of private men, and also in the manage of public affairs and policy; the which you shall understand to be of diverse natures, as I observed them, for some of them are of very great antiquity and long continuance; others more late and of less endurance; others daily growing and increasing continually as the evil occasions are every day offered.

EUDOXUS: Tell them then, I pray you, in the same order that you have now rehearsed them. For there can be no better method than this which the very matter itself offers, and when you have reckoned all the evils, let us hear your opinion for redressing of them, after which there will perhaps of itself appear some reasonable way to settle a sound and perfect rule of government by shunning the former evils and following the offered good. The which method we may learn of the wise physicians which first require that the malady be known thoroughly and discovered, afterwards do teach how to cure and redress it, and lastly do prescribe a diet with strait rules and orders to be daily observed, for fear of relapse into the former disease or falling into some other more dangerous than it.

IRENIUS: I will then according to your advisement begin to declare the evils which seem to be most hurtful to the common weale[9] of that land, and first those which I said were most ancient and long grown; and they are also of three kinds: the first in the laws, the second in customs, and last in religion.

EUDOXUS: Why, Irenius, can there be any evil in the laws? Can the things which are ordained for the safety and good of all turn to the evil and hurt of them? This well I note, both in that state and in all other, that were they not contained in duty with fear of law which restraineth offences, and inflicteth sharp punishment to misdoers, no man should enjoy anything; every man's hand would be against another. Therefore in finding fault with the laws I doubt me you shall much overshoot yourself, and make me the more dislike your other dislikes of that government.

IRENIUS: The laws, Eudoxus, I do not blame for themselves, knowing right well that all laws are ordained for the good of the commonwealth, and for repressing of licentiousness and vice: but it falleth out in laws no otherwise than it doth in physic,[10] which was at first devised and is yet daily meant and ministered for the health of the patient, but nevertheless we often see that either through ignorance of the disease, or unseasonableness of the time, or other accidents coming between, instead of good it worketh hurt, and out of one evil, throweth the patient into many miseries. So the laws were at first intended for the formation of abuses and peaceable continuance of the subjects, but are since either disannulled or quite prevaricated[11] through change and alteration of times; yet are they good still in themselves, but to that Commonwealth which is ruled by them they work not that good which they should, and sometimes also perhaps that evil which they would not.

EUDOXUS: Whether do you mean this by the Common Law of the realm, or by the statute laws and acts of Parliaments?

IRENIUS: Surely by them both. For even the Common Law, being that which William of Normandy[12] brought in with his conquest and laid upon the neck of England, though it perhaps fitted well with the state of England then being, and was readily obeyed through the power of the commander which had before subdued the people to him and made easy way to the settling of his will; yet with the state of Ireland peradventure it doth not so well agree, being a people altogether stubborn and untamed, and if it were ever tamed, yet now lately having quite shaken off their yoke and broken the bands of their obedience. For England before the entrance of the Conqueror was a peaceable kingdom, and but lately enured[13] to the mild and godly government of King Edward surnamed the Confessor,[14] besides now lately grown unto a loathing and detestation of the unjust and tyrannous rule of Harold,[15] an usurper, which made them the more willing to accept of any reasonable conditions and order of the new victor, thinking surely that it could be no worse than the latter, and hoping well it would be as good as the former; yet what the proof of the first bringing in and

9. the common welfare or commonwealth.

10. medicine.
11. annulled or abolished.
12. William the Conqueror, king of England 1066-87.
13. accustomed to.
14. Edward, king of England 1042-66, was famed for his asceticism and piety. He was canonized in 1161.
15. Harold II became king of England on the death of Edward the Confessor, but ruled for just ten months. He was killed at the battle of Hastings (1066).

establishing of those laws was, was to many full bitterly made known. But with Ireland it is far otherwise. For it is a nation ever acquainted with wars though but amongst themselves, and in their own kind of military discipline trained up even from their youths, which they have never yet been taught to lay aside, nor made to learn obedience unto the law, scarcely to know the name of law, but instead thereof have always preserved and kept their own law which is the Brehon law.[16]

EUDOXUS: What is that which you call the Brehon law? It is a word to us altogether unknown. . . .

16. The law used in Gaelic Ireland, so called by the English from the Irish word *breitheamh*, meaning judge.

[At this point Eudoxus and Irenius identify the iniquities of Gaelic Brehon law and seek to explain why, in spite of the Anglo-Norman Conquest, this legal system still prevails over much of the island. The thrust of the discussion is that Brehon law is repugnant 'both to God's law and man's', and the speakers contend that the strategy favoured by the Old English councillors to bring the Gaelic Irish to obedience through a process of surrender and re-grant has consolidated rather than weakened the position of Brehon law. Since they agree that this strategy has failed, Eudoxus seeks a different course.]

EUDOXUS: What remedy is there, then, or means to avoid this inconvenience, for without first cutting off this dangerous custom, it seemeth hard to plant any sound ordinance, or reduce them to a civil government, since all their evil customs are permitted unto them?

IRENIUS: Surely nothing hard; for by this act of parliament, whereof we speak, nothing was given to King Henry,[1] which he had not before from his ancestors, but only the bare name of a king. For all other absolute power of principality he had in himself before derived from many former kings, his famous progenitors and worthy conquerors of that land; the which since they first conquered and by force subdued unto them, what need afterwards to enter into any such idle terms with them to be called their king when as it is in the power of the conqueror to take upon himself what title he will over his dominions conquered? For all is the conqueror's, as Tully[2] to Brutus saith; therefore meseems instead of so great and meritorious a service as they boast they performed to the king in bringing all the Irish to acknowledge him for their liege, they did great hurt unto his title, and have left a perpetual gall in the mind of that people, who before being absolutely bound to his obedience, are now tied but with terms, whereas both their lives, their lands, and their liberties were in his free power to appoint what tenures, what laws, what conditions he would over them, which were all his, against which there could be no rightful resistance; or if there were, he might, when he would, establish them with a stronger hand.

EUDOXUS: Yea, but perhaps it seemed better unto that noble king to bring them by their own accord to his obedience and to plant a peaceable government amongst them, than by such violent means to pluck them under. Neither yet hath he thereby lost anything that he formerly had, for having all before absolutely in his own power, it remaineth so still unto him, he having neither forgiven nor forgone anything thereby unto them, but having received something from them; that is, a more voluntary and loyal subjection; so as Her Majesty may yet, when it shall please her, alter anything of those former ordinances, or appoint other laws that may be more both for her own behoof[3] and for the good of that people.

IRENIUS: Not so, for it is not so easy now that things are grown into an habit and have their certain course, to change the channel, and turn their streams another way: for they may have now a colourable pretence[4] to withstand such innovation, having accepted of other laws and rules already.

EUDOXUS: But you say they do not accept of them but delight rather to lean to their old customs and Brehon laws, though they be much more unjust and also more inconvenient for the common people, as by your late relation of them I gathered. As for the laws of England they are surely most just and most agreeable both with the government and with the nature of the people. How falls it out, then, that you seem to dislike of them, as not so meet for that realm of Ireland, and not only the common law but also the statutes and acts of parliament which were specially provided and intended for the only benefit thereof?

1. Henry VIII. An Act that the Kings of England be Kings of Ireland, 1542.

2. Cognomen for Cicero.
3. advantage, profit.
4. plausible excuse.

IRENIUS: I was about to have told you my reason therein, but that you yourself drew me away with other questions; for I was showing you by what means and in what sort the positive laws were first brought in and established by the Norman conqueror, which were not by him devised nor applied unto the state of the realm then being, nor as it might best be (as should by lawyers principally be regarded), but were indeed the very laws of his own country of Normandy, the condition whereof how far it differeth from this of England, is apparent to every least judgement; but to transfer the same laws for the governing of the realm of Ireland was much more inconvenient and unmeet, for he found a better advantage of the time than was in the planting of them in Ireland, and followed the execution of them, with more severity, and was also present in person to overlook the magistrates, and to overawe the subjects with the terror of his sword and countenance of his majesty. But not so in Ireland: for they were otherwise affected, and yet do so remain, so as the same laws, me seems, can ill fit with their disposition or work that reformation that is wished, for laws ought to be fashioned unto the manners and condition of the people to whom they are meant, and not to be imposed upon them according to the simple rule of right, for then as I said instead of good they may work ill, and pervert justice to extreme injustice: for he that would transfer the laws of the Lacedemonians[5] to the people of Athens should find a great absurdity and inconvenience: For those laws of Lacedemon were devised by Lycurgus,[6] as most proper and best agreeing with that people, whom he knew to be inclined altogether to wars, and therefore wholly trained them up even from their cradles in arms and military exercises clean contrary to the institution of Solon,[7] who in his laws to the Athenians laboured by all means to temper their warlike courages with sweet delights of learning and sciences, so that as much as the one excelled in arms the other exceeded in knowledge. The like regard and moderation ought to be had in tempering and managing of this stubborn nation of the Irish, to bring them from their delight of licentious barbarism unto the love of goodness and civility.

EUDOXUS: I cannot see how that may better be than by the discipline of the laws of England. For the English were at first as stout and warlike a people as ever were the Irish, and yet you see are now brought to that civility, that no nation in the world excelleth them in all goodly conversation, and all the studies of knowledge and humanity.

IRENIUS: What they now be, both you and I see very well; but by how many thorny and hard ways they are come thereunto, by how many civil brawls, by how many tumultuous rebellions, that even hazarded oftentimes the whole safety of the kingdom, may easily be considered, all which they nevertheless fairly overcame by reason of the continual presence of the king, whose only person is oftentimes instead of an army to contain the unruly people from a thousand evil occasions, which that wretched kingdom is for want thereof daily carried into: the which when so they make head, no laws, no penalties can restrain, but that they do in the violence of that fury tread down and trample underfoot all both divine and human things, and the laws themselves they do specially rage at and rend in pieces as most repugnant to their liberty and natural freedom, which in their madness they effect.

EUDOXUS: It is then a very unseasonable time to plead law, when swords are in the hands of the vulgar,[8] or to think to retain them with fear of punishments, when they look after liberty and shake off all government.

IRENIUS: Then so it is with Ireland continually, for the sword was never yet out of their hand, but when they are weary with wars and brought down to extreme wretchedness; then they creep a little perhaps and sue for grace, till they have gotten new breath and recovered strength again: so as it is in vain to speak of planting of laws and plotting of policies till they be altogether subdued.

EUDOXUS: Were they not so at the first conquering of them by Strongbow[9] in the time of King Henry the Second? Was there not a through way then made by the sword, for the imposing of the laws upon them, and were they not then executed with such a mighty hand as you say was used by the Norman Conqueror? What odds is there then in this case? Why should not the same laws take as good effect in that people as they did here, being in

5. The inhabitants of Sparta.
6. The traditional founder of the Spartan constitution.
7. The Athenian statesman and poet who reformed the constitution.
8. the multitude.
9. Richard de Clare (died 1176), earl of Pembroke, who led the Anglo-Norman invasion of Ireland before the arrival of King Henry II in 1172.

like sort prepared by the sword and brought under by extremity, and why should they not continue in as good force and vigour for the containing of the people?

IRENIUS: The case yet is not like, but there appears great odds between them, for by the conquest of Henry the Second, true it is that the Irish were utterly vanquished and subdued, so as no enemy was able to hold up head against his power, in which their weakness he brought in his laws and settled them as now they there remain, like as William the Conqueror did, so as in this much they agree, but in the rest, that is in the chiefest, they vary. For to whom did King Henry the Second impose those laws? Not to the Irish, for the most part of them fled from his power into deserts and mountains, leaving the wide country to the Conqueror, who in their stead eftsones[10] placed Englishmen who possessed all the land and did quite shut out the Irish or the most part of them; and to those new inhabitants and colonies he gave his laws to wit, the same laws under which they were born and bred, the which it was not difficult to place amongst them, being formerly well inured thereunto; unto whom afterwards there repaired diverse of the poor distressed people of the Irish for succour and relief, of whom such as they thought fit for labour and industriously disposed, as the most part of their baser sort are, they received unto them as their vassals, but scarcely vouchsafed[11] to impart unto them the benefit of those laws under which themselves lived, but everyone made his will and commandment a law unto his own vassal. Thus was not the law of England ever properly applied unto the Irish nation as by a purposed plot[12] of government, but as they could insinuate and steal themselves under the same by their humble carriage and submission.

EUDOXUS: How comes it then to pass that having been once so low brought and thoroughly subjected, they afterwards lifted themselves so strongly up again, and since do stand so stiffly against all rule and government? . . .

10. soon afterwards.
11. condescended.
12. a clearly thought-out plan.

[The answer to this query of Eudoxus is provided by means of a historical discourse, which shows how the outbreak of civil strife in England provided the Gaelic Irish with the opportunity to revive their fortunes. Account is also taken of the leadership provided to the Gaelic Irish by Edward Bruce and to the falling away from obedience of some Irish lords of Norman descent, most notably Thomas Fitzgerald (Silken Thomas) in 1536 and Gerald, earl of Desmond, in 1579. This last point provides the speakers with the opportunity to praise the service of Arthur Lord Gray de Wilton who, by suppressing Desmond's revolt, had, they believed, pre-empted a general revolt against crown authority in Ireland. Following these diversions, the discussion returns to the identification of the defects and inconveniences of the laws, customs and religion of Ireland, and Irenius leads the way by considering the shortcomings of the English common law as it is practised in Ireland.]

IRENIUS: The Common Law is (as I before said) of itself most rightful and very convenient, I suppose, for the kingdom for which it was first devised; for this I think (as it seems reasonable) that out of the manners of the people and abuses of the country for which they were invented, they took their first beginning. For else they should be most unjust, for no laws of man according to the strait rule of right,[1] are just, but as in regard of the evils which they prevent, and the safety of the common weale which they provide for. As for example, in the true balancing of justice, it is a flat wrong to punish the thought or purpose of any before it be enacted; for true justice punisheth nothing but the evil act or wicked word. Yet by the laws of all kingdoms it is a capital crime to devise or purpose the death of the king. The reason is for that when such a purpose is effected it should be too late to devise of the punishment thereof, and should turn that common weal to more hurt by such loss of their prince, than such punishment of the malefactors could remedy; and therefore the law in that case punisheth his thought: for better is a mischief than an inconvenience, so that *Jus Politicum*,[2] though it be not of itself just, yet by application, or rather necessity, is made just, and this only respect maketh all laws just. Now then, if those laws of Ireland be not likewise applied and fitted for that realm, they are sure very inconvenient.

EUDOXUS: You reason strongly, but what unfitness do you find in them for that realm? Show us some particulars.

IRENIUS: The Common Law appointeth that all

1. strict entitlement.
2. Literally 'political law', but what is meant is the rule of expediency.

trials, as well of crimes as titles and rights, shall be made by verdict of jury chosen out of the honestest and most substantial freeholders. Now all the freeholders of that realm are Irish, which, when the cause shall fall between an Irishman and an English, or between the Queen and any freeholder of that country, they make no more scruple to pass against the Englishman or the Queen, though it be to strain their oaths, than to drink milk unstrained,[3] so that before the jury go together, it is all to nothing what their verdict will be. The trial thereof have I so often seen, that I dare confidentially avouch the abuse thereof: yet is the law of itself (as I said) good, and the first institution thereof being given to all Englishmen very rightful, but now that the Irish have stepped into the rooms of the English, who are now become so heedful and provident to keep them out from henceforth, that they make no scruple of conscience to pass against them, it is good reason that either that course of the law for trials be altered, or other provision for juries be made.

EUDOXUS: In sooth,[4] Irenius, you have discovered a point worth the consideration, for hereby not only the English subject findeth no indifference[5] in deciding of his cause, be it never so just, but also the Queen as well in all pleas of the Crown, as also for all inquiries for escheates, lands, attainted wardships, concealments,[6] and all such like is abused, and exceedingly endamaged.

IRENIUS: You say very true: for I dare undertake that at this day, there are more attainted lands[7] concealed from Her Majesty, than she now hath possessions in all Ireland, and that is no small inconvenience: for besides that, she loseth so much land as should turn her to great profit, she besides loseth so many good subjects which might be assured to her, as those lands would yield inhabitants and living unto.

EUDOXUS: But does that people, say you, make no more conscience to perjure themselves in their verdicts and to damn their souls?

IRENIUS: Not only so in their verdicts, but also in all other their dealings. Specially with the English they are most wilfully bent, for though they will not seem manifestly to do it, yet will some one or other subtle-headed fellow amongst them pick some quirk, or devise some subtle evasion, whereof the rest will lightly take hold, and suffer themselves easily to be led by him to that themselves desired; for in the most apparent matter that may be, the least question or doubt that can be moved will make a stop unto them, and put them quite out of the way, besides that of themselves they are for the most part, so cautelous[8] and wily headed, especially being men of so small experience and practice in law matters, that you would wonder whence they borrow such subtleties and sly shifts.

EUDOXUS: But methinks this inconvenience might be much helped in the judges and chief magistrates which have the choosing and nominating of those jurors, if they would have care to appoint either most Englishmen, or such Irishmen as were of the soundest disposition; for no doubt but some there be incorruptible.

IRENIUS: Some there be indeed, as you say. But then would the Irish party[9] cry out of partiality, and complain he hath not justice, he is not used as a subject, he is not suffered to have the free benefit of the law. And these outcries the magistrates there do much shun, as they have cause, since they are so readily harkened unto here, neither can it indeed, although the Irish party would be content, to be so compassed, that such English freeholders which are but few, and such faithful Irishmen which are indeed as few, shall always be chosen for trials. For being so few they should soon be made weary of their freehold, and therefore a good care is to be had by all good occasions, to increase their number, and to plant more by them, but were it so that the juries could be picked out of such choice men as you desire, there would nevertheless be as bad corruption in the trial, for the evidence being brought in by the base Irish people will be as deceitful as the verdicts, for they care much less than the others what they swear, and sure their lords may compel them to say anything. For myself have heard, when one of that base sort which they call Churls,[10] being challenged and reproved for his false oath, have answered confidently, that his Lord commanded him, and that it was the least thing he could do for his Lord to swear for him, so inconscionable are

3. Spenser is here punning on the word 'strain' while alluding to the Irish reputation for drinking filthy milk.
4. truly.
5. impartiality.
6. These terms refer to lands that should rightfully fall to the crown according to the procedures of feudal tenure.
7. Lands that should be rightfully confiscated to the crown.
8. deceitful and crafty.
9. The Old English politicians.
10. cultivators of the soil.

these common people, and so little feeling have they of God or their own souls' health.

EUDOXUS: It is a most miserable case, but what help then can there be in this? For though the manner of the trial should be altered, yet the proof of everything must needs be by testimonies of such persons as the parties shall produce; which if they shall be corrupt, how can there ever any light of the truth appear? What remedy is there for this evil, but to make heavy laws and penalties against perjurers?

IRENIUS: I think sure that will do small good; for when a people are inclined to any vice or have no touch of conscience, nor sense of their evil doing, it is bootless[11] to think to restrain them by any penalties or fear of punishment; but either the occasion is to be taken away, or a more understanding of the right and shame of the fault is to be imprinted. For if Lycurgus should have made it death for the Lacedemonians to steal, they being a people which naturally delighted in stealth, or if it should be made a capital crime for the Flemings to be taken in drunkenness, there should have been few Lacedemonians soon left, and fewer Flemings. So impossible it is to remove any fault so general in a people with terror of laws, or most sharp restraints.

EUDOXUS: What means may there then be to avoid this inconvenience, for the case sure seems very hard?

IRENIUS: We are not yet come to that point to devise remedies for the evils, but only have now to recount them, of the which this that I have told you is one defect in the Common Law.

EUDOXUS: Tell us then, I pray you further, have you any more of this sort in the Common Law? . . .

11. useless.

[In response to this overture, Irenius lists further deficiencies that he has witnessed in the operation of the common law in Ireland. The most serious of these is that the common law provides would-be rebels with a facility whereby they can entrust their property to nominees, who hold it in trust for their heirs if their rebellion proves to be a failure. In this way the rebels stood to lose only their lives in the attempt, and the crown was defrauded of the property that would otherwise have been declared forfeit. This example, with others, satisfies Eudoxus that the preferred Old English scheme for extending the benefits of common law to all elements of the Irish population does not provide a remedy for the country's social ills.

The speakers then consider statute law as a possible instrument of social reform, but they reject this too because judges are still given excessive scope to interpret statutes. Moreover, they find that statutes that pass through parliament frequently result in the consolidation rather than in the weakening of the position of Irish lords. Irenius cites one such example.]

IRENIUS: Another statute I remember: which having been an ancient Irish custom, is now upon advisement made an English law, and that is called the Custom of Kincogish,[1] which is that every head of every sept and every chief of every kindred or family should be answerable and bound to bring forth every one of that kindred or sept under him at all times to be justified when he should be required or charged with any treason, felony or other heinous crime.

EUDOXUS: Why, surely this seems a very necessary law, for considering that many of them be such losels and scatterlings,[2] as that they cannot easily by any sheriff, constable, bailiff, or other ordinary officer, be gotten when they are challenged for any such fact, this is a very good means to get them to be brought in by him, that is the head of the sept or chief of that house; wherefore I wonder what just exception ye can make against the same.

IRENIUS: True, Eudoxus, in the pretence of the good of this statute ye have nothing erred, for it seemeth very expedient and necessary, but the hurt which comes thereby is greater than the good, for whilst every chief of a sept standeth so bound to the law for every man that is of his blood or sept that is under him, inclusive every one of his sept is put under him, and he made great by the commanding of them all. For if he may not command them, then that law doth wrong that bindeth him to bring them forth to be justified, and if he may command them then he may command them as well to ill as to good; hereby the lords and captains of countries, the principals and heads of septs are made stronger, whom it should be a most special care in policy to weaken, and to set up and strengthen diverse of his underlings against him, which whensoever he shall offer to swerve from duty, may be able to beard him, for it is very dangerous to leave the command of so many as some septs are, being 5 or 6 thousand

1. The word derives from the Irish *cin comfocuis*, 'responsibility for a relative or legal connection'.

2. scoundrels and vagrants.

persons, to the will of one man, who may lead them to what he will as he himself shall be inclined.

EUDOXUS: In very deed, Irenius, it is very dangerous, especially seeing the disposition of those people, not always inclinable to the best, and therefore I hold it no wisdom to leave unto them too much command over their kindred, but rather to withdraw their followers from them as much as may be, and to gather them under the command of law by some better mean, than this Custom of Kincogish, the which word I would be glad to know what it namely signifieth, for the meaning thereof, I seem to understand reasonably well.

IRENIUS: It is a word mingled of English and Irish together, so as I am partly led to think that the custom thereof was first English, and afterwards made Irish, for such another law they had here in England as I remember made by King Alured,[3] that every gentleman should continually bring forth his kindred and followers to the law, so, *kyn* is English and *coghish* signifieth affinity in Irish....

3. King Alfred the Great (849-99), king of Wessex 871-99.

[Having thus discredited the notion, which was particularly favoured by the Old English, that the Irish could be reformed by legal measures alone, Eudoxus and Irenius proceed, according to their initial plan, to detail the customs of Ireland that are in need of drastic reform.]

EUDOXUS: Syth[1] then that we have thus reasonably handled the inconveniences in the laws, let us now pass unto your second part, which was, as I remember, of the abuses of customs, in which me seems yet have a fair champion[2] laid open unto you, in which ye may at large stretch out your discourse into many sweet remembrances of antiquities, from whence it seemeth that the customs of that nation proceeded.

IRENIUS: Indeed, Eudoxus, you say very true, for all the customs of the Irish which I have very often noted and compared with that I have read would minister occasion of most ample discourse of the first original of them, and the antiquity of that people which, in truth, I do think to be more ancient than most that I know in this end of the world; so as if it were in the handling of some man of

1. Seeing that, since.
2. Literally 'open ground'.

sound judgement and plentiful reading it would be most pleasant and profitable, but it may be, we may at some other time of meeting, take occasion to treat thereof more at large, here only it shall suffice to touch such customs of the Irish as seem offensive and repugnant to the good government of that realm.

EUDOXUS: Follow then your own course, for I shall the better content myself, to forbear my desire, now in hope that you will as you say some other time more abundantly satisfy it.

IRENIUS: Before we enter into the treatise of their customs it is first needful to consider from whence they first sprung, for from the sundry manners of the nations from whence that people which are now called Irish were derived, some of the customs which now remain amongst them have been fetched, and since have been continued amongst them. For not of one nation was it peopled as it is, but of sundry people of different conditions and manners, but the chiefest which have first possessed and inhabited it, I suppose to be Scythians,[3] which at such time as the Northern nations overflowed all Christendom, came down to the sea coast, where inquiring for other countries abroad and getting intelligence of this country of Ireland, finding shipping convenient, passed over thither and arrived in the North part thereof, which is now called Ulster; which first inhabiting, and afterwards stretching themselves forth into the land as their numbers increased, named it all of themselves Scuttenland — which more briefly is called Scutlande or Scotland....

3. The Greek name for the inhabitants of the country lying between the Carpathians and the river Don. These were accepted in sixteenth-century ethnology as prototype barbarians, as in Olaus Magnus, *Historia de Gentium Septentrionalium Variis Conditionibus* (1567).

[This introduction provides the occasion for a lengthy discourse on the original settlement of Ireland. The speakers conclude from the evidence cited by Irenius that most inhabitants of the province of Ulster were of Scythian descent, that most inhabitants in the west and south of the country were of Gaullish ancestry, and that those inhabiting the mountainous areas of Leinster were descended from the ancient Britons, who had once been dominant in England and Wales. These original inhabitants, it is concluded, subsequently were joined by Saxon and then Anglo-Norman migrants from England and Wales, who in turn had left a cultural residue in Ireland. This historical account serves to explain the diversity of customs that have been witnessed in Ireland, but the authors are agreed that the Scythian influence is the most potent one and that all the inhabitants of Ireland, regardless of their origins, have been attracted by Scythian customs. This point, which is essential to an understanding of the text, is introduced by Eudoxus.]

EUDOXUS: What is this that ye say of so many as remain English of them? Why are not they that were once English abiding English still?

IRENIUS: No, for the most part of them are degenerated and grown almost mere Irish,[1] yea and more malicious to the English than the very Irish themselves.

EUDOXUS: What hear I? And is it possible that an Englishman brought up naturally in such sweet civility as England affords could find such liking in that barbarous rudeness that he should forget his own nature and forgo his own nation? How may this be, or what, I pray you, may be the cause hereof?

IRENIUS: Surely nothing but the first evil ordinance and institution of that commonwealth. But thereof now is here no fit place to speak, lest by the occasion thereof offering matter of a long discourse, we might be drawn from this that we have in hand, namely the handling of abuses in the customs of Ireland.

EUDOXUS: In truth, Irenius, ye do well remember the plot of your first purpose, but yet from that meseems ye have much swerved in all this long discourse of the first inhabiting of Ireland, for what is that to your purpose?

IRENIUS: Truly very material, for if you marked the course of all that speech well it was to show by what means the customs that now are in Ireland being some of them indeed very strange and almost heathenish, were first brought in, and that was as I said by those nations from whom that country was first peopled; for the difference of manners and customs doth follow the difference of nations and people, the which I have declared unto you to have been three special, which seated themselves there: to wit, first the Scythians, then the Gauls and lastly the English; notwithstanding that I am not ignorant, that there were sundry other nations which got footing in that land, of which there yet remain diverse great families and septs of whom I will also in their proper places make mention.

1. pure Irish.

EUDOXUS: Ye bring yourself, Irenius, very well into the way again, notwithstanding that it seemeth that ye were never out of the way, but now that ye have passed through those antiquities which I could have wished not so soon ended, begin when ye please to declare what customs and manners have been derived from those nations to the Irish, and which of them ye find fault withal. . . .

[There follows a detailed description of those customs to which Irenius most objects. These include the practice of transhumance, the wearing of mantles and long glibs of hair, the use of loud cries when entering battle, and the employment of 'immoderate wailings' at funerals. This litany enables the speakers to dwell upon these elements in Irish society, such as professional fighting men (known to the English as 'kerne') and bardic poets, who, it is asserted, would have to be 'cut off' before any reformation could take place. This was so because these elements were known to have a professional interest in fostering those customs that seemed reprehensible to Irenius and Eudoxus. Of equal concern to both are those practices, such as fostering and intermarriage, which served to accelerate the degeneration of the previously civil population towards the social condition of those who derived from Scythian ancestors. This point is pursued as follows:]

EUDOXUS: Ye have very well run through such customs as the Irish have derived from the first old nations which inhabited that land, namely the Scythians, the Spaniards, the Gauls, the Britons. It now remaineth that you take in hand the customs of the old English[1] which are amongst the Irish, of which I do not think that ye shall have much to find fault with any, considering that by the English most of the old bad Irish customs were abolished, and more civil fashions brought up in their stead.

IRENIUS: You think otherwise, Eudoxus, than I do, for the chiefest abuses which are now in that realm are grown from the English, and the English that were are now much more lawless and licentious than the very wild Irish, so that as much care as was then by them had to reform the Irish, so much and more must now be used to reform them so much time doth alter the manners of men.

EUDOXUS: That seemeth very strange which you say, that men should so much degenerate from their first natures as to grow wild.

1. Spenser here means the descendants of the Anglo-Norman settlers in Ireland. This is the first known use of the term 'Old English' in an unqualified fashion.

IRENIUS: So much can liberty and ill example do.

EUDOXUS: What liberty had the English there, more than they had here at home? Were not the laws planted amongst them at the first, and had they not governors to curb and keep them still in awe and obedience?

IRENIUS: They had, but it was for the most part such as did more hurt than good, for they had governors for the most part of themselves, and commonly out of the two families of the Geraldines and the Butlers, both adversaries and co-rivals one against the other, who though for the most part they were but deputies under some of the kings of England's sons, brethren, or other near kinsmen who were the king's lieutenants, yet they swayed so much as they had all the rule and the others but the title; of which the Butlers and Geraldines, albeit I must confess there were very brave and worthy men, as also of other the peers of that realm made Lord Deputies and Lords Justices at sundry times, yet through greatness of their late conquests and seignories they grew insolent, and bent both that regal authority and also their private powers one against another, to the utter subversion of themselves and strengthening of the Irish again. This ye may read plainly discovered by a letter written from the citizens of Cork out of Ireland to the Earl of Shrewsbury then in England and remaining yet upon record both in the Tower of England, also amongst the Chronicles of Ireland, wherein it is by them complained that the English lords and gentlemen who then had great possessions in Ireland began, through pride and insolence, to make private wars one against another, and when either part was weak they would wage and draw in the Irish to take their part, by which means they both greatly encouraged and enabled the Irish, which till that time had been shut up within the Mountain of Slewlougher,[2] and weakened and disabled themselves insomuch that their revenues were wonderfully impaired, and some of them which are there reckoned to have been able to have spent twelve or fourteen hundred pounds per annum of old rent (that I may say no more) besides their commodities of creeks and havens, were now scarce able to dispend the third part; from which disorder, and through other huge calamities which have come upon them thereby, they are now grown to be almost as lewd as the Irish; I mean of such English as were planted above towards the west, for the English pale hath preserved itself through nearness of their state in reasonable civility, but the rest which dwell above in Connaught and Munster, which is the sweetest soil of Ireland, and some in Leinster and Ulster, are degenerate and grown to be as very patchocks[3] as the wild Irish, yea and some of them have quite shaken off their English names and put on Irish, that they might be altogether Irish.

2. The mountains of Sliabh Luachra in County Kerry.

EUDOXUS: Is it possible that any should so far grow out of frame that they should in so short space quite forget their country and their own names? That is a most dangerous lethargy, much worse than that of Messala Corvinus,[4] who being a most learned man, through sickness forgot his own name. . . .

3. This is the only known use of this word; various derivations have been suggested and it clearly means a base person.
4. Roman soldier, orator and statesman (64 B.C.-8 A.D.), who had a reputation as a historian and also dabbled in poetry and philosophy.

[Having thus had the opportunity to expose the excessive authority that was conceded by the crown to Old English lords and the evils that derived therefrom, the speakers conclude their consideration of evil customs by considering the malconsequences of the power enjoyed by all lords in Ireland.]

IRENIUS: Now we will proceed to other like defects, among which there is one general inconvenience which reigneth almost throughout all Ireland, and that is of the lords of lands and freeholders, who do not there use to set out their lands in farm or for term of years to their tenants, but only from year to year, and some during pleasure; neither indeed will the Irish tenant or husband otherwise take his land than so long as he list[1] himself. The reason hereof in the tenant is for that the landlords there use most shamefully to rack[2] their tenants, laying upon him coignie and livery[3] at pleasure, and exacting of him, besides his

1. as long as he wants or desires.
2. To raise rents exorbitantly.
3. From Irish *coinnmid* (right to free quarters) and Latin *liber* (free); the term described the methods used by Anglo-Norman lords in Ireland for billeting their soldiers and horses upon their tenants. The equivalent in Gaelic lordships was known as *buannacht*, or 'bonnaght' in its anglicized form.

covenant, what he please, so that the poor husbandman either dare not bind himself to him for longer time, or that he thinketh by his continual liberty of change to keep his landlord the rather in awe from wronging him; and the reason why the landlord will no longer covenant with him is for that he daily looketh after change and alteration, and hovereth in expectation of new worlds.

EUDOXUS: But what evil cometh hereby to the commonwealth, or what reason is it that any landlord should not set, nor any tenant take his land as himself list?

IRENIUS: Marry, the evils which cometh thereby are great, for by this mean both the landlord thinketh that he hath his tenant more at command to follow him into what action soever he will enter. And also the tenant, being left at his liberty, is fit for every variable occasion of change that shall be offered by time, and so much also the more willing and ready is he to run into the same, for that he hath no such estate in any his holding, no such building upon any farm, no such costs employed in fencing and husbanding the same, as might withhold him from any such wilful course as his lord's cause and his own lewd disposition may carry him unto. All which he hath forborne and spared so much expense, for that he had no former estate in his tenement, but was only a tenant at will or little more, and so at will may leave it. And this inconvenience may be reason enough to ground any ordinance for the good of a commonwealth against the private behoof or will of any landlord that shall refuse to grant any such tenure or estate unto his tenant as may tend to the good of the whole realm.

EUDOXUS: Indeed, meseems, it is a great wilfulness in any such landlord, to refuse to make any longer farms unto their tenants, as may besides the general good of the realm, be also greatly for their own profit and avail. For what reasonable man will not think that the tenement shall be made much the better for the lord's behoof, if the tenant may by such means be drawn to build himself some handsome habitation thereon, to ditch and enclose his ground, to manure and husband it as good farmers use; for when his tenant's term shall be expired, it will yield him in the renewing his lease, both a good fine[4] and also a better rent, and also it shall be for the good of the tenant likewise, who by such buildings and enclosures, shall receive many benefits. First by the handsomeness of his house, he shall take great comfort of his life, more safe dwelling, and a delight to keep his said house neat and cleanly, which now being (as they commonly are) rather swinesteads than houses, is the chiefest cause of his so beastly manner of life and savage condition, lying and living together with his beast in one house in one room and in one bed, that is the clean straw, or rather the foul dunghill; and to all these other commodities he shall in short time find a greater added, that is his own wealth and riches increased and wonderfully enlarged by keeping his cattle in enclosures, where they shall always have fresh pasture, that now is all trampled and overrun, warm cover, that now lieth open to all weather, safe being, that now are continually filched and stolen.

IRENIUS: Ye have well, Eudoxus, accounted the commodities of this one good ordinance amongst which this that ye named last is not the least; for all the other being most beneficial both to the landlord and the tenant, this chiefly redowndeth to the good of the commonwealth, to have the land thus enclosed and well fenced. For it is both a principal bar and impeachment unto thieves from stealing of cattle in the night, and also a gall against all rebels and outlaws that shall rise up in any numbers against that government, for the thief thereby shall have much ado, first to bring forth, and afterwards to drive, his stolen prey, but through the common highways, where he shall soon be discried and met withal; and the rebel or open enemy, if any such shall happen, either at home or from abroad shall easily be found when he cometh forth, and also be well encountered withal by a few, in so strait passages and strong enclosures. This therefore when we come to the reforming of all these evil customs before mentioned is needful to be remembered. But now by this time, meseems, that I have well run through the evil uses, which I have observed in Ireland. Nevertheless, I well wot[5] that many more there be, and infinitely many more in the private abuses of men, but these that are most general and tending to the hurt of the commonwealth as they have come to my remembrance I have as briefly as I could rehearsed unto you, and therefore now I think best that we pass to our third part, in which we noted inconveniences that is in religion....

4. An entry fine or fee paid by a tenant when he was granted a tenancy for a specified period.

5. I well know.

[In accordance with their initial plan, the two speakers proceed to identify the religious obstacles to reform.]

EUDOXUS: Surely ye have very well handled these two former, and if you shall as well go through the third likewise ye shall merit a very good meed.[1]

IRENIUS: Little have I to say of religion, both because the parts thereof be not many, itself being but one, and myself have not been much conversant in that calling, but as lightly passing by I have seen or heard. Therefore the fault which I find in religion is but one, but the same universal throughout all that country, that is that they are all Papists by their profession, but in the same so blindly and brutishly informed, for the most part as that you would rather think them atheists or infidels; but not one amongst an hundred knoweth any ground of religion and article of his faith, but can perhaps say his pater noster or his Ave Maria, without any knowledge or understanding what one word thereof meaneth.

EUDOXUS: This is truly a most pitiful hearing, that so many souls should fall into the Devil's jaws at once, and lack the blessed comfort of the sweet Gospel and Christ's dear passion. Aye me, how cometh it to pass that being a people as they are trading with so many nations, and frequented of so many, yet they have not tasted any part of those happy joys, nor once been lightened with the morning star of truth, but lie weltering in such spiritual darkness, hard by hell mouth, even ready to fall in, if God haply help not.

IRENIUS: The general fault cometh not of any late abuse either in the people or their priests, who can teach no better than they know, nor show no more light than they have seen but in the first institution and planting of religion in all that realm, which was, (as I read) in the time of Pope Celestine; who, as it is written, did first send over thither Palladius, who there deceasing, he afterwards sent over St. Patrick, being by nation a Briton, who converted the people, being then infidels, from paganism, and christened them; in which Pope's time and long before, it is certain that religion was generally corrupted with their Popish trumpery.[2] Therefore, what other could they learn than such trash as was taught them, and drink of that cup of fornication, with which the purple harlot had then made all nations drunken?[3]

EUDOXUS: What? Do you then blame and find fault with so good an act in that good Pope as the reducing of such a great people to Christendom, bringing so many souls to Christ, if that were ill what is good?

IRENIUS: I do not blame the christening of them, for to be sealed with the mark of the Lamb, by what hand soever it be done rightly, I hold it a good and gracious work; for the general profession which they then take upon them of the Cross and faith in Christ, I nothing doubt but through the powerful grace of that mighty Saviour, will work salvation in many of them. But nevertheless, since they drunk not from the pure spring of life, but only tasted of such troubled waters as were brought unto them, the dregs thereof have bred great contagion in their souls, the which daily increasing and being still augmented with their own lewd lives and filthy conversation, hath now bred in them this general disease, that cannot but only with very strong purgations be cleansed and carried away.

EUDOXUS: Then for this defect ye find no fault with the people themselves nor with the priests which take the charge of souls, but with the first ordinance and institution thereof?

IRENIUS: Not so, Eudoxus, for the sin or ignorance of the priest shall not excuse the people, nor the authority of their great pastor, Peter's successor, shall not excuse the priests, but they all shall die in their sins, for they have all erred and gone out of the way together.

EUDOXUS: But if this ignorance of the people be such a burden unto the Pope, is it not a like blot to them that now hold that place, in that they which now are in the light themselves,[4] suffer a people under their charge to wallow in such deadly darkness, for I do not see that the fault is changed but the fault's master?

IRENIUS: That which you blame, Eudoxus, is not, I suppose, any fault of will in these godly Fathers[5] which have charge thereof, nor any defect

1. recompense, reward.
2. Spenser's version of how Ireland was first converted to Christianity conforms closely to modern scholarly understanding of the subject. Celestine I was pope 422-32.
3. This is a classical protestant diatribe against the papacy — the purple harlot — which was held responsible for corrupting the pure Christianity that had first been instituted by Christ and the early fathers of the church.
4. The English, who have been brought to the light of true religion as a consequence of the success of the protestant Reformation.
5. The protestant clergy appointed in Ireland.

of zeal for reformation hereof, but the inconvenience of the time and troublous occasions wherewith that wretched realm hath been continually turmoiled. For instruction in religion needeth quiet times, and ere we seek to settle a sound discipline in the clergy, we must purchase peace unto the laity; for it is ill time to preach amongst swords, and most hard or rather impossible it is to settle a good opinion in the minds of men, for matters of religion doubtful, which have a doubtless evil opinion of ourselves: for ere a new be brought in, the old must be removed.

EUDOXUS: Then belike it is meet that some fitter time be attended, that God send peace and quietness there in civil matters, before it be attempted in ecclesiastical, I would rather have thought that, as it is said, correction should begin at the House of God, and that the care of the soul should have been preferred before the care of the body.

IRENIUS: Most true, Eudoxus. The care of the soul and soul matters[6] are to be preferred before the care of the body, in consideration of the worthiness thereof, but not in the time of reformation. For if you should know a wicked person dangerously sick, having now both soul and body greatly diseased, yet both recoverable, would ye not think it ill advisement to bring the preacher before the physician? For if his body were neglected, it is like that his languishing soul, being disquieted by his diseaseful body, would utterly refuse and loath all spiritual comfort. But if his body were first recured and brought to good frame, should there not then be found best time to recure his soul also? So it is in the state of a realm. Therefore, as I said, it is expedient first to settle such a course of government there, as thereby both civil disorders and ecclesiastical abuses may be reformed and amended whereto needeth not any such great distance of times as ye suppose I require, but one joint resolution for both that each might second and confirm the other.

EUDOXUS: That we shall see when we come thereto. In the meantime I consider thus much as you have delivered touching the general fault which ye suppose in religion, to weet[7] that it is Popish, but do you find no particular abuses therein, nor in the ministers thereof?

IRENIUS: Yes, verily, for whatever disorders ye see in the Church of England ye may find there, and many, many more, namely, gross symonie, greedy covetousness, fleshly incontinence, careless sloth, and generally all disordered life in the common clergymen, and besides all these, they have their own particular enormities, for all the Irish priests which now enjoy the church livings there, are in manner mere laymen, saving that they have taken holy orders, but otherwise they do like laymen, go like laymen, live like laymen, follow all kind of husbandry and other worldly affairs, as the common Irish laymen do. They neither read scriptures nor preach to the people, nor minister the sacrament of Communion, but the Baptism they do, for they christen yet after the Popish fashion, and with the Popish Latin ministration; only they take the tithes and offerings, and gather what fruits else they may of their livings, the which they convert as badly. And some of them, they say, pay as due tributes and shares of their livings to their Bishops, (I speak of those which are Irish) as they receive them duly.

EUDOXUS: But is it suffered amongst them? It is wonder but that the governors redress such shameful abuses.

IRENIUS: How can they, since they know them not? For the Irish Bishops have their clergy in such awe and subjection under them, that they dare not complain of them, so as they may do to them what they please, for they, knowing their own unworthiness and incapacity, and that they are therefore still removable at their Bishop's will, yield what pleaseth him, and he taketh what he listeth; yea, and some of them whose diocese are in remote parts, somewhat out of the world's eye, do not at all bestow the benefices which are in their own donation upon any, but keep them in their own hands and set their own servants and horseboys to take up the tithes and fruits[8] of them, with the which some of them purchase great lands and build fair castles upon the same; of which abuse, if any question be moved, they have a very seemly colour of excuse, they they have no worthy ministers to bestow them upon, but keep them so unbestowed, for any such sufficient person as any shall bring unto them.

EUDOXUS: But is there no law or ordinance to meet with this mischief? Nor hath it never before been looked into?

IRENIUS: Yes, it seems it hath, for there is a statute there enacted in Ireland, which seems to

6. spiritual matters.
7. to wit, to know.

8. spiritual livings.

have been grounded upon a good meaning, that whatsoever Englishman being of good conversation and sufficiently shall be brought unto any of those bishops and nominated unto any living within their diocese, that is presently void, that he shall without contradiction be admitted thereunto before any Irish.

EUDOXUS: This is surely a very good law and well provided for this evil whereof ye speak, and why is not the same observed?

IRENIUS: I think it is well observed, and that none of the bishops transgress the same, but yet it worketh no reformation hereof, for many respects. First, there are no such sufficient English ministers sent over, as might be presented to any bishop for any living, but the most part of such English as come over thither of themselves are either unlearned or men of some bad note, for which they have forsaken England, so as the bishop to whom they shall be presented may justly reject them as incapable and insufficient. Secondly, the bishop himself is perhaps an Irishman, who being made judge by that law of the sufficiency of the minister, may at his own will dislike of the Englishman as unworthy in his opinion, and admit of any other Irish whom he shall think more for his turn. And if he shall, at the instance of any Englishman of countenance there, whom he will not displease, accept of any such English minister as shall be tendered unto him, yet he will underhand carry such a hard hand over him, or by his officers wring him so sore that he will soon make him weary of his poor living. Lastly, the benefices themselves are so mean and of so small profit in those Irish counties, through the ill husbandry of the Irish people which inhabit them, that they will not yield any competent maintenance for any honest minister to live upon, scarcely to buy him a gown: And were all this redressed as happily it might be, yet what good shall any English minister do amongst them, by preaching or teaching, which either cannot understand him or will not hear him, or what comfort of life shall he have, when his parishioners are so unsociable, so intractable, so ill affected to him as they usually be to all the English? Or finally, how dare almost any honest minister that are peaceful civil men commit his safety into the hands of such neighbours as the boldest captains dare scarcely dwell by?

EUDOXUS: Little good then, I see, is by that statute wrought, however well intended; but the reformation thereof must grow higher and be brought from a stronger ordinance than the commandment or penalty of a law, which none dare inform or complain of, when it is broken. But have you any more of these abuses in the clergy?

IRENIUS: I could perhaps reckon more, but I perceive my speech to grow too long, and these may suffice to judge of the general disorders which reign amongst them. As for the particulars, they are too many to be reckoned, for the clergy there (except some few grave fathers which are in high place about the state, and some few others which are lately planted in their new college)[9] are generally bad, licentious and most disordered....

9. Trinity College, Dublin, founded in 1591 for the education of a protestant clergy to serve in Ireland.

[At this point Eudoxus expresses himself satisfied that Irenius has isolated the principal inconveniences 'in the laws, in the customs and in the religion of that land.' Before proceeding to a consideration of how reform might best be proceeded with, they both allude to the existence of corrupt practices among some of the English-born officials and captains serving in Ireland; they suggest that these people, like the Old English before them, are degenerating from their previous civil condition. Neither Irenius nor Eudoxus sees any resolution to this problem until the government in England decides on a coherent programme of reform that will be proceeded with by each successive governor of Ireland. It is only then, they believe, that individual governors will see the need to discipline their subordinates, whose misdeeds would otherwise cast doubt on their own effectiveness as rulers. Once they have agreed on this point, the two proceed to a consideration of the most appropriate reform for the conditions they have described.]

IRENIUS: Now that we have thus ended all the abuses and inconveniences of that government which was our first part, it followeth next that we pass unto the second part, which was of the means to cure and redress the same, which we must labour to reduce to the first beginning thereof.

EUDOXUS: Right so, Irenius, for by that which I have noted in all this your discourse, ye suppose that the whole ordinance and institute of that realm's government was both at first when it was placed evil plotted, and also since through other oversight, run more out of square, to that disorder which it is now come unto, like as two indirect lines, the further they are drawn out, the further they go asunder.

IRENIUS: I do so, Eudoxus, and as ye say, so think, that the longer that government thus continueth, in the worse case will that realm be, for it is all in vain that they now strive and endeavour by fair means and peaceable plots, to redress the same, without first removing all those inconveniences, and new framing as it were in the forge all that is worn out of fashion; for all other means will be but lost labour by patching up one hole to make many. For the Irish do strongly hate and abhor all reformation and subjection to the English, by reason that having been once subdued by them, they were thrust out of all their possessions. So as now they fear that if they were again brought under they should likewise be expelled out of all: which is the cause that they hate English government according to the saying, '*Quem metuunt Oderunt*,'[1] therefore the reformation must now be with the strength of a greater power.

EUDOXUS: But, methinks, that might be by making of good laws, and establishing of new statutes with sharp penalties and punishments for amending of all that is presently amiss, and not as ye suppose to begin all as it were anew and to alter the whole form of the government, which how dangerous a thing it is to attempt, you yourself must needs confess, and they which have the managing of the realm's whole policy cannot, without great cause, fear and refrain. For all innovation is perilous insomuch as, though it be meant for the better, yet so many accidents and fearful events may come between, as that it may hazard the loss of the whole.

IRENIUS: Very true, Eudoxus. All change is to be shunned, where the affairs stand in such state as that they may continue in quietness or be assured at all to abide as they are. But that in the realm of Ireland we see much otherwise, for every day we perceive the troubles growing more upon us, and one evil growing upon another, insomuch as there is no part sound nor ascertained, but all have their ears upright, waiting when the watchword shall come that they should all rise generally into rebellion and cast away the English subjection to which there now little wanteth, for I think the word be already given and there wanteth nothing but opportunity, which truly is the death of one noble person,[2] who being himself most steadfast to his sovereign Queen, his country coasting upon the South Sea, stoppeth the ingate of all that evil which is looked for, and holdeth in all those which are at his back with the terror of his greatness, and the assurance of his immovable loyalty. And therefore where you think that good and sound laws might amend and reform things amiss there you think surely amiss, for it is vain to prescribe laws where no man careth for keeping them, nor feareth the danger for breaking them, but all the realm is first to be reformed and laws are afterward to be made, for keeping and continuing it in that reformed estate.

EUDOXUS: How then do you think is the reformation thereof to be begun, if not by laws and ordinances?

IRENIUS: Even by the sword, for all those evils must first be cut away with a strong hand before any good can be planted, like as the corrupt branches and the unwholesome boughs are first to be pruned, and the foul moss cleansed or scraped away, before the tree can bring forth any good fruit.

EUDOXUS: Did you blame me even now for wishing kerne[3] horseboys and carrows[4] to be clean cut off as too violent a means, and do you yourself now prescribe the same medicine? Is not the sword the most violent redress that may be used for any evil?

IRENIUS: It is so, but yet where no other remedy may be devised, nor no hope of recovery had, there must needs this violent means be used, as for that loose kind of people which you would have cut off I blamed it for that they might otherwise perhaps be brought to good, as namely by this way which I set before you.

EUDOXUS: Is not your way all one with the former in effect which you found fault with, save only this odds, that I say by the halter and you say by the sword. What difference is there?

IRENIUS: There is surely great when you shall understand it. For by the sword which I named I do not mean the cutting off of all that nation with the sword, which far be it from me that ever I should think so desperately or wish so uncharitably, but by

1. They shall hate whom they fear.

2. Spenser can be referring only to Thomas Butler (1532-1614), tenth earl of Ormond. That earl was generally not liked or praised by English protestant officials in Ireland, but Spenser would have seen the need to honour a man whose opinion was always respected by Ormond's cousin, Queen Elizabeth I.

3. Irish professional footsoldiers; from the Irish *ceithreanach*.

4. professional gamblers; from the Irish *cearabhach*.

the sword I meant the royal power of the prince, which ought to stretch itself forth in her chief strength, to the redressing and cutting off of those evils which I before blamed, and not of the people which are evil; for evil people by good ordinance and government may be made good, but the evil that is of itself evil will never become good.

EUDOXUS: I pray you then, declare your mind at large how you would wish that sword which you mean, to be used to the reformation of all those evils....

[In response to this request, Irenius details the military subjugation of the country that, in his opinion, would precede any work of reform. The force that he considers necessary would be of the strength of 10,000 footmen and 1,000 horsemen, to be maintained in the government's pay for a year-and-a-half. These troops would be garrisoned in the several provinces of Ireland, with the largest being assigned to Ulster, which province presents the greatest threat to the government's authority. The very presence of troops in such numbers, it is believed, would overawe the population at large and force many to desert their leaders who had introduced them to disobedience. All but these leaders would be given the opportunity to surrender their arms and to submit themselves to mercy. This liberal offer of pardon is considered sufficient by Irenius to justify his describing the entire scheme as moderate. Then, in the most arresting and most frequently quoted passage of the text, Irenius describes the action that would be taken against those who reject this offer of clemency. This section of the discourse is employed both to justify the extreme actions taken by Lord Gray against the rebels in Munster and to point the way towards the country's comprehensive reform. Of those who would not submit themselves upon the first summons, Irenius asserts that he:]

IRENIUS: ... would have none received, but left to their fortune and miserable end. My reason is, for that those which will afterwards remain without are stout and obstinate rebels, such as will never be made dutiful and obedient, nor brought to labour or civil conversation, having once tasted that licentious life, and being acquainted with spoil and outrages, will ever after be ready for the like occasions, so as there is no hope of their amendment or recovery, and therefore needful to be cut off.

EUDOXUS: Surely of such desperate persons as wilfully follow the course of their own folly, there is no compassion to be had, and for the others ye have proposed a merciful means, much more than they have deserved. But what then shall be the conclusion of this war, for you have prefixed a short time of his continuance?

IRENIUS: The end I assure me will be very short and much sooner than can be in so great a trouble (as it seemeth) hoped for. Although there should none of them fall by the sword, nor be slain by the soldier, yet thus being kept from manurance,[1] and their cattle from running abroad by this hard restraint, they would quickly consume themselves and devour one another. The proof whereof I saw sufficiently ensampled[2] in those late wars in Munster, for notwithstanding that the same was a most rich and plentiful country, full of corn and cattle, that you would have thought they could have been able to stand long, yet ere one year and a half they were brought to so wonderful wretchedness, as that any stony heart would have rued the same. Out of every corner of the woods and glens they came creeping forth upon their hands, for their legs could not bear them. They looked anatomies of death, they spake like ghosts crying out of their graves, they did eat of the dead carrions, happy were they could find them, yea and one another soon after in so much as the very carcasses they spared not to scrape out of their graves. And if they found a plot of water cress or shamrocks, there they flocked as to a feast for the time, yet not able long to continue therewithal, that in short space there were none almost left and a most populous and plentiful country suddenly left void of man or beast. Yet sure in all that war there perished not many by the sword, but all by the extremity of famine, which they themselves had wrought.

EUDOXUS: It is wonder that you tell, and more to be wondered how it should so shortly come to pass.

IRENIUS: It is most true, and the reason also very ready; for ye must conceive that the strength of all that nation is the kern, gallowglass,[3] stocagh,[4] horseman and horseboy, the which having been never used to have anything of their own, and now living upon spoil of others, make no spare of anything, but havoc and confusion of all they meet with, whether it be their own friends' goods or their foes', and if they happen to get never so great spoils at any time the same they waste and consume in a trice, as naturally delighting in spoil, though it do

1. tilling the soil.
2. exemplified.
3. Scots mercenary soldier; from the Irish *galloglach*.
4. Probably from the Irish *stócach*, meaning an idle fellow, or foot-soldier.

themselves no good. And on the other side whatsoever they leave unspent, the soldier, when he cometh there, he havocketh and spoileth likewise, so that between them both nothing is very shortly left. And yet this is very necessary to be done, for the soon finishing of the war. And not only this in this wise, but also all those subjects which border upon those parts are either to be removed and drawn away or likewise to be spoiled, that the enemy may find no succour thereby, for what the soldier spares the rebel will surely spoil.

EUDOXUS: I do now well understand you. But now when all things are brought to this pass, and all filled with these rueful spectacles of so many wretched carcasses starving, goodly countries wasted, so huge a desolation and confusion, as even I that do but hear it from you and do picture it in my mind, do greatly pity and commiserate it, if it shall happen that the state of this misery, and lamentable image of things shall be told and feelingly presented to Her sacred Majesty, being by nature full of mercy and clemency, who is most inclinable to such pitiful complaints, and will not endure to hear such tragedies made of her people and poor subjects, as some about her may insinuate, then she perhaps for very compassion of such calamities, will not only stop the stream of such violence and return to her wonted mildness, but also con them little thanks[5] which have been the authors and counsellors of such bloody platforms. So I remember that in the late government of that good Lord Gray,[6] when after long travail and many perilous assays, he had brought things almost to this pass that ye speak of, that it was even made ready for reformation, and might have been brought to what Her Majesty would, like complaint was made against him, that he was a bloody man, and regarded not the life of her subjects, no more than dogs, but had wasted and consumed all, so as now she had almost nothing left but to reign in their ashes. Ear was soon lent thereunto, all suddenly turned topsy turvy, the noble Lord eftsoons was blamed, the wretched people pitied, and new counsels plotted, in which it was concluded that a general pardon should be sent over to all that would accept of it; upon which all former purposes were blanked,[7] the governor at a bay, and not only all that great and long charge which she had before been at quite lost and cancelled, but also all that hope of good which was even at the door put back and clean frustrate; all which whether it be true or no yourself can well tell.

IRENIUS: Too true, Eudoxus. The more the pity. For I may not forget so memorable a thing, neither can I be ignorant of that perilous device and of the whole means by which it was compassed and very cunningly contrived, by sowing first dissension between him and and another noble personage,[8] wherein they both at length found how notably they had been abused, and how thereby underhand this universal alteration of things was brought about; but then too late to stay the same, for in the meantime all that was formerly done with long labour and great toil was (as you say) in a moment undone, and that good lord blotted with the name of a bloody man, whom who that well knew, knew to be most gentle, affable, loving and temperate. But that the necessity of that present state of things enforced him to that violence, and almost changed his very natural disposition, but otherwise he was so far from delighting in blood, that oftentimes he suffered not just vengeance to fall where it was deserved, and even some of those which were afterwards his accusers had tasted too much of his mercy,[9] and were from the gallows brought to be his accusers. But his course indeed was this that he spared not the heads and principals of any mischievous practice or rebellion, but showed sharp judgement on them, chiefly, for ensample sake, that all the meaner sort, which also were then generally infected with that evil might by terror thereof be reclaimed and saved, if it were possible. For in that last conspiracy of the English Pale,[10] think you not that there were many more guilty than that felt the punishment, or was there any almost clear from the same? Yet he touched only a few of special note, and in the trial of them also even to prevent the blame of cruelty and partial proceeding, as seeking their blood, which he in his great wisdom, (as it seemeth) did foresee would be objected against him, he for avoiding thereof did use a singular discretion and

5. i.e. will not thank them at all.
6. Arthur Lord Gray de Wilton (1536-93), lord deputy of Ireland 1580-82, to whom Spenser had been personal secretary.
7. defeated or disappointed.
8. The reference here is to the jealousy that developed between Ormond and Lord Gray. Spenser is suggesting that this was deliberately fomented by a third party.
9. Spenser is referring to Old English politicians from the Pale whose position had been compromised by the Baltinglass revolt of 1580 and by the Nugent conspiracy that followed.
10. The Nugent conspiracy of 1581.

regard, for the jury that went upon their trial he made to be chosen out of their nearest kinsmen, and their judges he made, of some their own fathers, of others their uncles and dearest friends, who, when they could not but justly condemn them, yet uttered their judgement in abundance of tears. And yet he even herein was counted bloody and cruel. . . .

[The speakers concede that any governor who pursues such a policy would, like Lord Gray, expose himself to the denigration of the Old English community. Nonetheless, they strive to redeem Gray's reputation and seek to reveal the disastrous consequences that have derived from the alternate scheme of government pursued by Gray's successors. In this way, Irenius and Eudoxus make the case for a resumption of Gray's policy which, they believe, is the only one that will lead to a true and enduring reform. They further strengthen their case by asserting that the O'Neills of Tyrone, the most persistent opponents of English rule, are trespassers upon crown property and that Hugh O'Neill, recently created earl of Tyrone but now a rebel, is an ungrateful wretch who owes all he holds to the queen's benevolence. What holds true for the O'Neills is, it is contended, equally true for the ruling Gaelic septs in Leinster and elsewhere. This is advanced as a further reason why the queen should undertake a war designed both to recover crown property and to erect 'a perfect establishment and new commonwealth'. The various stages of the military endeavour are detailed, as are the components of a scheme for disbanding the native population and resettling them within the context of an English plantation in Ireland. Irenius suggests that a proclamation should be issued in the aftermath of war, to the effect:]

IRENIUS: . . . that whatsoever outlaws will freely come in and submit themselves to Her Majesty's mercy shall have liberty so to do, where they shall either find that grace they desire or return again in safety; upon which it is likely that so many as survive will come in to sue for grace, of which who so are thought meet[1] for subjection and fit to be brought to good may be received or else all of them, for I think that all will be but a very few, upon condition and assurance that they will submit themselves absolutely to Her Majesty's ordinance for them, by which they shall be assured of life and liberty and be only tied to such conditions as shall be thought by her meet, for containing them ever after in due obedience. To the which conditions I nothing doubt but that they will also most readily and upon their knees submit themselves, by the proof of that which I saw in Munster, for upon the like proclamation there they all came in, tag and rag, and when as afterwards many of them were denied to be received, they bade them do with them what they would, for they would by no means return again, nor go forth, for in that case who will not accept almost of any conditions, rather than die of hunger and misery?

EUDOXUS: It is likely so. But what then is the ordinance, and what be the conditions which you will propose unto them that shall reserve unto them an assurance of life and liberty?

IRENIUS: So soon then as they have given the best assurance of themselves which may be required, which must be, I suppose, some of their principal men to remain in hostage one of another, and some other for the rest (for other surety I reckon of none that may bind them, neither of wife nor of children, since then perhaps they would gladly be rid of both from the famine), I would have them first unarmed utterly, and stripped quite of all their warlike weapons, and then these conditions set down and made known unto them, that they shall be brought and removed with such creet[2] as they have into Leinster, where they shall be placed, and have land given them to occupy and live upon in such sort as shall become good subjects to labour thenceforth for their living, and to apply themselves unto honest trades of civility as they shall every one be found meet and able for.

EUDOXUS: Where then in God's name will ye place them in Leinster, or will you find out any new land there for them that is yet unknown?

IRENIUS: No, I will place them in all the country of the Byrnes and Tooles, which Hugh MacHugh hath, and in all the lands of the Cavanaghs[3] which are now in rebellion, and all the lands which will fall to Her Majesty thereabouts, which I know to be very spacious and large enough to contain them, being very near twenty or thirty miles wide.

EUDOXUS: But what then will ye do with all the Byrnes, the Tooles and the Cavanaghs, and all those that now are joined with them?

IRENIUS: At the very same time and in the same

1. thought by her fitting.

2. A rendition of the Irish word *creaght*, meaning herds of cattle, together with the accompanying herdsmen.

3. Gaelic septs that inhabited the mountainous areas of County Dublin and County Wicklow.

manner that I make that proclamation to them of Ulster, will I also have it made to these, and upon their submission thereunto I will take like assurance of them as of the other, after which I will translate all that remain of them into the places of the other, in Ulster, with all their creet and what else they have left them, the which I will cause to be divided amongst them in some meet sort as each may thereby have somewhat to sustain himself awhile withal, until by his further travail and labour of the earth he shall be able to provide himself better.

EUDOXUS: But will you then give the land freely unto them and make them heirs of the former rebels, so may you perhaps make them heirs also of their former villainies and disorders, or how else will you dispose of them?

IRENIUS: Not so, but all the lands I will give unto Englishmen whom I will have drawn thither, who shall have the same with such estates as shall be thought meet, and for such rent as shall eftsoons be rated. Under every of those Englishmen will I place some of those Irish to be tenants, for a certain rent according to the quantity of such land as every man shall have allotted unto him, and shall be found able to wield. Wherein this special regard shall be had, that in no place under any landlord there shall be many of them planted together, but dispersed wide from their acquaintances, and scattered far abroad through all the country. For that is the evil which I now find in all Ireland, that the Irish dwell altogether by their septs and several nations, so as they may practise or conspire what they will, whereas if there were English shed amongst them and placed over them they should not be able once to stir or murmur, but that it should be known, and they shortened according to their demerits.

EUDOXUS: Ye have good reason, but what rating of rents mean you? To what end do you purpose the same?

IRENIUS: My purpose is to rate the rent of all those lands of Her Majesty in such sort unto those Englishmen as shall take them as they may be well able to live thereupon, yielding Her Majesty a reasonable chiefery and also give a competent maintenance unto the garrisons which shall there be left amongst them. For these soldiers, (as I told you) remaining of the former garrisons, I cast to maintain upon the rent of those lands which shall be escheated,[4] and to have them divided through all Ireland, in such places as shall be thought most convenient, and occasion may require. And this was the course which the Romans observed in the conquest of England, for they planted some of their legions in all places convenient, the which they caused the country to maintain, cutting upon every portion of land a reasonable rent which they called *Romescot*, the which might not surcharge the tenant or freeholder, and defray the pay of the garrison. And this hath been always observed in all princes in all countries to them newly subdued, to set garrisons amongst them to contain them in duty, whose burden they made them to bear. And the want of this ordinance in the first conquest of Ireland, by Henry the Second, was the cause of the so short decay of that government, and the quick recovery again of the Irish. Therefore, by all means it is to be provided for. And this is that I would blame (if it should not misbecome me) in the late planting of Munster, that no care was had of this ordinance, nor any strength of a garrison provided for by a certain allowance out of all the said lands, but only the present profit looked unto, and the safe continuance thereof ever hereafter neglected. . . .

[Procedures are then described whereby the garrisons would be placed on a permanent footing and revenues would be raised within Ireland for their long-term maintenance. Eudoxus and Irenius also discuss the best means of inducing English colonists to take land in the proposed Irish plantations and to settle in the manufacturing towns that it is hoped will be established near the garrisons. Even when allowing for such civil concerns, Irenius cannot disguise the decidedly military aspect of his reform agenda, which provokes the protest of Eudoxus and the ensuing discussion.]

EUDOXUS: But as for these garrisons which ye have now so strongly planted throughout all Ireland, and every place swarming with soldiers; shall there be no end of them? For now thus being, meseemeth, I do see rather a country of war than of peace and quiet which ye erst[1] pretended to work in Ireland, for if you bring all things to that quietness which ye said, what need then to maintain so great forces as ye have charged upon it?

IRENIUS: I will unto you, Eudoxus, in private, discover the drift of my purpose. I mean (as I told you) and do well hope, hereby both to settle an eternal peace in that country, and also to make it

4. confiscated.

1. which you previously.

very profitable to Her Majesty, the which I see must be brought in by a strong hand, and so continued until it grow into a steadfast course of government; the which in this sort will neither be difficult nor dangerous, for the soldier, being once brought in for the service into Ulster, and having subdued it and Connaught, I will not have him to lay down his arms any more till he have effected that which I purpose. That is first to have a general composition[2] for the maintenance of these throughout the realm, in regard of the troublous times and daily danger which is threatened to this realm by the King of Spain, and thereupon to bestow all the soldiers in sort[3] as I have done, that no part of all Ireland shall be able to dare so much as quinch.[4] Then will I eftsoons[5] bring in my reformation, and thereupon establish such an order of government as I may think meetest for the good of that realm, which being once established and all things put into a right way, I doubt not but they will run on fairly, and though they would ever seek to swerve aside, yet shall they not be able without foreign violence once to remove, as you yourself shall soon, I hope, in your own reason, readily conceive, which if it shall ever appear, then may her Majesty at pleasure withdraw some of her garrison, and turn their pay into her purse, or if she will never please so to do (which I would rather wish), then shall she have a number of brave old soldiers always ready for any occasion that she will employ them unto, supplying their garrisons with fresh ones in their stead, the maintenance of whom shall be no more charge to her Majesty than now the realm is, for all the revenue thereof and much more she spendeth even in the most peaceable times that are there (as things now stand), and in time of war, which is once now sure every seventh year, she spendeth infinite treasure besides to small purpose.

EUDOXUS: I perceive your purpose, but now that you have thus strongly made way unto your reformation as that I see the people so humbled and prepared that they will and must yield to any ordinance that shall be given them, I do much desire to understand the same, for in the beginning you promised to show a mean[6] how to redress all those inconveniences and abuses which you showed to be in that state of government, which now stands there as in the laws, customs and religion, wherein I would gladly know first, whether instead of those laws, you would have new laws made, for now for ought that I see you may do what you please.

IRENIUS: I see, Eudoxius, that you well remember our first purpose, and do rightly continue the course thereof. First, therefore, to speak of laws, since we first began with them, I do not think it convenient (though now it be in the power of the prince) to change all the laws and make new; for that should breed a great trouble and confusion, as well in the English now dwelling, and to be planted, as also in the Irish. For the English, having been trained up always in the English government, will hardly be enured[7] unto any other, and the Irish will better be drawn to the English than the English to the Irish government. Therefore, since we cannot now apply laws fit to the people, as in the first institution of commonwealths it ought to be, we will apply the people and fit them to the laws, as it most conveniently may be. The laws, therefore, we resolve shall abide in the same sort that they do, both common law and statutes, only such defects in the common law, and inconveniences in the statutes, as in the beginning we noted and as men of deep insight shall advise, may be changed by some other new acts and ordinances to be by a parliament there confirmed, as those of trials of pleas of the Crown, and private rights between parties, colourable conveyances, accessories,[8] etc.

EUDOXUS: But how will those be redressed by parliament, when as the Irish which sway most in parliament as you said shall oppose themselves against them?

IRENIUS: That may now be well avoided, for now that so many freeholders of English shall be established, they together with burgesses of towns and such other loyal Irishmen as may be preferred to be knights of the shire, and such like, will be able to beard and counterpoise[9] the rest, who, also being now brought more in awe, will the more easily submit to any such ordinances as shall be for the good of themselves and that realm generally.

EUDOXUS: You say well, for the increase of the freeholders for their numbers will hereby be greatly

2. A monetary rent to be raised on land according to its worth, for the purpose of maintaining government forces and a civil administration.
3. to place all the soldiers in this way.
4. to move or stir.
5. soon afterwards.
6. a method.
7. accustomed.
8. i.e. questionable legal documents.
9. to oppose openly and contradict.

augmented. But how shall it pass through the higher house which will still consist all of Irish?

IRENIUS: Marry, that also may well be redressed by ensample of that which I have heard was done in the like case, by King Edward the Third as I remember, who, being greatly bearded and crossed by the lords of the clergy, they being then, by reason of the Lord Abbotts and others, too many and too strong for them, so he could not for their frowardness[10] order and reform things as he desired, was advised to direct forth his writs to certain gentlemen of best ability and trust, entitling them therein barons to serve and sit as barons in the next parliament, by which means he had so many barons in his parliament as were able to weigh down the clergy and their friends; the which barons they say were not afterwards lords, but only baronets, as sundry of them do yet retain the name, and by the like devise her Majesty may now likewise curb and cut short those Irish and unruly lords that hinder all good proceedings.

EUDOXUS: It seemeth no less than for reforming of all those inconvenient statutes which ye noted in the beginning and redressing of all those evil customs. And lastly for settling sound religion amongst them, methinks ye shall not need any more to overgo those particulars again, which you mentioned, nor any other which might besides be remembered, but to leave all to the reformation of such parliament, in which by the good care of the Lord Deputy, and Counsel they may all be amended. Therefore, now you may come to that general reformation which you spake of, and bringing in of all the establishment, by which you said all men should be contained in duty ever after, without the terror of warlike forces, or violent wresting of things by sharp punishment.

IRENIUS: I will so, at your pleasure, the which meseems by no means can be better plotted than by ensample of such other realms as have been annoyed with the like evils, that Ireland now is and useth still to be. And first in this our realm of England, it is manifest by report of the chronicles and other ancient writers, that it was greatly infested with robbers and outlaws which lurked in woods and fast[11] places, whence they used oftentimes to break forth into the highways, and sometimes into small villages to rob and spoil, for redress whereof it is written, that King Allured or Alfred, who then reigned, did divide the realm into shires, and the shires into hundreds,[12] and the hundreds into lathes or wapentakes,[13] and wapentakes into tithings, so that ten tithings made a hundred, and five made a lathe or wapentake, of which ten each one was bound for another. And the eldest or best of them, whom they called the tithingman or borsholder, that is the eldest pledge, became surety for all the rest, so that if any one of them did start into any undutiful action, the borsholder was bound to bring him forth, who joining eftsoons with all his tithing would follow that loose person through all places till they brought him in, and if all that tithing failed, all the lathe was charged for the tithing, and if that lathe failed, then all the hundred was demanded for them, and if the hundred then the shire, who joining eftsoons altogether would not rest till they had found out and delivered in that unlawful fellow which was not amenable to law. And herein it seemed that good Saxon king followed the counsel of Jethro to Moses, who advised him to divide the people into hundreds, and to set captains and wise men of trust over them which should take the charge of them, and ease him of that burthen.[14] And so did Romulus, as you may read, divide the Romans into tribes, and the tribes into centuries or hundreds. By this ordinance the king brought this realm of England, which before was most troublesome, unto that quiet state that no one bad person could stir, but that he was straight taken hold of by those of his own tithing and their borsholder who, being his neighbours or next kinsman, was privy to all his ways, and looked narrowly unto his life; the which institution, if it were observed in Ireland, would work that effect which it did then in England, and keep all men within the compass of duty and obedience.

EUDOXUS: This is contrary to that you said before, for as I remember ye said there was a great disproportion between England and Ireland, so as the laws which were fitting of the one would not fit the other. How comes it then now that ye would transfer a principal institution from England to Ireland?

IRENIUS: This law was made not by the Norman

10. stubbornness.
11. secure.
12. A subdivision of a county or shire.
13. Further subdivisions of certain shires, especially in the English Midlands and the North.
14. Exodus 18.

conqueror, but by a Saxon king, being at what time England was very like to Ireland as now it stands. For it was, as I told you, annoyed greatly with robbers and outlaws which troubled the whole state of the realm, every corner having in it a Robin Hood that kept the woods and spoiled all passengers and inhabitants as Ireland now hath, so as meseemeth this ordinance would fit very well and bring them all into awe.

EUDOXUS: Then when you have thus tithed the commonalty[15] as you say and set borsholder over them all, what would ye do when ye come to the gentlemen? Would you hold the same course?

IRENIUS: Yea, marry,[16] most specially; for this you must know, that all the Irish almost, boast themselves to be gentlemen, no less than the Welsh; for if he can derive himself from the head of a sept (as most of them can, they are so expert by their bards), then he holdeth himself a gentleman, and thereupon scorneth eftsoons to work or use any hand labour, which he sayth is the life of a peasant or churl, but thenceforth either becometh a horseboy or a stocagh to some kern,[17] enuring himself to his weapon and to his gentlemanly trade of stealing (as they count it); so that if a gentleman or any worthy yeoman of them have any children, the eldest perhaps shall be kept in some order, but all the rest shall shift for themselves and fall to this occupation. And it is a common use amongst some of their best gentlemen's sons that, so soon as they are able to use their weapons, they straight gather to themselves stragglers or kerns, with whom, wandering a while idly up and down the country, taking only meat,[18] he at last falleth into some bad action that shall be offered which, being once made known he is thenceforth counted a man of worth in whom there is courage, whereupon there draw to him many other like loose young men, which, stirring him up with encouragement, provoke him shortly to flat[19] rebellion. And this happens not only in the sons of gentlemen, but oftentimes also of their noblemen, specially their base borne sons as there are few without some of them, for they are not ashamed not only to acknowledge them, but also boast of them and use them in such secret services as they themselves will not be seen in, as to plague their enemies, spoil their neighbours, to oppress and crush some of his own too stubborn freeholders which are not tractable to their bad wills. Two such bastards of the Lord Roche's,[20] they are now out in Munster, whom he doth not only countenance, but also privily maintain and relieve nightly amongst his tenants, such other is there of the Earl of Clancarty's[21] in Desmond, and many others in many other places.

EUDOXUS: Then it seemeth that this ordinance of tithing them by the poll,[22] is not only fit for the gentlemen, but also for the noblemen, whom I would have thought to have been of so honourable minds as that they should not need such a base kind of living, being bound to their allegiance, who should rather have held in and stayed all others from undutifulness, than need to be forced thereunto themselves.

IRENIUS: Yet so it is, Eudoxus. But yet because the noblemen cannot be tithed, there being not many tithings in them, and also because a borsholder over them should not only be a great indignity but also a danger to add more power to them than they have, or to make one the commander of ten, I hold it meet that there were only sureties taken of them and one bound for another, whereby if any shall swerve,[23] his sureties shall for safeguard of their bonds bring him in, or seek to serve upon him. And besides this I would wish them all to be sworn to Her Majesty, which they never yet were but at the first creation, and that oath would sure contain them in duty greatly, or the breach of it bring them to shorter vengeance, for God useth to punish perjury sharply. So I read in the reign of Edward the Second, and also of Henry the Seventh, when the times were very broken, that there was a corporate oath taken of all the lords and best gentlemen, of fealty to the king, which now is no less needful because many of them are suspected to have taken another oath privily to some bad purpose, and thereupon to have received the sacrament and been sworn to a priest, which they think blindeth them more than their allegiance to their prince or love of their country.

15. taxed the common people.
16. to be sure.
17. cf. Irish *stócach*: youth or idler; kern: footsoldier or vagabond.
18. i.e. billeting men on the people.
19. outright.
20. A reference to one of the great Anglo-Norman families, Lords of Roche and Fermoy, probably John FitzEdmund Roche, who succeeded his father Maurice in 1593.
21. Probably a reference to Donald MacCarthy Mór, earl of Clancar, who died in 1597.
22. i.e. taxing each person.
23. do something wrong.

EUDOXUS: This tithing of the common people and taking sureties of lords and gentlemen I like very well, but that it will be very troublesome. Should it not be as well to have them all booked,[24] and the lords and gentlemen to take all the meaner sort upon themselves, for they are best able to bring them in whensoever any of them starteth out?

IRENIUS: This indeed, Eudoxus, hath been hitherto, and yet is, a common order amongst them, to have all the people booked by the lords and gentlemen, but it is the worst order that ever was devised, for by this booking of men all the inferior sort are brought under the command of their lords and forced to follow them into any action whatsoever. Now this ye are to understand, that all the rebellions which ye see from time to time happen in Ireland, are not begun by the common people, but by the lords and captains of countries upon pride or wilful obstinacy against the government; which whensoever they will enter into, they draw with them all their people and followers, which think themselves bound to go with them, because they have booked them and undertaken for them. And this is the reason that you have few such bad occasions here in England, by reason that the noblemen, however they should happen to be evil disposed, have no command at all over the commonalty, though dwelling under them, because every man standeth upon himself, and buildeth his fortunes upon his own faith and firm assurance, the which this manner of tithing the polls will work also in Ireland, for by this the people are broken into many small parts like little streams that they cannot easily come together into one head, which is the principal regard that is to be had in Ireland, to keep them from growing into such a head and adhering unto great men. . . .

24. Reference is being made here to the practice of 'booking', whereby the lord of a designated area was required to provide a list or book of those dwelling in his territory, for whose conduct he would be responsible. Anyone else found in the area would be liable to execution under martial law.

[Both parties to the debate recognize that all Irish lords, and particularly those of Old English origin, would resent and even oppose these well-meaning measures. Therefore, they engage in a renewed onslaught against the Old English and, in so doing, explain how the process whereby all previous English settlers in Ireland have degenerated from civility has finally been arrested.]

IRENIUS: Neither should their lands be taken away from them, nor the uttermost advantages enforced against them, but this by the discretion of the commissioners should be made known unto them, that it is not Her Majesty's meaning to use any such extremity but only to reduce things into order of English law and make them hold their lands of Her Majesty, and restore to her her due services, which they detain, out of those lands which were anciently held of her, and that they should not only not be thrust out, but also have estates and grants of their lands now made to them from Her Majesty so as they should thenceforth hold them rightfully which they now usurp most wrongfully. And yet withal I would wish that in all those Irish countries there were some land reserved to Her Majesty's free disposition, for the better containing of the rest and intermeddling them with English inhabitants and customs, that knowledge might still be had by them of all their doings, so as no manner of practice or conspiracy should be given thereof by one means or another, and their practices prevented.

EUDOXUS: Truly, neither can the Irish nor yet the English lords think themselves wronged or hardly dealt withal herein, to have that indeed which is none of their own at all but Her Majesty's absolutely given unto them with such equal conditions as that both they may be assured thereof better than they are, and also Her Majesty not defrauded of her right utterly; for it is a great grace in a prince to take that with conditions which is absolutely her own. Thus shall the Irish be well satisfied, and as for the great men which had such grant made them at first by the Kings of England it was in regard that they should keep out the Irish and defend the king's right and his subjects; but now seeing that instead of defending them they rob and spoil them, and instead of keeping out the Irish they do not only make the Irish their tenants in those lands and thrust out the English, but also they themselves become mere Irish with marrying with them, fostering with them and combining with them against the queen, what reason but those grants and privileges should be either revoked or at least reduced to their first intention for which they were granted? For surely in my opinion they are more sharply to be chastised and reformed than the rude Irish, which, being very wild at the first, are now become somewhat more civil, when as these from civility are grown to be wild and mere Irish.

IRENIUS: Indeed as ye say, Eudoxus. These do need a sharper reformation than the very Irish, for they are much more stubborn and disobedient to law and government than the Irish be, and more malicious against the English that daily are sent over.

EUDOXUS: Is it possible, I pray you? How comes it to pass what might be the reason thereof?

IRENIUS: Marry, they say that the land is theirs only by right, being first conquered by their ancestors, and that they are wronged by the new Englishmen's intruding thereinto, whom they call *Sassona*, that is, English, with as great reproach as they would rate a dog. And for that some of their ancestors were in times past, when they were civil and uncorrupted, deputies and justices of the land, they think that the like authority should be committed unto them, and the charge of the realm left in their hands which for that they see now otherwise disposed, and that trust not given them which their ancestors had, they think themselves greatly undignified and disgraced thereby, and so grow both discontented and undutiful.

EUDOXUS: In truth, Irenius, this is more than ever I heard, that the English Irish[1] there should be worse than the wild Irish. Lord, how quickly doth that country alter men's natures! It is not for nothing, I perceive, that I have heard the Council of England think it no good policy to have that realm reformed or planted with English, lest they should grow as undutiful as the Irish and become much more dangerous, as appeareth by the example of the Lacys, in the time of Edward the Second, which you spake of, that shook off their allegiance to their natural prince, and turned to the Scot,[2] devising to make him King of Ireland.

IRENIUS: No times have been without bad men; but as for that purpose of the Council of England which ye speak of, that they should keep the realm from reformation, I think they are most lewdly abused, for their great carefulness and earnest endeavour do witness the contrary, neither is the nature of the country to alter men's manners, but the bad minds of them who, having been brought up at home under a strait rule of duty and obedience, being always restrained by sharp penalties from lewd behaviour, so soon as they come thither, where they see law so slackly tended and the hard constraints which they were used unto now slacked, they grow more loose and careless of their duty, as it is the nature of all men to love liberty; so they become flat libertines and fall to all licentiousness of the Irish, more boldly daring to disobey the law through presumption of favour and friendship than any Irish dare.

EUDOXUS: Then if it be so, methinks your late advisement was very evil, whereby you wished the Irish to be sowed and sprinkled with the English in all the Irish countries, to have English planted amongst them, for to bring them to English fashions. Since the English be sooner drawn to the Irish than the Irish to the English, for, as you said before, they must run with the stream, the greater number will carry away the less, therefore meseems by this reason it should be better to part the Irish and English than to mingle them together.

IRENIUS: Not so, Eudoxus, but where there is no good stay of government and strong ordinances to hold them there indeed, the fewer will follow the more. But where there is due order of discipline and good rule, there the better shall go foremost, and the worse shall follow. And therefore, since Ireland is full of her own nation that may not be rooted out, and somewhat stored with English already and more to be, I think it best by an union of manners and conformity of minds, to bring them to be one people, and to put away the dislikeful concept both of the one and the other, which will be by no means better than by this intermingling of them, that neither all the Irish may dwell together, nor all the English, but by translating of them, and scattering them in small numbers amongst the English, not only to bring them by daily conversation unto better liking of each other, but also to make both of them less able to hurt. And therefore when I come to the tithing I will tithe them one with another, and for the most part will make the Irish man the tithing man, whereby he shall take the less exception to partiality, and yet be the more tied thereby. But when I come to the headborough which is the head of the lathe, him will I make an English man or Irishman of no small assurance; as also when I come to appoint the alderman that is the head of the hundred, him will I surely choose an Englishman of special regard, that may be a stay and pillar of all the boroughs under him....

[Returning to his main theme, Irenius stresses the need for continued watchfulness lest the Irish lords should

1. The Old English.
2. Those who joined with the Bruce invaders of Ireland.

recover power over their kinship groups. On this occasion he is able to detail the use that he will make of statute law and education once the English forces have gained the upper hand militarily.]

IRENIUS: Moreover for the better breaking of these heads and septs which I told you was one of the greatest strengths of the Irish, methinks it should do very well to renew that old statute that was made in the reign of Edward the Fourth in England, by which it was commanded that whereas all men then used to be called by the name of their septs according to their several nations, and had no surnames at all, that from thenceforth each one should take unto himself a several surname, either of his trade or faculty or of some quality of his body or mind, or of the place where he dwelt, so as every one should be distinguished from the other or from the most part; whereby they shall not only not depend upon the head of their sept as now they do, but also shall in short time learn quite to forget his Irish nation. And herewithal would I also wish all the Oes and the Macs which the heads of septs have taken to their names to be utterly forbidden and extinguished, for that the same being an ordinance (as some sayth) first made by O'Brien[1] for the strengthening of the Irish, the abrogating thereof will as much enfeeble them.

EUDOXUS: I like this ordinance very well, but now that you have thus divided and distinguished them, what other order will you take for their manner of life, for all this, though perhaps it may keep them from disobedience and disloyalty, yet will it not bring them from their barbarism and savage life.

IRENIUS: The next that I will do shall be to appoint to every one that is not able to live off his freehold a certain trade of life to which he shall find himself fittest and shall be thought ablest, the which trade he shall be bound to follow and live only thereupon. All trades therefore is [*sic*] to be understood to be of three kinds, manual, intellectual and mixed, the one containing all such as need the exercise of bodily labour to the performance of their profession, the other consisting only of the exercise of wit and reason, the third, part of bodily labour and part of the wit, but depending of industry and carefulness. Of the first sort be all handicrafts and husbandry labour, of the second be all sciences and those which are called the liberal arts, of the third is merchandry and chaffery,[2] that is buying and selling, and without all these three there is no commonwealth can almost consist, or at the least be perfect. But that wretched realm of Ireland wanteth the most principal of them, that is the intellectual. Therefore in seeking to reform her estate it is specially to be looked unto. But because of husbandry which supplyeth unto us all things necessary for food, whereby we chiefly live, therefore it is first to be provided for. The first thing then that we are to draw these new tithed men unto ought to be husbandry, first because it is the most easy to be learned, needing only the labour of the body, next because it is most general and most needful, then because it is most natural, and lastly because it is most enemy to war and most hateth unquietness, as the poet saith, *Bella execrata colonis*;[3] for husbandry being the nurse of thrift and the daughter of industry, and labour detesteth all that may work her scathe[4] and destroy the travail of her hands, whose hope is all her lives comfort. Unto the plough, therefore, are all those kerne, stocaghs, and horseboys to be driven, and made to employ that ableness of body which they wont to use to theft and villainy, henceforth to labour and husbandry; in the which by that time they have spent but a little pain, they will find such sweetness and happy contentment, that they will hardly afterwards be haled away from it or drawn to their wonted lewd life in thiefery and roguery. And being this once enured thereunto they are not only to be countenanced and encouraged by all good means, but also provided that their children after them may be brought up likewise in that same and succeed in the rooms of their fathers, to which end there is a statute in Ireland already well provided, which commandeth that all the sons of husbandmen shall be trained up in their fathers' trade, but it is, God wot,[5] very slenderly looked unto.

EUDOXUS: But do you not count in this trade of husbandry, pasturing of cattle and keeping of their cows, for that is reckoned as a part of husbandry?

IRENIUS: I know it is, and needfully to be used, but I do not mean to allow any of these able bodies

1. The reference is to Brian Boraimhe, who usurped the high kingship of Ireland in the tenth century.

2. haggling, bargaining.
3. Wars are hated by cultivators.
4. harm, damage.
5. God knows.

which are able to use bodily labour, to follow a few cows, grazing, but such impotent persons as being unable for strong travail, are yet able to drive cattle to and fro the pasture, for this keeping of cows is of itself a very idle life and a fit nursery for a thief; for which cause ye remember I disliked the Irish manner of keeping of bollies[6] in summer upon the mountain and living after that savage sort. But if they will algates[7] feed many cattle or keep them on the mountains, let them make some towns near to the mountain's side where they may dwell together with neighbours and be conversant in the view of the world. And to say truth, though Ireland be by nature counted a great soil of pasture, yet had I rather have fewer cows kept and men better mannered than to have such huge increase of cattle and no increase of good conditions. I would therefore wish that there were some ordinance made against them, that whosoever keepeth 20 kine should keep a plough going, for otherwise all men would fall to pasturage and none to husbandry, which is a great cause of this dearth[8] now in England, and a cause of the usual stealths in Ireland; for look into all countries that live in such sort by keeping of cattle, and you shall find that they are both very barbarous and uncivil and also greatly given to war, The Tartarians, the Muscovites, the Norways, the Goths, the Armenians and many other do witness the same. And therefore since now we purpose to draw the Irish from desire of wars and tumults to the love of peace and civility, it is expedient to abridge their custom of herding and augment their more trade of tilling and husbandry. As for other occupations and trades they need not to be enforced to, but every man bound only to follow one that he thinks himself aptest for. For other trades of artificers will be occupied for very necessity and constrained use of them, and so likewise will merchandise for the gain thereof. But learning and bringing up in liberal sciences will not come of itself, but must be drawn on with strait laws and ordinances; and therefore it were meet that such an act were ordained, that all the sons of lords and gentlemen and such others as are able to bring them up in learning should be trained up herein from their childhoods, and for that end every parish should be forced to keep one petty schoolmaster, adjoining unto the parish church, to be the more in view, which should bring up their children in the first rudiments of letters; and that in every cantred[9] or baronry they should keep another able schoolmaster, which should instruct them in grammar and in the principles of sciences, to whom they should be compelled to send their youth to be disciplined, whereby they will in short time grow up to that civil conversation, that both the children will loathe the former rudeness in which they were bred, and also their parents will, even by the ensample of their young children, perceive the foulness of their own brutish behaviour compared to theirs, for learning hath that wonderful power of itself that it can soften and temper the most stern and savage nature.

6. herds of cattle; from the Irish *buaile*. What Spenser refers to when he uses this term is the practice of transhumance, whereby flocks of livestock were driven into the hills and rough pastures for summer grazing.
7. in any case.
8. scarcity of food.

EUDOXUS: Surely I am of your mind that nothing will bring them from their uncivil life sooner than learning and discipline, next after the knowledge and fear of God. And therefore I do still expect that ye should come thereunto and set some order for reformation of religion, which is first to be respected according to the saying of Christ, 'First seek the Kingdom of Heaven and the righteousness thereof.' ...

9. A district containing a hundred townships.

[The subject of religious reform is again shelved by Irenius until he has made his case for the appointment of a provost marshal in each shire to execute those who would lapse from civility. Then, upon Eudoxus's insistence, he returns to the subject of religious reform — the ultimate objective of the reform programme.]

IRENIUS: For religion little have I to say myself, being (as I said) not professed therein, and itself being but one, so as there is but one way therein, for that which is true only is and the rest are not at all; yet in planting of religion thus much is needful to be observed, that it be not sought forcibly to be impressed into them with terror and sharp penalties, as now is the manner, but rather delivered and intimated with mildness and gentleness, so as it may not be hated before it be understood, and their professors despised and rejected. For this I know, that the most of the Irish are so far from understanding of the popish religion as they are of the protestants' profession, and yet do they hate it, though unknown, even for the very hatred which they have of the English and their government. Therefore it is expedient that some discreet ministers of their own countrymen be first sent amongst them, which, by their mild persuasions and instructions as also by their sober life and conversation, may draw them, first to understand and afterwards to embrace the doctrine of their salvation. For if that the ancient godly fathers which first converted them, being infidels, to the faith, were able to draw them from infidelity and paganism to the true belief in Christ as St. Patrick and St. Columb[1] did, how much more easily shall godly teachers bring them to the true understanding of that which they already profess, wherein it is great wonder to see the odds which is between the zeal of Popish priests[2] and ministers of the gospel, for they spare not to come out of Spain, from Rome, from Rheims, by long toil and dangerous travel hither, where they know peril of death awaiteth them and no reward nor riches is to be found, only to draw the people to the church of Rome; whereas our idle ministers,[3] having a way for credit and estimation thereby opened unto them, and having the livings of the country offered them, without pains, without peril, will neither for the same, nor for any love of God nor zeal of religion, nor for all the good which they might do by winning of so many souls to God, be drawn forth from their warm nests and their sweet love's side to look out into God's harvest which is even ready for the sickle, and all the fields yellow long ago. Doubtless these good old Godly fathers will, I fear me, rise up in the day of judgement to condemn them.

EUDOXUS: Surely it is great pity, Irenius, that there are none chosen out of the ministers of England good and sober discreet men which might be sent over thither to teach and instruct them, and that there is not as much care had of their souls as of their bodies; for the care of both lieth upon the Prince?

IRENIUS: Were there never so many sent over they should do small good till one enormity be taken away from them, that is, that both they be restrained from sending their young men abroad to other universities beyond seas as Rheims, Douai, Louvaine and the like, and that others from abroad be restrained from coming to them; for they, lurking secretly in their houses and in corners of the country, do more hurt and hindrance to religion with their private persuasions than all the others can do good with their public instruction. And though for these latter there be a good statute there ordained, yet the same is not executed, and as for the former, there is no law nor order for their restraint at all.

EUDOXUS: I marvel that it is no better looked unto, and not only this, but also that which I remember you mentioned in your abuses concerning the profits and revenues of the lands of fugitives in Ireland, which by pretence of certain colourable conveyances[4] are sent continually over unto them to the comforting of them and others against Her Majesty, for which here in England there is good order taken, and why not then as well in Ireland? For though there be no statute there yet enacted therefore, yet might Her Majesty, by her only prerogative, seize the fruits and profits of those fugitives' lands into her hands till they came over to testify their true allegiance.

IRENIUS: Indeed she might so do, but the cumbrous times do perhaps hinder the regard thereof and of many other good intentions.

EUDOXUS: But why did they not mind it in peaceable times?

IRENIUS: Leave we that to their grave considerations, but proceed we forward. Next care in religion is to build up and repair all the ruined churches, whereof the most part lie even with the ground, and some that have been lately repaired are so unhandsomely patched and thatched that men do even shun the places for the uncomeliness thereof. Therefore I would wish that there were order taken to have them built in some better form according to the Churches of England, for the outward show, assure yourself, doth greatly draw the rude people to the reverencing and frequenting thereof; and whatever some of our late too nice fools[5] say there is nothing in the seemly form and comely order of the church. And for so keeping and

1. St Columba (521-97), the Irish missionary who founded the monastery at Iona.
2. Irish priests trained in continental seminaries, established in the aftermath of the Council of Trent 1545-63.
3. Spenser is here joining with such as Barnaby Rich in faulting the protestant ministers in Ireland for their lack of zeal.
4. Legal devices, used by the Old English, whereby certain lands owned by those who proposed to go to the Continent to be trained as priests were conveyed to trustees, who transmitted the profits of those lands to the seminarians.
5. Puritans within the Church of England who attached little importance to the form and decor of churches.

continuing them there should likewise church wardens of the gravest men in the parish be appointed as there be here in England, which should take the yearly charge both hereof and also of the schoolhouses which I wished to be builded near to the said churches; for maintenance of both which it were meet that some several portion of land were allotted, seeing no more mortmains[6] are to be looked for.

EUDOXUS: Indeed, meseems it would be so convenient; but when all is done, how will you have your churches served or your ministers maintained, since the livings (as you said) are not sufficient scarce to make them a gown, much less to yield meet maintenance according to the dignity of their degree.

IRENIUS: There is no way to help that but to lay 2 or 3 of them together until such time as the country grow more rich and better inhabited, at which times the tithes and other obventions[7] will also be more augmented and better valued....

6. Lands held inalienably.
7. Occasional incoming revenues.

[Since religious reform is thus shown to be contingent upon economic advancement, Irenius itemizes the improvements in the infrastructure that are necessary before economic conditions can be bettered. Having disposed of these matters, he again returns to the qualities needed in the governor who would implement this programme, and the discourse concludes as follows.]

IRENIUS: Thus I have, Eudoxus, as briefly as I could, and as my remembrance would serve, run through the state of that whole country both to let you see what it now is, and also what it may be by good care and amendment. Not that I take upon me to change the policy of so great a kingdom or prescribe rules to such wise men as have the handling thereof, but only to show you the evils which in my small experience I have observed to be the chief hindrance of the reformation thereof. And by way of conference to declare my simple opinion for redress thereof, and establishing a good course for that government; which I do not deliver for a perfect plot of mine own invention to be only followed, but as I have learned and understood the same by the consultations and actions of very wise governors and counsellors whom I have sometimes heard treat thereof, so have I thought good to set down a remembrance of them for mine own good and your satisfaction, that who so list to overlook them, although perhaps much wiser than they which have thus advised of this estate, yet at least by comparison hereof, may perhaps better his own judgement, and by the light of others foregoing him may follow after with more ease, and haply find a fairer way thereunto than they which have gone before.

EUDOXUS: I thank you, Irenius, for this your gentle pains withal, not forgetting now in the shutting up to put you in mind of that which you have formerly half promised that hereafter, when we shall meet again upon the like good occasion, ye will declare unto us these your observations which ye have gathered of the antiquities of Ireland.

RICHARD BEACON

(*fl.* 1567-92)

from: SOLON HIS FOLLIE, OR A POLITICAL DISCOURSE TOUCHING THE REFORMATION OF COMMONWEALS CONQUERED, DECLINED, OR CORRUPTED (1594)

[This work is in the form of a dialogue between Epimenides, a religious teacher of Crete who lived about 500 B.C., and Solon, the Athenian war-leader, poet and law-giver, who was prominent in the war waged by Athens against Megara about 600 B.C. for control of the island of Salamis or Salamina. A third party to the discourse is Pisistratus, a tyrant of Athens, who also participated in the war for the possession of Salamina. Pisistratus was related to Solon through his mother, and he honoured the legal reforms of Solon once he had achieved power in Athens.

Beacon's text is a thinly disguised dialogue about the reform of Ireland: Athens represents England, Salamina stands for Ireland, and Megara represents Spain. It appears that Solon corresponds to Sir William Russell, who had just been appointed lord deputy of Ireland when the text was published in 1594 and who was expected to lead the war that would clear the way for the country's reform. The parallels are carefully preserved. Russell, like Solon, was responsible for conducting a war about which most of his countrymen had come to despair.]

EPIMENIDES PHAESTIAN:[1] Well met good Sir Pisistratus in this holy place of the temple of Venus, where though the sacrifices be finished yet notwithstanding your devotion is highly to be commended.

PISISTRATUS:[2] You also are happily well saluted right wise and famous Epimenides, and this devotion which you have friendly now commended is but a duty first unto the Gods and next unto my friends amongst whom I enumber you not the least.

EPIMENIDES: I am the least in power I must confess that is worthy of Pisistratus but not in good will: but what matter of importance hath caused your arrival so unexpected upon this coast and haven?

PISISTRATUS: We lead here a strong army by the commandment of the council of Athens unto Salamina[3] for the better repossessing and reforming thereof.

EPIMENIDES: What? Contrary to their former decrees and proclamations which were so straight and that upon pain of death that no citizen of Athens should be so hardy as once to move the question to the council of the city for the repossessing and reforming of Salamina?

PISISTRATUS: Yes verily: for when the Athenians did once behold that their long and troublesome wars, the which they had now sustained against the Megarians[4] for the repossessing and reforming of Salamina did arise unto them not from the nature of the people, nor from the difficulty of that action, but rather that they received all their advertisements for the advancement of those affairs from such as gave counsel therein more for their private profit than for the public good, but chiefly for that sundry governors there placed were found either negligent or ignorant in the managing of public affairs, they willingly revoked their public proclamations and made choice of Solon,[5] a most wise

1. Epimenides, a religious leader and wonder-worker of Crete. His inclusion in the discourse evidently suggests that the cause being fought for was a godly one.
2. Pisistratus was a tyrant of Athens who engaged in war for the control of Salamina (or Salamis). If we are to follow the logic of Beacon's reasoning, Pisistratus represents Queen Elizabeth I, although he can hardly have meant to suggest that she was a tyrant in domestic affairs.
3. In Greek antiquity Salamina (or Salamis) was an island in the Saronic Gulf of the Aegean Sea. It was colonized by Aegina and was temporarily occupied by Megara (*c.* 600 B.C.). It was then conquered by the Athenians and thereafter shared the fortunes of Athens from the age of Solon and Pisistratus. In this discourse, Salamina represents Ireland and Athens corresponds to England.
4. In Greek antiquity Megara was a town on the isthmus of Corinth, twenty miles west of Athens. Between 730 and 550 B.C., it displayed considerable colonizing energies and about 600 B.C., when it came under the rule of a tyrant, it became a threat to Athens. Subsequently it fell prey to domestic strife, lost its overseas possessions and lapsed into obscurity. In this discourse, Megara must represent Spain, which was seeking to advance its authority in Ireland, fomenting Irish rebellion against the authority of the English government.
5. Solon, the famous law-giver of Athens, but also the man who advocated the continuation of the war against Megara for the control of Salamina when others had despaired of the effort.

and expert governor, for leading and conducting their armies now here landed for the repossessing and reforming of Salamina.

EPIMENIDES: But who persuaded this first unto the Council of Athens?

PISISTRATUS: Solon, that faithful councillor of Athens.

EPIMENIDES: But how does Solon the wise offend their public laws and proclamations?

PISISTRATUS: Solon holding it for an open shame the which would be left unto all posterities if the city of Athens should not be able to repossess and reform Salamina, now commanding the most parts of Greece, feigned himself to be out of his wits and caused it to be given out that Solon was become a fool: and soon after on a day clothed with the habit, gesture and countenance of a fool or man possessed with lunacy, he ran suddenly out of his house with a garland on his head unto the market place where the people straight swarmed like bees about him, and raising himself upon the stone where all proclamations were made, did so effectually persuade the repossessing of Salamina unto the people as what with the weight of his reasons and the laud and praise everywhere spread by his friends of his proceeding therein their former proclamations were revoked and the wars for the repossessing and reforming of Salamina with greater fury than before were followed, they giving unto Solon, as I said before, the leading of the army and the whole managing of the action.

EPIMENIDES: After this manner did Brutus[6] by a feigned frenzy and lunacy, not only reform the mighty city of Rome but wisely acquitted himself thereby of the suspicion and jealousy of Tarquin,[7] by the which manner of proceeding he delivered as well the city of Rome as his own person from peril and danger, so as this common proverb did first arise *Simulare stultitiam non numquam sapientis est*.[8] But where remaineth Solon my dear and familiar friend, that I may salute him and give him the best comfort I may in this worthy action of reformation?

PISISTRATUS: He is newly landed with his whole army, and hath now for his better recreation withdrawn himself into a pleasant and solitary garden near unto the temple of Venus whereunto if your pleasure serve I will readily conduct you.

EPIMENIDES: I readily follow you.

PISISTRATUS: Sir, I go before as the best guide and not the best man and behold Solon in the most solitary place in the garden.

SOLON: Thrice welcome my dear and familiar friend Epimenides, behold this solitary and pleasant place as also the times, hath even newly conspired with my thoughts and desires to impose a great and weighty labour upon you.

EPIMENIDES: No labour may be thought ever so great as shall exceed the greatness of my goodwill I bear unto Solon. But what may the same be? Tell it unto me.

SOLON: As you have of late most friendly lent unto me your faithful counsel and best advice for the reformation of the city of Athens, greatly to the advancement of that estate, in like manner now I am earnestly to entreat your most friendly advice for the better reformation of Salamina.

EPIMENIDES: This labour and travail, I must confess, is due unto Solon, if there wanted not wisdom which should give strength for the performance thereof. But I have chosen at this time for our old familiarity and friendship to give you just cause rather to reprehend my skill than to accuse any part of that office and duty which in the highest manner belongeth unto Solon; so as when the fault appeareth you shall acknowledge the same to be imposed by yourself, and not received by me without your commandment.

SOLON: Then friendly Epimenides, before we enter into this large discourse for the reformation of Salamina, I will declare unto you a dream, which this last night amazed my thoughts.

EPIMENIDES: I pray thee tell it unto me.

SOLON: This night I seemed to behold fair Diana[9] with a beautiful dove glistering[10] like gold, placed upon her shoulder, sliding and wavering everywhere, in such sort as it seemed to me to be in great jeopardy of falling, but forthwith moved with compassion I stretched forth my right hand to better and reform the place of her standing: wherewith I might behold Diana with a sharp and sour countenance to threaten the loss of my hand.

6. The character being referred to is Lucius Junius Brutus, the traditional founder of the Roman Republic, who feigned idiocy in order to escape vengeance at the hands of the Tarquins, whom he had overthrown after the rape of Lucrece.
7. Tarquinius Sextus, son of the last king of Rome, who committed the rape on Lucrece.
8. Roughly translated this means: To simulate stupidity is sometimes the characteristic of a wise man.
9. An Italian goddess anciently identified with Artemis.
10. sparkling, glittering.

Wherat being amazed I did awake out of my drousy sleep.

EPIMENIDES: The people of Salamina, is the threatening Diana hating all reformation: the golden dove is the pleasant country of Salamina: the wavering of this dove from place to place is the frailty and mutability whereunto this country of Salamina hath ever been subject: the compassion which you have taken of this golden dove, is the love you bear unto Salamina: the moving of your body and hand to succour the golden dove is the ardent desire now newly kindled in you for the reformation thereof: the loss of hand threatened by Diana is the difficulties and dangers which shall from time to time oppose themselves against you in this action of reformation.

SOLON: Describe therefore unto us, first, what you intend by this word reformation, and then the difficulties and dangers that follow the same, and lastly the ways and means, whereby we may readily eschew these dangers and difficulties....

EPIMENIDES: A reformation of a declined common-weal is nothing else but an happy restitution unto his first perfection: this word Reformation being thus described may in like sort be divided into two parts and members: the one may be termed an absolute and a thorough reformation of the whole body of the common-weale, namely of the ancient laws, customs, governments and manners of the people: the other may be termed a reformation of particular mischiefs and inconveniences only, which like unto evil and superfluous humours daily arise to the annoyance and disturbance of this politic body.

. . . Such common-weale which in all the parts thereof are found corrupted and declined from their first institution may not by profitable laws made and established as occasion shall them require be reformed; whereof sometimes the city of Rome and now the state of Salamina may be unto us an example: since neither the one after her final declension, which did chiefly grow by a general corruption of manners in the people could be reformed by the laws against captainship, against *coigne and livery*,[11] or against the unlawful custom of supporting and maintaining of rebels or any other new law whatsoever: nor the other by their laws *sumptuarii ambitus*,[12] and such like, the reason whereof shall more at large appear in this discourse following.

SOLON: There remaineth now the discipline of laws as the second part and member of this particular reformation not as yet consulted of....

EPIMENIDES: This manner of reformation is nothing else but a fear to offend, bred in the hearts of the people by the true discipline of laws ... after this manner by a severe discipline of laws did the Lord Gray in times past, and now Sir R. Bingham[13] mightily reform and advance the government of Salamina so as we may truly say by such governors must this nation be reformed.

11. The term used for the means of billeting soldiers and raising provision for men and horses in the Hiberno-Norman lordships of Ireland. These practises were strongly discouraged by the government and were frequently forbidden by legislation.

12. The reference here is probably to the ineffectual efforts to reform political corruption in ancient Rome through the enactment of laws relating to the voting system.

13. Arthur Lord Gray de Wilton (1536-93) served as lord deputy of Ireland 1580-82 and then conducted the war against the Munster rebels. Sir Richard Bingham (1528-99) served as lord president in Connacht 1584-99. Each had a reputation for forceful action in the single-minded pursuit of an objective.

[The discussion then proceeds to show that such discipline by severe laws can occur only at opportune occasions, and even then at great risk to the reformer who proceeds with such measures. The dangers and difficulties that beset the governor are identified, as are the measures that the ruler must take to overcome them.]

SOLON: Therefore in such common-weales where the manners of the people are altogether corrupted for not applying in good time the discipline of laws it behoveth the judges, and such as shall revive the force of ancient laws by the exact discipline thereof, strongly to be guarded, according to the example of Cicero being accompanied with a strong guard of lusty men when as consul he was to convict and execute Lentulus and Cethegus for their conspiracies with Catiline....[1]

EPIMENIDES: In like manner, governors in cases of great extremities, for the avoiding of dangers and difficulties, may proceed against offenders without observing the usual ceremonies of law. After this

1. The Catiline conspiracy of 62 B.C. forced Cicero, as consul, to have five of the conspirators executed with the sanction of the Roman senate, without benefit of trial. This action won Cicero an immediate reputation as the saviour of Rome, but also earned him lasting unpopularity because his action was of doubtful legality and because Catiline had been a popular figure. Lentulus was one of those executed with Catiline; Cethegus was also involved in the conspiracy.

manner did Cicero proceed against Lentulus and Cethegus when as upon proof only in open senate without any lawful indictment or condemnation he commanded their delivery into the hands of the officers to be put to death.... This severe course and manner of proceeding in cases of extremity may not be deemed any part of tyranny if either we will give credit to the opinion of Caesar, or unto the fact of Cicero and the senate, or follow the custom of Rome, or deem Cato to be mild and just who then being in the senate did vehemently persuade the same, and whose heart was so far from cruelty as beholding the dead bodies slain in the camp of his enemies in the last skirmish betwixt Pompey and Caesar,[2] he covered his face and went away weeping.

SOLON: I call to remembrance one Sir R. Bingham provincial governor of Salamina, in my time a most valiant and honourable knight and withall a most wise and grave governor, being given to understand of a general rebellion with an intention not only to overthrow the state and government, but also to make deliverance of the principal rebels of the sect and nation of the Burkes,[3] then in prison and safeguard, did forthwith deliver those traitors and rebels to be put to death without lawful indictment or condemnation. For seeing himself fallen into these extremities that either he must spare the lives of open and manifest rebels to the damage of the common-weale or execute them without lawful indictment and other ceremonies, like a wise governor, two mischiefs offering themselves at once, made choice of the least, not being as then to learn that which Caesar sometimes taught Metellus,[4] 'The times of war and law are two things'. So as in this action and in all other parts of his government he hath shown himself to be the person which Archilocus[5] describeth in these his verses:

He is both champion stout of Mars his warlike band
And of the Muses eke, the arts doth understand.

EPIMENIDES: It seemeth also convenient for the better avoiding of difficulties and dangers that such heads and leaders as shall be found to give impediment unto this manner of reformation be committed to some safeguard or prison and there detained, all which Dionysius advised Dion[6] sometimes by his letters, wishing him thereby not to set them at liberty which hated him and the action which he had then undertaken of reformation.

SOLON: If the earl of Desmond, late of Salamina, committed to safeguard and prison for his sundry rebellions against the city of Athens had there been safely detained the wars of Salamina had neither been chargeable nor troublesome unto the city of Athens, and if James Fitzmaurice, in like manner being in safety and custody of officers to answer all accusations of high treason, had not been set at large by the justices for the time being he had not then wasted, burned and spoiled a great part of Salamina, neither had he put the city of Athens to so huge and mighty a charge nor yet combined with the enemy to the great danger of that estate.[7] Therefore it is a chief surety unto princes and great furtherance unto actions of importance to commit to safeguard and prison such as may give impediment thereunto.... But now since we have spoken at large of the first part and member of this reformation let us descend unto the other which you have termed a reformation absolute and universal....

EPIMENIDES: This reformation universal of the whole state and body of the commonwealth is nothing else but a thorough and absolute mutation and change of ancient laws, customs and manners of the people, and finally of the commonwealth itself unto a better form of government.

SOLON: It seemeth then, that this reformation respecteth three matters principally. First the mutation of ancient laws and customs; secondly the

2. Contemporaries in ancient Rome. The references are to Julius Caesar's own stated opinions in *De Bello Gallico*, to Cato's speech to the senate advocating the execution of the Catiline conspirators, and to the pitched battle of Pharsalus in 48 B.C. when Caesar routed Pompey.
3. The MacWilliam Burkes of County Mayo were among Bingham's principal adversaries; the O'Rourkes, lords of Breifne, were also opponents of Bingham.
4. Metellus Nepos, an ally of Caesar at the time of the Catiline conspiracies, was suspended from office with Caesar, but then served with Pompey (67-64 B.C.) against Caesar.
5. An iambic and elegiac poet of Paros, who is remembered principally for his epigrams about war and wine. He lived *c.* 714-676 B.C.
6. The reference is to the correspondence between the philosopher Dion (*c.* 408-*c.* 354 B.C.) and Dionysius II, ruler of Syracuse, and the attempt to make the latter a philosopher king.
7. The reference here is to Gerald, fourteenth earl of Desmond, and his cousin James Fitzmaurice Fitzgerald, whose dynastic rivalry was largely responsible for the outbreak of war in Munster. Successive governors in Ireland had wished to keep both men in prison, but had been overruled by the queen.

alteration and change of manners in the people; and, finally, a new institution and better form of government than before prescribed.

[At this point the speakers cite examples from the histories of Rome and Salamina to show how good laws can be put to evil purposes by wickedly inclined governors, such as the Great Earl of Kildare, and they identify those arts, skills and powers of persuasion that are essential attributes of the reforming magistrate. Examples from the historians of Greece, Rome and Florence are cited in support of the general propositions being advanced, and it is agreed that only governors such as Lord Gray and Sir William Russell, who have special expertise in military affairs, can rule successfully in Salamina because of the extreme corruption that prevails there. The speakers also conclude that any governor who is placed in such a situation must seek either to win the people by persuasion, so that they will not wish to oppose him, or to so intimidate them that they will not dare go against his wishes. Those governors who attempt to mix these modes are, it is asserted, doomed to failure; the experience of Salamina, which has never enjoyed stable government, is cited in support of this proposition. Consideration is then given to the general corruption of manners; how it occurs, how it can be prevented and what are its consequences. A definition is provided as follows:]

EPIMENIDES: We intend nothing else by a corruption of manners but a departure from the fear and reverence of God, from the honour and obedience due unto princes, governors and magistrates, from the love which we owe unto our country, and generally a declining from a just care and regard of public affairs and all heroical virtues into pleasures, wantonness, vices and other such private respects and regards.

SOLON: You have exactly described the same: for as the fatness and goodness of the earth is easily discerned by the large profit and benefit it yieldeth to the labouring hand, and the goodness of the tree by his pleasant fruit; so the corruption of manners in the people by his infinite evil, miseries, common calamities, ruins and destructions of states which every where it begetteth and bringeth forth, as by his several fruits and effects may be discerned. For it breedeth in men a base opinion and estimation of virtues and a contempt of magistrates.... From this fountain springeth ambition, desire of revenge, mutinies, sedition, treason and rebellion . . . so as generally it may be reputed the mother and nurse of all common calamities.

EPIMENIDES: That detestable custom and more detestable confirmation thereof for receiving and supporting of traitors, rebels and evil disposed persons coming and arriving into the land did first occasion so general a corruption of manners in Salamina . . . .

SOLON: Since then this general corruption of manners doth draw with it so many public miseries and calamities as are before remembered we cannot, except men be altogether void of humanity and reason, but abhor even the remembrance of these lamentable times and be forthwith kindled with a desire of reformation.

[Consideration is given here to the factors that can give rise to this corruption. It is found in the case of Salamina that corruption prevails not because good laws are absent, but rather because excessive power rests in the hands of local lords who will not permit these laws to take effect. This facilitates the following conclusion:]

EPIMENIDES: Lastly, the many and sundry privileges are found to give impediment unto the execution of profitable laws, and to nourish a corruption of manners in the subject as more at large it doth appear in the act of absentees, which is left unto us as a register of the fall and declination of the state of Salamina wherein it is manifest that the lords of the several countries of Carlow and Wexford[1] being places privileged may keep and hold all manor pleas within the same under colour whereof the king's laws, writs or other process be not obeyed, neither any other justice there administered for the quieting and good order of the subject, so as in the default thereof the king's enemies have them in servage,[2] all murders, robberies, thefts, treasons and other offences remaining there unpunished.

SOLON: But what magistrate may be found sufficient to establish a reformation of manners?

EPIMENIDES: A severe magistrate is herein required: for that a common-weale mightily corrupted in manners is squared and reformed only by the rule and line of justice which we call distributive, the which for the inequality thereof may not without great motions and sharp remedies reform the enormities and mischiefs of the

1. The ancient liberty of Wexford had been abolished in the early sixteenth century.
2. bondage, slavery.

common-weale. Lastly where the manners of the people remain corrupted there the laws . . . are found unprofitable unless by a severe and stout magistrate they be supported and maintained. For if Brutus had not severely proceeded, as well against his owns sons as against all other traitors he could not have reformed the corruptions of Tarquin and of his other confederates.[3]

SOLON: He that shall in these weighty actions of reformation proceed as you have said with lenity and softness shall never with Collatinus[4] be able to suppress a corruption of manners in the subject, but he shall by that course rather embolden and comfort traitors in their intended purposes.

3. The reference here, again, is to the rivalry between Brutus and the supporters of Tarquin.
4. The cognomen of Tarquin, who was outwitted by Brutus.

[Having agreed on this proposition, the speakers proceed to consider the relative merits of the different possible forms of government as instruments for the promotion of reform. They agree that monarchical rule is particularly suited to the government of servile commonwealths and those that are customarily subservient to others, as Salamina is to Athens.

In the third book of *Solon His Follie*, the speakers remark on the circumstances under which decline occurs in different commonwealths and again conclude that, in Salamina, this always results from excessive power being vested in the hands of great lords, such as was the case with the Earls of Kildare and Desmond at the point of their respective rebellions. This bring the speakers to consider how to reduce the power of the nobility. The measures that are agreed upon are the appointment of provincial governors, who shall hold superior authority over these lords and shall supervise the application of reform legislation, the raising of composition rents, which will make it possible for these provincial governors to maintain in good order soldiers for the protection of the subject, and the advancement of those subjects who show themselves amenable to reform. Most necessary of all, however, is that continued support be offered by the central government to its officers in Salamina, and particularly so whenever they meet with local resistance. This latter subject is introduced as follows:]

SOLON: There remain yet other occasions of the declining of common-weales worthy of remembrance.

EPIMENIDES: What may the same be?

SOLON: If Princes, Kings and states shall not publicly grace, countenance and support all governors and magistrates by them placed for reformation of any province or nation during the time of their government the subjects shall take thereby occasion of rebelling. For the Gauls understanding that Rome did conspire to disgrace Caesar raised themselves forthwith in arms under the leading of Ambiorix and Vercingetorix[1] in such sort as if they had not too hastily proceeded therein they had put all Italy in as great fear and danger as it was sometimes when the Cumbri[2] came to invade their city.

EPIMENIDES: We need not fetch foreign examples herein: for Salamina by this error committed was for many years vexed with the rebellions of the Burkes and the O'Rourkes until that famous knight Sir R. Bingham by his singular art and skill in military discipline as another Caesar suppressed at the last Vercingetorix and the rebelling Gauls.

SOLON: What governors were there that were found so unskilful in their charge?

EPIMENIDES: A late deputy of Salamina[3] whose name here I pass over with silence for that I may not say, *honoris causa nomine*.[4] But O you governors, princes, kings and emperors whatsoever, countenance all inferior governors and magistrates placed for the reformation of any nation or province.

1. Ambiorix (*fl.* 54 B.C.), chief of the Eburones, and Vercingetorix (died 46 B.C.), acclaimed king of the Arverni, were leading Gallic adversaries of Caesar.
2. Probably a reference to the Cimbri, a fierce Germanic tribe which invaded the Roman Empire.
3. Reference is being made here to Sir John Perrot, lord deputy of Ireland 1584-88, who was thought by his critics to have been excessively accommodating to Old English officials.
4. 'with all respect' (Cicero).

[Following this exhortation, the speakers detail the steps that must be followed if Salamina is to be recovered from its declined condition. These involve treating all inhabitants as a single people with one religion and one language, as prescribed by the state; the rigorous enforcement of a legal code; and the creation of conditions under which the population will apply themselves to productive occupations. This draws to the following conclusion:]

EPIMENIDES: There remaineth now that we deduct[1] colonies which is the last, but not the least, means to suppress this distemperature which of all others is the most beneficial for the containing of a nation conquered in their duty and obedience,

1. The verb is from the Latin *deduco*, to lead away.

wherein four matters are worthily considered: first the necessity of deducting colonies; secondarily the benefit that redoundeth thereby unto common-weales; thirdly what order and manner in deducting colonies is to be used and observed; lastly the impediments which are usually given unto the deducting of colonies.

SOLON: Show us the necessity of colonies?

EPIMENIDES: A nation conquered may not be contained in their obedience without the strength of colonies or garrisons: for may we be induced to believe that that people or nation who daily bewaileth and accuseth his present state and condition may persist therein longer than they be pressed thereunto by necessity . . . so as we may conclude that where colonies are not strongly and faithfully deducted there the end of the first way is the beginning of a second more dangerous than the first, the which may appear by the records of Salamina . . . . Now then if we be willing to cast off our former and manifold troubles, if we be desirous to dismiss ourselves of these infinite and perpetual charges, and lastly if we endeavour to be strong against the invaders and such as shall contend to occupy Salamina by force, let us lose no opportunity of deducting of colonies, for they be deducted and maintained with small or no charges and with no great offence but only to such whose lands and houses they possess.... And all others which find themselves free from their losses shall rest pacified, partly fearing lest they commit anything rashly or foolishly and partly doubting lest the like befalleth them as to those which remained spoiled for their offences. Again, being thus deducted with small or no discontentment, and maintained with far less charge they be found also more faithful and stout defenders of the confines of the country than garrisons . . . .

SOLON: Now since the necessity of colonies doth manifestly appear by infallible proofs and examples let us proceed unto the profit and benefit that groweth thereby.

EPIMENIDES: The benefits that hereby arise to the common-weale are sundry and diverse: first the people poor and seditious which were a burden to the common-weale are drawn forth, whereby the matter of sedition is removed out of the city . . . secondly by translating of colonies the people conquered are drawn and enticed by little and little to embrace the manners, laws and government of the conqueror; lastly the colonies being placed and dispersed abroad amongst the people, like beacons do foretell and disclose all conspiracies and as a garrison also are wont to suppress the mutinies of such as are desirous of alteration and change, . . . lastly they do yield a yearly rent, profit or service to the crown forever. . . .

SOLON: Now since as well the necessity as the profit of deducting colonies doth sufficiently appear unto us, let us proceed unto the manner and order of translating of colonies. . . .

EPIMENIDES: In the order and manner of deducting colonies certain rules are to be observed: first that the land be so divided as strength by great numbers may be deducted . . . . Secondly, we are to plant and place our colonies in the most rich and fruitful lands. . . . Thirdly, such as are to be deducted in the number of colonies, we shall wisely make them but proprietors of the land during life only . . . by which constitution three matters beneficial to the weale public shall arise. First, opportunity shall be lent from time to time to recompense servitors by these casual profits that shall arise, . . . secondly by the death of this tenant for life the profits thereof grow unto the prince until the lands be newly disposed by him; thirdly, the prince or state being to dispose these lands at his or their pleasure shall with this reward bind the proprietor of the land during life in all services to be loyal and faithful; lastly, by holding this course sundry inconveniences shall be eschewed which usually follow such as grant these lands in perpetuity; for in such cases they have been found in Salamina, especially after two or three descents to intermarry and foster with the meer native people and by that occasion decline sometimes from their obedience. . . .

SOLON: You have at large described unto us the necessity, the profit, and the order and manner of deducting of colonies, you shall orderly proceed if you intreat of the impediments which usually are given unto such actions.

EPIMENIDES: The impediments are sundry and diverse: the first is given by such as usually oppose themselves against all new orders for that they reap a benefit by the old disorders. The second is equal with the first and proceedeth from a general incredulity ingrafted in all sorts of persons which never yet have given assistance or confidence unto new attempts be they never so profitable. The third impediment ariseth greater than the rest when the authors of these new orders shall become faint defenders thereof and shall give leave and way to others which gave impediment thereunto. The last impediment is the great trouble and charge which followeth such as shall inhabit lands far removed . . . .

SOLON: Now you have at large discoursed of a reformation of declined common-weales, declare unto us what you intended by the subsequent words which follow in your general and first description where you term it a happy restitution unto his first perfection.

EPIMENIDES: I have termed it a happy restitution when the same is effected without bloodshed and spot of tyranny or cruelty; but yet it must be confessed that where *sanandi medicina* may not prevail there *execandi* is rightly used;[2] neither is nature said to hate those members and parts which she cutteth off for the preservation and safety of the whole body. And by this word perfection I intend nothing but that good which even from the first institution we did aim and shoot at, and this is the end and scope of all reformation.

2. What Beacon is saying is that if medicine does not prove efficacious, the surgeon's knife will have to effect a cure.

[The discourse ends with the arrival of a messenger, who summons Solon to muster his troops for the onset of war in Salamina. Solon offers the assurance that his war will be waged with the purpose of implementing the reform that Epimenides has outlined.]

FYNES MORYSON
(1566-1630)

from: OF THE COMMONWEALTH OF IRELAND (*c*.1620)

[Fynes Moryson's discourse was completed in 1619 or 1620, but the ideas it contained were probably worked out when he was serving in Ireland as secretary to Lord Deputy Mountjoy from 1600 to 1603. In the earlier part of the discourse, Moryson deplores the lack of continuity of purpose among governors in Ireland; he describes and bewails the barbaric customs of the Gaelic Irish, and argues that the Old English were unfit to hold office because they had degenerated from their civil condition and had become attached to the base customs and popish superstitions of the Gaelic Irish. This bitter onslaught is intended to be a justification of the harsh measures taken by Lord Mountjoy in his conduct of the last of the Elizabethan wars in Ireland. But while justifying the war, Moryson contends that it was not without a grander purpose and he makes the case for the pursuit of the reform objectives that had been intended by Mountjoy.

It is clear that the programme that Moryson (and presumably Mountjoy) favoured bears a close resemblance to that outlined in Spenser's *View*.

The work was not published until 1903, when it was included in Charles Hughes (ed.), *Shakespeare's Europe*.]

REFORMATION INTENDED AT THE END OF THE LAST REBELLION[1]

Having largely written of all mischiefs growne in the gouernment of Ireland, I will add something of the Reformation intended at the end of the last Rebellion. The worthy lord Mountjoy[2] (as I haue mentioned in the end of the second part of this woorke) having reduced Ireland from the most desperate estate, in which it had euer beene since the Conquest, to the most absolute subiection, being made as a fayre payre of Tables[3] wherein our State might write, what lawes best fitted it; yet knowing that he left that great woorke vnperfect, and subiect to relapse, except his Successors should finish the building, whereof he had layd the foundation, and should polish the stones, which he had only rough hewed. And fynding euery

1. The spelling of the original text has been used: 'haue' for 'have', 'vpon' for 'upon', 'subiection' for 'subjection', 'mutinus' for 'mutinous'. By 'the last Rebellion', Moryson means the wars in Ireland 1594-1603.
2. Charles Blount, lord Mountjoy (and subsequently earl of Devonshire), who served as lord deputy of Ireland 1600-03.
3. i.e. writing-tablets on which laws could be inscribed.

Rebellion in Ireland to haue beene more dangerous then the former, and the last to haue wanted litle of Casting the English out of that kingdome, was most carefull to preuent all future mischeefes. To which end (howsoeuer his diseignes were diuerted) I dare boldly say, both from his discourse with nearest frends, and from the papers he left, that he proiected many good poynts of Reformation, wherof these fewe that followe are worthy to be remembred.

First to establish the mantenance of some necessary Forts planted within land remote from Seas and Riuers, the warders whereof might cleare all paces[4] (or passages of Bogges and woodes) and might not only keepe the Irish in awe, but be to the State as it were spyes to advertise all mutinous and seditious inclinations. Also to plant like Garrysons vpon such hauens, as be easy and commodious for the discent of forayne enemyes. And because the Cittyes (espetially of Mounster) hauing large priuiledges graunted to the first English inhabitants (as namely the Profitt of Fynes and penall Statutes) had many wayes abused them in the last Rebellion to the preiudice of the Comonwealth (as namely in remitting to the delinquents all Fynes and penaltyes imposed on them, for transporting and importing Jesuits and Priests and prohibeted wares) and also because these Cittyes in the Rebellion[5] had nourished the same by secreet practises, and in the ende thereof, had by open sedition in the cause of Religion forfeited theire Charteres, his lordship purposed to procure the Cutting off many exorbitant priuiledges in the renewing of theire Charters, and likewise the establishing of Forts with strong garrysons vpon those Cittyes which had shewed themselues most false harted and Mutinus, more spetially Corke and Watterford, who had denyed entrance to the kings Forces, and were only reduced by a strong hand from theire obstinate sedition, without which Fortes he thought the Cittyes would nether be kept in obedience for the safetie of the Army, nor be brought to any due reformation in Religion. But howsoeuer Dublin was no lesse ill affected in the cause of Religion then the rest, yet he thought it sufficently restrayned by the residency of the Lord Deputy in the Castle, and great numbers of English that lodged in the Citty attending upon the State. For the Fortes within land, he hoped they would in shorte tyme become townes well inhabited, as was founde by experience in the old Fortes of Lease and Ophalia,[6] and in some newe Fortes in Vlster, and that they would much strengthen the State, so great Caution were had that only English soldyers shoulde keepe them, and that by faythfull Musters they were kept strong, so as the covetousnes of Captaynes might not lay them open to surprisall, ether by taking Irish soldyers seruing for lesse pay, or by wanting theire full numbere of warders, and that, as the garrysons were to haue land allotted and many priuiledges graunted to them so constant care were taken to kepe them from spoyling the Countrye by seuere disciplyne. Agayne for the Fortes, because he feared the soldyers could not be kept from making affinity by maryage with the neighboring Irish, and for that the Captaynes and officers were likely to intertayne the Irish for Soldyers and seruants as content with small or no wages, whereby the Fortes could not but be subiect to betraying, as likewise for that the Captaynes were likely in tyme by letters Pattens[7] from the State to apropriate to themselues the land allotted to each Forte for the publike vse of the garrysons, and for diuers like reasons, more spetially for that the Continuall sound of Drommes and Trumpitts was dissonant from a Commonwealth peaceably governed: His lordship thought these Fortes were not like to yeald such strength to the State as the planting of Faythfull Colonyes. And so his lordshipp in the second place purposed to perswade the Reformation of the old Colonyes, and the leading of newe into that kingdome, both to be planting of Faythfull Colonyes. And so his lordshipp in the second place purposed to perswade Irish to inhabitt the Countryes within land, whereby these Colonyes might be free or more safe from theire assaultes, and not only be easely releeued out of England, but growe rich with forrayne traffique. And to this purpose to exchange inland possessions pertayning to the old Colonyes or belonging to the king, with such Irish as then had

4. narrow paths.
5. Irish towns were reluctant to support the government war effort during the Nine Years' War (1594-1603). The corporations of Cork and Waterford were unwilling to proclaim King James I until they had been given an assurance that he would grant freedom of worship to catholics.
6. The chain of fortresses constructed in the mid-sixteenth century as part of the Leix-Offaly plantation.
7. letters patent (i.e. that can be opened for inspection).

theire lands vpon the Sea Coasts, Riuers, and lakes, giuing them greater proportions of ground, to make them better content with this exchange. Some aduised in this exchange, to giue the Irish also those spirituall liuings which they helde by Custody as vacant at that tyme, but this course was thought to ouerthrowe the foundation of all good reformation, that must beginn with Religion, which could not be established without settling a learned and honest Cleargy, nor they be mantayned without these liuinges. But because the Irish and English Irish[8] were obstinate in Popish superstition, great care was thought fitt to be taken, that these newe Colonyes should consist of such men, as were most vnlike to fall to the barbarous Customes of the Irish, or the Popish superstition of Irish and English Irish so as no lesse Cautions were to be obserued for vniting them and keeping them from mixing with the other, then if these newe Colonyes were to be ledd to inhabitt among the barbarous Indians. In which respect caution was thought fitt to be had, that these newe Colonyes, should not Consist of obstinate Papists, nor Criminall fugitiues, Cutt purses,[9] and infamous weomen, or persons rather drawne out to Clense England of ill members, then to reduce Ireland to Ciuility and true Religion, but of honest gentlemen and husbandmen to inhabitt the Country, and honest Cittisens and marchants to inhabitt the Cittyes, with weomen of good fame, and espetially learned and honest Preachers and ministers for them both. That the Cittisens consisting of noble and Plebean Familyes, should builde and fortifye Cittyes, vpon the riuers and lakes, to be thorughfayres for the whole kingdome, all other by passages through woodes and desert places being shutt vp, so as theeues and malefactors might more easily be apprehended, and all Catle, being not otherwise to be solde or bought then in the publike marketts of Cittyes, All theftes and Rapines[10] might easily be detected and the barbarous people seeing the Cittisens to liue plentifully vnder good gouernment, and to growe rich by trades and traffique, might in tyme be allured to imbrace theire Ciuill manners and profitable industrye. That the gentlemen inhabiting the adioyning Countryes, should dwell in Castles of stone, and not keepe there husbandmen vnder absolute Commaund as Tennants at will, but graunt them freeholds, Copieholdes,[11] and leases, with obligation to mantayne horse and Foote, and to rise vp with them for defence of the Country from thefts and incursions. And in case England was not able to supply these Colonyes, or the English (as lesse industrous) were not thought so fitt for this purpose, without others ioyned with them, then his lordship Judged the Netherlanders most fitt to be drawne to this worke, as a people most industrous, peaceable, and subiect to iust commaund, and abounding with inhabitants, but streaightend[12] by not hauing large teritoryes. Many other cautions were proiected for the quality of these Colonies, as that they should not dwell together in great numbers of one Sapt[13] or name, nor should Consist of bordering people, vsed to liue like outlawes vpon spoyle, and one Sept to haue deadly quarrells and hatred (as it were by inheritance) with an other. That they should be a Free people like the Flemings, and vsed to liue of themselues like them and the Italians, not vsed to the absolute Commandes of lordes after the seruile manner of Ireland, which dependancye makes them apt to followe their lords into Rebellion and priuate quarells. That they should be such, as were not vsed to liue in smoaky Cotages and Cabines, or to goe naked and in ragged apparrell, but in Commodious houses and decently attyred, that so they might not be apt to fall to the Irish manners, but rather to bring them to ciuility. That they should be planted in remote places from theire Natiue home, lest in seditions they might easily drawe theire neighboring frendes and Countrymen to take part with them. Finally and espetially, that they should be soundly affected to the Reformed Religion.

Thirdly because his lordship knewe all endeuours would be in vayne, if Ciuill Magistrates should thincke by fayre meanes without the sworde to reduce the Irish to due obedience (they hauing beene Conquered by the sword, and that Maxime being infallible, that all kingdomes must be preserued by the meanes by which they were first gayned, and the Irish espetially being by theire nature plyable to a harde hand, and Jadish[14] when

8. Another term for the Old English.
9. pickpockets.
10. plunderings, pillages.
11. estates held by tenure, evidenced by a copy of the court roll.
12. straitened or hindered.
13. i.e. sept: dynastic family with a common surname.
14. vicious.

vpon the least pricking of prouender the bridle is lett loose vnto them)[15] Therefore it was thought fitt that the Irish should not only beare no Armes in the pay of the State (which should euer be committed to the hands of most faithfull Subiects) but should also haue all priuate Armes taken from them till by Parliament it might be agreed, what vse of swordes or Peeces[16] were fitt to be graunted some men by priuiledge for grace and ornament or for necessary vse, as for fowling and like vses. And howsoeuer this disarming of the Irish could not well be done during the Rebellion, when the Counsell of England commaunded it, because the submitted Irish should thereby haue beene left a pray to the spoyling of those that were still in Rebellion, yet nothing seemed more fitt and easy to be done when the Rebellion was fully appeased, and our Conquering Army houered like Falcons ouer the heads of any that should dare to resist. And likewise that lawes of Reformation should be enacted by Parliament, if either the Irish would consent or could be ouertopped[17] by the voyces of the new Colonyes and Bishopps, or otherwise should be imposed by absolute power, as no doubt the king of Spaine would doe vppon any his Subiects in like case, to whose subiection the Irish seemed then strongly affected. Fourthly for the last alleged reason his lordshipp purposed to procure that the English Army should be continued in some strength, till Religion were reformed, whereof I shall treat in the last Chapter of the next Booke, and till the kings Reuenues Customes and Tributes were established, whereof something must here be added.

Of old the Customes of exported or imported marchandize, were very small, the people hauing fewe Commodityes to export, and desyring not to haue more imported then wynes and such things for necessity, vppon which things the ancient kings imposed small or no Customes, in regard the Conquered Irish were basely poore, and content with any apparrell, yet with nakednes, and with milke and butter for foode, and for that it was fitt the English Irish, should haue immunity from such burthens, thereby to drawe more Inhabitants into that kingdome. For which reason also the Tolles within land, and the Rents of the kings lands of Inheritance were of small value, and both they and the Customes, yea the very Fynes of penall Statutes, were for rewardes of seruice giuen or lett vppon a small Rent to the English Irish Cittyes, and lordes of Countryes. In the last Rebellion the whole Revenues of the kingdome amounting to some thirty thousand pounds yearely, were so farr from defraying the Charge of the Army, as it cost the State of England one yeare with an other, all Reckonings cast vpp betweene 200 and 300th thousand pounds yearely aboue the Reuenue. And the Rebellion being appeased, when the Army was reduced to 1200 Foote, and some 400 horse, yet the Charge of these small forces, and the Stipends of Magistrates and Judges, exceeded the Reuenes some 45 thousand pounds yearely. But due Courses being taken in this tyme of peace, it was thought the Reuenues might be much increased, then which nothing was more necessary. The Irish Cowes are so stubborne, as many tymes they will not be milked but by some one woman, when, how, and by whome they list. If their Calues be taken from them, or they otherwise grewe stubborne, the skinnes of the Calues stuffed with strawe must be sett by them to smell on, and many fooleries done to please them, or els they will yeilde no milke. And the Inhabitants of that tyme were no lesse froward[18] in their obedience to the State, then their beasts were to them. But I would gladly know from them by what right they challenge more priuiledge then England hath, why they should not beare the same tributes and Subsidyes that England beareth, and why so rich a kingdome should be so great a burthen to the State of England and not rather yeild profitt aboue the Charge thereof. One lord of the Countye of Carberie[19] being in Rebellion mantayned one thousand Rebells against the State, who after becoming a Subiect, was hardly drawne to serue the State with thirty foote, at the invasion of the Spaniards, and yet thought he deserued thankes and reward for that poore Supply. I cannot wonder inough, how the lordes of Ireland can be so blinde in their owne affections as having mantayned some 15,000 men in

15. i.e. because they are suffering from hunger, they are allowed a loose rein (to eat freely).
16. weapons, firearms.
17. outnumbered.
18. obstinate.
19. The lordship of Carbery in west County Cork, ruled by the Mac Carthy Reagh.

Rebellion, they should thinck much in tyme of peace to pay the Stipends of Magistrates and Judges, and to mantayne the small Remnant of the English Army being some 1200 Foote, and vnder 500 horse. Of old after the first Conquest, when Vlster was obedient to the State, that Prouince alone paid 30000 markes yearely into the Exchequer, and besides, (as many Relations witnes) mantayned some thousands of Foote for the States seruice, yeilding also Tymber to build the kings Shipps, and other helpes of great importance to the state. No doubt Ireland after the Rebellion appeased, was in short tyme like to be more rich, and happy in all aboundance, then euer it had bene, if the Subiects would delight in the Arts of peace, and the fertility of Ireland yeildeth not to England, if it had as many, and as industrious Inhabitants. In Sommer it hath lesse heat then England, which proceeding from the reflection of the sunne vppon the earth, is abated by the frequent Boggs and lakes, (which together with rawe or litle rosted meates, cause the Country diseases of Fluxes and Agues[20] fatall to the English) but this defect might be helped by the industry of Husbandmen drayning the grounds, and may hinder the ripening of some fruites, but no way hurtes the Corne, though perhapps it may cause a later Harvest then England hath. Againe in winter by the humiditye of Sea and land, Ireland is lesse subiect to Colde then England, so as the Pastures are greene, and the Gardens full of Rosemary, laurell and sweete hearbes, which the Colde of England often destroyeth. It passeth[21] England in Riuers, and frequent lakes abounding with fish, whereof one lake called the Bande,[22] yieldeth 500li yearely Rent by Fishing. The Hauens from Galloway to Calebeg[23] a third part of the kingdome, are fowerteene in number, whereof some will receiue 200th, some 300th, some 400th great shipps, and only two or three of them are barred,[24] and shallowe, and all these with the other Harbors, Creekes, and Seas, on all sydes of Ireland, abound with plenty of excellent fish, if the Inhabitants were industrious to gett them for foode and traffique.

20. bloody dysentery and fever.
21. surpasses.
22. The Bann in Northern Ireland, although it is a river, flowing through Lough Neagh.
23. Galway to Killybegs, Co. Donegal.
24. blocked by sand bars.

For the increasing of the kings Customes in tyme by vnsensible degrees, it was thought the Irish were not likely to repyne[25] much thereat, since that burthen greiueth none that are content with natiue Commoditwritten, and affect not forayne luxuryes, but they haue bene litle vsed to taxes and Tributes vppon their land, and haue euer kicked at the least burthen in that kinde for the seruice of the State, only bearing it chearefully for their owne ends, as to support the Popish Religion, and to mantayne Agents in England, to pleade for that, and other Clamorous greiuances. Howsoeuer the question is not how willingly they will yeilde profitt to the king, but how it may be most commodiously raysed. To which purpose in regard the Wealth of Ireland consists especially in Cattell and victualls, and wanted nothing more then mony, the best Relations of the Irish estate in those tymes of the Rebellion appeased, thought not so fitt to rayse it by new Compositions[26] of all Countryes, and increasing the old, as by making Ireland only to beare the Charge of the Magistrates, and Judges Stipends, and moreouer, to be (as it were) a nursery for some Competent English forces, extracting old Soldiers from thence vppon occasion of seruice, and sending new men to be trayned vpp in their place. This done whereas forayne Enemyes heretofore thought Ireland the weakest place wherein England might be annoyed, henceforward, they would rather dare to invade England, then Ireland thus armed. And the Rents by Compositions would be a trifle in respect of this profitt of Sessing soldiers.[27] By sessing I meane, the allotting of Certayne numbers to each Citty and shire to be mantayned by them, who would be as so many Spyes to obserue their Parleyes and Conspiracyes, and as Garisons in Townes to keepe them in awe, whether they might be sent in greater or lesse numbers as the publike seruice required. Prouided alwayes, that this Sessing should be to the kings profitt only, not (as it was in the last Rebellion) for the Captaynes profitt, who tooke all the profitt thereof without taking a penny lesse pay from the State, or making any satisfaction to the Subiects, though they had their hands to charge them. As this Sessing was thought to be most profitable to the State, (easing it of the Armyes

25. repine, to be low-spirited through discontent.
26. Rents to the state based on land valuation.
27. cessing or billeting soldiers.

charge, espetially for victualls, whereof the publike stores could neuer be replenished but with farr greater expence then any Compositions were like to yeilde), so was this kinde of Charge most easy for the Irish abounding in victualls. Prouided that the Soldiers were restrayned from extorting by violence more then should be due to them, and the due prouision were gathered by orderly course. For preuention whereof, and for the Soldiers safety, they should not lye scattered in the Country, but together in Garisons, yet not leaving it in the power of the Irish to starue them, but they fetching in victualls aforehand, if according to order it were not brought to them. Prouided also, that the Soldiers trauelling for any seruice, should in like sort be restrayned from extortions. When the Rebellion was ended, and the English Army in strength, this course was thought easy to be settled, and if at any tyme after, the State should thinck fitter to receiue yearely Rents, it was not doubted but this Course for a tyme would after make the people glad to raise their Compositions, so as the Sessing might be taken away. And by this practise we see that Fraunce hath of late raysed great Tributes, increasing them vppon new burthens of warr, and so making the most seditious to abhorr troubles, and loue peace.

Then it was proiected that Commissioners should be sent ouer out of England, To veiwe such lands, for which small or no rent had long bene payd to the king, vppon false pretence that they lay waste. To rayse the Rents of those vndertakers in Mounster, to whome the Queene having graunted to some 3000, to some more Acres of good land for small Rent, or they having bought it at second hand at so easy a price, as some of them raysed as much profitt in one yeare as payd the Purchase, and they hauing broken all their Couenants with the Queene, not peopling the land with English Tenants, nor having English seruants, but vsing the Irish for both, as seruing vppon base Conditions, and not building their Castles, but suffering the old Castles to goe to ruine, and so in the Rebellion being betrayde by their owne Irish men, and having no English to serue the State, or keepe their owne possessions, were forced vppon the first tumults to quitt their lands, or charge the Queene with warders to keepe their Castles, for which causes, if their estates were not taken from them vppon breach of Couenants, yet at least they deserued to be charged with greater rents. To tye them strictly to the obseruing hereafter of all Couenants for the publike good, vppon payne to forfeite their graunts. To dispose for the kings best profitt all concealed lands giuen to superstitious vses, which were thought of great value. To dispose of spirituall lands and livings by custody to the kings profitt, for a tyme till a learned Clergie might be setled. To rate the Sessing of Soldiers in Vlster where it was thought the people would willingly beare any reasonable burthen, so they might be freed from the great lords Tyranny. To doe the like in other parts of the kingdome, at least for a tyme, since if after yearely Rents were thought more commodious the people would more willingly rayse the Compositions to be freed from this Sessing, and mantayning of Garisons. Lastly to rayse the Customes[28] by degrees, and to consider what priuiledges of Cittyes, or of priuatemen, for that present deseruing litle of the State, were fitt to be cutt of, or restrayned.

By these meanes it was thought no difficult thing in fewe yeares, highly to rayse the kings Reuenues, and to reforme in some good measure the Ciuill and Ecclesiasticall policy. Prouided that these Commissioners being of the best sort, for Nobility, and experience, were after the first Reformation continued still in that imployment, and sent ouer once in fiue yeares, or like space of tyme, to visitt that kingdome especially for administration of Justice, yet by the way (with Arts of peace, and by degrees) for setling and increasing the kings Reuenues, which wee see daily and wisely to haue beene done in England. Thus the Irish bearing Common and equall burthen with the English, should haue no iust cause to complayne and finding Rebellions to increase their burthens, would be taught to loue peace, the English should be eased from bearing the wonted burthen of their seditions; the king should haue meanes in Ireland to reward his magistrates, and seruants in that kingdome. And it was hoped such treasure might in tyme be drawne out of Ireland, as might in some measure repay the great expences, England hath heretofore disbursed to keepe Ireland in peace, without raysing any least profitt from a Conquered kingdome.

28. to raise the tax on imports.

SIR JOHN DAVIES

(1569-1626)

from: A DISCOVERY OF THE TRUE CAUSES WHY IRELAND WAS NEVER ENTIRELY SUBDUED. . . . (1612)

[This text was composed by Davies in 1612 to celebrate the conquest of Ireland by the forces of Queen Elizabeth I and the promotion of civil conditions in Ireland by the civil servants appointed by King James I. When he suggests that Ireland has been reformed in civil matters, Davies is making the case for his own recall to serve his monarch in England. But while taking due credit for what has been accomplished, Davies, like Spenser before him, admits the possibility of a future relapse to barbaric conditions if the state does not remain constantly attentive to its responsibility to effect a thorough reform. For Davies, the most compelling lesson is the means by which the earlier Hiberno-English settlers in Ireland have lapsed from civility to the point where they have become 'the chief impediments of the final conquest of Ireland'. The details of this salutary example are spelled out in the passage included here.

The *Discovery* was an influential text throughout the seventeenth century and was frequently cited by constitutional theorists in the next century. A modernized version was included in Henry Morley, *Ireland Under Elizabeth and James I* (London, 1890) and a photo-offset of the original 1612 edition was published at Shannon by Irish University Press in 1969.]

. . . It is, then, manifest, by that which is before expressed, that the not communicating of the English laws to the Irish; the over-large grants of lands and liberties to the English; the plantation made by the English in the plains and open countries, leaving the woods and mountains to the Irish, were great defects in the civil policy, and hindered the perfection of the conquest very much. Howbeit, notwithstanding these defects and errors, the English colonies stood and maintained themselves in a reasonable good estate as long as they retained their own ancient laws and customs, according to that of Ennius, '*Moribus antiquis res stat Romana virisque*'.[1] But when the civil government grew so weak and so loose as that the English lords would not suffer the English laws to be put in execution within their territories and seigniories,[2] but in place thereof both they and their people embraced the Irish customs, then the estate of things, like a game at Irish, was so turned about as the English, which hoped to make a perfect conquest of the Irish, were by them perfectly and absolutely conquered, because *Victi victoribus leges dedere*,[3] a just punishment to our nation, that would not give laws to the Irish when they might; and therefore now the Irish gave laws to them. Therefore, this defect and failing of the English justice in the English colonies, and the inducing of the Irish customs in lieu thereof, was the main impediment that did arrest and stop the course of the conquest, and was the only mean that enabled the Irishry to recover their strength again.

For, if we consider the nature of the Irish customs, we shall find that the people which doth use them must of necessity be rebels to all good government, destroy the commonwealth wherein they live, and bring barbarism and desolation upon the richest and most fruitful land of the world. For, whereas by the just and honourable law of England, and by the laws of all other well-governed kingdoms and commonweals, murder, manslaughter, rape, robbery, and theft are punished with death, by the Irish custom, or Brehon Law,[4] the highest of these offences was punished only by fine, which they called an ericke.[5] Therefore, when Sir William Fitzwilliams,[6] being Lord-Deputy, told Maguire[7] that he was to send a sheriff into Fermanagh, being lately before made a county, 'Your sheriff,' said Maguire, 'shall be welcome to me; but let me know his ericke, or the price

1. 'The Roman Empire and its strength stands firm because of traditional values.' Quintus Ennius (239-169 B.C.) was regarded by the Romans as the father of Latin poetry.
2. feudal domains.
3. 'The conquered made laws for the conquerors.'
4. The laws of Ireland before the occupation by the English. They were abolished during the first half of the seventeenth century.
5. Pecuniary compensation for a violent crime.
6. Sir William Fitzwilliam (died 1577), lord justice of Ireland 1560 and 1561, lord deputy 1571-75.
7. Seán Maguire (died 1566), lord of the Maguires, who ruled the land that became County Fermanagh.

of his head, aforehand, that if my people cut it off I may cut the ericke upon the country.' As for oppression, extortion, and other trespasses, the weaker had never any remedy against the stronger; whereby it came to pass that no man could enjoy his life, his wife, his lands or goods in safety if a mightier man than himself had an appetite to take the same from him. Wherein they were little better than cannibals, who do hunt one another, and he that hath most strength and swiftness doth eat and devour all his fellows.

Again, in England and all well-ordered commonweals men have certain estates in their lands and possessions, and their inheritances descend from father to son, which doth give them encouragement to build and to plant and to improve their lands, and to make them better for their posterities. But by the Irish custom of tanistry[8] the chieftains of every country and the chief of every sept had no longer estate than for life in their chiefries, the inheritance whereof did rest in no man. And these chiefries, though they had some portions of land allotted unto them, did consist chiefly in cuttings and cosheries[9] and other Irish exactions, whereby they did spoil and impoverish the people at their pleasure; and when their chieftains were dead their sons or next heirs did not succeed them, but their tanists, who were elective and purchased their elections by strong hand. And by the Irish custom of gavelkind[10] the inferior tenantries were partible[11] amongst all the males of the sept, both bastards and legitimate; and after partition made, if any one of the sept had died, his portion was not divided among his sons, but the chief of the sept made a new partition of all the lands belonging to that sept, and gave every one his part according to his antiquity.

These two Irish customs made all their possessions uncertain, being shuffled and changed and removed so often from one to another by new elections and partitions, which uncertainty of estates hath been the true cause of such desolation and barbarism in this land as the like was never seen in any country that professed the name of Christ; for though the Irishry be a nation of great antiquity and wanted neither wit nor valour, and though they have received the Christian faith above twelve hundred years since, and were lovers of music, poetry, and all kind of learning, and possessed a land abounding with all things necessary for the civil life of man, yet, which is strange to be related, they did never build any houses of brick or stone, some few poor religious houses excepted, before the reign of King Henry the Second, though they were lords of this island for many hundred years before and since the conquest attempted by the English. Albeit, when they saw us build castles upon their borders they have only, in imitation of us, erected some few piles for their captains of the country; yet I dare boldly say that never any particular person, either before or since, did build any stone or brick house for his private habitation but such as have lately obtained estates according to the course of the law of England. Neither did any of them in all this time plant any gardens or orchards, enclose or improve their lands, live together in settled villages or towns, nor make any provision for posterity, which, being against all commonsense and reason, must needs be imputed to those unreasonable customs which made their estates so uncertain and transitory in their possessions.

For who would plant or improve or build upon that land which a stranger whom he knew not should possess after his death? For that, as Solomon noteth, is one of the strangest vanities under the sun. And this is the true reason why Ulster and all the Irish countries are found so waste and desolate at this day, and so would they continue till the world's end if these customs were not abolished by the law of England.

Again, that Irish custom of gavelkind did breed another mischief, for thereby every man being born to land, as well bastard as legitimate, they all held themselves to be gentlemen; and though their portions were never so small and themselves never so poor — for gavelkind must needs in the end make a poor gentility — yet did they scorn to descend to husbandry or merchandise or to learn any mechanical art or science. And this is the true cause why there were never any corporate towns erected in the Irish countries. As for the maritime cities and towns, most certain it is that they were

8. From Irish *tánaiste* (the second person): the ancient custom of choosing an heir apparent of a Celtic chieftain, during the chief's lifetime.
9. Entertainment for themselves and their followers exacted by Irish chiefs from their dependants.
10. A system of land tenure whereby the tenant paid rent (or *gafol*) to the lord instead of performing services for him. Under gavelkind, if a person died intestate, his property was divided equally among his sons.
11. divisible, especially of property or an inheritance.

built and peopled by the Oostmen or Easterlings,[12] for the natives of Ireland never performed so good a work as to build a city. Besides, these poor gentlemen were so affected unto their small portions of land as they rather chose to live at home by theft, extortion, and coshering than to seek any better fortunes abroad, which increased their septs or surnames into such numbers as there are not to be found in any kingdom of Europe so many gentlemen of one blood, family, and surname as there are of the O'Neills in Ulster, of the Bourkes in Connaught, of the Geraldines and Butlers in Munster and Leinster. And the like may be said of the inferior bloods and families. Whereby it came to pass in times of trouble and dissension that they made great parties and factions adhering one to another with much constancy because they were tied together *vinculo sanguinis*;[13] whereas rebels and malefactors which are tied to their leaders by no band, either of duty or blood, do more easily break and fall off one from another; and, besides, their cohabitation in one country or territory gave them opportunity suddenly to assemble and conspire and rise in multitudes against the Crown. And even now, in the time of peace, we find this inconvenience, that there can hardly be an indifferent trial had between the King and the subject, or between party and party, by reason of this general kindred and consanguinity.

But the most wicked and mischievous custom of all others was that of coigny and livery,[14] often before mentioned, which consisted in taking of man's-meat, horse-meat, and money of all the inhabitants of the country at the will and pleasure of the soldier, who, as the phrase of Scripture is, 'did eat up the people as it were bread,'[15] for that he had no other entertainment. This extortion was originally Irish, for they used to lay bonaght[16] upon their people and never gave their soldier any other pay. But when the English had learned it they used it with more insolency and made it more intolerable; for this oppression was not temporary or limited either to place or time, but because there was everywhere a continual war, either offensive or defensive, and every lord of a country and every marcher made war and peace at his pleasure, it became universal and perpetual, and was indeed the most heavy oppression that ever was used in any Christian or heathen kingdom. And therefore, *vox oppressorum*,[17] this crying sin did draw down as great or greater plagues upon Ireland than the oppression of the Israelites did draw upon the land of Egypt; for the plagues of Egypt, though they were grievous, were but of a short continuance, but the plagues of Ireland lasted four hundred years together. This extortion of coigny and livery did produce two notorious effects. First, it made the land waste; next it made the people idle. For when the husbandman had laboured all the year, the soldier in one night did consume the fruits of all his labour, *longique perit labor irritus anni*.[18] Had he reason then to manure[19] the land for the next year? Or rather might he not complain as the shepherd in 'Virgil':

Impius hæc tam culta novalia miles habebit?
Barbarus has segetes? En, quo discordia cives
Perduxit miseros! his nos consevimus agros![20]

And hereupon of necessity came depopulation, banishment, and extirpation of the better sort of subjects, and such as remained became idle and lookers-on, expecting the event of those miseries and evil times; so as this extreme extortion and oppression hath been the true cause of the idleness of this Irish nation, and that rather the vulgar sort have chosen to be beggars in foreign countries than to manure their own fruitful land at home.

Lastly, this oppression did of force and necessity make the Irish a crafty people; for such as are oppressed and live in slavery are ever put to their shifts, *Ingenium mala sæpe movent*;[21] and therefore in the old comedies of Plautus and Terence the bond-slave doth always act the cunning and crafty part. Besides, all the common people have a whining tune or accent in their speech, as if they did still smart or suffer some oppression. And this

12. The names given in Ireland to the Northmen or Danes and their descendants who settled on the east coast.
13. blood bond.
14. The right to free billeting and the provision of food and clothing.
15. This echoes Numbers 24.8.
16. From Irish *buanacht* (subsidy): a tax levied by Irish chieftains for the maintenance of their soldiers.
17. 'the voice of the oppressed'.
18. 'The toil of years vanishes to no purpose.'
19. Spreading animal excreta, usually mixed with straw, upon fields, as a fertilizer.
20. Virgil, *Eclogue* I, 70-72. Dryden translated it as:
Did we for these barbarians plant and sow?
On these, on these, our happy fields bestow?
Good heaven, what dire effects from civil discord flow!
21. 'Evil things often move genius.'

idleness, together with fear of imminent mischiefs which did continually hang over their heads, have been the cause that the Irish were ever the most inquisitive people after news of any nation in the world; as St. Paul himself made observation upon the people of Athens, that they were an idle people, and did nothing but learn and tell news. And because these news-carriers did by their false intelligence many times raise troubles and rebellions in this realm, the Statute of Kilkenny[22] doth punish news-tellers, by the name of skelaghes,[23] with fine and ransom.

This extortion of coigny and livery was taken for the maintenance of their men of war; but their Irish exactions, extorted by the chieftains and tanists by colour of their barbarous seigniory, were almost as grievous a burthen as the other, namely, cosherings, which were visitations and progresses made by the lord and his followers among his tenants, wherein he did eat them, as the English proverb is, out of house and home; cessings of the kern,[24] of his family, called kernety, of his horses and horse-boys, of his dogs and dog-boys, and the like; and lastly, cuttings, tallages, or spendings,[25] high or low, at his pleasure; all which made the lord an absolute tyrant and the tenant a very slave and villain,[26] and in one respect more miserable than bond-slaves. For commonly the bond-slave is fed by his lord, but here the lord was fed by his bond-slave.

Lastly, there were two other customs proper and peculiar to the Irishry, which being the cause of many strong combinations and factions, do tend to the utter ruin of a commonwealth; the one was fostering, the other gossipred,[27] both which have ever been of greater estimation among this people than with any other nation in the Christian world. For fostering, I did never hear or read that it was in that use or reputation in any other country, barbarous or civil, as it hath been and yet is in Ireland, where they put away all their children to fosterers, the potent and rich men selling, the meaner sort buying, the alterage[28] of their children. And the reason is because in the opinion of this people fostering hath always been a stronger alliance than blood, and the foster-children do love and are beloved of their foster-fathers and their sept more than of their own natural parents and kindred, and do participate of their means more frankly, and do adhere unto them in all fortunes with more affection and constancy. And though Tully in his book of Friendship[29] doth observe that children of Princes being sometimes, in cases of necessity, for saving of their lives, delivered to shepherds to be nourished and bred up, when they have been restored to their great fortunes have still retained their love and affection to their fosterers, whom for many years they took to be their parents; yet this was a rare case, and few examples are to be found thereof.

But such a general custom in a kingdom, in giving and taking children to foster, making such a firm alliance as it doth in Ireland, was never seen or heard of in any other country of the world besides.

The like may be said of gossipred or compaternity, which though by the Canon Law it may be a spiritual affinity, and a juror that was gossip to either of the parties might in former times have been challenged as not indifferent by our law, yet there was no nation under the sun that ever made so religious account thereof as the Irish.

Now, these two customs, which of themselves are indifferent in other kingdoms, became exceeding evil and full of mischief in this realm by reason of the inconveniences which followed thereupon. For they made, as I said before, strong parties and factions, whereby the great men were enabled to oppress their inferiors and to oppose their equals; and their followers were borne out and countenanced in all their lewd and wicked actions. For fosterers and gossips, by the common custom of Ireland, were to maintain one another in all causes lawful and unlawful, which, as it is a combination and confederacy punishable in all well-governed commonweals, so was it not one of the least causes of the common misery of this kingdom.

I omit their common repudiation of their wives;

22. Legislation passed at Kilkenny in 1366 by the Irish parliament. The purpose of the 35 statutes was to stem the assimilation of the Anglo-Normans into Irish society. They included a ban on intermarriage with the Irish and on the adoption of the Irish language, dress, or legal system. The statutes proved to be unenforceable and were repealed in 1613.
23. *scéalaithe*, 'storytellers' in modern Irish. cf. *scéalaigh* (newsbearing, gossiping).
24. Forcing a householder to supply a kern, or footsoldier, with provisions.
25. Tolls or taxes levied by a feudal lord upon his tenants.
26. villein: a serf or peasant who was bound to a lord, to whom he paid dues and services in return for land.
27. godparenting.
28. fostering, rearing.
29. Marcus Tullius Cicero (106-43 B.C.), known as Tully. He wrote various philosophical works, including *De amicitia* (On friendship).

their promiscuous generation of children; their neglect of lawful matrimony; their uncleanness in apparel, diet, and lodging; and their contempt and scorn of all things necessary for the civil life of man.

These were the Irish customs which the English colonies did embrace and use after they had rejected the civil and honourable laws and customs of England, whereby they became degenerate and metamorphosed like Nebuchadnezzar,[30] who, although he had the face of a man, had the heart of a beast; or like those who had drunk of Circe's cup,[31] and were turned into very beasts, and yet took such pleasure in their beastly manner of life as they would not return to their shape of men again; insomuch as within less time than the age of a man they had no marks or differences left amongst them of that noble nation from which they were descended. For, as they did not only forget the English language and scorn the use thereof, but grew to be ashamed of their very English names, though they were noble and of great antiquity, and took Irish surnames and nicknames. Namely, the two most potent families of the Bourkes in Connaught, after the House of the Red Earl failed of heirs-males, called their chiefs MacWilliam Eighter and MacWilliam Oughter.[32] In the same province, Bremingham, Baron of Athenrie, called himself MacYoris; Dexecester, or De'exon, was called MacJordan; Dangle, or De Angulo, took the name of MacCostelo. Of the inferior families of the Bourkes, one was called MacHubbard, another MacDavid. In Munster, of the great families of the Geraldines planted there, one was called Mac-Morice, chief of the House of Lixnaw; and another MacGibbon, who was also called the White Knight. The chief of the Baron of Dunboyne's house, who is a branch of the House of Ormond, took the surname of MacFeris. Condon, of the county of Waterford, was called MacMaioge; and the Archdeacon of the county of Kilkenny, MacOdo. And this they did in contempt and hatred of the English name and nation, whereof these degenerate families became more mortal enemies than the mere Irish. And whereas the State and Government, being grown weak by their defection, did, to reduce them to obedience, grant them many protections and pardons, the cheapness whereof in all ages hath brought great dishonour and damage to this commonweal, they grew so ungrateful and unnatural as in the end they scorned that grace and favour, because the acceptance thereof did argue them to be subjects, and they desired rather to be accounted enemies than rebels to the Crown of England.

Hereupon was that old verse made which I find written in the White-book of the Exchequer, in a hand as ancient as the time of King Edward the Third:

By graunting charters of peas
To false English, withouten leas,
    This land shall be mich undoo.
But gossipred, and alterage,
And leesing of our language,
    Have mickly holp[33] theretoo.

30. Nebuchadnezzar, the greatest king of Babylon, reigned from 604 to 541 B.C. See Daniel 4.32-33.

31. Circe, a sorceress in Greek mythology, lived on the island of Aeaea, upon which Ulysses was cast. His companions, whom he sent to explore the island, drank from the magic cup that Circe offered them, and were changed into swine, except for Eurylochus, who brought the news to Ulysses. See Milton, *Comus*, lines 50-53.

32. The Clanrickard branch of the family was known as the 'Upper MacWilliams', the Mayo one as the 'Lower MacWilliams'. Eighter = *íochtar* ('lower' in modern Irish); oughter = *uachtar* ('upper' in modern Irish).

33. great help.

SIR JOHN TEMPLE

(1600-77)

from:
THE IRISH REBELLION. . . .
(1646)

[John Temple's *The Irish Rebellion* was the first effort by an Irish protestant settler to provide a coherent account of what had occurred in 1641. The author was particularly well placed to compose such an account because he had been a senior official in the Dublin administration when the rising occurred and was one of those responsible for collecting depositions from protestants who had escaped the rebels and found refuge in Dublin. While acknowledging that the rising had been most bloody in Ulster, Temple could not accept that it had had its origin in that province. The present extract shows how he traced the original conspiracy to the Old English population of Leinster.

The Irish Rebellion was first published in London in 1646 and was an immediate success in stirring up public sentiment against those in Ireland who had engaged in insurrection. The book continued to be controversial throughout the seventeenth century, and was regularly reprinted in Ireland throughout the eighteenth century to remind the protestant population there of the menace of catholicism. There is no twentieth-century scholarly edition of the book.]

. . . The great instrument chiefly imployed in this work of drawing the meer *Irish* into a firm combination with the old English (as appears by the Lord *Mac Guire*'s relation before mentioned) was *Roger Moore* Esquire, a person of a broken fortune, by descent meerly *Irish*, and issued out of the chief family of the *O Moores* in the Country of *Leax*,[1] but by inter-marriages allied to some of the principal Gentlemen of the *Pale*;[2] He Treated with them about the Association; he first broke the design to the Northern *Irish*, he was the man that made several journeys in *Leinster*, into *Ulster* and *Conaught*: Sundry messages were interchangeably sent and returned the Summer before the breaking out of the Rebellion by his means and *entercourse between them*; And all things were so ordered for their agreement, as they were to go hand in hand together; some of the principal Gentlemen of the Pale, as Colonel *Plunket*, Captain *Fox*, and others, were designed to joyn with the Lord *Mac Guire*, *Mac Mahone*, *Brian O Neale*, *Con O Neale*, *Hugh Birne*, for the surprize of his Majesties Castle of *Dublin*. *Cartan*, Major Domi[3] to *Owen O Neale* in *Flanders*, in his Examination taken *February* 1641 tells, among many other remarkable passages, of several preparatives to this Rebellion; as that *Con O Neale*, brother to *Daniel O Neale*, was sent by *Owen O Neale* into *England*, and that while he resided there he received letters from the President *Rosse* (which was Sir *Phelim O Neale*) and that he assured him he went on very well in his business; for *Brabant* and *Valence* were joyned together, which as he affirms, signified in those Characters *Ulster* and *Leinster*, and that he expected the coming of *Lewes Lenoy*, viz. *Daniel O Neale*: Besides, as *James Talbot* Esq; testifies in his Letter of the 9 of *November* 1641 written to the Lords Justices out of the County of *Cavan*, that he understood from *Philip Mac Mulmore O Rely*, that there were certain Covenants passed between the Lords of the *Pale* and the Northern Irish, for the advancing of the Rebellion; and that the Remonstrance from the principal *Irish* in the County of *Cavan*, unto the Lords Justices and Council sent by Dean *Jones* and Master *Waldrone*, there then Prisoner, was framed in the Pale and brought unto the said *Irish* by Colonel *Plunket*, one of their own: And this was in the very beginning of the Rebellion, long before any jealousies were entertained by the State of the adherence or conjunction of the old *English* with the *Irish*. What those Covenants or Contracts were, I cannot say, but it is most certain, some there were, and some Covenants also entred into, between the Northern *Irish*, and the Lords and Gentlemen of the chief of both the other Provinces, as well as *Leinster*, and these were signed with their blood, as

1. Rory O'Moore was descended from the chiefs of Laois (Leax or Leix). A leading spirit in the rising of 1641, he was given command of rebel troops in Laois and Offaly.
2. The name given in the fourteenth century to that part of Ireland where English rule held sway: Louth, Meath, Trim, Dublin, Kilkenny, Wexford, Waterford and Tipperary. By the late fifteenth century, the Pale had shrunk to the four counties of Louth, Meath, Dublin and Kildare. The word derives from the Latin *palum* (a stake); hence, a fence, a territory within defined boundaries. 'Beyond the pale' means beyond the bounds of civilization.
3. From the medieval Latin *major domus*, the chief steward of a great household.

Doctor *Maxwell* testifies in his examination, he heard Sir *Phelim O Neale* say on the 19 of *December* 1641 in his own house, and in the hearing of Master *Joseph Travers* and others: If the Lords and Gentlemen (meaning the Papists of other Provinces) then not in Arms, would not rise, but leave him in the lurch for all, he would produce his Warrant, signed with their own hands, and written in their own blood, which should bring them to the Gallows. And certainly, had there not been some very strange and extraordinary engagements, and more than I can well imagine, it had not been possible that so many persons of quality, having great possessions and many Children, should have declared themselves, after they saw the main part of the plot for the surprize of the Castle of *Dublin* to fail, and the power of the Northern Rebels begin to decline, that the Parliament of *England* had with great alacrity and readiness undertaken the War, and not only engaged themselves to his Majesty to send over powerful supplies both out of *England* and *Scotland*, but by their publick Order of both Houses, sent over to the Lords Justices, and Printed at *Dublin* in the Month of *November*, fully declared their resolutions for the vigorous prosecution of the war of *Ireland*: Nay, the Cities of *Galway* and *Limeric*, kept their designs very covertly, not doing any open acts of hostility, till after the arrival of some Forces at *Dublin* out of *England*, and that the siege of *Drohedagh* or *Tredah* was raised, and those bold perfidious Traitors beaten back into the North, the Lords of the *Pale* banished by force of his Majesties Arms out of their own habitations, which were all spoiled and laid waste.

Now that then they should declare themselves, is more than a Miracle to me, and such a mysterie, as I should not know what to think of, but that I find in the Lord *Mac Guires* relation before mentioned, that they were acquainted with the first beginnings of this great Plot, and had a particular interest from time to time in the carriage of it on, so as I think I shall not wrong them positively to determine, that they were too deeply engaged slightly to retire; and that howsoever upon the failing of it in the main piece, they at first stood at a gaze, and were put to take up second Counsels; yet such was the strength of the conspiracy, and their great confidence in the power of their Arms, as made them appear in due time to entertain their several assignations, and act their parts with great diligence and industry. The wife of *Philip O Rely* in the County of *Cavan*, told *James Talbot* (as he openly related it to the Lords Justices at Council Board) that she wondered very much the Lords and Gentlemen of the *Pale* did not rise and join with them in the very beginning of this Rebellion, adding these words, or to this effect; that if they would have let us alone, and not set us on, we were so well at ease, as we would never have begun this troublesome work. It cannot certainly be imagined, that those of the *English Pale* (unless they had been the first projectors, or deep adventurers) would have yielded that the meer *Irish* should have seized upon the City and Castle of *Dublin*, places of refuge for them in all former troubles, and which would now have given them protection and safety against the incursions of the *Irish*.

But I hold it not necessary to produce further evidence in this particular; I purpose now to declare how those great Instruments of mischief, that were the supream conductors of this wicked design, moved forwards so successfully in the beginning, toward the accomplishment of their long intended extirpation of all the Brittish and Protestants out of the Kingdom. I find two sorts of persons who did most eminently appear in laying those main fundamentals whereupon their bloody superstructions were afterwards easily reared up: And these were such of the Popish Lawyers as were Natives of the Kingdom, and those of the Romish Clergy of several degrees and Orders. For the first, they had in regard of their knowledge in the Laws of the Land, very great reputation and trust, they now began to stand up like great Patriots for the vindication of the liberties of the Subject, and redress of their pretended grievances, and having by their bold appearing therein, made a great party in the house of Commons, here then sitting, some of them did there magisterially obtrude, as undoubted maximes of Law, the pernicious speculations of their own brain, which though plainly discerned to be full of virulency and tending to sedition, yet so strangely were many of the Protestants and well meaning men in the house blinded with an apprehension of ease and redress, and so stupified with their bold accusations of the Government, as most thought not fit, others durst not stand up to contradict their fond assertions; so as what they spake was received with great acclamation, and much applause by most of the Protestant Members of the house; many of which under specious pretences of publick zeal to this Country, they had inveigled into their party: And then it was, that having impeached Sir *Richard Bolton*, Lord Chancellour of *Ireland*, of high Treason, together with other prime Officers and Ministers of State that were of English birth, some of those great Masters took upon them with much confidence to declare the Law, to make new expositions of their own upon the Text, to frame their *Queres*,[4] challenges fitter to be taken to a long, wilfully, over-grown misgovernment, than to be made against an Authority, that had for many years struggled against the beloved irregularities of a stubborn people, and which had prevailed far beyond former times, towards the allaying of the long continued distempers of the Kingdom: they disdained the moderate qualifications of the Judges, who gave them modest answers, such as the Law and duty to their Soveraign would admit. But those would not serve their turn, they resolved upon on alteration in the Government, and drawing of it wholly into the hands of the Natives, which they knew they could not compass in a Parliamentary way, and therefore only made preparatives there, and delivered such desperate maximes, which being diffused abroad would sit and dispose the people to a change: As they declared it to be Law, that being killed in Rebellion, though found by matter of record, would give the King no forfeiture of estates; that though many thousands stood up in Arms in a Kingdom, working all manner of destruction, yet if they professed not to rise against the King, that it was no Rebellion: That if a man were out-lawed for Treason, and his Land thereby vested in the Crown or given away by the King, his heir might come afterwards and be admitted to reverse the Outlawry, and recover his Ancestors estate. And many other positions of a perilous consequence, tending to sedition and disturbance, did they continue to publish during that Session, and by the power and strength of their party, so far did they prevail at last, as they presumed to attempt a suspension of *Poynings* Act,[5] and indeed intended the utter abrogation of that Statute, which remains as one of the greatest tyes and best monuments the *English* have of their entire dominion over the *Irish* Nation, and the annexion of that Kingdom to the imperial Crown of *England*. They further assumed power of Judicature to the Parliament in criminal and capital offences: A right which no former age hath left any president[6] for, neither would this admit the example.

And thus carrying all things before them, they continued the Session of Parliament begun in *May*, till about two moneths before the first breaking out of this Rebellion; it being very ill taken, that even then they were adjourned. And this they have since aggravated as a high crime against the Lords Justices, and as one of the chief moving causes to the taking up of Arms generally throughout the Kingdom.

But to let those things pass, how finely soever these proceedings were carried on, and being covered over with pretences of zeal and publick affection, passed then currant without any manner of suspicion; yet now the eyes of all men are opened, and they are fully resolved that all these passages, together with the other high contestations in Parliament, not to have the newly raised *Irish* Army disbanded, the importunate solicitation of their Agents in *England*, to, have the old Army in *Ireland* cashiered,[7] and the Kingdom left to be defended by Trained Bands[8] of their own Nation. As likewise the Commissions procured by several of the most eminent Commanders now in Rebellion, for the raising men to carry into *Spain*, were all parts of this Plot, Prologues to this ensuing Tragedy, Preparatives, such as had been long laid to bring on the suddain execution of this most bloody design, all at one and the same time throughout the Kingdom.

Now for the Jesuits, Priests, Fryers, and all the rest of the viperous fraternity belonging to their holy Orders; who, as I said, had a main part to Act, and have not failed with great assiduity and diligence to discharge the same. They lost no time, but most dexterously applyed themselves in all parts of the Country to lay such other dangerous impressions in the minds, as well of the meaner sort as of the chief Gentlemen, as might make them ready to take fire upon the first occasion. And when this Plot was so surely, as they thought, laid, as it

4. queries, questions.
5. An act of 1494 (also known as the Drogheda statutes) named after Sir Edward Poynings (1459-1521), who was lord deputy of Ireland 1494-95. It stipulated that statutes passed by the Irish parliament were valid only if they were approved by the English privy council. The law was not repealed until 1782 when Henry Grattan's parliament met in Dublin.

6. precedent.
7. disbanded, dismissed with dishonour.
8. trained companies of citizens' militia.

could not well fail, and the day once prefixed for execution; they did in their publick Devotions long before, recommend by their Prayers; the good success of a great design, much tending to the prosperity of the Kingdom, and the advancement of the Catholick cause. And for the facilitating of the Work, and stirring up of the people with greater animosity and cruelty to put it on at the time prefixed; they loudly in all places declaimed against the Protestants; telling the people that they were Hereticks, and not to be suffered any longer to live among them; that it was no more sin to kill an *English-man*, then to kill a dog; and that it was a most mortal and unpardonable sin to relieve or protect any of them. Then also they represented with much acrimony the severe courses taken by the Parliament in *England*, for the suppressing of the *Romish* Religion in all parts of the Kingdom, and utter extirpation of all professors of it. They told the people that in *England* they had caused the Queens Priest to be hanged before her own face, and that they held her Majesty in her own person under a most severe Discipline: That the same cruel Laws against Popery were here ordered to be put suddainly in execution; and a design secretly laid for bringing and seizing upon all the principal Noblemen and Gentlemen in *Ireland* upon the 23 of *November* next ensuing, and so to make a general Massacre of all that would not desert their Religion and presently become Protestants.

And now also did they take occasion to revive their inveterate hatred and ancient animosities against the *English* Nation, whom they represented to themselves as hard Masters; under whole Government, how pleasant, comfortable and advantageous so ever it was, they would have the world believe they had endured a most miserable captivity and envassalage. They looked with much envie upon their prosperity, considering all the Land they possessed (though a great part bought at high rates of the Natives) as their own proper inheritance. They grudged at the great multitudes of their fair *English* Cattel; at their goodly Houses, though built by their own industry at their own charges; at the large improvements they made of their Estates, by their own travails and careful endeavours. They spake with much scorn and contempt of such as brought little with them into *Ireland*, and having there planted themselves, in a little time contracted great fortunes: they were much troubled, especially in the *Irish* Countries, to see the *English* live handsomely, and to have every thing with much decency about them, while they lay nastily buried, as it were, in mire and filthiness; the ordinary sort of people commonly bringing their Cattle into their own stinking Creates,[9] and there naturally delighting to lye among them. These malignant considerations made them with an envious eye impatiently to look upon all the *British* lately come over into the Kingdom. Nothing less than a general extirpation will now serve their turn; they must have restitution of all the Lands to the proper Natives, whom they take to be the ancient proprietors, and only true owners, most unjustly despoiled by the *English*, whom they hold to have made undue acquisitions of all the Land they possess by gift from the Crown, upon the attainder of any of their Ancestors.

And so impetuous were the desires of the Natives to draw the whole Government of the Kingdom into their own hands, to enjoy the publick profession of their Religion, as well as to disburden the Country of all the *British* inhabitants seated therein, as they made the whole body of the State to be universally disliked; represented the several members as persons altogether corrupt and ill affected; pretended the ill humours and distempers in the Kingdom to be grown to that height as required Cauteriers,[10] deep incisions; and indeed nothing able to work so great a cure, but an universal Rebellion. This was certainly the disease, as appears by all the symptoms, and the joynt concurrence in opinion of all the great Physitians that held themselves wise enough to propose remedies, and prescribe fit applications to so desperate a Malady. In those Instructions privately sent over into *England* by the Lord *Dillon* of *Costeloz*, presently after the breaking out of the Rebellion, the alteration of the Supream power in the government and setling of it in the hands of the Earl of *Ormond*, giving leave to the Grand Council of the Kingdom to remove such Officers of State, as they thought fit, and to recommend Natives to their places, were there positively laid down to be a more likely means to appease these tumults than a considerable Army. In the Remonstrance of the County of *Longford*, presented about the same time to the Lords Justices, by the same Lord *Dillon*, as

9. More commonly 'creaghts': nomadic herds of cattle that were driven along, in time of war, with their soldier owners.
10. burning with a hot iron.

also in the frame of the Common-wealth, found at Sir *John Dungars* House, not far from *Dublin*, and sent up thither out of *Conaught* to be Communicated to those to *Leinster*; pieces which publickly appeared soon after the breaking out of the Rebellion; the main points insisted upon in them and several others, were restauration of the Publick profession of the *Romish* Religion; restitution of all the Plantation Lands unto the Natives, and settlement of the present Government in their hands. All the Remonstrances from several parts, *and that came out of the several Provinces of the Kingdom* do concurre in these Propositions, with very little or no difference. . . .

II SPENSER THE POET

Although Edmund Spenser thought of himself as an Englishman in Ireland, as the preceding selections from his *A View of the Present State of Ireland* have shown, he chose to set important episodes of his major poetic work, *The Faerie Queene*, in Ireland. In doing so, he became the first English poet to make use of the Irish landscape and of Irish mythology. Many later Anglo-Irish writers have found themselves, consciously or unconsciously, imitating Spenser in this and other ways.

As a Renaissance gentleman, brought up in London and Cambridge and familiar with life at court, Spenser was obviously unsettled by the wildness of the Irish countryside. But the mountains behind his estate at Kilcolman, Co. Cork, — the Ballyhoura and Galtie ranges, which he called 'Old Father Mole' —provided him with a wild and lofty setting for a council of the Gods, an Irish Olympus. He was also fascinated by the many rivers that flowed through the country near his home, and by the myths associated with them. He could see obvious parallels between the countryside where he was living as he wrote *The Faerie Queene* and that of the classical world.

Kilcolman Castle itself was the setting for the famous passage in 'Colin Clouts Come Home Againe' in which Spenser entertains Sir Walter Ralegh in a pastoral poetic jousting, and the city of Cork itself was the probable scene of Spenser's own marriage to Elizabeth Boyle, celebrated in the 'Epithalamion', one of the most beautiful poems in the English language.

It is fitting to commemorate here the extended sojourn in Elizabethan Ireland of one of the finest of English poets.

from:
COLIN CLOUTS COME HOME AGAINE (1591)

[At the beginning of this autobiographical pastoral, the shepherd Colin (representing Spenser himself) has just agreed to tell the other shepherds about his recent visit to England. They gather round him to hear the tale. Colin recounts how, before he left for England, he was visited at his home at Kilcolman, Co. Cork by the 'shepheard of the Ocean' (Sir Walter Ralegh, the famous Elizabethan adventurer), and he tells the shepherds the mythological story, which he says he had then told Ralegh, concerning the rivers of the area. Spenser's own archaic spelling and punctuation have been retained.]

. . . One day (quoth[1] he) I sat, (as was my trade)
Vnder the foote of *Mole*[2] that mountaine hore,[3]
Keeping my sheepe amongst the cooly shade,
Of the greene alders by the *Mullaes*[4] shore:
There a straunge shepheard chaunst to find me out,
Whether allured with my pipes delight,
Whose pleasing sound yshrilled far about,
Or thither led by chaunce, I know not right:
Whom when I asked from what place he came,
And how he hight,[5] himselfe he did ycleepe,[6]

1. said.
2. Spenser uses this term (sometimes 'Old Father Mole') to refer to two mountain ranges north of his estate at Kilcolman, Co. Cork: the Ballyhoura mountains and the Galties, the highest peak of which is Galtymore.
3. = hoar = hoary: grey or white with age.
4. i.e. by the banks of the river Mulla. In the personification Spenser is using in this passage, 'Old Father Mole' (the mountain range) has a beautiful daughter named Mulla (i.e. the Awbeg river, which rises in the Ballyhoura mountains).
5. was named.
6. call.

The shepheard of the Ocean[7] by name,
And said he came far from the main-sea deepe.
He sitting me beside in that same shade,
Prouoked me to plaie some pleasant fit,[8]
And when he heard the musicke which I made,
He found himselfe full greatly pleasd at it:
Yet æmuling[9] my pipe, he tooke in hond[10]
My pipe before that æmuled of many,
And plaid thereon; (for well that skill he cond)[11]
Himselfe as skilfull in that art as any.
He pip'd, I sung; and when he sung, I piped,
By chaunge of turnes, each making other mery,
Neither enuying[12] other, nor enuied,
So piped we, vntill we both were weary.

There interrupting him, a bonie swaine,
That *Cuddy* hight,[13] him thus atweene bespake:[14]
And should it not thy readie course restraine,[15]
I would request thee *Colin*, for my sake,
To tell what thou didst sing, when he did plaie.
For well I weene[16] it worth recounting was,
Whether it were some hymne, or morall laie,[17]
Or carol made to praise thy loued lasse.

Nor of my loue, nor of my losse (quoth he).
I then did sing, as then occasion fell:
For loue had me forlorne, forlorne of me,[18]
That made me in that desart[19] chose to dwell.
But of my riuer *Bregogs*[20] loue I soong,
Which to the shiny *Mulla* he did beare,
And yet doth beare, and euer will, so long
As water doth within his bancks appeare.

Of fellow ship (said then that bony[21] Boy)
Record to vs that louely lay againe:
The staie whereof, shall nought these eares annoy,
Who all that *Colin* makes, do couet faine.[22]

Heare then (quoth he) the tenor of my tale,
In sort as I it[23] to that shepheard told:
No leasing new, nor Grandams fable stale,[24]
But auncient truth confirm'd with credence[25] old.

Old father *Mole*, (*Mole* hight that mountain gray
That walls the Northside of *Armulla* dale)[26]
He had a daughter fresh as floure of May,
Which gaue that name vnto that pleasant vale;
Mulla[27] the daughter of old *Mole*, so hight
The Nimph, which of that water course has charge,
That springing out of *Mole*, doth run downe right
To *Butteuant*,[28] where spreading forth at large,
It giueth name vnto that auncient Cittie,
Which *Kilnemullah*[29] cleped is of old:
Whose ragged ruines[30] breed great ruth[31] and pittie,
To trauailers, which it from far behold.
Full faine[32] she lou'd, and was belou'd full faine,
Of her owne brother riuer, *Bregog* hight,
So hight because of this deceitfull traine,[33]
Which he with *Mulla* wrought to win delight.
But her old sire[34] more carefull of her good,
And meaning her much better to preferre,[35]
Did thinke to match her with the neighbour flood,
Which *Allo* hight,[36] Broad water called farre:
And wrought so well with his continuall paine,
That he that riuer for his daughter wonne:
The dowre[37] agreed, the day assigned plaine,
The place appointed where it[38] should be doone.

7. Sir Walter Ralegh (*c.*1552-1618), soldier, diplomat, courtier, historian and poet.
8. part of a song.
9. imitating.
10. hand.
11. knew.
12. envying.
13. a lively young shepherd named Cuddy (unidentified).
14. spoke between (Colin's speeches).
15. hold back the flow of your story.
16. For I am sure.
17. = lay: song.
18. i.e. for love had forsaken me, destroyed by me.
19. = desert: i.e. Ireland.
20. The Bregoge river flows around what used to be Spenser's land and joins the Awbeg river (Mulla); the Bregoge used to appear to dry up in summertime near the confluence but, in fact, the remaining water flowed underground and rose again to join the larger river. Spenser plays on this natural phenomenon to invent a fanciful love-story about the two rivers. The Allo (now the river Blackwater, into which all these rivers eventually flow) is cast as the husband intended by Old Father Mole for his daughter Mulla. Her lover, Bregoge, outwits Father Mole by intertwining with Mulla before either river gets to the Blackwater. This tale, typical of topographical myths found widely in Europe, exists in several forms in Irish folk sources.
21. = bonny.
22. i.e. we shall not resent the time it takes to tell the story since we enjoy listening to every tale Colin tells.
23. i.e. in the way I told it.
24. i.e. no new falsehood or stale traditional fable.
25. trustworthiness.
26. Now known as the Vale of the Blackwater.
27. See above note 20.
28. Buttevant is a town in County Cork.
29. 'Kilnemullah' seems to be a name invented by Spenser. cleped = called.
30. The ruins of a Franciscan friary in Buttevant.
31. sorrow.
32. willingly.
33. treachery, deceit. Spenser is playing on the similarity between the name of the river Bregoge and the Irish word *bréagach* (lying or deceitful).
34. i.e. 'Old Father Mole', the mountain range.
35. i.e. to improve her status or rank (by marriage, in this case).
36. is named. The Allo river was also known as the Broadwater river; its modern name is the Blackwater. See above note 20.
37. dowry.
38. i.e. the marriage between the two rivers.

Nath lesse[39] the Nymph her former liking held;
For loue will not be drawne, but must be ledde,
And *Bregog* did so well her fancie weld,[40]
That her good will he got her first to wedde.
But for her father sitting still on hie,
Did warily[41] still watch which way she went,
And eke from far obseru'd with iealous eie,
Which way his course the wanton *Bregog* bent,
Him to deceiue for all his watchfull ward,
The wily louer did deuise this slight:[42]
First into many parts his streame he shar'd,
That whilest the one was watcht, the other might
Passe vnespide[43] to meete her by the way;
And then besides, those little streames so broken
He vnder ground so closely did conuay,
That of their passage doth appeare no token,
Till they into the *Mullaes* water slide.
So secretly did he his loue enioy:
Yet not so secret, but it was descride,
And told her father by a shepheards boy.
Who wondrous wroth[44] for that so foule despight,[45]
In great auenge[46] did roll downe from his hill
Huge mightie stones, the which encomber might
His passage, and his water-courses spill.[47]
So of a Riuer, which he was of old,
He none was made,[48] but scattred all to nought,
And lost emong those rocks into him rold,[49]
Did lose his name: so deare his loue he bought....[50]

39. nevertheless.
40. fasten tightly (to himself).
41. carefully.
42. trickery.
43. unseen. See above note 20.
44. angry.
45. outrage, insult.
46. vengeance.
47. Boulders and rocks still obstruct the river bed.
48. i.e. he was no longer a river.
49. rolled.
50. i.e. this was the high price he paid for his love.

from:
EPITHALAMION (1594)

[Spenser wrote this wedding song to celebrate his own marriage to Elizabeth Boyle, which took place on 11 June 1594, certainly in Ireland and probably in Cork city. In its form, the poem is based on the Italian *canzone* and, in its subject matter, Spenser combines traditional classical motifs for a wedding song with details from the Irish world in which the marriage took place. The poem has twenty-four stanzas, apparently representing the twenty-four hours of the wedding day; each stanza, except the final one, ends with an echoing refrain. The poem has been universally praised by critics as the highest poetic achievement of the most melodious of English poets.

We print below the central section of the poem, representing probably the middle of the day, and including the marriage ceremony itself. Spenser's own spelling and punctuation have been retained.]

... Now is my loue all ready forth to come,[1]
Let all the virgins[2] therefore well awayt,
And ye fresh boyes[3] that tend vpon her groome
Prepare your selues; for he is comming strayt.[4]
Set all your things in seemely good aray[5]
Fit for so ioyfull day,
The ioyfulst day that euer sunne did see.
Faire Sun, shew forth thy fauourable ray,
And let thy lifull[6] heat not feruent be
For feare of burning her sunshyny[7] face,
Her beauty to disgrace.
O fayrest Phœbus,[8] father of the Muse,
If euer I did honour thee aright,
Or sing the thing, that mote[9] thy mind delight,
Doe not thy seruants simple boone[10] refuse,
But let this day let this one day be myne,
Let all the rest be thine.
Then I thy souerayne prayses loud wil sing,
That all the woods shal answer and theyr eccho ring.

Harke how the Minstrels gin to shrill aloud[11]
Their merry Musick that resounds from far,
The pipe, the tabor, and the trembling Croud,[12]
That well agree withouten breach or iar.[13]
But most of all the Damzels doe delite,
When they their tymbrels[14] smyte,
And thereunto doe daunce and carrol[15] sweet,
That all the sences they doe rauish quite,
The whyles the boyes run vp and downe the street,

1. This is the seventh stanza of the poem. The bride and groom are now awake and the preparations for the marriage ceremony begin.
2. i.e. the girls attending the bride.
3. i.e. the young boys attending the groom.
4. immediately.
5. order.
6. lifegiving.
7. bright and happy. A weather-beaten or sun-browned complexion was considered 'unladylike' until comparatively recently.
8. The sun-god.
9. might.
10. request.
11. i.e. begin to make loud sounds with....
12. Three traditional Irish musical instruments, the pipe (whistle or flute), the drum (or perhaps the *bodhrán*) and the crowd or Celtic fiddle.
13. disharmony.
14. tambourines.
15. sing.

Crying aloud with strong confused noyce,
As if it were one voyce.
Hymen io Hymen,[16] Hymen they do shout,
That euen to the heauens theyr shouting shrill
Doth reach, and all the firmament doth fill,
To which the people standing all about,
As in approuance[17] doe thereto applaud
And loud aduaunce her laud,[18]
And euermore they Hymen Hymen sing,
That all the woods them answer and theyr eccho ring.

Loe where she comes along with portly pace[19]
Lyke Phœbe[20] from her chamber of the East,
Arysing forth to run her mighty race,
Clad all in white, that seemes[21] a virgin best.
So well it her beseemes[22] that ye would weene[23]
Some angell she had beene.
Her long loose yellow locks lyke golden wyre,[24]
Sprinckled with perle, and perling[25] flowres a tweene,
Doe lyke a golden mantle her attyre,
And being crowned with a girland[26] greene,
Seeme lyke some mayden Queene.
Her modest eyes abashed to behold
So many gazers, as on her do stare,
Vpon the lowly ground affixed are.
Ne[27] dare lift vp her countenance too bold,
But blush to heare her prayses sung so loud,
So farre from being proud.
Nathlesse[28] doe ye still loud her prayses sing.
That all the woods may answer and your eccho ring.

Tell me ye merchants daughters[29] did ye see
So fayre a creature in your towne before,
So sweet, so louely, and so mild as she,
Adornd with beautyes grace and vertues store,
Her goodly eyes lyke Saphyres shining bright,
Her forehead yuory white,
Her cheekes lyke apples which the sun hath rudded,[30]
Her lips lyke cherryes charming[31] men to byte,
Her brest like to a bowle of creame vncrudded,[32]
Her paps[33] lyke lyllies budded,[34]
Her snowie necke lyke to a marble towre,
And all her body like a pallace fayre,
Ascending vppe with many a stately stayre,
To honors seat and chastities sweet bowre.[35]
Why stand ye still ye virgins in amaze,
Vpon her so to gaze,
Whiles ye forget your former lay to sing,
To which the woods did answer and your eccho ring.

Bvt if ye saw that which no eyes can see,
The inward beauty of her liuely spright,[36]
Garnisht with heauenly guifts of high degree,
Much more then would ye wonder at that sight,
And stand astonisht lyke to those which red[37]
Medusaes mazeful hed.[38]
There dwels sweet loue and constant chastity,
Vnspotted fayth and comely womanhood,
Regard of honour and mild modesty,
There vertue raynes as Queene in royal throne,
And giueth lawes alone.
The which the base affections[39] doe obay,
And yeeld theyr seruices vnto her will,
Ne thought of thing vncomely euer may
Thereto approch to tempt her mind to ill.
Had ye once seene these her celestial threasures,[40]
And vnreuealed pleasures,
Then would ye wonder and her prayses sing,
That al the woods should answer and your echo ring.

Open the temple gates[41] vnto my loue,
Open them wide that she may enter in,
And all the postes adorne as doth behoue,[42]

16. Hymen was the classical god of marriage. The boys are shouting in celebration of the wedding.
17. approval.
18. praise.
19. i.e. in a stately fashion.
20. the moon.
21. suits.
22. suits.
23. think.
24. wire. The simile suggests that her hair is as exquisite as spun gold and that pearls are being used to decorate it.
25. winding.
26. garland.
27. Nor.
28. Nevertheless.
29. i.e. daughters of the shopkeepers of Cork.
30. made red or ruddy.
31. tempting.
32. uncurdled.
33. nipples.
34. lily buds.
35. i.e. the head, where the higher faculties of reason dwell. The preceding catalogue of the lady's beauties is a convention of Elizabethan love poetry.
36. soul.
37. saw.
38. Medusa, one of the Gorgons in classical mythology, had snakes instead of hairs on her head. Her head looked 'mazeful' — bewildering or maddening — to the beholder, who would, in any case, be turned to stone at the sight of her, according to the legend.
39. lower instincts, particularly lust.
40. treasures.
41. i.e. doors of the church.
42. i.e. as is proper. The doorposts were often decorated for weddings.

And all the pillours deck with girlands trim,[43]
For to recyue this Saynt with honour dew,
That commeth in to you.
With trembling steps and humble reuerence,
She commeth in, before th'almighties vew,
Of her ye virgins learne obedience,
When so ye come into those holy places,
To humble your proud faces:
Bring her vp to th'high altar, that she may
The sacred ceremonies there partake,
The which do endlesse matrimony make,
And let the roring Organs loudly play
The praises of the Lord in liuely notes,
The whiles with hollow throates
The Choristers the ioyous Antheme sing,
That al the woods may answere and their eccho ring.

Behold whiles she before the altar stands
Hearing the holy priest that to her speakes
And blesseth her with his two happy hands,
How the red roses flush vp in her cheekes,
And the pure snow with goodly vermill[44] stayne,
Like crimsin dyde in grayne,[45]
That euen th'Angels which continually,
About the sacred Altare doe remaine,
Forget their seruice[46] and about her fly,
Ofte peeping in her face that seemes more fayre,
The more they on it stare.
But her sad[47] eyes still fastened on the ground,
Are gouerned with goodly modesty,
That suffers not one looke to glaunce awry,
Which may let in a little thought vnsownd.
Why blush ye loue to giue to me your hand,
The pledge of all our band?[48]
Sing ye sweet Angels, Alleluya sing,
That all the woods may answere and your eccho ring.

Now al is done; bring home the bride againe,
Bring home the triumph of our victory,
Bring home with you the glory of her gaine,[49]
With ioyance[50] bring her and with iollity.
Neuer had man more ioyfull day then this,
Whom heauen would heape with blis.
Make feast therefore now all this liue long day,[51]

43. suitable garlands or decorations.
44. bright red.
45. dyed scarlet.
46. duty; i.e. to guard the high altar.
47. modest.
48. bond.
49. i.e. the glory of gaining her hand in marriage.
50. joy.
51. i.e. the whole day long.

This day for euer to me holy is,
Poure out the wine without restraint or stay,
Poure not by cups, but by the belly full,
Poure out to all that wull,[52]
And sprinkle all the postes and wals with wine,
That they may sweat, and drunken be withall.
Crowne ye God Bacchus[53] with a coronall,[54]
And Hymen also crowne with wreathes of vine,
And let the Graces[55] daunce vnto the rest;
For they can doo it best:
The whiles the maydens doe theyr carroll[56] sing,
To which the woods shal answer and theyr eccho ring.

Ring ye the bels, ye yong men of the towne,[57]
And leaue your wonted[58] labours for this day:
This day is holy; doe ye write it downe,
That ye for euer it remember may.
This day the sunne is in his chiefest hight,
With Barnaby the bright,[59]
From whence declining daily by degrees,
He somewhat loseth of his heat and light,
When once the Crab behind his back he sees.[60]
But for this time it ill ordained was,
To chose[61] the longest day in all the yeare,
And shortest night, when longest fitter weare:[62]
Yet neuer day so long, but late[63] would passe.
Ring ye the bels, to make it weare away,
And bonefiers[64] make all day,
And daunce about them, and about them sing:
That all the woods may answer, and your eccho ring....

52. want it.
53. The god of wine.
54. garland of flowers.
55. The sister goddesses of classical mythology.
56. song.
57. i.e. Cork.
58. accustomed.
59. St Barnabas's day was, in Spenser's time, at the summer solstice, the longest day of the year.
60. i.e. the constellation Cancer (the crab). As the sun passes through the zodiac (and the days get shorter), it leaves Cancer behind and progresses to Leo.
61. have chosen.
62. i.e. it would have been more appropriate to hold the wedding at a time of year when the nights were longer.
63. at last.
64. Bonfires were traditional at midsummer and also at weddings.

from: THE FAERIE QUEENE VII (1609)

[Although it is one of the longest poems in English, *The Faerie Queene* as we have it today is only just over half of the poem originally projected by Spenser. The six completed books are an enormous pageant of heroic and fairy tales woven around the adventures of simple allegorical figures who represent Christian virtues. A belief in ultimately stable moral, political and religious values seems to underpin each of the six books. But in the short 'Mutability Cantos', generally printed as fragments of an otherwise lost seventh book, the reader is presented with a different challenge from that of the rest of the poem. The theme of the Mutability Cantos is change, and they explore the very Renaissance paradox that man needs to accept both the idea of permanent perfection and the reality of often casual change and decay.

The main event of the Mutability Cantos is a grand trial at which the claims of the present world order — as presented by the existing gods — are challenged by a new, upstart goddess named Mutability, who wishes to supplant Jove as chief of the heavenly hierarchy. In the passage below, Spenser sets the scene for this contest in the mountains above his estate in County Cork. To give a sense of timelessness to this setting, he transfers a famous classical story to the Irish countryside.

The extract is from Book VII, Canto VI, Stanzas 36-55. Spenser's own archaic spelling and punctuation have been retained.]

. . . Eftsoones[1] the time and place appointed were,
Where all, both heauenly Powers, and earthly wights,[2]
Before great Natures[3] presence should appeare,
For triall of their Titles and best Rights:
That was, to weet,[4] vpon the highest hights
Of *Arlo-hill*[5] (Who knowes not *Arlo-hill*?)
That is the highest head (in all mens sights)
Of my old father *Mole*,[6] whom Shepheards quill
Renowmed hath with hymnes fit for a rurall skill.

And, were it not ill fitting for this file,[7]
To sing of hilles and woods, mongst warres and Knights,[8]
I would abate the sternenesse of my stile,
Mongst these sterne stounds[9] to mingle soft delights;
And tell how *Arlo* through *Dianaes*[10] spights[11]
(Beeing of old the best and fairest Hill
That was in all this holy-Islands hights)
Was made the most vnpleasant, and most ill.
Meane while, O *Clio*, lend *Calliope*[12] thy quill.

Whylome,[13] when *IRELAND* florished in fame
Of wealths and goodnesse, far aboue the rest
Of all that beare the *British* Islands name,
The Gods then vs'd (for pleasure and for rest)
Oft to resort there-to, when seem'd them best:
But none of all there-in more pleasure found,
Then *Cynthia*;[14] that is soueraine Queene profest[15]
Of woods and forrests, which therein abound,
Sprinkled with wholsom waters, more then most on ground.[16]

But mongst them all, as fittest for her game,[17]
Either for chace of beasts with hound or boawe,[18]
Or for to shroude in shade from *Phœbus*[19] flame,
Or bathe in fountaines that doe freshly flowe,
Or from high hilles, or from the dales belowe,
She chose this *Arlo*; where shee did resort
With all her Nymphes[20] enranged on a rowe,
With whom the woody Gods[21] did oft consort:
For, with the Nymphes, the Satyres loue to play and sport.

Amongst the which, there was a Nymph that hight[22]
Molanna;[23] daughter of old father *Mole*,
And sister vnto *Mulla*,[24] faire and bright:

1. Soon afterwards.
2. beings.
3. The goddess who is to decide whether Mutability should reign in heaven or not.
4. i.e. in fact.
5. Galtymore, the highest peak in the mountain ranges near Spenser's estate at Kilcolman, Co. Cork. See note 2 to 'Colin Clouts Come Home Againe' above.
6. Spenser gave the name 'Old Father Mole' to the Ballyhoura and Galtie mountains and, as the Shepherd Colin, praised them in 'Colin Clouts Come Home Againe'.
7. narrative.
8. The main subjects of *The Faerie Queene* have been chivalry and feats of valour.
9. clashes.
10. The classical goddess of hunting and of forests, Diana is also known in this passage as Cynthia.
11. spite.
12. The muses of history and epic poetry, respectively.
13. Formerly.
14. i.e. Diana.
15. acknowledged.
16. earth.
17. recreation.
18. bow.
19. the sun.
20. Classical goddesses of streams and trees.
21. The 'woody Gods' or satyrs (in classical mythology) were goat-footed, half-human gods of the woods, addicted to wine and to all sensual pleasures.
22. named.
23. The Behenna river, a shallow rocky river that rises in the mountains above Kilcolman Castle.
24. The river Awbeg: see note 20 to 'Colin Clouts Come Home Againe' above.

Vnto whose bed false *Bregog*[25] whylome stole,
That Shepheard *Colin* dearely did condole,[26]
And made her lucklesse loues well knowne to be.
But this *Molanna*, were she not so shole,[27]
Were no lesse faire and beautifull then shee:
Yet as she is, a fairer flood[28] may no man see.

For, first, she springs out of two marble Rocks,
On which, a groue of Oakes high mounted growes,
That as a girlond[29] seemes to deck the locks
Of som faire Bride, brought forth with pompous showes[30]
Out of her bowre,[31] that many flowers strowes:[32]
So, through the flowry Dales she tumbling downe,
Through many woods, and shady coverts[33] flowes
(That on each side her siluer channell crowne)
Till to the Plaine she come, whose Valleyes shee doth drowne.

In her sweet streames, *Diana* vsed oft
(After her sweatie chace and toilesome play)
To bathe her selfe; and after, on the soft
And downy grasse, her dainty limbes to lay
In couert[34] shade, where none behold her may:
For, much she hated sight of liuing eye.
Foolish God *Faunus*,[35] though full many a day
He saw her clad, yet longed foolishly
To see her naked mongst her Nymphes in priuity.[36]

No way he found to compasse[37] his desire,
But to corrupt *Molanna*, this her maid,
Her to discouer[38] for some secret hire:[39]
So, her with flattering words he first assaid;[40]
And after, pleasing gifts for her purvaid,[41]
Queene-apples,[42] and red Cherries from the tree,
With which he her allured and betraid,
To tell what time he might her Lady see
When she her selfe did bathe, that he might secret[43] bee.

There-to hee promist, if shee would him pleasure
With this small boone, to quit[44] her with a better;
To weet,[45] that where-as shee had out of measure
Long lov'd the *Fanchin*, who by nought did set her,[46]
That he would vndertake, for this to get her
To be his Loue, and of[47] him liked well:
Besides all which, he vow'd to be her debter
For many moe good turnes then he would tell;
The least of which, this little pleasure should excell.

The simple maid did yield to him anone;[48]
And eft[49] him placed where he close[50] might view
That[51] neuer any saw, saue onely one;
Who, for his hire to so foole-hardy dew,
Was of his hounds devour'd in Hunters hew.[52]
Tho, as her manner was on sunny day,
Diana, with her Nymphes about her, drew
To this sweet spring; where, doffing[53] her array,
She bath'd her louely limbes, for *Ioue*[54] a likely pray.

There *Faunus* saw that pleased much his eye,
And made his hart to tickle in his brest,
That for great ioy of some-what[55] he did spy,
He could him not containe in silent rest;
But breaking forth in laughter, loud profest
His foolish thought. A foolish *Faune* indeed,
That couldst not hold thy self so[56] hidden blest,
But wouldest needs thine owne conceit areed.[57]
Babblers vnworthy been of so diuine a meed.[58]

25. See note 20 to 'Colin Clouts Come Home Againe'.
26. earnestly lamented.
27. shallow.
28. river.
29. garland.
30. ceremonially.
31. bower.
32. decorates.
33. small woods.
34. hidden.
35. An invented deity who plays the part of Actaeon in this reworking of the classical story of Actaeon and Diana.
36. privacy.
37. accomplish.
38. reveal.
39. bribe.
40. tried.
41. purveyed, i.e. brought.
42. quinces or crab-apples.
43. hidden.
44. repay.
45. That is.
46. i.e. since, for a long time, she had been excessively in love with the riven Funsheon, who cared nothing for her. . . .
47. by.
48. in due course.
49. immediately.
50. secretly.
51. that which.
52. The one person who had previously seen Diana naked (i.e. Actaeon) had been (deservedly) devoured by his hunting dogs after being turned into a stag.
53. taking off.
54. Jove, Jupiter or Zeus, chief of the gods, was inclined, according to mythology, to pursue beautiful maidens, earthly as well as divine. For instance, he descended upon Danae as a shower of golden rain; she bore him Perseus as a result.
55. something.
56. thus.
57. i.e. declare what you thought.
58. reward.

The Goddesse, all abashed[59] with that noise,
In haste forth started from the guilty brooke;
And running straight where-as she heard his voice,
Enclos'd the bush about,[60] and there him tooke,
Like darred[61] Larke; not daring vp to looke
On her whose sight before so much he sought.
Thence, forth they drew him by the hornes, and shooke
Nigh all to peeces, that they left him nought;
And then into the open light they forth him brought.

Like as an huswife,[62] that with busie care
Thinks of her Dairie to make wondrous gaine,
Finding where-as some wicked beast vnware[63]
That breakes into her Dayr'house, there doth draine
Her creaming pannes, and frustrate all her paine;[64]
Hath in some snare or gin[65] set close behind,
Entrapped him, and caught into her traine,[66]
Then thinkes what punishment were best assign'd,
And thousand deathes deuiseth in her vengefull mind:

So did *Diana* and her maydens all
Vse silly *Faunus*, now within their baile:[67]
They mocke and scorne him, and him foule miscall;[68]
Some by the nose him pluckt, some by the taile,
And by his goatish beard some did him haile:[69]
Yet he (poore soule) with patience all did beare;
For, nought against their wils might countervaile:[70]
Ne ought he said what euer he did heare;
But hanging downe his head, did like a Mome[71] appeare.

At length, when they had flouted him their fill,
They gan to cast[72] what penaunce him to giue.
Some would haue gelt him, but that same would spill
The Wood-gods breed, which must for euer liue:[73]
Others would through the riuer him haue driue,
And ducked deepe: but that seem'd penaunce light;
But most agreed and did this sentence giue,
Him in Deares skin to clad; and in that plight,
To hunt him with their hounds, him selfe saue how hee might.

But *Cynthia's* selfe, more angry then the rest,
Thought not enough, to punish him in sport,
And of her shame to make a gamesome iest;
But gan examine him in straighter[74] sort,
Which of her Nymphes, or other close consort,[75]
Him thither brought, and her to him betraid?
He, much affeard, to her confessed short,
That 'twas *Molanna* which her so bewraid.[76]
Then all attonce[77] their hands vpon *Molanna* laid.

But him (according as they had decreed)
With a Deeres-skin they couered, and then chast
With all their hounds that after him did speed;
But he more speedy, from them fled more fast
Then any Deere: so sore him dread aghast.[78]
They after follow'd all with shrill out-cry,
Shouting as they the heauens would haue brast:[79]
That all the woods and dales where he did flie,
Did ring againe, and loud reeccho to the skie.

So they him follow'd till they weary were;
When, back returning to *Molann'* againe,
They, by commaund'ment of *Diana*, there
Her whelm'd with stones.[80] Yet *Faunus* (for her paine)[81]
Of her beloued *Fanchin* did obtaine,
That her he would receiue vnto his bed.
So now her waues passe through a pleasant Plaine,
Till with the *Fanchin* she her selfe doe wed,

59. disconcerted.
60. i.e. with her hunting net.
61. cowering.
62. housewife.
63. unseen.
64. effort (to make butter etc.).
65. trap.
66. snare.
67. custody.
68. i.e. revile him.
69. pull. Satyrs were depicted with beards like goats; these suggested their lustful nature.
70. reciprocate.
71. fool.
72. deliberate.
73. i.e. some would have castrated him, except that this would destroy the race of wood gods, who must live for ever.
74. stricter.
75. companion.
76. betrayed.
77. at once.
78. i.e. so terribly did they frighten him.
79. burst.
80. i.e. filled with stones. The river is still shallow and rocky.
81. trouble.

And (both combin'd) themselues in one faire riuer
    spred.[82]

Nath'lesse,[83] *Diana*, full of indignation,
  Thence-forth abandond her delicious brooke;
  In whose sweet streame, before that bad occasion,
  So much delight to bathe her limbes she tooke:
  Ne onely her, but also quite forsooke
  All those faire forrests about *Arlo* hid,
  And all that Mountaine, which doth over-looke
  The richest champian that may else be rid,[84]
And the faire *Shure*,[85] in which are thousand
    Salmons bred.

Them all, and all that she so deare did way,[86]
  Thence-forth she left; and parting from the place,
  There-on an heauy haplesse curse did lay,
  To weet,[87] that Wolues, where she was wont to
    space,[88]
  Should harbour'd be, and all those Woods deface,
  And Thieues should rob and spoile that Coast[89]
    around.
  Since which, those Woods, and all that goodly
    Chase,[90]
  Doth to this day with Wolues and Thieues
    abound:
Which too-too true that lands in-dwellers[91] since
    haue found.

82. The rivers mentioned all flow into the river Blackwater, a fine, slow-moving river.
83. Nevertheless.
84. the richest countryside that may be seen.
85. The river Suir.
86. esteem.
87. That is.
88. roam.
89. land.
90. hunting-ground.
91. inhabitants. Wolves were still found in that part of Ireland in Spenser's time.

NOTES ON THE TEXTS

Edmund Spenser, *A View of the Present State of Ireland*. The text used is a conflation of that edited by W. L. Renwick (second ed. Oxford: Clarendon Press, 1970) and that edited by Rudolf Gottfried (variorum edition of Spenser's *Works* (Baltimore: Johns Hopkins University Press, 1949), vol. X). Neither text is entirely satisfactory and the present text is an attempt to improve on both. It is a 'modern spelling' text. The texts of Spenser's poems in each case have been edited from the first editions.

Richard Beacon, *Solon His Follie* .... (Oxford, 1594).

Fynes Moryson, 'Of the Commonwealth of Ireland' in *Shakespeare's Europe* edited by Charles Hughes (London: Sherratt and Hughes, 1903).

Sir John Davies, *A Discovery of the True Causes why Ireland was Never Entirely Subdued* .... (London, 1612).

Sir John Temple, *The Irish Rebellion* .... (London, 1646).

Biographies/Bibliographies

Edmund Spenser

LIFE. Born in London about 1552 into modest circumstances, Spenser attended Merchant Taylors' School and proceeded from there to Pembroke Hall, Cambridge in 1569. At Cambridge, he distinguished himself as a classical scholar and also became conversant with French and Italian literature. Already an established literary figure, Spenser took an M.A. from Cambridge in 1576, and in 1579 was adopted into the household of the Earl of Leicester where he became associated with Sir Philip Sidney, Leicester's nephew. This connection certainly enhanced his literary reputation, but it also provided him with an introduction to Arthur Lord Gray de Wilton, who took up office as lord deputy of Ireland in July 1580. Spenser accompanied Lord Gray as his secretary; he remained close by him during the wars in Munster and the rising in Leinster with which Gray had to contend; and it was through Gray's influence that Spenser was appointed to official positions in Dublin and on the Munster provincial council. This latter placed him in a strategic position to advance claim to an estate in the Munster plantation of the 1580s and he spent most of his time in Ireland until 1598 seeking to establish himself as a planter in the seignory of Kilcolman, Co. Cork.

The difficulties he encountered with a hostile native population in Ireland, combined with the difficulties he had in retaining the attention of English literary patrons when residing at a distance, seem to have soured his outlook on life and this is reflected in *The Faerie Queene* and *A View of the Present State of Ireland*, which were both composed during this period. Spenser, his family and estate fell foul of a renewed rising in Munster in 1598 and one of his children was killed during it. Spenser himself returned a broken man to England, where he died in 1599. He is buried in Westminster Abbey.

CHIEF WRITINGS. Rudolf Gottfried (ed.), *The Works of Edmund Spenser: A Variorum Edition*, 10 vols (Baltimore: Johns Hopkins University Press, 1932-57).

BIOGRAPHY AND CRITICISM. *D.N.B.*; Paul Alpers, *The Poetry of 'The Faerie Queene'* (Princeton, N.J: Princeton University Press, 1967); Stephen Greenblatt, *Renaissance Self-Fashioning* (Chicago and London: University of Chicago Press, 1980); Nicholas Canny, 'Edmund Spenser and the Development of an Anglo-Irish Identity', *Yearbook of English Studies*, XIII (1983), pp. 1-19; Ciaran Brady, 'Spenser's Irish Crisis: Humanism and Experience in the 1590s', *Past & Present*, no. 111 (May 1986), 17-49.

Richard Beacon

LIFE. Richard Beacon, or Becon, was a native of Suffolk and matriculated at St John's College, Cambridge in 1567. He graduated with a B.A. (1572) and an M.A. (1575) and was incorporated at Oxford University in 1594. The law became his chosen profession and he was admitted as a student of Gray's Inn in 1577 and duly became a barrister in 1585. Employment in Ireland followed almost immediately, and Beacon served as attorney on the provincial council for Munster 1586-91.

This service placed him in a position to claim a portion of the Desmond lands that were then being allocated to suitable tenants, and he was involved until 1592 with each successive commission that dealt with the allocation and legal defence of the Munster plantation lands. Those estates assigned to Beacon himself were situated in the vicinity of Bantry, Co. Cork, and in west Waterford. The Waterford lands were soon lost to a legal claim advanced by the Old English lawyer, Nicholas Walshe, and settlement in Bantry was impeded by the physical as well as the legal assault of the Earl of Clancar and other members of the Mac Carthy sept. Consequently, Beacon made little progress as a planter and in 1592 he sold what remained to him to Henry Goldfinch of London. This experience may explain Beacon's bitterness towards all elements of the Irish population, as well as towards service in Ireland, and this is duly reflected in *Solon His Follie*. It is Beacon's only printed work and was published in Oxford in 1594 after he had severed his connection with Ireland. There was no subsequent printing.

CHIEF WRITINGS. *Solon His Follie, or a Political Discourse Touching the Reformation of Commonwealth Conquered, Declined, or Corrupted* (Oxford, 1594).

BIOGRAPHY AND CRITICISM. *D.N.B.*; John Venn and J. A. Venn (eds), *Alumnae Cantabrienses* (Cambridge: Cambridge University Press, 1922); Michael Mac Carthy-Morrogh, *The Munster Plantation: English Migration to Southern Ireland, 1583-1641* (Oxford: Clarendon Press, 1986).

Fynes Moryson

LIFE. Born in 1566 at Cadeby, Lincolnshire, into a comfortable family, Fynes Moryson studied at Peterhouse, Cambridge, where he took his degree in 1587. He chose to educate himself further by travel. During his first continental journey (1591-95) Moryson spent some time studying at Leyden University, and by the end of his second journey (1595-97) he had visited almost every jurisdiction in continental Europe, except Spain, Russia and Scandinavia. On his return to England in 1598, he journeyed to Scotland and throughout much of England, and finally took up employment in Ireland in November 1600.

In Ireland he soon became personal secretary to Charles Blount, lord Mountjoy, who was then lord deputy of Ireland and in charge of the military operations there. Moryson accompanied Mountjoy at the field of Kinsale in December 1601 and throughout the war of attrition in Ulster that continued until March 1603. Two months later he returned with Mountjoy to England and remained in his service until Mountjoy (by then earl of Devonshire) died in 1606. Thereafter, Moryson devoted himself to composing an account of his European travels, together with a detailed narrative of his service in Ireland. This was published in 1617 under the title *An Itinerary*. He revisited Ireland in 1613 and offered a critical appraisal of how the country had fared since his earlier service there. A brief element of this was included in *An Itinerary*, but a more detailed manuscript had not been published at his death in 1630.

CHIEF WRITINGS. *A History of Ireland, from the year 1599 to 1603*: with a short narration of the state of the kingdom from the year 1169; to which is added a description of Ireland (Dublin, 1735); *An Itinerary* (London, 1617; new edition in 4 vols, Glasgow: James Maclehose & Sons, 1907-08). Manuscript in Corpus Christi College, Oxford, partially published in C. Litton Falkiner, *Illustrations of Irish History and Topography* (London: Longman, 1904) and in Charles Hughes (ed.), *Shakespeare's Europe*. Unpublished chapters of Fynes Morison's *Itinerary* (London: Sherratt and Hughes, 1903). *Ireland under Elizabeth and James the First*, described by Edmund Spenser, by Sir John Davies and by Fynes Morison, edited by H. Morley (London: George Routledge & Sons, 1890).

BIOGRAPHY AND CRITICISM. *D.N.B.* and the introductions to the three modern collections mentioned above.

Sir John Davies

LIFE. Born in Tisbury, Wiltshire in 1569, the son of a tanner, Davies was educated at Winchester, Oxford and the Middle Temple, where he was admitted to the bar in 1595. A man of ungainly and even ugly appearance, Davies impressed by his keen intelligence as a lawyer and by his literary talents, which found expression principally in verse. His poems 'Nosce Teipsum' and 'Orchestra', published in the 1590s, earned him a considerable reputation, and his range of experience was broadened by a private visit to the Netherlands in 1592 and by an official expedition to Scotland in 1594 to attend the christening of Henry, son of King James VI. An apparently promising career was blighted by his expulsion from the Middle Temple as a punishment for a physical assault upon a colleague, but Davies gradually clawed his way back to favour through his contact with Sir Robert Cecil, later earl of Salisbury. His rehabilitation was marked by his restoration to the Middle Temple in 1601, by his return to the English parliament in that same year as the member for Corfe Castle, and by his appointments as solicitor general for Ireland 1603-06 and attorney general 1606-19.

In Ireland, Davies was one of the key administrators of the early seventeenth century. He organized the first modern circuits of assize as English common law was extended to those areas previously under Gaelic control. He promoted a series of statutes that served to underpin the Elizabethan military conquest of the country, was largely responsible for devising a plantation scheme in Ulster in 1609, and arranged a protestant majority in the Irish parliament of 1613. Davies became speaker of that parliament, and was also favoured by a knighthood in 1603 and by a substantial grant of land in the plantation of Ulster. Besides being an efficient administrator, Davies was a keen social observer and became Salisbury's most valuable informant on Irish affairs. At this stage, his ambition was to translate himself to a senior position in the English administration, but this eluded him until the day before his death in 1626 when he was nominated chief justice of the King's Bench. Before then he had served as a member in the English parliament in 1621, and these honours served as some compensation for a disastrous marriage to the hopelessly insane Eleanor Touchet, daughter of George, Baron Audley. Their only surviving child married Ferdinando Hastings, earl of Huntingdon.

CHIEF WRITINGS. Robert Krueger (ed.), *The Poems of Sir John Davies* (Oxford: Clarendon Press, 1975); *A Discovery of the True Causes why Ireland was Never Entirely Subdued....* (London, 1612); *Le Primer Report des Cases in les Courts del Ray* (Dublin, 1615).

BIOGRAPHY AND CRITICISM. *D.N.B.*; Hans S. Pawlisch, *Sir John Davies and the Conquest of Ireland: A Study in Legal Imperialism* (Cambridge: Cambridge University Press, 1985); T. L. Sanderson, 'Recent Studies in Sir John Davies', *English Literary Renaissance*, 4 (1974), 411-17.

Sir John Temple

LIFE. Born in Dublin in 1600, the son of Sir William Temple who became provost of Trinity College, Dublin, he was educated at that college before touring the Continent and entering the service of King Charles I. This led to his appointment in 1640 as master of the rolls in Ireland, a position he held until his death in 1677, except for the period 1643-55. Temple was outraged by the Irish catholic rising in 1641 and was the most articulate advocate of stern measures against all who had been involved. This explains his employment by the Cromwellian regime when it undertook a comprehensive plantation in Ireland. Temple acquired substantial estates in that confiscation. His services continued to be indispensable to the government of King Charles II, and he was advanced to the position of vice-treasurer in 1673. Among his children, by his wife Mary Hammond, were Sir John Temple, who became attorney general for Ireland, and Sir William Temple, the political writer and controversialist of late seventeenth-century England.

CHIEF WRITINGS. *The Irish Rebellion....* (London, 1646).

BIOGRAPHY AND CRITICISM. *D.N.B.*; *A New History of Ireland*, III, *1534-1691* (Oxford: Clarendon Press, 1976).

ANDREW CARPENTER and ALAN HARRISON, *Editors*

Ireland and Her Past: Topographical and Historical Writing to 1690

However impartial he claims to be, no historian writes of the past without being strongly influenced by the age in which he lives. During periods of change and conflict, objectivity is not only difficult for the historian but is sometimes deliberately rejected so that 'history' can be written specifically to further the cause of one political group or another. In Ireland, the period between the assumption of the lordship of Ireland by Henry VIII and the battle of the Boyne — a time of high tension between religious, racial and cultural factions — stands out for the polemic of its historians and for the bias of their histories. As the conflict between the native Irish and the English settler community ebbed and flowed, historians from the two sides neglected certain aspects of the Irish past or concentrated upon others in order to justify or defend the actions of those they supported in the present. As the settlers began to overcome the native Irish, it was their view of the Irish past that became the dominant one — in written history at any rate; but the native Irish, both those who were forced to emigrate to Europe and those who remained in Ireland, sought to conserve what they could of the Gaelic view of the past, to justify, among other things, their fight for survival. However, as the seventeenth century progressed, the Gaelic community in Ireland was gradually overwhelmed and in almost every decade of the century it received a further body blow from the settler community. The *coup de grâce* was the defeat of the Jacobite army at the battle of the Boyne in 1690 and the subsequent enactment of the Penal Laws against the catholic community.

The writing of topographical description, which often accompanied historical writing in the early modern period, is equally susceptible to political pressure. This is particularly so when the behaviour of the inhabitants is thought to have an effect on the landscape and countryside. Some of the descriptive writing below is nearly as biased as the historical work we have been discussing.

The people of Ireland have always been obsessed by the land in which they live and the history of their ancestors, and in the late sixteenth and seventeenth centuries all sections of the community felt a need to hear Irish history from their own point of view. The writing of history was by no means a new activity at this time. In fact, written history — one of the oldest of the arts in Ireland — had been in existence for almost one thousand years, first produced by monks in their *scriptoria* and, after the twelfth century, by members of the hereditary learned families of later medieval Ireland. The Irish word for this traditional history, *seanchas* (ancient lore) embraces not only the formal recording of history — annals, regnal lists, genealogies and laws — but also much that, in later generations, would be considered literature — sagas, origin legends, hagiography, political propaganda, stories associated with place-names, and even romantic tales concerning mythical figures. The dividing line between 'history' and 'literature' was never clear or distinct in early and medieval Irish culture, and this amalgamated lore and history of the Irish race was part of the living texture of the world and world view that differentiated the Gaelic race from their neighbours and from the invaders from England. Inevitably, however, the world based upon this vision of the past moved towards its demise from the moment of the arrival of the 'new English' settlers during the reigns of Henry VIII and Elizabeth I.

The political policy of these monarchs from outside Ireland, particularly in the sixteenth and seventeenth centuries, was to centralize and rationalize government in Ireland, and this naturally brought about conflict between the new order and the hereditary schools of learning. The *filí* — the poets and men of learning of medieval Ireland — were the strongest unifying feature of that politically fragmented world. They depended on the chieftains for patronage and the chieftains depended on them for their learning, especially their knowledge of the past and its practices, which confirmed the chieftains in their positions of power. In fact, the status of the poet often depended on his competence and dexterity in manipulating 'historical' sources. The incoming colonial officials soon realized, correctly, that such scholars would be against the anglicization of their chieftains. As it turned out, poets often encouraged nobles to resist attempts — whether bribes, threats or promises — to make them accept English ways. But as the sixteenth century drew to a close, it became clear that these methods of cultural pressure effectively had succeeded and that the patronage that had fostered the bardic schools and ensured the continuation of the power of the hereditary families had been undermined; the traditions, jealously guarded by the Irish poets for more than four hundred years, were dying. One by one, the schools closed and the scholars dispersed, some of them entering religious life and pursuing education in other ways, others apparently coming to terms with the changing times and acting as intercultural interpreters. In this latter capacity, they would have been minor officials in the country's administration, explaining the new regime and its laws to the natives and interpreting the customs and culture of the Irish to the 'new English', who were soldiers, government officials, landowners and planters.

This 'new English' community, as we have seen (pp. 171-74), justified its presence forcefully and confidently in the work of Spenser and his contemporaries. The arguments of this community, pointing to the benefits of its influence, served to justify its behaviour in its own eyes. This typically colonial point of view was supported and influenced by the topographical writings of the twelfth-century Giraldus Cambrensis (often known as Gerald of Wales), a Norman Welshman who had accompanied Henry II to Ireland and who had written two accounts of Ireland from the point of view of the conquering Normans. Since his purpose was to justify the actions of the Norman knights, Giraldus portrayed the Irish as an uncivilized and barbarous people. His remarks were picked up by all subsequent English commentators on Ireland and, by the seventeenth century, many of them had become clichés repeated by almost every English writer on Irish affairs.

Giraldus was the authority whom apologists for catholic, Gaelic Ireland sought to refute. By far the most influential of these apologists was Geoffrey Keating, whose *Foras Feasa ar Éirinn* (A Basis of Knowledge about Ireland) was completed in the early 1630s. Keating set out to refute the 'lies' written about Ireland by Giraldus and the Elizabethans, and to establish the antiquity, piety and courage of the Irish. He claimed that, since he was himself of Norman stock and because he could master all the sources — ancient classical authors and polemical contemporaries, as well as native manuscript material — he was uniquely placed to give a true and balanced picture of the history of the Irish people. From our point of view, Keating's work is important not so much as history but as the version of the past that most satisfied the Gaelic Irish and that sustained them in their view of themselves throughout the seventeenth and eighteenth centuries. The cultural importance of *Foras Feasa ar Éirinn* is that it filled the gaps in the transmission of *seanchas*, which inevitably occurred following the demise of the bardic schools, and that it informed the political attitudes of those who stood in opposition to the English domination of Ireland. This almost racial polarization in the writing of history is paralleled by the religious opposition between protestant and catholic historians. Thus the catholic writers praised Keating and condemned Cambrensis; those who followed Cambrensis and dismissed Keating were protestants.

Few of those writing history in this period were completely free from the biases mentioned above, but there were some efforts to write history according to more rigorous methods. By the seventeenth century, authors of such works had inherited the renaissance interest in original documents and they sought them out and proceeded to use them to authenticate their views of the past. Although the conclusions reached by scholars using these methods may differ, depending on their own sectarian position, the similarities in their use of source material and methodology are more significant than their differences. The catholic wing of this scholarly movement was represented by the Franciscans of Louvain, who numbered among their ranks many refugees from the Irish learned families, some of them traditional historians. The chief exponents of the 'scientific' movement among the protestants were James Ussher and James Ware, both working in Dublin. All these scholars were particularly interested in the history of the early church in Ireland, and it was the fact that so many documents concerning the early church remained in Ireland that prompted the lay brother Mícheál Ó Cléirigh to return from the Continent in 1620 and, under the general direction of Father John Colgan, he and other Franciscans collected the material necessary to compile the annals now known as *The Annals of the Four Masters*. These Franciscans also collected much material concerning the early Irish church and Irish saints which, although it does not appear in the *Annals*, was eventually published at Louvain.

James Ussher's interest in Irish history, like that of the Louvain friars, stemmed from a fascination with the early Irish church. He promoted the theory, still often used in sectarian politics, that the Irish church set up by St Patrick was fundamentally different from the church in the rest of the Roman empire. More significant than his theories about Irish Christianity, however, is the fact that Ussher brought together an immensely important collection of primary sources for the study of Irish history, including two of the great Gaelic manuscripts of medieval Ireland, the Book of Lecan and the Book of Ballymote. Although it is not clear who Ussher's informants were or who procured the books for him, he certainly employed native scholars to help in his research and to translate and copy the manuscripts he obtained. Similarly, Ussher's nephew, James Ware, collected manuscripts and employed native scholars to help decipher them, including the great genealogist An Dualtach Mac Fhirbhisigh (Duald mac Firbis or Dudley Forbes) and Tadhg Ó Rodaigh (Thady Rody). Ware's own historical work was written mainly in Latin, but most of his Irish manuscripts came into the possession of his son after his death. The son, Robert, has the reputation of being more careless and less tolerant of catholics than was his sober, scholarly father. However, he produced a translation of his father's works, which was published in 1705.

These scholars, working in Louvain and in Ireland, provided the basis upon which a new non-sectarian Irish historiography could have been built. It is unfortunate that the events of the seventeenth century, from 1641 onwards especially, ensured that little, if any, Irish history would be written upon these foundations; most historians, from this point onwards, interpreted the past in order to promote the ascendancy of one group or to defend the diminishing power-base of the other. Throughout the eighteenth and early nineteenth centuries, historical writing continued to be part of the polemical armoury of both sides.

In the section that follows, we have first printed the most famous passage from Giraldus Cambrensis's *Topographia Hiberniae* to give an idea of the comments that so annoyed Irishmen and that so comforted Englishmen. To balance this, we give selections from the work of seventeenth-century Gaelic historians, Keating, Conall Mac Geoghegan and the Four Masters. The contrasting views of Cambrensis and Keating are the bedrock upon which Irish historical writing of the age was built. Much of the edifice built on Cambrensis is to be found, however, not in this section but in that on Spenser and his contemporaries. There, Cambrensis is used extensively and his arguments repeated constantly. Here however, we concentrate upon the work of the more 'scientific' historians of the age — Ussher, Ware, Wadding and Colgan — and that of the Gaelic apologists who refuted Cambrensis, such as O'Sullivan-Beare, Lynch, Walsh and O'Flaherty.

As a body of work, Irish historical and topographical writing has been highly influential on later generations; for this reason, if for no other, its importance should be recognized.

The historical and topographical works in this section include many references to obscure persons, events and books cited to help prove the authority behind the writer's view of history or his veracity. To explain each allusion would have cluttered the text with detailed references unnecessary for an anthology such as this. The notes in this section have been deliberately reduced, therefore, and do not include identification of most historical or mythological figures or of most authors.

GIRALDUS CAMBRENSIS (GERALD OF WALES)

(*c.*1146-1223)

from: TOPOGRAPHIA HIBERNIAE (The History and Topography of Ireland) (*c.*1187)

[Giraldus Cambrensis was a member of one of the leading Norman families involved in the 'invasion' of Ireland in the late twelfth century. He visited Ireland twice: in 1183 he came with his uncle and his brother and assessed the land they were attempting to conquer; in 1185 he returned with the army led by Prince John, Henry II's son, and he stayed on for some time after that army had left.

Giraldus wrote two books on Ireland, a topography and an account of the conquest. Both are designed to justify the conquest and, since they were written from the position of the invaders, they make out the native Irish to be barbarous and uncivilized. Giraldus's text had immense influence and was referred to by every Englishman writing about Ireland for several hundred years. Irish commentators have found his work highly offensive and have cast serious doubts on its accuracy. However, Giraldus's parallel work on Wales is fairly accurate and it must be admitted that his books on Ireland are our only substantial source of information on the state of the country in the medieval period; they are still much consulted by modern historians. The translation is by John J. O'Meara, Penguin Books, 1982.]

The nature, customs and characteristics of the people

I have thought it not superfluous to say a few things about the nature of this people both in mind and body, that is to say, of their mental and physical characteristics.

To begin with: when they are born, they are not carefully nursed as is usual. For apart from the nourishment with which they are sustained by their hard parents from dying altogether, they are for the most part abandoned to nature. They are not put in cradles, or swathed;[1] nor are their tender limbs helped by frequent baths or formed by any useful art. The midwives do not use hot water to raise the nose, or press down the face, or lengthen the legs. Unaided nature according to her own judgement arranges and disposes without the help of any art the limbs that she has produced.

As if to prove what she can do by herself she continually shapes and moulds, until she finally forms and finishes them in their full strength with beautiful upright bodies and handsome and well-complexioned faces.

But although they are fully endowed with natural gifts, their external characteristics of beard and dress, and internal cultivation of the mind, are so barbarous that they cannot be said to have any culture.

They use very little wool in their dress and that itself nearly always black — because the sheep of that country are black — and made up in a barbarous fashion. For they wear little hoods, close-fitting and stretched across the shoulders and down to a length of about eighteen to twenty-two inches, and generally sewn together from cloths of various kinds. Under these they wear mantles instead of cloaks. They also use woollen trousers that are at the same time boots, or boots that are at the same time trousers, and these are for the most part dyed.

When they are riding, they do not use saddles or leggings or spurs. They drive on, and guide their horses by means of a stick with a crook at its upper end, which they hold in their hand. They use reins to serve the purpose both of a bridle and a bit.

1. Wrapped in long strips of bandage (swaddling clothes) to prevent movement.

These do not keep the horses, accustomed to feeding on the grass, from their food.

Moreover, they go naked and unarmed into battle. They regard weapons as a burden, and they think it brave and honourable to fight unarmed. They use, however, three types of weapons — short spears, two darts (in this they imitate the Basclenses),[2] and big axes well and carefully forged, which they have taken over from the Norwegians and the Ostmen,[3] about which we shall speak later.

They are quicker and more expert than any other people in throwing, when everything else fails, stones as missiles, and such stones do great damage to the enemy in an engagement.

They are a wild and inhospitable people. They live on beasts only, and live like beasts. They have not progressed at all from the primitive habits of pastoral living.

While man usually progresses from the woods to the fields, and from the fields to settlements and communities of citizens, this people despises work on the land, has little use for the money-making of towns, contemns the rights and privileges of citizenship, and desires neither to abandon, nor lose respect for, the life which it has been accustomed to lead in the woods and countryside.

They use the fields generally as pasture, but pasture in poor condition. Little is cultivated, and even less sown. The fields cultivated are so few because of the neglect of those who should cultivate them. But many of them are naturally very fertile and productive. The wealth of the soil is lost, not through the fault of the soil, but because there are no farmers to cultivate even the best land: 'the fields demand, but there are no hands'. How few kinds of fruit-bearing trees are grown here! The nature of the soil is not to be blamed, but rather the want of industry on the part of the cultivator. He is too lazy to plant the foreign types of trees that would grow very well here.

The different types of minerals too, with which the hidden veins of the earth are full, are not mined or put to any use, precisely because of the same laziness. Even gold, of which they are very desirous — just like the Spaniards — and which they would like to have in abundance, is brought here by traders that search the ocean for gain.

2. The Basques; Cambrensis obviously believed that they had been responsible for one of the earlier 'invasions' of Ireland.

3. Norsemen.

They do not devote their lives to the processing of flax or wool, or to any kind of merchandise or mechanical art. For given only to leisure, and devoted only to laziness, they think that the greatest pleasure is not to work, and the greatest wealth is to enjoy liberty.

This people is, then, a barbarous people, literally barbarous. Judged according to modern ideas, they are uncultivated, not only in the external appearance of their dress, but also in their flowing hair and beards. All their habits are the habits of barbarians. Since conventions are formed from living together in society, and since they are so removed in these distant parts from the ordinary world of men, as if they were in another world altogether and consequently cut off from well-behaved and law-abiding people, they know only of the barbarous habits in which they were born and brought up, and embrace them as another nature. Their natural qualities are excellent. But almost everything acquired is deplorable.

The incomparable skill of the people in musical instruments

It is only in the case of musical instruments that I find any commendable diligence in the people. They seem to me to be incomparably more skilled in these than any other people that I have seen.

The movement is not, as in the British instrument to which we are accustomed, slow and easy, but rather quick and lively, while at the same time the melody is sweet and pleasant. It is remarkable how, in spite of the great speed of the fingers, the music proportion is maintained. The melody is kept perfect and full with unimpaired art through everything — through quivering measures and the involved use of several instruments — with a rapidity that charms, a rhythmic pattern that is varied, and a concord achieved through elements discordant. They harmonize at intervals of the octave and the fifth, but they always begin with B flat and with B flat end, so that everything may be rounded with the sweetness of charming sonority. They glide so subtly from one mode to another, and the grace notes[4] so freely sport with such abandon and bewitching charm around the steady tone of the heavier sound, that the perfection of their art seems

4. Embellishments to the melody.

to lie in their concealing it, as if 'it were the better for being hidden. An art revealed brings shame.'

Hence it happens that the very things that afford unspeakable delight to the minds of those who have a fine perception and can penetrate carefully to the secrets of the art, bore, rather than delight, those who have no such perception — who look without seeing, and hear without being able to understand. When the audience is unsympathetic they succeed only in causing boredom with what appears to be but confused and disordered noise.

One should note that both Scotland and Wales, the former because of her affinity and intercourse, the latter as it were by grafting, try to imitate Ireland in music and strive in emulation. Ireland uses and delights in two instruments only, the harp, namely, and the timpanum. Scotland uses three, the harp, timpanum, and the crowd.[5] Wales uses the harp, the pipes, and the crowd. They also use strings made of bronze, and not from leather. In the opinion, however, of many, Scotland has by now not only caught up on Ireland, her instructor, but already far outdistances and excels her in musical skill. Therefore people now look to that country as to the fountain of the art.

5. Two early Celtic stringed instruments, the timpanum played with a plectrum and the crowd with a bow.

RICHARD STANIHURST
(1547-1618)

from:
THE HISTORIE OF IRELAND (1577)

[Richard Stanihurst's lively description of Ireland is the most entertaining Irish book of the sixteenth century. Stanihurst was a Dubliner, son of the recorder of the city and uncle of the famous archbishop, James Ussher. He wrote his history and description of Ireland at least partly under the influence of his Oxford tutor, Edmund Campion, who spent some time in Stanihurst's house in Dublin researching for his own history of Ireland. Stanihurst's work reflects not only a genuine enthusiasm for Ireland but also an infectious delight in the resources of language. The two passages that follow are representative of the best of his topographical work. The first has been rendered into modern English in full in the notes, which should make it possible for the reader who is armed with a little perseverence to work out the meaning of the second passage. The modern English rendering is by Alan Fletcher of University College, Dublin.]

Of the nature of the soyle, and other incidentes

The soyle is lowe and watrish, encludeth diuers little Islandes, enuironned wyth lakes and marrish. Highest hilles haue standyng pooles in theyr tops. Inhabitantes, especially new come, are subiect to distillations, reumes and flixes. For remedy wherof, they vse an ordinary drinke of *Aqua vitæ*, so quallified in the makyng that it dryeth more, and enflameth lesse then other whote confections. One *Theoricus* wrote a proper treatise of *Aqua vitæ*, wherein he prayseth it to the ninth degree. He destinguisheth three sortes therof, *Simplex*, *Composita*, and *Perfectissima*. He declareth the simples and ingrediences thereto belongyng. He wisheth it to be taken as well before meate as after. It dryeth vp the breakyng out of handes, and killeth the fleshe wormes, if you wash your handes therewith. It skoureth all skurfe and skaldes from the head, beyng therewith daily washte before meales. Beyng moderately taken, sayth he, it sloeth age, it strengtheneth youth, it helpeth digestion, it cutteth fleume, it abandoneth melancholy, it relisheth thc hart, it lighteneth the mynd, it quickeneth the spirites, it cureth the hydropsie, it healeth the strangury, it pounceth the stone, it expelleth grauell, it puffeth away all Ventositie, it kepeth and presereuth the hed from whirlyng, the eyes from dazelyng, the tongue from lispyng, the mouth from mafflyng, the teeth from chatteryng, the throte from ratling, the weasan from stieflyng, the stomacke from wambling, the harte from swellyng, the belly from wirtchyng, the guts from rumblyng, the handes from shiuering, the sinowes from shrinkyng, the veynes from crumpling, the bones from akyng, the marrow from soakyng. *Vlstadius* also ascribeth thereto a singuler prayse, and would haue it to burne, beyng kindled, which he taketh to be a token to know the goodnesse thereof. And truly it is a soueraigne liquour, if it be orderly taken.

The ayre is very holesome, not generally so cleare and subtill as that of Englande. The weather is more temperate, beyng not so warme in Sommer, nor colde in Winter, as it is in Englande and Flaunders. The countrye is stoared with Bees, contrarye to the opinion of some wryters, who both in this & other errours touching this countrye maye easily be excused, as those that wrote by heresay. No Vineyards, yet Grapes growe there as in Englande. They lacke the Roe buck, as *Polichronicon* writeth. They lack the Bird called the Pye. Howbeit in the Englishe pale[1] to thys daye, they vse to tearme a slye cosener, a wyly Pye. *Cambriense* in his time complaineth that Irelande had excesse of woode, and very little champayne grounde, but now the English pale is to naked. Turfe is their most fewell and seacoale. No venemous creeping beaste is brought forth, or nourished, or can liue in Irelande, being brought or sent. And therfore the spyder of Ireland is wel known not to be venemous; onely because a frogge was found lying in the medowes of Waterforde somewhat before the conquest they construed it to importe their ouerthrowe.

Bede[2] wryteth that serpentes conueighed to Irelande did presently die, beyng touched with the smell of the lande, that whatsoeuer came from Irelande was then of souereigne vertue against poyson. He exemplifieth in certayne men, stung of Adders, who dranke in water, the scrapings of bookes that had beene of Irelande, and were cured. Generally it is obserued, the farther west, the lesse annoiance of pestilent creatures. The want whereof is to Irelande so peculiar, that whereas it laye long in question to whether realme, Brytayne or Irelande, the Ile of Man should appertayne, the sayd controuersie was decyded: that forsomuch as venemous beastes were knowen to breede therein, it could not be a naturall part of Ireland. And contrarywise the Orchades are adiudged to be appendaunt to Irelande, because those Islandes neyther breede nor foster any venemous worme, as *Hector Boethus*[3] aduoucheth. *Giraldus Cambriense* writeth that he hearde certayne Merchaunts affirme that when they had vnladen theyr shippes in Irelande, they founde by hap some toades, vnder theyr balast. And they had no sooner cast them on the shore then they would puffe and swell vnmeasurably, & shortly after turning vp theyr bellyes, they would burst in sunder. And not onely the earth & dust of Irelande, but also the very thonges of Irishe leather, haue the same force and vertue. I haue sene it, saith *Cambriense,* experimented, that a toade being encompassed with a thong of Irishe leather, and creepyng thitherward, endeuouring to haue skipt ouer it, sodenly reculed backe, as though it had bene rapte in the hed: wherupon it began to spraule to the other side. But at length perceiuyng that the thong did embay it of all partes, it began to thyrle, and as it were to dig the earth where, findyng an hole, it sluncke away in the presence of sondry persons.

It happened also in my tyme, sayeth *Giraldus Cambriense*, that in the North of England a knot of yoongkers tooke a nap in the fieldes. As one of them lay snorting with his mouth gaping, as though he would haue caught flies, it happened that a Snake or Adder slipt into his mouth, and glyded downe into his bellye, where herboring it selfe, it beganne to roame vp and downe and to feede on the young man his entralles. The pacient being sore distracted and aboue measure tormented wyth the byting pangues of this greedie guest, incessantly prayed to God, that if it stoode wyth his gracious will, eyther wholly to berieue him of his lyfe, or else of his vnspeakable mercie to ease him of his payne. The worme woulde neuer cease from gnawing the pacient his carkasse, but when he had taken his repast. And his meate was no sooner digested then it woulde giue a freshe onset in boaring his guttes. Diuers remedies were sought, as medicines, pilgrimages to Sainctes: but all could not preuayle. Being at length schooled by the graue aduise of some sage and expert father, that willed him to make his speedie repayre to Ireland, he would tract no time, but busked himselfe ouersea, and arriued in Irelande. He dyd not sooner

1. The part of Ireland (centred on Dublin) in which English jurisdiction had been established.
2. The venerable Bede (673-735), English scholar and churchman.
3. Hector Boace (1465-1536), one of the founders of the University of Aberdeen, who published *Scottorum Historiae* in 1527.

drinke of the water of that Islande, and taken of the victuals of Ireland, but forthwith he kilde the Snake, auoyded it downewarde, and so being lustye and liuely he returned into Englande. Thus farre *Giraldus Cambriense*.

[The land of Ireland is low and waterlogged; it includes several little islands surrounded by lakes and marshes. Even the highest hills have standing pools at their summits. The inhabitants, especially those who have arrived recently, suffer from colds and discharges and, to remedy this, they usually drink Irish whiskey, made in such a way that it dries out the body more and heats it less than other hot mixtures. One Theoricus wrote a detailed treatise about Irish whiskey in which he praises it to the highest degree. He distinguishes three kinds of it: the simple, the blended, and the very best. He explains its recipe and ingredients exactly. He recommends it should be taken before meals as well as after them. If you wash your hands in it, it dries up any sores you may have on your hands and kills flesh-worms. If you wash your head with it daily before meals, it clears up all scurf and other infections. If it is drunk in moderation, says Theoricus, it slows down ageing, rejuvenates, helps digestion, breaks up catarrh, puts depression to flight, refreshes the heart, lightens the mind, enlivens the spirits, cures dropsy, heals hernia, dissolves stones in the gall bladder, helps one pass kidney stones, removes windiness, prevents attacks of dizziness, prevents the eye from being dazzled, the tongue from lisping, the mouth from stammering, the teeth from chattering, the throat from rattling, the windpipe from getting blocked, the stomach from rumbling, the heart from swelling, the belly from retching, the guts from rumbling, the hands from shivering, the sinews from shrinking, the veins from crumpling, the bones from aching, the marrow from soaking. Ulstadius also gives unique praise to whiskey and says that it will burn if it is kindled; this he takes to be a way of testing the quality of it. Truly it is a wonderful liquor if it is taken in an orderly manner.

The air is very wholesome, not generally so clear and delicate as that of England. The weather is more temperate, being not so warm in summer nor cold in winter as it is in England and Flanders. The country has many bees in it contrary to the opinion of some writers who both in this and other errors about the country may easily be excused since they wrote from hearsay. There are no vineyards yet grapes grow there as they do in England. They lack the roebuck as [Eusebius in his] *Polychronicon* writes; they lack the bird the English call 'the Pie'. However in the English pale, to this day, they use the term 'a wily pie' to describe somebody who cheats them slyly. Cambrensis in his time complained that Ireland had too much forest in it and very little open cultivated ground but now there are too few trees in the English pale. Turf and coal brought by sea are their most common fuels. No venomous creeping beast is born or nourished in Ireland nor can it live there if it is brought in or sent to the country. And therefore the Irish spider is well known not to be poisonous; it was because a frog was found lying in the meadows of Waterford just before the conquest that they thought it meant that they would be overthrown.

Bede writes that snakes brought to Ireland died as soon as the smell of the land touched them and that whatsoever came from Ireland was therefore a sovereign cure against poison. He gives the example of certain men stung by adders who drank water in which were scrapings of books that had been in Ireland, and were cured. Generally it is observed that the further west you go, the less you are troubled by poisonous creatures. But the lack of them in Ireland is so peculiar that, whereas there was for a long time a debate as to whether the Isle of Man should belong to the realm of Britain or to Ireland, it was decided that because poisonous creatures were known to breed there, it could not be a natural part of Ireland. And on the contrary, the Orkneys are judged to be dependent to Ireland because on those islands no venomous snakes breed or thrive, as Hector Boethus avers. Giraldus Cambrensis writes that he heard certain merchants say that when they had unloaded their ships in Ireland, they found by chance some toads under their ballast. And they had no sooner thrown them on to the shore than they would puff and swell up beyond all bounds and shortly afterwards would turn on their backs and their bellies would burst. And it is not only the earth and dust of Ireland that has this characteristic power and virtue but even thongs of Irish leather. I have seen, says Cambrensis, the following experiment; a toad was placed in a circle made by a thong of Irish leather; it crept towards it and tried to jump over it but suddenly recoiled as though it had been hit on the head. Upon which it crawled towards the other side. But at last, understanding that the thong was all round it, it began to bore the ground, and as it were to dig up the earth and, when it found a hole, slunk away. This happened in the presence of several people.

It also happened in my time, says Giraldus Cambrensis, that in the north of England a group of youngsters took a nap in the fields. As one of them lay snoring with his mouth wide open, as though he were trying to catch flies, it happened that a snake or adder slipped into his mouth and glided down into his belly where, settling itself in, it began to move around and to feed on the young man's entrails. The patient was in great pain and tormented almost beyond endurance with the biting pangs of this greedy guest. He prayed to God incessantly that if it were his gracious will, he would either allow him to die or else, of his ineffable mercy, ease him of his pain. The snake would never stop gnawing the patient's body except when he had eaten a meal. And his meal was no sooner digested that the snake would make a new onslaught, eating his entrails. Many remedies were tried, such as medicines and pilgrimages to shrines of saints. But none of them succeeded. At last, he was advised by a certain wise old priest to go as quickly as possible to Ireland. He wasted no time but went over the seas as quickly as he could and got to Ireland. No sooner did he drink Irish water and eat Irish food than he killed the snake and voided it downwards and so, returned to life and good health, he came back to England. Thus says Giraldus Cambrensis.]

Kilkenny

Kilkenny, the best vplandish towne, or, as they terme it, the proprest dry towne in Ireland. It is parted into the high towne & the Irishe towne. The Irish towne claymeth a corporation apart from the high town, wherby great factions growe daily betwene the inhabitants. True it is that the Irish towne is the auncienter, and was called the olde Kilkenny, beyng vnder the bishop his becke, as they are or ought to be at this present. The high town was builded by the Englishe after the conquest, and had a parcell of the Irishe towne therto vnited, by the bishop his graunt, made vnto the founders vpon their earnest request. In the yere 1400 Robert Talbot, a worthy gentleman, enclosed with walles the better part of this towne, by which it was greatly fortified. This gentleman deceased in the yeare 1415. In this towne in the chore of the Frier preachers, William Marshal, Erle Marshal and Erle of Penbroke was buried, who departed this lyfe in the yere 1231. Richard, brother to William, to whome the inheritaunce descended, within three yeres after deceased at Kilkenny, beyng wounded to death in a field giuen in the heath of Kyldare, in the yere 1234, the xij of Aprill, & was entumbed wyth hys brother, according to the olde epitaph.

Hic comes est positus Richardus vulnere fossus.
Cuius sub fossa Kilkenia continet ossa.[1]

This town hath thre churches, S. Kennies church, our Ladies churche, *alias* S. Maries church, and S. Patrikes church, with the abbey of S. Iohn. S. Kennies churche is theyr chiefe and cathedrall church, a worthy foundation as well for gorgeous buildinges as for notable liuyngs. In the West ende of the churchyard of late haue bene founded a Grammer schoole by the right honourable Pierce or Peter Butler Erle of Ormond and Ossory, and by his wife the countesse of Ormond, the lady Margarete fitz Girald, sister to Girald fitz Girald the Erle of Kyldare that last was. Out of which schoole haue sprouted such proper ympes through the painefull diligence and the laboursome industry of a famous lettered man M. Peter White (sometyme fellow of Oriall colledge in Oxford, and schoolemaister in Kilkenny) as generally the whole weale publike of Ireland, and especially the southerne partes of that Island are greatly therby furthered. This gentlemans methode in trayning vp youth was rare and singuler, framyng the education according to the scholers vaine. If he found him free, he would bridle hym like a wyse Isocrates from his booke; if her perceiued hym to be dull, he would spur hym forwarde; if he vnderstoode that he were the woorse for beating, he woulde win him with rewardes; finally, by interlacing study wyth recreation, sorrow with mirth, payne with pleasure, sowernesse with sweetenesse, roughnesse with myldenesse, he had so good successe in schooling his pupils, as in good sooth I may boldly byde by it, that in the realme of Ireland was no Grammar schoole so good, in Englande, I am well assured, none better. And because it was my happy happe (God & my parents be thanked) to haue bene one of his crewe, I take it to stand with my duety, sith I may not stretch myne habilitie in requiting hys good turnes, yet to manifest my goodwill in remembryng his paines. And certes, I acknowledge my selfe so much bound and beholding to him and his, as for his sake I reuerence the meanest stone cemented in the walles of that famous schoole. This town is named Kilkenny of an holy and learned Abbot called Kanicus, borne in the countie of Kilkenny, or (as it is in some bookes recorded) in Connaght. This prelate beyng in his suckling yeres fostered, through the prouidence of God, with the milk of a cow, and baptized and bishopped by one Luracus, thereto by Gods especiall appoyntment deputed, grew in tracte of tyme to such deuotion and learnyng as he was reputed of all men to be as well a mirrour of the one as a paragon of the other: whereof he gaue sufficient coniecture in hys minoritie. For beyng turned to the keepyng of

1. 'Here, pricked by a wound, is placed Sir Richard
Whose bones Kilkenny has in her moat.'
The point of the epitaph is the play on the words 'fossus' (pricked), 'ossa' (bones) and 'fossa' (ditch or moat).

sheepe, and hys fellow shepeheards wholy yelding themselues like luskish vagabonds to slouth and sluggishnesse, yet would he still fine himselfe occupied in framing with Osiars and twigs little woodden churches, and in fashioning the furnitures thereto appertaining. Beyng stepte further in yeares, he made his repayre into England, where cloystering himselfe in an abbey wherof one named *Doctus* was abbot, he was wholy wedded to his booke and to deuotion: wherein he continued so painefull and diligent, as being on a certaine time penning a serious matter and hauing not fully drawn the fourth vocall,[2] the abbey bell tingde to assemble the couent to some spirituall exercise. To which he so hastened, as he left the letter in semicirclewyse vnfinished, vntill he returned backe to his booke. Soone after being promoted to ecclesiasticall orders, he trauailed by the consent of his fellow monkes to Rome, and in Italy he gaue such manifest proofe of his pietie as to this day in some partes therof he is highly renowmed.

2. vowel.

FYNES MORYSON

(1566-1630)

from: AN ITINERARY ... CONTAINING HIS TEN YEERES TRAVELL.... (1617)

[Fynes Moryson's famous *Itinerary* is an important sourcebook for historians of Elizabethan Ireland. As secretary to the lord deputy, Moryson was closely involved with the suppression of Tyrone's rebellion and was at the battle of Kinsale in 1601; his account of military events of the period is invaluable. As a social historian, too, Moryson is important. His *Itinerary* contains an enormous amount of detailed information about life at all levels of Irish society of the time. The passage that follows gives a broad outline of the country.]

This famous Iland in the Virginian Sea, is by olde Writers called *Ierna, Inuerna,* and *Iris,* by the old Inhabitants *Eryn,* by the old Britans *Yuerdhen,* by thc English at this day *Ireland,* and by the Irish Bardes at this day *Banno,* in which sence of the Irish word, *Auicen* cals it the holy *Iland,* besides *Plutarch* of old called it *Ogigia,* and after him *Isidore* named it *Scotia.* This *Ireland* according to the Inhabitants, is deuided into two parts, the wild Irish, and the English Irish, liuing in the English Pale:[1] but of the old Kingdomes fiue in number, it is deuided into fiue parts.

1. The first is by the Irish called *Mowne,* by the English *Mounster,* and is subdeuided into sixe Counties, of *Kerry,* of *Limricke,* of *Corcke,* of *Tipperary,* of the *Holy Crosse,* and of *Waterford,* to which the seuenth County of *Desmond* is now added. The *Gangaui* a Scithean people comming into *Spaine,* and from thence into *Ireland,* inhabited the County of *Kerry,* full of woody mountaines, in which the Earles of *Desmond* had the dignity of Palatines,[2] hauing House in *Trailee,* a little Towne now almost vninhabited: Not farre thence lies Saint *Mary Wic,* vulgarly called *Smerwicke,* where the Lord *Arthur Gray,* being Lord Deputy, happily ouerthrew the aiding troopes sent to the Earle of *Desmond* from the Pope, and the King of *Spaine.* On the South side of *Kerry* lies the County of *Desmond,* of old inhabited by three kinds of people, the *Luceni* (being Spaniards), the *Velabri* (so called of their seate upon the Sea waters or Marshes), and the *Iberni,* called the vpper Irish, inhabiting about *Beerehauen* & *Baltimore,* two Hauens well known by the plentiful fishing of Herrings, and the late inuasion of the Spaniards in the yeere 1601. Next to these is the County of *Mac Carti More,* of Irish race, whom as enemy to the *Fitz-geralds,* Queene *Elizabeth* made Earle of *Glencar* in the yeere 1566.

1. The area (centred on Dublin) under English control.

2. A Palatine ruler possessed royal privileges within his territory.

For of the *Fitz-Geralds* of the Family of the Earles of *Kildare*, the Earles of *Desmond* descended, who being by birth English, and created Earles by King *Edward* the third, became hatefull Rebels in our time. The third County hath the name of the City *Corke*, consisting almost all of one long streete, but well known and frequented, which is so compassed with rebellious neighbours, as they of old not daring to marry their Daughters to them, the custome grew and continues to this day, that by mutuall marriages one with another, all the Citizens are of kinne in some degree of Affinity. Not farre thence is *Yoghall*, hauing a safe Hauen, neere which the Vicounts of *Barry* of English race are seated. In the fourth County of *Tipperary*, nothing is memorable, but that it is a Palatinate. The little Towne *Holy-Crosse*, in the County of the same name, hath many great priuiledges. The sixth County hath the name of the City *Limerike*, the seate of a Bishop, wherein is a strong Castle built by King *John*. Not farre thence is *Awne*[3] the seate of a Bishop, and the lower *Ossery*, giuing the title of an Earle to the *Butlers*, and the Towne *Thurles*, giuing them also the title of Vicount. And there is *Cassiles*,[4] now a poore City, but the seate of an Archbishoppe. The seuenth County hath the name of the City *Waterford*, which the Irish call *Porthlargi*, of the commodious Hauen, a rich and well inhabited City, esteemed the second to *Dublyn*. And because the Inhabitants long faithfully helped the English in subduing *Ireland*, our Kings gaue them excessiue priuiledges, but they rashly failing in their obedience, at King *James* his comming to the Crowne, could not in long time obtaine the confirmation of their old Charter.

2. *Leinster* the second part of *Ireland* is fertile, and yeelds plenty of Corne, and hath a most temperate mild Aire, being deuided into ten Counties, of *Catterlogh*, *Kilkenny*, *Wexford*, *Dublin*, *Kildare*, the *Kings* County, the *Queenes* County, the Counties of *Longford*, of *Fernes* and of *Wickle*. The *Cariondi* of old inhabited *Caterlogh* (or *Carloo*) County, and they also inhabited great part of *Kilkenny*, of vpper *Ossery* and of *Ormond*, which haue nothing memorable, but the Earles of *Ormond*, of the great Family of the *Butlers*, inferiour to no Earle in *Ireland*, (not to speake of *Fitz-patric* Baron of vpper *Ossery*.) It is rediculous, which some Irish (who will be beleeued as men of credit) report of Men in these parts yeerely turned into Wolues, except the aboundance of melancholy humour, transports them to imagine that they are so transformed. *Kilkenny* giuing name to the second County, is a pleasant Towne, the chiefe of the Townes, within Land, memorable for the ciuility of the Inhabitants, for the Husbandmens labour, and the pleasant Orchards. I passe ouer the walled Towne *Thomas-towne*, and the ancient City *Rheban*, now a poore Village with a Castle, yet of old giuing the title of Barronet. I passe ouer the Village and strong Castle of *Leighlin*, with the Countrey adioyning, vsurped by the Sept of the Cauanaghs, now surnamed *Omores*. Also I omit *Rosse*, of old a large City, at this day of no moment. The third County of *Wexford*, (called by the Irish County *Reogh*) was of old inhabited by the *Menappij*, where at the Towne called *Banna*, the English made their first discent into *Ireland*, and vpon that Coast are very dangerous flats in the Sea, which they vulgarly called *Grounds*. The City *Weshford*, *Weisford*, or *Wexford*, is the cheefe of the County, not great, but deseruing praise for their faithfulnesse towards the English, and frequently inhabited by Men of English race. The *Cauci*, (a Seabordering Nation of *Germany*), and the *Menappij* aforesaid, of old inhabited the territories now possessed by the *Omores* and *Obirns*. Also they inhabited the fourth County of *Kildare* a fruitfull soyle, hauing the cheefe Towne of the same name, greatlie honoured in the infancie of the Church by *Saint Briget*. King *Edward* the second, created the *Giralds* Earles of *Kildare*. The *Eblani* of old inhabited the territory of *Dublin* the fifth County, hauing a fertile soyle and rich pastures, but wanting wood, so as they burne Turffe, or Seacoale brought out of *England*. The City *Dublyn* called *Diuelin* by the English, and *Balacleigh* (as seated vpon hurdles) by the Irish, is the cheefe City of the Kingdome and seate of Iustice, fairely built, frequently inhabited, and adorned with a strong Castle, fifteene Churches, an Episcopall seate, and a faire Colledge, (an unhappy foundation of an Vniuersity laid in our Age), and indowed with many priuiledges, but the Hauen is barred and made lesse commodious by those hils of sands.[5] The adioyning Promontory

3. *recte* Ardfert (?).
4. Cashel.
5. The problem posed to shipping by the sandbar at the mouth of the river Liffey was not solved until the building of the Bull Wall in the eighteenth century.

Hoth-head, giues the title of a Barron to the Family of *Saint Laurence*: And towards the North lies *Fengall*, a little Territory, as it were the Garner[6] of the Kingdome, which is enuironed by the Sea and great Riuers, and this situation hath defended it from the incursion of Rebels in former ciuill warres. I omit the Kings and Queenes Counties, (namely *Ophaly* and *Leax*) inhabited by the *Oconnors* and *Omores*, as likewise the Counties of *Longford*, *Fernes*, and *Wicklo*, as lesse affoording memorable things.

3. The third part of *Ireland* is *Midia* or *Media*, called by the English *Methe*, in our Fathers memory deuided into *Eastmeath* and *Westmeath*. In *Eastmeath* is *Drogheda*, vulgarly called *Tredagh*, a faire and well inhabited Towne. *Trym* is a little Towne vpon the confines of *Vlster*, hauing a stately Castle, but now much ruinated, and it is more notable for being the ancient (as it were) Barrony of the *Lacies*. *Westmeath* hath the Towne *Deluin*, giuing the title of Baron to the English Family of the *Nugents*, and *Westmeath* is also inhabited by many great Irish Septs, as the *Omaddens*, the *Magoghigans*, *Omalaghlens*, and *MacCoghlans*, which seeme barbarous names. *Shannon* is a great Riuer, in a long course making many and great lakes (as the large Lake or *Lough Regith*), and yeeldes plentifull fishing, as doe the frequent Riuers and all the Seas of *Ireland*. Vpyn this Riuer lies the Towne *Athlon*, hauing a very faire Bridge of stone, (the worke of Sir *Henry Sidney* Lord Deputy) and a strong faire Castle.

4. *Connaght* is the fourth part of *Ireland*, a fruitfull Prouince, but hauing many Boggs and thicke Woods, and it is diuided into sixe Countyes, of *Clare*, of *Letrim*, of *Galloway*, of *Rosecomen*, of *Maio*, and of *Sligo*. The County of *Clare* or *Thowmond* hath his Earles of *Thowmond*, of the Family of the *Obrenes* the old Kings of *Connaght*, and *Toam*[7] is the seate of an Archbishop, onely part but the greatest of this County was called *Clare* of *Thomas Clare* Earle of *Glocester*. The adioyning Territory *Clan Richard* (the land of *Richards* sonnes) hath his Earles called *Clanricard* of the land, but being of the English Family *de Burgo*, vulgarly *Burck*, and both these Earles were first created by *Henry* the eight. In the same Territory is the Barony *Atterith*, belonging to the Barons of the English Family *Bermingham*, of old very warlike: but their posteritie haue degenerated to the Irish barbarisme. The city *Galway* giuing name to the County, lying vpon the Sea, is frequently inhabited with ciuill people, and fairely built. The Northern part of *Connaght* is inhabited by these Irish Septs, *O Conor*, *O Rorke*, and *Mac Diarmod*. Vpon the Westerne coast lyes the Iland *Arran*, famous for the fabulous long life of the inhabitants.

5. *Vlster* the fifth part of *Ireland* is a large Prouince, woody, fenny, in some parts fertile, in other parts barren, but in al parts greene and pleasant to behold, and exceedingly stoared with Cattell. The next part to the Pale, and to *England*, is diuided into three Countyes, *Lowth*, *Down*, and *Antrimme*, the rest containes seuen Counties, *Monaghan*, *Tyrone*, *Armach*, *Colrane*, *Donergall*, *Fermanagh*, and *Cauon*. *Lowth* is inhabited by English-Irish, (*Down* and *Antrimme* being contained vnder the same name), and the Barons thereof be of the *Berminghams* family, and remaine louing to the English. *Monaghan* was inhabited by the English family *Fitzursi*, and these are become degenerate and barbarous, and in the sense of that name are in the Irish tongue called *Mac Mahon*, that is, the sonnes of Beares. I forbeare to speake of *Tyrone*, and the Earle thereof, infamous for his Rebellion, which I haue at large handled in the second part of this work. *Armach* is the seate of an Archbishop, and the Metropolitan City of the whole Iland, but in time of the Rebellion was altogether ruinated. The other Countyes haue not many memorable things, therefore it shall suffice to speake of them briefely. The neck of land called *Lecale*, is a pleasant little territory, fertile, and abounding with fish, and all things for food, and therein is *Downe*, at this time a ruined Towne, but the seate of a Bishop, and famous for the buriall of S. *Patrick*, S. *Bridget*, and S. *Columb*. The Towne of *Carickfergus* is well knowne by the safe Hauen. The Riuer *Bann* running through the Lake *Euagh* into the Sea, is famous for the fishing of Salmons, the water being most cleare, wherein the Salmons much delight. The great Families (or Septs) of *Vlster*, are thus named, *O Neale*, *O Donnel*, (whereof the chiefe was lately created Earle of *Tirconnel*) *O Buill*, *Mac Guyre*, *O Cane*, *O Dogharty*, *Mac Mahown*, *Mac Gennis*, *Mac Sorleigh*, *&c*. The Lake *Ern*, compassed with thicke Woods, hath such plenty of fish, as the fishermen feare the breaking of their nets, rather then want of fish. Towards the

6. Granary.
7. Tuam.

North in the middest of vast woods (and as I thinke) in the County *Donergall* is a lake, and therein an Iland, in which is a Caue, famous for the apparition of spirits, which the inhabitants call *Ellanui-frugadory*, that is, The Iland of Purgatory, and they call it Saint *Patricks* Purgatory, fabling that hee obtained of God by prayer, that the Irish seeing the paines of the damned, might more carefully auoide sinne.

The land of *Ireland* is vneuen, mountanous, soft, watry, woody, and open to windes and flouds of raine, and so fenny, as it hath Bogges vpon the very tops of Mountaines, not bearing man or beast, but dangerous to passe, and such Bogs are frequent ouer all *Ireland*. Our Marriners obserue the sayling into *Ireland* to be more dangerous, not onely because many tides meeting, makes the sea apt to swell vpon any storme, but especially because they euer find the coast of *Ireland* couered with mists, whereas the coast of *England* is commonly cleare, and to be seene farre off. The ayre of *Ireland* is vnapt to ripen seedes, yet (as *Mela* witnesseth) the earth is luxurious in yeelding faire and sweete hearbs. *Ireland* is little troubled with thunders, lightnings, or earthquakes, yet (I know not vpon what presage) in the yeere 1601, and in the moneth of Nouember almost ended, at the siege of *Kinsale*, and few daies before the famous Battell, in which the Rebels were happily ouerthrowne, we did nightly heare and see great thundrings & lightnings, not without some astonishment what they should presage. The fields are not onely most apt to feede Cattell, but yeeld also great increase of Corne. I wil freely say, that I obserued the winters cold to be far more mild, then it is in *England*, so as the Irish pastures are more greene, and so likewise the gardens al winter time, but that in Summer, by reason of the cloudy ayre, and watry soyle, the heate of the Sunne hath not such power to ripen corne and fruits so as their haruest is much later then in *England*. Also I obserued, that the best sorts of flowers and fruits are much rarer in *Ireland*, then in *England*, which notwithstanding is more to bee attributed to the inhabitants, then to the ayre. For *Ireland* being oft troubled with Rebellions, and the Rebels not only being idle themselues, but in naturall malice destroying the labours of other men, and cutting vp the very trees of fruits for the same cause, or else to burne them. For these reasons the inhabitants take lesse pleasure to till their grounds, or plant trees, content to liue for the day in continuall feare of like mischiefes. Yet is not *Ireland* altogether destitute of these flowers and fruites, wherewith the County of *Kilkenny* seemes to abound more then any other part. And the said humility of aire and land; making the fruits for food more raw and moyst: hereupon the inhabitants and strangers are troubled with loosenes of body, the Country disease. Yet for the rawnes they haue an excellent remedy by their aquauity, vulgarly called *Vsquebagh*, which binds the belly, and drieth vp moysture, more then our Aquauity, yet inflameth not so much. Also inhabitants aswell as strangers are troubled there with an ague, which they call the Irish Ague, and they who are sick thereof, vpon a receiued custome, doe not vse the helpe of the Phisitian, but giue themselues to the keeping of Irish women, who starve the ague, giuing the sick man no meate, who takes nothing but milke, and some vulgarly knowne remedies at their hand....

PHILIP O'SULLIVAN-BEARE

(*c.*1590-*c.*1660)

from:
HISTORIAE CATHOLICAE HIBERNIAE COMPENDIUM (Chapters towards a Catholic History of Ireland) (1621)

[Philip O'Sullivan-Beare's account of the Elizabethan wars in Ireland is the only near-eyewitness account from the catholic side. It was printed in Lisbon; O'Sullivan-Beare had been living in the Iberian peninsula since he had been sent there as a boy after the Irish defeat at Kinsale. His informants, both on the Armada and on the flight of Donall O'Sullivan-Beare and his followers from Cork to Connaught in 1602, were almost certainly eye-witnesses of the events. O'Sullivan-Beare was determined to write a *catholic* history of Ireland to refute those being produced by English and Anglo-Irish protestant historians. The translation is by Matthew J. Byrne (1903).]

ON THE WRECK OF THE SPANISH FLEET, ALFONSUS LEIVA, O'ROURKE, MACSWEENY TUETH AND OTHERS

Philip II., that most far-seeing King of the Spains, pitying the misfortune and the darkened state of England, over which, having married Queen Mary, he had reigned for a short time, got together a splendid fleet and valiant army under the command of the Duke of Mitina Sidonia, and despatched them to that island, where undoubtedly they would have destroyed the deadly pest of heresy in its very cradle, if they had landed safely. But our sins rising against us, in the year of our Redeemer 1588, partly by the skill of the heretics, but principally by a storm which arose, the fleet was scattered far and wide and portion of it returned to Spain; part caught by the storm between England and Belgium was carried round Scotland and Ireland; while a great part of it was wrecked. Some ships were driven by the storm on the coasts of Ireland and Scotland, and these striking on jutting rocks and sinking, had some of their men drowned, while some narrowly escaped by swimming or scrambling. The English killed such of the strangers as they caught. Alfonsus Leiva, a Spanish nobleman, having sailed round these islands, became distressed for want of provisions, and took his ship, shaken as it was by the storm, into an Ulster port in the country of MacSweeny Tueth.[1] Three hundred other Spaniards, whose ship had been wrecked off Sligo, a part of Connaught, sought the protection of Brian O'Rourke, surnamed More, chief of Breffny, who was not far off. As soon as Elizabeth, Queen of England, and her Viceroy, John Perrott, had learned this, they required O'Rourke and MacSweeny Tueth to suffer the royalist ministers to try the Spaniards. To this requisition O'Rourke and Tueth replied that the Catholic religion, which they professed, would not allow them to hand over Catholics to death, and moreover that it would be incompatible with their honor to betray those who had fled to their protection. And hereupon O'Rourke provided a guide and provisions for the three hundred who had come to him and sent them to Tueth, with whom Leiva was staying while his ship was being repaired. Others also, who had been shipwrecked in different places in Ireland, flying from the English, flocked to him, the Irish supplying them with guides and provisions. Already there were with Tueth nearly 1,000 Spaniards under command of Leiva. Tueth, elated by the number of Spaniards, and relying on their valour, urged Leiva to declare war against the English in Ireland; that he would arm his mercenaries; that O'Rourke would do the same; that all the Irish would join in defence of the liberty of the Catholic faith; that the Queen had neither means nor sufficient forces nor fortified places; that having first gained Ireland, England might then be easily conquered. Leiva replied that this would not be at all right for him, as he had not received orders to that effect from his own king, but that when he got to Spain he would urge the king to send a stronger army to assert the freedom of Ireland. And so, being supplied with provisions by Tueth, he embarked all his soldiers in his ship, now repaired. But scarcely had he set sail, when in the sight of the mourning Tueth, the ship, burthened with the multitude of men, went to pieces and sank with all hands.

The Spaniards who afterwards escaped from the shipwreck to the Irish coast, were sent by the Irish to Scotland, to Earl Bothwell, commander of the Scottish fleet, and by him were sent to France or Belgium.

The Queen having ordered that O'Rourke's and Tueth's disobedience should be punished by force, Richard Bingham, an English knight, Governor of Connaught, proceeded to attack O'Rourke, and got together a few English and many Irishmen. Amongst others, Ulick Burke, Earl of Clanrickarde, accompanied him. O'Rourke had some time previously hired Murrough MacSweeney, surnamed Na-mart, with his band of two hundred Munstermen; and had, shortly before, armed many mercenaries, and he had no more forces when, in the village of Drumahaire, he was surrounded by the enemy's cavalry and gunmen to whose assistance a division of pikemen were coming up. Murrough, when it seemed as if he must not only suffer defeat, but even perish unavenged, if he gave battle with such scanty forces to so numerous an enemy, arranged his ranks and evacuated the village, he, himself, bringing up the rear, encouraging his men and sustaining the enemy's attack, in which he received a wound from a leaden bullet, which passing from the end of his nose across his cheek, put out his left eye. He suffered so much from this wound that he was unable to discharge his functions, and a panic seizing the rest, they seemed on the point of

1. Chief of the northern branch of the MacSweeney sept or clan.

breaking their ranks, when my uncle Roderic MacSweeny — a young man — quickly assumed the command and taking up the colours and arms from his kinsman Murrough rallied the panic-stricken and brought off the rear ranks.

When Murrough's wound had healed and the war seemed about to be renewed he was not able to do anything. For he had lost his left eye and was still more blinded by the beauty of Gorumplath[2] O'Rourke, O'Rourke's niece by his brother Conn, whom he abducted, violated, and then dismissed. O'Rourke, indignant at this foul deed, ever afterwards considered the author of this crime unpardonable. O'Rourke being about the same time deserted by Murrough and by his own mercenaries, was driven to Tueth, by whom he was received not only with kindness but with great and unheard of magnificence.

Tueth surrendered to his rule his towns and whole country, transferring to him the entire legal administration, and himself serving in the army as a captain under O'Rourke.

O'Rourke, having received this power, had two of MacSweeny's most intimate followers hanged, and when on account of so severe a punishment for a trivial offence, Tueth's friends remonstrated with him for having given all his authority to O'Rourke, 'Do not be surprised,' said Tueth, 'he is assuredly more worthy of a chieftaincy who knows how to execute justice, than I who, perhaps, should allow crimes to go unpunished.' The royalist army pursuing O'Rourke after he had been driven from his own country, turned the entire weight of the war against Tueth. This army was a large one, composed of some Englishmen but principally of Irishmen, who thought they would not be safe in disobeying the Queen when there appeared to be no means of resisting her. O'Rourke, worried and fretted by the loss of his possessions, went, against Tueth's wish and advice, to Scotland to hire Scots for the purpose of recovering his country. Here he was seized by James Stuart, King of Scotland, who afterwards became King of England also, and sent in chains to London, to Elizabeth Queen of England.

There he was brought before the Privy Council and asked by one of the Councillors, why he did not bend the knee, 'I am not accustomed to do so,' said he. 'But,' said the Councillor, 'do you not genuflect before images?' 'Certainly,' said he. 'Why then,' said the Councillor, 'not do the same now?' 'Because,' said he, 'between God and his saints, whose images I respect, and you, I have ever thought there was a great difference.' Shortly after he was put to death. When this became known, his son Brian was proclaimed O'Rourke, by the clansmen, and the war in Connaught being renewed, he endeavoured to recover this patrimony with the assistance of Tueth, in a successful campaign.

2. *recte* Gormlaith.

O'SULLIVAN'S VARIOUS ACTIONS AND ALMOST DAILY BATTLES DURING THE FIRST SEVEN DAYS OF HIS FLIGHT

Now let us see the fortunes and perils and trials which O'Sullivan[1] suffered in his flight from the hands of the enemy. He had to accomplish a long journey of about 100 leagues;[2] the winter weather was most unsuitable therefor. His soldiers little exceeded 400 in number, of whom thirteen were cavalry, the others infantry, pikemen, musketeers, and a few targets.[3] He had a large crowd of women and sutlers.[4] All the roads were beset with enemies, and a large sum of money was promised to whoever would slay him. Hence it came to pass that he endured almost incredible toils and faced tremendous risks. I will briefly relate these circumstances in their order.

On the 31st December, in the year of our Redeemer's birth, 1602, O'Sullivan set out from Glengariff, and at night pitched his tents twenty-six miles away in Muskerry country, at a place which the natives call Augeris.

On the next day, the 1st of January, 1603, starting off in the early morning, he reached, before midday, the populous village of Ballyvourney, dedicated to Saint Gobnata.

There the soldiers paid such vows as each one list,[5] gave vent to unaccustomed prayers, and made offerings, beseeching the saint for a happy journey. Advancing thence they were pursued by the sons of

1. Donall O'Sullivan-Beare (1560-1618), Philip O'Sullivan-Beare's uncle.
2. About 300 miles.
3. targeteers: foot-soldiers carrying shields.
4. camp-followers who sold provisions to the soldiers.
5. wished.

Thady MacCarthy with a band of natives, harassing their rear ranks with missiles, and again and again returning to the skirmish after being driven off by O'Sullivan's wings of marksmen. Four hours were spent in continual fighting of this kind, and some on both sides were wounded. At last O'Sullivan, by making an attack with his whole column and killing some, put the enemy to flight. Covering twenty-four miles in that day, he pitched his tents at nightfall in O'Keeffe's country. Sentinels being posted, the soldiers abandoned their way-worn limbs to rest, but the natives annoyed them throughout the whole night rather by yelling than hurting. Hunger also greatly weakened them, because they had had no food the whole day, the provisions which they had taken with them for only one day having been all consumed. On the following dawn O'Sullivan marched his men by the base of Slieve Lougher towards Limerick City. Not far from this road was an English garrison under Cuffe, who, with Viscount Barry's nephew, and a band of his dependents, occupied the ford of a river O'Sullivan had to cross. The ford was contested with red hot balls from both sides for about an hour, until Cuffe was forced to abandon the place. In this fight four of the Catholics fell; the royalists lost more, many were wounded, and perhaps more would have perished, although they were superior in numbers, were it not that the Catholics, through want and weariness, were unable to pursue them, The Catholics having buried their dead and in turns carrying the wounded in military litters,[6] accomplished a march of thirty miles that day, and on a stormy night pitched their camp in a desert place and vast solitude, near the woods of Aherlow, the guards being scarce able to keep awake through hunger, weariness, and fatigue. On the following day they refreshed themselves with cresses[7] and water and hastened along in a direct route before sunrise.

The inhabitants in the usual way pursued. The Gibbons, mercenaries of the White Knight, natives of Limerick City, and a few English superior in numbers, but very undisciplined, attacked, not in column, but in a mob. However, they charged boldly and fiercely in front, rear, and baggage, which was carried in the middle, attacking all at once. Both sides fought with guns. Such heavy showers of bullets rained on all sides that O'Sullivan could not, as usual, bury his dead or carry off his wounded. Such a cloud of smoke from gunpowder darkened the air that one party was often unable to see the other. After the contest had continued in this way for eight hours, O'Sullivan, reached at night Kilnamanagh, where fires were lit, for as soon as the fighting was over the cold of a very severe winter pinched. The soldiers, in whom want had produced starvation, fed on plants and roots and leaves of trees. As they proceeded on the following day, their rear ranks were engaged with the enemy's musketeers until they had reached Donohill fort, which the soldiers stormed for the sake of getting food. Whatever prepared food was there, the first who entered devoured right off. The rest set themselves to feed on meal, beans, and barley grains, like cattle. Carrying their packs, they covered about twenty miles, and halted in the village of Solloghod.

At this time Dermot, second son of O'Sullivan, aged two, was left in charge in unhappy Bear,[8] where he was secretly nursed for two years by some gentleman of rank, and afterwards sent into Spain. From thence, at break of day, they took the route to Slievefelim, where far larger forces sent by Ormond blocked the way. On learning this the Catholics were filled with terror, but as things were come to such a pass that the enemy could force them to fight against their wills, they resolved to attack the enemy first. When the enemy saw this they were stricken with greater fear and quitted the ground.

Hunger pinching them bitterly, Thomas Burke and Daniel O'Malley, by O'Sullivan's order, made a slight detour, with sixty men to look for booty and food.

These were suddenly attacked by the enemy, Daniel and twenty men killed, Thomas captured, and the rest routed, but saved by O'Sullivan coming to the rescue, and immediately he rescued Thomas flying from the enemy after having broken his bonds, his helmet on, but stripped of his sword, pike, and dagger. He halted in the village of Latteragh, and threw his men into a rather small church and its enclosure. There was in this village a fort from which he was annoyed the whole night

6. stretchers.
7. wild watercress and other edible plants.
8. i.e. the Bere peninsula in west Cork, home territory of the O'Sullivan-Beare family.

with firing and by sallies of the garrison. He withstood the attack from the fort and momentarily awaited with drawn sword, prepared muskets and couched[9] pikes a larger crowd of the enemy assembled not far from the camp; the men going on sentry and to sleep in turns.

It was now the 6th of January, when at dawn, a storm of red-hot balls blazed on O'Sullivan as he advanced. This was, indeed, a daily salutation with which the enemy honoured him; a farewell as they drew off at night; a greeting as they turned up in the morning.

Throughout the whole day his rear column was continually engaged in fight and some fell on both sides, nor was O'Sullivan's only disadvantage that with a few he had to meet many, but, in addition, he had to oppose, with wearied and wounded, fresh and staid enemies. The fighting was usually with missiles. Whenever O'Sullivan halted the enemy fled, when he advanced they quickly pursued. Night putting an end to the contest, O'Sullivan reached the village of Brosna.

9. held ready for attack.

JAMES USSHER
(1581-1656)

from:
A DISCOURSE OF THE RELIGION ANCIENTLY PROFESSED BY THE IRISH AND BRITISH (1631)

[Archbishop Ussher's *Discourse* on the ancient religions of Ireland and Britain had, as its ultimate goal, the proof that the Irish church was fundamentally different from that of Rome and that, therefore, protestantism was the 'true' religion of Ireland. But Ussher's scholarly method — the use of early documents — ensured that he remained more aloof from sectarian polemic than many of his contemporaries. He used the Irish annals and succession lists, as well as many documents of the early Irish church, to try and prove his case. In this passage, his many references to obscure sources have been omitted, but the general sense of scholarly detachment remains.]

This countrey was heretofore, for the number of holy men that lived in it, termed the *Iland of Saints*: of that innumerable companie of Saints, whose memorie was reverenced here; what one received anie solemne canonization from the *Pope*, before *Malachias* archbishop of *Ardmagh* and *Laurence* of *Dublin*? who lived as it were, but the otherday. We reade of sundry *Archbishops* that have beene in this land: betwixt the dayes of S. *Patrick* and of *Malachias*, what one of them can be named, that ever sought for *a Pall*[1] from *Rome*? *Ioceline* indeed a late Monke of the abbey of *Furnesse*, writeth of S. *Patrick*; that the Bishop of *Rome* conferred the *Pall* upon him, together with the execution of legatine[2] power in his roome. But he is well knowne to be a most fabulous author: and for this particular, *Bernard* (who was his ancient)[3] informeth us farre otherwise; that *from the very beginning until his time, the metropoliticall see of Ardmagh wanted the use of the Pall.* And therefore *Giraldus Cambrensis*, howsoever he acknowledgeth that S. *Patrick* did *choose Ardmagh for his seate and did appoint it to be as it were a metropoliticall see, and the proper place of the primacie of all Ireland*; yet doth he affirme withall, that in verie deed *there were no Archbishops in Ireland, but that Bishops onely did consecrate one another, untill Johannes Paparo the Popes legate brought foure palls thither*, in the yeare of our Lord 1152. *Gelasius* was then archbishop of *Ardmagh*, who dyed in the yeare 1174 at which, wee finde this note in our *Annales*. *This man is said to be the first Archbishop, because he used the first Pall. But others before him were called Archbishops and Primates in*

1. pall = pallium, the mantle or robe bestowed on a bishop by the pope. Hence the office of bishop bestowed by the pope.
2. i.e. authority to represent the pope.
3. standard-bearer or assistant.

name only; for the reverence and honour of S. Patrick, as the Apostle of that nation.

The same time that the foure Archbishopricks were established by *Iohannes Paparo*; our Bishopricks also were limited, & reduced unto a fewer number: where as at the beginning they were verie many (for we reade in *Nennius*,[4] that S. *Patrick* founded here 365 Churches, and ordayned 365 Bishops beside 3000 Presbyters) and in processe of time were daily *multiplied according to the pleasure of the Metropolitan, so farre that every Church almost had a severall Bishop*; whereof *Bernard* doth much complaine in the life of *Malachias*. For in erecting of new Bishopricks the Pope was no more sought unto here, then in the nomination and confirmation of the Bishops themselves: all matters of this kinde being done at home, without relation to anie forraine authoritie. The ancient forme of making a Bishop, is thus laid downe by *Bonifacius* archbishop of *Mentz*, in the life of *Livinus*. When *Menalchus the Archbishop was dead, Colomagnis the King of* Scotts, *and the troupe of his Officers with the under-courtiers, and the concourse of all that countrey, with the same affection of heart cryed out, that the holy Priest Livinus was most worthily to be advanced unto the honour of this order. The King (more devoute then all of them) consenting thereunto, three or foure times placed the blessed man in the chayre of the Archbishoprick with due honour, according to the will of the Lord.* In like manner also did King *Ecgfrid* cause our *Cuthbert* to be ordayned Bishop of the Church of *Lindisfarne*; and king *Pipin* granted the Bishoprick of *Salzburg* to our *Virgilius*: & Duke *Gunzo* would have conferred the Bishoprick of *Constance* upon our *Gallus*; but that hee refused it, and caused another upon his recommendation to be preferred thereunto.

As the Pope intermedled not with the making of our Bishops: so neyther can we finde by any approved record of antiquitie, that anie *Visitations* of the clergie were held here in his name; much lesse that any *Indulgences* were sought for by our people at his hands. For as for the *Charter* of S. *Patrick* (by some intituled, *De antiquitate Avalonica*) wherein *Phaganus* and *Deruvianus* are said to have purchased *ten* or *thirtie* yeares of Indulgences from Pope *Eleutherius*; and S. *Patrick* himselfe to have procured *twelve* yeares in his time from Pope *Celestinus*: it might easily be demonstrated (if this were a place for it) that it is a meere figment, devised by the Monkes of *Glastenbury*. Neyther doe I well know, what credite is to be given unto that stragling sentence, which I finde ascribed unto the same author (for I will still deale fairely, and conceale nothing that I meet withall in anie hidden part of antiquitie, that may tend to the true discoverie of the state of former times; whether it may seeme to make for me, or against me.) *If any questions doe arise in this Iland, let them be referred to the See Apostolick.* Onely this I will say, that as it is most likely, that S. *Patrick* had a speciall regard unto the Church of *Rome*, from whence he was sent for the conversion of this Iland: so if I my selfe had lived in his dayes, for the resolution of a doubtfull question I should as willingly have listened to the judgement of the Church of *Rome*, as to the determination of anie Church in the whole world; so reverend an estimation have I of the integritie of that Church, as it stood in those good dayes. But that S. *Patrick* was of opinion, that the Church of *Rome* was sure ever afterward to continue in that good estate, and that there was a perpetuall priviledge annexed unto that See, that it should never erre in judgement, or that the Popes sentences were alway to be held as infallible Oracles; that will I never beleeve: sure I am, that my countrey men after him were of a farre other beleefe; who were so farre from submitting themselves in this sort[5] to whatsoever should proceed from the See of *Rome*, that they oftentimes stood out against it, when they had little cause so to do. . . .

4. Nennius (*fl.* 796), a Welsh writer who wrote the *Historia Britonum*.

5. in this way.

CONALL MAC GEOGHEGAN

(*fl.* 1620-40)

from:
Translation of
THE ANNALS OF CLONMACNOISE (1627)

[This loose but vivid translation of *The Annals of Clonmacnoise* (the original of which is now lost) is one of the earliest translations from Irish into English. We have selected the dedicatory preface, which refers to the decline in the world of traditional learning in early seventeenth-century Ireland, and the entry for the year 996. This contains a description of the battle of Clontarf in 1014.]

To the worthy and of Great expectac̃on young gentlemen Mr. Terenc Coghlan his Brother Connell MaGeoghagan wisheth long health wth good success in all his affaires.

Among all the worthy & memorable Deeds of K. Bryan Borowe[1] sometime K. of his Kingdome, this is not of the least accoumpt, y[t] after he had shaken off the Intollarable Yoake & Bondage wherew[th] this land was cruelly tortured & harried by the Danes & Normans for the space of 219 yeares that they bore sway, & receaved tribute of the Inhabitants in Generall, & though they nor none of them euer had the name of K. or Monarch of the land yet they had that power as they executed what they pleased & behaued themselves soe cruell and pagan-like as well towards the eclesiasticall as Temporalls of the K. dome, that they broke downe theire churches and razed them to theire very foundations and burnt theire books of Cronicles & prayers to the end that there should be no memory left to theire posterityes & all Learninge should be quite forgotten, the said K. Bryan seeing into what rudenesse the kingdome was fallen, after settinge himselfe in the quite Governm[t] thereof, & restored each one to his auntient Patrimony, repayred theire Churches and houses of religion, he caused open schoole to be kept in the seuerall parrishes to Instruct theire youth, which by the s[d] Long warrs were growne rude and altogether illiterate, he assembled together all the nobility of the K.dome as well spirituall as temporall to Cashell in Mounster, & caused them to compose a booke contayning all the Inhabitants, euents and scepts that lived in this land from the first peopleing, Inhabitac̃on and Discouery thereof after the creac̃on of the world untill that present, which booke they caused to be called by the name of the psalter of Cashell,[2] signed it wth his owen hands together wth the hands of the K[s]. of the five provinces, & alsoe wth the hands of all the Bushops and prelates of the K.dome, caused seueral coppyes thereof to be given to the K[s] of the provinces, wth straight Charge, that there should be noe credit giuen to any other Chronicles thence-forth, but should be held as false, Disannulled & quite forbiden for ever. Since wch time there were many septs[3] in ye k.dome that liued by it, & whose profession was to Chronicle and keep in memory the state of the K.dome as well for the time past present & to come, & now because they cañot enjoy that respect & gaine by their said profession as heretofore they and theire auncestors receaved they set naught by the s[d] knowledg, neglect their Bookes, and choose rather to put their children to learne eng:[4] than their own native Language, in soe much that some of them suffer Taylors to cutt the leaves of the said Books (which their auncestors held in great accoumpt, & sliece them in long peeces to make theire measures off)[5] that the posterities are like to fall into meere Ignorance of any things hapened before theire tyme.

Ireland in ould time, in the raigne of the s[d] K. Bryan & before was well stored with learned men and colledges that people came from all partes of Christendome to learne therein, and among all other nations that came thither there was none soe much made of nor respected with the Irish as was the english & Welshmen, to whome they gave severall Collages to Dwell and Learne In, as to the englishmen a collage in the towne of Mayo in Coñaught, wch to this day is called Mayo of the

1. i.e. Brian Boru (*c.*941-1014), king of Ireland.

2. Ir. *Saltair Chaisil*, an old Irish chronicle in verse.
3. clans or tribes.
4. English.
5. i.e. to make tape-measures of.

english, & to the Welshmen the town of Gallen in the K^{s} County, wch is likewise called Gallen of the Welchmen or Wales, from whence these said twoo nations haue brought theire charactors, espetially the eng: saxons as by confering the old saxons Characters to the Irish (wch the Irish neuer change) you shall find little or no Difference at all.

The earnest Desire I understand you haue to know these things made me to undertake the translating of the ould Irish booke for you, wch by longe lying shutt & unused I could hardly read and left places, that I could not read because they were altogether growne illegible & put out; & if this my simple Labour shall any way pleasure you I shall hould myselfe thorough recompensed & my payne well Imployed, wch for your owene Reading I have done, & not for the reading of any other Curious fellow that would rather carp at my Phrace, then take any Delight in the History & In the meane time I bid you heartyly farewell. from Leyeuanchan the Twentyeth of Aprill Año Dñi 1627.

Y^{r} very Loveing Brother

CONELL MA GEOGHAGAN.

996.—Bryan Borowa[1] tooke the kingdome and government thereof out of the handes of king Moyleseachlin in such manner as I doe not Intend to Relate in this place. Hee was very well worthy of the place and government, and raigned 12 years, the most famous king for his time that ever was before or after him of the Irish nation for manhood, fortune, manners, laws, liberties, religion, and many other good partes, hee neuer had his peere amongst them all, though some chroniclers of the kingdome made comparisons between him and Conn Cedcahagh, Conairey more, and king Neale of the nine hostages.[2] Yett hee in regard of the state of the kingdome when hee came to the government thereof was judged to beare the bell away from[3] them all. At his first entry into the kingdom the whole realme was overrun and overspread by the Danes every where, the churches, abbyes, and other religious howses were by them quite Razed, and Debased, or otherwise turned to vile, base, servile, and abominable uses. Most of all, yea almost all the noblemen, gentlemen and those that were of any account were turned out of theire landes and liveings without any hopes of recovery or future redress; Yea some of the best sort were compelled to servitude and bounden slavery; both human lawe and Godes feare were set aside. In summe, it was strange how men of any fashion could use men as the Danes did use the Irish men at that time. King Bryan Borowa was a meet salve to cure such festred sores, all the phisick in the world could not cure it else, where in a small time he bannished the Danes, made up the churches and religious houses, restored the nobilityes to their auntient patrimonies and possessions, and in fine[4] brought all to a notable reformation. At lenth in the yeare of our Lord God 1007 the 22nd of march being good ffryday hee assembled together all his forces to give battle to the Danes at Clontarffe, and on the other side Brwader Earle of the Island of the Orcades called together and assembled all the Danes of Denmark out of all parts and kingdoms that owed them any service to that place as Generall and captain of the Danes, where there was a bloody battle between them fought at Clontarffe aforesaid. Brwader himself with his thousand men in shirtes of maile were slaine, the rest of his army were both slaine and drowned in the sea. Mulmurray m^{c}Murrogh m^{c}ffinn king of Leinster and m^{c}Brogaroann prince of Affaile[5] that partaked with the Danes with many Leinstermen about them were slaine alsoe in this battle, and of the other side king Bryan Borowa sonn of Kennedy m^{c}Lorckan then greatest monarch in these partes of Europe, then of the age of 88 years, his nephew Conyng m^{c}Don Cwan, prince Murrogh his son then of the age of 63 yeares, were killed, Terence the kings grand-child, then about the age of 15 yeares was found drowned neare the fishing wier of Clontarffe with both his hands fast bounde in the haire of a Danes head, whome he pursued to the sea at the time of the flight of the Danes, Mothlae m^{c}Donell m^{c}Foylan, prince of the Desies of Mounster, Eachy m^{c}Dawny, Neale o'Coyne, and Cowdaylye m^{c}Kennedy, 3 noblemen of the kings bed-chamber, Teig o'Kelly prince of Imanie, Moyleronye o'Hoynn prince of Ayny, Geveannagh m^{c}Dowagan king of Fearnmoy, m^{c}Beachy m^{c}Morreaye, Kloen, prince of Kerry Lawchra, Donnell m^{c}Dermott prince of Corka avaiskin, Scannlan m^{c}Cahall prince of Eonaght of Loghlyen, and Donnell m^{c}Evin

1. Brian Boru.
2. Three famous kings of Ireland in the prehistoric period.
3. i.e. be much the best of.
4. in short.
5. Offaly.

m^c^Caynich earle of Dombarr in Scottland, all which noblemen with many others were slaine in that battle, to the great greefe of the whole Realme. The o'Neales forsooke king Brian in this battle and soe did all Connaught except Ferall o'Roirch and o'Ferall. The Leinstermen did not onely forsake him but were the first that opposed themselves against him of the Danes side, onely o'Morey and o'Nolan excepted. Moyleseachlin that was late before king of Ireland (but at that time but king of Meath) all be it hee fought of his side, was his mortall enemie, and therefore for his evill will to king Brian, he was content rather to lose the field then win it.

Moyleseachlin, after king Bryan was thus slaine, succeeded againe king of Ireland and reigned 8 years, dureing which time hee fought 25 battles both great and small against his enemies, wherein he for the most part had the victory. Donnogh the son of king Bryan Borowe, went with an army to the west of Ireland, and there killed Cahall m^c^Donell and took hostages of Donell. Teige sonn of king Bryan, and his brother Donnogh, fell at debate and were against one another in the field where Donnogh had the worst, and Rory M^c^Donnagann prince of Arie, was slaine. Dowlenn m^c^Twahall king of Leinster died. Carbry m^c^Cahall, and Newman O'Seanchin, 2 anchorites, Died. O'Moyledorie prince of Tire Connell, and O'Royrck killed Donnell m^c^Cahall and destroyed all Connaught and tooke theire hostages. . . .

GEOFFREY KEATING

(*c.*1580-*c.*1650)

from: FORAS FEASA AR ÉIRINN (A Basis of Knowledge about Ireland) (*c.*1634)

[Geoffrey Keating undertook his *Foras Feasa ar Éirinn* (often referred to as his 'History of Ireland') to refute the calumnies that he considered had been perpetrated on Ireland by such 'historians' as Giraldus Cambrensis, Spenser, Stanihurst and Campion. In the preface to the work (part of which follows) he attacks these writers and in the third extract refutes, in detail, some of their 'facts'. In the second extract, Keating retells part of the Midas legend, and the fourth section shows the essentially topographical and local nature of much early Irish historiography. The translation is by David Comyn and P.S. Dinneen.]

[THE AUTHOR TO THE READER]

Whosoever proposes to trace and follow up the ancient history and origin of any country ought to determine on setting down plainly the method which reveals most clearly the truth of the state of the country, and the condition of the people who inhabit it: and forasmuch as I have undertaken to investigate the groundwork of Irish historical knowledge, I have thought at the outset of deploring some part of her affliction and of her unequal contest; especially the unfairness which continues to be practised on her inhabitants, alike the old foreigners[1] who are in possession more than four hundred years from the Norman invasion down, as well as the native Irish[2] who have had possession during almost three thousand years. For there is no historian of all those who have written on Ireland from that epoch that has not continuously sought to cast reproach and blame both on the old foreign settlers and on the native Irish.

Whereof the testimony given by Cambrensis, Spenser, Stanihurst, Hanmer, Camden, Barckly, Moryson, Davies, Campion,[3] and every other new foreigner[4] who has written on Ireland from that

1. *Sean-ghaill*: Keating refers to the first Norman invaders of Ireland in the twelfth century and their descendants. He distinguishes carefully between them and the *nua-ghaill*, the more recent English settlers and planters of the sixteenth and seventeenth centuries.
2. *Gaedhil*: the gael or native inhabitants of Ireland.
3. Writers in the list not included in this anthology are: Meredith Hanmer (1543-1604), author of a chronicle of Ireland; William Camden (1551-1621), author of *Brittania* (1586); John Barckly (1582-1621), Scottish satirist and poet; and Edmund Campion (1540-81), author of *A Historie of Ireland written in 1571.*
4. *Gall*: foreigner. Keating applies this word to Danes, French, Normans and English.

time, may bear witness; inasmuch as it is almost according to the fashion of the beetle they act, when writing concerning the Irish. For it is the fashion of the beetle, when it lifts its head in the summertime, to go about fluttering, and not to stoop towards any delicate flower that may be in the field, or any blossom in the garden, though they be all roses or lilies, but it keeps bustling about until it meets with dung of horse or cow, and proceeds to roll itself therein. Thus it is with the set above-named; they have displayed no inclination to treat of the virtues or good qualities of the nobles among the old foreigners and the native Irish who then dwelt in Ireland; such as to write on their valour and on their piety, on the number of abbeys they had founded, and what land and endowments for worship they had bestowed on them; on the privileges they had granted to the learned professors of Ireland, and all the reverence they manifested towards churchmen and prelates: on every immunity they secured for their sages, and the maintenance they provided for the poor and for orphans; on each donation they were wont to bestow on the learned and on petitioners, and on the extent of their hospitality to guests, insomuch that it cannot truthfully be said that there ever existed in Europe folk who surpassed them, in their own time, in generosity or in hospitality according to their ability. . . .

[THE LEGEND OF THE KING WITH HORSE'S EARS]

We read of Labhraidh Loingseach that his ears were like those of a horse; and hence he used to kill on the spot everyone who cut his hair, lest he or anyone else might be aware of this blemish. Now he was wont to have his hair cropped every year, that is, to have cut off the part of his hair that grew below his ears. It was necessary to cast lots to determine who should crop the king each year, since it was his wont to put to death everyone who cropped him. Now it happened that the lot fell on the only son of a widow who approached the close of her life, and who lived near the king's stronghold. And when she heard that the lot had fallen on her son, she came and besought the king not to put her only son to death, seeing he was her sole offspring. The king promised her that he would not put her son to death, provided he kept secret what he should see, and made it known to no one till death. And when the youth had cropped the king, the burden of that secret so oppressed his body that he was obliged to lie in the bed of sickness, and that no medicine availed him. When he had lain long in a wasting condition, a skilful druid came to visit him, and told his mother that the cause of his sickness was the burden of a secret, and that he would not be well till he revealed his secret to some thing; and he directed him, since he was bound not to tell his secret to a person, to go to a place where four roads met, and to turn to his right and to address the first tree he met, and to tell his secret to it. The first tree he met was a large willow, and he disclosed his secret to it. Thereupon the burden of pain that was on his body vanished; and he was healed instantly as he returned to his mother's house. Soon after this, however, it happened that Craiftine's harp got broken, and he went to seek the material for a harp, and came upon the very willow to which the widow's son had revealed the secret, and from it he took the material for his harp; and when the harp was made and set to tune, as Craiftine played upon it all who listened imagined that it sang, 'Dá ó phill ar Labhraidh Lorc,' that is, Labraidh Loingseach, meaning, 'Two horse's ears on Labhraidh Lorc'; and as often as he played on that harp, it was understood to sing the same thing. And when the king heard this story, he repented of having put so many people to death to conceal that deformity of his, and openly exhibited his ears to the household, and never afterwards concealed them. I think this part of the story is a romantic tale rather than history. This Labhraidh fell by Meilge son of Cobhthach Caol mBreagh.

Meilge Molbhthach son of Cobhthach Caol mBreagh, son of Ughaine Mór of the race of Eireamhon, held the sovereignty of Ireland seven years; and he fell by Mogh Corb son of Cobhthach Caomh.

Mogh Corb son of Cobhthach Caomh, son of Reachthaidh Ridhearg, son of Lughaidh Laighdhe, son of Eochaidh, son of Oilill Fionn, son of Art, son of Lugaidh Lamhdhearg, son of Eochaidh Uaircheas of the race of Eibhear, held the sovereignty of Ireland seven years. He was called Mogh Corb, because, as his son was one day in a chariot, a portion of the chariot got broken, and Mogh Corb repaired it, and through having done this service for his son whose name was Corb he was called Mogh Corb. He fell by Aonghus Ollamh.

[A REFUTATION OF CAMBRENSIS]

Cambrensis says, in his twenty-second chapter, that whenever the nobles of Ireland are making a compact with each other, in presence of a bishop, they kiss at that time a relic of some saint, and that they drink each other's blood, and at that same time they are ready to perpetrate any treachery on each other. My answer to him here [is], that there is not a lay nor a letter, of old record or of ancient text, chronicle or annals, supporting him in this lie: and, moreover, it is evident that it was obligatory on the antiquaries not to conceal the like of this evil custom, and even to put it in [their] manuscript on pain of losing their professorship, if it had been practised in Ireland. Wherefore it is clear that it is a lie Cambrensis has uttered here. Cambrensis says, in his tenth chapter, that the Irish are an inhospitable nation: here is what he says: — 'Moreover, this nation is an inhospitable nation' [says he]. However, I think Stanihurst sufficient in his history by way of reply to him in this matter; here is what he says, speaking of the generosity of the Irish: — 'Verily [he says], they are a most hospitable people; and there is no greater degree in which you may earn their gratitude, than freely, and of your own will, to make your resort to their houses.' Hence it may be inferred, without leave of Cambrensis, that they are hospitable people, [and] truly generous in regard to food....

Again, he says, in the twenty-fifth chapter of his narration concerning Ireland, that the king of *Cinéal Conaill*, i.e. O'Donnell, used to be inaugurated in this wise: an assembly being made of the people of his country on a high hill in his territory, a white mare being slain, and being put to boil in a large pot in the centre of the field, and, on her being boiled, he to drink up her broth like a hound or a beagle with his mouth, and to eat the flesh out of his hands without having a knife or any instrument for cutting it, and that he would divide the rest of the flesh among the assembly, and then bathe himself in the broth. It is manifest that this thing Cambrensis tells is false, according to the ancient record of Ireland, for it is thus it describes the mode in which O'Donnell was proclaimed, to wit, by his being seated in the midst of the nobles and of the council of his own territory; and a chief of the nobility of his district used to stand before him with a straight white wand in his hand, and on presenting it to the king of *Cinéal Conaill*, it is this he would say to him, to receive the headship of his own country, and to maintain right and equity between each division of his country: and, wherefore the wand was appointed to be straight and white, was to remind him that so ought he to be just in his administration, and pure and upright in his actions. I marvel at Cambrensis reporting this lie, and I conceive that it was through malice he inserted it in his work. For it is well known that they have been at all times devout and religious people; and that many of them forsook the world, and finished their lives under religious rule, and, moreover, that from them came many saints, such as Columcille, Baoithin, Adhamnan, and many other saints whom we shall not mention here. Besides, it is not credible that the nobility of Ireland would permit the king of *Cinéal Conaill* to have in use that barbarous custom which Cambrensis mentions, seeing that the Catholic religion has lived among them from the time of Patrick to the Norman invasion, and, accordingly, I consider that it is a malicious unwarranted lie Cambrensis has uttered here.

[THE TALE OF THE 'ROAD OF THE DISHES']

The seventh year of the reign of this Diarmaid, king of Ireland, a nun named Sineach Chro came to Diarmaid to make a complaint to him against Guaire, son of Colman, for having taken her only cow from her. Diarmaid assembled a numerous host with the object of obtaining satisfaction from Guaire for the nun's cow, and he at once marched to the Sionainn.[1] Now Guaire had assembled a host and multitude on the other side to oppose him, and he sent Cuimin Foda, son of Fiachna, to ask Diarmaid not to go westward beyond the Sionainn for the space of twenty-four hours. 'That is not a great request to grant thee,' said Diarmaid, 'and a greater would be granted thee had'st thou asked it.' Now they were on either side of the Sionainn, King Diarmaid on the east side and Guaire on the west side until the following morning. 'I wonder,' said Cuimin, 'at the smallness of this host of thine seeing how great the host is which is against thee.' 'Understand, O cleric,' said Diarmaid 'that a battle is not won by large armies, but according to God's will; and if thou contemnest my host, know that it is not

1. The river Shannon.

fair forms but stout hearts that win battles.'

The battle was set on foot between them, the king and his host on one side and Guaire, with the Connaught and Munster forces, on the other. But Guaire and his host were defeated, and many Connaught nobles and Munstermen were slain. And it was at the intercession of Caimin, who lived and blessed in Inis Cealltrach, that the battle went against Guaire; for Caimin fasted three days against Guaire in order that he might lose the battle. This St. Caimin is of the race of Fiachaidh Aiceadha, son of Cathaoir Mor. Now Guaire went to Caimin and paid him respect and homage and bowed down before him. 'There is no avoiding defeat in battle for thee,' said Caimin.

Now when Guaire had lost the battle he came alone to a little monastery, in which there was a solitary pious woman, and the woman asked who he was. 'I am a favourite with Guaire,' said he. 'I am very sorry,' said she, 'that defeat should have overtaken this king, who is the most charitable and humane and hospitable in Ireland, and that his followers should be visited with dreadful slaughter.' The pious woman went to a stream hard by and saw a salmon therein. She came back to Guaire with this news. Guaire went out to the stream and killed the salmon, and gave God thanks for having only the salmon that night, though he had often ten beeves[2] other nights. Guaire went the next day to meet his friends, and took counsel of them as to whether he should give battle again to the king of Ireland or swear submission to him on a javelin's point. What Guaire and his friends resolved on was that he should go to Diarmaid and make his submission to him. Now the way in which he made his submission to him was to put the point of the king's javelin or sword in his mouth, between his teeth, while on bended knees. And while Guaire was in this position the king said secretly to some of his own people: 'We will find out,' said he, 'whether it was through vain glory that Guaire practised such great generosity.' He caused a druid from among his friends to ask him for something for the sake of science, but Guaire did not heed him. He sent a leper to ask him for an alms for God's sake; he gave the poor man the gold bodkin that held his mantle. The poor man left him; and one of king Diarmaid's people met him and took the gold bodkin from him and gave it to Diarmaid. The poor man again came back to Guaire and complained of this to him, and Guaire gave him the gold belt that was round him, and Diarmaid's people took the belt also from the poor man; and he came again to Guaire, who had the point of Diarmaid's sword between his teeth, and, as Guaire beheld the poor man troubled, a flood of tears came from him. 'O, Guaire,' said the king, 'is it distress at being under my sway that makes thee thus weep?' 'I solemnly declare that it is not,' said he, 'but my distress at God's poor one being in want.' Thereupon Diarmaid told him to arise and that he would not be thenceforth under his own authority, and that the King of all the elements was over him if he were to make a submission, and that he considered that sufficient on his part. They made a treaty of peace with one another, and Diarmaid asked him to come to the fair of Taillte, into the presence of the men of Ireland; 'and,' added he, 'I will give thee my lordship to be thine from my death onwards.'

Guaire then went to the fair of Taillte, having with him a budget or bag of silver to dispense to the men of Ireland. Now Diarmaid charged the men of Ireland that none of them should ask anything of Guaire at the fair. Two days passed in this manner; on the third day, however, Guaire asked Diarmaid to send for a bishop for him that he might make his confession and be anointed. 'How is that?' enquired Diarmaid. 'As I am near death,' said Guaire. 'How dost thou know that?' asked Diarmaid. 'I know it,' said Guaire, 'for the men of Ireland are assembled and none of them asks me for anything.' Then Diarmaid gave Guaire leave to make gifts. Guaire proceeded to make gifts to everyone, and, if the tale be true, the hand with which he made gifts to the poor was longer than that with which he made gifts to the bards. Then Diarmaid made peace and agreement with Guaire in presence of the men of Ireland, and they were thenceforth on friendly terms with each other.

Now Guaire had a brother called Mochua, a holy virtuous man, and on a certain occasion he went to observe Lent to a well of spring water, which is a little to the south-west of Buirenn,[3] five miles from Durlus Guaire, attended only by one young cleric, who used to serve him at Mass, and neither himself nor the young cleric took more than a meal every day-and-night, and then they took only a little barley bread and spring water. And when Easter

2. carcasses of beef.

3. The Burren, Co. Clare.

day had come, and Mochua had said Mass a desire for meat seized the young cleric, and he said to St. Mochua that he would go to Durlus to visit Guaire in order to get enough of meat. 'Do not go,' said Mochua, 'stay with me, and let me pray to God for meat for thee.' And on this he knelt on the ground and prayed with fervour to God, asking for meat for the young cleric. At the same time while food was being served to the tables of Guaire's house, it came to pass through Mochua's prayer that the dishes and the meat they contained were snatched from the hands of those who were serving them and were carried out over the walls of the dwelling, and by direct route reached the desert in which Mochua was; and Guaire went with all his household on horseback in quest of the dishes; and when the dishes came into the presence of Mochua he set to praise and magnify the name of God, and told the young cleric to eat his fill of meat.

The latter thereupon looked up and saw the plain full of mounted men, and said that it was of no advantage to him to get the meat, seeing how many there were in pursuit of it. 'Thou needest not fear,' said Mochua, 'these are my brother and his household, and I beseech God to permit none of them to advance beyond that point until thou hast had thy fill.' And on this the horses' hoofs clung to the ground so that they could not go forward till the young cleric had had his fill. Then Mochua prayed God to set his brother and his household free. On this they were set free, and they came into Mochua's presence. Guaire knelt before St. Mochua and asked his forgiveness. 'Thou needest not fear, brother; but eat ye your meal here.' And when Guaire and his people had taken their meal they bade farewell to Mochua and returned to Durlus. It is a proof of the truth of this story that the Road of the Dishes is the name given to the five miles' path that lies between Durlus and the well at which Mochua then was.

MÍCHEÁL Ó CLÉIRIGH
(1575-1643)
and others

from: ANNÁLA RÍOGHACHTA ÉIREANN (The Annals of the Kingdom of Ireland, or The Annals of the Four Masters) (*c.*1636)

[In the early seventeenth century, Irish scholars exiled to Europe — particularly the Franciscans in Louvain — recognized that, if the history of Ireland and her saints was to be written, there was much material to be collected in Ireland itself. In the 1620s, Mícheál Ó Cléirigh, originally from County Donegal but by now a young Franciscan at Louvain, was sent back to Ireland to collect manuscript material for the lives of the Irish saints. His work developed and, with three principal assistants — all master historians like Ó Cléirigh — he compiled the *Annála Ríoghachta Éireann* ('The Annals of the Kingdom of Ireland' or 'The Annals of the Four Masters', after the four chief compilers). Like all annals, these are primarily a plain chronicle of facts and dates, as the extracts below confirm. From a historical point of view, however, *The Annals* are still of considerable importance. They help scholars to unravel the complex history of pre-Norman Ireland and constitute a unique synthesis of material from many disparate sources, many of which are now lost. Only in the latter years covered by *The Annals* do they contain any extended narrative. The translation is by John O'Donovan (1849).]

The Age of Christ, 915. The first year of Niall Glundubh, son of Aedh Finnliath, over Ireland in sovereignty. Maelgiric, Abbot of Cill-achaidh, died. The fair of Tailltin was renewed by Niall. Sitric, grandson of Imhar, with his fleet, took up at Ceann-fuait, in the east of Leinster. Raghnall, grandson of Imhar, with another fleet, went to the foreigners of Loch Dachaech.[1] A slaughter was

1. Danes.

made of the foreigners by the Munstermen. Another slaughter was made of the foreigners by the Eoghanachta, and by the Ciarraighi. The army of the Ui-Neill of the South and North was led by Niall, son of Aedh, King of Ireland, to the men of Munster, to wage war with the foreigners. He pitched his camp at Tobar-Glethrach, in Magh-Feimhin, on the 22nd of August. The foreigners went into the territory on the same day. The Irish attacked them the third hour before mid-day, so that one thousand one hundred men were slain between them; but more of the foreigners fell, and they were defeated. There fell here in the heat of the conflict the chief of Carraig-Brachaidhe, and Maelfinnen, son of Donnagan, chief of Ui-Cearnaigh; Fearghal, son of Muirigen, chief of Ui-Creamhthainn; and others besides them. Reinforcements set out from the fortress of the foreigners to relieve their people. The Irish returned back to their camp before [the arrival of] the last host, i.e. before [the arrival of] Raghnall, king of the black foreigners, who had an army of foreigners with him. Niall set out with a small force against the foreigners, so that God prevented their slaughter through him. Niall after this remained twenty nights encamped against the foreigners. He requested of the Leinstermen to remain in siege against the foreigners. [This they did, and continued the siege] until Sitric, the grandson of Imhar, and the foreigners, gave the battle of Ceannfuait to the Leinstermen, wherein six hundred were slain about the lords of Leinster, together with the king of Ugaire, son of Ailell. These are the names of some of their chiefs: Maelmordha, son of Muireagan, lord of Airther Life; Mughron, son of Cinneidigh, lord of the three Comainns and of Laighis; Cinaedh, son of Tuathal, lord of Ui-Feineachlais; and many other chieftains, with the archbishop Maelmaedhog, son of Diarmaid, who was one of the Ui-Conannla, Abbot of Gleann-Uisean, a distinguished scribe, anchorite, and an adept in the Latin learning and the Scotic language.[2] It was concerning the battle of Ceann-Fuaid the following lines were composed:

The expedition of the Leinstermen of many
 youths, upon a very fine road, royal the
  march;
Scarcely heard they the [sound of] the road;
 they received death at Ceann-Fuaid.
The chiefs of Liphe of broad deeds waged a
 battle with a sacred shrine.
There were cut off five hundred heads in the
 valley over Tigh-Moling.
Great its renown in every thing, rightly indeed,
 for celebrated is the spot,
Over the plain with thousands of hundreds,
 Leinster sends its troops of youths.

The plundering of Cill-dara by the foreigners of Ceann-Fuaid. Maelruanaidh, son of Niall, Tanist of the Deisi, was slain by Cormac, son of Mothla, lord of the Deisi. Culothair, son of Matudhan, chief of Ui-Ceallaigh-Cualann, [died]....

The Age of Christ, 1115. Diarmaid Ua Briain, King of Munster, was taken prisoner by Muircheartach Ua Briain; and Muircheartach Ua Briain assumed his kingdom again, and set out with an army into Leinster and Breagha. Muircheartach Ua Ciarmhaic, lord of Aine; Domhnall Ua Conchobhair Ciarraighe; Murchadh Ua Flainn; the son of Flannchadha, lord of Muscraighe, were slain. The Daimhliag [great stone church] of Ard-Breacain, with its full of people, was burned by the men of Munster, and also many other churches in [the country of the] Feara-Breagh. A great predatory excursion was made by Toirdhealbhach Ua Conchobhair and the Connaughtmen; and they plundered Thomond as far as Luimneach, and carried off countless spoils and many prisoners. A battle was gained by Domhnall Ua Briain and the foreigners of Ath-cliath over the Leinstermen, wherein fell Donnchadh Ua Mael-na-mbo, lord of Ui-Ceinnsealaigh, and Conchobhair Ua Conchobhair, lord of Ui-Failghe, with his sons, and many others besides them. Domhnall Ua Briain, i.e. the son of Tadhg, royal heir of Munster, was killed by the Connaughtmen. An onset was made at Ath-bo by the sons of Maeleachlainn, son of Aedh, son of Ruaidhri, upon Toirdhealbhach Ua Conchobhair, King of Connaught; and they wounded him, so that he was lying in the agonies of death. Maelruanaidh Ua Ciardha, lord of Cairbre, [died]. Maelseachlainn Ua Maeleachlainn, royal heir of Teamhair, was killed. Boisterous weather, frost, and snow, from the fifteenth of the Calends of January to the fifteenth of the Calends of March, or longer, which caused great destruction of cattle, birds, and men; whence grew a great dearth

2. i.e. the Irish language. The statement reflects the traditional belief that the Gaels were from Scythia in Asia Minor.

throughout all Ireland, and in Leinster particularly. A fleet was brought by Toirdhealbhach Ua Conchobhair, King of Connaught; and he plundered Domhnall, son of Cusleibhe Ua Fearghail, and Murchadh Ua Maeleachlainn came into his house; and he fortified Buidhi-an-bheithe. He made an offering of three jewels to St. Ciaran, i.e. a drinking-horn with gold, a cup with gold, and a mullog[3] of copper with gold. He afterwards divided Meath between the two sons of Domhnall Ua Maeleachlainn, [namely, Maelseachlainn and Murchadh], but Maelseachlainn fell by Murchadh immediately after....

3. A small vessel.

JOHN COLGAN

(*c.*1592-1658)

from: ACTA SANCTORUM ... HIBERNIAE.... (The Deeds of the Saints of Ireland) (1645)

[John Colgan's *Acta Sanctorum ... Hiberniae* contains the lives of Irish and Scottish saints whose feast-days are celebrated in January, February and March. It was intended to be merely the first volume of a series, but Colgan's work on lives of the major saints, Patrick, Brigid and Columba, preoccupied him. The *Acta Sanctorum*, even though it is incomplete, is an immensely valuable source of material on the early Irish church as well as on medieval saints. We have selected the entry on St Muranus but have omitted the discursive notes. The translation is by Andrew Smith of University College, Dublin.]

CONCERNING SAINT MURUS OR MURANUS

In the northern territory of Ulster on the isthmus or peninsula commonly called Inishowen, after the beginning of the seventh century, there flourished a holy man known by the name of Murus or Muranus, descended from a most noble family. He far excelled by the fame of his virtue the splendour of his family. And granting that, this man is held among the most esteemed of the saints of his province so that his cult flourishes there, ever fresh, and his feast is celebrated up to our own day. Nevertheless, because we have not yet seen the account of his life — which certainly once existed — I thought I would produce in the following few notes some things which it occurs to me should be recorded about him.

He was born into the most distinguished family of the O'Neills. His father was Feradach, the son of Ronan: Ronan's father was Eoghan — not that Eoghan who was the founder of the family, but his grandson, by his son Muireadach, and called by the surname Merchrom to distinguish him. However the mother of Saint Muranus was called Dairine and was from a family of the first rank; but she was more renowned because of the happy and blessed fecundity of her womb. Indeed this happy woman produced six children, all of whom were delivered into God's service and honoured by the veneration of the heavenly host and by the worship of posterity — although they were not all born from the same marriage. The names of these sons are Saint Muranus abbot of Fothad, Saint Mochumma abbot of Drumbo, Co. Down, Saint Killian of Aghakeel, Co. Down, Saint Domongart, son of Eochaidh, Saint Ailbhe [?] and Saint Aidan.

And if indeed the lack of ancient relics (because of the disturbances of time) has deprived us of the knowledge of the schooling and of the other deeds of Saint Muranus, nevertheless it is agreed that the abbot did exist and ruled a community of monks in the monastery of Fothad, in the diocese of Derry, five miles to the west of the see and city of Derry. That monastery was richly endowed with many fields and estates and was held in great reverence for many centuries both because of the respect shown to the saintly Muranus (to whom, as patron saint of the place, a basilica was dedicated), and also because of the splendid relics of antiquity which were preserved there until the arrival of the mad heretics who desecrated, demolished and plundered everything sacred. But thereafter that long-famous and noble monastery was laid waste and destroyed by the passage of time and the carelessness of those in charge. It was afterwards devastated and demolished and ended by being a parish church.

Among the other relics which were preserved in that monastery there was a book which Saint Muranus had written in a metre in his native language about the deeds of Saint Columba Cille. Fragments of this work survive today and are often cited in other accounts of the same saint; and there was another large, very old manuscript consisting of chronicles and of other histories of the whole country which was always held in great esteem by students of antiquity and greatly valued.

Until modern times, there also existed various relics of Saint Muranus and of other saints from the same area; but these have been removed from that place because of the fanaticism of the heretics and are still preserved, though their whereabouts are unknown to me who am today at a great distance — in fact, working in Belgium — though once I had considerable knowledge of that place. And there survives today and is preserved as a precious treasure, the pastoral staff or shepherd's crook of this holy man (which is commonly called Bachull-Mura or the staff of Muranus); it is covered and adorned with jewels and a layer of gilt. By this, many miracles occur. Pious people and nobles, particularly those sprung from the O'Neill clan, have grown accustomed to swearing by this staff (as if it were able to punish false swearing and clearly indicate virtue) whenever they want to remove any ambiguity from their statements or to settle any legal matter on sacred oath.

Also there was in existence, before these troubled times, the saint's own office, a fragment of which we have once seen, which contains accounts of many of his virtues and miracles. But because this fragment does not itself survive in my hands, nor any other relics from which we can make an account of his miracles or his deeds, let it suffice to note that Saint Muranus became the patron saint of the O'Neill clan from which he had traced his ancestry and that in the church of Fothad in the region of Inishowen, his feast is celebrated as the patron of that place on this very day, the twelfth of March.

LUKE WADDING

(1588-1657)

from: ANNALES ORDINIS MINORUM. . . . (Annals of the Friars Minors or Franciscans) (1625-54)

[Luke Wadding was not only the most influential Irish churchman on the Continent in the seventeenth century but also the most productive Irish scholar of the age. He undertook many scholarly projects, including the eight-volume history of the Franciscan order (of which he was a member) and a sixteen-volume edition of the works of Johannes Duns Scotus.

This entry from his history of the Franciscans refers to Wadding's older contemporary, Florence Conry, the founder of St Anthony's College, Louvain and titular archbishop of Tuam, whose death in 1629 came during the publication of *Annales Ordinis Minorum*. The entry follows the typical pattern of the age: some biographical facts are followed by a full bibliography and the whole is copiously noted and annotated. The translation is by Andrew Smith of University College, Dublin.]

FLORENCE CONRY

Florence Conry, an Irishman, a man of Connaught, Minister of the Irish province, founded at Louvain the College of Saint Anthony of Padua for the Irish brothers of strict observance. He was sent to Ireland by Pope Clement VIII to be at hand to give advice to the army which had been sent by the catholic king Philip II to help the catholics. Next, he was Archbishop of Tuam, and outlawed by the English.

He was exiled from his country first in Belgium and then in Spain, where I got to know him when he was staying in Madrid; there he was given help by a Spaniard. During this long exile, he devoted himself entirely to elucidating the works of Saint Augustine and with immense effort he attained an understanding of the most holy Doctor on the necessity and efficacy of grace. He read the whole mass of Augustine's works seven times, and he examined twenty times whatever Augustine had written on the controversy with Pelagius and other heretics about grace. When a passage gave him great difficulty or the words were particularly obscure, he applied prayer and fasting — this sometimes for several days — until he thought he had attained the real meaning. And so he wrote, in this way, most seriously and learnedly, always keeping to the meaning and words of Augustine.

'A Complete Volume on the Grace of Christ'; he wrote this intending it to be published whenever permission should be granted, on the removal by the Holy See of the prohibition on books on this subject; nevertheless, it did appear in Paris in 1646, long after his death.

'A compendium of the doctrine of Saint Augustine about grace'; this was composed by him in four parts.

'A treatise on the state of small children departing this life without baptism according to the opinion of Blessed Augustine', first printed in Louvain in 1624 and secondly by Henry Master in the same place in 1635; thirdly at Rouen in 1643. Dedicated to Gabriel, Cardinal of Trejo, eulogized by the praise of almost all learned men of the academies of Louvain and Douai.

A second book 'Concerning the Scourges of the Just, following the thought of this same Saintly Doctor,' which he himself cites at the beginning of the preceding treatise, which, as yet, I have not seen.

The third book, 'Concerning the miserable state of fallen nature, concerning the wounds inflicted by sin, concerning the necessity of a remedy and the remedy found in Christ.' The theme of this work is provided by the parable of the man who went down from Jerusalem to Jericho and fell into the hands of thieves who plundered him and inflicted wounds on him. Therefore he called the book 'A Pilgrim at Jericho'. Printed in Paris, 1644.

The fourth book, 'Concerning the opinion of Augustine about the Conception of the Blessed Virgin Mary,' to Anthony of Trejo, former Vicar-General of the Order of Friars Minor, Bishop of Carthage, spokesman of Philip II, king of Spain to Paul V, to deal with this dispute; printed by John Keeberg at Antwerp, 1619.

'The Mirror of a Christian Life', also called 'Desiderius — Ardent Desire' for the instruction of catholic Irishmen, exceedingly suitable; published at the College of the Friars Minor at Louvain, in Irish, 1626.

'An extended letter against those men who proposed in the Irish Parliament an act to confiscate the property of certain prominent catholics who had fought for the catholic faith against the heretical English'; Philip O'Sullivan [Beare] wrote this down in his Compendium of the History of Ireland, part four, book 12, chapter 9.

JAMES WARE

(1594-1666)

from: DE HIBERNIA ET ANTIQUITATIBUS EJUS ... DISQUISITIONES .... (Inquiries concerning Ireland and its antiquities, tr. Robert Ware, 1705) (1654)

[James Ware dedicated his life to the scholarly study of Irish history and antiquities; linking a recognition of the importance of ancient Irish manuscripts to knowledge of many other sources, he achieved the first objective view of the Irish secular past. The selected passage comes from his *De Hibernia et Antiquitatibus ejus . . . Disquisitiones . . . .* (1654) as translated by his son Robert Ware and published in 1705. In his interpretation of the Irish annals, Ware was assisted by members of the Irish learned classes including An Dualtach Mac Fhirbhisigh, the famous hereditary scholar and scribe.]

Of Cormac *Son of* Culinan, *who was both* King *and* Bishop *of* Cashel; *where by the way of others who were at the same time both Kings and Bishops*, or *Priests, and of the strange Tonsure introduced by* Æd *Called* Clericus Barbosus, *or the* Bearded Priest.

Historians do often make mention of some Kings who resigning their Kingdoms, became Monks or Bishops, So in *Ireland*, *Cormac* King of *Leinster*, resigning his Kingdom betook himself to a Monastick life in the Abby of *Banchor* under St. *Congallus*. So *Aid* the Black King likewise of *Leinster*, of a King was made Monk, Abbot and Bishop of *Killdare*, says *Jo. Colgan*,[1] and dyed on the Tenth of *May*, In the year of our Lord *DCXXVIII*. And so (to omit several others) in *England*, *Sigibert* King of the *East-Saxons*, resigning his Kingdom by the perswasion of *Fursius* an *Irish* man, became a Monk in the Abby of *Cnobersburg*, now called *Burgh-Castle* in *Suffolk*. But *Cormac* Son of *Culinan*, of whom we now speak, was at the same time both King and Bishop of *Cashel*, he derived himself (as we have elsewhere said) from *Engusa Nafrach* the first Son of the Kings of *Cashel* who embraced the Christian Faith. *Cormac* began his Reign in the year of our Lord 901. And (which may seem strange) exercised at the same time the Function of a Bishop. Historians do plainly shew that it was the custom of those times in *Ireland*, particularly among the Predecessors of *Cormac*. *Olchobar* who dyed in the year 851, And *Cenfelad* who dyed in 872, Were both Kings of *Cashel* and Bishops of *Emly*. Yet not without example; For among the *Jews*, *Jonathan*, *Simon* and *John Hircanus*, were both Rulers of the People and High-Priests; And those also among them who were Kings were at the same time High-Priests, as *Aristobulus, Alexander, Jannæus* others, among the heathens. Likewise we find that the *Roman* Emperors were sometimes High-Priests, and among their Kings, *Anius* was King of *Delos*, of whom *Virgil*,

> *Rex Anius, Rex idem hominum, Phœbique sacerdos.*[2]

And *Ovid*.

> *Hunc Anius, quo Rege homines, Antiste Phœbus*
> *Rite colebatur, temploque domoque recepit,*[3]

Likewise *Mercurius Trismegistus*, or *ter-maximus*, that is, *Thrice great* (if we may believe *Alexander ab Alexandro*) *had his Name from hence, that he was a great Philosopher, a great Priest, and a great King*. Of this, see *Plato*, *in Polit*.[4] But to our purpose *Caradocus Lhancarvanensis* mentions this *Cormac* in his Chronicle of *Wales*, but he, or whoever Publish'd him in *English*, mistakes and calls him *Carmot, Son of Cukeman, King and Bishop of Ireland*. In the year 906, *Flan* Son of *Melsechlin*, King of *Ireland*, with a great Army Invaded *Munster*, and destroyed it as far as *Limerick*, but *Cormac* who then fled, highly resented the injury,

1. John Colgan.

2. Virgil, *Aeneid*, Book III, 80: 'King Anius, who was both king of men and priest of Phoebus.'
3. Ovid, *Metamoirphoses*, Book XII, 632-33: 'Anius welcomed him [Aeneas] into his temple and home, Anius under whom, as king, men were reverenced and under whom, as priest, Phoebus was duly worshipped.'
4. Plato, *Philebus*, 18 (b); see also Plato, *Phaedrus*, 274 (c)-(d).

the year following entred *Meath* with an Army, overthrew *Flan* in Battle, had Pledges from him for the performance of Articles, and so return'd to *Cashel*: But in the year 908 *Flan* to revenge his loss, Confederates with the Kings of *Leinster* and *Conaght*, and with united Forces again Invades *Munster*. They came to a Battle in a place called *Moy-albe* on the XVI. of *August*; the Dispute was long and Bloody, but *Flan* at last had the Victory, and *Cormac* was there slain. There were also at the same time killed most of the Chief Leaders or Princes, among whom are reckon'd *Fogertach* of *Kerry*, and *Kellach* of *Ossory*. Thus the *Irish* Annals. But *Caradocus Lhancarvanensis* says that *Cormac* was at this time kill'd by the *Danes*. I remember likewise that I have Read in a certain MS. of *Cotton's* Library,[5] that he was kill'd by a Herdsman at *Beanree* near *Leghlin*, while he was on his knees at Prayers for the success of his Army then ingag'd. So Different are the opinions of his Death. His Body was convey'd to *Cashel*, and there Buried. He was a man learned and very knowing in the *Irish* Antiquities, and writ in his own Language the History commonly call'd *Psalter-Cashel*,[6] which is yet extent,[7] and in great esteem. I have some collections out of the said History in an antient Parchment Book call'd *Psalter-Narran*,[8] written above 300 years since, as appears by the antiquity of the Character.[9] In the same Book are many miscellanies, part *Irish* and part *Latin*, collected by *Oengusa Celide*, among which we have a bare Catalogue (*viz.* only the Names) of the Kings of Ireland, from *Heremon* to *Brien* Son of *Cined*, Sir-named *Boro*, of whom before, chap. 4. It is here to be observed, that *Cashel* was heretofore the chief Seat of the Kings of *Munster*, and one of the first Synods of *Ireland* was there held by S. *Patrick*, S. *Albeus*, and S. *Declan*, in the time of King *Engusa*, of whom before.

We may here add the Strange kind of Tonsure introduced by *Æd*, an *Irish* Man (from his long Beard commonly called *Æd the Bearded Priest*) had gain'd a great opinion for his Learning and Sanctity; but in the year 1053, or 1054, he was banish'd, because *in his School, where he had a great Number of Clerks, Maids and Laicks*,[10] *he would introduce a custom of shaving the Maids after the manner of the Clerks*, as appears out of *Marianus Scotus* and *Florence* of *Worcester*. Here I had thoughts of describing the various kinds of Tonsures used among the antient, both Clerks (or secular Priests) and Monks, and the original of them; for some shaved their heads in the form of our Saviours crown of thorns, others only on the fore-part of the head with a round Tonsure, but an imperfect Circle drawn from ear to ear, others with a little Circle on the Crown of the head, others almost about the whole head, leaving only a few hairs below in form of a Crown. But having observ'd that all these and many other things of like nature have been already deliver'd by the most learned later Arch-Bishop of *Armagh*[11] in his Antiquities of the *British* Churches, and by *Prosperus Stellartius* in his Book *de Coronis & Tonsuris Paganorum*, &c. I thought this enough for me, and refer the Reader to those Authors for further satisfaction.

5. The magnificent library of Sir Robert Cotton (1571-1631), often consulted by antiquaries during the seventeenth century. It later formed the basis of the British Library collection.
6. Ir. *Saltair Chaisil*, a verse chronicle concerning old Irish history.
7. i.e. extant.
8. Ir. *Saltair na Rann*, a verse version of biblical stories in Irish.
9. handwriting.

10. laymen.
11. James Ussher.

JOHN LYNCH

(*c.*1599-*c.*1673)

from: CAMBRENSIS EVERSUS. . . . (Or refutation of the authority of Giraldus Cambrensis on the History of Ireland. . . .) (1662)

[John Lynch's refutation of Giraldus Cambrensis is one of the most famous works of Irish historiography. It is a sustained attack on Giraldus's veracity and accuracy, and Lynch cites many interesting sources to discredit his opponent. The translator of Lynch's Latin text was the Rev. Matthew Kelly and the translation appeared in 1848-52.]

. . . . But he[1] states many things regarding our very remote history, which he could neither see with his eyes, nor learn from others, nor sanction even with the poor authority of his favorite popular reports. The gossipings of sailors, or the vague stories of the common soldiers, to which he was ever ready to give so willing an ear, could supply him with no glimpse of those facts which he has recorded regarding our ancient history. 'But, alas!' he cries, 'they had been,' before his own day 'either utterly unexplored, or known only to a few. For the Irish world, though not a perfectly maiden subject before him, was never before fully exhibited to the world.' Nay, 'in the two first parts of the Topography, he got no light whatsoever from Irish books, none from external aid, nothing but his own searching and diligent inquiry.' The two first parts of the Topography were, therefore, a compound of his own reveries and inquiries: the third was taken from the public records, of which he gives us the following account. 'In the third part alone,' he says, 'there are some sketches of the inhabitants of the isle, and the origin of the tribes, which I took from their chronicles. But as they were too diffuse and disorderly, and generally too frivolous and redundant, and thrown together in a rude and indigested way, it cost me a world of labor to select the more interesting parts, culling them like pearls from sea sand, and arranging them in the most lucid and compendious form in my present volume.' A moment ago he complained of the paucity of Irish writers and the poverty of Irish chronicles, whose vague and undefiled outlines had never been filled up until his master-hand moulded and colored them into a living picture. But now he complains that he is literally overwhelmed by the mass and variety of Irish materials; his great difficulty being to abridge 'their diffuseness,' and lop away their 'exuberant redundance.' The chronicles were an Augean stable demanding the full exertion of his expurgating powers; but his success has not corresponded with his industry. For his own work is strewn thick with the fetid refuse; and, instead of pruning down its rank luxuriance, he has put his sickle in the harvest of other men, and utterly destroyed the good seed with the weeds. The whole frame of his work, in all its members, is a compound of 'redundant,' incoherent, contradictory statements, flagrantly opposed to facts; and beyond a doubt it was he that destroyed the chronicles from which he compiled: they must have been in Latin, as he was utterly ignorant of the Irish language . . . .

But such censures on rashness and pertinacity could not deter Giraldus from patronizing other branches of superstition. As wave presses wave, rolling successively over each other, so, when he had once tasted the illicit sweets of superstition, he is urged by an insatiable passion to plunge deeper in the black art, and complete his knowledge of dreams by the kindred science of augury. But the result of his project was as unsatisfactory as its conception had been temerarious.[2] 'Not long,' he writes, 'or about two years before the descent of the English, a fish was found near Carlingford, in Ulster, which had three golden teeth, of about fifty ounces weight; an omen, perhaps, of the golden days of the impending and approaching conquest.' Such an interpretation of the prodigy is setting a saddle on a bull in the best style. Had it portended anything to the inhabitants of Ireland, or the Church of God, it must have portended evil, if the character of this omen is to be

1. i.e. Giraldus Cambrensis.

2. reckless, rash.

tested by the voice of history, for the Church was shockingly deformed, and the Irish were robbed of a large portion of their country. These facts Giraldus himself admits, — the former frequently, — the latter in all its vivid details; so that, out of his own mouth, those first days of the English robbers in Ireland were an age, not of gold but of iron, when the sword hewed down everything in its path. Listen to his own pathetic plaint on the sorrows of the Church: 'The clergy of this island are beggared; the cathedral churches mourn, despoiled of their ample lands and domains, the gift of the confiding and tender piety of former days. Thus has the exaltation of the Church ended in the spoliation of the Church.'

But, on the matter of fact, Giraldus is egregiously mistaken. Events which had occurred many centuries ago he brings near his own time, that the proximity might conveniently corroborate his false statement. This is how the case really stands. Not two, but more than 400 years before the English invasion, and while Fiacha Dubhdrochtech, the son of Aid Ronius, was King of Ulster, an enormous whale was drifted along by the tide, and cast up on the shore in Ulster. It had three teeth of gold, one of which was given by Fiacha as wages to some men whom he had employed in erecting a bridge over the rivers Fersus and Monidamh; the other two were presented to the church to make a reliquary-case, on which the inhabitants of that country were accustomed to purge or bind themselves by oath. Fiacha got his surname "Dubh-droichtech," from building bridges (for drochet means a bridge), the ancients having regarded the erection of a bridge as a meritorious act of religion, and instituted certain solemn pontifical rites to inaugurate the laying of the foundation stone; hence, if we believe Varro, pontiffs were so called from building bridges. Fiacha, moreover, was so ardent a lover of justice, that an ox having been stolen within his territory, he made a pilgrimage to the monastery of Bangor, and voluntarily expiated in his own person the penalty of that crime, probably because the robber had eluded or not satisfied the vengeance of the law. Was the whale then an omen of a far distant event — the English invasion of Ireland — and not an evident present sent from Heaven to a prince whose resources, perhaps, were not equal to his piety, to enable him to cover his expenditure, and decorate with a suitable shrine relics so highly revered by the inhabitants of that country? Tigernach, who died about the year 1088, states that this whale with the golden teeth was cast on shore in the year 743, and that each of the teeth, when tested in the scales, weighed fifty ounces. One of them, he adds, was for a long time after to be seen on the great altar of the monastery of Bangor. Perhaps it had been cast into a shrine containing the aforesaid relics.

Having seen what slight importance is due to this first augury of Giraldus, let us now follow him into the still more profound mysteries of the craft, to ascertain whether no truer oracle issued from him under the access of the Pythonic spirit:[3] 'It is in December,' he says, 'that wolves generally bring forth their cubs in Ireland, an omen of the horrors of treachery and rapine, which pullulate[4] precociously here.' Where is his tripod[5] now? Assuredly Apollo was unpropitious. Whatever thought enters his mind, it is instantly seized to brand infamy on Ireland, never reflecting that it is not every timber that makes a Mercury, nor every accusation a conviction. If I could trust my own opinion, I would say that this unseasonable parturition of the wolf is a more appropriate type of the cruelty of the Englishman coming to Ireland, and gorging himself with blood, than of any rapine or treachery of the Irish, who fought for their lives and their altars, their children and their wives, against the robber allies of a traitor to his country. Treachery and rapine can be charged more truly on the English than on the Irish. For the English came as auxiliaries of Dermod MacMurrough, who, according to Giraldus himself, 'oppressed his nobles, exalted upstarts, was a calamity to his countrymen, hated by the strangers, and, in a word, at war with the world.' Such was the man whom the English supported. They not only restored him to that throne which he had most justly forfeited by his crimes, but, by a hideous injustice, extended his dominion by a large accession of territory, and rioted like savage furies throughout Ireland, depopulating the country, burning the public buildings, and plundering cities. Giraldus himself confesses those facts in almost every page of his work, especially when he says, 'that this new and bloody conquest was defiled by an enormous effusion of blood, and the slaughter of a Christian

3. The spirit of a monstrous serpent — the first of several references to Greek mythology in this passage.
4. multiply, breed.
5. The three-legged seat used by the priestess at the shrine of Apollo at Delphi when delivering oracles.

people.' Had the English confined their cruelty to those whom Giraldus represents as their enemies, there might be some palliation; but, as if to secure their title to the infamy of the robber, they seized the property even of the Irish who assisted them. Giraldus himself exclaims: 'The lands even of the Irish who stood faithful to our cause from the first descent of Fitzstephen and the Earl, you have, in violation of a treaty, made over to your friends.' Who now were those traitors and robbers, whose crimes were appropriately prefigured by wolves' cubs coming to the world out of season?

PETER WALSH

(*c*.1618-88)

from: A PROSPECT OF THE STATE OF IRELAND . . . (1682)

[Peter Walsh's *A Prospect of the State of Ireland* is a strange book. It is based mainly on Keating's history but also on various Irish manuscripts. It has always been regarded with disfavour by historians: 'worthless' according to the *Dictionary of National Biography*, while it is not mentioned in the *New History of Ireland*. Yet Walsh writes with considerable energy and, since his work takes little or no account of the more scientific historiography of Ussher and Ware, it retains a sense of mystery and chronological chaos that reflects the atmosphere of much popular historiography of the seventeenth century.]

Ireland, before that fatal War broke out in the year 1641, had two different Nations, (like the Twins of *Rebecca*) strugling in its Womb perpetually, almost five hundred years, the one called by themselves the *Ancient Irish*, the other the *Old English*, or *English Irish*. And indeed the former may justly glory in the Epithet of *Ancient* since, as *Cambden* himself confesses, *they fetch the beginning of their Histories from the most profound and remote Records of Antiquity, so that in comparison of them, the Ancientness of all other Nations is but Novelty, and as it were, a matter of yesterday*. It is now at least 2988 years since their Fore-fathers, the Sons of *Mileadh* (alias *Milesius* the *Spaniard*) in a Fleet of three-score Sail, arrived in *Ireland* from *Gallicia* in *Spain*, conquer'd it, and left it to their Posterity. I say *at least*, Because, although *Polychronicon* and *Cambrensis* by their saying, That *from the Arrival of those Milesians in* Ireland, *till the death of S.* Patrick *their Apostle, were efflux'd* 1800 *years* agree exactly with *Ketings* Epocha here, yet the *Irish Book of Reigns*, makes the Arrival of those *Milesians* much earlier, that is, (to this present year of Christ 1680) e'en as long since as 3480 years compleat. But I follow *Ketings* Reformation of that *Book*, and his Account whereby he places the Milesian Conquest in the year of the World 2736, after the Floud 1086, after *Moses's* passing the *Red Sea* 192, and before the Birth of Christ 1308.

Were it to my main purpose, which is, or only, or at least mostly concern'd in those *Milesians*, I could insert here, out of *Keting*, the several Plantations and Conquests of that Countrey before they knew it.

How one *Ciocal*, about a hundred years after the Deluge, in a small Fleet of Vessels each Vessel having fifty Men, and fifty Women aboard, arriving there, was the First that planted it.

How *Bartholanus* and his three Sons *Languinus*, *Salanus*, and *Reterugus* with their Wives, and as Nennius writes, a thousand Fighting Men, about 300 years after the Flood, (*Anno Mundi* 1956, before the Birth of *Abraham* 95 years) invaded it, had many doughty Battels therein with those *Aborigines* the issue of *Ciocal*, and Progeny of *Cham*, who (come thither from *Afric*) were called *Gyants* because partly of their stature or corpulency (which yet was no way exceeding the tallest growth of other men) and partly of their wickedness, endeavouring to destroy every where the Descendants or Progeny of *Japhet*. And how this *Bartholanus*, alias *Partholan*, having Conquer'd at last those *Aborigines*, and *Affricans*, his issue after him were, at the end of three hundred years, consumed by a Pestilence, not one remaining of them. A just judgment from Heaven (without peradventure) on him, who had fled thither (as it were) from Heaven, for having in his own Countrey, in *Scythia*, kill'd both his Father and Mother, to make way for a Brother of his, and their Son, to come to the Royal Throne.

How, in the end of 30 years more, *Nemedus*, another *Scythian* (some of the *Irish* Chronologists say he was a son to *Bartholanus*, left by him in *Scythia* when himself had departed thence) with his four Sons, *Starius*, *Gervale*, *Annin*, and *Fergus*, in a Fleet of 34 Ships, and 30 Marriners in each of them, arriving in *Ireland*, overthrew in three Battels the remainder of those *Affrican Gyants*, but was overcome in the fourth. And how soon after this defeat, *Nemedus* being dead, his People rousing themselves, put it to the issue of one great Battel, fought at the same time both by Sea and by Land, they having 30 thousand at Land, and so many more at Sea: and the Fight proved so mortal, that albeit they had the Victory yet they could reap no benefit by it; the very Air being so corrupted by the stench of the Carcasses which lay unburied every where (for they kill'd promiscuously in every place after that Victory, Man, Woman, and Child of their Enemies) that all over the Land there was an universal Pestilence; which after seven years more made 'em depart and quit the whole Country, leaving only ten Captains to defend those of their People (that could not have Shipping) against the remainder of the Gygantick *Affricans*.

How these Children or Posterity of *Nemedus* (*Clanna Neimheadh*, the *Irish* call 'em) to avoid that dreadful and continual Pestilence, departing in a thousand Vessels, great and small under the Conduct of three Chieftains, *Simeon Breac*, *Ibaath*, and *Briotan*, the other two sailing to *Greece*, *Briotan* with his adherents Landed in the *North* of that Countrey, which we now call *Scotland*: and, with his and their Posterity remaining there, gave the denomination of *Brittain* to this whole Island, which is now called *Great Brittain*, as holy *Cormac*, the K. of *Mounster*, and Bishop of *Cashel*, in his Psalter of *Cashel*, together with all the Chronologers of *Ireland*, affirm. Wherein surely they have at least much more probability of their side, than any late Authors have, that derive that name from *Brutus*, of his Romantick History either in *Galfridus*, or in any other. For if from *Brutus*, besides other reasons, why not *Brutannia* rather than *Britannia*?...

RODERIC O'FLAHERTY
(1629-1718)

from: OGYGIA; or, A Chronological Account of Irish Events (1685)

[Roderic O'Flaherty's *Ogygia* is a curious mixture of fact and fiction, based primarily on the old Irish annals, written in Latin and dedicated to the future James II. O'Flaherty's aim was to make an appeal to the Stuart royal family and to the international community of the day for some understanding of Ireland and her political plight through a view of her history. Much of the book is taken up with dry chronological entries, but we have selected below a passage where O'Flaherty allows himself to develop a description — in this case of the boats of the Irish people. *Ogygia* was translated in 1793 by the Rev. James Hely.]

Achy Fuarch, the sixty-third king of Ireland: Containing also some account of the ancient ships of the Irish.

Achy, surnamed Fuarch, from the wicker hurdles that were covered with hides, which he used in putting his men on shore from the vessels, when he spent two years committing piratical depredations, of the Heberian descent,[1] was declared king of Ireland after the decease of his predecessor.

The ancient Irish had, besides, boats and canoes, which we even use yet in crossing ferries, these small wicker boats (for Fuarch, the surname of king

1. Descended from Heber Fionn, the eldest of the sons of King Milesius of Spain, whose descendants were said to have peopled Ireland. He, in turn, was descended from Japheth, son of Noah.

Achy, signifies a boat not well joined) which St. Isidore calls *Carabs*, and says they were made of twigs and covered with raw hides; which are made use of yet, in coasting along the shores and islands. They are called in Irish *Corach*, or *Noemhog*.

In such a vessel as this, Fabius Ethelwerd, the Anglo-saxon Annals, Florentius of Worcester, and Mathæus Florilegus relate, that three Irishmen, Dusslan, Macbeth, and Magulmumen, the last of whom, as Ethelward says, was 'a perfect master of arts, a man of great literary abilities, and a distinguished professor of the Scots,' came from Ireland to Alfred king of the English; who, desirous to lead a hermetical religious life, went on board a conoe, which was made of two or three ox hides, with provisions sufficient to support them for one week, and without sails or any other necessary tackling, failing wherever chance led them, landed at Cornwal; and were admitted to the presence of king Alfred, to be assured of the miraculous novelty of it.

Besides, it is very obvious our vessels were formerly large enough, and sufficiently commodious, being sheathed with bull's hides, which were stout enough to undergo the voyages of those ages, and to endure their naval engagements. St. Cormac, a disciple of St. Columba, of Hy, as St. Adamnan relates, undertook a wonderful and laborious voyage in a skiff covered with hides, which was furnished with a prow, stern, sails, keel, sides, oars and provisions, on board which there was a number of passengers. First weighing anchor from Irrosdamnonia, he ploughed along the ocean: secondly, with full sail, he coasted along the ocean, and, after many doubles, he arrived at the Orkney islands: his third voyage was from land, for fourteen long summer days and nights; with a south wind he sailed a direct course to the north, so that the voyage, beyond the limits of human excursion, (according to the nautical knowledge of those times) seemed not to be explored back again. So far Adamnan: but long before this, when the Roman power was in a declining state in Britain, the Scots from Ireland made a descent on Britain in a fleet of this kind, as Gildas says in his Destruction of Britain. 'They sprung out of their canoes with a spirit of emulation, in which multitudes of Scots and Picts sailed beyond the Scythian valley.' This invasion of the Scots on Britain happened in the year of Christ 431, in the reign of Theodosius the second, under whose father and uncle, who reigned jointly from the year 395 to the year 408. There was another expedition in a fleet of the same construction, of which Claudian introduces Britain thus speaking:

Me quoque vicinis pereuntem gentibus, inquit,
Munivit Stilico, totam cum Scotus Iernen
Movit, & infesto spumavit remige Tethys.[2]

We may conceive the structure and form of ships of this sort, although we can form no idea of the bulk, strength, or warlike apparatus of them, from the life of St. Brendan in a manuscript book of Carthusius Moguin, in the following manner:— They made a small ship, exceedingly light, lined with ribs and with timber formed like pillars, as it is the custom in these countries; afterwards they covered her with the hides of oxen, having made them red; then they daubed all the outside ligatures of the skins with butter, and they brought with them in the vessel two more hides prepared for use, and necessaries for forty days. They likewise took with them a quantity of butter, in order to prepare the skins for covering the vessel, and every implement and utensil, with the necessaries of life. They also fixed a mast in the middle of the ship, and sails, and all things necessary for steering the vessel. The description of another author of the life of St. Brendan, in the Insular Book, of the structure of these ships, coincides with the foregoing account. They fitted out a small ship, very light, made of the pine-tree, as is the custom of that country, and covered it with the hides of oxen, made red, and daubed all the outside joined parts of the skins, and took with them necessaries for fifty days, and every thing requisite for the use of the vessel. . . .

2. Claudian, *De laudibus Stilichonis* II, 250-52. 'Stilicho defended me, she [Britain] said, as I was perishing beneath the blows of neighbouring tribes, when the Scot roused the whole of Ireland and the sea foamed with hostile ships.'

Biographies/Bibliographies

NOTE: *A New History of Ireland,* III, *Early Modern Ireland, 1534-1691* (Oxford: Clarendon Press, 1976) (hereafter cited as *N.H.I.* III) provides the best modern account of the historiography of seventeenth-century Ireland. See particularly chapters 20-23 and the bibliography.

Giraldus Cambrensis

LIFE. Giraldus de Barri was born in west Wales about 1146. He is generally called 'Cambrensis' — of Wales — in tribute to his place of origin and to his family, the Fitzgeralds. An energetic and ambitious churchman and diplomat, he knew many of the most powerful figures of his day. Giraldus wrote books about Wales and Ireland. He died in 1223.

CHIEF WRITINGS. The best-known works of Giraldus Cambrensis, *Topographia Hiberniae* (*c.*1187), *Expugnatio Hibernica* (*c.*1188) and *Descriptio Kambriae* (*c.*1194), together with all his other writings, have been published in eight volumes. See S.J. Brewer, J.F. Dinock and G.F. Warner (eds), *Opera* (Rolls series, London: Longman Green, 1861-91). See also John J. O'Meara's translation *The History and Topography of Ireland* (Harmondsworth: Penguin Books, 1982).

BIOGRAPHY AND CRITICISM. There is no full biography of Giraldus Cambrensis. See Michael Richter, *Giraldus Cambrensis*: *The Growth of the Welsh Nation* (Aberystwyth: National Library of Wales, 1972). See, also, commentary and essays in *Expugnatio Hibernica*: *The Conquest of Ireland* by Giraldus Cambrensis, edited with translation and historical notes by A.B. Scott and F.X. Martin (Dublin: Royal Irish Academy, 1978).

For a list of critical works up to 1960, see E.A. Williams, 'A Bibliography of Giraldus Cambrensis', *National Library of Wales Journal*, 12 (1961-62), pp. 97-140.

Richard Stanihurst

LIFE. Born in Dublin in 1547, Richard Stanihurst (or Stanyhurst) was an uncle of James Ussher. The Stanihurst family had been active in Dublin's political and commercial life for generations, filling several posts in the administration. Richard was educated at University College, Oxford and returned to Ireland with his tutor, Edmund Campion, SJ. He became fascinated by Irish history and published a description of Ireland and a history of Ireland, both of which appeared in Raphael Holinshed's *Chronicle* in 1577. In 1579, on the death of his wife, Stanihurst went to the Netherlands where he became a catholic and, according to Barnaby Riche, 'professed Alchymy'. He translated Virgil's *Aeneid* into appalling English heroic verse. He died in Brussels in 1618.

CHIEF WRITINGS. *Harmonia seu catena dialectica in Porphyrianos institutiones* (London, 1570); *The third booke of the historie of Ireland, comprising the reigne of Henry the eight* in Raphael Holinshed, *Chronicles* (London, 1577); *A treatise containing a plain and perfect description of Ireland* .... in Raphael Holinshed, *Chronicles* (London, 1577); *The first four books of Virgil's* Aeneid *translated into English heroical verse* (Leyden, 1582); *De rebus in Hibernia gestis* (Antwerp, 1584); *De vita S. Patricii* (Antwerp, 1587); *Hebdomada Mariana* (Antwerp, 1609); *Hebdomada Eucharistica* (Douai, 1614); *Brevis praemunitio pro futura concertatione cum Jacobo Usserio* (Douai, 1615).

BIOGRAPHY AND CRITICISM. Colm Lennon, *Richard Stanihurst The Dubliner, 1547-1618* (Dublin: Irish Academic Press, 1981). See, especially, pp. 170-78 for a detailed bibliography. See, by the same author, 'Recusancy and the Dublin Stanihursts', *Archivium Hibernicum*, 33 (1975); and 'Richard Stanihurst (1547-1618) and Old English Identity', *Irish Historical Studies*, XXII, No. 82 (1978), pp. 121-43. See also *N.H.I.* III.

Fynes Moryson

For biography and bibliography, see p. 234.

Philip O'Sullivan-Beare

LIFE. Philip O'Sullivan-Beare, nephew of the famous Donall O'Sullivan-Beare, was born about 1590 in the castle of Dunboy in west Cork. After the defeat of the Irish forces at Kinsale in 1601, and when he was still a child, O'Sullivan-Beare was sent to Spain to be educated at Santiago de Compostela. He entered the Spanish army and served on board Spanish warships. His published works include a life of St Patrick, while his accounts of the Elizabethan wars and the flight of Donall O'Sullivan-Beare are particularly valuable since his sources were eye-witnesses of the events. He died in Spain about 1660.

CHIEF WRITINGS. *Historiae Catholicae Hiberniae Compendium*.... (Lisbon, 1621); new edition edited by Matthew Kelly (Dublin: O'Daly, 1850); T.J. O'Donnell (ed.), *Selections from the Zoilomastix of Philip O'Sullivan-Beare* (Dublin: Stationery Office, 1960); *Ireland under Elizabeth* ... being a portion of *The History of Catholic Ireland* by Don Philip O'Sullivan-Beare, translated by M.J. Byrne (Dublin: Sealy, Bryers & Walker, 1903).

BIOGRAPHY AND CRITICISM. *Vindiciae Hiberniae*, presented by A. Gwynn in *Analecta Hibernica*, 6 (1934). For a detailed bibliography, see Peter Somerville-Large, *From Bantry Bay to Leitrim*: *A Journey in Search of O'Sullivan Beare* (London: Gollancz, 1974). See also *N.H.I.* III.

James Ussher

LIFE. James Ussher, born in Dublin in 1581, was one of the first undergraduates to enter Trinity College, Dublin on its foundation in 1594. Ordained in 1601, he became a fellow of the college and was made professor of theological controversies in 1607. After fourteen years in this post, he was appointed bishop of Meath. In 1625 he became archbishop of Armagh. He was on a visit to England in 1640, and the momentous events of that decade prevented a return to Ireland. Although he was a royalist, he advised Charles I against the execution of Thomas Wentworth, earl of Strafford. After serving briefly as bishop of Carlisle, Ussher moved to Oxford and then to Wales. In 1646 he became the guest of the dowager Countess of Peterborough at Reigate, Surrey.

Ussher was a fine scholar in many disciplines, particularly church history, and a discerning collector of books and manuscripts. His system of chronology, which placed the date of the Creation at 4004 B.C., was the source of the dates in many English editions of the Bible. He died in Reigate, Surrey in 1656 and his fine library eventually came to Trinity College, Dublin.

CHIEF WRITINGS. *A Discourse of the Religion Anciently Professed by the Irish and British* (Dublin, 1631); *Veterum Epistolarum Hibernicarum Sylloge* (Dublin, 1632); *Britannicarum Ecclesiarum Antiquititates* (Dublin, 1639); *An Answer to a Challenge made by a Jesuite in Ireland* (4th edition, London, 1687). For a complete collection, see C.R. Elrington and J.H. Todd, *The Whole Works of* ... *James Ussher* .... 17 vols (Dublin, 1847-64).

BIOGRAPHY AND CRITICISM. The most recent biography is R. Buick Knox, *James Ussher*: *Archbishop of Armagh* (Cardiff: University of Wales Press, 1967), which includes a detailed bibliography. See also, Hugh Jackson Lawlor, 'Primate Ussher's Library before 1641', *Royal Irish Academy Proceedings*, 3rd series, 6 (1900-02), 216-64; T.C. Barnard, 'The Purchase of Archbishop Ussher's Library in 1657', *Longroom*, 2 (1970), 9-14; Seán O'Donnell, 'Early Irish Scientists', *Éire-Ireland*, Vol. 11, No. 1 (1976), 122-26. See also *N.H.I.* III.

Conall Mac Geoghegan

LIFE. Little is known of Conall Mac Geoghegan except that he appears to have been a scribe and translator of Irish texts and that he lived in or near Lismoyney, Co. Westmeath. He was active in the 1620s and 1630s. A passage in R.I.A. Catalogue 417 states that Mac Geoghegan made a transcript of the Book of Lecan in 1636 and that, at the time, this book was on loan to him from Archbishop Ussher. He also wrote an approbation for *Genealogiae Regum et Sanctorum Hiberniae* in 1630. His loose translation of the annals known as *The Annals of Clonmacnoise* (1627) is particularly valuable because the original Irish text of this portion of the annals is now lost.

CHIEF WRITINGS. *The Annals of Clonmacnoise from the earliest period to A.D. 1408*, translated into English by Conall Mac Geoghegan, A.D. 1627, edited by Denis Murphy (Dublin: Kilkenny Archaeological Society, 1896).

BIOGRAPHY AND CRITICISM. See *N.H.I.* III.

Geoffrey Keating

LIFE. Geoffrey Keating (Seathrún Céitinn) was born into a well-to-do Norman family in Burges, Co. Tipperary about 1580. He received his early education near the town of Cahir and almost certainly attended a bardic school for a time. He was sent to France to study for the secular priesthood and attended the University of Bordeaux. He returned to Ireland about 1610, a doctor of divinity, and became a parish priest in Tubrid near Cahir. It appears that he offended a local lady in a sermon and, in consequence, was pursued by the authorities. He went into hiding and is said to have composed *Foras Feasa ar Éirinn* (A Basis of Knowledge about Ireland) in the early 1630s. According to his early biographers, Keating travelled widely in quest of historical material, enjoying the protection of protestants while consulting manuscripts and even gaining access to the libraries of Trinity College, Dublin and of the protestant Archbishop of Cashel. *Foras Feasa ar Éirinn* remained in manuscript until Dermot O'Conor's translation of 1723. Keating was also a poet of note and wrote a memorable spiritual essay, *The Three Shafts of Death*. He is said to have been murdered by Cromwellian soldiers in St Nicholas's Church, Clonmel, probably in 1650. He is buried in the graveyard of Tubrid.

CHIEF WRITINGS. David Comyn and P.S. Dinneen (eds), *Foras Feasa ar Éirinn: A Complete History of Ireland* 4 vols (London: Irish Texts Society, 1902-14); *Foras Feasa ar Éirinn: Séathrún Céitinn athnua le Padraig de Barra* (Baile Átha Cliath: Foilseacháin Náisiúnta Teo, 1982-83); *Foras Feasa ar Éirinn*, translated by Dermot O'Connor (Dublin, 1723; reprinted Dublin, 1809 and Dublin: Duffy, 1854); Osborn Bergin (ed.), *Sgéalaigheacht Chéitinn: Stories from Keating's History of Ireland* (Dublin: Dublin School of Irish Learning, 1909); David Comyn (ed.), *Díonrbhrollach foras feasa ar Éirinn, or, Vindication of the Sources of Irish History*, being the introduction to 'Groundwork of Knowledge of Ireland' (Dublin: Gill, 1898); Patrick O'Brien (ed.), *Eochair-sgiath an Aifrinn*: an explanatory defence of the Mass, written in Irish, early seventeenth century (Dublin: O'Brien, 1898); *Dánta amhráin is caointe Shéathrúin Céitinn* (Baile Átha Cliath: Conradh na Gaedhilge, 1900); *Trí bior-ghaoithe an bháis: The Three Shafts of Death of Geoffrey Keating*, edited by R. Atkinson (Dublin: Royal Irish Academy, 1890). 2nd edition, edited by Osborn Bergin (Dublin: Hodges Figgis, 1931); Rev. F.W. O'Connell (ed.), *Selections from Keating's Three Shafts of Death* (Dublin, London: Maunsel & Co, 1910).

BIOGRAPHY AND CRITICISM. B. Ó Buachalla, '*Annála Ríoghachta Éireann* is *Foras Feasa ar Éirinn*: An Comhthéacs Comhaimseartha', *Studia Hibernica* 22 and 23 (1982-83), 60-105; D. Ó Corráin, 'Seathrún Céitinn (*c.*1580-*c.*1644): An Cúlra Stairiúil', *Dúchas 1983-85* (Dublin, 1986), 56-68. See also Diarmaid Ó Catháin, 'Dermot O'Connor, translator of Keating', *Eighteenth-Century Ireland* 2, (1987), 67-87.

Mícheál Ó Cléirigh

LIFE. Mícheál Ó Cléirigh, born into a family of traditional historians in Kilbarron, Co. Donegal in 1575, entered the Franciscan order as a lay brother in Louvain. He had already established a reputation as an antiquary when, in 1620, the guardian at Louvain, Aodh Mac an Bháird, sent him back to Ireland to collect manuscript material for the lives of the Irish saints. With the help of other scholars, he gathered an immense amount of information and compiled a list of kings and their pedigrees (*Réim Ríograidhe*, 1630). This, and subsequent works, were of great value to John Colgan in the compilation of *Acta Sanctorum... Hiberniae*. Ó Cléirigh died in Louvain in 1643.

CHIEF WRITINGS. Paul Walsh (ed.), *Genealogiae Regum et Sanctorum Hiberniae* (Dublin: Gill, 1918); *The Martyrology of Donegal: A Calendar of the Saints of Ireland*, translated by John O'Donovan, edited by J.H. Todd and W. Reeves (Dublin: Irish Archaeological and Celtic Society, 1864); Seamus Pender (ed.), *The O'Clery Book of Genealogies* in *Analecta Hibernica* 18 (1951). With Fear Feasa Ó Maoil Chonaire, Cú Choigeriche ó Duibhgeanháin and Cú Choigeríche Ó Cléirigh, he compiled the *Annála Ríoghachta Éireann* (*c.*1636) translated by John O'Donovan and published as *The Annals of the Four Masters* in 1849.

BIOGRAPHY AND CRITICISM. *N.H.I.* III; Rev. Sylvester O'Brien (ed.), *Measgra i gcuimhne Mhichíl Ui Chléirigh*: miscellany of historical and linguistic studies in honour of Brother Mícheál Ó Cléirigh, Chief of the Four Masters (Dublin: Assisi Press, 1944); B. Jennings, *Mícheál Ó Cléirigh, Chief of the Four Masters and his Associates* (Dublin: Talbot Press, 1936); Rev. Victor Sheppard, 'Michael O'Clery', in F.J. Sheed (ed.), *The Irish Way* (London: Sheed & Ward, 1932). B. Ó Buachalla (see reference under Keating above).

John Colgan

LIFE. John Colgan, born about 1592 near Carndonagh, Co. Donegal, left Ireland for the Continent as a young man and was ordained a priest in 1618. He entered the Franciscan order and became professor of theology at Louvain. Although he planned to write and publish lives of all the Irish saints, he completed work only on those whose feast-days occur in January, February and March. He also published valuable, detailed lives of Saints Patrick, Brigid and Columba, and a life of Johannes Scottus. He died at Louvain in 1658.

CHIEF WRITINGS. *Acta Sanctorum ... Hiberniae* (Louvain, 1645; reprinted Dublin: Stationery Office, 1948); *Acta Sanctorum Veteris et Maioris Scotiae, seu Hiberniae Sanctorum Insulae Bonus Primus....* 2 vols (Louvain, 1645; facsimile reprint, with foreword by Brendan Jennings, Dublin: Irish Manuscript Commission, 1948); *Triadis Thaumaturgae, seu divorum Patricii, Columbae, et Brigidae ... acta* (Louvain, 1647); *Tractatus de Iohannis Scoti....* (Antwerp, 1655).

BIOGRAPHY AND CRITICISM. Terence O'Donnell (ed.), *Father John Colgan, OFM: Essays in Commemoration of the Third Centenary of his Death* (Dublin: Assisi Press, 1959); William Reeves, 'Colgan's Works', *Ulster Journal of Archaeology*, 1 (1853), 295-302. See also *N.H.I.* III.

Luke Wadding

LIFE. Luke Wadding, born in County Waterford in 1588, was orphaned at the age of fourteen. He was sent to Lisbon to study in the Jesuit seminary, but soon moved on to Oporto. There, he joined the Franciscans and took vows in 1613. After preaching in different parts of Spain and Portugal, he arrived in Rome in 1618 and began work on his history of the Franciscan order. He also compiled a bibliography of the order. Considered an outstanding figure among the Franciscans of his era, he is said to have been regarded as worthy of the papacy. He founded the Irish Franciscan College of St Isidore in Rome and played an influential part in papal politics of the 1640s. Wadding persuaded Pope Innocent X to sent Archbishop Rinuccini to Ireland. Despite his influential position, Wadding refused all ecclesiastical honours. He died in Rome in 1657.

CHIEF WRITINGS. *Annales Ordinis Minorum....* 8 vols (Rome, 1625-54); (ed.), *Francisci Assisiati opuscula nunc primum collecta....* (Antwerp, 1623); (ed.), *Joannis Duns Scoti... opera omnia* 16 vols (Lyons, 1639); *Scriptores Ordinis Minorum* (Rome, 1650); B. Jennings (ed.), *Papers, 1614-38* (Dublin: Irish Manuscripts Commission, 1953); B. Jennings (ed.), *Some Correspondence . . . .*, *Collectanea Hibernica* 2 (1959), 66-94.

BIOGRAPHY AND CRITICISM. G. Cleary, *Fr Luke Wadding and St Isidore's College, Rome* (Rome: Bardi, 1925); Franciscan Fathers (eds), *Father Luke Wadding: Commemorative Volume* (Dublin: Dun Mhuire, Killiney, 1957); Canice Mooney, 'The Writings of Father Luke Wadding, OFM', *Franciscan Studies*, 18 (1958), 227-31. See also *N.H.I.* III.

James Ware

LIFE. Born in Dublin in 1594, James Ware was a son of the auditor general of Ireland. He was educated at Trinity College, Dublin and, encouraged by his uncle, James Ussher, dedicated himself to historical and antiquarian research. He was knighted in 1629 and succeeded his father as auditor general for Ireland in 1632. Ware was member of parliament for the University of Dublin and a privy counsellor in the 1630s. After suffering at the hands of the parliamentary forces, Ware lived in London in the 1650s, but he returned to Ireland on the restoration. A lifelong commitment to the collection and publication of Irish historical material marks him as one of the most significant figures in her historiography. He died in Dublin in 1666.

CHIEF WRITINGS. *De Praesulibus Hageniae, sive Provinciae Dublinensis* (Dublin, 1628); *Vitae archiepiscorum Casseliensum et Tumansium* (Dublin, 1628); (ed.), *Ancient Irish histories: The works of Spenser, Campion, Hanmer, and Marleburrough* (Dublin, 1633; reprinted in 2 vols Dublin, 1809); *De scriptoribus Hiberniae libri duo* (Dublin, 1639; facsimile reprint, Farnborough, Hants, 1966); *Librorum manuscriptorum bibliotheca Jacobi Waraei, equitus catalogus* (Dublin, 1648); *De Hibernia et Antiquitatibus ejus ... Disquisitiones ....* (London, 1654); *Rerum Hibernicarum annales ... 1485-1558 ....* (Dublin, 1664); *De praesulibus Hiberniae commentarius ....* (Dublin, 1665); *The Antiquities and History of Ireland: The Life of Sir James Ware Prefixed translated and edited by Robert Ware* (Dublin, 1705); Walker Harris (ed.), *The Whole Works of Sir James Ware concerning Ireland, revised and improved* (Dublin, 1739-64).

BIOGRAPHY AND CRITICISM. Kathleen Hughes, 'A Manuscript of James Ware: British Museum Additional 4788', *Royal Irish Academy Proceedings*, series C, 55 (1952-3), 111-16. See also *N.H.I.* III.

John Lynch

LIFE. John Lynch was born in Galway about 1599. He was educated by the Jesuits in the town and by 1618 was studying in France. Ordained about 1622, he returned to Ireland and taught at a school in Galway. He was later appointed titular archdeacon of Tuam. He opposed the catholic confederation of the 1640s on the grounds that it was too subservient to the church in Rome and he asserted loyalty to the English crown. During the siege of Galway by the parliamentary forces in 1652, he fled to France and seems to have lived there for the rest of his life. Lynch translated Keating's *Foras Feasa ar Éirinn* into Latin and wrote his famous refutation of Giraldus Cambrensis in the same language. He died, probably in St Malo, about 1673.

CHIEF WRITINGS. *Cambrensis Eversus ....* (St Malo? 1662); edited and translated by Rev. Matthew Kelly, 3 vols (Dublin: Celtic Society, 1848-52); Rev. J.F. O'Doherty (ed.), *De praesulibus Hiberniae, potissimis catholicae religionis in Hibernia serendae et propagande, et conservandae authoribus*, 2 vols (Dublin: Stationery Office, 1944); *Pii antistitis icon; sive, de vita et morte ... Francisci Kirovani* (St Malo, 1669); (Dublin, 1848; Dublin: Stationery Office, 1951); *Alithinologia ....* (St Malo, 1664) ... supplementum (1667).

BIOGRAPHY AND CRITICISM. See *N.H.I.* III.

Peter Walsh

LIFE. A controversial figure in seventeenth-century Irish history, Peter Walsh was born in County Kildare about 1618 and was educated at Louvain. After becoming a Franciscan, he returned to Ireland about 1646. He played an important political role for the next twenty years, obstinately urging loyalty to the crown in all circumstances. This earned him disapproval from many quarters, including the Vatican. After 1660 he urged the catholic clergy in Ireland to send a loyal address to the king and he worked for this against the wishes of Rome. He became extremely unpopular in church circles, although he was protected by the Duke of Ormonde. Towards the end of his life, Walsh wrote his history of Ireland. He died in London in 1688.

CHIEF WRITINGS. *Queries Concerning the Lawfulnesse of the Present Cessation* (Kilkenny, 1648); *The History and Vindication of the Loyal Formulary of Irish Remonstrance* (n.p., 1674); *Causa Valesiana epistolis ternis praelibata* (London, 1684); *A Prospect of the State of Ireland from the Year of the World 1756 to the Year of Christ 1652* (London, 1682); *Four Letters on Several Subjects* (London, 1686).

BIOGRAPHY AND CRITICISM. See *N.H.I.* III.

Roderic O'Flaherty

LIFE. Roderic O'Flaherty was born in Moycullen Castle, Co. Galway in 1629. He studied under John Lynch in Galway and also under the famous scholar, An Dualtach Mac Fhirbhisigh (anglicized as Dualtach Mac firbis or Dudley Forbes). His land was confiscated in the Cromwellian settlements and he lived in poverty for the rest of his life. In 1677 O'Flaherty managed to recover some part of his estate. His history of Ireland in Latin, *Ogygia*, was published in 1685. The book's extended dedication to the future James II begins: 'Ireland, the most ancient nursery of your ancestors, most humbly implores your highness's protection and patronage....' and proceeds to provide a genealogy for the Stuarts which makes them indubitably Irish. By the time Edward Lhuyd of Oxford visited him in 1700, O'Flaherty had been reduced to great poverty. He died in squalor, aged eighty-nine, in Connemara in 1718.

CHIEF WRITINGS. *Ogygia; seu, rerum Hibernicarum chronologia* (London, 1685); reprinted as *Ogygia; or, A Chronological Account of Irish Events*, translated by Rev. James Hely (Dublin, 1793); Charles O'Conor (ed.), *The Ogygia Vindicated....* (Dublin, 1775); *A Chronological Description of West or h-Iar Connaught*, written A.D. 1684 by Roderic O'Flaherty, edited by James Hardiman (Dublin, 1846).

BIOGRAPHY AND CRITICISM. K. Theodore Hoppen, *The Common Scientist in the Seventeenth Century: A Study of the Dublin Philosophical Society, 1683-1708* (London: Routledge and Kegan Paul, 1970), pp. 189-90, 194; Mícheál O'Duigeannáin, 'A Letter from Roderic O'Flaherty to William Molyneux, 29 January 1697', *Galway Archaeological Society Journal*, 18 (1938-39), 183-85; Ann de Valera, 'Antiquarian and Historical Investigations in Ireland in the Eighteenth Century' (unpublished MA thesis, National University of Ireland, 1978), pp. 18, 34, 41, 58n; Tomás Ó Concheanainn, 'Scríobhaithe Leacáin Mhic Fhirbhisigh', *Celtica* XIX (Dublin, 1987), 145 ff. See also *N.H.I.* III.

ALAN HARRISON, *Editor*

Literature in Irish 1600-1800

The poet Dáibhí Ó Bruadair (*c.* 1625-98) referred to the period in which he lived as that of 'briseadh an tseanghnáthaimh' (the break-up of the old custom), and this phrase expressed how he and many of the Irish men of learning viewed the events of the time, especially as they affected their own profession. All through the medieval period, the poets and scholars had been minor nobles patronized by Irish chieftains. Their exclusive position depended on this patronage, but it was progressively eroded as the Tudor policies for governing Ireland put pressure on the chieftains to give up their traditional ways. In a very short time, the poets lost the special position that they had guarded jealously for hundreds of years and they were compelled to adapt to the changing world. Some of them continued to operate as professional literary practitioners, but with diminishing support; some collaborated with the new authorities, acting as cultural interpreters between the English and the Irish; and others pursued another kind of learning by going to continental Europe and associating themselves with the intellectual movements of the post-Tridentine catholic church.

The story of Gaelic literature in the two centuries that followed the battle of Kinsale in 1601 is closely related to the ways in which the literary artists responded to the changing times. From the beginning, many of them saw and lamented the imminent catastrophe. Others tried to ignore it and stubbornly maintained their old ways. They sought to emulate the medieval Irish poets and constantly looked back on the Classical Irish era (*c.* 1200-1600) as a golden age. Some changes were forced on them. With the demise of the schools of traditional learning, the skills of composing in the standard literary language, which by the seventeenth century was quite different from the vernacular, had diminished. Nor were the poets able to maintain the expertise in prosody and the esoteric traditional lore or *seanchas*. The learning in the schools had been essentially oral — the students acquiring skills by rote over a number of years — and the written word and the formal written description of the language had become peripheral. Now these assumed an importance they had never had before. If the traditional learning was to last, it would have to be written down and passed on to succeeding generations in that form. Increasingly, Irish writers became scribes and teachers as well as literary artists. Even if they had managed to maintain the arcane language and the esoteric metrical forms, they no longer had a public of rich patrons who would pay for the 'praise poetry' that had been their stock-in-trade. They began to write for a wider public, using language that was closer to everyday speech and employing song metres that had been popular for some time among the ordinary people. Their own personal situations and feelings became part and parcel of their compositions and they reflect very much the attitudes and interests of many of their fellow Irishmen at the time.

Many poems contain an expression of a political or moral attitude to contemporary events. For example, some of the last of the traditional poets followed the fortunes of their O'Neill or O'Donnell patrons during and after the Nine Years' War (as the rebellion of Hugh O'Neill is sometimes called), in Ireland and on continental Europe. Eoghan Rua and Fearghal Óg Mac an Bhaird composed elegies in which the poets' feelings, the sad condition of the country and the sorrow of the womenfolk who were left alive, are interwoven themes. This intense personal feeling, combined with the trope of female sorrow, made a considerable impact on the development of national political attitudes expressed in Irish poetry for the next two hundred years. We have the basic paradigm from the early seventeenth century — leaders gone abroad and the women/Ireland left behind in desolation, hoping for the return of the heroes and the alleviation of their plight. As hope waned that the Gaelic chieftains would return, their place as potential saviours of the dispossessed Irish was taken over by successive members of the Stuart royal family. This was, of course, a gradual development and by no means universal. Thus, while Séamas Dall Mac Cuarta and Art Mac Cumhaigh were still looking for the return of an O'Neill, Aogán Ó Rathaille and Eoghan Rua Ó Súilleabháin were expressing hope in some incarnation of the Stuart kings. This political poetry explores the issues of religious, cultural and economic conflict.

The voices of exiled Irishmen are often heard in the literature of the period. Most of those who went to continental Europe entered the catholic church, where they continued their education and participated in the Counter Reformation. They understood well the cultural importance of the language in withstanding the efforts of protestant proselytizers in Ireland and they worked hard at preserving records, writing grammars, compiling dictionaries and fostering the use of the language for didactic and polemical purposes. The most significant development in this regard was the foundation of the Irish College of St Anthony by the Franciscan Flaithrí Ó Maolchonaire (Florence Conry) in 1603. Ó Maolchonaire himself was a member of a traditional family of historians who had become involved in the intrigues of the struggle between the two cultures from the end of the sixteenth century. He was assisted in setting up the College by Bonaventura Ó hEodhasa (O'Hussey) and Aodh Mac Aingil. Ó hEodhasa was also a member of one of the families of traditional poets, and Mac Aingil seems to have learned to write Irish from him. All three produced exile poetry and didactic devotional prose. The poetry often registers the intense feelings of exiles with a clarity of expression never attained during the Classical period. This set the pattern that later was followed to such good effect by Séathrún Céitinn (Geoffrey Keating) and Pádraigín Haicéad (Hackett). The prose gives us plenty of evidence of the influence of post-Council of Trent catholic theology, which was not only innovative and formative in Irish writing but also provided a moral basis for the descriptions of the political situation. This introduces a judgmental attitude; Ireland's troubles are often ascribed both to the perfidy of the English and to the waywardness of the Irish.

If we look closely at one poem from this selection, 'Óm sceol ar ardmhágh Fáil' by Séathrún Céitinn, we find examples of many of the themes of political poetry from the period. Like other poems composed in exile, this one starts with the poet abroad receiving news of the desolation of the country and the plight of the people. This is, of course, a similar scenario to that developed in the later *aisling* or dream poetry, in which the poet meets the beautiful maiden, Ireland, who proceeds to describe the state of the country. Céitinn is devastated by the news of the plight of the Irish and of how upstarts have despoiled the land. He then takes the common theme of Ireland as a woman and in this case accuses her of nurturing 'the litter of every alien sow', instead of the fine, modest sons of Milesius (the mythical ancestor of the Irish). The poet then claims that the English have gained the land without a struggle because the nobles have been dispersed and many have neglected their duties to God and each other. The only hope for the Irish will be the willingness of the Lord to help them. If He does not, it would be best to 'winnow them now without delay' and send them safely across the sea. This poem and others like it set the standard and tone that were followed stylistically, thematically and sometimes even verbally for the next two hundred years. They must have played their part not only in reflecting the political attitudes of many Irish people, but in forming and developing those same attitudes.

This patriotic theme in poetry reached its climax in the *aisling* of the Jacobite period. The word *aisling* means 'dream' or 'vision'. Dream literature had existed in Irish for a very long time. The *aisling*, where a man falls in love with an unattainable fairy woman (*spéirbhean* = literally, sky woman) is well-known in Irish literature, the earliest example occurring in the Old Irish *Aisling Oengusa*. This topos of the beautiful fairy woman was welded to the political motifs of seventeenth-century poetry. Indeed, we can see that some of the poems of that period that deal with female grief are embryonic political *aislings*. The period after 1690, when the Stuart claimants of the throne were abroad, lent itself to this development. The poet, usually in a rural setting, meets a beautiful woman in a dream. She is questioned by him and proceeds to tell him of her plight as a deserted spouse. She has several names that have become synonymous with Ireland — Síle Ní Ghadhra, Caitlín Ní Uallacháin and Róisín Dhubh among them. Her only hope is the return of her rightful husband — and it is clear that he is one of the Stuart pretenders. Certainly, in the early eighteenth century, for example in the *aislings* of Aogán Ó Rathaille, they represented a real, if romantic, political aspiration. However, many *aislings* were written in the same vein after the collapse of Stuart hopes in 1745 and these can only represent a romantic escape from the reality of the political situation. The genre reached its artistic peak with the poems of Eoghan Rua Ó Súilleabháin. These are technically and verbally exquisite, but still express a forlorn hope in the Stuart rescuer who never came and who, by that time, never would come. The swansong of the *aisling* poetry is, perhaps, the burlesque of it that was incorporated in the best known Irish poem from the period, Brian Merriman's *Cúirt an Mheón-Oíche* (The Midnight Court).

The schools of traditional learning declined, but, as we have seen, the poets sought to continue the pursuit of learning, using the language and, as far as they were able, the themes of the earlier period. One significant difference between the seventeenth- and eighteenth-century poets and their predecessors was that they did not need to belong to special families to practise the profession of writing and learning. Thus we find scholars with names not associated with the traditional families writing poems, transcribing manuscripts and teaching others to do the same from the early seventeenth century onwards; such poets as Céitinn, Haicéad, Ó Bruadair and Peadar Ó Doirnín. These most likely received some training from a scholar belonging to one of the learned families — training in language, metrics and *seanchas*. They still depended on some form of patronage and on the help and support of others in their particular part of the country who were drawn to literature by their inclinations or their talents. The existence of a coterie of such scholars in any district did not necessarily mean that it had been a centre of learning at an earlier time, but a previous tradition of learning would be both an inspiration for the later poets and would also create an atmosphere that was favourable for literary activity. We find such coteries in different parts of the country and each of them made a special contribution to the literature.

The most important areas for this activity were Munster, including Clare and Waterford, south-east Ulster and Dublin. In Munster the poets seem to have been highly mobile. We find Clare poets travelling to Cork and Kerry to meet with their counterparts. It was in Munster also that the political *aisling* came into being and reached its peak in the efforts of Eoghan Rua Ó Súilleabháin. Another poetical form was initiated in Munster: the poetical warrant, which gives us an insight into the organization of the literary brotherhood in that province. The poetical warrant is a burlesque treatment of the legal warrant that calls the poetic fraternity together to discuss a supposed crime against one of their number, and arranges for punishment of the guilty party and compensation of the aggrieved person. When, we see the crimes, we realize that this is an elaborate joke; sometimes a poet has been injured, his hat has been stolen, his land has been trespassed upon, or another poet has composed a satire against him. Although we cannot assume that each warrant concluded with a meeting of poets, we can say that they did meet from time to time and that this acted as a stimulus to them and established and disseminated the reputations of the best of the poets. The warrants and the 'courts' they inspired are important indicators of the extent and the quality of literary Munster in the eighteenth century. It must be admitted that, although the warrants are full of fraternal fun and sometimes earthy humour, very few of them are of great literary merit.

In south-east Ulster we have no evidence of a similar coordination. However, we can see signs of joint activity and indications of mutual respect among some of the major figures. This part of Ireland also produced a distinctive literary form: *trí rainn agus amhrán* (three verses in syllabic metre and one verse in accentual or song metre). The form is found mainly in this region, with some other examples from other places in Ulster and even as far south as Dublin. *Trí rainn agus amhrán* has the virtue of being relatively short and has often been described as 'the Irish sonnet'. It also lends itself to imitation, so that one poet can cleverly answer another by echoing exactly the other poet's technique. The best-known example of such a contention is the poem by Peadar Ó Doirnín in which he echoes poems by his elder colleagues, Séamas Dall Mac Cuarta and Pádraig Mac Giolla Fhiondáin (1665-1733), and in which he establishes his claim to be at least their equal. The district is rightly famous for Ó Doirnín's poetry, which is a delightful combination of traditional learning and passionate expressions of independence and love.

By the end of the seventeenth century, Dublin was the city of the ruling protestant ascendancy and in the following hundred years it became the cultural centre that produced Swift, Berkeley, Goldsmith, Burke and others. However from the middle of that century there were many Irish speakers in Dublin and in the early eighteen hundreds a coterie of scholars and writers were working there. These writers came from every part of Ireland and some of them belonged to the remnants of the traditional learned families; for example, Mac Cruitín (McCurtin/Curtin) from Clare, Ó Duinnín from Kerry, and Ó Luinín (Lyneger) from Fermanagh. Others, it seems, learned to read and write Irish in Dublin. Like their counterparts, these scholars transcribed manuscripts for their own or their patrons' pleasure, compiled and translated histories, and encouraged each other to produce works of creative literature. The pivotal members of this coterie were Seán Ó Neachtain (Naughton/Norton) and his son Tadhg. About 1726, Tadhg wrote a poem naming 26 scholars who were working in Dublin at this time. Although these writers did not produce any great works of literature, they did represent a writing and reading urban public; a study of their work shows us the literary potential of the tensions between the members of a bilingual community. Seán Ó Neachtain is by far the best literary artist from this group and his poetry and especially his prose works are lively and erudite in Irish, English and Latin. Several of his fellow writers also knew one or more continental languages.

We have been dealing so far mainly with poetry. From the beginning of the Classical Irish period and probably before that, poetry was more important that prose. Poems are often ascribed to particular individuals, but we do not know the names of the prose writers. A scribe could, and often did, interfere with the text of a piece of prose, 'correcting' it from another version or even altering it to suit his own point of view regarding the facts or style. Poetry was governed by stylistic, linguistic and metrical rules, which made it difficult to tamper with a text. It also was seen as an almost sacred text, especially when it involved the ritual praise of a chieftain. This view of the supremacy of poetry lasted into the post-Classical period, but we do have some noteworthy prose examples in the literature of the next two centuries.

We can divide the prose into the following categories: (a) devotional prose; (b) historical prose; (c) comic prose; and (d) versions of romantic tales or new compositions based on romantic tales. The didactic nature of devotional prose brought a directness of style that is very refreshing after the florid extravagance of some of the earlier literature. In the historical prose we have both a compendium of Irish literature and a synthesis of what had been passed down in the traditional schools for generations. The comic prose, in which *Pairlement Chloinne Tomáis* has pride of place, combines the best of previous humorous literature in Irish with some of the polemic techniques of Elizabethan pamphlet literature. This type of composition has left its mark on all Irish satire and comic literature down to the present day in both the oral and the written traditions. The versions of the perennially popular romantic tales are interesting because they give us an indication of our ancestors' taste for adventure stories. Many of them read like embryonic novels, but because the printing revolution left Gaelic Ireland relatively untouched, the novel in Irish did not flourish until the twentieth century.

We have dealt up to now practically exclusively with literature composed by those who could read and write Irish. We must realize that such writers were always in a small minority and each would be depending on his fellow writers as his public. Side by side with this tradition of reading and writing, there was another that fostered what we can call oral literature. This term is used to describe the great corpus of songs, stories, prayers and rhymes that have come down to the Irish-speaking communities of the present day. Many such pieces were first composed in the forms we have them now between 1600 and 1800, and they give us evidence of the life and leisure of the Irish people during the period. As will be apparent in some of the extracts selected below, it is sometimes very hard to draw the line between the literature of the writers and the oral compositions of the 'people'. There are many borrowings in both directions and these throw light on the real nature of Gaelic Ireland in the period from the battle of Kinsale to the Union of the two kingdoms in 1801.

Irish literary figures had always been able to adapt to the changing times that historical events brought into their world. In the twelfth century, when the reform of the church had broken the cultural cooperation between the church and secular systems of learning, they organized themselves to provide the system of education that gave us Classical Irish and its literature. When that broke up in the seventeenth century, they adapted and changed in response to the needs of the time. The literature they produced has had a profound effect in reflecting some attitudes of Gaelic Ireland and also in forming the view that Irish people have of themselves. The texts selected here attempt to give some insight into the way literature in Irish reflects the life and times of the Irish-speaking people in the period. The pieces have also been chosen because they have some literary merit. Such a choice is always subjective and can only be taken as a sample of all that was available in Irish from 1600 to 1800.

These editions and translations

Most of Irish literature from the period 1600-1800 was written and disseminated in manuscript form. The Irish texts in this selection have been produced by consulting modern editions and in some cases by examining the original manuscripts. An attempt has been made to render them intelligible to the reader who knows modern Irish, where such an approach is compatible with the original texts and the rules of Irish metrics. All the prose renderings are in direct and simple English. They are not meant to be literal translations, but they do attempt to convey both the sense and tone of the originals. Where not all the available stanzas of a poem have been used, this is indicated by the use of ellipses in the Irish text.

A note on metres

We can divide the metres in the poems in this selection into three categories: syllabic metre, stress or song metre, and rosc. *The syllabic metres are so called because there is a given number of syllables in each line and they are distinguished by this and by the number of syllables in the last word of each line. There are elaborate rules of rhyme and consonance. These metres were used during the Classical Irish period. In the seventeenth and eighteenth centuries we have often only loose forms of the syllabic metres. The stress or song metres are probably based on actual musical forms and in the latter period it is clear that many of the poems were composed to be sung. They are based on a correspondence between the stressed words in the verses. The word* rosc *has no real equivalent in English. It refers to a short rhythmical metre that was used for a variety of purposes, from nursery rhymes to the ritual keening of the dead. The main features are rhythm and usually short lines, all of which have the same stressed vowel at the end. This stress pattern can be changed from time to time. This metre probably has its origin in a musical chant. All these types of metres regularly use alliteration.*

EOCHAIDH Ó hEODHASA

(*c.*1565-1613)

from: THE WINTER CAMPAIGN

[This poem is well-known because of James Clarence Mangan's adaptation, 'O'Hussey's Ode to the Maguire'. The original poem was composed by Eochaidh Ó hEodhasa (O'Hussey) for his patron and friend Aodh Mag Uidhir (Hugh Maguire) during the Nine Years' War. Mag Uidhir was taking part in the winter campaign in Munster and the poem reflects Ó hEodhasa's anxiety for his safety. See Volume II, p. 28.]

Fuar liom an oidhche-se d'Aodh,
cúis truime a ciothbhraon;
mo thruaighe sein dar seise,
neimh-fhuaire na hoidcheise.

… … … … … …

Do hosgladh ós ochtaibh néill
doirse uisgidhe an aiéir:
Tug sé minlinnte 'na muir,
do sgé an fhirminnte a hurbhuidh.

… … … … … … …

Nárab aithreach leis ná leam
a thuras timcheall Éireann;

go ndeach tharainn — ná tí m'olc —
an ní fá ngabhaim guasacht.

Dá dtí ris an toisg do thriall,
do chur chuarta Chraoi Mhaicniadh —
ní tháirtheamar mar soin —
créad acht snáithghearradh saoghail.

... ...

Gidh eadh is adhbhar téighthe
dá ghnúis shuaithnidh shoiléirthe
slios gach múir ghormshaothraigh ghil
'na dhlúimh thonnghaothmhair theintigh.

... ...

Iomdha ó chuairt Aoidh Mhéig Uidhir
feadh iarthair fhóid fhionnfhuinidh,
cúirt 'na doighir, ní díoth nua,
críoch gan oighir, gan iarmhua.

TRANSLATION

Too cold I deem this night for Hugh;[1] the heaviness of its showerdrops is a cause of sadness; alas that our loved one must suffer the venom of this night's cold....

From above the tops of the clouds, the floodgates of heaven have been opened. It has turned small pools into seas; the firmament has spewed out its destruction....

May neither he nor I regret his journey around Ireland; may my calamity not come — may the thing that causes me peril pass from us.

If he should be harmed from the task he has attempted, namely to make a circuit of Munster[2] — we have found none like him — what is it but the thread-cutting of life itself.[3] ...

And yet his remarkable, clear countenance is warmed when the side of each bright stone-worked castle is changed into a fiery stormy mist....

Because of Maguire's circuit through the west of the land where the sun sets, there are many courts in flames; no new destruction this, and many the land without heir or great-grandson.

1. Chieftain of the Maguires of Fermanagh from *c.* 1590 until his death on campaign in Munster in 1600.
2. Cró Maicnia is a typical kenning for Munster.
3. Maguire was killed in a skirmish near Cork early in the year 1600.

AINDRIAS MAC MARCAIS

(*fl.* 1610)

from:
THE DESERTED LAND

[Many poems deal with the Irish chieftains who left for continental Europe in September 1607. This one concerns the plight of the country and her people after the leaders have gone.]

Anocht is uaigneach Éire,
do-bheir fógra a fírfhréimhe
gruaidhe a fear 's a fionnbhan fliuch,
treabh is iongnadh go huaigneach.

... ...

Ag triall gan locadh tar lear
uainn do roighnibh mac Míleadh;
gé daoineach aon fhádbhuig fhinn,
fágbhaid gan aoinneach Éirinn.

... ...

Gan gáire fá ghníomhaibh linbh,
cosg ar cheol, glas ar Ghaoidhilg,
mic ríogh, mar nach dual don dream,
gan luadh ar fhíon ná ar aifreann.

Gan imirt, gan ól fleidhe,
gan aithghearradh aimseire,
gan mhalairt, gan graifne greadh,
gan tabhairt aighthe in éigean.

Gan ŕadha rithlearg molta,
gan scaoileadh sceol gcodlata,
gan úidh ar fhaicsin leabhair,
gan chloistin nglúin gheinealaigh.

... ...

Rug orra, ní cóir a cheilt,
an bhroid do bhí san Éigeipt,
nó an líon fán dTraoi do thionóil,
nó an sníomh do bhaoi ar Bhaibiolóin.

... ...

Ó tá an cuan um chrích bhFeimhin,
an bhroid cionnas chuirfidhear
don fhréimh naoi-se chéibhfhinn Chuinn,
is gan Maoise in Éirinn againn.

Ní fhuil díobh fear a hiomchair
d'éis ar imthigh d'Éirionnchaibh;
ríoghhraidh Bhanbha fá bhroid troim
ag goid ar n-anma asainn.

TRANSLATION

Tonight Ireland is lonely. The banishment of her true race causes the cheeks of her men and her fair women to be wet — it is strange that this tribe should be lonely....

Away from us the choicest of the sons of Ireland are journeying without anyone stopping them. Though any fair, fertile land be full of people, these leave Ireland uninhabited....

There is no laughter at a child's deeds, music ceases, Irish is in chains. Princes, unusually for them, speak not of wine-feast nor Mass.

There is no playing, feasting, nor any pastime. There is no trading or riding horses or turning to face danger.

No praise poem is recited, no bedtime story told, no desire to see a book, no giving ear to the family pedigrees.[1] ...

The captivity that was in Egypt has overtaken them, let it not be concealed, or the host that gathered about Troy, or the affliction that was in Babylon....

Seeing that the land of Ireland is surrounded by sea, how shall the oppression be lifted from the bright fair-haired race of Conn,[2] since we have no Moses in Ireland?

There is none of them who can lift her up after all the Irish who have gone. The fact that the kingly lines are under heavy oppression is stealing our soul from us.

1. In this verse the poet lays emphasis on the way his own profession has been affected.
2. Conn Céadchathach (Conn of the Hundred Battles), eponymous ancestor of the people of Connacht in Irish mythology. Such figures are often used to signify the ancestors of all the Gaelic Irish.

BONAVENTURA Ó hEODHASA

(*c.*1570-1614)

from: A FRIEND'S CONSOLATION

[Bonaventura Ó hEodhasa (O'Hussey) was one of the many writers trained in a traditional poetical school who went to the European continent at the end of the sixteenth century. He joined the Franciscan order and was one of the founders of the Irish College of St Anthony in Louvain. This poem, lamenting the death of Richard Nugent, son of his friends William and Janet Nugent of Delvin, Co. Meath, has the rare combination of sincere feeling and the polished language and technique of Classical Irish poetry.]

Deacair suan ar chneidh gcarad:
gar d'airdheanaibh easgarad
an t-aos comtha nach geabh gráin
re horchra gcneadh a gcompáin.

Gidh bé uaibh do fhéadfadh soin,
codladh ar chneadh a chomhthaigh;
d'aos chomtha ní croidhe glan
gan orchra aroile d'iomchar.

Aos comtha an chumainn dearbhtha,
coitcheann cúis a mbuaidheartha,
ionann orchra, ionann ceas
ortha agus ionann áineas.

Mar sin damhsa, diochra an léan
fá d'orchra a inghean Uaitéar;
neimh na cneidhe rod' chreimse
'na chneidh eile ar m'intinnse.

Bíth d'osnadh do dhruim dheacra
ag clódh chéadfadh m'éisteachta;
bíth do dheor, a chnú chridhe,
ag deol chrú as ár gcridhe.

Dá gcoisginn cion mo thuirse
sunna dhíot dod'dhoghailse,
ar ndóigh ní budh dimbríogh linn,
ná a bhfuil d'imshníomh ar m'intinn.

… … … … … … … …

Rugadh uait, dia do dhoghra,
do mhac, oighre d'athardha,
do chosg bróin, t'aondalta ar n-éag,
do ghlóir shaoghalta, a Shinéad.

Saor an scoth do scar ruibhse,
ní hiongnadh d'fáth doghailse:
ba triall ráith, ba gaoth i ngal,
ba laoch, ba flaith, ba fealsamh.

Dia athar — ga huaisle ceard —
dó féin do-rinne Risteard:
ní huaibhse rug an nglaic ngloin
is ní duit tug ó thosaigh.

Doras beathadh bás an fhir,
ní cúis imshníomha a oighidh:
cia an neach i gcás budh cuirthe
dá ndeach le bás mbeannaighthe.

Glan budh-easd d'aghaidh dtuirsigh,
triomaigh do ghruaidh ngrianluisnigh,
an doigh do-chuaidh id chridhe,
ad-roigh uaibh a m'impidhe.

TRANSLATION

It is hard to sleep when a friend is hurt. For comrades not to hate the sorrow of a companion's injury is almost to be without the bonds of friendship.

Sleeping when a friend is hurt, who could do that? It does not show a pure heart to fail to carry each other's sorrow.

For comrades who love truly, the cause of their distress is common; they feel the same pain, the same wound and the same pleasure.

It is like that for me; the intensity of my affliction concerning your grief is great; the bitterness of the wound consuming you is another wound on my mind.

Your sighing because of sorrow stifles my sense of hearing; your tear, o loved one, sucks blood from my heart.

If only my portion of sorrow could remove from you your pain; indeed it would not be beyond my power with all the grief on my mind. . . .

He was taken from you (what great misery), your son, heir of your patrimony, he who dispelled sorrow, your only child, your worldly glory has died, Janet.

Noble was the youth who left you, no wonder for you to be sorrowful: he was a prosperous wayfarer, skilful in battle, a warrior, a leader, a sage.

God the Father — there is no greater creator — for Himself He fashioned Richard: it was not from you that He took the pure-handed one. And He did not give him to you in the beginning.

The man's death was the door to life; his passing is no cause for grief. Who can be compared to one who had died a blessed death?

Henceforth clear your sorrowful face, dry your bright shining cheek. The pain that entered your heart leaves you at my behest.

SÉATHRÚN CÉITINN

(*c.*1580-*c.*1650)

from: NEWS FROM IRELAND

[A familiar theme in seventeenth-century poetry is the effect that news of conditions in Ireland had on the poets who were in exile on the Continent. Much of the patriotic feeling that came into the verse of the period sets the formula for subsequent poets. In this poem Keating tells us first of the effect the bad news has on him. After alluding to the contamination of the Irish by renegades and strangers, he addresses Ireland as a fickle woman who has deserted her rightful family. He then talks of the rapacious foreigners, who, he says, would not have their wicked way if the noble Irish families were still strong. The only hope is in the mercy of the Almighty. If He does not help, the Irish may as well go abroad.

The translation of these stanzas is by Thomas Kinsella; see *An Duanaire*, pp. 85, 87.]

Óm sceol ar ardmhágh Fáil ní chodlaim oíche
'S do bhreoigh go bráth mé dála a pobail dílis;
gé rófhada atáid 'na bhfál ré broscar bíobha,
fá dheoidh gur fhás a lán den chogal tríothu.

A Fhódla phráis, is náir nach follas díbhse
gur córa tál ar sháirshliocht mhodhail Mhíle;
deor níor fágadh i gclár do bhrollaigh mhínghil
nár dheolsad ál gach cránach coigríche.

Gach treod gan tásc tar sál dá dtogair síneadh
go hóirlios álainn ársa Chobhthaigh Chaoil chirt,
is leo gan ghráscar lámh ár ndonna-bhruíne,
's gach fód is fearr dár n-áitibh eochar-aoibhne.

... ...

Dá mba beoga ardfhlaith Áine is Droma Daoile
's na leoghain láidre ón Máigh do bhronnadh maoine,
dar ndóigh níorbh áit don táinse in oscaill Bhríde
gan gheoin is gártha ós ard dá dtoghaildíbirt.

Muna bhfóiridh Ceard na n-ardreann pobal chrích Chuirc
ar fhoirneart námhad ndána n-ullamh ndíoltach
ní mór nárbh fhearr gan chairde a bhfoscaindíolaim
's a seoladh slán i bhfán tar tonnaibh Chlíodhna.

TRANSLATION

At the news from Fál's high plain I cannot sleep.
I am sick till doom at the plight of its faithful folk.
Long have they stood as a hedge against hostile trash
but a lot of the cockle has grown up through them at last.

O brazen Fódla, it is shameful you do not see
it were fitter to nourish Míle's[1] sweet high race.
Not a drop is left in the plain of your smooth bright breast
— drained dry by the litter of every alien sow.

Any worthless crew that thought to cross the sea
to the fair, gold, age-old *lios* of Cobhthach 'the just'
— theirs without struggle of hands our mighty mansions
and the choicest swards of our lovely-bordered places.

... ...

If that high prince lived, of Áine and Drom Daoile,[2]
or the great gift-generous lions of the Máigh,[3]
this horde would have no place in the bend of the Bríde[3]
— smashed, driven out, with outcry and loud wails.

If the Craftsman of Stars protect not Ireland's people
from violent vengeful enemies, bold and ready,
better gather and winnow them now without delay
and sail them out wandering safe on the waves of Clíona.[4]

1. Father of the first Gaels to come to Ireland, according to the mythological account of the invasions of Ireland.
2. Two hills in County Limerick. The verse refers to the earls of Desmond.
3. The Bríde and the Máigh are rivers in County Limerick.
4. In the last verse this is a popular kenning for the waters surrounding Ireland.

PÁDRAIGÍN HAICÉAD O.P.

(*c.*1600-54)

from: THE EMIGRANT'S LOVE FOR IRELAND

[In this poem Haicéad uses the language and style of love poetry to express his feelings for Ireland while he languishes on the Continent.]

Cuirim séad suirghe chum seise;
searc mo chléibh do dháileas dí,
Éire chliathbhras bhocht an bhánfhuinn,
an gort iathghlas — álainn í.

An ghlac rann so romham siarainn,
mo shéad suirghe dá sliocht mhín,
's mo chroidhe ronnta ar na rannaibh,
bronnta ar chlannaibh Toighe-an-Trír.

… … … … … … …

Ní tharla liom ar fheadh m'eachtra
éin-tír eile mar iath Néill,
an tulaigh ghlan bhrianach bhraonach,
an mhagh ghrianach raonach réidh.

… … … … … …

Mithigh dhamh-sa dul dá féachain;
fada liom mo chor ar cuairt;
aonráith Dhá-Thí, an ráith ríoghach,
is í mo sháith shíodhach shuairc.

… … … … … …

Ataim uait i gcríochaibh ciana,
a chláir aosda is óige i gcruith,
mar aon feacht i ngeimhlibh garbha
le seacht ngeimhribh marbha amuich.

… … … … … …

Tugas grádh dhuit d'fheabhas t'fhoirne,
d'fheabhas t'éigse an tsuaircis tsaoir,
d'fheabhas t'fhéinne, t'fhuinn is t'oinigh,
's do chléire i gcuing ndoiligh ndaoir.

… … … … … …

TRANSLATION

I send a love token to my beloved; I gave her my heart's affection, she is Ireland, the pure bright land of swift battles, the green field — she is beautiful.

This handful of verses going westwards before me is my love-token to the smooth-sided one. And my heart is dispersed among the verses and presented to the children of Ireland....

I did not meet in my journey any other country like Ireland, the varied, pure, well-watered hillside and the sunny, smooth plain full of roads....

It is time for me to go and see her; I've been away for a long time. The one and only rath of Dá Thí,[1] the regal rath, that satisfies and is peaceful and pleasant for me....

I am away from you in faraway lands, o ancient land, so youthful in form, and also I have been in harsh fetters for seven dead winters....

I loved you for the excellence of your people; your excellent poets of noble eloquence, your excellent warriors, the land and your generosity, and your clerics in hard bondage....

1. Dá Thí Mac Fiachrach, second high king of Ireland, according to the regnal lists.

THE MARIGOLD

[These two love poems to Máire Tóibín have been ascribed to the Dominican priest Pádraigín Haicéad. The first is a good example of the elaborate *amour courtois* style, using in this case an accentual song metre. The next poem, written on the occasion of her death, is not as stylish, but expresses a more personal feeling.]

Dála an nóinín — ó do-chí soilse i ngréin
is gearr go gcomhscaoil clólíon trilseach géag,
is tráth um nóin laoi, ar dtós dí i gcoim na néall,
fáiscidh fóichnín pórdhlaoi chruinn a craobh,

Mo dháil le hóigín oirní is milse méin,
Máire Tóibín, lóithnín lingthe laoch,
ghrámhar, ghlóirfhíor, ghnóchaoin, ghrinnghlic,
ghaoth;
tálaim óm chlí só sí is sinn láire.

'S mar fhágas m'óighbhríd gcóirchíoch gcoimseach
mé,
ní fhaghaim óm chroí cónaí i gcuing go gcéill,
ach trácht, ar nós tsíornóinín fhinn na raon,
rem bhá i mbrónchaoí ghleodhaoir ghoilseach ghéir.

... ...

Ní táire fóiscríob chló chaoilphinn go ngléas
ná a dhá corrbhraoi ar shnó an daoil chionnduibh
chéir,
os ardaibh borrbhlaosc mhórdhaí a lionnruisc léith,
láimh ré somplaíbh róis trí fhionn 'na gné.

... ...

Cé tharla slóighlíon d'óigshíol Ghoill is Ghaoidhil,
i gcásaibh cróilí ó a grís tinnsheirc tréimhse,
in áitibh óglaoich an ngeobhaidh sí spreill mar mé?
ní fearr mo bheo, 's ní móide í sinn iar n-éag.

TRANSLATION

Behold the marigold[1] — from the time she sees the sunlight she quickly opens out her network of petals and in the afternoon, as soon as the shadows fall, she folds up the blades tight to the stem.

I am like that with the beautiful maiden of the sweetest disposition; she who is the breeze that inspires warriors: she is loving, true-voiced, sweet, clever and wise. When I am with her, my heart opens up.

And when my pure girl, smooth-breasted and neat, leaves me, my heart gives me no respite in sensible repose, but rather engulfs me like the fair, eternal marigold by the wayside, in sharp, noisy, bitter lamentation. . . .

The skilful writing of a narrow pen is not as slender as her two eyebrows, black as beetles above the noble shells of her grey, sparkling eyes, surrounded by rosy samples mixing with the fairness of her face. . . .

Although great numbers of young men, both Gall and Gael, are laid low by the intensity of their love for her, will she take a wretch like me instead of a warrior? [If not] my life is no good to me and [anyway] it is no benefit to her if I die.

1. *nóinín* = daisy, or marigold in modern Irish. Haicéad's poem is probably based on an English version of a poem by Ovid, which used the same conceit. In this case the poem is a play on Máire's own name.

from: MÁIRE'S DEATH

A shuaircfhir sháimh, ní sámh do reacaireacht
sceoil;
ba thuaidh dá ngráin, ar scáthcheilt m'aingilse
dhóibh!
ar tuathal táid; dob'fhearr bheith balbh go mór,
ná buain le gáir ón gránna gafann do ghlór.

Beir uaimse a thásc, ní háil a chlaistin, ní heol
an t-uamhan gáibhtheach gránna garbh guirt gleo;
i dtuairim cháich má fágadh m'ainnir faoi fhód,
níor bhuaigh bás ar Mháire im mheabhairse fós.

... ...

Ní duairce rá ná a rá gur theastaigh roimh nóin,
ar dtuar a blátha, d'áille a hearraigh um thós,
m'uan beag cáidh gan ghnás, gan ghalar, gan ghó,
gan chluain, gan chnáid, gan cháith, gan chailg,
gan cheo.

... ...

Buaidhreadh, báthadh, bearnadh, bascadh is brón,
tug m'fhuathsa ar cheardaibh, d'ardchuir m'atuirse
ar phóit,
as cuasaibh cnámh ag tál na rabharta ndeor,
ón suaill nach snámhaid snáithe m'anma i neoll.

Mar luach ba táir in áit an cheana do-chóidh
an uair seo amháin chum báis dá ndeachainn 'na
deoidh;
ach fuaras grásta i lár na lasarghomh leoin,
bheith buan i bpáis go bráth dom mharú beo.

Mar ghluaiseas trá le táin a healtan gach corr,
do luathaigh Máire i ndáil na n-aingeal a seol;
go cuachaibh Parrthais slán lem sheabhac loin eoin;
dá gcuaine atá; ní bás ach beatha don óigh.

TRANSLATION

The tales you are telling are not pleasing, o gentle pleasant man. Keep their hatefulness away, protect my angel from them. They are wrong; it would be far better to be dumb than to have anything to do with that cry that makes your voice bitter as gall.

Take away from me the bad news, I don't wish to hear it; let the terrible, ugly, harsh, bitter, noisy fear be unknown. Even if in everyone's opinion my girl is beneath the clay, death has not triumphed over Máire in my mind yet....

There is no more unpleasant saying than to declare her absence before her noontide, in the promise of her flowering, at the beginning of her springtime. She, who was my revered little lamb, innocent without affliction, sincere without deception, mockery, blemish, malice or gloom....

Grief, drowning, splitting, beating and sorrow have made me hate occupations, and have heightened the heaviness of my sorrow, bringing forth a springtide of tears from the hollows of my bones, so that the threads of my life almost swim in a swoon!

It would be shameful after all my affection if I followed her in death only this one time now. But I have received grace in the midst of burning pain to be eternally tortured in living death.

Like as every heron follows her own flock, Máire has sped her sail to be with the angels. Farewell to my brave little blackbird as she goes to the embraces of heaven. She belongs in their company; this is not death but life for the maiden.

DÁIBHÍ Ó BRUADAIR

(*c.*1625-98)

from:
THE POET FALLS ON HARD TIMES

[It seems that Ó Bruadair was relatively well-off until some misfortune struck in 1674. He compares his carefree lifestyle with the hardships he encountered when he lost his livelihood.

The translation of these stanzas is by Thomas Kinsella; see *An Duanaire*, pp. 121, 123.]

Is mairg nár chrean le maitheas saoghalta
do cheangal ar gad sul ndeacha in éagantacht,
's an ainnise im theach ó las an chéadluisne
nach meastar gur fhan an dadamh céille agam.

An tamall im ghlaic do mhair an ghléphingin,
ba geanamhail gart dar leat mo thréithe-se —
do labhrainn Laidean ghasta is Béarla glic
's do tharrainginn dais ba cleas ar chléireachaibh.

Do bheannachadh dhamh an bhean 's a céile cnis,
an bhanaltra mhaith 's a mac ar céadlongadh;
dá ngairminn baile is leath a ngréithe-sean,
ba deacair 'na measc go mbainfeadh éara dhom.

Do ghabhainn isteach 's amach gan éad i dtigh
is níor aistear uim aitreabh teacht aréir 's aniogh;
dobh aitheasc a searc fá seach le chéile againn
'achainghim, ceadaigh blaiseadh ár mbéile-ne'.

D'athraigh 'na ndearcaibh dath mo néimhe anois
ar aiste nach aithnidh ceart im chéimeannaibh;
ó shearg mo lacht le hais na caomhdhroinge,
d'aithle mo cheana is marcach mé dem chois.

... ...

Is tartmhar mo thasc ag treabhadh im aonarsa
le harm nár chleachtas feacht ba mhéithe me;
d'atadar m'ailt de reath na crélainne
is do mhartra' an feac ar fad mo mhéireanna.

TRANSLATION

Woe to that man who leaves on his vagaries
without busying himself tying up some worldly
goods.
There is misery in my house from the first
dawn-light,
and no one believes I've got one tatter of sense.

For as long as the shining penny was in my fist
my ways were charming and cheerful, you would
think.
My speech was fluent Latin and cunning English!
I could describe a flourish to dazzle the scribes!

Wives and the mates of their flesh saluted me
and mothers and their boys before their breakfast.
If I were to ask for a village, with half its contents,
I'd find it hard to get a refusal among them.

I could enter and leave a house, and no complaint;
turn up at the same house night and day — it was
  nothing.
Jointly and several, the burthen of their love
was: 'Deign, I implore you, to take a taste of our
  meal!'

But I've taken a different colour now in their eyes
so that they see no right in my procedures.
To judge by this gentry now, my milk has turned
and after my time of respect I must ride on foot.

… … … … … … … … … …

It's a thirsty task, ploughing this lonely furrow,
with a weapon I never employed when I was rich:
this sword-play into the earth has swelled my ankles
and the shaft has martyred my fingers totally.

THE POET LAMENTS HIS LEARNING

[Ó Bruadair ironically praises boorishness and his lack of poetic elegance, seeing that learning and clever verse have availed him nothing. His lament is most clearly stated in the last two lines of the fourth stanza.

The translation is by Thomas Kinsella; see *An Duanaire*, pp. 113, 115.]

Mairg nach fuil 'na dhubhthuata,
  gé holc duine 'na thuata,
i ndóigh go mbeinn mágcuarda
  idir na daoinibh duarca.

Mairg nach fuil 'na thrudaire
  eadraibhse, a dhaoine maithe,
ós iad is fearr chugaibhse,
  a dhream gan iúl gan aithne.

Dá bhfaghainn fear mo mhalarta,
  leis do reacfainn an suairceas;
do-bhéarainn luach fallainge
  idir é 'gus an duairceas.

Ós mó cion fear deaghchulaith
  ná a chion de chionn bheith tréitheach,
truagh ar chaitheas le healadhain
  gan é a-niogh ina éadach.

Ós suairc labhartha is bearta gach buairghiúiste
gan uaim gan aiste 'na theangain ná suanúchas,
mo thrua ar chreanas le ceannaraic cruaphrionta
ó bhuaic mo bheatha nár chaitheas le tuatúlacht.

TRANSLATION

O it's best be a total boor
  (though it's bad be a boor at all)
if I'm to go out and about
  among these stupid people.

It's best to be, good people,
  a stutterer among you
since that is what you want,
  you blind ignorant crew.

If I found me a man to swap
  I'd give him my lovely skill.
He'd find it as good as a cloak
  around him against the gloom.

Since a man is respected more
  for his suit than for his talents
I regret what I've spent on my art,
  that I haven't it now in clothes.

Since happy in word and deed is each boorish clod
without music or metre or motherwit on his tongue,
I regret what I've wasted struggling with hard print
since the prime of life — that I might have spent as a
  boor.

LAST WORDS I
AOGÁN Ó RATHAILLE
(*c.*1670-1726)

[The following three poems all deal with death — the poets' own impending deaths. In the first, Aogán Ó Rathaille is defiant and proud to the end.

The translation is by Thomas Kinsella; see *An Duanaire*, pp. 164-67.]

Cabhair ní ghairfead (No help I'll call)

Cabhair ní ghairfead go gcuirthear mé i gcruinn-
chomhrainn —
dar an leabhar dá ngairinn níor ghaire-de an ní dhomh-sa;
ár gcodhnach uile, glac-chumasach shíl Eoghain,
is tollta a chuisle 'gus d'imigh a bhrí ar feóchadh.

Do thonnchrith m'inchinn, d'imigh mo phríomh-dhóchas,
poll im ionathar, biora nimh' trím dhrólainn,
ár bhfonn, ár bhfothain, ár monga 's ár mínchóngair
i ngeall le pingin ag foirinn ó chrích Dhóbhair.

Do bhodhar an tSionainn, an Life, 's an Laoi cheolmhar,
abhainn an Bhiorra Dhuibh, Bruice 'gus Bríd, Bóinne,
com Loch Deirg 'na ruide 'gus Toinn Tóime
ó lom an cuireata cluiche ar an rí coróinneach.

Mo ghlam is minic, is silimse síordheora,
is trom mo thubaist 's is duine mé ar míchomhthrom,
fonn ní thigeann im ghaire 's mé ag caoi ar bhóithre
ach foghar na Muice nach gontar le saigheadóireacht.

... ...

(Ceangal)

Stadfadsa feasta — is gar dom éag gan mhoill
ó treascradh dragain Leamhan, Léin is Laoi;
rachad 'na bhfasc le searc na laoch don chill,
na flatha fá raibh mo shean roimh éag do Chríost.

TRANSLATION

No help I'll call till I'm put in the narrow coffin.
By the Book, it would bring it no nearer if I did!
Our prime strong-handed prop, of the seed of Eoghan
— his sinews are pierced and his vigour is withered up.

Wave-shaken is my brain, my chief hope gone.
There's a hole in my gut, there are foul spikes through my bowels.
Our land, our shelter, our woods and our level ways
are pawned for a penny by a crew from the land of Dover.[1]

The Sionainn, the Life, the musical Laoi, are muffled
and the Biorra Dubh river, the Bruice, the Bríd, the Bóinn.
Reddened are Loch Dearg's narrows and the Wave of Tóim[2]
since the Knave[3] has skinned the crowned King in the game.

Incessant my cry; I spill continual tears;
heavy my ruin; I am one in disarray.
No music is nigh as I wail about the roads
except for the noise of the Pig[4] no arrows wound.

... ...

(The Binding)[5]

I will stop now — my death is hurrying near
now the dragons of the Leamhan, Loch Léin and the Laoi[6] are destroyed.
In the grave with this cherished chief I'll join those kings
my people served before the death of Christ.

1. A town on the south coast of England. This epithet is obviously taken from another context, since Dover does not face Ireland.
2. The wave at the mouth of Castlemaine Harbour, Co. Kerry. Traditionally it roars when Ireland is in danger. The rivers named here are the Shannon, the Liffey, the Lee, the Blackwater, the Brick, the Bride and the Boyne.
3. A reference to Oliver Cromwell (1599-1658).
4. Perhaps a reference to the Torc (torc = boar) Waterfall.
5. Irish poems in the eighteenth century often have such verses summarizing the spirit of the subject-matter of the rest of the poem.
6. Rivers in Counties Cork and Kerry.

LAST WORDS II
SÉAMAS DALL MAC CUARTA
(*c.*1650-1733)

[Séamas Dall Mac Cuarta (McCourt) looks forward to joining his loved ones.]

Is fada mé 'mo luí i Lúghaidh
  'mo scraiste brúite, mo mhíle crá!
Dúiscídh is cruinnídh na seabhaic lúfar'
  is iomchraidh an t-úrmhac i gcaol na gcnámh.

Dias is ochtar a theastaigh uaimse
  'tá 'na luí go suaimhneach sa mBaile Nua,
mar a bhfuil Mairghréad is Ruairí is Brian, mo chuallaí,
  is déantar uaigh dhamh ar ghar an triúir.

Síntear síos mo thaobh le Ruairí,
  mar a bhfuil mo chuallaí, Brian Bán;
tá siad a ndís ann 'na luí ar uaigneas
  'cuir idir fuacht mé 'gus cor den gclár.

Cha bhíonn Róis ann nó an dá Éamann,
  's ar son Mhairghréada, char chlaon a páirt;
tá an dá Bhríd ann le taobh a chéile,
  's cha bhíonn siad at éad fá mo chur san áit.

… … … … … … …

Is iomdha cúirt agus caisleán láidir
  i raibh mé ag ráfla 's ag déanamh spóirt,
ach má théim go Flaitheas, a Rí na ngrása,
  cérbh fhearr 'mo thámh mé ná ag déanamh ceoil?

Cha ndearna mé aithreachas ariamh mar 'chóir damh
  ach ag déanamh ceoltaí ar feadh mo shaoil,
ach anois ó tá mise tréithlag breoite,
  a Dhia, déan trócaire ar Shéamus Caoch.

TRANSLATION

Long I have been lying in Louth, a broken wretch, a thousand torments! Awake and gather lively men and bring your loved one to the narrow grave of bones.

I am missing ten persons who are lying peacefully in Baile Nua;[1] that's where Margaret, Rory and Brian my companion are. Let a grave be made for me close to the three of them.

Let me be laid down by Rory where my companion Fair Brian is. Both of them are lying in a lonely place, so put me down between the cold air and the edge of the coffin.

Rose is not alive nor the two Edwards and, as for Margaret, her love did not waver; the two Bríds are there beside each other and they do not begrudge me being put in that place....

There were many courts and mighty castles in which I chatted and made sport; and if I go to Heaven, O God of grace, would I have been better to have kept silent than to have made music?

I never repented as I should, but I spent my life composing songs; but now that I am sick and weak, O God have mercy on Blind Jim.

1. Newtown, beside Slane, Co. Meath.

LAST WORDS III
CATHAL BUÍ MAC GIOLLA GUNNA
(died *c.*1756)

[Cathal Buí Mac Giolla Gunna repents for his dissolute life.]

Marbhnaí Chathail Bhuí
(Lament of the Yellow-Haired Cathal)

A Rí na ngrása, is dána dhamh amharc ort suas
's nach bhfuil oíche nó lá nach dtairnim fuil as do
  ghruaidh;
d'fhuiling tú páis agus bás dár gceannach go cruaidh
's mur' dtille tú, a Athair, gan spás 'nois imeoidh mé
  uait.

… … … … … … … … …

A Rí na bhfeart, go nglaca tú mo chroí
's go mbeire tú leat gan stad mé mar 'bhfuil na
  haingil;

admhaim mo lochta anocht, cam agus claon:
gur thit mé i bpeaca crosta deamhnaí an tsaoil.

Fuair mé cúig ní ón Spioraid Naomh 's níorbh fhiú
mé a bhfáil:
amharc na slí. fa-raoir! agus cluinim a lán,
blas agus boladh, molaim thú, a Rí na ngrás,
's go n-aithneann mo chroí gach ní, míle altú leat,
a Athair.

… … … … … … … … … …

Is é mo chrá géar le toil Dé nachar rugadh mé dall,
bodhar gan radharc, gan aon phioc teanga in mo
cheann,
sul a dheachaigh mé i dtréas mar cheithearnach
coille 'ní feall;
is fa-raoir géar! ní dhearna mé an aithrí in am.

Nach trua mé Lá an tSléibhe ar thosach an tslóigh
's gur measa mé nó an té bhraith Críosta le póig;
gheobhaidh mé cré an dá aspal déag agus creidfear
mé, ar ndóigh,
agus déaraidh mé féin i láthair Dé '*I am guilty, my Lord*'.

TRANSLATION

O King of grace, it is forward of me to look up to you because day and night I draw blood on your cheek; you suffered and died in redeeming us and if you don't come back to me soon, I'll be a lost soul. . . .

O King of miracles, take my heart and bring me with you without delay to the place where the angels are; I admit my faults tonight, I am crooked and evil: and I have fallen into the forbidden devilish sins of this life.

Five things I received from the Holy Spirit that I was not worthy of; I can see my way alas! and I hear plenty, I can taste and smell, I praise you, King of grace, and my heart recognizes all things, a thousand blessings on you Father. . . .

It is my great distress that I was not born blind, and deaf and without a tongue in my head at all, by the will of God, before I committed treason like an outlaw doing evil; Alas alas! I never repented in time.

Won't it be pitiful for me on the Day of Judgment at the front of the mob; and me being worse than the one who betrayed Christ with a kiss. I shall have the creed of the twelve disciples and I shall be believed and I shall say in the presence of God '*I am guilty, my Lord*'.

THE LOVER'S INVITATION I

PEADAR Ó DOIRNÍN

(*c.*1700-69)

[A popular form of love song in Irish is the invitation the poet gives to his lover to come apart and enjoy the beauties of nature and solitude with him. The first song by Peadar Ó Doirnín is one of the best examples we have. Some versions also include the earthy rejection of the last verse, which is in contrast to the romantic terms of the invitation.]

A phlúr na maighdean is úire gné
thug clú le scéimh ón Ádhamhchlainn,
A chúl na bpéarlaí, a rún na héigse
dhúblaíos féile 's fáilte,
a ghnúis mar ghréin i dtús gach lae ghil
mhúchas léan le gáire,
's é mo chumhaidh gan mé 's tú, a shiúr, linn féin
sa dún sin Chéin mhic Cáinte.

Táim brúite i bpéin, gan suan gan néal,
de do chumhaidhse, a ghéag is áille,
's gur tú mo roghain i gcúigibh Éireann,
cúis nach séanaim ás de;
dá siúlfá, a réalt gan smúid, liom féin
ba súgach saor ár sláinte —

gheobhair plúr is méad is cnuasach craobh
 sa dún sin Chéin mhic Cáinte.

Cluinfir uaill na ngadhar ar luas i ndéidh
 Bhriain luaimnigh bhearnaigh mhásaigh
is fuaim guth béilbhinn cuach is smaolach
 go suairc ar ghéaga in altaibh;
i bhfuarlinn tséimh chífir slua-bhuíon éisc
 ag ruagadh a chéile ar snámh ann,
's an cuan go léir dhuit uait i gcéin
 ó nua-chnoc Chéin mhic Cáinte.

A rún mo chléibh, nach mar súd ab fhearr dhuit
 tús do shaoil a chaitheamh liom? —
's ní i gclúid faoi léan ag túirscín bréan
 i gcionn túirne 's péire cardaí;
gheobhair ciúl na dtéad le lúth na méar
 do do dhúscadh 's dréachta grá fós —
níl dún faoin ngréin chomh súgach aerach
 le hÚrchnoc Chéin mhic Cáinte.

A shuaircbhean tséimh na gcuachfholt péarlach,
 gluais liom féin ar ball beag,
tráth is buailte cléir is tuataí i néal
 'na suan faoi éadaí bána;
ó thuaidh go mbéam i bhfad uathu araon
 teacht nua-chruth gréine amárach,
gan ghuais le chéile in uaigneas aerach
 san uaimh sin Chéin mhic Cáinte.

(An Cailín)

Beir uaim do phléid cé gur luaigh tú céad ní —
 Nós a bhfuil spéis ag a lán ann —
Is an duais is fearr nó uallaí séad
 Níor chuala mé thú ag trácht air;
Tuatha saora, buaibh is caoraigh,
 Is cruacha péarlaí i bpálais
Mar luach ní ghéabhainn uait is gan gléas
 In am suain le ndéantar páiste.

TRANSLATION

Most beautiful of maidens with the fairest complexion, who has surpassed all others in beauty, O girl with the pearly-headed hair, beloved of poets, who increases generosity and welcome, your face, like the sun at the beginning of a bright day, quenches sorrow with a laugh, alas my girl that we are not together alone in the fort of Cian Mac Cáinte.[1]

I am in pain and unable to sleep because I am pining for you, most beautiful one, and you are my choice from all over Ireland, I do not deny it at all; O faultless star, if you would only walk away with me, fair and free would our state be — you'll have the best and plenty and fruit in the fort of Cian Mac Cáinte.

You'll hear the dogs bark as they follow the strong running hare, and the sweet-voiced singing of cuckoo and thrush merrily on branches in the glens; in a smooth cold lake you'll see a host of fish as they chase each other in swimming and the sea in front of you, far away from the fresh hill of Cian Mac Cáinte.

O my sweetheart, would you not like to spend the beginning of your life with me like that? — and not pine in a hovel with a stinking boor, spinning and carding wool. You'll have harp-music played with swift fingers to wake you and love songs — there is no fort under the sun as happy and full of fun as the fresh hill of Cian Mac Cáinte.

Gentle happy woman of the curling, pearly hair, come with me soon, while clergy and people are fast asleep under white bedclothes; let's be off to the north away from them all when the sun's new form rises tomorrow; we'll be far from danger in happy solitude in the hollow of Cian Mac Cáinte.

(The girl answers)

Away with your whining, though you mention a hundred things — a habit many people have — but the prize that is better than heaps of treasure I did not hear you talk about; I wouldn't accept noble lands, cattle, and sheep, or piles of pearls in palaces from you if you had no instrument to make a child at bedtime.

1. The hill or fort of Cian Mac Cáinte, hero of the tale 'The Death of the Sons of Tuireann', lies about two miles north-west of Dundalk, Co. Louth.

THE LOVER'S INVITATION II

SEÁN Ó NEACHTAIN

(*c.*1650-1729)

[This poem was said to have been composed for Una Ní Bhroin, who accepted Ó Neachtain and became his wife.]

Rachainn fón choill leat a mhaighdean na n-órfholt,
ag féachain ar éanlaith 's ag éisteacht a gceolghob.
Beidh fidil at caoinche, beidh píop ag an smólach,
londubh ag cur cana le cláirsigh go ceolmhar.

Beidh liú ag an dreolán is órgán ag céirseach,
an fhuiseog 's an meantán 's a dtiompán go gleasta,
gealbhan sa tom glas 's a thrumpa ina bhéal-san,
ag bualadh puirt damhsa ré ansacht a chléibh duit.

Beidh cuilm agus fearáin ag cronán ré chéile,
an truideog 's an sacán go cóngarach ag léimnigh,
cuach bheag na craoibhe go silleadh dod' fhéachain,
gearrghuirt is traona de shíor frat, a théagair.

... ...

Beidh an macalla inár n-aice-ne ag gáirí,
beidh na mná sí is braoine ar a gcláirsigh,
beidh an uile ní frat dar mian leat, a chathaigh,
go deo na díle ní scaoilfe mo pháirt leat.

Beidh dealramh na gréine ag sméideadh go
drithleach
orainne féachaint trí ghéagaibh na coille,
drúilíní ag súgradh, ba chiúl leat an t-uisce,
éisc agus dobhráin ag comhspairn go cliste.

(An Freagra)

Rachaidh mé féin leat gan éaradh go súgach,
ag féachain 's ag éisteacht na n-éan sin ag súgradh,
céad fearr liom féin sin ná féasta na cúirte;
a ailleáin, is a théagair súd mé leat gan diúltadh.

TRANSLATION

I would go to the wood with you, O golden-headed maiden, looking at the birds and listening to the music of their mouths. The nightingale will have a fiddle, the thrush will have a flute and the blackbird will be chanting melodiously accompanied by a harp.

The wren will have a lute and the hen-blackbird an organ, the lark and the titmouse will have their drums ready, a sparrow in the green bush will have his trumpet in his mouth, playing dance music because he loves you so much.

Pigeons and doves will be cooing together, the starling and the fieldfare will be hopping about close by, the little cuckoo on the branch will be seeking to look at you, and the corncrake will be always with you, my love....

The echo will be laughing beside us, the women from the fairy mounds and forts will play on harps; all you wish will be there beside you, my temptress, and till the end of time my love for you will never desert you.

The sunlight will pour down upon us through the branches of the wood, glittering droplets will play, the water will be your music while the otters and fish cleverly wrestle together.

(The reply)

I'll go with you merrily without refusing, looking and listening to the birds at play. I prefer that a hundred times to feasting at court; my pet, and my beloved, I come with you without resistance.

DREAMS OF LOVE AND FREEDOM I

[The concept of Ireland as a beautiful woman reaches its climax in the political *aisling* or vision poems of the eighteenth century. These are based on the love vision, where the poet sees a lovely but unattainable woman and his efforts to woo her are connected with the political themes of the deserted land and the hope of help from abroad. The following three examples give some idea of the range and scope of the genre. Typically the poet encounters the beautiful fairy woman, who tells him that she has been deserted and, while they talk, we can sense the hope or the despair of the poet's feelings.]

AOGÁN Ó RATHAILLE

['Mac an Cheannaí' ('The Merchant's Son', a title usually taken to mean the Stuart claimant to the throne) is one of the earliest political *aislings* and was composed by Aogán Ó Rathaille at a time when there was still the hope of a Jacobite rebellion. The translation is by Thomas Kinsella; see *An Duanaire*, pp. 157, 159, 161.]

Mac an Cheannaí

Aisling ghéar do dhearcas féin im leaba is mé go lagbhríoch,
ainnir shéimh darbh ainm Éire ag teacht im ghaor ar marcaíocht.
A súil ramhar ghlas, acúl trom cas, a com seang geal 's a malaí,
á mhaoímh go raibh ag tíocht 'na gar, le díograis, Mac an Cheannaí.

A beol ba bhinn, a glór ba chaoin, is ró-shearc linn an cailín,
céile Bhriain dár ghéill an Fhiann, mo léirchreach dhian a haicíd
fá shúistí Gall dá brú go teann, mo chúlfhionn tseang 's mo bhean ghaoil
níl faoiseamh seal le tíocht 'na gar go bhfillfidh Mac an Cheannaí.

Na céadta tá i bpéin de ghrá le géirshearc sháimh dá cneaschlí,
clanna ríthe, maca Míleadh, dragain fhíochda is gaiscígh.
Tá gnúis 'na gnaoi, ní mhúsclann sí; cé dubhach faoi scíos an cailín
níl faoiseamh seal le tíocht 'na gar go bhfillfidh Mac an Cheannaí.

... ...

A bráithre breaca táid thar lear, na táinte shearc an cailín,
níl fleá le fáil, níl gean ná grá ag neach dá cairdibh admhaím,
a gruanna fliuch, gan suan, gan sult, faoi ghruaim is dubh a n-aibíd:
Níl faoiseamh seal le tíocht 'na gar go bhfillfidh Mac an Cheannaí.

Dúrt-sa léi ar chlos na scéal 'na rún gur éag ar chleacht sí,
suas sa Spáinn go bhfuair an bás 's nar thrua le cach a haicíd.
Ar gclos mo ghotha i bhfogas dí do chorraigh a cruth 's do scread sí,
is d'éalaigh a hanam d'aon phreib aisti; mo léansa an bhean go lagbhríoch.

TRANSLATION

A bitter vision I beheld
in bed as I lay weary:
a maiden mild whose name was Éire
coming toward me riding,
with eyes of green hair curled and thick,
fair her waist and brows,
declaring he was on his way
— her loved one *Mac an Cheannaí*.

Her mouth so sweet, her voice so mild,
I love the maiden dearly,
wife to Brian, acclaimed of heroes
— her troubles are my ruin!

Crushed cruelly under alien flails
  my fair-haired slim kinswoman:
she's a dried branch, that pleasant queen,
  till he come, her *Mac an Cheannaí.*

Hundreds hurt for love of her
  — her smooth skin — in soft passion:
kingly children, sons of Míle,
  champions, wrathful dragons.
Her face, her countenance, is dead,
  in weariness declining,
and nowhere near is there relief
  till he come, her *Mac an Cheannaí.*

… … … … … … …

Her dappled Friars are overseas,
  those droves that she held dear;
no welcome, no regard or love,
  for her friends in any quarter.
Their cheeks are wet; no ease or sleep;
  dressed in black, for sorrow
— dried branch she'll stay, with no man lie,
  till he come, her *Mac an Cheannaí.*

I told her, when I heard her tale,
  in a whisper, he was dead,
that he had found death up in Spain,
  that no one heard her plaint.
She heard my voice beside her;
  her body shook; she shrieked;
her soul departed in a leap.
  Alas, that woman lifeless.

DREAMS OF LOVE AND FREEDOM II

ART MAC CUMHAIGH

(*c.*1738-73)

['Úirchill an Chreagáin' (Fair Churchyard of Cregan), like most *aislings* from the northern part of the country, is not political but rather reflects the poet's despair after the demise of his local chieftains, the O'Neills.

The translation is by Seamus Deane.]

Úirchill an Chreagáin

Ag Úirchill an Chreagáin a chadail mé aréir faoi bhrón
is le héirí na maidne thainig ainnir fá mo dhéin le póig;
bhí gríos-ghrua ghartha aici 'gus lainnir ina céibh mar ór
's gurb é íocshláinte an domhain bheith ag amharc ar an ríoghain óig.

'A fhialfhir charthanaigh, ná caitear thusa i ndealramh bróin
ach éirigh ' do sheasamh 'gus aistrigh liom siar sa ród
go tír dheas na meala nach bhfuair Gallaibh ann cead réim go fóill
mar ' bhfaighir aoibhneas ar hallaibh do do mhealladh le siansa ceoil.'

'Cha diúltfainn do chuireadh ar a gcruinníonn siad na ríthe d'ór
ach gur cladhartha liom scarúint le mo charaid 'tá sa tír go fóill;
an céile úd a mheallas le mo ghealltúint tráth bhí sí óg,
dá dtréigfinn anois í gur fiosach damh go mbeadh sí i mbrón.'

'Cha shílim gur caraid duit a maireann de do ghaoltaibh beo —
tá tú faofa, gan earra, bocht, earraoideach, baoth, gan dóigh;
nach mb'fhearr dhuitse imeacht le hainnir na maothchrobh meor
nó an tírse a bheith ag fanóid faoi gach rabhán dá ndéan tú ' cheol?'

'A ríoghain deas mhilis, an tú Helen fár treaghdadh sló
nó an de na naoi mná deasa thú ó Pharnassus bhí déanta i gcló?;
cá tír insa chruinne 'nar hoileadh thú, a réalt gan cheo,

lér mhian leat mo shamhailse a bheith ag cagarnaigh
leat siar sa ród?'

'Ná fiafraigh dhíom ceastaibh óir cha gcadlaim ar an
taobhsa ' Bhóinn;
is síogaí beag linbh mé a hoileadh le taobh Ghráinne
Óig';
i mbruín cheart na n-ollamh bím go follas ag
dúscadh an cheoil,
san oíche ag Teamhair 's ar maidin i gclár Thír
Eoghain.'

''S é mo ghéarghoin tinnis gur theastaigh uainn
Gaeil Thír Eoghain
agus oidhríbh an Fheadha gan seaghais faoi léig 'ár
gcóir,
géagaibh glandaite Néill Fhrasaigh nach
dtréigfeadh an ceol
is chuirfeadh éide fá Nollaig ar na hollaimh bheadh
ag géilleadh dóibh.'

'Ó treaghdadh na treabhaibh bhí in Eachroim is
fa-raoir! fán mBóinn,
sliocht Íre, na flathaibh bhéaradh fascadh do gach
draoi gan ghleo,
nach mb'fhearr dhuitse sna liosaibh agus mise le do
thaoibh gach neoin
ná saighde chlann Bhullaí a bheith ag tolladh fá do
chroí go deo?'

'A ríoghain deas mhilis, más cinniúin damh tú féin
mar stór,
tabhair léagsa is gealladh damh sul fá n-aistre mé
leat siar sa ród,
má éagaim fán tSeanainn, i gcrích Mhanainn nó san
Éiphte mhór
gurb i gcill chumhra an Chreagáin a leagfar mé i
gcré faoi fhód.'

TRANSLATION

At Cregan churchyard last night
I slept in grief.
And out of the dawnlight
That crimsoned her cheek
A maiden, gold fibre in her hair,
Came to kiss me. Just to stare
On that princess lifted the blight
From the world and gave it relief.

'Good-hearted man, don't be depressed,
Lighten that sorrowful glance;
Rise and come with me to the west
Where the land's not under the trance
Of the stranger; it's honey-sweet there,
And in the high halls the fair
Strains of the music will bless
Your ear and enchant.'

'I would not refuse you, not for the gold
Hoarded by all the kings
That lived since the days of old.
But the thought that stings
Is deserting my friends, for I care
For all that remain and more for my fair
Wife to whom in her youth I told
Promises to which her heart clings.'

'You have none left alive,
No family nor friends,
Not a jot or a jive
Do you own. You can't fend
For yourself, you are bare,
Hopeless, with nothing to share.
Instead of my filigree love, you'd abide
By your verses that all here deride?

'O princess, of royal line,
Are you the Helen that brought
Armies to ruin? Or one of the nine
From Parnassus, so sweetly wrought
In their beauty? Star in clear air,
In what land, by what or where
Did you find nurture? And why is mine
The voice you want, as we go west, in your
thought?'

'Don't question me; I do not sleep
On this side of the Boyne.
I'm a changeling; on the steep
Side of Grainneog,[1] from the loin
Of fairy race I'm sprung; all aver
It is I who stir music where
There are true poets — in Tara by deep
Night, by morning on the plains of Tyrone.'

'It stabs me to know
The Gaels of Tyrone are gone,

1. A place in County Westmeath. The moat there is sometimes taken to be a fairy mound.

The heirs of the Fews[2] are low
Under the slabbed stone;
Niall Frasach's[3] noble heirs
Who would not forsake verse
And at Christmas would bestow
Robes on those whose tribute was their song.'

Since the tribes were torn apart
At Aughrim and, alas, the Boyne,[4]
The Irish, who always gave support
To the learned, cannot again conjoin.
Wouldn't it be better, then, to be there
With us in the magic mounds where,
Instead of Orange arrows in your heart,
Each midday you'll have me, closely joined?'

'If it is foretold,
Princess, you are to be my love.
I would have to hold
You to an oath before we move
West on the road. Swear
That when I die, no matter where,
By the Shannon, the Isle of Man, in Egypt old,
I will be laid under in Cregan, its sweet soil above.'

2. A place in County Armagh.
3. High king of Ireland 763-70.
4. The Irish armies of James II (1633-1701) were defeated at the Boyne (1690) and at Aughrim (1691).

DREAMS OF LOVE AND FREEDOM III
EOGHAN RUA Ó SÚILLEABHÁIN
(*c.*1748-84)

['Ceo Draoíchta' (Magical Mist) is technically one of the finest examples of the political *aisling*, but its Jacobite message by that time was only a hollow pretence.

The translation is by Thomas Kinsella; see *An Duanaire*, pp. 187, 189, 191.]

Ceo Draíochta

Ceo draíochta i gcoim oíche do sheol mé
trí thíorthaibh mar óinmhid ar strae,
gan príomhcharaid díograis im chóngar,
is mé i gcríochaibh tar m'eolas i gcéin;
do shíneas go fíorturseach deorach
i gcoill chluthar, cnómhar, liom féin
ag guíochtain chum Rí gil na glóire,
is gan ní ar bith ach trócaire im bhéal.

Bhí líonrith im chroí-se, gan gó ar bith,
sa choill seo gan glór dhuine im ghaor,
gan aoibhneas ach binnguth na smólach
ag síorchantain cheoil ar gach géig.
Im thaobh gur shuigh síbhruinneall mhómharach,
i bhfioghair is i gclóchruth mar naomh,
'na gnaoi do bhí an lí gheal le rósaibh
i gcoimheasgar, is nárbh eol dom cé ghéill.

Ba trillseach tiugh buí casta ar órdhath
a dlaoifholt go bróig leis an mbé,
a braoithe gan teimheal is mar an ómra,
a claoinruisc do bheoghuin gach laoch.
Ba bhinn blasta fíormhilis ceolmhar,
mar shíochruit gach nóta óna béal,
is ba mhín cailce a cíoch cruinne i cóir chirt
dar linne nár leonadh le haon.

Feacht roimhe sin cé bhíos-sa gan treoir cheart,
do bhíogas le róshearc don bhé,
is do shíleas gurbh aoibhneas mór dom
an tsíbhean do sheoladh fám dhéin.
Im laoithibh do scríobhfad go deo dhuit
mar scaoileas mo bheol ar strae,
is gach caoinstair dar ríomhas don óigh dheis
is sinne sínte ar fheorainn an tsléibhe.

'A bhrídeach na rinnrosc do bhreoigh mé
le díograis dod shnó is dod scéimh,
an tú an aoilchneis trér díoscadh mórthruip,
mar scríobhtar i gcomhrac na Trae.
Nó an ríobhruinneall mhíonla d'fhúig comhlag
cathmhílidh na Bóirmhe is a thréad,
nó an ríon do dlighidh ar an mórfhlaith
ón mBeinn dul dá tóraíocht i gcéin.'

Is binn blasta caoin d'fhreagair domh-sa
is í ar síorshileadh deora tré phéin.
'Ní haon bhean dár mhaois mise id ghlórthaibh
is mar chím-se ní heol duit mo thréad.
Is mé an bhrídeach do bhí sealad pósta
fá aoibhneas i gcoróin chirt an Réics,
ag rí Chaisil Chuinn agus Eoghain,
fuair mírcheannas Fódla gan phlé.'

'Is dubhach bocht mo chúrsa 's is brónach,
dom dhúrchreimeadh ag cóirigh gach lae,
fa dhlúthsmacht ag búraibh, gan sóchas,
Is mo Phrionsa gur seoladh i gcéin.
Tá mo shúil le húrMhac na glóire
go dtabharfaidh mo leoin faoi réim
'na ndúnbhailtibh dúchais i gcóir mhaith
ag rúscadh na gcrónphoc le faobhar.'

'A chuilfhionn tais mhúinte na n-órfholt,
de chrú chirt na corónach gan bhréig,
do chúrsa-sa ag búraibh is brón liom,
fá smúit, cathach, ceomhar gan scléip,
'na ndlúthbhrughaibh dúchais dá seoladh
mac cúntach na glóire do Réics,
is súgach do rúscfainn-se crónphuic
go humhal tapaidh scópmhar le piléir.'

'Ar Stíobhard da dtigeadh chughainn tar sáile,
go crích Inis Fáilghe faoi réim,
le flít d'fhearaibh Laoisigh, is Spáinnigh,
is fíor le corp áthais go mbeinn.
Ar fíoreach mhear ghroí thapaidh chéafrach
ag síorchartadh cáich le neart faobhair,
is ní chloífinn-se m'intinn 'na dheaghaidh sin
chum luí ar sheasamh garda lem ré.'

TRANSLATION

Through the deep night a magic mist led me
like a simpleton roaming the land,
no friends of my bosom beside me,
an outcast in places unknown.
I stretched out dejected and tearful
in a nut-sheltered wood all alone
and prayed to the bright King of Glory
with 'Mercy!' alone on my lips.

My heart, I declare, full of turmoil
in that wood with no human sound nigh.
the thrush's sweet voice the sole pleasure,
ever singing its tunes on each bough.

Then a noble *sídh*-girl[1] sat beside me
like a saint in her figure and form:
in her countenance roses contended
with white — and I know not which lost.

Furrowed thick, yellow-twisting and golden
was the lady's hair down to her shoes,
her brows without flaw, and like amber
her luring eye, death to the brave.
Sweet, lovely, delicious — pure music —
the harp-notes of the *sídh* from her lips,
breasts rounded, smooth, chalk-white, most proper
— never married by another, I swear.

Though lost to myself till that moment,
with love for the lady I throbbed
and I found myself filled with great pleasure
that she was directed my way.
How it fell, I write out in these verses
— how I let my lips speak unrestrained,
the sweet things that I told the fair maiden
as we stretched on the green mountain slope:

'Are you, languid-eyed lady who pierced me
with love for your face and your form,
the Fair-One caused hordes to be slaughtered
as they write in the Battle of Troy?
Or the mild royal girl who let languish
the chief of Boru and his troop?[2]
Or the queen who decreed that the great prince
from Howth follow far in pursuit?'[3]

Delicious, sweet, tender, she answered,
ever shedding tears down in her pain:
'I am none of those women you speak of,
and I see that you don't know my clan.
I'm the bride wed in bliss for a season
— under right royal rule — to the King
over Caiseal of Conn and of Eoghan[4]
who ruled undisputed o'er Fódla.

1. *sídh* is a fairy, an otherworld being.
2. This is a reference to a romantic tale about the battle of Clontarf in 1014, in which Murchadh, Brian Boru's son, is delayed by an encounter with a fairy woman.
3. A reference to Finn Mac Cool, the leader of the Fiana, a band of warriors who traditionally defended Ireland. The story referred to is 'Tóraíocht Taise Taoibhghile' (The Pursuit of Taise Taoibhghile), in which the Fiana are drawn into adventures after being enticed to seek a beautiful maiden.
4. The ancestors of the Irish and the traditional kingdoms of Ireland (Fódla).

'Gloomy my state, sad and mournful,
  by horned tyrants daily devoured,
and heavy oppressed by grim blackguards
  while my prince is set sailing abroad.
I look to the great Son of Glory
  to send my lion back to his sway
in his strong native towns, in good order,
  to flay the swarth goats with his blades.'

'Mild, golden-haired, courteous fair lady,
  of true royal blood, and no lie,
I mourn for your plight among blackguards,
  sad and joyless, dark under a pall.

If your King to his strong native mansions
  the Son of Glory should send, in His aid,
those swarth goats — swift, freely and willing —
  with shot would I joyfully flay!'

'If our Stuart returned o'er the ocean
  to the lands of Inis Áilge in full course
with a fleet of Louis' men, and the Spaniard's,
  by dint of joy truly I'd be
on a prancing pure steed of swift mettle
  ever slucing them out with much shot
— after which I'd not injure my spirit
  standing guard for the rest of my life.'

BRIAN MERRIMAN

(*c.*1749-1805)

from:
THE MIDNIGHT COURT

['The Midnight Court' is perhaps the best known Irish poem from the eighteenth century. We have only one other short piece by Brian Merriman, but he was obviously well-versed in the themes and techniques of his fellow poets. Merriman uses an imaginary court of women to discuss many aspects of the relationship between men and women: from lack of marriage partners, to the difficulties of union between young lusty girls and wizened old men, from bastards to amorous priests. In form the poem is a parody of the *aislings*; it has a prologue, three speeches and an epilogue. This makes it more dramatic in its effects than most contemporary poetry. The first speech is given by a young girl, in which she puts the case for her sex. The passage here is from the reply to her by an old man. His *tour de force* is then answered by the girl, whereupon the judge, Aoibheall, a fairy goddess, gives her judgment on behalf of the women. The judgment involves the chastizing of the poet, who luckily wakes up before it can be carried out.

The translation of *Cúirt an Mheón-Oíche* is by Dennis Woulfe, a Clare schoolmaster, who wrote it in the 1820s. An expurgated version of this was published in *The Irishman* in 1880.]

. . Preabann anuas go fuadrach fíochmhar
Seanduine suarach is fuadach nimhe fé,
A bhaill ar luascadh is luas anáile air,
Draighean is duais ar fuaid a chnámha,
Ba dearóil an radharc go deimhin don chúirt é,
Ar bord 'na thaibhse im éisteacht dúirt sé:

'Dochar is díobháil is síorchrá cléibh ort,
A thoice le místáid 'o shíol gá is déirce.
Is dóch nách iongantas laigeacht na gréine
Is fós gach tubaist dár imigh ar Éirinn,
Mar mheath gach ceart gan reacht gan dlí againn,
Ár mba bhí bleacht gan lacht gan laoigh acu,
Is dá dtagadh níos mó do mhóirscrios tíortha
Is gach faisean dá nócht ar Mhóir 's ar Shíle.
A thoice gan chríoch nách cuimhin le táinte
Olcas na síolrach daoine ó dtángais
Gan focal le maíomh id shinsear gránna
Acht lopaigh gan bhrí, lucht míre is mála.
Is aithne dhúinne an snamhaire is athair dhuit,
Gan charaid gan chlú gan chúl gan airgead
'Na leibide liath gan chiall gan mhúnadh,
Gan mheidhir gan mhias gan bhia gan anlann,
Gan faic ar a dhrom 's a chabhail gan chóta
Acht gad ar a chom 's a bhonn gan bhróga.
Creididh, a dhaoine, dhá ndíoltaí ar aonach
Eisean 's a bhuíon, tar éis íoc gach éilimh,
Dar colann na naomh ba dícheall mór dho
Pota maith dí lena fhuílleach d'fhuascailt.
Nách mór an tóbhacht 's an gleo i measc daoine
Truaire 'od shórt gan bhó gan chaora

. . . .

Chonac lem shúile an chúil 'na luíonn tú:
Garbh ná mín ní síntear fút ann,
Barrach ná líon dár sníomhadh le tuirne,

Acht mata 'na smuirt gan chuilt gan chlúdadh,
Dealamh gan luid gan phluid gan tsúsa,
I gcomhar bhotháin gan áit chum suí ann,
Sú sileáin is fáscadh aníos ann,
Fiaile ag teacht go fras gan choimse
Is rian na gcearc air trasna scríofa,
Lag ina dhrom is na gabhla ag lúbadh
Is clagarnach dhonn go trom ag tuirlingt.
A Chumainn na bhFáidh nách ard do labhair sí,
Gustalach gálbhach gártha ghabhann sí
I ndathaibh i gcóir 's i gclóca síoda,
Faire go deo arú! fóill cár fríodh é?
Aithris cá bhfaigheann tú an radharc so mhaíonn tú
Is aithris cár thuill tú an leadhb gan bhrí seo?
Is deacair a shuíomh gur fríodh go cóir iad,
Is gairid ó bhís gan síol an orlaigh.
Aithris cá bhfuar tú luach do húda
Is aithris cá bhfuair tú luach do ghúna,
Acht leagaimid uainn mar ghluais an cóta
Is aithris cá bhfuair tú luach na mbróga?

'Aoibheall cheannasach charthanach chomhachtach
Guím thu, gairim thu, freagair is fóir me.
Is fíor gur feasach me farairí Fódla
Suíte greamaithe ag sladairí 'on tsórt seo.
Lámh mo charad! Is aithne dhom comharsa,
Láimh le baile agam, gairid do chóngar,
Buachaill soineanta, srimile sóntach
Is buaileadh duine acu chuige mar nóchar.
Is searbh lem chroí an uair chím im radhairc í,
A gradam, a críoch, a poimp 's a taibhse,
Sealbhach bó aici is eorna ag fás di
Is airgead póca is ór idir lámha aici.
Chonaic mé inné í ar thaobh na sráide,
Is cumasach tréan an léire mná í,
Malfaire másach mágach magúil,
Marbh le cámas, lán do ladús.
Marach gur claon liom éad do mhúscailt,
Scannal do scéamh ná scéalta scrúdadh,
B'fhurast dom insint cruinn mar chuala
An cuma 'na mbíodh sí sraoillte suaite
Stracaithe ar lár is gáir 'na timpeall,
Caite ar an sráid nó i stábla sínte.
Mairfidh a tásc is tráchtfar choíche
Ar mharbhna, ar cháil, ar gháir a gníomhartha
In Íbh Breacáin an aráin 's an fhíona,
I dTíortha 'Calláin na mbánta míne,
Ag ísle is ársa Mháinse is Inse,
Chill Bhreacáin, an Chláir is Chuinche,
Ag consaigh ainmhí Thradaí an phónra
Is fionsaigh fhalchaí Chreatlaí an chorda.
Faire ba claon í tar éis a ndúirt me,
Ghlacfainn gur saor í féna cionta,
Acht bheirim don phláigh í lá mar chínn í
Leagaithe láimh le Gáras sínte,
Caite ar an ród gan orlach fúithi
Ag gramaisc na móna ar bhóithre Dhúire.
M'iongantas ann os cheann mo chéille
Is crithim go fann le scanradh an scéil seo,
Ise bheith seang nuair theann gach éinne í
Is druidim le clann nuair shantaigh féin é.
Is mór na grásta é ag rá na mbriathra,
Nóimint spáis níor ghá le hiarraidh,
Ó léadh ar bord di os comhair na coinnle
An t*Ego Vos* so d'ordaigh Íosa,
Gur shéid sí lacht go bleacht 'na cíochaibh
Acht naoi mí beacht is seachtmhain chinnte.

Breathain gur baol don té tá scaoilte
Ceangal go héag fá thaobh don chuing seo,
I sealbh gach saoth is éad dá shuaitheadh,
In aisce, mo léan, mo léann ní bhfuair mé.
Is feasach don taobh seo den saol mar bhí mé
Sealad dom réim 's dom laethaibh roimhe seo,
Leitheadach láidir lán do shaibhreas,
Eisteas le fáil is fáilte im theaghlach,
Caraid i gcúirt is cúnamh dlí agam
Ceannas is clú agus comhar na saoithe,
Tathag im chaint is suim is éifeacht,
Talamh is maoin ag suíomh mo chéille,
M'aigne síoch is m'intinn sásta,
Chailleas le mnaoi mo bhrí is mo shláinte.
Ba taitneamhach leabhair an crobhaire mná í,
Bhí seasamh is com is cabhail is cnámha aici,
Casadh 'na cúl go búclach trilseach,
Lasadh 'na gnúis go lonrach soilseach,
Cuma na hóighe uirthi is só ina gáire
Is cuireadh ina cló chum póige is fáilte.
Acht chreathas le fonn gan chonn gan chairde
Ó bhaitheas go bonn go tabhartha i ngrá dhi.
Is dearbh gan dabhta ar domhan gur díoltas
Danartha donn, dom thabhairt ar m'aimhleas,
D'fhearthain go trom, ar bhonn mo ghníomhartha
Ó fhlaitheas le fonn, do lom 'na líon me.
Do snadhmadh suite snaidhm na cléire
Is ceangladh sinn i gcuing re chéile,
Ghlanas gan chinnteacht suim gach éilimh
Bhaineas le baois gan ghaois an lae sin.
Cothrom go leor, níor chóir mé cháineadh,
Stopas an gleo bhí ag cóip na sráide,
Bacaigh go léir, bhí an cléireach sásta,
An sagart ró-bhuíoch is b'fhéidir fáth leis.

Lasamair toirse is comharsain cruinn ann
Is leagadh ar bordaibh mórchuid bídh chúinn,
Clagarnach cheoil is ól gan choimse
Is chaitheadar cóisir mhórtach mhaíteach.

Mo dhíth gan easpa nár tachtadh le bia me
An oíche baisteadh nó as sin gur iarr me
Síneadh ar leabain le ainnir do liath me
Is scaoil le gealaigh gan charaid gan chiall me.
Is é tásc do gheobhainn ag óg 's ag aosta
Gur breallán spóirt ag ól 's ag glaoch í
I mbotháin ósta is boird dá bpléascadh,
Ar lár 'na lóiste ag pósta is aonta.
B'fhada dhá mheilt a teist 's a tuairisc,
B'fhada gur chreid me a bheag ná a mhór dhe,
B'eaglach le gach beirt dá gcuala é
Go rachainn im pheilt im gheilt gan tuairisc.
Fós ní ghéillfinn, caoch mar bhí me,
Do ghlór gan éifeacht éinne mhaígh é,
Acht magadh nó greim gan feidhm gan chéill
Gur aithris a broinn dom deimhin gach scéil.
Níor chúrsaí leamhais ná durdam bréige é,
Dúirt bean liom go ndúradh léithi é,
Acht labhair an bheart i gceart 's in éifeacht —
Bhronn sí mac i bhfad roimh ré orm.

Mo scanradh scéil, gan féith 'om chroí air,
Clann dá dtéamh dhom tar éis na hoíche,
Collóid anfach ainigí scólta,
Bunóc ceangailte is bean an tí breoite,
Posóid leagaithe ar smeachaidí teo acu,
Cuinneog bhainne dhá greadadh le fórsa
Is mullach ar láinmhiais, báinbhia is siúicre,
Ag Murainn Ní Cháimlaith, báinlia an chrúca.
Bhí coiste cruinnithe ag tuilleadh dem chomharsain
Chois na tine is ag siosarnach dhomhsa
Scaoilid cogar i bhfogas dom eisteacht —
"Míle moladh le Solas na Soilse,
Bíodh nách baileach a d'aibigh an chré seo
Chímse an t-athair 'na sheasamh 'na chéadfa,
An bhfeiceann tú, a Shaidhbh 'rú, luí a ghéaga
A dheilbh gan droinn, a bhaill 's a mhéaraibh,
Cumas na lámh ba dána doirne,
Cuma na gcnámh is fás na feola?"
Cheapadar cruinn gur shíolraigh an dúchas
Maise mo ghnaoi agus íor mo ghnúise,
Feilleadh mo shrón is glónradh m'éadain,
Deiseacht mo chló, mo shnó agus m'fhéachaint,
Leagadh mo shúl is fiú mo gháire
Is as sin do shiúil ó chúl go sála é.

Amharc ná radharc ní bhfaighinnse 'on chréice,
"Is baileach gan leigheas do mhillfeadh gaoth é",
Ag cuideachta an teaghlaigh i bhfeighil mo chaochta,
"Siolla dhá laghad di leagfaidh an créatúir".
Do labhras garg is d'agras Íosa,
Is stollta garbh do bhagras gríosach,
D'fhógras fearg le ainbhios cainte
Is dócha gur chreathadar cailleacha an tí romham.
Ar leisce an achrainn leagadar chúm é,
"Beir go haireach air, seachain ná brúigh é,
Is furas é shuaitheadh, luaisc go réidh é,
Turraing do fuair sí ruaig roimh ré é,
Seachain ná fáisc é, fág 'na luí é,
Is gairid an bás do is gearr do raghaidh sé,
Dá maireadh go lá idir lámha ina chló,
Is an sagart ar fáil, níorbh fhearr a bheith beo".
Do bhaineas an tsnaidhm dá chuibhreach cumhdaigh,
Bhreathain me cruinn é sínte ar ghlún liom,
Amuaireach, d'airigh me tathagach tamhanda é,
Fuair me feargach fearsadach lúfach,
Láidir leathan mo leanbh 'na ghuaille,
Sála daingeana is an-chuid gruaige air,
Cluasa cruinnithe is ingní fásta,
Chruadar a uilleanna, a chroibh is a chnámha,
D'aibigh a shúile is fiú a pholláirí
Is d'airigh me a ghlúine lúfach láidir,
Coileán cumasach cuisleannach córach,
Folláin fulangach fuinneamhach feolmhar.

Screadaim go hard le gáir na tíre
Is leagaim dod láthair cás na ndaoine,
Breathain go caoin is bí truamhéileach
Beannaibh a gcinn is suim a gcéille.
Athraigh an dlí seo, cuing na cléire,
Is ainic an bhuíon nár fríodh sa ngéibheann.
Má lagaigh an síolrach díonmhar daonna
I dtalamh dath-aoibhinn fhíorghlas Éireann,
Is furas an tír d'athlíonadh de lachaibh
D'uireasa a nguí gan bhrí gan éifeacht.
Ca bhfuil an gá le gáir na bainse,
Cartadh biotáille is pá lucht sainte,
Sumaigh ar bord go fóiseach taibhseach,
Glugar is gleo acu is ól dá shaighdeadh
Ó d'aibigh an t-ábhar do bhronn Mac Dé
Gan sagart ar domhan dá dtabhairt dá chéile?
Is leathanmhar láidir lánmhear léadmhar
Fairsing le fáil an t-álbach saor seo.
Is minic do chímse bríomhar borrtha
Cumasach líonta i gcroí 's i gcóir iad,
Créim ní fheicim ná doille ná caoiche

I léim ar leithre dár hoileadh ó mhnaoi ar bith,
Is mó is is mire is is teinne is is tréine
I gcló is i gclisteacht ná dlisteanaigh éinne.
Is furas a luaimse d'fhuascailt suíte
Is duine acu an uair seo ar fuaid an tí seo.
An bhfeiceann tú thall go ceansa ciúin é?
Deisigh anall i dteannta an bhuird é,
Breathain go cruinn é, bíodh gurab óg é,
Is dearfa suíte an píosa feola é,
Is preabaire i dtoirt i gcorp 's i gcnáimh é
Ca bhfuil a locht i gcois ná i láimh dhe?
Ní seirgtheach fann ná seandach feosach,
Leibide cam ná gandal geoiseach,
Meall gan chumadh ná sumach gan síneadh é
Acht lansa cumasach buinneamhach bríomhar.
Ní deacair a mheas nách spreas gan bhrí
Bheadh ceangailte ar nasc, ar teasc ag mnaoi,
Gan chnáimh gan chumas gan chuma gan chom
Gan ghrá gan chumann gan fuinneamh gan fonn
Do scaipfeadh i mbroinn aon mhaighre mná
Le catachas draighean an groighire breá,
Mar chuireann sé i bhfeidhm gan mhoill gan bhréig
Le cumas a bhaill 's le luí a ghéag
Gur crobhaire é crothadh go cothrom gan cháim
Le fonn na fola is le fothrom na sláinte.

Leis sin ná iarrsa a Ríoghain réaltach
Meilleadh mar iad le riail gan éifeacht,
Scaoil a chodladh gan chochall gan chuibhreach
Síol an bhodaigh 's an mhogallfhuil mhaíteach,
Scaoil fá chéile do réir nádúra
An síolbhach séad 's an braon lábúrtha,
Fógair féilteach tré gach tíortha
D'óg is d'aosta saorthoil síolraigh.
Cuirfidh an dlí seo gaois i nGaelaibh
Is tiocfaidh an brí mar bhí ina laochaibh,
Ceapfaidh sé com is drom is doirne
Ag fearaibh an domhain mar Gholl Mac Morna,
Gealfaidh an spéir, beidh éisc i líonta
Is talamh an tsléibhe go léir fá luibheanna,
Fir agus mná go brách dá bhíthin
Ag seinm do cháil le gardas aoibhnis'. . . .

TRANSLATION

. . . A Grey old man of feeble frame
With hasty steps straight forward came
His palsied limbs emaciated
His pallid phiz[1] quite desolated
The assembled court his port surveyed
Whilst thus he spoke with force essayed:
'May pains and darts thy heart pervade
Thou shameless sordid philbeg[2] jade.
No wonder that the sun has weakened
And Erin still to ills awakened
Our rights and laws have from us flown
Our kine uncalved and barren grown
Or yet if fire and famine raged
The newest style by Poll engaged.
The worthless flock from which you grew
Are well remarked thou filthy spew
No wealth or weal could they describe
A begging straying dreary tribe.
Your wretched sire full well we know
Possessing naught but abject woe
A senseless gray degraded fool
Bereft of fare dish chair or stool
His ragged robe the brogueless[3] hound
With gads enclosed as waistbands round.
Believe my words if he were sold
With all his household goods enrolled
All fees discharged by George I swear
A small Beerpot he could not spare.
A plaguing rout you hourly keep
Tho not endowed with cow or sheep.
No wonder that you brag so high

. . . .

I saw the wad whereon you lie
Coarse or fine you could not show
From flax derived soft wool or tow
A musty mat for years decayed
No coverlet your pelt to shade
Your cabin sluiced from soot and rain
And spring fluids that oozed amain[4]
Its weed-grown roof so rudely shaped
By hens at roost all scooped and scraped
Its hollow back with props contending
Unrelaxed foul drops descending.
Immortal Queen long venerated
Her dress and speech how elevated
In silken suits she moves distracted
You bilking[5] rook from whom abstracted?
Your boasted knowledge how procured
Or yet your mantles more obscured?
Tis hard to say no shameful store

1. face. A colloquial shortening of 'physiognomy'.

2. Probably from the Irish *filleadh beag* (skirt, kilt).
3. shoeless.
4. all over.
5. cheating, deceiving.

Your boots so bare not long before
Your hood now found come now declare
Your cotton gown without compare
Your cloak so gay I lay aside
Your shoes in haste I pray decide.
O Aovill[6] hail! our great safeguard
Now grant my prayer my tale regard.
The flower of Erin's bravest breed
To owls ill famed of late decreed.
I promptly swear my friends right hand
I knew a neighbour nigh at hand
A simple sober solvent swain
Who one of those exposed for gain.
My heart revolts when I review
Her pride her pranks and grandeur too
Milch cows in bawn and barley growing
Coffers large and all things flowing.
This flashy dame I did espy
On yesterday as I passed by
Her body big her limbs well freighted
With fat well fed and flesh conceded.
Were it not my love of Union
Hate of rough and fell disunion
I could review from true hearsay
How tripped abused and led astray
Tossed about with loud commotion
In stables, houses and crowds in motion.
Her fame will last for craft and crime
And shameless acts to end of time
In Ibrickan of wine and fare
In Timaclane of lawns so rare
In Mannish More and Ennis town
Kilbracken, Quin and old Clare town
In Tradree land of fruitful brains
In Cratloe long inured to chains.
Although depraved as here defined
I would be lenient still and kind
But plague be on her one day I viewed
By Garus Mills the game renewed
To Doora road she next retreated[7]
Where ass boys roared and rusticated.
No marvellous tale above my own
I do relate as will be shown
Her womb so light when primed by all
To swell so high at Hymen's call.
How vast the grace in Marriage rite
She would not claim a day or night
All minds composed and tapers lighted
With *Ego vos*[8] in fame recited
Her fruitfulness was highly praised
In nine months time an outcry raised.
Therefore the man from thraldom free
Should wisely act and cautious be
By practice proved from heartfelt pain
The truth alas I did obtain.
All around could now attest
The wealth and power I once possessed
My body straight and athletic
My acts proclaimed philanthropic
A friend in court my cause to plead
From Gentlefolks due honor paid
My words and wit with wisdom teemed
My land and store much more esteemed
My mind at ease in fair construction
Till woman sealed my soul's destruction.
Her graceful form looked divine
Her waist so small and limbs so fine
Her golden hair in braids descending
Her comely face sunbeams transcending
Her virgin bloom her courteous smile
Her looks demure ensured no guile.
My body shook from head to heel
Such ardent love I then did feel
Which hurried on so rapidly
That fate must plan my destiny.
Such evils then did me beset
As made me rue blind Cupid's net.
The nuptial knot was quickly tied
With mother church we soon complied
All expenses were discharged
Manfully if more enlarged
All approved and none dispraised
The voice of youth I soon appeased
Long tapers blazed the train assembled
With loaded fare the tables trembled
The priest confessed no selfish saving
The Clerk refreshed and beggars raving
Music playing ladies lauding
The sumptuous feast all grades commending.
I wish I died in infancy
When dandled on my mother's knee
Before my bed had been defiled
And wit and wealth from me exiled.
From young and old I tidings got
Which proved my wife a drunken sot

6. Ir. Aoibheall, the fairy goddess who presided over the court.
7. The placenames are baronies, townlands or villages in Counties Clare and Limerick.
8. A reference to the 'magical' qualities of the Latin liturgy.

Who tables rapped and draughts injected
And chastity esteemed rejected.
Her faults from proofs no longer doubted
But faults and proofs I scoffed and scouted,
It was feared by all in Evil hour
A naked elf unfelt I'd scour.
All in vain no tale I minded
My intellects so firmly blinded
Until her size the truth revealed
No barefaced lie for me retailed.
No foolish whim or fib untrue
Or she told me as I told you
Before due time my wife so fair
To me consigned a son and heir.
Oh dire deceit when least expected
A fine young babe in haste ejected
Tribes amazed my case contrasted
My child in swades[9] and mate exhausted
The posset pot[10] contained a potion
The churnstaff in lofty motion
The accouching dame from ancient rule
A dish prepared of sweetened gruel.
A jury sat of old beldames
In private chat close by the flames
A secret whisper they let fly
"Praises be to him on high
Although this babe non-aged evicted
I see his parents frame depicted
Hasten Sal his parts survey
His fine limbed dad they all display
No bone disjointed or joint deformed
His thumping fists and wrists well formed".
They all described a right connection
My visage bright and fine complexion
My handsome nose of bony size
My manly port and glowing eyes
Each member drew a view from nature
A similitude in every feature.
To see my child I importuned
"By air and wind he would be ruined"
So all my lying household said
And that one puff would strike him dead.
I ranted, stamped and swore outright
I should survey this baby bright
My boisterous words did so betake
That gossiping hags began to quake.
To end disputes they soon obeyed
And in my view the infant laid,
"Enforce no squall and squeeze him not
A sudden fall his mother got
Which caused so soon his visit here
But death will end his swift career
And if the Priest affixed his seal
His death would be of no avail".
His swaddling hands I then untied
And on my knee the bantling[11] eyed
I felt him lusty safe and sound
His limbs well braced and firmly bound
His shoulders brawny broad and fair
His head not bald but covered with hair
His ears well shaped his elbows tight
His heels full square and frame upright
His eyes were ripe with fine posteriors
His knees composed no slight inferiors
A sinewy lusty brave young blade
That health and height and might displayed.
With bitter cries I now invoke
This foolish rite you would evoke
For mad was he and empty pated
Who marriage first had contemplated.
Enriched are they in mind and soul
Who yielded not to its control
Tho human kind has blessed been
In this our isle of annual green
A race of heroes still would rise
Without this useless compromise.
From wedding dress we should refrain
Where Laity lose and Clergy gain
Where crowds repair to share the spoil
And end the day in great turmoil.
This gift so free has not been blighted
And yet no priest our flesh united,
The breed has spread and multiplied,
In spleen in wealth in pomp and pride
I often viewed them puffed and bloated
And grandly dressed with flesh well coated.
A further proof it plain appears
That one of them to me adheres.
Lo! yonder moves the blooming boy
A handsome youth demure and coy
With care inspect tho not matured
The heir elect for me procured
He's plump and prime in size and bone
His limbs combined all blights disown
No withered weak decaying wight
Deformed ape or gander light

9. pieces of cloth.
10. cup.
11. bastard; literally, a child conceived on a bench.

Misshapen lump or stunted lout
My brave young son so firm and stout
This hard to say or yet surmise
That weak was he in enterprise
In bone or might in application
In love in life in inclination
That did in time a child produce
From womankind so fair and spruce,
As here set down in true relation
Free from foul exaggeration
For nature has her gifts bestowed
And him with ruddy cheeks endowed.
Therefore Oh Queen this law repeal
Destruction to our common weal
And let the dusty dunghill race
With gentlefolks unite apace,
Let rich and poor without rejection
Join henceforth in stout connection
And let your mandate truly paint
That young and old with no restraint.
For marriage laws if abrogated
Our tribes would be invigorated
Our Irish heroes soon would spread
Like warlike Goll[12] who knew no dread
Our atmosphere would daily clear
And mountain daisies gay appear
Thousands would your actions praise
And crown you with immortals lays'....

12. Goll Mac Mórna, one of the strong men of the Fiana, the traditional defenders of Ireland.

TOMÁS MAC CAISIDE

(*fl. c.*1760)

from: THE SPOILT PRIEST

[Tomás Mac Caiside lived in the latter half of the seventeenth century. He entered holy orders, but, as he tells us in a semi-biographical work, he was banished and had many misadventures on account of an illicit association with a girl. The song that has come down to us is probably basically his own composition, but it has regional and temporal variations. This version was collected in County Galway at the beginning of the twentieth century.]

An Caisideach bán (Cassidy the white)

Thug mé an ruaig údan ó mhullach na Cruaiche
  chugat anuas chun an tSléibhe Bháin
ar thuairisc mo chailín a d'fhág m'intinn buartha
  agus rinne sí gual dubh de mo chroí i mo lár;
d'at mo ghuaillí go nuige mo chluasa
  agus fuair mé fuagra glan géar ón mbás,
is níl duine dá gcuala mo scéal an uair sin
  nach dúirt go mba trua bocht an Caisideach bán

Ar cheann an staighre tá plúr gach maighdin —
  's í siúd meidhreog an bhrollaigh bháin.
is trua nach liom í gan buaibh ná punt í
  is í a bheith gan chuntas liom ar láimh.
Dhéanfainn teach mór di ar shúil an bhóthair
  agus chuirfinn cóiste faoina clann,
is a chúilín ómra, dá mblitheá bó dhom,
  i do cheangal fómhair ní chuirfinn suim.

... ...

Agus bhí me sealad ag foghlaim Béarla,
  agus dúirt an chléir go mba mhaith mo chaint,
an fhaid úd eile gan únsa céille
  ach mar na héiníní faoi bharr na gcrann;
amuigh san oíche gan fascadh ná dídean,
  agus sneachta dá shíorchur faoi íochtar gleann;
is a chúilín donndeas ar chaill mé na grádha leat
  nár fhaighe tú na grástaí mara n-éalaír liom

Bhí mé i gcoláiste go ham mo bhearrtha
  agus san ardscoil ar feadh cúig bliana,
go bhfuair mé oideachas agus comhairle ón eaglais,
  ach faraoir cráite do bhris mé tríd!
is rímhór m'fhaitíos roimh Rí na ngrásta
  nach bhfuil sé i ndán go dtiocfad saor,
mar is mó mo pheacaí na leath Chruach Phádraig
  mar gheall ar ghrá a thug mé d'iníon mhaoir.

Siúd í tharainn an eala bhán deas
agus í chomh gléasta le bean ar bith;
trua mar a gineadh í mbroinn a máthar,
mar is le haghaidh mo bháis a rugadh í.
Níl bun cíbe na tulán timpeall,
na gleanntán aoibhinn a mbíonn mo ghrá,
nach bhfuil ceol á sheinm ann do ló is d'oíche;
is go bhfóire Críost ar an gCaisideach bán.

… … … … … … … …

Aisling bhréagach do chonacthas aréir dom
agus gheit sí mé trí lár mo shuain,
go raibh ainnirín chaoin deas na gcíoch cruinngheal
sínte síos liom taobh ar thaobh.
ar iontó tharm dom go tapaidh lúfar
chun breith ar chúl uirthi bhí tanaí tréan,
ní bhfuair mé agam ann ach binn an tsúsa
agus d'fhág sin brúite mé le mo shaol.

TRANSLATION

I hurried down from the top of Croagh Patrick to you at Sliabh Bán,[1] seeking my girl who bothered my mind, and she made my heart into black coal. My shoulders swelled up as far as my ears and I felt I was going to die, and there is no one who heard my story then who did not say it was a pity for Cassidy the white.

At the top of the stairs is the choicest maiden — and she is the merry one whose breast is fair. It is sad that she is not mine without cattle or money and for her to be at my side without any retribution. I would make a large house for her at the top of the road and I would have a coach for her children, and, my fair-haired one, if you would milk a cow for me, I'd not be worried if you could not help bind at harvest....

I was for a while learning English and the clergy said my speech was fine, the rest of the time without an ounce of sense but like the birds under the branches of the trees; out at night without shelter or cover and snow falling constantly at the bottom of the glen; and my fair one, for whom I gave up holy orders, may you not receive forgiveness if you do not come away with me.

I was at college until I shaved and, five years at the seminary, I received education and counsel from the church but alas alas I broke away from it! Great is my fear before the King of grace that I am not fated to escape, since my sins are more than half of Croagh Patrick because of the love I gave to a steward's daughter.

There she goes, the fine white swan dressed as well as any woman; it's a pity she was conceived in her mother's womb because she was born to bring about my death. There's no grass bank or hillock around or pleasant glen in which my love goes that music is not being played day and night; May Christ help Cassidy the white...

Last night I saw a false vision and I started in my sleep, that the gentle girl with the bright rounded breasts was lying down side by side with me. Turning around quickly and lively to hold her body, slim and strong, all I got was the edge of the rug and that left me broken for life.

1. Mountains in County Mayo.

ANONYMOUS

THE FAVOURITE SOUNDS OF FINN

[This nature lyric is associated with the literature of the Fenian cycle. It praises the sounds and sights of outdoor life and, by using local names, gives a spirit of place that pervades much of that literature. Such poems are ascribed to Oisín, Finn's son and bard of the Fiana, but in language and style they belong to the late Classical period and perhaps as late as the seventeenth century.]

Binn sin a luin Doire an Chairn;
ní chuala mé in aird san mbith
ceol ba bhinne ná do ghuth
agus tú i mbun do nid.

Aoncheol is binne fán mbith,
mairg nach éisteann go fóill,
a Mhic Alpruinn na gclog mbinn
's go mbéarthá arís ar do nóin.

Agat mar tá agam féin,
dá mbeith deimhin scéal an eoin,
do dhéanfá déara go dian,
's ní bhiadh d'aire ar Dhia go fóill.

I gcrích Lochlann na sreabh ngorm,
fuair Mac Cumhaill na gcorn ndearg
an t-éan do-chíthí anois,
ag sin a scéal duit go dearbh.

Doire an Chairn an choill úd thiar
mar a ndéanaidis an Fhiann fos,
ar áille 's ar chaoimhe a crann
isea do cuireadh ann an lon.

Scolghaire luin Doire an Chairn
búithre an daimh ó Aill na gCaor,
ceol le gcodladh Fionn go moch
lachain ó Loch na dTrí gCaol.

Cearca fraoich um Chruachain Chuinn,
feadghail dobhráin Druim Dhá Loch,
gotha fiolair Glinn na bhFuath,
longhaire cuach Chnuic na Scoth.

An tráth do mhair Fionn 's an Fhiann
dob ansa leo sliabh ná cill
Fá binn leo-san fuighle lon,
gotha na gclog leo níor bhinn.

TRANSLATION

That is sweet, blackbird from Doire an Chairn; I did not hear in any place music that was sweeter than the song you sing while you are nesting.

The sweetest music in the world, sad it is for any who do not listen still, O son of Alpronn[1] of the melodious bells, and sad for you to go back to your prayers.

If you knew for certain, as I do, the story of the bird, you would shed tears bitterly and you would not keep your attention on God.

In Norway of the azure streams, Mac Cumhaill of the wine-filled cups obtained the bird that is now seen and that's the story of its origin for you.

That wood there is Doire an Chairn where the *Fiana*[2] used to shelter and there the blackbird was put because of the beauty and loveliness of its trees.

The whistle of the blackbird of Doire an Chairn, the lowing of the stag from Aill na gCaor, and the noise of the ducks from Loch na dTrí gCaol, this was the music to which Finn slept until early morning.

The grouse about Cruachain Chuinn, the shrill cry of the otters of Druim Dá Loch, the shriek of the eagle of Gleann na bhFuath and the song of the cuckoo from Cnoc na Scoth.

When Finn and the Fiana were living, they preferred the mountainside to churchyard. Sweet to them was the song of blackbird and they did not enjoy the sound of church bells.

1. St Patrick.
2. The traditional defenders of Ireland, led by Finn.

AODH MAC GABHRÁIN

(*fl. c.*1720)

O'ROURKE'S FEAST

[Very few poems were famous in both Irish and English soon after their original composition. 'Pléaráca na Ruarcach' (O'Rourke's Feast) was probably acceptable to both communities because soon after it was composed by Aodh Mac Gabhráin (Hugh Magauran), the blind harper Turlogh Carolan put music to it. It somehow came to the attention of Jonathan Swift and he made an English version (see p. 399). The Irish text reprinted here appears in a contemporary manuscript, TCD MS 1325, the Irish verses preceding Swift's 'version'.]

Pléaráca na Ruarcach

Pléaráca na Ruarcach a gcuimnne an uile dhuine
dá dtiocfadh, dá bhfaca 's dá gcluinfeadh go deo.
Seacht bhfithchid muc, mart et caora/dá gcosgart
don ghasra gach aon lá,
Céad Pál uisge bheatha 'sna meadra dá líonadh.

Ag éirí ar maidin is againn do bhí sport;
'Do briseadh mo phíopasa,' 'sladadh mo phócasa,'
'do ghoideadh mo bhrístese,' 'loisgeadh mo chlócasa,'
'chaill mé mo bhirréad, m'fhalluing is m'fhilléad,
ó d'imthig 'na gcláréide ár seacht mbeannacht leo.'
'Spreag ar an gclairsigh sin, seinn an pléaráca sin,
Sgaird don digh sin, as í so an chuirm chóir.'

Lucht leanamhna na Ruarcach, ag crothadh a gcleití
tráth chuala siad tormán is troipléasg an cheoil,
gan fhaire ar a gcoisreagadh ag éirí as a leabthacha
a bhean féin ar leathláimh ag gach aon don chóip.
Budh láidir an seasamh don talamh do bhí fútha
gan raobadh le sodar agus glugar a mbróg.
'Sláinte agus Saoghal chugad a Mhaoilsheachluinn Uí Ionagáin,'
'Dar mo láimh is maith dhamhsas tú a Mhairsill ní Ghniodagáin,'
'Súd ort a mháthair,' 'go raibh maith agad a Phádraig,'
'Beir ar an scála is sgág é in do sceoig.'
'Croith fúinn an tsráideog sin, leathnaidh oruinn an cháiteog sin,'
'An bogsa sin 'Áine, agus gráideog le n-ól.'

A athair na ngrás gibé chífeadh an ghasradh
iar líonadh a gcraiceann síor-lasadh san ól;
Bhí cnáimhrí bacard, ar fad an gach sgiain aca,
Ag stabadh 's ag gearradh go leor leor,
Céad áithslisne darach le tine ag gabháil trína chéile
Ag cnagadh, ag leagadh, ag losgadh 's ag dó.
'A bhodaigh is é m'athairse chuir Mainistir na Búille suas
Sligioch is Gaillimh is Carruig Druim Rúsga fós.
As é Iarla Chill Dara is biatach Mhuighe Nealta
d'oil agus d'altraidh me, fiosraidh do Mhór.'
Leagaidh an t-adhmad sin, buailidh an stráiméad sin,
buille ina thárr is preab ina thóin.

'Cia thóg an t-alórm so', ar aon don Eaglais,
ag éirghe 'sna sheasamh 's ag bagairt go mór,
Ní hé an spargheis coisreagtha bhí leis chun racáin
acht bata maith cnapánach boglán doirinn.
An tráth shaoil sé na cabhail éguidhe do lasgadh 's do thiortháil.
do fágbhadh an sagart 'na mheall chasda faoi an mbord.
D'éirgheadar na bráithre do tharthái na bruighne sin
Do fágbhadh an t-athair gardian ar a thárr annsa ngríosaidh aco.
'An uair bhi misi thall ag glacadh na ngrádh
ag foghlaim chráibhtheacht ag an bPápa san Róimh,
As é an Seven Wise Masters do bhí ar chluais ar do thárr agad
is tú ag ithe na bputátaoi 's gan snáithe ar do thóin'.

[The fourth verse is not translated in the Swift version. The following translation is from a rare book entitled *Selected Irish Poems* by Charles Henry Wilson (Dublin, 1782).

Who raised this alarm?
Says one of the Clergy;
A threat'ning severely,
Cease fighting I charge ye.
A good knotted staff,
The full of his hand,
Instead of the spiradis[1]
Back'd his Command;
So falling to thresh
Fast as he was able,
A trip and a box
Stretch'd him under the table;
Then rose a big fryar
To settle them straight,
But the back of the fire
Was quickly his fate;
From whence he cry'd out,
Do ye thus treat your pastors?
Ye, who scarcely were bred
To the *Seven Wise Masters*,[2]
That when with the Pope
I was getting my lore,
Ye were roasting potatoes
Nor far from *Sheemôr*.[3]

1. The *aspergillum*, for sprinkling holy water.
2. The popular title for a pseudo-philosophical tract of late antiquity.
3. Sheemôr + Ir. Sí mór, a place in County Leitrim.

SÉAMAS DALL MAC CUARTA

THE CUCKOO'S RETURN

[This lyric by Séamas Dall Mac Cuarta (McCourt) is well-known. The form is *trí rainn agus amhrán*, three verses in syllabic metre and one in song metre. This was popular in south-east Ulster and, because of its structure, has been compared to the English sonnet.]

Fáilte don éan is binne ar chraoibh
  labhras ar chaoin na dtor le gréin;
damh-sa is fada tuirse an tsaoil
  nach bhfaicim í le tiacht an fhéir.

Gach neach dá bhfaiceann cruth na n-éan,
  amharc Éireann, deas is tuaidh,
bláth na dtulach ar gach taoibh,
  dóibh is aoibhinn bheith dá luadh.

Cluinim, cé nach bhfaicim gné,
  seinm an éin darb ainm cuach;
amharc uirthi i mbarraibh géag,
  mo thuirse ghéar nach mise fuair.

Mo thuirse nach bhfuaireas buaidh ar m'amharc a dh'fháil
  go bhfaicinn ar uaigneas uaisle an duilliúir ag fás;
cuid de mo ghruaim — ní ghluaisim chun cruinnigh' le cách
  le seinm na gcuach ar bhruach na coilleadh go sámh.

TRANSLATION

Welcome to the sweetest bird on the branch, who talks to the sun from the edge of the bush; for me life is wearisome because I don't see her when the grass begins to grow.

For everyone who sees the form of the birds, and the scenery of Ireland, south and north, and the flowers on the hillsides on every side, it is pleasant to talk about them.

I hear, though I don't see her shape, the bird's music, the bird called cuckoo; alas, alas I never saw her on the tops of the branches.

Alas that I did not get the power of sight so that I could see, when I am by myself, the beauty of the leaves growing; I can't go along with everyone else at the gentle singing of the cuckoo at the edge of the woods — this is part of my sorrow.

CEARBHALL Ó DÁLAIGH

(*fl.*1610)

LOVE'S BITTER SWEET

[Versions of Irish love songs are still extant and the stories associated with their composition continue to circulate. 'Eibhlín, a rún' is attributed to Cearbhall Ó Dálaigh. There are many poets of this name, and the figure in folklore stories is probably a composite of more than one. According to the tradition, he was renowned for his love poetry. When he was married to a beautiful woman, he overheard two men say that although she was beautiful, Eleanor Kavanagh was more beautiful. He then forsook his own wife for Eleanor, whom he wooed against her father's wishes. In some versions of the story, he and Eleanor lived happily ever after; in others he was killed for his audacity. The song was one of the earliest Irish songs to become popular among a non-Gaelic-speaking audience.]

Eibhlín, a rún

Le grá dhuit níl radharc im chionn,
  a Eibhlín, a rún!
Bheith ag trácht ort is saibhreas liom,
  a Eibhlín, a rún!
Mo mhóráil róghrinn is tú,
sólás na soillse is tú,
mo ghreann is mo mheidhir is tú,
  a Eibhlín, a rún!
Mo bhruinneall go deimhin is tú,
mo cholúr dá bhfuil sa gcoill is tú,

is ar mo chroí istigh níl leigheas gan tú,
a Eibhlín, a rún!

… … … … … … … …

Rachainn tar sáile leat,
a Eibhlín, a rún!
Is go deó ní fhágfainn tú,
a Eibhlín, a rún!
Le staraíocht do bhréagfainn tú,
do bhlaisfinn do bhéal go dlúth,
is shínfinn go séimh led chom,
a Eibhlín, a rún!
Thabharfainn aeraíocht duit cois abhann,
faoi ghéaga glasa crann,
ceól na n-éan os ár gceann,
a Eibhlín, a rún!

Le díograis tar bheatha dhuit,
a Eibhlín, a rún!,
do luífinn ar leaba leat,
a Eibhlín, a rún!
D'fháiscfinn im ghéaga thú,
choinneóinn go séanmhar thú,
ghráfainn tar éinneach thú,
a Eibhlín, a rún!
A réilteann mhaiseach mhodhail,
sul a mbéinn duit bun os ceann
och! éagadh ba thúisce leam,
a Eibhlín, a rún!

TRANSLATION

I have no sight in my head, Eileen aroon,[1] riches for me is to talk about you, Eileen aroon! My real glory you are, solace of light you are, my fun and my merriment you are, Eileen aroon! You are certainly my beautiful lady, you are my pigeon in the trees and without you there is no cure for my heart within, Eileen aroon!...

I would go over the sea with you, Eileen aroon! And never would I leave you, Eileen aroon! With joking I would entice you, I would taste your mouth firmly, and I would stretch gently by your waist, Eileen aroon! I would give you sport by the riverside, under the green boughs of trees, with the birdsong above us, Eileen aroon!

With diligence past existence, Eileen aroon! I would lie in bed with you, Eileen aroon! I would fold you in my arms, I would keep you happy, I would love you above all others, Eileen aroon! O beautiful gentle star, I would sooner die before you would be finished with me, Eileen aroon!

1. my love.

TOMÁS LÁIDIR MAC COISDEALBHA

(*fl.*1660)

THE LOVER'S LAMENT

['Úna bhán' is still a very popular song in Irish-speaking areas. Úna Nic Dhiarmada was the daughter of the Mac Diarmada (MacDermot) chieftain. He had forbidden the association she had with the poet Tomás Láidir Mac Coisdealbha (Costelloe). She pined for him and he was sent for. His visit helped her recovery. When he left, he delayed, hoping that a message would be sent to him before he went across a ford. He vowed that if he crossed the ford he would never return. The message arrived just as he reached the other side. He refused to break his vow and the story tells us that soon afterwards Úna expired of a broken heart.]

Úna bhán

A Úna chléibh, a ghéag na n-úrchíoch tais,
na nglas-shúl claon, is a chraobhfholt trom buí deas,
dá bhfaightí spré leat, céad bó, is chúig mhíle each,
b'fhearr thú féin ná gach séad dá dtabharfaí leat.

A Úna, a chara, a dhalta na ndaoine suairc,
is tú is so-chaideartha dá bhfaca mé riamh ar tuath;
do bhéilín tana is lasadh ón gcaoir id ghrua;
is buan mo ghean ort is ní rachaidh mé choíche ar cuairt.

Dá mbeadh a fhios agam go dtug tusa grá dhom féin,
bheinn dod mholadh go stopfadh an bás mo bhéal;
a phéarla an bhrollaigh ghil shochma is áille méin,
b'fhearr liom ' mo chodladh leat i bhfogas ná i láthair Dé.

… … … … … … … … … …

A Úna mhilis, is deimhin is éadáil thú
is ó aois an linbh a hoileadh mar bhréagán thú;
aon do gineadh ó bhile na ngéagán úr,
a phlúr na cruithneachta is tú d'ullmhaigh mo ghné
don úir.

A Úna, a rúin, is tú a mhearaigh mo chiall,
a Úna, a rúin, is tú a chuaidh eadar mé is Dia,
a Úna, a rúin, a lúib chumhra chasta na gciabh,
b'fhearr dhamhsa a bheith gan súile ná t'fhaicsint
ariamh.

... ...

Do chúl geal fáinneach bláthcheart ba órga
nár chuir spás i gcás na droch-chomhairle;
féachaidh, a mhná, cé b'fhearr ná an t-ochón seo
aon liú amháin ag Áth na Donóige?

TRANSLATION

Fair Úna my love, young girl with the fresh, smooth breasts, with languid, grey eyes and branching, heavy, fine, blonde hair, if riches were given with you, a hundred cows and five thousand horses, you yourself would surpass every treasure given as a dowry.

Úna my friend, young fosterling of the cheerful people; you are the friendliest person I ever met in the land; your slender mouth, and the berry's glow in your cheek; my affection for you is steadfast and I'll never visit you again.

If I knew that you loved me, I would praise you until death stopped my mouth; O pearl of the bright, pleasing bosom with the best disposition, I would prefer to sleep (in death) beside you than to be in the presence of God....

Sweet Una, certainly you are a prize worth having and from childhood you have been brought up as a pet; you are one who is descended from nobles, you are the best of the best and you have made my face ready for the grave.

Úna my love, you have set my senses astray, Úna my love, you came between me and God, Úna my love, girl with the curling, fragrant hair, it would have been better for me to have been without eyes than to have ever seen you....

Your bright flowing curls, golden like a flower, gave no respite when the bad advice was given;[1] look here you keening women, would not one cry have been better at Áth na Donóige[2] than all this wailing?

1. The reference to bad advice is either to the advice of Úna's family that she should have nothing to do with the poet or to the advice that was given to him not to turn back once he had crossed the ford.
2. Áth na Donóige is near Boyle, Co. Roscommon.

EIBHLÍN DHUBH NÍ CHONAILL

(*c.*1745-?)

from: THE LAMENT FOR ART O'LEARY

[In the Irish literature of the period, very few poems are attributed to women. This lament for her husband Art by Eibhlín Dhubh Ní Chonaill is the best known of such compositions. The story behind the poem is as follows. In 1767 Eibhlín, then a young widow, met Art O'Leary, a youthful Irishman who had served as a captain in the Hungarian army and, in spite of the disapproval of her family (the O'Connells of Derrynane), they married. Art quarrelled with a protestant named Abraham Morris. When Morris claimed Art's horse for £5, Art went into hiding. He was seen by a company of soldiers on 4 May 1774 and, when he resisted, he was killed. Art's horse is said to have returned, whereupon Eibhlín went to the place he was lying. The poem is supposed to have been started there and completed as he was waked and buried. In form it is a traditional *caoineadh* (keen) and was recited in a musical chant. Although it is traditional and formulaic, it also conveys a high degree of personal feeling.

The translation is by Frank O'Connor; see *Kings, Lords, & Commons* (Dublin: Gill and Macmillan, 1959).]

Mo ghrá go daingean tu!
Lá dá bhfaca thu
Ag ceann tí an mhargaidh,
Thug mo shúil aire dhuit,
Thug mo chroí taitneamh duit,

D'éalaíos óm charaid leat
I bhfad ó bhaile leat.

Is domhsa nárbh aithreach:
Chuiris parlús á ghealadh dhom
Rúmanna á mbreacadh dhom,
Bácús á dheargadh dhom,
Brící á gceapadh dhom,
Rósta ar bhearaibh dom,
Mairt á leagadh dhom;
Codladh i gclúmh lachan dom
Go dtíodh an t-eadartha
Nó thairis dá dtaitneadh liom.

Mo chara go daingean tu!
Is cuimhin lem aigne
An lá breá earraigh úd,
Gur bhreá thíodh hata dhuit
Faoi bhanda óir tarraingthe,
Claíomh cinn airgid —
Lámh dheas chalma —
Rompsáil bhagarthach —
Fír-chritheagla
Ar námhaid chealgach —
Tú i gcóir chun falaracht,
Is each caol ceannann fút.
D'umhlaídís Sasanaigh
Síos go talamh duit,
Is ní ar mhaithe leat
Ach le haon-chorp eagla,
Cé gur leo a cailleadh tu,
A mhuirnín mh'anama.
… … … … …

Mo chara thu go daingean!
Is nuair thiocfaidh chugham abhaile
Conchubhar beag an cheana
Is Fear Ó Laoghaire, an leanbh,
Fiafróid díom go tapaidh
Cár fhágas féin a n-athair.
'Neosad dóibh faoi mhairg
Gur fhágas i gCill na Martar.
Glaofaid siad ar a n-athair,
Is ní bheidh sé acu le freagairt.

Mo chara thu go daingean!
Is níor chreideas riamh dod mharbh
Gur tháinig chugham do chapall
Is a srianta léi go talamh,
Is fuil do chroí ar a leacain
Siar go t'iallait ghreanta
Mar a mbítheá id shuí 's id sheasamh.
Thugas léim go tairsigh,
An dara léim go geata,
An tríú léim ar do chapall.

Do bhuaileas go luath mo bhasa
Is do bhaineas as na reathaibh
Chomh maith is bhí sé agam,
Go bhfuaras romham tu marbh
Cois toirín ísil aitinn,
Gan Pápa gan easpag,
Gan cléireach gan sagart
Do léifeadh ort an tsailm,
Ach seanbhean chríonna chaite
Do leath ort binn dá fallaing —
Do chuid fola leat 'na sraithibh;
Is níor fhanas le hí ghlanadh
Ach í ól suas lem basaibh.

Mo ghrá thu go daingean!
Is éirigh suas id sheasamh
Is tar liom féin abhaile,
Go gcuirfeam mairt á leagadh,
Go nglaofam ar chóisir fhairsing,
Go mbeidh againn ceol á spreagadh,
Go gcóireod duitse leaba
Faoi bhairlíní geala,
Faoi chuilteanna breátha breaca,
A bhainfidh asat allas
In ionad an fhuachta a ghlacais.

Deirfiúr Airt
Mo chara is mo stór tu!
Is mó bean chumtha chórach
Ó Chorcaigh na seolta
Go Droichead na Tóime,
Do thabharfadh macha mór bó dhuit
Agus dorn buí-óir duit,
Ná raghadh a chodladh 'na seomra
Oíche do thórraimh.

Eibhlín Dhubh
Mo chara is m' uan tu!
Is ná creid sin uathu,
Ná an cogar a fuarais,
Ná an scéal fir fuatha,
Gur a chodladh a chuas-sa.
Níor throm suan dom:
Ach bhí do linbh ró-bhuartha,
'S do theastaigh sé uathu
Iad a chur chun suaimhnis.

A dhaoine na n-ae istigh,
'Bhfuil aon bhean in Éirinn,
Ó luí na gréine,
A shínfeadh a taobh leis,
Do bhéarfadh trí lao dho,
Ná raghadh le craobhacha
I ndiaidh Airt Uí Laoghaire
Atá anso traochta
Ó mhaidin inné agam?

M'fhada-chreach léan-ghoirt
Ná rabhas-sa taobh leat
Nuair lámhadh an piléar leat,
Go ngeobhainn é im thaobh dheas
Nó i mbinn mo léine,
Is go léigfinn cead slé' leat
A mharcaigh na ré-ghlac.

... ...

Mo chara thu is mo shearc-mhaoin!
Is gránna an chóir a chur ar ghaiscíoch
Comhra agus caipín,
Ar mharcach an dea-chroí
A bhíodh ag iascaireacht ar ghlaisíbh
Agus ag ól ar hallaíbh
I bhfarradh mná na ngeal-chíoch.
Mo mhíle mearaí
Mar a chailleas do thaithí.

Greadadh chughat is díth
A Mhorris ghránna an fhill!
A bhain díom fear mo thí
Athair mo leanbh gan aois:
Dís acu ag siúl an tí,
'S an tríú duine acu istigh im chlí,
Agus is dócha ná cuirfead díom.

... ...

Mo chara thu is mo chuid!
A mharcaigh an chlaímh ghil,
Éirigh suas anois,
Cuir ort do chulaith
Éadaigh uasail ghlain,
Cuir ort do bhéabhar dubh,
Tarraing do lámhainní umat.
Siúd í in airde t'fhuip;
Sin í do láir amuigh.
Buail-se an bóthar caol úd soir
Mar a maolóidh romhat na toir,
Mar a gcaolóidh romhat an sruth,
Mar a n-umhlóidh romhat mná is fir,
Má tá a mbéasa féin acu —
'S is baolach liomsa ná fuil anois.

Tá fhios ag Íosa Críost
Ná beidh caidhp ar bhathas mo chinn,
Ná léine chnis lem thaoibh,
Ná bróg ar thrácht mo bhoinn,

... ...

TRANSLATION

My love and my delight
The day I saw you first
Beside the markethouse
I had eyes for nothing else
And love for none but you.

I left my father's house
And ran away with you,
And that was no bad choice;
You gave me everything.
There were parlours whitened for me
Bedrooms painted for me,
Ovens reddened for me,
Loaves baked for me,
Joints spitted for me,
Beds made for me
To take my ease on flock
Until the milking time
And later if I pleased.

My mind remembers
That bright spring day,
How your hat with its band
Of gold became you,
Your silver-hilted sword,
Your manly right hand,
Your horse on her mettle
And foes around you
Cowed by your air;
For when you rode by
On your white-nosed mare
The English lowered their head before you
Not out of love for you
But hate and fear,
The English killed you.

... ...

My love and my darling
When I go home
The little lad, Conor,
And Fiach the baby
Will surely ask me
Where I left their father,
I'll say with anguish
'Twas in Kilnamartyr;[1]
They will call the father
Who will never answer.

My love and my mate
That I never thought dead
Till your horse came to me
With bridle trailing,
All blood from forehead
To polished saddle
Where you should be,
Either sitting or standing;
I gave one leap to the threshold,
A second to the gate,
A third upon its back.
And off at a gallop;
I never lingered
Till I found you lying
By a little furze-bush
Without pope or bishop
Or priest or cleric
One prayer to whisper
But an old, old woman,
And her cloak about you,
And your blood in torrents —
Art O'Leary —
I did not wipe it off,
I drank it from my palms.

My love and my delight
Stand up now beside me,
And let me lead you home
Until I make a feast,
And I will roast the meat
And send for company
And call the harpers in,
And I shall make your bed
Of soft and snowy sheets
And blankets dark and rough
To warm the beloved limbs
An autumn blast has chilled.

1. Near Macroom, Co. Cork.

(His sister speaks)
My love and treasure,
Where is the woman
From Cork of the white sails
To the bridge of Tomey
With her dowry gathered
And cows at pasture
Would sleep alone
The night they waked you?

(His wife replies)
My darling, do not believe
One word she is saying,
It is a falsehood
That I slept while others
Sat up to wake you —
But the children crying;
They would not rest
Without me beside them.

O people, do not believe
Any lying story!
There is no woman in Ireland
Who had slept beside him
And borne him three children
But would cry out
After Art O'Leary
Who lies dead before me
Since yesterday morning.

… … … … …

Destruction pursue you,
Morris the traitor
Who brought death to my husband!
Father of three children —
Two on the hearth
And one in the womb
That I shall not bring forth.

It is my sorrow
That I was not by
When they fired the shots
Or in my heart, who cares?
If you but reached the hills
Rider of the ready hands.

My love and my fortune
'Tis an evil portion
To lay for a giant —
A shroud and a coffin —

For a big-hearted hero
Who fished in the hill-streams
And drank in bright halls
With white-breasted women.

My comfort and my friend,
Master of the bright sword,
'Tis time you left your sleep;
Yonder hangs your whip,
Your horse is at the door,
Follow the lane to the east
Where every bush will bend
And every stream dry up,
And man and woman bow
If things have manners yet
That have them not I fear.

... ...

My rider of the bright eyes,
What happened you yesterday?
I thought you in my heart,
When I bought you your fine clothes,
A man the world could not slay.

'Tis known to Jesus Christ
Nor cap upon my head,
Nor shift upon my back
Nor shoe upon my foot,
Nor gear in all my house,
Nor bridle for the mare
But I will spend at law;
And I'll go oversea
To plead before the King,
And if the King be deaf
I'll settle things alone
With the black-blooded rogue
That killed my man on me.

... ...

But cease your weeping now,
Women of the soft, wet eyes
Till Art O'Leary drink
Ere he go to the dark school —
Not to learn music or song
But to prop the earth and the stone.

... ...

ANONYMOUS

from:
TÓRAÍOCHT DHIARMADA AGUS GHRÁINNE
(The Pursuit of Diarmaid and Gráinne)

[Stories about Finn mac Cumaill and the select band of warriors, the Fiana, are as old as the tenth century; some traditions go back even further. This cycle of stories, known as the Fenian cycle, were productive from the very beginning; they were continually reworked, retold, and new stories were created. The stories are full of all the ingredients of romantic adventure: heroes, villains, beautiful maidens, envy, love and constant exaggerated action. The version of *Tóraíocht Dhiarmada agus Ghráinne* that has come down to us was probably composed in the early fourteenth century. It was common in seventeenth- and eighteenth-century manuscripts.

Finn sees Gráinne and chooses her as his wife. She falls in love with Diarmaid and entices him to elope with her. They are pursued by Finn and pass through many adventures (during which, almost incidentally, the liaison is consummated) before they are reconciled to the Fiana again. In the final tragic episode told here, Diarmaid is persuaded to fight a deadly boar, which fatally wounds him. Finn is the only one who could help him, but he waits too long, thus ensuring Diarmaid's death. The text and translation are based on Nessa Ní Shéaghdha's edition (Dublin: Irish Texts Society, 1967).

'Na dhiaidh sin táinic an torc i n-aghaidh na Beinne aníos agus an Fhian ina diaigh, agus do sgaoil Diarmaid Mac an Chuill dá héill ina coinne, agus ní dhearnaidh sin tarbha dhó óir níor an sí risin torc acht do theith roimpe. Adubhairt Diarmaid: 'Is mairg nach déan comhairle dheagh-mhná, óir adubhairt Gráinne ream i mochrach an Móraltach agus an Ga Dearg do thabhairt leam.'

Rena chois sin do chuir méar i suaichneamh síoda an Gha Buidhe an Lámhaigh do bhí 'na láimh agus tuc rogha n-áitheasach n-urchair ar amus na muice dhe gur bhuail i gceart-lár a haithche agus a héadain í, agus níor ghearr aon-ruibe innte, agus níor mhó dhearg fuirre. Réna chois sin ro bhean a chloidheamh amach .i. an Beacaltach, agus do bhuail ina druim hí agus níor ghearr aon-ruibe ann, agus do-rinne dá chuid dá chloidheamh.

Rena chois sin tuc an torc sidhe nimhneach neimh-eaglach ar Diarmaid agus do bhean sí an fód do bhí fána chosuibh, agus tarla mullach a chinn faoi.

Agus ag éirghe dó tarla cos ar gach taobh don torc aige agus a aghaidh roimhe siar, agus do ghluais sí re fánaigh an chnuic síos agus níor fhéad sí Diarmaid do chur dhi. Agus do ghabh roimpe as sin nó go ráinic Eas Ruaidh mhic Bhadhoirn, agus mar do ráinic an t-eas ruc trí léimeanna lúith tar an eas anonn agus anall agus níor fhéad sí Diarmaid do chur dhi risin bhfeadh sin. Táinic roimpe i bhfrithing na conaire céadna agus i n-aghaidh aird na Beinne suas arís, agus ar tteacht ar mullach an chnuic anios di do chuir sí Diarmaid di, agus ag tuitim dochum láir dhó tuc sí sidhe nimhneach neimh-eaglach air gur leig sí a abach agus a ionathar ris. Agus ag fágbháil na tulcha dhi tuc Diarmaid urchar áitheasach do chobhail an chloidhimh do bhí 'na láimh dhi gur bhuail i n-oghar a himlinne hí, gur leig sé a habach agus a hionathar ria, gur fhág-uibh marbh gan anmain hí. Gurab Ráithín na hAbarnaigh ainm na rátha atá ar mullach na Beinne sin thuas ó sin a leith.

Rena chois sin táinig Fionn agus Fiana Éireann do láthair, agus do bhádar airgheana báis agus buan-éaga ag teacht do Dhiarmaid. Is ann sin adubhairt Fionn:

'Is maith leam t'fheicsin mar sin, a Dhiarmaid,' ar sé, 'agus is truagh leam nach bhfuilid mná Éireann uile dot fhéachain anois, ór tucais maise ar mhí-mhaise agus dealbh mhaith ar droch-dheilbh.'

'Atá ar cumus duit-si mise do leigheas uatha sin,' ar Diarmaid, 'madh áil leat féin hé.'

'Cionnus do leigheósainn-si thú?' ar Fionn.

'Co maith,' ar Diarmaid, 'óir do ghlacais an t-eó fis do bhí for Bóinn, agus gidh bé dá dtiubharthá deoch dot bhasuibh do bhiadh sé óghshlán ón uile ghalar dá éis.'

'Níor thuillis-si uaim-si an deoch sin do thabhairt duit,' ar Fionn.

'Ní fíor sin,' ar Diarmaid, 'óir is maith do thuilleas-sa uait í an oidhche do chuadhuis-si do thigh an Deirg mhic Dionnarthaigh, agus maithe agus mór-uaisle Fhian Éireann id fhochair, do thochaitheamh fleidhe. Agus táinic Cairbre Lif-eachair mac Cormaic agus fir Bhreagh agus Mhidhe agus Chearmna agus Colamhna tinniosnacha na Teamhrach timcheall na bruighne ort-sa, agus tucadar trí trom-ghárrtha ós aird ina timcheall, agus do chuireadar teinnte agus teannála innte, agus do éirghis-si it sheasamh, a Fhinn, agus dob áil leat a dhol amach, agus adubhart-sa riot-sa anmhain istigh id ionadh óil agus aoibhneasa agus go rachainn féin amach agus go ccoisgfinn iad sin. Agus do chuadhas amach agus do bhádhus na teinnte agus tucus trí dearg-ruathair timcheall na bruighne agus do mharbhas céad do gach ruathar dhíobh, agus do chuadhas féin isteach iomshlán uatha gan fhuiliughadh gan fhordeargadh orum. Agus do budh luathgháireach lán-mheanmnach do bhádhuis-si romham an oidhche sin, a Fhinn, agus tucais deoch dhamh an oidhche sin, agus níor chóra duit sin do thabhairt damh an uair sin ná anois.'

'Ní fíor sin,' ar Fionn, 'óir is olc do thuillis uaim-si deoch do thabhairt duit ná aon-ní maitheasa do dhénamh dhuit an oidhche tángais leam go Teamhraigh agus ruguis Gráinne leat uaim a Teamhraigh i bhfiaghnuise bhfear nÉireann, agus gurab tú féin dob fhear coimhéada agum-sa an oidhche sin i dTeamhraigh.'

'Ní fíor sin,' ar Diarmaid, 'óir níor chionntach mise leis sin acht geasa do chuir Gráinne orm, agus ní chaillfinn-si mo gheasa ar ór na cruinne. Is maith do thuilleas-sa uait deoch do thabhairt damh dá madh cumhain leat an uair do-rinne Mídheach mac Colgáin fleadh Bhruighne Caorrthainn fád chomhair. Agus do bhí bruighean ar tír agus bruighean ar tuinn aige, agus do tharraing sé Ríghe an Domhain agus trí rígh Innsi Tile gusan mbruighin do bhí ar muir aige fá chomhair do chinn do bhuain díot-sa. Agus do bhí an fhleadh dá tabhairt amach isin mbruigh-in do bhí ar tír aige, agus do chuadhuis-si agus drong do mhaithibh Fhian Éireann maille riot do chaitheamh na fleidhe sin go Bruighin in Chaorrthainn, agus do chuir Mídheach úir Innse Tile fúibh ionnus gur leandar bhur ccosa agus bhur lámha i n-aoineacht don talamh. Agus mar do fuair Rígh an Domhain sgéala thusa agus do mhuintir do bheith ceangailte cruaidh-chuibhrighthe mar sin do chuir sé taoiseach céad dá mhuintir féin d'iarraidh do chinn-si. Agus tucais-si th'ordóg fád dhéad fis agus do foillsigheadh fios agus eolus duit.

Agus as í sin uair agus aimsir fá dtánag-sa féin ad dheaghaidh-si go Bruighin an Chaorrthainn agus tucais-si aithne orum ag teacht dochum na bruighne damh, agus do fhoillsighis-si damh Mídhach mac Colgáin agus Ríghe an Domhain agus trí rígh Innse Tile do bheith i mBruighin an

Oiléain ar Sionainn, agus nach fada go dtiucfadh cuid éigin aca d'iarraidh do chinn féin agus dá bhreith go Ríghe an Domhain. Agus mar do chualas-sa sin do ghabhas cumairce th'anma-sa agus do chuirp orum féin go héirghe do ló arna mhárach.

Agus do-chuadhas ar an áth do bhí re taobh na bruighne dá chosnamh. Níor chian do bhádhus ann an tan táinic an taoiseach céad sin do mhuintir Rígh an Domhain chugum, agus do chomhraicsim re chéile agus do bheanus a cheann de féin agus do chuireas ár a mhuintire, agus do bheanus a cheann de féin agus do chuireas ár a mhuintire, agus do leanas iad go Bruighin an Oiléain, agus fuaras Rígh an Domhain i ndáil óil agus aoibhneasa ann sin agus trí rígh Innsi Tile ina fhochair. Agus do bheanas mo chloidheamh amach agus do bheanas a cheann do Rígh an Domhain don chéad-bhéim, agus ro bheanas i dtrí cinn dona trí ríoghuibh sin eile do bhí 'na fhochair agus do chuireas i gcobhraidh mo sgéithe iad. Agus do thógbhas an corn cloch-órrdha cumhdaigh gona lán do shean-mhiodh sho-óla do bhí a bhfiaghnuisi Rígh an Domhain im láimh chlí agus do-rinneas faobhar-chleas dom chloidheamh um thimcheall, agus tánag romham do thoradh mo ghoile agus mo ghaisgidh go Bruighin in Chaorrthainn. Agus tucas na cinn sin agus na cuirn duit-si, a Fhinn, mar chomhartha cosgair agus comhmaoite, agus do choimleas fuil mhéidhe na dtrí ríogh sin fút féin agus fán druing sin d'Fhianaibh Éireann do bhí ceangailte maille friot, ionnus gur leigeas luaghuil a lámh agus céim-niughadh a gcos ar a gcumas. Agus dá madh í an oidhche sin, a Fhinn, do iarrfuinn-si deoch ort-sa do-ghébhuinn í.'

Is ann sin adubhairt Osgar mac Oisín:

'A Fhinn,' ar sé, 'an fhuil a fhios agad gurab goire mo ghaol féin do Dhiarmaid ó Duibhne ná duit-si, agus nach leigfinn leat gan deoch do thabhairt dó.'

'Ní haithne damh-sa tobar ar an mBeinn si,' ar Fionn.

'Ní fíor sin,' ar Diarmaid, 'óir ní fhuil acht naoi spáis uait tobar fíor-áluinn fíor-uisge is fearr ar bith.'

Ina dhiaigh sin téid Fionn d'ionnsaighe an tobair agus do thógaibh lán a dhá bhas leis, agus ní mó ná leath sligheadh táinic an uair do leig sé an t-uisge trína bhasuibh síos, agus do innis nachar fhéad sé an t-uisge do thabhairt leis.

'Do-bheirim-si mo bhriathar,' ar Diarmaid, 'gurab dot dheóin féin do-ní tú sin.'

Téid Fionn ar ceann an uisge arís, agus ní mó ná an fad céadna tuc leis é an uair do leig tréna bhasuibh síos é.

'Dar mo bhréithir a bhfiaghnuise m'arm,' ar Osgar, 'muna dtucair an t-uisge leat go luath, a Fhinn, ní racha don láthair so dhínn 'nar ndís acht an tí bhus treise.'

Do thill Fionn an treas feacht ar ceann an uisge leis in gcomhrádh sin go Diarmaid, agus tuc lán a dhá bhos don uisge leis. Agus ag teacht do láthair dó do sgar a anam rena chorp ag Diarmaid. Agus do thógbhadar an drong do bhí ar an láthair sin d'Fhianuibh Éireann trí trom-ghárrtha adhbhal-mhóra acaoineacha ós aird ag caoineadh Diarmada uí Dhuibhne. Agus d'éirigh Osgar do bhorb-thulcha troim-fheirge iona sheasamh agus do bhreathnaigh a cheann do bhuain d'Fhionn ar an láthair sin go ndubhairt Oisín:

'A mhic,' ar sé, 'is fíor gur thuill sé sin uait-si agus ó Fhiannaibh Éireann go hiomlán tré gan Diarmaid d'fhóirighthin, agus ná déin-si an dá léan i n-aon-ló dhúinn, agus fágbham an tulach so anois ar eagla go dtiocfadh Aonghus chuguinn agus nách creidfeadh uainn nách sinn féin tug bás do Dhiarmaid gion gur chionntach Fionn rena bhás.'

TRANSLATION

After that the boar came up the Beann with the Fiana after it, and Diarmaid slipped Mac an Chuill from its leash against it, and that did not profit him for he did not wait for the boar but fled before it. Diarmaid said:

'Woe to him who does not follow the counsel of a good wife, for Gráinne told me at dawn to take the Móraltach and the Ga Dearg with me.'[1]

With that he put a finger in the silken loop of the Ga Buidhe an Lámhaigh which he had in his hand and he aimed a most successful cast at the pig so that he struck it right in the middle of its face and of its forehead, and he did not cut a single bristle on it and not even did he wound it. With that he took out his sword, namely, the Beagaltach, and he struck it on the back and he did not cut a single bristle on it, and his sword broke in two.

With that the boar made a venomous fearless spring on Diarmaid and it tripped him and he fell headlong.

1. It was common for the chief warriors of the Fiana to have special weapons with their own particular names.

And when he was rising up it happened that one leg was on either side of the boar and his face looking backward and it went down the slope of the hill without being able to put Diarmaid off [from its back]. And off it went from there until it reached Eas Ruaidh mhic Bhadhoirn, and when it reached the waterfall it gave three swift leaps across the fall hither and thither and it could not put Diarmaid off during that time. It came back the same way and uphill to the Beann again, and when it reached the top of the hill it put Diarmaid off, and when he was falling to the ground it gave a fearless spring on him and it let out his bowels and his entrails about him. And as it was leaving the mound Diarmaid aimed a successful cast at it with the stump of the sword which was in his hand, so that he struck it in the middle of the navel letting out its bowels and its entrails about it, so that he left it without life. Therefore Ráithín na hAbarnaigh is the name of the rath which is on top of that Beann since then.

With that Fionn and the Fiana of Ireland came to the place, and the signs of death and of lasting extinction were coming on Diarmaid. It was then Fionn said:

'I like to see you like that, Diarmaid,' said he, 'and I regret that all the women of Ireland are not looking at you now, for your beauty is turned to ugliness and your good form to deformity.'

'It is in your power to heal me from those,' said Diarmaid, 'if you yourself wish it.'

'How should I heal you?' said Fionn.

'Well indeed,' said Diarmaid, 'for you handled the salmon of knowledge which was on the Boyne, and to whomsoever you should give a drink from your palms would be perfectly sound from all diseases after that.'

'You have not deserved of me that I should give you that drink,' said Fionn.

'That is not true,' said Diarmaid, 'for well I earned it from you the night you went to the house of Dearg son of Dionnarthach,[2] and the chiefs and great nobles of the Fiana of Ireland with you, to partake of a banquet. And Cairbre Lifeachair son of Cormac and the men of Breagha and Meath and Cearmna, and the strong Pillars of Tara came around the hostel against you, and they uttered three mighty shouts out loud around it and they put fires and flames into it, and you rose up, Fionn, and it was your wish to go out and I told you to stay inside where you were drinking and enjoying yourself and that I myself would go out and that I would stop those. And I went out and quenched the fires and made three fierce attacks around the hostel and I killed a hundred in every attack of them, and I myself went in safe from them without loss of blood, without a wound on me. And you were joyous fill-spirited before me that night, Fionn, and you gave me a drink that night, and it was not more proper for you to give it to me that time than now.'

'That is not true', said Fionn, 'for you ill-deserved of me to give you a drink or to do any other goodness for you the night you came to Tara with me and took Gráinne with you from me out of Tara in the presence of the men of Ireland, and [considering] that you were my body-guard that night in Tara.'

'That is not true,' said Diarmaid, 'for I was not guilty of that, but Gráinne put injunctions on me and I would not violate my injunctions for the gold of the world. I have well deserved of you that you should give me a drink if you may remember when Míodhach son of Colgán made the feast of Bruidhean Chaorthainn for you.[3] And he had a hostel on land and a hostel on sea, and he brought the King of the World and the three kings of Inis Tile to the hostel which he had on sea in order to take your head off. And the feast was being given in the hostel which he had on land, and you went and a number of the chiefs of the Fiana of Ireland with you to Bruidhean an Chaorthainn to partake of that feast, and Míodhach put [some of] the soil of Inis Tile under you so that your feet and your hands stuck to the ground at the same time. And when the King of the World heard that you and your people were tied and hard-bound like that he sent a chief of a hundred [men] of his own people to seek your head. And you put your thumb under your tooth of knowledge, and knowledge and information were revealed to you.

And that was the occasion and time that I came myself after you to Bruidhean an Chaorthainn and you recognised me as I was coming towards the hostel, and you revealed to me that Míodhach son of Colgán and the King of the World and the three kings of Inis Tile were in Bruidhean an Oileáin on the Shannon, and that it would not be long before

2. A reference to another story about the Fiana.

3. This refers to another Fenian tale, 'Bruidhean Chaorthainn' (The Rowantree Fort), in which the Fiana are enticed to a fort from which they cannot escape.

some of them would come to seek your own head and to bring it to the King of the World. And when I heard that I took the protection of your life and your body on myself till daybreak on the morrow.

And I went to the ford which was by the hostel to defend it. I had not been long there when that chief of a hundred [men] of the people of the King of the World came to me, and we fought with each other and I cut his head off himself and made slaughter of his people, and I followed them to Bruidhean an Oileáin, and I found the King of the World occupied in drinking and pleasure there, and the three kings of Inis Tile with him. And I took my sword out and I cut the head off the King of the World with the first stroke, and I cut their three heads off those three other kings who were with him and I put them into the boss of my shield. And I took the golden-jewelled ornate goblet, being full of old mead pleasant to drink, which was before the King of the World in my left hand and I made an edge-feat[4] with my sword around me, and I came, as a result of my heroism and of my valour, to Bruidhean an Chaorthainn. And I gave those heads and those goblets to you, Fionn, as a sign of victory and triumph, and I rubbed the blood of the necks of those three kings on you and on that company of the Fiana of Ireland who were bound along with you, so that I restored to them the use of their hands and the movement of their feet. And had I asked a drink of you that night, Fionn, I would have got it.'

It was then Osgar son of Oisín said:

'Fionn,' said he, 'do you know that I am closer akin to Diarmaid ó Duibhne than to you, and that I would not allow you not to give him a drink.'

4. The Fiana were renowned for their martial prowess. This is obviously a feat of dexterity with a sword, but we have no exact description of it.

'I do not know of a well on this Beann,' said Fionn.

'That is not true,' said Diarmaid, 'for but only nine paces from you is the most truly beautiful, pure-watered well in the whole world.'

After that Fionn went towards the well and he took the full of his two palms with him, and he had not reached more than half-way when he let the water run down through his palms, and he said that he could not bring the water with him.

'I give my word,' said Diarmaid, 'that you are doing that purposely.'

Fionn went for the water again, and he had not brought it more than the same distance when he let it down through his palms.

'I swear before my arms,' said Osgar, 'that if you do not bring the water with you quickly, Fionn, there shall not leave this place of the two of us but he who is strongest.'

Fionn returned for the water the third time for Diarmaid because of that speech, and he brought with him the full of his two palms of water. And as he was coming to the place the life parted from the body of Diarmaid. And the company of the Fiana of Ireland that was at that place raised three mighty exceedingly great mournful shouts out loud mourning Diarmaid ó Duibhne. And Osgar rose up in a fierce attack of great anger and was about to cut his head off Fionn on that spot but that Oisín said:

'Son,' said he, 'it is true that he has deserved that of you and of all the Fiana of Ireland through not helping Diarmaid, but do not cause the two sorrows in one day for us, and let us leave this mound now for fear that Aonghus might come to us and that he would not believe from us that it was not we who brought death to Diarmaid although Fionn is guilty of his death.'

ANONYMOUS

from: PAIRLEMENT CHLOINNE TOMÁIS

[This extract is from *Pairlement Chloinne Tomáis* (The Parliament of Clan Thomas). The parliament burlesques the practice of the rustics in gathering together to discuss matters. This always leads to chaos and slapstick humour. It is one of the great works of satire and humour in Irish literature. The story derives from the native tradition of parody and burlesque, from medieval estate satire and from the Elizabethan and Jacobean pamphlet literature about vagabonds, thieves and other peripheral groups. The author, who was steeped in Irish literature, portrays Clann Tomáis (the family of Thomas, an archetypal boor) from the time of their dissemination from hell until the early seventeenth century. He is obviously using this device to lament the 'world turned upside down' in which the Irish nobles are driven from the country or are at best living in penury, while the uncouth, uncultured classes hold sway. In this passage, one of them tries to better himself by marrying into a family of 'good' blood.]

Do bhádar mar sin go haimsir Fheidhlime mhic Criomhthuin do bheith i bfhlaitheas Mumhan fá bhruth agus fá bhorradh; agus do bhí taoiseach do dhearrsgnuigh ar chách dena treabhuibh sin táinig ó Thomás, eadhon Murcha Maolchluasach Ó Multuaisgirt; agus is é baile iona n-áitreabhadh an Murcha sin: i gCluain Mhic Nóis. Agus re linn Fheidhlime mhic Criomhthuin do thabhairt chuarda timpcheall dá Chóige Mumhan, d'fhás fán am sin toice agus tromchonách leis an Murcha sin, agus do chuir teachta fá ollchóigibh Éireann do thionól gach a raibhe do lucht eoluis agus údaráis ionnta ar Chloinn Tomáis go Cluain Mhic Nóis; agus tángadar umorro go háit aonbhaile agus do fearadh fáilte riú ag Murcha. Do labhair riú agus as eadh adubhairt:

'A bhráithreacha ionmhuine', ar sé, 'agas a shliocht céillidhe cianradharcach caomhchonáig Thomáis Mhóir mhic Liobair Lobhtha mhic Lóbuis Laghruigh mhic Dracapéisde mhic Beilsebub, as uime do chuireas fios oraibh: chum comhairle do thabhairt damh cia an bhean dhiongmhála do-bhéarainn; óir is mithid damh bean do thabhairt a ndiaidh agus iar n-éag mo bhanchéile croidhe chumuinn .i. Brighid Ní Mhagarláin, inghean Mhathghamhna Bhreallaigh Í Mhagarláin agus Raighnuite Cosbhuidhe Ní Mheigiolláin ó Bhéal an dá Chab'.

Agus iar rádh na mbriathar sin dó, do thuit sruth smuguirleach deor uaidh, agus do ghlac racht agus tocht aigne é, go nár fhéad labhairt feadh uaire. 'agus do-chloinim', ar Murcha, 'go bhfuil taoiseach tromchonáig i gCóige chaomhálainn Chonnacht .i. Maghnus Ó Madagáin, agus ní beag linn a fhad atámaoid gan ar bhfuil d'uaisliughadh agus sinn fá dhaoirse agus ag foghnamh do chách gus aniugh; agus atá inghean álainn aontugha ag an Maghnus sin, agus do thograsa le bhur gcomhairlese teachta do chur dá hiarraidh for a hathair'.

Adubhradar cách gur cóir sin, agus is iad so do cuireadh ann .i. ceathrar éagsamhail ealadhanta do Chloinn Tomáis .i. Mathghamhuin Mórthónach, Bernard Brógfhada, Niall Ó Neanntanáin agus Conchubhar Cromcheannach Ó Craoinntiolláin. Is annsin do ghabhadur a gcead agus adubhairt Nial an laoi si ann:

'Slan agad, a Mhurcha mhóir,
a cheann slóig an phlub ó phlib,
as iomdha id dhún pónaire oirnéis,
fuil, tóirnéis agus glugram glig.

Slán d'fhoirinn na gcorrán ngéar,
d'itheadh brúcht le buan déas,
nach bíodh dian dúr dranntánach,
gruama garbhshálach ná géar.

Slán do Bhrian Ó Briolláin tshuairc,
fear crónain a gcluais a mhic;
slán do Mhurghuill is do Mheidhbh,
nár leig braidhm is nár ith min.

Mo shlán duit, a Bhearnáird bhuirb,
's a Lochluinn ghuirm nár chreim cnámh,
an drong ghlic nach caidréiseach,
sluagh aimléisioch na gcrios lán'.

Do mhol Murcha agus cách ar cheana an dán sin, agus tugsad muinntear agus matha an teaghluigh mionna agus mórbhriathar nach dearnadh a chom-math sin d'éigse ná d'ealadhain san domhan riamh roimhe sin. Is annsin táinig fáidh fírfheasach Chloinne Tomáis do láthair chuca .i. Brian Brusanta Ó Bloingidhe, agus ba mór tráth fios, foghlaim agus fíreolus an fhir sin, agus adubhairt gurab é príomhollamh airdrígh Éireann do chéadchum an aisde sin; agus is mór do moladh mar do hiadhadh an dán sin, agus is é ainm tug Brian ar an aisde sin, eadhon ceathramhna corra.

Gluaisid an drong dheadhbhéasach sin i ndíreach gacha conaire agus gacha caoimheolais nó go rángadur láimh re Ceapuig an Aráin agus do Bhealach na Bláthaighe, do Mhachaire na Meacan agus do Ráithín na Praisge, do Bhuailtín an Phónaire, do Chúil na Mine, do Lios na nGarbhán agus do Thuairín an Bhainne agus do Bhealach na Lótuighe, agus riompa bhu-thuaidh do leathimeal Mhachaire Chonnacht nó go dtángadur go tigh Mhaghnuis Í Mhadagáin; agus ar mbeith dóibh ag rásdáil go ramharbhrógach ar fhaiche an dúnaidh, táinig Maghnus 'na gcomhdháil agus fiafraigheas díobh cia hiad féin nó cá hionad asa dtángadar nó créad an toisg tugsad sonn. Ro inniseadar na teachta a dtoisg agus adubhairt Maghnus: 'Is aithnid dúinn bhur gcinéal agus is aithnid dúinn mar an gcéadna gurab duine saidhbhir bhur dtighearna'.

Do chuir Maghnus iar sin teachta ar a dhraoithibh agus ar a fhlathaibh. Tángadar umorro an lucht feasa sin agus do labhair Maghnus riú agus is eadh adubhairt:

'Is uime do chuirios féin fios oraibh .i. inghean chruthach chaomhálainn atá agamsa, agus táinig iarraidh uirrthe ó Mhurcha Mhaolchluasach Ó Mhultuaisgirt, agus is taoiseach tromthoiceach an Murcha sin'.

'Is feasach sinne', ar na draoithe, 'gur den chineadh chodrama an t-óglaoch sin, óir is iad na geinte ifreannda is sinnsir don Mhurcha chéanna; agus ní dhlighionn aonneach d'fhuil uasail ar bith measgadh ar fhuil anuasail; óir dá mhéid macnais agus foghlaim, onóir agus udarás do-gheibhid an aois anuasal, ní bhí modh ná measardhacht ionnta dhá réir, mar adeirid na heolaigh, *ut dixit poeta*:

Rustica progenies nescit habere modum.

Agus is dearbh dá réir sin, nach cóir duitse go deo ná go deireadh an domhain t'fhuil do shalcha le fuil mhoghuidh ná dhaoirsig, óir ní mianach maith iad, agus ní bhfuil cruth dá aoirde iona rachaid, nó oifig nó udarás do-ghéabhuid, nach é budh mian leo fola uaisle do mhaslughadh agus do mhilleadh, dá dtíosadh leo a dhéanamh'.

Gidheadh do bhí bean uaibhreach lántshanntach ag Maghnus, agus is eadh adubhairt: go madh fearr lé féin saidhbhreas agus socracht do bheith ag a hinghin an feadh do bhiadh beo, ná fuil agus foghlaim dá fheabhas. Do críochnuigheadh an cleamhnas leis an mnaoi sanntuig sin d'aimhdheoin na ndraoithe; agus do chuireadar feasa agus teachta d'iarraidh Murcha Mhaoilchluasaig Í Mhultuaisgirt, agus do pósadh an inghean fris .i. Meadhbh inghean Mhaghnuis a hainm; agus rug leis dá theagh féin í agus ro geineadh clann iomdha eaturra an oidhche sin.

TRANSLATION

They were thus in vigour and vitality until Feidhlim mac Criomhthain was king of Munster; and there was a leader who excelled all others of those kindreds that descended from Tomás, namely: droop-eared Murcha Ó Multuaisgirt; and the place that Murcha inhabited was Clonmacnois.[1]

1. An ancient monastic site in County Offaly. Its pristine sanctity contrasts with the vulgarity of its later inhabitants.

And while Feidhlim mac Criomhthain was making a circuit of the two provinces of Munster, the wealth and great prosperity of this Murcha increased, and he dispatched messengers to the mighty provinces of Ireland to assemble all men of wisdom and authority of Clan Thomas among them to Clonmacnois; they moreover came to one appointed spot and they were bidden welcome by Murcha. He addressed them and said:

'My beloved kinsmen', he said, 'and you intelligent, meticulous and prosperous progeny of Tomás Mór, son of Liobar Lobhtha, son of Lóbus Laghrach, son of Dracapéist, son of Beelzebub,[2] I have sent for you for this reason: so that you can advise me what worthy woman I should take to wife; for it is high time that I marry a woman after and since the death of my wife, the love of my heart, namely: Brighid Ní Mhagarláin, daughter of Mathghamhain Breallach Ó Magarláin and tawny-legged Raghnuit Ní Mheigiolláin from Ballydehob'.[3]

And when he had spoken these words, a mucous stream of tears fell from him and a seizure and sorrow of heart took hold of him, so that he could not speak for a while. 'Now I hear', said Murcha, 'that there is a prosperous chieftain in fair and lovely Connaught, namely: Maghnus Ó Madagáin, and it is long enough we have been without ennobling our blood, while we have been in slavery, serving everyone until today; and this same Maghnus has a beautiful, virgin daughter, and I have decided with your approval to send messengers to ask her father for her hand'.

Everyone said that that was fitting; and these are they who were sent thither, four outstanding and well-educated men of Clan Thomas, namely: Big-Bottomed Mathghamhain, Bernard Long-Shoe, Niall Ó Neanntanáin and stooping Conchubhar Ó Craointiolláin. Then they took their leave and Niall recited the following lay:

Farewell to you, great Murcha,
chief of the host of hubble-bubble,[4]
many in your fort are the horse-beans,[5]
the blood, the hubbub and the jingle-jangle.

2. Traditionally, one of the lords of Hell.
3. A town in County Cork.
4. An attempt to reproduce the nonsense of the Irish *an phlub ó phlib*.
5. A type of bean fed to animals.

Farewell to the men of sharp sickles,
who used to eat great amounts while reaping ears,
who were not harsh, surly, cantankerous,
gloomy, rough-heeled nor sour.

Farewell to affable Brian Ó Briolláin,
a man who croons in his son's ear;
farewell to Murgholl and to Meadhbh,
who did not fart, who ate no meal.

I bid you farewell, O impetuous Bernard,
and swarthy Lochluinn, who gnawed no bone,
the crafty group that are not nonsensical,
an untidy host with bulging belts.

Murcha and everyone else praised that poem, and the people and nobles of the household swore great oaths that its equal in poesy or poetic art had never before been composed in all the world. Then the truly knowledgeable seer of Clan Thomas, trim Brian Ó Bloingidhe, appeared before them, and this man's wisdom, learning and understanding were great indeed, and he said that it was the chief ollave[6] of the high king of Ireland who first composed in that metre; and the way in which the poem was concluded was greatly praised, and the name Brian gave the metre was 'odd quatrains'.[7]

This well-mannered party moved off straight along each path and route until they came to Ceapach an Aráin, to Bealach na Bláthaighe, to Machaire na Meacan, to Ráithín na Praisge, to Buailtín an Phónaire, to Cúil na Mine, to Lios na nGarbhán, to Tuairín an Bhainne and to Bealach na Lótuighe, and ahead northwards to the edge of the Plain of Connaught, until they came to the house of Maghnus Ó Madagáin; and when they had strode with their heavy boots upon the green of the fort, Maghnus came to meet them and asked them who they were or whence they had come or what message they had brought thither. The messengers declared their errand and Maghnus said: 'We know your kindred and we know likewise that your lord is a rich man'.

Maghnus straightway summoned his druids and nobles. These wise men indeed came and Maghnus addressed them and said:

'The reason for my having summoned you is this: I have a beautiful and lovely daughter, and a request has come for her hand from droop-eared Murcha Ó Multuaisgirt; and this Murcha is a chieftain of exceeding wealth'.

'We know', said the druids, 'that this warrior is of the race of barbarians, for the tribes of hell were this same Murcha's ancestors; and no-one of any noble blood at all should mix with ignoble blood; for however great the luxury and learning, honour and position the lower orders acquire, they do not accordingly exhibit breeding or moderation, as the learned say, *ut dixit poeta*:[8]

Rustica progenies nescit habere modum.[9]

It is obvious therefore that you should never until the end of the world sully your blood with the blood of serf or churl, for they are not a good breed, and it does not matter how high they reach, nor what office or standing they attain, they always desire to pollute and corrupt high-born kindreds, if only they are able'.

Nonetheless Maghnus had an ambitious and utterly avaricious wife, and she said that she would prefer her daughter to have riches and comfort all her life, rather than the best of breeding and education. The match was concluded by this avaricious woman in spite of the druids; and they sent messengers and emissaries for droop-eared Murcha Ó Multuaisgirt, and the girl was joined to him in marriage, namely, Meadhbh, daughter of Maghnus by name; and he took her off with him to his own house and many children were engendered by them that night.

6. Ir. *ollamh*: the chief rank of poet in Ireland; a poetical professor.
7. This is a parody of the name for proper verse, *dán díreach* (straight versification).
8. as the poet said.
9. Peasant stock does not know how to be moderate.

AODH MAC AINGIL

(*c.*1571-1626)

from: SCÁTHÁN SHACRAMUINTE NA hAITHRÍ (The Mirror of the Sacrament of Repentance)

[This is the best example of Irish recusant literature to come from the Franciscans at Louvain. The simplicity and clarity of the prose is evidence that it was intended to be used to instruct the ordinary people. In the following passage Mac Aingil, having already shown the hopeless, sinful state of mankind, sets down the reasons for writing such a treatise and the methods he uses.]

A PIOUS BOOK IN IRISH

Do chonacthas dúinn, dá bhrí seo, an leabhrán seo do scríobh do ghluaiseacht cháich chun an chláir seo do ghlacadh agus dá dteagasc chun a stiúrtha dá saoradh ar anfa ifrinn is dá dtreorú go port parthais. Cuirfimid síos údaráis, réasúin agus samplaí dá mbrostú chun na haithrí, agus múinfimid go soiléir conas is cóir dóibh doilíos do bheith orthu fána bpeacaí, admháil iomlán bhéil do dhéanamh iontu, an gléas ar a dtarraingeoid chun a gcuimhne iad, an leorghníomh agus an leasú a dhlíthear ar a son. . . .

Bíd leabhráin mar seo ag gach náisiún Caitliceach eile, agus atáid de riachtanas ar an náisiún dá bhfuilimidne go speisilta, de bhrí go bhfuil gan máistrí, gan prealáidí, gan searmóntaithe, leath amuigh de bheagán a bhíos i bhfolach d'eagla báis nó príosúin, mar do bhídís na haspail tar éis bháis Chríost d'eagla an chine Ghiúdaigh. Dá n-abraítí gur dána dúinn ní do scríobh i nGaeilge is nár shaothraíomar inti, is é ár bhfreagra air sin nach do mhúineadh Gaeilge a scríobhaimid ach do mhúineadh na haithrí, agus is leor linn go dtuigfear sinn gí nach mbeadh ceart na Gaeilge againn. Ábhar eile fós fár cóir ár leithscéal do ghabháil agus is é seo é: is gnáth leis na heiricigh, mar a deir an naomhathair uasal Athanasius, a n-uile dhícheall do dhéanamh chun iad féin a chuir i gcosúile éigin leis an Eaglais fhírinneach, mar a bhíd na hápaí dá gcur féin a gcosúile leis na daoine. Dá réir seo, mar atá leabhair aifrinn ag an Eaglais Chaitliceach, do chonacthas d'eiricigh na hÉireann gné leabhair aifrinn do bheith acu féin dá ngairid *'Leabhar an Chumainn'*, — agus níorbh olc an t-ainm sin dá gcuiridís 'falsa' leis. Ó nár chuireadar, ní leasainm dó 'Leabhar Ifrinn Eiriceachta' do thabhairt air. Do chuir siad an leabhar seo agus mórán den Bhíobla i nGaeilge, agus is leor a neamhchirte a scríobhtar iad. Do mheas mise nach córa fulaingt do thabhairt dóibhsean an leabhar sin do scríobh go héigeart . . . .

TRANSLATION

Therefore we decided to write this treatise so that everyone might be directed to accept this means of salvation, and to instruct them to steer themselves clear of the storm of hell and to guide them to the harbour of Paradise. We shall set down authorities, arguments and exempla for the purpose of inciting them to repent. We shall also teach them clearly how to be sad at heart because of their sins, how they can fully declare them with their mouths, how to remember them all and what repentance and reparation they must make on account of them. . . .

Every other Catholic nation has books like this, and it is especially necessary for our nation because it is without master, prelate or preacher, except for the few who are in hiding for fear of death or prison, just like the apostles after the death of Christ were for fear of the Jews. If anyone were to say that I have a nerve to write in Irish, seeing I have never used it (up to now),[1] my answer to that is that I am not trying to teach Irish but rather to teach repentance, and I am satisfied as long as I am understood, even though my Irish be faulty. There is another excuse we can give, and it's this: Heretics, as St Athanasius says,[2] try their best to make themselves like the true church, just like apes imitate humans. Accordingly, just as there is a Mass book for the Catholic Church, some of the heretics sought to have a kind of prayerbook of their own which they call 'The

1. Mac Aingil is alluding to the fact that he had not been trained in one of the traditional schools.
2. St Athanasius (*c.* 293-373) was one of the Christian church fathers who led the fight against the Arian heresy.

Common Book',[3] which would not be a bad name if they also put the word 'deceitful' with it. Seeing that they have not, it's not a bad name for it to be called 'The Hell Book of Heresy'. They have published this book and portions of the Bible, all written in fairly bad Irish. I felt that it was no more fit to put up with their badly written book than it was ... for me to write this one in simple, if inaccurate, Irish.

3. Word-play between the English 'common' and Irish *cumann* (association). Word-play between *aifreann* (mass) and *iffreann* (hell).

SÉATHRÚN CÉITINN

from: TRÍ BIORGHAOITHE AN BHÁIS (The Three Shafts of Death)

[*Trí Biorghaoithe an Bháis* is a devotional work in the tradition of Counter-Reformation literature. Unlike the work of Mac Aingil and other Franciscans, it is generally turgid both in style and subject-matter. It is interesting because of the way it combines church learning with the native traditions. The exemplum in this passage is obviously a contemporary story about the clash between English culture and Irish culture.]

THE UNPAID BILL

As so is iontuigthe nach fuil acht aoidheacht nó ósdóireacht ar an saoghal againn. Agus measaim dá réir sin gurab ionann dál dá gach n-aon ré ndol don domhan so agus don cheithearnach allta aineolach a hiarthar Mhumhan, do-chuaidh i luing chogaidh d'iarraidh éadála ar fairrge. Agus do cuireadh i dtír i Sagsaibh iad; agus an céad-bhaile 'na dtarla i dtír iad, tángadar lucht an bhaile do dhéanamh lúthghára rompa, agus dá mbreith leo dá dtighthibh féin ré tabhairt ósda dhóibh; óir fá lucht ósda do chomhéad an mhéid do bhí ag áitiughadh san bhaile sin. Agus fá hiongnadh leis an gceithearnach iad agá chuireadh féin, agus gan aithne ag aon-duine dhiobh air. Agus do-chuaidh féin agus drong don mhuinntir do bhí mar aon ris i dtigh dhuine aca ar ósda. Agus do bhádar muinntear an tighe go ró-mhaith riú ar feadh seachtmhaine, ionnus gur sháimh leis an gceithearnach an t-inneall ar a raibhe féin, ar ghloine an árais 'na dtarlaidh é, agus ar fheabhas a leaptha agus a bhídh agus a dhighe. Gidh eadh, ar mbeith dhó féin agus dá chuideachtain ag gabháil a gceada, do ghairm an t-ósdóir an fear cúntais do bhí aige, agá rádh ris *make reckoning* .i. 'déana cúntas.' Leis sin táinig fear an chúntais, agus do ghabh ag feannadh an cheithearnaigh agus na muinntire do bhí maille ris, gurbh éigean dóibh uile díolaidheacht iomlán do thabhairt uatha in gach ní dár chaitheadar san tigh an gcéin do bhádar ann, ionnus go rabhadar folamh ag imtheacht dóibh. Agus táinig dhe sin, cion a raibhe do shólás agus do mheanmain ré linn gach seasgaireachta dá bhfuaradar i dtigh an ósda, go raibhe sé do dhólás orra tré bheith folamh ag imtheacht. Dobudh iongnadh iomorra leis an gceithearnach créad an fáth fár feannadh é féin agus cách; óir níor chleacht sé biadh ná deoch do cheannach riamh roimhe sin. Agus ar dteacht go hÉirinn dó do ghabhadar a charaid ag fiafraighe thuarasgbhála na Sagsan de. Do ghabh-san ag innisin sgéal dóibh, agus adubhairt thrá nach facaidh talamh riamh budh fearr biadh agus deoch agus teine agus leabaidh, agus budh suilbhire daoine. 'Agus locht ar bioth, ar sé, ní haithnidh damh uirre, acht an tan bhíd na deoraidh ag ceileabhradh don druing do-bheir aoidheacht dóibh, tig trú dhuaibhseach dheamhnaidhe dá ngairthear Mac Raicín anuas, agus lámhuighidh go heasaontach na deóraidh, agus feannaidh agus foghbhaidh iad.'

TRANSLATION

From this it is to be understood that we are only guests lodging in this life. And so I think it is for everyone before they leave this world just as it was for the wild ignorant outlaw[1] from west Munster who went in a warship on the sea, seeking booty.

1. *ceithearnach* = footsoldier, outlaw. Anglicized as *kern*.

And they put in to land in England; and at the first town they came to, the people made a great fuss of them, bringing them to their houses and giving them hospitality; this was because the people who lived in that town were innkeepers. And the outlaw was surprised at his welcome, seeing that none of them knew him. Now the people of the household were very good to them, so that the outlaw was happy with the situation he was in; the house he was in was clean, the beds, food and drink were excellent. However, when he and his company were taking their leave, the innkeeper called in the accountant saying to him *make reckoning*[2] i.e. make up the bill. With that the accountant came and began to take from[3] the outlaw and his companions, so that they had to make full payment for everything they had had in the house while they were there, and they went away destitute. And because of that, their great grief because of their poverty was equal in proportion to their happiness and joy while they lived comfortably in the inn. The outlaw wondered why he and the others had been fleeced; because he had not been used to buying food and drink ever before that. When he arrived in Ireland, his friends began asking him to give an account of England. He began his tale and said that he never saw a land better for food and drink, material for heating and beds and with the pleasantest people. 'And I can discern no fault there, except when strangers are saying goodbye to those who have given them hospitality a boorish diabolic wretch comes; his name is Mac Raicín[4] and he manhandles strangers and attacks and fleeces them.'

2. These words are in English script in the text.
3. *feannadh* = flay; figuratively: criticize, take from, fleece.
4. In English this means 'make reckoning'.

from:
FORAS FEASA AR ÉIRINN (A Basis of Knowledge about Ireland) (*c.*1634)

[*Foras Feasa ar Éirinn* by Geoffrey Keating is not only the first attempt to provide a coherent version of the Irish past, it is also a valuable compendium of Irish literature written in Irish that does not present too many difficulties for a modern reader. Practically all Irish literature is there, from the Ulster and Fenian cycles, from the stories of famous kings and saints, and from stories of place-names and local history. This little tale about the two saints, Mo Chua and Colmcille, is a good example of the type of story we find in the history; these add to its charm, even if they take from its validity as history.]

THE THREE TREASURES

Fá lucht comhaimsire dá chéile Mo Chua agus Colam Cille, agus ar mbeith i ndíthreibh an fhásaigh do Mo Chua, nó Mac Duach, ní raibhe do spréidh shaoghalta aige acht coileach agus luchóg agus cuil. Is é feidhm do-níodh an coileach dhó, iairmhéirghe an mheadhóin oidhche do choimhéad. An luchóg iomorra, ní léigeadh dhó acht chúig uaire do chodladh san ló go n-oidhche, agus an tan do thogradh ní sa mhó do chodladh do dhéanamh, ar mbeith tuirseach dhó ó iomad crois-fhigheal agus sléachtan, do ghabhadh an luchóg ag slíobadh a chluas, go ndúsgadh amhlaidh sin é. An chuil cheana, is é feidhm do-níodh, bheith ag siubhal ar gach líne dá léaghadh 'na shaltair, agus an tan do-níodh sgíoth ó bheith ag cantain a shalm, do chomhnuigheadh an chuil ar an líne do fhágbhadh go tilleadh arís do rádh a shalm dhó.

Tarla go grod dá éis sin go bhfuaradar na trí seoide sin bás, agus sgríobhais Mo Chua leitir dá éis sin go Colam Cille ar mbeith i nÍi nAlbain dó, agus do-ní casaoid ar éag na healtan soin.

Sgríobhais Colam Cille chuige, agus is eadh adubhairt:—

A bhráthair, ar sé, ní cuirthe dhuit i n-iongantas éag na healtan do-chuaidh uait, óir ní bhí an tubaist acht mar a mbí an spréidh.

TRANSLATION

Mo Chua and Colmcille were contemporaries, and when Mo Chua, or Mac Duach, was alone in the wilderness, the only worldly wealth he had was a cock and a mouse and a fly. The cock's function used to be to wake him for midnight matins. As for the mouse, he only used to let him have five hours sleep, night or day, and whenever he used to wish for more sleep, because he was tired from all the cross vigils and prostrations, the mouse used to lick his ear and wake him like that. The fly also: its function was to walk along each line as he read his psalter, and when he rested from chanting his psalms it used to stay on the line he left until he came again to read his psalms. It happened soon after that those three treasures died, and Mo Chua wrote to Colmcille, who was in Iona in Scotland, complaining about the death of that little flock. Colmcille wrote to him and he said: 'My brother, you should not be surprised at the death of the flock that has departed from you because misfortune only strikes where there is wealth.'

SEÁN Ó NEACHTAIN

from: STAIR ÉAMAINN UÍ CHLÉIRE (The Story of Eamonn O'Clery)

[*Stair Éamainn Uí Chléire* is generally taken to be an amusing version of Ó Neachtain's own life. The eponymous hero travels from Roscommon to Dublin and takes up schoolmastering in County Meath. He has many adventures as he seeks to win his sweetheart, Una, and to defeat his many enemies, whose names make clear that they are different types of drink. The following passage comes from the period when Eamonn is a schoolmaster. He is approached by a prospective pupil who speaks Irish, except that he uses English words. The puns are explained in the notes.]

Do tháinig chum a scoile an deispóir cruaidh do tharla air, más cuimhneach leat é (a léighthoir), agus chomh doith agus do tháinig isteach do rinne lúta agus adubhairt le hÉamonn:[1]

Nine God to you, sold Winifred.

What sense is in that? ar Éamonn.

Sense enough, ar eisean, for Nine God to you is naoi Dia Dhuit, and sold Winifred is a dhiol Una.[2]

Od sankins, is that you? ar Éamonn.

Yes faith, ar eisean, is not simple question that,[3] sure everybody is himself?

Good lad, give me your hand, ar Éamonn.

No faith, ar eisean, if I did make that[4] I should have but one hand and you would have three hands, but I believe you have a mind to put a shew out, 'the man with the three hands'.

Give me your hand is séan do lámh,[5] ar Éamonn.

Séan do lámh,[6] that is John your hand, ar eisean.

I have no business to be with you, ar Éamonn.

But if you be in my face I have no business to come to school to you, ar eisean.[7]

Oh, I understand you; no, I will be kind to you, ar Éamonn . . . .

Go on your news, ar Éamonn.

I have no news, but yellow with God, bread is maudlin enough and butter is very carpenter. You get a barrel of round snow for two shillings died, you will get a rod of gentle cloth for half a market, you will get a barrel of corruption for six shillings; every thing is free enough but for that there is no king or standing with all that is asking of alms, and they have no might upon it.[8]

1. This passage in Irish is translated: The tough disputer that he had met came to the school, if you remember him, O reader, and as soon as he came he bowed and said to Eamonn.
2. The common greeting in Irish, *'go mbeannaí Dia duit'*, can have a phonetic realization that is close to the words *'naoi Dia dhuit'*, which is literally translated here.
3. Irish: *Nach ceist shimplí sin.*
4. Irish: *Dá ndéanfainn sin.* Here the verb *déanaim* (makes/do) is used.
5. *Séan do lámh* = *sín do lámh* (extend/proffer your hand).
6. The scholar confuses 'séan' above with the proper name Seán (John).
7. Irish: *Ach má tá tú im aghaidh níl aon ghnó agam teacht chun na scoile chugat.*
8. Irish: *Níl aon scéal agam, ach a bhuí le Dia* (*buí* = yellow *or* thanks), *tá arán measctha go leor* (*measctha* = drunk *or* mixed) *agus tá im an-saor* (*saor* = carpenter *or* cheap). *Faigheann tu baraille cruinneachta* (cruinneacht = wheat, *cruinn* = round + *sneachta* = snow) *ar dhá scilling déag* (*d'éag* = died, confused with *déag* = ten), *gheobhaidh tú slat mínéadaigh ar leathmhargadh* (*slat* = rod *or* yard; *margadh* = market *or* price), *gheobhaidh tú baraille bracha ar sé scillinge* (*bracha* = corruption *or* malt); *tá gach rud saor go leor ach ar a shon sin* (*ar a shon* = for that *or* nevertheless) *níl aon rian nó seasamh* (*rian* is a pun for *rí ann* = king there) *leo siúd atá ag iarraidh déirce, agus níl aon neart acu air* (*neart* = might, but the whole idiom means 'they can not help it').

This passage is now translated into English: I have no news, but thanks be to God bread is mixed enough and butter very cheap. You get a barrel of wheat for twelve shillings, and you will get a yard of smooth cloth for half-price, you will get a barrel of malt for six shillings; everything is cheap enough, but nevertheless there is no passage or space with all those who are asking for alms, and they cannot help it.

Biographies

The main biographical details of writers and poets to whom selected pieces have been ascribed are given here. Where it is appropriate (as has been done in the introduction to this section), an anglicized form of the name or surname will be given.

Eochaidh Ó hEodhasa (O'Hussey). Born *c.* 1565. Friend of Hugh Maguire, and poet of the Maguires from about 1590. He retained his lands in the plantation of Ulster and died esteemed by Gael and Gall in 1613.

Aindrias Mac Marcais. Date of birth uncertain. He probably belonged to the Mac Craith family of poets. Patronized by the O'Donnells.

Bonaventura Ó hEodhasa (O'Hussey). Born *c.* 1570. Younger relation of Eochaidh. Trained as a professional poet, but in the 1590s went to the Continent and took orders as a Franciscan. He wrote the first catholic catechism in Irish and is reputed to have compiled a grammar of Irish. He died at Louvain in 1614.

Séathrún Céitinn (Geoffrey Keating). For biography and bibliography, see p. 272.

Pádraigín Haicéad (Hackett). Born in County Tipperary *c.* 1600. Entered the Dominican order and spent seven years on the Continent. He appears in documents associated with the order and the events in Ireland in the 1640s. He was ordered to return to the Continent in 1651 to answer charges against him of acting against the interests of the Dominican order by his partisan interventions in the politics of the time. He died in 1654.

Dáibhí Ó Bruadair. Born in County Cork *c.* 1625. He was the first great scholar/scribe poet and his work presents a view of most of the second half of the seventeenth century. Ó Bruadair spent much of his life in County Limerick. He was relatively well-off until 1674 and from that time his poetry shows even more of the qualities that caused James Stephens to write of him: 'an unending rebellious bawl that would be the most desolating utterance ever made by man, if it were not also the most gleeful.' He died in 1698.

Aogán Ó Rathaille (Egan O'Rahilly). Born in the Sliabh Luachra district, near Killarney, Co. Kerry about 1670, Ó Rathaille was a scribe and poet and had the reputation of great learning. He laments the demise of the MacCarthy chieftains and in some poems looks to the ascendant Browne family for help. Like Ó Bruadair, he fell on bad times and had to live out the later part of his life in poverty in west Kerry. He is sometimes credited with the composition of the earliest political *aisling* and poetical warrant poems. He died in 1726 and is buried in Muckross Abbey.

Séamas Dall Mac Cuarta (McCourt). Born in County Louth *c.* 1650, Mac Cuarta spent most of his life in that county and in north County Meath. He died in 1733.

Cathal Buí Mac Giolla Gunna (Gunn). Probably born in south County Fermanagh. Not much is known about him that can be verified. He is well-known as a rake in the folklore of the region, and tradition also tells us that he had been a priest. His most famous poem (not included in this selection) is about the yellow bittern that he found dead with its beak stuck in ice as it looked for water. He died about 1756.

Peadar Ó Doirnín (Durnin). Born probably in south County Louth *c.* 1700. He spent most of his life in the area near Dundalk. He was a teacher and a scribe. His poetry is noted for its independence and freedom in dealing with his own love affairs. He died in 1769.

Seán Ó Neachtain (Naughton/Norton). Born *c.* 1650 in County Roscommon. Ó Neachtain and his family came to Dublin after 1690 and spent the rest of his life there and in County Meath as a schoolmaster. He was a competent scribe and poet. His prose work has many original features, not the least of which is his tendency to use bilingual, bicultural puns. He died in March 1729.

Art Mac Cumhaigh (McCooey). Born near Cregan, Co. Armagh *c.* 1738. He spent most of his life as a farm labourer and is the least 'educated' of the south-east Ulster poets. He had to leave his home district because of a quarrel with the local priest, but he was able to return later. He died in 1773.

Eoghan Rua Ó Súilleabháin (O'Sullivan). Born near Killarney, Co. Kerry *c.* 1748. He was a scribe and schoolmaster as well as a poet. He is still remembered as a rake and perhaps that is the explanation for his wandering life. Ó Suilleabháin seems to have spent some time in England and to have served in the navy. He died near his native district in 1784.

Brian Merriman. Not much is known about Merriman. He was probably born in County Clare about 1749. His poem *Cúirt an Mheon-Oíche* was composed in 1780 near Feakle, Co. Clare, and we only have one other small poem by him. He was a schoolmaster and small farmer. Merriman won prizes for crops from the Royal Dublin Society in 1797 and died in Limerick in 1805.

Tomás Mac Caiside (Cassidy). Belonged to the Cassidy family of County Fermanagh. It seems that he trained to be a priest, but he had to leave the priesthood because of his irregular behaviour. He then wandered around Ireland and joined the French army in the 1730s. Mac Caiside returned to Ireland, but the date of his death is unknown.

Aodh Mac Gabhráin (Hugh Magauran). Not much is known about Mac Gabhráin. He came from Connacht, according to a poem about Irish scholars in Dublin in the early eighteenth century. He was a friend of the blind harper, Turlogh Carolan.

Cearbhall Ó Dálaigh (Carroll O'Daly). There are several characters of this name in the Irish tradition and we have very little information about any of them. The poet involved with the poem 'Eileen aroon' probably lived at the beginning of the seventeenth century and had a reputation for his love poetry.

Tomás Láidir Mac Coisdealbha (Costelloe). A Connacht poet of the seventeenth century about whom little is known.

Eibhlín Dhubh Ní Chonaill (O'Connell). Born *c.* 1745, Eibhlin was one of the O'Connells of Derrynane, Co. Kerry. Her mother was known as a poet and there were other poets on that side of the family. She married a man named O'Connor, who died shortly afterwards. She then remained unmarried until 1767 when she met Art O'Leary at her sister's house, close to Macroom, Co. Cork. They married and in 1774 the events recounted in the 'The Lament for Art O'Leary' took place. The date of her death is not known.

Aodh Mac Aingil (Mac Caughwell). Born in Downpatrick, Co. Down *c.* 1571, Mac Aingil was educated in the Isle of Man. He was adviser to Hugh O'Neill and tutor to his sons. He went to Spain and entered the Franciscan order in 1603. He helped with the foundation of St Anthony's College, Louvain. Mac Aingil was famous for his work in theology and philosophy and was responsible for disseminating the work of Johannes Duns Scotus (*c.* 1265-1308), the great Franciscan medieval philosopher. He was in Rome from 1623 and three years later was appointed archbishop of Armagh, but he died before he could take up office.

Select Bibliography

General

Alspach, Russell K., *Irish Poetry from the English Invasion to 1798* (Philadelphia: University of California Press, 1943).

Breatnach, R.A., 'The End of a Tradition: A Survey of Eighteenth-century Gaelic Literature', *Studia Hibernica* I (Dublin, 1961), pp. 128-50.

Corkery, Daniel, *The Hidden Ireland* (Dublin: Gill & Son, 1924).

de Blácam, Aodh, *Gaelic Literature Surveyed* (Dublin: Talbot Press, 1929).

Hyde, Douglas, *A Literary History of Ireland* edited by Brian Ó Cuív (London: Barnes and Noble, 1967).

Leersen, Joseph Theodoor, *Mere Irish and Fíor-Gael: Studies in the Idea of Irish Nationality, Its Development and Literary Expression prior to the Nineteenth Century* (Amsterdam/Philadelphia: John Benhamin's Publishing Company, 1986).

Mercier, Vivian, *The Irish Comic Tradition* (Oxford: Oxford University Press, 1962).

Mooney, Canice, *Devotional Writings of the Irish Franciscans* (Killiney: Four Masters' Press, 1952).

O'Connor, Frank, *The Backward Look* (London: Macmillan, 1962).

Ó Cuív, Brian, 'The Irish Language in the Early Modern Period' in T.W. Moody, F.X. Martin, F.J. Byrne (eds), *A New History of Ireland* III (Oxford: Clarendon Press, 1976), pp. 509-42.

Ó Cuív, Brian, 'Irish Language and Literature 1691-1845' in T.W. Moody, W. Vaughan (eds), *A New History of Ireland* IV (Oxford): Clarendon Press, 1986), pp. 374-423.

Ó Cuív, Brian (ed.), *A View of the Irish Language* (Dublin: Stationery Office, 1969).

Ó Maonaigh, Cainneach, 'Scríbhneoirí Gaeilge an seachtú haois déag', *Studia Hibernica* II (Dublin, 1962), pp. 182-208.

Walsh, Paul, *Irish Men of Learning* (Dublin: The Sign of the Three Candles, 1947).

Texts

Bergin, Osborn (ed.), *The Three Shafts of Death* (Dublin: Royal Irish Academy, 1931).

Bergin, Osborn (ed.), *Sgéalaigheacht Chéitinn* (Dublin: Royal Irish Academy, 1925).

Bergin, Osborn (ed.), *Irish Bardic Poetry* [D. Greene, F. Kelly (eds)] (Dublin: Dublin Institute for Advanced Studies, 1970).

Dinneen, P.S., and T. Ó Donnchadha (eds), *The Poems of Egan O'Rahilly* (London: Irish Texts Society, 1911).

Harrison, Alan, and Ursula Ní Dhálaigh (eds), *Fios Feasa* III (Baile Átha Cliath: An Comhlucht Oideachais, 1970).

MacErlean, J.C. (ed.), *Duanaire Dháibhidh Uí Bhruadair* I, II, III (London: Irish Texts Society, 1910, 1913, 1917).

Ní Cheallacháin, Máire (ed.), *Filíocht Phádraigín Haicéad* (Baile Átha Cliath: An Institiúid Ardléinn, 1962).

Ní Fhaircheallaigh, Úna (ed.), *Filidheacht Sheagháin Uí Neachtain* (Baile Átha Cliath: Conradh na Gaedhilge, 1911).

Ní Shéaghdha, Nessa (ed.), *Tóruigheacht Dhiarmada agus Gráinne* (Dublin: Irish Texts Society, 1967).

Nic Philibín, Máire (ed.) *Na Caisidigh agus a gcuid Filidheachta* (Baile Átha Cliath: Oifig an tSoláthair, 1938).

Ó Buachalla, Breandán (ed.), *Peadar Ó Doirnín* (Baile Átha Cliath: An Clóchomhar, 1969).

Ó Buachalla, Breandán (ed.), *Nua-Dhuanaire* II (Baile Átha Cliath: An Institiúid Ardléinn, 1976).

Ó Concheanainn, Tomas, Breandán Ó Buachalla, Pádraig de Brún (eds), *Nua-Dhuanaire* I (Baile Átha Cliath: An Institiúid Ardléinn, 1971).

O'Connor, Frank, *Kings, Lords, & Commons: An Anthology from the Irish* (Dublin: Gill and Macmillan, 1959).

Ó Gallchóir, Seosamh (ed.), *Séamas Dall Mac Cuarta: Dánta* (Baile Átha Cliath: An Clóchomhar, 1971).

Ó Máille, Mícheál, and Tomás Ó Máille (eds), *Amhráin Chlainne Gaedheal* (Baile Átha Cliath: Conradh na Gaedhilge, 1905).

Ó Maonaigh, Cainneach (ed.), *Scáthán Shacramuinte na hAithridhe* (Baile Átha Cliath: Conradh na Gaedhilge, 1905).

Ó Murchú, Liam (ed.), *Cuirt an Mhéon-Oíche* (Baile Átha Cliath: An Clóchomhar, 1982).

Ó Neachtain, Eoin (ed.), *Stair Éamuinn Uí Chléire* (Baile Átha Cliath: Conradh na Gaedhilge, 1918).

Ó Tuama, Seán (ed.), *Caoineadh Airt Uí Laoghaire* (Baile Átha Cliath: An Clóchomhar, 1961).

Ó Tuama, Seán and Thomas Kinsella (eds), *An Duanaire, 1600-1900: Poems of the Dispossessed* (Dublin: Dolmen Press, 1981).

Ua Duinnín, Pádraig (ed.), *Amhráin Eoghain Ruaidh Uí Shúilleabháin* (Baile Átha Cliath: Conradh na Gaedhilge, 1902).

Williams, N.J.A. (ed.), *Pairlement Chloinne Tomáis* (Dublin: Dublin Institute for Advanced Studies, 1980).

ANDREW CARPENTER, *Editor*

Jonathan Swift

(1667-1745)

It is ironic that Swift, the most potent and recurrent symbolic presence in modern Irish writing, should have wished so fervently that he had not been born in Ireland. 'As to my native country,' he wrote, 'I happened indeed by a perfect accident to be born here, my mother being left here from returning to her house at Leicester . . . and thus I am a Teague, or an Irishman, or what people please . . . .'[1] His letters and prose writings are sprinkled with complaints about life in Ireland and, since Swift belonged to that group of protestants of English extraction we now call the Anglo-Irish, this attitude is not surprising. For them, at least during the period of Swift's lifetime, England was a *patria*, a homeland, and Ireland was a place of exile. But Swift, like many of his contemporaries, was far more deeply influenced by Ireland than he would publicly acknowledge. In obvious ways, much of his work is about Ireland; but, more subtly, the tone and mood of what he wrote is quite unlike that of English writers. His imagination has a fantastic, grotesque side closer to that of the Irish comic tradition than to anything in English literature.[2] His methods — dislocation, distortion of perspective, fantasy — are fundamentally different from those of Pope or Dryden, Gay, Defoe or Fielding. The only limit in *Gulliver's Travels*, *A Tale of a Tub*, or *A Modest Proposal* is the limit of the imagination. The English limit of reason, good sense and decorum is entirely missing.

This is because, as Carole Fabricant makes clear in her important recent study of Swift, both the actual features of the physical surroundings of his life and the mental features of his aesthetic, ideological and political landscape were specifically Irish.

> Born in Dublin in 1667, Swift spent eighteen of his first twenty-one years in Ireland and, except for several lengthy periods spent in England during the next twenty years, followed by four years in London (1710-1714) working for the Tory ministry and two brief (half-year) visits to England in 1726 and 1727, Swift lived out his long life in his native country. By the time of his death in 1745, he had been a resident of Ireland for well over half a century and a politically involved actor in its internal affairs for almost as long.[3]

Such a long residence in Ireland had its effect, and Swift was often influenced by the attitudes of the Anglo-Irish who surrounded him. The tone of his major work is profoundly un-English; specifically, it is full of rough energy and aggression, quite unlike that of even the most energetic of his English contemporaries. Swift's way of seeing things was that of the outsider, and his mind was always questioning and exploring, doubting the evidence of the senses and transferring this doubt to his readers.

This aggression, which is so noticeable a part of Swift's work, comes to a considerable extent from his own lack of cultural security. Although any English-speaking protestant in Ireland was physically secure during Swift's lifetime because of the presence of a substantial English standing army in the country, he was culturally insecure, constantly aware that he was surrounded by a

1. Harold Williams (ed.), *The Correspondence of Jonathan Swift*, 5 vols (Oxford: Clarendon Press, 1963-65) IV, 229; hereafter *Correspondence*.
2. For a full discussion of this point, see Vivian Mercier, *The Irish Comic Tradition* (Oxford: Oxford University Press, 1962).
3. Carole Fabricant, *Swift's Landscape* (Baltimore: Johns Hopkins University Press, 1982), p. 18.

healthy, living culture very alien to him. The language of the streets, markets and servants' quarters was Irish; the music and dancing in town and countryside alike was Irish music and dancing, and the ballad operas staged in Dublin during the 1720s and 1730s featured Irish tunes and songs;[4] thus, even the lord lieutenant heard them in the theatre. In addition, the English language as spoken in Ireland was different in many respects from that of England, influenced partly by the syntax and vocabulary of Irish, as Swift himself pointed out in his *Dialogue in Hybernian Stile.*[5] Finally, the religious allegiance of the bulk of the people was not to the protestant Church of Ireland — which they saw as a church imposed on them from England — but to the catholic or presbyterian churches; the former of these, with its use of Latin and Irish, was linguistically as well as doctrinally alien.

Behind Swift's actual experience of the Irish language and of Irish culture were the prejudices of his class and, indeed, of his race — prejudices inherited from Spenser, Sir John Temple and others of the new English landlord class.[6] Things Irish were inferior, the language best used for proselytizing the natives, the countryside best 'improved' into a copy of that of England, and the people made to work. But Swift's actions show that these prejudices wore thin on him. In 1720 for instance, he translated into English a poem from Irish, probably with the help of his friend Anthony Raymond, and, if the persistent voice of folklore is to be believed, he became good friends at about this time with the Irish harper Turlogh Carolan.[7] Certainly, when visiting his friend Thomas Sheridan in the wilds of County Cavan in 1722, he enjoyed encounters with blind harpers,[8] and his long journeys through the remoter parts of Ireland would have brought him into direct contact with the people and their way of life.

Of course, Swift always admired and envied the order and discipline of English culture, English landscape and English cities. But in time, particularly after his return to Dublin in 1714, he began to accept and enjoy the actual condition of life in Ireland, as many of his letters and poems testify. The paradoxes of his position are well shown in a letter he wrote to Pope in 1728 inviting his old friend to come and live in the deanery in Dublin. After remarking, characteristically, 'God forbid I should condemn you to Ireland', he continues:

> I say one thing, that both summers and winters are milder here than with you; all things for life in general better for a middling fortune; you will have an absolute command of your company, with whatever obsequiousness or freedom you may expect or allow. I have an elderly housekeeper, who has been my *Walpole* above thirty years, whenever I liv'd in this kingdom. I have the command of one or two villa's near this town: You have a warm apartment in this house, and two Gardens for amusement. I have said enough, yet not half. Except absence from friends, I confess freely that I have no discontent at living here. . . .[9]

But even if Swift mellowed towards the circumstances of his life in Ireland, the basic paradoxes of the Irish situation always plagued him, as they did most Irish writers of the eighteenth century. In effect, the paradoxes and distortions of the truth that made up life in Ireland gave Irish writers a kind of double perspective on everything, a double vision. All aspects of Irish life — political, ecclesiastical, legal and even social — were hedged around with irreconcilable contradictions. The Church of Ireland, for example, was not the church of the people of Ireland; the Irish parliament, with its grandeur and its speaker and its mace and its traditions, was actually subordinate to the English privy council in everything. Many laws were passed in the full knowledge that they could not be implemented. For example, one of the Penal Laws, designed to repress catholics, took account of actual human behaviour by regulating against 'too much conniving' at the existence of catholic schools — not against conniving at them at all, but against too much conniving. Another notorious law of 1697 declared that protestant maidens and women who take as husbands papists or popish persons ('to the great Dishonour of Almighty God') shall be deemed

4. See Frank Ll. Harrison, 'Music, Poetry and Polity in the Age of Swift', *Eighteenth-Century Ireland* I (1986), 37-63.
5. See Alan Bliss (ed.), *A Dialogue in Hybernian Stile and Irish Eloquence* by Jonathan Swift (Dublin: Cadenus Press, 1977).
6. See the section of work by Spenser and the Anglo-Irish above.
7. See Andrew Carpenter and Alan Harrison, 'Swift's "O'Rourke's Feast" and Sheridan's "Letter"' in Hermann J. Real and Heinz J. Vienken (eds), *Proceedings of the First Münster Symposium on Jonathan Swift* (Munich: W. Fink, 1985), 27-46.
8. *Correspondence* II, 441.
9. *Correspondence* III, 285-86.

dead in law: dead by one eye and alive by another.[10] Reality and fantasy were interwoven in the actual landscape and mindscape of Swift's Ireland and this interweaving had a deep effect on his writings and on those of his Irish contemporaries.

It is from this world of double standards and values impossible to reconcile that the profound questioning of *Gulliver's Travels* and *A Modest Proposal* springs; so does the savage indignation of *The Drapier's Letters* and *A Proposal for the Universal Use of* Irish *Manufacture*. But Swift's fierce originality of vision is less startling when seen in the context of other writers from Ireland than it is when he is compared with his English contemporaries. In fact, other writers in this anthology — Farquhar, Dunkin, Thomas Sheridan, Sterne — all show the same kind of daring. They seem determined to crack the mould of secure mental boundaries such as those which surrounded Pope and even Samuel Johnson. Anarchy of mind and technique mark Swift and the other Irish writers of the eighteenth century and their unsettled vision of the world brings forth writings absolutely different from those of eighteenth-century England.

The selections that follow are drawn from all periods of Swift's life. *A Tale of a Tub* comes from his early years when, between the ages of 23 and 32, he lived mostly in the household of Sir William Temple in Surrey, reading widely and testing his powers as a writer. He was ordained into the Church of Ireland in 1695 and by 1707 was sufficiently influential to be sent to England as the representative of the Irish church. By 1710, he had become a close confidant of the ministers of the English government and was at the centre of political power in London. From this period come the intimate letters to Esther Johnson, known as *The Journal to Stella*.

On the death of Queen Anne in 1714, Swift returned to Dublin where he had become dean of St Patrick's Cathedral. Within a few years, he became embroiled in Irish politics, and three Irish pamphlets from the 1720s are included in the selection below. So is the fourth part of *Gulliver's Travels*, Swift's most famous work, also written in the 1720s. From the last part of his life come *Verses on the Death of Dr Swift*.

An important and recurrent feature of Swift's work is the use of a persona. This device enables the real author to lurk behind an imagined one and so exploit aspects of double vision and double perspective. The madness of the imagined 'author' of *A Tale of a Tub* is that of the frenzied solipsist, determined to impose his self-perpetuating lunatic view of the world on all and sundry. Echoes of this cast of mind recur in the 'modest proposer', in Captain Gulliver and even in the apparently staid Dublin shopkeeper of *The Drapier's Letters*. Swift was fascinated by madness and the personae of all these works are to a greater or lesser extent mad. As one reads all this work, one becomes aware of the questions that hang over Swift's life and writing. What if the madness in the world becomes its dominant voice? What if true virtue and learning and honesty and humanity are shouted down by the strident self-important spokesmen of madness? The answer to these questions is in the books themselves, in the 'Tubbian' world of inverted values, or the stable where Gulliver lives at the end of his travels, or the kitchen of the modest proposer. Equally, it is in an Ireland prepared to accept the imposition of Wood's halfpence or laws prohibiting economic growth. Madness, after all, has been 'the Parent of all those mighty Revolutions, that have happened in *Empire*, in *Philosophy*, and in *Religion*.'[11]

Against this side of Swift's visionary work, one can set Swift the man. He was, as Ehrenpreis's masterly recent biography[12] has shown, a very private man, playful with a few close friends but haughty or austere with strangers. His closest intellectual friend was Alexander Pope, whom he grew to know well during his years in England. His closest personal friend was Esther Johnson, also known as Stella. Swift first met Stella when she was a girl at Sir William Temple's house in Surrey and there grew up between them a close friendship which became the talk of the town when Stella moved to Dublin, with her life-long companion Rebecca Dingley. The exact nature of the intriguing friendship between Swift and Stella has never been fully explained, but the relationship, which was the subject of much gossip in the early eighteenth century, was the most important of his private life.

10. *Statutes at Large (Ireland)* (Dublin, 1786), 7 William III, Chapter XIV.

11. *A Tale of a Tub*, A Digession on Madness.

12. Irvin Ehrenpreis, *Swift, the Man, his Works and the Age* 3 vols (London: Methuen, 1962-83).

But it is the public side of Swift that most concerns us here, and we are dealing with a writer of incomparable force, wit and savage indignation. It is small wonder that such energy, so closely related to the experiences of life in Ireland, should have been an inspiration for so many later Irish writers. For Swift's works themselves are unforgettable as, indeed, is the man. As you walk around Dublin today or leaf through the pages of an anthology such as this, you understand how appropriate were the words of W.B. Yeats: 'Swift haunts me: he is always just round the next corner.'[13]

13. W.B. Yeats, *The Words upon the Window Pane* (Dublin: Cuala Press, 1934), p. 3.

from:
A TALE OF A TUB (1704)

[Late in his life, Swift is said to have remarked of *A Tale of a Tub*, 'Good God! what a genius I had when I wrote that book'. It certainly is a young man's work, flamboyant, outrageous, daring and irreverent. The book appeared in 1704 anonymously, and this anonymity on the part of the author is in itself an important key to the nature of the work. There are, in effect, two levels of anonymity in the authorship of *A Tale of a Tub*. Swift himself, the real author, is hard to find in the book and, if he *is* present, it is by implication behind its irony. A much more obvious presence — but still an anonymous one — is that of an officious busybody who bustles about the book asserting that he is its author. He would seem to be a self-important hack author of the late 1690s, one of a new breed of men earning a living as a writer, willing and able to turn his hand to any subject. (Among the treatises he promises the reader in the near future are 'A panegyrical Essay upon the Number THREE' and 'A general History of Ears'.) He is, thus, a 'Modern', a man of the new world of cheap, quick books, rather than an 'Ancient' whose learning is based on the classics and on solid values. These Modern values, which are presented as ideal in the book, are entirely opposed to those of Swift himself, and the reader must realize that almost everything which is praised by the 'author' is really to be scorned and, of course, *vice versa*.

A Tale of a Tub is part of the late seventeenth-century dispute between the Ancient and the Moderns and was conceived and partly written when Swift, as a young man, was living in the household of Sir William Temple in Surrey. Sir William himself, a great upholder of traditional values, was one of the staunchest of the Ancients and Swift's own position was close to that of his patron. On the other side were the Moderns whom Swift described in section VII of the *Tale*, as men who have developed a 'prudent method to become scholars and wits without the fatigue of reading or of thinking'; among these Swift (rather unfairly) placed the scholars Richard Bentley and William Wotton, both of whom he satirized mercilessly in the *Tale*. These Moderns, Swift believed, had perverted true learning in the same way as the Roman catholic and presbyterian churches had perverted true Christianity: these two perversions are the subject of the satire of *A Tale of a Tub*.

The book is really in two parts which run concurrently, the tale proper and digressions; the latter, with the lengthy introductions and prefaces, take up much more than half the book and are, in themselves, satiric comments on the distortions of learning so clearly found in books put together by hacks. The distortions of the world of religion — the other main subject of the satire — are highlighted in the story itself. This is an allegory in which a father (God) leaves his three sons, Peter (the Roman catholic church), Martin (the anglican or established protestant church) and Jack (the non-conformist churches, particularly the presbyterian church), his will (the Bible); the aberrations of the catholic church are seen in Peter's behaviour, those of the presbyterians in that of Jack. Martin, the middle son (representing the church nearest to Swift's own ideal) distorts his father's will less than the other two brothers. Story and digressions are interwoven and often inseparable.

The style of the whole book is outrageous and much of the material is, on the surface, elaborate and learned nonsense, taken very seriously by the 'author'. Normal conventions are constantly flouted and serious arguments collapse at their most crucial moments into lines of asterisks while the author pretends that there is a gap in the manuscript. Only the reader who can enjoy the irony and relax into the joke will get anything worthwhile out of *A Tale of a Tub*. It is a book that makes fun of the whole idea of 'the book' as an exercise in communication.

The last two sections are reproduced below. Section XI, after a short digression, carries on the tale of Jack, the presbyterian son. Through the descriptions of his behaviour, Swift comments on excessive use of scriptural texts in everyday speech, presbyterians' belief in pre-destination, and their opposition to both the anglican church and the catholic church. In the Conclusion, the anonymous author comes to the fore, talking ceaselessly about his brilliant methods of writing until, almost imperceptibly, he drops out of sight, threatening to return at any moment.

Two sets of notes are printed below the text. The first set were added by Swift for the fifth edition (1710); notes prepared for the present edition are printed below the line or in square bracket after Swift's notes.]

SECT. XI

A TALE OF A TUB

After so wide a Compass as I have wandred,[1] I do now gladly overtake, and close in with my Subject, and shall henceforth hold on with it an even Pace to the End of my Journey, except some beautiful Prospect appears within sight of my Way; whereof, tho' at present I have neither Warning nor Expectation, yet upon such an Accident, come when it will, I shall beg my Readers Favour and Company, allowing me to conduct him thro' it along with my self. For in *Writing*, it is as in *Travelling*: If a Man is in haste to be at home, (which I acknowledge to be none of my Case, having never so little Business, as when I am there) if his *Horse* be tired with long Riding, and ill Ways, or be naturally a Jade,[2] I advise him clearly to make the straitest and the commonest Road, be it ever so dirty; But, then surely, we must own such a Man to be a scurvy Companion at best; He *spatters* himself and his Fellow-Travellers at every Step: All their Thoughts, and Wishes, and Conversation turn entirely upon the Subject of their Journey's End; and at every Splash, and Plunge, and Stumble, they heartily wish one another at the Devil.

On the other side, when a Traveller and his *Horse* are in Heart and Plight,[3] when his Purse is full, and the Day before him; he takes the Road only where it is clean or convenient; entertains his Company there as agreeably as he can; but upon the first Occasion, carries them along with him to every delightful Scene in View, whether of Art, of Nature, or of both; and if they chance to refuse out of Stupidity or Weariness; let them jog on by themselves, and be d——n'd; He'll overtake them at the next Town; at which arriving, he Rides furiously thro', the Men, Women, and Children run out to gaze, a hundred * *noisy Curs* run *barking* after him, of which, if he honors the boldest with a *Lash of his Whip*, it is rather out of Sport than Revenge: But should some *sourer Mungrel* dare too near an Approach, he receives a *Salute* on the Chaps[4] by an accidental Stroak from the Courser's Heels, (nor is any Ground lost by the Blow) which sends him yelping and limping home.

I now proceed to sum up the singular Adventures of my renowned *Jack*;[5] the State of whose Dispositions and Fortunes, the careful Reader does, no doubt, most exactly remember, as I last parted with them in the Conclusion of a former Section.[6] Therefore, his next Care must be from two of the foregoing, to extract a Scheme of Notions, that may best fit his Understanding for a true Relish of what is to ensue.

JACK had not only calculated the first Revolution of his Brain so prudently, as to give Rise to that Epidemick Sect of *Æolists*,[7] but succeeding also into a new and strange Variety of Conceptions, the Fruitfulness of his Imagination led him into certain Notions, which, altho' in Appearance very unaccountable, were not without their Mysteries and their Meanings, nor wanted Followers to countenance and improve them. I shall therefore be extreamly careful and exact in recounting such material Passages of this Nature, as I have been able to collect, either from undoubted Tradition, or indefatigable Reading; and shall describe them as graphically as it is possible, and as far as Notions of that Height and Latitude can be brought within the Compass of a Pen. Nor do I at all question, but they will furnish Plenty of noble Matter for such, whose converting Imaginations dispose them to reduce all Things in to *Types*;[8] who can make *Shadows*, no thanks to the Sun; and then mold them into Substances, no thanks to Philosophy; whose peculiar Talent lies in fixing Tropes and Allegories to the *Letter*, and refining what is Literal into Figure and Mystery.[9]

JACK had provided a fair Copy of his Father's *Will*,[10] engrossed in Form upon a large Skin of Parchment; and resolving to act the Part of a most dutiful Son, he became the fondest Creature[11] of it imaginable. For, altho', as I have often told the Reader, it consisted wholly in certain plain, easy Directions about the management and wearing of

*By these are meant what the Author calls, The *True Criticks*.

1. i.e. throughout the book.
2. a worn-out or worthless horse.
3. good condition.
4. jaws.
5. See headnote.
6. Section VI.
7. Section VIII of the *Tale* concerns the sect of Æolists, created by Jack, who worship wind in all its forms.
8. Interpreting the scriptures according to typology or symbolism was a characteristic of certain seventeenth-century puritan sects.
9. See John Toland's *Christianity Not Mysterious* (1697) for the full implications of this remark (p. 765).
10. In the main allegory, the father's will is the New Testament.
11. most foolish puppet.

their Coats, with Legacies and Penalties, in case of Obedience or Neglect; yet he began to entertain a Fancy, that the Matter was *deeper* and *darker*, and therefore must needs have a great deal more of Mystery at the Bottom. *Gentlemen*, said he, *I will prove this very Skin of Parchment to be Meat, Drink, and Cloth, to be the Philosopher's Stone, and the Universal Medicine.*† In consequence of which Raptures, he resolved to make use of it in the most necessary, as well as the most paltry Occasions of Life. He had a Way of working it into any Shape he pleased; so that it served him for a Night-cap when he went to Bed, and for an Umbrello in rainy Weather. He would lap a Piece of it about a sore Toe, or when he had Fits, burn two Inches under his Nose; or if any Thing lay heavy on his Stomach, scrape off, and swallow as much of the Powder as would lie on a silver Penny, they were all infallible Remedies. With Analogy to these Refinements, his common Talk and Conversation‡ ran wholly in the Phrase of his Will, and he circumscribed the utmost of his Eloquence within that Compass, not daring to let slip a Syllable without Authority from thence. Once at a strange House, he was suddenly taken short, upon an urgent Juncture, whereon it may not be allowed too particularly to dilate; and being not able to call to mind, with that Suddenness, the Occasion required, an Authentick Phrase for demanding the Way to the Backside; he chose rather as the more prudent Course, to incur the Penalty in such Cases usually annexed. Neither was it possible for the united Rhetorick of Mankind to prevail with him to make himself clean again: Because having consulted the Will upon this Emergency, he met with a §Passage near the Bottom (whether foisted in by the Transcriber, is not known) which seemed to forbid it.

He made it a Part of his Religion, never to say* Grace to his Meat, nor could all the World persuade him, as the common Phrase is, to† eat his Victuals *like a Christian.*

He bore a strange kind of Appetite to ‡ *Snap-Dragon*,[12] and to the livid Snuffs of a burning Candle, which he would catch and swallow with an Agility, wonderful to conceive; and by this Procedure, maintained a perpetual Flame in his Belly, which issuing in a glowing Steam from both his Eyes, as well as his Nostrils, and his Mouth; made his Head appear in a dark Night, like the Scull of an Ass, wherein a roguish Boy hath conveyed a Farthing Candle, *to the Terror of His Majesty's Liege Subjects.* Therefore, he made use of no other Expedient to light himself home, but was wont to say, That *a Wise Man was his own Lanthorn.*

He would shut his Eyes as he walked along the Streets, and if he happened to bounce his Head against a Post, or fall into the Kennel[13] (as he seldom missed either to do one or both) he would tell the gibing Prentices, who looked on, that *he submitted with entire Resignation, as to a Trip, or a Blow of Fate, with whom he found, by long Experience, how vain it was either to wrestle or to cuff; and whoever durst undertake to do either, would be sure to come off with a swinging Fall, or a bloody Nose. It was ordained,*[14] said he, *some few Days before the Creation, that my Nose and this very Post should have a Rencounter; and therefore, Nature thought fit to send us both into the World in the same Age, and to make us Country-men and Fellow-Citizens. Now, had my Eyes been open, it is very likely, the Business might have been a great deal worse; For, how many a confounded Slip is daily got by Man, with all his Foresight about him? Besides, the Eyes of the Understanding see best, when those of the Senses are out of the way; and therefore, blind Men are observed to tread their Steps with much more Caution, and Conduct, and Judgment, than those who rely with too much*

†The Author here lashes those Pretenders to Purity, who place so much Merit in using Scripture Phrase[s] on all Occasions.

‡The *Protestant Dissenters* use *Scripture Phrases* in their serious Discourses, and Composures more than the *Church of England-Men*, accordingly *Jack* is introduced making his common Talk and Conversation to run wholly in the Phrase of his WILL. *W. Wotton.* [William Wotton (1666-1726) a Cambridge clergyman, was the chief critic of *A Tale of a Tub.* In the course of his hostile *Observations . . . on The Tale of a Tub* (1705), he had explained several words in the allegory. Swift included these notes *verbatim* in the fifth edition of *A Tale* (1710) thus making his severest critic appear like a scholarly commentator. Ed.]

§I cannot guess the Author's meaning here, which I would be very glad to know, because it seems to be of Importance.

*The slovenly way of Receiving the Sacrament among the Fanaticks. [i.e. dissenters. Ed.]

†This is a common Phrase to express Eating cleanlily, and is meant for an Invective against that undecent Manner among some People in Receiving the Sacrament, so in the Lines before ['tis said, Jack *would never say Grace to his Meat*], which is to be understood of the Dissenters refusing to kneel at the Sacrament.

‡I cannot well find the Author's meaning here, unless it be the hot untimely, blind Zeal of Enthusiasts.

12. A game in which participants tried to catch and swallow raisins floating in flaming brandy.
13. gutter.
14. In both tone and subject matter, this passage is a parody of a Calvinist preacher.

Confidence, upon the Virtue of the visual Nerve, which every little Accident shakes out of Order, and a Drop, or a Film, can wholly disconcert; like a Lanthorn among a Pack of roaring Bullies, when they scower the Streets; exposing its Owner, and it self, to outward Kicks and Buffets, which both might have escaped, if the Vanity of Appearing would have suffered them to walk in the Dark. But, farther; if we examine the Conduct of these boasted Lights, it will prove yet a great deal worse than their Fortune: *'Tis true, I have broke my Nose against this Post, because Fortune either forgot, or did not think it convenient to twitch me by the Elbow, and give me notice to avoid it. But, let not this encourage either the present Age or Posterity, to trust their* Noses *into the keeping of their* Eyes, *which may prove the fairest Way of losing them for good and all. For, O ye Eyes, Ye blind Guides; miserable Guardians are Ye of our frail Noses; Ye, I say, who fasten upon the first Precipice in view, and then tow our wretched willing Bodies after You, to the very Brink of Destruction: But, alas, that Brink is rotten, our Feet slip, and we tumble down prone into a Gulph, without one hospitable Shrub in the Way to break the Fall; a Fall, to which not any Nose of mortal Make is equal, except that of the Giant** Laurcalco, *who was Lord of the* Silver Bridge.[15] *Most properly, therefore, O Eyes, and with great Justice, may You be compared to those foolish Lights, which conduct Men thro' Dirt and Darkness, till they fall into a deep Pit, or a noisom Bog.*[16]

**Vide* Don Quixot.

This I have produced, as a Scantling[17] of *Jack's* great Eloquence, and the Force of his Reasoning upon such abstruse Matters.

He was besides, a Person of great Design and Improvement in Affairs of *Devotion,* having introduced a new Deity, who hath since met with a vast Number of Worshippers; by some called *Babel,* by others, *Chaos*; who had an antient Temple of *Gothick* Structure upon *Salisbury*-Plain;[18] famous for its Shrine, and Celebration by Pilgrims.

§When he had some Roguish Trick to play, he would down with[19] his Knees, up with his Eyes, and fall to Prayers, tho' in the midst of the Kennel.

§The Villanies and Cruelties committed by Enthusiasts and Phanaticks among us, were all performed under the Disguise of Religion and long Prayers.

15. See *Don Quixote* I, 18. Silver was used to repair broken noses.
16. cf. the language of John Bunyan's *The Pilgrim's Progress.*
17. sample.
18. Stonehenge; 'gothic' here means old and exotic.
19. i.e. on.

Then it was that those who understood his Pranks, would be sure to get far enough out of his Way; And whenever Curiosity attracted Strangers to Laugh, or to Listen; he would of a sudden, with one Hand out with his *Gear,* and piss full in their Eyes, and with the other, all to bespatter them with Mud.

*In Winter he went always loose and unbuttoned, and clad as thin as possible, to let *in* the ambient Heat;[20] and in Summer, lapt himself close and thick to keep it *out.*

†In all Revolutions of Government, he would make his Court for the Office of *Hangman* General; and in the Exercise of that Dignity, wherein he was very dextrous, would make use of ‡ no other *Vizard*[21] than a long *Prayer.*

He had a Tongue so Musculous and Subtil, that he could twist it up into his Nose, and deliver a strange Kind of Speech[22] from thence. He was also the first in these Kingdoms, who began to improve the *Spanish* Accomplishment of *Braying;*[23] and having large Ears, perpetually exposed and arrect,[24] he carried his Art to such a Perfection, that it was a Point of great Difficulty to distinguish either by the View or the Sound, between the *Original* and the *Copy.*

He was troubled with a Disease, reverse to that called the Stinging of the *Tarantula;*[25] and would§ run Dog-mad, at the Noise of *Musick,* especially a *Pair of Bag-Pipes.* But he would cure himself again, by taking two or three Turns in *Westminster-Hall,* or *Billingsgate,* or in a *Boarding-School,* or the *Royal-Exchange,* or a *State Coffee-House.*[26]

He was a Person that ***feared* no *Colours,*[27] but

*They affect Differences in Habit and Behaviour.
†They are severe Persecutors, and all in a Form of Cant and Devotion.
‡Cromwell and his Confederates went, as they called it, *to seek God,* when they resolved to murther the King.
§This is to expose our Dissenters Aversion to Instrumental Musick in Churches. *W. Wotton.*
**They quarrel at the most Innocent Decency and Ornament, and defaced the Statues and Paintings on all the Churches in *England.*

20. i.e. the heat in the surrounding air.
21. A hangman normally wore a mask or visor.
22. i.e. the harsh nasal sounds popularly believed to be typical of Puritan preachers.
23. The reference is to Cervantes, *Don Quixote* II, 35 and 38, where a Spanish alderman tries to recover a lost ass by braying.
24. upright.
25. Anyone stung by a tarantula spider was thought to become infected with 'tarantism', a hysterical desire to dance. It could be cured by dancing the tarantella. Thus, those bitten by the spider sought music to be cured.
26. i.e. places frequented by those in mercantile society.
27. regimental flags.

mortally *hated* all, and upon that Account, bore a cruel Aversion to *Painters,* insomuch, that in his Paroxysms, as he walked the Streets, he would have his Pockets loaden with Stones, to pelt at the *Signs.*[28]

Having from this manner of Living, frequent Occasion to *wash* himself, he would often leap over Head and Ears into the Water,[29] tho' it were in the midst of the Winter, but was always observed to come out again much *dirtier,* if possible, than he went in.

He was the first that ever found out the Secret of contriving a ‡*Soporiferous* Medicine to be convey'd in at the *Ears;* It was a Compound of *Sulphur* and *Balm of Gilead,* with a little *Pilgrim's Salve.*[30]

He wore a large Plaister of artificial *Causticks*[31] on his Stomach, with the Fervor of which, he could set himself a *groaning,* like the famous *Board* upon Application of a red-hot Iron.[32]

*He would stand in the Turning of a Street, and calling to those who passed by, would cry to One; *Worthy Sir, do me the Honour of a good Slap in the Chaps:*[33] To another, *Honest Friend, pray, favour me with a handsom Kick on the Arse : Madam, shall I entreat a small Box on the Ear, from your Ladyship's fair Hands? Noble Captain, Lend a reasonable Thwack, for the Love of God, with that Cane of yours, over these poor Shoulders.* And when he had by such earnest Sollicitations, made a shift to procure a Basting sufficient to swell up his Fancy and his Sides, He would return home extremely comforted, and full of terrible Accounts of what he had undergone for the *Publick Good. Observe this Stroak,* (said he, shewing his bare Shoulders) *a plaguy* Janisary[34] *gave it me this very Morning at seven a Clock, as, with much ado, I was driving off the* Great Turk. *Neighbours mine, this broken Head deserves a Plaister; had poor* Jack *been tender of his Noddle,*[35] *you would have seen the* Pope, *and the* French *King, long before this time of Day, among your Wives and your Warehouses. Dear* Christians, *the* Great Mogul *was come as far as* White-Chappel,[36] *and you may thank these poor Sides that he hath not (God bless us) already swallowed up Man, Woman, and Child.*

†It was highly worth observing, the singular Effects of that Aversion, or Antipathy, which *Jack* and his Brother *Peter* seemed, even to an Affectation, to bear toward each other. *Peter* had lately done *some Rogueries,* that forced him to abscond; and he seldom ventured to stir out before Night, for fear of Bayliffs. Their Lodgings were at the two most distant Parts of the Town, from each other; and whenever their Occasions, or Humors called them abroad, they would make Choice of the oddest unlikely Times, and most uncouth Rounds they could invent; that they might be sure to avoid one another: Yet after all this, it was their perpetual Fortune to meet. The Reason of which, is easy enough to apprehend: For, the Phrenzy and the Spleen[37] of both, having the same Foundation, we may look upon them as two Pair of Compasses, equally extended, and the fixed Foot of each, remaining in the same Center; which, tho' moving contrary Ways at first, will be sure to encounter somewhere or other in the Circumference. Besides, it was among the great Misfortunes of *Jack,* to bear a huge Personal Resemblance with his Brother *Peter.* Their Humour and Dispositions were not only the same, but there was a close Analogy in their Shape, and Size and their Mien. Insomuch, as nothing was more frequent than a Bayliff to

‡Fanatick Preaching, composed either of Hell and Damnation, or a fulsome Description of the Joys of Heaven, both in such a dirty, nauseous Style, as to be well resembled to Pilgrims Salve.

*The Fanaticks have always had a way of affecting to run into Persecution, and count vast Merit upon every little Hardship they suffer.

†The Papists and Fanaticks, tho' they appear the most Averse to each other, yet bear a near Resemblance in many things, as has been observed by Learned Men.

Ibid. The Agreement of our Dissenters and the Papists in that which Bishop *Stillingfleet* called, *The Fanaticism of the Church of* Rome, is ludicrously described for several Pages together by *Jack*'s Likeness to *Peter,* and their being often mistaken for each other, and their frequent Meeting, when they least intended it. *W. Wotton.*

28. painted signs outside shops and coffee-houses.
29. i.e. baptism by total immersion.
30. Balm of Gilead is a soothing, antiseptic resin exuded from a small, rare tree of the same name; pilgrim's salve was an ointment made from swine's grease and isinglass, according to the nineteenth-century Shakespearean scholar, James O. Halliwell.
31. burning or corrosive substances.
32. In seventeenth-century England, large boards made of elm wood were occasionally exhibited as wonders because, when a red hot iron was applied to them, they would groan. The effect seems to have been caused by the rapid expansion of small air-pockets in the wood.
33. cheeks.
34. a confounded Turkish soldier.
35. 'cared about his head', i.e. not been prepared to risk himself in your defence.
36. i.e. The Great Mogul of Delhi had come as far as the Eastern edge of London.
37. bad temper.

seize *Jack* by the Shoulders, and cry, *Mr.* Peter, *You are the King's Prisoner.* Or, at other Times, for one of *Peter*'s nearest Friends, to accost *Jack* with open Arms, *Dear* Peter, *I am glad to see thee, pray send me one of your best Medicines for the Worms.* This we may suppose, was a mortifying Return of those Pains and Proceedings, *Jack* had laboured in so long; And finding, how directly opposite all his Endeavours had answered to the sole End and Intention, which he had proposed to himself; How could it avoid having terrible Effects upon a Head and Heart so furnished as his? However, the poor Remainders of his *Coat*[38] bore all the Punishment; The orient Sun never entred upon his diurnal Progress, without missing a Piece of it. He hired a Taylor to stitch up the Collar so close, that it was ready to choak him, and squeezed out his Eyes at such a Rate, as one could see nothing but the White. What little was left of the main Substance of the Coat, he rubbed every day for two hours, against a rough-cast Wall, in order to grind away the Remnants of *Lace* and *Embroidery*;[39] but at the same time went on with so much Violence, that he proceeded[40] a *Heathen Philosopher.* Yet after all he could do of this kind, the Success continued still to disappoint his Expectation. For, as it is the Nature of Rags, to bear a kind of mock Resemblance to Finery; there being a sort of fluttering Appearance in both, which is not to be distinguished at a Distance, in the Dark, or by short-sighted Eyes: So, in those Junctures, it fared with *Jack* and his Tatters, that they offered to the first View a ridiculous Flanting, which assisting the Resemblance in Person and Air, thwarted all his Projects of Separation, and left so near a Similitude between them, as frequently deceived the very Disciples and Followers of both.[41] * * *

* * * * * * * * * * *

* * * * * * * *

Desunt * * * * * * * *

non-nulla. * * * * * * * *

* * * * * * * * * * *

The old *Sclavonian* Proverb said well, That *it is with* Men, *as with* Asses; *whoever would keep them fast, must find a very good Hold at their Ears.*[42] Yet, I think, we may affirm, that it hath been verified by repeated Experience, that,

Effugiet tamen hæc sceleratus vincula Proteus.[43]

It is good therefore, to read the Maxims of our Ancestors, with great Allowances to Times and Persons: For, if we look into Primitive Records, we shall find, that no Revolutions have been so great, or so frequent, as those of human *Ears.* In former Days, there was a curious Invention to catch and keep them; which, I think, we may justly reckon among the *Artes Perditæ*:[44] And how can it be otherwise, when in these latter Centuries, the very Species is not only diminished to a very lamentable Degree, but the poor Remainder is also degenerated so far, as to mock our skilfullest *Tenure*? For, if the only slitting of one *Ear* in a Stag,[45] hath been found sufficient to propagate the Defect thro' a whole Forest; Why should we wonder at the greatest Consequences, from so many Loppings and Mutilations, to which the *Ears* of our Fathers and our own, have been of late so much exposed?[46] 'Tis true, indeed, that while this *Island* of ours, was under the *Dominion of Grace,* many Endeavours were made to improve the Growth of *Ears* once more among us. The Proportion of Largeness, was not only lookt upon as an Ornament of the *Outward* Man, but as a Type of Grace in the *Inward.* Besides, it is held by Naturalists, that if there be a Protuberancy of Parts in the *Superiour* Region of the Body, as in the *Ears* and *Nose,* there must be a Parity also in the *Inferior*:[47] And therefore in that truly pious Age, the *Males* in every Assembly, according as they were gifted, appeared very forward in exposing their

38. In the main allegory of the *Tale*, the father gave each son a 'coat' of the Gospels.
39. Jack the Puritan has been trying to strip his coat of the lace and embroidery ('spurious additions') made by his brother Peter, the catholic church.
40. advanced to the status of.
41. This pretence that there is a gap in the manuscript is frequent in the *Tale*, both for comic effect and also to show the specious nature of much 'logical' argument. Laurence Sterne used the same device.
42. The 'proverb' — like Sclavonia — is Swift's invention.
43. 'But Proteus, the villain, will still escape from these bonds.' Horace, *Satires* II. 3. 71.
44. lost arts.
45. Sir Thomas Browne (*Vulgar Errors* (1646) vi, 10) explains that Aristotle had observed that the deer of Arginusa had divided ears 'occasioned at first by slitting the ears of Deers'. See the note on this by A.C. Guthkelch and D. Nichol Smith in their edition of *A Tale of a Tub* (Oxford: Clarendon Press, 1958, second ed.).
46. Puritans cut their hair short, which made their ears prominent.
47. The sexual innuendoes in this paragraph are typical of much low anglican humour of the seventeenth century. 'Zeal' for righteousness was meant to be matched by 'zeal' for sexual matters. See Ben Jonson's *The Alchemist* for the best-known example.

Ears to view, and the Regions about them; because *Hippocrates tells us, that *when the Vein behind the Ear happens to be cut, a Man becomes a Eunuch*: And the *Females* were nothing backwarder in beholding and edifying by them: Whereof those who had already *used the Means*, lookt about them with great Concern, in hopes of conceiving a suitable Offspring by such a Prospect: Others, who stood Candidates for *Benevolence,* found there a plentiful Choice, and were sure to fix upon such as discovered the largest *Ears,* that the Breed might not dwindle between them. Lastly, the devouter Sisters, who lookt upon all extraordinary Dilatations of that Member, as Protrusions of Zeal, or spiritual Excrescencies, were sure to honor every Head they sat upon, as if they had been *Marks of Grace*; but, especially, that of the Preacher, whose *Ears* were usually of the prime Magnitude; which upon that Account, he was very frequent and exact in exposing with all Advantages to the People: in his Rhetorical *Paroxysms,* turning sometimes to *hold forth* the one, and sometimes to *hold forth* the other: From which Custom, the whole Operation of Preaching is to this very Day among their Professors, styled by the Phrase of *Holding forth.*

*Lib. de aëre locis & aquus. [50, 51]

Such was the Progress of the *Saints,* for advancing the Size of that Member; And it is thought, the Success would have been every way answerable, if in Process of time, a ‡ cruel King had not arose, who raised a bloody Persecution against all *Ears,* above a certain Standard: Upon which, some were glad to hide their flourishing Sprouts in a black Border, others crept wholly under a Perewig: some were slit, others cropt, and a great Number sliced off to the Stumps. But of this, more hereafter, in my *general History of Ears*; which I design very speedily to bestow upon the Publick.

From this brief Survey of the falling State of *Ears,* in the last Age, and the small Care had to advance their antient Growth in the present, it is manifest, how little Rcason we can have to rely upon a Hold so short, so weak, and so slippery; and that, whoever desires to catch Mankind fast, must have Recourse to some other Methods. Now, he that will examine Human Nature with Circumspection enough, may discover several *Handles,* whereof the **Six* Senses[48] afford one apiece, beside a great Number that are screw'd to the Passions, and some few riveted to the Intellect. Among these last, *Curiosity* is one, and of all others, affords the firmest Grasp: *Curiosity,* that Spur in the side, that Bridle in the Mouth, that Ring in the Nose, of a lazy, an impatient, and a grunting Reader. By this *Handle* it is, that an Author should seize upon his Readers; which as soon as he hath once compast, all Resistance and struggling are in vain; and they become his Prisoners as close as he pleases, till Weariness or Dullness force him to let go his Gripe.

*Including Scaliger's.

And therefore, I the Author of this miraculous Treatise, having hitherto, beyond Expectation, maintained by the aforesaid *Handle,* a firm Hold upon my gentle Readers; It is with great Reluctance, that I am at length compelled to remit my Grasp; leaving them in the Perusal of what remains, to that natural *Oscitancy*[49] inherent in the Tribe. I can only assure thee, Courteous Reader, for both our Comforts, that my Concern is altogether equal to thine, for my Unhappiness in losing, or mislaying among my Papers the remaining Part of these Memoirs; which consisted of Accidents, Turns, and Adventures, both New, Agreeable, and Surprizing; and therefore, calculated in all due Points, to the delicate Taste of this our noble Age. But, alas, with my utmost Endeavours, I have been able only to retain a few of the Heads. Under which, there was a full Account, how *Peter* got a *Protection* out of the *King's-Bench*; And of a §Reconcilement between *Jack* and Him, upon a Design they had in a certain *rainy Night,* to trepan[50] Brother *Martin* into a *Spunging-house,*[51] and there strip him to the Skin. How *Martin,* with much ado, shew'd them both a fair pair of Heels. How a *new Warrant* came out

‡This was King *Charles* the Second, who at his Restauration, turned out all the Dissenting Teachers that would not conform.

§In the Reign of King *James* the Second, the Presbyterians by the King's Invitation, joined with the Papists, against the Church of *England,* and Addrest him for Repeal of the Penal-Laws and Test. The King by his Dispensing Power, gave Liberty of Conscience, which both Papists and Presbyterians made use of, but upon the Revolution, the Papists being down of Course, the Presbyterians freely continued their Assemblies, by Virtue of King *James*'s Indulgence, before they had a Toleration by Law; this I believe the Author means by *Jack*'s stealing *Peter*'s Protection, and making use of it himself.

48. The sixth sense, according to J.C. Scaliger (*De Subtilitate* (1557), p. 358), is titillation.
49. drowsiness.
50. ensnare.
51. Bailiff's house for temporary lodging of an arrested debtor.

against *Peter*: upon which, how *Jack* left him in the lurch, *stole his Protection, and made use of it himself. How Jack's* Tatters came into Fashion in *Court* and *City*; How *he* **got upon a great Horse, and eat* †*Custard.* But the Particulars of all these, with several others, which have now slid out of my Memory, are lost beyond all Hopes of Recovery. For which Misfortune, leaving my Readers to condole with each other, as far as they shall find it to agree with their several Constitutions; but conjuring them by all the Friendship that hath passed between Us, from the Title-Page to this, not to proceed so far as to injure their Healths, for an Accident past Remedy; I now go on to the Ceremonial Part of an accomplish'd Writer, and therefore, by a Courtly *Modern*,[52] least of all others to be omitted.

THE CONCLUSION

Going *too long* is a Cause of Abortion as effectual, tho' not so frequent, as *Going too short*; and holds true especially in the *Labors* of the Brain. Well fare the Heart of that Noble **Jesuit*,[53] who first adventur'd to confess in Print, that Books must be suited to their several Seasons, like Dress, and Dyet, and Diversions; And better fare our noble Nation, for refining upon this, among other *French* Modes. I am living fast, to see the Time, when a *Book* that misses its Tide, shall be neglected, as the *Moon* by Day, or like *Mackarel* a Week after the Season.[54] No Man hath more nicely observed our Climate, than the Bookseller who bought the Copy of this Work; He knows to a Tittle what Subjects will best go off in a *dry Year,* and which it is proper to expose foremost, when the Weather-glass is fallen to *much Rain.* When he had seen this Treatise, and consulted his *Almanack* upon it; he gave me to understand, that he had manifestly considered the two Principal Things, which were the *Bulk*, and the *Subject*; and found, it would never *take,* but after a long Vacation,[55] and then only, in case it should happen to be a hard Year for Turnips. Upon which I desired to know, *considering my urgent Necessities,* what he thought might be acceptable this Month. He lookt *Westward,* and said, *I doubt we shall have a Fit of bad Weather; However, if you could prepare some pretty little* Banter (but not in Verse) *or a small Treatise upon the* —— *it would run like Wild-Fire. But,* if it hold up, *I have already hired an Author to write something against* Dr. B--tl-y,[56] *which, I am sure, will turn to Account.*

*Pere d'Orleans.

At length we agreed upon this Expedient; That when a Customer comes for one of these, and desires in Confidence to know the Author; he will tell him very privately, as a Friend, naming which ever of the Wits shall happen to be that Week in the vogue; and if *Durfy*'s last Play should be in Course,[57] I had as lieve[58] he may be the Person as *Congreve*. This I mention, because I am wonderfully well acquainted with the present Relish of Courteous Readers; and have often observed, with singular Pleasure, that a *Fly* driven from a *Honey-pot,* will immediately, with very good Appetite alight, and finish his Meal on an *Excrement.*

I have one Word to say upon the Subject of *Profound Writers,* who are grown very numerous of late; And, I know very well, the judicious World is resolved to list me in that Number. I conceive therefore, as to the Business of being *Profound,* that it is with *Writers,* as with *Wells*; A Person with good Eyes may see to the Bottom of the deepest, provided any *Water* be there; and, that often, when there is nothing in the World at the Bottom, besides *Dryness* and *Dirt,* tho' it be but a Yard and half under Ground, it shall pass, however, for wondrous *Deep,* upon no wiser a Reason than because it is wondrous *Dark.*

I am now trying an Experiment very frequent among Modern Authors; which is, to *write upon Nothing*;[59] When the Subject is utterly exhausted,

*Sir *Humphry Edwyn,* a Presbyterian, was some Years ago Lord-Mayor of *London,* and had the Insolence to go in his Formalities to a Conventicle, with the Ensigns of his Office. [conventicle: a non-conformist or dissenting meeting house. Ed.]

†Custard is a famous Dish at a Lord-Mayors Feast.

52. The author of the *Tale* is constantly asserting that he is a Modern rather than an Ancient. See headnote.
53. Father Pierre-Joseph d'Orleans (d.1734), who states in his *Histoire de M. Constance* (1690) that books, like fruit, have their season.
54. Except in Cornwall, where it was pickled, mackerel was eaten fresh in the seventeenth and eighteenth centuries. Since the flesh does not keep well, there would be no interest in it a week after the shoals had left English waters.
55. i.e. in the autumn.
56. Doctor Richard Bentley (1662-1742), a rather pedantic classical scholar and critic, a Modern and a favourite butt for Swift's sarcasm.
57. i.e. being staged at the moment.
58. am as willing.
59. Several writers tried to do this; the best known example is a poem by John Wilmot (1647-80), earl of Rochester.

to let the Pen still move on; by some called, the Ghost of Wit, delighting to walk after the Death of its Body. And to say the Truth, there seems to be no Part of Knowledge in fewer Hands, than That of Discerning *when to have Done*. By the Time that an Author has writ out a Book, he and his Readers are become old Acquaintants, and grow very loth to part: So that I have sometimes known it to be in Writing, as in Visiting, where the Ceremony of taking Leave, has employ'd more Time than the whole Conversation before. The Conclusion of a Treatise, resembles the Conclusion of Human Life, which hath sometimes been compared to the End of a Feast; where few are satisfied to depart, *ut plenus vitæ conviva*:[60] For Men will sit down after the fullest Meal, tho' it be only to *doze*, or to *sleep* out the rest of the Day. But, in this latter, I differ extreamly from other Writers; and shall be too proud, if by all my Labors, I can have any ways contributed to the *Repose* of Mankind in †Times so turbulent and unquiet as these. Neither do I think such an Employment so very alien from the Office of a *Wit*, as some would suppose. For among a very Polite Nation in **Greece*,[61] there were the *same* Temples built and consecrated to *Sleep* and the *Muses*, between which two Deities, they believed the strictest Friendship was established.

**Trezenii Pausan. l. 2.*

I have one concluding Favour, to request of my Reader; that he will not expect to be equally diverted and informed by every Line, or every Page of this Discourse; but give some Allowance to the Author's Spleen, and short Fits or Intervals of Dullness, as well as his own; And lay it seriously to his Conscience, whether, if he were walking the Streets, in dirty Weather, or a rainy Day; he would allow it fair Dealing in Folks at their Ease from a Window, to Critick his Gate,[62] and ridicule his Dress at such a Juncture.

In my Disposure of Employments of the Brain, I have thought fit to make *Invention* the *Master*, and give *Method* and *Reason*, the Office of its *Lacquays*. The Cause of this Distribution was, from observing it my peculiar Case, to be often under a Temptation of being *Witty*, upon Occasion, where I could be neither *Wise* nor *Sound*, nor any thing to the Matter in hand. And, I am too much a Servant of the *Modern* Way, to neglect any such Opportunities, whatever Pains or Improprieties I may be at, to introduce them. For, I have observed, that from a laborious Collection of Seven Hundred Thirty Eight *Flowers*,[63] and *shining Hints* of the best *Modern* Authors, digested with great Reading, into my Book of *Common-places*;[64] I have not been able after five Years to draw, hook, or force into common Conversation, any more than a Dozen. Of which Dozen, the one Moiety[65] failed of Success, by being dropt among unsuitable Company; and the other cost me so many Strains, and Traps, and *Ambages*[66] to introduce, that I at length resolved to give it over.[67] Now, this Disappointment, (to discover a Secret) I must own, gave me the first Hint of setting up for an *Author*; and, I have since found among some particular Friends, that it is become a very general Complaint, and has produced the same Effects upon many others. For, I have remarked many a *towardly*[68] *Word*, to be wholly neglected or despised in *Discourse*, which hath passed very smoothly, with some Consideration and Esteem, after its Preferment and Sanction in *Print*. But now, since by the Liberty and Encouragement of the Press, I am grown absolute Master of the Occasions and Opportunities, to expose the Talents I have acquired; I already discover, that the *Issues*[69] of my *Observanda*[70] begin to grow too large for the *Receipts*.[71] Therefore, I shall here pause awhile, till I find, by feeling the World's Pulse, and my own, that it will be of absolute Necessity for us both, to resume my Pen.

†This was writ before the Peace of *Riswick* [signed in September 1697 between France, Spain, England, Germany and Holland. Ed.]

60. 'Like a dinner guest full of life'. Lucretius, *De Rerum Natura*, III, 938.
61. the people of Troezen.
62. to criticize the way he walks.
63. the most attractive passages.
64. A commonplace book was a bound volume of blank sheets into which the owner copied passages he wished to remember or refer to later.
65. half.
66. roundabout routes.
67. to stop.
68. seasonable or suitable.
69. discharge of blood etc. from a wound or ulcer.
70. observations.
71. prescriptions.

from:
THE JOURNAL TO STELLA (1710-13)

[*The Journal to Stella* is a remarkable document that gives the reader a vivid insight into Swift's feelings and emotions at the time when he was at the centre of political life in London. From about 1704 onwards, when he was spending time in London, Swift developed the habit of keeping in touch with Esther Johnson (Stella) and Rebecca Dingley (her companion) in Dublin by writing a short daily journal describing his life and feelings. Every ten days or so, he posted the resulting 'letter': those written between 1710 and 1713 have survived and are known as *The Journal to Stella.* In these letters, Swift used various terms of endearment and also abbreviations for other words, phrases and names. For instance, 'MD' stood for 'My Dears', 'Presto' ('Swift' in Italian) was Swift's own name for himself, and many phrases from nursery-talk are incorporated. Swift obviously found, as Harold Williams put it in the introduction to his edition of the journal, 'happiness and refreshment of spirit' in this 'little language'.

A short glossary of unfamiliar words is printed after the text, and words listed there are marked thus.⁰]

LETTER XVIII

[Saturday London, March 10, 1710-11.[1]]

Pretty little MD must expect little from me till Mr. Harley[2] is out of danger. We hope he is so now; but I am subject to fear for my friends. He has a head full of the whole business of the nation, was out of order when the villain[3] stabbed him, and had a cruel contusion⁰ by the second blow. But all goes on well yet. Mr. Ford[4] and I dined with Mr. Lewis,[5] and we hope the best.

11. This morning Mr. Secretary[6] and I met at Court, where he went to the queen,[7] who is out of order and aguish:⁰ I doubt[8] the worse for this accident to Mr. Harley. We went together to his house, and his wound looks well, and he is not feverish at all, and I think it is foolish in me to be so much in pain as I am. I had the penknife[9] in my hand, which is broken within a quarter of an inch of the handle. I have a mind to write and publish an account of all the particularities of this fact:[10] it will be very curious, and I would do it when Mr. Harley is past danger.

12. We have been in terrible pain to-day about Mr. Harley, who never slept last night, and has been very feverish. But this evening I called there, and young Mr. Harley (his only son) tells me he is now much better, and was then asleep. They let no-body see him, and that is perfectly right. The parliament cannot go on till he is well, and are forced to adjourn their money businesses, which none but he can help them in. Pray God preserve him.

13. Mr. Harley is better to-day, slept well all night, and we are a little out of our fears. I send and call three or four times every day. I went into the city for a walk, and dined there with a private man; and coming home this evening broke[11] my shin in the Strand over a tub of sand left just in the way. I got home dirty enough, and went straight to bed, where I have been cooking it with gold-beaters skin,[12] and have been peevish enough with Patrick,[13] who was near an hour bringing a rag from next door. It is my right shin, where never any humour fell when t'other used to swell;[14] so I apprehend it less: however I shall not stir till 'tis well, which I reckon will be in a week. I am very careful in these sort of things; but I wish I had Mrs. J——s water:[15] she is out of town, and I must make a shift with⁰ allum.⁰ I will dine with Mrs. Vanhomrigh[16] till I am well, who lives but five doors off; and that I may venture.

14. My journals are like to be very diverting, now I cannot stir abroad, between accounts of Mr. Harley's mending, and of my broken shin. I just walkt to my neighbour Vanhomrigh at two, and came away at six, when little Harrison[17] the Tatler came to me, and begged me to dictate a paper to

1. i.e. 1711 (the new year began on 25 March).
2. Robert Harley (1661-1724), earl of Oxford, lord treasurer at this time.
3. Antoine de Guiscard (1658-1711), a French emigré who stabbed Harley with a penknife on 8 March 1711.
4. Charles Ford (1682-1741), a close friend of Swift.
5. Erasmus Lewis (1670-1754), first secretary to Lord Dartmouth and friend of Swift.
6. Henry St John (1678-1751), viscount Bolingbroke, secretary of state at this time.
7. Queen Anne (1665-1714), who ruled 1702-14.
8. i.e. do not doubt.
9. The penknife used by Guiscard in his attack on Harley; it later belonged to Swift.
10. See *The Examiner* No. 33.
11. i.e. cut and bruised.
12. A prepared animal membrane used to separate leaves of gold foil during the process of beating them (i.e. into thin gold foil from ingots of gold); occasionally used to cover wounds.
13. Swift's Irish man-servant.
14. i.e. which never gave me trouble when the other used to swell.
15. Probably a reference to a medicinal water made out of wild flowers by Stella's sister, Anne Johnson.
16. Mrs Vanhomrigh (died 1714), widow of Bartholomew Vanhomrigh, lord mayor of Dublin, and mother of Swift's friend Vanessa.
17. William Harrison (1685-1713), poet, journalist (editor of *The Tatler*) and protégé of Swift.

him, which I was forced in charity to do. Mr. Harley still mends; and I hope in a day or two to trouble you no more with him, nor with my shin. Go to bed and sleep, sirrahs,[18] that you may rise to-morrow and walk to Donnybrook,[19] and lose your money with Stoite[20] and the dean;[21] do so, dear little rogues, and drink Presto's[22] health. O, pray, don't you drink Presto's health sometimes with your deans, and your Stoites, and your Walls,[23] and your Manleys,[24] and your every body's, pray now? I drink MD's to myself a hundred thousand times.

15. I was this morning at Mr. secretary St. John's for all my shin, and he has given me for young Harrison, the Tatler, the prettiest employment in Europe; secretary to my lord Raby,[25] who is to be ambassador extraordinary at the Hague, where all the great affairs will be concerted; so we shall lose the *Tatlers* in a fortnight. I will send Harrison to-morrow morning to thank the secretary. Poor Biddy Floyd[26] has got the small-pox. I called this morning to see lady Betty Germain;[27] and when she told me so, I fairly[0] took my leave.[28] I have the luck of it; for about ten days ago I was to see lord Carteret;[29] and my lady was entertaining me with telling of a young lady, a cousin, who was then ill in the house of the small-pox, and is since dead: it was near lady Betty's, and I fancy Biddy took the fright by it. I dined with Mr. secretary, and a physician came in just from Guiscard, who tells us he is dying of his wounds, and can hardly live till to-morrow. A poor wench that Guiscard kept, sent him a bottle of sack;[0] but the keeper would not let him touch it, for fear it was poison. He had two quarts of old clotted blood come out of his side to-day, and is delirious. I am sorry he is dying; for they had found out a way to hang him. He certainly had an intention to murder the queen.

16. I have made but little progress in this letter for so many days, thanks to Guiscard and Mr. Harley; and it would be endless to tell you all the particulars of that odious fact. I do not yet hear that Guiscard is dead, but they say 'tis impossible he should recover. I walkt too much yesterday for a man with a broken shin; to-day I rested, and went no further than Mrs. Vanhomrigh's, where I dined; and lady Betty Butler[30] coming in about six, I was forced in good manners to sit with her till nine; then I came home, and Mr. Ford came in to visit my shin, and sat with me till eleven: so I have been very idle and naughty. It vexes me to the pluck[0] that I should lose walking this delicious day. Have you seen the *Spectator*[31] yet, a paper that comes out every day? 'Tis written by Mr. Steele,[32] who seems to have gathered new life, and have a new fund of wit; it is in the same nature as his *Tatlers*, and they have all of them had something pretty. I believe Addison[33] and he club.[34] I never see them; and I plainly told Mr. Harley and Mr. St. John,[35] ten days ago, before my lord keeper[36] and lord Rivers,[37] that I had been foolish enough to spend my credit with them in favour of Addison and Steele; but that I would engage and promise never to say one word in their behalf, having been used so ill for what I had already done. — So, now I have got into the way of prating[0] again, there will be no quiet for me. When Presto begins to prate, Give him a rap upon the pate.[0] — O Lord, how I blot;[38] 'tis time to leave off, &c....

19. I went to-day into the city, but in a coach, and sossed[0] up my leg on the seat; and as I came home I went to see poor Charles Barnard's[39] books, which are to be sold by auction, and I itch to lay out nine or ten pounds for some fine editions of fine

18. Like 'dear little rogues', this is an example of the affectionate 'little language' Swift used when writing to Stella and Rebecca.
19. A village about a mile from Dublin.
20. Mrs Stoyte, wife of a Dublin alderman, was a favourite card-playing companion of Stella and Rebecca.
21. John Stearne (1660-1745), dean of St Patrick's Cathedral 1704-13 and later the bishop of Clogher.
22. i.e. 'Swift' in Italian.
23. Archdeacon Thomas Walls (*c.*1672-1750), master of St Patrick's School; he and his wife were friends of both Swift and Stella.
24. Isaac Manley, postmaster-general in Ireland, another card player.
25. Thomas Wentworth (1672-1739) baron Raby.
26. A noted London beauty.
27. Lady Betty Germain was daughter of the second Earl of Berkeley.
28. Swift never caught small-pox, which was highly contagious.
29. Lord Carteret (1690-1763), statesman and friend of Swift.
30. Lady Betty Butler, daughter of the second Duke of Ormonde.
31. *The Spectator*, written by Addison and Steele, had started at the beginning of the month.
32. Sir Richard Steele (1672-1719), playwright and journalist.
33. Joseph Addison (1672-1719), author, statesman and secretary of the Irish government 1709-10.
34. i.e. are closely associated.
35. i.e. Lord Bolingbroke.
36. Sir Simon Harcourt (1661-1727), lord keeper.
37. Richard Savage (*c.*1654-1712), earl Rivers, constable of the Tower.
38. This refers to blots of ink on the writing paper.
39. Charles Bernard (died 1710), serjeant-surgeon to the Queen and a great book collector.

authors. But 'tis too far, and I shall let it slip, as I usually do all such opportunities. I dined in a Coffee-house with Stratford[40] upon chops, and some of his wine. Where did MD dine? Why, poor MD dined at home to-day, because of the archbishop,[41] and they could not go abroad, and had a breast of mutton and a pint of wine.... Oh, that we were at Laracor[42] this fine day! the willows begin to peep, and the quicks[0] to bud. My dream's out: I was a-dreamed last night that I eat ripe cherries. — And now they begin to catch the pikes, and will shortly the trouts (pox on these ministers), and I would fain know whether the floods were ever so high as to get over the holly bank or the river walk; if so, then all my pikes are gone; but I hope not. Why don't you ask Parvisol[43] these things, sirrahs? And then my canal, and trouts, and whether the bottom be fine and clear? But hearkee, ought not Parvisol to pay in my last year's rents and arrears out of his hands? I am thinking, if either of you have heads to take his accounts it should be paid in to you; otherwise to Mr. Walls. I will write an order on t'other side; and do as you will. Here's a world of business; but I must go sleep, I'm drowsy: and so good night, &c....

40. Francis Stratford, a school friend and regular dinner-companion of Swift.
41. William King (1650-1729), archbishop of Dublin.
42. Swift's house by the riverside in his parish of the same name in County Meath.
43. Isaiah Parvisol, Swift's steward and tithe collector.

Glossary

aguish: feverish.
allum: an astringent salt containing potassium.
contusion: bruise.
fairly: completely; *here*, 'quickly).
make a shift with: to make do with.
pate: top of the head.
pluck: heart.
prating: boasting.
quicks: white hawthorn bushes.
sack: spanish white wine or sherry.
soss: to rest softly.

A PROPOSAL FOR THE UNIVERSAL USE OF *IRISH* MANUFACTURE, &c. (1720)

[This important pamphlet, written in 1720, was Swift's first work on Irish affairs after his return to Ireland in 1713. Like *The Drapier's Letters*, it was designed to arouse the people of Ireland, protestant and catholic alike, to oppose the government's economic legislation. It was directed particularly to shopkeepers and merchants, whom Swift felt had an important role to play in opposing the seemingly endless acts forbidding free trade. Ireland was, in effect, being treated as an English colony, subservient to the mother country in all matters of commerce, whereas she was, legally at any rate, an equal kingdom which merely shared a monarch with England. The pamphlet was anonymous, but the government was so annoyed by it that the printer, Edward Waters, was arrested and prosecuted. The jury in the case refused to convict, despite the fact that the lord justice sent them back nine times to reconsider their verdict.]

It is the peculiar Felicity and Prudence of the People in this Kingdom, that whatever Commodities, or Productions, lie under the greatest Discouragements from *England*, those are what they are sure to be most industrious in cultivating and spreading. *Agriculture*, which hath been the principal Care of all wise Nations, and for the Encouragement whereof there are so many Statute-Laws in *England*, we countenance so well, that the Landlords are every where, by *penal Clauses*, absolutely prohibiting their Tenants from Plowing;[1] not satisfied to confine them within certain Limitations, as it is the Practice of the *English*; one Effect of which, is already seen in the prodigious Dearness of Corn, and the Importation of it from *London*, as the cheaper Market: And, because People are the *Riches of a Country*, and that our *Neighbours* have done, and are doing all that in them lie, to make our Wool a Drug to us,[2] and a Monopoly to them; therefore, the politick[3] Gentlemen of *Ireland* have depopulated vast Tracts of the best Land, for the feeding of Sheep.

I could fill a Volume as large as the *History of the wise Men of Goatham*,[4] with a Catalogue only of some *wonderful* Laws and Customs we have observed within thirty Years past. It is true, indeed, our beneficial Traffick of Wool with *France*,[5] hath been our only Support for several Years past; furnishing

1. Swift is drawing attention to legislation that adversely affected Irish agriculture, as a result of which landlords prohibited tenants from growing tillage crops.
2. A reference to the Woollen Bill of 1699, which prohibited the export of wool from Ireland except to England, where it was heavily taxed.
3. wise or shrewd.
4. A nursery and folk tale.
5. i.e. exported by smugglers.

us all the little Money we have to pay our Rents, and go to Market. But our Merchants assure me, *This Trade hath received a great Damp by the present fluctuating Condition of the Coin in* France; *and that most of their Wine is paid for in Specie,*[6] *without carrying thither any Commodity from hence.*

However, since we are so universally bent upon enlarging our *Flocks,* it may be worth inquiring, what we shall do with our Wool, in case *Barnstable*[7] should be over-stocked, and our *French* Commerce should fail?

I should wish the Parliament had thought fit to have suspended their Regulation of *Church* Matters, and Enlargements of the *Prerogative,*[8] until a more convenient Time, because they did not appear very pressing, (at least to the Persons *principally concerned*) and, instead of those great Refinements in *Politicks* and *Divinity,* had *amused* Themselves and their Committees, a little, with the *State of the Nation.* For Example: What if the House of Commons had thought fit to make a Resolution, *Nemine Contradicente,*[9] against wearing any Cloath or Stuff[10] in their Families, which were not of the Growth and Manufacture of this Kingdom? What if they had extended it so far, as utterly to exclude all Silks, Velvets, Calicoes, and the whole *Lexicon* of Female Fopperies; and declared, that whoever acted otherwise, should be deemed and reputed *an Enemy to the Nation*? What if they had sent up such a Resolution to be agreed to by the House of Lords; and by their own Practice and Encouragement, spread the Execution of it in their several Countries? What if we should agree to make *burying in Woollen a Fashion,* as our Neighbours have made it a *Law*?[11] What if the Ladies would be content with *Irish* Stuffs for the Furniture of their Houses, for Gowns and Petticoats to themselves and their Daughters? Upon the whole, and to crown all the rest, let a firm Resolution be taken, by *Male* and *Female*, never to appear with one single *Shred* that comes from *England*; and let all the People say, AMEN.

I hope, and believe, nothing could please his Majesty better than to hear that his loyal Subjects, of both Sexes, in this Kingdom, celebrated his *Birth-Day* (now approaching) *universally* clad in their own Manufacture.[12] Is there Vertue enough left in this deluded People to save them from the Brink of Ruin? If the Mens Opinions may be taken, the Ladies will look as handsome in Stuffs as Brocades, and, since all will be equal, there may be room enough to employ their Wit and Fancy in chusing and matching of Patterns and Colours. I heard the late Archbishop of *Tuam*[13] mention a pleasant Observation of some Body's; *that* Ireland *would never be happy 'till a Law were made for* burning *every Thing that came from* England, *except their* People *and their* Coals: I must confess, that as to the former, I should not be sorry if they would stay at home; and for the latter, I hope, in a little Time we shall have no Occasion for them.

Non tanti mitra est, non tanti Judicis ostrum.[14]

But I should rejoice to see a *Stay-Lace*[15] from *England* be thought *scandalous,* and become a Topick for *Censure* at *Visits* and *Tea Tables.*

If the unthinking Shopkeepers in this Town, had not been *utterly* destitute of common Sense, they would have made some *Proposal to the Parliament,* with a *Petition* to the Purpose I have mentioned; promising to improve the *Cloaths and Stuffs of the Nation, into all possible Degrees of Fineness and Colours, and engaging not to play the Knave, according to their Custom, by exacting and imposing upon the Nobility and Gentry either as to the Prices or the Goodness.* For I remember, in *London,* upon a general Mourning, the *rascally Mercers* and *Woollen Drapers,* would, in Four and Twenty Hours, raise their *Cloaths* and *Silks* to above a double Price; and if the Mourning continued long, then come whingeing with *Petitions* to the *Court, that they were ready to starve, and their Fineries lay upon their Hands.*

6. (gold) coins.
7. The port in Devon to which most exported Irish wool was sent.
8. The Irish parliament, in its most recent session, had passed the Toleration Act and other bills concerned with the Church of Ireland; it had also defied the English parliament which, in response, had passed the notorious *Act for the better Securing the Dependency of the Kingdom of Ireland upon the Crown of Great Britain,* known as the 'Declaratory Act'; this restated England's right to make acts in the parliament at Westminster which could 'bind the kingdom and people of Ireland'.
9. 'none voting against it'.
10. Irish woven textile or tweed.
11. An English law of the reign of Elizabeth I (designed to help the English woollen trade) made it mandatory for shrouds to be made of wool.
12. This potentially seditious pamphlet was timed to appear just before King George I's sixtieth birthday, 28 May 1720.
13. John Vesey (1638-1716).
14. 'A mitre is not worth so much; the robes of a judge are not of so much importance.'
15. A cord used to draw together a woman's stays or bodice.

I could wish our Shopkeepers would immediately think on this *Proposal,* addressing it to all Persons of Quality, and others; but first be sure to get some Body who can write Sense, to put it into Form.

I think it needless to exhort the *Clergy* to follow this good Example, because, *in a little Time, those among them who are so unfortunate to have had their Birth and Education in this Country, will think themselves abundantly happy when they can afford* Irish *Crape, and an* Athlone *Hat;*[16] and as to the others, I *shall not presume* to direct them. I have, indeed, seen the present Archbishop of *Dublin*[17] clad from Head to Foot in our own Manufacture; and yet, under the Rose[18] be it spoken, *his Grace deserves as good a Gown, as if he had not been born among us.*

I have not Courage enough to offer *one Syllable* on this Subject to *their Honours* of the Army: Neither have I sufficiently considered the great Importance of *Scarlet* and *Gold Lace.*

The Fable, in *Ovid,* of *Arachne* and *Pallas,*[19] is to this Purpose. The Goddess had heard of one *Arachne* a young Virgin, very famous for *Spinning* and *Weaving*: They both met upon a Tryal of Skill; and *Pallas* finding herself almost equalled in her own Art, stung with Rage and Envy, knockt her *Rival* down, turned her into a *Spyder,* enjoining her to *spin* and *weave* for ever, *out of her own Bowels,* and *in a very narrow Compass.* I confess, that from a Boy, I always pitied poor *Arachne,* and could never heartily love the Goddess, on Account of so *cruel and unjust a Sentence*; which, however, is *fully executed* upon *Us* by *England,* with further Additions of *Rigor* and *Severity.* For the greatest Part of *our Bowels and Vitals* is extracted, without allowing us the Liberty of *spinning* and *weaving* them.

The Scripture tells us, that *Oppression makes a wise Man mad;*[20] therefore, consequently speaking, the Reason why some Men are not *mad,* is because they are not *wise*: However, it were to be wished that *Oppression* would, in Time, teach a little *Wisdom* to *Fools.*

I was much delighted with a Person, who hath a great Estate in this Kingdom, upon his Complaints to me, *how grievously POOR* England *suffers by Impositions from* Ireland. *That we convey our own Wool to* France, *in Spight of all the* Harpies *at the Custom-House. That Mr.* Shutleworth, *and others on the* Cheshire *Coasts, are such Fools to sell us their* Bark *at a good Price, for tanning* our own Hydes *into Leather; with other Enormities of the like Weight and Kind.* To which I will venture to add more: *That the* Mayorality *of this City is always executed by an* Inhabitant, *and often by a* Native, *which might as well be done by a* Deputy, *with a moderate Salary, whereby POOR* England *loseth, at least, one thousand Pounds a Year upon the Ballance. That the Governing of this Kingdom costs the Lord Lieutenant three Thousand six Hundred Pounds a Year, so much* net *Loss to POOR* England. *That the People of* Ireland *presume to dig for Coals* in their own Grounds; *and the Farmers in the County of* Wicklow *send their Turf to the very Market of* Dublin, *to the great Discouragement of the Coal Trade at* Mostyn *and* White-haven.[21] *That the Revenues of the* Post-Office *here, so righteously belonging to the* English *Treasury, as arising chiefly from our own Commerce with each other, should be remitted to* London, *clogged with that grievous Burthen of Exchange,*[22] *and the Pensions paid out of the* Irish *Revenues to* English Favourites, *should lie under the same Disadvantage, to the great Loss of the Grantees. When a* Divine *is sent over to a* Bishoprick *here, with the Hopes of Five and Twenty Hundred Pounds a Year; upon his Arrival, he finds, alas! a dreadful Discount of Ten or Twelve* per Cent. *A* Judge, *or a* Commissioner *of the Revenue, has the same Cause of Complaint.* Lastly, *The Ballad upon* Cotter[23] *is vehemently suspected to be* Irish *Manufacture; and yet is allowed to be sung in our open Streets, under the very* Nose *of the* Government.

These are a *few* among the many Hardships we put upon that *POOR* Kingdom of *England*; for which, I am confident, every *honest* Man wisheth a

16. Crape was a thin worsted material often used for the dress of clergy in the eighteenth century, and Athlone was famous for hats. The implication is that Irish-born and educated clergy, since they would never be given such lucrative posts as those born in England, would be happy if they could afford the simplest Irish-made clothing.
17. William King (1650-1729), born in County Antrim, was leader of the 'Irish faction' in the Irish parliament.
18. sub rosa, i.e. privately, in strict confidence.
19. Ovid, *Metamorphoses* vi, 1.
20. Ecclesiastes 7.7.
21. Ports in Scotland and England.
22. i.e. the difference in value between the Irish pound and the pound sterling.
23. Sir James Cotter, a prominent catholic, had been executed for rape shortly before this pamphlet appeared and ballads about the case were circulating freely.

Remedy: And, I hear, there is a Project *on Foot* for transporting our best Wheaten *Straw,* by Sea and Land Carriage, to *Dunstable*;[24] and *obliging us by a Law,* to take off yearly so many *Tun of Straw-Hats,* for the Use of our Women; which will be a *great Encouragement* to the Manufacture of that industrious Town.

I would be glad to learn among the Divines, whether a Law *to bind Men without their own Consent,*[25] be obligatory *in foro Conscientiæ*;[26] because, I find *Scripture, Sanderson* and *Suarez,*[27] are wholly silent in the Matter. The Oracle of *Reason,* the great *Law of Nature,* and general Opinion of *Civilians,* wherever they treat of *limited Governments,* are, indeed, decisive enough.

It is wonderful to observe the Biass among our People in favour of *Things, Persons,* and *Wares* of all Kinds that come from *England.* The *Printer* tells his *Hawkers,* that *he has got an excellent new Song just brought from* London. I have somewhat of a Tendency that way my self; and upon hearing a *Coxcomb* from thence displaying himself, with great Volubility, upon the *Park,* the *Play-House,* the *Opera,* the *Gaming Ordinaries,*[28] it was apt to beget in me a Kind of Veneration for his Parts and Accomplishments. It is not many Years, since I remember a *Person* who, by his Style and Literature,[29] seems to have been *Corrector* of a Hedge-Press, in some *Blind-Alley* about *Little-Britain,*[30] proceed *gradually* to be an *Author,* at least a **Translator* of a lower Rate, although somewhat of a larger Bulk, than any that now *flourishes* in *Grub-street*; and, upon the Strength of this Foundation, came over *here*; erect himself up into an *Orator* and *Politician,* and lead a *Kingdom* after him. This, I am told, was the *very Motive* that prevailed on the †*Author* of a Play called, *Love in a Hollow-Tree*[31] to do us the *Honour* of a Visit; presuming, with very good Reason, *that he was a Writer of a superior Class.* I know *another,* who, for thirty Years past, hath been the *common Standard of Stupidity in England,* where he was never heard a Minute in any *Assembly,* or by any *Party,* with *common Christian Treatment*; yet, upon his Arrival hither, could put on a *Face of Importance and Authority,* talked more than Six, without either *Gracefulness, Propriety,* or *Meaning*; and, at the same Time, be admired and followed as the Pattern of *Eloquence* and *Wisdom.*

*Supposed to be *Cæsar's* Commentaries, dedicated to the D[uke] of *Marlborough.* [Swift's note]
†L. *G*[*ri*]*mst*[*o*]*n.* [Swift's note]

Nothing hath humbled me so much, or shewn a greater Disposition to a *contemptuous* Treatment of *Ireland* in some chief *Governors,* than that high Style of several Speeches from the *Throne,* delivered, as usual, after the *Royal Assent,* in *some Periods* of the two last *Reigns.* Such Exaggerations of the prodigious *Condescensions* in the Prince, to pass *those good Laws,* would have but an odd Sound at *Westminster*: Neither do I apprehend, how any *good Law* can pass, wherein the *King*'s Interest is not as much concerned as that of the *People.* I remember, after a Speech on the like Occasion, delivered by my Lord *Wharton,*[32] (I think it was his last) he desired Mr. *Addison*[33] to *ask my Opinion of it*: My Answer was, *That his Excellency had very honestly forfeited his Head, on Account of one Paragraph; wherein he asserted, by plain Consequence, a* dispensing Power *in the Queen.*[34] His Lordship owned *it was true,* but *swore* the Words were *put into his Mouth* by direct Orders from Court. From whence it is clear, that some *Ministers* in those Times, were apt, from their *high* Elevation, to look *down* upon this Kingdom, as if it had been one of their *Colonies* of *Out-casts* in *America.* And I observed a little of the same Turn of Spirit in *some great Men,* from whom I expected better; although, to do them Justice, it proved no Point of Difficulty to make them *correct their Idea,* whereof the *whole Nation* quickly found the Benefit. —— But that is *forgotten.* How the Style hath since run, I am wholly a Stranger; having never seen a Speech since the last of the Queen.

I would now expostulate a little with our Country Landlords; who, by unmeasurable *screwing* and *racking*[35] their Tenants all over the Kingdom, have

24. A town in Kent.
25. The phrase is an echo of the wording of the Declaratory Act.
26. 'before the tribunal of conscience', i.e. in a man's own conviction of what is just.
27. Robert Sanderson (1587-1663) and Francisco Suarez (1548-1617), writers on ethics, particularly on conscience.
28. The tables in gaming houses were known as 'ordinary' tables (*OED*).
29. Martin Bladen (1680-1746), soldier and minor writer.
30. An area of London which, like Grub Street, was frequented by second-rate writers and journalists.
31. Viscount Grimston.
32. Thomas Wharton, earl Wharton (1648-1715).
33. Joseph Addison (1672-1719), statesman and friend of Swift.
34. The Crown claimed the right to override certain statutes in special circumstances.
35. Two terms for the custom of raising rents excessively.

already reduced the miserable *People* to a *worse Condition* than the *Peasants* in *France*, or the *Vassals* in *Germany* and *Poland*; so that the whole *Species* of what we call *Substantial Farmers*, will, in a very few Years, be utterly at an End. It was pleasant to observe these Gentlemen, *labouring* with all their *Might*, for preventing the *Bishops* from letting their Revenues at a moderate half Value, (whereby the whole *Order* would, in an Age, have been reduced to manifest Beggary) at the very Instant, when they were every where *canting* their own Lands upon short Leases,[36] and sacrificing their *oldest Tenants for a Penny an Acre advance*. I know not how it comes to pass, (and yet, perhaps, I know well enough) that *Slaves* have a natural Disposition to be *Tyrants*; and that when my *Betters* give me a Kick, I am apt to revenge it with six upon my *Footman*; although, perhaps, he may be an honest and diligent Fellow. I have heard *great* Divines affirm, that *nothing is so likely to call down an universal Judgment from Heaven upon a Nation, as universal Oppression;* and whether this be not already verified in Part, *their Worships* the Landlords are *now* at full Leisure to consider. Whoever travels this Country, and observes the *Face* of Nature, or the *Faces*, and Habits, and Dwellings of the *Natives*, will hardly think himself in a Land where either *Law, Religion*, or *common Humanity* is professed.

I cannot forbear saying one Word upon a *Thing* they call a *Bank*,[37] which, I hear, is projecting in this Town. I never saw the *Proposals*, nor understand any one Particular of their Scheme: What I wish for, at present, is only a sufficient Provision of *Hemp*, and *Caps*, and *Bells*,[38] to distribute according to the several Degrees of *Honesty* and *Prudence* in *some Persons*. I *hear* only of a monstrous Sum already named; and, if OTHERS do not soon hear of it too, and *hear* it with a *Vengeance*, then am I a Gentleman of less Sagacity than my self, and very few besides, take me to be. And the Jest will be still the better, if it be true, as judicious Persons have assured me, that one Half of this Money will be *real*, and the other Half altogether imaginary. The Matter will be likewise much mended, if the Merchants continue to carry off our Gold, and our Goldsmiths to melt down our heavy Silver.

36. auctioning rents (so getting the maximum price).
37. A proposal to found a national bank in Ireland had recently been made; Swift was strongly opposed to it.
38. A 'hemp' was a rope for hanging; cap and bells were the distinguishing marks of a jester.

THE FIRST DRAPIER'S LETTER (1724)

[*The Drapier's Letters* controversy is the most famous Irish affair in which Swift was directly involved. In the 1720s, Ireland needed new coinage, but the contract to provide it was obtained, by bribery, for an Englishman named William Wood. His coins were, it was suspected, to be made of inferior metal so that he could make extra profit. Again, the Irish people were being imposed upon by an Englishman and, in this case, the issue was the emotive one of coinage.

Swift adopted the persona of a shopkeeper, M.B. Drapier, and published seven pamphlets supposedly written by the Drapier in 1724 and 1725. Partly as a result of Swift's work — but also because of other pressures — the patent was withdrawn. The credit for bringing about the government's change of heart was generally given to Swift and he became the hero of the people, publicly acknowledged as the Hibernian Patriot.

We print below the first letter in the controversy. The consummate skill with which Swift slips into the personality of a shopkeeper, using homely images and arithmetical calculations exactly appropriate, has made this one of the most enduring of his pamphlets, despite the local and ephemeral nature of the coinage issue itself.]

To the *Tradesmen*, *Shop-Keepers*, *Farmers*, and *Country-People* in General, of the Kingdom of Ireland.

Brethren, Friends, Countrymen, and *Fellow-Subjects.*

WHAT I intend now to say to you, is next to your Duty to God, and the Care of your Salvation, of the greatest Concern to your selves, and your Children; your *Bread* and *Cloathing*, and every common Necessary of Life entirely depend upon it. Therefore I do most earnestly exhort you as *Men*, as *Christians*, as *Parents*, and as *Lovers of your Country*, to read this Paper with the utmost Attention, or get it read to you by others; which that you may do at the less Expence, I have ordered the Printer to sell it at the lowest Rate.[1]

1. The price was two shillings for 36, an extremely low price. Coinage and weight values were as follows: 4 farthings to one penny, 2 half-pence to one penny, twelve pence to one shilling, 20 shillings to one pound. Twenty-one shillings equals one guinea. In weight, 16 ounces equals one pound (also known as a pound butter-weight).

IT is a great Fault among you, that when a Person writes with no other Intention than *to do you Good, you will not be at the Pains to read his Advices*: One Copy of this Paper may serve a Dozen of you, which will be less than a Farthing apiece. It is your Folly, that you have no common or general Interest in your View, not even the Wisest among you; neither do you know or enquire, or care who are your Friends, or who are your Enemies.

ABOUT four Years ago, a little Book was written to advise all People to wear the *Manufactures of this our own Dear Country*:[2] It had no other Design, said nothing against the *King* or *Parliament*, or *any* Person whatsoever, yet the POOR PRINTER was prosecuted two Years, with the utmost Violence; and even some WEAVERS themselves, for whose Sake it was written, being upon the JURY, FOUND HIM GUILTY.[3] This would be enough to discourage any Man from endeavouring to do you Good, when you will either neglect him, or fly in his Face for his Pains; and when he must expect only *Danger to himself*, and to be fined and imprisoned, perhaps to his Ruin.

HOWEVER, I cannot but warn you once more of the manifest Destruction before your Eyes, if you do not behave your selves as you ought.

I WILL therefore first tell you the *plain Story of the Fact*; and then I will lay before you, how you ought to act in common Prudence, and according to the *Laws of your Country*.

THE *Fact is thus*; It having been many Years since COPPER HALF-PENCE OR FARTHINGS were last Coined in this *Kingdom*, they have been for some Time very scarce, and many *Counterfeits* passed about under the Name of RAPS: Several Applications were made to *England*, that we might have Liberty to *Coin New Ones*, as in former Times we did; but they did not succeed. At last one Mr. WOOD, *a mean ordinary Man, a Hard-Ware Dealer*, procured a *Patent* under HIS MAJESTY'S BROAD SEAL, to coin 108000 *l.* in *Copper* for this *Kingdom*;[4] which Patent however did not oblige any one here to take them, unless they pleased. Now you must know, that the HALF-PENCE and FARTHINGS in *England* pass for very little more than they are worth: And if you should beat them to Pieces, and sell them to the *Brazier*, you would not lose much above a Penny in a Shilling. But Mr. WOOD made his HALF-PENCE of such *Base Metal*, and so much smaller than the *English* ones, that the *Brazier* would hardly give you above a *Penny* of good Money for a *Shilling* of his; so that this sum of 108000 *l.* in good Gold and Silver, must be given for TRASH that will not be worth above *Eight* or *Nine Thousand Pounds* real Value. But this is not the Worst; for Mr. WOOD, when he pleases, may by Stealth send over *another* 108000 *l.* and buy *all our Goods for Eleven Parts in Twelve*, under the Value. For Example, if a *Hatter* sells a Dozen of *Hats* for *Five Shillings* a-piece, which amounts to *Three Pounds*, and receives the Payment in Mr. WOOD'S Coin, he really receives only the Value of *Five Shillings*.

PERHAPS you will wonder how such an *ordinary Fellow* as this Mr. WOOD could have so much Interest as to get His MAJESTY'S Broad Seal for so great a Sum of bad Money, to be sent to this poor Country; and that all the *Nobility* and *Gentry* here could not obtain the same Favour, and let us make our own HALF-PENCE, as we used to do. Now I will make that Matter very plain. We are at a great Distance from the *King's Court*, and have no body there to solicit for us, although a great Number of *Lords* and *Squires*, whose Estates are here, and are our Countrymen, spend all their *Lives* and *Fortunes* there. But this same Mr. WOOD was able to attend constantly for his own Interest; he is an ENGLISHMAN and had GREAT FRIENDS,[5] and it seems knew very well *where to give Money*, to those that would speak to OTHERS that could speak to the KING, and would tell a FAIR STORY. And HIS MAJESTY, and perhaps the great Lord or Lords who advised him, might think it was for our *Country's Good*; and so, as the Lawyers express it, the KING was deceived in his Grant; which often happens in *all Reigns*. And I am sure if His MAJESTY knew that such a Patent, if it should take Effect according to the Desire of Mr. WOOD, would utterly ruin this Kingdom, which hath given such great Proofs of its *Loyalty*; he would immediately recall it, and perhaps shew his Displeasure to SOME BODY OR OTHER:[6] *But a Word to the Wise is enough.* Most of you must have heard with what Anger our *Honourable House of Commons* received an Account of this WOOD'S PATENT. There were several *Fine Speeches* made

2. Swift's *A Proposal for the Universal Use of Irish Manufacture* (1720).
3. See above headnote to *A Proposal*....
4. In fact, the patent was for £100,800.
5. i.e. George I's mistress, the Duchess of Kendal and Munster (1667-1743).
6. i.e. the prime minister, Sir Robert Walpole (1676-1745).

upon it, and plain Proofs; that it was all a WICKED CHEAT from the *Bottom to the Top*; and several *smart Votes* were printed, which that same WOOD had the Assurance to answer likewise in *Print*, and in so confident a Way, as if he were *a better Man than our whole Parliament* put together.

THIS WOOD, as soon as his *Patent* was passed, or soon after, sends over a great many *Barrels of those* HALF-PENCE, to *Cork* and other *Sea-Port Towns*, and to get them off, offered an *Hundred Pounds* in his *Coin* for *Seventy* or *Eighty* in *Silver*: But the *Collectors* of the KING'S Customs very honestly refused to take them, and so did almost every body else. And since the Parliament hath condemned them, and desired the KING that they might be stopped, all the *Kingdom* do abominate them.

BUT WOOD is still working *under hand* to force his HALF-PENCE upon us; and if he can by help of his *Friends* in *England* prevail so far as to get an Order that the *Commissioners* and *Collectors* of the *King's* Money shall receive them, and that the *Army* is to be paid with them, then he thinks *his Work shall be done*. And this is the Difficulty you will be under in such a *Case*: For the common Soldier when he goes to the *Market* or *Ale-house*, will offer this Money, and if it be refused, perhaps he will *swagger* and *hector*, and *threaten* to *beat* the *Butcher* or *Ale-wife*, or take the Goods by Force, and throw them the bad HALF-PENCE. In this and the like Cases, the *Shop-keeper*, or *Victualler*, or *any other Tradesman* has no more to do, than to demand ten times the Price of his Goods, if it is to be paid in WOOD'S Money; for Example, Twenty Pence of that Money for a *Quart of Ale*, and so in all things else, and not part with his Goods till he gets the *Money*.

FOR suppose you go to an *Ale-house* with that base Money, and the *Landlord* gives you a Quart for Four of these HALF-PENCE, what must the *Victualler* do? His *Brewer* will not be paid in that Coin, or if the *Brewer* should be such a Fool, the *Farmers* will not take it from them for their *Bere*,[7] because they are bound by their Leases to pay their Rents in Good and Lawful Money of *England*, which this is not, nor of *Ireland* neither, and the *Squire their Landlord* will never be so bewitched to take such *Trash* for his Land; so that it must certainly stop somewhere or other, and wherever it stops it is the same Thing, and we are all undone.

7. barley.

THE common Weight of these HALF-PENCE is between four and five to an *Ounce*; suppose five, then three Shillings and four Pence will weigh a Pound, and consequently *Twenty Shillings* will weigh *Six Pounds Butter Weight*. Now there are many hundred *Farmers* who pay Two hundred Pounds a Year Rent: Therefore when one of these *Farmers* comes with his Half-Year's Rent, which is One hundred Pound, it will be at least Six hundred Pound weight, which is Three Horses Load.

IF a *Squire* has a mind to come to Town to buy Cloaths and Wine and Spices for himself and Family, or perhaps to pass the Winter here; he must bring with him five or six Horses loaden with *Sacks* as the *Farmers* bring their Corn; and when his Lady comes in her Coach to our Shops, it must be followed by a Car loaded with Mr. WOOD'S Money. And I hope we shall have the Grace to take it for no more than it is worth.

THEY say SQUIRE CONNOLLY[8] has *Sixteen Thousand Pounds a Year*; now if he sends for his *Rent* to Town, *as it is likely he does*, he must have *Two Hundred and Fifty Horses* to bring up his *Half Year's Rent*, and two or three great *Cellars* in his House for Stowage. But what the Bankers will do I cannot tell. For I am assured, that some great Bankers keep by them *Forty Thousand Pounds* in ready Cash to answer all Payments, which Sum in Mr. WOOD'S Money, would require Twelve Hundred Horses to carry it.

FOR my own Part, I am already resolved what to do; I have a pretty good Shop of *Irish Stuffs*[9] and *Silks*, and instead of taking Mr. WOOD'S bad Copper, I intend to Truck[10] with my Neighbours the *Butchers*, and *Bakers*, and *Brewers*, and the rest, *Goods for Goods*, and the little *Gold* and *Silver* I have, I will keep by me like my *Heart's Blood* till better Times, or until I am just ready to starve, and then I will buy Mr. WOOD'S Money, as my Father did the Brass Money in King *James*'s Time;[11] who could buy *Ten Pound* of it with a *Guinea*,[12] and I hope to get as much for a *Pistole*,[13] and so purchase *Bread* from those who will be such Fools as to sell it me.

8. William Conolly (?-1729), Speaker of the Irish House of Commons.
9. tweeds.
10. barter.
11. In 1689-90, King James II issued base copper coins to pay his troops in Ireland. They were still remembered in the 1720s.
12. See note 1 above.
13. A Spanish gold coin worth about 18 shillings.

THESE *Half-pence,* if they once pass, will soon be *Counterfeit,* because it may be cheaply done, the *Stuff* is so *Base*. The *Dutch* likewise will probably do the same thing, and send them over to us to pay for our *Goods*; and Mr. WOOD will never be at rest, but coin on: So that in some Years we shall have at least five Times 108000 *l.* of this *Lumber*.[14] Now the current Money of this Kingdom is not reckoned to be above Four Hundred Thousand Pounds in all; and while there is a *Silver* Six-Pence left, these *Blood-suckers* will never be quiet.

WHEN once the *Kingdom* is reduced to such a Condition, I will tell you what must be the End: The *Gentlemen of Estates* will all turn off their *Tenants* for want of Payment; because, as I told you before, the *Tenants* are obliged by their Leases to pay *Sterling,* which is Lawful Current Money of *England*; then they will turn their own *Farmers, as too many of them do already,* run *all* into *Sheep*[15] where they can, keeping only such other *Cattle* as are necessary; then they will be their own *Merchants,* and send their *Wool,* and *Butter,* and *Hides,* and *Linnen* beyond Sea for ready *Money,* and *Wine,* and *Spices,* and *Silks.* They will keep only a few miserable *Cottagers*.[16] The *Farmers* must *Rob* or *Beg,* or leave their *Country*. The *Shop-keepers* in this and every other Town, must *Break*[17] and *Starve*: For it is the *Landed-man* that maintains the *Merchant,* and *Shop-keeper,* and *Handicrafts-Man.*

BUT when the *Squire* turns *Farmer* and *Merchant* himself, all the good Money he gets from abroad, he will hoard up to send for *England,* and keep some poor *Taylor* or *Weaver,* and the like, in his own House, who will be glad to get Bread at any Rate.

I SHOULD never have done, if I were to tell you all the Miseries that we shall undergo, if we be so *Foolish* and *Wicked* as to take this *Cursed Coin.* It would be very hard, if all *Ireland* should be put into *One Scale,* and *this sorry Fellow* WOOD *into the other*: That Mr. WOOD should weigh down *this whole Kingdom,* by which *England* gets above a Million of good Money every Year clear into their *Pockets*: And that is more than the *English* do by *all the World besides.*

BUT your *great Comfort is,* that, as his Majesty's *Patent* doth not oblige you to take this *Money,* so the *Laws* have not given the *Crown* a Power of forcing the *Subjects* to take what *Money* the *King* pleases: For then by the same Reason we might be bound to take *Pebble-stones,* or *Cockle-shells,* or *stamped Leather* for *Current Coin*; if ever we should happen to live under an ill *Prince*; who might likewise by the same Power makes a *Guinea* pass for Ten Pounds, a *Shilling* for Twenty Shillings, and so on; by which he would in a short Time get all the *Silver* and *Gold* of the *Kingdom* into his own Hands, and leave us nothing but *Brass* or *Leather,* or what he pleased. Neither is any thing reckoned more *Cruel* or *Oppressive* in the *French Government,* than their common Practice of calling in all their Money after they have sunk it very low, and then coining it a-new at much higher Value; which however is not the Thousandth Part so wicked as this *abominable Project* of Mr. *Wood.* For the *French* give their Subjects *Silver* for *Silver,* and *Gold* for *Gold*; but this *Fellow* will not so much as give us good *Brass* or *Copper* for our *Gold* and *Silver,* nor even a Twelfth Part of their Worth.

HAVING said this much, I will now go on to tell you the Judgments of some great *Lawyers* in this Matter; whom I fee'd on purpose for your Sakes, and got their *Opinions* under their *Hands,* that I might be sure I went upon good Grounds.

A Famous Law-Book *called the* Mirrour of Justice,[18] *discoursing of the Charters (or Laws) ordained by our* Ancient Kings, *declares the* Law *to be as follows: It was ordained that no* King *of this Realm should* Change, *or* Impair *the* Money, *or make any other* Money *than of* Gold *or* Silver *without the Assent of all the Counties, that is,* as my Lord *Coke* says,[19] *without the Assent of* Parliament.

THIS Book is very Ancient, and of great Authority for the Time in which it was wrote, and with that Character is often quoted by that great Lawyer my Lord *Coke.* By the Laws of *England,* the several Metals are divided into *Lawful* or *true Metal* and *unlawful* or *false Metal*; the Former comprehends *Silver* or *Gold,* the Latter all *Baser Metals*: That the Former is only to pass in Payments, appears by an Act of *Parliament* made the Twentieth Year of *Edward* the *First,* called the *Statute concerning the passing of Pence*; which I give

14. rubbish.
15. The keeping of sheep was increasing in Ireland; see note 1 to *A Proposal. . . .* above.
16. i.e. very poor tenants on annual leases of small plots.
17. go bankrupt.
18. *The Mirror of Justice* by Andrew Horne (died 1328).
19. Sir Edward Coke (1552-1634), a famous judge and author of law texts.

you here as I got it translated into *English*; For some of our *Laws* at that time were, as I am told, writ in *Latin: Whoever in Buying or Selling presumeth to refuse an Half-penny or Farthing of Lawful Money, bearing the Stamp which it ought to have, let him be seized on as a Contemner*[20] of the King's Majesty, and cast into Prison.

BY this *Statute*, no Person is to be reckoned a *Contemner* of the *King's Majesty*, and for that Crime to be *committed to Prison*; but he who refuseth to accept the King's Coin made of *Lawful Metal*: by which as I observed before, *Silver* and *Gold* only are intended.

THAT this is the true *Construction* of the *Act*, appears not only from the plain Meaning of the Words, but from my Lord *Coke*'s Observation upon it. By this Act (says he) it appears, that no Subject can be forced to take in *Buying* or *Selling* or other *Payments*, any Money made but of lawful Metal; that is, of *Silver* or *Gold*.

THE LAW of *England* gives the King all Mines of *Gold* and *Silver*, but not the Mines of other *Metals*; the Reason of which *Prerogative* or *Power*, as it is given by my Lord *Coke*, is because Money can be made of *Gold* and *Silver*; but not of other Metals.

PURSUANT to this Opinion, *Half-pence* and *Farthings* were anciently made of *Silver*, which is evident from the Act of *Parliament* of *Henry* the IVth. Chap. 4. whereby it is enacted as follows: *Item, for the great Scarcity that is at present within the Realm of* England *of Half-pence and Farthings of* Silver; *it is ordained and established, that the Third Part of all the* Money *of* Silver Plate *which shall be brought to the* Bullion,[21] *shall be made in* Half-pence *and* Farthings. This shews that by the Words *Half-penny* and *Farthing* of Lawful Money in that Statute concerning the *passing of* Pence, is meant a small Coin in *Half-pence* and *Farthings* of *Silver*.

THIS is further manifest from the Statute of the Ninth Year of *Edward* the IIId. Chap. 3. which enacts, *That no sterling* Half-penny *or* Farthing *be Molten for to make Vessels,*[22] *or any other thing by the Gold-smiths, nor others, upon Forfeiture of the* Money *somolten (or melted.)*

BY another Act in this *King*'s Reign, *Black Money* was not to be current in *England*. And by an Act made in the Eleventh Year of his Reign, Chap. 5. *Galley Half-pence* were not to pass: What kind of *Coin* these were I do not know; but I presume they were made of *Base Metal*. And these Acts were no New *Laws*, but further Declarations of the old *Laws* relating to the *Coin*.

THUS the *Law* stands in Relation to *Coin*. Nor is there any Example to the contrary, except one in *Davis*'s *Reports*;[23] who tells us, that in the time of *Tyrone*'s Rebellion, *Queen Elizabeth* ordered *Money* of *mixt Metal* to be coined in the Tower of *London*, and sent over hither for Payment of the *Army*; obliging all People to receive it; and Commanding, that all *Silver Money* should be taken only as *Bullion*, that is, for as much as it weighed. *Davis* tells us several Particulars in this Matter too long here to trouble you with, and that the *Privy Council* of this *Kingdom* obliged a *Merchant* in *England* to receive this *mixt Money* for Goods transmitted hither.

BUT this Proceeding is rejected by all the best Lawyers, as contrary to Law, the *Privy council* here having no such legal Power. And besides it is to be considered, that the *Queen* was then under great Difficulties by a Rebellion in this *Kingdom* assisted from *Spain*. And, whatever is done in great Exigences and dangerous Times, should never be an Example to proceed by in Seasons of *Peace* and *Quietness*.

I WILL now, my dear Friends, to save you the Trouble, set before you in short, what the *Law* obliges you to do; and what it does not oblige you to.

FIRST, you are obliged to take all Money in Payments which is coined by the *King*, and is of the *English* Standard or Weight; provided it to be of *Gold* or *Silver*.

SECONDLY, you are not obliged to take any Money which is not of *Gold* or *Silver*; not only the *Half-pence* or *Farthings* of *England*, but of any other Country. And it is meerly for Convenience, or Ease, that you are content to take them; because the Custom of coining *Silver Half-pence* and *Farthings* hath long been left off; I suppose, on Account of their being subject to be lost.

THIRDLY, Much less are we obliged to take those *Vile Half-pence* of that same *Wood*, by which you must lose almost *Eleven*-Pence in every Shilling.

THEREFORE, my Friends, stand to it One and All:

20. despiser.
21. The Royal Mint.
22. = silver plates and bowls.
23. Legal reports by Sir John Davies (1569-1626), attorney general of Ireland 1606-19.

Refuse this *Filthy Trash.* It is no Treason to rebel against Mr. *Wood.* His *Majesty* in his Patent obliges no body to take these *Half-pence*: Our *Gracious Prince* hath no such ill Advisers about him; or if he had, yet you see the Laws have not left it in the *King's* Power, to force us to take any Coin but what is Lawful, of right Standard, *Gold* and *Silver.* Therefore you have nothing to fear.

AND let me in the next Place apply my self particularly to you who are the poorer Sort of *Tradesmen*: Perhaps you may think you will not be so great Losers as the Rich, if these *Half-pence* should pass; because you seldom see any *Silver,* and your Customers come to your Shops or Stalls with nothing but *Brass*; which you likewise find hard to be got. But you may take my Word, whenever this Money gains Footing among you, you will be utterly undone. If you carry these *Half-pence* to a Shop for *Tobacco* or *Brandy,* or any other Thing you want; the Shop-keeper will advance his Goods accordingly, or else he must break and leave the *Key under the Door.* Do you think I will sell you a Yard of Ten-penny Stuff for Twenty of Mr. *Wood's Half-pence*? No, not under Two Hundred at least; neither will I be at the Trouble of counting, but weigh them in a Lump. I will tell you one Thing further; that if Mr. *Wood's* Project should take, it will ruin even our Beggars: For when I give a Beggar a Half-penny, it will quench his Thirst, or go a good Way to fill his Belly; but the Twelfth Part of Half-penny will do him no more Service than if I should give him three Pins out of my Sleeve.

IN short; these *Half-pence* are like the *accursed Thing,*[24] which, as the *Scripture* tells us, the *Children of Israel* were forbidden to touch. They will run about like the *Plague* and destroy every one who lays his Hands upon them. I have heard *Scholars* talk of a Man who told the King that he had invented a Way to torment People by putting them into a *Bull* of Brass with Fire under it:[25] But the *Prince* put the *Projector* first into his own *Brazen Bull* to make the Experiment. This very much resembles the Project of Mr. *Wood*; and the like of this may possibly be Mr. *Wood's* Fate; that the *Brass* he contrived to torment this *Kingdom* with, may prove his own Torment, and his Destruction at last.

24. Joshua 6.18.
25. Perillus of Athens, who invented a brazen bull in which the Sicilian tyrant Phalaris could torture his captives, was roasted in it and became its first victim.

N.B. The Author of this Paper is informed by Persons who have made it their Business to be exact in their Observations on the true Value of these *Half-pence*; that any Person may expect to get a Quart of Two-penny Ale for Thirty Six of them.

I DESIRE that all Families may keep this Paper carefully by them to refresh their Memories whenever they shall have farther Notice of Mr. *Wood's* Half-pence, or any other the like Imposture.

from: LETTER TO ALEXANDER POPE (1725)

[In this important letter, Swift explains to Alexander Pope the principle upon which *Gulliver's Travels* is founded — the revision of the old definition of man as a rational animal to one of him as an animal capable of reason. This very phrase occurs several times in *Gulliver's Travels* and explains clearly how Swift meant his readers to take the traveller's tale. The spelling and punctuation are Swift's.]

Sep. 29. 1725

. . . I am now returning to the noble Scene of Dublin[1] in to the Grande Monde, for fearing of burying my parts[2] to Signalise[3] my self among Curates and Vicars, and correct all Corruption crept in relating to the weight of Bread and Butter through those Dominions where I govern.[4] I have employd my time (besides ditching) in finishing correcting, amending, and Transcribing my Travells,[5] in four parts Compleat newly Augmented, and intended for the press when the world shall deserve them, or rather when a Printer shall be found brave enough to venture his Eares,[6] I like your Schemes of our meeting after Distresses

1. Swift had spent the summer at his house at Laracor in County Meath — hence the reference to ditching a few lines below.
2. abilities or talents.
3. to make conspicuous.
4. As dean of St Patrick's, Swift was secular administrator and governor of the dean's Liberty, the area of the city immediately around the cathedral.
5. i.e. *Gulliver's Travels.*
6. Those who printed seditious work were sometimes punished by having their ears cut off.

and dispertions but the chief end I propose to my self in all my labors is to vex the world rather then divert it, and if I could compass that designe without hurting my own person or Fortune I would be the most Indefatigable writer you have ever seen without reading. I am exceedingly pleased that you have done with Translations[7] Lord Treasurer Oxford often lamented that a rascaly World should lay under a Necessity of Misemploying your Genius for so long a time. But since you will now be so much better employd when you think of the World give it one lash the more at my Request. I have ever hated all Nations professions and Communityes and all my love is towards individualls for instance I hate the tribe of Lawyers, but I love Councellor such a one, Judge such a one for so with Physicians (I will not Speak of my own Trade) Soldiers, English, Scotch, French; and the rest but principally I hate and detest that animal called man, although I hartily love John, Peter, Thomas and so forth. this is the system upon which I have governed my self many years (but do not tell) and so I shall go on till I have done with them I have got Materials Towards a Treatis proving the falsity of that Definition *animal rationale*; and to show it should be only *rationis capax*.[8] Upon this great foundation of Misanthropy (though not Timons manner)[9] The whole building of my Travells is erected: And I never will have peace of mind till all honest men are of my Opinion: by Consequence you are to embrace it immediatly and procure that all who deserve my Esteem may do so too. The matter is so clear that it will admit little dispute. nay I will hold a hundred pounds that you and I agree in the Point.

I did not know your Odyssey was finished being yet in the Country, which I shall leave in three days I shall thank you kindly for the Present but shall like it three fourths the less from the mixture you mention of another hand,[10] however I am glad you saved yourself so much drudgery — I have been long told by Mr Ford[11] of your great Atchivements in building and planting and especially of your Subterranean Passage to your Garden whereby you turned a blunder into a beauty which is a Piece of Ars Poetica.[12]

I have almost done with Harridans[13] and shall soon become old enough to fall in love with Girls of Fourteen. The Lady whom you describe to live at Court,[14] to be deaf and no party Woman, I take to be Mythology but know not how to moralize it. She cannot be Mercy, for mercy is neither deaf nor lives at Court Justice is blind and perhaps deaf but neither is she a Court Lady. Fortune is both blind and deaf and a Court Lady, but then she is a most Damnable party Woman,[15] and will never make me easy as you promise. It must be riches which Answers all your description; I am glad she visites you but my voice is so weak that I doubt she will never[16] hear me.

Mr Lewis[17] sent me an Account of Dr Arbuthnett's[18] Illness which is a very sensible[19] Affliction to me, who by living so long out of the World have lost that hardness of Heart contracted by years and generall Conversation. I am daily loosing Friends, and neither seeking nor getting others. O, if the World had but a dozen Arbuthnetts in it I would burn my Travells but however he is not without Fault. There is a passage in Bede[20] highly commending the Piety and learning of the Irish in that Age, where after abundance of praises he overthrows them all by lamenting that, Alas, they kept Easter at a wrong time of the Year. So our Doctor has every Quality and virtue that can make a man amiable or usefull, but alas he hath a sort of Slouch in his Walk. I pray god protect him for he is an excellent Christian tho not a Catholick and as fit a man either to dy or Live as ever I knew.

I hear nothing of our Friend Gay,[21] but I find the Court keeps him at hard Meat I advised him to come over here with a Lord Lieutenant. Mr Tickell[22] is in a very good Office I have not seen

7. Pope had just finished his very lucrative translations of Homer.
8. *animal rationale* = rational animal; *rationis capax* = capable of reason.
9. The misanthropic Timon curses mankind in Lucian's dialogue.
10. Elijah Fenton (1683-1730), a minor poet and dramatist, helped Pope in his translation of Homer's *Odyssey*; the other assistant was the even lesser poet and translator William Broome (1689-1745).
11. Charles Ford (1682-1741), close friend of Swift.
12. Pope's house and his garden were on opposite sides of the road at Twickenham, near London; he gained access to the garden by building an underground passage and incorporating in it a grotto full of unusual stones. *Ars poetica* = the art of poetry.
13. haggard old women.
14. Henrietta Hobart, wife of Charles Howard (*c.*1688-1767), earl of Suffolk.
15. i.e. supporter of one political party.
16. i.e. ever.
17. Erasmus Lewis (1670-1754), statesman and friend of Swift.
18. Dr John Arbuthnot (1667-1735), Scotsman, physician and close friend of Swift.
19. keenly felt.
20. *A History of the English Church and People*, III, 3.
21. John Gay (1685-1732), dramatist and friend of Swift.
22. Thomas Tickell (1686-1740), poet.

Philips,[23] tho' formerly we were so intimate He has got nothing, and by what I can find will get nothing though he writes little Flams[24] (as Lord Leicester call'd those sort of Verses) on Miss Carteret[25] and others. it is remarkable and deserves recording that a Dublin Blacksmith a great poet hath imitated his manner in a Poem to the same Miss. Philips is a Complainer, and on this Occation I told Lord Carteret that Complainers never Succeed at Court though Railers do.

Are you altogether a Country Gentleman that I must Address to you out of London to the Hazard of your losing this pretious Letter, which I will now Conclude although so much Paper is left. I have an ill name and therefore shall not Subscribe it. but you will guess it comes from one who esteems and loves you about half as much as you deserve. I mean as much as he can.

I am in great concern at which I am just told is in some News Paper that Lord Bolingbroke[26] is much hurt by a fall in Hunting I am glad he has so much youth and Viger left of which he hath not been thrifty but I wonder he has no more Discretion.

23. Ambrose Philips (1674-1749), poet.
24. Verses with very short lines addressed to the children of nobility.
25. Daughter of John, Lord Carteret (1690-1763), friend of Swift.
26. Henry St John (1678-1751), viscount Bolingbroke, secretary of state 1710-14 and longstanding friend of Swift.

from: TRAVELS INTO SEVERAL REMOTE NATIONS OF THE WORLD *BY LEMUEL GULLIVER*

[Gulliver's Travels] (1726)

[In Swift's most famous work, known as *Gulliver's Travels,* the narrator, Captain Lemuel Gulliver, recounts his adventures on four separate voyages: he visits, successively, the kingdom of Lilliput which is inhabited by minute people, the kingdom of Brobdingnag which is inhabited by giants, the land of Laputa where the inhabitants are obsessed with abstract science, and Houyhnhnmland where rational horses rule degenerate humans called Yahoos. As he explained in his letter to Pope (printed above), Swift was redefining man in *Gulliver's Travels,* and Part IV, which we have selected for this anthology, gives the best demonstration of his technique and of its success.

A glossary of unfamiliar words and terms is printed at the end of the text (p. 386); words listed in the glossary are marked thus.[0]]

PART IV

A VOYAGE TO THE COUNTRY OF THE HOUYHNHNMS[1]

CHAPTER I

The Author sets out as Captain of a Ship. His Men conspire against him, confine him a long Time to his Cabbin, set him on Shore in an unknown Land. He travels up into the Country. The Yahoos, *a strange Sort of Animal, described. The Author meets two* Houyhnhnms.

I continued at home with my Wife and Children about five Months in a very happy Condition, if I could have learned the Lesson of knowing when I was well. I left my poor Wife big with Child, and accepted an advantageous Offer made me to be Captain of the *Adventure,* a stout Merchant-man of 350 Tuns: For I understood Navigation well, and being grown weary of a Surgeon's Employment at Sea, which however I could exercise upon Occasion, I took a skilful young Man of that Calling, one *Robert Purefoy* into my Ship. We set sail from *Portsmouth* upon the 7th Day of *September,* 1710; on the 14th we met with Captain *Pocock* of *Bristol,* at *Tenariff,*[2] who was going to the Bay of *Campeachy,*[3] to cut Logwood. On the 16th he was parted from us by a Storm: I heard since my Return, that his Ship foundered, and none escaped, but one Cabbin-Boy. He was an honest Man and a good Sailor, but a little too positive in his own Opinions, which was the Cause of his Destruction, as it hath been of several others. For if he had followed my Advice, he might at this Time have been safe at home with his Family as well as my self.

I had several Men died in my Ship of

1. Pronounced 'Whinnims', suggesting the sound made by horses.
2. Tenerife, one of the Canary Islands.
3. The bay of Campeche, on the west of the Yucatan peninsula, Mexico.

Calentures,[0] so that I was forced to get Recruits out of *Barbadoes,* and the *Leeward Islands,* where I touched by the Direction of the Merchants who employed me; which I had soon too much Cause to repent; for I found afterwards that most of them had been Buccaneers.[0] I had fifty Hands on Board; and my Orders were, that I should trade with the *Indians* in the *South-Sea*, and make what Discoveries I could. These Rogues whom I had picked up, debauched,[0] my other Men, and they all formed a Conspiracy to seize the Ship and secure me; which they did one Morning, rushing into my Cabbin, and binding me Hand and Foot, threatening to throw me overboard, if I offered to stir. I told them, I was their Prisoner, and would submit. This they made me swear to do, and then unbound me, only fastening one of my Legs with a Chain near my Bed; and placed a Centry at my Door with his Piece[0] charged, who was commanded to shoot me dead if I attempted my Liberty. They sent me down Victuals and Drink, and took the Government of the Ship to themselves. Their Design was to turn Pirates, and plunder the *Spaniards,* which they could not do, till they got more Men. But first they resolved to sell the Goods in the Ship, and then go to *Madagascar* for Recruits, several among them having died since my Confinement. They sailed many Weeks, and traded with the *Indians*; but I knew not what Course they took, being kept close Prisoner in my Cabbin, and expecting nothing less than to be murdered, as they often threatened me.

Upon the 9th Day of *May*, 1711, one *James Welch* came down to my Cabbin; and said he had Orders from the Captain to set me ashore. I expostulated with him, but in vain; neither would he so much as tell me who their new Captain was. They forced me into the Long-boat, letting me put on my best Suit of Cloaths, which were as good as new, and a small Bundle of Linnen, but no Arms except my Hanger;[0] and they were so civil as not to search my Pockets, into which I conveyed what Money I had, with some other little Necessaries. They rowed about a League;[0] and then set me down on a Strand. I desired them to tell me what Country it was: They all swore, they knew no more than my self, but said, that the Captain (as they called him) was resolved, after they had sold the Lading,[0] to get rid of me in the first Place where they discovered Land. They pushed off immediately, advising me to make haste, for fear of being overtaken by the Tide; and bade me farewell.

In this desolate Condition I advanced forward, and soon got upon firm Ground, where I sat down on a Bank to rest my self, and consider what I had best to do. When I was a little refreshed, I went up into the Country, resolving to deliver my self to the first Savages I should meet; and purchase my Life from them by some Bracelets, Glass Rings, and other Toys,[0] which Sailors usually provide themselves with in those Voyages, and whereof I had some about me: The Land was divided by long Rows of Trees, not regularly planted, but natural growing; there was great Plenty of Grass, and several Fields of Oats. I walked very circumspectly for fear of being surprised, or suddenly shot with an Arrow from behind, or on either Side. I fell into a beaten Road, where I saw many Tracks of human Feet, and some of Cows, but most of Horses. At last I beheld several Animals in a Field, and one or two of the same Kind sitting in Trees. Their Shape was very singular, and deformed, which a little discomposed me, so that I lay down behind a Thicket to observe them better. Some of them coming forward near the Place where I lay, gave me an Opportunity of distinctly marking their Form. Their Heads and Breasts were covered with a thick Hair, some frizzled and others lank; they had Beards like Goats, and a Long Ridge of Hair down their Backs, and the fore Parts of their Legs and Feet; but the rest of their Bodies were bare, so that I might see their Skins, which were of a brown Buff Colour. They had no Tails, nor any Hair at all on their Buttocks, except about the *Anus*; which, I presume Nature had placed there to defend them as they sat on the Ground; for this Posture they used, as well as lying down, and often stood on their hind Feet. They climbed high Trees, as nimbly as a Squirrel, for they had strong extended Claws before and behind, terminating on sharp Points, hooked. They would often spring, and bound, and leap with prodigious Agility. The Females were not so large as the Males; they had long lank Hair on their Heads, and only a Sort of Down on the rest of their Bodies, except about the *Anus,* and *Pudenda*. Their Dugs[0] hung between their fore Feet, and often reached almost to the Ground as they walked. The Hair of both Sexes was of several Colours, brown, red, black and yellow. Upon the whole, I never beheld in all my Travels so disagreeable an Animal, or one against which I naturally conceived so strong an Antipathy. So that thinking I had seen enough, full of Contempt and Aversion, I got up and pursued the beaten Road, hoping it might direct me to the Cabbin of some *Indian.* I had not gone far when I met one of these Creatures full in my Way, and coming up directly to me. The ugly Monster, when he saw me, distorted several Ways every Feature of his Visage, and stared as at an Object he had never seen before; then approaching nearer, lifted up his fore Paw, whether out of Curiosity or Mischief, I could not tell: But I drew my Hanger, and gave him a good Blow with the flat Side of it; for I durst not strike him with the Edge, fearing the Inhabitants might be provoked against me, if they should come to know, that I had killed or maimed any of their Cattle.[0] When the Beast felt the Smart, he drew back, and roared so loud, that a Herd of at least forty came flocking about me from the next Field, howling and making odious Faces; but I ran to the Body of a Tree, and leaning my Back against it, kept them off, by waving my Hanger. Several of this cursed Brood getting hold of the Branches behind, leaped up into the Tree, from whence they began to discharge their Excrements on my Head: However, I escaped pretty well, by sticking close to the Stem of the Tree, but was almost stifled with the Filth, which fell about me on every Side.

In the Midst of this Distress, I observed them all to run away on a sudden as fast as they could; at which I ventured to leave the Tree, and pursue the Road, wondering what it was that could put them into this Fright. But looking on my Left-Hand, I saw a Horse walking softly in the Field; which my Persecutors having sooner discovered, was the Cause of their Flight. The Horse started a little when he came near me, but soon recovering himself, looked full in my Face with manifest Tokens of Wonder: He viewed my Hands and Feet, walking round me several times. I would have pursued my Journey, but he placed himself directly in the Way, yet looking with a very mild Aspect, never offering the least Violence. We stood gazing at each other for some time; at last I took the Boldness, to reach my Hand towards his Neck, with a Design to stroak it; using the common Style and Whistle of Jockies when they are going to handle a strange Horse. But, this Animal seeming to receive my Civilities with Disdain, shook his Head, and bent his Brows, softly raising up his Left Fore-Foot to remove my Hand. Then he neighed three or four times, but in so different a Cadence, that I almost began to think he was speaking to himself in some Language of his own.

While He and I were thus employed, another Horse came up; who applying himself to[0] the first in a very formal Manner, they gently struck each others Right Hoof before, neighing several times by Turns, and varying the Sound, which seemed to be almost articulate. They went some Paces off, as if it were to confer together, walking Side by Side, backward and forward, like Persons deliberating upon some Affair of Weight; but often turning their Eyes towards me, as it were to watch that I might not escape. I was amazed to see such Actions and Behaviour in Brute Beasts; and concluded with myself, that if the Inhabitants of this Country were endued[0] with a proportionable Degree of Reason, they must needs be the wisest People upon Earth. This Thought gave me so much Comfort, that I resolved to go forward until I could discover some House or Village, or meet with any of the Natives; leaving the two Horses to discourse together as they pleased. But the first, who was a Dapple-Grey, observing me to steal off, neighed after me in so expressive a Tone, that I fancied myself to understand what he meant; whereupon I turned back, and came near him, to expect his farther Commands; but concealing my Fear as much as I could; for I began to be in some Pain, how this Adventure might terminate: and the Reader will easily believe I did not much like my present Situation.

The two Horses came up close to me, looking with great Earnestness upon my Face and Hands. The grey Steed rubbed my Hat all round with his Right Fore-hoof, and discomposed it so much, that I was forced to adjust it better, by taking it off, and settling it again; whereat both he and his Companion (who was a brown Bay) appeared to be much surprized; the latter felt the Lappet[0] of my Coat, and finding it to hang loose about me, they both looked with new Signs of Wonder. He stroked my Right Hand, seeming to admire the Softness, and Colour; but he squeezed it so hard between his Hoof and his Pastern,[0] that I was forced to roar; after which they both touched me with all possible Tenderness. They were under great Perplexity about my Shoes and Stockings, which they felt very often, neighing to each other, and using various

Gestures, not unlike those of a Philosopher,[4] when he would attempt to solve some new and difficult Phænomenon.

Upon the whole, the Behaviour of these Animals was so orderly and rational, so acute and judicious, that I at last concluded, they must needs be Magicians, who had thus metamorphosed themselves upon some Design; and seeing a Stranger in the Way, were resolved to divert themselves with him; or perhaps were really amazed at the Sight of a Man so very different in Habit, Feature and Complexion from those who might probably live in so remote a Climate.[0] Upon the Strength of this Reasoning, I ventured to address them in the following Manner: Gentlemen, if you be Conjurers, as I have good Cause to believe, you can understand any Language; therefore I make bold to let your Worships know, that I am a poor distressed *Englishman*, driven by his Misfortunes upon your Coast; and I entreat one of you, to let me ride upon his Back, as if he were a real Horse, to some House or Village, where I can be relieved. In return of which Favour, I will make you a Present of this Knife and Bracelet, (taking them out of my Pocket). The two Creatures stood silent while I spoke, seeming to listen with great Attention; and when I had ended, they neighed frequently towards each other, as if they were engaged in serious Conversation. I plainly observed, that their Language expressed the Passions very well, and the Words might with little Pains be resolved into an Alphabet more easily than the *Chinese*.

I could frequently distinguish the Word *Yahoo*, which was repeated by each of them several times; and although it were impossible for me to conjecture what it meant, yet while the two Horses were busy in Conversation, I endeavoured to practice this Word upon my Tongue; and as soon as they were silent, I boldly pronounced *Yahoo* in a loud Voice, imitating, at the same time, as near as I could, the Neighing of a Horse; at which they were both visibly surprized, and the Grey repeated the same Word twice, as if he meant to teach me the right Accent, wherein I spoke after him as well as I could, and found myself perceivably to improve every time, although very far from any Degree of Perfection. Then the Bay tried me with a second Word, much harder to be pronounced; but reducing it to the *English Orthography*, may be spelt thus, *Houyhnhnm*. I did not succeed in this so well as the former, but after two or three farther Trials, I had better Fortune; and they both appeared amazed at my Capacity.

After some farther Discourse, which I then conjectured might relate to me, the two Friends took their Leaves, with the same Compliment of striking each other's Hoof; and the Grey made me Signs that I should walk before him; wherein I thought it prudent to comply, till I could find a better Director. When I offered to slacken my Pace, he would cry *Hhuun, Hhuun*; I guessed his Meaning, and gave him to understand, as well as I could, that I was weary, and not able to walk faster; upon which, he would stand a while to let me rest.

CHAPTER II

The Author conducted by a Houyhnhnm *to his House. The House described. The Author's Reception. The Food of the* Houyhnhnms. *The Author in Distress for want of Meat, is at last relieved. His Manner of feeding in that Country.*

Having travelled about three Miles, we came to a long Kind of Building, made of Timber, stuck in the Ground, and wattled a-cross; the Roof was low, and covered with Straw. I now began to be a little comforted; and took out some Toys,[0] which Travellers usually carry for Presents to the Savage *Indians* of *America* and other Parts, in hopes the People of the House would be thereby encouraged to receive me kindly. The Horse made me a Sign to go in first; it was a large Room with a smooth Clay Floor, and a Rack and Manger extending the whole Length on one Side. There were three Nags, and two Mares, not eating, but some of them sitting down upon their Hams,[0] which I very much wondered at; but wondered more to see the rest employed in domestick Business: The last seemed but ordinary Cattle; however this confirmed my first Opinion, that a People who could so far civilize brute Animals, must needs excel in Wisdom all the Nations of the World. The Grey came in just after, and thereby prevented any ill Treatment, which the others might have given me. He neighed to them several times in a Style of Authority, and received Answers.

Beyond this Room there were three others,

4. i.e. a natural philosopher or scientist.

reaching the Length of the House, to which you passed through three Doors, opposite to each other, in the Manner of a Vista: We went through the second Room towards the third; here the Grey walked in first, beckoning me to attend:[5] I waited in the second Room, and got ready my Presents, for the Master and Mistress of the House; They were two Knives, three Bracelets of false Pearl, a small Looking Glass and a Bead Necklace. The Horse neighed three or four Times, and I waited to hear some Answers in a human Voice, but I heard no other Returns than in the same Dialect, only one or two a little shriller than his. I began to think that this House must belong to some Person of great Note among them, because there appeared so much ceremony before I could gain Admittance. But, that a Man of Quality should be served all by Horses, was beyond my Comprehension. I feared my Brain was disturbed by my Sufferings and Misfortunes: I roused my self, and looked about me in the Room where I was left alone; this was furnished as the first, only after a more elegant Manner. I rubbed mine Eyes often, but the same Objects still occurred. I pinched my Arms and Sides, to awake my self, hoping I might be in a Dream. I then absolutely concluded, that all these Appearances could be nothing else but Necromancy[0] and Magick. But I had no Time to pursue these Reflections; for the Grey Horse came to the Door, and made me a Sign to follow him into the third Room; where I saw a very comely Mare, together with a Colt and Fole, sitting on their Haunches, upon Mats of Straw, not unartfully made, and perfectly neat and clean.

The Mare soon after my Entrance, rose from her Mat, and coming up close, after having nicely[0] observed my Hands and Face, gave me a most contemptuous Look; then turning to the Horse, I heard the Word *Yahoo* often repeated betwixt them; the meaning of which Word I could not then comprehend, although it were the first I had learned to pronounce; but I was soon better informed, to my everlasting Mortification: For the Horse beckoning to me with his Head, and repeating the Word *Hhuun, Hhuun,* as he did upon the Road, which I understood was to attend him, led me out into a kind of Court, where was another Building at some Distance from the House. Here we entered, and I saw three of those detestable Creatures, which I first met after my landing, feeding upon Roots, and the Flesh of some Animals, which I afterwards found to be that of Asses and Dogs, and now and then a Cow dead by Accident or Disease. They were all tied by the Neck with strong Wyths,[0] fastened to a Beam; they held their Food between the Claws of their fore Feet, and tore it with their Teeth.

The Master Horse ordered a Sorrel[0] Nag,[0] one of his Servants, to untie the largest of these Animals, and take him into a Yard. The Beast and I were brought close together; and our Countenances diligently compared, both by Master and Servant, who thereupon repeated several Times the Word *Yahoo.* My Horror and Astonishment are not to be described, when I observed, in this abominable Animal, a perfect human Figure; the Face of it indeed was flat and broad, the Nose depressed, the Lips large, and the Mouth wide: But these Differences are common to all savage Nations, where the Lineaments of the Countenance are distorted by the Natives suffering their Infants to lie grovelling on the Earth, or by carrying them on their Backs, nuzzling with their Face against the Mother's Shoulders. The Fore-feet of the *Yahoo* differed from my Hands in nothing else, but the Length of the Nails, the Coarseness and Brownness of the Palms, and the Hairiness on the Backs. There was the same Resemblance between our Feet, with the same Differences, which I knew very well, although the Horses did not, because of my Shoes and Stockings; the same in every Part of our Bodies, except as to Hairiness and Colour, which I have already described.

The great Difficulty that seemed to stick with the two Horses, was, to see the rest of my Body so very different from that of a *Yahoo,* for which I was obliged to my Cloaths,[0] whereof they had no Conception: The Sorrel Nag offered me a Root, which he held (after their Manner, as we shall describe in its proper Place) between his Hoof and Pastern; I took it in my Hand, and having smelt it, returned it to him again as civilly as I could. He brought out of the *Yahoo*'s Kennel a Piece of Ass's Flesh, but it smelt so offensively that I turned from it with loathing; he then threw it to the *Yahoo,* by whom it was greedily devoured. He afterwards shewed me a Wisp of Hay, and a Fettlock[0] full of Oats; but I shook my Head, to signify, that neither of these were Food for me. And indeed, I now apprehended, that I must absolutely starve, if I did

5. i.e. made a sign to me to wait.

not get to some of my own Species: For as to those filthy *Yahoos,* although there were few greater Lovers of Mankind, at that time, than myself; yet I confess I never saw any sensitive Being so detestable on all Accounts; and the more I came near them, the more hateful they grew, while I stayed in that Country. This the Master Horse observed by my Behaviour, and therefore sent the *Yahoo* back to his Kennel. He then put his Forehoof to his Mouth, at which I was much surprized, although he did it with Ease, and with a Motion that appear'd perfectly natural; and made other Signs to know what I would eat; but I could not return him such an Answer as he was able to apprehend; and if he had understood me, I did not see how it was possible to contrive any way for finding myself Nourishment. While we were thus engaged, I observed a Cow passing by; whereupon I pointed to her, and expressed a Desire to let me go and milk her. This had its Effect; for he led me back into the House, and ordered a Mare-servant to open a Room, where a good Store of Milk lay in Earthen and Wooden Vessels, after a very orderly and cleanly Manner. She gave me a large Bowl full, of which I drank very heartily, and found myself well refreshed.

About Noon I saw coming towards the House a Kind of Vehicle, drawn like a Sledge by four *Yahoos.* There was in it an old Steed, who seemed to be of Quality; he alighted with his Hind-feet forward, having by Accident got a Hurt in his Left Fore-foot. He came to dine with our Horse, who received him with great Civility. They dined in the best Room, and had Oats boiled in Milk for the second Course, which the old Horse eat[0] warm, but the rest cold. Their Mangers were placed circular in the Middle of the Room, and divided into several Partitions, round which they sat on their Haunches upon Bosses[0] of Straw. In the Middle was a large Rack with Angles answering to every Partition of the Manger. So that each Horse and Mare eat their own Hay, and their own Mash of Oats and Milk, with much Decency and Regularity. The Behaviour of the young Colt and Fole appeared very modest; and that of the Master and Mistress extremely chearful and complaisant to their Guest. The Grey ordered me to stand by him; and much Discourse passed between him and his Friend concerning me, as I found by the Stranger's often looking on me, and the frequent Repetition of the Word *Yahoo.*

I happened to wear my Gloves; which the Master Grey observing, seemed perplexed; discovering Signs of Wonder what I had done to my Fore-feet; he put his Hoof three or four times to them, as if he would signify, that I should reduce them to their former Shape, which I presently did, pulling off both my Gloves, and putting them into my Pocket. This occasioned farther Talk, and I saw the Company was pleased with my Behaviour, whereof I soon found the good Effects. I was ordered to speak the few Words I understood; and while they were at Dinner, the Master taught me the Names for Oats, Milk, Fire, Water, and some others; which I could readily pronounce after him; having from my Youth a great Facility in learning Languages.

When Dinner was done, the Master Horse took me aside, and by Signs and Words made me understand the Concern he was in, that I had nothing to eat. Oats in their Tongue are called *Hlunnh.* This Word I pronounced two or three times; for although I had refused them at first, yet upon second Thoughts, I considered that I could contrive to make of them a Kind of Bread, which might be sufficient with Milk to keep me alive, till I could make my Escape to some other Country, and to Creatures of my own Species. The Horse immediately ordered a white Mare-servant of his Family to bring me a good Quantity of Oats in a Sort of wooden Tray. These I heated before the Fire as well as I could, and rubbed them till the Husks came off, which I made a shift to winnow from the Grain; I ground and beat them between two Stones, then took Water, and made them into a Paste or Cake, which I toasted at the Fire, and eat warm with Milk. It was at first a very insipid Diet, although common enough in many Parts of *Europe*, but grew tolerable by Time; and having been often reduced to hard Fare in my Life, this was not the first Experiment I had made how easily Nature is satisfied. And I cannot but observe, that I never had one Hour's Sickness, while I staid in this Island. It is true, I sometimes made a shift to catch a Rabbet, or Bird, by Springes[0] made of *Yahoos* Hairs; and I often gathered wholesome Herbs, which I boiled, or eat as Salades with my Bread; and now and then, for a Rarity, I made a little Butter, and drank the Whey. I was at first at a great Loss for Salt; but Custom soon reconciled the Want of it; and I am confident that the frequent Use of Salt among us is an Effect of Luxury, and was first introduced only as a Provocative to Drink; except where it is necessary for preserving of Flesh in long Voyages, or in Places remote from great Markets. For we observe no Animal to be fond of it but Man: And as to myself, when I left this Country, it was a great while before I could endure the Taste of it in any thing that I eat.

This is enough to say upon the Subject of my Dyet, wherewith other Travellers fill their Books, as if the Readers were personally concerned, whether we fare well or ill. However, it was necessary to mention this Matter, lest the World should think it impossible that I could find Sustenance for three Years in such a Country, and among such Inhabitants.

When it grew towards Evening, the Master Horse ordered a Place for me to lodge in; it was but Six Yards from the House, and separated from the Stable of the *Yahoos.* Here I got some Straw, and covering myself with my own Cloaths, slept very sound. But I was in a short time better accommodated, as the Reader shall know hereafter, when I come to treat more particularly about my Way of living.

CHAPTER III

The Author studious to learn the Language, the Houyhnhnm *his Master assists in teaching him. The Language described. Several* Houyhnhnms *of Quality come out of Curiosity to see the Author. He gives his Master a short Account of his Voyage.*

My principal Endeavour was to learn the Language, which my Master (for so I shall henceforth call him) and his Children, and every Servant of his House were desirous to teach me. For they looked upon it as a Prodigy, that a brute Animal should discover such Marks of a rational Creature. I pointed to every thing, and enquired the Name of it, which I wrote down in my *Journal Book* when I was alone, and corrected my bad Accent, by desiring those of the Family to pronounce it often. In this Employment, a Sorrel Nag, one of the under Servants, was very ready to assist me.

In speaking, they pronounce through the Nose and Throat, and their Language approaches nearest to the *High Dutch* or *German,* of any I know in *Europe*; but is much more graceful and significant. The Emperor *Charles V* made almost the same Observation when he said, That if he were to speak to his Horse, it should be in *High Dutch.*[6]

The Curiosity and Impatience of my Master were so great, that he spent many Hours of his Leisure to instruct me. He was convinced (as he afterwards told me) that I must be a *Yahoo*, but my Teachableness, Civility and Cleanliness astonished him; which were Qualities altogether so opposite to those Animals. He was most perplexed about my Cloaths, reasoning sometimes with himself, whether they were a Part of my Body; for I never pulled them off till the Family were asleep, and got them on before they waked in the Morning. My Master was eager to learn from whence I came; how I acquired those Appearances of Reason, which I discovered in all my Actions; and to know my Story from my own Mouth, which he hoped he should soon do by the great Proficiency I made in learning and pronouncing their Words and Sentences. To help my Memory, I formed all I learned into the *English* Alphabet, and writ the Words down with the Translations. This last, after some time, I ventured to do in my Master's Presence. It cost me much Trouble to explain to him what I was doing; for the Inhabitants have not the least Idea of Books or Literature.

In about ten Weeks time I was able to understand most of his Questions; and in three Months could give him some tolerable Answers. He was extremely curious to know from what Part of the Country I came, and how I was taught to imitate a rational Creature; because the *Yahoos,* (whom he saw I exactly resembled in my Head, Hands and Face, that were only visible,) with some Appearance of Cunning, and the strongest Disposition to Mischief, were observed to be the most unteachable of all Brutes. I answered; that I came over the Sea, from a far Place, with many others of my own Kind, in a great hollow Vessel made of the Bodies of Trees: That, my Companions forced me to land on this Coast, and then left me to shift for myself. It was with some Difficulty, and by the Help of many Signs, that I brought him to understand me. He replied, That I must needs be mistaken, or that I *said the thing which was not.* (For they have no Word in their Language to express Lying or Falshood.) He knew it was impossible that there could be a Country beyond the Sea, or that a Parcel of Brutes could move a wooden Vessel whither they pleased upon Water. He was sure no

6. German.

Houyhnhnm alive could make such a Vessel, or would trust *Yahoos* to manage it.

The Word *Houyhnhnm,* in their Tongue, signifies a *Horse*; and in its Etymology, *the Perfection of Nature.* I told my Master, that I was at a Loss for Expression, but would improve as fast as I could; and hoped in a short time I should be able to tell him Wonders: He was pleased to direct his own Mare, his Colt and Fole, and the Servants of the Family to take all Opportunities of instructing me; and every Day for two or three Hours, he was at the same Pains himself: Several Horses and Mares of Quality in the Neighbourhood came often to our House, upon the Report spread of a wonderful *Yahoo,* that could speak like a *Houyhnhnm,* and seemed in his Words and Actions to discover some Glimmerings of Reason. These delighted to converse with me; they put many Questions, and received such Answers, as I was able to return. By all which Advantages, I made so great a Progress, that in five Months from my Arrival, I understood whatever was spoke, and could express myself tolerably well.

The *Houyhnhnms* who came to visit my Master, out of a Design of seeing and talking with me, could hardly believe me to be a right *Yahoo,* because my Body had a different Covering from others of my Kind. They were astonished to observe me without the usual Hair or Skin, except on my Head, Face and Hands: But I discovered that Secret to my Master, upon an Accident, which happened about a Fortnight before.

I have already told the Reader, that every Night when the Family were gone to Bed, it was my Custom to strip and cover myself with my Cloaths: It happened one Morning early, that my Master sent for me, by the Sorrel Nag, who was his Valet; when he came, I was fast asleep, my Cloaths fallen off on one Side, and my Shirt above my Waste. I awaked at the Noise he made, and observed him to deliver his Message in some Disorder; after which he went to my Master, and in a great Fright gave him a very confused Account of what he had seen: This I presently discovered; for going as soon as I was dressed, to pay my Attendance upon his Honour, he asked me the Meaning of what his Servant had reported; that I was not the same Thing when I slept as I appeared to be at other times; that his Valet assured him, some Part of me was white, some yellow, at least not so white, and some brown.

I had hitherto concealed the Secret of my Dress, in order to distinguish myself as much as possible, from that cursed Race of *Yahoos*; but now I found it in vain to do so any longer. Besides, I considered that my Cloaths and Shoes would soon wear out, which already were in a declining Condition, and must be supplied by some Contrivance from the Hides of *Yahoos,* or other Brutes; whereby the whole Secret would be known. I therefore told my Master, that in the Country from whence I came, those of my Kind always covered their Bodies with the Hairs of certain Animals prepared by Art, as well for Decency, as to avoid Inclemencies of Air both hot and cold; of which, as to my own Person I would give him immediate Conviction, if he pleased to command me; only desiring his Excuse, if I did not expose those Parts that Nature taught us to conceal. He said, my Discourse was all very strange, but especially the last Part; for he could not understand why Nature should teach us to conceal what Nature had given. That neither himself nor Family were ashamed of any Parts of their Bodies; but however I might do as I pleased. Whereupon I first unbuttoned my Coat, and pulled it off. I did the same with my Wastecoat; I drew off my Shoes, Stockings and Breeches. I let my Shirt down to my Waste, and drew up the Bottom, fastening it like a Girdle about my Middle to hide my Nakedness.

My Master observed the whole Performance with great Signs of Curiosity and Admiration. He took up all my Cloaths in his Pastern, one Piece after another, and examined them diligently; he then stroaked my Body very gently, and looked round me several Times; after which he said, it was plain I must be a perfect *Yahoo*; but that I differed very much from the rest of my Species, in the Whiteness, and Smoothness of my Skin, my want of Hair in several Parts of my Body, the Shape and Shortness of my Claws behind and before, and my Affectation of walking continually on my two hinder Feet. He desired to see no more; and gave me leave to put on my Cloaths again, for I was shuddering with Cold.

I expressed my Uneasiness at his giving me so often the Appellation of *Yahoo,* an odious Animal, for which I had so utter an Hatred and Contempt. I begged he would forbear applying that Word to me, and take the same Order in his Family, and among his Friends whom he suffered to see me. I requested likewise, that the Secret of my having a false Covering to my Body might be known to none but himself, at least as long as my present Cloathing should last: For as to what the Sorrel Nag his Valet had observed, his Honour might command him to conceal it.

All this my Master very graciously consented to; and thus the Secret was kept till my Cloaths began to wear out, which I was forced to supply by several Contrivances, that shall hereafter be mentioned. In the mean Time, he desired I would go on with my utmost Diligence to learn their Language, because he was more astonished at my Capacity for Speech and Reason, than at the Figure of my Body, whether it were covered or no; adding, that he waited with some Impatience to hear the Wonders which I promised to tell him.

From thenceforward he doubled the Pains he had been at to instruct me; he brought me into all Company, and made them treat me with Civility, because, as he told them privately, this would put me into good Humour, and make me more diverting.

Every Day when I waited on him, beside the Trouble he was at in teaching, he would ask me several Questions concerning my self, which I answered as well as I could; and by those Means he had already received some general Ideas, although very imperfect. It would be tedious to relate the several Steps, by which I advanced to a more regular Conversation: But the first Account I gave of my self in any Order and Length, was to this Purpose:

That, I came from a very far Country, as I already had attempted to tell him, with about fifty more of my own Species; that we travelled upon the Seas, in a great hollow Vessel made of Wood, and larger than his Honour's House. I described the Ship to him in the best Terms I could; and explained by the Help of my Handkerchief displayed, how it was driven forward by the Wind. That, upon a Quarrel among us, I was set on Shoar on this Coast, where I walked forward without knowing whither, till he delivered me from the Persecution of those execrable *Yahoos*. He asked me, Who made the Ship, and how it was possible that the *Houyhnhnms* of my Country would leave it to the Management of Brutes? My Answer was, that I durst proceed no farther in my Relation, unless he would give me his Word and Honour that he would not be offended; and then I would tell him the Wonders I had so often promised. He agreed; and I went on by assuring him, that the Ship was made by Creatures like myself, who in all the Countries I had travelled, as well as in my own, were the only governing, rational Animals; and that upon my Arrival hither, I was as much astonished to see the *Houyhnhnms* act like rational Beings, as he or his Friends could be in finding some Marks of Reason in a Creature he was pleased to call a *Yahoo*; to which I owned my Resemblance in every Part, but could not account for their degenerate and brutal Nature. I said farther, That if good Fortune ever restored me to my native Country, to relate my Travels hither, as I resolved to do; every Body would believe that I *said the Thing which was not*; that I invented the Story out of my own Head: And with all possible Respect to Himself, his Family, and Friends, and under his Promise of not being offended, our Countrymen would hardly think it probable, that a *Houyhnhnm* should be the presiding Creature of a Nation, and a *Yahoo* the Brute.

CHAPTER IV

The Houyhnhnms *Notion of Truth and Falshood. The Author's Discourse disapproved by his Master. The Author gives a more particular Account of himself, and the Accidents of his Voyage.*

My Master heard me with great Appearances of Uneasiness in his Countenance; because *Doubting* or *not believing*, are so little known in this Country, that the Inhabitants cannot tell how to behave themselves under such Circumstances. And I remember in frequent Discourses with my Master concerning the Nature of Manhood, in other Parts of the World; having Occasion to talk of *Lying*, and *false Representation*, it was with much Difficulty that he comprehended what I meant; although he had otherwise a most acute Judgment. For he argued thus; That the Use of Speech was to make us understand one another, and to receive Information of Facts; now if any one *said the Thing which was not*, these Ends were defeated; because I cannot properly be said to understand him; and I am so far from receiving Information, that he leaves me worse than in Ignorance; for I am led to believe a Thing *Black* when it is *White*, and *Short* when it is *Long*. And these were all the Notions he had concerning that Faculty of *Lying*, so perfectly well understood, and so universally practised among human Creatures.

To return from this Digression; when I asserted

that the *Yahoos* were the only governing Animals in my Country, which my Master said was altogether past his Conception, he desired to know, whether we had *Houyhnhnms* among us, and what was their Employment: I told him, we had great Numbers; that in Summer they grazed in the Fields, and in Winter were kept in Houses, with Hay and Oats, where *Yahoo*-Servants were employed to rub their Skins smooth, comb their Manes, pick their Feet, serve them with Food, and make their Beds. I understand you well, said my Master; it is now very plain from all you have spoken, that whatever Share of Reason the *Yahoos* pretend to, the *Houyhnhnms* are your Masters; I heartily wish our *Yahoos* would be so tractable. I begged his Honour would please to excuse me from proceeding any farther, because I was very certain that the Account he expected from me would be highly displeasing. But he insisted in commanding me to let him know the best and the worst: I told him he should be obeyed. I owned, that the *Houyhnhnms* among us, whom we called *Horses*, were the most generous and comely Animal we had; that they excelled in Strength and Swiftness; and when they belonged to Persons of Quality, employed in Travelling, Racing, and drawing Chariots, they were treated with much Kindness and Care, till they fell into Diseases, or became foundered[0] in the Feet; but then they were sold, and used to all kind of Drudgery till they died; after which their Skins were stripped and sold for what they were worth, and their Bodies left to be devoured by Dogs and Birds of Prey. But the common Race of Horses had not so good Fortune, being kept by Farmers and Carriers, and other mean People, who put them to greater Labour, and feed them worse. I described as well as I could, our Way of Riding; the Shape and Use of a Bridle, a Saddle, a Spur, and a Whip; of Harness and Wheels. I added, that we fastened Plates of a certain hard Substance called *Iron* at the Bottom of their Feet, to preserve their Hoofs from being broken by the Stony Ways on which we often travelled.

My Master, after some Expressions of great Indignation, wondered how we dared to venture upon a *Houyhnhnm*'s Back; for he was sure, that the meanest Servant in his House would be able to shake off the strongest *Yahoo*; or by lying down, and rouling upon his Back, squeeze the Brute to Death. I answered, That our Horses were trained up from three or four Years old to the several uses we intended them for; That if any of them proved intolerably vicious, they were employed for Carriages; that they were severely beaten while they were young for any mischievous Tricks: That the Males, designed for the common Use of Riding or Draught, were generally *castrated* about two Years after their Birth, to take down their Spirits, and make them more tame and gentle: That they were indeed sensible of Rewards and Punishments; but his Honour would please to consider, that they had not the least Tincture of Reason any more than the *Yahoos* in this Country.

It put me to the Pains of many Circumlocutions to give my Master a right Idea of what I spoke; for their Language doth not abound in Variety of Words, because their Wants and Passions are fewer than among us. But it is impossible to express his noble Resentment at our savage Treatment of the *Houyhnhnm* Race; particularly after I had explained the Manner and Use of *Castrating* Horses among us, to hinder them from propagating their Kind, and to render them more servile. He said, if it were possible there could be any Country where *Yahoos* alone were endued with Reason, they certainly must be the governing Animal, because Reason will in Time always prevail against Brutal Strength. But, considering the Frame of our Bodies, and especially of mine, he thought no Creature of equal Bulk was so ill-contrived, for employing that Reason in the common Offices of Life; whereupon he desired to know whether those among whom I lived, resembled me or the *Yahoos* of his Country. I assured him, that I was as well shaped as most of my Age; but the younger and the Females were much more soft and tender, and the Skins of the latter generally as white as Milk. He said, I differed indeed from other *Yahoos,* being much more cleanly, and not altogether so deformed; but in point of real Advantage, he thought I differed for the worse. That my Nails were of no Use either to my fore or hinder Feet: As to my fore Feet, he could not properly call them by that Name, for he never observed me to walk upon them; that they were too soft to bear the Ground; that I generally went with them uncovered, neither was the Covering I sometimes wore on them, of the name Shape, or so strong as that on my Feet behind. That I could not walk with any Security; for if either of my hinder Feet slipped, I must inevitably fall. He then began to find fault with other Parts of my Body; the Flatness of my Face, the Prominence of my Nose, mine Eyes placed directly in Front, so that I could not look on either Side without turning my Head: That I was not able to feed my self, without lifting one of my fore Feet to my Mouth: And therefore Nature had placed those Joints to answer that Necessity. He knew not what could be the Use of those several Clefts and Divisions in my Feet behind; that these were too soft to bear the Hardness and Sharpness of Stones without a Covering made from the Skin of some other Brute; that my whole Body wanted a Fence against Heat and Cold, which I was forced to put on and off every Day with Tediousness and Trouble. And lastly, that he observed every Animal in this Country naturally to abhor the *Yahoos*, whom the Weaker avoided, and the Stronger drove from them. So that supposing us to have the Gift of Reason, he could not see how it were possible to cure that natural Antipathy which every Creature discovered against us; nor consequently, how we could tame and render them serviceable. However, he would (as he said) debate the Matter no farther, because he was more desirous to know my own Story, the Country, where I was born, and the several Actions and Events of my Life before I came hither.

I assured him, how extreamly desirous I was that he should be satisfied in every Point; but I doubted much, whether it would be possible for me to explain my self on several Subjects whereof his Honour could have no Conception, because I saw nothing in his Country to which I could resemble them. That however, I would do my best, and strive to express my self by Similitudes, humbly desiring his Assistance when I wanted proper Words; which he was pleased to promise me.

I said, my Birth was of honest Parents, in an Island called *England*, which was remote from this Country, as many Days Journey as the strongest of his Honour's Servants could travel in the Annual Course of the Sun. That I was bred a Surgeon, whose Trade is to cure Wounds and Hurts in the Body, got by Accident or Violence. That my Country was governed by a Female Man, whom we called *Queen*. That I left it to get Riches, whereby I might maintain my self and Family when I should return. That in my last Voyage, I was Commander of the Ship and had about fifty *Yahoos* under me, many of which died at Sea, and I was forced to supply them by others picked out from several Nations. That our Ship was twice in Danger of being sunk; the first Time by a great Storm, and the second, by striking against a Rock. Here my Master interposed, by asking me, How I could persuade Strangers out of different Countries to venture with me, after the Losses I had sustained, and the Hazards I had run. I said, they were Fellows of desperate Fortune, forced to fly from the Places of their Birth, on Account of their Poverty or their Crimes. Some were undone by Law-suits; others spent all they had in Drinking, Whoring and Gaming; others fled for Treason; many for Murder, Theft, Poysoning, Robbery, Perjury, Forgery, Coining false Money; for committing Rapes or Sodomy; for flying from their Colours,[0] or deserting to the Enemy; and most of them had broken Prison. None of these durst return to their native Countries for fear of being hanged, or of starving in a Jail; and therefore were under a Necessity of seeking a Livelihood in other Places.

During this Discourse, my Master was pleased often to interrupt me. I had made Use of many Circumlocutions in describing to him the Nature of the several Crimes, for which most of our Crew had been forced to fly their Country. This Labour took up several Days Conversation before he was able to comprehend me. He was wholly at a Loss to know what could be the Use or Necessity of practising those Vices. To clear up which I endeavoured to give some Ideas of the Desire of Power and Riches; of the terrible Effects of Lust, Intemperance, Malice, and Envy. All this I was forced to define and describe by putting of Cases, and making Suppositions. After which, like one whose Imagination was struck with something never seen or heard of before, he would lift up his Eyes with Amazement and Indignation. Power, Government, War, Law, Punishment, and a Thousand other Things had no Terms, wherein that Language could express them; which made the Difficulty almost insuperable to give my Master any conception of what I meant: But being of an excellent Understanding, much improved by Contemplation and Converse, he at last arrived at a competent Knowledge of what human Nature in our Parts of the World is capable to perform; and desired I would give him some particular Account of that Land, which we call *Europe*, especially, of my own Country.

CHAPTER V

The Author at his Master's Commands informs him of the State of England. *The Causes of War among the*

Princes of Europe. *The Author begins to explain the* English *Constitution.*

The Reader may please to observe, that the following Extract of many Conversations I had with my Master, contains a Summary of the most material Points, which were discoursed at several times for above two Years; his Honour often desiring fuller Satisfaction as I farther improved in the *Houyhnhnm* Tongue. I laid before him, as well as I could, the whole State of *Europe*; I discoursed of Trade and Manufactures, of Arts and Sciences; and the Answers I gave to all the Questions he made, as they arose upon several Subjects, were a Fund of Conversation not to be exhausted. But I shall here only set down the Substance of what passed between us concerning my own Country, reducing it into Order as well as I can, without any Regard to Time or other Circumstances, while I strictly adhere to Truth. My only Concern is, that I shall hardly be able to do Justice to my Master's Arguments and Expressions, which must needs suffer by my Want of Capacity, as well as by a Translation into our barbarous *English*.

In Obedience therefore to his Honour's Commands, I related to him the *Revolution* under the Prince of *Orange*; the long War with *France* entered into by the said Prince, and renewed by his Successor the present Queen; wherein the greatest Powers of *Christendom* were engaged, and which still continued: I computed at his Request, that about a Million of *Yahoos* might have been killed in the whole Progress of it; and perhaps a Hundred or more Cities taken, and five times as many Ships burnt or sunk.

He asked me what were the usual Causes or Motives that made one Country go to War with another. I answered, they were innumerable; but I should only mention a few of the chief. Sometimes the Ambition of Princes, who never think they have Land or People enough to govern: Sometimes the Corruption of Ministers, who engage their Master in a War in order to stifle or divert the Clamour of the Subjects against their evil Administration. Difference in Opinions hath cost many Millions of Lives:[7] For Instance, whether *Flesh* be *Bread*, or *Bread* be *Flesh*: Whether the Juice of a certain *Berry* be *Blood* or *Wine*: Whether *Whistling* be a Vice or a Virtue: Whether it be better to *kiss a Post*, or throw it into the Fire: What is the best Colour for a *Coat*, whether *Black*, White, Red or *Grey*; and whether it should be *long* or *short*, *narrow* or *wide*, *dirty* or *clean*; with many more. Neither are any Wars so furious and bloody, or of so long Continuance, as those occasioned by Difference in Opinion, especially if it be in things indifferent.

Sometimes the Quarrel between two Princes is to decide which of them shall dispossess a Third of his Dominions, where neither of them pretend to any Right. Sometimes one Prince quarrelleth with another, for fear of other should quarrel with him. Sometimes a War is entered upon, because the Enemy is too *strong*, and sometimes because he is too *weak*. Sometimes our Neighbours *want* the *Things* which we *have*, or *have* the Things which we want; and we both fight, till they take ours or give us theirs. It is a very justifiable Cause of War to invade a Country after the People have been wasted by Famine, destroyed by Pestilence, or embroiled by Factions amongst themselves. It is justifiable to enter into a War against our nearest Ally, when one of his Towns lies convenient for us, or a Territory of Land, that would render our Dominions round and compact. If a Prince send Forces into a Nation, where the People are poor and ignorant, he may lawfully put half of them to Death, and make Slaves of the rest, in order to civilize and reduce them from their barbarous Way of Living. It is a very kingly, honourable, and frequent Practice, when one Princes desires the Assistance of another to secure him against an Invasion, that the Assistant, when he hath driven out the Invader, should seize on the Dominions himself, and kill, imprison or banish the Prince he came to relieve. Allyance by Blood or Marriage, is a sufficient Cause of War between Princes; and the nearer the Kindred is, the greater is their Disposition to quarrel: *Poor* Nations are *hungry*, and *rich* Nations are *proud*; and Pride and Hunger will ever be at Variance. For these Reasons, the Trade of a *Soldier* is held the most honourable of all others: Because a *Soldier* is a *Yahoo* hired to kill in cold Blood as many of his own Species, who have never offended him, as possibly he can.

There is likewise a Kind of beggarly Princes in *Europe*, not able to make War by themselves, who hire out their Troops to richer Nations for so much a Day to each Man; of which they keep three Fourths to themselves, and it is the best Part of their

7. The references that follow are to disagreements between protestants and catholics.

Maintenance; such are those in many *Northern* Parts of *Europe*.

What you have told me, (said my Master) upon the Subject of War, doth indeed discover most admirably the Effects of that Reason you pretend to: However, it is happy that the *Shame* is greater than the *Danger*; and that Nature hath left you utterly uncapable of doing much Mischief: For your Mouths lying flat with your Faces, you can hardly bite each other to any Purpose, unless by Consent. Then, as to the Claws upon your Feet before and behind, they are so short and tender, that one of our *Yahoos* would drive a Dozen of yours before him. And therefore in recounting the Numbers of those who have been killed in Battle, I cannot but think that you have *said the Thing which is not*.

I could not forbear shaking my Head and smiling a little at his Ignorance. And, being no Stranger to the Art of War, I gave him a Description of Cannons, Culverins,[0] Muskets, Carabines, Pistols, Bullets, Powder, Swords, Bayonets, Sieges, Retreats, Attacks, Undermines, Countermines, Bombardments, Sea-fights; Ships sunk with a Thousand Men; twenty Thousand killed on each Side; dying Groans, Limbs flying in the Air: Smoak, Noise, Confusion, trampling to Death under Horses Feet: Flight, Pursuit, Victory; Fields strewed with Carcases left for Food to Dogs, and Wolves, and Birds of Prey; Plundering, Stripping, Ravishing, Burning and Destroying. And, to set forth the Valour of my own dear Countrymen, I assured him, that I had seen them blow up a Hundred Enemies at once in a Siege, and as many in a Ship; and beheld the dead Bodies drop down in Pieces from the Clouds, to the great Diversion of all the Spectators.

I was going on to more Particulars, when my Master commanded me Silence. He said, whoever understood the Nature of *Yahoos* might easily believe it possible for so vile an Animal, to be capable of every Action I had named, if their Strength and Cunning equalled their Malice. But, as my Discourse had increased his Abhorrence of the whole Species, so he found it gave him a Disturbance in his Mind, to which he was wholly a Stranger before. He thought his Ears being used to such abominable Words, might by Degrees admit them with less Detestation. That, although he hated the *Yahoos* of this Country, yet he no more blamed them for their odious Qualities, than he did a *Gnnayh* (a Bird of Prey) for its Cruelty, or a sharp Stone for cutting his Hoof. But, when a Creature pretending to Reason, could be capable of such Enormities, he dreaded lest the Corruption of that Faculty might be worse than Brutality itself.[8] He seemed therefore confident, that instead of Reason, we were only possessed of some Quality fitted to increase our natural Vices; as the Reflection from a troubled Stream returns the Image of an ill-shapen Body, not only *larger*, but more *distorted*.

He added, That he had heard too much upon the Subject of War, both in this, and some former Discourses. There was another Point which a little perplexed him at present. I had said, that some of our Crew left their Country on Account of being ruined by *Law*: That I had already explained the Meaning of the Word; but he was at a Loss how it should come to pass, that the *Law* which was intended for *every* Man's Preservation, should be any Man's Ruin. Therefore he desired to be farther satisfied what I meant by *Law*, and the Dispensers thereof, according to the present Practice in my own Country: Because he thought, Nature and Reason were sufficient Guides for a reasonable Animal, as we pretended to be, in shewing us what we ought to do, and what to avoid.

I assured his Honour, that *Law* was a Science wherein I had not much conversed, further than by employing Advocates, in vain, upon some Injustices that had been done me. However, I would give him all the Satisfaction I was able.

I said there was a Society of Men among us, bred up from their Youth in the Art of proving by Words multiplied for the Purpose, that *White* is *Black*, and *Black* is *White*, according as they are paid. To this Society all the rest of the People are Slaves.

For Example. If my Neighbour hath a mind to my *Cow*, he hires a lawyer to prove that he ought to have my *Cow* from me. I must then hire another to defend my Right; it being against all Rules of *Law* that any Man should be allowed to speak for himself. Now in this Case, I who am the true Owner lie under two great Disadvantages. First, my Lawyer being practiced almost from his Cradle in defending Falshood; is quite out of his Element when he would be an Advocate for Justice, which as an Office unnatural, he always attempts with great Awkwardness, if not with Ill-will. The second Disadvantage is, that my Lawyer must proceed

8. See Swift to Pope, 29 September 1725 (printed above).

with great Caution: Or else he will be reprimanded by the Judges, and abhorred by his Brethren, as one who would lessen the Practice of the Law. And therefore I have but two Methods to preserve my *Cow*. The first is, to gain over my Adversary's Lawyer with a double Fee; who will then betray his Client, by insinuating that he hath Justice on his Side. The second Way is for my Lawyer to make my Cause appear as unjust as he can; by allowing the *Cow* to belong to my Adversary; and this if it be skilfully done, will certainly bespeak the Favour of the Bench.

Now, your Honour is to know, that these Judges are Persons appointed to decide all Controversies of Property, as well as for the Tryal of Criminals; and picked out from the most dextrous Lawyers who are grown old or lazy: And having been byassed all their Lives against Truth and Equity, lie under such a fatal Necessity of favouring Fraud, Perjury and Oppression; that I have known some of them to have refused a large Bribe from the Side where Justice lay, rather than injure the *Faculty*, by doing any thing unbecoming their Nature or their Office.

It is a Maxim among these Lawyers, that whatever hath been done before, may legally be done again: And therefore they take special Care to record all the Decisions formerly made against common Justice and the general Reason of Mankind. These, under the Name of *Precedents*, they product as Authorities to justify the most iniquitous Opinions; and the Judges never fail of directing accordingly.

In pleading, they studiously avoid entering into the *Merits* of the Cause; but are loud, violent and tedious in dwelling upon all *Circumstances* which are not to the Purpose. For Instance, in the Case already mentioned: They never desire to know what Claim or Title my Adversary hath to my *Cow*; but whether the said *Cow* were Red or Black; her Horns long or short; whether the Field I graze her in be round or square; whether she were milked at home or abroad; what Diseases she is subject to, and the like. After which they consult *Precedents*, adjourn the Cause, from Time to Time, and in Ten, Twenty, or Thirty Years come to an Issue.

It is likewise to be observed, that this Society hath a peculiar Cant and Jargon of their own, that no other Mortal can understand, and wherein all their Laws are written, which they take special Care to multiply; whereby they have wholly confounded the very Essence of Truth and Falshood, of Right and Wrong; so that it will take Thirty Years to decide whether the Field, left me by my Ancestors for Six Generations, belong to me, or to a Stranger three Hundred Miles off.

In the Tryal of Persons accused for Crimes against the State, the Method is much more short and commendable: The Judge first sends to sound the Disposition of those in Power; after which he can easily hang or save the Criminal, strictly preserving all the Forms of Law.

Here my Master interposing, said it was a Pity, that Creatures endowed with such prodigious Abilities of Mind as these Lawyers, by the Description I gave of them must certainly be, were not rather encouraged to be Instructors of others in Wisdom and Knowledge. In Answer to which, I assured his Honour, that in all Points out of their own Trade, they were usually the most ignorant and stupid Generation among us, the most despicable in common Conversation, avowed Enemies to all Knowledge and Learning; and equally disposed to pervert the general Reason of Mankind, in every other Subject of Discourse, as in that of their own Profession.

CHAPTER VI

A Continuation of the State of England, *under Queen* Anne. *The Character of a first Minister in the Courts of* Europe.

My Master was yet wholly at a Loss to understand what Motives could incite this Race of Lawyers to perplex, disquiet, and weary themselves by engaging in a Confederacy of Injustice, merely for the Sake of injuring their Fellow-Animals; neither could be comprehend what I meant in saying they did it for *Hire*. Whereupon I was at much Pains to describe to him the Use of *Money*, the Materials it was made of, and the Value of the Metals: That when a *Yahoo* had got a great Store of this precious Substance, he was able to purchase whatever he had a mind to; the finest Cloathing, the noblest Houses, great Tracts of Land, the most costly Meats and Drinks; and have his Choice of the most beautiful Females. Therefore since *Money* alone, was able to perform all these Feats, our *Yahoos* thought, they could never have enough of it to spend or to save, as they found themselves inclined from their natural Bent either to Profusion or Avarice. That, the rich Man enjoyed the Fruit of the poor Man's Labour, and the latter were a Thousand to One in Proportion to the former. That the Bulk of our People was forced to live miserably, by labouring every Day for small Wages to make a few live plentifully. I enlarged myself much on these and many other Particulars to the same Purpose: But his Honour was still to seek: For he went upon a Supposition that all Animals had a Title to their Share in the Productions of the Earth; and especially those who presided over the rest. Therefore he desired I would let him know, what these costly Meats were, and how any of us happened to want them. Whereupon I enumerated as many Sorts as came into my Head, with the various Methods of dressing them, which could not be done without sending Vessels by Sea to every Part of the World, as well for Liquors to drink, as for Sauces, and innumerable other Conveniencies. I assured him, that this whole Globe of Earth must be at least three Times gone round, before one of our better Female *Yahoos* could get her Breakfast, or a Cup to put it in. He said, That must needs be a miserable Country which cannot furnish Food for its own Inhabitants. But what he chiefly wondered at, was how such vast Tracts of Ground as I described, should be wholly without *Fresh water*, and the People put to the Necessity of sending over the Sea for Drink. I replied, that *England* (the dear Place of my Nativity) was computed to produce three Times the Quantity of Food, more than its Inhabitants are able to consume, as well as Liquors extracted from Grain, or pressed out of the Fruit of certain Trees, which made excellent Drink; and the same Proportion in every other Convenience of Life. But, in order to feed the Luxury and Intemperance of the Males, and the Vanity of the Females, we sent away the greatest Part of our necessary Things to other Countries, from whence in Return we brought the Materials of Diseases, Folly, and Vice, to spend among ourselves. Hence it follows of Necessity, that vast Numbers of our People are compelled to seek their Livelihood by Begging, Robbing, Stealing, Cheating, Pimping, Forswearing,[0] Flattering, Suborning,[0] Forging, Gaming, Lying, Fawning, Hectoring, Voting, Scribling, Stargazing, Poysoning, Whoring, Canting, Libelling, Free-thinking, and the like Occupations: Every one of which Terms, I was at much Pains to make him understand.

That, *Wine* was not imported among us from foreign Countries, to supply the Want of Water or other Drinks, but because it was a Sort of Liquid which made us merry, by putting us out of Our Senses; diverted all melancholy Thoughts, begat wild extravagant Imaginations in the Brain, raised our Hopes, and banished our Fears; suspended every Office of Reason for a Time, and deprived us of the Use of our Limbs, untill we fell into a profound Sleep; although it must be confessed, that we always awaked sick and dispirited; and that the Use of this Liquor filled us with Diseases, which made our Lives uncomfortable and short.

But beside all this, the Bulk of our People supported themselves by furnishing the Necessities or Conveniencies of Life to the Rich, and to each other. For Instance, when I am at home and dressed as I ought to be, I carry on my Body the Workmanship of an Hundred Tradesmen; the Building and Furniture of my House employ as many more; and five Times the Number to adorn my Wife.

I was going to tell him of another Sort of People, who get their Livelihood by attending the Sick; having upon some Occasions informed his Honour that many of my Crew had died of Diseases. But here it was with the utmost Difficulty, that I brought him to apprehend what I meant. He could easily conceive, that a *Houyhnhnm* grew weak and heavy a few Days before his Death; or by some Accident might hurt a Limb. But that Nature, who worketh all things to Perfection, should suffer any Pains to breed in our Bodies, he thought impossible; and desired to know the Reason of so unaccountable an Evil. I told him, we fed on a Thousand Things which operated contrary to each other; that we eat when we were not hungry, and drank without the Provocation of Thirst: That we sat whole Nights drinking strong Liquors without eating a Bit; which disposed us to Sloth, enflamed our Bodies, and precipitated or prevented Digestion. That, prostitute Female *Yahoos* acquired a certain Malady, which bred Rottenness in the Bones of those, who fell into their Embraces: That this and many other Diseases, were propagated from Father to Son; so that great Numbers come into the World with complicated Maladies upon them: That, it would be endless to give him a Catalogue of all Diseases incident to human Bodies; for they could not be fewer than five or six Hundred, spread over every Limb, and Joynt: In short, every Part, external and intestine, having Diseases appropriated to each. To remedy which, there was a Sort of People bred among us, in the Profession or Pretence of curing the Sick. And because I had some Skill in the Faculty, I would in Gratitude to his Honour, let him know the whole Mystery and Method by which they proceed.

Their Fundamental is, that all Diseases arise from *Repletion*; from whence they conclude, that a great *Evacuation* of the Body is necessary, either through the natural Passage, or upwards at the Mouth. Their next Business is, from Herbs, Minerals, Gums, Oyls, Shells, Salts, Juices, Sea-weed, Excrements, Barks of Trees, Serpents, Toads, Frogs, Spiders, dead Mens Flesh and Bones, Beasts and Fishes, to form a Composition for Smell and Taste the most abominable, nauseous and detestable, that they can possibly contrive, which the Stomach immediately rejects with Loathing: And this they call a *Vomit*. Or else from the same Store-house, with some other poysonous Additions, they command us to take in at the Orifice *above* or *below*, (just as the Physician then happens to be disposed) a Medicine equally annoying and disgustful to the Bowels; which relaxing the Belly, drives down all before it: And this they call a *Purge*, or a *Clyster*. For Nature (as the Physicians alledge) having intended the superior anterior Orifice only for the *Intromission* of Solids and Liquids, and the inferior Posterior for Ejection; these Artists ingeniously considering that in all Diseases Nature is forced out of her Seat; therefore to replace her in it, the Body must be treated in a Manner directly contrary, by interchanging the Use of each Orifice; forcing Solids and Liquids in at the *Anus*, and making Evacuations at the Mouth.

But, besides real Diseases, we are subject to many that are only imaginary, for which the Physicians have invented imaginary Cures; these have their several Names, and so have the Drugs that are proper for them; and with these our Female *Yahoos* are always infested.

One great Excellency in this Tribe is their Skill at *Prognosticks*,[0] wherein they seldom fail; their Predictions in real Diseases, when they rise to any Degree of Malignity, generally portending *Death*, which is always in their Power, when Recovery is not: And therefore, upon any unexpected Signs of Amendment, after they have pronounced their Sentence, rather than be accused as false Prophets, they know how to approve their Sagacity to the World by a seasonable Dose.

They are likewise of special Use to Husbands and Wives, who are grown weary of their Mates; to eldest Sons, to great Ministers of State, and often to Princes.

I had formerly upon Occasion discoursed with my Master upon the Nature of *Government* in general, and particularly of our own *excellent Constitution*, deservedly the Wonder and Envy of the whole World. But having here accidentally mentioned a *Minister of State*; he commanded me some Time after to inform him, what Species of *Yahoo* I particularly meant by that Appellation.

I told him, that a *First* or *Chief Minister of State*, whom I intended to describe, was a Creature wholly exempt from Joy and Grief, Love and Hatred, Pity and Anger; at least makes use of no other Passions but a violent Desire of Wealth, Power, and Titles: That he applies his Words to all Uses, except to the Indication of his Mind; That he never tells a *Truth*, but with an Intent that you should take it for a *Lye*; nor a *Lye*, but with a Design that you should take it for a *Truth*; That those he speaks worst of behind their Backs, are in the surest way to Preferment; and whenever he begins to praise you to others or to your self, you are from that Day forlorn. The worst Mark you can receive is a *Promise*, especially when it is confirmed with an Oath; after which every wise Man retires, and gives over all Hopes.[9]

There are three Methods by which a Man may rise to be Chief Minister: The first is, by knowing how with Prudence to dispose of a Wife, a Daughter, or a Sister. The second, by betraying or undermining his Predecessor: And the third is, by a *furious Zeal* in publick Assemblies against the Corruptions of the Court. But a wise Prince would rather chuse to employ those who practise the last of these Methods; because such Zealots prove always the most obsequious and subservient to the Will and Passions of their Master. That, these *Ministers* having all Employments at their Disposal, preserve themselves in Power by bribing the Majority of a Senate or great Council; and at last by an Expedient called an *Act of Indemnity* (whereof I described the Nature to him) they secure themselves from After-reckonings, and retire from the Publick laden with the Spoils of the Nation.[10]

9. Swift's own experiences during the period 1710-13 lie behind this bitter remark.
10. In *The Examiner* (XXVII), Swift attacked the Duke of Marlborough in very similar terms.

The Palace of a *Chief Minister*, is a Seminary to breed up others in his own Trade: The Pages, Lacquies, and Porters, by imitating their Master, become *Ministers of State* in their several Districts, and learn to excel in the three principal *Ingredients*, of *Insolence, Lying*, and *Bribery*. Accordingly, they have a *Subaltern* Court paid to them by Persons of the best Rank; and sometimes by the Force of Dexterity and Impudence, arrive through several Gradations to be Successors to their Lord.

He is usually governed by a decayed Wench, or favourite Footman, who are the Tunnels through which all Graces are conveyed, and may properly be called, *in the last Resort*, the Governors of the Kingdom.

One Day, my Master, having heard me mention the *Nobility* of my Country, was pleased to make me a Compliment which I could not pretend to deserve: That, he was sure, I must have been born of some Noble Family, because I far exceeded in Shape, Colour, and Cleanliness, all the *Yahoos* of his Nation, although I seemed to fail in Strength, and Agility, which must be imputed to my different Way of Living from those other Brutes; and besides, I was not only endowed with the Faculty of Speech, but likewise with some Rudiments of Reason, to a Degree, that with all his Acquaintance I passed for a Prodigy.

He made me observe, that among the *Houyhnhnms*, the *White*, the *Sorrel*, and the *Iron-grey*, were not so exactly shaped as the *Bay*, the *Dapple-grey*, and the *Black*; nor born with equal Talent of Mind, or a Capacity to improve them; and therefore continued always in the Condition of Servants, without ever aspiring to match out of their own Race, which in that Country would be reckoned monstrous and unnatural.

I made his Honour my most humble Acknowledgements for the good Opinion he was pleased to conceive of me; but assured him at the same Time, that my Birth was of the lower Sort, having been born of plain, honest Parents, who were just able to give me a tolerable Education: That, *Nobility* among us was altogether a different Thing from the Idea he had of it; That, our young *Noblemen* are bred from their Childhood in Idleness and Luxury; that, as soon as Years will permit, they consume their Vigour, and contract odious Diseases among lewd Females; and when their Fortunes are almost ruined, they marry some Woman of mean Birth, disagreeable Person, and unsound Constitution, merely for the sake of Money, whom they hate and despise. That, the Productions of such Marriages are generally scrophulous,[0] rickety[0] or deformed Children; by which Means the Family seldom continues above three Generations, unless the Wife take Care to provide a healthy Father among her Neighbours, or Domesticks, in order to improve and continue the Breed. That, a weak diseased Body, a meager Countenance, and sallow Complexion, are the true Marks of *noble Blood*; and a healthy robust Appearance is so disgraceful in a Man of Quality, that the World concludes his real Father to have been a Groom or a Coachman. The Imperfections of his Mind run parallel with those of his Body; being a Composition of Spleen,[0] Dulness, Ignorance, Caprice, Sensuality and Pride.

Without the Consent of this illustrious Body,[11] no Law can be enacted, repealed, or altered: And these Nobles have likewise the Decision of all our Possessions without Appeal.

CHAPTER VII

The Author's great Love of his Native Country. His Master's Observations upon the Constitution and Administration of England, *as described by the Author, with parallel Cases and Comparisons. His Master's Observations upon human Nature.*

The Reader may be disposed to wonder how I could prevail on my self to give so free a Representation of my own Species, among a Race of Mortals who were already too apt to conceive the vilest Opinion of Human Kind, from that entire Congruity betwixt me and their *Yahoos*. But I must freely confess, that the many Virtues of those excellent *Quadrupeds* placed in opposite View to human Corruptions, had so far opened mine Eyes, and enlarged my Understanding, that I began to view the Actions and Passions of Man in a very different Light; and to think the Honour of my own Kind not worth managing; which, besides, it was impossible for me to do before a Person of so acute a Judgment as my Master, who daily convinced me of a thousand Faults in my self, whereof I had not the least Perception before, and which with us would never be numbered even among human Infirmities. I had likewise learned from his

11. i.e. the House of Lords.

Example an utter Detestation of all Falsehood or Disguise; and *Truth* appeared so amiable to me, that I determined upon sacrificing every thing to it.

Let me deal so candidly with the Reader, as to confess, that there was yet a much stronger Motive for the Freedom I took in my Representation of Things. I had not been a Year in this Country, before I contracted such a Love and Veneration for the Inhabitants, that I entered on a firm Resolution never to return to human Kind, but to pass the rest of my Life among these admirable *Houyhnhnms* in the Contemplation and Practice of every Virtue; where I could have no Example or Incitement to Vice. But it was decreed by Fortune, my perpetual Enemy, that so great a Felicity should not fall to my Share. However, it is now some Comfort to reflect, that in what I said of my Countrymen, I *extenuated* their Faults as much as I durst before so strict an Examiner; and upon every Article, gave as *favourable* a Turn as the Matter would bear. For, indeed, who is there alive that will not be swayed by his Byass and Partiality to the Place of his Birth?

I have related the Substance of several Conversations I had with my Master, during the greatest Part of the Time I had the Honour to be in his Service; but have indeed for Brevity sake omitted much more than is here set down.

When I had answered all his Questions, and his Curiosity seemed to be fully satisfied; he sent for me one Morning early, and commanding me to sit down at some Distance, (an Honour which he had never before conferred upon me) He said, he had been very seriously considering my whole Story, as far as it related both to my self and my Country: That, he looked upon us as a Sort of Animals to whose Share, by what Accident he could not conjecture, some small Pittance of *Reason* had fallen, whereof we made no other Use than by its Assistance to aggravate our *natural* Corruptions, and to acquire new ones which Nature had not given us. That, we disarmed our selves of the few Abilities she had bestowed; had been very successful in multiplying our original Wants, and seemed to spend our whole Lives in vain Endeavours to supply them by our own Inventions. That, as to my self, it was manifest I had neither the Strength or Agility of a common *Yahoo*; that I walked infirmly on my hinder Feet; had found out a Contrivance to make my Claws of no Use or Defence, and to remove the Hair from my Chin, which was intended as a Shelter from the Sun and the Weather. Lastly, That I could neither run with Speed, nor climb Trees like my *Brethren* (as he called them) the *Yahoos* in this Country.

That, our Institutions of *Government* and *Law* were plainly owing to our gross Defects in *Reason*, and by consequence, in *Virtue*; because *Reason* alone is sufficient to govern a *Rational* Creature; which was therefore a Character we had no Pretence to challenge, even from the Account I had given of my own People; although he manifestly perceived, that in order to favour them, I had concealed many Particulars, and often *said the Thing which was not.*

He was the more confirmed in this Opinion, because he observed, that as I agreed in every Feature of my Body with other *Yahoos*, except where it was to my real Disadvantage in point of Strength, Speed and Activity, the Shortness of my Claws, and some other Particulars where Nature had no Part; so, from the Representation I had given him of our Lives, our Manners, and our Actions, he found as near a Resemblance in the Disposition of our Minds. He said, the *Yahoos* were known to hate one another more than they did any different Species of Animals; and the Reason usually assigned, was, the Odiousness of their own Shapes, which all could see in the rest, but not in themselves. He had therefore begun to think it not unwise in us to *cover* our Bodies, and by that Invention, conceal many of our Deformities from each other, which would else be hardly supportable. But, he now found he had been mistaken; and that the Dissentions of those Brutes in his Country were owing to the same Cause with ours, as I had described them. For, if (said he) you throw among five *Yahoos* as much Food as would be sufficient for fifty, they will, instead of eating peaceably, fall together by the Ears, each single one impatient to *have all to it self*; and therefore a Servant was usually employed to stand by while they were feeding abroad, and those kept at home were tied at a Distance from each other. That, if a Cow died of Age or Accident, before a *Houyhnhnm* could secure it for his own *Yahoos*, those in the Neighbourhood would come in Herds to seize it, and then would ensue such a Battle as I had described, with terrible Wounds made by their Claws on both Sides, although they seldom were able to kill one another, for want of such convenient Instruments of Death as we had invented. At other Times the like Battles have been fought between the *Yahoos* of several

Neighbourhoods without any visible Cause: Those of one District watching all Opportunities to surprise the next before they are prepared. But if they find their Project hath miscarried, they return home, and for want of Enemies, engage in what I call a *Civil War* among themselves.

That, in some Fields of his Country, there are certain *shining Stones* of several Colours, whereof the *Yahoos* are violently fond; and when Part of these *Stones* are fixed in the Earth, as it sometimes happeneth, they will dig with their Claws for whole Days to get them out, and carry them away, and hide them by Heaps in their Kennels; but still looking round with great Caution, for fear their Comrades should find out their Treasure. My Master said, he could never discover the Reason of this unnatural Appetite, or how these Stones could be of any Use to a *Yahoo*; but now he believed it might proceed from the same Principle of *Avarice*, which I had ascribed to Mankind. That he had once, by way of Experiment, privately removed a Heap of these *Stones* from the Place where one of his *Yahoos* had buried it: Whereupon, the sordid Animal missing his Treasure, by his loud lamenting brought the whole Herd to the Place, there miserably howled, then fell to biting and tearing the rest; began to pine away, would neither eat nor sleep, nor work, till he ordered a Servant privately to convey the *Stones* into the same Hole, and hide them as before; which when his *Yahoo* had found, he presently recovered his Spirits and good Humour; but took Care to remove them to a better hiding Place; and hath ever since been a very serviceable Brute.

My Master farther assured me, which I also observed my self; That in the Fields where the *shining Stones* abound, the fiercest and most frequent Battles are fought, occasioned by perpetual Inroads of the neighbouring *Yahoos*.

He said, it was common when two *Yahoos* discovered such a *Stone* in a Field, and were contending which of them should be the Proprietor, a third would take the Advantage, and carry it away from them both; which my Master would needs contend to have some Resemblance with our *Suits at Law*; wherein I thought it for our Credit not to undeceive him; since the Decision he mentioned was much more equitable than many Decrees among us: Because the Plaintiff and Defendant there lost nothing beside the *Stone* they contended for; whereas our *Courts of Equity*, would never have dismissed the Cause while either of them had any thing left.

My Master continuing his Discourse, said, There was nothing that rendered the *Yahoos* more odious, than their undistinguishing Appetite to devour every thing that came in their Way, whether Herbs, Roots, Berries, corrupted Flesh of Animals, or all mingled together: And it was peculiar in their Temper, that they were fonder of what they could get by Rapine or Stealth at a greater Distance, than much better Food provided for them at home. If their Prey held out, they would eat till they were ready to burst, after which Nature had pointed out to them a certain *Root* that gave them a general Evacuation.

There was also another Kind of *Root* very *juicy*, but something rare and difficult to be found, which the *Yahoos* sought for with much Eagerness, and would suck it with great Delight: It produced the same Effects that Wine hath upon us. It would make them sometimes hug, and sometimes tear one another; they would howl and grin, and chatter, and roul,[0] and tumble, and then fall asleep in the Mud.

I did indeed observe, that the *Yahoos* were the only Animals in this Country subject to any Diseases; which however, were much fewer than Horses have among us, and contracted not by any ill Treatment they meet with, but by the Nastiness and Greediness of that sordid Brute. Neither has their Language any more than a general Appellation for those Maladies; which is borrowed from the Name of the Beast, and called *Hnea Yahoo*, or the *Yahoo's-Evil*; and the Cure prescribed is a Mixture of *their own Dung* and *Urine*, forcibly put down the *Yahoo*'s Throat. This I have since often known to have been taken with Success: And do here freely recommend it to my Countrymen, for the publick Good, as an admirable Specifick against all Diseases produced by Repletion.

As to Learning, Government, Arts, Manufactures, and the like; my Master confessed he could find little or no Resemblance between the *Yahoos* of that Country and those in ours. For, he only meant to observe what Parity there was in our Natures. He had heard indeed some curious *Houyhnhnms* observe, that in most Herds there was a Sort of ruling *Yahoo*, (as among us there is generally some leading or principal Stag in a Park) who was always more *deformed* in Body, and *mischievous in Disposition*, than any of the rest. That, this *Leader* had usually a Favourite as *like himself* as he could get, whose Employment was to *lick his Master's Feet and Posteriors, and drive the Female* Yahoos *to his Kennel*; for which he was now and then rewarded with a Piece of Ass's Flesh. This *Favourite* is hated by the whole Herd; and therefore to protect himself, keeps always *near the Person of his Leader*. He usually continues in Office till a worse can be found; but the very Moment he is discarded, his Successor, at the Head of all the *Yahoos* in that District, Young and Old, Male and Female, come in a Body, and discharge their Excrements upon him from Head to Foot. But how far this might be applicable to our *Courts* and *Favourites*, and *Ministers of State*, my Master said I could best determine.

I durst make no Return to this malicious Insinuation, which debased human Understanding below the Sagacity of a common *Hound*, who hath Judgment enough to distinguish and follow the Cry of the *ablest Dog in the Pack*, without being ever mistaken.

My Master told me, there were some Qualities remarkable in the *Yahoos*, which he had not observed me to mention, or at least very slightly, in the Accounts I had given him of human Kind. He said, those Animals, like other Brutes, had their Females in common; but in this they differed, that the She-*Yahoo* would admit the Male, while she was pregnant; and that the Hees would quarrel and fight with the Females as fiercely as with each other. Both which Practices were such Degrees of infamous Brutality, that no other sensitive Creature ever arrived at.

Another Thing he wondered at in the *Yahoos*, was their strange Disposition to Nastiness and Dirt; whereas there appears to be a natural Love of Cleanliness in all other Animals. As to the two former Accusations, I was glad to let them pass without any Reply, because I had not a Word to offer upon them in Defence of my Species, which otherwise I certainly had done from my own Inclinations. But I could have easily vindicated human Kind from the Imputation of Singularity upon the last Article, if there had been any *Swine* in that Country, (as unluckily for me there were not) which although it may be a *sweeter Quadruped* than a *Yahoo*, cannot I humbly conceive in Justice pretend to more Cleanliness; and so his Honour himself must have owned, if he had seen their filthy Way of feeding, and their Custom of wallowing and sleeping in the Mud.

My Master likewise mentioned another Quality, which his Servants had discovered in several *Yahoos*, and to him was wholly unaccountable. He said, a Fancy would sometimes take a *Yahoo*, to retire into a Corner, to lie down and howl, and groan, and spurn away all that came near him, although he were young and fat, and wanted neither Food nor Water; nor did the Servants imagine what could possibly ail him. And the only Remedy they found was to set him to hard Work, after which he would infallibly come to himself. To this I was silent out of Partiality to my own Kind; yet here I could plainly discover the true Seeds of *Spleen*,[12] which only seizeth on the *Lazy*, the *Luxurious*, and the *Rich*; who, if they were forced to undergo the *same Regimen*, I would undertake for the Cure.

His Honour had farther observed, that a Female *Yahoo* would often stand behind a Bank or a Bush, to gaze on the young Males passing by, and then appear, and hide, using many antick Gestures and Grimaces; at which time it was observed, that she had a most *offensive Smell*; and when any of the Males advanced, would slowly retire, looking often back, and with a counterfeit Shew of Fear, run off into some convenient Place where she knew the Male would follow her.

At other times, if a Female Stranger came among them, three or four of her own Sex would get about her, and stare and chatter, and grin, and smell her all over; and then turn off with Gestures that seemed to express Contempt and Disdain.

Perhaps my Master might refine a little in these Speculations, which he had drawn from what he observed himself, or had been told him by others: However, I could not reflect without some Amazement, and much Sorrow, that the Rudiments of *Lewdness*, *Coquetry*, *Censure*, and *Scandal*, should have Place by Instinct in Womankind.

I expected every Moment, that my Master would accuse the *Yahoos* of those unnatural Appetites in both Sexes, so common among us. But Nature it seems hath not been so expert a Schoolmistress; and these politer Pleasures are entirely the Productions of Art and Reason, on our Side of the Globe.

12. depression or melancholy, often referred to in the eighteenth century as 'the English malady'.

CHAPTER VIII

The Author relateth several Particulars of the Yahoos. *The great Virtues of the* Houyhnhnms. *The Education and Exercise of their Youth. Their general Assembly.*

As I ought to have understood human Nature much better than I supposed it possible for my Master to do, so it was easy to apply the Character he gave of the *Yahoos* to myself and my Countrymen; and I believed I could yet make farther Discoveries from my own Observation. I therefore often begged his Honour to let me go among the Herds of *Yahoos* in the Neighbourhood; to which he always very graciously consented, being perfectly convinced that the Hatred I bore those Brutes would never suffer me to be corrupted by them; and his Honour ordered one of his Servants, a strong Sorrel Nag, very honest and good-natured, to be my Guard; without whose Protection I durst not undertake such Adventures. For I have already told the Reader how much I was pestered by those odious Animals upon my first Arrival. I afterwards failed very narrowly three or four times of falling into their Clutches, when I happened to stray at any Distance without my Hanger. And I have Reason to believe, they had some Imagination that I was of their own Species, which I often assisted myself, by stripping up my Sleeves, and shewing my naked Arms and Breast in their Sight, when my Protector was with me: At which times they would approach as near as they durst, and imitate my Actions after the Manner of Monkeys, but ever with great Signs of Hatred; as a tame *Jack Daw* with Cap and Stockings, is always persecuted by the wild ones, when he happens to be got among them.

They are prodigiously nimble from their Infancy; however, I once caught a young Male of three Years old, and endeavoured by all Marks of Tenderness to make it quiet; but the little Imp fell a squalling, and scratching, and biting with such Violence, that I was forced to let it go; and it was high time, for a whole Troop of old ones came about us at the Noise; but finding the Cub was safe, (for away it ran) and my Sorrel Nag being by, they durst not venture near us. I observed the young Animal's Flesh to smell very rank, and the Stink was somewhat between a *Weasel* and a *Fox*, but much more disagreeable. I forgot another Circumstance, (and perhaps I might have the Reader's Pardon, if it were wholly omitted) that while I held the odious Vermin in my Hands, it voided its filthy Excrements of a yellow liquid Substance, all over my Cloaths; but by good Fortune there was a small Brook hard by, where I washed myself as clean as I could; although I durst not come into my Master's Presence, until I was sufficiently aired.

By what I could discover, the *Yahoos* appear to be the most unteachable of all Animals, their Capacities never reaching higher than to draw or carry Burthens. Yet I am of Opinion, this Defect ariseth chiefly from a perverse, restive Disposition. For they are cunning, malicious, treacherous and revengeful. They are strong and hardy, but of a cowardly Spirit, and by Consequence insolent, abject, and cruel. It is observed, that the *Red-haired* of both Sexes are more libidinous and mischievous than the rest, whom yet they much exceed in Strength and Activity.

The *Houyhnhnms* keep the *Yahoos* for present Use in Huts not far from the House; but the rest are sent abroad to certain Fields, where they dig up Roots, eat several Kinds of Herbs, and search about for Carrion, or sometimes catch *Weasels* and *Luhimuhs* (a Sort of *wild Rat*) which they greedily devour. Nature hath taught them to dig deep Holes with their Nails on the Side of a rising Ground, wherein they lie by themselves; only the Kennels of the Females are larger, sufficient to hold two or three Cubs.

They swim from their Infancy like Frogs, and are able to continue long under Water, where they often take Fish, which the Females carry home to their Young. And upon this Occasion, I hope the Reader will pardon my relating an odd Adventure.

Being one Day abroad[0] with my Protector the Sorrel Nag, and the Weather exceeding hot, I entreated him to let me bathe in a River that was near. He consented, and I immediately stripped myself stark naked, and went down softly into the Stream. It happened that a young Female *Yahoo* standing behind a Bank, saw the whole Proceeding; and inflamed by Desire, as the Nag and I conjectured, came running with all Speed, and leaped into the Water within five Yards of the Place where I bathed. I was never in my Life so terribly frighted; the Nag was grazing at some Distance, not suspecting any Harm: She embraced me after a most fulsome Manner: I roared as loud as I could, and the Nag came galloping towards me, whereupon she quitted her Grasp, with the utmost

Reluctancy, and leaped upon the opposite Bank, where she stood gazing and howling all the time I was putting on my Cloaths.

This was Matter of Diversion to my Master and his Family, as well as of Mortification to my self. For now I could no longer deny, that I was a real *Yahoo*, in every Limb and Feature, since the Females had a natural Propensity to me as one of their own Species: Neither was the Hair of this Brute of a Red Colour, (which might have been some Excuse for an Appetite a little irregular) but black as a Sloe, and her Countenance did not make an Appearance altogether so hideous as the rest of the Kind; for, I think, she could not be above Eleven Years old.

Having already lived three Years in this Country, the Reader I suppose will expect, that I should, like other Travellers, give him some Account of the Manners and Customs of its Inhabitants, which it was indeed my principal Study to learn.

As these noble *Houyhnhnms* are endowed by Nature with a general Disposition to all Virtues, and have no Conceptions or Ideas of what is evil in a rational Creature; so their grand Maxim is, to cultivate *Reason*, and to be wholly governed by it. Neither is *Reason* among them a Point problematical as with us, where Men can argue with Plausibility on both Sides of a Question; but strikes you with immediate Conviction; as it must needs do where it is not mingled, obscured, or discoloured by Passion and Interest. I remember it was with extreme Difficulty that I could bring my Master to understand the Meaning of the Word *Opinion*, or how a Point could be disputable; because *Reason* taught us to affirm or deny only where we are certain; and beyond our Knowledge we cannot do either. So that Controversies, Wranglings, Disputes, and Positiveness in false or dubious Propositions, are Evils unknown among the *Houyhnhnms*. In the like Manner when I used to explain to him our several Systems of *Natural Philosophy*, he would laugh that a Creature pretending to *Reason*, should value itself upon the Knowledge of other Peoples Conjectures, and in Things, where that Knowledge, if it were certain, could be of no Use. Wherein he agreed entirely with the Sentiments of *Socrates*, as *Plato* delivers them; which I mention as the highest Honour I can do that Prince of Philosophers. I have often since reflected what Destruction such a Doctrine would make in the Libraries of *Europe*; and how many Paths to Fame would be then shut up in the Learned World.

Friendship and *Benevolence* are the two principal Virtues among the *Houyhnhnms*; and these not confined to particular Objects, but universal to the whole Race. For, a Stranger from the remotest Part, is equally treated with the nearest Neighbour, and where-ever he goes, looks upon himself as at home. They preserve *Decency* and *Civility* in the highest Degrees, but are altogether ignorant of *Ceremony*. They have no Fondness[0] for their Colts or Foles; but the Care they take in educating them proceedeth entirely from the Dictates of *Reason*. And, I observed my Master to shew the same Affection to his Neighbour's Issue that he had for his own. They will have it that *Nature* teaches them to love the whole Species, and it is *Reason* only that maketh a Distinction of Persons, where there is a superior Degree of Virtue.

When the Matron *Houyhnhnms* have produced one of each Sex, they no longer accompany with their Consorts, except they lose one of their Issue by some Casualty, which very seldom happens: But in such a Case they meet again; or when the like Accident befalls a Person, whose Wife is past bearing, some other Couple bestows on him one of their own Colts, and then go together a second Time, until the Mother be pregnant. This Caution is necessary to prevent the Country from being over-burthened with Numbers. But the Race of inferior *Houyhnhnms* bred up to be Servants is not so strictly limited upon this Article; these are allowed to produce three of each Sex, to be Domesticks in the Noble Families.

In their Marriages they are exactly careful to chuse such Colours as will not make any disagreeable Mixture in the Breed. *Strength* is chiefly valued in the Male, and *Comeliness* in the Female; not upon the Account of *Love*, but to preserve the Race from degenerating: For, where a Female happens to excel in *Strength*, a Consort is chosen with regard to *Comeliness*. Courtship, Love, Presents, Joyntures,[0] Settlements, have no Place in their Thoughts; or Terms whereby to express them in their Language. The young Couple meet and are joined, merely because it is the Determination of their Parents and Friends: It is what they see done every Day; and they look upon it as one of the necessary Actions in a reasonable Being. But the Violation of Marriage, or any other Unchastity, was never heard of: And the married Pair pass their

Lives with the same Friendship, and mutual Benevolence that they bear to all others of the same Species, who come in their Way; without Jealousy, Fondness, Quarrelling, or Discontent.

In educating the Youth of both Sexes, their Method is admirable, and highly deserveth our Imitation. These are not suffered to taste a Grain of *Oats*, except upon certain Days, till Eighteen Years old; nor *Milk*, but very rarely; and in Summer they graze two Hours in the Morning, and as many in the Evening, which their Parents likewise observe; but the Servants are not allowed above half that Time; and a great Part of the Grass is brought home, which they eat at the most convenient Hours, when they can be best spared from Work.

Temperance, *Industry*, *Exercise* and *Cleanliness*, are the Lessons equally enjoyned to the young ones of both Sexes: And my Master thought it monstrous in us to give the Females a different Kind of Education from the Males, except in some Articles of Domestick Management; whereby, as he truly observed, one Half of our Natives were good for nothing but bringing Children into the World: And to trust the Care of their Children to such useless Animals, he said was yet a greater Instance of Brutality.

But the *Houyhnhnms* train up their Youth to Strength, Speed and Hardiness, by exercising them in running Races up and down steep Hills, or over hard stony Grounds; and when they are all in a Sweat, they are ordered to leap over Head and Ears into a Pond or a River. Four times a Year the Youth of certain Districts meet to shew the Proficiency in Running, and Leaping, and other Feats of Strength or Agility; where the Victor is rewarded with a Song made in his or her Praise. On this Festival the Servants drive a Herd of *Yahoos* into the Field, laden with Hay, and Oats, and Milk for a Repast to the *Houyhnhnms*; after which, these Brutes are immediately driven back again, for fear of being noisome to the Assembly.

Every fourth Year, at the *Vernal Equinox*, there is a Representative Council of the whole Nation, which meets in a Plain about twenty Miles from our House, and continueth about five or six Days. Here they inquire into the State and Condition of the several Districts; whether they abound or be deficient in Hay or Oats, or Cows or *Yahoos*? And where-ever there is any Want (which is but seldom) it is immediately supplied by unanimous Consent and Contribution. Here likewise the Regulation of Children is settled: As for instance, if a *Houyhnhnm* hath two Males, he changeth one of them with another who hath two Females: And when a Child hath been lost by any Casualty, where the Mother is past Breeding, it is determined what Family shall breed another to supply the Loss.

CHAPTER IX

A grand Debate at the General Assembly of the Houyhnhnms; *and how it was determined. The Learning of the* Houyhnhnms. *Their Buildings. Their Manner of Burials. The Defectiveness of their Language.*

One of these Grand Assemblies was held in my time, about three Months before my Departure, whither my Master went as the Representative of our District. In this Council was resumed their old Debate, and indeed, the only Debate that ever happened in their Country; whereof my Master after his Return gave me a very particular Account.

The Question to be debated was, Whether the *Yahoos* should be exterminated from the Face of the Earth. One of the *Members* for the Affirmative offered several Arguments of great Strength and Weight; alledging, That, as the *Yahoos* were the most filthy, noisome, and deformed Animal which Nature ever produced, so they were the most restive and indocible, mischievous and malicious: They would privately suck the Teats of the *Houyhnhnms* Cows; kill and devour their Cats, trample down their Oats and Grass, if they were not continually watched; and commit a Thousand other Extravagancies. He took Notice of a general Tradition, that *Yahoos* had not been always in their Country: But, that many Ages ago, two of these Brutes appeared together upon a Mountain; whether produced by the Heat of the Sun upon corrupted Mud and Slime, or from the Ooze and Froth of the Sea, was never known. That these *Yahoos* engendered, and their Brood in a short time grew so numerous as to over-run and infest the whole Nation. That the *Houyhnhnms* to get rid of this Evil, made a general Hunting, and at last inclosed the whole Herd; and destroying the Older, every *Houyhnhnm* kept two young Ones in a Kennel, and brought them to such a Degree of Tameness, as an Animal so savage by Nature can be capable of acquiring; using them for Draught and Carriage. That, there seemed to be much Truth in this Tradition, and that those Creatures could not be *Ylnhniamshy* (or *Aborigines* of the Land) because of the violent Hatred the *Houyhnhnms* as well as all other Animals, bore them; which although their evil Disposition sufficiently deserved, could never have arrived at so high a Degree, if they had been *Aborigines*, or else they would have long since been rooted out. That, the Inhabitants taking a Fancy to use the Service of the *Yahoos*, had very imprudently neglected to cultivate the Breed of *Asses*, which were a comely Animal, easily kept, more tame and orderly, without any offensive Smell, strong enough for Labour, although they yield to the other in Agility of Body; and if their Braying be no agreeable Sound, it is far preferable to the horrible Howlings of the *Yahoos*.

Several others declared their Sentiments to the same Purpose; when my Master proposed an Expedient to the Assembly, whereof he had indeed borrowed the Hint from me. He approved of the Tradition, mentioned by the *Honourable Member*, who spoke before; and affirmed, that the two *Yahoos* said to be first seen among them, had been driven thither over the Sea; that coming to Land, and being forsaken by their Companions, they retired to the Mountains, and degenerating by Degrees, became in Process of Time, much more savage than those of their own Species in the Country from whence these two Originals came. The Reason of his Assertion was, that he had now in his Possession, a certain wonderful *Yahoo*, (meaning myself) which most of them had heard of, and many of them had seen. He then related to them, how he first found me; that, my Body was all covered with an artificial Composure of the Skins and Hairs of other Animals: That, I spoke in a Language of my own, and had thoroughly learned theirs: That, I had related to him the Accidents which brought me thither: That, when he saw me without my Covering, I was an exact *Yahoo* in every Part, only of a whiter Colour, less hairy, and with shorter Claws. He added, how I had endeavoured to persuade him, that in my own and other Countries the *Yahoos* acted as the governing, rational Animal, and held the *Houyhnhnms* in Servitude: That, he observed in me all the Qualities of a *Yahoo*, only a little more civilized by some Tincture of Reason; which however was in a Degree as far inferior to the *Houyhnhnm* Race, as the *Yahoos* of their Country were to me: That, among other things, I mentioned a Custom we had of *castrating* *Houyhnhnms* when they were young, in order to render them tame; that the Operation was easy and safe; that it was no Shame to learn Wisdom from Brutes, as Industry is taught by the Ant, and Building by the Swallow. (For so I translate the Word *Lyhannh*, although it be a much larger Fowl) That, this Invention might be practiced upon the younger *Yahoos* here, which, besides rendering them tractable and fitter for Use, would in an Age put an End to the whole Species without destroying Life. That, in the mean time the *Houyhnhnms* should be *exhorted* to cultivate the Breed of Asses, which, as they are in all respects more valuable Brutes; so they have this Advantage, to be fit for Service at five Years old, which the others are not till Twelve.

This was all my Master thought fit to tell me at that Time, of what passed in the Grand Council. But he was pleased to conceal one Particular, which related personally to myself, whereof I soon felt the unhappy Effect, as the Reader will know in its proper Place, and from whence I date all the succeeding Misfortunes of my Life.

The *Houyhnhnms* have no Letters, and consequently, their Knowledge is all traditional. But there happening few Events of any Moment among a People so well united, naturally disposed to every Virtue, wholly governed by Reason, and cut off from all Commerce with other Nations; the historical Part is easily preserved without burthening their Memories. I have already observed, that they are subject to no Diseases, and therefore can have no Need of Physicians. However, they have excellent Medicines composed of Herbs, to cure accidental Bruises and Cuts in the Pastern or Frog[0] of the Foot by sharp Stones, as well as other Maims and Hurts in the several Parts of the Body.

They calculate the Year by the Revolution of the Sun and Moon, but use no Subdivisions into Weeks. They are well enough acquainted with the Motions of those two Luminaries, and understand the Nature of *Eclipses*; and this is the utmost Progress of their *Astronomy*.

In *Poetry* they must be allowed to excel all other Mortals; wherein the Justness of their Similes, and the Minuteness, as well as Exactness of their Descriptions, are indeed inimitable. Their Verses abound very much in both of these; and usually contain either some exalted Notions of Friendship and Benevolence, or the Praises of those who were Victors in Races, and other bodily Exercises. Their

Buildings, although very rude and simple, are not inconvenient, but well contrived to defend them from all Injuries of Cold and Heat. They have a Kind of Tree, which at Forty Years old loosens in the Root, and falls with the first Storm; it grows very strait, and being pointed like Stakes with a sharp Stone, (for the *Houyhnhnms* know not the Use of Iron) they stick them erect in the Ground about ten Inches asunder, and then weave in Oat-straw, or sometimes Wattles betwixt them. The Roof is made after the same Manner, and so are the Doors.

The *Houyhnhnms* use the hollow Part between the Pastern and the Hoof of their Fore-feet, as we do our Hands, and this with greater Dexterity, than I could at first imagine. I have seen a white Mare of our Family thread a Needle (which I lent her on Purpose) with that Joynt. They milk their Cows, reap their Oats, and do all the Work which requires Hands, in the same Manner. They have a Kind of hard Flints, which by grinding against other Stones, they form into Instruments, that serve instead of Wedges, Axes, and Hammers. With Tools made of these Flints, they likewise cut their Hay, and reap their Oats, which there groweth naturally in several Fields: The *Yahoos* draw home the Sheaves in Carriages, and the Servants tread them in certain covered Hutts, to get out the Grain, which is kept in Stores. They make a rude Kind of earthen and wooden Vessels, and bake the former in the Sun.

If they can avoid Casualties, they die only of old Age, and are buried in the obscurest Places that can be found, their Friends and Relations expressing neither Joy nor Grief at their Departure; nor does the dying Person discover the least Regret that he is leaving the World, any more than if he were upon returning home from a Visit to one of his Neighbours: I remember, my Master having once made an Appointment with a Friend and his Family to come to his House upon some Affair of Importance; on the Day fixed, the Mistress and her two Children came very late; she made two Excuses, first for her Husband, who, as she said, happened that very Morning to *Lhnuwnh*. The Word is strongly expressive in their Language, but not easily rendered into *English*; it signifies, *to retire to his first Mother*. Her Excuse for not coming sooner, was, that her Husband dying late in the Morning, she was a good while consulting her Servants about a convenient Place where his Body should be laid; and I observed she behaved herself at our House, as chearfully as the rest: She died about three Months after.

They live generally to Seventy or Seventy-five Years, very seldom to Fourscore: Some Weeks before their Death they feel a gradual Decay, but without Pain. During this time they are much visited by their Friends, because they cannot go abroad with their usual Ease and Satisfaction. However, about ten Days before their Death, which they seldom fail in computing, they return the Visits that have been made them by those who are nearest in the Neighbourhood, being carried in a convenient Sledge drawn by *Yahoos*; which Vehicle they use, not only upon this Occasion, but when they grow old, upon long Journeys, or when they are lamed by any Accident. And therefore when the dying *Houyhnhnms* return those Visits, they take a solemn Leave of their Friends, as if they were going to some remote Part of the Country, where they designed to pass the rest of their Lives.

I know not whether it may be worth observing, that the *Houyhnhnms* have no Word in their Language to express any thing that is *evil*, except what they borrow from the Deformities or ill Qualities of the *Yahoos*. Thus they denote the Folly of a Servant, an Omission of a Child, a Stone that cuts their Feet, a Continuance of foul or unseasonable Weather, and the like, by adding to each the Epithet of *Yahoo*. For Instance, *Hhnm Yahoo*, *Whnaholm Yahoo*, *Ynlhmnawihlma Yahoo*, and an ill contrived House, *Ynholmhnmrohlnw Yahoo*.

I could with great Pleasure enlarge farther upon the Manners and Virtues of this excellent People; but intending in a short time to publish a Volume by itself expressly upon that Subject, I refer the Reader thither. And in the mean time, proceed to relate my own sad Catastrophe.

CHAPTER X

The Author's Oeconomy and happy Life among the Houyhnhnms. *His great Improvement in Virtue, by conversing with them. Their Conversations. The Author hath Notice given him by his Master that he must depart from the Country. He falls into a Swoon for Grief, but submits. He contrives and finishes a Canoo, by the Help of a Fellow-Servant, and puts to Sea at a Venture.*

I had settled my little Oeconomy to my own Heart's Content. My Master had ordered a Room to be made for me after their Manner, about six Yards from the House; the Sides and Floors of which I plaistered with Clay, and covered with Rush-mats of my own contriving: I had beaten Hemp, which there grows wild, and made of it a Sort of Ticking:[0] This I filled with the Feathers of several Birds I had taken with Springes made of *Yahoos* Hairs; and were excellent Food. I had worked two Chairs with my Knife, the Sorrel Nag helping me in the grosser and more laborious Part. When my Cloaths were worn to Rags, I made my self others with the Skins of Rabbets, and of a certain beautiful Animal about the same Size, called *Nnuhnoh*, the Skin of which is covered with a fine Down. Of these I likewise made very tolerable Stockings. I soaled my Shoes with Wood which I cut from a Tree, and fitted to the upper Leather, and when this was worn out, I supplied it with the Skins of *Yahoos*, dried in the Sun. I often got Honey out of hollow Trees, which I mingled with Water, or eat it with my Bread. No Man could more verify the Truth of these two Maxims, *That, Nature is very easily satisfied*; and, *That, Necessity in the Mother of Invention.* I enjoyed perfect Health of Body, and Tranquility of Mind; I did not feel the Treachery or Inconstancy of a Friend, nor the Injuries of a secret or open Enemy. I had no Occasion of bribing, flattering or pimping, to procure the Favour of any great Man, or of his Minion. I wanted no Fence against Fraud or Oppression: Here was neither Physician to destroy my Body, nor Lawyer to ruin my Fortune: No Informer to watch my Words and Actions, or forge Accusations against me for Hire: Here were no Gibers, Censurers, Backbiters, Pickpockets, Highwaymen, Housebreakers, Attorneys, Bawds, Buffoons, Gamesters, Politicians, Wits, Spleneticks, tedious Talkers, Controvertists, Ravishers, Murderers, Robbers, Virtuoso's; no Leaders or Followers of Party and Faction; no Encouragers to Vice, by Seducement or Examples: No Dungeon, Axes, Gibbets, Whipping-posts, or Pillories; No cheating Shopkeepers or Mechanicks:[0] No Pride, Vanity or Affectation: No Fops, Bullies, Drunkards, strolling Whores, or Poxes: No ranting, lewd, expensive Wives: No stupid, proud Pedants: No importunate, over-bearing, quarrelsome, noisy, roaring, empty, conceited, swearing Companions: No Scoundrels raised from the Dust upon the Merit of their Vices; or Nobility thrown into it on account of their Virtues: No Lords, Fidlers, Judges or Dancing-masters.

I had the Favour of being admitted to several *Houyhnhnms*, who came to visit or dine with my Master; where his Honour graciously suffered me to wait in the Room, and listen to their Discourse. Both he and his Company would often descend to ask me Questions, and receive my Answers. I had also sometimes the Honour of attending my Master in his Visits to others. I never presumed to speak, except in answer to a Question; and then I did it with inward Regret, because it was a Loss of so much Time for improving my self: But I was infinitely delighted with the Station of an humble Auditor in such Conversations, where nothing passed but what was useful, expressed in the fewest and most significant Words: Where (as I have already said) the greatest *Decency* was observed, without the least Degree of Ceremony; where no Person spoke without being pleased himself, and pleasing his Companions: Where there was no Interruption, Tediousness, Heat, or Difference of Sentiments. They have a Notion, That when People are met together, a short Silence doth much improve Conversation: This I found to be true; for during those little Intermissions of Talk, new Ideas would arise in their Minds, which very much enlivened the Discourse. Their Subjects are generally on Friendship and Benevolence; on Order and Oeconomy; sometimes upon the visible Operations of Nature, or ancient Traditions; upon the Bounds and Limits of Virtue; upon the unerring Rules of Reason; or upon some Determinations, to be taken at the next great Assembly; and often upon the various Excellencies of *Poetry*. I may add, without Vanity, that my Presence often gave them sufficient Matter for Discourse, because it afforded my Master an Occasion of letting his Friends into the History of me and my Country, upon which they were all pleased to discant in a Manner not very advantageous to human Kind; and for that Reason I shall not repeat what they said: Only I may be allowed to observe, That his Honour to my great Admiration, appeared to understand the Nature of *Yahoos* much better than my self. He went through all our Vices and Follies, and discovered many which I had never mentioned to him; by only supposing what Qualities a *Yahoo* of their Country, with a small Proportion of Reason, might be capable of exerting: And concluded, with too much Probability, how vile as well as miserable such a Creature must be.

I freely confess, that all the little Knowledge I

have of any Value, was acquired by the Lectures I received from my Master, and from hearing the Discourses of him and his Friends; to which I should be prouder to listen, than to dictate to the greatest and wisest Assembly in *Europe*. I admired the Strength, Comeliness and Speed of the Inhabitants; and such a Constellation of Virtues in such amiable Persons produced in me the highest Veneration. At first, indeed, I did not feel that natural Awe which the *Yahoos* and all other Animals bear towards them; but it grew upon me by Degrees, much sooner than I imagined, and was mingled with a respectful Love and Gratitude, that they would condescend to distinguish me from the rest of my Species.

When I thought of my Family, my Friends, my Countrymen, or human Race in general, I considered them as they really were, *Yahoos* in Shape and Disposition, perhaps a little more civilized, and qualified with the Gift of Speech; but making no other Use of Reason, than to improve and multiply those Vices, whereof their Brethren in this Country had only the Share that Nature allotted them. When I happened to behold the Reflection of my own Form in a Lake or Fountain, I turned away my Face in Horror and detestation of my self; and could better endure the Sight of a common *Yahoo*, than of my own Person. By conversing with the *Houyhnhnms*, and looking upon them with Delight, I fell to imitate their Gait and Gesture, which is now grown into a Habit; and my Friends often tell me in a blunt Way, that *I trot like a Horse*; which, however, I take for a great Compliment: Neither shall I disown, that in speaking I am apt to fall into the Voice and manner of the *Houyhnhnms*, and hear my self ridiculed on that Account without the least Mortification.

In the Midst of this Happiness, when I looked upon my self to be fully settled for Life, my Master sent for me one Morning a little earlier than his usual Hour. I observed by his Countenance that he was in some Perplexity, and at a Loss how to begin what he had to speak. After a short Silence, he told me, he did not know how I would take what he was going to say: That, in the last general Assembly, when the Affair of the *Yahoos* was entered upon, the Representatives had taken Offence at his keeping a *Yahoo* (meaning my self) in his Family more like a *Houyhnhnm* than a Brute Animal. That, he was known frequently to converse with me, as if he could receive some Advantage or Pleasure in my Company: That, such a Practice was not agreeable to Reason or Nature, or a thing ever heard of before among them. The Assembly did therefore *exhort* him, either to employ me like the rest of my Species, or command me to swim back to the Place from whence I came. That, the first of these Expedients was utterly rejected by all the *Houyhnhnms*, who had ever seen me at his House or their own: For, they alledged, That because I had some Rudiments of Reason, added to the natural Pravity[0] of those Animals, it was to be feared, I might be able to seduce them into the woody and mountainous Parts of the Country, and bring them in Troops by Night to destroy the *Houyhnhnms* Cattle, as being naturally of the ravenous Kind, and averse from Labour.

My Master added, That he was daily pressed by the *Houyhnhnms* of the Neighbourhood to have the Assembly's *Exhortation* executed, which he could not put off much longer. He doubted, it would be impossible for me to swim to another Country; and therefore wished I would contrive some Sort of Vehicle resembling those I had described to him, that might carry me on the Sea; in which Work I should have the Assistance of his own Servants, as well as those of his Neighbours. He concluded, that for his own Part he could have been content to keep me in his Service as long as I lived; because he found I had cured myself of some bad Habits and Dispositions, by endeavouring, as far as my inferior Nature was capable, to imitate the *Houyhnhnms*.

I should here observe to the Reader, that a Decree of the general Assembly in this Country, is expressed by the Word *Hnhloayn*, which signifies an *Exhortation*; as near as I can render it: For they have no Conception how a rational Creature can be *compelled*, but only advised, or *exhorted*; because no Person can disobey Reason, without giving up his Claim to be a rational Creature.

I was struck with the utmost Grief and Despair at my Master's Discourse; and being unable to support the Agonies I was under, I fell into a Swoon at his Feet: When I came to myself, he told me, that he concluded I had been dead. (For these People are subject to no such Imbecillities of Nature) I answered, in a faint Voice, that Death would have been too great an Happiness; that although I could not blame the Assembly's *Exhortation*, or the Urgency of his Friends; yet in my weak and corrupt Judgment, I thought it might consist with Reason to have been less rigorous. That, I could not swim a

League, and probably the nearest Land to theirs might be distant above an Hundred: That, many Materials, necessary for making a small Vessel to carry me off, were wholly wanting in this Country, which however, I would attempt in Obedience and Gratitude to his Honour, although I concluded the thing to be impossible, and therefore looked on myself as already devoted to Destruction.[0] That, the certain Prospect of an unnatural Death, was the least of my Evils: For, supposing I should escape with Life by some strange Adventure, how could I think with Temper, of passing my Days among *Yahoos*, and relapsing into my old Corruptions, for want of Examples to lead and keep me within the Paths of Virtue. That, I knew too well upon what solid Reasons all the Determinations of the wise *Houyhnhnms* were founded, not to be shaken by Arguments of mine, a miserable *Yahoo*; and therefore after presenting him with my humble Thanks for the Offer of his Servants Assistance in making a Vessel, and desiring a reasonable Time for so difficult a Work, I told him, I would endeavour to preserve a wretched Being; and, if ever I returned to *England*, was not without Hopes of being useful to my own Species, by celebrating the Praises of the renowned *Houyhnhnms*, and proposing their Virtues to the Imitation of Mankind.

My Master in a few words made me a very gracious Reply, allowed me the Space of two *Months* to finish my Boat; and ordered the Sorrel Nag, my Fellow-Servant, (for so at this Distance I may presume to call him) to follow my Instructions, because I told my Master, that his Help would be sufficient, and I knew he had a Tenderness for me.

In his Company my first Business was to go to that Part of the Coast, where my rebellious crew had ordered me to be set on Shore. I got upon a Height, and looking on every Side into the Sea, fancied I saw a small Island, towards the *North-East*: I took out my Pocket-glass, and could then clearly distinguish it about five Leagues off, as I computed; but it appeared to the Sorrel Nag to be only a blue Cloud: For, as he had no Conception of any Country beside his own, so he could not be as expert in distinguishing remote Objects at Sea, as we who so much converse in that Element.

After I had discovered this Island, I considered no farther; but resolved, it should, if possible, be the first Place of my Banishment, leaving the Consequence to Fortune.

I returned home, and consulting with the Sorrel Nag, we went into a Copse at some Distance, where I with my Knife, and he with a sharp Flint fastened very artificially,[0] after their Manner, to a wooden Handle, cut down several Oak Wattles about the Thickness of a Walking-staff, and some larger Pieces. But I shall not trouble the Reader with a particular Description of my own Mechanicks:[0] Let it suffice to say, that in six Weeks time, with the Help of the Sorrel Nag, who performed the Parts that required most Labour, I finished a Sort of *Indian* Canoo, but much larger, covering it with the Skins of *Yahoos*, well stitched together, with hempen Threads of my own making. My Sail was likewise composed of the Skins of the same Animal; but I made use of the youngest I could get, the older being too tough and thick; and I likewise provided myself with four Paddles. I laid in a Stock of boiled Flesh, of Rabbets and Fowls; and took with me two Vessels, one filled with Milk, and the other with Water.

I tried my Canoo in a large Pond near my Master's House, and then corrected in it what was amiss; stopping all the Chinks with *Yahoos* Tallow, till I found it stanch, and able to bear me, and my Freight. And when it was as compleat as I could possibly make it, I had it drawn on a Carriage very gently by *Yahoos*, to the Sea-side, under the Conduct of the Sorrel Nag, and another Servant.

When all was ready, and the Day came from my Departure, I took Leave of my Master and Lady, and the whole Family, mine Eyes flowing with Tears, and my Heart quite sunk with Grief. But his Honour, out of Curiosity, and perhaps (if I may speak it without Vanity) partly out of Kindness, was determined to see me in my Canoo; and got several of his neighbouring Friends to accompany him. I was forced to wait above an Hour for the Tide, and then observing the Wind very fortunately bearing towards the Island, to which I Intended to steer my Course, I took a second Leave of my Master: But as I was going to prostrate myself to kiss his Hoof, he did me the Honour to raise it gently to my Mouth. I am not ignorant how much I have been censured for mentioning this last Particular. Detractors are pleased to think it improbable, that so illustrious a Person should descend to give so great a mark of Distinction to a Creature so inferior as I. Neither have I forgot, how apt some Travellers are to boast of extraordinary Favours they have received. But, if these Censurers were better acquainted with the noble and courteous

Disposition of the *Houyhnhnms,* they would soon change their Opinion.

I paid my Respects to the rest of the *Houyhnhnms* in his Honour's Company; then getting into my Canoo, I pushed off from Shore.

CHAPTER XI

The Author's dangerous Voyage. He arrives at New-Holland, *hoping to settle there. Is wounded with an Arrow by one of the Natives. Is seized and carried by Force into a* Portugueze *Ship. The great Civilities of the Captain. The Author arrives at* England.

I began this desperate Voyage on *February* 15, 1714/5,[13] at 9 o'Clock in the Morning. The Wind was very favourable; however, I made use at first only of my Paddles; but considering I should soon be weary, and that the Wind might probably chop about, I ventured to set up my little Sail; and thus, with the Help of the Tide, I went at the Rate of a League and a Half an Hour, as near as I could guess. My Master and his Friends continued on the Shoar, till I was almost out of Sight; and I often heard the Sorrel Nag (who always loved me) crying out, *Hnuy illa nyha maiah Yahoo,* Take Care of thy self, gentle *Yahoo.*

My Design was, if possible, to discover some small Island uninhabited, yet sufficient by my Labour to furnish me with Necessaries of Life, which I would have thought a greater Happiness than to be first Minister in the politest Court of *Europe*; so horrible was the Idea I conceived of returning to live in the Society and under the Government of *Yahoos.* For in such a Solitude as I desired, I could at least enjoy my own Thoughts, and reflect with Delight on the Virtues of those inimitable *Houyhnhnms,* without any Opportunity of degenerating into the Vices and Corruptions of my own Species.

The Reader may remember what I related when my Crew conspired against me, and confined me to my Cabbin. How I continued there several Weeks, without knowing what Course we took; and when I was put ashore in the Long-boat, how the Sailors told me with Oaths, whether true or false, that they knew not in what Part of the World we were. However, I did then believe us to be about ten Degrees *Southward* of the *Cape of Good Hope,* or about 45 Degrees *Southern* Latitude, as I gathered from some general Words I overheard among them, being I supposed to the *South-East* in their intended Voyage to *Madagascar.* And although this were little better than Conjecture, yet I resolved to steer my Course *Eastward,* hoping to reach the *South-West* Coast of *New-Holland,*[14] and perhaps some such Island as I desired, lying *Westward* of it. The Wind was full *West,* and by six in the Evening I computed I had gone *Eastward* at least eighteen Leagues; when I spied a very small Island about half a League off, which I soon reached. It was nothing but a Rock with one Creek, naturally arched by the Force of Tempests. Here I put in my Canoo, and climbing a Part of the Rock, I could plainly discover Land to the *East,* extending from *South* to *North.* I lay all Night in my Canoo; and repeating my Voyage early in the Morning, I arrived in seven Hours to the *South-East* Point of *New-Holland.* This confirmed me in the Opinion I have long entertained, that the *Maps* and *Charts* place this Country at least three Degrees more to the *East* than it really is; which Thought I communicated many Years ago to my worthy Friend Mr. *Herman Moll,*[15] and gave him my Reasons for it, although he hath rather chosen to follow other Authors.

I saw no Inhabitants in the Place where I landed; and being unarmed, I was afraid of venturing far into the Country. I found some Shell-Fish on the Shore, and eat them raw, not daring to kindle a Fire, for fear of being discovered by the Natives. I continued three Days feeding on Oysters and Limpits, to save my own Provisions; and I fortunately found a Brook of excellent Water, which gave me great Relief.

On the fourth Day, venturing out early a little too far, I saw twenty or thirty Natives upon a Height, not above five hundred Yards from me. They were stark naked, Men, Women and Children round a Fire, as I could discover by the Smoke. One of them spied me, and gave Notice to the rest; five of them advanced towards me, leaving the Women and Children at the Fire. I made what haste I could to the Shore, and getting into my Canoo, shoved off: The Savages observing me retreat, ran after me;

13. According to our calendar, the year was 1715. The new year began on 25 March in Swift's lifetime.

14. Australia.

15. A famous Dutch map-maker who settled in London.

and before I could get far enough into the Sea, discharged an Arrow, which wounded me deeply on the Inside of my left Knee (I shall carry the Mark to my Grave). I apprehended the Arrow might be poisoned; and paddling out of the Reach of their Darts (being a calm Day) I made a shift to suck the Wound, and dress it as well as I could.

I was at a Loss what to do, for I durst not return to the same Landing-place, but stood to the *North*, and was forced to paddle; for the Wind, although very gentle, was against me, blowing *North-West*. As I was looking about for a secure Landing-place, I saw a Sail to the *North North-East*, which appearing every Minute more visible, I was in some Doubt, whether I should wait for them or no; but at last my Detestation of the *Yahoo* Race prevailed; and turning my Canoo, I sailed and paddled together to the *South*, and got into the same Creek from whence I set out in the Morning; choosing rather to trust my self among these *Barbarians*, than live with *European Yahoos*. I drew up my Canoo as close as I could to the Shore, and hid my self behind a Stone by the little Brook, which, as I have already said, was excellent Water.

The Ship came within half a League of this Creek, and sent out her Long-Boat with Vessels to take in fresh Water (for the Place it seems was very well known) but I did not observe it until the Boat was almost on Shore; and it was too late to seek another Hiding-Place. The Seamen at their landing observed my Canoo, and rummaging it all over, easily conjectured that the Owner could not be far off. Four of them well armed searched every Cranny and Lurking-hole, till at last they found me flat on my Face behind the Stone. They gazed a while in Admiration at my strange uncouth Dress; my Coat made of Skins, my wooden-soaled Shoes, and my furred Stockings; from whence, however, they concluded I was not a Native of the Place, who all go naked. One of the Seamen in *Portugueze* bid me rise, and asked who I was. I understood that Language very well, and getting upon my Feet, said, I was a poor *Yahoo*, banished from the *Houyhnhnms*, and desired they would please to let me depart. They admired to hear me answer them in their own Tongue, and saw by my Complection I must be an European; but were at a Loss to know what I meant by *Yahoos* and *Houyhnhnms*, and at the same Time fell a laughing at my strange Tone in speaking, which resembled the Neighing of a Horse. I trembled all the while betwixt Fear and Hatred: I again desired Leave to depart, and was gently moving to my Canoo; but they laid hold on me, desiring to know what Country I was of? whence I came? with many other Questions. I told them, I was born in *England*, from whence I came about five Years ago, and then their Country and ours were at Peace. I therefore hoped they would not treat me as an Enemy, since I meant them no Harm, but was a poor *Yahoo*, seeking some desolate Place where to pass the Remainder of his unfortunate Life.

When they began to talk, I thought I never heard or saw any thing so unnatural; for it appeared to me as monstrous as if a Dog or a Cow should speak in *England*, or a *Yahoo* in *Houyhnhnm-Land*. The honest Portuguese were equally amazed at my strange Dress, and the odd Manner of delivering my Words, which however they understood very well. They spoke to me with great Humanity, and said they were sure their Captain would carry me *gratis* to *Lisbon*, from whence I might return to my own Country; that two of the Seamen would go back to the Ship, to inform the Captain of what they had seen, and receive his Orders; in the mean Time, unless I would give my solemn Oath not to fly, they would secure me by Force. I thought it best to comply with their Proposal. They were very curious to know my Story, but I gave them very little Satisfaction; and they all conjectured, that my Misfortunes had impaired my Reason. In two Hours the Boat, which went loaden with Vessels of Water, returned with the Captain's Commands to fetch me on Board. I fell on my Knees to preserve my Liberty; but all was in vain, and the Men having tied me with Cords, heaved me into the Boat, from whence I was taken into the Ship, and from thence into the Captain's Cabbin.

His Name was *Pedro de Mendez*; he was a very courteous and generous Person; he entreated me to give some Account of my self, and desired to know what I would eat or drink; said, I should be used as well as himself, and spoke so many obliging Things, that I wondered to find such Civilities from a *Yahoo*. However, I remained silent and sullen; I was ready to faint at the very Smell of him and his Men. At last I desired something to eat out of my own Canoo; but he ordered me a Chicken and some excellent Wine, and then directed that I should be put to Bed in a very clean Cabbin. I would not undress my self, but lay on the Bed-Cloaths; and in half an Hour stole out, when I thought the Crew was at Dinner; and getting to the Side of the Ship, was going to leap into the Sea, and swim for my Life, rather than continue among *Yahoos.* But one of the Seamen prevented me, and having informed the Captain, I was chained to my Cabbin.

After Dinner *Don Pedro* came to me, and desired to know my Reason for so desperate an Attempt; assured he only meant to do me all the Service he was able; and spoke so very movingly, that at last I descended to treat him like an Animal which had some little Portion of Reason. I gave him a very short Relation of my Voyage; of the Conspiracy against me by my own Men; of the Country where they set me on Shore, and of my five Years Residence there. All which he looked upon as if it were a Dream or a Vision; whereat I took great Offence: For I had quite forgot the Faculty of Lying, so peculiar to *Yahoos* in all Countries where they preside, and consequently the Disposition of suspecting Truth in others of their own Species. I asked him, Whether it were the Custom of his Country to *say the Thing was was not*? I assured him I had almost forgot what he meant by Falshood; and if I had lived a thousand Years in *Houyhnhnmland*, I should never have heard a Lie from the meanest Servant. That I was altogether indifferent whether he believed me or no; but however, in return for his Favours, I would give so much Allowance to the Corruption of his Nature, as to answer any Objection he would please to make; and he might easily discover the Truth.

The Captain, a wise Man, after many Endeavours to catch me tripping in some Part of my Story, at last began to have a better Opinion of my Veracity. But he added, that since I professed so inviolable an Attachment to Truth, I must give him my Word of Honour to bear him Company in this Voyage without attempting any thing against my Life; or else he would continue me a Prisoner till we arrived at *Lisbon.* I gave him the Promise he required; but at the same time protested that I would suffer the greatest Hardships rather than return to live among *Yahoos.*

Our Voyage passed without any considerable Accident. In Gratitude to the Captain I sometimes sate with him at his earnest Request, and strove to conceal my Antipathy against human Kind, although it often broke out; which he suffered to pass without Observation. But the greatest Part of the Day, I confined myself to my Cabbin, to avoid seeing any of the Crew. The Captain had often intreated me to strip myself of my savage Dress, and offered to lend me the best Suit of Cloaths he had. This I would not be prevailed on to accept, abhorring to cover myself with any thing that had been on the Back of a *Yahoo.* I only desired he would lend me two clean Shirts, which having been washed since he wore them, I believed would not so much defile me. These I changed every second Day, and washed them myself.

We arrived at *Lisbon, Nov.* 5, 1715. At our landing, the Captain forced me to cover myself with his Cloak, to prevent the Rabble from crouding about me. I was conveyed to his own House; and at my earnest Request, he led me up to the highest Room backwards.[0] I conjured him to conceal from all Persons what I had told him of the *Houyhnhnms*; because the least Hint of such a Story would not only draw Numbers of People to see me, but probably put me in Danger of being imprisoned, or burnt by the *Inquisition.* The Captain persuaded me to accept a Suit of Cloaths newly made; but I would not suffer the Taylor to take my Measure; however, Don *Pedro* being almost of my Size, they fitted me well enough. He accoutred me with other Necessaries all new, which I aired for Twenty-four Hours before I would use them.

The Captain had no Wife, nor above three Servants, none of which were suffered to attend at Meals; and his whole Deportment was so obliging, added to very good *human* Understanding, that I really began to tolerate his Company. He gained so far upon me, that I ventured to look out of the back Window. By Degrees I was brought into another Room, from whence I peeped into the Street, but drew my Head back in a Fright. In a Week's Time he seduced me down to the Door. I found my Terror gradually lessened, but my Hatred and Contempt seemed to increase. I was at last bold enough to walk the Street in his Company, but kept my Nose well stopped with Rue,[0] or sometimes with Tobacco.

In ten Days, Don *Pedro*, to whom I had given some Account of my domestick Affairs, put it upon me as a Point of Honour and Conscience, that I ought to return to my native Country, and live at home with my Wife and Children. He told me, there was an *English* Ship in the Port just ready to sail, and he would furnish me with all things necessary. It would be tedious to repeat his Arguments, and my Contradictions. He said, it was altogether impossible to find such a solitary Island as I had desired to live in; but I might command in my own House, and pass my time in a Manner as recluse as I pleased.

I complied at last, finding I could not do better. I left *Lisbon* the 24th Day of *November*, in an *English* Merchant-man, but who was the Master I never inquired. Don *Pedro* accompanied me to the Ship, and lent me Twenty Pounds. He took kind Leave of me, and embraced me at parting; which I bore as well as I could. During this last Voyage I had no Commerce with the Master, or any of his Men; but pretending I was sick kept close in my Cabbin. On the Fifth of *December*, 1715, we cast Anchor in the *Downs* about Nine in the Morning, and at Three in the Afternoon I got safe to my House at *Redriff*.

My Wife and Family received me with great Surprize and Joy, because they concluded me certainly dead; but I must freely confess, the Sight of them filled me only with Hatred, Disgust and Contempt; and the more, by reflecting on the near Alliance I had to them. For, although since my unfortunate Exile from the *Houyhnhnm* Country, I had compelled myself to tolerate the Sight of *Yahoos*, and to converse with Don *Pedro de Mendez*; yet my Memory and Imaginations were perpetually filled with the Virtues and Ideas of these exalted *Houyhnhnms*. And when I began to consider, that by copulating with one of the *Yahoo*-Species, I had become a Parent of more; it struck me with the utmost Shame, Confusion and Horror.

As soon as I entered the House, my Wife took me in her Arms, and kissed me; at which, having not been used to the Touch of that odious Animal for so many Years, I fell in a Swoon for almost an Hour. At the Time I am writing, it is five Years since my last Return to *England*: During the first Year I could not endure my Wife or Children in my Presence, the very Smell of them was intolerable; much less could I suffer them to eat in the same Room. To this Hour they dare not presume to touch my Bread, or drink out of the same Cup; neither was I ever able to let one of them take me by the Hand. The first Money I laid out was to buy two young Stone-Horses,[0] which I keep in a good Stable, and next to them the Groom is my greatest Favourite; for I feel my Spirits revived by the Smell he contracts in the Stable. My Horses understand me tolerably well; I converse with them at least four Hours every Day. They are Strangers to Bridle or Saddle; they live in great Amity with me, and Friendship to each other.

CHAPTER XII

The Author's Veracity. His Design in publishing this Work. His Censure of those Travellers who swerve from the Truth. The Author clears himself from any sinister Ends in writing. An Objection answered. The Method of planting Colonies. His Native Country commended. The Right of the Crown to those Countries described by the Author, is justified. The Difficulty of conquering them. The Author takes his last Leave of the Reader; proposeth his Manner of Living for the future; gives good Advice, and concludeth.

Thus, gentle Reader, I have given thee a faithful History of my Travels for Sixteen Years,[16] and above Seven Months; wherein I have not been so studious of Ornament as of Truth. I could perhaps like others have astonished thee with strange improbable Tales; but I rather chose to relate plain Matter of Fact in the simplest Manner and Style; because my principal Design was to inform, and not to amuse thee.

It is easy for us who travel into remote Countries, which are seldom visited by *Englishmen* or other *Europeans*, to form Descriptions of wonderful Animals both at Sea and Land. Whereas, a Traveller's chief Aim should be to make Men wiser and better, and to improve their Minds by the bad, as well as good Example of what they deliver concerning foreign Places.

I could heartily wish a Law were enacted, that every Traveller, before he were permitted to publish his Voyages, should be obliged to make Oath before the *Lord High Chancellor*, that all he intended to print was absolutely true to the best of his Knowledge; for then the World would no longer be deceived as it usually is, while some Writers, to make their Works pass the better upon the Publick, impose the grossest Falsities on the unwary Reader. I have perused several Books of Travels with great Delight in my younger Days; but, having since gone over most Parts of the Globe, and been able to contradict many fabulous Accounts from my own Observation; it hath given me a great Disgust against this Part of Reading, and some Indignation to see the Credulity of Mankind so impudently abused. Therefore since my Acquaintance were pleased to think my poor Endeavours might not be

16. i.e. since the beginning of the first voyage, 4 May 1699.

unacceptable to my Country; I imposed on myself as a Maxim, never to be swerved from, that I would *strictly adhere to Truth*; neither indeed can I be ever under the least Temptation to vary from it, while I retain in my Mind the Lectures and Example of my noble Master, and the other illustrious *Houyhnhnms*, of whom I had so long the Honour to be an humble Hearer.

> ——*Nec si miserum Fortuna Sinonem*
> *Finxit, vanum etiam, mendacemque improba finget.*[17]

I know very well, how little Reputation is to be got by Writings which require neither Genius nor Learning, nor indeed any other Talent, except a good Memory, or an exact *Journal*. I know likewise, that Writers of Travels, like *Dictionary*-Makers, are sunk into Oblivion by the Weight and Bulk of those who come last, and therefore lie uppermost. And it is highly probable, that such Travellers who shall hereafter visit the Countries described in this Work of mine, may by detecting my Errors, (if there be any) and adding many new Discoveries of their own, jostle me out of Vogue, and stand in my Place; making the World forget that ever I was an Author. This indeed would be too great a Mortification if I wrote for Fame: But, as my sole Intention was the *Publick Good*, I cannot be altogether disappointed. For, who can read of the Virtues I have mentioned in the glorious *Houyhnhnms*, without being ashamed of his own Vices, when he considers himself as the reasoning, governing Animal of his Country? I shall say nothing of those remote Nations where *Yahoos* preside; amongst which the least corrupted are the *Brobdingnagians*,[18] whose wise Maxims in Morality and Government, it would be our Happiness to observe. But I forbear descanting[0] further, and rather leave the judicious Reader to his own Remarks and Applications.

I am not a little pleased that this Work of mine can possibly meet with no Censurers: For what Objections can be made against a Writer who relates only plain Facts that happened in such distant Countries, where we have not the least Interest with respect either to Trade or Negotiations? I have carefully avoided every Fault with which common Writers of Travels are often too justly charged. Besides, I meddle not the least with any *Party*,[19] but write without Passion, Prejudice, or Ill-will against any Man or Number of Men whatsoever. I write for the noblest End, to inform and instruct Mankind, over whom I may, without Breach of Modesty, pretend to some Superiority,[20] from the Advantages I received by conversing so long among the most accomplished *Houyhnhnms*. I write without any View towards Profit or Praise. I never suffer a Word to pass that may look like Reflection, or possibly give the least Offence even to those who are most ready to take it. So that, I hope, I may with Justice pronounce myself an Author perfectly blameless; against whom the Tribes of Answerers, Considerers, Observers, Reflecters, Detecters, Remarkers, will never be able to find Matter for exercising their Talents.

I confess, it was whispered to me, that I was bound in Duty as a Subject of *England*, to have given in a Memorial to a Secretary of State, at my first coming over; because, whatever Lands are discovered by a Subject, belong to the Crown. But I doubt, whether our Conquests in the Countries I treat of, would be as easy as those of *Ferdinando Cortez*[21] over the naked *Americans*. The *Lilliputians* I think, are hardly worth the Charge of a Fleet and Army to reduce them; and I question whether it might be prudent or safe to attempt the *Brobdingnagians*: Or, whether an *English* Army would be much at their Ease with the Flying Island[22] over their Heads. The *Houyhnhnms*, indeed, appear not to be so well prepared for War, a Science to which they are perfect Strangers, and especially against missive Weapons. However, supposing myself to be a Minister of State, I could never give my Advice for invading them. Their Prudence, Unanimity, Unacquaintedness with Fear, and their Love of their Country would amply supply all Defects in the military Art. Imagine twenty Thousand of them breaking into the Midst of an *European* Army, confounding the Ranks, overturning the Carriages, battering the Warriors Faces into Mummy,[0] by terrible Yerks from their hinder Hoofs: For they would well deserve the Character

17. 'Nor, if cruel fortune has made Sinon miserable shall she also make him false and deceitful' (Virgil, *Aeneid*, ii, 79-80).
18. i.e. the giants of Part II of *Gulliver's Travels*.
19. i.e. political party.
20. cf. the last two paragraphs of this voyage.
21. Hernando Cortez (1485-1547), the Spaniard who conquered Mexico.
22. The Lilliputians are found in Part I and the Flying Island in Part III.

given to *Augustus*; *Recalcitrat undique tutus.*[23] But instead of Proposals for conquering that magnanimous Nation, I rather wish they were in a Capacity or Disposition to send a sufficient Number of their Inhabitants for civilizing *Europe*; by teaching us the first Principles of Honour, Justice, Truth, Temperance, publick Spirit, Fortitude, Chastity, Friendship, Benevolence, and Fidelity. The *Names* of all which Virtues are still retained among us in most Languages, and are to be met with in modern as well as ancient Authors; which I am able to assert from my own small Reading.

But, I had another Reason which made me less forward to enlarge his Majesty's Dominions by my Discoveries: To say the Truth, I had conceived a few Scruples with relation to the distributive Justice of Princes upon those Occasions. For Instance, A Crew of Pyrates are driven by a Storm they know not whither; at length a Boy discovers Land from the Top-mast; they go on Shore to rob and plunder; they see an harmless People, are entertained with Kindness, they give the Country a new Name, they take formal Possession of it for the King, they set up a rotten Plank or a Stone for a Memorial, they murder two or three Dozen of the Natives, bring away a Couple more by Force for a Sample, return home, and get their Pardon. Here commences a new Dominion acquired with a Title by *Divine Right*. Ships are sent with the first Opportunity; the Natives driven out or destroyed, their Princes tortured to discover their Gold; a free Licence given to all Acts of Inhumanity and Lust; the Earth reeking with the Blood of its Inhabitants: And this execrable Crew of Butchers employed in so pious an Expedition, is a *modern Colony* sent to convert and civilize an idolatrous and barbarous People.

But this Description, I confess, doth by no means affect the *British* Nation, who may be an Example to the whole World for their Wisdom, Care, and Justice in planting Colonies;[24] their liberal Endowments for the Advancement of Religion and Learning; their Choice of devout and able Pastors to propagate *Christianity*; their Caution in stocking their Provinces with People of sober Lives and Conversations from this the Mother Kingdom; their strict Regard to the Distribution of Justice, in supplying the Civil Administration through all their Colonies with Officers of the greatest Abilities, utter Strangers to Corruption: And to crown all, by sending the most vigilant and virtuous Governors, who have no other Views than the Happiness of the People over whom they preside, and the Honour of the King their Master.

But, as those Countries which I have described do not appear to have a Desire of being conquered, and enslaved, murdered or driven out by Colonies; nor abound either in Gold, Silver, Sugar or Tobacco; I did humbly conceive they were by no Means proper Objects of our Zeal, our Valour, or our Interest. However, if those whom it may concern, think fit to be of another Opinion, I am ready to depose,[0] when I shall be lawfully called, That no *European* did ever visit these Countries before me. I mean, if the Inhabitants ought to be believed.

But, as to the Formality of taking Possession in my Sovereign's Name, it never came once into my Thoughts; and if it had, yet as my Affairs then stood, I should perhaps in point of Prudence and Self-Preservation, have put it off to a better Opportunity.

Having thus answered the *only* Objection that can be raised against me as a Traveller; I here take a final Leave of my Courteous Readers, and return to enjoy my own Speculations in my little Garden at *Redriff*; to apply those excellent Lessons of Virtue which I learned among the *Houyhnhnms*; to instruct *the Yahoos* of my own Family as far as I shall find them docible[0] Animals; to behold my Figure often in a Glass, and thus if possible habituate my self by Time to tolerate the Sight of a human Creature: To lament the Brutality of *Houyhnhnms* in my own Country, but always treat their Persons with Respect, for the Sake of my noble Master, his Family, his Friends, and the whole *Houyhnhnm* Race, whom these of ours have the Honour to resemble in all their Lineaments, however their Intellectuals[0] came to degenerate.

I began last Week to permit my Wife to sit at Dinner with me, at the farthest End of a long Table; and to answer (but with the utmost Brevity) the few Questions I asked her. Yet the Smell of a *Yahoo* continuing very offensive, I always keep my Nose well stopt with Rue, Lavender, or Tobacco-Leaves. And although it be hard for a Man late in Life to remove old Habits; I am not altogether out of Hopes in some Time to suffer a Neighbour *Yahoo*

23. 'He kicks back, protected on every side' (Horace, *Satires* II. i. 20).
24. Swift's experience of the administration of Ireland lies behind the irony of this passage.

in my Company, without the Apprehensions I am yet under of his Teeth or his Claws.

My Reconcilement to the *Yahoo*-kind in general might not be so difficult, if they would be content with those Vices and Follies only which Nature hath entitled them to. I am not in the least provoked at the Sight of a Lawyer, a Pick-pocket, a Colonel, a Fool, a Lord, a Gamester, a Politician, a Whore-munger, a Physician, an Evidence,[0] a Suborner, an Attorney, a Traytor, or the like: This is all according to the due Course of Things: But, when I behold a Lump of Deformity, and Diseases both in Body and Mind, smitten with *Pride*, it immediately breaks all the Measures of my Patience; neither shall I be ever able to comprehend how such an Animal and such a Vice could tally together. The wise and virtuous *Houyhnhnms*, who abound in all Excellencies that can adorn a rational Creature, have no Name for this Vice in their Language, which hath no Terms to express any thing that is evil, except those whereby they describe the detestable Qualities of their *Yahoos*; among which they were not able to distinguish this of Pride, for want of thoroughly understanding Human Nature, as it sheweth it self in other Countries, where that Animal presides. But I, who had more Experience, could plainly observe some Rudiments of it among the wild *Yahoos*.

But the *Houyhnhnms*, who live under the Government of Reason, are no more proud of the good Qualities they possess, than I should be for not wanting a Leg or an Arm, which no Man in his Wits would boast of, although he must be miserable without them. I dwell the longer upon this Subject from the Desire I have to make the Society of an *English Yahoo* by any Means not insupportable; and therefore I here intreat those who have any Tincture[0] of this absurd Vice, that they will not presume to appear in my Sight.

Glossary

abroad: away from one's own house.
applying himself to: coming up to.
artificially: skilfully.
backwards: at the back of the house.
bosses: seats or hassocks of straw.
buccaneer: a pirate operating off the coast of South America.
calenture: fever during which a sailor, thinking the sea was a green field, would try to leap overboard into it.
cattle: all livestock (not merely 'cattle' in the modern sense).
climate: region.
cloaths: clothes.
colours: standards or regimental flags.
culverins: cannons used during the sixteenth and seventeenth centuries.
debauch: corrupt or encourage someone to turn away from his lawful employer.
depose: to make a deposition or testimony upon oath in a law court.
descanting: commenting or enlarging upon.
devoted to Destruction: consigned to destruction.
docible: able to be trained or taught.
dugs: breasts (a derogatory term).
eat: ate.
evidence: a witness.
fettlock = fetlock: the back of the lower part of a horse's front leg.
fondness: excessive affection.
forswearing: false swearing, perjury.
foundered: gone lame.
frog (of horse's foot): the sensitive centre of a horse's foot.
hams: the upper part of the back legs (of a horse).
hanger: a short sword that hangs from the belt.
intellectuals: intellects.
joynture = jointure: an estate held jointly by husband and wife.
lading: cargo or freight.
lappet: the 'skirt' of a coat, or the lapel.
league: three nautical miles.
mechanicks: a) workmen; b) manual labour.
mummy: pulp.
nag: a small horse or pony.
necromancy: enchantment, conjuring.
nicely: carefully.
pastern: the part of a horse's foot between the fetlock and the hoof.
piece: firearm.
pravity: depravity.
prognostic(k)s: prediction.
rickety: suffering from rickets.
roul: roll.
rue: a strong scented herb.
scrophulous = scrofulous: affected with scrofula, a disease of the lymph glands, known as the 'King's evil'.
sorrel: reddish brown in colour.
spleen: violent ill-temper or melancholy.
springe: a snare for catching small game.
stone-horses: stallions.
suborning: bribing or unlawfully procuring.
ticking: pillow or mattress cover.
tincture: tinge or taint.
toys: trinkets.
wyths = withes: halters made of tough flexible twigs, twisted or plaited together.

A MODEST PROPOSAL

FOR PREVENTING THE CHILDREN OF POOR PEOPLE IN *IRELAND,* FROM BEING A BURDEN TO THEIR PARENTS OR COUNTRY; AND FOR MAKING THEM BENEFICIAL TO THE PUBLICK (1729)

[This, the best known of Swift's shorter works, is also the most outrageous. Since Ireland's main problem is said to be overpopulation, the writer, who seems to be a genial, good-natured economic planner, proposes a simple solution: eat the children of the poor. There had been three years of famine before 1729 and this, coupled with England's continuing bleeding of Ireland's wealth, led to great hardship. The solution proposed, with terrible irony, was meant to shock readers into a realization of man's inhumanity to man in the Irish context. Although it had no effect on the government of the day, the deadly rhetoric of the pamphlet has made a lasting impact on many modern readers, who perceive it to be as relevant to our times as it was to Swift's.]

It is a melancholly Object to those, who walk through this great Town,[1] or travel in the Country; when they see the *Streets,* the *Roads,* and *Cabbin-doors* crowded with *Beggars* of the Female Sex, followed by three, four, or six Children, *all in Rags,* and importuning every Passenger[2] for an Alms. These *Mothers,* instead of being able to work for their honest Livelyhood, are forced to employ all their Time in stroling to beg Sustenance for their *helpless Infants*; who, as they grow up, either turn *Thieves* for want of Work; or leave their *dear Native Country, to fight for the Pretender*[3] *in* Spain, or sell themselves to the *Barbadoes.*[4]

I think it is agreed by all Parties, that this prodigious Number of Children in the Arms, or on the Backs, or at the *Heels* of their *Mothers,* and frequently of their *Fathers,* is *in the present deplorable State of the Kingdom,* a very great additional Grievance; and therefore, whoever could find out a fair, cheap, and easy Method of making these Children sound and useful Members of the Commonwealth, would deserve so well of the Publick, as to have his Statue set up for a Preserver of the Nation.

But my Intention is very far from being confined to provide only for the Children of *professed Beggars*: It is of a much greater Extent, and shall take in the whole Number of Infants at a certain Age, who are born of Parents, in effect as little able to support them, as those who demand our Charity in the Streets.

As to my own Part, having turned my Thoughts for many Years, upon this important Subject, and maturely weighed the several *Schemes of other Projectors,* I have always found them grosly mistaken in their Computation. It is true a Child, *just dropt from its Dam,* may be supported by her Milk, for a Solar Year with little other Nourishment; at most not above the Value of two Shillings; which the Mother may certainly get, or the Value in *Scraps,* by her lawful Occupation of *Begging*: And, it is exactly at one Year old, that I propose to provide for them in such a Manner, as, instead of being a Charge upon their *Parents,* or the *Parish,* or *wanting Food and Raiment* for the rest of their Lives; they shall, on the contrary, contribute to the Feeding, and partly to the Cloathing, of many Thousands.

There is likewise another great Advantage in my *Scheme,* that it will prevent those *voluntary Abortions,* and that horrid Practice of *Women murdering their Bastard Children*; alas! too frequent among us; sacrificing the *poor innocent Babes,* I doubt, more to avoid the Expence than the Shame; which would move Tears and Pity in the most Savage and inhuman Breast.

The Number of Souls in *Ireland* being usually reckoned one Million and a half;[5] of these I calculate there may be about Two hundred Thousand Couple whose Wives are Breeders; from which Number I subtract thirty thousand Couples, who are able to maintain their own Children; although I apprehend there cannot be so many, under *the present Distresses of the Kingdom*; but this being granted, there will remain an Hundred and Seventy Thousand Breeders. I again subtract Fifty Thousand, for those Women who miscarry, or whose Children die by Accident, or Disease, within the Year. There only remain an Hundred and Twenty Thousand Children of poor Parents, annually born: The Question therefore is, How this Number shall be reared, and provided for? Which, as I have already said, under the present Situation of Affairs, is utterly impossible, by all the Methods hitherto proposed: For we can *neither employ them in Handicraft* or *Agriculture*; we neither build Houses, (I mean in the Country) nor cultivate Land: They can very seldom pick up a Livelyhood *by Stealing* until they arrive at six Years old; except where they are of towardly Parts;[6] although, I confess, they learn the Rudiments much earlier; during which Time, they can, however, be properly

1. Dublin.
2. passer-by.
3. James Stuart (1688-1766), the 'Old Pretender', son of James II; he lived in exile in France and was a focus for the loyalty of Irish catholics.
4. Many Irish labourers sold themselves as indentured servants to the owners of West Indian sugar plantations. There they worked for low wages for an agreed number of years in exchange for bed and lodging.
5. For a cold and calculating assessment of Ireland's population and its problems, see William Petty's *A Treatise on Ireland* (1687).
6. unless they show promise and ability.

looked upon only as *Probationers*; as I have been informed by a principal Gentleman in the County of *Cavan*, who protested to me, that he never knew above one or two Instances under the Age of six, even in a Part of the Kingdom *so renowned for the quickest Proficiency in that Art*.

I am assured by our Merchants, that a Boy or a Girl before twelve Years old, is no saleable Commodity; and even when they come to this Age, they will not yield above Three Pounds, or Three Pounds and half a Crown at most, on the Exchange; which cannot turn to Account either to the Parents or the Kingdom; the Charge of Nutriment and Rags, having been at least four Times that Value.

I shall now therefore humbly propose my own Thoughts; which I hope will not be liable to the least Objection.

I have been assured by a very knowing *American* of my Acquaintance in *London*; that a young healthy Child, well nursed, at a Year old, a most delicious, nourishing, and wholesome Food; whether *Stewed, Roasted, Baked*, or *Boiled*; and, I make no doubt, that it will equally serve in a *Fricasie*, or *Ragoust*.[7]

I do therefore humbly offer it to *publick Consideration*, that of the Hundred and Twenty Thousand Children, already computed, Twenty thousand may be reserved for Breed; whereof only one Fourth Part to be Males; which is more than we allow to *Sheep, black Cattle*, or *Swine*; and my Reason is, that these Children are seldom the Fruits of Marriage, *a Circumstance not much regarded by our Savages*; therefore, *one Male* will be sufficient to serve *four Females*. That the remaining Hundred thousand, may, at a Year old, be offered in Sale to the *Persons of Quality* and *Fortune*, through the Kingdom; always advising the Mother to let them suck plentifully in the last Month, so as to render them plump, and fat for a good Table. A Child will make two Dishes at an Entertainment for Friends; and when the Family dines alone, the fore or hind Quarter will make a reasonable Dish; and seasoned with a little Pepper or Salt, will be very good Boiled on the fourth Day, especially in *Winter*.

I have reckoned upon a Medium,[8] that a Child just born will weigh Twelve Pounds; and in a solar Year, if tolerably nursed, encreaseth to twenty eight Pounds.

I grant this Food will be somewhat dear, and therefore very *proper for Landlords*; who, as they have already devoured most of the Parents, seem to have the best Title to the Children.

Infants Flesh will be in Season throughout the Year; but more plentiful in *March*, and a little before and after: For we are told by a grave Author,[9] an eminent *French* Physician, that *Fish being a prolifick Dyet*, there are more Children born in *Roman Catholick Countries* about Nine Months after *Lent*, than at any other Season: Therefore reckoning a Year after *Lent*, the Markets will be more glutted than usual; because the Number of *Popish Infants*, is, at least, three to one in this Kingdom; and therefore it will have one other Collateral Advantage, by lessening the Number of *Papists* among us.

I have already computed the Charge of nursing a Beggar's Child (in which List I reckon all *Cottagers, Labourers*, and Four fifths of the *Farmers*)[10] to be about two Shillings *per Annum*, Rags included; and I believe, no Gentleman would repine[11] to give Ten Shillings for the *Carcase of a good fat Child*; which, as I have said, will make four Dishes of excellent nutritive Meat, when he hath only some particular Friend, or his own Family, to dine with him. Thus the Squire will learn to be a good Landlord, and grow popular among his Tenants; the Mother will have Eight Shillings net Profit, and be fit for Work until she produceth another Child.

Those who are more thrifty (*as I must confess the Times require*) may flay the Carcase; the Skin of which, artificially dressed, will make admirable *Gloves for Ladies*, and *Summer Boots for fine Gentlemen*.

As to our City of *Dublin*; Shambles[12] may be appointed for this Purpose, in the most convenient Parts of it; and Butchers we may be assured will not be wanting; although I rather recommend buying the Children alive, and dressing them hot from the Knife, as we do *roasting Pigs*.

A very worthy Person, *a true Lover of his Country*, and whose Virtues I highly esteem, was lately pleased, in discoursing on this Matter, to offer a Refinement upon my Scheme. He said, that many

7. a highly seasoned stew.
8. on average.

9. François Rabelais (*c*.1494-1553), *Pantagruel*, V, xix. Since Lent was (and is) in March and April, 'Nine Months after *Lent*' would be at Christmas, not in March.
10. Swift is commenting on changing land-use in Ireland when he categorizes four-fifths of the farmers as beggars.
11. complain.
12. slaughter-houses.

Gentlemen of this Kingdom, having of late destroyed their Deer; he conceived, that the Want of Venison might be well supplied by the Bodies of young Lads and Maidens, not exceeding fourteen Years of Age, nor under twelve; so great a Number of both Sexes in every County being now ready to starve, for Want of Work and Service: And these to be disposed of by their Parents, if alive, or otherwise by their nearest Relations. But with due Deference to so excellent a Friend, and so deserving a Patriot, I cannot be altogether in his Sentiments. For as to the Males, my *American* Acquaintance assured me from frequent Experience, that their Flesh was generally tough and lean, like that of our School-boys, by continual Exercise, and their Taste disagreeable; and to fatten them would not answer the Charge. Then, as to the Females, it would, I think, with humble Submission, *be a Loss to the Publick,* because they soon would become Breeders themselves: And besides it is not improbable, that some scrupulous People might be apt to censure such a Practice (although indeed very unjustly) as a little bordering upon Cruelty; which, I confess, hath always been with me the strongest Objection against any Project, how well soever intended.

But in order to justify my Friend; he confessed, that this Expedient was put into his Head by the famous Salmanaazor,[13] a Native of the Island *Formosa,* who came from thence to *London,* above twenty Years ago, and in Conversation told my Friend, that in his Country, when any young Person happened to be put to Death, the Executioner sold the Carcase to *Persons of Quality,* as a prime Dainty; and that, in his Time, the Body of a plump Girl of fifteen, who was crucified for an Attempt to poison the Emperor, was sold to his Imperial *Majesty's prime Minister of State,* and other great *Mandarins* of the Court, *in Joints from the Gibbet,* at Four hundred Crowns. Neither indeed can I deny, that if the same Use were made of several plump young girls in this Town, who, without one single Groat to their Fortunes, cannot stir Abroad without a Chair,[14] and appear at the *Play-house,* and *Assemblies* in foreign Fineries, which they never will pay for; the Kingdom would not be the worse.

Some Persons of a desponding Spirit are in great Concern about that vast Number of poor People, who are Aged, Diseased, or Maimed; and I have been desired to employ my Thoughts what Course may be taken, to ease the Nation of so grievous an Incumbrance. But I am not in the least Pain upon that Matter; because it is very well known, that they are every Day *dying,* and *rotting,* by *Cold* and *Famine,* and *Filth,* and *Vermin,* as fast as can be reasonably expected. And as to the younger Labourers, they are now in almost as hopeful a Condition: They cannot get Work, and consequently pine away for Want of Nourishment, to a Degree, that if at any Time they are accidentally hired to common Labour, they have not Strength to perform it; and thus the Country, and themselves, are in a fair Way of being soon delivered from the Evils to come.

I have too long digressed; and therefore shall return to my Subject. I think the Advantages by the Proposal which I have made, are obvious, and many, as well as of the highest Importance.

For, *First,* as I have already observed, it would greatly lessen the *Number of Papists,* with whom we are yearly overrun; being the principal Breeders of the Nation, as well as our most dangerous Enemies; and who stay at home on Purpose, with a Design to *deliver the Kingdom to the Pretender*; hoping to take their Advantage by the Absence *of so many good Protestants,* who have chosen rather to leave their Country, than stay at home, and pay Tithes[15] against their Conscience, to an idolatrous *Episcopal Curate.*

Secondly, The poorer Tenants will have something valuable of their own, which, by Law, may be made liable to Distress,[16] and help to pay their Landlord's Rent; their Corn and Cattle being already seized, and *Money a Thing unknown.*

Thirdly, Whereas the Maintenance of an Hundred Thousand Children, from two Years old, and upwards, cannot be computed at less than ten Shillings a Piece *per Annum,* the Nation's Stock will be thereby encreased Fifty Thousand Pounds *per Annum*; besides the Profit of a new Dish, introduced to the Tables of all *Gentlemen of Fortune* in the Kingdom, who have any Refinement in Taste; and the Money will circulate among

13. George Psalmanazar wrote a spurious *History of Formosa* which includes this disgusting story.
14. i.e. a sedan chair.
15. Every property owner or tenant in Ireland, whatever his religious affiliation, had to pay tithes to the Church of Ireland curate of his parish. Tithes, originally one-tenth of all produce, were still levied in corn (as well as money) in Swift's day.
16. to be seized because of unpaid rent.

ourselves, the Goods being entirely of our own Growth and Manufacture.

Fourthly, The constant Breeders, besides the Gain of Eight Shillings *Sterling per Annum,* by the Sale of their Children, will be rid of the Charge of maintaining them after the first Year.

Fifthly, This Food would likewise bring great *Custom to Taverns,* where the Vintners will certainly be so prudent, as to procure the best Receipts for dressing it to Perfection; and consequently, have their Houses frequented by all the *fine Gentlemen,* who justly value themselves upon their Knowledge in good Eating; and a skilful Cook, who understands how to oblige his Guests, will contrive to make it as expensive as they please.

Sixthly, This would be a great Inducement to Marriage, which all wise Nations have either encouraged by Rewards, or enforced by Laws and Penalties. It would encrease the Care and Tenderness of Mothers towards their Children, when they were sure of a Settlement for Life, to the poor Babes, provided in some Sort by the Publick, to their annual Profit instead of Expence. We should soon see an honest Emulation among the married Women, *which of them could bring the fattest Child to the Market.* Men would become as *fond* of their Wives, during the Time of their Pregnancy, as they are now of their *Mares* in Foal, their *Cows* in Calf, or *Sows* when they are ready to farrow; nor offer to beat or kick them, (as it is too *frequent* a Practice) for fear of a Miscarriage.

Many other Advantages might be enumerated. For instance, the Addition of some Thousand Carcasses in our Exportation of barrelled Beef: The Propagation of *Swines Flesh,* and Improvement in the Art of making good *Bacon;* so much wanted among us by the great Destruction of *Pigs,* too frequent at our Tables, and are no way comparable in Taste, or Magnificence, to a well-grown fat yearling Child; which, roasted whole, will make a considerable Figure at a *Lord Mayor's Feast,* or any other publick Entertainment. But this, and many others, I omit; being studious of Brevity.

Supposing that one Thousand Families in this City, would be constant Customers for Infants Flesh; besides others who might have it at *merry Meetings,* particularly *Weddings* and *Christenings;* I compute that *Dublin* would take off, annually, about Twenty Thousand Carcasses; and the rest of the Kingdom (where probably they will be sold somewhat cheaper) the remaining Eighty Thousand.

I can think of no one Objection, that will possibly be raised against this Proposal; unless it should be urged, that the Number of People will be thereby much lessened in the Kingdom. This I freely own; and it was indeed one principal Design in offering it to the World. I desire the Reader will observe, that I calculate my Remedy *for this one individual Kingdom of* IRELAND, *and for no other that ever was, is, or I think ever can be upon Earth.* Therefore, let no man talk to me of other Expedients:[17] *Of taxing our Absentees at five Shillings a Pound: Of using neither Cloaths, nor Houshold Furniture except what is of our own Growth and Manufacture: Of utterly rejecting the Materials and Instruments that promote foreign Luxury: Of curing the Expensiveness of Pride, Vanity, Idleness, and Gaming in our Women: Of introducing a Vein of Parsimony, Prudence and Temperance: Of learning to love our Country, wherein we differ even from* LAPLANDERS, *and the Inhabitants of* TOPINAMBOO:[18] *Of quitting our Animosities, and Factions; nor act any longer like the* Jews, *who were murdering one another at the very Moment their City was taken:*[19] *Of being a little cautious not to sell our Country and Consciences for nothing: Of teaching Landlords to have, at least, one Degree of Mercy towards their Tenants.* Lastly, *Of putting a Spirit of Honesty, Industry, and Skill into our Shop-keepers; who, if a Resolution could not be taken to buy only our native Goods, would immediately unite to cheat and exact upon us in the Price, the Measure, and the Goodness; nor could ever yet be brought to make one fair Proposal of just Dealing, though often and earnestly invited to it.*

Therefore I repeat, let no Man talk to me of these and the like Expedients; till he hath, at least, a Glimpse of Hope, that there will ever be some hearty and sincere Attempt to put *them in Practice.*

But, as to my self; having been wearied out for many Years with offering vain, idle, visionary Thoughts; and at length utterly despairing of Success, I fortunately fell upon this Proposal; which, as it is wholly new, so it hath something *solid* and *real,* of no Expence, and little Trouble, full in our own Power; and whereby we can incur no

17. Swift had recommended all these expedients at various times; see *A Proposal for the Universal Use of* Irish *Manufacture* above.
18. Part of the Brazilian jungle.
19. When Jerusalem was under siege by the Emperor Titus in 70 A.D., the Jews used their energies in civil strife, rather than in defending the city.

Danger in *disobliging* ENGLAND: For, this Kind of Commodity will not bear Exportation; the Flesh being of too tender a Consistence, to admit a long Continuance in Salt; *although, perhaps, I could name a Country, which would be glad to eat up our whole Nation without it.*

After all, I am not so violently bent upon my own Opinion, as to reject any Offer proposed by wise Men, which shall be found equally innocent, cheap, easy, and effectual. But before something of that Kind shall be advanced, in Contradiction to my Scheme, and offering a better; I desire the Author, or Authors, will be pleased maturely to consider two Points. *First,* As Things now stand, how they will be able to find Food and Raiment, for a Hundred Thousand useless Mouths and Backs? And *secondly,* There being a round Million of Creatures in human Figure, throughout this Kingdom; whose whole Subsistence, put into a common Stock, would leave them in Debt two Millions of Pounds *Sterling*; adding those, who are Beggars by Profession, to the Bulk of Farmers, Cottagers, and Labourers, with their Wives and Children, who are Beggars in Effect; I desire those Politicians, who dislike my Overture, and may perhaps be so bold to attempt an Answer, that they will first ask the Parents of these Mortals, Whether they would not, at this Day, think it a great Happiness to have been sold for Food at a Year old, in the Manner I prescribe; and thereby have avoided such a perpetual Scene of Misfortunes, as they have since gone through; by the *Oppression of Landlords*; the Impossibility of paying Rent, without Money or Trade; the Want of common Sustenance, with neither House nor Cloaths, to cover them from the Inclemencies of Weather; and the most inevitable Prospect of intailing the like, or greater Misers upon their Breed for ever.

I profess, in the Sincerity of my Heart, that I have not the least personal Interest, in endeavouring to promote this necessary Work; having no other Motive than the *publick Good of my Country, by advancing our Trade, providing for Infants, relieving the Poor, and giving some Pleasure to the Rich.* I have no Children, by which I can propose to get a single Penny; the youngest being nine Years old, and my Wife past Child-bearing.

from: VERSES ON THE DEATH OF DR. SWIFT, D.S.P.D. (1731)

[Swift placed a maxim from La Rochefoucauld at the head of this poem:

> *Dans l'adversité de nos meilleurs amis, nous trouvons quelque chose, qui ne nous deplaist pas.*
>
> In the adversity of our best friends, we find something that doth not displease us.

This poem, written in 1731, foresees the comments of Swift's friends on his death. It is written in the easy, relaxed tetrameter that Swift used for most of his verse. The selection below includes some of Swift's most acute remarks on himself. The notes above the rule are by Swift himself.]

. . . The Time is not remote, when I
Must by the Course of Nature dye:
When I foresee my special Friends,
Will try to find their private Ends:
Tho' it is hardly understood,
Which way my Death can do them good;
Yet, thus methinks, I hear 'em speak;
See, how the Dean begins to break:
Poor Gentleman, he droops apace,
You plainly find it in his Face:
That old Vertigo[1] in his Head,
Will never leave him, till he's dead:
Besides, his Memory decays,
He recollects not what he says;
He cannot call his Friends to Mind;
Forgets the Place where last he din'd:
Plyes you with Stories o'er and o'er,
He told them fifty Times before.
How does he fancy we can sit,
To hear his out-of-fashion'd Wit?
But he takes up with younger Fokes,
Who for his Wine will bear his Jokes:
Faith, he must make his Stories shorter,
Or change his Comrades once a Quarter:
In half the Time, he talks them round;
There must another Sett be found.

For Poetry, he's past his Prime,
He takes an Hour to find a Rhime:
His Fire is out, his Wit decay'd,
His Fancy sunk, his Muse a Jade.[2]

1. Swift suffered from Ménière's syndrome, an ailment that brought him recurrent bouts of deafness and giddiness.
2. worn-out old horse.

I'd have him throw away his Pen;
But there's no talking to some Men.

And, then their Tenderness appears,
By adding largely to my Years:
'He's older than he would be reckon'd,
And well remembers *Charles* the Second.
He hardly drinks a Pint of Wine;
And that, I doubt, is no good Sign.
His Stomach too begins to fail:
Last Year we thought him strong and hale;
But now, he's quite another Thing;
I wish he may hold out till Spring.'

Then hug themselves, and reason thus;
'It is not yet so bad with us.'
. . . .

'Behold the fatal Day arrive!
How is the Dean? He's just alive.
Now the departing Prayer is read:
He hardly breathes. The Dean is dead.
Before the Passing-Bell[3] begun,
The News thro' half the Town has run.
O, may we all for Death prepare!
What has he left? And who's his Heir?
I know no more than what the News is,
'Tis all bequeath'd to publick Uses.
To publick Use! A perfect Whim!
What had the Publick done for him!
Meer Envy, Avarice, and Pride!
He gave it all: — But first he dy'd.
And had the Dean, in all the Nation,
No worthy Friend, no poor Relation?
So ready to do Strangers good,
Forgetting his own Flesh and Blood?'

Now Grub-Street Wits[4] are all employ'd;
With Elegies, the Town is cloy'd:
Some Paragraph in ev'ry Paper,
To *curse* the *Dean*, or *bless* the *Drapier*.*

The Doctors tender of their Fame,
Wisely on me lay all the Blame:

* The Author imagines, that the Scriblers of the prevailing Party, which he always opposed, will libel him after his Death; but that others will remember him with Gratitude, who consider the Service he had done to *Ireland*, under the Name of *M. B.* Drapier, by utterly defeating the destructive Project of *Wood*'s Halfpence, in five Letters to the People of *Ireland*, at that Time read universally, and convincing every Reader.

3. The church bell tolled when a death occurred.
4. 'the tribe of literary hacks' (*OED*).

'We must confess his Case was nice;[5]
But he would never take Advice:

Had he been rul'd, for ought appears,
He might have liv'd these Twenty Years:
For when we open'd him we found,
That all his vital Parts were sound.'

From *Dublin* soon to *London* spread,
'Tis told at Court, the Dean is dead.†
King Lady *Suffolk*** in the Spleen,
Runs laughing up to tell the Queen.[6]
The Queen, so Gracious, Mild, and Good,
Cries, 'Is he gone? 'Tis time he shou'd.
He's dead you say; why let him rot;
I'm glad the Medals‡ were forgot.
I promis'd them, I own; but when?
I only was the Princess then;

But now as Consort of the King,
You know 'tis quite a different Thing.'
. . . .

My female Friends, whose tender Hearts
Have better learn'd to act their Parts.
Receive the News in *doleful Dumps*,
'The Dean is dead, (*and what is Trumps?*)[7]
Then Lord have Mercy on his Soul.
(Ladies I'll venture for the *Vole.*)[8]

† The Dean supposeth himself to dye in *Ireland*.

** Mrs. *Howard*, afterwards Countess of *Suffolk*, then of the Bed-chamber to the Queen, professed much Friendship for the Dean. The Queen then Princess, sent a dozen times to the Dean (then in *London*) with her Command to attend her; which at last he did, by Advice of all his Friends. She often sent for him afterwards, and always treated him very Graciously. He taxed her with a Present worth Ten Pounds, which she promised before he should return to *Ireland*, but on his taking Leave, the Medals were not ready.

‡ The Medals were to be sent to the Dean in four Months, but she forgot them, or thought them too dear. The Dean, being in *Ireland*, sent Mrs. *Howard* a Piece of *Indian* Plad made in that Kingdom: which the Queen seeing took from her, and wore it herself, and sent to the Dean for as much as would cloath herself and Children, desiring he would send the Charge of it. He did the former. It cost thirty-five Pounds, but he said he would have nothing except the Medals. He was the Summer following in *England*, was treated as usual, and she being then Queen, the Dean was promised a Settlement in *England*, but returned as he went, and, instead of Favour or Medals, hath been ever since under her Majesty's Displeasure.

5. strange or difficult.
6. Queen Caroline (1683-1737), wife of George II.
7. The suit of cards which, for the game being played, ranks higher than all other cards.
8. In quadrille and ombre, two fashionable card games of the day, a player who has won five tricks may choose to play for 'the vole', i.e. the rest of the outstanding tricks.

Six Deans they say must bear the Pall.[9]
(I wish I knew what *King* to call.)
Madam, your Husband will attend
The Funeral of so good a Friend.
No Madam, 'tis a shocking Sight,
And he's engag'd To-morrow Night!
My Lady *Club* wou'd take it ill,
If he shou'd fail her at *Quadrill*.[10]
He lov'd the Dean. (*I lead a Heart.*)
But dearest Friends, they say, must part.
His Time was come, he ran his Race;
We hope he's in a better Place.'
. . . .

Suppose me dead; and then suppose
A Club assembled at the *Rose*;[11]
Where from Discourse of this and that,
I grow the Subject of their Chat:
And, while they toss my Name about,
With Favour some, and some without;
One quite indiff'rent in the Cause,
My Character impartial draws:
'The Dean, if we believe Report,
Was never ill receiv'd at Court:
As for his Works in Verse and Prose,
I own my self no Judge of those:
Nor, can I tell what Criticks thought 'em;
But, this I know, all People bought 'em;
As with a moral View design'd
To cure the Vices of Mankind:
His Vein, ironically grave,
Expos'd the Fool, and lash'd the Knave:
To steal a Hint was never known,
But what he writ was all his own.'
. . . .

'Perhaps I may allow, the Dean
Had too much Satyr in his Vein;
And seem'd determin'd not to starve it,
Because no Age could more deserve it.
Yet, Malice never was his Aim;
He lash'd the Vice but spar'd the Name.
No Individual could resent,
Where Thousands equally were meant.
His Satyr points at no Defect,
But what all Mortals may correct;
For he abhorr'd that senseless Tribe,
Who call it Humour when they jibe:

9. The cloth spread over a coffin during a funeral.
10. A card game played by four people; cf. ombre, which is played by three people.
11. A famous London tavern.

He spar'd a Hump or crooked Nose,
Whose Owners set not up for Beaux.
True genuine Dulness mov'd his Pity,
Unless it offer'd[12] to be witty,
Those, who their Ignorance confess'd,
He ne'er offended with a Jest;
But laugh'd to hear an Idiot quote,
A Verse from *Horace*, learn'd by Rote.

He knew an hundred pleasant Stories,
With all the Turns of *Whigs* and *Tories*:
Was chearful to his dying Day,
And Friends would let him have his Way.

He gave the little Wealth he had,
To build a House for Fools and Mad:[13]
And shew'd by one satyric Touch,
No Nation wanted it so much:
That Kingdom* he hath left his Debtor,
I wish it soon may have a Better.'

* Meaning, *Ireland*, where he now lives, and probably may dye.

12. tried.
13. Swift left his money for the foundation of St Patrick's Hospital, one of Ireland's most important psychiatric hospitals.

Biography/Bibliography

LIFE. Swift was born in Dublin in 1667, of English parents. His father died some months before his birth and his mother employed an English nurse who, apparently, took the child to England with her for three years. He returned to Ireland aged four and was sent as a boarder to Kilkenny School when he was six. From there he entered Trinity College, Dublin in 1682 and graduated in 1686. He stayed at college to earn an M.A. but left Ireland in 1689 during 'the troubles' associated with the reign of James II. In England, he entered the service of the retired diplomat Sir William Temple, for whom he acted as secretary and amanuensis and in whose library he read widely. He was ordained into the Church of Ireland in 1695 and returned to Ireland to live in his parish in County Antrim for a short period. After a further stay in the household of Sir William Temple, he came to Ireland in 1699 and by 1704 was sufficiently trusted to be sent to London as emissary of the Church of Ireland to seek remission of the First Fruits from Queen Anne. This he eventually obtained in 1710 through the intervention of Robert Harley, the Tory 'prime minister'. Swift became a close confidant of Harley and of Henry St John, viscount Bolingbroke, the secretary of state, for the next three years. With the death of Queen Anne and the fall of the ministry, Swift returned to Ireland, where he had been appointed dean of St Patrick's Cathedral, Dublin. Apart from two short visits to England, he remained in Ireland until his death in 1745.

CHIEF WRITINGS. *A Tale of a Tub* (London, 1704); *An Argument against Abolishing Christianity* (1708; published London, 1711); *The Examiner* (London, 1710-11); *The Journal to Stella* (1710-13); *A Proposal for the Universal Use of Irish Manufacture* (Dublin, 1720); *The Drapier's Letters* (Dublin, 1724-25); *Gulliver's Travels* (London, 1726); *A Modest Proposal* (Dublin, 1729); *Verses on the Death of Dr Swift* (1731; published London, 1739).

The standard editions of Swift's works are: Herbert Davis et al (eds), *The Prose Works of Jonathan Swift* 14 vols (Oxford: Basil Blackwell, 1939-68); Harold Williams (ed.), *The Poems of Jonathan Swift* 2nd edition, 3 vols (Oxford: Clarendon Press, 1958); Harold Williams (ed.), *The Correspondence of Jonathan Swift* 5 vols (Oxford: Clarendon Press, 1963-68); Harold Williams (ed.), *Swift's Journal to Stella* (Oxford: Clarendon Press, 1948).

BIOGRAPHY AND CRITICISM. The best biography is Irvin Ehrenpreis, *Swift, the Man, his Works and the Age* 3 vols (London: Methuen, 1962-83). An excellent one-volume biography is David Nokes, *Jonathan Swift: A Hypocrite Reversed. A Critical Biography* Oxford: Oxford University Press, 1985); see also A.C. Elias Jr, *Swift at Moor Park* (Philadelphia: University of Pennsylvania Press, 1982) and Louis Landa, *Swift and the Church of Ireland* (Oxford: Clarendon Press, 1954).

An enormous amount has been written on Swift, particularly in the last 25 years. Rather than a list of critical works, a list of the most significant modern critics is given below: W.B. Carnochan, Herbert Davis, Michael V. DePorte, Denis Donoghue, Irvin Ehrenpreis, A.C. Elias Jr., Frank Ellis, Carole Fabricant, Oliver W. Ferguson, Phillip Harth, Louis Landa, Ronald Paulson, Clive Probyn, Ricardo Quintana, Claude Rawson, Angus Ross, Harold Williams, Kathleen Williams, and James Woolley. Useful publications include the journal *Swift Studies*, and mention should also be made of the important bibliographical work of David Woolley, Hermann Real and Heinz Vienken.

BRYAN COLEBORNE, *Editor*

Anglo-Irish Verse 1675-1825

During the eighteenth century, Dublin was second only to London in the English-speaking world as a centre for the printing of poetry. Between 1675 and 1825, hundreds of poets were active in Ireland and innumerable broadsheets and collections of poetry were published in the capital. Swift was the greatest of these poets, but there were many other good (and some very fine) poets besides. Few modern scholars have paid attention to eighteenth-century Anglo-Irish verse and no modern anthology contains more than a few of its major poems. The section that follows is designed therefore to correct this critical imbalance and to direct attention to the work of a number of significant — and hitherto unregarded — Anglo-Irish poets of the eighteenth century; grouping their poems by theme rather than in chronological order, it aims to provide a cultural context for the reading of the better-known poems and useful standards of comparison for the lesser-known.

The selection consists of nearly one hundred items, ranging chronologically from 'Lilli burlero', the anti-Jacobite song of the 1680s, to orange and green poems published in the aftermath of the 1798 Rebellion. The poetry of the period was embedded fundamentally in its social context; much of it was occasional, and the most interesting way of viewing it is by event or theme, rather than by date of composition. This explains why this section departs from the normal format of the anthology and presents headnotes for groups of poems, rather than headnotes introducing each individual poem. The Irish literary milieu that gave rise to this poetry has received no critical attention and, as the poems emerge from their groups to stand in comparison with each other, they reveal much of interest about eighteenth-century Irish literary and social life. Poems like *The Irish Hudibras*, for example, or Swift's 'The Description of an *Irish-Feast*', suggest a greater degree of contact between Irish- and English-speaking cultures, or between catholics and protestants, than might be expected. Music and theatre, too, broke down the religious and social divides; even in the political sphere, some of the underlying forces in play, as Ireland moved from apparent peace at the beginning of the century to open conflict at the end, may be traced through the tone and subject-matter of the verse.

Broadly, of course, Anglo-Irish verse of this period corresponds in form and tone to the English verse of the times. Some Anglo-Irish poets followed classical norms and wrote mock-heroic or neo-classical epistles and odes; others sought more personal or sentimental voices. *The Irish Hudibras* and Samuel Whyte's 'The New Ferry', for example, are full of Graeco-Roman references; William Dunkin's *The Murphæid* and Matthew Pilkington's 'The Progress of Music in *Ireland*' show the influence of English Augustanism. Social and political life similar to that of London appears in Thomas Sheridan's 'To the *Dean*' or Jonathan Smedley's 'Verses, *Fix'd on the Cathedral Door* . . . .'. Some of the later eighteenth-century Anglo-Irish poets, however, tend to be more sentimental than their English counterparts, as James Orr's 'The Irishman' or the famous Irish Volunteer songs prove; but there are sound political reasons for this.

Foreign influences and literary norms, however, did nothing to dampen the native genius and inventiveness of eighteenth-century Anglo-Irish poets. Popular song and balladry are major elements in the output of the age, reflecting the energy — often the rebellious energy — of the people of Ireland. Popular emotion and popular verse forms came together at certain moments during the century; for instance, at the time of the protest against Wood's Halfpence in the 1720s. Political outrage was spurred into action on the streets of Dublin with the help of rousing songs, many the work of Swift, set to popular tunes. Much later, during the Regency crisis of 1788-89, Mary O'Brien used popular metres to rebuke the English government — and William Pitt in particular — for the part it had played during the commercial and political negotiations of the 1780s.

Although the structural patterns of eighteenth-century rhetoric exercised a strong influence on the Anglo-Irish poetry of the time, they did not always have a restricting force. William Dunkin, perhaps the most notable among the lesser-known poets whose work appears below, forged his own style. His work combines intellectual and formal discipline with remarkable freedom and flexibility of language. Dunkin paraded his formidable scholarship in his verse; for many of his poems, including the extended *Poetical Mirror* and *The Murphæid*, Latin and English texts face each other throughout. For others, *Faulkner's Nativity* for instance, Greek text faces Latin text and each is translated into English (the translation of the Greek text is into unrhymed iambic pentameter and that of the Latin text into heroic couplets). Surprisingly, the English poetry in all these exercises stands out for its liveliness, colour and ironic, self-deprecatory wit. Such dazzling versatility appears in a different guise in Dunkin's long poem *The Parson's Revels*, a veritable *tour de force* of energetic dialogue and lively description, which exploits to the full a popular song stanza. Dunkin's skilful, ironic manipulation of the poet's persona makes his verse as attractive to a modern audience as it was to Swift, the master of this mode. In 1738 Swift described Dunkin as 'a Gentleman of much Wit and the best English as well as Latin Poet in this Kingdom' (Swift to John Barber, 17 January 1737-8).

Two other versatile poets were Laurence Whyte and John Winstanley. In his '*Dissertation on* Italian *and* Irish *Musick*', Whyte provides significant details of the musical culture of Swift's Ireland; and in his poem on Swift in 1735, he presents an important interpretation of the reception of the first collected edition of Swift's *Works.* John Winstanley could produce the racy verses of the 'Song *upon an intended Jaunt to* Power's-court . . . .' and the clever tetrameter couplets of the '*An* Inventory *of the* Furniture *of a* Collegian's Chamber'. Winstanley's work is far less consistent than that of Dunkin, but his verse — like that of the eccentric Richard Pockrich — is included here because of the vivid insight it provides into life in early eighteenth-century Dublin.

Whatever their technical accomplishments, though, it is for their interpretation of the experience of life in Ireland that we read these poets today. Few of them were uncritical of their subjects — James Ward's '*Phoenix* Park' is perhaps the only example of uncritical panegyric in the poems below; most writers saw Ireland, her life and people, with the double, almost endemically ironic, vision that became established in the eighteenth century as the Anglo-Irish mode of seeing the world. As such they worked within a tradition divergent from that of England — one that requires serious analysis. Some poets, such as the anonymous author of *Hesperi-neso-graphia*, which refers to Geoffrey of Monmouth, the romantic historiographer of the twelfth century, appeared to make a self-conscious rejection of '*British* authors'. Others, such as the writer of 'A Description of the County of Kerry', seemed to adapt emerging Anglo-Irish models. Swift and Goldsmith, whose experience spans the worlds of both Ireland and England, dip into either culture at will. These last figures create difficulties for the literary historian who would separate them from one culture or the other.

Yet as the pattern of Anglo-Irish verse in the eighteenth century emerges, an important theme becomes the search for personal and institutional stability in a world of change. This theme pervades the entire selection, from the poems of Swift and his circle to those on Wood's Halfpence or Irish domestic politics, from accounts of the social and political divisions of the early eighteenth century to poems on the Volunteers. The effect of *The Deserted Village* is greatly heightened if it is read alongside poems written in Ireland on the theme of the lack of stability in Irish social and cultural life; poets in Ireland, too, saw traditional values weakening in the face of forces that seemed to threaten the survival of a humane society. The critical orthodoxy that asserts that the picture of rural life in *The Deserted Village* is generic is surely open to doubt when the poem is read in this context. Conversely, of course, it deepens the reading of the Irish poems to approach them from the perspectives afforded by *The Deserted Village*.

Inevitably, many of the poems make use of the vocabulary and constructions of Hiberno-English, sometimes for comic effect, sometimes because they are the linguistic material at hand. Swift was more delighted by words and nuances than any other writer of the age and his poems exploit joyfully the multiple resources of wit and word-play. William Dunkin also deserves recognition for his accomplishments in this field and some of the poets late in the century are equally inventive. But the duality that is inherent in word-play is best seen in the poems of Swift, where it informs his whole perspective. In 'Verses *said to be written on the* Union', for example, the 'Commonweal' becomes 'A Vessel with a double Keel' in which 'tossing Faction will o'erwhelm/Our crazy double-bottom'd Realm'. Ireland, not a member of the Union, faces the dilemma of establishing political stability in a world of political ambiguity. The negative that emerges here comes to be crucial both to Ireland and to Swift. Ireland did not have legislative independence: it could not control its own economy, it could not reform its own currency. As Swift well knew, the force of the negative could be exploited to turn an Irish audience against its political masters, as he did when he advised his readers to refuse Wood's Halfpence. The sense of the negative that Swift presented could also be comic. In 'A Serious Poem upon William Wood, *Brasier, Tinker, Hard-Ware-Man, Coiner, Counterfeiter, Founder* and *Esquire*', Swift established a dichotomy between truth and falsehood, and proposed that Wood be drilled into with an auger in order to discover 'What *Stuff* he is made on'. In fact, Swift developed, in this and other poems, a sense of comic fantasy, which is one of the distinguishing features not only of his own imagination but also of that of many of the other poets whose work is presented below. The reader has only to glance at *Hesperi-neso-graphia*, *The Irish Hudibras*, 'The Description of an *Irish-Feast*' or *The Old Westmeath-Ballad* to see this comic fantasy in many different forms. In effect, it is a distinguishing feature of much Anglo-Irish poetry and is deserving of study.

While Swift dominates the first half of the eighteenth century in Anglo-Irish writing, another subject — the impact of his presence in Irish culture — begins to grow out of that domination. The most important writer of his day became a subject for others to address and, whether they attacked him or praised him, a sense of his presence became indelibly fixed in the Irish mind. In 1740, Francis Bindon painted his last portrait of Swift. In his poem on this painting, Dunkin presented an awesome picture of the tragic figure of Swift in old age. 'And what remains against the storm/Of malice, but an empty form?' What, indeed, did remain when Swift had gone, a figure who had dominated Anglo-Irish culture in a way no other writer has ever done?

The answer is, of course, a body of less outrageous, less whimsical but increasingly political poetry. The leisurely world of the early eighteenth century — with its Sheelahs and Dermots, and Phoenix Park in apparent peace — was gradually transformed to the world of the Volunteers, Henry Grattan and 1798. The poets reflected all this and, as Irish life became more overtly political after about 1750, so did Anglo-Irish poetry. Eventually, as the Jacobite white became the revolutionary green, and orange acquired its political significance, figures such as William Blacker and James Orr took over from John Winstanley and Matthew Pilkington; Irish poetry began moving towards that political intimacy that would characterize it in the more openly propagandist conditions of the next century.

Poetry as closely tied to context as is that of eighteenth-century Ireland may easily be dismissed as minor poetry, available to those with the inclination and time to pursue it, but hardly essential reading for most. But all literary forms — fiction and drama as well as poetry — derive from social and political contexts and in Ireland they reproduce the ambivalence and sense of double vision that was increasingly a part of the Irish experience. The military defeat of Irish catholicism in 1690 led not to abrupt emigration or annihilation but to the slow assimilation and absorption of one culture in another; and this, of course, ushered in a period of extended cultural and political uncertainty. 'What ish my nation?' was a question of vital importance not only to Swift and Goldsmith, but also to Blacker and Orr, Winstanley, Pockrich, Mary Barber and indeed to almost all the people of eighteenth-century Ireland. The lack of a secure identity, linked as it was, ironically, to a determination to celebrate life in all its forms, produced verse with a peculiar flavour, full of energy and ambivalence, quite unlike that of eighteenth-century England or Scotland. From one point of view, Ireland's political problems might seem to have been 'solved' by the battle of the Boyne, but her cultural problems were exacerbated by it and by the settlement that followed. Furthermore, as the century progressed, the Anglo-Irish rightly felt themselves to be increasingly abandoned and made fun of by the English of England. It is little wonder that a large proportion of the poetry of eighteenth-century Anglo-Ireland is ironic and critical. There is nothing complacent or comfortable about most of the poems below. On the contrary, they range from the uneasy to the querulous, from the outrageously grotesque to the aggressively bantering. The reader is constantly aware of the pressure of confrontation between the demands of different backgrounds and cultures.

And yet, as much of the poetry celebrates life, nature and human activity, it also celebrates Ireland itself. Although they wrote in English and were proud of distant forbears in England, almost all these poets thought of themselves as Irishmen and of Ireland as their country. England was 'across the water', and 'parliament' meant their Irish parliament rather than the overlord body at Westminster. Pride in Irish achievements, despite the mercantile and military burdens imposed by Britain, was real enough; and national fervour, as it rose towards the end of the century, was based on foundations genuinely laid by such events as the defeat of Wood's Halfpence. This poetry, then, is the product of a society culturally unsure of itself but conscious that it was, at any rate, distinct from English culture and from England.

At another level, these poets might pretend to themselves and their gentle readers that their Irish world was stable and secure as they celebrated the building of bridges or monuments, the enclosure of parks or the exchange of birthday gifts; but they were aware that the language they used was often not easily reconciled to fact. Although they might publicly celebrate the belief that, in County Kerry, for instance, 'Every man's a monarch in his mind', such a claim to personal autonomy may have been no more than a consolatory gesture for the loss of national autonomy and responsibility. For, Ireland — official Ireland of the English language at any rate — throughout the eighteenth century showed itself unwilling to pay any attention to the voice of intelligent criticism, to the values of natural justice or to the wishes of most of its people, even those who held the franchise. If British rule and eventual integration with Britain had been able to bring economic or political security, Ireland might have thrown up a James Thomson or a William Collins to celebrate enthusiastically its achievement or allow its landscape to work upon the open imagination. But the brooding nostalgia and intellectual hesitancy that so pervade Goldsmith's work are typical features of serious Anglo-Irish writing of the eighteenth century. The contrast between what was publicly stated and what was privately experienced in Ireland was so marked that poets were driven to irony and satire from praise and description, to invective and burlesque rather than to outright celebration. In the church, the theatre, the world of music, the city and the countryside, the celebration is tinged with insecurity and regret.

Irony and a deep-seated fear of facing reality — of self-knowledge, in fact — are probably the hallmarks of Anglo-Irish poetry of the eighteenth century and yet, as the groupings below indicate, outwardly the poems are mostly celebratory, witty, full of life. The paradox of eighteenth-century Ireland may be seen here in microcosm, and the selection perhaps shows how, in poems on many different themes, there was a slow emergence during the period from cultural ambiguity and uneasy joking towards a sense of political and literary identity, even maturity. The poets thus reflected an important strand of Anglo-Irish life.

For its own political reasons, the nineteenth century chose to neglect this period of Irish cultural history or to dismiss it with curt generalizations; some twentieth-century scholars, even very recently, have felt equally able to do so. The selection below is presented in the hope that it may stimulate fresh examination not only of the poets whose works are printed here but also of the cultural milieu in which they worked. Such an examination is long overdue.

I

'A monarch in his mind'

The title for this first selection of poetry from the Irish eighteenth century comes from a line in 'A Description of the County of Kerry', first published pseudonymously in Dublin in 1726: 'Here every man's a monarch in his mind'. The recurrent theme of the poems that follow is the celebration of life in its many different forms.

The poems have been grouped by subject-matter, so that those connected with specific aspects of daily life, such as eating and drinking, the theatre, or music, appear together. Poems are included which present social types, such as William Dunkin's schoolmaster or parson, and others in which real figures, such as Turlogh Carolan or George Frideric Handel, appear. Throughout, the selection is designed to present different facets of eighteenth-century Irish life and to show how energetically and enthusiastically — if ironically — it was embraced by the poets of the age.

The 'noble Fare'

[Eating and drinking were popular subjects for the poets of eighteenth-century Ireland and these four poems are representative of many others. Perhaps the best-known description of an Irish feast is Swift's translation of the Irish poem 'Pléaráca na Ruarcach', which tells of a famous feast given by Brian O'Rourke, a chieftain of County Leitrim, in the sixteenth century. The original Irish poem was probably by Hugh Mac Gauran, a friend of the harper Turlogh Carolan, who composed the air 'O'Rourke's Feast' for it. (For the Irish text, with an early early version of Swift's translation, see p. 305.)

Laurence Whyte's poem, a satiric description of a miserly host who deceived his guests, dates from 1725, and Matthew Concanen's drinking song, which uses the generally known eighteenth-century meaning of 'October' as 'ale', appeared in his comedy *Wexford Wells* in 1721. Thomas Dermody's comic epitaph for his drinking companion John Baynham provides a brief glimpse into the gay and intoxicated way of life that led to his own death at the age of twenty-seven.]

JONATHAN SWIFT
(1667-1745)

THE DESCRIPTION OF AN *IRISH-FEAST*, TRANSLATED ALMOST LITERALLY OUT OF THE ORIGINAL *IRISH*

O Rourk's noble Fare
 Will ne'er be forgot,
By those who were there.
 Or those who were not.
His Revels to keep,
 We sup and we dine,
On seven Score Sheep,
 Fat Bullocks and Swine.
Usquebagh[1] to our Feast
 In Pails was brought up,
An Hundred at least,
 And a Madder[2] our Cup.
O there is the Sport,
 We rise with the Light,
In disorderly Sort,
 From snoring all Night.
O how was I trick't,
 My Pipe it was broke,
My Pocket was pick't,
 I lost my new Cloak.
I'm rifled, quoth *Nell*,
 Of Mantle and Kercher,[3]
Why then fare them well,
 The De'el take the Searcher.[4]
Come, Harper, strike up,
 But first by your Favour,
Boy, give us a Cup;
 Ay, this has some Savour:
O *Rourk*'s jolly Boys
 Ne'er dream't of the Matter,
Till rowz'd by the Noise,
 And musical Clatter,
They bounce from their Nest,
 No longer will tarry,
They rise ready drest,
 Without one *Ave Mary*.
They dance in a Round,
 Cutting Capers and Ramping,[5]
A Mercy the Ground
 Did not burst with their stamping.
The Floor is all wet
 With Leaps and with Jumps,

1. whiskey.
2. wooden vessel.
3. A variant of kerchief, a headcloth worn by women.
4. Possibly an officer searching for smuggled or illegally distilled liquor. 'De'el' = Devil.
5. romping.

While the Water and Sweat,
Splish, splash in their Pumps.
Bless you late and early,
Laughlin O Enagin,
By my Hand, you dance rarely,
Margery Grinagin.
Bring Straw for our Bed,
Shake it down to the Feet,
Then over us spread,
The winnowing Sheet.
To show, I don't flinch,
Fill the Bowl up again,
Then give us a Pinch
Of your Sneezing; *a Yean*.[6]
Good Lord, what a Sight,
After all their good Cheer,
For People to fight
In the Midst of their Beer:
They rise from their Feast,
And hot are their Brains,
A Cubit at least
The Length of their Skeans.[7]
What Stabs and what Cuts,
What clatt'ring of Sticks,
What Strokes on Guts,
What Bastings and Kicks!
With Cudgels of Oak,
Well harden'd in Flame,
An hundred Heads broke,
An hundred struck lame.
You Churle, I'll maintain
My Father built *Lusk*,[8]
The Castle of *Slain*,[9]
And *Carrickdrumrusk*:[10]
The Earl of *Kildare*,[11]
And *Moynalta*,[12] his Brother,
As great as they are,
I was nurs'd by their Mother.[13]
Ask that of old *Madam*,
She'll tell you who's who,
As far up as *Adam*,
She knows it is true,
Come down with that Beam,
If Cudgels are scarce,
A Blow on the Weam,[14]
Or a Kick on the A-se.

6. Probably based on a form of the Irish word for 'Ann'.
7. 'daggers, or short swords' (Swift's editor, George Faulkner).
8. A village thirteen miles north of Dublin.
9. i.e. Slane, Co. Meath.
10. Carrick-on-Shannon, Co. Leitrim.
11. It is not clear which Earl of Kildare is referred to here.
12. A place or area in County Meath.
13. 'It is the custom in *Ireland* to call nurses foster-mothers; their husbands foster-fathers; and their children foster-brothers or foster-sisters; and thus the poorest claim kindred to the richest.' (Swift's editor, John Hawkesworth).
14. A jocular term for belly.

LAURENCE WHYTE

(*c.* 1700-55)

THE HUE AND CRY AFTER THE CLIEVE-BOY[1]

Dublin Feb. 22d. 1725

Last *Saturday* a *French* Ale-Drapier,
To Market gave a nimble Caper,
To buy provisions for they say,
That *Sunday* is his Kettle Day;[2]
And once a Week did treat his Guest,
With boiled and roasted of the best,
His Pockets were well lin'd with Gold,
But *Meat* was dear that Day I'm told,
This with the Scarcity of Bread,
Made frugal *Peter* scratch his Head.
Quoth he I'm loth to give offence —
But Ale won't Ballance this Expence,
I must contrive some cunning Scheme,
To save my Money and my Fame,
Then I must draw a Bill of Fare,
To make this Project look more clear.
First then a Turky, Sprouts and Bacon,
Next comes a Sallad and fat Capon,
And then a stately Leg of Mutton,
Enough for twelve at least to glut on,
For sure the Thoughts of such a Treat,
May serve for once instead of Meat.
Next night his Friends together met,
And each Man in his Post being set,
To chat and drink had equal right,
Which was the bus'ness of that Night;
Pipes and Tobacco on the Table,
To smoak and drink while they were able;
At Eight a Clock, by Watch and Chimes,
The Cup went round just twenty times,
And just so many Chalks were scor'd
In parallels upon the Board.

1. The servant whose job it was to cleave the meat; two forms of the word are used in the poem.
2. Presumably a variant of the sense of 'kettle' as a cooked meal. On the host's kettle day, it becomes his turn to entertain his guests.

The Parish Clerk took up his Place,
And, came, as usual, to say Grace,
The Hour was past, and all did wait,
But lo! there was no smell of Meat,
No Sign of *Catty's*[3] lay'ng the Cloth,
To bring us either Meat or Broth,
No noise of Plates or Knives cou'd hear,
As true forerunners of good Chear.
Then *Peter* comes, and to be brief,
Tells how his Cleave-boy had turn'd Thief
Took leg and ran away with all
That he bought for the Carnival,
The Capon and the Turkey too,
Took Wings, and both together flew,
The very Sallad, Sprouts and Bacon,
Cou'd never more be overtaken.
In vain let *Peter* for them seek,
Soop Meager[4] be his Food this Week,
Let him do Penance and repent,
Then fast the forty days of *Lent*,
Lest Vengeance fall upon his Head
Who sent us supperless to Bed.

3. The servant girl. An abbreviation of Catherine.
4. *soupe maigre* = vegetable soup.

MATTHEW CONCANEN
(1701-49)

OCTOBER ALE

How void of ease
He spends his days
Who wastes his time in thinking?
How like a beast,
That ne'er can taste
The pleasures of good drinking?
May curses light upon the sot
That ever kennels sober,
Or rises e'er without a pot
Of lovely brown October.[1]

Let others raise
Their voice to praise
The Rhenish[2] or the Sherry,
The sparkling white
Champaign so bright,
The Claret or Canary.[3]
'Tis true they'd thaw the freezing blood,
And hinder our being sober;
But what for that was e'er so good
As lovely brown October?

What knaves are they
Who cross the sea
To bring such stuff among us?
How blind are we,
Who will not see
How grievously they wrong us?
They spoil the products of the land,
And of her coin disrobe her;
And yet their dregs can never stand
Against our brave October.

My jolly boys,
Let us rejoice,
And cast away all sorrow;
Let's never think,
While thus we drink,
What may fall out tomorrow.
Let's waste our wealth, enjoy content,
And never more live sober:
By Jove, the coin is rightly spent,
That's melted in October.

1. i.e. ale brewed in October.
2. Wine from the region of the river Rhine.
3. A light, sweet wine from the Canary Islands.

THOMAS DERMODY
(1775-1802)

JOHN BAYNHAM'S EPITAPH

Here lieth Hercules the Second,
A penman fine by critics reckon'd;[1]
With back so huge, and brawny neck on't,
And shrewdish head,
Which oft to smoking hotpot[2] beckon'd:
John Baynham's dead.

Woe's me! no more shall younkers[3] crowd
About thy hearth, and gabble loud;

1. Baynham was the parish clerk of Killeigh, Co. Offaly. Obviously he was employed by some of the parishioners to write letters for them; he was also a drinking companion of the poet.
2. A hot alcoholic drink, or a stew.
3. fashionable young men, probably sons of the local gentry.

Where thou, in magistracy proud,
Nought humbly said:
Alas! we never thought thee good
Till thou wast dead.

Though, by my soul! still sober, mellow,
I ken'd[4] thee aye a special fellow,
Catches or psalm-staves[5] prompt to bellow,
O pious breed!
I ween[6] thou'rt fixt 'tween heav'n and hell: oh!
Our comfort's dead.

But for that plaguy profligate,[7]
We early might enjoy and late
The knowledge of thy teeming pate[8]
From board to bed:
But now thou'rt 'neath a puny slate:
Droll Johnny's dead.

Full many a hard bout hast thou weather'd:
By merry Bob severely tether'd;
More sadly than if tarr'd and feather'd,
Like bull-dog led:
Now all my tools are fairly gather'd;
Blythe Baynham's dead.

Heav'n lend thy soul its surest port,
And introduce thee to the court;
Revive again thy earthly sport,
And melt thy lead!
Alas! we mourn; for, by the mort![9]
John Baynham's dead.

No curate now can work thy throat,
And alter clean thy jocund note;
Charon[10] has plump'd thee in his boat,
And run a-head:
My curse on death, the meddling sot!
Gay Johnny's dead.

With gills[11] of noblest usquebaugh[12]
Will we anoint thy epitaph;
While thou at the full bowl shalt laugh,
A precious meed:[13]
At last thou liest in harbour safe;
Sage Johnny's dead.

News shall no more thy mornings muzzle,
Or schemes good spirit-punch to guzzle;
Wounds! thou art past this mortal bustle.
With manna[14] fed;
Satan and thou hadst a long tussel;
At last thou'rt dead.

May blessings light upon thy gloom,
And geese grow fat upon thy tomb![15]
While no rash scribbler's impious thumb
Shall maul thy head;
But greet thee soft 'in kingdom come,'
Though thou art dead.

Postscript

After inditing these sad stories,
I happed to hear some brother tories[16]
Ranting and roaring loud at Lory's,[17]
Not quite well bred;
I enter'd, and exclaim'd, 'Ye glories,
John Baynham's dead.'

Scarce had I spoke, when 'neath the table
Something sigh'd out most lamentable:
Anon, to make my song a fable,
Starts out brave John;
Sitting, by Jove above! most stable
On wicked throne.

They press'd my sitting:[18] marv'lous dull,
I gap'd at Banquo like a fool,[19]
And cried 'Good Sirs, the table's full,
And there's a spirit,'
'Come reach,' quote sprite, 'an easy stool':
And lent a wherret.[20]

4. knew.
5. verses of psalms (probably of the metrical psalms common in the eighteenth century).
6. think.
7. death (?).
8. head.
9. death.
10. In Greek mythology, the ferryman who rowed the dead across the river Styx to Hades.
11. A gill is a measure of one-quarter or one-half pint of liquid.
12. whiskey.
13. reward (cf. mead: an alcoholic drink made of honey).
14. i.e. heavenly food; manna was the food that fell from heaven to the Israelites in the wilderness. Wounds = by God's wounds.
15. Eighteenth-century clergymen had the right to keep sheep and geese in the churchyard.
16. i.e. other drinkers. The term 'tory' actually referred to those turned off their land by the English; they often became outlaws.
17. The name of the friend who owned the public house where Baynham, Dermody and their friends met.
18. i.e. made me sit down.
19. cf. *Macbeth*, III. 4, where the ghost of the murdered Banquo enters the dining hall and is seen only by the terrified Macbeth.
20. i.e. gave me a box on the ear.

'You rogue,' said he, 'how dare you write
Such stuff on me, as dead outright;....[21]

21. The poem breaks off at this point.

'Grammar is but fit for slaves'

[The three poems below direct attention to a body of eighteenth-century Irish writing that satirized aspects of contemporary education. William Dunkin presents the 'modish' schoolmaster, who spurns the rules of grammar and lives by his own shrewdness. In time, perhaps, some of his pupils will progress to create the disarray of the 'Collegian's chamber', the contents of which are so wittily listed in John Winstanley's polished satire, or evade the porter, like Dunkin's undergraduates, as they slip out of college in search of the life of the city.

The Murphæid, which first appeared in 1728 and was widely read in Dublin for generations, is the most important work in this body of writing. A mock-heroic poem that reveals Dunkin's remarkable knowledge of antiquity, *The Murphæid* presents a drama through its varying narratives and descriptions; eighteenth-century readers must have found themselves looking back, with affectionate laughter, on the experiences of their student days.]

WILLIAM DUNKIN
(*c*.1709-65)

THE MODISH SCHOOL-MASTER

'Well!' said Hopkins, on the lurch,[1]
When a coffin pass'd his church:
'Turn, good people, turn the bier,
You had better bury here;
For you cannot find around
Finer mould on christian ground.'
So, when Bubo,[2] lucky man,
Open'd school, he thus began:
Gentlemen, and ladies fair,
—— is a special air,
Most commodious for your boys,
Free from all the daily noise,
And the vices of the town;
Prithee send them hither down.

1. i.e. hidden or lying in wait. Hopkins, the clergyman, lies in wait for passing funerals and directs them into his own churchyard, presumably so that he can gain the extra fee for the burial.
2. Owl (Latin).

Dublin, barring all disasters,
Has too many idle masters:
I may say, without aspersions,
They mind only their diversions.

As for me, you need not fear,
I'm not absent thrice a year.
Then I have a short, unknown,
Charming method of my own.

I DESPISE the musty rules,
Practis'd in your city-schools.
Others dig, to lay foundations
For their future habitations;
But, indignant of a prop,
I begin my house a-top.

GRAMMAR is but fit for slaves,
Laws were only made for knaves.
Link your asses with your collars,
I shall never yoke my scholars:
They shall want no other model,
Than what issues from this noddle.[3]
Garrans[4] on the common roads
Jog along with heavy loads:
But the steed, which travels faster,
Bears no burthen, save — his master.
Thus he said, and men of sense
Even favour'd his pretence.
So the queen of wisdom bright
Fain would shew her love for night,
And from all the flocks of fowl
Gravely chose the boding owl.

3. head.
4. = garrons: small Irish horses used for carrying loads.

from:
THE ART OF GATE-PASSING:
OR,
THE MURPHÆID
[from Book I]

... And now to bring expanded on the stage
A scene surprising, and display the Sage
In all his various attitudes, behold
A dreadful monster of uncommon mould:[1]

1. i.e. Murphy, the under-porter in Trinity College, Dublin, who was obviously fond of tracing his descent to the original 'O Murphy' and to the ancient kings of Ireland.

From great O MURPHY'S thickest blood he springs,
August descendant of Hibernian kings,
Second in Porter's pension, as in place,
Proud of his post, but prouder of his race.
How stern his visage! how uncouth his hairs!
How black! how shaggy, and how like a Bear's!
Mark well his figure, and imagine then,
You see dread Polyphemus[2] in his den:
High in his lodge he stands, although a sub,[3]
Nor grander look'd the Cynic[4] in his tub.

Full five-and-twenty years the radiant Sun,
His annual journey through the signs hath run,
Since PADDY first assum'd the gate-command,
Content for ever with his narrow stand....

Not thou, Priapus,[5] who art set to fright
The timid birds by day, and thieves by night,
Can'st half infuse the panic, though a God,
That Freshmen suffer at his angry nod.
The very youths, observant of the laws,
Whose long deportment merits fair applause,
Wax pale at his approach with icy fright,
Their inmost vitals shudder at the sight.
His baleful front, his awful beard combin'd,
And all the tyrant rushes on their mind,
This for the present, and for future times
The vengeance due to yet unacted crimes.

Before the lodge two trusty vassals wait,
Assistant guardians of the bolted gate,
Lest any fugitive disfigur'd roam
Beyond the wooden barriers of the dome:
But PADDY, much more vigilant and wise,
Darting around his unremitting eyes,
Notes, as he sits and drains his liquid urns,
Their silent exits, and their sly returns.

Behold then all the porter here complete,
And strictly mark his implements of fate,
Decently rang'd each find a proper class,
Ah, too well known to novel eyes! his glass,[6]
Pens, ink, and paper; paper light, but lo!
The pregnant harbinger of heavy woe,
His ink, whose drops like Stygian[7] waters fall,
His pens, that speak in characters of gall,[8]
His monitory-glass,[9] that stands to show,
How fleet the moments of duration flow:
With this he regulates his portal pow'rs,
And measures out the sand-devolving hours;
With those, respective to the various times,
Denotes delinquents, and records their crimes.

Hence, hem'd with rocky perils night and day,
A thousand wily stratagems we lay,
Revolving hence our fabricable parts,[10]
We beat our brains, and forge a thousand arts,
And many hence, as guided by the clew
Of Dædalus,[11] their mazy paths pursue,
Inventing methods to deceive his ken,
And mock the strictures of his rigid pen.

Such as escape with rapture bound abroad,
Triumphant felons, and themselves applaud,
As if, victorious from the tedious toil
Of Mars,[12] returning to their native soil.
Then free they rove, unfetter'd scud away,
Joys usher in, and circling close the day;
Whether each winding street they traverse o'er,
Eblana,[13] rifling thy promiscuous store,
Or, more transported with a rural scene,
They court calm pleasures on the flow'ry plain,
Supinely stretch'd along the tender grass,
Forget their cares, and quaff the genial glass,
With snowy sillabub[14] revive the heart,
Or slake inclement thirst with cyder tart;
While all the songsters of the forest greet
Their ears with notes, irregularly sweet,
And arbours arch with interwoven sprays
A grateful gloom, and cool the sunny rays.
Or, if they trust to painted gallies gay,
And painted nymphs with painted loose array,
And, gliding down the Liffey's glassy tide,

2. The one-eyed giant in Homer's *Odyssey*.
3. The porters' lodge overlooked the gate into Trinity College. A 'sub' was an under-porter, as is explained in the Latin text of the poem, which matches the English line for line.
4. Diogenes, the chief proponent of the Cynic school of philosophy in ancient Athens, taught his pupils from inside a tub.
5. The Greek god of fertility, originally of gardens and property; his image was sometimes set up to scare birds and thieves.
6. i.e. hour-glass. The point of the next few lines is that students were permitted to leave the college only for a certain fixed period of time; the 'monitory-glass' would warn of the amount of time that was left to them.
7. Black, like the waters of the mythological river Styx.
8. i.e. bitter letters.
9. i.e. the hour-glass.
10. i.e. turning our creative powers to the problem.
11. The Athenian craftsman who constructed a labyrinth for King Minos. clew = ball of thread or twine.
12. The god of war in Roman mythology.
13. The Latin name for Dublin.
14. A drink made of sweetened milk and wine or cider.

With bending oars the curling waves divide;
The breezes gently chide the flying sails,
The flying streamers to the chiding gales
Re-murmur gently; wanton as they fly,
The nymphs as gently to their music sigh,
And soft, to fan the lover's youthful fire,
The sails, light gales, and lighter nymphs
  conspire....

A certain Freshman, who had spent the day
In the loose freaks of ev'ry idle play,
From town returning in the evening late,
With silent rapture smiling pass'd the gate,
Mistaken hugg'd himself with secret pride,
That, as he pass'd, he had re-pass'd unspy'd:
But when to view the fatal book he came,
And found in sable characters[15] his name,
Aghast he stood, quite thunder-struck with fear,
The baulk was instant, and the mulct[16] was near.
With speeches bland and deprecating face
He sues to PADDY, and bemoans his case;
To Heav'n uplifting both his hands and eyes,
Some way reverse the cruel doom he cries.
PADDY contracts his brow, then grimly leers
Both at the Freshman's posture and his fears,
Shook the rough honours of his matted head,
Snarl'd an enormous grin, and mockful said:
What could you think me such a stupid ass
To let your worship unregarded pass?
What break through all restraints, these bars
  despise,
Nor dread the searches of these piercing eyes?
Submit with patience to the mulct assign'd;
The next elopement more success may find....

15. black letters.
16. penalty, i.e. fine or 'gating'.

[from Book II]

... If therefore, Freshman, thou wouldst fain
  unbend
Thy graver studies, to my lays attend:
Where e'er it suits thy genius best to roam,
Indignant of the gate and guarded dome; ...
Then hear what arts, what stratagems defeat
The prying guardian of the dreadful gate.

The rest apart, that lucky minute catch,
When the rude monster stands alone to watch:
Like sage Ulysses,[1] oily to deceive,
Then all your wiles and artifices weave.
Paddy with serpent ken will stare around,
And strictly traverse all the hostile ground,
True Epidaurian snake[2] in double skill,
Not more acute to see, than prompt to kill:
But thou, the more he darts a piercing glance,
The more in subtle stratagems advance.

If haply therefore you should spy a pair
Of friends, distinguish'd by their awkward air,
Their Teaguish[3] tone and clownly[4] garb, engage
These, thy best actors for the doubtful stage.
In Attic Irish[5] let them greeting pray
To know with favour but the time of day:
By compliments like this, when grown more free,
Let them cull out his birth and pedigree,
Assume his name, recount their fathers o'er
And sons, descended from O MURPHY-MORE,[6]
O MURPHY-MORE, who held the regal reins
Of Munster fair, and rul'd the vassal swains,
Who daily slaughter'd, for his guests to dine,
Thrice ten fat wethers,[7] and as many swine,
His whisky burn'd with purifying flame,
And pour'd, like water from the running stream.
Proud of their cousin, let them lift their eyes
With sudden rapture to the vaulted skies,
And bless their happy stars, as much astoun'd,
As at a pot of bury'd treasure found;
With fists full heavy let them then attack,
And kindly thump him on the brawny back,
Shake hands alternate, and with eager dint
Ambrosial kisses on his lips imprint.

PADDY will straight on this occasion run
Through all the tribe from father down to son,
Sum all his ancestors with gallant pride,[8]
Hibernian chiefs, in feats of arms well try'd,

1. i.e. Odysseus.
2. See Horace, *Satires* I, iii, 25-27 for a reference to the sharp-eyed snake of the Greek state of Epidaurus.
3. From Teague, an English form of the Irish name Tadhg; used in English with derogatory overtones.
4. countryman's.
5. Attic Greek was the common language of Greece; Attic Irish, therefore, means the common Irish language.
6. This name in Irish means 'the grandsons of Murphy the Great'. Many Gaelic surnames are derived in this fashion from an eponymous ancestor.
7. castrated rams.
8. Murphy is indulging in the (by this time almost stage-Irish) custom of recalling his genealogy and listing his noble ancestors.

Whom, Oh sad sentence and severe decree!
Jack Ketch's hand with dire dexterity
Exalted,[9] rapt from weeping friends beneath,
To dance in æther, which they could not breathe,
To swing, alas! before the stated time,
Green in their years, and blooming in their prime,
With art adapted to the noosy rope,
Their parent's comfort, and their country's hope,
With twirling jerk their vital thread, I wot,[10]
Toss'd, and cut off with soul-absolving knot.
While thus they[11] hold the monster at a bay,
Clear as the coast appears, then slink away:
But flying cautious cast a backward eye,
Lest any porter should your steps espy.
When you have pass'd the pinching gates,[12] employ
The flying moments in excess of joy;
Freed from the galling yoke, and Paddy's beck,
Use pliant limbs, and bear aloft your neck:
Exhaust the spirit of Sabæan[13] blooms,
To wound the nymphs with breezes of perfumes,
And give with graceful negligence behind
Your dusty locks to wanton with the wind....

9. i.e. they were hanged. Jack Ketch was a famous hangman.
10. know.
11. i.e. the countrymen who are distracting the porter's attention.
12. Very narrow gates allowing only one person to pass at a time.
13. i.e. perfumed. Saba, the ancient kingdom in Arabia, was renowned for its perfumes.

JOHN WINSTANLEY

(*c.*1678-1750)

AN INVENTORY *OF THE* FURNITURE *OF A* COLLEGIAN'*S CHAMBER*

Imprimis,[1] there's a *Table* blotted;
A tatter'd *Hanging* all besnotted;
A *Bed* of Flocks,[2] as one may rank it,
Reduc'd to *Rug*, and half a *Blanket*;
A *Tinder-box*, as People tell us;
A broken-winded pair of *Bellows*.
A pair of *Tongs*, bought from a Broker,[3]
A *Fender*, and a rusty *Poker*.
A *Penny-pot*, and *Bason*, this
Design'd for Water, that for Piss.
A *Trencher*,[4] and a *College-bottle*[5]
Riding on *Locke*, or *Aristotle*:
A smutty *Ballad*, musty *Libel*,
A *Burgersdiscius*,[6] and a *Bible*:
A *Prayer-book*, he seldom handles;
Item, a Pound of *Farthing-candles*.
A rusty *Fork*, a blunted *Whittle*,[7]
To cut his *Table*, and his *Vittle*.[8]
There is likewise a pair of *Breeches*,
But patch'd, and fallen in the Stitches.
Item, a *Surplice*,[9] not unmeeting
Either for *Chappel*, or for *Sheeting*,
Hung up in Study very little,
Plaister'd with Cobwebs, Ink, and Spittle,
With lofty *Prospect*, all so pleasing,
And *Sky-light window* without Glazing.
Item, if I am not mistaken,
A *Mouse-trap*, with a Bit of *Bacon*.
A *Candlestick*, without a *Snuffer*,
Whereby his Fingers often suffer;
And *Chairs* a couple, (I forgot 'em)
But each of them without a *Bottom*.
A *Bottle-Standish*,[10] *Pen* unmended,
His inventory thus is ended.

1. First in a list; cf. later 'items' at lines 16, 21, 27.
2. Coarse wool or cotton used as stuffing for mattresses.
3. pawnbroker or general dealer.
4. plate or platter.
5. A wine bottle with the seal of Trinity College, Dublin on it.
6. The standard logic textbook in Trinity College was by Francis Burgersdyk (1590-1629).
7. knife, especially a large carving knife.
8. victuals, food.
9. A loose, white linen vestment, compulsory wear in the college chapel and sometimes able to double as bed linen.
10. A stand containing ink-bottle, pen and pencils. 'To mend a pen' meant to trim a worn quill pen.

'True to the text, his doctrines would he preach'

[For most of the eighteenth century, the established Church of Ireland was an embattled and embittered organization, threatened by dissenters, cynically manipulated by the English government and weakened from within by many lazy, incompetent and self-interested clergy, particularly in the upper ranks. It is this side of church life that is the butt of Swift's epigram in the section below.

At lower levels, however, churches of all denominations in Ireland contained individuals who strove to uphold higher spiritual values, such as those reflected in the other poems in this section. There is the well-known simple Christmas hymn by Nahum Tate, one of the many graduates of Trinity College, Dublin who were forced to seek a living in England, and Bishop Berkeley's poem on the college he attempted to found in America — a clear statement of the high ideals that motivated him. Finally, William Dunkin's imitation of Geoffrey Chaucer's description of the good parson could well have applied to some of the rural clergy of the day, catholic or protestant.]

JONATHAN SWIFT

EPIGRAM

On seeing a worthy Prelate go out of Church in the Time of *Divine Service*, to wait on his Grace the D. of *D*....

Lord *Pam*[1] in the Church[2] (cou'd you think it) kneel'd down,
When told the Lieutenant[3] was just come to Town,
His *Station* despising, unaw'd by the *Place*,[4]
He flies from his *God*, to attend on his *Grace*:
To the *Court* it was fitter to pay his *Devotion*,
Since *God* had no Hand in his Lordship's *Promotion*.[5]

1. A term for the knave of clubs, here referring to Dr Josiah Hort (*c*. 1674-1751), bishop of Kilmore at the time this poem was written (1732).
2. St Ann's Church, Dublin.
3. The Duke of Dorset (1688-1765), lord lieutenant of Ireland 1730-37 and 1750-55.
4. i.e. the church.
5. To his bishopric.

NAHUM TATE

(1652-1715)

WHILE SHEPHERDS WATCHED THEIR FLOCKS BY NIGHT

While shepherds watched their flocks by night,
All seated on the ground,
The angel of the Lord came down,
And glory shone around.

'Fear not,' said he, for mighty dread
Had seized their troubled mind;
'Glad tidings of great joy I bring
To you and all mankind.

'To you, in David's town, this day
Is born of David's line,
The Saviour, who is Christ the Lord,
And this shall be the sign:

'The heavenly babe you there shall find
To human view displayed,
All meanly wrapped in swaddling bands,
And in a manger laid.'

Thus spake the seraph;[1] and forthwith
Appeared a shining throng
Of angels, praising God, who thus
Addressed their joyful song:

'All glory be to God on high,
And to the earth be peace;
Goodwill henceforth from Heaven to men
Begin and never cease.'

1. angel.

GEORGE BERKELEY

(1685-1753)

ON THE PROSPECT OF PLANTING ARTS AND LEARNING IN AMERICA

The Muse, disgusted at an age and clime
Barren of every glorious theme,
In distant lands now waits a better time
Producing subjects worthy fame:

In happy climes, where from the genial sun
And virgin earth such scenes ensue,
The force of art by nature seems outdone,
And fancied beauties by the true.

In happy climes, the seat of innocence,
Where nature guides and virtue rules;
Where men shall not impose for truth and sense
The pedantry of courts and schools;

There shall be sung another golden age,
The rise of empire and of arts,
The good and great inspiring epic rage
The wisest heads and noblest hearts.

Not such as Europe breeds in her decay—
Such as she bred when fresh and young,
When heavenly flame did animate her clay,
By future poets shall be sung.

Westward the course of empire takes its way,
  The four first acts already past;
A fifth shall close the drama with the day —
  Time's noblest offspring is the last.

WILLIAM DUNKIN

THE CHARACTER OF A GOOD PARSON

From Chaucer[1]

There was (so Chaucer hands the story down)
A good old man, the Parson of a town,
Meetly array'd in humble, sable weeds,[2]
And poor in purse, but rich in holy deeds.
Pure was his heart, and able was his head,
Deep-vers'd in books, but most in scripture read.
True to the text, his doctrines would he preach,
And each parishioner devoutly teach
Without the help of puzzling gloss absurd,
Benign in thought, and affable in word,
Of heart undaunted, in demeanor mild,
A man of God, but of the world a child.
Few minutes from his office would he spare,
His patience only could surpass his care,
Through frequent trials of distress approv'd,
Distress, true touch-stone of the faith he lov'd.
Full loth was he, although he wanted shoes,
To breathe anathemas,[3] for unpaid dues:
But rather from his own domestic store
With pious hands reliev'd the parish poor.
Though much he gave, on little wont to live,
He only liv'd, that many more might live.
Wide was his parish, and the houses stood
Asunder; yet thro' thunder, hail, or flood
At morning by the dawn, or ev'ning late
He steer'd his journey to the sick man's gate,
Uncheck'd by fevers of infectious rage.
He walk'd: A staff sustain'd his awful[4] age.
This good example to his flock he brought,
That first he gave, and afterwards he taught.

1. An 'imitation' of lines 477-97 of the General Prologue to Geoffrey Chaucer's *The Canterbury Tales* (1387-92).
2. black clothes.
3. to denounce, condemn.
4. i.e. inspiring awe or respect.

The 'Persuasive Charms' of Music

[Matthew Pilkington's 'The Progress of Music in *Ireland*. To Mira', published in 1725, and Laurence Whyte's '*A Dissertation on* Italian *and* Irish *Musick, with some Panegyrick on* Carrallan *our late* Irish Orpheus', which appeared in his *Poems on Various Subjects, Serious and Diverting, Never before Published* in 1740, create complementary pictures of the musical culture of Dublin and the world beyond the capital in the first half of the eighteenth century. Pilkington's neo-classical poem, which makes elegant transitions from subject to subject, and Whyte's remarkable narrative, with its abrupt movement and sudden conclusion, approach their subjects from widely different perspectives. While Pilkington reveals the influence of Pope in the mechanics of his verse and in his choice of diction, Whyte sets his own course with a lively and dramatic tetrameter; and while Pilkington surveys his subject in a narrative and philosophical fashion, Whyte draws on musical terminology for the arrangement of his poem and reveals a sense of involvement with its movement. In contrast to Pilkington, who begins with echoes of the pastoral tradition and who then moves gradually towards the Irish elements of his theme, Whyte writes with a strong sense of the moment and captures the abstractions of his subject in personal terms as he seeks 'something new not sung before,/That shall demand a loud *Encore!*'

Whyte, who was born in County Westmeath and became a teacher of mathematics in Dublin, was a friend of John and William Neal, the father and son who were the leading publishers of music in Dublin in Swift's day. His poem, which contains important details of contemporary popular music in Ireland, creates a more comprehensive picture than does Pilkington's. Each presents unique images, however. Pilkington has William Viner, the Master of the State Music in Dublin, making 'new Transports rise in ev'ry Breast', and creates a picture of Nicolini (Nicolo Grimaldi), the greatest male singer of the early eighteenth century. Whyte, who has the eye of a social satirist, creates a comic image of Irish music in flight before the advancing fashion for the Italian. It should be noted, however, that his reference to '*Hendal's* Notes' predates the famous visit that Handel made to Dublin in 1741-42, during which his *Messiah* was performed for the first time at the Neals' fashionable Music Hall in Fishamble Street.

Despite the differences between these two poems, both Pilkington and Whyte address the subject of foreign influence, which is revealed either in imported music or in the performances of foreigners in the country. There are other references in common too, such as the accounts of Lorenzo Bocchi, a little-known Italian musician who was active in Dublin in the 1720s, although it is left to Whyte to establish the irony of an Italian's making Irish music newly stimulating. The most important image these poems share, however, is that of Turlogh Carolan, the most renowned harper of his day. Carolan, who was born in 1670 and who lived as an itinerant composer and performer, was at the height of his fame when Pilkington described him in 1725 as 'The Vagrant *Bard*' who 'charms the Villages with venal Lays'. While Pilkington celebrates Carolan's playing, presenting his performance as one aspect of 'the progress of music' in Ireland, Whyte, whose poem belongs to the period between Carolan's death in 1738 and the publication of his *Poems* in 1740, writes '*some Panegyrick*' on him as he laments his death, ending his poem with a question that cannot be answered. Both compare him with Orpheus, but Whyte's image is the more poignant, for now the Irish Orpheus himself is dead and there is no replacing him.

The editor acknowledges the invaluable assistance in annotating these two poems of Professor Brian Boydell, Trinity College, Dublin, and Nicholas Carolan, Irish Traditional Music Archive, Dublin.]

MATTHEW PILKINGTON

(*c*.1701-74)

THE PROGRESS OF MUSIC IN *IRELAND*. TO MIRA

By thee enjoyn'd th'obsequious *Muse* obeys,
Yet trembling, dreads the Danger she surveys,
But vain are Infant Fears, I plead in vain,
The Task too Noble, too Sublime the Strain,
The *Fancy*'s wing'd, and springs to bolder Flights,
When *Beauty* bids, and *Harmony* invites;
For each, our Passions pleasingly controuls;
Love's but the purer Harmony of Souls:
Musick and Love the savage World refin'd,
Reform'd the Manners, while they rais'd the Mind,
Gave Man a Foretaste of the Joys above;
For what is Heav'n but *Harmony* and *Love*?

Hibernia long beheld, with Sorrow fill'd,
Her Poets and her Sons in Arts unskill'd:
Sons! dead to Fame, nor comely to the Sight,
Their Customs wild, their Manners unpolite;
Nor yet could *Musick* boast persuasive Charms,
To tempt one sprightly Genius to her Arms:
The *Muse*, in mournful Pomp, laments her Case,
Pale Grief and Anguish painted in her Face;
To lonely Woods retire the tuneful Throng,
Uncharm'd by Sound, and negligent of Song:
The silent *Lark* forgets to wake the Dawn
With early Song, suspended o'er the Lawn,
On Earth he pines, and droops his useless Wings
With dumb Concern, and neither Soars nor Sings.

At length a *Swain*, long tortur'd with Despair,
The Scorn of some inexorable Fair,[1]
Haunted each Grove, each dark Retreat of Grief,
Bereft of Ease, and hopeless of Relief;
Nightly he heard sad *Philomel*[2] complain,
And wish'd to copy so divine a Strain,
So clear, so soft the plaintive Warbler sung,
The Groves, and Hills with plaintive *Echoes* rung.
Her Notes so mournfully melodious flow,
They calm his Soul, and mitigate his Woe,
Distressful Passion both alike bewail,
He sighs his Grief, she chants her piteous Tale.

Fain would he Sing; his Voice was still suppress
By swelling Sighs, which struggled from his Breast.
Despair, whose Sting can haughtiest Minds controul,
Unstrings his Nerves, and quite unmans his Soul,
Breathes a wild Horror into ev'ry Part,
Restrains his Tongue, and preys upon his Heart.

But near the Grove, where comfortless he lies,
The spiky Reeds in waving Clusters rise,
He models one, and his Invention tires,
Varying its Form as Art or Chance inspires:
Then gives it Breath to sing: With gentle Mirth
It strikes the Ear, as conscious of its Birth.
With sharpen'd Steel he lanc'd its tender Skin,
In Order ranged the op'ning Wounds are seen,
Wounds! less than he received, with piercing Smart,
In that soft Instrument of Love, the *Heart*:
To these his active Fingers he applies,
Which bid the changing *Musick* fall, and rise,
While in the Road of *Harmony* they guide
Each infant Sound, and o'er the Notes preside.

But o'er his Airs a gloomy Sorrow hung;
For still he lov'd, and Love distress'd he sung,
His Heart in ev'ry Accent seem'd to bleed,
And Grief harmonious trembled from the Reed,

And still the Tenor of *Hibernian* Strains,
Those pleasing Labours of enamour'd Swains,
From his a melancholly Turn receive,
The Airs are moving, and the Numbers grieve.

1. young woman.
2. Tereus, the king of Thrace and husband of Procne, raped her sister Philomel. When his crime was discovered, he tried to kill both his wife and her sister, but Procne turned into a swallow and Philomel into a nightingale.

Musick thus wak'd to Life, fair Child of Love!
Time's rip'ning Touch, and growing Arts improve,
While to the feeble Voice of slender Reeds,
The manlier Musick of the *Fife*[3] succeeds.
Alike in Form, but of a larger Mold,
More durable its Frame, its Tone more bold;
Now lively Numbers, born on willing Gales,
Flow to the Hills, and echo in the Vales;
The rural Throng now chearful croud around,
And catch, enamour'd, the inspiring Sound,
They walk and move with correspondent Mien,
And Dance exulting on the level Green:
No Secret now the raptur'd Heart conceals,
The conscious Maid her hidden Flames reveals,
In glowing Blushes on her Cheeks they rise,
Burst from her Tongue, and kindle in her Eyes.

But secret Pleasures once disclos'd to Sight,
Give Birth to fresh Successions of Delight.
On Objects new the restless Fancy strays,
And wantons in the Search of nobler Lays.
Extended Strings at length Experience found,
Start at the Touch, and tremble into Sound;
Of which a Vocal Multitude conspire,
In shining Order plac'd to form the *Lyre*:
And thus the Strings, as in a Choir combin'd,
Have each their Parts of Harmony assign'd:
Some heavenly Sounds transportingly create,
Like *Echo* some the heav'nly Sounds repeat,
Those plac'd above, rejoice in sprightly Tones,
Below the rough, hoarse *Base*, responsive, groans.

If the judicious Artist bids them play,
The dancing Chords in silver Sounds obey;
But struck with Hands unskill'd, they spring to War,
Hiss out their Rage, and in harsh Discords jar.

Musick henceforward more Domestick grew,
Courts the throng'd Towns, and from the Plains withdrew:
The Vagrant *Bard*[4] his circling Visits pays,
And charms the Villages with venal[5] Lays.
The solemn *Harp*, beneath his Shoulder plac'd,
With both his Arms is earnestly embrac'd,
Sweetly irregular, now swift, now slow,
With soft Variety his Numbers flow,
The shrill, the deep, the gentle, and the strong,
With pleasing Dissonance adorn his Song;
While thro' the Chords his Hands unweary'd range,
The Music changing as his Fingers change.

The Crowd transported in Attention hung,
Their Breath in Silence sleeps upon the Tongue,
The *Wheels* forget to turn, the Labours cease,
And ev'ry Sound but *Music* sinks to Peace.
So when the *Thracian*[6] charm'd the Shades below,
And brought down Raptures to the Realms of Woe,
Despairing Ghosts from Labour stand releas'd,
Each Wheel, each Instrument of Torture ceas'd;[7]
The *Furies*[8] drop their Whips, afflictive Pain
Suspends, with ghastly Smiles, her Iron Reign,
All Groans were still'd, all Sorrow lull'd to Rest,
And ev'ry Care was hush'd in ev'ry Breast.

Joy spreads her Wings o'er all the raptur'd *Isle*,
And bids each Face be brighten'd to a Smile.
Now Nature, pleas'd, her Gifts profusely pours,
To paint the chearful Earth with od'rous Flow'rs,
So chang'd a Scene she wonders to survey,
And bids ev'n Things inanimate look gay.

The *Muses* now from *Albion's Isle*[9] retreat,
And here with kind Indulgence fix their Seat:
Then *Viner*[10] rose, with all their Warmth inspir'd,
A Bard caress'd by all, by all admir'd;
He choral Strings, in sleepy Silence bound,
Touch'd into Voice, and waken'd into Sound;
Then taught those Sounds to flow with easy Art,
To wooe the Soul, and glide into the Heart,
In Notes, untry'd before, his Fancy drest,
And bid new Transports rise in ev'ry Breast.

While round in Crowds the fair Creation stand,
The polish'd *Viol*[11] trembling in his Hand,

3. 'A small cylindrical transverse flute, but with a narrower bore and hence a louder, shriller sound than the flute proper' (*The New Grove Dictionary of Music and Musicians*).
4. Turlogh Carolan (1670-1738), the famous Irish composer and harper.
5. Probably the rare and obsolete sense of venal, meaning 'of the blood', 'contained in the veins'.
6. Orpheus of Thrace, the famed musician of Greek mythology, whose playing on the lyre charmed even the wild animals.
7. Orpheus visited the underworld in search of his wife Eurydice, who was released on condition that he did not look back upon her on their journey to the world of the living. Overcome by his longing, he turned to see her and consequently lost her forever. Although he was able to captivate the world of the dead with his music, he was unable to defeat the force of his love. The dead are tortured in the underworld.
8. The pursuing avengers of Greek mythology, who inflicted pain upon their victims.
9. Britain.
10. William Viner (died 1716), English violinist and composer, who was Master of the State Music in Dublin 1703-16.
11. 'A bowed string instrument with frets. It is usually played held

While swift as Thought, from Note to Note he
  springs,
Flies o'er th'unerring Tones, and sweeps the
  sounding Strings,
The Old, the Young, the Serious, and the Gay,
With ravish'd Ears devour the 'witching Lay,
The *Lover*'s Eyes now languishingly roll,
And speak the Dictates of the raptur'd Soul;
Foes, in whose Breasts the wildest Passion strove,
Forget their Rage, and soften into Love:
The prideful *Beauty*, feels with new Surprize
Her Bosom swell, and wonders why she sighs,
Each Passion acts as he affects the Heart,
And Nature answers ev'ry stroke of Art.

But now refin'd *Hibernia*'s ravish'd Throng,
With Wonder dwell on *Nicolini*'s[12] Song,
Whose warbling Voice and tuneful Tongue
  dispense,
The blended Harmony of Sound and Sense:
With these he knew the list'ning Soul to charm,
And ev'ry Torment of its Sting disarm,
Cou'd calm the harsh disturber *Care*, to Ease,
With Fear delight us, and with Sorrow please;
Cou'd warm the kindling Soul with am'rous Fire,
And Raptures, which he never felt, inspire.

While *Music* thus its native Beauty shows,
And from its living Spring delightful flows,
How does it raise! how gladden ev'ry Heart!
How far transcend the mimic Voice of *Art!*

So, when *Belinda*'s[13] heav'nly Beauties stand,
Wrought into Life by *Kneller*'s[14] magic Hand,
Her Face, her Shape, have all that *Art* can give,
Start from the animated Paint, and Live;
But, when the real Nymph, divinely bright,
Array'd in native Lustre, strikes our Sight,
Some nameless Transport in our Bosom plays,
That Shade and Colour want the Force to raise.

Dubourg[15] next sways the Soul with nicest Art,
And binds in airy Chains the captive Heart,
While from the vocal Strings, and shifting *Bow*,
At his nice Touch th'obsequious Numbers flow.
With easy Toil he swells the Notes aloud,
Now on the Ear precipitant they croud,
Now, scarcely heard, they gradually decay,
And with melodious *Cadence* waste away,
While at his melting Falls, and dying Notes,
Around the Heart the liquid Rapture floats.

With martial Ardour if he boldly warms,
The animated *Hero* pants for Arms,
With guiltless Rage th'impetuous Spirit glows,
And prostrates *Legions* of imagin'd Foes.

But if to Mirth a sprightly Strain inclines,
With Humour fraught his quick'ning Genius
  shines,
Then smiling Joys thro' ev'ry Aspect fly,
Glow in the Lips, and wanton in the Eye.

Next *Bocchi*[16] reigns, whom Art and Nature grace
To smooth the Roughness of the sullen *Base*,
Directs his Notes distinct to rise or fall,
Tries ev'ry *Tone* to charm, and charms in all.

Th'awaken'd *Muse* thus rises, thus refines,
Improves with *Time*, and in Perfection shines;
The first rude Lays are now but meanly priz'd,
As rude, neglected, as untun'd, despis'd:
Dead — (in Esteem too dead) the *Bards* that sung,
The *Fife* neglected, and the *Harp* unstrung.

So when the *Thrush* exalts his chearful Throat,
To glad the Fields with many an artless Note,

---

downwards on the lap or between the legs (hence the name "viola de gamba", literally "leg viol") .... As a solo instrument, it continued to flourish until the middle of the 18th century' (*The New Grove Dictionary*).

12. Nicolo Grimaldi (1673-1732), Italian alto castrato and the outstanding male singer of the early eighteenth century. After an early career in Italy, he established himself in London 1708-17; he also became known in Dublin, and returned to Italy for his final years on the stage. Joseph Addison wrote that he was 'the greatest performer in dramatic Music that is now living, or that perhaps ever appeared on a stage' (*Spectator*, 14 June 1712).
13. The heroine of Alexander Pope's *The Rape of the Lock* (1712, 1714).
14. Sir Godfrey Kneller (1646-1723), the German artist who came to England in 1675 and who subsequently became the leading portrait painter of his generation.
15. Matthew Dubourg (1703-67), English violinist and musical director, who visited Dublin in 1724. As Master and Composer of State Music in Ireland 1728-52, Dubourg was a dominant figure in the musical culture of Dublin.
16. An Italian musician who was renowned as 'the second master of the violoncello in Europe', Lorenzo Bocchi came to Edinburgh in 1720. By 1724 he was known in Dublin, where he was associated with John and William Neal, the foremost publishers of music in the city, and where his compositions and performances attracted considerable attention. He returned to Edinburgh in 1729. Pilkington's 'An Hymn to Sleep', which appeared in his *Poems on Several Occasions* in 1731, was 'Set to Musick by Mr. Lorenzo Bocchi'. He is unknown to the *Dizionario Biografico Degli Italiani* and *The New Grove Dictionary*.

With rude Delight the List'ner's Breast he warms,
Wild tho' he sings, his sylvan Wildness charms;
But if the warbling *Nightingale* prepares
Her softer Voice, that melts with thrilling Airs,
The Winds are hush'd, still Silence reigns around,
And list'ning *Echo* dwells upon the Sound;
Harsh seem the Strains which gave Delight before,
And far excell'd, those Strains delight no more.

The pausing *Muse* now shuts her vent'rous Wings,
And, anxious of Success, distrustful sings;
O! might her Lays to thy Esteem succeed,
For whom she tun'd her artless Voice and Reed,
Thy Smiles would swell her Heart with honest Pride,
Approv'd by thee she scorns the World beside.

LAURENCE WHYTE

A DISSERTATION ON ITALIAN *AND* IRISH *MUSICK, WITH SOME PANEGYRICK ON* CARRALLAN *OUR LATE* IRISH ORPHEUS

A Prelude, or Voluntary

Begin my *Muse*, with tuneful *Stanza's*
Concerto's, or *Extravaganza's*,
With something new not sung before,
That shall demand a loud *Encore!*
Overture, Symphony, or *Solo*,
Goes down with universal *Volo*;[1]
Some brisk *Alegro's, Fuges*, and *Jiggs*
Will please young *Ladies*, and young *Priggs*,
Your *Echo*'s may be soft or loud,
With *Gavots*[2] to amuse the *Crowd*;
Courants[3] and *Minutes*[4] *French*, and *Spanish*,
That may our Cares and Sorrows banish.
Play *Voluntaries* smooth and free,
From *E* in *alt*[5] to double *B*,
Spin out your Thoughts on ev'ry Strain,
Da Capo,[6] then begin again,
Then some *Adagio's* — with your Leave,
To please the sober and the grave;
Some dying Notes, soft and complaining,
Notes full of Energy and Meaning,
Which all the Passions strangely move,
To Joy, or Grief, to Mirth, or Love.
Sounds elevate the Soul to Prayers,
They mitigate our Toils, and Cares,
Rouse and excite us all to Arms,
Allay our Fury by their Charms,
Compose the Mind, lull us to sleep,
And mollify or make us weep.

Adagio

Corelly's,[7] or *Vivaldi's*[8] Stile,
Shall from *Corinna*[9] force a Smile,
Which does her Aspect more adorn,
Than all her Cruelty and Scorn,
Thus while you hold her by the Ear,
She catches others in her Snare:
The longer she is kept in Tune,
The more her Charms have Power to ruin.
Then *Hendal's*[10] Notes shall make her thrill,
When *Raffa*[11] warbles them with Skill,
And if *Dub—ge*[12] but touch the String,
To hear him play, and *Raffa* sing,
In Extasies — she sounds away,
Revives again to hear him play.

Jigg

The *Beaus* who watch *Corinna's* Eyes,
Encore! and clap them to the Skies,

1. speed, in the sense of approbation, from the Italian verbal substantive of the same spelling.
2. dances that resemble a lively minuet.
3. running dances.
4. minuets, dances that are slow and stately in triple measure, for two dancers.
5. The E above the treble clef, a high E.
6. Italian for 'from the beginning', *Da Capo* is used in music as a direction, meaning 'repeat from the beginning'.
7. Arcangelo Corelli (1653-1713), Italian composer and violinist, was widely influential in his own lifetime and beyond.
8. Antonio Vivaldi (1678-1741), Italian composer, regarded as the most original and influential of his generation.
9. A popular name in madrigal literature, Corinna may refer to a well-known singer in Whyte's Dublin.
10. George Frideric Handel (1685-1759), the German-born composer who became an English subject; initially he used the form 'Hendel' in England. One of the greatest composers of the baroque age, in both vocal and instrumental music, Handel came to Dublin on 18 November 1741 and stayed until 13 August 1742.
11. Mrs Raffa, a soprano and scholar of Matthew Dubourg's, who made her debut at the Crow Street Music Hall on 28 November 1733 and who was active in the musical world of the city 1733-35.
12. i.e. Dubourg. See note 15 in Pilkington above. An old friend of Handel's, Dubourg led the orchestra for him during his visit to the city.

The Country *Squire* dress'd like a *Hero*,
Who'd rather hear *Lill'bolero*,[13]
And having neither Air nor Voice,
Of *Bobbin Joan*[14] wou'd make his Choice,
Now joins in *Chorus* with the rest,
And cries *Encore!* to crown the Jest,
Then out of time he gives a Clap!
Huzza's![15] and then throws up his Cap!
Cries damn you! play up the *Black Joke*,[16]
Or else you'll get your Fiddles broke,
Then play *Jack Lattin*[17] my dear Honey!
Hey! *Larry Grogan*[18] for my Money!
Then rushes out with seeming Haste,
And leaves that Sample of his Taste.

Recitativo

Some *Solo's* Songs,[19] and merry Lays,
These are which will for ever please,
When well perform'd or sung with Art,
With graces proper for each Part.
Some old ones we have oft reviv'd,
For modern Opera's contriv'd,
Instead of those *Italian* Airs,
So much in Vogue for many Years;
Poor *Ireland*, like *old England* doats
On Multiplicity of Notes,[20]
And with few *Words* she can dispense,
Sometimes with little or no Sense,
And those spun out so very long,
A *Word* or two wou'd make a *Song*,
Thro' various *Bars* they rise and fall;
They might as well have none at all;
But to begin with ha, ha, ha,
And to conclude with fa, la, la,
The Words are vanish'd quite away,
Whilst they in such Meanders stray,
Or swell'd so high, so long and loud,
They burst like Thunder from a Cloud,
That from *Olympus*[21] down is cast,
And at the Bottom breath their last.
  A *Word's* sufficient to the wise,
But *Words* exotick bear the Prize,
Whatever has a *Foreign* Tone,
We like much better than our own,
'Tis often said, *few Words are best*,
To trace their meaning is a Jest,
And such as cannot well be scan'd,
What need have we to understand.
  'Tis well the *Vulgar*[22] now of late,
Can relish *Sounds* articulate,
There's scarce a *Forthman*[23] or *Fingallion*,[24]
But sings or whistles in *Italian*,
Instead of good old *Barley Mow*,[25]
With *Tamo tanto*[26] drive the Plow,
They o'er their Cups can sing, *Si caro*,[27]
And dare prophane it at the *Harrow*,[28]
There's *Ariadne*[29] cross'd the *Shannon*,[30]

13. 'Lilli burlero', the famous ballad attacking the appointment of Richard Talbot, earl of Tyrconnell, as lord deputy in 1687. It was sung throughout the eighteenth century with memories of his 'patriot parliament' of 1689, in which there was a substantial catholic majority. 'The Orange Lily was the symbol of the Irish supporters of William of Orange and the words *Lilliburlero Bullenala* are apparently a corruption of . . . *An lile ba léir é ba linn an lá* (the lily was triumphant and we won the day)' (*Brewer's Dictionary of Phrase and Fable*).
14. Known also as 'Bob and Joan', 'Bobbing Joan', 'Bobbing Joe' and 'Bob in Joe'. There are two unrelated tunes with the name of 'Bobbin Joan', one in John Playford's *English Dancing Master* (1651), the other in undated Irish collections, probably of the second half of the eighteenth century.
15. shouts, showing support and pleasure.
16. A popular tune of the early eighteenth century, 'The Black Joke' appeared in Charles Coffey's *The Beggar's Wedding* (1729) and was published by John and William Neal in 1730.
17. A tune composed by or named after a fiddle player of this name, who was active in Dublin in the 1720s, 'Jack Lattin' was published by the Neals in their third collection of country dances in 1734.
18. Laurence Grogan, of Johnstown Castle, Co. Wexford, a 'gentleman piper' and composer, who was active in the mid-1720s and whose tune 'Ally Croker' was widely popular (W.H. Grattan Flood). A tune with the title 'Larry Grogan' was published by the Neals in their third collection of country dances in 1734.
19. songs sung as solos.
20. See Jonathan Swift's 'A Cantata', written in order to satirize those who attempted to find counterparts in music for the meaning and variety of the sounds of words. Swift's words were set to music by the Rev. John Echlin (died 1763), his adviser on the cathedral choir, who was appointed vicar-general of Tuam in 1734.
21. The mountain in Greece that is the traditional home of the gods in Greek mythology and religion.
22. the common people.
23. A man from Forth, a barony in the south-east of County Wexford, which was settled in the wake of the Norman invasion of 1169 by a mixture of Normans, Flemings, Welsh and English. Various forms of twelfth-century English, which survived until recently in Forth and the adjoining barony of Bargy, are now referred to as the dialect of Forth and Bargy.
24. A man from Fingal, 'the land of the Norsemen, or foreigner', an area of very early settlement to the north of Dublin, where the dialect which survived until recently was similar to the dialect of Forth and Bargy. The term 'Fingallian' came to be used of the inhabitants of the Pale, the area of settlement extending from Dublin (Russell K. Alspach).
25. An English folk song.
26. Possibly an Italian aria.
27. An Italian aria.
28. A heavy frame of timber (or iron) set with iron teeth or tines, dragged over ploughed land to break clods, pulverize and stir the soil, root up weeds, or cover in the seed.
29. There were numerous operas of this title in the period.
30. The river that flows south from County Leitrim and reaches the sea once it has passed Limerick. 'To cross the Shannon' has special significance, meaning 'to enter the west of Ireland'.

She sings in *Gallaway*,[31] *Tuam*,[32] and *Mannin*,[33]
And in her Progress to and fro,
Expels a sweeter Song, *Speak Shoy*,[34]
She travels down to *Portaferry*,[35]
To *Omy*[36] and to *London-derry*,[37]
Where People hears[38] her with more Pleasure,
Than highland *Lilt*, or *Scottish Measure*,
She, of the *Truagh*,[39] has taken place,
And *Meu Vin Yall*,[40] of *Irish* Race.[41]
She flies to *Munster*[42] for the Air,
To clear her pipes and warble there,
Poor *Cronaan*,[43] being turn'd out of Play,
With *Rinke Mueenagh*[44] flew away,
To the remotest part of *Kerry*,[45]
In hopes to make the Vulgar merry,
But scarce one Cabbin in their Flight,
Wou'd give them Lodging for a Night,
So taken up with foreign Jingle,
Tralee[46] despis'd them, likewise *Dingle*.[47]
But *Drimin duh*[48] is still in favour,
Since we from *Murphy*,[49] beg, and crave her,
Of him alone we must require
To do her Justice on the Lyre,
She, and old *Eveleen a Rune*,[50]
Are by the *Muses* kept in Tune,
Who many Centuries have thriv'd,
And doom'd by fate to be long liv'd,
With many others we know well,
Which do in harmony excel.
Dub—g[51] improves them in our Days,
And never from the subject strays,
Nor by Extravagance perplext,
Will let them wander from the text.
Mac—n,[52] on the *Coal Black Joke*,[53]
(To his great Credit be it spoke)
Has multiply'd upon that Strain,
To shew his vast extensive Vein.
Sweet *Bocchi*[54] thought it worth his while,
In doing honour to our *Isle*,
To build on *Carallan's*[55] Foundation,
Which he perform'd to Admiration,
On his Pheraca's[56] went to work,
With long Divisions on *O Rowrk*.[57]
A *Dean*[58] the greatest Judge of Wit,
That ever wrote amongst us yet,
Gave us a Version of the Song,
Verbatim from the *Irish* Tongue.[59]

---

31. Galway.
32. A town in County Galway.
33. Mannin Bay, near Clifden, Co. Galway, or possibly Mannin Lake, near Ballyhaunis, Co. Mayo.
34. In modern Irish 'Spéic Seoigheach', an Irish tune whose title is obscure and which has been variously translated as 'Joices' Tune', 'The Joyces' Cry' and 'The Humours of Joyces' Country'.
35. A town in County Down.
36. Omagh, Co. Tyrone.
37. Known in the Republic of Ireland and by nationalists in Northern Ireland as Derry, most loyalists refer to the city as Londonderry.
38. An Hiberno-English form.
39. A tune with the title 'Ye Trugh' appeared in John and William Neal's *A Collection of the Most Celebrated Irish Tunes* (1724). In modern Irish this title is 'An Triúch', 'a word denoting a cantred or district. Truagh is the most northerly barony of County Monaghan, and the words of a poem in its praise to this tune survive' (Nicholas Carolan).
40. The title of an Irish tune; its meaning is obscure.
41. The sense is 'She has taken the place of both the *Truagh* and *Meu Vin Yall*, of *Irish* Race.'
42. The largest province in Ireland, Munster lies in the south-west and comprises the counties of Clare, Cork, Kerry, Limerick, Tipperary and Waterford.
43. In modern Irish *crónán*, a word denoting humming or crooning, and therefore a song of that type.
44. In modern Irish 'Rince Muimhneach', a Munster dance.
45. The county to the far south-west of Munster.
46. A town in County Kerry, to the north of the Dingle Peninsula.
47. A town in County Kerry, on the southern side of the Dingle Peninsula.
48. In modern Irish, 'Druimin dubh' (Black Cow), an ancient tune whose author and date are unknown. It is a lament for a drowned cow.
49. The well-known harper, who is referred to in the Irish newspapers of the 1720s to the 1740s as 'Mr Murphy'.
50. In modern Irish 'Eibhlín a rún' (Eileen my darling), popularly known as 'Eileen Aroon'. A famous love song, which is one of the oldest, authenticated Irish tunes, 'Eileen Aroon' may have originated in County Wexford in the early seventeenth century. It was the outstandingly popular Irish tune in the eighteenth century, and it became the established practice for singers to perform it. It was first published in Coffey's *The Beggar's Wedding* and Dubourg wrote variations on it for the harpsichord. See pp. 307-08.
51. Dubourg.
52. Possibly Aodh Mac Gabhráin or Hugh MacGauran, the Irish poet of the early eighteenth century who wrote the poem 'Pléaráca na Ruarcach', which Swift rendered as 'The Description of an *Irish-Feast*', and which inspired Turlogh Carolan, MacGauran's close friend, to compose the air 'The O'Rourke's Feast'.
53. Another title of 'The Black Joke'; see note 16.
54. Lorenzo Bocchi, the Italian musician, who was known in Dublin by 1724, when John and William Neal gave him special prominence on the title page of their *Collection of the Most Celebrated Irish Tunes*.
55. Carolan, who is also 'Carrollan', 'Carrallan' and 'Signor Carrollini' in the Neals' *Collection*.
56. In modern Irish 'Pheraca' is 'Pléaráca', a word of disputed meaning that has been derived from 'play-raking' and which here means tunes of revelry.
57. The central piece of the Neals' *Collection* was Bocchi's 'Plea Rarkeh na Rourkough or ye Irish weding improved with diferent divitions after ye Italian maner with A bass and Chorus'. In modern Irish 'Pléaráca na Ruarcach' means 'The revels of the O'Rourke's'. 'The English title here seems to arise from a misunderstanding of the subject. The simple unfigured bass may be for Bocchi's instrument, the cello, the instrumental chorus probably for violins' (Carolan).
58. Jonathan Swift (1667-1745), dean of St Patrick's Cathedral, Dublin 1713-45.
59. 'The Description of an *Irish-Feast*', which Swift appears to have written with the help of his friend Anthony Raymond (1675-1726), the only one of his circle who had a detailed knowledge of Irish. See Andrew Carpenter and Alan Harrison 'Swift's "O'Rourke's Feast" and Sheridan's "Letter": Early Transcripts by Anthony Raymond' in

Ta me ma choll,[60] and *Candun dilish*,[61]
For Ages have preserv'd their Relish,
Together with *Da mihi Manum*,[62]
Which we may reckon an *Arcanum*,[63]
With all the *Planksty's*[64] and *Pleracca's*,
By *Carallan* in his Sonata's,
The greatest *Genius* in his way,
An *Orpheus*,[65] who cou'd sing and play,
So great a *Bard* where can we find,
Like him illiterate, and blind.[66]

Hermann J. Real and Heinz J. Vienken (eds.), *Proceedings of the First Münster Symposium on Jonathan Swift* (Munich: Wilhelm Fink Verlag, 1985), pp. 27-46.

60. The Neals' *Collection* included 'Ta me ma Chulla's na doushe me', which in modern Irish is 'Tá mé i mo chodladh is ná dúisigh mé' (I am asleep and don't waken me). 'The composer is unknown, but the tune here is probably a song air, and several later texts are found to versions of it' (Carolan).
61. The Neals' *Collection* included 'Can duh Dilish', which in modern Irish is 'Ceann dubh dílis' (Dear dark head). 'The composer is unknown, but the tune was evidently popular earlier in the century.' The version in the Neals' *Collection* 'is the air of a love song' (Carolan).
62. Latin for 'Give me your hand'. The Neals' *Collection* included this tune, which is said to have been composed by Ruairí Dall Ó Catháin (Blind Rory O'Cahan or O'Kane) and which was probably written in the early seventeenth century. Ó Catháin wrote the tune for a Lady Eglinton in Scotland after she had apologized to him for not according him the status that he considered was his due (Carolan).
63. a deep secret.
64. Celebratory tunes and lively instrumental airs. A planksty is not necessarily a dance.
65. The celebrated musician of Greek mythology, Orpheus's playing on the lyre charmed all who heard it, including wild animals and the spirits of the underworld.
66. The sense is 'now that he is dead, where can we find another like him, especially since he was illiterate and blind.'

The 'Play-House Kings' and 'hauty Queen'

[When Swift published his *A Proposal for the Universal Use of* Irish *Manufacture* in 1720, he broke his six-year-old resolution not to become involved in Irish politics. Acutely aware of the effects of English mercantilist restrictions on Irish trade and industry, and angered by the Declaratory Act of 1720, which had reinforced the English claim to control Ireland, Swift retaliated by adopting the argument that his domestic audience should buy products of Irish manufacture. Economic conditions deteriorated in 1721, and distressed weavers began to beg in the streets of Dublin. When it was decided to perform *Hamlet* at the Theatre Royal to raise money for the relief of suffering, Swift seized the opportunity to reinforce the argument of his pamphlet. The importance of 'An Epilogue', however, surpasses the connexion between dramatic performance and social or political action. As Swift directs his attention to the relationship between the actors and the weavers, he alludes to the idea from antiquity, which he was to draw upon so effectively within a few years in *The Drapier's Letters*: the concept of cloth as a metaphor for speech.

The actor Thomas Griffith, who was well-known in Dublin, spoke both Swift's 'An Epilogue' and the one written by Ambrose Philips for a performance before the lord lieutenant and his wife, the Duke and Duchess of Grafton, at the Theatre Royal in October 1721. The theme has now become the theatre itself, for although the Theatre Royal was the main playhouse in Dublin, its sixty-year-old building had begun to fall into serious disrepair.]

JONATHAN SWIFT

AN EPILOGUE, TO BE SPOKE AT THE THEATRE-ROYAL

This present Saturday being *April* the 1st. In the Behalf of the Distressed *Weavers*

Who dares affirm this is no pious age,
When Charity begins to tread the Stage:
When Actors who at best are hardly Savers,
Will give a Night of Benefit to Weavers.
Stay — But let me see how finely will it Sound,
Imprimis:[1] From his Grace[2] a Hundred pound.
Peers, Clergy, Gentry, all are Benefactors;
And then Comes in the Item of the Actors.
Item the Actors, freely gave a Day,
The Poet had no more who made the Play.

But whence this Wonderous Charity, in Play'rs,
They learnt it not at Sermons or at pray'rs.
Under the Rose[3] since here are none but friends;
To own the truth we have some private Ends.[4]
Since Waiting Women like Exacting Jades,
Hold up the prices of their Old *Brocades*.
We'll dress in *Manufactures*, made at home?
Equip our *KINGS*, and *Generalls* at the Comb.[5]
We'll Rigg in Meath-Street,[6] *Egypt's* hauty *Queen*,[7]
And *Anthony* shall Court her in *Ratteen*.[8]
In *blew shalloon*,[9] shall *Hanniball*[10] be Clad,

1. First in a list; other 'items' are listed below.
2. William King (1650-1729), archbishop of Dublin 1703-29.
3. *sub rosa*, in strict confidence.
4. reasons.
5. The Coombe, an area near St Patrick's Cathedral, was the neighbourhood of the Dublin weavers.
6. A street adjoining the Coombe.
7. Cleopatra. The dramatic characters named were all popular on the Dublin stage.
8. Thick tweed woven in Ireland.
9. A woven material.
10. Hannibal and Scipio are characters in Nathaniel Lee's *Sophonisba* (1675).

And *Scipio*, trail an *Irish purple Plad.*[11]
In Drugget[12] drest of Thirteen Pence a Yard,
See *Philip*'s Son[13] amidst his *Persian* Guard;
And proud *Roxana*[14] fir'd with jealous Rage,
With fifty Yards of Crape,[15] shall sweep the Stage.
In short our Kings and Princesses within,
Are all resolv'd the Project to begin;
And you, our Subjects, when you here resort,
Must Imitate the Fashion of the Court.

O! Cou'd I see this Audience Clad in *Stuff*,[16]
Tho' Moneys scarce we shou'd have Trade enough;
But *Chints*,[17] *Brocades*, and *Lace* take all away,
And scarce a Crown is left to see the Play:
Perhaps you wonder whence this Friendship Springs,
Between the *Weavers* and us Play-House Kings.
But Wit and Weaving had the same beginning,
Pallas[18] first taugh[t] us Poetry and Spinning;
And next Observe how this Alliance fits,
For *Weavers* now are just as poor as Wits;
Their Brother Quill-Men Workers for the Stage,
For sorry *Stuff*,[19] can get a Crown a Page;
But *Weavers* will be Kinder to the *Players*,
And Sell for Twenty Pence a Yard [of] theirs;
And to your knowledge there is often less in,
The *Poets* Wits, than in the *Players* Dressing.

11. Twill or cloth woven in a checkered or tartan design.
12. Thick, cheap woven cloth.
13. i.e. Alexander the Great, a character in Nathaniel Lee's *The Rival Queens* (1677).
14. Another character in *The Rival Queens*.
15. crepe: thin woven material, usually black.
16. Heavy woven material.
17. i.e. chintz, a printed cotton fabric which, like brocade and lace, was imported into Ireland. The contrast is between these imported materials and the more homely ones, listed above, which were made by the weavers of Dublin.
18. Pallas Athene, Greek goddess of spinning and weaving, among other things.
19. worthless writing. The 'Quill-Men Workers' are hack playwrights.

AMBROSE PHILIPS
(1674-1749)

AN EPILOGUE *TO THEIR GRACES THE DUKE AND DUTCHESS OF* GRAFTON *at the* Theatre *in* Dublin ... Spoken by Mr. *Griffith*[1]

1. This is the form of the title in Matthew Concanen's *Miscellaneous Poems* (1724). The poem first appeared in the *Dublin Courant* of 4 October 1721 and also on a separate broadsheet, where it is attributed to Philips. 'The Theatre' was the Theatre Royal, Smock Alley.

Illustrious Pair! the Blessings of this Isle,
Who, gracious, on our humble Labours smile;
To you, thus low, your Servants bow; — to you,
Their only Hope, they for Protection sue,
And beg your Aid against th'Assaults of Time,
We suffer by that *old Offender's*[2] Crime:
These Walls impair'd by *him*, disclos'd such Flaws,
The Ladies trembled at a loud Applause.
When in soft Scenes we exercis'd our Calling,
We mov'd their Terror, — lest the Roof was falling:
Scarce durst we represent a Tragick Battle,
And, struck with Dread, they heard our Thunder rattle.
But for a while we now suspend our Fear,
And can securely bid you welcome here:
Nor shall the Crack of one disjointed Rafter,
Disturb the Scene, or interrupt your Laughter.

This Pile, the Temple of *Apollo*,[3] rose,
When *Charles*[4] return'd, to give his Realms Repose:
So true is what our fam'd *Roscommon*[5] sings,
Who joyns the Muses to the Fate of Kings:
'By secret Influence of indulgent Skies,
Empire and Poesy together rise.'
This House, we hope, is not of long Duration, —
The Hint suffices to a gallant Nation:[6]
Let not the Ladies Fears their Joys restrain,
Nor with their Pleasures mix perpetual Pain,
With a new *Theatre* oblige the Fair,
Who else, will all to *London*-Plays repair;
With one Consent, like Swallows, bid adieu t'ye,
And leave poor *Dublin* destitute of Beauty.

The greatest Patriots have in every Age
Made it their Glory to support the Stage:
Your Ancestors, to raise this Dome combin'd,
Improv'd our Pleasures, and our Taste refin'd:
May you, like them, the Arts of Peace maintain,
Since *George*,[7] like *Charles*, renews a peaceful Reign.

2. i.e. time, since the theatre building was now sixty years old. In 1670, the galleries had collapsed during a performance, which explains the series of references to the building falling down.
3. The god of reason in Greek mythology, patron of poetry and by extension, of Diana.
4. Charles II, whose reign (1660-85) marked the reopening of the Dublin theatre after the Commonwealth period. In 1662, Dublin had received one of the royal patents, created by Charles, authorizing theatrical performances; only three were issued for Britain and Ireland.
5. Wentworth Dillon (*c.* 1633-85), fourth earl of Roscommon, poet, translator and critic. The lines are from his 'Essay on Translated Verse' (1684), lines 354-55.
6. i.e. Ireland. The 'hint' is to subscribe to the fund for a new theatre building.
7. George I, king of Britain and Ireland 1714-27.

'The Poet's Prayer' for Himself

[Dunkin's 'The Poet's Prayer' and Dermody's 'An Ode to Myself' share the traditional theme of the poet's awareness of his creative integrity. While Dunkin prays to Apollo, Dionysus is the god behind Dermody's recognition that he is his own 'muse and patron', and while Dunkin's sense of reason directs him to list a series of potential 'disasters' that threaten the poet in the contemporary world, Dermody, who is 'Reckless' of all such disasters, recognizes that he is driven by forces that make him a 'prince' who may sit 'With clown or peer'. Each represents the other's creative or cultural enemy, for Dermody is one of 'the triflers in rhyme' against whom Dunkin seeks protection, and Dunkin's allegiance is to the works that Dermody sees as 'classics sleeping on the shelf', and, beyond them, to the Muses on Mount Olympus or Mount Helicon, which Dermody dismisses as 'that hill'.

While Dunkin's analysis of the different kinds of contemporary falsehood inevitably gives rise to a poem that is more comprehensive than Dermody's ode, both poets share a sense of the transforming power of art, manifest in the adoption of original poetic forms. Dunkin's twelve-syllable line, which works substantially with anapaestic rhythms, suggests a voice that dwells on the objects of satire, while Dermody's inventive stanzaic pattern, which adopts lines of varied pace, creates a distinctive emphasis on the central ideas. If Dunkin's wish to be 'honest' seems similar to Dermody's 'lingering honour', then the differences that remain are the traditional ones between Apollonian and Dionysian conceptions of the self.]

WILLIAM DUNKIN

THE POET'S PRAYER

If e'er in thy sight I found favour, Apollo,[1]
Defend me from all the disasters, which follow:
From the knaves, and the fools, and the fops of the
time,
From the drudges in prose, and the triflers in
rhyme:
From the patch-work, and toils of the royal
sack-bibber,[2]
Those dead birth-day odes, and the farces of
CIBBER:[3]
From servile attendance on men in high places,
Their worships, and honours, and lordships, and
graces:
From long dedications to patrons unworthy,
Who hear, and receive, but will do nothing for thee:
From being caress'd, to be left in the lurch,
The tool of a party, in state, or in church:
From dull thinking blockheads, as sober, as Turks,
And petulant bards, who repeat their own works:
From all the gay things of a drawing-room show,
The sight of a Belle, and the smell of a Beau:
From busy back-biters, and tatlers, and carpers,
And scurvy acquaintance with fiddlers, and
sharpers:
From old politicians, and coffee-house lectures,
The dreams of a chymist, and schemes of
projectors:[4]
From the fears of a jail, and the hopes of a pension,
The tricks of a gamester, and oaths of an ensign:
From shallow free-thinkers, in taverns disputing,
Nor ever confuted, nor ever confuting:
From the constant good fare of another man's
board,
My lady's broad hints, and the jests of my lord:
From hearing old chymists prelecting[5] *de oleo*,[6]
And reading of Dutch commentators in folio:
From waiting, like GAY,[7] whole years at Whitehall:
From the pride of great wits, and the envy of small:
From very fine ladies with very fine incomes,
Which they finely lay out on fine toys, and fine
trincums:[8]
From the pranks of ridottoes,[9] and court-
masquerades,
The snares of young jilts, and the spite of old maids:
From a saucy dull stage, and submitting to share
In an empty third night with a beggarly play'r:
From CURL,[10] and such Printers, as would have me
curst
To write second parts, let who will write the first:
From all pious patriots, who would, to their best,

1. The god of reason in Greek mythology.
2. The place-seeker who drinks in the circles of the court.
3. Colley Cibber (1671-1757), dramatist and poet laureate 1730-57, whom Pope made the ridiculed hero of *The Dunciad* (1743).
4. Speculators, cheats and, especially, the promoters of wildly impracticable projects.
5. lecturing upon.
6. The subject of fuming sulphuric acid.
7. John Gay (1685-1732), poet and dramatist, who came to prominence with his *Fables* (1727) and *The Beggar's Opera* (1728) and who was disappointed in his search for a suitable position.
8. A dialectal or colloquial form that is 'a humorous alteration of *trinket*, with latinized ending' (*OED*).
9. An entertainment or social assembly consisting of music and dancing.
10. Edmund Curll (1675-1747), bookseller, publisher and pirate printer, who was attacked by numerous writers, especially Swift and Pope.

Put on a new tax, and take off an old test:[11]
From the faith of informers, the fangs of the law,
And the great rogues, who keep all the lesser in awe:
From a poor country-cure,[12] that living interment,
With a wife, and no prospect of any preferment:
From scribbling for hire, when my credit is sunk,
To buy a new coat, and to line an old trunk:
From 'squires, who divert us with jokes at their tables,
Of hounds in their kennels, and nags in their stables:
From the nobles and commons, who bound in strict league are
To subscribe for no book, yet subscribe to Heidegger:[13]
From the cant of fanatics, the jargon of schools,
The censures of wise men, and praises of fools:
From critics, who never read Latin, or Greek,
And pedants, who boast they read both all the week:
From borrowing wit, to repay it like BUDGEL,[14]
Or lending, like POPE, to be paid by a cudgel.
If ever thou didst, or wilt ever befriend me,
From these, and such evils, APOLLO, defend me;
And let me be rather but honest with no-wit,
Than a noisy, nonsensical, half-witted poet.

11. An allusion to the various oaths and declarations that were listed in the different Test Acts from 1673, including the Irish Test Act of 1704, which were aimed at catholics and nonconformists.
12. parish.
13. John James Heidegger (*c.* 1659-1749), the wealthy and fashionable manager of the opera in London. He had a chequered career and his involvement with scandalous performances prompted a grand jury in Middlesex to present him in 1729 'as the principal promoter of vice and immorality' (*DNB*).
14. Eustace Budgell (1686-1737), miscellaneous writer, who held various positions in the early years of the Irish administration of George I and who was member of parliament for Mullingar 1715-27.

THOMAS DERMODY

AN ODE TO MYSELF

Thrice hail, thou prince of jovial fellows,
Tuning so blithe thy lyric bellows,
Of no one's brighter genius jealous;
Whose little span
Is spent 'twixt poetry and alehouse,
'Twixt quill and cann!

Reckless howe'er the world may fadge,[1]
Variety thy only badge:
Now courting Susan, Kate, or Madge,
Or black-eyed Molly;
For living in one sullen lodge
Is downright folly.

Thy classics sleeping on the shelf,
Thou'rt muse and patron to thyself:
Aye frolic when profuse of pelf;[2]
Grim as the gallows
When dunned by that obstreperous elf,
False-scoring Alice.

Long may'st thou punch ambrosial swill,
Drinking no water from that hill[3]
By temperate bards recorded still
In tasteless rhime;
For noble punch shall sweetly fill
The thought sublime.

By many wrong'd, gay bloom of song,
Thou yet art innocent of wrong,
Virtue and truth to thee belong,
Virtue and truth;
Though Pleasure led thy step along,
And trapp'd thy youth.

With Baynham,[4] social spring of wit,
Thou hadst full many a merry fit;
And whether haply thou shalt sit
With clown or peer,
Never shall lingering honour quit
Thy heart sincere.

1. agree.
2. money.
3. Alluding to the fountain Hippocrene on Mount Helicon in Boeotia, traditionally associated with poetic inspiration.
4. See Thomas Dermody's 'John Baynham's Epitaph' (p. 401).

'As I strole the City ....'

[Dublin expanded dramatically during the eighteenth century and became a city of great houses and squares, fashionable walks and fine public buildings. Two of the poems below refer to Dublin public monuments of the time: to the newly rebuilt Essex Bridge, about which Dunkin wrote some elegant if uncritical lines, and to the statue of George II, erected in St Stephen's Green in 1758, about which Thomas Newburgh was considerably less enthusiastic.

Members of Dublin 'society' made no secret of their disdain for life in the country, as Constantia Grierson, the brilliant wife of a celebrated Dublin printer, shows in her verse letter to Laetitia van Lewen, the beauty who married the Rev. Matthew Pilkington in 1729. But even the delights of Dublin might pall, in which case the fashionable set in the city could easily escape by coach to Templeogue, south-west of Dublin, where a spa had been established in the 1720s. There, as Richard Pockrich, the eccentric 'inventor' of the musical glasses, makes clear in his Templeogue ballad, beaux and belles could enjoy the delights of social intrigue and malicious gossip with the added attractions of pure air and water.

In Dublin itself, the two most imposing buildings were Trinity College and the new Parliament House. The latter is the setting for 'The Legion Club', now regarded as one of Swift's most powerful works. The poem, with its blend of classical allusion and vitriolic attacks on individual members of parliament, inevitably dominates whatever poems serve to provide a sense of its Irish context. That context must include the subject of the finances of the Church of Ireland, which had been threatened by moves in the House of Commons in 1734-36 to abolish certain tithes. Drawing a metaphor from Aeneas's descent into hell, Swift directs his bitterness towards all those whose loss of direction in government had led them to hate the clergy, to defy various court decisions, and to disregard the voice of opposition in the House of Commons itself.

The section ends with two of the many squibs current in eighteenth-century Dublin.]

WILLIAM DUNKIN

ON THE NEW BRIDGE[1] BUILT ON THE EASTERN SIDE OF DUBLIN

Swift rushes Liffey to the main, afloat
Against the stream slow tugs the lab'ring boat.
The waving multitude promiscuous flow
Through streets in air, and spurn the tide below.
Hence learn what labour's persevering part
Performs, attended with her hand-maid, art:
The wit of man, superior to the might
Of nature, bade the distant banks unite.

1. Essex Bridge, named for Arthur Capel, earl of Essex, lord lieutenant of Ireland 1672-76, the period of its planning and construction by Sir Humphrey Jervis. In disrepair in 1751, the bridge was rebuilt by George Semple on the model of Westminster Bridge and was reopened in 1755. Enlarged in 1874, it is now known as Grattan Bridge.

THOMAS NEWBURGH

(*c.* 1695-1779)

THE *BEAU WALK*,[1] IN *STEPHEN'S-GREEN*

'Mid Trees of stunted Growth, unequal Roes,
On the coarse Gravel, trip the Belles and Beaus.
Here, on one Side, extends a length of Street,
Where Dirt-bespattering Cars and Coaches meet.
On t'other, in the Ditches[2] lazy Flood,
Dead Cats and Dogs lie bloated; drench'd in Mud.
But lo! a Statue from afar salutes your Eyes,
To which th'Inclosure all Access denies.
So distant, whose, or whom, no Eye can ken,
Plac'd in the Centre of a marshy Fen.
But know, 'tis Royal George[3] on whom you stare,
Tho' oft mistaken for some good Lord Mayor:
And tho' his Charger foams in ductile[4] Brass,
The Charger for an ambling Pad[5] may pass;
The whole equestrian Statue for a Toy,
A Horse of Hobby, mounted by a Boy.
For shame ye Cits,[6] where meet th'assembl'd Fair,
Fill up your Dikes[7] and purge th'unwholsome Air.
Let George's royal Form be fairly shewn,
And like his Virtues, be reveal'd and known.

1. 'The Green was then surrounded on each side by a tree-lined walk (Beaux Walk on the north, Monks's Walk on the east, Leeson's Walk on the south, and French Walk on the west)' (Edward McParland).
2. The ha-ha, a sunken-fence in the Green, 'the practical purpose of which was to protect the Corporation's grazing' (McParland).
3. George II, king of Britain and Ireland 1727-60.
4. worked or beaten into shape.
5. a slow riding horse.
6. Citizens, usually applied, more or less contemptuously, to townsmen or shopkeepers.
7. i.e. fill the ditch (the ha-ha).

CONSTANTIA GRIERSON

(*c.*1704-32)

TO MISS LAETITIA VAN LEWEN IN A COUNTRY-TOWN AT THE TIME OF THE ASSIZES

The fleeting Birds may soon in Ocean swim,
And *Northern* Whales thro' liquid Azure skim,
The *Dublin* Ladies their Intrigues forsake,
To Dress and Scandal an Aversion take;
When you can in the lonely Forrest walk,

And with some serious Matron gravely talk
Of Possets,[1] Poultices, and Waters still'd,
And monstrous Casks with Mead[2] and Cider fill'd;
How many Hives of Bees she has in Store,
And how much Fruit her Trees this *Summer* bore;
Or Home returning in the Yard can stand,
And feed the Chickens from your bounteous Hand:
Of each one's Top-knot tell, and hatching pry,
Like *Tully*[3] waiting for an Augury.
When Night appoaches, down to Table sit,
With a great Crowd, choice Meat, and little Wit;
What Horse won the last Race, how mighty *Tray*,[4]
At the last famous hunting, caught the Prey;
Surely, you can't, but such Discourse despise,
Methinks, I see Displeasure in your Eyes:
O my *Laetitia*, stay no longer there,
You'll soon forget, that you yourself are fair;
Why will you keep from us, from all that's gay,
There in a lonely Solitude to stay?
Where not a Mortal thro' the Year you view,
But Bob-wigg'd Hunters,[5] who their Game pursue
With so much Ardor, they'd a Cock or Hare,
To thee, in all thy blooming Charms, prefer.
You write of Belles and Beaux that there appear,
And gilded Coaches, such as glitter here;
For gilded Coaches, each estated Clown
That gravely slumbers on the Bench[6] has one;
But Beaux! they're young Attorneys! sure you Mean!
Who thus appear to your romantick Brain.
Alas! no Mortal there can talk to you,
That Love, or Wit, or Softness ever knew:
All they can speak of's *Capias*'s[7] and Law,
And Writs to keep the Country Fools in Awe.
And, if to Wit, or Courtship they pretend,
'Tis the same Way that they a Cause defend;
In which they give of Lungs a vast Expence,
But little Passion, Thought or Eloquence:
Bad as they are, they'll soon abandon you,
And Gain, and Clamour, in the Town pursue.
So haste to Town, if ev'n such Fools you prize;
O haste to Town! and bless the longing Eyes
Of your Constantia.

1. A rural (rather than a city) drink composed of hot milk curdled with ale or wine, often with sugar and spices.
2. An alcoholic drink made by fermenting a mixture of honey and water.
3. Marcus Tullius Cicero (106-43 B.C.), Roman orator, statesman and philosopher.
4. The name of a hunting dog or hound.
5. i.e. huntsmen wearing old-fashioned wigs.
6. i.e. in the House of Lords.
7. A writ ordering an arrest. From Latin: You must take.

RICHARD POCKRICH

(*c.*1690-1759)

THE TEMPLE-OGE BALLAD

To the tune of, To you fair ladies now at land, *&c.*

Ye *Dublin Ladies* that attend,
This Place of Mirth and Fame,
My Song, or Praise or Discommend,
As you approve my Theme.
'Tis you, that make the *Poet* Sing;
The Subject's but a trivial thing.
With a Fal, lal, la,

Those *Damsels* that were us'd of late,
To rise when some had Din'd,
Now leave their Toilets pleasing Seat,
For Air that's unconfin'd;
On *Mondays*[1] rise by Six — O strange!
What stubborn Hearts can't Musick change?
With a Fal, &c.

At Breakfast what a Buzz is made,
What Scandal runs about;
What him, and her, and they, have said,
Or who's that, that went out.
Such Prating round each Table fly,
For one Word Truth, there's Ten a —,
With a Fal, &c.

The *Cockscombs* that officious wait,
With Kettles in their Hands,
And Walk about from Seat to Seat,
To see who 'tis Commands;
If Smiles won't Pay for all their Pain,
Another time *the Rest they'll gain,*
With a Fal, &c.

The Fiddles now with sprightly Grace,
Invite them to the Jigg,
And Pleasure sparkles in each Face;
With their own Praise they're big,
A Captive Heart or two must fall,
To *Chloe*'s Share — or none at all,
With a Fal, &c.

1. The day the social group met at the spa on the lands of Sir Compton Domvile (died 1768) at Templeogue, a journey of an hour or so to the south-west of Dublin.

The Rival Queens,[2] with equal Charms,
Attract the Standers Eyes,
And strike the Soul with wild Alarms,
Of Love and deep Surprize;
Yet raise, by their prevailing Art,
The chastest Wish in th' lewdest Heart,
With a Fal, &c.

How pleasant 'tis to View the Fair?
How sweetly we are caught?
With gentle Smiles they spread their Snare,
We're their's, as soon as thought.
Who can withstand when *W—mys*'s[3] Face
Heightens the *Lustre* of the Place.
With a Fal, &c.

The greatest Crime 'twould be to miss
A celebrated *Toast*,
In future Ages — as in this,
She'll be *Hibernia*'s Boast;
Miss *Wh—te* for ever, then must shine,
Whilst we revere all that's Divine.
With a Fal, &c.

Miss *Sm—y* whose Exploits renown'd,
Have run where Fame can go:
With Bays full oft she has been Crown'd,
And prais'd from Top to Toe;
She Loves a *Soldier*'s honest Name,
By the Major,[4] she acquir'd Fame,
With a Fal, &c.

Oh could the Muse her Shape but Span,
And shew her Brilliant Eyes,
But that no Human Creature can
Behold them but he Dies.
Bless'd as th' Immortal Gods is he,
The Youth who fondly sits by thee.[5]
With a Fal, &c.

When all prepare their Legs to Prance,
Each Sex in Rows apart;
They long to blend them in the Dance,
And shew their hopping Art;

2. A play (1677) by Nathaniel Lee.
3. The names of well-known beauties, thinly disguised.
4. A well-known dance.
5. An echo of lines from a poem by Sappho, quoted in Longinus, *On the Sublime*.

A Tune they want, and can't agree,
Moll bids them play, The best in Three.[6]
With a Fal, &c.

Thrice happy *Lee*,[7] whose forming Hands
First taught her the Coupee,[8]
Which e'ry Heart at once Commands;
She owes her Fame to thee,
To thee, the grateful Muses sing,
For raising such a pretty thing.
With a Fal, &c.

To shift the Scene and Paint the Men,
And eke the Beaus also:
O Muse prepare thy flowing Pen,
With Justice let it glow.
To Lash at *Vice*, but *Honour* Praise,
Be that the Subject of thy Lays.
With a Fal, &c.

From Foreign Climes[9] the worst of Vice,
By *C——m*[10] is brought,
To mention which, infects Advice,
Tho' artfully 'tis wrought.
His awkard Grin, and Scull of Lead,
Shews *Mother Dulness*[11] crown'd his Head.
With a Fal, &c.

Among the Throng, where Follies dwell,
Conspicuous *R—lly* Glares,
His silly Tongue does Sense expell,
His Toss[12] his Meaning shares;
No more the Vacuum shall confound,
Search but his Head, the Vacuum's found.
With a Fal, &c.

The *Freakish* Knight with splendid Dress,
(If Wh—s don't Interpose)
Is there by Eight, his Sight to bless,
With Girls that Charms disclose,

6. 'a most famous Country-Dance' (Pockrich).
7. 'a noted little Dancing-Master' (Pockrich).
8. 'a dance step, in which the dancer rests on one foot and passes the other forward or backward, making a sort of salutation' (*OED*).
9. 'the Taverns, Play and Opera Houses in *France* and *Italy*' (Pockrich).
10. Again, contemporaries would have recognized those intended in this part of the poem.
11. cf. Dryden's *Mac Flecknoe* (*c.* 1679) and Pope's *The Dunciad* (1728-42).
12. An affected toss of the head when the speaker is at a loss for words (Pockrich).

No Wonder he the Dance declin'd;
His Bones were not too close combin'd.
With a Fal, &c.

Fain would my Song more Courtly grow,
When *F—s—ter* I name,
With *Wit* like his to overflow
My Lines, and raise my Fame.
Words are too feeble to Rehearse
Sufficient Praise for him in Verse.
With a Fal, &c.

The Smoak of Vice will soon infect
A Youth, tho' well inclin'd,
Their glowing Blood, they should Correct,
Their Intellectuals mind.
I speak to *B—y—le* and *H—sen* to[o],
You shou'd your Parts[13] with warmth pursue.
With a Fal, &c.

My Brother *Bard*[14] whose honest Heart,
Still props our falling State,[15]
And strives with Judgment and with Art,
T' avert impending Fate.
Who Spends so much, so little gains,
Just Honour claims, for all his Pains.
With a Fal, &c.

To him[16] O *Temple-Oge*, is due
Thy Praise and Fame renown'd;
Had he not been thy *Patron* True,
Thy Well had ne'er been found:
Thy *Waters* might have silent sprung,
Nor yet by him, nor me be Sung.[17]
With a Fal, &c.

His Fluent Speech runs smoothly out,
Each Word is fraught with Sense:
The Powder'd Fops, are piqu'd no doubt,
With Fops he must Dispence.

13. abilities, characteristics.
14. The pamphleteer John Browne (*c.* 1695-1762), who was attacked by Swift for the role he played in the controversy over Wood's Halfpence, and who became known as 'Halfpenny Browne'.
15. ''Tis not to be doubted, but the publick Spirit which Mr. *B*[*ro*]*wn*[*e*] expresses in his Writings, on the Affairs of our poor Country, has, in a great Measure, prevented, and still continues to prevent, many evil Purposes fram'd by wicked M[anage]rs for our Ruin' (Pockrich).
16. Browne 'was the first Encourager of this Well' and constantly sought to make it 'as agreeable as may be' (Pockrich).
17. See 'his *Temple-Oge* Intelligencer' (Pockrich). Seven issues of *The Temple-Oge Intelligencer* appeared in Dublin in 1728, and were published with Browne's *The Plain-Dealer* as *The Lucubrations of Sallmanazor Histrum, Esq;* (Dublin, 1730).

B—wn's an Exception to Old Rules;
That Men of Sense can't herd with Fools.
With a Fal, &c.

Ye *Dublin Citts*[18] whose thoughtless Souls,
Incline ye to be Blind,
Whose Knowledge ends in brimming Bowls,
These my last Sayings mind:
Where Fops unnumber'd pay their Court,
Let not your pretty Girls resort.
With a Fal, &c.

18. Citizens, usually applied, more or less contemptuously, to townsmen or shopkeepers.

JONATHAN SWIFT

A CHARACTER, PANEGYRIC, AND DESCRIPTION OF THE LEGION[1] CLUB

Written in the Year, 1736

As I strole the City, oft I
Spy a Building[2] large and lofty,[3]
Not a Bow-shot from the College,[4]
Half the Globe from Sense and Knowledge.
By the prudent Architect[5]
Plac'd against the Church[6] direct;
Making good my Grandames Jest,
Near the Church — you know the rest.[7]

Tell us, what this Pile contains?
Many a Head that holds no Brains.
These Demoniacs[8] let me dub
With the Name of *Legion Club.*

1. Recalling Luke 8.30: 'Jesus then asked him, "What is your name?" And he said, "Legion"; for many demons had entered him' (Swift's editor, Pat Rogers).
2. The Parliament House, whose architect was Sir Edward Lovett Pearce, the member of parliament for Ratoath, Co. Meath. Begun in 1728, it was completed in 1739.
3. From an architectural point of view, it was 'one of the most important buildings of the early eighteenth century in Europe' (Edward McParland), and 'incomparably the most splendid Parliament House in the Empire, even eclipsing Westminster' (Edith Mary Johnston).
4. The building faced Trinity College, Dublin across College Green.
5. 'Pearce ... had been voted £2,000 as an *ex gratia* payment by parliament' (Rogers).
6. St Andrew's Church, generally known as the Round Church, which actually looks down towards College Green from the corner of Suffolk Street and St Andrew Street.
7. The proverbial saying concludes 'and far from God' (Rogers).
8. madmen.

Such Assemblies, you might swear,
Meet when Butchers bait a Bear;[9]
Such a Noise, and such haranguing,
When a Brother Thief is hanging.
Such a Rout and such a Rabble
Run to hear Jackpudding[10] gabble;
Such a Croud their Ordure throws[11]
On a far less Villain's Nose.[12]

Could I from the Building's Top
Hear the rattling Thunder drop,
While the Devil upon the Roof,
If the Devil be Thunder Proof,
Should with Poker fiery-red
Crack the Stones, and melt the Lead;
Drive them down on every Scull,
While the Den of Thieves[13] is full,
Quite destroy that Harpies[14] Nest,
How might then our Isle be blest?
For Divines allow, that God
Sometimes makes the Devil his Rod:
And the Gospel will inform us,
He can punish Sins enormous.

Yet should *Swift* endow the Schools
For his Lunatics and Fools,
With a Rood[15] or two of Land,
I allow the Pile may stand.
You perhaps will ask me, why so?
But it is with this Proviso,
Since the House is like to last,
Let a royal Grant be pass'd,
That the Club have Right to dwell
Each within his proper Cell;
With a Passage left to creep in,
And a Hole above for peeping.

Let them, when they once get in
Sell the Nation for a Pin;
While they sit a picking Straws
Let them rave of making Laws;
While they never hold their Tongue,
Let them dabble in their Dung;
Let them form a grand Committee,
How to plague and starve the City;
Let them stare and storm and frown,
When they see a Clergy-Gown.
Let them, 'ere they crack a Louse,
Call for th'Orders of the House;
Let them with their gosling Quills,[16]
Scribble senseless Heads of Bills;[17]
We may, while they strain their Throats,
Wipe our Arses with their Votes.[18]

Let Sir *Tom*,[19] that rampant Ass,
Stuff his Guts with Flax and Grass;[20]
But before the Priest he fleeces
Tear the Bible all to Pieces.
At the Parsons,[21] *Tom*, Halloo[22] Boy,
Worthy Offspring of a Shoeboy,
Footman, Traytor, vile Seducer,
Perjur'd Rebel, brib'd Accuser;
Lay thy paltry Priviledge aside,
Sprung from Papists and a Regicide;[23]
Fall a Working like a Mole,
Raise the Dirt about your Hole.

Come, assist me, Muse obedient,
Let us try some new Expedient;
Shift the Scene for half an Hour,
Time and Place are in thy Power.
Thither, gentle Muse, conduct me,
I shall ask, and you instruct me.

See, the Muse unbars the Gate;
Hark, the Monkeys, how they prate!

9. Referring to the roles played by butchers in the sports where bears were baited (Rogers).
10. A buffoon or clown.
11. Crowds used to pelt condemned criminals with rubbish.
12. 'That is, criminals who went to be executed were less guilty men' (Rogers).
13. See Matthew 21.13: 'He said to them, "It is written, 'My house shall be called a house of prayer'; but you make it a den of robbers"' (Rogers).
14. Rapacious, plundering, or grasping monsters.
15. A measure of land; pile = a large building.
16. Quill pens made with the feathers of young geese, implying that those who are using them are no better than young geese.
17. The Irish parliament was only able to 'submit "Heads of Bills" to England for approval. There the Privy Council could delete, add, or reject as it saw fit. When — and if — the bill was returned to the Irish Parliament, it had to be passed with whatever alterations it had met with in England, or be rejected *in toto*' (Oliver W. Ferguson).
18. 'The printed "votes" were among the few official records of parliamentary affairs available to the public' (Rogers).
19. Sir Thomas Prendergast (died 1760), postmaster-general for Ireland 1733.
20. 'On which the graziers allegedly grew fat' (Rogers).
21. 'An injunction, like a cry in the hunting field' (Rogers).
22. A huntsman's call to encourage the hounds.
23. Prendergast's father (*c.* 1660-1709), a Jacobite soldier, 'supplied information to the government of a plot to assassinate William III at Turnham Green in 1696, and gave evidence against the conspirators' (Rogers).

All ye Gods,[24] who rule the Soul
Styx,[25] through Hell whose Waters roll!
Let me be allow'd to tell
What I heard in yonder Hell.

Near the Door[26] an entrance gapes,
Crouded round with antic Shapes;
Poverty, and *Grief*, and *Care*,
Causeless *Joy*, and true *Despair*;
Discord[27] periwigg'd with Snakes,
See the dreadful Strides she takes.

By this odious Crew beset,[28]
I began to rage and fret
And resolv'd to break their Pates,
'Ere we enter'd at the Gates;
Had not *Clio*[29] in the Nick,
Whisper'd me, let down your Stick;
What, said I, is this the Mad-House?
These, she answer'd, are but Shadows,
Phantoms, bodiless and vain,
Empty Visions of the Brain.

In the Porch *Briareus*[30] stands,
Shews a Bribe in all his Hands:
Briareus the Secretary,
But we Mortals call him *Cary*.[31]
When the Rogues their Country fleece,
They may hope for Pence a Piece.

24. Swift's editor George Faulkner notes a lengthy allusion to Virgil, *Aeneid* VI, 264 ff., an account of Aeneas in the underworld: 'Ye gods, who hold the domain of spirits! ye voiceless shades! Thou, Chaos, and thou, Phlegethon, ye broad, silent tracts of night! Suffer me to tell what I have heard; suffer me of your grace to unfold secrets buried in the depths and darkness of the earth!' (Virgil's editor, H. Rushton Fairclough).
25. The main river of the underworld in Greek mythology.
26. *Aeneid* VI, 273-74: 'Just before the entrance, even within the very jaws of Hell, Grief and Avenging Cares have made their bed' (Fairclough).
27. *Aeneid* VI, 280-81: 'and savage Strife, her snaky locks entwined with bloody fillets' (Fairclough). There is an image here of Megaera, one of the three Eumenides, the so-called Kindly Ones who were known as the Furies. Playing the role of avengers, they were often represented with writhing snakes in their hair (Rogers).
28. *Aeneid* VI, 290-91: 'Here on a sudden, in trembling terror, Aeneas grasps his sword, and turns the naked edge against their coming' (Fairclough).
29. One of the nine Muses of Greek mythology, Clio was associated with history. See also *Aeneid* VI, 292: 'and did not his wise companion warn him that these were but faint, bodiless lives' (Fairclough).
30. *Aeneid* VI, 287: 'and the hundredfold Briareus' (Fairclough). He was also known as 'Aegeon, a giant with fifty heads and a hundred hands' (Rogers).
31. Walter Carey (1685-1757), secretary to the Duke of Dorset, lord lieutenant of Ireland 1730 and supporter of the Whig administration.

Clio, who had been so wise
To put on a Fool's Disguise,
To bespeak some Approbation,
And be thought a near Relation;
When she saw three hundred Brutes,[32]
All involv'd in wild Disputes;
Roaring till their Lungs were spent,
Privilege of Parliament,
Now a new Misfortune feels,
Dreading to be laid by th' Heels.[33]
Never durst a Muse before
Enter that Infernal Door;
Clio stifled with the Smell,
Into Spleen and Vapours[34] fell;
By the *Stygian*[35] Steams that flew,
From the dire infectious Crew.
Not the Stench of Lake *Avernus*,[36]
Could have more offended her Nose;
Had she flown but o'er the Top,
She would feel her Pinions drop,
And by Exhalations dire,
Though a Goddess must expire.
In a Fright she crept away,
Bravely I resolved to stay.

When I saw the Keeper frown,
Tipping him with Half a Crown;
Now, said I, we are alone,
Name your Heroes one, by one.

Who is that Hell-featur'd Brawler,
Is it Satan? No 'tis *Waller*.[37]
In what Figure can a Bard dress
Jack, the Grandson of Sir *Hardress*?[38]
Honest Keeper, drive him further,
In his Looks are Hell and Murther;
See the Scowling Visage drop,
Just as when he murther'd *Throp*.[39]

32. There were three hundred members of the parliament.
33. 'Arrested, imprisoned. They were immune from arrest for anything said in parliament' (Rogers).
34. 'hysteria' (Rogers).
35. Alluding to the river Styx.
36. A lake near Naples, close to the cave through whch Aeneas entered the underworld. See *Aeneid* VI, 201-02: 'then, when they came to the jaws of noisome Avernus, they swiftly rise'.
37. John Waller, member of parliament for Doneraile, Co. Cork.
38. Waller was a grandson of Sir Hardress Waller (*c.* 1604-*c.* 1666), who sat in judgment on Charles I in 1649.
39. The Rev. Roger Throp, of Kilcorman, Co. Limerick, who was involved in legal conflict with Waller. He died in 1736, shortly after a parliamentary committee had made a decision in his favour.

Keeper, shew me where to fix
On the Puppy Pair of *Dicks*;[40]
By their lanthorn Jaws[41] and Leathern,[42]
You might swear they both are Brethren:
Dick Fitz-Baker,[43] *Dick* the Player,[44]
Old Acquaintance, are you there?
Dear Companions hug and kiss,
Toast *old Glorious*[45] in your Piss.
Tye them Keeper in a Tether,
Let them stare and stink together;
Both are apt to be unruly,
Lash them daily, lash them duly,
Though 'tis hopeless to reclaim them,
Scorpion Rods perhaps may tame them.

Keeper, yon old Dotard smoke,[46]
Sweetly snoring in his Cloak.
Who is he? 'Tis hum-drum *Wynne*,[47]
Half encompass'd by his Kin:
There observe the Tribe of *Bingham*,[48]
For he never fails to bring 'em;
While he sleeps the whole Debate,
They submissive round him wait;
Yet would gladly see the Hunks[49]
In his Grave, and search his Trunks.
See they gently twitch his Coat,
Just to yawn, and give his Vote;
Always firm in his Vocation,
For the Court against the Nation.

Those are *Allens, Jack* and *Bob*,[50]
First in every wicked Jobb,
Son and Brother to a Queer,
Brainsick Brute, they call a Peer.[51]
We must give them better Quarter,
For their Ancestor trod Mortar;[52]
And at *Hoath* to boast his Fame,
On a Chimney cut his Name.[53]

There sit *Clements*,[54] *Dilkes*,[55] and *Harrison*,[56]
How they swagger from their Garrison.
Such a Triplet could you tell
Where to find on this Side Hell?
Harrison, and *Dilkes*, and *Clements*,
Souse them in their own Ex-crements.[57]
Every Mischief in their Hearts,
If they fail 'tis Want of Parts.

Bless us, *Morgan!*[58] Art thou there Man?
Bless mine Eyes! Art thou the Chairman?
Chairman to yon damn'd Committee!
Yet I look on thee with Pity.
Dreadful Sight! What learned *Morgan*
Metamorphos'd to a Gorgan![59]
For thy horrid Looks, I own,
Half convert me to a Stone.[60]
Hast thou been so long at School,
Now to turn a factious[61] Tool!
Alma Mater[62] was thy Mother,
Every young Divine thy Brother.
Thou a disobedient Varlet,
Treat thy Mother like a Harlot!

40. Richard Tighe (*c.* 1678-1736), member of parliament for Belturbet, Co. Cavan and member of the Irish privy council; and Richard Bettesworth (1689-1741), member of parliament for Midleton, Co. Cork and an influential lawyer.
41. lantern jaws.
42. like leather.
43. Tighe's ancestor had contracted to supply bread to Cromwell's armies.
44. Bettesworth is 'termed "the Player", it is said, on account of his pompous manner and enunciation' (Swift's editor, Harold Williams).
45. William III, king of Britain and Ireland 1689-1702.
46. 'Find out who he is, identify him' (Rogers).
47. There were three Wynnes in the parliament: Owen Wynne, member for County Sligo, Owen Wynne, member of the borough of Sligo, and John Wynne, member for the borough of Castlebar, Co. Mayo.
48. Sir John Bingham (*c.* 1690-1749), member for County Mayo, and his brother Henry Bingham, member for the borough of Castlebar, Co. Mayo.
49. Surly, crusty old people.
50. John Allen, member for the borough of Carysfort, Co. Wicklow, and Robert Allen, member for County Wicklow.
51. John was the son and Robert the brother of Joshua, second viscount Allen.
52. Their ancestor, John Allen, had been the architect of some of the big houses built in Ireland when Sir Thomas Wentworth, first earl of Strafford (1593-1641) was lord lieutenant 1632-41.
53. Howth Castle was one of the places where the architect John Allen had worked.
54. Either Henry Clements, member for the borough of Cavan, or Nathaniel Clements, member for the borough of Duleek, Co. Meath. They were brothers.
55. Michael O'Brien Dilkes, member for the borough of Castlemartyr, Co. Cork.
56. William Harrison, member for Bannow, Co. Wexford.
57. The orthography draws attention to the stress on the second syllable.
58. Dr Mark Antony Morgan (born 1702/03), member for Athy, Co. Kildare, who was the chairman of the committee that received 'the petition of the graziers for relief from the tithe of agistment. On the 17th of April, 1736, that committee reported in favour of the case put forward, and the Commons passed a resolution, on the following day, in support of the graziers' (Williams).
59. There were three Gorgons — hideously ugly sisters with writhing snakes in their hair, who had the power to turn anyone who saw them into stone. Medusa, the most famous one, was slain by Perseus, who used her severed head to petrify his enemies.
60. A comic effect, since the power of the Gorgon was absolute.
61. The emphasis on party faction denies the value of education.
62. The Latin for a bounteous mother, in reference to the role education plays in nurturing talent.

Thou, ungrateful to thy Teachers,
Who are all grown reverend Preachers!
Morgan! Would it not surprise one?
Turn thy Nourishment to Poison!
When you walk among your Books,
They reproach you with their Looks;
Bind them fast, or from the Shelves
They'll come down to right themselves:
Homer, *Plutarch*, *Virgil*, *Flaccus*,[63]
All in Arms prepare to back us:[64]
Soon repent, or put to Slaughter
Every *Greek* and *Roman* Author.
While you in your Faction's Phrase
Send the Clergy all to graze;
And to make your Project pass,
Leave them not a Blade of Grass.[65]

How I want thee, humorous *Hogart*?[66]
Thou I hear, a pleasant Rogue art;
Were but you and I acquainted,
Every Monster should be painted;
You should try your graving Tools
On this odious Group of Fools;
Draw the Beasts as I describe 'em,
Form their Features, while I gibe them;
Draw them like, for I assure you,
You will need no *Car'catura*;[67]
Draw them so that we may trace
All the Soul in every Face.
Keeper, I must now retire,
You have done what I desire:
But I feel my Spirits spent,
With the Noise, the Sight, the Scent.

Pray be patient, you shall find
Half the best are still behind:
You have hardly seen a Score,
I can shew two hundred more.
Keeper, I have seen enough,
Taking then a Pinch of Snuff;
I concluded, looking round 'em,
May their God, the Devil confound 'em.

63. Scholarly controversy surrounds Homer's dates and identity, but the *Iliad* and the *Odyssey* have made him the unrivalled, powerfully influential figure at the beginnings of western culture. Plutarch (*c.* 46-*c.* 120 A.D.) is best known for his *Lives* of the great figures from ancient Greece and Rome. The great epic poet of the beginnings of the Roman empire, Virgil (70-19 B.C.) is best known for the *Aeneid*. Quintus Horatius Flaccus (65-8 B.C.), generally known as Horace, whose satires, odes and literary criticism have ensured his abiding reputation.
64. Swift aligns himself with four of the literary immortals from antiquity, two Greek and two Roman, whose works and pervasive influence would have been central to Morgan's education at Trinity College, Dublin.
65. Alluding to the role Morgan played in undermining one of the established sources of income for the clergy of the Church of Ireland.
66. William Hogarth (1697-1764), whose skill as an artist and engraver would have served to create graphic counterparts of Swift's satire.
67. 'Then a new and slightly exotic word, which survived alongside "caricature" throughout the eighteenth century' (Rogers).

EPIGRAM

Behold! a proof of *Irish* sense!
Here *Irish* wit is seen!
When nothing's left, that's worth defence,
We build a magazine.[1]

1. 'The magazine for arms and powder, for the security of the city' (Swift's physician Dr Kingsbury, cited by his editor, John Nichols). The Magazine Fort in the Phoenix Park 'was the favourite point for general views of Dublin. . . . built in about 1735, it is still there and still in military occupation' (Maurice Craig).

ANONYMOUS

(*c.* 1710)

ON THE COLLEGE OF PHYSICIANS[1] IN DUBLIN

Who, haveing brought to life a malefactor that was given from the Gallows to be dissected, Redelivered him To the Sherif to be Executed

Whoe'er wou'd life preserve, Let him beware
How he confides in Dublin Doctors' Care.

Taught by me, let him banefull Physick hate,
The vile Dissectors shun, as his own Fate;

Spared by the Rope, and Hangman's cruell Hand,
My Life I lost by Gallen's's[2] Guessing Band.

And to their shame lett after Ages say,
That those the Gallows save, the Doctors slay.

1. Founded in 1654.
2. A jocular term for a physician, from Galen (*c.* 129-99 A.D.), born at Pergamum, Asia Minor, the renowned physician of antiquity, who wrote extensively on medicine.

'Where more can boundless Nature please?'

[While the growth of Dublin provided metaphors for the poets throughout the eighteenth century, the world of nature continued to exert its own influence. These poems, written within a period of twenty-five years in the first half of the century, reveal the conflicting forces already evident in Anglo-Irish literary culture. James

Ward, whose '*Phoenix* Park' appeared in 1718, adopts a romantic view of nature and an uncritical approach to the society to which it is related. Dutifully celebrating the city's answer to Windsor Forest, he delights in the hidden spaces and the distant views. As the Liffey flows past the Royal Hospital at Kilmainham, where the military veterans from the Duke of Marlborough's campaigns have retired, Ward recalls '*Britain*'s Glory'; as his eye takes in the ships in the harbour, 'By whose kind Aid we num'rous Blessings share,/In Peace our Riches, and our Strength in War', he chooses to ignore the English mercantilist restrictions on Irish commerce, trade and shipping. His sense of the Liffey as masculine, which probably arose from the classical influence of Father Tiber, contrasts with his romantic perception of the landscape, where he discovers 'a ruin'd Tow'r' on a distant 'Mount', which he imagines is inhabited by a 'Fairy Monarch' with attendant 'Elfs unseen'.

In the extract from Henry Brooke's *Universal Beauty*, however, there is a consistent classical influence. The 'deepest art' of these lines belongs both to Minerva, the goddess of wisdom, whom Brooke sees as representing the originating power of the universe, and to Venus Urania, who symbolizes the creating force of perfection in nature. In the six books of his long philosophical poem, which was published in 1735, Brooke demonstrates the nature of God and surveys the creation of the universe, the forms of knowledge and the nature of man; he concludes by contemplating the beauty of the overall design.

In his '*A* Thought, *in the Pleasant* Grove *at* Cabragh', which appeared in his *Poems Written Occasionally* in 1742, John Winstanley presents nature as a refuge from the burdens of everyday life. His sense of 'wicked *Dublin*' is far more convincing than Ward's reference to the city's 'Vice and Follies', but neither has the pithy urgency of Swift, who presents a witty sense of country life in two short verses from 1725, which adopt the voices of the servants in the house of his friend Thomas Sheridan at Quilca, Co. Cavan.]

JAMES WARD
(*fl.* 1710-20)

from:
PHOENIX PARK[1]

. . . Shall *Windsor* Forrest win immortal Praise,
It self outlasting in its Poets Lays?[2]
And thou, O *Phoenix* Park! remain so long
Unknown to Fame, and unadorn'd in Song?. . . .

What Scene more lovely, and more form'd for Bliss,
What more deserves the Muse's Strain than this?
Where more can boundless Nature please, and where
In Shapes more various, and more sweet appear?

Now when the Centre of the Wood is found,
With goodly Trees a spacious Circle bound,
I stop my wandring — while on ev'ry Side,
Glades op'ning to the Eye, the Grove divide,
To distant Objects stretch my lengthen'd View,
And make each pleasing Prospect charm anew.

The Mountain here heaves up his airy Height,
A short Horizon to my bounded Sight,
Whose Caverns treasure up descending Show'rs,
Nor Heav'n on him in vain its Plenty pours;
When sultry Seasons scorch the rivel'd[3] Earth,
His Bounty gives a thousand Fountains Birth:
Prolifick Moisture swells the smiling Grain,
And double Harvests load the grateful Plain.

Deep in the Vale old *Liffy* rolls his Tides,
Romantick Prospects crown his rev'rend Sides;
Now thro' wild Grotts,[4] and pendant[5] Woods he strays,
And ravish'd at the Sight, his Course delays,
Silent and calm — now with impetuous Shock
Pours his swift Torrent down the steepy Rock;
The tumbling Waves thro' airy Channels flow,
And loudly roaring, smoak, and foam below.

Fast by his Banks stands, high above the Plain,
A Fabrick rais'd in peaceful *Charles*'s[6] Reign,
Where vet'ran Bands, discharg'd from War, retire,
Feeble their Limbs, extinct their martial Fire:
I hear methinks, I hear the gallant Train,
Recount the Wonders of each past Campaign:
Conquests, and Triumphs in my Bosom roll,
And *Britain*'s Glory fills my wid'ning Soul:

1. A city park, one of the biggest in Europe, on the western side of Dublin.
2. lyric or narrative poems; the reference is to Pope's poem 'Windsor Forest' (1704-13).
3. shrivelled by heat.
4. grottoes.
5. Referring to trees with low-hanging branches.
6. The Royal Hospital at Kilmainham, completed in 1684 during Charles II's reign, was for military veterans. In the seventeenth century, its site was part of the Phoenix Park.

Here blest with Plenty, and maintain'd at Ease,
They boast th'Adventures of their youthful Days;
Repeat exhausted Dangers o'er again,
And sigh to speak of faithful Comrades slain.
Silent the list'ning Audience sit around,
Weep at the Tale, and view the Witness Wound:
What mighty Things each for his Country wrought
Each tells, — and all how bravely *Marlbro'*[7] fought.

There, o'er wide Plains, my lab'ring Sight extends,
And fails itself e'er the long Landskape ends:
Where Flocks around the rural Cottage seen,
Brouze[8] the young Buds, or graze the tufted Green;
And Fields bespread with golden Crops appear,
Ensuring Plenty for the following Year.

There on a Mount a ruin'd Tow'r I spy,
A sweet Amusement to the distant Eye;
Forward it starts, approaching to be seen,
And cheats me of the sinking Lands between.
Within this Mount, as some old Matron tells,
In all his Pomp, the Fairy Monarch dwells;
To his wide Treas'ry here, his Elfs unseen,
Convey whate'er is lost on Earth by Men;
With endless Stores the gloomy Caverns fill,
And as their Sums increase, distend their Hill.

There the broad Ocean spreads his Waves around,
With anchor'd Fleets a faithful Harbour crown'd:
By whose kind Aid we num'rous Blessings share,
In Peace our Riches, and our Strength in War.
While thus retir'd, I on the City look,
A Groupe of Buildings in a Cloud of Smoak;
(Where various Domes for various Uses made,
Religion, Revels, Luxury and Trade;
All undistinguish'd in one Mass appear,
And widely diff'ring are united here)
I learn her Vice and Follies to despise,
And love that Heav'n which in the Country lies.
The Sun in his Meridian mounted high,
Now warns me to the covert Bow'r to fly;
Where Trees officious croud around my Head,
And twisted Woodbine forms a fragrant Shade.
No noisy Ax thro' all the Grove resounds,
No cruel Steel the living Branches wounds:
Rev'rend in Age the wide-spread Beech appears,
The lofty Oak lives his long Date of Years.

Here careless on some mossy Bank reclin'd,
Lull'd by the murm'ring Stream, and whistling Wind;
Nor poys'nous Asp I fear, nor savage Beast,
That wretched Swains in other Lands infest:
Fir'd with the Love of Song, my Voice I raise,
And woo the Muses to my Country's Praise.

7. John Churchill (1650-1722), duke of Marlborough, chief commander of the English and Dutch forces during the War of the Spanish Succession.
8. browse, i.e. crop or eat.

HENRY BROOKE

(*c.* 1703-83)

from: UNIVERSAL BEAUTY

[from Book I]

. . . With deepest art, her[1] skilful plan she lays;
With equal scale, the least advantage weighs;
How apt, for time, place, circumstance, and use,
She culls[2] all means, that to all ends conduce!
Nice[3] to a point, each benefit selects;
As prudent, every mischief she rejects;
In due proportions, time, and motion, metes,[4]
Advances to a hair, and to a hair retreats:
Constant to Good, for that alone she veers,
And with the varying beam her offspring chears;
Cools all beneath her equinoctial[5] line,
And gives the day throughout the world to shine;
The nitre[6] from the frozen pole unseals,
And to the tropic speeds the pregnant gales;
Here, leaves the exhausted fallow to recruit;
Here, plumps and burnishes the ripening fruit;
Superfluous hence withdraws the sultry beam,
Here drinks anew the vivifying flame;

1. i.e. the earth, created by Minerva, the goddess of wisdom, and Venus Urania, who represents nature or the creation 'rising out of chaos in the perfection of beauty' (Brooke). In the preceding passage, the poet has invited those who will not acknowledge the existence of 'infinite wisdom' to approach their 'parent earth' and observe its wonders.
2. gathers.
3. accurate.
4. measures.
5. When day and night are of equal length. Brooke implies that half the world ('beneath her equinoctial line') is always cooler than the other half.
6. saltpetre. It was believed that there was nitrous matter in air, plants and ice.

Returns, still faithful to the labouring steer —
Wide waves the harvest of the golden year;
Trades universal on from pole to pole,
Inspires, revives, and cultivates the whole;
Frugal, where lack, supplies with what redounds,[7]
And here bestows what noxious there abounds;[8]
This with the gift, and that with giving, blest,
Alike, throughout, of every wish possest.
Wrapt in her airy car,[9] the matron[10] glides,[11]
And o'er the firmament ascending rides;
The subtile mass its copious mantle spreads,
Its mantle wove of elemental[12] threads;
The elastick flue[13] of fluctuating air,
Transfused invisible, enfolds the sphere;[14]
With poinance[15] delicate pervades the whole,[16]
Its ear, eye, breath, and animating soul;
Active, serene, comprest, rare, cool'd, or warm'd,
For life, health, comfort, pleasure, business, form'd;
Useful around, throughout, above, beneath![17]
By this, the quadrupeds, the reptiles breath;
This gives the bloom of vegetative life;
Corrects the seeds of elemental strife;[18]
Broods o'er the eggs, in airy caverns laid,
Warm'd in the down of their etherial bed;
Gives motion to the swimmers of the flood;
Gives musick to the warblers of the wood;
Rebounds in echo from the doubling vale,
And wafts to heaven the undulating gale:
Here hush'd, translucid[19] smiles the gentle calm;
And here impearld,[20] sheds meek the showery balm;
Salubrious here, a lively rapture claims,
And winnows pure the pestilential steams;

7. i.e. frugal where something is lacking, she supplies what is needed to remedy the deficiency.
8. i.e. and gives *here* things which, in excess *there*, are unwholesome.
9. chariot (poetic).
10. the earth mother.
11. At this point, Brooke draws attention in a note to 'the wonderful texture of the air or atmosphere'.
12. Referring to the four traditional elements: earth, air, fire and water.
13. fluency or copiousness.
14. Written in the context of complex notions of the earth, the planets and the universe, 'the sphere' carries the sense of the distant reaches of the universe within the visible heavens.
15. poignancy, in the sense of the quality of being stimulating.
16. Brooke's note on this line is 'its surprizing subtilty, penetrating even deep below the surface of the earth'.
17. There are many echoes of Pope's *An Essay on Man*, epistle 1 (1733-34) in this and in the following passage.
18. The peculiarity of Brooke's views on nature and generation is heightened by his note to this line: 'raising harmony from disorder, and friendship from enmity, by fermenting and reconciling heat and cold, the fiery and watery particles, for the better conception and genial production of the beauties of nature.'
19. translucent, shining through.
20. Drops of dew like pearls.

Here buoys the bird high on the chrystal wave,
Whose level plumes the azure concave shave;
Here sits voluptuous in the swelling sail,
The vessel dancing to the sprightly gale!
Its varied power to various uses tends,[21]
And qualities occult atchieve contrarious ends;
With generative warmth fomenting breed,
Or alimental with nutrition feed;
In opposition reconciled to good,
Alike the menstruum, as sustaining food:
Or here restorative, destructive here;
Here nature's cradle, here her funeral bier;
With keen dispatch on all corruption preys,
And grateful, from our aching sense conveys;
Returns the bane[22] into its native earth,
And there revives it to a second birth,
Renew'd and brighten'd like the minted ore,
To shoot again to life, more gorgeous than
  before!. . . .

21. Again, Brooke's peculiar footnote is worth quoting in full: 'The various influence of the air on all bodies animate or inanimate: first, in the generation of particular beings; then, in their nutrition; thirdly, affording a healing balsam to the hurts or wounds of all creatures, when recoverable; but if past remedy, fourthly, hastening their dissolution, to rid the world of the nuisance, by restoring the matter to its original principle of nativity; fifthly, to send again the new modelled being blooming afresh in animal life or vegetation.'
22. poison or destructive matter.

JOHN WINSTANLEY

A THOUGHT, *IN THE PLEASANT* GROVE *AT* CABRAGH[1]

As, off the Sea, the chearful *Eastern* Gales,
Loos'd from the welcome Vessel's furling[2] Sails,
(By diff'rent Winds, and boyst'rous Waves long
  toss'd,
Now safely anchor'd on the pleasing Coast)
With careless Speed blow o'er the open Meads,[3]
To stop, and wanton in these closer Shades;
Here gaily revel; while the joyful Trees,
With dancing Leaves salute each sprightly Breeze;
Till charm'd to Rest, nor farther pleas'd to rove,
They fall expiring in the silent Grove.

1. Now a suburb of Dublin to the north-west of the city centre, Cabra is close to the present borders of the Phoenix Park.
2. rolled or bound up.
3. meadows.

So I, retiring to this pleasant Shade,
(My toilsome, worldly Voyage, almost made)
Reflect with Scorn, on all my Troubles past,
The low'ring Clouds, that still my Joys o'ercast,
My Friend's lukewarmness, or my Foes dire Hate,
And all the ruffling Storms of adverse Fate:
Here free from all the num'rous ills of Life;
From Care, Pain, Envy, Pride, Design, or Strife;
From wicked *Dublin* happily remov'd,
And all it's Follies (once too dearly lov'd,)
This quiet, calm, and lonely Seat I chuse,
Bless'd with my Innocence, and harmless Muse:
In this Retreat, could make a lasting stay,
Till Sense, to Dotage, Life to Death, gave way.

JONATHAN SWIFT

THE BLESSINGS OF A COUNTRY LIFE

Far from our Debtors,[1]
No *Dublin* Letters,
Not seen by our Betters.

1. Alluding to the most celebrated financial scandal of Dublin in the 1720s, in which Captain John Pratt (born *c.* 1670), the deputy vice-treasurer of Ireland and constable of Dublin Castle, was imprisoned in 1725 for embezzlement. Swift, who was able to recover most of the money he was owed by Pratt, reverses the notion of being far from creditors.

THE PLAGUES OF A COUNTRY LIFE

A Companion with News,
A great want of Shoes;
Eat lean Meat, or chuse,[1]
A Church without Pews.
Our Horses astray,
No Straw, Oats, or Hay;
December in *May*.
Our Boys run away,
All Servants at play.

1. i.e. choose not to eat meat.

'Looking for chance . . . .'

[Lawlessness was a feature of many Irish towns and cities in the eighteenth century and the first song in this section celebrates the bravado of the boys of Garryowen, an area of Limerick city. By 1813, when Henry Code's song appeared in his musical drama, *The Russian Sacrifice; or, The Burning of Moscow*, the roving, fighting blade had taken to the stage and had become a romantic cliché. Sung to the popular country dance tune of 'Langolee' (recorded in 1775), Code's song of 'smack'em' and 'whack'em' Irishmen is as valid a part of the cultural landscape of the period as the anonymous street ballad 'The Happy Beggarman' or Charles O'Flaherty's 'The Humours of Donnybrook Fair'.]

ANONYMOUS

(*c.* 1775)

GARRYOWEN

Let Bacchus's[1] sons be not dismayed,
But join with me each jovial blade;
Come booze and sing, and lend your aid
  To help me with the chorus:—
    Instead of Spa[2] we'll drink brown ale,
    And pay the reckoning on the nail,[3]
    No man for debt shall go to gaol
      From Garryowen in glory!

We are the boys that take delight in
Smashing the Limerick lamps when lighting,[4]
Through the streets like sporters[5] fighting,
  And tearing all before us.
      Instead, &c.

We'll break windows, we'll break doors,
The watch[6] knock down by threes and fours;
Then let the doctors work their cures,
  And tinker up[7] our bruises.
      Instead, &c.

We'll beat the bailiffs, out of fun,
We'll make the mayor and sheriffs run;

1. Bacchus was one of the names of Dionysus, the Greek god of vegetation, drink and creativity.
2. i.e. spa water. There was a popular spa at Castle Connell, some six miles from Limerick, at the time of this song.
3. Arising from the custom of placing money on round pieces of metal in the exchange, the phrase 'to pay the reckoning on the nail' means to pay at once, on the spot.
4. Lamps were erected in the streets of Limerick in 1696 (Thomas Crofton Croker, citing John Ferrar's *History of Limerick*, 1766, 1787).
5. sportsmen, gamesters.
6. watchmen, who guarded and patrolled the streets.
7. patch up.

We are the boys no man dares dun,[8]
If he regards a whole skin.
Instead, &c.

Our hearts, so stout, have got us fame,
For soon 'tis known from whence we came;
Where'er we go they dread the name
Of Garryowen in glory.
Instead, &c.

Johnny Connell's[9] tall and straight,
And in his limbs he is complete;
He'll pitch a bar of any weight,
From Garryowen to Thomond Gate.[10]
Instead, &c.

Garryowen is gone to rack
Since Johnny Connell went to Cork,
Though Darby O'Brien[11] leapt over the dock
In spite of judge and jury.[12]
Instead, &c.

8. press for the payment of money.
9. A young squire, the son of a brewer (Croker, citing Sir Charles O'Donnell).
10. The well-known gate on the north side of the city. Hence, from Garryowen on the southern side to Thomond Gate was 'from one side of Limerick to the other' (Croker).
11. Connell's companion, another young squire, and also the son of a brewer (Croker, citing O'Donnell).
12. An alternative reads 'In spite of all the soldiers' (Croker).

HENRY BRERETON CODE

(*fl.* 1810-30)

SONG

If you'd search the world round, all from Howth[1] to Killarney,[2]
An Irishman's fellow[3] you never could meet!
Och! for love he's the lad, with a touch of his blarney,[4]
On all the dear creatures himself is so sweet.
And then for a row, or a small taste of fighting,
By day and by night he is never for slighting,
Love and war all the same, for in both still delighting,
With his Smack'em! and Whack'em! so ready and free.

At patron,[5] or fair, or in England when hay-making,
Recruiting,[6] foes-shooting, or other neat fun;
For coaxing the girls, or trifles of head-breaking,
On Pat you may reckon as sure as a gun.
Oh then for a row, or a small share of fighting,
By day and by night he is never for slighting,
Love and war all the same, for in both still delighting,
With his Smack'em! and Whack'em! so ready and free.

Och! good luck to the boys of the neat little island,
At home and abroad, or wherever they go!
May they always be first, on the sea or on dry land,
In pleasing the ladies, or trouncing the foe!
And sure for a row, or a small taste of fighting,
By day or by night Pat is never for slighting,
Love and war, all the same, for in both still delighting,
With his Smack'em! and Whack'em! so ready and free.

1. The fashionable suburb of Dublin on the north side of the bay.
2. Killarney, long renowned for its beauty, is in County Kerry.
3. equal, match.
4. Smooth, flattering speech, often having a persuasive force.
5. An obsolete form of 'pattern', which in Ireland is the day of a patron saint, and hence the celebrations of the day.
6. Forcing recruits into the British forces.

ANONYMOUS

(*c.* 1820)

THE HAPPY BEGGARMAN

Of all trades agoing, begging it is my delight;
My rent it is paid and I lay down my bags ev'ry night:
I'll throw away care and take a long staff in my hand,
And I'll flourish each day courageously looking for chance.

With my belt round my shoulder and down my bags they do hang;
With a push and a joult it's quickly I'll have them yoked on;

With my horn by my side, likewise my skiver[1] and can;
With my staff and long pike to fight the dogs as I gang.[2]

To patterns[3] and fairs I'll go round for collection[4] along,
I'll seem to be lame and quite useless of one of my hands;
Like a pilgrim I'll pray each day with my hat in my hand,
And at night in the alehouse I'll stay and pay like a man.

1. skewer, which keeps pieces of meat together while cooking.
2. go.
3. Celebrations on the days of patron saints.
4. Collecting money for his own use.

CHARLES O'FLAHERTY

(*c*.1794-*c*.1828)

THE HUMOURS OF DONNYBROOK FAIR

To Donnybrook[1] steer, all you sons of Parnassus[2] —
Poor painters, poor poets, poor newsmen, and knaves,
To see what the fun is, that all fun surpasses —
The sorrow and sadness of green Erin's slaves.
Oh, Donnybrook, jewel! full of mirth is your quiver,
Where all flock from Dublin to gape and to stare
At two elegant bridges, without e'er a river:[3]
So, success to the humours of Donnybrook Fair!

O you lads that are witty, from famed Dublin city,
And you that in pastime take any delight,
To Donnybrook fly, for the time's drawing nigh
When fat pigs are hunted, and lean cobblers fight;
When maidens, so swift, run for a new shift;[4]
Men, muffled in sacks,[5] for a shirt they race there;
There jockeys well booted, and horses sure-footed,
All keep up the humours of Donnybrook Fair.

The mason does come, with his line and his plumb;
The sawyer and carpenter, brothers in chips;
There are carvers and gilders, and all sort of builders,
With soldiers from barracks and sailors from ships.
There confectioners, cooks, and printers of books,
There stampers of linen, and weavers, repair;
There widows and maids, and all sort of trades,
Go join in the humours of Donnybrook Fair.

There tinkers and nailers,[6] and beggars and tailors,
And singers of ballads, and girls of the sieve;[7]
With Barrack Street rangers,[8] the known ones and strangers,
And many that no one can tell how they live:
There horsemen and walkers, and likewise fruit-hawkers,
And swindlers, the devil himself that would dare.
With pipers and fiddlers, and dandies and diddlers,[9]—
All meet in the humours of Donnybrook Fair.

'Tis there are dogs dancing, and wild beasts a-prancing,
With neat bits of painting in red, yellow, and gold;
Toss-players[10] and scramblers, and showmen and gamblers,
Pickpockets in plenty, both of young and of old.
There are brewers, and bakers, and jolly shoemakers,
With butchers, and porters, and men that cut hair;
There are mountebanks grinning, while others are sinning,
To keep up the humours of Donnybrook Fair.

Brisk lads and young lasses can there fill their glasses
With whisky, and send a full bumper[11] around;
Jig it off in a tent till their money's all spent,
And spin like a top till they rest on the ground.

1. A village about two miles south-east of Dublin; the celebrated fair came to an end in 1868.
2. i.e. poets and songsters. Parnassus, a mountain near Delphi in Greece, came to be regarded as the seat of poetry and music.
3. Perhaps a reference to bridges over the Dodder river, which flows through Donnybrook and could be low in dry weather (the fair took place in August).
4. nightdress or loose cotton garment.
5. Possibly referring to sack races.
6. nail-makers.
7. i.e. who cannot keep a secret.
8. Prostitutes who usually frequented the street near the Royal Barracks.
9. swindlers, cheats — from Jeremy Diddler in James Kenney's farce, *Raising the Wind* (1803).
10. Toss was a throwing game.
11. A large cup or glass used for drinking toasts.

Oh, Donnybrook capers, to sweet catgut-scrapers,
 They bother the vapours,[12] and drive away care;
And what is more glorious — there's naught more
 uproarious —
 Huzza for the humours of Donnybrook Fair!

12. depression.

The traveller's 'Prospect'

[As travel became easier during the eighteenth century, so its effects became a subject of interest to prose writers and to poets. Some, like Swift, journeying from London to Dublin in 1727 and held up at Holyhead by contrary winds, considered travel a frustrating necessity. Others, such as Goldsmith, saw leisurely travel as an opportunity for philosophical reflection and meditative self-examination. This latter attitude was widely shared and partly accounts for the long-lasting popularity of Goldsmith's *The Traveller* (1764).

A more urgent and pragmatic response to the effects of travel came from Samuel Whyte, who, with his children, passed through his native Liverpool on the way from Dublin to London in 1787; so disgusted was he at the changes he saw in Liverpool that he sent the poem printed below to the mayor of Liverpool in the hope, presumably, that he would take note of his views.

Yet all eighteenth-century travellers considered themselves lucky to escape a meeting with the hereditary foe of those on the roads: a highwayman such as Willie Brennan, the terror of travellers on the borders of Counties Cork and Tipperary. It is worth noting that the emphasis, in the well-known ballad below, is placed on his popular support and on the danger he faced from the authorities.]

JONATHAN SWIFT

HOLYHEAD[1]

Sept. 25. 1727

Lo here I sit at holy head
With muddy ale and mouldy bread
All Christian vittals[2] stink of fish
I'm where my enemyes would wish
Convict[3] of lyes is every sign,
The Inn has not one drop of wine
I'm fasnd[4] both by wind and tide
I see the ship at anchor ride
The Captain swears the sea's too rough
He has not passengers enough.
And thus the Dean is forc't to stay
Till others come to help the pay
In Dublin they'd be glad to see
A packet[5] though it brings in me.
They cannot say the winds are cross
Your Politicians at a loss
For want of matter swears and fretts,
Are forced to read the old gazettes.
I never was in hast before
To reach that slavish hateful shore
Before, I always found the wind
To me was most malicious kind
But now, the danger of a friend[6]
On whom my fears and hopes depend
Absent from whom all Clymes[7] are curst
With whom I'm happy in the worst
With rage impatient makes me wait
A passage to the land I hate.
Else, rather on this bleaky shore
Where loudest winds incessant roar
Where neither herb nor tree will thrive,
Where nature hardly seems alive.
I'd go in freedom to my grave,
Than Rule yon Isle[8] and be a Slave.

1. The port in Anglesey, Wales that traditionally has been used by travellers to Ireland.
2. victuals, provisions.
3. 'Convicted (rare by Swift's day)' (Swift's editor, Pat Rogers).
4. fastened, i.e. imprisoned here.
5. The packet-boat, which travelled regularly between Holyhead and Dublin with mail, passengers and goods.
6. Stella (Esther Johnson).
7. climes, regions.
8. Ireland.

OLIVER GOLDSMITH

(1728-74)

from:

THE TRAVELLER, OR A PROSPECT OF SOCIETY

Remote, unfriended, melancholy, slow,
Or by the lazy Scheld,[1] or wandering Po;[2]

1. The river Scheldt rises in Picardy, France and flows through Belgium and the Netherlands, reaching the North Sea near Walcheren Island.
2. The river Po, the main river of Italy, rises in the Cottian Alps near the French border and flows across the northern regions into the Adriatic.

Or onward, where the rude Carinthian[3] boor
Against the houseless stranger shuts the door;[4]
Or where Campania's plain[5] forsaken lyes,
A weary waste expanding to the skies.
Where'er I roam, whatever realms to see,
My heart untravell'd fondly turns to thee;
Still to my brother[6] turns, with ceaseless pain,
And drags at each remove a lengthening chain.[7]

Eternal blessings crown my earliest friend,
And round his dwelling guardian saints attend;
Blest be that spot, where chearful guests retire
To pause from toil, and trim their ev'ning fire;
Blest that abode, where want and pain repair,
And every stranger finds a ready chair;
Blest be those feasts with simple plenty crown'd,
Where all the ruddy[8] family around
Laugh at the jests or pranks that never fail,
Or sigh with pity at some mournful tale,
Or press the bashful stranger to his food,
And learn the luxury of doing good.[9]

But me, not destin'd such delights to share,
My prime of life[10] in wand'ring spent and care:
Impell'd, with steps unceasing, to pursue
Some fleeting good, that mocks me with the view;
That, like the circle bounding earth and skies,
Allures from far, yet, as I follow, flies;
My fortune leads to traverse realms alone,
And find no spot of all the world my own.

Even now, where Alpine solitudes ascend,
I sit me down a pensive hour to spend;
And, plac'd on high above the storm's career,
Look downward where an hundred realms appear;
Lakes, forests, cities, plains extending wide,
The pomp of kings, the shepherd's humbler pride.

When thus Creation's charms around combine,
Amidst the store, should thankless pride repine?
Say, should the philosophic mind disdain
That good, which makes each humbler bosom
vain?
Let school-taught pride dissemble all it can,
These little things are great to little man;
And wiser he, whose sympathetic mind
Exults in all the good of all mankind.
Ye glitt'ring towns, with wealth and splendour
crown'd,
Ye fields, where summer spreads profusion round,
Ye lakes, whose vessels catch the busy gale,
Ye bending swains, that dress the flow'ry vale,
For me your tributary stores combine;
Creation's heir, the world, the world is mine.

As some lone miser visiting his store,
Bends at his treasure, counts, recounts it o'er;
Hoards after hoards his rising raptures fill,
Yet still he sighs, for hoards are wanting still:
Thus to my breast alternate passions rise,
Pleas'd with each good that heaven to man supplies:
Yet oft a sigh prevails, and sorrows fall,
To see the hoard of human bliss so small;
And oft I wish, amidst the scene, to find
Some spot to real happiness consign'd,
Where my worn soul, each wand'ring hope at rest,
May gather bliss to see my fellows blest.

But where to find that happiest spot below,
Who can direct, when all pretend to know?
The shudd'ring tenant of the frigid zone
Boldly proclaims that happiest spot his own,
Extols the treasures of his stormy seas,
And his long nights of revelry and ease;
The naked negroe, panting at the line,[11]
Boasts of his golden sands and palmy wine,
Basks in the glare, or stems the tepid wave,
And thanks his Gods for all the good they gave.
Such is the patriot's boast, where'er we roam,
His first best country ever is at home.
And yet, perhaps, if countries we compare,
And estimate the blessings which they share;
Tho' patriots flatter, still shall wisdom find
An equal portion dealt to all mankind,

3. A region in northern Italy, Carinthia was on the route of Goldsmith's travels in 1755.
4. In his *Life of Oliver Goldsmith* (1837), James Prior notes that Goldsmith, tired after walking for a day, was 'obliged to quit a house he had entered for shelter, and pass part or the whole of the night in seeking another.'
5. The Campagna di Roma, stretching from the south of Rome to Terracina, a town on the coast to the north of Naples.
6. Goldsmith addressed the poem to his brother, the Rev. Henry Goldsmith.
7. In *The Citizen of the World* (1762), Letter III, Goldsmith refers to 'the pain of separation' from his country, saying that 'By every remove, I only drag a greater length of chain'.
8. healthy-looking.
9. Prior notes a similar line in Sir Samuel Garth's *Claremont* (1715): 'Hard was their Lodging, homely was their Food,/For all their Luxury was doing Good.'
10. During his travels in Europe in 1755, which ended early the the following year, Goldsmith was in his mid-twenties.
11. the equator.

As different good, by Art or Nature given,
To different nations makes their blessings even.

Nature, a mother kind alike to all,
Still grants her bliss at Labour's earnest call;
With food as well the peasant is supply'd
On Idra's[12] cliffs as Arno's[13] shelvy side;
And though the rocky crested summits frown,
These rocks, by custom, turn to beds of down.

From Art more various are the blessings sent;
Wealth, commerce, honour, liberty, content:
Yet these each other's power so strong contest,
That either seems destructive of the rest.
Where wealth and freedom reign contentment fails,
And honour sinks where commerce long prevails.
Hence every state, to one lov'd blessing prone,
Conforms and models life to that alone.
Each to the favourite happiness attends,
And spurns the plan that aims at other ends;
'Till, carried to excess in each domain,
This favourite good begets peculiar pain....

12. Probably Idria in Carniola, formerly in Italy and since 1947 in Yugoslavia, where it is known as Idrija. A mining town situated in mountainous country, Idrija was known to Goldsmith as Idra. He refers to it and its mines in *An History of the Earth and Animated Nature* (1774).
13. Rising in the Etruscan Apennines, the river Arno flows into the Ligurian Sea near Pisa.

SAMUEL WHYTE

(1733-1811)

THE NEW FERRY,[1] ADDRESSED TO THE MAYOR OF LIVERPOOL[2]

Sunday, July 29th, 1787

In early youth o'er Mersey's[3] tide
By wayward fortune trick'd,
While sleep my weary eyelids clos'd,
I got my pockets pick'd.[4]

Twice fifteen years elaps'd, again
The skippers mock'd my care;
For, tho' I kept a good look-out,
They robb'd me in the fare.[5]

The ferry much improv'd I found,
The port, the docks, the streets;[6]
But, O! curst thirst of lucre![7] still
Disgrac'd with rogues and cheats.

Yet partial to this goodly town,
It flatters native pride,[8]
That though I suffer'd and was vex'd,
'Twas from the farther side.[9]

Nor mean I all should wear the cap
Full well befitting one,
By fellow swabbers[10] Henry hight,[11]
An imp[12] of Chatterton.[13]

Hard is his visage, hard his heart,
Uncouth his speech and chuff;[14]
The squalid waterman of Styx[15]
Had scarce a mien so gruff.[16]

Did he, the souls to ferry o'er,
For Charon[17] take the helm,

1. Whyte notes that the boatman of the ferry, 'about three miles above Liverpool, on the Cheshire side', made 'exorbitant demands' on an occasion when he had his children with him. In the following year there was another incident, in which the poet and his children 'were near being overset in the same boat, by one of the passengers, a drunken blade, insisting upon taking the helm.'
2. When he reached Liverpool, Whyte wrote the poem to the mayor from his hotel 'at the corner of Lord-street'. The Dublin to Liverpool route, which is longer than the passage to Holyhead, is another traditional crossing from Ireland.
3. The river Mersey flows into the Irish Sea just below Liverpool.
4. Whyte notes an incident in December 1754 when he landed in Liverpool from Ireland and had to walk to London because his pockets had been picked.
5. Wary after the incident in 1754, in 1787 Whyte found himself being overcharged.
6. Substantial development had occurred in Liverpool in the second half of the eighteenth century.
7. money, in the derogatory sense of gain, profit and advantage.
8. Whyte explains that he was 'born on ship-board approaching the entrance of the Mersey' and that he remembers Liverpool with affection because it 'was the first land' he ever touched.
9. The incident that prompted the poem occurred on the Cheshire side of the Mersey.
10. Members of a ship's crew who swabbed the decks; sailors.
11. called, named.
12. offspring, in the sense of a little devil or demon.
13. Thomas Chatterton (1752-70), who produced various false documents in support of his claim to have made literary discoveries.
14. Dialectal usage, meaning churlish, gruff or morose.
15. The Styx was the main river of the underworld in Greek mythology.
16. See Virgil, *Aeneid* VI, 298-301 and the following context (Whyte): 'A grim warden guards these waters and streams, terrible in his squalor — Charon, on whose chin lies a mass of unkempt, hoary hair; his eyes are staring orbs of flame; his squalid garb hangs by a knot from his shoulders' (Virgil's editor, H. Rushton Fairclough).
17. The ferryman who rowed the dead across the Styx to Hades.

Not one, tho' of Elysium[18] sure,
Would visit Pluto's[19] realm. —

Tho' born in storms, to objects loath'd,[20]
And storms in life inur'd,
Even at his aspect I recoil'd,
And scarce his sight endur'd. —

I tread the ground, where, blithe and free
In thoughtless years I stray'd,
And trace the haunts, to memory dear,
Where oft my childhood play'd.

Around the place fond, anxious looks
At every turn I threw,
In hopes, nor vain my hopes at last,
To meet some face I knew.

I stop at each remembered spot,
And on the prospect dwell;
Then of some boyish incident
My sweet companions[21] tell.

Here, the prompt champion of my friend,
I check'd his saucy[22] foes;
And here a hardy conquest gain'd,
And here a bloody nose.

Here Leadbetter kept school — here
Hughes,[23]
By death long since remov'd;
A tear, affection's tribute, shows
Their pains not thankless prov'd.

As recollection livelier grew,
From place to place I rang'd;
See palaces where oxen grazed,
And huts to churches chang'd.

18. In Greek mythology, the place where the deserving enjoyed bliss after death.
19. The god of the underworld.
20. Whyte's note redirects attention to Virgil's account of Charon.
21. Whyte's note explains that they were Edward Athenry Whyte and Martha-Ann Whyte, his 'youngest son and daughter, who were going with him to London'. Edward, who later taught at his father's grammar school in Grafton Street, Dublin, edited his father's work.
22. presumptuous, impertinent.
23. Schoolmasters whom Whyte remembers with gratitude.

St. Peter's, George's, Nicholas'[24] too,
The seaman's ancient trust;[25]
Each object with delight I view;
Yet still intrudes disgust.

Why should a foul, imposing elf[26]
My soul's serene o'er-cast?
Keep clear your wharfs, ye sons of trade!
For first impressions last.

'Tis meet the labourer to reward,
And 'tis as strictly true,
Integrity's the safest plan,
And wisest to pursue.

Frenchman or Dutch, or friend or foe,
By name whatever call'd,
He'll scarce the mooring recommend,
Who has his hawser gall'd.[27]

To see this town, their father's boast,
Oft would my children crave,
And, lo! the poor young travellers greet
A rude designing knave.

Weeds are produc'd in every soil;
But that's a lame excuse,
And justly censure they incur[28]
Who tolerate abuse.

Are there no laws, no magistrates,
Extortion to correct,
That strangers who your wealth admire,
Your justice may respect?

24. Whyte notes that these were 'the only churches there in the Author's time': St George's, consecrated in 1734, the year he was born, St Peter's, consecrated in 1704, and St Nicholas's, 'of very ancient date'.
25. Whyte notes that near St Nicholas's there was once a statue of St Nicholas, 'to which the sailors used to present a propitiatory offering at their going out to sea'.
26. A personification of the trickery and commercial greed which Whyte feels has destroyed his native city.
27. i.e. whose visit is marred by trickery. hawser = mooring-rope; galled = made sore by rubbing.
28. i.e. and those who tolerate abuse justly incur censure.

ANONYMOUS
(*c*. 1805)

BRENNAN ON THE MOOR

It's of a famous highway-man a story I will tell;
His name was Willie Brennan, and in Ireland he did
dwell;

And on the Kilworth mountains[1] he commenced
his wild career,
Where many a wealthy gentleman before him
shook with fear.

Brennan on the Moor, Brennan on the Moor,
A brave undaunted robber was bold Brennan on
the Moor.

A brace of loaded pistols he carried night and day;
He never robbed a poor man upon the king's
highway;
But what he'd taken from the rich, like Turpin and
Black Bess,[2]
He always did divide it with the widow in distress.
Brennan on the Moor &c.

One night he robbed a packman[3] by name of Pedlar
Bawn;
They travelled on together till the day began to
dawn;
The pedlar seeing his money gone, likewise his
watch and chain,
He at once encountered Brennan and he robbed
him back again.
Brennan on the Moor &c.

One day upon the highway, as Willie he went down,
He met the Mayor of Cashel[4] a mile outside the
town:
The Mayor he knew his features; 'I think, young
man,' said he,
'Your name is Willie Brennan; you must come
along with me.'
Brennan on the Moor &c.

As Brennan's wife had gone to town, provisions for
to buy,
And when she saw her Willie, she began to weep
and cry;
He says, 'Give me that tenpenny'; as soon as Willie
spoke,

1. In County Cork.
2. Dick Turpin (1706-39), the highwayman who became a legendary figure. He was celebrated for a famous ride he made to York on his horse, Black Bess. Charged with horse-stealing, Turpin was executed at York.
3. An itinerant who sold wares from packs.
4. A town in County Tipperary.

She handed him a blunderbuss from underneath
her cloak.
Brennan on the Moor &c.

Then with his loaded blunderbuss, the truth I will
unfold,
He made the Mayor to tremble, and robbed him of
his gold;
One hundred pounds was offered for his
apprehension there,
So he with horse and saddle to the mountains did
repair.
Brennan on the Moor &c.

Then Brennan being an outlaw upon the mountains
high,
When cavalry and infantry to take him they did try;
He laughed at them with scorn, until at length, 'tis
said,
By a false-hearted young man he basely was
betrayed.
Brennan on the Moor &c.

In the county of Tipperary, in a place they call
Clonmore,
Willie Brennan and his comrade that day did suffer
sore;
He lay amongst the fern, which was trick[5] upon the
field,
And nine deep wounds he did receive before that he
did yield.
Brennan on the Moor &c.

So they were taken prisoners, in irons they were
bound,
And both conveyed to Clonmel[6] jail, strong walls
did them surround;
They were tried and there found guilty, the judge
made this reply:
'For robbing on the king's highway you're both
condemned to die.'
Brennan on the Moor &c.

Farewell unto my dear wife and to my children
three,
Likewise my aged father, he may shed tears for me;

5. = thick (?).
6. A town in County Tipperary.

And to my loving mother, who tore her locks and cried,
Saying, 'I wish, my Willie Brennan, in your cradle you had died!'

Brennan on the Moor, Brennan on the Moor,
A brave undaunted robber was bold Brennan on the Moor.

'A Description of the Western Isle'

[*The Irish Hudibras, or Fingallian Prince, Taken from the Sixth Book of Virgil's Aenaeids, and Adapted to the Present Times*, published in London in 1689, is the third version of a seventeenth-century poem (elsewhere called *The Fingallian Burlesque*), which parodies Book VI of Virgil's *Aeneid* in an Irish setting. This version belongs to the Williamite period, when the protestant ascendancy began to strengthen its control on the country and when the influence of the English on Ireland became increasingly pervasive. Written in the Hiberno-English of the late seventeenth century, *The Irish Hudibras* depicted an English sense of Ireland and appealed to English expectations of Irish customs and behaviour. Set in Fine Gall, or Finis Galliae, the territory of the 'foreigners' in Ireland, which came to be known as Fingal, the district to the north of Dublin, the poem adapts to the Irish context the story of Aeneas's descent into the underworld, creating equivalent characters and events and exploring the use of parody as a form of satire on the native Irish.

Hesperi-neso-graphia: *Or, a Description of the Western Isle*, first published in 1716, appeared in numerous editions in the eighteenth and early nineteenth centuries. By 1755 'The Irish Hudibras' was added to the title, evidently becoming its primary name. Creating a satiric picture of Irish life with its burlesque forms and parodic names, it appeared in both Ireland and England, and by 1755 was attributed to a William Moffet, a schoolmaster whose initials had been used in the 1716 edition. This name, however, may be a pseudonym for a member of the Jones family, but the existing bibliographical confusion over which one has not yet been resolved.

'A Description of the County of Kerry', published for the first time in 1726 as an addition to another work, 'A Pastoral in Imitation of the First Eclogue of Virgil: Inscrib'd to the Provost, Fellows, and Scholars, of Trinity College, Dublin', which had originally appeared in 1719, came to attention in the context of reference to the tenancy of lands in County Kerry, which had been granted to Trinity College, Dublin in 1666. The author of these pieces was given from the outset as a Murroghoh O Connor, a name which has been taken as a pseudonym; but Murroghoh O Connor and Owen Sullivan, whose dialogue with O Connor was also added to the 1726 edition, both occur on numerous occasions in the records of Trinity College, Dublin. These references may indicate that, although they are commonly used names, in this case they are not inventions. Whatever the truth, however, 'A Description of the County of Kerry' contains several elements which place it apart from *The Irish Hudibras* and *Hesperi-neso-graphia*. While its account of the fighting between the O Donaghoos and the O Sullivans may appear to appeal to a preconceived notion of the Irish, its literary model is Sir John Denham's poem *Cooper's Hill*, which became a prototype of what Samuel Johnson called 'local poetry' and whose first two lines it recalls as it directs attention to the beauty of the Dingle peninsula.

Dunkin's 'Carbery *Rocks in the County of* Cork, Ireland', a translation of his own Latin poem, appeared with the version in Latin at the end of the volume devoted to poetry in the 1735 edition of Swift's *Works*. Swift, who described Dunkin in 1738 as 'the best English as well as Latin Poet' in Ireland, had visited south-west Cork in 1723; seemingly, he so much admired Dunkin's description of the rugged scenery that he wanted it included in his own *Works*.

Dunkin first came to attention in the verse warfare of the Dublin Grub Street in the 1730s, but his reputation now rests substantially on his long poems, such as *The Parson's Revels*, published in the second volume of his *Select Poetical Works* in 1770. A burlesque narrative which is set at a feast given by a country squire, *The Parson's Revels* employs the device of assembling a set of characters who represent the different forces at work in contemporary Anglo-Irish society. The excerpts present two of the central figures of this feast, the worldly and unscrupulous Father Fegan, who clashes with the presbyterian Denison, and the harper O Murphy, who clashes with another presbyterian, the landlord Oaf. Both the priest and the harper boast of their lineage as they proclaim their Irish identity, but whereas Father Fegan has come to his own accommodation with the protestant ascendancy, saying 'Gaad blish king Gaarge and hish Lutterians', O Murphy performs 'much against his heart' as he cunningly celebrates the Williamite victory.

If Dunkin's theme is the tensions within Anglo-Irish society, and if his contemporary audience existed primarily within that society, then Goldsmith's *The Deserted Village*, also published in 1770, moves beyond those tensions and that audience as it creates a generic picture of village life before the widespread impact of the various forces in eighteenth-century social and economic life which led to the depopulation of the countryside in both Ireland and England. While Dunkin creates satiric portraits of social types whom he compares and contrasts, Goldsmith recalls the influential figures of the preacher and the schoolmaster, whose images act as fusions of personal and collective memory and who represent the theme of the vanished goodness in humanity. If Dunkin burlesques a society which is, at least, alive with its own divisions, then Goldsmith laments the passing of a cohesive and harmonious social order; and if Dunkin's characters revel in the society they have inherited on the one hand and served to shape on the other, then Goldsmith's vision directs attention to the disruptive force of materialism and to the ruin which accompanies the pursuit of luxury.]

ANONYMOUS

(*c.* 1689)

from: THE IRISH HUDIBRAS. OR, FINGALLIAN PRINCE

. . . Mean while the Rout[1] to work do fall,
To Celebrate the Funeral.[2]
And first with Turff from Bog, and Blocks,
They made a Fire wou'd roast an Oxe.
Some lay the Pipkins[3] on, and some
With Holy-water bathe his Bum.
There was the Priest forgiving Sins,
Busie as Hen with two Chick-eens,
'Nointing his Forehead, and his Nose,
And downwards to his Pettitoes;[4]
After the Method of his Function,
With Holy Oyl of Extreme Unction.

Which Office decently perform'd,
The Guests, with Usquebagh[5] well warm'd,
They raise the Cry. And so they fout[6] him
Unto a Crate,[7] to howl about him;
Built without either Brick or Stone,
Or Couples[8] to lay Roof upon:
With Wattlets[9] unto Wattles ty'd,
(Fixt in the ground on either side)
Did like a shaded Arbour show,
With Seats of Sods, and Roof of Straw.
The Floor beneath with Rushes laid, stead
of Tapestry; no Bed nor Bedstead;[10]
No Posts, nor Bolts, nor Hinges in door,
No Chimney, Kitchin, Hall, or Windor;[11]
But narrow Dormants stopt with Hay
All night, and open in the day.
On either side there was a door
Extent from Roof unto the floor,
Which they, like Hedg-hogs, stop with straw,
Or open, as the Wind does blow:
And tho they reach from top to floor,
His Grace[12] crept in upon all four.
Betwixt the door there was a spot
I' th' middle, to hang o're the pot;
And had an Engine[13] in the nick,[14]
For pair of Tongues,[15] a broken stick.
I' th' presence was no stool, but one
Old Creel,[16] for *Nees* to sit upon:
For all the rest, as they did come,
Made Stools and Cushions of their Bum.

In this so rich and stately Cabbin,
To lie in state came this Sea-Crab[17] in,
Dy'd for the nonce in liquid Sable,[18]
And laid him underneath the Table;
Where in one end the parted Brother
Was laid to rest, the Cows in t' other,
With all his Followers and Kin,
Who far and near came crowding in,
With *Hub-bub-boos*,[19] besides what Cryers
For greater state his Highness hires;[20]
Who all come crowding in; and in comes
Monk Coron[21] too, with all his Trinkums;[22]
Who when he had his Office paid,

1. company.
2. Macshane (Misenus), piper to 'prince' Nees (Aeneas), has just been killed and his funeral is about to occur.
3. large earthenware cooking pots.
4. feet.
5. whiskey.
6. carried.
7. cabin.
8. rafters or roof beams (set in pairs).
9. boughs or twigs bound together and interlaced to form wattle-work, used in the construction of the cabin.
10. The poet has some difficulty with metre, rhyme and syntax at this point.
11. window; 'Dormants' in the next line are dormer windows which project vertically from a sloping roof; here, of course, they are just holes in the fabric of the cabin.
12. i.e. 'prince' Nees.
13. a (wooden) frame.
14. = niche.
15. tongs. A marginal note here reads 'Madda brist', Ir. *maide briste* (a broken stick), which is used to signify fire tongs.
16. A large wickerwork basket.
17. Sea-Crab; a sailor, referring to the fact that Macshane (like his prototype Misenus) had died by drowning.
18. A reference to the saffron cloaks typically worn by the native Irish. According to Elizabethan writers, the colour was achieved by dyeing them in urine.
19. wailing and crying.
20. i.e. professional mourners.
21. Or Father O Corin; cf. Corinaeus, who presides over the funeral ceremonies for Misenus (cf. Macshane) in Virgil's *Aeneid*.
22. A colloquial form of trinkets.

And for the Dead a while had pray'd,
To their own Sports, (the *Masses* ended,)
The Mourners now are recommended.

Some for their pastime count their Beads,[23]
Some scratch their Breech, some louse their Heads;
Some sit and chat, some laugh, some weep;
Some sing *Cronans*,[24], and some do sleep;
Some pray, and with their prayers mix curses;
Some Vermin pick, and some pick Purses;
Some court, some scold, some blow, some puff,
Some take Tobacco, some take Snuff;
Some play the Trump, some trot the Hay,[25]
Some at *Macham*,[26] some *Noddy*[27] play;
With all the Games they can devise;
And (when occasion serves him) cries.

Thus did they mix their grief and sorrow,
Yesterday bury'd, kill'd to morrow;
And mounted him upon a Beer;[28]
Through which the Wattles did appear;
Like Ribbs on either side made fast,
With a White Velvet[29] over-cast:
So poor *Macshane*, Good rost his Shoul,
Was after put him in a hole;
In which, with many sighs and scrietches,
They throw his Trouses and his Breeches;
And tattar'd Brogue[30] was after throw,
With a new heel-piece on the toe;
And Stockins Fine as *Friez*[31] to feel,
Worn out with praying at the heel;
And in his mouth, 'gainst he took Wherry,[32]
Dropt a white Groat[33] to pay the Ferry.
Thus did they make this last hard shift,[34]
To furnish him for a dead lift.[35]

23. The marginal note reads 'An *Irish* Wake'.
24. Ir. *cronán*: 'droning, humming, singing'.
25. Irish Hay is glossed at the end of *The Irish Hudibras* as 'a dance'.
26. A card game.
27. Another card game, similar to cribbage.
28. bier, a frame of wattles on which the body is placed before burial.
29. blanket.
30. shoe.
31. Woven woollen cloth.
32. 'in readiness for the time that he would take the wherry'. A wherry was a small rowing boat. The reference is to the boat in which Charon rowed newly dead souls across the river Styx.
33. A silver coin, worth four (old) pennies.
34. difficult but successful effort.
35. A combination of the meaning of 'dead lift', an emergency, with the dialectal meaning of 'lift', the removal of a corpse from the house for burial.

Last having done his *Ave Mary*'s,
And all his *Drollans* and Boldaries,[36]
The Priest, Father *O Corin*, gi's 'em
His Blessing too; calls for the Besom,[37]
Which dipt in Salt and Holy Water,
He does their Coxcombs[38] all bespatter;
And while they for the Blessing stickle,[39]
Did leave them all in sacred pickle.[40]....

36. The marginal note glosses these unusual words as 'Fopperies and Trumperies'.
37. A broom, i.e. the aspergillum or little brush used to sprinkle holy water.
38. caps or heads.
39. strive or contend.
40. a) condition; b) cf. Swift, *A Tale of a Tub* (1704) where holy water is described (section IV) as 'universal pickle', able to preserve anything.

ANONYMOUS
(*c.* 1716)

HESPERI-NESO-GRAPHIA:[1] OR, A DESCRIPTION OF THE WESTERN ISLE

Canto I

In Western isle renown'd for bogs,
For tories,[2] and for great wolf-dogs,
For drawing hobbies by the tail,[3]
And threshing corn with fiery flail;[4]
Where beer, and curds,[5] for truth I tell it,
Are made without a pot or skellet,[6]
And without pan, and without kettle,
Or any thing that's made of mettle;
Where, in some places, cows shite fire,
And hogs such soap as some desire;

1. From the Greek 'graphein' (to write), 'hesperos' (western) and 'nesos' (island).
2. cf. Ir. *tóraí* = literally, a pursuer, later bandit, outlaw. In its anglicized form, it refers to Irish rebels.
3. 'hobbies' are small to medium-sized horses, which were commonly secured head to tail by traces for ploughing and for pulling carts. A textual note to the 1755 edition refers to the custom 'of ploughing, not with such gears or harness as in other places' but by 'tying the hindmost horse's head to the tail of the foremost'.
4. A device for threshing corn by hand. A textual note to the 1755 edition refers to the custom 'of burning their straw (rather than put themselves to the pains to thresh it) by that means to part it from the corn.'
5. A textual note to the 1755 edition records that the Irish would put 'several large stones into the fire till they were red hot, and then put them into their brewing vessels, and milk to make curds.'
6. skillet, a cooking pot, generally used for boiling and stewing.

And where in bowels of the ground
There are great heaps of butter found,[7]
Of which with blood of living beast,
The natives make a dainty[8] feast;
And where in leathern hairy boat,[9]
O'er threatening waves bold mortals float,
Like *gulls*, who never yet were found,
By strength of water to be drown'd,
And free from fear and danger ride
On back of waves 'gainst wind and tide;
And where the mountains once a year,
In flames, like *Aetna*,[10] do appear,
And burn (believe me) day and night,
To strangers a most dreadful sight;
One *Gillo*[11] liv'd, the son of *Shane*,[12]
Who was the son of *Patrick Bane*,[13]
Who was the son of *Teigue*[14] the *Tory*,
Who, to his great and endless glory,
Out of a bush a shot let fly,
And kill'd a man that passed by,
For which he was advanced high.
This *Teigue* was son of *Gilli-Christ*,[15]
And he the son of *Hugh* the priest;
For priests in *Shambroghshire*,[16] they say,
Can women kiss, as well as pray.
This *Hugo*, rampant priest, was son,
And only heir to *Dermot Dun*,[17]
Who was the son of *Teigue Mc Shane*,[18]
Who was the son of *Terlaugh Greane*,[19]
Who was the son of *Phelim Fad*,[20]
Who on each hand six fingers had,
Could twist horse-shoes, and at one meal
With ease could eat the greatest veal;
With head instead of hammer cou'd
Knock nail into a piece of wood,
And with his teeth, without least pain,
Could pull the nail from thence again:
This monster sprung from *Laughlin Crone*,[21]
A greater thief was never known;
For in his trade he had such skill,
That he a stolen cow could kill,
For shift[22] with mantle and a stone,
A way to former thieves unknown.
And *Laughlin* sprung from *Manus Row*,[23]
Who valu'd neither frost nor snow;
His feet they were so callous grown,
That he could kick at ice or stone;
And therefore in the coldest weather,
Did never wear one bit of leather.
This *Manus* from *Mulrooney*[24] came,
A man of no ignoble fame;
For begging learning in the schools,
He learnt at length the grammar rules,
And, without doubt had so much sense,
To form a verb through mood and tense;
Nay, some do say that he was able
To moralize on *Aesop*'s[25] fable!
And tho' he had *Corderius*[26] read,
He often broke poor *Priscian*'s[27] head;
And yet the mob admir'd his sense,
His *Latin* and his eloquence;
Because at fairs he did dispute,
Where he some school-boys did confute.
Of him this also can be said,
That near *Benbolben*[28] he was bred,
Where *Phin Mc Cool*[29] was buried;
Who kill'd more mighty giants, than
Were ever kill'd by mortal man.
This learn'd *Mulroony* was the son
Of *Bryan Mirgah*[30] of *Crooncun*;
Who was admir'd for nothing more,
Than for the kindness, which he bore

7. Quantities of butter, hidden or stored by earlier generations, are still sometimes found in the bogs of Ireland.
8. tasty, pleasing to eat. A textual note to the 1755 edition records that the Irish would bleed 'their kine [cattle] once a year, which they boiled and eat with their butter, and made boats of cows', and horses' hides.'
9. Probably a currach, a light boat with a wooden frame covered with hides.
10. Mount Etna, a volcano in Sicily.
11. Ir. *giolla*, a servant, attendant.
12. Ir. Seán (John).
13. Ir. *bán*, white.
14. Ir. Tadhg.
15. Ir. Giolla Chríost, servant of Christ, a common ecclesiastical name.
16. A burlesque name for Ireland.
17. Ir. Diarmaid donn, brown(-haired) Dermot.
18. Ir. Tadhg Mac Seáin, Teigue son of Seán.
19. Ir. Toirealach gránna, ugly Turlagh.
20. Ir. Féilim fada, tall Phelim. The whole passage is a burlesque treatment of the Irish propensity for genealogies.
21. Ir. Lochlann crón, swarthy Laughlin.
22. an expedient.
23. Ir. Mánus rua, red(-haired) Manus.
24. Ir. Maol Ruanaidh, servant of Rooney.
25. Aesop (died *c.* 564 B.C.), Greek author of fables about animals, in which human weaknesses are satirized.
26. Mathurin Cordier (*c.* 1479-1564), French grammarian and educator, whose *Colloquia* ran to many editions and was used widely as a standard school textbook.
27. Priscianus Caesariensis (late 5th, early 6th centuries A.D.), a grammarian whose work was well-known in the Middle Ages. 'To break Priscian's head' meant to violate the rules of grammar.
28. Benbulben, the famous, distinctively shaped mountain to the north of Sligo town.
29. Ir. Fionn Mac Cumhail, the main hero of the Fenian or Ossianic cycle of legends.
30. Ir. Brian meirgeach, freckled Brian.

To butter'd meal and blood-raw meat,
Which he for constant food did eat;
Affirming that all meat was spoil'd
That either roasted was or boil'd.
His *ostrich* stomach[31] had such heat,
It could digest the hardest meat.
I could as well trace out the blood
Of *Gillo* up to *Noah*'s flood,[32]
As *British* authors, who pretend
That they from *Trojans* did descend;[33]
But that would be a tedious task,
Therefore your pardon I must ask,
And leav't to be performed by
Some tracer of antiquity.

31. Alluding to the belief that the ostrich has indiscriminate voracity and likes hard substances.
32. Many Irish genealogies go back to Noah and the flood.
33. Geoffrey of Monmouth (died 1155) in his *Historia Regum Britanniae* (*c.* 1136) claimed the authority of an ancient record in British for the story that Brut, or Brutus, was the founder of ancient Britain. The great-grandson of Aeneas, this Brutus came to Britain with a small group of Trojans after the sack of Troy and founded a line of kings. Geoffrey drew on earlier writers and traditions; the legend he formulated was related and discussed beyond his own time.

ANONYMOUS
(1726)

from: A DESCRIPTION OF THE COUNTY OF KERRY

Sure there are poets who did never dream,
On Brandon hill,[1] nor taste the gentle stream,
Which from the glitt'ring summit daily flows:
And the bright pebbles in its fair bosom shews:
From thy clear height I take my lofty flight,
Which opens all the country to my sight:
Both rocks and woods are from thy prospect seen,
Blake[2] in the winter, in the summer green:
Where e'er I turn'd my eyes new scenes appear,
Adorn'd with all the blessings of the year:
On one side Dingle[3] forms a goodly bay,
Well known to mariners that cross the sea.

1. Mount Brandon on the Dingle peninsula, from which there is a commanding view, notably of the Blasket Islands and Dingle Bay. A textual note to the 1740 edition records that this is 'An high hill ... [which is] remarkable for a bright stone, which by the reflection of the sun shews at a great distance the time of the day.'
2. Dialectal usage, meaning pale, yellow.
3. On the southern side of the Dingle peninsula, the town of Dingle has its own harbour, which opens into Dingle Bay.

Tho' choice[4] of wines are wreck'd upon the coast,
It can of a much nobler liquor boast;
Bulcawn,[5] that strong support to sons of earth,
Can elevate the soul to nobler mirth;
Milesian[6] Bards are by its force inspir'd,
When from the labours of the day retir'd:
The Indies[7] here point out sufficient store,
Of all their riches on this distant shore:
Lough-Layn[8] the next sweet object of my sight,
Can add new wonders and my verse invite;
Smooth are thy waters and thy fountains deep,
Whilst precious stones[9] upon the bottom sleep;
Stones, that give lustre in the dead of night,
Out-shine the stars in their apparent light;
Here pearls intermix'd with common sand,
Neglected lye upon the bord'ring strand.
With such our lord[10] in foreign courts appear'd,
To polish them he no expenses spar'd;
Admir'd by all for such a costly dress,
They thought him king, nor cou'd they think him less.
And thou smooth Leawn,[11] which by its borders flows,
And guards Ross castle[12] 'gainst our monarch's[13] foes;

4. the best.
5. An anglicized form of the Irish *bolcán*, which means 'fiery spirits, rot-gut' (*Foclóir Gaeilge-Béarla*).
6. Irish, from Milesius, a fabulous Spanish king whose sons are said to have conquered Ireland about 1300 B.C.
7. The East or the West Indies, used as an emblem of enormous wealth.
8. Lough Leane, immediately to the west and south-west of Killarney. Containing about thirty islands, it is also known as the Lower Lake of the three Lakes of Killarney.
9. Possibly cobalt, which has been found at Muckross, in the south-east of Lough Leane. Copper has been mined on Ross Island, on the eastern side of the lough, and also at Muckross (Samuel Lewis, *A Topographical Dictionary of Ireland*, 1837). A textual note to the 1740 edition records that the 'lough [is] remarkable for a number of precious stones, which shine very much by night, and it is imagin'd by all People that there's a Carbuncle concealed in it.' See also the extract from Charles Smith, *The Antient and Present State of the County of Kerry* (Dublin, 1756), on p. 974.
10. Alluding to one of the Fitzgeralds of Desmond, one of the major Irish families in the late Middle Ages, who controlled extensive areas of Munster. Gerald Fitzgerald (died 1583), fifteenth earl of Desmond, visited the court of Elizabeth I in 1559 with a retinue of one hundred gentlemen, and other Fitzgeralds were known in England and Europe.
11. The river Laune, which flows from Lough Leane into Castlemaine Harbour, near Killorglin.
12. On the eastern shore of Lough Leane, Ross Castle dates from the fifteenth century, when it was founded by the O'Donoghues. The notion of the water guarding the castle is wishful thinking, since it was besieged from the lough by the Cromwellian commander Edmund Ludlow (*c.* 1617-92) in 1652, when it was surrendered by Donagh MacCarthy (1594-1665), second viscount Muskerry, who was created earl of Clancarty in 1658.
13. George I, king of Britain and Ireland 1714-27.

Thy gentle stream deserves uncommon praise,
Which thro' the winding valleys gladly strays;
Close on thy confines is that fruitful land,
Where ever happy lives the Desmond Band;[14]
Sprung from the loins of kings this noble race,
As high as Thales[15] can their parents trace:
No foreign customs do their lands invade,
Nor will their antient custom ever fade;
No tea nor coffee is among them us'd,
And stranded claret is for ale refus'd;
Their cleanly dishes are of wooden ware,
Best suited to their strong and homely fare;
Here every man's a monarch in his mind,
And ev'ry traveller will admittance find:
Their constant dress is made of home-spun frize,[16]
No more they covet than will just suffice.
Now Glownayalth[17] approaches to my view,
Daily resorted[18] by a crack-brain'd crew;
Whose herbage[19] never fails to cure the mind,
When folks thro' guilt of madness are inclin'd:
Now to Tralee[20] I'll guide my wand'ring eye,
Where rocks and mountains seem to reach the sky;
Here great O Connor[21] monarch of the west,
Sway'd[22] uncontroul'd, with peace and plenty blest;
If lawless subjects mutter'd at his laws,
Then green oak cudgels did decide the cause;
No pike[23] nor military art was us'd,
To conquer those that wholesome laws refus'd;
But well dry'd saplins[24] ended the debate,
From those whole thousands met untimely fate;
And still this antient custom is observ'd,
By strong Desmonians,[25] even by force preserv'd.
The Highlands[26] sooner wou'd give up their right
Of Arms, and gladly quit th'unequal fight,
Before Desmonians wou'd their cudgels yield,
With saplins they wou'd try the doubtful field;
No scymeter[27] can pierce that harden'd wood,
Which many a fight at fairs and patrons[28] stood;
A broken scull ensues at ev'ry stroak,
They'll bend with blows, but never can be broke.
Oft have I seen two landlords at a fair,
Where tenants with their sheep and cows repair;
A quarrel first betwixt themselves create,
Then urge their clans to end the fierce debate;
Off go the hats and coats, the fight begins,
Some strike the heads whilst others strike the shins;
The winding cudgels round their foreheads play
They need no leaders to begin the fray.
Where e'er the brave O Donaghoos[29] engage,
Well known with cudgels such brave fights to wage;
All must submit unto their stiff'ning blows,
Unless th' O Sullivans[30] their sticks oppose;
Then victory on either side divides:
'Till night alone the eager clans divides;
No enmity in either party's seen,
Till the next meeting on some neighb'ring green;
'Tis then the honour of the day depends,
On him who best the sally gole[31] defends;
The winning side assumes his dear bought right,
And bears the trophies of the former fight.
What land can such a store of jewels boast,
As daily shine upon our plenteous coast:
Rome in her grandeur, never cou'd produce,
Such stones as we in common houses use;
Her Gothick structures and her marble domes,
Were far inferior to our Kerry stones;

14. A romanticized view, since the Fitzgeralds rebelled against Elizabeth I in the periods 1569-73 and 1579-83, and after Gerald Fitzgerald, the fifteenth earl of Desmond, was killed in 1583, his entire territory, almost 600,000 acres in Munster, was confiscated so that a plantation could be established.
15. Thales (*c.* 624-*c.* 546 B.C.), Greek philosopher, astronomer and mathematician, who held that everything consists of water, and who is said to have foretold the solar eclipse that occurred in 585 B.C.
16. Coarse, locally woven cloth or tweed.
17. Ir. Gleann na ngealt (Madmen's Glen), between Tralee and Dingle.
18. frequented.
19. herbs, plants that are sought for cooking and medicine.
20. A mile inland from Tralee Bay on the north side of the Dingle peninsula, Tralee is the county town of Kerry.
21. The high-king Rory O'Connor, whom Henry II (king of England 1154-89) recognized in the Treaty of Windsor (1175) as king of Connacht, the north-western province of Ireland.
22. ruled.
23. A medieval weapon of war, still in use in the eighteenth century. It consisted of a long pole with a metal spearhead, axe and hook attached to it, and was used by English and continental soldiers rather than by Irishmen.
24. saplings.
25. Those who lived under the Fitzgeralds of Desmond, who had controlled extensive territory in Munster before it was confiscated in 1586 after the Desmond rebellion. The term comes to mean the inhabitants of Kerry.
26. The Highlands of Scotland, territory that the Gaelic clans had formerly occupied and which was central to Scottish concepts of freedom and independence.
27. scimitar: a short, curved sword.
28. An obsolete form of 'patterns' — in Ireland, the days of patron saints, and hence the celebrations of those days.
29. An anglicized form of the Irish Ó Donnchadha: 'An important sept in Desmond: they were driven from their original habitat in County Cork to County Kerry where their name was perpetuated in the territory called Onaght O'Donoghue' (Edward MacLysaght).
30. The anglicized form of the Irish Ó Súileabháin, the most frequently encountered surname in Munster. The O'Sullivans, originally of south Tipperary, were forced westwards by the Anglo-Norman invaders and eventually became one of the leading septs in the southern parts of Munster.
31. Willow or sallow, used to make the goal posts for a ball game, probably an early version of modern Gaelic football or hurling.

Lexshnaw[32] thou goodly pile for ever blest,
No monarch ever such a seat possest;
Plenty for ever dwells within thy walls,
Each day an ox beneath the hatchet falls;
Whole herds of deer upon thy mountains stray,
Thy ponds abounding with the finny frey;[33]
Surrounded with the springs of gentle Fale,[34]
The winding Cashin[35] and the lympid Geal;[36]
Plenty and peace in ev'ry house abound,
Such happiness can no where else be found;
I who desires to live an easy life,
Absent from faction and remote from strife;
In Kerry only must expect to find,
Those lasting blessings sought by human kind.

32. Probably Lixnaw, between Tralee and Listowel in the north of County Kerry. It was the seat of the Fitzmaurices, lords of Kerry and barons Lixnaw. Thomas Fitzmaurice (1574-1630), eighteenth lord Kerry and baron Lixnaw, had rebelled in 1598 with his father, who had supported the Desmond rebellion in 1580. pile = a substantial building.
33. fish, particularly salmon.
34. The river Feale, which rises in the mountains that stand on the borders of Counties Kerry, Limerick and Cork.
35. The Feale flows through Listowel and then becomes the river Cashen, which flows into the Atlantic on the southern side of the mouth of the Shannon.
36. The river Galey rises in the west of County Limerick and flows into the Cashen five miles from its mouth.

WILLIAM DUNKIN

CARBERY *ROCKS IN THE COUNTY OF CORK, IRELAND*

Lo! from the Top of yonder Cliff, that shrouds
Its airy Head amidst the azure Clouds,
Hangs a huge Fragment; destitute of props
Prone on the Waves the rocky Ruin drops.
With hoarse Rebuff the swelling Seas rebound,
From Shore to Shore the Rocks return the Sound:
The dreadful Murmur Heav'n's high Convex
 cleaves,
And *Neptune*[1] shrinks beneath his Subject Waves;
For, long the whirling Winds and beating Tides
Had scoop'd a Vault into its nether[2] Sides.
Now yields the Base, the Summits nod, now urge
Their headlong Course, and lash the sounding
 Surge.

1. The god of the sea in Roman mythology.
2. lower.

Not louder Noise could shake the guilty World,
When *Jove*[3] heap'd Mountains upon Mountains
 hurl'd,
Retorting *Pelion*[4] from his dread abode,
To crush Earth's rebel Sons beneath the Load.

Oft too with hideous yawn the Cavern wide
Presents an Orifice on either Side,
A dismal[5] Orifice from Sea to Sea
Extended, pervious[6] to the God of Day:[7]
Uncouthly[8] joyn'd, the Rocks stupendous form
An Arch, the Ruin of a future Storm:
High on the Cliff their Nests the *Woodquests*[9] make,
And Sea calves[10] stable in the oozy Lake.

But when bleak Winter with her sullen Train
Awakes the Winds, to vex the watry Plain;
When o'er the craggy Steep without Controul,
Big with the Blast, the raging Billows rowl;
Not Towns beleaguer'd, not the flaming Brand
Darted from Heav'n by *Jove*'s avenging Hand,
Oft as on impious Men his Wrath he pours,
Humbles their Pride, and blasts their gilded Tow'rs,
Equal the Tumult of this wild Uproar:
Waves rush o'er Waves, rebellows[11] Shore to Shore.
The neighb'ring Race, tho' wont to brave the
 Shocks,
Of angry Seas, and run along the Rocks,
Now pale with Terror, while the Ocean foams,
Fly far and wide, nor trust their native Homes.

The Goats, while pendent from the Mountain
 top
The wither'd Herb improvident they crop,
Wash'd down the Precipice with sudden Sweep,
Leave their sweet Lives beneath th' unfathom'd
 Deep.

The frighted Fisher with desponding[12] Eyes,
Tho' safe, yet trembling in the Harbour lies,

3. Jupiter, the father of the gods in Roman mythology.
4. A mountain in Thessaly, Greece. The giants Otus and Ephialtes attacked the gods by trying to heap the mountains of Ossa on Mount Olympus, the home of the gods, and then Pelion on Ossa, in order to reach heaven itself. Jove retaliated, as the poem has it, by crushing them to death.
5. dire, in the sense of being full of dread and inspiring awe.
6. allowing passage, open.
7. i.e. the sun.
8. awkwardly, gracelessly.
9. wood-pigeons.
10. seals.
11. echoes loudly.
12. losing heart or confidence.

Nor hoping to behold the Skies serene,
Wearies with Vows the Monarch of the Main.[13]

13. i.e. Neptune.

from: THE PARSON'S REVELS

[from Canto II]

... But enters now the Parish Priest,[1]
Who was by Patrick[2] and by Chreest,
As great a wolf, as ever fleec'd
The laity.

Although but little known to fame,
By birth and breeding he would claim
Profound respect; for why? his name
Was Fegan:[3]

He swore, he travell'd many a league
To Paris, Antwerp, and the Hague,[4]
And was descended from Sir Teague
O Regan:[5]

His body-coat was fac'd with fat,
His head as grey, as any cat,
And belly big, to cupboard what
He gathers.

His wit and humour much he smothers,
But numerates his learned brothers,
And quotes his venerable mothers,
The fathers.

Quoth he, 'I am vwell boarn and brid,[6]
Shur Teague O Regan vwash my hid,
Aldough, deer joay, I nivir rid
Your Nhomars;

Yit Fegan can confabulaat[7]
In Frinch and Laatin, dher mey faat,
And hild a Teshis at dhe graat
Shaint Omars.[8]

Yit, bey dhe bilt,[9] fhwich Franshis[10] vwoar,
Dhe crass ov Chreest, fhwich Paatrick boar,
Dhe Baads ov Bridgit,[11] and fwhat's moar
Mey Vistimints,

I louv your clargymin indeed,
Fwho bovw to Jeshuz in dhe creed,
Aldough dhey lit dheir laamin reed
Dhe Tistimints.

Gaad blish king Gaarge and hish Lutterians,
But cursh upon dhe Proshpiterians,
Dhe knaaves are oogly Nolliverians,[12]
And apish —'

But Denison[13] began to chase here:
A Turk, or Pagan must be safer
Than thee with all thy Gods of wafer,
Vile Papish![14]

Thy brethren, void of faith, and hope,
And charity, deserve the rope;
Old Antichrist is but the Pope
In scarlet:[15]

The rock,[16] which you would rest upon,
As I shall fairly prove anon,
Is but the spawn of Babylon,[17]
A harlot,

1. Father Fegan joins the extended, riotous party that is the subject of *The Parson's Revels.*
2. St Patrick.
3. Fegan or Fagan is a name of Norman origin, known in Dublin, County Meath and County Louth.
4. Surprisingly, these are protestant rather than catholic centres of learning in northern Europe.
5. A composite name comprising the anglicized form of the Irish Tadhg, commonly applied to catholics, and the anglicized form of the Irish Ó Réagáin, a name from County Waterford.
6. Father Fagan's speech may be roughly 'translated':

'I am well born and bred,/Sir Tadhg Ó Réagáin was my head,/Although, dear joy, I never read your Homers;

Yet Fegan can confabulate/in French and Latin, they're my fate (?),/And held a thesis(?) at the great St Omers.

Yet by the belt which Francis wore,/The cross of Christ which Patrick bore,/The beads of Brigid, and what's more my vestments,

I love your clergymen indeed,/Who bow to Jesus in the creed,/Although they let their laymen read the testaments.

God bless King George and his Lutherans,/But curse upon the Presbyterians,/The knaves are ugly Nolliverians, and like apes.'

7. converse.
8. St Omer, a cathedral town in north-west France, famous for its Jesuit college, which was founded *c.* 1592.
9. According to English writers, oaths such as these were common among the Irish.
10. St Francis of Assisi (1181-1226).
11. St Brigid (died *c.* 525), abbess of Kildare.
12. = nullifidians (?), sceptics.
13. One of the guests at the feast, a presbyterian.
14. papist.
15. i.e. the pope dressed in scarlet robes is nothing but the devil.
16. The rock of St Peter, i.e. the catholic church.
17. Babylon was the city in Mesopotamia where the Jews were held

Who curses with her blessings mixes,
Trick'd up with painted babies,[18] pyxies,[19]
Indulgencies,[20] and crucifixes,
Her trapping.

A church, upheld by lying rumours,
Long bloated with unhealthy tumours,
And ripe (if you would purge her humours)
For tapping.[21]

He said, and in his fury collar'd
The Priest, who cry'd, 'I am a scollard,[22]
Na Manichæan, Arian, Lollard,[23]
Or pagan'....

Thus Fegan, fraught with Latin, huffs,
And Presbyter as proudly puffs,
Preparing for conclusive cuffs
Their thumpers.

But B——, with pacific grace
Uprising, splits the doubtful case,
And reconciles them with a brace
of bumpers[24] ....

At flowing bumpers who can carp,
Or in his jovial humour warp?[25]
Then fill your glasses: — tune your harp,
O Murphy.

This Murphy, strolling up and down,
Had been a harper of renown,
And Bard as eloquent, as Crown,
Or Durfy.[26]

About O Neal[27] he kept a pother,[28]
For why, he was his foster-brother,
Begotten on a base-born mother,
A Spinster;

But, though reduc'd to live by strings,
Greater than great O Neal[29] he brings
His father's blood from antient kings
Of Leinster.

As ladies fair, of taste refin'd,
Their petted linnets often blind
To make them sing the sweeter, kind-
ly cruel:

To strike his mind with visions bright,
And give his hearers more delight,
Melpomene[30] depriv'd of sight
This jewel.

Quoth Oaf,[31] I hate him, and his kin,
To hear his music is a sin:
For bringing such a rebel in
Small thanks t'ye.

His harp is hollow; so is he;
Both make one popish jubilee:
What can he play, but Garran-buoy,
Or Plankstv?[32]

At this O Murphy, like a nag
Spurr'd to his mettle, would not lag:
Quoth he, 'I am na ribil rag-
A-muffin,

But ov dhe reight Hibarnian seed,
Aldough mey fadhir cud nat reed,
Nat lek yur black[33] fanaatic breed,
You puffin'....

His voice was brazen, deep, and such,
As well accorded with High-dutch,[34]

prisoner under Nebuchadnezzar (604-562 B.C.). Protestants often described the catholic church as 'the whore of Babylon', since, for them, Babylon was a symbol of corruption.
18. Angels in painting and statues.
19. The pyx is the container in which the Hosts for the Eucharist are kept on the altar.
20. Documents issued by the church, giving remission of punishments due for sin on earth.
21. i.e. draining off supposedly diseased blood in order to cure a patient; bleeding.
22. A scholar; a comic term, normally applied by the totally illiterate to the partially literate.
23. Three heresies are referred to in this line: Manichaeus (*c.* 216-76 A.D.) stressed the conflict between light and darkness, good and evil, on a cosmic scale; Arius (*c.* 250-*c.* 336 A.D.) denied the divinity of Christ; the followers of John Wycliffe (*c.* 1330-84), who attacked abuses in the church, were called Lollards, from the Dutch word 'lollen' to mumble (prayers).
24. large glasses or tankards.
25. turn aside from.
26. Probably references to the minor playwrights John Crowne (*c.* 1640-*c.* 1703) and Thomas D'Urfey (1653-1723).
27. One of the O'Neills of Ulster.
28. kept making a bother or fuss.
29. Hugh O'Neill (1550-1616).
30. One of the nine muses of Greek mythology, Melpomene was associated with tragedy.
31. One of the main guests, a presbyterian and a landlord.
32. A lively dance tune and an instrumental air, respectively.
33. cf. the phrase 'black protestant'.
34. German.

Or Attic Irish,[35] and his touch
Was pliant:

Dubourgh[36] to him was but a fool;
He play'd melodious without rule,
And sung the feats of Fin Macool,[37]
The giant.

He sounds in more majestic strains,
How brave Milesians[38] with their skanes[39]
Had butcher'd all the bloody Danes
Like weathers.[40]

While Bryan Borough[41] with a yell
Flat on the bed of honour fell,
When he might sleep at home as well
On feathers:

He celebrates with lofty tone
Tyrconnel, Desmond, and Tyrone,[42]
Renown'd O Neal, who shook the throne
Of Britain;

O Donnel, fam'd for whisky rare,
And then, O Rowrk,[43] thy noble fare
Of sheep and oxen, with — no chair
To sit on[44] ....

At last, though much against his heart,
His tongue and fingers act their part,
Displaying with Orphean[45] art,
And cunning,

35. Common Irish (since the Greek of Attica became the most common form of Greek).
36. Matthew Dubourg (1703-67), an English violinist and conductor who became the dominant figure in the musical culture of Dublin in the 1730s and 1740s.
37. Ir. Fionn Mac Cumhail, the hero of the Fenian or Ossianic cycle of legends.
38. Irish, from Milesius, a fabulous Spanish king whose sons are said to have conquered Ireland about 1300 B.C..
39. knives or daggers.
40. weathers = wethers, castrated rams.
41. Brian Boru, the high king of Ireland who defeated the Vikings at the battle of Clontarf in 1014.
42. Rory O'Donnell (1575-1608), first earl of Tyrconnel, the Fitzgerald family of Desmond and Hugh O'Neill (*c.* 1540-1616), second earl of Tyrone.
43. Alluding to the Irish poem 'Pléaráca na Ruarcach', which celebrates a famous feast, said to have been given by Brian O'Rourke, a chieftain of County Leitrim, towards the end of the sixteenth century, which Swift reworked as 'The Description of an *Irish-Feast*' (see p. 399).
44. Referring to a particular incident in the 'Pléaraca na Ruarcach', which Swift did not include in his version, in which 'the friars rose up to save the battle, and the Father guardian was left on his rump in the ashes'.
45. Orpheus was the most famous lyre-player in Greek mythology.

How WILLIAM[46] cross'd the Boyn to fight,
And how King James had beaten quite
His hot pursuers out of sight —
By running.

He plays, and sings it o'er and o'er,
Encore, quoth Denison, encore!
One Williamite would rout a score
Of trimmers:[47]

Nassau,[48] with bays[49] immortal crown'd,
Nassau, Nassau the guests resound;
The GLORIOUS MEMORY[50] flows round
In brimmers.[51]

46. William of Orange, king of England 1689-1702, who defeated James II at the battle of the Boyne in July 1690.
47. Those who change sides depending on who is winning.
48. William III was not only prince of Orange but also count of Nassau, a territory in Germany.
49. laurels — the victor's symbol in ancient Greece.
50. The words of a typical Orange toast were: 'To the glorious, pious and immortal memory of the great and good King William.'
51. Huge tankards or glasses filled to the brim ready for the drinking of toasts.

OLIVER GOLDSMITH

THE DESERTED VILLAGE

Sweet Auburn,[1] loveliest village of the plain,
Where health and plenty cheared the labouring swain,
Where smiling spring its earliest visit paid,
And parting summer's lingering blooms delayed,
Dear lovely bowers of innocence and ease,
Seats of my youth, when every sport could please,
How often have I loitered o'er thy green,
Where humble happiness endeared each scene;
How often have I paused on every charm,
The sheltered cot,[2] the cultivated farm,
The never failing brook, the busy mill,
The decent[3] church that topt the neighbouring hill,

1. Although there is a town of this name in Wiltshire, and while Auburn has been associated with Lissoy, a village in County Westmeath that Goldsmith knew in his childhood, the picture of Auburn is a composite one, drawn from Goldsmith's experience of England and Ireland.
2. small cottage.
3. proper, not ostentatious.

The hawthorn bush, with seats beneath the shade,
For talking age and whispering lovers made.
How often have I blest the coming day,
When toil remitting lent its turn to play,
And all the village train from labour free
Led up their sports beneath the spreading tree,
While many a pastime circled in the shade,
The young contending as the old surveyed;
And many a gambol frolicked o'er the ground,
And slights[4] of art and feats of strength went round.
And still as each repeated pleasure tired,
Succeeding sports the mirthful band inspired;
The dancing pair that simply sought renown
By holding out to tire each other down,
The swain mistrustless of his smutted face,
While secret laughter tittered round the place,[5]
The bashful virgin's side-long looks of love,
The matron's glance that would those looks reprove.
These were thy charms, sweet village; sports like these,
With sweet succession, taught even toil to please;
These round thy bowers their chearful influence shed,
These were thy charms — But all these charms are fled.

Sweet smiling village, loveliest of the lawn,
Thy sports are fled, and all thy charms withdrawn;
Amidst thy bowers the tyrant's hand is seen,
And desolation saddens all thy green:
One only master grasps the whole domain,[6]
And half a tillage[7] stints[8] thy smiling plain;
No more thy glassy brook reflects the day,
But choaked with sedges, works its weedy way.
Along thy glades, a solitary guest,
The hollow sounding bittern[9] guards its nest;
Amidst thy desert walks the lapwing flies,
And tires their ecchoes with unvaried cries.
Sunk are thy bowers in shapeless ruin all,
And the long grass o'ertops the mouldering wall,
And trembling, shrinking from the spoiler's hand,
Far, far away thy children leave the land.

Ill fares the land, to hastening ills a prey,
Where wealth accumulates, and men decay;
Princes and lords may flourish, or may fade;
A breath can make them, as a breath has made.[10]
But a bold peasantry, their country's pride,
When once destroyed, can never be supplied.

A time there was, ere England's griefs began,
When every rood[11] of ground maintained its man;
For him light labour spread her wholesome store,
Just gave what life required, but gave no more.
His best companions, innocence and health;
And his best riches, ignorance of wealth.

But times are altered; trade's unfeeling train
Usurp the land and dispossess the swain;
Along the lawn, where scattered hamlets rose,
Unwieldy wealth, and cumbrous pomp repose,
And every want to oppulence allied,
And every pang that folly pays to pride.
These gentle hours that plenty bade to bloom,
Those calm desires that asked but little room,
Those healthful sports that graced the peaceful scene,
Lived in each look, and brightened all the green;
These far departing seek a kinder shore,
And rural mirth and manners are no more.

Sweet AUBURN! parent of the blissful hour,
Thy glades forlorn confess the tyrant's power.
Here as I take my solitary rounds,
Amidst thy tangling walks, and ruined grounds,
And, many a year elapsed, return to view
Where once the cottage stood, the hawthorn grew,
Here, as with doubtful, pensive steps I range,
Trace every scene, and wonder at the change,
Remembrance wakes with all her busy train,
Swells at my breast, and turns the past to pain.

In all my wanderings round this world of care,
In all my griefs — and GOD has given my share —
I still had hopes my latest hours[12] to crown,
Amidst these humble bowers to lay me down;
To husband out life's taper[13] at the close,
And keep the flame from wasting by repose.

4. sleights.
5. A practical joke has been played on the villager, who does not know that soot has been placed on his face (Donald Davie).
6. Referring to the various enclosure acts passed in the eighteenth century, allowing the enclosure of 'common' land and forcing the departure of villagers and farmers to the cities or to the New World.
7. The new owner ploughs only half of the land.
8. limits, confines.
9. A wading bird related to the heron, with a distinctive, booming call.
10. Playing with the meanings of 'breath', referring to the vagaries and vicissitudes of life on the one hand and suggesting the myths of the origin of life on the other.
11. An old English unit of measurement, an area equal to a quarter of an acre.
12. i.e. my last years.
13. to manage the end of life carefully.

I still had hopes, for pride attends us still,
Amidst the swains to shew my book-learned skill,
Around my fire an evening groupe to draw,
And tell of all I felt, and all I saw;
And, as an hare whom hounds and horns pursue,
Pants to the place from whence at first she flew,
I still had hopes, my long vexations past,
Here to return — and die at home at last.

O blest retirement, friend to life's decline,
Retreats from care that never must be mine,
How happy he who crowns in shades like these,
A youth of labour with an age of ease;
Who quits a world where strong temptations try,
And, since 'tis hard to combat, learns to fly.[14]
For him no wretches, born to work and weep,
Explore the mine, or tempt the dangerous deep;
No surly porter stands in guilty state
To spurn imploring famine from the gate,
But on he moves to meet his latter end,
Angels around befriending virtue's friend;
Bends to the grave with unperceived decay,
While resignation gently slopes the way;
And all his prospects brightening to the last,
His Heaven commences ere the world be past!

Sweet was the sound when oft at evening's close,
Up yonder hill the village murmur rose;
There as I past with careless steps and slow,
The mingling notes came softened from below;
The swain responsive as the milk-maid sung,
The sober herd that lowed to meet their young;
The noisy geese that gabbled o'er the pool,
The playful children just let loose from school;
The watch-dog's voice that bayed the whispering wind,
And the loud laugh that spoke the vacant mind,[15]
These all in sweet confusion sought the shade,
And filled each pause the nightingale had made.
But now the sounds of population fail,
No chearful murmurs fluctuate in the gale,
No busy steps the grass-grown foot-way tread,
For all the bloomy flush of life is fled.
All but yon widowed, solitary thing
That feebly bends beside the plashy spring;
She, wretched matron, forced, in age, for bread,
To strip the brook with mantling cresses[16] spread,
To pick her wintry faggot from the thorn,
To seek her nightly shed, and weep till morn;
She only left of all the harmless train,
The sad historian of the pensive plain.

Near yonder copse, where once the garden smil'd,
And still where many a garden flower grows wild;
There, where a few torn shrubs the place disclose,
The village preacher's[17] modest mansion rose.
A man he was, to all the country dear,
And passing rich with forty pounds a year;
Remote from towns he ran his godly race,
Nor ere had changed, nor wish'd to change his place;[18]
Unpractised he to fawn, or seek for power,
By doctrines fashioned to the varying hour;
Far other aims his heart had learned to prize,
More skilled to raise the wretched than to rise.
His house was known to all the vagrant train,
He chid their wanderings, but relieved their pain;
The long remembered beggar was his guest,
Whose beard descending swept his aged breast;
The ruined spendthrift, now no longer proud,
Claimed kindred there, and had his claims allowed;
The broken soldier,[19] kindly bade to stay,
Sate by his fire, and talked the night away;
Wept o'er his wounds, or tales of sorrow done,
Shouldered his crutch, and shewed how fields were won.
Pleased with his guests, the good man learned to glow,
And quite forgot their vices in their woe;
Careless their merits, or their faults to scan,
His pity gave ere charity began.

Thus to relieve the wretched was his pride,
And even his failings leaned to Virtue's side;
But in his duty prompt at every call,
He watched and wept, he prayed and felt, for all.
And, as a bird each fond endearment tries,
To tempt its new fledged offspring to the skies;
He tried each art, reproved each dull delay,
Allured to brighter worlds, and led the way.

Beside the bed where parting life was layed,
And sorrow, guilt, and pain, by turns dismayed,

14. flee.
15. i.e. free from the cares of life.
16. Covered with (edible) watercress.
17. Goldsmith's sister identified the village preacher with his father (see Goldsmith's *Collected Letters* ed. K. Balderston (Cambridge: Cambridge University Press, 1928), p. 162).
18. Appointment in the church.
19. The demobilized soldier, now a beggar.

The reverend champion stood. At his control,
Despair and anguish fled the struggling soul;
Comfort came down the trembling wretch to raise,
And his last faultering accents whispered praise.

At church, with meek and unaffected grace,
His looks adorned the venerable place;
Truth from his lips prevailed with double sway,
And fools, who came to scoff, remained to pray.
The service past, around the pious man,
With steady zeal each honest rustic ran;
Even children followed with endearing wile,
And plucked his gown, to share the good man's smile.
His ready smile a parent's warmth exprest,
Their welfare pleased him, and their cares distrest;
To them his heart, his love, his griefs were given,
But all his serious thoughts had rest in Heaven.
As some tall cliff that lifts its awful[20] form
Swells from the vale, and midway leaves the storm,
Tho' round its breast the rolling clouds are spread,
Eternal sunshine settles on its head.

Beside yon straggling fence that skirts the way,
With blossomed furze[21] unprofitably gay,
There, in his noisy mansion, skill'd to rule,
The village master[22] taught his little school;
A man severe he was, and stern to view,
I knew him well, and every truant knew;
Well had the boding tremblers learned to trace
The day's disasters in his morning face;[23]
Full well they laugh'd with counterfeited glee,
At all his jokes, for many a joke had he;
Full well the busy whisper circling round,
Conveyed the dismal tidings when he frowned;
Yet he was kind, or if severe in aught,
The love he bore to learning was in fault;
The village all declared how much he knew;
'Twas certain he could write, and cypher[24] too;
Lands he could measure, terms[25] and tides[26] presage,
And even the story ran that he could gauge.[27]
In arguing too, the parson owned his skill,
For even tho' vanquished, he could argue still;
While words of learned length, and thundering sound,
Amazed the gazing rustics ranged around,
And still they gazed, and still the wonder grew,
That one small head could carry all he knew.

But past is all his fame. The very spot
Where many a time he triumphed, is forgot.
Near yonder thorn, that lifts its head on high,
Where once the sign-post caught the passing eye,
Low lies that house[28] where nut-brown draughts inspired,
Where grey-beard mirth and smiling toil retired,
Where village statesmen talked with looks profound,
And news much older than their ale went round.
Imagination fondly stoops to trace
The parlour splendours of that festive place;
The white-washed wall, the nicely sanded floor,
The varnished clock that clicked behind the door;
The chest contrived a double debt to pay,
A bed by night, a chest of drawers by day;
The pictures placed for ornament and use,
The twelve good rules,[29] the royal game of goose;[30]
The hearth, except when winter chill'd the day,
With aspen boughs, and flowers, and fennel gay,
While broken tea-cups, wisely kept for shew,
Ranged o'er the chimney, glistened in a row.

Vain transitory splendours! Could not all
Reprieve the tottering mansion[31] from its fall!
Obscure it sinks, nor shall it more impart
An hour's importance to the poor man's heart;
Thither no more the peasant shall repair
To sweet oblivion of his daily care;
No more the farmer's news, the barber's tale,
No more the wood-man's ballad shall prevail;
No more the smith his dusky brow shall clear,
Relax his ponderous strength, and lean to hear;
The host himself no longer shall be found
Careful to see the mantling[32] bliss go round;

20. inspiring awe.
21. gorse.
22. Identified by Goldsmith's sister (*Collected Letters*, p. 164) as the village schoolmaster of Lissoy.
23. The trembling pupils were able to predict the disasters of the day by examining the schoolmaster's face in the morning.
24. perform arithmetical calculations.
25. Times for which a particular thing, such as a natural phenomenon, would last, periods of limited time, days when payments were due.
26. tides = the movable feasts of the Christian calendar, such as Easter.
27. measure proportions, make calculations, such as the volume of a vessel.
28. The public house of the village.
29. Referring to a broadside, 'King Charles's Twelve Good Rules', which listed twelve homely maxims under a woodcut of the execution of Charles I (Davie).
30. A game with counters, moved according to the throw of dice.
31. i.e. the public house.
32. frothing.

Nor the coy maid, half willing to be prest,
Shall kiss the cup to pass it to the rest.

Yes! let the rich deride, the proud disdain,
These simple blessings of the lowly train,
To me more dear, congenial to my heart,
One native charm, than all the gloss of art;
Spontaneous joys, where Nature has its play,
The soul adopts, and owns their first born sway,
Lightly they frolic o'er the vacant mind,
Unenvied, unmolested, unconfined.
But the long pomp, the midnight masquerade,
With all the freaks of wanton wealth arrayed,
In these, ere trifflers[33] half their wish obtain,
The toiling pleasure sickens into pain;
And, even while fashion's brightest arts decoy,
The heart distrusting asks, if this be joy.

Ye friends to truth, ye statesmen who survey
The rich man's joys encrease, the poor's decay,
'Tis yours to judge, how wide the limits stand
Between a splendid and an happy land.
Proud swells the tide with loads of freighted ore,
And shouting Folly hails them from her shore;
Hoards, even beyond the miser's wish abound,
And rich men flock from all the world around.
Yet count our gains. This wealth is but a name
That leaves our useful products still the same.
Not so the loss. The man of wealth and pride,
Takes up a space that many poor supplied;
Space for his lake, his park's extended bounds,
Space for his horses, equipage, and hounds;
The robe that wraps his limbs in silken sloth,
Has robbed the neighbouring fields of half their growth;
His seat, where solitary sports are seen,
Indignant spurns the cottage from the green;
Around the world each needful product flies,
For all the luxuries the world supplies.
While thus the land adorned for pleasure all
In barren splendour feebly waits the fall.

As some fair female unadorned and plain,
Secure to please while youth confirms her reign,
Slights every borrowed charm that dress supplies,
Nor shares with art the triumph of her eyes.
But when those charms are past, for charms are frail,
When time advances, and when lovers fail,
She then shines forth sollicitous to bless,
In all the glaring impotence of dress.
Thus fares the land, by luxury betrayed,
In nature's simplest charms at first arrayed,
But verging to decline, its splendours rise,
Its vistas strike, its palaces surprize;
While scourged by famine from the smiling land,
The mournful peasant leads his humble band;
And while he sinks without one arm to save,
The country blooms — a garden, and a grave.

Where then, ah, where shall poverty reside,
To scape the pressure of contiguous pride;
If to some common's fenceless limits strayed,
He drives his flock to pick the scanty blade,
Those fenceless fields the sons of wealth divide,
And even the bare-worn common is denied.

If to the city sped — What waits him there?
To see profusion that he must not share;
To see ten thousand baneful arts combined
To pamper luxury, and thin mankind;
To see those joys the sons of pleasure know,
Extorted from his fellow-creature's woe.
Here, while the courtier glitters in brocade,
There the pale artist[34] plies the sickly trade;
Here, while the proud their long drawn pomps display,
There the black gibbet[35] glooms beside the way.
The dome[36] where pleasure holds her midnight reign,
Here richly deckt admits the gorgeous train,
Tumultuous grandeur crowds the blazing square,
The rattling chariots clash, the torches glare;
Sure scenes like these no troubles ere annoy!
Sure these denote one universal joy!
Are these thy serious thoughts — Ah, turn thine eyes
Where the poor houseless shivering female lies.
She once, perhaps, in village plenty blest,
Has wept at tales of innocence distrest;
Her modest looks the cottage might adorn,
Sweet as the primrose peeps beneath the thorn;
Now lost to all; her friends, her virtue fled,
Near her betrayer's door she lays her head,

33. triflers.

34. artisan, tradesman.
35. gallows, on which the bodies of the executed were left hanging to public view.
36. building.

And pinch'd with cold, and shrinking from the shower,
With heavy heart deplores that luckless hour,
When idly first, ambitious of the town,
She left her wheel[37] and robes of country brown.

Do thine, sweet AUBURN, thine, the loveliest train,
Do thy fair tribes participate her pain?[38]
Even now, perhaps, by cold and hunger led,
At proud men's doors they ask a little bread!

Ah, no. To distant climes, a dreary scene,
Where half the convex world intrudes between,
Through torrid tracts with fainting steps they go,
Where wild Altama[39] murmurs to their woe.
Far different there from all that charm'd before,
The various terrors of that horrid shore.
Those blazing suns that dart a downward ray,
And fiercely shed intolerable day;
Those matted woods where birds forget to sing,
But silent bats in drowsy clusters cling,
Those poisonous fields with rank luxuriance crowned
Where the dark scorpion gathers death around;
Where at each step the stranger fears to wake
The rattling terrors of the vengeful snake;
Where crouching tigers[40] wait their hapless prey,
And savage men more murderous still than they;
While oft in whirls the mad tornado flies,
Mingling the ravaged landschape with the skies.
Far different these from every former scene,
The cooling brook, the grassy vested green,
The breezy covert of the warbling grove,
That only sheltered thefts of harmless love.

Good Heaven! what sorrows gloom'd that parting day,
That called them from their native walks away;
When the poor exiles, every pleasure past,
Hung round their bowers, and fondly looked their last,
And took a long farewell, and wished in vain
For seats like these beyond the western main;
And shuddering still to face the distant deep,
Returned and wept, and still returned to weep.
The good old sire, the first prepared to go
To new found worlds, and wept for others woe.
But for himself, in conscious virtue brave,
He only wished for worlds beyond the grave.
His lovely daughter, lovelier in her tears,
The fond companion of his helpless years,
Silent went next, neglectful of her charms,
And left a lover's for a father's arms.
With louder plaints the mother spoke her woes,
And blest the cot where every pleasure rose;
And kist her thoughtless babes with many a tear,
And claspt them close in sorrow doubly dear;
Whilst her fond husband strove to lend relief
In all the silent manliness of grief.

O luxury! Thou curst by heaven's decree,
How ill exchanged are things like these for thee!
How do thy potions with insidious joy,
Diffuse their pleasures only to destroy!
Kingdoms by thee, to sickly greatness grown,
Boast of a florid vigour not their own.
At every draught more large and large they grow,
A bloated mass of rank unwieldy woe;
Till sapped their strength, and every part unsound,
Down, down they sink, and spread a ruin round.

Even now the devastation is begun,
And half the business of destruction done;
Even now, methinks, as pondering here I stand,
I see the rural virtues leave the land.
Down where yon anchoring vessel spreads the sail
That idly waiting flaps with every gale,
Downward they move a melancholy band,
Pass from the shore, and darken all the strand.[41]
Contented toil, and hospitable care,
And kind connubial tenderness, are there;
And piety with wishes placed above,
And steady loyalty, and faithful love.
And thou, sweet Poetry, thou loveliest maid,
Still first to fly where sensual joys invade;
Unfit in these degenerate times of shame,
To catch the heart, or strike for honest fame;
Dear charming nymph,[42] neglected and decried,
My shame in crowds, my solitary pride.
Thou source of all my bliss, and all my woe,
That found'st me poor at first, and keep'st me so;

37. spinning wheel.
38. i.e. Do some of the fair people, Auburn, share sufferings like hers?
39. The river Altamaha or Alatamaha in the American state of Georgia, whose region the English had attempted to settle in 1732 and where they had founded a colony three years later.
40. cougars.
41. beach.
42. The muse of poetry.

Thou guide by which the nobler arts excell,
Thou nurse of every virtue, fare thee well.
Farewell, and O where'er thy voice be tried,
On Torno's cliffs,[43] or Pambamarca's[44] side,
Whether where equinoctial fervours glow,[45]
Or winter wraps the polar world in snow,
Still let thy voice prevailing over time,
Redress the rigours of the inclement clime;

43. The river Torneälv rises in the north of Sweden, forms part of Sweden's border with Finland, and flows into the Gulf of Bothnia.
44. A mountain near Quito, Ecuador.
45. Referring to the heat of the equatorial regions.

Aid slighted truth, with thy persuasive strain
Teach erring man to spurn the rage of gain;
Teach him that states of native strength possest,
Tho' very poor, may still be very blest;
That trade's proud empire hastes to swift decay,
As ocean sweeps the labour'd mole[46] away;
While self dependent power can time defy,
As rocks resist the billows and the sky.[47]

46. The breakwater, which man has built and which lacks the 'self dependent power' of nature.
47. Samuel Johnson wrote the last four lines sometime before 1783.

II

'St Patrick's Dean'

On 16 August 1714, a fortnight after the death of Queen Anne, Jonathan Swift left London to return to Dublin, where he had been installed as dean of St Patrick's Cathedral the previous year. The collapse of the Tories, for whom he had worked on *The Examiner* from 1710 to 1714, and the prospect of making his career in Ireland, with his political enemies in power in London, filled him with a deep gloom. Despite his work for the Church of Ireland, which had resulted in the removal of the tax of the First Fruits, there were those who did not welcome Swift's promotion, and as he confronted his predicament in his poem 'In Sickness', evidently in October 1714, he began to slip into despondency, thinking himself trapped in a land he hated. Events combined to enforce his silence and, as the years wore on, he kept to the 'Resolution' he had described to his friend Charles Ford in August 1714 'of never medling with Irish politicks'.

By 1725, however, a number of fundamental changes had occurred. The passage of the Declaratory Act in 1720 — in which the Whigs of Westminster had declared that England possessed the power to legislate directly for Ireland — and Swift's own perception of the country's economic situation had led him to write his *Proposal for the Universal Use of Irish Manufacture* (1720). Two years later, the granting of a patent to William Wood, an influential English iron-merchant, to mint a copper coinage for Ireland, had led to the creation of his most famous Irish role, that of M. B. Drapier, the lowly shopkeeper who defied the government in England. As the crowds in Dublin protested against the coinage in 1724 or celebrated the victory of the Drapier in 1725, the Hibernian patriot was born. The success he achieved, however, created fresh burdens for Swift, for there were those who looked to him to cure the various ills of Ireland and who approached him time and again to endorse one scheme or another. If the publication of *Gulliver's Travels* (1726) and *A Modest Proposal* (1729) offset the image of Swift as the Drapier, and if some of the gloom of 1714 disappeared as he achieved new fame, then his ambivalence towards Ireland was always present; and if his circle of friends, which did not enter his reckoning in the despondency of 1714, served to make the burdens of life more tolerable, then the passage of time brought fresh pain, such as the death of 'Stella' (Esther Johnson) in 1728.

The compliments of friends, such as Matthew Pilkington and Patrick Delany, the poems given to him on his various birthdays, such as those by Stella and by Mary Barber, and the witty verse-letter by Thomas Sheridan, who wrote to Swift in 1726 when he was in London on his important visit with the manuscript of *Gulliver's Travels*, create glimpses of his private life and testify to the impact of his friendship, which was resented by those who looked on from afar at a circle from which they felt excluded.

If this group of poems from the 1720s and early 1730s draws attention to the presence of Swift in a personal sense, then his influence in Anglo-Irish culture in Dublin was the more significant force. In 1713 Jonathan Smedley had attacked him as an opportunist, and in 1734 James Sterling reinforced the theme of Barber's witty couplet on *The Battle of the Books* (1704) — that Swift's defence of the ancient authors had paradoxically demonstrated the superiority of the modern ones, for whom he had unwittingly fought. The most severe attack on Swift, however, was made by James Arbuckle, the poet, philosopher and journalist who edited *The Dublin Weekly Journal* from 1725 to 1727 and who was ridiculed again and again by the literati between 1725 and 1736. Swift had used the figure of Momus as the patron of the 'moderns' in *The Battle of the Books*. In 1735 Arbuckle made him identify Swift as '*Apollo* in Disguise' and used him to attack Swift's private life, leaving it to Mercury, a thief, 'Pimp' and 'Black-guard Crier of the News', to make an unconvincing tribute to Swift at the end of the poem. The occasion of Arbuckle's attack — the publication of the edition of Swift's collected works — was also marked by Laurence Whyte, whose poem to Swift paid him the compliment of repeating some of the central images of *The Drapier's Letters* (1724-25), and of associating him favourably with Apollo, in terms reminiscent of Delany's '*News from* Parnassus'. In his shorter poem on the celebration of the feast of St Patrick, Whyte extends Swift the greatest of compliments by making him St Patrick's own dean.

The most powerful poem in this group, however, is William Dunkin's 'An Epistle to R[o]b[er]t N[u]g[en]t, Esquire, with a Picture of Doctor Swift', which apparently dates from 1740, when Swift was seventy-three, and which creates an awesome image of him in the last years of his life. Swift has become 'an empty form', 'a shell without the gem', a tragic figure deserted by those who danced attendance on him and at the mercy of those who once served him and who now 'Attempt to stigmatize his morals'. Such was the force he exerted, however, that Dunkin, his closest friend among the younger generation of poets, recalled the two most important elements of Swift's presence in Ireland in this powerful lament: the role he had played as 'the bulwark of this isle' and the identification of him with the gods of inspiration themselves.

Whether we allow Swift to speak for himself or listen to his friends and enemies, his presence, from his sense of himself to the life of his circle, the criticism of his enemies, his role as the Hibernian patriot, the impact of the publication of his collected works, and the vision of him at the end of his life, becomes a subject that continues to make demands upon our scrutiny.

JONATHAN SWIFT

IN SICKNESS

Written soon after the Author's coming to live in Ireland, *upon the Queen's Death,* October 1714

'Tis true, — then why should I repine,
To see my Life so fast decline?
But, why obscurely here alone?
Where I am neither lov'd nor known.
My State of Health none care to learn;
My Life is here no Soul's Concern.
And, those with whom I now converse,
Without a Tear will tend my Herse.
Remov'd from kind *Arbuthnot*'s[1] Aid,
Who knows his Art but not his Trade;[2]
Preferring his Regard for me
Before his Credit or his Fee.
Some formal Visits, Looks, and Words,
What meer Humanity affords,
I meet perhaps from three or four,
From whom I once expected more;
Which those who tend the Sick for pay
Can act as decently as they.
But, no obliging, tender Friend
To help at my approaching End,
My Life is now a Burthen grown
To others, e'er it be my own.

Ye formal Weepers for the Sick,
In your last Offices be quick:
And spare my absent Friends the Grief
To hear, yet give me no Relief;
Expir'd To-day, entomb'd To-morrow,
When known, will save a double Sorrow.

1. John Arbuthnot (1667-1735), physician and author, and member of Pope's and Swift's circle. Pope addressed his *Epistle to Dr Arbuthnot* (1735) to him, and he was a close friend of Swift's from their meeting about 1710.
2. A skilful physician ('his Art'), Arbuthnot did not promote himself in pursuing his career ('his Trade'). Nevertheless, he had been appointed physician to Queen Anne in 1705.

JONATHAN SMEDLEY

(1671-*c.*1729)

VERSES, *FIX'D ON THE CATHEDRAL DOOR, THE DAY OF* DEAN GULLIVER'S *INSTALLMENT*

Today,[1] this Temple gets a *Dean*,
  Of Parts and Fame, uncommon;

1. Swift was installed as dean of St Patrick's Cathedral, Dublin on 13 June 1713. The title of the poem is taken from the version of it published in Smedley's *Gulliveriana* in 1728, two years after *Gulliver's Travels*.

Us'd, both to Pray, and to Prophane,
To serve both *God* and *Mammon*.[2]

When *Wharton*[3] reign'd, a *Whig* he was;
When *Pembroke*,[4] that's Dispute, Sir:
In *Oxford*'s[5] Time, what *Oxford* pleas'd;
Non-Con,[6] or *Jack*,[7] or *Neuter*.[8]

This Place He got by Wit and Rhime,
And many Ways most odd;
And might a Bishop be, in Time,
Did he believe in God.

For High-Churchmen and Policy
He swears he prays, most hearty;
But wou'd pray back again, wou'd be
A *Dean* of any Party.

Four *Lessons!*[9] *Dean*, all, in one Day,
Faith! it is hard, that's certain:
'Twere better hear *thy'own Peter* say,
G-d d—n the *Jack* and *Martin*.[10]

Hard! to be plagu'd with Bible, still,
And Prayer-Book before thee;
Hadst thou not Wit, to think, at Will,
On some diverting Story?

Look down, St. *Patrick*, look, we pray,
On thine own *Church and Steeple*;
Convert thy *Dean*, on this *Great Day*;
Or else God help the People!

2. wealth, personified as a false god.
3. Thomas Wharton (1648-1715), first earl of Wharton 1706, lord lieutenant of Ireland 1708-10, and Whig politician.
4. Thomas Herbert (*c.* 1656-1733), eighth earl of Pembroke 1683, lord lieutenant of Ireland 1707-08. Some of his contemporaries thought him closer to the Tories than to the Whigs.
5. Robert Harley (1661-1724), first earl of Oxford 1711, lord treasurer 1711-14, under whose Tory administration of England, the tax of the First Fruits on the Church of Ireland was remitted.
6. Nonconformist, a person who did not make the various oaths and declarations listed in the different Test Acts from 1673, including the Irish Test Act of 1704.
7. A presbyterian, from John Calvin (1509-64), French theologian and reformer, who established presbyterianism in Switzerland and whose ideas influenced John Knox (*c.* 1505-72), the Scottish theologian and historian.
8. Someone not belonging to any religious denomination.
9. i.e. four readings from the Bible during the service of installation.
10. Alluding to Peter, Jack and Martin, who represented the catholic, presbyterian and anglican denominations in Swift's *A Tale of a Tub* (1704).

And now, whene'er his *Deanship* dies,
Upon his Tomb be 'graven;
A Man of God here buried lies,
Who never thought of Heaven.

MARY BARBER
(1690-1757)

AN EPIGRAM ON THE *BATTLE OF THE BOOKS*

SWIFT for the Antients has argu'd so well,[1]
'Tis apparent from thence, that the Moderns excel.

1. In *The Battle of the Books* (1704) Swift favoured the ancients (authors of the classical period) over the moderns, but his persuasive argument — that of a modern, of course — proves the moderns actually superior.

JAMES STERLING
(1701-63)

AN EPIGRAM
On a certain great Author's asserting the superiority of the *Ancients* over the *Moderns*[1]

While the *Dean* with more wit than man ever wanted,
Or than heav'n to any man else ever granted,
Endeavours to prove, how the *Ancients* in knowledge
Have excell'd our adepts[2] of each *Modern* college;
How by heroes of old our chiefs are surpass'd
In each useful science, true learning, and taste:
While thus he behaves, with more courage than manners,
And fights for the foe, deserting our banners:
While *Bentley*[3] and *Wotton*,[4] our champions, he foils;

1. See note to previous poem.
2. skilled, proficient persons.
3. Richard Bentley (1662-1742), clergyman and one of the foremost classical scholars of his age, a 'modern' whom Swift attacked in *A Tale of a Tub* (1704) and *The Battle of the Books* (1704).
4. William Wotton (1666-1727), clergyman and scholar, another 'modern', whom Swift also attacked in *A Tale of a Tub* and *The Battle of the Books*.

And wants neither *Temple*'s[5] assistance, nor
Boyle's;[6]
In spite of his learning, fine reasons, and stile,
— Wou'd you think it? — he favours our cause all
the while:
We raise by his conquest our glory the higher,
And from our defeat to a triumph aspire:
Our great *Brother-Modern*, the *Boast* of our days,
Unconscious, has gain'd for our party the bays:[7]
St. *James*'s[8] old authors, so fam'd on each shelf,
Are vanish'd by what he has written himself.

5. Sir William Temple (1628-99), statesman and patron of Swift. His 'Essay upon the Ancient and Modern Learning' (1690), which praised the learning of the 'ancients', drew criticism from Bentley and Wotton.
6. Charles Boyle (1676-1731), fourth earl of Orrery 1703, became involved in the controversy over the 'ancients' and the 'moderns'.
7. laurels, the rewards or honours for the victors.
8. The battle of the books, as Swift told it, was fought between the ancient and modern volumes in St James's Library — the royal library housed in St James's Palace, London — where Bentley was keeper of the books.

MATTHEW PILKINGTON

THE GIFT

Oppress'd *Hibernia*, in Despair,
Complains to *Jove*[1] in fervent Pray'r
How fast her Liberties decay,
How fast her Honours fade away;
Her *Sons* to no Preferment rise
Tho' Earth can boast of few so Wise;
How Poor, how Desolate she grows,
And begs Redress of all her Woes.

Then *Jove*: '*Hibernia* sues too late,
Her Sorrows are decreed by Fate;
But Heav'n those Sorrows shall Repay
With Blessings in a nobler Way.
Let Haughty *Britain* boast no more,
With scornful Pride, her golden Store,
That distant Worlds her Name revere,
That Arts and Learning flourish there;
To raise thy glory, we design
To bless thee with a *Gift* Divine,
A *Gift* by which thy injur'd Name
Shall fill th' immortal voice of Fame,

1. Jupiter, the Roman counterpart of the Greek Zeus, the father of the gods.

That *Albion*[2] may with Envy see
Her Glories far surpass'd by thee.'

Hibernia thanks him for the Gift,
And owns, She's overpaid in *Swift*.

2. An ancient name for Britain.

PATRICK DELANY
(*c.* 1685-1768)

NEWS FROM PARNASSUS

Parnassus,[1] *February* the twenty-seventh,
The *Poets* assembled here on the Eleventh;
Conven'd by *Apollo*,[2] who gave them to know,
He'd have a *Vicegerent* in his Empire below;
But declar'd that no *Bard* shou'd this Honour
inherit,
'Till the rest had agreed he surpass'd them in Merit:
Now this you'll allow was a difficult Case,
For each *Bard* believ'd he had a Right to the Place;
So finding the Assembly grow warm in Debate,
He put 'em in Mind of his *Phaeton*'s[3] Fate:
'Twas urged to no Purpose, the Dispute higher rose,
Scarce *Phœbus*[4] himself cou'd their Quarrels
compose.
'Till at length he determin'd that every *Bard*
Shou'd (each in their Turn) be patiently heard.

First, one who believ'd he excell'd in Translation,[5]
Founds his Claim on the Doctrine of
Transmigration:[6]
'Since the Soul of great *Milton*[7] was given to me,
I hope the Convention will quickly agree —'

1. The mountain range in Greece sacred to Dionysus and associated with Apollo and the Muses, Parnassus becomes a metaphor for the sources of inspiration for poetry and song.
2. The god of light, reason and the arts in Greek mythology.
3. Alluding to the identification, in Greek mythology, of Apollo with the sun, whose god is Helios, the charioteer. His son Phaeton sought permission to drive the chariot of the sun for one day, but he was unable to control it. The horses bolted and the earth was in danger of being consumed by fire until Zeus, the father of the gods, intervened and transfixed Phaeton with a thunderbolt.
4. An epithet for Apollo, meaning 'the bright'.
5. Dr Joseph Trapp (1679-1747), first professor of poetry at Oxford University 1708-18, chaplain to Henry St John (1678-1751), 1st viscount Bolingbroke and Tory versifier and translator.
6. The teaching that the souls of the dead pass into other bodies.
7. John Milton (1608-74).

'Agree,' quoth *Apollo*, 'from whence is this Fool?
Is he just come from reading *Pythagoras*[8] at School?
Begone, Sir, you've got your Subscriptions in
Time,
And giv'n in Return neither Reason nor Rhyme.'[9]

'To the *next*,'[10] says the God, 'tho' now I
won't chuse you,
I'll tell you the Reason for which I refuse you;
Love's Goddess has oft to her Parent complain'd,
Of my fav'ring a *Bard* who her Empire disdain'd,
That at my Instigation a Poem you writ,
Which to Beauty and Youth prefer'd Judgment and
Wit;
That to make you a Laureat I gave the first Voice,
Inspiring the *Britons* t'approve of my Choice.
Jove[11] sent her to me her Power to try;
The Goddess of *Beauty* what God can deny?
She forbids your Preferment, I grant her Desire,
Appease the fair Goddess, you then may rise
higher.'

The *next*[12] that appear'd, had good Hopes of
succeeding,
For he merited much for his Wit and his Breeding.
'Twas wise in the *Britons* no favour to shew him,
He else might expect they shou'd pay what they
owe him.
And therefore they prudently chose to discard
The Patriot, whose Merits they wou'd not reward.
The God with a Smile bid his Fav'rite advance,
'You were sent by *Astrea*[13] her Envoy to *France*.
You bent your Ambition to rise in the *State*,
I refuse you, because you cou'd stoop to be great.'

Then a *Bard*,[14] who had been a successful
Translator,
'The Convention allows me a Versificator.'

8. Greek philosopher and mathematician of the sixth century B.C., who believed in the transmigration of souls.
9. i.e. you have solicited advance subscriptions for your works, but have not given the subscribers either reason or rhyme in the works themselves.
10. Probably Laurence Eusden (1688-1730), poet laureate 1718-30.
11. Jupiter, the Roman counterpart of the Greek Zeus, the father of the gods.
12. Matthew Prior (1664-1721), English poet, who joined the Tory party and who was sent in 1711 on a secret mission to Paris during the negotiations that culminated in the Treaty of Utrecht (1713).
13. The constellation Virgo, known as the 'Starry Maid'; i.e. Queen Anne.
14. Alexander Pope (1688-1744), English poet, whose translation of Homer's *Iliad* was completed in 1720, the year before Delany's poem was published. His *Odyssey* appeared in 1725-26.

Says *Apollo*, 'You mention the least of your Merit,
By your Works it appears you have much of my
Spirit;
I esteem you so well, that to tell you the Truth,
The greatest Objection against you's your Youth;[15]
Then be not concern'd you are now laid aside,
If you live you shall certainly one Day preside.'

Another,[16] low bending, *Apollo* thus greets,
''Twas I taught your Subjects to walk thro' the
Streets.'
'You taught 'em to walk, why they knew it before,
But give me the *Bard* that can teach them to soar;
Whenever he claims his Right, I'll confess
Who lately attempted my Style with Success;
Who writes like *Apollo*, has most of his Spirit,
And therefore 'tis just I distinguish his Merit;
Who makes it appear by all he has writ,
His Judgment alone can set Bounds to his Wit;
Like *Virgil*[17] correct, with his own Native Ease,
But excels ev'n *Virgil* in elegant Praise;
Who admires the Ancients,[18] and knows 'tis their
due,
Yet writes in a Manner entirely new;
Tho' none with more Ease their Depths can explore,
Yet whatever he wants he takes from my Store;
Tho' I'm fond of his Virtues, his Pride I can see,
In scorning to borrow from any but me;
'Tis owing to this, that like *Cynthia*,[19] his Lays[20]
Enlighten the World by reflecting my Rays.'
This said, the whole Audience soon found out his
Drift,
The Convention was summon'd in Favour of
Sw—t.

15. Pope was then thirty-three.
16. John Gay (1685-1732), English poet and dramatist, whose *Trivia: or, the Art of Walking the Streets of London* appeared in 1716.
17. The great epic poet of the beginnings of the Roman Empire, Virgil (70-19 B.C.) is best known for the *Aeneid*.
18. The authors of the Graeco-Roman world.
19. The moon, a name given to Artemis, the sister of Apollo.
20. ballads, narrative poems, particularly those meant to be sung.

ESTHER JOHNSON ('STELLA')

(1681-1728)

TO DR. SWIFT *ON HIS BIRTH-DAY*

November 30, 1721

St. Patrick's dean, your country's pride,
My early and my only guide,[1]
Let me among the rest attend,
Your pupil and your humble friend,
To celebrate in female strains
The day that paid your mother's pains;
Descend to take that tribute due
In gratitude alone to you.
When men began to call me fair,
You interpos'd your timely care;
You early taught me to despise
The ogling of a coxcomb's[2] eyes;
Shew'd where my judgment was misplac'd;
Refin'd my fancy and my taste.
Behold that beauty just decay'd,
Invoking art to nature's aid;
Forsook by her admiring train
She spreads her tatter'd nets in vain;
Short was her part upon the stage;
Went smoothly on for half a page;
Her bloom was gone, she wanted art,
As the scene chang'd, to change her part:
She, whom no lover could resist,
Before the second act was hiss'd.
Such is the fate of female race
With no endowments but a face;
Before the thirti'th year of life
A maid forlorn, or hated wife.
STELLA to you, her tutor, owes
That she has ne'er resembled those;
Nor was a burthen to mankind
With half her course of years behind.[3]
You taught how I might youth prolong
By knowing what was right and wrong;
How from my heart to bring supplies
Of lustre to my fading eyes;
How soon a beauteous mind repairs
The loss of chang'd or falling hairs;
How wit and virtue from within
Send out a smoothness o'er the skin:
Your lectures cou'd my fancy fix,
And I can please at thirty-six.[4]
The sight of CHLOE[5] at fifteen
Coquetting, gives not me the spleen;[6]
The idol now of every fool
'Till time shall make their passions cool;
Then tumbling down time's steepy hill,
While STELLA holds her station still.
Oh! turn your precepts into laws,
Redeem the women's ruin'd cause,
Retrieve lost empire to our sex,
That men may bow their rebel necks.
Long be the day that gave you birth
Sacred to friendship, wit, and mirth;
Late dying may you cast a shred
Of your rich mantle o'er my head;
To bear with dignity my sorrow,
One day *alone, then die to-morrow.*

1. Swift had evidently known Stella since 1689, when he joined the household of Sir William Temple at Moor Park, Surrey. One of his duties was to act as her tutor.
2. An excessively fashionable young man.
3. Stella, born on 13 March 1681, was now forty.
4. A playful reference to her age.
5. A favourite contemporary romantic name, derived from the shepherdess in the Greek pastoral romance *Daphnis and Chloe*.
6. melancholy.

MARY BARBER

ON SENDING MY SON, AS A PRESENT, TO DR. *SWIFT*, DEAN OF ST. *PATRICK*'S, ON HIS BIRTH-DAY[1]

A Curious Statue, we are told,
Is priz'd above its Weight in Gold;
If the fair Form the Hand confess
Of *Phidias*,[2] or *Praxiteles*:[3]
But if the Artist could inspire
The smallest Spark of heav'nly Fire,
Tho' but enough to make it walk,
Salute the Company, or talk;
This would advance the Price so high,
What Prince were rich enough to buy?
Such if *Hibernia* could obtain,
She sure would give it to the *Dean*:[4]
So to her Patriot should she pay
Her Thanks upon his Natal Day.

A RICHER Present I design,
A finish'd Form, of Work divine,
Surpassing all the Pow'r of Art,
A thinking Head, and grateful Heart,

1. This poem was written for Swift's birthday, 30 November 1726. It was published in Barber's *Poems on Several Occasions* (1734).
2. Phidias (*c.* 500-*c.* 432 B.C.), Athenian sculptor and architect.
3. Athenian sculptor, *fl. c.* 370-*c.* 330 B.C.
4. The rhyme with 'obtain' suggests the Hiberno-English pronunciation of '*Dean*'.

An Heart, that hopes, one Day, to show
How much we to the *Drapier* owe.[5]

KINGS could not send a *nobler* Gift;
A *meaner* were unworthy *Swift*.

5. i.e. for his part in forcing the withdrawal of the patent for Wood's Halfpence in 1725.

THOMAS SHERIDAN

(1687-1738)

TO THE *DEAN*, WHEN IN ENGLAND, IN 1726[1]

You will excuse me, I suppose,
For sending rhyme instead of prose,
Because hot weather makes me lazy,
To write in metre is more easy.

While you are trudging London town,
I'm stroling Dublin, up and down;
While you converse with lords and dukes,
I have their betters here, my books:
Fix'd in an elbow chair at ease,
I chuse companions as I please.
I'd rather have one single shelf,
Than all my friends, except your self;
For after all that can be said,
Our best acquaintance, are the dead.
While you're in raptures with Faustina,[2]
I'm charm'd at home, with our Sheelina;[3]
While you are starving there in state,
I'm cramming here with butcher's meat:
You say, when with those Lords you dine,
They treat you with the best of wine;
Burgundy, Cyprus, and Tockay,[4]
Why so can we, as well as they.
No reason, my dear Dean,
But you should travel home again.
What tho' you mayn't in Ireland hope,
To find such folk as Gay and Pope:[5]
If you with rhymers here would share,
But half the wit, that you can spare;
I'd lay twelve eggs, that in twelve days,
You'd make a doz'n of Popes and Gays.

Our weather's good, our sky is clear,
We've ev'ry joy, if you were here;
So lofty, and so bright a skie,
Was never seen by *Ireland's-Eye!*[6]
I think it fit to let you know,
This week I shall to Quilca[7] go;
To see McFayden's[8] horny brothers,
First suck, and after bull their mothers.
To see alas, my wither'd trees!
To see what all the country sees!
My stunted quicks,[9] my famish'd beeves,[10]
My servants such a pack of thieves;
My shatter'd firs, my blasted oaks,
My house in common to all folks:
No cabbage for a single snail,
My turnips, carrots, parsnips, fail;
My no green pease, my few green sprouts,
My mother always in the pouts:
My horses rid, or gone astray,
My fish all stol'n, or run away:
My mutton lean, my pullets old,
My poultry starv'd, the corn all sold.

A man come now, from Quilca says,
They've[11] stolen the locks from all your keys:
But what must fret and vex me more,
He says, they stole the keys before.
They've stol'n the knives from all the forks,
And half the cows from half the sturks;[12]
Nay more, the fellow swears and vows,
They've stol'n the sturks from half the cows.

1. Swift was in England from March to August 1726, after an absence of twelve years. He saw much of Pope, and made arrangements for the publication of *Gulliver's Travels*, which appeared that October.
2. Faustina Bordoni (1700-81), an Italian mezzo-soprano, who made her London debut in Handel's *Alessandro* at the King's Theatre, London in May 1726.
3. A playful variant of Sheila, Sheela or Shelagh, anglicized forms of the Irish Síle; i.e. a local, Irish girl.
4. Tokaj (Tokay) is a wine-producing town in Hungary.
5. John Gay (1685-1732), English poet and dramatist, and Alexander Pope (1688-1744), English poet, translator and editor, were the most prominent members of Swift's London circle.
6. A small island in the Irish Sea just north of Dublin.
7. In County Cavan, where Sheridan maintained a house.
8. Evidently the name of one of Sheridan's cattle, possibly inspired by a local farmer.
9. quicksets, plants or cuttings, especially of hawthorn, set so as to form a hedge.
10. The plural of beef; i.e. cattle.
11. 'They, is the grand thief of the county of Cavan; for whatever is stolen, if you enquire of a servant about it, the answer is, *They* have stolen it' (Swift's editor, George Faulkner).
12. An obsolete form of stirks: young bullocks or heifers.

With many more accounts of woe,
Yet tho' the devil be there, I'll go:
'Twixt you and me, the reason's clear,
Because, I've more vexation here.

JAMES ARBUCKLE

(*c.*1700-42)

MOMUS MISTAKEN: A FABLE, OCCASIONED BY THE PUBLICATION OF THE WORKS OF THE REVD. DR. SWIFT, D.S.P.D. IN DUBLIN[1]

One Day, as is his Wont, the Dean
Was sauntr'ing through a dirty Lane,
And snugly laughing in his Sleeve
At what would graver Mortals grieve,
The Crowds of Fools, both Low, and High,
Passing, in idle Hurry, by,
Merc'ry,[2] 'tis said to aid his Laughter,
Follow'd some little Distance after,
Not in the Shape he wears above,
Or brings down Messages from Jove,[3]
But in a Form, true Politicks,
Will own much fitter for those Tricks
Of Theft, the God did whilome use;
A Black-guard Crier of the News.[4]

What Conversation pass'd between
This merry Pair in such a Scene,
What Waggish Jokes, and sly Remarks
Between the Damsels and their Sparks,[5]
The Muse at present hath forgot;
Nor is't essential to her Plot:
But sure, 'twould form of Mirth a Tale
Might *Pope*,[6] and all his Friends regale.
Not He, nor They would blush to sit,
And shake at such strange Turns of Wit.

Scarce had they half a Street trudg'd through,
Ere *Momus*[7] met them full in View;
A Fellow said to be a God,
But of a Temper somewhat odd,
Addicted much to Jeers, and Gybes;
Eternal Foe to tender Kybes;[8]
And, with but slender Skill in Letters,
Was always carping at his Betters.

But Gods themselves, whatever Wonders
We Mortals think them, can make Blunders.
To put which Doctrine past all Doubt,
Momus himself shall make it out.
For tho' he critically ey'd
Our Drapier's human Shape and Hide,
Yet, 'tis prodigious[9] to relate
What a strange Maggot[10] seiz'd his Pate,[11]
'An old Acquaintance this,' he cries,
'Faith, 'tis *Apollo*[12] in Disguise,
What need of further Proof? Depend on't,
It is the Rascal, by's[13] Attendant.'
Then instantly resolved to roast[14] him,
Thus, with a Sneer, he did accost him.
'Your Godship's Servant! So, I find
You've got some *Daphne*[15] in the Wind.
Why else in such a scurvy Place;
Disguis'd too in that Garb of Grace;[16]
And with your Scoundrel Pimp[17] equipp'd,
So well deserving to be whipp'd,
What! will a God of Wit and Learning
For ever thus be deaf to Warning?
Can no Misfortunes in Amours[18]
Suffice to put an End to yours?

1. The four-volume edition of Swift's works, which was the first collected edition of his writings and which carried the imprint of George Faulkner, Dublin, 1735, was released between November 1734 and January 1735. 'D.S.P.D.' stands for Dean of St Patrick's, Dublin.
2. The Roman counterpart of the Greek Hermes, Mercury was the messenger of the gods.
3. Jupiter, the Roman counterpart of the Greek Zeus, was the father of the gods.
4. Mercury, a successful thief, came to be the god of trade, commerce, thieves and pickpockets. He also attended to the interests of travellers, herdsmen and orators, and was particularly associated with carrying news and information. He is cast here as a newsboy.
5. smart, fashionable young men, suitors.
6. Alexander Pope (1688-1744), the foremost verse satirist of the age, and a member of Swift's London circle.
7. The god of ridicule, Momus was particularly associated with fault-finding.
8. feelings; 'kibes' are chilblains.
9. amazing.
10. fancy or whim.
11. head.
12. The god of light, in the sense of reason, in Greek mythology.
13. by his.
14. ridicule.
15. i.e. lover. Apollo loved Daphne, who escaped his advances when she was turned into a laurel tree. Swift's own relationships with Stella and Vanessa had been the subject of gossip fifteen or twenty years before this poem appeared.
16. clerical attire.
17. i.e. Mercury.
18. Apollo, like other gods, had numerous loves and misfortunes. Again, cf. Swift.

Perhaps, you think, you're Woman-proof,
And always will come safely off;
Or hope to be no worse affronted,
Than when you after *Daphne* hunted,
Where Fortune, to prevent a Quarrel,
Your Misadventure crown'd with Lawrel,
But let me tell you as a Friend,
(Indeed 'tis seldom known to mend)
This lower World is strangely chang'd,
Since with *Admetus'*[19] Sheep you rang'd,
For should you now a Nymph pursue,
Instead of turning into Yew,
Or Birch, or Bays, 'tis, by my Soul, as
Likely, she might become a Bolus.[20]
Then think, how would the Gods endure
To see you spawl[21] their azure Floor?
And must you not at once sustain
The bitterest Pangs of Rage and Pain,
When ev'ry giggling Girl above
Shall smirk, and tip the Wink on Jove,
To smoke[22] your Honour sadly chewing,
The filthy Rags of Caterwawling?'

The Dean look'd gruff, and pass'd him by;
Leaving his Lacquey[23] to reply.
'For once, Friend *Momus*, fairly bit;[24]
No longer now pretend to Wit.
He, whom you see, and make your Jest,
No God is, but a mortal Priest.
And ev'n a Priest of such a Make
As scarce excuses the Mistake;
The God you fancy'd him to be,
'Tis true, hath not more Wit than He;
But herein still a Difference lies,
Your God was once kick'd from the Skies;[25]
And by the righteous Laws of Fate
Was doom'd to fall from God's Estate.
But he, whom proud I call my Master
Is subject to no such Disaster.
These Volumes in my Hand behold!
(In *Faulkner's*[26] Shop they're to be sold)
These shall to future Ages tell,
The Drapier never sunk, or fell.'

19. After he had killed the Cyclops, Apollo sentenced Zeus to work for a year as a herdsman of King Admetus.
20. Medicine unpleasant to take.
21. spit on.
22. ridicule.
23. lackey, attendant.
24. deceived.
25. Alluding to Zeus's sentencing Apollo to work for King Admetus.
26. As George Faulkner's imprint recorded, his shop was in Dublin's '*Essex-Street*, opposite to the Bridge'.

LAURENCE WHYTE

TO THE REV. DR. *JONATHAN SWIFT*, DEAN OF ST *PATRICK'S*, *DUBLIN*, ON THE PUBLISHING OF A NEW EDITION OF HIS WORKS IN FOUR VOLUMES[1]

Pardon, great *Swift*, the Freedom of a Bard!
Who writes for neither Interest, or Reward;
Whose Head cou'd never Politicks distil,
Nor for Preferment prostitute his Quill.

Thou great *Vicegerent*[2] of the sacred *Nine*![3]
To judge of Wit, and Language to refine;
Around the *Globe* their Empire to advance,
And dissipate the Clouds of Ignorance:
To cherish *Virtue*, and her friends caress,
To scourge her Foes, in all their pompous Dress.
To stop the wicked in their full Career,
And to direct them in what path to steer.
To punish Varlets, who dare utter Treason
Against the *Muses* without Rhime or Reason:
With all the Bands of Byblows[4] in Alliance,
For ever warring with the Sons of Science;
Where Laureat *Asses* gravest Nonsense bray,[5]
And greatest *Dunces* have the greatest Pay.[6]

Since you, with open Purse, relieve the Poor,[7]
And by their frequent Blessings, Heav'n insure;

1. The 1735 edition of Swift's works, published by George Faulkner in Dublin for the subscribers, formed the basis of subsequent, expanded editions for the book trade.
2. vice-regent, deputy.
3. The nine Muses of Greek mythology who, as goddesses of literature and the arts, were associated with Pieria near Mount Olympus and with Mount Helicon.
4. bastards. Whyte's note directs attention to the '*scurrilous*' poem, 'A Panegyric on the Reverend Dean Swift in Answer to the Libel on Dr Delany, and a certain Great Lord' (1730), which Harold Williams attributed to Swift, but which recent scholars (D. F. Foxon, Aubrey Williams, James Woolley and Pat Rogers) have suggested should be assigned to James Arbuckle.
5. Alluding to various minor poets who were appointed to the laureateship, such as Laurence Eusden (1688-1730), poet laureate 1718-30.
6. Whyte's note directs attention to Pope's *The Dunciad* (1728) and to Paul Whitehead's 'State Dunces' (1733).
7. The poor were everywhere to be seen in the streets of Dublin, particularly in the Liberty of St Patrick's, and Swift's philanthropy was a matter of public knowledge.

Do not exclude the Brethren of the Quill,[8]
Who stand in need of thy superior skill:
The least Supply from thy *Pierian*[9] Store,
They deem more precious than the *Indian* Ore.[10]
Inspire thy Suppliant to adjust his Thoughts,
Assist his Weakness, and correct his Faults:
Whilst he attempts to sing thy *Works*, and *Thee*,
Let every Line be musical and free.
You best can judge the merits of his Cause,
When he transgresses, or maintains your Laws:
Tho' he obeys the *Muses*, when they call,
'Tis by your Sentence he must stand or fall.

In vain I strive to climb the arduous Hill,[11]
Alas! for want of Genius, Strength and Skill:
My low Productions, and my humble Lays,
No more can raise thy Merits, or thy Praise,
Than he, who bless'd with Benefit of Sight,
Can add new Lustre to the Rays of Light.
Yet with the Nation let me raise my Voice,
And in thy Works, with Millions more rejoice.

These Sheets must raise the Printer's Wealth
and Fame,
Since they receive a Sanction from thy *Name*;
Since every Volume, Page, and nervous[12] Line
Declare their Lineage from a Stock Divine:
These are thy Off-spring, which the Wise
admire,
And shew the Beauties of a learned Sire,
Whether diffus'd in Metre or in Prose,
The Stile is easy, and the Reasons close;
The Thoughts extensive, free, and unconfin'd,
To entertain and cultivate the Mind.

When summon'd by *Apollo*[13] to retire
From publick Cares, to touch the warbling Lyre;
The *Nine* with all the *Graces* thee attend,
Admire thy Lays, and ev'ry Strain commend;
Whether thy Theme be moral or divine,
True Wit and Spirit in each Period[14] shine;

Whilst *Merit* in the clearest Light is shewn,
You still remain unmindful of your own.

Here *Virtue* soars triumphant in the Skies;
There *Vice*[15] is damn'd in ev'ry Shape and Size.
No Grandeur guards the Vicious from thy
Stings,
Who scorn to flatter Statesmen, Lords, or
Kings.
No reigning Folly of the present Age
But you've severely lash'd with pious Rage:
And thus you labour to reform our Isle
By sharp Invectives, Irony, or Smile.

Good Sense will ever bear the Test of Time,
When richly clad like *yours*, in Prose or Rhime;
And like the Products of old *Greece* and
Rome,
Yours must continue in perpetual Bloom.

Here may the Learned chuse their Bills of
Fare,
To serve for all the Seasons of the Year:
For ev'ry Palate they may find a Page,
For either Sex, of any Rank or Age.
And in thy Volumes find a sumptuous Feast,
A choice Regale[16] for Men of Wit and Taste,
For ever new, when rightly understood,
And when digested, proves delightful Food.

Thy Works are Mirrours, where Mankind
may see
Their Portraitures in perfect Symmetry.
Some laugh to find their Vanities display'd,
And others of their Pictures are afraid.
The Hypocrite's astonish'd without doubt,
When he beholds himself turn'd Inside out.
My Lord starts back — and from his Shadow
flies;
'Am I that Monster? — Heav'n forbid,' he cries,
'It must be so — if I may trust my Sight,
An evil Genius, — or some hideous Sprite.'
Turns on his Heel, and takes a Pinch of Snuff,
Cry's, 'Damn the Author, — 'tis but horrid
Stuff.
Get me a Bottle to allay my Grief,
If that won't do it, — there is no Relief.'

8. Swift looked on the contemporary writers in Dublin, as he said in *The Drapier's Letters* (1745-25), as his '*Brethren*, the Makers of *Songs* and *Ballads*' (*Letter to Molesworth*), although there were other occasions when he rejected their approaches.
9. An allusion to the inspiration of the Pierian Muses; see note 3.
10. An emblem for the wealth of the New World.
11. Either Mount Olympus or Mount Helicon, the two mountains in Greece sacred to the Muses.
12. vigorous, forcible.
13. The god of light, in the sense of reason, in Greek mythology, Apollo is presented here as the supreme being.
14. sentence.
15. Whyte's note directs attention to Swift's 'The Place of the Damned' (1731).
16. Choice article of food or drink.

When in Disguise a *Gulliver*, or *Drapier*,
The Author's Steps we trace on ev'ry Paper,
Apollo's Rays we easily descry
Diffus'd thro' gloomy Regions of the Sky.
The Bird of *Jove*[17] by his superior Flight,
A brilliant Star, from *Luna*'s[18] borrow'd Light,
And the whole Frame of *Hercules*[19] compute
By the Impression of the Hero's Foot.
Where'er thy Fancy leads us, we pursue,
And view the world, still as we follow you,
To Climes we sail, unheard of heretofore,
From *British* Isles, to *Lilliputian*[20] Shore;
Pigmies and Giants in our Travels meet,
With strange Adventures starting from each Sheet,
The Pencil's lively Draught thy Pen supplies,
And ev'ry Leaf's a Landskip[21] to our Eyes.

What grateful Tribute can be paid by Men,
Who owe their safety to thy matchless Pen;
A *Pen*, which had the Power to reconcile
The jarring Sects, and Parties of our Isle
To strictest Union, for the Common Good,
Against the Torrent of a brazen Flood,[22]
Which had destroy'd, and overspread our Land,
If not prevented by the *Drapier*'s Hand;
Who, like a Guardian-Angel, did preside,
And by his Influ'nce stem'd the rapid Tide.
Thus *Moses*[23] made the Waters to give Way,
And led his *People* thro' the raging Sea.
Behold thy *Pen* exceeds the Prophet's Wand,
That from a second Deluge sav'd our Land.

Long may our Isle with such a sage be blest,
Who has her Int'rest ever in his Breast;
When Death, at length, shall close our *Patriot*'s Eyes,
And fir'd with *Zeal*, his Soul transcends the Skies,
A second *Swift* must from his Ashes rise.[24]

17. Jupiter, the Roman counterpart of the Greek Zeus, the father of the gods. His bird was the eagle.
18. The Roman goddess of the moon.
19. The Roman counterpart of the Greek Heracles, the hero of the ancient world who performed a series of twelve labours.
20. From Lilliput, one of the imaginary countries in Swift's *Gulliver's Travels* (1726).
21. i.e. page is a landscape.
22. Referring to the unity of opposition in Ireland to the proposal to circulate Wood's Halfpence. During the campaign against the coinage, Swift in *The Drapier's Letters* repeatedly raised the prospect that Ireland would be deluged with debased money, which he dismissed as being composed of brass.
23. The Old Testament prophet who led the Israelites away from Egypt to the safety of the Promised Land and who revealed God's laws to them. With divine help, the waters of the Red Sea gave way before the Israelites, enabling them to escape from the pursuing Egyptians.
24. '*Alluding to the* Phoenix, *an* Arabian *Bird, said to live alone for many Years, and then to burn herself in a Nest of Spices; from whose Ashes springs a young One*' (Whyte).

ON *ST*. PATRICK'S-EVE

Dublin, Friday March *the* 16*th*, 1738

All over *Ireland*, 'tis the common Way,
To drink St. *Patrick*'s Pot on *Patrick*'s Day,
A greater Scope to Merriment we give,
Who, at the *Bull's-Head*, celebrate the Eve.
Heaven bless'd the Saint, let *Ireland* bless his *Dean*,
Let all his Days be happy and serene,
Who draws his Pen, her Welfare to support,
'Gainst Bosom Foes, and Managers at Court,
Whilst all the *Saints* that Whilom[1] bless'd our *Isle*,
Look down with Joy, and on our *Patriot* Smile,
Bless'd with a *Genius*, and a fruitful Vein,
With such a Turn peculiar to his *Strain*,
To lash at *Vice*, the *Pest* of ev'ry reign.

1. once.

WILLIAM DUNKIN

AN EPISTLE TO R[O]B[ER]T N[U]G[EN]T, ESQUIRE,[1] WITH A PICTURE OF DOCTOR SWIFT

To gratify thy long desire,
(So love and piety require)
From B[i]nd[o]n's[2] colours you may trace
The PATRIOT'S venerable face,
The last, O N[u]g[e]nt! which his art
Shall ever to the world impart;[3]

1. Robert Nugent (1702-88), viscount Clare and baron Nugent 1766, politician in both England and Ireland, and minor poet. In December 1733 the legal arrangements were finalized for his lease of Deane Swift's property at Castlerickard, Co. Meath, in which Swift had a financial interest. Swift visited him at Castlerickard in May 1735.
2. Francis Bindon (died 1765), painter and architect, who painted Swift's portrait in 1735, 1739 and apparently also *c.* 1740.
3. Dunkin appears to be referring here to the portrait of Swift that Bindon painted for Nugent. In 1740 Nugent mentioned it in a letter

For know, the prime of mortal men,
That matchless monarch of the pen,
(Whose labours, like the genial sun,
Shall through revolving ages run,
Yet never, like the sun, decline,
But in their full meridian shine)
That ever-honour'd, envy'd sage,
So long the wonder of his age,
Who charm'd us with his golden strain,
Is not the shadow of the Dean:
He only breathes Bœothian[4] air —
'Oh! what a falling off was there?'

Hibernia's Helicon[5] is dry,
Invention, wit and humour die,
And what remains against the storm
Of malice, but an empty form?
The nodding ruins of a pile,[6]
That stood the bulwark of this isle?
In which the sisterhood was fix'd
Of candid honour, truth unmix'd,
Imperial reason, thought profound,
And charity, diffusing round
In cheerful rivulets the flow
Of fortune to the sons of woe?

Such once, my N[u]g[en]t, was thy Swift,
Endu'd[7] with each exalted gift.
But, lo! the pure ætherial flame
Is darken'd by a misty steam:
The balm exhausted breathes no smell,
The rose is wither'd, ere it fell.
That godlike supplement of law,
That held the wicked world in awe,
And could the tide of faction stem,
Is but a shell without the gem.

Ye sons of genius, who would aim
To build an everlasting fame,
And, in the field of letter'd arts,
Display the trophies of your parts,[8]
To yonder mansion turn aside,
And mortify your growing pride.
Behold the brightest of the race,
And nature's honour in disgrace:
With humble resignation own,
That all your talents are a loan,
By Providence advanc'd for use,
Which you should study to produce.
Reflect, the mental stock, alas!
However current now it pass,
May haply be recall'd from you,[9]
Before the grave demands his due.
Then, while your morning-star proceeds,
Direct your course to worthy deeds,
In fuller day discharge your debts;
For, when your sun of reason sets,
The night succeeds, and all your schemes
Of glory vanish with your dreams.

Ah! where is now the supple train,
That danc'd attendance on the Dean?
Say, where are those facetious folks,
Who shook with laughter at his jokes,
And with attentive rapture hung
On wisdom, dropping from his tongue?
Who look'd with high disdainful pride
On all the busy world beside,
And rated his productions more
Than treasures of Peruvian ore?[10]

Good Christians! they with bended knees
Ingulph'd[11] the wine, but loath the lees,[12]
Averting (so the text commands)
With ardent eyes and upcast hands,
The cup of sorrow from their lips,
And fly, like rats from sinking ships.
While some, who by his friendship rose
To wealth, in concert with his foes
Run counter to their former track,
Like old Actæon's[13] horrid pack
Of yelling mungrils, in requitals[14]

from Bath to Mrs Whiteway: 'I must beg that you will let Mr. *Bindon* know I would have the picture no more than a head upon a three-quarter cloth, to match one which I now have of Mr. *Pope*.'

4. Alluding to the fact that Mount Helicon, one of the two mountains in ancient Greece that were sacred to the Muses, was in Boeotia. 'Bœothian air', then, suggests the air of the Muses themselves.
5. Alluding to the two springs on Mount Helicon that were sacred to the Muses: Aganippe, near the base, and Hippocrene, near the summit; i.e. the source of Ireland's poetic inspiration.
6. great building.
7. endowed.
8. abilities.
9. i.e. reflect that your mental powers, however genuine they are at present, may well be taken from you before . . . .
10. An emblem for the wealth of the New World, recalling the riches of Peru.
11. swallowed up.
12. sediment, dregs.
13. Actaeon fell foul of Artemis, the sister of Apollo, either because he claimed to be a better hunter than she was or because he happened to see her bathing. She turned him into a stag and he was then savaged to death by his own hounds.
14. revenge.

To riot on their master's vitals,
And, where they cannot blast his laurels,
Attempt to stigmatize his morals:
Through scandal's magnifying glass
His foibles view, but virtues pass,
And, on the ruins of his fame,
Erect an ignominious name.
So vermin foul of base extraction,
The spawn of dirt and putrefaction,
The sounder members traverse o'er,
But fix, and fatten on a sore.
Hence! peace, ye wretches, who revile
His wit, his humour, and his style,
Since all the monsters, which he drew
Were only meant to copy you,
And, if the colours be not fainter,
Arraign yourselves, and not the painter.

But, O! that He, who gave him breath,
Dread arbiter of life and death,
That He, the moving soul of all,
The sleeping spirit would recall,
And crown him with triumphant meeds,[15]
For all his past heroic deeds,
In mansions of unbroken rest,
The bright republic of the bless'd!
Irradiate his benighted mind
With living light of light refin'd,
And there the blank of thought employ
With objects of immortal joy!

Yet, while he drags the sad remains
Of life, slow-creeping through his veins,
Above the views of private ends,
The tributary[16] Muse attends,
To prop his feeble steps, or shed
The pious tear around his bed.

So pilgrims, with devout complaints,
Frequent the graves of martyr'd saints,
Inscribe their worth in artless lines,
And, in their stead, embrace their shrines.

15. rewards.
16. i.e. paying tribute.

III

'My love ... is ... firmly fixt'

There is, as the selection that follows shows clearly, no unity of approach to the subject of love among eighteenth-century Anglo-Irish poets. Their poems range from the neoclassical to the earthy, from the elegance of Thomas Parnell's lyric to Samuel Whyte's piece of myth-making or Henry Code's stage song of the innocent Irishman. The traditions of the Renaissance, which are echoed in Parnell's imagery of the beloved and in Laetitia Pilkington's suggestion of some of the conventions of pastoral literature, disappear as the various satiric elements of the period come to the fore; these may be seen in John Winstanley's use of mimicry in '*A* Song, *by a* Cumberland-Lass', with its hints of a regional dialect, in Swift's use of burlesque in 'A Pastoral Dialogue', in James Dalacourt's 'On his Brother's Marriage' and in Laurence Whyte's '*The Old* Westmeath-Ballad'. Yet the satiric, which was never divorced from the ballad tradition, as Pilkington's 'The Happy Pair' or Whyte's '*The Old* Westmeath-Ballad' reveal, eventually gave way to the song-lyric, which reasserted itself as the eighteenth century advanced, as George Ogle's 'Mailligh a Stór' demonstrates.

If there is a recurrent element in these poems, then it is clearly the tradition of song, which invigorates the different forms that appear throughout the eighteenth century. Some poems, such as Samuel Whyte's 'The Hone', an extended pun on 'hone' and 'ohone', which weaves a story around the local myths of the properties of the water of Lough Neagh, lie outside this tradition, but others, such as the anonymous ballad 'The Boys of Kilkenny' and Code's 'Song', direct us to consider love as a social phenomenon. Code's poem, which was written some years before it was published in *The Russian Sacrifice*; *or*, *The Burning of Moscow* (1813), and which develops the theme of the first verse of 'The Boys of Kilkenny', makes the lover into the representative of the national character. Code moves beyond love and into international politics, however, since he supports the Duke of Wellington and the wish of Spain to be freed from French control in 1813.

JOHN WINSTANLEY

A SONG, *BY A* CUMBERLAND-LASS

What tho' I came from *Cumberland*![1]
  Yet I can write and read-*a*,
By which you well may understand,
  I came of a good *Breed-a*.
What tho' my Voice be not so sweet,
  As those bred in a *City*,
Yet in my Cloaths, I am as neat,
  And in my Thoughts as pretty,
As any of the *Dublin Dames*,
  Who Powder, or wear Patch-*a*,[2]
And boast of their creating Flames,[3]
  With Sonnet or a Catch-*a*.[4]
I think I have ten thousand Charms,
  Of which I now may boast-*a*,
I've often caus'd as great Alarms,
  Nay more than any *Toast-a*.[5]
I think myself an equal Match
  For *Parson* or for *Poet*,
The one or t'other, I hope to catch,
  And I care not who does know it.
For I can bake, and I can brew,
  And can raise a Pye-*a*,
And I know how to milk a Cow,
  I'm sure this is no Lye-*a*.
I can almost do any thing,
  Fit for a *Maid* or *Wife-a*,
I hitherto have had my swing,
  And hope for't all my *Life-a*.

1. Formerly a county of north-west England, and now part of Cumbria, Cumberland faces Ireland across the Irish Sea.
2. A small piece of black or coloured silk, worn on the face as a beauty spot.
3. strong passions.
4. A round of a song, in which one singer catches at the words of another, producing sometimes ludicrous effects.
5. An attractive woman to whom toasts of good health were frequently drunk.

A *SONG* UPON AN INTENDED JAUNT TO *POWER*'S-*COURT*[1] TO SEE MISS P——— *L*———

To the Tune of, Which no Body can deny[2]

1. A large house about ten miles to the south of Dublin in County Wicklow, Powerscourt lies in attractive hilly country.
2. 'Which nobody can deny' came to be the title by which a short version of the popular late sixteenth-century air 'Greensleeves' was known

I'll sing you a Song, on a comical Theme,
Of a whimsical Jaunt, or a Jaunt like a Dream,
Or of no Jaunt at all, which you'll say's much the
  same.
  Which no Body can deny.

There's a Place near a Vale, a Mountain, or Glin,[3]
I can't tell you which, having never there been,
But, they say it's ten Miles from fair *Dublin*.
  Which, *&c*.

This Place, of a late Lord deceas'd,[4] was the Seat;
But by his Demise, (as next Heir to th' Estate)
Is fall'n to one, tho' no Lord, yet as great.
  Which, *&c*.

Who welcomes his Friends so kindly, (I hear)
With all Sorts of Wine, and other good Chear,
Enough to make any one long to be there.
  Which, *&c*.

Here a Spark[5] had intended a Jaunt to be merry;
Some may think to drink Claret, Hock, White-wine
  or Sherry,
But, in Truth, for a Taste of a Cask of sweet *Perry*.[6]
  Which, *&c*.

A Liquor he lov'd, and fancy'd so dear,
That (tho' he despair'd of broaching[7] it there)
Yet, he'd took with a Lick of the Cask for his Share.
  Which, *&c*.

The Morn' was appointed, this same Spark, and I,
With a jolly gay Friend, one *George Willoughby*,
Were to ride there on Horseback, or in Chair[8] to fly.
  Which, *&c*.

from the middle of the seventeenth century. This version was particularly suited to a stanza with three lines and a refrain, each line containing eleven or twelve syllables, which were arranged to create a predominantly anapaestic tetrameter (Claude M. Simpson).
3. glen.
4. Sir Richard Wingfield (*c*. 1550-1634), viscount Powerscourt, who had no direct descendants. His property passed through various members of the Wingfield family to Richard Wingfield (1697-1751), member of parliament for Boyle, County Roscommon 1727-44, who was created baron Wingfield and viscount Powerscourt in 1743. Winstanley's poem was published in his *Poems Written Occasionally* . . . (1742).
5. A smart, fashionable young man.
6. The woman's first name; also a cider made of pears.
7. Tapping the cask to draw off the wine.
8. A light carriage drawn by two horses, a chaise.

Now, whether the Horses were plagu'd with sore
Heels,
Or a Fracture had happ'd to the Chair, or the
Wheels,
But the Jaunt was broke off by a Trick of the De'ils.[9]
Which, *&c.*

A curs'd Disappointment this, by the by,
To see neither *Powers-court*, nor Miss *P——y*
Both which I may yet do, before that I dye.
Which, *&c.*

9. devils.

THOMAS PARNELL

(1679-1718)

SONG

When thy Beauty appears
In its Graces and Airs,
All bright as an Angel new dropt from the Sky;
At distance I gaze, and am aw'd by my Fears,
So strangely you dazzle my Eye!

But when without Art,
Your kind Thoughts you impart,
When your Love runs in Blushes thro' ev'ry Vein;
When it darts from your Eyes, when it pants in
your Heart,
Then I know you're a Woman again.

There's a Passion and Pride
In our Sex, (she reply'd,)
And thus (might I gratify both) I wou'd do:
Still an Angel appear to each Lover beside,
But still be a Woman to you.

JONATHAN SWIFT

A PASTORAL DIALOGUE

DERMOT, SHEELAH[1]

A Nymph and Swain, *Sheelah* and *Dermot* hight,[2]
Who wont to weed the Court of *Gosford Knight*,[3]
While each with stubbed[4] Knife remov'd the Roots
That rais'd between the Stones their daily Shoots;
As at their Work they sate in counterview,[5]
With mutual Beauty smit, their Passion grew.
Sing heavenly Muse in sweetly flowing Strain,
The soft Endearments of the Nymph and Swain.

DERMOT

My Love to *Sheelah* is more firmly fixt
Than strongest Weeds that grow these Stones
betwixt:
My Spud[6] these Nettles from the Stones can part,
No Knife so keen to weed thee from my Heart.

SHEELAH

My Love for gentle *Dermot* faster grows
Than yon tall Dock[7] that rises to thy Nose.
Cut down the Dock, 'twill sprout again: but O!
Love rooted out, again will never grow.

DERMOT

No more that Bry'r[8] thy tender Leg shall rake:
(I spare the Thistle for Sir *Arthur*'s sake.)[9]
Sharp are the Stones, take thou this rushy Matt;
The hardest Bum will bruise with sitting squat.

SHEELAH

Thy Breeches torn behind, stand gaping wide;
This Petticoat shall save thy dear Back-side;
Nor need I blush, although you feel it wet;
Dermot, I vow, 'tis nothing else but Sweat.

DERMOT

At an old stubborn Root I chanc'd to tug,
When the Dean[10] threw me this Tobacco-plug:

1. The anglicized form of the Irish Diarmait or Diarmaid, recalling Diarmait úa Duibne, the greatest lover in Irish literature and the hero of the story, 'The Pursuit of Diarmuid and Gráinne'. Sheelah (Ir. Síle) was considered a typical Irish country-girl's name.
2. called.
3. Sir Arthur Acheson (1688-1749), viscount Gosford, member of parliament for Mullingar, Co. Westmeath 1727-49, who lived at Market Hill, Co. Armagh and whom Swift knew well. His family's seat was at Gosford in Scotland.
4. short.
5. facing each other.
6. The weeding-knife of line 3.
7. A weed with broad leaves.
8. briar.
9. Alluding to the thistle as the symbol of Scotland and hence to Sir Arthur's Scottish ties.
10. Referring to the time Swift spent visiting Sir Arthur and Lady Acheson at Market Hill. He bought land from the Achesons with the intention of building on it, but eventually decided against doing so.

A longer half-p'orth[11] never did I see;
This, dearest *Sheelah*, thou shalt share with me.

SHEELAH

In at the Pantry-door this Morn I slipt,
And from the Shelf a charming Crust I whipt:
Dennis[12] was out, and I got hither safe;
And thou, my dear, shalt have the bigger half.

DERMOT

When you saw *Tady*[13] at long-bullets[14] play,
You sat and lows'd[15] him all the Sun-shine Day.
How could you, *Sheelah*, listen to his Tales,
Or crack such Lice as his betwixt your Nails?

SHEELAH

When you with *Oonah*[16] stood behind a Ditch,
I peept, and saw you kiss the dirty Bitch.
Dermot, how could you touch those nasty Sluts!
I almost wisht this Spud were in your Guts.

DERMOT

If *Oonah* once I kiss'd, forbear to chide:
Her Aunt's my Gossip[17] by my Father's Side:
But, if I ever touch her Lips again,
May I be doom'd for Life to weed in Rain.

SHEELAH

Dermot, I swear, tho' *Tady*'s Locks could hold
Ten thousand Lice, and ev'ry Louse was gold,
Him on my Lap you never more should see;
Or may I loose my Weeding-knife — and Thee.

DERMOT

O, could I earn for thee, my lovely Lass,
A pair of Brogues to bear thee dry to Mass!
But see, where *Norah*[18] with the Sowins[19] comes —
Then let us rise, and rest our weary Bums.

11. The quantity a halfpenny would purchase. A tobacco-plug was a piece of tobacco pressed and twisted so that it could be chewed.
12. 'Sir Arthur's butler' (Swift's editor, George Faulkner).
13. An anglicized form of the Irish Tadhg.
14. A bowling game, now known as road bowling, which is played with an iron ball or 'bullet' on public roads or lanes.
15. cleaned from lice.
16. An anglicized form of the Irish Úna.
17. godmother.
18. The kitchen maid, whose name is an anglicized form of the Irish Onóra.
19. A porridge-like food.

LAETITIA PILKINGTON

(1712-50)

THE HAPPY PAIR. A BALLAD

At Dewy Dawn
As o'er the Lawn,
Young *Roger* early stray'd,
He chanc'd to meet
With *Jenny* sweet,
That blooming Country Maid;
Her Cheeks so red
With Blushes spread,
Shew'd like the breaking Day,
Her modest Look
The Shepherd took;
She stole his Heart away.

With tender Air,
He woo'd the Fair,
And movingly addrest;
For Love divine,
Can Clowns[1] refine,
And warm the coldest Breast;
Her Eyes he prais'd,
And fondly gaz'd,
On her inchanting Face,
Where Innocence,
And Health dispence,
Each winning rosy Grace.

Young *Jenny*'s Breast,
Love's Pow'r confest,
And felt an equal Fire;
Nor had she Art,
To hide her Smart,
Or check the soft Desire.
Hymen[2] unites,
In blissful Rites,
The fair, the matchless two;
And Wedlock ne'er
Could boast a Pair
More lovely or more true.

Ye Rich and Great,
How seldom Fate
Gives you so mild a Doom;

1. countrymen; the term often occurs in pastoral poetry alongside shepherds, swains and fair damsels.
2. The god of marriage in the classical world.

Whose wand'ring Flames,
And wanton Dames,
A mutual Plague become;
While Coach and Six
Your Passions fix,
You buy your State too dearly:
Ah! courtly Folks!
You're but the Jokes
Of those who love sincerely.

JAMES DALACOURT
(*c.* 1710-*c.* 1785)

ON HIS BROTHER'S MARRIAGE

How comes it, neighbour Bob,
That you should thus surmount us,
And all the nobles rob,
By wedding a rich countess?
Happy Bob.

'Twas first believ'd a lie,
Upon my word and honour,
None thought you'd soar so high,
Or dare to look upon her.
Happy Bob.

A countess! haughty boy,
That name should fright a merchant;
Her trunk[1] was in your eye —
Dear bargain! you'd the search on't.
Happy Bob.

No doubt but you have found
Therein an immense treasure,
So deep you'd scarce get ground,
Though ne'er so long a measure.
Happy Bob.

Had you but pick'd the lock,
A treasure you would hit on;
But Hymen's[2] key's a rock
That many lover's split on.
Happy Bob.

A license and a priest
Are words that bear no evil,
But stolen joys are sweet,
And marriage is the Devil.
Wretched Bob.

But what to call this prize,
This great, this precious jewel,
I' faith I can't surmise
Whether new good or new-ill.
Happy Bob.

Her noble blood was sure
Above thy birth so humble;
How could her pride endure
So very great a tumble?
Happy Bob.

Her fortune, vastly high,
For thee was ne'er design'd;
The prince may have an eye
To treasure so refined.
Happy Bob.

Then surely thou art blest,
When kings and princes woo'd her,
To undermine the rest,
And cunningly delude her.
Happy Bob.

But 'twill be null'd, of course,
Her friends will ne'er allow it;
They'll put the act in force,
For nobles can undo it.
Happy Bob.

For prizes sailors roam,
For this their cannons thunder;
You've got a prize at home,
E'en Vernon[3] may knock under.[4]
Happy Bob.

Permit us, bridegroom, then,
To wish thee joy in wedlock,
May no malicious pen
Presume to call it padlock.
Happy Bob.

1. torso; perhaps also trunk full of treasure.
2. The Greek and Roman god of marriage.
3. Admiral Edward Vernon (1684-1757), whose capture of Portobello, now in Panama, from the Spaniards in 1739 made him a national hero in England in the early stages of the period of hostilities that became known as the War of Jenkins's Ear.
4. knock under board: acknowledge himself beaten, yield.

LAURENCE WHYTE

THE OLD WESTMEATH-BALLAD; *OR, YOUNG* BOBB'S *LAMENTATION FOR THE DEATH OF OLD* SARAH

To the Tune of, Ye Commons and Peers, &c.

Come listen a while, you friends of our Isle,
Tho' perhaps you will scarcely believe,
How *Sarah M[orga]n* cou'd think of a Man,
When she had been past seventy five.

To her Credit be't said, she liv'd a stale Maid,
Before *Thomas* fell into her Snare,
Tho' he till'd up the Ground, to his Sorrow he found
The Fruits did not answer his Care.

Of Wealth he had store, tho' he coveted more,
And *Sarah,* still cry'd she was poor;
For what she did gather, scarce one was the better,
Her Looks scar'd all Guests from her Door.

In the height of his Wealth, *Tom* fail'd in his Health,
The last Debt with Reluctance he paid;
His Life then he ends, leaving all to rich Friends;
And with Pomp in his Tomb he was laid.

To his Brother most dear, left twelve hundred a Year,
And to *Sarah,* two hundred and fifty,
To fat *Robbin* a Lot, and to *D[ic]k* a good Spot,
Because they were thriving and thrifty.

Poor *Hall* was forgot, and his Hopes gone to Pot,[1]
And Long-*Tom* who is wonderful witty,
Who travel'd so far, and was famous in War,
But was slighted, and 'twas a great Pity.

Then Old *Sarah* grew stout, and wou'd have t'other Bout,
Cry'd, Poor *Tom* is now dead and gone!
I no longer can mourn, but will take t'other Turn,[2]
For I'm fearful to lie thus alone.

Which *Bobb* over-heard, and for Action prepar'd,
When he found her inclin'd to surrender,
By a private Intrigue, he with her fell in League,
And the Citadel[3] boldly did enter.

1. gone to ruin.
2. Referring to her sexual intentions.
3. Literally a stronghold; figuratively referring to his sexual conquest.

Some took an Alarm, and grew very warm,[4]
On her Conduct they made much Reflection;
But to tell you the Truth, she lik'd the brisk Youth
Who kiss'd her, and won her Affection.

Of Guineas good Store, five hundred and more,
She gave him with other large Fees;
Besides Lumber[5] enough of good household Stuff,
With a Stock of old Blankets and Cheese.

By so noble a Feat, *B[ob]*b grew very great,
And got a Religion to Boot:[6]
Now he freely may own, that before he had none,
Since it sprung from his Wife's Petticoat.

But alas! cruel Death too soon stopt her Breath,
In the midst of her Transports and Pleasure,
Poor *R[obbi]n* is crost,[7] for the Jointure[8] is lost,
Which he now may lament at his Leisure.

Then his head was Intent on an Experiment,
Which he try'd in the Sight of the People,
He mounted her high that to Heaven she might fly,
And then flung her over the Steeple.

Now *Morgan* rejoice, and raise up your Voice,
As the happiest Man of this Age,
Give *Bobb* a good Fee, he deserves it of thee,
For he tickled her quite off the Stage.

4. angry.
5. household articles.
6. as well, in addition.
7. thwarted.
8. The property that a husband settles upon his wife when they are married, in order to provide for her in the event of his death.

SAMUEL WHYTE

THE HONE:[1] A PIECE OF IRISH MYTHOLOGY

Grifolia,[2] fairest of O Connor's[3] race,
Of spotless virtue, and angelic face,

1. 'A species of stone found at Lough Neagh in the province of Ulster, of which Hones for whetting Razors are made, supposed to be Holly converted into that substance by a singular petrifying quality attributed to the Lake' (Whyte).
2. An invented name.
3. A name particularly associated with County Kerry.

Was by O Neil,[4] a youth of princely blood,
With wanton fire, and loveless courtship woo'd;
He watch'd her steps, by lawless passion sway'd,
And once, alone, surprised the pious maid.

On the green banks of Neagh's[5] peaceful sea,
The chaste Grifolia had retir'd to pray:
Here, the base prince, with more than savage power,
Assail'd the vestal[6] in her sacred hour.
He talk'd — he pleaded of love's darts and fires;
Of his warm wishes, and his strong desires;
Of time, and place — of his long suit refus'd;
Of wealth; of title; patience; — all abused!
At length, he seiz'd the fair, resistless prize,
While fires indignant darted from her eyes;
He grasped — he press'd the virgin to his breast,
And urged her yielding to his high behest.

'Tyrant!' she cried, 'thy vain attempt forbear;
My strength may fail; but heaven will hear my prayer:
O! may the sacred guardian of this land
Protect a maid from thy polluting hand!
May he, whose power expell'd the prowling wolf,
Save virtue from perdition's fatal gulph!
May he, who purg'd this Isle from poisonous air,
Blast thee! or snatch me to his saintly care!'[7]

She pray'd — He still invades her blushing charms —
When, lo! a prickly *Holly* fills his arms!
Wounded, and stung with disappointed pride,
He drew a faulchion[8] from his trembling side,
And smote the new-rais'd Holly as it grew,
When to the lake the sever'd fragment flew;
It sunk, and, as it disappear'd, the flood
Was crimson'd o'er with drops of virgin blood;
Groanings were heard; and, what is still more strange,
A plaintive voice succeeds the wonderous change!
From the deep lake, in words articulate,
Thus mourn'd Grifolia her disasterous Fate:

'O cruel prince! transform'd, and turn'd to stone,
My honour's safe!' she cried, then sigh'd —
'*O hōn*!'[9]
O Honour! Half dissolv'd in liquid air
Was the last breathing of this hapless fair.
Thus, Myrrha,[10] victim of a former time,
Shar'd thy sad fate; but how unlike thy crime!

Amaz'd the prince gaz'd o'er the silent flood,
And grew a burning nettle[11] as he stood:
Rank as his thoughts, and fiery as his lust,
Chang'd to that weed, his punishment how just!
While chaste Grifolia constantly is seen
Rob'd in a vesture of eternal green;
Each leaf in military form appears
Arm'd with a range of vegetable spears.
Thus nature shows in emblematic sense
Her persevering virtue and defence.

The rude, unletter'd natives of this land,
When struck by power, or pain's oppressive hand,
In accents slow and sad, express their moan,
And, to this hour, sob out and cry, 'Oh *hone*!'
But those, whom arts and education fire,
Who into nature's curious laws enquire,
Place portions of this ever-verdant tree
In Neagh's peaceful petrifying sea,
Where, steeped a time, it hardens into stone,
And thus becomes the edge-bestowing *hone*.

4. A name particularly associated with Counties Tyrone and Antrim.
5. A freshwater lake of almost 400 square kilometres in central Northern Ireland.
6. Alluding to the vestal virgins of ancient Rome, who tended the sacred fire in the temple of Vesta, the goddess of the hearth.
7. A reference to St Patrick.
8. sword.
9. 'The customary plaintive ejaculation of the native Irish' (Whyte).
10. An obscure allusion. The name 'Mira' or 'Myra' does not occur in classical literature, and does not appear in English poetry until the Renaissance and neoclassical periods.
11. stinging nettle.

GEORGE OGLE

(1742-1814)

MAILLIGH A STÓR[1]

As down by Banna's banks I strayed,
One evening in May,
The little birds, in blithest notes,
Made vocal every spray;
They sung their little notes of love,
They sung them o'er and o'er.

1. 'My darling Molly'.

Ah! grá mo chroí, mo chailín óg,
Mailligh a stór.[2]

The daisy pied,[3] and all the sweets
The dawn of Nature yields —
The primrose pale, and violet blue,
Lay scattered o'er the fields;
Such fragrance in the bosom lies
Of her whom I adore.
Ah! grá mo chroí, etc.

I laid me down upon a bank,
Bewailing my sad fate,
That doomed me thus the slave of love
And cruel Molly's hate;
How can she break the honest heart
That wears her in its core?
Ah! grá mo chroí, etc.

You said you loved me, Molly dear!
Ah! why did I believe?
Yet who could think such tender words
Were meant but to deceive?
That love was all I asked on earth —
Nay, heaven could give no more.
Ah! grá mo chroí, etc.

Oh! had I all the flocks that graze
On yonder yellow hill,
Or lowed for me the numerous herds
That yon green pasture fill —
With her I love I'd gladly share
My kine and fleecy store.[4]
Ah! grá mo chroí, etc.

Two turtle-doves, above my head,
Sat courting on a bough;
I envied them their happiness,
To see them bill and coo.
Such fondness once for me was shewn,
But now, alas! 'tis o'er.
Ah! grá mo chroí, etc.

Then fare thee well, my Molly dear!
Thy loss I e'er shall moan;
Whilst life remains in my poor heart,
'Twill beat for thee alone:

2. 'Love of my heart, my young girl, My darling Molly'.
3. two-coloured.
4. my cattle and sheep.

Though thou art false, may heaven on thee
Its choicest blessings pour.
Ah! grá mo chroí, etc.

GEORGE NUGENT REYNOLDS
(*c.* 1770-1802)

KATHLEEN O'MORE

My love, still I think that I see her once more,
But, alas! she has left me her loss to deplore —
My own little Kathleen, my poor little Kathleen,
My Kathleen O'More!

Her hair glossy black, her eyes were dark blue,
Her colour still changing, her smiles ever new —
So pretty was Kathleen, my sweet little Kathleen,
My Kathleen O'More!

She milked the dun[1] cow, that ne'er offered to stir;
Though wicked to all, it was gentle to her —
So kind was my Kathleen, my poor little Kathleen,
My Kathleen O'More!

She sat at the door one cold afternoon,
To hear the wind blow, and to gaze on the moon, —
So pensive was Kathleen, my poor little Kathleen,
My Kathleen O'More!

Cold was the night-breeze that sighed round her bower,
It chilled my poor Kathleen, she drooped from that hour,
And I lost my poor Kathleen, my own little Kathleen,
My Kathleen O'More!

The bird of all birds that I love the best
Is the robin that in the churchyard builds his nest;
For he seems to watch Kathleen, hops lightly o'er Kathleen,
My Kathleen O'More.

1. brownish-grey.

ANONYMOUS
(*c.* 1775)

THE BOYS OF KILKENNY

O! The boys of Kilkenny are brave roving blades,
And if ever they meet with the nice little maids,
They'll kiss them, and coax them, and spend their
money free,
Of all the towns in Ireland Kilkenny for me.

In the town of Kilkenny there runs a clear stream,
In the town of Kilkenny there lives a pretty dame,
Her lips are like roses, and her mouth much the
same,
Like a dish of fresh strawberries smothered in
cream.

Her eyes are as black as Kilkenny's famed coal,[1]
Which through my poor bosom have burnt a big
hole,
Her mind, like its river, is mild, clear, and pure,
But her heart is more hard than its marble, I'm sure.

1. Coal and marble were mined north of Kilkenny.

HENRY BRERETON CODE

SONG — SPRIG OF SHILLELA[1]

Och! love is the soul of a neat Irishman;
He loves all that's lovely, loves all that he can,
With his sprig of Shillela, and shamrock so green.
His heart is right honest, it's open and sound,
No malice nor envy is there to be found;
He courts and he marries, he drinks and he fights,
He loves — Och! he loves, for in that he delights,
With his sprig of Shillela and shamrock so green.

Who has e'er had the luck to see Donnybrook fair?[2]
An Irishman all in his glory is there,
With his sprig of Shillela and shamrock so green:
His clothes spick and span new, without e'er a speck,
A nice Barcelona[3] tied round his neat neck;
He goes to a tent, and he spends half a crown,[4]
Comes out, meets a friend, and for love knocks him
down,
With his sprig of Shillela and shamrock so green.

In the ev'ning returning, as homeward he goes,
His heart soft with whiskey, his head soft with
blows,
With a sprig of Shillela and shamrock so green;
He meets with his Shelagh, who frowning a smile,
Cries, 'Get you gone Pat,' yet consents all the while;
To church they soon go, and nine months after that,
A young baby cries — 'How do you do, Father Pat,
With your sprig of Shillela and shamrock so
green.'

Long life to the land that gave Patrick his birth,
To the land of the oak, and its neighbouring earth,
With a sprig of Shillela, and shamrock so green:
May the sons of the Thames, the Tweed, and the
Shannon,[5]
Thrash the foes that would plant on their confines a
cannon;
United and happy at Liberty's shrine,
May the rose and the thistle[6] long flourish and twine
Round the sprig of Shillela, and shamrock so
green.

Nor here shall the wish of an Irishman end,
All the wide world round he will stand by his friend,
With his sprig of Shillela, and shamrock so green:
May the Milesian[7] tide which still flows in his veins,
Swell high at the clank of his forefathers' chains;
And may WELLINGTON[8] brave, a true son of
the sod,
Find freedom for Spain[9] — for her Tyrant[10] a rod,
In a sprig of Shillela, and shamrock so green.

1. Shillelagh, the name of a town and barony in County Wicklow, gave its name in the eighteenth century to the shillelagh or shillala, the club or cudgel shaped from the oak or blackthorn trees of the area. The reference here is to the shoots or sprays of the trees, which were worn like shamrock, pinned to the coat lapel, to symbolize loyalty to Ireland.
2. The famous August fair at Donnybrook, just to the south of Dublin, which became so disorderly in the early nineteenth century that the authorities moved to close it down.
3. A piece of ornamental silk worn around the neck, a custom thought to have arisen in the Spanish city.
4. i.e. spent several days' wages on drink.
5. The three rivers symbolize England, Scotland and Ireland.
6. Symbols of England and Scotland.
7. From Milesius, a fabulous Spanish king whose sons are said to have conquered Ireland about 1300 B.C.; hence Irish.
8. Arthur Wellesley (1769-1852), first duke of Wellington, the Irish-born military hero of England, who defeated Napoleon at the battle of Waterloo in 1815.
9. Alluding to the hope that Spain, which was invaded in 1808 and occupied by France in the Peninsula War, when Britain and Spain were allies, would be freed from French control. Code noted that since the Irish claimed 'through Milesius, descent from the Spanish nation, [they] should naturally feel a more than common interest in the present glorious struggle for her independence.'
10. Joseph Bonaparte (1768-1844), brother of Napoleon I, was placed on the Spanish throne in 1808 and ruled until 1813, the year Code published this poem in *The Russian Sacrifice*.

IV

'How's poor ould Ireland, and how does she stand?'

In 'The Wearin' of the Green', one of the best-known Irish street-ballads, the narrator meets Napper Tandy, the Dublin intellectual and member of the United Irishmen who fought in the uprising of 1798 and who subsequently lived in France. 'How's poor ould Ireland', he asks, 'and how does she stand?' The question, which reverberates throughout Irish history, is particularly pertinent to the eighteenth century, which opens with the aftermath of the defeat of the Jacobites in 1689-91, and ends with the failure of the rebellion of 1798 and the collapse of the revolutionary movement. While there were fundamental changes in the nature of Irish opposition to English authority from the late seventeenth to the early nineteenth centuries, the position of the English, as expressed in 1784, remained essentially unchanged, that 'Ireland is too great to be unconnected with us, and too near us to be dependent on a foreign state, and too little to be independent'.

In 'Lilli burlero', the anti-Jacobite song that possibly was written by Thomas Wharton, the catholics are taunted with their sense of victory in the late 1680s. Widely popular throughout the eighteenth century, its words and tune became a mark of social identity, as the country squire in Laurence Whyte's '*A Dissertation on* Italian *and* Irish *Musick, with some Panegyrick on* Carrallan *our late* Irish Orpheus' reveals. In contrast, the Jacobite song 'The Blackbird', which appears to date from the early eighteenth century, is a sentimental lament that employs both the conventional device of the poet's discovering the grieving figure of Erin and the code of the Old Pretender, James Francis Edward Stuart, in the disguise of a bird. Sung throughout the period when the hopes of the Jacobites were still alive, 'The Blackbird' became ambiguous, referring to the Old Pretender in 1715, and the Young Pretender, Charles Edward Stuart, in 1745.

The five poems by Swift direct attention to the complexity of the issues debated in Ireland in the early years of the protestant ascendancy. When the Union of England and Scotland was effected in 1707, Swift, who strongly opposed it, reminded his audience of the inherently unstable order in Ireland, and when it was planned to establish a bank in Dublin in 1720, he praised Archbishop William King for his opposition to it. In 'A Serious Poem upon William Wood, *Brasier, Tinker, Hard-Ware-Man, Coiner, Counterfeiter, Founder* and *Esquire*', he attacked the English iron-merchant William Wood, who had come into possession of a patent to mint a new copper coinage for Ireland. In the defeat of the plan to issue Wood's Halfpence, Swift, who led the Irish objections to the patent, achieved the greatest victory of his career; but the Ireland he faced for the remainder of his life was the Ireland he endured, as he demonstrates in his image of the perilous condition of the ship of state in '*Horace*. Book I. Ode XIV. Paraphrased and inscribed to *Ireland*' and in his denunciation of the timeserver in 'Ireland'.

Two of the poems that Swift inspired in his role as the Drapier, Richard Witheral's 'A New Song Sung at the Club at Mr. Taplin's . . . .' and Charles Shadwell's 'A Second Song . . . .' create a sense of the temporary unity which emerged in Ireland as the factions united to protect their common interest; they also lead to a comparison with 'Love and Whiskey', the anonymous song of the Volunteer movement in the late 1770s and early 1780s. Founded to meet the need for a force to maintain civil and even military order once the British had withdrawn troops from Ireland during the American War of Independence, the Volunteers rose to the height of their power in 1782, when they demanded parliamentary reform at their Convention in Dungannon, Co. Tyrone. By 1784, however, the movement had foundered, and the unity achieved in Henry Grattan's parliament in the 'constitution of 1782', when the goal of legislative independence had been secured, collapsed in the face of the growing isolation of parliament from the community and fresh difficulties in Anglo-Irish relationships. These difficulties, which lie behind Mary O'Brien's two poems, 'The Freedom of John Bull' and 'Paddy's Opinion. An Irish Ballad', grew out of the hostility of English merchants and manufacturers to the prospect of Irish commercial independence and the Irish parliament's support of the Prince of Wales and the opposition party during the Regency crisis of 1788-89.

In the early 1790s another movement, that of the United Irishmen, was born, more as a result of the influence of the French Revolution than of the remnants of the Volunteers or of the Catholic Committee, which had fought for civil rights and religious toleration. In 'The Wake of William Orr', William Drennan, who was one of the founders of the United Irishmen and who is the most important poet of the 1798 rebellion, mourned the death of the Ulster farmer who was executed in 1797 for administering an illegal oath. Many of the poems and songs of the 1790s became more popular and politically even more potent after the mid-century. Thus, 'The Shan Van Vocht' and 'The Wearin' of the Green' are included in the 'Popular Songs' section of 'Poetry 1800-1975'. It was their revival then that gave them an extension of life in the popular tradition into the present century.

Whether the poets of the 1790s lamented death or dreamed of rescue, whether they retreated into sentiment or deplored violence, the nationalistic and revolutionary movement of the decade, whose colour was now the Irish green, collapsed in the face of military defeat. James Orr, a member of the United Irishmen, who had fought in the battle of Antrim in 1798, went into temporary exile in America and later wrote 'The Irishman', a sentimental and controversial description of the national character of his countryman, the figure who was generous to his foe. William Blacker, the Orange poet, found inspiration in 'Oliver's Advice' in the words of Oliver Cromwell, where he argued that the divine power that had led the Israelites out of slavery in Egypt would guide all those who confronted the surviving participants in the rebellion of 1798. More than a hundred years had passed, and the spirit of 'Lilli burlero' and 'The Blackbird' was still alive.

ANONYMOUS

(*c.* 1687)

LILLI BURLERO[1]

Ho! brother Teague,[2] dost hear de decree,
    Lilli burlero bullen a la;[3]
Dat we shall have a new debittie,[4]
    Lilli burlero bullen a la.
  Lero, lero, lero, lero, Lilli burlero bullen a la.
  Lero, lero, lero, lero, Lilli burlero bullen a la.

Ho! by my shoul[5] it is a Talbot,
    Lilli, &c.
And he will cut all the English throat,
    Lilli, &c. &c.

Though by my shoul de English do prat,[6]
    Lilli, &c.
De law's on dare side, and Chreist knows what,
    Lilli, &c. &c.

But if dispense[7] do come from de pope,
    Lilli, &c.
We'll hang Magno Carto[8] and demselves in a rope,
    Lilli, &c. &c.

And the good Talbot is made a lord,[9]
    Lilli, &c.
And he with brave lads is coming aboard,[10]
    Lilli, &c. &c.

Who all in France[11] have taken a swear,
    Lilli, &c.
Dat dey will have no Protestant heir,[12]
    Lilli, &c. &c.

O! but why does he[13] stay behind?
    Lilli, &c.
Ho by my shoul 'tis a Protestant wind,[14]
    Lilli, &c. &c.

Now Tyrconnell is come ashore,[15]
    Lilli, &c.
And we shall have commissions gillore,[16]
    Lilli, &c. &c.

And he dat will not go to mass
    Lilli, &c.
Shall turn out and look like an ass,
    Lilli, &c. &c.

Now, now de heretics all go down,
    Lilli, &c.

1. In fact, Thomas Wharton (1648-1715), lord lieutenant of Ireland 1708-10, is now accepted as the author of this Williamite song. It was an attack on Richard Talbot (1630-91), earl of Tyrconnell, who restored offices and rights to Irish catholics. The 'Lilli' refers to William Lilly (1602-81), the English astrologist. The refrain, which is a garbled version of Irish, means 'Lilly will be manifest: the day will be ours.' See Brendan Ó Buachalla, 'Lillibulero agus Eile', *Comhar,* Vol. 46, Nos. 3-7 (Mairt-Iúl, 1987).
2. An anglicized form of the Irish Tadhg, which protestants used pejoratively to refer to catholics.
3. 'The words of distinction used among the Irish Papists at the time of their massacre of the Protestants in 1641' (Bishop Thomas Percy, *Reliques of Ancient English Poetry*, 4th ed., 1794).
4. Tyrconnell's appointment as lord deputy or lord lieutenant of Ireland was announced in January 1687.
5. soul.
6. prate.
7. dispensation.
8. Magna Carta.
9. Talbot had been made earl of Tyrconnell and given a major commission in the Irish army in 1685. By 1686 he was in command of the army, whose composition he quickly made predominantly catholic.
10. Alluding to the traditional metaphor of the ship of state.
11. Alluding to the French support of the Jacobite cause. Sung in the aftermath of the Williamite victory in 1691, 'Lilli burlero' taunted the French and Irish Jacobites who left Ireland for France under the military articles of the Treaty of Limerick.
12. A mocking reference to one of the chief matters of contention between catholics and protestants: the transfer of the ownership of land. After the various Williamite confiscations, most of the remaining land in catholic hands passed to protestants.
13. James II, king of England, Scotland and Ireland 1685-88, came to Ireland in March 1689.
14. A wind blowing from a country of protestant Europe towards England was referred to as a protestant wind, and one blowing in the opposite direction was referred to as a catholic wind. Thus William of Orange came to England on a protestant wind, and it was a protestant wind that kept James II from Ireland.
15. A continuation of the allusion to the metaphor of the ship of state.
16. galore, in great numbers.

By Chreist and St. Patrick de nation's our own,
Lilli, &c. &c.

There was an old prophecy found in a bog,
Lilli, &c.
That Ireland should be rul'd by an ass and a dog:
Lilli, &c. &c.

And now this prophecy is come to pass,
Lilli, &c.
For Talbot's[17] the dog, and Tyrconnell's the ass,
Lilli, &c. &c.

17. Peter Talbot (1620-80), the catholic, and hence titular, archbishop of Dublin, who was Richard Talbot's brother and who was renowned for defending the interests of his faith. 'The line appears intended to satirize the heads of church and state' (Croker).

ANONYMOUS

(*c.* 1715)

THE BLACKBIRD[1]

Upon a fair morning, for soft recreation,
I heard a fair lady[2] was making her moan,
With sighing and sobbing, and sad lamentation,
Saying, my *blackbird* most royal is flown.
My thoughts they deceive me,
Reflections do grieve me,
And I am o'erburden'd with sad misery;
Yet, if death should blind me,
As true love inclines me,
My *blackbird* I'll seek out, wherever he be.[3]

Once in fair England my *blackbird* did flourish,
He was the chief flower that in it did spring;
Prime ladies of honour his person did nourish,
Because he was the true son of a king:[4]
But since that false fortune,
Which still is uncertain,
Has caused this parting between him and me,[5]
His name I'll advance
In Spain and in France,
And seek out my *blackbird* wherever he be.

The birds of the forest all met together,
The turtle has chosen to dwell with the dove;[6]
And I am resolved, in foul or fair weather,
Once in the spring to seek out my love.
He's all my heart's treasure,
My joy and my pleasure;
And justly (my love) my heart follows thee,
Who art constant and kind,
And courageous of mind,
All bliss to my *blackbird* wherever he be.

In England my *blackbird* and I were together,
Where he was still noble and gen'rous of heart;
Ah! wo to the time that first he went thither,
Alas! he was forc'd from thence to depart.
In Scotland he's deem'd,
And highly esteem'd,
In England he seemeth a stranger to be;
Yet his fame shall remain
In France and in Spain;
All bliss to my *blackbird*, wherever he be.

What if the fowler[7] my *blackbird* has taken,
Then sighing and sobbing will be all my tune;
But if he is safe, I'll not be forsaken,
And hope yet to see him in May or in June.
For him through the fire,
Through mud and through mire,
I'll go; for I love him to such a degree,
Who is constant and kind,
And noble of mind,
Deserving all blessings, wherever he be.

It is not the ocean can fright me with danger,
Nor though, like a pilgrim, I wander forlorn,
I may meet with friendship of one is a stranger,[8]
More than of one that in Britain is born.
I pray heaven so spacious,
To Britain be gracious,
Tho' some there be odious to both him and me;
Yet joy and renown,
And laurels shall crown
My *blackbird* with honour, wherever he be.

1. The Old Pretender, or claimant to the throne of England, James Francis Edward Stuart (1688-1766), the son of James II.
2. The figure of Erin, a poetic name for Ireland.
3. After the failure of the Jacobite rebellion of 1715, the Old Pretender, who had landed in Scotland and had been proclaimed James VIII of Scotland and James III of England, fled to France and subsequently lived in Italy and Spain.
4. Born on 10 June 1688, the Old Pretender was taken to France by his mother in December 1688.
5. The failure of the Jacobite rebellion of 1715, and the collapse of later hopes of an uprising to regain the throne.
6. Turtledoves, traditional emblems of lovers, arising from their mutual devotion.
7. A shooter and trapper of birds.
8. The sense is 'I may meet with the friendship of one who is a stranger.'

JONATHAN SWIFT

VERSES *SAID TO BE WRITTEN ON THE* UNION[1]

The Queen has lately lost a Part[2]
Of her entirely-*English* Heart,
For want of which by way of Botch,
She piec'd it up again with *Scotch.*
Blest Revolution, which creates
Divided Hearts, united States.
See how the double Nation lies;
Like a rich Coat with Skirts of Frize:[3]
As if a Man in making Posies
Should bundle Thistles up with Roses.[4]
Whoever yet a Union saw
Of Kingdoms, without Faith or Law.
Henceforward let no Statesman dare,
A Kingdom to a Ship compare;
Lest he should call our Commonweal,
A Vessel with a double Keel:[5]
Which just like ours, new rigg'd and man'd,[6]
And got about a League from Land,
By Change of Wind to Leeward Side
The Pilot knew not how to guide.
So tossing Faction will o'erwhelm
Our crazy double-bottom'd Realm.

1. The Union of England and Scotland took effect on 1 May 1707.
2. The Anglo-Irish. The Irish parliament had rejected the proposal for a Union between England and Ireland in 1703.
3. frieze: coarse woollen cloth.
4. Traditional symbols of Scotland and England.
5. Sir William Petty's experiments with a double-keeled boat or catamaran in Dublin bay in 1684 (when Swift was a student at Trinity College) ended in disaster.
6. After the battle of the Boyne in 1690, Ireland was under new laws and a new administration.

PART OF THE 9TH *ODE* OF THE 4TH *BOOK* OF *HORACE,* ADDRESS'D TO DOCTOR *WILLIAM KING,* LATE LORD ARCHBISHOP OF *DUBLIN*[1]

Virtue conceal'd within our Breast
Is Inactivity at best:
But, never shall the Muse endure
To let your Virtues lye obscure,
Or suffer Envy to conceal
Your Labours for the Publick Weal.[2]
Within your Breast all Wisdom lyes,
Either to govern or advise;
Your steady Soul preserves her Frame
In good and evil Times the same.
Pale Avarice and lurking Fraud
Stand in your sacred Presence aw'd;
Your Hand alone from Gold abstains,
Which drags the slavish World in Chains.

Him for an happy Man I own,
Whose Fortune is not overgrown;
And, happy he, who wisely knows
To use the Gifts, that Heav'n bestows;
Or, if it please the Powers Divine,
Can suffer Want, and not repine.
The Man, who Infamy to shun,
Into the Arms of Death would run,
That Man is ready to defend
With Life his Country, or his Friend.

1. William King (1650-1729), archbishop of Dublin 1703-29, who opposed the proposal to establish a bank in Ireland in 1720. Swift, also against the plan, believed that it had been conceived by various financial operators. It was rejected by the Irish parliament in 1721. The poem, which dates from that time, was published in 1730.
2. interest, in the sense of prosperity, well-being.

A SERIOUS POEM UPON WILLIAM WOOD, *BRASIER, TINKER, HARD-WARE-MAN, COINER, COUNTERFEITER, FOUNDER* AND *ESQUIRE*[1]

When Foes are o'ercome, we preserve them from
Slaughter,
To be *Hewers* of WOOD[2] and *Drawers* of *Water,*[3]
Now, although to *Draw Water* is not very good,
Yet we all should Rejoyce to be *Hewers* of WOOD.
I own it hath often provok'd me to Mutter,
That, a Rogue so *Obscure* should make such a
Clutter,
But antient *Philosophers* wisely Remark,
That old rotten WOOD will *Shine* in the *Dark.*
The *Heathens,* we Read, had *Gods* made of WOOD,
Who could do them no Harm, if they did them no
Good:

1. William Wood (1671-1730), Wolverhampton ironmonger, and receiver general of taxes for Shropshire 1715-19, which entitled him to be known as 'Esquire'. In 1722 he secured a patent to mint a copper coinage for Ireland. One of the main Irish objections to this patent was that it would lead to the debasement of the currency, which could be easily counterfeited, possibly even by Wood himself.
2. The beginning of a sustained pun on Wood.
3. Edward Waters (*fl.* 1707-40), the Dublin printer of Swift's *A Proposal for the Universal Use of Irish Manufacture* (1720); he was charged with sedition. The line carries echoes of Joshua 9. 21.

But this Idol WOOD may do us great Evil,
Their Gods were of WOOD, but our WOOD is the DEVIL:
To cut down fine WOOD is a very bad Thing,
And yet we all know much *Gold* it will bring,
Then if cutting down WOOD brings Money good Store,[4]
Our Money to keep, let us *Cut down* ONE *more.*

Now hear an old Tale. There antiently stood
(I forget in what Church) an Image of *Wood*;
Concerning this Image there went a Prediction,
It would Burn a whole *Forest*; nor was it a Fiction;
'Twas cut into Faggots, and put to the Flame,
To burn an old Fryer, one *Forrest* by Name.
My Tale is a wise one if well understood,
Find you but the *Fryer*, and I'll find the WOOD.

I hear among Scholars there is a great Doubt
From what Kind of Tree this WOOD was Hewn out.
Teague[5] made a good PUN by a *Brogue*[6] in his Speech,
And said: *By my Shoul*[7] *he's the Son of a* BEECH:[8]
Some call him a *Thorn*, the Curse of a Nation,
As *Thorns*[9] were design'd to be from the Creation.
Some think him cut out from the Poisonous *Yew*,
Beneath whose ill Shade no Plant ever grew.
Some say he's a *Birch*, a Thought very odd,
For none but a *Dunce* would come under his *Rod*.[10]
But I'll tell you the Secret, and pray do not Blab,
He is an old *Stump* cut out of a *Crab*,[11]
And *England* has put this *Crab*[12] to hard Use,
To Cudgel our Bones, and for Drink give us *Verjuice*;[13]
And therefore his *Witnesses*[14] justly may boast
That none are more properly Knights of the POST.[15]

But here Mr. *Wood* complains that we Mock,
Though he may be a *Block*-head, he is no real *Block*.
He can Eat, Drink and Sleep; now and then for a Friend
He'll not be too proud an old Kettle to mend;[16]
He can *Lye* like a *Courtier*, and think it no Scorn,
When *Gold*'s to be got, to FORSWEAR and SUBORN.[17]
He can RAP his own RAPS,[18] and has the true Sapience[19]
To turn a *Good* Penny to Twenty *Bad* Ha'pence.[20]
Then in Spight of your Sophistry,[21] Honest WILL. WOOD
Is a Man of this World all true Flesh and Blood;
So you are but in Jest, and you will not I hope
Un-man the poor Knave for sake of a *Trope*.[22]
'Tis a *Metaphor* known to ev'ry plain Thinker.
Just as when we say, *the Devil's a Tinker*
Which cannot in Literal Sense be made Good,
Unless by the *Devil* we mean Mr. WOOD.

But some will object, that the *Devil* oft spoke
In *Heathenish* Times from the *Trunk* of an *Oak*:
And, since we must grant, there never were known
More *Heathenish* Times than those of our own;
Perhaps you will say, 'tis the *Devil* that puts
The Words in WOOD's Mouth, or speaks from his Guts:
And then your old Argument still will return:
Howe'er let us try him and see how he'll burn.
You'll pardon me Sir, your Cunning I smoak,[23]
But WOOD I assure you is no *Heart of* OAK;[24]
And instead of the *Devil*, this Son of Perdition[25]
Hath joyn'd with himself two HAGS in Commission:[26]

4. in plenty.
5. An anglicized form of the Irish Tadhg, used as a name for the stock figure of the Irishman.
6. An Irish way of speaking.
7. soul.
8. The beech tree, used as a pun on 'bitch'.
9. cf. the phrase, 'a thorn in the flesh'; in rural Ireland, it is considered unlucky to cut down a hawthorn tree, the branches of which are said to have been used for Christ's crown of thorns.
10. The birch cane of the schoolmaster.
11. The crab-apple, whose wild fruit, often sour, could not be eaten; a stick or cudgel cut from such a tree.
12. An irritable, ill-tempered person.
13. The acid juice of unripe crab-apples or other sour fruit.
14. Four Irish witnesses testified at the English privy council's inquiry into the coinage in 1724 that Ireland had a shortage of small coins. They were Coleby, a clerk in the Irish treasury, John Browne of County Mayo, later a pamphleteer and essayist, Robert Finlay, a merchant and banker, and Thomas Bailey, a trader.
15. Professional witnesses, who gave evidence for payment; a continuation of the pun on 'wood'.
16. Alluding to Wood's early career in the iron industry, and continuing the attack on him in the title as a tinker.
17. commit perjury and bribe.
18. counterfeit his own counterfeit coins.
19. wisdom.
20. i.e. melt down the copper in a good penny and use it to make twenty debased halfpence — so making money for himself.
21. trickery.
22. A figure of speech, such as a metaphor.
23. observe.
24. A person of strong and resolute spirit — particularly a true Englishman.
25. damnation. cf. John 17.12.
26. The Duchess of Kendal, the older mistress of George I, who has been traditionally named as having sold the patent for the coinage to Wood

I ne'er could endure my Talent to smother,
I told you one Tale, I will tell you another.
A *Joyner* to fasten a *Saint* in a *Nitch*,
Bor'd a large *Augre-hole*[27] in the Image's Breech;[28]
But finding the *Statue* to make no Complaint,
He would ne'er be convinc'd it was a *True Saint*:
When the *True* WOOD[29] arrives, as he soon will no doubt,
(For that's but a Sham WOOD[30] they carry about)
What *Stuff* he is made on you quickly may find,
If you make the same Tryal, and *Bore* him *Behind*;
I'll hold[31] you a Groat,[32] when you *wimble*[33] his Bumm,
He'll Bellow as loud as the *Dee'l*[34] *in a Drum*:
From me I declare you shall have no Denial,
And there can be no Harm in making a Tryal;
And when to the Joy of your Hearts he has Roar'd,
You may shew him about for a new *Groaning Board*.[35]

Now ask me a Question. How came it to pass
WOOD got so much Copper? He got it by BRASS;[36]
This BRASS was a Dragon (observe what I tell ye)
This *Dragon* had gotten two *Sows* in it's Belly;[37]
I know you will say, this is all *Heathen Greek*;[38]
I own it, and therefore I leave you to seek.

I often have seen two Plays very Good,
Call'd, LOVE IN A TUB, and LOVE IN A WOOD.[39]
These Comedies twain Friend *Wood* will contrive
On the *Scene* of this *Land* very soon to *revive*.
First, LOVE IN A TUB: 'Squire[40] *Wood* has in Store
Strong *Tubs* for his *Raps*, Two thousand and more;
These *Raps* he will honestly dig out with Shovels,
And sell them for Gold, or he can't shew his Love else,
WOOD swears he will do it for *Ireland*'s Good,
Then can you deny it is *Love in a* WOOD?[41]
However, if Criticks find Fault with the Phrase,
I hope you will own it is *Love in a Maze*;[42]
For when you express a Friend's Love we are willing,
We never say more than, your *Love is a Million*;
But with honest WOOD's *Love* there is no contending,
'Tis Fifty round *Millions* of *Love*, and a *Mending*.[43]
Then in his First *Love* why should he be crost?
I hope he will find that *no Love is lost*.[44]

Hear one Story more and then I will stop.
I dream't WOOD was told he should Dye by a *Drop*[45]
So methought, he resolv'd no Liquor to taste,
For fear the *First Drop* might as well be his *Last*:
But *Dreams* are like *Oracles*, hard to explain 'em,
For it prov'd that he dy'd of a DROP at *Killmainham*:[46]
I wak'd with Delight, and not without Hope,
Very soon to see WOOD *Drop* down from *a Rope*.
How he and how we at each other should grin!
'Tis Kindness to hold a Friend up by the Chin;[47]
But soft says the Herald,[48] I cannot agree;
For *Metal on Metal is false Heraldry*:[49]
Why that may be true, yet WOOD upon WOOD,[50]
I'll maintain with my Life, is *Heraldry*[51] Good.

---

for £10,000, and presumably the younger mistress, the Countess of Darlington, who is not known to have been involved with the coinage but who becomes guilty here by association. Both ladies were German by birth.

27. A hole made with an auger, a tool for boring.
28. anus.
29. To be compared with the 'Sham WOOD', but also, in the context of the references to religion and testing for authenticity, an ironic allusion to the True Cross.
30. The Dublin mob marched with an effigy of Wood and carried out a mock execution on 7 September 1724. Wood was paraded and burnt in effigy on other occasions at this time.
31. wager.
32. A small English silver coin.
33. bore into.
34. Devil.
35. A large board which 'groaned' when heat was applied to it. Often displayed as a 'wonder'.
36. One of the nicknames for Sir Robert Walpole, the chief minister of the English Whig government 1715-17 and 1721-42, who was known as Sir Robert Brass, an allusion to his reputation as a financial manipulator and to the moral connotations of 'brass' and 'brazen'.
37. Probably an allusion to the 'two HAGS' of note 26. The reference to the *Dragon* is obscure.
38. incomprehensible talk.
39. George Etherege's comedy, *The Comical Revenge, or Love in a Tub* (1664) and William Wycherley's comedy, *Love in a Wood, or* St James's Park (1671).
40. A taunting, derisive reference to Wood's use of 'Esquire', a title of respect.
41. A pun on the titles of the plays mentioned and the meaning of 'in a wood', i.e. 'bewildered or in a confused state'.
42. James Shirley's comedy, *Changes, or Love in a Maze* (1632). The allusion plays with the meanings of *'in a Maze'* and 'in amaze'.
43. Evidently a pun on 'amending'; possibly an ironic reference to the debasement of the coinage.
44. cf. Shakespeare's *Love's Labour's Lost*.
45. Punning on the meanings of 'drop' as liquor and death by hanging.
46. The village to the west of Dublin, the site of a gaol and a gallows.
47. i.e. to save him from drowning; but used here ironically.
48. Announcer of news, heraldic officer.
49. Playing with the proverbial saying, which took its meaning from the sense of what was inappropriate in heraldic design, and with the sense of *'Metal on Metal'* as 'coin upon coin', that is, to excess.
50. Playing with the parallel to *'Metal on Metal'* and with the sense of 'wood' both as gallows and as surname.
51. news.

HORACE
BOOK I. ODE XIV

Paraphrased and inscribed to *Ireland*

THE INSCRIPTION

Poor floating Isle, tost on ill Fortune's Waves,
Ordain'd by Fate *to be the Land of Slaves:*[1]
Shall moving Delos[2] *now deep-rooted stand,*
Thou, fixt of old, be now the moving Land?
Altho' the Metaphor be worn and stale
Betwixt a State, and Vessel under Sail;
Let me suppose thee for a Ship a-while,
And thus address thee in the Sailor Stile.

Unhappy Ship, thou art return'd in Vain:
New Waves shall drive thee to the Deep again.
Look to thy Self, and be no more the Sport
Of giddy Winds, but make some friendly Port.
Lost are thy Oars that us'd thy Course to guide,
Like faithful Counsellors on either Side.
Thy Mast, which like some aged Patriot stood
The single Pillar for his Country's Good,
To lead thee, as a Staff directs the Blind,
Behold, it cracks by yon rough *Eastern* Wind.[3]
Your Cable's burst, and you must quickly feel
The Waves impetuous entring at your Keel.
Thus, Commonwealths receive a foreign Yoke,
When the strong Cords of Union once are Broke.
Torn by a sudden Tempest is thy Sail,
Expanded to invite a milder Gale.
As when some Writer in a public Cause,
His Pen to save a sinking Nation draws,
While all is Calm, his Arguments prevail,
The People's Voice expands his Paper Sail;
'Till Pow'r, discharging all her stormy Bags,
Flutters the feeble Pamphlet into Rags.
The Nation scar'd, the Author doom'd to Death,
Who fondly put his Trust in pop'lar Breath.

A larger Sacrifice in Vain you vow;
There's not a Pow'r above will help you now:
A Nation thus, who oft Heav'ns Call neglects,
In Vain from injur'd Heav'n Relief expects.
'Twill not avail, when thy strong Sides are broke,
That thy Descent is from the *British* Oak:[4]
Or when your Name and Family you boast,
From Fleets triumphant o'er the *Gallick*[5] Coast.
Such was *Ierne*'s[6] Claim, as just as thine,
Her Sons descended from the *British* Line;
Her matchless Sons; whose Valour still remains
On *French* Records for twenty long Campains;[7]
Yet from an Empress, now a Captive grown,
She saved *Britannia*'s Right, and lost her own.

In Ships decay'd no Mariner confides,
Lur'd by the gilded Stern, and painted Sides.
So, at a Ball, unthinking Fools delight
In the gay Trappings of a Birth-Day Night:[8]
They on the Gold Brocades and Satins rav'd,
And quite forgot their Country was enslav'd.

Dear Vessel, still be to thy Steerage[9] just,
Nor, change thy Course with ev'ry sudden Gust:
Like supple Patriots of the modern Sort,
Who turn with ev'ry Gale that blows from Court.

Weary and Sea-sick when in thee confin'd,
Now, for thy Safety Cares distract my Mind,
As those who long have stood the Storms of State,
Retire, yet still bemoan their Country's Fate.
Beware, and when you hear the Surges roar,
Avoid the Rocks on *Britain*'s angry Shore:
They lye, alas, too easy to be found,
For thee alone they lye the Island round.

1. After the Declaratory Act of 1720, known in Ireland as the Enslaving Act, Swift came to refer to life in Ireland as a form of slavery.
2. An island in the Cyclades in the Aegean Sea, Delos was created by Neptune, who made it float. It was the birthplace of Apollo, Swift's favourite god, and of his twin sister Artemis.
3. Similar imagery occurs in the Drapier's fifth *Letter*, where the '*cold* Easterly *Winds*' are the winds of the tyranny which blows from England. The previous lines seem to refer to Alan Brodrick (*c.* 1656-1728), first viscount Midleton 1717, lord chancellor for Ireland 1714-25, who resigned in 1725; to Thomas Lindsay (died 1724), archbishop of Armagh and primate of Ireland 1714-24, who died in office; and to William King (1650-1729), archbishop of Dublin 1703-29, who was nearing the end of his life.
4. Conventionally the timber of ships, with implications of strength and virtue.
5. French.
6. Ireland's.
7. Either alluding to conflict between the Irish and the Normans in the eleventh and twelfth centuries or to the presence of Irish officers in many regiments of the French army.
8. The celebrations of a birthday in the court.
9. A course that has been set.

IRELAND

Remove me from this land of slaves,[1]
Where all are fools, and all are knaves;

1. Imagery of slavery was common in Swift's writing of this time, and reflected the influence of the Declaratory Act of 1720, known in Ireland as the Enslaving Act.

Where every knave and fool is bought,
Yet kindly sells himself for nought;
Where Whig and Tory fiercely fight
Who's in the wrong, who in the right;
And when their country lyse at stake
They only fight for fighting sake,
While English sharpers[2] take the pay,
And then stand by to see fair play.
Mean time the whig[3] is always winner
And for his courage gets — a dinner.
His Excellency[4] too perhaps
Spits in his mouth and stroaks his Chaps.[5]
The humble whelp[6] gives ev'ry vote:
To put the question strains his throat.[7]
His Excellency's condescension
Will serve instead of place or pension,
When to the window he's trepan'd,[8]
When my Lord shakes him by the hand,
Or in the presence of beholders,
His arms upon the booby's shoulders,
You quickly see the gudgeon[9] bite;
He tells his brother fools at night
How well the Governor's inclined,
So just, so gentle and so kind:
'He heard I kept a pack of hounds,
And longed to hunt upon my grounds;
He said our Ladyes were so fair,
The Court had nothing to compair.
But that indeed which pleased me most,
He called my Dol a perfect toast.[10]
He whispered publick things at last,
Askt me how our elections past.
Some augmentation,[11] Sir, You know,
Would make at least a handsome show.
New Kings[12] a compliment expect;
I shall not offer to direct —

2. swindlers.
3. Swift's idea of a gullible Anglo-Irish MP, completely taken in by the flattery of the lord lieutenant, who advises him to act in ways totally against Ireland's interest. He is both 'slave' and 'knave'.
4. More likely a generalized lord lieutenant than the actual holder, Lord Carteret.
5. cheeks. i.e. has an intimate, close conversation with him.
6. puppy (used contemptuously).
7. strains himself voting for the government.
8. tricked or enticed.
9. A fish that will swallow any bait; hence a gullible person.
10. An attractive woman who would be the ideal toast of the gentlemen of the day. 'Dol' is a name typical of a country rather than a city lady.
11. increase; the MP is asking for an increase in the money available to him for bribery.
12. George II, king of England, Scotland and Ireland 1727-60, whose recent accession had been accompanied by substantial political bribery.

There are some prating folks in town,
But, Sir, we must support the Crown.
Our Letters[13] say a Jesuit[14] boasts
Of some Invasion on your coasts;
The King is ready, when you will,
To pass another Popery bill;[15]
And for dissenters[16] he intends
To use them as his truest friends.
I think they justly ought to share
In all employments we can spare.
Next for encouragement of spinning,
A duty might be layd on linnen;[17]
An act for laying down the Plough,[18]
England will send you corn enough.
Another act that absentees
For licences shall pay no fees.[19]
If England's friendship you would keep,
Feed nothing in your lands but sheep,[20]
But make an act secure and full
To hang up all who smuggle wool.[21]
And then he kindly give me hints
That all our wives should go in Chints.[22]
To morrow I shall tell you more,
For I'm to dine with him at four.'

This was the Speech, and here's the jest:
His arguments convinc't the rest.
Away he runs with zealous hotness
Exceeding all the fools of Totness,[23]
To move that all the Nation round
Should pay a guinnea in the pound.[24]

13. reports in newspapers.
14. Alluding to the possibility of a Jacobite invasion, aimed at establishing on the throne the Old Pretender, James Francis Edward Stuart (1688-1766), the son of James II.
15. i.e. another anti-catholic bill for Ireland.
16. Chiefly presbyterians, who dissented from the obligations imposed by the various Sacramental Test Acts. The English Whigs favoured the dissenters.
17. The lord lieutenant advises the Irish MP on actions that would favour English mercantile interests and damage those of Ireland.
18. i.e. for reducing tillage — to the benefit of English exporters.
19. A piece of sarcasm, since the system of licences and fees was designed to contain the problem of absentees, who were subsequently attacked by Thomas Prior (*c.* 1682-1751) in his *A List of the Absentees of Ireland* (1729).
20. An additional sarcastic joke since the Irish woollen industry had been severely controlled under English legislation.
21. to execute wool smugglers. In fact, the only profitable way to dispose of Irish wool was by smuggling it to France.
22. chintz: expensive, imported fabrics.
23. The people of Totnes, Devon, made an address of loyalty to the king, which was satirized in some verses which appeared in Dublin in 1727 (Swift's editor, Pat Rogers).
24. i.e. should pay a tax of 110 per cent.

Yet should this Blockhead beg a Place
Either from Excellence or Grace[25]
'Tis pre-engaged[26] and in his room[27]
Townshend's cast Page or Walpole's groom.[28]

25. i.e. from the lord lieutenant or from an archbishop.
26. granted to someone else.
27. place.
28. i.e. Townshend's dismissed pageboy or Walpole's [dismissed] groom. Charles Townshend (1674-1738), second viscount 1687, secretary of state 1714-16, 1721-30 and leading Whig, who fell from power in 1730. Sir Robert Walpole (1676-1745), first earl of Orford 1742, chief minister and chancellor of the exchequer 1715-17, 1721-42, and Swift's greatest political enemy.

RICHARD WITHERAL

(*fl.* 1720-30)

A NEW SONG SUNG AT THE CLUB AT MR. TAPLIN'S THE SIGN OF THE DRAPIER'S HEAD IN *TRUCK-STREET*[1]

To the Tune of The Apprentices Song in Massonary[2]

With brisk merry Lays[3]
We'll sing to the Praise
Of that honest Patriot, the DRAPIER;
Who, all the World knows,
Confounded our Foes,
With Nothing but Pen, Ink and Paper.

A Spirit Divine,
Ran through ev'ry Line,
And made all our Hearts for to caper:
He sav'd us our Goods,
And Dumfounder'd *Woods*;[4]
Then long Life and Health to the DRAPIER.

We ne'er shall forget,
His Judgment, or Wit,
But Life, you must know, is a Vapour;
In Ages to come,
We well may Presume,
They'll Monuments raise to the DRAPIER.

When Senators meet,
They'll surely think fit,
To Honour and Praise the good DRAPIER;
Nay Juries shall join,
And Sheriffs Combine,
To thank him in well written Paper.

You Men of the *Comb*,[5]
Come lay by your *Loomb*,[6]
And go to the Sign of the DRAPIER;
To TAPLIN Declare,
You one and all are,
Kind Loving good Friends to his Paper.[7]

Then join Hand in Hand,
T'each other firm stand,
All Health to the CLUB and the DRAPIER;
Who merrily meet,
And sing in *Truck-Street*,
In Praise of the well written Paper.

1. The Club was probably a public house (perhaps legally named 'The Drapier's Head'), owned by a Mr Taplin. Outside hung a portrait of Swift as 'The Drapier'. Truck Street is now Brabazon Street, a small street off the Coombe, to the west of St Patrick's Cathedral and near the Drapier's supposed shop in Francis Street.
2. Probably the tune known as 'Come let us prepare' or 'The Freemason's Song', which may be found in Claude M. Simpson, *The British Broadside Ballad and its Music* (1966), tune 147.
3. tunes, songs.
4. Probably echoing Swift, who misspelled the name of the patentee, William Wood, as Woods, in the original versions of the Drapier's first and second *Letters*, as part of the attack on him.
5. The street near St Patrick's Cathedral which was, at this time, the centre of the depressed weaving industry in Dublin.
6. loom.
7. i.e. *The Drapier's Letters.*

CHARLES SHADWELL

(*fl.* 1710-25)

A SECOND SONG, SUNG AT THE CLUB AT MR. TAPLIN'S THE SIGN OF THE DRAPIER'S-HEAD IN TRUCK-STREET[1]

Since the *Drapier*'s set up, and *Wood* is cry'd down,
Let *Ballads* be made by the *Bards* of this Town;
To thank the brave *Drapier* for what he has done.
Which no Body can deny, brave Boys, which no Body can deny.[2]

1. See note 1 to previous poem.
2. See note 2 to John Winstanley's 'A *Song* Upon an Intended Jaunt to *Power*'s-*court* to see Miss *P*—— *L*——' (p. 466).

When a Project to ruin this Nation was laid,
To Drain all our *Gold*, and give *Brass* in its stead;
The *Drapier* he *writ*, and knock'd all on the Head.
Which no Body can deny, &c.

His Advice he address'd to Men of all Ranks,[3]
Which Timely supported our *Trade* and our *Banks*.
And no doubt the next *Session*[4] he'll have publick *Thanks*,
Which no Body can deny, &c.

But who could imagine that some *Men* in *Place*,[5]
Were for bringing this *Drapier* to *Shame* and *Disgrace*;
Because he had writ upon too nice a Case:
Which no Body can deny, &c.

That a *J[udge]*[6] of this Country should use all his *Skill*,
To prevail on a *J[ur]y* for finding a *Bill*;
And dissolve them because they thwarted his will.
Which no Body can deny, &c.

In vain are all Offers the *Drapier* to take,
This Kingdom ne'er cherish'd a *poisonous Snake*,
And *Informers* are *Wretches* all Men will forsake.
Which no Body can deny, &c.

And for the good Things he has brought to pass,
We here for a Sign have set up his Face;[7]
And wish we cou'd set up his Statue in *Brass*.
Which no Body can deny, &c.

Then, *Taplin*, fill out a Glass of the best,
And let the King's[8] Health be drank by each Guest,
Let it shine in his Face and glow in his Breast.
Which no Body can deny, &c.

3. Alluding to the audience of *The Drapier's Letters*, which were directed to all sections of the community.
4. i.e. of parliament. This was a fanciful suggestion. The Irish parliament met on 21 September 1725, to hear that the patent for the coinage had been surrendered.
5. On 27 October 1724, the Irish privy council issued a proclamation against the Drapier, with a reward of £300 for information leading to his arrest and conviction.
6. William Whitshed (*c.*1656-1727), chief justice of the king's bench in Ireland 1714-27, who, on 21 November 1724, urged the grand jury that had been empanelled to hear charges against Swift's printer, John Harding, to make a presentment of Swift's *Seasonable Advice to the Grand-Jury* (1724), which advised the jury to find Harding innocent. When the members of the jury refused to make this presentment, Whitshed discharged them.
7. as an inn-sign.
8. George I, king of England, Scotland and Ireland 1714-27.

For *Carteret*'s[9] Merit a Bumper[10] prepare,
Whose faithful Report of our Loyalty here,
Has baffled our Foes and remov'd all our Fear.
Which no Body can deny, &c.

The Protestant Int'rest Abroad and at Home,
Our Friends in this City, and those on the *Comb*,[11]
Shall be pledg'd by all Members in this Club and Room.
Which no Body can deny, &c.

Make haste, honest *Taplin*, and bring t'other Pot,[12]
The *Drapier*'s good Friends must not be forgot,
While you have good Liquor, or we have a Groat.[13]
Which no Body can deny, brave Boys, which no Body can deny.

9. Lord Carteret, lord lieutenant 1724-30.
10. glass, tankard.
11. See note 5 to previous poem.
12. tankard.
13. English silver coin.

LAETITIA PILKINGTON

ADVICE TO THE PEOPLE OF DUBLIN, *IN THEIR CHOICE OF A* RECORDER[1]

Is there a Man, whose fix'd and steady Soul
No Flatt'ry can seduce, no Fear controul;
Constant to Virtue, resolutely just,
True to his Friend his Country, and his Trust;
Like *Tully*,[2] Guardian of the *Roman* State,
Is Patriot, Lawyer, Orator compleat;
If such there be, O! let your noble Zeal
Advance him to defend the Public Weal.[3]

Painters and Poets are in this alike,
Mean Artists oft a strong Resemblance strike;
And who can this unfinish'd Picture see,
But owns, O STANNARD![4] it was drawn for thee.

1. The legal official who maintained the rolls of the city and the records of the courts of quarter sessions.
2. Marcus Tullius Cicero (106-43 B.C.), Roman orator, statesman and philosopher.
3. interest, in the sense of prosperity, well-being.
4. Eaton Stannard (*c.* 1685-1755), barrister and member of parliament for Midleton, Co. Cork, who was elected to the position of recorder in 1733, and who was one of the executors of Jonathan Swift's will.

JAMES DALACOURT

ON DISBANDING A TROOP OF DRAGOON[1] VOLUNTEERS

Who were assembled on the Parade, Cork, at the end of the American War[2]

From your saddles to your straddles[3] prepare;
From your boots to your brogues,
To the mountains you rogues —
As you were.[4]

1. Infantrymen who fought either on foot or on horseback.
2. The American War of Independence was formally concluded with the Treaty of Paris in 1783.
3. styles of walking, standing or sitting.
4. Play on the military command 'As you were' and the implication that men who have been soldiers will now be free to return to the mountains and become rebels again.

ANONYMOUS

(*c.* 1778)

LOVE AND WHISKEY[1]

Air — 'Bobbin Joan'[2]

Love and whiskey both,
Rejoice an honest fellow;
Unripe joys of life
Love and whiskey mellow.
Both the head and heart
Set in palpitation;
From both I've often found
A mighty sweet sensation.
Love and whiskey's joys,
Let us gaily twist 'em,
In the thread of life,
Faith, we can't resist 'em.

But love's jealous pang,
In heartache oft we find it;
Whiskey, in its turn,
A headache leaves behind it.
Thus, of love or drink,
We curse th' enchanted cup, sir;
All its charms forswear,
Then take another sup, sir.
Love and whiskey's joys,
Let us gaily twist 'em,
In the thread of life,
Faith, we can't resist 'em.

Love and whiskey can
To anything persuade us;
No other power we fear
That ever can invade us.[3]
Should others dare intrude,
They'll find our lads so frisky,
By none can be subdued,
Excepting love and whiskey.
May the smiles of love
Cheer our lads so clever;
And, with whiskey, boys,
We'll drink King George[4] for ever.

1. This was one of the most popular songs among the Irish Volunteers.
2. Known also as 'Bob and Joan', 'Bobbing Joan', 'Bobbing Joe' and 'Bob in Joe', this English tune is first recorded in the middle of the seventeenth century.
3. The allusion recalls the constant threat of French invasion in the late eighteenth century and probably refers directly to the capture of Carrickfergus, Co. Antrim, by the French commander François Thurot in 1760.
4. George III, king of England, Scotland and Ireland 1760-1820.

EDWARD LYSAGHT

(1763-1811)

THE MAN[1] WHO LED THE VAN[2] OF IRISH VOLUNTEERS

The gen'rous sons of Erin, in manly virtue bold,
With hearts and hands preparing our country to uphold,
Tho' cruel knaves and bigot slaves disturbed our isle some years,
Now hail the man, who led the van of Irish Volunteers.

Just thirty years are ending, since first his glorious aid,
Our sacred rights defending, struck shackles from our trade;[3]

1. Henry Grattan (1746-1820).
2. vanguard, the leading group.
3. Grattan entered the Irish parliament in 1775; among other things, he fought for the removal of restrictions on Irish trade, securing initial success in 1779.

To serve us still, with might and skill, the vet'ran now appears,
That gallant man, who led the van of Irish Volunteers.

He sows no vile dissensions; good will to all he bears;
He knows no vain pretensions, no paltry fears or cares;
To Erin's and to Britain's sons his worth his name endears;
They love the man, who led the van of Irish Volunteers.

Opposed by hirelings sordid,[4] he broke oppression's chain;[5]
On statute-books recorded his patriot acts remain;[6]
The equipoise his mind employs of Commons, King and Peers,
The upright man, who led the van of Irish Volunteers.

A British constitution — to Erin ever true —
In spite of state pollution, he gained in 'Eighty-two';[7]
'He watch'd it in its cradle, and bedew'd its hearse with tears,'[8]
This gallant man, who led the van of Irish Volunteers.

While other nations tremble, by proud oppressors gall'd,
On hustings[9] we'll assemble, by Erin's welfare call'd;
Our Grattan, there we'll meet him, and greet him with three cheers;
The gallant man, who led the van of Irish Volunteers.

4. Alluding to the opposition to Grattan in the Irish parliament, particularly to his early attempts to secure legislative independence in 1780-82.
5. Alluding to Grattan's role in the Irish parliament of 1782, in moving the Declaration of Irish Rights, which was supported unanimously by both houses and which led to the English parliament's repealing the Declaratory Act of 1720.
6. The Irish parliament passed bills to repeal Poynings's Law of 1494, which severely limited the power of the Irish parliament, and to secure other Irish freedoms in 1782.
7. The 'constitution of 1782', in which the Irish parliament declared its independence.
8. Echoing Grattan's words on his career in the Irish parliament: 'Of that assembly I have a parental recollection. I sate by her cradle, I followed her hearse.'
9. election platforms.

JOHN PHILPOT CURRAN
(1750-1817)

THE DESERTER'S MEDITATION

If sadly thinking, with spirits sinking,
  Could, more than drinking, my cares compose,
A cure for sorrow from sighs I'd borrow,
  And hope to-morrow would end my woes.
But as in wailing there's nought availing,
  And Death unfailing will strike the blow,
Then for that reason, and for a season,
  Let us be merry before we go.

To joy a stranger, a wayworn ranger,
  In ev'ry danger my course I've run;
Now hope all ending, and death befriending,
  His last aid lending, my cares are done.
No more a rover, or hapless lover,
  My griefs are over — my glass[1] runs low;
Then for that reason, and for a season,
  Let us be merry before we go.

1. From 'hourglass', suggesting that the sands of time have almost run from one chamber to the other.

MARY O'BRIEN
(*fl.* 1783-90)

THE FREEDOM OF JOHN BULL[1]

As poets write, and painters tell,
In form some heads are like a well;
Round as scoop'd pumpkins in the hull,[2]
Fat brains, thick sinews form a skull,
With every wit so near a kin,[3]
You'd swear, if swearing was no sin,
Genius was in a *fog* within.
A face! for so the stories run,
Resembling much a mid-day sun;
Broad chin, plump cheeks ascending rise,
Sinking the twinkling of two eyes:
Such Jacky Bull, so soft and mellow
He's a mere woolsack[4] of a fellow.

1. The personification of England. The name was established in Dr John Arbuthnot's satire, *Law is a Bottomless Pit* (1712).
2. i.e. as round as the outer casing of a pumpkin.
3. i.e. with every part of the mind so similar to every other part.
4. bulky, but lacking the corresponding weight. The epithet also taunts the English with one of their national images: the seats of the judges and, in particular, that of the lord chancellor, in the House of Lords, were originally cushioned with woolsack.

With belly not unlike a butt,[5]
Behold him oft in elbow strut,[6]
Discoursing on Britannia's[7] laws,
A counsellor in freedom's cause;
As Bacchus[8] on a barrel rides
So he on liberty bestrides,
Trotting with hobby horse's motion[9]
To mount the cliffs of mother ocean.
Firm on a rock, a Briton born,
A foreign coast he views with scorn;
There 'tween roast beef and porter[10] hung,
Each sense suspended, but the tongue,
Free 'midst a load of ills he reigns,
Tax'd at all points except his brains.
Were Billy Pitt[11] but to propose,
A tax on breathing thro' the nose,
Compliant to the youth's[12] intent,
He'd snuffle freedom in his scent;
So proud of his politic fate,
He'd boast tho' sinking with the weight.
Thus Billy, happily befriended,
Patches that fame but last year mended;[13]
As prudes in thread-bare estimation,
Clout up[14] their worn out reputation.

5. target, object of ridicule; also a barrel.
6. swagger aggressively.
7. The female warrior who acts as the personification of Britain.
8. One of the names of Dionysus, the Greek god of vegetation, drink and creativity.
9. i.e. obsessively.
10. The dark, sweet ale which, with roast beef, is traditional fare in England.
11. William Pitt the Younger (1759-1806), English chief or prime minister 1783-1801, 1804-06.
12. Pitt became the leader of the government at the age of twenty-four.
13. When the Regency crisis developed in 1788, Pitt delayed direct action, in the hope that George III would regain his health. The crisis passed in 1789 when the king recovered. Mary O'Brien's poem was published in 1790.
14. patch, repair awkwardly.

PADDY'S[1] OPINION. AN IRISH BALLAD

Since your fame, my dear Billy,[2]
Is burn'd to a snuff,[3]
And your wisdom looks silly,
For want of a puff;[4]
Now, instead of a better,
Take me for your minion,[5]
Without law or letter,
I'll state my opinion:

And to strengthen my case too,
Thro' the maze of my journey,
By my *shoul*[6] I'll take Fraud
To be my Attorney;

And just to a hair[7] too,
So keen is my wit,
Without study or reas'ning
The subject I've hit.

Thus stands my brief[8] now,
Of ev'ry gay light,
That shines by the day,
Or burns by the night,

From the bright fiery beam,
That gilds up your windows,[9]
To the fat greasy taper,
That's burning within doors;

All[10] receive without murmur,
In humble devotion,
(Except the late titles
Made by your promotion,)[11]

Without any cavil,
The *badge* of taxation;
In compliment civil
It's worn thro' the nation.

Since then, haughty Sol,[12]
But darts in his flashes
Thro' the casement, my jewel,
Of your silver sashes:[13]

1. The stock figure of the Irishman, formed from Patrick, the anglicized form of the Irish Pádraig, and employed here against the British with ironic echoes of its derisive use, by them, against Irishmen.
2. William Pitt (1759-1806), English chief or prime minister 1783-1801, 1804-06, whose handling of Anglo-Irish commercial relationships in 1785 aroused hostility in Ireland.
3. The burnt wick of a candle; to be read in the context of the English prohibiton on imports of candles from Ireland.
4. inflated speech, to bolster it up.
5. favourite, especially a servile or fawning one.
6. soul.
7. exactly.
8. (legal) case.
9. i.e. from the sun, the reflection of which makes the windows shine like gold.
10. everybody.
11. Probably alluding to Pitt's creation of new peers and baronets.
12. The personification of the sun.
13. The window tax, which applied mainly to the wealthy, became

Ergo,[14] the argument
Sure will hold good,
All light, my dear joy,
Of coal, grease, or wood,

From hay or from straw,
From rush[15] or from thatch;
Or spark that rekindles
The sulphur of match,

Or vapour that tends
By its light to illume
A crevice or cobweb,
That hangs in a room.

For light is a Critic
No Premier can shun;
Your wit shines the brighter
By taxing the sun.

Arrah,[16] who then can blame you,
By way of a joke,
To tax, without scruple,
Tobacco[17] and smoke.

But beware now, dear *crature*,[18]
Since wisdom may fail ye,
To smoke out our brains,[19]
In the land of Shillelah;[20]

Lest Hibernia's high notions
To anger should rise,
And smoke out your taxes,
And blast your excise.[21]

Arrah, then, my dear Billy,
It might prove in the pull,[22]
Paddy's not quite so silly
As your Jacky Bull.[23]

increasingly important in England's finances. In 1792 it was abolished for houses which had up to seven windows, and in 1797 it was trebled. Sash-windows (the largest kind) generated 'silver' for the government through the tax.

14. therefore.
15. The rush, a grasslike plant, generally used in the plural. Its pith, dipped in tallow, was used to make the narrow candles known as rush candles.
16. An Hiberno-English expletive.
17. Imported into England from America and subject to taxation.
18. Familiar Irish pronunciation of 'creature' — an ironic term of endearment here.
19. make our brains appear. cf. smoking rabbits out of their burrows.
20. Shillelagh, the stick or cudgel, often used derogatively of Ireland.
21. i.e. drive away your taxes and blow away your excise duties. (From 1784 onwards, Pitt was reconstructing the taxation system.)
22. in the act of exercising force.
23. While 'Billy', 'Paddy' and 'Jacky' are congruent forms, the effect of 'Jacky Bull' is incongruous and contemptuous.

WILLIAM DRENNAN
(1754-1820)

THE WAKE OF WILLIAM ORR[1]

Here our murdered brother lies —
Wake him not with women's cries;
Mourn the way that manhood ought;
Sit in silent trance of thought.

Write his merits on your mind —
Morals pure and manners kind;
In his head, as on a hill,
Virtue placed her citadel.

Why cut off in palmy[2] youth?
Truth he spoke, and acted truth —
Countrymen, 'Unite!' he cried,
And died — for what his Saviour died.

God of Peace, and God of Love,
Let it not thy vengeance move!
Let it not thy lightnings draw —
A Nation guillotin'd by law!

Hapless nation! rent and torn,
Thou wert early taught to mourn,
Warfare of six hundred years[3] —
Epochs marked with blood and tears!

Hunted thro' thy native grounds,
Or flung reward to human hounds;
Each one pull'd and tore his share,
Heedless of thy deep despair.

Hapless Nation — hapless Land,
Heap of uncementing sand!

1. A member of the United Irishmen, Orr was executed in 1797 under the terms of the Insurrection Act of 1796, which made the administration of an illegal oath a capital offence.
2. flourishing.
3. i.e. since the 'conquest' of Ireland by the Normans in the late twelfth century.

Crumbled by a foreign weight,
And, by worse, domestic hate.

God of Mercy! God of Peace!
Make the mad confusion cease;
O'er the mental chaos move,
Through it speak the light of love.

Monstrous and unhappy sight,
Brothers' blood will not unite;
Holy oil and holy water,
Mix, and fill the world with slaughter.

Who is she with aspect wild?
The widow'd mother with her child —
Child new stirring in the womb!
Husband waiting for the tomb!

Angel of this sacred place,
Calm her soul and whisper peace,
Cord, or axe, or guillotin'
Make the sentence — not the sin.[4]

Here we watch our brother's sleep;
Watch with us, but do not weep;
Watch with us thro' dead of night,
But expect the morning light.

Conquer fortune — persevere! —
Lo! it breaks, the morning clear!
The cheerful cock awakes the skies,
The day is come — arise! — arise!

4. The sense is 'The separate methods of execution effect the sentence, which the offence, the sin, does not justify.'

ANDREW CHERRY

(1762-1812)

THE GREEN LITTLE SHAMROCK[1] OF IRELAND

There's a dear little plant that grows in our isle,
'Twas Saint Patrick[2] himself, sure, that set[3] it;
And the sun on his labor with pleasure did smile,
And with dew from his eye often wet it.
It thrives through the bog, through the brake,[4]
through the mireland;[5]
And he called it the dear little shamrock of Ireland,
The sweet little shamrock, the dear little shamrock,
The sweet little, green little, shamrock of Ireland.

This dear little plant still grows in our land,
Fresh and fair as the daughters of Erin,
Whose smiles can bewitch, whose eyes can
command,
In each climate that they may appear in;
And shine through the bog, through the brake,
through the mireland;
Just like their own dear little shamrock of Ireland,
The sweet little shamrock, the dear little shamrock,
The sweet little, green little, shamrock of Ireland.

This dear little plant that springs from our soil,
When its three little leaves are extended,
Denotes from one stalk we together should toil,
And ourselves by ourselves be befriended;
And still through the bog, through the brake,
through the mireland,
From one root should branch, like the shamrock of
Ireland,
The sweet little shamrock, the dear little shamrock,
The sweet little, green little, shamrock of Ireland.

1. The shamrock became 'a religious emblem and a badge of nationality about 1700'. After the late 1770s it came to be associated, through its colour, with the emergence of the patriotic movements (G.-D. Zimmermann).
2. Alluding to the traditional but comparatively recent story that St Patrick used the shamrock to demonstrate the mysterious unity of the Holy Trinity.
3. planted.
4. thicket.
5. An area of bogs or marshes.

JAMES ORR

(1770-1816)

SONG

Composed on the Banks[1] of Newfoundland

In Ireland 'tis ev'ning. From toil my friends hie[2] all,
And weary walk home o'er the dew-sprinkled lea;
The shepherd in love tunes his grief-soothing viol,
Or visits the maid that his partner will be:

1. Fishing banks. Orr went into exile in America after the battle of Antrim in 1798 and wrote this poem near the end of his voyage.
2. Archaic and poetic usage, meaning hasten, make speed.

The blythe milk-maids trip to the herd that stands
lowing,
The West[3] finely smiles, and the landscape is
glowing,
The sad-sounding curfew,[4] and torrent fast-flowing,
Are heard by my fancy,[5] tho' far, far at sea.

What has my eye seen since I left the green valies
But ships as remote as the prospect could be?
Unwieldy huge monsters, as ugly as *malice*?
And planks of some wreck, which with sorrow I
see?
What's seen but the fowl that his lonely flight urges?
The light'ning that darts thro' the sky-meeting
surges?
And the sad scouling sky, that with bitter rain
scourges
This cheek, Care sits drooping on, far, far at sea.

How hideous the hold is! — Here, children are
screaming,
There dames faint, thro' thirst, with their babes
on their knee;
Here, down ev'ry hatch the big breakers are
streaming,
And, there, with a crash, half the fixtures break
free:
Some court — some contend — some sit dull
stories telling —
The mate's mad and drunk, and the tar's task'd
and yelling:
What sickness and sorrow, pervade my rude
dwelling! —
A huge floating lazar-house,[6] far, far at sea.

How chang'd all may be when I seek[7] the sweet
village!
A hedge-row may bloom where its street us'd to
be;
The floors of my friends may be tortur'd by tillage,[8]
And the upstart be serv'd by the fallen grandee:[9]

3. The west of Ireland, traditionally associated with the inspiration of creativity; also, the sunset makes the landscape 'glow'.
4. evening-bell.
5. Imagination and 'opinion bred rather by the imagination than the reason' (Samuel Johnson).
6. From 'lazar', a diseased person, and hence a place for the diseased, a hospital.
7. The poet imagines the sights he may see if he returns after some while has passed. cf. Goldsmith's *The Deserted Village*.
8. Referring to the possibility of dispossession and the use of acquired ground for the raising of crops.
9. an eminent person. i.e. the new landlord served by the dispossessed, hereditary landowner.

The axe may have humbled the grove that I haunted,
And shades be my shield that as yet are unplanted;
Nor one comrade live, who repin'd when he wanted
The sociable suff'rer, that's far, far at sea.

In Ireland 'tis night. On the flow'rs of my setting[10]
A parent may kneel, fondly praying for me:
The village is smokeless, the red moon is getting
The hill for a throne, which I yet hope to see:
If innocence thrive, many more have to grieve for,
Success, slow but sure, I'll contentedly live for —
Yes, Sylvia![11] we'll meet, and your sigh cease to
heave for
The swain, your fine image haunts, far, far at sea.

10. Home and its surroundings.
11. A Roman name, popular in the Renaissance, derived from 'silva', a wood, orchard, or grove, and hence appropriate to the evocation of the rural world; a generalized name for a maiden/lover.

THE IRISHMAN

The savage loves his native shore,
Though rude[1] the soil and chill the air;
Well then may Erin's sons adore
Their isle, which Nature formed so fair!
What flood reflects a shore so sweet,
As Shannon great, or past'ral Bann?[2]
Or who a friend or foe can meet,
So gen'rous as an Irishman?

His hand is rash, his heart is warm,
But principle is still his guide —
None more regrets a deed of harm,
And none forgives with nobler pride.
He may be duped, but won't be dared; —
Fitter to practise than to plan,
He dearly earns his poor reward,
And spends it like an Irishman.

If strange or poor, for you he'll pay,
And guide to where you safe may be;
If you're his guest, while e'er you stay,
His cottage holds a jubilee:
His inmost soul he will unlock,
And if he should *your* secrets scan,

1. coarse.
2. The river Shannon, the largest river in Ireland, and the river Bann, which rises in the Mourne mountains and flows through Lough Neagh to the sea.

Your confidence he scorns to mock,
For faithful is an Irishman.

By honour bound in woe or weal,[3]
Whate'er she bids he dares to do;
Tempt him with bribes, he will not fail;
Try him in fire, you'll find him true.
He seeks not safety: let his post
Be where it ought, in danger's van;[4]
And if the field of fame be lost,
'Twill not be by an Irishman.

Erin, loved land! from age to age,
Be thou more great, more fam'd and free!
May peace be thine, or, should'st thou wage
Defensive war, cheap victory!
May plenty flow in every field;
With gentle breezes softly fan,
And cheerful smiles serenely gild,
The breast of every Irishman!

3. prosperity, well-being.
4. vanguard, the leading group.

WILLIAM BLACKER

(1777-1855)

OLIVER'S[1] ADVICE

The night is gathering gloomily, the day is closing fast —
The tempest flaps his raven wings in loud and angry blast;
The thunder clouds are driving athwart the lurid sky —
But 'put your trust in God, my boys, and keep your powder dry.'[2]

There was a day when loyalty was hailed with honour due,[3]
Our banner the protection waved to all the good and true —
And gallant hearts beneath its folds were linked in honour's tie,
We put our trust in God, my boys, and kept our powder dry.

When Treason bared her bloody arm, and maddened round the land,
For King, and laws, and order fair, we drew the ready brand;[4]
Our gathering spell was William's[5] name — our word was, 'Do or die.'
And still we put our trust in God, and kept our powder dry.

But now, alas! a wondrous change has come the nation o'er,
And worth and gallant services remembered are no more;
And, crushed beneath oppression's weight, in chains of grief we lie —
But put your trust in God, my boys, and keep your powder dry.

Forth starts the spawn of Treason, the 'scaped of Ninety-eight,[6]
To bask in courtly favour, and seize the helm of state —
E'en they whose hands are reeking yet with murder's crimson dye;
But put your trust in God, my boys, and keep your powder dry.

They come, whose deeds incarnadined[7] the Slaney's[8] silver wave —
They come, who to the foreign foe[9] the hail of welcome gave;
He comes, the open rebel fierce — he comes, the Jesuit sly;[10]

1. Oliver Cromwell (1599-1658), whose savage campaign in Ireland in 1649-50 led to the subjugation of the country by 1652. The poet evokes the spirit of this archetypal protestant avenger to encourage protestants dispirited by the rise of catholic influence after the Act of Union.
2. A remark attributed to Cromwell, whose troops were about to cross a river before making an attack.
3. i.e. under Cromwell.
4. flaming torch, sword. These two lines refer to the Jacobite period, 1685-90.
5. William of Orange, king of England 1689-1702, who defeated James II at the battle of the Boyne in 1690.
6. Alluding to those who escaped being brought to 'justice' after the uprising in 1798, some of whom may have had political influence after the Act of Union.
7. dyed with blood, possibly echoing Shakespeare, *Macbeth*, II. 2. 60-62.
8. Referring to one of the last battles of 1798, when the insurgents were defeated at Vinegar Hill, near Enniscorthy, Co. Wexford.
9. The French, who supported the uprising and who fought with the insurgents in various battles.
10. The cliché of the Jesuit priest, who was held to be devious and equivocal.

But put your trust in God, my boys, and keep your
powder dry.

They come, whose counsels wrapped the land in
foul rebellious flame,
Their hearts unchastened by remorse, their cheeks
untinged by shame.
Be still, be still, indignant heart — be tearless, too,
each eye,
And put your trust in God, my boys, and keep your
powder dry.

The Power that led his chosen, by pillared cloud
and flame,[11]
Through parted sea and desert waste,[12] that Power
is still the same;
He fails not — He, the loyal hearts that firm on him
rely —
So put your trust in God, my boys, and keep your
powder dry.

The Power that nerved the stalwart arms of
Gideon's chosen few,[13]
The Power that led great William, Boyne's[14]
reddening torrent through —
In his protecting aid confide, and every foe defy —
Then put your trust in God, my boys, and keep
your powder dry.

Already see the star of hope emits its orient[15] blaze,
The cheering beacon of relief it glimmers thro' the
haze.
It tells of better days to come, it tells of succour
nigh —
Then put your trust in God, my boys, and keep
your powder dry.

See, see along the hills of Down[16] its rising glories
spread,

11. Alluding to Exodus 13. 20-22, where the Lord led the Israelites out of bondage in Egypt, appearing in front of them as a pillar of cloud by day and as a pillar of flame by night.
12. Alluding to Exodus 14. 15-31, where the Lord made the waters of the Red Sea part in front of the Israelites in the desert, and then flood back again to engulf the pursuing Egyptians.
13. Alluding to Judges 6.11-8.35, the account of Gideon, who was visited by the angel of the Lord and who selected a band of three hundred men, with which he defeated the army of the Midianites.
14. William of Orange at the battle of the Boyne.
15. Irish protestants looked to the east (Britain) for support.
16. The Mountains of Mourne in County Down.

But brightest beams its radiance from Donard's[17]
lofty head.
Clanbrassil's[18] vales are kindling[19] wide, and
'Roden' is the cry[20] —
Then put your trust in God, my boys, and keep
your powder dry.

Then cheer, ye hearts of loyalty, nor sink in dark
despair,
Our banner shall again unfold its glories to the air.
The storm that raves the wildest the soonest passes
by;
Then put your trust in God, my boys, and keep
your powder dry.

For 'happy homes,' for 'altars free,'[21] we grasp the
ready sword —
For freedom, truth, and for our God's unmutilated
word.[22]
These, these the war-cry of our march, our hope
the Lord on high;
Then put your trust in God, my boys, and keep
your powder dry.

17. Slieve Donard, the commanding peak that overlooks the sea to the east of the Mountains of Mourne.
18. The Hamiltons, earls of Clanbrassil in the seventeenth and eighteenth centuries, were associated with various places in Counties Down, Armagh and Louth.
19. being aroused, inflamed.
20. Alluding to the Jocelyns, earls of Roden in the late eighteenth and early nineteenth centuries. Robert Jocelyn (1756-1820), second earl of Roden 1797, member of parliament for Dundalk 1783-97, and auditor general of the exchequer 1797-1820, fought against the insurgents at Rathfarnham, Co. Dublin, and at Castlebar, Co. Mayo in 1798 as the commander of the First Fencible Light Dragoons.
21. The dreams of the Israelites, cast as the political slogans of the Orange Order.
22. Asserting the traditional protestant argument of the right of interpretation of the Scriptures based on the biblical languages, instead of on the Vulgate.

CHECKLIST OF POEMS AND SOURCES

Abbreviations Used

Cabinet — Charles A. Read (ed.), *The Cabinet of Irish Literature*, new ed. by Katharine Tynan Hinkson, 4 vols (London: Gresham Publishing, 1903).

Dublin Book — John Cooke (ed.), *The Dublin Book of Irish Verse 1728-1909* (Dublin: Hodges, Figgis, 1924).

Foxon — David F. Foxon (ed.), *English Verse 1701-1750: A Catalogue of Separately Printed Poems* .... 2 vols (Cambridge: Cambridge University Press, 1975).

Irish Literature — Justin McCarthy et al (eds), *Irish Literature* 10 vols (New York: Bigelow, Smith & Co., 1911; reprinted New York and London: Johnson Reprint Corporation, 1970).

Teerink — Herman Teerink (ed.), *A Bibliography of the Writings of Jonathan Swift*, revised edition (Philadelphia: University of Pennsylvania Press, 1963).

1000 Years — Kathleen Hoagland (ed.), *1000 Years of Irish Poetry. The Gaelic and Anglo-Irish Poets from Pagan Times to the Present* (New York: Devin-Adair, 1947).

Poems and Sources

Anon. 'On the College of Physicians in Dublin', from Andrew Carpenter (ed.), *Irish Writings from the Age of Swift*, II (Monkstown, Co. Dublin: The Cadenus Press, 1973), p. 18.

Anon. 'Garryowen', from T. Crofton Croker (ed.), *Popular Songs of Ireland* (London: H. Colburn, 1839).

Anon. 'The Happy Beggarman', from *1000 Years*, p. 265.

Anon. 'Brennan on the Moor', from *1000 Years*, pp. 250-52.

Anon. 'The Boys of Kilkenny', from H. Halliday Sparling (ed.), *Irish Ministrelsy. A Selection of Irish Songs and Ballads; Original and Translated*, 2nd edition, revised (London and New York: Walter Scott, n.d.).

Anon. [Thomas Wharton?] 'Lilli burlero', from T. Crofton Croker (ed.), *The Historical Songs of Ireland . . . .*, pp. 6-9.

Anon. 'The Blackbird', from Allan Ramsay (ed.), *The Tea-Table Miscellany: A Collection of Choice Songs Scots & English*, reprinted from the 14th edition, 2 vols (Glasgow, 1876) I, 107-08.

Anon. 'Love and Whiskey', from T. Crofton Croker (ed.), *Popular Songs of Ireland*.

Anon. *The Irish Hudibras, or Fingallian Prince* (London, 1689), pp. 31-37.

Anon. ['William Moffet'] — Canto I of *Hesperi-neso-graphia* (1716), Foxon H162, from *The Irish Hudibras. Hesperi-neso-graphia: Or, a Description of the Western Isle* (London, 1755), pp. 1-4.

Anon. ['Murrough O'Connor'] — 'A Description of the County of Kerry' (Dublin, 1726), Foxon 011, from *The Petition of Murroghoh O Connor to the Provost and Senior Fellows of Trinity College, near Dublin. To which are added, I. An Eclogue, in Imitation of the First Eclogue of Virgil. Inscrib'd to the Provost and Fellows of Trinity College, &c. with additional Notes. II. Two Dialogues between Murroghoh O Connor and his Friend. III. The County of Kerry. A Poem* (Dublin, 1740), Foxon 013, pp. 24-28.

James Arbuckle — 'Momus Mistaken . . . .' (Dublin, 1735), Foxon A282, from Swift's *Works* (Dublin: Faulkner, 1768), XVII, iii-vi (Teerink 53).

Mary Barber — *Poems on Several Occasions* (London, 1734). 'On sending my Son, as a Present, to Dr. *Swift* . . . .', pp. 71-72. 'An Epigram on the *Battle of the Books*', p. 164.

George Berkeley — 'On the Prospect of Planting Arts and Learning in America', from *Irish Literature*, Vols I and II reprinted in one volume. pp. 180-81.

William Blacker — 'Oliver's Advice', from *Dublin Book*, pp. 29-32.

Henry Brooke — Extract from *Universal Beauty: A Philosophical Poem* (1735), from *The Poetical Works of Henry Brooke, Esq*, 4 vols, ed. Charlotte Brooke, 3rd ed. (Dublin, 1792), II, 18-22.

Andrew Cherry — 'The Green Little Shamrock of Ireland' from *Irish Literature*, Vols I and II reprinted in one volume, pp. 587-88.

Henry Brereton Code — from Code's *The Russian Sacrifice; or, The Burning of Moscow. As Performed at the Theatre-Royal, Dublin* (Dublin, 1813). 'Song — Air, Langolee', pp. 17-18; 'Song — Sprig of Shillela', pp. 14-16.

Matthew Concanen — 'October Ale', from *Cabinet*, Vol. II, p. 104.

John Philpot Curran — 'The Deserter's Meditation' from *Dublin Book*, pp. 5-6.

James Dalacourt — from *Poetry and Legendary Ballads of the South of Ireland by various writers, with biographical notices, notes etc.* (First series) (1894), published in *The Journal of the Cork Historical and Archaeological Society* (Cork: Guy & Co. Ltd., 1894). 'On his Brother's Marriage', pp. 277-78; 'On disbanding a Troop of Dragoon Volunteers . . . .', p. 270. (Dalacourt material edited by John O'Mahony.)

Patrick Delany — '*News from* Parnassus' (Dublin, 1721), Foxon D202 from Harold Williams (ed.), *The Poems of Jonathan Swift*, I, 266-69. Also in Matthew Concanen's *Miscellaneous Poems* (London, 1724), p. 215.

Thomas Dermody — 'John Baynham's Epitaph', from *1000 Years*, pp. 369-71; 'An Ode to Myself' from *1000 Years*, pp. 372-73.

William Drennan — 'The Wake of William Orr' from *Dublin Book*, pp. 12-14.

William Dunkin — 'Carbery *Rocks* . . . .', from Swift, *Poems* (ed. Harold Williams), I, 318-19. All other Dunkin poems from his *Select Poetical Works*, 2 vols (Dublin, 1769-70).

Oliver Goldsmith — *The Deserted Village* (1770) and the extract from *The Traveller* (1764) from Arthur Friedman (ed.), *The Collected Works of Oliver Goldsmith*, 5 vols (Oxford: Clarendon Press, 1966).

Constantia Grierson — '*To Miss* Laetitia van Lewen . . . . from *The Memoirs of Mrs. Laetitia Pilkington* (Dublin, 1776), pp. 25-26.

Esther Johnson ('Stella') — '*To* Dr. Swift *on his Birth-day, November 30,* 1721' from Swift, *Poems*, II, 737-38.

Edward Lysaght — 'The Man who Led the Van of Irish Volunteers', from *Dublin Book*, pp. 16-17.

Thomas Newburgh — 'The *Beau Walk*, in *Stephen's-Green*', from [Thomas Newburgh], *Essays Poetical, Moral and Critical* (Dublin, 1769).

Mary O'Brien — from O'Brien's *The Political Monitor; or Regent's Friend. Being a Collection of Poems Published in England during the Agitation of the Regency: Consisting of Curious, Interesting, Satyrical and Political Effusions of Poetry* (Dublin, 1790). 'The Freedom of John Bull' and 'Paddy's Opinion. An Irish Ballad', pp. 27-32.

Charles O'Flaherty — 'The Humours of Donnybrook Fair' from *1000 Years*, pp. 265-67.

George Ogle — 'Mailligh a Stór', from *Dublin Book*, pp. 3-5.

James Orr — 'Song Composed on the Banks of Newfoundland', from *Poems on Various Subjects* by James Orr, new ed. (Belfast: William Mullan & Son, 1936) (reprint of *Poems on Various Subjects* [Belfast, 1804]), pp. 167-68; 'The Irishman', from *The Posthumous Works of James Orr, of Ballycarry: with a Sketch of his Life* (Belfast, 1817), pp. 132-34.

Thomas Parnell — 'Song', from his *Poems on Several Occasions . . . .* (London, 1722), pp. 18-19.

Ambrose Philips — 'An Epilogue . . . .' (Dublin, 1721), Foxon P203, from Concanen's *Miscellaneous Poems*, pp. 274-76.

Laetitia Pilkington — Text from *The Memoirs of Mrs. Laetitia Pilkington* (Dublin, 1776). 'The Happy Pair', pp. 174-75, and '*Advice to the People of* Dublin . . . .', p. 93.

Matthew Pilkington — from his *Poems on Several Occasions* (London, 1731) (Foxon, I, 575). 'The Progress of Music in *Ireland*', pp. 1-17 (this is Foxon P282, first published Dublin, 1725); 'The Gift', p. 74.

Richard Pockrich — 'The Temple-Oge Ballad' (Rathfarnham, 1730), Foxon P516.

George Nugent Reynolds — 'Kathleen O'More', from *Dublin Book*, pp. 22-23.

Charles Shadwell — 'A Second Song. . . .' (Dublin, 1725), Foxon S381, from *The Hibernian Patriot* (London, 1730), pp. 256-57 (Teerink 22).

Thomas Sheridan — 'To the *Dean*, when in England, in 1726', from Swift, *Poems*, III, 1042-44.

Jonathan Smedley — 'Verses, *Fix'd on the Cathedral Door* . . . .' from *Gulliveriana* (London, 1728), pp. 77-79 (Teerink 32).

James Sterling — from *The Poetical Works of the Rev. James Sterling* (Dublin, 1734). 'An Epigram . . . .', pp. 22-23.

Jonathan Swift — All poems from Harold Williams (ed.), *The Poems of Jonathan Swift*, 3 vols (Oxford: Clarendon Press, 2nd ed. 1958).

Nahum Tate — 'While Shepherds Watched their Flocks by Night', *1000 Years*, p. 322.

James Ward — Extract from '*Phoenix* Park' from Concanen's *Miscellaneous Poems* (London, 1724), pp. 378-88.

Laurence Whyte — from his *Poems on Various Subjects, Serious and Diverting, Never before Published* (Dublin, 1740). 'The Hue and Cry after the Clieve-Boy', pp. 168-69; '*A Dissertation on* Italian *and* Irish *Musick*', pp. 154-59; 'To the Rev. Dr. *Jonathan Swift* . . . .', pp. 181-85; 'On *St.* Patrick's-Eve . . . .', p. 204; '*The Old* Westmeath-Ballad', pp. 206-08.

Samuel Whyte — from his *Poems on Various Subjects*, 3rd ed., rev. Edward Athenry Whyte (Dublin, 1795). 'The New Ferry . . . .', pp. 204-08, 332-35; 'The Hone', pp. 255-57, 258.

John Winstanley — from his *Poems Written Occasionally. Interspers'd with many others, by Several Ingenious Hands* (Dublin, 1742). '*An* Inventory . . . .', pp. 86-87; '*A* Thought, *in the Pleasant* Grove *at* Cabragh', pp. 184-45; '*A* Song, *by a* Cumberland-Lass', pp. 155-56; 'A *Song* upon an Intended Jaunt to *Power's-court* . . . .', pp. 197-99.

Richard Witheral — 'A New Song . . . .' (Dublin, 1724), Foxon D428.

General Bibliography

Russell K. Alspach, *Irish Poetry from the English Invasion to 1798*, 2nd ed. (Philadelphia: University of Pennsylvania Press, 1959).

J.C. Beckett, 'Literature in English 1691-1800', Chapter XIV of T.W. Moody and W.E. Vaughan (eds), *Eighteenth-Century Ireland 1691-1800*, Vol. IV of F.X. Martin et al (eds), *A New History of Ireland* (Oxford: Clarendon Press, 1986).

Anne M. Brady and Brian Cleeve, *A Biographical Dictionary of Irish Writers* (Mullingar: The Lilliput Press, 1985).

Andrew Carpenter and Alan Harrison, 'Swift's "O'Rourke's Feast" and Sheridan's "Letter": Early Transcripts by Anthony Raymond' in Hermann J. Real and Heinz J. Vienken (eds), *Proceedings of the First Münster Symposium on Jonathan Swift* (Munich: Wilhelm Fink, 1985), pp. 27-46.

Brian Cleeve, *Dictionary of Irish Writers*, 2 vols (Cork: Mercier Press, 1967-69).

Bryan Coleborne, 'Jonathan Swift and the Dunces of Dublin', unpublished Ph.D. thesis, National University of Ireland, 1982.

Bryan Coleborne, 'The Dublin Grub Street: The Documentary Evidence in the Case of John Browne', *Swift Studies* 2 (1987), 12-24.

Bryan Coleborne, 'Jonathan Swift and the Voices of Irish Protest against Wood's Halfpence', in Clive T. Probyn and Bryan Coleborne (eds.), *Monash Swift Papers* 1 (1988), 66-86.

Bryan Coleborne, 'Jonathan Swift and the Literary World of Dublin', *Englisch Amerikanische Studien* 1 (1988), 6-28.

Matthew Concanen (ed.), *Miscellaneous Poems* (London, 1724); (contains poems by Delany, Parnell, Philips, Sheridan, Smedley, Sterling, Swift and Ward).

T. Crofton Croker (ed.), *Popular Songs of Ireland* (London: H. Colburn, 1839).

T. Crofton Croker (ed.), *The Historical Songs of Ireland: Illustrative of the Revolutionary Struggle between James II and William III* (London: The Percy Society, 1841).

T. Crofton Croker, *Popular Songs, Illustrative of the French Invasions of Ireland* (London: The Percy Society, 1845-47).

Donald Davie (ed.), *The Late Augustans: Longer Poems of the Later Eighteenth Century* (London: Heinemann, 1968).

Joseph C. Day, 'William Dunkin: "Best Poet" in the Kingdom? A New Look at his Augustan Burlesque', unpublished M.A. thesis, National University of Ireland, 1978.

Oliver W. Ferguson, *Jonathan Swift and Ireland* (Urbana, Illinois: University of Illinois Press, 1962).

W.H. Grattan Flood, *A History of Irish Music* (Dublin: Browne & Nolan, 1905).

Folk Music Society of Ireland, *Popular Music in Eighteenth-Century Dublin* (Dublin: Folk Music Society of Ireland, 1985).

John Hewitt, *Rhyming Weavers and Other Country Poets of Antrim and Down* (Belfast: Blackstaff Press, 1974).

Robert Hogan (ed.), *Dictionary of Irish Literature* (Westport, Connecticut: Greenwood Press; Dublin: Gill and Macmillan, 1979).

E.M. Johnston, *Ireland in the Eighteenth Century* (Dublin: Gill and Macmillan, 1974).

Arno Löffler, 'The End of a Satirist's Career: "The Legion Club"....', *Englisch Amerikanische Studien* 1 (1988), 70-82.

James Malton, *Georgian Dublin: Twenty-Five Aquatint Views in Colour*, ed. Maurice Craig (Dublin: Dolmen Press, 1984).

Roger McHugh, 'Anglo-Irish Poetry 1700-1850' in Seán Lucy (ed.), *Irish Poets in English* (Cork: Mercier Press, 1973).

Edward McParland, 'Sir Edward Lovet Pearce's Parliament House: Some Architectural Observations', paper delivered to the American Society for Eighteenth-Century Studies Conference, Williamsburg, Virginia, 1986.

John and William Neal, *A Collection of the Most Celebrated Irish Tunes Proper for the Violin, German Flute or Hautboy* (Dublin, 1724), facsimile edition by Nicholas Carolan (Dublin: Folklore Society of Ireland, 1986).

D.J. O'Donoghue, *The Poets of Ireland: A Biographical and Bibliographical Dictionary of Irish Writers of English Verse* (Dublin: Hodges, Figgis, 1912).

Hugh Shields et al (eds), *Irish Folk Music Studies* 4 (1982-85) (Dublin: Folk Music Society of Ireland, 1985).

Claude M. Simpson, *The British Broadside Ballad and Its Music* (New Brunswick, New Jersey: Rutgers University Press, 1966).

Janet Todd (ed.), *A Dictionary of British and American Women Writers 1660-1800* (London: Methuen, 1984).

J.M. Treadwell, 'William Wood and the Company of Ironmasters of Great Britain', *Business History* 16, No. 2 (July 1974), 97-112.

J.M. Treadwell, 'Swift, William Wood, and the Factual Basis of Satire', *The Journal of British Studies* 15, No. 2 (Spring 1976), 76-91.

T.J. Walsh, *Opera in Dublin 1705-1797: The Social Scene* (Dublin: Allen Figgis, 1973).

H.A. Wheeler and M.J. Craig, *The Dublin City Churches of the Church of Ireland: An Illustrated Handbook* (Dublin: APCK, 1948).

G.-D. Zimmermann, *Irish Political Street Ballads and Rebel Songs 1780-1900* (Dublin: Allen Figgis, 1967), published in America as *Songs of Irish Rebellion: Political Street Ballads and Rebel Songs 1780-1900* (Hatboro, Pennsylvania: Folklore Associates Inc., 1967).

Biographies/Bibliographies

[In this section, the bio/bibliographical entries are in alphabetical order to facilitate reference to the authors of specific poems.]

James Arbuckle

LIFE. The son of the Rev. James Arbuckle (?-1720), a presbyterian minister in Dublin, James Arbuckle was born about 1700. He studied at the University of Glasgow, where he became a friend of Allan Ramsay, the Scottish poet. In Dublin, he moved in presbyterian circles and was a member of the literary group around Viscount Molesworth and the philosopher Francis Hutcheson, whose work he published in *The Dublin Weekly Journal*, which he edited (1725-27) as 'Hibernicus'. Arbuckle was frequently attacked and lampooned by the literati of Dublin. At the time of his death in 1742 he held two positions in the bureaucracy in Dublin: clerk in the quitrents and forfeitures section, and clerk in the postage section of the Office of the Commissioners of the Revenue and Excise. (He should not be confused with James Arbuckle, a prominent physician specializing in midwifery in Dublin at the same time, who died in 1746.)

CHIEF WRITINGS. 'Snuff, a Poem' (Glasgow, 1717); 'An Epistle to the Right Honourable Thomas Earl of Hadington, on the Death of Joseph Addison, Esq.' (London, 1719); 'Glotta, a Poem humbly inscribed to the Right Honourable the Marquess of Carnarvon' (Glasgow, 1721); 'Momus Mistaken: A Fable, Occasioned by the Publication of the Works of the Revd. Dr. Swift, D.S.P.D. in Dublin' (Dublin, 1735); 'A Poem Inscribed to the Dublin Society' (Dublin, 1737); [James Arbuckle and others], *A Collection of Letters and Essays on Several Subjects, Lately Publish'd in the Dublin Journal*, 2 vols (London, 1729); [James Arbuckle and others], *Hibernicus's Letters: or, a Philosophical Miscellany*. 2nd ed. 2 vols (London, 1734).

BIOGRAPHY AND CRITICISM. 'The Bibliographical Society of Ireland' [Report of paper on Arbuckle by T.P.C. Kirkpatrick], *The Irish Book Lover*, 26 (May 1939), 103-04; Bryan Coleborne, 'James Arbuckle and Jonathan Swift: New Light on Swift's Biography', *Studies in the Eighteenth Century* 6, ed. Colin Duckworth and Homer Le Grand, published in *Eighteenth-Century Life*, 11, n.s. 1 (February 1987), 170-80; M.A. Stewart, 'John Smith and the Molesworth Circle', *Eighteenth-Century Ireland*, 2 (1987); 89-102; Aubrey L. Williams, '"A Vile Encomium": That "Panegyric on the Reverend D--n S---t"' in John Irwin Fisher and Donald C. Mell (eds), *Contemporary Studies of Swift's Poetry*, (Newark: University of Delaware Press, 1981), pp. 178-90; James Woolley, 'Arbuckle's "Panegyrick" and Swift's Scrub Libel: The Documentary Evidence' in *Contemporary Studies of Swift's Poetry*, pp. 191-209.

Mary Barber

LIFE. Mary Barber was born in Dublin in 1690. She married a Dublin tailor and clothier, and became a member of Swift's circle, where she was known as 'Sapphira'. Her friends included Laetitia and Matthew Pilkington, Constantia Grierson, and Dr Patrick Delany. Swift advised and supported her, giving her the manuscript of his *Polite Conversation*, which was published in 1738. She died in Dublin in 1757.

BIOGRAPHY AND CRITICISM. Andrew Carpenter, 'On a manuscript of poems catalogued as by Mary Barber in the Library of T.C.D.', *Hermathena*, 109 (1969), 54-64; Oliver W. Ferguson, 'The Authorship of "Apollo's Edict"', *PMLA* 70 (1955), 433-40; Joyce Fullard, 'Mary Barber [Sapphira]' in Janet Todd (ed.), *A Dictionary of British and American Women Writers 1660-1800* (London: Methuen, 1984), p. 38.

George Berkeley

For biography and bibliography, see pp. 804-05.

William Blacker

LIFE. A native of County Armagh, William Blacker was born in 1777. He was educated at Trinity College, Dublin and wrote for *The Dublin University Magazine*. He entered the army and rose to the rank of colonel. Blacker became known as a military versifier and for his Orange ballads, especially 'Oliver's Advice'. He died in 1855. Little is known of his life, and his poems have not been collected.

CHIEF WRITINGS. Poems not collected.

BIOGRAPHY AND CRITICISM. There is passing reference to him, and explanation of the context for some of his verse, in G.-D. Zimmermann, *Irish Political Street Ballads and Rebel Songs 1780-1900* (Dublin: Allen Figgis, 1967).

Henry Brooke

For biography and bibliography, see p. 759.

Andrew Cherry

LIFE. Little is known about the background of Andrew Cherry, except that he was born in 1762 in Limerick, where his father was a printer and bookseller. He became an actor, song-writer and dramatist, well-known in Dublin and London. He is remembered today for his songs 'The Green Little Shamrock of Ireland' and 'The Bay of Biscay'. He died, apparently in Monmouth, Wales, in 1812.

CHIEF WRITINGS. *The Soldier's Daughter* (London, 1804) (comedy); *The Travellers; or Music's Fascination* (London, 1806) (operatic drama); *Spanish Dollars; or, The Priest of the Parish* (London, 1806) (operatic drama); *Peter the Great; or, The Wooden Walls* (London, 1807) (operatic drama).

BIOGRAPHY AND CRITICISM. Noted in Robert Hogan (ed.), *Dictionary of Irish Literature* (Westport, Connecticut: Greenwood Press, 1979), p. 154.

Henry Brereton Code

LIFE. Henry Brereton Code was a dramatist, song-writer and editor, of whom very little is known. His musical dramas were performed in Dublin and London and he edited the *The Warder*, a Dublin Tory journal, in the 1820s. He worked for the government in Dublin in the late 1790s and died about 1830.

CHIEF WRITINGS. *The Patriot* (Dublin, 1811) (musical drama); *Spanish Patriots* (London, 1812) (historical drama); *The Russian Sacrifice; or, The Burning of Moscow* (Dublin, 1813) (drama, with songs).

BIOGRAPHY AND CRITICISM. Noted in D.J. O'Donoghue, *The Poets of Ireland* (Dublin: Hodges, Figgis, 1912).

Matthew Concanen

LIFE. Matthew Concanen was born in Ireland in 1701 and initially trained as a lawyer. He moved to London, where his collection *Miscellaneous Poems* was published in 1724. Concanen became involved with London literary and journalistic circles, and criticized Pope after *The Dunciad* appeared in 1728; Pope subsequently attacked him in 1729. He was appointed attorney general of Jamaica in 1732. Concanen returned to England in 1743, a very rich man. He died of consumption, in London, in 1749.

CHIEF WRITINGS. *Wexford Wells* (comedy) (1721); 'A Match at Football: A Poem. In Three Cantos' (Dublin, 1720); *Poems upon Several Occasions* (Dublin, 1722); *Miscellaneous Poems* (London, 1724) (important as the first — it appears — anthology of Anglo-Irish poetry, including the work of Patrick Delany, Swift, Smedley, Dr Thomas Sheridan, Sterling, Parnell, Philips and Ward).

BIOGRAPHY AND CRITICISM. Noted in D.J. O'Donoghue, *The Poets of Ireland* and *The Dictionary of National Biography (D.N.B.)*.

John Philpot Curran

For biography and bibliography, see p. 959.

James Dalacourt

LIFE. James Dalacourt, whose name appears in various forms, was the son of a soldier. He was born in County Cork in 1709 or 1710 and educated at Trinity College, Dublin. His first poems were published while he was still a student; he also became involved in a literary skirmish with his friend Charles Carthy and their adversary, William Dunkin. Dalacourt became a clergyman in 1737 and moved from Dublin to Cork, where he presented an eccentric figure. He was curate of Ballinaboy 1744-55. He died in either 1781 or 1785.

CHIEF WRITINGS. 'Abelard to Eloisa, in Answer to Mr. Pope's fine piece of Eloisa to Abelard' (Dublin, 1730); 'The Progress of Beauty. A Poem' (Dublin, 1732); 'A Prospect of Poetry: Address'd to the Right

Honourable John, Earl of Orrery. To which is added, a Poem to Mr. Thomson on his Seasons' (Dublin, 1734 [1733?]); *Poems* (Cork, 1778).

BIOGRAPHY AND CRITICISM. Entry in D.J. O'Donoghue, *The Poets of Ireland*; discussion of his Dublin years and writings in Bryan Coleborne, 'Jonathan Swift and the Dunces of Dublin'; brief notice in J.C. Beckett, 'Literature in English 1691-1800', Chapter XIV of T.W. Moody and W.E. Vaughan (eds), *Eighteenth-Century Ireland 1691-1800*, Vol. IV of *A New History of Ireland* (Oxford: Clarendon Press, 1986), pp. 424-70. See also Andrea von Dietrich, 'Satirische Techniken in den persönlicken Schmähschriften der Dubliner "University Wits", James Delacourt, Charles Carthy, William Dunkin und Ambrose Philips', unpublished Staatsexamen thesis, Technical University of Berlin, 1985.

Patrick Delany

LIFE. Patrick Delany was born in Ireland in 1685 or 1686. He was educated at Trinity College, Dublin, where he became fellow and tutor, Archbishop King's lecturer (1722) and professor of oratory and history (1724). He was appointed chancellor of Christ Church Cathedral in 1728 and of St Patrick's Cathedral in 1730 before becoming dean of Down in 1744. Delany was a prominent member of Swift's circle in Dublin, well-known for his preaching, his stimulating conversation, and his controversial writings on such diverse subjects as preferment, polygamy and Jewish history and customs. He was one of the earliest of Swift's biographers. In 1743, he married Mary Pendarves, the famous 'Mrs Delany'. He was a cheerful, hospitable man, who usually lived beyond his means. Delany died in Bath, where he had gone to take the waters, in 1768.

CHIEF WRITINGS. *Observations upon Lord Orrery's Remarks on the Life and Writings of Dr. Jonathan Swift* (London, 1754) (also Dublin, 1754).

BIOGRAPHY AND CRITICISM. Delany is considered in all the major biographies of Swift and in editions of Swift's poetry and correspondence. See also Robert W. Uphaus, 'Swift's "whole character": The Delany Poems and "Verses on the Death of Dr. Swift"', *Modern Language Quarterly* 34, No. 4 (December 1973), 406-16. There is a passing reference to Delany in J.C. Beckett's chapter in *A New History of Ireland*, IV. See also *D.N.B.*

Thomas Dermody

LIFE. Thomas Dermody was born in 1775 in Ennis, Co. Clare, the son of a schoolmaster, who taught him Latin and Greek at an early age. A child prodigy, Dermody was teaching in his father's school at the age of nine, but ran away to Dublin when he was ten. There he attracted and then alienated various influential patrons, resisted all attempts to have him educated, and resorted to heavy drinking. He spent a period in Killeigh, Co. Offaly, where a Rev. Boyd attempted to rescue him from himself. Dermody was briefly in the army and served in France. He lived out the rest of his short life in London, and died in Sydenham, Kent in 1802.

CHIEF WRITINGS. *Poems* (Dublin, 1789); *Poems, Consisting of Essays, Lyrics, Elegiac, &c. Written between the 13th and 16th Year of His Age* (Dublin, 1792); *Poems, Moral, and Descriptive* (London, 1800); *Poems on Various Subjects* (London, 1802); *The Harp of Erin*, ed. James Grant Raymond, 2 vols (London, 1807).

BIOGRAPHY AND CRITICISM. Robert Hogan (ed.), *Dictionary of Irish Literature*; James Grant Raymond, *The Life of Thomas Dermody: Interspersed with Pieces of Original Poetry . . . and Containing a Series of Correspondence* . . . . 2 vols (London, 1806); Peter Somerville-Large, *Irish Eccentrics: A Selection* (London: Hamish Hamilton, 1975), pp. 127-36. There is a passing reference to Dermody in J.C. Beckett's chapter in *A New History of Ireland*, IV.

William Drennan

LIFE. William Drennan, the son of a dissenting clergyman, was born in Belfast in 1754. He was educated at Glasgow University and at the University of Edinburgh. In 1789 he settled as a doctor in Dublin. Drennan was one of the founders of the Society of United Irishmen and was tried for sedition in 1794, but was acquitted. He was also probably the best nationalist poet of the age and coined the term 'the emerald isle' in his poem 'When Erin First Rose'. In 1807 he returned to Belfast and founded the Academical Institution and the *Belfast Magazine*. He died in Belfast in 1820.

CHIEF WRITINGS. *Fugitive Pieces in Verse and Prose* (Belfast, 1815); *The Electra of Sophocles* (Belfast, 1817); *Glendalloch and Other Poems*, 2nd ed., with additional verses by William and John Swanwick Drennan (Dublin: W. Robertson, 1859); *The Drennan Letters*, ed. D.A. Chart (Belfast: HMSO, 1931).

BIOGRAPHY AND CRITICISM. Passing reference in J.C. Beckett's chapter in *A New History of Ireland*, IV; also in John Hewitt, *Rhyming Weavers and Other Country Poets of Antrim and Down* (Belfast: Blackstaff Press, 1974); entry in Robert Hogan (ed.), *Dictionary of Irish Literature*; passing reference, and context for his verse, in G.-D. Zimmermann, *Irish Political Street Ballads and Rebel Songs 1780-1900*.

William Dunkin

LIFE. William Dunkin was born in Dublin about 1709 and was educated at Trinity College, Dublin. He was involved in literary skirmishes in Dublin in his student days and in the early 1730s. Dunkin came to Swift's attention as a brilliant young poet and scholar, and joined his circle in the mid- to late 1730s. He taught at St Michael-le-Pole School, Dublin, and was appointed headmaster of Portora Royal School, Enniskillen, in 1746. Dunkin died in Dublin in 1765. He is probably the most underrated poet of eighteenth-century Ireland.

CHIEF WRITINGS. *Select Poetical Works*, 2 vols (Dublin, 1769-70); *The Poetical Works of William Dunkin*, 2 vols (London, 1774).

BIOGRAPHY AND CRITICISM. Discussed in Bryan Coleborne, 'Jonathan Swift and the Dunces of Dublin'; Joseph C. Day, 'William Dunkin: "Best Poet" in the Kingdom? A New Look at his Augustan Burlesque', unpublished M.A. thesis, National University of Ireland, 1978. See also Andrea von Dietrich, 'Satirische Techniken in den persönlicken Schmähschriften der Dubliner "University Wits", James Delacourt, Charles Carthy, William Dunkin und Ambrose Philips', unpublished Staatsexamen thesis, Technical University of Berlin, 1985.

Oliver Goldsmith

For biography and bibliography, see p. 656.

Constantia Grierson

LIFE. Constantia Grierson was born in Ireland between 1703 and 1705. When in her teens she was apprenticed to Dr Van Lewen, the Dublin physician and father of Laetitia (later Laetitia Pilkington), to train in midwifery. She attracted attention as a poet and scholarly editor and soon married George Grierson, the king's printer and a colleague of George Faulkner. She was closely involved, as editor and proofreader, with Grierson's editions of classical authors, including Terence (1727) and Tacitus (1730), and her scholarly work has been highly praised. She was a member of Swift's circle and was among those who advised Mary Barber; some of her poems were included in Mary Barber's *Poems on Several Occasions* (London, 1734). Constantia Grierson died in Dublin in 1732.

CHIEF WRITINGS. Poems uncollected. Some published in: Mary Barber, *Poems on Several Occasions* (London, 1734); Laetitia Pilkington, *The Memoirs of Mrs. Laetitia Pilkington*, 3 vols (Dublin, 1748-54).

BIOGRAPHY AND CRITICISM. A.C. Elias, 'A Manuscript Book of Constantia Grierson's', *Swift Studies* 2 (1987), 33-56; Ruth Perry, 'Constantia Grierson' in Janet Todd (ed.), *A Dictionary of British and American Women Writers 1660-1800*, pp. 140-41. Myra Reynolds, *The Learned Lady* (Gloucester, Massachusetts: P. Smith, 1964 [1920]), pp. 222-25.

Esther Johnson

LIFE. Esther (or Hester, as she was christened) Johnson, Swift's closest friend, was born in England in 1681, the daughter of Bridget and Edward Johnson, housekeeper and steward to Sir William Temple. She first met Swift in 1689 when he became Temple's secretary; he acted as her tutor 1689-94 and 1696-99. Bequeathed property in Ireland by Temple, Esther Johnson moved there and lived close to Swift, who knew her as 'Stella' and whose correspondence to her and her companion, Rebecca Dingley, in 1710-13 forms *The Journal to Stella*. Her death, in Dublin in 1728, affected Swift deeply.

CHIEF WRITINGS. Only three poems have been attributed to Stella. Two were published in Matthew Concanen's *Miscellaneous Poems* (London, 1724) and the third in Deane Swift's *Essay upon the Life, Writings, and Character of Dr. Jonathan Swift* (London, 1755). See also Harold Williams (ed.), *The Poems of Jonathan Swift* (Oxford: Clarendon Press, 1958), pp. 736-39.

BIOGRAPHY AND CRITICISM. Herbert Davis, *Stella: A Gentlewoman of the Eighteenth Century* (New York: Macmillan, 1942); Margaret Duggan, 'Esther Johnson', in Janet Todd (ed.), *A Dictionary of British and American Women Writers 1660-1800,* pp. 180-81.

Edward Lysaght

LIFE. Edward Lysaght, poet, lawyer and politician, was born at Brickhill, Co. Clare in 1763, and educated at Trinity College, Dublin and at Oxford. Initially he practised law, but later he turned to politics. He supported Henry Grattan and strongly opposed the Act of Union. He was widely popular as a *bon vivant* and writer of songs. He died in Dublin in 1811.

CHIEF WRITINGS. *Poems* (Dublin: Gilbert and Hodges, 1811).

BIOGRAPHY AND CRITICISM. Brief notes on him in: Robert Hogan (ed.), *Dictionary of Irish Literature*, pp. 385-86, and D.J. O'Donoghue, *The Poets of Ireland.*

Thomas Newburgh

LIFE. Thomas Newburgh was born in Dublin about 1695, the son of Brockhill Newburgh (*c.*1678-1760), chairman of the Dublin Linen Board. He was a cousin of Richard Pockrich. He was educated at Oxford and came into his father's estate in County Cavan. The volume *Essays Poetical, Moral and Critical*, from which the poem 'The *Beau Walk*' is taken, traditionally has been ascribed to Brockhill Newburgh. However, recent scholarship suggests that C.H. Wilson was right (in *Brookiana*, 1804) to consider the volume and the poem to be the work of Thomas Newburgh. He died, probably in Dublin, in 1779.

CHIEF WRITINGS. *Essays Poetical, Moral and Critical* (Dublin, 1769).

BIOGRAPHY AND CRITICISM. Bibliographical reference in C.H. Wilson, *Brookiana* (London, 1804), I, 2-4. Brief reference in Edward McParland, 'A Note on George II and St Stephen's Green', *Eighteenth-Century Ireland*, 2 (1987), 187-95. Brief entry in D.J. O'Donoghue, *The Poets of Ireland*.

Mary O'Brien

LIFE. Very little is known of the life of the poet, novelist and dramatist, Mary O'Brien. She is said to have been the wife of a Patrick O'Brien. Her collection of poems, *The Political Monitor*, was inspired by the political situation in Ireland at the time of the Regency crisis in the late 1780s. The date of her death is not recorded.

CHIEF WRITINGS. *The Political Monitor; or Regent's Friend. Being a Collection of Poems Published in England during the Agitation of the Regency: Consisting of Curious, Interesting, Satyrical and Political Effusions of Poetry* (Dublin, 1790).

BIOGRAPHY AND CRITICISM. Elizabeth Nelson, 'Mary O'Brien', in Janet Todd (ed.), *A Dictionary of British and American Women Writers 1660-1800* (London: Methuen, 1984), p. 236. Brief entry in D.J. O'Donoghue, *The Poets of Ireland* (Dublin: Hodges, Figgis, 1912).

Charles O'Flaherty

LIFE. Practically nothing is known of Charles O'Flaherty. He is said to have been born around 1794 and to have been apprenticed to a bookseller. He wrote verse, became a journalist, and died about 1828.

CHIEF WRITINGS. *Poems* (Dublin, 1813); *Poems and Songs* (Dublin, 1821).

BIOGRAPHY AND CRITICISM. Brief entry in D.J. O'Donoghue, *The Poets of Ireland.*

George Ogle

LIFE. George Ogle was born in Ireland in 1742, the son of the translator George Ogle (1704-46). He was a prominent politician and served in the Irish House of Commons for over thirty years. He was a colonel in the Irish Volunteers and actively supported the cause of legislative independence for Ireland. Described by the *D.N.B.* as 'a man of wealth and fashion', Ogle was also the author of several popular songs. He died in County Wexford in 1814.

CHIEF WRITINGS. Poems uncollected. Several were published in: T. Crofton Croker (ed.), *Popular Songs of Ireland* (London: Henry Colburn, 1839).

BIOGRAPHY AND CRITICISM. Brief note in D.J. O'Donoghue, *The Poets of Ireland*. See also *D.N.B.*

James Orr

LIFE. James Orr, the only son of a weaver, was born at Broad Island, Co. Antrim, in 1770. He had little education and himself started life as a weaver. He later joined the United Irishmen and contributed poetry to *The Northern Star*. He fought in the battle of Antrim in 1798, after which he went into a brief exile in America. He returned to County Antrim in the early 1800s and died in 1816.

CHIEF WRITINGS. *Poems on Various Subjects* (Belfast, 1804); *The Posthumous Works of James Orr, of Ballycarry: with a Sketch of his Life* (Belfast, 1817); *Poems on Various Subjects* (Belfast: Mullan, 1935).

BIOGRAPHY AND CRITICISM. Donald Harman Akenson and W.H. Crawford, *Local Poets and Social History: James Orr, Bard of Ballycarry* (Belfast: Public Record Office of Northern Ireland, 1977); John Hewitt, *Rhyming Weavers and Other Country Poets of Antrim and Down*; Robert Hogan (ed.), *Dictionary of Irish Literature*; Linde Connolly Lunney, 'Attitudes to Life and Death in the Poetry of James Orr, an Eighteenth-Century Ulster Weaver', *Ulster Folklore* 31 (1985), 1-12. There is a passing reference to Orr, and context for some of his verse, in G.-D. Zimmermann, *Irish Political Street Ballads and Rebel Songs 1780-1900*. Brief entry in D.J. O'Donoghue, *The Poets of Ireland*.

Thomas Parnell

LIFE. Thomas Parnell was born in 1679 in Dublin. He was educated at Trinity College, Dublin and was ordained into the Church of Ireland in 1700. He was appointed archdeacon of Clogher in 1706. Parnell frequently visited London and became friendly with Swift, Pope and other members of the Scriblerus Club — to which he was elected. He died at Chester (on his way back to Ireland from visiting friends in London) in 1718. Pope edited his poems posthumously and Goldsmith wrote a life of Parnell, which was published in 1770 with an edition of his poems.

CHIEF WRITINGS. *An Essay on the Different Stiles of Poetry* (London, 1713); reprinted in Robert Mahony (ed.), *Different Styles of Poetry* (Monkstown, Co. Dublin: The Cadenus Press, 1978); *Poems on Several Occasions* .... edited by Pope (London, 1722); *The Posthumous Works of Dr. Thomas Parnell* (London, 1758).

BIOGRAPHY AND CRITICISM. *D.N.B.*; brief reference in J.C. Beckett's chapter in *A New History of Ireland*, IV; entry in D.J. O'Donoghue, *The Poets of Ireland*; C.J. Rawson, 'Swift's Certificate to Parnell's "Posthumous Works"', *Modern Language Review* 57 (1962) 179-82.

Ambrose Philips

LIFE. Ambrose Philips was born in England in 1674 and educated at Cambridge. He became known as a poet and miscellaneous writer in London and started the Whig periodical, *The Freethinker*, in 1718. He came to Ireland as secretary to Archbishop Hugh Boulter in 1724. Philips was known (rather unfairly) by Swift and his circle as 'Namby Pamby', for his charming but sentimental verses on children. He was MP for Armagh from 1727 until his death in 1749, and he also held various government positions. His collected poems were published in London in 1748 and his editions of Archbishop Boulter's correspondence appeared in 1769-70.

CHIEF WRITINGS. *Pastorals* (London, 1710); *The Distrest Mother* (London, 1712) (drama); *Poems by Mr. Philips* (Dublin, 1725); *Pastorals, Epistles, Odes, and other Original Poems, with Translations from Pindar, Anacreon, and Sappho* (London, 1748); M.G. Segar (ed.), *The Poems of Ambrose Philips* (Oxford: Blackwell, 1937).

BIOGRAPHY AND CRITICISM. *D.N.B.*; referred to in Bryan Coleborne, 'Jonathan Swift and the Dunces of Dublin'; M.G. Segar, Introduction to *The Poems of Ambrose Philips* (Oxford: Blackwell, 1937), pp. xiii-liii. See also Staatsexamen thesis by Andrea von Dietrich, listed under Dalcourt above.

Laetitia Pilkington

For biography and bibliography, see p. 1009.

Matthew Pilkington

LIFE. Matthew Pilkington, diminutive husband of the famous Laetitia, was born about 1701, the only son of a clockmaker in Ballyboy, Co. Offaly (then King's County). He was educated at Trinity College, Dublin and was ordained into the Church of Ireland. From about 1724 until his death, he was vicar of Donabate and Portrane. He was a good classical scholar and musician. After their marriage, the Pilkingtons were among Swift's favourite companions. Later, however, their marital infidelities and dishonesty forced Swift to disown them. Pilkington died in 1774.

CHIEF WRITINGS. *Poems on Several Occasions* (Dublin, 1730); *Poems on Several Occasions* (London, 1731) containing additional poems.

BIOGRAPHY AND CRITICISM. Mentioned in D.J. O'Donoghue, *The Poets of Ireland*. See also Irvin Ehrenpreis, *Swift: The Man, his Works and the Age*, Vol. III 'Dean Swift' (London: Methuen, 1983); and an article by Elrington Ball in *Notes and Queries*, 11th series, 6 (1912).

Richard Pockrich

LIFE. Richard Pockrich, one of the most memorable eccentrics of the eighteenth century, was born about 1690 of a wealthy English family settled on a large estate in County Monaghan. He spent his fortune on a succession of scatterbrained schemes, all of which failed. Pockrich was involved with the social life of Dublin and of the spa at Templeogue, which provided the subject-matter for some of his verse. He is remembered today for 'inventing' the musical glasses — goblets of varying pitch which he struck to create music — and a new kind of dulcimer. In 1759, while on a visit to London, he was suffocated in a fire at his lodging near the Royal Exchange.

CHIEF WRITINGS. *The Miscellaneous Works of Richard Pockrich, Esq*; (Dublin, 1755).

BIOGRAPHY AND CRITICISM. D.J. O'Donoghue, *An Irish Musical Genius: The Inventor of the Musical Glasses* (Dublin: M.H. Gill, 1899); Peter Somerville-Large, *Irish Eccentrics: A Selection* (London: Hamish Hamilton, 1975), pp. 188-95. Entries in D.J. O'Donoghue, *The Poets of Ireland* and *D.N.B.*

George Nugent Reynolds

LIFE. George Nugent Reynolds was born about 1770 in County Leitrim, where his father had an estate. From about 1790, he published poems and songs in various Dublin literary magazines. After the Act of Union, he went to England, intending to study law, but died there suddenly in 1802.

CHIEF WRITINGS. *The Panthead* (Dublin, 1794) (poem); *Bantry Bay* (London, 1797) (musical piece).

BIOGRAPHY AND CRITICISM. *D.N.B.*; D.J. O'Donoghue, *The Poets of Ireland*.

Charles Shadwell

LIFE. Little is known about the life of Charles Shadwell. Like his father Thomas Shadwell (*c.* 1642-92), he was a poet and dramatist. His plays were performed and published in London and Dublin between 1710 and 1720. His *Works* appeared, in two volumes, in Dublin in 1720. He joined in the popular attack on Wood's Halfpence and died, possibly in Dublin, in 1726.

CHIEF WRITINGS. *The Works of Charles Shadwell* 2 vols (Dublin, 1720).

BIOGRAPHY AND CRITICISM. Included in *Dictionary of National Biography* under entry for Thomas Shadwell. Referred to in Bryan Coleborne, 'Jonathan Swift and the Dunces of Dublin', unpublished Ph.D. thesis, National University of Ireland, 1982.

Thomas Sheridan (the Elder)

LIFE. Thomas Sheridan (the Elder) was born in County Cavan in 1687. He was educated at Trinity College, Dublin and was ordained into the Church of Ireland by Archbishop King. He set up a school for boys in Dublin and soon became, according to Swift, 'the best instructor of youth in these kingdoms, or perhaps in Europe.' He was one of Swift's closest Irish friends and together they wrote and published *The Intelligencer* in 1728-29. Many verse letters passed between them, although they became estranged towards the end of Sheridan's life. Among Sheridan's nine children was Thomas Sheridan (the Younger), playwright, lexicographer, husband of Frances Sheridan the novelist and father of Richard Brinsley Sheridan. The elder Thomas Sheridan died in 1738.

CHIEF WRITINGS. *The Intelligencer* (with Jonathan Swift) (Dublin, 1728-29; a new edition by James Woolley is forthcoming from Oxford University Press. 'A Selection of Dr Sheridan's Poems' edited by Robert Hogan, in *The Journal of Irish Literature* (Newark, Delaware: Proscenium Press), Vol. XVI, No. 1 (January 1987), 33-60 and Vol. XVI, No. 2 (May 1987), 19-48.

BIOGRAPHY AND CRITICISM. The standard biographies of Swift all carry adequate coverage of Sheridan; see also *Dictionary of National Biography* and Robert Hogan (ed.), *A Dictionary of Irish Literature*. Two important recent articles are James Woolley, 'Thomas Sheridan and Swift', *Studies in Eighteenth-Century Culture*, Vol. 9 (Madison: University of Wisconsin Press for the American Society for Eighteenth-Century Studies, 1979), pp. 93-114, and Bricriu Dolan, 'Tom the Punman: Dr Thomas Sheridan, the Friend of Swift', in *The Journal of Irish Literature* (Newark, Delaware: Proscenium Press), Vol. XVI, No. 1 (January 1987), 3-32.

Jonathan Smedley

LIFE. Born in Ireland in 1671, Jonathan Smedley was educated at Trinity College, Dublin and was ordained into the Church of Ireland. He was a prominent supporter of the Whigs in Dublin and attacked Swift on his appointment to the deanery of St Patrick's. They became enemies and poetic sparring adversaries. Smedley was appointed dean of Killala in 1718, and dean of Clogher in 1724. His attacks on Swift and Pope in *Gulliveriana* in 1728 led to Pope's inserting him in *The Dunciad*. He sailed for Madras in 1729 and presumably died in India soon afterwards.

CHIEF WRITINGS. *Poems on Several Occasions* (London, 1721) (reissued 1723, 1730); *Gulliveriana: or, a Fourth Volume of Miscellanies* (London, 1728).

BIOGRAPHY AND CRITICISM. Referred to in Bryan Coleborne, 'Jonathan Swift and the Dunces of Dublin'. See also Edward Graham, 'Smedley and Swift — "Further Reasons for their Enmity"', *Philological Quarterly* 48, No. 3 (July 1969), 416-20. Also in *D.N.B.* and D.J. O'Donoghue, *The Poets of Ireland*.

James Sterling

LIFE. James Sterling was born in Ireland in 1701 and educated at Trinity College, Dublin. He contributed to Matthew Concanen's *Miscellaneous Poems* in 1724, but was ridiculed by the Dublin literati for his poetic attempts. He went to London with Concanen in 1733 to try and make his living there as a miscellaneous writer. All his efforts seem to have failed, however, and in 1737 he emigrated to America, where he became a Church of England minister in Maryland. He died there in 1763.

CHIEF WRITINGS. *The Rival Generals* (London, 1722) (drama); *The Loves of Hero and Leander . . . .* (London and Dublin, 1728); *The Poetical Works* (Dublin, 1734); *The Parricide* (London, 1736) (drama).

BIOGRAPHY AND CRITICISM. Referred to in Bryan Coleborne, 'Jonathan Swift and the Dunces of Dublin'. See also Lawrence C. Wroth, 'James Sterling: Poet, Priest and Prophet of Empire', *Proceedings of the American Antiquarian Society* (Worcester, Massachusetts: 1932), Vol. 41, pp. 25-76. Entries in *D.N.B.* and D.J. O'Donoghue, *The Poets of Ireland*.

Jonathan Swift

For biography and bibliography, see p. 393.

Nahum Tate

For biography and bibliography, see p. 1009.

James Ward

LIFE. Very little is known of James Ward, although he was probably born in Ireland about 1691. He was educated at Trinity College, Dublin and was ordained into the Church of Ireland. He contributed to *A New Miscellany of Poems and Translations* (Dublin, 1716) and to Matthew Concanen's *Miscellaneous Poems* (London, 1724); nothing can be discovered about his life after 1724.

CHIEF WRITINGS. *A New Miscellany of Poems and Translations* (Dublin, 1716); *Phoenix Park* (Dublin, 1718), later reprinted in Matthew Concanen's *Miscellaneous Poems* (London, 1724).

BIOGRAPHY AND CRITICISM. Entry in D.J. O'Donoghue, *The Poets of Ireland*.

Laurence Whyte

LIFE. Little is known of the life of Laurence Whyte. He was born in County Westmeath, perhaps around 1700, and lived in Dublin where he became a teacher of mathematics. He was associated with John and William Neal, father and son, leading publishers of music in Dublin in Swift's day. Whyte appears to have been active in writing poetry between the mid-1720s and the early 1740s. He died in 1755.

CHIEF WRITINGS. *Poems on Various Subjects, Serious and Diverting, Never before Published* (Dublin, 1740); *Original Poems on Various Subjects, Serious, Moral and Diverting* (Dublin, 1742) (second edition, but with some new poems).

BIOGRAPHY AND CRITICISM. Referred to in Russell K. Alspach, *Irish Poetry from the English Invasion to 1798*, 2nd ed. (Philadelphia: University of Pennsylvania Press, 1959). Context for some of his poems, and some reference to him, in John and William Neal, *A Collection of the Most Celebrated Irish Tunes Proper for the Violin, German Flute or Hautboy* (Dublin, 1724), facsimile edition by Nicholas Carolan (Dublin: Folklore Society of Ireland, 1986). Brief entry in D.J. O'Donoghue, *The Poets of Ireland*.

Samuel Whyte

LIFE. Samuel Whyte was born in 1733 aboard a ship; as he put it, 'Liverpool was the first land I touched'. He was brought up by the

Sheridan family in Dublin; his first cousin was Frances Sheridan, the novelist and mother of R.B. Sheridan. The school he opened in 1758 in Grafton Street, Dublin became very famous and many Dublin families sent their sons and daughters to Whyte's Academy, from which a large proportion of the boys went to Trinity College, Dublin. Whyte published essays on education and rhetoric, as well as poetry and a junior encyclopaedia. He died in Dublin in 1811.

CHIEF WRITINGS. *The Shamrock; or, Hibernian Cresses* (Dublin, 1772) edited by Whyte: about two-thirds of the poetry in the book is by him; *Poems on Various Subjects* (Dublin, 1795).

BIOGRAPHY AND CRITICISM. *D.N.B.*; mentioned in D.J. O'Donoghue, *The Poets of Ireland.* Reference also in Russell K. Alspach, *Irish Poetry from the English Invasion to 1798.*

John Winstanley

LIFE. Little is known about John Winstanley. He was presumably of Irish extraction and, since he states in his *Poems* (1751) that he was sixty-seven years of age in 1745, seems to have been born in 1678. He also described himself as '*a* Doctor, *tho without* Degrees ... *Apollo's and the* Muses *Licens'd* Doctor'. He died in Dublin in 1750.

CHIEF WRITINGS. *Poems Written Occasionally. Interspers'd with many others, by Several Ingenious Hands* (Dublin, 1742); *Poems Written Occasionally. Interspers'd with many others, by Several Ingenious Hands*, Vol. II (Dublin, 1751).

BIOGRAPHY AND CRITICISM. Noticed in *D.N.B.* and D.J. O'Donoghue, *The Poets of Ireland.*

Richard Witheral

LIFE. Nothing is known about Richard Witheral, except that he was one of the popular versifiers on the subject of Wood's Halfpence. He may be the Richard Witheral who subscribed to Charles Coffey's *Poems and Songs upon Several Occasions* (Dublin, 1724).

CHIEF WRITINGS. His one known poem, ' A New Song Sung at the Club at Mr. Taplin's the Sign of the Drapier's Head in *Truck-Street*' (Dublin, 1724), was reprinted in *Fraud Detected: or, The Hibernian Patriot* (Dublin, 1725) and *The Hibernian Patriot: Being a Collection of the Drapier's Letters to the People of Ireland, Concerning Mr. Wood's Brass Half-Pence* (London, 1730).

BIOGRAPHY AND CRITICISM. Referred to in Bryan Coleborne, 'Jonathan Swift and the Dunces of Dublin'.

CHRISTOPHER MURRAY, *Editor*

Drama 1690-1800

Wherever theatre has flourished, in various civilizations from the Greek onwards, it has flourished in urban communities. In Ireland the towns were built by the invaders — the Danes, Normans and English. It follows that drama in Ireland was from its earliest times an art form which had little to do with the native, Gaelic-speaking population. It was imported by the conquerors. Moreover, the native literary tradition was bardic and oral, and did not include drama among its forms. There are no Gaelic plays as there are Gaelic epics, sagas, lyrics and other poetic forms.

It is therefore impossible to consider Irish drama apart from its relationship to England and the English dramatic tradition. Before the seventeenth century, drama existed intermittently in Ireland, in Dublin and in various other towns and garrisons around the country. But it was not until the 1630s that the first professional theatre was opened, providing the possibility of establishing continuity and development. The question is, what kind of relationship existed between this theatre and the Irish people? If by 'Irish people' is meant the majority, catholic, Gaelic-speaking and (since 1603) dispossessed, the answer must be, 'very little'. This theatre, and its successors, the theatres royal, were manifestations of colonial rule. Indeed, one scholar, W. J. Lawrence, has called the Dublin theatre of the seventeenth and eighteenth centuries a 'semi-governmental institution'. Whereas this theatre was never under the jurisdiction of the British lord chamberlain, it owed its origin to and depended on the support of the lord lieutenant, the king's viceroy in Ireland.

The founder of the Irish theatre was not an Irishman at all but a Scot. John Ogilby (1600-76), a dancing master and in later years a publisher in London, somehow got the idea that Dublin stood in need of a theatre as a fashionable social amenity. An opportunist with an eye to his own advancement, Ogilby found a patron in Thomas Wentworth, earl of Strafford, lord lieutenant of Ireland and a man eager to build up a little court around himself in Dublin. Little detail is known about the theatre Ogilby found a patron in Thomas Wentworth, earl of Strafford, lord lieutenant of Ireland and a man structures of London theatres of the day, for London styles and taste were to guide the Irish theatre from the beginning. A plague in London during 1636-37 helped Ogilby's recruiting of personnel, for at such times the London theatres were officially closed and the actors and musicians had to look elsewhere for employment. Ogilby managed to engage enough of these to form a stock company, and he was doubly fortunate in attracting to Dublin the playwright James Shirley (1595-1666) as what would today be termed writer-in-residence. The Werburgh Street theatre opened in autumn 1637, and lasted for about four years, until the war of 1641 led to its demise. During that time the repertory was largely made up of plays well established on the London stage: not Shakespeare's at this point, but Jonson's, Middleton's and Fletcher's, as well as Shirley's own plays. The new prologues which Shirley wrote for his plays indicate the nature of the problem facing Ogilby and his successors, namely how to win audiences in a town where taste was fickle and unformed. Shirley also wrote a new play for Werburgh Street, *Saint Patrick for Ireland* (1639)*, which has the distinction of being the first modern (as distinct from medieval) play in English to receive its première in Dublin. Once again Shirley lamented the audience's shortcomings, in his prologue:

We know not what will take; your pallats are
Various, and many of them sick I feare:

As if in desperation to please all tastes, the play itself is a strange mixture of intrigue, romance and

* All dates of plays are of first production.

spectacle, with some hope riding on the Irish historical subject. Most interesting to the student of Irish drama, however, is the Ascendancy ideology which underlies the conflict between Patrick and the Druids. Had Yeats written the play 260 years later, the Druids would have been the heroes. In Shirley's play, Saint Patrick is depicted as triumphing over the power of Irish paganism, symbolized by the snakes which he banishes from the land at the end. His is the voice of reason, overcoming superstition and barbarism. The native culture, seen as steeped in Druidic darkness, yields finally to the enlightened stranger. Patrick's final prophecy of Ireland's greatness, as the land of saints and scholars, is somehow transformed in the presence of the Earl of Strafford and his little court, into a colonialist statement:

You are, Sir, reserv'd
To blesse this Kingdome with your pious government,
Your Crowne shall flourish, and your bloud possesse
The Throne you shall leave glorious: This Nation
Shall in a faire succession thrive, and grow
Up the world's Academie . . . .

Available in a modern edition by John P. Turner (New York: Garland, 1979) *Saint Patrick for Ireland* is well worth studying by anyone who wants a fuller introduction to the issues underlying early Irish drama.

The same interest does not attach to the only known play by an Irish author to have been staged at Werburgh Street, namely *Landgartha* (1640), by one Henry Burnell from Castleknock. Printed in Dublin in 1641, this may have been the last play to have been staged at Werburgh Street. Reading it, one is not surprised. It is a gallimaufry of the most extraordinary kind, with a story out of Danish history about an Amazonian warrior of Norway (Landgartha) who marries Regnar, king of Denmark and acts as his protectress, against lust as much as against various Scandinavian enemies. At one point there is a masque scene to provide much-needed light relief, and here Burnell introduced some local (Irish) colour: Marsisa, cousin to Landgartha, does a dance in '*an Irish Gowne tuck'd up to mid-legge, with a broad basket-hilt Sword on, hanging in a great Belt, Broags on her feet, her hayre disshevell'd, and a payre of long neck'd big-rowell'd Spurs on her heels.*' One may infer that Ogilby, a dancing-master after all, thought to win Dublin audiences by interpolating Irish dances and a dash of spectacle into quite foreign material.

By contrast, *Saint Patrick for Ireland* provides a coherent dramatization of a cultural attitude. It is to be found overtly or covertly in all serious drama emanating from Ireland after 1637. Another example is to be found in Charles Shadwell's *Rotherick O'Connor, King of Connaught, or The Distress'd Princess* (1720), in which the victory of the Norman Strongbow over the (villainous) last high king of Ireland in the late twelfth century is presented as the victory of enlightenment over barbarism. The point of view is also identical with that expressed in countless prologues delivered in the Dublin theatres all through the eighteenth century, namely, that refinement, reason and good taste were the hallmarks of the ruling aristocracy, striving under the guidance of the lord lieutenant to bring peace and prosperity to a troubled land. It was not until the end of the nineteenth century that this ideology was questioned and opposed, when the Irish Literary Theatre was established by Yeats, Lady Gregory and Edward Martyn.

EXPATRIATE WRITERS

Once the Irish theatre was firmly established professionally, through the granting of a royal patent to John Ogilby to build a new theatre to replace the one in Werburgh Street, which had fallen into decay during the years after the outbreak of rebellion in 1641, it prospered to quite an extraordinary degree. The Theatre Royal — Smock Alley, as it was called — from its opening in 1662 as the first Restoration theatre in either England or Ireland grew in reputation until by the 1740s it was recognized as on a par with its two London equivalents, the theatres royal at Drury Lane and at Covent Garden. As it built up a tradition for good acting and production, whether of Shakespeare and his contemporaries or of playwrights more recently successful on the London stage, Smock Alley became something of a nursery of talent. Whereas when Ogilby first set up the professional theatre in Dublin the traffic was all one way, from London, towards the end of the seventeenth century actors, actresses (first introduced after the Restoration) and playwrights began to move from Dublin to London. The era of the expatriate Irish dramatist had begun.

Very many of the writers during the period 1690 to 1800 were alumni of Trinity College, Dublin (founded in 1592). That immediately places them in a social category, since Roman catholics were not allowed to register at the college. From William Congreve to Oscar Wilde the profile of the expatriate Irish playwright is of the polished man of letters, as eager for social status in England as for literary fame. Once he had made the transition from Dublin to London, he usually had nothing to do with the Dublin stage. He wrote primarily to please the English arbiters of taste, the managers, performers and discerning playgoers, and he took particular pains to impress and court the approval of men such as Dryden, Johnson and Hazlitt, in the hope of penetrating and irradiating their literary circles.

Irish playwrights did not, as a rule, distinguish themselves in tragedy. This was not because they did not try, but more because of the nature of tragedy in English from the time of Dryden on. It remained a stiff, artificial medium, whether in blank verse or in rhyme. Modern readers may sample the style by reading through the most famous adaptation of *King Lear* in literary history, the work of Nahum Tate from Dublin. Its standards may be neoclassical but its effect is utterly dismaying. William Congreve and Thomas Southerne fared rather better with *The Mourning Bride* (1697) and *Oroonoko* (1695) respectively, but even these are plays never staged in modern times, and are therefore doomed to the exclusive interest of the literary historian. There seems little point in supplying excerpts from such plays for this anthology, since they have nothing to offer in clarification of the Irish sensibility. The same may be said of Irish tragedies in general, with the possible exception of the plays of Henry Brooke (*c.* 1703-83), whose *Gustavus Vasa,* refused permission for staging in London by order of the lord chamberlain, found an eager audience in Dublin when it was staged under the new title of *The Patriot* in the early 1740s. Banned for its alleged slander of Prime Minister Robert Walpole, this play was perceived by Dublin audiences, ever alert to political undertones, as having application to Ireland. Although he wrote seven other tragedies, Brooke did not follow up in this form his political intuitions, saving these instead for his 'Farmer's Letters'. Like the rest of his fellow-playwrights, Brooke viewed tragedy as a literary exercise, clearly indebted to Shakespeare.

It was in comedy, accordingly, that Irish writers made the most significant contribution to the flowering of drama in English from the end of the seventeenth to the end of the eighteenth centuries, and even after that time. We are talking here about a body of drama which, for all its colonial origins, constitutes a tradition of its own. It is really neither Irish nor English, but something uneasily in between, for which the term Anglo-Irish seems just about adequate.

William Congreve does not really answer to the description of an Anglo-Irish playwright, and consequently his work is not represented in this anthology. Congreve was born in Yorkshire, and although he was educated in Ireland and held an M.A. from Trinity College, he left Ireland in 1688, fearing the direction Irish political life was taking. In all his plays, the wit he exhibits has a serenity and a security of tone entirely lacking from most Anglo-Irish writers, whose ability to use the English language brilliantly masks an unease. Neither is Congreve autobiographical, as Anglo-Irish playwrights usually are, exploiting their personalities or their backgrounds for the entertainment of their English audiences. Moreover, Congreve was content to work within the conventions of his day, whereas the Anglo-Irish playwright usually shows a certain impatience or irreverence for established norms and tries instead for new ideas or new forms. In all of Congreve, finally, there is nothing about Ireland, if one excludes the lines in *Love for Love* (1695) about a woman being as hard to decipher as an Irish manuscript: 'you may pore till you spoil your eyes, and not improve your knowledge'. But he invokes only to dismiss.

A far more typical Anglo-Irish playwright was George Farquhar, Congreve's contemporary. His father being a clergyman of Scottish extraction, Farquhar grew up among Ulster planter stock, soon to issue their famous cry of 'no surrender' to the catholic forces led by Richard Talbot, earl of Tyrconnell. The siege of Derry took place in 1689 when the apprentice boys shut the gates against the advancing army of King James II, and ever after the gesture became an emblem of Ulster protestant defiance. (The victorious siege is commemorated still, every year, in Derry.) Farquhar's family endured this siege and, it seems, lost everything by it. That was not the sort of thing a twelve-year-old boy would forget. Moreover, Farquhar is said to have fought at the battle of the Boyne in 1690, that other great landmark in modern Irish political history. The victory of protestant King William over catholic King James was not merely historical: in the minds and imaginations of Irish protestants ever since, it is mythological. The glorious twelfth of July is still a red-letter day in the north of Ireland, celebrating deliverance from the threat of catholic domination. George Farquhar was of this victorious party. He marked the occasion with an ode on the death of General Schomberg, William's Dutch general who was killed at the Boyne. Farquhar was not without roots, then, when he eventually became an expatriate Irish writer.

Yet if such experience as Farquhar had of political struggles in the north of Ireland left their mark on his psyche, they left very little impression on his temperament. So far as one can judge, he was an ebullient, devil-may-care personality. While a student at Trinity College he facetiously turned an assignment on Christ's walking on the water into an argument that 'the man born to be hanged will never be drowned', a piece of blasphemy that landed him in considerable trouble. He abandoned Trinity College for Smock Alley, where he became a professional actor and learned first-hand about the theatre. He was never to become anything like as good an actor as his Dublin friend Robert Wilks, whom he followed to London in 1698 and for whom he then began to write comedies. Farquhar left Dublin abruptly, having wounded a fellow-actor on stage through his carelessness. His career up to this point hardly suggested a man whom political history was going to weigh down too much. Accordingly, residence in London revealed in Farquhar a detachment which fuelled his plays with gaiety and unusual high spirits.

Because he set the pattern for many Irish playwrights who made London their home, it is worth giving special attention to Farquhar's plays. He not only influenced those who came after him, particularly Sir Richard Steele and Oliver Goldsmith, but helped to alter the style and tone of English comedy by abandoning the usual city setting for (in his best plays) a rural setting where a more uninhibited study of human nature could be undertaken. There was also the matter of autobiography. In Farquhar's first play, *Love and a Bottle,* presented at Drury Lane in 1698, the hero is an Irishman in London named George Roebuck, and when another character in the play says that 'the Hero in Comedy is always the Poet's Character ... A Compound of practical Rake, and speculative Gentleman', we realize that Farquhar was deliberately being autobiographical. Even where the hero of his plays is not actually an Irishman, they all resemble Roebuck and Farquhar himself. They are all warm-hearted, rather down-at-heel opportunists, like Sir Harry Wildair in *The Constant Couple* (1699) or Captain Plume in *The Recruiting Officer* (1706) or Archer in *The Beaux' Stratagem* (1707). Whereas it would be foolish to claim that every Irish playwright writing for the London stage exploited his own personality in the way Farquhar seems to have done, it is certain that such exploitation tended to be a significant characteristic of Anglo-Irish drama. For example, one finds this in Arthur Murphy's *The Apprentice* (1756), in Goldsmith's *The Good Natur'd Man* (1768) and even in his masterpiece, *She Stoops to Conquer* (1773), where the central incident was based on a personal experience. As a young man at home in County Longford, Goldsmith was misled into believing a country house to be an inn, where he grandly availed himself of the 'landlord's' hospitality before calling loudly for his bill the next morning. Characteristically, the Irish playwright turned the joke against himself when he transformed the experience into art, indeed into a parable about identity.

So also with Richard Brinsley Sheridan. It is well known that the details of the duel in *The Rivals* (1775) and the whole atmosphere of romance and family deception were drawn from Sheridan's own experience at Bath. Further, *The Duenna* (1775) drew upon details of Sheridan's elopement, whereas *The School for Scandal* (1777) used differences between Sheridan and his brother Charles as the basis for the characterization of Charles and Joseph Surface. Perhaps this phenomenon is bound up with the Irishman's need to be amusing by exaggerating experience, but is also bound up with the very process of art itself. In other words, the argument here may be circular: Irish plays of the eighteenth century were autobiographical because they attained the status of great art. In any case, this is suggested by Oscar Wilde's remark in an interview given in 1895: 'In the case of a dramatist also an artist it is impossible not to feel that the work of art, to be a work of art, must be dominated by the artist. Every play of Shakespeare is dominated by Shakespeare. Ibsen and Dumas dominate their works. My works are dominated by myself.'

THE STAGE IRISHMAN

By mutual agreement with the London audience, the expatriate Irish playwright portrayed his own countrymen as amusing and harmless. Very occasionally he portrayed one of them as sinister and dangerous, as Farquhar depicts Foigard in *The Beaux' Stratagem*. The point here is sectarian. Foigard, masquerading as a Frenchman, is actually an Irish priest who is a spy; his unmasking displays him as totally untrustworthy and a coward as well. At the time, and for most of the eighteenth century, the English feared a French invasion, and since the discontented native Irish were catholics like the French, they were constantly regarded as Jacobites and conspirators. Perhaps this was one further reason why the playwrights, instead of directly exposing catholics as traitors like Foigard, introduced them instead as bungling, innocent and loyal. Such a characterization was better suited to the comic form; it also served, like all ethnic jokes, to release and dissipate real fears on the part of insecure masters.

There were two types of stage Irishman. One, the uneducated servant whose mistakes, verbal and logical alike, provide the basis of popularity, is found for the first time in Sir Robert Howard's *The Committee* (1662), where he is given the name Teague. In *The Twin Rivals* (1702) Farquhar, who had acted in Howard's play at Smock Alley, also names his stage Irishman Teague, which was to become the habitual name of the Irish footman, the counterpart, perhaps, of the black man on the American stage. Teague is the Irish for Timothy, but it is ironic that in modern times it has become a sectarian term for 'catholic' in Northern Ireland. Farquhar's Teague is from Carrickfergus, in County Antrim. He is presented with a broad accent, spelt phonetically, and a tendency to contradict himself foolishly, using what became known as Irish bulls. For example, he says: 'Dear Maishter, have a care upon your shelf; now they know you are dead, by my Shoul they may kill you.' Or when he is told he will be hanged: 'Hanged! Dat is nothing, dear Joy; — we are us'd to't'. Teague the servant was immensely popular on the English stage in the eighteenth century, often found in plays not by Irish authors at all and acted by men who had never set foot in Ireland in their lives. The comic Irishman was simply a stereotype who offered a variation on the Shakespearian fool. The type persisted down to the founding of the Irish Literary Theatre, part of whose manifesto was to show that Ireland is not the home of 'buffoonery and of easy sentiment'.

It has to be said, however, that the major playwrights after Farquhar, such as Steele, Goldsmith and Sheridan, do not employ this particular version of the stage Irishman. But proof that he was a continuing temptation is seen in Kelly's *The School for Wives* (1773), where Connolly, a servant with very little part in the plot, regales the audience with such mispronunciations as 'spake', 'hould', 'kilt' (for 'killed'), 'Gintlemin', 'cretur' (for 'creature'), and treats them to such bulls as (about pistols), 'the more I clane [clean] them, the dirtier they are, honey', or, 'I don't believe for all that, that there's a word of a lie in the truth he speaks.' Yet Kelly's purpose, according to the preface, was to rescue Irishmen from the charge of 'barbarous ferocity'. It appears that Kelly merely wanted to stress the 'well known humanity' of the Irish, and ignored the fact that he was depicting them as vacuous.

John O'Keeffe, a writer more of ballad operas and farcical afterpieces than of full-length comedies, tried to integrate the stage Irishman more fully into the plot, as in *The Poor Soldier* (1783) and *The Wicklow Goldmines* (1796), both set in Ireland. Yet O'Keeffe lived to be described (by William Hazlitt) as the *English* Molière, and this emphasizes for us the virtual impossibility of an Irish playwright's escaping from the necessity of presenting his countrymen as essentially amusing by standards that were English.

The second version of the stage Irishman was more socially elevated. He was a landowner, a man of means, with military experience. As a soldier, indeed, he may well have had his roots in Shakespeare's Captain Macmorris, the fighting Irishman in *Henry V* (1599). Like his cousin Teague, the captain was ignorant by English standards and used the language inefficiently and at times ridiculously, with Gaelicisms sprinkled throughout his speech. Physically he was a big man; he carried not only a long sword but a big cudgel or shillelagh; and his costume tended to be equally distinctive: an old red coat, a pinched hat and a great pair of jackboots. Such was the description of the first noteworthy soldier-version, Captain O'Blunder, in Thomas Sheridan's farce, *The Brave Irishman* (1743). This play told of the Irishman's love adventures in London, where he was regarded as a freak, although at the same time as generous and loveable. Such portraits must have been rather common, because by 1759 we have an attempt by Charles Macklin to redress the disparaging image. In *Love à la Mode* (1759) there is an Irish soldier named Sir Callaghan O'Brallaghan who is baited with the question: 'how many might you kill in a battle?' He is obviously expected (after a mighty oath) to answer according to stereotype, but he replies coolly: 'Why, I generally kill more in a battle than a coward would choose to look upon, or than an impertinent fellow would be able to eat.' It is clear that Macklin was deliberately combating the concept of the stage Irishman here. He tried even harder in *The Trueborn Irishman* (1762), which first played in Dublin, for Macklin was one of the few significant writers who came back to Ireland to present some of his work (in which he also acted). When this play transferred to London, however, it failed miserably. 'I believe', said Macklin, 'there's a geography in humour as well as in morals, which I had not previously considered.' Correcting the image of Irishman on the Dublin stage was one thing, but to expect Londoners to be interested could be another. The market was still for the loveable stage Irishman, found again in Richard Cumberland's Major O'Flaherty in *The West Indian* (1771). It may be recalled also that Richard Brinsley Sheridan seriously miscalculated the public taste on this point when first he presented *The Rivals* (1775). The audience objected strongly to the portrayal of Sir Lucius O'Trigger. Sheridan took off the play, rewrote the role and changed his actor.

The fighting Irishman lived on, wherever motley was worn, into the nineteenth century. But he forsook comedy for melodrama, where his fighting qualities were better appreciated and given political motivation. In the Irish plays of another Dubliner, Dion Boucicault (1820-90) the two versions of stage Irishman were happily combined. The ignorant servant became a roguish, heroic helpmate of the patriotic Irish soldier carrying on a dignified, gentlemanly opposition to English rule in Ireland. Boucicault found a formula for buffoonery and sentimentality which it became the mission of writers such as J. M. Synge, W. B. Yeats and even Bernard Shaw, in *John Bull's Other Island* (1904), to counteract and to replace with an authentic picture of, in Shaw's phrase, 'the real old Ireland'.

WIT

It is something of a cliché that Irish dramatists writing in English display a characteristic wit. Hackneyed though it may be, however, it remains true that the best writers who wrote for an English public, from Farquhar to George Bernard Shaw, consistently achieved a style that allows one to describe their wit as Anglo-Irish. Because the Irishman in London is a stranger, he has a perspective denied to the native Englishman; because he is fluent in English he has an advantage over other ethnic representatives. His attitude to society is ambivalent, intent simultaneously on mocking its solemnity and formality and also envious of its security. The result is a more subversive style of wit than is to be found among English writers.

To give a few examples, starting once again with Farquhar: in *The Constant Couple* (1699) Sir Harry Wildair coolly refuses to fight a duel with a man because he sensibly recognizes that this man is a professional soldier. He is not in the least interested in the question of honour, which would have been the conventional concern, and he says: 'I can't conceive how running you through the Body shou'd contribute one Jot more to my Gentility.' And so he will not fight. That cool indifference to the conventional view is peculiarly Irish. It may be more familiar to us in the style of Wilde and Shaw but it is discernible from the very outset of the Anglo-Irish tradition. The wit often takes the form of a surprising reversal of expected associations, resulting in an amusing paradox which is also a social comment. For example, in Farquhar's *The Recruiting Officer*: 'I'm a free-born *Englishman*, and will be a Slave my own way.' In Goldsmith's *She Stoops to Conquer*, Tony Lumpkin asks who the strangers outside the tavern might be: 'Do they seem to be Londoners?' And the Landlord replies: 'I believe they may. They look woundily like Frenchmen.' He means that if they look like Frenchmen they must be Londoners, which is a sly commentary on contemporary fashions. The wit is not content to be merely verbal; it contains within its absurdity a comment, sometimes a radical one, on manners and customs. Behind Farquhar's last play, *The Beaux' Stratagem* (1707), for all its high spirits and witty exchanges, lies a serious examination of the question of divorce, and the play ends with the unusual event of a husband and wife agreeing to part forever, since they were never more than 'two Carcasses join'd unnaturally together.'

Using comedy to explore some serious social issue, accordingly, is another feature of Irish playwriting. Sir Richard Steele explored the fashion for duelling in his day, and he said himself that he wrote *The Conscious Lovers* (1722) mainly for the scene in the fourth act which sets up an argument against duelling. Of course, Steele was also continuing in drama what he had already achieved in the essay form. In *The Tatler,* numbers 25 and 31 (June 1709), he had condemned duelling as both foolish and dangerous. Hazlitt exaggerated when he described Steele's plays as 'homilies in prose', but it is true that *The Lying Lover* (1703) and *The Tender Husband* (1703) resemble his best-known play, *The Conscious Lovers,* in having an earnest moral point to make as well as offering comic entertainment. In this matter, however, Steele was responding to a change in public taste. He is often credited with creating the vogue for sentimental comedy in the eighteenth century, but this claim needs serious qualification. Ever since the middle of the 1690s a reaction was setting in against the sex-orientated plots and libertine characters of Restoration comedy. When the major attack came, in Jeremy Collier's *A Short View of the Immorality and Profaneness of the English Stage* (1698), it had such an impact because it was pushing at an open door. The new merchant classes were more interested in improving themselves when they went to the theatre than had been the more aristocratic and courtly audiences of the generation just passing. Both Farquhar and Steele refer to Collier in prefaces to their plays, and make clear that it is their intention to write comedy that will avoid smuttiness and will condemn vice. Farquhar was really too jovial a personality to do much in this vein, although the last act of *The Beaux' Stratagem* certainly has sentimental features, especially when the rogue-hero Aimwell becomes conscience-stricken and confesses his deception to the heroine Dorinda. Steele went much further, since he believed that the stage should offer exemplary characters and should promote refined feelings.

Whereas it may be no great boast to claim that the Irish playwrights gave the lead in sentimental comedy in the eighteenth century, the point becomes more meaningful if we understand that traditionally the Irish playwright is interested in ways in which comedy can combine didacticism with either satire or warm-hearted joy in life. Sentimentalism is thus only an episode in the history of comedy. It did not kill laughter, as Goldsmith later claimed, and it is foolish to argue that Goldsmith and Sheridan successfully turned the tide by reviving pure comedy in their own plays. Nowadays, it is better understood that pure comedy existed side by side with sentimental comedy all through the eighteenth century. The comedies of Arthur Murphy, for example, stand out as evidence that the Restoration comedy of manners was still a viable model in the 1760s. Goldsmith's essay on theatre (1773), reprinted in this anthology, makes clear his objections to sentimental or weeping comedy, anticipating the attitude taken by Sheridan in his prologue, added on the tenth night of *The Rivals* (1775); and yet both authors display vestiges of sentimentalism in their major plays. The fact was that both writers were constrained by certain norms of taste, according to which Goldsmith's love of farcical or 'low' scenes had to be tempered and Sheridan's impulse for satire had to bow to gentility. For this reason they introduced no radical change in the history of English comedy; they merely brought back the qualities of 'nature' and 'humour' found so refreshingly in the plays of Farquhar and Congreve.

CONCLUSION

It has been argued here that from George Farquhar onwards, through Steele, Macklin, Goldsmith and Sheridan, the expatriate Irish writer was drawn to London by what we might call the market situation. We have seen that, with whatever degree of irony, he exploited his own personality, his Irishness and his biography in the material of his plays. He usually took liberties with the existing dramatic forms and was reluctant to write entirely within the norms in vogue. Moreover, he displayed, characteristically, a form of wit, born of his peculiar position in London society as at once stranger and aspiring entrant. Although this wit often involved absurdities, reversals and paradoxes, it usually conveyed a serious idea, perhaps subversive of conventional morality or social customs. In this regard, behind the mask of the laughing Irishman, be it Farquhar or Goldsmith or Shaw or Wilde, lay the determined enemy of English falsity.

In all of this, however, political questions hardly entered the picture at all before the arrival on the scene of W. B. Yeats. Prior to Yeats, expatriate Irish writers could write of 'our country' and mean England, because they were writing mainly for an English audience. One finds this in Goldsmith, in *An Enquiry into the Present State of Polite Learning in Europe* (1759), as in Farquhar before him, in his essay on comedy (in *Love and Business*, 1702). But Yeats consciously reversed the tradition of the expatriate writer by returning to Dublin to set up the Irish Literary Theatre in 1899. It was then that the political questions were raised, concerning national identity, artistic sincerity, and the nature of Ireland's linguistic relationship to England. Obviously, the development of a national theatre meant opposition to the traditional theatre, the colonial theatre, founded by John Ogilby in 1637. There was now be a building up of native talent and of a native tradition, as playwrights came back to Ireland to assist in the establishment of a new drama, intensely preoccupied with making an Irish audience think in terms of differentiation from, rather than identification with, English culture.

Once the Abbey Theatre opened its doors in 1904 the expatriate Irish playwright practically disappeared. Thereafter, expatriates tended primarily to be writers of fiction, such as George Moore (after his brief appearance as a playwright), James Joyce and Samuel Beckett, and they tended more towards Paris than London. Irish writers were learning to 'fly by the nets' of colonialist appropriation. After 1922, when the Irish Free State was established, expatriation tended to be a political decision, a conscious repudiation or at least a scorning of the national theatre. According to his autobiography, Seán O'Casey left Dublin as a result of the riots which greeted *The Plough and the Stars* (1926). Even if the reasons were more complicated, this was how O'Casey later saw the matter. It was simply 'time to go'. But his presence in Britain was never on a par with Shaw's. He never played the game of expatriate. He stood in undisguised hostility to what he saw as British cultural depravity. It is because Brendan Behan was much more easygoing, more ready to play the game of eighteenth-century stage Irishman who sings for his supper, that he created the illusion he was fighting the battle of the Boyne all over again, in a surreal encounter with George Farquhar. Behan knew he was playing a game, and that the reality, especially the political reality, was simply too terrible to take seriously. Thus in his short career as expatriate, Brendan Behan serves, in spite of the recklessness of his whole approach to drama, to put into focus the problem of identity which for the Irish writer exists still as it has existed in some form for three hundred years. Not even the foundation of the Abbey Theatre has changed that.

GEORGE FARQUHAR

(1677-1707)

from: THE RECRUITING OFFICER (1706)

[Whether or not Farquhar may be identified with Captain Plume, it is plain that he was in sympathy with his roguery. In the first excerpt below, Plume arrives to back up in a subtle way the unscrupulous conscription methods of Sergeant Kite, working on the rustic innocents Costar and Thomas. Although a real and costly war lies in the background — the War of the Spanish Succession, in which England fought against France — this play refuses to take it seriously, and by that very lightness of touch succeeds in making the reader or spectator aware of a day of reckoning for this 'food for powder'.]

ACT II, SCENE 3

The Street

Enter KITE, *with* COSTAR PEARMAIN *and* THOMAS APPLETREE, *one in each hand, drunk.*[1]

KITE *sings*

1. In the early editions (1706-28), the stage directions call for a 'Mob' and identify 1st Mob and 2nd Mob later in the scene. Following modern practice, the present text, based on the Dublin edition of 1722, supplies the two names from the start of the scene.

Our Prentice TOM *may now refuse*
To wipe his scoundrel Master's Shoes;
For now he's free to sing and play,
Over the Hills, and far away ——— *Over,* &c.
(COSTAR *and* THOMAS *sing the Chorus*)
We shall lead more happy Lives,
By getting rid of Brats and Wives,
That scold and brawl both Night and Day:
Over the Hills, and far away ——— *Over,* &c.

KITE: Hey Boys! Thus we Soldiers live: Drink, sing, dance, play: We live, as one should say — we live — 'Tis impossible to tell how we live — We are all Princes — Why — Why you are a King — You are an Emperor, and I'm a Prince — Now — an't we?

COSTAR: No, Serjeant; I'll be no Emperor.

KITE: No!

COSTAR: No, I'll be a Justice of Peace.

KITE: A Justice of Peace, Man!

COSTAR: Ay, wauns[2] will I; for since this Pressing-Act,[3] they are greater than any Emperor under the Sun.

KITE: Done: You are a Justice of Peace, and you are a King, and I am a Duke, and a Rum Duke, an't I?

THOMAS: Ay, but I'll be no King.

KITE: What then?

THOMAS: I'll be a Queen.

KITE: A Queen!

THOMAS: Ay, Queen of *England*,[4] that's greater than any King of 'em all.

KITE: Bravely said, Faith: Huzza for the Queen: (*Huzza*!) But Hark'ee, you Mr. Justice, and you Mr. Queen, did you never see the Queen's Picture?

COSTAR, THOMAS: No, no, no.

KITE: I wonder at that. I have two of 'em set in Gold, and as like her Majesty, God Bless the Mark. See here, they are in Gold.

(*Takes two Broad Pieces*[5] *out of his Pocket, gives one each to* COSTAR *and* THOMAS)

COSTAR: *(Looking at it)* The wonderful Works of Nature!

THOMAS: What's this written about? Here's a Posy, I believe. *Ca-ro-lus* — What's that, Serjeant?

2. 'By God's wounds'.
3. The Act for Raising Recruits (1704), to provide troops for the war against the French. Justices of the Peace were empowered to raise troops in their locality.
4. Queen Anne had come to the throne of England in 1702.
5. Gold sovereigns from the reign of Charles II (1660-85).

KITE: O! *Carolus*![6] — Why *Carolus* is Latin for Queen *Ann*; that's all.

THOMAS: 'Tis a fine thing to be a Scollard[7] — Serjeant, will you part with this? I'll buy it on you, if it come within the Compass of a Crown.[8]

KITE: A Crown! never talk of buying; 'tis the same thing among Friends, you know; I'll present them to you both: You shall give me as good a thing. Put 'em up, and remember your old Friend, when I'm *singing* over the Hills, and far away!

(*They sing, and put up*[9] *the Money*)

Enter PLUME *singing.*

Over the Hills, and o'er the Main,
To Flanders, Portugal, *or* Spain:
The Queen commands, and we'll obey,
Over the Hills, and far away.

Come on my Men of Mirth, away with it, I'll make one among ye. Who are these hearty Lads?

KITE: Off with your Hats; Ounds off with your Hats: This is the Captain, the Captain.

COSTAR: We have seen Captains afore-now, mun.

THOMAS: Ay, and Lieutenant-Captains too: 'Sflesh![10] I'll keep on my Nab.[11]

COSTAR: And I'se scarcely doff mine for any Captain in *England*: My Vether's a Freeholder.[12]

PLUME: Who are these jolly Lads, Serjeant?

KITE: A couple of honest brave Fellows, that are willing to serve the Queen: I have entertain'd 'em just now, as Volunteers under your Honour's Command.

PLUME: And good Entertainment they shall have: Volunteers are the Men I want; those are the Men fit to make Soldiers, Captains, Generals.

COSTAR: Wounds,[13] *Tummas*, what's this! are you listed?[14]

THOMAS: Flesh! Not I: Are you, Costar?

COSTAR: Wounds, not I.

KITE: What! not listed! ha, ha, ha! a very good Jest, faith.

COSTAR: Come, *Tummas*, we'll go Home.

THOMAS: Ay, ay, come.

6. Charles.
7. scholar (dialect).
8. i.e. if it can be bought for five shillings.
9. away.
10. 'By God's flesh'.
11. hat.
12. i.e. My father has the freehold to his farm for life (and so has social status).
13. 'By God's wounds'.
14. enlisted.

KITE: Home! For shame, Gentlemen, behave yourselves better before your Captain: Dear *Tummas*, honest *Costar*.

THOMAS: No, no, we'll be gone. (*Going*)

KITE: Nay then, I command you to stay: I place you both Centinels in this Place, for two Hours, to watch the Motion of St. *Mary's* Clock, you; and you the Motion St. *Chad's*:[15] And he that dares stir from his Post, till he be reliev'd, shall have my Sword in his Guts the next Minute.

PLUME: What's the matter, Serjeant? I'm afraid you are too rough with these Gentlemen.

KITE: I'm too mild, Sir: They disobey Command, Sir; and one of 'em shou'd be shot for an Example to the other.

COSTAR: Shot, *Tummas*!

PLUME: Come, Gentlemen, what's the Matter?

COSTAR: We don't know; the noble Serjeant is pleas'd to be in a Passion, Sir —— but —

KITE: They disobey Command, they deny their being listed.

THOMAS: Nay, Serjeant, we don't downright deny it neither; that we dare not do, for fear of being Shot. But we humbly conceive in a civil way, and begging your Worship's Pardon, that we may go Home.

PLUME: That's easily known: Have either of you receiv'd any of the Queen's Money?

COSTAR: Not a Brass Farthing, Sir.

KITE: Sir, they have each of them receiv'd three and twenty Shillings and Six pence, and 'tis now in their Pockets.

COSTAR: Wounds, if I have a Penny in my Pocket but a bent Six-pence I'll be content to be listed, and shot into the Bargain.

THOMAS: And I, look ye here, Sir.

COSTAR: Ay, here's my Stock too: Nothing but the Queen's Picture, that the Serjeant gave me just now.

KITE: See there, a Broad-piece, three and twenty Shillings and Six-pence, the t'other has the Fellow on't.

PLUME: The Case is plain, Gentlemen, the Goods are found upon you: Those Pieces of Gold are worth Three and Twenty [shillings] and Six-pence each.

COSTAR: So it seems that *Carolus* is Three and Twenty Shillings and Six-pence in *Latin*.

THOMAS: 'Tis the same thing in *Greek*, for we are listed.

COSTAR: Flesh! but we an't *Tummas*: I desire to be carry'd before the Mayor, Captain.

(*Captain and Serjeant whisper the while*)

PLUME: 'Twill never do, *Kite*, — Your damn'd Tricks will ruin me at last — I won't lose the Fellows tho', if I can help it — Well, Gentlemen, there must be some Trick in this, my Serjeant offers to take his Oath that you are fairly listed.

COSTAR: Why, Captain, we know that you soldiers have more Liberty of Conscience than other Folks; but for me, or Neighbour *Tummas* here to take such an Oath, 'twould be downright Perjuration.

PLUME: Look'e, Rascal, you Villain; if I find that you have impos'd upon these two honest Fellows, I'll trample you to Death, you Dog — Come, how was't?

THOMAS: Nay then, we will speak: Your Serjeant, as you say, is a Rogue, begging your Worship's Pardon — and —

COSTAR: Nay, *Tummas*, let me speak; you know I can read — And so, Sir, he gave us those two Pieces of Money for Pictures of the Queen, by way of a Present.

PLUME: How! by way of a Present! The Son of a Whore! I'll teach you to abuse honest Fellows, like you: Scoundrel, Rogue, Villain!

(*Beats the Serjeant off the stage, and follows him out*)

COSTAR, THOMAS: O Brave noble Captain! Huzza! a brave Captain, Faith.

COSTAR: Now, *Tummas*, *Carolus* is Latin for a Beating: This is the Bravest Captain I ever saw — Wauns, I have a Month's Mind[16] to go with him.

Re-enter PLUME

PLUME: A Dog! to abuse two such honest Fellows as you — Look'e, Gentlemen, I love a pretty Fellow; I come among you as an Officer to list Soldiers, not as a Kidnapper to steal Slaves.

COSTAR: Mind that, *Tummas*.

PLUME: I desire no Man to go with me but as I went my self: I went a Volunteer, as you, or you may do; for a little time carry'd a Musket; and now I command a Company.

THOMAS: Mind that, *Costar*: A sweet Gentleman.

15. Actual landmarks in Shrewsbury, a town in the English west midlands close to the border with Wales, where the play is set. The river Severn runs through Shrewsbury.

16. a strong intention.

PLUME: 'Tis true, Gentlemen, I might take an Advantage of you; the Queen's Money was in your Pockets; my Serjeant was ready to take his Oath you were listed; but I scorn to do a base thing; you are both of you at your Liberty.

COSTAR: Thank you, noble Captain — I cod,[17] I can't find in my Heart to leave him, he talks so finely.

THOMAS: Ay *Costar*, wou'd he always hold in this Mind.

PLUME: Come, my Lads, one thing more I'll tell you: You're both young tight Fellows, and the Army is the Place to make you Men for ever: Every Man has his Lot, and you have yours. What think you now of a Purse of *French* Gold out of a *Monsieur's* Pocket, after you have dash'd out his Brains with the Butt of your Firelock? eh! —

COSTAR: Wauns! I'll have it, Captain — Give me a Shilling, I'll follow you to the End of the World.

THOMAS: Nay, dear *Costar*, do'na; be advis'd.

PLUME: Here, my Hero, here are two Guineas for thee, as Earnest of what I'll do farther for thee.

THOMAS: (*Crys, and pulls back his Arm*) Do'na take it, do'na dear *Costar*.

COSTAR: I wull — I wull — Waunds, my Mind gives me,[18] that I shall be a Captain my self — I take your Money, Sir, and now I am a Gentleman.

PLUME: Give me thy Hand. And now you and I will travel the World o'er, and command it wherever we tread — (*Aside*) Bring your Friend with you, if you can.

COSTAR: Well, *Tummas*, must we part?

THOMAS: No, *Costar*, I canno' leave thee — Come; Captain, (*Crying*) I'll e'en go along too; and if you have two honester, simpler Lads in your Company than we two have been, I'll say no more.

PLUME: Here, my Lad, (*Gives him Money*). Now your Name?

THOMAS: *Tummas Appletree.*

PLUME: And yours?

COSTAR: *Costar Pearmain.*

PLUME: Born where?

COSTAR: Both in *Herefordshire.*

PLUME: Very well: Courage, my Lads — Now we'll sing, *Over the Hills, and far away.*

Courage, brave Boys, 'tis One to Ten,
But we return all Gentlemen, &c.

Exeunt

17. By God.
18. I think that.

ACT III, SCENE 2

The Walk, by the Severn Side

[The love interest runs side by side with the military. Captain Plume loves Sylvia, but since her father forbids the match she disguises herself as a soldier and enlists unrecognized. Plume's friend Worthy loves Melinda, Sylvia's cousin, who is too proud and affected to accept his sincere proposals and accepts instead the advances of the delightfully foolish Captain Brazen, a version of the braggart soldier with social pretensions. In this excerpt, the theatrical potential of *The Recruiting Officer* comes through clearly in the use of disguise and the splendid characterization of Captain Brazen.]

... MELINDA: And from all the Men I ever saw, I never had so fine a Complement; but you Soldiers are the best bred Men, that we must allow.

BRAZEN: Some of us, Madam — But there are Brutes among us too; very sad Brutes; For my own Part, I have always had the good Luck to prove agreeable — I have had very considerable Offers, Madam, — I might have marry'd a *German* Princess, worth fifty thousand Crowns a Year; but her Stove[1] disgusted me. — The Daughter of a *Turkish* Bashaw fell in Love with me too, when I was Prisoner among the Infidels: She offer'd to rob her Father of his Treasure, and make her Escape with me; but I don't know how, my Time was not come; Hanging and Marriage, you know, go by Destiny: Fate has reserv'd me for a *Shropshire* Lady[2] with twenty thousand Pound — Do you know any such Person, Madam?

MELINDA: (*Aside*) Extravagant Coxcomb! to be sure a great many Ladies of that Fortune wou'd be proud of the Name of Mrs. *Brazen.*

BRAZEN: Nay, for that matter, Madam, there are Women of very good Quality of the Name of *Brazen.*

Enter WORTHY

MELINDA: O! Are you there, Gentleman? — Come, Captain, we'll walk this Way; give me your Hand.

BRAZEN: My Hand, Heart's Blood and Guts, are at your Service — Mr. *Worthy,* your Servant, my Dear.

Exit leading MELINDA

WORTHY: Death and Fire! this not to be borne.

1. Her furnace, overheating her boudoir. Bashaw = Turkish military commander.
2. Melinda herself, whose fortune is the main attraction for Captain Brazen.

Enter PLUME

PLUME: No more it is, Faith.

WORTHY: What?

PLUME: The *March*-Beer at the *Raven*:[3] I have been doubly serving the Queen, — raising Men, and raising the Excise — Recruiting and Elections are rare Friends to the Excise.[4]

WORTHY: You an't drunk.

PLUME: No, no; whimsical only: I cou'd be mighty foolish, and fancy my self mighty witty: Reason still keep its Throne; but it nods a little, that's all.

WORTHY: Then you're just fit for a Frolick?

PLUME: As fit as close Pinners[5] for a Punk in the Pit.[6]

WORTHY: There's your Play then, recover me that Vessel from that *Tangerine*.[7]

PLUME: She's well rigg'd; but how is she mann'd?

WORTHY: By Captain *Brazen*, that I told you of to Day; She's Call'd the *Melinda*, a first Rate, I can assure you; She sheer'd off with him just now on purpose to affront me; but, according to your Advice, I wou'd take no Notice, because I wou'd seem to be above a Concern for her Behaviour; But have a care of a Quarrel.

PLUME: No, no, I never quarrel with anything in my Cups but an Oyster-Wench, or a Cook-Maid; and if they been't civil, I knock 'em down. But hark'e, my Friend, I'll make Love, and I must make Love. I tell you what, I'll make Love like a Platoon.

WORTHY: Platoon, how's that?

PLUME: I'll kneel, stoop and stand, Faith; Most Ladies are gain'd by Platooning.

WORTHY: Here they come; I must leave you.

Exit

PLUME: Soh! Now must I look as sober, and as demure as a Whore at a Christening.

Enter BRAZEN *and* MELINDA

BRAZEN: Who's that, Madam?

MELINDA: A Brother Officer of yours, I suppose, Sir.

BRAZEN: Ay! — (*to* PLUME) my Dear.

PLUME: My Dear.

([*They*] *Run and embrace*)

BRAZEN: My dear boy, how is't? Your Name, my Dear? if I be not mistaken I have seen your Face.

PLUME: I never see yours in my Life, my Dear — But there's a Face[8] as well known as the Sun that shines on all, and is by all ador'd.

BRAZEN: Have you any Pretensions Sir?

PLUME: Pretensions!

BRAZEN: That is, Sir, have you ever serv'd Abroad?

PLUME: I have serv'd at Home, Sir, for Ages serv'd this cruel Fair — And that will serve the Turn, Sir.

MELINDA: (*Aside*) So between the Fool and the Rake, I shall bring a fine spot of Work upon my Hands — I see *Worthy* yonder — I cou'd be content to be Friends with him wou'd he come this way.

BRAZEN: Will you fight for the Lady, Sir?

PLUME: No, Sir, but I'll have her notwithstanding.

Thou Peerless Princess of Salopian *Plains,*
Envy'd by Nymphs, and worshipp'd by the Swains.

BRAZEN: Oons, Sir, not fight for her!

PLUME: Prithee be quiet — I shall be out[9] —
Behold how humbly does the SEVERN *glide*
To greet Thee, Princess of the SEVERN*-side.*

BRAZEN: Don't mind him, Madam. — If he were not so well drest, I shou'd take him for a Poet. — But I'll shew the Difference presently — Come, Madam, — we'll place you between us; and now the longest Sword carries her.

(*Draws,* MELINDA *shrieks*)

Enter WORTHY

MELINDA: Oh! Mr *Worthy*! save me from these Madmen.

Exit with WORTHY

PLUME: Ha, ha, ha! Why don't you follow, Sir, and fight the bold Ravisher?

BRAZEN: No, Sir, you are my Man.

PLUME: I don't like the Wages, and I won't be your Man.

BRAZEN: Then you're not worth my Sword.

PLUME: No! pray what did it cost?

BRAZEN: It cost me twenty Pistoles in *France*, and my Enemies thousands of Lives in *Flanders*.

3. Strong beer made at the end of the brewing season. 'The Raven' was the tavern in Shrewsbury where Captain Plume had his recruiting station.
4. government duty or tax.
5. close-fitting caps.
6. a prostitute at the playhouse.
7. A pirate-ship from Tangiers (referring here to Captain Brazen, who has 'captured' Melinda).
8. i.e. Melinda's.
9. i.e. forget my lines.

PLUME: Then they had a dear Bargain.

Enter SILVIA *in Man's Apparel*

SILVIA: Save ye, save ye, Gentlemen.

BRAZEN: My Dear, I'm yours.

PLUME: Do you know the Gentleman?

BRAZEN: No; but I will presently — Your Name, my Dear.

SILVIA: *Wilful; Jack Wilful*, at your Service.

BRAZEN: What, the *Kentish Wilfuls*, or those of *Staffordshire*?

SILVIA: Both, sir, both; I'm related to all the *Wilfuls* in *Europe*, and I'm Head of the Family at present.[10]

PLUME: Do you live in this Country, Sir?

SILVIA: Yes, Sir, I live where I Stand; I have neither Home, House, nor Habitation beyond this Spot of Ground.

BRAZEN: What are you, Sir?

SILVIA: A Rake.

PLUME: In the Army, I presume.

SILVIA: No; but I intend to list immediately. — Look'e, Gentlemen, he that bids me fairest has me.

BRAZEN: Sir, I'll prefer you; I'll make you a Corporal this Minute.

PLUME: Corporal! I'll make you my Companion; you shall eat with me.

BRAZEN: You shall drink with me.

PLUME: You shall lie with me, you young Rogue *(Kisses her)*

BRAZEN: You shall receive your Pay, and do no Duty.

SILVIA: Then you must make me a Field Officer.

PLUME: Pho, pho! I'll do more than all this; I'll make you a Corporal, and give you a Brevet[11] for Serjeant.

BRAZEN: Can you read and write, Sir?

SILVIA: Yes.

BRAZEN: Then your Business is done. — I'll make you Chaplain to the Regiment.

SILVIA: Your Promises are so equal, that I'm at a loss to chuse: There is one *Plume*, that I hear much commended in Town; pray, which of you is Captain *Plume*?

PLUME: I am Captain *Plume*.

BRAZEN: No, no I'm Captain *Plume*.

SILVIA: Hey Day!

PLUME: Captain *Plume*! I'm your Servant, my Dear.

BRAZEN: Captain Brazen! I am yours — The Fellow dare not fight.

Enter KITE

KITE: Sir, if you please — *(Goes to whisper* [*to*] PLUME)

PLUME: No, no, there's your Captain. Captain *Plume*, your Serjeant has got so drunk, he mistakes me for you.

BRAZEN: He's an incorrigible Sot. — Here, my *Hector* of *Holbourn*,[12] forty Shillings for you.

PLUME: I forbid the Banes[13] — Look'e, Friend, you shall list with Captain *Brazen*.

SILVIA: I will see Captain *Brazen* hang'd first; I will list with Captain *Plume*; I am a free-born *Englishman*, and will be a Slave my own Way[14] — (*To* BRAZEN) Look'e, Sir, will you stand by me?

BRAZEN: I warrant you, my Lad.

SILVIA: Then I will tell you, Captain *Brazen*, (*To* PLUME) that you are an ignorant, pretending, impudent Coxcomb.

BRAZEN: Ay, ay, a sad Dog.

SILVIA: A very sad Dog: Give me the Money, noble Captain *Plume*.

PLUME: Then you won't list with Captain Brazen.

SILVIA: I won't.

BRAZEN: Never mind him, Child, I'll end the Dispute presently. — Hark'e, my Dear.

(*Takes* PLUME *to one Side of the Stage, and entertains him in dumb Show*)[15]

KITE: Sir, he in the plain Coat is Captain *Plume*. I am his Serjeant and will take my oath on't.

SILVIA: What! you are Serjeant *Kite*.

KITE: At your Service.

SILVIA: Then I wou'd not take your Oath for a Farthing.

KITE: A very understanding Youth of his Age! Pray, Sir, let me look you full in your Face.

SILVIA: Well, Sir, what have you to say to my Face?

KITE: The very Image of my Brother; two Bullets of the same Caliver[16] were never so like: Sure it must be *Charles, Charles* —

SILVIA: What d'ye mean by *Charles*?

10. This, at least, is true. In II.2 news was brought of the death of Silvia's brother, making her sole heiress of the Balance estate. At this point her father insisted that she must 'think no more of Captain Plume'.
11. A document giving higher rank, though not the right to higher pay. Farquhar is satirizing army practice.
12. A district of London known for its rowdiness.
13. banns. Plume means he objects to this proposed arrangement.
14. The sort of 'bull' only an Irish writer can sire.
15. mimes a conversation.
16. calibre.

KITE: The Voice too, only a little Variation in *F fa ut* flat.[17] My dear Brother, for I must call you so, if you shou'd have the Fortune to enter into the most noble Society of the Sword, I bespeak you for a Comrade.

SILVIA: No, Sir, I'll be the Captain's Comrade, if any Body's.

KITE: Ambition there again! 'Tis a noble Passion for a Soldier; by that I gain'd this glorious Halberd. Ambition! I see Commission in his Face already. Pray, noble Captain,[18] give me leave to salute you. (*Offers to kiss her*)

SILVIA: What, Men kiss one another!

KITE: We Officers do: 'tis our Way; we live together like Man and Wife, always either kissing or fighting: — But I see a Storm a coming.[19]

SILVIA: Now, Serjeant, I shall see who is your Captain, by your knocking down the other.

KITE: My Captain scorns Assistance, Sir.

BRAZEN: How dare you[20] contend for any thing, and not dare to draw your Sword? But you are a young Fellow, and have not been much Abroad; I excuse that, but prithee resign the Man, prithee do; you are a very honest Fellow.

PLUME: You lye; and you are a Son of a Whore. (*Draws and makes up to* BRAZEN)

BRAZEN: (*Retiring*) Hold, hold, did not you refuse to fight for the Lady?

PLUME: I always do — But for a Man I'll fight Knee deep; so you lie again.

(PLUME *and* BRAZEN *fight a Traverse*[21] *or two about the Stage:* SILVIA *draws, who is held by* KITE, *who sounds to Arms with his Mouth. Takes* SILVIA *in his Arms, and carries her off the Stage*)

BRAZEN: Hold, where's the Man?

PLUME: Gone.

BRAZEN: Then what do we fight for? (*Puts up*)[22] Now let's embrace, my Dear.

PLUME: With all my Heart, my Dear. (*Putting up*) I suppose *Kite* has listed him by this time. (*Embrace*)

17. The musical key of F minor. 'It was associated with extremes of passion and stormy feeling, so Kite is poking fun at Silvia's indignant tone' (Peter Dixon).
18. Kite has promoted Silvia instantly.
19. Plume and Brazen have finished their private conversation and must suggest a 'stormy' outcome.
20. Addressed to Plume.
21. brief passage of arms.
22. i.e. his sword.

BRAZEN: You are a brave Fellow. I always fight with a Man before I make him my Friend; and if once I find he will fight, I never quarrel with him afterwards. — And now I'll tell you a Secret, my dear Friend, That Lady[23] we frighted out of the Walk just now, I found in Bed this Morning — So beautiful, so inviting — I presently lock'd the Door — But I am a Man of Honour — But I believe I shall marry her nevertheless — Her twenty thousand Pound, you know, will be a pretty Conveniency — I had an Assignation with her here; but your coming spoil'd my Sport. Curse you, my Dear; but don't do so again —

PLUME: No, no, my Dear, Men are my Business at present.

Exeunt

23. i.e. Melinda. Brazen tells one of his many lies.

from:
THE BEAUX' STRATAGEM (1707)

[In his last and probably best comedy, Farquhar puts side by side the disguise and deception born of young men's desperation with genteel poverty and the disguise and deception of hard-nosed criminals and (in the political sense) traitors. Thus contrasted, the stratagem of the two *beaux* or young bucks, Archer and Aimwell, has more high spirits about it than immorality, and it serves to open up more serious issues in which Farquahar wanted to interest his audience, such as the basis of marriage in mutual love and the case for divorce where a marriage has, to coin a phrase, failed. The latter was a new and daring theme for comedy.

In the first excerpt below, Archer and Aimwell explain what their stratagem involves: fortune hunting. Little do they know that the curious landlord, Boniface, operates a gang of dangerous thieves from this inn.]

ACT I, SCENE I

An Inn

...*Enter* ARCHER/*to* BONIFACE *and* AIMWELL

ARCHER: Landlord, there are some *French* Gentleman below that ask for you.

BONIFACE: I'll wait on 'em: — (*To* ARCHER) Does your Master stay long in Town, as the Saying is?

ARCHER: I can't tell, as the Saying is.[1]

BONIFACE: Come from *London*?

ARCHER: No.

BONIFACE: Going to *London*, may hap?

ARCHER: No.

BONIFACE: An odd Fellow this. I beg your Worship's Pardon, I'll wait on you in half a Minute. *Exit*

AIMWELL: The Coast's clear, I see, —— Now, my dear *Archer*, welcome to *Litchfield*.[2]

ARCHER: I thank thee, my dear Brother in Iniquity.

AIMWELL: Iniquity! prithee, leave Canting;[3] you need not change your Style with your Dress.

ARCHER: Don't mistake me, *Aimwell*, for 'tis still my Maxim, that there is no Scandal like Rags, nor any Crime so shameful as Poverty.[4]

AIMWELL: The World Confesses it every Day in its Practice, tho' Men won't own it for their Opinion: Who did that worthy Lord, my Brother, single out of the Side-box[5] to sup with him t'other Night?

ARCHER:: *Jack Handcraft*, a handsome, well-dress'd, mannerly, sharping[6] Rogue, who keeps the best Company in Town.

AIMWELL: Right; and, pray, who marry'd my Lady *Manslaughter* t'other Day, the great Fortune?

ARCHER: Why, *Nick Marrabone*, a profess'd Pick-pocket, and a good Bowler;[7] but he makes a handsome Figure, and rides in his Coach that he formerly used to ride behind.

AIMWELL: But did you observe poor *Jack Generous* in the Park last Week?

ARCHER: Yes, with his Autumnal Perriwig, shading his melancholy Face, his Coat older than any thing but its Fashion, with one Hand idle in his Pocket, and with the other picking his useless Teeth; and tho' the Mall was crowded with Company, yet was poor *Jack* as single and solitary as a Lyon in a Desart.

AIMWELL: And as much avoided, for no Crime upon Earth but the want of Money.

ARCHER: And that's enough; Men must not be poor; Idleness is the Root of all Evil;[8] the World's wide enough, let 'em bustle; Fortune has taken the Weak under her Protection, but Men of Sense are left to their Industry.

AIMWELL: Upon which Topick we proceed, and, I think, luckily hitherto: Wou'd not any Man swear now, that I am a Man of Quality, and you my Servant, when if our intrinsick value were known —

ARCHER: Come, come, we are the Men of intrinsick Value, who can strike our Fortunes out of ourselves, whose Worth is independent of Accidents in Life, or Revolutions in Government; we have Heads to get Money, and Hearts to spend it.

AIMWELL: As to our Hearts, I grant ye, they are as willing Tits[9] as any within twenty Degrees; but I can have no great Opinion of our Heads from the Service they have done us hitherto, unless it be that they brought us from *London* hither to *Litchfield*, made me a Lord and you my Servant.

ARCHER: That's more than you cou'd expect already. But what Money have we left?

AIMWELL: But two hundred Pound.

ARCHER: And our Horses, Cloaths, Rings, *etc.* why, we have very good Fortunes now for moderate People; and let me tell you, that this two hundred Pound, with the Experience that we are now Masters of, is a better Estate than the Ten Thousand we have spent. —— Our Friends indeed began to suspect, that our Pockets were low, but we came off with flying Colours, shew'd no Signs of Want either in Word or Deed.

AIMWELL: Ay, and our going to *Brussels* was a good Pretence enough for our sudden disappearing; and, I warrant you, our Friends imagine, that we are going a Volunteering.

ARCHER: Why, 'faith, if this Prospect fails, it must e'en come to that. I am for venturing one of the Hundreds if you will upon this Knight-Errantry; but in case it should fail, we'll reserve the

1. A tag-phrase used by Boniface to win the confidence of his guests; Archer has seen through the usage and mocks it by repeating it. Farquhar was very good at this subtle use of linguistic combat.
2. Lichfield, the town in Staffordshire where the play is set. As with *The Recruiting Officer*, this play was based on Farquhar's actual knowledge of people and places in the English midlands.
3. hypocritical talk.
4. An interesting anticipation of George Bernard Shaw's argument that poverty is a crime, to be found in *Mrs Warren's Profession* (1893) and *Major Barbara* (1905), for example.
5. A compartment in a theatre or coffee-house.
6. cheating.
7. a heavy drinker.
8. A witty reversal of the Biblical saying, 'The love of money is the root of all evil' (First Epistle to Timothy, 6.10). Farquhar is saying, satirically, that money is the measure of good and lack of it construed as a sign of idleness.
9. nags or serviceable horses. Degrees = steps.

other to carry us to some Counterscarp,[10] where we may die as we liv'd, in a Blaze.

AIMWELL: With all my Heart; and we have liv'd justly, *Archer*; we can't say that we have spent our Fortunes, but that we have enjoy'd 'em.

ARCHER: Right; so much Pleasure for so much Money; we have had our Pennyworths; and had I Millions, I wou'd go to the same Market again. O *London, London*! well, we have had our Share, and let us be thankful: Past Pleasures, for ought I know, are best, such as we are sure of; those to come may disappoint us.

AIMWELL: It has often griev'd the Heart of me, to see how some inhumane Wretches murther their kind Fortunes; those that by sacrificing all to one Appetite, shall starve all the rest. —— You shall have some that live only in their Palates, and in their Sense of Tasting shall drown the other Four: Others are only Epicures[11] in Appearances, such who shall starve their Nights to make a Figure a Days, and famish their own to feed the Eyes of others: A contrary Sort confine their Pleasures to the Dark, and contract their spacious Acres to the Circuit of a Must-string.

ARCHER: Right; but they find the *Indies* in that Spot where they consume 'em, and I think, your kind Keepers have much the best on't; for they indulge the most Senses by one Expence, there's the Seeing, Hearing, and Feeling, amply gratify'd; and some Philosophers will tell you, that from such a Commerce, there arises a Sixth Sense, that gives infinitely more Pleasure than the other five put together.[12]

AIMWELL: And to pass to the other Extremity, of all Keepers, I think those the worst that keep their Money.

ARCHER: Those are the most miserable Wights[13] in being, they destroy the Rights of Nature, and disappoint the Blessings of Providence: Give me a man that keeps his five Senses keen and bright as his Sword, that has 'em always drawn out in their just Order and Strength, with his Reason as Commander at the Head of 'em, that detaches 'em by turns upon whatever Party of Pleasure agreeably offers, and commands 'em to retreat upon the least Appearance of Disadvantage or Danger: —— For my part, I can stick to my Bottle, while my Wine, my Company, and my Reason hold good; I can be charm'd with *Sappho*'s Singing,[14] without falling in Love with her Face; I love Hunting, but wou'd not, like *Acteon*,[15] be eaten up by my own Dogs; I love a fine House, but let another keep it; and just so I love a fine Woman.

AIMWELL: In that last Particular you have the better of me.

ARCHER: Ay, you're such an amorous Puppy, that I'm afraid you'll spoil our Sport; you can't counterfeit the Passion without feeling it.

AIMWELL: Tho' the whining Part be out of Doors in Town, 'tis still in Force with the Country Ladies; —— And let me tell you, *Frank*, the Fool in that Passion shall out-do the Knave at any time.

ARCHER: Well, I won't dispute it now; you command for the Day, and so I submit: —— At *Nottingham* you know I am to be Master.

AIMWELL: And at *Lincoln* I again.

ARCHER: Then, at *Norwich*, I mount, which, I think, shall be our last Stage; for, if we fail there, we'll embark for *Holland*, bid adieu to *Venus*, and welcome *Mars*.

AIMWELL: A Match! (*Enter* BONIFACE) Mum.[16]

BONIFACE: What will your Worship please to have for Supper?

AIMWELL: What have you got?

BONIFACE: Sir, we have a delicate Piece of Beef in the Pot, and a Pig at the Fire.

AIMWELL: Good Supper-meat, I must confess —— I can't eat Beef, Landlord.

ARCHER: And I hate Pig.

AIMWELL: Hold your prating, Sirrah, do you know who you are?

10. A term from fortification: outer wall or slope of ditch.
11. Farquhar is analyzing philosophies of pleasure, to which the rake/hero of Restoration comedy was conventionally dedicated. Aimwell implies that he and Archer are genuine pleasure-seekers, unlike some who either discipline themselves just to look well or restrict their pleasures to some fetish or sexual obsession. The major irony of this play is that in the end Aimwell cannot go through with his stratagem, and live by pleasure alone: conscience, his moral sense, forces him to tell the girl he has wooed for her money that he is 'all a lie'. Thus Farquhar is actually providing a critique of Restoration comedy and its epicurean values. This passage and those following should be read as a discussion on this topic, rather as Shaw later introduced philosophical discussions into his comedies.
12. The 'sixth sense' was said to be titillation. See Robert Burton's *The Anatomy of Melancholy*, I, i, 2, subsection 6.
13. creatures.
14. The love poetry of 'burning' Sappho, Greek female poet of the seventh century B.C.; Archer is arguing that he can order and control sensual pleasure by power of reason. He is colder and more calculating than Aimwell.
15. In Greek mythology, Actaeon was the man who saw Artemis naked while hunting in the woods and in punishment was turned into a stag and attacked by his own hounds.
16. i.e. Be quiet!

BONIFACE: Please to bespeak[17] something else; I have every thing in the House.

AIMWELL: Have you any Veal?

BONIFACE: Veal! Sir, we had a delicate Loin of Veal on *Wednesday* last.

AIMWELL: Have you got any Fish or Wildfowl?

BONIFACE: As for Fish, truly, Sir, we are an inland Town, and indifferently provided with Fish, that's the Truth on't; and then for Wildfowl —— We have a delicate Couple of Rabbets.

AIMWELL: Get me the Rabbets fricasy'd.

BONIFACE: Fricasy'd! Lard, Sir, they'll eat much better smother'd with Onions.

ARCHER: Pshaw! damn your Onions.

AIMWELL: Again, Sirrah! —— Well, Landlord, what you please; but hold, I have a small Charge of Money, and your House is to full of Strangers, that I believe it may be safer in your Custody than mine; for when this Fellow of mine gets drunk, he minds nothing. —— Here, Sirrah, reach me the strong Box.

ARCHER: Yes, sir, (*Aside*) this will give us a Reputation. (*Brings the Box*)

AIMWELL: Here, Landlord, the Locks are sealed down both for your Security and mine; it holds somewhat above Two hundred Pound; if you doubt it, I'll count it to you after Supper; but be sure you lay it where I may have it at a Minute's Warning; for my Affairs are a little dubious at present; perhaps I may be gone in half an Hour, perhaps I may be your Guest till the best part of that be spent; and pray order your Ostler to keep my Horses always sadled; but one thing above the rest I must beg, that you would let this Fellow have none of your *Anno Domini*,[18] as you call it —— for he's the most insufferable Sot —— Here, Sirrah, light me to my Chamber.

Exit, lighted by ARCHER

BONIFACE: *Cherry*, Daughter *Cherry*.

Enter CHERRY

CHERRY: D'ye call, Father?

BONIFACE: Ay, Child, you must lay by this Box for the Gentleman, 'tis full of Money.

CHERRY: Money! all that Money! why sure, Father, the Gentleman comes to be chosen Parliament-man. Who is he?

BONIFACE: I don't know what to make of him; he talks of keeping his Horses ready sadled, and of going perhaps at a Minute's Warning, or of staying perhaps till the best part of this be spent.

CHERRY: Ay! ten to one, Father, he's a Highway-man.

BONIFACE: A Highway-man! upon my Life, Girl, you have hit it, and this Box is some new purchased Booty. —— Now, cou'd we find him out, the Money were ours.

CHERRY: He don't belong to our Gang.

BONIFACE: What Horses have they?

CHERRY: The Master rides upon a Black.

BONIFACE: A Black! ten to one the Man upon the black Mare; and since he don't belong to our Fraternity, we may betray him with a safe Conscience: I don't think it lawful[19] to harbour any Rogues but my own. —— Look'ye, Child, as the Saying is, we must go cunningly to work; Proofs we must have; the Gentleman's Servant loves Drink, I'll ply him that way; and ten to one loves a Wench, you must work him t'other way.

CHERRY: Father, wou'd you have me give my Secret[20] for his?

BONIFACE: Consider, Child, there's Two hundred Pound to boot. (*Ringing without*) Coming, coming: —— Child, mind your Business.

Exit

CHERRY: What a Rogue is my Father! my Father! I deny it. —— My Mother was a good, generous, Free-hearted Woman, and I can't tell how far her good Nature might have extended for the good of her Children. This Landlord of mine, for I think I can call him no more, would betray his Guest, and debauch his Daughter into the Bargain, —— by a Footman too!

Enter ARCHER

ARCHER: What Footman, pray, Mistress, is so happy as to be the Subject of your Contemplation?

CHERRY: Whoever he is, Friend, he'll be but little the better for't.

ARCHER: I hope so, for I'm sure you did not think of me.

CHERRY: Suppose I had?

ARCHER: Why then you're but even with me; for the Minute I came in, I was considering in what Manner I should make Love to you.

CHERRY: Love to me, Friend!

17. order.
18. strong, old ale.

19. An anticipation of the kind of humour to be found in J.M. Synge's *The Playboy of the Western World* (1907), e.g. Christy Mahon's insistence that, although a murderer, he 'never used weapons. I've no licence, and I'm a law-fearing man.'
20. sexual favours.

ARCHER: Yes, Child.

CHERRY: Child! Manners; if you kept a little more distance, Friend, it would become you much better.

ARCHER: Distance! good Night, Sauce-box. (*Going*)

CHERRY: A pretty Fellow! I like his Pride, —— Sir, pray Sir, you see, Sir (ARCHER *returns*) I have the Credit to be intrusted with your Master's Fortune here, which sets me a Degree above his Footman; I hope, Sir, you an't affronted.

ARCHER: Let me look you full in the Face, and I'll tell you whether you can affront me or no. —— S'death, Child you have a Pair of delicate Eyes, and you don't know what to do with 'em.

CHERRY: Why, Sir, don't I see every body?

ARCHER: Ay, but if some Women had 'em, they wou'd kill every body. —— Prithee instruct me, I wou'd fain make Love to you, but I don't know what to say.

CHERRY: Why, did you never make Love to any body before?

ARCHER: Never to a person of your Figure, I can assure you, Madam; my Addresses have been always confin'd to People within my own Sphere, I never aspir'd so high before. (*Sings*)

But you look so bright,
And are dress'd so tight, &c.

CHERRY: (*Aside*) What can I think of this Man? Will you give me that Song, Sir?

ARCHER: Ay, my Dear, take it while it is warm. (*Kisses her*) Death and Fire! her Lips are Honey-combs.

CHERRY: And I wish there had been Bees too, to have stung you for your Impudence.

ARCHER: There's a swarm of *Cupids*, my little *Venus*, that has done the Business much better.

CHERRY: (*Aside*) This Fellow is misbegotten[21] as well as I. What's your Name, Sir?

ARCHER: (*Aside*) Name! I gad, I have forgot it. Oh! *Martin*.

CHERRY: Where were you born?

ARCHER: In St. *Martin's* Parish.

CHERRY: What was your Father?

ARCHER: St. *Martin's* Parish.

CHERRY: Then, Friend, good night.

ARCHER: I hope not.

CHERRY: You may depend upon't.

ARCHER: Upon what?

21. illegitimate. She means he must be nobly born.

CHERRY: That you're very impudent.

ARCHER: That you're very handsome.

CHERRY: That you're a Footman.

ARCHER: That you're an Angel.

CHERRY: I shall be rude.

ARCHER: So shall I.

CHERRY: Let go my Hand.

ARCHER: Give me a Kiss. (*Kisses her*)

(*Call without* 'Cherry, Cherry')

CHERRY: I'm-m —— My Father calls; you plaguy Devil, how durst you stop my Breath so? —— Offer to follow me one Step, if you dare.

Exit

ARCHER: A fair Challenge, by this Light; this is a pretty fair opening of an Adventure; but we are Knight-Errants, and so Fortune be our Guide.

Exit

ACT IV, SCENE I

A Gallery in LADY BOUNTIFUL's *House*

[Archer and Aimwell, having marked out their prey, namely the heiress Dorinda and her sister-in-law Mrs. Sullen, set about putting their 'stratagem' into operation by gaining entrance to the stately home presided over by Dorinda's mother, Lady Bountiful. In this scene another stratagem begins to unfold, that of the Jacobite Irishman, Foigard, masquerading as a French priest. Eventually, in Act V, Farquhar plays one stratagem off against the other.]

Enter MRS. SULLEN

MRS. SULLEN: Were I born an humble *Turk*, where Women have no Soul nor Property, there I must sit contented —— But in *England*, a Country whose Women are its Glory, must Women be abus'd? Where Women rule,[1] must Women be enslav'd?[2] Nay, cheated into Slavery? mock'd by a Promise of comfortable Society into a wilderness of Solitude? —— I dare not keep the Thought about me —— O, here comes something to divert me ——

Enter a COUNTRY WOMAN

WOMAN: I come, an't please your Ladyship; you're my Lady *Bountiful*, a'n't ye?

MRS. SULLEN: Well, good Woman, go on.

WOMAN: I come seventeen long Mail[3] to have a Cure for my Husband's sore Leg.

1. A reference to Queen Anne, queen of England, Scotland and Ireland 1702-14.
2. i.e. in marriage.
3. miles.

MRS. SULLEN: Your Husband! What, Woman cure your Husband![4]

WOMAN: Ay, poor Man, for his sore Leg won't let him stir from Home.

MRS. SULLEN: There, I confess, you have given me a Reason. Well good Woman, I'd tell you what you must do —— You must lay your Husband's Leg upon a Table, and with a Chopping-Knife you must lay it open as broad as you can, then you must take out the Bone, and beat the Flesh soundly with a Rolling-pin, then take Salt, Pepper, Cloves, Mace and Ginger, some Sweet-Herbs, and season it very well, then roll it up like a Brawn, and put it into the Oven for two Hours.

WOMAN: Heaven reward your Ladyship —— I have two little Babies too that are pitious bad with the Graips,[5] a'n't please ye.

MRS. SULLEN: Put a little Pepper and Salt in their Bellies, good Woman.

Enter LADY BOUNTIFUL

I beg your Ladyship's Pardon for taking your Business out of your Hands, I have been a tampering here a little with one of your Patients.

LADY BOUNTIFUL: Come, good Woman, don't mind this mad Creature; I am the Person that you want, I suppose —— What wou'd you have, Woman?

MRS. SULLEN: She wants something for her Husband's sore Leg.

LADY BOUNTIFUL: What's the matter with his Leg, Goody?[6]

WOMAN: It came first, as one might say, with a sort of Dizziness in his Foot, then he had a kind of Laziness in his Joints, and then his Leg broke out, and then it swell'd, and then it clos'd again, and then it broke out again, and then it fester'd, and then it grew better, and then it grew worse again.

MRS. SULLEN: Ha, ha, ha.

LADY BOUNTIFUL: How can you be merry with the Misfortunes of other People?

MRS. SULLEN: Because my own make me sad, Madam.

LADY BOUNTIFUL: The worst Reason in the World, Daughter; your own Misfortunes should teach you to pity others.

MRS. SULLEN: But the Woman's Misfortunes and mine are nothing alike; her Husband is sick, and mine, alas! is in Health.

LADY BOUNTIFUL: What! wou'd you wish your Husband sick?

MRS. SULLEN: Not of a sore Leg, of all things.

LADY BOUNTIFUL: Well, good Woman, go to the Pantry, get your Belly-full of Victuals, then I'll give you a Receipt[7] of Diet-drink for your Husband —— But d'ye hear, Goody, you must not let your Husband move too much.

WOMAN: No, no, Madam, the poor Man's inclinable enough to lie still.

Exit

LADY BOUNTIFUL: Well, Daughter *Sullen*, tho' you laugh, I have done Miracles about the Country here with my Receipts.

MRS. SULLEN: Miracles indeed, if they have cur'd any Body; but I believe, Madam, the Patient's Faith goes farther toward the Miracle than your Prescription.

LADY BOUNTIFUL: Fancy helps in some Cases; but there's your Husband, who has as little Fancy as any Body, I brought him from Death's Door.

MRS. SULLEN: I suppose, Madam, you made him drink plentifully of Ass's Milk.

Enter DORINDA, *runs to* MRS. SULLEN

DORINDA: News, dear Sister, News, News.

Enter ARCHER *running*

ARCHER: Where, where is my Lady *Bountiful*? —— Pray, which is the old Lady of you three?

LADY BOUNTIFUL: I am.

ARCHER: O, Madam, the Fame of your Ladyship's Charity, Goodness, Benevolence, Skill and Ability have drawn me hither to implore your Ladyship's Help in behalf of my unfortunate Master, who is this Moment breathing his last.

LADY BOUNTIFUL: Your Master! where is he?

ARCHER: At your Gate, drawn by the Appearance of your handsome House to view it nearer, and walking up the Avenue within five Paces of the Court-Yard, he was taken ill of a sudden with a sort of I know not what, but down he fell, and there he lies.

LADY BOUNTIFUL: Here, *Scrub*, *Gipsey*, all run, get my easie Chair down Stairs, put the Gentleman in it, and bring him in quickly, quickly.

ARCHER: Heaven will reward your Ladyship for this charitable Act.

LADY BOUNTIFUL: Is your Master us'd to these Fits?

4. Mrs Sullen is so disenchanted with her own marriage that she cannot envisage any woman's wanting to preserve the health of her husband.
5. gripe.
6. (colloquial) good wife.
7. recipe, prescription.

ARCHER: O yes, Madam, frequently —— I have known him have five or six of a Night.

LADY BOUNTIFUL: What's his Name?

ARCHER: Lord, Madam, he's a dying; a Minute's Care or Neglect may save or destroy his Life.

LADY BOUNTIFUL: Ah, poor Gentleman; come, Friend shew me the way; I'll see him brought in myself.

Exit with ARCHER

DORINDA: O, Sister, my Heart flutters about strangely, I can hardly forbear running to his Assistance.

MRS. SULLEN: And I'll lay my Life, he deserves your Assistance more than he wants it: Did not I tell you that my Lord wou'd find a way to come at you? Love's his Distemper, and you must be the Physician; put on all your Charms, summon all your Fire into your Eyes, plant the whole Artillery of your Looks against his Breast, and down with him.

DORINDA: O, Sister, I'm but a young Gunner, I shall be afraid to shoot, for fear the Piece shou'd recoil, and hurt myself.

MRS. SULLEN: Never fear, you shall see me shoot before you, if you will.

DORINDA: No, no, dear Sister, you have miss'd your Mark so unfortunately, that I sha'n't care for being instructed by you.

Enter AIMWELL *in a Chair, carry'd by* ARCHER *and* SCRUB, LADY BOUNTIFUL, GIPSEY. AIMWELL *counterfeiting a Swoon*

LADY BOUNTIFUL: Here, here, let's see the Hartshorn Drops[8] —— *Gipsey*, a Glass of fair Water,[9] his Fit's very strong. —— Bless me, how his Hands are clinch'd.

ARCHER: For shame, Ladies, what d'ye do? why don't you help us? —— Pray, Madam (*To* DORINDA) take his Hand, and open it, if you can, whilst I hold his Head.

(DORINDA *takes his Hand*)

DORINDA: Poor Gentleman —— Oh —— he has got my Hand within his, and squeezes it unmercifully ——

LADY BOUNTIFUL: 'Tis the Violence of his Convulsion, Child.

ARCHER: O, Madam, he's perfectly possess'd in these Cases —— he'll bite you if you don't have a care.

DORINDA: Oh, my Hand, my Hand.

LADY BOUNTIFUL: What's the matter with the foolish Girl? I have got this Hand open, you see, with a great deal of Ease.

ARCHER: Ay, but Madam, your Daughter's Hand is somewhat warmer than your Ladyship's, and the Heat of it draws the Force of the Spirits that way.

MRS. SULLEN: I find, Friend, you're very learned in these Sorts of Fits.

ARCHER: 'Tis no wonder, Madam, for I'm often troubled with them myself; I find myself extremely ill at this Minute. (*Looking hard at* MRS. SULLEN)

MRS. SULLEN: (*Aside*) I fancy I cou'd find a way to cure you.

LADY BOUNTIFUL: His Fit holds him very long.

ARCHER: Longer than usual, Madam, —— Pray, young Lady, open his Breast, and give him Air.

LADY BOUNTIFUL: Where did his Illness take him first, pray?

ARCHER: To Day at Church, Madam.

LADY BOUNTIFUL: In what manner was he taken?

ARCHER: Very strangely, my Lady. He was of a sudden touch'd with something in his Eyes, which at the first he only felt, but could not tell whether 'twas Pain or Pleasure.

LADY BOUNTIFUL: Wind, nothing but Wind.

ARCHER: By soft Degrees it grew and mounted to his Brain, there his Fancy caught it; there form'd it so beautiful, and dress'd it up in such gay, pleasing Colours, that his transported Appetite seiz'd the fair Idea, and straight convey'd it to his Heart. That hospitable Seat of Life sent all its sanguine Spirits forth to meet, and open'd all its sluicy Gates to take the Stranger in.

LADY BOUNTIFUL: Your Master shou'd never go without a Bottle to smell to —— Oh! —— he recovers —— the Lavender-Water —— some Feathers to burn under his Nose —— *Hungary* Water[10] to rub his Temples —— O, he comes to himself. Hem a little, Sir, hem —— *Gipsey*, bring the Cordial-Water.

(AIMWELL *seems to awake in amaze*)

DORINDA: How d'ye, Sir?

AIMWELL: (*Rising*) Where am I?

Sure I have pass'd the Gulph of silent
Death,

8. smelling salts.
9. pure water.
10. A distilled water, made of rosemary flowers infused in rectified spirit of wine.

And now I land on the *Elisian*[11] Shore ——
Behold the Goddess of those happy Plains,
Fair *Proserpine*[12] —— let me adore thy
bright Divinity.

(*Kneels to* DORINDA, *and kisses her Hand*)

MRS. SULLEN: So, so, so, I knew where the Fit wou'd end.

AIMWELL: *Euridice*[13] perhaps ——
How cou'd thy *Orpheus* keep his Word,
And not look back upon thee;
No Treasure but thyself cou'd sure have
brib'd him
To look one Minute off thee.

LADY BOUNTIFUL: Delirious, poor Gentleman.

ARCHER: Very delirious, Madam, very delirious.

AIMWELL: *Martin*'s Voice, I think.

ARCHER: Yes, my Lord —— How do's your Lordship?

LADY BOUNTIFUL: Lord! did you mind[14] that Girls?

AIMWELL: Where am I?

ARCHER: In very good Hands, Sir, —— You were taken just now with one of your old Fits, under the Trees, just by this good Lady's House, her Ladyship had you taken in, and has miraculously brought you to yourself, as you see ——

AIMWELL: I am so confounded with Shame, Madam, that I can now only beg Pardon — And refer my Acknowledgments for your Ladyship's Care, till an Opportunity offers of making some Amends —— I dare be no longer troublesome —— *Martin*, give two Guineas to the Servants.

(*Going*)

DORINDA: Sir, you may catch cold by going so soon into the Air; you don't look, Sir, as if you were perfectly recovered. (*Here* ARCHER *talks to* LADY BOUNTIFUL *in dumb shew*)[15]

AIMWELL: That I shall never be, Madam; my present Illness is so rooted, that I must expect to carry it to my Grave.

MRS. SULLEN: Don't despair, Sir, I have known several in your Distemper shake it off, with a Fortnight's Physick.

LADY BOUNTIFUL: Come, Sir, your Servant has been telling me that you're apt to relapse if you go into the Air —— Your good Manners shan't get the better of ours —— You shall sit down again, Sir: —— Come, Sir, we don't mind Ceremonies[16] in the Country: —— Here, Sir, my Service t'ye —— You shall taste my Water; 'tis a Cordial I can assure you, and of my own making —— Drink it off, Sir. (AIMWELL *drinks*) And how d'ye find yourself, now, Sir?

AIMWELL: Somewhat better — tho' very faint still.

LADY BOUNTIFUL: Ay, ay, People are always faint after these Fits. —— Come, Girls, you shall shew the Gentleman the House; 'tis but an old Family Building, Sir, but you had better walk about, and cool by degrees, than venture immediately into the Air —— You'll find some tolerable Pictures. —— *Dorinda*, shew the Gentleman the way; I must go to the poor Woman below.

Exit

DORINDA: This way Sir.

AIMWELL: Ladies, shall I beg leave for my Servant to wait on you, for he understands Pictures very well.

MRS. SULLEN: Sir, we understand Originals, as well as he do's Pictures, so he may come along.

Exeunt DORINDA, MRS. SULLEN, AIMWELL, ARCHER, [GIPSEY]; AIMWELL *leads* DORINDA.

Enter FOIGARD *and* SCRUB, *meeting*

FOIGARD: Save you,[17] Master *Scrub*.

SCRUB: Sir, I won't be sav'd your way —— I hate a Priest,[18] I abhor the *French* and I defie the Devil —— Sir, I'm a bold *Briton*, and will spill the last Drop of my Blood to keep out Popery and Slavery.

FOIGARD: Master *Scrub*, you wou'd put me down in Politicks, and so I wou'd be speaking with Mrs. *Shipsey*.[19]

SCRUB: Good Mr. Priest, you can't speak with her; she's sick, Sir, she's gone abroad, Sir; she's —— dead two Months ago, Sir.

Enter GIPSEY

GIPSEY: How, now Impudence! How dare you

11. Of Elysium, the happy fields of the underworld in classical mythology. Aimwell launches into blank verse and a high style.
12. Beautiful daughter of Jupiter and Ceres, captured by Pluto, god of the underworld.
13. Wife of the musician Orpheus, who failed to bring her back from the underworld when he looked behind him as he was forbidden to do.
14. notice.
15. making significant gestures, but silently.
16. formalities. Aimwell's 'stratagem' exploits this rural informality, which lies at the heart of Farquhar's comic style.
17. God save you!
18. Foigard, the Irish spy, is disguised as a French priest.
19. Gipsey, thus (suddenly and with effect) revealed as one of his 'contacts'. Foigard's accent is suggested in the spelling; later editions have *'Gipsey'*.

talk so saucily to the Doctor? Pray, Sir, don't take it ill; for the Common People of *England* are not so civil to Strangers, as ——

SCRUB: You lie, you lie; —— 'tis the Common People that are civilest to Strangers.

GIPSEY: Sirrah, I have a good mind to —— Get you out, I say.

SCRUB: I won't.

GIPSEY: You won't, Sauce-box —— Pray, Doctor, what is the Captain's Name that came to your Inn last Night?

SCRUB: The Captain![20] ah, the Devil, there she hampers me again; —— The Captain has me on one side, and the Priest on t'other: —— So between the Gown and the Sword, I have a fine time on't —— But, *Cedunt Arma togae*[21] (*Going*).

GIPSEY: What, Sirrah, won't you march?

SCRUB: No, my Dear, I won't march —— but I'll walk —— And I'll make bold to listen a little too.

(*Goes behind the Side-scene and listens*)

GIPSEY: Indeed, Doctor, the Count[22] has been barbarously treated, that's the Truth on't.

FOIGARD: Ah, Mrs. *Gipsey*, upon my Shoul, now, *Gra*,[23] his Complainings would mollifie the Marrow[24] in your Bones, and move the Bowels of your Commiseration; he veeps, and he dances, and he fistles, and he swears, and he laughs, and he stamps, and he sings: In conclusion, Joy, he's afflicted, *à la François*,[25] and a Stranger wou'd not know whider to cry, or to laugh with him.

GIPSEY: What wou'd you have me do, Doctor?

FOIGARD: Nothing, Joy, but only hide the Count in Mrs. *Sullen*'s Closet, when it is dark.

GIPSEY: Nothing! Is that nothing? It wou'd be both a Sin, and a Shame, Doctor.

FOIGARD: Here is twenty *Lewidores*,[26] Joy, for your Shame; and I will give you an Absolution for the Shin.

GIPSEY: But won't that Money look like a Bribe?

FOIGARD: Dat is according as you shall tauk it. —— If you receive the Money before-hand, 'twill be *Logicè*[27] a Bribe; but if you stay till afterwards, 'twill be only a Gratification.

GIPSEY: Well, Doctor, I'll take it *Logicè* —— But what must I do with my Conscience, Sir?

FOIGARD: Leave dat vid me, Joy; I am your Priest, *Gra*; and your Conscience is under my Hands.

GIPSEY: But shou'd I put the Count into the Closet ——

FOIGARD: Vell, is there any Shin for a Man's being in a Closhet? one may go to Prayers in a Closet.

GIPSEY: But if the Lady shou'd come into her Chamber, and go to Bed?

FOIGARD: Vel, and is dere any Shin in going to Bed Joy?

GIPSEY: Ay, but if the Parties shou'd meet, Doctor?

FOIGARD: Vel den —— the Parties must be responsable. —— Do you be after putting[28] the Count in the Closhet; and leave the Shins wid themselves —— I will come with the Count to instruct you[29] in your Chamber.

GIPSEY: Well, Doctor, your Religion is so pure —— Methinks I'm so easie after an Absolution, and can sin afresh with so much Security, that I'm resolv'd to die a Martyr to't — Here's the Key of the Garden-door; come in the Back-way, when 'tis late —— I'll be ready to receive you; but don't so much as whisper, only take hold of my Hand; I'll lead you, and do you lead the Count, and follow me.

Exeunt

Enter SCRUB

SCRUB: What Witchcraft now have these two Imps of the Devil been a hatching here? —— There's twenty *Lewidores*, I heard that, and saw the Purse: But I must give room to my Betters.

Exit

Enter AIMWELL *leading* DORINDA, *and making Love in dumb Shew* —— MRS. SULLEN *and* ARCHER

MRS. SULLEN: (*to* ARCHER) Pray, Sir, how d'ye like that Piece?[30]

ARCHER: O, 'tis *Leda* —— You find, Madam, how *Jupiter* comes disguis'd to make Love ——

MRS. SULLEN: But what think you there of *Alexander*'s Battles?

20. Actually Gibbet, a highwayman.
21. i.e. the military yields to the civic power (Cicero, *Officia*).
22. The Frenchman, Count Bellair, who is in love with Mrs Sullen.
23. (Irish) my love. Foigard speaks a stage-Irish dialect here, with accompanying pronunciation (e.g. 'shoul' for soul).
24. Proof that alliterative phrasing of rhythmic Anglo-Irish prose did not begin with Sean O'Casey. 'veeps' = weeps; 'fistles' = whistles.
25. in the French style (of love).
26. French gold coins.
27. by logic. Farquhar satirizes the casuistry of catholic morality.
28. A version of Gaelic syntax. Puzzled English printers subsequently inserted 'gone' between 'be' and 'after'.
29. It is implied, to make love.
30. painting. In this scene Mrs Sullen is showing Archer around the gallery, well decked with amorous paintings, which give him his cue.

ARCHER: We want only a *Le Brun*,[31] Madam, to draw greater Battles, and a greater General of our own. —— The *Danube*, Madam, wou'd make a greater Figure in a Picture than the *Granicus*; and we have our *Ramelies* to match their *Arbela*.[32]

MRS. SULLEN: Pray, Sir, what Head is that in the Corner there?

ARCHER: O, Madam, 'tis poor *Ovid*[33] in his Exile.

MRS. SULLEN: What was he banish'd for?

ARCHER: His ambitious Love, Madam. (*Bowing*) His Misfortune touches me.

MRS. SULLEN: Was he successful in his Amours?

ARCHER: There he has left us in the dark. —— He was too much a Gentleman to tell.

MRS. SULLEN: If he were secret, I pity him.

ARCHER: And if he were successful, I envy him.

MRS. SULLEN: How d'ye like that *Venus* over the Chimney?

ARCHER: *Venus*![34] I protest, Madam, I took it for your Picture; but now I look again, 'tis not handsome enough.

MRS. SULLEN: Oh, what a Charm is Flattery! if you wou'd see my Picture, there it is, over that Cabinet —— How d'ye like it?

ARCHER: I must admire any thing, Madam, that has the least Resemblance of you —— But, methinks, Madam —— (*He looks at the Picture and* MRS. SULLEN *three or four times, by turns*) Pray, Madam, who drew it?

MRS. SULLEN: A famous Hand, Sir.

(*Here* AIMWELL *and* DORINDA *go off*)

ARCHER: A famous Hand, Madam —— Your Eyes, indeed, are featur'd there; but where's the sparkling Moisture, shining Fluid, in which they swim? The Picture, indeed, has your Dimples; but where's the Swarm of killing *Cupids* that shou'd ambush there? The Lips too are figur'd out; but where's the Carnation-Dew, the pouting Ripeness that tempts the Taste in the Original?

MRS. SULLEN: (*Aside*) Had it been my Lot to have match'd with such a Man!

ARCHER: Your Breasts too, presumptuous Man! what! paint Heaven! *Apropa*, Madam, in the very next Picture is *Salmoneus*,[35] that was struck dead with Lightning, for offering to imitate *Jove*'s Thunder; I hope you serv'd the painter so, Madam?

MRS. SULLEN: Had my Eyes the Power of Thunder, they shou'd employ their Lightning better.

ARCHER: There's the finest Bed in that Room, Madam, I suppose 'tis your Ladyship's Bed-Chamber?

MRS. SULLEN: And what then, Sir?

ARCHER: I think the Quilt is the richest that ever I saw —— I can't, at this distance, Madam, distinguish the Figures of the Embroidery: Will you give me leave, Madam?

MRS. SULLEN: [*Aside*] The Devil take his Impudence —— Sure, if I gave him an Opportunity, he durst not offer it —— (*Going*) I have a great mind to try —— (*Returns*) 'Sdeath, what am I doing? —— And alone too! —— Sister, Sister. (*Runs out*)

ARCHER: I'll follow her close ——
For where a Frenchman[36] *durst attempt to storm,*
A Briton, *sure, may well the Work perform.*

(*Going*)

Enter SCRUB

SCRUB: *Martin*, Brother[37] *Martin*.

ARCHER: O Brother *Scrub*, I beg your Pardon, I was not a going. Here's a Guinea my Master order'd you.

SCRUB: A Guinea; hi, hi, hi, a Guinea! eh —— by this Light it is a Guinea; but I suppose you expect one and twenty Shillings in change.[38]

ARCHER: Not at all, I have another for *Gipsey*.

SCRUB: A Guinea for her! Faggot and Fire for the Witch! —— Sir, give me that Guinea, and I'll discover a Plot.

ARCHER: A Plot!

SCRUB: Ay, Sir, a Plot, a horrid Plot —— First, it must be a Plot, because there's a Woman in't: Secondly, it must be a Plot, because there's a Priest

31. Charles Le Brun (1619-90), French court painter.
32. Archer sets up a comparison between Alexander the Great's military victories over the Persians and those of the Duke of Marlborough, who defeated the French in the Danube valley in 1704 and again at Ramillies in 1706.
33. The Latin love poet, banished from Rome to the Black Sea by the Emperor Augustus in A.D. 1.
34. Compare Fluther Good's reaction to *The Sleeping Venus*: 'Oh, that's a terrible picture; oh, that's a shockin' picture! Oh, th' one that got that taken, she must have been a prime lassie!' Sean O'Casey, *The Plough and the Stars* (1926), Act 1.
35. A son of Aeolus and brother of Sisyphus, who built the town of Salmone in Elis. His arrogance was so great that he ordered sacrifices to be offered to himself and imitated the thunder of Zeus, who killed him with a thunderbolt and destroyed his town.
36. A reference to Count Bellair, who has already (in III.iii) made an attempt to seduce Mrs Sullen. Farquhar plays a lot, in this scene, on the contemporary dislike of everything French, because of the war still going on (until the Treaty of Utrecht in 1713).
37. Because Archer is, he thinks, a fellow-servant.
38. Exactly the value of a guinea.

in't: Thirdly, it must be a Plot, because there's *French* Gold in't: And fourthly, it must be a Plot, because I don't know what to make on't.

ARCHER: Nor any Body else, I'm afraid, Brother *Scrub*.

SCRUB: Truly, I'm afraid so too; for where there's a Priest and a Woman, there's always a Mystery and a Riddle. —— This I know, that here has been the Doctor with a Temptation in one Hand, and an Absolution in the other, and *Gipsey* has sold herself to the Devil; I saw the Price paid down, my Eyes shall take their Oath on't.

ARCHER: And is all this Bustle about *Gipsey*?

SCRUB: That's not all; I cou'd hear but a Word here and there; but I remember they mention'd a Count, a Closet, a Back-door, and a Key.

ARCHER: The Count! Did you hear nothing of Mrs. *Sullen*?

SCRUB: I did hear some Word that sounded that way: But whether it was *Sullen* or *Dorinda*, I cou'd not distinguish.

ARCHER: You have told this Matter to no Body, Brother?

SCRUB: Told! No, Sir, I thank you for that; I'm resolv'd never to speak one Word *pro* nor *con*, till we have a Peace.

ARCHER: You're i' th' right, Brother *Scrub*; here's a Treaty afoot between the Count and the Lady —— The Priest and the Chamber-maid are the Plenipotentiaries —— It shall go hard, but I find a way to be included in the Treaty. —— Where's the Doctor now?

SCRUB: He and *Gipsey* are this Moment devouring my Lady's Marmalade in the Closet.

AIMWELL: (*From without*) *Martin! Martin!*

ARCHER: I come, Sir, I come.

SCRUB: But you forget the other Guinea, Brother *Martin*.

ARCHER: Here I give it with all my Heart.

Exit

SCRUB: And I take it with all my Soul —— I'cod I'll spoil your Plotting, Mrs. *Gipsey*; and if you shou'd set the Captain upon me, these two Guineas will buy me off.

Exit

Enter MRS. SULLEN *and* DORINDA, *meeting*

MRS. SULLEN: Well, Sister.[39]

DORINDA: And well, Sister.

MRS. SULLEN: What's become of my Lord?

DORINDA: What's become of his Servant?

MRS. SULLEN: Servant! He's a prettier Fellow, and a finer Gentleman by fifty Degrees than his Master.

DORINDA: O' my Conscience, I fancy you cou'd beg that Fellow at the Gallows-foot.[40]

MRS. SULLEN: O' my Conscience I cou'd, provided I cou'd put a Friend of yours in his room.[41]

DORINDA: You desir'd me, Sister, to leave you, when you trangress'd the Bounds of Honour.

MRS. SULLEN: Thou dear censorious Country Girl —— What dost mean? You can't think of the Man without the Bedfellow, I find.

DORINDA: I don't find any thing unnatural in that Thought; while the Mind is conversant with Flesh and Blood, it must conform to the Humours of the Company.

MRS. SULLEN: How a little Love and good Company improves a Woman! Why Child, you begin to live —— you never spoke before.

DORINDA: Because I was never spoke to —— My Lord[42] has told me, that I have more Wit and Beauty than any of my Sex; and truly I begin to think the Man is sincere.

MRS. SULLEN: You're in the right, *Dorinda*; Pride is the Life of a Woman, and Flattery is our daily Bread; and she's a Fool that won't believe a Man there, as much as she that believes him in any thing else —— But I'll lay you a Guinea, that I had finer things said to me than you had.

DORINDA: Done —— What did your Fellow say to ye?

MRS. SULLEN: My Fellow took the Picture of *Venus* for mine.

DORINDA: But my Lover took me for *Venus* herself.

MRS. SULLEN: Common Cant! Had my Spark call'd me a *Venus* directly, I should have believed him a Footman in good earnest.

DORINDA: But my Lover was upon his Knees to me.

MRS. SULLEN: And mine was upon his Tiptoes to me.

DORINDA: Mine vow'd to die for me.

MRS. SULLEN: Mine swore to die with me.

DORINDA: Mine spoke the softest moving things.

39. Dorinda is half-sister to Sullen (Lady Bountiful is their mother).

40. save a condemned man by an offer of marriage.

41. place. Presumably she means her (detested) husband.

42. Aimwell.

MRS. SULLEN: Mine had his moving things too.

DORINDA: Mine kiss'd my Hand ten thousand times.

MRS. SULLEN: Mine has all that Pleasure to come.

DORINDA: Mine offer'd Marriage.

MRS. SULLEN: O Laird! D'ye call that a moving thing?

DORINDA: The sharpest Arrow in his Quiver, my dear Sister: —— Why, my ten thousand Pounds may lie brooding here this seven Years, and hatch nothing at last but some ill-natur'd Clown like yours: —— Whereas, if I marry my Lord *Aimwell*, there will be a Title, Place, and Precedence, the Park, the Play, and the Drawing-Room, Splendor, Equipage, Noise, and Flambeaux. —— Hey, my lady *Aimwell*'s Servants there —— Lights, Lights to the Stairs —— My Lady *Aimwell*'s Coach, put forward —— Stand by; make room for her Ladyship —— Are not these things moving? What! Melancholy of a sudden?

MRS. SULLEN: Happy, happy Sister! Your Angel has been watchful for your Happiness, whilst mine has slept regardless of his Charge —— Long smiling Years of circling Joys for you, but not one Hour for me! *(Weeps)*[43]

DORINDA: Come, my Dear, we'll talk of something else.

MRS. SULLEN: O *Dorinda*, I own myself a Woman, full of my Sex, a gentle, generous Soul, —— easy and yielding to soft Desires; a spacious Heart, where Love and all his Train might lodge. And must the fair Apartment of my Breast be made a Stable for a Brute[44] to lie in?

DORINDA: Meaning your Husband, I suppose.

MRS. SULLEN: Husband! No, —— Even Husband is too soft a Name for him —— But come, I expect my Brother here to Night or to Morrow; he was abroad when my Father marry'd me, perhaps he'll find a way to make me easy.[45]

DORINDA: Will you promise not to make yourself easy in the mean time with my Lord's Friend?

MRS. SULLEN: You mistake me, Sister —— It happens with us, as among the Men, the greatest Talkers are the greatest Cowards, and there's a Reason for it; those Spirits evaporate in Prattle, which might do more Mischief if they took another Course —— Tho', to confess the Truth, I do love that Fellow; —— And if I met him drest as he shou'd be, and I undrest as I should be —— Look'ye, Sister, I have no supernatural Gifts; —— I can't swear I cou'd resist the Temptation, —— tho' I can safely promise to avoid it; and that's as much as the best of us can do.

Exit MRS. SULLEN *and* DORINDA

Enter AIMWELL *and* ARCHER *laughing*

ARCHER: And the awkward Kindness of the good motherly old Gentlewoman[46] ——

AIMWELL: And the coming Easiness of the young one —— 'Sdeath, 'tis pity to deceive her.

ARCHER: Nay, if you adhere to those Principles, stop where you are.

AIMWELL: I can't stop; for I love her to Distraction.

ARCHER: 'Sdeath, if you love her a Hair's breadth beyond Discretion, you must go no farther.

AIMWELL: Well, well, anything to deliver us from sauntering away our idle Evenings at *White*'s, *Tom*'s, or *Will*'s,[47] and be stinted to bear looking at our old Acquaintance, the Cards; because our impotent Pockets can't afford us a Guinea for the mercenary Drabs.[48]

ARCHER: Or be obliged to some Purse-proud Coxcomb for a scandalous Bottle,[49] where we must not pretend to our Share of the Discourse, because we can't pay our Club o' th' Reckoning:[50] —— Damn it, I had rather spunge upon *Morris*,[51] and sup upon a Dish of Bohea[52] scor'd behind the Door.[53]

AIMWELL: And there expose our want of Sense by talking Criticisms, as we should our Want of Money by railing at the Government.

ARCHER: Or be oblig'd to sneak into the Side-box, and between both Houses, steal two Acts of a Play;[54] and because we ha'n't Money to see the other three, we come away discontented, and damn the whole five.

43. An indication that Farquhar wanted a deeper-sounding kind of comedy than the conventional Restoration romp.
44. Her husband. His 'brutishness' has already been shown in II.i and III.iii.
45. Sir Charles Freeman does, in fact, arrange for her divorce in V.iv.
46. Lady Bountiful.
47. London coffee-houses.
48. whores.
49. This passage bears the ring of Farquhar's personal experience: the humiliation of being under a compliment to a foul-mouthed coxcomb or conceited fool in a tavern.
50. share of the bill.
51. The keeper of a coffee-house.
52. China tea.
53. on credit.
54. At this time one could gain admission to a side-box free, up to the second act of a play.

AIMWELL: And ten thousand such rascally Tricks —— had we out-liv'd our Fortunes among our Acquaintance —— But now —

ARCHER: Ay, now, is the Time to prevent all this —— Strike while the Iron is hot —— This Priest is the luckiest part of our Adventure —— He shall marry you, and pimp for me.

AIMWELL: But I shou'd not like a Woman that can be so fond of a *Frenchman*.[55]

ARCHER: Alas, Sir, Necessity has no Law; the Lady may be in Distress; perhaps she has a confounded Husband, and her Revenge may carry her farther than her Love. —— I gad, I have so good an Opinion of her, and of myself, that I begin to fancy strange things; and we must say this for the Honour of our Women, and indeed of ourselves, that they do stick to their Men, as they do to their *Magna Charta*. —— If the Plot lies as I suspect, —— I must put on the Gentleman. —— But here comes the Doctor:[56] —— I shall be ready.

Exit . . . .

55. Aimwell thinks Mrs Sullen is suspect because of her apparent regard for Count Bellair.

56. Foigard, the 'priest'.

SIR RICHARD STEELE

(1672-1729)

from: THE CONSCIOUS LOVERS (1722)

[If George Farquhar was innovative for returning comedy to a rural setting in place of urban sophistication, and in replacing the cynicism of much Restoration comedy with the humanity of his rake-heroes, Steele went much farther in promoting a new, romantic comedy in reaction to the harsh realism of the Restoration comedy of manners. It is common to credit Steele with the initiation of sentimental comedy in eighteenth-century England, but this is actually a mistake. The trend towards a 'drama of sensibility' was there since Cibber's *Love's Last Shift* (1696) and merely accelerated following the timely attack on Restoration comedy launched by Jeremy Collier in his book, *A Short View of the Immorality and Profaneness of the English Stage* (1698). Steele, the 'maker and reflector of his era's taste' (Shirley Kenny) found the ground well prepared for him when he gave the world the improving comedy of *The Conscious Lovers*. Otherwise, the popularity of its stiff-necked moralizing would be incredible. It paved the way for the predominance in the English theatre of morality over wit in eighteenth-century comedy. Steele wanted comedy to move audiences to virtue by providing them with examples of sober-minded, though young, characters who survive various trials and temptations. His high-minded hero and heroine may seem less off-putting today if we see them as attempting to define anew the role of 'the gentleman' and 'the lady' in society: even though he idealized his creations, Steele wanted to bring literature close to life, and above all to the questions of choice and value raised by romantic situations in which the pressures (economic as well as ethical) were very much those which faced young men and women in real life at this time. It is no accident that Sealand, the father of Lucinda and Indiana, is a rich merchant: as a model member of the new middle class he is the key figure in the whole action. Through him, as much as through his serious lovers, Steele was making a new bridge between drama and life.

In the first extract below, Bevil Junior, the hero, convinces the heroine, Indiana, of the nobility of his intentions. She, an orphan cared for by her aunt Isabella, who takes the worldly and suspicious view of Bevil's generosity towards Indiana, is much indebted to Bevil and feels strongly that he is sincere. Bevil, for his part, wishes to keep his feelings detached, so as to keep faith with his father, who wants him to marry Lucinda. If the heart is sincere, Steele seems to be saying, intuitions may be trusted as a sound guide to good behaviour.]

ACT II, SCENE 3

[*A Room in* INDIANA'*s Lodgings*]

Re-enter INDIANA *speaking to a* SERVANT

INDIANA: Desire Mr. *Bevil* to walk in ——

Exit SERVANT

Design! impossible![1] A base designing Mind cou'd never think of what he hourly puts in practice ——

1. Indiana is reflecting on her aunt Isabella's warning that Bevil's generosity is all geared towards seduction.

And yet, since the late Rumour of his Marriage, he seems more reserved than formerly — he sends in too, before he sees me, to know if I am at leisure —— such new Respect may cover Coldness in the Heart —— it certainly makes me thoughtful —— I'll know the worst, at once; I'll lay such fair Occasions in his way, that it shall be impossible to avoid an Explanation —— for these Doubts are insupportable! —— But see! he comes, and clears them all.

Enter BEVIL

BEVIL: Madam, your most Obedient —— I am afraid I broke in upon your Rest last Night —— 'twas very late before we parted; but 'twas your own Fault: I never saw you in such agreeable Humour.

INDIANA: I am extremely glad we were both pleas'd; for I thought I never saw you better Company.

BEVIL: Me, Madam! you rally;[2] I said very little.

INDIANA: But I am afraid you heard me say a great deal; and when a Woman is in the talking Vein, the most agreeable thing a Man can do, you know, is to have Patience to hear her.

BEVIL: Then 'tis pity, Madam, you should ever be silent, that we might be always agreeable to one another.

INDIANA: If I had your Talent, or Power, to make my Actions speak for me, I might indeed be silent, and yet pretend to something more than the Agreeable.

BEVIL: If I might be vain of any thing, in my Power, Madam, 'tis that my Understanding, from all your Sex, has mark'd you out, as the most deserving Object of my Esteem.

INDIANA: Should I think I deserve this, 'twere enough to make my Vanity forfeit the very Esteem you offer me.

BEVIL: How so, Madam?

INDIANA: Because Esteem is the Result of Reason, and to deserve it from good Sense, the Height of Human Glory: Nay, I had rather a Man of Honour should pay me that, than all the Homage of a sincere and humble Love.

BEVIL: You certainly distinguish right, Madam; Love often kindles from external Merit only ——

INDIANA: But Esteem arises from a higher Source, the Merit of the Soul ——

BEVIL: True —— And great Souls only can deserve it. (*Bowing respectfully*)

2. tease.

INDIANA: Now, I think, they are greater still, that can so charitably part with it.

BEVIL: Now, Madam, you make me vain, since the utmost Pride, and Pleasure of my Life is, that I esteem you —— as I ought.

INDIANA: (*Aside*) As he ought! still more perplexing! he neither saves, nor kills my Hope.

BEVIL: But Madam, we grow grave methinks —— Let's find some other Subject —— Pray how did you like the Opera last Night?

INDIANA: First give me leave to thank you, for my Tickets.

BEVIL: O! your Servant, Madam —— But pray tell me, you now, who are never partial to the Fashion, I fancy, must be the properest Judge of a mighty Dispute among the Ladies, that is, whether *Crispo* or *Griselda*[3] is the more agreeable Entertainment.

INDIANA: With submission now, I cannot be a proper Judge of this Question.

BEVIL: How so, Madam?

INDIANA: Because I find I have a Partiality for one of them.

BEVIL: Pray which is that?

INDIANA: I do not know —— there's something in that Rural Cottage of *Griselda*, her forlorn Condition, her Poverty, her Solitude, her Resignation, her innocent Slumbers, and that lulling *Dolce Sogno*[4] that's sung over her; it had an Effect upon me, that —— in short I never was so well deceiv'd, at any of them.

BEVIL: Oh! Now then, I can account for the Dispute: *Griselda*, it seems, is the Distress of an injur'd innocent Woman: *Crispo*, that only of a Man in the same Condition; therefore the Men are mostly concern'd for *Crispo*, and by a Natural Indulgence, both Sexes for *Griselda*.

INDIANA: So that Judgment, you think, ought to be for one, tho' Fancy and Complaisance have got ground for the other. Well! I believe you will never give me leave to dispute with you on any Subject; for I own *Crispo* has its Charms for me too: Though in the main, all the Pleasure the best Opera gives us, is but meer Sensation.[5] —— Methinks it's Pity the Mind can't have a little more Share in the Entertainment. —— The Musick's certainly fine;

3. Two operas by Bononcini, which were sung in London in 1722.

4. sweet dream.

5. A common view, since Italian opera was new to England and had enemies among intellectuals, e.g. Joseph Addison in *The Spectator*, No. 18, 21 March 1711.

but in my Thoughts, there's none of your Composers come up to Old *Shakespear* and *Otway*.[6]

BEVIL: How, Madam! why if a Woman of your Sense were to say this in the Drawing-room. ——

Enter a SERVANT

SERVANT: Sir, here's Signior *Carbonelli*[7] says he waits your Commands, in the next Room.

BEVIL: A propos! You were saying Yesterday, Madam, you had a mind to hear him —— will you give him leave to entertain you now?

INDIANA: By all means: desire the Gentleman to walk in.

Exit SERVANT

BEVIL: I fancy you will find something in this Hand, that is uncommon.

INDIANA: You are always finding ways, Mr. *Bevil*, to make Life seem less tedious to me. ——

Enter MUSICK MASTER

When the Gentleman pleases.

(*After a Sonata*[8] *is play'd,* BEVIL *waits on the* MASTER *to the Door, &c.*)

BEVIL: You smile, Madam, to see me so Complaisant[9] to one, whom I pay for his Visit: Now, I own, I think it is not enough barely to pay those, whose Talents are superior to our own (I mean such Talents, as would become our Condition, if we had them). Methinks we ought to do something more, than barely gratify them, for what they do at our Command, only because their Fortune is below us.

INDIANA: You say I smile: I assure you it was a Smile of Approbation; for indeed I cannot but think it the distinguishing part of a Gentleman, to make his Superiority of Fortune as easy to his Inferiors, as he can —— (*Aside*) Now once more to try him. —— I was saying just now, I believed you would never let me dispute with you, and I dare say, it will always be so: However, I must have your Opinion upon a Subject, which created a Debate between my Aunt and me, just before you came hither; she would needs have it, that no Man ever does any extraordinary Kindness or Service for a Woman, but for his own sake.

BEVIL: Well, Madam! Indeed I can't but be of her Mind.

INDIANA: What, tho' he should maintain, and support her, without demanding any thing of her, on her part?

BEVIL: Why Madam, is making an Expence, in the Service of a Valuable Woman (for such I must suppose her) though she should never do him any Favour, nay, though she should never know who did her such Service, such a mighty Heroick Business?

INDIANA: Certainly! I should think he must be a Man of an uncommon Mold.

BEVIL: Dear Madam, why so? 'tis but, at best, a better Taste in Expence: To bestow upon one, whom he may think one of the Ornaments of the whole Creation, to be Conscious, that from his Superfluity, an Innocent, a Virtuous Spirit is supported above the Temptations and Sorrows of Life! That he sees Satisfaction, Health and Gladness in her Countenance, while he enjoys the Happiness of seeing her (as that I will suppose too, or he must be too abstracted, too insensible) I say, if he is allowed to delight in that Prospect; alas! what mighty matter is there, in all this?

INDIANA: No mighty matter, in so disinterested a Friendship!

BEVIL: Disinterested! I can't think him so; your Hero, Madam, is no more, than what every Gentleman ought to be, and I believe very many are —— He is only one, who takes more delight in Reflections, than in Sensations: He is more pleased with Thinking than Eating; that's the utmost you can say of him —— Why, Madam, a greater Expence, than all this, Men lay out upon an unnecessary Stable of Horses.

INDIANA: Can you be sincere, in what you say?

BEVIL: You may depend upon it, if you know any such Man, he does not love Dogs inordinately.

INDIANA: No, that he does not.

BEVIL: Nor Cards, nor Dice.

INDIANA: No.

BEVIL: Nor Bottle Companions.

INDIANA: No.

BEVIL: Nor loose Women.

INDIANA: No, I'm sure he does not.

BEVIL: Take my Word then, if your admired Hero is not liable to any of these kind of Demands, there's no such Preheminence in this, as you imagine: Nay, this way of Expence you speak of, is

6. Thomas Otway (1652-85), author of *Venice Preserved* (1682), a popular tragedy.
7. A violinist then popular on the London stage. In the Preface to *The Conscious Lovers*, Steele says that in performance a song he had written was omitted here. As a result, the musical interlude was criticized, since it left Bevil and Indiana simply exchanging glances.
8. At this time, 'a Sonata' meant any musical composition for instruments.
9. polite.

what exalts and raises him, that has a Taste for it; And, at the same time, his Delight is incapable of Satiety, Disgust, or Penitence.

INDIANA: But still I insist his having no private Interest in the Action, makes it Prodigious, almost Incredible.

BEVIL: Dear Madam, I never knew you more mistaken: Why, who can be more an Usurer, than he, who lays out his Money in such Valuable Purchases? If Pleasure be worth purchasing, how great a Pleasure is it to him, who has a true Taste of Life, to ease an Aking Heart, to see the human Countenance lighted up, into Smiles of Joy, on the Receipt of a Bit of Oar,[10] which is superfluous, and otherwise useless in a Man's own Pocket? What could a Man do better with his Cash? This is the Effect of an human Disposition, where there is only a general Tye of Nature, and common Necessity. What then must it be, when we serve an Object of Merit, of Admiration!

INDIANA: Well! The more you argue against it, the more I shall admire the Generosity.

BEVIL: Nay, nay —— Then, Madam, 'tis time to fly, after a Declaration, that my Opinion strengthens my Adversary's Argument —— I had best hasten to my Appointment with Mr. *Myrtle*, and be gone, while we are Friends, and —— before things are brought to an Extremity ——

Exit carelessly

Enter ISABELLA

ISABELLA: Well, Madam, what think you of him now pray?

INDIANA: I protest, I begin to fear he is wholly disinterested, in what he does for me. On my Heart, he has no other View, but the meer Pleasure of doing it, and has neither Good or Bad Designs upon me.

ISABELLA: Ah! dear Neice! don't be in fear of both! I'll warrant you, you will know time enough, that he is not indifferent.

INDIANA: You please me when you tell me so: For, if he has any Wishes towards me, I know he will not pursue them, but with Honour.

ISABELLA: I wish I were as confident of one, as t'other —— I saw the respectful Downcast of his Eye, when you catcht him gazing at you during the Musick: He, I warrant, was surpriz'd, as if he had been taken stealing your Watch. O! the undissembled Guilty Look!

10. ore, gold.

INDIANA: But did you observe any such thing, Really? I thought he look'd most Charmingly Graceful! How engaging is Modesty, in a Man, when one knows there is a great Mind within —— So tender a Confusion! and yet, in other Respects, so much himself, so collected, so dauntless, so determin'd!

ISABELLA: Ah! Neice! there is a sort of Bashfulness, which is the best Engine to carry on a shameless Purpose: some Men's Modesty serves their Wickedness, as Hypocrisy gains the Respect due to Piety: But I will own to you, there is one hopeful Symptom, if there could be such a thing, as a disinterested Lover; But 'tis all a Perplexity, —— till —— till —— till ——

INDIANA: Till what?

ISABELLA: Till I know whether Mr. *Myrtle* and Mr. *Bevil* are really Friends or Foes —— And that I will be convinced of, before I sleep: For you shall not be deceiv'd.

INDIANA: I am sure, I never shall, if your Fears can guard me: In the mean Time, I'll wrap my self up in the Integrity of my own Heart, nor dare to doubt of his.

As Conscious Honour all his Actions steers:
So Conscious Innocence dispels my Fears

Exeunt

ACT IV, SCENE 1

BEVIL'S *Lodgings*

BEVIL *with a Letter in his Hand, follow'd by* TOM

[Myrtle, Bevil's best friend, has come to believe that Bevil's marriage to Lucinda will go forward on this day, even though he is well aware that Bevil has only pretended to agree to the match. Because he discovers a letter written by Bevil to Lucinda, he suddenly suspects that he has been deceived, and challenges Bevil to a duel. Steele says in his Preface that the whole play was written for the sake of this scene.]

TOM: Upon my Life, Sir, I know nothing of the Matter: I never open'd my Lips to Mr. *Myrtle*, about any Thing of your Honour's Letter[1] to Madam *Lucinda*.

1. Dispatched in I.i. Bevil needed to assure Lucinda that his agreeing to marry her on this day was only a pretence (since he loves Indiana); but Myrtle (who loves Lucinda) was not told of the letter.

BEVIL: (*Aside*) What's the Fool in such a Fright for? I don't suppose you did: What I would know is, whether Mr. *Myrtle* shew'd any Suspicion, or ask'd you any Questions, to lead you to say casually, that you had carry'd any such Letter, for me, this Morning.

TOM: Why, Sir, if he did ask me any Questions, how could I help it?

BEVIL: I don't say you could, Oaf! I am not questioning you, but him: What did he say to you?

TOM: Why, Sir, when I came to his Chambers, to be dress'd for the Lawyer's Part,[2] your Honour was pleas'd to put me upon, he ask'd me, if I had been at Mr. *Sealand*'s this Morning —— So I told him, Sir, I often went thither —— because, Sir, if I had not said that, he might have thought, there was something more, in my going now, than at another Time.

BEVIL: Very well! —— (*Aside*) The Fellow's Caution, I find, has given him this Jealousy. Did he ask you no other Questions?

TOM: Yes, Sir —— now I remember, as we came away in the Hackney Coach, from Mr. *Sealand*'s, *Tom*, says he, as I came in to your Master, this Morning, he bid you go for an Answer to a Letter he had sent. Pray did you bring him any? says he —— Ah! says I, Sir, your Honour is pleas'd to joke with me, you have a mind to know whether I can keep a Secret, or no?

BEVIL: And so, by shewing him you could, you told him you had one?

TOM: Sir —— (*confus'd*)

BEVIL: What mean Actions does Jealousy make a Man stoop to? How poorly has he us'd Art, with a Servant, to make him betray his own Master? Well! and when did he give you this Letter for me?

TOM: Sir, he writ it, before he pull'd off his Lawyer's Gown, at his own Chambers.

BEVIL: Very well; and what did he say, when you brought him my Answer to it?

TOM: He look'd a little out of Humour, Sir, and said, it was very well.

BEVIL: I knew he would be grave upon't, —— wait without.

TOM: Humh! 'gad, I don't like this; I am afraid we are all in the wrong Box here. ——

Exit TOM

2. In Act III, Myrtle and Tom dressed up as lawyers, supposedly representing the case of Cimberton, a foolish rival for the hand of Lucinda. This decoy was Bevil's idea, and now Myrtle thinks he has been double-crossed.

BEVIL: I put on a Serenity, while my Fellow was present: But I have never been more thoroughly disturb'd; This hot Man! to write me a Challenge, on supposed artificial Dealing, when I profess'd myself his Friend! I can live contented without Glory; but I cannot suffer Shame. What's to be done? But first let me consider Lucinda's Letter again. (*Reads*)

SIR,

I hope it is consistent with the Laws a Woman ought to impose upon herself, to acknowledge, that your Manner of declining a Treaty of Marriage in our Family, and desiring the Refusal may come from me, has something more engaging in it, than the Courtship of him, who, I fear, will fall to my Lot; except your Friend exerts himself, for our common Safety, and Happiness: I have Reasons for desiring Mr. Myrtle *may not know of this Letter, till hereafter, and am your most obliged humble Servant,*

Lucinda Sealand.

Well, but the Postscript,

I won't, upon second Thoughts, hide any Thing from you. But my Reason for concealing this is, that Mr. Myrtle *has a Jealousy in his Temper, which gives me some Terrors; but my Esteem for him inclines me to hope that only an ill Effect, which sometimes accompanies a Tender Love; and what may be cur'd, by a careful and unblameable Conduct.*

Thus has this Lady made me her Friend and Confident, and put her self, in a kind, under my Protection: I cannot tell him immediately the Purport of her Letter, except I could cure him of the violent and untractable Passion of Jealousy, and so serve him, and her, by disobeying her, in the Article of Secrecy, more than I should by complying with her Directions —— But then this Duelling[3] which Custom has impos'd upon every Man, who would live with Reputation and Honour in the World: —— How must I preserve my self from Imputations there? He'll, forsooth, call it, or think it Fear, if I explain without Fighting —— But his Letter —— I'll read it again ——

SIR,

You have us'd me basely, in corresponding, and carrying on a Treaty, where you told me you were indifferent: I have chang'd my Sword since I saw you; which Advertisement I thought proper to send you

3. In *The Tatler*, No. 25, 7 June 1709, Steele vigorously attacked the practice of duelling and stripped it 'of all its false Pretences to Credit and Reputation amongst Men.'

against the next Meeting, between you and the injur'd
Charles Myrtle.

Enter TOM

TOM: Mr. *Myrtle*, Sir: would your Honour please to see him?

BEVIL: Why you stupid Creature! Let Mr. *Myrtle* wait at my Lodgings! shew him up.

Exit TOM

Well! I am resolv'd upon my Carriage[4] to him —— He is in Love, and in every Circumstance of Life a little distrustful, which I must allow for —— but here he is.

Enter TOM *introducing* MYRTLE

Sir, I am extremely oblig'd to you for this Honour —— But, Sir, you, with your very discerning Face, leave the Room.

Exit TOM

Well, Mr. *Myrtle*, your Commands with me?

MYRTLE: The Time, the Place, our long Acquaintance, and many other Circumstances, which affect me on this Occasion, oblige me, without farther Ceremony, or Conference, to desire you would not only, as you already have, acknowledge the Receipt of my Letter, but also comply with the Request in it. I must have farther Notice taken of my Message than these half Lines, —— I have yours, —— I shall be at home ——

BEVIL: Sir, I own, I have receiv'd a Letter from you, in a very unusual Style; But as I design every thing, in this Matter, shall be your own Action, your own Seeking, I shall understand nothing but what you are pleas'd to confirm, Face to Face, and I have already forgot the Contents of your Epistle.

MYRTLE: This cool Manner is very agreeable to the Abuse you have already made of my Simplicity and Frankness; and I see your Moderation tends to your own Advantage, and not mine; to your own Safety, not Consideration of your Friend.

BEVIL: My own Safety, Mr. *Myrtle*!

MYRTLE: Your own Safety, Mr. *Bevil*.

BEVIL: Look you Mr. *Myrtle*, there's no disguising that I understand what you would be at —— But, Sir, you know, I have often dared to disapprove of the Decisions a Tyrant Custom has introduc'd, to the Breach of Laws, both Divine and Human.

MYRTLE: Mr. *Bevil*, Mr. *Bevil*, it would be a good first Principle, in those who have so tender a Conscience that way, to have as much Abhorrence of doing Injuries, as ——

BEVIL: As what?

MYRTLE: As Fear of answering for them.

BEVIL: As Fear of answering for 'em! But that Apprehension is just or blameable, according to the Object of that Fear —— I have often told you in Confidence of Heart, I abhorr'd the Daring to offend the Author of Life, and rushing into his Presence —— I say by the very same Act, to commit the Crime against him, and immediately to urge on to his Tribunal.

MYRTLE: Mr. *Bevil*, I must tell you, this Coolness, this Gravity, this Shew of Conscience, shall never cheat me of my Mistress. You have, indeed, the best Excuse for Life, the Hopes of possessing *Lucinda*: But consider, Sir, I have as much Reason to be weary of it, if I am to lose her; and my first Attempt to recover her, shall be to let her see the Dauntless Man, who is to be her Guardian and Protector.

BEVIL: Sir, shew me but the least Glimpse of Argument, that I am authoriz'd, by my own Hand, to vindicate any lawless Insult of this nature, and I will shew thee —— to chastise thee —— hardly deserves the Name of Courage —— slight, inconsiderate Man! —— There is, Mr. *Myrtle*, no such Terror in quick Anger; and you shall, you know not why, be cool, as you have, you know not why, been warm.

MYRTLE: Is the Woman one loves, so little an Occasion of Anger? You perhaps, who know not what 'tis to love, who have your Ready, your Commodious, your Foreign Trinket, for your loose Hours; and from your Fortune, your specious outward Carriage, and other lucky Circumstances, as easie a Way to the Possession of a Woman of Honour; you know nothing of what it is to be alarm'd, to be distracted, with Anxiety and Terror of losing more than Life: Your Marriage, happy Man! goes on like common Business, and in the Interim, you have your Rambling Captive, your *Indian* Princess, for your soft Moments of Dalliance, your Convenient, your ready *Indiana*.

BEVIL: You have touch'd me beyond the Patience of a Man; and I'm excusable in the Guard of Innocence (or from the Infirmity of Human Nature, which can bear no more) to accept your Invitation, and observe your Letter —— Sir, I'll attend you.

Enter TOM

TOM: Did you call, Sir? I thought you did: I heard you speak aloud.

4. attitude.

BEVIL: Yes, go call a Coach.

TOM: Sir, —— Master —— Mr. *Myrtle*, —— Friends —— Gentlemen —— what d'ye mean? I am but a Servant, or ——

BEVIL: Call a Coach.

Exit TOM

(*A long Pause, walking sullenly by each other*)

BEVIL: (*Aside*) Shall I (though provok'd to the Uttermost) recover my self at the Entrance of a third Person, and that my Servant too, and not have respect enough to all I have ever been receiving from Infancy, the Obligation to the best of Fathers, to an unhappy Virgin too, whose Life depends on mine? (*Shutting the Door*)

(*To* MYRTLE) I have, thank Heaven, had time to recollect my self, and shall not, for fear of what such a rash Man as you think of me, keep longer unexplain'd the false Appearances, under which your Infirmity of Temper makes you suffer; when, perhaps, too much Regard to a false Point of Honour, makes me prolong that Suffering.

MYRTLE: I am sure, Mr. *Bevil* cannot doubt, but I had rather have Satisfaction from his Innocence, than his Sword.

BEVIL: Why then would you ask it first that Way?

MYRTLE: Consider, you kept your Temper your self no longer than till I spoke to the Disadvantage of her you lov'd.

BEVIL: True. But let me tell you, I have sav'd you from the most exquisite Distress, even tho' you had succeeded in the Dispute: I know you so well, that I am sure, to have found this Letter about a Man you had kill'd, would have been worse than Death to your self —— Read it. —— (*Aside*) When he is thoroughly mortify'd, and Shame has got the better of Jealousie, when he has seen himself thoroughly, he will deserve to be assisted towards obtaining *Lucinda*.

MYRTLE: With what a Superiority has he turn'd the Injury on me, as the Aggressor? I begin to fear, I have been too far transported —— *A Treaty in our Family!* is not that saying too much? I shall relapse —— But, I find (on the Postscript) *something like Jealousie* —— with what Face can I see my Benefactor? my Advocate? whom I have treated like a Betrayer. —— Oh! *Bevil*, with what Words shall I ——

BEVIL: There needs none; to convince, is much more than to conquer.

MYRTLE: But can you ——

BEVIL: You have o'erpaid the Inquietude you gave me, in the Change I see in you towards me: Alas! what Machines are we! thy Face is alter'd to that of another Man; to that of my Companion, my Friend.

MYRTLE: That I could be such a precipitant Wretch!

BEVIL: Pray no more.

MYRTLE: Let me reflect how many Friends have died, by the Hands of Friends, for want of Temper; and you must give me Leave to say again, and again, how much I am beholden to that Superior Spirit you have subdu'd me with —— what had become of one of us, or perhaps both, had you been as weak as I was, and as incapable of Reason?

BEVIL: I congratulate to us both the Escape from our selves, and hope the Memory of it will make us Dearer Friends than ever.

MYRTLE: Dear *Bevil*, your Friendly Conduct has convinc'd me that there is nothing manly, but what is conducted by Reason, and agreeable to the Practice of Virtue and Justice. And yet, how many have been sacrific'd to that Idol, the Unreasonable Opinion of Men! Nay, they are so ridiculous in it, that they often use their Swords against each other, with Dissembled Anger and Real Fear.

Betray'd by Honour, and compell'd by Shame,
They hazard Being, to preserve a Name:
Nor dare enquire into the dread Mistake,
'Till plung'd in sad Eternity they Wake.

Exeunt

THOMAS SHERIDAN

(1719-88)

THE BRAVE IRISHMAN;
or, CAPTAIN O'BLUNDER (1743)

[In the theatre of the eighteenth and nineteenth centuries, farces and afterpieces formed an important part of the bill of entertainment. *Hamlet* and *Macbeth* were all very well, but they could never stand on their own at this time. Audiences demanded and received, besides, comic, musical, or pantomimic diversion. To the modern reader, a piece such as *The Brave Irishman* may seem slight and even contemptible, but if the reader takes it as one dish on a pretty hearty menu, an entrée to a more substantial course comprising the generous nightly fare of another age, he or she may see it in the proper light. Taken as a one-act romp, it entertainingly reveals the stage Irishman in London, ultimately winning all stakes in spite of his apparent disadvantages. Although it is not to be taken very seriously, since it was meant as farce, *The Brave Irishman* nevertheless records in exaggerated form some social and cultural attitudes obtaining between Ireland and England in the eighteenth century. Furthermore, the piece demands to be seen as theatrical rather than as literary material, and the role of Captain O'Blunder was a star part in its day. From its first production in Dublin in 1743, this farce remained a popular favourite, in London as well as in Dublin.]

PROLOGUE

Spoken by Capt. O'BLUNDER

Oagh, brilliant shircle, shease to vend your spleen
On ush, poor Irish *'till our faults are sheen;*
My business here, I'll swear, you ne'er would guesh;
But come, — my duty 'tish, first to confesh;
To keep you then no longer in suspince,
To wed a fair one ish my whole pretince.

Phoo, now d'ye hear — the titter ne'er will shease,
I plainly see the curl in each merry faash.

Well then, 'tish strange that 'fronts we here reshave,
Ven tish by us the English spalpeens[1] *live.*
Have we not fought your battles — bravely too;
And yet, ungrateful boors, all that wont do.
Oagh, would the heroes of Hibernia's blood,
Who lately in their caush[2] *uprightly stood,*
But shay with me, they'll mix their noble breed
With Britain's daughters! Then we should be freed.[3]
Hark the bell rings – I therefore must obey,
So smooth your brows, and calmly hear the play.

Dramatis Personae

MEN
CAPTAIN O'BLUNDER
MR. TRADER, A MERCHANT
CHEATWELL
SCONCE
JERRY, CAPTAIN'S SERJEANT
DR. CLYSTER
DR. GALLYPOT
MONSIEUR RAGOU
WOMEN
LUCY, DAUGHTER TO TRADER
BETTY, MAID TO LUCY
MOB, KEEPERS, &C

SCENE: LONDON.

ACT I, SCENE 1

A Chamber

LUCY *repeating;*

'Tis not the Marriage, but the man we hate;
'Tis there we reason and debate:
For, give us but the Man we love,
We're sure the Marriage to approve.

Well, this same barbarous Marriage-Act[4] is a great Draw-back on the Inclinations of young People.

BETTY: Indeed and so it is, Mem; for my Part I'm no Heiress, and therefore at my own Proposal! and

1. From the Gaelic, *spailpín*, itinerant hired labourer.

2. cause. Presumably the 1715 Jacobite rebellion.
3. A disarming political comment.
4. Passed in 1754. 'Its main purpose was to end the confusion about what constituted a legal marriage' (Ian Watt). It seems odd that a woman should describe the Act as 'barbarous', since it offered her more protection from cheats and deceivers. Since this is clearly a topical reference, it dates the text at around 1754, even though the farce had been staged in 1743.

if I was under the Restraint of the Act, and kept from Men, I would run to Seed, so I wou'd — but la! Mem, I had forgot to acquaint you, I verily believes that I saw your *Irish* Lover the Captain; and I conceits[5] it was he and no other, so I do — and I saw him go into the Blue Postices,[6] so I did.

LUCY: My *Irish* Lover, Miss Pert; I never so much as saw his Potato Face in all my born Days; but I hear he's a strange Animal of a Brute — Pray had he his Wings on? I suppose they saved him in his Passage.

BETTY: Oh! Mem, you mistakes the *Irishmen*; they deny that they've *Wings,* but they all confess and boast of their *Tails.*[7]

LUCY: Oh Tawdry! but see who's at the Door.

Exit BETTY *and returns with* CHEATWELL

CHEATWELL: Miss! Your most humble and obedient — I came to acquaint you of our Danger: Our common Enemy is just imported hither, and is enquiring for your Father's House thro' every Street —— The *Irish* Captain, in short, is come to *London;* such a Figure! and so attended by the Rabble ——

LUCY: (*Aside*) I long to see him —— we love Variety; and *Irishmen*, I hear, are not so despicable; besides, the Captain may be misrepresented. Mr *Cheatwell*, you know my Father's Design is to have as many Suitors as he can, in order to have a Choice of them all.

CHEATWELL: I have nothing but your Professions and Sincerity to depend on —— Oh! here's my trusty Mercury.

Enter SCONCE

So — Well, have you dogg'd the Captain?

SCONCE: Yes, yes, I left him snug at the *Blue Posts*; he's just pat for our Purpose, easily humm'd;[8] as simple and as undesigning as we would have him. Well, and what do you propose?

CHEATWELL: Propose! why, to drive him back to his native Bogs as fast as possible.

LUCY: Oh! Mr. *Cheatwell* — pray let's have a Sight of the *Creature* ——

CHEATWELL: Oh! Female Curiosity —— Why, Child, he'd frighten thee — he's above six Feet high ——

LUCY: (*Aside*) A fine Size —— I like a tall Man.

SCONCE: A great huge Back and Shoulders.

LUCY: (*Aside*) We women love Length and Breadth in Proportion.

SCONCE: Wears a great long Sword, which he calls his *Andrew Ferara* ——

LUCY: I hear the *Irish* are naturally brave ——

SCONCE: And carries a large Oaken Cudgel, which he calls his *Shillela.*

LUCY: (*Aside*) Which he can make Use of on Occasions, I suppose.

SCONCE: Add to this a great Pair of Jackboots, a *Cumberland* Pinch to his Hat, an old red Coat, and a damn'd Potato Face.

LUCY: He must be worth seeing truly ——

CHEATWELL: Well, my dear Girl, be constant, wish me Success; for I shall so hum, so roast, and so banter this same *Irish* Captain, that he'll scarce wish himself in *London* again these seven Years to come.

LUCY: About it — Adieu — I hear my Father.

Exeunt severally

ACT 1, SCENE 2

A Street

Enter CAPTAIN O'BLUNDER *and* JERRY

CAPTAIN: And so you tells me, Cherjeant, that *Terence M'Gloodterry* keeps a Goon?[1]

SERJEANT: Yes, Sir.

CAPTAIN: Monomundioul![2] but if I catches any of these Spalpeen Brats keeping a Goon to destroy the Game, but I'll have 'em chot first, and phipt[3] thorough the Regiment afterwards.

SERJEANT: One wou'd think that they should be whipp'd first, and then shot.

CAPTAIN: Well, isn't it the same Thing? Fat the Devil magnifies[4] that? — 'Tis but phipping and shooting all the time —— 'Tis the same Thing in the End, sure, after all your Cunning, but still you'll be a Wiseacre: But that *Terence M'Gloodterry* is an old Pocher, he shoots all the Rabbits in the Country to stock his own Burrough with 'em.

Enter a MOB *who stare at him*

1st MOB: Twig[5] his Boots.

5. i.e. I conceive or consider. Betty speaks non-standard English. In the Belfast edition, she is called Maid in this part of the play, and is named at the end.
6. Betty's pronunciation of 'Posts', the tavern mentioned by Sconce, below.
7. coat-tails, with a strong hint, besides, of sexual conquests.
8. tricked.

1. i.e. a gun. The Captain's pronunciation is mocked throughout.
2. An Irish oath, *m'anam don diabhal* (my soul to the devil).
3. whipped.
4. for 'signifies'. The Captain's verbal absurdities are part of his character.
5. Look at.

2nd MOB: Smoke[6] his Sword, &c. &c.

CAPTAIN: Well, you Scoundrels, did you never see an *Irish* Shentleman before?

Enter SCONCE

SCONCE: Oh! fie! Gentlemen are not you asham'd to mock a Stranger after this rude Manner.

CAPTAIN: (*Aside*) This is a shivil Short of a little Fellow enough.

SCONCE: If[7] he is an *Irishman*; you may see by his Dress and Behaviour, that he's a Gentleman.

CAPTAIN: Yesh, you Shons of Whores, don't you see by my Dress and Behaviour, that I'm a Shentleman-Stranger —— By my Shoul if I take *Shillela* to you, I'll make you all smoke.[8]

MOB *runs off*

(*To* SCONCE) Shir, your humble Sharvant; you seem to be a shivil mannerly Shentleman, and I shall be glad to be gratified with your nearer Acquaintance. (*Salutes*)

Enter CHEATWELL

CHEATWELL: Captain *O'Blunder*; Sir, you are extremely welcome to *London* —— Sir, I'm your most sincere Friend and devoted humble Servant.

CAPTAIN: Yara! then how well every Body knows me in *London* —— to be sure they read of my Name in the Papers, and they know my Faas ever since. —— Shir, your affected humble Sharvant. (*Salutes*)

CHEATWELL: Well, and Captain, tell us, how long are you arrived; I hope you had a good Passage?

CAPTAIN: By my Shoul, my own Bones are shore after it —— We were on the Devil's own Turnpike for eight and forty Hours —— to be sure, we were all in a comical Pickle. —— 'Twas Old Nick's Race Horse we rode, and tho' I bid the Landlord of the Ferry-boat to stop it, he took no more Notice of me, than if I was one of the Spalpeens that was going over to reap the Harvest.[9]

CHEATWELL: No, Captain! —— The unmannerly Fellow; and what brought you to *London*.

CAPTAIN: Faith, my Jewel, I came in the Stage-Coach from *Chester*.

CHEATWELL: I mean, what Business?

CAPTAIN: (*Aside*) How damn'd inquisitive they are here! but I'll be as cunning as no Man alive. By my shoul, my Jewel, I'm going over to *Whirginny*[10] to beat the *Frinch* —— They say they have driven our Countrymen out of their Plantaations; by my Shoul, my Jewel, if our Troops get vonse among them, we'll cut them all in Pieces, and then bring 'em over Prisoners of War besides.

CHEATWELL: Indeed, Captain, you are come upon an honourable Expedition —— but pray, how is[11] the old Gentleman your Father? I hope you left him in good Health?

CAPTAIN: Oh! by my Shoul, he's very well, my Jewel; for he's dead these four Years.

CHEATWELL: And the old Gentleman, your Uncle?

CAPTAIN: My Uncle! —— You mean my Shister's Hushband, you Fool you, that's my Brother-in-law ——

CHEATWELL: Ay, a handsome Man ——

CAPTAIN: Ha, ha, a handsome Man? ay, for he's a damn'd crooked Fellow; he's crooked Shoulder'd, and has a Hump upon his Nose, and a Pair of Huckle Backs upon his Shins, if you call that handsome —— Ha, ha, ha.

CHEATWELL: And pray is that merry, joking Gentleman alive still —— He that used to make us laugh so —— Mr. —— Mr. —— a.

CAPTAIN: Phoo, I'll tell you who you mean —— You mean *Sheela Shaghnassy*'s Husband the Exshizeman.

CHEATWELL: The very same.

CAPTAIN: Oh! my dear Jewel, he's as merry as my Lord Chief Joke[12] in *Dublin*; tho' he's not very wise phin I'm by; for I took him down —— Ara, my Jewel, I'll tell you the whole Story —— We took a walk together, and the Wind was very high, considering 'twas a fine calm Morning —— 'Twas in our Back going, but, by my Shoul, as we returned, it was in our Faash coming home —— and yet I could never persuade him that the Wind was turn'd.

CHEATWELL: Oh the Fool ——

CAPTAIN: Ara, so I told him, my Jewel; you great Oaf, says I —— If the Wind blows in your Back going, and blows in your Faash coming, sure the Wind is turn'd —— No, if I was to preach, and to preach, till last Year come Twelvemonth, I cou'd not dissuade him that the Wind was turn'd.

CHEATWELL: He had not common Sense ——

6. Look at.
7. i.e. 'even if': note the condescension.
8. suffer severely.
9. Irish itinerant labourers used to travel to England to get work at harvest-time.
10. The colony in Virginia.
11. In this passage the satire is turned on the polite Englishman, whose inquiries are patently insincere.
12. = Justice(?). A topical allusion, now obscure. The Belfast edition has 'Joaker'. phin = when.

Well, and does the old Church stand where it did?

CAPTAIN: The old Church —— the Devil a Church within ten Mile of us. ——

CHEATWELL: I'm sure there was a kind of an old Building like a Church or a Castle. ——

CAPTAIN: Phoo, my Jewel, I know what you call a Church —— by my Shoul, 'tis old lame *Will Hurley*'s Mill you mean. (*Talk aside*)

Enter SCONCE *with* MONSIEUR RAGOU

SCONCE: Consider, Monsieur, he's your Rival, and is come purely, and with an Intent to rob you of your Mistress.

MONSIEUR: Is he —— Le Fripon[13] —— Le grand Fripon! Parbleu, me no endure dat! icy l'Epee —— vat you call —— my Sword —— Est bien assuré —— he may take my Vord for dat. ——

SCONCE: And he's the greatest of all Cowards —— tho' he carries that great swaggering broad Sword —— believe me Monsieur, he wou'd not fight a Cat —— he'd run away if you drew upon him. ——

MONSIEUR: You be bien assuré that he be de grand Coward —— Mon Ami —— Eh bien —— vel den —— I'll have his Blood —— (*Aside*) my Heart dance de pit a pit. Je n'avois pas la Courage. I have not de good Courage.

SCONCE: Tut, Man, only affront him —— go up to him.

MONSIEUR: Me sal shew him de bon Addresse —— Helas —— (*goes up to the* CAPTAIN). Monsieur le Capitaine vous etes le grand Fripon. ——

CAPTAIN: *Wel Gelun a gud,*[14] have you any *Irish*?

MONSIEUR: *Ireland*! me be no such outlandish Country: —— You smell of de Potato. ——

CAPTAIN: Do I —— by my Shoul I did not taast a Praty since I left *Ireland*; (*To* CHEATWELL) May be he has a mind to put the Front upon me.[15]

CHEATWELL: It looks like it, very like it, Captain.

CAPTAIN: Faith, my Jewel, I don't know a more peaceable Companion than *Andrew Ferara* here —— (*showing his Sword*) but if he's provok'd —— he's no Slouch at it —— do you mean to front me, you *French* Bogre[16] —— Eh? ——

MONSIEUR: Affront —— you be de Teague, de vild *Irishman* —— de Potato Face —— me no think it vorth my while to notice you. Otez vous, je dis[17] —— go about your Business ——

CAPTAIN: Oh, ho, are you there? —— come out my trusty *Andrew Ferara* —— here take *Shillela* —— (*Gives his Cudgel to* CHEATWELL).

SCONCE: (*To the* FRENCHMAN) Draw, for he won't fight.

MONSIEUR: He be de terrible Countenance —— he be fort enrage, dev'lish angry.

CAPTAIN: Come on, you Soup Maigre.[18]

(*They fight* —— MONSIEUR *falls*)

CAPTAIN: After that you're easy —— who smells of Pratys now? you Refugee Son of a Whore —— Affront an *Irish* Shentlemen!

SCONCE: The Man's dead.

CAPTAIN: Is he? —— what magnifies that; I killed him in the fair duelling Way.

CHEATWELL: But, Captain, 'tis Death by the Law to duel in *England* —— and this Place is not so safe a Place for you —— I'm heartily sorry for this Accident.

CAPTAIN: Ara, my Jewel, they don't mind it in *Ireland* one Trawneen.[19]

CHEATWELL: Come, come, Captain, safe's the Word —— the Street will be soon alarm'd —— you can come to my House till the Danger's over —— and I will get you Bail.

CAPTAIN: By my Shoul, I believe 'tis the best Way, for fear of the Boners.[20]

CHEATWELL: Here's my Friend will shew you the Way to my House; I'll be with you in a minute.

Exit CAPTAIN *with* SCONCE

CHEATWELL: Are you dead, Monsieur, Eveillez-vous —— get up, Man.

(MONSIEUR *rises*)

MONSIEUR: Parbleu —— il avoit de long Rapier —— he be de terrible *Irishman* —— 'tis well me fall in time, or he make me fall so dat me never resusciter —— never get up again.

CHEATWELL: Well, I'm glad there's no more Mischief done ——

Come, never mind the *Irishman* a Rush.
You and the Captain shall have t'other Brush.

MONSIEUR: Parbleu —— me kis de Book —— me just have swore,

13. the rascal.
14. Irish, *an bhfuil Gaelainn agat?* The Captain gives the English translation immediately, but the Frenchman misunderstands 'Irish' as referring to place rather than language.
15. i.e. to affront me.
16. bugger.
17. Remove yourself, I say.
18. vegetable soup.
19. From the Irish, *traithnin*, a straw.
20. To 'bone' was 'to seize, arrest' (Eric Partridge, *The Routledge Dictionary of Historical Slang*). 'Boners', therefore, presumably means the constables. The word is not recorded.

Never to fight an *Irishman*, no more.[21]

CHEATWELL: Come, come along, you Son of a *French* whore.

Exeunt

21. Added from the Belfast edition.

ACT I, SCENE 3

A Mad House

Enter CAPTAIN *and* SCONCE

SCONCE: Captain, this is your Cousin's House: I'll go and get proper Things for your Accommodation —— Sir, your humble Servant for a Moment or so —— give me your Things. (*Takes his Sword and Cudgel*)

CAPTAIN: Shir, your most humble Sharvant. (*Looks about*) Faith my Cousin's House is a brave[1] large Place —— tho' it is not so very well furnish'd —— but I suppose the Maid was cleaning out the Rooms: So —— who are these now? —— Some Acquaintance of my Cousin's to be sure.

Enter DR. CLYSTER *and* DR. GALLYPOT (*Both salute the* CAPTAIN)

CAPTAIN: Shentlemen, your most humble Sharvant —— but where's my Cousin?

CLYSTER: (*To* DR. GALLYPOT) His Cousin —— what does he mean?

GALLYPOT: What should a Madman mean? Sir, we come to treat you in a regular Manner.

CAPTAIN: O, dear Shentlemen, 'tis too much Trouble —— you need not be over regular, a single Joint of Meat, and a good Glass of Ale, will be a very good Treat without any needless Expences.

CLYSTER: Do you mind that Symptom —— the canine Appetite.

CAPTAIN: Nine Appetites —— no, my Jewel; I have an Appetite like other People; a Couple of Pounds will serve me if I was ever so hungry —— phat the Devil do they talk of nine Appetites; do they think I'm a Cat, that has as many Stomachs as Lives?

GALLYPOT: He looks a little wild, Brother.

CAPTAIN: Fat! are you Brothers?

BOTH: Pray, Sir, be seated; we shall examine methodically into the Nature of your Case.

(*They sit —* CAPTAIN *in the Middle — they feel his Pulse — he stares at them*)

CAPTAIN: Fat the Devil do they mean by taking me by the Wrists —— may be 'tis the Fashion of Compliment in *London*.

1. i.e. fine.

CLYSTER: Brother, you plainly perceive that the Systole and Diastole are obstructed.

CAPTAIN: My Piss-hole and Arse-hole —— Fat the Devil ails them? Eh! sure de're mad.

GALLYPOT: First, Brother, let us examine the Symptoms.

CAPTAIN: By my Shoul, the Fellows are Fools.

CLYSTER: Pray, Sir, how do you rest?

CAPTAIN: In a good Feather-bed, my Jewel —— and sometimes I take a Nap in an Arm-chair.

CLYSTER: But do you sleep sound?

CAPTAIN: Faith I sleep and snore all Night; and when I awake in the Morning, I find myself fast asleep.

GALLYPOT: The *Cerebrum* or *Cerebellum* is affected.

CAPTAIN: The Devil a Sir Abram, or Bell either, I mind.

GALLYPOT: How do you eat, Sir?

CAPTAIN: Width my Mouth —— how the Devil should I eat d'ye think.

CLYSTER: Pray, Sir, have you a good Stomach, d'ye eat heartily?

CAPTAIN: Oh, my Jewel, I am no Slouch at that, tho' a clumsy Beef-stake, or the Leg and Arm of a Turkey with a Griskin[2] under his Oxter[3] would sharve my Turn.

GALLYPOT: Do you generally drink much?

CAPTAIN: Oh my Jewel, a Couple of Quarts of Ale and Porter would not choke me; but fat the Devil magnifies so many Questions about eating and drinking? —— If you have a mind to order any Thing, do it as soon as you can, for I'm almost famish'd.

CLYSTER: I am for treating him regularly, methodically, and *secundum Artem.*[4]

CAPTAIN: Secundum Fartem? —— I don't see any Sign of treating at all —— Ara, my Jewel, send for a Mutton Chop, and don't trouble yourself about my Stomach.

CLYSTER: I shall give you my Opinion, concerning this Case, Brother —— *Galen*[5] says ——

CAPTAIN: *Wel Gelun a gud?*

2. The lean part of a loin of pork.
3. 'The armpit or the under-side of the upper arm' (*OED*). The phrase means 'with sore lean meat under its side'.
4. 'according to the art' [of medicine].
5. Galen (*c.* 130-200 A.D.) was a Greek physician and medical authority.

CLYSTER: I say that *Galen* is of Opinion, that in all adust[6] Complexions.

CAPTAIN: Well, and who has a dusty Complexion?

CLYSTER: A little Patience, Sir.

CAPTAIN: I think I have a great deal of Patience; that People can't eat a Morsel without so many impertinent Questions.

CLYSTER: *Qui habet vultum adustum,*
Habet caninum Gustum.[7]

CAPTAIN: I'm sure 'tis an ugly Custom to keep a Man fasting so long after pretending to treat him.

GALLYPOT: Ay, Brother, but *Hippocrates*[8] differs from *Galen* in this Case.

CAPTAIN: Well, but my Jewels, let there be no Difference, nor falling out between Brothers about me, for a small Matter will sharve my Turn.

CLYSTER: Sir, you break the Thread of our Discourse; I was observing that in gloomy opaque Habits, the Rigidity of the Solids causes a continual Friction in the Fluids, which, by being constantly impeded, grow thick and glutinous, by which means they cannot enter the Capillary Vessels, nor the other finer Ramifications of the Nerves.

GALLYPOT: Then, Brother, from your Position, it will be deducible that the *Primæ Viæ* are to be clear'd, which must be effected by frequent Emeticks.

CLYSTER: Sudorificks.[9]

GALLYPOT: Catharticks.

CLYSTER: Pneumaticks.

GALLYPOT: Restoratives.

CLYSTER: Corrosives.

GALLYPOT: Narcoticks.

CLYSTER: Cephalicks.[10]

GALLYPOT: Pectorals.

CLYSTER: Stypticks.[11]

GALLYPOT: Specificks.

CLYSTER: Causticks.

CAPTAIN: How naturally they answer one another, like the Parish Minister and the Clerk —— By my Shoul, Jewels, thish Gibberish will never fill a Man's Belly.

CLYSTER: And thus to speak *Summatim* and *Articulatim*, or categorically to recapitulate the several Remedies in the Aggregate, the Emetics will clear the first passages, and restore the Viscera to their pristine Tone, and regulate their lost peristaltick or vermicular Motion, so that from the Oesophagus to the Rectum I am for potent Emeticks.

GALLYPOT: And next for Sudorificks, as they open the Pores, or rather the porous Continuity of the cutaneous Dermis and Epidermis: thence to convey the noxious and melancholy Humours of the Blood.

CLYSTER: With Catharticks to purge him.

GALLYPOT: Pneumaticks to scourge him.

CLYSTER: Narcoticks to doze him.

GALLYPOT: Cephalicks to pose him.

CAPTAIN: These are some of the Dishes they are to treat me with —— Why, my Jewels, there's no need for all this Cookery —— upon my Shoul this is to be a grand Entertainment. Well, they'll have their own Way.

CLYSTER: Suppose we use Phlebotomy, and take from him thirty Ounces of Blood.

CAPTAIN: Flay my Bottom, d'ye say?

GALLYPOT: His Eyes roll —— call in the Keepers.

Enter KEEPERS

CAPTAIN: Flay my Bottom —— Oh, my *Andrew Ferara* and *Shillela*, I want ye now —— but here's a Chair —— Flay my Bottom —— Ye Sons of Whores —— ye Gibberish Scoundrels. (*Drives them out*)

Oh! this Son of a Whore of a Cousin of mine, to bring me to these Thieves to flay my Bottom —— If I meet him, I'll flay his Bottom.

Exit

ACT I, SCENE 4

The Street

Enter SERJEANT

I have been seeking my Master every where, and cannot find him; I hope nothing has happened him —— I think that was one of the Gentlemen I saw with him.

Enter SCONCE

Sir, Sir, pray did you see the Captain, my Master, Captain *O'Blunder*, the *Irish* Gentleman?

SCONCE: Not I, indeed, my Friend —— I left him last with Mr. *Cheatwell* —— I suppose they're

6. melancholy.
7. 'He who has a melancholy face, has the appetite of a dog.'
8. Hippocrates (*c.* 460-370 B.C.) was a Greek physician, recognized as the father of medicine.
9. Drugs that cause one to sweat. This use of comic verbal 'snap', or stichomythia, is probably indebted to the French playwright Molière, whose farce *Monsieur de Pourceaugnac* was a source here.
10. Drugs for the head.
11. Drugs that stop bleeding.

taking a Bottle together —— Oh, No! here's the Captain.

Enter CAPTAIN

CAPTAIN: Oh! my dear Friend, I had like to be lost, to be ruinated by that Scoundrel my Coushin —— Well I'm so out of Breath, I ran away with my Life from the Thieves —— You know you left me at my Coushin's House —— Well, I walk'd about for some Time, to be sure I thought it an odd sort of a House, when I saw no Furniture —— There I expected my Coushin every Moment; and, dear Honey,[1] there came in two Bird-lime Sons of Whores, with great Wigs —— they look'd like Conjurers and Fortune-tellers —— one takes hold of one of my Wrists, and the other catches hold of my other Wrist; I thought by Way of Compliment. I sat down betwixt them; they did chatter such Gibberish, like a Couple of old Baboons; and all this Discourse was conchaarning me —— they talk'd at first of treating me, and ask'd me, Had I a good Stomach? —— one of 'em said, I had nine Appetites; but at length, my Jewels, what should come of the Treat, but they agreed before my Face to flay my Bottom —— Oh! if I tell you a Word of Lie, I'm not here —— My Dear, they calls in the Keepers to tie me; I up with the Chair; for I gave you my *Shillela* and *Andrew Ferara,* and drove them out, and made my Escape.

SCONCE: I am sorry to see that your Cousin has behaved so rudely towards you; but any thing that lies in my Power ——

CAPTAIN: Oh! Sir, you're a very worthy Shentleman; but Cherjeant, I must go to see Mr. *Trader* the Merchant, and his fair Daughter. —— Has the Taylor brought home my Clothes?

SERJEANT: Yes, Sir, and the old Gentleman expects you immediately, and sent a Man in Livery for you. ——

CAPTAIN: Come, my good Friend, I won't part with you —— I'll step to my Lodgings, and just slip on my Clothes, that I may pay my due Regards to my Mishtress.

Exeunt

1. 'my dear Jewel' (Belfast edition).

ACT I, SCENE 5

The Mad House

CHEATWELL, CLYSTER *and* GALLYPOT

CHEATWELL: I'm sorry for this Accident.

CLYSTER: In troth, Mr. *Cheatwell,* he was the most furious Madman that ever I met with during the whole Course of my Practice.

GALLYPOT: I am now surpris'd how he sat so long quiet.

CHEATWELL: He'll run riot about the Streets; but I hope he'll be taken —— Oh! here's *Sconce.*

Enter SCONCE

Well, What News of the Captain?

SCONCE: I just ran to let you know of his Motions; he is preparing to dress, in order to pay a visit to Miss *Lucy,* and to pay his Respects to *Trader*; and worse News for you, 'tis whispered on 'Change,[1] that *Trader* is broke.

CHEATWELL: If that shou'd fall out so, I shall easily resign my Pretensions to the Captain. 'Twas *Lucy*'s Purse, and not her Beauty, that I courted.

SCONCE: I must run back to the Captain, and keep in with him, to serve a Turn; do you at a Distance watch us, and proceed accordingly.

Exit

CHEATWELL: Well, Gentlemen, I shall take Care to acknowledge your Trouble the first Time I see you again; so adieu.

Exeunt

1. The London Exchange.

ACT I, SCENE 6

The CAPTAIN's *Lodgings*

CAPTAIN: Arrah but who the Divil do you think I met Yesterday fullbut[1] in the Street but *Thady Shaghnassy*?

SERJEANT: Well, and how is he?

CAPTAIN: Arrah stay till I tell you; he wash at todther Side of the Way, and when I came up, it wash not him. Tell me, dosh my new Regimentals become me?

SERJEANT: Yes indeed, Sir, I think they do.

CAPTAIN: This pocket is too high; I must be forced to stoop for my Snuff-box.

Enter SCONCE

SCONCE: Ha! upon my Word, Captain, you look as spruce as a young Bridegroom.

CAPTAIN: All in good Time —— and does it fit easy?

SCONCE: Easy, Sir, it fits like your Shirt.

CAPTAIN: I think it's a little too wide here in the Sleeve: I'm afraid the Fellow has not left Cloth

1. point-blank or face-to-face.

enough to take it in;[2] tho' I can't blame the Fellow neither; for I was not by when he took Measure of me —— Cherjeant, here, go, take this Sixpence Halfpenny, and buy me a Pair of white Gloves.

SERJEANT: I don't think you can get a pair for Six-pence.

CAPTAIN: Why how much will the Leatherman have?

SCONCE: Two Shillings.

CAPTAIN: Two Thirteens![3]

SERJEANT: Indeed, Sir, you won't get them less in *London*.

CAPTAIN: Not less than two Thirteens! *Monomondioul!* but I'd rather my Hands shou'd go barefoot all the Days of their Lives, than give Two Thirteens for a Pair of Gloves —— Come, come along, I'll go without 'em; my Mishtress must excuse me.

Exeunt

2. As so often, the Captain uses an Irish 'bull' as absurdity here.
3. Irish money was worth less than English; it took thirteen pence, instead of twelve, to make a shilling.

ACT I, SCENE 7

Scene *changes to* TRADER's *House*

Enter TRADER *and* LUCY

TRADER: Well, Daughter, I have been examining into the Circumstances of *Cheatwell*, and find he is not worth a Six-pence; and as for your *French* Lover, he is some run-away Dancing-master or Hair-cutter from *Paris*; so that really, among them all, I cannot find any one to come up to your *Irish* Lover, either for Birth, Fortune, or Character.

LUCY: Sir, you're the best Judge in the disposing of me; and indeed I have no real Tendre[1] for any one of them —— As to the *Irish* Captain, I have not seen him as yet.

TRADER: You'll see him presently; I sent to his Lodgings, and expect him every Moment —— Oh! here's *Monsieur*.

Enter MONSIEUR RAGOU

TRADER: Well, Monsieur, I have been trying my Daughter's Affections in Regard to you, and as she is willing to be guided by me in this Affair, I wou'd willingly know by what visible Means you intend to maintain her like a Gentlewoman, as she is both by Birth and Education?

MONSIEUR: Me have de grand Acquaintance with the Beau Monde; and, si vous plais, to do me the Honour of making me your Son-in-Law, me transact your Negotiations with all possible Care and Belle Air.

Enter CAPTAIN O'BLUNDER

TRADER: You're welcome to my House —— Sir, this is my Daughter —— this, Child, is Captain *O'Blunder*, whom I hope you will receive as he deserves.

CAPTAIN: Fairest of Creatures, will you gratify me with a Taste of your sweet delicate Lips. (*Kisses*) By my Shoul a neat Creature, and a good Bagoorah[2] Girl —— Oh! oh! I see my *Frenchman*! and, Faith, I have a Praty ready for him now.

MONSIEUR: Oh! Le Diable —— he espy me —— me better go off while I am well.

CAPTAIN: (*Goes up to* MONSIEUR) I thought, Monsieur *Ragou*, that you were dead —— Do I smell of the Praty now, you Soupe Maigre Son of a *French* Boogre?

TRADER: The Captain has a Mind to be merry with the *Frenchman*.

CAPTAIN: By my Shoul, my Jewel, I have got a Praty for you now —— here eat it. Eat this —— Oh, oh, come forth. (*Draws*) Eat that Praty this Minute. I'm sure 'tis better nor your Garlick nor Ingyons in *France*.

Frenchman eats it

Enter a SERVANT *to* TRADER

SERVANT: Oh! Sir —— there are certain Accounts come —— but these Letters will better inform you.

TRADER: (*Reads*) Oh! Captain, I am ruin'd, undone —— broke ——

CAPTAIN: Broke! what have you broke?

TRADER: Oh! Sir, my Fortune's broke; I am not a Penny above a Beggar.

MONSIEUR: Oh! den me be of de Amour —— me have no Dealings with Beggars; me have too many of de Beggar in my own Country; so me better slip away in good Time.

Exit

TRADER: So now, Captain, I have not concealed my Misfortunes from you; you are at Liberty to choose a happier Wife, for my poor Child is miserable.

CAPTAIN: I thought your Ribs was broke; I am no Surgeon; but if 'tis only a little Money that broke

1. tenderness.

2. cf. begorra — Irish corruption of 'by God'. The Captain is implying that Lucy is as good as an Irish girl.

you; give me this sweet Lady's Lily-white Hand, and, as far as a good Estate in Land and Stock will go, I'll share it with her, and with yourself —— Ara, never mind the Thieves, my Jewel, I'll break their Necks before they shall break your little Finger. Come, I'll give you a Song of my own Composition.

Wherever I am going, and all the Day long,
Abroad and at Home, or alone in a Throng,
I find that my Passions so lively and strong,
That your name, when I'm silent, runs still in my song.[3]

Sing Balinamone oro, Balinamone oro, Balinamone oro,
A Kiss of your sweet Lips for me.

Since the first time I saw you, I took[4] *no Repose,*
I sleep all the Day to forget half my Woes;
So strong is the Flame in my bosom which glows
By St. Patrick[5] *I'm afraid it would burn thro' my Cloaths.*

Sing Balinamone oro, &c.
Your pretty black Hair for me.

On that happy Day when I make you my bride,
With a swinging long Sword, how I'll strut and I'll stride,
In a Coach and six Horses with Honey I'll ride.
As before you I walk to the Church by your Side.

Sing Balinamone oro, &c.
Your little white Fist for me.[6]

Enter CHEATWELL

CHEATWELL: Gentlemen, I beg pardon for this Intrusion.

CAPTAIN: Oh, by my Shoul, this is my friendly Coushin that bid the old Conjurers flay my Bottom.

CHEATWELL: Sir, I beg your Pardon in particular, and hope you'll grant me it; nothing but Necessity was the Cause of my ungenteel Behaviour —— This Lady I had an Esteem for; but since Things have turn'd out as they have, my Pretensions are without Foundation;[7] and therefore rais'd the Report of your Ships being lost at Sea, in hopes that this Gentleman would decline his Addresses to your Daughter, when he found she had no Fortune.

CAPTAIN: Oagh, my Dear, we play no such dirty Tricks in our Country.

CHEATWELL: And now, Captain, I hope you'll grant me your Pardon, and look upon me in the Light of an unfortunate Man rather than of a bad Man.

CAPTAIN: Faath, my dear Coushin, since Love is the Cause of your Mourning, I shall forgive you with all my Heart. (*Shakes hands*)

CHEATWELL: Sir, I shall always look upon your Friendship as an Honour; and hope you'll look upon me as a poor unfortunate young Fellow, that has not a Shilling, nor the Means of getting one upon the Face of the Earth.

CAPTAIN: Oh! upon my Shoul, then, Cousin *Cheatwell*, I pity your Condition with all my Heart; and since Things are so bad with you, if you'll take a Trip to my *Irish* Plantations with me and my dear Creature here, I'll give you 500*l.* to stock a Farm upon my own Eshtate, at *Ballmascushlain*, in the County of *Monaghan*, and the Barony of *Coogafighy* — Fait, and here's *Betty*, a tight Girl; and since you cou'd not get the Mistress, if you'll take up with the Maid, my Dear here, shall give her a couple of Hundred to fortune her off.[8]

BETTY: Captain, I'm very much obliged to you, for getting me a Husband; if Mr. *Cheatwell* has any Tendre for me, I have a thousand Pounds[9] at his Service of my own saving.

CAPTAIN: Oagh, dear Joy,[10] a Servant-maid with a thousand Pounds! Phy, in my Country, there is many a fine Lady has not half the Money, and goes to the Plays, and the Balls, and the Reddottos,[11] and won't make her own Smock.

CHEATWELL: I should be blind to my own Interest not to accept of such valuable Proposals; and with Gratitude take your Hand, promising for the future to lead a Life which shall be a Credit both to myself and my Benefactor.

CAPTAIN: Well then, without Compliments, I am glad to have made one poor Man happy; and since we have made a double Match of it, hey for *Ireland*, where we will all live like the Sons of *Irish* Kings.

3. The order of the first and second verses was reversed in the Belfast edition.
4. 'take' (Belfast edition).
5. 'By my Shoul' (Belfast edition).
6. This line was not in the Belfast edition.
7. The next 7/8 lines are not in the Belfast edition.
8. to supply her with a dowry.
9. 'a hundred Pounds' (Belfast edition).
10. These lines of the Captain's are not in the Belfast edition.
11. public dances, cf. Fr. *redoute*.

LUCY: This Generosity amazes me, and greatly prejudices me in the Honesty and Goodness of the *Irish.*

CAPTAIN: Oagh, my dear little Charmer, I've another Song just *a propos.*

Of all the Husbands living an Irishman's *the best,*

With my fal, lal, &c.

No Nation on the Globe, oagh like him can stand the test,

With my fal, lal, &c.

The English *are all Drones, as you may plainly see,*
But we're all brisk and airy, and lively as a Bee,

With my fal, lal, &c.

LUCY: Sir, your generous Behaviour so frankly shewn on so melancholy an Accident, has entirely gained my Heart, nor do I value your Estate, when set in Composition[12] with your noble Soul.

Thus, let all Women judge and thus decide,
Be Beauty still to noble Worth ally'd;
Nor glittering Wealth shou'd blind the Fair-one's Eyes,
Which, not with Honour join'd, we shou'd despise.

Exeunt

EPILOGUE

Spoken by LUCY

Tut! tut! I was mistaken —— ne'er believe me,
If any Scandal shall again deceive me:
For now I find, they made me but a Child,
To tell me that the Irish *all were wild:*
My Captain is as gentle as a Dove,
As innocent, and quite as full of Love ——
Ye British *Fair, if ye would wed the* TRUTH,
You'll only find it in the IRISH *Youth.*
The Irish *to our Hearts have found the Way.*
I ne'er believ'd it till I saw the —— Key.
Our dearest Secret best such Youth Rewards,
Who find the Key-hole *quick, and hit so true the* Wards.[13]

12. 'Competition' (Belfast edition).

13. Young persons under the control of guardians.

CHARLES MACKLIN
(1699-1797)

from: THE TRUE-BORN IRISHMAN; or, THE IRISH FINE LADY (1762)

[Although the irreversible trend among Irish playwrights was to write for the London stage, there were those who from time to time deliberately wrote for the Dublin stage. Since the motive was ostentatiously patriotic, the work of such authors provides an interesting exemplification of what has been termed Irish cultural nationalism. William Philips, for example, wrote *St Stephen's-Green; or, The Generous Lovers* (1700) for the Smock Alley theatre, and made a character in it comment: 'I have observ'd that none Despise *Ireland* so much as those who thrive best in it. And none are so severe in their Reflections upon it, as those who owe their Birth and Fortune to it; I have known many of 'em, when they come first to *London,* think there is no way so ready to purchase the Title of a Wit, as to Ridicule their own Country' (IV.1.17-23).

Charles Shadwell was another who tried to counter anglophilic tastes by setting his plays in Ireland and by calling repeatedly in his prologues for support for the Irish theatre. His best comedy, *Irish Hospitality; or, Virtue Rewarded* (1720), stands out as a worthy successor to Philips's *St Stephen's-Green.*

Charles Macklin continued this trend of writing with a sense of Ireland and its traditions. Behind this trend, strengthened by Swift's Irish writings, was a search for dignity in the face of oppressive British influence. It was not a paying proposition, and this, more than anything else, probably explains why the fashion did not lead to the burgeoning of a (significant) native Irish drama at this time. It is true that in the 1780s, when Irish nationalism was vibrant, Robert Owenson attempted to found a national theatre at Fishamble Street, Dublin, but it was soon suppressed by government application of the 'patent' laws controlling theatres.

Macklin's farce must be seen in this political context. Intrinsically, it is rather a tame, conventional tale of an errant wife who reforms very abruptly once it is pointed out to her that her infatuation for an English lover threatens her ruin at his (perfidious) hands. The main point Macklin wishes to make, however, is that excessive regard for things English is a form of affectation that is both ridiculous and morally dangerous.

In the first scene, O'Dogherty, the 'true-born Irishman', complains about his wife's affectation, which he puts into perspective as a national failing.]

ACT I

. . . *Enter* WILLIAM *shewing in* COUNSELLOR HAMILTON

WILLIAM: Counsellor Hamilton.

Exit

O'DOGHERTY: Counsellor, you are welcome to Dublin.

COUNSELLOR HAMILTON: Brother, I am extremely glad to see you.

O'DOGHERTY: By my faith, and so am I you. Odzooks give us a kiss, man: I give you my honour I am as glad to see you in Dublin at this juncture, as I should to see a hundred head of fat bullocks upon my own land, all ready for Ballinasloe Fair.[1]

COUNSELLOR HAMILTON: Sir, your humble servant. That is a great compliment from you, brother, I know.

O'DOGHERTY: It is a very true one I assure you.

COUNSELLOR HAMILTON: Well, I see by the news-papers that my sister is returned from her coronation frolic,[2] and in health I suppose, or you would have wrote me word had it been otherwise.

O'DOGHERTY: Yes, yes, she is in health indeed, and returned with a vengeance.

COUNSELLOR HAMILTON: Pray what is the matter?

O'DOGHERTY: Ogho! enough is the matter, the devil an inhabitant[3] in Swift's Hospital for Lunatics,[4] is in a worse pickle than she is.

COUNSELLOR HAMILTON: You surprise me![5] —— in what respect, pray?

O'DOGHERTY: Why, with a distemper that she has brought over with her from England, which will, in a little time, I am afraid, infect the whole nation.

COUNSELLOR HAMILTON: Pray, what may that be?

O'DOGHERTY: Sir, it is called the Irish Fine Lady's delirium, or the London vertigo; if you were to hear her when the fit is upon her —— oh, she is as mad —— the devil a thing in this poor country but what gives her the spleen, and the vapours —— then such a phrenzy of admiration for every thing in England —— and, among the rest of her madness, she has brought over a new language with her.

COUNSELLOR HAMILTON: What do you mean by a new language?

O'DOGHERTY: Why a new kind of a London English, that's no more like our Irish English, than a coxcomb's fine gilded chariot like a Glassmanogue noddy[6] —— Why what name do you think she went by when she was in England?

COUNSELLOR HAMILTON: Why, what name dare she go by but Dogherty?

O'DOGHERTY: Dogherty! —— ogho —— upon my honour she startles when she hears the name of Dogherty, and blushes, and is as much ashamed as if a man had spoke bawdy to her. —— No, no, my dear, she is no longer the plain, modest, good-natured, domestic, obedient Irish Mrs. O'Dogherty, but the travelled, rampant, high-lif'd, prancing English Mrs. Diggerty.

COUNSELLOR HAMILTON: Ha, ha, ha! Mrs. Diggerty! ridiculous!

O'DOGHERTY: Ay, ridiculous indeed! to change her name —— was there ever such impertinence? But do you know, brother, among the rest of your sister's whims and madnesses, that she is turned a great politician too concerning my name.

COUNSELLOR HAMILTON: Ha, ha, ha! a

1. A cattle and horse fair still held in Ballinasloe, Co. Galway. Note how Macklin uses local details in the manner that later became such a characteristic of the dialogue in J. M. Synge's plays.
2. A topical reference to the coronation of George III in 1761.
3. (colloquialism) no inhabitant.
4. St Patrick's Hospital in Dublin, founded on the bequest of Jonathan Swift (1667-1745). cf. Swift's own lines:
   He gave the little Wealth he had,
   To build a House for Fools and Mad:
   And shew'd by one satyric Touch,
   No Nation wanted it so much.
5. The reader should remember that Counsellor Hamilton is Mrs O'Dogherty's brother.
6. A Dublin cart. Glassmanogue was the name of a district on the north side of Dublin city.

politician! —— Why how in the name of wonder and common sense can politics and the name of Dogherty be connected?

O'DOGHERTY: O it's a wonder indeed! —— but strange as it is, they are connected —— but very ridiculously as you may imagine.

COUNSELLOR HAMILTON: But, prithee, by what means?

O'DOGHERTY: Why, you must know, we are to have an election shortly for the county that I live in, which young Lord Turnabout wants to carry for one of his own gang; and as the election in a great measure depends upon my interest, the young fox, knowing the conceit and vanity of my wife, has taken her by her favourite foible, and tickled it up, by telling her that if I direct my interest properly, it would not be difficult to procure me a title. Now, sir, this piece of flattery has stirred up such a rage of quality and title in her giddy head, that I cannot rest night or day for her importunity —— in short, she would have me desert my friends, and sell myself, my honour, and my country, as several others have done before me, merely for a title, only that she may take place of a parcel of foolish idle women, and sink the antient name of Dogherty in the upstart title of Lady Thingum, my Lady Fiddle Faddle, or some such ridiculous nonsense.

COUNSELLOR HAMILTON: But, sir, pray pause a little upon this business —— my sister's vanity, I grant you, may be ridiculous —— but though you despise titles and ostentation, yet, as your interest can certainly make the member, were I in your circumstances, I would have a voice in the senate of my country —— go into parliament for the county yourself.

O'DOGHERTY: Ogh, I have been among them already, and I know them all very well. What signifies my sitting among hundreds of people with my single opinion all alone. When I was there before I was stigmatized as a singular blockhead, an impracticable fellow, only because I would not consent to sit like an image, and when the master of the puppets pulled the string of my jaw on one side, to say aye, and on t'other side, to say no, and to leap over a stick backwards and forwards, just as the faction of party and jobbers, and leaders, and political adventurers directed —— ah, brother, brother, I have done with them all —— oh, I have done with them all.

COUNSELLOR HAMILTON: What, and after all your expence of opposing government right or wrong, and supporting your patriots, will you give them all up?

O'DOGHERTY: Indeed I will —— I was patriot mad I own, like a great many other fools in this distracted country —— sir, I was so mad that I hated the very name of a courtier as much as an illiterate lay-swaddling methodist does that of a regular clergyman. But I am cured of that folly; for now I find that a courtier is just as honest a man as a patriot —— my dear, they are both made of the same stuff; ah, I have at last found out what sort of an animal a patriot is.

COUNSELLOR HAMILTON: Ay! —— and pray, brother, what sort of an animal is he?

O'DOGHERTY: Why, he is a sort of a political weathercock, that is blown about by every wind of society, which the foolish people are always looking up at, and staring, and distracting themselves with the integrity of its vicissitudes —— to-day it is blown by the rough, rattling, tempest of party; next day by the trade-wind of sly, subtle, veering faction; then by the headlong hurricane of the people's hot foggy breath; huzza boys, down with the courtier, up with the patriot, 'till at last the smooth, soft, gentle warm breeze of interest blows upon it, and from that moment it rusts to a point, and never stirs after —— so there is your puff patriot for you —— ogh, to the devil I pitch them all.

COUNSELLOR HAMILTON: Ha, ha, ha! I am glad to find, brother, that you are come to that way of thinking at last, and I wish you had had the same notions years ago, it would have saved you many thousands.

O'DOGHERTY: Indeed, and that it would —— however experience is an excellent tutor, and as you are a young man, and just coming into the world, mine may be of some service to you; take this judgment from me then, and remember that an honest quiet country gentleman who out of policy and humanity establishes manufactories, or that contrives employment for the idle and the industrious, or that makes but a blade of corn grow where there was none before,[7] is of more use to this poor country than all the courtiers, and patriots, and politicians, and prodigals that are unhanged; —— so there let us leave them and return to my wife's business.

COUNSELLOR HAMILTON: With all my heart, I long to have a particular account of her conduct. . . .

7. An echo of a famous passage from *Gulliver's Travels*, II, vii.

[Mrs O'Dogherty, who prefers to be known as Mrs Diggerty, displays her superior refinement to her husband and brother, while her prospective English lover, Mushroom, who —— as the name implies —— is an upstart, applauds her taste.]

Enter MRS DIGGERTY *and* MUSHROOM

MRS DIGGERTY: Brother, I am veestly[1] glad to see you.

COUNSELLOR HAMILTON: Welcome from England, sister.

MRS DIGGERTY: I am imminsely obligated to you, brother.

COUNSELLOR HAMILTON: I hope it answered your expectation, sister.

MRS DIGGERTY: Transcendantly.

COUNSELLOR HAMILTON: I am glad it pleased you.

MRS DIGGERTY: Ravishingly.

COUNSELLOR HAMILTON: Indeed!

MRS DIGGERTY: Beyond all degrees of compirison.

O'DOGHERTY: O yes —— beyond all degrees of compirison.

MRS DIGGERTY: Veest! imminse! extatic! I never knew life before —— every thing there is high, tip top, the grand monde, the bun tun —— and quite teesty.

O'DOGHERTY: O yes, every thing there is quite teesty, brother.

MRS DIGGERTY: Well, Count, do you know that you pleased me veestly last night; I never saw you in such high humour —— brother, I believe you do not know Mr. Mushroom, an English gentleman; pray let me have the honour of introducing him to you.

COUNSELLOR HAMILTON: I have had that honour already, sister.

MUSHROOM: Yes, madam, Hamilton and I are old acquaintance.

O'DOGHERTY: O yes they are old acquaintance, they have known each other above these two minutes.

COUNSELLOR HAMILTON: Pray how do you like London, sister?

MRS DIGGERTY: O the place of the world, brother.

COUNSELLOR HAMILTON: Then Dublin I suppose ——

1. vastly. Macklin reproduces Mrs O'Dogherty's 'refined' pronunciation throughout this scene.

MRS DIGGERTY: O, dear brother, don't neem them together.

O'DOGHERTY: O no, you must not neem them together.

MRS DIGGERTY: Upon my honour, Dublin, after seeing London, looks like Irish-Town or Ring's-End:[2] Oh, every thing I set my eyes on here gives me the ennui, and the countre cure.

O'DOGHERTY: O yes, every thing here gives her the contre coeur; that is a disease she has brought over with her from London that we know nothing of here.

MRS DIGGERTY: The streets are so narrow, the houses so dirty, and the people so ridiculous! then the women, Count! ha, ha, ha! —— I can't help laughing when I think of them. Well, I am convinced that the women of this here country who have never travelled, have nothing of that —— a —— a —— non-chalance, and that jenny-see-quee[3] that we have in London.

O'DOGHERTY: O no, brother! the women have nothing of that jenny-see-quee, that she has brought over with her from London.

MRS DIGGERTY: But, Mushroom —— I don't know if what I am going to tell you be conceit[4] or real; but, upon my honour, when I first came from England —— you must know, brother, I came over in the picket.[5]

O'DOGHERTY: O yes, brother, she came over in the picket.

MRS DIGGERTY: Yes, sir, I came over in the picket, and we had a great orage —— I don't believe, Mr Diggerty, you know what an orage is.

O'DOGHERTY: Indeed you may take your oath I don't, my dear.

MRS DIGGERTY: That is, sir, becase you have not been in foreign parts —— then I will tell you what an orage is —— sir, an orage is a storum.[6]

O'DOGHERTY: Madam, I thank you for your intelligence[7] —— indeed you are very learned and very obliging.

MRS DIGGERTY: And so, as I was saying, Count, we had a great storum, and the picket —— I shall never forget it —— the picket landed us about

2. Villages on the south side of Dublin bay, now part of Dublin city.
3. *Je ne sais quoi*: (literally) 'I don't know what': the indefinable grace of style.
4. imagined.
5. The packet or ferry between Dublin and England (or Wales).
6. storm. The pronunciation is perhaps less refined than she imagines. cf. the pronunciation 'fillum' for 'film' in modern Ireland.
7. information.

twenty miles from Dublin —— and so, do you know, I say, Mushroom, that I fancied, being just come from England, that the very dogs here when they barked, had the brogue, ha, ha, ha!

OMNES: Ha, ha, ha!

MUSHROOM: Why then, by all that's gothic, madam, I have thought so a thousand times.

MRS DIGGERTY: You have!

MUSHROOM: I have, upon honour.

MRS DIGGERTY: Have you ever observed it, brother? Mr Diggerty, what do you think? Hav'n't the dogs of this here country the brogue?

O'DOGHERTY: Indeed and that they have, my dear, and the cows too, and the sheep, and the bullocks, and that as strong as ever your own mother had it, who was an O'Gallagher.

MRS DIGGERTY: Oh!

O'DOGHERTY: Not two of whose ancestors could ever speak three words of English to be understood.

MRS DIGGERTY: You are a strange rude man, Mr Diggerty, to tell me of my mother's family —— you know I always despised my mother's family —— I hate the very name of Gallagher, and all the old Irish whatever.

COUNSELLOR HAMILTON: The present company excepted, sister —— your husband, you know ——

MRS DIGGERTY: O, I never think of him.

COUNSELLOR HAMILTON: Ha, that's polite indeed.

O'DOGHERTY: O no, she never thinks of me.

COUNSELLOR HAMILTON: Well, but sister, you have given us no account of the coronation, no doubt you were there. . . .

ACT II

[A chastened wife is reminded of the dignity of her native, Irish origins.]

KATTY and O'DOGHERTY *without*

O'DOGHERTY: I shall be in here with the counsellor, Katty, and the moment he comes, bring me word.

KATTY: I shall, sir.

COUNSELLOR HAMILTON: Here your husband comes.

MRS DIGGERTY: I am ashamed to see him.

Enter O'DOGHERTY

O'DOGHERTY: Well, brother, have you spoke to her?

COUNSELLOR HAMILTON: There she is, sir —— and as she should be —— bathed in the tears of humility and repentance.

O'DOGHERTY: Ogh! I am sorry to see this[1] indeed —— I am afraid you have gone too far. If I had been by, I assure you, brother, you should not have made her cry. —— Yerrow, Nancy, child, turn about, and don't be crying there.

MRS DIGGERTY: Sir, I am asham'd to see your face —— my errors I acknowledge —— and for the future ——

O'DOGHERTY: Pooh, pooh —— I will have no submissions nor acknowledgments; if you have settled every thing with your brother, that is sufficient.

MRS DIGGERTY: I hope he is satisfied —— and it shall be the business of my life ——

O'DOGHERTY: Pooh, pooh! say no more I tell you, but come, give me a kiss, and let us be friends at once —— there —— so, in that kiss, now, let all tears and uneasiness subside with you, as all fears and resentment shall die with me.

COUNSELLOR HAMILTON: Come, sister, give me your hand, for I must have my kiss of peace too. I own I have been a little severe with you, but your disease required sharp medicines.

O'DOGHERTY: Now we are friends, Nancy, I have a favour or two to beg of you.

MRS DIGGERTY: Pray, command them.

O'DOGHERTY: Why, then, the first thing that I ask, is, that you will send away that French rascal the cook, with his compots and combobs, his alamodes and aladobes, his crapandoes and frigandoes, and a thousand outlandish kickshaws,[2] that I am sure were never designed for Christian food; and let the good rough rumps of beef, the jolly surloins, the geese and turkies, cram fowls, bacon and greens; and the pies, puddings and pasties, that used to be perfectly shoving one another off of[3] the table, so that there was not room for the people's plates; with a fine large cod too, as big as a young alderman —— I say, let all those French kickshaws be banished from my table, and these good old Irish dishes be put in their places; and then the poor every day will have something to eat.

MRS DIGGERTY: They shall, sir.

O'DOGHERTY: And as to yourself, my dear

1. Mrs O'Dogherty is, presumably, in floods of tears.
2. fancy dishes.
3. off (Irish usage).

Nancy, I hope I shall never have any more or your London English; none of your this here's, your that there's, your winegars, your weals, your vindors, your toastesses, and your stone postesses; but let me have our own good plain, old Irish English, which I insist upon is better than all the English English that ever coquets and coxcombs brought into the land.

MRS DIGGERTY: I will get rid of these as fast as possible.

O'DOGHERTY: And pray, above all things, never call me Mr Diggerty —— my name is Murrogh O'Dogherty, and I am not ashamed of it; but that damn'd name Diggerty always vexes me whenever I hear it.

MRS DIGGERTY: Then, upon my honour, Mr O'Dogherty, it shall never vix you again.

O'DOGHERTY: Ogh, that's right, Nancy —— O'Dogherty for ever —— O'Dogherty! —— there's a sound for you —— why they have not such a name in all England as O'Dogherty —— nor as any of our fine sounding Milesian[4] names —— what are your Jones and your Stones, your Rice and your Price, your Heads and your Foots, and Hands and your Wills, and Hills and Mills, and Sands, and a parcel of little pimping names that a man would not pick out of the street, compared to the O'Donovans, O'Callaghans, O'Sullivans, O'Brallaghans, O'Shaghnesses, O'Flahertys, O'Gallaghers, and O'Doghertys, —— Ogh, they have courage in the very sound of them, for they come out of the mouth like a storm; and are as old and as stout as the oak at the bottom of the bog of Allen, which was there before the flood —— and though they have been dispossessed by upstarts and foreigners, buddoughs and sassanoughs,[5] yet I hope they will flourish in the Island of Saints, while grass grows or water runs.

4. pre-Christian. The Milesians were one of the earliest groups to invade Ireland.
5. (Irish) *bodaigh agus Sassanaigh* (oafs and Englishmen).

ARTHUR MURPHY

(1727-1805)

from:
ALL IN THE WRONG
(1761)

[Although later eclipsed by Goldsmith and Sheridan, Arthur Murphy was very highly regarded in his own day as a writer of comedy. He had a gift for presenting farcical situations, extended to breaking point, thereby revealing and mocking human frailty and folly. He had no time for sentimentalism and belonged instead to what has been called the 'laughing tradition'. This means that he was firmly on the side of the older, more vigorous style of comedy of Ben Jonson and William Congreve: indeed, comedy of humours combined with comedy of manners was what Murphy offered as antidote to the sentimental variety.

All in the Wrong offers a good example of Murphy's style. Borrowing the theme of jealousy from Molière's farce, *Cocu Imaginaire*, he maximizes the complications it can cause by combining a married and an unmarried couple as victims. Making the woman, Lady Restless, jealous, as well as her husband, Sir John, exaggerates the situation nicely. The characterization is farcical rather than realistic; it is two-dimensional and eccentric, but the dialogue is very lively and naturalistic. The tendency of the action to swell from a negligible source to an almost disastrous crisis ('They have got into a rare puzzle', a servant comments in Act V) is typical of Murphy's comedy. In this respect he can be said not only to look back to Ben Jonson but forward to Lady Gregory.]

ACT I

The Park

Enter SIR JOHN RESTLESS *and* ROBERT, *from a House in the Side Scene*[1]

SIR JOHN: Sir John Restless! —— Sir John Restless! thou hast play'd the fool with a vengeance. —— What devil whispered thee to marry such a woman? —— Robert, —— you have been a faithful servant in my family, Robert, and I value you ——

1. The wings. A direction later in this scene makes clear that this was a practicable setting, with an upper window, perhaps similar to the scene designed by John Inigo Richards for Isaac Bickerstaffe's comic opera, *The Maid of the Mill* (1765), reproduced by Sybil Rosenfeld, *A Short History of Scene Design in Great Britain* (Oxford: Blackwell, 1973), p. 81.

Did your lady go out at this door here into the park, or did she go out at the street door? ——

ROBERT: This door, Sir.

SIR JOHN: Robert, I will never live in a house again that has two doors to it.

ROBERT: Sir!

SIR JOHN: I will give warning to my landlord instantly. — The eyes of Argus are not sufficient to watch the motions of a wife, where there is a street door, and a back door, to favour her escapes.

ROBERT: Upon my word, Sir, I wish — you will pardon my boldness, Sir, — I wish you would shake off this uneasiness that preys upon your spirits — It grieves me to the heart, — it does, indeed, Sir, to see you in this way — Banish your suspicions, Sir — you have conceived some strange aversion, I am afraid, to my lady, Sir.

SIR JOHN: No, Robert; no aversion — in spite of me I doat upon her still —

ROBERT: Then why will you not think generously, Sir, of the person you love? — my lady, I dare be sworn —

SIR JOHN: Is false to me. — That embitters my whole life — I love her, and she repays me with ingratitude, with perfidy, — with falsehood, — with —

ROBERT: I dare be sworn, Sir, she is a woman of honour.

SIR JOHN: Robert, I have considered you as a friend in my house — Don't you betray me too — Don't justify her — don't —

ROBERT: Dear Sir, if you will but give me leave — you have been an indulgent master to me, and I am only concerned for your welfare — You married my lady for love, and I have heard you so warm in her praise — why will you go back from those sentiments? —

SIR JOHN: Yes, I married her for love — Oh! love! love! — What mischief dost thou not occasion in this world? — Yes, Robert, I married her for love. — When first I saw her I was not so much struck with her beauty, as with that air of an ingenuous mind that appeared in her countenance; — her features did not so much charm me with their symmetry, as that expression of sweetness, that smile that indicated affability, modesty, and compliance. — But, honest Robert, I was deceived — I was not a month married, when I saw her practising those very smiles at her glass — I saw thro' the artifice; plainly saw there was nothing natural in her manner, but all forced, all studied, put on with her head-dress — I was alarmed; I resolved to watch her from that moment, and I have seen such things —

ROBERT: Upon my word, Sir, I believe you wrong her, and wrong yourself — you build on groundless surmises; — you make yourself unhappy, and my lady too; and by being constantly uneasy, and never shewing her the least love, — you'll forgive me, Sir, — you fill her mind with strange suspicions, and so —

SIR JOHN: Suspicions, Robert!

ROBERT: Yes, Sir; strange suspicions! — My lady finds herself treated with no degree of tenderness; she infers that your inclinations are fixed elsewhere, and so she is become — you will pardon my blunt honesty — she is become downright jealous, — as jealous as yourself, Sir.

SIR JOHN: Oh! Robert, you are little read in the arts of women; you little know the intricacies of their conduct; the mazes thro' which they walk, shifting, turning, winding, running into devious paths, but tending all thro' a labyrinth to the temple of Venus; — you cannot see, Robert, that all her pretences to suspect me of infidelity are merely a counter-plot to cover her own loose designs; — 'tis but a gauze-covering, tho'. — it is seen thro' and only serves to shew her guilt the more.

ROBERT: Upon my word, Sir John, I cannot see.

SIR JOHN: No, Robert; I know you can't — her suspicions of me all make against her; they are but female stratagems, and yet it is but too true that she still is near my heart. — Oh! Robert, Robert, when I have watched her at a play, or elsewhere, — when I have counted her oglings, and her whisperings, her stolen glances, and her artful leer, with the cunning of her sex, she has pretended to be as watchful of me — dissembling, false, deceitful woman!

ROBERT: And yet, I dare assure you.

SIR JOHN: No more; I am not to be deceived; I know her thoroughly, and now — now — has not she escaped out of my house, even now? —

ROBERT: But with no bad design.

SIR JOHN: I am the best judge of that — which way did she go? —

ROBERT: Across the Park, Sir — that way, Sir — towards the Horse-guards —[2]

SIR JOHN: Towards the Horse-guards! — there,

2. Horse Guards Parade, at the western extremity of St James's Park, where the Admiralty and other government offices are situated.

— there, — there — the thing is evident; — you may go in, Robert.

ROBERT: Indeed, Sir, I ——

SIR JOHN: Go in, I say: go in ——

ROBERT: There is no persuading him to his own good.

Exit

SIR JOHN *alone*

Gone towards the Horse-guards! — my head aches, — my forehead burns — I am cutting my horns[3] — Gone towards the Horse-guards! — I'll pursue her thither; if I find her, her usual artifice will fail her — the time, the place, will all inform against her. — Sir John! Sir John! you were a madman to marry such a woman.

Exit

Enter BEVERLEY *and* BELLMONT *at opposite Sides*

BEVERLEY: Ha! my dear Bellmont —

BELLMONT: Beverley! — I rejoice to see you.

BEVERLEY: Well! I suppose the same cause has brought us both into the Park; both come to sigh amorous vows in the friendly gloom of yonder walk; — Belinda keeps a perpetual war of love and grief, and hope and fear in my heart — and let me see — (*lays his hand on* BELLMONT*'s breast*) how fares all here? I fancy my sister is a little busy here —

BELLMONT: Busy! she makes a perfect riot there — not one wink the whole night — Oh! Clarissa, Clarissa! her form so animated! her eyes so —

BEVERLEY: Prithee! truce; I have not leisure to attend to her praise — a sister's praise too! Faith, the greatest merit I ever could see in Clarissa is, that she loves you freely and sincerely.

BELLMONT: And to be even with you, Sir, — your Belinda, upon my soul, notwithstanding all your lavish praises, her highest perfection, in my mind, is her sensibility to the merit of my friend.

BEVERLEY: Oh! Bellmont, don't talk profanely — Such a girl!

Scarce can I to heav'n excuse
The devotion which I use
Unto that adored dame;

But, my dear Bellmont, tell me honestly now, do you think she has ever betrayed the least regard for me? —

BELLMONT: How can you, Beverley, you that have such convincing proofs, how can you ask such a question — that uneasiness of yours,[4] that inquietude of mind —

BEVERLEY: Prithee now don't fix that character upon me —

BELLMONT: It is your character, my dear Beverley; and instead of enjoying the object before you, you are ever looking back to something past, or conjecturing about something to come, and are your own self-tormentor.

BEVERLEY: No, no, no; don't say so; I hate the very notion of such a temper: the thing is, when a man loves tenderly as I do, sollicitude and anxiety are natural; and when Belinda's father opposes my warmest wishes —

BELLMONT: Why yes, the good Mr. Blandford is willing to give her in marriage to me.

BEVERLEY: The senseless old dotard! —

BELLMONT: Thank you for the compliment! — and my father, the wise Sir William Bellmont ——

BEVERLEY: Is a tyrannical, positive, headstrong ——

BELLMONT: There again I thank you — But in short, the old couple, Belinda's father and mine, have both agreed upon the match, and they insist upon compliance from their children; so that, according to them, I am to be married off-hand to your mistress, and you and your sister, poor Clarissa, are to be left to shift for yourselves.

BEVERLEY: Racks and torment!

BELLMONT: Racks and torment! — Seas of milk and ships of amber, man! — we are sailing to our wished for harbour, in spite of their machinations — I have settled the whole affair with Clarissa.

BEVERLEY: Have you?

BELLMONT: I have, and to-morrow morning makes me possessor of her charms.

BEVERLEY: My dear boy, give us your hand; — and then, thou dear rogue, and then Belinda's mine — (*sings*), Loll-toll-loll ——

BELLMONT: Well may you be in raptures, Sir; for here, here, here they both come ——

Enter BELINDA, *and* CLARISSA

BEVERLEY: Grace was in all her steps; heav'n in her eye; In every gesture, dignity and love.

BELINDA: A poetical reception truly! — But can't your passion inspire you to a composition of your own, Mr. Beverley?

3. The old image persists of the cheated husband's being made identifiable by his horns. cf. Pinchwife in William Wycherley's *The Country Wife* (1675).

4. A characteristic later found also in Sheridan's Faulkland in *The Rivals*, possibly indebted to Murphy's characterization.

BEVERLEY: It inspires me with sentiments, Madam, which I can't find words to express. — Suckling,[5] Waller,[6] Landsdown,[7] and all our dealers in love-verses, give but a faint image of a heart touched like mine.

BELINDA: Poor Gentleman! what a terrible taking you are in! But if the sonneteers cannot give an image of you, Sir, have you had recourse to a painter, as you promised me ——

BEVERLEY: I have, Belinda, and here, — here is the humble portrait of your adorer.

BELINDA: (*Takes the Picture*) Well! there is a likeness — but after all, there is a better painter than this gentleman, whoever he be.

BEVERLEY: (*Aside*) A better! — now she is discontented. Where, Madam, can a better be found? — if money can purchase him ——

BELINDA: Oh! Sir, when he draws for money he never succeeds — But when pure inclination prompts him, then his colouring is warm indeed —— He gives a portrait that endears the original.

BEVERLEY: Such an artist is worth the Indies.

BELINDA: You need not go so far to seek him — he has done your business already — The limner I mean is a certain little blind god, called Love, and he has stamped such an impression of you here——

BEVERLEY: Madam, your most obedient, — and I can tell you, that the very same gentleman has been at work for you too.

BELLMONT: (*Who had been talking apart with Clarissa*) Oh! he has had a world of business upon his hands, for we two have been agreeing what havock he has made with us.

CLARISSA: Yes, but we are but in a kind of fool's paradise here; all our schemes are but mere castle-building, which your father, Mr. Bellmont, — and my dear Belinda, — yours too are most obstinately determined to destroy.

BELLMONT: Why as you say, they are determined that I shall have the honour of Belinda's hand in the country dance of matrimony.

BELINDA: Without considering that I may like another partner better ——

BEVERLEY: And without considering that I, forlorn as I am, and my sister, there — who is as well inclined to a matrimonial game of romps as any girl in Christendom, must both of us sit down, and lead apes in hell,[8] in spite of our strongest inclinations to mingle in the groupe.

BELLMONT: But we have planned our own happiness, and with a little resolution we shall be successful in the end, I warrant ye. — Clarissa, my angel, let us take a turn this way, and leave that love-sick pair to themselves — they are only fit company for each other, and we can find where-withal to entertain ourselves.

CLARISSA: Ay! let us turn this way.

BELINDA: What are you going to leave us, Clarissa?

CLARISSA: Only just sauntering into this side-walk — we shan't lose one another.

BELINDA: Oh! you are such a tender couple — you are not tired I see of saying pretty soft things to each other. — Well! well! take your own way.

CLARISSA: And if I guess right, you are glad to be left together — Belinda.

BELINDA: Who I? —

CLARISSA: You, my dear ——

BELINDA: Not I truly — let us walk together.

CLARISSA: No, no, by no means — you shall be indulged — adieu! — we shall be within call.

Exeunt BELLMONT *and* CLARISSA

BEVERLEY: My sister is frankly in love with Bellmont — (*Aside*) I wish Belinda would act as openly towards me. — I wish she has not a lurking inclination for Bellmont.

BELINDA: Well, Sir! — Thoughtful! — Oh! I'll call Mr. Bellmont back, if that is the case.

BEVERLEY: (*Aside*) She will call Mr. Bellmont back.

BELINDA: Well, Sir; am I to entertain you, or you me? ——

BEVERLEY: Madam! ——

BELINDA: Madam! — ha! ha! why you look as if you were frightened — are you afraid of being left alone with me? ——

BEVERLEY: Oh! Belinda, you know that is the happiness of my life; — but ——

BELINDA: But what, Sir? ——

BEVERLEY: I am afraid I have done something to offend you.

5. Sir John Suckling (1609-42), cavalier poet and dramatist.
6. Edmund Waller (1606-87), poet.
7. George Granville, lord Lansdown (*c.* 1667-1735). Compared to Suckling and Waller, a very minor figure indeed. Samuel Johnson included him without enthusiasm in his *The Lives of the Most Eminent Poets*, commenting, 'He seems to have had no ambition above the imitation of Waller.'

8. A proverb: unmarried girls, i.e. old maids, were doomed to lead apes in hell. cf. Beatrice's rejection of marriage and her acceptance that she will 'even take sixpence in earnest of the bearward [keeper] and lead his apes into hell', *Much Ado About Nothing*, II.1. 36-37.

BELINDA: To offend me! ——

BEVERLEY: Yes, Belinda; I should have been of the party last night; I own I should; it was a sufficient inducement for me that you was to be there; it was my fault, and you I see are piqued at it.

BELINDA: I piqued!

BEVERLEY: I see you are; and you was so last night too — I have heard it all, and in mere resentment you directed all your discourse to Mr. Bellmont.

BELINDA: If I did, it was merely accidental.

BEVERLEY: No, it was deliberately done; — forgive my rash folly in refusing the invitation — I meant no manner of harm ——

BELINDA: Who imagines you did, Sir?

BEVERLEY: I beg your pardon, Belinda, you take offence too lightly ——

BELINDA: Ha! ha! what have you taken into your head now? — this uneasiness is of your own making — I have taken nothing ill, Sir ——

BEVERLEY: You could not but take it ill; but by all that's amiable about you, I meant not to incur your displeasure — forgive that abrupt answer I sent — I should have made a handsomer apology.

BELINDA: Apology! — what occasion was there for any thing more? — you said you was pre-engaged, did not you?

BEVERLEY: I said so; I own it, and beg your pardon ——

BELINDA: Beg my pardon! for what? ha! ha!

BEVERLEY: I only meant ——

BELINDA: Ha! ha! can you think I see any thing in your message to be offended at, Sir?

BEVERLEY: Where you were concerned, I own I should have expressed myself with more delicacy, than those hasty words. I am engaged, and can't wait upon you to-night. I should have told you that my heart was with you, though necessity dragged me another way — but this omission you resented — I could learn, since, the spirits you were in the whole evening, though I enjoyed nothing in your absence — I could hear the sallies of your wit, the sprightliness of your conversation, and on whom your eyes were fixed the whole night.

BELINDA: They were fixed upon Mr. Bellmont, you think!

BEVERLEY: Ay! and fixed with delight upon him; seemed negociating the business of love before the whole company.

BELINDA: Upon my word, Sir, whoever is your author, he has misinformed you; and let me tell you, you alarm me with these fancies, and you know I have often told you that you are of too refining a temper — you create for yourself imaginary misunderstandings, and then are ever entering into explanations — I assure you, Mr. Beverley, this watching for intelligence, from the spies and misrepresenters of conversation, betrays the symptoms of jealousy, and I would not be married to a jealous man for the world.

BEVERLEY: (*Aside*) Now she is seeking occasion to break off. — Jealousy, Ma'am, can never get admission into my breast, I am of too generous a temper; a certain delicacy[9] I own I have; I value the opinion of my friends, and when there are circumstances of a doubtful aspect, I am glad to set things in their true light; — and surely, Belinda, if I do so with others, surely with you on whom my happiness depends to desire a favourable interpretation of my words and actions ——

BELINDA: But these little humours[10] may grow up, and gather into the fixed disease of Jealousy at last. — (LADY RESTLESS *crosses the stage, and rings a bell at the door*) And there now, — there goes a lady who is a victim to her own fretful imagination ——

BEVERLEY: Who is the lady pray?

BELINDA: My lady Restless; — walk this way, and I will give you her whole character — I am not acquainted with her ladyship, but I have heard much of her — this way — this way ——

Exeunt BELINDA *and* BEVERLEY

LADY RESTLESS: (*Ringing at the door*)[11] What do these servants mean? — there is something going forward here — I will be let in or I will know the reason why — (*rings again*) but in the mean time, Sir John can let any body he pleases out at the street door — I'll run up the steps here,[12] and observe.

Exit

TATTLE *opens the door,* MARMALET *follows her*

TATTLE: Who rang this bell? — I don't see any body — and yet I am sure the bell rung — Well, Mrs. Marmalet, you will be going, I see.

MARMALET: Yes, Mrs. Tattle; I must be going; I'll run across the Park, and I shall soon get to

9. It is obviously closer to what Belinda calls 'too refining a temper'. This is the fault Hugh Kelly explores in depth in *False Delicacy*, below.

10. In the older sense of 'inclinations, obsessions', as in Ben Jonson's *Every Man in His Humour* (1598).

11. Obviously, a real bell was hung on the side scene (see opening stage direction and note 1 above).

12. The steps may have been painted on the wings, since Lady Restless actually exits here.

Grosvenor-Square — when shall I see you at our house?

TATTLE: Oh! the Lord knows when I shall be able to get out — my lady leads us all such lives — Oh! I wish I had such another place as you have of it.

MARMALET: Heaven be praised! I have nothing to complain of.

TATTLE: No, that you have not: Lord! when shall I get such a gown as that you have on by my lady — She will never fling off such a thing, and give it to a poor servant. — Worry, worry, worry herself, and every body else too ——

Re-enter LADY RESTLESS

LADY RESTLESS: No; there is nobody stirring that way — what do I see? — a hussy coming out of my house!

MARMALET: Well, I must be gone, Mrs. Tattle — fare you well ——

LADY RESTLESS: She is dizened[13] out too! Madam is! why did not you open the door, Tattle, when I rung?

TATTLE: I came as soon as possible, madam.

LADY RESTLESS: Who have you with you here? (*To* MARMALET) what is your business, mistress?

MARMALET: My business, madam!

LADY RESTLESS: In confusion too! — the case is plain — you come here after Sir John, I suppose ——

MARMALET: I come after Sir John, madam!

LADY RESTLESS: Guilt in her face! yes, after Sir John; and Tattle, you are in the plot against me; you were favouring her escape, were you?

TATTLE: I favour her escape, madam! — there is no occasion for that. — This is Mrs. Marmalet, madam, an acquaintance of mine, madam, that is come to see me ——

LADY RESTLESS: Oh! very fine, mistress! you bring your creatures after the vile man, do you?

MARMALET: I assure you, madam, I am a very honest girl ——

LADY RESTLESS: Oh! I dare say so — where did you get that gown?

MARMALET: La! ma'am — I came by it honestly — my lady Conquest gave it to me — I live with my lady Conquest, madam ——

LADY RESTLESS: What a complexion she has! — how long have you lived in London?

MARMALET: Three years, madam.

LADY RESTLESS: In London three years with that complexion! it can't be — but perhaps she is painted — all these creatures paint — you are all so many painted dolls (*rubs her face with a white handkerchief*) no — it does not come off — so, Mrs. Tattle, you bring your fresh country girls here to my house, do you?

TATTLE: Upon my credit, ma'am ——

LADY RESTLESS: Don't tell me — I see thro' this affair — Go you about your business, mistress, and let me never see you about my doors again — go — go ——

MARMALET: Lord, ma'am I shan't trouble your house — Mrs. Tattle, a good day — here's a deal to do, indeed — I have as good a house as her's to go to.

Exit

LADY RESTLESS: There, there, there; — see there; — she goes off in a huff! the way with them all — ay! I see how it is, Tattle, — you false, ungrateful — that gown was never given her by a woman — she had that from Sir John. — Where is Sir John?

TATTLE: Sir John an't at home, ma'am.

LADY RESTLESS: Where is he? — where is he gone? — when did he go out?

TATTLE: I really don't know, ma'am ——

LADY RESTLESS: Tattle, I know you fib now — But I'll sift this to the bottom — I'll write to my Lady Conquest to know the truth about that girl that was here but now.

TATTLE: You will find I told you truth, madam.

LADY RESTLESS: Very well, Mrs. Pert, — I'll go and write this moment, — send Robert to me to give me an account of his master — Sir John, Sir John, you will distract me ——

Exeunt

Re-enter BELINDA *and* BEVERLEY

BELINDA: Ay! but that quickness, and that extreme sensibility is what I am afraid of. — I positively would not have a jealous husband for the world ——

BEVERLEY: By heaven! no earthly circumstances shall ever make me think injuriously of you — Jealousy! — ha! ha! — it is the most ridiculous passion — ha! ha!

BELINDA: You may laugh, Sir; but I know your over-refining temper too well, and I absolutely will have it in our marriage-articles,[14] that I must not be

13. decked, adorned. Spelled 'dizoned' in the first edition, London, 1761.

14. The following exchange brings to mind William Congreve's famous *proviso* scene between Millamant and Mirabell in *The Way of the World* (1700), IV.v.

plagued with your suspicions.

BEVERLEY: I subscribe, ma'am ——

BELINDA: I will have no enquiries where I am going to visit; no following me from place to place; and if we should chance to meet, and you should perceive a man of wit, or a pretty fellow, speaking to me, I will not have you fidgeting about on your chair, knitting your brow, and looking at your watch — 'My dear, is it not time to go home? — my love, the coach is waiting:' — and then, if you are prevailed upon to stay, I will not have you converse with a 'yes, Sir,' and a 'no, Sir,' for the rest of the evening, and then wrangle with me in the chariot all the way home, and not be commonly civil to me for the rest of the night — I positively will have none of this ——

BEVERLEY: Agreed, ma'am, agreed ——

BELINDA: And then you shan't tell me you are going out of town, and then sneak in privately to the play, or to Ranelagh,[15] merely to be a spy upon me — and I positively will admit no curiosity about my letters — if you were to open a letter of mine, I should never forgive you — I do verily believe, if you were to open my letters I should hate you ——

BEVERLEY: I subscribe to every thing you can ask — you shall have what female friends you please; lose your money to whom you please; dance with what beau you please; ride out with whom you please; go to what china shop you please; and, in short, do what you please, without my attempting to bribe your footman, or your maid to —

BELINDA: Oh! lud! Oh! lud! that is in the very strain of jealousy — Heaven deliver me! — there is my father yonder, and Sir William Bellmont with him — Fly — this instant, fly, Mr. Beverley, down that walk — any where ——

BEVERLEY: You promise then ——

BELINDA: Don't talk to me now — what would you be at? — I am yours, and only yours; unalterably so — Fly — Mr. Beverley, be gone, and leave me ——

BEVERLEY: I obey, madam — I am gone.

Exit

BELINDA: Now are they putting their wise heads together to thwart all my schemes of happiness — but love, imperious love, will have it otherwise ——

Enter MR. BLANDFORD *and* SIR WILLIAM

MR. BLANDFORD: Sir William, since we have agreed upon every thing ——

SIR WILLIAM: Why yes, Mr. Blandford, I think every thing is settled ——

MR. BLANDFORD: Why then we have only to acquaint the young people with our intentions, and to conclude the affair ——

SIR WILLIAM: That is all, Sir.

MR. BLANDFORD: As to my girl, I don't mind her nonsense about Beverley — she must do as I will have her.

SIR WILLIAM: And my son too, he must follow my directions. — As to his telling me of his love for Clarissa, it is all a joke to me — Children must do as their Parents will have them.[16]

MR. BLANDFORD: Ay! ay! so they must; and so they shall — hey! here is my daughter — So Belinda! — well, my girl, Sir William and I have agreed, and so you are to prepare for Marriage, that's all ——

BELINDA: Marriage with Mr. Beverley, Sir?

MR. BLANDFORD: Mr. Beverley!

BELINDA: You know you encouraged him yourself, Sir ——

MR. BLANDFORD: Well, well! I have changed my mind on that head — my friend, Sir William, here offers you his son — do as I would have you — have a care, Belinda —

BELINDA: But, Sir ——

MR. BLANDFORD: But, madam, I will be obeyed —— You don't like him, you say — but I like him — and that's sufficient for you ——

SIR WILLIAM: And so it is, Mr. Blandford; — if my son pretended to have a will of his own, I should let him know to the contrary ——

BELINDA: And can you, Sir William, against our inclination force us both?

MR. BLANDFORD: Hold your tongue, Belinda; don't provoke me — What makes you from home? go your ways back to Queen's-Square directly, and settle your mind; for I tell you once for all I will have my own way. —— Come, Sir William, we will step to the lawyer's chambers. —— Go home, Belinda, and be observant of my commands. —— Come along, Sir William — what did you say? — you mutiny, do you? — don't provoke me — You know, Belinda, I am an odd sort of a man when provok'd — Look ye here — mind what I say; I won't reason with you about the matter; my power is absolute, and if you offer to rebel, you shall have

15. The site of pleasure gardens in London.

16. The starting-point of most comedies lies in the unacceptability of this 'law' to the children themselves.

no husband at all with my consent — I'll cut you off with a shilling;[17] I'll see you starve — beg an alms — live miserable — die wretched —— in short, suffer any calamity without the least compassion from me —— if I should find you an undutiful girl at last — so there's one word for all ——

Exeunt[18]

BELINDA: What will become of me? — his inhumanity overcomes me quite — I can never consent —the very sight of this picture is enough to forbid it —— Oh! Beverley, — you are the master of my heart — I'll go this instant — and — heavens! I can scarce move.

Enter SIR JOHN

SIR JOHN: No tidings of her far or near ——

BELINDA: How I tremble! I shall fall — no help ——

SIR JOHN: What do I see! — a young lady in distress!

BELINDA: Oh! — (*faints in his arms, and drops the picture*)

SIR JOHN: She is fallen into a fit — Would my servants were in the way.

LADY RESTLESS: (*At her Window*) Where can this barbarous man be gone to? — Ha! — under my very window!

SIR JOHN: How cold she is! (*lays his hand to her cheek*) — quite cold.

LADY RESTLESS: How familiar he is with her!

SIR JOHN: And yet she looks beautiful still.

LADY RESTLESS: Does she so?

SIR JOHN: Her eyes open — how lovely they look!

LADY RESTLESS: Traitor!

SIR JOHN: Her cheek begins to colour — well, young lady, how fare you now? — my dear.

LADY RESTLESS: My dear, too.

BELINDA: Heavens! where am I? — In a strange gentleman's arms all this time!

SIR JOHN: Repose yourself there, or will you step into my house?

LADY RESTLESS: No, truly, shan't she — vile man! — But I will spoil your sport — I will come down to you directly, and flash confusion in your face.

Exit from above

SIR JOHN: Where do you live, madam?

BELINDA: In Queen's-Square, Sir.

SIR JOHN: I will wait upon you — trust yourself with me — you look much better now. — Lean on my arm — there, there, I will conduct you.

Exeunt

Enter LADY RESTLESS

LADY RESTLESS: Now I'll make one among ye, — ha! fled! gone! which way? — is not that he, yonder? — no — he went into my house, I dare say, as I came down stairs. —— Tattle, Tattle, Robert, — will nobody answer.

Enter TATTLE

LADY RESTLESS: Where is Sir John?

TATTLE: La! ma'am, how should I know?

LADY RESTLESS: Did not he go in this moment?

TATTLE: No, ma'am.

LADY RESTLESS: To be sure you say so — I'll follow him thro' the world, or I'll find him out — so, so — what is here? — this is her picture, I suppose — I will make sure of this at least — this will discover her to me, tho' she has escaped now — The cruel, false, deceitful man!

Exit

TATTLE: Poor lady! I believe her head is turned, for my part. — Well! I am determined I'll look out for another place, that's a sure thing I will.

Exit

ACT II

In SIR JOHN's *House*

Enter SIR JOHN *and* ROBERT

SIR JOHN: Robert, where is your lady?

ROBERT: In her own room, Sir.

SIR JOHN: Any body with her?

ROBERT: I can't say, Sir — my lady is not well.

SIR JOHN: Not well! fatigued with rioting about this town, I suppose — how long has she been at home?

ROBERT: About an hour, Sir.

SIR JOHN: About an hour! — very well, Robert, you may retire — (*Exit* ROBERT) — now will I question her closely — so — so — so — she comes, leaning on her maid — finely dissembled! — finely dissembled! But this pretended illness shall not shelter her from my strict enquiry — Soft a moment! — If I could overhear what passes between 'em, it might lead to the truth — I'll work by stratagem — Oh! the hypocrite! how she acts her part!

Exit

Enter LADY RESTLESS *and* TATTLE

TATTLE: How are you now, madam?

LADY RESTLESS: Somewhat better, Tattle —

17. i.e. disinherit you.

18. So also the first edition, but presumably Blandford and Sir William *exeunt* together here.

reach that chair — Tattle, tell me honestly, does that girl live with Lady Conquest?

TATTLE: She does, madam, upon my veracity.

LADY RESTLESS: Very well! you will be obstinate, I see, but I shall know the truth presently; I shall have an answer from her ladyship, and then all will come out.

TATTLE: You will hear nothing, ma'am, but what I have told you already.

LADY RESTLESS: Tattle, Tattle, I took you up in the country in hopes gratitude would make you my friend — but you are as bad as the rest of them — conceal all you know, do; — it is of very little consequence — I now see through the whole affair — though it is the picture of a man — yet I am not to be deceived — I understand it all. — This is some former gallant — the creature gave this to Sir John, as a proof that she had no affection for any but himself. — What art he must have had to induce her to this! — I have found him out at last.

SIR JOHN: (*Peeping in*)[1] What does she say?

LADY RESTLESS: I have seen enough to convince me what a man he is — the fate of us poor women is hard — we all wish for husbands, and they are the torments of our lives.

TATTLE: There is too much truth in what you say, ma'am.

SIR JOHN: You join her, do you, Mrs. Iniquity?

LADY RESTLESS: What a pity it is, Tattle, that poor women should be under severer restraints than the men are!

SIR JOHN: You repine for want of freedom, do you?

LADY RESTLESS: Cruel laws of wedlock! — The tyrant-husband may triumph in his infidelity, may securely trample upon all laws of decency and order, and it redounds to his credit — gives him a fashionable air of vice, while a poor woman is obliged to submit to his cruelty —— and remains tied to him for life —— even though she has reason to entertain a mortal hatred for him.

SIR JOHN: Oh! very well argued, madam!

LADY RESTLESS: What a pity it is, Tattle, that we cannot change our husbands, as we do our ear-rings or our gloves!

SIR JOHN: There is a woman of spirit!

LADY RESTLESS: Tattle! will you own the truth to me about that girl?

1. From here until his entrance '*on tiptoe*' 52 lines later, Sir John comments half-hidden in the wings.

TATTLE: I really have told you the truth, madam.

LADY RESTLESS: You won't discover, I see — very well! — you may go down stairs ——

TATTLE: I assure your ladyship —

LADY RESTLESS: Go down stairs —

TATTLE: Yes, ma'am.

Exit

LADY RESTLESS: Would I had never seen my husband's face!

SIR JOHN: I am even with you — I have as good wishes for you, I assure you.

LADY RESTLESS: This picture here — Oh the base man!

SIR JOHN: The picture of her gallant, I suppose.

LADY RESTLESS: This is really a handsome picture — what a charming countenance! — It is perfumed I fancy — the scent is agreeable —

SIR JOHN: Oh! the jade, how eagerly she kisses it!

LADY RESTLESS: Why had not I such a dear, dear man, instead of the brute, the monster —

SIR JOHN: Monster! — She does not mince the matter, but speaks plain downright English — I must contain my rage, and steal upon her meditations — so — so — so ——

Enter on tiptoe

LADY RESTLESS: There is no falsehood in this look.

SIR JOHN: (*Looking over her shoulder*) Oh! what a handsome dog she has chosen for herself!

LADY RESTLESS: With you, I could be for ever happy —

SIR JOHN: You could, could you? (*Snatches the picture*)

LADY RESTLESS: (*Screams out*) Mercy on me! Oh! is it you, Sir?

SIR JOHN: Now, madam, now false one, have I caught you?

LADY RESTLESS: You are come home at last, I find, Sir.

SIR JOHN: My lady Restless, my lady Restless, what can you say for yourself now?

LADY RESTLESS: What can I say for myself, Sir John!

SIR JOHN: Ay! Madam! this picture —

LADY RESTLESS: Yes, Sir, that picture.

SIR JOHN: Will be an evidence —

LADY RESTLESS: Of your shame, Sir John.

SIR JOHN: Of my shame! — 'tis very true what she says; — yes, madam, it will be an evidence of my shame; I feel that but too sensibly; — but —

LADY RESTLESS: You own it then, do you?

SIR JOHN: Own it! I must own it, madam, though confusion cover me, I must own it; — it is what you have deserved at my hands —

LADY RESTLESS: I deserve it, Sir John! — but find excuses if you will — cruel, cruel man! — to make me this return at last — I cannot bear it — Oh! oh! *(Cries)*

SIR JOHN: Oh! you may weep; but your tears are lost; they will fall without effect. —— I now renounce you for ever — this picture will justify me to the wide world; it will shew what a base woman you have been.

LADY RESTLESS: What does the man mean?

SIR JOHN: The picture of your gallant, madam! — the darling of your amorous hours, — who gratifies your luxurious appetities abroad, and —

LADY RESTLESS: Scurrilous wretch! Oh! Sir, you are at your old stratagem I find, — recrimination, you think, will serve your turn.

SIR JOHN: It is a pity you know, madam, that a woman should be tied to a man for life, even though she has a mortal hatred for him.

LADY RESTLESS: Artful hypocrite!

SIR JOHN: That she can't change her husband as she does her ear-rings or her gloves.

LADY RESTLESS: Po! Sir John, this is your old device, this won't avail you.

SIR JOHN: Had the original of this fallen to your lot, you could kiss the picture for ever.

LADY RESTLESS: Oh! Sir John —

SIR JOHN: You can gloat upon it, madam, glue your very lips to it.

LADY RESTLESS: Shallow artifice!

SIR JOHN: With him you could be for ever happy.

LADY RESTLESS: This is all in vain, Sir John.

SIR JOHN: Had such a dear, dear man fallen to your lot, instead of the brute, the monster — Am I a monster? — I am, — and you have made me so — the world shall know your infamy.

LADY RESTLESS: Oh! brave it out, Sir, brave it out to the last — harmless, innocent man! — you have nothing to blush for, nothing to be ashamed of — you have no intrigues, no private amours abroad — I have not seen any thing, not I ——

SIR JOHN: Madam, I have seen, and I now see your paramour.

LADY RESTLESS: Oh! that air of confidence will be of great use to you, Sir — for you have no convenient to meet you under my very window, to loll softly in your arms —

SIR JOHN: Hey! how! —

LADY RESTLESS: Her arm thrown carelessly round your neck — your hand tenderly applied to her cheek.

SIR JOHN: *(Aside)* S'death! that's unlucky — she will turn it against me.

LADY RESTLESS: Oh! you are in confusion, are you, Sir? — but why should you? you meant no harm — 'You are safe with me, my dear — will you step into my house, my love?' — yes, Sir, you would fain bring her into my very house —

SIR JOHN: My Lady Restless, this evasion is mean and paultry — you beheld a young lady in distress.

LADY RESTLESS: Oh! I know it, Sir, — and you, tender-hearted man, could caress her out of meer compassion; — gaze wantonly on her out of charity, and, out of pure benevolence of disposition, convey her to come convenient dwelling — Oh! Sir John, Sir John —

SIR JOHN: Madam, this well-acted passion —

LADY RESTLESS: Don't imagine she has escaped me, Sir.

SIR JOHN: Oh! you may talk and rave, ma'am; but depend upon it, I shall spare no pains to do myself justice on this occasion — nor will I rest till —

LADY RESTLESS: Oh! fie upon you, Sir John; these artifices —

SIR JOHN: Nor will I rest, madam, until I have found, by means of this instrument here in my hand, who your darling is. I will go about straight — ungrateful, treacherous woman!

Exit

LADY RESTLESS: Yes, go now, under that pretext, in pursuit of your licentious pleasures. — This ever has been his scheme to cloak his wicked practices — abandoned man! — To face me down too, after what my eyes so plainly beheld — I wish I could wring that secret out of Tattle — I'll step to my own room directly, and try by menaces, by wheedling, by fair means, by foul means, by every means, to wrest it from her.

Exit

HUGH KELLY

(1739-77)

from: FALSE DELICACY (1768)

[Sentimental comedy, following its early development by Sir Richard Steele (see *The Conscious Lovers* above) in the early part of the eighteenth century, underwent a fresh influence in the 1760s. French refinement and the beginnings of French romanticism left their mark on English taste at this time. It would be a mistake, however, to think that English comedy was dominated by sentimentality; on the contrary, what Goldsmith was to call 'laughing comedy' continued to dominate the repertory of the two main London theatres. Sentimental comedy made an impact because, rather than in spite of, its concentration on lovers' distress, anguish and even tears; its gentility and artificiality, though narrowing the scope of comedy, had more appeal to the novel-reading public than to seasoned men of the theatre, such as Garrick.

Kelly's *False Delicacy* offers an excellent example of the new form of sentimental comedy. It deals with lovers sensitive and refined to a degree far beyond the native, robust traditions of English comedy. It seems plain from the text, however, that Kelly was not endorsing this new sensibility, or excess 'delicacy'. By showing the complications it could make in people's lives, he was mocking adherence to a code of behaviour that he exposed as 'false'. Thus Kelly had it both ways: he mocked what he presented as fashionable. So popular was his mix, so unerring his judgment of literary taste, that three thousand copies of his play were sold before 2 pm on the day of publication. No wonder Goldsmith, whose *The Good-Natur'd Man* (1768) was eclipsed by *False Delicacy*, conceived an inordinate dislike for Kelly and an exaggerated fear of the threat to his own, more vulgar, style of comedy.

In Act II, Lady Betty Lambton's 'delicacy' is defined: a widow, she has turned down Lord Winworth merely because she thought remarriage indelicate. Now, three years later, she has her regrets. Does he still love her and want her, however? Why else would he be trying to see her? The stuff of romance is somewhat punctured by the heroine's high-minded scruples, which may be morally admirable, but from the worldly point of view (always that of comedy) are also laughable. In this act she finds herself in a ridiculous situation of her own making.]

ACT II, SCENE 1

A Garden

Enter LADY BETTY and MRS. HARLEY

MRS. HARLEY: Lord, Lord, my dear, you're enough to drive one out of one's wits. — I tell you, again and again, he's as much yours as ever; and was I in your situation, he should be my husband to-morrow morning.

LADY BETTY: Dear Emmy, you mistake the matter strangely. — Lord Winworth is no common man, nor wou'd he have continued his silence so long upon his favourite subject; if he had the least inclination to renew his addresses. — His pride has justly taken the alarm at my insensibility, and he will not, I am satisfied, run the hazard of another refusal.

MRS. HARLEY: Why then, in the name of wonder, if he was so dear to you, cou'd you prodigally trifle with your own happiness, and repeatedly refuse him?

LADY BETTY: I have repeatedly told you because I was a fool, Emmy. — Till he withdrew his addresses I knew not how much I esteemed him; my unhappiness in my first marriage, you know, made me resolve against another. — And you are also sensible I have frequently argued that a woman of real delicacy shou'd never admit a second impression on her heart.

MRS. HARLEY: Yes, and I always thought you argued very foolishly. — I am sure I ought to know, for I have been twice married; — and though I lov'd my first husband very sincerely, there was not a woman in England who could have made the second a better wife. — Nay, for that matter, if another was to offer himself to-morrow, I am not altogether certain that I should refuse listening —

LADY BETTY: You are a strange creature.

MRS. HARLEY: And aren't you a much stranger, in declining to follow your own inclinations, when you cou'd have consulted them so highly, to the credit of your good sense, and the satisfaction of your whole family? — But it isn't yet too late; and if you will be advised by me every thing shall end as happily as you can wish.

LADY BETTY: Well, let me hear your advice.

MRS. HARLEY: Why this, then: — My Lord you know has requested that you wou'd indulge him with half an hour's private conversation some time this morning.

LADY BETTY: Well!

MRS. HARLEY: This is a liberty he hasn't taken

these three months — and he must design something by it; — now as he can design nothing but to renew his addresses, I wou'd advise you to take him at the very first word, for fear your delicacy, if it has time to consider, shou'd again shew you the strange impropriety of second marriages.

LADY BETTY: But suppose this should not be his business with me?

MRS. HARLEY: Why then we'll go another way to work: — I, as a sanguine friend[1] of my Lord's, can give him a distant hint of matters, exacting at the same time a promise of the most inviolable secrecy; and assuring him you wou'd never forgive me, if you had the least idea of my having acquainted him with so important a ——

LADY BETTY: And so you wou'd have me —?

MRS. HARLEY: Why not? — This is the very step I shou'd take myself, if I was in your situation.

LADY BETTY: May be so: — But it's a step which I shall never take. — What! wou'd you have me lost to all feeling? Wou'd you have me meanly make use of chambermaid artifices for a husband?

MRS. HARLEY: I would only have you happy my dear: — And where the man of one's heart is at stake I don't think we ought to stand so rigidly upon trifles.

LADY BETTY: Trifles, Emmy! do you call the laws of delicacy trifle? — She that violates these ——

MRS. HARLEY: Poh! poh! she that violates: — What a work there is with your sentimental folks — Why, don't I tell you that my Lord shall never know any thing of your concern in the design?

LADY BETTY: But shan't I know it myself, Emmy! — and how can I escape the justice of my own reflections!

MRS. HARLEY: Well, thank heav'n my sentiments are not sufficiently refin'd to make me unhappy.

LADY BETTY: I can't change my sentiments, my dear Emmy — nor wou'd I, if I cou'd. — Of this, however, be certain, that unless I have Lord Winworth without courting him, I shall never have him at all. — But be silent to all the world upon this matter I conjure you: — Particularly to Miss Marchmont;[2] for she has been so strenuous an advocate for my Lord, that the concealment of it from her might give her some doubts of my friendship; and I shou'd be continually uneasy for fear my reserve shou'd be consider'd as an indirect insult upon her circumstances.

MRS. HARLEY: Well, the devil take this delicacy; I don't know any thing it does besides making people miserable. — And yet somehow, foolish as it is, one can't help liking it. — But yonder I see Sir Harry and Mr. Cecil.

LADY BETTY: Let us withdraw then my dear; they may detain us; and till this interview is over, I shall be in a continual agitation; yet I am strangely apprehensive of a disappointment, Emmy — and if — (*going*).

MRS. HARLEY: Lady Betty.

LADY BETTY: What do you say?

MRS. HARLEY: Do you still think there is any thing extremely preposterous in second marriages?

LADY BETTY: You are intolerably provoking. —

Exeunt

ACT II, SCENE 2

[A little later, Lord Winworth tracks down Lady Betty, and she thinks he is going to propose once again.]

An apartment in LADY BETTY'S *house*

Enter LADY BETTY *and* MRS. HARLEY

LADY BETTY: You can't think, Emmy, how my spirits are agitated! — I wonder what my Lord can want with me?

MRS. HARLEY: Well, well, try and collect yourself a little — he is just coming up —— I must retire. —— Courage, my dear creature, this once —— and the day's our own, I warrant you.

Exit

Enter WINWORTH *bowing very low*

LADY BETTY: Here he is! — Bless me, what a flutter I am in!

WINWORTH: Your Ladyship's most obedient.

LADY BETTY: Won't your Lordship be seated? (*Aside*) He seems excessively confus'd.

WINWORTH: I have taken the liberty, Madam — (*Aside*) How she awes me now I am alone with her!

LADY BETTY: My Lord!

WINWORTH: I say, Madam, I have taken the liberty to —

LADY BETTY: I beg my Lord, you won't consider an apology in the least ——

WINWORTH: Your Ladyship is extremely obliging — and yet I am fearful —

LADY BETTY: I hope your Lordship will consider

1. blood relation.
2. Lady Betty's friend and ward.

me as a friend — and therefore lay aside this unnecessary ceremony.

WINWORTH: I do consider you Madam, as a friend; — as an inestimable friend — and I am this moment come to solicit you upon a subject of the utmost importance to my happiness.

LADY BETTY: (*Aside*) Lord, what is he going to say?

WINWORTH: Madam —

LADY BETTY: I say, my Lord, that you cannot speak to me on any subject of importance without engaging my greatest attention.

WINWORTH: You honour me too much, Madam.

LADY BETTY: Not in the least, my Lord — for there is not a person in the world who wishes your happiness with greater cordiality.

WINWORTH: You eternally oblige me, Madam — and I can now take courage to tell you, that my happiness, in a most material degree, depends upon your Ladyship.

LADY BETTY: On me, my Lord? — Bless me!

WINWORTH: Yes, Madam, on your Ladyship.

LADY BETTY: (*Aside*) Mrs. Harley was right, and I shall sink with confusion.

WINWORTH: 'Tis on this business, Madam, I have taken the liberty of requesting the present interview, — and as I find your Ladyship so generously ready —

LADY BETTY: Why, my Lord, I must confess — I say, I must acknowledge; my Lord, — that if your happiness depends upon me — I should not be very much pleas'd to see you miserable.

WINWORTH: Your Ladyship is benignity itself; — but as I want words to express my sense of this obligation, I shall proceed at once to my request, nor trespass upon your patience by an ineffectual compliment to your generosity.

LADY BETTY: If you please, my Lord.

WINWORTH: Then, Madam, my request is, that I may have our consent —

LADY BETTY: This is so sudden my Lord! — so unexpected!

WINWORTH: Why, Madam, it is so; — yet, if I cou'd but engage your acquiescence — I might still think of a double union on the day which makes my cousin happy.

LADY BETTY: My Lord — I really don't know how to answer; — Doesn't your Lordship think this is rather precipitating matters!

WINWORTH: No man, Madam, can be too speedy in promoting his happiness: — If, therefore, I might presume to hope for your concurrence, I wou'dn't altogether —

LADY BETTY: My concurrence, my Lord! Since it is so essentially necessary to your peace I cannot refuse any longer. — Your great merit will justify so immediate a compliance — and I shall stand executed of all.

WINWORTH: Then, Madam, I don't despair of the Lady's —

LADY BETTY: My Lord?

WINWORTH: I know your Ladyship can easily prevail upon her to overlook an immaterial punctilio,[1] and therefore —

LADY BETTY: The Lady, my Lord?

WINWORTH: Yes, Madam. Miss Marchmont, if she finds my addresses supported by your Ladyship, will, in all probability, be easily induced to receive them — and then, your Ladyship knows —

LADY BETTY: Miss Marchmont! my Lord?

WINWORTH: Yes, Madam, Miss Marchmont. — Since your final disapprobation of those hopes which I was once presumptuous enough to entertain of calling your Ladyship mine, the anguish of a rejected passion has render'd me inconceivably wretched, and I see no way of mitigating the severity of my situation but in the esteem of this amiable woman, who knows how tenderly I have been attached to you, and whose goodness will induce her, I am well convinced, to alleviate, as much as possible, the greatness of my disappointment.

LADY BETTY: Your Lordship is undoubtedly right in your opinion — and I am infinitely concern'd to have been the involuntary cause of uneasiness to you; — but Miss Marchmont, my Lord — she will merit your utmost ——

WINWORTH: I know she will, Madam — and it rejoices me to see you so highly pleas'd with my intention.

LADY BETTY: O, I am quite delighted with it!

WINWORTH: I knew I should please you by it. —

LADY BETTY: You can't imagine how you have pleas'd me!

WINWORTH: How noble is this goodness! — Then, Madam, I may expect your Ladyship will be my advocate? — The injustice which fortune has done Miss Marchmont's merit, obliges me to act

1. point of ceremony.

with a double degree of circumspection;[2] — for, when virtue is unhappily plung'd into difficulties, 'tis entitled to an additional share of veneration.

LADY BETTY: (*Aside*) How has my folly undone me!

WINWORTH: I will not trespass any longer upon your Ladyship's leisure, than just to observe, that though I have solicited your friendship on this occasion, I must, nevertheless, beg you will not be too much my friend. — I know Miss Marchmont would make any sacrifice to oblige you; — and if her gratitude should appear in the least concerned[3] — This is a nice point,[4] my dear Lady Betty, and I must not wound the peace of any person's bosom to recover the tranquillity of my own.

Exit

Enter MRS. HARLEY, *who speaks*

Well, my dear, is it all over?

LADY BETTY: It is all over indeed, Emmy.

MRS. HARLEY: But why that sorrowful tone — and melancholly countenance? Mustn't I wish you joy?

LADY BETTY: O, I am the most miserable woman in the world! — Would you believe it? — The business of this interview was to request my interest in his favour with Miss Marchmont.

MRS. HARLEY: With Miss Marchmont! — Then there is not one atom of sincere affection in the universe.

LADY BETTY: As to that, I have reason to think his sentiments for me are as tender as ever.

MRS. HARLEY: He gives you a pretty proof of his tenderness, truly, when he asks your assistance to marry another woman.

LADY BETTY: Had you but seen his confusion —

MRS. HARLEY: He might well be confused, when, after courting you these three years, he cou'd think of another, and that too at the very moment in which you were ready to oblige him.

LADY BETTY: There has been a sort of fatality in the affair — and I am punish'd but too justly: — The woman that wants[5] candour where she is address'd by a man of merit, wants a very essential virtue, and she who can delight in the anxiety of a worthy mind, is little to be pitied when she feels the sharpest stings of anxiety in her own.

2. Because Miss Marchmont is poor, Winworth feels doubly obliged to be careful over her feelings.
3. If she should consent only out of gratitude (to Lady Betty).
4. a delicate point.
5. lacks.

MRS. HARLEY: But what do you intend to do with regard to this extraordinary request of Lord Winworth; — will you really suffer him to marry Miss Marchmont?

LADY BETTY: Why what can I do? If it was improper for me, before I knew any thing of his design in regard to Miss Marchmont, to insinuate the least desire of hearing him again on the subject of his heart, 'tis doubly improper now, when I see he has turn'd his thoughts on another woman, and when this woman, besides, is one of my most valuable friends.

MRS. HARLEY: Well, courage Lady Betty — we aren't yet in a desperate situation — Miss Marchmont loves you — as himself — and wou'dn't, I dare say, accept the first man in the world, if it gave you the least uneasiness. — I'll go to her therefore this very moment — tell her at once how the case is — and my life on it, her obligations to you —

LADY BETTY: Stay, Emmy — I conjure you stay — and as you value my peace of mind be for ever silent on this subject — Miss Marchmont has no obligations to me; — since our acquaintance I have been the only person obliged; she has given me a power of serving the worthiest young creature in the world, and so far has laid me under the greatest obligation.

MRS. HARLEY: Why my dear —

LADY BETTY: But suppose I could be mean enough to think an apartment in my house, a place in my chariot, a seat at my table, and a little annuity in case of my decease, were obligations, when I continually enjoy such a happiness as her friendship and her company. — Do you think they are obligations which should make a woman of her fine sense, reject the most amiable man existing, especially in her circumstances, where he has the additional recommendation of an elevated rank and an affluent fortune? — This would be exacting interest with a witness for trifles, and, instead of having any little merit to claim from my behaviour to her, I shou'd be the most inexorable of all usurers.

MRS. HARLEY: Well, but suppose Miss Marchmont shou'd not like my Lord?

LADY BETTY: Not like him — why will you suppose an impossibility?

MRS. HARLEY: But let us suppose it for argument sake.

LADY BETTY: Why I cannot say but it would

please me above all things: — For still, Emmy, I am a woman, and feel this unexpected misfortune with the keenest sensibility: — It kills me to think of his being another's, but if he must, I would rather see him hers than any woman's in the universe. — But I'll talk no more upon this subject, 'till I acquaint her with this proposal; and yet, Emmy, how severe a trial must I go through.

MRS. HARLEY: Ay, and you most richly deserve it.

Exeunt

ACT III, SCENE 2

[But Lord Winworth's new choice, Miss Marchmont, loves another, as first the ageing Mr. Cecil finds out rather pathetically and then Lady Betty is told but fails to take advantage of. It is hard to say who has the greater amount of false delicacy in this scene, Miss Marchmont or Lady Betty; each is ready to complicate matters by self-sacrificing melodramatics.]

An Apartment in LADY BETTY's *house*

Enter MISS MARCHMONT and CECIL

MISS MARCHMONT: Nay, now, Sir, I must tax you with unkindness, — know something that may possibly be of consequence to my welfare, — and yet decline to tell me! — Is this consistent with the usual friendship which I have met with from Mr. Cecil?

CECIL: Look'ye, Hortensia, 'tis because I set a very great value on your esteem that I find this unwillingness to explain myself.

MISS MARCHMONT: Indeed, Sir, you grow every moment more and more mysterious. —

CECIL: Well then, Hortensia, if I thought you wou'dn't be offended — I —

MISS MARCHMONT: I am sure, Sir, you will never say any thing to give me a reasonable cause of offence. — I know your kindness for me too well, Sir, —

CECIL: Where is the need of Sirring me at every word? — I desire you will lay aside this ceremony, and treat me with the same freedom you do every body else, — these Sirs are so cold, and so distant.

MISS MARCHMONT: Indeed, Sir, I can't so easily lay aside my respect as you imagine, for I have long considered you as a father.

CECIL: As a father! — but that's a light in which I don't want to be consider'd. — (*Aside*) As a father indeed! — O she's likely to think me a proper husband for her, I can see that already.

MISS MARCHMONT: Why not Sir? — your years, — your friendship for my father, and your partiality for me, sufficiently justify the propriety of my epithet.

CECIL: (*Aside*) My years! — Yes; I thought my years would be an invincible obstacle.

MISS MARCHMONT: But pray, Sir, — to the business upon which you wanted to speak with me. — You don't consider I am all this time upon the rack of my sex's curiosity.

CECIL: Why then, Hortensia, — I will proceed to the business — and ask you, in one word, — if you have any disinclination to be married?

MISS MARCHMONT: This is proceeding to business indeed, Sir, — but ha — ha — ha! pray who have you designed me as a husband?

CECIL: Why, what do you think of a man about my age?

MISS MARCHMONT: Of your age, Sir?

CECIL: Yes, of my age —

MISS MARCHMONT: Why, Sir, what wou'd you advise me to think of him?

CECIL: That isn't the question, for all your arch significance of manner, Madam.

MISS MARCHMONT: O I am sure you wou'd never recommend him to me as a husband, Sir.

CECIL: So! — and why not, pray?

MISS MARCHMONT: Because I am sure you have too great a regard for me.

CECIL: (*Aside*) She gives me rare encouragement. — But do you imagine it impossible for such a husband to love you very tenderly?

MISS MARCHMONT: No — Sir, — But do you imagine it possible for me to love him very tenderly? — You see I have caught your own frankness, Sir, — and answer with as much ease as you question me.

CECIL: (*Aside*) How lucky it was that I did not open myself directly to her. — O! I should have been most purely contemptible.

MISS MARCHMONT: But pray, Sir, — have you, in reality, any meaning by these questions? — Is there actually any body who has spoken to you on my account?

CECIL: Hortensia, there is a fellow, a very foolish fellow, for whom I have some value, that entertains the sincerest affection for you.

MISS MARCHMONT: Then, indeed, Sir, I am very unhappy, — for I cannot encourage the addresses of any body.

CECIL: No?

MISS MARCHMONT: O, Sir! I had but two friends in the world, — yourself and Lady Betty, — and I am, with justice, apprehensive that neither will consider me long with any degree of regard. — Lady Betty has a proposal from Lord Winworth of the same nature with yours, in which I fear she will strongly interest herself, — and I must be under the painful necessity of disobliging you both, from an utter impossibility of listening to either of your recommendations.

CECIL: I tell you, Hortensia, not to alarm yourself.

MISS MARCHMONT: Dear Sir, I have always considered you with reverence, and it would make me inconceivably wretched if you imagin'd I was actuated upon this occasion by any ridiculous singularity of sentiment. — I wou'd do much to please you, — and I scarcely know what I should refuse to Lady Betty's request; — but, Sir, though it distresses me exceedingly to discover[1] it, — I must tell you I have not a heart to dispose of.

CECIL: How's this?

MISS MARCHMONT: At the same time, I must however, tell you, that my affections are so plac'd as to make it wholly impossible for me ever to change my situation[2] — This acknowledgment of a prepossession, Sir, may be inconsistent with the nice reserve which is proper for my sex, — but it is necessary to justify me in a case where my gratitude might be reasonably suspected, and when I recollect to whom it is made, I hope it will be doubly entitled to an excuse.

CECIL: Your candour, Hortensia, needs no apology, — but as you have trusted me thus far with your secret, — mayn't I know why you can have no prospect of being united to the object of your affections?

MISS MARCHMONT: Because, Sir, he is engaged to a most deserving young lady, and will be married to her in a few days: — In short, Mr. Sidney is the man for whom I entertain this secret partiality: — You see, therefore, that my partiality is hopeless, — but you see, at the same time, how utterly improper it would be for me to give a lifeless hand to another while he is entirely master of my affections. — It would be a meanness of which I think myself incapable, and I should be quite unworthy the honour of any deserving hand, if circumstanc'd in this manner, I could basely stoop to accept it.

CECIL: You interest me strangely in your story, Hortensia: — But has Sidney any idea?

MISS MARCHMONT: None in the least. — Before the match with Miss Rivers was in agitation[3] he made addresses to me, though privately; and, I must own, his tenderness, join'd to his good qualities, soon gave me impressions in his favour. — But, Sir, I was a poor orphan, wholly dependent upon the generosity of others; and he was a younger brother of a family, great in his birth, but contracted in his circumstances.[4] — What cou'd I do? — It was not in my power to make his fortune, — and I had too much pride, or too much affection, to think of destroying it.

CECIL: You are a good girl, — a very good girl; — but surely if Lady Betty knows any thing of this matter there can be no danger of her recommending Lord Winworth so earnestly to your attention. —

MISS MARCHMONT: There, Sir, is my principal misfortune. — Lady Betty is, of all persons, the least proper to be made acquainted with it. — Her heart is in the marriage between Miss Rivers and Mr. Sidney; and, had she the least idea of my sentiments for him, or of his inclination for me, I am positive it would immediately frustrate the match. — On this account, Sir, I have carefully concealed the secret of my wishes, — and, on this account, I must still continue to conceal it. — My heart shall break before it shall be worthless; — and I should detest myself for ever if I was capable of establishing my own peace at the expence of my benefactress's first wish, and the desire of her whole family.

CECIL: Zounds, what can be the matter with my eyes![5]

MISS MARCHMONT: My life was mark'd out early by calamity, — and the first light I beheld was purchas'd with the loss of a mother. — The grave snatched away the best of fathers just as I came to know the value of such a blessing; — and hadn't it been for the exalted goodness of others, I, who once experienc'd the unspeakable pleasure of relieving the necessitous, had myself, perhaps, felt the immediate want of bread; — and shall I ungratefully sting the bosom which has thus

1. reveal.
2. i.e. marry.
3. discussion, motion.
4. financially limited.
5. The tears associated with sentimental comedy are now flowing.

benevolently cherished me? — Shall I basely wound the peace of those who have rescu'd me from despair, — and stab at their tranquility in the very moment they honour me with protection? —— O, Mr. Cecil! they deserve every sacrifice which I can make. — May the benignant hand of Providence shower endless happiness upon their heads, and may the sweets of a still-encreasing felicity be their portion, whatever becomes of me!

CECIL: Hortensia, — I can't stay with you: — My eyes are exceedingly painful of late; — what the devil can be the matter with them? — But, let me tell you before I go, that you shall be happy after all; — that you shall, I promise you; — but I see Lady Betty coming this way — and I cannot enter into explanations, — yet, do you hear, don't suppose I am angry with you for refusing my friend, —— don't suppose such a thing, I charge you; — for he has too much humanity to make any woman miserable. — He is besides a very foolish fellow, and it doesn't signify ——

Exit

Enter LADY BETTY

LADY BETTY: Well, my dear Hortensia, I am come again to ask you what you think of Lord Winworth. — We were interrupted before, — and I want, as soon as possible, for the reason I hinted, to know your real opinion of him.

MISS MARCHMONT: You have long known my real opinion of him, Lady Betty. — You know I always thought him a very amiable man.

LADY BETTY: (*With impatience*) Do you think him an amiable man?

MISS MARCHMONT: The whole world thinks as I do in this respect, — yet, ——

LADY BETTY: (*Aside*) Ay, she loves him, 'tis plain; and there is no hope after this declaration —— His Lordship merits your good opinion, I assure you, Miss Marchmont.

MISS MARCHMONT: (*Aside*) Yes, I see by this ceremony that she is offended at my coolness to the proposal.

LADY BETTY: I have hinted to you, Miss Marchmont, that my Lord requested I would exert my little interest with you in his favour.

MISS MARCHMONT: The little interest your Ladyship has with me, — the little interest.

LADY BETTY: Don't be displeased with me, my dear Hortensia, — I know my interest with you is considerable. — I know you love me.

MISS MARCHMONT: I would sacrifice my life for you, Lady Betty: For what had that life been without your generosity — ?

LADY BETTY: If you love me, Hortensia, never mention any thing of this nature.

MISS MARCHMONT: You are too good.

LADY BETTY: But to my Lord Winworth. — He has earnestly requested I would become his advocate with you. — He has entirely got the better of his former attachments, and there can be no doubt of his making you an excellent husband.

MISS MARCHMONT: His Lordship does me infinite honour, — nevertheless.

LADY BETTY: (*Eagerly*) Nevertheless, what, my dear?

MISS MARCHMONT: I say, notwithstanding I think myself highly honour'd by his sentiments in my favour; — 'tis utterly impossible for me to return his affection.

LADY BETTY: (*Surprized*) Impossible for you to return his affection!

MISS MARCHMONT: (*Aside*) I knew what an interest she wou'd take in this affair.

LADY BETTY: And do you really say you can't give him a favourable answer? — (*Aside*) How fortunate!

MISS MARCHMONT: I do, my dear Lady Betty, — I can honour, I can reverence him, — but I cannot feel that tenderness for his person which I imagine to be necessary both for his happiness and my own.

LADY BETTY: Upon my word, my dear, you are extremely difficult in your choice, and if Lord Winworth is not capable of inspiring you with tenderness — I don't know who is likely to succeed; for, in my opinion, there is not a man in England possessed of more personal accomplishments.

MISS MARCHMONT: And yet, great as these accomplishments are, my dear Lady Betty, they never excited your tenderness.[6]

LADY BETTY: Why, all this is very true, my dear, — but, though I felt no tenderness, — yet I — to be sure, I — that is — I say, nevertheless. — (*Aside*) This is beyond my hopes.

MISS MARCHMONT: (*Aside*) She's distress'd that I decline the proposal. — Her friendship for us both is generously warm, — and she imagines I am equally insensible to his merit, and my own interest.

6. affection. With the stress on 'your', the charge takes on a slightly aggressive and dramatic tone.

LADY BETTY: Well, my dear, I see your emotion — and I heartily beg your pardon for saying so much. — I should be inexpressibly concern'd if I thought you made any sacrifice on this occasion to me. — My Lord, to be sure, possesses a very high place in my esteem, — but ——

MISS MARCHMONT: Dear Lady Betty, what can I do? — I see you are offended with me, — and yet ——

LADY BETTY: I offended with you, my dear! — far from it; I commend your resolution extremely, since my Lord is not a man to your taste. — Offended with you! why should I take the liberty to be offended with you? — A presumption of that nature ——

MISS MARCHMONT: Indeed, Lady Betty, this affair makes me very unhappy.

LADY BETTY: Indeed, my dear, you talk very strangely; — so far from being sorry that you have refus'd my Lord — I am pleas'd, — infinitely pleas'd, — that is, since he was not agreeable to you. — Be satisfied your acceptance of him would have given me no pleasure in the world, — I assure you it wou'dn't, — on the contrary, as matters are situated, I wou'dn't for the world have you give him the smallest encouragement.

Exit

MISS MARCHMONT: (*Alone*) I see she's greatly disappointed at my refusal of an offer so highly to my advantage, — I see, moreover, she's griev'd that his Lordship should meet with a second repulse, and from a quarter, too, where the generosity of his proposal might be reasonably expected to promise it success. — How surpriz'd she seem'd when I told her he cou'dn't make an impression on my heart, and how eagerly she endeavour'd to convince me that she was pleas'd with my conduct; not considering that this very eagerness was a manifest proof of her dissatisfaction. — She is more interested in this affair than I even thought she would be, — and I should be completely miserable if she cou'd suspect me of ingratitude. — As she was so zealous for the match I was certainly to blame in declining it. — 'Tis not yet, however, too late. — She has been a thousand parents to me, — and I will not regard my own wishes, when they are any way opposite to her inclinations. —— Poor Mr. Cecil! — Make me happy after all! — How? — Impossible! — for I was born to nothing but misfortune.

Exit

ACT IV, SCENE 1

An Apartment at LADY BETTY'S *House*

Enter LADY BETTY *and* MRS. HARLEY

LADY BETTY: Thus far, my dear Emmy, there is a gleam of hope. — She determined, positively determined, against my Lord: — And even suspected so little of my partiality for him, that she appeared under the greatest anxiety lest I should be offended with her refusing him: — And yet, shall I own my folly to you?

MRS. HARLEY: Pray do, my dear; — you'll scarcely believe it, — but I have follies of my own sometimes.[1]

LADY BETTY: Why you quite surprize me!

MRS. HARLEY: 'Tis very true for all that. — But to your business.

LADY BETTY: Why then, greatly as I dreaded her approbation of the proposal, — I was secretly hurt at her insensibility to the personal attractions of his Lordship.

MRS. HARLEY: I don't doubt it, my dear. — We think all the world should love what we are in love with ourselves.

LADY BETTY: You are right. — And though I was happy to find her resolution so agreeable to my wishes, my pride was not a little piqu'd to find it possible for her to refuse a man upon whom I had so ardently plac'd my own affection. — The surprize which I felt on this account threw a warmth into my expressions, and made the generous girl apprehensive that I was offended with her.

MRS. HARLEY: Well, this is a strange world we live in. —— That a woman without a shilling shou'd refuse an Earl with a fine person and a great estate is the most surprizing affair I ever heard of. — Perhaps, Lady Betty, my Lord may take it in his head to go round the family: — If he should, my turn is next, and, I assure you, he shall meet with a very different reception.

LADY BETTY: Then you wou'dn't be cruel, Emmy!

MRS. HARLEY: Why no! — Not very cruel. — I might give myself a few airs at first. — I might blush a little, and look down. — Wonder what he cou'd find in me to attract his attention: — Then

1. Mrs Harley's role in the play is to be the voice of reason and to officiate, as she says at the end, at 'the triumph of good sense over delicacy'.

pulling up my head, with a toss of disdain, — desire him, if ever he spoke to me on that subject again, ——

LADY BETTY: Well!

MRS. HARLEY: To have a licence in his pocket, — that's all. — I would make sure work of it at once, and leave it to your elevated minds to deal in delicate absurdities. — But I have a little anecdote for you, which proves beyond a doubt that you are as much as ever in possession of Lord Winworth's affection.

LADY BETTY: What is it, my dear Emmy?

MRS. HARLEY: Why about an hour ago, my woman, it seems, and Arnold, my Lord's man, had a little conversation on this unexpected proposal to Miss Marchmont; in which Arnold said, — 'Never tell me of your Miss Marchmonts, Mrs. Nelson; — between ourselves — but let it go no farther — Lady Betty is still the woman, and a sweet creature she is, that's the truth on't, but a little fantastical, and doesn't know her own mind.'

LADY BETTY: I'll assure you! — Why Mr. Arnold is a wit.

MRS. HARLEY: Well, but hear him out: — 'Mrs. Nelson, I know as much of my Lord's mind as any body; let him marry whom he pleases, he'll never be rightly happy but with her Ladyship; and I'd give a hundred guineas, with all my soul, that it cou'd be a match.' — These Nelson tells me were his very words. — Arnold is an intelligent fellow, and much in the confidence of his master.

LADY BETTY: Indeed I always thought my Lord happy in so excellent a servant. — This intelligence[2] is worth a world, my dear Emmy ——

Enter MISS MARCHMONT

MISS MARCHMONT: I have been looking for your Ladyship.

LADY BETTY: Have you any thing particular, my dear Hortensia? — But why that gloom upon your features? — What gives you uneasiness, my sweet girl? Speak, and make me happy by saying it is in my power to oblige you.

MISS MARCHMONT: 'Tis in your power, my dear Lady Betty, to oblige me highly — by forgiving the ungrateful disregard which I just now shew'd to your recommendation of Lord Winworth.

MRS. HARLEY: (*Aside*) Now will I be hang'd if she does not undo every thing by a fresh stroke of delicacy.

LADY BETTY: My dear!

MISS MARCHMONT: And by informing his Lordship that I am ready to pay a proper obedience to your commands.

MRS. HARLEY: (*Aside*) O the devil take this elevation of sentiment!

LADY BETTY: A proper obedience to my commands my dear! I really don't understand you.

MISS MARCHMONT: I see how generously you are concerned, for fear I shou'd, upon this occasion, offer violence to my inclination: —— But, Lady Betty, I shou'd be infinitely more distress'd by the smallest act of ingratitude to you, than by any other misfortune. — I am therefore ready, in obedience to your wishes, to accept of his Lordship, and if I can't make him a fond wife, I will, at least, make him a dutiful one.

MRS. HARLEY: (*Aside*) Now her delicacy is willing to be miserable.

LADY BETTY: How cou'd you ever imagine, my dear Hortensia, that your rejection of Lord Winworth cou'd possibly give me the smallest offence? — I have a great regard for his Lordship 'tis true, but I have a great regard for you also; and wou'd by no means wish to see his happiness promoted at your expence; — think of him therefore no more, and be assur'd you oblige me in an infinitely higher degree by refusing than accepting him.

MISS MARCHMONT: The more I see your Ladyship's tenderness and delicacy, the more I see it necessary to give an affirmative to Lord Winworth's proposal. — Your generosity must not get the better of my gratitude.

MRS. HARLEY: (*Aside*) Did ever two fools plague one another so heartily with their delicacy and sentiment? —— Dear Lady Betty, why don't you deal candidly with her?

LADY BETTY: Her happiness makes it necessary now, and I will.

MRS. HARLEY: Ay, there's some sense in this.

LADY BETTY: Your uncommon generosity, my dear Hortensia, has led you into an error.

MISS MARCHMONT: Not in the least, Lady Betty.

LADY BETTY: Still, Hortensia, you are running into very great mistakes. — My esteem for Lord Winworth, let me now tell you ——

Enter WINWORTH

WINWORTH: Ladies, your most obedient! — As I enter'd, Lady Betty, I heard you pronounce my name: — May I presume to ask, if you were talking

2. news.

to Miss Marchmont on the business I took the liberty of communicating to you this morning?

MRS. HARLEY: (*Aside*) Ay, now it's all over I see.

LADY BETTY: Why, to be candid, my Lord, I have mentioned your proposal ——

WINWORTH: Well, my dear Miss Marchmont, and may I flatter myself that Lady Betty's interposition will induce you to be propitious to my hopes? — The heart now offered to you, Madam, is a grateful one, and will retain an eternal sense of your goodness. — Speak, therefore, my dear Miss Marchmont, and kindly say you condescend to accept it.

MRS. HARLEY: (*Aside*) So — here will be a comfortable piece of work. — I'll e'en retire and leave them to the consequences of their ridiculous delicacy.

Exit

MISS MARCHMONT: I know not what to say, my Lord, — you have honoured me, greatly honoured me — but Lady Betty will acquaint you with my determination.

LADY BETTY: I acquaint him my dear — surely you are yourself the most proper to — (*Aside*) I shall run distracted!

MISS MARCHMONT: Indeed, Madam, I can't speak to his Lordship on this subject.

LADY BETTY: And I assure you, Hortensia, 'tis a subject upon which I do not chuse to enter.

WINWORTH: If you had a kind answer from Miss Marchmont, Lady Betty, I am sure you would enter upon it readily: — But I see her reply very clearly in your reluctance to acquaint me with it. ——

MISS MARCHMONT: Why, Madam, will you force me to ——

LADY BETTY: And why Hortensia? (*Aside*) What am I going to say?

WINWORTH: Don't my dear Ladies, suffer me to distress you any longer. (*Addressing himself to* LADY BETTY) To your friendship, Madam, I am as much indebted as if I had been successful, — and I sincerely wish Miss Marchmont that happiness with a more deserving man, which I find it impossible for her to confer on me. (*Going*)

LADY BETTY: (*Aside*) Now I have some hope ——

MISS MARCHMONT: My Lord I entreat your stay.

LADY BETTY: Don't call his Lordship back, my dear, it will have an odd appearance.

Enter LORD WINWORTH

MISS MARCHMONT: He is come back. — And I must tell him what your unwillingness to influence my inclinations, makes you decline.

LORD WINWORTH: Your commands[3] Madam.

LADY BETTY: (*Aside*) Now I am undone again!

MISS MARCHMONT: I am in such a situation, my Lord, that I can scarcely proceed — Lady Betty is cruelly kind to me — but as I know her wishes ——

LADY BETTY: My wishes, Miss Marchmont! — indeed, my dear, there is such a mistake.

MISS MARCHMONT: There is no mistaking your Ladyship's goodness, you are fearful to direct my resolution, and I should be unkind to distress your friendship any longer.

LADY BETTY: (*Half aside and sighing*) You do distress me indeed, Miss Marchmont.

LORD WINWORTH: I am all expectation, Madam!

MISS MARCHMONT: I am compell'd by gratitude to both, and from affection to my dear Lady Betty, to break through the common forms impos'd on our sex, and to declare that I have no will but her Ladyship's.

LADY BETTY: (*Aside*) This is so provoking.

LORD WINWORTH: Ten thousand thanks for this condescending goodness, Madam — a goodness which is additionally dear to me, as the result of your determination is pronounc'd by your own lips.

MISS MARCHMONT: Well, Lady Betty, I hope I have answer'd your wishes now.

LADY BETTY: You cannot conceive how sensibly I am touch'd with your behaviour my dear. (*Sighs*)

MISS MARCHMONT: You feel too much for me Lady Betty.

LADY BETTY: Why I do feel something my dear —— this unexpected event has fill'd my heart — and I am a little agitated. — But come, my dear, let us now go to the company.

MISS MARCHMONT: How generously, Madam, do you interest yourself for my welfare!

LORD WINWORTH: And for the welfare of all her friends.

LADY BETTY: Your Lordship is too good ——

LORD WINWORTH: But the business of her life is to promote the happiness of others, and she is constantly rewarded in the exercise of her own benignity.

LADY BETTY: You can't imagine how I am

3. Since Miss Marchmont has called back Lord Winworth, he wishes to know what he may do for her.

rewarded upon the present occasion, I assure your Lordship.

Exeunt

from: THE SCHOOL FOR WIVES (1773)

[To some readers, excerpts from another play by Kelly may appear questionable. Surely, they may feel, Kelly is a minor writer who may be given an indulgent smile or two (for his naïveté) and left aside. But Kelly's work has been unfairly neglected in modern times and deserves more attention. What he was doing was, to some extent, new. He did not rest content with formulaic comedy, like Arthur Murphy, or go for amusing mistakes, like Goldsmith. He studied the characters of young people as these are formed or screened by the trends of the day. He exposed the abuses that contemporary manners allowed, and analyzed the ways in which these abuses injure relationships and jeopardize the happiness of dependants — especially women. He had an eye for the vulnerability of those exploited by the approved rhetoric of the day. Above all, his plots were concerned with perception, bringing characters to a better vision of the way things are, so that what should be can flow from a proper perception of what is. As Miss Willoughby remarks in *A Word to the Wise* (1770), after she sees the folly of her intended elopement: 'Unknowing in the ways of the world, I could not distinguish between the language of sincerity, and the voice of dissimulation.' It was Kelly's function to bring his audiences also to this kind of discrimination.

The preface to *The School for Wives* is included below because it has several important things to say about Kelly's aims. Discounting any indebtedness to Molière, he says that he wanted to steer a course between 'sentimental gloom' and 'the excesses of uninteresting levity'. He wanted a moral drama that would be at the same time entertaining. Had he lived in the nineteenth century, he would have written problem plays. The preface also includes a rare statement by an eighteenth-century Irish playwright on the stage Irishman.]

PREFACE

The Author of the following performance cannot commit it to the press, without acknowledging the deepest sense of gratitude, for the uncommon marks of approbation with which he has been honoured by the Public.

Tho' he has chosen a title us'd by MOLIÈRE he has neither borrowed a single circumstance from that great poet, nor to the best of his recollection from any other writer. — His chief study has been to steer between the extremes of sentimental gloom, and the excesses of uninteresting levity; he has some laugh, yet he hopes he has also some lesson; and fashionable as it has been lately for the wits, even with his friend Mr. Garrick[1] at their head, to ridicule the Comic Muse, when a little grave, he must think that she degenerates into farce, where the grand business of instruction is neglected, and consider it as a heresy in criticism, to say that one of the most arduous tasks within the reach of literature, shou'd, when executed, be wholly without utility.[2]

The Author having been presumptuous enough to assert, that he has not purloin'd a single sprig of bays from the brow of any other writer, he may, perhaps, be ask'd, if there are not several plays in the English language, which before his, produced Generals, Lawyers, Irishmen, Duels, Masquerades, and Mistakes? He answers, yes; and confesses moreover, that all the Comedies before his, were compos'd not only of men and women, but that before his, the great business of comedy consisted in making difficulties for the purpose of removing them; in distressing poor young lovers; and in rendering a happy marriage the object of every catastrophe.

Yet tho' the Author of the School for Wives, pleads guilty to all these charges, still, in extenuation of his offence, he begs leave to observe, that having only men and women to introduce upon the stage, he was oblig'd to compose his Dramatis Personae of mere flesh and blood; if, however, he has thrown this flesh and this blood, into *new* situations; if he has given a *new* fable, and plac'd his characters in a point of light hitherto unexhibited: — he flatters himself he may call his play, a *new* play, and tho' it did not exist before the creation of the world, like the famous Welch pedigree, that he may have some small pretensions to originality.

Two things besides the general moral inculcated thro' his piece, the Author has attempted; the first,

1. David Garrick (1717-79), actor, playwright and manager of Drury Lane Theatre Royal, where *The School for Wives* was first staged. Garrick had written the prologue to *False Delicacy* (1768), in which he described Kelly's play as 'quite a sermon'.
2. At the end of *False Delicacy*, a character says that the stage 'should be a school of morality', and this seems to represent Kelly's own view. It is interesting to note that, just over a hundred years later, 'utility' was for George Bernard Shaw the major criterion for the assessment of dramatic merit.

to rescue the law, as a profession, from ridicule or obliquy; and the second, to remove the imputation of a barbarous ferocity, which dramatic writers, even meaning to compliment the Irish nation, have connected with their Idea of that gallant people: — The law, like every other profession, may have members who occasionally disgrace it; but to the glory of the British name, it is well known that in the worst of times, it has produced numbers whose virtues reflected honour upon human nature; many of the noblest privileges the constitution has to boast of, were derived from the integrity, or the wisdom of lawyers: Yet the stage has hitherto cast an indiscriminate stigma upon the whole body, and laboured to make the profession either odious or contemptible in the theatre, which, if the laws are indeed dear to good Englishmen, can never be too much respected in this kingdom. There is scarcely a play in which a lawyer is introduced, that is not a libel upon the long robe; and so ignorant have many dramatic writers been, that they have made no distinction whatever, between the characters of the first Barristers in Westminster-Hall, and the meanest solicitors at the Old Bailey.

With respect to the gentlemen of Ireland, where even an absolute attempt is manifested, to place them in a favourable point of view, they are drawn with a brutal promptitude to quarrel, which is a disgrace to the well known humanity of their country. — The gentlemen of Ireland have doubtless a quick sense of honour, and, like the gentlemen of England, as well as like the gentlemen of every other high-spirited nation, are perhaps unhappily too ready to draw the sword, where they conceive themselves injured. — But to make them proud of a barbarous propensity to Duelling; to make them actually delight in the effusion of blood, is to fasten a very unjust reproach upon their general character, and to render them universally obnoxious to society. The author of the School for Wives therefore, has given a different picture of Irish manners, though in humble life, and flatters himself that those who are really acquainted with the original, will acknowledge it to be at least a tolerable resemblance.

It would be ungrateful in the highest degree to close this preface, without acknowledging the very great obligations which the author has to Mr. Garrick. Every attention, which either as a manager, or as a man, he could give to the interest of the following play, he has bestowed with the most generous alacrity; but universally admired as he is at present, his intrinsic value will not be known, till his loss is deplored; and the public have great reason to wish, that this may be a very distant event in the annals of the theatre. . . .

Jan. 1, 1774.

ACT I, SCENE 2

[The hero plans his revenge against the man who seduced his sister.]

Scene Changes to LEESON's *Chambers in the Temple*[1]

Enter LEESON

LEESON: Where is this clerk of mine? Connolly!

CONNOLLY: (*Behind*)[2] Here, Sir!

LEESON: Have you copied the marriage settlement, as I corrected it?

CONNOLLY: (*Enters with pistols*) Ay, honey, an hour ago.

LEESON: What, you have been trying those pistols?

CONNOLLY: By my soul, I have been firing them this half hour, without once being able to make them go off.

LEESON: They are plaguy dirty.

CONNOLLY: In troth, so they are: I strove to brighten them up a little, but some misfortune attends every thing I do, for the more I clane them, the dirtier they are, honey.

LEESON: You have had some of our usual daily visitors for money, I suppose?

CONNOLLY: You may say that; and three or four of them are now hanging about the door, that I wish handsomely hang'd any where else, for bodering[3] us.

LEESON: No joking, Connolly! my present situation is a very disagreeable one.

CONNOLLY: Faith, and so it is; but who makes it disagreeable? Your Aunt Tempest would let you have as much money as you please, but you won't condescend to be acquainted with her, though people in this country can be very intimate friends, without seeing one another's faces for seven years.

LEESON: Do you think me base enough to receive

1. Where London's law schools are situated.
2. Off-stage.
3. bothering.

a favour from a woman, who has disgraced her family, and stoops to be a kept mistress? you see, my sister is already ruin'd by a connection with her.

CONNOLLY: Ah, Sir, a good guinea isn't the worse for coming through a bad hand; if it was, what would become of us lawyers?[4] and by my soul, many a high head in London would, at this minute, be very low, if they hadn't received favours even from much worse people than kept mistresses.

LEESON: Others, Connolly, may prostitute their honour, as they please; mine is my chief possession, and I must take particular care of it.

CONNOLLY: Honour, to be sure, is a very fine thing, Sir; but I don't see how it is to be taken care of, without a little money; your honour, to my knowledge, hasn't been in your own possession these two years, and the devil a crum can you honestly swear by, till you get it out of the hands of your creditors.

LEESON: I have given you a licence to talk, Connolly, because I know you faithful; but I hav'n't given you a liberty to sport with my misfortunes.

CONNOLLY: You know I'd die to serve you, Sir; but of what use is your giving me leave to spake, if you oblige me to hould my tongue? 'tis out of pure love and affection that I put you in mind of your misfortunes.

LEESON: Well, Connolly, a few days will, in all probability, enable me to redeem my honour, and to reward your fidelity; the lovely Emily, you know, has half consented to embrace the first opportunity of flying with me to Scotland,[5] and the paltry trifles I owe, will not be miss'd in her Fortune.

CONNOLLY: But, dear Sir, consider you are going to fight a duel this very evening, and if you shou'd be kilt, I fancy you will find it a little difficult, to run away afterwards with the lovely Emily.

LEESON: If I fall, there will be an end to my misfortunes.

CONNOLLY: But surely it will not be quite genteel, to go out of the world without paying your debts?

LEESON: But how shall I stay in the world, Connolly, without punishing Belville for ruining my sister?

CONNOLLY: O, the devil fly away with this honour; an ounce of common sense, is worth a whole ship load of it, if we must prefer a bullet or a halter, to a fine young lady and a great fortune.

LEESON: We'll talk no more on the subject at present. Take this letter to Mr. Belville; deliver it into his own hand, be sure; and bring me an answer: make haste; for I shall not stir out till you come back.

CONNOLLY: By my soul, I wish you may be able to stir out then, honey. — O, but that's true!

LEESON: What's the matter?

CONNOLLY: Why, Sir, the gentleman I last liv'd clerk with, died lately and left me a legacy of twenty guineas —

LEESON: What! is Mr. Stanley dead?

CONNOLLY: Faith, his friends have behav'd very unkindly if he is not, for they have buried him these six weeks.

LEESON: And what then?

CONNOLLY: Why, Sir, I received my little legacy this morning, and if you'd be so good as to keep it for me, I'd be much oblig'd to you.

LEESON: Connolly, I understand you, but I am already shamefully in your debt: you've had no money from me this age. —

CONNOLLY: O, Sir, that does not signify; if you are not kilt in this damn'd duel, you'll be able enough to pay me: if you are, I shan't want it.

LEESON: Why so, my poor fellow?

CONNOLLY: Because, tho' I am but your clerk, and tho' I think fighting the most foolish thing upon earth, I'm as much a gentleman as yourself, and have as much right to commit a murder in the way of duelling.

LEESON: And what then? You have no quarrel with Mr. Belville?

CONNOLLY: I shall have a damn'd quarrel with him tho' if you are kilt: your death shall be reveng'd, depend upon it, so let that content you.

LEESON: My dear Connolly, I hope I shan't want such a proof of your affection. — How he distresses me!

CONNOLLY: You will want a second, I suppose, in this affair: I stood second to my own brother, in the Fifteen Acres,[6] and tho' that has made me detest the very thought of duelling ever since; yet if you want a friend, I'll attend you to the field of death with a great deal of satisfaction.

LEESON: I thank you, Connolly, but I think it extremely wrong in any man who has a quarrel, to

4. Leeson is a law student, Connolly is his clerk.
5. They are eloping, to Gretna Green.
6. A secluded part of the Phoenix Park, Dublin, well known as a venue for duels.

expose his friend to difficulties; we shou'dn't seek for redress, if we are not equal to the task of fighting our own battles; and I choose you particularly, to carry my letter, because, you may be supposed ignorant of the contents, and thought to be acting only in the ordinary course of your business.

CONNOLLY: Say no more about it, honey; I will be back with you presently. (*Going, returns*) I put the twenty guineas in your pocket, before you were up, Sir; and I don't believe you'd look for such a thing there, if I wasn't to tell you of it.

Exit

LEESON: This faithful, noble-hearted creature! — but let me fly from thought; the business I have to execute, will not bear the test of reflection.

Exit

Re-enter CONNOLLY

CONNOLLY: As this is a challenge, I shou'dn't go without a sword; come down, little tickle-pitcher. (*Takes a sword*) Some people may think me very conceited now; but as the dirtiest black legs[7] in town can wear one without being stared at, I don't think it can suffer any disgrace by the side of an honest man.

Exit

7. clerks.

ACT II, SCENE 2

[Connolly delivers the challenge to the rake, Belville, who has seduced Miss Leeson. Belville's friend, the Captain, is also present.]

BELVILLE's *Apartment*

. . . *Enter* SPRUCE

SPRUCE: Sir, there is an Irish gentleman below with a letter for you, who will deliver it to nobody but yourself.

BELVILLE: Shew him up then.

SPRUCE: Yes, Sir.

Exit

CAPTAIN: It may be on business Belville, I'll take my leave of you.

BELVILLE: O, by no means; I can have no business which I desire to keep from you, tho' you are the arrant'st[1] miser of your confidence upon earth, and wou'd rather trust your life in any body's hands, then even a paltry amour with the apprentice of a millener.

1. most wicked.

Enter CONNOLLY

CONNOLLY: Gintlemin, your most obedient; pray which of you is Mr. Belville?

BELVILLE: My name is Belville, at your service, Sir.

CONNOLLY: I have a little bit of a letter for you, Sir.

BELVILLE: (*Reads*)

SIR.

The people where Miss Leeson lately lodg'd, asserting positively that you have taken her away in a fictitious character, the brother of that unhappy girl, thinks himself oblig'd to demand satisfaction, for the injury which you have done his family; tho' a stranger to your person, he is sufficiently acquainted with your reputation for spirit, and shall, therefore, make no doubt of seeing you with a case of pistols, near the Ring in Hyde Park, at eight o'clock this evening, to answer the claims of

George Leeson.

To Craggs Belville, Esq;

CAPTAIN: Eight o'clock in the evening! 'tis a strange time![2]

CONNOLLY: Why so, honey? A fine evening is as good a time for a bad action as a fine morning; and if a man of sense can be such a fool as to fight a duel, he shou'd never sleep upon the matter, for the more he thinks of it, the more he must feel himself asham'd of his resolution.

BELVILLE: A pretty letter!

CONNOLLY: O yes, an invitation to a brace of bullets is a very pretty thing.

BELVILLE: For a challenge, however, 'tis very civilly written!

CONNOLLY: Faith, if it was written to me, I shou'dn't be very fond of such civility; I wonder he doesn't sign himself, your most obedient servant.[3]

CAPTAIN: I told you Leeson's character, and what wou'd become of this damn'd business; but your affairs — are they settled, Belville?

BELVILLE: O they are always settled — for as this is a country where people occasionally die, I take constant care to be prepared for contingencies.

CONNOLLY: Occasionally die! — I'll be very much oblig'd to you, Sir, if you tell me the country

2. From Kelly's point of view, this is the most dramatic time. The action of his play takes but one day, and the climax must, therefore, take place at night.

3. An echo of Sir Richard Steele's essay against duelling, in *The Tatler*, no. 25, 7 June 1709. Compare also Act IV of Steele's *The Conscious Lovers*, above.

where people do not die, for I'll immediately go and end my days there.

BELVILLE: Ha! ha! ha!

CONNOLLY: Faith, you may laugh gintlemin, but tho' I am a foolish Irishman, and come about a foolish piece of business, I'd prefer a snug birth in this world, bad as it is, to the finest coffin in all Christendom.

BELVILLE: I am surpris'd, Sir, that thinking in this manner, you would be the bearer of a challenge.

CONNOLLY: And well you may, Sir. — But we must often take a pleasure in serving our friends, by doing things that are very disagreeable to us.

CAPTAIN: Then you think Mr. Leeson much to blame, perhaps, for hazarding his life, where he can by no means repair the honour of his sister.

CONNOLLY: Indeed and I do — But I shall think this gintleman, begging his pardon, much more to blame for meeting him.

BELVILLE: And why so, Sir — You wou'dn't have me disappoint your friend?

CONNOLLY: Faith, and that I wou'd — He, poor lad, may have some reason at present to be tir'd of the world, but you have a fine estate, a fine wife, a fine parcel of children. — In short, honey, you have every thing to make you fond of living, and the devil burn me, was I in your case, if I'd stake my own happiness against the misery of any man.

BELVILLE: I am very much oblig'd to your advice, Sir, tho' on the present occasion I cannot adopt it; be so good as to present my compliments to your friend, and tell him I shall certainly do myself the honour of attending his appointment.

CONNOLLY: Why then upon my soul I am very sorry for it.

CAPTAIN: 'Tis not very customary, Sir, with gentlemen of Ireland to oppose an affair of honour.

CONNOLLY: They are like the gintlemin of England, Sir, they are brave to a fault; yet I hope to see the day that it will be infamous to draw the swords of either, against any body but the enemies of their country. *Exit*

OLIVER GOLDSMITH

(1728-74)

SHE STOOPS TO CONQUER;

or, THE MISTAKES OF A NIGHT
(1773)

[Goldsmith detested sentimental comedy, even though there is a certain amount of sentimentalism in his first play, *The Good Natur'd Man* (1768), not to mention his novel *The Vicar of Wakefield* (1766). There is something puzzlingly defensive about Goldsmith's attitude towards sentimental drama, as is evidenced by his 'An Essay on the Theatre; or, A Comparison between Laughing and Sentimental Comedy', published anonymously in the *Westminster Magazine* less than three months before the première of *She Stoops to Conquer* (15 March 1773). It is now the view among commentators that Goldsmith's attack in this essay greatly exaggerated the contemporary popularity of sentimental comedy, as if he feared for the fate of his own new play. Once the reader is aware that Goldsmith was probably preparing the public for the appearance of *She Stoops to Conquer*, his essay (for nobody now doubts that it was his) may be adjusted, for its bias and distortion, and the sheer brilliance of Goldsmith's attack may be enjoyed as a mark of his genius rather than as a measure of his reliability as a critic. Thus Goldsmith's conclusion must be seen as a subjective response to the current theatrical repertory:

> Humour at present seems to be departing from the Stage, and it will soon happen, that our Comic Players will have nothing left for it but a fine Coat and a Song. It depends upon the Audience whether they will actually drive those poor Merry Creatures from the Stage, or sit at a Play as gloomy as at the Tabernacle. It is not easy to recover an art when once lost; and it would be but a just punishment that when, by our being too fastidious, we have banished Humour from the Stage, we should ourselves be deprived of the art of Laughing.

It is interesting to note, further, that the actor-manager David Garrick, who had already written the prologue to Kelly's *False Delicacy* (1768), jibing at sentimentalism, now wrote the prologue to Goldsmith's *She Stoops to Conquer,* in which he made the point that *'The Comic muse, long sick, is now a dying!'* The point is further made that Goldsmith, as doctor, is about to tend the patient and bring her back to her former vigour. If Garrick had really believed that sentimental comedy was killing off 'real' comedy, he would hardly have staged Kelly's play. It sounds as if the theatre was quite willing to exploit this controversy between a newer and an older style of entertainment, and that Garrick was capable of having his own little joke by casting Goldsmith as the 'doctor', when there was considerable doubt whether, in real life, he actually had a medical degree.

In the event, *She Stoops to Conquer* was an immediate success on stage, and although some critics found fault with its farcical scenes and what they saw as a lack of moral purpose, the general view may be summed up in Dr Johnson's response: 'I know of no comedy for many years that has so exhilarated an audience; that has answered so much the great end of comedy, making an audience merry.' Goldsmith need not have worried. Fortunately for Irish authors, English audiences still retained a sense of humour.]

DEDICATION
To SAMUEL JOHNSON, L.L.D.[1]

Dear Sir,

... I have, particularly, reason to thank you for your partiality to this performance. The undertaking a comedy, not merely sentimental,[2] was very dangerous; and Mr. Colman,[3] who saw this piece in its various stages, always thought it so. However I ventured to trust it to the public; and though it was necessarily delayed till late in the season, I have every reason to be grateful.

I am, Dear Sir,

Your most sincere friend,

And admirer,

OLIVER GOLDSMITH

PROLOGUE

By David Garrick, Esq.

Enter Mr. WOODWARD,[4] *Dressed in Black, and holding a Handkerchief to his Eyes.*

Excuse me, Sirs, I pray — I can't yet speak —
I'm crying now — and have been all the week!
'Tis not alone this mourning suit,[5] *good masters,*
I've that within[6] —— *for which there are no plaisters!*
Pray wou'd you know the reason why I'm crying?
The Comic muse, long sick, is now a dying!
And if she goes my tears will never stop;
For as a play'r, I can't squeeze out one drop:
I am undone, that's all — shall lose my bread —
I'd rather, but that's nothing — lose my head.
When the sweet maid is laid upon the bier,
Shuter[7] *and* I *shall be chief mourners here.*
To her *a mawkish drab of spurious breed,*
Who deals in sentimentals *will succeed!*
Poor Ned *and* I *are dead to all intents,*
We can as soon speak Greek *as* sentiments!
Both nervous grown, to keep our spirits up,
We now and then take down a hearty cup.
What shall we do? —— *If Comedy forsake us!*
They'll turn us out, and no one else will take us,
But why can't I be moral? —— *Let me try* ——
My heart thus pressing —— *fix'd my face and eye* —
With a sententious look, that nothing means,
(Faces are blocks, in sentimental scenes)
Thus I begin —— All is not gold that glitters,
Pleasure seems sweet, but proves a glass of bitters.
When ign'rance enters, folly is at hand;
Learning is better far than house and land.
Let not your virtue trip, who trips may stumble,
And virtue is not virtue, if she tumble.
I give it up —— *morals won't do for me;*
To make you laugh I must play tragedy.
One hope remains —— *hearing the maid was ill,*
A doctor *comes this night to shew his skill.*
To cheer her heart, and give your muscles motion,
He in five draughts *prepar'd, presents a potion:*
A kind of magic charm —— *for be assur'd,*
If you will swallow *it, the maid is cur'd:*
But desp'rate the Doctor, and her case is,
If you reject the dose, and make wry faces!
This truth he boasts, will boast it while he lives,
No pois'nous drugs *are mix'd in what he gives;*
Should he succeed, you'll give him his degree;
If not, within he will receive no fee!

1. Samuel Johnson (1709-84), the great lexicographer and man of letters, who befriended Goldsmith in London. He wrote the prologue to *The Good Natur'd Man* (1768).
2. Another indication that Goldsmith felt that he was going against public taste.
3. George Colman, the Elder (1732-94), manager of the Theatre Royal, Covent Garden, where *She Stoops*.... was first staged. Actually, Colman thought that the play would be a flop, and staged it only under considerable pressure.
4. Harry Woodward (1717-77), comic actor. He was joint manager (with Spranger Barry) of Crow Street Theatre, Dublin, from 1758 to 1763, and afterwards returned to act at Covent Garden. He created the role of Captain Absolute in Sheridan's *The Rivals* in 1775 (see below, p. 603).
5. A variation on Hamlet's line, ''Tis not alone my inky cloak, good mother', *Hamlet,* I.2.77.
6. Again, a reference to Hamlet's speech, 'But I have that within which passes show', *Hamlet,* I.2.85.
7. Ned Shuter (1728-76), comic actor, mentioned again at line 15. He played Hardcastle in *She Stoops*...., and later played Sir Anthony Absolute in *The Rivals.*

The college you, *must his pretensions back,*
Pronounce him regular, *or dub him* quack.

DRAMATIS PERSONAE

Men

SIR CHARLES MARLOW
YOUNG MARLOW *(his son)*
HARDCASTLE
HASTINGS
TONY LUMPKIN
DIGGORY[1]

Women

MRS. HARDCASTLE
MISS HARDCASTLE
MISS NEVILLE
MAID
Landlord, Servants, etc. etc.

ACT I, SCENE 1

A chamber in an old-fashioned house
Enter MRS. HARDCASTLE *and* MR. HARDCASTLE

MRS. HARDCASTLE: I vow, Mr. Hardcastle, you're very particular. Is there a creature in the whole country, but ourselves, that does not take a trip to town now and then, to rub off the rust a little? There's the two Miss Hoggs, and our neighbour, Mrs. Grigsby, go to take a month's polishing every winter.

HARDCASTLE: Ay, and bring back vanity and affectation to last them the whole year. I wonder why London cannot keep its own fools at home. In my time, the follies of the town crept slowly among us, but now they travel faster than a stage-coach. Its fopperies come down, not only as inside passengers, but in the very basket.[1]

MRS. HARDCASTLE: Ay, *your* times were fine times, indeed; you have been telling us of *them* for many a long year. Here we live in an old rumbling mansion, that looks for all the world like an inn, but that we never see company. Our best visitors are old Mrs. Oddfish, the curate's wife, and little Cripplegate, the lame dancing-master: And all our entertainment your old stories of Prince Eugene and the Duke of Marlborough. I hate such old-fashioned trumpery.

HARDCASTLE: And I love it. I love every thing that's old: old friends, old times, old manners, old books, old wine; and, I believe, Dorothy, (*taking her hand*) you'll own I have been pretty fond of an old wife.

MRS. HARDCASTLE: Lord, Mr. Hardcastle, you're for ever at your Dorothy's and your old wife's. You may be a Darby, but I'll be no Joan, I promise you. I'm not so old as you'd make me, by more than one good year. Add twenty to twenty, and make money of that.

HARDCASTLE: Let me see; twenty added to twenty, makes just fifty and seven.

MRS. HARDCASTLE: It's false, Mr. Hardcastle: I was but twenty when I was brought to bed of Tony, that I had by Mr. Lumpkin, my first husband; and he's not come to years of discretion yet.

HARDCASTLE: Nor ever will, I dare answer for him. Ay, you have taught *him* finely.

MRS. HARDCASTLE: No matter, Tony Lumpkin has a good fortune. My son is not to live by his learning. I don't think a boy wants much learning to spend fifteen hundred a year.

HARDCASTLE: Learning, quotha! a mere composition of tricks and mischief.

MRS. HARDCASTLE: Humour, my dear: nothing but humour. Come, Mr. Hardcastle, you must allow the boy a little humour.

HARDCASTLE: I'd sooner allow him an horse-pond. If burning the footmen's shoes, frighting the maids, and worrying the kittens, be humour, he has it. It was but yesterday he fastened my wig to the back of my chair, and when I went to make a bow, I popt my bald head in Mrs. Frizzle's face.

MRS. HARDCASTLE: And am I to blame? The poor boy was always too sickly to do any good. A school would be his death. When he comes to be a little stronger, who knows what a year or two's Latin may do for him?

HARDCASTLE: Latin for him! A cat and fiddle. No, no, the ale-house and the stable are the only schools he'll ever go to.

MRS. HARDCASTLE: Well, we must not snub the poor boy now, for I believe we shan't have him long

1. This name was added in the second impression, 1773. It is not in the Dublin printing, used here, which was based on the first London printing.
2. The overhanging back compartment on the outside of a stage-coach.

among us. Any body that looks in his face may see he's consumptive.

HARDCASTLE: Ay, if growing too fat be one of the symptoms.

MRS. HARDCASTLE: He coughs sometimes.

HARDCASTLE: Yes, when his liquor goes the wrong way.

MRS. HARDCASTLE: I'm actually afraid of his lungs.

HARDCASTLE: And truly so am I; for he sometimes whoops like a speaking trumpet —— (*Tony hallooing behind the scenes*) —— O there he goes —— A very consumptive figure, truly.

Enter TONY, *crossing the Stage*

MRS. HARDCASTLE: Tony, where are you going, my charmer? Won't you give papa and I a little of your company, lovee?

TONY: I'm in haste, mother, I cannot stay.

MRS. HARDCASTLE: You shan't venture out this raw evening, my dear: You look most shockingly.

TONY: I can't stay, I tell you. The Three Pigeons expects me down every moment. There's some fun going forward.

HARDCASTLE: Ay; the ale-house, the old place: I thought so.

MRS. HARDCASTLE: A low, paltry set of fellows.

TONY: Not so low neither. There's Dick Muggins the exciseman, Jack Slang the horse doctor, Little Aminadab that grinds the music box, and Tom Twist that spins the pewter platter.

MRS. HARDCASTLE: Pray, my dear, disappoint them for one night at least.

TONY: As for disappointing *them,* I should not so much mind; but I can't abide to disappoint *myself.*

MRS. HARDCASTLE: (*Detaining him*) You shan't go.

TONY: I will, I tell you.

MRS. HARDCASTLE: I say you shan't.

TONY: We'll see which is strongest, you or I.

Exit, hawling her out

HARDCASTLE (*Solus*) Ay, there goes a pair that only spoil each other. But is not the whole age in a combination to drive sense and discretion out of doors? There's my pretty darling Kate; the fashions of the times have almost infected her too. By living a year or two in town, she is as fond of gauze, and French frippery, as the best of them.

Enter MISS HARDCASTLE

HARDCASTLE: Blessings on my pretty innocence! Drest out as usual my Kate. Goodness! What a quantity of superfluous silk has thou got about thee, girl! I could never teach the fools of this age, that the indigent world could be cloathed out of the trimmings of the vain.

MISS HARDCASTLE: You know our agreement, Sir. You allow me the morning to receive and pay visits, and to dress in my own manner; and in the evening, I put on my housewife's dress to please you.

HARDCASTLE: Well, remember I insist on the terms of our agreement; and, by the bye, I believe I shall have occasion to try your obedience this very evening.

MISS HARDCASTLE: I protest, Sir, I don't comprehend your meaning.

HARDCASTLE: Then, to be plain with you, Kate, I expect the young gentleman I have chosen to be your husband from town this very day. I have his father's letter, in which he informs me his son is set out, and that he intends to follow himself shortly after.

MISS HARDCASTLE: Indeed! I wish I had known something of this before. Bless me, how shall I behave? It's a thousand to one I shan't like him; our meeting will be so formal, and so like a thing of business, that I shall find no room for friendship or esteem.

HARDCASTLE: Depend upon it, child, I'll never controul your choice; but Mr. Marlow, whom I have pitched upon, is the son of my old friend, Sir Charles Marlow, of whom you have heard me talk so often. The young gentleman has been bred a scholar, and is designed for an employment in the service of his country. I am told he's a man of an excellent understanding.

MISS HARDCASTLE: Is he?

HARDCASTLE: Very generous.

MISS HARDCASTLE: I believe I shall like him.

HARDCASTLE: Young and brave.

MISS HARDCASTLE: I'm sure I shall like him.

HARDCASTLE: And very handsome.

MISS HARDCASTLE: My dear Papa, say no more (*kissing his hand*) he's mine, I'll have him.

HARDCASTLE: And to crown all, Kate, he's one of the most bashful and reserved young fellows in all the world.

MISS HARDCASTLE: Eh! you have frozen me to death again. That word reserved, has undone all the rest of his accomplishments. A reserved lover, it is said, always makes a suspicious husband.

HARDCASTLE: On the contrary, modesty seldom resides in a breast that is not enriched with nobler virtues. It was the very feature in his character that first struck me.

MISS HARDCASTLE: He must have more striking features to catch me, I promise you. However, if he be so young, so handsome, and so every thing, as you mention, I believe he'll do still. I think I'll have him.

HARDCASTLE: Ay, Kate, but there is still an obstacle. It's more than an even wager, he may not have *you.*

MISS HARDCASTLE: My dear Papa, why will you mortify one so? — Well, if he refuses, instead of breaking my heart at his indifference, I'll only break my glass for its flattery. Set my cap to some newer fashion, and look out for some less difficult admirer.

HARDCASTLE: Bravely resolved! In the mean time I'll go prepare the servants for his reception; as we seldom see company they want as much training as a company of recruits, the first day's muster.

Exit

MISS HARDCASTLE: (*Sola*) Lud, this news of Papa's, puts me all in a flutter. Young, handsome; these he put last; but I put them foremost. Sensible, good-natured; I like all that. But then reserved, and sheepish, that's much against him. Yet can't he be cured of his timidity, by being taught to be proud of his wife? Yes, and can't I —— But I vow I'm disposing of the husband, before I have secured the lover.

Enter MISS NEVILLE

MISS HARDCASTLE: I'm glad you're come, Neville, my dear. Tell me, Constance, how do I look this evening? Is there any thing whimsical about me? Is it one of my well looking days, child? Am I in face to day?

MISS NEVILLE: Perfectly, my dear. Yet now I look again —— bless me! —— sure no accident has happened among the canary birds or the gold fishes. Has your brother or the cat been meddling? Or has the last novel been too moving?

MISS HARDCASTLE: No; nothing of all this. I have been threatened —— I can scarce get it out —— I have been threatened with a lover.

MISS NEVILLE: And his name ——

MISS HARDCASTLE: Is Marlow.

MISS NEVILLE: Indeed!

MISS HARDCASTLE: The son of Sir Charles Marlow.

MISS NEVILLE: As I live, the most intimate friend of Mr. Hastings, *my* admirer. They are never asunder. I believe you must have seen him when we lived in town.

MISS HARDCASTLE: Never.

MISS NEVILLE: He's a very singular character, I assure you. Among women of reputation and virtue, he is the modestest man alive; but his acquaintance give him a very different character among creatures of another stamp: you understand me.

MISS HARDCASTLE: An odd character, indeed. I shall never be able to manage him. What shall I do? Pshaw, think no more of him, but trust to occurrences for success. But how goes on your own affair my dear, has my mother been courting you for my brother Tony, as usual?

MISS NEVILLE: I have just come from one of our agreeable tête-a-têtes. She has been saying a hundred tender things, and setting off her pretty monster as the very pink of perfection.

MISS HARDCASTLE: And her partiality is such, that she actually thinks him so. A fortune like yours is no small temptation. Besides, as she has the sole management of it, I'm not surprized to see her unwilling to let it go out of the family.

MISS NEVILLE: A fortune like mine, which chiefly consists in jewels, is no such mighty temptation. But at any rate if my dear Hastings be but constant, I make no doubt to be too hard for her at last. However, I let her suppose that I am in love with her son, and she never once dreams that my affections are fixed upon another.

MISS HARDCASTLE: My good brother holds out stoutly. I could almost love him, for hating you so.

MISS NEVILLE: It is a good-natured creature at bottom, and I'm sure would wish to see me married to any body but himself. But my aunt's bell rings for our afternoon's walk round the improvements. Allons. Courage is necessary as our affairs are critical.

MISS HARDCASTLE: Would it were bed time and all were well.

Exeunt

ACT I, SCENE 2

An Alehouse Room

Several shabby fellows, with Punch and Tobacco.
TONY *at the head of the Table, a little higher than the rest: A mallet in his hand*

OMNES: Hurrea, hurrea, hurrea, bravo.

FIRST FELLOW: Now, gentlemen, silence for a

song. The 'Squire is going to knock himself down for a song.[1]

OMNES: Ay, a song, a song.

TONY: Then I'll sing you, gentlemen, a song I made upon this ale-house, the Three Pigeons.

SONG

Let school-masters puzzle their brain,
With grammar and nonsense, and learning;
Good liquor, I stoutly maintain,
Gives genus *a better discerning.*
Let them brag of their Heathenish Gods,
Their Lethes, their Styxes, and Stygians;
Their Quis, and their Quae, and their Quods,
They're all but a parcel of Pigeons.
Toroddle, toroddle, toroll.

When Methodist preachers come down,
A preaching that drinking is sinful,
I'll wager the rascals a crown,
They always preach best with a skinful.
But when you come down with your pence,
For a slice of their scurvy religion,
I'll leave it to all men of sense,
But you my good friend are the pigeon.
Toroddle, toroddle, toroll.

Then come, put the jorum about,
And let us be merry and clever,
Our hearts and our liquors are stout,
Here's the Three Jolly Pigeons for ever.
Let some cry up woodcock or hare,
Your bustards, your ducks, and your widgeons;
But of all the birds in the air,
Here's a health to the Three Jolly Pigeons.
Toroddle, toroddle, toroll.

OMNES: Bravo, bravo.

FIRST FELLOW: The 'Squire has got spunk in him.

SECOND FELLOW: I loves to hear him sing, bekeays[2] he never gives us nothing that's *low.*

THIRD FELLOW: O damn any thing that's *low,* I cannot bear it.

FOURTH FELLOW: The genteel thing is the genteel thing at any time. If so be that a gentleman bees in a concatenation accordingly.

THIRD FELLOW: I like the maxum of it, Master Muggins. What, tho' I am obligated to dance a bear, a man may be a gentleman for all that. May this be my poison if my bear ever dances but to the very genteelest of tunes. Water Parted,[3] or the minuet in Ariadne.[4]

SECOND FELLOW: What a pity it is the 'Squire is not come to his own. It would be well for all the publicans within ten miles round of him.

TONY: Ecod and so it would Master Slang. I'd then shew what it was to keep choice of company.

SECOND FELLOW: O he takes after his own father for that. To be sure old 'Squire Lumpkin was the finest gentleman I ever set my eyes on. For winding the streight horn, or beating a thicket for a hare, or a wench, he never had his fellow. It was a saying in the place, that he kept the best horses, dogs and girls in the whole county.

TONY: Ecod, and when I'm of age I'll be no bastard I promise you. I have been thinking of Bet Bouncer and the miller's gray mare to begin with. But come, my boys, drink about and be merry, for you pay no reckoning. Well Stingo, what's the matter?

Enter LANDLORD

LANDLORD: There be two gentlemen in a post-chaise at the door. They have lost their way upo' the forest; and they are talking something about Mr. Hardcastle.

TONY: As sure as can be one of them must be the gentleman that's coming down to court my sister. Do they seem to be Londoners?

LANDLORD: I believe they may. They look woundily[5] like Frenchmen.

TONY: Then desire them to step this way, and I'll set them right in a twinkling. (*Exit* LANDLORD) Gentlemen, as they mayn't be good enough company for you, step down for a moment, and I'll be with you in the squeezing of a lemon.

Exeunt MOB

TONY: (*Solus*) Father-in-law has been calling me whelp, and hound, this half year. Now if I pleased, I could be so revenged upon the old grumbletonian. But then I'm afraid —— afraid of what! I shall soon be worth fifteen hundred a year, and let him frighten me out of *that* if he can.

1. A pun: the phrase usually refers to selling at auction for a low price. The First Fellow, with a sly sense of humour, refers to the mallet that Tony wields to keep order and suggests that Tony is determined to sell himself cheaply.
2. because. Goldsmith uses phonetic spellings in this scene to suggest the realism of rustic speech.
3. A song in Thomas Arne's opera *Artaxerxes* (1762).
4. An opera by Handel, first staged in 1734.
5. (dialect) exceedingly.

Enter LANDORD, *conducting* MARLOW and HASTINGS

MARLOW: What a tedious uncomfortable day have we had of it! We were told it was but forty miles across the country, and we have come above threescore.

HASTINGS: And all, Marlow, from that unaccountable reserve of yours, that would not let us enquire more frequently on the way.

MARLOW: I own, Hastings, I am unwilling to lay myself under an obligation to every one I meet; and often, stand the chance of an unmannerly answer.

HASTINGS: At present, however, we are not likely to receive any answer.

TONY: No offence, gentlemen. But I'm told you have been enquiring for one Mr. Hardcastle, in these parts. Do you know what part of the country you are in?

HASTINGS: Not in the least Sir, but should thank you for information.

TONY: Nor the way you came?

HASTINGS: No, Sir; but if you can inform us ——

TONY: Why, gentlemen, if you know neither the road you are going, nor where you are, nor the road you came, the first thing I have to inform you is, that — You have lost your way.

MARLOW: We wanted no ghost to tell us that.[6]

TONY: Pray, gentlemen, may I be so bold as to ask the place from whence you came?

MARLOW: That's not necessary towards directing us where we are to go.

TONY: No offence; but question for question is all fair, you know. Pray, gentlemen, is not this same Hardcastle a cross-grain'd, old-fashion'd, whimsical fellow, with an ugly face; a daughter, and a pretty son?

HASTINGS: We have not seen the gentleman, but he has the family you mention.

TONY: The daughter, a tall trapesing, trolloping, talkative maypole — The son, a pretty, well-bred, agreeable youth, that every body is fond of.

MARLOW: Our information differs in this. The daughter is said to be well bred and beautiful; the son, an aukward booby, reared up, and spoiled at his mother's apron-string.

TONY: He-he-hem — Then, gentlemen, all I have to tell you is, that you won't reach Mr. Hardcastle's house this night, I believe.

HASTINGS: Unfortunate!

TONY: It's a damn'd long, dark, boggy, dirty, dangerous way. Stingo, tell the gentlemen the way to Mr. Hardcastle's. (*Winking upon the* LANDLORD) Mr. Hardcastle's, of Quagmire Marsh, you understand me.

LANDLORD: Master Hardcastle's! Lock-a-daisy, my masters, you're come a deadly deal wrong! When you came to the bottom of the hill, you should have cross'd down Squash-lane.

MARLOW: Cross down Squash-lane!

LANDLORD: Then you were to keep streight forward, 'till you came to four roads.

MARLOW: Come to where four roads meet!

TONY: Ay; but you must be sure to take only one of them.

MARLOW: O Sir, you're facetious.

TONY: Then keeping to the right, you are to go side-ways till you come upon Crack-skull common: there you must look sharp for the track of the wheel, and go forward, 'till you come to farmer Murrain's barn. Coming to the farmer's barn, you are to turn to the right, and then to the left, and then to the right about again, till you find out the old mill ——

MARLOW: Zounds, man! we could as soon find out the longitude!

HASTINGS: What's to be done, Marlow?

MARLOW: This house promises but a poor reception; though perhaps the Landlord can accommodate us.

LANDLORD: Alack, master, we have but one spare bed in the whole house.

TONY: And to my knowledge, that's taken up by three lodgers already. (*After a pause, in which the rest seem disconcerted*) I have hit it. Don't you think, Stingo, our landlady could accommodate the gentlemen by the fire-side, with —— three chairs and a bolster?

HASTINGS: I hate sleeping by the fire-side.

MARLOW: And I detest your three chairs and a bolster.

TONY: You do, do you? — then let me see — what — if you go on a mile further, to the Buck's Head; the old Buck's Head on the hill, one of the best inns in the whole county?

HASTINGS: O ho! so we have escaped an adventure for this night, however.

LANDLORD: (*Apart to* TONY) Sure, you ben't sending them to your father's as an inn, be you?

TONY: Mum, you fool you. Let *them* find that out. (*To them*) You have only to keep on streight

6. cf. *Hamlet* (I.5.125-26), 'There needs no ghost, my lord, come from the grave/To tell us this.'

forward, till you come to a large old house by the road side. You'll see a pair of large horns over the door. That's the sign. Drive up the yard, and call stoutly about you.

HASTINGS: Sir, we are obliged to you. The servants can't miss the way?

TONY: No, no: But I'll tell you though, the landlord is rich, and going to leave off business; so he wants to be thought a Gentleman, saving your presence, he, he, he. He'll be for giving you his company, and ecod if you mind him, he'll persuade you that his mother was an alderman, and his aunt a justice of peace.

LANDLORD: A troublesome old blade to be sure; but a keeps[7] as good wines and beds as any in the whole county.

MARLOW: Well, if he supplies us with these, we shall want no further connexion. We are to turn to the right, did you say?

TONY: No, no; streight forward. I'll just step myself, and shew you a piece of the way. (*To the* LANDLORD) Mum.

LANDLORD: Ah, bless your heart, for a sweet, pleasant — damn'd mischievous son of a whore.

Exeunt

7. he keeps.

ACT II

An old-fashioned house
Enter HARDCASTLE, *followed by three or four aukward Servants*

HARDCASTLE: Well, I hope you're perfect in the table exercise I have been teaching you these three days. You all know your posts and your places, and can shew that you have been used to good company, without ever stirring from home.

OMNES: Ay, ay.

HARDCASTLE: When company comes, you are not to pop out and stare, and then run in again like frighted rabbits in a warren.

OMNES: No, no.

HARDCASTLE: You, Diggory, whom I have taken from the barn, are to make a shew at the side-table; and you, Roger, whom I have advanced from the plow, are to place yourself behind *my* chair. But you're not to stand so, with your hands in your pockets. Take your hands from your pockets, Roger; and from your head, you blockhead you. See how Diggory carries his hands. They're a little too stiff, indeed, but that's no great matter.

DIGGORY: Ay, mind how I hold them. I learned to hold my hands this way, when I was upon drill for the militia. And so being upon drill ——

HARDCASTLE: You must not be so talkative, Diggory. You must be all attention to the guests. You must hear us talk, and not think of talking; you must see us drink, and not think of drinking; you must see us eat, and not think of eating.

DIGGORY: By the laws, your worship, that's parfectly unpossible. Whenever Diggory sees yeating going forward, ecod he's always wishing for a mouthful himself.

HARDCASTLE: Blockhead! Is not a belly full in the kitchen as good as a belly full in the parlour? Stay your stomach with that reflection.

DIGGORY: Ecod I thank your worship, I'll make a shift to stay my stomach with a slice of cold beef in the pantry.

HARDCASTLE: Diggory, you are too talkative. Then if I happen to say a good thing, or tell a good story at table, you must not all burst out a-laughing, as if you made part of the company.

DIGGORY: Then ecod your worship must not tell the story of Ould Grouse in the gun-room: I can't help laughing at that — he! he! he! — for the soul of me. We have laughed at that these twenty years — ha! ha! ha!

HARDCASTLE: Ha! ha! ha! The story is a good one. Well, honest Diggory, you may laugh at that — but still remember to be attentive. Suppose one of the company should call for a glass of wine, how will you behave? A glass of wine, Sir, if you please (*to* DIGGORY) — Eh, why don't you move?

DIGGORY: Ecod, your worship, I never have courage till I see the eatables and drinkables brought upo' the table, and then I'm as bauld as a lion.

HARDCASTLE: What, will no body move?

FIRST SERVANT: I'm not to leave this pleace.

SECOND SERVANT: I'm sure it's no pleace of mine.

THIRD SERVANT: Nor mine, for sartain.

DIGGORY: Wauns, and I'm sure it canna be mine.

HARDCASTLE: You numbskulls! and so while, like your betters, you are quarrelling for places, the guest must be starved. O you dunces! I find I must begin all over again. —— But don't I hear a coach drive into the yard? To your posts, you blockheads.

I'll go in the meantime and give my old friend's son a hearty reception at the gate.

Exit HARDCASTLE

DIGGORY: By the elevens, my pleas is gone quite out of my head.

ROGER: I know that my pleas is to be every where.

FIRST SERVANT: Where the devil is mine?

SECOND SERVANT: My pleas is to be no where at all; and so Ize go about my business.

Exeunt SERVANTS, *running about as if frighted, different ways*

Enter SERVANTS *with Candles, shewing in* MARLOW *and* HASTINGS

SERVANT: Welcome, gentlemen, very welcome. This way.

HASTINGS: After the disappointments of the day, welcome once more, Charles, to the comforts of a clean room and a good fire. Upon my word, a very well-looking house, antique, but creditable.

MARLOW: The usual fate of a large mansion. Having first ruined the master by good housekeeping, it at last comes to levy contributions as an inn.

HASTINGS: As you say, we passengers are to be taxed to pay all these fineries. I have often seen a good side-board, or a marble chimney-piece, tho' not actually put in the bill, enflame a reckoning confoundedly.

MARLOW: Travellers, George, must pay in all places. The only difference is, that in good inns, you pay dearly for luxuries; in bad inns, you are fleeced and starved.

HASTINGS: You have lived pretty much among them. In truth, I have been often surprized, that you who have seen so much of the world, with your natural good sense, and your many opportunities, could never yet acquire a requisite share of assurance.

MARLOW: The Englishman's malady. But tell me, George, where could I have learned that assurance you talk of? My life has been chiefly spent in a college, or an inn, in seclusion from that lovely part of the creation that chiefly teach men confidence. I don't know that I was ever familiarly acquainted with a single modest woman — except my mother —— But among females of another class you know —

HASTINGS: Ay, among them you are impudent enough of all conscience.

MARLOW: They are of *us* you know.

HASTINGS: But in the company of women of reputation I never saw such an ideot, such a trembler; you look for all the world as if you wanted an opportunity of stealing out of the room.

MARLOW: Why man that's because I *do* want to steal out of the room. Faith, I have often formed a resolution to break the ice, and rattle away at any rate. But I don't know how, a single glance from a pair of fine eyes has totally overset my resolution. An impudent fellow may counterfeit modesty, but I'll be hanged if a modest man can ever counterfeit impudence.

HASTINGS: If you could but say half the fine things to them that I have heard you lavish upon the bar-maid of an inn, or even a college bed-maker —

MARLOW: Why, George, I can't say fine things to them. They freeze, they petrify me. They may talk of a comet, or a burning mountain, or some such bagatelle. But to me, a modest woman, drest out in all her finery, is the most tremendous object of the whole creation.

HASTINGS: Ha, ha, ha. At this rate, man, how can you ever expect to marry!

MARLOW: Never, unless as among kings and princes, my bride were to be courted by proxy. If, indeed, like an Eastern bridegroom, one were to be introduced to a wife he never saw before, it might be endured. But to go through all the terrors of a formal courtship, together with the episode of aunts, grand-mothers and cousins, and at last to blurt out the broad staring question, of, *madam will you marry me?* No, no, that's a strain much above me I assure you.

HASTINGS: I pity you. But how do you intend behaving to the lady you are come down to visit at the request of your father?

MARLOW: As I behave to all other ladies. Bow very low, answer yes, or no, to all her demands — But for the rest, I don't think I shall venture to look in her face, till I see my father's again.

HASTINGS: I'm surprized that one who is so warm a friend can be so cool a lover.

MARLOW: To be explicit, my dear Hastings, my chief inducement down was to be instrumental in forwarding your happiness, not my own. Miss Neville loves you, the family don't know you, as my friend you are sure of a reception, and let honour do the rest.

HASTINGS: My dear Marlow! But I'll suppress the emotion. Were I a wretch, meanly seeking to carry off a fortune, you should be the last man in the world I would apply to for assistance. But Miss Neville's person is all I ask, and that is mine, both from her deceased father's consent, and her own inclination.

MARLOW: Happy man! You have talents and art to captivate any woman. I'm doom'd to adore the sex, and yet to converse with the only part of it I despise. This stammer in my address, and this aukward prepossessing visage of mine, can never permit me to soar above the reach of a milliner's 'prentice, or one of the dutchesses of Drury-lane.[1] Pshaw! this fellow here to interrupt us.

Enter HARDCASTLE

HARDCASTLE: Gentlemen, once more you are heartily welcome. Which is Mr. Marlow? Sir, you're heartily welcome. It's not my way, you see, to receive my friends with my back to the fire. I like to give them a hearty reception in the old stile at my gate. I like to see their horses and trunks taken care of.

MARLOW: (*Aside*) He has got our names from the servants already. (*To him*) We approve your caution and hospitality, Sir. (*To* HASTINGS) I have been thinking, George, of changing our travelling dresses in the morning. I am grown confoundedly ashamed of mine.

HARDCASTLE: I beg, Mr. Marlow, you'll use no ceremony in this house.

HASTINGS: I fancy, Charles, you're right: the first blow is half the battle. I intend opening the campaign with the white and gold.

HARDCASTLE: Mr. Marlow — Mr. Hastings — gentlemen —— pray be under no constraint in this house. This is Liberty-hall, gentlemen. You may do just as you please here.

MARLOW: Yet, George, if we open the campaign too fiercely at first, we may want ammunition before it is over. I think to reserve the embroidery to secure a retreat.

HARDCASTLE: Your talking of a retreat, Mr. Marlow, puts me in mind of the Duke of Marlborough, when he went to besiege Denain.[2] He first summoned the garrison.

MARLOW: Don't you think the *ventre dor*[3] waistcoat will do with the plain brown?

HARDCASTLE: He first summoned the garrison, which might consist of about five thousand men ——

HASTINGS: I think not: Brown and yellow mix but very poorly.

HARDCASTLE: I say, gentlemen, as I was telling you, he summoned the garrison, which might consist of about five thousand men ——

MARLOW: The girls like finery.

HARDCASTLE: Which might consist of about five thousand men, well appointed with stores, ammunition, and other implements of war. Now, says the Duke of Marlborough to George Brooks, that stood next to him — you must have heard of George Brooks; I'll pawn my Dukedom, says he, but I take that garrison without spilling a drop of blood. So ——

MARLOW: What, my good friend, if you gave us a glass of punch in the mean time, it would help us to carry on the siege with vigour.

HARDCASTLE: Punch, Sir! (*Aside*) This is the most unaccountable kind of modesty I ever met with.

MARLOW: Yes, Sir, Punch. A glass of warm punch, after our journey, will be comfortable. This is Liberty-hall, you know.

HARDCASTLE: Here's cup,[4] Sir.

MARLOW: (*Aside*) So this fellow, in his Liberty-hall will only let us have just what he pleases.

HARDCASTLE: (*Taking the Cup*) I hope you'll find it to your mind. I have prepared it with my own hands, and I believe you'll own the ingredients are tolerable. Will you, be so good as to pledge me, Sir? Here, Mr. Marlow, here is to our better acquaintance. (*Drinks*)

MARLOW: (*Aside*) A very impudent fellow this! but he's a character, and I'll humour him a little. Sir, my service to you. (*Drinks*)

HASTINGS: (*Aside*) I see this fellow wants to give us his company, and forgets that he's an innkeeper, before he has learned to be a gentleman.

MARLOW: From the excellence of your cup, my old friend, I suppose you have a good deal of business in this part of the country. Warm work, now and then, at elections, I suppose.

HARDCASTLE: No, Sir, I have long given that work over. Since our betters have hit upon the

1. prostitutes.
2. A village in north-eastern France; the French defeated the Allies there in July 1712 during the war of the Spanish Succession. The Duke of Marlborough had been recently dismissed and was not present.
3. gold-fronted.

4. A drink of spiced wine: cf. punch (above), a more expensive drink because it was made of whiskey or brandy with fruit and spices.

expedient of electing each other, there's no business *for us that sell ale.*[5]

HASTINGS: So, then you have no turn for politics I find.

HARDCASTLE: Not in the least. There was a time, indeed, I fretted myself about the mistakes of government, like other people; but finding myself every day grow more angry, and the government growing no better, I left it to mend itself. Since that, I no more trouble my head about *Heyder Ally*, or *Ally Cawn*, than about *Ally Croaker*.[6] Sir, my service to you.

HASTINGS: So that with eating above stairs, and drinking below, with receiving your friends within, and amusing them without, you lead a good pleasant bustling life of it.

HARDCASTLE: I do stir about a great deal, that's certain. Half the differences of the parish are adjusted in this very parlour.

MARLOW: (*After drinking*) And you have an argument in your cup, old gentleman, better than any in Westminster-hall.

HARDCASTLE: Ay, young gentleman, that, and a little philosophy.

MARLOW: (*Aside*) Well, this is the first time I ever heard of an innkeeper's philosophy.

HASTINGS: So then, like an experienced general, you attack them on every quarter. If you find their reason manageable, you attack it with your philosophy; if you find they have no reason, you attack them with this. Here's your health, my philosopher. (*Drinks*)

HARDCASTLE: Good, very good, thank you; ha, ha. Your Generalship puts me in mind of Prince Eugene, when he fought the Turks at the battle of Belgrade. You shall hear.

MARLOW: Instead of the battle of Belgrade, I believe it's almost time to talk about supper. What has your philosophy got in the house for supper?

HARDCASTLE: For Supper, Sir! (*Aside*) Was ever such a request to a man in his own house?

MARLOW: Yes, Sir, supper Sir; I begin to feel an appetite. I shall make devilish work to-night in the larder, I promise you.

HARDCASTLE: (*Aside*) Such a brazen dog sure never my eyes beheld. (*To him*) Why really, Sir, as for supper I can't well tell. My Dorothy, and the cook maid, settle these things between them. I leave these kind of things entirely to them.

MARLOW: You do, do you?

HARDCASTLE: Entirely. By-the-bye, I believe they are in actual consultation upon what's for supper this moment in the kitchen.

MARLOW: Then I beg they'll admit *me* as one of their privy council. It's a way I have got. When I travel, I always chuse to regulate my own supper. Let the cook be called. No offence I hope, Sir.

HARDCASTLE: O no, Sir, none in the least; yet I don't know how: our Bridget, the cook maid, is not very communicative upon these occasions. Should we send for her, she might scold us all out of the house.

HASTINGS: Let's see your list of the larder then. I ask it as a favour. I always match my appetite to my bill of fare.

MARLOW: (*To* HARDCASTLE, *who looks at them with surprize*) Sir, he's very right, and it's my way too.

HARDCASTLE: Sir, you have a right to command here. Here, Roger, bring us the bill of fare for to-night's supper. I believe it's drawn out. Your manner, Mr. Hastings, puts me in mind of my uncle, Colonel Wallop. It was a saying of his, that no man was sure of his supper till he had eaten it.

HASTINGS: (*Aside*) All upon the high ropes! His uncle a Colonel! We shall soon hear of his mother being a justice of peace. But let's hear the bill of fare.[7]

MARLOW: (*Perusing*) What's here? For the first course; for the second course; for the dessert. The devil, Sir, do you think we have brought down the whole Joiners Company, or the Corporation of Bedford, to eat up such a supper? Two or three little things clean and comfortable, will do.

HASTINGS: But, let's hear it.

MARLOW: (*Reading*) For the first course at the top, a pig and pruin[8] sauce.

HASTINGS: Damn your pig, I say.

MARLOW: And damn your pruin sauce, say I.

HARDCASTLE: And yet, gentlemen, to men that are hungry, pig, with pruin sauce, is very good eating.

5. i.e. ordinary people. The phrase is ironically misunderstood here.

6. *Heyder Ally*, or *Ally Cawn*: a maharaja and nabob, respectively, in the news around 1760. *Ally Croaker*, by contrast, was a character in a popular Irish song.

7. Presumably Roger has now entered with the menu, has given it to Hardcastle, who has handed it to Marlow, and Roger has then exited. Goldsmith does not seem to have provided the necessary stage directions.

8. prune.

MARLOW: At the bottom, a calve's tongue and brains.

HASTINGS: Let your brains be knock'd out, my good Sir; I don't like them.

MARLOW: Or you may clap them on a plate by themselves. I do.

HARDCASTLE: (*Aside*) Their impudence confounds me. (*To them*) Gentlemen, you are my guests, make what alterations you please. Is there any thing else you wish to retrench or alter, gentlemen?

MARLOW: Item. A pork pie, a boiled rabbet and sausages, a florentine,[9] a shaking pudding, and a dish of tiff—taff—taffety cream!

HASTINGS: Confound your made dishes, I shall be as much at a loss in this house as at a green and yellow dinner at the French ambassador's table. I'm for plain eating.

HARDCASTLE: I'm sorry, gentlemen, that I have nothing you like, but if there be any thing you have a particular fancy to ——

MARLOW: Why, really, Sir, your bill of fare is so exquisite, that any one part of it is full as good as another. Send us what you please. So much for supper. And now to see that our beds are air'd, and properly taken care of.

HARDCASTLE: I entreat you'll leave all that to me. You shall not stir a step.

MARLOW: Leave that to you! I protest, Sir, you must excuse me, I always look to these things myself.

HARDCASTLE: I must insist, Sir, you'll make yourself easy on that head.

MARLOW: You see I'm resolved on it. (*Aside*) A very troublesome fellow this, as ever I met with.

HARDCASTLE: Well, Sir, I'm resolved at least to attend you. (*Aside*) This may be modern modesty, but I never saw any thing look so like old-fashioned impudence.

Exeunt MARLOW *and* HARDCASTLE

HASTINGS: (*Solus*) So I find this fellow's civilities begin to grow troublesome. But who can be angry at those assiduities which are meant to please him? Ha! what do I see? Miss Neville, by all that's happy!

Enter MISS NEVILLE

MISS NEVILLE: My dear Hastings! To what unexpected good fortune? to what accident am I to ascribe this happy meeting?

HASTINGS: Rather let me ask the same question, as I could never have hoped to meet my dearest Constance at an inn.

MISS NEVILLE: An inn! sure you mistake! my aunt, my guardian, lives here. What could induce you to think this house an inn?

HASTINGS: My friend Mr. Marlow, with whom I came down, and I, have been sent here as to an inn, I assure you. A young fellow whom we accidentally met at a house hard by directed us hither.

MISS NEVILLE: Certainly it must be one of my hopeful cousin's tricks, of whom you have heard me talk so often, ha! ha! ha! ha!

HASTINGS: He whom your aunt intends for you? He of whom I have such just apprehensions?

MISS NEVILLE: You have nothing to fear from him, I assure you. You'd adore him if you knew how heartily he despises me. My aunt knows it too, and has undertaken to court me for him, and actually begins to think she has made a conquest.

HASTINGS: Thou dear dissembler! You must know, my Constance, I have just seized this happy opportunity of my friend's visit here to get admittance into the family. The horses that carried us down are now fatigued with their journey, but they'll soon be refreshed; and then if my dearest girl will trust in her faithful Hastings, we shall soon be landed in France, where even among slaves the laws of marriage are respected.[10]

MISS NEVILLE: I have often told you, that though ready to obey you, I yet should leave my little fortune behind with reluctance. The greatest part of it was left me by my uncle, the India Director, and chiefly consists in jewels. I have been for some time persuading my aunt to let me wear them. I fancy I'm very near succeeding. The instant they are put into my possession you shall find me ready to make them and myself yours.

HASTINGS: Perish the baubles! Your person is all I desire. In the meantime, my friend Marlow must not be let into his mistake. I know the strange reserve of his temper is such, that if abruptly informed of it, he would instantly quit the house before our plan was ripe for execution.

MISS NEVILLE: But how shall we keep him in the deception? Miss Hardcastle is just returned from walking; what if we still continue to deceive him? —— This, this way —— (*They confer*)

9. meat pie.

10. A remark received at the time as Goldsmith's criticism of the Royal Marriage Act of 1772.

Enter MARLOW

MARLOW: The assiduities of these good people teize me beyond bearing. My host seems to think it ill manners to leave me alone, and so he claps not only himself but his old-fashioned wife on my back. They talk of coming to sup with us too; and then, I suppose, we are to run the gauntlet thro' all the rest of the family. — What have we got here! ——

HASTINGS: My dear Charles! Let me congratulate you! — The most fortunate accident! — Who do you think is just alighted?

MARLOW: Cannot guess.

HASTINGS: Our mistresses boy, Miss Hardcastle and Miss Neville. Give me leave to introduce Miss Constance Neville to your acquaintance. Happening to dine in the neighbourhood, they called, on their return to take fresh horses, here. Miss Hardcastle has just stept into the next room, and will be back in an instant. Wasn't it lucky? eh!

MARLOW: (*Aside*) I have just been mortified enough of all conscience, and here comes something to complete my embarrassment.

HASTINGS: Well! but wasn't it the most fortunate thing in the world?

MARLOW: Oh! yes. Very fortunate — a most joyful encounter —— But our dresses, George, you know, are in disorder — What if we should postpone the happiness 'till to-morrow? —— To-morrow at her own house —— It will be every bit as convenient —— And rather more respectful —— To-morrow let it be. (*Offering to go*)

MISS NEVILLE: By no means, Sir. Your ceremony will displease her. The disorder of your dress will shew the ardour of your impatience. Besides, she knows you are in the house, and will permit you to see her.

MARLOW: O! the devil! how shall I support it? Hem! hem! Hastings, you must not go. You are to assist me, you know. I shall be confoundedly ridiculous. Yet, hang it! I'll take courage. Hem!

HASTINGS: Pshaw man! it's but the first plunge, and all's over. She's but a woman, you know.

MARLOW: And of all women, she that I dread most to encounter!

Enter MISS HARDCASTLE: *as returned from walking, a Bonnet, &c.*

HASTINGS: (*Introducing them*) Miss Hardcastle, Mr. Marlow, I'm proud of bringing two persons of such merit together, that only want to know, to esteem each other.

MISS HARDCASTLE: (*Aside*) Now, for meeting my modest gentleman with a demure face, and quite in his own manner. (*After a pause, in which he appears very uneasy and disconcerted*) I'm glad of your safe arrival, Sir — I'm told you had some accidents by the way.

MARLOW: Only a few, Madam. Yes, we had some. Yes, Madam, a good many accidents, but should be sorry — Madam — or rather glad of any accidents — that are so agreeably concluded. Hem!

HASTINGS: (*To him*) You never spoke better in your whole life. Keep it up, and I'll insure you the victory.

MISS HARDCASTLE: I'm afraid you flatter, Sir. You that have seen so much of the finest company can find little entertainment in an obscure corner of the country.

MARLOW: (*Gathering courage*) I have lived, indeed, in the world, Madam; but I have kept very little company. I have been but an observer upon life, Madam, while others were enjoying it.

MISS NEVILLE: But that, I am told, is the way to enjoy it at last.

HASTINGS: (*To him*) Cicero never spoke better. Once more, and you are confirm'd in assurance for ever.

MARLOW: (*To him*) Hem! Stand by me then, and when I'm down, throw in a word or two to set me up again.

MISS HARDCASTLE: An observer, like you, upon life, were, I fear, disagreeably employed, since you must have had much more to censure than to approve.

MARLOW: Pardon me, Madam, I was always willing to be amused. The folly of most people is rather an object of mirth than uneasiness.

HASTINGS: (*To him*) Bravo, Bravo. Never spoke so well in your whole life. Well! Miss Hardcastle, I see that you and Mr. Marlow are going to be very good company. I believe our being here will but embarrass the interview.

MARLOW: Not in the least, Mr. Hastings. We like your company of all things. (*To him*) Zounds! George, sure you won't go? How can you leave us?

HASTINGS: Our presence will but spoil conversation, so we'll retire to the next room. (*To him*) You don't consider, man, that we are to manage a little tête-à-tête of our own. *Exeunt*

MISS HARDCASTLE: (*After a pause*) But you have not been wholly an observer, I presume, Sir: The ladies I should hope have employed some part of your addresses.

MARLOW: (*Relapsing into timidity*) Pardon me, Madam, I — I — I as yet have studied — only — to — deserve them.

MISS HARDCASTLE: And that, some say, is the very worst way to obtain them.

MARLOW: Perhaps so, Madam. But I love to converse only with the more grave and sensible part of the sex. —— But I'm afraid I grow tiresome.

MISS HARDCASTLE: Not at all, Sir; there is nothing I like so much as grave conversation myself; I could hear it for ever. Indeed I have often been surprized how a man of *sentiment* could ever admire those light airy pleasures, where nothing reaches the heart.

MARLOW: It's —— a disease —— of the mind, Madam. In the variety of tastes there must be some who wanting a relish —— for —— um — a — um.

MISS HARDCASTLE: I understand you, Sir. There must be some who wanting a relish for refined pleasures, pretend to despise what they are incapable of tasting.

MARLOW: My meaning, Madam, but infinitely better expressed. And I can't help observing —— a ——

MISS HARDCASTLE: (*Aside*) Who could ever suppose this fellow impudent upon some occasions. (*To him*) You were going to observe, Sir ——

MARLOW: I was observing, Madam — I protest, Madam, I forget what I was going to observe.

MISS HARDCASTLE: (*Aside*) I vow and so do I. (*To him*) You were observing, Sir, that in this age of hypocrisy — something about hypocrisy, Sir.

MARLOW: Yes, Madam. In this age of hypocrisy there are few who upon strict enquiry do not — a — a — a —

MISS HARDCASTLE: I understand you perfectly, Sir.

MARLOW: (*Aside*) Egad! and that's more than I do myself.

MISS HARDCASTLE: You mean that in this hypocritical age there are few that do not condemn in public what they practise in private, and think they pay every debt to virtue when they praise it.

MARLOW: True, Madam; those who have most virtue in their mouths, have least of it in their bosoms. But I'm sure I tire you, Madam.

MISS HARDCASTLE: Not in the least, Sir; there's something so agreeable and spirited in your manner, such life and force — pray, Sir, go on.

MARLOW: Yes, Madam, I was saying —— that there are some occasions — when a total want of courage, Madam, destroys all the — and puts us — upon a — a — a —

MISS HARDCASTLE: I agree with you entirely, a want of courage upon some occasions assumes the appearance of ignorance, and betrays us when we most want to excel. I beg you'll proceed.

MARLOW: Yes, Madam. Morally speaking, Madam — But I see Miss Neville expecting us in the next room. I would not intrude for the world.

MISS HARDCASTLE: I protest, Sir, I never was more agreeably entertained in all my life. Pray go on.

MARLOW: Yes, Madam. I was — But she beckons us to join her. Madam, shall I do myself the honour to attend you?

MISS HARDCASTLE: Well then, I'll follow.

MARLOW: (*Aside*) This pretty smooth dialogue has done for me.

Exit

MISS HARDCASTLE: (*Sola*) Ha! ha! ha! Was there ever such a sober sentimental interview? I'm certain he scarce look'd in my face the whole time. Yet the fellow, but for his unaccountable bashfulness, is pretty well too. He has good sense, but then so buried in his fears, that it fatigues one more than ignorance. If I could teach him a little confidence, it would be doing somebody that I know of a piece of service. But who is that somebody? — that, faith, is a question I can scarce answer.

Exit

Enter TONY *and* MISS NEVILLE, *followed by* MRS. HARDCASTLE *and* HASTINGS

TONY: What do you follow me for, cousin Con? I wonder you're not ashamed to be so very engaging.[11]

MISS NEVILLE: I hope, cousin, one may speak to one's own relations, and not be to blame.

TONY: Ay, but I know what sort of a relation you want to make me though; but it won't do. I tell you, cousin Con, it won't do; so I beg you'll keep your distance, I want no nearer relationship. (*She follows, coquetting him to the back scene*)

MRS. HARDCASTLE: Well, I vow, Mr. Hastings, you are very entertaining. There's nothing in the world I love to talk of so much as London, and the fashions, though I was never there myself.

HASTINGS: Never there! You amaze me! From your air and manner, I concluded you had been

11. persuasive.

bred all your life either at Ranelagh, St. James's, or Tower-wharf.[12]

MRS. HARDCASTLE: O! Sir, you're only pleased to say so. We country persons can have no manner at all. I'm in love with the town, and that serves to raise me above some of our neighbouring rustics; but who can have a manner, that has never seen the Pantheon, the Grotto Gardens, and Borough, and such places where the Nobility chiefly resort? All I can do, is to enjoy London at second-hand. I take care to know every tête-à-tête from the Scandalous Magazine, and have all the fashions, as they come out, in a letter from the two Miss Rickets of Crooked-lane. Pray how do you like this head, Mr. Hastings?

HASTINGS: Extremely elegant and degagée,[13] upon my word, Madam. Your Friseur[14] is a Frenchman, I suppose?

MRS. HARDCASTLE: I protest I dressed it myself from a print in the Ladies Memorandum-book for the last year.

HASTINGS: Indeed! Such a head in a side-box, at the Playhouse, would draw as many gazers as a Lady-May'ress at a City Ball.

MRS. HARDCASTLE: I vow, since inoculation[15] began, there is no such thing to be seen as a plain woman; so one must dress a little particular or one may escape in the crowd.

HASTINGS: But that can never be your case, Madam, in any dress. (*Bowing*)

MRS. HARDCASTLE: Yet, what signifies *my* dressing, when I have such a piece of antiquity by my side as Mr. Hardcastle: all I can say will never argue down a single button from his cloaths. I have often wanted him to throw off his great flaxen wig, and where he was bald, to plaister it over like my Lord Pately, with powder.

HASTINGS: You are right, Madam; for, as among the ladies there are none ugly, so among the men there are none old.

MRS. HARDCASTLE: But what do you think his answer was? Why, with his usual Gothic vivacity, he said I only wanted him to throw off his wig to convert it into a tête[16] for my own wearing.

HASTINGS: Intolerable! At your age you may wear what you please, and it must become you.

MRS. HARDCASTLE: Pray, Mr. Hastings, what do you take to be the most fashionable age about town?

HASTINGS: Some time ago, forty was all the mode; but I'm told the ladies intend to bring up fifty for the ensuing winter.

MRS. HARDCASTLE: Seriously. Then I shall be too young for the fashion.

HASTINGS: No lady begins now to put on jewels 'till she's past forty. For instance, Miss there, in a polite circle, would be considered as a child, as a mere maker of samplers.

MRS. HARDCASTLE: And yet Mrs. Niece thinks herself as much a woman, and is as fond of jewels as the oldest of us all.

HASTINGS: Your niece, is she? And that young gentleman, a brother of yours, I should presume?

MRS. HARDCASTLE: My son, Sir. They are contracted to each other. Observe their little sports. They fall in and out ten times a day, as if they were man and wife already. (*To them*) Well Tony, child, what soft things are you saying to your cousin Constance this evening?

TONY: I have been saying no soft things; but that it's very hard to be followed about so. Ecod! I've not a place in the house now that's left to myself but the stable.

MRS. HARDCASTLE: Never mind him, Con, my dear. He's in another story behind your back.

MISS NEVILLE: There's something generous in my cousin's manner. He falls out before faces to be forgiven in private.

TONY: That's a damned confounded —— crack.

MRS. HARDCASTLE: Ah! he's a sly one. Don't you think they're like each other about the mouth, Mr. Hastings? The Blenkinsop mouth to a T. They're of a size too. Back to back, my pretties, that Mr. Hastings may see you. Come, Tony (*measuring*).

TONY: You had as good not make me, I tell you.

MISS NEVILLE: O lud! he has almost cracked my head.

MRS. HARDCASTLE: O the monster! For shame, Tony. You a man, and behave so!

TONY: If I'm a man, let me have my fortin.[17] Ecod! I'll not be made a fool of no longer.

12. A dubious area, in contrast to the other two, fashionable places. The joke is on Mrs Hardcastle.
13. (French) unconstrained.
14. (French) hairdresser.
15. i.e. against smallpox. Inoculation was introduced into England in 1718, but this did not save Goldsmith himself from the effects of the disease.
16. A woman's head of hair or wig, in fashion in the later eighteenth century.
17. fortune.

MRS. HARDCASTLE: Is this, ungrateful boy, all that I'm to get for the pains I have taken in your education? I that have rock'd you in your cradle, and fed that pretty mouth with a spoon! Did not I work that waistcoat to make you genteel? Did not I prescribe for you every day, and weep while the receipt was operating?

TONY: Ecod! you had reason to weep, for you have been dosing me ever since I was born. I have gone through every receipt in the complete houswife ten times over; and you have thoughts of coursing me through *Quincy*[18] next spring. But, Ecod! I tell you, I'll not be made a fool of no longer.

MRS. HARDCASTLE: Wasn't it all for your good, viper? Wasn't it all for your good?

TONY: I wish you'd let me and my good alone then. Snubbing[19] this way when I'm in spirits. If I'm to have any good, let it come of itself; not to keep dinging it, dinging it into one so.

MRS. HARDCASTLE: That's false; I never see you when you're in spirits. No, Tony, you then go to the alehouse or kennel. I'm never to be delighted with your agreeable wild notes, unfeeling monster!

TONY: Ecod! Mamma, your own notes are the wildest of the two.

MRS. HARDCASTLE: Was ever the like? But I see he wants to break my heart, I see he does.

HASTINGS: Dear Madam, permit me to lecture the young gentleman a little. I'm certain I can persuade him to his duty.

MRS. HARDCASTLE: Well! I must retire. Come, Constance, my love. You see, Mr. Hastings, the wretchedness of my situation: Was ever poor woman so plagued with a dear, sweet, pretty, provoking, undutiful boy.

Exeunt MRS. HARDCASTLE *and* MISS NEVILLE

TONY: (*Singing*) *There was a young man riding by, and fain would have his will. Rang do didlo dee.* Don't mind her. Let her cry. It's the comfort of her heart. I've seen her and sister cry over a book for an hour together, and they said, they liked the book the better the more it made them cry.

HASTINGS: Then you're no friend to the ladies, I find, my pretty young gentleman?

TONY: That's as I find 'um.

HASTINGS: Not to her of your mother's chusing, I dare answer? And yet she appears to me a pretty well-tempered girl.

TONY: That's because you don't know her as well as I. Ecod! I know every inch about her; and there's not a more bitter cantanckerous toad in all Christendom.

HASTINGS: (*Aside*) Pretty encouragement this for a lover!

TONY: I have seen her since the height of that. She has as many tricks as a hare in a thicket, or a colt the first day's breaking.

HASTINGS: To me she appears sensible and silent!

TONY: Ay, before company. But when she's with her play-mates she's as loud as a hog in a gate.

HASTINGS: But there is a meek modesty about her that charms me.

TONY: Yes, but curb her never so little, she kicks up, and you're flung in a ditch.

HASTINGS: Well, but you must allow her a little beauty. — Yes, you must allow her some beauty.

TONY: Bandbox![20] She's all a made up thing, mun. Ah! could you but see Bet Bouncer of these parts, you might then talk of beauty. Ecod, she has two eyes as black as sloes, and cheeks as broad and red as a pulpit cushion. She'd make two of she.

HASTINGS: Well, what say you to a friend that would take this bitter bargain off your hands?

TONY: Anon.

HASTINGS: Would you thank him that would take Miss Neville and leave you to happiness and your dear Betsy?

TONY: Ay; but where is there such a friend, for who would take *her*?

HASTINGS: I am he. If you but assist me, I'll engage to whip her off to France, and you shall never hear more of her.

TONY: Assist you! Ecod I will, to the last drop of my blood. I'll clap a pair of horses to your chaise that shall trundle you off in a twinkling, and may be get you a part of her fortin beside, in jewels, that you little dream of.

HASTINGS: My dear 'Squire, this looks like a lad of spirit.

TONY: Come along then, and you shall see more of my spirit before you have done with me (*singing*). *We are the boys that fears no noise where the thundering cannons roar.*

Exeunt

18. A book of medical prescriptions by John Quincy, *Pharmacopoeia Officinalis et Extemporanea* (1718).
19. reproving.

20. A box for keeping collars, bands or ruffs — here an oath.

ACT III

Enter HARDCASTLE *solus*

HARDCASTLE: What could my old friend Sir Charles mean by recommending his son as the modestest young man in town? To me he appears the most impudent piece of brass that ever spoke with a tongue. He has taken possession of the easy chair by the fire-side already. He took off his boots in the parlour, and desired me to see them taken care of. I'm desirous to know how his impudence affects my daughter. — She will certainly be shocked at it.

Enter MISS HARDCASTLE, *plainly dress'd*

HARDCASTLE: Well, my Kate, I see you have changed your dress as I bid you; and yet, I believe, there was no great occasion.

MISS HARDCASTLE: I find such a pleasure, Sir, in obeying your commands, that I take care to observe them without ever debating their propriety.

HARDCASTLE: And yet, Kate, I sometimes give you some cause, particularly when I recommended my *modest* gentleman to you as a lover to-day.

MISS HARDCASTLE: You taught me to expect something extraordinary, and I find the original exceeds the description.

HARDCASTLE: I was never so surprized in my life! He has quite confounded all my faculties!

MISS HARDCASTLE: I never saw any thing like it. And a man of the world too!

HARDCASTLE: Ay, he learned it all abroad, — what a fool was I, to think a young man could learn modesty by travelling. He might as soon learn wit at a masquerade.

MISS HARDCASTLE: It seems all natural to him.

HARDCASTLE: A good deal assisted by bad company and a French dancing-master.

MISS HARDCASTLE: Sure you mistake, papa! a French dancing-master could never have taught him that timid look — that aukward address — that bashful manner ——

HARDCASTLE: Whose look? whose manner? child!

MISS HARDCASTLE: Mr. Marlow's: his meauvaise honte,[1] his timidity struck me at the first sight.

HARDCASTLE: Then your first sight deceived you; for I think him one of the most brazen first sights that ever astonished my senses.

MISS HARDCASTLE: Sure, Sir, you rally![2] I never saw any one so modest.

HARDCASTLE: And can you be serious! I never saw such a bouncing swaggering puppy since I was born. Bully Dawson was but a fool to him.

MISS HARDCASTLE: Surprizing! He met me with a respectful bow, a stammering voice, and a look fixed on the ground.

HARDCASTLE: He met me with a loud voice, a lordly air, and a familiarity that made my blood freeze again.

MISS HARDCASTLE: He treated me with diffidence and respect; censured the manners of the age; admired the prudence of girls that never laughed; tired me with apologies for being tiresome; then left the room with a bow, and, Madam, I would not for the world detain you.

HARDCASTLE: He spoke to me as if he knew me all his life before. Asked twenty questions, and never waited for an answer. Interrupted my best remarks with some silly pun, and when I was in my best story of the Duke of Marlborough and Prince Eugene, he asked if I had not a good hand at making punch. Yes, Kate, he ask'd your father if he was a maker of punch!

MISS HARDCASTLE: One of us must certainly be mistaken.

HARDCASTLE: If he be what he has shewn himself, I'm determined he shall never have my consent.

MISS HARDCASTLE: And if he be the sullen thing I take him, he shall never have mine.

HARDCASTLE: In one thing then we are agreed — to reject him.

MISS HARDCASTLE: Yes. But upon conditions. For if you should find him less impudent, and I more presuming; if you find him more respectful, and I more importunate —— I don't know —— the fellow is well enough for a man — Certainly we don't meet many such at a horse race in the country.

HARDCASTLE: If we should find him so — But that's impossible. The first appearance has done my business. I'm seldom deceived in that.

MISS HARDCASTLE: And yet there may be many good qualities under that first appearance.

HARDCASTLE: Ay, when a girl finds a fellow's outside to her taste, she then sets about guessing the rest of his furniture. With her, a smooth face stands for good sense, and a genteel figure for every virtue.

1. (French) false shame.

2. joke.

MISS HARDCASTLE: I hope, Sir, a conversation begun with a compliment to my good sense won't end with a sneer at my understanding?

HARDCASTLE: Pardon me, Kate. But if young Mr. Brazen can find the art of reconciling contradictions, he may please us both, perhaps.

MISS HARDCASTLE: And as one of us must be mistaken, what if we go to make further discoveries?

HARDCASTLE: Agreed. But depend on't I'm in the right.

MISS HARDCASTLE: And depend on't I'm not much in the wrong.

Exeunt

Enter TONY *running in with a Casket*

TONY: Ecod! I have got them. Here they are. My Cousin Con's necklaces, bobs[3] and all. My mother shan't cheat the poor souls out of their fortune neither. O! my genus, is that you?

Enter HASTINGS

HASTINGS: My dear friend, how have you managed with your mother? I hope you have amused her with pretending love for your cousin, and that you are willing to be reconciled at last? Our horses will be refreshed in a short time, and we shall soon be ready to set off.

TONY: And here's something to bear your charges by the way (*giving the Casket*). Your sweetheart's jewels. Keep them, and hang those, I say, that would rob you of one of them.

HASTINGS: But how have you procured them from your mother?

TONY: Ask me no questions, and I'll tell you no fibs. I procured them by the rule of thumb. If I had not a key to every drawer in mother's bureau, how could I go to the alehouse so often as I do? An honest man may rob himself of his own at any time.

HASTINGS: Thousands do it every day. But to be plain with you; Miss Neville is endeavouring to procure them from her aunt this very instant. If she succeeds, it will be the most delicate way at least of obtaining them.

TONY: Well, keep them, till you know how it will be. But I know how it will be well enough; she'd as soon part with the only sound tooth in her head.

HASTINGS: But I dread the effects of her resentment, when she finds she has lost them.

TONY: Never you mind her resentment, leave me to manage that. I don't value her resentment, the bounce of a cracker. Zounds! here they are. Morrice.[4] Prance.

Exit HASTINGS

Enter MRS. HARDCASTLE *and* MISS NEVILLE

MRS. HARDCASTLE: Indeed, Constance, you amaze me. Such a girl as you want jewels? It will be time enough for jewels, my dear, twenty years hence, when your beauty begins to want repairs.

MISS NEVILLE: But what will repair beauty at forty, will certainly improve it at twenty, Madam.

MRS. HARDCASTLE: Yours, my dear, can admit of none. That natural blush is beyond a thousand ornaments. Besides, child, jewels are quite out at present. Don't you see half the ladies of our acquaintance, my Lady Kill-daylight, and Mrs. Crump, and the rest of them, carry their jewels to town, and bring nothing but Paste and Marcasites[5] back.

MISS NEVILLE: But who knows, Madam, but somebody that shall be nameless would like me best with all my little finery about me?

MRS. HARDCASTLE: Consult your glass, my dear, and then see, if with such a pair of eyes, you want any better sparklers. What do you think, Tony, my dear, does your cousin Con want any jewels, in your eyes, to set off her beauty?

TONY: That's as hereafter may be.

MISS NEVILLE: My dear aunt, if you knew how it would oblige me.

MRS. HARDCASTLE: A parcel of old fashioned rose and tablecut things.[6] They would make you look like the court of king Solomon at a puppet shew. Besides, I believe I can't readily come at them. They may be missing for aught I know to the contrary.

TONY: (*Apart to* MRS. HARDCASTLE) Then why don't you tell her so at once, as she's so longing for them. Tell her they're lost. It's the only way to quiet her. Say they're lost, and call me to bear witness.

MRS. HARDCASTLE: (*Apart to* TONY) You know, my dear, I'm only keeping them for you. So if I say they're gone, you'll bear me witness, will you? He! he! he!

TONY: Never fear me. Ecod! I'll say I saw them taken out with my own eyes.

MISS NEVILLE: I desire them but for a day,

3. pendants, earrings.

4. Dance away, move off quickly.

5. paste: imitation precious stone; marcasites: crystals used as ornaments.

6. rose-cut or table-cut diamonds.

Madam. Just to be permitted to shew them as relicks, and then they may be lock'd up again.

MRS. HARDCASTLE: To be plain with you, my dear Constance; if I could find them you should have them. They're missing, I assure you. Lost, for aught I know; but we must have patience wherever they are.

MISS NEVILLE: I'll not believe it; this is but a shallow pretence to deny me. I know they're too valuable to be so slightly kept, and as you are to answer for the loss.

MRS. HARDCASTLE: Don't be alarm'd, Constance. If they be lost, I must restore an equivalent. But my son knows they are missing and not to be found.

TONY: That I can bear witness to. They are missing, and not to be found, I'll take my oath on't.

MRS. HARDCASTLE: You must learn resignation, my dear; for tho' we lose our fortune, yet we should not lose our patience. See me, how calm I am.

MISS NEVILLE: Ay, people are generally calm at the misfortunes of others.

MRS. HARDCASTLE: Now, I wonder a girl of your good sense should waste a thought upon such trumpery. We shall soon find them; and, in the mean time, you shall make use of my garnets till your jewels be found.

MISS NEVILLE: I detest garnets.

MRS. HARDCASTLE: The most becoming things in the world to set off a clear complexion. You have often seen how well they look upon me. You *shall* have them.

Exit

MISS NEVILLE: I dislike them of all things. You shan't stir. — Was ever any thing so provoking to mislay my own jewels, and force me to wear her trumpery.

TONY: Don't be a fool. If she gives you the garnets, take what you can get. The jewels are your own already. I have stolen them out of her bureau, and she does not know it. Fly to your spark,[7] he'll tell you more of the matter. Leave me to manage *her*.

MISS NEVILLE: My dear cousin.

TONY: Vanish.[8] She's here, and has missed them already. Zounds! how she fidgets and spits about like a Catharine wheel.

Enter MRS. HARDCASTLE

MRS. HARDCASTLE: Confusion! thieves! robbers! We are cheated, plundered, broke open, undone.

TONY: What's the matter, what's the matter, mamma? I hope nothing has happened to any of the good family!

MRS. HARDCASTLE: We are robbed. My bureau has been broke open, the jewels taken out, and I'm undone.

TONY: Oh! is that all? Ha, ha, ha. By the laws, I never saw it better acted in my life. Ecod, I thought you was ruin'd in earnest, ha, ha, ha.

MRS. HARDCASTLE: Why boy, I *am* ruin'd in earnest. My bureau has been broke open, and all taken away.

TONY: Stick to that; ha, ha, ha; stick to that. I'll bear witness, you know, call me to bear witness.

MRS. HARDCASTLE: I tell you, Tony, by all that's precious, the jewels are gone, and I shall be ruin'd for ever.

TONY: Sure I know they're gone, and I am to say so.

MRS. HARDCASTLE: My dearest Tony, but hear me. They're gone, I say.

TONY: By the laws, mamma, you make me for to laugh, ha, ha. I know who took them well enough, ha, ha, ha.

MRS. HARDCASTLE: Was there ever such a blockhead, that can't tell the difference between jest and earnest? I tell you I'm not in jest, booby.

TONY: That's right, that's right: You must be in a bitter passion, and then nobody will suspect either of us. I'll bear witness that they are gone.

MRS. HARDCASTLE: Was ever such a cross-grain'd brute, that won't hear me! Can you bear witness that you're no better than a fool? Was ever poor woman so beset with fools on one hand, and thieves on the other?

TONY: I can bear witness to that.

MRS. HARDCASTLE: Bear witness again, you blockhead you, and I'll turn you out of the room directly. My poor niece, what will become of *her*! Do you laugh you unfeeling brute, as if you enjoy'd my distress?

TONY: I can bear witness to that.

MRS. HARDCASTLE: Do you insult me, monster? I'll teach you to vex your mother, I will.

TONY: I can bear witness to that. (*He runs off, she follows him*)

Enter MISS HARDCASTLE *and* MAID

MISS HARDCASTLE: What an unaccountable

7. beau, lover, suitor.
8. Presumably Miss Neville exits here.

creature is that brother of mine, to send them to the house as an inn, ha, ha. I don't wonder at his impudence.

MAID: But what is more, madam, the young gentleman as you passed by in your present dress, ask'd me if you were the bar maid? He mistook you for the bar maid, madam.

MISS HARDCASTLE: Did he? Then as I live I'm resolved to keep up the delusion. Tell me, Pimple, how do you like my present dress. Don't you think I look something like Cherry in the Beaux Stratagem?[9]

MAID: It's the dress, madam, that every lady wears in the country, but when she visits or receives company.

MISS HARDCASTLE: And are you sure he does not remember my face or person?

MAID: Certain of it.

MISS HARDCASTLE: I vow I thought so; for though we spoke for some time together, yet his fears were such, that he never once looked up during the interview. Indeed if he had, my bonnet would have kept him from seeing me.

MAID: But what do you hope from keeping him in his mistake?

MISS HARDCASTLE: In the first place, I shall be *seen*, and that is no small advantage to a girl that brings her face to market. Then I shall perhaps make an acquaintance, and that's no small victory gained over one who never addresses any but the wildest of her sex. But my chief aim is to take my gentleman off his guard, and like an invincible[10] champion of romance examine the giant's force before I offer to combat.

MAID: But are you sure you can act your part, and disguise your voice, so that he may mistake that, as he has already mistaken your person?

MISS HARDCASTLE: Never fear me. I think I have got the true bar cant.[11] — Did your honour call? —— Attend the Lion there. —— Pipes and tobacco for the Angel. — The Lamb has been outrageous this half hour.[12]

MAID: It will do, madam. But he's here.

Exit MAID

9. The landlord's daughter in George Farquhar's *The Beaux' Stratagem* (1707). See above, p. 516. This reference provides an important key to the tone of Goldsmith's comedy.
10. Usually 'invisible', but this reading in the Dublin edition is attractive.
11. Language used in a bar.
12. Rooms in a tavern had such names. cf. *The Beaux' Stratagem*, I.1, and *The Good Natur'd Man*, the start of Act V.

Enter MARLOW

MARLOW: What a bawling in every part of the house; I have scarce a moment's repose. If I go to the best room, there I find my host and his story. If I fly to the gallery, there we have my hostess with her curtesy down to the ground. I have at last got a moment to myself, and now for recollection. (*Walks and muses*)

MISS HARDCASTLE: Did you call, Sir? did your honour call?

MARLOW: (*Musing*) As for Miss Hardcastle, she's too grave and sentimental for me.

MISS HARDCASTLE: Did your honour call? (*She still places herself before him, he turning away*)

MARLOW: No, child. (*Musing*) Besides from the glimpse I had of her, I think she squints.

MISS HARDCASTLE: I'm sure, Sir, I heard the bell ring.

MARLOW: No, No. (*Musing*) I have pleased my father, however, by coming down, and I'll to-morrow please myself by returning. (*Taking out his tablets,*[13] *and perusing*)

MISS HARDCASTLE: Perhaps the other gentleman called, Sir.

MARLOW: I tell you, no.

MISS HARDCASTLE: I should be glad to know, Sir. We have such a parcel of servants.

MARLOW: No, no, I tell you. (*Looks full in her face*) Yes, child, I think I did call. I wanted —— I wanted —— I vow, child you are vastly handsome.

MISS HARDCASTLE: Oh la, Sir, you'll make one asham'd.

MARLOW: Never saw a more sprightly malicious eye. Yes, yes, my dear, I did call. Have you got any of your — a — what d'ye call it in the house?

MISS HARDCASTLE: No, Sir, we have been out of that these ten days.

MARLOW: One may call in this house, I find, to very little purpose. Suppose I should call for a taste, just by way of trial, of the nectar of your lips; perhaps I might be disappointed in that too.

MISS HARDCASTLE: Nectar! nectar! that's a liquor there's no call for in these parts. French, I suppose. We keep no French wines here, Sir.

MARLOW: Of true English growth, I assure you.

MISS HARDCASTLE: Then it's odd I should not know it. We brew all sorts of wines in this house, and I have lived here these eighteen years.

MARLOW: Eighteen years! Why one would think,

13. notebook.

child, you kept the bar before you were born. How old are you?

MISS HARDCASTLE: O! Sir, I must not tell my age. They say women and music should never be dated.

MARLOW: To guess at this distance, you can't be much above forty (*approaching*). Yet nearer I don't think so much (*approaching*). By coming close to some women they look younger still; but when we come very close indeed (*attempting to kiss her*).

MISS HARDCASTLE: Pray, Sir, keep your distance. One would think you wanted to know one's age as they do horses, by mark of mouth.

MARLOW: I protest, child, you use me extremely ill. If you keep me at this distance, how is it possible you and I can be ever acquainted?

MISS HARDCASTLE: And who wants to be acquainted with you? I want no such acquaintance, not I. I'm sure you did not treat Miss Hardcastle that was here awhile ago in this obstropalous[14] manner. I'll warrant me, before her you look'd dash'd, and kept bowing to the ground, and talk'd, for all the world, as if you was before[15] a justice of peace.

MARLOW: (*Aside*) Egad! she has hit it, sure enough. (*To her*) In awe of her, child? Ha! ha! ha! A mere, aukward, squinting thing, no, no. I find you don't know me. I laugh'd, and rallied her a little; but I was unwilling to be too severe. No, I could not be too severe, *curse me!*

MISS HARDCASTLE: O! then, Sir, you are a favourite, I find, among the ladies?

MARLOW: Yes, my dear, a great favourite. And yet, hang me, I don't see what they find in me to follow. At the Ladies Club in town, I'm called their agreeable Rattle. Rattle, child, is not my real name, but one I'm known by. My name is Solomons. Mr. Solomons, my dear, at your service. (*Offering to salute her*)

MISS HARDCASTLE: Hold, Sir; you were introducing me to your club, not to yourself. And you're so great a favourite there you say?

MARLOW: Yes, my dear. There's Mrs. Mantrap, Lady Betty Blackleg, the Countess of Sligo, Mrs. Langhorns, old Miss Biddy Buckskin, and your humble servant, keep up the spirit of the place.

MISS HARDCASTLE: Then it's a very merry place, I suppose.

MARLOW: Yes, as merry as cards, suppers, wine, and old women can make us.

MISS HARDCASTLE: And their agreeable Rattle, ha! ha! ha!

MARLOW: (*Aside*) Egad! I don't quite like this chit. She looks knowing, methinks. You laugh, child!

MISS HARDCASTLE: I can't but laugh to think what time they all have for minding their work or their family.

MARLOW: (*Aside*) All's well, she don't laugh at me. (*To her*) Do *you* ever work, child?

MISS HARDCASTLE: Ay, sure. There's not a screen or a quilt in the whole house but what can bear witness to that.

MARLOW: Odso! Then you must shew me your embroidery. I embroider and draw patterns myself a little. If you want a judge of your work you must apply to me. (*Seizing her hand*)

MISS HARDCASTLE: Ay, but the colours don't look well by candle light. You shall see all in the morning. (*Struggling*)

MARLOW: And why not now, my angel? Such beauty fires beyond the power of resistance. — Pshaw! the father[16] here! my old luck: I never nick'd seven that I did not throw ames ace[17] three times following.

Exit MARLOW

Enter HARDCASTLE, *who stands in surprize*

HARDCASTLE: So, madam! So I find *this* is your *modest* lover. This is your humble admirer that kept his eyes fixed on the ground, and only ador'd at humble distance. Kate, Kate, art thou not asham'd to deceive your father so?

MISS HARDCASTLE: Never trust me, dear papa, but he's still the modest man I first took him for, you'll be convinced of it as well as I.

HARDCASTLE: By the hand of my body I believe his impudence is infectious! Didn't I see him seize your hand? Didn't I see him hawl you about like a milk maid? and now you talk of his respect and his modesty, forsooth!

MISS HARDCASTLE: But if I shortly convince you of his modesty, that he has only the faults that will pass off with time, and the virtues that will improve with age, I hope you'll forgive him.

14. obstreperous.
15. 'before' is omitted in the Dublin edition.
16. Marlow is not supposed to know that Hardcastle is her father. Is this a slip on Goldsmith's part?
17. Terms in dice playing, seven being the highest score in the game of hazard and ace being the lowest.

HARDCASTLE: The girl would actually make one run mad! I tell you I'll not be convinced. I am convinced. He has scarcely been three hours in the house, and he has already encroached on all my prerogatives. You may like his impudence, and call it modesty. But my son-in-law, Madam, must have very different qualifications.

MISS HARDCASTLE: Sir, I ask but this night to convince you.

HARDCASTLE: You shall not have half the time, for I have thoughts of turning him out this very hour.

MISS HARDCASTLE: Give me that hour then, and I hope to satisfy you.

HARDCASTLE: Well, an hour let it be then. But I'll have no trifling with your father. All fair and open, do you mind me.

MISS HARDCASTLE: I hope, Sir, you have ever found that I considered your commands as my pride; for your kindness is such, that my duty as yet has been inclination.

Exeunt

ACT IV

Enter HASTINGS *and* MISS NEVILLE

HASTINGS: You surprise me! Sir Charles Marlow expected here this night? Where have you had your information?

MISS NEVILLE: You may depend upon it. I just saw his letter to Mr. Hardcastle, in which he tells him he intends setting out a few hours after his son.

HASTINGS: Then, my Constance, all must be completed before he arrives. He knows me; and should he find me here, would discover my name, and perhaps my designs, to the rest of the family.

MISS NEVILLE: The jewels, I hope, are safe?

HASTINGS: Yes, yes. I have sent them to Marlow, who keeps the keys of our baggage. In the mean time, I'll go to prepare matters for our elopement. I have had the 'Squire's promise of a fresh pair of horses; and, if I should not see him again, will write him further directions.

Exit

MISS NEVILLE: Well! Success attend you. In the mean time, I'll go amuse my aunt with the old pretence of a violent passion for my cousin.

Exit

Enter MARLOW, *followed by a* SERVANT

MARLOW: I wonder what Hastings could mean by sending me so valuable a thing as a Casket to keep for him, when he knows the only place I have is the seat of a post-coach at an inn-door. Have you deposited the Casket with the landlady, as I ordered you? Have you put it into her own hands?

SERVANT: Yes, your honour.

MARLOW: She said she'd keep it safe, did she?

SERVANT: Yes, she said she'd keep it safe enough; she ask'd me how I came by it? and she said she had a great mind to make me give an account of myself.

Exit SERVANT

MARLOW: Ha! ha! ha! They're safe however. What an unaccountable set of beings have we got amongst! This little bar-maid though runs in my head most strangely, and drives out the absurdities of all the rest of the family. She's mine, she must be mine, or I'm greatly mistaken.

Enter HASTINGS

HASTINGS: Bless me! I quite forgot to tell her that I intended to prepare at the bottom of the garden. Marlow here, and in spirits too!

MARLOW: Give me joy, George! Crown me, shadow me with laurels! Well, George, after all, we modest fellows don't want for success among the women.

HASTINGS: Some women you mean. But what success has your honour's modesty been crown'd with now, that it grows so insolent upon us?

MARLOW: Didn't you see the tempting, brisk, lovely, little thing that runs about the house with a bunch of keys to its girdle?

HASTINGS: Well! and what then?

MARLOW: She's mine, you rogue you. Such fire, such motion, such eyes, such lips — but, egad! she would not let me kiss them though.

HASTINGS: But are you so sure, so very sure of her?

MARLOW: Why man, she talk'd of shewing me her work above-stairs, and I am to improve the pattern.

HASTINGS: But can *you*, Charles, go about to rob a woman of her honour?

MARLOW: Pshaw! pshaw! we all know the honour of the bar-maid of an inn. I don't intend to *rob* her, take my word for it, there's nothing in this house I shan't honestly *pay* for.

HASTINGS: I believe the girl has virtue.

MARLOW: And if she has, I should be the last man in the world that would attempt to corrupt it.

HASTINGS: You have taken care, I hope, of the Casket I sent you to lock up? It's in safety?

MARLOW: Yes, yes. It's safe enough. I have taken

care of it. But how could you think the seat of a post-coach at an inn-door a place of safety? Ah! numbskull! I have taken better precautions for you than you did for yourself. —— I have ——

HASTINGS: What!

MARLOW: I have sent it to the landlady to keep for you.

HASTINGS: To the landlady!

MARLOW: To the landlady.

HASTINGS: You did?

MARLOW: I did. She's to be answerable for its forthcoming, you know.

HASTINGS: Yes, she'll bring it forth with a witness.

MARLOW: Wasn't I right? I believe you'll allow that I acted prudently upon this occasion?

HASTINGS: (*Aside*) He must not see my uneasiness.

MARLOW: You seem a little disconcerted though, methinks. Sure nothing has happened?

HASTINGS: No, nothing. Never was in better spirits in all my life. And so you left it with the landlady, who, no doubt, very readily undertook the charge?

MARLOW: Rather too readily. For she not only kept the Casket; but, thro' her great precaution, was going to keep the messenger too. Ha! ha! ha!

HASTINGS: He! he! he! They're safe however.

MARLOW: As a guinea in a miser's purse.

HASTINGS: (*Aside*) So now all hopes of fortune are at an end, and we must set off without it. (*To him*) Well, Charles, I'll leave you to your meditations on the pretty bar-maid, and, he! he! he! may you be as successful for yourself as you have been for me.

Exit

MARLOW: Thank ye, George! I ask no more. Ha! ha! ha!

Enter HARDCASTLE

HARDCASTLE: I no longer know my own house. It's turned all topsey-turvey. His servants have got drunk already. I'll bear it no longer, and yet, from my respect for his father, I'll be calm. (*To him*) Mr. Marlow, your servant, I'm your very humble servant (*Bowing low*).

MARLOW: Sir, your humble servant. (*Aside*) What's to be the wonder now?

HARDCASTLE: I believe, Sir, you must be sensible, Sir, that no man alive ought to be more welcome than your father's son, Sir. I hope you think so?

MARLOW: I do from my soul, Sir. I don't want much intreaty. I generally make my father's son welcome wherever he goes.

HARDCASTLE: I believe you do, from my soul, Sir. But tho' I say nothing to your own conduct, that of your servants is insufferable. Their manner of drinking is setting a very bad example in this house, I assure you.

MARLOW: I protest, my very good Sir, that's no fault of mine. If they don't drink as they ought *they* are to blame. I ordered them not to spare the cellar. I did, I assure you. (*To the side scene*)[1] Here, let one of my servants come up. (*To him*) My positive directions were, that as I did not drink myself, they should make up for my deficiencies below.

HARDCASTLE: Then they had your orders for what they do! I'm satisfied!

MARLOW: They had, I assure you. You shall hear from one of themselves.

Enter SERVANT *drunk*

MARLOW: You, Jeremy! Come forward, sirrah! What were my orders? Were you not told to drink freely, and call for what you thought fit, for the good of the house?

HARDCASTLE: (*Aside*) I begin to lose my patience.

JEREMY: Please your honour, liberty and Fleet-street for ever![2] Tho' I'm but a servant, I'm as good as another man. I'll drink for no man before supper, Sir, dammy! Good liquor will sit upon a good supper, but a good supper will not sit upon —— hiccup —— upon my conscience, Sir.

MARLOW: You see, my old friend, the fellow is as drunk as he can possibly be. I don't know what you'd have more, unless you'd have the poor devil soused in a beer-barrel.

HARDCASTLE: Zounds! He'll drive me distracted if I contain myself any longer. Mr. Marlow, Sir; I have submitted to your insolence for more than four hours, and I see no likelihood of its coming to an end. I'm now resolved to be master here, Sir, and I desire that you and your drunken pack may leave my house directly.

MARLOW: Leave your house! — Sure you jest, my good friend? What, when I'm doing what I can to please you.

HARDCASTLE: I tell you, Sir, you don't please me; so I desire you'll leave my house.

1. i.e. the wings.
2. An allusion to the freedom of the press, vindicated in 1763.

MARLOW: Sure you cannot be serious? At this time o'night, and such a night. You only mean to banter me?

HARDCASTLE: I tell you, Sir, I'm serious; and, now that my passions are rouzed, I say this house is mine, Sir; this house is mine, and I command you to leave it directly.

MARLOW: Ha! ha! ha! A puddle in a storm.[3] I shan't stir a step, I assure you. (*In a serious tone*) This, your house, fellow! It's my house. This is my house. Mine, while I chuse to stay. What right have you to bid me leave this house, Sir? I never met with such impudence, curse me, never in my whole life before.

HARDCASTLE: Nor I, confound me if ever I did. To come to my house, to call for what he likes, to turn me out of my own chair, to insult the family, to order his servants to get drunk, and then to tell me *This house is mine, Sir.* By all that's impudent it makes me laugh. Ha! ha! ha! Pray, Sir (*Bantering*) as you take the house, what think you of taking the rest of the furniture? There's a pair of silver candlesticks, and there's a fire-screen, and here's a pair of brazen nosed bellows, perhaps you may take a fancy to them?

MARLOW: Bring me your bill, Sir, bring me your bill, and let's make no more words about it.

HARDCASTLE: There are a set of prints too. What think you of the rake's progress[4] for your own apartment?

MARLOW: Bring me your bill, I say; and I'll leave you and your infernal house directly.

HARDCASTLE: Then there's a mahogany table, that you may see your own face in.

MARLOW: My bill, I say.

HARDCASTLE: I had forgot the great chair, for your own particular slumbers, after a hearty meal.

MARLOW: Zounds! bring me my bill, I say, and let's hear no more on't.

HARDCASTLE: Young man, young man, from your father's letter to me, I was taught to expect a well-bred modest man, as a visitor here, but now I find him no better than a coxcomb and a bully; but he will be down here presently, and shall hear more of it.

Exit

MARLOW: How's this! Sure I have not mistaken the house! Every thing looks like an inn. The servants cry, coming. The attendance is aukward; the barmaid too to attend us. But she's here, and will further inform me. Whither so fast, child. A word with you.

Enter MISS HARDCASTLE

MISS HARDCASTLE: Let it be short then. I'm in a hurry. (*Aside*) I believe he begins to find out his mistake, but it's too soon quite to undeceive him.

MARLOW: Pray, child, answer me one question. What are you, and what may your business in this house be?

MISS HARDCASTLE: A relation of the family, Sir.

MARLOW: What! A poor relation?

MISS HARDCASTLE: Yes, Sir. A poor relation appointed to keep the keys, and to see that the guests want nothing in my power to give them.

MARLOW: That is, you act as the bar-maid of this inn.

MISS HARDCASTLE: Inn! O law — What brought that in your head? One of the best families in the county keep an inn! Ha! ha! ha! Old Mr. Hardcastle's house an inn.

MARLOW: Mr. Hardcastle's house! Is this house Mr. Hardcastle's house, child!

MISS HARDCASTLE: Ay, sure. Whose else should it be?

MARLOW: So then all's out, and I have been damnably imposed on. O, confound my stupid head, I shall be laugh'd at over the whole town. I shall be stuck up in caricatura[5] in all the print-shops. The Dullissimo Maccaroni.[6] To mistake this house of all others for an inn, and my father's old friend for an inn-keeper. What a swaggering puppy must he take me for. What a silly puppy do I find myself. There again, may I be hanged, my dear, but I mistook you for the barmaid.

MISS HARDCASTLE: Dear me! dear me! I'm sure there's nothing in my *behaviour* to put me upon a level with one of that stamp.

MARLOW: Nothing, my dear, nothing. But I was in for a list of blunders, and could not help making you a subscriber. My stupidity saw every thing the wrong way. I mistook your assiduity for assurance, and your simplicity for allurement. But its over — This house I no more shew *my* face in.

3. i.e. 'a storm in a teacup'.
4. The title of a set of engravings by William Hogarth, published in 1753.
5. The print-shops were full of caricatures of well-known characters.
6. A Macaroni was a dandy who was fond of foreign clothes; 'Dullissimo' is a mock-Italian coinage which would mean 'an extremely dull man'.

MISS HARDCASTLE: I hope, Sir, I have done nothing to disoblige you. I'm sure I should be sorry to affront any gentleman who has been so polite, and said so many civil things to me. I'm sure I should be sorry (*pretending to cry*) if he left the family upon my account. I'm sure I should be sorry, people said any thing amiss, since I have no fortune but my character.

MARLOW: (*Aside*) By heaven, she weeps. This is the first mark of tenderness I ever had from a modest woman, and it touches me. (*To her*) Excuse me, my lovely girl, you are the only part of the family I leave with reluctance. But to be plain with you, the difference of our birth, fortune and education, make an honourable connexion impossible; and I can never harbour a thought of seducing simplicity that trusted in my honour, or bringing ruin upon one, whose only fault was being too lovely.

MISS HARDCASTLE: (*Aside*) Generous man.[7] I now begin to admire him. (*To him*) But I am sure my family is as good as Miss Hardcastle's, and tho' I'm poor, that's no great misfortune to a contented mind, and, until this moment, I never thought that it was bad to want fortune.

MARLOW: And why now, my pretty simplicity?

MISS HARDCASTLE: Because it puts me at a distance from one, that if I had a thousand pound I would give it all to.

MARLOW: (*Aside*) This simplicity bewitches me, so that if I stay I'm undone. I must make one bold effort, and leave her. (*To her*) Your partiality in my favour, my dear, touches me most sensibly, and were I to live for myself alone, I could easily fix my choice. But I owe too much to the opinion of the world, too much to the authority of a father, so that — I can scarcely speak it — it affects me. Farewel.

Exit

MISS HARDCASTLE: I never knew half his merit till now. He shall not go, if I have power or art to detain him. I'll still preserve the character in which I stoop'd to conquer, but will undeceive my papa, who, perhaps, may laugh him out of his resolution.

Exit

Enter TONY, MISS NEVILLE

TONY: Ay, you may steal for yourselves the next time. I have done my duty. She has got the jewels again, that's a sure thing; but she believes it was all a mistake of the servants.

MISS NEVILLE: But, my dear cousin, sure you won't forsake us in this distress. If she in the least suspects that I am going off, I shall certainly be locked up, or sent to my aunt Pedigree's, which is ten times worse.

TONY: To be sure, aunts of all kinds are damn'd bad things. But what can I do? I have got you a pair of horses that will fly like Whistlejacket, and I'm sure you can't say but I have courted you nicely before her face. Here she comes, we must court a bit or two more, for fear she should suspect us. (*They retire, and seem to fondle*)

Enter MRS. HARDCASTLE

MRS. HARDCASTLE: Well, I was greatly fluttered, to be sure. But my son tells me it was all a mistake of the servants. I shan't be easy, however, till they are fairly married, and then let her keep her own fortune. But what do I see! Fondling together, as I'm alive. I never saw Tony so sprightly before. Ah! have I caught you, my pretty doves! What, billing, exchanging stolen glances, and broken murmurs. Ah!

TONY: As for murmurs, mother, we grumble a little, now and then, to be sure. But there's no love lost between us.

MRS. HARDCASTLE: A mere sprinkling, Tony, upon the flame, only to make it burn brighter.

MISS NEVILLE: Cousin Tony promises to give us more of his company at home. Indeed, he shan't leave us any more. It won't leave us, cousin Tony, will it?[8]

TONY: O! it's a pretty creature. No, I'd sooner leave my horse in a pound,[9] than leave you when you smile upon one so. Your laugh makes you so becoming.

MISS NEVILLE: Agreeable cousin! Who can help admiring that natural humour, that pleasant, broad, red, thoughtless, (*patting his cheek*) ah! it's a bold face.

MRS. HARDCASTLE: Pretty innocence.

TONY: I'm sure I always lov'd cousin Con's hazle eyes, and her pretty long fingers, that she twists this way and that, over the haspicholls,[10] like a parcel of bobbins.[11]

7. The conventional tribute of the heroine once the hero of comedy changed from rake to man of conscience. See Farquhar's *The Beaux' Stratagem*, V.4, where Dorinda cries, 'Matchless honesty!' at Aimwell's similar confession.

8. 'it' as a term of endearment for 'you'. Tony responds accordingly.

9. An enclosure where stray animals were 'impounded'.

10. harpsichord.

11. i.e. a bundle of the wooden bobbins used by lace-makers — an insult when applied to Constance's fingers.

MRS. HARDCASTLE: Ah, he would charm the bird from the tree. I was never so happy before. My boy takes after his father, poor Mr. Lumpkin, exactly. The jewels, my dear Con, shall be yours incontinently.[12] You shall have them. Isn't he a sweet boy, my dear? You shall be married to-morrow, and we'll put off the rest of his education, like Dr. Drowsy's sermons, to a fitter opportunity.

Enter DIGGORY

DIGGORY: Where's the 'Squire? I have got a letter for your worship.

TONY: Give it to my mamma. She reads all my letters first.

DIGGORY: I had orders to deliver it into your own hands.

TONY: Who does it comes from?

DIGGORY: Your worship mun ask that o' the letter itself.

TONY: I could wish to know tho' (*turning the letter, and gazing on it*).

MISS NEVILLE: (*Aside*) Undone, undone. A letter to him from Hastings. I know the hand. If my aunt sees it, we are ruined for ever. I'll keep her employ'd a little if I can. (*To Mrs. Hardcastle*) But I have not told you, Madam, of my cousin's smart answer just now to Mr. Marlow. We so laugh'd —— You must know, Madam —— this way a little, for he must not hear us. (*They confer*)

TONY: (*Still gazing*) A damn'd cramp piece of penmanship, as ever I saw in my life. I can read your print-hand very well. But here there are such handles, and shanks, and dashes, that one can scarce tell the head from the tail. *To Anthony Lumpkin, Esquire*. It's very odd, I can read the outside of my letters, where my own name is, well enough. But when I come to open it, it's all — buzz. That's hard, very hard; for the inside of the letter is always the cream of the correspondence.

MRS. HARDCASTLE: Ha, ha, ha. Very well. Very well. And so my son was too hard for the philosopher.

MISS NEVILLE: Yes, Madam; but you must hear the rest, Madam. A little more this way, or he may hear us. You'll hear how he puzzled him again.

MRS. HARDCASTLE: He seems strangely puzzled now himself, methinks.

TONY: (*Still gazing*) A damn'd up and down hand, as if it was disguised in liquor. (*Reading*) Dear Sir, Ay, that's that. Then there's an *M*, and a *T*, and an *S*, but whether the next be an *izzard*[13] or an *R*, confound me, I cannot tell.

MRS. HARDCASTLE: What's that, my dear. Can I give you any assistance?

MISS NEVILLE: Pray, aunt, let me read it. Nobody reads a cramp hand better than I. (*Twitching the letter from her*) Do you know who it is from?

TONY: Can't tell, except from Dick Ginger the feeder.

MISS NEVILLE: Ay, so it is. (*Pretending to read*) Dear 'Squire, Hoping that you're in health, as I am at this present. The gentlemen of the Shake-bag club has cut the gentlemen of Goose-green quite out of feather.[14] The odds — um — odd battle — um — long fighting — um here, here, it's all about cocks, and fighting; it's of no consequence, here, put it up, put it up. (*Thrusting the crumpled letter upon him*)

TONY: But I tell you, Miss, it's of all the consequence in the world. I would not lose the rest of it for a guinea. Here, mother, do you make it out. Of no consequence! (*Giving Mrs. Hardcastle the letter*)

MRS. HARDCASTLE: How's this! (*Reads*) Dear 'Squire, I'm now waiting for Miss Neville, with a post-chaise and pair, at the bottom of the garden, but I find my horses yet unable to perform the journey. I expect you'll assist us with a pair of fresh horses, as you promised. Dispatch is necessary, as the *hag* (ay the hag) your mother will otherwise suspect us. Your's, Hastings. Grant me patience. I shall run distracted. My rage choaks me.

MISS NEVILLE: I hope, Madam, you'll suspend your resentment for a few moments, and not impute to me any impertinence, or sinister design that belongs to another.

MRS. HARDCASTLE: (*Curtesying very low*) Fine spoken, Madam, you are most miraculously polite and engaging, and quite the very pink of curtesy and circumspection, Madam. (*Changing her tone*) And you, you great ill-fashioned oaf, with scarce sense enough to keep your mouth shut. Were you too joined against me? But I'll defeat all your plots in a moment. As for you, Madam, since you have got a pair of fresh horses ready, it would be cruel to disappoint them. So, if you please, instead of running away with your spark, prepare, this very

12. at once.

13. the letter 'Z'.

14. The jargon in this passage is that of cock-fighting and betting.

moment, to run off with *me*. Your old aunt Pedigree will keep you secure, I'll warrant me. You too, Sir, may mount your horse, and guard us upon the way. Here, Thomas, Roger, Diggory, I'll shew you, that I wish you better than you do yourselves.

Exit

MISS NEVILLE: So now I'm completely ruined.

TONY: Ay, that's a sure thing.

MISS NEVILLE: What better could be expected from being connected with such a stupid fool, and after all the nods and signs I made him.

TONY: By the laws, Miss, it was your own cleverness, and not my stupidity, that did your business. You were so nice and so busy with your Shake-bags and Goose-greens, that I thought you could never be making believe.

Enter HASTINGS

HASTINGS: So, Sir, I find by my servant, that you have shewn my letter, and betray'd us. Was this well done, young gentleman?

TONY: Here's another. Ask Miss there who betray'd you. Ecod, it was her doing, not mine.

Enter MARLOW

MARLOW: So, I have been finely used here among you. Rendered contemptible, driven into ill manners, despised, insulted, laugh'd at.

TONY: Here's another. We shall have old Bedlam broke loose[15] presently.

MISS NEVILLE: And there, Sir, is the gentleman to whom we all owe every obligation.

MARLOW: What can I say to him, a mere boy, an ideot, whose ignorance and age are a protection.

HASTINGS: A poor contemptible booby, that would but disgrace correction.

MISS NEVILLE: Yet with cunning and malice enough to make himself merry with all our embarrassments.

HASTINGS: An insensible cub.

MARLOW: Replete with tricks and mischief.

TONY: Baw! damme, but I'll fight you both one after the other —— with baskets.[16]

MARLOW: As for him, he's below resentment. But your conduct, Mr. Hastings, requires an explanation. You knew of my mistakes, yet would not undeceive me.

HASTINGS: Tortured as I am with my own disappointments, is this a time for explanations? It is not friendly, Mr. Marlow.

MARLOW: But, Sir.

MISS NEVILLE: Mr. Marlow, we never kept on your mistake, till it was too late to undeceive you. Be pacified.

Enter SERVANT

SERVANT: My mistress desires you'll get ready immediately, Madam. The horses are putting to. Your hat and things are in the next room. We are to go thirty miles before morning.

Exit SERVANT

MISS NEVILLE: Well, well; I'll come presently.

MARLOW: (*To Hastings*) Was it well done, Sir, to assist in rendering me ridiculous? To hang me out for the scorn of all my acquaintance? Depend upon it, Sir, I shall expect an explanation.

HASTINGS: Was it well done, Sir, if you're upon that subject, to deliver what I entrusted to yourself, to the care of another, Sir?

MISS NEVILLE: Mr. Hastings. Mr. Marlow. Why will you increase my distress by this groundless dispute? I implore, I intreat you ——

Enter SERVANT

SERVANT: Your cloak, Madam. My mistress is impatient.

MISS NEVILLE: I come. Pray be pacified. If I leave you thus, I shall die with apprehension.

Enter SERVANT

SERVANT: Your fan, muff, and gloves, Madam. The horses are waiting.

MISS NEVILLE: O, Mr. Marlow; if you knew what a scene of constraint and ill-nature lies before me, I'm sure it would convert your resentment into pity.

MARLOW: I'm so distracted with a variety of passions, that I don't know what I do. Forgive me, Madam. George, forgive me. You know my hasty temper, and should not exasperate it.

HASTINGS: The torture of my situation is my only excuse.

MISS NEVILLE: Well, my dear Hastings, if you have that esteem for me that I think, that I am sure you have, your constancy for three years will but increase the happiness of our future connexion. If ——

MRS. HARDCASTLE: (*Within*) Miss Neville. Constance, why Constance, I say.

MISS NEVILLE: I'm coming. Well, constancy. Remember, constancy is the word.

Exit

15. i.e. as much noise as if the inmates of Bedlam (the London lunatic hospital) had broken loose.

16. sword-sticks, the handles of which were protected by basketwork guards.

HASTINGS: My heart. How can I support this? To be so near happiness, and such happiness.

MARLOW: (*To Tony*) You see now, young gentleman, the effects of your folly. What might be amusement to you, is here disappointment, and even distress.

TONY: (*From a reverie*) Ecod, I have hit it. It's here. Your hands. Yours and yours, my poor Sulky. My boots there, ho. Meet me two hours hence at the bottom of the garden; and if you don't find Tony Lumpkin a more good-natur'd fellow than you thought for, I'll give you leave to take my best horse and Bet Bouncer into the bargain. Come along. My boots, ho.

Exeunt

ACT V

Scene continues

Enter HASTINGS *and* SERVANT

HASTINGS: You saw the Old Lady and Miss Neville drive off, you say?

SERVANT: Yes, your honour. They went off in a post-coach, and the young 'Squire went on horseback. They're thirty miles off by this time.

HASTINGS: Then all my hopes are over.

SERVANT: Yes, Sir. Old Sir Charles is arrived. He and the Old Gentleman of the house have been laughing at Mr. Marlow's mistake this half hour. They are coming this way.

HASTINGS: Then I must not be seen. So now to my fruitless appointment at the bottom of the garden. This is about the time.

Exeunt

Enter SIR CHARLES *and* HARDCASTLE

HARDCASTLE: Ha, ha, ha. The peremptory tone in which he sent forth his sublime commands.

SIR CHARLES: And the reserve with which I suppose he treated all your advances.

HARDCASTLE: And yet he might have seen something in me above a common inn-keeper, too.

SIR CHARLES: Yes, Dick, but he mistook you for an uncommon inn-keeper, ha, ha, ha.

HARDCASTLE: Well, I'm in too good spirits to think of any thing but joy. Yes, my dear friend, this union of our families will make our personal friendships hereditary; and tho' my daughter's fortune is but small ——

SIR CHARLES: Why, Dick, will you talk of a fortune to *me*? My son is possessed of more than a competence already, and can want nothing but a good and virtuous girl to share his happiness and encrease it. If they like each other, as you say they do ——

HARDCASTLE: *If*, man, I tell you they *do* like each other. My daughter as good as told me so.

SIR CHARLES: But girls are apt to flatter themselves, you know.

HARDCASTLE: I saw him grasp her hand in the warmest manner myself; and here he comes to put you out of your *iffs*, I warrant him.

Enter MARLOW

MARLOW: I come, Sir, once more, to ask pardon for my strange conduct. I can scarce reflect on my insolence without confusion.

HARDCASTLE: Tut, boy, a trifle. You take it too gravely. An hour or two's laughing with my daughter will set all to rights again. She'll never like you the worse for it.

MARLOW: Sir, I shall be always proud of her approbation.

HARDCASTLE: Approbation is but a cold word, Mr. Marlow; if I am not deceived, you have something more than approbation thereabouts. You take me.

MARLOW: Really, Sir, I have not that happiness.

HARDCASTLE: Come, boy, I'm an old fellow, and know what's what, as well as you that are younger. I know what has past between you; but mum.

MARLOW: Sure, Sir, nothing has past between us but the most profound respect on my side, and the most distant reserve on her's. You don't think, Sir, that my impudence has been past upon all the rest of the family.

HARDCASTLE: Impudence. No, I don't say that —— Not quite impudence — Tho' girls like to be play'd with, and rumpled a little too sometimes. But she has told no tales, I assure you.

MARLOW: I never gave her the slightest cause.

HARDCASTLE: Well, well, I like modesty in its place well enough. But this is over-acting, young gentleman. You *may* be open. Your father and I will like you the better for it.

MARLOW: May I die, Sir, if I ever ——

HARDCASTLE: I tell you, she don't dislike you; and as I'm sure you like her ——

MARLOW: Dear Sir — I protest, Sir ——

HARDCASTLE: I see no reason why you should not be joined as fast as the parson can tie you.

MARLOW: But hear me, Sir ——

HARDCASTLE: Your father approves the match, I

admire it, every moment's delay will be doing mischief, so —

MARLOW: But why won't you hear me? By all that's just and true, I never gave Miss Hardcastle the slightest mark of my attachment, or even the most distant hint to suspect me of affection. We had but one interview, and that was formal, modest and uninteresting.

HARDCASTLE: (*Aside*) This fellow's formal modest impudence is beyond bearing.

SIR CHARLES: And you never grasp'd her hand, or made any protestations!

MARLOW: As heaven is my witness, I came down in obedience to your commands. I saw the lady without emotion, and parted without reluctance. I hope you'll exact no further proofs of my duty, nor prevent me from leaving a house in which I suffer so many mortifications.

Exit

SIR CHARLES: I'm astonished at the air of sincerity with which he parted.

HARDCASTLE: And I'm astonished at the deliberate intrepidity of his assurance.

SIR CHARLES: I dare pledge my life and honour upon his truth.

HARDCASTLE: Here comes my daughter, and I would stake my happiness upon her veracity.

Enter MISS HARDCASTLE

HARDCASTLE: Kate, come hither, child. Answer us sincerely, and without reserve; has Mr. Marlow made you any professions of love and affection?

MISS HARDCASTLE: The question is very abrupt, Sir! But since you require unreserved sincerity, I think he has.

HARDCASTLE: (*To* SIR CHARLES) You see.

SIR CHARLES: And pray, Madam, have you and my son had more than one interview?

MISS HARDCASTLE: Yes, Sir, several.

HARDCASTLE: (*To* SIR CHARLES) You see.

SIR CHARLES: But did he profess any attachment?

MISS HARDCASTLE: A lasting one.

SIR CHARLES: Did he talk of love?

MISS HARDCASTLE: Much, Sir.

SIR CHARLES: Amazing! And all this formally?

MISS HARDCASTLE: Formally.

HARDCASTLE: Now, my friend, I hope you are satisfied.

SIR CHARLES: And how did he behave, Madam?

MISS HARDCASTLE: As most profest admirers do. Said some civil things of my face, talked much of his want of merit, and the greatness of mine; mentioned his heart, gave a short tragedy speech, and ended with pretended rapture.

SIR CHARLES: Now I'm perfectly convinced, indeed. I know his conversation among women to be modest and submissive. This forward canting ranting manner by no means describes him, and I am confident, he never sate for the picture.

MISS HARDCASTLE: Then what, Sir, if I should convince you to your face of my sincerity? If you and my papa, in about half an hour, will place yourselves behind that screen, you shall hear him declare his passion to me in person.

SIR CHARLES: Agreed. And if I find him what you describe, all my happiness in him must have an end.

Exit

MISS HARDCASTLE: And if you don't find him what I describe — I fear my happiness must never have a beginning.

Exeunt

ACT V, SCENE 2

Scene changes to the Back of the Garden

Enter HASTINGS

HASTINGS: What an ideot am I, to wait here for a fellow, who probably takes a delight in mortifying me. He never intended to be punctual, and I'll wait no longer. What do I see! It is he, and perhaps with news of my Constance.

Enter TONY, *booted and spurred*

HASTINGS: My honest 'Squire, I now find you a man of your word. This looks like friendship.

TONY: Ay, I'm your friend, and the best friend you have in the world, if you knew but all. This riding by night, by the bye, is cursedly tiresome. It has shook me worse than the basket of a stage-coach.

HASTINGS: But how? Where did you leave your fellow-travellers? Are they in safety? Are they housed?

TONY: Five and twenty miles in two hours and a half is no such bad driving. The poor beasts have smoaked for it:[1] Rabbet me,[2] but I'd rather ride forty miles after a fox, than ten after such *varment*.[3]

1. steamed and sweated because of it.
2. Confound me! from the French 'rabattre', to beat again.
3. vermin.

HASTINGS: Well, but where have you left the ladies? I die with impatience.

TONY: Left them? Why where should I leave them, but where I found them?

HASTINGS: This is a riddle.

TONY: Riddle me this then. What's that goes round the house, and round the house, and never touches the house?

HASTINGS: I'm still astray.

TONY: Why that's it, mon. I have led them astray. By jingo, there's not a pond or slough within five miles of the place but they can tell the taste of.

HASTINGS: Ha, ha, ha, I understand; you took them in a round, while they supposed themselves going forward. And so you have at last brought them home again.

TONY: You shall hear. I first took them down Feather-bed-lane, where we stuck fast in the mud. I then rattled them crack over the stones of Up-and-down-hill — I then introduc'd them to the gibbet on Heavy-tree-heath, and from that, with a circumbendibus,[4] I fairly lodged them in the horse-pond at the bottom of the garden.

HASTINGS: But no accident, I hope.

TONY: No, no. Only mother is confoundedly frightened. She thinks herself forty miles off. She's sick of the journey, and the cattle[5] can scarce crawl. So if your own horses be ready, you may whip off with cousin, and I'll be bound that no soul here can budge a foot to follow you.

HASTINGS: My dear friend, how can I be grateful?

TONY: Ay, now its dear friend, noble 'Squire. Just now, it was all ideot, cub, and run me through the guts. Damn *your* way of fighting, I say. After we take a knock in this part of the country, we kiss and be friends. But if you had run me through the guts, then I should be dead, and you might go kiss the hangman.[6]

HASTINGS: The rebuke is just. But I must hasten to relieve Miss Neville: if you keep the old lady employed, I promise to take care of the young one.

Exit HASTINGS

TONY: Never fear me. Here she comes. Vanish. She's got from the pond, and draggled up to the waist like a mermaid.

Enter MRS. HARDCASTLE

MRS. HARDCASTLE: Oh, Tony, I'm killed. Shook. Battered to death. I shall never survive it. That last jolt that laid us against the quickset hedge has done my business.

TONY: Alack, mama, it was all your own fault. You would be for running away by night, without knowing one inch of the way.

MRS. HARDCASTLE: I wish we were at home again. I never met so many accidents in so short a journey. Drenched in the mud, overturned in a ditch, stuck fast in a slough, jolted to a jelly, and at last to lose our way. Whereabouts do you think we are, Tony?

TONY: By my guess we should be upon Crackskull-common, about forty miles from home.

MRS. HARDCASTLE: O lud! O lud! the most notorious spot in all the country. We only want a robbery to make a complete night on't.

TONY: Don't be afraid, mama, don't be afraid. Two of the five that kept here are hanged, and the other three may not find us. Don't be afraid. Is that a man that's galloping behind us? No; it's only a tree. Don't be afraid.

MRS. HARDCASTLE: The fright will certainly kill me.

TONY: Do you see any thing like a black hat moving behind the thicket?

MRS. HARDCASTLE: O death!

TONY: No, it's only a cow. Don't be afraid, mama; don't be afraid.

MRS. HARDCASTLE: As I'm alive, Tony, I see a man coming towards us. Ah! I'm sure on't. If he perceives us we are undone.

TONY: (*Aside*) Father-in-law,[7] by all that's unlucky, come to take one of his night-walks. (*To her*) Ah, it's a highwayman, with pistols as long as my arm. A damn'd ill-looking fellow.

MRS. HARDCASTLE: Good heaven defend us! He approaches.

TONY: Do you hide yourself in that thicket, and leave me to manage him. If there be any danger I'll cough and cry hem. When I cough be sure to keep close.[8] (MRS. HARDCASTLE *hides behind a tree in the back scene*)

Enter HARDCASTLE

HARDCASTLE: I'm mistaken, or I heard voices of people in want of help. Oh, Tony, is that you? I did not expect you so soon back. Are your mother and her charge in safety?

4. A made-up Latin word meaning a roundabout way.
5. horses.
6. Condemned criminals often forgave the hangman with a kiss.
7. Step-father.
8. hidden.

TONY: Very safe, Sir, at my aunt Pedigree's. Hem.

MRS. HARDCASTLE: (*From behind*) Ah death! I find there's danger.

HARDCASTLE: Forty miles in three hours; sure, that's too much, my youngster.

TONY: Stout horses and willing minds make short journies, as they say. Hem.

MRS. HARDCASTLE: (*From behind*) Sure he'll do the boy no harm.

HARDCASTLE: But I heard a voice here; I should be glad to know from whence it came?

TONY: It was I, Sir, talking to myself, Sir. I was saying that forty miles in four hours was very good going. Hem. As to be sure it was. Hem. I have got a sort of cold by being out in the air. We'll go in, if you please. Hem.

HARDCASTLE: But if you talk'd to yourself, you did not answer yourself. I am certain I heard two voices, and am resolved (*raising his voice*) to find the other out.

MRS. HARDCASTLE: (*From behind*) Oh! he's coming to find me out. Oh!

TONY: What need you go, Sir, if I tell you? Hem! I'll lay down my life for the truth — hem — I'll tell you all, Sir (*detaining him*).

HARDCASTLE: I tell you, I will not be detained. I insist on seeing. It's in vain to expect I'll believe you.

MRS. HARDCASTLE: (*Running forward from behind*) O lud, he'll murder my poor boy, my darling. Here, good gentleman, whet your rage upon me. Take my money, my life, but spare that young gentleman, spare my child, if you have any mercy.

HARDCASTLE: My wife, as I'm a Christian. From whence can she come, or what does she mean!

MRS. HARDCASTLE: (*Kneeling*) Take compassion on us, good Mr. Highwayman. Take our money, our watches, all we have, but spare our lives. We will never bring you to justice, indeed we won't, good Mr. Highwayman.

HARDCASTLE: I believe the woman's out of her senses. What, Dorothy, don't you know *me*?

MRS. HARDCASTLE: Mr. Hardcastle, as I'm alive! My fears blinded me. But who, my dear, could have expected to meet you here, in this frightful place, so far from home? What has brought you to follow us?

HARDCASTLE: Sure, Dorothy, you have not lost your wits. So far from home, when you are within forty yards of your own door. (*To him*) This is one of your old tricks, you graceless rogue you. (*To her*) Don't you know the gate, and the mulberry-tree; and don't you remember the horse-pond, my dear?

MRS. HARDCASTLE: Yes, I shall remember the horse-pond as long as I live; I have caught my death in it. (*To* TONY) And is it to you, you graceless varlet, I owe all this? I'll teach you to abuse your mother, I will.

TONY: Ecod, mother, all the parish says you have spoil'd me, and so you may take the fruits on't.

MRS. HARDCASTLE: I'll spoil you, I will.

Follows him off the stage. Exit

HARDCASTLE: There's morality, however, in his reply.

Exit

Enter HASTINGS *and* MISS NEVILLE

HASTINGS: My dear Constance, why will you deliberate thus? If we delay a moment, all is lost for ever. Pluck up a little resolution, and we shall soon be out of the reach of her malignity.

MISS NEVILLE: I find it impossible. My spirits are so sunk with the agitations I have suffered, that I am unable to face any new danger. Two or three years' patience will at last crown us with happiness.

HASTINGS: Such a tedious delay is worse than inconstancy. Let us fly, my charmer. Let us date our happiness from this very moment. Perish fortune. Love and content will encrease what we possess beyond a monarch's revenue. Let me prevail.

MISS NEVILLE: No, Mr. Hastings; no. Prudence once more comes to my relief, and I will obey its dictates. In the moment of passion, fortune may be despised, but it ever produces a lasting repentance. I'm resolved to apply to Mr. Hardcastle's compassion and justice for redress.

HASTINGS: But tho' he had the will, he has not the power to relieve you.

MISS NEVILLE: But he has influence, and upon that I am resolved to rely.

HASTINGS: I have no hopes. But since you persist, I must reluctantly obey you.

Exeunt

ACT V, SCENE 3

Scene changes [*to the interior of* HARDCASTLE'S *house*]

Enter SIR CHARLES *and* MISS HARDCASTLE

SIR CHARLES: What a situation am I in? If what

you say appears, I shall then find a guilty son. If what he says be true, I shall then lose one that, of all others, I most wish'd for a daughter.

MISS HARDCASTLE: I am proud of your approbation, and to shew I merit it, if you place yourselves as I directed, you shall hear his explicit declaration. But he comes.

SIR CHARLES: I'll to your father, and keep him to the appointment.

Exit SIR CHARLES

Enter MARLOW

MARLOW: Tho' prepar'd for setting out, I come once more to take leave, nor did I, till this moment, know the pain I feel in the separation.

MISS HARDCASTLE: (*In her own natural manner*) I believe these sufferings cannot be very great, Sir, which you can so easily remove. A day or two longer, perhaps, might lessen your uneasiness, by shewing the little value of what you now think proper to regret.

MARLOW: (*Aside*) This girl every moment improves upon me. (*To her*) It must not be, Madam. I have already trifled too long with my heart. My very pride begins to submit to my passion. The disparity of education and fortune, the anger of a parent, and the contempt of my equals, begin to lose their weight; and nothing can restore me to myself, but this painful effort of resolution.

MISS HARDCASTLE: Then go, Sir. I'll urge nothing more to detain you. Tho' my family be as good as hers you came down to visit, and my education, I hope, not inferior, what are these advantages without equal affluence? I must remain contented with the slight approbation of imputed merit; I must have only the mockery of your addresses, while all your serious aims are fix'd on fortune.

Enter HARDCASTLE *and* SIR CHARLES *from behind*

SIR CHARLES: Here, behind this screen.

HARDCASTLE: Ay, ay, make no noise. I'll engage my Kate covers him with confusion at last.

MARLOW: By heavens, Madam, fortune was ever my smallest consideration. Your beauty at first caught my eye; for who could see that without emotion. But every moment that I converse with you, steals in some new grace, heightens the picture, and gives it stronger expression. What at first seem'd rustic plainness, now appears refin'd simplicity. What seem'd forward assurance, now strikes me as the result of courageous innocence, and conscious virtue.

SIR CHARLES: What can it mean? He amazes me.

HARDCASTLE: I told you how it would be. Hush.

MARLOW: I am now determined to stay, Madam, and I have too good an opinion of my father's discernment, when he sees you, to doubt his approbation.

MISS HARDCASTLE: No, Mr. Marlow, I will not, cannot detain you. Do you think I could suffer a connexion, in which there is the smallest room for repentance? Do you think I would take the mean advantage of a transient passion, to load you with confusion? Do you think I could ever relish that happiness, which was acquired by lessening yours?

MARLOW: By all that's good, I can have no happiness but what's in your power to grant me. Nor shall I ever feel repentance, but in not having seen your merits before. I will stay, even contrary to your wishes; and tho' you should persist to shun me, I will make my respectful assiduities atone for the levity of my past conduct.

MISS HARDCASTLE: Sir, I must entreat you'll desist. As our acquaintance began, so let it end, in indifference. I might have given an hour or two to levity; but seriously, Mr. Marlow, do you think I could ever submit to a connexion, where *I* must appear mercenary, and *you* imprudent? Do you think I could ever catch at the confident addresses of a secure admirer?

MARLOW: (*Kneeling*) Does this look like security? Does this look like confidence? No, Madam, every moment that shews me your merit, only serves to encrease my diffidence and confusion. Here let me continue ——

SIR CHARLES: I can hold it no longer. Charles, Charles, how hast thou deceived me. Is this your indifference, your uninteresting conversation!

HARDCASTLE: Your cold contempt; your formal interview. What have you to say now?

MARLOW: That I am all amazement. What can it mean?

HARDCASTLE: It means that you can say and unsay things at pleasure. That you can address a lady in private, and deny it in public; that you have one story for us, and another for my daughter.

MARLOW: Daughter! — this lady your daughter!

HARDCASTLE: Yes, Sir, my only daughter. My Kate, whose else should she be?

MARLOW: Oh, the devil.

MISS HARDCASTLE: Yes, Sir, that very identical tall squinting lady you were pleased to take me for (*curtesying*). She that you addressed as the mild, modest, sentimental man of gravity, and the bold forward agreeable rattle of the ladies club; ha, ha, ha.

MARLOW: Zounds, there's no bearing this; it's worse than death.

MISS HARDCASTLE: In which of your characters, Sir, will you give us leave to address you? As the faultering gentleman, with looks on the ground, that speaks just to be heard, and hates hypocrisy; or the loud confident creature, that keeps it up with Mrs. Mantrap, and old Miss Biddy Buckskin, till three in the morning; ha, ha, ha.

MARLOW: O, curse on my noisy head. I never attempted to be impudent yet, that I was not taken down. I must be gone.

HARDCASTLE: By the hand of my body, but you shall not. I see it was all a mistake, and I am rejoiced to find it. You shall not, Sir, I tell you. I know she'll forgive you. Won't you forgive him, Kate? We'll all forgive you. Take courage, man.

(*They retire, she tormenting him to the back Scene*)

Enter MRS. HARDCASTLE *and* TONY

MRS. HARDCASTLE: So, so, they're gone off. Let them go, I care not.

HARDCASTLE: Who gone?

MRS. HARDCASTLE: My dutiful niece and her gentleman, Mr. Hastings, from Town. He who came down with our modest visitor here.

SIR CHARLES: Who, my honest George Hastings? As worthy a fellow as lives, and the girl could not have made a more prudent choice.

HARDCASTLE: Then, by the hand of my body, I'm proud of the connexion.

MRS. HARDCASTLE: Well, if he has taken away the lady, he has not taken her fortune, that remains in this family to console us for her loss.

HARDCASTLE: Sure, Dorothy, you would not be so mercenary?

MRS. HARDCASTLE: Ay, that's my affair, not yours.

HARDCASTLE: But you know, if your son, when of age, refuses to marry his cousin, her whole fortune is then at her own disposal.

MRS. HARDCASTLE: Ay, but he's not of age, and she has not thought proper to wait for his refusal.

Enter HASTINGS *and* MISS NEVILLE

MRS. HARDCASTLE: (*Aside*) What! returned so soon? I begin not to like it.

HASTINGS: (*To* HARDCASTLE) For my late attempt to fly off with your niece, let my present confusion be my punishment. We are now come back, to appeal from your justice to your humanity. By her father's consent, I first paid her my addresses, and our passions were first founded in duty.

MISS NEVILLE: Since his death, I have been obliged to stoop to dissimulation to avoid oppression. In an hour of levity, I was ready even to give up my fortune to secure my choice. But I'm now recovered from the delusion, and hope from your tenderness what is denied me from a nearer connexion.

MRS. HARDCASTLE: Pshaw, pshaw, this is all but the whining end of a modern novel.

HARDCASTLE: Be it what it will, I'm glad they're come back to reclaim their due. Come hither, Tony boy. Do you refuse this lady's hand whom I now offer you?

TONY: What signifies my refusing? You know I can't refuse her till I'm of age, father.

HARDCASTLE: While I thought concealing your age, boy, was likely to conduce to your improvement, I concurred with your mother's desire to keep it secret. But since I find she turns it to a wrong use, I must now declare, you have been of age these three months.

TONY: Of age! Am I of age, father?

HARDCASTLE: Above three months.

TONY: Then you'll see the first use I'll make of my liberty. (*Taking* MISS NEVILLE'S *hand*) Witness all men by these presents, that I, Anthony Lumpkin, Esquire, of BLANK place, refuse you, Constantia Neville, spinster, of no place at all, for my true and lawful wife. So Constance Neville may marry whom she pleases, and Tony Lumpkin is his own man again.

SIR CHARLES: O brave 'Squire.

HASTINGS: My worthy friend.

MRS. HARDCASTLE: My undutiful offspring.

MARLOW: Joy, my dear George, I give you joy sincerely. And could I prevail upon my little tyrant here to be less arbitrary, I should be the happiest man alive, if you would return me the favour.

HASTINGS: (*To* MISS HARDCASTLE) Come, Madam, you are now driven to the very last scene of all your contrivances. I know you like him, I'm sure he loves you, and you must and shall have him.

HARDCASTLE: (*Joining their hands*) And I say so too. And Mr. Marlow, if she makes as good a wife as she has a daughter, I don't believe you'll ever repent your bargain. So now to supper, to-morrow we shall gather all the poor of the parish about us, and the Mistakes of the Night shall be crowned with a merry morning; so, boy, take her; and as you have been mistaken in the mistress, my wish is, that you may never be mistaken in the wife.

FINIS

EPILOGUE

By DR. GOLDSMITH.

Well, *having stoop'd to conquer with success,*
And gain'd a husband without aid from dress,
Still as a Bar-maid, I could wish it too,
As I have conquer'd him to conquer you:
And let me say, for all your resolution,
That pretty Bar-maids have done execution.
Our life is all a play, compos'd to please,
'We have our exits and our entrances.'[1]
The first act shews the simple country maid,
Harmless and young, of ev'ry thing afraid;
Blushes when hir'd, and with unmeaning action,
I hopes as how to give you satisfaction.
Her second act displays a livelier scene, —
Th' unblushing Bar-maid of a country inn.
Who whisks about the house, at market caters,
Talks loud, coquets the guests, and scolds the waiters.
Next the scene shifts to town, and there she soars,
The chop-house toast of ogling connoisseurs.
On 'Squires and Cits[2] *she there displays her arts,*
And on the gridiron broils her lover's hearts —
And as she smiles her triumphs to compleat,
Even Common Councilmen forget to eat.
The fourth act shews her wedded to the 'Squire,
And Madam now begins to hold it higher;
Pretends to taste, at Operas cries caro,[3]
And quits her Nancy Dawson,[4] *for* Che Faro.[5]
Doats upon Dancing, and in all her pride,
Swims round the room, the Heinel[6] *of Cheapside:*
Ogles and leers with artificial skill,
Till having lost in age the power to kill,
She sits all night at cards, and ogles at spadille.[7]
Such, thro' our lives, the eventful history ——
The fifth and last act still remains for me.
The Bar-maid now for your protection prays,
Turns Female Barrister, and pleads for Bayes.[8]

1. From *As You Like It*, II.7.141: 'They have their exits and their entrances.' The rest of the epilogue toys with the basic idea in that speech by Jacques, 'All the world's a stage'.
2. citizens or shop-keepers, mockingly contrasted with squires, or country gentlemen.
3. dear.
4. A popular song.
5. An aria in Glück's *Orfeo* (1764).
6. Miss Heinel was one of the most noted dancers of the day. She performed at the Haymarket theatre in ballet sequences, either between acts or after performances.
7. The ace of spades in the card games of ombre or quadrille.
8. The poet or author. The reference goes back to the caricature of John Dryden as Mr Bayes in *The Rehearsal* (1671) by George Villiers, 2nd duke of Buckingham.

RICHARD BRINSLEY SHERIDAN

(1751-1816)

THE RIVALS (1775)

[It is often the function of comedy to bring an audience to a fresh judgment regarding common assumptions. By exaggerating fairly ordinary or conventional situations to the point of distortion, comedy encourages laughter and thereby the detachment necessary to judgment. But it is always a hazardous enterprise; there is a thin line between offending an audience through grossness or obviousness and sparking that recognition of human absurdity that enlightens understanding. It is one of the strangest stories in the history of comedy that Sheridan first got it wrong when *The Rivals* was staged (17 January 1775, at Covent Garden) and then, having rewritten, cut, and made changes in the casting of the play, got it gloriously right eleven days later.

What was wrong with *The Rivals* on its first showing? The prompt copy has not survived, but a manuscript exists, even though it is not in Sheridan's hand. It has been edited by Richard L. Purdy. The first edition of *The Rivals* was based on the revised text. There are the first reviews, however, to offer guidance on what went wrong on the night, and there is Sheridan's preface, printed below, which is really a defence. It seems clear that, with a running time of over three hours, Sheridan must have overtaxed his audience's endurance. But, more important, he misjudged his audience's taste in the characterizations, especially that of Sir Lucius O'Trigger, who offended not just the Irish but the judicious critics as well; Mrs Malaprop was given too much time and became tedious; and Faulkland and Julia were found to be 'even beyond the pitch of *sentimental* comedy'. Moreover, the language was too self-congratulatory, with too many puns and too much coarseness. And, finally, a number of the actors were badly rehearsed and did not know their lines — which is not a matter for which the playwright can be held responsible, of course, although it is something about which he must do something if he is given a second chance. The reviewers were very pleased when Sheridan came back with the revised script and an altered cast on 28 January, and one of them summed up the matter well: 'We heartily wish it was the general custom for authors to withdraw their pieces after a first performance, in order to remove the objectionable passages, heighten the favourite characters, and generally amend the play.' In every way, *The Rivals* was now a better comedy, better adjusted to the taste of the day, better calculated to amuse and delight, and, by all accounts, better acted. The result was a triumph for Sheridan, and the launching of a comedy of manners that has held the stage ever since.

The Rivals is mainly a play about young love, where ardour and common sense are very much at odds. Using material not only from his own love life (his jealousy, the duel), but also from his mother's unstaged comedy, *A Journey to Bath* (where the germ of Mrs Malaprop is to be found), Sheridan provides lively variations on such familiar comic themes as parental interference, mistaken identity, affectation, and love imperilled. To what extent he meant the Julia-Faulkland plot to appear satirical is not clear. Certainly, the liveliness of the play is increased if Faulkland's excess of feeling is perceived as an appeal to the audience's common sense, or is seen as comparable to Lydia's bookish romanticism. In the end, true love is distinguished from false imaginings, and Sheridan reasserts for the audience the primacy of natural feeling, thus fulfilling the function of comedy as he saw it, 'with every graceful art/To charm the fancy and yet reach the heart.']

PREFACE

A Preface to a Play seems generally to be considered as a kind of Closet-prologue, in which — if his Piece has been successful — the Author solicits that indulgence from the Reader which he had before experienced from the Audience: But as the scope and immediate object of a Play is to please a mixed assembly in *Representation* (whose judgment in the Theatre at least is decisive) its degree of reputation is usually as determined as public, before it can be prepared for the cooler tribunal of the Study. Thus any farther solicitude on the part of the Writer becomes unnecessary at least, if not an intrusion; and if the Piece has been condemned in the Performance, I fear an Address to the Closet, like an Appeal to Posterity, is constantly regarded as the procrastination of a suit, from a consciousness of the weakness of the cause. From these considerations, the following Comedy would certainly have been submitted to the Reader, without any further introduction than what it had in the Representation, but that its success has probably been founded on a circumstance which the Author is informed has not before attended a theatrical trial, and which consequently ought not to pass unnoticed.

I need scarcely add, that the circumstance alluded to, was the withdrawing of the Piece, to remove those imperfections in the first Representation which were too obvious to escape reprehension, and too numerous to admit of a hasty correction. There are few writers, I believe, who, even in the fullest consciousness of error, do not wish to palliate the faults which they acknowledge; and, however trifling the performance, to second their confession of its deficiencies, by whatever plea seems least disgraceful to their ability. In the present instance, it cannot be said to amount either to candour or modesty in me, to acknowledge an extreme inexperience and want of judgment on matters, in which, without guidance from practice, or spur from success, a young man should scarcely boast of being an adept. If it be said, that under such disadvantages no one should attempt to write a play — I must beg leave to dissent from the position, while the first point of experience that I have gained on the subject is, a knowledge of the candour and judgment with which an impartial Public distinguishes between the errors of inexperience and incapacity, and the indulgence which it shews even to a disposition to remedy the defects of either.

It were unnecessary to enter into any farther extenuation of what was thought exceptionable in this Play, but that it has been said, that the Managers should have prevented some of the defects before its appearance to the Public — and in particular the uncommon length of the piece as represented the first night. — It were an ill return for the most liberal and gentlemanly conduct on their side, to suffer any censure to rest where none was deserved. Hurry in writing has long been exploded as an excuse for an Author; — however, in the dramatic line, it may happen, that both an Author and a Manager may wish to fill a chasm in the entertainment of the Public with a hastiness not altogether culpable. The season was advanced when I first put the play into

Mr. Harris's[1] hands: — it was at that time at least double the length of any acting comedy. — I profited by his judgment and experience in the curtailing of it — 'till, I believe, his feeling for the vanity of a young Author got the better of his desire for correctness, and he left many excrescences remaining, because he had assisted in pruning so many more. Hence, though I was not uninformed that the Acts were still too long, I flatter'd myself that, after the first trial, I might with safer judgment proceed to remove what should appear to have been most dissatisfactory. — Many other errors there were, which might in part have arisen from my being by no means conversant with plays in general, either in reading or at the theatre. — Yet I own that, in one respect, I did not regret my ignorance: for as my first wish in attempting a Play, was to avoid every appearance of plagiary,[2] I thought I should stand a better chance of effecting this from being in a walk which I had not frequented, and where consequently the progress of invention was less likely to be interrupted by starts of recollection: for on subjects on which the mind has been much informed, invention is slow of exerting itself. — Faded ideas float in the fancy like half-forgotten dreams; and the imagination in its fullest enjoyments becomes suspicious of its offspring, and doubts whether it has created or adopted.

With regard to some particular passages which on the First Night's Representation seemed generally disliked, I confess, that if I felt any emotion of surprise at the disapprobation, it was not that they were disapproved of, but that I had not before perceived that they deserved it. As some part of the attack on the Piece was begun too early to pass for the sentence of *Judgment*, which is ever tardy in condemning, it has been suggested to me, that much of the disapprobation must have arisen from virulence of Malice, rather than severity of Criticism. But as I was more apprehensive of there being just grounds to excite the latter, than conscious of having deserved the former, I continue not to be believe that probable, which I am sure must have been unprovoked. However, if it was so, and I could even mark the quarter from whence it came, it would be ungenerous to retort; for no passion suffers more than malice from disappointment. For my own part, I see no reason why the Author of a Play should not regard a First Night's Audience, as a candid and judicious friend attending, in behalf of the Public, at his last Rehearsal.[3] If he can dispense with flattery, he is sure at least of sincerity, and even though the annotation be rude, he may rely upon the justness of the comment. Considered in this light, that Audience, whose *fiat* is essential to the Poet's claim, whether his object be Fame or Profit, has surely a right to expect some deference to its opinion, from principles of Politeness at least, if not from Gratitude.

As for the little puny Critics, who scatter their peevish strictures in private circles, and scribble at every Author who has the eminence of being unconnected with them, as they are usually spleen-swoln from a vain idea of increasing their consequence, there will always be found a petulance and illiberality in their remarks, which should place them as far beneath the notice of a Gentleman, as their original dulness had sunk them from the level of the most unsuccessful Author.

It is not without pleasure that I catch at an opportunity of justifying myself from the charge of intending any national reflection in the character of Sir *Lucius O'Trigger*. If any Gentlemen opposed the Piece from that idea, I thank them sincerely for their opposition; and if the condemnation of this Comedy (however misconceived the provocation) could have added one spark to the decaying flame of national attachment to the country supposed to be reflected on, I should have been happy in its fate; and might with truth have boasted, that it had done more real service in its failure, than the successful morality of a thousand stage-novels will ever effect.

It is usual, I believe, to thank the Performers in a new Play, for the exertion of their several abilities. But where (as in this instance) their merit has been so striking and uncontroverted, as to call for the warmest and truest applause from a number of judicious Audiences, the Poet's afterpraise comes like the feeble acclamation of a child to close the shouts of a multitude. The conduct, however, of the Principals in a Theatre cannot be so apparent to the Public. — I think it therefore but justice to declare, that from this Theatre (the only one I can speak of from experience) those Writers who wish to try the

1. Thomas Harris (died 1820), who took over management of Covent Garden from George Colman the elder (1723-94) in 1774.
2. plagiarism or using another's writing as one's own.
3. A surprisingly naive statement, considering that Sheridan's own father was a theatre manager.

Dramatic Line, will meet with that candour and liberal attention, which are generally allowed to be better calculated to lead genius into excellence, than either the precepts of judgment, or the guidance of experience.

THE AUTHOR.

PROLOGUE.[1]

BY THE AUTHOR.

Spoken by MR. WOODWARD[2] *and* MR. QUICK.[3]

Enter SERJEANT AT LAW, *and* ATTORNEY

SERJEANT AT LAW: What's here! —— a vile cramp hand! I cannot see
Without my spectacles.
ATTORNEY: He means his fee.
Nay, Mr. Serjeant, good Sir, try again.
Gives money
SERJEANT AT LAW: The scrawl improves (*more*) O come, 'tis pretty plain.
How's this! The Poet's Brief *again*! O ho!
Cast, I suppose?
ATTORNEY: O pardon me — No — No —
We found the Court, o'erlooking stricter laws,
Indulgent to the *merits* of the Cause;
By *Judges* mild, unus'd to harsh denial,
A Rule was granted for *another trial*.[4]
SERJEANT AT LAW: Then heark'e, *Dibble*, did you *mend* your *Pleadings*,
Errors, no few, we've *found* in our *Proceedings*.
ATTORNEY: Come, courage, Sir, we did *amend* our *Plea*,
Hence your *new Brief*, and this *refreshing Fee*.
Some Sons of Phoebus[5] *— in the Courts we meet,*
SERJEANT AT LAW: And fifty Sons of Phoebus in the Fleet![6]
ATTORNEY: Nor pleads he worse, who with a decent sprig
Of Bays[7] — adorns his legal waste of wig.
SERJEANT AT LAW: Full-bottom'd Heroes thus, on signs, unfurl
A leaf of laurel —— in a grove of curl!
Yet tell your Client, that, in adverse days,
This Wig is warmer than a bush of Bays.
ATTORNEY: Do you then, Sir, my Client's place supply,
Profuse of robe, and prodigal of tye ——
Do you, with all those blushing pow'rs of face,
And wonted bashful hesitating grace,
Rise in the Court, and flourish on the Case.
Exit
SERJEANT AT LAW: For practice then suppose —— this Brief will shew it, ——
Me, Serjeant *Woodward*, —— Counsel for the Poet,
Us'd to the ground —— I know 'tis hard to deal
With this dread *Court*,[8] from whence there's *no appeal*;
No *Tricking* here, to blunt the edge of *Law*,
Or, damn'd in *Equity* —— escape by *Flaw*:
But *Judgment* given — *your Sentence* must remain;
— No *Writ of Error* lies — to *Drury-lane*!
Yet when so kind you seem — 'tis past dispute
We gain some favour, if not *Costs of Suit*.
No spleen is here! I see no hoarded fury;
— I think I never fac'd a milder Jury!
Sad else our plight! — where frowns are transportation,
A hiss the gallows, — and a groan, damnation!
But such the public candour, without fear
My Client waves all *right of challenge* here.
No Newsman from *our* Session is dismiss'd,
Nor Wit nor Critic *we* scratch off the list;
His faults can never hurt another's ease,
His crime at worst — *a bad attempt* to please:
Thus, all respecting, he appeals to all,
And by the general voice will *stand* or *fall*.

1. The prologue was later revised for the tenth night of performance, and was printed in the third edition, corrected in 1776.
2. Harry Woodward (1717-77), comic actor. He also spoke the prologue to Goldsmith's *She Stoops to Conquer* (above, p. 571). He played Captain Absolute in *The Rivals*, although he was fifty-eight at the time.
3. John Quick (1748-1831), comic actor. He played Tony Lumpkin in the first production of *She Stoops to Conquer*, and Bob Acres in *The Rivals*.
4. A reference to the second performance, with the revised text, on 28 January 1775.
5. i.e. poets.
6. A debtors' prison.
7. bay leaves, ancient symbol of poetic merit.
8. i.e. held by the audience. The whole 'conceit' of the prologue is that *The Rivals* is on (re)trial.

DRAMATIS PERSONAE

Men

SIR ANTHONY ABSOLUTE
CAPTAIN ABSOLUTE [his son]
FAULKLAND
ACRES
SIR LUCIUS O'TRIGGER
FAG
DAVID
COACHMAN

Women

MRS. MALAPROP
LYDIA LANGUISH [her niece]
JULIA
LUCY

MAID, BOY, SERVANTS, &c.

SCENE: *Bath*

Time of Action, Five Hours

ACT I, SCENE 1

A Street in Bath

COACHMAN *crosses the stage.* —— *Enter* FAG, *looking after him*

FAG: What! — Thomas! Sure 'tis he? — What! — Thomas! — Thomas!

COACHMAN: Hay! —— Odd's life! —— Mr. Fag! —— give us your hand, my old fellow-servant.

FAG: Excuse my glove, Thomas: —— I'm dev'lish glad to see you, my lad: why, my prince of charioteers, you look as hearty! —— but who the deuce thought of seeing you in Bath!

COACHMAN: Sure, Master, Madam Julia, Harry, Mrs. Kate, and the postillion be all come!

FAG: Indeed!

COACHMAN: Aye! Master thought another fit of the gout was coming to make him a visit: —— so he'd a mind to gi't the slip, and whip we were all off at an hour's warning.

FAG: Aye, aye! hasty in every thing, or it would not be Sir Anthony Absolute!

COACHMAN: But tell us, Mr. Fag, how does young Master? Odd! Sir Anthony will stare to see the Captain here!

FAG: I do not serve Capt. Absolute now. ——

COACHMAN: Why sure!

FAG: At present I am employ'd by Ensign Beverley.

COACHMAN: I doubt, Mr. Fag, you ha'n't changed for the better.

FAG: I have not changed, Thomas.

COACHMAN: No! why didn't you say you had left young Master?

FAG: No —— Well, honest Thomas, I must puzzle you no farther: —— briefly then —— Capt. Absolute and Ensign Beverley are one and the same person.

COACHMAN: The devil they are!

FAG: So it is indeed, Thomas; and the *Ensign* half of my master being on guard at present —— the *Captain* has nothing to do with me.

COACHMAN: So, so! —— what, this is some freak, I warrant! —— Do, tell us, Mr. Fag, the meaning o't —— you know I ha' trusted you.

FAG: You'll be secret, Thomas.

COACHMAN: As a coach-horse.

FAG: Why then the cause of all this is — LOVE, — Love, Thomas, who (as you may get read to you) has been a masquerader ever since the days of Jupiter.

COACHMAN: Aye, aye; —— I guessed there was a lady in the case: —— but pray, why does your Master pass only for *Ensign*? —— now if he had shamm'd *General* indeed ——

FAG: Ah! Thomas, there lies the mystery o'the matter. —— Hark'ee, Thomas, my Master is in love with a lady of a very singular taste: a lady who likes him better as a *half-pay Ensign* than if she knew he was son and heir to Sir Anthony Absolute, a baronet with three thousand a-year!

COACHMAN: That is an odd taste indeed! ——but has she got the stuff, Mr. Fag; is she rich, hey?

FAG: Rich! —— why, I believe she owns half the stocks! —— Z— ds! Thomas, she could pay the national debt as easy as I could my washerwoman! — She has a lap-dog that eats out of gold, — she feeds her parrot with small pearls, — and all her threadpapers are made of bank-notes!

COACHMAN: Bravo! —— faith! —— Odd! I warrant she has a set of thousands at least: —— but does she draw kindly with the Captain!

FAG: As fond as pigeons.

COACHMAN: May one hear her name?

FAG: Miss Lydia Languish. — But there is an old

tough aunt in the way; — though by the bye — she has never seen my Master — for he got acquainted with Miss while on a visit in Gloucestershire.

COACHMAN: Well — I wish they were once harness'd together in matrimony. — But pray, Mr. Fag, what kind of a place is this Bath? — I ha' heard a deal of it — here's a mort[1] o' merry-making — hey?

FAG: Pretty well, Thomas, pretty well — 'tis a good lounge. Though at present we are, like other great assemblies, divided into parties — High-roomians and Low-roomians; however, for my part, I have resolved to stand neuter; and so I told Bob Brush at our last committee.

COACHMAN: But what do the folks do here?

FAG: Oh! there are little amusements enough —[2] in the morning we go to the pump-room (though neither my Master nor I drink the waters); after breakfast we saunter on the parades or play a game at billiards; at night we dance: but d—n the place, I'm tired of it: their regular hours stupify me —— not a fiddle nor a card after eleven! —— however Mr. Faulkland's gentleman and I keep it up a little in private parties; — I'll introduce you there, Thomas — you'll like him much.

COACHMAN: Sure I know Mr. Du-Peigne — you know his Master is to marry Madam Julia.

FAG: I had forgot. — But, Thomas, you must polish a little — indeed you must: — here now — this wig! —— what the devil do you do with a *wig*, Thomas? —— none of the London whips of any degree of Ton[3] wear *wigs* now.

COACHMAN: More's the pity! more's the pity, I say. —— Odd's life! when I heard how the lawyers and doctors had took to their own hair, I thought how 'twould go next: —— Odd rabbit it![4] when the fashion had got foot on the Bar, I guess'd 'twould mount to the Box! —— but 'tis all out of character, believe me, Mr. Fag: and look'ee, I'll never gi' up mine —— the lawyers and doctors may do as they will.

1. (dialect) great amount.
2. The lines from 'Though at present . . .' were cut in the third edition, corrected (1776). Sheridan's modern editor, Cecil Price, says that one cannot be sure whether or to what extent Sheridan himself corrected the third edition, and adds: 'The accidentals of the first edition are, in that case, likely to be closer to what he originally wrote than those of the third edition' (*Dramatic Works*, I, 65). Therefore, the present text retains the passages that subsequently were cut, and notes these where they occur.
3. taste.
4. An oath, as in 'God blast it'. 'Rabbit' may be a corruption of the French 'rebattre', to beat again.

FAG: Well, Thomas, we'll not quarrel about that.

COACHMAN: Why, bless you, the gentlemen of they professions ben't all of a mind —— for in our village now tho'ff[5] *Jack Gauge* the *exciseman*, has ta'en to his carrots,[6] there's little Dick the farrier swears he'll never forsake his *bob*,[7] tho' all the college should appear with their own heads!

FAG: Indeed! well said, Dick! but hold —— mark! mark! Thomas.

COACHMAN: Zooks! 'tis the Captain —— Is that the lady with him?

FAG: No! no! that is Madam Lucy —— my Master's mistress's maid. —— They lodge at that house —— but I must after him to tell him the news.

COACHMAN: Odd! he's giving her money! —— well, Mr. Fag ——

FAG: Good bye, Thomas —— I have an appointment in Gydes' Porch this evening at eight; meet me there, and we'll make a little party.

Exeunt severally

5. although.
6. taken to appearing in public in his own (red) hair.
7. bob-wig, with short curls.

ACT I, SCENE 2

A Dressing-room in MRS. MALAPROP's *lodgings*

LYDIA *sitting on a sopha with a book in her hand* —— LUCY, *as just returned from a message*

LUCY: Indeed, Ma'am, I transferr'd[1] half the town in search of it: —— I don't believe there's a circulating library[2] in Bath I ha'n't been at.

LYDIA: And could not you get *The Reward of Constancy*?[3]

LUCY: No, indeed, Ma'am.

LYDIA: Nor, *The Fatal Connection*?

LUCY: No, indeed, Ma'am.

1. Corrected in the third edition to 'travers'd', but Cecil Price suggests that the compositor misread Sheridan's writing of 'traips'd' (*Dramatic Works*, I, 64).
2. A new development in the eighteenth century was the growth of shops where, for a fee, books (mainly popular novels) could be read and borrowed. The age of free lending libraries had not yet arrived. Sheridan is satirizing a craze for fiction destructive of common sense.
3. Like most of the titles which follow, this refers to a popular novel of the day which Sheridan regarded as trash. The mischievous exceptions are *Peregrine Pickle* (1751) and *Humphry Clinker* (1771), both by the eminent novelist Tobias Smollett (1721-71), *The Sentimental Journey* (1768) by Laurence Sterne (1713-68) and the serious religious tome, *The Whole Duty of Man* (1659) by Richard Allestree (1618-91).

LYDIA: Nor *The Mistakes of the Heart*?

LUCY: Ma'am, as ill-luck would have it, Mr. Bull said Miss Sukey Saunter had just fetch'd it away.

LYDIA: Heigh-ho! —— Did you inquire for *The Delicate Distress*? ——

LUCY: —— Or *The Memoirs of Lady Woodford*? Yes indeed, Ma'am. —— I ask'd every where for it; and I might have brought it from Mr. Frederick's, but Lady Slattern Lounger, who had just sent it home, had so soiled and dog's-ear'd it, it wa'n't fit for a christian to read.

LYDIA: Heigh-ho! —— Yes, I always know when Lady Slattern has been before me. —— She has a most observing thumb; and I believe cherishes her nails for the convenience of making marginal notes. —— Well, child, what *have* you brought me?

LUCY: Oh! here Ma'am. (*Taking books from under her cloke, and from her pockets*) This is *The Gordian Knot*, —— and this *Peregrine Pickle*. Here are *The Tears of Sensibility* and *Humphry Clinker*. This is *The Memoirs of a Lady of Quality, written by herself*, —— and here the second volume of *The Sentimental Journey*.

LYDIA: Heigh-ho! —— What are those books by the glass?

LUCY: The great one is only *The whole Duty of Man* —— where I press a few blonds,[4] Ma'am.

LYDIA: Very well —— give me the *sal volatile*.

LUCY: Is it in a blue cover, Ma'am?

LYDIA: My smelling bottle, you simpleton!

LUCY: O, the drops! —— here Ma'am.

LYDIA: No note, Lucy?

LUCY: No indeed, Ma'am —— but I have seen a certain person ——

LYDIA: What, my Beverley! —— well Lucy?

LUCY: O Ma'am! he looks so desponding and melancholic![5]

LYDIA: Hold, Lucy! —— here's some one coming — quick, see who it is. ——

Exit LUCY

Surely I heard my cousin Julia's voice!

Re-enter LUCY

LUCY: Lud! Ma'am, here is Miss Melville.

LYDIA: Is it possible! ——

Enter JULIA

LYDIA: My dearest Julia, how delighted am I! —— (*Embrace*) How unexpected was this happiness!

JULIA: True, Lydia —— and our pleasure is the greater: —— but what has been the matter? —— you were denied to me at first!

LYDIA: Ah! Julia, I have a thousand things to tell you! —— but first inform me, what has conjur'd you to Bath? —— Is Sir Anthony here?

JULIA: He is —— we are arrived within this hour —— and I suppose he will be here to wait on Mrs. Malaprop as soon as he is dress'd.

LYDIA: Then before we are interrupted, let me impart to you some of my distress —— I know your gentle nature will sympathize with me, tho' your prudence may condemn me! —— My letters have inform'd you of my whole connexion with Beverley; —— but I have lost him, Julia —— my aunt has discover'd our intercourse by a note she intercepted, and has confin'd me ever since! —— Yet, would you believe it? she has fallen absolutely in love with a tall Irish baronet she met one night since we have been here, at Lady Macshuffle's rout.[6]

JULIA: You jest, Lydia!

LYDIA: No, upon my word. —— She absolutely carries on a kind of correspondence with him, under a feigned name though, till she chuses to be known to him; —— but it is a *Delia* or a *Celia*, I assure you.

JULIA: Then, surely, she is now more indulgent to her niece.

LYDIA: Quite the contrary. Since she has discovered her own frailty, she is become more suspicious of mine. Then I must inform you of another plague! —— That odious Acres is to be in Bath to-day; so that I protest I shall be teased out of all spirits!

JULIA: Come, come, Lydia, hope the best. —— Sir Anthony shall use his interest with Mrs. Malaprop.

LYDIA: But you have not heard the worst. Unfortunately I had quarrell'd with my poor Beverley, just before my aunt made the discovery, and I have not seen him since, to make it up.

JULIA: What was his offence?

LYDIA: Nothing at all! —— But, I don't know how it was, as often as we had been together, we had never had a quarrel! — And, somehow I was afraid he would never give me an opportunity. — So, last Thursday, I wrote a letter to myself, to inform myself that Beverley was at that time paying his

4. blond laces, produced from unbleached silk.

5. The lines from 'No note . . .' were cut in the third edition.

6. A large evening party or reception.

addresses to another woman. —— I sign'd it *your Friend unknown,* shew'd it to Beverley, charg'd him with his falsehood, put myself in a violent passion, and vow'd I'd never see him more.

JULIA: And you let him depart so, and have not seen him since?

LYDIA: 'Twas the next day my aunt found the matter out. I intended only to have teased him three days and a half, and now I've lost him for ever.

JULIA: If he is as deserving and sincere as you have represented him to me, he will never give you up so. Yet consider, Lydia, you tell me he is but an ensign, and you have thirty thousand pounds!

LYDIA: But you know I lose most of my fortune, if I marry without my aunt's consent, till of age; and that is what I have determin'd to do, ever since I knew the penalty. —— Nor could I love the man, who would wish to wait a day for the alternative.

JULIA: Nay, this is caprice!

LYDIA: What, does Julia tax me with caprice? —— I thought her lover Faulkland had enured her to it.

JULIA: I do not love even *his* faults.

LYDIA: But a-propos —— you have sent to him, I suppose?

JULIA: Not yet, upon my word —— nor has he the least idea of my being in Bath. —— Sir Anthony's resolution was so sudden, I could not inform him of it.

LYDIA: Well, Julia, you are your own mistress, (though under the protection of Sir Anthony) yet have you, for this long year, been the slave to the caprice, the whim, the jealousy of this ungrateful Faulkland, who will ever delay assuming the right of a husband, while you suffer him to be equally imperious as a lover.

JULIA: Nay, you are wrong entirely. —— We were contracted before my father's death. —— *That,* and some consequent embarrassments, have delay'd what I know to be my Faulkland's most ardent wish. —— He is too generous to trifle on such a point. —— And for his character, you wrong him there too. —— No, Lydia, he is too proud, too noble to be jealous; if he is captious, 'tis without dissembling; if fretful, without rudeness. —— Unus'd to the foppery of love, he is negligent of the little duties expected from a lover —— but being unhackney'd in the passion, his love is ardent and sincere; and as it engrosses his whole soul, he expects every thought and emotion of his mistress to move in unison with his. —— Yet, though his pride calls for this full return — his humility makes him undervalue those qualities in him, which shou'd entitle him to it; and not feeling why he should be lov'd to the degree he wishes, he still suspects that he is not lov'd enough: — This temper, I must own, has cost me many unhappy hours; but I have learn'd to think myself his debtor, for those imperfections which arise from the ardour of his love.

LYDIA: Well, I cannot blame you for defending him. —— But tell me candidly, Julia, had he never sav'd your life, do you think you should have been attach'd to him as you are? — Believe me, the rude blast that overset your boat was a prosperous gale of love to him.

JULIA: Gratitude may have strengthened my attachment to Mr. Faulkland, but I lov'd him before he had preserv'd me; yet surely that alone were an obligation sufficient.

LYDIA: Obligation! —— Why a water-spaniel would have done as much. —— Well, I should never think of giving my heart to a man because he could swim!

JULIA: Come, Lydia, you are too inconsiderate.

LYDIA: Nay, I do but jest —— What's here?

Enter LUCY *in a hurry*

LUCY: O Ma'am, here is Sir Anthony Absolute just come home with your aunt.

LYDIA: They'll not come here —— Lucy, do you watch.

Exit LUCY

JULIA: Yet I must go —— Sir Anthony does not know I am here, and if we meet, he'll detain me, to shew me the town. —— I'll take another opportunity of paying my respects to Mrs. Malaprop, when she shall treat me, as long as she chooses, with her select words so ingeniously *misapplied,* without being *mispronounced.*

Re-enter LUCY

LUCY: O Lud! Ma'am, they are both coming up stairs.

LYDIA: Well, I'll not detain you, Coz —— Adieu, my dear Julia, I'm sure you are in haste to send to Faulkland. —— There — through my room you'll find another stair-case.

JULIA: Adieu. — (*Embrace*)

Exit JULIA

LYDIA: Here, my dear Lucy, hide these books — Quick, quick. — Fling *Peregrine Pickle* under the toilet — throw *Roderick Random* into the closet — put *The Innocent Adultery* into *The Whole Duty of*

Man — thrust *Lord Aimworth* under the sopha —— cram *Ovid* behind the bolster — there — put *The Man of Feeling* into your pocket — so, so, now lay *Mrs. Chapone* in sight, and leave *Fordyce's Sermons* open on the table.

LUCY: O burn it, Ma'am, the hair-dresser has torn away[7] as far as *Proper Pride*.

LYDIA: Never mind — open at *Sobriety*. — Fling me *Lord Chesterfield's Letters*. —— Now for 'em.

Enter MRS. MALAPROP *and* SIR ANTHONY ABSOLUTE

MRS. MALAPROP: There, Sir Anthony, there sits the deliberate Simpleton, who wants to disgrace her family, and lavish herself on a fellow not worth a shilling!

LYDIA: Madam, I thought you once ——

MRS. MALAPROP: You thought, Miss! —— I don't know any business you have to think at all —— thought does not become a young woman; the point we would request of you is, that you will promise to forget this fellow — to illiterate[8] him, I say, quite from your memory.

LYDIA: Ah! Madam! our memories are independent of our wills. — It is not so easy to forget.

MRS. MALAPROP: But I say it is, Miss; there is nothing on earth so easy as to *forget*, if a person chooses to set about it. — I'm sure I have as much forgot your poor dear uncle as if he had never existed — and I thought it my duty so to do; and let me tell you, Lydia, these violent memories don't become a young woman.

SIR ANTHONY: Why sure she won't pretend to remember what she's order'd not! — aye, this comes of her reading!

LYDIA: What crime, Madam, have I committed to be treated thus?

MRS. MALAPROP: Now don't attempt to extirpate[9] yourself from the matter; you know I have proof controvertible[10] of it. — But tell me, will you promise to do as you're bid? — Will you take a husband of your friend's choosing?

LYDIA: Madam, I must tell you plainly, that had I no preference for any one else, the choice you have made would be my aversion.

MRS. MALAPROP: What business have you, Miss, with *preference* and *aversion*? They don't become a young woman; and you ought to know, that as both always wear off, 'tis safest in matrimony to begin with a little *aversion*. I am sure I hated your poor dear uncle before marriage as if he'd been a black-a-moor — and yet, Miss, you are sensible what a wife I made! — and when it pleas'd Heav'n to release me from him, 'tis unknown what tears I shed! — But suppose we were going to give you another choice, will you promise us to give up this Beverley?

LYDIA: Could I belie my thoughts so far, as to give that promise, my actions would certainly as far belie my words.

MRS. MALAPROP: Take yourself to your room. — You are fit company for nothing but your own ill-humours.

LYDIA: Willingly, Ma'am — I cannot change for the worse.

Exit LYDIA

MRS. MALAPROP: There's a little intricate[11] hussy for you!

SIR ANTHONY: It is not to be wonder'd at, Ma'am —— all this is the natural consequence of teaching girls to read. — Had I a thousand daughters, by Heavens! I'd as soon have them taught the black-art as their alphabet!

MRS. MALAPROP: Nay, nay, Sir Anthony, you are an absolute misanthropy.[12]

SIR ANTHONY: In my way hither, Mrs. Malaprop, I observed your niece's maid coming forth from a circulating library! —— She had a book in each hand — they were half-bound volumes, with marbled covers! —— From that moment I guess'd how full of duty I should see her mistress!

MRS. MALAPROP: Those are vile places, indeed!

SIR ANTHONY: Madam, a circulating library in a town is, as an ever-green tree, of diabolical knowledge! —— It blossoms through the year! —— And depend on it, Mrs. Malaprop, that they who are so fond of handling the leaves, will long for the fruit at last.

MRS. MALAPROP: Well, but Sir Anthony, your wife, Lady Absolute, was fond of books.

SIR ANTHONY: Aye — and injury sufficient they were to her, Madam. —— But were I to chuse

7. In these days ladies curled their hair with waste paper. In William Congreve's *The Way of the World* (1700), Millamant claimed that she pinned up her hair with poetry only, never with prose.
8. for 'obliterate'.
9. for 'extricate'.
10. for 'incontrovertible'.
11. for 'intrepid' or possibly 'intriguing'. It is not always clear what precise word Mrs Malaprop is abusing.
12. for 'misogynist', woman hater.

another helpmate, the extent of her erudition should consist in her knowing her simple letters, without their mischievous combinations; — and the summit of her science be —— her ability to count as far as twenty. — The first, Mrs. Malaprop, would enable her to work *A. A.* upon my linen; —— and the latter would be quite sufficient to prevent her giving me a shirt, No. 1. and a stock No. 2.[13]

MRS. MALAPROP: Fie, fie, Sir Anthony, you surely speak laconically![14]

SIR ANTHONY: Why, Mrs. Malaprop, in moderation, now, what would you have a woman know?

MRS. MALAPROP: Observe me, Sir Anthony. —— I would by no means wish a daughter of mine to be a progeny[15] of learning; I don't think so much learning becomes a young woman; for instance —— I would never let her meddle with Greek, or Hebrew, or Algebra, or Simony, or Fluxions, or Paradoxes,[16] or such inflammatory[17] branches of learning — neither would it be necessary for her to handle any of your mathematical, astronomical, diabolical instruments; —— But, Sir Anthony, I would send her, at nine years old, to a boarding-school, in order to learn a little ingenuity and artifice.[18] —— Then, Sir, she should have a supercilious[19] knowledge in accounts; —— and as she grew up, I would have her instructed in geometry,[20] that she might know something of the contagious[21] countries; —— but above all, Sir Anthony, she should be mistress of orthodoxy,[22] that she might not mis-spell, and mis-pronounce words so shamefully as girls usually do; and likewise that she might reprehend[23] the true meaning of what she is saying —— This, Sir Anthony, is what I would have a woman know; —— and I don't think there is a superstitious[24] article in it.

SIR ANTHONY: Well, well, Mrs. Malaprop, I will dispute the point no further with you; though I must confess, that you are a truly moderate and polite arguer, for almost every third word you say is on my side of the question. —— But, Mrs. Malaprop, to the more important point in debate, — you say, you have no objection to my proposal.

MRS. MALAPROP: None, I assure you. — I am under no positive engagement with Mr. Acres, and as Lydia is so obstinate against him, perhaps your son may have better success.

SIR ANTHONY: Well, Madam, I will write for the boy directly. — He knows not a syllable of this yet, though I have for some time had the proposal in my head. He is at present with his regiment.

MRS. MALAPROP: We have never seen your son, Sir Anthony; but I hope no objection on his side.

SIR ANTHONY: Objection! — let him object if he dare! — No, no , Mrs. Malaprop, Jack knows that the least demur puts me in a frenzy directly. — My process was always very simple — in their younger days, 'twas 'Jack, do this;' — if he demur'd — I knock'd him down — and if he grumbled at that — I always sent him out of the room.

MRS. MALAPROP: Aye, and the properest way, o' my conscience! — nothing is so conciliating[25] to young people as severity. —— Well, Sir Anthony, I shall give Mr. Acres his discharge, and prepare Lydia to receive your son's invocations; — and I hope you will represent *her* to the Captain as an object not altogether illegible.[26]

SIR ANTHONY: Madam, I will handle the subject prudently. — Well, I must leave you — and let me beg you, Mrs. Malaprop, to enforce this matter roundly to the girl; — take my advice — keep a tight hand — if she rejects this proposal — clap her under lock and key: — and if you were just to let the servants forget to bring her dinner for three or four days, you can't conceive how she'd come about!

Exit SIR ANTHONY

MRS. MALAPROP: Well, at any rate I shall be glad to get her from under my intuition.[27] —— She has somehow discovered my partiality for Sir Lucius O'Trigger — sure, Lucy can't have betray'd me,

13. The lines from 'Well, but Sir Anthony . . .' were cut in the third edition.
14. for 'ironically'.
15. for 'prodigy'. Sheridan is here indebted to his mother's comedy, *A Journey to Bath*, where Mrs Tryfort calls a man 'a perfect progeny'. See Robert Hogan and Jerry C. Beasley (eds), *The Plays of Frances Sheridan* (Newark: University of Delaware Press, 1984), p. 175.
16. Perhaps, 'syntax, or fractions, or paradigms'.
17. i.e. that would arouse passions. Compare Miss Prism's view on the study of political economy: 'The chapter on the Fall of the Rupee you may omit. It is somewhat too sensational. Even these metallic problems have their melodramatic side.' Oscar Wilde, *The Importance of Being Earnest* (1895), Act II.
18. She means the opposite: ingenuousness (politeness) and artistry.
19. for 'superficial'.
20. for 'geography'.
21. for 'contiguous', neighbouring.
22. for 'orthography'.
23. for 'apprehend'.
24. for 'superfluous'.
25. for 'humiliating'.
26. for 'ineligible'.
27. for 'tuition'.

—— No, the girl is such a simpleton, I should have made her confess it. — Lucy! — Lucy! — (*calls*). Had she been one of your artificial ones, I should never have trusted her.

Enter LUCY

LUCY: Did you call, Ma'am?

MRS. MALAPROP: Yes, girl. —— Did you see Sir Lucius while you was out?

LUCY: No, indeed, Ma'am, not a glimpse of him.

MRS. MALAPROP: You are sure, Lucy, that you never mention'd ——

LUCY: O Gemini! I'd sooner cut my tongue out.

MRS. MALAPROP: Well, don't let your simplicity be impos'd on.

LUCY: No, Ma'am.

MRS. MALAPROP: So, come to me presently, and I'll give you another letter to Sir Lucius; —— but mind, Lucy — if ever you betray what you are entrusted with — (unless it be other people's secrets to me) you forfeit my malevolence[28] for ever: — and your being a simpleton shall be no excuse for your locality.[29]

Exit MRS. MALAPROP

LUCY: Ha! ha! ha! — So, my dear *simplicity*, let me give you a little respite —— (*altering her manner*) — let girls in my station be as fond as they please of appearing expert, and knowing in their trusts; — commend me to a mask of *silliness*, and a pair of sharp eyes for my own interest under it! —— Let me see to what account I have turn'd my *simplicity* lately —— (*looks at a paper*) For *abetting Miss Lydia Languish in a design of running away with an Ensign! —— in money —— sundry times —— twelve pound twelve —— gowns, five —— hats, ruffles, caps* &c. &c. ——*numberless! —— From the said Ensign, within this last month, six guineas and a half.* —— About a quarter's pay! —— Item, *from Mrs. Malaprop, for betraying the young people to her* —— when I found matters were likely to be discovered —— *two guineas, and a black paduasoy*[30] —— Item, *from Mr. Acres, for carrying divers letters* —— which I never deliver'd — *two guineas, and a pair of buckles.* —— Item, *from Sir Lucius O'Trigger* —— *three crowns* —— *two gold pocket-pieces* —— *and a silver snuff-box*! —— Well done, *simplicity*! — yet I was forced to make my Hibernian believe, that he was corresponding, not with the *Aunt*, but with the *Niece*: for, though not over rich, I found he had too much pride and delicacy to sacrifice the feelings of a gentleman to the necessities of his fortune.

Exit

ACT II, SCENE 1

CAPTAIN ABSOLUTE's Lodgings

CAPTAIN ABSOLUTE *and* FAG

FAG: Sir, while I was there, Sir Anthony came in: I told him, you had sent me to inquire after his health, and to know if he was at leisure to see you.

CAPTAIN ABSOLUTE: And what did he say, on hearing I was at Bath?

FAG: Sir, in my life I never saw an elderly gentleman more astonished! He started back two or three paces, rapt out a dozen interjectoral oaths, and asked, what the devil had brought you here!

CAPTAIN ABSOLUTE: Well, Sir, and what did you say?

FAG: O, I lied, Sir —— I forgot the precise lie, but you may depend on't; he got no truth from me. Yet, with submission, for fear of blunders in future, I should be glad to fix what *has* brought us to Bath: in order that we may lie a little consistently. —— Sir Anthony's servants were curious, Sir, very curious indeed.

CAPTAIN ABSOLUTE: You have said nothing to them ——?

FAG: O, not a word, Sir —— not a word. —— Mr. Thomas, indeed, the coachman (whom I take to be the discreetest of whips) ——

CAPTAIN ABSOLUTE: S'death! —— you rascal! you have not trusted him!

FAG: O, *no*, Sir — no — no —— not a syllable, upon my veracity! — He was, indeed, a little inquisitive; but I was sly, Sir —— devilish sly! — My Master (said I) honest Thomas (you know, Sir, one says *honest* to one's inferiors) is come to Bath to *recruit* —— Yes, Sir — I said, *to recruit* —— and whether for men, money, or constitution, you know, Sir, is nothing to him, nor any one else.

CAPTAIN ABSOLUTE: Well — *recruit* will do — let it be so ——

FAG: O, Sir, recruit will do surprisingly — indeed, to give the thing an air, I told Thomas, that your Honour had already inlisted five disbanded chairmen, seven minority waiters, and thirteen billiard markers.

28. for 'benevolence'.
29. for 'loquacity'.
30. A strong corded silk fabric used for garments.

CAPTAIN ABSOLUTE: You blockhead, never say more than is necessary.

FAG: I beg pardon, Sir —— I beg pardon —— But with submission, a lie is nothing unless one supports it —— Sir, whenever I draw on my invention for a good current lie, I always forge *indorsements*, as well as the bill.

CAPTAIN ABSOLUTE: Well, take care you don't hurt your credit, by offering too much security. —— Is Mr. Faulkland returned?

FAG: He is above, Sir, changing his dress.

CAPTAIN ABSOLUTE: Can you tell whether he has been informed of Sir Anthony's and Miss Melville's arrival?

FAG: I fancy not, Sir; he has seen no one since he came in, but his gentleman, who was with him at Bristol —— I think, Sir, I hear Mr. Faulkland coming down ——

CAPTAIN ABSOLUTE: Go, tell him, I am here.

FAG: Yes, Sir —— (*going*) I beg pardon, Sir, but should Sir Anthony call, you will do me the favour to remember, that we are *recruiting*, if you please.

CAPTAIN ABSOLUTE: Well, well.

FAG: And in tenderness to my character, if your Honour could bring in the chairmen and waiters, I shall esteem it as an obligation; — for though I never scruple a lie to serve my Master, yet it *hurts* one's conscience, to be found out.

Exit

CAPTAIN ABSOLUTE: Now for my whimsical friend —— if he does not know that his mistress is here, I'll tease him a little before I tell him ——

Enter FAULKLAND

Faulkland, you're welcome to Bath again; you are punctual in your return.

FAULKLAND: Yes; I had nothing to detain me, when I had finished the business I went on. Well, what news since I left you? How stand matters between you and Lydia?

CAPTAIN ABSOLUTE: Faith, much as they were; I have not seen her since our quarrel, however I expect to be recalled every hour.

FAULKLAND: Why don't you persuade her to go off with you at once?

CAPTAIN ABSOLUTE: What, and lose two-thirds of her fortune? You forget that, my friend. — No, no, I could have brought her to that long ago.

FAULKLAND: Nay then, you trifle too long —— if you are sure of *her*, propose to the aunt *in your own character*, and write to Sir Anthony for his consent.

CAPTAIN ABSOLUTE: Softly, softly, for though I am convinced my little Lydia would elope with me as Ensign Beverley, yet am I by no means certain that she would take me with the impediment of our friend's consent, a regular humdrum wedding, and the reversion of a good fortune on my side; no, no, I must prepare her gradually for the discovery, and make myself necessary to her, before I risk it. —— Well, but Faulkland, you'll dine with us to-day at the Hotel?

FAULKLAND: Indeed I cannot: I am not in spirits to be of such a party.

CAPTAIN ABSOLUTE: By Heavens! I shall forswear your company. You are the most teasing, captious, incorrigible lover! — Do love like a man.

FAULKLAND: I own I am unfit for company.

CAPTAIN ABSOLUTE: Am not *I* a lover; aye, and a romantic one too? Yet do I carry every where with me such a confounded farago of doubts, fears, hopes, wishes, and all the flimsy furniture of a country Miss's brain!

FAULKLAND: Ah! Jack, your heart and soul are not, like mine, fixed immutably on one only object. —— You throw for a large stake, but losing — you could stake, and throw again: — but I have set my sum of happiness on this cast, and not to succeed, were to be stript of all.

CAPTAIN ABSOLUTE: But for Heav'ns sake! what grounds for apprehension can your whimsical brain conjure up at present? Has Julia miss'd writing this last post? or was her last too tender, or too cool; or too grave, or too gay; or ——[1]

FAULKLAND: Nay, nay, Jack.

CAPTAIN ABSOLUTE: Why, her love — her honour — her prudence, you cannot doubt.

FAULKLAND: O! upon my soul, I never have; —— but what grounds for apprehension did you say? Heavens! are there not a thousand! I fear for her spirits — her health — her life. —— My absence may fret her; her anxiety for my return, her fears for me, may oppress her gentle temper. And for her health — does not every hour bring me cause to be alarmed? If it rains, some shower may even then have chilled her delicate frame! —— If the wind be keen, some rude blast may have affected her! The heat of noon, the dews of the evening, may endanger the life of her, for whom only I value mine. O! Jack, when delicate and feeling souls are separated, there is not a feature in

1. The lines from 'Has Julia . . .' were cut in the third edition.

the sky, not a movement of the elements, not an aspiration of the breeze, but hints some cause for a lover's apprehension!

CAPTAIN ABSOLUTE: Aye, but we may choose whether we will take the hint or no. — Well then, Faulkland, if you were convinced that Julia was well and in spirits, you would be entirely content.

FAULKLAND: I should be happy beyond measure —— I'm anxious only for that.

CAPTAIN ABSOLUTE: Then to cure your anxiety at once —— Miss Melville is in perfect health, and is at this moment in Bath.

FAULKLAND: Nay, Jack — don't trifle with me.

CAPTAIN ABSOLUTE: She is arrived here with my father within this hour.

FAULKLAND: Can you be serious?

CAPTAIN ABSOLUTE: I thought you knew Sir Anthony better than to be surprised at a sudden whim of this kind — Seriously then, it is as I tell you — upon my honour.

FAULKLAND: My dear friend! — Hollo, Du — Peigne! my hat — my dear Jack — *now nothing on earth can give me a moment's uneasiness.*

Enter FAG

FAG: Sir, Mr. Acres just arrived is below.

CAPTAIN ABSOLUTE: Stay, Faulkland, this Acres lives within a mile of Sir Anthony, and he shall tell you how your mistress has been ever since you left her. — Fag, shew the gentleman up.

Exit FAG

FAULKLAND: What, is he much acquainted in the family?

CAPTAIN ABSOLUTE: O, very intimate: I insist on your not going: besides, his character will divert you.

FAULKLAND: Well, I should like to ask him a few questions.

CAPTAIN ABSOLUTE: He is likewise a rival of mine —— that is of my *other self's,* for he does not think his friend Capt. Absolute ever saw the lady in question; —— and it is ridiculous enough to hear him complain to me of *one Beverley* a concealed sculking rival, who ——

FAULKLAND: Hush! — He's here.

Enter ACRES

ACRES: Hah! my dear friend, noble captain, and honest Jack, how do'st thou? just arrived faith, as you see. — Sir, your humble servant. Warm work on the roads, Jack — Odds, whips and wheels, I've travelled like a Comet, with a tail of dust all the way as long as the Mall.

CAPTAIN ABSOLUTE: Ah! Bob, you are indeed an excentric Planet, but we know your attraction hither — give me leave to introduce Mr. Faulkland to you: Mr. Faulkland, Mr. Acres.

ACRES: Sir, I am most heartily glad to see you: Sir, I solicit your connections — Hey, Jack — what this is Mr. Faulkland, who ——

CAPTAIN ABSOLUTE: Aye, Bob, Miss Melville's Mr. Faulkland.

ACRES: Od'so! she and your father can be but just arrived before me — I suppose you have seen them. — Ah! Mr. Faulkland, you are indeed a happy man.

FAULKLAND: I have not seen Miss Melville yet, Sir, —— I hope she enjoyed full health and spirits in Devonshire.

ACRES: Never knew her better in my life, Sir, —— never better. —— Odd's Blushes and Blooms! she has been as healthy as the German Spa.

FAULKLAND: Indeed! — I did hear that she had been a little indisposed.

ACRES: False, false, Sir —— only said to vex you: quite the reverse I assure you.

FAULKLAND: There, Jack, you see she has the advantage of me; I had almost fretted myself ill.

CAPTAIN ABSOLUTE: Now are you angry with your mistress for not having been sick.

FAULKLAND: No, no, you misunderstand me: — yet surely a little trifling indisposition is not an unnatural consequence of absence from those we love. —— Now confess — isn't there something unkind in this violent, robust, unfeeling health?

CAPTAIN ABSOLUTE: O, it was very unkind of her to be well in your absence to be sure!

ACRES: Good apartments, Jack.

FAULKLAND: Well, Sir, but you were saying that Miss Melville has been so *exceedingly* well — what then she has been merry and gay I suppose? —— Always in spirits — hey?

ACRES: Merry, Odds Crickets! she has been the bell and spirit of the company wherever she has been —— so lively and entertaining! so full of wit and humour!

FAULKLAND: There, Jack, there. —— O, by my soul! there is an innate levity in woman, that nothing can overcome. — What! happy and I away!

CAPTAIN ABSOLUTE: Have done: how foolish this is! just now you were only apprehensive for your mistress's *spirits.*

FAULKLAND: Why, Jack, have I been the joy and spirit of the company?

CAPTAIN ABSOLUTE: No indeed, you have not.

FAULKLAND: Have I been lively and entertaining?

CAPTAIN ABSOLUTE: O, upon my word, I acquit you.

FAULKLAND: Have I been full of wit and humour?

CAPTAIN ABSOLUTE: No, faith, to do you justice, you have been confounded stupid indeed.

ACRES: What's the matter with the gentleman?

CAPTAIN ABSOLUTE: He is only expressing his great satisfaction at hearing that Julia has been so well and happy —— that's all —— hey, Faulkland?

FAULKLAND: Oh! I am rejoiced to hear it —— yes, yes, she has a *happy* disposition!

ACRES: That she has indeed —— then she is so accomplished —— so sweet a voice —— so expert at her Harpsichord — such a mistress of flat and sharp, squallante, rumblante, and quiverante! — there was this time month — Odds Minnums and Crotchets! how she did chirup at Mrs. Piano's Concert.

FAULKLAND: There again, what say you to this? you see she has been all mirth and song — not a thought of me!

CAPTAIN ABSOLUTE: Pho! man, is not music the food of love?[2]

FAULKLAND: Well, well, it may be so. — Pray Mr. —— what's his d—d name? —— Do you remember what Songs Miss Melville sung?

ACRES: Not I, indeed.

CAPTAIN ABSOLUTE: Stay now, they were some pretty, melancholy, purling stream airs, I warrant; perhaps you may recollect: — did she sing — '*When absent from my soul's delight?*'

ACRES: No, that wa'n't it.

CAPTAIN ABSOLUTE: Or —— '*Go, gentle Gales!*' —— '*Go, gentle Gales!*' (*Sings*)

ACRES: O no! nothing like it. — Odds slips? now I recollect one of them —— '*My heart's my own, my will is free.*' (*Sings*)

FAULKLAND: Fool! fool that I am! to fix all my happiness upon such a trifler! S'death! to make herself the pipe and ballad-monger of a circle! to soothe her light heart with catches and glees! — What can you say to this, Sir?

CAPTAIN ABSOLUTE: Why, that I should be glad to hear my mistress had been so merry, *Sir*.

FAULKLAND: Nay, nay, nay —— I am not sorry that she has been happy — no, no, I am glad of that — I would not have had her sad or sick — yet surely a sympathetic heart would have shewn itself even in the choice of a song — she might have been temperately healthy, and somehow, plaintively gay; —— but she has been dancing too, I doubt not!

ACRES: What does the gentleman say about dancing?

CAPTAIN ABSOLUTE: He says the lady we speak of dances as well as she sings.

ACRES: Aye truly, does she — there was at our last race-ball ——

FAULKLAND: Hell and the devil! There! there! — I told you so! I told you so! Oh! she thrives in my absence! —— Dancing! — but her whole feelings have been in opposition with mine! —— I have been anxious, silent, pensive, sedentary — my days have been hours of care, my nights of watchfulness. — She has been all Health! Spirit! Laugh! Song! Dance! —— Oh! d—n'd, d—n'd levity!

CAPTAIN ABSOLUTE: For Heaven's sake! Faulkland, don't expose yourself so. — Suppose she has danced, what then? — does not the ceremony of society often oblige ——

FAULKLAND: Well, well, I'll contain myself — perhaps, as you say — for form sake. — What, Mr. Acres, you were praising Miss Melville's manner of dancing a *minuet* — hey?

ACRES: O I dare insure her for that —— but what I was going to speak of was her *country dancing*: —— Odds swimmings! she has such an air with her! —

FAULKLAND: Now disappointment on her! — defend this, Absolute, why don't you defend this? —— Country-dances! jiggs, and reels! am I to blame now? A Minuet I could have forgiven —— I should not have minded that — I say I should not have regarded a Minuet — but *Country-dances*! Z—ds! had she made one in a *Cotillon* —— I believe I could have forgiven even that — but to be monkey-led for a night! — to run the gauntlet thro' a string of amorous palming puppies! — to shew paces like a managed filly! —— O Jack, there never can be but *one* man in the world, whom a truly modest and delicate woman ought to pair with in a *Country-dance*; and even then, the rest of the couples should be her great uncles and aunts!

CAPTAIN ABSOLUTE: Aye, to be sure! — grand-fathers and grand-mothers!

FAULKLAND: If there be but one vicious mind in the Set, 'twill spread like a contagion —— the action of their pulse beats to the lascivious

2. According to Shakespeare, *Twelfth Night*, I.1.1.

movement of the jigg — their quivering, warm-breath'd sighs impregnate the very air — the atmosphere becomes electrical to love, and each amorous spark darts thro' every link of the chain! —— I must leave you — I own I am somewhat flurried — and that confounded looby[3] has perceived it. (*Going*)

CAPTAIN ABSOLUTE: Aye, aye, you are in a hurry to throw yourself at Julia's feet.[4]

FAULKLAND: I'm not in a humour to be trifled with —— I shall see her only to upbraid her. (*Going*)

CAPTAIN ABSOLUTE: Nay, but stay Faulkland, and thank Mr. Acres for his good news.

FAULKLAND: D—n his news!

Exit FAULKLAND

CAPTAIN ABSOLUTE: Ha! ha! ha! poor Faulkland five minutes since — 'nothing on earth could give him a moment's uneasiness!'

ACRES: The gentleman wa'n't angry at my praising his mistress, was he?

CAPTAIN ABSOLUTE: A little jealous, I believe, Bob.

ACRES: You don't say so? Ha! ha! jealous of me — that's a good joke.

CAPTAIN ABSOLUTE: There's nothing strange in that, Bob: let me tell you, that sprightly grace and insinuating manner of your's will do some mischief among the girls here.

ACRES: Ah! you joke —— ha! ha! mischief — ha! ha! but you know I am not my own property, my dear Lydia, has forestalled me. —— She could never abide me in the country, because I used to dress so badly — but odds frogs and tambours! I shan't take matters so here — now ancient Madam has no voice in it — I'll make my old clothes know who's master — I shall straitway cashier the hunting-frock — and render my leather breeches incapable —— My hair has been in training some time.

CAPTAIN ABSOLUTE: Indeed!

ACRES: Aye —— and tho'ff the side-curls are a little restive, my hind-part takes to it very kindly.

CAPTAIN ABSOLUTE: O, you'll polish, I doubt not.

ACRES: Absolutely I propose so — then if I can find out this Ensign Beverley, odds triggers and flints! I'll make him know the difference o't.

CAPTAIN ABSOLUTE: Spoke like a man — but pray, Bob, I observe you have got an odd kind of a new method of swearing ——

ACRES: Ha! ha! you've taken notice of it —— 'tis genteel, isn't it? — I didn't invent it myself though; but a commander in our militia —— a great scholar, I assure you —— says that there is no meaning in the common oaths, and that nothing but their antiquity makes them respectable; — because, he says, the ancients would never stick to an oath or two, but would say By Jove! or by Bacchus! or by Mars! or by Venus! or by Pallas! according to the sentiment —— so that to swear with propriety, says my little Major, the 'oath should be an echo to the sense;'[5] and this we call the *oath referential,* or *sentimental swearing* — ha! ha! ha! 'tis genteel, isn't it?

CAPTAIN ABSOLUTE: Very genteel, and very new indeed —— and I dare say will supplant all other figures of imprecation.

ACRES: Aye, aye, the best terms will grow obsolete —— D—ns have had their day.

Enter FAG

FAG: Sir, there is a gentleman below, desires to see you — shall I shew him into the parlour?

CAPTAIN ABSOLUTE: Aye — you may.

ACRES: Well, I must be gone ——

CAPTAIN ABSOLUTE: Stay; who is it, Fag?

FAG: Your father, Sir.

CAPTAIN ABSOLUTE: You puppy, why didn't you shew him up directly?

Exit FAG

ACRES: You have business with Sir Anthony —— I expect a message from Mrs. Malaprop at my lodgings —— I have sent also to my dear friend Sir Lucius O'Trigger — Adieu, Jack, we must meet at night — Odds bottles and glasses![6] you shall give me a dozen bumpers to little Lydia.

CAPTAIN ABSOLUTE: That I will, with all my heart.

Exit ACRES

CAPTAIN ABSOLUTE: Now for a parental lecture —— I hope he has heard nothing of the business that has brought me here — I wish the gout had held him fast in Devonshire, with all my soul!

3. silly fellow.
4. The lines from 'Aye, aye . . .' were cut in the third edition.

5. A variation on Alexander Pope's line on onomatopoeia in *An Essay on Criticism* (1711): 'The sound must seem an echo to the sense' (line 365).
6. This sentence was cut in the third edition; 'bumpers': brim-full glasses.

Enter SIR ANTHONY

CAPTAIN ABSOLUTE: Sir, I am delighted to see you here; and looking so well! — your sudden arrival at Bath made me apprehensive for your health.

SIR ANTHONY: Very apprehensive, I dare say, Jack. — What, you are recruiting here, hey?

CAPTAIN ABSOLUTE: Yes, Sir, I am on duty.

SIR ANTHONY: Well, Jack, I am glad to see you, tho' I did not expect it, for I was going to write to you on a little matter of business. —— Jack, I have been considering that I grow old and infirm, and shall probably not trouble you long.

CAPTAIN ABSOLUTE: Pardon me, Sir, I never saw you look more strong and hearty; and I pray frequently that you may continue so.

SIR ANTHONY: I hope your prayers may be heard with all my heart. Well then, Jack, I have been considering that I am so strong and hearty, I may continue to plague you a long time. — Now, Jack, I am sensible that the income of your commission, and what I have hitherto allowed you, is but a small pittance for a lad of your spirit.

CAPTAIN ABSOLUTE: Sir, you are very good.

SIR ANTHONY: And it is my wish, while yet I live, to have my Boy make some figure in the world. — I have resolved, therefore, to fix you at once in a noble independence.

CAPTAIN ABSOLUTE: Sir, your kindness overpowers me — such generosity makes the gratitude of reason more lively than the sensations even of filial affection.

SIR ANTHONY: I am glad you are so sensible of my attention — and you shall be master of a large estate in a few weeks.

CAPTAIN ABSOLUTE: Let my future life, Sir, speak my gratitude: I cannot express the sense I have of your munificence. — Yet, Sir, I presume you would not wish me to quit the army?

SIR ANTHONY: O, that shall be as your wife chooses.

CAPTAIN ABSOLUTE: My wife, Sir!

SIR ANTHONY: Aye, aye, settle that between you — settle that between you.

CAPTAIN ABSOLUTE: A *wife,* Sir, did you say?

SIR ANTHONY: Aye, a wife — why; did not I mention her before?

CAPTAIN ABSOLUTE: Not a word of it, Sir.

SIR ANTHONY: Odd so! — I mustn't forget *her* tho'. —— Yes, Jack, the independence I was talking of is by a marriage — the fortune is saddled with a wife — but I suppose that makes no difference.

CAPTAIN ABSOLUTE: Sir! Sir! — you amaze me!

SIR ANTHONY: Why, what the d——l's the matter with the fool? Just now you were all gratitude and duty.

CAPTAIN ABSOLUTE: I was, Sir, — you talked to me of independence and a fortune, but not a word of a wife.

SIR ANTHONY: Why — what difference does that make? Odd's life, Sir! if you have the estate, you must take it with the live stock on it, as it stands.

CAPTAIN ABSOLUTE: If my happiness is to be the price, I must beg leave to decline the purchase. —— Pray, Sir, who is the lady?

SIR ANTHONY: What's that to you, Sir! — Come, give me your promise to love, and to marry her directly.

CAPTAIN ABSOLUTE: Sure, Sir, this is not very reasonable, to summon my affections for a lady I know nothing of!

SIR ANTHONY: I am sure, Sir, 'tis more unreasonable in you to *object* to a lady you know nothing of.

CAPTAIN ABSOLUTE: Then, Sir, I must tell you plainly, that my inclinations are fix'd on another.

SIR ANTHONY: They are, are they? well, that's lucky — because you will have more merit in your obedience to me.

CAPTAIN ABSOLUTE: Sir,[7] my heart is engaged to an Angel.

SIR ANTHONY: Then pray let it send an excuse. —— It is very sorry — but *business* prevents its waiting on her.

CAPTAIN ABSOLUTE: But my vows are pledged to her.

SIR ANTHONY: Let her foreclose, Jack; let her foreclose; they are not worth redeeming: besides, you have the Angel's vows in exchange, I suppose; so there can be no loss there.

CAPTAIN ABSOLUTE: You must excuse me, Sir, if I tell you, once for all, that in this point I cannot obey you.

SIR ANTHONY: Hark'ee Jack; —— I have heard you for some time with patience — I have been cool, —— quite cool; — but take care — you know I am compliance itself — when I am not thwarted; — no one more easily led — when I have my own way; — but don't put me in a phrenzy.

7. The lines from 'They are . . .' were cut in the third edition.

CAPTAIN ABSOLUTE: Sir, I must repeat it —— in this I cannot obey you.

SIR ANTHONY: Now, d—n me! if ever I call you *Jack* again while I live!

CAPTAIN ABSOLUTE: Nay, sir, but hear me.

SIR ANTHONY: Sir, I won't hear a word — not a word! not one word! so give me your promise by a nod — and I'll tell you what, Jack — I mean, you Dog — if you don't, by ——

CAPTAIN ABSOLUTE: What, Sir, promise to link myself to some mass of ugliness! to ——

SIR ANTHONY: Z——ds! sirrah! the lady shall be as ugly as I choose; she shall have a hump on each shoulder; she shall be as crooked as the Crescent; her one eye shall roll like the Bull's in Coxe's Musæum — she shall have a skin like a mummy, and the beard of a Jew —— she shall be all this, sirrah! — yet I'll make you ogle her all day, and sit up all night to write sonnets on her beauty.

CAPTAIN ABSOLUTE: This is reason and moderation indeed!

SIR ANTHONY: None of your sneering, puppy! no grinning, jackanapes!

CAPTAIN ABSOLUTE: Indeed, Sir, I never was in a worse humour for mirth in my life.

SIR ANTHONY: 'Tis false, Sir! I know you are laughing in your sleeve: I know you will grin when I am gone, sirrah!

CAPTAIN ABSOLUTE: Sir, I hope I know my duty better.

SIR ANTHONY: None of your passion, Sir! none of your violence! if you please, — It won't do with me, I promise you.

CAPTAIN ABSOLUTE: Indeed, Sir, I never was cooler in my life.

SIR ANTHONY: 'Tis a confounded lie! — I know you are in a passion in your heart; I know you are, you hypocritical young dog! but it won't do.

CAPTAIN ABSOLUTE: Nay, Sir upon my word.

SIR ANTHONY: So you will fly out! can't you be cool, like me? What the devil good can *Passion* do! —— *Passion* is of no service, you impudent, insolent, overbearing Reprobate! — There you sneer again! — don't provoke me! —— but you rely upon the mildness of my temper —— you do, you Dog! you play upon the weakness of my disposition! Yet take care — the patience of a saint may be overcome at last! — but mark! I give you six hours and a half to consider of this: if you then agree, without any condition, to do every thing on earth that I choose, why — confound you! I may in time forgive you —— If not, z——ds! don't enter the same hemisphere with me! don't dare to breathe the same air, or use the same light with me; but get an atmosphere and sun of your own! I'll strip you of your commission; I'll lodge a five-and-threepence in the hands of trustees, and you shall live on the interest. —— I'll disown you, I'll disinherit you, I'll unget you! and —— d——n me, if ever I call you Jack again!

Exit SIR ANTHONY

CAPTAIN ABSOLUTE, *solus*

CAPTAIN ABSOLUTE: Mild, gentle, considerate father — I kiss your hands. —— What a tender method of giving his opinion in these matters Sir Anthony has! I dare not trust him with the truth. —— I wonder what old, wealthy Hag it is that he wants to bestow on me! —— yet he married himself for love! and was in his youth a bold Intriguer, and a gay Companion!

Enter FAG

FAG: Assuredly, Sir, our Father is wrath to a degree; he comes down stairs eight or ten steps at a time —— muttering, growling, and thumping the bannisters all the way: I, and the Cook's dog, stand bowing at the door —— rap! he gives me a stroke on the head with his cane; bids me carry that to my master, then kicking the poor Turnspit into the area, d—ns us all, for a puppy triumvirate! —— Upon my credit, Sir, were I in your place, and found my father such very bad company, I should certainly drop his acquaintance.

CAPTAIN ABSOLUTE: Cease your impertinence, Sir, at present. —— Did you come in for nothing more? —— Stand out of the way!

Pushes him aside, and Exit

FAG, *solus*

FAG: Soh! Sir Anthony trims my Master; He is afraid to reply to his Father —— then vents his spleen on poor Fag! —— When one is vexed by one person, to revenge one's self on another, who happens to come in the way —— is the vilest injustice! Ah! it shews the worst temper —— the basest ——

Enter ERRAND-BOY

ERRAND-BOY: Mr. Fag! Mr. Fag! your Master calls you.

FAG: Well, you little, dirty puppy, you need not baul so! —— The meanest disposition! the ——

ERRAND-BOY: Quick, quick, Mr. Fag.

FAG: *Quick, Quick,* you impudent Jackanapes!

am I to be commanded by you too? you little, impertinent, insolent, kitchen-bred ——

Exit, kicking and beating him

ACT II, SCENE 2

The North Parade

Enter LUCY

LUCY: So —— I shall have another Rival to add to my mistress's list —— Captain Absolute, —— However, I shall not enter his name till my purse has received notice in form. Poor Acres is dismissed! —— Well, I have done him a last friendly office, in letting him know that Beverley was here before him. —— Sir Lucius is generally more punctual, when he expects to hear from his *dear Dalia,* as he calls her: —— I wonder he's not here! —— I have a little scruple of conscience from this deceit; tho' I should not be paid so well, if my hero knew that *Delia* was near fifty, and her own mistress. —— I could not have thought he would have been so nice, when there's a golden egg in the case, as to care whether he has it from a pullet or an old hen![1]

Enter SIR LUCIUS O'TRIGGER

SIR LUCIUS O'TRIGGER: Hah! my little embassadress —— upon my conscience I have been looking for you; I have been on the South Parade this half-hour.

LUCY: (*Speaking simply*) O gemini! and I have been waiting for your worship here on the North.

SIR LUCIUS O'TRIGGER: Faith! —— may be, that was the reason we did not meet; and it is very comical too, how you could go out and I not see you —— for I was only taking a nap at the Parade Coffee-house, and I chose the *window* on purpose that I might not miss you.

LUCY: My stars! Now I'd wager a six-pence I went by while you were asleep.

SIR LUCIUS O'TRIGGER: Sure enough it must have been so —— and I never dreamt it was so late, till I waked. Well, but my little girl, have you got nothing for me?

LUCY: Yes, but I have: —— I've got a letter for you in my pocket.

SIR LUCIUS O'TRIGGER: O faith! I guessed you weren't come empty-handed —— well —— let me see what the dear creature says.

LUCY: There, Sir Lucius. (*Gives him a letter*)

SIR LUCIUS O'TRIGGER: (*Reads*) 'Sir — *there is often a sudden incentive impulse in love, that has a greater induction than years of domestic combination: such was the commotion I felt at the first superfluous*[2] *view of Sir Lucius O'Trigger.*' Very pretty, upon my word. '*As my motive is interested, you may be assured my love shall never be miscellaneous.*' Very well.[3] '*Female punctuation*[4] *forbids me to say more; yet let me add, that it will give me joy infallible*[5] *to find Sir Lucius worthy the last criterion*[6] *of my affections — Yours, while meretricious.*[7] —— DELIA.' Upon my conscience! Lucy, your lady is a great mistress of language. —— Faith, she's quite the queen of the dictionary! —— for the devil a word dare refuse coming at her call — though one would think it was quite out of hearing.

LUCY: Aye, Sir, a lady of her experience.

SIR LUCIUS O'TRIGGER: Experience! what, at seventeen?

LUCY: O true, Sir —— but then she reads so —— my stars! how she will read off-hand!

SIR LUCIUS O'TRIGGER: Faith, she must be very deep read to write this way —— tho' she is rather an arbitrary writer too —— for here are a great many poor words pressed into the service of this note, that would get their *habeas corpus*[8] from any court in Christendom. —— However, when affection guides the pen, Lucy, he must be a brute who finds fault with the style.[9]

LUCY: Ah! Sir Lucius, if you were to hear how she talks of you!

SIR LUCIUS O'TRIGGER: O tell her, I'll make her the best husband in the world, and Lady O'Trigger into the bargain! —— But we must get the old gentlewoman's consent — and do every thing fairly.

LUCY: Nay, Sir Lucius, I thought you wa'n't rich enough to be so nice!

SIR LUCIUS O'TRIGGER: Upon my word, young woman, you have hit it: —— I am so poor that I

1. The lines from 'I could not . . .' were cut in the third edition.

2. for 'superficial', casual.
3. The lines from 'As my motive . . .' were cut in the third edition.
4. for 'punctiliousness', modesty.
5. for 'ineffable'.
6. Possibly 'lasting assertion'.
7. These three words were cut in the third edition; *meretricious*: for 'meritorious'.
8. i.e. release. Sir Lucius means that 'Delia' offends by using an excess of words.
9. This sentence was cut in the third edition.

can't afford to do a dirty action — If I did not want money I'd steal your mistress and her fortune with a great deal of pleasure. — However, my pretty girl, (*gives her money*) here's a little something to buy you a ribband; and meet me in the evening, and I'll give you an answer to this. So, hussy, take a kiss beforehand, to put you in mind. (*Kisses her*)

LUCY: O lud! Sir Lucius —— I never seed such a gemman! My lady won't like you if you're so impudent.

SIR LUCIUS O'TRIGGER: Faith she will, Lucy —— that same —— pho! what's the name of it? —— *Modesty!* —— is a quality in a lover more praised by the women than liked; so, if your mistress asks you whether Sir Lucius ever gave you a kiss, tell her *fifty* —— my dear.

LUCY: What, would you have me tell her a lie?

SIR LUCIUS O'TRIGGER: Ah then, you baggage! I'll make it a truth presently.

LUCY: For shame now; here is some one coming.

SIR LUCIUS O'TRIGGER: O faith, I'll quiet your conscience! (*Sees* FAG. —— *Exit, humming a Tune*)

Enter FAG

FAG: So, so, Ma'am. I humbly beg pardon.

LUCY: O lud! — now, Mr. Fag — you flurry one so.

FAG: Come, come, Lucy, here's no one bye — so a little less simplicity, with a grain or two more sincerity, if you please. —— You play false with us, Madam. —— I saw you give the baronet a letter. — My master shall know this — and if he don't call him out — I will.

LUCY: Ha! ha! ha! you gentlemen's gentlemen are so hasty. —— That letter was from Mrs. Malaprop, simpleton. —— She is taken with Sir Lucius's address.

FAG: What tastes some people have! —— Why I suppose I have walked by her window an hundred times. —— But what says our young lady? Any message to my master?

LUCY: Sad news! Mr. Fag. —— A worse Rival than Acres! —— Sir Anthony Absolute has proposed his son.

FAG: What, Captain Absolute?

LUCY: Even so. — I overheard it all.

FAG: Ha! ha! ha! — very good, faith. — Good-bye, Lucy, I must away with this news.

LUCY: Well — you may laugh — but it is true, I assure you. (*Going*) But — Mr. Fag — tell your master not to be cast down by this.

FAG: O, he'll be so disconsolate!

LUCY: And charge him not to think of quarrelling with young Absolute.

FAG: Never fear! — never fear!

LUCY: Be sure — bid him keep up his spirits.

FAG: We will — we will.

Exeunt severally

ACT III, SCENE 1

The North Parade

Enter CAPTAIN ABSOLUTE

CAPTAIN ABSOLUTE: 'Tis just as Fag told me indeed. — Whimsical enough, faith! My Father wants to *force* me to marry the very girl I am plotting to run away with! —— He must not know of my connection with her yet a-while. —— He has too summary a method of proceeding in these matters — and Lydia shall not yet lose her hopes of an elopement.[1] —— However, I'll read my recantation instantly. —— My conversion is something sudden, indeed — but I can assure him it is very *sincere*. —— So, so — here he comes. — He looks plaguy gruff.

Steps aside

Enter SIR ANTHONY

SIR ANTHONY: No — I'll die sooner than forgive him. — *Die,* did I say? I'll live these fifty years to plague him. —— At our last meeting, his impudence had almost put me out of temper. — An obstinate, passionate, self-willed boy! — Who can he take after? This is my return for getting him before all his brothers and sisters! — for putting him, at twelve years old, into a marching regiment, and allowing him fifty pounds a year, beside his pay ever since! — But I have done with him; — he's any body's son for me. — I never will see him more, — never — never — never — never.

CAPTAIN ABSOLUTE: Now for a penitential face.

SIR ANTHONY: Fellow, get out of my way.

CAPTAIN ABSOLUTE: Sir, you see a penitent before you.

SIR ANTHONY: I see an impudent scoundrel before me.

CAPTAIN ABSOLUTE: A sincere penitent. —— I am come, Sir, to acknowledge my error, and to submit entirely to your will.

SIR ANTHONY: What's that?

1. The lines 'and Lydia . . .' were cut in the third edition.

CAPTAIN ABSOLUTE: I have been revolving, and reflecting, and considering on your past goodness, and kindness, and condescension to me.

SIR ANTHONY: Well, Sir?

CAPTAIN ABSOLUTE: I have been likewise weighing and balancing what you were pleased to mention concerning duty, and obedience, and authority.

SIR ANTHONY: Well, Puppy?

CAPTAIN ABSOLUTE: Why then, Sir, the result of my reflections is — a resolution to sacrifice every inclination of my own to your satisfaction.

SIR ANTHONY: Why now, you talk sense — absolute sense — I never heard any thing more sensible in my life. — Confound you; you shall be *Jack* again.

CAPTAIN ABSOLUTE: I am happy in the appellation.

SIR ANTHONY: Why, then, Jack, my dear Jack, I will now inform you — who the lady really is. —— Nothing but your passion and violence, you silly fellow, prevented my telling you at first. Prepare, Jack, for wonder and rapture — prepare. —— What think you of Miss Lydia Languish?

CAPTAIN ABSOLUTE: Languish! What, the Languishes of Worcestershire?

SIR ANTHONY: Worcestershire! No. Did you never meet Mrs. Malaprop and her Niece, Miss Languish, who came into our country just before you were last ordered to your regiment?

CAPTAIN ABSOLUTE: Malaprop! Languish! I don't remember ever to have heard the names before. Yet, stay —— I think I do recollect something. —— *Languish! Languish!* She squints, don't she? —— A little, red-haired girl?

SIR ANTHONY: Squints! —— A red-haired girl! —— Z——ds, no.

CAPTAIN ABSOLUTE: Then I must have forgot; it can't be the same person.

SIR ANTHONY: Jack! Jack! what think you of blooming, love-breathing seventeen?

CAPTAIN ABSOLUTE: As to that, Sir, I am quite indifferent. — If I can please you in the matter, 'tis all I desire.

SIR ANTHONY: Nay, but Jack, such eyes! such eyes! so innocently wild! so bashfully irresolute! Not a glance but speaks and kindles some thought of love! Then, Jack, her cheeks! her cheeks, Jack! so deeply blushing at the insinuations of her tell-tale eyes! Then, Jack, her lips! — O Jack, lips smiling at their own discretion; and if not smiling, more sweetly pouting; more lovely in sullenness!

CAPTAIN ABSOLUTE: That's she indeed. —— Well done, old gentleman!

SIR ANTHONY: Then, Jack, her neck. —— O Jack! Jack!

CAPTAIN ABSOLUTE: And which is to be mine, Sir, the Niece or the Aunt?

SIR ANTHONY: Why, you unfeeling, insensible Puppy, I despise you. When I was of your age, such a description would have made me fly like a rocket! The *Aunt,* indeed! — Odds life! when I ran away with your mother, I would not have touched any thing old or ugly to gain an empire.

CAPTAIN ABSOLUTE: Not to please your father, Sir?

SIR ANTHONY: To please my father! —— Z——ds! not to please —— O my father! —— Oddso! —— yes — yes! if my father indeed had desired —— that's quite another matter. —— Tho' he wa'n't the indulgent father that I am, Jack.

CAPTAIN ABSOLUTE: I dare say not, Sir.

SIR ANTHONY: But, Jack, you are not sorry to find your mistress is so beautiful.

CAPTAIN ABSOLUTE: Sir, I repeat it; if I please you in this affair, 'tis all I desire. Not that I think a woman the worse for being handsome; but, Sir, if you please to recollect, you before hinted something about a hump or two, one eye, and a few more graces of that kind — now, without being very nice,[2] I own I should rather chuse a wife of mine to have the usual number of limbs, and a limited quantity of back: and tho' *one* eye may be very agreeable, yet as the prejudice has always run in favour of *two,* I would not wish to affect a singularity in that article.

SIR ANTHONY: What a phlegmatic sot it is! Why, sirrah, you're an anchorite! — a vile insensible stock. — You a soldier! — you're a walking block, fit only to dust the company's regimentals[3] on! —— Odds life! I've a great mind to marry the girl myself!

CAPTAIN ABSOLUTE: I am entirely at your disposal, Sir; if you should think of addressing Miss Languish[4] yourself, I suppose you would have me marry the *Aunt*; or if you should change your mind,

2. fastidious. Charles Dickens echoed the lines about the popular prejudice running in favour of two eyes in chapter 4 of *Nicholas Nickleby* (1838-39).
3. [*sic*] in Dublin edition. This shows that it took account of the Errata in the first (London) edition, correcting 'regiment' here.
4. [*sic*]. Here the Dublin edition corrects 'Anguish'.

and take the old lady — 'tis the same to me — I'll marry the *Niece*.

SIR ANTHONY: Upon my word, Jack, thou'rt either a very great hypocrite, or —— but, come, I know your indifference on such a subject must be all a lie — I'm sure it must — come, now — d—n your demure face! — come, confess, Jack — you have been lying ha'n't you? You have been lying, hey? I'll never forgive you, if you ha'n't: — so now, own, my dear Jack,[5] you have been playing the hypocrite, hey! I'll never forgive you, if you ha'n't been lying and playing the hypocrite.

CAPTAIN ABSOLUTE: I'm sorry, Sir, that the respect and duty which I bear to you should be so mistaken.

SIR ANTHONY: Hang your respect and duty! But, come along with me, I'll write a note to Mrs. Malaprop, and you shall visit the lady directly.

CAPTAIN ABSOLUTE: Where does she lodge, Sir?

SIR ANTHONY: What a dull question! — only on the Grove here.

CAPTAIN ABSOLUTE: O! then I can call on her in my way to the coffee-house.

SIR ANTHONY: In your way to the coffee-house! You'll set your heart down in your way to the coffee-house, hey? Ah! you leaden-nerv'd, wooden-hearted dolt! But come along, you shall see her directly; her eyes shall be the Promethean torch to you — come along, I'll never forgive you, if you don't come back, stark mad with rapture and impatience — if you don't, egad, I'll marry the girl myself!

Exeunt

5. The lines from 'You have been lying . . .' were cut in the third edition.

ACT III, SCENE 2

JULIA's *Dressing-room*

FAULKLAND, *solus*

FAULKLAND: They told me Julia would return directly; I wonder she is not yet come! — How mean does this captious, unsatisfied temper of mine appear to my cooler judgment! Yet I know not that I indulge it in any other point: — but on this one subject, and to this one object, whom I think I love beyond my life, I am ever ungenerously fretful, and madly capricious! — I am conscious of it — yet I cannot correct myself! What tender, honest joy sparkled in her eyes when we met! — How delicate was the warmth of her expressions! —— I was ashamed to appear less happy — though I had come resolved to wear a face of coolness and upbraiding. Sir Anthony's presence prevented my proposed expostulations: — yet I must be satisfied that she has not been so *very* happy in my absence. — She's coming! — Yes! — I know the nimbleness of her tread, when she thinks her impatient Faulkland counts the moments of her stay.[1]

Enter JULIA

JULIA: I had not hop'd to see you again so soon.

FAULKLAND: Could I, Julia, be contented with my first welcome — restrained as we were by the presence of a third person?

JULIA: O Faulkland, when your kindness can make me thus happy, let me not think that I discovered more coolness in your first salutation than my long-hoarded joy could have presaged.[2]

FAULKLAND: 'Twas but your fancy, Julia. — I *was* rejoiced to see you — to see you in such health — Sure I had no cause for coldness?

JULIA: Nay, then, I see you have taken something ill. — You must not conceal from me what it is.

FAULKLAND: Well then — shall I own to you — but you will despise me, Julia — nay, I despise myself for it. —— Yet I *will* own,[3] that my joy at hearing of your health and arrival here, by your neighbour Acres, was something damped, by his dwelling much on the high spirits you had enjoyed in Devonshire — on your mirth — your singing — dancing, and I know not what! — For such is my temper, Julia, that I should regard every mirthful moment in your absence as a treason to constancy: — The mutual tear that steals down the cheek[4] of parting lovers is a compact, that no smile shall live there till they meet again.

JULIA: Must I never cease to tax my Faulkland with this teasing minute caprice? — Can the idle reports of a silly boor weigh in your breast against my tried affection?

FAULKLAND: They have no weight with me, Julia: no, no — I am happy if you have been so — yet only say, that you did not sing with *mirth* — say

1. delay.
2. forecast. Although the balance of 'more . . . than' is pleasing, this phrasing was altered in the third edition simply to: 'I discovered something of coldness in your first salutation.'
3. The lines from 'but you will . . .' were cut in the third edition.
4. Faulkland's use of the singular number underlines the absurdity of his pathetic picture.

that you *thought* of Faulkland in the dance.

JULIA: I never can be happy in your absence. —— If I wear a countenance of content, it is to shew that my mind holds no doubt of my Faulkland's truth. —— If I seem'd sad — it were to make malice triumph; and say, that I had fixed my heart on one, who left me to lament his roving, and my own credulity. —— Believe me, Faulkland, I mean not to upbraid you, when I say, that I have often dressed sorrow in smiles, lest my friends should guess whose unkindness had caused my tears.

FAULKLAND: You were ever all goodness to me — O, I am a brute, when I but admit a doubt of your true constancy!

JULIA: If ever, without such cause from you, as I will not suppose possible, you find my affections veering but a point, may I become a proverbial scoff for levity, and base ingratitude.

FAULKLAND: Ah! Julia, that *last* word is grating to me. I would I had no title to your *gratitude*! Search your heart, Julia; perhaps what you have mistaken for Love, is but the warm effusion of a too thankful heart!

JULIA: For what quality must I love you?

FAULKLAND: For no quality! To regard me for any quality of mind or understanding, were only to *esteem* me. And for person[5] — I have often wish'd myself deformed, to be convinced that I owed no obligation *there* for any part of your affection.

JULIA: Where nature has bestowed a shew of nice attention in the features of a man, he should laugh at it, as misplaced. I have seen men, who in this vain article perhaps might rank above you; but my heart has never asked my eyes if it were so or not.

FAULKLAND: Now this is not well from *you,* Julia — I despise person in a man. —— Yet if you lov'd me as I wish, though I were an Æthiop,[6] you'd think none so fair.

JULIA: I see you are determined to be unkind. — The *contract* which my poor father bound us in gives you more than a lover's privilege.

FAULKLAND: Again, Julia, you raise ideas that feed and justify my doubts. —— I would not have been more free — no — I am proud of my restraint. —— Yet — yet — perhaps your high respect alone for this solemn compact has fettered your inclinations, which else had made worthier choice. — How shall I be sure, had you remained unbound in thought and promise, that I should still have been the object of your persevering love?

JULIA: Then try me now. — Let us be free as strangers as to what is past: — *my* heart will not feel more liberty!

FAULKLAND: There now! so hasty, Julia! so anxious to be free! — If your love for me were fixed and ardent, you would not loose your hold, even tho' I wish'd it!

JULIA: O, you torture me to the heart! — I cannot bear it.

FAULKLAND: I do not mean to distress you. — If I lov'd you less, I should never give you an uneasy moment. — But hear me. — All my fretful doubts arise from this — Women are not used to weigh, and separate the motives of their affections: the cold dictates of prudence, gratitude, or filial duty, may sometimes be mistaken for the pleadings of the heart. —— I would not boast — yet let me say, that I have neither age, person, or character, to found dislike on; — my fortune such as few ladies could be charged with *indiscretion* in the match. — O Julia! when *Love* receives such countenance from *Prudence,* nice minds will be suspicious of its *birth.*

JULIA: I know not whither your insinuations would tend: — as they seem pressing to insult me — I will spare you the regret of having done so. — I have given you no cause for this!

Exit in tears

FAULKLAND: In Tears! stay, Julia: stay but for a moment. —— The door is fastened! — Julia! — my soul — but for one moment: — I hear her sobbing! — 'Sdeath! what a brute am I to use her thus! Yet stay. — Aye — she is coming now; — how little resolution there is in woman! — how a few soft words can turn them ! —— No, faith! — she is *not* coming either. —— Why, Julia — my love — say but that you forgive me — come but to tell me that — now, this is being *too* resentful: — stay! she *is* coming too — I thought she would — no *steadiness* in any thing! her going away must have been a mere trick then — she sha'n't see that I was hurt by it. — I'll affect indifference —— (*hums a tune: then listens*) — No — Z—ds! she's *not* coming! — nor don't intend it, I suppose. — This is not *steadiness,* but *obstinacy*! Yet I deserve it. — What, after so long an absence, to quarrel with her tenderness! — 'twas barbarous and unmanly! —— I should be ashamed to see her now. — I'll wait till her just resentment is abated — and when I distress her so again, may I lose her for ever! and be linked instead to some antique virago, whose gnawing passions,

5. physique.
6. i.e. an Ethiopian.

and long-hoarded spleen, shall make me curse my folly half the day, and all the night!

Exit

ACT III, SCENE 3

MRS. MALAPROP's *Lodgings*

MRS. MALAPROP, *with a letter in her hand, and* CAPTAIN ABSOLUTE

MRS. MALAPROP: Your being Sir Anthony's son, Captain, would itself be a sufficient accommodation;[1] — but from the ingenuity[2] of your appearance, I am convinced you deserve the character here[3] given of you.

CAPTAIN ABSOLUTE: Permit me to say, Madam, that as I never yet have had the pleasure of seeing Miss Languish, my principal inducement in this affair at present, is the honour of being allied to Mrs. Malaprop; of whose intellectual accomplishments, elegant manners, and unaffected learning, no tongue is silent.

MRS. MALAPROP: Sir, you do me infinite honour! —— I beg, Captain, you'll be seated. — (*Sit*) — Ah! few gentlemen, now a days, know how to value the ineffectual[4] qualities in a woman! few think how a little knowledge becomes a gentlewoman! Men have no sense now but for the worthless flower, beauty!

CAPTAIN ABSOLUTE: It is but too true, indeed, Ma'am; — yet I fear our ladies should share the blame — they think our admiration of *beauty* so great, that *knowledge* in *them* would be superfluous. Thus like garden-trees, they seldom shew fruits, till time has robb'd them of the more specious blossom. — Few, like Mrs. Malaprop and the Orange-tree, are rich in both at once!

MRS. MALAPROP: Sir — you overpower me with good-breeding. — He is the very Pine-apple[5] of politeness! You are not ignorant, Captain, that this giddy girl has somehow contrived to fix her affections on a beggarly, strolling, eve's-dropping[6] Ensign, whom none of us have seen, and nobody knows any thing of.

CAPTAIN ABSOLUTE: O I have heard the silly affair before. —— I'm not at all prejudiced against her on *that* account.

MRS. MALAPROP: You are very good, and very considerate, Captain. — I am sure I have done every thing in my power since I exploded the affair! long ago I laid my positive conjunction[7] on her never to think on the fellow again; — I have since laid Sir Anthony's preposition[8] before her; — but I'm sorry to say she seems resolved to decline every particle[9] that I enjoin her.

CAPTAIN ABSOLUTE: It must be very distressing indeed, Ma'am.

MRS. MALAPROP: It gives me the hydrostatics[10] to such a degree! — I thought she had persisted[11] from corresponding with him; but behold this very day, I have interceded[12] another letter from the fellow! I believe I have it in my pocket.

CAPTAIN ABSOLUTE: (*Aside*) O the devil! my last note.

MRS. MALAPROP: Ay, here it is.

CAPTAIN ABSOLUTE: (*Aside*) Ay, my note indeed! O the little traitress, Lucy.

MRS. MALAPROP: There, perhaps you may know the writing. (*Gives him the letter*)

CAPTAIN ABSOLUTE: I think I have seen the hand before — yes, I *certainly must* have seen this hand before: ——

MRS. MALAPROP: Nay, but read it, Captain.

CAPTAIN ABSOLUTE: (*Reads*) *'My soul's idol, my ador'd Lydia!'* — Very tender indeed!

MRS. MALAPROP: Tender! aye, and prophane too, o' my conscience!

CAPTAIN ABSOLUTE: *'I am excessively alarmed at the intelligence you send me, the more so as my new rival'* ——

MRS. MALAPROP: That's *you*, Sir.

CAPTAIN ABSOLUTE: *'has universally the character of being an accomplished gentleman, and a man of honour.'* —— Well, that's handsome enough.

MRS. MALAPROP: O, the fellow had some design in writing so ——

1. for 'recommendation', actually used in one Dublin printing, 1773.
2. for 'ingenuousness', innocence.
3. i.e. in the letter she has in her hand. The first edition failed to include that information in the opening stage direction, but it was added in the third and is adopted here. Presumably, Mrs Malaprop hands back to Captain Absolute his letter of introduction.
4. for 'intellectual'.
5. for 'pinnacle'.
6. eaves-dropping.
7. for 'injunction', command.
8. for 'proposition'.
9. for 'article'.
10. for 'hysterics'.
11. for 'desisted'.
12. for 'intercepted'.

CAPTAIN ABSOLUTE: That he had, I'll answer for him, Ma'am.

MRS. MALAPROP: But go on, Sir — you'll see presently.

CAPTAIN ABSOLUTE: *'As for the old weather-beaten she-dragon who guards you,'* — Who can he mean by that?

MRS. MALAPROP: *Me,* Sir — *me* — he means *me* there — what do you think now? — but go on a little further.

CAPTAIN ABSOLUTE: Impudent scoundrel! — *'it shall go hard but I will elude her vigilance, as I am told that the same ridiculous vanity, which makes her dress up her coarse features, and deck her dull chat with hard words which she don't understand'* ——

MRS. MALAPROP: There, Sir! an attack upon my language! what do you think of that? —— an aspersion upon my parts of speech! was ever such a brute! save if I reprehend[13] any thing in this world, it is the use of my oracular[14] tongue, and a nice derangement of epitaphs![15]

CAPTAIN ABSOLUTE: He deserves to be hang'd and quartered! let me see —— *'same ridiculous vanity'* ——

MRS. MALAPROP: You need not read it again, Sir.

CAPTAIN ABSOLUTE: I beg pardon, Ma'am *'does also lay her open to the grossest deceptions from flattery and pretended admiration'* — an impudent coxcomb! *'so that I have a scheme to see you shortly with the old Harridan's consent, and even to make her a go-between in our interviews.'* — Was ever such assurance!

MRS. MALAPROP: Did you ever hear any thing like it? —— he'll elude my vigilance, will he? —— yes, yes! ha! ha! he's very likely to enter these floors![16] — we'll try who can plot best!

CAPTAIN ABSOLUTE: Ha! ha! ha! a conceited puppy, ha! ha! ha! —— Well, but Mrs. Malaprop, as the girl seems so infatuated by this fellow, suppose you were to wink at her corresponding with him for a little time — let her even plot an elopement with him — then do you connive at her escape — while *I,* just in the nick, will have the fellow laid by the heels, and fairly contrive to carry her off in his stead.

MRS. MALAPROP: I am delighted with the scheme, never was any thing better perpetrated![17]

CAPTAIN ABSOLUTE: But, pray, could not I see the lady for a few minutes now? —— I should like to try her temper a little.

MRS. MALAPROP: Why, I don't know — I doubt she is not prepared for a first visit of this kind. —— There is a decorum in these matters.

CAPTAIN ABSOLUTE: O Lord! she won't mind *me* — only tell her Beverley ——

MRS. MALAPROP: Sir! ——

CAPTAIN ABSOLUTE: (*Aside*) Gently, good tongue.

MRS. MALAPROP: What did you say of Beverley?

CAPTAIN ABSOLUTE: O, I was going to propose that you should tell her, by way of jest, that it was Beverley who was below — she'd come down fast enough then — ha! ha! ha!

MRS. MALAPROP: 'Twould be a trick she well deserves — besides you know the fellow tells her he'll get my consent to see her — ha! ha! — Let him if he can, I say again — Lydia, come down here! (*Calling*) — He'll make me *a go-between in their interviews!* — ha! ha! ha! Come down, I say, Lydia! — I don't wonder at your laughing, ha! ha! ha! his impudence is truly ridiculous.

CAPTAIN ABSOLUTE: 'Tis very ridiculous, upon my soul, Ma'am, ha! ha! ha!

MRS. MALAPROP: The little hussy won't hear. —— Well, I'll go and tell her at once who it is —— she shall know that Captain Absolute is come to wait on her. — And I'll make her behave as becomes a young woman.

CAPTAIN ABSOLUTE: As you please, Ma'am.

MRS. MALAPROP: For the present, Captain, your servant — Ah! you've not done laughing yet, I see —— *elude my vigilance!* yes, yes, ha! ha! ha!

Exit

CAPTAIN ABSOLUTE: Ha! ha! ha! one would think now that I might throw off all disguise at once, and seize my prize with security —— but such is Lydia's caprice, that to undeceive were probably to lose her. — I'll see whether she knows me. (*Walks aside, and seems engaged in looking at the pictures*)

Enter LYDIA

LYDIA: What a scene am I now to go thro'! surely nothing can be more dreadful than to be obliged to listen to the loathsome addresses of a stranger to one's heart. —— I have heard of girls persecuted as

13. for 'apprehend'.
14. for 'vernacular'.
15. for 'arrangement of epithets'.
16. for 'doors'.
17. for 'instigated'.

I am, who have appealed in behalf of their favoured lover to the generosity of his rival: suppose I were to try it — there stands the hated rival — an officer too! — but O how unlike my Beverley! —— I wonder he don't begin —— truly he seems a very negligent wooer! — quite at his ease, upon my word! I'll speak first —— Mr. Absolute.

CAPTAIN ABSOLUTE: Madam. (*Turns round*)

LYDIA: O Heav'ns! Beverley!

CAPTAIN ABSOLUTE: Hush! — hush, my life! —— softly! be not surprised!

LYDIA: I am so astonished! and so terrified! and so overjoy'd! —— for Heav'n's sake! how came you here?

CAPTAIN ABSOLUTE: Briefly —— I have deceived your Aunt — I was informed that my new rival was to visit here this evening, and contriving to have him kept away, have passed myself on *her* for Captain Absolute.

LYDIA: O, charming! — And she really takes you for young Absolute?

CAPTAIN ABSOLUTE: O, she's convinced of it.

LYDIA: Ha! ha! ha! I can't forbear laughing to think how her sagacity is over-reached!

CAPTAIN ABSOLUTE: But we trifle with our precious moments —— such another opportunity may not occur —— then let me now conjure my kind, my condescending angel, to fix the time when I may rescue her from undeserved persecution, and with a licensed warmth plead for my reward.

LYDIA: Will you then, Beverley, consent to forfeit that portion of my paltry wealth? —— that burthen on the wings of love?

CAPTAIN ABSOLUTE: O come to me — rich only thus — in loveliness —— Bring no portion to me but thy love — 'twill be generous in you, Lydia —— for well you know, it is the only dower your poor Beverley can repay.

LYDIA: How persuasive are his words! — how charming will poverty be with him!

CAPTAIN ABSOLUTE: Ah! my soul, what a life will we then live? Love shall be our idol and support! we will worship him with a monastic strictness; abjuring all worldly toys, to center every thought and action there. —— Proud of calamity, we will enjoy the wreck of wealth; while the surrounding gloom of adversity shall make the flame of our pure love show doubly bright. —— By Heav'ns! I would fling all goods of fortune from me with a prodigal hand to enjoy the scene where I might clasp my Lydia to my bosom, and say, the world affords no smile to me — but here —— (*Embracing her*) (*Aside*) If she holds out now the devil is in it!

LYDIA: Now could I fly with him to the Antipodes! but my persecution is not yet come to a crisis.

Enter MRS. MALAPROP, *listening*

MRS. MALAPROP: (*Aside*) I'm impatient to know how the little huzzy deports herself.

CAPTAIN ABSOLUTE: So pensive, Lydia! — is then your warmth abated?

MRS. MALAPROP: *Warmth abated!* — so! — she has been in a passion, I suppose.

LYDIA: No — nor ever can while I have life.

MRS. MALAPROP: An ill-temper'd little devil! —— She'll be *in a passion all her life* —— will she?

LYDIA: Think not the idle threats of my ridiculous aunt can ever have any weight with me.

MRS. MALAPROP: Very dutiful, upon my word!

LYDIA: Let her choice be *Captain Absolute*, but Beverley is mine.

MRS. MALAPROP: I am astonished at her assurance! —— *to his face* —— *this to his face!*

CAPTAIN ABSOLUTE: Thus then let me enforce my suit. (*Kneeling*)

MRS. MALAPROP: Aye — poor young man! —— down on his knees entreating for pity! —— I can contain no longer. —— Why, huzzy! huzzy! —— I have overheard you.

CAPTAIN ABSOLUTE: (*Aside*) O confound her vigilance!

MRS. MALAPROP: Captain Absolute —— I know now how to apologize for her shocking rudeness.

CAPTAIN ABSOLUTE: (*Aside*) So —— all's safe, I find.

I have hopes, Madam, that time will bring the young lady ——

MRS. MALAPROP: O, there's nothing to be hoped for from her! she's as head-strong as an allegory[18] on the banks of Nile.

LYDIA: Nay, Madam, what do you charge me with now?

MRS. MALAPROP: Why, thou unblushing rebel —— didn't you tell this gentleman to his face that you loved another better? —— didn't you say you never would be his?

LYDIA: No, Madam — I did not.

MRS. MALAPROP: Good Heav'ns! what assurance! —— Lydia, Lydia, you ought to know that

18. for 'alligator'.

lying don't become a young woman! — Didn't you boast that Beverley —— that stroller Beverley, possessed your heart? —— Tell me that, I say.

LYDIA: 'Tis true, Ma'am, and none but Beverley ——

MRS. MALAPROP: Hold; —— hold, Assurance! — you shall not be so rude.

CAPTAIN ABSOLUTE: Nay, pray Mrs. Malaprop, don't stop the young lady's speech: —— she's very welcome to talk thus —— it does not hurt *me* in the least, I assure you.

MRS. MALAPROP: You are *too* good, Captain —— *too* amiably patient —— but come with me, Miss — let us see you again soon, Captain —— remember what we have fixed.

CAPTAIN ABSOLUTE: I shall, Ma'am.

MRS. MALAPROP: Come, take a graceful leave of the gentleman.

LYDIA: May every blessing wait on my Beverley, my lov'd Bev ——

MRS. MALAPROP: Huzzy! I'll choak the word in your throat! —— come along —— come along.

Exeunt severally

CAPTAIN ABSOLUTE *kissing his hand to* LYDIA —— MRS. MALAPROP *stopping her from speaking*

ACT III, SCENE 4

ACRES's *lodgings*

ACRES *and* DAVID

ACRES *as just dress'd*

ACRES: Indeed, David — do you think I become it so?

DAVID: You are quite another creature, believe me Master, by the Mass! an' we've any luck we shall see the Devon monkeyrony[1] in all the print-shops in Bath!

ACRES: Dress *does* make a difference, David.

DAVID: 'Tis all in all, I think —— difference! why, an' you were to go now to Clod-Hall, I am certain the old lady wouldn't know you: Master Butler wouldn't believe his own eyes, and Mrs. Pickle would cry, 'Lard presarve me!' our dairy-maid would come giggling to the door, and I warrant Dolly Tester, your Honour's favourite, would blush like my waistcoat. —— Oons! I'll hold a gallon, there an't a dog in the house but would bark, and I question whether *Phillis* would wag a hair of her tail!

ACRES: Aye, David, there's nothing like *polishing*.

DAVID: So I says of your Honour's boots; but the boy never heeds me!

ACRES: But, David, has Mr. De-la-Grace been here? I must rub up my balancing, and chasing, and boring.[2]

DAVID: I'll call again, Sir.

ACRES: Do —— and see if there are any letters for me at the post-office.

DAVID: I will —— By the Mass, I can't help looking at your head! —— if I hadn't been by at the cooking, I wish I may die if I should have known the dish again myself!

Exit

ACRES *comes forward, practising a dancing step*

ACRES: Sink, slide —— coupee —— Confound the first inventors of cotillons! say I —— they are as bad as algebra to us country gentlemen — I can walk a Minuet easy enough when I'm forced! — and I have been accounted a good stick in a Country-dance —— Odd's jiggs and tabors! —— I never valued your cross-over two couple — figure in — right and left — and I'd foot it with e'er a captain in the county! —— but these outlandish heathen Allemandes and Cotillons are quite beyond me! —— I shall never prosper at 'em, that's sure — mine are true-born English legs — they don't understand their curst French lingo! —— their *Pas* this, and *Pas* that, and *Pas* t'other! —— d—n me, my feet don't like to be called Paws! no, 'tis certain I have most Antigallican[3] Toes!

Enter SERVANT

SERVANT: Here is Sir Lucius O'Trigger to wait on you, Sir.

ACRES: Shew him in.

Enter SIR LUCIUS

SIR LUCIUS O'TRIGGER: Mr. Acres, I am delighted to embrace you.

ACRES: My dear Sir Lucius, I kiss your hands.

SIR LUCIUS O'TRIGGER: Pray, my friend, what has brought you so suddenly to Bath?

ACRES: Faith! I have followed Cupid's Jack-a-Lantern, and find myself in a quagmire at last. ——

1. for 'macaroni', a fop who affects Italian fashion. The reference is to Acres, so dressed.

2. practise my dancing — but Acres seems to confuse a dancing term, 'balancing', with terms from gun maintenance ('chasing', 'boring').

3. unFrench; hence 'awkward'.

In short, I have been very ill used, Sir Lucius. —— I don't choose to mention names, but look on me as on a very ill-used gentleman.

SIR LUCIUS O'TRIGGER: Pray, what is the case? — I ask no names.

ACRES: Mark me, Sir Lucius, I falls as deep as need be in love with a young lady —— her friends take my part —— I follow her to Bath —— send word of my arrival; and receive answer, that the lady is to be otherwise disposed of. —— This, Sir Lucius, I call being ill-used.

SIR LUCIUS O'TRIGGER: Very ill, upon my conscience —— Pray, can you divine the cause of it?

ACRES: Why, there's the matter: she has another lover, *one* Beverley, who, I am told, is now in Bath. —— Odds slanders and lies! he must be at the bottom of it.

SIR LUCIUS O'TRIGGER: A rival in the case, is there? —— and you think he has supplanted you unfairly.

ACRES: *Unfairly!* — to be sure he has. —— He never could have done it fairly.

SIR LUCIUS O'TRIGGER: Then sure you know what is to be done!

ACRES: Not I, upon my soul!

SIR LUCIUS O'TRIGGER: We wear no swords here,[4] but you understand me.

ACRES: What! fight him!

SIR LUCIUS O'TRIGGER: Aye, to be sure: what can I mean else?

ACRES: But he has given me no provocation.

SIR LUCIUS O'TRIGGER: Now, I think he has given you the greatest provocation in the world. —— Can a man commit a more heinous offence against another than to fall in love with the same woman? O, by my soul, it is the most unpardonable breach of friendship!

ACRES: Breach of *friendship*! Aye, aye; but I have no acquaintance with this man. I never saw him in my life.

SIR LUCIUS O'TRIGGER: That's no argument at all — he has the less right then to take such a liberty.

ACRES: 'Gad that's true — I grow full of anger, Sir Lucius! —— I fire apace! Odds hilts and blades! I find a man may have a deal of valour in him, and not know it! But couldn't I contrive to have a little right of my side?

SIR LUCIUS O'TRIGGER: What the d——l signifies *right*, when your *honour* is concerned? Do you think *Achilles*, or my little *Alexander the Great* ever inquired where the right lay? No, by my soul, they drew their broad swords, and left the lazy sons of peace to settle the justice of it.

ACRES: Your words are a grenadier's march to my heart! I believe courage must be catching! —— I certainly do feel a kind of valour rising as it were —— a kind of courage, as I may say —— Odds flints, pans, and triggers! I'll challenge him directly.

SIR LUCIUS O'TRIGGER: Ah, my little friend! if we had *Blunderbuss-Hall* here —— I could shew you a range of ancestry, in the O'Trigger line, that would furnish the new room;[5] every one of whom had killed his man! —— For though the mansion-house and dirty acres have slipt through my fingers, I thank God our honour, and the family-pictures, are as fresh as ever.

ACRES: O Sir Lucius! I have had ancestors too! every man of 'em colonel or captain in the militia! —— Odds balls and barrels! say no more —— I'm brac'd for it —— my nerves are become catgut! my sinews wire! and my heart Pinchbeck![6] The thunder of your words has soured the milk of human kindness[7] in my breast! — Z——ds! as the man in the play says, 'I could do such deeds!'[8]

SIR LUCIUS O'TRIGGER: Come, come, there must be no passion at all in the case —— these things should always be done civilly.

ACRES: I must be in a passion, Sir Lucius —— I must be in a rage —— Dear Sir Lucius let me be in a rage, if you love me. —— Come, here's pen and paper. (*Sits down to write*) I would the ink were red! —— Indite, I say, indite! — How shall I begin? Odds bullets and blades! I'll write a good *bold hand*, however.

SIR LUCIUS O'TRIGGER: Pray compose yourself.

ACRES: Come —— now shall I begin with an oath? Do, Sir Lucius, let me begin with a damme.

SIR LUCIUS O'TRIGGER: Pho! pho!— do the thing *decently* and like a Christian. Begin now, —— '*Sir*' ——

ACRES: That's too civil by half.

4. Swords were prohibited in Bath.

5. The Upper Assembly Rooms in Bath, opened in 1771.

6. The lines from 'my nerves ...' were cut in the third edition. 'Pinchbeck' is ironically inappropriate: an alloy of copper and zinc, it also means 'sham, counterfeit'.

7. Lady Macbeth's phrase, *Macbeth*, I.5.18.

8. Possibly Hamlet: 'now could I drink hot blood,
And do such bitter business as the day
Would quake to look on', *Hamlet*, III. 2. 408-10.

SIR LUCIUS O'TRIGGER: *'To prevent the confusion that might arise.'*

ACRES: Well ——[9]

SIR LUCIUS O'TRIGGER: *'From our both addressing the same lady.'*

ACRES: Aye — there's the reason — *'same lady'* —— Well ——

SIR LUCIUS O'TRIGGER: *'I shall expect the honour of your company'* —

ACRES: Z—ds! I'm not asking him to dinner.

SIR LUCIUS O'TRIGGER: Pray be easy.

ACRES: Well then, 'honour of your company,'

SIR LUCIUS O'TRIGGER: *'To settle our pretensions.'*

ACRES: Well.

SIR LUCIUS O'TRIGGER: Let me see, aye, *King's Mead-fields* will do. —— *'In King's Mead-fields.'*

ACRES: So that's done —— Well, I'll fold it up presently; my own crest —— a hand and dagger shall be the seal.

SIR LUCIUS O'TRIGGER: You see now this little explanation will put a stop at once to all confusion or misunderstanding that might arise between you.

ACRES: Aye, we fight to prevent any misunderstanding.

SIR LUCIUS O'TRIGGER: Now, I'll leave you to fix your own time. —— take my advice, and you'll decide it this evening if you can; then let the worst come of it, 'twill be off your mind to-morrow.

ACRES: Very true.

SIR LUCIUS O'TRIGGER: So I shall see nothing more of you, unless it be by letter, till the evening. —— I would do myself the honour to carry your message; but, to tell you a secret, I believe I shall have just such another affair on my own hands. There is a gay captain here, who put a jest on me lately, at the expence of my country, and I only want to fall in with the gentleman, to call him out.[10]

ACRES: By my valour, I should like to see you fight first! Odds life! I should like to see you kill him, if it was only to get a little lesson.

SIR LUCIUS O'TRIGGER: I shall be very proud of instructing you. — Well for the present —— but remember now, when you meet your antagonist, do every thing in a mild and agreeable manner. —— Let your courage be as keen, but at the same time as polished as your sword.

Exeunt severally

9. We are to understand that Acres is writing to Sir Lucius's dictation, and calling for more material.

10. meet and challenge him.

ACT IV, SCENE 1

ACRES's *Lodgings*

ACRES *and* DAVID

DAVID: Then, by the Mass, Sir! I would do no such thing — ne'er a Sir Lucius O'Trigger in the kingdom should make me fight, when I wa'n't so minded. Oons! what will the old lady say, when she hears o't!

ACRES: Ah! David, if you had heard Sir Lucius! —— Odds sparks and flames! he would have rous'd your valour.

DAVID: Not he, indeed. I hates such bloodthirsty cormorants. Look'ee, Master, if you'd wanted a bout of boxing, quarter-staff, or short-staff, I should never be the man to bid you cry off: But for your curst sharps[1] and snaps,[2] I never knew any good come of 'em.

ACRES: But my *honour,* David, my *honour*! I must be very careful of my honour.

DAVID: Aye, by the Mass! and I would be very careful of it; and I think in return my *honour* could not do less than to be very careful of *me.*

ACRES: Odds blades! David, no gentleman will ever risk the loss of his honour!

DAVID: I say then, it would be but civil in *honour* never to risk the loss of the *gentleman.* —— Lookee, Master, this *honour* seems to me to be a marvellous false friend; aye, truly, a very courtier-like servant. —— Put the case, I was a gentleman (which, thank God, no one can say of me); well — my honour makes me quarrel with another gentleman of my acquaintance. — So — we fight. (Pleasant enough that) Boh! —— I kill him. —— (the more's my luck). Now, pray who gets the profit of it? — Why, my *honour.* —— But put the case that he kills me! —— by the Mass! I go to the worms, and my honour whips over to my enemy!

ACRES: No, David — in that case! —— Odds crowns and laurels! your honour follows you to the grave.

DAVID: Now, that's just the place where I could make a shift to do without it.

ACRES: Z—ds, David! you're a coward! —— It doesn't become my valour to listen to you —— What, shall I disgrace my ancestors? — Think of that, David — think what it would be to disgrace my ancestors!

1. swords.

2. pistols.

DAVID: Under favour, the surest way of not disgracing them, is to keep as long as you can out of their company. Look'ee now, Master, to go to them in such haste —— with an ounce of lead in your brains — I should think might as well be let alone. Our ancestors are very good kind of folks; but they are the last people I should choose to have a visiting acquaintance with.

ACRES: But David, now, you don't think there is such very, very, *very* great danger, hey? —— Odds life! people often fight without any mischief done!

DAVID: By the Mass, I think 'tis ten to one against you! —— Oons! here to meet some lion-headed fellow, I warrant, with his d—n'd double-barrell'd swords, and cut and thrust pistols! Lord bless us! it makes me tremble to think o't! —— Those be such desperate bloody-minded weapons! Well, I never could abide 'em! —— from a child I never could fancy 'em — I suppose there a'n't so merciless a beast in the world as your loaded pistol!

ACRES: Z—ds! I *won't* be afraid — Odds fire and fury! you shan't make me afraid. —— Here is the challenge, and I have sent for my dear friend Jack Absolute to carry it for me.

DAVID: Aye, I' the name of mischief, let *him* be the messenger. — For my part, I wouldn't lend a hand to it for the best horse in your stable. By the Mass! it don't look like another letter! —— It is, as I may say, a designing and malicious-looking letter! — and I warrant smells of gunpowder like a soldier's pouch! — Oons! I wouldn't swear it mayn't go off!

ACRES: Out, you poltroon! —— you ha'n't the valour of a grass-hopper.

DAVID: Well, I say no more — 'twill be sad news, to be sure, at Clod-Hall! — but I ha' done —— How Phyllis will howl when she hears of it! —— Aye, poor bitch, she little thinks what shooting her Master's going after! — And I warrant old Crop, who has carried your honour, field and road, these ten years, will curse the hour he was born. (*Whimpering*)

ACRES: It won't do, David — I am determined to fight — so get along, you Coward, while I'm in the mind.

Enter SERVANT

SERVANT: Captain Absolute, Sir.

ACRES: O! shew him up.

Exit SERVANT

DAVID: Well, Heaven send we be all alive this time to-morrow.

ACRES: What's that! — Don't provoke me, David!

DAVID: Good bye, Master. (*Whimpering*)

ACRES: Get along, you cowardly, dastardly, croaking raven.

Exit DAVID

Enter CAPTAIN ABSOLUTE.

CAPTAIN ABSOLUTE: What's the matter, Bob?

ACRES: A vile, sheep-hearted blockhead! —— If I hadn't the valour of St. George and the dragon to boot ——

CAPTAIN ABSOLUTE: But what did you want with me, Bob?

ACRES: O! — There — (*Gives him the challenge*)

CAPTAIN ABSOLUTE: *'To Ensign Beverley.'* (*Aside*) So —— what's going on now! Well, what's this?

ACRES: A challenge!

CAPTAIN ABSOLUTE: Indeed! —— Why, you won't fight him; will you, Bob?

ACRES: 'Egad but I will, Jack. —— Sir Lucius has wrought me to it. He has left me full of rage —— and I'll fight this evening, that so much good passion mayn't be wasted.

CAPTAIN ABSOLUTE: But what have I to do with this?

ACRES: Why, as I think you know something of this fellow, I want you to find him out for me, and give him this mortal *defiance.*

CAPTAIN ABSOLUTE: Well, give it to me, and trust me he gets it.

ACRES: Thank you, my dear friend, my dear Jack; but it is giving you a great deal of trouble.

CAPTAIN ABSOLUTE: Not in the least — I beg you won't mention it. — No trouble in the world, I assure you.

ACRES: You are very kind. —— What it is to have a friend! —— You couldn't be my second —— could you, Jack?

CAPTAIN ABSOLUTE: Why no, Bob —— not in *this* affair — it would not be quite so proper.

ACRES: Well then I must fix on my friend Sir Lucius. I shall have your good wishes, however, Jack.

CAPTAIN ABSOLUTE: Whenever he meets you, believe me.

Enter SERVANT

SERVANT: Sir Anthony Absolute is below, inquiring for the Captain.

CAPTAIN ABSOLUTE: I'll come instantly. —— Well, my little hero, success attend you. (*Going*)

ACRES: Stay —— stay, Jack. —— If Beverley should ask you what kind of a man your friend Acres is, do tell him I am a devil of a fellow — will you, Jack?

CAPTAIN ABSOLUTE: To be sure I shall. —— I'll say you are a determined dog — hey, Bob!

ACRES: Aye, do, do — and if that frightens him, 'egad perhaps he mayn't come. So tell him I generally kill a man a week; will you, Jack?

CAPTAIN ABSOLUTE: I will, I will; I'll say you are call'd in the country *'Fighting Bob!'*

ACRES: Right, right — 'tis all to prevent mischief; for I don't want to take his life if I clear my honour.

CAPTAIN ABSOLUTE: No! — that's very kind of you.

ACRES: Why, you don't wish me to kill him — do you, Jack?

CAPTAIN ABSOLUTE: No, upon my soul, I do not. — But a devil of a fellow, hey? (*Going*)

ACRES: True, true — but stay — stay, Jack — you may add that you never saw me in such a rage before — a most devouring rage!

CAPTAIN ABSOLUTE: I will, I will.

ACRES: Remember, Jack —— a determined dog!

CAPTAIN ABSOLUTE: Aye, aye, *'Fighting Bob!'*

Exeunt severally

ACT IV, SCENE 2

MRS. MALAPROP'S *Lodgings*

MRS. MALAPROP *and* LYDIA

MRS. MALAPROP: Why, thou perverse one! — tell me what you can object to him? —— Isn't he a handsome man? — tell me that. — A genteel man? a pretty figure of a man?

LYDIA: (*Aside*) She little thinks whom she is praising! — So is Beverley, Ma'am.

MRS. MALAPROP: No caparisons,[1] Miss, if you please! — Caparisons don't become a young woman. — No! Captain Absolute is indeed a fine gentleman.

LYDIA: (*Aside*) Aye, the Captain Absolute *you* have seen.

MRS. MALAPROP: Then he's *so* well bred; — *so* full of alacrity, and adulation! — and has *so much* to say for himself: — in such good language too! — His physiognomy so grammatical![2] — Then his presence is so noble! — I protest, when I saw him, I thought of what Hamlet says in the Play: — 'Hesperian curls! — the front of *Job* himself! — an eye, like *March,* to threaten at command! — a Station, like Harry Mercury, new—'[3] Something about kissing — on a hill — however, the similitude struck me directly.

LYDIA: (*Aside*) How enraged she'll be presently when she discovers her mistake.

Enter SERVANT

SERVANT: Sir Anthony, and Captain Absolute are below, Ma'am.

MRS. MALAPROP: Shew them up here.

Exit SERVANT

Now, Lydia, I insist on your behaving as becomes a young woman. — Shew your good breeding at least, though you have forgot your duty.

LYDIA: Madam, I have told you my resolution; — I shall not only give him no encouragement, but I won't even speak to, or look at him. (*Flings herself into a chair, with her face from the door*)

Enter SIR ANTHONY *and* CAPTAIN ABSOLUTE

SIR ANTHONY: Here we are, Mrs. Malaprop; come to mitigate the frowns of unrelenting beauty — and difficulty enough I had to bring this fellow. — I don't know what's the matter; but if I hadn't held him by force, he'd have given me the slip.

MRS. MALAPROP: You have infinite trouble, Sir Anthony, in the affair. — I am ashamed for the cause. (*Aside to her*) Lydia, Lydia, rise I beseech you! — pay your respects.

SIR ANTHONY: I hope, Madam, that Miss Languish has reflected on the worth of this gentleman, and the regard due to her Aunt's choice, and *my* alliance (*Aside to him*). — Now, Jack, speak to her!

CAPTAIN ABSOLUTE: (*Aside*) — What the d——l shall I do! — You see, Sir, she won't even look at me, whilst you are here. — I knew she wouldn't. — I told you so — Let me intreat you, Sir, to leave us together! (CAPTAIN ABSOLUTE *seems to expostulate with his Father*)

LYDIA: (*Aside*) I wonder I ha'n't heard my Aunt exclaim yet: sure she can't have look'd at him? — perhaps their regimentals are alike, and she is something blind.

SIR ANTHONY: I say, Sir, I won't stir a foot yet.

MRS. MALAPROP: I am sorry to say, Sir Anthony,

1. for 'comparisons'.
2. for 'symmetrical'.
3. Ludicrously misquoting Hamlet's description of his dead father, *Hamlet*, III. 4. 56-59.

that my affluence[4] over my Niece is very small (*Aside to her*) — Turn round, Lydia, I blush for you!

SIR ANTHONY: May I not flatter myself that Miss Languish will assign what cause of dislike she can have to my son (*Aside to him*) — Why don't you begin, Jack? — Speak, you puppy — speak!

MRS. MALAPROP: It is impossible, Sir Anthony, she can have any. —— She will not *say* she has. —— (*Aside to her*) Answer, huzzy! why don't you answer?

SIR ANTHONY: Then Madam, I trust that a childish and hasty predilection will be no bar to Jack's happiness. — (*Aside to him*) Z—ds!sirrah! why don't you speak?

LYDIA: (*Aside*) I think my lover seems as little inclined to conversation as myself. —— How strangely blind my Aunt is!

CAPTAIN ABSOLUTE: Hem! hem! — Madam — hem! (CAPTAIN ABSOLUTE *attempts to speak, then turns to* SIR ANTHONY) — Faith! Sir, I am so confounded — and so — so — confused — I told you I should be so, Sir, — I knew it — The — the tremor of my passion, entirely takes away my presence of mind.

SIR ANTHONY: But it don't take away your voice, fool, does it? — Go up, and speak to her directly!

CAPTAIN ABSOLUTE *makes signs to* MRS. MALAPROP *to leave them together*.

MRS. MALAPROP: Sir Anthony, shall we leave them together? — (*Aside to her*) Ah! you stubborn, little vixen!

SIR ANTHONY: Not yet, Ma'am, not yet! — (*Aside to him*) What the d—l are you at? unlock your jaws, sirrah, or —

CAPTAIN ABSOLUTE *draws near* LYDIA

CAPTAIN ABSOLUTE: (*Aside*) Now Heav'n send she may be too sullen to look round! — I must disguise my voice — (*Speaks in a low hoarse tone*) Will not Miss Languish lend an ear to the mild accents of true love? — Will not ——

SIR ANTHONY: What the d——l ails the fellow? —— Why don't you speak out? — not stand croaking like a frog in a quinsey!

CAPTAIN ABSOLUTE: The — the — excess of my awe, and my — my — my modesty, quite choak me!

SIR ANTHONY: Ah! your *modesty* again! — I'll tell you what, Jack; if you don't speak out directly, and glibly too, I shall be in such a rage! — Mrs. Malaprop, I wish the lady would favour us with something more than a side-front.

MRS. MALAPROP *seems to chide* LYDIA

CAPTAIN ABSOLUTE: So! — all will out I see! (*Goes up to* LYDIA, *speaks softly*) Be not surprised, my Lydia, suppress all surprise at present.

LYDIA: (*Aside*) Heav'ns! 'tis Beverley's voice! — Sure he can't have impos'd on Sir Anthony too! — (*Looks round by degrees, then starst up*) Is this possible! — my Beverley! — how can this be? — my Beverley?

CAPTAIN ABSOLUTE: (*Aside*) Ah! 'tis all over.

SIR ANTHONY: Beverley! — the devil — Beverley! — What can the girl mean? — This is my son, Jack Absolute!

MRS. MALAPROP: For shame, huzzy! for shame! — your head runs so on that fellow, that you have him always in your eyes! — Beg Captain Absolute's pardon directly.

LYDIA: I see no Captain Absolute, but my lov'd Beverley!

SIR ANTHONY: Z—ds! the girl's mad! — her brain's turn'd by reading!

MRS. MALAPROP: O' my conscience, I believe so! — what do you mean by Beverley, huzzy? — You saw Captain Absolute before to-day; there he is — your husband that shall be.

LYDIA: With all my soul, Ma'am — when I refuse my Beverley ——

SIR ANTHONY: O! she's as mad as Bedlam! — or has this fellow been playing us a rogue's trick? — Come here, sirrah! who the d—l are you?

CAPTAIN ABSOLUTE: Faith, Sir, I am not quite clear myself; but I'll endeavour to recollect.

SIR ANTHONY: Are you my son, or not? — answer for your mother, you dog, if you won't for me.

MRS. MALAPROP: Aye, Sir, who are you? O mercy! I begin to suspect! —

CAPTAIN ABSOLUTE: (*Aside*) Ye powers of Impudence befriend me! Sir Anthony, most assuredly I am your wife's son; and that I sincerely believe myself to be *your's* also, I hope my duty has always shewn. — Mrs. Malaprop, I am your most respectful admirer — and shall be proud to add *affectionate nephew.* — I need not tell my Lydia, that she sees her faithful Beverley, who, knowing the singular generosity of her temper, assum'd that name, and a station, which has proved a test of the

4. for 'influence'.

most disinterested love, which he now hopes to enjoy in a more elevated character.

LYDIA: (*Sullenly*) So! — there will be no elopement after all!

SIR ANTHONY: Upon my soul, Jack, thou art a very impudent fellow! to do you justice, I think I never saw a piece of more consummate assurance.

CAPTAIN ABSOLUTE: O, you flatter me, Sir — you compliment — 'tis my *modesty* you know, Sir — my *modesty* that has stood in my way.

SIR ANTHONY: Well, I am glad you are not the dull, insensible varlet you pretended to be, however — I'm glad you have made a fool of your father, you dog — I am. —— So this was your *penitence,* your *duty,* and *obedience*! — I thought it was d—n'd sudden! — You *never heard their names before,* not you! — *What, Languishes of Worcestershire,* hey? — *if you could please me in the affair, 'twas all you desired* — Ah! you dissembling villain! — What! (*pointing to* LYDIA) *she squints, don't she? — a little red-hair'd girl* — hey? — Why, you hypocritical young rascal — I wonder you a'n't asham'd to hold up your head.

CAPTAIN ABSOLUTE: 'Tis with difficulty, Sir — I *am* confus'd — very much confus'd, as you must perceive.

MRS. MALAPROP: O Lud! Sir Anthony! — a new light breaks in upon me! — hey! how! what! Captain, did *you* write the letters then? — What! — I am to thank *you* for the elegant compilation of '*an old weather-beaten she-dragon*' — hey? — O mercy! — was it *you* that reflected on my parts of speech?

CAPTAIN ABSOLUTE: Dear Sir! my modesty will be overpower'd at last, if you don't assist me. — I shall certainly not be able to stand it.

SIR ANTHONY: Come, come, Mrs. Malaprop, we must forget and forgive — odds'life! matters have taken so clever a turn all of a sudden, that I could find in my heart, to be so good-humour'd! and so gallant! — hey! Mrs. Malaprop!

MRS. MALAPROP: Well, Sir Anthony, since *you* desire it, we will not anticipate[5] the past; — so mind, young people — our retrospection[6] will now be all to the future.

SIR ANTHONY: Come, we must leave them together; Mrs. Malaprop, they long to fly into each other's arms, I warrant! — Jack — is'n't the *cheek* as I said, hey? — and the eye, you dog! — and the lip — hey? Come, Mrs. Malaprop, we'll not disturb their tenderness — their's is the time of life for happiness! —— '*Youth's the season made for joy*' — (*sings*) — hey! — Odds'life! I'm in such spirits, — I don't know what I couldn't do! — Permit me, Ma'am — (*gives his hand to* MRS. MALAPROP) (*sings*) Tol-de-rol — 'gad I should like a little fooling myself — Tol-de-rol! de-rol!

Exit singing, and handing MRS. MALAPROP
LYDIA *sits sullenly in her chair*

CAPTAIN ABSOLUTE: (*Aside*) So much thought bodes me no good — So, grave, Lydia!

LYDIA: Sir!

CAPTAIN ABSOLUTE: (*Aside*) So! — egad! I thought as much! — that d—n'd monosyllable has froze me! — What, Lydia, now that we are as happy in our *friends consent,* as in our *mutual vows* ——

LYDIA: (*Peevishly*) *Friends consent*, indeed!

CAPTAIN ABSOLUTE: Come, come, we must lay aside some of our romance — a little *wealth* and *comfort* may be endur'd after all. And for your fortune, the lawyers shall make such settlements as ——

LYDIA: *Lawyers!* I *hate* lawyers!

CAPTAIN ABSOLUTE: Nay then, we will not wait for their lingering forms, but instantly procure the licence, and —

LYDIA: The *licence!* — I *hate* licence!

CAPTAIN ABSOLUTE: O my Love! *be* not so unkind! — thus let me intreat —— (*Kneeling*)

LYDIA: Pshaw! — what signifies kneeling, when you know I *must* have you?

CAPTAIN ABSOLUTE: (*Rising*) Nay, Madam, there shall be no constraint upon your inclinations, I promise you. — If I have lost your *heart,* — I resign the rest. —— (*Aside*) 'Gad, I must try what a little *spirit* will do.

LYDIA: (*Rising*) Then, Sir, let me tell you, the interest you had there was acquired by a mean, unmanly imposition, and deserves the punishment of fraud. — What, you have been treating *me* like a *child*! — humouring my romance! and laughing, I suppose, at your success!

CAPTAIN ABSOLUTE: You wrong me, Lydia, you wrong me —— only hear ——

LYDIA: So, while *I* fondly imagined we were deceiving my relations, and flatter'd myself that I should outwit and incense them *all* — behold! my hopes are to be crush'd at once, by my Aunt's

5. She means the opposite, possibly 'contemplate'.
6. Again, she means the opposite, possibly 'concentration'; but the joke here, as in the preceding line, is in the 'bull' or absurdity of the phrase, rather than in the particular word misused.

consent and approbation! — and *I* am *myself,* the only dupe at last! (*Walking about in heat*)

CAPTAIN ABSOLUTE: Nay, but hear me ——

LYDIA: No, Sir, you could not think that such paltry artifices could please me, when the mask was thrown off! — But I suppose since your tricks have made you secure of my *fortune,* you are little solicitous about my *affections.*[7] — But here, Sir, here is the picture — Beverley's picture! (*taking a miniature from her bosom*) which I have worn, night and day, in spite of threats and entreaties! — There, Sir, (*flings it to him*) and be assured I throw the original from my heart as easily!

CAPTAIN ABSOLUTE: Nay, nay, Ma'am, we will not differ as to that. — Here, (*taking out a picture*) *here* is Miss Lydia Languish. — What a difference! —— aye, *there* is the heav'nly assenting smile, that first gave soul and spirit to my hopes! —— those are the lips which seal'd a vow, as yet scarce dry in Cupid's calendar! — and *there* the *half* resentful blush, that *would* have check'd the ardour of my thanks — Well, all that's past — all over indeed! — There, Madam — in *beauty,* that copy is not equal to you, but in my mind its merit over the original, in being still the same, is such —— that —— I cannot find in my heart to *part with* it. (*Puts it up again*)

LYDIA: (*Softening*) 'Tis *your own* doing, Sir — I, I, I suppose you are perfectly satisfied.

CAPTAIN ABSOLUTE: O, most certainly — sure now this is much better than being in love! — ha! ha! ha! — there's some spirit in *this*! — What signifies breaking some scores of solemn promises, half an hundred vows, under one's hand, with the marks of a dozen or two angels to witness[8] — all that's of no consequence you know. — To be sure people will say, that Miss didn't know her own mind — but never mind that: — or perhaps they may be ill-natured enough to hint, that the gentleman grew tired of the lady and forsook her — but don't let that fret you.

LYDIA: There's no bearing his insolence. (*Bursts into tears*)

Enter MRS. MALAPROP *and* SIR ANTHONY

MRS. MALAPROP: (*Entering*) Come, we must interrupt your billing and cooing a while.

LYDIA: *This* is *worse* than your treachery and deceit, you base ingrate! (*Sobbing*)

SIR ANTHONY: What the devil's the matter now! — Z—ds! Mrs. Malaprop, this is the *oddest billing* and *cooing* I ever heard! — but what the deuce is the meaning of it? — I'm quite astonish'd!

CAPTAIN ABSOLUTE: Ask the lady, Sir.

MRS. MALAPROP: O mercy! — I'm quite analys'd[9] for my part! — why, Lydia, what is the reason of this!

LYDIA: Ask the *gentleman,* Ma'am.

SIR ANTHONY: Z—ds! I shall be in a phrenzy! — why Jack, you scoundrel, you are not come out to be any one else, are you?

MRS. MALAPROP: Are, Sir, there's no more *trick,* is there? — you are not like Cerberus,[10] *three* Gentlemen at once, are you?

CAPTAIN ABSOLUTE: You'll not let me speak — I say the *lady* can account for *this* much better than I can.

LYDIA: Ma'am, you once commanded me never to think of Beverley again — *there* is the man — I now obey you: — for, from this moment, I renounce him for ever.

Exit LYDIA

MRS. MALAPROP: O mercy! and miracles! what a turn here is — why sure, Captain, you haven't behaved disrespectfully to my Niece.

SIR ANTHONY: Ha! ha! ha! — ha! ha! ha! — now I see it — Ha! ha! ha! — now I see it —— you have been too lively, Jack.

CAPTAIN ABSOLUTE: Nay, Sir, upon my word ——

SIR ANTHONY: Come, no lying, Jack — I'm sure *'twas* so.

MRS. MALAPROP: O Lud! Sir Anthony! —— O fie, Captain!

CAPTAIN ABSOLUTE: Upon my soul, Ma'am ——

SIR ANTHONY: Come, no excuses, Jack; — why, your father, you rogue, was so before you: — the blood of the Absolutes was always impatient. — Ha! ha! ha! poor little Lydia! — why, you've frighten'd her, you Dog, you have.

CAPTAIN ABSOLUTE: By all that's good, Sir ——

SIR ANTHONY: Z—ds! say no more, I tell you. —— Mrs. Malaprop shall make your peace. —— You must make his peace, Mrs. Malaprop! —— you must tell her 'tis Jack's way —— tell her 'tis all

7. The lines from 'Nay, but hear me . . .' were cut in the third edition.
8. The lines from 'half a hundred vows . . .' were cut in the third edition.
9. for 'surprised'.
10. The mythological watchdog guarding the entrance to Hades. He was usually represented as having three heads.

our ways —— it runs in the blood of our family! —— Come, get on, Jack, —— ha! ha! ha! Mrs. Malaprop —— a young villain!

Pushing him out

MRS. MALAPROP: O! Sir Anthony! —— O fie, Captain!

Exeunt severally

ACT IV, SCENE 3

The North-Parade

Enter SIR LUCIUS O'TRIGGER

SIR LUCIUS O'TRIGGER: I wonder where this Capt. Absolute hides himself. —— Upon my conscience! —— these officers are always in one's way in love-affairs: —— I remember I might have married Lady Dorothy Carmine, if it had not been for a little rogue of a Major, who ran away with her before she could get a sight of me. —— And I wonder too what it is the ladies can see in them to be so fond of them — unless it be a touch of the old serpent in 'em, that makes the little creatures be caught, like vipers with a bit of red cloth. —— Hah! —— isn't this the Captain coming? —— faith it is! —— There is a probability of succeeding about that fellow, that is mighty provoking. —— Who the devil is he talking to?

Steps aside

Enter CAPTAIN ABSOLUTE

CAPTAIN ABSOLUTE: To what fine purpose I have been plotting! a noble reward for all my schemes, upon my soul! — a little gypsey! — I did not think her romance could have made her so d—n'd absurd either — S'death, I never was in a worse humour in my life! — I could cut my own throat, or any other person's, with the greatest pleasure in the world!

SIR LUCIUS O'TRIGGER: O, faith! I'm in the luck of it —— I never could have found him in a sweeter temper for my purpose — to be sure I'm just come in the nick! now to enter into conversation with him, and so quarrel genteelly.

SIR LUCIUS *goes up to* CAPTAIN ABSOLUTE

—— With regard to that matter, Captain, I must beg leave to differ in opinion with you.

CAPTAIN ABSOLUTE: Upon my word then, you must be a very subtle disputant: —— because, Sir, I happen'd just then to be giving no opinion at all.

SIR LUCIUS O'TRIGGER: That's no reason. —— For give me leave to tell you, a man may *think* an untruth as well as *speak* one.

CAPTAIN ABSOLUTE: Very true, Sir, but if the man never utters his thoughts, I should think they *might* stand a *chance* of escaping controversy.

SIR LUCIUS O'TRIGGER: Then, Sir, you differ in opinion with me, which amounts to the same thing.

CAPTAIN ABSOLUTE: Hark'ee, Sir Lucius, —— if I had not before known you to be a gentleman, upon my soul, I should not have discovered it at this interview: — for what you can drive at, unless you mean to quarrel with me, I cannot conceive.

SIR LUCIUS O'TRIGGER: I humbly thank you, Sir, for the quickness of your apprehension (*bowing*), — you have nam'd the very thing I would be at.

CAPTAIN ABSOLUTE: Very well, Sir, — I shall certainly not baulk your inclinations: —— but I should be glad you would please to explain your motives.

SIR LUCIUS O'TRIGGER: Pray, Sir, be easy — the quarrel is a very pretty quarrel as it stands — we should only spoil it, by trying to explain it. — However, your memory is very short —— or you could not have forgot an affront you pass'd on me within this week. —— So no more, but name your time and place.

CAPTAIN ABSOLUTE: Well, Sir, since you are so bent on it, the sooner the better; let it be this evening —— here, by the Spring-Gardens. —— We shall scarcely be interrupted.

SIR LUCIUS O'TRIGGER: Faith, that same interruption in affairs of this nature, shews very great ill-breeding. —— I don't know what's the reason, but in England, if a thing of this kind gets wind, people make such a pother, that a gentleman can never fight in peace and quietness. — However, if it's the same to you, Captain, I should take it as a particular kindness, if you'd let us meet in King's-Mead-Fields, as a little business will call me there about six o'clock, and I may dispatch both matters at once.

CAPTAIN ABSOLUTE: 'Tis the same to me exactly. — A little after six, then we will discuss this matter more seriously.

SIR LUCIUS O'TRIGGER: If you please, Sir, there will be very pretty small-sword light, tho' it won't do for a long shot. — So that matter's settled, and my mind's at ease.

Exit SIR LUCIUS

Enter FAULKLAND, *meeting* CAPTAIN ABSOLUTE

CAPTAIN ABSOLUTE: Well met — I was going to look for you. —— O, Faulkland, all the Dæmons of spite and disappointment have conspired against me! I'm so vex'd, that if I had not the prospect of a resource in being knock'd o' the head by and bye, I should scarce have spirits to tell you the cause.

FAULKLAND: What can you mean? —— Has Lydia chang'd her mind? —— I should have thought her duty and inclination would now have pointed to the same object.

CAPTAIN ABSOLUTE: Aye, just as the eyes do of a person who squints: — when her *love-eye* was fix'd on *me* —— t'other —— her *eye* of *duty*, was finely obliqued: — but when duty bid her point *that* the same way — off t'other turn'd on a swivel, and secured its retreat with a frown.

FAULKLAND: But what's the resource you ——

CAPTAIN ABSOLUTE: O, to wind up the whole, a good natured Irishman here has (*mimicking* SIR LUCIUS) beg'd leave to have the pleasure of cutting my throat —— and I mean to indulge him — that's all.

FAULKLAND: Prithee, be serious.

CAPTAIN ABSOLUTE: 'Tis fact, upon my soul. —— Sir Lucius O'Trigger —— you know him by sight —— for some affront, which I am sure I never intended, has obliged me to meet him this evening at six o'clock: —— 'tis on that account I wish'd to see you —— you must go with me.

FAULKLAND: Nay, there must be some mistake sure —— Sir Lucius shall explain himself —— and I dare say matters may be accommodated: —— but this evening, did you say? —— I wish it had been any other time.

CAPTAIN ABSOLUTE: Why? —— there will be light enough: —— there will (as Sir Lucius says) 'be very pretty small-sword light, tho' it won't do for a long shot.' — Confound his long shots!

FAULKLAND: But I am myself a good deal ruffled, by a difference I have had with Julia — my vile tormenting temper has made me treat her so cruelly, that I shall not be myself till we are reconciled.

CAPTAIN ABSOLUTE: By Heav'ns, Faulkland, you don't deserve her.

Enter SERVANT, *gives* FAULKLAND *a letter*

FAULKLAND: O Jack! this is from Julia — I dread to open it — I fear it may be to take a last leave — perhaps to bid me return her letters — and restore — O how I suffer for my folly!

CAPTAIN ABSOLUTE: Here — let me see. (*Takes the letter and opens it*) Aye, a final sentence indeed! — 'tis all over with you, faith!

FAULKLAND: Nay, Jack — don't keep me in suspence.

CAPTAIN ABSOLUTE: Hear then. — *'As I am convinced that my dear* Faulkland's *own reflections have already upbraided him for his last unkindness to me, I will not add a word on the subject. — I wish to speak with you as soon as possible. — Your's ever and truly,* Julia.' — There's stubbornness and resentment for you! (*Gives him the letter*) Why, man, you don't seem one whit the happier at this.

FAULKLAND: O, yes, I am —— but —— but ——

CAPTAIN ABSOLUTE: Confound your *buts*. — You never hear any thing that would make another man bless himself, but you immediately d—n it with a *but*.

FAULKLAND: Now, Jack, as you are my friend, own honestly — don't you think there is something forward — something indelicate in this haste to forgive? —— Women should never sue for reconciliation: — *that* should *always* come from us. — *They* should retain their coldness till *woo'd* to kindness — and their *pardon*, like their *love*, should 'not unsought be won.'[1]

CAPTAIN ABSOLUTE: I have not patience to listen to you: —— thou'rt incorrigible! —— so say no more on the subject. — I must go to settle a few matters — let me see you before six — remember — at my lodgings. — A poor industrious devil like me, who have toil'd, and drudg'd, and plotted to gain my ends, and am at last disappointed by other people's folly — may in pity be allowed to swear and grumble a little; — but a captious sceptic in love, — a slave to fretfulness and whim —— who has no difficulties but of *his own* creating — is a subject more fit for ridicule than compassion.

Exit ABSOLUTE

FAULKLAND: I feel his reproaches! —— yet I would not change this too exquisite nicety, for the gross content with which *he* tramples on the thorns of love. — His engaging me in this duel, has started an idea in my head, which I will instantly pursue. — I'll use it as the touch-stone of Julia's sincerity and disinterestedness — if her love prove pure and sterling ore —— my name will rest on it with honour! — and once I've stamp'd it there, I lay aside my doubts for ever: — but if the dross of

1. Milton, *Paradise Lost*, VIII, 503. It is Adam's description of Eve: 'That would be wooed, and not unsought be won.'

selfishness, the allay[2] of pride predominate —— 'twill be best to leave her as a toy for some less cautious Fool to sigh for.

Exit FAULKLAND

2. (obsolete) alloy.

ACT V, SCENE 1

JULIA's *Dressing-Room*

JULIA, *sola*

JULIA: How this message has alarmed me! what dreadful accident can he mean! why such charge to be alone? — O Faulkland! — how many unhappy moments! — how many tears have you cost me!

Enter FAULKLAND, *muffled up in a Riding-coat*

JULIA: What means this? —— why this caution, Faulkland?

FAULKLAND: Alas! Julia, I am come to take a long farewell.

JULIA: Heav'ns! what do you mean?

FAULKLAND: You see before you a wretch, whose life is forfeited. —— Nay, start not! —— the infirmity of my temper has drawn all this misery on me. —— I left you fretful and passionate — an untoward accident drew me into a quarrel — the event is, that I must fly this kingdom instantly. — O Julia, had I been so fortunate as to have call'd you mine intirely, before this mischance had fallen on me, I should not so deeply dread my banishment! — But no more of that — your heart and promise were given to one happy in friends, character, and station! they are not bound to wait upon a solitary, guilty exile.[1]

JULIA: My soul is oppress'd with sorrow at the *nature* of your misfortune: had these adverse circumstances arisen from a less fatal cause, I should have felt strong comfort in the thought that I could *now* chase from your bosom every doubt of the warm sincerity of my love. — My heart has long known no other guardian — I now entrust my person to your honour — we will fly together. — When safe from pursuit, my Father's will may be fulfilled — and I receive a legal claim to be the partner of your sorrows, and tenderest comforter. Then on the bosom of your wedded Julia, you may lull your keen regret to slumbering; while virtuous love, with a Cherub's hand, shall smooth the brow of upbraiding thought, and pluck the thorn from compunction.

1. The lines from 'But no more ...' were cut in the third edition.

FAULKLAND: O Julia! I am bankrupt in gratitude! but the time is so pressing, it calls on you for so hasty a resolution. — Would you not wish some hours to weigh the advantages you forgo, and what little compensation poor Faulkland can make you beside his solitary love?

JULIA: I ask not a moment. —— No, Faulkland, I have lov'd you for yourself: and if I now, more than ever, prize the solemn engagement which so long has pledged us to each other, it is because it leaves no room for hard aspersions on my fame, and puts the seal of duty to an act of love. — But let us not linger. — Perhaps this delay ——

FAULKLAND: 'Twill be better I should not venture out again till dark. —— Yet am I griev'd to think what numberless distresses will press heavy on your gentle disposition!

JULIA: Perhaps your fortune may be forfeited by this unhappy act. — I know not whether 'tis so — but sure that alone can never make us unhappy. — The little I have will be sufficient to *support* us; and *exile* never should be splendid.

FAULKLAND: Aye, but in such an abject state of life, my wounded pride perhaps may increase the natural fretfulness of my temper, till I become a rude, morose companion, beyond your patience to endure. Perhaps the recollection of a deed, my conscience cannot justify, may haunt me in such gloomy and unsocial fits, that I shall hate the tenderness that would relieve me, break from your arms, and quarrel with your fondness!

JULIA: If your thoughts should assume so unhappy a bent, you will the more want some mild and affectionate spirit to watch over and console you: — One who, by bearing *your* infirmities with gentleness and resignation, may teach you *so* to bear the evils of your fortune.

FAULKLAND: O Julia, I have proved you to the quick! and with this useless device I throw away all my doubts. How shall I plead to be forgiven this last unworthy effect of my restless, unsatisfied disposition?

JULIA: Has no such disaster happened as you related?

FAULKLAND: I am ashamed to own that it was all pretended; yet in pity, Julia, do not kill me with resenting a fault which never can be repeated: But sealing, this once, my pardon, let me to-morrow, in the face of Heaven, receive my future guide and monitress, and expiate my past folly, by years of tender adoration.

JULIA: Hold, Faulkland! — that you are free from a crime, which I before fear'd to name, Heaven knows how sincerely I rejoice! — These are tears of thankfulness for that! But that your cruel doubts should have urged you to an imposition that has wrung my heart, gives me now a pang more keen than I can express!

FAULKLAND: By Heav'ns! Julia ——

JULIA: Yet hear me. —— My Father lov'd you, Faulkland: and you preserv'd the life that tender parent gave me; in his presence I pledged my hand —— *joyfully* pledged it —— where before I had given my heart. When, soon after, I lost that parent, it seem'd to me that Providence had, in Faulkland, shewn me whither to transfer without a pause, my grateful duty, as well as my affection: Hence I have been content to bear from you what pride and delicacy would have forbid me from another. — I will not upbraid you, by repeating how you have trifled with my sincerity. ——

FAULKLAND: I confess it all! yet hear ——

JULIA: After such a year of trial — I might have flattered myself that I should not have been insulted with a new probation of my sincerity, as cruel as unnecessary! A trick of such a nature, as to shew me plainly, that when I thought you lov'd me best, you even then regarded me as a mean dissembler; an artful, prudent hypocrite.

FAULKLAND: Never! never![2]

JULIA: I now see it is not in your nature to be content, or confident in love. With this conviction — I never will be yours. While I had hopes that my persevering attention, and unreproaching kindness might in time reform your temper, I should have been happy to have gain'd a dearer influence over you; but I will not furnish you with a licensed power to keep alive an incorrigible fault, at the expence of one who never would contend with you.

FAULKLAND: Nay, but Julia, by my soul and honour, if after this ——

JULIA: But one word more. — As my faith has once been given to you, I never will barter it with another. —— I shall pray for your happiness with the truest sincerity; and the dearest blessing I can ask of Heaven to send you, will be to charm you from that unhappy temper, which alone has prevented the performance of our solemn engagement. — All I request of *you* is, that you will yourself reflect upon this infirmity, and when you number up the many true delights it has deprived you of —— let it not be your *least* regret, that it lost you the love of one —— who would have follow'd you in beggary through the world!

Exit

FAULKLAND: She's gone! —— for ever! —— There was an awful resolution in her manner, that rivetted me to my place. —— O Fool! —— Dolt! —— Barbarian! —— Curst as I am, with more imperfections than my fellow-wretches, kind Fortune sent a heaven-gifted cherub to my aid, and, like a ruffian, I have driven her from my side! — I must now haste to my appointment. —— Well my mind is tuned for such a scene. — I shall wish only to become a principal in it, and reverse the tale my cursed folly put me upon forging here. — O Love! — Tormentor! — Fiend! — whose influence, like the Moon's, acting on men of dull souls, makes ideots of them, but meeting subtler spirits, betrays their course, and urges sensibility to madness!

Exit

Enter MAID *and* LYDIA

MAID: My Mistress, Ma'am, I know, was here just now — perhaps she is only in the next room.

Exit MAID

LYDIA: Heigh ho! — Though he has used me so, this fellow runs strangely in my head. I believe one lecture from my grave Cousin will make me recall him.

Enter JULIA

LYDIA: O Julia, I am come to you with such an appetite for consolation. —— Lud! Child, what's the matter with you? —— You have been crying! —— I'll be hanged, if that Faulkland has not been tormenting you.

JULIA: You mistake the cause of my uneasiness. — Something *has* flurried me a little. — Nothing that you can guess at. —— (*Aside*) I would not accuse Faulkland to a Sister!

LYDIA: Ah! whatever vexations you may have, I can assure you mine surpass them —— You know who Beverley proves to be?

JULIA: I will now own to you, Lydia, that Mr. Faulkland had before inform'd me of the whole affair. Had young Absolute been the person you took him for, I should not have accepted your confidence on the subject, without a serious endeavour to counteract your caprice.

LYDIA: So, then, I see I have been deceived by every one! — but I don't care — I'll never have him.

2. The lines from 'A trick ...' were cut in the third edition.

JULIA: Nay, Lydia ——

LYDIA: Why, is it not provoking; when I thought we were coming to the prettiest distress imaginable, to find myself made a mere Smithfield bargain[3] of at last —— There had I projected one of the most sentimental elopements! — so becoming a disguise! —— so amiable a ladder of Ropes! — Conscious Moon —— four horses — Scotch parson — with such surprise to Mrs. Malaprop — and such paragraphs in the News-papers![4] —— O, I shall die with disappointment.

JULIA: I don't wonder at it!

LYDIA: Now — sad reverse! — what have I to expect, but, after a deal of flimsy preparation with a bishop's licence, and my Aunt's blessing, to go simpering up to the Altar; or perhaps be cried three times in a country-church, and have an unmannerly fat clerk ask the consent of every butcher in the parish to join John Absolute and Lydia Languish, *Spinster*! O, that I should live to hear myself called Spinster!

JULIA: Melancholy, indeed!

LYDIA: How mortifying, to remember the dear delicious shifts I used to be put to, to gain half a minute's conversation with this fellow! —— How often have I stole forth, in the coldest night in January, and found him in the garden, stuck like a dripping statue! —— There would he kneel to me in the snow, and sneeze and cough so pathetically! he shivering with cold, and I with apprehension! and while the freezing blast numb'd our joints, how warmly would he press me to pity his flame, and glow with mutual ardour! —— Ah Julia! that was something like being in love.

JULIA: If I were in spirits, Lydia, I should chide you only by laughing heartily at you: but it suits more the situation of my mind at present, earnestly to entreat you, not to let a man, who loves you with sincerity, suffer that unhappiness from your *caprice*, which I know too well caprice can inflict.

LYDIA: O Lud! what has brought my Aunt here!

Enter MRS. MALAPROP, FAG, *and* DAVID

MRS. MALAPROP: So! so! here's fine work, —— here's fine suicide, paracide,[5] and salivation[6] going on in the fields! and Sir Anthony not to be found to prevent the antistrophe![7]

JULIA: For Heaven's sake, Madam, what's the meaning of this?

MRS. MALAPROP: That gentleman can tell you —— 'twas he enveloped[8] the affair to me.

LYDIA: (*To* FAG) Do, Sir, will you inform us.

FAG: Ma'am, I should hold myself very deficient in every requisite that forms the man of breeding, if I delay'd a moment to give all the information in my power to a lady so deeply interested in the affair as you are.

LYDIA: But quick! quick, Sir!

FAG: True, Ma'am, as you say, one should be quick in divulging matters of this nature; for should we be tedious, perhaps while we are flourishing on the subject, two or three lives may be lost.

LYDIA: O patience! —— Do, Ma'am, for Heaven's sake, tell us what is the matter?

MRS. MALAPROP: Why, murder's the matter! slaughter's the matter! killing's the matter! —— but he can tell you the perpendiculars.[9]

LYDIA: Then prythee, Sir, be brief.

FAG: Why then, Ma'am — as to murder — I cannot take upon me to say — and as to slaughter, or manslaughter, that will be as the jury finds it.

LYDIA: But who, Sir — who are engaged in this?

FAG: Faith, Ma'am, one is a young gentleman whom I should be very sorry any thing was to happen to —— a very pretty behaved gentleman! —— We have lived much together, and always on terms.

LYDIA: But who is this? who, who, who!

FAG: My Master, Ma'am — my Master — I speak of my Master.

LYDIA: Heavens, what, Captain Absolute!

MRS. MALAPROP: O, to be sure, you are frightened now.

JULIA: But who are with him, Sir?

FAG: As to the rest, Ma'am, this gentleman can inform you better than I.

JULIA: (*To* DAVID): Do speak, friend.

DAVID: Look'ee, my Lady — by the Mass, there's mischief going on. —— Folks don't use to meet for amusement with fire-arms, firelocks, fire-engines, fire-screens, fire-office, and the devil knows what other crackers besides! — This, my Lady, I say, has an angry favour.

3. A marriage of interest, in which money is the chief consideration. Smithfield was the great cattle-market in London.
4. Lydia's imagination is full of romantic images of elopement. 'Scotch parson' implies a quick and easy marriage ceremony.
5. for 'homicide'.
6. Changed to 'simulation' in the third edition.
7. for 'catastrophe'.
8. for 'disclosed'.
9. for 'particulars'.

JULIA: But who is there beside Captain Absolute, friend?

DAVID: My poor Master —— under favour, for mentioning him first. — You know me, my Lady — I am David — and my Master of course is, or *was* Squire Acres. — Then comes Squire Faulkland.

JULIA: Do, Ma'am, let us instantly endeavour to prevent mischief.

MRS. MALAPROP: O fie — it would be very inelegant in us: — we should only participate[10] things.

DAVID: Ah, do, Mrs Aunt, save a few lives — they are desperately given, believe me. — Above all, there is that blood-thirsty Philistine, Sir Lucius O'Trigger.

MRS. MALAPROP: Sir Lucius O'Trigger, —— O mercy, have they drawn poor little dear Sir Lucius into the scrape? — why, how you stand, girl, you have no more feeling than one of the Derbyshire Putrefactions.[11]

LYDIA: What are we to do, Madam?

MRS. MALAPROP: Why, fly with the utmost felicity[12] to be sure, to prevent mischief: — here, friend — you can shew us the place?

FAG: If you please, Ma'am, I will conduct you. — David, do you look for Sir Anthony.

Exit DAVID

MRS. MALAPROP: Come, girls, — this gentleman will exhort[13] us. — Come, Sir, you're our envoy —— lead the way, and we'll precede.[14]

FAG: Not a step before the ladies for the world.

MRS. MALAPROP: You're sure you know the spot.

FAG: I think I can find it, Ma'am; and one good thing is, we shall hear the report of the pistols as we draw near, so we can't well miss them; never fear, Ma'am, never fear.

Exeunt, he talking

10. for 'precipitate', hurry up.
11. for 'petrefactions', stalactites.
12. for 'celerity', speed.
13. for 'escort'.
14. for the opposite, 'follow'.

ACT V, SCENE 2[1]

South-Parade

Enter CAPTAIN ABSOLUTE, *putting his sword under his great-coat*

CAPTAIN ABSOLUTE: A sword seen in the streets of Bath would raise as great an alarm as a mad-dog.[2] —— How provoking this is in Faulkland! —— Never punctual! I shall be obliged to go without him at last. —— O, the devil, here's Sir Anthony! —— how shall I escape him? (*Muffles up his face, and takes a circle to go off*)

Enter SIR ANTHONY

SIR ANTHONY: How one may be deceived at a little distance! only that I see he don't know me, I could have sworn that was Jack! — Hey! — 'Gad's life; it is — Why, Jack, you Dog, — what are you afraid of? — hey! sure I'm right. — Why Jack — Jack Absolute! (*Goes up to him*)

CAPTAIN ABSOLUTE: Really, Sir, you have the advantage of me: — I don't remember ever to have had the honour — my name is Saunderson, at your service.

SIR ANTHONY: Sir, I beg your pardon —— I took you —— hey! — why, z—ds! it is —— Stay —— (*Looks up to his face*) So, so, —— your humble servant, Mr. Saunderson! — Why, you scoundrel, what tricks are you after now?

CAPTAIN ABSOLUTE: O! a joke, Sir, a joke! —— I came here on purpose to look for you, Sir.

SIR ANTHONY: You did! well, I am glad you were so lucky: — but what are you muffled up so for? —— what's this for? — hey?

CAPTAIN ABSOLUTE: 'Tis cool, Sir; isn't it? — rather chilly somehow: — but I shall be late — I have a particular engagement.

SIR ANTHONY: Stay — why, I thought you were looking for me? — Pray, Jack, where is't you are going?

CAPTAIN ABSOLUTE: Going, Sir!

SIR ANTHONY: Aye — where are you going?

CAPTAIN ABSOLUTE: Where am I going?

SIR ANTHONY: You unmannerly puppy!

CAPTAIN ABSOLUTE: I was going, Sir, to — to — to — to Lydia —— Sir, to Lydia — to make matters up if I could; —— and I was looking for you, Sir, to — to ——

SIR ANTHONY: To go with you, I suppose — Well, come along.

1. This scene was omitted from early performances at Covent Garden in response to criticism that it was unnecessary to the plot, but it was restored by Sheridan when, as manager, he brought out *The Rivals* at Drury Lane in January 1777. The fact that the scene was included in the third edition (1776) inclines Sheridan's editor, Cecil Price, to believe that Sheridan 'seems to have paid little attention to actors' cuts' (*Dramatic Works*, I, 63). If this is right, then the third edition, corrected, must not be regarded as the *stage* version of the play.
2. The prohibition against wearing swords in Bath was introduced by Richard 'Beau' Nash (1674-1761).

CAPTAIN ABSOLUTE: O! z—ds! no, Sir, not for the world! —— I wish'd to meet with you, Sir, to — to — to —— You find it cool, I'm sure, Sir —— you'd better not stay out.

SIR ANTHONY: Cool! — not at all —— Well, Jack —— and what will you say to Lydia?

CAPTAIN ABSOLUTE: O, Sir, beg her pardon, humour her —— promise and vow: —— but I detain you, Sir —— consider the cold air on your gout.

SIR ANTHONY: O, not at all! —— not at all! —— I'm in no hurry. —— Ah! Jack, you youngsters when once you are wounded here. (*Putting his hand to* ABSOLUTE's *breast*) Hey! what the deuce have you got here?

CAPTAIN ABSOLUTE: Nothing, Sir —— nothing.

SIR ANTHONY: What's this? —— here's something d—d hard!

CAPTAIN ABSOLUTE: O, trinkets, Sir! trinkets —— a bauble for Lydia!

SIR ANTHONY: Nay, let me see your taste. (*Pulls his coat open, the sword falls*) Trinkets! —— a bauble for Lydia! — z—ds! sirrah, you are not going to cut her throat, are you?

CAPTAIN ABSOLUTE: Ha! ha! ha! —— I thought it would divert you, Sir, tho' I didn't mean to tell you till afterwards.

SIR ANTHONY: You didn't? —— Yes this is a very diverting trinket, truly.

CAPTAIN ABSOLUTE: Sir, I'll explain to you. —— You know, Sir, Lydia is romantic —— dev'lish romantic, and very absurd of course: —— now, Sir, I intend, if she refuses to forgive me —— to unsheath this sword —— and swear — I'll fall upon its point, and expire at her feet!

SIR ANTHONY: Fall upon fiddle-stick's end! —— why, I suppose it is the very thing that would please her — Get along, you Fool. ——

CAPTAIN ABSOLUTE: Well, Sir, you shall hear of my success —— you shall hear. — 'O, Lydia! — forgive me, or this pointed steel' —— says I.

SIR ANTHONY: 'O, Booby! stab away, and welcome' — says she — Get along! and d—n your trinkets!

Exit CAPTAIN ABSOLUTE

Enter DAVID, *running*

DAVID: Stop him! stop him! Murder! Thief! Fire! — Stop fire! Stop fire! — O! Sir Anthony! — call! call! bid 'em stop! Murder! Fire!

SIR ANTHONY: Fire! Murder! where?

DAVID: Oons! he's out of sight! and I'm out of breath, for my part! O, Sir Anthony, why didn't you stop him? why didn't you stop him?

SIR ANTHONY: Z—ds! the fellow's mad! — Stop whom? stop Jack?

DAVID: Aye, the Captain, Sir! —— there's murder and slaughter ——

SIR ANTHONY: Murder!

DAVID: Aye, please you, Sir Anthony, there's all kinds of murder, all sorts of slaughter to be seen in the fields: there's fighting going on, Sir — bloody sword and gun fighting!

SIR ANTHONY: Who are going to fight, Dunce?

DAVID: Every body that I know of, Sir Anthony: — every body is going to fight, my poor Master, Sir Lucius O'Trigger, your son, the Captain ——

SIR ANTHONY: O, the Dog! — I see his tricks: — do you know the place?

DAVID: King's-Mead-Fields.

SIR ANTHONY: You know the way?

DAVID: Not an inch; — but I'll call the Mayor —— Aldermen — Constables — Church-wardens — and Beadles — we can't be too many to part them.

SIR ANTHONY: Come alone — give me your shoulder! we'll get assistance as we go — the lying villain! —— Well, I shall be in such a phrenzy — So — this was the history of his d—d trinkets! I'll bauble him!

Exeunt

ACT V, SCENE 3

King's-Mead-Fields

SIR LUCIUS *and* ACRES, *with pistols*

ACRES: By my valour! then, Sir Lucius, forty yards is a good distance — Odds levels and aims! — I say it is a good distance.

SIR LUCIUS O'TRIGGER: Is it for muskets or small field-pieces? upon my conscience, Mr. Acres, you must leave those things to me. — Stay now — I'll shew you. (*Measures paces along the stage*) There now, that is a very pretty distance —— a pretty gentleman's distance.

ACRES: Z—ds! we might as well fight in a sentry-box —— I tell you, Sir Lucius, the farther he is off, the cooler I shall take my aim.

SIR LUCIUS O'TRIGGER: Faith, then, I suppose you would aim at him best of all if he was out of sight.

ACRES: No, Sir Lucius — but I should think forty or eight and thirty yards ——

SIR LUCIUS O'TRIGGER: Pho! pho! nonsense! three or four feet between the mouths of your pistols is as good as a mile.

ACRES: Odds bullets, no, by my valour! there is no merit in killing him so near: —— do, my dear Sir Lucius, let me bring him down at a long shot. —— a long shot, Sir Lucius, if you love me!

SIR LUCIUS O'TRIGGER: Well — the gentleman's friend and I must settle that. — But tell me now, Mr. Acres, in case of an accident, is there any little will or commission I could execute for you?

ACRES: I am much obliged to you, Sir Lucius —— but I don't understand ——

SIR LUCIUS O'TRIGGER: Why, you may think there's no being shot at without a little risk —— and if an unlucky bullet should carry a *Quietus* with it —— I say it would be no time then to be bothering you about family matters.

ACRES: A *Quietus*!

SIR LUCIUS O'TRIGGER: For instance, now —— if that should be the case —— would you chuse to be pickled and sent home? —— or would it be the same to you to lie here in the Abbey? —— I'm told there is very snug lying in the Abbey.

ACRES: Pickled! —— Snug lying in the Abbey! — Odds tremors! Sir Lucius, don't talk so!

SIR LUCIUS O'TRIGGER: I suppose, Mr. Acres, you never were engaged in an affair of this kind before?

ACRES: No, Sir Lucius, never before.

SIR LUCIUS O'TRIGGER: Ah! that's a pity! —— there's nothing like being used to a thing —— Pray now, how would you receive the gentleman's shot?

ACRES: Odds files! —— I've practised that —— there, Sir Lucius —— there. (*Puts himself in an attitude*) —— a side-front, hey? —— Odd! I'll make myself small enough: —— I'll stand edge-ways.

SIR LUCIUS O'TRIGGER: Now —— you're quite out —— for if you stand so when I take my aim —— (*Levelling at him*)

ACRES: Z—nds! Sir Lucius — are you sure it's not cock'd?

SIR LUCIUS O'TRIGGER: Never fear.

ACRES: But —— but —— you don't know — it may go off of its own head!

SIR LUCIUS O'TRIGGER: Pho! be easy — Well, now, if I hit you in the body, my bullet has a double chance —— for if it misses a vital part on your right side —— 'twill be very hard if it don't succeed on the left.

ACRES: A vital part! O, my poor vitals![1]

SIR LUCIUS O'TRIGGER: But, there —— fix yourself so —— (*Placing him*) let him see the broad side of your full front —— there — now a ball or two may pass clear thro' your body, and never do any harm at all.

ACRES: Clean thro' me! —— a ball or two clean thro' me!

SIR LUCIUS O'TRIGGER: Aye —— may they —— and it is much the genteelest attitude into the bargain.

ACRES: Look'ee! Sir Lucius —— I'd just as lieve be shot in an aukward posture as a genteel one —— so, by my valour, I will stand edge-ways.

SIR LUCIUS O'TRIGGER: (*Looking at his watch*) Sure they don't mean to disappoint us —— Hah? —— no faith — I think I see them coming.

ACRES: Hey! —— what! —— coming! ——

SIR LUCIUS O'TRIGGER: Aye —— Who are those yonder getting over the stile?

ACRES: There are two of them, indeed; —— well — let them come —— hey, Sir Lucius! —— we — we — we — we — won't run. ——

SIR LUCIUS O'TRIGGER: Run!

ACRES: No —— I say —— we *won't* run, by my valour!

SIR LUCIUS O'TRIGGER: What the devil's the matter with you?

ACRES: Nothing —— nothing —— my dear friend —— my dear Sir Lucius —— but —— I — I — I don't feel quite so bold, somehow —— as I did.

SIR LUCIUS O'TRIGGER: O fie! —— consider your honour.

ACRES: Aye —— true —— my honour —— Do, Sir Lucius, edge in a word or two every now and then about my honour.

SIR LUCIUS O'TRIGGER: Well, here they're coming. (*Looking*)

ACRES: Sir Lucius —— if I wa'n't with you, I should almost think I was afraid —— if my valour should leave me! —— Valour will come and go.

SIR LUCIUS O'TRIGGER: Then, pray keep it fast, while you have it.

ACRES: Sir Lucius —— I doubt it is going —— yes —— my valour is certainly going! —— it is sneaking off! —— I feel it oozing out as it were at the palms of my hands!

SIR LUCIUS O'TRIGGER: Your honour —— your honour —— Here they are.

1. The last sentence was cut in the third edition.

ACRES: O mercy! —— now —— that I were safe at *Clod-Hall*! or could be shot before I was aware!

Enter FAULKLAND *and* CAPTAIN ABSOLUTE

SIR LUCIUS O'TRIGGER: Gentlemen, your most obedient —— hah! —— what Captain Absolute! —— So, I suppose, Sir, you are come here, just like myself —— to do a kind office, first for your friend —— then to proceed to business on your own account.

ACRES: What, Jack! —— my dear Jack! —— my dear friend!

CAPTAIN ABSOLUTE: Hark'ee, Bob, Beverley's at hand.

SIR LUCIUS O'TRIGGER: Well, Mr. Acres —— I don't blame your saluting the gentleman civilly. —— So, Mr. Beverley, *(to* FAULKLAND) if you'll chuse your weapons, the Captain and I will measure the ground.

FAULKLAND: *My* weapons, Sir.

ACRES: Odds life! Sir Lucius, I'm not going to fight Mr. Faulkland; these are my particular friends.

SIR LUCIUS O'TRIGGER: What, Sir, did not you come here to fight Mr. Acres?

FAULKLAND: Not I, upon my word, Sir.

SIR LUCIUS O'TRIGGER: Well, now, that's mighty provoking! But I hope, Mr. Faulkland, as there are three of us come on purpose for the game —— you won't be so cantanckerous as to spoil the party by sitting out.

CAPTAIN ABSOLUTE: O pray, Faulkland, fight to oblige Sir Lucius.

FAULKLAND: Nay, if Mr. Acres is so bent on the matter.

ACRES: No, no, Mr. Faulkland —— I'll bear my disappointment like a Christian —— Look'ee, Sir Lucius, there's no occasion at all for me to fight; and if it is the same to you, I'd as lieve let it alone.

SIR LUCIUS O'TRIGGER: Observe me, Mr. Acres —— I must not be trifled with. You have certainly challenged somebody — and you came here to fight him — Now, if that gentleman is willing to represent him — I can't see, for my soul, why it isn't just the same thing.

ACRES: Z—ds, Sir Lucius — I tell you, 'tis one Beverley I've challenged —— a fellow, you see, that dare not shew his face! If *he* were here, I'd make him give up his pretensions directly. ——

CAPTAIN ABSOLUTE: Hold, Bob — let me set you right — there is no such man as Beverley in the case. —— The person who assumed that name is before you; and as his pretensions are the same in both characters, he is ready to support them in whatever way you please.

SIR LUCIUS O'TRIGGER: Well, this is lucky —— Now you have an opportunity —

ACRES: What, quarrel with my dear friend Jack Absolute — not if he were fifty Beverley's! Z—ds, Sir Lucius, you would not have me be so unnatural.

SIR LUCIUS O'TRIGGER: Upon my conscience, Mr. Acres, your valour has *oozed* away with a vengeance!

ACRES: Not in the least! Odds Backs and Abbettors! I'll be your second with all my heart — and if you should get a *Quietus*, you may command me entirely. I'll get you a *snug lying* in the *Abbey here*; or *pickle* you, and send you over to Blunderbuss-hall, or any thing of the kind with the greatest pleasure.

SIR LUCIUS O'TRIGGER: Pho! pho! you are little better than a coward.

ACRES: Mind, gentlemen, he calls me a *Coward*; Coward was the word, by my valour!

SIR LUCIUS O'TRIGGER: Well, Sir?

ACRES: Look'ee, Sir Lucius, 'tisn't that I mind the word Coward — *Coward* may be said in joke. — But if you had call'd me a *Poltroon,* Odds Daggers and Balls!

SIR LUCIUS O'TRIGGER: Well, Sir?

ACRES: —— I should have thought you a very ill-bred man.

SIR LUCIUS O'TRIGGER: Pho! you are beneath my notice.

CAPTAIN ABSOLUTE: Nay, Sir Lucius, you can't have a better second than my friend Acres — He is a most *determined dog* —— call'd in the country, *Fighting Bob.* —— He generally *kills* a *man a week*; don't you, Bob?

ACRES: Aye — at home.

SIR LUCIUS O'TRIGGER: Well then, Captain, 'tis we must begin — so come out my little counsellor (*draws his sword*) and ask the gentleman, whether he will resign the lady, without forcing you to proceed against him?

CAPTAIN ABSOLUTE: Come on then, Sir; (*draws*) since you won't let it be an amicable suit, here's *my reply*.

Enter SIR ANTHONY, DAVID, *and the* WOMEN

DAVID: Knock 'em all down, sweet Sir Anthony, knock down my Master in particular — and bind his hands over to their good behaviour.

SIR ANTHONY: Put up, Jack, put up, or I shall be

in a frenzy — how came you in a duel, Sir?

CAPTAIN ABSOLUTE: Faith, Sir, that gentleman can tell you better than I; 'twas he call'd on me, and you know, Sir, I serve his Majesty.

SIR ANTHONY: Here's a pretty fellow; I catch him going to cut a man's throat, and he tells me, he serves his Majesty! —— Zounds, sirrah, then how durst you draw the King's sword against one of his subjects?

CAPTAIN ABSOLUTE: Sir, I tell you! That gentleman call'd me out, without explaining his reasons.

SIR ANTHONY: Gad! Sir, how came you to call my son out, without explaining your reasons?

SIR LUCIUS O'TRIGGER: Your son, Sir, insulted me in a manner which my honour could not brook.

SIR ANTHONY: Zounds! Jack, how durst you insult the gentleman in a manner which his honour could not brook?

MRS. MALAPROP: Come, come, let's have no Honour before ladies — Captain Absolute, come here — How could you intimidate us so? —— Here's Lydia has been terrified to death for you.

CAPTAIN ABSOLUTE: For fear I should be kill'd, or escape, Ma'am?

MRS. MALAPROP: Nay, no delusions[2] to the past —— Lydia is convinc'd; speak child.

SIR LUCIUS O'TRIGGER: With your leave, Ma'am, I must put in a word here —— I believe I could interpret the young lady's silence —— Now mark. —

LYDIA: What is it you mean, Sir?

SIR LUCIUS O'TRIGGER: Come, come, Delia, we must be serious now —— this is no time for trifling.

LYDIA: 'Tis true, Sir; and your reproof bids me offer this gentleman my hand, and solicit the return of his affections.

CAPTAIN ABSOLUTE: O! my little angel, say you so? —— Sir Lucius —— I perceive there must be some mistake here —— with regard to the affront which you affirm I have given you —— I can only say, that it could not have been intentional —— And as you must be convinced, that I should not fear to support a real injury —— you shall now see that I am not ashamed to atone for an inadvertency —— I ask your pardon. —— But for this lady, while honour'd with her approbation, I will support my claim against any man whatever.

SIR ANTHONY: Well said, Jack, and I'll stand by you, my Boy.

ACRES: Mind, I give up all my claim —— I make no pretensions to any thing in the world —— and if I can't get a wife, without fighting for her, by my Valour! I'll live a bachelor.

SIR LUCIUS O'TRIGGER: Captain, give me your hand —— an affront handsomely acknowledged becomes an obligation — and as for the Lady — if she chuses to deny her own hand writing here — (*Taking out letters*)

MRS. MALAPROP: O, he will dissolve[3] my mystery! — Sir Lucius, perhaps there's some mistake — perhaps, I can illuminate —

SIR LUCIUS O'TRIGGER: Pray, old gentlewoman, don't interefere, where you have no business. — Miss Languish, are you my Delia, or not?

LYDIA: Indeed, Sir Lucius, I am not.

LYDIA and CAPTAIN ABSOLUTE *walk aside*

MRS. MALAPROP: Sir Lucius O'Trigger —— ungrateful as you are —— I own the soft impeachment —— pardon my blushes, I am Delia.

SIR LUCIUS O'TRIGGER: You Delia —— pho! pho! be easy.

MRS. MALAPROP: Why, thou barbarous Vandyke.[4] —— those letters are mine —— When you are more sensible of my benignity —— perhaps I may be brought to encourage your addresses.

SIR LUCIUS O'TRIGGER: Mrs. Malaprop, I am extremely sensible of your condescension; and whether you or Lucy have put this trick upon me, I am equally beholden to you. —— And to shew you I'm not ungrateful, Captain Absolute! since you have taken that lady from me, I'll give you my Delia into the bargain.

CAPTAIN ABSOLUTE: I am much obliged to you, Sir Lucius; but here's our friend, fighting Bob, unprovided for.

SIR LUCIUS O'TRIGGER: Ha! little Valour —— here, will you make your fortune?

ACRES: Odds Wrinkles! No. —— But give us your hand, Sir Lucius, forget and forgive: but if ever I give you a chance of *pickling* me again, say Bob Acres is a Dunce, that's all.

SIR ANTHONY: Come, Mrs. Malaprop, don't be cast down —— you are in your bloom yet.

MRS. MALAPROP: O Sir Anthony! —— men are all barbarians —

2. for 'allusions'.

3. for 'resolve'.

4. Possibly 'vandal'.

All retire but JULIA *and* FAULKLAND

JULIA: He seems dejected and unhappy — not sullen —— there was some foundation, however, for the tale he told me —— O woman! how true should be your judgment, when your resolution is so weak!

FAULKLAND: Julia! — how can I sue for what I so little deserve? I dare not presume —— yet Hope is the child of Penitence.

JULIA: Oh! Faulkland, you have not been more faulty in your unkind treatment of me, than I am now in wanting[5] inclination to resent it. As my heart honestly bids me place my weakness to the account of love, I should be ungenerous not to admit the same plea for your's.

FAULKLAND: Now I shall be blest indeed!

SIR ANTHONY *comes forward*

SIR ANTHONY: What's going on here? —— So you have been quarrelling too, I warrant. —— Come, Julia, I never interfered before; but let me have a hand in the matter at last. —— All the faults I have ever seen in my friend Faulkland, seemed to proceed from what he calls the *delicacy* and *warmth* of his affection for you —— There, marry him directly, Julia, you'll find he'll mend surprisingly!

The rest come forward

SIR LUCIUS O'TRIGGER: Come now, I hope there is no dissatisfied person, but what is content; for as I have been disappointed myself, it will be very hard if I have not the satisfaction of seeing other people succeed better ——

ACRES: You are right, Sir Lucius. — So, Jack, I wish you joy — Mr. Faulkland the same. — Ladies, —— come now, to shew you I'm neither vex'd nor angry, Odds Tabors and Pipes! I'll order the fiddles in half an hour, to the New Rooms — and I insist on you all meeting me there.

SIR ANTHONY: Gad! Sir, I like your spirit; and at night we single lads will drink a health to the young couples, and a husband to Mrs. Malaprop.

FAULKLAND: Our partners are stolen from us, Jack — I hope to be congratulated by each other — yours for having checked in time, the errors of an ill-directed Imagination, which might have betray'd an innocent heart; and mine, for having, by her gentleness and candour, reformed the unhappy temper of one, who by it made wretched whom he loved most, and tortur'd the heart he ought to have ador'd.

5. lacking.

CAPTAIN ABSOLUTE: Well, Faulkland, we have both tasted the Bitters, as well as the Sweets, of Love — with this difference only, that *you* always prepared the bitter cup for yourself, while *I* ——

LYDIA: Was always obliged to *me* for it, hey! Mr. Modesty? —— But come, no more of that — our happiness is now as unallay'd as general.

JULIA: Then let us study to preserve it so: and while Hope pictures to us a flattering scene of future Bliss, let us deny its pencil those colours which are too bright to be lasting. —— When Hearts deserving Happiness would unite their fortunes, Virtue would crown them with an unfading garland of modest, hurtless flowers; but ill-judging Passion will force the gaudier Rose into the wreath, whose thorn offends them, when its Leaves are dropt!

FINIS

EPILOGUE

By the author

Spoken by Mrs. BULKLEY[1]

Ladies, for *You* — I heard our Poet say —
He'd try to coax some *Moral* from his Play:
'One moral's plain' — cried I — 'without more fuss;
Man's social happiness all rests on Us —
Thro' all the Drama — whether d—n'd or not —
Love gilds the *Scene*, and *Women* guide the *plot*.
From every rank — obedience is our due —
D'ye doubt? — The world's great stage shall prove it true.'
The Cit[2] — well skill'd to shun domestic strife —
Will sup abroad; — but first — he'll ask his *wife*:
John Trot,[3] his friend — for once will do the same,
But then — he'll just *step home to tell my dame*. —
The *surly 'Squire* — at noon resolves to rule,
And half the day — Zounds! Madam is a fool!
Convinc'd at night — the vanquish'd Victor says,
Ah! Kate! *you women have such coaxing ways!* —
The *jolly Toper* chides each tardy blade, —
Till reeling Bacchus calls on Love for aid:
Then with each Toast, he sees fair bumpers swim,
And kisses Chloe on the sparkling Brim!

1. Mary Bulkley (1748-92), the actress, who played Julia in the first production; she had also played Kate Hardcastle in *She Stoops to Conquer* in 1773.
2. citizen, a type commonly satirized in English comedy.
3. i.e. an awkward fellow. In George Etherege's *The Man of Mode* (1676), Sir Fopling Flutter has a footman called John Trott, of whom he remarks: 'There's nothing so barbarous as the names of our English servants' (III.3).

Nay, I have heard, that Statesmen — great and wise —
Will *sometimes* counsel with a Lady's eyes;
The servile suitors — watch her various face,
She smiles preferment — or she frowns disgrace,
Curtsies a pension here — there nods a place.
Nor with less awe, in scenes of humbler life,
Is *view'd* the *mistress,* or is *heard* the *wife.*
The poorest Peasant of the poorest soil,
The child of Poverty, and heir to Toil —
Early from radiant Love's impartial light,
Steals one small spark, to cheer his world of night:
Dear spark! — that oft thro' winter's chilling woes,
Is all the warmth his little cottage knows!
The wand'ring *Tar*[4] — who, not for *years,* has press'd
The widow'd Partner of his *day* of rest —
On the cold deck — far from her arms remov'd —
Still hums the ditty which his Susan lov'd:
And while around the cadence rude is blown,
The Boatswain whistles in a softer tone.
The *Soldier,* fairly proud of wounds and toil,
Pants for the *triumph* of his Nancy's smile;
But ere the battle should he list' her cries,
The Lover trembles — and the Hero dies!
That heart, by war and honour steel'd to fear,
Droops on a sigh, and sickens at a tear!
But ye more cautious — ye nice judging few,
Who give to Beauty only Beauty's due,
Tho' friends to Love — *Ye* view with deep regret
Our conquests marr'd — our triumphs incomplete,
'Till polish'd Wit more lasting charms disclose,
And Judgment fix the darts which Beauty throws!
— In female breasts did Sense and Merit rule,
The Lover's mind would ask no other school;
Sham'd into sense — the Scholars of our eyes,
Our Beaux from *Gallantry* would soon be wise;
Would gladly light, their homage to improve,
The Lamp of Knowledge at the Torch of Love!

4. sailor.

JOHN O'KEEFFE

(1747-1833)

from: TONY LUMPKIN IN TOWN (1780)

[Drawing both on Goldsmith's established characterization and on the experience familiar in comedy ever since Farquhar's *Love and a Bottle* (1698) of the awkward countryman let loose in polite London society, O'Keeffe manages tactfully to sidestep the stage Irishman in order to create a jolly little farce, enlivened by Tony Lumpkin's boorishness.]

ACT I, SCENE 2

A Chamber

MR. JONQUIL *discovered in a morning undress,* FRANK *attending with chocolate*

MR. JONQUIL: Frank, has your lady quitted her apartment?

FRANK: Yes, sir, I think I heard Mrs. Lavender say —— Oh, sir, here is my lady.

Exit

Enter MRS. JONQUIL *and* LAVENDER

MR. JONQUIL: A good morning to you, my dear.

MRS. JONQUIL: Thank you, love. Lavender, give those cards to Pompey, and desire him to deliver them agreeable to[1] their address. I have an immensity of visits, but must pay them this morning in paper;[2] or, (*to a lap-dog, which* LAVENDER *carries under her arm*) Shock you dear polite toad, will you take the chair, and be my representative to the ladies?

Exit LAVENDER

Oh, my head! such a night! Mr. Jonquil, when did you break up at the masquerade?

MR. JONQUIL: I fancy, my dear, 'twas five.

MRS. JONQUIL: I might as well have accompanied you there, for I counted the clock 'till four. A masquerade to this house[3] last night, was a quaker's meeting. Such a noise and uproar!

MR. JONQUIL: Uproar! what was the matter?

MRS. JONQUIL: Only your cousin Tony holding his nocturnal revels.

MR. JONQUIL: Tony! So, so, 'twas here he came,

1. according to.
2. in curlers.
3. compared to.

when he slipped from me at the Pantheon.[4]

MRS. JONQUIL: Yes, here he came indeed; and such a ball as he held with the bear and the servants, and the mob out of the street, I believe!

Enter LAVENDER

LAVENDER: Madam, I'm sorry I'm obliged to complain of a servant, but don't blame me, ma'am; but indeed there's no such thing as living in the house.

MRS. JONQUIL: What's all this?

LAVENDER: Why ma'am, Mr. Diggory, 'Squire Lumpkin's man, ran into your ladyship's dressing-room, and snatched your cold cream off the toilet.[5]

MR. JONQUIL: Ha! ha! ha! what in the name of delicacy could Diggory want with the cold cream?

LAVENDER: He said it would do to oil his wig, sir.

MR. JONQUIL: Ha! ha! ha! ha!

MRS. JONQUIL: Nay, but Mr. Jonquil, this is beyond bearing. I'll assure you I'll ——

MR. JONQUIL: Come, my dear, don't be discomposed, 'twill soon be at an end.

Exit LAVENDER

Let me see what time his mother proposes to be in town, for I think she says she'll take a house for him. I have her letter here. I wish he was in a house of his own, from my soul, for in a fortnight I should not know mine from a carrier's inn.

MRS. JONQUIL: What gives me most singular amazement, is that you chuse to be seen in public with him.

MR. JONQUIL: I grant he is not the most eligible companion for a man of fashion: but at a masquerade I was safe from censure, for every body imagined the uncouthness of his appearance, and rusticity of his manners, merely the effect of his imitative genius. The company thought his behaviour all assumed, put on *pour l' occasion*; for he threw off his domino,[6] and I'll assure you, simple nature got him infinite reputation. He gaped at the masks, roared most stentoriously discordant with the music; overset the pyramids, pocketed the sweetmeats, broke the glasses, made love to an Arcadian dairy maid, tripped up the heels of a harlequin, beat a hermit, who happened to be a captain in the guards, and gave a bishop a black eye.

4. One of the best-known late-eighteenth-century assembly rooms, where masquerades and light entertainments were held. Under the patent laws, it was refused permission to hold theatrical productions.

5. dressing table.

6. eye-mask.

MRS. JONQUIL: But his mother's epistle; I languish to hear it.

MR. JONQUIL: I ask your pardon; here it is.

Takes out a letter and reads

'Dear Cousin,

In the bearer of this, I introduce to your care and friendship my dear son Tony. I'll assure you, cousin, Tony with your help will make a bright man, as he's already humoursome and comical. I shall be in town myself in about a fortnight, or three weeks, and then I intend taking a house for him, in some airy, fashionable part, somewhere near Duke's Place, as I'd have him near the King's Palace. No more at present from your loving cousin,

DOROTHEA HARDCASTLE

P.S. Mr. Hardcastle's and my love to cousin Emilia. I request you'll take Tony to Sadler's Wells,[7] as I'm sure he'll like operas'.

A horn sounds without

MRS. JONQUIL: Bless me, what's that?

MR. JONQUIL: Oh, that's Tony's summons for his man; he says he hates the ringing of bells, therefore has invented that polite substitute.

TONY *calls without*

TONY: Hollo, Diggory, hollo.

MR. JONQUIL: Oh, here he comes.

TONY: (*Without*) Hollo! slap up the bear here.

MRS. JONQUIL: Heaven defend us, sure he won't drive in a bear here!

MR. JONQUIL: No, no, my dear, don't be alarmed.

TONY: (*Without*) Come along Bruin.

Enter TONY LUMPKIN

Come in; I long to introduce Bruin to my relations. Cousin Milly, will you see the bear, ma'am, if you please?

MRS. JONQUIL: Bear! oh heavens! *Runs off*

TONY: Cousin Milly's very timbersome, sure; Bruin is a mighty civil beast; why he's as gentle as the good-natured lion in the Tower, that lets the dog lie in his den with him.

MR. JONQUIL: I don't entertain a doubt of his politeness or good-nature; but you'll eternally oblige me by sending him down.

TONY: Now would it oblige you in downright earnest?

MR. JONQUIL: Beyond measure.

7. Not an opera house but a 'minor' theatre, one licensed only for non-legitimate theatre and also, notoriously, for the sale of alcohol.

TONY: Tim, walk Bruin down again: bid him first make his honours at the door tho'. Come here — only, cousin, look —— only look at him. Servant, sir;[8] why he learned among the grown gentlemen at Hatton-garden. Ah do now let him in, and he, and I, and you, will dance the hay.[9] He's muzzled! Tim, an't he muzzled?

TIM: (*Without*) Yes, Sir.

TONY: Oh! then there's no danger; you see he cou'dn't bite you, if he had a mind; he can only scratch you a little.

MR. JONQUIL: Gads curse, but I'm not dispos'd to be scratch'd this morning.

TONY: Oh! very well; any other time. Only say the word, and Bruin's the boy for it. Slap him down, lad.

MR. JONQUIL: I wish the Devil had you and him together. Such a fellow! —— Mr. Lumpkin, have you a fancy for this house?

TONY: Anan?[10]

MR. JONQUIL: I say, do you like this house?

TONY: Like it? for certain I do.

MR. JONQUIL: Then to you and the bear, I must absolutely resign it.

TONY: I thank you for your kind offer; but if you was to give me your house, and your pyebalds, and your visee vie,[11] I would not thank you; because them that give all, give nothing at all. But indeed if you'd let me bring in a little queen with me some night or other, unknown to cousin Milly, you'd make me as happy as a king.

MR. JONQUIL: Oh, fie!

TONY: Oh fie! Baw! shake hands! Why don't you get drunk sometimes? It's mighty pleasant! ay, and very wholesome, once a week. Dr. What-d'ye call-um says so, in the book that lies in my mama's window: what say you to a bout, cousin, ha?

MR. JONQUIL: Excuse me; drinking is, in my opinion, the most savage and barbarous method, that ever brutality invented, to murder time and intellects.

TONY: By jingo, then mama is the first time-killer within ten miles of Quagmire Marsh:[12] Oh! she loves a sup dearly.

MR. JONQUIL: For shame! Mr. Lumpkin.

TONY: Oh! take me, it's all in the genteel way, tho'; for my mama alway's sipp'd her cordial out of a tea-pot; and then, before folks, it was only a drop of cold tea, you know.

MR. JONQUIL: Ha, ha, ha!

TONY: Ay, and Cousin Con, Miss Nevill, that was courting me, used to drink like a glass-blower, all in the sentimental way: Over a love-story book, she and my mama wou'd read and sip till it came out of their eyes. Sure Cousin Con was in love with me; Oh! how sweetly she'd kiss me after a chapter of Mildmay,[13] and a twist of the tea-pot.

MR. JONQUIL: Yes, yes, what I've always found; curse me! if there's a woman in the world easier had, than the die-away romantic novelist.

TONY: (*Aside*) How fine I tell lies! he swallows them like syllabub.[14]

MR. JONQUIL: But you gave me the slip last night, at the Pantheon; why did not you wait for supper?

TONY: Why, I love my supper as well as any body, especially after a day's hunting; because then we have something to talk of. But the snug way for my money;[15] and we had our own gig[16] here at home: I never saw the bear so airy.

MR. JONQUIL: But what think you of the splendour of the Pantheon? Is'n't it the temple of Elegance? an Olympus hall, worthy the gods to revel in?

TONY: Gods do you call 'em? I took some of 'em for rascals. A fool of a fellow would have it, that I was a lady; now I am sure I have not a bit of the lady about me, except the softness of my voice: but the monkey was a macaroni;[17] and those beaux, I fancy, make as much use of a woman, as they do of a sword; they keep both merely for shew. Oh, now I talk of that, by jingo, I saw a power of fine shews yesterday, o'top of Ludgate-hill.

MR. JONQUIL: Shews?

TONY: Ay, I believe I've seen all the fine shews now; aye, Gog and Magog, St. Paul's and the Tower, and the high post near the bridge, that's going to fall upon the neighbours' heads; and I've seen a hanging, and a house on fire; and I paid a

8. Tony returns a bow to the (offstage) bear.
9. 'A country dance having a winding or serpentine movement, or being of the nature of a reel' (*OED*).
10. An interrogation: 'What did you say?'
11. vis-à-vis: a fashionable horse-drawn carriage.
12. In *She Stoops to Conquer*, I. 2., Tony Lumpkin tells Marlow and Hastings that Hardcastle lives at Quagmire Marsh. See p. 576.
13. Hugh Kelly, *Memoirs of a Magdalen, or, The History of Louisa Mildmay* (2 vols, 1767).
14. A dish made of cream or milk flavoured, sweetened, and whipped to thicken it.
15. (dialect) the comfortable way is my preference.
16. (dialect) fun or frolic.
17. fop.

halfpenny to walk over the Thames at Blackfriars; and I eat calves-head turtle, opposite the Bank: and saw Lord Thingumme's fine coach, and the Lilliputian Patagonians, and the stock-brokers on 'Change; the mad folks in Bedlam, and the actor folks at the play-houses; one of the play men at What-d'ye-call-it play-house was very like you, and ——

MR. JONQUIL: But, Mr. Lumpkin, I imagine 'tis time for you to begin to dress. (*Aside*) Some of the *Scavoir Vivre*[18] and *Dilettanti* dine with me to-day, and you'll be a precious exhibition.

TONY: Ay, ay, I'll be as fine as the sheriff's horse, by-and-by.

Enter DIGGORY *in a new livery; and struts in an awkward conceited manner, across the stage.* TONY *leads him by the arm back to the door*

Get out!

DIGGORY: Why, sure, 'Squire, you'll be proud enough yourself of your new clothes when you get into them.

TONY: Yes; but there's difference between the miller and his dog. (*Aside*) Pray know your distance; and I desire, Diggory, you'll never dare to be so superstitious[19] with me, before company.

DIGGORY: Well, I won't.

TONY: You won't? —— I think you might call me, my honour; and not waste much of your manners.

DIGGORY: If that's the case, there's all kinds of nice tradesfolks, and ingenious learners,[20] of all sizes, waiting below for My Honour.

TONY: Your Honour, you cuckold, it's my honour they want.

DIGGORY: I'll tell them so, sir; your honour, I mean.

Exit

TONY: Well, now, cousin, I'll go; and ——

MR. JONQUIL: Sir, Mr. Lumpkin, I have a trifling request to make.

TONY: What is it? I'll give you any thing you ask.

MR. JONQUIL: That you will dress with all possible celerity; for I languish to see you one of us.

TONY: Hollo, for lace and powder. Hollo, Diggory; hey, for grandeur — yoics[21] — hark forward, taylors, milliners, and glorious haberdashers! hollo, hollo!

MR. JONQUIL: Such a fellow! — makes more noise than a kennel of hounds.

Exit

18. know-it-alls.
19. superior, extraordinary.
20. i.e. willing to learn Tony's wishes; or else, 'teachers', e.g. of dancing etc.
21. A hunting cry.

from: THE POOR SOLDIER (1783)

[This may not be an inappropriate piece with which to conclude the present survey of Irish drama before 1800. At one extreme there is Farquhar's *The Recruiting Officer,* vigorous, combative, fully alive; at the other there is *The Poor Soldier,* innocuous, sentimental, somewhat artificial. O'Keeffe's *Wild Oats* (1791) might have served also to make this contrast, and it is a play that was rescued from obscurity by the Royal Shakespeare Company in 1976. But *Wild Oats,* for all its theatricality, is not a musical, and O'Keeffe is best understood as a writer of musical farces.

Ever since the outstanding success of John Gay's *The Beggar's Opera* (1728), eighteenth-century audiences clamoured for musicals and ballad operas. O'Keeffe, a Dubliner, was but one of dozens of authors in the second half of the century who endeared himself to the London public by his farces set to music. These were afterpieces, meant to bolster up the repertory of legitimate drama, but they supply a key, nevertheless, to public taste. Because O'Keeffe sometimes used Irish airs in his farces, it is possible to describe him as the equivalent of the poet Thomas Moore, another charmer in his own day but now rather out of fashion. Even that comparison, however, may be to set O'Keeffe too high in esteem: he was essentially, and willingly, a popular hack.

If O'Keeffe's work was slight, however, it nevertheless was transitional. In the lilting rhythms of his dialogue one may discern the Irish facility with language, and the Irish love of pastoral, here somewhat debased. In the nineteenth century, Dion Boucicault (1820-90) was to build on these popular traits and lead Irish drama on to its next phase, romantic melodrama.

In this extract, Pat, the 'poor soldier', returns from the wars (in colonial America) to meet his sweetheart Norah and all his carefree but apparently musical friends.]

ACT I, SCENE 1

The Country

View of two Cottages

DARBY, *without*

Now what harm, Dermot?

DERMOT, *without*

Why 'tis harm, so stay where you are.

Enter DERMOT *and* DARBY

DARBY: Upon my faith, I won't say a word.

DERMOT: Go along back, I tell you.

DARBY: Lud, I never saw such a man as you are; sure I'll only stand by.

DERMOT: But I tell you it's not proper for any one to be by, when one's along with one's sweetheart.

DARBY: Well, I always like to be by when I'm along with my sweetheart, — she's asleep, — I'll call her up, —— Hollo, Kathleen!

Calls at the Cottage

DERMOT: Will you be quiet, Darby? Can't you go make a noise there under Father Luke's Window?

DARBY: Ecod if I do, he'll put me in the Bishop's Court.

DERMOT: If I wasn't so fond of Kathleen, I should think Norah, his niece there, a very handsome girl.

DARBY: Why so she is; but since her own sweetheart Patrick, full of ale and vexation, went for a soldier, she don't care a pin for the prettiest of us; by the law, she even turned up her nose at me.

DERMOT: Well, well, you'll see how it will be; somebody I know. —

DARBY: Aye, you mean the foreign serving man to the strange officer, that's just come from America, and is now above at my Lord's —— Eh! why faith, Dermot, it would indeed be a shame to let a black muzzled Mounseer of a Frenchman, carry off a pretty Girl from a parcel of tight Irish boys of us.

DERMOT: So 'twou'd, Darby: but my sweet Kathleen is fast asleep, and never dreams that her poor Dermot is here under her Window.

DARBY: Ay, never dreams that poor Darby's under her Window; but I'll have her up, —— Kathleen, — Kathleen ——

DERMOT: Hush.

AIR I

Sleep on, sleep on, my Kathleen dear,
May peace possess thy breast;
Yet dost thou dream thy true love's here,
Depriv'd of peace and rest?

II

The birds sing sweet, the morning breaks,
Those joys are none to me;
Tho' sleep is fled, poor Dermot wakes,
To none but love and thee.

Exit DERMOT

DARBY: What a dull dog that is! — Ah! poor Dermot, ha, ha; why such a song cou'dn't wake an owl out of his sleep; let alone a pretty girl that's dreaming of me! Upon my conscience I'll —— yes, I'll rouse her.

AIR II

Dear Kathleen, you, no doubt,
Fine sleep how very sweet 'tis;
Dogs bark, and cocks have crowed out,
You never dream how late 'tis.
This morning gay,
I post away,
To have with you a bit of play,
On two legs rid
Along to bid
Good morrow to your night cap.

II

Last night a little bowzy,
With whiskey, ale, and cyder,
I ask'd young Betty Blowsey,
To let me sit beside her,
Her anger rose,
And sour as sloes,
The little gipsy cock'd her nose:
Yet here I've rid,
Along to bid,
Good morrow to your night cap.

(KATHLEEN *opens her Window,* DARBY *looks up*)

DARBY: Ay there she is — Oh, I'm the Boy for it!

KATHLEEN: Is that Dermot?

DARBY: Oh, dear me, she takes me for Dermot, he, he.

KATHLEEN: Who's there?

DARBY: Sure it's only I.

KATHLEEN: What, Dermot?

DARBY: Yes, I am, —— (*Aside*) Darby.

KATHLEEN: Stay a bit, I'm coming down. (*Retires*)

DARBY: I'll bring her down; I'm a nice marksman.

Enter KATHLEEN, *from the Cottage*

KATHLEEN: Where are you my dear Dermot?

DARBY: (*Comes forward*) 'Good morrow to your night cap.'

KATHLEEN: Darby! now, hang you for an impudent fellow.

DARBY: Then hang me about your neck, my sweet Kathleen.

KATHLEEN: It's a fine thing that people can't take their rest of a morning, but you must come roaring under their Windows.

DARBY: Now, what need you be so cross with a body, when you know I love you too?

KATHLEEN: Well, let me alone, Darby? for once for all, I tell you, I will not have you.

DARBY: No!

KATHLEEN: No; as I hope for man, I won't.

DARBY: Ha, ha, ha, hope for man, and yet won't have me!

KATHLEEN: Yes, but I'll tell you what sort of a man; then look in the river, and see if you are he.

DARBY: And if not, I'll pop in head foremost.

KATHLEEN: Do, Darby, and then you may whistle for me.

DARBY: How can I whistle when the speak's out of me?

KATHLEEN:

AIR III

Since love is the plan,
I'll love if I can,
But first let me tell you what sort of a man;
In address how compleat
And in dress spruce and neat.
No matter how tall, so he's over five feet:
Not dull nor too witty,
His eyes I'll think pretty,
If sparkling with pleasure whenever we meet.

II

Tho's gentle he be
His man he shall see,
Yet never be conquer'd by any but me.
In a song bear a bob,
In a glass a hob nob,
Yet drink of his reason his noddle ne'er rob.
This is my Fancy,
If such a man can see,
I'm his if he's mine; until then I am free.

DARBY: So then you won't have me?

KATHLEEN: No, that I won't.

DARBY: Why, I'm a better match for you than Dermot.

KATHLEEN: No.

DARBY: No! hav'n't I every thing comfortable about me? cows, sheep, geese, and turkeys, for you to look after the week days, and a pretty pad[1] for you to ride to chapel on a Sunday; a nice little cabin for you to live in, and a neat bit of a potato garden for you to walk in, and for a husband, I'm as pretty a lad as you'd meet with of a long Summer's day.

KATHLEEN: Get along; don't talk to me of your geese, and your turkeys, man, with your conceit and your nonsense. —— You know, Darby, I'm an heiress, and so take your answer, you're no match for me.

1. a road-horse, a nag.

DARBY: An heiress! why tho' your father, old Jorum, that kept the Harp and Crown, left you well enough in the world, as a body may say, yet ——

KATHLEEN: Well enough! you disparaging Fellow! didn't my Father leave me a fortune of eleven pounds, a barrel of Ale upon draught, the dappled Mare, besides the furniture of the whole House which prais'd to a matter of thirty-eight shillings? Well enough, indeed!

DARBY: Nay, but Kathleen ——

KATHLEEN: Well enough! And didn't he leave me the bald filley, you puppy?

DARBY: Ay, now she is got upon the bald filley, the devil wou'dn't take her down.

DARBY *and* KATHLEEN ——*Duett*

AIR IV

KATHLEEN: *Out of my sight, or I'll box your ears.*
DARBY: *I'll fit you soon for your jibes and jeers.*
KATHLEEN: *I'll cock my cap at a smart young man.*
DARBY: *Another I'll wed this day if I can.*
KATHLEEN: —— *In courtship funny,*
DARBY: —— *One sweet as honey!*
KATHLEEN: —— *You drone.*
DARBY: *No, Kate, I am your humble bee,*
KATHLEEN: *Go dance your dogs with your fiddle dee dee.*
For a sprightly lad is the man for me.
DARBY: *You'll never meet such a kind soul as me.*

II

KATHLEEN: *Like sweet milk turn'd, to me now seems love.*
DARBY: *The fragrant rose does a nettle prove.*
KATHLEEN: *Sour curds I taste, tho' sweet cream I chuse.*
DARBY: *And with a flow'r I sting my nose.*
In courtship, &c.

Exeunt severally

Enter CAPTAIN FITZROY

FITZROY: Aye, here's Father Luke's house. — I doubt if his charming niece is up yet. — I shall be back before the family are stirring; the beauty and freshness of the morning exhilarates and delights. (*Horns sound at a distance*) Going out with the hounds; — but my game lies another way.

AIR V

The twins of Latona, so kind to my boon,
Arise to partake of the chase,
And Sol lends a ray to chaste Dian's fair moon,
And a smile to the smiles of her face.
For the sport I delight in, the bright Queen of love
With myrtles my brows shall adorn;

While Pan breaks his chaunter and skulks in the grove,
Excell'd by the sound of the Horn.
The dogs are uncoupled, and sweet is their cry,
Yet sweeter the notes of sweet Echo's reply:
Hard forward, my honies, the game is in view,
But love is the game that I wish to pursue.

II

The Stag from his Chamber of woodbine peeps out,
His sentence he hears in the Gale;
Yet flies, 'till entangled in fear and in doubt,
His courage and constancy fail.
Surrounded by foes he prepares for the fray,
Despair taking place of his fear;
With antlers erected, a while stands at bay,
Then surrenders his life with a tear.
The dogs are uncoupled, &c.

FATHER LUKE's *door opens*

FITZROY: 'Tis she. — I fear to speak, lest I should be observed by some of the Villagers.

Retires

Enter NORAH *from the House*

AIR VI

The meadows look chearful, the birds sweetly sing,
So gaily they carrol the praises of spring;
Tho' nature rejoices, poor Norah shall mourn,
Until her dear Patrick again shall return.

II

Ye lasses of Dublin, ah, hide your gay charms,
Nor lure her dear Patrick, from Norah's fond arms;
Tho' sattins and ribbons, and laces are fine,
They hide not a heart with such feelings as mine,

NORAH: If the grass is not too wet, perhaps Kathleen will take a walk with me. — Ah! she's gone to walk with her sweetheart Dermot: well, if Patrick hadn't forsook me, I should'n't now want a companion. — Oh, dear! here's the Gentleman that my uncle's always teizing me about.

FITZROY: A fine morning, madam; but your presence gives an additional lustre to the beauties of this charming scene.

NORAH: Sir!

FITZROY: Nay, do not avert those lovely eyes, — look kindly on me.

BAGATELLE: (*Without*) Oh, mon maitre! mon maitre!

NORAH: Do, Sir, permit me to withdraw; our village is very censorious; and a gentleman's being seen with me, will neither add to your honour nor my reputation.

Exit into the House

Scene, *another View of the Country*

Enter PATRICK

PATRICK: Well, here I am after all the dangers of war return'd to my native village, two years older than I went — not much wiser, up to the heart in love, and not a sixpence in my pocket. (DARBY *sings without*) Isn't that Darby? It is indeed, and as foolish as ever.

Enter DARBY

DARBY: Is it Pat? — my dear boy, you're welcome — you're welcome, my dear boy.

PATRICK: Thank you, Darby, but how are all friends since I left 'em?

DARBY: Finely, except one. —

PATRICK: Who's that?

DARBY: A cow of mine that died last Michaelmas.

PATRICK: But tell me, how is my dear Norah?

DARBY: As pretty as ever — *(Aside)* I must'n't tell him of the Mounseer that's about her house. 'Twas a shame for you Pat to turn soldier, and run away from her.

PATRICK: Cou'd I help it when her ill natur'd uncle refus'd me his consent, and she woud'nt marry me without it?

DARBY: Why, Father Luke's very cross, indeed, to us young lovers ? eh, Pat! But let's look at you — egad, you make a tight little Soldier enough.

PATRICK: Ay, Darby, a Soldier's the finest thing in the world.

AIR VIII

[*Tune, Little House under the Hill*]

How happy the Soldier who lives on his pay,
And spends half-a-crown out of six-pence a day!
Yet fears neither justices, warrants, nor bums,[2]
But pays all his debts with the roll of his drums.
With a row de-row, &c.

II

He cares not a marvedy[3] *how the world goes,*
The King finds him Quarters, and money and cloaths;
He laughs at all Sorrow whenever it comes,
And rattles away with the roll of his drums.
With a row de-row, &c.

III

The drum is his glory, his joy and delight,
It leads him to pleasures as well as to fight,
No girl when she hears it, tho' ever so glum,
But packs up her tatters, and follows the drum.
With a row de-row, &c.

2. bum-bailiffs (who arrested debtors).
3. maravedi — an old Spanish coin.

DARBY: Ah, you'll have Norah with your row de-dow. — Od, if I thought I could get Kathleen by turning soldier, I'd list[4] to-morrow morning.

PATRICK: Well, do, and I'll introduce you to the serjeant.

DARBY: Aye, do if you please — I think I'd look very pretty in a red coat, he! he! he! — Let's see how the Hat becomes me! (*takes* PAT's *hat off*) What's that?

Seeing the scar on PAT's *forehead*

PATRICK: Only a wound I got in battle.

DARBY: Take your hat, I don't think regimentals would become me at all.

PATRICK: Ha! ha! ha! What, terrified at a scar, eh Darby?

DARBY: Me terrified! not I — I don't mind twenty scars, only it looks so conceited for a man to have a black patch upon his face — But how did you get that beauty spot?

PATRICK: In my attempt to save the life of an officer, and there I was left for dead upon the field, bleeding in my country's cause.

DARBY: Left for dead!

PATRICK: There was glory for you, my boy.

DARBY: So, there they found you bleeding in your glory.

PATRICK: Come, now, I'll introduce you to the serjeant.

DARBY: Hem! yes I'm coming, sir.

PATRICK: Oh, yonder's the serjeant. — Where are you going?

DARBY: To meet him — I'll be with you presently, sir. — Glory — (*looking at* PAT) row de-row, &c.

Exit

PATRICK: Ha! ha! ha! — the sight of a wound is enough for poor Darby — but now to see my sweet Norah, and then for a pitcher of friendship with all my old companions. . . .

4. enlist.

TEXTUAL NOTE

Throughout this section, the first Dublin editions have been taken as copy-texts. They are as follows: George Farquhar, *The Recruiting Officer*, Dublin, 1722; *The Beaux' Stratagem*, Dublin, 1729; Richard Steele, *The Conscious Lovers*, Dublin, 1725; Thomas Sheridan, *The Brave Irishman*, Dublin, n.d.; Charles Macklin, *The True-Born Irishman*, Dublin, 1783; Arthur Murphy, *All in the Wrong*, Dublin, 1762; Hugh Kelly, *False Delicacy*, Dublin, 1768; *The School for Wives*, Dublin, 1774; Oliver Goldsmith, *She Stoops to Conquer*, Dublin 1773; Richard Sheridan, *The Rivals*, Dublin, 1773; John O'Keeffe, *Tony Lumpkin in Town*, Dublin, 1780; *The Poor Soldier*, Dublin, 1789.

Biographies/Bibliographies

George Farquhar

LIFE. Born in Derry, Northern Ireland, in 1677, the son of a clergyman; educated in Derry, at the Free Grammar School, under Ellis Walker. His father was burned out during the siege of Derry in 1689. It is said that Farquhar then joined the Williamite army in a spirit of revenge and fought at the battle of the Boyne in 1690. After further education, he entered Trinity College, Dublin, in 1694, as a sizar or servant-student. After about two years he left without a degree, to take up acting, at the Theatre Royal, Smock Alley, in Dublin. He made his debut as Othello, a role for which he was physically too slight, and thereafter was confined to minor roles, in one of which, Guyomar in John Dryden's *The Indian Emperor,* he forgot to change a sword for a foil and injured a fellow actor in a stage duel. This accident effectively ended his career as an actor, since he left Dublin for London soon afterwards (in late 1697) and returned to Smock Alley only once, in 1704, to act in one of his own plays.

In London he visited the coffee-houses and made himself acquainted with the literary figures of the day, while also beginning to write comedies, persuaded by his fellow-Dubliner Robert Wilks, the actor, that he had talent. His first play, *Love and a Bottle*, was staged at Drury Lane in December 1698. This was less successful than Farquhar's next play, *The Constant Couple*, staged almost one year later. Its hero, Sir Harry Wildair, is often taken to be Farquhar's ideal of himself. The part was played by Wilks, whose friendship benefited the careers of both men. In 1700 Farquhar made a trip to Holland, where he worked on an unsuccessful sequel, *Sir Harry Wildair.*

When two more plays failed, Farquhar tried to mend his fortunes in 1703 by marrying a rich widow, but Margaret Pemell turned out, after marriage, to be as poor as himself and to have three children by a former marriage. Two more children, both girls, were born of Farquhar's marriage, which seems to have been unhappy. In 1704 he joined the army, and as lieutenant in an infantry regiment was sent on a recruiting campaign to the English midlands. This gave him the subject of *The Recruiting Officer* (1706). His financial affairs did not improve and he fell into ill health. He deserted his family. Wilks found him close to death, and persuaded him to write his last play, *The Beaux' Stratagem.* Farquhar died in London in May 1707, barely one month after that play had its successful première. The cause of his death is unknown, but may have been tuberculosis.

CHIEF WRITINGS. *The Adventures of Covent Garden* (London, 1698); *Love and a Bottle* (London, 1699); *The Constant Couple; or, A Trip to the Jubilee* (London, 1699); *Sir Harry Wildair, Being the Sequel of 'A Trip to the Jubilee'* (London, 1701); *The Inconstant; or, The Way to Win Him* (London, 1702), based on John Fletcher's *The Wild-Goose Chase* (London, 1621); *Love and Business* (London, 1702), miscellaneous verse and prose, including 'A Discourse upon Comedy in Reference to the English Stage'; *The Twin Rivals* (London, 1703); *The Stage Coach* (London, 1704), a farce adapted from the French by Jean de la Chapelle; *The Recruiting Officer* (London, 1706); *The Beaux' Stratagem* (London, 1707).

Standard editions: Charles Stonehill (ed.), *The Complete Works of George Farquhar* 2 vols (London: Nonesuch Press, 1930; reprinted New York: Gordian Press, 1967); Shirley Strum Kenny (ed.), *The Works of George Farquhar* 2 vols (Oxford: Clarendon Press, 1988).

BIOGRAPHY AND CRITICISM. 'Life' in Charles Stonehill (ed.), *The Complete Works of George Farquhar* (London: Nonesuch Press, 1930; reprinted New York: Gordian Press, 1967) Vol. 1, pp. xi-xxxiii; Peter Kavanagh, 'George Farquhar', in *The Irish Theatre* (Tralee: Kerryman, 1946), pp. 195-233; Willard Connely, *Young George Farquhar: Restoration Drama at Twilight* (London: Cassell, 1949); Eric Rothstein, *George Farquhar* (New York: Twayne, 1967); A. J. Farmer, *George Farquhar* (London: Longmans, 1972); Eugene Nelson James, *The Development of George Farquhar as a Comic Dramatist* (The Hague: Mouton, 1972); A. N. Jeffares (ed.), *The Beaux' Stratagem,* Critical Introduction (Edinburgh: Oliver & Boyd, 1972); Raymond A. Anselment (ed.), *Farquhar: 'The Recruiting Officer' and 'The Beaux' Stratagem': A Casebook* (London:

Macmillan, 1977); Peter Dixon (ed.), *The Recruiting Officer*, Introduction (Manchester: Manchester University Press, 1986); Eugene Nelson James, *George Farquhar: A Reference Guide* (Boston: G. K. Hall, 1986).

Sir Richard Steele

LIFE. Born in Dublin about the end of February 1672. Educated at Charterhouse, London, 1684-89, where he met Joseph Addison; studied at Oxford, but left in 1694 without taking a degree. Enlisted in the Life Guards as a trooper and rose to the rank of captain by 1700; left the army in 1705. Married twice: Margaret Ford Stretch in 1705 (died 1706), Mary Scurlock in 1707, and had four children. Began writing for the theatre in 1701, with *The Funeral*, to restore his reputation after publishing a moralistic tract, *The Christian Hero*. Manager of *The Gazette*, official government publication, 1707-10, and commissioner of stamps 1710-13. In April 1709 he founded the periodical *The Tatler*, a major influence on taste, for which Addison and Swift also wrote. After it closed in 1711, Steele founded *The Spectator* with Joseph Addison. Was Member of Parliament for Stockbridge, Hampshire, in 1713, but was expelled for anti-government views. In 1714 was appointed justice of the peace, deputy lieutenant for the County of Middlesex, surveyor of the royal stables at Hampton Court, and supervisor of the Drury Lane Theatre, London; granted life-patent of Drury Lane in 1715. Knighted 9 April 1715. Member of Parliament for Boroughbridge, Yorkshire, 1715, and for Wendover, Buckinghamshire, 1722. Edited various periodicals 1715-20, including *The Theatre*, 1720. Presented the first noteworthy sentimental comedy in English, *The Conscious Lovers*, at Drury Lane, November 1722. Retired to Wales in 1724, and died in Carmarthen on 1 September 1729.

CHIEF WRITINGS. *The Funeral; or, Grief-à-la-Mode* (London, 1702); *The Lying Lover; or, The Ladies' Friendship* (London, 1704), a comedy based on *Le Menteur* by Pierre Corneille; *The Tender Husband; or, The Accomplished Fools* (London, 1705); *The Tatler*, with Joseph Addison, 4 vols (London, 1710-11); *The Spectator*, with Joseph Addison, 8 vols (London, 1712-15); *The Conscious Lovers* (1722).

Standard edition (plays): Shirley Strum Kenny (ed.), *The Plays of Richard Steele* (Oxford: Clarendon Press, 1971).

BIOGRAPHY AND CRITICISM. Peter Kavanagh, 'Richard Steele', in *The Irish Theatre* (Tralee: Kerryman, 1946), pp. 252-62; John Loftis, *Steele at Drury Lane* (Berkeley & Los Angeles: University of California Press, 1952); Calhoun Winton, *Captain Steele: The Early Career of Richard Steele* (Baltimore: Johns Hopkins University Press, 1964); Calhoun Winton, *Sir Richard Steele, M.P.: The Later Career* (Baltimore & London: Johns Hopkins University Press, 1970); Malcolm Kelsall, 'Terence and Steele', in Kenneth Richards and Peter Thomson (eds), *Essays on the Eighteenth-Century English Stage* (London: Methuen, 1972); Simon Trussler, 'Richard Steele' in *Great Writers Student Library: Restoration and 18th-Century Drama*, with introduction by Arthur H. Scouten (London & Basingstoke: Macmillan, 1980).

Thomas Sheridan

LIFE. Born in 1719, either at his father's house and school in Capel Street, Dublin, or in his mother's home in Quilca, County Cavan. His father, Dr Thomas Sheridan, was a noted scholar and friend of Jonathan Swift, who was godfather to Thomas the Younger. At the age of thirteen he went to Westminster School, and three years later entered Trinity College, Dublin; took his BA in 1739 and MA before 1743. The death of his father in 1738 turned his attention to the theatre, as a means of making money and of learning the art of elocution. He made his debut as an actor at Theatre Royal, Smock Alley, on 29 January 1743, in the role of Richard III, and one week later presented a farce, *Captain O'Blunder*, later retitled *The Brave Irishman*. In 1747 he married Frances Chamberlaine and they had several children, including the future playwright, Richard Brinsley.

In 1745 he became manager of Smock Alley, and remained actor-manager almost continuously until 1758. During this time he introduced several reforms to the stage. More than once he encountered opposition from the Dublin audience, and it was a riot in the theatre that brought his managerial career to an end. Sheridan then went to live in London, where he acted with David Garrick. He also taught and wrote books on elocution, and published a pronouncing dictionary. In 1763 he returned to Dublin as an actor, last appearing on stage on 14 March 1777. From that date he assisted his son with the management of Drury Lane Theatre in London. He died and was buried in Margate in August 1788.

CHIEF WRITINGS. *A Full Vindication of the Conduct of the Manager of the Theatre-Royal. Written by Himself* (Dublin, 1747); *The Brave Irishman; or, Captain O'Blunder* [revised by another hand] (Dublin, n.d.): a portion of this text is included in Alan J. Bliss (ed.), *Spoken English in Ireland 1600-1740* (Monkstown, Co. Dublin: The Cadenus Press, 1976), pp. 166-71; *A Course of Lectures on Elocution* (London, 1762); *Lectures on the Art of Reading* (2 parts, London, 1775); *The Life of the Rev. Dr Jonathan Swift* (London, 1784); *A Complete Dictionary of the English Language*. 2nd edition (London, 1789).

BIOGRAPHY AND CRITICISM. Esther K. Sheldon, *Thomas Sheridan of Smock-Alley* (Princeton: Princeton University Press, 1967); Mary Rose Callaghan, 'Sheridan, Thomas (The Younger)', in Robert Hogan et al (eds), *The [Macmillan] Dictionary of Irish Literature* (Westport, Connecticut: Greenwood Press, 1979; London & Basingstoke: Macmillan, 1980).

Charles Macklin

LIFE. Born in 1699, probably at Culdaff in Inishowen, County Donegal. The family name seems originally to have been Mac Lochláinn, and Macklin was bilingual from an early age. In contrast to Farquhar's, Macklin's family suffered from the defeat of James II's forces in Ireland, and consequently Macklin was a member of the old dispossessed catholic-Gaelic gentry. His widowed mother married a protestant in Dublin, but Macklin remained a catholic until about 1740. Educated in Dublin, he may have worked for a time in Trinity College in 1713. Became a professional actor about 1717 in Bristol and made his first appearance on the London stage about 1725. Married the actress Ann Grace in 1739 and had a daughter, Maria, and a son, John. Married again, Elizabeth Jones, in 1778.

A disputatious man, Macklin inadvertently killed a fellow actor at Drury Lane in 1735 and was convicted of manslaughter. Had a dispute with David Garrick in 1743, who alone surpassed him as an actor at this time. Macklin restored Shakespeare's Shylock to the stage in 1741 by playing him with complete Jewish authenticity. Later he brought realism to the costuming of *Macbeth*. In 1754 he abandoned the stage for a time to become a teacher of acting, and offered the first public lectures on Shakespeare. Began writing for the stage in 1746 and had his first major success with *Love à la Mode* at Drury Lane on 12 December 1759. In 1748-50 and again in 1762 he acted in Dublin, and presented a new play there, *The True-born Irishman*. After 1762 he often acted in Dublin and his plays were staged there, as well as in London. He was unusual in his loyalty to the Irish stage. Macklin remained an actor into old age, last appearing on stage, as Shylock, on 7 May 1789. He died in London in 1797 and was buried in St Paul's, Covent Garden.

CHIEF WRITINGS. *King Henry VII; or, The Popish Impostor* (London, 1746); *A Will and No Will; or, A Bone for the Lawyers* (staged 1746, not printed); *The New Play Criticized; or, the Plague of Envy* (staged 1747, not printed); *The Club of Fortune-Hunters; or, The Widow Bewitched* (staged 1748, not printed); *Covent Garden Theatre; or, Pasquin Turned Drawcansir* (staged 1752, printed 1965); **Love à la Mode* (London, 1793); **The School for Husbands; or, The Married Libertine* (staged 1761, printed 1968); **The Man of the World* (London, 1793); **The True-born Irishman; or, The Irish Fine Lady* (Dublin, 1793).

Standard edition: *Four Comedies by Charles Macklin*, edited and with a biographical and critical sketch of Macklin by J. O. Bartley (Hamden, Connecticut: Archon Books; London: Sidgwick & Jackson, 1968). *represents inclusion in *Four Comedies* (1968).

BIOGRAPHY AND CRITICISM. William W. Appleton, *Charles Macklin: An Actor's Life* (Cambridge, Massachusetts: Harvard University Press, 1961); J. O. Bartley, 'A Biographical and Critical Sketch' in J. O. Bartley (ed.), *Four Comedies by Charles Macklin* (Hamden, Connecticut: Archon Books; London: Sidgwick & Jackson, 1968); R. W. Bevis,

'Macklin, Charles', in *Great Writers Student Library: Restoration and 18th-Century Drama*, with introduction by Arthur H. Scouten (London & Basingstoke: Macmillan, 1980).

Arthur Murphy

LIFE. Born in Clooniquin, Co. Roscommon, in 1727, at the house of his uncle. Lived with his mother in Dublin after his father's death in 1729 and went to London in 1735. Studied at the English (Jesuit) College in St Omer, France, from 1738 to 1744. Returning to Ireland about 1747, he became clerk to a merchant in Cork, but in 1749 went to work in a bank in London. Left the bank in 1751 and began to write, founding the *Gray's Inn Journal* (1752-54) on the lines of Addison's *The Spectator*. When his uncle died without leaving him the expected legacy, Murphy tried acting for two years and wrote a farce, *The Apprentice*, which Garrick produced in 1756. Became a member of Johnson's literary circle. Gave up acting and entered Lincoln's Inn to study law and was called to the bar. Subsequently he carried on a career in law while also writing plays. He also edited the works of Henry Fielding, and wrote biographies of Samuel Johnson and David Garrick. Murphy retired from the bar in 1788, and published translations of Latin authors. He died in London in 1805.

CHIEF WRITINGS. *The Apprentice* (London, 1756); *The Upholsterer; or, What News?* (London, 1758); *The Orphan of China* (London, 1759); *The Way to Keep Him* (London, 1760); *All in the Wrong* (London, 1761); *The Old Maid* (London, 1761); *The Citizen* (London, 1763); *No One's Enemy but his Own* (London, 1764); *What We Must All Come To* (London, 1764), later revised as *Three Weeks after Marriage* (London, 1776); *The School for Guardians* (London, 1767); *The Grecian Daughter* (London, 1772); *Know Your Own Mind* (London, 1778). For a modern reprint edition, see *The Plays of Arthur Murphy*, 4 vols, edited by Richard B. Schwartz (New York: Garland Publishing Inc., 1979).

BIOGRAPHY AND CRITICISM. Peter Kavanagh, 'Arthur Murphy', in *The Irish Theatre* (Tralee: Kerryman, 1946), pp. 337-47; Howard Hunter Dunbar, *The Dramatic Career of Arthur Murphy* (New York: Modern Language Association of America; London: Oxford University Press, 1946); Robert Donald Spector, *Arthur Murphy* (Boston: Twayne, 1979); George Taylor (ed.), introduction to *Plays by Samuel Foote and Arthur Murphy* (Cambridge: Cambridge University Press, 1984).

Hugh Kelly

LIFE. Born near Killarney, Co. Kerry, in 1739, but moved to Dublin where his father had bought a tavern. Received little education and was made apprentice to a maker of ladies' stays (corsets). Met theatrical people in his father's tavern and formed an interest in theatre and in books. Went to London in 1760 and worked as a copying-clerk to an attorney. Wrote for newspapers, became editor of the *Court Magazine*, the *Ladies' Museum*, and *The Public Ledger*, and wrote various essays and pamphlets. Married in 1761. In 1766 published a satirical poem on the contemporary theatre, *Thespis*, which attracted the interest of David Garrick, who staged Kelly's *False Delicacy* at Drury Lane on 23 January 1768. Garrick intended that Kelly's play should upstage Goldsmith's *The Good Natur'd Man*, scheduled to open at the rival theatre, Covent Garden, in six days. It did just that, to Goldsmith's chagrin. For political reasons, Kelly's next play, *A Word to the Wise*, was violently opposed in the theatre (Drury Lane), in March 1770. Later, Kelly brought out *The School for Wives* under a pseudonym and it was a success. This play had nothing to do with Molière's comedy of the same name. It was Kelly's last success, although he wrote one other play, *The Man of Reason* (unpublished). In 1774 he was called to the bar and gave up literature for law. He died in 1777, aged thirty-eight.

CHIEF WRITINGS. *L'Amour-à-la-Mode; or, Love-à-la Mode* (London, 1760); *Memoirs of a Magdalen; or, The History of Louisa Mildmay* (London, 1767) — a novel; *False Delicacy* (London, 1768); *A Word to the Wise* (London, 1770); *Clementina* (London, 1771); *The School for Wives* (London, 1774); *The Romance of an Hour* (London, 1774); *The Man of Reason* (staged 9 February 1776 but not printed). For a modern reprint edition, see *The Plays of Hugh Kelly*, edited by Larry Carver (New York: Garland Publishing Inc., 1980).

BIOGRAPHY AND CRITICISM. No full-scale biography has yet been published. The following references provide the major details and/or offer critical assessments: Ernest Bernbaum, *The Drama of Sensibility* (Boston & London: Ginn, 1915; reprinted Gloucester, Massachusetts: Peter Smith, 1958), pp. 226-48; Peter Kavanagh, 'Hugh Kelly', in *The Irish Theatre* (Tralee, Kerryman, 1946), pp. 329-36; Sven Eric Molin, 'Hugh Kelly' in Robert Hogan (ed.), *The [Macmillan] Dictionary of Irish Literature* (Westport, Connecticut: Greenwood Press, 1979; London & Basingstoke: Macmillan, 1980); Jean-Michel Lacroix, *L'Oeuvre de Hugh Kelly (1739-1777): Contribution à L'Etude du Sentimentalisme Anglais* 2 vols (undated, Bordeaux; thesis, University of Paris III, 1978).

Oliver Goldsmith

LIFE. Born in 1728 in Pallas, Co. Longford, the son of a clergyman. The family soon moved to Lissoy, the probable setting of Goldsmith's *The Deserted Village* (1770). Goldsmith was educated here and at the diocesan school at Elphin, Co. Roscommon. He contracted smallpox, which marked his face for life. Entered Trinity College, Dublin, as a sizar (like Farquhar, above), in June 1745. Frequented Theatre Royal, Smock Alley. Graduated 1749, after certain difficulties. Went to Edinburgh to study medicine in 1752 and then to Leyden in Holland. After much travelling in Europe, settled in London in 1756. May have been awarded a medical degree by Trinity College, Dublin, but this remains unproven. Began as a physician in London in 1756, supplementing his income with hack writing. Gradually abandoned medicine for literature, becoming essayist, editor, historian, novelist, poet and playwright. Accepted into the literary circle of Samuel Johnson. First of two plays staged in 1768, the other on 15 March 1773. Goldsmith died in 1774 after treating himself for a kidney complaint. Buried privately in London, but a monument to him was erected in Westminster Abbey, with an epitaph by Johnson.

CHIEF WRITINGS. Dr Johnson's epitaph on Goldsmith can be translated: 'There was almost no subject he did not write about, and he wrote about nothing without enhancing it.' The following is a selection of Goldsmith's works: *An Enquiry into the Present State of Polite Learning in Europe* (London, 1759); *The Bee* (London, 1759); *The Citizen of the World; or, Letters from a Chinese Philosopher, Residing in London, to his Friends in the East* (London, 1762); *The Traveller; or, A Prospect of Society* (London, 1764); *Essays* (London, 1765); *The Vicar of Wakefield* (Salisbury, 1766); *The Good Natur'd Man* (London, 1768); *The Deserted Village* (London, 1770); *She Stoops to Conquer; or, The Mistakes of a Night* (London, 1773).

The standard edition: Arthur Friedman (ed.), *The Collected Works of Oliver Goldsmith* 5 vols (Oxford: Clarendon Press, 1966).

BIOGRAPHY AND CRITICISM. Ralph M. Wardle, *Oliver Goldsmith* (Lawrence: University of Kansas Press; London: Constable, 1957); Ricardo Quintana, *Goldsmith: A Georgian Study* (New York: Macmillan, 1967; London: Weidenfeld & Nicolson, 1969); Clara M. Kirk, *Oliver Goldsmith* (New York: Twayne, 1967); A. Lytton Sells, *Oliver Goldsmith* (London: Allen & Unwin, 1974); George Sebastian Rousseau (ed.), *Goldsmith: The Critical Heritage* (London: Routledge and Kegan Paul, 1974); John Ginger, *The Notable Man: The Life and Times of Oliver Goldsmith* (London: Hamish Hamilton, 1977); J. B. Lyons, *The Mystery of Oliver Goldsmith's Medical Degree* (Blackrock: Carraig Books, 1978); Samuel J. Woods, Jr, *Oliver Goldsmith: A Reference Guide* (Boston: G. K. Hall, 1982); Andrew Swarbrick (ed.), *The Art of Oliver Goldsmith* (Totowa, New Jersey: Barnes & Noble; London: Vision Press, 1984); Seán Lucy (ed.), *Goldsmith: The Gentle Master* (Cork: Cork University Press, 1984).

Richard Brinsley Sheridan

LIFE. Born in Dublin in 1751, the third son of Thomas the actor-manager at Theatre Royal, Smock Alley, and Frances Chamberlaine, novelist and playwright. Educated in Dublin and Harrow 1762-68. The family moved to Bath in 1770. Further studies at Waltham Abbey School and at Middle Temple, London. In 1773 married Elizabeth Ann Linley, by whom he had one son; she died in 1795 and another son was born in a second marriage in 1795 to Esther Jane Ogle. *The Rivals*, his first play, was staged in 1775. Owner and manager of Theatre Royal, Drury Lane, from 1776 until its demolition by fire in 1809. Wrote very little for the stage after he turned to political life, apart from the successful adaptation of *Pizarro* in 1799. Member of Parliament 1780-1812, under-secretary of state for foreign affairs 1782, secretary of the treasury 1783; speaker in the trial of Warren Hastings by parliament 1788-94; treasurer of the navy 1806. Died in London in 1816 and was buried in Westminster Abbey.

CHIEF WRITINGS. *The Rivals* (London, 1775); *The Duenna* (London, 1775); *The School for Scandal* (Dublin, 1780); *A Trip to Scarborough* (London, 1781), adapted from Sir John Vanbrugh's *The Relapse* (London, 1696); *The Critic; or, A Tragedy Rehearsed* (London, 1781); *St Patrick's Day; or, The Scheming Lieutenant* (Dublin, 1788); *The Camp* (London, 1795); *The Glorious First of June*, with James Cobb (London, 1794, songs only; 1973 in Price below, Vol. II); *Pizarro*, from a play by August Friedrich von Kotzebue (London, 1799).

Standard edition: Cecil Price (ed.), *The Dramatic Works of Richard Brinsley Sheridan* 2 vols (Oxford: Clarendon Press, 1973).

BIOGRAPHY AND CRITICISM. Walter Sichel, *Sheridan* 2 vols (London: Constable, 1909); Richard L. Purdy (ed.), *The Rivals* (Oxford: Clarendon Press, 1935); Robert D. Hume, 'Goldsmith and Sheridan and the Supposed Revolution of "Laughing" against "Sentimental" Comedy', in Paul J. Korshin (ed.), *Studies in Change and Revolution: Aspects of English Intellectual History 1640-1800* (Menton, Yorkshire: Scolar Press, 1972), pp. 237-76; Madeleine Bingham, *Sheridan: The Track of a Comet* (London: Allen & Unwin, 1972); Jack D. Durant, *Richard Brinsley Sheridan* (Boston: Twayne, 1975); John Loftis, *Sheridan and the Drama of Georgian England* (Oxford: Blackwell, 1976); Mark S. Auburn, *Sheridan's Comedies: Their Contexts and Achievements* (Lincoln, Nebraska: University of Nebraska Press, 1977); Richard Bevis, *The Laughing Tradition: Stage Comedy in Garrick's Day* (Athens, Georgia: University of Georgia Press, 1980); Stanley Ayling, *A Portrait of Sheridan* (London: Constable, 1985); James Morwood, *The Life and Works of Richard Brinsley Sheridan* (Edinburgh: Scottish Academic Press, 1985); Peter Davison (ed.), *Sheridan: Comedies: A Selection of Critical Essays* (Basingstoke: Macmillan, 1986).

John O'Keeffe

LIFE. Born in Abbey Street, Dublin in 1747, of a catholic family that had once fought for King James II and was thereafter dispossessed. Educated in Dublin and later attended the Royal Academy of Art. In 1762 went to live for two years with an aunt in London, and took an interest in the theatre. Back in Dublin, he went on stage as an actor, under Henry Mossop at Theatre Royal, Smock Alley. During twelve years as an actor, he wrote minor pieces for the stage. Married Mary Heaphy in 1774, from whom he separated in 1780; they had two sons and a daughter. Although he went to London around 1777 and wrote for the theatres there, his work was always equally if not more popular in Dublin. Much of it was musical, and he used traditional Irish airs long before Thomas Moore made such music popular in London. Following an accident in 1780, O'Keeffe began to go blind and used an amanuensis for his writings. He retired from the theatre in 1799 and in November 1803 received an annuity from the management of Covent Garden. In January 1826 he was awarded a pension by George IV. He died at Southampton in 1833.

CHIEF WRITINGS. O'Keeffe's most noted works are his comedy, *Wild Oats* (London, 1791, reprinted London: Heinemann, 1977) and his memoirs, *Recollections* 2 vols (London, 1826). He wrote some seventy-seven plays, operas, farces and afterpieces. For a full description, see Peter Kavanagh, *The Irish Theatre* (Tralee: Kerryman, 1946), pp. 348-49, and the *CBEL*, II (Cambridge: Cambridge University Press, 1969), 479-81. The following is a brief selection: *The Shamrock; or St Patrick's Day* (staged 1777, unpublished); *Tony Lumpkin in Town* (Dublin, 1780); *The Castle of Andalusia* (London, 1782); *The Son-in-Law* (Dublin, 1783); *The Dead Alive* (Dublin, 1783); *The Agreeable Surprise* (Newry, 1783); *The Poor Soldier* (Dublin, 1785); *Love in a Camp; or, Patrick in Prussia* (Dublin, 1786); *Wild Oats; or, The Strolling Gentleman* (Dublin, 1791); *Valentine and Orson; or, The Wild Man of Orleans* (London, 1795); *The Wicklow Gold Mines; or, The Lads of the Hills* (Dublin, 1814); *Recollections of the Life of O'Keeffe*, written by himself (London, 1826). For a modern reprint edition, see *The Plays of John O'Keeffe*, 4 vols, edited by Frederick M. Link (New York: Garland Publishing Inc., 1981).

BIOGRAPHY AND CRITICISM. No biography has been written. The best extant account is Peter Kavanagh, 'John O'Keeffe', in *The Irish Theatre* (Tralee: Kerryman, 1946), pp. 348-61. Invaluable also are O'Keeffe's own *Recollections*, written with his daughter, Adelaide, as amanuensis. See Karen J. Harvey and Kevin B. Pry, 'John O'Keeffe as an Irish Playwright within the Theatrical, Social and Economic Context of his Time', *Eire-Ireland*, XXII: 1 (Spring 1987), 19-43.

SEAMUS DEANE, *Editor*

Oliver Goldsmith

Miscellaneous Writings 1759–74

Three members of the Literary Club, founded by Samuel Johnson, were forced to earn their living for a time by hack journalism: Johnson himself, Burke in his labours with the *Annual Review*, and Oliver Goldsmith most of all. He wrote for almost every magazine of distinction and for many whose only ultimate distinction was that he wrote for them. He turned out reviews, prefaces, introductions, histories, addresses to ladies, short biographies and surveys; he edited selections of poems and even was editor and compiler of a magazine of his own, *The Bee*, which survived for only eight numbers, from September to November 1759. In addition, Goldsmith also wrote *The Citizen of the World*, a satirical work in the epistolary mode so much favoured in Europe since the 1720s. There is no doubt that much of this miscellaneous writing is slight. Goldsmith was concerned to fill space and earn his guineas, although the ratio between these things was never satisfactory. Nevertheless, for all his fecklessness in practical matters, Goldsmith was rarely less than competent in what he had to say and was always able to say it with remarkable fluency and ease. 'No man was more foolish when he had not a pen in his hand, or more wise when he had', according to Johnson. His admirers have talked of the ease, limpidity, order and amenity of his style. These virtues are as obvious in his essays as in his great works. In his Preface to *A General History of the World*, included below, he gives his credo in a single sentence: 'Writers are unpardonable who convert our amusement into labour, and divest knowledge of one of its most pleasing allurements.'

Goldsmith was a popularizer of general knowledge and, as such, he repeatedly insisted on the obligation on the part of the writer to communicate to the public at large in a pleasing and readily comprehensible manner. 'True learning and true morality', he wrote in the Introduction to *An Enquiry Into The Present State of Polite Learning in Europe*, 'are closely connected; to improve the head will insensibly influence the heart, a deficiency of taste and a corruption of manners are sometimes found mutually to produce each other.'

Learning should be 'polite'. In Goldsmith's day that meant that it should be accessible, as well as elegant and polished. Politeness was lost when learning became pedantry, specialized to such a degree that it had to produce a jargon of its own that shut it off from people of a general education. It was a live issue in the first great age of cylopaedias, encyclopaedias and digests of every conceivable kind. The accumulated information that had been produced by the new sciences, and the new attitudes of mind that they promoted, had to find some new mode of dissemination. The journal, magazine, review, along with the digest and the cyclopaedia, were the available means, and the writer, as journalist, popularizer and purveyor, was the technician who availed of them. The work was badly paid, but the booksellers and entrepreneurs who ran the magazines and the printing shops could afford to pay relatively low rates in a market where the appetite of an expanding readership was increasing by the decade, and the level of writing required was so low that the numbers of those who could claim to be writers was increasing at an even faster rate. It was in this situation that Goldsmith, and many of his famous contemporaries, had to make their way.

Goldsmith was fighting a losing battle, because knowledge was becoming increasingly specialized and the need for specialist terminology was becoming ever more apparent. He still clung to the notion that, with effort, an educated person could still command the whole field of knowledge and thereby become a citizen of the intellectual world. This was a classic ideal of the Enlightenment, which tended to regard those forms of knowledge that were cast in obscure language as more akin to the inane disputes of theologians and old prejudice than to the arcane arguments of the new sciences. Goldsmith sees knowledge as a mode of moral development. It clears the mind of falsehood and the heart of bigotry. It is a light that casts warmth on those who receive it. Therefore it should be made available in the most genial form possible. Otherwise it would not pervade the social system, and its benefits would be reduced or lost.

Yet, as his remarks in the Preface to *A General History of the World* show, Goldsmith was aware that too great an accumulation of knowledge could so confuse the mind that no supervening conception would survive. The organization of his longer works, like *An Enquiry into the Present State of Polite Learning in Europe* or *The History of England*, is effective only to the extent that his materials remain illustrative of some general theme or themes. As a consequence, he tends towards sententiousness. History is a series of moral lessons. These are elicited by the skill of the writer and given memorable point and clarity by the subtly turned antitheses and parallels that structurally dominate his sentences. He is very much part of the literary world of Pope and Voltaire, although he has the acerbity of neither.

From about 1760 to 1780, one of the most persistent arguments in pamphlets and journals concerned the merits or demerits of the claim that England and Europe in general were undergoing a period of decline and degeneracy. Those who supported this claim tended to blame 'luxury' as one of the prime causes and to look back with nostalgia to more frugal, sterner times when the moral life was simpler and England was not the loser in wars against the French or, later, the Americans. Goldsmith sometimes supported this view, as in *The Deserted Village*, and sometimes rebuked it, as in his introduction to the *Enquiry*. When he tried to give an extended account of the issue, as in his 1762 essay 'The Revolution of Low Life', he was inept, seeing only that the new wealth from the Empire had increased the gap between the very rich and the very poor and had led to an increasingly rapid proliferation of fads and fashions, which Goldsmith deplored as a symptom of a profound instability. He was as far from understanding the economics of Mandeville as those of Adam Smith. But in a moral sense, he clung to one essential principle. All these social changes, all this accumulation of wealth and knowledge, threatened to upset, even disprove, the doctrine of benevolence, which he, following Shaftesbury and his compatriot Hutcheson, as well as some of the greatest of the English novelists, believed to be the basis of the ideal social life. It was in the spirit of benevolence that he wrote with such lucidity. His obligation to his reader was both to inform and to please; by doing both, he also managed to improve mankind morally. Like Burke, Goldsmith believed in the importance of affection in the preservation of social systems and, like many before and since, thought that the 'new' systems of selfishness were leading to economic development at the expense of moral decay. In his essays, this note is struck time after time. That combination of sentiment with a sense of moral obligation did not appear again in English essay writing until Hazlitt.

Goldsmith was aware that the contrast between England and Ireland was one of the most painful examples of the discrepancy between rich and poor which modern Europe had to offer. Yet he inclined to see this as deriving from the different national characteristics of the two races, never for a moment envisaging them as conceivably distinct political entities. His vision of Europe as a community embracing a number of distinct races while remaining a cultural entity, readily identifiable as such in comparison to China, Persia or any other part of the world, is standard for the time. A number of admired authorities, like Montesquieu, had pondered the differences that climate, religion, habit, racial origin and other such factors could have on the political and economic disposition of a given country. Goldsmith follows this line, seeing in this diversity, as Hutcheson had done before him and Burke would do after him, a fundamental unity. The relationship between these should be preserved, although it does seem that Goldsmith believed that England was especially fortunate in its historical fate and was therefore in many ways an exemplary country. His native land he viewed almost with the eyes of a foreigner, seeing it as attractive and cultured in ways not usually noticed or accepted by English commentators, yet also perceiving it as a slightly exotic variation on the English norm. Of all the Irish writers of the eighteenth century, he is perhaps the least affected by any specifically national sentiment. Ireland is the occasion for a nostalgia that is important precisely because it is associated with what he first knew and is therefore in some sense a radical feeling. Yet, ultimately, Goldsmith was sufficiently of the Enlightenment to see Ireland, England, France and all the other European countries as sharing in that general advancement that would lead to the triumph of reason and feeling throughout the world.

Yet there is a degree of blandness in Goldsmith's attitudes towards Ireland, which disguises his success in effacing from his occasional writings on the country — two samples of which are included here — the drastic effects of English misrule there. This is not the Ireland of the penal laws and of occasional famines, agrarian disturbances and judicial murders. It is an idyll, comparable to his view of Irish society of which *The Deserted Village* is the appealing remnant. It is therefore not surprising that the Victorian commentators on Goldsmith and, later, Yeats and many other Irish writers were able to use this pastoral version of Ireland to support the notion of the Anglo-Irish honeymoon which had intervened between the seventeenth century wars and the rise of nationalism in the nineteenth century. Blandness is converted to sweetness and the nostalgia is believed to refer to an actual society, English or Irish, that had been degraded by the onset of the new world of the agricultural and industrial revolutions. As the following selection from his miscellaneous writings demonstrates, Goldsmith was anxious to support the idea that the form of liberty gained in England in 1688 was a commodity that had been exported to Ireland. Its sluggish reception there, he claims, is a consequence of the Irish national character, governed, indeed, by Irish conditions. If he has a national sentiment that could be said to override his rather naive Enlightenment faith, it is British, not Irish, in origin.

The elegance of Goldsmith's writing is never achieved at the expense of warmth in his address. He is a fine journalist, as well as a great playwright and memorable novelist, because he appeals to a shared moral sense, or common set of assumptions, which binds him with his audience. He was one of the last writers to assume that degree of shared interest and a belief in the moral usefulness of popular discourse. This is one of the features that makes even the most casual of his writings readable.

from: AN ENQUIRY INTO THE PRESENT STATE OF POLITE LEARNING IN EUROPE (1759)

[The *Enquiry* was so unfavourably reviewed that it was fifteen years before a new and revised edition appeared. The current objections to it are well-grounded. Goldsmith did not provide any substantial account of the state of learning in Europe and he was as guilty as any other hack writer of producing a book that would have been briefer had he not been paid for it by the page. Nevertheless, the opening and conclusion of the work demonstrate Goldsmith's general attitude towards the new vogue for 'learning' and information and the question of the relationship between taste and morality.]

CHAPTER I

INTRODUCTION

It has been so long the practice to represent literature as declining,[1] that every renewal of this complaint now comes with diminish'd influence. The publick has been often excited by a false alarm, so that at present the nearer we approach the threatned period of decay, the more our fatal security increases.

To deplore the prostitution of learning, and despise cotemporary merit, it must be owned, have too often been the resource of the envious or disappointed, the dictates of resentment not impartiality. The writer, possessed of fame, is willing to enjoy it without a rival, by lessening every competitor; the unsuccessful author is desirous to turn upon others the contempt which is levelled at himself, and being convicted at the bar of literary justice, vainly hopes for pardon by accusing every brother of the same profession.

Sensible of this; the writer of the following essay is at a loss where to find an apology for his conduct, in still persisting to arraign the merit of the age; for

1. This was a common complaint. See John D. Scheffer, 'The Idea of Decline in Literature and the Fine Arts in Eighteenth-century England', *Modern Philology* XXXIV (1936), 155-78.

joining in a cry which the judicious have long since left to be kept up by the vulgar, and for adopting the sentiments of the multitude in a performance that at best can please only the Few.

Complaints of our degeneracy in literature as well as in morals, I own have been frequently exhibited of late;[2] but seem to be enforced more with the ardour of devious declamation, than the calmness of deliberate enquiry. The dullest critic, who strives at a reputation for delicacy, by shewing he cannot be pleased, may pathetically assure us that our taste is upon the decline, may consign every modern performance to oblivion, and bequeath nothing to posterity except the labours of our ancestors, and his own. Such general invective, however, conveys no instruction; all it teaches is, that the writer dislikes an age by which he is probably disregarded. The manner of being useful on the subject would be to point out the symptoms, to investigate the causes, and direct to the remedies of the approaching decay. This is a subject hitherto unattempted in criticism, perhaps it is the only subject in which criticism can be useful.

To mark out, therefore, the corruptions that have found way into the republick of letters, to attempt the rescuing of genius from the shackles of pedantry and criticism, to distinguish the decay, naturally consequent on an age like ours grown old in literature, from every erroneous innovation which admits a remedy, to take a view of those societies which profess the advancement of polite learning, and by a mutual opposition of their excellencies and defects to attempt the improvement of each, is the design of this essay.

How far the writer is equal to such an undertaking the reader must determine; but this may be asserted without the imputation of vanity, that he enters the lists with no disappointments to biass his judgment, nor will he ever reprove but with a desire to reform. The defects of his execution may be compensated by the usefulness of his design, his observations may be just, tho' his manner of expressing them should only serve as an example of the errors he undertakes to reprove.

If the present enquiry were a topick of speculative curiosity, calculated to fill up a few vacant moments in literary indolence, I should think my labour ill bestowed. To rank in the same despicable class with the dissertations, ænigma's[*sic*], problems, and other periodical compilations with which even idleness is cloyed at present, is by no means my ambition. True learning and true morality are closely connected; to improve the head will insensibly influence the heart, a deficiency of taste and a corruption of manners are sometimes found mutually to produce each other.[3]

Dissenting from received opinions may frequently render this essay liable to correction, yet the reader may be assured that a passion for singularity never gives rise to the error. Novelty is not permitted to usurp the place of reason; it may attend, but shall not conduct the enquiry. The more original however any performance is, the more it is liable to deviate; for cautious stupidity is always in the right. In literature as in commerce the value of the acquisition is generally proportioned to the hazard of the adventure. I shall think therefore with freedom, and bear correction with candour. It is but just that he who dissents from others should not be displeased if others differ from him. The applause of a few, a very few, will satisfy ambition, and even ill-nature must confess that I have been willing to advance the reputation of the age at the hazard of my own.

CHAPTER XIV

THE CONCLUSION

Every subject acquires an adventitious importance to him who considers it with application. He finds it more closely connected with human happiness, than the rest of mankind are apt to allow; he sees consequences resulting from it, which do not strike others with equal conviction, and still pursuing speculation beyond the bounds of reason, too

2. John 'Estimate' Brown's *An Estimate of the Manners and Principles of the Times* (1757) was the most famous of contemporary attacks on 'luxury', 'effeminacy' and the decline in literary taste. Burke reviewed it favourably in the *Annual Register* (1758), pp. 445 ff. The theme was to survive until the end of the century. See John Bowles, *Reflections on the Political and Moral State of Society at the Close of the Eighteenth Century* (London, 1800-01).

3. This too was a commonplace in the discussions of Taste, the main lines of which had been laid down by Joseph Addison in his *Spectator* papers of 1712 (nos. 409, 411-21). The chief signs of 'taste' were considered to be an ability to discriminate differences of quality and to take pleasure in excellence.

frequently becomes ridiculously earnest in trifles, or absurdity.

It will, perhaps, be incurring this imputation, to deduce an universal degeneracy of manners, from so slight an origin as the depravation of taste; to assert, that as a nation grows dull, it sinks into debauchery. Yet such, probably, may be the consequence of literary decay; or, not to stretch the thought beyond what it will bear, vice and stupidity are always mutually productive of each other.

Life at the greatest and best, has been compared to a froward[1] child, that must be humoured, and play'd with, till it falls asleep, and then all the care is over.[2] Our few years are laboured away in varying its pleasures; new amusements are pursued with studious attention; the most childish vanities are dignified with titles of importance; and the proudest boast of the most aspiring philosopher is no more than that he provides his little playfellows the greatest pastime with the greatest innocence.

Thus the mind ever wandering after amusement, when abridged of happiness on one part, endeavours to find it on another, when intellectual pleasures are disagreeable, those of sense will take the lead. The man, who, in this age, is enamoured of the tranquil joys of study and retirement, may, in the next, should learning be fashionable no longer, feel an ambition of being foremost at an horse-course; or if such could be the absurdity of the times, of being himself a jockey. Reason and appetite are therefore masters of our revels in turn; and as we incline to the one, or pursue the other, we rival angels, or imitate the brutes. In the pursuit of intellectual pleasure, lies every virtue; of sensual, every vice.

It is this difference of pursuit, which marks the morals and characters of mankind; which lays the line between the enlightened philosopher, and the half-taught citizen; between the civil citizen and the illiterate peasant; between the law-obeying peasant, and the wandering savage of Africa, an animal less mischievous indeed, than the tyger, because endued with fewer powers of doing mischief. The man, the nation, must therefore be good, whose chiefest luxuries consist in the refinement of reason; and reason can never be universally cultivated unless guided by Taste, which may be considered as the link between science and common sense, the medium through which learning should ever be seen by society.

Taste will, therefore, often be a proper standard, when others fail, to judge of a nation's improvement, or degeneracy in morals. We have often no permanent characteristics by which to compare the virtues or the vices of our ancestors with our own; a generation may rise and pass away, without leaving any traces of what it really was, and all complaints of our deterioration, may be only topics of declamation, or the cavillings of disappointment: but in taste, we have standing evidence, we can, with precision, compare the literary performances of our fathers with our own, and from their excellence, or defects, determine the moral, as well as the literary merits of either.

If then, there ever comes a time, when taste is so far depraved among us, that critics shall load every work of genius with unnecessary comment, and quarter their empty performances, with the substantial merit of an author, both for subsistence and applause; if there comes a time, when censure shall speak in storms, but praise be whispered in the breeze, while real excellence often finds shipwreck in either; if there be a time, when the muse shall seldom be heard, except in plaintive elegy, as if she wept her own decline, while lazy compilations supply the place of original thinking; should there ever be such a time, may succeeding critics, both for the honour of our morals as well as our learning, say, that such a period bears no resemblance to the present age.

1. obstinate, contrary.
2. Adapted from the close of Sir William Temple's essay 'Of Poetry' (1690).

from: THE BEE (27 OCTOBER 1759)

[A later version of this piece appeared as Letter CXVIII of *The Citizen of the World*. As is often the case with Goldsmith's occasional writings, a number of borrowings are discernible, many of them from French sources. Nevertheless, he still manages to provide us with a description of London low-life in the eighteenth century and an account of the sentimental observer, increasingly appalled and moved by the environing misery. This figure recurs throughout Goldsmith's work and that of his contemporaries.]

A CITY NIGHT-PIECE

Ille dolet vere qui sine teste dolet. MART.[1]

The clock has struck two, the expiring taper rises and sinks in the socket, the watchman forgets the hour in slumber, the laborious and the happy are at rest, and nothing now wakes but guilt, revelry and despair. The drunkard once more fills the destroying bowl, the robber walks his midnight round, and the suicide lifts his guilty arm against his own sacred person.

Let me no longer waste the night over the page of antiquity, or the sallies of cotemporary genius, but pursue the solitary walk, where vanity, ever changing, but a few hours past, walked before me, where she kept up the pageant, and now, like a froward child, seems hushed with her own importunities.

What a gloom hangs all around! the dying lamp feebly emits a yellow gleam, no sound is heard but of the chiming clock, or the distant watch-dog. All the bustle of human pride is forgotten, and this hour may well display the emptiness of human vanity.

There may come a time when this temporary solitude may be made continual, and the city itself, like its inhabitants, fade away, and leave a desart in its room.

What cities, as great as this, have once triumph'd in existence, had their victories as great as ours, joy as just, and as unbounded as we, and with short-sighted presumption, promised themselves immortality. Posterity can hardly trace the situation of some. The sorrowful traveller wanders over the awful ruins of others, and as he beholds, he learns wisdom, and feels the transience of every sublunary possession.

Here stood their citadel, but now grown over with weeds; there their senate-house, but now the haunt of every noxious reptile; temples and theatres stood here, now only an undistinguished heap of ruin. They are fallen, for luxury and avarice first made them feeble. The rewards of state were conferred on amusing, and not on useful members of society. Thus true virtue languished, their riches and opulence invited the plunderer, who, though once repulsed, returned again, and at last swept the defendants into undistinguished destruction.

How few appear in those streets, which but some few hours ago were crowded; and those who appear, no longer now wear their daily mask, nor attempt to hide their lewdness or their misery.

But who are those who make the streets their couch, and find a short repose from wretchedness at the doors of the opulent? These are strangers, wanderers, and orphans, whose circumstances are too humble to expect redress, and their distresses too great even for pity. Some are without the covering even of rags, and others emaciated with disease; the world seems to have disclaimed them; society turns its back upon their distress, and has given them up to nakedness and hunger. These poor shivering females, have once seen happier days, and been flattered into beauty. They have been prostituted to the gay luxurious villain, and are now turned out to meet the severity of winter in the streets. Perhaps now lying at the door of their betrayers they sue to wretches whose hearts are insensible to calamity, or debauchees who may curse, but will not relieve them.

Why, why was I born a man, and yet see the sufferings of wretches I cannot relieve! Poor houseless creatures! the world will give you reproaches, but will not give you relief. The slightest misfortunes, the most imaginary uneasinesses of the rich, are aggravated with all the power of eloquence, and engage our attention; while you weep unheeded, persecuted by every subordinate species of tyranny, and finding enmity in every law.

Why was this heart of mine formed with so much sensibility! or why was not my fortune adapted to its impulse! Tenderness, without a capacity of relieving, only makes the heart that feels it more wretched than the object which sues for assistance.

But let me turn from a scene of such distress to the sanctified hypocrite, *who has been talking of virtue till the time of bed*,[2] and now steals out, to give a loose to his vices under the protection of midnight; vices more attrocious, because he attempts to conceal them. See how he pants down the dark alley, and, with hastening steps, fears an acquaintance in every face. He has passed the whole day in company he hates, and now goes to prolong the night among company that as heartily hate him. May his vices be detected; may the morning rise

1. Martial, *Epigrams* i.33.4. 'He truly grieves who grieves without witness [unseen].'

2. Thomas Parnell, 'The Hermit' (1722): 'Then talk'd of Virtue till the time of Bed.'

upon his shame: yet I wish to no purpose; villainy, when detected, never gives up, but boldly adds impudence to imposture.

A DESCRIPTION OF THE MANNERS AND CUSTOMS OF THE NATIVE *IRISH*. IN A LETTER FROM AN *ENGLISH* GENTLEMAN[1] (1759)

[This piece first appeared in the *Weekly Magazine* (29 December 1759). Goldsmith's authorship is not beyond dispute, but it is highly probable. The account is interesting, not least for its description of the relationships between protestants and catholics in the Ireland of the time. Goldsmith is at once insulated from and deeply influenced by the 'original natives' and characteristically deals with this paradox by attributing a great deal to national character and by using the conventional contrast between 'polite' and 'savage' society. Antiquaries and other writers reread this distinction later in the century, with 'wildness' and 'naturalness' replacing the term 'savage'.]

DEAR JACK.

While our travellers are busied in studying the manners, the soil, and produce of distant countries, there are several which are at our very doors possessed of peculiarities hitherto unknown, and yet quite neglected; like conquerors who have been too eagerly employed in foreign conquests, we leave our native dominions without notice or regard.

Perhaps our conquered kingdom of Ireland is as strong an instance of this as any that may be found, since whether we regard its natural history, or the manners of its original inhabitants, we may in both find matter for speculation and curiosity. Many wonders in the former are still left undescribed, as the mountain of Case Corin in the western division of the kingdom,[2] and several peculiarities of the latter have been injuriously or injudiciously represented.

The present inhabitants may be divided into two sorts, the Protestants and Papists; the Protestants are almost all originally from England, and have adopted the manners of their mother-country, though at the same time it must be acknowledged that they have superinduced over the rough English character a degree of ceremony and politeness which may sufficiently serve to distinguish the two nations.

The English for instance are rough, prudently generous, and sincere, the Irish protestants are on the contrary affable, foolishly prodigal, hospitable, and often not to be depended upon. This difference from their ancestors they have acquired by long conversation with the original natives, who carry all these faults to a vicious extreme. The original Irish are therefore, frequently found fawning, insincere, and fond of pleasure, prodigality makes them poor, and poverty makes them vicious, such are their faults, but they have national virtues to recompence these defects. They are valiant, sensible, polite, and generally beautiful. Their women have exquisite complexions, though their features are a little broad somewhat approaching that turn of visage which we are told of the Tartars, from whom they pretend to be originally descended.

Whatever beauty they may have in their faces their persons are not equally irreprehensible, for the women are generally too tall for beauty, and are found to have thick legs. But then though there are no where men more lascivious than these, perhaps no country upon earth produces women more modest, we frequently find Irish men turn fortune hunters, but a fortune hunting Irish woman, even in her own country is one of the scarcest of characters.

It must be owned indeed, that no climate in the world is more apt to fan desire than that. The weather is almost always as our spring, and it is scarce known that the water is frozen sufficiently to bear a man's weight. So that if Venus were to fix a temple in any part of the world it might be here in the land of Honeys and Joys. Fanned by luxuriant airs what shepherd refuses to sing, or what nymph disdains to hear.

From hence their manners, their language, and all their poetry is turned to love. On this subject their language otherwise barren is excessively copious,[3] and for one term of endearment in ours, they have ten in theirs.

1. For the evidence of Goldsmith's authorship, see Arthur Friedman (ed.), *Collected Works of Oliver Goldsmith* (Oxford: Clarendon Press, 1966), III, p. 24.
2. Keshcorran in County Sligo, a mountain about forty-five miles from Lissoy, where Goldsmith spent his boyhood. It was renowned for its caves and appears in several literary legends.
3. Goldsmith's ignorance of Irish poetry is painfully obvious here. Much of the love poetry, which was extremely ornate, had a political dimension that seems to have escaped his notice.

The manners of the original inhabitants, which they to this day preserve unvaried, are entirely different from those of the English, and partake somewhat of the ancient Scythian, and modern Spanish customs, as described by travellers and historians, for from these two nations the country was at different periods inhabited. Their burials, pattons,[4] and cakes, their houses, furniture and dress, all partake somewhat of these two different nations, and sufficiently mark the original from whence they sprung.

But in order to give you a more minute description of the inhabitants, I shall present you with one month's adventures in the country, where I was invited from Dublin by a Gentleman who had a handsome country seat upon the western shore. I set out on horseback attended only with one servant, and he an English man, being resolved to observe the manners of the inhabitants more minutely than they had been examined before.

When I had got about forty miles from the capital, I found the country begin to wear a different appearance from what it before appeared to me in. The neat inclosures, the warm and well built houses, the fine cultivated grounds, were no more to be seen, the prospect now changed into, here and there a gentleman's seat, grounds ill cultivated, though seemingly capable of cultivation, little irregular fences made of turf, and topped with brush wood, cut from some neighbouring shrub, and the peasants houses wearing all the appearance of indigence and misery. You will not be surprized, sir, as you know me, that I had curiosity enough to enter one of those mansions, which seemed by its appearance to be the habitation of despair: ordering my servant therefore to walk his horses to a neighbouring inn, I alighted and walked into the peasant's hovel. The first sight that struck me was a cow, tied by the horns at one end of the cottage, and a fire of turf without any chimney in the midst. By this sat the mistress of the house, and her daughter knitting stockings, the first seemed about fifty, her eyes bleared with smoak, the daughter about fifteen, and beautiful as an angel. To say the truth, I was surprized to the last degree to see so much beauty where I expected nothing but objects of compassion. For only conceive an hut the walls of which were about four feet high, and made of clay, thatched only with rushes, dirt, and straw, with a door which I was obliged to stoop to enter, conceive this I say, and how could it be expected to find the goddess of beauty lodged so meanly.

In every thing however I was greatly disappointed, for though nothing seemed more wretched than their situation, both seemed alert and lively, and quite insensible of their uncomfortable way of living. They both desired I might be seated upon a straw truss placed by the fire side, probably designed for the husband against his return. The daughter who could speak a little English was excessively chearful and no way surprized at the appearance of a stranger, for by her mother's directions she invited me to supper.

Though I could not imagine where they could procure any thing fit to be eaten, yet in order to see life I complied with their request; for had I refused, it would have been looked upon by the Irish as the highest affront, and the most unpardonable piece of ill breeding. The daughter and I therefore, immediately entered into conversation till the husband's return, who was by trade a labourer, by which occupation he earned four pence a day without meat and drink, but then as he had two sons and they put their profits into one stock, the daughter assured me they all contrived to live pretty comfortably.

The father and his two sons soon returned, and all instead of surprize testified the sincerest satisfaction at the arrival of their new guest, informing me at the same time that nothing was more common than for great folks to lodge a night in their house, when the neighbouring inn could hold no more. The pot was therefore put down with potatoes, and the whole family were busily employed in providing supper; all but the father who it seems is ever exempted from domestic occupations. Supper was soon upon the table, which consisted of nothing more than potatoes and milk, for the rest of the family, but for the father and me, we were honoured each with a wooden knife, and a print of butter.

We accordingly fell to, and as I had a good appetite, I assure you I never made a more comfortable meal. In order however to do things genteely I offered my landlord half a crown when supper was over for my entertainment, but this he refused with the utmost indignation, telling me at the same time that he scorned to keep an inn, and was resolved never to be such a disgrace to his family. It was with the utmost entreaties therefore,

4. Usually spelt 'patterns', celebrations on the days of patron saints.

that I was permitted to send to the neighbouring alehouse for a shilling's worth of beer, which the daughter ran and fetched in a moment. The circulation of the beer soon threw us all into tip top spirits, I could not behold without the utmost satisfaction the faces of my fellow creatures which were but a little before wrinkled with fatigue and labour, expanding gradually into smiles, and forgetting those miseries which I had before foolishly deemed insupportable. My landlord offered to tell me the story of Kaul Kroodareg,[5] but continues he it will be nothing in English, but in Irish it is finer than fine itself. I declined his offer, pretending to have heard it before, for I had a greater inclination to have some conversation (such Jack is the fraility of us mortals) with the daughter. I therefore attempted to prelude my discourse by a kiss, but guess my surprize, when a favour which the English girls think nothing of bestowing, was denied me. I was therefore obliged in spite of me to let the conversation take a general turn, and answer the news of the day, which was asked me by every one of the family. To these questions I answered to the best of my power, but I found they looked upon my answers as no way satisfactory, they wanted something *strange*, and I had only *news*, to tell them. 'Lord my dear Soul, says my landlord. Taking Quebec, burning the French fleet, ruining what d'ye call him, Tierconneldrago,[6] what signifies all that, where is the wonder there, we have been told here that the king of Prussia, took the whole French army, and fifty pieces of cannon prisoners of war, there is something in such news as that; between ourselves my dear soul, I hate the doubled hearted French, for they have always deceived the Irish, but for all that my dear I love king James in my heart, and God knows I have a good right for my father lost a very good estate by him.' With such discourse it began to grow late, and I thought it time to go to my inn; to this my host objected, for says he, we shall have some clean straw, and you may lie by the fire side, as for us here, we all lie together, my wife, my daughter, and I, at the head of the bed, and Laughlin, and Thady, and our dog at the feet. I thanked him for his offer, and went to my inn where the servant had secured me the best and perhaps the only feather-bed in the house.

Before I left that part of the country, I went to see a wake or funeral, which is entirely peculiar to these people. As soon as a person dies he is immediately carried out into the best appartment, and the bed on which he died is burned at the door. The body is wrapped in linnen all but the face, and thus laid upon the door of the house, which on this occasion is taken off the hinges, and claped[7] under their large square table. Beer, pipes, and tobacco are immediately procured, and all the neighbours are invited to sit up the ensuing night, with the corpse, which they call waking it.

Upon this occasion all the old men and women who are generally fond of beer and tobacco, and all the young ones of both sexes, who are equally fond of diversion assemble at the house of the deceased, in order to howl, to romp, and to tell stories. If the deceased was of any substance there is always employed on this occasion a man whose only employment is story telling, and a woman whose only business is to bear a chorus in every howl. At night fall the plays begin, the young folks no way terrified at the scene of death before them, toy and play tricks and have twenty pastimes suited to the occasion, the old ones smoak, guzzle, and upon the appearance of every stranger, howl in the most dismal manner, to a particular tune which you may have seen set to music. This custom of rejoicing instead of sorrow upon the death of a relation, is still preserved among the Tartars, and I fancy from them it is that the native Irish have taken it. When they have thus watched one night for they never keep the body two, it is next day carried upon men's shoulders to the churchyard, and the women continue howling all the way.

Their cakes also are another peculiarity unknown among the English. Upon certain festivals a large cake is procured made of flower, sugar, spices, &c. and placed upon a pole adorned with ribbons and garlands of flowers. Round this the men and women dance in pairs, and that woman that holds out longest wins the cake, and divides it as she thinks proper. Of all entertainments perhaps this is the most rational, for here they may be literally said to dance for their bread.

Their patrons also I have seen in no other Popish

5. Col Cró-dhearg, meaning 'red-handed violator', the name of an outlaw figure in folk legend.
6. The English took Quebec from the French on 6 October 1759. The British navy burned French ships in August and November of that year. 'Tierconneldrago' refers to the siege of Fort Ticonderoga in New York state in 1758-59, which the British, after severe losses, finally took from the French.

7. slammed (of a door or window).

country in Europe; this is a term perhaps you do not understand, almost every fountain in this country is under the patronage of some saint, where the people once a year meet to shew their strength and best cloaths, drink muddy ale, dance with their mistresses, get drunk, and beat each other with cudgels most unmercifully, these religious meetings are never known to pass without blood shed and battery, and their priests often put themselves at the head of the opposite parties, and gain more renown by cudgel-playing than by piety.

But while I thus describe the lower sort of people, you must not suppose but that the gentry have as much politeness, good-nature, and humanity as those of any other country whatsoever; easy in their manners, excessively fond of the English, hospitable in their houses, and fond of shew. In short I spent a month in a part of the kingdom where I expected to meet nothing but savages in as good company, with as good cheer, and as hearty a reception as I ever remember to have seen. They sit however too long at their meals, I have sometimes staid at the table where we dined for several hours, until the servant came to inform us that supper was served in the next room. They still drink too much which is a certain sign they have not yet arrived at true politeness, since every country is more drunken in proportion as it is barbarous.

I am, &c.

THE HISTORY OF CAROLAN, THE LAST IRISH BARD (1760)

[Goldsmith's account of Turlogh Carolan (1670-1738) is the earliest of the published material on this famous composer and harper. Although it is unreliable in many of its details, the elements of folklore indicate something of Carolan's status and give a sense of the ways in which the Gaelic and Anglo-Irish civilizations touched upon one another.]

There can be perhaps no greater entertainment than to compare the rude Celtic simplicity with modern refinement. Books, however, seem incapable of furnishing the parallel; and to be acquainted with the ancient manners of our own ancestors, we should endeavour to look for their remains in those countries, which, being in some measure retired from an intercourse with other nations, are still untinctured with foreign refinement, language, or breeding.

The Irish will satisfy curiosity in this respect preferably to all other nations I have seen. They, in several parts of that country, still adhere to their ancient language, dress, furniture, and superstitions; several customs among them that still speak their original; and, in some respect, Caesar's description of the Ancient Britons is applicable to these.[1]

Their bards, in particular, are still held in great veneration among them; those traditionary heralds are invited to every funeral, in order to fill up the intervals of the howl with their songs and harps.[2] In these they rehearse the actions of the ancestors of the deceased, bewail the bondage of their country under the English government, and generally conclude with advising the young men and maidens to make the best use of their time, for they will soon, for all their present bloom, be stretched under the table, like the dead body before them.

Of all the bards this country ever produced, the last and the greatest was Carolan the blind.[3] He was at once a poet, a musician, a composer, and sung his own verses to his harp. The original natives never mention his name without rapture; both his poetry and music they have by heart; and even some of the English themselves who have been transplanted there, find his music extremely pleasing. A song beginning *O Rourke's noble fare will ne'er be forgot*, translated by Dean Swift, is of his composition;[4] which though perhaps by this means the best known of his pieces, is yet by no means the most deserving. His songs, in general, may be compared to those of Pindar, as they have frequently the same flights of imagination, and are composed (I don't say written,

1. Caesar, *De Bello Gallico* 4. 20-36; 5. 8-23.
2. The 'howl' is the traditional keening of the women.
3. Turlogh Carolan, the most famous of the itinerant Irish harper/composers. For a full account, see Donal O'Sullivan, *Carolan: The Life and Times of an Irish Harper* 2 vols (London: Routledge & Kegan Paul, 1958; reprinted Celtic Music, Louth, Lincolnshire, 1983). Goldsmith's essay is, according to O'Sullivan, 'the earliest mention of Carolan in literature'.
4. 'The Description of an *Irish-Feast*, translated almost literally out of the original *Irish*', published by Swift in 1735. See Harold Williams (ed.), *The Poems of Jonathan Swift* (Oxford: Clarendon Press, 1937), pp. 243-47. The original, entitled 'Pléaráca na Ruarcach', was by Aodh Mac Gabhráin (Hugh Magauran). See O'Sullivan, I, pp. 83-86; and A. Carpenter and A. Harrison, 'Swift's "O'Rourke's Feast" and Sheridan's "Letter": Early Transcripts by Anthony Raymond' in H. J. Real and H. J. Vienken (eds), *Proceedings of the First Münster Symposium on Jonathan Swift* (Munich: Wilhelm Fink Verlag, 1985), pp. 27-46.

for he could not write) merely to flatter some man of fortune upon some excellence of the same kind. In these one man is praised for the excellence of his stable, as in Pindar, another for his hospitality, a third for the beauty of his wife and children, and a fourth for the antiquity of his family. Whenever any of the original natives of distinction were assembled at feasting or revelling, Carolan was generally there, where he was always ready with his harp, to celebrate their praises. He seemed by nature formed for his profession; for as he was born blind, so also he was possessed of a most astonishing memory, and a facetious turn of thinking, which gave his entertainers infinite satisfaction. Being once at the house of an Irish nobleman, where there was a musician present, who was eminent in the profession, Carolan immediately challenged him to a trial of skill. To carry the jest forward, his lordship persuaded the musician to accept the challenge, and he accordingly played over on his fiddle the fifth concerto of Vivaldi. Carolan, immediately taking his harp, played over the whole piece after him, without missing a note, though he had never heard it before: which produced some surprize; but their astonishment increased, when he assured them he could make a concerto in the same taste himself, which he instantly composed,[5] and that with such spirit and elegance, that it may compare (for we have it still) with the finest compositions of Italy.

His death was not more remarkable than his life. Homer was never more fond of a glass than he; he would drink whole pints of Usquebaugh,[6] and, as he used to think, without any ill consequence. His intemperance, however, in this respect, at length brought on an incurable disorder, and when just at the point of death, he called for a cup of his beloved liquor. Those who were standing round him, surprised at the demand, endeavoured to persuade him to the contrary; but he persisted, and when the bowl was brought him, attempted to drink but could not; wherefore, giving away the bowl, he observed with a smile, that it would be hard if two such friends as he and the cup should part at least without kissing; and then expired.

5. This improbable story is repeated later by other commentators on Carolan (see O'Sullivan, I, pp. 144-48). The tune known as Carolan's Concerto is one of the many he wrote for patrons and is more properly known as 'Mrs Power', the wife of a Galway landowner, David Power.

6. whiskey (Irish, *uisce bheatha*, 'water of life').

from: A COMPARATIVE VIEW OF RACES AND NATIONS (1760)

[These two pieces were published in the *Royal Magazine* in June and September 1760. Much of what Goldsmith says of the influence of climate upon races, of the difference between Europe and the Orient, and of the nature and quality of British liberty, derives from French sources, such as Montesquieu and the Marquis d'Argens, as well as any number of English tracts on the liberty England had gained in 1688. The piece is a good example of Goldsmith's skill in reproducing, in bland terms, a powerful political and racial ideology.]

To the Author of the ROYAL MAGAZINE

SIR,

O Felices Nimium, bona si sua Norint Anglicani![1] The Traveller, who after an absence of fifteen years revisits his native country, feels a joy which it is impossible to express. That spot which gave him birth, how rude, how barbarous soever, has beauties beyond the most charming scene that ever art improved or fancy painted. Placed on his native mountain, the returning wanderer feels an happiness beyond whatever the vales of Caprea, or the orange-groves of Naples, could afford; finds more solid satisfaction in cultivating his little kitchen-garden at home, than when indolently stretched beneath the luxuriant shades of Pisa.

The Scotchman who wish'd for an estate in Arno's vale,[2] that he might sell it and buy one at home in the highlands, was not so ignorant as we at first might be apt to imagine: those dear relatives he had left behind, might have enhanced the value of his country.[3] To grow old in the same fields where we once were young; to be capable of every moment beholding objects that recal [*sic*] our early pleasures;

1. Virgil, Georgics ii. 458-59: 'O fortunatos nimium bona si sua norint agricolas.' Goldsmith adapts the quotation to read 'O happy Englishmen; too happy should they come to know their blessings.'

2. The upper valley of the river Arno in Tuscany is famous for its beautiful countryside.

3. Arthur Friedman quotes Goldsmith writing to an Irish friend as follows: 'Unaccountable [fond]ness for country, this maladie du Pays, as the french [call] it. Unaccountable, that he should have an affec[tion for] a place, who never received when in it above civil [contem]pt, who never brought out of it, except his brogue [an]d his blunders; sure my affection is equally ridiculous with the Scotchman's, who refused to be cured of the itch because it made him unco' [i.e. very] thoughtful of his wife and bonny Inverary.'

to measure our own years by the trees that our hands have planted, are more truly pleasing than may at first be imagined. We entertain for every mountain, stream, or cottage, that we have been accustomed to see, an habitual fondness; and each is capable of improving our sensations. 'Methinks, says the sensible Menage, I would not wish to see even an old post removed with which I had been long acquainted.'[4]

After a life of the most dissipated variety, after having strayed through so many countries without being regarded, or known, with what enthusiasm do I again visit the happy island where I drew my first breath, and received the early pleasures and institutions of life? After so many fatigues, dangers, discontents; after seeing so many millions of faces, without finding one friend among the number, to be again restored to my country, my friends, my relations, to a competency for life; what rapture, what poignant satisfaction? here let me spend the small remainder of my days in tranquillity and content: here let the rest of my life be passed in attempts to improve my fellow-creatures: let the last running of that current be useful, which has hitherto been exhausted in a vain search for something new, in restless and unsatisfying curiosity!

Hail Britain, happiest of countries! happy in thy climate, fertility, situation, and commerce; but still happier in the peculiar nature of thy laws and government. Examine every state in Europe, and you will find the people either enjoying a precarious freedom under monarchical government, or what is worse, actually slaves in a republic, to laws of their own contriving. What constitutes the peculiar happiness of Britain, is, that laws may be overlooked without endangering the state. In a mere republic, which pretends to equal freedom, every infringement upon law is a dissolution of government, and must consequently be punished with the most unremitting severity; but in England, laws may be sometimes overlooked without danger. A King who has it in his power to pardon, gives the government at once the strength of the oak, and the flexibility of the yew.

England is not less happy with respect to climate: the almost continual spring of Italy, does not indeed adorn our fields; but if we want their spring, we are also without their sultry summer. We have no occasion to pant after the valleys of Hæmus, or wish for the deep embowering shade:[5] our summers are less warm, and our winters are to the senses less cold, than those of any other country.

These are some of the many advantages we enjoy above the rest of mankind; nature pours her gifts round us, and we only want a proper temper to enjoy them. I should esteem it my greatest happiness, could my travels conduce to form such a temper; could they make one individual more happy in himself, or more useful to society; could I enlarge one mind, and make the man who now boasts his patriotism, a citizen of the world;[6] could I level those distinctions which separate mankind; could I teach the English to allow strangers to have their excellencies; could I mend that country in which I reside, by improvements from those which I have left behind.

'In whatever part of the world fortune pleases to throw me, whatever character she gives me to act, says the Tyanean of old, let me consider mankind as my friends, and think myself at home. The brown Indian and the pallid Gaul, in my eyes, only differ in external covering: the polished Athenian and the savage Thracian have their peculiar virtues, and what one attains by refinement, the other makes up by sincerity. Where-ever I turn, I find the earth peopled with many fools, some villains, and but few that are wise.'[7]

In all the circle of knowledge, there is not perhaps a more pleasing employment, than that of comparing countries with each other; if the traveller happens to be possessed of talents equal to the enquiry; who knows where to dilate, and where to be concise; who with a well-directed understanding passes hastily through the howling wilderness or sandy desart, but enjoys the cultivated spot, the peopled valley, with an abiding delectation.

Come then, and let us take a view of this earth in which providence has placed us; let us at least

4. Not found in *Ménagiana* 3 vols (Paris, 1715) (Friedman).

5. Haemus is a mountain, separating Thrace from Thessaly and commanding a view of the Euxine and Adriatic seas. On 'imbower', cf. Milton, *Paradise Lost*, I, 303-04:

'. . . where the Etrurian shades
High over-arch'd embower.'

Some lines earlier, Milton refers to the river Arno, on which Florence stands.

6. The phrase, used as the equivalent to a philosopher, was widely used before Goldsmith adopted it. See H. J. Smith, *Oliver Goldsmith's 'The Citizen of the World': A Study* (New Haven: Yale University Press, 1926).

7. Flavius Philostratus (born *c.* 170 A.D.), wrote the *Life of Appolonius of Tyana*, a philosophizing mystic of the first century. A.D. Friedman reports that the quotation cannot be traced there.

examine the out-lines of the universal plan; let us survey the various customs of the inhabitants. To compare the individuals of one nation with each other, has been performed by others: to consider nations in the same light as individuals, and to improve our native customs by whatever appears praiseworthy among foreigners, has been hitherto unattempted; it makes a subject at once replete with instruction and entertainment....

THE SAME SUBJECT CONTINUED

To the Author of the ROYAL MAGAZINE

SIR,
If we compare the inhabitants of Europe with those of the other parts of the globe, the latter will appear not much superior to the fabled satyrs of antiquity, and possessed of little more of humanity than the appearance. It is true, the Turks, Persians, and Indians, have their schools for learning as well as we: in Constantinople, Grand Cairo, Ispahan, and Agra, there are professors appointed by the state to instruct the nobility in astronomy, geometry, arithmetic, poetry, and the Arabic language; but their learning, instead of opening the mind, only adds obstinacy and vanity to their ignorance: so that they labour under all the errors of falsehood, and all the pride of pedantry.

It is a subject worthy consideration, how it comes to pass that those countries which enjoy so much fertility, and so happy a climate, where the inhabitants have not only leisure to cultivate philosophy, but have frequent admonitions to that purpose, in many of the books of their law: it is a matter of surprise, I say, how these countries, which were the first to nurse infant science, and to divulge it to the world; who, after a long succession of ignorance, once more under the Arabian caliphs emerged into politeness; it is surprising how they have relapsed into more than the pristine barbarity.

The kingdoms of Asia Minor are by no means so populous now as formerly, and that from the defects of its government; while one part of the country is too closely inhabited, another part is seen without any inhabitants at all; a country becomes steril by too much or too little cultivation, hence the whole face of nature is changed at length, here into spots worn out by too frequent tillage, there into tracts grown wild and barren from want of human culture. As every country becomes barren, it is proportionably depopulated; and as the people diminish, so do the love, and even the utility of the sciences diminish also.

Hence we see how the inhabitants of Asia are more savage than those of Europe; where the whole domain is divided into small districts, and governed with equity; where the inhabitants are more equably diffused, and where all find in mutual distrust mutual security.

The difference between the Asiatics and Europeans is striking and obvious; and even the natives of the east themselves acknowledge our mental superiority. But it is a more difficult task, and requires a more acute discernment, to be able well to describe the minute differences which obtain among the respective countries of Europe, compared with each other; to ascertain the genius and character of each, how far it proceeds from accident, climate, government, or religion; and to represent the whole uninfluenced by resentment, and unbiassed by national partiality.

To begin with Ireland, the most western part of the continent, the natives are particularly remarkable for the gaiety and levity of their dispositions: the English, transplanted there, in time lose their melancholy serious air, and become gay and thoughtless, more fond of pleasure, and less addicted to reasoning. This difference of disposition cannot properly be said to arise from climate or soil, which is in general the same as in England; but merely from the nature of their government. They live in a fruitful country, sequestered from the rest of mankind, protected by a powerful nation from foreign insult; and regardless of neighbouring greatness, they have no important national concerns to make them anxious, or cloud their tempers with the solemnity of pride. In such circumstances they are contented with indolence and pleasure, take every happiness as it presents, are easily excited to resent, and as easily induced to submission.[8]

Scotland, till of late, had in itself the power as well of foreign as domestic administration; a consciousness of power, and a long continued government, always produces a love of one's country. The Scotch therefore are still partial to their countrymen, and jealous of their country's honour. The cause of these passions first implanted among them,

8. Compare this with the equally idyllic view given in *A Description of the Manners and Customs of the Native* Irish.

has ceased with the discontinuance of national administration; but the effects are still visible, and may continue so for several ages. Their country is barren, and consequently the people are frugal; it would be absurd for the natives to indulge the same desire for pleasure, that those of the country before-mentioned entertain; for this would be to create wants which it is not in the power of nature to satisfy. Their frugality brings several other virtues in its train; they have fortitude in adversity, because they have from their youth been taught to suffer; and they have moderation in prosperity, for it is seldom that those who have been bred frugally during the younger part of life, after a certain age gain new tastes for luxury and refinement.

The English are not less divided from the rest of the world by the circumfluent seas, than differing from them in their manners, dispositions, and turn of thinking: and these peculiarities may be ascribed partly to the government, and partly to the climate and soil. As the government is charged with the most important concerns of Europe, and as every man has some share in the government, he by this means acquires a conscious importance, and this superinduces that gloom of solid felicity which foreigners have mistaken in some for melancholy and spleen: the soil is fruitful, and this prompts to luxury; but as those necessaries which are eaten are produced in greater plenty and delicacy than those which are drank, in other words, as the soil produces the most excellent meats, but no wine, the inhabitants are more apt to indulge an excess of eating than drinking; and this has a mechanical effect upon the tempers: it encreases their seeming severity, so that they are grave without phlegm, and apparently ill-natured with hearts sympathising with every distress. They are distinguished from the rest of Europe by their superior accuracy in reasoning, and are in general called the nation of philosophers by their neighbours of the continent; this superiority of reason is only the consequence of their freedom; they pursue truth wherever it may lead, regardless of the result; and unawed by power, give a loose to the most hidden workings of the mind: wherever philosophy takes root in a country of freedom and solemnity, it must certainly flourish; the one gives courage to pursue the literary adventure, and the other gives perseverance in the journey.

It has long however been a doubt, whether the passion for liberty, now implanted among the English, be merely the result of accident; or whether it proceeds from the influence of external causes, or whether an Englishman is naturally more fond of freedom than others, who are unacquainted with the happiness of its effects.

If we regard some other animals which the country produces, and consider their impetuosity, their fierceness, their courage, and how they lose those qualities when they leave the soil, we shall be apt to attribute that impatience of servitude, which the English are so very remarkable for, to physical causes.

They have ever been noted for a jealousy of their privileges, and even in the times of the Romans were remarkable for treating strangers with severity, whom they fancied were only spies upon their liberties and constitution.

This principle of liberty, of impatience under restraint, probably proceeds from their happy situation; as they have no foreign foes to distract their attention, every care is fixed upon internal happiness, and as they know no external enemies that are truly dreadful, none can be so great a foe as he who would restrain that freedom of which strangers leave them in quiet possession.

from:
THE CITIZEN OF THE WORLD (1762)

[The one hundred and nineteen Chinese letters, which first appeared in the daily newspaper, *The Public Ledger*, in late January 1760 and weekly thereafter until 14 August 1761, were collected, with additions, in two volumes, published in 1762 under the title *The Citizen of the World; or, Letters from a Chinese Philosopher, Residing in London, to his Friends in the East*. In this work, Goldsmith treats with irony the theme of misplaced benevolence, which was to play such an important role in his novel *The Vicar of Wakefield* (1766) and his play *The Good Natur'd Man* (1768). The fiction of the foreign traveller allowed the author to comment on established convention by making it seem strange and thereby questioning its security. Much of the comment in the work is reserved for recent developments in the English social structure, including alterations in the profession of writing. With the decline of patronage, the writer grew dependent on the bookseller and the bookseller in turn became dependent upon, although he also helped to form, the public taste. The number of books increased by the year; the writer began to perform functions previously carried out by the preacher. Yet, despite his increased importance, the writer was badly paid for his important ameliorative and instructional role.

All of this has a direct bearing on the hard life Goldsmith lived in the London of the day. Even so, his distinctive suavity of manner does not desert him. As always, he manages, through the figure of his Chinese visitor, Lien Chi Altangi, to create a measurable distance between himself and the oddities and injustices that he addresses.]

LETTER LXXV

[The necessity of amusing each other with new books, insisted upon.]

From Lien Chi Altangi, to Fum Hoam, first president of the Ceremonial Academy at Pekin, in China

There are numbers in this city who live by writing new books, and yet there are thousands of volumes in every large library unread and forgotten. This, upon my arrival, was one of those contradictions which I was unable to account for. Is it possible, said I, that there should be any demand for new books, before those already published are read? Can there be so many employed in producing a commodity with which the market is already overstocked; and with goods also better than any of modern manufacture.

What at first view appeared an inconsistence, is a proof at once of this people's wisdom and refinement. Even allowing the works of their ancestors better written than theirs, yet those of the moderns acquire a real value, by being marked with the impression of the times. Antiquity has been in the possession of others, the present is our own; let us first therefore learn to know what belongs to ourselves, and then if we have leisure, cast our reflections back to the reign of *Shouou*, who governed twenty thousand years before the creation of the moon.

The volumes of antiquity like medals, may very well serve to amuse the curious, but the works of the moderns, like the current coin of a kingdom, are much better for immediate use; the former are often prized above their intrinsic value, and kept with care, the latter seldom pass for more than they are worth, and are often subject to the merciless hands of sweating critics, and clipping compilers; the works of antiquity were ever praised, those of the moderns read, the treasures of our ancestors have our esteem, and we boast the passion, those of cotemporary genius engage our heart altho' we blush to own it. The visits we pay the former resemble those we pay the great; the ceremony is troublesome, and yet such as we would not chuse to forego; our acquaintance with modern books, is like sitting with a friend; our pride is not flattered in the interview, but it gives more internal satisfaction.

In proportion as society refines, new books must ever become more necessary. Savage rusticity is reclaimed by oral admonition alone; but the elegant excesses of refinement are best corrected by the still voice of studious enquiry. In a polite age, almost every person becomes a reader, and receives more instruction from the press than the pulpit. The preaching Bonse[1] may instruct the illiterate peasant; but nothing less than the insinuating address of a fine writer can win its way to an heart already relaxed in all the effeminacy of refinement. Books are necessary to correct the vices of the polite, but those vices are ever changing, and the antidote should be changed accordingly; should still be new.

Instead therefore of thinking the number of new publications here too great, I could wish it still greater, as they are the most useful instruments of reformation. Every country must be instructed either by *writers* or *preachers*; but as the number of readers encreases, the number of hearers is proportionably diminished, the writer becomes more useful, and the preaching Bonse less necessary.

Instead, therefore, of complaining that writers are overpaid, when their works procure them a bare subsistence, I should imagine it the duty of a state not only to encourage their numbers, but their industry. A Bonse is rewarded with immense riches for instructing only a few, even of the most ignorant, of the people; and sure the poor scholar should not beg his bread, who is capable of instructing a million!

Of all rewards, I grant, the most pleasing to a man of real merit, is fame; but a polite age, of all times, is that in which scarce any share of merit can acquire it. What numbers of fine writers in the latter empire of Rome, when refinement was carried to the highest pitch, have missed that fame and immortality which they had fondly arrogated to themselves? How many Greek authors, who wrote at that period when Constantinople was the refined

1. A European term for a Buddhist monk of Japan or China.

mistress of the empire, now rest either not printed, or not read, in the libraries of Europe! Those who came first, while either state as yet was barbarous, carried all the reputation away. Authors, as the age refined, became more numerous, and their numbers destroyed their fame. It is but natural, therefore, for the writer, when conscious that his works will not procure him fame hereafter, to endeavour to make them turn out to his temporal interest here.

Whatever be the motives which induce men to write, whether avarice or fame, the country becomes most wise and happy, in which they most serve for instructors. The countries where sacerdotal instruction alone is permitted, remain in ignorance, superstition, and hopeless slavery. In England where there are as many new books published as in all the rest of Europe together, a spirit of freedom and reason reigns among the people; they have been often known to act like fools, they are generally found to think like men.

The only danger that attends a multiplicity of publications, is that some of them may be calculated to injure, rather than benefit society. But where writers are numerous, they also serve as a check upon each other, and perhaps a literary inquisition is the most terrible punishment that can be conceived, to a literary transgressor.

But to do the English justice, there are but few offenders of this kind, their publications in general aim at mending either the heart, or improving the common weal. The dullest writer talks of virtue, and liberty, and benevolence with esteem; tells his true story, filled with good and wholesome advice; warns against slavery, bribery, or the bite of a mad dog, and dresses up his little useful magazine of knowledge and entertainment, at least with a good intention. The dunces of France, on the other hand, who have less encouragement, are more vicious. Tender hearts, languishing eyes, Leonora in love at thirteen, ecstatic transports, stolen blisses, are the frivolous subjects of their frivolous memoirs. In England, if a bawdy blockhead thus breaks in on the community, he sets his whole fraternity in a roar; nor can he escape, even though he should fly to nobility for shelter.

Thus even dunces, my friend, may make themselves useful. But there are others whom nature has blest with talents above the rest of mankind; men capable of thinking with precision, and impressing their thought with rapidity. Beings who diffuse those regards upon mankind, which others contract and settle upon themselves. These deserve every honour from that community of which they are more peculiarly the children, to such I would give my heart, since to them I am indebted for its humanity!

Adieu

LETTER LVII

[The difficulty of rising in literary reputation, without intrigue or riches.]

From Lien Chi Altangi, to Fum Hoam, first president of the Ceremonial Academy at Pekin, in China

I have frequently admired the manner of criticising in China, where the learned are assembled in a body to judge of every new publication; to examine the merits of the work without knowing the circumstances of the author, and then to usher it into the world with the proper marks of respect or reprobation.

In England there are no such tribunals erected; but if a man thinks proper to be a judge of genius, few will be at the pains to contradict his pretensions. If any chuse to be critics, it is but saying they are critics; and from that time forward they become invested with full power and authority over every caitiff[2] who aims at their instruction or entertainment.

As almost every member of society has by this means a vote in literary transactions; it is no way surprizing to find the rich leading the way here as in other common concerns of life, to see them either bribing the numerous herd of voters by their interest, or brow beating them by their authority.

A great man says, at his table, that such a book *is no bad thing.* Immediately the praise is carried off by five flatterers to be dispersed at twelve different coffee-houses, from whence it circulates, still improving as it proceeds, through forty-five houses, where cheaper liquors are sold, from thence it is carried away by the honest tradesman to his own fire-side, where the applause is eagerly caught up by his wife and children, who have been long taught to regard his judgment as the standard of perfection. Thus when we have traced a wide extended literary reputation up to its original source, we shall find it derived from some great

2. A base, despicable wretch.

man, who has, perhaps, received all his education and English from a tutor of Berne, or a dancing master of Picardie.

The English are a people of good sense; and I am the more surprized to find them sway'd in their opinions, by mean who often from their very education, are incompetent judges. Men who being always bred in affluence, see the world only on one side, are surely improper judges of human nature: they may indeed describe a ceremony, a pageant, or a ball; but how can they pretend to dive into the secrets of the human heart, who have been nursed up only in forms, and daily behold nothing but the same insipid adulation smiling upon every face. Few of them have been bred in that best of schools, the school of adversity; and by what I can learn, fewer still have been bred in any school at all.

From such a description one would think, that a droning Duke, or a Dowager Dutchess, was not possessed of more just pretensions to taste than persons of less quality; and yet, whatever the one or the other may write or praise, shall pass for perfection without farther examination. A nobleman has but to take pen, ink, and paper, and write away through three large volumes, and then sign his name to the title page, tho' the whole might have been before more disgusting than his own rent roll, yet signing his name and title gives value to the deed; title being alone equivalent to taste, imagination, and genius.

As soon as a piece therefore is published, the first questions are, Who is the author? Does he keep a coach? Where lies his estate? What sort of a table does he keep? If he happens to be poor and unqualified for such a scrutiny, he and his works sink into irremediable obscurity; and too late he finds, that having fed upon turtle is a more ready way to fame than having digested Tully.

The poor devil, against whom fashion has set its face, vainly alledges, that he has been bred in every part of Europe where knowledge was to be sold; that he has grown palc in the study of nature and himself; his works may please upon the perusal, but his pretensions to fame are entirely disregarded; he is treated like a fidler, whose music, though liked, is not much praised, because he lives by it; while a gentleman performer, though the most wretched scraper alive, throws the audience into raptures. The fidler indeed may in such a case console himself by thinking, that while the other goes off with all the praise, he runs away with all the money: but here the parallel drops; for while the nobleman triumphs in unmerited applause, the author by profession steals off with — *Nothing*.

The poor, therefore, here, who draw their pens auxiliary to the laws of their country,[3] must think themselves very happy if they find, not fame but forgiveness; and yet they are hardly treated; for as every country grows more polite, the press becomes more useful; and writers become more necessary, as readers are supposed to increase. In a polished society, that man, though in rags, who has the power of enforcing virtue from the press, is of more real use than forty stupid brachmans,[4] or bonzes, or guebres,[5] though they preached never so often, never so loud, or never so long. That man, though in rags, who is capable of deceiving even indolence into wisdom, and who professes amusement while he aims at reformation, is more useful in refined society than twenty cardinals with all their scarlet, and tricked out in all the fopperies of scholastic finery.

3. By this the correspondent means that the writer helps the legislature. He prevents crimes; he does not punish them.
4. An obsolete form of 'brahmin'.
5. A Zoroastrian or Parsee.

from: A GENERAL HISTORY OF THE WORLD FROM THE CREATION TO THE PRESENT TIME . . .

By William Guthrie, Esq; John Gray, Esq;
And others eminent in this Branch of Literature
(1764)

[The twelve-volume work *A General History of the World*, to which Goldsmith contributed this preface, was a typical piece of bookmaking by the publisher John Newbery and a group of other booksellers. It is, despite what Goldsmith says here, a dreary compilation. But his plea for simplicity, accessibility and for the painless imparting of knowledge to the audience, allies him with those writers of the Enlightenment who sought to inform and please at once, thereby improving the condition of mankind.]

PREFACE

Experience every day convinces us, that no part of learning affords so much wisdom upon such easy terms as history. Our advances in most other studies are slow and disgusting, acquired with effort, and retained with difficulty; but in a well written history, every step we proceed only serves to encrease our ardour: we profit by the experience of others without sharing their toils or misfortunes; and in this part of knowlege in a more particular manner study is but relaxation.

Of all histories however, that, which not confined to any particular reign or country, but which extends to the transactions of all mankind, is the most useful and entertaining. As in geography, we can have no just idea of the situation of one country without knowing that of others, so in history, it is in some measure necessary to be acquainted with the whole, thoroughly to comprehend a part. There is a constant, tho' sometimes concealed, concatenation in events by which they produce each other, and without a knowledge of which they cannot be comprehended separately. The rise of one kingdom is often found owing to political defects in some other. The arts and learning of succeeding states take a tincture from those countries from whence they were originally derived. Some nations have been applauded for plans of government, which an acquaintance with general history would have shewn were not their own; while others have been reproached for barbarities which were not natural to them, but the result of erroneous imitation. Thus no one part of the general picture can be thoroughly conceived alone; but by taking in the whole of history at one view, we can trace every cause to its remotest source, observe how far every nation was indebted to its own efforts for its rise or decline, how far to accident or the particular circumstances of the country around it. We may here trace the gradations of its improvement or decay, mark in what degree conquerors introduced refinement among those they subdued, or how far they conformed to the soil and put on barbarity. By such reflections as these, and by applying the transactions of past times to our own, we may become more capable of regulating our private conduct, or directing that of others in society.

A knowledge of universal history is therefore highly useful, nor is it less entertaining. *Tacitus* complains, that the transactions of a few reigns could not afford him a sufficient stock of materials to please or interest the reader;[1] but here that objection is entirely removed; an history of the world presents the most striking events, with the greatest variety. In fact, what can be more entertaining than thus reviewing this vast theatre where we ourselves are performers, to converse with those who have been great or famous, to condemn the vices of tyrants without fearing their resentment, or praise the virtues of the good without conscious adulation, to constitute ourselves judges of the merit of even kings, and thus to anticipate what posterity will say of such as now hear only the voice of flattery. These are a part of the many advantages which universal history has over all others, and which have encouraged so many writers to attempt compiling works of this kind, among the ancients as well as the moderns. Each of them seems to have been invited by the manifest utility of the design; yet it must be owned, that many of them have failed through the great and unforeseen difficulties of the undertaking.

Nor will the reader be surprized if he considers how many obstructions an historian, who embarks in a work of this nature, has to interrupt his progress. The barrenness of events in the early periods of history, and their fertility in modern times, equally serve to encrease his embarrasments. In recounting the transactions of remote antiquity, there is such a defect of materials, that the willingness of mankind to supply the chasm, has given birth to falsehood and invited conjecture. The farther we look back into those distant periods, all the objects seem to become more obscure, or are totally lost by a sort of perspective diminution. In this case, therefore, when the eye of truth could no longer discern clearly, fancy undertook to form the picture, and fables were invented where truths were wanting. So that were an historian to relate all that has been conjectured concerning the transactions before the flood, it would be found to compose by no means the smallest part of universal history, a composition equally voluminous, obscure, and disgusting.

In the work, therefore, which is here presented to the public, we have been very concise in relating these fictions and conjectures, which have been the result of idleness, fraud, or superstition. Nor yet would the task have been difficult to amaze the ignorant, as some have done before us, with obscure erudition and scholastic conjecture. The regions of conjectural erudition are wide and extensive; in them there is room for every new adventurer, and

1. An adaptation of the comparison Tacitus draws between himself, as imperial historian, and the republican historians. See *Annals*, 4.32-33.

immense loads of neglected learning still remain to be carried from thence into our own language. There, as in those desolate and remote countries that are colonized by sickening states, every stranger who thinks proper may enter and cultivate; there is much room; but after much labour he will most probably find it an ungrateful soil....

Man, while yet unreduced by laws, and struggling with the beasts of the forest for divided dominion, while yet savage and solitary, was scarce an object whose actions were worth transmitting to posterity. The value of history arises from the necessary diversity of laws, arts, and customs among men, which inform the understanding, and produce an agreeable variety; but savage life is the same in every climate and every age, presenting the observer only with one uniform picture, a life of suspicion, indolence, improvidence, and rapacity. Besides, the nearer history comes home to the present times, the more it is our interest to be acquainted with it, the accounts of ancient ages being only useful as introductory to our own; wherefore it happens well that those parts of which we know the least, are the least necessary to be known.

Sensible, therefore, how liable we are to redundancy in this first part of our design, it has been our endeavour to unfold ancient history with all possible conciseness; and, solicitous to improve the reader's stock of knowlege, we have been indifferent as to the display of our own. We have not stopt to discuss or confute all the absurd conjectures men of speculation have thrown in our way. We at first had even determined not to embarrass the page of truth with the names of those whose labours had only been calculated to encumber it with falsehood and vain speculation. However, we have thought proper, upon second thoughts, slightly to mention them and their opinions, quoting the author at the bottom of the page, so that the reader who is curious about such particularities, may know where to have recourse for fuller information. But critical philology of this kind, is pretty much and justly exploded in the present age: at the revival of letters, indeed, when all the stores of antiquity were as yet unexplored, the learned, as might naturally be expected, made greater use of their memory than their judgment, and exhausted their industry in examining opinions not yet well known. But all that could conduce to enlighten history, has been since often examined, and placed in every point of view; it now only remains to shew a skill rather in selecting than collecting, to discover a true veneration for the works of the ancients, not by compiling their sentiments, but by imitating their elegant simplicity.

As in the early part of history a want of real facts hath induced many to spin out the little that was known with conjecture, so in the modern department the superfluity of trifling anecdotes was equally apt to introduce confusion. In one case history has been rendered tedious from our want of knowing the truth, in the other, from knowing too much of truths not worth our notice. Every year that is added to the age of the world, serves to lengthen the page of its history; so that to give this branch of learning a just length in the circle of human pursuits, it is necessary to abridge several of the least important facts. It is true we often at present see the annals of a single reign, or even the transactions of a single year, occupying folios: But can the writers of such tedious journals ever hope to reach posterity? Or do they think that our descendants, whose attention will naturally be turned to their own concerns, can exhaust so much time in the examination of ours? Though a late elegant writer has said much in favour of abridgments, we neither approve nor contend for them; but even such mutilated accounts are better than to have that short duration alloted us here below entirely taken up with minute details and uninteresting events. There are many other useful branches of knowlege as well as history to share our industry; but from the extent of some late works of this kind, one would be led to suppose, that this study alone were recommended to fill up all the vacuities of life, and that to contemplate what others had done, was all we had to do.

A plan of general history rendered too extensive, deters us from a study that is perhaps of all others the most useful, by rendering it too laborious; and instead of alluring our curiosity, excites our despair. A late work has appeared to us highly obnoxious in this respect. There have been already published of that performance not less than fifty four volumes, and it still remains unfinished,[2] and perhaps may continue to go on *finishing* while it continues to find purchasers, or till time itself can no longer furnish

2. Friedman identifies this as referring to *An Universal History, from the Earliest Account of Time*, continued as *The Modern Part of Universal History*. By 1763, it had reached its sixty-first volume.

new materials. Already, as *Livy* hath exprest it upon a different occasion, *eo crevit ut magnitudine laboret sua*,[3] it is grown to such a size, as actually to seem sinking under the weight of its own corpulence. In fact, where is the reader possest of sufficient fortitude to undertake the painful task of travelling through such an immense tract of compilation, particularly if thro' the greatest part of his journey he should find no landschapes to amuse nor pleasing regions to invite, but a continued uniformity of dreary prospects, shapeless ruins, and fragments of mutilated antiquity. Writers are unpardonable who convert our amusement into labour, and divest knowlege of one of its most pleasing allurements. The ancients have represented history under the figure of a woman, easy, graceful, and inviting; but we have seen her in our days converted like the virgin of Nabis[4] into an instrument of torture. But in truth, such as read for profit, and not for ostentation, seldom have any thing to do with such voluminous productions, which are utterly unsuited to human talents and time; they are at first usually caught up by vanity, and admired by ignorance; from their weight they naturally descend into the lower shelves of a large library, and ever after keep their stations there in unmolested obscurity.

How far we have retrenched these excesses, and steered between the opposites of exuberance and abridgment, the judicious are left to determine. We here offer the public an history of mankind from the earliest account of time to the present age, in twelve volumes, which, upon mature deliberation, appeared to us the proper mean. For as some have lengthened similar undertakings to ten times that size, so others have comprized the whole in one tenth of our compass. Thus, for instance, *Turselinus, Puffendorf, Bossuet*, and *Holberg*,[5] have each reduced universal history into a single volume. But as the former are found fatiguing from their prolixity, so the latter are unsatisfactory from the necessary brevity to which they are confined. It has been therefore our endeavour to give every fact its full scope; but at the same time to retrench all disgusting superfluity, to give every object the due proportion it ought to maintain in the general picture of mankind without crowding the canvas; such an history should, in one respect, resemble a well formed dictionary of arts and sciences; both should serve as a complete library of science or history to every man, except in his own profession, in which more particular tracts or explanations may be wanted. We flatter ourselves, therefore, that this will be found both concise and perspicuous, tho' it must be candidly confessed, that we sate down less desirous of making a succinct history than a pleasing one; we sought after elegance alone, but accidentally found conciseness in our pursuit.

But to attain a just elegance, order was requisite; it was necessary, in so complex a subject, to be very careful both of the method and the connexion. This is a point in which all writers of general history have usually vied with their predecessors, every last attempt discovering the defects in the former: and indeed to do each justice, every last attempt seems to have been the best in this respect. Method, in very complex subjects, is one of those attainments which is gained only by the successive application of different talents to the same pursuit; it is mended by repeated effort, and refines as it flows; so that from the times of the first writer of this kind among the moderns that we remember, down to that of the late Universal History published in fifty four volumes, the distribution of the parts has gone on improving. It would therefore be the height of injustice not to acknowlege our obligations to those writers last-mentioned for their assistance in this particular. We have, however, laid hold of every opportunity that offered of improvement, particularly by proscribing all such foreign matter as tended to lead the reader away from the principal subject. Uniformity in a work of this kind should be principally attended to; in a subject like this, consisting of heterogeneous parts that are at best feebly

3. Livy, *History*, Book I, Preface: 'it has gradually increased to such an extent that it is distressed by its own bulk.'
4. Nabis, a celebrated tyrant of Lacedaemon, made a statue resembling his wife. When anyone refused to surrender his riches to him, Nabis had him taken to the statue which, moved by secret springs, seized the victim in its arms and tormented him with an array of sharp points and prickles hidden under the splendid clothes with which it was bedecked.
5. Orazio Torsellino wrote a single volume history of the world, *Historiarum, ab origine mundi* (1710).

Samuel Puf(f)endorf (1632-94) was one of the greatest exponents of international law. His most renowned work is *De Jure Naturae et Gentium* (1688).

Jacques Bénigne Bossuet (1627-1704), the greatest preacher of seventeenth-century France, was the author of *Discours sur l'histoire universelle* (1681).

Baron Ludwig Holberg wrote a *General History of Christianity* (1749-77).

held together, we should never render the connexion still more feeble by the insinuation of new materials; or, to express it in a different manner, where there is already danger of embarrasment from multitude, the introduction of foreign members would but necessarily encrease the tumult. We hope, therefore, that the reader will here see the revolutions of empires without confusion, and trace arts and laws from one kingdom to another, without losing his interest in the narrative of their other transactions.

To attain these ends with greater certainty of success, we have taken care in some measure to banish that late, and we may add, gothic practice of using a multiplicity of notes; a thing as much unknown to the ancient historians as it is disgusting in the moderns. *Balzac* somewhere calls vain erudition the baggage of antiquity;[6] might we in turn be permitted to make an apothegm, we would call notes the baggage of a bad writer. Scarce any other reason has been assigned for this practice, but that if such were inserted into the body of the work, they might impede the rapidity of the narration. It is not easy, however, to conceive in what manner a reader is less interrupted whose eye is invited down to the note at the bottom of the page, which was certainly placed there in order to be read, than he would be by a proper insertion of the same into the body of the work. Will they persuade us that an animal will move with less ease and swiftness who carries its load upon its back, than if he dragg'd it along at the tail. It certainly argues a defect of method, or a want of perspicuity, when an author is thus obliged to write notes upon his own works; and it may assuredly be said, that whoever undertakes to write a comment upon himself, will for ever remain without a rival his own commentator. We have therefore lopt off such excrescencies, tho' not to any degree of affectation; as sometimes an acknowleged blemish may be admitted into works of skill either to cover a greater defect, or to take a nearer course to beauty.

Having mentioned the danger of affectation, it may be proper to observe, that as this, of all defects, is most apt to insinuate itself into such a work, we have therefore been upon our guard against it. From the natural biass which every historian has to some favourite profession or science, he is apt to introduce phrases or topics drawn from thence upon every occasion, and thus not unfrequently tinctures a work otherwise valuable with absurdity. *Menage*[7] tells us of a chymist, who writing an history, used upon every occasion the language of an adept, and brought all his allusions from the laboratory. *Polybius*,[8] who was a soldier, has been reprehended for taking up too much time in the history of a siege, or the description of a battle. *Guicciardin*,[9] on the other hand, who was a secretary, has been tedious in disserting upon trifling treaties and dull negotiations. In like manner we have known writers, who being somewhat acquainted with oriental languages, have filled a long history with long *Arabic* names and uncouth spellings. Were we disposed to the same affectations, it would have been easy enough through the course of our work to have written *Mohammed* for *Mahomet*, *Tatar* for *Tartar*, *Wazir* for *Visier*, or *Timur* for *Tamerlane*;[10] we might even have outgone our predecessors, and have written *Stamboul* for *Constantinople*, or *Ganga* for *Ganges*, with true exotic propriety. But tho' we have the proper reverence for *Arabic* and *Malayan* also, of which we profess our ignorance, we have thought it expedient to reject such peculiarities....

With respect to chronology and geography, the one of which fixes actions to time, while the other assigns them to place, we have followed the most approved methods among the moderns. All that was requisite in this, was to preserve one system of each invariably, and permit such as chose to adopt the plans of others, to rectify our deviations to their own standard. If actions and things are made to preserve their due distances of time and place mutually with respect to each other, it matters little as to the duration of them all with respect to eternity, or their situation with regard to the universe.

Thus much (perhaps some will think too much) we have thought proper to premise concerning a work which, however executed, has cost much

6. Jean-Louis Guez de Balzac (1597-1654) in *Le Socrate Chrétien* (1562).

7. Gilles Ménage (1613-92), French poet and philologist, author of *Ménagiana* 3 vols (Paris, 1715).

8. Polybius (*c.* 203-*c.*120 B.C.), the Greek historian of Rome who wrote a *Universal History* in forty books.

9. Francesco Guiccardin(i) (1483-1540), one of the greatest Italian historians of the fourteenth century and an acute commentator on the writings of his great contemporary, Machiavelli. His *Storia d'Italia* appeared posthumously in 1567.

10. Goldsmith is here ridiculing the spellings used in *The Modern Part of an Universal History*.

labour and great expence. Had we for our judges the unbiassed and judicious alone, few words would have served, or even silence would have been our best address; but when it is considered that we have wrought for the public, that miscellaneous being, at variance within itself from the differing influence of pride, prejudice, or incapacity, a public already sated with attempts of this nature, and in a manner unwilling to find out merit till forced upon its notice, we hope to be pardoned for thus endeavouring to shew where it is presumed we have had a superiority. An History of the World to the present time, at once satisfactory and succinct, calculated rather for use than curiosity, to be read rather than consulted, seeking applause from the reader's feelings, not from his ignorance of learning, or affectation of being thought learned; an history that may be purchased at an easy expence, yet that omits nothing material, delivered in a style correct yet familiar, was wanting in our language; and tho' sensible of our own insufficiency, this defect we have attempted to supply. Whatever reception the present age or posterity may give this work, we rest satisfied with our own endeavours to deserve a kind one. The completion of our design has for some years taken up all the time which we could spare from other occupations, of less importance indeed to the public, but probably more advantageous to ourselves. We are unwilling therefore to dismiss this subject without observing, that the labour of so great a part of life should at least be examined with candour, and not carelessly confounded in that multiplicity of daily publications which, being conceived without effort, are produced without praise, and sink without censure. Were he who now particularly entreats the reader's candid examination to mention the part he has had in this work himself, he is well convinced, and that without any affected modesty, that such a discovery would only shew the superiority of his associates in this undertaking: but it is not from his friendship or his praise, but from their former labours in the learned world, that they are to expect their reward. Whatever be the fate of this history, their reputation is in no danger, but will still continue rising; for they have found by its gradual encrease already, that the approbation of folly is loud and transient; that of wisdom, still but lasting.

AN ESSAY ON THE THEATRE; or, A COMPARISON BETWEEN LAUGHING AND SENTIMENTAL COMEDY (1773)

[Goldsmith probably wrote this essay, published anonymously in *The Westminster Magazine* on 1 January 1773, to prepare his audience for his own comedy, *She Stoops to Conquer*, which came out less than three months later. Its importance goes beyond that immediate occasion. Goldsmith attacked the prevailing sentimentalism of the London stage and restored to it what Samuel Foote, a contemporary dramatist, called its 'usual laugh and good humour'. It is useful to be reminded, here as elsewhere, of Goldsmith's alertness to the sickly sentiment of prevailing fashion, for it helps a modern audience to notice the irony which, suavely but unmistakably, pervades most of his writing.]

The Theatre, like all other amusements, has its Fashions and its Prejudices; and when satiated with its excellence, Mankind begin to mistake Change for Improvement. For some years, Tragedy was the reigning entertainment; but of late it has entirely given way to Comedy, and our best efforts are now exerted in these lighter kinds of composition. The pompous Train, the swelling Phrase, and the unnatural Rant, are displaced for that natural portrait of Human Folly and Frailty, of which all are judges, because all have sat for the picture.

But as in describing Nature it is presented with a double face, either of mirth or sadness, our modern Writers find themselves at a loss which chiefly to copy from; and it is now debated, Whether the Exhibition of Human Distress is likely to afford the mind more Entertainment than that of Human Absurdity?

Comedy is defined by Aristotle to be a picture of the Frailties of the lower part of Mankind, to distinguish it from Tragedy, which is an exhibition of the Misfortunes of the Great.[1] When Comedy therefore ascends to produce the Characters of Princes or Generals upon the Stage, it is out of its walk, since Low Life and Middle Life are entirely

1. Aristotle, *The Poetics*, 1449a.

its object. The principal question therefore is, Whether in describing Low or Middle Life, an exhibition of its Follies be not preferable to a detail of its Calamities? Or, in other words, Which deserves the preference? The Weeping Sentimental Comedy, so much in fashion at present, or the Laughing and even Low Comedy, which seems to have been last exhibited by Vanburgh and Cibber?[2]

If we apply to authorities, all the Great Masters in the Dramatic Art have but one opinion. Their rule is, that as Tragedy displays the Calamities of the Great; so Comedy should excite our laughter by ridiculously exhibiting the Follies of the Lower Part of Mankind. Boileau, one of the best modern Critics, asserts, that Comedy will not admit of Tragic Distress.

Le Comique, ennemi des soupirs et des pleurs,
N'admet point dans ses vers de tragiques doleurs.[3]

Nor is this rule without the strongest foundation in Nature, as the distresses of the Mean by no means affect us so strongly as the Calamities of the Great. When Tragedy exhibits to us some Great Man fallen from his height, and struggling with want and adversity, we feel his situation in the same manner as we suppose he himself must feel, and our pity is increased in proportion to the height from whence he fell. On the contrary, we do not so strongly sympathize with one born in humbler circumstances, and encountering accidental distress: so that while we melt for Belisarius,[4] we scarce give halfpence to the Beggar who accosts us in the street. The one has our pity; the other our contempt. Distress, therefore, is the proper object of Tragedy, since the Great excite our pity by their fall; but not equally so of Comedy, since the Actors employed in it are originally so mean, that they sink but little by their fall.

Since the first origin of the Stage, Tragedy and Comedy have run in different channels, and never till of late encroached upon the provinces of each other. Terence, who seems to have made the nearest approaches, yet always judiciously stops short before he comes to the downright pathetic; and yet he is even reproached by Caesar for wanting the *vis comica*.[5] All the other Comic Writers of antiquity aim only at rendering Folly or Vice ridiculous, but never exalt their characters into buskined[6] pomp, or make what Voltaire humourously calls a *Tradesman's Tragedy*.[7]

Yet, notwithstanding this weight of authority, and the universal practice of former ages, a new species of Dramatic Composition has been introduced under the name of *Sentimental* Comedy, in which the virtues of Private Life are exhibited, rather than the Vices exposed; and the Distresses, rather than the Faults of Mankind, make our interest in the piece. These Comedies have had of late great success, perhaps from their novelty, and also from their flattering every man in his favourite foible. In these Plays almost all the Characters are good, and exceedingly generous; they are lavish enough of their *Tin* Money on the Stage, and though they want Humour, have abundance of Sentiment and Feeling. If they happen to have Faults or Foibles, the Spectator is taught not only to pardon, but to applaud them, in consideration of the goodness of their hearts; so that Folly, instead of being ridiculed, is commended, and the Comedy aims at touching our Passions without the power of being truly pathetic: in this manner we are likely to lose one great source of Entertainment on the Stage; for while the Comic Poet is invading the province of the Tragic Muse, he leaves her lovely Sister quite neglected. Of this, however, he is noway solicitous, as he measures his fame by his profits.

But it will be said, that the Theatre is formed to amuse Mankind, and that it matters little, if this end be answered, by what means it is obtained. If Mankind find delight in weeping at Comedy, it would be cruel to abridge them in that or any other

2. Sir John Vanbrugh (not Vanburgh) (1664-1726), dramatist and architect. His plays include *The Relapse* (1696), *The Provok'd Wife* (1697) and *The Provok'd Husband*, unfinished at his death and completed by Cibber. Colley Cibber (1671-1757), dramatist and hackwriter, remembered for his autobiography, for Pope's ridicule of him in the final edition of *The Dunciad*, and for his plays, *She Wou'd and She Wou'd Not* (1702) and *The Careless Husband* (1704).
3. Nicolas Boileau-Despreaux (1636-1711), poet and critic, whose *L'Art Poétique* (1674), a treatise in verse, achieved international status. The quotation is from canto III:
   'Comedy, to sighs and tears averse,
   Admits no tragic sorrows in its verse.'
4. Jean François Marmontel's romance *Bélisaire* (1767) was an appeal for a purer and simpler Christianity. It was condemned by the Sorbonne and successfully defended by Voltaire.
5. Terence (*c.*195-159 B.C.), Roman dramatist, was criticized by Caesar in an epigram for lacking comic force or vigour (*vis comica*). See *Fragmenta Poetarum Latinorum epicorum et lyricorum*, ed. W. Morel (1927).
6. Buskins were the high, thick-soled boots worn by actors in ancient Athenian tragedy. The word 'buskined' therefore means, figuratively, to be concerned with tragedy.
7. In the article 'Art dramatique' (1770) in the *Dictionnaire Philosophique* (1764).

innocent pleasure. If those Pieces are denied the name of Comedies; yet call them by any other name, and if they are delightful, they are good. Their success, it will be said, is a mark of their merit, and it is only abridging our happiness to deny us an inlet to Amusement.

These objections, however, are rather specious than solid. It is true, that Amusement is a great object of the Theatre; and it will be allowed, that these Sentimental Pieces do often amuse us: but the question is, Whether the True Comedy would not amuse us more? The question is, Whether a Character supported throughout a Piece with its Ridicule still attending, would not give us more delight than this species of Bastard Tragedy, which only is applauded because it is new?

A friend of mine who was sitting unmoved at one of these Sentimental Pieces, was asked, how he could be so indifferent. 'Why, truly,' says he, 'as the Hero is but a Tradesman, it is indifferent to me whether he be turned out of his Counting-house on Fish-street Hill, since he will still have enough left to open shop in St. Giles's.'

The other objection is as ill-grounded; for though we should give these Pieces another name, it will not mend their efficacy. It will continue a kind of *mulish* production, with all the defects of its opposite parents, and marked with sterility. If we are permitted to make Comedy weep, we have an equal right to make Tragedy laugh, and to set down in Blank Verse the Jests and Repartees of all the Attendants in a Funeral Procession.

But there is one Argument in favour of Sentimental Comedy which will keep it on the Stage in spite of all that can be said against it. It is, of all others, the most easily written. Those abilities that can hammer out a Novel, are fully sufficient for the production of a Sentimental Comedy. It is only sufficient to raise the Characters a little, to deck out the Hero with a Ribband, or give the Heroine a Title; then to put an Insipid Dialogue, without Character or Humour, into their mouths, give them mighty good hearts, very fine cloaths, furnish a new sett of Scenes, make a Pathetic Scene or two, with a sprinkling of tender melancholy Conversation through the whole, and there is no doubt but all the Ladies will cry, and all the Gentlemen applaud.

Humour at present seems to be departing from the Stage, and it will soon happen, that our Comic Players will have nothing left for it but a fine Coat and a Song. It depends upon the Audience whether they will actually drive those poor Merry Creatures from the Stage, or sit at a Play as gloomy as at the Tabernacle. It is not easy to recover an art when once lost; and it would be but a just punishment that when, by our being too fastidious, we have banished Humour from the Stage, we should ourselves be deprived of the art of Laughing.

Biography/Bibliography

Goldsmith's biography can be found on p. 656. The following is a brief selection of commentaries not previously mentioned: H. J. Smith, *Oliver Goldsmith's 'The Citizen of the World': A Study* (New Haven: Yale University Press, 1926); M. P. Conant, *The Oriental Tale in England in the Eighteenth Century* (New York: Random House, 1908); C. A. Moore, *Backgrounds of English Literature, 1700-1776* (Minneapolis: University of Minnesota Press, 1953); G. Sherburn, 'The Periodicals and Oliver Goldsmith' in A. C. Baugh (ed.), *A Literary History of England* 2nd ed. (New York: Knopf, 1957), pp. 1057-58; J. Dussinger, 'Oliver Goldsmith, Citizen of the World', *Studies in Voltaire and the Eighteenth Century*, 55 (1967), 445-61.

IAN CAMPBELL ROSS, *Editor*

Fiction to 1800

No Irish literature in English has suffered more critical neglect than eighteenth-century prose fiction. The repeated privileging of Maria Edgeworth's *Castle Rackrent* (1800) as 'the first Irish novel' has not merely obscured those works of fiction published during the previous century but has frequently seemed to deny their very existence. *Castle Rackrent* (a masterpiece entirely *un*typical of its author's enormous output) has been taken as a starting point in Irish fiction. Published in the same year as the Act of Union, the novel has perhaps too conveniently suggested that Irish fiction, from the beginning, showed the deep involvement with issues of nationality and cultural identity that subsequently — in the works of Lady Morgan, the Banims, Gerald Griffin and William Carleton — came to be thought characteristic of it.

The sense in which *Castle Rackrent* might legitimately be considered 'the first Irish novel' is, however, problematic. It is not the first novel by an Irish-born writer, nor the first novel written in Ireland, nor the first novel about Ireland. For at least fifty years before its publication, Irish men and women, most of them from a background much like Maria Edgeworth's, had produced a substantial and varied body of fiction, published mainly in Dublin and London, for an audience both in Ireland and England. Throughout that period, Ireland was possessed of an important, if frequently piratical, publishing trade (Ireland was not covered by the English Copyright Act of 1709) and its first home-produced novel dates from at least the early 1750s. The result was that half a century before the Act of Union initiated the slow decline of Dublin as a cultural centre of European importance, the novel-reading public began to develop a taste for fiction which, while related to that of England, was also to a degree independent of it. The history of eighteenth-century Irish fiction reveals not only instances of novels by Irish writers published first in London and subsequently in Dublin (or Cork), but of novels that appeared first in Dublin and which were only later taken up by English publishers, and of novels published in Dublin alone. Most significantly, in the light of future developments, the relative independence of the Irish reading public allowed for the emergence, from the late 1770s onwards, of 'patriotic' novels. Eschewing the cosmopolitanism of earlier writers, the authors of such novels preferred, however awkwardly, to fill their Irish settings, however nominal, with Irish characters, however implausible. In so doing, they helped provide an audience for the notable upsurge of fiction on Irish subjects which appeared after 1800.

Comparatively little eighteenth-century Irish fiction deals predominantly with Irish subject-matter. Nevertheless, there is almost no feature of the early nineteenth-century Irish novel which is not significantly anticipated somewhere in the eighteenth century, whether we consider writers' concern with issues of nationality and Ireland's cultural complexity, their use of humour and the grotesque, or the significance of anecdote and the role of the story-teller. Eighteenth-century fiction (in Ireland or elsewhere) should not be judged finally, however, by criteria appropriate to the nineteenth- and twentieth-century novel, much less by the narrow criteria appropriate to Romantic nationalist literature. What a reading of Irish fiction between 1750 and 1800 reveals is the thematic and structural variety of that fiction, the confident authorial placing of the novel in European contexts, both literary and intellectual, and a sense of what was lost as well as gained by the narrowing of the novelist's range in the early years of the nineteenth century.

National and cultural identity are issues very much at the heart of one of the earliest of all Irish novels, *The History of Jack Connor* (1752) by William Chaigneau (1709-81). *Jack Connor* is a picaresque novel whose eponymous hero is forced to leave Ireland as a young man to pursue a peripatetic existence as apprentice, servant, and soldier in England, France, the Low Counties and Spain, before he is able to return to a more settled and prosperous life in Ireland. Behind Chaigneau's only work of prose fiction lie the Spanish *novelas picarescas* of the sixteenth and seventeenth centuries, as also eighteenth-century works within the picaresque tradition such as Alain-René Le Sage's *Gil Blas* (1715-47) or Tobias Smollett's *Roderick Random* (1748). The influence of Henry Fielding's comic epic *Tom Jones* (1749) is acknowledged by Chaigneau himself. Like other *pícaros*, Jack finds himself largely at the mercy of an indifferent society, and throughout his varied adventures is primarily concerned with his own survival in a morally disordered universe, described in a narrative voice that is frequently satiric in tone.

The moral, social, and geographical exploration of the hero's world is familiar from other picaresque narratives, while the conclusion, in which Jack is revealed as the natural son of an Irish landowner, derives from contemporary comic romance. *Jack Connor*, though, is much more than an imitation of fashionable European prose fiction. It is also a conscious attempt at writing a specifically Irish novel. Forced to abandon Ireland precipitately as a youth, Jack Connor is able to attain the social and moral stability he desires only by his return to Ireland. Chaigneau, meanwhile, engages the reader's interest both in the hero's progress and in his own attempts to define Ireland's ills and to suggest a remedy. In the novel's conclusion, these twin concerns are resolved in Jack's recognition of his own identity as a protestant Irishman. *Jack Connor*, as a result, is especially noteworthy for its detailed examination of the question of national identity at a time when little cogent discussion of such matters was to be found anywhere.

Born of a protestant father and a Roman catholic mother, Jack Connor is perhaps unique among Irish fictional heroes before Maria Edgeworth's Ormond in straddling two cultures, whose often opposed values are at times inextricably linked in his own person. Although he holds unswerving allegiance to both his protestant faith and a belief in liberty, conceived of in terms of a post-Williamite political rhetoric, Jack is notably impatient of English interference in Ireland, and a sympathetic and perceptive advocate on behalf of that part of the Irish people not always deemed worthy of notice by contemporary political commentators writing in English. Hence Jack's sympathy (and evidently that of the Huguenot Chaigneau) is not only for the Irish peasantry but also for those descendants of the Wild Geese whom the hero encounters in France, sentimentally attached to a land they have never seen and outspokenly critical of the Penal Laws. The intolerance Jack Connor experiences as an Irishman in England itself contributes to the hero's moral and political education and enables him finally to consider his own cultural identity as a protestant Irishman.

Recognized by contemporary reviewers as an attempt to write an *Irish* novel, *The History of Jack Connor* also belongs recognizably to an important strand within European prose fiction. Not all early Irish novels are so easily assimilated into even a European, still less an English, tradition. The comparative neglect of *The Life of John Buncle, Esq.* (1756-66) by Thomas Amory (*c.*1691-1788) is at least in part attributable to its unconventional form, which has tended to push it, at best, to the periphery of accounts of the eighteenth-century novel in English. *John Buncle* is in fact an early example of an Irish novel founded on anecdote and the told tale, a kind most obviously represented within the early phase of Irish fiction by *Castle Rackrent*, but which (it has been argued) lies at the centre of Irish fiction.

An enthusiastic, even incorrigible, story-teller, John Buncle is a Unitarian who defies worldly success for his beliefs and who takes in rapid succession eight remarkably beautiful and devout wives, and who principally delights in abstruse learning, religious controversy and the sublime landscape of the English Lake and Peak districts through which he travels. (The recurrent concern with the 'sublime' in landscape not only predates Lady Morgan by half a century but even, by a year, Burke's essay on the sublime.) While all these elements have their interest, the novel's most persistent and fascinating concern is with Ireland and her inhabitants — English- and Irish-speaking alike. Though the author's knowledge of the Irish language or of Ireland's history and culture is not beyond reproach, there is greater evidence of interest in all these than is found elsewhere in fiction before 1800. Thirty years before the scholarly revival of interest in the Irish language got really under way, and half a century before the emergence of Romantic nationalism in fiction, *John Buncle* offers a view of both Anglo-Irish and Gaelic Ireland which anticipates the work of Maria Edgeworth and Sydney Owenson, Lady Morgan, while remaining happily as free of the moral earnestness of the former as of the enervating sentiment of the latter.

Amory's novel reveals its Irish origins not only in what is said, however, but in how it is said. Although *John Buncle* is, like many eighteenth-century novels, an autobiography, its most characteristic narrative technique is the use of the anecdote, a self-contained and frequently fantastic tale avowedly based on the narrator's personal experience. This narrator is an inveterate story-teller whose voice is heard throughout, button-holing an audience whose presence is acutely felt. What is unfamiliar in the English novel of the mid-eighteenth century is less so if considered in an Irish context. The form of the tale on which Amory repeatedly draws is *seanchas*. While the *scéal* is acknowledged by teller and audience alike to be invention — its events far removed from those of daily life — the events related in *seanchas* are purported by the story-teller to be true and, as part of the narrative convention, accepted as such by his audience. Buncle's life-story is then told in no linear fashion but by means of frequently isolated episodes which take him from Astrakhan to Peru via Ringsend and Kerry. The result is a fusion of plausible autobiography, whose truthfulness is frequently alleged, and the wildest fantasy. Offering the contemporary novel an alternative means of narrative organization, Amory simultaneously controls the Gaelic oral tradition on which he draws by setting it within a culture both English and typographic.

Although Amory, who insisted on the importance of his Irish background to his work, was read abroad (in Germany by Lessing, for example) and would be rediscovered by English writers like William Hazlitt, he has been largely ignored in Ireland. A rather different fate has befallen Laurence Sterne (1713-68) whose concept of narrative — 'writing ... is but a different name for conversation' — recalls Amory's in its emphasis on the importance of the speaking voice. Born at Clonmel into an English family with strong Irish links, Sterne left Ireland at the age of nine and thereafter paid little attention to his Irish roots. Usually considered an English writer whose masterpiece, *Tristram Shandy* (1759-67), is one of the great works of world literature, Sterne has nonetheless been occasionally claimed back for Ireland by writers and critics alike. If such cultural imperialism has little to recommend it, we may at least pause to consider the fact that while Sterne's influence has been widely felt in Europe (on Diderot, Gogol or Milan Kundera, for instance) his most notable imitators in English have been Irish — Richard Griffith in *The Triumvirate* (1765) and *The Posthumous Works of a Late Celebrated Genius* (1770) and Flann O'Brien. Most significant among those who more fully assimilated Sterne's influence was James Joyce who both considered Sterne his 'fellow-countrym[a]n' and said of *Finnegans Wake* that the book's elements were 'exactly what every novelist might use: man and woman, birth, childhood, night, sleep, marriage, prayer, death [the list is peculiarly appropriate to *Tristram Shandy*]. . . . Only I am trying to build many planes of narrative within a single aesthetic purpose. Did you ever read Laurence Sterne?' If, as Borges has argued, each writer creates his own precursors, we may feel justified in acknowledging Sterne's place, if not in *the* then at least in *one* Irish fictional tradition.

The question of an Irish tradition in fiction is a vexed one. The work of certain Irish writers of the eighteenth century does engage with issues of central significance to their successors in later centuries or use narrative devices of recurring importance in subsequent fiction. Other eighteenth-century Irish fiction looks deliberately away from Ireland, or indeed any single country. The classical tradition, which would give rise most notably in Irish fiction to *Ulysses*, underlies the work of several writers of the eighteenth century, among them Charles Johnstone (*c.* 1719-*c.* 1800). A satirist, compared with Juvenal, Johnstone portrayed a world characterized, always and everywhere, by man's propensity to vice — to moral failings which 'are not particular in this age or country [but] are the weeds which, in every age and clime, have always, and always will, over-run the human heart'. His work informed by this pessimistic humanist vision, Johnstone avoided excessive particularity, offering, in his best-known work, *Chrysal; or, The Adventures of a Guinea* (1760-65), a panoramic view of human nature throughout all ranks of society in a wide variety of geographical settings — North and South America,

England, Holland, Germany and Portugal. Neither Ireland nor the Irish make more than the occasional appearance, though when they do it is very much as Johnstone believed the English saw them, as a land and a people to be exploited and degraded. There is little evidence, though, that Johnstone was especially sympathetic to his fellow-countrymen or women. Most of his novels do, like *Chrysal*, contain Irish characters, such as the sympathetic Dr. Macshane in *The History of John Juniper, Esq.* (1781), while *The Adventures of Anthony Varnish* (1786) has an Irish hero and includes extended descriptions of Irish scenes. The unchanging struggle between vice and virtue is Johnstone's primary concern throughout his work, however. If the former is abundant, the latter is rarely to be found, at least in developed societies. In marked contrast to the dominant humanist view of man as irremediably flawed, in *Chrysal* Johnstone eulogizes the American Indians. These, though 'savages', are 'our fellow-creatures; and in general above our level, in the virtues which give real preheminence'. Without the advantages of learning, they see by the light of natural reason and are strangers to the dissimulation that passes for politeness among the civilized nations of Europe.

Such Rousseauesque intrusions into Johnstone's fictional world are as notable as they are inconsistent, for they indicate the increasing importance of sentimentalism — the single most significant influence on Irish fiction from the 1760s to 1800 and even beyond. Among the most accomplished writers of sentimental fiction was Frances Sheridan (1724-66), author of the long and long-popular *Memoirs of Miss Sidney Bidulph* (1761). Influenced both by Samuel Richardson's *Clarissa* (1747-48) and the work of such French sentimentalists as the Abbé Prévost, Baculard d'Arnaud and Madame Riccoboni, *Sidney Bidulph* received the compliment of being quickly translated into French, as *Mémoires pour servir à l'histoire de la virtu* (1761), by Prévost himself. In her novel, Sheridan is concerned to examine the effect of extreme suffering on apparently irreproachable virtue. In exploring the heroine's response to the misfortune of a ruined love affair and unhappy marriage, the fiction not only questions the place of ideal virtue in a corrupt world but offers a critical examination of the role assigned to women in eighteenth-century society. Like Richardson, Sheridan is less concerned to comfort than confront the sentimental reader. 'We are indeed so much used to what they call poetical justice,' she writes, 'that we are disappointed in the catastrophe of a fable, if every body concerned in it be not disposed of according to the sentence of that judge which we have set up in our own breasts. The contrary we know happens in real life....' Upon this premiss, Sheridan founds her remorseless probing of female virtue, both in her first published novel and, for those many readers whose appetite for vicarious suffering was not yet sated, in the *Conclusion of the Memoirs of Miss Sidney Bidulph* (1767).

Sentimentalism of a different kind is much in evidence in *The Fool of Quality; or, The History of Henry, Earl of Moreland* (1765-70) by Henry Brooke (*c.* 1703-83). Beginning to appear three years after the publication of *Émile*, Brooke's work is a thesis-novel directly inspired by Rousseau's *traité d'éducation.* Though owing much to other contemporary fiction, notably *Tristram Shandy*, *The Fool of Quality* describes the education of the boy-hero (the fool of the title whose soubriquet derives from his admirable simplicity) by his merchant uncle via a varied collection of sentimental set-pieces, lengthy anecdotes and digressive disquisitions on literature, politics and religion. The story of Harry's progress from birth to marriage is notable for being the first extended account of boyhood in fiction in English. Like Rousseau, Brooke believed the purpose of education to be the fostering of those natural virtues that society tended to destroy. Believing also that true education must take place in the world, however, Brooke has ample scope for a great variety of setting and dramatic action alongside the intellectual speculation in which his novel abounds.

As a novelist, Brooke was pre-eminently a sentimentalist, as the title of a subsequent work, *Juliet Grenville; or, The History of the Human Heart* (1774), most clearly suggests. Supplementing Shaftesbury's sensibility with a moral dimension inspired by Adam Smith's *Theory of Moral Sentiments* (1759), Brooke suggests, in *The Fool of Quality*, that feeling is worth cultivating not primarily for its own sake but as a spur to active benevolence. Tears — the sentimental index of individual sensibility — flow in abundance but they are here the prelude either to demonstrations of practical charity or an authorial irony, which suggests that Brooke's attachment to a sentimental view of life is never uncritical. Where authorial irony is less in evidence in later volumes of the work is in the portrayal of the hero. Early interpolated dialogues between the Author and the Reader enable Brooke to maintain ironic distance between himself and Harry; after one instance of the latter's precocious benevolence, the Reader interjects laconically: 'Sir, your Hero is indeed a Hero. He must be every body's Hero.' Finally, though, the irony is dissipated; Harry, affectionate, good-natured and pious *is* everybody's hero, the idealized product of an enlightened educational system.

Henry Brooke's deep concern with the actual state of Ireland is indicated by, among much else, his work entitled *The Tryal of the Cause of the Roman Catholics* (1761). *The Fool of Quality* is, by contrast, not greatly concerned with Irish settings and characters, nor with themes of peculiarly Irish interest. Doubtless his desire to address an audience beyond Ireland partly persuaded him to avoid excessively national concerns and (like other Irish authors of prose fiction) to take advantage instead of the freedom the novel form offered in the eighteenth century to blend narrative and discursive writing, almost at will. The lack of the Irish dimension found in Chaigneau or Amory should not be taken as the evasiveness of a displaced writer whose loyalties were essentially to England. (The 'English' setting of *The Fool of Quality* is nominal, both historically and geographically.) It derives rather from a positive preference — though one perhaps fostered on Brooke's part by a sense of belonging wholly to no one country — for themes not national but cosmopolitan.

Brooke was not unique in this, and an elected cosmopolitanism may be thought a dominant trait of eighteenth-century Irish literature in English. 'It is the duty of the learned to unite society more closely and to persuade men to become citizens of the world,' declares Lien Chi Altangi in *Letters from a Chinese Philosopher, Residing in London, to his Friends in the East* (1760-61). The sentiments are those of the author of those letters, Oliver Goldsmith (1728-74), who collected them in 1762 under the title *The Citizen of the World*. The cosmopolitanism of Goldsmith was not just a matter of the influences on his own work, though, like Chaigneau, Sheridan or Brooke before him, he looked as much to French as to English literature. It is evident also in *The Vicar of Wakefield* (1766), whose setting is notably drained of geographical specificity. (Like *The Deserted Village* (1770), Goldsmith's fiction is remarkably resistant to attempts to prove its locations either authentically English or nostalgically Irish.) Around the slender narrative thread provided by the highly symmetrical and formal tale of Dr Primrose and his disaster-prone family, Goldsmith weaves a varied fabric of digressive, discursive prose (at home equally with politics, punishment or poetry), interpolated tales, and original songs and ballads.

Goldsmith's sentimentalism, like that of Sterne or Brooke, is equivocal. For all its affection, the portrait of the Vicar is a critical as well as an admiring one. Through his own narration, the Vicar reveals himself as possessed of a simplicity at once laudable in theory and dangerous in practice. Admirable in his benevolence, Primrose suffers from an excess of simplicity, which makes him both ineffectual and too easily the dupe of those he encounters in a world altogether less amiable than he perceives it to be. Goldsmith is interested finally not in the theory but in the practice of life. An insistence on the complexity of often intractable experience and a corresponding mistrust of systems of all kinds, disallowing facile solutions to the problems experience raises, may be thought to have contributed greatly to the enduring fascination Goldsmith's slim book has held for readers. Such qualities may be thought equally to characterize a notable line of conservative Irish writing in English from Swift to Burke.

Not all eighteenth-century Irish fiction has proved as durable as *The Vicar of Wakefield*, often with good reason. Nonetheless, there are — amid the substantial output of fiction of the last three or four decades of the century — works at once diverting and indicative of the mentality of the country and of its writers. Irish authors produced — at home and in England — examples of most varieties of contemporary fiction. The novel of sentiment was most popular, in Ireland as elsewhere in Europe. Richard (*c.* 1714-88) and Elizabeth (*c.*1720-93) Griffith enjoyed success both jointly and individually. In *Memoirs of a Magdalen; or, The History of Louisa Mildmay* (1767), Hugh Kelly (1739-77), better known as a dramatist, produced a novel whose exploration of the contemporary double-standard in sexual morality is as engrossing as it is extreme. Like Frances Sheridan, Kelly was influenced by Richardson; later writers in the sentimental mode, such as the anonymous author of *The Triumph of Benevolence* (1772) would look to

Goldsmith or else to Henry Mackenzie's *The Man of Feeling* (1771) or Rousseau's *La Nouvelle Héloïse* (1761). In *Longsword, Earl of Salisbury* (1762), Thomas Leland (1722-85) wrote what has been claimed as the first historical novel in English. There is little sense, however, either here or in subsequent examples of the genre, of the past as other than a quaintly accoutred present and such novels merged easily into the sentimental on the one hand or the gothic on the other. Of more developed gothic fiction, the amazingly durable *The Children of the Abbey* (1796), by Regina Maria Roche (1765-1845), gave a foretaste of the use to which later Anglo-Irish writers like Maturin or Le Fanu would put the gothic. If gothic fiction provided one possibility for Irish writers who preferred to engage obliquely with the life of their own country, the oriental tale provided another means of dealing with substantial issues — moral or political — without the need for the overt depiction of a land whose nature they might not fully comprehend. In *The History of Nourjahad* (1767), Frances Sheridan developed her obsessive concern with virtue under stress and produced in the process what was once the most admired oriental tale in English after Samuel Johnson's *Rasselas.* Charles Johnstone's *Arsaces, Prince of Betlis* (1774) meanwhile provides, in allegorical form, an account of colonial America's struggle with England. Though sympathetic to the American side, Johnstone is unable or unwilling, unlike some slightly later contemporaries, to perceive directly the analogous situation developing in Ireland.

A willingness to locate fiction in Ireland, to portray Irish characters, and even to consider national political issues is evident in some, albeit isolated, works of Irish fiction. From the 1770s onwards, Anglo-Irish readers evinced an interest in reading about themselves and their country in fiction. Novels with titles like *The Irish Guardian* (1776) or *The Irish Heiress* (1797) began to appear. Though rarely making much of their national settings or characters — the Irish locations seem often as nominal as earlier English or European ones — such works give evidence of an increasing willingness on the part of readers to accept Irish subject-matter and doubtless helped also to foster that willingness. In *The Fair Hibernian* (1789), for instance, there is little sustained attempt at a detailed setting, but the young heroine, Valeria O'Bryen, gives constant voice to suitably patriotic sentiments. When Valeria is introduced, in France, as *'la belle Angloise,'* her aunt 'with a kind of national pride, insisted upon its being changed into — *Irlandoise'*. If most such novels are likely to appeal only to literary historians, some are of continuing interest. *The Triumph of Prudence over Passion* (1781) is an epistolary novel, published anonymously by 'An Irish Lady'. Set in the years between the Free Trade debate and the 1782 Constitution, the novel includes detailed accounts of Dublin and a landed estate, informed by the sensibility of a patriotic member of the Anglo-Irish gentry at a time when protestant nationalist feeling was running high. Notable for its extreme anti-English sentiment, *The Triumph of Prudence over Passion* manages to show a sustained concern with political and feminist themes within the improbable context of a novel of sensibility.

The Triumph of Prudence over Passion appeared in London in 1783 as *The Reconciliation . . . An Hibernian Novel.* On *its* title-page, Maria Edgeworth's *Castle Rackrent* is denominated 'An Hibernian Tale'. The latter is an altogether more accomplished work of fiction and will, no doubt, continue to provide a convenient starting-point for thumbnail sketches of the 'Irish novel'. Yet it is no mere pedantry to insist that since the year 1800 is not the first year of the nineteenth century but the last of the eighteenth, so *Castle Rackrent* may represent not simply the beginning of a century of fictional experiment in Ireland but a culmination of (at least) a previous half-century of such experiment. Those interested in literary traditions, as in literary history, may find the burgeoning early-nineteenth century novels of Maria Edgeworth, Lady Morgan, the Banims or Charles Robert Maturin deriving sustenance through roots buried deep in the eighteenth century.

The early Irish novel has been considered to be inextricably bound up with questions of nationality and cultural complexity. A reading of Irish fiction before 1800 reveals the novel rather to include that preoccupation within a wider range of characteristic themes and forms. Eighteenth-century fiction notably possesses exuberance, humour, sentiment and an openness to experimentation, alongside a concern with national identity. Irish novelists, in their confident awareness of Ireland's place in Europe, produced fiction with an imaginative variety that can be ignored only at the expense of an impoverished awareness of literary history and literary tradition.

WILLIAM CHAIGNEAU

(1709-81)

from: THE HISTORY OF JACK CONNOR (1752)

[Chaigneau's picaresque novel begins, as it ends, in Ireland. The first three chapters describe the hero's birth and childhood.]

CHAPTER I

The Rise, the Progress, of the human Heart,
The real Honour, *the* Disguise *of* Art;
The Wise, *the* Good, *the* Vicious; — *all I sing,*
Oh Thou! from whom our ev'ry Actions spring,
Not the poor Author, but the World inspire,
If not the Stile, — the Moral to admire.
Learn from the Child, he places in your Sight,
To act with Justice, and to judge aright.

ANONIMOUS[1]

The Actions of *Monarchs*, the Intrigues of *Ministers*, the History of *Battles* and *Slaughter*, and the Revolutions of *Kingdoms*, are Subjects that rather surprise and astonish the Generality of Readers, than *improve* or *amend* the Heart. A great, wicked, or virtuous Man, plung'd into the utmost Distress, must raise our Pity and Compassion: A Glorious and a Wise *Prince*, triumphing over *Foreign* or *Domestick* Enemies, and fixing his Crown in the *Affections* of his People, must warm the rational Mind, and give Delight and Pleasure; but what have the Bulk of Mankind to do with their Greatness? Their Misfortunes or Successes may make us cry out, *'Tis strange! — 'Tis wondrous strange!*[2] But how can we make the Application to ourselves? The wide Difference in our Situations, almost renders it impossible, and, if by Chance, something like a Parallel should arise, it must be stript of all pompous Terms; — the Rubbish of State and Parade must be removed; and the Whole levell'd to the Sphere we act in.

Perhaps, Reflections of this Nature, gave Rise to Biography. The Story of the *Calamities*, or *good Fortune* of *private Persons*, must sensibly affect every *private Reader*, and, as the Incidents are natural, and what *every Man* is subject to, he with Ease applies the Inferences, and, in some Measure, may be said to *read himself.*[3]

The *Papers* and *Memorandums*, committed to my Care, give Rise to the following Account of John Connor. — I will not affirm that I have acted *impartially*, because I will not presume doing, what, I am afraid, no Historian *ever did.* If I assure my Readers I am quite *unbias'd*, yet I hope to be indulg'd, like the rest of my Brethren, when I sometimes act *otherwise.* I cannot avoid saying, I have consulted the Ease of my Reader as much as possible, by not swelling this Work into *Twenty Volumes.* As a Proof of my Indulgence, I have shortened my Prefatory Discourse and this Introduction, above *One Hundred Pages*, and shall proceed directly to the History.

Jeremiah Connor, the Father of John, whose Story I now write, had been a well made, athletic Man, and a Soldier in *King* William's Army in the War in *Ireland.*[4] When that Matter was settled, he quitted that sort of Life, and passing through sundry Services, at last settled with Sir *Roger Thornton*, a Gentleman of great Honour and Fortune, in the County of *Limerick*, in *Ireland.* He liv'd here in the humble Station of a *Footman*, and by good Usage and good Victuals, nourish'd some *Scars of Credit*, which furnish'd him a large Fund of Conversation. He found the Happiness of being virtuous in the *Cause of Liberty* and *Common-Sense.* Though he was one of the famous *Enniskilliners* that joyn'd *King William*, yet his Reward, like other

1. *Jack Connor* is the first novel in English to make use of mottoes for chapter-headings, a device which became very popular in the nineteenth century; the quotations marked 'anonimous' are probably by Chaigneau himself.
2. *Hamlet*, V. 4. 190.
3. Chaigneau's consideration of the novel form as a new kind of writing is close to that of other contemporary writers of fiction, including Henry Fielding in *Joseph Andrews* (1742) and *Tom Jones* (1749) and Tobias Smollett in the 'Preface' to *Roderick Random* (1748).
4. i.e. the protestant William III in his Irish campaign of 1689-90 against the Roman catholic James II, which ended with William's victory at the battle of the Boyne on 1 July 1690.

great Men, was confin'd to the secret Pleasure of having done *his Duty*.

In this Family liv'd Dolly Bright, who perform'd the Function of *Laundry-Maid*; she was young and handsome; and *Jerry* observing, she had a docile and tractable Turn, he encourag'd her in it. Being himself a Man of *Learning*, he took some Pains to inculcate all his Knowledge, and taught her to *Read* and *Write*. The Fame of her Erudition a little hightened her Vanity, especially when *Sir Roger* examined her himself, and declaring her a very surprising Genius, gave her a Kiss and *two Guineas* to buy a Gown and Linen. — This unfortunate Present, and a few more of the same Nature, at last alarm'd *Lady Thornton*, and brought on some Altercation, in which the Lady seem'd in the Right. All *Sir Roger's* Affirmations were of no Effect; my Lady most violently protested the impudent *Slut* should quit the House, or she would —. Sir *Roger* knew the World, and what's more, he knew himself and his Wife, which determined him to make all this easy. He told *Jerry Connor*, that if he would marry *Dolly Bright*, he would give him a Farm at a small Rent, and compleat his Happiness, who had been so careful of her Education.

Lady Thornton objected to this, but finding Sir *Roger* grow warm and somewhat peremptory, she acquiesced. — Though *Jerry Connor* was thirty Years older than *Dolly*, they willingly consented to the Match, and Peace was restor'd to the Family.

Thus *Jack's* Parents were fix'd in a Farm about twenty Miles from *Thornton-Castle*. *Jerry* was Fifty-five and *Dolly* Twenty four Years of Age. To compleat their Joy, the *Hero of this History* stepp'd forth, and was usher'd into the World the 15th Day of *December* 1720, just *seven Months* after their Nuptials, a fine healthy Boy, and the *very* Picture of *Jerry Connor*.

Whether it was from the *frequent* Visits Sir *Roger* paid them, or from some other Motive, my *Lady Thornton* never rested till she had persuaded him to remove his Family to *England*. This was a mighty Loss, and poor *Connor* felt it more and more every Day. They were much in Arrear, and as the Steward could no longer indulge them, they were put to vast Difficulties. This shagrin'd Mrs. *Connor*, and her Husband was sometimes peevish. Every Misfortune was imputed to *one* or the *other*, consequently many bitter Invectives passed between them, and sometimes *Blows*. Mrs. *Connor* generally conquer'd, for an *old Wound* broke out in *his Knee* and lam'd him. The good Woman had always *great Spirits*, which rais'd itself on certain Occasions, to that noble Ardour, which the Vulgar call *Termagant*, in which her *Neighbours* and *Husband*, gave her Opportunities to *improve*.

At last another Wound appear'd in *his Head*, and oblig'd him to have Recourse to the Surgeon of the next Town, though ill able to bear the Expence of, at least a *Shilling* a Day. However, the *Surgeon* was a *skillful Man*, and so managed his Patient, that in a Month he brought a Humour into *his Eyes*, and in *six Weeks*, he was *quite Blind*. The *Surgeon* declared his sorrow for the Accident, but believed, that had it not *providentially* happen'd, it must have cost him *his Life*. The Wound at last heal'd, but *Connor* thought, and his *Wife* saw, they were ruin'd; which the Seizing their two remaining *Cows*, and a Barrel of *Potatoes*, completed, finish'd; and next Night the good Woman threw *Jack* on her Back, took her *blind Husband* by the Hand, and march'd off, with about *six Shillings*, to seek better Fortune.

CHAPTER II

> *He tells us*,
> 'When one Sense is suprest,
> It but retires into the rest.'
> *So* Poverty, *against the Will*,
> *Gives* Cunning *to assuage the Ill*.
>
> ANONIMOUS

Sullen and *silent* were their Travels all that Night, but when Day appeared, they determin'd, to repose themselves at the first Inn that seem'd proper to entertain such Guests, mutually agreeing to postpone all Talk of Affairs, till their Bodies were a little refresh'd. At length a *Cabin* appear'd, to which they bended their Steps, and, by the Information of a *Linen Rag* over the Door, and a *Pipe* stuck in the *Thatch*, they boldly enter'd and call'd for *Milk* and *Bread*. Before this could be had, the Woman of the House demanded *three Half pence*, and Mrs. *Connor* pulling out a Piece of an *old Glove*, which contained all her *Treasure*, paid for the approaching Breakfast.

At this Repast the *good Creature* seem'd very tender of Mrs. *Connor*, whose Eyes were swell'd with Crying. She ask'd many Questions, as, *Where they came from*, and *whither going*; to which she received a melancholy Account of the past, but not of what they intended to do, being ignorant of it themselves. The poor Woman sympathiz'd with her Guest, who, by a change of Fortune grew *strangely humble*, and was now all *Humility* and *Meekness.* — *God Almighty* help you, *said the Landlady*, 'I'm sure you've Troubles enough; — I pray the *sweet Jesus* to comfort you, and send you safe in your Journey; — but *my dear sowle, added she, rocking herself*, you must not set Grief too much about your Heart, for my poor *dear Man* in his Grave (God be with his Sowle) left me the Mother of *three Children*, and one in my *Belly*, and the *Devil* a Farthing to bless myself, but three Shillings and Five pence in *Silver and Brass.* To be sure it was the *Holy Virgin* put it into my Head to speak to the *Quality* that travell'd the Road, and by my own Sowle I got Pence enough, and bred my poor *little Creturs* to get their Bread as well as myself; for *Thady* is a fine Boy, and a *poor Scolard*, and speaks his *Latin*, and brings home many a *Happenny*; *sweet Jesus* bless him! and send me once to hear him *say* Mass! for my *dear Child* will be nothing but a *Priest*, and *Father O'Shoughnesy* will send him to *France* on his own Means; God's Blessing on the *sweet Man*! — Then my *dear little Terence*, drives the *Cows* out and home for Mr. *Flaherty*, and brings me *broken Meat*, and a *Bottle of good Ale* when he finds it after the Servants; for the *Rogue* is as cunning as a Fox. — *Pray Jesus* I could see him a *Priest* too! — And my Daughter *Noragh*, poor Sowle, is always busy enough, and minds the *Hens* and the *Turf*, and digs the *Potatoes*, and serves the *Carryers* very well ever since *Father O'Shoughnesy* got me this good House.'

She was going on, but finding Mr. *Connor* was more inclin'd to Sleep than Hear, she call'd to her Daughter *Noragh* to settle the *Straw* in the other Room, and advis'd the Travellers to rest for a few Hours; assuring them, that the *Cow* and the *Pigs* at one End of it, kept it *pure and warm.* Mrs. *Connor* conducted her Husband to the Apartment, where, in Spite of every Calamity, *Sleep* attended and diverted every anxious Thought.

'Twas about Twelve o'Clock at Noon when they join'd the Landlady. Mrs. *Connor* was putting her Hand in her Pocket to pay for her *Bed*, but the *kind Woman* held it fast and prevented her, swearing she would not take a *Farthing*, and order'd *Noragh* to give them a large *Bowl of Milk*; and putting some *boil'd Potatoes* into her Apron, she fix'd the *Child* on her Back, and with a *sweet Jesus be with you*, let them depart.

Jerry greatly prais'd the *Tenderness* of the poor Woman, and a Conversation ensu'd on their present Circumstances. 'To be sure, *said his Wife*, since *God Almighty* has made you *stone blind*, and given me this *helpless Infant*, you can't *Work*, nor can I go into Service, *God help me*; so, to be sure, *myself* can't find out a better Way than to speak to the *Quality* on the Road, as the *Landlady* did, though to be sure none of my *Kiff* or *Kin* ever did so before; but you know *Jerry*, *God's* will must be done,' — and then she cry'd heartily.

'Don't cry, *said Connor*, for what Good will that do us? — Though we never begg'd yet, 'tis *a Trade* soon learn'd, and *God knows*, our *Poverty* ought to make us set up very soon. — I formerly mimick'd an *old blind Man* for *Sport*, and now I must do it for *Profit*. — Take care of the Child *Dolly*, and don't leave your poor *Jerry*, and I warrant we shall *eat* and *drink* well enough, — and, *what more can any body do?*'

The *Transition* from an *Irish Farmer* to a *Beggar*, is very *natural* and common in the Country. The many Examples of that Sort, enabled the *poor Couple* to *bear*, and in some Measure *lighten'd* their Afflictions. — They now seriously determin'd to begin this new Occupation on the first *proper Object*, resolving with themselves, not to touch the *Capital Stock*, but at the last Extremity.

They had march'd about seven Miles without meeting any Passengers, but what seem'd as *poor* as themselves; at last she cry'd out, that a Gentleman in Scarlet appear'd, with two Servants well-mounted. This put them into some Confusion, but *Jerry*, boldly raising his Spirits, assisted his Voice, and in the most pathetick Manner, begg'd *a little Charity to a poor blind, old Soldier, who once serv'd most faithfully his King and Country*. — His *Help-mate* was not *Eloquent* on this Occasion, but the Abundance of her *Tears*, supply'd her want of Speech; and perhaps inclin'd the Gentleman to throw them a few *Half-pence*, which he did in a hasty Manner; and riding smartly on, was followed by a Million of *Blessings*: But how great was her Surprise and Joy, when she pick'd up *Three Half pence*, and a *Shilling*? — She kiss'd the *Silver* a thousand Times, and in her Transport, as often kiss'd the *Child* and *Jerry*, who were now *squatted* in the *Ditch*. She talk'd of *Providence* and the *blessed Virgin*; and in Rapture concluded, *that please God they cheer their Hearts by a Pot of Ale, at the first House.* — The poor Man objected to this, and begg'd of her only to spend the *Brass*, but to put the

Shilling in the Glove with the rest. — After much Dispute, and sundry Dissertations on *Extravagance* and *Stinginess*, she consented. — But, who can *paint* the *Wildness of her Looks*, and the *frantick* Motion of her Limbs, or describe her dreadful *Shrieks* and *Exclamations*, when she neither found *Glove* or *Pocket*? — They were fairly cut off. — *Heaven*, and *Hell*, and *Purgatory*, and all *Mankind*, were in an Instant engaged in her *Quarrel*, till *fatigu'd* and *tir'd* with the Violence of her *Passion*, she threw herself on the Ground, and in a Torrent of *Tears* assuaged the *Storm* in her swelling Breast.

Connor bore this Misfortune with great *Patience*, and comforted his Wife out of the *Proverbs*. He gave her many on this Occasion; and concluded, that *Solomon, who was a wise Man, told us, that Riches made themselves Wings and flew away.* —[5] 'Don't tell me *Jerry, said she*, of such *Stuff*. I say again and again, our poor matter of Money would have been safe enough in my Pocket, if we had not slept at that *cursed Inn*, and as for your *Wings*, I'm sure they must have been in the *old B—'s Fingers,'*——'Or, *said Jerry*, in her Daughters — But, hang it, *'tis gone. — What can't be cur'd must be endur'd. — A Pound of Sorrow never paid an Ounce of Debt.* — I've heard a wise Man say, *that when the worst has happen'd, we ought to be content, because we know the worst. — Many a cloudy Morning turns out a fine Day.* — We are now Beggars *Dolly*, and 'twould be a Sin to be Rich; for, *sufficient to the Day is the Evil thereof,*[6] — and St. Paul says — Hold your foolish Tong, *cry'd Dolly*, — this is fine *prating* indeed! — Will your *Solomon* provide a *Bed* for us to Night? Or will St. Paul pay for our Supper? — Not they by my *Sowle*; — They'll *talk* and make a fine *Story*, but the *Devil a bit* will they give to fill a *hungry Belly*? — Come, come, *said he*, we have a *Shilling* still left; let us keep that and our Wits, and my Life for it, we shall pick up a *pretty Living.'* — So saying, *Jack* took his Post on his Mother's Back, and got safe to the next Village. They finish'd the Remainder of their *Potatoes*, had their Pint of *Ale*, and went to *Rest* pretty much as in the former Manner.

CHAPTER III

Begging is not so vile a Trade
As some imagine — some have made.
Vary the Stile, or change the Dress,
You'll find 'tis what we all profess;
The Difference lies 'twixt Rich and Poor,
One begs for little —— th' other more.

HUDIBRASTICK

The good People continued their daily Travels, and wander'd through many Countries, and greatly improv'd in the *Art* and *Mystery*, that was to furnish them with Bread; and indeed, every Day produc'd its Supply. Three Months past in this Manner, till the *old Man* complain'd of the Fatigue, and most ardently wish'd for a settled Habitation. They were now in the great Road, and within a few Miles of *Clonmel*,[7] on a pretty Eminence that commanded a good Prospect. 'Twas agreed to fix here, and lodge about a Quarter of a Mile from the Road; where was an *old Hut*, which a few Boughs cover'd well enough for the present.

The Venerableness of *Jerry's* Beard, which no *Razor* was suffer'd to visit, had a very good Effect, and the *tatter'd* Condition of *Dolly's* Cloaths; Her *Hair* hanging about her *Eyes*, a *dirty Clout* on her Head, and *Face* and *Hands* almost of the same Colour, made her look near *as old* as her *Husband*, and procur'd the Charity of *well-dispos'd Christians* so amply, that they had no Reason to repent of their Situation. — In a short Time, the Hut was better cover'd; and they provided themselves with *two Caddows*,[8] a *small Pot, two woodden Platters, two Trenchers, one Knife*, and *two Horn Spoons.* However, this Abode being so distant from what they might call *their Shop*, made it very inconvenient, and lost them many *Customers*. This determin'd them to double Diligence, and to save as much as would build *a Cabin* by the Road Side, on the *Common*. A few *Shillings* compleated this Structure, and their Effects were soon remov'd.

Thus were they fix'd in a more comfortable Manner than could be imagined, from the Appearance of the *Hovel*. Business went on in a very prosperous Way; and, as Money came in, they increas'd their Conveniencies and Utensils; but every Thing was added *externally* that gave an Idea of *Misery* and *Wretchedness*. — They often drank *Ale*, eat *Bread*, and sometimes *Meat*, which many Farmers in the *Kingdom* are utter Strangers to. In short, they lived as happily as the Impetuosity of *Dolly's* Temper would admit, which, at some

5. Proverbs 23:5.
6. Matthew 6:34.
7. County town of County Tipperary.
8. Rough woollen rugs or mantles.

Seasons, vented itself on *Jerry*, in *old Rogue* and *old Scoundrel*, and such *affectionate* Epithets, which he bore with the Calmness of a *Philosopher*, seldom answering but in *Proverbs*.

Scarcely had they been settled three Months, before some of their Neighbours *smoak'd a Pipe* with *blind Connor* and *poor Doll*. Their great Knowledge, surpriz'd them, particularly when they found *She* could *both Read and Write*. The *Priest* of the Parish who was a young Man, being at last made acquainted with this *Prodigy*, determin'd to pay her a Visit. One Morning, when she was *cleaner* dress'd than usual, she was *sweetly singing* on the Ditch Side, and *his Reverence* surpriz'd her in the Act of *giving Suck*. As she knew him, she blush'd, and was going to cover her *Neck*, which the *holy Man* prevented with his Hand, saying, '*God speed your Work, my dear Child. — Don't be asham'd at what God has given you. — I'm well enough us'd to such Sights!*' — Perhaps he was; but Mrs. *Connor* had a *Skin* of such an wholesome *Sanguineness*, and *Breasts* so *prominent and firm*, as puzzled his *Reverence*, and made his *Blood* rise in his Face, and his *Speech* to faulter.

As Mrs. *Connor* durst not disoblige the *Priest*, she made all the fine Speeches in her Power, and told him almost as much, as if she had been at *Confession*. His *Reverence* spoke very compassionately on her unhappy Circumstances, and, in a *tender Manner*, insinuated the hard Fortune, that *so young* and *well-spoken a Woman*, should be reduced to *ask a Favour* of any *Man*; when, if she had *her due*, they ought to *ask Favours* of her. — 'Not, my *dear Child, said he*, that I would be after finding Fault with your *Industry*, or putting *bad Thoughts* in your Head. No! no! God forbid! But as you are a *sensible Woman*, I may tell you, we ought to know *Good* as well as *Bad*, that we may avoid the *one*, and follow the *other*: But when we make *a Slip*, as we are all *frail Mortals*, it must be great Comfort to a *good Catholick*, to have a *Holy Priest* to pray for, and *absolve us.*' — At this, he put on a Countenance of *primitive Piety*, or at least, so much of it, as his *Eyes* would permit, which still sparkled, and being fixed on the *beautiful Part*, before mentioned, spoke a Language *truly Universal*.

Jack's Mother was quite confounded at all these fine Words; and not perfectly understanding *Logical* Distinctions, was afraid the *Holy Father* was endeavouring to make her Proof against *good* or *bad Fortune*, not against *good* or *bad Morals*. Father *Kelly* soon solv'd her Doubts; for as the *Child* still continued at the *Breast*, he prais'd its *Beauty*, patted its *Cheeks*, and uttered every *infantine* Expression, which Mothers are so naturally fond to hear. — 'The sweet little Fellow, *said he*, it looks like an Angel, I must *kiss it*, were it but for the Sake of the Nurse.' — He kept his Word; but guiding his *Head* a little more on *one Side*, he feasted his Lips (as if by Accident) on *these Charms* his Eyes has been Witness of for half an Hour.

His Reverence recover'd himself at last, and — I ask your Pardon, good Mrs. *Connor*, said he, for by my *own Conscience* I had no Harm in my Thoughts, but God forgive me! in troth I was going to t'other Side, for fear it would be jealous; tho' if I had, you know, there would be no *Sin* in it, neither; for what is a *Breast* but *Flesh*? and so is *your Hand*; and what *Sin*, my Dear, in touching a *Hand*?' — This Reasoning was so strong that Conviction sat on Mrs. *Connor's* Countenance; which the *good Man* perceiving, he very fervently transported his *Kisses* from *one Side* to *the other*.

Some Travellers appearing and *Jerry* being summon'd to his Post, the charitable *Priest* slipt Sixpence into her Hand, and gave the old Man a Yard of good Tobacco; so wishing them *good Luck*, added his *Benediction*, and promis'd to call in his Walks.

It would be endless to point out the Virtues of this *good Man*. He visited frequently, and always left *something* behind him. He mentioned to *Dolly* the most charitable Families in the Country; and taught *Jerry* how to tell the weary Traveller the *Hour of the Day*. He repair'd the *first Hut*, where she always cook'd the Victuals when he *honour'd* them with his Company. He put a Door to it, and sent in good Store of *Whisky* and *Straw*, with *two Caddows*. This serv'd *his Reverence* for a Country Retreat; and answered every End of a *Confessional*. His Conversation was *truly pious*, and his Pains were great to convert *Jerry* to the *Bosom of that Church* out of which there is *no Salvation*. Sometimes, indeed, his *Zeal* was rather too great; for, when Mr. *Connor* made strong Objections, he *most charitably*, and with a *truly Christian Spirit*, hurry'd poor *Jerry*'s Soul *to the Devil and all his Angels*; in which Journey, his Wife always added an hearty *Amen*.

About the Age of Five Years, Jack remembers his daily sitting on a Ditch with his *Father* and *Mother*, industriously employ'd in that *most antient* and *most noble* Profession of *Begging*. The Situation was well contriv'd, and three Roads terminated just at their Mansion, and, as it were, empty'd themselves into the *great one*. Besides the Beauty of the Prospect, I apprehend *his Parents* had some *Regard* and *Love* to Society; for no Traveller could pass, but were attack'd with all the *Oratory* in their Power. Without Vanity, I may say, few People of *their Distinction* enjoy'd that *Talent* to greater Perfection, especially Mrs. *Connor*. When she was determin'd to *extract* a *Penny* from a *good Christian*, she mounted the Ditch, and with Eyes rais'd to Heaven, and uplifted Hands, she bespoke his Favour: She saluted him with every *tender, moving* Expression. The *Tear* was ready; and sometimes she pleaded a *numerous Family of Orphans*, and sometimes an *antient helpless Husband*. — Did his *hard Heart* pass by *untouch'd*, she follow'd him with her rais'd Voice, invoking every *Saint* to prosper his Journey, and to commiserate her *wretched Condition*. — Many a Time, and oft', has she compelled the most *obdurate Lawyer* or *Parson* to *Rein-back*, and fumble for *Farthings*.

Jerry had his Excellence: He was really advanc'd in Years; was infirm and *blind*. The Loss of Sight, so dreadful to many, was to them of infinite Use. From this he drew the *Pity* of the *Good-natur'd*, and the *Compassion* of most Travellers; but his being an *old Soldier, who had serv'd by Sea and Land*, afforded an Addition to his *Revenue*; to which a *red Coat* contributed not a little.

Young as our *Hero* was, his Employment had its Use; for whilst his dear Parents were solacing themselves in *their Castle*, and enjoying the Comforts of *Ale*, *Tobacco*, and the Conversation of *Friends*, he was on the Watch for the Approach of Passengers; when his *Father* or *Mother*, and sometimes *both*, sally'd out, and he always attended to join in the *Cry*, and pick up the *Copper* that Humanity threw them.

Jack now grew a sturdy Fellow, of Six Years old. As his Mother had been so good to teach him to *read*, he was a great Comfort to his *Father*, and entertained him out of *The whole Duty of Man*,[9] which he took particular Care of, ever since Mrs. *Connor* had sold his *Bible*. The Child read so frequently, that at last he was very *expert*, and began to relish the Subject. One Day, he asked his Father, *if there was any more Books in the World, for he would read them all*. 'God bless you, poor Child, *said Jerry*, and give you *Grace* to *learn*, and *practice* all good Things.'
— Then, folding him in his Arms, with many Tears, and uplifted Hands, beseech'd the *Almighty* to succour his helpless Age, and guide his Steps, that he might live by *Honesty* and *Labour*. — Tho' *Jack* knew not what he meant, yet his Words made so great an Impression, that he *cry'd* most heartily. — In this Situation the Mother found them, which soon chang'd the Scene: She storm'd like a Fury, and swore he was sending the Boy to the Devil, as well as himself: 'But, *continued she*, with all my Heart, an obstinate Bastard as he is; but I'll take Care, I warrant, of your *damn'd Book*.' —— She then *curs'd herself* most bitterly, for teaching *Jack* to *read*; and mutter'd something of *sending him far enough out of his Reach*.

'No, *Dolly*, *said her Husband*, you need not do that; for *Father Kelly* and *You*, will soon send me to my *long Home!*' — 'Tis too good News to be true, — *said she*. — 'Well, well, *reply'd Jerry*, I shan't trouble you long; — you may let me have a little Peace whilst I live.' — Some Passengers interrupted this Conversation; and the common Occurrences of the Day, gave *Jerry* some Respite till Dinner. — He said *Grace* as usual, but could not eat. At Supper 'twas the same Way; and in the Night a *Fever* came on, which open'd his Wounds, and, for want of *proper Care*, a *Mortification* ensued; and the fourth Day, *he slept with his Fathers*. — The pious *Priest* was determin'd to have the better of the *Argument* at last, and make him a good Catholick, by performing the final *Rites of the Church*, before the *Body* was *quite cold*.

On this melancholy Occasion, it must be confess'd, the poor Widow behav'd as the most fashionable of her Sex. — She *shriek'd* and *wrung her Hands*, and call'd on *Death* to ease her *Misery*. — She *fainted*, and fell into *Fits*; and the Neighbours, with great Difficulty brought her to herself. — When recover'd, she bore her *Fate* with great *Resignation*, and gave Directions about the *Funeral* with much Composure of Mind, except when more Friends dropt in, which renew'd her *Sorrows*; and then the whole Company sympathiz'd in the *most doleful Cadences*.

The Deceas'd being stripp'd and wash'd, was laid out on some *Straw*, cover'd with a Sheet that

9. A protestant handbook of religious instruction, of disputed authorship, first published in 1658 but much reprinted in the late-seventeenth and eighteenth centuries.

was formerly white. On his *Breast* was a large Dish fill'd with Salt, which undoubtedly had its Use. The good People, three Miles round, flock'd to *blind Connor's Wake*, with Loads of *Whisky* and *Tobacco*; *Pipers* were in Abundance; and sundry *Gentlemen* amused the Company with the *sweet Harmony* of their *Trumps* or *Jews-harps*. — When *Father Kelly* had declared that *Jerry Connor* died a *True Son of the Church*, being by him converted almost by a *Miracle*, a *Buzz* of Content ran through the whole Assembly; and he finished a few Prayers for the *Repose of his Soul*.

The *common Irish* are chearful at a *Wedding*; but, at a *Wake*, their *Joy* and *Mirth* is seemingly *extravagant*. *Ill Nature*, and the Want of *Compassion* and *Tenderness*, are not placed amongst their *natural Vices*. If the Moral of this antient Custom be examin'd, and found to proceed from their Pleasure, in believing, that their *Friend* or *Companion* has quitted all *human Infirmities*, and now enjoys a Fulness of *Bliss*, we cannot think the Practice *irrational* or *absurd*.

Mirth in every Shape abounded; but *Jack* seem'd to drop all the romping Sporters. He listen'd with great Attention to a Knot of *Old Ladies*, who entertain'd each other with true *Stories of Giants* and *Witches*, and *Spirits*, and *Kings of Ireland*. — From these he went to another Cluster, who spoke of the Deceased, like the *Egyptian Priests*. They magnify'd his *supposed Virtues*, and gave him *Vices*, to which he was a *Stranger*. —— *Scandal* and *Malice*, and *Envy*, were present! Some hinted, that *Dolly* was not *his Wife*; some call'd her his *Niece*, and some his *Daughter*; but *all* agreed, in wondering, what the Devil *Father Kelly* could see, to make him so *civil to her*. — I much fear many grand Societies are but *humble* Imitators of this *equally polite* Assembly.

At last the *Funeral* set out, directing their Course to a *ruin'd Monastery*, about Six Miles distant. The March was solemn; and ever and anon a *Sacred Dirge* was rais'd, that shook the *Hills* and eccho'd through the *Vales*. The Company still encreas'd from the neighbouring Cabins, whose Inhabitants having walk'd two or three Miles, and rais'd their *Notes* of Condolance with the rest; perhaps would at last find Time to ask, *who is dead?*

The necessary *Rites* being finish'd, Mr. *Kelly*, with some of the Company, return'd to the *Hut*, where *Jack* soon found he wanted a *Father*, and had not a *Mother*.

THOMAS AMORY

(*c.* 1691-1788)

from: THE LIFE OF JOHN BUNCLE, ESQ.; CONTAINING VARIOUS OBSERVATIONS AND REFLECTIONS, MADE IN SEVERAL PARTS OF THE WORLD, AND MANY EXTRAORDINARY RELATIONS (1756-66)

[This curious compendium novel opens with a preface in which the actual author, Thomas Amory, and the fictional character, John Buncle, become hopelessly confused (William Hazlitt was later to refer, symptomatically, to the author as 'John Amory'). Amory's principal concerns with Ireland, free-thinking, and Unitarianism are here all in evidence.]

TO THE

CRITICKS,

THIS

JOURNAL

Is most humbly DEDICATED,

BY

Their most humble Servant,

The AUTHOR.

A PREFACE By WAY of DEDICATION

GENTLEMEN,

This book is not addressed to you, in order to ask your protection for its faults; or in hopes, that such valuable names at the head of it, may preserve it. Things in print must stand by their own worth. But it is offered to you, to let the world see I had that confidence in the goodness of my design in writing it, as to submit it to such great and impartial judges; and that I believe you will report your opinion in such a manner, as to procure me the esteem of the virtuous; when you find that my principal intention in this piece, is to serve the interests of truth, liberty, and religion, and to advance useful learning, to the best of my abilities: --- that I have the happiness of mankind at heart, and attempt, in a historical manner, to encrease their knowledge in general; and in particular, to lead them to a pious contemplation and acknowledgment of God's unspeakable wisdom and goodness manifested in the works of the creation; --- shew them the truth of the testimony of *Jesus Christ* concerning a divine providence, immortality, and a future state; and that as virtue advances and improves, human felicity augments, and becomes a sure prognostick of that fulness of bliss, which men of goodness and integrity are to enjoy, without interruption, frailty, and infirmity, in an unchangeable and everlasting life. This was my scheme. These things I had principally in view, when, to vindicate my character from misrepresentation and idle stories, and to illustrate my *memoirs of several ladies of Great-Britain,*[1] I sat down to write a true history of my life and notions. You will see at once, gentlemen, that this is the labored part of my work. Were I able to write so as to persuade even a few to alter their way of living, and employ their time for the future, in forming and training up their moral powers to perfection, I should think myself more fortunate and glorious than the greatest genius in the temple of Fame. Indeed, gentlemen, fame or name, in this world, is not the thing I think of. *Non est mortale quod opto,* I can say with *Lactantius*:[2] and were it within my power to choose, sure I am, that I would be for ever unknown. But that was impossible. In justice to myself, as before observed, and that tradition might not hand me down, when I am gone, in that variety of bad and foolish characters, which a malice, that known nothing of me, whispers while I am living; it was necessary I should tell my own story. The relation was likewise requisite, to render the memoirs before mentioned intelligible. The volumes of that work, which are to be published, would be quite dark, and not so grateful as intended, without a previous account of the author's life.

This, gentlemen, is the truth of the case, and as I say as little of myself, in my relations, as I can; and as much for true religion and useful learning, as I was able, I hope, from your rectitude and judgment, that you will get me a fair hearing; and I call upon you as my patrons, and the friends to learning and truth, for your approbation of my good and pious intentions, tho' you should not be able to say one word of any excellencies in my writings. This is all I ask. As I wish well to your cause, the cause of virtue and letters, and have chiefly endeavoured, according to my abilities, to make my readers acquainted with the *majesty of the Deity, and his kingdom,* and *the greatness of his excellency*, before whom all the inhabitants of the earth, all powers and principalities, are as nothing; I hope you will, in return, favour me with your best wishes.

As to some strange things you will find in the following journal; and a life, in various particulars, quite contrary to the common course of action, I can assure you, gentlemen, in respect of the strange things, that however wonderful they may appear to you, yet they are, exclusive of a few decorations and figures, (necessary in all works), strictly true: and as to the difference of my life, from that of the generality of men, let it only be considered, that I was born in London, and carried an infant to Ireland, where I learned the Irish language, and became intimately acquainted with its original inhabitants: — that I was not only a lover of books from the time I could spell them to this hour; but read with an extraordinary pleasure, before I was

1. Thomas Amory published *Memoirs of Several Ladies of Great Britain* in 1755.

2. 'There is nothing mortal that I want.' Lucius Caecilius Firminianus Lactantius (*c.* 240-*c.* 320) was an early Christian apologist. I have not identified the source of the quotation.

twenty, the works of several of the fathers,[3] and all the old romances; which tinged my ideas with a certain piety and extravagance, that rendered my virtues as well as my imperfections particularly mine: — that by hard measure, I was compelled to be an adventurer, when very young, and had not a friend in the universe but what I could make by good fortune, and my own address: — that my wandering life, wrong conduct, and the iniquity of my kind, with a passion for extraordinary things and places, brought me into several great distresses; and that I had quicker and more wonderful deliverances from them than people in tribulation generally receive: --- that the dull, the formal, and the visionary, the hard-honest man, and the poor-liver, are a people I have had no connexion with; but have always kept company with the polite, the generous, the lively, the rational, and the brightest freethinkers of this age: — that beside all this, I was in the days of my youth, one of the most active men in the world, at every exercise; and to a degree of rashness, often venturous, when there was no necessity for running any hazards: in diebus illis,[4] I have descended head-foremost from a high cliff into the ocean, to swim, when I could, and ought, to have gone off a rock not a yard from the surface of the deep. — I have swam near a mile and a half out in the sea, to a ship that lay off, went on board, got clothes from the mate of the vessel, and proceeded with them to the next port; while my companion I left on the beach concluded me drowned, and related my sad fate in the town. — I have taken a cool thrust over a bottle, without the least animosity on either side; but both of us depending on our skill in the small sword, for preservation from mischief. ——— Such things as these I now call wrong, and mention them only as samples of a rashness I was once subject to, as an opportunity happened to come in the way. Let all these things be taken into the account, and I imagine, gentlemen, that what may at first sight seem strange, and next to incredible, will, on considering these particulars, not long remain so, in your opinion; though you may think the relator an odd man. As to that, I have nothing to say. And if oddness consists in spirit, freedom of thought, and a zeal for the divine unity; in a taste for what is natural, antique, romantic, and wild; in honouring women, who are admirable for goodness, letters, and arts; and in thinking, after all the scenes I have gone through, that every thing here is vanity; except that *virtue* and *charity*, which gives us a right to *expect beyond the grave*; and procures us, in this world, the direction of infinite wisdom, the protection of infinite power, and the friendship of infinite goodness; — then, may it be written on my stone, — *Here lies an odd man*.

Thus much, gentlemen, I thought proper to say to you, that by being acquainted with the particulars relative to the complexion, and design of the author, you might the easier and the better comprehend the various things you will find in the work he dedicates to you.

I have only to add, that I wish you all happiness; that your heads may lack no ointment, and your garments be always white and odoriferous: but especially, may you press on, like true critics, towards perfection; and may bliss, glory, and honour, be your reward and your Portion.

Barbican,[5]
Aug. 1. 1756.

[Buncle leaves Ireland for England]

[May 1, 1725. I left my father's house.] 15. On the first day of May then, early in the morning, as the clock struck one, I mounted my excellent mare, and with my boy, O'Fin, began to journey as I had projected, on seeing how things went. I did not communicate my design to a soul, nor take my leave of any one, but in the true spirit of adventure, abandoned my father's dwelling, and set out to try what fortune would produce in my favor. I had the world before me, and Providence my guide.[6] As to my substance, it consisted of a purse of gold, that contained fifty Spanish pistoles,[7] and half a score moidores;[8] and I had one bank note for five hundred pounds, which my dear Miss *Noel*[9] left me by her will, the morning she sickened; and it was all she had of her own to leave to any one. With this I set forward, and in five days time arrived from the Western extremity of Ireland at a village called Rings-end, that lies on the Bay of Dublin. Three

3. i.e. fathers of the Church, Christian writers of the first five centuries A.D.
4. in those days.
5. A street slightly to the north of Cripplegate in the City of London.
6. Milton, *Paradise Lost*, XII, 646-47.
7. Spanish gold coins (of various values).
8. A Portuguese gold coin current in Britain and Ireland during the eighteenth century.
9. Harriot Noel, who died of smallpox just before she and John Buncle were to be married.

days I rested there, and at the *Conniving-House*,† and then got my horses on board a ship that was ready to sail, and bound for the land I was born in, I mean Old England.

[My departure from Rings end, and what happened at sea.] 16. The wind, in the afternoon, seemed good and fair, and we were in hopes of getting to *Chester*[10] the next day: but at midnight, a tempest arose, which held in all the horrors of hurricane, thunder and lightning, for two nights and a day, and left us no hope of escape. It was a dreadful scene indeed, and looked as if the last fatal assault was making on the globe. As we had many passengers, their cries were terrible, and affected me more then the flashing fires and the winds. For my part, I was well reconciled to the great change, but I confess that nature shrunk at the frightful manner of my going off, which I expected every moment the second night. At last however, we got into *Whitehaven.*[11] It pleased the great King of all the earth to bid the storm, *Have done*.

[The case of Dean Whaley.] Four remarkable things I noticed while the tempest lasted. One was, that the *Dean* of *Derry*, Dr. *Whaley*, whom we had on board, (who had nineteen hundred a year from the church, for teaching the people to be Christians) was vastly more afraid than one young lady of the company, who appeared quite serene. The Dean, tho' a fine Orator at land, was ridiculous in his fears at sea. He screamed as loud as any of the people: But this young lady behaved, like an angel in a storm. She was calm and resigned, and sat with the mate and me, the second night, discoursing of the divine power, and the laws of nature, in such uproars. By the way, neither mate, nor master, nor hand, could keep the deck. The ship was left to the mercy of the winds and waves.

[The Case of Miss Melmoth.] The second remarkable thing is, that as this young lady went into naked bed in her cabbin, the first night, before the tempest began to stir, it was not many hours till a sea struck us upon the quarter, and drove in one of our quarter, and one of our stern dead lights, where we shipped great quantities of water, that put us under great apprehensions of foundering, and filled so suddenly the close wooden bed in which Miss *Melmoth* lay, that had not I chanced to be then leaning against the partition, and snatched her out, the moment I found my self all over wet, and half covered with the breaking sea, she must inevitably have perished. I ran up on deck with her in my arms, and laid her almost senseless and naked there: and as there was no staying many minutes in that place, I threw my great coat over her, and then brought her down to my own birth, which I gave her, and got her dry cloaths from her trunk, and made her drink a large glass of brandy, which saved her life. She got no cold, which I thought very strange, but was hurt a little in the remove. When all was over, she protested she would never go into naked bed, on board ship, again.

[The case of some officers in the storm.] The third particular is, that there were some officers on board, most monstrously wicked men, and when we were given over by the captain, and no hope he thought of being saved, these warriors lamented like young children, and were the most dismal, disturbing howlers on board: yet, when we got on land, they had done with *O Lord, O Lord*, and began again their obscene talk, and to damn themselves at every word to the center of hell.

[The cases of Gavan and Henley.] The fourth thing was this. There was on board with us a young gentleman of my acquaintance, one *Pierce Gavan*, who had been a fellow-commoner in my time of Trinity, Dublin. The first day of the storm, he was carried over-board by a rolling sea, and fairly lodged in the ocean, at above twenty yards distance from the ship; but the next tumbling billow brought him back again. He was laid on the deck without any hurt. On the contrary, one *Charles Henley*, a young merchant, was beat over, and we never saw him more.

[Henley's character.] *Henley* was not only a man of sense and prudence, who had an honest mind, and a cultivated understanding, but by search and

† The *Conniving-House*, (as the gentlemen of Trinity called it in my time, and long after) was a little public house, kept by *Jack Macklean*, about a quarter of a mile beyond Rings-end, on the top of the beach, within a few yards of the sea. Here we used to have the finest fish at all times; and in the season, green peas, and all the most excellent vegetables. The ale here was always extraordinary, and every thing the best; which, with its delightful situation, rendered it a delightful place of a summer's evening. Many a delightful evening have I passed in this pretty thatched house with the famous *Larrey Grogan*, who played on the bag-pipes extreme well; dear *Jack Lattin*, matchless on the fiddle, and the most agreeable of companions; that ever charming young fellow, *Jack Wall*, the most worthy, the most ingenious, the most engaging of them, the son of councellor *Maurice Wall*; and many other delightful fellows; who went in the days of their youth to the shades of eternity. When I think of them and their evening songs — *We will go to Johnny Macklean's — to try if his ale be good or not*, etc. and that years and infirmities begin to oppress me — What is life!

10. Chester, on the river Dee, was an important eighteenth-century disembarkation point from Ireland.
11. A port in Cumberland.

enquiries into the doctrines, institutions and motives of reveled religion, had the highest regard for the truths of genuine Christianity, and chose the best means in his power to make himself acceptable to God.

[Gavan's character.] *Gavan*, on the contrary, had no sense of religion, nor did he ever think of the power and goodness of God. He was a most prophane swearer, drank excessively, and had the heart to debauch every pretty woman he saw, if it had been possible for him to do so much mischief. — Yet this man, who never reformed that I heard, and whose impieties have shocked even young fellows who were no saints, was astonishingly preserved; and *Henley*, who had the justest natural notions, and listened to Revelation, perished miserably? How shall we account for such things? By saying, that the world that now is, and the world that is to come, are in the hands of God, and every transaction in them is quite right, tho' the reason of the procedure may be beyond our view. We cannot judge certainly of the ends and purposes of Providence, and therefore to pass judgment on the ways of God, is not only impious, but ridiculous to the last degree. This we know for certain, that whenever, or however, a good man falls, he falls into the hand of God, and since we must all die, the difference as to time and manner, signifies very little, when there is an infinite wisdom to distinguish every case, and an infinite goodness to compensate all our miseries. This is enough for a Christian. Happy is the man, and for ever safe, let what will happen, who acts a rational part, and has the fear and love of God in his thoughts. With pleasure he looks into all the scenes of futurity. When storms and earthquakes threaten calamity, distress, and death, he maintains an inward peace.

[This brief anecdote is as typical of the principal narrative as the copious footnoting is characteristic of the novel's typographical appearance.]

[A great deliverance.] 31. As I travelled once in the county of *Kerry* in *Ireland*, with the *White Knight*, and the *Knight of the Glin*,† we called at *Terelah O Crohanes*, an old Irish gentleman, our common friend, who kept up the hospitality of his ancestors, and shewed how they lived, when *Cormac Mac Cuillenan*, the *Generous*, (from whose house he descended) was king of *Munster* and *Archbishop of Cashel*, in the year 913.‡ There was no end of eating and drinking there, and the famous

† Such *knights* were honourable creations made by the *Irish kings*. We have an account of them in the *psalter of Tarah*, before the reigns of *Conaire* the *Great*, A.M. 3970, ante *Christum* 34; *Cormac Ulfadda*, A.D. 230; and the glorious *Brien Boiroimhe*, A.D. 1027; the three greatest monarchs that ever *Ireland* had: *Fitzgerald*, the first *knight of Glin*, was so made by the immortal *Brien Boiroimhe*, who fell in the bloody fight, A.D. 1239, that was fought by him with *Maolmorda king* of *Leinster*, who joined with the *Danes*. The *king* of *Ireland* and the *king* of *Leinster* slew each other; and with *Brien Boiroimhe* set the glory of Ireland. The states from this time began to decay; and *Roderick O Connor*, who came to the crown, A.D. 1168, was the *last king* of *Ireland*. Our *Henry the Second*, got the kingdom A.D. 1172, by two means; one of which was a *grant* the *pope* made of it to him; who was allowed by the natives to be *supreme Lord* of the *island* in *temporals*, and the nobility had by commission resigned it to him, after the death of *Brien Boiroimhe*. —— The other mean, and what effectually did the work, was the *king* of *Leinster*'s joining with *Strangwell*, who was at the head of the *English* forces, and had married that king's daughter. An old chronicle says she was the most beautiful woman upon earth of her time, and very learned: but inferior nevertheless in beauty and learning to the six princesses we read of in the *psalter of Tarah*, who were fair beyond all mortals that ever lived, and wonderful in the extent of their knowledge; to wit,

The princess *Mac Diarmuid.*
The princess *Mac Reagien.*
The princess *Mac Faolain.*
The princess *Mac Kennedy.*
The princess *O Heyn.*
The princess *O Flaherty.*

These six were *Druidesses*, says the *psalter of Tarah.*

By the way, reader, let me tell you, that from this same *psalter of Tarah*, I writ out one of the finest and most improving *love stories* that ever I read. It is called *the adventure of Terlagh Mac Shain and the beautiful Gara O Mulduin; which happened in the reign of Cormac Ulfada, king of Ireland, in the year of salvation* 213, *that Faon Maccumhail, commonly called Fian Maccul, the mighty champion, beat the Picts, and brought off among other prisoners, the beautiful Ciarnuit, (daughter to the king of the Picts) whom Cormac Ulfada took for his concubine.* This story is likewise more shortly told in the *red book of Mac Eogane*, a very valuable old Irish manuscript: and from both those books I will give my reader the best part of this adventure as soon as I can see a proper place to bring it in. [Amory's principal source of information in this note seems to be not the manuscripts he mentions but the *Foras Feasa ar Éirinn* (*c.* 1634) of Geoffrey Keating (*c.* 1580-*c.* 1650), in the English translation, *General History of Ireland* (1723) by Dermod O'Connor, especially Book I, pp. 123ff. Ed.]

‡ This *Cormac Cuillenan* writ the famous *psalter* of *Cashel*, a very extraordinary and valuable book, which he composed from antient poems of the bards, who thus writ their history, and from venerable records, as this king and prelate declares in his will. The clause is this — *My psalter, which preserves the antient records and monuments of my native country, which are transcribed with great fidelity, I leave to Ronal Cashel, to be preserved to after-times and ages yet to come.* —— There is another remarkable clause in this great man's will, to wit, —— *My soul for mercy I commit to heaven; my body leave to dust and rottenness.* There is not a word of any saint in it; and of consequence, there was *no saint-worship then in Ireland.*

Cormac writ his will the day before he fought the bloody battle of *Maghailbe* with the king of *Leinster*, and therein fell. It begins in this manner:——

Summon'd away by death, which I perceive
Approaches; for by prophetic skill,
I find that short will be my life and reign:
I solemnly appoint that my affairs
Shall thus be settled after I am dead;
And thus I constitute my latest will:

Downe Falvey played on the harp. For a day and a night we sat to it by candle-light, without shirts or cloaths on; naked, excepting that we had our breeches and shoes and stockings on; and I drank so much burgundy in that time, that the sweat ran of a red colour down my body; and my senses were so disordered, that when we agreed to ride out for a couple of hours to take a little air, I leaped my horse into a dreadful quarry, and in the descent was thrown into a large deep water that was in a part of the frightful bottom, and by that means saved my life. When I came above water, I swam very easily out of the pit, and walked up the low side of the quarry as sober as if I had not drank a glass. This is a fact, whatever the critics may say of the thing. All I can say to it is, my hour was not come.

My royal robe embroider'd o'er with gold,
And sparkling with the rays of costly jewels;
Well suited to a state of majesty,
I do bequeath, etc. ——— ———
My coat of mail of bright and polish'd steel
Will well become the martial king of Ulster,
To whom I give it: and my golden chain
Shall the most pious *Muchuda* enjoy
As a reward, etc. ——— ———
My golden vestment for most sacred use,
And my royal wardrobe I hereby give
To etc. ——— ——— ——— ———

Now from this antique piece verbally translated, I think it is evident, that the kings of the four provinces of Ireland were not such poor and ignorant chiefs as they are generally imagined to be; and of consequence, that one of the four, to whom the other three did homage, and who was therefore called the king of Ireland, was always a potent prince, and could do great matters, when they were all united. This consideration, I fansy, (and the *address* let me add of *Anselm*, archbishop of Canterbury, and of Lanfranc, archbishop of the same see, to *Mortogh O Brien* king of *Ireland*, and *Terlah O Brien* king of *Ireland*, *Moriardacho Glorioso* and *Terdelucho Magnifico*, To the *most magnificent Terlagh O Brien, king of Ireland*, our benediction, etc. as you may read them at large in *Usher's Primordia**) ought to give some credit to *O Flaherty's Ogygia*, *Keating's History*, and *MacCurtins' Annals*; which those writers really took from very antient records, and principally from the very valuable manuscripts, called the *psalters* of *Cashel* and *Tarah*.

What the *psalter* of *Cashel* was I have told you, reader; and as to the *psalter* of *Tarah*, the history of it is this. — On a tract of land called *Tarah*, that was taken from the province of *Leinster*, and added to the county of *Meath*, stood the largest of the four vast palaces of the kings of *Ireland*, and at that grand fabric there was a triennial meeting of the states of the kingdom, called the *royal assembly of Tarah*. There they enacted laws, examined the antient chronicles and records, and purged them from all false and spurious relations, settled genealogies, and considered noble exploits. All the things that received the assembly's approbation were registered, and transcribed into the royal records, and they called this journal the *psalter of Tarah*. [O'Connor's translation of Keating is again the source, particularly Book II, pp. 65ff. Ed.]

* These letters were written by the English archbishops to the Irish kings, *Turlogh* and *Murtogh*, in the years 1098 and 1110.

[Chance encounters with Irish friends, even in the remotest parts of England, characterize Buncle's experience. Here, he meets no fewer than six of them, at the popular Harrogate Spa in Yorkshire.]

[The author meets at *Harrogate* six gentlemen of his acquaintance from *Dublin*.]

§. 4. Among the company I found at this agreeable place, were six *Irish* gentlemen, who had been my contemporaries in Trinity-College, *Dublin*, and were right glad to see me, as we had been *Sociorums*, (a word of *Swift's*) at the conniving-house at *Ringsend*, for many a summer's evening, and their regard for me was great. They thought I had been long numbered with the dead, as they could not get any account of me for so many years; and when they saw me, at their entring the public room, sitting by a beauty, in deep discourse, God-zounds, (says one of them), there he is, making love to the finest woman in the world. These gentlemen were Mr. *Gollogher*, Mr. *Gallaspy*, Mr. *Dunkley*, Mr. *Makins*, Mr. *Monaghan*, and Mr. *O'Keefe*, descended from the *Irish* kings, and first cousin to the great *O'Keefe*, who was buried not long ago in *Westminster* Abby. They were all men of large fortunes, and, Mr. *Makins* excepted, were as handsome, fine fellows as could be picked out in all the world. *Makins* was a very low, thin man, not four feet high, and had but one eye, with which he squinted most shockingly. He wore his own hair,[12] which was short and bad, and only drest by his combing it himself in the morning, without oyl or powder. But as he was matchless on the fiddle, sung well, and chatted agreeably, he was a favourite with the ladies. They preferred ugly *Makins* (as he was called) to many very handsome men. I will here give the public the character of these *Irish* gentlemen, for the honour of *Ireland*, and as they were curiosities of the human kind.

[The characters of six *Irish* gentlemen. *O'Keefe's* character.]

§. 5. *O'Keefe* was as distinguished a character as I have ever known. He had read and thought, travelled and conversed, was a man of sense, and a scholar. He had a greatness of soul, which shewed a pre-eminence of dignity, and by conduct and behaviour, the faithful interpreters of the heart, always attested the noblest and most generous sentiments. He had an extreme abhorrence of meanness of all kinds, treachery, revenge, envy,

12. i.e. instead of a wig, as was usual at the time.

littleness of mind, and shewed in all his actions the qualities that adorn a man. — His learning was of the genteel and useful kind; a sort of agreeable knowledge, which he acquired rather from a sound taste and good judgment than from the books he had read. He had a right estimation of things, and had gathered up almost every thing that is amusing or instructive. This rendered him a master in the art of pleasing: and as he had added to these improvements the fashionable ornaments of life, languages and bodily exercises, he was the delight of all that knew him.

[Character of Mr. *Makins.*] *Makins* was possessed of all the excellent qualities and perfections that are within the reach of human abilities. He had received from nature the happiest talents, and he made singular improvements of them by a successful application to the most useful and most ornamental studies. Music, as before observed, he excelled in. His intellectual faculties were fine, and, to his honour I can affirm, that he mostly employed them, as he did his great estate, to the good of mankind, the advancement of morality, and the spread of *pure theism*, the worship of God *our Saviour*, who raised and sent Christ to be a Redeemer. This gentleman was a zealous *Unitarian*, and, though but five and twenty, (when we met at *Harrogate*) a religious man: but his religion was without any melancholy; nor had it any thing of that severity of temper, which diffuses too often into the hearts of the religious a morose contempt of the world, and an antipathy to the pleasures of it. He avoided the assemblies of fools, knaves, and blockheads, but was fond of good company, and condemned that doctrine which taught men to retire from human society to seek God in the horrors of solitude. He thought the Almighty may be best found among men, where his goodness is most active, and his providence most employed.

[Character of Mr. *Gallaspy.*] *Gallaspy* was the tallest and strongest man I have ever seen, well made, and very handsome. He had wit and abilities, sung well, and talked with great sweetness and fluency, but was so extremely wicked, that it were better for him, if he had been a natural fool. By his vast strength and activity, his riches and eloquence, few things could withstand him. He was the most prophane swearer I have known: fought every thing, whored every thing, and drank seven in a hand; that is, seven glasses so placed between the fingers of his right hand, that in drinking, the liquor fell into the next glasses, and thereby he drank out of the first glass seven glasses at once. This was a common thing, I find from a book in my possession, in the reign of *Charles* the Second, in the madness that followed the restoration of that profligate and worthless prince. But this gentleman was the only man I ever saw who could or would attempt to do it; and he made but one gulp of whatever he drank; he did not swallow a fluid like other people, but if it was a quart, poured it in as from pitcher to pitcher. When he smoaked tobacco, he always blew two pipes at once, one at each corner of his mouth, and threw the smoak of both out of his nostrils. He had killed two men in duels before I left *Ireland*, and would have been hanged, but that it was his good fortune to be tried before a Judge, who never let any man suffer for killing another in this manner. (This was the late Sir *John St. Leger.*) He debauched all the women he could, and many whom he could not corrupt, he ravished. I went with him once in the stage-coach to *Kilkenny*, and seeing two pretty ladies pass by in their own chariot, he swore in his horrible way, having drank very hard after dinner, that he would immediately stop them, and ravish them: nor was it without great difficulty that I hindered him from attempting the thing; by assuring him I would be their *protector*, and he must pass through my heart before he could proceed to offer them the least rudeness. In sum, I never saw his equal in impiety, especially when inflamed with liquor, as he was every day of his life, though it was not in the power of wine to make him drunk, weak, or senseless. He set no bounds or restrictions to mirth and revels. He only slept every third night, and that often in his cloaths in a chair, where he would sweat so prodigiously as to be wet quite through; as wet as if come from a pond, or a pail of water had been thrown on him. While all the world was at rest, he was either drinking or dancing, scouring the bawdy-houses, or riding as hard as he could drive his horse on some iniquitous project. And yet, he never was sick, nor did he ever receive any hurt or mischief. In health, joy, and plenty, he passed life away, and died about a year ago at his house in the county of *Galway*, without a pang or any kind of pain. This was *Jack Gallaspy*. There are however some things to be said in his favour, and as he had more regard for me than any of his acquaintance, I should be ungrateful if I did not do him all the justice in my power.

He was in the first place far from being quarrelsome, and if he fought a gentleman at the small-sword, or boxed with a porter or coachman, it was because he had in some degree been ill used, or fancied that the laws of honour required him to call an equal to an account, for a transaction. His temper was naturally sweet.

In the next place, he was the most generous of mankind. His purse of gold was ever at his friend's service: he was kind and good to his tenants: to the poor a very great benefactor. He would give more money away to the sick and distressed in one year, than I believe many rich pious people do in seven. He had the blessings of thousands, for his charities, and, perhaps, this procured him the protection of heaven.

As to *swearing*, he thought it was only criminal, when it was false, or men lyed in their affirmations: and for *whoring*, he hoped there would be mercy, since men will be men while there are women. *Ravishing* he did not pretend to justify, as the laws of his country were against it; but he could not think the woman was a sufferer by it, as she enjoyed without sinning the highest felicity. He intended her happiness; and her saying *No*, kept her an *innocent*.

How far all this can excuse Mr. *Gallaspy*, I pretend not to determine: but as I thought it proper to give the world the picture of so extraordinary a man, it was incumbent on me, as his friend, to say all I could, with truth, in his vindication.

[Character of Mr. *Dunkley*.] *Dunkley* had an extensive capacity, an exquisite taste, and a fine genius. Besides an erudition which denominates what we call a man of learning, he happily possessed a social knowledge, which rendered him agreeable to every body. He was one of the men that are capable of touching every note. To all the variety of topics for conversation, the diversity of occurrences and incidents, the several distinctions of persons, he could adapt himself. He would laugh like *Democritus*: weep like *Heraclitus*.[13] He had the short, pert trip of the affected; the haughty, tragic stalk of the solemn; and the free, genteel gait of the fine gentleman. He was qualified to please all tastes, and capable of acting every part. He was grave, gay, a philosopher, and a trifler. He had a time for all things, relative to society, and his own true happiness, but none for any thing repugnant to honour and conscience. He was a surprising and admirable man.

[Character of Mr. *Monaghan*.] *Monaghan* had genius and knowledge, had read many books, but knew more of mankind. He laughed at the men who lost among their books the elegancy of mind so necessary in civil society. He had no relish but for nice studies and fine literature, and despised too serious and abstruse sciences. This was reckoned a fault in him by several judges: but with me it is a quere,[14] if he was much to blame. Politeness is certainly preferable to dry knowledge and thorny enquiries. This gentleman's was such as rendered him for ever agreeable and engaging. He was continually an improving friend, and a gay companion. In the qualities of his soul, he was generous without prodigality, humane without weakness, just without severity, and fond without folly. He was an honest and charming fellow. This gentleman and Mr. *Dunkley* married ladies they fell in love with at *Harrogate* Wells: *Dunkley* had the fair *Alcmena*, Miss *Cox* of *Northumberland*; and *Monaghan*, *Antiope*[15] with haughty charms, Miss *Pearson* of *Cumberland*: They lived very happy many years, and their children I hear are settled in *Ireland*.

[Character of Mr. *Gollogher*.] *Gollogher* was a man of learning and extraordinary abilities. He had read very hard for several years, and during that time, had collected and extracted from the best books more than any man I ever was acquainted with. He had four vast volumes of commonplace, royal paper, bound in rough calf, and had filled them with what is most curious and beautiful in works of literature, most refined in eloquent discourses, most poignant in books of criticism, most instructive in history, most touching and affecting in news, catastrophes, and stories; and with aphorisms, sayings, and epigrams. A prodigious memory made all this his own, and a great judgment enabled him to reduce every thing to the most exact point of truth and accuracy. A rare man! Till he was five and twenty, he continued this studious life, and but seldom went into the mixed and fashionable circles of the world. Then, all at once, he sold every book he had, and determined to read no more. He spent his every day in the best company of every kind; and as he had the happy talent of manner, and possessed

13. Democritus of Abdera (460/457-*c*.356), was known as the 'laughing philosopher', while Heraclitus (*c*.540-*c*.480) received the epithet of the 'weeping philosopher'.

14. i.e. query.

15. Like Alcmene, Antiope attracted the attention of Zeus himself by her beauty.

that great power which strikes and awakens fancy, by giving every subject the new dress and decoration it requires; — could make the most common thing no longer trivial, when in his hand, and render a good thing most exquisitely pleasing; — as he told a story beyond most men, and had, in short, a universal means towards a universal success, it was but natural that he should be every where liked and wished for. He charmed wherever he came. The specific I have mentioned made every one fond of him. With the ladies especially he was a great favourite, and more fortunate in his amours than any man I knew. Had he wanted the fine talents he was blest with, yet his being an extremely handsome man, and a master on the fiddle, could not but recommend him to the sex. He might, if he had pleased, have married any one of the most illustrious and richest women in the kingdom. But he had an aversion to matrimony, and could not bear the thought of a wife. Love and a bottle were his taste. He was however the most honourable of men in his amours, and never abandoned any woman to distress, as too many men of fortune do, when they have gratified desire. All the distressed were ever sharers in Mr. *Gollogher's* fine estate, and especially the girls he had taken to his breast. He provided happily for them all, and left nineteen daughters he had by several women a thousand pounds each. This was acting with a temper worthy of a man; and to the memory of the *benevolent Tom Gollogher* I devote this memorandum.

Having said above, that too many men of fortune abandon the girls they have ruined, I will here relate a very remarkable story, in hopes it may make an impression on some rake of fortune, if such a man should ever take this book in his hand.

[The history of the unfortunate Miss *Hunt*.]

§. 6. As I travelled once in the county of *Kildare* in *Ireland*, in the summer-time, I came into a land of flowers and blossoms, hills, woods, and shades: I saw upon an eminence a house, surrounded with the most agreeable images of rural beauties, and which appeared to be on purpose placed in that decorated spot for retirement and contemplation. It is in such silent recesses of life, that we can best enjoy the *noble* and *felicitous* ideas, which more immediately concern the attention of man, and in the *cool hours* of reflection, secreted from the fancies and follies, the business, the faction, and the pleasures of an engaged world, thoroughly consider the wisdom and harmony of the works of nature, the important purposes of providence, and the various reasons we have to adore that ever glorious *Being*, who formed us for rational happiness here, and after we have passed a few years on this sphere, in a *life* of *virtue* and *charity*, to translate us to the realms of endless bliss. Happy they who have a taste for these silent retreats, and when they please, can withdraw for a time from the world.

[The picture of Miss *Hunt*.]

The owner of this sweet place was Mr. *Charles Hunt*, a gentleman of a small estate and good sense, whom I knew many years before fortune led me to his house. His wife was then dead, and he had but one child left, his daughter *Elizabeth*. The beauties of this young lady were very extraordinary. She had the finest eyes in the world, and she looked, she smiled, she talked with such diffusive charms, as were sufficient to fire the heart of the morosest woman-hater that ever lived, and give his soul a softness it never felt before. Her father took all possible pains to educate her mind, and had the success to render her understanding a wonder, when she was but twenty years old. She sung likewise beyond most women, danced to perfection, and had every accomplishment of soul and body that a man of the best taste could wish for in a wife or a mistress. She was all beauty, life, and softness.

Mr. *Hunt* thought to have had great happiness in this daughter, though it was not in his power to give her more than five hundred pounds for a fortune, and she would have been married to a country-gentleman in his neighbourhood of a good estate, had not death carried off both her father and lover in a few days, just as the match was agreed on. This was a sad misfortune, and opened a door to a long train of sorrows. For two years however after the decease of her father, she lived very happily with an old lady, her near relation, and was universally admired and respected. I saw her many times during that term, at the old lady's villa within a few miles of *Dublin*, and took great delight in her company. If I had not been then engaged to another, I would most certainly have married her.

In this way I left *Eliza* in *Ireland*, and for several years could not hear what was become of her. No one could give me any information: but, about a twelvemonth ago, as I was walking in *Fleet-street*,[16] I saw a woman who cleaned shoes, and seemed to be an object of great distress. She was in rags and dirt

16. An important London thoroughfare to the west of Ludgate and St Paul's Cathedral.

beyond all I had ever seen of the profession, and was truly skin and bone. Her face was almost a scull, and the only remaining expression to be seen was despair and anguish. The object engaged my attention, not only on account of the uncommon misery that was visible; but, as her eyes, though sunk, were still extraordinary, and there were some remains of beauty to be traced. I thought I had somewhere seen that face in better condition. This kept me looking at her, unnoticed, for near a quarter of an hour; and as I found she turned her head from me, when she saw me, with a kind of consciousness, as if she knew me, I then asked her name, and if she had any where seen me before? —— The tears immediately ran plentifully from her eyes, and when she could speak, she said, I am *Elizabeth Hunt*. —— What, Mr. *Hunt*'s daughter of *Rafarlin*! I replied with amazement, and a concern that brought the tears into my eyes. I called a coach immediately, and took her to the house of a good woman, who lodges and attends sick people: ordered her clean cloaths, and gave the woman a charge to take the greatest care of her, and let her want for nothing proper, till I called next day.

When I saw her again, she was clean and whole, and seemed to have recovered a little, though very little, of what she once was: but a more miserable spectacle my eyes have not often seen. She told me, that soon after I went to *England*, Mr. *R.* a gentleman of my acquaintance of great fortune, got acquainted with her, courted her, and swore in the most solemn manner, by the supreme power, and the everlasting gospel, that he would be her husband, and marry her as soon as a rich dying uncle had breathed his last, if she would consent, in the mean while, to their living in secret as man and wife; for his uncle hated matrimony, and would not leave him his vast fortune, if he heard he had a wife; and he was sure, if he was married by any of the church, some whisperer would find it out, and bring it to his ear. But notwithstanding this plausible story, and that he acted the part of the fondest and tenderest man that ever lived, yet, for several months, she would not comply with his proposal. She refused to see him any more, and for several weeks he did not come in her sight.

The fatal night however at last arrived, and from the Lord Mayor's ball, he prevailed on her, by repeated vows of sincerity and truth, to come with him to his lodgings. She was undone, with child, and at the end of two months, she never saw him more. When her relations saw her big belly, they turned her out of doors; her friends and acquaintance would not look at her, and she was so despised, and ashamed to be seen, that she went to *England* with her little one. It fortunately died on the road to *London*, and as her five hundred pounds were going fast by the time she had been a year in the capital, she accepted an offer made her by a great man to go into keeping. Three years she lived with him in splendor, and when he died, she was with several in high life, 'till she got a cancer in her breast; and after it was cut off, an incurable abscess appeared. This struck her out of society, and as she grew worse and worse every day, what money she had, and cloaths, were all gone in four years time, in the relief she wanted and in support. She came the fifth year to a garret and rags, and at last, to clean shoes, or perish for want. She then uncovered the upper part of her body, which was half eaten away, so as to see into the trunk, and rendered her, in the emaciated condition she was in, an object shocking to behold. She lived in torment, and had no kind of ease or peace, but in reflecting, that her misery and distress might procure her the mercy of heaven hereafter, and in conjunction with her true repentance bring her to rest, when she had passed through the grave and gate of death.

Such was the case of that *Venus* of her sex, Miss *Hunt*. — When first I saw her, it was rapture to be in her company: her person matchless, and her conversation as charming as her person: both easy, unconstrained, and beautiful to perfection. — When last I saw her, she was grim as the skeleton, horrid, loathsome, and sinking fast into the grave by the laws of corruption. What a change was there! She lived but three months from the time I put her into a lodging, and died as *happy a penitent* as she had lived an *unhappy woman.* I gave her a decent private funeral; a *hearse*, and one *mourning-coach*, in which I alone attended her *remains* to the *earth*; the great *charnel-house*, where all the *human race* must be *deposited.* Here ends the story of Miss *Hunt*.

[A word or two to Mr. *R.* who debauched Miss *Hunt.*]

And now a word or two to the man who ruined her. *Bob R.* is still living, the master of thousands, and has thought no more of the *wretched Eliza*, than if her ruin and misery were a trifle. He fancies his riches and power will screen him from the hand of justice, and afford him lasting satisfaction: but, *cruel man*, after this short day, the present life, the night of death cometh, and your unrelenting soul must then appear before a judge, infinitely knowing and righteous; who is not to be imposed upon, and cannot be biassed. The sighs and groans of *Eliza* will then be remembred, and *confound* and *abash* you for your falshood and *inhumanity* to this *unhappy woman.* In your last agony, her *ghost* will haunt you, and at the sessions of righteousness appear against you, execrable *R. R.*

[The author falls in love with Miss *Spence.*]

§. 7. But to return to *Harrogate.* While I was there, it was my fortune to dance with a lady, who had the head of *Aristotle*, the *heart* of a *primitive christian*, and the *form* of *Venus de medicis.* This was Miss *Spence*, of *Westmoreland.* I was not many hours in her company, before I became most passionately in love with her. I did all I could to win her heart, and at last asked her the question. But before I inform my readers what the consequence of this was, I must take some notice of what I expect from the critical reviewers.[17] These gentlemen will attempt to raise the laugh. Our *moralist*, (they will say) has buried three wives running, and they are hardly cold in their graves, before he is dancing like a buck at the Wells, and plighting vows to a fourth girl, the beauty, Miss *Spence.* An *honest fellow*, this *Suarez*, as *Pascal* says of that *Jesuit*, in his provincial letters.[18]

[An apology for the author's marrying so often.]

To this I reply, that I think it unreasonable and impious to grieve immoderately for the dead. A decent and proper tribute of tears and sorrow, humanity requires; but when that duty has been payed, we must remember, that to lament a dead woman is not to lament a wife. A wife must be a living woman. The wife we lose by death is no more than a sad and empty object, formed by the imagination, and to be still devoted to her, is to be in love with an idea. It is a mere chimerical passion, as the deceased has no more to do with this world, than if she had existed before the flood. As we cannot restore what nature has destroyed, it is foolish to be faithful to affliction. — Nor is this all. If the woman we marry has the seven qualifications which every man would wish to find in a wife, beauty, discretion, sweetness of temper, a sprightly wit, fertility, wealth, and noble extraction, yet death's snatching so amiable a wife from our arms can be no reason for accusing fate of cruelty, that is, providence of injustice; nor can it authorise us to sink into insensibility, and neglect the duty and business of life. This wife was born to die, and we receive her under the condition of mortality. She is lent but for a term, the limits of which we are not made acquainted with; and when this term is expired, there can be no injustice in taking her back: nor are we to indulge the transports of grief to distraction, but should look out for another with the seven qualifications, as it is not good for man to be alone, and as he is by the *Abrahamic* covenant bound to carry on the *succession*, in a regular way, if it be in his power. — Nor is this all; if the woman adorned with every natural and acquired excellence is translated from this gloomy planet to some better world, to be a sharer of the *divine favour*, in that peaceful and happy state which God hath prepared for the *virtuous* and *faithful*, must it not be senseless for me to indulge melancholy and continue a mourner on her account, while she is breathing the balmy air of paradise, enjoying pure and radiant vision, and beyond description happy?

In the next place, as I had forfeited my father's favour and estate, for the sake of *christian-deism*,[19] and had nothing but my own honest industry to secure me daily bread, it was necessary for me to lay hold of every opportunity to improve my fortune, and of consequence do my best to gain the heart of the first rich young woman who came in my way, after I had buried a wife. It was not fit for me to sit snivelling for months, because my wife died before me, which was, at least, as probable, as that she should be the survivor; but instead of solemn affliction, and the inconsolable part, for an event I foresaw, it was incumbent on me, after a little decent mourning, to consecrate myself to virtue and good fortune united in the form of a woman. Whenever she appeared, it was my business to get her if I could. This made me sometimes a dancer at the Wells, in the days of my youth.

17. i.e. the writers of the *Critical Review*, to which Amory's preface is addressed; see above pp. 694-696.

18. Blaise Pascal (1623-62), mathematician, scientist, and religious writer, whose works include *Les Provinciales ou les lettres écrites par Louis de Montalte à un provincial* (1656), i.e. letters written to a provincial of the Jesuit order.

19. Buncle holds steadfastly to Unitarianism (a denial of the Athanasian creed, concerning the Trinity) and to a belief in natural rather than revealed religion — a conviction that God does not reveal himself through mysteries but may be apprehended by men through the proper use of their reason.

LAURENCE STERNE
(1713-68)

from:
THE LIFE AND OPINIONS OF TRISTRAM SHANDY, GENTLEMAN (1759-67)

[Like many eighteenth-century novels, *Tristram Shandy* is an autobiography. Unlike other fictional autobiographers, however, Tristram does not begin his life-story with his birth (which occurs only in Volume III).]

VOLUME I

CHAPTER I

I WISH either my father or my mother, or indeed both of them, as they were in duty both equally bound to it, had minded what they were about when they begot me; had they duly consider'd how much depended upon what they were then doing; — that not only the production of a rational Being was concern'd in it, but that possibly the happy formation and temperature of his body, perhaps his genius and the very cast of his mind; — and, for aught they knew to the contrary, even the fortunes of his whole house might take their turn from the humours[1] and dispositions which were then uppermost: —— Had they duly weighed and considered all this, and proceeded accordingly, —— I am verily persuaded I should have made a quite different figure in the world, from that, in which the reader is likely to see me. — Believe me, good folks, this is not so inconsiderable a thing as many of you may think it; — you have all, I dare say, heard of the animal spirits,[2] as how they are transfused from father to son, &c. &c. — and a great deal to that purpose: — Well, you may take my word, that nine parts in ten of a man's sense or his nonsense, his successes and miscarriages in this world depend upon their motions and activity, and the different tracks and trains you put them into; so that when they are once set a-going, whether right or wrong, 'tis not a halfpenny matter, — away they go cluttering like hey-go-mad; and by treading the same steps over and over again, they presently make a road of it, as plain and as smooth as a garden-walk, which, when they are once used to, the Devil himself sometimes shall not be able to drive them off it.

Pray, my dear, quoth my mother, *have you not forgot to wind up the clock*? —— *Good G—*! cried my father, making an exclamation, but taking care to moderate his voice at the same time, —— *Did ever woman, since the creation of the world, interrupt a man with such a silly question*? Pray, what was your father saying? —— Nothing.

CHAPTER II

—— Then positively, there is nothing in the question, that I can see, either good or bad. —— Then let me tell you, Sir, it was a very unseasonable question at least, — because it scattered and dispersed the animal spirits, whose business it was to have escorted and gone hand-in-hand with the *HOMUNCULUS*,[3] and conducted him safe to the place destined for his reception.

The HOMUNCULUS, Sir, in how-ever low and ludicrous a light he may appear, in this age of levity, to the eye of folly or prejudice; — to the eye of reason in scientifick research, he stands confess'd — a BEING guarded and circumscribed with rights: —— The minutest philosophers, who, by the bye, have the most enlarged understandings, (their souls being inversely as their enquiries) shew us incontestably, That the HOMUNCULUS is created by the same hand, —engender'd in the same course of nature, — endowed with the same loco-motive powers and faculties with us: —— That he consists, as we do, of skin, hair, fat, flesh, veins, arteries, ligaments, nerves, cartileges, bones, marrow, brains, glands, genitals, humours, and articulations; —— is a Being of as much activity, —— and, in all senses of the word, as much and as truly our fellow-

1. In ancient physiology, the balance of the cardinal humours — blood, phlegm, choler (yellow bile) and melancholy (black bile) — was thought to determine an individual's character.
2. Supposedly an agent in human physiology determining muscular motion and sensation; like the humours, their very existence was regarded with scepticism by eighteenth-century science.
3. Diminutive of Latin 'homo' — 'little man'; here, the miniature human figure which early microscopists believed they saw in a spermatozoon.

creature as my Lord Chancellor of England. — He may be benefited, he may be injured, — he may obtain redress; — in a word, he has all the claims and rights of humanity, which *Tully, Puffendorff,*[4] or the best ethick writers allow to arise out of that state and relation.

Now, dear Sir, what if any accident had befallen him in his way alone? —— or that, thro' terror of it, natural to so young a traveller, my little gentleman had got to his journey's end miserably spent; —— his muscular strength and virility worn down to a thread; — his own animal spirits ruffled beyond description, — and that in this sad disorder'd state of nerves, he had laid down a prey to sudden starts, or a series of melancholy dreams and fancies for nine long, long months together. —— I tremble to think what a foundation had been laid for a thousand weaknesses both of body and mind, which no skill of the physician or the philosopher could ever afterwards have set thoroughly to rights.

CHAPTER III

TO my uncle Mr. *Toby Shandy* do I stand indebted for the preceding anecdote, to whom my father, who was an excellent natural philosopher,[5] and much given to close reasoning upon the smallest matters, had oft, and heavily, complain'd of the injury; but once more particularly, as my uncle *Toby* well remember'd, upon his observing a most unaccountable obliquity, (as he call'd it) in my manner of setting up my top,[6] and justifying the principles upon which I had done it, — the old gentleman shook his head, and in a tone more expressive by half of sorrow than reproach, — he said his heart all along foreboded, and he saw it verified in this, and from a thousand other observations he had made upon me, That I should neither think nor act like any other man's child: —— *But alas!* continued he, shaking his head a second time, and wiping away a tear which was trickling down his cheeks, *My Tristram's misfortunes began nine months before ever he came into the world.*

—— My mother, who was sitting by, look'd up, — but she knew no more than her backside what my father meant, -- but my uncle, Mr. *Toby Shandy*, who had been often informed of the affair, — understood him very well.

CHAPTER IV

I KNOW there are readers in the world, as well as many other good people in it, who are no readers at all, — who find themselves ill at ease, unless they are let into the whole secret from first to last, of every thing which concerns you.

It is in pure compliance with this humour of theirs, and from a backwardness in my nature to disappoint any one soul living, that I have been so very particular already. As my life and opinions are likely to make some noise in the world, and, if I conjecture right, will take in all ranks, professions, and denominations of men whatever, — be no less read than the *Pilgrim's Progress*[7] itself --- and, in the end, prove the very thing which *Montaigne*[8] dreaded his essays should turn out, that is, a book for a parlour-window; — I find it necessary to consult every one a little in his turn; and therefore must beg pardon for going on a little further in the same way: For which cause, right glad I am, that I have begun the history of myself in the way I have done; and that I am able to go on tracing every thing in it, as *Horace*[9] says, *ab Ovo*.

Horace, I know, does not recommend this fashion altogether; But that gentleman is speaking only of an epic poem or a tragedy; — (I forget which) — besides, if it was not so, I should beg Mr. *Horace*'s pardon; — for in writing what I have set about, I shall confine myself neither to his rules, nor to any man's rules that ever lived.

To such, however, as do not choose to go so far back into these things, I can give no better advice, than that they skip over the remaining part of this Chapter; for I declare before hand, 'tis wrote only for the curious and inquisitive.

———— Shut the door. ————

I was begot in the night, betwixt the first *Sunday* and the first *Monday* in the month of *March*, in the year of our Lord one thousand seven hundred and

4. Marcus Tullius Cicero (106-43 B.C.) and Samuel Pufendorf (1632-94) were both noted for their influence on the philosophy of natural law.
5. The development of experimental science in the seventeenth century gave rise to a concept of natural philosophy which included astronomy, physics and chemistry, as well as biology.
6. i.e. a child's spinning top.
7. John Bunyan's *The Pilgrim's Progress* (1678) was one of the most widely read books in the eighteenth century.
8. Michel de Montaigne (1533-92), French essayist; the reference is to the *Essays*, III. v, 'Upon some verses of Virgil'.
9. Quintus Horatius Flaccus (65-8 B.C.), author of *Ars Poetica,* to which Tristram misleadingly refers. Horace commends Homer for *not* starting his tale of the Trojan War *ab ovo* — that is, from the birth of Helen from Leda's egg.

eighteen. I am positive I was. — But how I came to be so very particular in my account of a thing which happened before I was born, is owing to another small anecdote known only in our own family, but now made public for the better clearing up this point.

My father, you must know, who was originally a *Turky* merchant,[10] but had left off business for some years, in order to retire to, and die upon, his paternal estate in the county of ———, was, I believe, one of the most regular men in every thing he did, whether 'twas matter of business, or matter of amusement, that ever lived. As a small specimen of this extreme exactness of his, to which he was in truth a slave, — he had made it a rule for many years of his life, — on the first *Sunday night* of every month throughout the whole year, — as certain as ever the *Sunday night* came, —— to wind up a large house-clock which we had standing upon the back-stairs head, with his own hands: — And being somewhere between fifty and sixty years of age, at the time I have been speaking of, — he had likewise gradually brought some other little family concernments to the same period, in order, as he would often say to my uncle *Toby*, to get them all out of the way at one time, and be no more plagued and pester'd with them the rest of the month.

It was attended but with one misfortune, which, in a great measure, fell upon myself, and the effects of which I fear I shall carry with me to my grave; namely, that, from an unhappy association of ideas which have no connection in nature, it so fell out at length, that my poor mother could never hear the said clock wound up, — but the thoughts of some other things unavoidably popp'd into her head, — *& vice versâ:* — which strange combination of ideas, the sagacious *Locke*,[11] who certainly understood the nature of these things better than most men, affirms to have produced more wry actions than all other sources of prejudice whatsoever.

But this by the bye.

Now it appears, by a memorandum in my father's pocket-book, which now lies upon the table, "That on *Lady-Day*, which was on the 25th of the same month in which I date my geniture, — my father set out upon his journey to *London* with my eldest brother *Bobby*, to fix him at *Westminster* school;" and, as it appears from the same authority, "That he did not get down to his wife and family till the *second week* in *May* following," — it brings the thing almost to a certainty. However, what follows in the beginning of the next chapter puts it beyond all possibility of doubt.

—— But pray, Sir, What was your father doing all *December*, — *January*, and *February?* —— Why, Madam, — he was all that time afflicted with a Sciatica.

CHAPTER V

ON the fifth day of *November*, 1718, which to the æra fixed on, was as near nine kalendar months as any husband could in reason have expected, — was I *Tristram Shandy*, Gentleman, brought forth into this scurvy and disasterous world of ours. — I wish I had been born in the Moon, or in any of the planets, (except *Jupiter* or *Saturn*, because I never could bear cold weather) for it could not well have fared worse with me in any of them (tho' I will not answer for *Venus*) than it has in this vile, dirty planet of ours, — which o' my conscience, with reverence be it spoken, I take to be made up of the shreds and clippings of the rest; —— not but the planet is well enough, provided a man could be born in it to a great title or to a great estate; or could any how contrive to be called up to publick charges, and employments of dignity or power; — but that is not my case; ---- and therefore every man will speak of the fair as his own market has gone in it; — for which cause I affirm it over again to be one of the vilest worlds that ever was made; --- for I can truly say, that from the first hour I drew my breath in it, to this, that I can now scarce draw it at all, for an asthma I got in scating against the wind in *Flanders*; -- I have been the continual sport of what the world calls Fortune; and though I will not wrong her by saying, She has ever made me feel the weight of any great or signal evil; --- yet with all the good temper in the world, I affirm it of her, That in every stage of my life, and at every turn and corner where she could get fairly at me, the ungracious Duchess has pelted me with a set of as pitiful misadventures and cross accidents as ever small HERO sustained.

CHAPTER VI

IN the beginning of the last chapter, I inform'd you exactly *when* I was born; — but I did not inform

10. i.e. a trader to Asia Minor.

11. John Locke (1632-1704), whose view of the association of ideas, expressed in the *Essay Concerning Human Understanding* (4th ed., 1700), gave rise, in a parodic form, to much of *Tristram Shandy*'s structure.

you, *how*. *No*; that particular was reserved entirely for a chapter by itself; — besides, Sir, as you and I are in a manner perfect strangers to each other, it would not have been proper to have let you into too many circumstances relating to myself all at once. — You must have a little patience. I have undertaken, you see, to write not only my life, but my opinions also; hoping and expecting that your knowledge of my character, and of what kind of a mortal I am, by the one, would give you a better relish for the other: As you proceed further with me, the slight acquaintance which is now beginning betwixt us, will grow into familiarity; and that, unless one of us is in fault, will terminate in friendship, —— *O diem præclarum!*[12] —— then nothing which has touched me will be thought trifling in its nature, or tedious in its telling. Therefore, my dear friend and companion, if you should think me somewhat sparing of my narrative on my first setting out, — bear with me, — and let me go on, and tell my story my own way: —— or if I should seem now and then to trifle upon the road, —— or should sometimes put on a fool's cap with a bell to it, for a moment or two as we pass along, -- don't fly off, — but rather courteously give me credit for a little more wisdom than appears upon my outside; — and as we jogg on, either laugh with me, or at me, or in short, do any thing, —— only keep your temper.

[The story of Le Fever, which reveals the good nature of Tristram's Uncle Toby, is one of the most celebrated sentimental set-pieces in Sterne's work. Having been invalided out of the army after being wounded at the siege of Namur, Uncle Toby has taken up playing war-games (following the progress of the allied armies in the War of the Spanish Succession, 1701-13) in his garden, aided by his servant, Corporal Trim.]

VOLUME VI

CHAPTER VI

The Story of LE FEVER.

IT was some time in the summer of that year in which *Dendermond*[13] was taken by the allies, — which was about seven years before my father came into the country, — and about as many, after the time, that my uncle *Toby* and *Trim* had privately decamped from my father's house in town, in order to lay some of the finest sieges to some of the finest fortified cities in *Europe* —— when my uncle *Toby* was one evening getting his supper, with *Trim* sitting behind him at a small sideboard, — I say, sitting — for in consideration of the corporal's lame knee (which sometimes gave him exquisite pain) — when my uncle *Toby* dined or supped alone, he would never suffer the corporal to stand; and the poor fellow's veneration for his master was such, that, with a proper artillery, my uncle *Toby* could have taken *Dendermond* itself, with less trouble than he was able to gain this point over him; for many a time when my uncle *Toby* supposed the corporal's leg was at rest, he would look back, and detect him standing behind him with the most dutiful respect: this bred more little squabbles betwixt them, than all other causes for five and twenty years together —— But this is neither here nor there — why do I mention it? —— Ask my pen, — it governs me, — I govern not it.

He was one evening sitting thus at his supper, when the landlord of a little inn in the village came into the parlour with an empty phial in his hand, to beg a glass or two of sack;[14] 'Tis for a poor gentleman, — I think, of the army, said the landlord, who has been taken ill at my house four days ago, and has never held up his head since, or had a desire to taste any thing, till just now, that he has a fancy for a glass of sack and a thin toast, —— *I think*, says he, taking his hand from his forehead, *it would comfort me.* ——

—— If I could neither beg, borrow, or buy such a thing, — added the landlord, — I would almost steal it for the poor gentleman, he is so ill. —— I hope in God he will still mend, continued he, — we are all of us concerned for him.

Thou art a good natured soul, I will answer for thee, cried my uncle *Toby*; and thou shalt drink the poor gentleman's health in a glass of sack thyself, — and take a couple of bottles with my service, and tell him he is heartily welcome to them, and to a dozen more if they will do him good.

Though I am persuaded, said my uncle *Toby*, as the landlord shut the door, he is a very compassionate fellow — *Trim*, — yet I cannot help entertaining a high opinion of his guest too; there must be something more than common in him, that

12. O splendid day!
13. Dendermond, in Flanders, was taken by the Duke of Marlborough in 1706, during the War of the Spanish Succession.
14. Sweet Spanish wine.

in so short a time should win so much upon the affections of his host; —— And of his whole family, added the corporal, for they are all concerned for him. —— Step after him, said my uncle *Toby*, — do *Trim*, — and ask if he knows his name.

—— I have quite forgot it, truly, said the landlord, coming back into the parlour with the corporal, — but I can ask his son again: —— Has he a son with him then? said my uncle *Toby*. — A boy, replied the landlord, of about eleven or twelve years of age; — but the poor creature has tasted almost as little as his father; he does nothing but mourn and lament for him night and day: —— He has not stirred from the bedside these two days.

My uncle *Toby* laid down his knife and fork, and thrust his plate from before him, as the landlord gave him the account; and *Trim*, without being ordered, took away without saying one word, and in a few minutes after brought him his pipe and tobacco.

—— Stay in the room a little, said my uncle *Toby*. ——

Trim! —— said my uncle *Toby*, after he lighted his pipe, and smoak'd about a dozen whiffs. —— *Trim* came in front of his master and made his bow; — my uncle *Toby* smoak'd on, and said no more. —— Corporal! said my uncle *Toby* —— the corporal made his bow. —— My uncle *Toby* proceeded no farther, but finished his pipe.

Trim! said my uncle *Toby*, I have a project in my head, as it is a bad night, of wrapping myself up warm in my roquelaure,[15] and paying a visit to this poor gentleman. —— Your honour's roquelaure, replied the corporal, has not once been had on, since the night before your honour received your wound, when we mounted guard in the trenches before the gate of St. *Nicholas*; —— and besides it is so cold and rainy a night, that what with the roquelaure, and what with the weather, 'twill be enough to give your honour your death, and bring on your honour's torment in your groin. I fear so; replied my uncle *Toby*, but I am not at rest in my mind, *Trim*, since the account the landlord has given me. —— I wish I had not known so much of this affair, — added my uncle *Toby*, — or that I had known more of it: —— How shall we manage it? Leave it, an't please your honour, to me, quoth the corporal; —— I'll take my hat and stick and go to the house and reconnoitre, and act accordingly; and I will bring your honour a full account in an hour. —— Thou shalt go, *Trim*, said my uncle *Toby*, and here's a shilling for thee to drink with his servant. —— I shall get it all out of him, said the corporal, shutting the door.

My uncle *Toby* filled his second pipe; and had it not been, that he now and then wandered from the point, with considering whether it was not full as well to have the curtain of the tennaile[16] a straight line, as a crooked one, — he might be said to have thought of nothing else but poor *Le Fever* and his boy the whole time he smoaked it.

15. A knee-length cloak.

CHAPTER VII

The Story of LE FEVER *continued.*

IT was not till my uncle *Toby* had knocked the ashes out of his third pipe, that corporal *Trim* returned from the inn, and gave him the following account.

I despaired at first, said the corporal, of being able to bring back your honour any kind of intelligence concerning the poor sick lieutenant — Is he in the army then? said my uncle *Toby* —— He is: said the corporal —— And in what regiment? said my uncle *Toby* —— I'll tell your honour, replied the corporal, every thing straight forwards, as I learnt it. — Then, *Trim*, I'll fill another pipe, said my uncle *Toby*, and not interrupt thee till thou has done; so sit down at thy ease, *Trim*, in the window seat, and begin thy story again. The corporal made his old bow, which generally spoke as plain as a bow could speak it — *Your honour is good*: —— And having done that, he sat down, as he was ordered, — and begun the story to my uncle *Toby* over again in pretty near the same words.

I despaired at first, said the corporal, of being able to bring back any intelligence to your honour, about the lieutenant and his son; for when I asked where his servant was, from whom I made myself sure of knowing every thing which was proper to be asked, — That's a right distinction, *Trim*, said my uncle *Toby* — I was answered, an' please your honour, that he had no servant with him; —— that he had come to the inn with hired horses, which, upon finding himself unable to proceed, (to join, I

16. In the science of fortification, a tenaille was a small, angled outwork between two bastions; the curtain, the wall between the bastions.

suppose, the regiment) he had dismissed the morning after he came. — If I get better, my dear, said he, as he gave his purse to his son to pay the man, — we can hire horses from hence. —— But alas! the poor gentleman will never get from hence, said the landlady to me, — for I heard the death-watch[17] all night long; —— and when he dies, the youth, his son, will certainly die with him; for he is broken-hearted already.

I was hearing this account, continued the corporal, when the youth came into the kitchen, to order the thin toast the landlord spoke of; —— but I will do it for my father myself, said the youth. —— Pray let me save you the trouble, young gentleman, said I, taking up a fork for the purpose, and offering him my chair to sit down upon by the fire, whilst I did it. —— I believe, Sir, said he, very modestly, I can please him best myself. —— I am sure, said I, his honour will not like the toast the worse for being toasted by an old soldier. —— The youth took hold of my hand, and instantly burst into tears. —— Poor youth! said my uncle *Toby*, — he has been bred up from an infant in the army, and the name of a soldier, *Trim*, sounded in his ears like the name of a friend; — I wish I had him here.

—— I never in the longest march, said the corporal, had so great a mind to my dinner, as I had to cry with him for company: — What could be the matter with me, an' please your honour? Nothing in the world, *Trim*, said my uncle *Toby*, blowing his nose, — but that thou art a good natured fellow.

When I gave him the toast, continued the corporal, I thought it was proper to tell him I was Captain *Shandy*'s servant, and that your honour (though a stranger) was extremely concerned for his father; — and that if there was any thing in your house or cellar —— (And thou might'st have added my purse too, said my uncle *Toby*) —— he was heartily welcome to it: —— He made a very low bow, (which was meant to your honour) but no answer, — for his heart was full — so he went up stairs with the toast; — I warrant you, my dear, said I, as I opened the kitchen door, your father will be well again. —— Mr. *Yorick*'s curate was smoaking a pipe by the kitchen fire, — but said not a word good or bad to comfort the youth.—— I thought it wrong; added the corporal —— I think so too, said my uncle *Toby*.

When the lieutenant had taken his glass of sack and toast, he felt himself a little revived, and sent down into the kitchen, to let me know, that in about ten minutes he should be glad if I would step up stairs. —— I believe, said the landlord, he is going to say his prayers, —— for there was a book laid upon the chair by his bedside, and as I shut the door, I saw his son take up a cushion.——

I thought, said the curate, that you gentlemen of the army, Mr. *Trim*, never said your prayers at all. —— I heard the poor gentleman say his prayers last night, said the landlady, very devoutly, and with my own ears, or I could not have believed it. —— Are your sure of it? replied the curate. —— A soldier, an' please your reverence, said I, prays as often (of his own accord) as a parson; —— and when he is fighting for his king, and for his own life, and for his honour too, he has the most reason to pray to God, of any one in the whole world —— 'Twas well said of thee, *Trim*, said my uncle *Toby*. —— But when a soldier, said I, an' please your reverence, has been standing for twelve hours together in the trenches, up to his knees in cold water, — or engaged, said I, for months together in long and dangerous marches —— harrassed, perhaps, in his rear to-day; — harrassing others to-morrow; — detached here; — countermanded there; — resting this night out upon his arms; — beat up in his shirt the next; — benumbed in his joints; — perhaps without straw in his tent to kneel on; — must say his prayers *how* and *when* he can. — I believe, said I, — for I was piqued, quoth the corporal, for the reputation of the army, — I believe, an' please your reverence, said I, that when a soldier gets time to pray, — he prays as heartily as a parson, — though not with all his fuss and hypocrisy. —— Thou shouldst not have said that, *Trim*, said my uncle *Toby*, — for God only knows who is a hypocrite, and who is not: —— At the great and general review of us all, corporal, at the day of judgment, (and not till then) — it will be seen who has done their duties in this world, — and who has not; and we shall be advanced, *Trim*, accordingly. —— I hope we shall, said *Trim*. —— It is in the Scripture, said my uncle *Toby*; and I will shew it thee to-morrow: — In the mean time we may depend upon it, *Trim*, for our comfort, said my uncle *Toby*, that God Almighty is so good and just a governor of the world, that if we have but done our duties in it, — it will never be enquired into, whether we have done them in a red coat or a black one: —— I hope not; said the corporal —— But go on, *Trim*, said my uncle *Toby*, with thy story.

17. i.e. death-watch beetle.

When I went up, continued the corporal, into the lieutenant's room, which I did not do till the expiration of the ten minutes, — he was lying in his bed with his head raised upon his hand, with his elbow upon the pillow, and a clean white cambrick handkerchief beside it: —— The youth was just stooping down to take up the cushion, upon which I supposed he had been kneeling, — the book was laid upon the bed, — and as he rose, in taking up the cushion with one hand, he reached out his other to take it away at the same time. —— Let it remain there, my dear, said the lieutenant.

He did not offer to speak to me, till I had walked up close to his bed-side: — If you are Captain *Shandy*'s servant, said he, you must present my thanks to your master, with my little boy's thanks along with them, for his courtesy to me; — if he was of *Leven's*[18] — said the lieutenant. — I told him your honour was — Then, said he, I served three campaigns with him in *Flanders*, and remember him, — but 'tis most likely, as I had not the honour of any acquaintance with him, that he knows nothing of me. —— You will tell him, however, that the person his good nature has laid under obligations to him, is one *Le Fever*, a lieutenant in *Angus*'s —— but he knows me not, — said he, a second time, musing; —— possibly he may my story — added he — pray tell the captain, I was the ensign at *Breda*,[19] whose wife was most unfortunately killed with a musket shot, as she lay in my arms in my tent. —— I remember the story, an't please your honour, said I, very well. —— Do you so? said he, wiping his eyes with his handkerchief, — then well may I. — In saying this, he drew a little ring out of his bosom, which seemed tied with a black ribband about his neck, and kiss'd it twice —— Here, *Billy*, said he, —— the boy flew across the room to the bed-side, — and falling down upon his knee, took the ring in his hand, and kissed it too, — then kissed his father, and sat down upon the bed and wept.

I wish, said my uncle *Toby*, with a deep sigh, — I wish, *Trim*, I was asleep.

Your honour, replied the corporal, is too much concerned; — shall I pour your honour out a glass of sack to your pipe? —— Do, *Trim*, said my uncle *Toby*.

I remember, said my uncle *Toby*, sighing again, the story of the ensign and his wife, with a circumstance his modesty omitted; — and particularly well that he, as well as she, upon some account or other, (I forget what) was universally pitied by the whole regiment; — but finish the story thou art upon: — 'Tis finished already, said the corporal, — for I could stay no longer, — so wished his honour a good night; young *Le Fever* rose from off the bed, and saw me to the bottom of the stairs; and as we went down together, told me, they had come from *Ireland*, and were on their route to join the regiment in *Flanders*. —— But alas! said the corporal, — the lieutenant's last day's march is over. — Then what is to become of his poor boy? cried my uncle *Toby*.

CHAPTER VIII

The Story of LE FEVER *continued.*

IT was to my uncle *Toby*'s eternal honour, —— though I tell it only for the sake of those, who, when coop'd in betwixt a natural and a positive law,[20] know not for their souls, which way in the world to turn themselves —— That notwithstanding my uncle *Toby* was warmly engaged at that time in carrying on the siege of *Dendermond*, parallel with the allies, who pressed theirs on so vigorously, that they scarce allowed him time to get his dinner —— that nevertheless he gave up *Dendermond*, though he had already made a lodgment upon the counterscarp; — and bent his whole thoughts towards the private distresses at the inn; and, except that he ordered the garden gate to be bolted up, by which he might be said to have turned the siege of *Dendermond* into a blockade, — he left *Dendermond* to itself, — to be relieved or not by the *French* king, as the *French* king thought good; and only considered how he himself should relieve the poor lieutenant and his son.

—— That kind BEING, who is a friend to the friendless, shall recompence thee for this.

Thou hast left this matter short, said my uncle *Toby* to the corporal, as he was putting him to bed, —— and I will tell thee in what, *Trim*. —— In the first place, when thou madest an offer of my

18. i.e. regiment (understood). See also *Angus*'s below.
19. A town in Brabant, a province in central Belgium.
20. Respectively, a law based on man's innate moral feeling and a formally enacted law.

services to *Le Fever*, — as sickness and travelling are both expensive, and thou knowest he was but a poor lieutenant, with a son to subsist as well as himself, out of his pay, — that thou didst not make an offer to him of my purse; because, had he stood in need, thou knowest, *Trim*, he had been as welcome to it as myself. —— Your honour knows, said the corporal, I had no orders; —— True, quoth my uncle *Toby*, — thou didst very right, *Trim*, as a soldier, — but certainly very wrong as a man.

In the second place, for which, indeed, thou hast the same excuse, continued my uncle *Toby*, —— when thou offeredst him whatever was in my house, — thou shouldst have offered him my house too: —— A sick brother officer should have the best quarters, *Trim*, and if we had him with us, — we could tend and look to him: —— Thou art an excellent nurse thyself, *Trim*, — and what with thy care of him, and the old woman's, and his boy's, and mine together, we might recruit him again at once, and set him upon his legs.——

—— In a fortnight or three weeks, added my uncle *Toby*, smiling, — he might march. —— He will never march, an' please your honour, in this world, said the corporal: —— He will march; said my uncle *Toby*, rising up from the side of the bed, with one shoe off: —— An' please your honour, said the corporal, he will never march, but to his grave: —— He shall march, cried my uncle *Toby*, marching the foot which had a shoe on, though without advancing an inch, — he shall march to his regiment. —— He cannot stand it, said the corporal; —— He shall be supported, said my uncle *Toby*; —— He'll drop at last, said the corporal, and what will become of his boy? —— He shall not drop, said my uncle *Toby*, firmly. —— A-well-o'day, — do what we can for him, said *Trim*, maintaining his point, — the poor soul will die: —— He shall not die, by G—, cried my uncle *Toby*.

— The ACCUSING SPIRIT which flew up to heaven's chancery with the oath, blush'd as he gave it in; — and the RECORDING ANGEL as he wrote it down, dropp'd a tear upon the word, and blotted it out for ever.

CHAPTER IX

—— MY uncle *Toby* went to his bureau, — put his purse into his breeches pocket, and having ordered the corporal to go early in the morning for a physician, — he went to bed, and fell asleep.

CHAPTER X

The Story of LE FEVER *concluded.*

THE sun looked bright the morning after, to every eye in the village but *Le Fever*'s and his afflicted son's; the hand of death press'd heavy upon his eye-lids, —— and hardly could the wheel at the cistern turn round its circle, — when my uncle *Toby*, who had rose up an hour before his wonted time, entered the lieutenant's room, and without preface or apology, sat himself down upon the chair by the bed-side, and independantly of all modes and customs, opened the curtain in the manner an old friend and brother officer would have done it, and asked him how he did, — how he had rested in the night, — what was his complaint, — where was his pain, — and what he could do to help him: —— and without giving him time to answer any one of the enquiries, went on and told him of the little plan which he had been concerting with the corporal the night before for him.——

—— You shall go home directly, *Le Fever*, said my uncle *Toby*, to my house, — and we'll send for a doctor to see what's the matter, — and we'll have an apothecary, — and the corporal shall be your nurse; —— and I'll be your servant, *Le Fever*.

There was a frankness in my uncle *Toby*, — not the *effect* of familiarity, — but the *cause* of it, — which let you at once into his soul, and shewed you the goodness of his nature; to this, there was something in his looks, and voice, and manner, superadded, which eternally beckoned to the unfortunate to come and take shelter under him; so that before my uncle *Toby* had half finished the kind offers he was making to the father, had the son insensibly pressed up close to his knees, and had taken hold of the breast of his coat, and was pulling it towards him. —— The blood and spirits of *Le Fever*, which were waxing cold and slow within him, and were retreating to their last citadel, the heart, — rallied back, — the film forsook his eyes for a moment, — he looked up wishfully in my uncle *Toby*'s face, — then cast a look upon his boy, —— and that *ligament*, fine as it was, — was never broken.——

Nature instantly ebb'd again, —— the film returned to its place, —— the pulse fluttered —— stopp'd —— went on —— throb'd —— stopp'd again —— moved —— stopp'd —— shall I go on? —— No.

[The Widow Wadman has matrimonial designs on her neighbour, Uncle Toby. Before committing herself to marriage, however, she is naturally anxious to discover exactly *where* Uncle Toby was wounded in the groin.]

VOLUME IX

CHAPTER XXVI

IT is natural for a perfect stranger who is going from London to Edinburgh, to enquire before he sets out, how many miles to York; which is about the half way —— nor does any body wonder, if he goes on and asks about the Corporation, &c.--

It was just as natural for Mrs. Wadman, whose first husband was all his time afflicted with a Sciatica, to wish to know how far from the hip to the groin; and how far she was likely to suffer more or less in her feelings, in the one case than in the other.

She had accordingly read *Drake*'s anatomy from one end to the other. She had peeped into *Wharton* upon the brain, and borrowed * Graaf[21] upon the bones and muscles; but could make nothing of it.

She had reason'd likewise from her own powers —— laid down theorems —— drawn consequences, and come to no conclusion.

To clear up all, she had twice asked Doctor Slop, 'if poor captain Shandy was ever likely to recover of his wound ——?'

—— He is recovered, Doctor Slop would say——

What! quite?

—— Quite: madam ——

But what do you mean by a recovery? Mrs. Wadman would say.

Doctor Slop was the worst man alive at definitions; and so Mrs. Wadman could get no knowledge: in short, there was no way to extract it, but from my uncle Toby himself.

There is an accent of humanity in an enquiry of this kind which lulls SUSPICION to rest —— and I am half persuaded the serpent got pretty near it, in his discourse with Eve; for the propensity in the sex to be deceived could not be so great, that she should have boldness to hold chat with the devil, without it —— But there is an accent of humanity —— how shall I describe it? — 'tis an accent which covers the part with a garment, and gives the enquirer a right to be as particular with it, as your body-surgeon.

'—— Was it without remission? —

—— Was it more tolerable in bed?

—— Could he lie on both sides alike with it?

— Was he able to mount a horse?

— Was motion bad for it?' et cætera, were so tenderly spoke to, and so directed towards my uncle Toby's heart, that every item of them sunk ten times deeper into it than the evils themselves —— but when Mrs. Wadman went round about by Namur[22] to get at my uncle Toby's groin; and engaged him to attack the point of the advanced counterscarp, and *pêle mêle* with the Dutch to take the counterguard of St. Roch[23] sword in hand — and then with tender notes playing upon his ear, led him all bleeding by the hand out of the trench, wiping her eye, as he was carried to his tent —— Heaven! Earth! Sea! — all was lifted up — the springs of nature rose above their levels — an angel of mercy sat besides him on the sopha — his heart glow'd with fire — and had he been worth a thousand, he had lost every heart of them to Mrs. Wadman.

— And whereabouts, dear Sir, quoth Mrs. Wadman, a little categorically, did you receive this sad blow? —— In asking this question, Mrs. Wadman gave a slight glance towards the waistband of my uncle Toby's red plush breeches, expecting naturally, as the shortest reply to it, that my uncle Toby would lay his fore-finger upon the place —— It fell out otherwise —— for my uncle Toby having got his wound before the gate of St. Nicolas, in one of the traverses of the trench, opposite to the salient angle of the demi-bastion of St. Roch; he could at any time stick a pin upon the identical spot of ground where he was standing when the stone struck him: this struck instantly upon my uncle Toby's sensorium[24] —— and with it, struck his large map of the town and citadel of Namur and its environs, which he had purchased

*This must be a mistake in Mr. Shandy; for Graaf wrote upon the pancreatick juice, and the parts of generation. [Sterne's note.]

21. James Drake (1667-1707), author of *Anthropologia Nova, or a new system of Anatomy* (1707); Thomas Wharton (1614-73), author of *Adenographia; sive glandularum totius corporis descriptio* (1656); Reinier de Graaf (1641-73), Dutch physician and author of both the *Tractatus anatomico-medicus de succi pancreati natura & usu* (1671) and of *De virorum organis generationi inservientibus* (1668).

22. An important fortified town at the confluence of the Maes and Sambre rivers to the south-east of Brussels.

23. The name of a bastion at Namur.

24. brain.

and pasted down upon a board by the Corporal's aid, during his long illness —— it had lain with other military lumber in the garret ever since, and accordingly the Corporal was detached into the garret to fetch it.

My uncle Toby measured off thirty toises,[25] with Mrs. Wadman's scissars, from the returning angle before the gate of St. Nicolas; and with such a virgin modesty laid her finger upon the place, that the goddess of Decency, if then in being — if not, 'twas her shade — shook her head, and with a finger wavering across her eyes — forbid her to explain the mistake.

Unhappy Mrs. Wadman! ——

—— For nothing can make this chapter go off with spirit but an apostrophe to thee —— but my heart tells me, that in such a crisis an apostrophe is but an insult in disguise, and ere I would offer one to a woman in distress — let the chapter go to the devil; provided any damn'd critick *in keeping* will be but at the trouble to take it with him.

CHAPTER XXVII

MY uncle Toby's Map is carried down into the kitchen.

CHAPTER XXVIII

—— AND here is the *Maes* — and this is the *Sambre*; said the Corporal, pointing with his right hand extended a little towards the map, and his left upon Mrs. Bridget's shoulder[26] — but not the shoulder next him — and this, said he, is the town of Namur — and this the citadel — and there lay the French — and here lay his honour and myself —— and in this cursed trench, Mrs. Bridget, quoth the Corporal, taking her by the hand, did he receive the wound which crush'd him so miserably *here* —— In pronouncing which he slightly press'd the back of her hand towards the part he felt for —— and let it fall.

We thought, Mr. Trim, it had been more in the middle —— said Mrs. Bridget ——

That would have undone us for ever — said the Corporal.

—— And left my poor mistress undone too — said Bridget.

The Corporal made no reply to the repartee, but by giving Mrs. Bridget a kiss.

Come — come — said Bridget — holding the palm of her left-hand parallel to the plane of the horizon, and sliding the fingers of the other over it, in a way which could not have been done, had there been the least wart or protuberance —— 'Tis every syllable of it false, cried the Corporal, before she had half finished the sentence ——

— I know it to be fact, said Bridget, from credible witnesses.

—— Upon my honour, said the Corporal, laying his hand upon his heart, and blushing as he spoke with honest resentment — 'tis a story, Mrs. Bridget, as false as hell —— Not, said Bridget, interrupting him, that either I or my mistress care a halfpenny about it, whether 'tis so or no —— only that when one is married, one would chuse to have such a thing by one at least ——

It was somewhat unfortunate for Mrs. Bridget, that she had begun the attack with her manual exercise; for the Corporal instantly *.

CHAPTER XXIX

IT was like the momentary contest in the moist eyelids of an April morning, 'Whether Bridget should laugh or cry.'

She snatch'd up a rolling-pin —— 'twas ten to one, she had laugh'd ——

She laid it down —— she cried; and had one single tear of 'em but tasted of bitterness, full sorrowful would the Corporal's heart have been that he had used the argument; but the Corporal understood the sex, a *quart major to a terce*[27] at least, better than my uncle Toby, and accordingly he assailed Mrs. Bridget after this manner.

I know, Mrs. Bridget, said the Corporal, giving her a most respectful kiss, that thou art good and modest by nature, and art withal so generous a girl in thyself, that if I know thee rightly, thou wouldst not wound an insect, much less the honour of so gallant and worthy a soul as my master, wast thou

25. A French measure of about 6½ft.

26. Bridget is Mrs. Wadman's maid; the title 'mistress' was still used of unmarried women in the eighteenth century.

27. In piquet, a quart major is the sequence of ace, king, queen, jack, while a tierce is a sequence of three cards, in any suit.

sure to be made a countess of —— but thou has been set on, and deluded, dear Bridget, as if often a woman's case, 'to please others more than themselves ——'

Bridget's eyes poured down at the sensations the Corporal excited.

—— Tell me —— tell me then, my dear Bridget, continued the Corporal, taking hold of her hand, which hung down dead by her side, —— and giving a second kiss —— whose suspicion has misled thee?

Bridget sobb'd a sob or two —— then open'd her eyes —— the Corporal wiped 'em with the bottom of her apron —— she then open'd her heart and told him all.

CHAPTER XXX

MY uncle Toby and the Corporal had gone on separately with their operations the greatest part of the campaign, and as effectually cut off from all communication of what either the one or the other had been doing, as if they had been separated from each other by the *Maes* or the *Sambre.*

My uncle Toby, on his side, had presented himself every afternoon in his red and silver, and blue and gold alternately, and sustained an infinity of attacks in them, without knowing them to be attacks — and so had nothing to communicate ——

The Corporal, on his side, in taking Bridget, by it had gain'd considerable advantages —— and consequently had much to communicate —— but what were the advantages —— as well, as what was the manner by which he had seiz'd them, required so nice an historian that the Corporal durst not venture upon it; and as sensible as he was of glory, would rather have been contented to have gone barehead and without laurels for ever, than torture his master's modesty for a single moment——

—— Best of honest and gallant servants! —— But I have apostrophiz'd thee, Trim! once before —— and could I apotheosize thee also (that is to say) with good company —— I would do it *without ceremony* in the very next page.

CHAPTER XXXI

NOW my uncle Toby had one evening laid down his pipe upon the table, and was counting over to himself upon his finger ends, (beginning at his thumb) all Mrs. Wadman's perfections one by one; and happening two or three times together, either by omitting some, or counting others twice over, to puzzle himself sadly before he could get beyond his middle finger —— Prithee, Trim! said he, taking up his pipe again, —— bring me a pen and ink: Trim brought paper also.

Take a full sheet —— Trim! said my uncle Toby, making a sign with his pipe at the same time to take a chair and sit down close by him at the table. The Corporal obeyed —— placed the paper directly before him —— took a pen and dip'd it in the ink.

— She has a thousand virtues, Trim! said my uncle Toby ——

Am I to set them down, an' please your honour? quoth the Corporal.

—— But they must be taken in their ranks, replied my uncle Toby; for of them all, Trim, that which wins me most, and which is a security for all the rest, is the compassionate turn and singular humanity of her character — I protest, added my uncle Toby, looking up, as he protested it, towards the top of the ceiling —— That was I her brother, Trim, a thousand fold, she could not make more constant or more tender enquiries after my sufferings —— though now no more.

The Corporal made no reply to my uncle Toby's protestation, but by a short cough — he dip'd the pen a second time into the inkhorn; and my uncle Toby, pointing with the end of his pipe as close to the top of the sheet at the left hand corner of it, as he could get it —— the Corporal wrote down the word HUMANITY - - - - thus.

Prithee, Corporal, said my uncle Toby, as soon as Trim had done it —— how often does Mrs. Bridget enquire after the wound on the cap of thy knee, which thou received'st at the battle of Landen?[28]

She never, an' please your honour, enquires after it at all.

That, Corporal, said my uncle Toby, with all the triumph the goodness of his nature would permit —— That shews the difference in the character of the mistress and maid —— had the fortune of war allotted the same mischance to me, Mrs. Wadman would have enquired into every circumstance relating to it a hundred times —— She would have enquired, an' please your honour, ten times as often about your honour's groin —— The pain, Trim, is equally excruciating, —— and Compassion has as much to do with the one as the other ——

28. The Battle of Landen, or Neerwinden, was fought on 19 July 1693, and marked a significant defeat for the allies under William III.

—— God bless your honour! cried the Corporal —— what has a woman's compassion to do with a wound upon the cap of a man's knee? had your honour's been shot into ten thousand splinters at the affair of Landen, Mrs. Wadman would have troubled her head as little about it as Bridget, because, added the Corporal, lowering his voice and speaking very distinctly, as he assigned his reason ——

'The knee is such a distance from the main body — whereas the groin, your honour knows, is upon the very *curtin* of the *place*.'

My uncle Toby gave a long whistle —— but in a note which could scarce be heard across the table.

The Corporal had advanced too far to retire —— in three words he told the rest ——

My uncle Toby laid down his pipe as gently upon the fender, as if it had been spun from the unravellings of a spider's web ——

—— Let us go to my brother Shandy's, said he.

CHAPTER XXXII

THERE will be just time, whilst my uncle Toby and Trim are walking to my father's, to inform you, that Mrs. Wadman had, some moons before this, made a confident of my mother; and that Mrs. Bridget, who had the burden of her own, as well as her mistress's secret to carry, had got happily delivered of both to Susannah[29] behind the garden-wall.

As for my mother, she saw nothing at all in it, to make the least bustle about —— but Susannah was sufficient by herself for all the ends and purposes you could possibly have, in exporting a family secret; for she instantly imparted it by signs to Jonathan —— and Jonathan by tokens to the cook, as she was basting a loin of mutton; the cook sold it with some kitchen-fat to the postilion for a groat,[30] who truck'd it with the dairy-maid for something of about the same value —— and though whisper'd in the hay-loft, FAME caught the notes with her brazen trumpet and sounded them upon the house-top — In a word, not an old woman in the village or five miles round, who did not understand the difficulties of my uncle Toby's siege, and what were the secret articles which had delay'd the surrender.——

29. Like Jonathan (see below), Susannah is a servant in the Shandy household.

30. A coin of small value.

My father, whose way was to force every event in nature into an hypothesis, by which means never man crucified TRUTH at the rate he did —— had but just heard of the report as my uncle Toby set out; and catching fire suddenly at the trespass done his brother by it, was demonstrating to Yorick,[31] notwithstanding my mother was sitting by —— not only, 'That the devil was in women, and that the whole of the affair was lust;' but that every evil and disorder in the world of what kind or nature soever, from the first fall of Adam, down to my uncle Toby's (inclusive) was owing one way or other to the same unruly appetite.

Yorick was just bringing my father's hypothesis to some temper, when my uncle Toby entering the room with marks of infinite benevolence and forgiveness in his looks, my father's eloquence rekindled against the passion —— and as he was not very nice in the choice of his words when he was wroth —— as soon as my uncle Toby was seated by the fire, and had filled his pipe, my father broke out in this manner.

CHAPTER XXXIII

—— THAT provision should be made for continuing the race of so great, so exalted and godlike a Being as man — I am far from denying — but philosophy speaks freely of every thing; and therefore I still think and do maintain it to be a pity, that it should be done by means of a passion which bends down the faculties, and turns all the wisdom, contemplations, and operations of the soul backwards —— a passion, my dear, continued my father, addressing himself to my mother, which couples and equals wise men with fools, and makes us come out of our caverns and hiding-places more like satyrs and four-footed beasts than men.

I know it will be said, continued my father (availing himself of the *Prolepsis*[32]) that in itself, and simply taken —— like hunger, or thirst, or sleep —— 'tis an affair neither good or bad — or shameful or otherwise. —— Why then did the delicacy of *Diogenes* and *Plato* so recalcitrate against it? and wherefore, when we go about to make and plant a man, do we put out the candle? and for what

31. The local curate (and in Volume I, a partial self-portrait of Sterne himself).

32. A rhetorical figure in which a speaker anticipates a future stage in an argument.

reason is it, that all the parts thereof — the congredients — the preparations — the instruments, and whatever serves thereto, are so held as to be conveyed to a cleanly mind by no language, translation, or periphrasis whatever?

—— The act of killing and destroying a man, continued my father raising his voice — and turning to my uncle Toby — you see, is glorious — and the weapons by which we do it are honourable —— We march with them upon our shoulders —— We strut with them by our sides —— We gild them —— We carve them —— We in-lay them —— We enrich them —— Nay, if it be but a *scoundril* cannon, we cast an ornament upon the breech of it. —

—— My uncle Toby laid down his pipe to intercede for a better epithet —— and Yorick was rising up to batter the whole hypothesis to pieces ——

—— When Obadiah[33] broke into the middle of the room with a complaint, which cried out for an immediate hearing.

The case was this:

My father, whether by ancient custom of the manor, or as improprietor of the great tythes,[34] was obliged to keep a Bull for the service of the Parish, and Obadiah had led his cow upon a *pop-visit*[35] to him one day or other the preceding summer —— I say, one day or other — because as chance would have it, it was the day on which he was married to my father's house-maid —— so one was a reckoning to the other. Therefore when Obadiah's wife was brought to bed — Obadiah thanked God——

—— Now, said Obadiah, I shall have a calf: so Obadiah went daily to visit his cow.

She'll calve on Monday — on Tuesday — or Wednesday at the farthest——

The cow did not calve —— no — she'll not calve till next week —— the cow put it off terribly —— till at the end of the sixth week Obadiah's suspicions (like a good man's) fell upon the Bull.

Now the parish being very large, my father's Bull, to speak the truth of him, was no way equal to the department; he had, however, got himself, somehow or other, thrust into employment — and as he went through the business with a grave face, my father had a high opinion of him.

—— Most of the townsmen, an' please your worship, quoth Obadiah, believe that 'tis all the Bull's fault——

—— But may not a cow be barren? replied my father, turning to Doctor Slop.

It never happens: said Dr. Slop, but the man's wife may have come before her time naturally enough —— Prithee has the child hair upon his head? — added Dr. Slop———

—— It is as hairy as I am; said Obadiah. —— Obadiah had not been shaved for three weeks —— Wheu-- u ---- u -------- cried my father; beginning the sentence with an exclamatory whistle —— and so, brother Toby, this poor Bull of mine, who is as good a Bull as ever p–ss'd, and might have done for Europa[36] herself in purer times —— had he but two legs less, might have been driven into Doctors Commons[37] and lost his character —— which to a Town Bull, brother Toby, is the very same thing as his life ———

L--d! said my mother, what is all this story about? ——

A COCK and a BULL, said Yorick —— And one of the best of its kind, I ever heard.

The END of the NINTH VOLUME.

33. A servant in the Shandy household.
34. An impropriator was a layman to whom pre-Reformation ecclesiastical tithes were subsequently paid.
35. A short visit.
36. In Greek mythology, Europa was carried off to Crete by Zeus, who appeared in the form of a bull.
37. The college of doctors of civil law in London, where divorce proceedings took place.

CHARLES JOHNSTONE

(*c.*1719-*c.*1800)

from:
CHRYSAL; OR, THE ADVENTURES OF A GUINEA.
WHEREIN ARE EXHIBITED VIEWS OF SEVERAL STRIKING SCENES, WITH CURIOUS AND INTERESTING ANECDOTES.... (1760-65)

[The opening chapter explains the nature of Chrysal, the spirit of gold, who is the novel's principal narrator.]

BOOK I

CHAPTER I

The Apparition of CHYRSAL *to an* ADEPT, *in the very moment of projection. His account of himself, and the cause of his appearing to the author.*

On a day, when long and strict abstinence had purified my body from every *terrene* incumbrance, and intense contemplation wound up my mind to an enthusiasm fit for *empyreal* conversation, as I stood with my eyes riveted on the *obstetrick* flame, in strong expectation of the birth of the *mystick child, the first-born of the morning*, ready to seize the happy moment, *when the earth sufficiently impregnated with the water, ascendeth white and splendent, that I might compound the pure elements, before they fly from the fire, and so perfect the great work*; my eyes began to dazzle, and the power of imagination overwhelmed my soul. ——— I saw a blue effulgence break from the liquid gold, and play about the genial vase! — I was astonished! I thought it the *substantial form of the son of the sun!* I thought the happy moment was come, when the *rose of the east should bloom in the desart*, and mine the favoured hand to cultivate its growth! I indulged the pleasing thought! I melted in the virtuous joy! and in obedience to the divine impulse, I kneeled to receive the reward of all my labours, *the radiant crown of wisdom and glory*, from the hand of nature, with every sense and faculty suspended, for fear of interrupting the mysterious process.

As my soul hung in this extasy, the flame which wrapped the *sacred birth in the bed of purification*, arose with a glory too strong for mortal sense, and filled the room. My senses sunk under the pressure, and I was dissolved into a trance, when a voice, celestially harmonious, encouraged me to raise my eyes, and I beheld *the body of the effulgence condense into an incorporeal substance in the form of a spirit*, while a placid shade softened the fierceness of the radiance, and made it tolerable to human sense.

An holy horror curdled all my blood; but the melody of the same voice, which had before emboldened me to look up, reassured my fainting heart with these words; 'Son of pains and votary of science! thy unwearied perseverance has prevailed, and I am sent to crown thee with the virgin rose! I am CHRYSAL, the spirit of that incorruptible mass now glowing in that vase before thee, who in reward of thy noble constancy in offering this thy last mite, on the shrine of knowledge, am come to reveal the mysteries of nature to thee, and satisfy that raging thirst for wisdom, which has so long excrutiated thy soul, and thus emaciated thy body! And that thou mayest the better comprehend the greatness of this honour vouchsafed unto thee, I shall trace the operations of nature through her most secret recesses, and illustrate the truth of what I say, by a detail of the various incidents of my being, in my present state, to prepare thee for the reception and proper use of that *grand secret*, which I shall afterwards communicate!

I can see your thoughts; and will answer every doubt which may arise in your mind at the wonders of my relation, without the interruption of your inquiries, as *awful silence is the essence of my converse*, the least breach of which puts an end to it for ever! listen then in mute attention, nor let a breath disturb the mystick tale!' —

The works of nature are infinitely various, and her methods of operation inscrutable to the curiosity of that vain intruder Reason, which has of late presumed to pry into her ways, and to doubt, if not deny, the reality of all effects, which her short-sighted eye cannot trace to their causes! a presumption that has justly shortened the line of human knowledge, and condensed the mist of ignorance which overspreads the world! Some noble efforts though I see the nature of man preparing to make, to recover that eminence of conjecture and credulity which alone can merit such a communication of extraordinary knowledge as is now indulged to you. Some of the most hidden truths which I shall here unfold, has unassisted genius discovered already; and more shall curious penetration make learned guesses at, even in this sceptick age.*

Know then, that in the economy of nature, to ease the trouble, and keep up the state of its great authour,† a subordination of ministerial spirits executes the system of his government in all its degrees; one of whom, for the greater order and expedition, is made to actuate every divided particle of matter in this immense universe. In this distribution, *that* portion of gold was assigned to my charge, upon its first feeling the influence of the‡ etherial fire of the sun, the general minister of the divine commands. This happened in *Peru*, where *that* body of which I then became the spirit, was torn from its peaceful bed 200 fathoms deep in the bowels of the earth.

I shall not describe my surprize, at my first plunging into those realms of darkness, nor shall I satisfy the curiosity I see rising in you, whether that period was the beginning of my existence, or whether I was, either as a punishment or reward for a past, or a preparation for a future life, thrown into this. These are mysteries not yet discovered, though often most learnedly guessed at. All I shall unfold to you are points already known, or such as I see ready to be found out by human industry, as it would put an end to learning to make a revelation of the objects of its enquiries! such matters, I say, I shall explain to you, and farther, relate some occurrences, the knowledge of which will be equally useful and entertaining, which happened to the several persons with whom I have had intercourse, in the various stages of my present state.

And as you may be at a loss, to know how I could arrive at the knowledge of such facts, many of which happened long before my converse with those persons, I shall inform you, that besides that *intuitive knowledge* common to all spirits, we of superior orders, who animate this universal monarch GOLD, have also a power of entering into the hearts of the immediate possessors of our bodies, and there reading all the secrets of their lives. And this will explain to you, the cause of that love of gold, which is so remarkable in all who possess any quantity of that metal.* For the operation of every material cause, is in proportion to the strength of the spirit actuating that cause; as the strength of the spirit is reciprocally in proportion to the quantity of his material body: and consequently, when the mighty spirit of a large mass of gold takes possession of the human heart, it influences all its actions, and overpowers, or banishes, the weaker impulse of those immaterial, unessential notions called *virtues.* And this intuition, and power of transmigration I have thus explained, to remove every shadow of doubt of what I shall relate.

* See all the modern hypothetical philosophy.
† Essay on Spirit.[1]
‡ Siris.[2] —— Would not these, and many other passages of the same nature which support the systems of those celebrated works, almost tempt us to think, that the writers of them must have had a communication with this or some such spirit, to come at knowledge so supernatural?

1. *An Essay on Spirit* (1750) by Robert Clayton, bishop of Clogher.
2. *Siris ... Concerning the Virtues of Tar-Water* (1744) was the work of the philosopher George Berkeley, bishop of Cloyne.

[In the form of the guinea of the title, Chrysal has come briefly into the possession of an army officer. The following episode — characteristic of Johnstone's harshly satirical depiction of the immorality of contemporary society — concludes with a more general reflection on the universal corruption of human nature.]

BOOK II

CHAPTER I

CHRYSAL *enters into the service of the gentleman of a general. Gratitude in high and low life. The modern way of rising in the world, and the happiness of dependance. Influence of* CHRYSAL'S *master, with his curious manner of supporting it.*

You may judge that my stay with this owner was but short: he gave me directly to the general's *gentleman*, with a letter to be presented to his excellency next morning, as he could not find courage to speak to him in person.

* Essay on Spirit.

The case of this person, though not uncommon among men, I own affected me. He was the son of an officer of distinguished merit, the services of whose life had, in the 80th year of it, been rewarded with the command of a regiment, and the hopes of his son crowned with a pair of colours; which, on the death of his father, in six months after his elevation, he found to be his whole inheritance; the fees of office, and the equipage for his new rank, having exhausted all the savings of the old man's subaltern frugality. —— The most exemplary duty, in five warm campaigns, had advanced the son to the rank of a lieutenant, when the exaltation of the person to whom he now applied, raised his hopes to a company, which was vacant in the regiment, and his right by seniority: for such was his ignorance of mankind, that he built sanguine expectations on the very reasons that should have deprived him of any, *the obligations of the person, to whom he applied, to his father*, who had taken him up, the poor friendless orphan of a young ensign, educated him at his own expence, procured him his first commission, and afterwards lent him the money with which he had purchased his company: a debt which the son was weak enough to expect a friendship from, though it, and much more, had long since been cleared at play.

But though the character of the son, and the general's known intimacy with the father, in a manner obliged him to promise him his friendship, yet nothing was farther from his thoughts than ever to do him any real service; as he imagined that would be acknowledging the obligations which his very attendance seemed to upbraid him with: a dinner now and then being the only favour he ever had or ever meant to give him. You may perhaps have experienced the misery of a dependant's dining at the table of his patron, where the tortures of *Tantalus*[3] are aggravated by anxiety of giving offence. I shall therefore hasten over this, and the other scenes of that evening, which were but the common occurrences of military greatness, and ended in a deep debauch, as soon as all but the *chosen few* had retired, to come to the conclusion of my *late* master's story, in which my *present* bore a considerable part.

3. In Greek myth, a son of Zeus who was punished in Hades for crimes against the gods by having to stand up to his neck in water, which receded when he attempted to drink, and under fruits that the wind blew away when he tried to eat.

As soon as the general had slept off the fumes of his wine, and awoke next morning, my master's hour of influence arrived, which he never failed to improve. After a prelude of coughing and spitting, the scene opened thus, *'Who's there? William!'* —— 'Sir,' — *'William, was not I very drunk last night? my head achs most confoundedly.'* —— 'Your excellency was a little cut, but you broke up much the strongest of the company.' — *'Aye, I wonder at that, I spend myself with talking, when I begin to go, and that helps a man on damnably: that story of the battle, where I was taken prisoner, is a bottle in my way always.'* — 'That foreign gentleman, who never speaks a word, has a great advantage then' — *'Aye, so he has; but he is a damned honest fellow, and a very good companion; he always fills a bumper and never speaks a word. — But my head.'* — 'Perhaps your excellency had better take something' — *'No, I have taken too much already; though that's right; give me a glass of the old Geneva; I am to go to council to day, and must settle my head — Aye, that will do, I am much better now; there is nothing like a hair of the old dog'.*

This conversation continued till he was seated to breakfast, when my master turned to a new topic. 'I was very sorry (said he) that your *excellency* happened to sit in last night, as Mrs. *Motherly* was to call' — *'Why that's true, William; I did not think of one engagement when I made the other; and when she called me out, I was not in cue; I was too far gone. We old fellows are not sparrows; the spirit is often willing, when the flesh is weak; ha, ha, ha'.*

'Your *excellency* is pleased to be merry, but to my thinking, the youngest fellow of the age has not more vigour' — *'Aye, William, do you think so indeed? But why do you think so William?'* — 'Because your *excellency* always chuses such green things: now I should think a ripe woman would be better; I am sure she would give less trouble.' — *'Ha, ha, ha, why that's your taste; but youth is mine; and while I have powers (and I do not think mine quite gone yet) I will please my taste. But what had Mrs. Motherly last night?'* — 'A very fine girl as your *excellency* could wish to see' — *'How old?'* — 'About sixteen.' — *'Psha, mellow pears; I loath such trash.'* — 'But Mrs. *Motherly* said she could swear she was untouched. She came from the country but yesterday, a relation of her own: the poor thing knew nothing of the matter, and thought she came to be hired for a laundry-maid!' — *'Why that is something; but I wish she were younger'* — 'If your *excellency* pleases but to wait a little, I have one in my eye that will suit your taste exactly; a sweeter child is not in all England' — *'Aye, good William* (spitting once or twice, and wriggling in his chair) *Aye, that is something, but how old?'* —— 'Just ten, and finely grown' —— *'Right, the right age. That's true! I'll speak this very day for that place for your brother. Tell him to come to-morrow; I will not be refused.'* — We are both obliged to your *excellency* for all your favours' —— *'But when shall I see this girl? Give Motherly some excuse with her ripe fruit. Sixteen! sixty! psha!'* — 'Sir I shall go about it this very evening.' A letter from captain *Standard*; will your *excellency* please to read it'? ——— *'Damn him and his letter: throw it into the fire! What would the unreasonable scoundrel have? Did I not give him his dinner yesterday? Has he not been introduced to good company at my table? If he had any industry or spirit, with these advantages, he would have learned to play, and made his fortune as others do. Since he grows troublesome on encouragement, I'll starve him into better manners. Bid the porter strike him off the dinner list.'* — 'I beg your *excellency*'s pardon, for mentioning him, but the manner I have heard you talk to him made me imagine you really did design to provide for him; and he says there is a vacancy in the regiment just now' — *'Damn his impudence! a vacancy indeed! I shall never think there is a good one till he makes it at Tyburn.'*[4] ——— 'I beg your *excellency*'s pardon: I shall never mention him more. Would you have me go about the *child* this evening; it is a little angel to be sure' ——— *'This moment if you think you can succeed.'* — 'I shall try at any rate: but there is one obstacle' — *'What is that? you know I never grudge money on these occasions. How much will do?'* —— 'That is not the difficulty here; money will not do, and I hardly know what will' ——— *'Money not do? Why what the devil can it be, that money will not do?* — 'I scarce know how to mention it to your *excellency*, but the little cherub is neice to captain *Standard*, his sister's daughter, and while he is in the way, there will be no possibility of getting at her' —— *'Is that all? He shall join the regiment to-morrow.'* —— 'But then he will leave such an impression of your unkindness upon his sister, if there is nothing done for him, after waiting so long, that it will be impossible for any person belonging to you to gain access.' — *'What would you have me do? I never will bear to have the fellow get a company in my regiment: that would be acknowledging the obligations he has the impudence to say I received from his father; I never will bear it'* — 'I beg your *excellency*'s pardon, I did not presume to point out any such thing, and indeed the possession of such a *baby* (though my eyes never beheld her fellow) is not worth your giving yourself so much trouble about; she is quite too young, though so well grown' — *'You say she is but just ten! and such a beauty!'* —— 'I wish your *excellency* could but see her, for I am unable to describe her' — *'But cannot some way be found out, beside fixing this fellow under my nose?'* —— 'That was just what I was going to take the liberty of hinting to your *excellency*. There are several gentlemen of fortune, in the troops just ordered to *America*, who have no liking to the voyage. Now I think, with submission, that you would oblige some of them, with an exchange into your regiment, and let captain *Standard* go in his place. And this will oblige him too; for I have often heard him wish to go there, in hopes of rising, when they come into action.' — *'A good thought! and so I will. Let the fellow go to* America *and get scalped; his hot head wants to be cooled: such poor wretches as he are just fit to be transported there. Tell him to prepare directly. I long to be rid of him. But when shall I see the dear little creature?'* — 'In twenty-four hours after he is gone, I'll undertake to have her eating sugar-plumbs, and sobbing in your bosom. It cannot possibly be sooner, for you know the captain's spirit, and that he would cut the throat of a prince, who should dishonour his family, as he calls it.' — *'Aye, damn his spirit, that is true; that is what has kept me civil to the fellow so long: I know he has all the romantic madness about honour, and such stuff that made his fool of a father live and die a beggar'.*

By this time his *excellency* was dressed, to go to council, for which another dram settled his head.

I *see* your surprise, at the brutal behaviour of the master, and the infamous designs of the man. The former is beyond aggravation; but the latter were only an honest artifice in favour of his friend, who had no such neice in the world.

CHAPTER II

The history of Mr. William. *Some odd circumstances in his conduct accounted for. . . .*

William was a son of the regiment, born of one of the general wives that followed it. He was about the

4. A celebrated place of execution in eighteenth-century London, near the site of the present Marble Arch.

same age with *Standard*, who had taken such a liking to him, when they were boys, that he shared his allowance with him, gave him his old cloaths, and taught him what he learned at school. A natural acuteness of genius improved these advantages so well, that *William* could read and write enough for a gentleman; dance, fence, and scrape on the violin, before his friend's power of serving him was put an end to, by the death of his father; and his spirit and appetites were too great, to accept of his offer, of the best support an ensign could spare him, to maintain him as a *cadet*, till his merit should get him a commission. But though he would not accept, he did not forget the offer, nor make his obligations a cause of hatred, now that it was in his power to make some return; a way of thinking, that proved the meanness of his birth; for quitting the barren paths of military honour, he had turned his genius to the more thriving profession of a footman; through the various ascents of which, he had risen to his present rank, of his *excellency*'s gentleman; in which he had the unfashionable gratitude to return the favours of his former benefactor in the above manner, which his experience and knowledge of his master's temper convinced him to be the only one he could hope to succeed in. As to his promise about the child, he was in no pain about that, there being no person who could contradict whatever excuse he should please to give.

There is one circumstance, which I see puzzles you, in the character of this man, and that is his taking *me* from his friend, when he must be sensible how badly he could spare such a sum. But you must consider the power of nature when strengthened by habit.

From his mother, *William* had inherited venality, which the bribery of vails,[5] in his present profession, had confirmed beyond all possibility of correction; so that it was no more in his power to refuse a guinea when offered to him, than to change his stature or complexion. And attention to this observation would take off the wonder, and ease the world from the trouble of the exclamations that are daily made against the rapacity of persons in office, for as such are generally taken from the class of *William*, it cannot be expected but they must act from the same natural principles with him.

I *see* the depravity of human nature, when stripped of disguise and ornament, affects your unexperienced heart too strongly. But consider, that *we* see things as they really are, and to represent them otherwise to you, would invert the design of my mission, and confirm, rather than remove the prejudices that lead astray the mind of man.

However, this consolation I can give you, that the vices I have already drawn, and may hereafter draw to your view, are not particular to this age or country: they are the weeds which in every age and clime, have always, and always will, over-run the human heart.

Nor is it just to call them vices (though in compliance with the language of men I do call them so) which *perhaps* are but * necessary parts of this universal system; and though in a particular instance, and viewed by themselves, they may appear deformed, yet when thrown into the general representation of things, they may have their beauty and use, if only to diversify the scene: and with respect to men in particular, be as † advantagious to the community as they are prejudicial to individuals. . . .

[The guinea now belongs to a magistrate, whose dispensing of justice suggests Johnstone's perception of the potentially fatal consequences of English prejudice against Irish immigrants.]

BOOK II

CHAPTER X

An instance of his worship's exemplary justice on a shop-lifter. The unfashionable compassion and generosity of a sailor. . . .

It was now pretty late, and my master was just retiring to supper, pleased with having made so good a day, when he was stopped by more business. A woman who kept a chandler's shop, in the next street, had dragged before him one of her poor neighbours, whom she had caught in the very fact of stealing a pound of cheese off her counter, as she

* From hence it should seem, the hint of a late treatise, on the origin of evil, was borrowed or else dictated by the same spirit.[6]

† Fable of the bees.[7]

5. Gratuities given to servants (often providing a large part of their total wages).

6. *De Origine Mali* (1702), by William King, archbishop of Dublin, translated into English as *An Essay on the Origin of Evil* (1731). See p. 772.

7. Bernard Mandeville's *The Fable of the Bees* (1714 with later additions), whose argument is indicated by its subtitle, 'Private Vices, Publick Benefits'.

was reaching her a two-penny loaf from the shelf: a crime that was heightened by ingratitude too, as she was giving her the loaf on trust; the thief having owned to her, that she had not a farthing in the world to pay for it, nor a morsel to give her three small children, who had been fasting the whole day.

Enraged at the heinousness of the crime, and at being kept from supper, while the chickens and asparagus were cooling on the table, his worship, knitting his brows, and putting on all the magistrate, asked the trembling wretch, with a voice that pierced her soul, — 'What she had to say for herself, and whether she was guilty of the crime laid to her charge, or not.' —

The poor creature, almost dead with wretchedness, want, and fear, threw herself at his feet, and pouring out a flood of tears, that for some moments choaked her utterance, 'O mercy! mercy! (said she) for the love of the sweet *Jesus*, have mercy on a poor wretch, whom want alone compelled to this first offence, to save the lives of three poor infants, who are this moment perishing with hunger. Oh, send, and prove the truth of what I say; send and learn their misery, and it will move you to relieve them, and then I care not what becomes of me.' —— *'Very fine truely! if we admit such excuses for shop-lifting, there will be enough ready to plead them. Here, make her* mittimus;[8] *she confesses the fact; as for her brats, bastards too, I suppose, let them be sent to the work-house'* ——— 'Oh the poor creatures! they are not bastards; and they have no parish to be sent to. My husband is a sailor, who was pressed on board a man of war six years ago, and has been in the *West-Indies* ever since, till this summer, when the ship was ordered home to be laid up. Poor soul! he thought he should be paid off, and so wrote me word to *Corke*, to come to him, for he meant to go and settle in *Scotland*, his own country; but the moment he came to *Portsmouth*, he was *turned over* into another ship, without getting a shilling of his six years wages or prize-money, and sent away directly to *America*; so that, after spending every penny I had in the world, to come to him from *Ireland*, as he desired, I am left here with my poor children, to starve in a strange place, where nobody has any compassion for me, though my husband wrote me word, that he had above 300l. due to him for wages and prize-money; here is his letter! I never go without it! it is all the comfort I have in my distress.'

'Aye, I thought so! I thought you were one of those Irish *thieves that came to rob us, and cut our throats! but I shall take care of you! I shall make you wish you had continued eating potatoes at home. I wish I could provide as well for every one of your country! we shall never be well, till we have hang'd you all.'* — 'Oh good your worship! I am no thief; I never stole any thing before. And this woman, who has brought me before you, knows the truth of every thing I have told your worship, and that I have always paid her honestly while I had a penny in the world; for I have dealt with her ever since I came to *London*; but hunger, and the cries of three starving children, forced me to this! Oh my children, my children!' — *'Peace, woman! all you can say signifies nothing; you were taken in the fact, and to* Newgate *you shall go directly. And as for your brats, it is better for them to die of hunger now, than to live to be hanged like their mother.'* —

By this time, the *mittimus* was ready, which he signed without the least hesitation or pity, and then hurried away to his supper, having almost fretted his bowels out, to think it was spoiled by waiting so long.

But though the Justice's compassion could not be moved, by such a *poor* wretch, his clerk was not so inexorable, but yielded to the persuasion of an honest *tar*, who seeing a croud at the door, had given six-pence to go in, and see the *fun*; and for two guineas, *which barely paid the fees*, ventured to make up the affair, and let her go about her business, *though he did not know what might be the consequence, if it should ever come to his worship's knowledge.* — *Jack* took no notice of what he said, but taking the poor creature, who was just sinking under the agitations of fear, joy, and gratitude, by the hand, 'Chear away, sister (said he) chear away; we'll bring up all this lee-way, next trip. Damn my eyes and limbs, if I'll see a brother seaman's family at short allowance, while I have a shilling! come, heave a-head; I'll rig and victual you and your children, against your husband comes, to man you for a voyage home. I'll swing my hammock in the next birth, and you shall cook the kettle, while I stay ashore.' — Saying which words, he led her off in triumph. — This the clerk told his worship, when he come in to supper, giving him one of the guineas, as his share of the composition....

8. A warrant signed by a justice of the peace directed to the keeper of a prison, ordering him to receive a prisoner into custody and later deliver him or her to court.

[*Chrysal* is a *roman à clef* — a fictionalized account of real people or circumstances. The guinea is now 'the favourite of the favourite of a mighty monarch,' and this passage contains an unflattering portrait of Amalie Wallmoden, German-born countess of Yarmouth, and mistress to George II, who had close financial connections with the Irish administration.]

BOOK III

CHAPTER VI

An odd visitor to a lady. The mystery of stock-jobbing. Charity begins at home. Her Grace's kind intentions for honest Aminadab. Another visitor. The worth of honour. The best salve for a broken character.

As soon as the mysteries of the toilet were over, and my mistress's face finished for the day, a person entered to her, whose appearance was far from promising such an intimacy with a female of her rank.

The most shabby, squallid dress covered a distorted carcass, not much above four feet high, but so gross, that, laid upon his back, he would have cast a shadow nearly as long as when he stood upright. A deep olive complexion, an Aquiline nose, and a mouth from ear to ear, fringed round with a greasy, curled beard, made the beauty of his face correspond with the elegance of his figure.

This extraordinary person approached her *Grace*, without introduction or ceremony, and entering immediately upon business, told her, 'that he came to know if she meant to *buy in* that day, for the report raised in *the Alley*,[9] by their express from abroad, had given such a stroke to the funds, that they had tumbled to the ground; but would most certainly rise again the next day, as soon as the news, which had arrived that morning, should be known; which could not be kept a secret, as the people wanted some thing to keep up their spirits, among so many miscarriages, and divert them from making too close enquiries into the conduct of affairs.'

'Why! my honest friend *Aminadab*! (replied her *Grace*) I must be directed in these matters by you. If you think there is any thing to be got, by *buying in* to day, with all my heart: though I must own I cannot conceive why you should *sell out*, the very last week, to *buy in* this.'

'Ah! my lady (returned *Aminadab*) there is a mystery in all business, and in none greater than ours. The *Bulgarian* King's success last week raised people's spirits so high, that they thought the world was to be all their own, and therefore bought at any price. Now that was the time for a prudent person to *sell*, as I advised your *Grace*; which we had no sooner done, than instantly come an express, *(of our own)* with an account that the enemy had turned upon him in their retreat, and entirely vanquished the vanquishers.

This news quite overthrew the spirits raised by the former, and made every one eager to sell out at any loss, for fear the enemy should *get wings and fly over*, to take all they had. Now as this was but a terror raised by ourselves, we take the advantage of it, and so buy in when others are selling out 20 *per cent.* cheaper than we ourselves sold out last week, when the madness bent the other way; and may perhaps *sell* again the next, when another packet shall set things right, and bring the people back their senses. For the senses of the people of this country are more inconstant than the *Moon*, depending entirely upon the winds that blow them news.'

'But is it really possible that any people can be such fools?' — 'O, please your *Grace*, they are only too rich! They have more money than they know what to do with; that is all' — *'Then Aminadab, we will ease them of some of the burthen. But would it not be better to conceal this news for another day; might not that make them fall still lower?'* — 'But, my lady, the people want the good news.' —— *'The people may hang themselves in despair, I care not, so I get money.'* — 'The government though' — *'What is the government to me; I will get all I can, and then leave them to themselves, to sink or swim as they will; it is all one to me.'* —— 'That is true; your *Grace* says right. A people who do not know, or at least, will not follow their own interest, are not worth any person's care, longer than while he can make something of them. But we must reserve that stroke for another time. This news has got into the offices, and nothing there is a secret you know. Besides the *Pannick* was too violent to last; it begins to wear off already: in another day they would recover their senses of themselves. I think, therefore, with your *Grace*'s approbation, to *buy in* all I can to day;

9. i.e. 'Change (or Exchange) Alley, a small street opposite the Royal Exchange in the City of London, much frequented by merchants and brokers.

without you had rather lay out your money in the supplies, for the Protestants of *Germany.*' —— '*With all my heart, if you can make as much of it that way as in the funds: but not otherwise. I would not lose one shilling for any people under heaven!*'

'Your *Grace* has a just notion of the world, and of the value of money that governs it. Indeed, I must say, that the terms for these supplies are very unreasonable, considering how such things have been done, for some time past. It is expected that people should bring in their money, without any *premium*, or other advantage, than what was publickly calculated for, at the granting them. But these œconomists will find themselves mistaken. The world is wiser now a-days, than to give up advantages which they have once got possession of. As to that affair, therefore, I should think it better to let it stand a little longer, 'till the necessity becomes more urgent, and then they will be glad to come into our terms, if it were not that the poor people may be ruined in the mean time; so that indeed I am at a loss what to advise your *Grace* to do, in so nice[10] an affair.'

'*Why let them be ruined then: it is not my fault nor my business to save them; nor will I part with a shilling to do it. Besides, if they do suffer by the delay, those who gave them this supply to prevent their ruin, may give them another to repair it.*' — 'I cannot but admire your *Grace*'s judgment in all things. You are above the foolish weaknesses of nature, and have the noble resolution to see your own family perish, rather than injure your own interest, to relieve them. I shall obey your *Grace* in all things. I go now to *the Alley*, where business will soon begin.' — '*Do honest Aminadab, and fear not; though I could not procure an establishment for your whole nation,*[11] *as I would have done, I certainly will for your family, and that is enough for you. Your son shall be made a* BARONET *at least; you have riches enough to support the title.*'

'Your *Grace* is very good; our people are all satisfied of your kind intentions: but, alas, that was a severe disappointment to us, after costing us so much money. The children of the Lord weep over it in their synagogues, and the daughters of *Sion* lament it in their songs; but my household shall rejoice in thy favour, and the labours of my life prove my gratitude for it.'

Honest *Aminadab* was no sooner gone, than there entered an agent, seemingly of another nature, this dealing in honours as the other did in money; but the difference between them was only in appearance, the end of both being ultimately the same.

'May it please your *Grace*, (said he, advancing with due reverence and ceremony) I come to wait upon you, about that place in the ————: that gentleman will not, indeed cannot, give one shilling more for it.' — '*Then let the other have it; I will not lose five pence, much less 500l. for him.*' — 'But, please your *Grace*, you know what grounds he has to expect it on; besides your promise, which cannot well be broken through, it was so positive.' — '*My promise was only conditional (in my own intention) that he should give me as much as another, and in no other sense will I keep it. As for his grounds of expectation I regard them not: let him make the most of them, where he can.*' — 'Just as your *Grace* pleases; I only took the liberty of speaking my own opinion, but always in submission to your's. Not but I must own I am apprehensive of this gentleman's resentment, though not immediately for myself, so much as for your Grace's character, with which he may be provoked to make too free upon such an affair.' — '*Aye! that is liberty, your boasted English liberty, to speak disrespectfully of your superiors. But I despise whatever he can say; nor will I give up my own way for fear of his impertinence.*' — 'Very right; your *Grace* is very right. It were by no means fit that you should: but then it is to be considered, whether this breach of promise may not be attended with inconveniencies, that may overballance the advantage, as it may make others afraid to deal with you another time.' — '*I will venture that: none come to me but for their own advantage, and while they can find that, they will scarce stay away for punctilio's. So let me hear no more of this, but close with the other directly.*'

'Will not your *Grace* please to abate of your demand for that place in *Ireland?* I really fear you rate it too high.' — '*Not a shilling! I will not abate a shilling! Surely I ought to know the value of things in* IRELAND *by this time! I have had sufficient dealings there, to teach me; it has been my privy purse for many years.*'[12] — 'But what I fear is, that if your *Grace*

10. i.e. delicate.
11. Johnstone is alluding to the Jewish Naturalization Act (the so-called 'Jew Bill') of 1753, a controversial (and rapidly repealed) measure which sought to allow individual Jews to become naturalized British citizens by Act of Parliament.
12. The Countess of Yarmouth had close dealings with Nathaniel Clements, the teller of the exchequer in Ireland.

does not fix upon some one directly the lord deputy may, and that would disappoint you; for this place has ever been immediately in his gift, and it would reflect a kind of dishonour on him, to give it up.' — '*Dishonour indeed! I am much concerned for his honour certainly! And as for his naming any one to contradict me, I believe he will be cautious how he does that. The example of his predecessor will teach him.*' —— 'However, if your *Grace* pleases, to prevent any disputes, I will wait on him, and tell him that you have a friend, whom you design to recommend.' — '*With all my heart; you may if you will. But as to the price, I will not abate one shilling, as I said before. Do not I know that places in that country are either mere pensions, without any thing to do, or even necessity of ever going there at all, or where that can not be dispensed with, from the nature of the place, that no learning, no abilities are requisite. If it was here indeed, where knowledge in a profession is absolutely necessary to a place in it, there might be something in higling*[13] *about the price, but for a coward to scruple paying for being made a general, or a blockhead a judge, there can be nothing more unreasonable; and I will not hear another word about it. — But what have you done about those titles, which I gave you to dispose of.*' — 'Really I do not know what to say to your *Grace* about them: the bent of the people does not seem to incline to honours of late.' — '*No; I thought they were always as good as ready money; especially with those who have more money than sense, and think it easier to buy, than earn honour by merit. An* IRISH *title was the constant refuge of those sons of fortune, who not being born in the rank of gentlemen, or having forfeited it, by their villainies, were desirous of changing their names for sonorous titles, to hide their disgrace, as it were, under an heap of honours, which in reality only make them the more exposed to the view, and consequently to the censure, of the world. —— But I find, even that imaginary sense of honour is gone out of fashion, and the shadow is in no more request than the substance, at present. But since they are grown such a drug, even make the most you can of them: sell them to whoever will buy; I shall take no exceptions to persons.*'

'I shall certainly do the best I can for your *Grace*, though they have been so oddly given away of late, that I verily believe people are ashamed of taking them, for fear of being laughed at. Rattles are given to children, but titles to old men to divert them; to some, in reward for not doing *the very worst* possibly in their power; and to others, for doing *nothing at all*'....

13. i.e. haggling.

FRANCES SHERIDAN

(1724-66)

from: MEMOIRS OF MISS SIDNEY BIDULPH (1761)

[Framed by an elaborate 'Editor's Introduction' testifying to the supposed authenticity of the 'Memoirs', *Sidney Bidulph* begins with a brief expository section before to the opening of the heroine's journal.]

Mrs. Catharine Sidney Bidulph[1] was the Daughter of Sir Robert Bidulph of Wiltshire. Her father died when she was very young; and of ten children none survived him but this lady, and his eldest son, afterwards Sir George Bidulph. The family estate was not very considerable; and Miss Bidulph's portion was but four thousand pounds; a fortune however at that time not quite contemptible: it was in the beginning of queen Ann's reign.[2]

Lady Bidulph was a woman of plain sense, but exemplary piety; the strictness of her notions (highly commendable in themselves) now and then gave a tincture of severity to her actions, though she was ever esteemed a truly good woman.

She had educated her daughter, who was one of the greatest beauties of her time, in the strictest

1. 'Mistress' was a title still commonly given to unmarried women in the eighteenth century.

2. Anne ruled Britain and Ireland from 1702 to 1714.

principles of virtue; from which she never deviated, through the course of an innocent, though unhappy life.

Sir George Bidulph was nine or ten years older than his sister. He was a man of good understanding, moral as to his general conduct, but void of any of those refined sentiments, which constitute what is called *delicacy*. Pride is sometimes accounted laudable; that which Sir George possessed (for he had pride) was not of this kind.

He was of a weakly constitution, and had been ordered by the physicians to Spa[3] for the recovery of a lingering disorder, which he had laboured under for some time. It was just on his return to England that the busy scene of his sister's life opened. An intimate friend of hers, of her own sex, to whom she revealed all the secrets of her heart, happened at this juncture to go abroad, and it was for her perusal only the following journal was intended. That friend has carefully preserved it, as she thinks it may serve for an example, to prove that neither prudence, foresight, nor even the best disposition that the human heart is capable of, are of themselves sufficient to defend us against the inevitable ills that sometimes are allotted, even to the best. 'The race is not to the swift, nor the battle to the strong.'[4]

The JOURNAL

[Sidney Bidulph has received a proposal of marriage from the Anglo-Irish hero, Orlando Faulkland, with whom she is in love. She here resumes her journal after a serious illness.]

[London]

July 27 [1705]. — After a fortnight's, a dreadful fortnight's intermission, I reassume my pen. I have often told you, Cecilia, I was not born to be happy. Oh! I prophesied when I said so, though I knew not why I said it.

I will try to recollect all the circumstances of this miserable interval, and relate them as well as I can. The last line in my journal (which I have not yet ventured to send you, as your stay at Paris is so uncertain) informs you that I was ill. I was let blood;[5] but my disorder increased, and I was in a high fever before next morning. I remember what my reflections were, and am sure my apprehensions of death were not on my *own* account afflicting, but grievously so at the thoughts of what those should feel whom I was to leave behind.

My mother and Mr. Faulkland, I believe, chiefly engaged my mind: but I did not long continue capable of reflection. The violence of my disorder deprived me of my senses on the fourth day, and they tell me I raved of Mr. Faulkland. I remember nothing, but that, in my intervals of reason, I always saw my poor mother in tears by my bedside. I was in the utmost danger, but it pleased God to restore me to the ardent prayers of my dear parent. In about ten days I began to shew some symptoms of amendment, and inquired how Mr. Faulkland did. My mother answered, he is well, my dear, and gone out of town, but I believe will return in a day or two. Gone out of town, said I, and leave me dying! Indeed that was not kind of Mr. Faulkland, and I shall tell him so. My mother was sitting on the bedside, and had hold of my hand; my brother was standing with his back to the fireplace. I observed they looked at one another, but neither made me any answer. Pray, Sir George, I cried, would you serve the woman so whom you were so near making your wife? My brother was going to reply, but my mother frowned at him; he looked displeased, and went out of the room. Dear madam, said I, there is something the matter with Mr. Faulkland; don't keep me in suspence. I *know* there is something, which you and my brother would conceal from me. Is Mr. Faulkland sick? Not that I know of, I assure you, answered my mother; he was well yesterday, for we had a message from him to enquire after your health, as we have had every day, for he is but at Richmond; and you know, if he were in town, he could receive no other satisfaction than hearing from you, as you are too ill to admit of any visits. My mother rang the bell immediately, and asked me to take something; I saw she wanted to turn the conversation. My maid Ellen came into the room, and I asked no more questions.

My mother staid with me till it was time for her to go to rest; but avoided mentioning Mr. Faulkland's name, or giving me any opportunity of doing it; for she tenderly conjured me to keep myself quite

3. Health resort in modern Belgium, already famous in the seventeenth century.
4. Ecclesiastes 9.11.
5. Bleeding was a common medical treatment for many ailments in the eighteenth century.

composed, and not to talk. The doctor assured her this night that he thought me out of danger; and she retired with looks of cordial delight.

She was no sooner gone, than I called Ellen to my bedside, and charged her to tell me all she knew concerning Mr. Faulkland. The poor girl looked concerned, and seemed to study for an answer. Lord bless me, madam! what should I know of him more than my lady has told you? When did you see him? said I: Not for several days, she answered. Where is he? At Richmond, I heard Sir George say; but I suppose he will come to town as soon as he hears you are well enough to receive him. I catched hold of her hand; 'Ellen, I know there is something, relative to Mr. Faulkland, which you all want to hide from me; don't attempt to deceive me; you may be sure, whatever it be, I must soon be informed of it; in the mean while, my doubts make me very unhappy.'

The good-natured girl's trouble and confusion increased as I spoke; My dear madam, she replied, when you are better, my lady will tell you all: 'No, no, Ellen, I must know it now; tell it me this minute, or you must never expect to see me better under such uncertainty. What is the *all*, the frightful *all*, that I am to be told? How you have shocked me with that little word!' I know nothing, madam, answered Ellen, but what I gathered from Sir George's loud angry talk with my lady; and I should be undone if her ladyship were to know I mentioned it to you. I assured her my mother should not know it. Why then, madam, (speaking lower) I am afraid that Mr. Faulkland has misbehaved, or has been belied to my lady—She stopped at this — How? how? cried I eagerly; what has she heard of him? Something of another courtship, she replied; but I hope it is all false — You trifle with me — speak out, and say all you know. The poor creature started at my impatience: 'I know no more, madam, than that I heard my lady say to Sir George, I had rather Sidney were in her grave than married to him. Sir George said, But why will you not let Mr. Faulkland justify himself, madam? Justify himself! my lady answered; what can he say? is it not plain that he is false to another woman? They talked lower; but at last Sir George raised his voice, and said, he would give half his estate to have the villain punished; — All this, madam, I over-heard by mere accident. Sir George was going abroad; his linen was lying ready for him in his dressing-room; and his man desired me to put a stitch in one of his master's point ruffles, which was a little ripped in the gathering. I had come up the back stairs into the dressing-room, just as my lady (who was with Sir George in the bed-chamber) said the words I first repeated; and while I stood doing the ruffle, I heard the rest. There was a great deal more said, but I could not distinguish any thing besides, except a word here and there, which Sir George seemed to speak in a very angry tone. This was the second day of your illness. Mr. Faulkland had been here in the morning to enquire how you did; my lady saw him, and I thought they parted very friendly. I met Mr. Faulkland coming down stairs; he looked full of grief; my lady stood at the dining-room door and wished him a good morning. About an hour after came a letter directed to you; it was brought by a porter, who said it required no answer. As you were too ill to read it, I gave it to my lady; and it was soon after this, that I heard the conversation between Sir George and her ladyship. Mr. Faulkland came again in the evening. Sir George was not at home; but my lady had him above an hour in the drawing-room; and the footman, who let him out, said, he looked as if he were in sad trouble. He has never been here since, but sends constantly every day to know how you do. My lady ordered me, if any letters came for you, to deliver them to her.' 'And has there any come to me?' 'No, madam, word was always sent to Mr. Faulkland of your being so ill that to be sure he thought it would be in vain for him to write to you.'

This was all I could gather from the maid. What a night did I pass! I scarce closed my eyes. Ellen lay in a field-bed by me; she had watched several nights, and I obliged her now to undress and go into bed. She slept soundly; how I envied her tranquillity! If I forgot myself for a few minutes, my slumbers were distracted, and I started at the recollection of what I had already heard, and the dread of what I had *still* to hear. Mr. Faulkland absenting himself from the house so long; my mother wishing me in the grave, rather than be his wife; my brother denouncing vengeance on the *villain*! These were the terrible ideas that haunted me till morning. What can he have done? I cried aloud several times. I summoned to my aid all the fortitude I was mistress of, and resolved not to sink under the calamity, be it of what nature it would.

My mother, ever kind and tender, came early the next morning into my room. She enquired after my health, and looked as if she *pitied* me. I was ready to cry at her compassionate glances; they mortified me, but I was determined not to let her perceive it. I told her I was much better; and, what is surprising, I was really so, notwithstanding the uneasy state of my mind. She talked of indifferent things, and said, she hoped I should soon be able to go into the country for a few days, to recover a little strength. I answered, I hope so too, madam. We were both silent for a while; my mother had her indulgent eyes fixed upon me; mine were cast down: at last I resolved to speak out. Madam, said I, looking steadfastly at her, what is the cause of your coldness towards Mr. Faulkland? Its in vain for you to hide it longer; you say he is *well*, and gone out of town. If he has shewn any slight towards me, tell me so at once; and do not entertain so mean an opinion of your daughter, as to suppose she cannot bear the news. Your tenderness, I see, would conceal *something* from me; but believe me, madam, I am prepared for the worst.

My dear, replied my mother, it gives me great pleasure to hear you say so. I pray God preserve my child, and grant her a better lot than she could hope for in a union with Mr. Faulkland. What has he done, madam? My dearest Sidney, she answered, this is the first trial you have ever had of your patience; but I have no doubt that your goodness and discretion will teach you to act as becomes your character.

I did not intend to have spoken to you on the subject, till you were better able to bear the knowledge of what I am going to acquaint you with; but your prudence, I think, makes you equal to every thing; and I hope your health will not be endangered by the discovery of Mr. Faulkland's baseness. (What a dreadful preface!)

The day after you were taken ill, a letter, directed to you, was brought hither by a porter, which your maid (very discreetly) delivered to me. As you were not in a condition to read it yourself, I thought proper to open it. The cover contained a few lines addressed to you; and in it was inclosed a letter directed to Mr. Faulkland. Good God, added she, taking the papers out of her pocket, how little reliance ought we to have on a fair out-side!

Here are the letters; read what is in the cover first. I did so; it was ill writ, and worse spelt. These were the contents:

Madam,

I hear you are soon to be married to Mr. Faulkland; but as I think it a great pity that so virtuous a young Lady should be thrown away, this is to inform you, that he does not deserve you.

The inclosed letter, wrote to him by a fine and beautiful young lady that he decoyed, shews you how false he is. When you tax him with it, he will know from whence you got your information; but let him deny it if he can.

I am, madam,
Your unknown friend,
and humble servant.

The letter to Mr. Faulkland, in a very pretty female hand, and the date but a week old (from the time it was sent to me) was as follows:

'Oh! Mr. Faulkland, I am the most unfortunate woman in the world! Fatal have you been to me, and I am undone for ever. — I was in hopes that our mutual fault might have been concealed; for, while we stayed at Bath, I kept my aunt entirely ignorant of what passed between us, though she often pressed me to confess the truth; but it can now no longer be concealed. I am but too sensibly reminded of the unhappy consequences of my own weakness, and your ungoverned (would I could call it) love. I never meant to trouble you with complaints, but my present condition calls loudly for your compassion. Are you then really going to be married? There wants but this to complete my destruction! Oh! Sir, before it is too late, take pity on me! I dare not continue in the house with my uncle much longer. My aunt says, that, when my affliction becomes so conspicuous as not to be any longer hid, she will form a pretence, on account of my health, for me to be absent for some months, under colour of going to Bath, or to London, for better advice than I can have here. But what will this avail me? I have no relations, no friends, nor acquaintance, that I can trust with the secret of my miserable situation. To whom then can I fly, but to you, the cause of all my sorrow? I beseech you for heaven's sake, write to me, and tell me, if indeed you are going to give yourself away for ever! If you are, your intended bride, perhaps may have no other advantage of me, but what you in an evil hour deprived me of. Write to me, dear, though cruel as you are; and think of some place of refuge for your unhappy

A. B.'

When I had read these letters, my mother asked me, what I thought of Mr. Faulkland? Indeed, I was so astonished, that I scarce knew what answer to make; but replied, madam, are you satisfied that this letter is not forged, with a design to injure Mr. Faulkland? Ah! my dear, said she, I am sorry you strive to catch at so slender a twig; you may be sure I am but too well convinced that the letter is genuine, or you should never have had a moment's uneasiness by the knowledge of it. Mr. Faulkland himself does not deny it, and it is with his permission that I kept it. I promised to return it, but desired leave to retain it for a few days. He could not refuse me this, though he might easily imagine I designed to shew it to you. That, indeed, *was* my intention, when I desired to keep it a little while in my hands, and I did so, that I might have your judgment on the letter itself, as well as fully to justify my own proceedings in what I have done. Ah! dear madam, cried I, scarce knowing what I said, I rely on your maternal goodness; I am sure you have done what is proper. Yet has Mr. Faulkland nothing to say for himself? ——— But I will ask no more questions — I know too much already — My love, said my mother, you have a right to know every thing relative to this affair.

I shewed the letters to your brother, as soon as I received them. Sir George at first seemed quite confounded, but afterwards, to my very great surprize, he smiled and said, he knew of that foolish business before. I asked him if he knew of it before, how he could answer it to his honour, his conscience, or the love he ought to bear his sister, not to divulge it immediately? Why, said he, I assure you it is a *trivial* affair, that ought not to make you uneasy.

What, George! answered I, a trivial matter for a man to ruin a fine young lady, forsake her, and dare to involve an innocent creature in his crimes! Do you call this a *trivial* affair? If you knew the *circumstances*, said he, you would not view it in so disadvantageous a light. Faulkland certainly gained the affections of a young lady, though without seeking to do so; he never courted her, never attempted to please her, much less to win her heart, and least of all to ruin her virtue. I know that is an action he is not capable of committing. How comes it to pass then that he *did* so, said I, interrupting him? Why, the girl was silly, and she was thrown in his way by a vile designing woman that had the care of her. 'And was he (again stopping him) to take advantage of her folly, and join with that *vile designing* woman, to destroy a poor young creature's honour?' The *best* men, said he confidently, may fall into an error; and if you expect to find a man entirely free from them, you look for what is not possible in human nature.

I may expect to find a man without flagrant crimes to answer for, I hope; and I believe I spoke it with warmth. Do you call *this* one, madam? said he, with still more assurance: I hope Sidney will not be such a chit[6] as to think in this manner, when she comes to hear the affair explained. I really grew down-right angry, and could not forbear saying, I would rather see you married to your grave than to such a man. Your brother then begged I would hear Mr. Faulkland *justifi'd*, and be a little cool till that was done. I told him there was a terrible fact alledged, of which I could not conceive it possible for him to acquit himself.

George said, he had a letter to shew me on the subject, which he had received from Mr. Faulkland while he was at Bath, and which he was sure would convince me, that the whole affair was so trifling, it ought by no means to be objected to Mr. Faulkland, nor, in his opinion, even mentioned to him.

I told him, I was sorry to find that he and I thought so differently; for that I was determined to speak to Mr. Faulkland immediately about it, and, if he could not satisfy me entirely on the score of the injured lady, that he must never think of Sidney more.

Your brother said, that the letter which was sent to you had come from the revengeful dog who had robbed his master, and that he would give half his estate to have the villain punished as he deserved. Mr. Faulkland, it seems, had told him this himself. The fellow found it in the pocket-book which he had taken out of the escrutore,[7] and his disappointment, perhaps, at not getting a better booty (for he found but twenty moidores[8] besides) joined to his malice against his master, incited him to make the use he did of this letter. Now, continued my mother, though the fellow is undoubtedly a vile creature, yet, my dear, I think *we* are obliged to him for this discovery, providentially as it has come, to save you from what, in my opinion, would be the worst of misfortunes.

6. A silly young girl.
7. = escritoire, writing cabinet.
8. Portuguese gold coins.

The loss of this letter had alarmed Mr. Faulkland so much, that he put an advertisement into the papers next day, worded in so particular a manner, as shewed how very fearful he was of that letter's coming to light; for, no doubt, he suspected the man might make a dangerous use of it. The advertisement said, that if the servant, who had absconded from his master's house in St. James's Square the night before, would restore the papers which he took with him, they should be received without any questions being asked, and a reward of twenty guineas paid to any person who should bring them back. This advertisement, which, to be sure, the fellow either did not see at all, or had not time enough to avail himself of it, shews you to what sad resources people are driven, who, having done unwarrantable actions, are often in the power of the lowest wretches. I own this circumstance gave me a very ill impression of Mr. Faulkland. Your brother says, he remembers this man was one of the servants he took with him to Bath, and, without doubt, he knew of his amour. The advertisement has since been changed, by Sir George's advice. I find the man is named, his person described, and a reward of fifty pounds offered for the apprehending him; but I take it for granted he has got out of reach.

Though this little digression was very pertinent, I was impatient to know what had passed between my mother and Mr. Faulkland on the fatal subject, and could not forbear asking her.

I shall tell you, said she, in order. Your brother and I had some farther altercations; and indeed, my dear, it amazes me to find, that a young man, educated as Sir George was, in the early part of life, in the strictest principles of virtue, and the son of parents, who, thank God, always gave him the best example, should have so far deviated from the sober paths he was brought up in, as to treat the most glaring vices with a levity that shocked me. But, I suppose, the company he kept abroad, among whom this hypocrite Faulkland was his chief, has quite perverted him. He gave me the letter to read, which he had received from his friend whilst he was at Bath; and which, he said, was to convince me that it was such a *trifling* affair, that we ought not to take the least notice of it. And all his reason for this was, truly, because that loose man treats the subject as lightly as he does. I am afraid Sir George is no better than himself, or he would not have ventured to make him the confidant of his wild amours; and that at a time too when he was encouraged to address you. He tells him of a very pretty young lady (innocent he says too) that he got acquainted with, who came to Bath under the care of an aunt and uncle; he talks some idle stuff of avoiding her, when he found she liked him, and that the aunt (wicked woman!) contrived to leave them together one evening, when, I understand, the poor young creature fell into the snare that was prepared for her. For, would you believe it, my dear, the monstrous libertine, notwithstanding his pretences, owned that he had paid a price for the girl to her aunt. The betrayed creature herself knew not of this.

I own I had not patience to read the letter through. To say the truth, I but run my eye in a cursory manner over it; I was afraid of meeting, at every line, something offensive to decency. And *this* was the account, which, in your brother's opinion, was entirely to exculpate Mr. Faulkland. I think I never was so angry. I threw the letter to George with indignation, telling him, I was ashamed to find, that he, after knowing an incident of this kind, had so little regard to the honour of his sister, as to promote a marriage between her and such a rake. He answered, if I kept you unmarried till I found such a man as *I* should *not* call a rake, you were likely to live and die a maid. That for his part, he was very sorry, as well for Mr. Faulkland's sake as yours, he had ever proposed an union, which he found was likely to be overthrown by unseasonable scruples. And the gentleman, in a violent passion, flung out of the room, without deigning even to take up the letter, which had fallen on the floor.

I presume he went directly to his friend Faulkland, and told him all that had passed; for the plausible man came to me in the evening, and with looks, full of pretended sorrow, but *real* guilt, begged I would hear him on the subject of a letter which, he said, he found had unfortunately prejudiced me against him. To be sure he was prepared, and had, with George's help, contrived an artful story to impose on me. He took me unawares; but I was resolved not to give him the advantage of arguments, but proceed to ask him a few plain questions. I therefore cut him short at once, by saying, Mr. Faulkland, I am extremely concerned and shocked at what has happened; I will say but a few words to you; and desire to hear nothing more than answers to my questions: he bowed, and remained silent.

I then asked him, taking the young lady's letter

out of my pocket, whether that was from the same person, of whom he had written an account to my son whilst he was at Bath? He answered, it is, madam; and I hoped from that letter, which I find Sir George has shewn you, you would be induced to believe that I never formed a thought of injuring that young lady, till some unfortunate circumstances combined, and suddenly surprized me into the commission of a fault that has made us both unhappy. Sir, said I, I don't pretend to know people's hearts, I can only judge of them from their actions. You acknowledge that she was a fine young woman, and you believe innocent: What excuse can you offer for being her destroyer? Dear madam, don't use so severe an expression ——— Sir, I can use no other: how can you extenuate the fault, by which you merit so severe an appellation? To a lady of your rigid delicacy, madam, said he, perhaps what youth could offer, in extenuation of the fault, might appear but a weak plea: yet 'tis most certain, that I was surprized into the fatal error: I am under no promises, no ties, no engagements whatsoever to the lady. No ties, Sir! (interrupting him) is your own honour no tie upon you, supposing you free from any other obligation? You see the consequence of this fatal error, as you call it: here is a young person, of fashion, perhaps (I don't enquire who she is, but she seems to have had no mean education) who is likely to bring a child into the world, to the disgrace of herself and her family. On you, Sir, she charges her dishonour, and mentions your marrying another, as the blow which is to complete her ruin. Mr. Faulkland, is not all this truth? Be so good as to give me a direct answer. Madam, I cannot deny it; you have the proof of it in your hands: from all that appears to you, I am indeed very blameable; nay, I do not pretend to vindicate my folly; but, madam, do not aggravate my fault in your own thoughts, by considering the affair in a more unfavourable light than what even her letter puts it. I conjure you, madam, to suffer Sir George to be my advocate on this occasion; he is acquainted with every particular of the transaction, and can give you a detail that I will not presume to do. Be pleased, Sir, replied I, to tell me what you mean to do in regard to this lady? I mean to do all that I *can* do, answered he; I shall provide a place of retreat for her, where she will meet with the utmost care, tenderness, and respect; and where she may continue with privacy till she is in a condition to return home again to her friends. You may be sure, madam, as to the rest, I shall acquit myself consistently with honour. That is as much as to say, Sir, said I, that you will take care of the maintenance of your poor babe. He looked as if he had a mind to smile, forward man! but constrained it. Doubtless, madam, I shall do all that is now in my power to do, in every circumstance relating to her.

I felt myself exceedingly displeased with him; I was so disappointed in my opinion of him, that it increased my resentment. Sir, I proceeded, I must inform you, that there is as much *now* in your power as ever there was. You are still unmarried; the way is open to you to repair the mischief you have done: I will never bring down the curses of an injured maid upon my daughter's head, nor purchase her worldly prosperity at the expence of the shame and sorrow of another woman, for aught I know, as well born, as tenderly bred, and, till she knew you, perhaps as innocent as herself. For heaven's sake, madam! he cried, don't, don't, I beseech you, pronounce my fate so hastily — You must pardon me, Sir, said I, if I beg to hear no more on this subject. Sir George has already said every thing you could expect of your friend to say in your justification, and more than became him to utter. All I can find by either you or him, is, that you think the loss of honour to a young woman is a trifle, which a man is not obliged to repair, because truly he did not *promise* to do so. This young creature, I understand, is a gentlewoman, very charming in her person, by your own account; one who loves you tenderly, and will shortly make you a father. Is not all this so? I grant it, madam, said the criminal. Then, Sir, what reason can you urge in your conscience for not doing her justice? None — but your own inconstant inclinations, which happen now to be better pleased with another woman, whom, perhaps, you might forsake in a few months.

I cannot pretend to repeat to you all he said upon this last article: words of course you may be sure. He entreated, over and over again, that I would permit Sir George to plead for him. I told him, that after the facts he had granted, it was impossible that either he or Sir George could make the affair better; that I was very sorry to find myself disappointed in a person of whom I had conceived so high an opinion; and added, that as your illness made it very improper to let you know any thing of the matter for the present, I should take it as a favour if he would permit me to retain the lady's letter to him for a few days, or till you were in a condition to have the matter broke to you. In the mean while, I requested that he would dispense with my receiving any more visits from him.

He said some frantic things (for the man seems of a violent temper;) but finding me peremptory, took his leave with respect.

I understand from Sir George, that he flew directly down to Richmond, to a little house he has there, where he has remained ever since; but sends every day to enquire after your health. Sir George, I am sure, sees him often; for he frequently goes out early in the morning, and stays abroad till night. The increase of your illness, from the time I received the last visit from Mr. Faulkland, to such a degree as to alarm us for your life, I suppose, prevented your brother from reassuming the subject; though I can perceive he is full of anger and vexation on the occasion. You are now, my dear, God be praised, in a hopeful way of recovery, and I expect that George (who has, by espousing this man's interests so warmly, very much offended me) that George, I say, will renew his sollicitations in his favour. What do you say, my child? I should be glad to know your thoughts, with regard to the part I have acted, as well as with respect to Mr. Faulkland's conduct.

Shall I own my weakness to you, my dear Cecilia? I was ready to melt into tears; my spirits, exhausted by sickness, were not proof against this unexpected blow; a heavy sigh burst from my heart, that gave me a little relief. You know my mother is rigid in her notions of virtue; and I was determined to shew her that I would endeavour to imitate her. I therefore suppressed the swelling passion in my breast, and, with as much composure as I could assume, told her, I thought she acted as became her; and that, with regard to Mr. Faulkland, my opinion of his conduct was such, that I never desired to see him more. This answer, dictated perhaps by female pride (for I will not answer for the feelings of my heart at that instant) was so agreeable to my mother, that she threw her arms about my neck, and kissed me several times; blessing, and calling me by the most endearing names at every interval. Her tenderness overcame me; or, to deal with sincerity, I believe I was willing to make it an excuse for weeping. Oh! my dear mother, cried I, I have need of your indulgence; but indeed your goodness quite over-powers me. My dear love, said she, you deserve it all, and more than it is in your mother's power to shew you. What a blessed escape have you had, my sweet child, of that wild man! Little did I think, my Sidney, when I told you the story of my first disappointment, that a case so parallel would soon be your own. With respect to you and me indeed, the incidents are nearly alike; but there is a wide difference between the two men. My lover had the grace to repent, and would have returned to his first engagements, if a dreadful malady had not overtaken him; but this graceless Faulkland persists in his infidelity, and would make you as culpable as himself. I own to you, daughter, that the recollection of that melancholy event which happened to me, has given me a sort of horror at the very thoughts of an union between you and Mr. Faulkland. You remember the sad consequences which I related to you of an infidelity of this kind; the poor forsaken woman died of grief, and the dishonest lover ran mad. Think of this, my child, and let it encourage you to banish such an unworthy man from your heart. I was afraid your regard for him might make this a difficult task; but I rejoice to find your virtue is stronger than your passion. *I* loved as well as you, but I overcame it when I found it a duty to do so; and I see your mother's example is not lost upon you.

The honest pride that my mother endeavoured to inspire me with, had a good effect, and kept up my spirits for a time.

She told me, she was sure that Sir George would quarrel with us both, when we came to talk upon the subject of the marriage; but she was entirely easy as to that, now she knew that my sentiments corresponded with her own.

You know my mother has ever been despotic in her government of me; and had I even been inclined to dissent from her judgment in a matter of this importance, it would have been to no purpose; but this was really far from my thoughts.

I was as much disgusted with Mr. Faulkland as she was, and as heartily pitied the unhappy young creature whom he had undone.

You may recollect, my dear, that my mother, tho' strictly nice in every particular, has a sort of partiality to her own sex, and where there is the least room for it, throws the whole of the blame upon the *man*'s side; who, from her own early prepossessions, she is always inclined to think are deceivers of women. I am not surprized at this bias in her; her early disappointment, with the attending circumstances, gave her this impression. She is warm, and sometimes *sudden*, in her attachments; and yet it is not always difficult to turn her from them. The integrity of her own heart makes her liable to be imposed on by a plausible outside; and yet the dear good woman takes a sort of pride in her sagacity. She had admired and esteemed Mr. Faulkland prodigiously; her vexation was the greater, in finding her expectations disappointed; and could I have been so unjust to the pretensions of another, or so indelicate in regard to myself, as to have overlooked Mr. Faulkland's fault, I knew my mother would be inflexible. I therefore resolved in earnest to banish him from my thoughts. I found my mother was mightily pleased with her own management of the conversation she had held with Mr. Faulkland. I think I talked pretty *roundly* to him, said she; but there was no other way; he is an artful man, and I was resolved not to let him wind me about. He would make a merit of having *formed no designs* upon the young lady; why, possibly, he did not, till he found the poor soul was so smitten with him, that he thought she would be an easy prey. Sir George impudently insinuated, that a man *must* not reject a lady upon these occasions. I was ashamed to hint to Mr. Faulkland at the circumstance of his having actually paid a price for the girl; it was too gross; and I think, had I mentioned it, must have struck him dumb: though very likely he might have had some subterfuge, even for that aggravating part of the story.

How I am shock'd, my Cecilia, to think of this! I was glad my mother had spared his confusion on this particular; for though probably, as she observed, he had come prepared with some evasion to this charge, yet what a mean figure must a man make, who is reduced to disingenuous shifts, to excuse or palliate an action, despicable as well as wicked!

My brother came in, during our discourse, to ask me how I did. My mother answered his question before I had time to speak. She is pretty well, thank God! and not likely to break her heart, though she *knows* your friend Mr. Faulkland's story (and she spoke it scornfully.) My brother said, Sidney, Are *you* as averse to Mr. Faulkland as my mother is? I replied, brother, I wonder you can ask me that question, after what you have been just now told. I always said, answered he, that you did not know the value of the man, and now I am convinced of it. I wish he had never seen you! I wish so too, said I. Sir George walked about the room, and seemed vexed to death. For Heaven's sake, madam, (turning to my mother) now my sister is tolerably recovered, suffer her to see Mr. Faulkland; let her hear what he has to say in his own vindication: I think you may trust to her honour, and her discretion; and if the affair appears to her in so heinous a light as it does to you, I will be contented to give Mr. Faulkland up; but don't shut your own ears, and your daughter's too, against conviction.

Sir, you are disrespectful, said my mother angrily. Dear brother, I cried, I beg you will spare me on this subject; my mother *has* given me leave to judge for myself; she has repeated all that you have said, and all that Mr. Faulkland has been able to urge on the occasion; and I am sorry to tell you, that I think myself bound never to have any farther correspondence with him; therefore you must excuse me for not seeing him. And so the match is broke off, cried Sir George. *It is*, said my mother peremptorily. It is, echoed I faintly. Why then, replied Sir George, (and he swore), you will never get such another whilst you live. A pretty figure you'll make in the world, when you give it for a reason that you refused *such* a man, after every thing was concluded upon, because truly you found that he had had an intrigue! Why, Sidney, you'll be so laugh'd at! He addressed himself to me, though I knew he meant the reproof for my mother. Sir, answered she, neither your sister nor I shall trouble ourselves much about the opinion of people who *can* laugh at such things. You may put the matter into as ridiculous a light as you please; but this was no common intrigue; you *know* it was not, however you may affect to speak of it. I don't suppose *any* of you are *Saints*, but, I trust in Heaven, some are better than others. Oh! madam, madam, said my brother, if you knew the world as well as *I* do, you would think that Mr. Faulkland is one of the best. God forbid! my mother answered coolly. Well, well, madam, cried Sir George, I see it is to no purpose to argue; there are many families of more consequence than ours, and ten times the fortune, that will be very proud of Faulkland's alliance; and will hardly make it an objection to him, that he was led into a foolish scrape by the wickedness of one woman, and the folly of another. If you make my sister wait for a husband, till you find a man who never offended in that way, I think, mother, you had better take a little boy from his nurse, breed him up under your own eye, and by the time Sidney is a good motherly gentlewoman, you may give her the baby to make a play-thing of. For my own part, I am heartily sorry I ever interfered. — People of such nice scruples had better chuse for themselves; but I cannot help thinking, that both Faulkland and I are very ill used. I told you (said my mother to me) how he would behave. Sir George, I desire you will not distress your sister thus (she saw me sadly cast down: I was ill and weak:) if you have no respect for *me*, have a little tenderness for her. ——— I beg your pardon, child, said he, I did not mean to distress you, I pity *you*, indeed Sidney. I could have cried at his using that expression, it humbles one so. Madam (to my mother,) you shall be troubled no farther by my friend or myself; all I shall say is this, that whenever my sister gets a husband of your ladyship's chusing, I wish he may have half the worth of the poor rejected Faulkland.

My brother left the room with these words. My mother was downright in a passion, but soon cooled on his withdrawing.

My spirits were quite fatigued; and my mother left me, that I might take a little rest.

What a strange alteration have a few days produced! our domestic peace broke in upon by the unlucky difference between my mother and my brother. My near prospect of ——— of ——— oh! let me be ingenuous, and say Happiness, vanished — Poor Mr. Faulkland! *Poor* do I call him? for shame, Sidney — but let the word go; I will not blot it. Mr. Faulkland forbid the house, myself harrassed by a cruel disorder, and hardly able to crawl out of bed. All this has fallen on me within these last fourteen black days. Then I dread the going abroad, or seeing company, I shall look so silly; for the intended wedding began to be talked of; — and the curiosity of people to know the cause of it's being broke off ——— What wild guesses will be made by some, and what lies invented by others! Then the ill-natured mirth of one half of the girls of my acquaintance, and the *as* provoking condolements of the other half ——— I am fretted at the thoughts of it — but it cannot be helped; I must bear it all ——— I wish I were well enough to get into the country, to be out of the reach of such impertinence.

I long to know who this ill-fated girl is, that has been the cause of all this. *A gentlewoman, and very pretty; one that loves Mr. Faulkland, and will shortly make him a parent.* Thus my mother described her to Mr. Faulkland, and he assented to it. Oh! fie, fie, Mr. Faulkland, how could you be so cruel to *her*? How could you use *me* so ill? and Sir George knew of all this, and makes light of it! it is a strange story! My mother is severe in her virtue, but she is in the right ——— My brother would sacrifice every consideration to aggrandize his family ——— To make a purchase of the unhappy creature, and that without her knowledge too, it is horrid! Away, away from my thoughts, thou vile intruder ——— Return to your Bath mistress, she has a better right to you than I have; she implores your pity; she has no refuge but you; and she may be every way preferable to me ——— I wish I knew her name, but what is it to me; *mine* will never be Faulkland, *hers* ought. Perhaps Mr. Faulkland may be induced to marry her, when he sees her in her present interesting situation. He says he will provide a retreat for her; to be sure he will have the compassion to visit her: and then who knows what may happen? If I know my own heart, I think I do most sincerely wish he may make her his wife; but then I would not chuse to have it known suddenly; that might look as if he forsook me for her. *That,* I own, would a little hurt my pride. I wish not the truth to be known, for Mr. Faulkland's sake; but then I should not like to have a slur thrown on me.

I will add no more to this, but send the packet off at all events; I think it will find you at Paris....

[Married to the dull and unfaithful Mr. Arnold, the heroine begins to learn the truth about the woman, Miss Burchell, whom she has compelled her admirer to marry. This passage marks the beginning of the heroine's questioning of her behaviour and her troubled progress towards self-knowledge, by means of which Frances Sheridan explores the role eighteenth-century society imposed on women.]

October 29 [1706]. — Ah, my Cecilia, what an aggravation is here to the already too deep regret I began to feel on Mr. Faulkland's account! His triumph over me is now complete!

In sorting my mother's papers (as I am to leave these lodgings to-morrow) I found that letter which Mr. Faulkland wrote to my brother from Bath. You may remember I told you my mother had, in her resentment, flung it to Sir George, and that, as it happened to fall on the ground, he had quitted the room in a passion without taking it up. My mother, I suppose, when she cooled, laid it by, though I dare say she never looked into it afterwards. Read it, and see by what a fatality we have been governed.

Mr. Faulkland's letter to Sir George Bidulph.

Bath, May 9, 1703.

How you mortify me, my dear Bidulph, when you tell me of the happiness I lose by staying so long at Bath! *The ladies are impatient to see me,* say you? Ah! Sir George, thou hast spoke better of me than I deserve, I fear.

I am sadly out of humour with myself at present. I have got into a very foolish sort of a scrape here. My wrist is quite well, and I should have thrown myself at Miss Bidulph's feet before now, but to tell you a secret, my virtue not being proof against temptation, I have been intercepted.

'Tis but a slight lapse, however, a flying affair; neither my honour, nor my heart in the question. A little vagrant Cupid has contented himself with picking my pocket, just lightly fluttering through my breast, and away.

Are you fallen so low as that, Faulkland, say you? to *buy* the favour of the fair? No, George, no; not quite so contemptible as that neither: and yet, faith, I did *buy* it too, for it cost me three hundred pounds; but the lady to whom I am obliged knows nothing of this part of her own history; at least, I hope so, for my credit sake. The case in short is this: an old gouty officer, and his wife (a very notable dame; a fine woman too) happened to lodge in the same house with me. The man came hither to get rid of his aches; the lady of her money, and her virtue, if she has any, for she is eternally at the card tables.

Under the conduct of this hopeful guide, came a niece of the husband's; an extremely fine girl, innocent too, I believe, and the best dancer I ever saw. I don't know how it happened, but she took a fancy to me, which, upon my word, and I am sure you have no doubts of me, I was far from wishing to improve. You know I always despise the mean triumph of gaining a heart, for which I could not give another in return. I saw with pain her growing inclination for me; but as we lived in the same house, and met every day in the rooms, it was impossible for me to avoid her as much as I wished to do. The aunt I found, had her eyes upon me, and took some pains to promote a liking on my side. I saw her design, and was so much upon my guard, that she, who I soon found was an adept in love-matters, almost despaired of gaining her ends. The young lady's inclination however seemed to increase; a pair of fine blue eyes told me so every day; and I was upon the point of flying to avoid the soft contagion, when an accident happened that totally overthrew all my good resolutions.

I had not seen the young lady for two or three days; I enquired for her, and her aunt answered, with a mysterious smile. She is ill, poor thing, why don't you look in upon her, and ask her how she does? I replied, if the lady will permit me, I will do myself that honour, and intended literally to have kept my word, by just asking her at her chamber door how she did.

You are very cruel, said the aunt; would you persuade me that you don't know the girl is in love with you? Oh, your Servant, Madam; if you think me vain, I thank you for the reprimand. Come, come, said she, this is all affectation, we'll drink tea with her this evening. Upon my word, said I, if I am to believe what you say, I think you ought not to desire me. I am not blind to the young lady's merit, but am so unfortunate as not to have it in my power to make such returns as she deserves. I found the occasion required my being serious.

If you have not love, said she, you may at least have a little complaisance. Was there ever such a barbarian, not to go and see a woman that is dying for him? I promised to bring you, and she expects you. What is the pretty creature afraid of (patting my cheek). I'll stay by it all the while. There was no withstanding this; I promised to wait on her.

She knocked at my door about six o'clock, and looking in, asked if the coy Narcissus[9] was ready? I went with her, and she led me directly to her niece's chamber. The young lady looked pale and languishing, but very pretty. I was really grieved to see her, and enquired with an unaffected concern after her health. The tea-things were set, and I tried to force something like conversation, but I believe I was rather formal.

When we had done tea, the aunt looked at her watch, started off her chair, said she had outstaid her appointment with the party she was to meet at cards, and turning to me, I hope, Sir, you will have the *Charity* to stay with my niece; and then hurried out of the room. I begged leave to hand her to her chair, intending to take that opportunity of slipping away, and resolved to quit the house the next morning. But the determined gipsey was prepared for this motion, and insisting that I should not stir,

9. In Greek myth, a youth who fell in love with his own reflection.

thrust me back from the door, which she shut, and flew down stairs.

What was to become of me now, George? My situation was dangerous, and really critical. To be short, I forgot my prudence, and found the young lady's heart too, too tender.

I never felt remorse before. I never had cause. I accuse myself of indiscretion, but I have not the aggravating addition to my fault of oaths and promises to fly in my face. I made none — love, foolish love did all, and led a willing victim to his altar, who asked nothing in return for the sacrifice she offered; and received nothing but unavailing repentance on my side.

I know not any thing now that would give me so much pleasure as to find that the girl hated me heartily, though I have given her no cause.

A just reparation I cannot make her. Every thing forbids that thought. I do not consider myself as free; but if I were so, I am not a seducer, and therefore do not think myself bound to carry my penitence to such lengths. The damned aunt has been the serpent. And here let me explain to you what I call buying the lady's favour. You must know the aunt one night, (the greatest part of which she had spent at hazard)[10] lost two hundred pounds; at least she told me so the next morning, and with tears in her eyes besought me, in the most earnest manner, to lend her that sum. She said, she should be undone if her husband were to know it, and that she would pay me in a very few days, as she had as much due to her from different people who had lost to her at play. Though our short acquaintance could hardly warrant her making such a request, I nevertheless did not hesitate, but gave her the money directly. She meant indeed to pay me, but it was in a different coin, and this I suppose was the price she set on the unhappy girl's honour.

My reflections on this unlucky affair make me very grave. I have explained my situation to the young lady, and expressed my concern at not having it in my power to be any other than a friend to her. She blames her own weakness, and her aunt's conduct, but does not reproach me. She cannot with justice, yet I wish she would, for then I should reproach myself less.

'Tis a foolish business, and I must get off as handsomely as I can. Prithee, Bidulph, say something to encourage me, and put me into more favour with myself. You have often been my confessor, but I never wanted absolution so much as now; nor ever was so well entitled to it, for I am really full of penitence, and look *so* mortified, you would pity me. I am ashamed of having been surprised into a folly; I who *ought* to have been upon my guard, knowing the natural impetuosity of my temper.

I must not conclude without telling you, that this very morning, the precious aunt, instead of paying me the two hundred pounds she had of me before, very modestly requested I would oblige her with another hundred, to redeem a pair of diamond earrings which she had been obliged to part with for the supply of some other necessary demands; and with abundance of smooth speeches, she assured me, in a fortnight she would pay me all together, having notes to that value which would then become due to her. I was such a booby as to give it to her. — Why, fare it well! I never expect to see a shilling of it. She thinks, perhaps, there is value received for it. Vile woman! The affair fortunately for us all, has not taken wind; and for me, the names of both aunt and niece, may ever stand enrolled amongst those of chaste matrons and virgins. The family quits this place soon, as the old gentleman is better.

I thank you for your care, in relation to my house. I hope to take possession of it in a week or ten days; you are very good in fixing me so near yourself. Adieu.

I am, &c.

What do you think of this letter, my Cecilia, written in confidence to my brother? Mr. Faulkland could not conceive it probable that any body but Sir George should ever see it; he had no reason therefore to gloss over any of the circumstances, *Had* I seen it but in time — Oh what anguish of heart might we all have been spared! Miss Burchell singly as she *ought,* would have borne the punishment of her folly.

My mother had not patience to read this letter through; nice and punctilious as her virtue was, she passed a censure on the crime in gross, without admitting any palliating circumstance. But I blame her not; the excellence of her own morals, made her scrupulous in weighing those of others; she read the letter in a cursory way, and it is plain but half of it; prepossessed as she was before, by knowing the material point.

The account was given with levity at the *first* mention of the young lady. Then she understood he

10. A dice game.

had *bought* her of her aunt; there is a paragraph which *looks* like it, and to be sure she attended not to the explanation. Fatal oversight! she read not far enough to have this matter cleared up. She took nothing but the bare facts into her account. A young lady dishonoured, her disgrace likely to be public, then her tenderness for the man who had undone her, and that man rejecting her, and on the point of marrying another. These were the only points of view in which my mother beheld the story. Her justice, her humanity, and her religion prompted her to act as she did; and her conduct stands fully acquitted to my judgment, though my heart must upon this full conviction of Mr. Faulkland's honour, sigh at recollecting the past.

I know that the memory of my mother's own first disastrous love wrought strongly on her mind. She was warm in her passions, liable to deep impressions, and always adhered strictly to those opinions she first imbibed. Her education had been severe and recluse; and she had drawn all her ideas of mankind from her own father and mine, who, I have been told, were both men of exemplary lives. From all these considerations, I must again say, that I entirely acquit my dear mother, in regard to her whole conduct, however I have suffered by it....

HENRY BROOKE

(*c.* 1703–83)

from:
THE FOOL OF QUALITY;
OR, THE HISTORY OF HENRY, EARL OF MORELAND (1765-70)

[The 'Preface', like the novel's second chapter, shows Brooke's peculiar fusion of a Rousseau-inspired concern with education, religious enthusiasm, and a playful conception of novelistic form, heavily influenced by Laurence Sterne's *Tristram Shandy.* Though Brooke's sentiment can seem excessive to a modern reader, the book was enormously admired by, among others, John Wesley, the founder of Methodism, who produced a very successful abridged version of it, and, in the nineteenth century, by the clergyman and novelist, Charles Kingsley, who thought that readers might learn from the book 'more which is pure, sacred, and eternal, than from any which has been published since Spenser's Fairy Queen'.]

PREFACE

I Hate Prefaces. I never read them, and why should I write them? They stand like Pales[1] about a Park, I always overleap 'em, if I am told there is any thing, within, worth seeing. But, what can I do? I am likely to lead a fine Life with this Performance, when People begin to quarrel with me, upon reading the first Word, of the first Page, of my Works.

This Friend, and that Friend, and t'other Friend asks me, and here sits Another, who is mighty curious to know, why I entitle my Hero the FOOL OF QUALITY.

Pray, was it not more decent to impute Folly to one Man, than to Mankind, if I found myself under the Necessity of doing the One or the Other?

Perhaps I call him a Fool, in Complaisance to a World that will, certainly, honour him with the same Title, when they find his Wisdom of a Size not suited to their Own —— Why, pray, what is Wisdom? — Tell me, first, what is Folly? I will, then, tell you what is Wisdom, if I find any Smattering of it in your Definition.

I wonder, was there ever an Age of Wisdom, or a Land of Wisdom? — Look about You. The World will answer for Itself. — Does not every Age and Nation grow wiser and wiser? And have not all Fathers, from the Flood downward, been accounted, no better than Fools, by their Posterity? — I wish I had not been born for some Centuries to come. What a Prodigy of Wisdom should I then be, in comparison of what I am, at this Day.

Indeed, I should be glad to be wise, if I thought I could get any thing by It. — Right, that is all the Use that the World makes of It; it is the very End, Purpose, Goal, and Business of all the Wisdom

1. fencing.

upon Earth. — If a Man has Length enough of Sense to outreach all about him, by a Yard and a Half; He is, by a Yard and Half, wiser than all his Neighbours.

But, was not *Solomon* then a Fool to neglect Riches,[2] which he might have had with a Wish: and to ask for Wisdom, whose only Use is the obtaining of Riches? Was not this wishing to mend a round-about Road, when a Quarter of an Hour would have carried him, by a short Cut, to the End of his Journey? — I fancy, my dear Friend, it would be no great Matter of additional Burden to take the Folly of *Solomon* upon your own Shoulders. For, in case he had taken the Riches, how the pox should he keep them, while any neighbouring Power was wiser than himself?

Paris was not five Years younger than *Solomon*, when he, also, might have chosen either Riches or Wisdom, and yet preferred a pretty Wench to the One and to the Other.[3] I am not so young as *Paris*, by five times five Years, and would, therefore, prefer the One or the Other to the Wench — You then allow that *Paris* was a Blockhead in the present Case — Sir, I allow any Man to be so, in every Case, where he happens to differ in Opinion from myself — Why pray, sage Sir, have You got all the Wisdom of the World to yourself, or what Quantity thereof, think you, may there be upon Earth? — Less, by five Scruples, than any Man in judiciary Robes and a full bottom'd Wig, conceives to have fallen to his own Share. — But Folly you take to be multiplied and various — Of two Sorts, quoth an eminent Author, That which belongs to the Writer, and That which belongs to the Reader of these Works.

Sir, this is wild Discourse, and very wide from the Purpose. Let me tell you the World was never so wise as now. It is filled with Men of deep Erudition, and Science — True, my Monitor, but are they a Jot the wiser for all their Knowledge?

At the Rate that you talk, in the Times of ancient Ignorance, there might have been a competent Modicum of wise Folk in the World — possible — And, by the same Rule, in these our enlightened Days of Connoissieurship and Erudition, nearly, all our Literati may turn out Fools — more than probable — These are Riddles — that might be solved — Explain 'em, I beseech you — Not at present. I will tell you a Story and pray listen. It is worth the hearing.

Fifty and five Pilgrims met, one Evening, at a great Inn, that led to more Roads than there are Points in the Compass. They supped merrily together, in a large Hall; and found, upon enquiry, that they were, all, bound to the *Castle of final Repose*, appointed for the Reception of the Sons of Science. When the Cloth was removed, Gentlemen, quoth the Pilgrim who first entered, I rejoice to be joined, by so much good Company, on these my honourable Travels; and, I am still better pleased to have it in my Power to conduct every Man of ye, the shortest and surest Way, to your Journey's End. Here, Gentlemen, here is my Map of infallible Directions, the most accurate Extract, that ever was taken, of all Inquiries, Observations, and Informations for the Nonce.[4] Pardon me, Brother, said the Pilgrim who sat next, your Map must be erroneous by, at least, five Degrees; by five, did I say? by seven, as I hope to get to my Journey's End. Look here at my Map, and believe your own Eyes. I'll be damned, cried a third Pilgrim, (peering over the Maps of his Neighbours, and taking out his own Parchment) I'll be damned if the Geographers, who designed the one or the Other, were any better than Adventurers; They never reached the Place of Destination I'll be sworn. Gentlemen, said a Fourth, with wonderful good Temper, I do not swear; but I have, critically, remarked all the Charts produced. There's a blind Beggar, in our Town, who is led by his Dog, and if he does not arrive at the Place we are bound to, with better Speed, and greater Certainty, than any of you Three, I give myself, do you see, and all my Goods to the Devil, save a small Perpetuity, in Remainder, to my Son. That may be, exclaimed a Fifth, but, look ye here, my Friends, here are the Quotations, here are the Authorities. Authorities! quoth a Sixth, a Fiddlestick for a Hobby! are they unquestionable, unassailable, like these in my Hand? Thus, every Man's Chart, throughout the Fifty and Five, was, like the Hand of the Son of *Hagar*,[5] against the Chart of every Man. Each insisted on being accompanied, in his own Way, as a Matter of mere

2. The story of Solomon's choice of wisdom over riches or the lives of his enemies is told in I Kings 3. 5-15 and II Chronicles 1. 1-12.
3. In Greek myth, Paris chose Aphrodite as more beautiful than Hera or Athena in order to obtain Helen, promised him by Hermes; the story is very similar to that of Solomon's choice.
4. for the particular purpose.
5. Hagar, the handmaid of Sarah, bore Sarah's husband, Abraham, a son of whom the Angel of the Lord said (in part): 'And he will be a wild man; his hand will be against every man, and every man's hand against him' (Genesis 16.12).

Charity to all the rest. They set out, the next Morning, on as many different Roads as there were Persons at Table; and, yet, no One of them ever arrived at the Place proposed, if any Dependance may be had on those customary Posts, whom the World, from Age to Age, has paid for Intelligence.

I don't clearly apprehend the Application of your Story. — If that is not your Fault, it must be my Own. It is at least a Dozen of the Twelve Labours[6] to beat any thing into the Head of some People. — I will give you the Chance of another Tale.

A certain Prince sent an Invitation, to two distant Personages, to come to his Court. He, further, sent such Directions as could not be mistaken by any One, living, who was willing to find the Way. And he, further, sent a written Promise, signed, and sealed by the Seal royal, of the most happy Accommodations, upon their Arrival.

The One, of the Parties invited, was a purblind Man, who, barely, saw sufficient to discern his Road. He, accordingly, was fearful of Error. He cautiously held on his Way; and, thereby, reached his Journey's End, the Place of happy Destination to which he was appointed.

The other was a Man who had all his Eyes about him; but, he was a Genius, had vast Invention, and thought it a Disparagement to tread in any Path that had been beaten by others. He was for contriving short Cuts, and opening new Discoveries. He made Excursions on all Hands. He grew impatient of the Accommodations, appointed and reserved for him, at the Court of the Prince. He expected them on his Journey, and sought for them at every Turn. He found them not. He, therefore, travelled and strayed this way, and that way, in Search of them. This led him, still, further and further from his Road. Till, maimed by Accident, and stiff with Age, he grew, equally, ashamed and unable to return.

— As plain as my Nose — You can the readier follow — But, talk to me, no more, about the World and its Wisdom. I detest Wisdom, I avoid it, I would not be bit by it. It is the *Tarantula* that spins a Web, whereby Innocence is entangled. It is a Politician who opens a Gulph for the swallowing up of a People. It is a Lawyer who diggs a Grave for the Burial of Equity. It is the Science, of *Hocus Pocus,* that bids Happiness come and pass, by the Virtue of Cups and Balls. It is a Syllabub of fasting-Spittle for the Fattening of the *Virtuosi.*[7]

It is a Robe with a pompous Train. A Wig spread to the Rump. A Beard lengthened to the Girdle. It is a Ditch of Puddle, with a hoary Mantle, that will not be moved to Merriment by any Wind that blows. It is an Ass in a Sumpter-Cloth.[8] An Owl, solemnly perched, amidst solemn Ruins, on a solemn Night.

Descend to me, sweet Folly! if thou hast not, as I suspect, been my constant Companion. Be, thou, my Sister, my Playfellow, thou Kitten of the solemn Cats of State and Learning. But, no. Thou never wert the Offspring of such stupid Progenitors. Thou art ever joyous, ever young, although coeval, in Paradise, with our first Parents, ere, (a Pox upon their Ambition) they wished for the Knowledge of Good and Evil. Pride pretends to spurn thee; Science affects to look down upon thee; but they sigh for thee when no one sees, they have frowned thee away, and when they seek they shall not find thee. Come, Folly! for even thy Petulance and little Wickednesses become delightful, when thou incitest the yearling Kids and cooing Turtles to Combat. Thou art not captious, thou art not testy, they laugh at thee, and thou laughest with them for Company. The Hours dance before thee, the Graces smile in thy Train. Thou art a Companion for Conquerors, a Play-fellow for crowned Heads. But, alas! thou art not respected, as heretofore; when the Monarch of all Asia sent his Ambassadors to wait upon thee, they came, with a mighty Train, even from *Persepolis* into *Laconia,* to see thee riding upon Switches, with *Agesilaus* and his little Son.[9]

By — my pleasant Friend, thou almost persuadest me to be a Fool, during the Remainder of my Pilgrimage through the Wisdom of this World. But, is there no such thing as true Wisdom in Nature? — Sir, I have written a whole Chapter upon the Subject; but it lies a great way on, toward the End of my Book, and you have much Folly to wade through, before you come at it. — Give me a Peep, I beseech you. — No, Sir, you shall not

6. i.e. the labours of Hercules.

7. Compare the learned nonsense in this paragraph with parts of Swift's *A Tale of a Tub* and Sterne's *Tristram Shandy*.

8. A cloth to protect a pack-ass from his burden.

9. Agesilaus II (444-360 B.C.), king of Sparta (or Laconia), received numerous embassies from the Persian monarch, Artaxerxes II; the story of Agesilaus riding a stick and playing horse with his children is told by Plutarch in his 'Life' of Agesilaus, XXV.

anticipate. Do you Want to be in Port, without making any Voyage? — If I must win my way to Wisdom, Inch by Inch, let me set out directly. — Here then, begin. And pray, let me have your Remarks, unpremeditated, as you proceed. I will answer you, as Whim or Judgment shall happen to dictate.

[Unlike his cossetted elder brother, Dick, the hero, Harry, has been sent out from his family to a foster-home for four years. On his return, he strikes Dick, in defence of his nurse or 'mammy', and is promptly sent back by his enraged mother. On his way, he meets a stranger.]

CHAPTER II

The old Gentleman turned and gazed at the Child, as on some sudden Apparition. His Tears stopped. He returned the Picture, which he held, into his Bosom. And, lifting up his Eyes, Great Power, he cried, is this the One, of all the World, who has any Feelings for me? Is it this Babe, this Suckling, whom thou hast sent, to be a Partaker in my Griefs, and the Sharer of my Afflictions? Welcome, then, my little Friend, said he, tenderly turning and caressing the Child, I will live the longer for thy Sake, and endeavour to repay the Tears thou hast shed in my Behalf.

The Language of true Love is understood by all Creatures, and was that of which *Harry* had, almost, the only Perception. He returned his Friend's Caresses with unaffected Ardour, and no Two could be more highly gratified in the Endearments of each Other.

What is your Name, my Dear? said the old Gentleman. *Harry Clinton,* Sir. *Harry Clinton!* repeated the Old Man, and started. And pray who is your Father? The Child, then looking tenderly at him, replied; I'll have you for a Father, if you please, Sir. The Stranger, then caught him up in his Arms, and passionately exclaim'd, You shall, you shall, my Darling, for the tenderest of Fathers, never to be torn asunder, till Death shall part us.

Then asking him where he lived, and *Harry* pointing to the Town before them, they both got up and went towards it. Our Hero was now again all Glee, all Action; he sprung from and to his Friend, and play'd and gambol'd about him, like a young Spaniel in a Morning, just loos'd from his Chain, and admitted to accompany his Master to the Field. As his two Dogs frisked about him, he would now mount upon One, then bound upon t'other, and each pranced and paraded under him as delighted with the Burden. The old Gentleman beheld all with a Pleasure that had long been a Stranger to his Breast, and shared in the Joys of his young Associate.

Being arrived near the Farm House, Nurse, who stood at the Door, saw them approaching, and cried out, *Gaffer, Gaffer,* here comes our *Harry* with the dumb Gentleman. When they were come up, Good People, says the Stranger, is this your Child! No, no, Sir, answered the Nurse, we are but his Fosterers. And, pray, who is his Father? He is second Son, Sir, to the Earl of *Moreland.* The Earl of *Moreland*! you amaze me greatly, is this all the Notice and Care they take of such a Treasure? Sir, replied the Nurse, they never sent for him but once; they don't mind him, they take him for a Fool. For a Fool? cried he, and shook his Head in Token of Dissent. I am sure he has the wisest of all human Hearts. I wish it may be so, Sir, said the Nurse, but he behaved very sadly, some Time ago, at the great House. She then made a Recital of all our young Hero's Adventures in the Mansion-Parlour; whereat the old Gentleman inwardly chuckled, and, for the first Time, of some Years, permitted his Features to relax into a Smile of Chearfulness.

Nurse, said he, every Thing that I hear and see of this Child serves the more to endear and bind me to him. Pray, be so good as to accompany us to my House, we will try to equip him better both as to Person and Understanding.

As this Stranger's Seat made Part of the Village, they were soon there. He first whispered his old Domestic, who, then, looked upon the Child with Surprise and Pleasure. The Footman was next sent to bring the Taylor, and some light Stuffs from the Town Shop. Matters being thus dispatched, with respect to our Hero's first Coat and Britches,[10] Nurse was kept to Dinner; and after this Gentleman had entertained his young Guest with a Variety of little Tricks, childish Plays, and other Fooleries, toward Evening, he dismissed him and his Nurse, with a Request that she would send him every Day, and a Promise that he should be returned every Night if she desired it.

Harry, being thus furnished with the external

10. Breeching was an important rite of passage in the eighteenth century, marking the moment when education for adulthood began.

Tokens of a Man Child, having been born into the World, became an inseparable Friend and Play-fellow to his Patron. At Times of Relaxation, the old Gentleman, with the most winning and insinuating Address, endeavoured to open his Mind and cultivate his Morals, by a thousand little Fables, such as of bold Sparrows, and naughty Kids, that were carried away by the Hawk, or devoured by the Wolf, and of good Robbins, and innocent Lambs, that the very Hawks and Wolves themselves were fond of. For he never proposed any Encouragement or Reward to the Heart of our Hero, save that of the Love and Approbation of Others. At the Times of such Instruction, *Harry,* who knew no other Dependance, and beheld his Patron as his Father and as his God, would hang upon his Knee, look up to his Face, delighted, and greedily imbibe the Sweetness of those Lessons whose Impressions neither Age, nor any Occurrence, could ever after erase: so prevalent are the Dictates of Lips that are beloved.

At other Times, the Stranger would enter, with our Hero, into all his little Frolicks and childish Vagaries, would run and wrestle with him, ride the Rods, roll down the Slope, and never felt such sweet Sensations and inward Delight, as when he was engaged in such Recreations.

There was a Cock at *Harry*'s Nurse's, the Lord of the Dunghill, between whom and our Hero a very particular Intimacy and Friendship had been contracted. *Harry*'s Hand was his daily Caterer; and *Dick,* for the Cock was so called, would hop into the Child's Lap and pick his Cloaths, and rub his Feathers against him, and court *Harry* to tickle and stroak and play with him.

Upon a *Shrove-Tuesday,* while *Harry* was on his Road, from his Patron's, intending a short Visit to his Nurse and Foster Father, a Lad came to their Door and offer'd *Gaffer* a double Price for *Dick*; the Bargain was quickly made, the Lad bore off his Prize in Triumph, and *Gaffer* withdrew to the manuring of a back Field. Just at that Crisis *Harry* came up, and enquired of the Maid for his Daddy and Mammy, but was answered that neither of them was within. He then asked after his favourite Cock, but was told that his Daddy had, that Minute, sold him to yonder Man who was almost out of Sight.

Away sprung our Hero, like an Arrow from a Bow, and held the Man in View till he saw him enter a great Crowd, at the upper end of the Street. Up he comes, at last, quite out of Breath, and making way through the Assembly, perceived his Cock, at some Distance, tied to a short Stake, and a Lad preparing to throw at him with a Stick. Forward he rushed, again, and stopped resolutely before his Bird, to ward the Blow with his own Person, at the Instant that the Stick had taken its Flight, and that all the People cried out, hold! hold! One End of the Stick took *Harry* in the left Shoulder, and bruised him sorely, but, not regarding that, he instantly stooped, delivered his captive Favourite, whipt him under his Arm, caught up the Stick, flourish'd it, as in Defiance of all Opponents, made Homeward thro' the Crowd, and was followed by the Acclamations of the whole Assembly.

The old Gentleman was standing before his Court Door when his Favourite arrived, all in a Sweat; what's the Matter, my Dear, says he, what made you put yourself into such a Heat? what Cock is that you have under your Arm? In Answer to these several Questions *Harry* ingenuously confessed the whole Affair. And, when his Patron with some Warmth, cried, why, my Love, did you venture your Life for a silly Cock? why did I? repeated the Child, why, Sir, because he loved me. The Stranger, then, stepping back and gazing upon him with Eyes of tender Admiration; may Heaven for ever bless thee, my little Angel, he exclaimed, and continue to utter from thy Lips the Sentiments that it inspires. Then, catching him up in his Arms, he bathed him with his Tears, and almost stifled him with his Caresses.

In a few Days, our Hero was again restored, by frequent Fomentations, to the Use of his Arm; and his Dada, as he called him, and he returned to their old Recreations.

As *Harry*'s Ideas began to open and expand, he grew ambitious of greater Power and Knowledge. He wished for the Strength of that Bull, and for the Swiftness of yonder Horse. And, on the Close of a solemn and serene Summer's Evening, while he and his Patron walked in the Garden, he wished for Wings that he might fly up and see what the Sky, and the Stars, and the rising Moon were made of.

In order to reform this Inordinancy of his Desires, his Patron addressed him in the following Manner.

I will tell you a Story, my *Harry.* On the other Side of yonder Hill there runs a mighty clear River, and in that River, on a Time, there lived three silver

Trouts, the prettiest little Fishes that any one ever saw. Now God took a great liking and love to these pretty silver Trouts, and he let them want for nothing that such little Fishes could have occasion for. But two of them grew sad and discontented; and the One wished for this Thing, and the Other wished for that Thing, and neither of them could take Pleasure in any Thing that they had, because they were always longing for something that they had not.

Now, *Harry*, you must know that all this was very naughty in those two little Trouts; for God had been exceedingly kind to them; he had given them every Thing that was fittest for them; and he never grudged them any Thing that was for their Good; but instead of thanking him for all his Care and his Kindness, they blamed him, in their own Minds, for refusing them any Thing that their silly Fancies were set upon. In short there was no End of their wishing, and longing, and quarrelling, in their Hearts, for this Thing and t'other.

At last, God was so provoked, that he resolved to punish their Naughtiness by granting their Desires, and to make the Folly of those two little stubborn Trouts an Example to all the foolish Fish in the whole World.

For this Purpose, he called out to the three little silver Trouts, and told them they should have whatever they wished for.

Now, the Eldest of these Trouts was a very proud little Fish, and wanted, forsooth, to be set up above all other little Fishes. May it please your Greatness, says he, I must be free to tell you that I do not, at all, like the Way in which you have placed me. Here you have put me into a poor, narrow, and troublesome River, where I am straitened on the right Side, and straitened on the left Side, and can neither get down into the Ground, nor up into the Air, nor go where, nor do any one Thing I have a mind to. I am not so blind, for all, but that I can see, well enough, how mighty kind and bountiful you can be to Others. There are your favourite little Birds, who fly this Way and that Way, and mount up to the very Heavens; and do whatever they please, and have every Thing at Command, because you have given them Wings. Give me such Wings, also, as you have given to them, and then I will have something for which I ought to thank you.

No sooner ask than have. He felt the Wings he wished for growing from either Side, and, in a Minute, he spread them abroad, and rose out of the Water. At first he felt a wonderful Pleasure in finding himself able to fly. He mounted high into the Air, above the very Clouds, and he looked down with Scorn on all the Fishes in the World.

He now resolved to travel, and to take his Diversion far and wide. He flew over Rivers, and Meadows, and Woods, and Mountains; till, growing faint with Hunger and Thirst, his Wings began to fail him, and he thought it best to come down to get some Refreshment.

The little Fool did not consider that he was now in a strange Country, and many a Mile from the sweet River, where he was born and bred, and had received all his Nourishment. So, when he came down, he happened to alight among dry Sands and Rocks, where there was not a Bit to eat nor a Drop of Water to drink; and so there he lay faint and tired, and unable to rise, gasping and fluttering, and beating himself against the Stones, till at length he died in great Pain and Misery.

Now, the second silver Trout, though he was not so high minded as the first little proud Trout; yet he did not want for Conceit enough, and he was moreover a narrow hearted and very selfish little Trout, and, provided he himself was snug and safe, he did not care what became of all the Fishes in the World. So he says to God:

May it please your Honour. I don't wish, not I, for Wings to fly out of the Water, and to ramble into strange Places, where I don't know what may become of me. I lived contented and happy enough till the other Day, when, as I got under a cool Bank from the Heat of the Sun, I saw a great Rope coming down into the Water, and it fastened itself, I don't know how, about the Gills of a little Fish that was basking beside me, and he was lifted out of the Water, struggling and working in great Pain, till he was carried, I know not where, quite out of my Sight. So I thought in my own Mind, that this Evil, some Time or other, may happen to myself, and my Heart trembled within me, and I have been very sad and discontented ever since. Now, all I desire of you, is, that you would tell me the Meaning of this, and of all the other Dangers to which you have subjected us poor little mortal Fishes; for then I shall have Sense enough to take Care of my own Safety, and I am very well able to provide for my own Living, I warrant you.

No sooner said than done. God immediately opened his Understanding; and he knew the Nature and Meaning of Snares, Nets, Hooks, and Lines, and of all the Dangers to which such little Trouts could be liable.

At first he greatly rejoiced in this his Knowledge; and he said to himself, now surely I shall be the happiest of all Fishes; for, as I understand and am forewarned of every Mischief that can come near me, I'm sure I love myself too well not to keep out of Harm's Way.

From this Time forward, he took Care not to go into any deep Holes, for fear that a Pike, or some other huge Fish might be there, who would make nothing of swallowing him up at one Gulp. He also kept away from the shallow Places, especially in hot Weather, lest the Sun should dry them up and not leave him Water enough to swim in. When he saw the Shadow of a Cloud coming and moving upon the River, A ha! said he to himself, here are the Fishermen with their Nets, and immediately he got on one Side and skulked under the Banks, where he kept trembling in his Skin, till the Cloud was past. Again when he saw a Fly skimming on the Water, or a Worm coming down the Stream, he did not dare to bite, however hungry he might be; no no, said he to them, my honest Friends, I am not such a Fool as that comes to neither; go your ways and tempt those who know no better, who are not aware that you may serve as Baits to some treacherous Hook, that lies hid for the Destruction of those ignorant and silly Trouts that are not on their Guard.

Thus, this over careful Trout kept himself, in continual Frights and Alarms, and could neither eat, nor drink, nor sleep in Peace, lest some Mischief should be at Hand, or that he might be taken napping. He daily grew poorer and poorer, and sadder and sadder, for he pined away with Hunger, and sigh'd himself to Skin and Bone; till, wasted almost to nothing with Care and Melancholy, he at last died, for fear of dying, the most miserable of all Deaths.

Now, when God came to the youngest silver Trout, and asked him what he wished for. Alas (said this darling little Trout) you know, may it please your Worship, that I am but a very foolish and good for nothing little Fish; and I don't know, not I, what is good for me or what is bad for me; and I wonder how I came to be worth bringing into the World, or what you could see in me to take any thought about me. But, if I must wish for something, it is that you would do with me whatsoever you think best; and that I should be pleased to live, or die, even just as you would have me.

Now, as soon as this precious Trout made this Prayer in his good and his humble little Heart, God took such a Liking and a Love to him, as the like was never known. And God found it in his own Heart, that he could not but take great Care of this sweet little Trout, who had trusted himself so wholly to his Love and good Pleasure, and God went wheresoever he went, and was always with him and about him, and was to him as a Father and Friend and Companion; and he put Contentment into his Mind and Joy into his Heart; and so this little Trout slept always in Peace, and wakened in Gladness; and whether he was full or hungry, or whatever happened to him, he was still pleased and thankful; and he was the happiest of all Fishes that ever swam in any Water.

Harry at the close of this Fable, looked down and grew thoughtful, and his Patron left him to himself to ruminate on what he had heard. Now, *Harry* had often heard talk of God, and had some general though confused Notions of his Power.

The next Day, he requested his Patron to repeat the Story of the three little silver Trouts. When he had ended, Dada, says *Harry,* I believe I begin to guess a little at what you mean. You wou'dn't have me wish for any Thing, but leave every Thing to God; and, if I thought that God loved me half as well as you love me, I would leave every Thing to himself, like the good little Trout. He does, my *Harry,* he loves you a thousand Times better than I love you, nay a thousand Times better than you love yourself. God is all Love; it is he who made every Thing, and he loves every Thing that he has made. Ay, but Dada, I can't, for the Heart of me, help pitying the two poor little naughty Trouts. If God loves every Thing, why did he make any Thing to dye? You begin to think too deeply, *Harry*; we will speak more of these Matters another Time. For the present, let it suffice to know that, as he can kill, he can also make alive, again, at his own Pleasure.

Harry, had now remained about twelve Months with his Patron, when it was intimated to the Earl and his Lady that the dumb Man had taken a Fancy to their Child, and, that he was almost constantly resident at his House. Alarmed at this News, and apprehending that this Man might be some Imposter or Kidnapper, they, once more, sent Orders to the Nurse to bring the Boy home.

Nurse run in a Hurry to the Stranger's, and, having informed him of the Necessity she was under to take away the Child, many mutual Tears were shed at Parting, but *Harry* was the sooner pacified when Nurse told him that it was but for a short Visit, as before.

When they came to the Castle, there was no Company in the Parlour, but the Earl and his Lady, with Lord *Richard* and some other Masters of Quality, about his Age and Size. *Harry,* however, looked about with a Brow of Disgust; and, when my Lady desired him to come and kiss her, maybe you'll whip me, he answer'd sullenly; No, she replied, if you don't strike your Brother *Dicky* any more. I won't beat him, says *Harry,* if he won't beat Mammy. Come then and kiss me, my Dear, said my Lady, whereon *Harry* advanced with a slow Caution, and held up his little Mouth to receive her Salute. He was then kiss'd by his Father, his Brother, and the little Masters, and all Things promised future Reconcilement and Amity.

A Number of glittering Toys were then presented to *Harry* on all Sides; he received them, indeed, in good Part, but laid them all aside again as Things of whose Use he yet was not wise enough to be apprehensive.

Friend. Is it not too early for your Hero to shew a Contempt of Toys?

Author. My Lady, as you will see, imputed it to his Folly, not to his Philosophy.

Friend. But Children have a natural Fondness for fine Things.

Author. How so, is there a natural Value in them?

Friend. No. But ——

Author. Education, indeed, has made the Fondness next to natural. The Coral and Bells, teach Infants, on the Breast, to be delighted with Sound and Glitter. Has the Child of an Inhabitant of *Monomotapa*[11] a natural Fondness for Garbage?

Friend. I think not.

Author. But when he is instructed to prize them, and sees that it is the Fashion to be adorned with such Things, he prefers them to the Glister of Gold and Pearl. Tell me, was it the Folly, or Philosophy, of the Cock in the Fable, that spurned the Diamond and wished for the Barley Corn?

Friend. The Moral says it was his Folly, that did not know how to make a right Estimate of Things.

Author. A wiser Moral would say it was his Philosophy, that did know how to make a right Estimate of Things; for, of what Use could the Diamond be to the Cock? In the Age of Acorns, antecedent to *Ceres*[12] and the royal Ploughman *Triptolemus,*[13] a single Barley Corn had been of more Value, to Mankind, than all the Diamonds that glowed in the Mines of *India.*

Friend. You see, however, that Age, Reflection, and Philosophy can hardly wean People from their early Fondness for Shew.

Author. I see on the contrary, that the older they grow and the wiser they think themselves, the more they become attached to Trifles. What would you think of a sage Minister of State, who should make it the utmost Height of his Wishes and Ambition to be mounted on a Hobby-horse?

Friend. You can't be serious for the Soul of you.

Author. It has been seriously, and truly, and literally the Fact. For *Haman*[14] being asked, by the greatest Monarch upon Earth, what should be done most desirable for the Man whom the King delighted to honour? He answered (in the Persuasion that he himself was the Person) *Let the royal Apparel be brought and let him be arrayed therewith, and let him be put upon the Horse that the King useth to ride, and let him be brought through the Street, and have it proclaimed before him, thus shall it be done to the Man whom the King delighteth to honour.* What shall we say here? could the sage and ambitious *Haman* think of nothing better than what would have suited the Request of a Child of five Years old? Or was it that the Emperor of *Asia,* or this World itself, had nothing more valuable to bestow than a fine Coat and a Hobbyhorse?

Friend. How many Volumes do you expect this Work will contain?

Author. Sir, a Book may be compared to the Life of your Neighbour. If it be good, it cannot last too long; if bad, you cannot get rid of it too early.

Friend. But, how long, I say, do you propose to make your Story?

Author. My good Friend, the Reader may make it as short as he pleases.

11. Roman name for the ancient African kingdom of Zimbabwe.

12. The Roman corn-goddess.
13. A ploughman figure in Greek myth.
14. The story of Haman the Agagite is told in the Book of Esther. Brooke refers to an episode in Chapter 6 (paraphrasing vv. 8-9) in which the honour Haman thought for himself was intended by King Ahasuerus for Mordecai the Jew. Haman was subsequently hanged on the gallows he had prepared for Mordecai.

OLIVER GOLDSMITH

(1728-74)

from: THE VICAR OF WAKEFIELD

A TALE SUPPOSED TO BE WRITTEN BY HIMSELF (1766)

[Goldsmith's complex irony is immediately in evidence at the beginning of Dr Primrose's ingenuous narrative.]

CHAPTER I

The description of the family of Wakefield; in which a kindred likeness prevails as well of minds as of persons.

I was ever of opinion, that the honest man who married and brought up a large family, did more service than he who continued single, and only talked of population. From this motive, I had scarce taken orders a year before I began to think seriously of matrimony, and chose my wife as she did her wedding gown, not for a fine glossy surface, but such qualities as would wear well. To do her justice, she was a good-natured notable woman; and as for breeding, there were few country ladies who could shew more. She could read any English book without much spelling, and for pickling, preserving, and cookery, none could excel her. She prided herself much also upon being an excellent contriver in house-keeping; yet I could never find that we grew richer with all her contrivances.

However, we loved each other tenderly, and our fondness encreased with age. There was in fact nothing that could make us angry with the world or each other. We had an elegant house, situated in a fine country, and a good neighbourhood. The year was spent in moral or rural amusements; in visiting our rich neighbours, and relieving such as were poor. We had no revolutions to fear, nor fatigues to undergo; all our adventures were by the fire-side, and all our migrations from the blue bed to the brown.

As we lived near the road, we often had the traveller or stranger come to taste our gooseberry wine, for which we had great reputation; and I profess with the veracity of an historian, that I never knew one of them find fault with it. Our cousins too, even to the fortieth remove, all remembered their affinity, without any help from the Herald's office, and came very frequently to see us. Some of them did us no great honour by these claims of kindred; for literally speaking, we had the blind, the maimed, and the halt amongst the number. However, my wife always insisted that as they were the same *flesh and blood* with us, they should sit with us at the same table. So that if we had not very rich, we generally had very happy friends about us; for this remark will hold good thro' life, that the poorer the guest, the better pleased he ever is with being treated: and as some men gaze with admiration at the colours of a tulip, and others are smitten with the wing of a butterfly, so I was by nature an admirer of happy human faces. However, when any one of our relations was found to be a person of very bad character, a troublesome guest, or one we desired to get rid of, upon his leaving my house for the first time, I ever took care to lend him a riding coat, or a pair of boots, or sometimes an horse of small value, and I always had the satisfaction of finding he never came back to return them. By this the house was cleared of such as we did not like; but never was the family of Wakefield known to turn the traveller or the poor dependant out of doors.

Thus we lived several years in a state of much happiness, not but that we sometimes had those little rubs which Providence sends to enhance the value of its other favours. My orchard was often robbed by school-boys, and my wife's custards plundered by the cats or the children. The 'Squire would sometimes fall asleep in the most pathetic parts of my sermon, or his lady return my wife's civilities at church with a mutilated curtesy. But we soon got over the uneasiness caused by such accidents, and usually in three or four days began to wonder how they vext us.

My children, the offspring of temperance, as they were educated without softness, so they were at once well formed and healthy; my sons hardy and active, my daughters dutiful and blooming. When I stood in the midst of the little circle, which promised to be the supports of my declining age, I could not avoid repeating the famous story of Count Abensberg, who, in Henry II's progress through Germany, while other courtiers came with their treasures, brought his thirty-two children, and presented them to his sovereign as the most valuable offering he had to bestow.[1] In this manner, though I had but six, I considered them as a very valuable present made to my country, and consequently looked upon it as my debtor. Our eldest son was named George, after his uncle, who left us ten thousand pounds. Our second child, a girl, I intended to call after her aunt Grissel; but my wife, who during her pregnancy had been reading romances, insisted upon her being called Olivia. In less than another year we had a daughter again, and now I was determined that Grissel should be her name; but a rich relation taking a fancy to stand godmother, the girl was, by her directions, called Sophia; so that we had two romantic names in the family; but I solemnly protest I had no hand in it. Moses was our next, and after an interval of twelve years, we had two sons more.

It would be fruitless to deny my exultation when I saw my little ones about me; but the vanity and the satisfaction of my wife were even greater than mine. When our visitors would usually say, 'Well, upon my word, Mrs. Primrose, you have the finest children in the whole country.' ---- 'Ay, neighbour,' she would answer, 'they are as heaven made them, handsome enough, if they be good enough; for handsome is that handsome does.' And then she would bid the girls hold up their heads; who, to conceal nothing, were certainly very handsome. Mere outside is so very trifling a circumstance with me, that I should scarce have remembered to mention it, had it not been a general topic of conversation in the country. Olivia, now about eighteen, had that luxuriancy of beauty with which painters generally draw Hebe;[2] open, sprightly, and commanding. Sophia's features were not so striking at first; but often did more certain execution; for they were soft, modest, and alluring. The one vanquished by a single blow, the other by efforts successfully repeated.

The temper of a woman is generally formed from the turn of her features, at least it was so with my daughters. Olivia wished for many lovers, Sophia to secure one. Olivia was often affected from too great a desire to please. Sophia even represt excellence from her fears to offend. The one entertained me with her vivacity when I was gay, the other with her sense when I was serious. But these qualities were never carried to excess in either, and I have often seen them exchange characters for a whole day together. A suit of mourning has transformed my coquet into a prude, and a new set of ribbands given her younger sister more than natural vivacity. My eldest son George was bred at Oxford, as I intended him for one of the learned professions. My second boy Moses, whom I designed for business, received a sort of a miscellaneous education at home. But it would be needless to attempt describing the particular characters of young people that had seen but very little of the world. In short, a family likeness prevailed through all, and properly speaking, they had but one character, that of being all equally generous, credulous, simple, and inoffensive.

[Olivia has been lured away from home and seduced. In notable contrast to many eighteenth-century fathers of seduced daughters, the Vicar searches out Olivia to bring her home. The chapters that follow give a good sense of the extreme and continual reversal of fortune which characterizes the Vicar's experience, in accord with the motto on the tale's title-page, *'sperate miseri, cavete faelices'* — 'take heart, you who are heavy, take heed, you who are happy'.]

CHAPTER XXII

Offences are easily pardoned where there is love at bottom.

The next morning I took my daughter behind me, and set out on my return home. As we travelled along, I strove, by every persuasion, to calm her sorrows and fears, and to arm her with resolution to bear the presence of her offended mother. I took every opportunity, from the prospect of a fine country, through which we passed, to observe how much kinder heaven was to us, than we to each other, and that the misfortunes of nature's making were very few. I assured her, that she should never perceive any change in my affections, and that during my life, which yet might be long, she might depend upon a guardian and an instructor. I armed

1. Professor Arthur Friedman noted the story in Louis Moréri, *Le Grand Dictionaire historique* (1670).
2. In Greek legend, Hebe was cup-bearer to the gods.

her against the censures of the world, shewed her that books were sweet unreproaching companions to the miserable, and that if they could not bring us to enjoy life, they would at least teach us to endure it.

The hired horse that we rode was to be put up that night at an inn by the way, within about five miles from my house, and as I was willing to prepare my family for my daughter's reception, I determined to leave her that night at the inn, and to come for her, accompanied by my daughter Sophia, early the next morning. It was night before we reached our appointed stage: however, after seeing her provided with a decent apartment, and having ordered the hostess to prepare proper refreshments, I kissed her, and proceeded towards home. My heart caught new sensations of pleasure the nearer I approached that peaceful mansion. As a bird that had been frighted from its nest, my affections outwent my haste, and hovered round my little fireside, with all the rapture of expectation. I called up the many fond things I had to say, and anticipated the welcome I was to receive. I already felt my wife's tender embrace, and smiled at the joy of my little ones. As I walked but slowly, the night wained apace. The labourers of the day were all retired to rest; the lights were out in every cottage; no sounds were heard but of the shrilling cock, and the deep-mouthed watch-dog, at hollow distance. I approached my little abode of pleasure, and before I was within a furlong of the place, our honest mastiff came running to welcome me.

It was now near mid-night that I came to knock at my door: all was still and silent: my heart dilated with unutterable happiness, when, to my amazement, I saw the house bursting out in a blaze of fire, and every apperture red with conflagration! I gave a loud convulsive outcry, and fell upon the pavement insensible. This alarmed my son, who perceiving the flames, instantly waked my wife and daughter, and all running out, naked, and wild with apprehension, recalled me to life with their anguish. But it was only to objects of new terror; for the flames had, by this time, caught the roof of our dwelling, part after part continuing to fall in, while the family stood, with silent agony, looking on, as if they enjoyed the blaze. I gazed upon them and upon it by turns, and then looked round me for my two little ones; but they were not to be seen. O misery! 'Where,' cried I, 'where are my little ones?' — 'They are burnt to death in the flames,' says my wife calmly, 'and I will die with them.' — That moment I heard the cry of the babes within, who were just awaked by the fire, and nothing could have stopped me. 'Where, where, are my children?' cried I, rushing through the flames, and bursting the door of the chamber in which they were confined, 'Where are my little ones?' — 'Here, dear papa, here we are,' cried they together, while the flames were just catching the bed where they lay. I caught them both in my arms, and snatched them through the fire as fast as possible, while just as I was got out, the roof sunk in. 'Now,' cried I, holding up my children, 'now let the flames burn on, and all my possessions perish. Here they are, I have saved my treasure. Here, my dearest, here are our treasures, and we shall yet be happy.' We kissed our little darlings a thousand times, they clasped us round the neck, and seemed to share our transports, while their mother laughed and wept by turns.

I now stood a calm spectator of the flames, and after some time, began to perceive that my arm to the shoulder was scorched in a terrible manner. It was therefore out of my power to give my son any assistance, either in attempting to save our goods, or preventing the flames spreading to our corn. By this time, the neighbours were alarmed, and came running to our assistance; but all they could do was to stand, like us, spectators of the calamity. My goods, among which were the notes I had reserved for my daughters fortunes, were entirely consumed, except a box, with some papers, that stood in the kitchen, and two or three things more of little consequence, which my son brought away in the beginning. The neighbours contributed, however, what they could to lighten our distress. They brought us cloaths, and furnished one of our outhouses with kitchen utensils; so that by daylight we had another, tho' a wretched, dwelling to retire to. My honest next neighbour, and his children, were not the least assiduous in providing us with every thing necessary, and offering what ever consolation untutored benevolence could suggest.

When the fears of my family had subsided, curiosity to know the cause of my long stay began to take place; having therefore informed them of every particular, I proceeded to prepare them for the reception of our lost one, and tho' we had nothing but wretchedness now to impart, yet to procure her a welcome to what we had. This task would have been more difficult but for our recent calamity, which had humbled my wife's pride, and blunted it by more poignant afflictions. Being unable to go for my poor child myself, as my arm now grew very painful, I sent my son and daughter, who soon returned, supporting the wretched delinquent, who had not courage to look up at her mother, whom no instructions of mine could persuade to a perfect reconciliation; for women have a much stronger sense of female error than men. 'Ah, madam,' cried her mother, 'this is but a poor place you are come to after so much finery. My daughter Sophy and I can afford but little entertainment to persons who have kept company only with people of distinction. Yes, Miss Livy, your poor father and I have suffered very much of late; but I hope heaven will forgive you.' — During this reception, the unhappy victim stood pale and trembling, unable to weep or to reply; but I could not continue a silent spectator of her distress, wherefore assuming a degree of severity in my voice and manner, which was ever followed with instant submission, 'I entreat, woman, that my words may be now marked once for all: I have here brought you back a poor deluded wanderer; her return to duty demands the revival of our tenderness. The real hardships of life are now coming fast upon us, let us not therefore encrease them by dissention among each other. If we live harmoniously together, we may yet be contented, as there are enough of us to shut out the censuring world, and keep each other in countenance. The kindness of heaven is promised to the penitent, and let ours be directed by the example. Heaven, we are assured, is much more pleased to view a repentant sinner, than many persons who have supported a course of undeviating rectitude.[3] And this is right; for that single effort by which we stop short in the down-hill path to perdition, is itself a greater exertion of virtue, than an hundred acts of justice.'

CHAPTER XXIII

None but the guilty can be long and completely miserable.

Some assiduity was now required to make our present abode as convenient as possible, and we were soon again qualified to enjoy our former serenity. Being disabled myself from assisting my son in our usual occupations, I read to my family from the few books that were saved, and particularly from such, as, by amusing the imagination, contributed to ease the heart. Our good neighbours too came every day with the kindest condolence, and fixed a time in which they were all to assist at repairing my former dwelling. Honest farmer Williams was not last among these visitors; but heartily offered his friendship. He would even have renewed his addresses to my daughter; but she rejected them in such a manner as totally represt his future solicitations. Her grief seemed formed for continuing, and she was the only person of our little society that a week did not restore to chearfulness. She now lost that unblushing innocence which once taught her to respect herself, and to seek pleasure by pleasing. Anxiety now had taken strong possession of her mind, her beauty began to be impaired with her constitution, and neglect still more contributed to diminish it. Every tender epithet bestowed on her sister brought a pang to her heart and a tear to her eye; and as one vice, tho' cured, almost ever plants others where it has been, so her former guilt, tho' driven out by repentance, left jealousy and envy behind. I strove a thousand ways to lessen her care, and even forgot my own pain in a concern for her's, collecting such amusing passages of history, as a strong memory and some reading could suggest. 'Our happiness, my dear,' I would say, 'is in the power of one who can bring it about a thousand unforeseen ways, that mock our foresight. If example be necessary to prove this, I'll give you a story, my child, told us by a grave, tho' sometimes a romancing, historian.

'Matilda was married very young to a Neapolitan nobleman of the first quality, and found herself a widow and a mother at the age of fifteen. As she stood one day caressing her infant son in the open window of an apartment, which hung over the river Volturna, the child, with a sudden spring, leaped from her arms into the flood below, and disappeared in a moment. The mother, struck with instant surprize, and making an effort to save him, plunged in after; but, far from being able to assist the infant, she herself with great difficulty escaped to the opposite shore, just when some French soldiers were plundering the country on that side, who immediately made her their prisoner.

'As the war was then carried on between the French and Italians with the utmost inhumanity, they were going at once to perpetrate those two extremes, suggested by appetite and cruelty. This base resolution, however, was opposed by a young

3. Matthew 18. 12-14.

officer, who, tho' their retreat required the utmost expedition, placed her behind him, and brought her in safety to his native city. Her beauty at first caught his eye, her merit soon after his heart. They were married; he rose to the highest posts; they lived long together, and were happy. But the felicity of a soldier can never be called permanent: after an interval of several years, the troops which he commanded having met with a repulse, he was obliged to take shelter in the city where he had lived with his wife. Here they suffered a siege, and the city at length was taken. Few histories can produce more various instances of cruelty, than those which the French and Italians at that time exercised upon each other. It was resolved by the victors, upon this occasion, to put all the French prisoners to death; but particularly the husband of the unfortunate Matilda, as he was principally instrumental in protracting the siege. Their determinations were, in general, executed almost as soon as resolved upon. The captive soldier was led forth, and the executioner, with his sword, stood ready, while the spectators in gloomy silence awaited the fatal blow, which was only suspended till the general, who presided as judge should give the signal. It was in this interval of anguish and expectation, that Matilda came to take her last farewell of her husband and deliverer, deploring her wretched situation, and the cruelty of fate, that had saved her from perishing by a premature death in the river Volturna, to be the spectator of still greater calamities. The general, who was a young man, was struck with surprize at her beauty, and pity at her distress; but with still stronger emotions when he heard her mention her former dangers. He was her son, the infant for whom she had encounter'd so much danger. He acknowledged her at once as his mother, and fell at her feet. The rest may be easily supposed: the captive was set free, and all the happiness that love, friendship, and duty could confer on each, were united.'

In this manner I would attempt to amuse my daughter; but she listened with divided attention; for her own misfortunes engrossed all the pity she once had for those of another, and nothing gave her ease. In company she dreaded contempt; and in solitude she only found anxiety. Such was the colour of her wretchedness, when we received certain information, that Mr. Thornhill[4] was going to be married to Miss Wilmot, for whom I always suspected he had a real passion, tho' he took every opportunity before me to express his contempt both of her person and fortune. This news only served to encrease poor Olivia's affliction; such a flagrant breach of fidelity, was more than her courage could support. I was resolved, however, to get more certain information, and to defeat, if possible, the completion of his designs, by sending my son to old Mr. Wilmot's, with instructions to know the truth of the report, and to deliver Miss Wilmot a letter, intimating Mr. Thornhill's conduct in my family. My son went, in pursuance of my directions, and in three days returned, assuring us of the truth of the account; but that he had found it impossible to deliver the letter, which he was therefore obliged to leave, as Mr. Thornhill and Miss Wilmot were visiting round the country. They were to be married, he said, in a few days, having appeared together at church the Sunday before he was there, in great splendour, the bride attended by six young ladies drest in white, and he by as many gentlemen. Their approaching nuptials filled the whole country with rejoicing, and they usually rode out together in the grandest equipage that had been seen in the country for many years. All the friends of both families, he said, were there, particularly the 'Squire's uncle, Sir William Thornhill, who bore so good a character. He added, that nothing but mirth and feasting were going forward; that all the country praised the young bride's beauty, and the bridegroom's fine person, and that they were immensely fond of each other; concluding, that he could not help thinking Mr. Thornhill one of the most happy men in the world.

'Why let him if he can,' returned I: 'but, my son, observe this bed of straw, and unsheltering roof; those mouldering walls, and humid floor; my wretched body thus disabled by fire, and my children weeping round me for bread; you have come home, my child, to all this, yet here, even here, you see a man that would not for a thousand worlds exchange situations. O, my children, if you could but learn to commune with your own hearts, and know what noble company you can make them, you would little regard the elegance and splendours of the worthless. Almost all men have been taught to call life a passage, and themselves the travellers. The similitude still may be improved when we observe that the good are joyful and serene, like travellers that are going towards home; the wicked

4. The young landowner with whom Olivia eloped.

but by intervals happy, like travellers that are going into exile.'

My compassion for my poor daughter, overpowered by this new disaster, interrupted what I had farther to observe. I bade her mother support her, and after a short time she recovered. She appeared from this time more calm, and I imagined had gained a new degree of resolution: but appearances deceived me; for her tranquility was the langour of over-wrought resentment. A supply of provisions, charitably sent us by my kind parishioners, seemed to diffuse new chearfulness amongst the rest of the family, nor was I displeased at seeing them once more sprightly and at ease. It would have been unjust to damp their satisfactions, merely to condole with resolute melancholy, or to burthen them with a sadness they did not feel. Once more, therefore, the tale went round and the song was demanded, and chearfulness condescended to hover round our little habitation.

ANONYMOUS

from: THE TRIUMPH OF PRUDENCE OVER PASSION; OR, THE HISTORY OF MISS MORTIMER AND MISS FITZGERALD (1781)

[The principal characters and the social and political realities of the society in which they live are introduced in the opening letter of this epistolary novel.]

Miss MORTIMER, to Miss FITZGERALD

LETTER I.

Nov. 4. 1779.

According to my promise, made this morning at our parting, I shall dedicate all my leisure moments to my dear Eliza, and amuse her with the little occurrences, or observations of the day, just as they present themselves to my pen; I say, just as they present themselves, by way of giving you warning, that you are not to expect much order or method in my Letters: but I fancy our former correspondence may have given you some idea that my style is not renowned for either. However, if you are diverted, that is the chief point with me, for I have my fears that great part of your time will pass but heavily, as I am very apprehensive your mother's health will suffer by going from a very warm house in town, to a very cold one (surrounded by ponds and lakes) in the country, at this dreary season, you know what bad effect it had on her last winter, though the weather was uncommonly mild; and I really think it was very unnecessary for her to run any hazard, as the chief purpose of her going could have been accomplished as well, had she staid in town; it is, I allow, a very laudable custom to be kind to the tenants, to entertain them, and make them happy at the approaching season; but I think, as she is so delicate, Mr. Skeffington might as well have done the honours of Christmas to your tenants as his own, since it must be done in his house, your's being sett.[1] I hope, however, my fears may prove without foundation, both for her sake and yours; for then I know you will be happy any where with her, and another person that shall be nameless. —— You contrived mighty ill to leave town to-day, for by so doing you lost a most glorious sight; a large body of our Volunteers[2] assembled, to honour the memory of King William,[3] who made a very fine appearance, and fired several vollies, even better than the Regulars, who performed the same ceremony an hour or two after. Every one looked delighted, except some few, who want to be thought friends to Government, but for me who am an enthusiast in the cause of Liberty and my country, I was wonderfully delighted to see our men of the first rank and property, as well as our most eminent

1. rented.
2. The Volunteer Movement was formed by members of the protestant gentry in 1778 to protect Ireland against foreign invasion. As a military force outside the control of England or the Irish administration, the Volunteers soon became an important support for Irish attempts to achieve a Free Trade and constitutional independence.
3. i. e. William III.

citizens, voluntarily arming in defence of both: I think it warms one's heart, and I really pity your lukewarm souls, who can see such a sight without emotion.—

November 5th. I had wrote thus far yesterday, and should perhaps have expatiated for some time on the love of our country, but that I was agreeably interrupted by the arrival of an unexpected visitor; a thundering rap at the door, threw all the family into consternation, as it was a very unusual hour for company: I, who sat by the window, stood up, and looking through the glass, saw a post-chaise and four horses up to their bellies in mud, the postilions and servants all in black: the door was soon opened, and out stepped the prettiest young widow I ever saw; I believe you will easily recollect this description suits but one of our acquaintance; it was no other than our dear Emily: I flew to welcome her, and in a minute a thousand questions were asked by each, without either waiting for an answer: however, when we were seated, and began to be more coherent, I told her she should be my guest, as I had spare beds for her and her maid, and the men might go with their horses, for I had not room for them; and if I had, she knew, I could not abide to run foul of a servant fellow every step I took about my house: she smiled at the expression, but said, she had as little liking to them as I, when they could be dispensed with, and that she would gladly accept my invitation, that she might have as much of my company as possible while she staid. Gertrude, who, you know, is the mother of this family, no sooner heard this affair regulated, than she quitted the room to give the necessary orders; for that is a trouble she takes entirely on herself, and indeed she makes a much better figure in the office than I should do, so I am mighty willing to indulge her in it. Emily and I being left quite to ourselves till tea-time, you may imagine we had no lack of chat; I found the business that hurried her to town was to administer to her husband's will; it seems her tender care of him, during an illness of six months, touched his conscience, and by way of amends for the very unkind treatment he had given her, all the while she was his wife, he made a will, to which he appointed her Executrix, and left her the interest of a large sum of ready money during her life, in addition to her jointure, and some part of the principal at her disposal: she is also to be guardian to the child, and have the care of the estate; I know no one more capable of managing it for the child's advantage: the man certainly meant well at last, but I think the greatest favour he could confer on her was his dying; for her own fortune is so large, that she only wanted to be allowed to enjoy it in comfort, and what he has left her, will, I am sure, be no great addition to her happiness, for I know few that value riches less than she, nor none that make a better use of them. Lovely as she was when last you saw her, you can scarce have an idea of what she is now! She is of the middle size, elegantly formed, and has a feminine sweetness in her air and manner, that is easier imagined than described; her weeds become her amazingly; and there is a langour in her countenance, contracted during the two unhappy years she was a wife, so peculiarly suited to her habit, that it interests one, you cannot think how much, in her favour. I cannot with any degree of patience reflect on her being sacrificed to a man, with whom it was impossible she could be happy, merely because his estate and her father's were contiguous:[4] it is astonishing to think, that such ridiculous motives can actuate rational creatures, in the most material circumstances of life: I cannot say I should have been quite so obedient as Emily was; for a child has a natural right to a negative voice, when it concerns the happiness of her life. I do not mean by that to justify all the pretty masters and misses who in direct opposition to the will of their parents, as well as to every dictate of reason and discretion, are daily performing the tragedy of, All for Love;[5] and indeed, it usually turns out a very deep tragedy to them; for whatever they may think before marriage, they soon after discover, that a competency, according to their rank in life, is absolutely necessary to matrimonial felicity: but I think in chusing a husband for a girl, her friends should be careful to fix on one, whose qualities of mind and temper, are such as would be capable of inspiring her with that tender esteem, which, according to my notions, is much more likely to be lasting than fierce flaming love; for that being more a passion than a sentiment, is, like all other violent passions, very apt to subside, and leave no traces but what are unpleasing.

I took the opportunity of Emily's being out on

4. Emily's situation is very like that of Clarissa Harlowe in Samuel Richardson's *Clarissa* (1747-48), whose family want her to marry a neighbouring landowner, Roger Solmes.

5. *All for Love; or, The World Well Lost* (1678) is Dryden's version of Shakespeare's *Antony and Cleopatra.*

business, to finish my letter for the post, as I think you will be uneasy if I defer it longer. I hear her carriage stop, so shall conclude, for as her stay will be but short in town, I would not wish to leave her when she is at home; she is come up and bid me say a thousand kind things for her, to dear Eliza: Gertrude expresses herself much in the same manner. But I hope you have more conscience than to expect I should impart all they say: I shall therefore leave you to suppose them; and subscribe myself,

Your's,
in sincerest friendship,
LOUISA MORTIMER.

Mr. Fitzgerald and Charles know how much I esteem them; so I need not trouble you to tell them.

[The following extract suggests how comment on both national and sexual politics is introduced into letters predominantly concerned with domestic or sentimental matters. The idealized portrayal of life on a country estate in Letter XIX should be compared not only with the picture of rural distress in the subsequent excerpt but with Arthur Young's very different account of the Ireland he observed in *A Tour of Ireland* (1780).]

Miss MORTIMER, to Miss FITZGERALD.

LETTER XVIII.

Dec. 18.—

. . . I have forborn to mention political transactions this some time, as I know you have the most material occurrences from Mr. Fitzgerald, and the public prints: by them you are informed our commons have demanded a FREE TRADE; I do not however give them the credit of it, except those few who have uniformly been actuated by love of their country; as for the rest they were impelled to it, by the spirit that at present pervades all degrees of people, and which they dare not set themselves against: the same reason will oblige England to comply, because she is not in a situation to refuse; but I am clear of opinion, that if we do not watch her with unremitting attention, she will, by some artifice, the first convenient opportunity, contrive to render every thing she grants of no effect, for they are selfish, illiberal people, and look with a jealous eye on every advantage enjoyed by their fellow subjects, either envying their prosperity, or looking on it as so much taken from them; like some individuals, who are as anxious to detract from other people's merit, as if they thought it would add any thing to their own. To repine at another's prosperity is a most odious disposition, even in private persons; but it is still worse, when it is the temper of a whole nation, because it then affects millions of people, who are connected with, or dependant on them; and who in consequence, are sure to be oppressed.

The uniform conduct of the English towards this kingdom, as well as to America,[6] justifies my opinion of them; and I dare say, a little time will shew what dependance we can have on their affection, that is, provided we give them an opportunity; for no doubt they will dissemble till they are sure of carrying their point.

How some of the wise heads would laugh at a girl pretending to give an opinion in politics; it is not, I believe, a very usual subject for young ladies to correspond on; but I know you have been taught to think, the welfare of our country is of as much consequence to women as men; and when public affairs are the general topic, to write on them is an agreeable variety, and at least as improving as intrigue or scandal, which the men generously allow us to talk of as much as we please, and indeed make no bad figure in such conversation themselves.

We go on here just as usual: cousin James as attentive as ever to our fair widow; and Harry Maunsell a constant attendant on your humble servant. If Gertrude had her young count here, three such swains would make us the envy of every female circle we frequented.

I observe when we meet Mr. Fitzgerald at a drum,[7] which often happens, all eyes are cast on him and Emily, for the town has already made a match between them, and his behaviour confirms the idea, as it is really very particular.

These men, Eliza, with all their sense, have mighty little discretion in those sort of matters: we women have it all to nothing; now Emily behaves with the greatest composure and indifference, while your cousin is unable to conceal his chagrin if he cannot play at the same table she does, and yet I am sure she likes him. ——— What an unmerciful letter here is! I am half dead with writing.

Adieu,
LOUISA MORTIMER.

6. Louisa is referring to the American War of Independence, fought from 1776 onwards, in which the colonists battled for political independence from England.

7. A fashionable evening assembly in a private house.

Miss FITZGERALD, to Miss MORTIMER.

LETTER XIX.

Dec. 26.—

My dear Louisa's very agreeable epistle of the 18th had all the effect you could wish in restoring my spirits; for you point out the folly, and I may say, impiety of sinking under every trivial distress in such forcible language, that I grew ashamed of my own weakness while I read, and have ever since manifested such resignation and composure, though my mother is confined with the rheumatism, and Charles did not arrive till the 22nd, that I am sure you would be astonished at my improvement in your Philosophic Doctrines, joking a-part. I wish you were always near, to teach me to support disagreeable accidents with some degree of resolution: I fear I shall very soon stand in need of all your arguments on that head, as the time for Charles going to England advances fast, and there is little probability that my mother will be able to go to town before then, as she intended. But I will not anticipate uneasiness, if I can help it.

Yesterday, according to ancient custom, Charles's tenants were entertained in the Great Hall, with roast beef and plumb-pudding; mine were treated in the same manner the day before, the Steward and House-keeper doing the honours of the table. My mother was not able to come amongst them, which was a great mortification to her; but I went, dispensed my usual present of a guinea to each of the young girls who was cloathed in her own housewifery; and that, you may be sure, was every one that was present; but if on enquiry I found any of them so industrious as to help to cloath the younger children of the family, I added a second guinea, by way of encouragement to her, and to inspire the rest with emulation: a cap and ribbon to each of the little ones, makes them attend both to their book and their needle; and my approbation makes them all compleatly happy; for I often call in at each of their houses, when I take an airing, and then the mothers inform me how they go on at school, and I praise or chide them, according to the account I hear.

I pay for the schooling of those whose parents cannot well afford it, because I think reading and writing may be useful to them, if they should happen to be hereafter in any sort of business: besides, they can be better instructed in religion, if they are able to read the Bible.

Charles accompanied me into the Hall, and chatted with the old folks, while I was distributing my favours amongst the young ones. A large bowl of punch[8] was brought in for them to drink my health, and one of the old men made me look very silly, by adding a wish, that their next meeting might be to rejoice on my ladyship's marriage with his honour: you may think I could not answer such a speech, but Charles relieved me by thanking him for his wish, and hoping he should see them very shortly on that happy occasion. The girls simpered, and their mothers smiled: I recovered from my confusion enough to say something kind to them all, and then left them to enjoy their mirth the rest of the evening; and diverted my mother with what had passed, who was rather inclined to be low-spirited at being unable to go down to them, for she used to take great delight in seeing them all so happy; and has made it a request, that I will never drop the custom, which I could easily promise, as it is quite agreeable to my inclination.

Charles's behaviour, since he returned from Hamilton-Hall, is just what it used to be, before he discovered any symptoms of that unhappy failing, which has this while past interrupted our peace; but I dare not flatter myself his present disposition will hold, as his letter to Mr. Maunsell shews, how doubtful he is about it.

I rejoice to hear Gertrude's little Novel is likely to conclude to her satisfaction; though to be sure, his absence will give her much uneasiness; but something may happen to occasion his return sooner than she expects; there may be a peace, or cessation, not that there is now any appearance of it; but she must hope the best. She will, indeed, be a great loss to you; you should think of some one to supply her place; for it will not be pleasing for you to be alone, nor you need not, as you have several young relations, who, I dare say, would like well to be with you.

Your bit of Poetry was happily chosen to illustrate your own sentiments; I am convinced you are perfectly right, not to let your sensibility run away with your happiness, and sincerely wish, I could follow your example, but fear I have not strength of mind sufficient for the purpose.

I am of your opinion, both as to our own Parliament and the English nation, and I find cousin James thinks as you do; for in one of his

8. Wine or whiskey mixed with water, sugar, lemons, spices, etc.

letters, he says, 'There is no doubt but our demands will be granted, as it would be too dangerous to refuse them; but I am sure England will seize the first opportunity to render her concessions abortive.' I hope we may all find ourselves mistaken; yet I am afraid we shall prove too good politicians in that respect.

I know most men disapprove of women pretending to any opinion on these subjects; but the men of your family and mine were above that vulgar prejudice, and took pains to make us capable of judging with some degree of precision; and I think we are obliged to them for it, since it enables us to converse sometimes on matters of importance, and not be always confined to trifles; a little of each is agreeable.

I wonder the men are not more discreet in their behaviour before strangers, for I should think it not pleasing to themselves to have their attachments public, before they know how they will be received: most men look on it as very mortifying to be refused, and would think themselves very ill treated if the lady should publish it; though they scarce ever fail of making it known to every body, they make very little use of their understanding on those occasions. James is a striking proof of it, for by what you say, a giddy lad could not be more foolish; and yet in every other circumstance of life, he is quite a pattern of propriety of manners; and it certainly is far from that to draw people's eyes on Emily, and set them telling of her second marriage, before she is out of her weeds: why do not you speak to him about it? but indeed, as it is a fault, or a folly (call it which you please) most of them are guilty of, I suppose they cannot help it.

Charles has just got a letter from England, which, he says, will hasten his departure; he talks of going in two or three days, and all your lessons are insufficient to make me hear it with any composure; all I could do was, to restrain my tears till he had quitted the room. I can only add, that I am your's,

with much affection,

ELIZA FITZGERALD.

Miss Fitzgerald, to Miss Mortimer.

LETTER XXX.

Jan. 28.—

I think this last jaunt of mine to the country has produced nothing but disagreeable events. In the first place, it separated me from my Louisa; then it deprived me of meeting Emily; of seeing the Volunteers; gave occasion for Charles's jealousy to break out; and to sum up all, the coldness of the place brought on my mother's illness, which will now detain me from Gertrude's wedding; and that, I acknowlege, is a very great mortification to me; and what is still worse, I have no one pleasing reflection to make me amends for all my disappointments, except that my mother continues tolerably, and I have hopes we shall get to town in less than a month.

I never liked the Country in winter, and from this time, I believe I shall hate the sight of it.

My acquaintance with the Miss Boyle's is the only agreeable circumstance that has occurred since I left Dublin: I fancy they will be in town before me, as the servants they left in the house, tell our's, they expect their master soon; and I know he was to come home when his daughters set out for town. When I come, I will introduce them to you.

I have been trying the experiment you recommended to me, Louisa, and it has succeeded to the utmost of your wishes. I am ashamed of having ever been so unthankful for the many blessings I enjoy; as to overlook them all, and make myself unhappy with the apprehension of evils, that, perhaps, may never come to pass; and if they did, would not be equal to half the miseries which I have seen one family patiently suffering; but people bred up in ease and affluence, have no idea of what real misfortune is; and therefore lament as such, trifles that ought not to give a reasonable creature a moment's pain.

The day after I wrote to you last, I took Kitty with me in the chaise, and went about three miles off, where she told me there were several poor Cottagers on the estate of a young gentleman now on his travels; for thank Heaven, the lower class of tenants on Charles's estate, or mine, are none of them in want. We had turned into a bye-road that led to a few scattered cabbins, and were driving towards the nearest, when I saw a pretty girl, about nine years old, run out, and clapping her hands together, in an agony of grief, cried out, 'Oh! my mammy! my mammy!' and without seeming to hear the carriage, in a manner flew across the road to a cottage at the other side, into which she went. The child's exclamation raised both my pity and curiosity, as I guessed it must be occasioned by some distress she had left her mother in; and calling

John to stop, I stepped out, followed by Kitty, and went directly into the house: but what a scene of woe presented itself! at one side of the room lay the corpse of a man, on a bed; at the other, near the dying embers of a turf fire, lay the woman on a bed of straw, in a fainting fit; an infant about three days old, sleeping at her side. With Kitty's assistance I raised her, and applied my Eau de Luce[9] to her nose, which soon revived her, and she looked wildly round; when casting her eyes on her dead husband, she clapped her hands over them, as if unable to bear the sight, and cried out, who was so cruel as to bring me back to a life of misery! I bid her be comforted, as I hoped she and her children would yet be happy. The strange voice struck her ear, (for I believe she never observed my appearance) and she took down her hand to view me, just as the little girl came in, followed by an old woman.

They all looked astonished, and seemed at a loss to account for what they saw; when I, who was supporting the poor woman, and apprehensive she would faint again, asked if they had any thing fit to give her? The old woman with tears in her eyes, answered, she feared there was nothing but a little buttermilk, and a few potatoes, which the poor neighbours brought in. I then called for some water, and geve her a little, with Eau de Luce in it, which recovered her from the faintishness; and tears flowing plentifully, she was much relieved, and we laid her down again.

I sent John to an Inn about half a mile off, for a bottle of Wine, and some other refreshments; and while he was away, enquired of the old woman, how the people came into such distress. She told me the man had been a Linen-Weaver, near Armagh; and lived very comfortably, till he fell into a lingering illness; which disabled him from working, and having nothing to support him but what his wife earned by spinning, they were forced to sell most of their furniture, to pay their rent, and brought the small remainder to the place they were now in, where they had been but a few months; they made a shift to maintain themselves by the woman's industry, and what little the child could do, till the man grew so bad, his wife could do nothing but attend him, and they were reduced to the greatest distress, when to add to it, she was brought to bed a few days ago; that she staid with them as much as she could, and had not left them half an hour, when the child ran to tell her, her father was dead, and her mother dying; she concluded with saying, she hoped Heaven had sent me that way for their relief.

John returned sooner than I could have expected, and I gave the woman some warm Wine and Water, and gave directions for a Chicken he had brought to be made into broth for her, and the old woman undertook to stay and do every thing that was proper, to whom I gave some money to provide firing, and whatever was necessary for that night: promising to send a supply from our house next day.

You may be sure I rewarded her for her trouble, in a manner that will secure her attendance while it is wanted; and as soon as the woman is well enough, I intend to bring her to a neat little house that is now unoccupied on my lands, where she shall be rent-free, till she can, by her industry (for I do not wish to encourage idleness) get a few guineas to lay by, and then I will let her have it at a very easy rent: the garden is now well cropped, so that she will have nothing to do but attend her spinning for some time.

I am now convinced that the wise man's saying, 'It is better to go to the house of mourning,' provided one makes a proper use of the lesson it teaches; for those poor people's distress has engrossed all my thoughts; and relieving them, given me more pleasing reflections than ever I enjoyed before on doing a charitable action: because till now, I never saw the wretchedness from which I relieved the objects of my compassion.

While I stay in the country, I shall often step into the little huts, and see what way the poor inhabitants are in, and in Dublin the news-papers frequently furnish us with notice where to find the distressed: for the future I shall always visit them myself; it will teach me to set a proper value on the blessings that are extended to me, and to bear light evils without repining.

I will not again pretend to blame you in regard to Mr. Maunsell, for I acknowlege you are uncommonly circumstanced; nor do I know a woman, except yourself, that would act with such propriety in the same situation: but I cannot help pitying him. No doubt, the Count, who has so much sensibility, is quite affected with his melancholy tale.

I hope soon to hear from Charles in London, for then his stay in England will not be very much longer; perhaps we may reach Dublin nearly at the

9. A medicinal preparation of alcohol, ammonia, and oil of amber, used as smelling salts.

same time. Do you think James has made any declaration to Emily yet? I find all our family look on it as a match very likely to take place: I hope it may.

Tell Gertrude how mortified I am that I cannot fill the office of Bride-Maid at her nuptials, which I had promised myself I should. Who is she to have beside you. Believe me, dear Louisa,

Your affectionate,

ELIZA FITZGERALD.

[Charles Skeffington's uncomplimentary account of London life is characteristic of the novel's strongly patriotic and anti-English values. Miss Freeman, introduced in the course of the letter, is the novel's (English) villainess.]

Mr. SKEFFINGTON, to Mr. MAUNSELL.

LETTER XXXIV.

London, Feb. 12 —

DEAR MAUNSELL,

I have been about three weeks in this centre of Amusements, and so borne down by the torrent of dissipation with which people here are overwhelmed, that I could not find time to perform my promise of writing to you, till this day, that a violent cold has obliged me to stay at home and nurse myself; I got it by walking home late from a Tavern.

To confess the truth, raking does not agree with me, but it is scarce possible to withstand the temptations that are continually thrown in one's way, in a place where vice puts on the most alluring form, and covers her deformity with the spacious appearance of pleasure, which one must be almost insensible to resist; at least, till experience has taught us wisdom.

You cautioned me against Sharpers, and I was on my guard; but you did not tell me, I might be in as much danger from those whose birth intitled them to be called Gentlemen; but perhaps you never met with such, I would hardly believe it myself, if I had not purchased my knowledge at the extravagant rate of two thousand pounds. I did not at first suspect, but latterly I perceived the cheat, and rising, gave the gentleman a draft on my Banker for the money, informing him at the same time, I did not chuse to play any longer with one who understood all the game; and instantly quit the room, expecting he would follow to demand an explanation, as there was a deal of company present, who all heard what I said.

It happened as I thought, for I had not gone ten yards when he came up with me, and asking what my words meant, I answered, the meaning was so very obvious it could scarcely be mistaken; on which he drew his sword, and bid me defend myself: I did it so effectually, that in less than a minute I wounded him in the sword arm, and the weapon dropped from his hand; as he bled fast, I advised him to return to the house we had just left, and send for a Surgeon; then bidding him good night, stepped into a Chair[10] I met, and went home very much dissatisfied with myself.

I had no apology for playing so deep, because my fortune is already too large to receive any advantage from winning that sum, and though the loss is no way material to me, yet since I had it to spare, I might have disposed of it in a way that would have made several happy: the event too, might have been fatal, and duelling, you know, I greatly disapprove; but when his unfair practices were so plain, that I must see it, I should have been looked on either as a fool or a coward, if I had not taken notice of it.

I took great care, however, not to wound him in a dangerous place, for I soon perceived he had very little skill: his is recovering fast, but I shall always chuse to avoid his company, as I must dislike the man; besides, I am determined never to play again, but for a few guineas, which will not be worth any one's while to cheat for.

My intercourse with the other Sex has been more agreeable; for affairs of Gallantry have offered every day without my seeking. I should be sorry my lovely Eliza knew how I have been led astray, though they were only venial transgressions, in which the heart was no way concerned, and indeed, the man must be void of all passion that could withstand such temptations.

The women have such a fund of vivacity, that they are the most agreeable mistresses in the world; but for a wife, I would prefer the more reserved chearfulness of my pretty country-women. That, perhaps, may be prejudice; for it is likely an English-man would think them insipid.

I have paid pretty high for my amusements in this way, though I assure you, it was not with those who set their charms to sale; but presents must be

10. i. e. sedan chair.

made, and of value according to the rank of the fair one.

In all my dealings here, I find money is the Idol of the place, and the whole force of the people's genius is turned towards the different methods of obtaining it.

I often think if a medium could be struck between the English and the Irish, it would just produce a proper standard whereby to regulate our œconomy; for one loves Gold too much for their eternal welfare, the other too little for their temporal peace; as their total disregard of it keeps their domestic affairs in continual embarrassment: I speak of the general character of the two nations; for I know there are many exceptions in each.

I made an acquaintance in Sussex, with a Miss Freeman, who was in a visit with a family where I was intimate; she lives in London, and when she was coming to town, a few days before me, gave me an invitation to her aunt's house in Jermyn-street, where she lives. I availed myself of it, and have passed several agreeable evenings there.

They are genteel people, and very pleasing. Miss Freeman is a pretty lively girl, about nineteen; her aunt's daughter something younger, and handsomer, but more serious than her cousin. I find the former has a large fortune at her own disposal: I believe the aunt gave me that hint with some view, but my heart is already fixed, and if Eliza's sentiments remain unaltered at my return, I have nothing more to wish for, except being at age, as I cannot marry till then; but I have a very short time to wait for that.

I shall not expect to hear from you, since I mean to set out for Ireland in less than a week, and hope to find you and all those I most wish to see, in Dublin.

My best compliments to Miss Mortimer, but do not tell her I am indisposed, for I shall write to Eliza this post, and will not mention it, lest she should be uneasy.

Tell Fitzgerald, I have just received his letter, and will answer it if I have time, before I quit London.

Adieu, dear Maunsell:

Your's,

C. SKEFFINGTON.

Biographies/Bibliographies

Fiction to 1800

Very little has been written on eighteenth-century Irish fiction, although see: Klaus Lubbers, *Geschichte der irischen Erzahlprosa I: von den anfangen bis zum ausgehenden 19. Jahrhundert* (Munich: Wilhelm Fink Verlag, 1985), chapter I, and Ian Campbell Ross, 'Rewriting Irish literary history: the case of the Irish novel', *Etudes Anglaises,* XXXIX, 4 (1986), 385-99. Discussion of some works by eighteenth-century Irish writers is to be found, however, in the following: Ernest A. Baker, *The History of the English Novel,* 10 vols (London: H. F. & G. Witherby, 1924-39), esp. vol. iv (1930), 'Intellectual Realism from Richardson to Sterne', and vol. v (1934), 'The Novel of Sentiment and the Gothic Romance'; J. M. S. Tompkins, *The Popular Novel in England 1700-1800* (London: Constable, 1932); John Butt and Geoffrey Carnall, *The Oxford History of English Literature VIII: The Mid-Eighteenth Century* (Oxford: Clarendon Press, 1979), esp. chapters x and xi; Dale Spender, *Mothers of the Novel* (London and New York: Pandora, 1986); James M. Cahalan, *The Irish Novel* (Dublin: Gill and Macmillan, 1989).

William Chaigneau

LIFE. Born in Ireland in 1709, of Huguenot descent. Subsequent to serving in the army, he acted as agent to many Irish regiments. *Jack Connor,* for which, it was reported, he declined to accept any 'pecuniary Indulgence' from the bookseller, was published in Dublin and London in 1752, going into at least two English and four Irish editions. Otherwise, Chaigneau is known to have written only one work, 'Harlequin Soldier', an adaptation from the French of a farce, performed in Edinburgh on 22 March 1765, for the benefit of the actor Tate Wilkinson, whom, along with many other leading members of the theatrical profession, Chaigneau had known well in Dublin. He died in 1781.

CHIEF WRITINGS. *The History of Jack Connor,* 2 vols (1752).

BIOGRAPHY AND CRITICISM. *D.N.B.;* Ian Campbell Ross, 'An Irish Picaresque Novel: William Chaigneau's *The History of Jack Connor*', *Studies,* LXXI, no. 283 (Autumn 1982), 270-79.

Thomas Amory

LIFE. By his quasi-autobiographical account in *John Buncle,* Amory was born in England around 1691, and taken to Ireland as a child. This account was disputed within Amory's own lifetime, however, and it is possible he was born in Ireland, where his father owned an estate in County Clare. Very little is known of Amory's life and he does not seem to have studied at Trinity College, Dublin, as he claimed. His alleged personal acquaintance with such prominent Irishmen as John Toland and Jonathan Swift is also suspect. By the mid-1750s, Amory was living in London where he died in 1788.

CHIEF WRITINGS. *Memoirs of Several Ladies of Great Britain* (1755); *The Life and Opinions of John Buncle, Esq.* (1756, 66).

BIOGRAPHY AND CRITICISM. *D.N.B.*; William Hazlitt, 'On John Buncle' in *The Round Table* (1817); Ian Campbell Ross, 'Thomas Amory, *John Buncle,* and the Origins of Irish Fiction', *Eire-Ireland,* XVIII, 3 (Fall 1983), 71-85.

Laurence Sterne

LIFE. Born in Clonmel, Co. Tipperary in 1713, Sterne left Ireland to go to school near Halifax in England at the age of nine. He was educated at

Jesus College, Cambridge, and spent most of his life in Yorkshire as an obscure priest in the Church of England. In 1760, at the age of forty-six, he found enormous fame with the publication of the first two volumes of *Tristram Shandy*, the ninth and final volume of which eventually appeared in 1767. From January 1762 to May 1764, Sterne lived in France, where he travelled in hope of arresting the consumption from which he suffered and which would finally kill him. *A Sentimental Journey* appeared the month before his death. Sterne also published several volumes of sermons and wrote a lightly fictionalized version of his celebrated sentimental friendship, during the last year of his life, with the twenty-three-year old Mrs Elizabeth Draper, eventually published as the *Journal to Eliza*. He died in London on 22 March 1768.

CHIEF WRITINGS. *Chrysal; or, the Adventures of a Guinea* (1760-65; *Gentleman* (1759-67; Ian Campbell Ross (ed.), Oxford: Clarendon Press and London and New York: Oxford University Press, 1983); *The Sermons of Mr. Yorick* (1760-69); *A Sentimental Journey through France and Italy* (1768; Gardner D. Stout, Jr., (ed.) Berkeley and Los Angeles: University of California Press, 1967).

BIOGRAPHY AND CRITICISM. Wilbur L. Cross, *The Life and Times of Laurence Sterne* (1909; 3rd. rev. ed. New Haven: Yale University Press, 1929); Lodwick Hartley, *Laurence Sterne: A Biographical Essay* (1943; repr. Chapel Hill: University of North Carolina Press, 1968); Arthur H. Cash, *Laurence Sterne: The Early and Middle Years* (London: Methuen, 1975). Among many critical works, the following are of particular interest: John Traugott, *Tristram Shandy's World: Sterne's Philosophical Rhetoric* (Berkeley and Los Angeles: University of California Press, 1954); Alan B. Howes, *Yorick and the Critics: Sterne's Reputation in England 1760-1868*, Yale Studies in English, vol. 139 (New Haven: Yale University Press, 1958); John M. Stedmond, *The Comic Art of Laurence Sterne* (Toronto: University of Toronto Press, 1967); John Traugott (ed.), *Laurence Sterne; A Collection of Critical Essays* (Englewood Cliffs, N.J.: Prentice-Hall, Inc., 1968); Arthur H. Cash and John M. Stedmond (eds), *The Winged Skull: Papers from the Laurence Sterne Bicentenary Conference* (London: Methuen, 1971); Richard A. Lanham, *'Tristram Shandy': The Games of Pleasure* (Berkeley, Los Angeles, London: University of California Press, 1973); Mark Loveridge, *Laurence Sterne and the Argument about Design* (London: Macmillan, 1982); Valerie Grosvenor Myer (ed.), *Laurence Sterne: Riddles and Mysteries* (London and Totowa, New Jersey: Vision and Barnes & Noble, 1984); Max Byrd, *Tristram Shandy* (London; George Allen & Unwin, 1985).

Charles Johnstone

LIFE. Born at Carrigogunnel in Co. Limerick in 1719, Johnstone studied at Trinity College, Dublin. Before embarking on a writing career, he practised as a lawyer. In 1782, Johnstone left England, where he had lived for some years, to settle in India. Here he became a journalist and later a newspaper proprietor. He died in Calcutta about 1800.

CHIEF WRITINGS.*Chrysal; or the Adventures of a Guinea* (1760-65; repr. New York and London: Garland, 1979); *The Reverie* (1762; Ronald Paulson (ed.), New York and London: Garland, 1974); *Arsaces, Prince of Betlis* (1774; Michael F. Shugrue (ed.), New York and London: Garland, 1975), *The Pilgrim; or a Picture of Life* (1775; repr. New York and London: Garland, 1974); *The History of John Juniper, Esq.* (1781); *The Adventures of Anthony Varnish* (1786).

BIOGRAPHY AND CRITICISM. *D.N.B.*; Sir Walter Scott, 'Charles Johnstone' in *The Lives of the Novelists* (1821-24).

Frances Sheridan

LIFE. Born in Dublin in 1724, Frances Sheridan was the daughter of the Rev. Dr. Philip Chamberlaine, whose prejudice against women's education was such that Frances was only taught to write in secret by her older brother. Despite this unpromising beginning, Frances Chamberlaine wrote her first (though only posthumously published) novel, *Eugenia and Adelaide*, at the age of fifteen. In 1747, she married the actor and theatre-manager Thomas Sheridan. Four children were born of the marriage, including Richard Brinsley Sheridan and Alicia, later LeFanu, author of a memoir of her mother. Admired and encouraged by such established writers as Samuel Richardson and Samuel Johnson, Frances Sheridan made a name for herself as both a dramatist and a novelist. David Garrick put on two of her plays at Drury Lane in 1763, though, to her great disappointment, he turned down a third. Frances Sheridan died in France in 1766.

CHIEF WRITINGS. *Memoirs of Miss Sidney Bidulph* (1761); *The Discovery* (1763) and *The Dupe* (1764), collected, with *A Journey to Bath* in Robert Hogan and Jerry C. Beasley (eds), *The Plays of Frances Sheridan* (Newark: University of Delaware Press, and London and Toronto: Associated University Presses, 1984); *Continuation of the Memoirs of Miss Sidney Bidulph* (1767); *The History of Nourjahad* (1767).

BIOGRAPHY AND CRITICISM. Alicia LeFanu, *Memoirs of the Life and Writings of Mrs. Frances Sheridan* (1824); *D.N.B.*; Robert Hogan and Jerry C. Beasley, op. cit., 'Introduction', esp. pp. 13-31.

Henry Brooke

LIFE. Born around 1703, the son of a clergyman, Henry Brooke was educated at Trinity College, Dublin, subsequently studying law in London. In the 1730s, Brooke began to establish a reputation for himself as a poet, with the philosophical poem *Universal Beauty*, and as a dramatist, particularly with his celebrated tragedy, *Gustavus Vasa*, whose London performance was banned by the prime minister, Robert Walpole, who regarded the play as critical of himself. The play was later successfully acted in Dublin as *The Patriot*. Various literary projects on Irish fable and history proved abortive, but Brooke wrote important political and economic pamphlets on Irish affairs, including *The Tryal and Cause of the Roman Catholics*, in which he reversed his earlier position and argued for a relaxation of the penal laws. Brooke lived most of the latter part of his life on his small estate in County Cavan. He died in Dublin in 1783.

CHIEF WRITINGS. *Universal Beauty* (1735); *Tasso's Jerusalem . . . translated* (1738); *Gustavus Vasa* (1739); *The Farmer's Letters to the Protestants of Ireland* (1745); *The Interests of Ireland considered* (1759); *The Tryal and Cause of the Roman Catholics* (1761); *The Earl of Essex* (1761); *The Fool of Quality; or, the History of Henry, Earl of Moreland* (1765-70; Ronald Paulson (ed.), New York and London: Garland, 1979); *Juliet Grenville; or, The History of the Human Heart* (1774).

BIOGRAPHY AND CRITICISM. *D.N.B.*; John Wesley, 'Preface' to his abridged edition of *The Fool of Quality* (1781); Charles Kingsley, 'Preface' to his edition of *The Fool of Quality* (1859); H. M. Scurr, *Henry Brooke* (Minneapolis: University of Minnesota Press, 1927).

Oliver Goldsmith

For biography and bibliography, see p. 656.

Anonymous

The Triumph of Prudence Over Passion (1781)

The author of the novel is unknown, but she is described on the title-page as an 'Irish lady' and as the author of an earlier novel, *Emeline*.

CRITICISM. Ian Campbell Ross, '*The Triumph of Prudence over Passion:* Nationalism and Feminism in an Eighteenth-century Irish Novel', *Irish University Review*, Vol. X (1980), 232-40.

DAVID BERMAN and ANDREW CARPENTER, *Editors*

Eighteenth-Century Irish Philosophy

It has often been said — with some truth — that Irish writers have been drawn more to the world of the imagination than to that of abstract ideas, more to poetry and fiction than to philosophy. The eighteenth century, however, provides an exception to this general rule; between 1696 and 1757, a remarkable number of important philosophical and theological books were produced in Ireland. The Penal Laws made it almost inevitable that those who wrote philosophy in Ireland at this time were all protestants; most of them were, in fact, members of the Church of Ireland. The work of their catholic counterparts on the Continent is considered elsewhere in this anthology.

Both liberal and conservative minds were drawn to philosophical speculation in eighteenth-century Ireland; the liberals, espousing the world of reasonable enquiry and toleration — usually leaning towards free-thinking and deism — began with John Toland and ended with Robert Clayton. The conservatives, many of them initially taking up the cudgels to defend traditional Christianity against Toland's rationalism, began with three bishops of the Church of Ireland — Peter Browne, William King and Edward Synge (the elder) — and continued with such figures as Philip Skelton and eventually, and perhaps surprisingly, Edmund Burke. George Berkeley, by far the most important eighteenth-century Irish philosopher, absorbs the concerns of both groups and towers above all factions.

Eighteenth-century Irish philosophy — both wings of it — derived its impetus and inspiration from two related events: the publication of John Locke's major philosophical works in the years 1687-93 and the accession of William and Mary to the thrones of England, Scotland and Ireland in 1689. Locke stood for toleration and moderation, for government by contract and respect for property — for what became, in fact, the English Whig point of view. Unfortunately, things had to be seen rather differently by the Whigs in Ireland after the battle of the Boyne; for, whereas the arrival of William and Mary led to toleration and liberalism in England, it led to repression in Ireland. Thus the response of members of the Irish ascendancy — though they might call themselves Whigs — to the liberalism of Locke and to the type of government developing in England was of necessity different from that of Englishmen and English Whigs. A little toleration might, even if only theoretically, be permissible in England: but the suspicion of toleration in Ireland would threaten the very foundations upon which the country was governed. The Irish political world was profoundly unlike that of England; the basis for political power itself was dissimilar and the theoretical structures for religious and political life had to be articulated in an entirely different way.

What is interesting about the Irish philosophy of the eighteenth century is that, although it is addressing theoretical problems of the nature of experience and the nature of language — which seem to lie in the domain of pure philosophy — its approach to these subjects reflects the political position of those who were writing. In other words, the contribution made by the protestant Irish philosophers to the study of philosophy in the eighteenth century was based on a view of the universe which had to be maintained for political reasons. This makes Irish eighteenth-century philosophy, in a most unexpected and interesting way, a reflection of the political climate of the country itself.

Ostensibly, the philosophers whose works we consider in this section were concerned initially with questions of perception, belief and language that had been raised by Descartes, Malebranche and, most of all, Locke in the latter part of the seventeenth century. But Irish thinkers of this period, in common with those in all European countries, were often polymaths, whose concern with matters of philosophy was an aspect of their interest in, for example, natural philosophy, medicine, theology, economics and politics. In the selections that follow, we have concentrated on the philosophical and theological side of the work of these Irish thinkers, although in doing so we have necessarily excluded many important aspects of their work, particularly in the case of Berkeley and Toland. However, our selection will show the philosophers' recurrent interest in certain major themes, and the reader is encouraged to pursue other aspects of eighteenth-century Irish philosophy in the works listed in the bibliography.

* * *

Two of the earliest of the Irish eighteenth-century philosophers were John Toland and William Molyneux. Both had personal contact with Locke and were avowed admirers of his views on liberty and toleration. Molyneux, a keen scientist and political writer, made some use of Locke's ideas in his political treatise *The Case of Ireland . . . Stated* (1698) and he corresponded with Locke for several years. It was to Locke that Molyneux proposed the philosophical problem that bears his name: he asked whether a blind man suddenly able to see would recognize, by sight alone, a sphere and a cube that formerly he had known only by touch. This question has a bearing on Locke's theories of knowledge, for the English philosopher maintained that all our knowledge is derived from experience and that there are no such things as innate principles. The Molyneux problem was to be taken up in Ireland by Berkeley, Synge and Francis Hutcheson, among others, and it became the root metaphor for much eighteenth-century Irish philosophy.

John Toland was one of the most colourful figures of the age. He was a native Irish-speaker from the Inishowen peninsula in County Donegal. Although he was born a catholic, Toland had left the catholic church by the age of fifteen, had become a dissenter and had moved to Scotland. He soon became involved in promoting the more radical positions of his day, not only in England but also on the Continent. The liberal aspects of Locke's philosophy in particular attracted Toland's interest and were at least partly behind his famous book *Christianity Not Mysterious*, which caused a major controversy when it appeared in England in 1696. Locke immediately dissociated himself from the work and when Toland, who had returned to Ireland hoping for preferment, found that his book was condemned to be burned by the common hangman, he hurriedly left the country.

Toland's book retained its influence and is normally seen as the foundation stone of the deist controversy that played such an important part in eighteenth-century theological and philosophical life in Europe. Certainly *Christianity Not Mysterious* is the loudest call for a radical rethinking of traditional Christianity issued in the late seventeenth century; it is probably the first philosophical work of any note by an Irishman since Ériugena and its significance can hardly be overestimated. In the same decade another Irishman, Robert, Viscount Molesworth, issued his *Account of the State of Denmark* (London, 1694), which asserted that clergy of the reformed churches could be as violent in their oppression of the people as those of the catholic church; while Toland's call for a rational re-examination of Christianity seemed to threaten the basis of anglican belief, Molesworth's *Account* seemed to question the rationale for an anglican religious establishment or indeed for any link between church and state. It is interesting that these two calls for a fundamental rethinking of the principles of political and religious life came from Irishmen.

Toland's countrymen felt the implications of his work acutely, and, interwoven with the controversies surrounding Locke's empirical theories and their importance in matters theological, was the constant need, on the part of the mainstream of Irish philosophers, to refute Toland's position. *Christianity Not Mysterious* carried the radical subtitle 'that there is nothing in the Gospel contrary to reason nor above it'; thus, Toland argued, there are no 'mysteries' in Christianity. This challenge struck at the heart of the hierarchical, exclusive, conservative traditions of the Church of Ireland and, indeed, at the heart of the arguments that sustained the Irish protestant establishment. The irony of the position was as follows: in an age that was moving away from belief in mysteries and towards belief in reason, away from the supernatural and towards the natural, Irish philosophers (though many of them were keen natural scientists and intellectually drawn to the new learning) found themselves forced into anti-enlightenment positions. They could not support toleration, sympathy for natural religion, or any form of anti-clericalism. The philosophical positions that went with such views — rationalism particularly — were equally suspect for them. Of course, such views emerged even in Ireland, and again one sees the paradox of the Irish situation: political and ecclesiastical establishment needs in Ireland led bishops and thinkers to attack the very ideas that seemed to be gaining ground elsewhere. These liberal ideas came to be associated in Ireland with the circle of writers connected with Lord Molesworth. By the 1720s, such views are to be found most clearly expressed in the work of Francis Hutcheson, who spent the years 1720-30 teaching at a dissenting academy in Dublin. Hutcheson went on to become the father of Scottish philosophy and a major inspiration for the American Revolution and constitution.

But toleration of any kind threatened the status quo in Ireland, and it is significant that Toland was answered by three ecclesiastics. Peter Browne wrote a direct ... *Answer to ... Christianity Not Mysterious* (1697) and Edward Synge's *Appendix* to his *Gentleman's Religion* (1698) was another rebuttal. In their refutations, Browne and Synge both used an illustration closely associated with the Molyneux problem: moving from pure theology towards philosophy, they consider the case of the blind man who is told about light and who must try and understand it in terms of some other sense; thus, writes Browne, he might think of it as 'wondrous soft and smooth', but he should not refuse to believe in it just because he cannot experience it himself. Initially, the same blind man might think than those who spoke of colours were imposing upon him, as Toland held that priests were imposing their mysteries on the laity. But after certain experiments, as Synge maintained, the blind man can be brought to believe that there are such things as colour and light. In the same way, Synge asserts, we should assent to the existence of mystery in religion even though we cannot, with our imperfect senses and mental faculties, know precisely what such mysteries are. William King's 1709 sermon on *Predestination and Foreknowledge* employs the same illustration in the passage given below.

In answering the rationalist challenge of Toland and other freethinkers or deists, the Irish philosophers of this counter-enlightenment movement developed a novel and influential philosophical theory that has been called theological representationalism. To explain the nature of man's knowledge of God, they proposed a theory of knowledge analagous to that developed within the new scientific movement of the age. According to Locke and other 'new' scientists, we perceive the qualities of a physical object only through our ideas or immediate experiences of it: colour or smell, for instance, are not in the object as such but in our experience of it. In much the same way, King, Browne and Synge strove to show that we can know God's attributes only indirectly, through what we experience of God in our lives. God's attributes are actually beyond our understanding, but we can get some idea answering to them by concentrating on our anthropomorphic representations of them, particularly as revealed in the Scriptures. Our representations of the workings of God, writes King, may not accurately reflect His attributes, but they do enable us to relate successfully to Him. So a map, although it is different from the land it represents, does enable us to find our way in that land. King tries to put his readers into the state of mind of someone who, though confronted with a representation that is totally different from what it is supposed to represent, can yet pragmatically bridge the gap between these two things. He wants us to appreciate that if we wish to relate successfully to God, we have only to try and see Him represented in ourselves and the natural world. God, though impossible to comprehend, is nevertheless able to be understood in the same way as secondary qualities, such as colour or smell, enable us to experience the real nature of a flower.

If this development of Locke's original ideas was pragmatic, it was so in a way entirely consistent with the conservative churchmanship of the Church of Ireland in the eighteenth century. Peter Browne, probably the most original of those who answered Toland, developed a further refinement of this philosophical position in *The Procedure, Extent and Limits of Human Understanding* (London, 1728) and in *Things Divine and Supernatural conceived by Analogy with things Natural and Human* (London, 1733); there he argued that all our ideas are derived from sensation, so our concepts of emotions, for example, are not essentially different from our ideas of colours. Browne, even more than Locke, was a full-blooded sensationalist with regard to the mind, and made it clear that we cannot possibly *understand* things divine or supernatural; so Christianity is indeed mysterious and it is reasonable to hold that it is so. There is a need for a church to explain the mysteries and also a need for bishops and hierarchies. The political status quo is justified, by implication, by the 'truths' of philosophy.

★ ★ ★

George Berkeley, Ireland's most original and influential philosopher — as well as one of the great prose stylists of the eighteenth century — opposed the theological representationalism of King, Browne and Synge. He held that such arguments, though they might indeed defend God's mysteries, made Him unintelligible; but Berkeley did not support Toland either, for Toland had tried to reduce Christianity to rational theology, while Berkeley, as a strong-minded Christian, believed that Christianity was rational, yet also contained mysterious elements. He centred his investigation more on the basic questions of how we actually use language, how we know what we know, and how we experience what we experience. For Berkeley, religious mysteries are not cognitive but emotive; in other words, faith is not an act of the understanding but one of the emotions and attitudes. Thus, talk of the Trinity is able to produce love, hope and gratitude, grace is likely to evoke piety, and original sin may well produce a salutary sense of one's unworthiness. Berkeley disagreed with the view of King and Browne that God's wisdom is in itself unknowable, holding instead that we know it just as we know that other men are wise — by inferring analogically from their associated sensible effects. As orderly human effects imply a human mind, so the infinite orderliness of nature implies an infinite divine mind. Thus Berkeley clearly rejected the excesses of Toland on the one side and those of the theological representationalists on the other; he retained, in the centre, both reason and faith.

Berkeley is best known for his theory of immaterialism — the view that objects only exist as they are being perceived; this he first published in his *Treatise Concerning the Principles of Human Knowledge* (Dublin, 1710), written when he was a young fellow of Trinity College, Dublin. But his earliest major work on the problems of perception had been *A New Theory of Vision* (Dublin, 1709), in which he analysed the foundations of our judgments of distance, size and position. The Molyneux problem, which Berkeley considers in passages printed below, was central to any investigation of the perception of objects by sight or by touch. So was the question of language, and Berkeley devoted much thought to the meanings of abstract terms. For him, everything perceived is, in effect, an idea that must exist in a mind. So the existence of a mind or spirit is essential for the existence of any 'thing'. And, since the vast world of sensible things can hardly be sustained by human minds, there must be a mind or spirit that enables everything to exist, and this spirit is 'God'. In effect, by saying this, Berkeley was affirming that physical appearance and physical reality are the same thing and that they exist in the mind or spirit only; this view, Berkeley felt, enabled him to refute sceptics and unbelievers.

★ ★ ★

The originality of Berkeley's ideas has long been acknowledged and it is significant for Irish philosophy not only that he was — as he often asserted himself to be — an Irishman, but also that many of the ablest philosophical minds of the age were to be found in Ireland. Among these, William King was perhaps the best-known among his contemporaries, particularly on the Continent, for his treatise on the origin of evil, *De Origine Mali* (Dublin, 1702); this important work was criticized at length by Leibniz, Bayle and other important European thinkers. Although the work was not made available in English until Edmund Law translated it in the 1730s, its influence entered the mainstream of English literature in an unusual way; Alexander Pope, having read King's theories in the work of Henry St John, viscount Bolingbroke (who had in turn read of them in Leibniz), used them for the philosophy of *An Essay on Man*, the most widely read poem of the age.

The ideas of King, like those of Browne and Synge, remained the dominant ones in eighteenth-century Irish philosophy. A generation later, they surfaced in the works of Philip Skelton, a clergyman from the diocese of Clogher, who was one of the most lively and vigorous defenders of the Church of Ireland. Skelton's vigour drew a perceptive comment from Samuel Taylor Coleridge, who wrote in his copy of Skelton's works: 'By the bye, the Rev. Phil. Skelton is one of the true Irish Breed — i.e. a *brave* fellow but a *Bit* of a *Bully*. "E.g. by St. Patrick but I shall make cold mutton of you, Mister Arian."'

Skelton's contemporary and bishop, Robert Clayton, is an altogether more considerable figure in Irish philosophy. He had been a bishop for twenty years when he published his rebellious *An Essay on Spirit* (1750). This caused an uproar and led to calls for Clayton's resignation and even for his excommunication; his rationalism seemed to revive the spirit of Toland and to be opposed to the conservative theological views of Browne, King and others. Furthermore, Clayton was not only a rationalist but also an eloquent pleader for toleration — a highly inappropriate position for a bishop of the Church of Ireland. Only Clayton's death in 1758 saved him from some appallingly ignominious fate at the hands of zealous defenders of the fideistic position essential for the eighteenth-century Church of Ireland.

But the representationalists were obviously in the majority and it is the dominance of their views which lends interest to the early aesthetic theories of Edmund Burke, formed while he was an undergraduate at Trinity College, Dublin in the 1740s. Burke's commitment to the theological position of Browne, King and Synge is clear in his *A Philosophical Enquiry into the Origin of our Ideas of the Sublime and Beautiful* (London, 1757). Here, when considering our understanding of God's attributes, Burke writes that it is 'stretched to a degree far exceeding the bounds of our comprehension.... Thus when we contemplate the Deity, His attributes and their operation coming united on the mind, form a sort of sensible image, and as such are capable of affecting the imagination.' It is worth noting that Burke was also one of the very few eighteenth-century thinkers to accept Berkeley's emotive theory of language: for Burke, as for Berkeley, words may be used significantly without their necessarily representing ideas. This view does not seem to reappear until C.K. Ogden and I.A. Richards's famous book *The Meaning of Meaning* (1923).

* * *

Behind these debates on Christian mysteries, on the nature of knowledge or on language, was a sense of political insecurity. Members of the established Church of Ireland felt themselves threatened by views such as those promulgated by Toland and Clayton and by any suggestion, even of a purely philosophical nature, that might undermine the ideas of hierarchy and exclusivity on which the Irish ascendancy was based. In effect, we are suggesting that political realities lay, at least to a significant extent, behind this burst of philosophical and theological speculation in early eighteenth-century Ireland. Certainly, after 1690, the Irish anglicans were in an insecure and precarious position. They were faced with a hostile, dispossessed majority and a treaty that did not seem to go far enough in restricting the catholics. The presbyterians also seemed a dangerous minority because William III was known to favour them; yet from this insecure position, the Irish anglicans developed a remarkably successful *modus operandi* whose foundation was the penal legislation against both catholics and presbyterians. This legislation, which came into being in the 1690s and 1700s, established the ascendancy just as it repressed the two other religious classes politically, economically and socially.

Even if individual churchmen — and William King was one of these — sometimes opposed the penal legislation on the grounds that to oppress a man because of his religion was against natural law, the actual situation was different once the Penal Laws had been enacted. In any case, at about the same time, Toland's *Christianity Not Mysterious* cast the gauntlet before the anglicans of Ireland as it did before the Church of England. His attack on Christian mysteries and his defence of natural religion represented a challenge to the political status quo. For if there were no Christian mysteries, then there could be nothing to separate the rival Christian religions or sects, and then there could be no basis for the penal code. The success of deism or natural religion would be fatal to the ascendancy; deism's belief in a few fundamental religious doctrines and little or no ritual, as well as its emphasis on morality and toleration, could hardly fail to soften or erode penal codes. If we allow that Toland's deistic thinking represented a threat to the material well-being of the ascendancy, then we can explain the fury unleashed against him, and later against Clayton as well, and also the distinctively counter-enlightenment character of most eighteenth-century Irish philosophy.

It would be wrong, however, to claim that the Irish philosophers who took up these positions were aware of their political implications or that such indirect political motivation invalidates in any way the truth of their philosophical writings. It merely reveals the underlying cause or occasion.

JOHN TOLAND

(1670-1722)

from: CHRISTIANITY NOT MYSTERIOUS (1696)

[*Christianity Not Mysterious* was the seminal work of Irish philosophy. In the chapter that follows, Toland presents the philosophical underpinning of his attack on Christian mysteries, drawing on John Locke's theories of meaning and essence.]

SECTION III

CHAPTER II

That nothing ought to be called a Mystery, *because we have not an adequate Idea of all its Properties, nor any at all of its Essence.*

8. I shall discuss this Point with all the Perspicuity I am able. And, first, I affirm, *That nothing can be said to be a Mystery, because we have not an adequate Idea of it, or a distinct View of all its Properties at once; for then every thing would be a Mystery.* The Knowledge of finite Creatures is gradually progressive, as Objects are presented to the Understanding. *Adam* did not know so much in the twentieth as in the hundredth Year of his Age; and *Jesus Christ* is expressly recorded to have *encreas'd in Wisdom as well as in Stature.* We are said to know a thousand things, nor can we doubt of it; yet we never have a full Conception of whatever belongs to them. I understand nothing better than this *Table* upon which I am now writing: I conceive it divisible into Parts beyond all Imagination; but shall I say it is *above my Reason* because I cannot count these Parts, nor distinctly perceive their Quantity and Figures? I am convinc'd that *Plants* have a regular Contexture, and a Multitude of Vessels, many of them equivalent or analogous to those of *Animals*, whereby they receive a Juice from the Earth, and prepare it, changing some into their own Substance, and evacuating the excrementitious Parts. But I do not clearly comprehend how all these Operations are perform'd, though I know very well what is meant by a *Tree.*

9. The Reason is, because *knowing nothing of Bodies but their Properties, God has wisely provided we should understand no more of these than are useful and necessary for us*; which is all our present Condition needs. Thus our Eyes are not given us to see all Quantities, nor perhaps any thing as it is in itself, but as it bears some Relation to us. What is too minute, as it escapes our Sight, so it can neither harm nor benefit us: and we have a better View of Bodies the nearer we approach them, because then they become more convenient or inconvenient; but as we remove farther off we lose their Sight with their Influence. I'm perswaded there's no Motion which does not excite some Sound in Ears dispos'd to be affected with proportionable Degrees of Force from the Air; and, it may be, the small Animals concern'd can hear the Steps of the *Spider*, as we do those of Men and Cattel. From these and Millions of other Instances it is manifest, that we have little Certainty of any thing but as it is noxious or beneficial to us.

10. Rightly speaking then, we are accounted to

comprehend any thing when its chief Properties and their several Uses are known to us: for *to comprehend* in all correct Authors is nothing else but *to know*; and as of what is not knowable we can have no Idea, so it is nothing to us. It is improper therefore to say a thing is above our Reason, because we know no more of it than concerns us, and ridiculous to supersede our Disquisitions about it upon that score. What should we think of a Man that would stifly maintain *Water* to be above his Reason, and that he would never enquire into its Nature, nor employ it in his House or Grounds, because he knows not how many Particles go to a Drop; whether the Air passes through it, is incorporated with it, or neither? This is for all the World as if I would not go because I cannot fly. Now, feeling *the Denominations of things are borrow'd from their known Properties*, and *that no Properties are knowable but what concern us, or serve to discover such as do*, we cannot be accountable for comprehending no other, nor justly requir'd more by reasonable Men, much less by the all-wise *DEITY*.

11. The most compendious Method therefore to acquire sure and useful Knowledg, *is neither to trouble our selves nor others with what is useless, were it known; or what is impossible to be known at all*. Since I easily perceive the good or bad Effects of Rain upon the Earth, what should I be the better did I comprehend its Generation in the Clouds? for after all I could make no Rain at my Pleasure, nor prevent its falling at any time. A probable Hypothesis will not give Satisfaction in such Cases: The Hands, for Example, of two Dials may have the same Motion, tho the Disposition of the latent Springs which produce it should be very different. And to affirm this or that to be the Way, will not do, unless you can demonstrate that no other possible Way remains. Nay, should you hit upon the real Manner, you can never be sure of it, because the Evidence of Matters of Fact solely depends upon Testimony: And it follows not that such a thing is so, because it may be so.

12. The Application of this Discourse to my Subject admits of no Difficulty; and it is, first, *That no Christian Doctrine, no more than any ordinary Piece of Nature, can be reputed a Mystery, because we have not an adequate or compleat Idea of whatever belongs to it*. Secondly, *That what is reveal'd in Religion, as it is most useful and necessary, so it must and may be as easily comprehended, and found as consistent with our common Notions, as what we know of Wood or Stone, of Air, of Water, or the like*. And, Thirdly, *That when we do as familiarly explain such Doctrines, as what is known of natural things*, (which I pretend we can) *we may then be as properly said to comprehend the one as the other*.

13. They trifle then exceedingly, and discover a mighty Scarcity of better Arguments, who defend their *Mysteries* by this pitiful Shift of drawing Inferences from what is unknown to what is known, or of insisting upon adequate Ideas; except they will agree, as some do, to call every Spire of Grass, Sitting and Standing, Fish or Flesh, profound *Mysteries*. And if out of a pertinacious or worse Humour they will be still fooling, and call these things *Mysteries*, I'm willing to admit as many as they please in *Religion*, if they will allow me likewise to make mine as intelligible to others as these are to me.

14. But to finish this Point, I conclude, that neither God himself, nor any of his Attributes, are *Mysteries* to us for want of an adequate Idea: No, not *Eternity*. The *mysterious Wits* do never more expose themselves than when they treat of *Eternity* in particular. Then they think themselves in their impregnable Fortress, and strangely insult over those dull Creatures that cannot find a thing where it is not. For if any Bounds (as Beginning or End) could be assign'd to *Eternity*, it ceases immediately to be what it should; and you frame only a finite, or rather *a negative Idea*, which is the Nature of all Limitation. Nor can it be said, that therefore *Eternity is above Reason* in this Respect, or that it is any Defect in us not to exhaust its Idea; for what greater Perfection can be ascrib'd to *Reason* than to know precisely the Nature of things? And does not all its Errors lie in attributing those Properties to a thing which it has not, or taking any away that it contains? *Eternity* therefore is no more above Reason, *because it cannot be imagin'd*, than a Circle, *because it may*; for in both Cases *Reason* performs its Part according to the different Natures of the Objects, whereof the one is essentially imaginable, the other not.

15. Now it appears that the pretended *Mysteriousness* of *Eternity* do's not consist in the want of an adequate Notion, which is all that we consider in it at present. The Difficulties rais'd from its Duration, as, that *Succession seems to make it finite*, and that *all things must exist together if it be instantaneous*, I despair not of solving very easily;

and rendring *Infinity* also (which is inseparable from it, or rather a different Consideration of the same thing) as little *mysterious* as that *three and two make five*. But this falls naturally into my *second Discourse*, where I give a particular Explication of the *Christian* Tenets, according to the general Principles I am establishing in this.[1]

16. As we know not all the Properties of things, so we can never conceive the *Essence* of any Substance in the World. To avoid Ambiguity, I distinguish, after an excellent modern Philosopher, the *Nominal* from the *Real Essence* of a thing. *The nominal Essence is a Collection of those Properties or Modes which we principally observe in any thing, and to which we give one common Denomination or Name.*[2] Thus *the nominal Essence* of the *Sun* is a bright, hot, and round Body, at a certain Distance from us, and that has a constant regular Motion. Whoever hears the word *Sun* pronounc'd, this is the Idea he has of it. He may conceive more of its Properties, or not all these; but it is still a Collection of Modes or Properties that makes his Idea. So the *Nominal Essence* of *Honey* consists in its Colour, Taste, and other known Attributes.

17. But *the real Essence is that intrinsick Constitution of a thing which is the Ground or Support of all its Properties, and from which they naturally flow or result.*[3] Now tho we are perswaded that the Modes of things must have such a Subject to exist in, (for they cannot subsist alone) yet we are absolutely ignorant of what it is. We conceive nothing more distinctly than the mention'd Properties of the Sun, and those whereby Plants, Fruits, Metals, *&c.* are known to us; but we have no manner of Notion of the several Foundations of these Properties, tho we are very sure in the mean time, that some such thing must necessarily be. The observable Qualities therefore of things is all that we understand by their Names, for which Reason they are call'd their *Nominal Essence*.

18. It follows now very plainly, that *nothing can be said to be a Mystery, because we are ignorant of its real Essence, since it is not more knowable in one thing than in another, and is never conceiv'd or included in the Ideas we have of things, or the Names we give 'em.* I had not much insisted upon this Point, were it not for the so often repeated Sophistry of some that rather merit the Encomiums of great Readers than great Reasoners. When they would have the most palpable Absurdities and Contradictions go down with others, or make them place Religion in Words that signify nothing, or what they are not able to explain, then they wisely tell them, that they are ignorant of many things, especially the *Essence* of their own Souls; and that therefore they must not always deny what they cannot conceive. But this is not all; for when they would (instead of confuting them) make those pass for ridiculous or arrogant Pretenders, who maintain that *only intelligible and possible things are the Subject of Belief*, they industriously represent them as presuming to define the *Essence* of God with that of created Spirits. And after they have sufficiently aggravated this Presumption of their own coining, they conclude, that if the Contexture of the smallest Pebble is not to be accounted for, then they should not insist upon such rigorous Terms of Believing, but sometimes be content to submit their Reason to their Teachers, and the Determinations of the Church.

19. Who perceives not the Weakness and Slight of this Reasoning? We certainly know as much of the *SOUL* as we do of any thing else, if not more. We form the clearest Conceptions of Thinking, Knowing, Imagining, Willing, Hoping, Loving, and the like Operations of the Mind. But we are Strangers to the *Subject* wherein these Operations exist. So are we to that upon which the Roundness, Softness, Colour, and Taste of a Grape depend. There is nothing more evident than the Modes or Properties of *BODY*, as to be extended, solid, divisible, smooth, rough, soft, hard, *&c.* But we know as little of the internal Constitution, which is the Support of these sensible Qualities, as we do of that wherein the Operations of the *SOUL* reside. And, as the great Man I just now mention'd observes, *we may as well deny the Existence of* Body, *because we have not an Idea of its real Essence, as call the Being of the* Soul *in question for the same Reason.* The Idea of the *Soul* then is every whit as clear and distinct as that of the *Body*; and had there been (as there is not) any Difference, the *Soul* must have carried the Advantage, because its Properties are more immediately known to us, and are the Light whereby we discover all things besides.

20. As for *GOD*, we comprehend nothing better

1. In the preface (p. xxviii), Toland says that he plans to issue three books or discourses, of which the present work is the first. In the event, it was the only one published.
2. See Locke's *Essay concerning Human Understanding* (London, 1690) IV. vi. 69 [Toland's note].
3. See Locke's *Essay on Human Understanding*, II. iii. 17 [Toland's note].

than his Attributes. We know not, it's true, the Nature of that eternal *Subject* or *Essence* wherein Infinite Goodness, Love, Knowledg, Power and Wisdom co-exist; but we are not better acquainted with the *real Essence* of any of his Creatures. As by the Idea and Name of *GOD* we understand his known Attributes and Properties, so we understand those of all things else by theirs; and we conceive the one as clearly as we do the other. I remark'd in the Beginning of this Chapter, that we knew nothing of things but such of their Properties as were *necessary* and *useful*. We may say the same of *God*; for every Act of our Religion is directed by the Consideration of some of his Attributes, without ever thinking of his *Essence*. Our Love to him is kindled by his Goodness, and our Thankfulness by his Mercy; our Obedience is regulated by his Justice; and our Hopes are confirm'd by his Wisdom and Power.

21. I think I may now warrantably conclude, that nothing is a *Mystery*, because we know not its *Essence*, since it appears that it is neither knowable in it self, nor ever thought of by us: So that the *Divine Being* himself cannot with more Reason be accounted *mysterious* in this Respect, than the most contemptible of his Creatures. Nor am I very much concern'd that these *Essences* escape my Knowledg: for I am fix'd in the Opinion, that *what Infinite Goodness has not been pleas'd to reveal to us, we are either sufficiently capable to discover our selves, or need not understand it at all.*

WILLIAM MOLYNEUX

(1656-98)

from: TWO LETTERS TO JOHN LOCKE

1. 2 MARCH 1692/93
2. 14 MARCH 1695/96 (WITH A LETTER BY EDWARD SYNGE TO DR QUAYL, DATED 6 SEPTEMBER 1695)

[The first publication of the celebrated Molyneux problem was in the 1694 (second) edition of Locke's *Essay concerning Human Understanding*, II. ix. 8. It was prompted by William Molyneux's letter of 2 March 1692/3. With the second letter to Locke printed below, dated 14 March 1695/96, Molyneux enclosed a letter on the same subject written by Edward Synge to a Dr Quayl. Edward Synge seems to have been the first to offer a positive answer to Molyneux's problem. The letters were published in Locke's *Familiar Letters* (London, 1708).]

1

... I will conclude my tedious Lines with a jocose Problem, that upon Discourse with several concerning your Book[1] and Notions, I have proposed to divers very ingenious Men, and could hardly ever meet with one, that, at first dash, would give me the Answer to it which I think true, till by hearing my Reasons they were convinced. 'Tis this: 'Suppose a Man born blind, and now adult, and taught by his Touch to distinguish between a Cube and a Sphere (suppose) of Ivory, nighly[2] of the same Bigness, so as to tell when he felt one and t'other, which is the Cube, which the Sphere. Suppose then, the Cube and Sphere placed on a Table, and the blind Man to be made to see; Query, whether by his Sight, before he touch'd them, he could now distinguish and tell which is the Globe, which the Cube? I answer, not; for tho' he has obtained the Experience of how a Globe, how a Cube affects his Touch; yet he has not yet attain'd the Experience, that what affects his Touch so or so, must affect his Sight so or so; or that a protuberant Angle in the Cube, that press'd his Hand unequally, shall appear to his Eye as it does in the Cube.' But of this enough; perhaps you may find some Place in your *Essay*, wherein you may not think it amiss to say Something of this Problem....

2

I herewith send you inclosed the Copy of a Letter from an ingenious Man, on the Problem which you

1. i.e. Locke's *Essay concerning Human Understanding.*

2. nearly.

have honour'd with a Place in *pag. 67.* of your *Essay.*[3] You will find thereby, that what I say of its puzzling some ingenious Men, is true; and you will easily discover by what false Steps this Gentleman is led into his Error. The Letter was communicated to me by the Party to whom it was writ, Dr. *Quayl.* And the Writer of the Letter, Mr. *Edw. Synge*, is the Author of a little Book call'd the *Gentleman's Religion*, which is vended as your's.[4] The Gentleman is on a second Part, which he will shew me before he sends it to the Press. But this only between our selves, and the Bookseller, who has been lately informed of thus much already. For tho' the Book shews not that Freedom of Thought as you or I, perhaps, may expect; yet it shews enough to incense his own Herd against him, for there is little of *Mystery* or *Enthusiastick* in it, and yet the Author is a Clergy-man. And you know that, in a Writer on a religious Subject, 'tis an high Offence, even to be silent on those abstruse Points. The Clergy are not dissatisfied only with those that plainly *oppose* them, but are inraged also, even at those that omit zealously to *advance* them; as we have had a late Instance in him that writes against the *Reasonableness of Christianity*.[5]

'... Mr. *Molyneux*'s ingenious Question, of which you gave me an Account at Mr. *Lukey*'s Yesterday, has run so much in my Mind ever since, that I could scarce drive it out of my Thoughts. To be reveng'd on you therefore for putting my Brains into such a Ferment, I have resolved to be so Impertinent as to send you the Result of my Meditations upon the Subject.

The Case is this: A Man born perfectly blind has a Globe and a Cube given into his Hands, and instructed, as much as he is capable of, in the Notion of each of these Figures, and the Difference between them. Let us now suppose this Man suddenly to be endowed with the Sense of Seeing, and the Question is, whether, the Globe and the Cube being placed before his Eyes, he would be able, by his Sight alone, and without touching them, to tell which was the Globe, and which the Cube?

For the better Understanding of what I shall say on this Question, I desire you to take Notice, that I call every Notion of any Thing which a Man entertains, an *Idea*; but that Notion only, which a Man entertains of a visible Thing, as it is visible, I call an *Image*.

This being premised, I lay down these Propositions.

1. A Man born Blind may have a true (though perhaps not a perfect) *Idea* of a Globe and of a Cube, and of some Difference which is between them.

This evidently appears, because he will certainly be able by his Touch to distinguish them one from the other.

2. A Man who has ever been perfectly Blind, and whilst he so remains, can have no *Image* in his Mind, either of a Cube or Globe.

This, in my Opinion, is very evident, because there is no Passage but the Organs of Sight (of which we suppose him to be deprived) for such an Image to enter; and I take it for granted, that such Images are not innate in Men's Apprehensions.

3. Such a Man, as soon as he is endowed with the Sense of Seeing, will immediately have a different *Image* in his Mind, of a Globe, and of a Cube, as soon as they are exposed to his Sight.

This must needs be so, if his Sight, and the Organs thereof be such as our's, which we suppose.

4. And if immediately, upon the Sight of the Globe and Cube, there be Grounds enough for such a Person clearly to perceive the Agreement, and the Difference between his pre-conceived *Ideas*, and newly conceived *Images* of those Figures, then may he be able to know which is the Globe, and which the Cube, without touching them again after he has seen them.

For the Agreement which he may find between his *Idea* and his *Image* of a Globe, and the Difference of the *Idea* of a Globe from the *Image* of a Cube (*& sic vice versâ*) will be a sufficient Direction to him. (If, I say, there be sufficient Ground immediately to perceive the said Agreement and Difference.)

5. The Idea which such a blind Man must needs, by his Touch alone, form of a Globe, will be this, that it is a Body which is exactly alike on all Sides.

For let him rowl it as often as he will between his Hands, and he can find no manner of Difference

3. *Essay concerning Human Understanding*, second edition (1694).
4. *A Gentleman's Religion* was first published in 1693; two further parts were added in 1697 and an Appendix (see below) in 1698. It was frequently reprinted in the eighteenth century.
5. Locke's *Reasonableness of Christianity* was published anonymously in 1695. Molyneux is probably alluding to John Edwards, *Thoughts concerning ... atheism ... and a book, The Reasonableness of Christianity* .... (London, 1695).

between the one Side and the other.

6. Part of the *Idea* which such a Man must needs, by his Touch, conceive of a Cube, will be, that it is a Body which is not alike in every Part of its Superficies.[6]

For in one Part he feels a smooth Flat, in another the sharp Point of an Angle, and in a third a long Ridge, which reaches from one Angle to another.

7. The *Image*, which at the first Sight such a Man will form of a Globe, must needs represent it as a Body which is alike on all Sides, which consequently must be agreeable to the *Idea* which he before had of it, and different from that *Idea* which he had of a Cube.

For turn a Globe ten thousand ways, and it still carries the same Aspect, if it be all of the same Colour which we now suppose.

6. surface, outward form.

8. The *Image*, which upon the first View such a Man will frame of a Cube, must needs be this, that it is a Body which is not alike in all the Parts of its Superficies, which consequently must be agreeable to the *Idea* which before he had of it, and different from that *Idea* which he had of a Globe.

For a Cube does not carry the same Aspect when it is exposed to our Sight in different Positions.

Since then the *Image*, which such a Man would have of a Globe, would be agreeable to the *Idea* which before he had conceiv'd of it, and different from that *Idea* which before he had entertain'd of a Cube (*& sic vice versâ*) it follows, that by his Sight alone he might be able to know which was the Globe, and which the Cube.

I have no more, but to wish you a good Journey, and tell you, that if you call me Impertinent for sending you my Thoughts upon such a Speculation, I will retort, and tell that it was your self who put the Question. . . .'

EDWARD SYNGE

(1659-1741)

from: AN APPENDIX TO A GENTLEMAN'S RELIGION (1698)

[In this work, a direct response to Toland's *Christianity Not Mysterious*, Synge draws on elements of the Molyneux problem. Although he was an opponent of Toland, Synge's views were closer to Toland's rationalism and deism than to the fideism of Browne, King or Skelton.]

XII. *No Man can possibly believe or give his Assent to any Doctrine or Proposition which appears to him to be contrary to Reason* (see § 9.)[1] For to own a Proposition to be self-evident, or built upon Reason, and yet at the same time to believe another, which mediately or immediately is contradictory to it, is absolutely impossible.

1. The sections referred to throughout this extract (e.g. § 9) are those of Toland's *Christianity Not Mysterious.*

XIII. *If a Proposition be reconcilable to Reason,* (§ 8.) *and the Truth of it also testified by such Persons whose Veracity is beyond all Doubt or Exception; such a Proposition cannot but be believed by any one unto whom it comes so testified.* For if it be reconcilable to Reason, then it may possibly be true, (§ 8.) and if I am actually convinc'd of the Veracity of the Person or Persons who relate it, I cannot chuse but believe that it is true. From whence I think it evidently follows, that Revelation, or the Testimony of another, may justly be looked upon, not only as *a Means of Information*, but also as *a Motive of Persuasion*, whatever a late Author says to the contrary.[2]

XIV. But that which is most material in this present Controversy, is what I am now going to make appear, *viz.* That *a Man may have most sufficient and cogent Arguments, to give his Assent to such Propositions as are not only in part, but wholly and altogether above his Reason,* (§ 10.) For the clear and plain evincing of which, I shall crave leave to

2. See *Christianity Not Mysterious*, section 1, chapters 3 and 4.

make a Relation of a Conference which once I had with a blind Man; to whom, when I understood that he had been quite blind from his Infancy, and never could remember to have seen the least glimmering of Light, I had the Curiosity to put several Questions. I ask'd him, first of all, Whether ever he had endeavour'd to frame any Notion or Conception of Light or Colours, of which, I suppose, he had often heard mention to be made in common Discourse? To which he answer'd me, That he had often endeavour'd it with the greatest Application of his Mind that possibly he could. And to that End and Purpose he had made it his Business to ask all the Questions he could think of, whereby to get Information, but all to no purpose; for that he was still altogether as ignorant of the Nature of Light and Colours, and as unable to frame any Conception of them, as if he had never before heard the Names of them. He told me moreover, that he was a long time before he would or could believe, that other Men had any Faculty at all which he wanted. For, says he, I was sensible of no Defect or Imperfection in my self, but believ'd myself to be altogether as perfect as all other Men with whom I convers'd; and therefore when they told me that I was blind, and talk'd to me of Light and Colours, I apprehended, for a great while, that they did it only to impose upon me. But are you now convinced, said I, that you are blind; and that other Men have the Faculty of Sight, which you want? Yes, reply'd he, I am fully satisfy'd and convinc'd of it. How can that be, said I, when you can frame no manner of Notion of Light or Colours, which are the Objects of Sight? Thus, answer'd he, I was convinc'd of it: They would put me at a Distance from them, and yet would tell me every thing that I did; as whether I stood or sate, or held up my Hand or let it down, or the like; Whereas I could not discover any thing which they did, except I were close to to them, and felt them carefully with my Hands. Now by this, continued he, I am fully convinc'd, that other Men have a Faculty which I want, whereby they can discover and distinguish things at a distance, which they call *Sight*: And I am told by all Men, that there is something call'd *Light*, which is diffus'd thro' the Air, and is the Instrument whereby they are enabled to exercise this Faculty; and also that the *Colour* and *Shape* of things are the Objects upon which the same is employ'd. But altho' I can by my Touch distinguish between the different shapes of some things, and so can frame a Notion of *Shape*: Yet what *Light* is, or what *Colours* are, I have not the least Conception; altho' I am, as I have told you, sufficiently convinc'd, that some such things there are. Now, this Relation being (for the Substance of it) true, to my own Knowledge; or at least (as every Man will own it to be) possible and rational, it will evidently follow, without any further Proof, that this Man had very good and unquestionable Grounds to believe some things that were altogether above his Reason; for what Sight, Light or Colours were, he was utterly uncapable of framing, or receiving any Idea. But yet that there were such things, and that all he heard Men discourse about them was not mere Fiction, (as he for some time apprehended) was plainly prov'd to him by such Arguments as every reasonable Man must allow to have been abundantly sufficient to move his Assent. Nor was this Assent of his, which he gave unto these things, a bare implicit Belief, (§ 11.) as if he had been told that something did exist, which was called *Blictri*;[3] but was altogether ignorant of what was signify'd by that Word, (as Mr. *Toland* speaks). For altho' it was absolutely impossible for him to frame any direct Notion, or Conception, of the things themselves, yet by those analogous Representations which were made to him of them, he well might be and was accordingly, not only fully convinced that what was spoken concerning them, was not insignificant Nonsense; but also enabled to frame some sort of representative Conception of them, which is more than a Man can do of *Blictri*, of which he hears only the Sound, but knows not the Signification. For, supposing a Man at the very Time of his Birth, to be utterly depriv'd of his Organs of Sight; yet by the use of his other four Senses, he may well conceive what a Faculty of Sensation is; and how a sensible Quality, or the small Particles of Matter flowing or rebounding from a Body, and striking upon the proper Organ of Sense, do make such a peculiar Impression upon it, as to affect our Understanding with some particular Knowledge of the Body itself, whereby we are enabled to distinguish it from other Bodies. And as he can directly apply all this to the Senses of

3. The word *Blictri* was a stock example of a nonsense word. Malebranche had recently used it in his *Dialogues*, but it goes back to the Schoolmen and the ancient Greeks. In section 3, chapter 4, Toland writes: 'Could that Person justly value himself upon being wiser than his Neighbours, who having infallible Assurance that something call'd *Blictri* had a Being in Nature, in the Mean time knew not what this *Blictri* was?'

Hearing, Smelling, Tasting, and Touching, of which he may be as good, or a better Master than other Men; so, by way of Analogy from these Senses he will be able to make some imperfect sort of Representation to himself, what sort of thing Sight is, and what Light and Colours are; tho' directly, and particularly, he knows no more of them, than if he had never heard of them. Sir *Kenelm Digby*, in his Treatise of Bodies, *Chap.* 28.[4] tells us of a *Spanish* Nobleman who was born so absolutely Deaf, that if a Gun were shot off, close by his Ear, he could not hear it; and yet was taught to speak very distinctly; and, by the Motion of any Man's Mouth, so perfectly to understand what he said, as that he would not lose a Word in a whole Day's Conversation. Now, the Doctrine of Sounds and Musick must of necessity have been as much above this Man's Reason, as that of Light and Colours was above the blind Man's, of whom I but now spoke; and yet there might very good Assurance have been given to the one, that there was such a Sense as Hearing, and such a thing as a Sound, as well as there was unto the other, in the Case of Light and Colours.

4. See K. Digby, *Two Treatises: in one of which the Nature of Bodies . . . is looked into* . . . . (London, 1658), pp. 307-08.

WILLIAM KING

(1650-1729)

SUMMARY OF THE CHIEF PRINCIPLES OF *DE ORIGINE MALI* (1702)

[Archbishop King's famous philosophical work on the origin of evil, *De Origine Mali*, was first published in 1702 and was criticized by Leibniz, Bayle and Berkeley. Some time after its original appearance, King made this summary, first printed by Edmund Law in his translation of King's work, *An Essay on the Origin of Evil* (London, 1731). King argues that there is no positive evil in the world.]

1. All Creatures are necessarily imperfect and at infinite distance from the Perfection of the Deity, and if a negative Principle were to be admitted, such as the PRIVATION of the PERIPATETICS,[1] it might be said that every created Being consists of Existence and Non-Existence; for it is nothing in respect both of those perfections which it wants, and of those which others have. And this Defect, or as may say, Mixture of NON-ENTITY in the constitution of created Beings is the necessary Principle of all Natural Evils, and of a possibility of Moral ones; as will appear in the sequel.

2. An Equality of Perfection in the Creatures is impossible, (as our Adversaries allow) I add, neither wou'd it be so convenient to place all in the same state of Perfection.

3. It is agreeable to Divine Wisdom and Goodness to have created not only the more perfect Beings, but also the most imperfect, such as Matter, so long as they are better than nothing, and no impediment to the more perfect ones.

4. Admitting Matter and Motion there necessarily follows Composition and Dissolution of Bodies, that is Generation and Corruption; which some may look upon as defects in the Divine work; and yet it is no Objection to his Goodness or Wisdom to create such things as are necessarily attended with these Evils. Allowing therefore God to be infinitely powerful, good and wise, yet it is manifest that some Evils, *viz.* Ge[ne]ration and Corruption, and the necessary Consequences of these, might have place in his Works; and if even one Evil cou'd arise without the ill Principle, why not many? And if we knew the nature and circumstances of all things as well as we do those of Matter and Motion, it may be presum'd that we cou'd account for them without any imputation of the Divine Attributes. For there's the same reason for them all, and one Instance to the contrary destroys an universal Proposition.

5. It is not inconsistent with the Divine Attributes to have created some Spirits or thinking

1. For the peripatetics, or followers of Aristotle, privation in natural philosophy was the principle of change or becoming.

Substances, which are dependant on Matter and Motion in their Operations, and being united to Matter may both move their Bodies and be affected with certain Passions and Sensations by their Motion, and stand in need of a certain disposition of Organs for the proper exercise of their thinking faculty; supposing the number of those that are quite separate from Matter to be as compleat as the System of the whole Universe wou'd admit, and that the lower order is no inconvenience to the higher.

6. It cannot be conceiv'd but that some sensations thus excited by Matter and Motion shou'd be disagreeable and tend to dissolve the union between Soul and Body, as well as others agreeable. For 'tis impossible as well as inconvenient that the Soul shou'd feel itself to be losing its faculty of thinking, which alone can make it happy, and not be affected with it. Now disagreeable sensation is to be reckon'd among natural Evils, which yet cannot be avoided without removing such kind of Animals out of nature. If any one ask why such a Law of Union was establish'd? Let this be his answer; Because there cou'd be no better. For such a necessity as this flows from the very nature of the union of things, and considering the circumstances and conditions under which, and which only they cou'd have existence, they cou'd neither be placed in a better State, nor govern'd by more commodious Laws. These Evils therefore are not inconsistent with the Divine Attributes, provided that the Creatures which are subject to them enjoy such benefits as over-balance them. 'Tis to be observ'd also that these Evils do not properly arise from the Existence which God gave to the Creatures, but from hence that they had not more of Existence given them, which nevertheless their State and the place they fill in the great Machine of the World cou'd not admit. This Mixture therefore of Non-existence supplies the place of an ill Principle in the Origin of Evil, as was said before.

7. The Happiness and Perfection of every thing or Agent arises from the due Exercise of those Faculties which God has given it, and the more Faculties and Perfections any thing has, 'tis capable of the greater and more perfect Happiness.

8. The less dependent on external things, the more self-sufficient any Agent is, and the more it has the principle of its Actions in itself, 'tis so much the more perfect; Since therefore we may conceive two Sorts of Agents, one which do not act, unless impell'd and determin'd by external force the other which have the Principle of their Actions within themselves and can determine themselves to action by their own natural Power: 'tis plain that the latter are much more perfect than the former. Nor can it be deny'd but that God may create an Agent with such a power as this, which can exert itself into action, without either the concourse of God or the determination of external Causes, so long as God by a general Concourse preserves the Existence, Powers and Faculties of that Agent.

9. Such an Agent may prescribe to itself an End, and prosecute it by proper Means and take delight in the prosecution of it, tho' that end might be perfectly indifferent to it before it was proposed, and be no more agreeable than any other of the same or a different kind wou'd be, if the Agent had once resolv'd to prosecute it. For since all the pleasure or happiness which we receive, arises from the due exercise of our Faculties, every thing which is equally commodious for the exercise of our faculties, will give us the same delight. The reason therefore why one thing pleases above another is founded in the Act of the Agent himself, *viz.* his Election. This is largely explain'd in the Book itself, together with the limits within which it is confined, and shall be illustrated more fully hereafter.

10. It is impossible that all things shou'd agree to all, that is be good; for since the things are limited, distinct and different one from another, and are endow'd with finite, distinct and different appetites, it necessarily follows that the relations of convenient and inconvenient must arise from this diversity. Since therefore every created being is from the imperfection of its nature necessarily limited, and from that limitation there necessarily follows distinction and diversity, it follows that a possibility at least of Evil is a necessary attendant on all Creatures, and cannot be separated from them by any Power, Wisdom or Goodness whatsoever. For when a thing is applied to an Appetite or Being to which it is not appropriated, as it is not agreeable to it, it necessarily affects it with uneasiness; nor was it possible that all things shou'd be appropriated to every Being, where the things themselves and the appetites are various and different, as they must necessarily be, if created, even in the most perfect manner.

11. Since some Agents have a power over their Actions, as above, and can please themselves in the choice of such things as may exercise their faculties;

and since there are some ways of exercising them which may be prejudicial to themselves or others; 'tis plain that from this power there arises a possibility of choosing amiss, and they may exercise themselves to their own prejudice or that of others.

12. And since in such a variety of things those that are beneficial or hurtful cannot be known by an intelligent Being which is in its own nature limited and imperfect, it was agreeable to the Divine Wisdom and Goodness to prescribe some Rules and Directions to such agents, in order to inform them of what wou'd benefit or incommode them and their Fellow Creatures, *i.e.* what wou'd be good or evil; that they might choose the one and avoid the other.

13. Since therefore, as was said before, an Equality of Perfections in the Creatures is impossible, neither wou'd it be convenient for them to be placed in the same State of Perfection, it follows that there are various Orders and Degrees even among intelligent Creatures; and since some of the inferior Orders and Degrees are capable of those benefits which the superior ones enjoy, and since there are as many placed in those superior Orders as the System of the Universe allow'd, it follows that the inferior ones, as a more convenient place cou'd not be left for them, ought to be content with a lower portion of Happiness, which their nature makes them capable of, and to a higher than which they cou'd not aspire without detriment to the superior which possesses that Station. For he must quit his place before another can ascend to it; and it seems hard and very inconsistent with the nature of God to degrade a Superior as long as he has done nothing to deserve it. But if one of a superior Order shall by his own act, without any violence or compulsion, voluntarily quit his place, or freely choose such things as deserve a Degradation, God wou'd seem unjust to those who are in an inferior Degree and by a good use of their Liberty become fit and qualify'd for a superior State, if he shou'd refuse them the free use of their Choice. It seems unjust for God to condemn or degrade any one arbitrarily, but he is not to be blamed for suffering one to degrade himself by his own act and choice, especially when the use of that elective power belongs to the nature of an intelligent Being, and cou'd not in the present state be prohibited without detriment to some other.

Here the Wisdom and Goodness of God seem to have exerted themselves in a most glorious manner, the contrivance appears to be the effect of the highest Policy and Prudence. For by this means God has shewn himself most equitable to his Creatures; so that no one can complain of or glory in his lot. He that is in a less convenient Situation has no room for complaint, since he is endow'd with faculties and has power to use them in such a manner as to acquire a more commodious one; and he must be forced to own himself only in the fault if he continues deprived of it: and he that is now in a superior State may learn to fear lest he fall from it by an unlawful use of his faculties. The Superior therefore has a Dread that may in some measure diminish his happiness, and the inferior Hope that may increase it; by which means they are both brought nearer to an equality, and in the mean time have the utmost provocation and incitement to choose the best, and make the most beneficial use of their faculties. This Contest, if I mistake not, makes for the good of the Universe, and much more than if all things were fix'd by Fate and Necessity, and absolutely confined to their present State. Either God must have created no free Agents to be govern'd by the hope of rewards and fear of punishments, or this will be the fittest means to that end, and worthy of a God. For what ground is there to complain of the Deity in this whole affair; except that when an equal share of happiness cou'd not befal every one, he bestows the best on such as use their faculties aright, and takes away what he had given from those that abuse them? But more of this hereafter.

14. If what is laid down above be true, from thence 'tis manifest that all kinds of Evil, *viz.* that of IMPERFECTION, PAIN and SIN may enter into a world made by the most wise good and powerful Author, and that its Origin may be accounted for without calling in the assistance of an Evil Principle.

15. 'Tis plain that we are tied down to this Earth and confined in it, as in a Prison, and that our Knowledge does not extend beyond the Ideas which we receive from the Senses; and who knows not how small a part we understand even of those Elements about which we are conversant? But since the whole Mass of Elements is as a Point in regard to the whole Universe, is it any wonder if we mistake when we are forming a judgment, or rather a conjecture, concerning the beauty, order and Goodness of the Whole from this contemptible Particle? This Earth of ours may be the Dungeon of

the Universe, an Hospital of Madmen or a Work-house of reprobates, and yet such as it is, there is much more both of natural and Moral Good than Evil to be found in it. . . .

from:
PREDESTINATION AND FOREKNOWLEDGE . . . . (1709)

[In this important sermon, King tries to answer some of the traditional problems faced by those who believe in God by explaining in what sense we know God's attributes. The theory, previously outlined by Peter Browne in his *Letter* against Toland, is the theological equivalent of Locke's theory of representationalism, according to which we know the physical world indirectly by means of ideas.]

§ XII. *Lastly*, It is observable, that no Care, Industry or Instruction can ever give a Person born and continuing blind, any Notion of Light; nor can he ever have any Conception, how Men, who have Eyes, discern the Shape and Figure of a Thing at a Distance, nor imagine what *Colours* mean: And yet he would, I believe readily (on the Account he receives from others of the Advantage of knowing these Things) endure Labour and Pain, and submit to the most difficult and tormenting Operations of *Physick* or *Chirurgery*,[1] in Order to obtain the Use of Eyes, if any reasonable Hope could be given him of the Success of such an Undertaking. And why then should not we as willingly submit to those easy Methods, which God has prescribed to us, in Order to obtain that Knowledge of his Nature and Attributes, in which our eternal Satisfaction and Happiness hereafter are in a very great Measure to consist? And 'tis certain, we now know as much of them as the Blind-man, in the Case supposed, does of *Lights* or *Colours*, and have better Reason to seek and more certain Hope of attaining in the next Life, to a fuller and more compleat Knowledge, than such a Man can have with Relation to the Use of his Eyes, and the Advantage of seeing: And then will not he rise up in Judgment against us, and condemn us? since he does endure so much to obtain Sight, on the imperfect Representations of it, that are made to him by other Men, whilst we will not believe and endure as much for eternal Happiness on the Testimony of God.

§ XIII. If it be asked, why these Things are not made clearer to us? I answer, for the same Reasons, that *Light* and *Colours* are not clear to one, who is born *blind*, even because in this imperfect State, we want Faculties to discern them; and we cannot expect to reach the Knowledge of them in this World for the same Reason, that a Child during his Childhood, cannot speak and discourse, as he doth when he is arrived to Manhood; there is a Time and Season for every Thing, and we must wait for that Season. There is another State and Life for the clear discerning of these Matters, but in the mean Time, we ought to take the Steps and Methods proper for our present Condition, and if we will not do so, we can no more expect to arrive at the Knowledge of these necessary Truths, or that State, which will make them plain to us, than a Child can hope, that he ever shall be able to read and write, who will not be perswaded to go to School and obey his Master.

This *Analogical Knowledge* of God's Nature and Attributes is all, we are capable of at present, and we must either be contented to know him thus, or sit down with an intire Ignorance and Neglect of God, and finally Despair of future Happiness. But it concerns us frequently to call to Mind the Apostle's Observation I. Cor. 13. 12. *For now we see through a Glass darkly; but then Face to Face: Now I know in Part; but then I shall know even as I am known.* Though our present Knowledge of Divine Things be very imperfect, however it is enough to awaken our Desire of more, and though we do not understand the Enjoyments of the Blessed, yet the Description we have of them, is sufficient to engage us to seek after them, and to prosecute the Methods prescribed in Scripture for attaining them.

§ XIV. And therefore let me offer it as a second Reason, why God and Divine Things are thus represented to us in Scripture, *viz.* that such Knowledge is sufficient to all Intents and Purposes of Religion. The Design whereof is to lead us in the Way to eternal Happiness, and in Order thereunto, to teach and oblige us to live reasonably, to perform our Duty to God, our Neighbours and our selves, to conquer and mortify our Passions and Lusts, to make us beneficent and charitable to Men, and to oblige us to love, obey and depend upon God.

Now it is easy to shew, that such a Knowledge, as I have described, is sufficient to obtain all those

1. An archaic word for 'surgery'.

Ends, for altho I know not what God is in himself, yet if I believe, that he is able to hurt or help me, to make me happy or miserable, this Belief is sufficient to convince me, that it is my Duty to fear him. If I be assured, that all his Works are done with Regularity, Order, and Fitness, that Nothing can surprize or disappoint him, that he can never be in any Doubt, or at a Loss what is proper for him to do, though I do not comprehend the Faculties by which he performs so many admirable and amazing Things, yet I know enough to make me adore and admire his Conduct. If I be satisfied that I can no more expect to escape free, when I break the Laws and Rules he has prescribed me, than a Subject can who assaults his Prince in the midst of all his Guards, this is enough to make me cautious about every Word I speak, and every Action I perform, and to put me out of all hope of escaping when I offend him....

§ XIX. Let me in the 4th Place observe, that as we transfer the Actions of our own Minds, our Powers and Virtues by *Analogy* to God, and speak of him, as if he had the like, so we proceed the same Way in the Representations we make to one another, of the Actions of our own Minds, and ascribe the Powers and Faculties of Bodies to the Transactions that pass in them. Thus to *weigh* Things, to *penetrate*, to *reflect*, are proper Actions of Bodies, which we transfer to our *Understandings*, and commonly say, that the Mind *weighs* or *penetrates* Things, that it *reflects* on it self, or Actions; thus, to *imbrace*, or *reject*, to *retain*, or let *slip*, are corporeal Performances, and yet we ascribe the first to the *Will*, and the last to the *Memory*. And it is manifest, that it do's not cause any Confusion in our Notions, though none will deny, but there is a vast Difference between *weighing* a Piece of Money in a *Scale*, and considering a Thing in our *Minds*, between one Body's passing through another, which is properly *penetrating*, and the Understanding's obtaining a clear Notion of a Thing hard to be comprehended. And so in all the rest, there is indeed a Resemblance and *Analogy* between them, which makes us give the same Names to each, but to compare them in all Particulars, and expect they should exactly answer, would run us into great Absurdities. As for Example, it would be ridiculous to think, that *weighing* a Thing in our *Minds*, should have all the Effects, and be accompanied with all the Circumstances that are observable in *weighing* a Body.

§ XX. Now to apply this, let us consider, that *Love*, *Hatred*, *Wisdom*, *Knowledge* and *Fore-Knowledge*, are properly Faculties or Actions of our Minds, and we ascribe them to God after the same Manner as we do *Reflection, Penetrating, Discovering, embracing* or *Rejecting*, to our intellectual Actions and Faculties, because there is some *Analogy* and Proportion between them. But then we ought to remember, that there is as great a Difference between these, when attributed to God, and as they are in us, as between *weighing* in a *Ballance* and *thinking*, in Truth infinitely greater, and we ought no more to expect, that the one should in all Respects and Circumstances answer the other, than that *thinking* in all Things should correspond to *weighing*. Would you not be surprized to hear a Man deny and obstinately persist in denying, that his Mind can reflect upon it self, because it is impossible, that a Body from whence the Notion is originally taken, should move or act on its self? And is it not equally absurd to argue, that what we call *Foreknowledge* in God, cannot consist with the *Contingency* or *Freedom* of Events, because our *Prescience*, from whence we transfer the Notion to the Divine Understanding could not, if it were certain? And is it not equally a sufficient Answer to both, when we say, that the *Reflection* of Bodies, though in many Circumstances it resemble that Action of the Mind, which we call so, yet in other Particulars is mighty unlike? And though the *Fore-knowledge* we have in some Things resembles what we term so in God, yet the Properties and Effects of these in other Particulars are infinitely different.

Nor can we think, that whatever is impossible in the one, must be likewise so in the other. It is impossible *Motion* should be in a Body, except it be moved by another, or by some other external Agent, and it requires a *Space* in which it is performed, and we can Measure it by *Feet* and *Yards*; but we should look on him as a very weak Reasoner, who would deny any *Motion* to be in the Mind, because he could find none of those there. And we should think, we had sufficiently answered his Objection, by telling him, that these two *Motions* are of very different Natures, though there be some *Analogy* and Proportion between them. And shall not the same Answer satisfy those who argue against the Divine *Fore-knowledge, Predestination*, and other *Actions* attributed to God, because many things are supposed possible to him which are impossible to us? . . .

GEORGE BERKELEY

(1685-1753)

from:
A NEW THEORY OF VISION
(1709)

[This was Berkeley's first major work. Its thesis is that what we see is mind-dependent. Berkeley uses the Molyneux problem as evidence that the objects of vision and touch are entirely different.]

132 A farther confirmation of our tenet may be drawn from the solution of Mr. Molyneux's problem, published by Mr. Locke in his *Essay*: Which I shall set down as it there lies, together with Mr. Locke's opinion of it, ' "Suppose a man born blind, and now adult, and taught by his touch to distinguish between a cube and a sphere of the same metal, and nighly of the same bigness, so as to tell, when he felt one and t'other, which is the cube and which the sphere. Suppose then the cube and sphere placed on a table, and the blind man to be made to see: *Quaere*, Whether by his sight, before he touched them, he could now distinguish and tell which is the globe, which the cube?" To which the acute and judicious proposer answers: "Not. For though he has obtained the experience of how a globe, how a cube, affects his touch, yet he has not yet attained the experience that what affects his touch so or so must affect his sight so or so: Or that a protuberant angle in the cube that pressed his hand unequally shall appear to his eye as it doth in the cube." I agree with this thinking gentleman, whom I am proud to call my friend, in his answer to this his problem; and am of opinion that the blind man at first sight would not be able with certainty to say which was the globe which the cube, whilst he only saw them.'[1]

133 Now, if a square surface perceived by touch be of the same sort with a square surface perceived by sight, it is certain the blind man here mentioned might know a square surface as soon as he saw it: It is no more but introducing into his mind by a new inlet an idea he has been already well acquainted with. Since, therefore, he is supposed to have known by his touch that a cube is a body terminated by square surfaces, and that a sphere is not terminated by square surfaces: upon the supposition that a visible and tangible square differ only *in numero* it follows that he might know, by the unerring mark of the square surfaces, which was the cube, and which not, while he only saw them. We must therefore allow either that visible extension and figures are specifically distinct from tangible extension and figures, or else that the solution of this problem given by those two thoughtful and ingenious men is wrong.

134 Much more might be laid together in proof of the proposition I have advanced: but what has been said is, if I mistake not, sufficient to convince any one that shall yield a reasonable attention: And as for those that will not be at the pains of a little thought, no multiplication of words will ever suffice to make them understand the truth, or rightly conceive my meaning.

135 I cannot let go the above-mentioned problem without some reflexion on it. It hath been made evident that a man blind from his birth would not, at first sight, denominate any thing he saw by the names he had been used to appropriate to ideas of touch, *vid.* sect. 106. Cube, sphere, table are words he has known applied to things perceivable by touch, but to things perfectly intangible he never knew them applied. Those words in their wonted application always marked out to his mind bodies or solid things which were perceived by the resistance they gave: But there is no solidity, no resistance or protrusion, perceived by sight. In short, the ideas of sight are all new perceptions, to which there be no names annexed in his mind: he cannot therefore understand what is said to him concerning them: And to ask of the two bodies he saw placed on the table which was the sphere, which the cube? were to him a question downright bantering and unintelligible; nothing he sees being able to suggest to his thoughts the idea of body, distance, or in general of any thing he had already known.

136 It is a mistake to think the same thing affects both sight and touch. If the same angle or square which is the object of touch be also the object of vision, what should hinder the blind man at first

1. *Essay on Human Understanding*, B.ii.C.9.S.8. [Berkeley's note].

sight from knowing it? For though the manner wherein it affects the sight be different from that wherein it affected his touch, yet, there being beside this manner or circumstance, which is new and unknown, the angle or figure, which is old and known, he cannot choose but discern it.

137 Visible figure and extension having been demonstrated to be of a nature intirely different and heterogeneous from tangible figure and extension, it remains that we inquire concerning motion. Now that visible motion is not of the same sort with tangible motion seems to need no farther proof, it being an evident corollary from what we have shewn concerning the difference there is between visible and tangible extension: But for a more full and express proof hereof we need only observe that one who had not yet experienced vision would not at first sight know motion. Whence it clearly follows that motion perceivable by sight is of a sort distinct from motion perceivable by touch. The antecedent I prove thus: By touch he could not perceive any motion but what was up or down, to the right or left, nearer or farther from him; besides these and their several varieties or complications, it is impossible he should have any idea of motion. He would not therefore think any thing to be motion, or give the name motion to any idea which he could not range under some or other of those particular kinds thereof. But from sect. 95 it is plain that by the meer act of vision he could not know motion upwards or downwards, to the right or left, or in any other possible direction. From which I conclude he would not know motion at all at first sight. As for the idea of motion in abstract, I shall not waste paper about it, but leave it to my reader to make the best he can of it. To me it is perfectly unintelligible.

138 The consideration of motion may furnish a new field for inquiry: But since the manner wherein the mind apprehends by sight the motion of tangible objects, with the various degrees thereof, may be easily collected from what hath been said concerning the manner wherein that sense doth suggest their various distances, magnitudes, and situations, I shall not enlarge any farther on this subject, but proceed to consider what may be alledged, with greatest appearance of reason, against the proposition we have shewn to be true: For where there is so much prejudice to be encountered, a bare and naked demonstration of the truth will scarce suffice. We must also satisfy the scruples that men may raise in favour of their preconceived notions, shew whence the mistake arises, how it came to spread, and carefully disclose and root out those false persuasions that an early prejudice might have implanted in the mind.

139 *First*, therefore, it will be demanded how visible extension and figures come to be called by the same name with tangible extension and figures, if they are not of the same kind with them? It must be something more than humour or accident that could occasion a custom so constant and universal as this, which has obtained in all ages and nations of the world, and amongst all ranks of men, the learned as well as the illiterate.

140 To which I answer, we can no more argue a visible and tangible square to be of the same species from their being called by the same name than we can that a tangible square and the monosyllable consisting of six letters whereby it is marked are of the same species because they are both called by the same name. It is customary to call written words and the things they signify by the same name: For words not being regarded in their own nature, or otherwise than as they are marks of things, it had been superfluous, and beside the design of language, to have given them names distinct from those of the things marked by them. The same reason holds here also. Visible figures are the marks of tangible figures, and from sect. 59 it is plain that in themselves they are little regarded, or upon any other score than for their connexion with tangible figures, which by nature they are ordained to signify. And because this language of nature doth not vary in different ages or nations, hence it is that in all times and places visible figures are called by the same names as the respective tangible figures suggested by them, and not because they are alike or of the same sort with them.

141 But, say you, surely a tangible square is liker to a visible square than to a visible circle: It has four angles and as many sides: so also has the visible square: but the visible circle has no such thing, being bounded by one uniform curve without right lines or angles, which makes it unfit to represent the tangible square but very fit to represent the tangible circle. Whence it clearly follows that visible figures are patterns of, or of the same species with, the respective tangible figures represented by them: that they are like unto them, and of their own nature fitted to represent them, as being of the same sort: and that they are in no respect arbitrary signs, as words.

142 I answer, it must be acknowledged the visible square is fitter than the visible circle to represent the tangible square, but then it is not because it is liker, or more of a species with it, but because the visible square contains in it several distinct parts, whereby to mark the several distinct corresponding parts of a tangible square, whereas the visible circle doth not. The square perceived by touch hath four distinct, equal sides, so also hath it four distinct equal angles. It is therefore necessary that the visible figure which shall be most proper to mark it contain four distinct equal parts corresponding to the four sides of the tangible square, as likewise four other distinct and equal parts whereby to denote the four equal angles of the tangible square. And accordingly we see the visible figures contain in them distinct visible parts, answering to the distinct tangible parts of the figures signified or suggested by them.

143 But it will not hence follow that any visible figure is like unto, or of the same species with, its corresponding tangible figure, unless it be also shewn that not only the number but also the kind of the parts be the same in both. To illustrate this, I observe that visible figures represent tangible figures much after the same manner that written words do sounds. Now, in this respect words are not arbitrary, it not being indifferent what written word stands for any sound: But it is requisite that each word contain in it so many distinct characters as there are variations in the sound it stands for. Thus the single letter *a* is proper to mark one simple uniform sound; and the word *adultery* is accommodated to represent the sound annexed to it, in the formation whereof there being eight different collisions or modifications of the air by the organs of speech, each of which produces a difference of sound, it was fit the word representing it should consist of as many distinct characters, thereby to mark each particular difference or part of the whole sound: And yet no body, I presume, will say the single letter *a*, or the word *adultery*, are like unto, or of the same species with, the respective sounds by them represented. It is indeed arbitrary that, in general, letters of any language represent sounds at all: but when that is once agreed, it is not arbitrary what combination of letters shall represent this or that particular sound. I leave this with the reader to pursue, and apply it in his own thoughts.

144 It must be confessed that we are not so apt to confound other signs with the things signified, or to think them of the same species, as we are visible and tangible ideas. But a little consideration will shew us how this may be without our supposing them of a like nature. These signs are constant and universal, their connexion with tangible ideas has been learnt at our first entrance into the world; and ever since, almost every moment of our lives, it has been occurring to our thoughts, and fastening and striking deeper on our minds. When we observe that signs are variable, and of human institution; when we remember there was a time they were not connected in our minds with those things they now so readily suggest; but that their signification was learned by the slow steps of experience: This preserves us from confounding them. But when we find the same signs suggest the same things all over the world; when we know they are not of human institution, and cannot remember that we ever learned their signification, but think that at first sight they would have suggested to us the same things they do now: All this persuades us they are of the same species as the things respectively represented by them, and that it is by a natural resemblance they suggest them to our minds.

145 Add to this that whenever we make a nice survey of any object, successively directing the optic axis to each point thereof, there are certain lines and figures described by the motion of the head or eye, which being in truth perceived by feeling, do nevertheless so mix themselves, as it were, with the ideas of sight, that we can scarce think but they appertain to that sense. Again, the ideas of sight enter into the mind several at once, more distinct and unmingled than is usual in the other senses beside the touch. Sounds, for example, perceived at the same instant, are apt to coalesce, if I may so say, into one sound: But we can perceive at the same time great variety of visible objects, very separate and distinct from each other. Now tangible extension being made up of several distinct coexistent parts, we may hence gather another reason that may dispose us to imagine a likeness or analogy between the immediate objects of sight and touch. But nothing, certainly, doth more contribute to blend and confound them together than the strict and close connexion they have with each other. We cannot open our eyes but the ideas of distance, bodies, and tangible figures are suggested by them. So swift and sudden and unperceived is the transition from visible to tangible ideas that we can

scarce forbear thinking them equally the immediate object of vision.

146 The prejudice which is grounded on these, and whatever other causes may be assigned thereof, sticks so fast that it is impossible without obstinate striving and labour of the mind to get intirely clear of it. But then the reluctancy we find in rejecting any opinion can be no argument of its truth to whoever considers what has been already shewn with regard to the prejudices we entertain concerning the distance, magnitude, and situation of objects; prejudices so familiar to our minds, so confirmed and inveterate, as they will hardly give way to the clearest demonstration.

147 Upon the whole, I think we may fairly conclude that the proper objects of vision constitute an universal language of the Author of nature, whereby we are instructed how to regulate our actions in order to attain those things that are necessary to the preservation and well-being of our bodies, as also to avoid whatever may be hurtful and destructive of them. It is by their information that we are principally guided in all the transactions and concerns of life. And the manner wherein they signify and mark unto us the objects which are at a distance is the same with that of languages and signs of human appointment, which do not suggest the things signified by any likeness or identity of nature, but only by an habitual connexion that experience has made us to observe between them.

148 Suppose one who had always continued blind be told by his guide that after he has advanced so many steps he shall come to the brink of a precipice, or be stopt by a wall; must not this to him seem very admirable and surprizing? He cannot conceive how it is possible for mortals to frame such predictions as these, which to him would seem as strange and unaccountable as prophesy doth to others. Even they who are blessed with the visive faculty may (though familiarity make it less observed) find therein sufficient cause of admiration. The wonderful art and contrivance wherewith it is adjusted to those ends and purposes for which it was apparently designed, the vast extent, number, and variety of objects that are at once with so much ease and quickness and pleasure suggested by it: All these afford subject for much and pleasing speculation, and may, if any thing, give us some glimmering, analogous prænotion[2] of things which are placed beyond the certain discovery and comprehension of our present state.

2. foreknowledge; compare below the extract from *The Guardian*.

from: TREATISE CONCERNING THE PRINCIPLES OF HUMAN KNOWLEDGE (1710)

[In this work, Berkeley sketches his emotive theory of meaning and outlines his ontology. For him, only two things exist: minds and ideas. Berkeley also begins to argue the case for immaterialism — that matter does not exist, because it is either meaningless or involves a contradiction.]

INTRODUCTION

20 Besides, the communicating of ideas marked by words is not the chief and only end of language, as is commonly supposed. There are other ends, as the raising of some passion, the exciting to, or deterring from an action, the putting the mind in some particular disposition; to which the former is in many cases barely subservient, and sometimes entirely omitted, when these can be obtained without it, as I think doth not infrequently happen in the familiar use of language. I entreat the reader to reflect with himself, and see if it doth not often happen either in hearing or reading a discourse, that the passions of fear, love, hatred, admiration, disdain, and the like arise, immediately in his mind upon the perception of certain words, without any ideas coming between. At first, indeed, the words might have occasioned ideas that were fit to produce those emotions; but, if I mistake not, it will be found that when language is once grown familiar, the hearing of the sounds or sight of the characters is oft immediately attended with those passions, which at first were wont to be produced by the intervention of ideas, that are now quite omitted. May we not, for example, be affected with the promise of a *good thing*, though we have not an idea of what it is? Or is not the being threatened with danger sufficient to excite a dread, though we think not of any particular evil likely to befall us, nor yet frame to our selves an idea of danger in abstract? If any one shall join ever so little reflection of his own to what has been said, I believe it will evidently

appear to him, that general names are often used in the propriety of language without the speaker's designing them for marks of ideas in his own, which he would have them raise in the mind of the hearer. Even proper names themselves do not seem always spoken, with a design to bring into our view the ideas of those individuals that are supposed to be marked by them. For example, when a Schoolman tells me *Aristotle hath said it*, all I conceive he means by it, is to dispose me to embrace his opinion with the deference and submission which custom has annexed to that name. And this effect may be so instantly produced in the minds of those who are accustomed to resign their judgment to the authority of that philosopher, as it is impossible any idea either of his person, writings, or reputation should go before. Innumerable examples of this kind may be given, but why should I insist on those things, which every one's experience will, I doubt not, plentifully suggest unto him? . . .

PART I

1 It is evident to any one who takes a survey of the objects of human knowledge, that they are either ideas actually imprinted on the senses, or else such as are perceived by attending to the passions and operations of the mind, or lastly ideas formed by help of memory and imagination, either compounding, dividing, or barely representing those originally perceived in the aforesaid ways. By sight I have the ideas of light and colours with their several degrees and variations. By touch I perceive, for example, hard and soft, heat and cold, motion and resistance, and of all these more and less either as to quantity or degree. Smelling furnishes me with odours; the palate with tastes, and hearing conveys sounds to the mind in all their variety of tone and composition. And as several of these are observed to accompany each other, they come to be marked by one name, and so to be reputed as one thing. Thus, for example, a certain colour, taste, smell, figure and consistence having been observed to go together, are accounted one distinct thing, signified by the name *apple*. Other collections of ideas constitute a stone, a tree, a book, and the like sensible things; which, as they are pleasing or disagreeable, excite the passions of love, hatred, joy, grief, and so forth.

2 But besides all that endless variety of ideas or objects of knowledge, there is likewise something which knows or perceives them, and exercises divers operations, as willing, imagining, remembering about them. This perceiving, active being is what I call *mind, spirit, soul* or *my self*. By which words I do not denote any one of my ideas, but a thing entirely distinct from them, wherein they exist, or, which is the same thing, whereby they are perceived; for the existence of an idea consists in being perceived.

3 That neither our thoughts, nor passions, nor ideas formed by the imagination, exist without the mind, is what every body will allow. And it seems no less evident that the various sensations or ideas imprinted on the sense, however blended or combined together (that is, whatever objects they compose) cannot exist otherwise than in a mind perceiving them. I think an intuitive knowledge may be obtained of this, by any one that shall attend to what is meant by the term *exist* when applied to sensible things. The table I write on, I say, exists, that is, I see and feel it; and if I were out of my study I should say it existed, meaning thereby that if I was in my study I might perceive it, or that some other spirit actually does perceive it. There was an odour, that is, it was smelled; there was a sound, that is to say, it was heard; a colour or figure, and it was perceived by sight or touch. This is all that I can understand by these and the like expressions. For as to what is said of the absolute existence of unthinking things without any relation to their being perceived, that seems perfectly unintelligible. Their *esse* is *percipi*,[1] nor is it possible they should have any existence, out of the minds or thinking things which perceive them.

4 It is indeed an opinion strangely prevailing amongst men, that houses, mountains, rivers, and in a word all sensible objects have an existence natural or real, distinct from their being perceived by the understanding. But with how great an assurance and acquiescence soever this principle may be entertained in the world; yet whoever shall find in his heart to call it in question, may, if I mistake not, perceive it to involve a manifest contradiction. For what are the forementioned objects but the things we perceive by sense, and what do we perceive besides our own ideas or sensations; and is

1. i.e. their existence consists in being perceived.

it not plainly repugnant that any one of these or any combination of them should exist unperceived? . . .

from: THE GUARDIAN, NO. 27 (1713)

[In this essay in *The Guardian*, Berkeley uses his views on vision to illustrate the doctrine of immortality.]

But as this manner of reasoning [against immortality] proceeds from a poverty of imagination and narrowness of soul in those that use it, I shall endeavour to remedy those defects, and open their views, by laying before them a case which, being naturally possible, may perhaps reconcile them to the belief of what is supernaturally revealed.

Let us suppose a person blind and deaf from his birth, who, being grown to man's estate, is, by the dead palsy or some other cause, deprived of his feeling, tasting, and smelling, and at the same time has the impediment of his hearing removed, and the film taken from his eyes. What the five senses are to us, that the touch, taste and smell were to him. And any other ways of perception, of a more refined and extensive nature, were to him as inconceivable as to us those are which will one day be adapted to perceive those things which 'eye hath not seen, nor ear heard, neither hath it entered into the heart of man to conceive.'[1] And it would be just as reasonable in him to conclude, that the loss of those three senses could not possibly be succeeded by any new inlets of perception, as in a modern Freethinker to imagine there can be no state of life and perception without the senses he enjoys at present. Let us further suppose the same person's eyes, at their first opening, to be struck with a great variety of the most gay and pleasing objects, and his ears with a melodious consort of vocal and instrumental musick: Behold him amazed, ravished, transported; and you have some distant representation, some faint and glimmering idea of the exstatic state of the soul in that article in which she emerges from this sepulchre of flesh into Life and Immortality. . . .

1. This is Berkeley's favourite scriptural quotation; it is from I Corinthians 2.9.

from: ALCIPHRON, OR THE MINUTE PHILOSOPHER (Dialogue VII) (1732)

[Berkeley's account of language, particularly his emotive theory, is here used to explain religious mysteries. Euphranor and Crito (standing for Berkeley) argue against Alciphron (whose views are very close to those of Toland).]

5. EUPHRANOR: Be the use of words or names what it will, I can never think it is to do things impossible. Let us then inquire what it is, and see if we can make sense of our daily practice. Words, it is agreed, are signs: it may not therefore be amiss to examine the use of other signs, in order to know that of words. Counters, for instance, at a card-table are used, not for their own sake, but only as signs substituted for money, as words are for ideas. Say now, Alciphron, is it necessary every time these counters are used throughout the progress of a game, to frame an idea of the distinct sum or value that each represents?

ALCIPHRON: By no means: it is sufficient the players at first agree on their respective values, and at last substitute those values in their stead.

EUPHRANOR: And in casting up a sum, where the figures stand for pounds, shillings, and pence, do you think it necessary, throughout the whole progress of the operation, in each step to form ideas of pounds, shillings, and pence?

ALCIPHRON: I do not; it will suffice if in the conclusion those figures direct our actions with respect to things.

EUPHRANOR: From hence it seems to follow, that words may not be insignificant, although they should not, every time they are used, excite the ideas they signify in our minds; it being sufficient that we have it in our power to substitute things or ideas for their signs when there is occasion. It seems also to follow that there may be another use of words besides that of marking and suggesting distinct ideas, to wit, the influencing our conduct and actions, which may be done either by forming rules for us to act by, or by raising certain passions, dispositions, and emotions in our minds. A discourse, therefore, that directs how to act or excites to the doing or forbearance of an action may, it seems, be useful and significant, although the words whereof it is composed should not bring each a distinct idea into our minds.

ALCIPHRON: It seems so.

EUPHRANOR: Pray tell me, Alciphron, is not an idea altogether inactive?

ALCIPHRON: It is.

EUPHRANOR: An agent therefore, an active mind or spirit, cannot be an idea, or like an idea. Whence it should seem to follow that those words which denote an active principle, soul, or spirit do not, in a strict and proper sense, stand for ideas. And yet they are not insignificant neither; since I understand what is signified by the term *I*, or *myself*, or know what it means, although it be no idea, nor like an idea, but that which thinks, and wills, and apprehends ideas, and operates about them. Certainly it must be allowed that we have some notion that we understand, or know what is meant by, the terms *myself, will, memory, love, hate,* and so forth; although, to speak exactly, these words do not suggest so many distinct ideas.

ALCIPHRON: What would you infer from this?

EUPHRANOR: What hath been inferred already — that words may be significant, although they do not stand for ideas. The contrary whereof having been presumed seems to have produced the doctrine of abstract ideas.

ALCIPHRON: Will you not allow then that the mind can abstract?

EUPHRANOR: I do not deny it may abstract in a certain sense, inasmuch as those things that can really exist, or be really perceived asunder, may be conceived asunder, or abstracted one from the other; for instance, a man's head from his body, colour from motion, figure from weight. But it will not thence follow that the mind can frame abstract general ideas, which appear to be impossible.

ALCIPHRON: And yet it is a current opinion that every substantive name marks out and exhibits to the mind one distinct idea separate from all others.

EUPHRANOR: Pray, Alciphron, is not the word *number* such a substantive name?

ALCIPHRON: It is.

EUPHRANOR: Do but try now whether you can frame an idea of number in abstract, exclusive of all signs, words, and things numbered. I profess for my own part I cannot.

ALCIPHRON: Can it be so hard a matter to form a simple idea of number, the object of a most evident demonstrable science? Hold, let me see if I can't abstract the idea of number from the numerical names and characters, and all particular numerable things. — [Upon which Alciphron paused a while, and then said,] To confess the truth I do not find that I can.

EUPHRANOR: But, though it seems neither you nor I can form distinct simple ideas of number, we can nevertheless make a very proper and significant use of numeral names. They direct us in the disposition and management of our affairs, and are of such necessary use that we should not know how to do without them. And yet, if other men's faculties may be judged of by mine, to attain a precise simple abstract idea of number is as difficult as to comprehend any mystery in religion. . . .

10. CRITO: It seems that what hath been now said may be applied to other mysteries of our religion. Original sin, for instance, a man may find it impossible to form an idea of in abstract, or of the manner of its transmission; and yet the belief thereof may produce in his mind a salutary sense of his own unworthiness, and the goodness of his Redeemer: from whence may follow good habits, and from them good actions, the genuine effects of faith; which, considered in its true light, is a thing neither repugnant nor incomprehensible, as some men would persuade us, but suited even to vulgar capacities, placed in the will and affections rather than in the understanding, and producing holy lives rather than subtle theories. Faith, I say, is not an indolent perception, but an operative persuasion of mind, which ever worketh some suitable action, disposition or emotion in those who have it; as it were easy to prove and illustrate by innumerable instances taken from human affairs. And, indeed, while the Christian religion is considered as an institution fitted to ordinary minds, rather than to the nicer talent, whether improved or puzzled, of speculative men; and our notions about faith are accordingly taken from the commerce of the world, and practice of mankind, rather than from the peculiar systems of refiners; it will, I think, be no difficult matter to conceive and justify the meaning and use of our belief of mysteries against the most confident assertions and objections of the minute philosophers, who are easily to be caught in those very snares which they have spun and spread for others. And that humour of controversy, the mother and nurse of heresies, would doubtless very much abate, if it was considered that things are to be rated, not by the colour, shape, or stamp, so truly as

by the weight. If the moment of opinions had been by some litigious divines made the measure of their zeal, it might have spared much trouble both to themselves and others. Certainly one that takes his notions of faith, opinion, and assent from common sense, and common use, and has maturely weighed the nature of signs and language, will not be so apt to controvert the wording of a mystery, or to break the peace of the church, for the sake of retaining or rejecting a term.

But, to convince you by a plain instance of the efficacious necessary use of faith without ideas: we will suppose a man of the world, a minute philosopher, prodigal and rapacious, one of large appetites and narrow circumstances, who shall have it in his power at once to seize upon a great fortune by one villainous act, a single breach of trust, which he can commit with impunity and secrecy. Is it not natural to suppose him arguing in this manner? All mankind in their senses pursue their interest. The interests of this present life are either of mind, body, or fortune. If I commit this fact my mind will be easy (having nought to fear here or hereafter); my bodily pleasures will be multiplied; and my fortune enlarged. Suppose now, one of your refined theorists talks to him about the harmony of mind and affections, inward worth, truth of character, in one word, the beauty of virtue; which is the only interest he can propose to turn the scale against all other secular interests and sensual pleasures; would it not, think you, be a vain attempt? I say, in such a juncture what can the most plausible and refined philosophy of your sect offer to dissuade such a man from his purpose, more than assuring him that the abstracted delight of the mind, the enjoyments of an interior moral sense, the *το καλον*,[1] are what constitute his true interest? And what effect can this have on a mind callous to all those things, and at the same time strongly affected with a sense of corporeal pleasures, and the outward interest, ornaments, and conveniences of life? Whereas that very man, do but produce in him a sincere belief of a Future State, although it be a mystery, although it be what eye hath not seen, nor ear heard, nor hath it entered into the heart of man to conceive, he shall, nevertheless, by virtue of such belief, be withheld from executing his wicked project: and that for reasons which all men can comprehend, though nobody can be the object of them. I will allow the points insisted on by your refined moralists to be as lovely and excellent as you please to a reasonable, reflecting, philosophical mind. But I will venture to say that, as the world goes, few, very few, would be influenced by them. We see, therefore, the necessary use, as well as the powerful effects of faith, even where we have not ideas. . . .

1. moral beauty.

from:
THE QUERIST (1752)

[*The Querist*, which comprised nearly six hundred questions in the last (1752) authorized edition, ranges widely. Here Berkeley draws on his emotive theory to attack mercantilism (the theory that money had value only in so far as it was necessarily connected with gold or silver).]

23. Whether money is to be considered as having an intrinsic value, or as being a commodity, a standard, a measure, or a pledge, as is variously suggested by writers? And whether the true idea of money, as such, be not altogether that of a ticket or counter? . . .

25. Whether the terms crown, livre, pound sterling, etc., are not to be considered as exponents or denominations of such proportion? And whether gold, silver, and paper are not tickets or counters for reckoning, recording, and transferring thereof?

26. Whether the denominations being retained, although the bullion were gone, things might not nevertheless be rated, bought, and sold, industry promoted, and a circulation of commerce maintained? . . .

29. What makes a wealthy people? Whether mines of gold and silver are capable of doing this? And whether the negroes, amidst the gold sands of Afric, are not poor and destitute?

30. Whether there be any virtue in gold or silver, other than as they set people at work, or create industry? . . .

32. Whether if there was no silver or gold in the kingdom, our trade might not, nevertheless, supply bills of exchange, sufficient to answer the demands of absentees in England or elsewhere? . . .

34. Provided the wheels move, whether it is not the same thing, as to the effect of the machine, be this done by the force of wind, or water, or animals?

35. Whether power to command the industry of others be not real wealth? And whether money be not in truth tickets or tokens for conveying and

recording such power, and whether it be of great consequence what materials the tickets are made of? . . .

46. Whether, in order to understand the true nature of wealth and commerce, it would not be right to consider a ship's crew cast upon a desert island, and by degrees forming themselves to business and civil life, while industry begot credit, and credit moved to industry?

47. Whether such men would not all set themselves to work? Whether they would not subsist by the mutual participation of each other's industry? Whether, when one man had in his way procured more than he could consume, he would not exchange his superfluities to supply his wants? Whether this must not produce credit? Whether, to facilitate these conveyances, to record and circulate this credit, they would not soon agree on certain tallies, tokens, tickets, or counters? . . .

134. Whether, if there was a wall of brass a thousand cubits high round this kingdom, our natives might not nevertheless live cleanly and comfortably, till the land, and reap the fruits of it? . . .

440. Whether paper doth not by its stamp and signature acquire a local value, and become as precious and as scarce as gold? And whether it be not much fitter to circulate large sums, and therefore preferable to gold? . . .

441. Whether it doth not much import to have a right conception of money? And whether its true and just idea be not that of a ticket, entitling to power, and fitted to record and transfer such power? . . .

445. Whether in the rude original of society the first step was not the exchanging of commodities; the next a substituting of metals by weight as the common medium of circulation; after this the making use of coin; lastly, a further refinement by the use of paper with proper marks and signatures? And whether this, as it is the last, so it be not the greatest improvement? . . .

461. Whether to oil the wheels of commerce be not a common benefit? And whether this be not done by avoiding fractions and multiplying small silver? . . .

475. As wealth is really power, and coin a ticket conveying power, whether those tickets which are the fittest for that use ought not to be preferred? . . .

476. Whether those tickets which singly transfer small shares of power, and, being multiplied, large shares, are not fitter for common use than those which singly transfer large shares? . . .

477. Whether the public is not more benefited by a shilling that circulates than a pound that lies dead? . . .

480. Whether facilitating and quickening the circulation of power to supply wants be not the promoting of wealth and industry among the lower people? And whether upon this the wealth of the great doth not depend? . . .

484. Whether the natural body can be in a state of health and vigour without a due circulation of the extremities, even in the fingers and toes? And whether the political body, any more than the natural, can thrive without a proportionable circulation through the minutest and most inconsiderable parts thereof? . . .

568. Whether it is not a great point to know what we would be at? And whether whole States, as well as private persons, do not often fluctuate for want of this knowledge? . . .

570. Whether means are not so far useful as they answer the end? And whether, in different circumstances, the same ends are not obtained by different means? . . .

572. Whether, therefore, it would not be highly expedient if our money were coined of peculiar values, best fitted to the circumstances and uses of our own country; and whether any other people could take umbrage at our consulting our own convenience, in an affair entirely domestic, and that lies within ourselves?

FRANCIS HUTCHESON

(1694-1746)

LETTER TO WILLIAM MACE (1727)

[In this letter, Hutcheson comments on topics contained in his two most important philosophical works, *An Inquiry into the Original of our Ideas of Beauty and Virtue* (London, 1725) and *An Essay on the Nature and Conduct of the Passions and Affections* (London, 1728). He also discusses the Molyneux problem, offering an answer similar to that of Leibniz.)

SIR, *Dublin, Sept. 6,* 1727.

I was very agreeably entertained this day se'nnight[1] with your ingenious letter. The reason of my not answering you immediately was what you seem in the close of your letter to be apprized of, that the alterations you proposed would be unpopular, and not so fit for so inconsiderable a name as mine to venture upon in a treatise upon a subject equally concerning all mankind. I therefore sent you a letter by my old friend Mr. Mairs, that I had some reasons requiring haste in the printing of those papers,[2] and that I dared not venture upon publishing some alterations, according to your remarks, which agree with my own sentiments, and that in some others I differed from you, of which I would apprize you as soon as I had leisure: but as our distance makes correspondence very slow in its returns, I fear I cannot expect, in any tolerable time, to have your sentiments upon any doubtful points, so that I could make proper alterations according to them. I am extremely obliged to you for your kind offer of your good offices in this matter, and should be proud of having it in my power to make any grateful returns for it.

I was well apprized of the scheme of thinking you are fallen into, not only by our Dr. Berkly's [*sic*] books, and by some of the old academics, but by frequent conversation with some few speculative friends in Dublin. As to your notion of our mind as only a system of perceptions, I imagine you'll find that every one has an immediate simple perception of *self*; to which all his other perceptions are some way connected, otherwise I cannot conceive how I could be any way affected with pleasure or pain from any past action, affection, or perception, or have any present uneasiness or concern about any future event or perception; or how there could be any unity of person, or any desire of future happiness or aversion to misery. My past perceptions or future ones are not my present, but would be as distinct as your perceptions are from mine: that it is otherwise I believe every one is conscious. As to material *substrata*, I own I am a sceptic; all the phænomena might be as they are, were there nothing but perceptions, for the phænomena are perceptions. And yet, were there external objects, I cannot imagine how we could be better informed of them than we are. I own I cannot see the force of the arguments against external objects, *i.e.* something like, or proportional, to our concomitant ideas, as I call extension, figure, motion, self, solidity.

Figure and *bounded colour* are not to me the same. Figure accompanies bounded colour, but the same or perfectly like idea may arise by touch, without any idea of colour, along with the ideas of hard, cold, smooth. A man born blind might learn mathematics with a little more trouble than one who saw, had he figures artfully cut in wood. Messrs. Locke and Molyneux are both wrong about the cube and sphere proposed to a blind man restored to sight. He would not at first view know the sphere from a shaded plane surface by a view from above; but a side view would discover the equal uniform round relievo in one, and the cubic one in the other. We can all by touch, with our eyes shut, judge what the visible extension of a body felt shall be when we shall open our eyes; but cannot by feeling judge what the colour shall be when we shall see it; which shews visible and tangible extension to be really the same idea, or to have one idea common, viz. the extension; though the purely tangible and visible perceptions are quite disparate. If one should alledge that the two extensions,

1. i.e. a week ago.
2. Presumably *An Essay on the Nature and Conduct of the Passions and Affections.*

abstracted from the colours, are different ideas, but that by long observation we find what changes in the visible arise from any change of the tangible extension, and *vice versa*; and hence from groping a figure we know what its visible extension shall be; I think upon this scheme, it would be impossible that one who had only the idea of tangible extension could ever apprehend any reasonings formed by one who argued about the visible; whereas blind men may understand mathematics. To illustrate this, suppose a person paralytic and blind, with an acute smell, who had no idea of either extension; suppose there were a body whose smell continually altered with every change of its figure; one man seeing the several figures changing in a regular course foresees which shall come next, so the other knows the course of smells; he agrees with the blind man about names; the one noting by them the various figures, the other the various smells. The seer reasons about the figures, or forms one of Euclid's propositions concerning the proportion of the sides: is it possible the blind man could ever assent to this, or know his meaning from the smells? And yet men may so far agree, one of whom had only the idea of tangible extension. Or suppose a man had never seen sounding strings, but heard the several sounds, not knowing any thing of length or tension, that he was taught names for notes, such as dupla, sesquialtera: should one who saw the strings say, 'the square of the cause of the octave was but a quarter of the square of the other cause,' could the other ever apprehend him in this point from his ideas of sounds? And yet a man born blind could perceive this point, and agree with one who only had ideas of sight.

Duration and number seem to me as real perceptions as any; and I can have no other idea of your words for explaining duration, (viz. the order of our ideas) than this, a perception of the connexion or relation of our several ideas to several parts of duration. What is order or succession of our ideas, unless duration be a real distinct idea accompanying them all? or how could the succession of ideas give us ideas of duration, if a part of duration were not connected with each of them? Number is also a real idea; the words are artificial symbols about which different nations differ, but agree in all their reasonings about the ideas of number, which are really the same. Numbers are the clearest ideas we have, and their relations are the most distinct, but often have nothing to do with wholes or parts, and are alike applicable to heterogeneous as homogeneous quantities.

I still cannot take *desire* to denote a complex idea. The Epicurean desire I am confident I should have myself as I mention it.

The prospect of interest is not desire, but something immediately preceding it, either *tempore* or *natura*,[3] if you can bear such stuff: the prospect is an opinion or perception of relation, *i.e.* a judgment. The desire is as different from a judgment as sound from colour, as far as I can apprehend. One may wish he had *desire*, but you see I own a volition cannot directly raise desire. Volition is perhaps to be called the proper action, but I imagine we have volitions about ideas in compounding, comparing, attention, recalling, enlarging, diminishing, as well as about bodily motion; so that an universal palsy would not take away all volition: and beside, I am not fully convinced, though I have heard it alledged, that there can be no volition without effect, as well as desires which are not gratified. Desire and volition are distinct from each other, and both distinct from what we commonly call perceptions; though we have also an idea or consciousness of volition and desire. Quere, Is there not here plainly an idea, viz. that of desire or volition, and an object, viz. the desire or volition distinct from this perception of it? May there not be the same as to the ideas I call the concomitant?

As to the main point in your letter about our activity, we are very much of the same opinion. But you know how sacred a point human liberty and activity, in the common notions, are to the generality of men, and how prejudicial any singularity on these heads might be to one whose business depends upon a character of orthodoxy. I am very sensible that the truest ideas of human virtue and of the divine goodness may be given on your scheme; but how few are there whom we could convince on these points.

Vel quia turpe putant parere minoribus, et quae
Imberbes didicere, senes perdenda fateri.[4]

I have some nearer touches at these points in another set of papers, which I shall send over very

3. i.e. either in time or in nature or logic.
4. From Horace, Epistles II, 1, 84-85: 'Or because they think it shameful to yield to their juniors and to confess that, when they are old, the things they learned as children should best be forgotten.' (We are grateful to Vincent Denard for identifying and translating these lines.)

soon to be joined with the other. But I am still on my guard in them.

I heartily wish you may find your new correspondent any way agreeable to you; I can only assure you of his hearty zeal for truth and virtue, and his particular regard and gratitude to you for your civilities.

I am, Sir,
Your most obliged humble servant,
FRANCIS HUTCHESON.

To Mr. William Mace,
at Mr. Osborn's,
bookseller,
Paternoster-Row.

PETER BROWNE

(*c.* 1665-1735)

from: THE PROCEDURE, EXTENT AND LIMITS OF HUMAN UNDERSTANDING (1728)

[In this extract from his introduction to the *Procedure*, Browne lays the ground for this and his other major book, *Things Divine and Supernatural conceived by Analogy with things Natural and Human* (London, 1733). He quotes extensively from his own earlier work against Toland, *A Letter in answer to a Book, entitled Christianity not mysterious* (Dublin, 1697).]

INTRODUCTION

Some years past a small Treatise was publish'd with this Title, *A Letter in answer to a Book, entitled, Christianity not mysterious; as also to all those who set up for Reason and Evidence, in opposition to Revelation and Mysteries.* It plainly appears to have been written in haste, and with the incorrectness of a youthful and as yet unformed stile; but the Foundation the Author all along proceeds upon, for the confutation of his Adversary; and for laying open the fallacy of mens Arguments against Divine Revelation and our Christian Mysteries, drawn from the Topics of strict Reason, Certainty, and Evidence seems to be solid and just; and indeed the only one upon which such a firm and unshaken Superstructure can be rais'd, as may be Proof against all the Arguments and Objections of Unbelievers.

That Letter proceeds intirely upon a Distinction at first laid down between a *Proper* and *Immediate* Idea or Conception of a Thing; such as we have of the things of this world, which are the proper and immediate Objects of our Senses and our Reason; and that Idea or Conception which is *Mediate* only and *Improper*, such as we necessarily form of the things of another world. It is there asserted as a sure and incontestable Truth, that we have no immediate proper Idea at all of God, or any of his Attributes as they are in themselves; or of any thing else in another world: and consequently, that we are under a necessity of conceiving all things supernatural by *Analogy*; that is, by the Mediation and Substitution of those Ideas we have of our selves, and of all other things of Nature.

This Distinction is there affirmed to be absolutely necessary, for the ascertaining and settling the Bounds and Measure of our Knowledge; for shewing the true Limits, and utmost Extent of human Understanding, that we may clearly and distinctly apprehend where mere *Knowledge* ends, and *Faith* begins: where it is they meet again, and inseparably combine together for the inlargement of our Understanding vastly beyond its native sphere; for opening to the Mind a new and immense scene of things otherwise imperceptible; and for a rational well-grounded Assent to such Truths concerning them, as are a solid Foundation for all Religion Natural and Revealed.

The nature of this *Analogy* the Author explains by a similitude in this following Paragraph.[1]

'And thus it is plain, that tho' we may be said to have Ideas of God and Divine things, yet they are not immediate or proper ones, but a sort of Com-

1. The passage is from *A Letter* .... (1697), pp. 50-51.

position we make up from our Ideas of worldly Objects; which at the utmost amounts to no more than a Type or Figure, by which something in another world is signified, of which we have no more notion than a blind man hath of Light. And now that I am fallen into this Similitude, which seems well to explain the nature of the thing, let us pursue it a little; and suppose, that to a Man who had never seen or heard any thing of it, it were to be reveal'd that there was such a thing as Light. This Man as yet hath neither a Name nor a Notion for it, nor any Capacity of conceiving what it is in it self. 'Tis plain therefore God would not reveal this to him by the name of Light, a word wholly unknown to him; nor by stamping on his Mind any immediate Idea of the thing it self: for then it were utterly impossible for him to communicate this Revelation to others as blind as himself; since nothing but the same Almighty Impression cou'd do that; so that this Revelation must be made by Words and Notions which are already in him. And accordingly when he is told, that it is a thing which can diffuse it self in an instant many thousands of miles round; and enable him to know in a moment in what Order all things lay at a great distance from him, and what Proportion they bore one to another; nay, that it could make him know where the Heavens lay; and that by the help of this he shou'd there discern at once, a vast and almost infinite number of very pleasant Bodies; and, in short, that without the help of his Stick or his Hand he shou'd know every thing that lay before him: After all, 'tis plain this Man wou'd form to himself an Idea of Light from his Touch; he wou'd think it very like Feeling, and perhaps call it by that name; because this was the best way he had of distinguishing one thing from another; and therefore wou'd conclude, that those Bodies he heard of must needs be wondrous soft and smooth. Just thus do we conceive the things of another World; so that we may rack our Invention, and turn and wind all those Ideas we have into ten thousand different shapes, and yet never make up any true likeness or similitude of the *Real* Nature of those Objects of another World.'

From hence the Author proceeds to the application of this Distinction to the Points in controversy between him and that famed Unbeliever [Toland] he had to deal with; and particularly to the explaining the true manner of our conceiving the Mysteries of Christianity, and that of the ever blessed Trinity in particular.

Now tho' the proceeding upon this foot of *Analogy* may seem something strange and new, yet it is as old as the earliest Fathers of the Church; who did not indeed expressly lay down this Distinction, and pursue it Logically thro' all the particulars of our knowledge human and divine; or apply it to the exact stating the Limits and Extent of human understanding in general. But however the sum and substance of all their Answers to the Arguments and Objections of Heretics and Unbelievers might be resolved into this, *That the true and real Nature of God and his Attributes, and of all things in another World were utterly incomprehensible and ineffable; and consequently that all mens Reasonings from the Real Nature of things in this world, to the* Real true *state and condition of things Supernatural, were precarious and inconclusive.*

It is now upwards of twenty-five years since that Treatise was published; and considering it underwent several Editions; that it met with the approbation of some men of greatest note, and highest station in the Church; and never was answered any otherwise than by some personal Reflections in a Pamphlet against the Author; but chiefly considering of what universal use and application the abovementioned Distinction is in all our Controversies with Arians, and Socinians,[2] and Deists; how necessary it is for reducing all matters in debate between them and us, to a Point under every head, so that they may admit of a clear and easy solution. It cannot be sufficiently admired, that in this interval (wherein so much hath been written on all sides concerning Revelation and Mystery, and the Doctrine of the Holy Trinity) the many pious and learned Defenders of our Faith have either intirely declined proceeding upon the foundation there laid; or have given only some general, short, and imperfect Hints of this Analogy. Insomuch that our Adversaries have not yet found themselves under a necessity of joining issue upon that foot; and consequently obliged either flatly to deny and disprove our Conceptions of God, and his Attributes, and of all things in another World to be Analogous; or to acknowledge that all their Inferences and Conclusions drawn from the Nature of Man and Things material, to the *Real* internal Nature of God and

2. Adherents of the beliefs of Faustus and Laelius Socinus, who refused to accept the divinity of Christ, the Trinity, and original sin. They maintained that those who heed Christ's virtues will be saved.

Things supernatural, are false and deceitful.

But our wonder will cease, when we consider the no small difficulty of applying this Distinction between proper and improper Ideas to the Mysteries of Christianity; and to the several difficulties and objections which have been raised concerning them, even after it is allowed and thoroughly digested; besides the great danger of pursuing it thro' all the instances which will every where occur: For without a judicious and cautious application of *Analogy*, men will be apt to mistake it for pure *Metaphor*, and by that means resolve all Religion into nothing more than mere Figure and Allusion. . . .

from: THINGS DIVINE AND SUPERNATURAL CONCEIVED BY ANALOGY WITH THINGS NATURAL AND HUMAN (1733)

[This selection is from the long eighth chapter of the *Divine Analogy*, most of which Browne devotes to an attack on Berkeley's *Alciphron* IV. However, this passage deals with divine analogy and here Browne criticizes Berkeley's novel theory of emotive meaning. Browne's incomprehension and scorn clearly reflect the effect that the radical nature of Berkeley's theory must have had on his contemporaries.]

The last and most extraordinary Step taken by our Author[1] for solving the preceding grand Objection of Infidels is, by telling them *That the true End of Speech, Reason, Science, Faith, Assent; is not always the imparting or acquiring of Ideas: But something of an operative Nature, tending to a conceived Good; which may be obtained — Altho' there should be no Possibility of offering or exhibiting any such Idea to the Mind.*[2] Surely more Confusion and Absurdity could not possibly have been crowded into the Compass of one short Period. *The End of Speech is not always the imparting or acquiring Ideas,* Conceptions, or Notions; tho' without some of these affixed to the Words or excited by them as *Signs*, it is no *Speech*, but insignificant empty *Noise*. Tho' it be evidently plain that Speech could serve no rational End; if it did not suggest and impart some of these: Tho' this is the very Point, wherein human Language differs from the irrational instinctive Sounds of Birds and Beasts, and even of Insects. And tho' if you exclude this Use, no Man living can assign any other for Words or Speech: In which it would be impossible there should be either Propriety or Figure; or any thing tending to excite us to a rational *Operation*. Insomuch that our conversing like Mutes, and denoting the Ideas and Conceptions of the Mind by Signs upon the Fingers; would, according to his Notion, be of more real Advantage to Mankind, and upon all Accounts vastly preferable to any Sounds variously articulated by the different Organs of Voice. *The true End of Reason.* But surely one true End and Use of Reason, is to acquire and impart a Perception of the Agreements and Disagreements of our Ideas Conceptions and Notions; which it could never perform, unless the *Ideas* Conceptions and Notions themselves are acquired, or exhibited to the Mind: Without this it could never Influence us to *Act* or *Operate* like Men; nor to obtain our ultimate End, which is true rational Happiness. *The true End of Science.* But surely each rational Science must be conversant about some *Ideas* Conceptions or Notions of things; and these must be acquired or exhibited to the Mind, and imparted by the Terms and Signs used in it: Or it would be impossible to understand or teach any of the Sciences; or to render them useful to any rational *End* or *Operation*. Otherwise the true End of all Science would be to talk much, but to learn and know and practice nothing: There would be in Reality but one Science in the World; that is a very learned Method of multiplying such Marks and Words only, as were most agreeable to the Eye and harmonious to the Ear. Upon this Author's Principle, there might be some Use of *Singing* indeed; but it would be to no purpose for any Man to speak who could not perform it melodiously. *The true End of Faith.* Religion then is placed upon the same absurd Foot with Science; Faith (according to him) may answer a true and excellent and operative End, without our always acquiring any Idea or Conception or Notion of *What* we believe, or having it any way exhibited to the Mind; and *We may believe* (as this Author himself words it) *Where we do not understand.* The

1. i.e. Berkeley.
2. The words in italics are directly quoted from *Alciphron*, dialogue VII, section 17.

bare Words in which we express our Faith, may be vital ruling Principles to rational Creatures; tho' they are not always animated by any Ideas or Conceptions affixed to them, and exhibited to the Mind: And tho' Faith in Words only for its Object, is no other than believing in certain Sounds and Syllables. You may profess indeed to believe in *Father, Son*, and *Spirit*; in the *Grace* of God; and in the *Mediation* and *Intercession* of Christ; but yet it is not always *Necessary* or *Possible* for you to acquire, or exhibit to your Mind, any *Ideas* Conceptions or Notions of the things marked out by those Words: Tho' by this Rule you may as well be said to have Faith in the Noise of sounding Brass or a tinkling Cymbal.[3] Nay your believing a God would be very useful; tho' upon his Scheme it may be no more than Faith in a Monosyllable. You may commendably believe in what you *Hear*, tho' you do not *Understand* any thing of it. Thus all Faith would terminate in the Ear; and no Point of it could ever reach the Head or the Heart, or Influence us to any rational Action. *The true End of Assent*. The *End* of Assent indeed is not the imparting or acquiring Ideas Conceptions or Notions: But surely some of these must necessarily be acquired or exhibited to the Mind for the *Object* of our Assent; otherwise it would be just such another useful Assent as one *Parrot* may yield to another.

Well then; Words do not always impart or exhibit Ideas or Conceptions to the Mind: But they may be very useful, says he, to another End; in producing or imparting something else without a particular Name, *Something of an Operative Nature*. Then surely the Words must impart something more than the bare Sounds of Syllables: And it cannot be they themselves which thus *Operate* alone upon us, but that *Something* which they impart to the Mind. Now since he will not have any Ideas Conceptions or Notions always imparted by them; it must be *Something*, says he, *that tends to a conceived Good, which may be obtained tho' the Ideas* or Conceptions *Marked* by the Terms, in order to our obtaining it, *Cannot be offered or exhibited to the Mind*: Something tending to a *Conceived* Good, *tho' there should be no Possibility of exhibiting such an Idea* or Conception *To the Mind*. Change the Syntax of this unaccountable Sentence into all the Forms and Varieties it can bear; and yet it will not produce any intelligible Truth.

Not *always the imparting Ideas*. But surely if Words, in Religious Doctrines especialy, do sometimes impart Ideas, and sometimes none; it was highly proper for him to have distinguished those Words, and to have informed the World which of them can have Ideas and Conceptions affixed to them and imparted by them, and which not: For now he hath left his Readers in an endless Uncertainty in relation to the *Grace* of God in particular; and upon the same Foot of Reasoning, in relation to all the Attributes of God and Mysteries of Christianity in general. *No Possibility of offering or exhibiting any Idea to the Mind*. Had he taken the word *Idea* in the true logical Sence, as limited to the *Direct* and *Immediate Perception* of external and sensible Objects only; and affirmed that there was no Possibility of our having any *Such* Perception or Ideas of things divine and purely spiritual: And that it was as ridiculous for Men to insist upon such Ideas of them, as to demand a full View and Prospect of them with their Eyes. Had he affirmed moreover, not only that such *Ideas* are impossible to us; but that it is equaly impossible for the Mind of Man to obtain an *Immediate Consciousness* of them, or of any thing the same in Kind with them; and consequently to frame even any *Direct Conceptions* or *Complex Notions* of them: And that we are therefore under a Necessity of conceiving them by *Analogy* with things natural and human, or else of denying the Truth and Reality even of the divine Attributes as well as the Mysteries of Christianity; or at least of disclaiming any Capacity in Mankind of obtaining an *Useful* Knowlege of either. Had he done this, I say, he had asserted an evident and important Truth; and thereby have inevitably reduced the Adversaries of Revelation to the palpable Absurdity of disbelieving the *Reality*, or denying the *Useful Knowlege* of every thing in the Universe, whereof they have not a direct Sensation or immediate Consciousness, either from the thing it self or from something the same in Kind: Nay of rejecting all things divine and supernatural for no other Reason; but because they have no such Conceptions of them, as would be directly inconsistent with their very Nature and Existence. He should have granted them that *Some* Idea Conception or Notion must necessarily be affixed to every Word expressive of each Doctrine in Christianity, and of every one of God's Attributes: Or else that it could have no Use and Signification; nor could otherwise impart or suggest any thing to the Mind for an

3. I Corinthians 13.1.

Object either of our *Knowlege* or *Faith*; and consequently for a Principle of rational *Action* or *Operation*. But what involved him in all this complicated Absurdity, was his having a strong Suspicion that we can obtain no *Direct* and *Immediate* Ideas or Conceptions, to annex to Words expressive of things divine and purely spiritual; together with his Reluctance at the same time to acknowlege that we may and must have *Analogical* Conceptions to annex to them, or else that they would be utterly useless: To avoid which he ran blindfold and headlong into the other Extreme, of maintaining a most pernicious Tenet; That Words and Doctrines may be significant and useful, and productive of Action, *Tho' there should be no Idea affixed to them or imparted by them; nay no Possibility of offering or exhibiting any such Idea* (Conception or Notion) *to the Mind.*[4]

The main Scope and Design of that obscure Dissertation, was to shew how impossible it is to affix any *Distinct* Idea or Conception to the word *Grace*:[5] But that however the Term it self, without any such Idea or Conception annexed to it or imparted by it, may have a useful Tendency and excite us to Action. Whereas without the Conception of human *Favour* annexed to it or imparted by it, when taken in the General; and without the Idea or Conception of the Influence of a natural and human Cause, when it is taken in particular; and so applyed with those *Clear* and *Distinct* Conceptions to God and the divine Spirit, by *Analogy*: It would have been a Word altogether senceless insignificant and useless in Religion; it would have imparted nothing to the Mind for an Object either of Knowlege or Faith; nor could it have been any rational Principle, or have afforded any Motive or spring of Action. Now to prove that the word Grace is not *Insignificant* tho' no *Determinate* Idea or Conception is annexed to it or imparted by it; he instances in the word *Number*, as being in this Point exactly parallel. *You can form no Idea of Number*, says he, *Abstracted from all things numbred.*[6] No surely, but it is for this Reason: Because there is no such *Thing* as Number abstracted from all things numbred: Exclude these from Number, and it can have no Existence or Reality. It is equaly true that we can form no Idea or Conception of Grace; exclusive of the Mind of Man, the divine Spirit, and the Effects. But why is this impossible? For no other Reason, but because Grace is then resolved into *Nothing*; insomuch that the very mention of such a Conception or Idea of it, is trifling and ridiculous. And much more such a tedious Dissertation about what is then but a mere *Sound*, and no *Sign* of any thing *True* and *Real* in respect either of God or Man. The Truth of the Matter is this: As we can form a clear and distinct Idea or Conception of Number in the *Concrete*, which is as *Direct* and *Immediate* as the Ideas or Conceptions we have of the *Objects numbred* by us: So we can form a clear and distinct Idea or Conception of Grace, in the *Concrete* likewise; but which is as necessarily and as truly *Analogical*, as that Conception we form of the divine *Spirit*, and its supernatural *Power*. And here I shall once more observe to this Author, what he seems to be wholy ignorant of; That we cannot form any *Direct* and *Immediate* Conception or Idea of Number, either in the *Abstract* or in the *Concrete*, in respect of things divine and supernatural: Because we can obtain no direct Conception or Idea of such *Objects* in any Degree; and consequently the Mind of Man cannot *Distinguish* them from one another as they are *In themselves*, or *In their own Kind*. And therefore it is, that the *Distinction* between the divine Persons is revealed to us by *Analogy* with that which is *Personal* among Men; who are easily numbred, and directly distinguishable from one another.

The other parallel Instance from which he argues, is that of *Force*; exclude, says he, Body the Subject of it, and Motion, and the sensible Effects of it, and then it is impossible to frame any Idea or Conception of it.[7] Yes surely; it is the same senceless Ridicule as if you bid a Man try to form a Conception of *Thinking* or *Willing*, exclusive of any *Object* of Thought or Desire, and of a Mind operating. So say I of *Grace*; exclude the divine Spirit, the Mind of Man, and the Effects of it: And then there is nothing left whereof to form even any Analogical Idea or Conception. About that same chimerical abstract Idea of *Force* or *Impetus*, he observes learned Men have had mighty Contests; and great variety of Opinions there are about what is in Truth but an airy empty Nothing: And therefore it is no Wonder that they are so much at a loss for such an Idea; and that the Searches of the

4. *Alciphron* VII. 17.
5. Compare *Alciphron* VII. 4.
6. *Alciphron* VII. 5.
7. *Alciphron* VII. 9.

Ingenious among them should amount to this at last, That it was but a *Subtil Abstract*, or *Spiritual Quintessence*; and that they knew not what to make of it.

Well, but notwithstanding all this waste of Learning is nothing to the Stress of the Objection; yet as our Author hath been very profuse in reciting the particular Disputes and curious Dissertations concerning Force or *Impetus*: So hath he blazoned out a large Field of Mechanics, to display the many Uses which have been made of it, to the great Benefit and Conveniency of Mankind; altho' Men could never fix upon any precise *Distinct* Idea to be annexed to that Term. Even so then, his Inference is, Infidels need not wonder that the word *Grace* hath occasioned so many different Opinions and Controversies; and that it is of so great Use in Religion; tho' it be impossible to frame any precise distinct Idea of it. But certainly Men could have had no Disputes or Dissertations about *Force*; or have deduced any convincing Consequences in relation to it for the Benefit and Advantage of Mankind, and their Improvement in the Knowlege of Mechanics; if they had not first formed *Some* clear and *Distinct* Idea of it in the *Concrete*. This clear and distinct Idea annexed to that Word, was the true Ground and Foundation of all those Dissertations; and without it they could not have made one Step towards any solid and useful Knowlege concerning it. And thus it is with *Grace*; without a *Distinct* Idea or Conception in the *Concrete* of some obvious natural Operation or Influence, affixed to that Term; and transfered together with it to *Represent* the supernatural Influence of the divine Spirit: It would be no distinct Object of our Knowlege Faith or Opinion; there would be no intelligible Dissertations or Contests about it; there could be no useful Conclusions drawn from it, or satisfactory Propositions formed with relation to it. And without *Any* Idea or Conception affixed, it could have no more real Signification than if you spelled the Word backward.

By this Author's thus placing *Physical Force* and *Divine Grace* upon the same Level, as to an Impossibility of forming any *Determinate* or *Distinct* Idea or Conception of either of them; he puts it intirely out of his Power and the Power of any Man living, to make a clear and effectual Reply to the strongest Part of the Infidels Objection, as he himself hath stated it; and that by which they clinch their main Argument against all Revelation. For says his Minute Philosopher, *You take your Idea of Grace from things Corporeal, from Motion and the Force of Bodies which are obvious and sensible; and this you substitute in the Place of the other, which is spiritual and incomprehensible, but this is manifest Delusion. For tho' the Idea of corporeal Force be ever so clear and intelligible; it will not therefore follow that the Idea of Grace, a thing perfectly incorporeal, must be so too: And tho' we may reason distinctly, perceive, assent, and form Opinions about Force; it will by no Means follow that we can do so about Grace.*[8] Tho' he hath prudently declined making any Reply to this *Pinch*[9] of the Argument; it will not however be amiss to shew the only way of performing it upon his Principle. We must first positively deny that we take our Idea or Conception of Grace from the Force or Influence of any thing material, or human: Which is a manifest Falsity; for if we did not take it from some of these (by Analogy) we could have no Idea or Conception at all of Grace, which is altogether spiritual and incomprehensible as it is in it self; and thus the Word would be completely insignificant and useless. Then we must go about to persuade Unbelievers out of their *Senses*, and convince them that they can form no *Determinate* and *Distinct* Idea or Conception of natural Force or human Influence; than which nothing is more obvious and sensible, and which they see and feel and clearly perceive every Day of their Lives: And out of their *Reason* likewise; so as to make them believe they can as easily form a *Direct* Idea of Grace, or the Influence of the divine Spirit on the Mind of Man, in the *Concrete*; as they can of any natural Force or human Influence: Whereas it is impossible to form any such *Direct* Idea of it; either general or particular, determinate or indeterminate, distinct or indistinct, in the Abstract or in the Concrete. And from these Premises we must at last draw this wild Conclusion, That tho' it may be as impossible to affix a *Distinct*, or even *Any* Idea or Conception to Grace, as to Force: Yet that Term may be *Significant* and *Useful*, and excite us to Operation; and we can assent to it, and reason and form Opinions about it, as we can about Physical *Force* or Influence.

Now therefore may I not appeal to the Reader, in this Author's own Words, *Whether this is taking his Notions of Faith Opinion and Assent from common*

8. *Alciphron* VII. 4.
9. crucial point.

Sence and common Use; and from maturely weighing the Nature of Signs and Language?[10] And whether he had any wrong done him when I asserted, that upon his Principle there could be but two Terms in the preceding Syllogism of *Grace*; or in any other Syllogism relating to the Attributes of God or the Mysteries of Christianity? Since nothing is more evident than that no Word can be a *Syllogistic Term* without *Some Idea* Conception or Complex Notion annexed to it; either direct and immediate, or Analogical: And that unless this is *Clear* and *Distinct*, nothing can be concluded with any *Determinate* Truth and *Satisfactory* Certainty. Was he any way injured or misrepresented, when I said he intirely gave up the whole Cause of Christian Mysteries? And may I not now justly add, that his notional Method of proceeding thro' that tedious obscure and perplexed Dissertation upon Number and Force and Grace, unwarily tends to sap the very Foundation of Religion natural and revealed? And to resolve it all at last into nothing more than a blind implicit Faith, and an empty Senceless Sound of Syllables without any real Meaning Use or Signification: By granting to Unbelievers the very Principle upon which their grand Objection proceeds, and by making them the only Concession they wanted; namely that it is not always *Necessary* or *Possible* to annex *Distinct*, nay *Any* Ideas Conceptions or Notions, to the main Terms by which we express our Faith in the Doctrines of the Gospel; and to the words *Grace* and *Trinity* in particular. For then all the vile Consequences which he hath put into the Mouth of his *Minute Philosopher* inevitably follow. *That those Terms are altogether insignificant; that there can be no Assent and consequently Faith, where there are no Ideas* Conceptions or Notions; *that then we pronounce hard Words without a Meaning; that thus there can be no Argument or Belief; nor any thing in Faith farther than a mere verbal Trifling. That those Terms are merely Forms of Speech, and express empty Sounds which mean nothing and are of no Use to Mankind; that they are Names only instead of Ideas and Things, and thought intelligible only because they are familiar.* In short, *That Doctrines and Propositions composed of them cannot regulate our Wills Passions and Conduct; or be lively Principles influencing the Mind and operating upon it: And that their Method of Reasoning concerning* GRACE *may be applyed, by any Man of Sence, to the confuting all other the most essential Articles of the Christian Faith.*[11]

The true Answer to the Stress of that Objection of Unbelievers in this latter Form is; by granting them *That we do realy take our Idea or Conception of divine Grace from things* natural and human and obvious (tho' not from things *Merely material*, as they unaccurately word it) *and these we substitute in the Place of the other*: And that for the very Reason mentioned in the Objection; because Grace is *Spiritual* and *Incomprehensible* as it is in it self, and therefore it is impossible for us to do otherwise. And this is so far from being *A manifest Delusion*, that it is a highly rational Method of proceeding; and effectualy answers all the present Ends of Morality and Religion. For our Case in short is this; As natural and human Force or Influence is a thing obviously and directly perceptible, we can frame a *Direct* and *Immediate* Idea or Conception of it: And as Grace is a thing of quite a different Kind, purely spiritual and imperceptible; we can form no direct and immediate Idea or Conception of it in any Degree. And therefore we substitute the clear, and distinct, and direct Idea or Conception of natural and human Force or Influence in the Concrete; as a clear *Analogical Conception* and distinct *Representation* of a *Correspondent* Operation of the divine Spirit upon the Mind of Man. So that the Idea or Conception is one and the same, as well as the Word: Nor are either of them to be otherwise distinguished, than by the different *Use* and *Application* of them to human, or divine Grace and Favour; and to natural, or supernatural Influence. Thus the *Perspicuity, Distinctness,* and *Usefulness* both of the Term and of the Idea or Conception annexed to it, are still the same; whether you apply those Terms to one or the other of those Things. If the Idea or Conception of natural and human Influence or Operation annexed to the Term is *Clear* and *Distinct*, as the Objection supposeth; it is not the less clear or *Useful* when the Word is used Analogicaly, to express that which is *Correspondent* and *Similar* in supernatural and spiritual Objects; for these two plain Reasons. Because no new and different Idea or Conception, obtained directly from the *Thing it self* (or from any thing *Of the same Kind*) can then be affixed to it; this being utterly imperceptible and incomprehensible after that Manner, and no otherwise conceivable than by some Analogical

10. *Alciphron* VII. 13.

11. *Alciphron* VII. 2-3.

Representation: And because we are *Obliged* to *Understand* and *Believe* nothing more beyond what we thus conceive by that distinct and intelligible *Correspondent Resemblance;* except that the supernatural Original is *Real* and *True*, but in no Degree conceivable or intelligible by us *As it is in its own Nature*.

Now then; If supernatural and divine Objects be totaly *Different in Kind* from any thing directly and immediately conceivable by us: And consequently there can be no other *Possible* way of *Thinking* or *Speaking* of them, but by the same Conceptions and Terms we use for *Correspondent* and *Similar* worldly Objects. Accordingly if we are not *Concerned* and *Obliged* to *Apprehend* or *Believe* the former, as they are in their own *Real Nature*; but only as they are *Represented* by such clear and distinct and intelligible Analogical Resemblances. If the *Word* and the *Idea* or *Conception* annexed to it are the very *Same*, for Instance, in respect of a natural and human; and a supernatural and divine Operation or Influence: And that it is impossible to affix any new and different Idea or Conception, when the Term is transfered to the latter. If the *Idea* or Conception is *Equaly Clear* and *Distinct*; and the *Word* equaly plain and *Intelligible* when they are applyed to either. If the *Things* for which that one and the same Idea or Conception stands in the Mind; and which are expressed by one and the same Word, are or may be equaly *True* and *Real*. If we conceive and express the divine *Grace*, and all *Gospel* Doctrines of Mystery, after no other Manner than we *Necessarily* do the *Attributes of God* known even by the Light of Nature. And lastly, If this only Method we have of conceiving them be perfectly *Useful*; effectualy answering all the Ends of *Religion*, and most strongly *Influencing* our *Moral Practice*.

If these things, I say, are firm substantial Truths; established upon a solid Foundation, never to be shaken by the utmost Efforts of mistaken Believers, or obstinate Unbelievers. Then, since I am in a Station which obligeth me to fence on both Sides, and ward against Friends as well as Enemies; here I fix my Foot, with open and resolute Defiance to any Man living to assign a good or even plausible Reason; why we may not *Understand* the divine *Grace* as clearly and distinctly; and believe the *Truth* and *Reality* of it as surely, firmly, and usefully, as we can conceive and believe any thing in this World, for which we have the utmost moral Evidence and Certainty? And why we may not *Reason as distinctly, assent, and form Opinions about* the supernatural Influence of the divine Spirit upon the Mind of Man; as we do about the Force or Influence of natural Causes? To which I shall add in the Style of this Author's Minute Philosopher, *That the same Method of Reasoning may be applyed by any Man of Sence* to establish all the *Attributes* of God known by the Light of Nature or Revelation, as well as all the *Mysteries* of the Gospel; against the strongest Objections of Infidels and Heretics: And he may thereby make it plainly appear to be *Manifest Delusion*, and a shameful Want not only of common Logic, but of common Sence and Reason in Men; either to explode the *Truth* and *Reality*, or to deny the *Useful Knowlege* of things divine and supernatural; only for want of such *Direct* Ideas or Conceptions of them, as they have of things natural and human. Which is no other than by plain Implication destroying the very Nature of the things themselves, and then requiring some Ideas or Conceptions of them. The Absurdity is no less than demanding a *Direct Apprehension* in some Degree, of things in every Degree *Incomprehensible* to us *As they are in themselves*; an *Immediate Perception* of things, totaly *Different in Kind* from all Objects *Immediately perceptible* by us; and *Purely spiritual* Ideas, in a Mind composed of *Matter and Spirit*: Which is a Knowlege of them utterly impossible to human Understanding; as well as intirely inconsistent with their very Nature, Properties, and Existence.

PHILIP SKELTON

(1707-87)

from:
OPHIOMACHES: OR, DEISM REVEALED (1749)

[In the following passage from the second dialogue of *Ophiomaches*, Skelton, a fervent anti-deist and one of Browne's followers, tries to show the limitations of reason in order to enhance faith and revelation.]

SHEPERD: This, I think, is evident, that altho' reason should be so strong in one man, or in a few, as to find out the being of some superior power, yet this would not, probably, happen, till after many ages, spent in vain attempts to account for the origin and regularity of the world; and when some notion of this kind should once be struck out, it would be so imperfect, so uncertain, and blended with so much absurdity and error, that it would scarcely be worth the propagating, which would be also a matter of infinite difficulty. But supposing it to prevail in some nations, or all over the world, having once preoccupied the minds of men, the improvements made by others in after-times on the first imperfect discovery, instead of having the notions, derived from that discovery, as a basis to build on, would find them, and the prejudices accompanying them, an infinite obstacle to their propagation. What is said of the first improvement, would be as true of all the subsequent ones. The old notions would be so many bars against the new; and, considering the great difficulty of the inquiry, and the vast room for conceit and imagination to graft their wild scions on the fruitful stock, it would require an almost infinite number of debates, refinements, and improvements, each of which must have a course thro' the world before they could be examined, in order to settle the right idea of God, and support it with demonstrations universally convincing. Reason labours under a yet greater difficulty in finding out the right notion of God. Reason, if I be not mistaken, is that faculty by which we form propositions out of ideas already conceived, and, laying those together, the terms of which have a necessary and self-evident connexion or dissonance, draw conclusions from thence. It is that power of the mind by which we hold, as it were, the light of clear and incontestable truths to dark and disputable questions, and endeavour by that means to discover on which side of the latter we ought to fix our assent. He whose ideas of things represent their objects in true and determinate lights, and whose faculty of reason is strong and clear, is called a judicious man. When this faculty is properly and judiciously exercised on a knowable proposition, the result should be called right reasoning, rather than right reason. As the office of reason is not to supply the mind with ideas, but to judge of the connexion or disagreement between those already received; so it can only exercise itself on such materials, as those other faculties, that hold intelligence with objects, supply it with. This latter is the function of the senses alone, which, for that purpose, are turned outward towards their proper objects, and set upon as so many avenues and inlets to the ingredients of all our knowlege. It is vain to say we have any proper or immediate idea of spirit, and its operations, or that we have any other source of notions than sensation. If *Brown[e]'s Procedure and extent of the understanding* had not clearly demonstrated this, the trials every man may make in his own mind would do it effectually. When we look into ourselves with a sharp and unprejudiced eye, we plainly perceive spirit represented there analogically by our idea of some subtil matter, its operations by those of body, and both, not only in our external, but internal speech, by terms and signs appropriated to sensible objects. If then all our ideas are derived from sensation, if reason can operate no farther than it hath ideas to work on, and if the Divine Being is not the object of any one sense, how much at a loss must reason be to fix our way of thinking concerning that which it is furnished with no idea of?

DECHAINE: Were this argument of yours capable of proving any thing, it would prove too much for your purpose, and reduce us to absolute Atheism, thro' an impossibility of forming any idea of God.

SHEPERD: I did not say, Sir, that it was impossible to form any idea of God; but only, that reason, left to itself, having no power of its own to form any ideas at all, and being supplied with ideas to work on only thro' the senses, could hardly form a right idea of God. This, however, it might be enabled to do by him who taught it to believe, that the soul of man is formed in the image of God; and that as we represent our souls to our own conceptions by a similitude or analogy to matter, so we ought to represent him in our thoughts by the analogy between him and our souls. . . .

ROBERT CLAYTON
(1695-1758)

from: A VINDICATION OF THE HISTORIES OF THE OLD AND NEW TESTAMENT, PART III (1757)

[Clayton, the last notable Irish rationalist, here shows his affinity with Toland on mystery and meaning.]

. . . But there is a Distinction made between believing Things that are contradictory to our Reason, and believing Things that are only above our Comprehension. Let it be so. And then let us see how far we ought to believe Things that are above, or beyond, our Comprehension. Now Things may be above, or beyond, our Comprehension, either as to the *Matter* or the *Manner* of them. They may be above or beyond our Comprehension as to the *Matter* of them, when the Terms of the Proposition are unintelligible; and they may be above or beyond our Comprehension, as to the *Manner*, when the Reason of the Thing, or the *Manner how*, is not made intelligible to us. Let us consider each of these separately, and first as to *the Manner how*.

And let us suppose that an Angel from Heaven, of the Divinity of whose Mission there was no Doubt, should appear to a Person in *Africa*, who had never seen any Ice or Snow, and should inform him, that in the northern Parts of this Globe, at certain Seasons of the Year, the Waters of the Rivers congealed into so hard and solid a Substance, that whole Armies of Men, with all their Cannon and other heavy Baggage, passed over them with the same Ease as they did over dry Land.[1] It is certain that this *African* ought to believe the Matter of Fact as related by the Angel, because he can so far comprehend him, as he understands what is meant by Armies marching as it were on dry Ground. But *how* or in what Manner the fluid Waters are so far congealed as to lose their Fluidity and become a solid and fixed Substance, as that is the *Mystery* which he cannot comprehend, that is no Object of his Faith; not only because he cannot comprehend it, but, indeed, because it was not revealed unto him. He may form Conjectures about it, or some of his own Species may help him to reason on the Subject, and he may believe those Conjectures to be true; but that is no Part of his Faith. For by the Word *Faith* I would, to avoid all Cavils, be understood to mean only our Belief in a GOD or in a divine Revelation. And therefore, as the Manner *how* the Waters are turned into Ice was not revealed to him by the Angel, it is therefore no Object of his Faith.

Let us again suppose this Angel should inform this *African* or any other Man, that there were three Persons in Heaven, called Father, Son, and Holy Ghost, and that these three were *one*. There is no Manner of Doubt but that the Person to whom the Revelation was made ought to believe that what the Angel said was true, though he could not comprehend the Manner *How*. For though he is certain that three Persons cannot be one Person in the same Sense of the Word, yet he may be sure that their being *one* is true in some Sense or other. But as that Sense was not revealed, this Part which is the *Mystery*, and which he therefore does not compre-

1. The idea that ice would seem incredible or miraculous to those in warm climates was common in the contemporary debates on miracles and mysteries; it was discussed by Locke, among others.

hend, is no Object of his Faith. And although he and his Friend may believe their own Conjectures about the Explanation of it; yet surely these human Conjectures, or Decisions, ought not to be imposed either upon themselves, or others, as Articles of Faith.

Thus far I have instanced in a Revelation where the Terms of it are intelligible, though the Manner *how* is not: But if we come to consider our Belief in any Proposition which we do not comprehend, because the Terms of it are unintelligible; then the Argument will appear so much the stronger.

Let us therefore suppose that an Angel should reveal unto any Man, that there was such a Thing in Heaven as an *Abdolubeden*; and that there was no Doubt to be made of the divine Mission of the Angel, or of his having spoken these Words. And then the Question will be, what is this Man to believe, and how far are these Words the Object of his Faith? To which the Answer is, just so far as his Reason can comprehend them, and no further. For as here is nothing revealed that is contradictory to his Reason, but only something the Meaning whereof he cannot comprehend; all that can possibly be required of him to believe is, that the Angel spoke these Words, and that there is such a Thing in Heaven as an *Abdolubeden*. But what that *Abdolubeden* is, whether it is one Substance or two; whether it is a material or spiritual Existence, he is neither obliged to believe, nor indeed ought he to determine any Thing about it. This Part which was not revealed, continueth to be a *Mystery*, and is therefore no Object of his Faith, and must continue such until it pleaseth GOD to make some further Revelation about it. He may very readily believe the Angel and the Revelation, that is, he may believe that what the Angel said was true; but what the Word *Abdolubeden* means, which is the *Mystery*, as that was not revealed, he is not obliged to believe any Thing about it. And if any uninspired Person should presume to explain it to him, he is surely at Liberty to reject all such Explanations; unless such Person can prove himself to be infallible.

However as this is the great Subterfuge of the Defenders of the Athanasian Doctrine concerning the Trinity, I must beg your Lordship's[2] Patience till, for your Satisfaction and my own, I endeavour to put this Question in another Light. And let us suppose that an Angel from Heaven should say these Words to an illiterate Man, *γνῶθι σγαυτόν*[3] this would be a *Mystery* to him; though there would be no *Mystery* in these Words to any one who understand *Greek*. He might believe that what the Angel said was true; but the Meaning of these Words would continue to be a *Mystery* to him, till they were explained, or revealed, unto him, and then they would be no longer a *Mystery*. In like Manner every Proposition, the Terms of which we do not understand, contains what is a Mystery to those who do not understand them; and it is impossible for such Persons reasonably to form any Notion, or Belief about them.

So that the common Expression of *believing a Mystery*, seems to be a very improper one. We may believe that there are Mysteries in Religion, or that certain Words contain a Mystery; but our Belief cannot reach the Mystery any more than our Knowledge can. Let us but change one Word for another, as we do Letters of the same Value in *Algebra*, and this Problem will, only by stating of it properly, work out its own Solution. Thus, for Example, if we insert the Word *Secret* instead of *Mystery*, we shall readily see the Impropriety of Speech in saying, that *we believe a Secret*. For while a Thing continues to be an absolute Secret, it is impossible for any one to believe any Thing about it. We may indeed believe that there is a Secret; but we cannot properly be said to believe the Secret. Guesses and Conjectures may be formed, just so far as People imagine they know something about it; but, as far as it continueth a Secret, Belief can not. . . .

2. Clayton may be addressing the second Earl of Egmont, the son of a close friend of George Berkeley. The subtitle of Clayton's work was 'a series of letters to a young noble man'.

3. Know thyself.

EDMUND BURKE

(1729-97)

from: A PHILOSOPHICAL ENQUIRY INTO THE ORIGIN OF OUR IDEAS OF THE SUBLIME AND BEAUTIFUL (1757)

[In these passages, from the third and fifth parts of the *Philosophical Enquiry*, Burke, the last important Irish philosopher, applies theological representationalism to the study of aesthetics and Berkeley's emotivism to illuminate poetry.]

PART III

SECTION XXIV

The beautiful in FEELING

The foregoing description of beauty, so far as is taken in by the eye, may be greatly illustrated by describing the nature of objects, which produce a similar effect through the touch. This I call the beautiful in *Feeling*. It corresponds wonderfully with what causes the same species of pleasure to the sight. There is a chain in all our sensations; they are all but different sorts of feeling, calculated to be affected by various sorts of objects, but all to be affected after the same manner. All bodies that are pleasant to the touch, are so by the slightness of the resistance they make. Resistance is either to motion along the surface, or to the pressure of the parts on one another; if the former be slight, we call the body, smooth; if the latter, soft. The chief pleasure we receive by feeling, is in the one or the other of these qualities; and if there be a combination of both, our pleasure is greatly increased. This is so plain, that it is rather more fit to illustrate other things, than to be illustrated itself by any example. The next source of pleasure in this sense, as in every other, is the continually presenting somewhat new; and we find that bodies which continually vary their surface, are much the most pleasant, or beautiful, to the feeling, as any one that pleases may experience. The third property in such objects is, that though the surface continually varies its direction, it never varies it suddenly. The application of any thing sudden, even though the impression itself have little or nothing of violence, is disagreeable. The quick application of a finger a little warmer or colder than usual, without notice, makes us start; a slight tap on the shoulder, not expected, has the same effect. Hence it is that angular bodies, bodies that suddenly vary the direction of the outline, afford so little pleasure to the feeling. Every such change is a sort of climbing or falling in miniature; so that squares, triangles, and other angular figures, are neither beautiful to the sight nor feeling. Whoever compares his state of mind, on feeling soft, smooth, variated, unangular bodies, with that in which he finds himself, on the view of a beautiful object, will perceive a very striking analogy in the effects of both; and which may go a good way towards discovering their common cause. Feeling and sight in this respect, differ in but a few points. The touch takes in the pleasure of softness, which is not primarily an object of sight; the sight on the other hand comprehends colour, which can hardly be made perceptible to the touch; the touch again has the advantage in a new idea of pleasure resulting from a moderate degree of warmth; but the eye triumphs in the infinite extent and multiplicity of its objects. But there is such a similitude in the pleasures of these senses, that I am apt to fancy, if it were possible that one might discern colour by feeling, (as it is said some blind men have done) that the same colours, and the same disposition of colouring, which are found beautiful to the sight, would be found likewise most grateful to the touch. But setting aside conjectures, let us pass to the other sense; of hearing.

PART V

SECTION V

Examples that WORDS may affect without raising IMAGES

I find it very hard to persuade several that their passions are affected by words from whence they have no ideas; and yet harder to convince them, that in the ordinary course of conversation we are sufficiently understood without raising any images of the things concerning which we speak. It seems to be an odd subject of dispute with any man, whether he has ideas in his mind or not. Of this at first view, every man, in his own forum, ought to judge without appeal. But strange as it may appear, we are often at a loss to know what ideas we have of things, or whether we have any ideas at all upon some subjects. It even requires a good deal of attention to be thoroughly satisfied on this head. Since I wrote these papers I found two very striking instances of the possibility there is, that a man may hear words without having any idea of the things which they represent, and yet afterwards be capable of returning them to others, combined in a new way, and with great propriety, energy and instruction. The first instance, is that of Mr. Blacklock,[1] a poet blind from his birth. Few men blessed with the most perfect sight can describe visual objects with more spirit and justness than this blind man; which cannot possibly be attributed to his having a clearer conception of the things he describes than is common to other persons. Mr. Spence,[2] in an elegant preface which he has written to the works of this poet, reasons very ingeniously, and I imagine for the most part very rightly upon the cause of this extraordinary phenomenon; but I cannot altogether agree with him, that some improprieties in language and thought which occur in these poems have arisen from the blind poet's imperfect conception of visual objects, since such improprieties, and much greater, may be found in writers even of an higher class than Mr. Blacklock, and who, notwithstanding, possessed the faculty of seeing in its full perfection. Here is a poet doubtless as much affected by his own descriptions as any that reads them can be; and yet he is affected with this strong enthusiasm by things of which he neither has, nor can possibly have any idea further than that of a bare sound; and why may not those who read his works be affected in the same manner that he was, with as little of any real ideas of the things described? The second instance is of Mr. Saunderson,[3] professor of mathematics in the university of Cambridge. This learned man had acquired great knowledge in natural philosophy, in astronomy, and whatever sciences depend upon mathematical skill. What was the most extraordinary, and the most to my purpose, he gave excellent lectures upon light and colours; and this man taught others the theory of those ideas which they had, and which he himself undoubtedly had not. But it is probable, that the words red, blue, green, answered to him as well as the ideas of the colours themselves; for the ideas of greater or lesser degrees of refrangibility[4] being applied to these words, and the blind man being instructed in what other respects they were found to agree or to disagree, it was as easy for him to reason upon the words as if he had been fully master of the ideas. Indeed it must be owned he could make no new discoveries in the way of experiment. He did nothing but what we do every day in common discourse. When I wrote this last sentence, and used the words *every day* and *common discourse*, I had no images in my mind of any succession of time; nor of men in conference with each other; nor do I imagine that the reader will have any such ideas on reading it. Neither when I spoke of red, blue, and green, as well as of refrangibility; had I these several colours, or the rays of light passing into a different medium, and there diverted from their course, painted before me in the way of images. I know very well that the mind possesses a faculty of raising such images at pleasure; but then an act of the will is necessary to this; and in ordinary conversation or reading it is very rarely that any image at all is excited in the mind. If I say, 'I shall go to Italy next summer,' I am well understood. Yet I believe no body has by this painted in his imagination the exact figure of the speaker passing by land or by water, or both; sometimes on horseback, sometimes in a carriage; with all the particulars of the journey. Still less has he any idea of Italy, the country to which I proposed to go; or of the greenness of the fields, the ripening of the fruits, and the warmth of the air, with the change to this from a different season, which are the ideas for which the word *summer* is substituted; but least of all has he any image from the word *next*; for this word stands for the idea of many summers, with the exclusion of all but one: and surely the man who says *next*

1. Thomas Blacklock (1721-91), a blind Scottish poet.
2. Joseph Spence (1699-1768), professor of poetry and of modern history at Oxford, who wrote an account of Thomas Blacklock.
3. Dr Nicholas Saunderson (1682-1739), professor of mathematics at Cambridge, who had lost his sight at an early age.
4. refraction (as of light), i.e. deflection from its course as it passes through a substance such as a prism or water.

summer, has no images of such a succession, and such an exclusion. In short, it is not only of those ideas which are commonly called abstract, and of which no image at all *can* be formed, but even of particular real beings, that we converse without having any idea of them excited in the imagination; as will certainly appear on a diligent examination of our own minds. Indeed so little does poetry depend for its effect on the power of raising sensible images, that I am convinced it would lose a very considerable part of its energy, if this were the necessary result of all description. Because that union of affecting words which is the most powerful of all poetical instruments, would frequently lose its force along with its propriety and consistency, if the sensible images were always excited. There is not perhaps in the whole Eneid a more grand and laboured passage, than the description of Vulcan's cavern in Etna, and the works that are there carried on. Virgil dwells particularly on the formation of the thunder which he described unfinished under the hammers of the Cyclops. But what are the principles of this extraordinary composition?

Tres imbris torti radios, tres nubis aquosæ
Addiderant; rutili tres ignis et alitis austri;
Fulgores nunc terrificos, sonitumque, metumque
Miscebant operi, flammisque sequacibus iras.[5]

This seems to me admirably sublime; yet if we attend coolly to the kind of sensible image which a combination of ideas of this sort must form, the chimeras of madmen cannot appear more wild and absurd than such a picture. '*Three rays of twisted showers, three of watery clouds, three of fire, and three of the winged south wind; then mixed they in the work terrific lightnings, and sound, and fear, and anger, with pursuing flames.*' This strange composition is formed into a gross body; it is hammered by the Cyclops, it is in part polished, and partly continues rough. The truth is, if poetry gives us a noble assemblage of words, corresponding to many noble ideas, which are connected by circumstances of time or place, or related to each other as cause and effect, or associated in any natural way, they may be moulded together in any form, and perfectly answer their end. The picturesque connection is not demanded; because no real picture is formed; nor is the effect of the description at all the less upon this account. What is said of Helen by Priam and the old men of his council, is generally thought to give us the highest possible idea of that fatal beauty.

They cry'd, no wonder such celestial charms
For nine long years have set the world in arms;
What winning graces! what majestic mien!
She moves a goddess, and she looks a queen.[6]
POPE

Here is not one word said of the particulars of her beauty; no thing which can in the least help us to any precise idea of her person; but yet we are much more touched by this manner of mentioning her than by these long and laboured descriptions of Helen, whether handed down by tradition, or formed by fancy, which are to be met with in some authors. I am sure it affects me much more than the minute description which Spenser has given of Belphebe;[7] though I own that there are parts in that description, as there are in all the descriptions of that excellent writer, extremely fine and poetical. The terrible picture which Lucretius has drawn of religion, in order to display the magnanimity of his philosophical hero in opposing her, is thought to be designed with great boldness and spirit.

Humana ante oculos fædè cum vita jaceret,
In terris, oppressa gravi sub religione,
Quæ caput e cæli regionibus ostendebat
Horribili desuper visu mortalibus instans;
Primus Graius homo mortales tollere contra
Est oculos ausus.[8] —

What idea do you derive from so excellent a picture? none at all most certainly; neither has the poet said a single word which might in the least serve to mark a single limb or feature of the phantom, which he intended to represent in all the horrors imagination can conceive. In reality poetry and rhetoric do not succeed in exact description so well as painting does; their business is to affect rather by

5. Virgil, *Aeneid*, VIII, 429-32.

6. Pope's translation of the *Iliad*, III, 1, 205-08.
7. Edmund Spenser, *The Faerie Queene*, II, iii, 21-31.
8. Lucretius, *De Rerum Naturae*, I, 62-67. Creech's translation (1682) of these lines reads:

Long time Men lay oppress'd with slavish fear;
Religion's Tyranny did domineer,
And being plac'd in Heav'n look'd proudly down,
And frighted abject Spirits with her Frown.
At length a mighty Man of Greece began
T'assert the nat'ral Liberty of Man ....

sympathy than imitation; to display rather the effect of things on the mind of the speaker, or of others, than to present a clear idea of the things themselves. This is their most extensive province, and that in which they succeed the best.

SECTION VI

POETRY not strictly an imitative art

Hence we may observe that poetry, taken in its most general sense, cannot with strict propriety be called an art of imitation. It is indeed an imitation so far as it describes the manners and passions of men which their words can express; where *animi motus effert interprete lingua*.[9] There it is strictly imitation; and all merely *dramatic* poetry is of this sort. But *descriptive* poetry operates chiefly by *substitution*; by the means of sounds, which by custom have the effect of realities. Nothing is an imitation further than as it resembles some other thing; and words undoubtedly have no sort of resemblance to the ideas for which they stand.

SECTION VII

How WORDS influence the passions

Now, as words affect, not by any original power, but by representation, it might be supposed, that their influence over the passions should be but light; yet it is quite otherwise; for we find by experience that eloquence and poetry are as capable, nay indeed much more capable of making deep and lively impressions than any other arts, and even than nature itself in very many cases. And this arises chiefly from these three causes. First, that we take an extraordinary part in the passions of others, and that we are easily affected and brought into sympathy by any tokens which are shewn of them; and there are no tokens which can express all the circumstances of most passions so fully as words; so that if a person speak upon any subject, he can not only convey the subject to you, but likewise the manner in which he is himself affected by it. Certain it is, that the influence of most things on our passions is not so much from the things themselves, as from our opinions concerning them; and these again depend very much on the opinions of other men, conveyable for the most part by words only. Secondly; there are many things of a very affecting nature, which can seldom occur in the reality, but the words which represent them often do; and thus they have an opportunity of making a deep impression and taking root in the mind, whilst the idea of the reality was transient; and to some perhaps never really occurred in any shape, to whom it is notwithstanding very affecting, as war, death, famine, &c. Besides, many ideas have never been at all presented to the senses of any men but by words, as God, angels, devils, heaven and hell, all of which have however a great influence over the passions. Thirdly; by words we have it in our power to make such *combinations* as we cannot possibly do otherwise. By this power of combining we are able, by the addition of well-chosen circumstances, to give a new life and force to the simple object. In painting we may represent any fine figure we please; but we never can give it those enlivening touches which it may receive from words. To represent an angel in a picture, you can only draw a beautiful young man winged; but what painting can furnish out any thing so grand as the addition of one word, 'the angel of the *Lord*?' It is true, I have here no clear idea, but these words affect the mind more than the sensible image did, which is all I contend for. A picture of Priam dragged to the altar's foot, and there murdered, if it were well executed would undoubtedly be very moving; but there are very aggravating circumstances which it could never represent.

Sanguine fœdantem quos ipse sacraverat *ignes*.[10]

As a further instance, let us consider those lines of Milton, where he describes the travels of the fallen angels through their dismal habitation,

——O'er many a dark and dreary vale
They pass'd, and many a region dolorous;
O'er many a frozen, many a fiery Alp;
Rock, caves, lakes, fens, bogs, dens and
shades of death,
A universe of death.[11]

9. Horace, *Ars Poetica*, line 111. (misquoted) '[Nature] expresses the emotions of the heart with the tongue as interpreter.'

10. Virgil, *Aeneid*, II, 502. 'I saw him [Priam] polluting with his blood the fires which he himself had consecrated.'

11. John Milton, *Paradise Lost*, II, 618-22. The passage begins: 'Through many a dark and dreary vale . . . .'

Here is displayed the force of union in

Rocks, caves, lakes, fens, bogs, dens and shades;

which yet would lose the greatest part of their effect, if they were not the

Rocks, caves, lakes, fens, bogs, dens and
shades——
——*of* Death.

This idea or this affection caused by a word, which nothing but a word could annex to the others, raises a very great degree of the sublime; and this sublime is raised yet higher by what follows, a '*universe of Death*'. Here are again two ideas not presentable but by language; and a union of them great and amazing beyond conception; if they may properly be called ideas which present no distinct image to the mind;— but still it will be difficult to conceive how words can move the passions which belong to real objects, without representing these objects clearly. This is difficult to us, because we do not sufficiently distinguish, in our observations upon language, between a clear expression, and a strong expression. These are frequently confounded with each other, though they are in reality extremely different. The former regards the understanding; the latter belongs to the passions. The one describes a thing as it is; the other describes it as it is felt. Now, as there is a moving tone of voice, an impassioned countenance, an agitated gesture, which affect independently of the things about which they are exerted, so there are words, and certain dispositions of words, which being peculiarly devoted to passionate subjects, and always used by those who are under the influence of any passion; they touch and move us more than those which far more clearly and distinctly express the subject matter. We yield to sympathy, what we refuse to description. The truth is, all verbal description, merely as naked description, though never so exact, conveys so poor and insufficient an idea of the thing described, that it could scarcely have the smallest effect, if the speaker did not call in to his aid those modes of speech that mark a strong and lively feeling in himself. Then, by the contagion of our passions, we catch a fire already kindled in another, which probably might never have been struck out by the object described. Words, by strongly conveying the passions, by those means which we have already mentioned, fully compensate for their weakness in other respects. It may be observed that very polished languages, and such as are praised for their superior clearness and perspicuity, are generally deficient in strength. The French language has that perfection, and that defect. Whereas the oriental tongues, and in general the languages of most unpolished people, have a great force and energy of expression; and this is but natural. Uncultivated people are but ordinary observers of things, and not critical in distinguishing them; but, for that reason, they admire more, and are more affected with what they see, and therefore express themselves in a warmer and more passionate manner. If the affection be well conveyed, it will work its effect without any clear idea; often without any idea at all of the thing which has originally given rise to it.

It might be expected from the fertility of the subject, that I should consider poetry as it regards the sublime and beautiful more at large; but it must be observed that in this light it has been often and well handled already. It was not my design to enter into the criticism of the sublime and beautiful in any art, but to attempt to lay down such principles as may tend to ascertain, to distinguish, and to form a sort of standard for them; which purposes I thought might be best effected by an enquiry into the properties of such things in nature as raise love and astonishment in us; and by shewing in what manner they operated to produce these passions. Words were only so far to be considered, as to shew upon what principle they were capable of being the representatives of these natural things, and by what powers they were able to affect us often as strongly as the things they represent, and sometimes much more strongly.

Biographies/Bibliographies

John Toland

LIFE. Toland was born in Inishowen, Co. Donegal in 1670. 'Educated from the cradle in the grossest superstition', as he says in his *Apology* (1697), he rejected Roman catholicism at the age of fifteen. After attending Glasgow, Leyden and Oxford Universities, he decided against becoming a dissenting minister. His controversial work, *Christianity Not Mysterious* (1696), gave rise to the dispute between deists and orthodox believers. The book, which argued for a rational religion, was burned in Dublin by order of the House of Commons. Toland was forced to abandon a stay in Ireland in 1697. In later years he visited Berlin and Hanover and published political and theological pamphlets. He wrote a life of Milton (published in 1698) and in 1705 coined the term 'pantheist'. A native Irish speaker, Toland used his knowledge of the language in *A History of the Druids*, which appeared in print in 1726, four years after his death at Putney, near London.

CHIEF WRITINGS. *Two Essays in a letter from Oxford* (London, 1695); *Christianity Not Mysterious* (London, 1696); 2nd ed. 1697; 3rd ed. 1702; *An Apology for Mr. Toland* (London, 1697); *Amyntor; or, a defence of Milton's Life* (1699); *Clito: a poem on the force of eloquence* (London, 1700); *The Art of Governing by Partys* (1701); *Vindicius Liberius* (London, 1702); *Letters to Serena* (London, 1704); *Nazarenus; or, Jewish, Gentile, and Mahometan Christianity* (London, 1718); *Pantheisticon* (1720); *Tetradymus* (London, 1720); *A Collection of several pieces of Mr. Toland, now first published from his original manuscripts* (London, 1726) — this contains a memoir of Toland by P. Desmaizeaux, Toland's *History of the Celtic Religion* and correspondence.

BIOGRAPHY AND CRITICISM. Giancarlo Carabelli, *Tolandiana meteriali bibliografici* (Firenze: La Nuova Italia, 1975 and 1978); Robert E. Sullivan, *John Toland and the Deist Controversy* (Cambridge, Mass.: Harvard University Press, 1982); Stephen H. Daniel, *John Toland: His Methods, Manners and Mind* (Kingston, Canada: McGill-Queen's University Press, 1984). The following three works are of general use: Hiroshi Takemoto, *A Bibliography of the Irish Writers in the 17th and 18th Centuries* (Tokyo, 1985); Leslie Stephen, *History of English Thought in the Eighteenth Century* (London, 1876); D. Berman, 'The Irish Counter-Enlightenment' in R. Kearney (ed.), *The Irish Mind* (Dublin: Wolfhound Press, 1985).

William Molyneux

LIFE. Born in Dublin in 1656, and educated at Trinity College, Dublin, Molyneux quickly showed a distaste for traditional curricular studies and a marked interest in the new sciences, especially in the activities of the Royal Society of London. He became a mathematician and astronomer, and was one of the founding members of the Dublin Philosophical Society in 1684. In 1689, he left Ireland for England and there wrote his work on optics, *Dipotrica Nova* (1692). This led to the beginning of a friendship with John Locke which was to alter Molyneux's life and turn him towards political philosophy. Between 1692 and 1698 he and Locke exchanged letters. Molyneux studied Locke's *Two Treatises of Government* (1690) and was deeply influenced by Locke's contract theory of government. In 1692 and 1695, Molyneux was elected to the Irish parliament as the member for Dublin University. In 1697, two controversies arose, one concerning English legislation on Irish woollen exports and the other concerning the supremacy of the English and Irish parliaments in an appellate jurisdiction case. These led Molyneux to write his *The Case of Ireland Stated* in the early part of 1698. The reaction of the English parliament was extremely hostile. In July of that year, after the fracas had died down, Molyneux spent five weeks in England with John Locke. On his return to Dublin, he became ill and died in October 1698.

CHIEF WRITINGS. *Dioptrica Nova* (London, 1692); *The Case of Ireland's Being Bound by Acts of Parliament in England, Stated* (Dublin: Joseph Ray, 1698). There were further Dublin editions in 1706, 1719, 1720, 1725, 1749, 1770, 1773, 1776 and 1782. The bulk of Molyneux's philosophical views are in his letters to Locke, published in *Some Familiar Letters between Mr. Locke and Several of his Friends* (London, 1708).

BIOGRAPHY AND CRITICISM. Sir Capel Molyneux, *Anecdotes of the life of ... Molyneux* (Dublin, 1803); J.G. Simms (ed.), *The Case of Ireland Stated*, with an afterword by Denis Donoghue, (Monkstown, Co. Dublin: The Cadenus Press, 1977); J.G. Simms, *William Molyneux of Dublin: A Life of the Seventeenth-century Political Writer and Scientist*, (Dublin: Irish Academic Press, 1982); J.G. Simms, *Colonial Nationalism, 1698-1776* (Cork: Mercier Press, 1976); C. Robbins, *The Eighteenth-Century Commonwealth Man* (Cambridge, Mass.: Harvard University Press, 1959); P.H. Kelly, 'Locke and Molyneux', *Hermathena* CXXVI (Summer 1979), 38-53; M.J. Morgan, *Molyneux's Question* (Cambridge: Cambridge University Press, 1977).

Edward Synge (the elder)

LIFE. Born in Cork in 1659, Synge was a churchman and theological writer. His numerous religious pamphlets were often reprinted. He became bishop of Raphoe in 1714 and archbishop of Tuam in 1716. The son of a bishop, Synge had two sons who also became bishops — one of whom, Edward, was a friend of both Berkeley and Hutcheson and a member of the Molesworth circle. Edward Synge (the elder) died in 1741.

CHIEF WRITINGS. *A Gentleman's Religion* (part one London, 1693; parts two and three London, 1697); *An Appendix to a Gentleman's Religion* (London, 1698); *A Plain and Easy Method* (London, 1715); *Freethinking in matters of religion stated and recommended* (London, 1727).

BIOGRAPHY AND CRITICISM. Robert Sullivan, *John Toland and the Deist Controversy* (Cambridge, Mass.: Harvard University Press, 1982), chapters 2 and 8.

William King

LIFE. Born in Antrim in 1650, King was educated as a presbyterian. He came to Dublin, attended Trinity College and was ordained into the Church of Ireland. King became dean of St Patrick's Cathedral in Dublin and acted a joint head of the Church of Ireland (with Bishop Anthony Dopping) during the period 1688-90. After the battle of the Boyne, he was appointed bishop of Derry and played a leading role in the Irish parliaments of the 1690s. King became archbishop of Dublin in 1703 and spent the rest of his life striving to improve the Church of Ireland and to minimize the destructive effects of English rule in Ireland. He was a close acquaintance of Swift. King died in Dublin in 1729, 'universally lamented'.

CHIEF WRITINGS. *The State of the Protestants in Ireland* (London, 1691); *De Origine Mali* (Dublin, 1702); translated into English as *An Essay on the Origin of Evil* with notes by Edmund Law (London, 1731); *Predestination and Foreknowledge consistent with the freedom of man's will: in a Sermon* (Dublin, 1709); reprinted with notes by Archbishop Whately (London, 1821) and D. Berman and A. Carpenter (Monkstown, Co. Dublin: The Cadenus Press, 1976).

BIOGRAPHY AND CRITICISM. C.S. King, *A Great Archbishop of Dublin: William King. His Autobiography ... and ... Correspondence* (London: Longmans, 1906); A. Carpenter, *Archbishop King and Dean Swift* (University College, Dublin, PhD thesis, 1970); D. Berman, 'Berkeley and King', *Notes and Queries* Vol. 29, No. 6 (December 1982), 528-30; A. Lovejoy, *The Great Chain of Being* (Cambridge, Mass.: Harvard University Press, 1936), chapter VII. (Lovejoy describes King's *Origin* as 'perhaps ... the most influential of eighteenth-century theodicies'.)

George Berkeley

LIFE. Berkeley, Ireland's most famous philosopher, was born at Kilkenny in March 1685 and grew up at Dysart Castle, two miles from Thomastown. After attending Kilkenny College, he entered Trinity College, Dublin in 1700, and was elected a fellow in 1707. At this time he developed his immaterialistic philosophy, which he published partly in *A New Theory of Vision* (Dublin, 1709), more fully in *Treatise Concerning the Principles of Human Knowledge* (Dublin, 1710), and more popularly in the *Three Dialogues between Hylas and Philonous* (London, 1713).

Although Berkeley's association with Trinity College lasted until 1724, when he was appointed dean of Derry, most of his time from 1713 was spent either in England — where he became friendly with Swift, Pope, Steele and Addison — or in Italy, where he travelled widely. By 1722, however, he had determined to found a college in Bermuda to educate the American colonists and to train missionaries to the Indians. During the next decade he gathered support for his project, obtained a royal charter and was promised funds by the British government.

In 1729 Berkeley set sail for Rhode Island, where he lived for nearly three years, waiting in vain for the promised grant. Although unsuccessful, his idealistic venture gave substance to Pope's tribute: 'To Berkeley every virtue under heaven.' In late 1731 he returned to Britain, where he issued *Alciphron* (London, 1732), composed in America, and *The Analyst* (London, 1734), which attacked Newton's mathematics in the interest of Christian mysteries.

In 1734 he became bishop of Cloyne, where he spent the next seventeen years. His social and economic recommendations are outlined in *The Querist* (Dublin, 1735-37). In *Siris* (Dublin, 1744) 'the good bishop' championed the drinking of tar water, a medicine he learned of from America, and to which he ascribed great curative powers. He left Cloyne in late 1752 for Oxford, where he died in January 1753.

CHIEF WRITINGS. There have been five separate collected editions of Berkeley's works, the best and most recent is that edited by A.A. Luce and T.E. Jessop, *The Works of George Berkeley* (London: Nelson, 1948-1957), 9 volumes. Apart from the individual works mentioned above, Berkeley also published: *Passive obedience, or the Christian doctrine of not resisting the supreme power, proved ... In a discourse delivered at the College Chappel* (Dublin, 1712); *An Essay towards preventing the ruine of Great Britain* (1721); *De Motu* (London, 1721); *A Proposal for the better supplying of churches in our foreign plantations, and for converting the savage Americans to Christianity* (London, 1724); *The Theory of Vision Vindicated and Explained* (London, 1733); *The Analyst* (London, 1734); *A Defence of Freethinking in Mathematics* (Dublin, 1735); *A Discourse addressed to magistrates and men in authority. Occasioned by the enormous license, and irreligion of the times* (Dublin, 1738); Two Letters to Prior on tar-war, in Prior's *Authentic Narrative of the Success of Tar-water* (Dublin, 1746); *A Word to the Wise* (1749); *Maxims concerning Patriotism* (1750). In 1752 Berkeley published his *Miscellany* in which he included, among other items, his 'Verses ... on the prospect of planting Arts and Learning in America'. Among the works which were either left by him in manuscript or have been identified as being by him are: *The Philosophical Commentaries* (London: Nelson, 1944), or philosophical notebooks Berkeley kept *c.* 1707; 'Of Infinites' (1707); Journals of Travels in Italy, 1717-18; Letter to Peter Browne on Divine Analogy (London, 1733); *The Ladies Library* (*c.*1714), 3 vols.

BIOGRAPHY AND CRITICISM. T.E. Jessop, *A Bibliography of George Berkeley ... with Inventory of Berkeley's Manuscript Remains* by A.A. Luce (2nd end. The Hague: Martinus Nijhoff, 1973); Geoffrey Keynes, *A Bibliography of Berkeley* (Oxford: Clarendon Press, 1976). Among the numerous works on Berkeley's life and thought are: A.A. Luce, *The Life of George Berkeley* (London: Nelson, 1949); A.A. Luce, *Berkeley's Immaterialism* (London: Nelson, 1945); H.M. Bracken, *The Early Reception of Berkeley's Immaterialism 1710-1733* (The Hague: Martinus Nijhoff, revised ed. 1965); Ian Tipton, *The Philosophy of Immaterialism* (London, Methuen, 1974); C.M. Turbayne, *Myth or Metaphor* (New Haven: Yale University Press, 1962); George Pitcher, *Berkeley* (London: Routledge and Kegan Paul, 1977); J.M. Hone and M.M. Rossi, *Bishop Berkeley* (London: Faber and Faber, 1931), with an Introduction by W.B. Yeats; G.J. Warnock, *Berkeley* (London: Pelican Books, 1953); H. M. Bracken, *Berkeley* (London: Macmillan, 1974); D. Berman, 'Rational Theology and Emotive Mysteries in Berkeley's *Alciphron*', *Proceedings of the Royal Irish Academy* Vol. 81(1981), 219-29; D. Berman, 'The Jacobitism of Berkeley's *Passive Obedience*', *Journal of the History of Ideas* Vol. XLVII (1986), 309-19. The *Berkeley Newsletter* has been published annually since 1977.

Francis Hutcheson

LIFE. Born in County Down in 1694, Hutcheson was educated at Glasgow University, where he also taught philosophy. Most of his famous works were written during the 1720s, while he was teaching at a dissenting academy in Dublin. He was a protégé of Molesworth and the inspiring teacher of Adam Smith. He died in Ireland in 1746.

CHIEF WRITINGS. *An Inquiry into the Original of our Ideas of Beauty and Virtue* (London, 1725); *An Essay on the Nature and Conduct of the Passions and Affections* (London, 1728); essays in *A Collection of Letters and Essays on Several Subjects* (London, 1729), edited by J. Arbuckle; *Letters between ... Burnet and ... Hutcheson, concerning the Time Foundations of ... Moral Goodness* (London, 1735); *A System of Moral Philosophy* (Glasgow, 1755); *A Short Introduction to Moral Philosophy* (Dublin, 1787).

BIOGRAPHY AND CRITICISM. T.E. Jessop, *A Bibliography of Hume and of Scottish Philosophy from Francis Hutcheson to Lord Balfour* (London: A. Brown & Sons, 1938); W.R. Scott, *Francis Hutcheson: His Life, Teaching and Position in the History of Philosophy* (Cambridge: Cambridge University Press, 1900); T. Fowler, *Shaftesbury and Hutcheson* (London, 1882); H. Jensen, *Motivation and the Moral Sense in Hutcheson's Ethical Theory* (The Hague: Martinus Nijhoff, 1971); D. Berman, 'Francis Hutcheson on Berkeley and the Molyneux Problem', *Proceedings of the Royal Irish Academy* Vol. 74 (1974), 259-65; P. Kivy, *The Seventh Sense. A Study of Francis Hutcheson's Aesthetics and its Influence in Eighteenth-century Britain* (New York: B. Franklin, 1976).

Peter Browne

LIFE. Born in 1664 or 1665, Browne was educated at Trinity College, Dublin, where he became a fellow in 1692 and provost in 1699. He owed this early success largely to his 1697 *Letter* in answer to Toland and to the support of Archbishop Marsh, who encouraged him to write the *Letter*. Browne was appointed bishop of Cork in 1709, now with the support of Archbishop King (although Toland slyly boasted that he (Toland) had made Browne a bishop). Browne engaged in a theological controversy with Edward Synge (the elder) in 1715-16, with Berkeley in 1732-33, and even more bitterly with a number of opponents between 1713 and 1722 over the propriety of drinking in memory of the dead. He died in Cork in 1735.

CHIEF WRITINGS. *A Letter in Answer to a book entitled Christianity Not Mysterious* (Dublin, 1697); *Faith Distinguished from Opinion and Science; The Procedure, Extent and Limits of Human Understanding* (London, 1728); *Things Divine and Supernatural conceived by Analogy with things Natural and Human* (London, 1733).

BIOGRAPHY AND CRITICISM. A. R. Winnett, *Bishop Browne: Provost, Bishop and Metaphysician* (London: SPCK, 1974); John Yolton, *John Locke and the Way of Ideas* (Oxford: Clarendon Press, 1956); J.P.. Pittion, D. Berman, A.A. Luce, 'A New Letter by Berkeley to Browne on Divine Analogy', *Mind*, LXXVIII (1969), 375-92; D. Berman, 'Enlightenment and Counter-Enlightenment in Irish Philosophy', *Archiv für Geschichte der Philosophie*, 64 (1982), 148-65; D. Berman, 'Berkeley's Semantic Revolution: 19 November 1707-11 January 1708', *History of European Ideas*, 7 (1986), 603-07.

Philip Skelton

LIFE. Born in Derriaghy, Co. Antrim in 1707, Skelton was educated at Trinity College, Dublin. He was a clergyman and writer, mostly on religious and satirical subjects. He spent much of his life as rector of Templecarn, Pettigo, Co. Donegal, the parish that contains St Patrick's Purgatory, and wrote a *Description of Lough Derg* (1759). Skelton lived a live of remarkable saintliness and was renowned for his charity. He retired to Dublin in 1780 and died there in 1787.

CHIEF WRITINGS. *A Vindication of ... the Bishop of Winchester, against the malicious aspersions of those who uncharitably ascribe the book ... A Plain Account ... to his Lordship* (Dublin, 1736); *A letter to the author of the Divine Analogy and the Minute Philosopher* (1734); *Ophiomaches: or, Deism Revealed* (London, 1749); *The Censor Censured* (Dublin, 1750). Skelton's works have twice been edited, once in 1770 and again in 1824.

BIOGRAPHY AND CRITICISM: S. Burdy, *Memoirs of Rev. Philip Skelton* (London, 1792), also prefixed to the 1824 edition of Skelton's *Works*. D. Berman, 'The Culmination and Causation of Irish Philosophy', *Archiv für Geschichte der Philosophie*, 64 (1982), 257-79.

Robert Clayton

LIFE. Born in Dublin in 1695, Clayton was educated at Westminster School in London and Trinity College, Dublin, where he became a fellow in 1714. Appointed to the bishopric of Killala in 1730, Clayton was transferred in 1735 to the see of Cork and Ross, and from there in 1745 to the lucrative bishopric of Clogher. He was a fellow of the Royal Society and of the Society of Antiquaries. In the 1720s he was closely associated with George Berkeley's Bermuda scheme; and when in 1733 Berkeley became bishop of Cloyne, it was Clayton who introduced him in the Irish House of Lords. However, Berkeley strongly disapproved of *An Essay on Spirit* (1750), in which Clayton first presents his heterodox views on the Trinity. This outspokenness led eventually to his near prosecution for heresy; this precipitated his death, which was caused by a nervous illness, in February 1758 in Dublin.

CHIEF WRITINGS. *An Essay on Spirit* (Dublin, 1750); *A Defence of An Essay on Spirit* (London, 1752); *A Vindication of the Histories of the Old and New Testament* (Dublin, 1752, 1754, 1757); *Some Thoughts on Self-Love, Innate Ideas, Free Will, occasioned by reading Mr. Hume's works* (London, 1753).

BIOGRAPHY AND CRITICISM. M. Halpin, *A Bibliography of Robert Clayton* (M. Phil. thesis, Trinity College, Dublin, 1985); A. Kippis's article on Clayton in the *Biographia Britannica* (London, 1784), 2nd ed. vol. 3, pp. 620-28; *Bishop Clayton on the Nicene and Athanasian Creeds, Republished with a Memoir* (Dublin, 1876) (the Trinity College Dublin copy contains manuscript additions and biography by W. Reeves); D. Berman, 'Berkeley, Clayton, and *An Essay on Spirit*', *Journal of the History of Ideas* Vol. XXXII (1971), pp. 367-78; A.R. Winnett, 'An Irish Heretic Bishop: Robert Clayton of Clogher' in *Studies in Church History*, Vol. 9 (1972), 311-21.

Edmund Burke

For biography and bibliography, see p. 853.

SEAMUS DEANE, *Editor*

Edmund Burke

(1729-97)

Edmund Burke was the most remarkable political philosopher of eighteenth-century Ireland. Although his reputation has been subjected to many assaults, then and since, it remains secure because of his unsurpassed articulation, in the last seven years of his life, of a conservative, counter-revolutionary philosophy. In attacking the French Revolution, Burke left himself open to the accusation that he was betraying those principles that had been the ground of his support for the American Revolution, for the cause of the Irish catholics, of the Indian princes against Warren Hastings and the East India Company, and of the Polish and Corsican rebellions. The inconsistency is not as glaring as it seems to be. The late expression of his thought in philosophical terms can best be understood in the light of his earlier, more pragmatic writings. For Burke, the French Revolution was an event for which scarcely any analogy or parallel existed in modern or ancient history; even the Reformation had been less cataclysmic. It was his resolve to identify and attack the new combination of forces that had entered European political life in 1789-90 before they gained ground and exercised their powerful missionary appeal. This resolve gave his *Reflections on the Revolution in France* its passionate, crusading tone. Even though he was far too much taken by the idea that the Revolution was the direct result of a deliberately fomented conspiracy, he was right in seeing it as an unprecedented event. On that basis, his hostility to it can be seen to be in accord with his earlier political views.

His writings on Ireland are in line with the general contour of his career. From the *Tracts on the Popery Laws* (written in 1763) to the second letter to Sir Hercules Langrishe (1795), Burke consistently defended the Irish catholic cause and pleaded for the admission of catholics to citizenship and to the benefits of the English Revolution settlement of 1688. For him, the moral obligation to yield these rights to the catholics was matched by the political wisdom of doing so. It was both right and useful that it should be done. After 1789, it became right and necessary; otherwise Ireland, in its profound disaffection, would be open to the revolutionary infection, and a residually Jacobite country would be transformed into a revolutionary Jacobin territory.

Although an Irish protestant, Burke was uncharacteristic of his class and faith in having important family ties with catholics. His mother and wife were catholic and it is not surprising, therefore, that he should be more than usually alert to the grievances of the great majority of his countrymen. Further, his natural sympathy and respect for the catholic faith was stimulated in the 1790s by the spectacle of the emigrant French clergy, many of whom received hospitality at his Beaconsfield home, and by the recognition that the catholic church was a formidable obstacle to the Revolution on the continent. He increasingly came to stress the common cause of all the Christian churches against this so-called 'atheistical' conspiracy. Burke was, then, less inclined than others to see the protestant/catholic distinction as politically defensible or wise. It prohibited the benign influence of the English Revolution in Ireland and promoted the malign ends of the French Revolution's missionary appeal.

However, Burke ultimately found it impossible to persuade his English or his Irish protestant audience and correspondents that substantial concessions to the catholics would have to be made if the English political system in Ireland was to be successfully maintained. Despite the gradual relaxation of the Penal Code and the new generosity of spirit that was prevalent in 1782 after a measure of legislative independence had been won, the exclusion and disaffection of the catholics remained as severe as they had ever been. Burke believed that this sense of unmerited exclusion was the less bearable because the ruling group in Ireland was not an aristocracy, but merely an ascendancy whose claim to supremacy was entirely based on its religious persuasion. A 'natural' aristocracy, as in England, could have the affection and respect of those who occupied a lowly position in the political structure. But the 'plebeian aristocracy' of Ireland was an anomaly. Its exercise of power and privilege, sternly and oppressively pursued, aroused only resentment and loathing. As a result, the political system in Ireland lacked the crucial element that, in Burke's view, made for endurance. It lacked the affection of the people who lived within it. In addition, the traditions, beliefs and cultural habits of the catholics were scorned or violated. The society in which traditional habits were so reduced or denied was ripe for doctrinaire revolution, since the revolutionaries too, although on different grounds, wished to amputate the present from the past and dispense with all those ties and loyalties that were characteristic of the old European system.

Thus Burke's pleas on behalf of the Irish catholics were a local application of his defence of the integrity of traditional society. It is more surprising to find that his ultimate response to the protestant ascendancy attitude was contrastingly severe. By 1795, he had come to see the ascendancy as a faction within the country, governing it against the interest of the many and for the interest of the few. This was for him the very definition of modern Jacobinism. It hardly needs saying that he did not believe that the protestant ascendancy had the same opinions as the Parisian radicals. What Burke did observe was a formal property which they had in common and which they shared with other factional groups against whom he had fought — the king's friends, the clique of men who, in his view, had subverted parliamentary authority in the 1770s, and the East Indian Company, which had been used by Warren Hastings as an instrument of annexation, aggrandizement and violence in India. Where the mass of the people was disaffected through exclusion and injustice, the principles of English liberty were denied and an opportunity was offered for the new French principles.

Just as he wanted Jacobinism exterminated (and he urged England to declare war on France for that purpose), Burke wished for the abolition of the protestant junta in Ireland and urged England to move in that direction too. Ironically, his advice was taken, but under very different conditions, by William Pitt the Younger when he pushed through the Act of Union in the aftermath of the 1798 rebellion, thus bringing to an ignoble end the first phase of Anglo-Ireland's political history. Burke was dubious about the advantages of a Union, but we may suppose that at least he would have welcomed its abolition of the Dublin junta. However, the interval between the Catholic Relief Act of 1793 and catholic emancipation in 1829, each of which had been granted only when it could not be refused, demonstrated the desolate weight of prejudice against which Burke had fought in his campaign for justice to the Irish catholics and in his appeal to the practical wisdom of bestowing upon them the benefits of British citizenship. It should be added, however, that his hostility to the repeal of the Test Acts against dissenters was not wholly inconsistent with his support for the catholics. The dissenters were clearly identified as among the most vocal and enthusiastic supporters of the French Revolution. To alter the constitution in the midst of revolution was, Burke believed, foolish in itself and doubly so to alter it in favour of those who supported the modern doctrines of the rights of man, equality, and all the rest of the resonant slogans by which the Revolution advertised itself throughout the world. But to alter it in favour of the catholics was to take a preservative measure, to bring a numerous and strategic population within the traditional fold.

Burke was so unlike the other 'patriot' writers of eighteenth-century Ireland that it seems rather odd to associate him with them in some version of a protestant Anglo-Irish tradition of the kind that Yeats was to invent in the 1920s. It may be that his defence of the old monarchical system in Europe was the last brilliant flare of the Irish Jacobite dream of a restored monarchy, in which catholic Ireland would play its full part and regain its lost privileges. Yet this Jacobite strain in Burke coexists with an unstinted, perhaps extravagant, admiration for the British constitution as established in 1688 — the Revolution that Burke was able to interpret as an evolution, in which Magna Carta and the accumulations of jurisprudential wisdom, embodied in the writings of Coke, Bracton and others, had been decisive early stages. This peculiarly British history was never separate, in Burke's mind, from continental developments. Montesquieu's description of the British Constitution in *L'Esprit des Lois* (1748) seemed to him a characteristic contribution to the cause of European civilization that had the great international lawyers like Grotius and Pufendorf among its outstanding names. In other words, he saw society as a system of laws that gave form to and was protected by political systems. The danger represented by French writers like Rousseau or revolutionaries like the Abbé Sieyès was that their political systems were predicated on abstract theories about rights and were ignorant of the actual experience of the human race in its providentially guided journey towards freedom. Ireland was a tragic example of a country that had had an opportunity to avail of the laws and of the political system that were the most perfectly congruent with each other and that were the almost miraculous result of an infinitely complex historical process, yet which had failed to do so. Burke realized that the claim of the British constitution to excellence and the admiration of others was questioned by its failure to transfer its much-vaunted benefits across St George's channel. The reason for that failure lay with the governing group in Ireland, not in the sacred constitution itself. That failure was a signal one, for it threatened the comity of old Europe by providing conditions for the dread emergence of the new Europe. No other Irish writer had such frequent recourse to a continental ideal in trying to envisage a solution to the Irish political impasse.

In 1881, Matthew Arnold published a selection of Burke's writings entitled *Edmund Burke on Irish Affairs*. This was meant to bring to the notice of the English government the wisdom that Arnold deemed to have been hidden from view since the end of the previous century. The volume did in fact launch Burke's posthumous career on its liberal phase, just as, in the 1950s, he would play his role in providing the conservative American intelligentsia with its fundamental principles in the Cold War with the Soviet Union. Yet Arnold was mistaken in at least one respect. Burke had remained a powerful influence in Irish political thinking throughout the nineteenth century; John Wilson Croker, Samuel Ferguson, Isaac Butt and others reveal this plainly. Predictably, his counter-revolutionary stance was popular among those who feared Irish republicanism or even Irish nationalism. His attacks on the protestant ascendancy were largely forgotten and his crusade against doctrinaire revolution remembered. But his influence was more diverse than this. His recognition of the power of the press and of the urban intelligentsia was noted. Many of those who felt his influence most keenly turned to periodical literature and the intellectual circle as agencies for the propagation of those traditional values that Burke had dwelt upon so lavishly. In Ireland, this meant the recovery of traditions of a cultural kind that were held in common by all sects. In fact, Burke's traditionalism, his emphasis upon familial, local and regional affections and loyalties gave a strong impulse to romantic nationalism and, most especially, promoted the aspirations of those protestant writers who wished to find in culture that bond with their fellow-countrymen which was still not achievable within the political system. More than his 'patriot' contemporaries, most of whom were men of the Enlightenment, Burke became the father of Irish national sentiment. He was the only Irish writer to envisage a place for that sentiment within a wider political philosophy, which was both European in its range and protean in its applicability to various situations. His writings on Irish affairs are a part of that broadly based political stance. They are in accord with his better-known writings on France and America. Ireland was one of the crusades that dominated Burke's passionate career. In these public and private letters and pamphlets he treats the problems of his native land both in their specific detail and in their application to larger issues. This is one of the reasons for their importance in the history of Irish writing.

from: TRACTS RELATIVE TO THE LAWS AGAINST POPERY IN IRELAND (*c.*1763)

[Burke's unfinished treatise on the Penal Laws was not published in his lifetime. It would have been damaging to his political career, launched under the patronage of the Earl of Rockingham in 1765, to have been associated with such a pro-catholic treatise. In fact, throughout his career, Burke had to defend himself against accusations that he was a secret catholic. Yet this early work is of a piece with his later writings on Ireland. Burke believed that better treatment of the Irish catholics would help to stabilize Ireland's position within the Empire.

The *Tracts* probably were written between 1759 and 1765.]

CHAPTER III

PART I

The system which we have just reviewed, and the manner in which religious influence on the public is made to operate upon the laws concerning property in Ireland, is in its nature very singular, and differs, I apprehend, essentially, and perhaps to its disadvantage, from any scheme of religious persecution now existing in any other country in Europe, or which has prevailed in any time, or nation, with which history has made us acquainted. I believe it will not be difficult to show that it is unjust, impolitic, and inefficacious; that it has the most unhappy influence on the prosperity, the morals, and the safety of that country; that this influence is not accidental, but has flowed as the necessary and direct consequence of the laws themselves, first on account of the object which they effect, and next by the quality of the greatest part of the instruments they employ. Upon all these points, first upon the general, and then on the particular, this question will be considered with as much order as can be followed in a matter of itself as involved and intricate as it is important.

The first and most capital consideration with regard to this, as to every object, is the extent of it; and here it is necessary to premise, this system of penalty and incapacity has for its object no small sect, or obscure party, but a very numerous body of men — a body which comprehends at least two-thirds of that whole nation; it amounts to 2,800,000 souls, a number sufficient for the materials constituent of a great people. Now it is well worthy of a serious and dispassionate examination, whether such a system, respecting such an object, be in reality agreeable to any sound principles of legislation, or any authorized definition of law; for if our reasons or practices differ from the general informed sense of mankind, it is very moderate to say that they are at least suspicious....

A law against the majority of the people is in substance a law against the people itself; its extent determines its invalidity; it even changes its character as it enlarges its operation: it is not particular injustice, but general oppression; and can no longer be considered as a private hardship, which might be borne, but spreads and grows up into the unfortunate importance of a national calamity....

In reality there are two, and only two, foundations of law; and they are both of them conditions without which nothing can give it any force; I mean equity and utility. With respect to the former, it grows out of the great rule of equality, which is grounded upon our common nature, and which Philo, with propriety and beauty, calls the Mother of Justice.[1] All human laws are, properly speaking, only declaratory; they may alter the mode and application, but have no power over the substance of original justice. The other foundation of law, which is utility, must be understood, not of partial or limited, but of general and public, utility, connected in the same manner with, and derived directly from, our rational nature; for any other utility may be the utility of a robber, but cannot be that of a citizen; the interest of the domestic enemy, and not that of a member of the commonwealth. This present equality can never be the foundation of statutes, which create an artificial difference between men, as the laws before us do, in order to induce a consequential inequality in the distribution of justice. Law is a mode of human action respecting society, and must be governed by the same rules of equity which govern every private action; and so Tully considers it, in his Offices, as the only utility agreeable to that nature; *unum debet esse omnibus propositum, ut eadem sit utilitas uniuscujusque et universorum; quam si ad se quisque rapiat, dissolvetur omnis humana consortio.*[2]

If any proposition can be clear in itself, it is this; that a law, which shuts out from all secure and valuable property the bulk of the people, cannot be made for the utility of the party so excluded. This, therefore, is not the utility which Tully mentions. But if it were true (as it is not) that the real interest

1. Philo, or Philo Judaeus (*c.* 20 B.C.-*c.* 50 A.D.), an Alexandrian Jewish philosopher.
2. Cicero, *De Officiis*, III, 26: 'This ought to be the chief end of all men, to make the interest of each individual and of the whole body politic identical. For, if the individual appropriates to selfish ends what should be devoted to the common good, all human fellowship will be destroyed.'

of any part of the community could be separated from the happiness of the rest, still it would afford no just foundation for a statute providing exclusively for that interest at the expense of the other; because it would be repugnant to the essence of law, which requires that it be made as much as possible for the benefit of the whole. If this principle be denied or evaded, what ground have we left to reason on? We must at once make a total change in all our ideas, and look for a new definition of law. Where to find it I confess myself at a loss....

But I flatter myself that not a few will be found who do not think that the names of Protestant and Papist can make any change in the nature of essential justice. Such men will not allow that to be proper treatment to the one of these denominations which would be cruelty to the other; and which converts its very crime into the instrument of its defence: they will hardly persuade themselves that what was bad policy in France can be good in Ireland;[3] or that what was intolerable injustice in an arbitrary monarch becomes, only by being more extended and more violent, an equitable procedure in a country professing to be governed by law. It is however impossible not to observe with some concern that there are many also of a different disposition; a number of persons whose minds are so formed, that they find the communion of religion to be a close and an endearing tie, and their country to be no bond at all; to whom common altars are a better relation than common habitations and a common civil interest; whose hearts are touched with the distresses of foreigners, and are abundantly awake to all the tenderness of human feeling on such an occasion, even at the moment that they are inflicting the very same distresses, or worse, on their fellow-citizens, without the least sting of compassion or remorse. To commiserate the distresses of all men suffering innocently, perhaps meritoriously, is generous, and very agreeable to the better part of our nature — a disposition that ought by all means to be cherished. But to transfer humanity from its natural basis, our legitimate and homebred connexions; to lose all feeling for those who have grown up by our sides, in our eyes, of the benefit of whose cares and labours we have partaken from our birth, and meretriciously to hunt abroad after foreign affections, is such a disarrangement of the whole system of our duties, that I do not know whether benevolence so displaced is not almost the same thing as destroyed, or what effect bigotry could have produced that is more fatal to society. This no one could help observing, who has seen our doors kindly and bountifully thrown open to foreign sufferers for conscience, whilst through the same ports were issuing fugitives of our own, driven from their country for a cause which to an indifferent person would seem to be exactly similar, whilst we stood by, without any sense of the impropriety of this extraordinary scene, accusing, and practising injustice. For my part, there is no circumstance, in all the contradictions of our most mysterious nature, that appears to be more humiliating than the use we are disposed to make of those sad examples which seem purposely marked for our correction and improvement. Every instance of fury and bigotry in other men, one should think, would naturally fill us with a horror of that disposition. The effect, however, is directly contrary. We are inspired, it is true, with a very sufficient hatred for the party, but with no detestation at all of the proceeding. Nay, we are apt to urge our dislike of such measures as a reason for imitating them; and, by an almost incredible absurdity, because some powers have destroyed their country by their persecuting spirit, to argue, that we ought to retaliate on them by destroying our own. Such are the effects, and such I fear has been the intention, of those numberless books which are daily printed and industriously spread, of the persecutions in other countries and other religious persuasions. These observations, which are a digression, but hardly, I think, can be considered as a departure from the subject, have detained us some time; we will now come more directly to our purpose.

It has been shown, I hope with sufficient evidence, that a constitution against the interests of the many is rather of the nature of a grievance than of a law; that of all grievances it is the most weighty and important; that it is made without due authority, against all the acknowledged principles of jurisprudence, against the opinions of all the great lights in that science; and that such is the tacit sense even of those who act in the most contrary manner. These points are indeed so evident, that I apprehend the abettors of the penal system will ground their defence on an admission, and not on a

3. A reference to Louis XIV's revocation of the Edict of Nantes (1685) and the subsequent persecution of protestants in France, many of whom emigrated to England and Ireland.

denial, of them. They will lay it down as a principle, that the Protestant religion is a thing beneficial for the whole community, as well in its civil interests as in those of a superior order. From thence they will argue, that, the end being essentially beneficial, the means becomes instrumentally so; that these penalties and incapacities are not final causes of the law, but only a discipline to bring over a deluded people to their real interest; and therefore, though they may be harsh in their operation, they will be pleasant in their effects; and, be they what they will, they cannot be considered as a very extraordinary hardship, as it is in the power of the sufferer to free himself when he pleases; and that only by converting to a better religion, which it is his duty to embrace, even though it were attended with all those penalties from whence in reality it delivers him: if he suffers, it is his own fault; *volenti non fit injuria.*[4]

I shall be very short, without being, I think, the less satisfactory, in my answer to these topics, because they never can be urged from a conviction of their validity; and are, indeed, only the usual and impotent struggles of those who are unwilling to abandon a practice which they are unable to defend. First then I observe, that if the principle of their final and beneficial intention be admitted as a just ground for such proceedings, there never was, in the blamable sense of the word, nor ever can be, such a thing as a religious persecution in the world. Such an intention is pretended by all men, who all not only insist that their religion has the sanction of Heaven, but is likewise, and for that reason, the best and most convenient to human society. All religious persecution, Mr. Bayle well observes, is grounded upon a miserable *petitio principii.*[5] You are wrong, I am right; you must come over to me, or you must suffer. Let me add, that the great inlet by which a colour for oppression has entered into the world, is by one man's pretending to determine concerning the happiness of another, and by claiming a right to use what means he thinks proper in order to bring him to a sense of it. It is the ordinary and trite sophism of oppression. But there is not yet such a convenient ductility in the human understanding, as to make us capable of being persuaded, that men can possibly mean the ultimate good of the whole society by rendering miserable for a century together the greater part of it; or that any one has such a reversionary benevolence as seriously to intend the remote good of a late posterity, who can give up the present enjoyment which every honest man must have in the happiness of his contemporaries. Everybody is satisfied, that a conservation and secure enjoyment of our natural rights is the great and ultimate purpose of civil society; and that therefore all forms whatsoever of government are only good as they are subservient to that purpose to which they are entirely subordinate. Now, to aim at the establishment of any form of government by sacrificing what is the substance of it; to take away, or at least to suspend, the rights of nature, in order to [alter] an approved system for the protection of them; and, for the sake of that about which men must dispute for ever, to postpone those things about which they have no controversy at all, and this not in minute and subordinate, but large and principal, objects, is a procedure as preposterous and absurd in argument as it is oppressive and cruel in its effect. For the Protestant religion, nor (I speak it with reverence, I am sure,) the truth of our common Christianity, is not so clear as this proposition; that all men, at least the majority of men in the society, ought to enjoy the common advantages of it. You fall, therefore, into a double error; first, you incur a certain mischief for an advantage which is comparatively problematical, even though you were sure of obtaining it; secondly, whatever the proposed advantage may be, were it of a certain nature, the attainment of it is by no means certain; and such deep gaming for stakes so valuable ought not to be admitted: the risk is of too much consequence to society. If no other country furnished examples of this risk, yet our laws and our country are enough fully to demonstrate the fact; Ireland, after almost a century of persecution, is at this hour full of penalties and full of Papists. This is a point which would lead us a great way; but it is only just touched here, having much to say upon it in its proper place. So that you have incurred a certain and an immediate inconvenience for a remote and for a doubly uncertain benefit. Thus far as to the argument which would sanctify the injustice of these laws by the benefits which are proposed to arise from them, and as to that liberty which by a new political chemistry was to be extracted out of a system of oppression.

4. To a person who consents, no injustice is done.
5. Pierre Bayle (1647-1706), author of the *Dictionnaire historique et critique* (1695), one of the seminal works of the European Enlightenment. *Petitio principii* is the fallacy of taking for granted a premiss that is either equivalent to, or itself depends upon, the conclusion.

Now as to the other point, that the objects of these laws suffer voluntarily: this seems to me to be an insult rather than an argument. For, besides that it totally annihilates every characteristic, and therefore every faulty, idea of persecution, just as the former does; it supposes, what is false in fact, that it is in a man's moral power to change his religion whenever his convenience requires it. If he be beforehand satisfied that your opinion is better than his, he will voluntarily come over to you, and without compulsion; and then your law would be unnecessary; but if he is not so convinced, he must know that it is his duty in this point to sacrifice his interest here to his opinion of his eternal happiness, else he could have in reality no religion at all. In the former case, therefore, as your law would be unnecessary; in the latter, it would be persecuting; that is, it would put your penalty and his ideas of duty in the opposite scales; which is, or I know not what is, the precise idea of persecution. If then you require a renunciation of his conscience, as a preliminary to his admission to the rights of society, you annex, morally speaking, an impossible condition to it. In this case, in the language of reason and jurisprudence, the condition would be void, and the gift absolute; as the practice runs, it is to establish the condition, and to withhold the benefit. The suffering is, then, not voluntary. And I never heard any other argument, drawn from the nature of laws and the good of human society, urged in favour of those prospective statutes, except those which have just been mentioned.

from: CHAPTER IV

The great prop of this whole system is not pretended to be its justice or its utility, but the supposed danger to the state which gave rise to it originally, and which, they apprehend, would return if this system were overturned. Whilst, say they, the Papists of this kingdom were possessed of landed property, and of the influence consequent to such property, their allegiance to the Crown of Great Britain was ever insecure; the public peace was ever liable to be broken; and Protestants never could be a moment secure either of their properties or of their lives. Indulgence only made them arrogant, and power daring; confidence only excited and enabled them to exert their inherent treachery; and the times which they generally selected for their most wicked and desperate rebellions were those in which they enjoyed the greatest ease and the most perfect tranquillity.

Such are the arguments that are used both publicly and privately in every discussion upon this point. They are generally full of passion and of error, and built upon facts which in themselves are most false. It cannot, I confess, be denied, that those miserable performances which go about under the names of Histories of Ireland, do indeed represent those events after this manner; and they would persuade us, contrary to the known order of nature, that indulgence and moderation in governors is the natural incitement in subjects to rebel. But there is an interior History of Ireland, the genuine voice of its records and monuments, which speaks a very different language from these histories, from Temple and from Clarendon;[1] these restore nature to its just rights, and policy to its proper order. For they even now show to those who have been at the pains to examine them, and they may show one day to all the world, that these rebellions were not produced by toleration, but by persecution; that they arose not from just and mild government, but from the most unparalleled oppression. These records will be far from giving the least countenance to a doctrine so repugnant to humanity and good sense, as that the security of any establishment, civil or religious, can ever depend upon the misery of those who live under it, or that its danger can arise from their quiet and prosperity. God forbid, that the history of this or any country should give such encouragement to the folly or vices of those who govern. If it can be shown that the great rebellions of Ireland have arisen from attempts to reduce the natives to the state to which they are now reduced, it will show that an attempt to continue them in that state will rather be disadvantageous to the public peace than any kind of security to it. These things have, in some measure, begun to appear already; and, as far as regards the argument drawn from former rebellions, it will fall

1. Sir John Temple (1600-77), author of the highly prejudiced histories, *The Irish Rebellion* (1646) and *Ormond's Curtain Drawn* (attributed). The Irish parliament of 1689 ordered *The Irish Rebellion* to be burned by the common hangman because it had so enflamed popular prejudice against the Irish in England. Edward Hyde (1609-74), earl of Clarendon, wrote *The True Historical Narrative of the Rebellion and Civil Wars in England* (1702-04), generally known as *The History of the Rebellion*. He also wrote a *History of the Irish Rebellion* (1721).

readily to the ground. But, for my part, I think the real danger of every state is, to render its subjects justly discontented; nor is there in politics or science any more effectual secret for their security, than to establish in their people a firm opinion, that no change can be for their advantage. It is true that bigotry and fanaticism may, for a time, draw great multitudes of people from a knowledge of their true and substantial interest. But upon this I have to remark three things; first, that such a temper can never become universal, or last for a long time. The principle of religion is seldom lasting; the majority of men are in no persuasion bigots; they are not willing to sacrifice, on every vain imagination that superstition or enthusiasm holds forth, or that even zeal and piety recommend, the certain possession of their temporal happiness. And if such a spirit has been at any time roused in a society, after it has had its paroxysm it commonly subsides and is quiet, and is even the weaker for the violence of its first exertion; security and ease are its mortal enemies. But, secondly, if anything can tend to revive and keep it up, it is to keep alive the passions of men by ill usage. This is enough to irritate even those who have not a spark of bigotry in their constitution to the most deperate enterprises; it certainly will inflame, darken, and render more dangerous the spirit of bigotry in those who are possessed by it. Lastly, by rooting out any sect, you are never secure against the effects of fanaticism; it may arise on the side of the most favoured opinions; and many are the instances wherein the established religion of a state has grown ferocious, and turned upon its keeper, and has often torn to pieces the civil establishment that had cherished it, and which it was designed to support; France–England–Holland.

from:
SPEECH IN SUPPORT OF RESOLUTIONS FOR CONCILIATION WITH THE AMERICAN COLONIES (22 March 1775)

[The First Continental Congress of 1774 had its offer of conciliation rebuffed by the king and parliament. In 1775, the British parliament debated motions designed to prohibit trade between the American colonies and other parts of the Empire. In this speech, Burke offered instead his own scheme of conciliation.

Most of his arguments are based on utilitarian grounds. He had no doubt that the parliament in London had the right to tax the colonies, but he did not think it prudent that this right should be insisted upon when the risks of damage to the Empire at large were so great. Moreover, he feared the increase in the arbitrary power of the crown that might be a consequence of the defeat of the colonists; he feared French or Spanish intervention; above all, he feared that the imperial system would be seen to be incompatible with the principles of the Revolution of 1688. At all times, Burke understood the American situation from the point of view of a Whig. He seems never to have appreciated that the American Revolution was based on abstract principles of universal rights, which were radically at odds with his conception of colonial privileges and British rights.

Nevertheless, practical issues — the distances involved, the effects on the British soldiers who would come home after the revolution was over, the character of the Americans, the conditions that fostered the spirit of liberty in the colonies — did not wholly engross his thinking. Throughout the American war, Burke was developing a vision of the imperial system that would combine central control, admitted as of right, with delegation of power to the local government, conceded as a prudent recognition of the great diversity of circumstances obtaining throughout the various territories. It should be said that Burke did not at this stage apply to Ireland the principles that he applied to America. But within a year of the French Revolution, which he did recognize as ideologically distinct from anything in the British tradition as he understood it, his attitude changed. The necessity of conceding to the American colonists in 1775, and to the Irish catholics in 1795, was borne in upon him by circumstances. In each case, the consequences of not doing so would be, as he guessed, serious indeed for the Empire and for the Whig idea of liberty. Yet, with that, he constantly indicates that political necessities of this kind are enforced when there is something morally unjust in the situation that preceded the crisis.]

In this character of the Americans, a love of freedom is the predominating feature which marks and distinguishes the whole: and as an ardent is always a jealous affection, your colonies become suspicious, restive, and untractable, whenever they see the least attempt to wrest from them by force, or shuffle from them by chicane, what they think the only advantage worth living for. This fierce spirit of liberty is stronger in the English colonies probably than in any other people of the earth; and this from a great variety of powerful causes; which, to understand the true temper of their minds, and the direction which this spirit takes, it will not be amiss to lay open somewhat more largely.

First, the people of the colonies are descendants of Englishmen. England, Sir, is a nation, which still I hope respects, and formerly adored, her freedom. The colonists emigrated from you when this part of your character was most predominant; and they took this bias and direction the moment they parted from your hands. They are therefore not only devoted to liberty, but to liberty according to English ideas, and on English principles. Abstract liberty, like other mere abstractions, is not to be found. Liberty inheres in some sensible object; and every nation has formed to itself some favourite point, which by way of eminence becomes the criterion of their happiness. It happened, you know, Sir, that the great contests for freedom in this country were from the earliest times chiefly upon the question of taxing. Most of the contests in the ancient commonwealths turned primarily on the right of election of magistrates; or on the balance among the several orders of the state. The question of money was not with them so immediate. But in England it was otherwise. On this point of taxes the ablest pens, and most eloquent tongues, have been exercised; the greatest spirits have acted and suffered. In order to give the fullest satisfaction concerning the importance of this point, it was not only necessary for those who in argument defended the excellence of the English constitution, to insist on this privilege of granting money as a dry point of fact, and to prove, that the right had been acknowledged in ancient parchments, and blind usages, to reside in a certain body called a House of Commons. They went much farther; they attempted to prove, and they succeeded, that in theory it ought to be so, from the particular nature of a House of Commons, as an immediate representative of the people; whether the old records had delivered this oracle or not. They took infinite pains to inculcate, as a fundamental principle, that in all monarchies the people must in effect themselves, mediately or immediately, possess the power of granting their own money, or no shadow of liberty could subsist. The colonies draw from you, as with their life-blood, these ideas and principles. Their love of liberty, as with you, fixed and attached on this specific point of taxing. Liberty might be safe, or might be endangered, in twenty other particulars, without their being much pleased or alarmed. Here they felt its pulse; and as they found that beat, they thought themselves sick or sound. I do not say whether they were right or wrong in applying your general arguments to their own case. It is not easy indeed to make a monopoly of theorems and corollaries. The fact is, that they did thus apply those general arguments; and your mode of governing them, whether through lenity or indolence, through wisdom or mistake, confirmed them in the imagination, that they, as well as you, had an interest in these common principles....

Religion, always a principle of energy, in this new people is no way worn out or impaired; and their mode of professing it is also one main cause of this free spirit. The people are Protestants; and of that kind which is the most adverse to all implicit submission of mind and opinion. This is a persuasion not only favourable to liberty, but built upon it. I do not think, Sir, that the reason of this averseness in the dissenting churches, from all that looks like absolute government, is so much to be sought in their religious tenets, as in their history. Every one knows that the Roman Catholic religion is at least coeval with most of the governments where it prevails; that it has generally gone hand in hand with them, and received great favour and every kind of support from authority. The Church of England too was formed from her cradle under the nursing care of regular government. But the dissenting interests have sprung up in direct opposition to all the ordinary powers of the world; and could justify that opposition only on a strong claim to natural liberty. Their very existence depended on the powerful and unremitted assertion of that claim. All Protestantism, even the most cold and passive, is a sort of dissent. But the religion most prevalent in our northern colonies is a refinement on the principle of resistance; it is the dissidence of dissent, and the Protestantism of the Protestant religion. This religion, under a variety of denominations agreeing in nothing but in the communion of the spirit of liberty, is predominant in most of the northern provinces; where the Church of England, notwithstanding its legal rights, is in reality no more than a sort of private sect, not composing most probably the tenth of the people. The colonists left England when this spirit was high, and in the emigrants was the highest of all; and even that stream of foreigners, which has been constantly flowing into these colonies, has, for the greatest part, been composed of dissenters from the establishments of their several countries, and have brought with them a temper and character far from alien to that of the people with whom they mixed....

Perhaps, Sir, I am mistaken in my idea of an empire, as distinguished from a single state or kingdom. But my idea of it is this; that an empire is the aggregate of many states under one common head; whether this head be a monarch, or a presiding republic. It does, in such constitutions, frequently happen (and nothing but the dismal, cold, dead uniformity of servitude can prevent its happening) that the subordinate parts have many local privileges and immunities. Between these privileges and the supreme common authority the line may be extremely nice. Of course disputes, often, too, very bitter disputes, and much ill blood, will arise. But though every privilege is an exemption (in the case) from the ordinary exercise of the supreme authority, it is no denial of it. The claim of a privilege seems rather, *ex vi termini*,[1] to imply a superior power. For to talk of the privileges of a state, or of a person, who has no superior, is hardly any better than speaking nonsense. Now, in such unfortunate quarrels among the component parts of a great political union of communities, I can scarcely conceive anything more completely imprudent, than for the head of the empire to insist, that, if any privilege is pleaded against his will, or his acts, his whole authority is denied; instantly to proclaim rebellion, to beat to arms, and to put the offending provinces under the ban. Will not this, Sir, very soon teach the provinces to make no distinctions on their part? Will it not teach them that the government, against which a claim of liberty is tantamount to high treason, is a government to which submission is equivalent to slavery? It may not always be quite convenient to impress dependent communities with such an idea....

Such is stedfastly my opinion of the absolute necessity of keeping up the concord of this empire by a unity of spirit, though in a diversity of operations, that, if I were sure the colonists had, at their leaving this country, sealed a regular compact of servitude; that they had solemnly abjured all the rights of citizens; that they had made a vow to renounce all ideas of liberty for them and their posterity to all generations; yet I should hold myself obliged to conform to the temper I found universally prevalent in my own day, and to govern two millions of men, impatient of servitude, on the principles of freedom. I am not determining a point of law; I am restoring tranquillity; and the general character and situation of a people must determine what sort of government is fitted for them. That point nothing else can or ought to determine.

My idea, therefore, without considering whether we yield as matter of right, or grant as matter of favour, is *to admit the people of our colonies into an interest in the constitution*; and, by recording that admission in the journals of parliament, to give them as strong an assurance as the nature of the thing will admit, that we mean for ever to adhere to that solemn declaration of systematic indulgence.

1. from the force of the term.

from:
LETTER TO A PEER OF IRELAND (1782)

[Most of this letter, written to Viscount Kenmare on 21 February 1782, was published in 1783 under the title *A Letter from a Distinguished English Commoner to a Peer in Ireland* and has been printed in Burke's *Works* under the title *Letter to a Peer of Ireland.* Thomas Browne (1726-95), 4th viscount Kenmare, was to become the rather timid and ineffective leader of the Catholic Committee in 1783, but his lethargic behaviour in that position was to lead to his replacement in 1790 by the much more energetic John Keogh. Burke is here writing about a timid measure of relief contained in a new bill brought forward by an Irish MP, Luke Gardiner. Burke wanted to concentrate on the extension of the franchise to catholics, rather than to further measures of religious toleration. Gardiner's bill made no provision for the franchise, but Burke did succeed in having the educational clauses removed. Yet all this was merely a prelude to the constitutional crisis of 1782, in which the relationship between England and Ireland was reshaped by the granting of constitutional independence. Burke played no part in the government's handling of this affair. He did not like the threatened use of force represented by the Irish Volunteers; he disliked the parallel between Ireland and America; he foresaw many difficulties in the new system and believed that it had breached the integrity of the Empire and had left the Irish catholics at the mercy of an ascendancy faction.]

. . . . To look at the Bill in the abstract, it is neither more nor less than a renewd act of universal, unmitigated, indispensible, exceptionless, disqualification. One would imagine, that a Bill inflicting such a multitude of incapacities, had followd on the heels of a conquest made by a very fierce Enemy under the impression of recent animosity and resentment. No man, in reading that Bill, could imagine he was reading an act of amnesty and indulgence, following a recital of the good behaviour of those who are the Objects of it, which recital stood at the head of this Bill as it was first introduced, but, I suppose, for its incongruity with the body of the piece, was afterwards omitted. This I say on memory. It however still recites the oath; and, that Catholics 'ought to be considerd as being good and loyal Subjects to his Majesty, his Crown and Government'. Then follows an universal exclusion 'of those good and loyal Subjects' from every, even the lowest Office of Trust or profit, from any Vote at an election, from any privelege in a Town Corporate from being even a Freeman of such corporation, from serving on Grand Juries, from a Vote at a *Vestry*, from having a Gun in his house, from being Barrister Attorney or Solicitor &c &c &c. This has surely much more the air of a Table of proscription than of an act of Grace. What must we suppose the laws concerning those good subjects to have been of which this is a relaxation!

I know well enough, that there is a Cant current about the difference between an exclusion from employments, even to the most rigorous extent, and an exclusion from the natural Benefits arising from a mans own industry. I allow, that under some Circumstances, the difference is very material in point of justice; and that there are considerations, which may render it advisable for a wise Government to keep the leading parts of every Branch of civil and military administration in hands of the best Trust. But a *total* exclusion from the commonwealth is a very different thing. When a Government subsists, as Governments formerly did, on an *Estate of its own*, with but few and inconsiderable revenues drawn from the Subject, then, the few offices which subsisted were naturally at the disposal of those who paid the salaries out of their *own* pocket, and there, an exclusive preference could hardly merit the name of a proscription. Almost the whole produce of a mans industry remaind in his own purse to maintain his family. When a very great portion of the Labour of individuals goes to the State, and is by the State again refunded to individuals, through the medium of Offices, and in this circuitous progress from the publick to the private fund, indemnifies the families from whom it is taken, an equitable Ballance between the Government and the Subject is established. But if a great body of the people who contribute to this State Lottery are excluded from all the prizes, the stopping the Circulation with regard to them may be a most cruel hardship, amounting, in effect, to being double and trebled Taxed; and will be felt as such, to the very quick, by all the families high and low of those hundreds of thousands, who are denied their chance, in the returned fruits of their own Industry. This is the thing meant, by those who look upon the publick Revenue only as a spoil; and will naturally wish to have as few as possible concerned in the division of the Booty. If a State should be so unhappy as to think it cannot subsist without such a barbarous proscription, the persons so proscribed ought to be indemnified by the remission of a large part of their Taxes, by an immunity from Offices of publick burthen, by an exemption from being pressed into any military or naval service. Common sense and common justice dictate, this at least, as some sort of compensation for their slavery. How many families are incapable of existing, if the little Offices of the revenue, and little military commissions are denied them? To deny them at home, and to make the happiness of acquiring some of them somewhere else, felony or high Treason, is a piece of cruelty in which, till very lately, I did not suppose this age capable of persisting. Formerly a similarity of religion made a sort of Country for a man in some quarter or other. A refugee for religion was a protected Character. Now their reception is cold indeed; and therefore as the asylum abroad is destroyd, the hardship at home is doubled.

This hardship is the more intollerable, because the professions are shut up. The Church is so of Course. Much is to be said on that subject with regard to them and to the protestant dissenters. But that is a chapter by itself. I am sure I wish well to that Church and think its Ministers among the very best Citizens of your Country. However such as it is, a great walk of Life is forbidden Ground to seventeen hundred thousand of the Inhabitants of Ireland. Why are they excluded from the Law? do not they expend money in their suits? why may not they indemnifye themselves by profiting, in the persons of some, for the losses incurred by others? Why may not they have persons of confidence, whom they may if they please, employ in the Agency of their affairs. The exclusion from the Law, from Grand Juries, from Sheriffships, and under sheriffships, as well from freedom in any corporation, may subject them to dreadful hardships; as it may exclude them wholly from all that is beneficial, and expose them to all that is mischievous, in a Trial by Jury. This was manifestly within my own observation; for I was three times in Ireland from the year 1760 to the year 1767; where I had sufficient means of information concerning the inhuman proceedings, (among which were many cruel murders, besides an infinity of other outrages and oppressions, unknown before in a civilized age) which prevailed during that period, in consequence of a pretended conspiracy among Roman Catholicks against the Kings Government.[1] I could dilate on the mischiefs that *may* happen, from those which *have* happend, upon this head of disqualification, if it were at all necessary.

The head of the exclusion from *Votes* for Members of Parliament is closely connected with the former. When you cast your Eye on the Statute book, you will see, that no Catholick, even in the ferocious act of Queen Anne, was disabled from Voting on account of his *religion*.[2] The only [conditions] required for that privelege, were the oaths of allegiance and abjuration; both oaths relative to a *civil* concern. Parliament has since added another oath of the same kind;[3] .... The taking away of a Vote is the taking away the Shield which the subject has, not only against the oppressions of power, but of that worst of all oppressions, the persecutions of private Society, and private manners. No candidate for parliamentary influence is obliged to the least attention towards them, either in Cities or Counties; on the contrary, if they should become obnoxious to any bigotted, or any malignant people among whom they live, it will become the Interest of those who court popular favour, to use the numberless means, which always reside in Magistracy and influence, to oppress them. The proceedings in a certain County in Munster, during that unfortunate period I have mentiond, reads a Strong Lecture on the cruelty of depriving men of that Shield, on account of their speculative opinions. The protestants of Ireland feel well and naturally on the hardship of their being bound by Laws for which they do not directly or indirectly Vote. The bounds of those matters are Nice[4] and hard to settle in Theory; and perhaps they have been pushed too far. But how they can avoid the necessary application in the Case of others towards them I know not. It is true, the words of this act do not create a disability, but they clearly and evidently suppose it. There are few Catholick Freeholders to take the Benefit of the privelege, if they were admitted to partake it: but the manner in which this very right in Freeholders at large is defended, is not on the Idea, that they do really and truly represent the people, but that all people being capable of obtaining freeholds, all those, who by their industry and sobriety merit this privelege, have the means of arriving at Votes. It is the same with the Corporations.

The Laws against foreign Education, I find are reenacted.[5] They are clearly, the very worst part of the old Code. Besides your Laity, you have the Succession to about four thousand Clergymen to provide for. These, having no lucrative livings in Prospect, are taken very much out of the Lower orders of the people. At home, they have no means whatsoever provided for their obtaining a *clerical* Education, or indeed any Education at all.... Whilst this restraint of foreign and domestick Education, was a part of an horrible and impious System of Servitude, the Member was well fitted to the body. To render men patient under a deprivation of all the rights of human nature, every thing which could give them the knowledge or feeling of these rights, was rationally forbidden. To render humanity fit to be insulted, it was fit that it should

1. Agrarian disturbances in Tipperary, Cork and neighbouring areas in the early 1760s led to memorably vicious official reactions and the claims that the disturbances were inspired by French sympathizers. The marauding bands called themselves Whiteboys. The most notorious case of judicial murder was that of Father Nicholas Sheehy, a catholic priest who was hanged, drawn and quartered after a trial that was scandalous even by the standards of the judicial system of that time in Ireland. The Sheehy case infuriated Burke, members of whose wife's family were also implicated in charges arising from these disturbances. The incident remained a focus of resentment into the next generation and beyond. Daniel O'Connell refers to it on several occasions in his speeches.
2. An act of 1704 allowed Irish catholics to vote only if they took the oath of abjuration. They were deprived entirely of the franchise in 1728.
3. By an act of 1774.
4. subtle.
5. Luke Gardiner (1745-98), 1st baron Mountjoy, had drafted the bill. The first draft may have contained these proposals. Burke's arguments against the educational clauses were effective.

be degraded. But when we profess to restore men to the capacity for property, it is equally irrational and unjust, to deny them the power of improving their minds, as well as their fortunes. Indeed I have ever thought that the prohibition of the means of improving our rational Nature to be the worst species of Tyranny, that the insolence and perverseness of mankind ever dared to exercise. This goes to all men in all situations, to whom Education can be denied. Your Lordship mentions a proposal which came from my friend the Provost, whose benevolence and enlarged spirit, I am perfectly convinced of, which is the proposal of erecting a few sizarships[6] in the College for the education, I suppose, of Roman Catholick Clergymen. He certainly meant it well. But coming from such a man as he is, it is a strong instance of the danger of suffering any description of men to fall into entire contempt. The charities intended for them, are not perceivd to be fresh insults; and the true Nature of their wants and necessities being unknown, remedies wholly unsuitable to the nature of their complaint are provided for them.... If the other parts of the university were open to them, as well on the foundation as otherwise, the offering of sizarships would be a proportiond part of a *general* kindness. But when every thing liberal is withheld, and only that which is servile is permitted, it is easy to conceive upon what footing they must be in such a place. Mr Hutchinson must well know, the regard and honour I have for him, and he does not think my dissenting from him in this particular, arises from a disregard of his opinions; It only shews, that, I think, he has lived in Ireland. To have any respect for the Character and person of a popish priest there — Oh! it is an uphill work indeed! But until we come to respect what stands in a respectable light with *others*, we are very deficient in the Temper which qualifies us to make any Laws or regulations about them. It even disqualifies us from being charitable towards them with any Effect or Judgment.[7]

When we are to provide for the Education of any body of men, we ought seriously to consider the particular functions they are to perform in Life. A Roman Catholick Clergyman is the Minister of a very ritual Religion; and by his profession subject to many restraints. His Life, is a life full of strict observances; and his Duties of a laborious nature towards himself, and of the highest possible trust towards others. The duty of *confession* alone is sufficient to set in the strongest light, the necessity of his having an appropriated mode of Education. The Theological opinions and the pecular Rites of one religion never can be properly taught in Universities founded for the purposes, and on the principles of another, which in many points is directly opposite. If a Roman Catholick Priest, intended for Celibacy, and the Function of confession, is not strictly bred, in a seminary where these things are respected, inculcated, and enforced, as sacred, and not made the subject of derision and obloquy, he will be ill fitted for the former, and the Latter will be indeed, in his hands, a terrible Instrument.... The Council of Trent has wisely introduced the discipline of *Seminaries*, by which Priests are not trusted for a Clerical institution even to the severe discipline of their own Colleges; but after they pass through them, are frequently, if not for the greater part, obliged to pass through peculiar methods, having their particular ritual Function in View. It is in a great measure to this, and to similar methods used in *foreign education*, that the Popish Clergy of Ireland, miserably provided for, living among *low* and ill regulated people, without any discipline of sufficient force to secure good manners, have been hinderd from becoming an intollerable nuisance to the Country, instead of being, as, I conceive, they generally are, of very great Service to it. The Ministers of Protestant Churches require a different mode of education, more Liberal, and more fit for the ordinary intercourse of Life, and having little hold on the minds of the people by external Ceremonies, extraordinary observances, or seperate habits of Living, they make up the deficiency, by cultivating their minds by all kinds of ornamental Learning, to which the Liberal provision made in England and Ireland for the parochial Clergy, and the comparative lightness of parochial Duties, enables the greater part of them, in some considerable degree to accomplish; to say nothing of the ample Church preferments with little or no Duties annexed. This learning, which I believe to be pretty general, together with

6. A system at Trinity College, Dublin whereby undergraduates received a maintenance grant.

7. John Hely-Hutchinson (1724-94), provost of Trinity College and MP for Cork, rightly remonstrated with Burke over these remarks. Hely-Hutchinson was a staunch defender of the Irish catholics and was in favour of opening Trinity College to them on as broad a front as possible.

an higher situation, and more chastened by the opinions of mankind, forms a sufficient security or their morals, and their sustaining their Clerical Character with dignity. It is not necessary to observe, that all these things are however collateral to their function; and that except in preaching, which may be, and is supplied, and often best supplied, out of printed Books, little else is necessary to a protestant Minister than to be able to read the English Language; I mean for the exercise of his Function, not to the scrutiny at his admittance. But a popish parson in Ireland, may do very well without any considerable Classical erudition, or any proficiency in pure or mixed Mathematics, or any knowledge of civil History. Even if they should possess these acquisitions (as at first many of them do) they soon lose them in the painful Course of professional and parochial Duties; but they must have all the *knowlege*, and what is to them more important than the Knowlege, the *discipline* necessary to those Duties. All modes of Education conducted by those, whose minds are cast in another mold, as I may say, and whose original ways of thinking are formed upon the reverse pattern, must be, to *them*, not only useless, but mischeivous — just as I should suppose the Education in a popish ecclesiastical Seminary would be ill fitted for a protestant Clergyman. Here it would be much more so, as in the Case of the Protestant it only requires to *reject*, in the other little for his purpose is *acquired*.

All this, my Lord, I know very well, will pass for nothing with those who *wish*, that the popish Clergy should be illiterate, dissolute, and in a Situation to produce contempt and detestation. Their minds are wholly taken up with party squabbles, and I have neither leisure nor inclination to apply any part of what I have to say, to those, who never think of religion, or of the commonwealth, in any other light, than as they tend to the prevalence of some Faction in either. I speak, on a supposition, that there is a disposition, — *to take the State in the Condition in which it is found*, — and to improve it *in that State*, to the best advantage. Hitherto the plan for the Government of Ireland has been to sacrifice the civil prosperity of the Nation to its religious improvement. But if people in power there, are, at length, come to entertain other Ideas, they will consider the good order, decorum, Virtue, and morality, of every *description* of men among them, as of infinitely greater importance, than the struggle (for it is nothing better) to change those *descriptions*, by means, which put to hazard Objects, which, in my poor opinion, are of more importance to religion and the State, than all the polemical matter which has ever been agitated among men from the beginning of the world to this hour....

Before I had written thus far, I learned more at large, than I had it from your Lordship, of the Scheme for giving to the Castle the patronage of the presiding Members of the Catholick Clergy. At first I could scarcely credit it; for I believe it is the first time, that the presentation to other peoples Alms has been desired in any Country. If the State provides a suitable maintenance and Temporality to those governing members, and to the Clergy under them, I should think the project, however improper in other respects, to be by no means unjust; But to deprive a *poor* people, who maintain a *second set of Clergy* out of the miserable remains of what is left after Taxing and Tything, to deprive them of the disposition of their own Charities among their own Communion, would in my opinion be an intollerable hardship. Never were the Members of one religious Sect fit to appoint the Pastors to another. Those who have no regard to their welfare, reputation, or internal quiet, will not appoint such as are proper.... It is a great deal, to suppose, that even the present Castle would nominate Bishops for the Roman Church of Ireland with a religious regard for its welfare. Perhaps they cannot, perhaps they dare not do it. But suppose them as well inclined, as I know, that *I* am, to do them all kind of Justice, I declare *I* would not, if it were in my power, take it upon myself. I know I ought not to do it. *I belong to another community*; and it would be an intollerable usurpation in me to affect such an authority where I conferred no Benefit, or even if I did confer, (as in some degree the Seraglio[8] does) temporal advantages. But allowing, that the present Castle finds itself fit, to administer the Government of a Church, which they solemnly forswear, and forswear with very hard words, and many evil Epithets, and that as often as they qualifye themselves for the power, which is to give this very patronage, or to give any thing else that they desire; yet they cannot ensure themselves, that a man like the late Lord Chesterfield[9] will not succeed to them. This man, whilst he

8. The harem of a Muslim palace.
9. Philip Dormer Stanhope (1694-1773), 4th earl of Chesterfield, had been lord lieutenant of Ireland 1745-46.

was duping the Credulity of Papists with fine words in private, and commending their good behaviour during a rebellion in Great Britain, as it well deserved to be commended and rewarded was capable, of urging penal Laws against them in a Speech from the Throne, and stimulating with provocatives, the wearied and half exhausted bigottry of the then parliament of Ireland.[10] They set to work, but they were at a loss what to do; for they had already almost gone through every contrivance which could waste the vigour of their Country; but after much struggling they produced[11] a child of their old Age the shocking and unnatural act about Marriages, which tended to finish the Scheme for making the people, not only two distinct parties for ever, but keeping them as two distinct species, in the same Land. Mr Gardiners humanity was shocked with it,[12] as one of the worst parts of that truly barbarous System, if one could well settle the preference where almost all the parts were outrages on the rights of humanity and the Laws of Nature.

Suppose an atheist, playing the Part of a Bigot, should be in power again in that Country, do you believe, that he would faithfully and religiously administer the trust of appointing Pastors to a Church, which wanting every other support, stands in tenfold need of Ministers, who will be dear to the people committed to their charge, and who will exercise a really paternal authority amongst them? But if the superior power were always in a disposition to dispense conscientiously, and like an upright Trustee and Guardian these rights which he holds for those, with whom he is at variance, has he the capacity and means of doing it? How can the Lord Lieutenant form the least judgment on their merits, so as to discern, which of the Popish priests is fit to be made a Bishop? It cannot be; the Idea is ridiculous. He will hand them over to Lords Lieutenants of Counties, Justices of peace and other persons, who for the purpose of vexing and turning to derision this miserable people, will pick out the worst and most obnoxious they can find among the Clergy, to set over the rest. Whoever is a complainant against his Brethren will always be considerd as persecuted; whoever is censured by his superiors will be looked upon as oppressed; whoever is careless in his opinions, and loose in his morals — will be called a Liberal man, and will be supposed to have incurred hatred because he was not a Bigot. Informers, Talebearers, perverse and obstinate men, flatterers, who turn their back upon their flock, and court the protestant Gentlemen of the Country — will be the Object of preferment. And then I run no risque in foretelling that whatever other quiet and Morality you have in the Country, will be lost. *A popish Clergy, who are not restraind by the most austere subordination, will become a Nuisance, a real publick Grievance of the heaviest kind in any Country that entertains them*; and instead of the great Benefit which Ireland does, and has long derived from them, if they are educated without any Idea of discipline and obedience, and then put under Bishops, who do not owe their station to their Good opinion, and whom they cannot respect, that Nation will see disorders, of which, bad as things are, it has yet no Idea. I do not say this, as thinking the leading men in Ireland would exercise this Trust worse than others. Not at all. No man, no set of men living, are fit to administer the affairs, or regulate the interior œconomy of a Church to which they are Enemies.

As to Government, if I might recommend a prudent caution to them, it would be to innovate, as little as possible, upon speculation, in establishments, from which as they stand, they experience no material inconvenience to the repose of the Country. *Quieta non movere.*[13] . . .

Thinking over this matter more maturely, I see no reason for altering my opinion in any part. The act, as far as it goes, is good undoubtedly. It amounts I think very nearly to a toleration with respect to religious Ceremonies. But it puts a new bolt on Civil Rights; and rivetts it I am afraid to the Old one in such a manner, that neither, I fear, will be easily loosend. What I could have wished would be to see the *civil advantages* take the lead. The other I conceive would follow, in a manner, of Course. For by what I have observed, it is pride, arrogance, and a spirit of domination, and not a bigotted spirit of religion, that has caused and kept up these oppressive Statutes. I am sure I have known those, who have oppressed papists in their civil rights, exceedingly indulgent to their religious ceremonies; who even wished them to continue, in

10. In 1745, Chesterfield had suggested that the Irish parliament should consider strengthening the Penal Laws.
11. The statute of 1747 enacted that every marriage between a Roman catholic and a protestant, or between two protestants if celebrated by a catholic priest, should be null and void.
12. Intermarriage was permitted under Gardiner's bill.

13. Let sleeping dogs lie.

order to furnish pretences for oppression; and who never saw a man, by converting, escape out of their power, but with grudging and regret. I have known men to whom, I am not uncharitable in saying, (though they are dead,) that they would become papists, in order to oppress protestants; if by being protestants, it was not in their power [to oppress] papists. It is [injustice, and not a] mistaken conscience, that has been the principle of persecution, at least so far as it has fallen under my observation.... However as I begun; so I end.

I have the honour to be with high regard and Esteem.

My Lord your Lordships most obedient and humble Servant

EDM BURKE

from: REFLECTIONS ON THE REVOLUTION IN FRANCE (1790)

[The most famous of Burke's writings, the *Reflections* is a powerful defence of traditional society and an analysis of the leading features of the French Revolution. The following passage, frequently attacked as a characteristic piece of bombast and as often praised as a historic moment in the development of English political prose, demonstrates how Burke used three central images — of the family, the mob, and the conspiratorial cabal — to develop his attack on the Revolution and mount his defence of affection as the bonding principle within a political system. As always, he claims a direct relationship between the selfish interests of a powerful faction and general anarchy in the society as a whole.]

It is now sixteen or seventeen years since I saw the queen of France, then the dauphiness, at Versailles; and surely never lighted on this orb, which she hardly seemed to touch, a more delightful vision. I saw her just above the horizon, decorating and cheering the elevated sphere she just began to move in, — glittering like the morning-star, full of life, and splendour, and joy. Oh! what a revolution! and what a heart must I have to contemplate without emotion that elevation and that fall! Little did I dream when she added titles of veneration to those of enthusiastic, distant, respectful love, that she should ever be obliged to carry the sharp antidote against disgrace concealed in that bosom; little did I dream that I should have lived to see such disasters fallen upon her in a nation of gallant men, in a nation of men of honour, and of cavaliers. I thought ten thousand swords must have leaped from their scabbards to avenge even a look that threatened her with insult. But the age of chivalry is gone. That of sophisters, economists, and calculators, has succeeded; and the glory of Europe is extinguished for ever. Never, never more shall we behold that generous loyalty to rank and sex, that proud submission, that dignified obedience, that subordination of the heart, which kept alive, even in servitude itself, the spirit of an exalted freedom. The unbought grace of life, the cheap defence of nations, the nurse of manly sentiment and heroic enterprise, is gone! It is gone, that sensibility of principle, that chastity of honour, which felt a stain like a wound, which inspired courage whilst it mitigated ferocity, which ennobled whatever it touched, and under which vice itself lost half its evil, by losing all its grossness.

This mixed system of opinion and sentiment had its origin in the ancient chivalry; and the principle, though varied in its appearance by the varying state of human affairs, subsisted and influenced through a long succession of generations, even to the time we live in. If it should ever be totally extinguished, the loss I fear will be great. It is this which has given its character to modern Europe. It is this which has distinguished it under all its forms of government, and distinguished it to its advantage, from the states of Asia, and possibly from those states which flourished in the most brilliant periods of the antique world. It was this, which, without confounding ranks, had produced a noble equality, and handed it down through all the gradations of social life. It was this opinion which mitigated kings into companions, and raised private men to be fellows with kings. Without force or opposition, it subdued the fierceness of pride and power; it obliged sovereigns to submit to the soft collar of social esteem, compelled stern authority to submit to elegance, and gave a dominating vanquisher of laws to be subdued by manners.[1]

But now all is to be changed. All the pleasing illusions, which made power gentle and obedience liberal, which harmonized the different shades of

1. The text seems to be corrupt here. Perhaps it should read 'and gave a Domitian, vanquisher of laws, to be subdued by manners'.

life, and which, by a bland assimilation, incorporated into politics the sentiments which beautify and soften private society, are to be dissolved by this new conquering empire of light and reason. All the decent drapery of life is to be rudely torn off. All the superadded ideas, furnished from the wardrobe of a moral imagination, which the heart owns, and the understanding ratifies, as necessary to cover the defects of our naked, shivering nature, and to raise it to dignity in our own estimation, are to be exploded as a ridiculous, absurd, and antiquated fashion.

On this scheme of things, a king is but a man, a queen is but a woman; a woman is but an animal, and an animal not of the highest order. All homage paid to the sex in general as such, and without distinct views, is to be regarded as romance and folly. Regicide, and parricide, and sacrilege, are but fictions of superstition, corrupting jurisprudence by destroying its simplicity. The murder of a king, or a queen, or a bishop, or a father, are only common homicide; and if the people are by any chance, or in any way, gainers by it, a sort of homicide much the most pardonable, and into which we ought not to make too severe a scrutiny.

On the scheme of this barbarous philosophy, which is the offspring of cold hearts and muddy understandings, and which is as void of solid wisdom as it is destitute of all taste and elegance, laws are to be supported only by their own terrors, and by the concern which each individual may find in them from his own private speculations, or can spare to them from his own private interests. In the groves of *their* academy, at the end of every vista, you see nothing but the gallows. Nothing is left which engages the affections on the part of the commonwealth. On the principles of this mechanic philosophy, our institutions can never be embodied, if I may use the expression, in persons; so as to create in us love, veneration, admiration, or attachment. But that sort of reason which banishes the affections is incapable of filling their place. These public affections, combined with manners, are required sometimes as supplements, sometimes as correctives, always as aids to law. The precept given by a wise man, as well as a great critic, for the construction of poems, is equally true as to states: — *Non satis est pulchra esse poemata, dulcia sunto.*[2] There ought to be a system of manners in every nation, which a well-formed mind would be disposed to relish. To make us love our country, our country ought to be lovely.

But power, of some kind or other, will survive the shock in which manners and opinions perish; and it will find other and worse means for its support. The usurpation which, in order to subvert ancient institutions, has destroyed ancient principles, will hold power by arts similar to those by which it has acquired it. When the old feudal and chivalrous spirit of *fealty*, which, by freeing kings from fear, freed both kings and subjects from the precautions of tyranny, shall be extinct in the minds of men, plots and assassinations will be anticipated by preventive murder and preventive confiscation, and that long roll of grim and bloody maxims, which form the political code of all power, not standing on its own honour, and the honour of those who are to obey it. Kings will be tyrants from policy, when subjects are rebels from principle.

When ancient opinions and rules of life are taken away, the loss cannot possibly be estimated. From that moment we have no compass to govern us; nor can we know distinctly to what port we steer. Europe, undoubtedly, taken in a mass, was in a flourishing condition the day on which your revolution was completed. How much of that prosperous state was owing to the spirit of our old manners and opinions is not easy to say; but as such causes cannot be indifferent in their operation, we must presume, that, on the whole, their operation was beneficial.

We are but too apt to consider things in the state in which we find them, without sufficiently adverting to the causes by which they have been produced, and possibly may be upheld. Nothing is more certain, than that our manners, our civilization, and all the good things which are connected with manners and with civilization, have, in this European world of ours, depended for ages upon two principles; and were indeed the result of both combined; I mean the spirit of a gentleman, and the spirit of religion. The nobility and the clergy, the one by profession, the other by patronage, kept learning in existence, even in the midst of arms and confusions, and whilst governments were rather in their causes, than formed. Learning paid back what it received to nobility and to priesthood; and paid it with usury, by enlarging their ideas, and by furnishing their minds. Happy if they had all continued to know their indissoluble union, and their

2. Horace, *Ars Poetica*, 99; 'It is not enough that poems be beautiful, they must also have tenderness.'

proper place! Happy if learning, not debauched by ambition, had been satisfied to continue the instructor, and not aspired to be the master! Along with its natural protectors and guardians, learning will be cast into the mire, and trodden down under the hoofs of a swinish multitude.[3]

If, as I suspect, modern letters owe more than they are always willing to own to ancient manners, so do other interests which we value full as much as they are worth. Even commerce, and trade, and manufacture, the gods of our economical politicians, are themselves perhaps but creatures; are themselves but effects, which, as first causes, we choose to worship. They certainly grew under the same shade in which learning flourished. They too may decay with their natural protecting principles. With you, for the present at least, they all threaten to disappear together. Where trade and manufactures are wanting to a people, and the spirit of nobility and religion remains, sentiment supplies, and not always ill supplies, their place; but if commerce and the arts should be lost in an experiment to try how well a state may stand without these old fundamental principles, what sort of a thing must be a nation of gross, stupid, ferocious, and, at the same time, poor and sordid, barbarians, destitute of religion, honour, or manly pride, possessing nothing at present, and hoping for nothing hereafter?

I wish you may not be going fast, and by the shortest cut, to that horrible and disgustful situation. Already there appears a poverty of conception, a coarseness and vulgarity, in all the proceedings of the Assembly and of all their instructors. Their liberty is not liberal. Their science is presumptuous ignorance. Their humanity is savage and brutal.

It is not clear, whether in England we learned those grand and decorous principles and manners, of which considerable traces yet remain, from you, or whether you took them from us. But to you, I think, we trace them best. You seem to me to be — *gentis incunabula nostræ*.[4] France has always more or less influenced manners in England; and when your fountain is choked up and polluted, the stream will not run long, or not run clear, with us, or perhaps with any nation. This gives all Europe, in my opinion, but too close and connected a concern in what is done in France. Excuse me, therefore, if I have dwelt too long on the atrocious spectacle of the 6th of October, 1789,[5] or have given too much scope to the reflections which have arisen in my mind on occasion of the most important of all revolutions, which may be dated from that day, I mean a revolution in sentiments, manners, and moral opinions. As things now stand, with everything respectable destroyed without us, and an attempt to destroy within us every principle of respect, one is almost forced to apologize for harbouring the common feelings of men.

Why do I feel so differently from the Reverend Dr. Price,[6] and those of his lay flock who will choose to adopt the sentiments of his discourse? — For this plain reason — because it is *natural* I should; because we are so made, as to be affected at such spectacles with melancholy sentiments upon the unstable condition of mortal prosperity, and the tremendous uncertainty of human greatness; because in those natural feelings we learn great lessons; because in events like these our passions instruct our reason; because when kings are hurled from their thrones by the Supreme Director of this great drama, and become the objects of insult to the base, and of pity to the good, we behold such disasters in the moral, as we should behold a miracle in the physical, order of things. We are alarmed into reflection; our minds (as it has long since been observed) are purified by terror and pity; our weak, unthinking pride is humbled under the dispensations of a mysterious wisdom. Some tears might be drawn from me, if such a spectacle were exhibited on the stage. I should be truly ashamed of finding in myself that superficial, theatric sense of painted distress, whilst I could exult over it in real life. With such a perverted mind, I could never venture to show my face at a tragedy. People would think the

3. The phrase 'the swinish multitude' was to be used against Burke in the pamphlet war that followed the publication of the *Reflections*.
4. Virgil, *Aeneid*, III, 105: 'gentis cunabula nostrae' (the cradle of our race).

5. On that date, the French royal family was escorted from Versailles, led to the palace of the Tuileries at the demand of the Parisian crowd and kept under guard.
6. Dr Richard Price (1723-91), a leading dissenter and philosopher. Price delivered a famous sermon, *A Discourse on the Love of Our Country*, published as a pamphlet, to the Revolution Society on 4 November 1789. The Revolution Society had been founded by dissenters to celebrate the English Revolution ('The Glorious Revolution') of 1688. Price believed the French Revolution to be the beginning of a process that would complete what 1688 had begun. After the sermon, Price moved a congratulatory address from the Revolution Society to the French National Assembly.

tears that Garrick[7] formerly, or that Siddons[8] not long since, have extorted from me, were the tears of hypocrisy; I should know them to be the tears of folly.

Indeed the theatre is a better school of moral sentiments than churches, where the feelings of humanity are thus outraged. Poets who have to deal with an audience not yet graduated in the school of the rights of men, and who must apply themselves to the moral constitution of the heart, would not dare to produce such a triumph as a matter of exultation. There, where men follow their natural impulses, they would not bear the odious maxims of a Machiavelian policy, whether applied to the attainment of monarchical or democratic tyranny. They would reject them on the modern, as they once did on the ancient stage, where they could not bear even the hypothetical proposition of such wickedness in the mouth of a personated tyrant, though suitable to the character he sustained. No theatric audience in Athens would bear what has been borne, in the midst of the real tragedy of this triumphal day; a principal actor weighing, as it were in scales hung in a shop of horrors, — so much actual crime against so much contingent advantage, — and after putting in and out weights, declaring that the balance was on the side of the advantages. They would not bear to see the crimes of new democracy posted as in a ledger against the crimes of old despotism, and the book-keepers of politics finding democracy still in debt, but by no means unable or unwilling to pay the balance. In the theatre, the first intuitive glance, without any elaborate process of reasoning, will show, that this method of political computation would justify every extent of crime. They would see, that on these principles, even where the very worst acts were not perpetrated, it was owing rather to the fortune of the conspirators, than to their parsimony in the expenditure of treachery and blood. They would soon see, that criminal means once tolerated are soon preferred. They present a shorter cut to the object than through the highway of the moral virtues. Justifying perfidy and murder for public benefit, public benefit would soon become the pretext, and perfidy and murder the end; until rapacity, malice, revenge, and fear more dreadful than revenge, could satiate their insatiable appetites. Such must be the consequences of losing, in the splendour of these triumphs of the rights of men, all natural sense of wrong and right.

But the reverend pastor exults in this 'leading in triumph,' because truly Louis the Sixteenth was 'an arbitrary monarch'; that is, in other words, neither more nor less than because he was Louis the Sixteenth, and because he had the misfortune to be born king of France, with the prerogatives of which, a long line of ancestors, and a long acquiescence of the people, without any act of his, had put him in possession. A misfortune it has indeed turned out to him, that he was born king of France. But misfortune is not crime, nor is indiscretion always the greatest guilt. I shall never think that a prince, the acts of whose whole reign was a series of concessions to his subjects, who was willing to relax his authority, to remit his prerogatives, to call his people to a share of freedom, not known, perhaps not desired, by their ancestors; such a prince, though he should be subjected to the common frailties attached to men and to princes, though he should have once thought it necessary to provide force against the desperate designs manifestly carrying on against his person, and the remnants of his authority; though all this should be taken into consideration, I shall be led with great difficulty to think he deserves the cruel and insulting triumph of Paris, and of Dr. Price. I tremble for the cause of liberty, from such an example to kings. I tremble for the cause of humanity, in the unpunished outrages of the most wicked of mankind. But there are some people of that low and degenerate fashion of mind, that they look up with a sort of complacent awe and admiration to kings, who know to keep firm in their seat, to hold a strict hand over their subjects, to assert their prerogative, and, by the awakened vigilance of a severe despotism, to guard against the very first approaches of freedom. Against such as these they never elevate their voice. Deserters from principle, listed with fortune, they never see any good in suffering virtue, nor any crime in prosperous usurpation....

If the French king, or king of the French, (or by whatever name he is known in the new vocabulary of your constitution,) has in his own person, and that of his queen, really deserved these unavowed, but unavenged, murderous attempts, and those frequent indignities more cruel than murder, such a

7. David Garrick (1717-79), the leading actor of the time and a friend of Burke.
8. Sarah Siddons (1755-1831), the best-known actress of the time, particularly famous for her playing of the role of Lady Macbeth.

person would ill deserve even that subordinate executory trust, which I understand is to be placed in him; nor is he fit to be called chief in a nation which he has outraged and oppressed. A worse choice for such an office in a new commonwealth, than that of a deposed tyrant, could not possibly be made. But to degrade and insult a man as the worst of criminals, and afterwards to trust him in your highest concerns, as a faithful, honest, and zealous servant, is not consistent with reasoning, nor prudent in policy, nor safe in practice. Those who could make such an appointment must be guilty of a more flagrant breach of trust than any they have yet committed against the people. As this is the only crime in which your leading politicians could have acted inconsistently, I conclude that there is no sort of ground for these horrid insinuations. I think no better of all the other calumnies.

In England, we give no credit to them. We are generous enemies: we are faithful allies. We spurn from us with disgust and indignation the slanders of those who bring us their anecdotes with the attestation of the flower-de-luce[9] on their shoulder. We have Lord George Gordon fast in Newgate;[10] and neither his being a public proselyte to Judaism, nor his having, in his zeal against catholic priests and all sorts of ecclesiastics, raised a mob (excuse the term, it is still in use here) which pulled down all our prisons, have preserved to him a liberty, of which he did not render himself worthy by a virtuous use of it. We have rebuilt Newgate, and tenanted the mansion. We have prisons almost as strong as the Bastile, for those who dare to libel the queens of France. In this spiritual retreat, let the noble libeller remain. Let him there meditate on his Thalmud, until he learns a conduct more becoming his birth and parts, and not so disgraceful to the ancient religion to which he has become a proselyte; or until some persons from your side of the water, to please your new Hebrew brethren, shall ransom him. He may then be enabled to purchase, with the old hoards of the synagogue, and a very small poundage on the long compound interest of the thirty pieces of silver, (Dr. Price has shown us what miracles compound interest will perform in 1790 years,) the lands which are lately discovered to have been usurped by the Gallican church. Send us your Popish archbishop of Paris, and we will send you our Protestant Rabbin.[11] We shall treat the person you send us in exchange like a gentleman and an honest man, as he is; but pray let him bring with him the fund of his hospitality, bounty, and charity; and, depend upon it, we shall never confiscate a shilling of that honourable and pious fund, nor think of enriching the treasury with the spoils of the poor-box.

To tell you the truth, my dear Sir, I think the honour of our nation to be somewhat concerned in the disclaimer of the proceedings of this society of the Old Jewry and the London Tavern.[12] I have no man's proxy. I speak only for myself, when I disclaim, as I do with all possible earnestness, all communion with the actors in that triumph, or with the admirers of it. When I assert anything else, as concerning the people of England, I speak from observation, not from authority; but I speak from the experience I have had in a pretty extensive and mixed communication with the inhabitants of this kingdom, of all descriptions and ranks, and after a course of attentive observation, began early in life, and continued for nearly forty years. I have often been astonished, considering that we are divided from you but by a slender dyke of about twenty-four miles, and that the mutual intercourse between the two countries has lately been very great, to find how little you seem to know of us. I suspect that this is owing to your forming a judgment of this nation from certain publications, which do, very erroneously, if they do at all, represent the opinions and dispositions generally prevalent in England. The vanity, restlessness, petulance, and spirit of intrigue, of several petty cabals, who attempt to hide their total want of consequence in bustle and noise, and puffing, and mutual quotation of each other, makes you imagine that our contemptuous neglect of their abilities is a mark of general

9. The *fleur-de-lis*, the emblem of French royalty, was worn by many French émigres, some of whom were spreading scandal about Queen Marie Antoinette.
10. Lord George Gordon (1751-93), a fanatic who led serious riots in 1780 against the Catholic Relief Act of 1778. Burke was himself threatened by the mob. Hundreds were killed, Newgate prison was burned, but Gordon was acquitted of high treason. He later converted to Judaism and was finally committed to Newgate, where he died.
11. A sardonic reference to Gordon. The Gallican Church was the Roman Catholic Church of France.
12. The Old Jewry was the church in which the Revolution Society gathered on 4 November 1789, the birthday of William of Orange, to hear Price's sermon. Thereafter they repaired to the 'Crown and Anchor' tavern to celebrate.

acquiescence in their opinions. No such thing, I assure you. Because half a dozen grasshoppers under a fern make the field ring with their importunate chink, whilst thousands of great cattle, reposed beneath the shadow of the British oak, chew the cud and are silent, pray do not imagine that those who make the noise are the only inhabitants of the field; that, of course, they are many in number; or that, after all, they are other than the little, shrivelled, meagre, hopping, though loud and troublesome, insects of the hour.

I almost venture to affirm, that not one in a hundred amongst us participates in the 'triumph' of the Revolution Society. If the king and queen of France, and their children, were to fall into our hands by the chance of war, in the most acrimonious of all hostilities, (I deprecate such an event, I deprecate such hostility,) they would be treated with another sort of triumphal entry into London. We formerly have had a king of France in that situation; you have read how he was treated by the victor in the field; and in what manner he was afterwards received in England.[13] Four hundred years have gone over us; but I believe we are not materially changed since that period. Thanks to our sullen resistance to innovation, thanks to the cold sluggishness of our national character, we still bear the stamp of our forefathers. We have not (as I conceive) lost the generosity and dignity of thinking of the fourteenth century; nor as yet have we subtilized ourselves into savages. We are not the converts of Rousseau; we are not the disciples of Voltaire; Helvetius has made no progress amongst us.[14] Atheists are not our preachers; madmen are not our lawgivers. We know that *we* have made no discoveries, and we think that no discoveries are to be made, in morality; nor many in the great principles of government, nor in the ideas of liberty, which were understood long before we were born, altogether as well as they will be after the grave has heaped its mould upon our presumption, and the silent tomb shall have imposed its law on our pert loquacity. In England we have not yet been completely embowelled of our natural entrails; we still feel within us, and we cherish and cultivate, those inbred sentiments which are the faithful guardians, the active monitors of our duty, the true supporters of all liberal and manly morals. We have not been drawn and trussed, in order that we may be filled, like stuffed birds in a museum, with chaff and rags and paltry blurred shreds of paper about the rights of man. We preserve the whole of our feelings still native and entire, unsophisticated by pedantry and infidelity. We have real hearts of flesh and blood beating in our bosoms. We fear God; we look up with awe to kings; with affection to parliaments; with duty to magistrates; with reverence to priests; and with respect to nobility.§ Why? Because when such ideas are brought before our minds, it is *natural* to be so affected; because all other feelings are false and spurious, and tend to corrupt our minds, to vitiate our primary morals, to render us unfit for rational liberty; and by teaching us a servile, licentious, and abandoned insolence, to be our low sport for a few holidays, to make us perfectly fit for, and justly deserving of, slavery, through the whole course of our lives.

You see, Sir, that in this enlightened age I am bold enough to confess, that we are generally men of untaught feelings; that instead of casting away all our old prejudices, we cherish them to a very considerable degree, and, to take more shame to ourselves, we cherish them because they are prejudices; and the longer they have lasted, and the more generally they have prevailed, the more we cherish them. We are afraid to put men to live and trade each on his own private stock of reason; because we suspect that this stock in each man is small, and that the individuals would do better to avail themselves of the general bank and capital of nations and of ages. Many of our men of speculation, instead of exploding general prejudices, employ their sagacity to discover the latent wisdom which prevails in them. If they find what they seek, and they seldom fail, they think it more wise to continue the prejudice, with the reason involved, than to cast away the coat of prejudice, and to leave

13. John II of France (1319-64), captured at the battle of Poitiers (1356) and imprisoned for four years in England.
14. Voltaire (1694-1778) and Jean-Jacques Rousseau (1712-78) were the most famous writers in Europe; Claude Adrien Helvétius (1715-71) was the author of *De L'esprit* (1758). Burke regarded them all as members of one consolidated group of subversive thinkers, although Rousseau was out of sympathy with the others.

§The English are, I conceive, misrepresented in a letter published in one of the papers, by a gentleman thought to be a dissenting minister. — When writing to Dr. Price of the spirit which prevails at Paris, he says, 'The spirit of the people in this place has abolished all the proud *distinctions* which the *king* and *nobles* had usurped in their minds; whether they talk of *the king, the noble, or the priest*, their whole language is that of the most *enlightened and liberal amongst the English*.' If this gentleman means to confine the terms *enlightened and liberal* to one set of men in England, it may be true. It is not generally so. [Burke's note.]

nothing but the naked reason; because prejudice, with its reason, has a motive to give action to that reason, and an affection which will give it permanence. Prejudice is of ready application in the emergency; it previously engages the mind in a steady course of wisdom and virtue, and does not leave the man hesitating in the moment of decision, sceptical, puzzled, and unresolved. Prejudice renders a man's virtue his habit; and not a series of unconnected acts. Through just prejudice, his duty becomes a part of his nature.

Your literary men, and your politicians, and so do the whole clan of the enlightened among us, essentially differ in these points. They have no respect for the wisdom of others; but they pay it off by a very full measure of confidence in their own. With them it is a sufficient motive to destroy an old scheme of things, because it is an old one. As to the new, they are in no sort of fear with regard to the duration of a building run up in haste; because duration is no object to those who think little or nothing has been done before their time, and who place all their hopes in discovery. They conceive, very systematically, that all things which give perpetuity are mischievous, and therefore they are at inexpiable war with all establishments. They think that government may vary like modes of dress, and with as little ill effect: that there needs no principle of attachment, except a sense of present conveniency, to any constitution of the state. They always speak as if they were of opinion that there is a singular species of compact between them and their magistrates, which binds the magistrate, but which has nothing reciprocal in it, but that the majesty of the people has a right to dissolve it without any reason, but its will. Their attachment to their country itself is only so far as it agrees with some of their fleeting projects; it begins and ends with that scheme of polity which falls in with their momentary opinion.

These doctrines, or rather sentiments, seem prevalent with your new statesmen. But they are wholly different from those on which we have always acted in this country.

I hear it is sometimes given out in France, that what is doing among you is after the example of England. I beg leave to affirm, that scarcely anything done with you has originated from the practice or the prevalent opinions of this people, either in the act or in the spirit of the proceeding. Let me add, that we are as unwilling to learn these lessons from France, as we are sure that we never taught them to that nation. The cabals here, who take a sort of share in your transactions, as yet consist of but a handful of people. If unfortunately by their intrigues, their sermons, their publications, and by a confidence derived from an expected union with the counsels and forces of the French nation, they should draw considerable numbers into their faction, and in consequence should seriously attempt anything here in imitation of what has been done with you, the event, I dare venture to prophesy, will be, that, with some trouble to their country, they will soon accomplish their own destruction. This people refused to change their law in remote ages from respect to the infallibility of popes; and they will not now alter it from a pious implicit faith in the dogmatism of philosophers; though the former was armed with the anathema and crusade, and though the latter should act with the libel and the lamp-iron.

Formerly your affairs were your own concern only. We felt for them as men; but we kept aloof from them, because we were not citizens of France. But when we see the model held up to ourselves, we must feel as Englishmen, and feeling, we must provide as Englishmen. Your affairs, in spite of us, are made a part of our interest; so far at least as to keep at a distance your panacea, or your plague. If it be a panacea, we do not want it. We know the consequences of unnecessary physic. If it be a plague, it is such a plague that the precautions of the most severe quarantine ought to be established against it.

I hear on all hands that a cabal, calling itself philosophic, receives the glory of many of the late proceedings; and that their opinions and systems are the true actuating spirit of the whole of them. I have heard of no party in England, literary or political, at any time, known by such a description. It is not with you composed of those men, is it? whom the vulgar, in their blunt, homely style, commonly call atheists and infidels? If it be, I admit that we too have had writers of that description, who made some noise in their day. At present they repose in lasting oblivion. Who, born within the last forty years, has read one word of Collins, and Toland, and Tindal, and Chubb, and Morgan, and that whole race who called themselves Freethinkers?[15] Who now reads Bolingbroke?[16] Who

15. Anthony Collins (1676-1729), militant freethinker and author of *Discourse of Free-thinking* (1713); John Toland (1670-1722), Irish

ever read him through? Ask the booksellers of London what is become of all these lights of the world. In as few years their few successors will go to the family vault of 'all the Capulets.'[17] But whatever they were, or are, with us, they were and are wholly unconnected individuals. With us they kept the common nature of their kind, and were not gregarious. They never acted in corps, or were known as a faction in the state, nor presumed to influence in that name or character, or for the purposes of such a faction, on any of our public concerns. Whether they ought so to exist, and so be permitted to act, is another question. As such cabals have not existed in England, so neither has the spirit of them had any influence in establishing the original frame of our constitution, or in any one of the several reparations and improvements it has undergone. The whole has been done under the auspices, and is confirmed by the sanctions, of religion and piety. The whole has emanated from the simplicity of our national character, and from a sort of native plainness and directness of understanding, which for a long time characterized those men who have successively obtained authority amongst us. This disposition still remains; at least in the great body of the people.

We know, and what is better, we feel inwardly, that religion is the basis of civil society, and the source of all good and of all comfort.§ In England we are so convinced of this, that there is no rust of superstition, with which the accumulated absurdity of the human mind might have crusted it over in the course of ages, that ninety-nine in a hundred of the people of England would not prefer to impiety. We shall never be such fools as to call in an enemy to the substance of any system to remove its corruptions, to supply its defects, or to perfect its construction. If our religious tenets should ever want a further elucidation, we shall not call on atheism to explain them. We shall not light up our temple from that unhallowed fire. It will be illuminated with other lights. It will be perfumed with other incense, than the infectious stuff which is imported by the smugglers of adulterated metaphysics. If our ecclesiastical establishment should want a revision, it is not avarice or rapacity, public or private, that we shall employ for the audit, or receipt, or application of its consecrated revenue. Violently condemning neither the Greek nor the Armenian, nor, since heats are subsided, the Roman system of religion, we prefer the Protestant; not because we think it has less of the Christian religion in it, but because, in our judgment, it has more. We are Protestants, not from indifference, but from zeal.

We know, and it is our pride to know, that man is by his constitution a religious animal; that atheism is against, not only our reason, but our instincts; and that it cannot prevail long. But if, in the moment of riot, and in a drunken delirium from the hot spirit drawn out of the alembic of hell, which in France is now so furiously boiling, we should uncover our nakedness, by throwing off that Christian religion which has hitherto been our boast and comfort, and one great source of civilization amongst us, and amongst many other nations, we are apprehensive (being well aware that the mind will not endure a void) that some uncouth, pernicious, and degrading superstition might take place of it. . . .

§Sit igitur hoc ab initio persuasum civibus, dominos esse omnium rerum ac moderatores, deos; eaque, quae gerantur, eorum geri vi, ditione, ac numine; eosdemque optime de genere hominum mereri; et qualis quisque sit, quid agat, quid in se admittat, qua mente, qua pietate colat religiones intueri; piorum et impiorum habere rationem. His enim rebus imbutae mentes haud sane abhorrebunt ab utili et à vera sententia. Cic. de Legibus, l. 2.[18]

---

author of *Christianity Not Mysterious* (1696); Matthew Tindal (1657-1733), author of *Christianity as Old as Creation* (1730); Thomas Chubb (1679-1747); Thomas Morgan (died 1743), author of *A Defence of Natural and Revealed Religion* (1728), were all freethinkers or deists whose works had aroused great hostility in England.

16. Henry St John Bolingbroke (1678-1751), statesman and author, friend of Swift, Pope and Voltaire. Burke had read Bolingbroke; his *Vindication of Natural Society* (1756) was a parody of Bolingbroke's ideas of natural religion.
17. *Romeo and Juliet*, IV. 1. 112: 'That same ancient vault/Where all the kindred of the Capulets lie.'
18. 'So let our citizens be convinced of this at the outset: that the gods are the lords and rulers of all things, that all that is done is done by their might, dominion and authority, and that they have treated mankind very well; that they also observe what sort of man each individual is, what he does, of what wrong he is guilty, with what intention, with what piety, he keeps ritual observances; and that they take cognizance of the pious and the impious. For minds imbued with these beliefs will surely not reject useful or true doctrine.' Cicero's passage is imperfect in Burke's rendering.

from:
FIRST LETTER TO SIR HERCULES LANGRISHE (1792)

[Published in London in January 1792, and in March in Dublin, with a second London edition in the same month, this Letter, for all its importance as a statement of

Burke's position in Ireland, was too late to have any effect on the very restricted relief bill voted through by the Irish parliament in February 1792. The Catholic Committee was displeased and the defeat of its aspirations did not reflect well on Burke's son Richard, who was its London agent and a tactless advocate on its behalf. It is evident from the Letter that Burke despaired of his Irish Whig friends, like Langrishe, ever having the necessary vision to include the catholics wholly in the political system and thus saving Ireland from potential revolution in this dangerous period.]

A LETTER
to
SIR H. LANGRISHE, BART. MP
on the subject of the
ROMAN CATHOLICS OF IRELAND,
and
the propriety of admitting them to the elective franchise, consistently with the principles of the constitution as established at the revolution

3 Jan., 1792.

. . . . You, who have looked deeply into the spirit of the Popery laws, must be perfectly sensible, that a great part of the present mischief, which we abhor in common, (if it at all exists,) has arisen from them. Their declared object was to reduce the Catholics of Ireland to a miserable populace, without property, without estimation, without education. The professed object was to deprive the few men who, in spite of those laws, might hold or obtain any property amongst them, of all sort of influence or authority over the rest. They divided the nation into two distinct bodies, without common interest, sympathy, or connexion. One of these bodies was to possess *all* the franchises, *all* the property, *all* the education: the other was to be composed of drawers of water and cutters of turf for them. Are we to be astonished, when, by the efforts of so much violence in conquest, and so much policy in regulation, continued without intermission for nearly an hundred years, we had reduced them to a mob; that whenever they came to act at all, many of them would act exactly like a mob, without temper, measure, or foresight? Surely it might be just now a matter of temperate discussion, whether you ought not to apply a remedy to the real cause of the evil. If the disorder you speak of be real and considerable, you ought to raise an aristocratic interest; that is, an interest of property and education amongst them; and to strengthen, by every prudent means, the authority and influence of men of that description. It will deserve your best thoughts, to examine whether this can be done without giving such persons the means of demonstrating to the rest, that something more is to be got by their temperate conduct, than can be expected from the wild and senseless projects of those who do not belong to their body, who have no interest in their well being, and only wish to make them the dupes of their turbulent ambition.

If the absurd persons you mention find no way of providing for liberty, but by overturning this happy constitution, and introducing a frantic democracy, let us take care how we prevent better people from any rational expectations of partaking in the benefit of that constitution *as it stands*. The maxims you establish cut the matter short. They have no sort of connexion with the good or the ill behaviour of the persons who seek relief, or with the proper or improper means by which they seek it. They form a perpetual bar to all pleas, and to all expectations.

You begin by asserting, that 'the Catholics ought to enjoy all things *under* the state, but that they ought not to *be the state*.' A position which, I believe, in the latter part of it, and in the latitude there expressed, no man of common sense has ever thought proper to dispute; because the contrary implies, that the state ought to be in them *exclusively*. But before you have finished the line, you express yourself as if the other member of your proposition, namely, that 'they ought not to be *a part* of the state,' were necessarily included in your first — Whereas I conceive it to be as different as a part is from the whole; that is, just as different as possible. I know, indeed, that it is common with those who talk very differently from you, that is, with heat and animosity, to confound those things, and to argue the admission of the Catholics into any, however minute and subordinate, parts of the state, as a surrender into their hands of the whole government of the kingdom. To them I have nothing at all to say.

Wishing to proceed with a deliberative spirit and temper in so very serious a question, I shall attempt to analyze, as well as I can, the principles you lay down, in order to fit them for the grasp of an understanding so little comprehensive as mine. — 'State' — 'Protestant' — 'Revolution.' These are terms, which, if not well explained, may lead us into many errors. In the word *State*, I conceive there is much ambiguity. The state is sometimes used to signify *the whole commonwealth*, comprehending all its orders, with the several privileges belonging to each. Sometimes it signifies only *the higher and ruling part* of the commonwealth; which we commonly call *the Government*. In the first sense, to be under the state, but not the state itself, *nor any part of it*, that is, to be nothing at all in the commonwealth, is a situation perfectly intelligible: but to those who fill that situation, not very pleasant, when it is understood. It is a state of *civil servitude* by the very force of the definition. *Servorum non est respublica*,[1] is a very old and a very true maxim. This servitude, which makes men *subject* to a state without being *citizens*, may be more or less tolerable from many circumstances: but these circumstances, more or less favourable, do not alter the nature of the thing. The mildness by which absolute masters exercise their dominion, leaves them masters still. We may talk a little presently of the manner in which the majority of the people of Ireland (the Catholics) are affected by this situation; which at present undoubtedly is theirs, and which you are of opinion ought so to continue for ever.

In the other sense of the word *State*, by which is understood the *Supreme Government* only, I must observe this upon the question: that to exclude whole classes of men entirely from this *part* of government, cannot be considered as *absolute slavery*. It only implies a lower and degraded state of citizenship; such is (with more or less strictness) the condition of all countries in which an hereditary nobility possess the exclusive rule. This may be no bad mode of government; provided that the personal authority of individual nobles be kept in due bounds, that their cabals and factions are guarded against with a severe vigilance, and that the people (who have no share in granting their own money) are subjected to but light impositions, and are otherwise treated with attention, and with indulgence to their humours and prejudices....

Between the extreme of *a total exclusion*, to which your maxim goes, and *an universal unmodified capacity*, to which the fanatics pretend, there are many different degrees and stages, and a great variety of temperaments, upon which prudence may give full scope to its exertions. For you know that the decisions of prudence (contrary to the system of the insane reasoners) differ from those of judicature; and that almost all the former are determined on the more or the less, the earlier or the later, and on a balance of advantage and inconvenience, of good and evil.

In all considerations which turn upon the question of vesting or continuing the state solely and exclusively in some one description of citizens, prudent legislators will consider, how far the *general form and principles of their commonwealth render it fit to be cast into an oligarchical shape, or to remain always in it*. We know that the government of Ireland (the same as the British) is not in its constitution *wholly* aristocratical; and, as it is not such in its form, so neither is it in its spirit. If it had been inveterately aristocratical, exclusions might be more patiently submitted to. The lot of one plebeian would be the lot of all; and an habitual reverence and admiration of certain families might make the people content to see government wholly in hands to whom it seemed naturally to belong. But our constitution has *a plebeian member*, which forms an essential integrant part of it. A plebeian oligarchy is a monster: and no people, not absolutely domestic or predial[2] slaves, will long endure it. The Protestants of Ireland are not *alone* sufficiently the people to form a democracy; and they are *too numerous* to answer the ends and purposes of *an aristocracy*. Admiration, that first source of obedience, can be only the claim or the imposture of the few. I hold it to be absolutely impossible for two millions of plebeians, composing certainly a very clear and decided majority in that class, to become so far in love with six or seven hundred thousand of their fellow-citizens, (to all outward appearance plebeians like themselves, and many of them tradesmen, servants, and otherwise inferior to some of them,) as to see with satisfaction, or even with patience, an exclusive power vested in them, by which *constitutionally* they become the absolute masters; and, by the *manners* derived from their circumstances, must be capable of exercising upon them, daily and hourly, an insulting and vexatious superiority. Neither are the majority of the Irish indemnified (as in some aristocracies) for

1. 'There is no republic for slaves.'

2. 'Predial' services relate to the land and the obligations of tenants.

this state of humiliating vassalage, (often inverting the nature of things and relations,) by having the lower walks of industry wholly abandoned to them. They are rivalled, to say the least of the matter, in every laborious and lucrative course of life; while every franchise, every honour, every trust, every place down to the very lowest and least confidential, (besides whole professions,) is reserved for the master cast.

Our constitution is not made for great, general and proscriptive exclusions; sooner or later it will destroy them, or they will destroy the constitution. In our constitution there has always been a difference made between *a franchise* and *an office*, and between the capacity for the one and for the other. Franchises were supposed to belong to the *subject*, as *a subject*, and not *as a member of the governing part of the state*. The policy of government has considered them as things very different; for whilst parliament excluded by the test acts (and for a while these test acts were not a dead letter, as now they are in England) Protestant dissenters from all civil and military employments, they *never touched their right of voting for members of parliament or sitting in either House*; a point I state, not as approving or condemning, with regard to them, the measure of exclusion from employments, but to prove that the distinction has been admitted in legislature, as, in truth, it is founded in reason.

I will not here examine, whether the principles of the British [the Irish] constitution be wise or not. I must assume that they are; and that those, who partake the franchises which make it, partake of a benefit. They who are excluded from votes (under proper qualifications inherent in the constitution that gives them) are excluded, not from the *state*, but from *the British constitution*. They cannot by any possibility, whilst they hear its praises continually rung in their ears, and are present at the declaration which is so generally and so bravely made by those who possess the privilege — that the best blood in their veins ought to be shed, to preserve their share in it; they, the disfranchised part, cannot, I say, think themselves in a *happy* state, to be utterly excluded from all its direct and all its consequential advantages. The popular part of the constitution must be to them by far the most odious part of it. To them it is not *an actual*, and, if possible, still less a *virtual*, representation. It is indeed the direct contrary. It is power unlimited, placed in the hands of *an adverse* description, *because it is an adverse description*. And if they who compose the privileged body have not an interest, they must but too frequently have motives of pride, passion, petulance, peevish jealousy or tyrannic suspicion, to urge them to treat the excluded people with contempt and rigour.

This is not a mere theory; though whilst men are men, it is a theory that cannot be false. I do not desire to revive all the particulars in my memory; I wish them to sleep for ever; but it is impossible I should wholly forget what happened in some parts of Ireland, with very few and short intermissions, from the year 1761 to the year 1766, both inclusive.[3] In a country of miserable police, passing from the extremes of laxity to the extremes of rigour, among a neglected, and therefore disorderly, populace — if any disturbance or sedition, from any grievance real or imaginary, happened to arise, it was presently perverted from its true nature, often criminal enough in itself to draw upon it a severe, appropriate punishment; it was metamorphosed into a conspiracy against the state, and prosecuted as such. Amongst the Catholics, as being by far the most numerous and the most wretched, all sorts of offenders against the laws must commonly be found. The punishment of low people for the offences usual among low people would warrant no inference against any description of religion or of politics. Men of consideration from their age, their profession, or their character; men of proprietary landed estates, substantial renters, opulent merchants, physicians, and titular bishops; could not easily be suspected of riot in open day, or of nocturnal assemblies for the purpose of pulling down hedges, making breaches in park walls, firing barns, maiming cattle, and outrages of a similar nature, which characterize the disorders of an oppressed or a licentious populace. But when the evidence, given on the trial for such misdemeanours, qualified them as overt acts of high treason, and when witnesses were found (such witnesses as they were) to depose to the taking of oaths of allegiance by the rioters to the king of France, to their being paid by his money, and embodied and exercised under his officers, to overturn the state for the purposes of that potentate; in that case, the rioters might (if the witness was believed) be supposed only the troops and persons more reputable, the leaders and commanders in

3. On the 1761-66 disturbances, see *Letter to a Peer of Ireland*, note 1.

such a rebellion. All classes in the obnoxious description, who could not be suspected of the lower crime of riot, might be involved in the odium, in the suspicion, and sometimes in the punishment, of a higher and far more criminal species of offence. These proceedings did not arise from any one of the Popery laws since repealed, but from this circumstance, that when it answered the purposes of an election party, or a malevolent person of influence, to forge such plots, the people had no protection. The people of that description have no hold on the gentlemen who aspire to be popular representatives. The candidates neither love, nor respect, nor fear them, individually or collectively. I do not think this evil (an evil amongst a thousand others) at this day entirely over; for I conceive I have lately seen some indication of a disposition perfectly similar to the old one; that is, a disposition to carry the imputation of crimes from persons to descriptions, and wholly to alter the character and quality of the offences themselves.

This universal exclusion seems to me a serious evil — because many collateral oppressions, besides what I have just now stated, have arisen from it. In things of this nature, it would not be either easy or proper to quote chapter and verse; but I have great reason to believe, particularly since the octennial act,[4] that several have refused at all to let their lands to Roman Catholics; because it would so far disable them from promoting such interests in counties as they were inclined to favour. They who consider also the state of all sorts of tradesmen, shopkeepers, and particularly publicans, in towns, must soon discern the disadvantages under which those labour who have no votes. It cannot be otherwise, whilst the spirit of elections, and the tendencies of human nature, continue as they are. If property be artificially separated from franchise, the franchise must in some way or other, and in some proportion, naturally attract property to it. Many are the collateral disadvantages amongst a *privileged* people, which must attend on those who have *no* privileges.

Among the rich each individual, with or without a franchise, is of importance; the poor and the middling are no otherwise so, than as they obtain some collective capacity and can be aggregated to some corps. If legal ways are not found, illegal will be resorted to; and seditious clubs and confederacies, such as no man living holds in greater horror than I do, will grow and flourish in spite, I am afraid, of anything which can be done to prevent the evil. Lawful enjoyment is the surest method to prevent unlawful gratification. Where there is property, there will be less theft; where there is marriage, there will always be less fornication.

I have said enough of the question of state, *as it affects the people merely as such*. But it is complicated with a political question relative to religion, to which it is very necessary I should say something; because the term *Protestant*, which you apply, is too general for the conclusions which one of your accurate understanding would wish to draw from it; and because a great deal of argument will depend on the use that is made of that term.

It is *not* a fundamental part of the settlement at the Revolution, that the state should be Protestant without *any qualification of the term*. With a qualification it is unquestionably true; not in all its latitude. With the qualification, it was true before the Revolution. Our predecessors in legislation were not so irrational (not to say impious) as to form an operose[5] ecclesiastical establishment, and even to render the state itself in some degree subservient to it, when their religion (if such it might be called) was nothing but a mere *negation* of some other — without any positive idea either of doctrine, discipline, worship, or morals, in the scheme which they professed themselves, and which they imposed upon others, even under penalties and incapacities — No! No! This never could have been done even by reasonable atheists. They who think religion of no importance to the state, have abandoned it to the conscience, or caprice, of the individual; they make no provision for it whatsoever, but leave every club to make, or not, a voluntary contribution towards its support, according to their fancies. This would be consistent. The other always appeared to me to be a monster of contradiction and absurdity. It was for that reason, that, some years ago, I strenuously opposed the clergy who petitioned, to the number of about three hundred, to be freed from the subscription to the Thirty-nine Articles,[6] without proposing to substitute any other in their place. There never has been a religion of the state, (the few

4. The Octennial Act (1768) limited the duration of the parliament in Dublin, which met in alternate years, to an eight-year term.

5. laborious, painstaking.

6. A series of formulas, issued in 1563, defining the doctrinal position of the Church of England.

years of the parliament only excepted,) but that of *the episcopal church of England*; the episcopal church of England, before the Reformation, connected with the see of Rome, since then, disconnected and protesting against some of her doctrines, and against the whole of her authority, as binding in our national church: nor did the fundamental laws of this kingdom (in Ireland it has been the same) ever know, at any period, any other church *as an object of establishment*; or in that light, any other Protestant religion. Nay, our Protestant *toleration* itself at the Revolution, and until within a few years, required a signature of thirty-six, and a part of the thirty-seventh, out of the Thirty-nine Articles. So little idea had they at the Revolution of *establishing* Protestantism indefinitely, that they did not indefinitely *tolerate* it under the name. I do not mean to praise that strictness, where nothing more than merely religious toleration is concerned. Toleration, being a part of moral and political prudence, ought to be tender and large. A tolerant government ought not to be too scrupulous in its investigations; but may bear without blame, not only very ill-grounded doctrines, but even many things that are positively vices, where they are *adulta et prævalida*.[7] The good of the commonwealth is the rule which rides over the rest; and to this every other must completely submit.

The church of Scotland knows as little of Protestantism *undefined*, as the church of England and Ireland do. She has by the articles of union secured to herself the perpetual establishment of *the Confession of Faith*,[8] and the *Presbyterian* church government. In England, even during the troubled interregnum,[9] it was not thought fit to establish a *negative* religion; but the parliament settled the *presbyterian*, as the church *discipline*; the *Directory*, as the rule of public *worship*; and the *Westminster Catechism*, as the institute of *faith*. This is to show, that at no time was the Protestant religion, *undefined*, established here or anywhere else, as I believe. I am sure that when the three religions were established in Germany, they were expressly characterized and declared to be the *Evangelic*, the *Reformed*, and the *Catholic*; each of which has its confession of faith and its settled discipline; so that you always may know the best and the worst of them, to enable you to make the most of what is good, and to correct, or to qualify, or to guard against whatever may seem evil or dangerous.

As to the coronation oath, to which you allude, as opposite to admitting a Roman Catholic to the use of any franchise whatsoever, I cannot think that the king would be perjured if he gave his assent to any regulation which parliament might think fit to make with regard to that affair. The king is bound by law, as clearly specified in several acts of parliament, to be in communion with the church of England. It is a part of the tenure by which he holds his crown; and though no provision was made till the Revolution, which could be called positive and valid in law, to ascertain this great principle, I have always considered it as in fact fundamental, that the king of England should be of the Christian religion, according to the national legal church for the time being. I conceive it was so before the Reformation. Since the Reformation it became doubly necessary; because the king is the head of that church; in some sort an ecclesiastical person; and it would be incongruous and absurd, to have the head of the church of one faith, and the members of another. The king may *inherit* the crown as a *Protestant*, but he cannot *hold it*, according to law, without being a Protestant *of the church of England*. . . .

For reasons forcible enough at all times, but at this time particularly forcible with me, I dwell a little the longer upon this matter, and take the more pains, to put us both in mind that it was not settled at the Revolution, that the state should be Protestant, in the latitude of the term, but in a defined and limited sense only, and that in that sense only the king is sworn to maintain it. To suppose that the king has sworn with his utmost power to maintain what it is wholly out of his power to discover, or which, if he could discover, he might discover to consist of things directly contradictory to each other, some of them perhaps impious, blasphemous, and seditious upon principle, would be not only a gross, but a most mischievous, absurdity. If mere dissent from the church of Rome be a merit, he that dissents the most perfectly is the most meritorious. In many points we hold strongly with that church. He that dissents throughout with that church will dissent with the church of England, and then it will be a

7. 'adulta et praevalida (vitia)', (vigorous and full-blown vices)): Tacitus, *The Annals*, III, 53, 8.
8. The Confession of Faith, prepared by the Westminster Assembly of Divines in 1646, set out the doctrinal position of the presbyterian churches with a strong Calvinist emphasis.
9. In the period 1648-60, presbyterianism was made the established form of church government in England and Scotland.

part of his merit that he dissents with ourselves: — a whimsical species of merit for any set of men to establish. We quarrel to extremity with those, who we know agree with us in many things, but we are to be so malicious even in the principle of our friendships, that we are to cherish in our bosom those who accord with us in nothing, because, whilst they despise ourselves, they abhor, even more than we do, those with whom we have some disagreement. A man is certainly the most perfect Protestant, who protests against the whole Christian religion. Whether a person's having no Christian religion be a title to favour, in exclusion to the largest description of Christians who hold all the doctrines of Christianity, though holding along with them some errors and some superfluities, is rather more than any man, who has not become recreant[10] and apostate from his baptism, will, I believe, choose to affirm. The countenance given from a spirit of controversy to that negative religion may, by degrees, encourage light and unthinking people to a total indifference to everything positive in matters of doctrine; and, in the end, of practice too. If continued, it would play the game of that sort of active, proselytizing, and persecuting atheism, which is the disgrace and calamity of our time, and which we see to be as capable of subverting a government, as any mode can be of misguided zeal for better things.

Now let us fairly see what course has been taken relative to those, against whom, in part at least, the king has sworn to maintain a church, *positive in its doctrine and its discipline*. The first thing done, even when the oath was fresh in the mouth of the sovereigns, was to give a toleration to Protestant dissenters, *whose doctrines they ascertained*. As to the mere civil privileges which the dissenters held as subjects before the Revolution, these were not touched at all. The laws have fully permitted, in a qualification for all offices, to such dissenters, *an occasional conformity*; a thing I believe singular, where tests are admitted. The act called the Test Act itself, is, with regard to them, grown to be hardly anything more than a dead letter. Whenever the dissenters cease by their conduct to give any alarm to the government, in church and state, I think it very probable that even this matter, rather disgustful than inconvenient to them, may be removed, or at least so modified as to distinguish the qualification to those offices which really *guide the state*, from those which are *merely instrumental*; or that some other and better tests may be put in their place.

So far as to England. In Ireland you have outrun us. Without waiting for an English example, you have totally, and without any modification whatsoever, repealed the test as to Protestant dissenters. Not having the repealing act by me, I ought not to say positively that there is no exception in it; but if it be what I suppose it is, you know very well, that a Jew in religion, or a Mahometan, or even *a public, declared atheist*, and blasphemer, is perfectly qualified to be lord-lieutenant, a lord justice, or even keeper of the king's conscience; and by virtue of his office (if with you it be as it is with us) administrator to a great part of the ecclesiastical patronage of the crown.

Now let us deal a little fairly. We must admit, that Protestant dissent was one of the quarters from which danger was apprehended at the Revolution, and against which a part of the coronation oath was peculiarly directed. By this unqualified repeal, you certainly did not mean to deny that it was the duty of the crown to preserve the church against Protestant dissenters; or taking this to be the true sense of the two revolution acts of King William, and of the previous and subsequent union acts of Queen Anne, you did not declare by this most unqualified repeal, by which you broke down all the barriers, not invented indeed, but carefully preserved at the Revolution; you did not then and by that proceeding declare, that you had advised the king to perjury towards God, and perfidy towards the church. No! far, very far from it! you never would have done it, if you did not think it could be done with perfect repose to the royal conscience, and perfect safety to the national established religion. You did this upon a full consideration of the circumstances of your country. Now if circumstances required it, why should it be contrary to the king's oath, his parliament judging on those circumstances, to restore to his Catholic people, in such measure, and with such modifications as the public wisdom shall think proper to add, *some part* in these franchises which they formerly had held without limitation at all, and which, upon no sort of urgent reason at the time, they were deprived of? If such means can with any probability be shown, from circumstances, rather to add strength to our mixed ecclesiastical and secular constitution, than to weaken it; surely they

10. disloyal.

are means infinitely to be preferred to penalties, incapacities, and proscriptions continued from generation to generation....

This way of proscribing men by whole nations as it were, from all the benefits of the constitution to which they were born, I never can believe to be politic or expedient, much less necessary for the existence of any state or church in the world. Whenever I shall be convinced, which will be late and reluctantly, that the safety of the church is utterly inconsistent with all the civil rights whatsoever of the far larger part of the inhabitants of our country, I shall be extremely sorry for it; because I shall think the church to be truly in danger. It is putting things into the position of an ugly alternative, into which I hope in God they never will be put.

First, I cannot possibly confound in my mind all the things which were done at the Revolution, with the *principles* of the Revolution. As in most great changes, many things were done from the necessities of the time, well or ill understood, from passion or from vengeance, which were not only not perfectly agreeable to its principles, but in the most direct contradiction to them. I shall not think that the *deprivation of some millions of people of all the rights of citizens, and all interest in the constitution, in and to which they were born,* was a thing conformable to the *declared principles* of the Revolution. This I am sure is true relatively to England, (where the operation of these *anti-principles* comparatively were of little extent,) and some of our late laws, in repealing acts made immediately after the Revolution, admit that some things then done were not done in the true spirit of the Revolution. But the Revolution operated differently in England and Ireland, in many, and these essential, particulars. Supposing the principles to have been altogether the same in both kingdoms, by the application of those principles to very different objects, the whole spirit of the system was changed, not to say reversed. In England it was the struggle of the *great body* of the people for the establishment of their liberties against the efforts of a very *small faction,* who would have oppressed them. In Ireland it was the establishment of the power of the smaller number, at the expense of the civil liberties and properties of the far greater part; and at the expense of the political liberties of the whole. It was, to say the truth, not a revolution, but a conquest; which is not to say a great deal in its favour. To insist on everything done in Ireland at the Revolution, would be to insist on the severe and jealous policy of a conqueror, in the crude settlement of his new acquisition, as a *permanent* rule for its future government. This, no power, in no country that ever I heard of, has done or professed to do — except in Ireland; where it is done, and possibly by some people will be professed. Time has, by degrees, in all other places and periods, blended and coalited the conquered with the conquerors....

For a much longer period than that which had sufficed to blend the Romans with the nation to which of all others they were the most adverse,[11] the Protestants settled in Ireland, consider themselves in no other light than that of a sort of a colonial garrison, to keep the natives in subjection to the other state of Great Britain. The whole spirit of the Revolution in Ireland, was that of not the mildest conqueror. In truth, the spirit of those proceedings did not commence at that æra, nor was religion of any kind their primary object. What was done, was not in the spirit of a contest between two religious factions; but between two adverse nations. The statutes of Kilkenny[12] show, that the spirit of the Popery laws, and some even of their actual provisions, as applied between Englishry and Irishry, had existed in that harassed country before the words Protestant and Papist were heard of in the world. If we read Baron Finglass, Spenser, and Sir John Davis,[13] we cannot miss the true genius and policy of the English government there before the Revolution, as well as during the whole reign of Queen Elizabeth. Sir John Davis boasts of the benefits received by the natives, by extending to them the English law, and turning the whole kingdom into shire ground. But the appearance of things alone was changed. The original scheme was never deviated from for a single hour. Unheard-of confiscations were made in the northern parts, upon grounds of plots and conspiracies, never proved upon their supposed authors. The war of chicane succeeded to the war of arms and of hostile statutes;

11. The reference is to the Gauls.

12. The Statutes of Kilkenny (1366) were passed by the parliament of Ireland at Kilkenny in a bid to halt the assimilation of Anglo-Normans into Gaelic society. Among the 35 statutes, there were prohibitions against intermarriage with the Irish, against the use of the Irish language, dress and legal system.

13. Elizabethan writers on Ireland. John Davies, *A Discovery of the True Causes why Ireland was Never Entirely Subdued* .... (1612); Edmund Spenser, *A View of the Present State of Ireland* (1596).

and a regular series of operations was carried on, particularly from Chichester's[14] time, in the ordinary courts of justice, and by special commissions and inquisitions; first under pretence of tenures, and then of titles in the crown, for the purpose of the total extirpation of the interest of the natives in their own soil — until this species of subtle ravage, being carried to the last excess of oppression and insolence under Lord Stafford, it kindled the flames of that rebellion which broke out in 1641.[15] By the issue of that war, by the turn which the Earl of Clarendon gave to things at the Restoration, and by the total reduction of the kingdom of Ireland in 1691, the ruin of the native Irish, and, in a great measure too, of the first races of the English, was completely accomplished.[16] The new English interest was settled with as solid a stability as anything in human affairs can look for. All the penal laws of that unparalleled code of oppression, which were made after the last event, were manifestly the effects of national hatred and scorn towards a conquered people; whom the victors delighted to trample upon, and were not at all afraid to provoke. They were not the effect of their fears, but of their security. They who carried on this system looked to the irresistible force of Great Britain for their support in their acts of power. They were quite certain, that no complaints of the natives would be heard on this side of the water, with any other sentiments than those of contempt and indignation. Their cries served only to augment their torture. Machines which could answer their purposes so well must be of an excellent contrivance. Indeed, in England, the double name of the complainants, Irish and Papist, (it would be hard to say which singly was the most odious,) shut up the hearts of every one against them. Whilst that temper prevailed, and it prevailed in all its force to a time within our memory, every measure was pleasing and popular, just in proportion as it tended to harass and ruin a set of people who were looked upon as enemies to God and man; and, indeed, as a race of bigoted savages who were a disgrace to human nature itself.

However, as the English in Ireland began to be domiciliated, they began also to recollect that they had a country. The *English interest*, at first by faint and almost insensible degrees, but at length openly and avowedly, became an *independent Irish interest*; full as independent as it could ever have been, if it had continued in the persons of the native Irish; and it was maintained with more skill, and more consistency, than probably it would have been in theirs. With their views, the *Anglo-Irish* changed their maxims — it was necessary to demonstrate to the whole people, that there was something, at least, of a common interest, combined with the independency, which was to become the object of common exertions. The mildness of government produced the first relaxation towards the Irish; the necessities, and, in part too, the temper that predominated at this great change, produced the second and the most important of these relaxations. English government, and Irish legislature, felt jointly the propriety of this measure. The Irish parliament and nation became independent.

The true revolution to you, that which most intrinsically and substantially resembled the English Revolution of 1688, was the Irish Revolution of 1782. The Irish parliament of 1782 bore little resemblance to that which sat in that kingdom, after the period of the first of these revolutions. It bore a much nearer resemblance to that which sat under King James.[17] The change of the parliament in 1782 from the character of the parliament which, as a token of its indignation, had burned all the journals indiscriminately of the former parliament in the council-chamber, was very visible. The address of King William's parliament, the parliament which assembled after the Revolution, amongst other causes of complaint, (many of them sufficiently just,) complains of the repeal by their predecessors of Poyning's law;[18] no absolute idol with the parliament of 1782.

Great Britain, finding the Anglo-Irish highly animated with a spirit, which had indeed shown

14. Arthur Chichester (1563-1625), a ruthless sergeant major general of the English army in Ireland 1600-05, in the wars against the Earl of Tyrone; lord deputy of Ireland 1605-14. He oversaw the plantation of Ulster.
15. Thomas Wentworth (1593-1641), 1st earl of Strafford, lord deputy of Ireland 1633-41. In 1641 both Gaelic and Old English catholics combined to rid the country of its settler population.
16. Edward Hyde (1609-74), earl of Clarendon, author of *The History of the Rebellion* (1702-04), lord-lieutenant of Ireland 1685-87. The wars of 1690-91 completed the destruction of the Gaelic civilization and of the power of the Old English, the descendants of the Anglo-Normans who had arrived in the twelfth century.
17. The Irish parliament, which sat under King James II, was, like that of 1782, 'Grattan's parliament', anxious to assert its independence of the parliament in London.
18. Poynings's Law (1494), a statute that made the Irish parliament subservient to the English crown.

itself before, though with little energy and many interruptions, and therefore suffered a multitude of uniform precedents to be established against it, acted, in my opinion, with the greatest temperance and wisdom. She saw that the disposition of the *leading part* of the nation would not permit them to act any longer the part of a *garrison*. She saw that true policy did not require that they ever should have appeared in that character; or if it had done so formerly, the reasons had now ceased to operate. She saw that the Irish of her race were resolved to build their constitution and their politics upon another bottom. With those things under her view, she instantly complied with the whole of your demands, without any reservation whatsoever. She surrendered that boundless superiority, for the preservation of which, and the acquisition, she had supported the English colonies in Ireland for so long a time, and at so vast an expense (according to the standard of those ages) of her blood and treasure.

When we bring before us the matter which history affords for our selection, it is not improper to examine the spirit of the several precedents, which are candidates for our choice. Might it not be as well for your statesmen, on the other side of the water, to take an example from this latter, and surely more conciliatory, revolution, as a pattern for your conduct towards your own fellow-citizens, than from that of 1688, when a paramount sovereignty over both you and them was more loftily claimed, and more sternly exerted, than at any former, or at any subsequent period? Great Britain, in 1782, rose above the vulgar ideas of policy, the ordinary jealousies of state, and all the sentiments of national pride and national ambition. If she had been more disposed than, I thank God for it, she was, to listen to the suggestions of passion than to the dictates of prudence; she might have urged the principles, the maxims, the policy, the practice of the Revolution, against the demands of the leading description in Ireland, with full as much plausibility, and full as good a grace, as any amongst them can possibly do, against the supplications of so vast and extensive a description of their own people.

A good deal too, if the spirit of domination and exclusion had prevailed in England, might have been excepted against some of the means then employed in Ireland, whilst her claims were in agitation. They were, at least, as much out of ordinary course, as those which are now objected against admitting your people to any of the benefits of an English constitution. Most certainly, neither with you, nor here, was any one ignorant of what was at that time said, written, and done. But on all sides we separated the means from the end: and we separated the cause of the moderate and rational, from the ill-intentioned and seditious; which on such occasions are so frequently apt to march together. At that time, on your part, you were not afraid to review what was done at the Revolution of 1688; and what had been continued during the subsequent flourishing period of the British empire. The change then made was a great and fundamental alteration. In the execution, it was an operose business on both sides of the water. It required the repeal of several laws, the modification of many, and a new course to be given to an infinite number of legislative, judicial, and official practices and usages in both kingdoms. This did not frighten any of us. You are now asked to give, in some moderate measure, to your fellow-citizens, what Great Britain gave to you, without any measure at all. Yet, notwithstanding all the difficulties at the time, and the apprehensions which some very well meaning people entertained, through the admirable temper in which this revolution (or restoration in the nature of a revolution) was conducted in both kingdoms, it has hitherto produced no inconvenience to either; and I trust, with the continuance of the same temper, that it never will. I think that this small, inconsiderable change (relative to an exclusive statute not made at the Revolution) for restoring the people to the benefits from which the green soreness of a civil war had not excluded them, will be productive of no sort of mischief whatsoever. Compare what was done in 1782, with what is wished in 1792; consider the spirit of what has been done at the several periods of reformation; and weigh maturely, whether it be exactly true that conciliatory concessions are of good policy only in discussions between nations; but that among descriptions in the same nation, they must always be irrational and dangerous. What have you suffered in your peace, your prosperity, or, in what ought ever to be dear to a nation, your glory, by the last act by which you took the property of that people under the protection of the *laws*? What reason have you to dread the consequences of admitting the people possessing that property to some share in the protection of the *constitution*?

I do not mean to trouble you with anything to

remove the objections, I will not call them arguments, against this measure, taken from a ferocious hatred to all that numerous description of Christians. It would be to pay a poor compliment to your understanding or your heart. Neither *your* religion, nor *your* politics, consists 'in odd perverse antipathies.'[19] You are not resolved to persevere in proscribing from the constitution so many millions of your countrymen, because, in contradiction to experience and to common sense, you think proper to imagine, that their principles are subversive of common human society. To that I shall only say, that whosoever has a temper which can be gratified by indulging himself in these good-natured fancies ought to do a great deal more. For an exclusion from the privileges of British subjects is not a cure for so terrible a distemper of the human mind, as they are pleased to suppose in their countrymen. I rather conceive a participation in those privileges to be itself a remedy for some mental disorders.

As little shall I detain you with matters that can as little obtain admission into a mind like yours; such as the fear, or pretence of fear, that, in spite of your own power, and the trifling power of Great Britain, you may be conquered by the pope; or that this commodious bugbear (who is of infinitely more use to those who pretend to fear, than to those who love him) will absolve his Majesty's subjects from their allegiance, and send over the Cardinal of York to rule you as his viceroy; or that, by the plenitude of his power, he will take that fierce tyrant, the king of the French, out of his jail, and arm that nation (which on all occasions treats his Holiness so very politely) with his bulls and pardons, to invade poor old Ireland, to reduce you to Popery and slavery, and to force the free-born, naked feet of your people into the wooden shoes of that arbitrary monarch.[20] I do not believe that discourses of this kind are held, or that anything like them will be held, by any who walk about without a keeper. Yet, I confess, that on occasions of this nature, I am the most afraid of the weakest reasonings; because they discover the strongest passions. These things will never be brought out in indefinite propositions. They would not prevent pity towards any persons; they would only cause it for those who were capable of talking in such a strain. But I know, and am sure, that such ideas as no man will distinctly produce to another, or hardly venture to bring in any plain shape to his own mind — he will utter in obscure, ill-explained doubts, jealousies, surmises, fears, and apprehensions; and that, in such a fog, they will appear to have a good deal of size, and will make an impression; when, if they were clearly brought forth and defined, they would meet with nothing but scorn and derision.

There is another way of taking an objection to this concession, which I admit to be something more plausible, and worthy of a more attentive examination. It is, that this numerous class of people is mutinous, disorderly, prone to sedition, and easy to be wrought upon by the insidious arts of wicked and designing men; that, conscious of this, the sober, rational, and wealthy part of that body, who are totally of another character, do by no means desire any participation for themselves, or for any one else of their description, in the franchises of the British constitution.

I have great doubt of the exactness of any part of this observation. But let us admit that the body of the Catholics are prone to sedition, (of which, as I have said, I entertain much doubt,) is it possible that any fair observer, or fair reasoner, can think of confining this description to them only? I believe it to be possible for men to be mutinous and seditious who feel no grievance; but I believe no man will assert seriously, that, when people are of a turbulent spirit, the best way to keep them in order, is to furnish them with something substantial to complain of.

You separate very properly the sober, rational, and substantial part of their description from the rest. You give, as you ought to do, weight only to the former. What I have always thought of the matter is this — that the most poor, illiterate, and uninformed creatures upon earth are judges of a *practical* oppression. It is a matter of feeling; and as such persons generally have felt most of it, and are not of an over-lively sensibility, they are the best judges of it. But for the *real cause*, or the *appropriate remedy*, they ought never to be called into council about the one or the other. They ought to be totally shut out; because their reason is weak; because, when once roused, their passions are ungoverned; because they want information; because the smallness of the property, which individually they possess, renders them less attentive to the con-

19. Samuel Butler, *Hudibras* (1663), Part I, Canto 1, line 206.
20. Wooden shoes were associated with the miserable condition of the European peasantry and, by extension, with catholicism. The phrase survives in Orange Order toasts.

sequence of the measures they adopt in affairs of moment. When I find a great cry amongst the people who speculate little, I think myself called seriously to examine into it, and to separate the real cause from the ill effects of the passion it may excite; and the bad use which artful men may make of an irritation of the popular mind. Here we must be aided by persons of a contrary character; we must not listen to the desperate or the furious; but it is therefore necessary for us to distinguish who are the *really* indigent, and the *really* intemperate. As to the persons who desire this part in the constitution, I have no reason to imagine that they are men who have nothing to lose and much too look for in public confusion. The popular meeting, from which apprehensions have been entertained, has assembled. I have accidentally had conversation with two friends of mine, who know something of the gentleman who was put into the chair upon that occasion; one of them has had money transactions with him; the other, from curiosity, has been to see his concerns; they both tell me he is a man of some property; but you must be the best judge of this, who by your office are likely to know his transactions. Many of the others are certainly persons of fortune; and all, or most, fathers of families, men in respectable ways of life, and some of them far from contemptible, either for their information, or for the abilities which they have shown in the discussion of their interests. What such men think it for their advantage to acquire, ought not, *prima facie*, to be considered as rash or heady, or incompatible with the public safety or welfare....

It is known, I believe, that the greater, as well as the sounder, part of our excluded countrymen have not adopted the wild ideas, and wilder engagements, which have been held out to them; but have rather chosen to hope small and safe concessions from the legal power, than boundless objects from trouble and confusion. This mode of action seems to me to mark men of sobriety, and to distinguish them from those who are intemperate, from circumstance or from nature. But why do they not instantly disclaim and disavow those who make such advances to them? In this, too, in my opinion, they show themselves no less sober and circumspect. In the present moment, nothing short of insanity could induce them to take such a step. Pray consider the circumstances. Disclaim, says somebody, all union with the dissenters: — right — But, when this your injunction is obeyed, shall I obtain the object which I solicit from *you*? — Oh, no, nothing at all like it! — But, in punishing us by an exclusion from the constitution through the great gate, for having been invited to enter into it by a postern, will you punish by deprivation of their privileges, or mulct in any other way, those who have tempted us? — Far from it — we mean to preserve all *their* liberties and immunities, as *our* life-blood. We mean to cultivate *them*, as brethren whom we love and respect — with *you* we have no fellowship. We can bear with patience their enmity to ourselves; but their friendship with you we will not endure. But mark it well! All our quarrels with *them* are always to be revenged upon you. Formerly, it is notorious, that we should have resented with the highest indignation, your presuming to show any ill-will to them. You must not suffer them, now, to show any goodwill to you. Know — and take it once for all — that it is, and ever has been, and ever will be, a fundamental maxim in our politics, that you are not to have any part, or shadow, or name of interest whatever in our state. That we look upon you as under an irreversible outlawry from our constitution — as perpetual and unalliable aliens.

Such, my dear sir, is the plain nature of the argument drawn from the revolution maxims, enforced by a supposed disposition in the Catholics to unite with the dissenters. Such it is, though it were clothed in never such bland and civil forms, and wrapped up, as a poet says, in a thousand 'artful folds of sacred lawn.'[21] For my own part, I do not know in what manner to shape such arguments, so as to obtain admission for them into a rational understanding. Everything of this kind is to be reduced, at last, to threats of power. — I cannot say *væ victis*,[22] and then throw the sword into the scale. I have no sword; and if I had, in this case most certainly I would not use it as a make-weight in political reasoning.

Observe, on these principles, the difference between the procedure of the parliament and the dissenters, towards the people in question. One employs courtship, the other force. The dissenters offer bribes, the parliament nothing but the *front negatif* of a stern and forbidding authority. A man may be very wrong in his ideas of what is good for

21. This quotation cannot be traced.
22. 'Woe to the conquered', as said by Brennus to the Romans (Livy, *History*, Book V).

him. But no man affronts me, nor can therefore justify my affronting him, by offering to make me as happy as himself, according to his own ideas of happiness. This the dissenters do to the Catholics. You are on the different extremes. The dissenters offer, with regard to constitutional rights and civil advantages of all sorts, *everything* — you refuse *everything*. With them there is boundless, though not very assured, hope; with you, a very sure and very unqualified despair. The terms of alliance, from the dissenters, offer a representation of the Commons, chosen out of the people by the head. This is absurdly and dangerously large, in my opinion; and that scheme of election is known to have been, at all times, perfectly odious to me. But I cannot think it right of course to punish the Irish Roman Catholics by an universal exclusion, because others, whom you would not punish at all, propose an universal admission. I cannot dissemble to myself, that, in this very kingdom, many persons who are not in the situation of the Irish Catholics, but who, on the contrary, enjoy the full benefit of the constitution as it stands, and some of whom, from the effect of their fortunes, enjoy it in a large measure, had some years ago associated to procure great and undefined changes (they considered them as reforms) in the popular part of the constitution. Our friend, the late Mr. Flood, (no slight man) proposed in his place, and in my hearing, a representation not much less extensive than this, for England; in which every house was to be inhabited by a voter — *in addition* to all the actual votes by other titles (some of the corporate) which we know do not require a house, or a shed. Can I forget that a person of the very highest rank, of very large fortune, and of the first class of ability, brought a bill into the House of Lords, in the head-quarters of aristocracy, containing identically the same project, for the supposed adoption of which by a club or two, it is thought right to extinguish all hopes in the Roman Catholics of Ireland? I cannot say it was very eagerly embraced or very warmly pursued. But the Lords neither did disavow the bill, nor treat it with any disregard, nor express any sort of disapprobation of its noble author, who has never lost, with king or people, the least degree of the respect and consideration which so justly belongs to him.

I am not at all enamoured, as I have told you, with this plan of representation; as little do I relish any bandings or associations for procuring it. But if the question was to be put to you and me — *universal* popular representation, or *none at all for us and ours* — we should find ourselves in a very awkward position. I do not like this kind of dilemmas [*sic*], especially when they are practical.

Then, since our oldest fundamental laws follow, or rather couple, freehold with franchise; since no principle of the Revolution shakes these liberties; since the oldest and one of the best monuments of the constitution demands for the Irish the privilege which they supplicate; since the principles of the Revolution coincide with the declarations of the Great Charter; since the practice of the Revolution, in this point, did not contradict its principles; since, from that event, twenty-five years had elapsed, before a domineering party, on a party principle, had ventured to disfranchise, without any proof whatsoever of abuse, the greater part of the community; since the king's coronation oath does not stand in his way to the performance of his duty to all his subjects; since you have given to all other dissenters these privileges without limit, which are hitherto withheld, without any limitation whatsoever, from the Catholics; since no nation in the world has ever been known to exclude so great a body of men (not born slaves) from the civil state, and all the benefits of its constitution; the whole question comes before parliament as a matter for its prudence. I do not put the thing on a question of right....

The whole being at discretion, I beg leave just to suggest some matters for your consideration — Whether the government in church or state is likely to be more secure by continuing causes of grounded discontent, to a very great number (say two millions) of the subjects? or, Whether the constitution, combined and balanced as it is, will be rendered more solid, by depriving so large a part of the people of all concern, or interest, or share, in its representation, actual or *virtual*? I here mean to lay an emphasis on the word *virtual*. Virtual representation is that in which there is a communion of interests, and a sympathy in feelings and desires, between those who act in the name of any description of people, and the people in whose name they act, though the trustees are not actually chosen by them. This is virtual representation. Such a representation I think to be, in many cases, even better than the actual. It possesses most of its advantages, and is free from many of its inconveniences; it corrects the irregularities in the literal representation, when the shifting current of human affairs, or the acting of public interests in different ways, carry it obliquely from its first line of direction. The people may err in their choice; but common interest and common sentiment are rarely mistaken. But this sort of virtual representation cannot have a long or sure existence, if it has not a substratum in the actual. The member must have some relation to the constituent. As things stand, the Catholic, as a Catholic, and belonging to a description, has no *virtual* relation to the representative; but the *contrary*. There is a relation in mutual obligation. Gratitude may not always have a very lasting power; but the frequent recurrence of an application for favours will revive and refresh it, and will necessarily produce some degree of mutual attention. It will produce, at least, acquaintance. The several descriptions of people will not be kept so much apart as they now are, as if they were not only separate nations, but separate species. The stigma and reproach, the hideous mask, will be taken off, and men will see each other as they are. Sure I am, that there have been thousands in Ireland, who have never conversed with a Roman Catholic in their whole lives, unless they happened to talk to their gardener's workmen, or to ask their way, when they had lost it, in their sports; or at best, who had known them only as footmen, or other domestics, of the second and third order: and so averse were they, some time ago, to have them near their persons, that they would not employ even those who could never find their way beyond the stable. I well remember a great, and in many respects a good, man, who advertised for a blacksmith; but at the same time added, he must be a Protestant. It is impossible that such a state of things, though natural goodness in many persons will undoubtedly make exceptions, must not produce alienation on the one side, and pride and insolence on the other....

Suppose the people of Ireland divided into three parts; of these (I speak within compass) two are Catholic. Of the remaining third, one half is composed of dissenters. There is no natural union between those descriptions. It may be produced. If the two parts Catholic be driven into a close confederacy with half the third part of Protestants, with a view to a change in the constitution in church or state, or both; and you rest the whole of their security on a handful of gentlemen, clergy, and their dependants; compute the strength *you have in Ireland*, to oppose to grounded discontent, to capricious innovation, to blind popular fury, and to ambitious, turbulent intrigue.

You mention that the minds of some gentlemen are a good deal heated: and that it is often said, that, rather than submit to such persons having a share in their franchises, they would throw up their independence, and precipitate an union with Great Britain. I have heard a discussion concerning such an union amongst all sorts of men ever since I remember anything. For my own part, I have never been able to bring my mind to anything clear and decisive upon the subject. There cannot be a more arduous question. As far as I can form an opinion, it would not be for the mutual advantage of the two kingdoms. Persons, however, more able than I am, think otherwise. But, whatever the merits of this union may be, to make it a *menace*, it must be shown to be an *evil*; and an evil more particularly to those who are threatened with it, than to those who hold it out as a terror. I really do not see how this threat of an union can operate, or that the Catholics are more likely to be losers by that measure than the churchmen.

The humours of the people, and of politicians too, are so variable in themselves, and are so much under the occasional influence of some leading men, that it is impossible to know what turn the public mind here would take on such an event. There is but one thing certain concerning it. Great divisions and vehement passions would precede this union, both on the measure itself and on its terms; and particularly, this very question of a share in the representation for the Catholics, from whence the project of an union originated, would form a principal part in the discussion; and in the temper in which some gentlemen seem inclined to throw themselves, by a sort of high, indignant passion, into the scheme, those points would not be deliberated with all possible calmness.

From my best observation, I should greatly doubt, whether, in the end, these gentlemen would obtain their object, so as to make the exclusion of two millions of their countrymen a fundamental article in the union. The demand would be of a nature quite unprecedented. You might obtain the union: and yet a gentleman, who, under the new union establishment, would aspire to the honour of representing his county, might possibly be as much obliged, as he may fear to be under the old separate establishment, to the unsupportable mortification of asking his neighbours, who have a different opinion concerning the elements in the sacrament, for their votes.

I believe, nay, I am sure, that the people of Great Britain, with or without an union, might be depended upon, in cases of any real danger, to aid the government of Ireland, with the same cordiality as they would support their own, against any wicked attempts to shake the security of the happy constitution in church and state. But before Great Britain engages in any quarrel, the *cause of the dispute* would certainly be a part of her consideration. If confusions should arise in that kingdom, from too steady an attachment to a proscriptive, monopolizing system, and from the resolution of regarding the franchise, and in it the security of the subject, as belonging rather to religious opinions than to civil qualification and civil conduct, I doubt whether you might quite certainly reckon on obtaining an aid of force from hence, for the support of that system. We might extend your distractions to this country, by taking part in them. England will be indisposed, I suspect, to send an army for the conquest of Ireland. What was done in 1782 is a decisive proof of her sentiments of justice and moderation. She will not be fond of making another American war in Ireland. The principles of such a war would but too much resemble the former one. The well-disposed and the ill-disposed in England would (for different reasons perhaps) be equally averse to such an enterprise. The confiscations, the public auctions, the private grants, the plantations, the transplantations, which formerly animated so many adventurers, even among sober citizens, to such Irish expeditions, and which possibly might have animated some of them to the American, can have no existence in the case that we suppose.

Let us form a supposition, (no foolish or ungrounded supposition,) that in an age when men are infinitely more disposed to heat themselves with political than religious controversies, the former should entirely prevail, as we see that in some places they have prevailed, over the latter; and that the Catholics of Ireland, from the courtship paid them on the one hand, and the high tone of refusal on the other, should, in order to enter into all the rights of subjects, all become Protestant dissenters; and as the others do, take all your oaths. They would all obtain their civil objects; and the change, for anything I know to the contrary, (in the dark as I am about the Protestant dissenting tenets,) might be of use to the health of their souls. But, what security our constitution, in church or state, could derive from that event, I cannot possibly discern. Depend upon it, it is as true as nature is true, that if you force them out of the religion of habit, education, or opinion, it is not to yours they will ever go. Shaken in their minds, they will go to that where the dogmas are fewest; where they are the most uncertain; where they lead them the least to a consideration of what they have abandoned. They will go to that uniformly democratic system, to whose first movements they owed their emancipation. I recommend you seriously to turn this in your mind. Believe that it requires your best and maturest thoughts. Take what course you please — union or no union; whether the people remain Catholics or become Protestant dissenters, sure it is, that the present state of monopoly *cannot* continue.

If England were animated, as I think she is not, with her former spirit of domination, and with the strong theological hatred which she once cherished for that description of her fellow-Christians and fellow-subjects; I am yet convinced, that after the fullest success in a ruinous struggle, you would be obliged to abandon that monopoly. We were obliged to do this, even when everything promised success in the American business. If you should make this experiment at last, under the pressure of any necessity, you never can do it well. But if, instead of falling into a passion, the leading gentlemen of the country themselves should undertake the business cheerfully, and with hearty affection towards it, great advantages would follow. What is forced, cannot be modified: but here you may measure your concessions. . . .

It is one excellence of our constitution, that all our rights of provincial election regard rather property than person. It is another, that the rights which approach more nearly to the personal are most of them corporate, and suppose a restrained and strict education of seven years in some useful occupation. In both cases the practice may have slid from the principle. The standard of qualification in both cases may be so low, or not so judiciously chosen, as in some degree to frustrate the end. But all this is for your prudence in the case before you. You may raise, a step or two, the qualification of the Catholic voters. But if you were, tomorrow, to put the Catholic freeholder on the footing of the most favoured forty-shilling Protestant dissenter, you know that such is the actual state of Ireland, this would not make a sensible alteration in almost any *one* election in the kingdom. The effect in their favour, even defensively, would be infinitely slow. But it would be healing; it would be satisfactory and protecting. The stigma would be removed. By admitting settled, permanent substance in lieu of the numbers, you would avoid the great danger of our time, that of setting up number against property. The numbers ought never to be neglected; because (besides what is due to them as men) collectively, though not individually, they have great property: they ought to have therefore protection: they ought to have security: they ought to have even consideration: but they ought not to predominate....

You hated the old system as early as I did. Your first juvenile lance was broken against that giant. I think you were even the first who attacked the grim phantom. You have an exceedingly good understanding, very good humour, and the best heart in the world. The dictates of that temper and that heart, as well as the policy pointed out by that understanding, led you to abhor the old code. You abhorred it, as I did, for its vicious perfection. For I must do it justice: it was a complete system, full of coherence and consistency; well digested and well composed in all its parts. It was a machine of wise and elaborate contrivance; and as well fitted for the oppression, impoverishment, and degradation of a people, and the debasement, in them, of human nature itself, as ever proceeded from the perverted ingenuity of man. It is a thing humiliating enough, that we are doubtful of the effect of the medicines we compound. We are sure of our poisons. My opinion ever was, (in which I heartily agreed with those that admired the old code,) that it was so constructed, that if there was once a breach in any essential part of it, the ruin of the whole, or nearly of the whole, was, at some time or other, a certainty. For that reason I honour, and shall for ever honour and love you, and those who first caused it to stagger, crack, and gape. — Others may finish; the beginners have the glory; and, take what part you please at this hour, (I think you will take the best,) your first services will never be forgotten by a grateful country. Adieu! Present my best regards to those I know, and as many as I know in our country, I honour. There never was so much ability, nor, I believe, virtue, in it. They have a task worthy of both. I doubt not they will perform it, for the stability of the church and state, and for the union and the separation of the people: for the union of the honest and peaceable of all sects; for their separation from all that is ill-intentioned and seditious in any of them.

Beaconsfield, January 3, 1792.

from: LETTER TO RICHARD BURKE, ESQ. (1793)

[After the passage of the Catholic Relief Act in 1793, Burke hoped that the catholics would go on to win the right to sit in parliament. He credited his son with helping to bring about the improvement of 1793, through his importunity with government ministers. Now, writing to Richard (who was to die very suddenly the next year), Burke tries to indicate to him the forces that he faced in trying to win further concessions for the catholics. This is the first extended analysis of what was meant by the newly minted phrase 'protestant ascendancy'.]

MY DEAR SON,

We are all again assembled in town, to finish the last, but the most laborious, of the tasks which have been imposed upon me during my parliamentary service. We are as well as at our time of life we can expect to be. We have, indeed, some moments of anxiety about you. You are engaged in an undertaking similar in its principle to mine. You are engaged in the relief of an oppressed people. In that service you must necessarily excite the same sort of passions in those who have exercised, and who wish to continue, that oppression that I have had to struggle with in this long labour. As your father has done, you must make enemies of many of the rich, of the proud, and of the powerful. I and you began in the same way. I must confess, that, if our place was of our choice, I could wish it had been your lot to begin the career of your life with an endeavour to render some more moderate, and less invidious, service to the public. But being engaged in a great and critical work, I have not the least hesitation about your having hitherto done your duty as becomes you....

I am sorry to find that pride and passion, and that sort of zeal for religion which never shows any wonderful heat but when it afflicts and mortifies our neighbour, will not let the ruling description perceive, that the privilege for which your clients contend is very nearly as much for the benefit of those who refuse it, as those who ask it. I am not to examine into the charges that are daily made on the administration of Ireland. I am not qualified to say how much in them is cold truth, and how much rhetorical exaggeration. Allowing some foundation to the complaint, it is to no purpose that these people allege that their government is a job in its administration. I am sure it is a job in its constitution; nor is it possible a scheme of polity which, in total exclusion of the body of the community, confines (with little or no regard to their rank or condition in life) to a certain set of favoured citizens the rights which formerly belonged to the whole, should not, by the operation of the same selfish and narrow principles, teach the persons who administer in that government to prefer their own particular, but well understood, private interest to the false and ill calculated private interest of the monopolizing company they belong to. Eminent characters, to be sure, overrule places and circumstances. I have nothing to say to that virtue, which shoots up in full force by the native vigour of the seminal principle, in spite of the adverse soil and climate that it grows in. But, speaking of things in their ordinary course, in a country of monopoly there *can* be no patriotism. There may be a party spirit — but public spirit there can be none. As to a spirit of liberty, still less can it exist, or anything like it. A liberty made up of penalties! a liberty made up of incapacities! a liberty made up of exclusion and proscription, continued for ages, of four-fifths, perhaps, of the inhabitants of all ranks and fortunes! In what does such liberty differ from the description of the most shocking kind of servitude?

But, it will be said, in that country some people are free — why this is the very description of despotism! *Partial freedom is privilege and prerogative, and not liberty.* Liberty, such as deserves the name, is an honest, equitable, diffusive, and impartial principle. It is a great and enlarged virtue, and not a sordid, selfish, and illiberal vice. It is the portion of the mass of the citizens; and not the haughty licence of some potent individual, or some predominant faction.

If anything ought to be despotic in a country, it is its government; because there is no cause of constant operation to make its yoke unequal. But the dominion of a party must continually, steadily, and by its very essence, lean upon the prostrate description. A constitution formed so as to enable a party to overrule its very government, and to overpower the people too, answers the purposes neither of government nor of freedom. It compels that power which ought, and often would be disposed, *equally* to protect the subjects, to fail in its trust, to counteract its purposes, and to become no better than the instrument of the wrongs of a faction. Some degree of influence must exist in all governments. But a government which has no interest to please the body of the people, and can neither support them, nor with safety call for their support, nor is of power to sway the domineering faction, can only exist by corruption; and, taught by that monopolizing party which usurps the title and qualities of the public, to consider the body of the people as out of the constitution, they will consider those who are in it in the light in which they choose to consider themselves. The whole relation of government and of freedom will be a battle, or a traffic.

This system in its real nature, and under its proper appellations, is odious and unnatural, especially when a constitution is admitted which not only, as all constitutions do profess, has a regard to the good of the multitude, but in its theory makes profession of their power also. But of late this scheme of theirs has been new christened — *honestum nomen imponitur vitio.*[1] A word has been lately struck in the mint of the Castle of Dublin; thence it was conveyed to the Tholsel,[2] or city-hall, where, having passed the touch of the corporation, so respectably stamped and vouched, it soon became current in parliament, and was carried back by the Speaker of the House of Commons in great pomp, as an offering of homage from whence it came. The word is *Ascendency*. It is not absolutely new. But the sense in which I have hitherto seen it used was to signify an influence obtained over the minds of some other person by love and reverence, or by superior management and dexterity. It had, therefore, to this its promotion no more than a

1. 'an honourable name is used to cover vice.' cf. Horace, *Satires* 1, 3.41-42.
2. The term 'protestant Ascendancy' was first used in a letter from the Earl of Westmoreland, the lord lieutenant in Dublin Castle, to the Home Secretary, Henry Dundas, on 14 January 1792. On the following day, the city corporation met in the Exhibition House (the 'tholsel' or town hall), William Street, Dublin to prepare an address to the king in support of the status quo, which was defined as the preservation of the interests of the 'protestant Ascendancy'. For a full account, see W.J. Mc Cormack, *Ascendancy and Tradition in Anglo-Irish Literary History from 1789 to 1939* (Oxford: Clarendon Press, 1985), pp. 61-96.

moral, not a civil or political, use. But I admit it is capable of being so applied; and if the Lord Mayor of Dublin, and the Speaker of the Irish parliament, who recommend the preservation of the Protestant ascendency, mean to employ the word in that sense, that is, if they understand by it the preservation of the influence of that description of gentlemen over the Catholics by means of an authority derived from their wisdom and virtue, and from an opinion they raise in that people of a pious regard and affection for their freedom and happiness, it is impossible not to commend their adoption of so apt a term into the family of politics. It may be truly said to enrich the language. Even if the Lord Mayor and Speaker mean to insinuate that this influence is to be obtained and held by flattering their people, by managing them, by skilfully adapting themselves to the humours and passions of those whom they would govern, he must be a very untoward critic who would cavil even at this use of the word, though such cajoleries would perhaps be more prudently practised than professed. These are all meanings laudable, or at least tolerable. But when we look a little more narrowly, and compare it with the plan to which it owes its present technical application, I find it has strayed far from its original sense. It goes much further than the privilege allowed by Horace. It is more than *parcè detortum*.[3] This Protestant ascendency means nothing less than an influence obtained by virtue, by love, or even by artifice and seduction; full as little an influence derived from the means by which ministers have obtained an influence, which might be called, without straining, an *ascendency* in public assemblies in England, that is, by a liberal distribution of places and pensions, and other graces of government. This last is wide indeed of the signification of the word. New *ascendency* is the old mastership. It is neither more nor less than the resolution of one set of people in Ireland to consider themselves as the sole citizens in the commonwealth; and to keep a dominion over the rest by reducing them to absolute slavery under a military power, and, thus fortified in their power, to divide the public estate, which is the result of general contribution, as a military booty solely amongst themselves.

The poor word ascendency, so soft and melodious in its sound, so lenitive[4] and emollient in its first usage, is now employed to cover to the world the most rigid, and perhaps not the most wise, of all plans of policy. The word is large enough in its comprehension. I cannot conceive what mode of oppression in civil life, or what mode of religious persecution, may not come within the methods of preserving an *ascendency*. In plain old English, as they apply it, it signifies *pride and dominion* on the one part of the relation, and on the other *subserviency and contempt* — and it signifies nothing else. The old words are as fit to be set to music as the new; but use has long since affixed to them their true signification, and they sound, as the other will, harshly and odiously to the moral and intelligent ears of mankind.

This ascendency, by being a *Protestant* ascendency, does not better it from the combination of a note or two more in this anti-harmonic scale. If Protestant ascendency means the proscription from citizenship of by far the major part of the people of any country, then Protestant ascendency is a bad thing; and it ought to have no existence. But there is a deeper evil. By the use that is so frequently made of the term, and the policy which is ingrafted on it, the name Protestant becomes nothing more or better than the name of a persecuting faction, with a relation of some sort of theological hostility to others, but without any sort of ascertained tenets of its own, upon the ground of which it persecutes other men; for the patrons of this Protestant ascendency neither do, nor can, by anything positive, define or describe what they mean by the word Protestant. It is defined, as Cowley defines wit, not by what it is, but by what it is not.[5] It is not the Christian religion as professed in the churches holding communion with Rome, the majority of Christians; that is all which in the latitude of the term is known about its signification. This makes such persecutors ten times worse than any of that description that hitherto have been known in the world. The old persecutors, whether Pagan or Christian, whether Arian or Orthodox, whether Catholics, Anglicans, or Calvinists, actually were, or at least had the decorum to pretend to be, strong

3. The full quotation is 'Graeco fonte cadent parce *detorta*', Horace, *Ars Poetica*, 53. Horace is saying that new words will win acceptance 'if they are drawn from a Greek fount *and are drawn therefrom but sparingly*.'

4. Soothing pain or distress.

5. Abraham Cowley (1618-67), *Ode of Wit* (1656), lines 55-56:
'What is it then, which like the power Divine
We only can be negatives define?'

dogmatists. They pretended that their religious maxims were clear and ascertained, and so useful, that they were bound, for the eternal benefit of mankind, to defend or diffuse them, though by any sacrifices of the temporal good of those who were the objects of their system of experiment.

The bottom of this theory of persecution is false. It is not permitted to us to sacrifice the temporal good of any body of men to our own ideas of the truth and falsehood of any religious opinions. By making men miserable in this life they counteract one of the great ends of charity; which is, inasmuch as in us lies, to make men happy in every period of their existence, and most in what most depends upon us. But give to these old persecutors their mistaken principle, in their reasoning they are consistent, and in their tempers they may be even kind and good-natured. But whenever a faction would render millions of mankind miserable, — some millions of the race co-existent with themselves, and many millions in their succession, without knowing, or so much as pretending to ascertain, the doctrines of their own school, (in which there is much of the lash and nothing of the lesson,) the errors which the persons in such a faction fall into are not those that are natural to human imbecility, nor is the least mixture of mistaken kindness to mankind an ingredient in the severities they inflict. The whole is nothing but pure and perfect malice. It is, indeed, a perfection in that kind belonging to beings of a higher order than man, and to them we ought to leave it.

This kind of persecutors, without zeal, without charity, know well enough that religion, to pass by all questions of the truth or falsehood of any of its particular systems, (a matter I abandon to the theologians on all sides,) is a source of great comfort to us mortals in this our short but tedious journey through the world. They know that to enjoy this consolation men must believe their religion upon some principle or other, whether of education, habit, theory, or authority. When men are driven from any of those principles on which they have received religion, without embracing with the same assurance and cordiality some other system, a dreadful void is left in their minds, and a terrible shock is given to their morals. They lose their guide, their comfort, their hope. None but the most cruel and hard-hearted of men, who had banished all natural tenderness from their minds, such as those beings of iron, the atheists, could bring themselves to any persecution like this. Strange it is, but so it is, that men, driven by force from their habits in one mode of religion, have, by contrary habits, under the same force, often quietly settled in another. They suborn their reason to declare in favour of their necessity. Man and his conscience cannot always be at war. If the first races have not been able to make a pacification between the conscience and the convenience, their descendants come generally to submit to the violence of the laws, without violence to their minds. As things stood formerly, they possessed a *positive* scheme of direction, and of consolation. In this men may acquiesce. The harsh methods in use with the old class of persecutors were to make converts, not apostates only. If they perversely hated other sects and factions, they loved their own inordinately. But in this Protestant persecution there is anything but benevolence at work. What do the Irish statutes? They do not make a conformity to the *established* religion, and to its doctrines and practices, the condition of getting out of servitude. No such thing. Let three millions of people but abandon all that they and their ancestors have been taught to believe sacred, and to forswear it publicly in terms the most degrading, scurrilous, and indecent for men of integrity and virtue, and to abuse the whole of their former lives, and to slander the education they have received, and nothing more is required of them. There is no system of folly, or impiety, or blasphemy, or atheism, into which they may not throw themselves, and which they may not profess openly, and as a system, consistently with the enjoyment of all the privileges of a free citizen in the happiest constitution in the world.

Some of the unhappy assertors of this strange scheme say they are not persecutors on account of religion. In the first place they say what is not true. For what else do they disfranchise the people? If the man gets rid of a religion through which their malice operates, he gets rid of all their penalties and incapacities at once. They never afterwards inquire about him. I speak here of their pretexts, and not of the true spirit of the transaction, in which religious bigotry, I apprehend, has little share. Every man has his taste; but I think, if I were so miserable and undone as to be guilty of premeditated and continued violence towards any set of men, I had rather that my conduct was supposed to arise from wild conceits concerning their religious advantages than from low and ungenerous motives relative to my own selfish interest. I had rather be thought insane in my charity than rational in my malice. This much, my dear son, I have to say of this Protestant persecution; that is, a persecution of religion itself.

A very great part of the mischiefs that vex the world arises from words. People soon forget the meaning, but the impression and the passion remain. The word Protestant is the charm that locks up in the dungeon of servitude three millions of your people. It is not amiss to consider this spell of potency, this abracadabra, that is hung about the necks of the unhappy, not to heal, but to communicate disease. We sometimes hear of a Protestant *religion*, frequently of a Protestant *interest*. We hear of the latter the most frequently, because it has a positive meaning. The other has none. We hear of it the most frequently, because it has a word in the phrase, which, well or ill understood, has animated to persecution and oppression at all times infinitely more than all the dogmas in dispute between religious factions. These are indeed well formed to perplex and torment the intellect; but not half so well calculated to inflame the passions and animosities of men.

I do readily admit, that a great deal of the wars, seditions, and troubles of the world did formerly turn upon the contention between *interests* that went by the names of Protestant and Catholic. But I imagined that at this time no one was weak enough to believe, or imprudent enough to pretend, that questions of Popish and Protestant opinions, or interest, are the things by which men are at present menaced with crusades by foreign invasion, or with seditions which shake the foundations of the state at home. It is long since all this combination of things has vanished from the view of intelligent observers. The existence of quite another system of opinions and interests is now plain to the grossest sense. Are these the questions that raise a flame in the minds of men at this day? If ever the church and the constitution of England should fall in these islands, (and they will fall together,) it is not Presbyterian discipline, nor Popish hierarchy, that will rise upon their ruins. It will not be the Church of Rome nor the Church of Scotland — not the Church of Luther, nor the Church of Calvin. On the contrary, all these Churches are menaced, and menaced alike. It is the new fanatical religion, now in the heat of its first ferment, of the Rights of Man, which rejects all establishments, all discipline, all ecclesiastical, and in truth all civil, order, which will triumph, and which will lay prostrate your church; which will destroy your distinctions, and which will put all your properties to auction, and disperse you over the earth. If the present establishment should fall, it is this religion which will triumph in Ireland and in England, as it has triumphed in France. This religion, which laughs at creeds, and dogmas, and confessions of faith, may be fomented equally amongst all descriptions, and all sects; amongst nominal Catholics, and amongst nominal churchmen, and amongst those dissenters who know little, and care less, about a presbytery, or any of its discipline, or any of its doctrine.

Against this new, this growing, this exterminatory system, all these churches have a common concern to defend themselves. How the enthusiasts of this rising sect rejoice to see you of the old churches play their game, and stir and rake the cinders of animosities sunk in their ashes, in order to keep up the execution of their plan for your common ruin!

I suppress all that is in my mind about the blindness of those of our clergy, who will shut their eyes to a thing which glares in such manifest day. If some wretches amongst an indigent and disorderly part of the populace raise a riot about tithes, there are of these gentlemen ready to cry out that this is an overt act of a treasonable conspiracy. Here the bulls, and the pardons, and the crusade, and the pope, and the thunders of the Vatican, are everywhere at work. There is a plot to bring in a foreign power to destroy the church. Alas! it is not about popes, but about potatoes, that the minds of this unhappy people are agitated. It is not from the spirit of zeal, but the spirit of whiskey, that these wretches act. Is it then not conceived possible that a poor clown can be unwilling, after paying three pounds rent to a gentleman in a brown coat, to pay fourteen shillings to one in a black coat for his acre of potatoes, and tumultously to desire some modification of the charge, without being supposed to have no other motive than a frantic zeal for being thus double-taxed to another set of landholders, and another set of priests? Have men no self-interest? no avarice? no repugnance to public imposts? Have they no sturdy and restive minds? no undisciplined habits? Is there nothing in the whole mob of irregular passions which might precipitate some of the common people, in some places, to quarrel with a legal, because they feel it to be a burdensome, imposition? According to these gentlemen, no offence can be committed by Papists but from zeal to their religion. To make room for the vices of Papists, they clear the house of all the vices of men....

I do not pretend to take pride in an extravagant attachment to any sect. Some gentlemen in Ireland affect that sort of glory. It is to their taste. Their piety, I take it for granted, justifies the fervour of their zeal, and may palliate the excess of it. Being myself no more than a common layman, commonly informed in controversies, leading only a very common life, and having only a common citizen's interest in the church, or in the state, yet to you I will say, in justice to my own sentiments, that not one of those zealots for a Protestant interest wishes more sincerely that I do, perhaps not half so sincerely, for the support of the Established Church in both these kingdoms. It is a great link towards holding fast the connexion of religion with the state; and for keeping these two islands, in their present critical independence of constitution, in a close connexion of *opinion and affection*. I wish it well, as the religion of the greater number of the primary land-proprietors of the kingdom, with whom all establishments of church and state, for strong political reasons, ought in my opinion to be warmly connected. I wish it well, because it is more closely combined than any other of the church-systems with the *Crown*, which is the stay of the mixed constitution; because it is, as things now stand, the sole connecting *political* principle between the constitutions of the two independent kingdoms. I have another, and infinitely a stronger, reason for wishing it well; it is, that in the present time I consider it as one of the main pillars of the Christian religion itself. The body and substance of every religion I regard much more than any of the forms and dogmas of the particular sects. Its fall would leave a great void, which nothing else of which I can form any distinct idea might fill. I respect the Catholic hierarchy, and the Presbyterian republic. But I know that the hope or the fear of establishing either of them is, in these kingdoms, equally chimerical, even if I preferred one or the other of them to the Establishment, which certainly I do not.

These are some of my reasons for wishing the support of the Church of Ireland as by law established. These reasons are founded as well on the absolute as on the relative situation of that kingdom. But is it because I love the church, and the king, and the privileges of parliament, that I am to be ready for any violence, or any injustice, or any absurdity, in the means of supporting any of these powers, or all of them together? Instead of prating about Protestant ascendencies, Protestant parliaments ought, in my opinion, to think at last of becoming patriot parliaments.

The legislature of Ireland, like all legislatures, ought to frame its laws to suit the people and the circumstances of the country, and not any longer to make it their whole business to force the nature, the temper, and the inveterate habits of a nation to a conformity to speculative systems concerning any kind of laws. Ireland has an established government, and a religion legally established, which are to be preserved. It has a people who are to be preserved too, and to be led by reason, principle, sentiment, and interest to acquiesce in that government. Ireland is a country under peculiar circumstances. The people of Ireland are a very mixed people; and the quantities of the several ingredients in the mixture are very much disproportioned to each other. Are we to govern this mixed body as if it were composed of the most simple elements, comprehending the whole in one system of benevolent legislation? or are we not rather to provide for the several parts according to the various and diversified necessities of the heterogeneous nature of the mass? Would not common reason and common honesty dictate to us the policy of regulating the people in the several descriptions of which they are composed, according to the natural ranks and classes of an orderly civil society, under a common protecting sovereign, and under a form of constitution favourable at once to authority and to freedom; such as the British constitution boasts to be, and such as it is, to those who enjoy it?

You have an ecclesiastical establishment, which, though the religion of the prince, and of most of the first class of landed proprietors, is not the religion of the major part of the inhabitants, and which, consequently, does not answer to *them* any one purpose of a religious establishment. This is a state of things which no man in his senses can call perfectly happy. But it is the state of Ireland. Two hundred years of experiment show it to be unalterable. Many a fierce struggle has passed between the parties. The result is — you cannot make the people Protestants — and they cannot shake off a Protestant government. This is what experience teaches, and what all men of sense, of all descriptions, know. Today the question is this — are we to make the best of this situation which we cannot alter? The question is — shall the condition of the body of the people be alleviated in other things, on account of their necessary suffering from their being subject to the burdens of two religious establishments, from one of which they do not partake the least, living or dying, either of instruction or of consolation; or shall it be aggravated by stripping the people thus loaded of everything which might support and indemnify them in this state, so as to leave them naked of every sort of right, and of every name of franchise; to outlaw them from the constitution, and to cut off (perhaps) three millions of plebeian subjects, without reference to property or any other qualification, from all connexion with the popular representation of the kingdom?

As to religion, it has nothing at all to do with the proceeding. Liberty is not sacrificed to a zeal for religion; but a zeal for religion is pretended and assumed, to destroy liberty. The Catholic religion is completely free. It has no establishment; but it is recognised, permitted, and in a degree protected by the laws. If a man is satisfied to be a slave, he may be a Papist with perfect impunity. He may say mass, or hear it, as he pleases; but he must consider himself as an outlaw from the British constitution. If the constitutional liberty of the subject were not the thing aimed at, the direct reverse course would be taken. The franchise would have been permitted, and the mass exterminated. But the conscience of a man left, and a tenderness for it hypocritically pretended, is to make it a trap to catch his liberty.

So much is this the design, that the violent partisans of this scheme fairly take up all the maxims and arguments, as well as the practices, by which tyranny has fortified itself at all times. Trusting wholly in their strength and power, (and upon this they reckon, as always ready to strike wherever they wish to direct the storm,) they abandon all pretext of the general good of the community. They say that if the people, under any given modification, obtain the smallest portion or particle of constitutional freedom, it will be impossible for them to hold their property. They tell us that they act only on the defensive. They inform the public of Europe, that their estates are made up of forfeitures and confiscations from the natives: — that if the body of people obtain votes, any number of votes, however small, it will be a step to the choice of members of their own religion: — that the House of Commons, in spite of the influence of nineteen parts in twenty of the landed interest now in their hands, will be composed in the whole, or in far the major part, of Papists; that this Popish House of Commons will instantly pass a law to confiscate all their estates, which it will not be in their power to save even by entering into that Popish party themselves, because there are prior claimants to be satisfied; — that as to the House of Lords, though neither Papists nor Protestants have a share in electing them, the body of the peerage will be so obliging and disinterested as to fall in with this exterminatory scheme, which is to forfeit all their estates, the largest part of the kingdom; and, to crown all, that his Majesty will give his cheerful assent to this causeless act of attainder[6] of his innocent and faithful Protestant subjects: — that they will be or are to be left without house or land, to the dreadful resource of living by their wits, out of which they are already frightened by the apprehension of this spoliation with which they are threatened: — that therefore they cannot so much as listen to any arguments drawn from equity or from national or constitutional policy; the sword is at their throats; beggary and famine at their door. See what it is to have a good look-out, and to see danger at the end of a sufficiently long perspective!

This is indeed to speak plain, though to speak nothing very new. The same thing has been said in all times and in all languages. The language of tyranny has been invariable; the general good is inconsistent with my personal safety. Justice and liberty seem so alarming to these gentlemen, that they are not ashamed even to slander their own titles; to calumniate, and call in doubt, their right to their own estates, and to consider themselves as novel disseizors,[7] usurpers, and intruders, rather than lose a pretext for becoming oppressors of their fellow-citizens, whom they (not I) choose to describe themselves as having robbed....

6. The extinction of a person's civil rights resulting from a sentence of death or outlawry on conviction for treason or felony.
7. Those who dispossess another of his lands.

from: SECOND LETTER TO SIR HERCULES LANGRISHE (1795)

[The debacle over the recall of Earl Fitzwilliam in 1795, who had come to Ireland with the promise of catholic emancipation and was replaced as lord lieutenant by the most bigoted members of the ascendancy whom he had sacked, left Burke in no doubt that the position of Ireland was now almost hopeless. The benefits of the proposed settlement were so great and had appeared so close that their disappearance was, in his view, tragic. He is speaking in the tones of a man who sees revolution in Ireland as almost inevitable, just after it had seemed, at last, avoidable.]

MY DEAR SIR,

.... In the Catholic Question I considered only one point. Was it at the time, and in the circumstances, a measure which tended to promote the concord of the citizens? I have no difficulty in saying it was; and as little in saying that the present concord of the citizens was worth buying, at a critical season, by granting a few *capacities*, which probably no one man now living is likely to be served or hurt by. When any man tells *you* and *me* that, if these places were left in the discretion of Protestant Crown, and these memberships in the discretion of Protestant electors, or patrons, we should have a Popish official system, and a Popish representation, capable of overturning the establishment, he only insults our understandings. When any man tells this to *Catholics*, he insults their understandings and he galls their feelings. It is not the question of the places and seats; it is the real hostile disposition, and the *pretended* fears, that leave stings in the minds of the people. I really thought that in the total of the late circumstances, with regard to persons, to things, to principles, and to measures, was to be found a conjunction favourable to the introduction, and to the perpetuation, of a general harmony, producing a general strength which to that hour Ireland was never so happy as to enjoy. My sanguine hopes are blasted, and I must consign my feeling on that terrible disappointment to the same patience in which I have been obliged to bury the vexation I suffered on the defeat of the other great, just, and honourable causes in which I have had some share; and which have given more of dignity than of peace and advantage to a long, laborious life. Though, perhaps, a want of success might be urged as a reason for making me doubt of the justice of the part I have taken, yet, until I have other lights than one side of the debate has furnished me, I must see things, and feel them too, as I see and feel them. I think I can hardly overrate the malignity of the principles of Protestant ascendency, as they affect Ireland; or of Indianism, as they affect these countries, and as they affect Asia; or of Jacobinism, as they affect all Europe, and the state of human society itself. The last is the greatest evil. But it readily combines with the others, and flows from them. Whatever breeds discontent at this time will produce that great master-mischief most infallibly. Whatever tends to persuade the people that the *few*, called by whatever name you please, religious or political, are of opinion that their interest is not compatible with that of the *many*, is a great point gained to Jacobinism. Whatever tends to irritate the talents of a country, which have at all times, and at these particularly, a mighty influence on the public mind, is of infinite service to that formidable cause. Unless where Heaven has mingled uncommon ingredients, of virtue in the composition — *quos meliore luto finxit præcordia Titan*[1] — talents naturally gravitate to Jacobinism. Whatever ill humours are afloat in the state, they will be sure to discharge themselves in a mingled torrent in the *cloacâ maximâ*[2] of Jacobinism. Therefore people ought well to look about them. First, the physicians are to take care that they do nothing to irritate this epidemical distemper. It is a foolish thing to have the better of the patient in a dispute. The complaint, or its cause, ought to be removed, and wise and lenient arts ought to precede the measures of vigour. They ought to be the *ultima*, not the *prima*, not the *tota* ratio[3] of a wise government. God forbid, that on a worthy occasion authority should want the means of force, or the disposition to use it. But where a prudent and enlarged policy does not precede it, and attend it too, where the hearts of the better sort of people do not go with the hands of the soldiery, you may call your constitution what you will, in effect it will consist of three parts, (orders, if you please,) —

1. 'Souls made of better clay by the kindlier art of the Titan.' Juvenal, *Satire* XIV, line 34.
2. The city sewers in Rome.
3. The final, not the primary nor total reason.

cavalry, infantry, and artillery, — and of nothing else or better.

I agree with you in your dislike of the discourses in Francis Street; but I like as little some of those in College Green.[4] I am even less pleased with the temper that predominated in the latter, as better things might have been expected in the regular family mansion of public discretion, than in a new and hasty assembly of unexperienced men, congregated under circumstances of no small irritation. After people have taken your tests, prescribed by yourselves as proofs of their allegiance, to be marked as enemies, traitors, or at best as suspected and dangerous persons, and that they are not to be believed on their oaths, we are not to be surprised if they fall into a passion, and talk, as men in a passion do, intemperately and idly.

The worst of the matter is this: you are partly leading, partly driving, into Jacobinism that description of your people whose religious principles — church polity, and habitual discipline — might make them an invincible dyke against that inundation. This you have a thousand mattocks and pick-axes lifted up to demolish. You make a sad story of the pope! — *O seri studiorum!*[5] — It will not be difficult to get many called Catholics to laugh at this fundamental part of their religion. Never doubt it. You have succeeded in part; and you may succeed completely. But in the present state of men's minds and affairs do not flatter yourselves that they will piously look to the head of our church in the place of that pope whom you make them forswear; and out of all reverence to whom you bully, and rail, and buffoon them. Perhaps you may succeed in the same manner with all the other tenets of doctrine, and usages of discipline, amongst the Catholics. But what security have you that in the temper and on the principles on which they have made this change, they will stop at the exact sticking-places you have marked in *your* articles? You have no security for anything, but that they will become what are called *Franco-Jacobins*, and reject the whole together. No converts now will be made in a considerable number from one of our sects to the other upon a really religious principle. Controversy moves in another direction.

Next to religion, *property* is the great point of Jacobin attack. Here, many of the debaters in your majority, and their writers, have given the Jacobins all the assistance their hearts can wish. When the Catholics desire places and seats, you tell them that this is only a pretext (though Protestants might suppose it just *possible* for men to like good places and snug boroughs for their own merits); but that their real view is to strip Protestants of their property. To my certain knowledge, till those Jacobin lectures were opened in the House of Commons, they never dreamt of any such thing; but now the great professors may stimulate them to inquire (on the new principles) into the foundation of that property, and of all property. If you treat men as robbers, why, robbers sooner or later they will become.

A third part of Jacobin attack is on *old traditionary constitutions*. You are apprehensive for yours, which leans from its perpendicular, and does not stand firm on its theory. I like parliamentary reforms as little as any man who has boroughs to sell for money, or for peerages, in Ireland. But it passes my comprehension, in what manner it is, that men can be reconciled to the *practical* merits of a constitution, the theory of which is in litigation, by being *practically* excluded from any of its advantages. Let us put ourselves in the place of these people, and try an experiment of the effects of such a procedure on our own minds. Unquestionably we should be perfectly satisfied when we were told that houses of parliament, instead of being places of refuge for popular liberty, were citadels for keeping us in order as a conquered people. These things play the Jacobin game to a nicety. Indeed, my dear Sir, there is not a single particular in the Francis Street declamations which has not, to your and to my certain knowledge, been taught by the jealous ascendants, sometimes by doctrine, sometimes by example, always by provocation. Remember the whole of 1781 and 1782 — in parliament and out of parliament; at this very day, and in the worst acts and designs, observe the tenor of the objections with which the College green orators of the ascendency reproach the Catholics. You have observed, no doubt, how much they rely on the affair of Jackson.[6] Is it not pleasant to hear Catholics

4. The Catholic Convention, sometimes called the 'Back Lane Parliament', was organized by Wolfe Tone and met in December 1792 at the Tailors' Hall in Francis Street, Dublin, to press for relief of the Penal Laws against catholics. The official Irish Houses of Parliament met at College Green, in the centre of Dublin.

5. 'O ye late learners!' Horace, *Satires*, I, x, 21.

6. Rev. William Jackson (1737-95), United Irishman. He was found guilty of high treason and poisoned himself in the dock.

reproached for a supposed connexion — with whom? — with Protestant clergymen! with Protestant gentlemen! with Mr. Jackson! — with Mr. Rowan,[7] &c. &c.! But *egomet mi ignosco*.[8] Conspiracies and treasons are privileged pleasures, not to be profaned by the impure and unhallowed touch of Papists. Indeed, all this will do, perhaps, well enough with detachments of dismounted cavalry and fencibles[9] from England. But let us not say to Catholics by way of *argument*, that they are to be kept in a degraded state, because some of them are no better than many of us Protestants. The thing I most disliked in some of their speeches (those I mean of the Catholics) was what is called the spirit of liberality, so much and so diligently taught by the ascendants, by which they are made to abandon their own particular interests, and to merge them in the general discontents of the country. It gave me no pleasure to hear of the dissolution of the committee.[10] There were in it a majority, to my knowledge, of very sober, well-intentioned men; and there were none in it but such who, if not continually goaded and irritated, might be made useful to the tranquillity of the country. It is right always to have a few of every description, through whom you may quietly operate on the many, both for the interests of the description, and for the general interest. Excuse me, my dear friend, if I have a little tried your patience. You have brought this trouble on yourself, by your thinking of a man forgot, and who has no objection to be forgot, by the world. These things we discussed together four or five and thirty years ago. We were then, and at bottom ever since, of the same opinion on the justice and policy of the whole, and of every part, of the penal system. You and I and everybody must now and then ply and bend to the occasion, and take what can be got. But very sure I am, that whilst there remains in the law any principle whatever which can furnish to certain politicians an excuse for raising an opinion of their own importance, as necessary to keep their fellow-subjects in order, the obnoxious people will be fretted, harassed, insulted, provoked to discontent and disorder, and practically excluded from the partial advantages from which the letter of the law does not exclude them.

Adieu! my dear Sir, and believe me very truly

Yours,

EDMUND BURKE.

Beaconsfield, May 26, 1795.

7. Archibald Hamilton Rowan (1751-1834), United Irishman. Sentenced to a term of imprisonment for sedition in 1794, he escaped to France, where he befriended Mary Wollstonecraft. The next year he went to America, where he was joined by Wolfe Tone and Napper Tandy.
8. 'I take no note of myself.' Horace, *Satires*, I, iii, 23.
9. Citizens who undertook military service in defence of their homeland.
10. The reference here is to the effective takeover of the old Catholic Committee by the Dublin Society of United Irishmen in 1792. Wolfe Tone took over from Richard Burke as agent for the committee.

Biography/Bibliography

LIFE. Born in Dublin, 1729. Entered Trinity College, 1744; helped found the Trinity College Historical Society; graduated 1749. In 1750, Burke went to London to study law at the Middle Temple. His career as author began in 1756. Married Jane Nugent in 1757 and became editor of the *Annual Register* in the following year, a post he retained until 1764. In 1759, Burke returned to Dublin as secretary to the Irish chief secretary, and stayed in this position until 1764, when he returned to London. In that year he became one of the original members of the Literary Club, founded by Samuel Johnson and including Goldsmith and Joshua Reynolds among its members. Introduced to the Marquis of Rockingham in 1765, Burke became his private secretary; after Rockingham became prime minister in 1765, he arranged that Burke be elected to parliament in January 1766. Although the government fell six months later, Burke had become the leading intelligence of the Rockingham Whig faction in opposition and quickly made his reputation as a political pamphleteer and speaker. In 1773, he visited Paris, where, besides seeing the Queen of France at a levee, he met some of the French intellectuals and was shocked by their atheism and licentiousness. He became the member for Bristol in 1774 and was much praised for his opposition to the government's American policy in the years 1775-81. At the end of this period he turned his attention to India and began his long pursuit of Warren Hastings, leading to the latter's trial and impeachment in the years 1788-95. Burke had a brief spell in government as paymaster-general, but his parliamentary reputation declined after the general election of 1784 and the entry of a new generation to the House of Commons. With the outbreak of the French Revolution, Burke began his last great campaign, earning a European reputation and irrevocably splitting the Whigs. France and Ireland preoccupied him in the last years of his life, darkened by his political fears and by the death of his son Richard in 1794. He died on 9 July 1797 at his house, Beaconsfield, near London.

CHIEF WRITINGS. *A Vindication of Natural Society* (1756); *A Philosophical Enquiry into the Origin of our Ideas of the Sublime and Beautiful* (1756; enlarged edition 1757); *An Account of the European Settlements in America* (1757); *Thoughts on the Causes of the Present Discontents* (1770); *Speech on American Taxation* (1774); *Speech on Conciliation with America* (1775, 1778); *Reflections on the Revolution in France* (1790); *Appeal from the Old to the New Whigs* (1791); *Speeches on the Impeachment of Warren Hastings*, with Introduction (1792).

Burke's writings on Ireland are usefully collected in Matthew Arnold (ed.), *Edmund Burke on Irish Affairs* (London: Macmillan, 1881). See also T. W. Copeland et al (eds), *The Correspondence of Edmund Burke* 10 vols (Cambridge University Press and Chicago University Press, 1958-71). Among the Collected Works, the best are *The Works of Edmund Burke* 8 vols (London: Bohn's British Classics, 1854-89) and *The Works of Edmund Burke*, rev. ed. 12 vols (Boston: Little, Brown, 1865-67).

BIOGRAPHY AND CRITICISM. Six biographies of Burke were published between 1798 and 1927, the best of which is that by James Prior, *The Life of the Right Honourable Edmund Burke*, 2nd ed. 2 vols (London,

1826). Of more modern biographies, the best are Philip Magnus, *Edmund Burke: A Life* (London: John Murray, 1939); Isaac Kramnick, *The Rage of Edmund Burke: Portrait of an Ambivalent Conservative* (New York: Basic Books, 1977); Stanley Ayling, *Edmund Burke: His Life and Opinions* (London: John Murray, 1988). Special studies include Thomas H. D. Mahoney, *Edmund Burke and Ireland* (Cambridge, Mass.: Harvard University Press, 1960); Thomas W. Copeland, *Our Eminend Friend Edmund Burke* (New Haven: Yale University Press, 1949); Donald C. Bryant, *Edmund Burke and His Literary Friends* (St Louis: Washington University Studies, New Series, Language and Literature, no. 9, 1939); Wecter Dixon, *Edmund Burke and His Kinsmen: A Study of the Statesman's Financial Integrity and Private Relationships* (Boulder, Colorado: University of Colorado Press, 1939).

Out of an immense bibliography, the following selection is recommended: J. T. Boulton, *The Language of Politics in the Age of Wilkes and Burke* (London: Routledge and Kegan Paul; Toronto: University of Toronto Press, 1963); F. P. Canavan, *The Political Reason of Edmund Burke* (Durham, North Carolina: Duke University Press, 1960); A. B. C. Cobban, *Edmund Burke and the Revolt Against the Eighteenth Century*, 2nd ed. (London: Allen and Unwin, 1929); C. B. Cone, *Burke and the Nature of Politics*, 2 vols (Lexington: University of Kentucky Press, 1957); C. P. Courtney, *Montesquieu and Burke* (Oxford: Oxford University Press, 1963); C. Parkin, *The Moral Basis of Burke's Political Thought* (Cambridge: Cambridge University Press, 1956); B. T. Wilkins, *The Problem of Burke's Political Philosophy* (Oxford: Oxford University Press, 1967).

ANDREW CARPENTER, SEAMUS DEANE, W.J. Mc CORMACK, *Editors*

Political Prose: Cromwell to O'Connell

In this section we can watch the evolution of a mentality that was to dominate all reflection on Irish political and cultural matters for over two centuries. The curse of Cromwell has hung more heavily on Irish memories than any other catastrophe, even including 1798 and the Famine. In part this was because he was so lethally effective, in part because he ratified protestant dominance with God's blessing and thereby imbued Irish life with a deep sectarian coloration which it has never entirely lost. Although this did not originate with Cromwell, he made it a permanent and inescapable feature of Irish experience. His success may have depended, in a practical sense, on artillery and superior military discipline. But in a deeper sense it came to be understood by the victors as a triumph of good over evil, of the civilized over the barbarous and, in brief, as a fulfilment of God's plan in Ireland.

This conviction consorted rather oddly with the protestant English claim to liberty and toleration. On paper, freedom of conscience might well be permitted and even encouraged in Ireland, but such toleration would not extend, as Cromwell makes clear, so far as to allow people to celebrate the Mass, for that would constitute permission to violate the tenets of protestantism by giving consent to the practice of evil superstition and idolatry. Similarly, to put men and women to the sword is not of itself a gratifying occupation — or so it is claimed — but it is justified if it prevents further sedition and acts as an awful example and warning to those who would persist in their wilful opposition to God's will. Thus, the appeal of the earlier rationale for colonialism is intensified by the Cromwellian campaign into a crusade on behalf of the divine plan for Ireland and against an opposition that is literally seen as diabolic. The catholic reaction to this, under Tyrconnell, and the subsequent protestant counter-reaction to the failed catholic attempt at revenge and restitution in those years, both derive from the furies, theological as well as military, of the Cromwellian campaign.

The turbulence of the years between 1640 and 1690 did produce a politically decisive settlement, although the question of land forfeiture and the larger question of the role and function of the colonists in Ireland continued to create a sense of insecurity that periodically intensified as the economy faltered and the constitutional arrangements were questioned. The conquest was in many ways complete. William Petty's 'Down Survey' (1673) and his *The Political Anatomy of Ireland* (1691) were the most discriminating responses to the new situation. Ireland was mapped and analysed so that it might be incorporated the more efficiently into the new scheme of things. Petty, like many others after him, supported a moderate line towards the catholics of Ireland because he recognized the advantages that would be gained from their conciliation and the equally great disadvantages that their hostility might create. Yet his writings, like those of Richard Cox, are generally free of any hint of such an emollient policy. If there was to be conciliation, it would be thinkable only after a harsh and well-organized campaign of dispossession. We can hear the note of anti-catholic bigotry in the polemics of Cox, whose vision of events in Ireland is characteristic of the fanatical London Whigs of 1689-90.

When the Irish parliament introduced the Penal Laws in the 1690s, it seemed that Irish society would remain wholly sectarian in its structure. Certainly, their effect was grievously felt throughout the century and their provisions created a political problem that grew even as the force of the laws receded. London was less inclined than Dublin to insist on the necessity of retaining the Penal Laws in anything like full force, but that itself was a signal indication of the failure in mutual understanding — which conditions in both countries conspired to aggravate — between the imperial and the colonial parliaments. The protestants of Ireland were still involved in the long colonizing enterprise that had begun at least as far back as the days of Elizabeth I. Yet it seemed that no organized view was ever formulated of what this enterprise required. The catholics were to be distrusted because they were catholics; but was any concerted effort to convert them to the reformed faith ever to be undertaken? They were to be distrusted because they still hankered after the dream of a Stuart restoration, to be brought about with the help of a foreign power that would invade Ireland. Yet was there any plan to convert them to the recognition of the virtues of the British system? Was their language to be suppressed or was it to be learned, if only for proselytizing purposes? None of these questions was clearly answered. In the absence of such answers, the colonists, or a powerful group among them, decided to provide one themselves. London's failure to hearken to them aroused their anger and they proceeded to negotiate for themselves a position that would bestow upon them a degree of independence sufficient to allow them to master their own destiny without ever entirely throwing off the protection of the neighbouring island. This protection, it was realized, was in the last resort necessary to secure their survival. It was a delicate, even impossible, political manoeuvre upon which the colonists embarked, from the days of Molyneux and Swift to those of Flood and Grattan. In the end, under the pressure of the great revolution in France, the situation was so transformed that the effort had to be abandoned. With the rebellion of 1798, it seemed to many protestants as though 1641 had come again. There never would be security, and liberty had become a dangerous revolutionary concept, French rather than English, with the power to mobilize the catholic populace to an unprecedented degree.

It was convenient for the victors to have a religious endorsement for their newly acquired wealth, property and power. Bigotry found in this a ready defence then and for a long time afterwards; but, within this set of sectarian considerations, there were other impulses and forces antithetical to such a degrading attitude. It was possible to believe in the necessity for the Penal Laws and, at the same time, to uphold the ideal of liberty and toleration won in the Glorious Revolution of 1688. Without penal legislation, the gains of that revolution could not be held. The gifts it provided were available to those who accepted the revolution settlement, to those who were, in a real sense, citizens of the commonwealth. After all, the belief that liberty and toleration, prosperity and cultural advancement were natural consequences of the revolution was not easily confined to the narrow purpose of justifying the expropriation and humiliation of the catholic Irish — or of their dissenting brethren, most of whom, their numbers swollen by a heavy emigration from a famished Scotland in the late 1690s, were to be found in the north of the island. That belief could and did take on a more generous and ample application.

The achievement of England in 1688 gave heart to the European continent throughout the eighteenth century in the various battles between the new enlightenment and the old despotisms — of which the Cromwellian kind was often cited as one example. The idea of citizenship was universalized. Man could become, in Goldsmith's famous (if not original) phrase, a citizen of the world. His claim to that citizenship rested in his desire to improve the human lot, by example or by exhortation. In protestant Ireland, that claim became both a proud and a troublesome possession. It was not only that a system of religious intolerance could not be compatible with the principles of the Enlightenment. For some it seemed that the constitutional arrangement between England and Ireland was equally incompatible with those principles, because it was an enslaving, rather than a liberating, relationship. The old arguments of men like Patrick Darcy and William Domville in favour of Irish parliamentary independence took on a fresh force and impetus in the changing conditions in which Molyneux wrote, and later was read, and in which Toland, Molesworth, Swift, Hutcheson, Lucas, Flood, Grattan and Burke all queried the basis of English rule in Ireland. In effect, these men wanted to modify, rather than to destroy, the basis of that rule. But the constitutional relationship could not be wholly separated from the political question of the catholics and their role in the nation. The failure to combine these questions, or to separate them, was to lead Anglo-Ireland far from its Enlightenment heritage.

Nevertheless, the right of the English parliament to legislate for Ireland and the exclusive claim to citizenship by any one religious faction were both assumptions that would be severely scrutinized by Irish protestant intellectuals. Francis Hutcheson, whose writings were to play such an important role later in the century in the Thirteen Colonies of America, described the link between sectarianism and despotism. Robert Molesworth refused to accept the conventional association between catholicism and despotism, citing protestant instances of this association to prove his case. Along with John Toland, these writers began to subvert the protestant claim to supremacy in Ireland in so far as that was based on religious grounds. Despite, or perhaps because of, their Irish origins and experience, they made a serious effort to secularize the idea of liberty and to detach it from the apocalyptic Cromwellian inheritance. To improve human existence as such, and to do it within the confines of one's own country first, became the avowed aim of that patriot group of Irish writers, orators and philosophers from Toland to Wolfe Tone. They adumbrated a noble programme of action, but existing conditions were altogether too limiting to allow for any hope of its being successfully translated into practice.

As for the catholic Irish, they had little choice but to find ways of surviving. In this they were moderately successful; something like an Irish catholic middle-class did emerge in the eighteenth century and, with that, a willingness to accept the new political order. Yet to enter into the political system, the catholics had to persuade their protestant counterparts (and sometimes themselves) that they too were members of an ancient traditional culture and, as such, were sufficiently 'civil' to be given political recognition. Their history and culture had been slandered and misunderstood as barbarous. It was necessary for them to disprove this widespread notion, current in Ireland since the sixteenth century, but recently given a new and brutal revision in the 'histories' of men like Sir John Temple and in the fundamentalist convictions of the Cromwellians and their descendants. The essentially aristocratic nature of the Gaelic order permitted many of its remaining bards and annalists to regard the new settlers with contempt, as people of no blood, as 'carpetbaggers', who had, nonetheless, taken over with an undeniable and irresistible completeness. But by mid-century, with the formation of the Catholic Committee and the early labours of Charles O'Conor of Belnagare, the catholics had found the double-barrelled argument, which was to be repeatedly fired for the next century. One barrel contained the antiquarian argument; the other contained the political plea. Supported by the continentally trained priests and by the Irish foundations at Louvain and Paris, the Irish catholics were able to claim for themselves a hallowed tradition that gave them cultural priority in the island and a veneration for the new political system that they believed should allow them political equality within it. Although this argument was conducted at first with tentativeness and caution, by Cornelius Nary, Charles O'Conor, Lord Kenmare and others, it gradually became more assertive and found full-blown articulation in the writings of the protestant radical, Wolfe Tone. And even though this version of the catholic cause was to be dismissed at that stage, it re-emerged, through a variety of antiquarian sidetracks, in the early crusades of Daniel O'Connell, the first great politician to exploit and organize the catholic superiority in numbers.

The anxiety of the catholics to prove, in petitions and pamphlets, that they were indeed the inheritors of a civilized tradition and therefore deserving of civic status, was both relentless and piteous. A much more aggressive and millennial tone dominates the literature in the Irish language, particularly the poetry. But in trying to display to others the record of Gaelic civilization, catholic intellectuals and writers were forced to recover some of the achievements of the past and thus to set in train a long series of investigations into Ireland's distant past, which were to bear strange fruit in the increasingly nationalistic atmosphere of late eighteenth-century romanticism. The uniqueness of the old civilization had to be stressed for polemical purposes. At first, this accorded with the century's growing, if troubled, interest in the diversity of human cultures, manifest in its fondness for travel literature and in its readiness to adopt various fads and fashions of exotic dress, furniture and the like — Chinese, Japanese, Celtic, even Red Indian. The Gaelic culture, like these, began by having the appeal of the exotic, but the study of it, conducted at times with professional skill and at times with a breathtaking amateurism and insouciance, culminated politically in making possession of or access to the Gaelic culture the foundation of the claim to be truly native. Antiquarianism was one of the sources of nationalism and its defence of cultural difference eventually became the source of those who began to speak of a corresponding political separatism. In effect, the exotic features of the Irish past gravitated more and more to the centre. Nationalism dealt in essences, fidelities, intuitive or ancestrally governed modes of identification. This was far removed from the more pragmatic and precise version of enlightenment citizenship. Wolfe Tone was as distant from this as, say, Swift or Molyneux. But nationalism, thoroughly identified with catholicism, became the domineering force, and the first catholic victory was to win cultural centrality long before achieving anything like political equality. The site of the later stages of that battle was the nineteenth and early twentieth centuries.

It would be possible to divide the selections given below into various categories. All those from Domville and Molyneux up to Grattan and Flood, who argued against the constitutional arrangements enshrined in Poynings's Law and the Declaratory Act, could be embraced under a heading such as 'Colonial Nationalism'. The defenders of the catholic position — MacCurtin, O'Conor, Nary and others — could be grouped together, as could all of those from Cromwell to Petty, Cox and others, as the expounders of the colonizing position. Tone, Emmet and O'Connell, perhaps Curran as well, exhibit a more militant spirit and could be seen as a group that had at least in common a militant hostility to the settlement established in 1688-89. Yet these groupings are at once too obvious and too exclusive. The interweaving of the various positions is too fine to allow for violent or sharp categorizations. A chronological sequence has at least the merit of showing a variety of positions without privileging any one. All these writings are, in one sense or another, about power and the retention or the regaining of it. It is possible to see a movement within the language from a theological-political vocabulary, belonging primarily to the seventeenth century, to the language of abstract rights and freedoms which became predominant in the era of the American and French Revolutions.

The rhetorical features of the prose represented in this section seem to embody in miniature some of the conventional accounts of the development in English prose style between the late seventeenth and the early nineteenth centuries. The reaction against the densely figurative prose of the seventeenth century, replete with political implications, leads to the plain style of the more 'enlightened' eighteenth century, in which the appeal to reason and the common reader is so strong that the language achieves a luminous ease and lucidity, entirely free of the jargon of extremists, specialists and fanatics, and unburdened by heavily allegorical figures and ingenious conceits. Yet, by the close of the century — and especially among orators, parliamentarians, advocates, condemned men like Robert Emmet — that easy simplicity of address, once so admired as the mark of the educated gentleman, has given way to a more complex style, in which classical references, opulent Ciceronian periods, elaborately pointed and frilled arguments, repetitive flourishes and self-consciously cadenced perorations seem to be the new order of the day. This appears to be even more the case in Ireland than in England. In part, the change can be explained in political terms.

By the 1780s, and most certainly by the 1790s, simplicity of address had begun to be suspect because it was so akin to the blunt forthrightness of the radical pamphleteer. It became a point of honour to indicate one's awareness of the endless complexity of human affairs by registering this in a prose of a comparable intricacy. Anything so delicate and complex had to be treated with circumspection before it could be interfered with; for the radical, whether he be a Wilkes, a Paine, a Cobbett or any one of a hundred others, rational inquiry dissolved the mystique of complexity, and action was as straightforward as words. The pedantically weighted style of the last decades of the century flourished in parliament and at the bar more vigorously than elsewhere. In Ireland, this general tendency was accentuated by the strong theatrical tradition, visible in Irish drama as in Irish oratory, and possibly the more vivid because it was, in each case, originating in a position of felt powerlessness. Neither Flood nor Grattan made much impression in the English parliament; the oratorical traditions there were quite different. Even Burke, especially in the late 1780s, had the gift of clearing the House as he embarked on one of his labyrinthine speeches. Sheridan is, perhaps, the figure in whom the dramatic and oratorical traditions are most happily embodied; but Emmet's performance in the dock and O'Connell's performances in court share the same self-conscious features of display. Only Tone preserves anything close to what was then already beginning to be called the 'democratic' style. However the phenomenon is understood, it is clear that the relationship between writing and speaking styles and the political position and context of the writer and speaker is an intimate one. It would be surprising if it were otherwise, especially in a country that had undergone so many prolonged crises over such a relatively short period. Further, the various forms of famous speeches, such as those of Grattan or Emmet, indicate to us the readiness with which such material could be reshaped for political purposes, either by the author or by his supporters. The style of greeting Ireland's independence or of greeting execution for Ireland's sake had, in the end, a great deal to do with the conception of Ireland which the later audiences for such speeches were thereby persuaded to reinvent for themselves.

OLIVER CROMWELL

(1599-1658)

from: LETTERS FROM IRELAND

RELATING THE SEVERAL GREAT SUCCESSES IT HATH PLEASED GOD TO GIVE UNTO THE PARLIAMENTS FORCES THERE, IN THE TAKING OF *DROGHEDA*, *TRYM*, *DUNDALK*, *CARLINGFORD*, AND THE NURY ....

(1649)

[When Oliver Cromwell landed in Ireland in July 1649, he brought not only a substantial army of foot and horse soldiers but also a train of modern artillery. This latter force was easily able to batter down the medieval walls of Irish towns, and the lightening progression of Cromwell's army of conquest throughout Ireland in 1649 and 1650 was due in no small part to it. Cromwell kept the English parliament posted on his progress, in order to solicit a continuation of supplies, and this letter is one of a series he sent to the speaker of the English parliament for this purpose. The vividness of Cromwell's own description of the siege of Drogheda is unparalleled in his writings; but more chilling is his justification for the indiscriminate massacre of the inhabitants as well as the defenders of the town: 'I am perswaded that this is a righteous Judgement of God upon these Barbarous wretches, who have imbrued their hands in so much innocent blood, and that it will tend to prevent the effusion of blood for the future ....' Since the ordinary inhabitants of Drogheda could not, by any stretch of the imagination, be considered guilty of imbruing their hands with innocent blood, it is clear that, in his progress through Ireland, Cromwell saw himself in the role of an avenging angel.]

For the Honorable *William Lenthal* Esq;
Speaker of the Parliament of *England*

SIR,

Your Army being safely arrived at *Dublin*, and the Enemy endeavouring to draw all his Forces together about *Trym* and *Tecroghan*[1] (as my Intelligence gave me;) from whence endeavors were used by the Marquis of *Ormond*, to draw *Owen Roe O Neal* with his Forces to his Assistance, but with what success I cannot yet learn.[2] I resolved after some refreshment taken for our weather beaten Men and Horses, and accommodations for a march, to take the Field; and accordingly upon Friday the Thirtieth of *August* last, Rendezvouzed with Eight Regiments of Foot, and Six of Horse, and some Troops of Dragoons, three miles on the Northside of *Dublin*; the Design was, To endeavor the Regaining of *Drogheda*, or tempting the Enemy, upon his hazard of the loss of that place, to fight. Your Army came before the Town upon Munday following, where having pitched, as speedy course

1. Town and townland in County Meath.
2. James Butler (1610-88), twelfth earl of Ormonde, the dominant figure in Irish political life between the reigns of Charles I and James II. As Charles I's chief representative in Ireland during the 1640s, Ormonde was opposed by the Catholic Confederation (including Owen Roe O'Neill (*c.* 1590-1649); by this time, however, the two sides had combined against the threat of the English parliamentary forces.

as could be was taken to frame our Batteries, which took up the more time, because divers of the Battering Guns were on Ship board: Upon Munday the Ninth of this instant, the Batteries began to play; whereupon I sent Sir *Arthur Ashton* the then Governor a Summons, To deliver the Town to the use of the Parliament of *England*; to the which I received no satisfactory Answer, but proceeded that day to beat down the Steeple of the Church on the Southside of the Town, and to beat down a Tower not far from the same place, which you will discern by the Card enclosed: Our Guns not being able to do much that day, It was resolved to endeavor to do our utmost the next day to make Breaches assaultable, and by the help of God to Storm them: The places pitched upon, were that part of the Town wall next a Church, called *St. Maries*; which was the rather chosen, because we did hope that if we did enter and possess that Church, we should be the better able to keep it against their Horse and Foot,[3] until we could make way for the entrance of our Horse, which we did not conceive that any part of the Town would afford the like advantage for that purpose with this. The Batteries planted were two, one was for that part of the Wall against the East end of the said Church, the other against the Wall on the Southside; being somewhat long in Battering, the Enemy made six Retrenchments, three of them from the said Church to Duleek Gate, and three from the East end of the Church to the Town wall, and so backward. The Guns after some two or three hundred shot, beat down the Corner Tower, and opened two reasonable good Breaches in the East and South wall. Upon Tuesday the tenth of this instant, about five of the clock in the evening, we begun the Storm, and after some hot Dispute, we entred about Seven or Eight hundred men, the Enemy disputing it very stifly with us; and indeed through the advantages of the place, and the courage God was pleased to give the Defenders, our men were forced to retreat quite out of the Breach, not without some considerable loss; Colonel *Cassel* being there shot in the Head, whereof he presently dyed, and divers Soldiers and Officers doing their duty, killed and wounded: There was a Tenalia[4] to flanker the South-wall of the Town, between *Duleek* Gate, and the Corner Tower before mentioned, which our men entred, wherein they found some forty or fifty of the Enemy, which they put to the sword, and this they held; but it being without[5] the Wall, and the Sally part[6] through the Wall into that Tenalia being choaked up, with some of the Enemy which were killed in it, it proved of no use for our entrance into the Town that way. Although our men that stormed the Breaches were forced to recoil, as before is expressed, yet being encouraged to recover their loss, they made a second attempt, wherein God was pleased to animate them, that they got ground of the Enemy, and by the goodness of God, forced him to quit his Entrenchments; and after a very hot dispute, the Enemy having both Horse and Foot, and we onely Foot within the Wall, the Enemy gave ground, and our men became masters; but of their Retrenchments and the Church, which indeed although they made our entrance the more difficult, yet they proved of excellent use to us, so that the Enemy could not annoy us with their Horse, but thereby we had advantage to make good the ground, that so we might let in our own Horse, which accordingly was done, though with much difficulty; the Enemy retreated divers of them into the Mill-Mount, a place very strong and of difficult access, being exceeding high, having a good graft[7] and strongly Pallisadoed;[8] the Governor Sir *Arthur Ashton*, and divers considerable Officers being there, our men getting up to them, were ordered by me to put them all to the Sword; and indeed being in the heat of action, I forbade them to spare any that were in Arms in the Town, and I think that night they put to the sword about two thousand men, divers of the Officers and Soldiers being fled over the Bridge into the other part of the Town, where about One hundred of them possessed St. *Peters* Church Steeple, some the West Gate, and others, a round strong Tower next the Gate, called St. *Sundays*: These being summoned to yield to mercy, refused; whereupon I ordered the Steeple of St. *Peters* Church to be fired, where one of them was heard to say in the midst of the flames, *God damn me, God confound me, I burn, I burn*; the next day the other two Towers were summoned,[9] in one of which was

3. i.e. horse- and foot-soldiers.
4. A low fortification to protect the south wall from the side.
5. i.e. outside.
6. Usually spelled 'sallyport': an opening in a fortified place for troops to pass through.
7. A ditch or moat.
8. defended with a pallisade, a strong fence of pointed stakes.
9. surrendered.

about six or seven score, but they refused to yield themselves; and we knowing that hunger must compel them, set onely good Guards to secure them from running away, until their stomacks were come down: from one of the said Towers, notwithstanding their condition, they killed and wounded some of our men; when they submitted, their Officers were knockt on the head, and every tenth man of the Soldiers killed, and the rest Shipped for the *Barbadoes*; the Soldiers in the other Town[10] were all spared, as to their lives onely, and Shipped likewise for the *Barbadoes*. I am perswaded that this is a righteous Judgement of God upon these Barbarous wretches, who have imbrued their hands in so much innocent blood, and that it will tend to prevent the effusion of blood for the future, which are the satisfactory grounds to such Actions, which otherwise cannot but work remorse and regret. The Officers and Soldiers of this Garison, were the flower of all their Army; and their great expectation was, That our attempting this place, would put fair to ruine us; they being confident of the Resolution of their men, and the advantage of the place; if we had divided our Force into two quarters, to have Besieged the North Town and the South Town, we could not have had such a correspondency between the two parts of our Army, but that they might have chosen to have brought their Army, and have fought with which part they pleased, and at the same time have made a Salley[11] with two thousand men upon us, and have left their walls manned, they having in the Town the numbers specified in this inclosed, by some say near Four thousand. Since this great Mercy vouchsafed to us, I sent a Party of Horse and Dragoons to *Dundalk*, which the Enemy quitted, and we are possessed of; as also another Castle they deserted between *Trym* and *Drogheda*, upon the *Boynes*. I sent a Party of horse and Dragoons to a House within five miles of *Trym*, there being then in *Trym* some Scots Companies which the Lord of *Ardes*[12] brought to assist the Lord of *Ormond*; but upon the News of *Drogheda* they ran away, leaving their great Guns behinde them, which we also have possessed. And now give me leave to say how it comes to pass that this work is wrought; It was set upon some of our hearts, that a great thing should be done, not by power, or might, but by the Spirit of God; and is it not so clear? That which caused your men to Storm so couragiously, it was the Spirit of God, who gave your men Courage, and took it away again, and gave the Enemy Courage, and took it away again, and gave your men Courage again, and therewith this happy Success; and therefore it is good that God alone have all the Glory. It is remarkable, that these people at the first set up the Mass in some places of the town that had been Monasteries; but afterwards grew so insolent, that the last Lords day before the Storm,[13] the Protestants were thrust out of the great Church, called *St. Peters*, and they had publique Mass there; and in this very place near One thousand of them were put to the Sword, flying thither for safety: I believe all their Fryers were knockt on the head promiscuously, but two, the one of which was Father *Peter Taaff* (Brother to the Lord *Taaff*)[14] whom the Soldiers took the next day, and made an end of; the other was taken in the Round Tower, under the repute of Lieutenant, and when he understood that the Officers in that Tower had no quarter, he confessed he was a Fryer, but that did not save him. A great deal of loss in this business, fell upon Col: *Hewson*, Col: *Cassel*, and Colonel *Ewers* Regiments; Colonel *Ewers* having two Field-Officers in his Regiment shot, Colonel *Cassel* and a Captain of his Regiment slain, Colonel *Hewsons* Captain-Lieutenant slain; I do not think we lost One hundred men upon the place, though many be wounded. I most humbly pray, the Parliament will be pleased this Army may be maintained, and that a consideration may be had of them, and of the carrying on of the Affairs here, as may give a speedy issue to this work, to which there seems to be a marvellous fair opportunity offered by God. And although it may seem very chargeable to the State of *England* to maintain so great a Force, yet surely to stretch a little for the present, in following Gods Providence, in hope the charge will not be long, I trust it will not be thought by any (that have no irreconcileable or malicious Principles) unfit for me to move for a

10. A misprint for 'tower'.
11. Usually spelled 'sally': a sudden rush.
12. Hugh Montgomery (*c.*1623-63), 3rd viscount of Ards.

13. i.e. Cromwell's storming of the town.
14. Theobald, 2nd viscount (Taaff (died 1677). An uncle of Lord Taaff, Lucas, as governor of New Ross, was forced to surrender the town to Cromwell in October 1649. It was to him that Cromwell wrote (in reply to a request that the townspeople of New Ross should have liberty of conscience): 'For that which you mention concerning liberty of conscience, I meddle not with any mans conscience; But if by liberty of conscience, you mean a liberty to exercise the Mass, I judge it best to use plain dealing, and to let you know, Where the Parliament of *England* have power, that will not be allowed of.'

constant supply, which in humane probability, as to outward means, is most likely to hasten and perfect this work; and indeed, if God please to finish it here, as he hath done in *England*, the War is like to pay itself. We keep the Field much, our Tents sheltring us from the wet and cold, but yet the Country sickness[15] overtakes many, and therefore we desire recruits, and some fresh Regiments of Foot may be sent us; for it is easily conceived by what the Garisons already drink up, what our field Army will come to, if God shall give more Garisons into our hands.[16] Craving pardon for this great trouble, I rest,

Your most humble Servant,
Dublin, Sept. 17. 1649 O. CROMWEL

15. Probably dysentery.

16. Every time a new garrison was needed to man a captured fort, Cromwell's army was depleted by that number.

WILLIAM DOMVILLE

(died 1689)

from: A DISQUISITION . . . CONCERNING AN ACT IN *ENGLAND* BINDING *IRELAND* . . . . (1660)

[The relationship between the legislatures of England and Ireland was a major issue during the whole period of English rule in Ireland. The key question was whether Ireland had been conquered by Henry II in 1171, in which case its parliament had no rights, or whether the country had voluntarily accepted Henry as its king, in which case the Irish parliament did have rights. Poynings's Law of 1497, which asserted that the heads of all bills debated in the Irish parliament had to be approved by the English privy council, seemed to settle the question in practical terms since it gave the English parliament an effective right of veto over the Irish parliament. Yet this right was constantly challenged by historians, judicial experts and political leaders of both the 'English in Ireland' and the native Irish themselves.

In the early 1640s the matter became a burning issue, and a number of pamphlets appeared, including Patrick Darcy's important *Argument delivered . . . by the express order of the House of Commons* (Waterford, 1643). Cromwell's reconquest of Ireland, of course, put the matter out of immediate concern, but on the restoration of the monarchy in 1660, the new attorney general, William Domville, immediately wrote a *Disquisition* on 'the great question' of whether an act passed by the English parliament was to be considered binding on Ireland. His work was never published, but the manuscript was used by his son-in-law, William Molyneux, in his famous *The Case of Ireland* . . . . (1698). Domville, like Molyneux, was much exercised by constitutional precedents, but also (again like Molyneux) allowed himself to question the morality of the English position.

The text is taken from TCD MS. 890.]

In 10: H.4 it was Enacted in Ireland that Statutes made in England should not be of force in Ireland unless they were allowed & published by the parliament of Ireland & the like Statute was made 29:H.6 (*vide* the Collection of Irish Statutes p. 67.) In the Tenth year of H:7: the parliament which was then lately held at Drogheda before Sr Christopher Preston, Deputy to Jasper Duke of Bedford, Lieutenant of Ireland was Declared void for this reason that there was noe generall summons to all the Countyes of Ireland to meet at that parliament but onely to foure, for which cause amongst others it was adjudged void and of noe effect, . . . & if actes of parliament made in Ireland shall not bind that people because some Countyes were omitted, how much less shall those actes made in England bind either their persons or estates whereat noe one County or persons of that Kingdome is present. . . .

Can the king make actes of parliament in England to bind his subjectes of Ireland without theire consent, & can hee make noe actes in Ireland with theire consent which may priviledge them in any Sorte? This were to argue the parliament of Ireland to be wholy Illusory & of noe force, though the king has as absolute power to priviledge his subjectes by his consent in the parliament of Ireland as he hath in this Kingdome, & amongst the people of England.

CHARLES II

(1630-85)

from: HIS MAJESTY'S GRACIOUS DECLARATION FOR THE SETTLEMENT OF HIS KINGDOM OF IRELAND .... (1662)

[The restoration of Charles II in 1660 was accompanied by the restoration of the Church of Ireland to the position of established church and by a new land settlement. It was hoped that the latter would clarify the confusions of a situation in which land had been constantly granted and forfeited, and regranted and reforfeited over the preceding thirty years. However, despite the resounding rhetoric of the 'gracious declaration', it is clear that the complexities of Irish land tenure proved too much for the legislators of the time, as is implied in the last paragraph.]

His Majesty's gracious declaration for the settlement of his kingdom of Ireland, and satisfaction of the several interests of adventurers, soldiers, and other his subjects there.

Charles the second, by the grace of God, King of England, Scotland, France and Ireland, defender of the faith, etc. To all our loving subjects of our kingdom of Ireland, of what degree or quality soever, greeting. It having pleased Almighty God out of His great mercy and compassion towards us, and all our subjects, to restore us in so wonderful a manner to each other, and with so wonderful circumstances of affection and confidence in each other as must for ever fill our hearts (if we are in any degree sensible of such blessings) with an humble and grateful acknowledgment of the obligation we owe to His Divine Providence, that He would vouchsafe to work that miracle for us Himself, which no endeavours of our own could bring to pass. We think it agreeable to the just sense we have, and ought to have of the good affection of all our good subjects, who have contributed so much in bringing this unspeakable blessing upon us and themselves, that we acknowledge that our good subjects in our kingdom of Ireland have born a very good part in procuring this happiness, ... however it was not easy for us to make any public declaration with reference to that our kingdom, there being many difficulties in the providing for, and complying with the several interests and pretences there, which we were bound in honour and justice in some degree to take care of, and which were different from the difficulties we were to contend within this kingdom; we well knew the acts of parliament which had formerly past for the security of the adventurers in that kingdom, and had heard of the proceedings which had been thereupon, by which very many officers, soldiers, and others, as well of this, as that our kingdom were in possession of a great part of the lands of that our kingdom, and of whose interests we resolve to be very careful.

II. We well remember the cessation, and the peace which our royal father of blessed memory had been forced, during the late troubles, to make with the Irish subjects of that our kingdom, by which he was compelled to give them a full pardon for what they had before done amiss upon their return to their duties, and their promise of giving his majesty a vigorous assistance, and that from that time divers persons of honour and quality had not (that we know or have heard of) swerved from their allegiance towards him or us. We could not forget the peace that ourself was afterwards necessitated to make with our said subjects, in the time when they who wickedly usurped the authority in this kingdom, had erected that odious court for the taking away of the life of our dear father; and then no body can wonder that we were desirous, though upon difficult conditions, to get such an united power of our own subjects, as might have been able, with God's blessing, to have prevented that infamous and horrible parricide.

III. And therefore we could not but hold ourself obliged to perform what we owe by that peace, to those who had honestly and faithfully performed what they had promised to us, though we and they were miserably disappointed of the effect of those promises, by an unhappy part of them which foolishly forfeited all the grace which they might have expected from us....

VI. And therefore in the first place, in order to a settlement of that interest claimed by the adventurers, although the present estates and possessions they enjoy, if they were examined by the strict letter of the law, would prove very defective and invalid, as being no ways pursuant to those acts of parliament upon which they pretend to be founded, but rather seem to be a structure upon their subsequent assent, both to different mediums and ends than the observance of those, yet we being always more ready to consult (where the prejudice can only reflect upon ourself) with our natural inclinations to mercy (we praise God we can say so) than with the positive reason of law, we do hereby declare, that all the lands, tenements and hereditaments, of which all or any of the adventurers were possessed [on] 7 May 1659 having been allotted or set out to them or enjoyed by them as adventurers in satisfaction of and for their adventures, shall be confirmed and made good to them, their heirs and assigns for ever....

XVI. And whereas we understand, that by the late usurped powers, during the distempers, of these times, several Irish proprietors of the popish religion, have been dispossessed of their estates merely for being papists, and have sued out decrees, and are possessed of lands in the province of Connaught, and county of Clare, in compensation of their former estates, ... we declare, that all innocent papists, being such as shall prove themselves to have been faithful and loyal unto, and never acted against our royal father or ourself since 22 October, 1641, though they have sued out decrees, and are possessed of lands in the province of Connaught, or county of Clare, in lieu of their former estates, shall notwithstanding be restored to their said estates by 2 May 1661....

XVII. Provided also, that whatsoever adventurer or soldier that shall be removed from his present possession, to make room for any such papist, shall forthwith have a reprise of equal value ... in other forfeited lands.

XVIII. Provided always, that whereas the corporations of Ireland are now planted with English, who have considerably improved at their own charges, and brought trade and manufacture into that our kingdom and by their settlement there do not a little contribute to the peace and settlement of that country, the disturbing or removal of which English would in many respects be very prejudicial, that all such of the popish religion, of any corporations in Ireland, who have been for public security dispossessed of their estates within any corporation, shall be forthwith reprised in forfeited lands, tenements and hereditaments, near the said corporations, ...

XXVIII. And though some, not sensible of the great perplexities we have laboured under to reconcile these jarring interests, may infer that we judge persons fitting to be restored to their estates, yet the limitation of a previous reprisal may eclipse much of our grace, to this we say, that the laying of the foundations is not now before us, when we might design the model of the structure answerable to our own thoughts; ...

WILLIAM PETTY

(1623-87)

from:
THE POLITICAL ANATOMY OF IRELAND (1672; published 1691)

[The best-known account of Ireland in the reign of Charles II is without a doubt William Petty's *The Political Anatomy of Ireland*. Petty, a child prodigy who had obtained a number of academic appointments at Oxford at an early age, first came to Ireland in 1652 as physician general to the parliamentary army. From then until his death, he lived partly in Ireland and had a considerable influence on many aspects of Irish life since his skills encompassed most branches of learning, including map-making and experimental science. (He was the first president of the Dublin Philosophical Society.)

Petty, like most of his fellow countrymen, regarded Ireland as an English colony, and the solutions he proposed to Ireland's problems in the *Anatomy* are those of a manager. In many ways, his thinking and rhetoric are inherited from the world of Spenser's contemporaries, but his proposals for bringing about union between England and Ireland by forced migration between the two countries are extreme even by the standards of the earlier Anglo-Irish colonists.]

CHAP. V

Of the future Settlement of Ireland, *Prorogation of Rebellions, and its Union with* England

The *English* invaded *Ireland* about 500 years since; at which time, if the *Irish* were in number about 1,200,000 *Anno* 1641, they were but 600,000 in number, 200 years ago, and not above 300,000 at the same time of their Invasion; for 300,000 People will, by the ordinary course of Generation, become 1,200,000 in 500 years; allowance being made for the extraordinary Effects of epidemical Diseases, Famines, Wars, &c.

There is at this Day no Monument or real Argument that, when the *Irish* were first invaded, they had any Stone-Housing at all, any Money, any Foreign Trade, nor any Learning but the Legend of the Saints, Psalters, Missals, Rituals, *&c. viz.* nor Geometry, Astronomy, Anatomy, Architecture, Enginery, Painting, Carving, nor any kind of Manufacture, nor the least use of Navigation; or the Art Military.

Sir *John Davys*[1] hath expressed much Wit and Learning, in giving the Causes why *Ireland* was in no measure reduced to *English* Government, till in Queen *Elizabeth*'s Reign, and since; and withal offers several means, whereby what yet remains to be done, may be still effected.

The Conquest made by the *English*, and described in the Preamble of the Act of Parliament past *Ann.* 1662. for the Settlement of *Ireland*, gave means for any thing that had been reasonable of that kind; but their Forfeiters being abroad, and suffering with His Majesty from the same usurping hands, made some diversion.

Wherefore (*Rebus sic stantibus*)[2] what is now to be done is the Question, *viz.* What may be done by natural possibility, if Authority saw it fit?

Some furious Spirits have wished, that the *Irish* would rebel again, that they might be put to the Sword. But I declare, that motion to be not only impious and inhumane, but withal frivolous and pernicious even to them who have rashly wish'd for those occasions.

That the *Irish* will not easily rebel again, I believe from the memory of their former Successes, especially of the last, had not many Providences interpos'd; and withal from the consideration of these following Particulars, *viz.*

1. That the *British Protestants* and *Church* have three Fourths of all the Lands; five Sixths of all the Housing; nine Tenths of all the Housing in wall'd Towns and Places of Strength, two Thirds of the Foreign Trade. That 6 of 8 of all the *Irish* live in a brutish, nasty Condition, as in Cabins, with neither Chimney, Door, Stairs, nor Window, feed chiefly upon Milk and Potatoes, whereby their Spirits are not dispos'd for War. And that although there be in *Ireland* 8 *Papists* for 3 others; yet there are far more Soldiers, and Soldier-like Men of this latter and lesser Number, than of the former.

2. That his Majesty, who formerly could do nothing for, and upon *Ireland*, but by the help of *England*, hath now a Revenue upon the Place, to maintain, if he pleases, 7000 Men in Arms, besides a Protestant Militia of 25000 more, the most whereof are expert in War.[3]

3. That the *Protestants* have Housing enough within Places of strength within 5 Miles of the Seafide, to receive and protect, and harbour every Man, Woman, and Child belonging to them, and have also places of strength of their own properly so situate in all parts of *Ireland*, to which they can easily travel the shortest day of the year.

4. That being able to secure their Persons, even upon all sudden Emergencies, they can be easily supplied out of *England* with Food sufficient to maintain them, till they have burnt 160,000 of their afore-described Cabins, not worth 50,000 *l.* destroy'd Stacks and Haggards[4] of Corn, and disturbed their Tillage, which the embody'd *British* can soon and easily atchieve.

5. That a few Ships of War, whereof the *Irish* have none, nor no skill or Practice of Navigation, can hinder their relief from all Foreign help.

6. That few Foreigners can help them if they

1. See above p. 216.
2. 'as things stand.'

3. Following the restoration of Charles II, the Irish finances were restructured and internal excise revenue was granted in perpetuity to the king. This raising of funds in Ireland in theory enabled the monarch to maintain an Irish army there at the expense of Irish taxpayers; previously Irish armies had been paid for by Westminster.
4. Sheds or yards full of stacked corn or hay.

would. But that none, not the King of *France*, can gain advantage by so doing, even tho' he succeeded. For *England* hath constantly lost these 500 years by their medling with *Ireland*. And at this day, than when *Ireland* was never so rich and splendid, it were the advantage of the *English* to abandon their whole Interest in that Country; and fatal to any other Nation to take it, as hath been elsewhere (as I think) demonstrated; and the advantage of the Landlords of *England*, to give them the Equivalent of what they should so quit out their own Estates in *England*.

Lastly, Let the *Irish* know, that there are, ever were, and will be men discontented with their present Conditions in *England*, and ready for any Exploit and Change, more than are sufficient to quell any Insurrection they can make and abide by.

Wherefore, declining all Military means of settling and securing *Ireland* in peace and plenty, what we offer shall tend to the transmuting one People into the other, and the thorough union of Interests upon natural and lasting Principles; of which I shall enumerate several, tho' seemingly never so uncouth and extravagant.

1. If *Henry* the IId. had or could have brought over all the People of *Ireland* into *England*, declining the Benefit of their Land; he had fortified, beautified, and enrich'd *England*, and done real Kindness to the *Irish*. But the same Work is near four times as hard now to be done as then; but it might be done, even now, with advantage to all Parties.

2. Whereas there are now 300,000 *British*, and 800,000 *Papists*, whereof 600,000 live in the wretched way above mentioned: If an Exchange was made of but about 200,000 *Irish*, and the like number of *British* brought over in their rooms,[5] then the natural strength of the *British* would be equal to that of the *Irish*; but their Political and Artificial strength three times as great; and so visible, that the *Irish* would never stir upon a National or Religious Account.

3. There are among the 600,000 above-mentioned of the poor *Irish*, not above 20,000 of unmarried marriageble Women; nor would above two thousand *per Ann*,[6] grow and become such. Wherefore if one half of the said Women were in one year, and the other half the next transported into *England*, and disposed one to each Parish, and as many *English* brought back and married to the *Irish*, as would improve their Dwelling but to an House and Garden of *3 l.* value, the whole Work of natural Transmutation and Union would in 4 or 5 years be accomplished.

The Charge of making the Exchange would not be 20,000 *l. per Ann.* which is about 6 Weeks Pay of the present or late Armies in *Ireland*.

If the *Irish* must have Priests, let the number of them, which is now between 2 and 3 thousand Secular and Regulars, be reduced to the competent number of 1000, which is 800 Souls to the pastorage of each Priest; which should be known persons, and *English-men*, if it may be. So as that when the Priests, who govern the Conscience, and the Women, who influence other powerful Appetites, shall be *English*, both of whom being in the Bosom of the Men, it must be, that no massacring of *English*, as heretofore, can happen again. Moreover, when the Language of the Children shall be *English*, and the whole Oeconomy of the Family *English*, *viz.* Diet, Apparel, *&c.* the Transmutation will be very easy and quick.

Add hereunto, That if both Kingdoms were under one Legislative Power and Parliament, the Members whereof should be proportionable in Power and Wealth of each Nation, there would be no danger such a Parliament should do any thing to the prejudice of the *English* Interest in *Ireland*; nor could the *Irish* ever complain of partiality, when they shall be freely and proportionably represented in all Legislatures.

5. i.e. in exchange.

6. i.e. per annun.

RICHARD COX
(1650-1733)

from:

HIBERNIA ANGLICANA:
OR THE HISTORY OF IRELAND FROM THE CONQUEST THEREOF BY THE ENGLISH TO THIS PRESENT TIME
(1689-90)

[Even before the death of Charles II in 1685, Irish catholics were hoping that his brother, the Duke of York, who was to succeed to the throne as James II and who was openly a catholic, would reverse the excesses of protestant rule in Ireland and restore rights to catholics. However, when James did succeed, he moved very slowly to improve the lot of his Irish catholic subjects, and it was not until 1687, and the appointment of Richard Talbot, earl of Tyrconnell, as lord lieutenant, that matters began to change. Tyrconnell began to shift the balance of power and appointed catholics to many positions of authority within the country. In 1688, James II was forced to flee from England to France and was succeeded on the English throne by the protestant William of Orange, ruling jointly with James's protestant daughter, Mary. From his exile in France, James planned to use Ireland as a base from which to recapture England, and Tyrconnell hastened the arming of Irish catholics to prepare for this possibility. From 1687 to 1690, Irish protestants became hysterically alarmed at the rapidly improving position of Irish catholics and at their own decline. Many Irish protestants fled to London and joined the increasing pressure that was being put upon William to invade Ireland with a protestant army and defeat James's catholic supporters. This pressure became even stronger when James himself landed in Ireland in March 1689.

One of the most vocal of those urging William to conquer Ireland at this time was Richard Cox, an English MP who later became attorney general of Ireland. His *Hibernia Anglicana* is of considerable interest for its use of Irish history as a base from which to justify political arguments in the present. In his book, Cox set out to prove that history showed Ireland to have been totally uncivilized before the arrival of the English, and the Irish to be merely barbarous savages; thus it was the pious duty of a civilized protestant prince to deliver the Irish from, as it were, themselves. 'The Irish are', as he repeated in one of the most memorable phrases of Irish historiography, 'beholding to God for being conquered.']

TO THEIR
MOST EXCELLENT MAJESTIES
WILLIAM
AND
MARY,
BY THE GRACE OF GOD,
KING AND QUEEN
OF
ENGLAND, SCOTLAND, FRANCE AND
IRELAND;
DEFENDERS OF THE FAITH, *&C.*

May it please Your Majesties,

I should not presume to lay this Treatise at Your Royal Feet, but that it concerns a Noble Kingdom, which is one of the most considerable Branches of Your Mighty Empire.

It is of great Advantage to it, that it is a *Subordinate* Kingdom to the Crown of *England*; for it is from that Royal Fountain that the Streams of Justice, Peace, Civility, Riches and all other Improvements have been derived to it; so that the Irish are (as *Campion*[1] says) beholding to God for being conquered: And yet *Ireland* has been so blind in this Great Point of its true Interest, that the Natives have managed almost a continual War with the English, ever since the first Conquest thereof; so that it has cost Your Royal Predecessors an unspeakable Mass of Blood and Treasure to preserve it in due Obedience.

But no Cost can be too great where the Prize is of such Value; and whoever considers the Situation, Ports, Plenty, and other Advantages of *Ireland*, will confess, That it must be retained at what rate soever; because if it should come into an Enemy's Hands, *England* would find it impossible to *flourish*; and perhaps difficult to *subsist* without it.

To demonstrate this Assertion, it is enough to say, That *Ireland* lies in the *Line of Trade*, and that all the English Vessels that sail to the *East, West* and *South*, must, as it were, *run the Gauntlet* between the

1. A misquotation from chapter 6 of Edmund Campion's history of Ireland (1571), edited and published by James Ware (Dublin, 1633).

Harbours of *Brest* and *Baltimore*:[2] And I might add, That the Irish Wool being transported, would soon ruine the English-Clothing-Manufacture....

But it is needless to tell your Majesties, That *Ireland* must not be separated from *England*; or to solicit your speedy Reduction of that Kingdom, since the loss of it is incompatible with Your *Glory*; and to suffer the Ruin of four hundred thousand Irish Protestants, meerly for their adherence to Your Majesties and their Religion, is inconsistent with your *Goodness*.

But, in Truth, the Recovery of *Ireland* was not proper for Your Majesty's Undertaking, until it became difficult beyond the Hopes of others; any Body can do easie things, but it is Your Majesty's peculiar Talent to atchieve what all the rest of the World think Impossible: Your Majesty did so, in buoying up a sinking *State*,[3] and restoring it to a more Glorious Condition than ever it was in before: And Your Majesty did so again, in retrieving from Ruine two expiring Kingdoms, that were at their last Gasp;[4] and the Recovery of the third, is all that remains to consummate your *Glory*, and make You the Darling both of Fame and of Fortune.

And when that is done, *Madam*, the bright Example of your Majesty's Virtue and Piety will influence that degenerate Nation to such a degree of Reformation and Religion, as will restore that Kingdom to its ancient Appellation, and *Ireland* will again be called, *Insula Sacra*.[5]

That Your Majesty's Glorious Designs, for the Advantage of *England*, and the Recovery of *Ireland*, for the Propagation of the Protestant Religion, and for the Good of Mankind, may be blessed with Success, suitable to Your Majesty's Generous and Pious Intentions: And that Your Majesties long and happy Reign here may be crowned with Everlasting Happiness hereafter, shall be the fervent as well as daily Prayers of,

May it please Your Majesties,
Your Majesties most Dutiful,
most Loyal,
and most devoted Subject,
R. COX

2. Brest: a port in Brittany; Baltimore: a small port in County Cork, in the south-west of Ireland.
3. i.e. England under the rule of James II.
4. i.e. Scotland and Wales.
5. Sacred Island.

WILLIAM KING

(1650-1729)

from: THE STATE OF THE PROTESTANTS OF IRELAND .... (1691)

[If the battle of the Boyne (July 1690) re-established protestant hegemony in Ireland, it also left a question-mark over the loyalty of those protestants who had remained in the country during the reign of James II. While they argued that they had remained to prepare for the return of a protestant monarch, they could be seen as traitors or, at the very least, collaborators. William King, at this time dean of St Patrick's, Dublin, and later bishop of Derry and archbishop of Dublin, undertook to vindicate the behaviour of these Irish protestants in a book that appeared in London in 1691, *The State of the Protestants of Ireland under the late King James's Government*. King's method was to collect many thousands of detailed incidences of unlawful, aggressive or threatening behaviour by catholics towards protestants during the previous four years and to draw general conclusions from his examples. In the following passage (Chapter III, section vii), he is concerned with 'King James's destructive proceedings against the liberties of his Protestant subjects'.]

There is no worldly thing more valuable to Man than Liberty. Many prefer it to life; and few can live long without it. 'Tis the Darling of our Laws, and there is nothing of which they are more tender. But the Protestants of *Ireland* from the very beginning of King *James*'s Reign, had their Liberties invaded, and at last intirely destroyed. 'Twas observable, that at his coming to the Crown he made no Proclamation for a general Pardon, as has been usual with Kings; neither did he pass any Act of Grace in his first Parliament, which gave a fair opportunity to the Papists of *Ireland* to revenge themselves on their Protestant Neighbors. No sooner had they gotten Judges and Juries that would believe them, but they began a Trade of Swearing, and ripping up what they pretended their Neighbors had said of His late Majesty, whilst Duke of *York* some years before, especially in time of the Popish Plot.[1] The new Justices of the Peace were eager to exercise their Offices, and therefore on the slightest occasion, bound over and committed their Protestant Neighbors, many times without any reason at all; at least, without any given in their Warrants: it was time enough to invent some against the next Assizes....

Upon this account Perjuries became so common, that if a Tenant owed his Protestant Landlord his Rent, he payed him by swearing him into a Plot, or by fixing on him some Treasonable or Seditious Words. If a Papist had any former Quarrel with his Protestant Neighbor, or owed him Money, he paid him in the same Coin. Many were indicted by these Contrivances; many found guilty, and excessively fin'd; some were imprisoned for their Fines, not being able to satisfie the King, who seised both their Bodies and Estates. Hardly any County in *Ireland* was free from numerous Indictments of this kind, and very few Country Gentlemen escaped being accused. Great numbers were indicted and found guilty in the Counties of *Wexford* and *Wicklow*, to the number at least of sixty; the most considerable Gentlemen in the County of *Meath* were indicted, but had better luck; the Perjury of their Accusers being made so manifest, that even a Popish Bench had not the confidence to countenance it, nor a Popish Jury to find it.... A great many in the County of *Tipperary*, were likewise brought into Trouble, but escaped the first time by a kind of Miracle; one of the Jurors was so maliciously bent against them, that he swore he would die before he would acquit them: It happened to him according to his own desire; he fell dead in the place, whilst they were disputing about returning the Verdict, which saved the Gentlemen for that time....

1. Titus Oates and Israel Tonge fabricated the Popish Plot in 1678, a supposed catholic conspiracy to assassinate Charles II, burn London, massacre protestants, and place James on the throne. Oates's perjury caused the execution of many innocent catholics, including Oliver Plunket, primate of Ireland.

The new Mayors and Justices of the Peace were no less troublesome to Protestants in their Employments; they made no scruple to send their Tokens and Warrants for Persons of the best Quality. And where-ever a Papist and Protestant had any difference, there needed no more but a complaint to procure a Committal, and to be sure it was done with all the indignity and affronting Circumstances imaginable. Sir *Thomas Hackett*,[2] whilst Lord Mayor of *Dublin*, did so many brutish and barbarous things of this nature, that it were endless to recount them; taking example from the Lord *Tyrconnel*,[3] who made him Mayor, he treated every body with Oaths, Curses, ill Names, and barbarous Language. The Lord Primate *Boyles*[4] Family could not escape his Warrants; he (or his Clerk, as he afterwards pretended) sent one for Mr. *Francis Cuff*, and Mr. *Jephson*, who lived in my Lords Family, being his Son in Law and Nephew: their Crime was, refusing to Contribute to the maintenance of two begging Fryars; one of them was one *Magee*, a Debauchee and Renegado, who had the impudence to have demanded it from my Lord Primate if he had been permitted access. The Fryars vexed that they should be repulsed, procured a Warrant for the two Gentlemen that refused them, and attempted the Execution of it in my Lord Primates House, with a Rabble of near two hundred. Sir *Thomas* was not content to Execute his Authority within his own Precincts, but extended it where the Mayors Power was never owned.[5] He sent his Warrant and committed the Officers of *Christs Church, Dublin*, to the Stocks, because he fancied they did not make the Bells ring *merrily enough* for the Birth of the Prince of *Wales*.[6] It was in vain for the Officers to tell him, that their Church and Persons were not subject to his Jurisdiction; that if the Bells did not ring *merrily enough*

2. Lord mayor of Dublin in 1687.
3. Richard Talbot (1630-91), earl and titular duke of Tyrconnell, viceroy of Ireland 1687-89.
4. Michael Boyle (*c.*1610-1702), archbishop of Armagh 1678-1702.
5. The reference is to the 'Liberties' of Dublin, an area near St Patrick's Cathedral. The deans of St Patrick's and Christ Church (like other church dignitaries) had legal jurisdiction in the areas around their cathedrals; the lord mayor's powers were not meant to extend to these 'Liberties'.
6. The birth of a son (later known as the 'Old Pretender' or the 'Chevalier de St George') to James II in 1687 provided him with a catholic heir. The protestants of Ireland, like all the king's subjects, were expected to show joy at the royal birth but, for obvious reasons, they considered it a disaster and, presumably, rang the bells with little enthusiasm.

as he alledged, it was the Ringers fault, not theirs. That no body, besides his Lordship, could observe any such thing in their Ringing. His brutish Passion would not give him leave to hearken to Reason; but upon all occasions he proceeded in the same method; which made every body, that valued his Liberty, get out of his Power; and prevailed with a great many to leave their Estates and Concerns, and Transport themselves, and what Effects they could carry with them into *England*. It was unsafe and uneasie living both in the City and in the Country, and he reckoned himself happy that could get out of them at any rate....

It may be thought that these things were unknown to King *James*, and therefore are not to be imputed to him: but it is certain, that if he did not Contrive and Order them, he yet consented to them; neither did he seem to have the least resentment or pity for their Sufferings; as appeared from his Carriage to the Bishop of *Lymerick*. His Lordship, by his Majesties Command, on a particular Service waited often on him; he took one of those Opportunities that seemed most favourable, to lay before his Majesty the manifold hardships which were put on the Clergy, and the Protestants in General, of his Diocess. He represented to him how they were first Robbed of all, and then laid in Goal; and that they had no way offended his Majesty, or disturbed his Government; and begged his favour in their behalf. His Majesty heard him, but made him no answer; instead thereof, he fell into discourse of another Affair, with a Papist that chanced to be by, and that with an Air more than ordinarily pleasant and unconcerned. Indeed his Majesty had by one general Order and Proclamation, dated *July* 26. 1689, confined all Protestants, without distinction of Age or Sex, to their Parishes and Cities, though their Occasions were such that he very well knew that this alone, without any more, was a very great encroachment on their Liberty, and a mighty inconveniency to their Affairs; especially when it was continued without Reason or Limitation. No body knew when this would be relaxed; and it was Executed with great strictness, till his present Majesties success put an end to it, and to the Power that imposed it.

ROBERT MOLESWORTH

(1656-1725)

from: AN ACCOUNT OF DENMARK AS IT WAS IN THE YEAR 1692 (1694)

[Robert Molesworth, later Viscount Molesworth of Swords, Co. Dublin, was one of the most important anti-clerical figures of his day and a radical Whig. His *Account of Denmark* is a thinly disguised attack on the power of churches in general and that of the protestant established church in particular. It startled its readers who, though they were used to the idea that the catholic church was authoritarian, had never considered that such could be said of any protestant church. The work played a considerable part in establishing an atmosphere, in London especially, in which the views of disaffected churchmen — some of whom became deists — could be heard. Molesworth's friends included John Toland, William Molyneux and (surprisingly, and late in life) Jonathan Swift.]

THE CONCLUSION

It has been a general Mistake among us, That the Popish Religion is the only one, of all the Christian Sects, proper to introduce and establish Slavery in a Nation, insomuch that Popery and Slavery have been thought inseparable: not to derogate from the merit of the Roman Catholick Perswasion, which has been the Darling of so many Monarchs upon that account; I shall make bold to say that other Religions, and particularly the *Lutheran*, has succeeded as effectually in this Design as ever Popery did. 'Tis confest indeed that Popery would certainly introduce Slavery, but 'tis denied that the last cannot come in without the assistance of the former; and whoever takes the pains to visit the Protestant Countries abroad, who have lost their Liberty even since they changed their Religion for a better, will be convinced that it is not Popery as such, but the

Doctrine of a blind Obedience in what Religion soever it be found, that is the destruction of the Liberty, and consequently of all the Happiness of any Nation. Nay, I am perswaded that many are satisfied the late King *James*'s Attempts to bring in Popery were the principal thing which rescued our Liberties from being entirely swallowed up; there seeming in his Reign, through the Interest and Dishonesty of some, the Dissoluteness, Laziness, and Ignorance of others, to have been (in many mens Opinions) a general tendency towards Slavery, which would scarcely have been vigorously enough opposed, had he left the business of Religion untouched; and if once introduced, it had been maintained more effectually than in the days of Popery, I say more effectually, because the dependance which the Romish Clergy and Monks have on the Church of *Rome*, causes often a clashing of Interests, and derogates from that intire Obedience the Subjects owe to the Prince, and which is preached up by that Church, as often as the Soveraign acts according to their direction, and down again whenever he displeases them; whereof we have had frequent Examples in this Kingdom of *England*, where there have been Bishops and Abbots in the days of Popery, as zealous Assertors of the Liberties of the People, as any Laymen could be, whether out of a true Principle, or not, I will not determine; but Occasions have been taken by them to raise Tumults and Wars, and in the Scuffle the Liberties of the People (of which both King and Church-men strove who should be the Masters) have escaped untouched: but in *Denmark*, as well as other Protestant Countries of the North, through the entire and sole dependance of the Clergy upon the Prince, without the interfering of the Authority of any Spiritual Superiour, such as that of the Pope among the Romanists, through their Principles and Doctrine, which are those of unlimited Obedience; through the Authority they have with the Common People, *&c.* slavery seems to be more absolutely established than it is in *France*; as in effect it is more practised; for that King's Subjects are better treated; there is a Name of a Parliament at *Paris*, and other great Towns, though they meet for no other end, than to verifie the King's Edicts; there is a formal Demand made of a Benevolence, or *Don Gratuit*[1] in some Provinces, which probably they have not the power to deny; there is an encouragement of Trade, Manufactures, Learning, *&c.* all tending to the good of the People. Besides, we see by experience, that that King often has great quarrels with the Court of *Rome*, which whensoever his power is reduced to a lower ebb, that his Clergy are not over-awed by it, may produce such Divisions and Disturbances as possibly some Sparks of the People's Liberty may again proceed from the collision of two such hard Rocks: but in the Countries I have spoken of, there is no hope of any such resource; all is swallowed up in the King; Temporals and Spirituals, Soul, Body, Estate, and Conscience; the Army and the Priests are two sure Cards: the Prince that has one of them on his side, can hardly fail; but he that has both depending on him, need fear nothing from his own Subjects, let him use them never so ill....

1. free gift.

WILLIAM MOLYNEUX

(1656-98)

from: THE CASE OF IRELAND'S BEING BOUND BY ACTS OF PARLIAMENT IN ENGLAND, STATED (1698)

[This, one of the most famous treatises in Irish political history, was the result of a jurisdictional wrangle between the parliaments of England and Ireland. William Molyneux, an enthusiastic natural scientist who wrote an important treatise on optics and was one of the founders of the Dublin Philosophical Society, was also MP for Dublin University in the Irish parliament. He appears to have believed that this treatise, based as it was as much on the assertion of the natural rights of the Irish people as upon legal precedent, would appeal to the English parliament; it fitted closely the popular ideas of his friend

John Locke, and Molyneux dedicated to the work to King William III.

However, the English parliament considered any document that questioned its right to legislate for Ireland an outrage, and it condemned Molyneux's book as seditious. Although it is often stated that *The Case of Ireland* was burned by the common hangman, there is no contemporary evidence of this. The insubordinate Irish parliament was the real object of English anger, rather than Molyneux himself. The work strongly states the case for Irish legislative independence and was reprinted in Ireland many times throughout the eighteenth century at moments of friction between England and Ireland. Two sections of the work are presented here, part of the introduction and the conclusion.]

[INTRODUCTION]

I have ever been so fully perswaded of the strict Justice of the Parliament of *England*, that I could never think that any of Their Proceedings, which might seem to have the least Tendency to Hardship on their Neighbours, could arise from any thing but want of Due Information, and a right State of the Business under their Consideration. The want of which, in Matters wherein another People are chiefly Concern'd, is no Defect in the Parliament of *England*, but is highly Blameable in the Persons whose Affair is Transacting, and who permit that Illustrious Body of Senators to be Mis-inform'd, without giving them that Light that might Rectifie them.

I could never Imagine that those Great *Assertors* of their *Own Liberties* and *Rights*, could ever think of making the least Breach in the *Rights* and *Liberties* of their *Neighbours*, unless they thought that they had *Right* so to do; and this they might well surmise, if their Neighbours quietly see their Inclosures Invaded, without *Expostulating* the Matter at least, and shewing Reasons, why they may think that Hardships are put upon them therein.

The Consideration hereof has Excited me to undertake this Disquisition, which I do with all Imaginable Diffidence of my own Performance, and with the most profound Respect and Deference to that August Senate. The present Juncture of Affairs, when the Business of *Ireland* is under the Consideration of both Houses of the English Parliament,[1] seems to require this from some Person; and seeing all Others silent, I venture to Expose my own Weakness, rather than be wanting at this time *to my Country*. I might say indeed *to Mankind*; for 'tis the Cause of the whole Race of *Adam*, that I Argue: *Liberty* seems the Inherent Right of all *Mankind*; and on whatsoever Ground any one Nation can Challenge it to themselves, on the same Reason may the Rest of *Adam's* Children expect it.

If what I Offer herein seems to carry any Weight, in relation to my own Poor Country, I shall be abundantly happy in the Attempt: But if after all, the Great Council of *England* Resolve the contrary, I shall then believe my self to be in an Error, and with the lowest Submission ask Pardon for my Assurance. However, I humbly presume I shall not be hardly Censur'd by them, for offering to lay before them a fair State of our Case, by such Information as I can procure; especially when at the same time I declare my Intention of a Submissive Acquiescence in whatever they Resolve for or against what I Offer.

The Subject therefore of our present Disquisition shall be, *How far the Parliament of* England *may think it Reasonable to intermeddle with the Affairs of* Ireland, *and Bind us up by Laws made in their House.*

And seeing the *Right* which *England* may pretend to, for Binding us by their Acts of Parliament, can be founded only on the *Imaginary Title of Conquest* or *Purchase*, or on *Precedents* and *Matters of Record*; We shall Enquire into the following Particulars.

(1) *First*, How *Ireland* became a Kingdom *Annex'd* to the Crown of *England*. And here we shall at large give a faithful Narrative of the *First Expedition of the Britains* into this Country, and King *Henry* the Second's Arrival here, such as our best Historians give us.

(2) *Secondly*, We shall Enquire, Whether this Expedition, and the English Settlement that afterwards follow'd thereon, can properly be call'd a *Conquest*? Or whether any Victories obtain'd by the English, in any succeeding Ages in this Kingdom, upon any *Rebellion*, may be call'd a *Conquest* thereof?

(3) *Thirdly*, Granting that it were a *Conquest*, we shall Enquire what *Title* a Conquest gives.

1. Molyneux inserted a note of his own at this point, in reference to the two wrangles between the English and Irish parliaments: one was a case in which the Bishop of Derry appealed to the Irish House of Lords to reverse a decision of the English House of Lords; the other concerned Irish objections to the English parliament's prohibition of the export from Ireland of Irish wool.

(4) *Fourthly*, We shall Enquire what *Concessions* have been from time to time made to *Ireland*, to take off what even the most Rigorous Assertors of a Conqueror's Title do pretend to. And herein we shall shew by what Degrees the English Form of Government, and the English Statute-Laws, came to be received among us: And this shall appear, to be wholly by the *Consent* of the People and Parliament of *Ireland*.

(5) *Fifthly*, We shall Enquire into the Precedents and Opinions of the Learned in the Laws, relating to this Matter, with Observations thereon.

(6) *Sixthly*, We shall Consider the Reasons and Arguments that may be farther Offered on one side and t'other; and shall Draw some General Conclusions from the Whole....

[CONCLUSION]

To conclude all, I think it highly *Inconvenient* for *England* to *Assume* this *Authority* over the Kingdom of *Ireland*: I believe there will need no great Arguments to convince the Wise Assembly of English Senators, how *inconvenient* it may be to *England*, to do that which may make the *Lords* and *People of Ireland* think that they are not *Well Used*, and may drive them into *Discontent*. The *Laws* and *Liberties of England* were granted above five hundred years ago to the People of *Ireland*, upon their Submissions to the Crown of *England*, with a Design to make them *Easie* to *England*, and to keep them in the Allegiance of the King of *England*. How Consistent it may be with True Policy, to do that which the People of *Ireland* may think is an *Invasion* of their Rights and Liberties, I do most humbly submit to the Parliament of *England* to Consider. They are Men of *Great Wisdom, Honour* and *Justice*: and know how to prevent all future *Inconveniencies*. We have heard Great Out-cries, and deservedly, on Breaking the *Edict of Nantes*,[2] and other Stipulations; How far the Breaking our Constitution, which has been of Five Hundred years standing, exceeds that, I leave the World to judge. It may perhaps be urg'd, That 'tis *convenient* for the State of *England*, that the *Supream Council* thereof should make their Jurisdiction as *Large* as they can. But with Submission, I conceive that if this *Assumed Power* be not *Just*, it cannot be *convenient* for the State. What *Cicero* says in his *Offices*, *Nihil est Utile, nisi idem sit Honestum*,[3] is most certainly true. Nor do I think, that 'tis any wise *necessary* to the *Good of England* to *Assert* this High Jurisdiction over *Ireland*. For since the Statutes of this Kingdom are made with such *Caution*, and in such *Form*, as is prescribed by *Poyning's Act* 10 *H*. 7.[4] and by the 3d and 4th of *Phil*. and *Mar*.[5] and whilest *Ireland* is in *English hands*, I do not see how 'tis possible for the Parliament of *Ireland* to do any thing that can be in the least *prejudicial* to *England*. But on the other hand, If *England assume a Jurisdiction* over *Ireland*, whereby they think their *Rights* and *Liberties* are *taken away, That their Parliaments are rendred meerly nugatory*, and that their Lives and Fortunes Depend on the Will of a *Legislature* wherein they are *not Parties*; there may be ill Consequences of this. *Advancing* the Power of the Parliament of *England*, *by breaking the Rights* of an *other*, may in time have ill Effects.

The *Rights of Parliament* should be preserved *Sacred* and *Inviolable*, wherever they are found. This kind of Government, once so *Universal* all over *Europe*, is now almost *Vanished* from amongst the Nations thereof. Our Kings Dominions are the only Supporters of this noble *Gothick Constitution*, save only what little remains may be found thereof in *Poland*. We should not therefore make so light of that sort of Legislature, and as it were Abolish it in One Kingdom of the Three, wherein it appears; but rather Cherish and Encourage it wherever we meet it.

2. To restore peace in France, Henry IV signed this edict, which set forth the rights of French protestants: liberty of conscience and worship; full civil rights; royal subsidies for protestant schools; and protestant control of some two hundred cities then held by the Huguenots. Louis XIV revoked the edict in 1685, declaring that the majority of French protestants had been converted to catholicism. No protestant was allowed to leave the country, although thousands did flee. In his ruthless application of his objective — to make France a catholic state — Louis became a detested figure in England and in the German protestant states.

3. 'Nothing is useful unless the same thing is honest.'

4. i.e. of 1495, the tenth year of the reign of Henry VII.

5. i.e. 'An Act declaring how Ponings acte shall be exponed and taken' passed in the Irish parliament of 1556, which sat in the third and fourth years of the reign of Queen Mary; her marriage to Philip II of Spain had made him legally the joint ruler of England, Wales and Ireland, and all parliamentary acts of the reign contain his name as well as that of his wife.

from: THE PENAL LAWS

[During the fifteen years following the battle of the Boyne, the Irish parliament passed a series of measures designed as far as possible to repress the catholic population of Ireland. Although several members of the parliament refused to support these 'Penal Laws' and despite the fact that they were not always enforced or enforceable, they remained on the statute books for most of the eighteenth century. Their existence has had a profound influence on Irish political thinking from the date of their enactment to the present day.

Three have been selected for this anthology: the first banishing all catholic clergy, the second dealing with the property of a protestant woman who marries a catholic (she is to be deemed 'Dead in Law'), and the third a more comprehensive act, which includes the Oaths of Abjuration. These statutes were not repealed until the Catholic Relief Act of 1778.]

An Act for Banishing all Papists *exercising any Ecclesiastical Jurisdiction, and all Regulars*[1] *of the* Popish Clergy *out of this Kingdom* (1697)

Whereas, it is Notoriously known, that the late Rebellions in this Kingdom have been Contrived, Promoted and Carried on by Popish Arch-Bishops, Bishops, Jesuits, and other Ecclesiastical Persons of the Romish Clergy. And forasmuch as the Peace and Publick Safety of this Kingdom is in Danger, by the great number of the said Arch-Bishops, Bishops, Jesuits, Friers and other Regular Romish Clergy, now residing here, and settling in Fraternities and Societies, contrary to Law, and to the great Impoverishing of many of His Majesty's Subjects of this Kingdom, Who are forc'd to maintain and support them; which said Romish Clergy do, not only endeavour to Withdraw His Majesty's Subjects from their Obedience, but do daily stir up, and move Sedition, and Rebellion, to the great hazard of the Ruine and Desolation of this Kingdom. For the prevention of all which Mischiefs, his Majesty is Graciously Pleased that it be Enacted.

And be it Enacted by the King's Most Excellent Majesty, by, and with the Advice and Consent of the Lords Spiritual and Temporal, and Commons in this present Parliament Assembled, and by Authority of the Same, That all Popish Arch-Bishops, Bishops, Vicars-General, Deans, Jesuits, Monks, Friers, and all other Regular Popish Clergy, and all Papists exercising any Ecclesiastical Jurisdiction, shall depart out of this Kingdom before the first day of May, which shall be in the Year of Our Lord, One thousand, Six hundred, Ninety eight: And if any of the said Ecclesiastical Persons, shall be at any time after the said First day of May, within this Kingdom, they, and every of them shall suffer Imprisonment, and remain in Prison, without Bail or Mainprize,[2] till he or they shall be Transported beyond seas, out of his Majesty's Dominions, wherever his Majesty, his Heirs or Successors, or the Chief Governor or Governors of this kingdom, for the time being, shall think fit: And if any person so Transported shall return again into this kingdom, they, and every of them, shall be Guilty of High-Treason; and every person so Offending, shall for his Offence, be adjudged a Traitor, and shall suffer, lose and forfeit[3] as in Case of High-Treason....

1. Members of religious orders.

2. suretyship. A prisoner could sometimes be released if someone else went surety for him and guaranteed his appearance in court.
3. i.e. suffer death and forfeit all his property.

An Act to Prevent Protestants Inter-Marrying with Papists (1697)

Whereas many Protestant Maidens and Women, as well such as be heirs Apparent to their Ancestors, as others, having left unto them by their Father, or other Ancestor or Friends, Mannors, Lands, Tenements, and Hereditaments,[1] or other great Substances in Goods or Chattels, Real or Personal, for their Advancement in Marriage; or having had considerable Estates for Life, by Dower or Jointure,[2] or having had the Tuition or Guardianship of Protestant Children Intituled to such Estates, or Interests, as aforesaid, by Flattery and other Crafty Insinuations of Popish Persons, have been Seduced and Prevailed upon, to Contract Matrimony with, and take to Husband, Papists or Popish Persons; which Marriages have not only

1. Any property that can be inherited.
2. Two ways by which women inherited estates after their husbands' deaths.

Tended to the Ruine and Destruction of such Estates and Interests, and to the great Loss and Damage of many Protestant Persons, to whom the same might Descend or Come, but as well to the Corrupting and Perverting such Protestants to Marrying, and the Protestant Persons in their Tuition and Guardianship, as aforesaid, that they forsake their Religion, and become Papists, to the great Dishonour of Almighty God, the great Prejudice of the Protestant Interest, and the heavy Sorrow and Displeasure of all their Protestant Friends. For remedy whereof, Be it Enacted by the King's Most Excellent Majesty, by, and with the Advice and Consent of the Lords Spiritual and Temporal, and the Commons in this present Parliament Assembled, and by the Authority of the same; That if any Protestant Maid, or Woman Unmarryed, being heir Apparent to her Ancestor or having a Sole or Joynt Estate ... or Intituled to any Personal Estate, either in Money, Stock, Plate, Jewels, or other Goods and Chattels in Law or Equity, to the Value of five hundred Pounds sterling, or more, shall at any time after the First Day of January next, Marry, or take to Husband any Person whatsoever, without having first obtained a Certificate in Writing under the Hand of the Minister of the Parish, Bishop of the Diocese, and some Justice of the Peace Living near the Place, or any two of them, where such Person shall be Resident at the time of such Marriage, that he is a known Protestant; ... that then and from the time of such Marriage, such Protestant person so Marrying, and the person she shall so Marry, shall be for ever afterwards Disabled and Rendered Incapable of having, holding, or Enjoying, all, or any of the aforesaid Estates or Interests, ... and that at any time after such Protestant Maid or Woman, shall Marry without such Certificate, as aforesaid, it shall, and may be Lawful, to, and for [any] Protestant person or Persons, to whom all, or any of the said Estates or Interests, shall come by such Marriage, as aforesaid, by any Action at Law, or other Legal means whatsoever, to Sue for, and Recover all, or any of the said Estates or Interests, as if such Protestant person or persons so marrying, as aforesaid, and all other Intervening Popish Heirs, Executors, or Administrators, were really Dead, and Intestate, as aforesaid, and as if such person or persons, who shall so Sue for, and Recover all or any of such Estates or Interests, were Rightfully and legally Intituled thereto, as Heir, Executor or Administrator to such Protestant Maid or Woman Marrying, as aforesaid; such Maid or Woman, being by such marriage, to be Deemed and Esteemed Dead in Law, to the aforesaid Intents, Constructions and Purposes.

An Act to Prevent the Further Growth of Popery (1704)

I. Whereas divers emissaries of the church of Rome, popish priests, and other persons of that persuasion, taking advantage of the weakness and ignorance of some of her majesty's subjects, or of the extreme sickness and decay of their reason and senses, in the absence of friends and spiritual guides, do daily endeavour to persuade and pervert them from the protestant religion, to the great dishonour of Almighty God, the weakening of the true religion, by His blessing so happily established in this realm, to the disquieting the peace and settlement, and discomfort of many particular families thereof; and in further manifestation of their hatred and aversion to the said true religion, many of the said persons so professing the popish religion in this kingdom, have refused to make provision for their own children for no other reason but their being of the protestant religion; and also by cunning devices and contrivances found out ways to avoid and elude the intents of an act of parliament, made in the ninth year of the reign of the late King William the Third for preventing protestants intermarrying with papists, and of several other laws made for the security of the protestant religion; and whereas many persons so professing the popish religion have it in their power to raise division among protestants, by voting in elections for members of parliament, and also have it in their power to use other ways and means tending to the destruction of the protestant interest in this kingdom; for remedy of which great mischiefs, and to prevent the like evil practices for the future be it enacted ... that if any person or persons from and after the twenty-fourth day of March, in this present year of our Lord 1703, shall seduce, persuade or pervert any person or persons professing, or that shall profess, the protestant religion, to renounce, forsake, or adjure the same, and to profess the popish religion, or reconcile him or them to the church of Rome, then and in such case every such person or persons do seducing, as also every such protestant or protestants who shall be so seduced, perverted and reconciled to popery, shall for the said offences, being thereof lawfully convicted, incur the danger and penalty of praemunire,[1] mentioned in the statute of praemunire made in England in the sixteenth year of the reign of King Richard the Second; ...

X. And further be it enacted ... that all lands tenements and hereditaments, whereof a papist now is, or hereafter shall be, seized in fee-simple or fee-tail,[2] shall from henceforth, so long as any papist shall be seized of or entitled to the same in fee-simple or fee-tail, be of the nature of gavelkind;[3] and if not sold, aliened, or disposed of by such papist in his life time for good and valuable consideration of money really and *bona fide* paid for such estate, shall from such papist descend to, and be inherited by, all and every the sons of such papist any way inheritable to such estate, share and share alike, and not descend on or come to the eldest of such sons only, being a papist, as heir-at-law; and shall in like manner from such respective sons, being papists, descend to and be inherited by all and every the sons of such sons, share and share alike, and not descend to the eldest of such sons, being a papist, as heir-at-law only; and that for want of issue male of such papist, the same shall descend to all his daughters any way inheritable to such estate in equal proportions; and for want of such issue, among the collateral kindred[4] of such papist, of the kin of his father, any way inheritable to such estate in equal degree; and for want of such kindred, to the collateral kindred of such papist of the kin of his mother, any way inheritable to such estate, and not otherwise; ...

XII. Provided always, that if the eldest son or heir-at-law of such papist shall be a protestant at the time of the decease of such papist, ... the lands whereof such papist shall be seized, shall descend to such eldest son or heir-at-law according to the rules of the common law of this realm, ... and if the eldest son or heir-at-law of any such papist, who shall at the time of the decease of such papist, whose heir he is, be of the age of one and twenty years, shall become a protestant and conform himself to the church of Ireland, as by law established, within one year after such decease of such papist, or being then under the age of one and twenty years, shall within one year after he shall attain that age become a protestant, and conform himself as aforesaid, ... he shall be entitled to, and shall have, and enjoy from thenceforth the whole real estate of such papist....

XV. Provided always, that no person shall take benefit by this act as a protestant within the intent and meaning hereof, that shall not conform to the church of Ireland as by law established, and subscribe the declaration, and also take and subscribe the oath of adjuration following, viz. I A.B.[5] do solemnly and sincerely, in the presence of God, profess, testify and declare, that I do believe, that in the sacrament of the Lord's-supper, there is not any transubstantiation of the elements of bread and wine into the body and blood of Christ, at or after the consecration thereof by any person whatsoever, and that the adoration or invocation of the Virgin Mary, or any other saint, and the sacrifice of the mass, as they are now used in the church of Rome, are superstitious and idolatrous. And I do solemnly, in the presence of God, profess, testify, and declare, that I do make this declaration, and every part thereof, in the plain and ordinary sense of the words read unto me, as they are commonly understood by protestants, without any evasion, equivocation or mental reservation whatsoever; and without any dispensation already granted me for this purpose by the pope, or any other authority or person whatsoever, or without any hope of dispensation from any person or authority whatsoever, or without believing that I am, or can be acquitted before God or man, or absolved of this declaration, or any part thereof, although the pope, or any other person or persons, or power whatsoever should dispense with or annul the same, or declare that it was null and void from the beginning.

I A.B. do truly and sincerely acknowledge, profess, testify and declare in my conscience, before God and the world, that our sovereign lady Queen Anne is lawful and rightful queen of this realm, and of all other her majesty's dominions and countries thereunto belonging. And I do solemnly and sincerely declare, that I do believe in my conscience,

1. Introducing a foreign power (particularly that of the pope) into England or Ireland. The penalties include forfeiture of goods and life imprisonment.
2. In legal possession to him and his heirs for ever or to him and specified heirs.
3. A system of land tenure by which land is divided between the sons of a landowner after his death.
4. Those descended from the same ancestor but in a different line, e.g. cousins.
5. At this point the person swearing inserts his own name.

that the person pretending to be Prince of Wales,[6] during the life of the late King James, and since his decease pretending to be, and taking upon himself the style and title of King of England by the name of James III, hath not any right or title whatsoever to the crown of this realm, or any other the dominions thereto belonging, and I do renounce, refuse and abjure any allegiance or obedience to him. And I do swear that I will bear faith and true allegiance to her majesty Queen Anne, and her will defend to the utmost of my power against all traiterous conspiracies and attempts whatsoever, which shall be made against her person, crown, or dignity. And I will do my best endeavour to disclose and make known to her majesty, and her successors, all treasons and traiterous conspiracies, which I shall know to be against her or any of them. And I do faithfully promise to the utmost of my power to support, maintain and defend the limitation and succession of the crown against him the said James, and all other persons whatsoever, as the same is and stands limited by an act, entitled, *An act declaring the rights and liberties of the subject, and settling the succession of the crown*, to her present majesty, and the heirs of her body being protestants; and as the same by one other act, entitled, *An act for the further limitation of the crown, and better securing the rights and liberties of the subject*, is and stands limited, after the decease of her majesty, and for default of issue of her majesty, to the Princess Sophia, electress and duchess dowager of Hanover,[7] and the heirs of her body being protestants. And all these things I do plainly and sincerely acknowledge and swear, according to the express words by me spoken, and according to the plain and common sense and understanding of the same words, without any equivocation, mental evasion or secret reservation whatsoever. And I do make this recognition, acknowledgement, abjuration, renunciation and promise, heartily, willingly, and truly, upon the true faith of a Christian. So help me God. . . .

6. James Stuart (1688-1766), son of James II. He was called James III by the Jacobites on his father's death in 1701.

7. Sophia Dorothea (1666-1762), cousin and wife of George Louis (later George I of England). They were divorced in 1694 and he imprisoned her for life on a charge of adultery.

WILLIAM KING

LETTER TO THE REVD. EDWARD NICOLSON (1712)

[The English parliament, not surprisingly, supported the Irish parliament in its penal legislation against catholics, but on other matters, economic and political, the two parliaments clashed throughout the eighteenth century — or rather the English ministry clashed with the Irish parliament — as England enforced its will on Ireland. Thoughtless, malicious or non-resident landlords were a further problem in Ireland, as Archbishop King made clear to a correspondent in 1712.

The source of this extract is TCD MS. 2532.]

Dublin, December 20th 1712

Revd. Sir,

Your son was with me today and gave me an account of your health, and that you are now a Grand-father by his having a son — on both which I congratulate you. He likewise gave me your book concerning charity schools,[1] of which I very much approve.

There's one thing I wish you had taken notice of, and it is that poverty of the people and neglect of education of children do not always proceed from the Laziness of the people or their unwillingness to give them learning, but much more from the cruelty of the Landlords who rack[2] their Tenants so that they can neither render to God, to the publick or their children what is due to them. And when I inquire of Beggars how they came to that condition, their answer is 'The Landlord came and took away all I had for his rent'; and on inquiry, I generally find it is so. I am perswaded neither the Peasants in France nor the Common Turks live so miserably as the Tenants in Ireland. Nor is it, as things stand now, to any purpose to set a good Lease: for he that

1. Edward Nicolson, *A Method of Charity Schools* . . . . (Dublin, 1712).
2. To raise rent above a fair or normal amount.

has it, sets it to another, and he to another, and the tenants often hold from the fourth, who screws and racks them to death. Here is the original of the Beggary of Ireland, and if we take the children of the poor people and ease them of their education, the effect is that the Landlord supposes they may pay more rent and screws them accordingly — so that the effect of all our charity go's finally to him. I wish I cou'd perswade them out of this wicked practice. But I do not remember that any has observ'd it. I have taken some pains to make people sensible of it, but to very lit[t]le purpose; they have no ears for anything that lessen[s] their profit.

There's another Source of the poverty of Ireland, and it is the great Stock Masters, who ingross[3] the land and, making more of it that way than Tenants can pay, will not allow them any place in the earth, but force them to Barren places and Mountains, where they are miserably starved or oblige them to pay greater rents for course Lands than it is possible for them to pay.

A Gentleman gave me a visit 'tother Day and entertained me with discourse how he had improved his Estate. He told me he had a farm on which there lived about an 100 familys that paid him rent very ill and he lost much every year: that he turned them off and set it dearer to one man who stocked it, lived well upon it and paid his rent punctually. I asked what came of the 100 familys he turned off it; he answered that he did not know. My reply was that those 100 family had at least 500 souls belonging to them, and with what conscience cou'd he send them a begging. He seemed surprized at this, but said that it was their own fault: why did they not pay their rent? I desired him to consider that those 500 souls had no other support than what the farms yeilded [*sic*] them, and when their maintenance was deducted, it was impossible so much shou'd remain for the Landlord as when only perhaps 10 souls were to be maintained by the produce thereof, and I desired him to consider whether it cou'd be agreable to equity or reason that 490 persons shou'd be turn'd out of their Livlihood without any manner of provision merely that the Landlord might get more rent: that this was just as if an heir shou'd be allowed to murther all his Brothers and Sisters that his Estate might be greater and less incumbered: that this seem'd to me to be the case, or very like the case, of those to whom the Prophet Isayah pronounces a wo. (Is. 5. 8).[4] But the Gentleman still insisted that he might make the best of his own Estate. I answered he might by all Lawful means, but oppressing the poor, ruining familys and sending the familys of whole Baronys to begg were absolutely unlawfull, and so declared by God (Is. 3. 14 & 15)[5] and in many other places of Scripture; but I did not find this had any consequence.

It is farther worth the observing that about one third of the Lands in Ireland are in the hands of Landlords that live in England, [and] that the higher our rents are raised, the more will live there. For a man that has an Estate of £500 with a family, must live in Ireland; but if he make it a £1,000, he is enabled to live in England, and generally do's so — of which there are innumerable instances. The improvement of Ireland therefore only contributes to enrich those that live out of it, and encourage others to follow their example, & helps to oppress those that live in it, and encrease their Labour and poverty. Those that live in England contribute not one shilling, either to support the poor they make or the Government by taxes; and to propose, as you do, to raise a penny or half penny an acre for the poor, were to encrease the Tenants rent, that all are already unreasonably racked so much. For assure yourself that the Landlords wou'd covenant with tenants to pay that tax as they do all others without abateing any thing of the price of the Lands, and this wou'd break more than it wou'd relieve.

As for trading, 'tis another source of oppression; for most of all our trading is with commodities that are the necessarys of life — such are Beef, Butter, fish and Grain — by which means persons are incouraged to keep great stocks and great quantities of Lands, the poor are debarred of the necessarys of Life and forced to feed on offals and the refuse of things — fit only for dogs — and kept from profitable and fruitfull farms; and none have the profit of our trade but the Landlords and a few Merchants, the rest being fed like Beasts, whilst these few ingross the fat of the Land.

'Tis a very pardonable mistake in you to think

3. engross: to buy up in large quantities.

4. 'Woe unto them that join house to house, that lay field to field, till there be no place, that they may be placed alone in the midst of the earth!'

5. 'The Lord will enter into judgment with the ancients of his people, and the princes thereof: for ye have eaten up the vineyard; the spoil of the poor is in your houses.

What mean ye that ye beat my people to pieces, and grind the faces of the poor? saith the Lord God of hosts.'

great Citys are in a better condition as to this matter than the Countrey, for so it must appear to any one that do's not thoroughly know both; but the case is truly much otherwise. Both Vice and Beggary are more predominant in the City than in the Countrey. A man that is rich employs perhaps 200 pair of hands: he has the profit of their labour and they a bare subsistance. One of these dys and leaves a family, or is sick and unable to labour, and then immediately his wife and children are on the parish. This is the constant fate of all Journeymen[6] that have familys, and hence it is observed in England that where the greatest Manufacturys are, beggar[s] most abound. A Million per annum do's not pay the poor taxes, and yet to see the multitude of miserable, vagrant beggars in London, and other places, you wou'd think no care were taken of the poor.

These are the Floodgates that let in Beggary and the attendant vices upon us, and to go about to supply the poor made by them, whilst they are left open, is to begin at the wrong end — and like applying a Strengthening plaster to the Toe when a man is in a fit of the appoplexy.

Yet since this is all we can do, we must not neglect it, and God will reward us according to our good intentions not according to our success. I will add no more but my hearty prayers for you, etc,

Will: Dublin

6. Tradesman or workmen hired by the day.

HUGH MacCURTIN

(*c.*1680-1755)

from:
A BRIEF DISCOURSE IN VINDICATION OF THE ANTIQUITY OF IRELAND (1717)

[The opinion of the catholics of Ireland, defeated at the battle of the Boyne, subjected to Penal Laws and to legal and commercial restraints of all kinds, is seldom heard in the early eighteenth century, at least not in print. However, Hugh MacCurtin, a member of one of the hereditary learned families of Ireland, ventured to publish his *Brief Discourse* in 1717.

MacCurtin, himself well-versed in the ancient Irish chronicles and histories, was aware of the gross inaccuracies of the 'histories' of Ireland written by Englishmen over the preceding centuries. He objected particularly to Richard Cox's *Hibernia Anglicana* and set out to refute Cox point by point.

The preface to the *Discourse*, in which MacCurtin places his work in historiographical context, stresses his objectivity and starts his demolition of Cox.]

THE PREFACE

I am confident, there is no indifferent Reader vers'd in the genuine Part of Antiquity now living, but will be surpriz'd at the many fabulous Relations written of the Kingdom of Ireland *these five hundred and odd Years past, all by Foreign Writers, and stiling them Histories of* Ireland, *without any Regard to the Antient State and Affairs of that Nation before the Year of Salvation* 1171, *when the* English *first got Footing therein. And tho' every one of those Historians pretends to write of the Origin, Monarchy, Custom, Language, &c. of the* Gadelians,[1] *yet you shall not find two of 'em to agree, and will discover in some of them much Malice and Hatred towards the Antient Inhabitants and their Posterity; insomuch, that setting by the Nobility almost in general, they write only of the Customs and Manners of the Common People; and in the same, collecting several Pages full of Stuff never found in History, but either invented by themselves, or had from others ignorant in the true Antiquity of the Nation, and setting the same to the Press, under the Title of* The History of IRELAND.

This is the Reason that moves me to give the following Account of the Antient Irish *before the Year above-mentioned. And tho' I confess my self not sufficient to write correctly in the* English *Language,*[2] *yet I promise my self the Favour of all serious indifferent Readers, that wou'd value Truth in a plain*

1. Gaedelians: belonging to the Gaelic branch of the Celtic race.
2. MacCurtin was a native Irish speaker.

poor Dress; more than the fabulous Narrations of some Foreign Writers, whose Safeguards are Power and Strength of Eloquence, in the most Part of their Tractates of the Ancient Gadelians *before the Coming of the* English *into* Ireland.

I doubt not, but it will be counted Presumption in me, to attempt the Vindication of the Antiquity of Ireland, *against a Number of Honourable, Learned, Foreign Writers, who have erroniously written thereof:*[3] *Whereas, Sir* Richard Cox *has given the following Opinions of those that wrote of the same before his Time. As to Doctor* Keting, *he says thus of his Manuscript History of* Ireland, *that,* It is an ill-digested Heap of very silly Fictions. *And of* Peter Walsh *says, that his,* will never pass for more than an *Utopian* Atchievement. *He says, the Learned* Flaherty's Ogygia must expect the same Fate. *And (meaning the Foreign Authors) says,* The Tractates which have been written of latter Times, have most of them another Fault, tho' they generally write true, *but not* observing Chronology, they Jumble Times, Persons, and Things together, and so confound the Story. *He says also, that* Campion *and the Rest,* have but a Scrap here and there, and that it self very imperfectly. *That* Camden's Annals, Fryer Clynn's, *and others* were very Faulty, and have no Coherence. *He liketh* Spencer's View *of* Ireland, *and Sir* John Davis*'s Discourse, but says at last, that* they are rather Commentaries *than Histories. When Sir* Richard *is pleas'd to judge thus of those Authors, Men of Learning, Distinction, and Quality, what shall I expect, who am inferior to 'em? tho' not to any Foreign Writer in the true Knowledge of the* Irish *Antiquity before King* Henry *the Second of* England*'s Time.*

The Honourable Sir James Ware, *tho' misled in some Matters of the* Antiquity of Ireland, *in the Beginning of his History, I believe it's no voluntary Fault; for he took Pains to Collect many true Copies which inform'd him much of the Clergy and Writers of* Ireland, *of the Churches, Monasteries, and their Founders, wherein he shew'd his Love to Truth and Knowledge in what he undertook to write of* Ireland *before and after the coming of the* English.

Sir Richard *says, in his Introductory Discourse, that it were in vain to guess, who were the* Aborigines or first *Inhabitants of* Ireland, *and says further, that,* the *Irish* Historians are of no Credit in this Matter. *If he wou'd be pleas'd to read the Authentick Antiquity Books of the Kingdom, he might find what assiduous Care was constantly taken by the* Gadelians *before they came into* Spain, *in pursuing their own Histories; and since the* Milesians *came into* Ireland, *how industriously they advanced and preserv'd their Antiquity and Records thro' many Ages, by revising and rectifying their Histories, Genealogies, and Annals, as I shall shew in this following* Discourse. *And tho' the learned* Camden *in his* Brittania Camdeni *never spar'd to wash and wind his Pen in the Antient* Irish *Blood in some other Matters, yet he confess'd their Histories ought to have Credit, touching their own Antiquity, where he says,* In his detur fuæ Antiquitati venia; In those Matters let their own Antiquity be allow'd. *Contrary to the unfavourable Opinions of some Modern Writers.*

Josephus contra Appion (*as* Peter Walsh *observes in his Preface) says, that the* Phænicians, Egyptians, Caldeans, *and* Chineses *in the Limits of* Asia, *with great Truth and Certainty have written of the Reigns of their own Kings, and other memorable Things happening in their Countries many hundred Years before the first Olympiad; and this is a Rule to conclude that other Nations like those* Phænicians, Egyptians, *and* Chaldeans, *and also the* Chineses *towards the Rising Sun, as the Antient* Irish *in the farthest Part of* Europe *towards the Setting Sun, may be careful in preserving their Genealogies, Kings, Adventures, Wars, and other memorable Deeds on Record for Posterity.*

Sir Richard *says, that the* Irish are a Mixture of People, *for which Reason they were call'd* Scots, *i.e.* Acerva, *which signifies* A Heap consisting of many Grains. Keting, Flaherty, Lucius, Walsh, *and Sir* James Ware, *all agree in the Name* Scots *given the* Irish, *because they were Scythians; Sir* James Ware *quotes* Radulphus, Reinerius, Nennius, *and* Hen. Hutington, *all Foreign Authors for the same. All the* Irish *Authors say, that the* Irish *are call'd* Scots, *because they are Originally* Scythians, *descended from* Feniusa-farsa *King of* Scythia, *and Grand-Father to* Gaoidheal *or* Gadelus; *and that* Scota *the Daughter*

3. The Irish histories mentioned in this and the following paragraphs are: Sir Richard Cox, *Hibernia Anglicana* (London, 1689-90); Geoffrey Keating, *Foras Feasa ar Éirinn* (*c.* 1634, available only in manuscript before 1723); Peter Walsh, *A Prospect of ... Ireland* (London, 1682); Roderic O'Flaherty, *Ogygia* (London, 1685); William Camden, *Britannia* (London, 1607 edition) and *Annales rerum Anglicarum et Hibernicum* (London, 1615-25); Edmund Spenser, *A View of the Present State of Ireland* (1596, published Dublin, 1633); Sir John Davies, *A Discovery of the True Causes why Ireland was Never Entirely Subdued* (London, 1612); Sir James Ware, *De Hibernia ...* (London, 1654); and John Lynch, *Cambrensis Eversus ....* (St Malo (?), 1662). Lynch's pseudonym was Gratianus Lucius; MacCurtin refers to him simply as 'Lucius'.

of the King of Egypt, *and Mother of* Gadelus, *was so call'd, because she was the Wife of* Niul *Son of* Feniusa-farsa; *likewise* Scota *the Wife of* Milesius *had her Name so call'd, because she was Wife to* Milesius *a* Scythian: *All the* Irish *generally are call'd* Scots, *as being originally descended from* Gadelus *and* Milesius, *which gave a Beginning to the* Gadelian *and* Milesian *Race. I leave the Reader to judge, whether it be a difficult Matter to remove or impugn this known* Truth, *so well back'd by Learned Historians, both Domestick and Foreign, in order to prove the Antient* Irish *to be* a Mixture or a Heap *of many Sorts, contrary to the Authorities aforesaid.*

Sir Richard *says,* the Brigantes of Ireland are undoubtedly descended from the Brigantes of England. *That he may be rightly informed of the Truth of that Matter, let him read* Giolla-caoimhghin*'s Annals,*[4] Cionn-fhaola*'s Chronology and History of* Ireland, Aimhergin*'s Poems, and* Keting*'s Manuscript History, all undoubted* Irish *Authors,* &c. *and he shall find, that those People call'd* Brigantes *were so call'd as being descended from* Breogan *King of* Galisia *in* Spain, *and Grand-Father to* Milesius; *for many of the Sons and Grand-Sons of* Breogan *had Issue besides* Milesius, *and when they came into* Ireland, *to distinguish them from the Issue of* Milesius, *they were call'd* Brigantes *from* Breogan; *and whosoever pleases to read* Muircheartach mor mac Earca*'s Reign, will believe that the* Brigantes *of* England *came thither from* Ireland *and* Spain, *where many of the Posterity of* Breogan *liv'd for many Ages, and perhaps to this Day.*

Sir Richard, *in his* Introductory Discourse, *says, that* the *Irish* Language is a Mixture of other Languages, *and that* Com estato *is an* Irish *Word borrowed from the* Spanish, *and is as much with us, as,* how do you do; *I refer my self to any indifferent Man whatsoever that can write the* Irish *in its true Orthography, or understandeth the common* Irish *Language, in what I object herein; for, I say that* Com estato *is no way us'd in the* Irish *Language, and has no Affinity to it in Orthography, or otherwise that I can find; and the same I say of all the other Words which he mentions in his* Apparatus, *or* Introductory Discourse, *to prove the* Irish *Language to be a Mixture of other Languages; and whosoever will be pleas'd to read the most Authentick* Irish *Histories, he shall find sufficient Reasons to believe that the* Scythian *Language (and consequently the* Irish *which is no other but the same) is one of the Antientest in the World, as I shall shew in this following Discourse.*

Sir Richard *says, in his said Introductory Discourse, that,* it is exceeding difficult to distinguish which is the History, and which is the Fable; *speaking of the* Irish *Antiquity. And this is what confounds the Foreign Authors in general, touching the Antiquity of* Ireland; *for they cannot distinguish the true Histories which are Authentick, from the School-Books, and other Romances that were written for Pastime. And if they take the one for the other (as commonly they do) they pervert the true Antiquity into Fables, as far as their Writings can make it so. Other Reasons they have for so doing; The first is, they cannot read the old Parchment Books of Antiquity, nay, if they were read before them they can't understand them; and those School-Books, and Pastime-Books were written in a plain and easy Character and Language, much different from the former: And there are but few Men living in this Age, that can read, or understand our Antiquity-Books, Annals, or Antient Records; for the many intestine Feuds and Commotions which of late Ages happen'd here among the Inhabitants, were such, that the* Irish *Antiquaries and Chronologers had neither Leasure, nor Reward, for teaching or following their Calling in that Matter; tho' some few meerly out of Love and Nature to the Country, did from Time to Time endeavour to study and learn the same. The second Reason is, because some of those Authors wrote not for the Advantage of the* Milesians, *or their Posterity, but altogether the contrary; and if they found any Thing favourable to the Antient Inhabitants, in those Books or fabulous Fragments, which they us'd on this Purpose, they wou'd omit it, and endeavour to perswade the World that the* Irish *had no other Account of their Antiquity, but what they thought fit to deliver of them....*

I do not give the following Discourse *as a full History or Antiquity of* Ireland: *For, any one Antient Princely* Irish *Family being truly pursu'd, according to what is written of them, as their warlike Spirits, Conquests Abroad, unparalell'd Hospitality, Piety, good Qualities, and great Actions, wou'd swell up a greater Volume in it self, than what I design at present. And though I give no Genealogy of any Family in the* First *or* Second *Part, yet I bring the Chiefest of them to their several Stocks. And among the rest the Noble Families* Eustace, Plunket, Power, Barnaval, *and* Arthur, *which I cou'd not well omit, because the three*

4. Giolla Caoimhghin wrote several important historical and genealogical poems. His works are often used as an authority for the origin of the Gaels.

first are mention'd in Miles Brodin*'s Poem, and in the* Munster *Book of Genealogy to have descended from* Donogh *Son of* Brian Borovey. *The fourth I find in Mr.* Thady Rody*'s Book of Genealogy*[5] *to have descended from* Brian *Son of* Eocha-muidhmheadhoin, *from whom also sprung the Kings of* Connacht, *and some Monarchs, as I shall shew hereafter. The Fifth, I find in Doctor* Keting*'s Manuscript History, and in other Books of Genealogy, to be of the Race of* Cormuc-Cas *King of* Munster; *Yet because I find other Opinions against those I have mention'd, I humbly submit my self to the Will, and better Judgment of the Nobles aforesaid: And if I have offended any of those great Families in this Matter, I beg Pardon; and shall endeavour to pursue the said Families in my* Third Part, *according to the most convincing Authorities I can find.*

To the latter End of the Third Part *I shall affix a Table of Synchronism, shewing what Monarchies, Monarchs, great Kings of the World in other Parts, and (since Christianity) what general Councils were contemporary with the various Revolutions, and Kings of* Ireland, *from the coming of the* Milesians *to this Time. Together with a large* Index.

5. Thady Rody, Tadhg Ó Rodaigh (1623-1706), a poet and scholar from County Leitrim who worked for James Ware and was friendly with Duald Mac Firbis and Roderick O'Flaherty. He had in his possession many important manuscripts.

THE 'DECLARATORY' ACT
(1720)

[This notorious piece of legislation was passed by the English parliament to try and put an end, once and for all, to the claims of the Irish parliament and people that they were in any way independent of the parliament at Westminster. The cause of friction between the parliaments had been (as indeed it had been at the time of William Molyneux's *The Case of Ireland*), the question of whether the Irish House of Lords had the right to overturn judgments concerning Ireland made by the English House of Lords. The act unambiguously defined Ireland's status as that of a dependent kingdom.]

An Act for the better Securing the Dependency of the Kingdom of Ireland *upon the Crown of* Great Britain.

Whereas the House of Lords of Ireland have of late, against Law, Assumed to themselves a Power and Jurisdiction to Examine, Correct, and Amend the Judgements and Decrees of the Courts of Justice in the Kingdom of Ireland: Therefore for the better Securing of the Dependency of Ireland upon the Crown of Great Britain, May it please your most Excellent Majesty that it may be Declared; And be it Declared by the Kings most Excellent Majesty, by and with the Advice and Consent of the Lords Spiritual and Temporal, and Commons, in this present Parliament Assembled, and by the Authority of the same, That the said kingdom of Ireland hath been, is, and of Right ought to be Subordinate unto and Dependent upon the Imperial Crown of Great Britain, as being inseparably United and Annexed thereunto; And that the Kings Majesty, by and with the Advice and Consent of the Lords Spiritual and Temporal, and Commons of Great Britain in Parliament Assembled, had, hath, and of Right ought to have full Power and Authority to make Laws and Statutes of sufficient force and Validity, to bind the kingdom and People of Ireland.

And be it further Declared and Enacted by the Authority aforesaid, That the House of Lords of Ireland have not, nor of Right ought to have any Jurisdiction to Judge of, Affirm or Reverse any Judgement, Sentence, or Decree, given or made in any Court within the said Kingdom; And that all Proceedings before the said House of Lords upon any such Judgement, Sentence, or Decree, are, and are hereby Declared to be utterly Null and Void to all Intents and Purposes whatsoever.

CORNELIUS NARY

(*c*.1660-1738)

from:
THE CASE OF THE ROMAN CATHOLICKS OF IRELAND .... (1724)

[The articles of the Treaty of Limerick, concluded in 1691 between the defeated Jacobites and the victorious Williamites, allowed for limited freedom of worship and land-tenure by catholics. But when the time came for the Irish parliament to ratify these articles, it refused to allow the articles on freedom of worship and passed only a radically altered form of the other articles. Catholics rightly felt themselves betrayed and perhaps were not surprised when the Penal Code was enacted to complete their ruin. Hugh Reilly, writing in 1695, bravely asserted that the rights of catholics under the Treaty of Limerick had been basely betrayed; but the most coherent and effective printed protest against the Penal Laws was made by Cornelius Nary, priest of St Michan's church, Dublin. His much reprinted *The Case of the Roman Catholicks of Ireland* puts, better than any other eighteenth-century catholic protest, the circumstances of the betrayal over the articles of the Treaty of Limerick and the case against the oaths of allegiance required by the Irish government.]

The case of the Roman Catholicks of Ireland *Humbly Represented to both Houses of* Parliament 1724; *in Relation to a Bill now under Consideration, by which the said* Roman Catholicks *conceive they are very much aggrieved shou'd it pass into a Law.*

Tho' the Case of these unfortunate People (in my humble Opinion) may not improperly be liken'd to the Roll of a Book, given to the Prophet *Ezekiel* to eat, which was written within and without; and there was written therein Lamentation and Mourning, and Wo.[1] *Qui erat Scriptus intus & foris; et Scripta erant in eo Lamentationes, et Carmen, et Va?* Yet they comfort themselves very much upon this Consideration, that their Fate is in the Hands of noble Peers, and Honourable Senators,[2] whose Goodness and Pitty they had often experienced upon the like Occasion; and look upon it as the greatest of their Happiness, that our Constitution has set them as a Barrier between the Prince and the People, that the Prince might not oppress the People, nor the People invade the Prerogative of the Prince.

The *Roman Catholicks* of *Ireland*, when the Revolution happen'd[3] did conceive and believe it to be undeniably true, that by the antient fundamental Laws, and Statutes of *England* and *Ireland*, the Imperial Crown of *England* was Monarchical and Hereditary, Lineally and Gradually descending by Inherent Indefeazible and Unalienable Right of *Primo Geniture*,[4] and Proximity of Blood, to the next true Heir, upon the Death or voluntary Abdication of the Preceding lawful Monarch, without any Intervening Formality, Call, Authority, Recognition, Coronation oath, or other Ceremony, whatsoever; whether the Heir shou'd happen to be, at the Time of such Death or Abdication, in, or out of the Kingdom, as it did to *James* the Sixth of *Scotland*, and first of *England*, on the Death of Q. *Elizabeth*; and to *Charles* the Second residing in *Holland*, upon the Murder of the King his Royal Father; which verifies the Maxim in Law, affirming that the King never dies. *Rex nunquam Moritur.*

The *Roman Catholicks* of *Ireland*, Grounding their Belief upon these Laws, and Statutes, thought then at least, they were bound in Conscience to keep the Faith and Allegiance, which they gave and swore to King *James* the 2*d*. And therefore concluded, they cou'd not transfer the same unto any other Prince so long as the said King *James* was alive; notwithstanding the Revolution which happen'd in *England*, in the Year 1688. And the rather, that they believed the Abdication, which was voted (in the Convention of *London*) to have been made by the said King, was not voluntary; Considering the Restraint he was under, and the Abuses offer'd to him, when he attempted to make his Escape. And they were further confirmed in this Belief, by the Letter, which he wrote to the Lords of his Privy Council, when he arrived at *Callice*[5] in

1. Ezekiel 2.10 and 3. 1-3.
2. i.e. the Irish Houses of Parliament.
3. In 1688.
4. Inheritance by the eldest child.
5. Calais.

France, desiring them to propose safe Methods for his Return, and giving among other Reasons for his withdrawing or leaving his Kingdoms, a Saying which he had heard of his Royal Father; *that the Prison and Grave of a Prince are not far asunder.*

Upon these Considerations, the *Roman Catholicks* of *Ireland* took up Arms in Defence of his Crown and Dignity, received himself in Person at their Head and fought for him till they were reduced to Extremities by King *William*'s Armies. And even then did not listen to any Terms of Peace, till they had King *James* his Consent, upon his Departure from *Ireland*, to make the best Condition they cou'd for themselves. Being then, the next Campaign after the Battle of *Aughrim*,[6] and surrender of *Galway*, Distressed at the Second Siege of *Limerick*, they Capitulated with the Generals of King *Williams* Troops, and the Lords Justices of *Ireland*; and obtained Articles commonly called the Articles of *Limerick* upon valuable Considerations; *viz.* First, the avoiding the further Effusion of human Blood. Secondly, the Surrendering of the City of *Limerick*, and all the Garrison Towns in the Countys of *Cork*, of *Clare*, of *Kerry*, of *Mayo*, and of *Sligo*. For the Religious[7] Performance of which Articles, according to the true Intent and meaning of the same, the said Lords Justices and Generals, under the Sanction of Publick Faith, solemnly plighted their Words and Honours, and promised to get the same ratified by King *William*, which they accordingly did, *King William* ratifying them in Council under the Broad Seal of *England*.

Now by the first of these Articles, the *Roman Catholicks* of *Ireland* were to enjoy such Privileges in the Exercise of their Religion, as they did in the Reign of King *Charles* the Second; in whose Reign it is manifest, the *Roman Catholicks* had Bishops, Dignitaries, Priests, and Religious Orders of their own Communion to instruct and govern them in Religious Matters.

By the Second Article, all the *Roman Catholicks* of *Ireland* (except those who left the Kingdom, and submitted not to King *William*'s Government) were to enjoy all their Real and Personal Estates, and all the Right Titles, and Interest, Privileges, and Immunities, which they, and every, or any of them held or enjoyed in the Reign of King *Charles* the Second; in whose Reign it is also manifest that all the *Roman Catholick* Peers and Gentlemen of *Ireland* and all others, who wou'd or cou'd purchase them, carried Arms; and that some of them were in Posts of Honours, as that of Sheriffs, Justices of the Peace and other Posts of Profit, and Trust. That their Lawyers, Attorneys, and Sollicitors, practised their respective Callings, with the same Freedom and Liberty as the Protestants. As also that the *Roman Catholick* Merchants, Dealers and Tradesmen were Aldermen and Burgesses in Citys and Freemen in Towns, and Corporations, over all the Kingdom.

By the ninth Article, the Oath to be administred to such *Roman Catholicks*, as submitted to King *William*, was the Oath of Allegiance, and no other.

In Confidence of this sacred Tye of Publick Faith solemnly given to them under the Hands and Seals of the said Lords Justices and Generals, the said *Roman Catholicks* Surrendered the City of *Limerick* and all the Towns and Garrisons then in their Possession, and have ever since to this Day, lived peaceably and quietly under the Government of the respective Kings, and Queens of *Great Britain*, without ever attempting to molest or disturb, or raise any Rebellion or Tumult, in it, as is evident to all the World.

But how well the said Articles and this sacred Tye have been kept to them; or rather how manifestly they have been broken in upon, and violated, is a Theme, which the *Roman Catholicks* cannot with Tears of Blood sufficiently lament, *Hinc illa Lachrima.*[8]

It would be tedious to recite all the Acts of Parliament since made in this Kingdom to that Purpose; Let it suffice to say, that by Laws since made, all and every *Roman Catholick* of the Kingdom (bateing[9] a few Lords and three or four Colonels, of the Troops that were actually in *Limerick* and *Galway*, at the Time they Surrendered) are disabled under severe Penalties, to carry Arms offensive or defensive for their own, or the Defence of their Houses and Goods, other than Pitch Forks, or such Instruments as the Peasants till the Earth with; Nay many Gentlemen, who formerly made a considerable Figure in the Kingdom, are now a Days, when they walk with Canes or Sticks only in their Hands, insulted by

6. Fought in July 1691 at Aughrim, Co. Galway. William III's army, under de Ginkel, scattered a Jacobite army of Irish and French troops.
7. exact.
8. 'From hence proceed those tears.'
9. except.

Men Armed with Swords and Pistols, who of late rose from the very Dregs of the People. *Servi Dominati Sunt nobis! Lamenta Jeremia.*[10]

All *Roman Catholick* Lawyers, Attorny's, and Soliciters, are disabled to practice their respective Callings, except they take the Oath of Abjuration, the Oath of Supremacy and the Test, that is, become Protestants.[11] So that of about an Hundred *Roman Catholick* Lawyers, and Attorneys, that attended the Courts in *Dublin*, and in the Country, not one of them is allowed to get a Morsel of Bread by those Studies upon which they spent their Youth and their Time.

All the *Roman Catholicks* of the Kingdom in general without any Exception or Saving, are disabled to purchase any Lands or Tenements, to take Mortages for Security of Money: or even to take any Lease or Farm exceeding the Term of 31 Years, and that at no less than two Thirds of the improv'd Rent. So that all Encouragement for natural Industry is taken away from them, and are left under an Impossibility of ever being other than Slaves. By the same Laws, their Children tho' never so profligate or undutiful to their Parents, upon their becoming Protestants, are Encouraged to compell their Parents to give them a Maintenance such as the Lord Chancellor, for the Time being shall think fit. And all Heirs apparent of such Parents upon their becoming Protestants, make their Fathers Tenants for Life; So that the Fathers cannot, may not provide for their other dutiful Children, or other extraordinary Exigences of Life. Now if this be not encouraging Children to transgress Gods Law, I own I know not what is. And will not the great Legislator of Heaven require this at Men's Hands?

By another Law, all the Registered *Roman Catholick* Priests of this Kingdom are required to take the Oath of Abjuration by a certain Day, under the Penalty of being reputed Regulars[12] and punished as such. And all the Laity, without Exception to be summon'd thereunto, and upon their Refusal[13] the third Time, to be guilty of a *Premunire*[14] which is Forfeiture and Confiscation of all their Real and Personal Estate, and perpetual Imprisonment. Notwithstanding that they had stipulated by the Articles of *Limerick*; and had the publick Faith given them, that no other Oath, but that of Allegiance shou'd be required of them, which Oath they were always ready to take....

By the Oath of Allegiance all Persons whatsoever, who take the same are bound in Conscience and by the sacred Tye of calling God to bear Witness of the sincerity of their Hearts (as all the Divines, Legislators and Lawyers, in the Christian World agree) not to have a Hand directly or Indirectly in any Plot or Conspiracy against the Prince or Government, to whom they take this Oath; and to discover to him or them, or to some of their Magistrates all such Plots or Conspiracies, as they shall have any Knowledge of; Yea and to be Aiding and assisting with their Lives and Fortunes in suppressing them in their respective Stations and Qualifications. Can there be any Thing more sacred to bind Men's Consciences? Can the Oath of Abjuration do more? If Men break this Oath, will they not break all other Oaths whatsoever? Is not any Government the most Tyranical, or the most unjustly acquired in the World, Safe under such a Tye, from Men whose Love and Affections they suspect, if this Oath be kept? or if it be not, what other Oath will they keep?

As to the Oath of Abjuration there is a vast Difference between it and this: For there are some Clauses in it to the Truth of which I think no *Roman Catholick* at least I am convinced, I cannot in Conscience swear, I shall single out three. *First*, I am required by this Oath to swear that I believe in my Conscience the late King *James* or the Pretender, have no Right or Title whatsoever to the Crown of *England:* Now, I am so far a Stranger to the Right and Titles of Kings and Princes (and I am sure most of my Profession, if not all, in this Kingdom are so) that I wou'd not take such an Oath to any King, Prince, or Potentate in *Europe* with Respect to all such Pretenders, to their Crowns as they shou'd require me to Abjure. For to be able to swear it, I must have sure and certain Motives to ground my Belief upon, else I perjure myself. But

10. 'Slaves rule over us.' Jeremiah in Lamentations 5.8.
11. The Oath of Abjuration required a disclaimer of the rights of the Old Pretender to the English or Irish thrones (cf. the Oath of Allegiance which merely required loyalty to the existing monarch). The Oath of Supremacy referred to the position of the monarch as supreme head on earth of the Churches of England and Ireland. The Test Act of 1673 required all holders of public office to take the sacraments according to the rites of the established church and to repudiate the catholic doctrine of transubstantiation. This last act disabled presbyterians as well as catholics.
12. Members of the household, or fellow-countrymen.
13. i.e. to take the Oath of Abjuration.
14. praemunire: the crime of attempting to introduce the rule of a foreign prince (particularly the pope) into England or Ireland.

this is what I cou'd never yet find in any thing that I read, or from any Person with whom I conversed. Nay many Divines, and Persons of Note and Learning of the Church of *England*, and of the Church of *Scotland*, and *Ireland* by Law Established, have believ'd and so still believe, that neither the late King *James* nor the Pretender have forfeited their Right to the Crown of *England*. And I am sure all the Divines and Lawyers in *France, Spain* and *Italy* are of the same Opinion. How can I then, or any other, *Roman Catholick* in this Kingdom ground my Belief, so as to swear that he has not? But whether he has, or has not, I am no Ways concern'd in taking the Oath of Allegiance, which the Law of Nature and the common Practice of all Nations allow me to take with a safe Conscience to any Prince who conquers me, and the Country of which I am a Member, tho' he be never so great a Tyrant or Usurper, even to *Zar* of *Muscovy*[15] or the Grand Turk. But surely I cou'd not swear, that I believed King *George* hath no Right to the Crown of *England*, or *Ireland*, should either of these conquer me. In a Word, what I swear in the Oath of Allegiance is in my Power to keep, that is, not to be in any Plot or Conspiracy against King *George* or his Government. Or if I hear of any to discover it. And if I do not I perjure my self; But it is not in my Power to found a Belief by which I shou'd swear[16] to the Truth of this Clause in the Oath of Abjuration, and therefore I think I cannot in Conscience take it.

Secondly, there is another Clause in the Oath of Abjuration, requiring Men to swear they will maintain the Succession to the Crown in the Protestant Line *&c.* Now how any *Roman Catholick* continuing such can in Conscience take such an Oath I own I do not understand. For by this Clause I am sworn (shou'd I take the said Oath) to withdraw my Obedience from (And the Allegiance I swore before to) King *George* and his Successors, in Case he or his Successors shou'd become *Roman Catholicks*, nor is this an imaginary Case: For what was, may be. The King of *Navar Henry* the 4*th* was once a Protestant, and became *Roman Catholick*. The Duke of *Saxony* now King of *Poland* was a Protestant, but is now a *Roman Catholick*; And to come nearer Home King *Charles* the Second, and King *James* his Brother were both Protestants, and became *Roman Catholicks*. Now if it shou'd so happen to the Royal Family in *Great Britain* in Time to come, and that they shou'd embrace the Religion which I profess; cou'd I in Conscience, violate my Oath of Allegiance to them, and to my Power be Aiding and Assisting in Dethroning them for doing that, which it is my Opinion and Belief they ought to do? No surely!

I wou'd willingly beg those Gentlemen who press us to take this Oath, to turn the Tables, and allow me for Argument Sake to put a Case. Suppose a *Roman Catholick* Prince sitting on his Throne in *England*, shou'd get an Oath fram'd by Act of Parliament, in which there shou'd be a Clause requiring all the Subjects to swear they wou'd maintain the Succession in the *Roman Catholick* Line. Cou'd any honest Protestant take this Oath with a safe Conscience? If not, I beseech you Gentlemen practice that *Golden Rule. Do as you wou'd be done by*. The third Clause I remark'd in the Oath runs thus. *And I make this Recognition, Declaration &c. Heartily, Freely, and willingly.* I shall only remark upon this Clause, that to my certain Knowledge, many a Man as well *Protestant* as *Catholick*, have taken the Oath of Abjuration with akeing Hearts, and no other Way willingly than as a Merchant or Sailor in a Storm, throws his Goods over Board into the Sea, to save his Life; Now whether such Men do not perjure themselves (since the Laws of God require we shou'd not only part with our Goods, but even lay down our Lives rather than sin, against Conscience) I leave the World to judge.

By this Time, I hope it is pritty plain, that no *Roman Catholick* can, with a safe Conscience take the Oath of Abjuration; and also that their Obedience and Fidelity to the Government, is as well secured by the Oath of Allegiance, as by it. But let us suppose that the takeing of the Oath of Abjuration, is a further Security of the Subjects Fidelity; what have the *Roman Catholicks* of *Ireland* to do with that? They laid down their Arms and gave up their Garrison Towns, and Cities with their Stores and Ammunition upon the solemn Promise, and under the Sanction of Publick Faith, ratified by Royal Authority, that no other Oath shou'd be required of them, but that of Allegiance. Is there no Regard to be had for that Publick Faith and Law of Nations, which were held so sacred by the very Heathens, that they used to denounce the Wrath

15. The Czar of Moscow.
16. i.e. create a situation that will relieve me so that I can swear....

and Vengeance of their false Gods, against such as violated them? . . .

King *William* of happy Memory had other Notions of the Publick Faith, when he went with his Army to besiege *Limerick*. He offered the *Roman Catholicks* Conditions; which they did not think good enough, tho' they were ready to submit, and lay down their Arms, had he condescended to give them better Terms. He besieged the Town in Form,[17] made a large Breach in the Wall, and assaulted it three several[18] Times. But cou'd not carry the Place: Would not his Majesty then give the *Roman Catholicks* any Terms they cou'd in Reason desire, rather than suffer the Check of being obliged to raise[19] the Siege as he was, if he thought he might in Honour or Conscience break his Promise, when the besieged were in his Power? So far from it that during his Reign, he did not suffer the least Attempt to be made upon the Articles which his Generals made the Year following with the *Roman Catholick* Army at *Limerick*, of which we have a pregnant Instance. For in the 3*d* Year of his Reign when an Act of Parliament passed in *England*, intituled an Act for the obrogating[20] the Oath of Supremacy, and appointing other Oaths, requiring all Officers, Magistrates, Lawyers, *&c.* in *Ireland* to take the same, there was a saving for such *Roman Catholicks* as were intituled to the Benefit of the Articles of *Limerick*; and it was expresly provided by the said Act that they shou'd be obliged to take the Oath of Allegiance and no other.

But alas! This great Monarch was no sooner laid up, with his Fathers, but the *Roman Catholicks* began to feel the dire Effects of some Mens Spleen. I say some Men: For God Almighty be thanked. We have always had many worthy Gentlemen of great Honour and Integrity in the House of Commons, and many also in the House of Lords, without whose help we would have been long since consumed. But our Misfortune hitherto was that, as every Thing in Parliament is carried by a Majority of Votes; and those, who did not wish us well, being generally the greater in Number, there was scarce a Session of Parliament in this Kingdom, during the Reign of Queen *Anne*, in which one Point or other has not been Invaded of the Articles and Conditions upon which we submitted to King *William*; and which are in themselves no more than what was natural for Subjects and Free born Men to expect; Nay much less than our Neighbouring Nation the *Scots* obtain'd upon their submitting to the Crown of *England*. But there is this Difference; that not one Title of the Conditions promised to these, was ever yet violated; whereas there is scarce an Article of the Conditions upon which the *Roman Catholicks* submitted, but has been broken by severe Laws. And yet we Challenge all the World to shew us one Instance in which we have not demeaned ourselves, as dutiful and as loyal Subjects as the *Scots*, if not more; so that it is plain the Design of those our Enemies who had no Regard to the sacred Bands by which all Nations are in a manner ty'd together was to destroy and exterminate us from off the Face of the Earth. But I wou'd beg of them to consider, that there is a God in Heaven, an Avenger of Wrongs, a God of Vengeance to those who violate Publick Faith, a Crime which never fails to bring visible Judgments from Heaven, especially when it is Publick and National, as may be manifestly seen both in Sacred and Prophane History. . . .

This Bill, this Fatal Bill! provides that no *Roman Catholick* Priest under the Penalty of High Treason shall say Mass in the Kingdom, Except those who have taken the Oath of Abjuration (a manifest Violation of the ninth Article of the Capitulation of *Limerick*) and that no Man, under the Penalty of Felony,[21] without Benefit of Clergy,[22] shall Aid, Assist, or Harbour any such Priest, and to make sure Work, it provides also, that the Informer of such Priest or lay Man Assisting, Aiding, or Harbouring him, shall have an Hundred Pounds Reward, and another hundred Pounds are to be given to the Prosecutor, of such Priest (or lay Man Aiding or Assisting the Priest) in Order to his Conviction.

Now it is certain that of Eleven Hundred *Roman Catholick* Priests, who were Registred Pursuant to an Act of Parliament to that Purpose,[23] not above 33 Priests ever took the Oath of Abjuration, and of these 33 one half are now dead; And of the Registred Priests more than two Thirds. What shall so many Thousands of *Roman Catholicks*, in every

17. in military formation.
18. separate.
19. lift.
20. abrogating, repealing.
21. A more serious class of crime than misdemeanour.
22. Clergy who broke the law had the right to be tried by an ecclesiastical rather than a secular court.
23. Passed in 1704.

Province of the Kingdom do then, to serve God in their own Way? (I beg I may not be understood, as if I intended to magnifie their Numbers to give an Umbrage[24] to the Government. For I say nothing but what every Protestant in the Nation knows as well as my self, and very well knows also, that they are in no Capacity to molest, and give any Disturbance; And I dare ingage they have no Intention or Design so to do) what shall they do when sick or dying? to send for Priest (if any can be had, for they must all quit the Kingdom, or expose themselves to inevitable Death) its to themselves certain Death, considering the Greatness of the Reward offer'd to the Informer, who doubtless will be one of their own Domesticks.[25] *O unspeakable Cruelty! O Faith of Men!* Surely to treat them as the *French* King did the *Hugenots*[26] would be much more tolerable; that is, to banish them the Kingdom, and to allow them a reasonable Time to sell their Estates and dispose of their Effects as he did.

To pass by many other severe Clauses in this Bill, I beg leave to offer my humble Opinion, that it is Unpolitick, and against the Interest of the Government, that such a Bill should pass into a Law.

First, it is Unpolitick to persecute the *Roman Catholicks* in this Kingdom, when the King is labouring to get a Toleration for *Protestants* from *Roman Catholick* Princes.

Secondly, it is Unpolitick, because it will drain the Kingdom of the greatest Part of the People; Especially of that Part which we call in Scripture Phrase *Heivers of Wood and Drawers of Water*.[27] For if this Bill passes into a Law, all the Estated *Roman Catholicks*, all the Merchants, Dealers, Shopkeepers, all the Trades Men and Farmers with their respective Clans will dispose of their Effects and quit the Kingdom, as will also the little People who are able to purchase their Passage, and such as are not, will become Thieves and Robbers, having no Clergy Men to teach or instruct, or to keep them within bounds. And I may very well presume there are few *Protestants* in the Kingdom, who do not know that the *Roman Catholicks* big and little taken together are more than half the Number of the People of *Ireland*. Besides all these, at least their Children may be trained up to Arms Abroad and furnish the *Pretender* with a numerous Army, who doubtless will have Stomach[28] enough to recover their native Country, and vindicate the Wrongs which they conceive to have been done to themselves and their Parents. And here I cannot but Reflect upon what I have often heard the greatest and wisest Statesmen in *France* say, that the *French* King never made a more Unpolitick Step than that of Banishing the *Hugenots*: For they were the most fierce, the most desperate, and the most Prodigal of their Lives, of all other Enemies, dureing the whole Course of his Wars.

Thirdly, it is Unpolitick to Dispeople a Nation which must of Necessity be supply'd by Foreigners and Strangers; how else shall we Plow our Land, Reap and Thress our Corn, Draw Stones or Water, *&c*. . . .

Lastly, it is against the Interest of the Government, For it is well known, that the *Roman Catholick* Merchants and Dealers carry on more than half the Trade of the Kingdom, and pay more Custom and Duty for Imported Goods, than all the Protestants in it. Now if this Bill shou'd pass, all these Merchants and Dealers would be necessitated to leave the Kingdom, to the great Diminution of the Revenue; and God knows in how many Years this cou'd be retrieved, if ever!

This is the lamentable Case, Right Reverend Fathers in God, Right Honourable Lords, and most excellent Senators,[29] of the unfortunate *Roman Catholicks* of *Ireland*; who wou'd have dyed to the last Man with their Swords in their Hands, cou'd they imagine that the Publick Faith so solemnly given them should be violated, or themselves reduced without Cause to so intollerable Servitude; Their Behaviour being so even, their Demeanor so peaceable, and their Loyalty so untainted, that they challenge the very worst of their Enemies from the Day they submitted, to this, to find the least Flaw or Blemish in their Conduct. . . .

24. offence.
25. Members of the household, or fellow-countrymen.
26. The Calvinist protestants of France were persecuted by Francis II and Louis XIII, but here Nary is referring to their treatment by Louis XIV. Entire provinces were depopulated and the Huguenots fled to England, Ireland, the Netherlands, Germany, Switzerland and America.
27. Joshua 9.21.
28. courage.
29. Nary is addressing the spiritual lords, the temporal lords and the House of Commons.

FRANCIS HUTCHESON
(1694-1746)

from:
AN INQUIRY INTO THE ORIGINAL OF OUR IDEAS OF BEAUTY AND VIRTUE (4th edition 1738)

[These passages from Hutcheson's *Inquiry*, first published in London in 1725, display the political implications of his doctrine of benevolence. Taking up the contemporary fad for travellers' tales (instanced in the popularity of *Robinson Crusoe* and *Gulliver's Travels*), Hutcheson argues that the exotic or incredible elements in these do not prove anything more than that different conditions can alter the form which benevolence takes. He goes on to say that the failure of benevolence leads to factionalism and sectarianism; these in turn prepare the way for despotism. His description of despotism and his definition of liberty were widely popular in the American colonies before the American revolution. Hutcheson was also one of the founding figures of eighteenth-century Scottish philosophy, but it is obvious, even from these extracts, how tellingly his Shaftesburian version of benevolence bore on the sectarianized situation in the Ireland in which he had received his philosophical training.]

SECTION 4

AN INQUIRY CONCERNING MORAL GOOD AND EVIL

III. From what has been said, we may easily account for the *vast Diversity* of *moral Principles*, in *various Nations* and *Ages*; and the Grounds of *this Diversity* are principally these:

1st. Different Opinions of *Happiness*, or *natural Good*, and of the most effectual Means to advance it. Thus in one Country, where there prevails a *courageous Disposition*, where *Liberty* is counted a *great Good*, and *War* an *inconsiderable Evil*, all Insurrections in Defence of Privileges will have the Appearance of *moral Good* to our *Sense*, because of their appearing *benevolent*; and yet the *same Sense* of *moral Good* in *Benevolence*, shall in another Country, where the Spirits of Men are more *abject* and *timorous*, where *Civil War* appears the *greatest natural Evil*, and *Liberty* no *great Purchase*, make the same Actions appear *odious*. So in SPARTA, where thro' Contempt of Wealth the Security of Possessions was not much regarded, but the Thing chiefly desir'd, as *naturally good to the State*, was to abound in a *hardy shifting Youth*, *Theft*, if dexterously perform'd, was so little odious, that it receiv'd the Countenance of a Law to give it Impunity.

But in these, and all other Instances of the like Nature, the Approbation is founded on *Benevolence*, because of some real, or apparent Tendency to the *publick Good*. For we are not to imagine, that this *Sense* should give us, without Observation, Ideas of complex Actions, or of their natural Tendencys to *Good* or *Evil*: it only determines us to approve *Benevolence*, whenever it appears in any Action, and to hate *the contrary*. So our *Sense* of *Beauty* does not, without Reflection, Instruction or Observation, give us Ideas of the *regular Solids, Temples, Cirques*, and *Theatres*; but determines us to approve and delight in *Uniformity amidst Variety*, where-ever we observe it. Let us read the *Preambles* of any Laws we count unjust, or the Vindications of any disputed Practice by the *Moralists*, and we shall find, no doubt, that Men are often mistaken in computing the Excess of the *natural good* or *evil Consequences* of certain Actions; but the Ground on which any Action is approv'd, is still some Tendency to the *greater natural Good* of others, apprehended by those who approve it.

The same Reason may remove also the Objections against the *Universality of this Sense*, from some Storys of Travellers, concerning *strange Crueltys* practis'd toward the *Aged*, or *Children*, in certain Countrys. If such Actions be done in such angry Passions, they only prove, that other Motives, or Springs of Action, may overpower *Benevolence* in its *strongest Ties*: and if they really be universally allow'd, look'd upon as innocent, and vindicated; it is certainly under some Appearance of *Benevolence*; such as to secure them from Insults of Enemys, to avoid the Infirmity's of Age, which perhaps appear greater Evils than Death, or to free the vigorous and useful Citizens from the Charge of maintaining them, or the Troubles of Attendance upon them. A Love of Pleasure and Ease, may in the immediate Agents be stronger in some Instances, than *Gratitude* toward Parents, or *natural Affection* to Children. But that such Nations are continu'd, notwithstanding all the Toil in educating their Young, is still a sufficient Proof of *natural Affection*: For I fancy we are not to imagine any nice Laws in such Places, compelling Parents to a proper Education of some certain Number of their Offspring. We know very well that an Appearance of *publick Good* was the Ground of Laws equally barbarous, enacted by LYCURGUS and SOLON,[1] of killing the Deform'd, or Weak, to prevent a burdensome Croud of useless Citizens.

A late ingenious Author[2] has justly observ'd the Absurdity of the *monstrous Taste*, which has possess'd both the *Readers* and *Writers* of *Travels*. They are sparing enough in Accounts of the *natural Affections, the Familys, Associations, Friendships, Clans*, of the *Indians*; and as transiently do they mention their Abhorrence of *Treachery* among themselves; their *Proneness*, to mutual Aid, and to the Defence of their several *States*; their Contempt of Death in Defence of their Country, or upon Points of *Honour*. 'These are but *common Storys.* — No need to travel to the *Indies* for what we see in *Europe* every Day.' The Entertainment therefore in these ingenious Studys consists chiefly in exciting *Horror*, and making Men *stare*. The ordinary Employment of the Bulk of the *Indians* in Support of their Wives and Offspring, or Relations, has nothing of the *Prodigious*: But a *Human Sacrifice*, a Feast upon Enemys Carcases, can raise an Horror and Admiration of the wondrous Barbarity of *Indians*, in Nations no Strangers to the *Massacre* at *Paris*, the *Irish Rebellion*, or the Journals of the *Inquisition*. These they behold with religious Veneration; but the *Indian Sacrifices*, flowing from a like Perversion of *Humanity* by *Superstition*, raise the highest Abhorrence and Amazement. What is most surprizing in these Studys, is the wondrous *Credulity* of some Gentlemen of great Pretensions in other Matters to Caution of Assent, for these *marvellous Memoirs* of Monks, Friars, Sea-Captains, Pirates; and for the *Historys, Annals, Chronologys*, receiv'd by oral Tradition, or Hieroglyphicks.

Men have *Reason* given them, to judge of the Tendencys of their Actions, that they may not stupidly follow the first Appearance of *publick Good*; but it is still some Appearance of *Good* which they pursue. And it is strange, that *Reason* is universally allow'd to Men, notwithstanding all the stupid ridiculous Opinions receiv'd in many Places; and yet absurd Practices, founded upon those very *Opinions*, shall seem an Argument against any *moral Sense*, altho' the bad Conduct is not owing to any Irregularity in the *moral Sense*, but to a wrong *Judgment* or *Opinion*. If putting the *Aged* to Death, with all its Consequences, really tends to the *publick Good*, and the *lesser Misery* of the *Aged*, it is, no doubt, *justifiable*; nay, perhaps the *Aged* choose it, in Hopes of a *future State*. If a *deform'd* or *weak Race* could never, by Ingenuity and Art, make themselves useful to Mankind, but should grow an absolutely unsupportable Burden, so as to involve a whole State in Misery, it is *just* to put them to Death. This all allow to be *just*, in the Case of an over-loaded Boat in a Storm. And as for *killing* of their Children, when Parents are sufficiently stock'd, it is perhaps practis'd, and allow'd from *Self-Love*; but I can scarce think it passes for a good Action any-where. If *Wood* or *Stone*, or *Metal* be DEITIES, have *Government*, and *Power*, and have been the *Authors* of *Benefits* to us; it is *morally amiable* to praise and worship them. Or if the true DEITY be pleas'd with Worship before *Statues*, or any *other Symbol* of some more *immediate Presence* or *Influence*; *Image-Worship* is *virtuous*. If *he* delights in *Sacrifices, Penances, Ceremonys, Cringings*; they are *all laudable*. Our *Sense* of *Virtue* generally leads us exactly enough according to our Opinions; and therefore the absurd Practices which prevail in the World, are much better Arguments that Men have no *Reason*, than that they have no *moral Sense* of *Beauty* in Actions.

IV. The next *Ground* of *Diversity* in Sentiments is the *Diversity* of *Systems*, to which Men, from foolish Opinions, confine their *Benevolence*. We intimated above, that it is *regular* and *beautiful*, to have *stronger Benevolence* toward the *morally good* Parts of Mankind, who are *useful* to the *Whole*, than

1. Lycurgus, the founder of the Spartan constitution, first referred to in Herodotus and usually associated with the 7th century B.C. when he led a reform movement to set up a machine of war that would preclude a revolt of the helots.

Solon (*c.* 638-*c.* 559 B.C.), an Athenian statesman and law-giver, generally acknowledged as the founder of the Athenian democracy.

2. Anthony Ashley Cooper (1671-1713), 3rd earl of Shaftesbury, whose chief work, *Characteristicks of Men, Manners, Opinions, Times*, 2 vols (London, 1711; rev. ed. 1714) exercised a dominant influence over Hutcheson. The reference here is to Shaftesbury's discussion of *Travel Tales* in Vol. I, pp. 346 ff.

toward the *useless* or *pernicious*. Now, if Men receive a *low* or *base Opinion* of any *Body*, or *Sect* of Men; if they imagine them bent upon the Destruction of the more valuable Parts, or but useless *Burdens* of the Earth; *Benevolence* itself will lead them to neglect the Interests of such, and to suppress them. This is the Reason why, among Nations who have high Notions of *Virtue*, every Action toward an Enemy may pass for *just*; why ROMANS and GREEKS could approve of making those they call'd *Barbarians, Slaves.*

A late ingenious Author[3] justly observes, 'That the various *Sects, Partys, Factions, Cabals* of Mankind in larger Societys, are all influenc'd by a *publick Spirit*: That some generous Notions of *publick Good*, some strong friendly Dispositions, raise them at first, and excite Men of the same *Faction* or *Cabal* to the most disinterested mutual Succour and Aid: That all the Contentions of the different Factions, and even the fiercest Wars against each other, are influenc'd by a sociable *publick Spirit* in a limited System.' But certain it is, that Men are little oblig'd to those, who often artfully raise and foment this Party Spirit; or cantonize them into several Sects for the Defence of very trifling Causes. Associations for innocent *Commerce*, or *Manufactures*; Cabals for Defence of *Liberty*, against a *Tyrant*; or even lower Clubs for *Pleasantry*, or *Improvement* by Conversation, are very amiable and good. But when Mens Heads are filled with some trifling Opinions; when designing Men raise in their Minds some unaccountable Notion of *Sanctity* and *Religion*, in Tenets or Practices, which neither increase our Love to GOD, or our own *Species*; when the several Factions are taught to look upon each other as *odious, contemptible, profane*, because of different Tenets or Opinions; even when these Tenets, whether true or false, are perhaps perfectly useless to the publick Good; when the keenest Passions are rais'd about such Trifles, and Men begin to hate each other for what, of itself, has no Evil in it; and to love the Zealots of their own Sect for what is no way valuable; nay, even for their Fury, Rage, and Malice against opposite Sects; (which is what all Partys commonly call *Zeal*) 'tis then no Wonder, if our *moral Sense* be much impair'd, and our *natural Notions* of *Good* and *Evil* almost lost, when our *Admiration*, and *Love* or *Contempt*, and *Hatred*, are thus perverted from their natural Objects.

If any Mortals are so happy as never to have heard of the *Party-Tenets* of most of our Sects; or, if they have heard of them, have either never espous'd any Sect, or all equally; they bid fairest for a truly *natural* and *good* Disposition, because their *Tempers* have never been soured about vain Trifles; nor have they contracted any *Sullenness* or *Rancour* against any Part of their own *Kind*. If any *Opinions* deserve to be contended for, they are those which give us lovely Ideas of the DEITY, and of our *Fellow-Creatures*: If any Opinions deserve Opposition, they are such as raise Scruples in our Minds about the *Goodness* of PROVIDENCE, or represent our Fellow-Creatures as *base* and *selfish*, by instilling into us some ill-natur'd, cunning, shrewd Insinuations, 'That our most generous Actions proceed wholly from *selfish Views*.' This wise *Philosophy* of some *Moderns*, after EPICURUS,[4] must be fruitful of nothing but *Discontent, Suspicion*, and *Jealousy*; a State infinitely worse than any little transitory *Injurys*, to which we might be expos'd by a good-natur'd *Credulity*. But Thanks be to the kind AUTHOR of our Nature, that in spite of such Opinions, our *Nature* itself leads us into *Friendship, Trust*, and *mutual Confidence*.

Were we freely conversant with *Robbers*, who shew a *moral Sense* in the *equal* or *proportionable Division* of their Prey, and in *Faith* to each other, we should find they have their own sublime *moral Ideas* of their Party, as *generous, courageous, trusty*, nay *honest* too; and that those we call *honest* and *industrious*, are imagin'd by them to be *mean-spirited, selfish, churlish*, or *luxurious*; on whom that Wealth is ill bestow'd, which therefore they would apply to better Uses, to maintain gallanter men, who have a Right to a Living as well as their Neighbours, who are their profess'd Enemys. Nay, if we observe the Discourse of our *profess'd Debauchees*, our *most dissolute Rakes*, we shall find their Vices cloath'd, in their Imaginations, with some amiable Dress of *Liberty, Generosity, just Resentment* against the

3. From Shaftesbury's 'Essay on Wit and Humour', included in *Characteristicks. . . .*, Vol. I, p. 110.

4. Epicurus (341-279 B.C.), the Greek philosopher whose ideas were most fully expressed by Lucretius in his poem *De Rerum Natura*. By the late seventeenth century, Epicureanism had come to be regarded as a selfish, pleasure-seeking philosophy. The French critic, Saint-Evrémond (1613-1703), who lived in England for some time, was the most influential proponent of this view. His works were translated into English in 1714.

Contrivers of artful Rules to enslave Men, and rob them of their Pleasures.

Perhaps never any Men pursu'd Vice long with Peace of Mind, without some such deluding Imagination of *moral Good*, while they may be still inadvertent to the *barbarous* and *inhuman Consequences* of their Actions. The Idea of an *ill-natur'd Villain* is too frightful ever to become familiar to any Mortal. Hence we shall find, that the *basest Actions* are dress'd in some *tolerable Mask*. What others call *Avarice*, appears to the *Agent* a *prudent Care* of a *Family*, or *Friends*; *Fraud*, *artful Conduct*; Malice and *Revenge*, a *just Sense* of *Honour*, and a *Vindication* of our Right in Possessions, or Fame; *Fire* and *Sword*, and *Desolation*, among Enemys, a *just thorow*[5] *Defence* of *our Country; Persecution*, a *Zeal* for the *Truth*, and for the *eternal Happiness* of Men, which *Hereticks* oppose. In all these Instances, Men generally act from a *Sense* of *Virtue* upon *false Opinions*, and *mistaken Benevolence*; upon *wrong* or *partial Views* of *publick Good*, and the Means to promote it; or upon very *narrow Systems* form'd by like *foolish Opinions*. It is not a *Delight* in the Misery of others, or *Malice*, which occasions the horrid Crimes which fill our Historys; but generally an *injudicious, unreasonable Enthusiasm* for some kind of *limited Virtue*. . . .

X. From *Art*. vii. it follows, 'That all human *Power*, or *Authority*, must consist in *a Right transferr'd to any Person or Council, to dispose of the alienable Rights of others*; and that consequently, there can be no Government so absolute, as to have even an *external Right* to do or command every thing.' For where-ever any Invasion is made upon *unalienable Rights*, there must arise either a *perfect*, or *external Right* to *Resistance*. The only Restraints of a moral Kind upon Subjects in such Cases, are, when they foresee that, thro' their want of Force, they shall probably by Resistance occasion greater Evils to the Publick, than those they attempt to remove; or when they find that *Governors*, in the main very useful to the Publick, have by some unadvised Passion, done an Injury too small to overbalance the Advantages of their Administration, or the Evils which Resistance would in all likelihood occasion; especially when the Injury is of a private Nature, and not likely to be made a Precedent to the Ruin of others. *Unalienable Rights* are *essential Limitations* in all Governments.

But by *absolute Government*, either in *Prince* or *Council*, or in *both jointly*, we understand *a Right to dispose of the natural Force, and Goods of a whole People, as far as they are naturally alienable, according to the Prudence of the Prince, Council, or of both jointly, for the publick Good of the State, or whole People; without any Reservation as to the Quantity of the Goods, Manner of Levying, or the Proportion of the Labours of the Subject, which they shall demand*. But in all States this *tacit Trust* is presuppos'd, 'That the Power conferr'd shall be employ'd according to the best Judgment of the Rulers for the publick Good.' So that, whenever the Governors openly profess a Design of destroying the State, or act in such a manner as will necessarily do it; the *essential Trust*, suppos'd in all Conveyance of *Civil Power*, is violated, and the *Grant* thereby made void.

A Prince, or Council, or both jointly, may be variously limited; *either when the Consent of the one may be necessary to the Validity of the Acts of the other; or when, in the very Constitution of this supreme Power, certain Affairs are expressly exempted from the Jurisdiction of the Prince, or Council, or both jointly*: as when several independent States uniting, form a general Council, from whose Cognizance they expressly reserve certain Privileges, in the very Formation of this Council; or when, in the very Constitution of any State, a certain Method of *Election* of the Person of the Prince, or of the Members of the supreme Council, is determin'd, and the *Intention* of their Assembling declar'd. In all such Cases, it is not in the Power of such Prince, Council, or both jointly, to alter the very *Form of Government*, or to take away that Right which the People have to be govern'd in such a manner, by a Prince or Council thus elected, without the universal Consent of the very People who have subjected themselves to this Form of Government. So that there may be a very *regular State*, where there is no universal absolute Power, lodg'd either in one Person, or Council, or in any other Assembly beside that of the whole People associated into that State. To say, that upon a Change attempted in the very *Form of the Government*, by the *supreme Power*, the People have no Remedy according to the Constitution itself, will not prove that the *supreme Power* has such a *Right*; unless we confound all Ideas of *Right* with those of *external Force*. The only Remedy indeed in that Case, is an universal Insurrection against such *perfidious Trustees*.

5. thorough.

Despotick Power, is *that which Persons injur'd may acquire over those Criminals, whose Lives, consistently with the publick Safety, they may prolong, that by their Labours they may repair the Damages they have done; or over those who stand oblig'd to a greater Value, than all their Goods and Labours can possibly amount to.* This Power itself is limited to the Goods and Labours only of the Criminals or Debtors; and includes no Right to *Tortures, Prostitution,* or any Rights of the Governed which are *naturally unalienable*; or to any thing which is not of some Moment toward *Repair of Damage, Payment of Debt,* or *Security against future Offences.* The Characteristick of *Despotick Power,* is this, 'That it is solely intended for the Good of the Governors, without any *tacit Trust* of consulting the Good of the *Governed.*' Despotick Government, in this Sense, is directly inconsistent with the Notion of Civil Government.

From the Idea of *Right*, as above explain'd, we must necessarily conclude, 'That there can be no *Right*, or *Limitation of Right*, inconsistent with, or opposite to the greatest publick Good.' And therefore in Cases of *extreme Necessity*, when the State cannot otherwise be preserv'd from Ruin, it must certainly be *just* and *good* in limited Governors, or in any other Persons who can do it, to use the Force of the State for its own Preservation, beyond the Limits fix'd by the *Constitution*, in some *transitory Acts*, which are not to be made *Precedents*. And on the other hand, when an *equal Necessity* to avoid Ruin requires it, the Subjects may justly resume the Powers ordinarily lodg'd in their Governors, or may counteract them. This Privilege of *flagrant Necessity* we all allow in Defense of the most perfect *private Rights*: And if *publick Rights* are of more extensive Importance, so are also *publick Necessitys*. These Necessitys must be very grievous and flagrant, otherwise they can never overbalance the *Evils* of violating a tolerable Constitution, by *an arbitrary Act of Power*, on the one hand; or by an Insurrection, or Civil War, on the other. No Person, or State can be happy, where they do not think their *important Rights* are secure from the *Cruelty, Avarice, Ambition*, or *Caprice* of their Governors. Nor can any *Magistracy* be safe, or effectual for the Ends of its Institution, where there are frequent Terrors of *Insurrections*. Whatever *temporary Acts* therefore may be allow'd in extraordinary Cases; whatever may be lawful in the *transitory Act* of a bold Legislator, who without previous Consent should rescue a slavish Nation, and place their Affairs so in the Hands of a *Person* or *Council, elected* or *limited* by themselves, that they should soon have Confidence in their own Safety, and in the Wisdom of the Administration; yet, as to the fixed State which should ordinarily obtain in all Communitys, since no *Assumer* of Government can so demonstrate his superior Wisdom or Goodness to the Satisfaction and Security of the Governed, as is necessary to their Happiness; this must follow, 'That except when Men, for their *own Interest*, or out of *publick Love*, have by *Consent* subjected their Actions, or their Goods, within certain Limits to the Disposal of others; no Mortal can have a *Right* from his *superior Wisdom*, or *Goodness*, or any other *Quality*, to give Laws to others without their *Consent, express* or *tacit*; or to dispose of the *Fruits* of their Labours, or of any other *Right* whatsoever.' And therefore *superior Wisdom*, or *Goodness*, gives no *Right* to Men to govern others. . . .

JONATHAN SWIFT

(1667-1745)

LETTER TO THE EARL OF PETERBOROUGH (1726)

[From an Anglo-Irish perspective, no short document explains the predicament of eighteenth-century Ireland under English control better than this letter written by Swift during his visit to London in 1726. The administrative, commercial and economic injustices under which Ireland laboured are here presented in a form that even Walpole could have understood.]

April 28, 1726

My Lord,

Your Lordship having at my request, obtained

for me an hour from Sir *Robert Walpole*,[1] I accordingly attended him yesterday at eight o'clock in the morning, and had somewhat more than an hour's conversation with him. Your Lordship was this day pleased to inquire what passed between that great Minister and me, to which I gave you some general answers, from whence you said you could comprehend little or nothing.

I had no other design in desiring to see Sir *Robert Walpole*, than to represent the affairs of *Ireland* to him in a true light, not only without any view to myself, but to any party whatsoever: and, because I understood the affairs of that kingdom tolerably well, and observed the representations he had received were such as I could not agree to, my principal design was to set him right, not only for the service of *Ireland*, but likewise of *England*, and of his own administration.

I failed very much in my design; for, I saw, he had conceived opinions from the examples and practices of the present and some former governors, which I could not reconcile to the notions I had of liberty, a possession always understood by the *British* nation to be the inheritance of a human creature.

Sir *Robert Walpole* was pleased to enlarge very much upon the subject of Ireland, in a manner so alien from what I conceived to be rights and privileges of a subject of *England*, that I did not think proper to debate the matter with him so much as I otherwise might, because I found it would be in vain. I shall, therefore, without entering into dispute, make bold to mention to your Lordship some few grievances of that kingdom, as it consisteth of a people, who, beside a natural right of enjoying the privileges of subjects, have also a claim of merit from their extraordinary loyalty to the present King and his Family.

First, That all persons born in *Ireland* are called and treated as *Irishmen*, although their fathers and grandfathers were born in *England*; and their predecessors having been conquerors of *Ireland*, it is humbly conceived they ought to be on as good a foot as any subjects of *Britain*, according to the practice of all other nations, and particularly of the *Greeks* and *Romans*.

Secondly, That they are denied the natural liberty of exporting their manufactures to any country which is not engaged in a war with *England*.

Thirdly, That whereas there is a University in *Ireland*, founded by Queen *Elizabeth*,[2] where youth are instructed with a much stricter discipline than either in *Oxford* or *Cambridge*, it lieth under the greatest discouragements, by filling all the principal employments, civil and ecclesiastical, with persons from *England*, who have neither interest, property, acquaintance, nor alliance, in that kingdom; contrary to the practice of all other States in *Europe* which are governed by viceroys, at least what hath never been used without the utmost discontents of the people.

Fourthly, That several of the bishops sent over to *Ireland*, having been clergymen of obscure condition, and without other distinction than that of chaplains to the governors, do frequently invite over their old acquaintance or kindred, to whom they bestow the best preferments in their gift. The like may be said of the judges, who take with them one or two dependents, to whom they give their countenance, and who, consequently, without other merit, grow immediately into the chief business of their courts. The same practice is followed by all others in civil employments, if they have a cousin, a valet, or footman, in their family, born in *England*.

Fifthly, That all civil employments, grantable in reversion, are given to persons who reside in *England*.

The people of *Ireland*, who are certainly the most loyal subjects in the world, cannot but conceive that most of these hardships have been the consequence of some unfortunate representations (at least) in former times; and the whole body of the gentry feel the effects in a very sensible part, being utterly destitute of all means to make provision for their younger sons, either in the Church, the law, the revenue, or, of late, in the army: and, in the desperate condition of trade, it is equally vain to think of making them merchants. All they have left is, at the expiration of leases, to rack their tenants; which they have done to such a degree, that there is not one farmer in a hundred through the kingdom who can afford shoes or stockings to his children, or to eat flesh, or drink anything better than sour milk or water, twice in a year; so that the whole country, except the *Scotch* plantation in the north, is a scene

1. Sir Robert Walpole (1676-1745), 1st earl of Orford, became first lord of the treasury and effectively prime minister in 1721.

2. Trinity College, Dublin, founded in 1591.

of misery and desolation, hardly to be matched on this side *Lapland*.

The rents of *Ireland* are computed to be about a million and a half, whereof one half million at least is spent by lords and gentlemen residing in *England*, and by some other articles too long to mention.

About three hundred thousand pounds more are returned thither on other accounts: and, upon the whole, those who are the best versed in that kind of knowledge, agree, that *England* gaineth annually by *Ireland* a million at least, which even I could make appear beyond all doubt.

But, as this mighty profit would probably increase, with tolerable treatment, to half a million more; so it must of necessity sink, under the hardships that kingdom lieth at present.

And whereas Sir *Robert Walpole* was pleased to take notice how little the King gets by *Ireland*, it ought, perhaps, to be considered, that the revenues and taxes, I think, amount to above four hundred thousand pounds a year; and reckoning the riches of *Ireland*, compared with *England*, to be as one to twelve, the King's revenues there would be equal to more than five millions here; which, considering the bad payment of rents, from such miserable creatures as most of the tenants in *Ireland* are, will be allowed to be as much as such a kingdom can bear.

The current coin of *Ireland* is reckoned, at most, but five hundred thousand pounds; so that above four-fifths are paid every year into the exchequer.

I think it manifest, that whatever circumstances can possibly contribute to make a country poor and despicable, are all united with respect to *Ireland*. The nation controled by laws to which they do not consent, disowned by their brethren and countrymen, refused the liberty not only of trading with their own manufactures but even their native commodities, forced to seek for justice many hundred miles by sea and land, rendered in a manner incapable of serving their King and country in any employment of honour, trust, or profit; and all this without the least demerit: while the governors sent over thither can possibly have no affection to the people, further than what is instilled into them by their own justice and love of mankind (which do not always operate); and whatever they please to represent hither is never called in question.

Whether the representatives of such a people, thus distressed and laid in the dust, when they meet in a Parliament, can do the public business with that chearfulness which might be expected from freeborn subjects, would be a question in any other country, except that unfortunate island, the *English* inhabitants whereof have given more and greater examples of their loyalty and dutifulness than can be shown in any other part of the world.

What part of these grievances may be thought proper to be redressed by so wise and great a minister as Sir *Robert Walpole*, he perhaps will please to consider; especially because they have been all brought upon that kingdom since the Revolution, which, however, is a blessing annually celebrated there with the greatest zeal and sincerity.

I most humbly entreat your Lordship to give this paper to Sir *Robert Walpole*, and desire him to read it, which he may do in a few minutes. I am, with the greatest respect, my Lord.

Your Lordship's,
Most obedient humble servant,
Jon. Swift.

JOHN BROWNE

(*c*.1700-62)

from: REFLECTIONS UPON THE PRESENT UNHAPPY CIRCUMSTANCES OF IRELAND .... (1731)

[The Declaratory Act of 1720 ushered in a decade during which many important pamphlets were published in Dublin on the subject of Ireland's political and economic ills, including Swift's *Drapier's Letters*. One of the more interesting of the lesser pamphleteers was John Browne, the owner of land and an ironworks in County Mayo, whose rather chequered career included being forced to flee from Ireland on a charge of attempted murder.

The passage below comes from a paper in which Browne was putting forward a proposal for the establishment of public granaries to alleviate the suffering caused by the shortage of grain in some parts of Ireland. In the course of his argument, Browne achieves a useful assessment — from the point of view of the English in Ireland — of the problems inherent in the relationship between the two nations.]

The Misunderstanding between the two Nations arises mostly from Prejudice. Our Predecessors have been in perpetual Wars and Enmity with the old *Irish*, who inhabited this Island: There were here frequent Rebellions and bloody Massacres, and in the last Strugles for their expiring Liberties, nothing was left undone which a desperate People could undertake, in Defence of the most valuable Blessings; this laid a strong and a lasting Foundation for Hatred and ill Blood, between the contending Parties, and it has taken so deep a Root in *England*, that they even forget how that People are no more, how we are here no longer their Enemies, but their Sons and their Brethren, and how we must ever be studious to support the Glory of that People, from whom we are every one of us descended, and from whom we derive the most valuable of our Rights and Possessions.

This, is one great Cause of that Prejudice which is so conspicuous in the Behaviour, and even in the Councils of our Neighbours of *Britain*: By our Migration into this Island we have acquired the Name of *Irish-Men*: The Sons have heard their Fathers tell of the barbarous Cruelties, and of the bloody Murthers committed upon their Friends in *Ireland*; This has begot a Prejudice in the Children against *Irish-Men* in general, and as we, by our Situation, have got that Name, thè Prejudice is transfer'd to us, and tho' we are really the very People, of whose Sufferings, they have heard their Fathers complain, yet they, unaccountably lay to our Charge the Blame and the Infamy of the whole; not remembering that, as the Poet beautifully Expresses it, *Cælum non animum mutant qui transmare Currunt*.[1]

But, *my Lord*, there is a Prejudice of another kind which they have also imbibed, and which tho' not of so extraordinary a Nature, is yet altogether as hurtful to us, I mean, *my Lord*, the Prejudice which has long prevail'd amongst them, against the *Irish* Trade....

1. 'Those who cross the seas change their climate, but not their mind.' Horace, *Epistles* I, 11, 27.

Thus, *my Lord*, the whole People of *England*, were put in a Flame upon the Article of *Irish* Beef, to the great Loss of *England*, and to the more extraordinary Profit of the *French*, who at this very time, take most of our Beef, and export it by long and gainful Channels to *America*: This poor Country of ours, labouring under so many Disadvantages, that they have not a Stock[2] left to carry on any Branch of Trade ...

Such a private, designing, interested Spirit has prevail'd, in most of the Commercial Laws of *Great-Britain*, to the unspeakable Loss of that Nation, as well as of this; but a more unhappy Prejudice yet has taken Root there, from the great Expence which our Neighbours have been at, for the Reduction of this Country, and the large Remittances, which they have been oblig'd in antient Times to make, for even the Support of the *Irish Establishment*, insomuch, that I have often with Astonishment heard it said, by Men of otherwise very good Understandings, *That it had been happy for* England, *if* Ireland *had been sunk under the Sea*....

These are the Prejudices which stand in our way, upon every Application for an Encouragement of our Commerce, and these in particular are the Reasons why we have so long solicited among other things, for proper Laws for the Encouragement of our Tillage: But, *my Lord*, if this Matter were by some able hand laid in a proper Light before them ... it is impossible that a wise Nation disengaged from Prejudice, should any longer remain Blind to the Interests of their Country, and defer to raise us up into such a Station in Trade, as without breaking in upon their own Business, wou'd enable us to recover (for them) the Commerce which they have lost, and to furnish them with a Treasure, which until that is done, must remain a Wealth and a Power in the Hands of their Enemies.

2. a capital sum.

from:
THE BENEFITS WHICH ARISE TO A TRADING PEOPLE FROM NAVIGABLE RIVERS .... (1729)

[Another of Browne's pamphlets was concerned with the

sensible plan to encourage inland water transport in Ireland, particularly on the Shannon, where he proposed the establishment of a company to develop the river.]

Our whole inland Carriage is at present performed by small feeble Cattle,[1] either in high Loads, which scarcely exceed two hundred Weight; or on truckle Cars, of which, a Horse and Car in Summertime, when the Roads are dry, and the Cattle strong, may, one with another, carry about 4 C. Weight; but in other Seasons of the Year, there is little or no Land-carriage; for those little Machines are swallowed up in bad Roads: The Cattle (which are in themselves very small) are for want of proper Food and Care unable to encounter the Road, and the Wetness and Uncertainty of the Seasons make it unsafe to send any choice Goods by Carriages so ill defended; so that the whole, or at least, the most considerable Part of the Land-carriage must be hurried on in one Quarter of the Year, and the Consequence is, that on the one hand, the Price of carrying to Market, by being so greatly inhanced, becomes a Burthen upon all our Exports and Imports; and on t'other hand, the want of Carriages in the other three Quarters, confining all the Produce of Art and Labour, for so long a time, to the respective Places of their Growth and Production, must necessarily be a great Discouragement to the Industry of the Inland Countries, and a great Clog upon our Trade in general.

I can instance this Misfortune in no matter more obvious to all Capacities, than the late Scarcity of Corn, and I will suppose, that there might have been a great Plenty of Corn in the inland Parts of *Ireland*, whilst the Scarcity thereof in *Dublin* was almost insupportable, or *Vice Versa*, a Plenty at the Sea-ports and a Famine in the Inland Countries. Corn is a bulky Commodity, Cattle are weak, the Roads bad, how should we be the better here in the *Winter* or Spring, for such a Plenty in the very Heart of our Country? would it not be easier for us to have our Bread from *Egypt*, than from the Counties of *Roscommon, Longford*, &c? and how would it, in the other Case, be possible to relieve the Wants of the Inland Countries by imported Grain, unless the whole People had travelled up to eat it? There are few People, sure, who have seen the Price of Corn in *Dublin*, reduced by an Importation from the *Mediterranean*, but will readily allow it; and what can be the Reason of this, but the want of a proper Communication, and a convenient Vehicle to carry our Goods to Market.

Man is perhaps the only Creature that does not yield to the Inclemency of the Seasons, and lose or recover Strength by the Recess or Approach of the grand Luminary; and this is due to that Reason and Foresight with which our Creator has been pleased to endow us: By this we are taught to prepare our Hovels, and lay in our Stores, for that which would otherwise be the most helpless and the least comfortable Season of the Year, and by this we are led out early in the *Spring* again, to labour and till the Soil for such another Crop; so that by his Providence we are qualified alike for Labour and Industry, either in the *Winter* or the *Summer* Seasons, and are therefore the only Carriers to be relied upon. The Frame of our Bodies, 'tis true, does not fit us out for great Burthens, but this Defect is however abundantly supplied by our Craft and Ingenuity: By these, Ships and Barges are launched out, which by the Assistance of a few Hands, can perform the Business of many hundreds of Horses and Oxen: By such Helps as these we have seen the Scarcity of *Europe* for many Years furnished by the Labours of the innermost Parts of *Poland*, the River Vistula affording them a Passage to the Ocean, and by that to our Markets....

And that it may not for ever remain a Reproach to the People of *Ireland*, that being furnished by Nature, with one of the finest Rivers in the World, ... they shall yet suffer it to remain of no Account, ... I make bold to offer to the Publick, a Scheme, for the Establishment of a Company, and a reasonable Stock for the Undertaking, which is so contrived, that every Person concern'd, shall have an Influence in the Company, in Proportion to the Interest he has in it, and that, with such a Regard to the Welfare of the whole, that neither can the designing Man injure, or circumvent his Brethren, nor the tardy become a Remora,[2] to delay or postpone the Business, in which, I am far from designing any particular Advantage to my self, excepting only, the Honour of being instrumental in bringing about, an Undertaking so advantagious to my Country.

1. livestock (i.e. oxen or dray horses).

2. A fish with a sucking disc on the top of its head, enabling it to attach itself to ships or rocks. Hence, figuratively, an impediment, obstacle.

THOMAS PRIOR

(1682-1751)

from: A LIST OF THE ABSENTEES OF IRELAND .... (1730 edition)

[Thomas Prior's *Absentees* was one of the most frequently reprinted books of eighteenth-century Ireland. Its popularity was probably due to the fact that it not only stated the economic arguments against absentee landlords but listed these landlords and their incomes. It is worth nothing that modern economic historians are inclined to mistrust some of Prior's figures and his arguments against absenteeism. (See *A New History of Ireland*, IV (Oxford: Clarendon Press, 1986), pp. 172-73.)]

... 'Tis notorious, that some have drawn out of the Kingdom 100,000, some 200,000, and others above 300,000 *l.* the last 20 Years; and yet the said Persons have not contributed to the Support of the publick Charges, as much as the meanest Persons who pay *the least part of our Taxes.*

It cannot be supposed, that our *Irish* Landlords, who live abroad, and consume no Part of the Produce or Manufacture of their Country, pay the least Share of the Duties or Taxes thereof, or relieve any of its Poor, whose Miseries they never see, or make any Improvements, who never mean to live among us. Nay, their living abroad seems to have so far alienated their Affections from their Country, and hardened their Tempers towards it, that they above all others, are remarkable for setting their Estates at a *Rack-Rent*, so as hardly to allow a Livelihood to their poor Tenants, by whom they are supported.

There is no Country in *Europe*, which produces and exports so great a Quantity of *Beef, Butter, Tallow, Hydes* and *Wool*, as *Ireland* does; and yet our common People are very poorly cloath'd, go bare-legged half the Year, and very rarely taste of that Flesh-meat, with which we so much abound. We pinch our selves in every Article of Life, and export more than we can well spare, with no other Effect or Advantage, than to enable our Gentlemen and Ladies to live more luxuriously abroad.

And *They* are not content to treat us thus, but add Insult to ill Usage; *they* reproach us with our Poverty, at the same Time, that *they* take away our Money; and can tell us, we have no Diversions or Entertainments in *Ireland* for them, when they themselves disable us from having better, by withdrawing from us.

But 'tis to be hoped, that our Legislature will take care, that those Gentlemen who spend their Fortunes abroad, and are thereby the greatest, and almost only Cause of its Poverty and Distress, shall not be the only Persons favoured, and exempted from paying the Taxes thereof.

A Tax of four Shillings in the Pound, on the Estates of *Absentees*, would in all Likelihood remove the Evils complain'd of, by stopping in a great measure those wasteful Drains of our Money; and would, in all Respects, answer the Occasions of the Government: for if these Gentlemen will, notwithstanding, still live abroad, then a considerable Fund will arise out of their Estates to defray the publick Charges; and if they should return home, then the publick Revenue will encrease by a greater Produce in the Excise and Customs, in Proportion as the home Consumption would be enlarg'd by the spending of so much more Money among us: either Way the publick Occasions would be supply'd; and the People reliev'd.

We may farther observe by the said List, that the great and continual Drain of Money out of this Kingdom, is from the large Estates; few Gentlemen of small Fortunes, do, or can live abroad.

An Act of Gavelkind, whereby all Estates above 500 *l. per Ann.* should descend, and be divided in equal Proportion, among all the Sons, as Coheirs, (with certain Reservation, in favour of those, who have Titles of Honour, of all present Family Settlements, and of eldest Sons, if it should be thought adviseable) would, in a great measure, prevent so much living and spending abroad, and induce all the Sons to sit down on their own respective Patrimonies, and improve them.

Such a Descent of Estates is certainly agreeable to the Law of Nature, for Children equally related to their Parents ought to be equally their Care; but our Law and Custom, that gives the whole real Estate to the eldest Son, serves indeed no other Purpose, but to gratify the *Pride* and *Vanity* of

Families, and leaves to the younger Children (often the most deserving) a poor scanty Provision, or perhaps no Provision at all; whilst the eldest Son is tempted, by the largeness of his Estate, to spend all luxuriously abroad, to the utter Ruin of the Family, and great Loss of the Kingdom. *The Pride of Names and Families, is despised by all People of Sense, and is rarely to be found but in poor Countrys, or Persons of reduc'd Fortunes, and is generally accompany'd with the Want of real Merit.*

'Tis true Policy, and would tend much to the Benefit of remote Provinces, if Property were more equally divided among the Inhabitants; large overgrown Estates are generally consumed, either abroad or at the Capital, and may be reckon'd as so much Tribute, in effect, drawn from the Provinces; while small Fortunes are spent in the Place where they arise, with more Vertue and Advantage to the Country.

And till we can be so happy as to obtain such an Act of Parliament, which would be greatly to the benefit of this Kingdom; 'tis to be hoped, that Gentlemen of large Estates, out of Regard to their Posterity, and the Good of their Country, will in their Marriage-Settlements, or last Wills, choose rather to bring in their younger Sons for a Share of their Lands, and so make many thriving young Families, than by giving all to one Son, to tempt him, by extravagant living abroad, to put an End to the Family at once, as it hath often happened of late within the Knowledge and Observation of every one.

We must own, that there are many of our *Gentlemen* abroad, who wish well to their Country, and abhor all Thoughts of having a hand in the Ruin of it; who yet are not sensible how much this Kingdom is distressed, and suffers by their living and spending their Estates in other Countries: but when they come to reflect on the Consequences thereof, and see the Poverty and Miseries we labour under by their Means, and that they themselves must at last share therein, 'tis not to be doubted, but that they will, out of Regard to themselves, and Compassion to their Country, change their Conduct, and act as becomes them.

We must not forget, that as on the one hand we suffer extremely by many, who have abdicated their Country, and have no Sense of its Miseries; so on the other hand, we lie under the greatest Obligations to those Lords and Gentlemen, who constantly live, and spend their Fortunes among us. If the Earl of *Kildare*, and others of our Nobility; Mr. *Conolly*,[1] and others of our Commons, had not all along resided among us, we should long since have been exhausted of all our Treasure, and reduced to the greatest Distress.

I can't forbear, on this Occasion, to take Notice of one remarkable Instance, among many others, which Mr. *John Damer*, one of our richest Commoners, has lately given us, of the just Sense he has of the Good of this Country, and how much he has the Interest thereof at heart. This Gentleman having no Prospect of Issue to inherit his great Estate, in order to engage his Brother, (who, we may suppose, is design'd to be his Heir, and has several Children, and a large Fortune in *England*,) to settle in this *Kingdom*, has agreed to make over to him at present a considerable Estate, with a fine House well furnished thereon, upon this *express Condition* and *Consideration*, that he shall immediately bring over his Family and reside among us: And I am inform'd his Brother has agreed thereto. By this means he has provided, that his Estate shall continue to be spent in the Kingdom, which otherwise would, in all probability, be constantly carry'd off after his Decease; and it is to be hoped, that other Gentlemen, moved by the same Spirit, will shew themselves the same Spirit, will shew themselves the same true *Patriots*, and by their last Wills oblige their Heirs to reside among us.

The Love of one's Country is seldom found in any remarkable Degree, but in those, who live long in it, agreeable to the Intention of *Nature*, which disposes all Men, and other Creatures, to a Fondness for those Places in which they live; if this be the Case, I fear we can expect but little Good from those, who, by forsaking their Country, must have lost almost all natural Affection towards it; and this may teach us, who still retain a Sense of the Duty we owe our Country, to be very cautious, on all future Elections of Parliament-Men, or on any other Occasions, how we pay any Regard to those, who do not live constantly among us. It must be of Service, to take publick Notice of those Actions, which tend both to the Good and Hurt of one's Country; in order to excite us to the Practice of the First, and prevent our being guilty of the Second.

1. William Conolly (died 1729) was appointed speaker of the Irish parliament in 1715. He built Castletown in Celbridge, Co. Kildare, the largest and one of the most splendid houses in Ireland.

HENRY BROOKE

(*c.*1703-83)

from: THE FARMER'S LETTERS TO THE PROTESTANTS OF IRELAND (1745)

[The Jacobite rising of 1745, although confined to Scotland and the north of England, alarmed many Irish protestants, and several strong anti-catholic pamphlets exhorting protestants to protect their nation and their interests appeared at this time. The liveliest series of pamphlets, ostensibly by an outraged protestant farmer, was actually written by the landlord, playwright and novelist, Henry Brooke, the father of Charlotte Brooke. The rhetorical flourishes in these pamphlets are important in the history of eighteenth-century writing, coming half-way between Swift's use of such full-blown rhetoric for satiric purposes in the 1720s and the florid verbal excesses of the later eighteenth-century Irish parliament and bar. Ornate language was often the mark of a self-conscious conservatism in the last decade of the century.]

Countrymen and Fellow Protestants,

I shall make neither Preface nor Apology for this Address; could I vent my Thoughts to you in any other Way, I would not chuse this; but the Backwardness of better Pens, and the Necessity of the Times, urges the very Stones to Utterance: This is not the Season for fine Flourishes and Rhetorick, but for plain Truth, and Manhood; and I hope my Want of Capacity as a Writer, will be attoned by the Warmth and Honesty of my Heart.

It is not many Weeks since I my self was looked upon as a Kind of Malecontent among my few Acquaintance, and used to harangue, very learnedly, as I thought, upon Corruptions in *England* and Grievances in *Ireland*; for I had borrowed some useless Books from the neighbouring 'Squires, and did believe that a Man who held himself to be free-born, ought to give a plain Account of his Faith in *Politicks*, as well as *Religion*, to all who asked him.

I make no Doubt but there are many others of the same Turn of Thought and Spirit who yet love his Majesty's Person, and would stand by his Government, as firmly, as those who flatter his Power, or share his Favours.

It is not any Disaffection to his *Majesty*, but our Affection to the *Constitution*, that gives us this wrangling Disposition; and I think we shall be the likeliest of all Men, to spill the last of our Blood in the Defence of *both*; for sure the Miser who grumbles to part with a *Penny*, will *struggle* hard before he parts with his *Plumb*.[1]

Perhaps there never was a Constitution upon Earth that would not admit of Improvement, nor a Ministry that did not leave room for Reproof; and I am often captious with my best Friends, at the same Time that I wish their Health, and act for their Interest. Such little Jealousies and Exceptions are often Instances of the strongest Attachment, at the worst they only ruffle the Surface of Loyalty, and, like Family Disputes, always cease on the Approach of a common *Enemy*.

This common *Enemy*[2] is now at hand. He is our Enemy by *Nature* as well as *Education*; and my Intent is to prove, that were it possible for him to prevail, the Consequence to us would be the same, as if this whole Frame of Heaven and Earth was to be broken, and thrown into its first Darkness and Confusion; for such is the Antipathy between a *Popish* Prince and *Protestant* Subjects, and such would be the Ruin of all our Interests, and the utter Subversion of our State.

In the late Readiness and Chearfulness with which you assembled throughout the several Counties and Baronies of this Kingdom, you expressed a brave and a loyal Resolution, a Resolution of defending his Majesty's Person, with your Lives and Fortunes, against the impudent Attempt of a Popish Pretender to his Throne, and against the united Power of all his Enemies.

Indeed we can do do no less, for his Government has been mild, and his Subjects have prospered under it.

But, my Countrymen, this is not the Cause for which his Majesty has called us, he is known to be a brave Man, and his late glorious *Declarations* in Parliament, as well as his frequent Contempt of

1. Plumb = plum: the titbit or best thing he possesses.
2. The Young Pretender, Charles Edward Stuart (1720-88), popularly known as Bonnie Prince Charlie.

Dangers, assure us, that his Fears are not for himself, but for his Subjects.

France and *Spain*, two of the most powerful States in *Europe*, threaten us with *Popery* and *Slavery*: and his Majesty, who is the Father of his People, has summoned us together, as one Family united in Interest and Affection, to preserve ourselves from the most utter Ruin that ever came upon any Nation.

The Oaths of Allegiance, which we have taken on this Summons, are quite different in their Nature from those taken by most other People upon Earth.

Where the Will of Rulers either makes or dispences with the Law, the Obligation of such an Oath commenceth but from the Taking, and is binding no further than the Letter; because it is an *Obligation* of Constraint, and not of Reason: But the Oaths we have so newly and voluntarily taken, are a Recognition of former Ties, their Obligation is of eternal *Force*, it has lain upon our Forefathers, and I trust will lie upon our Children from Generation to Generation, while *Great-Britain* or *Ireland* have a Name.

Whatever regards this World, or that which is to come; all that is sacred in Heaven, or valuable on Earth, is included in this Obligation; our Duty to GOD, to our King, to our Country, to Truth, to Reason, to Interest, to Ourselves, to our Honours, to the Memory of our valiant Ancestors, and the Consideration of that everlasting Infamy which must brand us, should we degenerate from their Actions.

But is that possible? can we prove recreant[3] to so noble, so fresh an Example? —— I think not —— some of the Eyes that saw those Times are still open among us, and many of us are the Kindred and immediate Descendants of those glorious Men, to whom we owe that we are now living, that we are Protestants, that we are Free, and to whom, perhaps, the World is indepted that there is such a Thing as Liberty now left upon the Earth.

The Talk of our Fathers was as difficult as it was important, it was to recover from those in Possession the Blessings already lost: ours is merely to preserve the great Inheritance they have left us....

Is the Nature of Things reversed? are *Protestants* become enamoured of *Popery*? and do the *Free-born* of these Kingdoms call out for *Chains*? shall the *Children invite* that very Evil, which the *Fathers* laid down their Lives to *reject*? —— No, my Countrymen —— as we received so great a Trust from our wise and brave Ancestors, we will deliver it down safe and inviolate to our Posterity, we will, to the Death, preserve that Liberty which alone can make Life valuable, and the Purity of that Religion, which will best qualify us for Immortality.

While ever there is a Church in *Rome*, that claims a Power to dispense with *Lay* Obligations, and arrogates supreme Authority over Sovereign Princes and Civil Rights, it is utterly incompatible with our Constitution, and absurd to common Sense, to trust one of her Votaries on the Throne. She will ever look on our *Reformation* in Religion as *Heresy*, and on the *Supremacy* of our King as the *Usurpation* of her Right; she will therefore leave no Machinations, nor Means unattempted, to reclaim us to our former Sphere of Superstition and Slavery; and what Method so proper, nay what Method possible? save the Imposition of some royal *Tool* on the State, who may secretly work for the Restoration of the *Papal Hierarchy*. For this supreme Purpose, the Sense of Revelation is perverted, and the Authority of Heaven profaned....

During the last fifty Years, and upward, this Kingdom has possessed the Advantages of Liberty, Property, and a profound Peace. Such long Tranquility naturally produceth Indolence, a Forgetfulness of former Ills, and an Insensibility of present Enjoyments. Human Life is like the Picture in my Neighbour's Parlour, where the Lights are in a great Measure relative, and recommended by the Shading. It is just so, that the Memory or Sense of Affliction, giveth us the higher Relish of any succeeding Pleasure; let us then look back, and by the Prospect of what our Fathers have *suffered*, be taught to feel, and defend the Blessings we *possess*.

For this Purpose we need not go beyond the *mild* and *favourite* Line of the *Stuarts*; nor there, beyond the Memory of the present Age, and the supposed Grandfather of this *young Adventurer*.

I first beg Leave to premise, that the very Essence and vital Strength of Civil *Liberty*, in every Constitution, is *the Right of being governed by Laws to which the People give their own Consent*; and this Right is derived from the natural Constitution of Man, in which no Obedience is required, even to Divine Commands, before the Examination and Assent of Reason; and under such rational Government, the *Principle of Freedom* is left uncontrouled,

3. unfaithful.

even by GOD himself; and who is that Prince, that has a Right to Jurisdiction, beyond what INFINITE POWER and WISDOM has prescribed to his own Authority?

Agreeable to this *just*, and *Godlike Institution*, *England* had her *Magna Charta*[4] and her Parliamentary Laws; all foreign Usurpations were exploded from Religion and Liberty, nor could the Life or Property of the meanest *Briton* be affected, but by the Tryal and Verdict of his Peers.

To maintain these Privileges, and to defend these Rights, was *James* the Second placed upon the Throne. He first calls a Parliament, he attempts to threaten them into his Measures, he then dissolves them, and rules alone. He taxes the People by his sole Authority, they murmur, he overawes them by Force, and raises a Standing Army in Midst of Peace. He compels all Cities and Corporations to deliver up their Charters and Franchises, he turns out the Protestants from every Place of Power, and fills the Benches with Papists, and all Places of Trust with his own Creatures, to whom he shares his Power that they may support his Tyranny. Hereupon he sends abroad his arbitrary Inquisitions and Commissioners, a thousand Tyrants are made out of one; they dispose of Life and Property at Pleasure; in one Place the Bodies of the Free-born are drawn to Execution without Tryal, in another pack'd Juries are impanelled, or the Verdicts rejected, and overruled by the Court —— Where then was Trade, Where was Art, where was Industry? Where then was the Law, the Religion, and the Liberty? Where the Arms and the Honour of a *British* Constitution? All was crushed, all was abolished, the three Kingdoms trembled, but did not dare to groan under their Calamities.

But, O, my Countrymen! while the Lightning blasted other Places, the Bolt itself fell upon Us. I cannot recollect such Scenes without Horror and Indignation. May we all perish, before we suffer the like again! and herein I only wish to you, what I resolve for my self.

Our Arms, and every Instrument of Defence was seized; we were debarred all Friendship and Society with each other; our Smiles and Tears became equally dangerous, and every Word and Action was interpreted to our Disadvantage. No Place was a Refuge, no Conduct was a Sanction to us; if we appealed to Law, we encountered with Power; and if we applied for Justice, we met with Condemnation. An Army of Sixty Thousand Free-booters[5] was let loose upon us, whose only Pay was the Pillage and Plunder of the Protestants, on whom they were appointed for free Quarters. Those Wretches seized our Properties as of Right, and entered our Houses by Violence; they insulted our Misery, and perpetrated all Kinds of Villainy; they invaded the Marriage Bed, they compelled the Parents to behold the Rape of their Daughters; our Submission encouraged them to proceed to new Injuries, and if we resisted, we were dragged to Execution for Rebellion.

The Traces of those Times, my Countrymen, are not yet worn out, the Scars of those Wounds are still evident, and the Memory of them bleeds to this Day.

If we are Freemen, if we are Men —— if we are Husbands, if we are Parents —— if we have Families to defend, or Properties to preserve —— if Liberty and Religion are more than Names —— if there is any Sense of Honour, or even of Interest left among us —— if an universal Lethargy does not prevail, if Cowardice has not quelled a Kingdom — we will arise! we will seize every Man his Sword! we will turn upon these Destroyers! these Enemies of Mankind! nor will we be appeased, till we have swept this Invader with his Slavish Rout, from the very Face of the Earth that they incumber.

4. The Great Charter of liberties extorted by the barons from King John in 1215. It secured the liberties of the church, the rights of the barons and freemen, and restricted the abuses of royal power. Parliamentarians in the sixteenth century saw it as a milestone in British constitutional history.

5. plunderers.

CHARLES LUCAS
(1713-71)

from:
A SECOND ADDRESS TO THE FREE CITIZENS AND FREE-HOLDERS OF THE CITY OF DUBLIN
(3rd edition 1748)

[Charles Lucas, a Dublin apothecary and doctor, was the architect of an important extra-parliamentary agitation in Dublin in the late 1740s. In his candidature for parliament, he espoused the principles of Swift and Molyneux and opposed the power of Dublin Corporation. The government, under the viceroy, the Earl of Harrington, declared Lucas to be an enemy of the country and, in so doing, aroused the Dublin mob that supported him. The pamphlet from which the following extracts are taken demonstrates Lucas's style and technique: rhetorical generalizations about liberty are interspersed with attacks on the Dublin Corporation and appeals for support of his own candidacy.]

Every *good Member of Society* must always be mindful of the indispensible *Debt* he owes to the *Public*, and, therefore, constantly sollicitous for the *Freedom* and *Wealth* of all *Mankind*, in general, but, more especially, of that *Body of Men* to which he is inviolably Bound by Law, as well, as by every moral and religious Consideration.

Next to his Duty to his CREATOR, *Man's* chief Obligation is to *Man*. We are not born for ourselves alone. We have a mutual relation to, and Dependance upon, each other; and *self-Love*, tho' the most active Principle in the Mind of Man, is but a Branch of *Social Love*; Insomuch, that by this alone, the purity and real Value of the former are to be proved and ascertained.

The truly sensible, who must ever be a good, Man, looks upon himself, not only as a Limb or Member of the great Society, but as a *Trustee* or *Servant* to the PUBLIC. His *first* and *great Obligation* is to *serve* the *Community*, in his *allotted Station*, to the utmost of his Power. He knows that every *Individual* is, by the *great, unerring* LAW of NATURE, as well, as by that of *Man*, indispensably *Subservient* and *Ministerial* to, as well, as dependent on, the WHOLE COMMUNITY, and that, therefore, all *selfish* or *private Interest* must ever be freely, and readily sacrificed to the *Public*. Such a Man cannot, unmoved, see the most slight and distant Incroachment made, or threatened, on the *Privileges* and *Rights* of his *Neighbours*. His Heart and Hand must ever be *raised* to oppose all *Degrees* of, and *Tendencies* to, *Oppression* and *Tyranny*, executed or attempted by the *highest* upon the *lowest* and *most remote*: And much less, can an *immediate Member* of the *Community*, receive the *slightest Wound* or *Injury*, which the good Man does not Feel and Bleed for, in a double Sense; first, from universal Benevolence and Brotherly Love; and secondly, from good Policy.

While any Sense of Liberty is left, the good Man, let his Sphere in Life be what it may, must ever be able, as well, as willing, to give some check to the *highest Oppressors* and *evil Doers*, and some comfort or solace to *injured Innocence* and *Virtue*. He cannot, therefore, grow *weary in well-doing*. He must persevere with *Zeal, Courage* and *Fortitude*.

This Character every Man should adopt. For this is but a short Sketch of what Man should be, I am sorry to say, not what Man is. But I must insist, that that Man is best qualified for every Office of public Trust, who best fullfills this Character.

Yet, melancholly Consideration! Such is the depravity of the Times, that no Man wades with more, real difficulties, thro' Life, than the generous, public spirited Man. His Conduct is ever a Reproach to the Multitude; their *Envy, Hatred* and *Malice* will, therefore, upon all Occasions, boil over upon him, and shew it self in various Shapes. — *The Virtues of the most Eminent are*, at best, *obscured, by the Ignorance, Prejudice or Envy of their Beholders. — Some Men cannot*, or if they can, will not, *Discern*, or distinguish, *a noble from a base Action. Others are apt to attribute them to some false End or Intention; and others purposely mis-represent, or put a wrong Interpretation upon them. But a solid and substantial Greatness of Soul looks down with a generous Neglect on the Censures and Applauses of the* misguided *Multitude, and places a Man beyond the little noise and strife of Tongues.*

If these Positions be true, and these Considerations just, nothing should deter the Man, who has established these Principles in his Mind, from steadily pursuing the virtuous Course, which a well informed Conscience Directs. His Mind must ever be bent on doing all possible Good. Nor is he to be discouraged by all the Obstacles that can be thrown in his way; his Intentions are all that he is accountable for, to Heaven; and, when he has done, or endeavoured to do, all the good in his Power, not till then, can he content himself with the comfortable Consideration of having discharged his Duty; he is not answerable for the Event, that must be left to Providence.

However short of this Character, I may be found to have fallen, if I know my self, I can, of a Truth, say, it has ever been uppermost in my View, and that it is from these Principles alone, I am now prompted, to offer my self for an *high Station* among you. Could I have means of laying my Bosom open to you, I should not fear being able to acquit myself of Undertaking this *arduous Talk*, for you, thro' *Pride* or unbecoming *Ambition*. I assure you, I am most perfectly contented with being cast among the *lower Class* of Men, with regard to *Station* and *Grandeur*; for there, in all Nations, at this, nay, at all Times, do we find most Freedom and Virtue. It is my utmost Pride that I am a *Tradesman* and *Citizen of* DUBLIN, and that I am neither of *Family, Fortune, Education*, or *Principle* to recommend me, to what the World falsely calls, *Great Men*, that is, *Men in Power*; or *modern*, that is, *new-fashioned Gentlemen*. Do but reflect, who have restored, and now, uphold the Freedom and Rights of *Sweden*. You will find they were the *poor, despised Tradesmen* and *Peasants*, whose *Representatives*, in their *Parliament*, tho' called from their *Trades*, their *Shops* or their *Ploughs*, are now the principal *Opponents* of the Incroachments on PUBLIC LIBERTY, and its *boldest* and *best Assertors*. Who long preserved the sinking States of *Holland* from *impending Slavery*, and lately restored the *original Frame of Government*, against the Power of many *corrupt Tyrants, grown great* by the Spoils of their Country? Was not this done by the *Tradesmen*, headed, at first, by no more considerable Persons, than a *Black-Smith* and a *Wheel-Wright*? What has often prevented the Ruin of a neighbouring Nation, when a *Minister practised* in *Perfidy* and *Corruption, packed Place-Men*,[1] *Pensioners* and other *venal Slaves* and *Prostitutes*, in such Crowds, into Parliament, that he could gain every End he proposed there? — It was the *Virtue* and *Freedom* of the TRADESMEN of LONDON, alone, which prevented many *anticonstitutional Bills* being carried into Execution, that had passed both Houses of Parliament. — In this Class my Pride would Place me, if my Fortune had not. Here I contentedly, gladly cast my Anchor. — Judge of the Truth of this by my Conduct, thro' all the Offices in which I have already served you. And as a Bond for future Behaviour, accept these public Declarations. — It is time to lay *Self* aside; but let me first inform you, that tho' I have publickly offered myself a Candidate for the Place of a CITIZEN to represent you in Parliament, it is but to let you See my Intention and Desire, however weak and insufficient you may find me, to serve the Sinking Cause of LIBERTY and my COUNTRY. From the same Motive, incapable as I am of the Talk, if the *Citizens* of *Dublin* Commanded me, on any Emergency, to lead an Army for them, I should certainly obey them. Their *Free Choice* shall ever determine me in all Matters. And to shew my *inviolable* Regard to their *Freedom*, I scorn, disdain and detest all the little *base anticonstitutional* Arts of *modern Candidates*, to gain the *Voices* of Men and if any *mistaken* Friend should attempt to influence *any Man* to *Vote* for me, on any other Principle, than FREE CHOICE, let it not be looked upon, as my Act, I *renounce*, and *protest* against it — The Man who acts on Constitutional Principles cannot, *in any instance, invade* or *restrain* the LIBERTIES of his *Neighbour*. He must think it, therefore *designing*, if not *Criminal* to *influence* a *Voice* to bring him into Parliament, as it would be to influence a *Sheriff* to put him on a *Jury*. — Suppose yourselves, then, *Sheriffs*, and any Man Sollicited you to be put on a *Pannel*, would you not, therefore, *Suspect* and *Reject* him? You could not avoid it. — In the Case of an *Election*, you act in a *judicial Capacity*, as much as a Sheriff does. Your Vote is not entirely your own. You cannot without *Perfidy*, a Breach of Trust to Society, give it, thro' *Interest* or *Complement* to any Man. He is a *Wicked, low Tyrant* that Demands, or accepts of it, on these Terms, and cannot therefore be fit to *represent*, nor, indeed, to

1. Persons who hold or aspire to hold public office for self-interested motives or as a reward for political support. From 1718 to 1772, Sweden had a parliamentary government in which the aristocratic element was predominant. In the 1730s, other factions arose and the opposition was provided by the merchant classes. The Dutch Merchant class was almost as powerful as the aristocracy.

be *represented* by, any Body. And the only difference between *him*, and *those* that comply with him, can be no more, than that between the *Tempter* and the *Tempted*, *both*, at best, are *criminal*. — It is an Honor to represent FREE-MEN, but not but a *Slave* can Submit to be the *Representative* of *Slaves*....

You cannot be altogether insensible how YOU and YOUR COMMONS are treated by the Board of *Aldermen*. Tho' you cannot see all their *Impositions*, all their *Oppressions*, all their *Perfidy* and *unnatural Usurpations*, at one View, you must know, that they *confessedly*, *unlawfully*, and *unjustly*, with-hold from you, YOUR UNQUESTIONABLE RIGHT of *electing Aldermen*, *Coroners*, and other Officers of the City: That they look upon your COMMONS as *Beasts of Burden*, and transact matters without their consent: That they *withhold* the *Government* and every *Benefit* of the *Hospital*, *founded* and *erected* by the *City*, for *reduced Citizens*, and *their Children*, from the *Commons* and *Citizens*, and *their Issue*: That, in *Spight* to the *Commons*, they prefer their *menial Servants* and *their Bastards*, to *Places* for which many *poor Citizens Petition*, and for want of which, *they* and the *abandoned Orphans* of the City are left exposed to all the *Miseries* of a wretched, degenerate state, where *Poverty* is deemed the *worst*, the only *unpardonable Crime*. That YOUR GREAT COURT OF DAREIN HUNDRED,[2] where you have a *negative* upon *all* the *Acts of Assembly*, is set at nought: That your CUSTOMS are given up without asking the Commons Consent: That the Entertainments instituted and set apart for You, on all Public Days, are taken from You and bestowed upon *Great Men*, and *Favourites* of the Board; while YOU and YOUR COMMONS are treated with the *Fragments* of their Feasts, at the *Stairs* of the *Tholsel*,[3] or at the *Door* of the *Mayoralty-house*, like *Beggars*. These are but a few of the *Grievances* I could, and may hereafter, recite. Nothing can give these Abuses Sanction but your having *Aldermen* for your Representatives. If you have *disinterested Citizens* to represent you, your *Grievances*, of every kind, may be brought before the COMMON-COUNCIL of the Realm, the Parliament, and you must have Redress. — Have you any reason to judge that an *Alderman* will bring in any Petition, and much less, one against *himself* and the Board? And consider, will not returning an *Alderman* be such a consenting to, and approving of, the *Tyranies*, under which you *groan*, that it will, hereafter, be vain to make any *struggle* for your *Liberties*. I am too inconsiderable an Example for any body, but as I shall ever act as a *Free Agent*, before I should be looked upon as *One* of the Members of a Body, that could return *such a Representative*, I shall chuse to be *cut off* from all Communion with them, by *Disfranchisement*.

One thing more, which I had like to have forgot. Every Man, that is Born the Son of a *free-Man*, Every Man, that serves an *Apprenticeship* to a *free-Man*, and every Man that Marries the Daughter of a *free-Man*, is intituled to his *Freedom* of *Dublin*. This later *Right* the *Aldermen*, for Reasons best known to themselves, have, for several Years passed, cut off; but, all such may Claim their Freedom at any Assembly; and tho' they be refused, yet their Votes are as good, as these of any other *Freemen*, or of the *Free-holders*.

While you deserve the Name of *Free-men*, I shall ever think it an Honor to be, and declare myself,

BRETHREN AND FELLOW-CITIZENS,

Your truly affectionate Brother,
and
most faithful Servant,

C. Lucas

Dublin
Aug. 27th, 1748

2. The court of Darein Hundred was a general assembly of the free or enfranchised citizens of Dublin city, and was probably of medieval origin. By the eighteenth century the court was used to proclaim publicly the decisions of the council of the city's corporation, but Lucas claimed that the court also had the power to veto council decisions and attempted to revive this power. See Sean Murphy, 'The Lucas Affair: A Study of Municipal and Electoral Politics in Dublin 1742-49', unpublished MA thesis, University College. Dublin, 1981, pp. 13-14, 98-99.

3. City hall.

GEORGE BERKELEY
(1685-1753)

from: THE QUERIST (1753)

[Bishop George Berkeley, though best known as a philosopher, was influential also for his economic and political queries. A short selection of those dealing specifically with Ireland is included here to indicate Berkeley's awareness of the underlying causes of Ireland's problems in the mid-eighteenth century.]

89 Whether our hankering after our woollen trade be not the true and only reason which hath created a jealousy in England towards Ireland? And whether anything can hurt us more than such jealousy?

90 Whether it be not the true interest of both nations to become one people? And whether either be sufficiently apprised of this?

91 Whether the upper part of this people are not truly English, by blood, language, religion, manners, inclination, and interest?

92 Whether we are not as much Englishmen as the children of old Romans, born in Britain, were still Romans?

93 Whether it be not our true interest not to interfere with them; and, in every other case, whether it be not their true interest to befriend us?

94 Whether a mint in Ireland might not be of great convenience to the kingdom; and whether it could be attended with any possible inconvenience to Great Britain? And whether there were not mints in Naples and Sicily, when those kingdoms were provinces to Spain or the house of Austria?

95 Whether anything can be more ridiculous than for the north of Ireland to be jealous of a linen manufacturer in the south?

96 Whether the county of Tipperary be not much better land than the county of Armagh; and yet whether the latter is not much better improved and inhabited than the former?

97 Whether every landlord in the kingdom doth not know the cause of this? And yet how few are the better for such their knowledge?

98 Whether large farms under few hands, or small ones under many, are likely to be made most of? And whether flax and tillage do not naturally multiply hands, and divide land into small holdings, and well-improved.

99 Whether, as our exports are lessened, we ought not to lessen our imports? And whether these will not be lessened as our demands, and these as our wants, and these as our customs or fashions? Of how great consequence therefore are fashions to the public?

100 Whether it would not be more reasonable to mend our state than to complain of it; and how far this may be in our own power?

101 What the nation gains by those who live in Ireland upon the produce of foreign countries?

102 How far the vanity of our ladies in dressing, and of our gentlemen in drinking, contributes to the general misery of the people?

103 Whether nations, as wise and opulent as ours, have not made sumptuary[1] laws; and what hinders us from doing the same?

104 Whether those who drink foreign liquors, and deck themselves and their families with foreign ornaments, are not so far forth to be reckoned absentees?

105 Whether, as our trade is limited, we ought not to limit our expenses; and whether this be not the natural and obvious remedy?

106 Whether the dirt, and famine, and nakedness of the bulk of our people might not be remedied, even although we had no foreign trade? And whether this should not be our first care; and whether, if this were once provided for, the conveniences of the rich would not soon follow?

107 Whether comfortable living doth not produce wants, and wants industry, and industry wealth? . . . .

115 Whether, if the arts of sculpture and painting were encouraged among us, we might not furnish our houses in a much nobler manner with our own manufactures?

116 Whether we have not, or may not have, all the necessary materials for building at home?

117 Whether tiles and plaster may not supply the place of Norway fir for flooring and wainscot?

118 Whether plaster be not warmer, as well as

1. Controlling expenditure or extravagance.

more secure, than deal? And whether a modern fashionable house, lined with fir, daubed over with oil and paint, be not like a fire-ship, ready to be lighted up by all accidents?

119 Whether larger houses, better built and furnished, a greater train of servants, the difference with regard to equipage and table between finer and coarser, more and less elegant, may not be sufficient to feed a reasonable share of vanity, or support all proper distinctions? And whether all these may not be procured by domestic industry out of the four elements, without ransacking the four quarters of the globe?

120 Whether anything is a nobler ornament, in the eye of the world, than an Italian palace, that is, stone and mortar skilfully put together, and adorned with sculpture and painting; and whether this may not be compassed without foreign trade?

121 Whether an expense in gardens and plantations would not be an elegant distinction for the rich, a domestic magnificence employing many hands within, and drawing nothing from abroad?

122 Whether the apology which is made for foreign luxury in England, to wit, that they could not carry on their trade without imports as well as exports, will hold in Ireland?

123 Whether one may not be allowed to conceive and suppose a society or nation of human creatures, clad in woollen cloths and stuffs, eating good bread, beef and mutton, poultry and fish, in great plenty, drinking ale, mead, and cider, inhabiting decent houses built of brick and marble, taking their pleasure in fair parks and gardens, depending on no foreign imports either for food or raiment? And whether such people ought much to be pitied?

124 Whether Ireland be not as well qualified for such a state as any nation under the sun?

125 Whether in such a state the inhabitants may not contrive to pass the twenty-four hours with tolerable ease and cheerfulness? And whether any people upon earth can do more? ....

132 Whether there be upon earth any Christian or civilized people so beggarly, wretched, and destitute as the common Irish?

133 Whether, nevertheless, there is any other people whose wants may be more easily supplied from home?

134 Whether, if there was a wall of brass a thousand cubits high round this kingdom, our natives might not nevertheless live cleanly and comfortably, till the land, and reap the fruits of it?

135 What should hinder us from exerting ourselves, using our hands and brains, doing something or other, man, woman, and child, like the other inhabitants of God's earth? ....

141 Whether a woman of fashion ought not to be declared a public enemy?

142 Whether it be not certain that from the single town of Cork were exported, in one year, no less than one hundred and seven thousand one hundred and sixty-one barrels of beef; seven thousand three hundred and seventy-nine barrels of pork; thirteen thousand four hundred and sixty-one casks, and eighty-five thousand seven hundred and twenty-seven firkins[2] of butter? And what hands were employed in this manufacture?

143 Whether a foreigner could imagine that one half of the people were starving, in a country which sent out such plenty of provisions?

144 Whether an Irish lady, set out with French silks and Flanders lace, may not be said to consume more beef and butter than a hundred of our labouring peasants? ....

175 Whether she would not be a very vile matron, and justly thought either mad or foolish, that should give away the necessaries of life from her naked and famished children, in exchange for pearls to stick in her hair, and sweetmeats to please her own palate?

176 Whether a nation might not be considered as a family?

2. A small cask for liquids, fish or butter.

CHARLES O'CONOR

(1710-91)

from: DISSERTATIONS ON THE ANTIENT HISTORY OF IRELAND (1753)

[Charles O'Conor, a catholic landlord from Belnagare, Co. Roscommon, was one of the most active supporters of Irish learning in the eighteenth century. His knowledge of the Irish language led him to attempt a history of Ireland based on old sources, as he explains in the introduction to *Dissertations*. This work laid the foundation for later Irish historical writing and encouraged the growing interest in Irish antiquities and history which became so noticeable in late eighteenth-century Dublin.]

INTRODUCTION

The History of the old Inhabitants of this Country is so important, and, at the same Time, so edifying to a free People, that few Subjects merit more their Attention, and hardly any can afford more political Instruction: To attain a tolerable Idea of it, we must necessarily enter into the Genius of the People; what we will find, in all Ages, invariable, with regard to their Manners and Polity: An Inflexibility confirmed by Habit, proceeding, partly, from their Original, and partly, from the Remoteness of their Situation: Descended from the most humane and knowing Nation of all the old *Celts*, they imported, very early, the Elements of Letters and Arts into *Ireland*: Here they improved those Elements into Systems of Government and Philosophy, which their undisturbed State from foreign Ambition left them at full Liberty to cultivate, thorough[1] a long Succession of Ages: Their Theology, grafted upon the Religion of Nature, and, partly, deduced from the clearest Fountains of the old Patriarchal Worship, influenced their Manners; rendering them a benevolent, whilst their Researches in Philosophy rendered them a wise, People: It can, therefore, be no Admiration to find this lettered Nation, so long studied in Arts peculiar to themselves, extremely retentive of them, and paying but little Deference to the Learning of the Continent, introduced, comparatively, but lately among them.

It is next to impossible that the Laws and Polity of this Nation should hold out long, after the Reception of Christianity, had they not been founded in their first Principles, and erected, in their Progress, on the Plan of Nature and Wisdom: In a Country where lettered Merit obtained the highest Reward; where Luxury never deranged, nor Conquest stunned, the Intellects of Men, useful Discoveries must be made, and several important Truths unfolded: Principles, thus established, can never be shaken in the Times of Liberty; nor exchanged for worse, but in Times of Ignorance and Servitude: And thus it was, that, during the sixth and seventh Centuries; when *Ireland* was acknowledged as the prime Seat of Learning and Liberty in *Europe*, we had no Attempts made to Alter her Constitution, Laws or Customs, notwithstanding the Introduction of all the *Greek* and *Roman* Refinements.

We shall not anticipate, in this Place, what we have delivered in the subsequent Sections on the Government, Learning and Manners, of this People: We will observe, in the general, That the History of *Ireland* may be denominated, either that of *Liberty* itself; or of (what ought, perhaps, to be as edifying to our Readers) the ABUSE of it. That its Constitution, however excellent in other Respects, gave, or was necessitated to give, too great a Price for the popular Arts, and administered inadequate Means to the noblest Ends; a Contention for rational Liberty and for those Endowments of Body and Mind, without which neither Preferments nor Honors could be obtained in the State. The Thread of their Story will suggest the dangerous Alternative to which this Institution was Subject; and how Power, even on these Terms of Merit, was seldom yielding enough to the Virtue, or, more frequently, that Semblance of Virtue, which both created and endowed it.

The Novelty of this Subject, hardly yet known in our Language by the *faintest* Idea, may recommend it. The Author of the following Essays, like the Explorator of an unknown Region, may claim the Merit of a *first Discoverer*, leaving the Honour, as well as Advantage, of Cultivation to his *Successors*: Whatever the Fate of his Labours may be, it is

1. i.e. through.

doubtless, a Shame ... that Persons, who take great Pains to know as much as possible of the History of *every other* Nation, should be utter Strangers to that of their *own*.

Before he entered on this Subject, he endeavoured to make himself Master of the Language of the People he treats of; what he found *absolutely necessary*, to gain any competent Knowledge of their Antiquities, Literature and Customs. When this Task was partly over, he was under the Necessity of stopping short, until several Friends furnished him with Manuscripts, which took some Time to collect. It were to be wished that this Collection was more complete; although considering how the old *Scotish* Records have been dispersed in *England*, *France*, and other Parts at home and abroad, he could not but reckon himself lucky in the Acquisitions he hath made....

The Study and Knowledge of this ancient People, through all the Stages of their Story, can hardly fail of being edifying to the present Times. Truth is a Mark set up for all Mankind, and if we render Society unhappy by missing it, we may blame ourselves. We inertly take our Aim from a Point, which is generally the worst we can be placed in; that of *Education* and *Custom*, *the Source of almost every moral Evil*: we seek *no farther*; and perhaps never less, than in Times rendered unbenevolent by a Memory of former Contests, about Power and Property. Many among us, and we gratulate[2] the Nation upon it, have quitted this Point of View, and emancipated themselves. Others may improve by a Retrospect to Times and Ages, as well as by the Force of such Examples. The Contrast between Liberty and Faction can be found in no History better illustrated than in that of *Ireland*. Let us take it in Review. A careful Attention on so variegated a Prospect may teach some of us a great deal of that Wisdom whose Place is taken up by mere local Judgments, and political Anomalies; Sores, productive of national Phrenzies, but absolutely perversive of national Happiness whenever they rankle in the Breasts of Governors and Legislators.

Whatever Evils of this Nature we may still labour under, it is certain that the untoward Fortune of *Ireland*, for several Ages past, hath at length happily relented. The first Men of the Nation have distinguished themselves throughout *Europe*, by the Encouragement of every Art extensive of its Happiness and Reputation: They have expelled its evil Genius, by weeding *Prejudice* from *Patriotism*, hateful Distinctions from the common interest, and all Schemes of Engrossment from Liberty....

This Effort should be considered only as the rude Draught of an extensive Landschape [*sic*]; the mere Out-lines of which must tempt an abler Hand to touch it over, and give the whole some Life and Colouring. It is easy to conceive the Disadvantages of an Author, *alone* in this Subject, and remote from Persons who could correct him, both in the Matter and Style: For these Reasons, he has Confidence enough that the Public will spare his Failings on the score of the *several Truths* which attend them: Truths very important, and to which the Right of the Public is indisputable. If the Author should obtain this fair Quarter, it will be easy hereafter, supposing a second Impression, to alter or expunge some few Passages (for we hope they are but *few*) which may be found weak in *Reason*, or false in *Fact*.

2. compliment, salute.

HENRY BROOKE

from: THE TRYAL AND CAUSE OF THE ROMAN CATHOLICS.... (1761)

[Henry Brooke here appears as a champion of the Irish catholics, who, by 1760, were publicly asserting their loyalty to the British crown at every opportunity, and petitioning for repeal of the Penal Laws. In this pamphlet, an imaginary lawsuit is in progress: Counsellor Candour is pleading the catholic case before Lord Chief Justice Reason, Lord Chief Baron Interest and Mr Justice Clemency.]

... Let us now, my Lords, take a Prospect of the

Situation of Protestants in that Country.[1] Let us take it in the natural Occurrence of Objects, and in the Light that Common-Sense may cast upon them.

I purposely pass over, in the Way of our View, the Danger that *Irish* Protestants may be in, or the Jealousies they may still entertain of a People who are very little interested in their Prosperity or Preservation. Supposing that nothing of this required any Matter of Prevention or Remedy; let us behold all the *Irish* as Inhabitants of the same Country; as Members, of one Community, who ought to be united, in Prospects, Attachments, Operations, and Pursuits.

But, is that the Light, my Lords, in which you see them? No so, not so. You behold *Irish* Papists, as a Body of Men retained within the Bowels of the Public, and yet rejected from any personal Service thereto, or any real Interest, or durable Property, therein. You behold them as an independent and unnatural Fœtus within the Womb of their Mother Country. Or as so many internal Parts, of a great Machine, that are *legally* clogged and retarded in their Offices, and, thence, obstruct or counteract that Movement which is necessary to the Intention of the Whole. You behold their Industry as a Shell-Snail that, slowly, draggs along its unavoidable Incumbrance. You behold their Arts and Inventions as a Flock of tamed Poultry, with Weights at their Legs, to prevent the Use of Wings and keep them from soaring. You behold them listless and bound on the Backs of their Protestant Brethren, as *Mezentius*[2] bound the Bodies of the Dead to the Living! Is it, then, to be wondered that all the Wisdom and Patriotism, of our succeeding Legislators, neither have availed, nor can avail, for the Cure of a Malady so constitutional and inherent, till the Cause, from whence the Malady proceeds, is attempted?

My Lords. When Mr. Serjeant asked me, upon the Word of a Man of Integrity, if I thought that *Irish* Catholics were to be depended upon; I answered that I thought they were not to be depended upon. I then spoke, my Lords, from the Jealously that naturally arises in the Mind of Man, on the most remote Apprehension or Possibility of Danger. And, indeed, I then spoke in direct Contradiction to repeated Trial and Experience, long approved.

About six Generations have now passed away, according to the Rates of Purchase and Estimate of the Life of Man, since these People have offended in Word or in Deed. No Riotings have been heard in their Houses, no Complainings in their Streets; they have been silent and harmless as the Flocks on the Hill of *Croghan*.[3] Our Parties, Factions, and Insurrections, as they are merrily stiled here in *England*, have been all, among *Irish* Protestants; this People were neither Actors nor Partakers therein. They have offered themselves to our Fleets and to our Armies, to tend our Persons, to till our Grounds, to hew our Wood, and to draw our Water. Where we admit them to fight for us, they have ever proved valiant; where we admit them to serve us, they are ever found loving, observant, and faithful. Temptations have come to their Doors and called them forth; the Contagion of Rebellion hath several Times broken out among their Neighbours; they have yet remained quiet, and continued untainted; still loyal to their Sovereign, ameneable to Government, and submissive to Law, through a long and trying Succession of upward of seventy Years, they have scarce appeared to repine in the Midst of Calamity.

What, then, do we look for further? What Proofs do we yet require, of Peacefulness and Attachment at the Hands of these our Brethren? Is no Period to be put to their State of Probation? Must they *for ever* keep out upon *Quarantine*,[4] without Harbour or Hopes of Rest or Reconciliation? Or is it possible that *Irish* Catholics, who have so long and so loyally demeaned themselves as Friends, while considered as Enemies; is it possible I say, my Lords, that they should become our Enemies, on account of their being treated by us, and attached to us, and interested in us as Friends? A People, my Lords, who, through a Winter of seventy Years Continuance, have never failed, or forsaken, or given us Cause of Offence, surely merit some Consideration, some grateful and chearful Ray, to warm them to a Sense that Protestants are not, by Choice, of a cruel, unforgiving, or malevolent Nature.

With what a Strengthening to his Majesty's Throne and Government! With what an Assurance

1. i.e. Ireland.
2. The ruthless Etruscan king in Virgil's *Aeneid*, Book VII, lines 647 et seq. See note 9 to Wolfe Tone's *Argument*, p. 927 below.
3. A mountain in County Wicklow.
4. From the Italian *quaranta* (forty). The period, originally forty days, that a ship suspected of being infected with a contagious disease was compelled to lie off port.

of Safety to *Irish* Protestants! With what an Encrease of Wealth and Prosperity to *Ireland*! With what Ease and Honour to our Legislature might this be done! It is but *interesting* this People in the Defence of the State, in the Safety of their Protestant Brethren, and in the Culture and Preservation of the Country wherein their Treasures will then be deposited; and, as surely as Matter must gravitate to its Center, these People will adhere to the Interests of those, with whom their own shall be united, against Men and Angels, against Pretenders, Popes, or Devils. No Seductions, no Persuasions, could then tempt them to permit, and much less to assist, toward the Overthrow of a Constitution, wherein their Stake lay, and whose Equal they could not hope to find upon Earth.

It were to be wished, I confess, that these People were reclaimed from their ecclesiastical Errors, at least, provided they might not, thereafter, become worse Men, or worse Subjects, then they are at present; provided they should, thereafter, retain a sufficient Sense of any Religion at all.

Two Thirds, of the Inhabitants of *Ireland*, are at this Day Roman Catholics. And yet, my Lords, it is remarkable, that there are fewer Robberies, Thefts, Murders, Maims or Riotings, in that Kingdom, than in any Nation, equally numerous, in *Europe*.

I once intimated to your Lordships, that speculative or religious Errors, in certain Cases might be politically useful, with respect to civil Government. That auricular Confessions, Purgatories, Fasts, and Penances, are to the Members of the Church of *Rome*, what Discipline is in the military Department, by preserving Roman Catholics in the familiar Use and Practise of daily Obedience. That this Habit of Respect and Submission to ecclesiastical Discipline, is, not unnaturally, attended with Respect and Submission to the secular Powers. And, that the Obedience of these People, to the Authority of their Church, is an Earnest[5] of their Obedience to the Authority of all States under which they live. But, my Lords, this is not all. Nineteen in Twenty, of *Irish* Papists, though naturally the most sensible and apprehensive of all People, are wholly illiterate; and their Priests are to them, in the Place of Letters, of Instructors, of Parents, of Governors, of their Church, and of their GOD.

Those same Priests, my Lords, are, also, extremely zealous and sedulous in their Functions. They visit from Village to Village and House to House. They call in Question the most ancient and the most respectable of their Communion. They take hold of the Souls of Infants, as you would of sprouting Twiggs, and bend them, during their State of Pliancy, to the desired Direction. They preserve their Authority, over their People, not only by the Threats of future, but by the Infliction of present Punishments. And, indeed, we cannot say, during these seventy Years and upward, but that the Influence of this Priesthood, hath been exercised and directed to the Quiet of the Nation, to the Benefit of the Public, to the Observance of legal Ordinances, and to the Safety of the State....

This, my Lords, is the Case of the Catholics of *Ireland*. They look upon us as Enemies, as well to their civil Interests as religious Opinions, and this gives them an equal Prejudice to our Persons and Principles, and mainly helps to continue them obstinate in Error. Give them Cause, then, to think us Friends to their civil Interests, and they will no longer be averse to our religious Opinions; they will listen, they will like, and, in Time, they will reform.

And now, my Lords, as the Good of Society is the only rational End and Intent of all Laws; where any Laws, on Experience, are found detrimental to that very Society, for whose Emolument they were enacted; can Wisdom make it a Question, whether they should continue or be repealed?

Were Protestants enriched, and strengthened, and exalted, in Proportion, as Papists are impoverished, debilitated, and depressed. Did we derive any Wealth from their yearly Exportations of the current Cash of that Kingdom. Did we derive any Safety from their Discontent and Disaffection. Did we gain any Power, by their being divided from us, while they are continued among us. Were our national Products encreased by their Want of Motives to Industry. Were our Bogs and Wastes better reclaimed by their Want of Incitement to Labour. Were our Coasts the better secured from foreign Invasion, because two Parts in Three of the Inhabitants of *Ireland*, are no Way concerned in the Defence thereof. Were our internal Dangers lessened, by giving ourselves Cause to be jealous of such Numbers. Could we hope to gain their Friendship by the public Acts and Expressions of our own Distrust. Or, could we expect that their having different Interests and Attachments would engage them to wish our Welfare or to promote our

5. pledge or sign.

Prosperity. I would be the first Man in *Ireland* to remonstrate and petition against the smallest Abatement of the Popery Laws.

But, as a seventy Years Experience hath proved and continues to prove, that the Reverse of all such happy Consequences is, permanently, and palpably, and perniciously the Fact. I would humbly propose: That, for the better Security of his Majesty's Crown and Government in the Kingdom of *Ireland*, by interesting *Irish* Catholics in the Guardianship thereof; for stopping the perpetual Drain of the Specie[6] or political Blood of that Nation; for deriving Strength to *Irish* Protestants from the good Will and Assistance of *Irish* Papists, with whom they are unavoidably though discontentedly associated; for acquiring immediate and inconceivable Opulence to the State from the animated Industry of two Thirds of the People; for doubling the yearly and natural Value of *Ireland*, by giving Papists an Interest in the reclaiming of our Lands; for giving them Cause to oppose our common Enemies by giving them a common Stake to retain and defend; for giving them Cause to contribute to our Prosperity by admitting them to a legal Participation thereof; it is humbly proposed, I say, that our Patriot Legislature, so studious in other Respects for the Advancement of their Country, should make such an Abatement or Alteration, of the said disabling Laws, as, to their superior Wisdom and Discernment shall appear requisite, for lessening the many Evils that are thereby created; and for restoring the many Benefits that are thereby suppressed. — — — —

I had carried my Notes thus far, when I was called away on a very interesting Affair, and cannot say, whether the Jury brought in a formal Verdict, or left Matters to the better Judgment of our Legislature.

6. Money in the form of coins.

from:
THE FREEMAN'S JOURNAL
(Vol. I, September 1763)

[*The Freeman's Journal*, founded in 1763 by Charles Lucas (among others), was probably the most influential newspaper in eighteenth-century Ireland. It mirrored the opinions of the 'independent interest' in Dublin politics at a time when democracy was having its first success over the oligarchical system that the inhabitants of Ireland had come to take for granted. *The Freeman's Journal* proclaimed itself the enemy of riot but the watchdog of liberty, the champion of parliamentary democracy and the scourge of anarchy. It gave ordinary protestant freeholders — and, to some extent, their catholic counterparts — a feeling that they could influence the governance of city and of state and, coming as it did at a time when newspapers had an unparalleled influence on the inhabitants of Dublin, and on members of the Irish parliament, *The Freeman's Journal* must be considered one of the major political organs of eighteenth-century Ireland. This essay on liberty and lawlessness appeared in the newspaper's first issue.]

The TRUE FRIENDS of LIBERTY: To the WHITE-BOYS of the South; The OAK BOYS of the North; and the LIBERTY-BOYS of Dublin.[1]

Countrymen, Fellow-Citizens!

There are several among us who are true lovers of LIBERTY, who wish well to the PEOPLE, and to the CAUSE OF THE PEOPLE; who would heartily join with you in reclaiming any of your RIGHTS, in redressing any of your GRIEVANCES, if any such there be; and yet who greatly disapprove of your present Excesses.

LIBERTY is like a CANNON, when it is temperately charged and duly directed, it hath its fullest Power and Efficacy, it must attain its Point, and can hurt None but the Enemies at whom it is levelled: But when it is overcharged, it bursts its Bounds, misses wholly of its Aim, slaughters none but Friends, and from that Moment becomes powerless

1. During the early 1760s, organized agrarian societies dedicated to the remedy of specific grievances sprang up in several parts of Ireland. The Whiteboys operated in the north Munster between 1761 and 1763, while the Oakboys were active in Ulster for a short period in 1763. The Liberty Boys of Dublin can be dated back to the 1730s and took their name from the Earl of Meath's Liberty in the city. Entirely protestant in composition, they feuded regularly with the catholic Ormonde Boys and occasionally became involved in political demonstrations such as the anti-union riots of 1759. [The editors are grateful to Mr James Maguire for the information in this note.]

and useless, till broken and bruised to Pieces, and melted and cast anew.

LIBERTY, again, may be likened to a fine managed and mettled Horse. While he continues under Government, he keeps to the Road of Law, reaches the appointed Journey, and is carefully dressed and fed at every Stage: But, when he discharges himself from the Rein and the Rider, he leaps the adjoining Fences, flies wantonly abroad, tears up the Meadows and Corn-Fields that were intended for his own Sustenance, and becomes the Companions of the wild and bleak Elements; till, being caught, or reduced to Submission by Famine, he is no longer trusted, pampered, or spared; but chained to the galling Yoke, and driven forward by the Goad and the Lash.

What are you about, Friends, or what would you be at? Are you agreed in these Matters among Yourselves? Or, why did You not address your Complaints to Government, before You arrogated all Power to your own Hands, and cast off all Allegiance and Respect to your Rulers?

What, think You, is likely to be the Consequence of these your Tumults and Riots? of your trampling on the Laws by which You look to be protected, and of your destroying the Peace of the Country and of the City wherein you dwell?

Had Any of our Governors, or Great-Men, daringly entered on your Liberties with a high and powerful Hand; had they broke open your Houses; demolished the Instruments of your Trade; cut the Products of your Industry and Ingenuity to Pieces; violently seized and abused your Fellows; dragged some through the Mire; and hanged up Others, without Examination, Trial, or Hearing; would You not have cired out, to Heaven and Earth, against such Tyranny and Barbarity, against these Breaches of every Law, and Outrages on every Duty, whether human or divine?

And yet, Countrymen and Fellow-Citizens, All This, in every Article, is what You have actually done or attempted to do, though no Worse could be done or attempted by any Hottentots or Savages that ever inhabited the Wilds of *Africa*, who never entered a Court of Justice, or heard the Toll of a Bell.

What sort of a Land is this we live in? Have we no Humanity, no Urbanity, no Government among Us? Can the Name of a Country, or Rights of a Constitution be now said to remain to *Ireland*? Or how shall we expect to have our own Lives, Liberties, and Properties protected by Law; while in avowed Violation of every Law, we openly assail the Lives, Liberties, and Properties of our Fellow-Subjects?

There are no Men upon Earth, Friends, who *love* and who *hate* LIBERTY so much as we do. Who have so much to be free from the Encroachment of Others who hate so much that Others should be free from our own Encroachments. The People are like the smaller Tyrants of the Waters; while, with a Conscience undisturbed, they devour the Spawn of their Species yet they abhor any Trespass on their own Persons, and piously petition the Goddess LIBERTY to preserve them from the wicked Jaws of the mightier Shark and Crocodile.

What then can LIBERTY do on this contradictory Occasion? For she cannot possibly grant *a Privilege from Oppression*, and at the same Time grant *a Privilege to oppress.*

Know you not, Friends, that LIBERTY can only lie, where All are restrained from doing Injury to Any? For, if Licence may be permitted to Any, why not therefore to All? And, where All would encroach, All would likewise be encroach'd upon; and Freedom and Property would cease throughout the Earth.

Wherefore, whoever openly trespasses, on the Privileges of Others, declares himself an Enemy to the Laws of Society, and the Rights of Mankind.

But, let it be! —— Since nothing but Riot, Uproar, and utter Anarchy can please; let us no longer have any Country, any Constitution! —— Let the Bloody and madding Spirit, of the First-Born *Cain* breathe through the South, through the North, enflame Country and Capital!

Gracious Heaven prevent, or, at least defer those Days.

When *Até*, hot from Hell,
Shall in these Confines, with a Monarch's Voice,
Cry Havock? and let slip the Dogs of War;
That these foul Deeds shall smell, above the Earth,
With Carrion-Men, groaning for Burial![2]

Countrymen, Countrymen! at this Moment are we forging, at this Moment are we preparing double Bitts for own Mouths, and double Burdens for our own Backs. At this pernicious Moment are we framing and soliciting new RIOT-ACTS, and new MILITARY ESTABLISHMENTS for wretched *Ireland*;

2. Shakespeare, *Julius Caesar*, III. 1. 271-75.

new Restraints and Grievances for an unruly People whom their King cannot govern, and whom their God cannot please.

Often have you heard us utter the SACRED NAME OF LIBERTY, often have we instructed you in the due Sense of your Rights and Privileges, often have we inspired you with a Detestation and Rejection of all such Tyrants and Oppressors as should dare to break in on that glorious Constitution, that inviolable Fence *of human Law divine*, which our Ancestors had built up, *for the Guardianship of the People*.

But, what is now to be done?

The chaste Name of LIBERTY, through the Country and Capital, is profaned and vilely strumpeted by an outrageous Rabble. The Scale of *Justice* is rent from the Hand of Magistracy. All Power is arrogated by the Spirit of Wrath and Riot. New Oaths are imposed; new Institutions dictated; new Threatnings denounced; and new Contributions raised; by Mobs, who, themselves, have cast off all Obedience; and no Law remains to *Ireland*, save what lies in the Will of a wild and frantic Populace.

Is not this to invite, to pull upon us, All who are Enemies to the Rights and Liberties of the Poor; Who shall come with a mighty and military Hand, not to fence us for our Protection, but to impound us for our Restraint; to enter at the Breach of LAW which we, ourselves, have made; not to guard, but to invade us; to bind us when we struggle, and to lash us when we dare to complain. Then shall every Friend of *Ireland*, every Patriot and Lover of Liberty, hang down his shamed Face, nor presume to utter a Sentence, or breathe a Sigh in your Behalf, lest he be accounted a Disturber, a licentious Incendiary, who would again stir up your Minds to Sedition and Anarchy.

When a Nation is oppressed, when it hath any general Evil or Injury to complain of, when there is any general Grievance that ought to be redressed, the Voice of the People then becomes the Voice of GOD, it is consistent, unanimous and persevering. It is accompanied by the Voice of Reason, by the Voice of the Friends of Liberty, Society, and Virtue; and it will be heard, it will not rest till it is attended to.

But, when the People wrest to themselves the Legislative Authority from the Hands of their Representatives; when they wring the executive Power from the Hand of Majesty and his lawful Magistrates; there is an End, at once, of all Government, all Law, and civil Society. And no one hath any Remedy, Redress, or Appeal, save to a tumultuous Number of Men, agreed in no one Article of Religion, Law, or Liberty; and only united in a frantic Propensity, to judge without deliberating, and to executive without listening.

History proves to us, in every Age and in every Nation, that the Power of such a Populace may be great and irresistable. It is great, indeed, in pulling down and bringing to Ruin; it may lay waste the most prosperous Nation; it may destroy the best established Constitution upon Earth; but it never was yet known to erect the Compass of a Cottage, for the Habitation of Law or Liberty, of Plenty or of Peace.

Remember, Friends, what we have told you before, and what we now repeat! Engrave it on your Minds, bear it constantly in your Memories, That, from the Beginning of Time to the End thereof, TRUE LIBERTY never did, nor ever can lodge POWER in the Hands of the PEOPLE. Your's, indeed, is the Appointment and Disposition of Power, but, whenever you reclaim it, your Perdition ensues.

You are, it is true, the Originals and Fountains of all *Power*, and of all *Law*. But, in order to prevent Confusion and total Anarchy, your Numbers make it necessary to depute the Framing of LAW, and the Execution of POWER, to the Few whom you imagine to be best qualified for the Discharge of those important and popular Trusts.

Wherefore, if the Few, to whom you have entrusted your Power, shall suffer Bashaws[3] in the Country, to levy Taxes for By-Ends; or clandestine Dealers in Town, to hurt the fair Trade and Manufactures of your Country, the Way is open to lawful Suits, Addresses, Remonstrances; the Speaking-Trumpet is ever ready to the Voice of a People, it must bring Delinquents to Shame, and must assure Redress to the Sufferers. But, remember and mark well, beloved Countrymen, that, through all Nations and all Ages, when the People have resumed their deputed Authority, they never fail'd to become the Victims of their own Folly; that Oppression ever attended their grasping at Power, and that SLAVERY is the inevitable Offspring of LICENTIOUSNESS.

3. Bashaw is an early form of 'Pasha' — a Turkish grandee.

RICHARD WOODWARD

(1726-94)

from: AN ARGUMENT IN SUPPORT OF THE RIGHT OF THE POOR IN THE KINGDOM OF IRELAND TO A NATIONAL PROVISION (1768)

[One of the causes of the harsh circumstances of life for the Irish poor in the eighteenth century was the lack of a poor law. The English poor law of 1602 had provided a rudimentary but universal system of relief for the poor there, but nothing comparable existed in Ireland. Richard Woodward, at the time dean of Clogher, argued in this pioneering and influential pamphlet that there should be a tax of one percent of income, the proceeds of which would be used to relieve the poor. The Irish parliament passed an act, probably based on his ideas, in 1772. In later sections of the work, Woodward appeals to the duty of the rich to provide a competent maintenance for the poor; in this first section he contents himself with giving an account of the conditions in which the Irish poor found themselves in the 1760s.]

POSITION I

That the Poor are so inadequately provided for by Voluntary *Contributions in this Kingdom, as to stand in* need *of some* Legal *Title to a Maintenance.*

That the lower Class of our People are very ill accommodated with Lodging, Rayment, and even Food, is but too manifest to all who are acquainted with their manner of Living. That their Poverty is likely to continue, with but little Mitigation, will be as evident to any intelligent Man, who reflects on the following, amongst other, Causes of it: The exorbitant Rent extorted from the poorer Tenants, ever loth and afraid to quit their antient Habitations, by the general Method of setting Farms to the highest Bidder without any Allowance for a Tenant-Right; the System, as prejudicial to the Landlord as to the Under-tenant, of letting large Tracts of Land to Undertakers[1] inured to Tyranny and Extortion; the Oppression of Duty-Work, which calls the Cottager arbitrarily from the Tillage of the little Spot which he holds at so dear a Rent; and the low Rate of Wages for Labour. These Circumstances, combined with some others, reduce the *Irish* Cottager below the Peasant of almost every Country in Europe. Such is his hard Condition in the most plentiful Season, and in the prime of his Health and Strength: What then must be his State in time of Dearth, under the Pressure of Years, Infirmities, or even a very numerous young Family? His Expences admit of no Retrenchment. He is a Stranger to Luxury, or even to decent Accommodation, and yet his Wages seldom afford any Reserve. On the Death of such a Father of a Family, dependent on his Labour for their main, or perhaps entire Support, how forlorn must be the Situation of his Widow and Orphan Children! It would shock a tender Mind to imagine (if Imagination could paint) the Miseries, to which the Bulk of the Inhabitants of this Kingdom are constantly exposed by the slightest Reverse of Fortune: By a single bad Season, by an accidental Loss, by an occasional Disease, and even by the gradual Decay of Nature. Nor are these affecting Scenes confined to Seasons of Scarcity; they must always exist in a great, though not equal, Number. They present themselves but too often to every country Gentleman, (and still more to the Clergy, in the Exercise of their parochial Duties, to whose Experience we appeal) to need a Proof. They cannot be doubted or denied by any, but those who shut their Eyes or steel their Hearts against them.

So numerous, so urgent, and so well known are the Distresses of the Poor: Let us now fairly estimate the Sufficiency of the Resources, at present subsisting for their Relief. Our Eyes will be naturally turned *first* to the Landed Gentlemen, who derive their Wealth and Importance from the Labour of these Men. Of these, many, perhaps a Majority, of the most Considerable, constantly reside in another Kingdom; and though some of them may cast back a Part of their Superfluity on those to whose Industry they owe their *All*, yet it is to be feared, that such Instances are comparatively very rare. On the contrary, it is too frequently urged as a Recommendation of *Irish* Property, that it is not

1. Holders of crown lands in Ireland.

encumbered with any Tax for the Maintenance of the Poor. A singular instance this of the Inadvertence (one would only hope of the Inadvertence, lest we should be forced to impute it to the Depravity) of Mankind, that such a Phrase could be rendered so familiar to the Ear of any wise and good Man, as to lose its genuine Horror! If the Sentiment were developed, surely few would entertain, and still fewer avow it: And therefore, no ingenuous Reader will think it either invidious or unnecessary in this interesting Argument to lay open its plain Import, which is this, 'An estate in this Kingdom is represented to be peculiarly advantagious to the Landlord, because, though he may, and generally does avail himself of the utmost Profit that can be drawn from the Labour of his Tenant,' (leaving him in Truth too scanty a *present* Maintenance,) 'he is nevertheless at Liberty to abandon that Labourer to perish, when he is unable to work any longer.' Is this boasted Privilege either Honourable or Desiraable? A wise Man would not glory in such an Exemption, a good Man would not claim it, and he who wishes to enjoy, doth not deserve it.

But it will be replied, that notwithstanding the Absence of many great Proprietors of Land in *Ireland*, there is yet a large Number of Persons of distinguished Property, and a still greater of respectable Gentry, who reside on their Estates, (a part of the Year at least) administring Employment to the Industrious, and Charity to the Distressed. Granted! There are many such valuable Characters amongst us, who are an Ornament and Blessing to their Country. To such, every Mark of publick Regard is due. We pay Homage to their Virtues with Alacrity, we perceive and unveil their Imperfections with Regret. But it is the Duty of an Advocate for the Poor to ask even *them*, whether their Bounty be not confined too much, if not entirely, to the Neighbourhood of their own Residence. Does their Liberality extend equally to their distant Estates? How few can truly say, that they ever have it in their Contemplation, what may be the Condition of their lower Tenants on Lands remote from their own Mansions! Yet those Tenants are unquestionably of equal Service to them and the Publick, equally entitled to their Attention, and the more likely to stand in need of their Charity, because from those Estates they are *Absentees*, almost as fatally as if they resided in another Kingdom. On the whole it cannot be denied, that by far the greater Part of our Lands do not enjoy the Benefit of the Proprietor's Residence, and in general the Poor of those Estates partake not of his Charity. Now when we have weighed, on one Side, the extraordinary Indigence of the whole Peasantry; and allowed, on the other, for the Number of Absentees from the Kingdom, the Remoteness of many Estates from the Mansions of the resident Gentry, (which together render it no uncommon Case to find a Tract of Country containing some Scores of square Miles without one Family of Note) it will be intuitively clear, that there can be no Balance, nor indeed any the least Proportion, between the Necessities of the poor Tenants, and the Alms of their Landlords.

To compensate for this Inequality, let no one lay the smallest Stress on the Collections in the Places of divine Worship. For however considerable they may be in some particular Churches fortunately circumstanced, the Average of them through the Kingdom is too trivial to be worth mentioning. In a Word, however harsh or unpalatable it may be, it is but too notorious a Truth, that the Poor in the Country draw little of their Support from the Gentry; the vagrant Beggar excepted, who is generally a Disgrace to the Name, and an Injury to the Cause of Charity. They depend principally upon the neighbouring Farmer, or even Cottager, the Poorest of whom are humane enough to communicate with them, and thereby lessen, their little Stock. Can there be a Spectacle more edifying, and at the same time more reproachful to an affluent Landlord, than to see (and it is his own Neglect if he does not see or know it) one of his poor Tenants feeding another, with Bread taken as it were out of the Mouth of his own Children; whilst he who is Feasting on the Labour of both, attends to the Miseries of neither: but throws the whole Burthen of relieving them on those, whom no reasonable By-stander could think equal to bear the smallest Part of it. But to return to the Argument, (if this Observation be thought a Digression) what can such Wretches give? What can they who are themselves so ill defended from Cold and Hunger, be supposed to spare to another for Food, much less for Cloathing? As to Education for the Infant, or Medicine for the sick Poor, such Relief seemed to have been never thought of, till the latter were considered in a late Act for County Infirmaries, which does Honour to the Legislature. Yet honourable as this Beginning of Good is to our Governors, it can be regarded only as a Sample of what they approve, a kind of Earnest of Public Benevolence. For it is clear at first Sight, that the Income of those Infirmaries is in no Degree adequate to the Number of sick Poor in a whole County; the Orphan, the Aged, and a vast Majority of the Sick, (who from Distance of Situation, or the Extremity of their Cases, cannot be removed, or from the Contagiousness of their Distempers, or want of Room, cannot be admitted to the County Hospital) are still without Relief; and therefore no more is necessary to place out of the Reach of Cavil the first Position: 'That the Poor are so inadequately provided for by *Voluntary* Contributions in this Kingdom, as to stand in *need* of some *Legal* Title to a Maintenance.'

CHARLES H. WILSON

(1757-1808)

from: A COMPLEAT COLLECTION OF THE RESOLUTIONS OF THE VOLUNTEERS, GRAND JURIES ETC. OF IRELAND .... (1782)

[Corps of volunteers, predominantly protestants of the middle classes, were formed throughout Ireland in the 1770s as the British army, needed in North America, was partially withdrawn from the country. They soon became an influential element in Irish political life and, after the American declaration of independence, a clear military threat to English power in Ireland. The Volunteer corps adopted splendid uniforms and were much given to parading and to debating the age-old theme of Irish liberty. Charles H. Wilson's introduction to his history of Volunteering expresses clearly the mood of the day.]

The plains are yet warm with the blood of Irishmen in defence of Britain,[1] which, if yet faithful to us, our veins are ready to bleed afresh in the same cause; if not, we shine the centre of our own interest, and danger is a cloud that mocks at a distance. The King of England is also King of Ireland; the liberty of England, is the liberty of Ireland. But why deduce from her the Heavenly gift? It is the privilege of individuals, breathed with our breath, and wrote on the heart by the finger of God! Let no little party-spirit disunite you; twigs gather strength from combination; the dignity of your prince, the aggrandisement of your kingdom, and the welfare of Britain is your object; discuss your affairs with spirit and moderation!

Persevere; your cause is good; your sufferings have been great; your complaints just; your spirit is roused, and you *cannot* be enslaved.

It is a maxim that the *King can do no wrong*; let it be now, that he *shall* do no wrong.

Watch over the sacred freedom of the press that great medium of information, through which we think aloud; friends will not be wanting on all occasions to wield the pen:

> O sacred weapon, left for Truth's defence,
> Sole dread of folly, vice, and insolence.

> Quid de reliquis republicæ malis? Licet-ne dicere? Mihi vero licet et semper licebit dignitatem tueri; mortem contemnere. Protestas modo veniendi in hunc locum fit, dicendi periculum non recuso. Cic. Orat.[2]

I contemplate with joy, and wait with impatience, the happy moment that is to crown your glorious exertions with something more than human felicity, when the unwearied Newenham[3] is to exert himself for the more due representation of the people; when the discerning and comprehensive Flood,[4] with irresistable eloquence, shall help to fix our liberties on the most durable basis; when

1. In the American war of independence.

2. 'But to resume. Am I permitted to speak of the remaining ills of the State? I permit, and shall always permit, myself to protect my reputation to despise death. Only let me have the power of coming into this place, the peril of speaking I do not shrink from.' Cicero, *The Philippics* I, vi, 14.
3. Sir Edward Newenham (1732-1814), MP for Dublin County.
4. Henry Flood (1732-91), statesman and orator, who had been removed from his post as vice-treasurer of Ireland in the year before Wilson's history was published.

an *Irish Bill of Rights* shall shine as the rainbow of our political sky; when the placemen and pensioners sink beneath public execration, and the voice of virtue resound in the senate; when the transactions of the bishops, those expletives[5] of society, and other lumber of the church, shall be more duly examined: to doubt of these would be to doubt of our existence! to mistrust that Providence, which has smiled on our endeavours, and the disinterested flame, that pervades the most inanimate bosom. Your progression to perfection is quick, and I see you will not cease till you attain it; the wide, the unbounded prospect lies before you,

Nor 'shadows, clouds, nor darkness rest upon it.'

Then shall the sun of freedom rush forth as a bridegroom out of his chamber, and rejoice as a giant to run his course. May it go forth from the uttermost part of the Heaven, and run about to the end of it again, and nothing be hid from the heat thereof.[6]

5. Those who serve merely to fill up space.
6. cf. Book of Common Prayer, translation of Psalm 19. 5-6.

Before I part the reader, I must make another observation or two, which is, that whoever attempts to suppress Volunteering, or but whispers, that it ought to be done, let his rank or situation be what it may; let him do it with a tongue dipt in oil, and with a countenance dressed by the graces; or with lightening in his eye, and thunder leaping from his brow; whether he does it in the senate or out of the senate; whether tyrannically to a set of trembling dependents, or servilely cringing to some lordly superior, he is equally the detested enemy of Ireland, and should be looked upon with abhorrence; and if we are anxious to have our constitution and liberty fully ascertained, and the extention of our commerce indisputably established on a lasting foundation, there is no other means under Heaven of doing so, but by persevering in the present spirit, and keeping up, unimpaired, our Volunteer army. For, O my country! should your *chosen sons* put off their warlike attire, you may dress in sable,[7] and mourn indeed!

7. Black mourning garments.

HENRY GRATTAN

(1746-1820)

from: SPEECH IN THE IRISH PARLIAMENT, 16 APRIL 1782 (later revised)

[The late 1770s and early 1780s were the outstanding period for high-flown rhetoric in the Irish parliament. The themes of the great speeches delivered in those years by Grattan, Flood, Yelverton, Bushe and Hussey Burgh were great themes — Ireland and liberty. Time after time, Ireland's past was invoked, her people's loyalty stressed, her right to liberty and constitutional freedom asserted. Rhetorical flourishes that would have done credit to Cicero or Demosthenes were commonplace in the Irish parliament, and legislative independence, when it came in a limited form in 1782, arrived on a cloud of syntactical glory.

The most impressive orator of all was Henry Grattan, the leader of the faction seeking Irish legislative independence. The speech below, though it enjoys the distinction of being the most famous in Irish parliamentary history, was not delivered in the form in which it was finally printed. When revising his speeches for publication in his old age, Grattan appears to have written up the speech as he would have liked to have delivered it, but the text, with its memorable rhetoric and sense of historical perspective, is a later fabrication. However, this text, as amended, has contributed not a little to Grattan's posthumous reputation.]

Mr. Grattan rose, and spoke as follows:

I am now to address a free people: ages have passed away, and this is the first moment in which you could be distinguished by that appellation.

I have spoken on the subject of your liberty so often, that I have nothing to add, and have only to admire by what Heaven-directed steps you have proceeded until the whole faculty of the nation is braced up to the act of her own deliverance.

I found Ireland on her knees, I watched over her with a paternal solicitude; I have traced her progress from injuries to arms, and from arms to liberty. Spirit of Swift! spirit of Molyneux! your genius has prevailed! Ireland is now a nation! in that new character I hail her! and bowing to her august presence, I say, *Esto perpetua*![1]

She is no longer a wretched colony, returning thanks to her governor for his rapine, and to her king for his oppression; nor is she now a squabbling, fretful sectary,[2] perplexing her little wits, and firing her furious statutes with bigotry, sophistry, disabilities, and death, to transmit to posterity insignificance and war.

Look to the rest of Europe, and contemplate yourself, and be satisfied. Holland lives on the memory of past achievements; Sweden has lost liberty;[3] England has sullied her great name by an attempt to enslave her colonies. You are the only people — you, of the nations in Europe, are now the only people who excite admiration, and in your present conduct you not only exceed the present generation, but you equal the past. I am not afraid to turn back and look antiquity in the face: the revolution[4] — that great event, whether you call it ancient or modern I know not, was tarnished with bigotry: the great deliverer (for such I must ever call the Prince of Nassau)[5] was blemished with oppression; he assented to, he was forced to assent to, acts which deprived the Catholics of religious, and all the Irish of civil and commercial rights, though the Irish were the only subjects in these islands who had fought in his defence. But you have sought liberty on her own principle: see the Presbyterians of Bangor petition for the freedom of the Catholics of Munster. You, with difficulties innumerable, with dangers not a few, have done what your ancestors wished, but could not accomplish, and what your posterity may preserve, but will never equal: you have moulded the jarring elements of your country into a nation, and have rivalled those great and ancient commonwealths, whom you were taught to admire, and among whom you are now to be recorded: in this proceeding you had not the advantages which were common to other great countries; no monuments, no trophies, none of those outward and visible signs of greatness, such as inspire mankind, and connect the ambition of the age which is coming on with the example of that going off, and forms the descent and concatenation of glory: no, you have not had any great act recorded among all your misfortunes, nor have you one public tomb to assemble the crowd, and speak to the living the language of integrity and freedom.

Your historians did not supply the want of monuments; on the contrary, these narrators of your misfortunes, who should have felt for your wrongs, and have punished your oppressors with oppressions, natural scourges, the moral indignation of history, compromised with public villainy and trembled; they excited your violence, they suppressed your provocation, and wrote in the chain which entrammelled their country. I am come to break that chain, and I congratulate my country, who, without any of the advantages I speak of, going forth as it were with nothing but a stone and a sling, and what oppression could not take away — the favour of Heaven, accomplished her own redemption, and left you nothing to add and everything to admire.

You want no trophy now; the records of Parliament are the evidence of your glory: I beg to observe, that the deliverance of Ireland has proceeded from her own right hand; I rejoice at it, for had the great requisition of your freedom proceeded from the bounty of England, that great work would have been defective both in renown and security: it was necessary that the soul of the country should have been exalted by the act of her own redemption, and that England should withdraw her claim by operation of treaty, and not of mere grace and condescension; a gratuitous act of Parliament, however express, would have been revocable; but the repeal of her claim under operation of treaty is not: in that case, the legislature is put in covenant, and bound by the law of nations — the only law that can legally bind Parliament. Never did this country stand so high. England and Ireland treat *ex æquo*.[6] Ireland transmits to the King her claim of right, and requires of the Parliament of England the repeal of her claim of

1. May she last for ever!
2. A zealous adherent of one point of view.
3. By the treaties of Stockholm (1720) and Nystad (1721), Sweden ceded part of her lands to Russia, Hanover and Prussia.
4. Of 1688-89.
5. William III, king of England, Scotland and Ireland 1689-1702 and stadtholder of the Netherlands 1672-1702.

6. from equal positions.

power, which repeal the English Parliament is to make under the force of a treaty which depends on the law of nations — a law which cannot be repealed by the Parliament of England.

I rejoice that the people are a party to this treaty, because they are bound to preserve it. There is not a man of forty shillings freehold that is not associated in this our claim of right, and bound to die in its defence; cities, counties, associations, Protestants and Catholics; it seems as if the people had joined in one great national sacrament; a flame has descended from Heaven on the intellect of Ireland, plays round her head, and encompasses her understanding with a consecrated glory.

There are some who think, and a few who declare, that the associations to which I refer are illegal: come, then, let us try the charge, and state the grievance. And first, I ask, What were the grievances? an army imposed on us by another country, that army rendered perpetual; the privy-council of both countries made a part of our legislature; our legislature deprived of its originating and propounding power; another country exercising over us supreme legislative authority; that country disposing of our property by its judgments, and prohibiting our trade by its statutes: these were not grievances, but spoliations, which left you nothing. When you contended against them, you contended for the whole of your condition; when the minister asked, by what right? we refer him to our Maker: we sought our privileges by the right which we have to defend our property against a robber, our life against a murderer, our country against an invader, whether coming with civil or military force — a foreign army, or a foreign legislature. This is a case that wants no precedent; the *revolution* wanted no precedent; for such things arrive to reform a course of bad precedents, and, instead of being founded on precedent, become such: the gazing world, whom they come to save, begins by doubt and concludes by worship. Let other nations be deceived by the sophistry of courts: Ireland has studied politics in the lair of oppression, and, taught by suffering, comprehends the rights of subjects and the duty of kings. Let other nations imagine that subjects are made for the monarch; but we conceive that kings, and parliaments like kings, are made for the subjects. The House of Commons, honourable and right honourable as it may be; the Lords, noble and illustrious as we pronounce them, are not original, but derivative. Session after session they move their periodical orbit about the source of their being, the nation; even the King's Majesty must fulfil his due and tributary course round that great luminary; and, created by its beam and upheld by its attraction, must incline to that light, or go out of the system.

Ministers, we mean the ministers who have gone out (I rely on the good intentions of the present), former ministers, I say, have put questions to us; we beg to put questions to them. They desired to know by what authority this nation has acted. This nation desires to know by what authority they have acted. By what authority did Government enforce the articles of war? By what authority does Government establish the post-office? By what authority are our merchants bound by the charter of the East India Company? By what authority has Ireland for near one hundred years been deprived of her export trade? By what authority are her peers deprived of their judicature? By what authority has that judicature been transferred to the peers of Great Britain, and our property in its last resort referred to the decision of a non-resident, unauthorized, and unconstitutional tribunal? Will ministers say it was the authority of the British Parliament? On what ground, then, do they place the question between the Government on one side, and the volunteers on the other? According to their own statement, the Government has been occupied in superseding the lawgiver of the country; and the volunteers are here to restore him. The Government has contended for the usurpation, and the people for the laws. His Majesty's late ministers imagined they had quelled the country when they had bought the newspapers; and they represented us as wild men, and our cause as visionary; and they pensioned[7] a set of wretches to abuse both: but we took little account of them or their proceedings, and we waited and we watched, and we moved, as it were, on our native hills, with the minor remains of our parliamentary army, until that minority became Ireland. Let those ministers now go home, and congratulate their king on the redemption of his people. Did you imagine that those little parties whom three years ago you beheld in awkward squads parading in the streets,[8] should have now arrived to such distinction and effect? What was the cause? for it was not the sword of the volunteer, nor

7. i.e. secretly gave wages to.
8. The Volunteers.

his muster,[9] nor his spirit, nor his promptitude to put down accidental disturbance or public disorder, nor his own unblamed and distinguished deportment. This was much; but there was more than this: the upper orders, the property, and the abilities of the country, formed with the volunteer; and the volunteer had sense enough to obey them. This united the Protestant with the Catholic, and the landed proprietor with the people. There was still more than this; there was a continence which confined the corps to limited and legitimate objects; there was a principle which preserved the corps from adultery with French politics; there was a good taste which guarded the corps from the affection of such folly: this, all this, made them bold; for it kept them innocent, it kept them rational: no vulgar rant against England; no mysterious admiration of France; no crime to conceal — no folly to be ashamed of. They were what they professed to be; and that was nothing less than the society asserting her liberty according to the frame of the British constitution, her inheritance to be enjoyed in perpetual connection with the British empire.

I do not mean to say that there were not divers violent and unseemly resolutions; the immensity of the means was inseparable from the excess.

Such are the great works of nature; such is the sea: but, like the sea, the waste and excess were lost in the advantage: and now, having given a parliament to the people, the volunteers will, I doubt not, leave the people to Parliament, and thus close, specifically and majestically, a great work, which will place them above censure and above panegyric. These associations, like other institutions, will perish: they will perish with the occasion that gave them being, and the gratitude of their country will write their epitaph, and say: 'This phenomenon, the departed volunteer, justified only by the occasion, the birth of spirit and grievances, with some alloy of public evil, did more public good to Ireland than all her institutions; he restored the liberties of his country, and thus from the grave he answers his enemies.' Connected by freedom as well as by allegiance, the two nations, Great Britain and Ireland, form a constitutional confederacy as well as one empire; the crown is one link, the constitution another; and, in my mind, the latter link is the more powerful.

You can get a king anywhere, but England is the only country with whom you can participate a free constitution. This makes England your natural connexion, and her king your natural as well as your legal sovereign. This is a connexion, not as Lord Coke[10] has idly said, not as Judge Blackstone[11] has foolishly said, not as other judges have ignorantly said, by conquest; but, as Molyneux has said, and as I now say, by compact; and that compact is a free constitution.[12] Suffer me now to state some of the things essential to that free constitution; they are as follow: the independency of the Irish Parliament; the exclusion of the British Parliament from any authority in this realm; the restoration of the Irish judicature, and the exclusion of that of Great Britain. As to the perpetual mutiny bill, it must be more than limited — it must be effaced; that bill must fall, or the constitution cannot stand; that bill was originally limited by this House to two years, and it returned from England without the clause of limitation. What! a bill making the army independent of Parliament, and perpetual! I protested against it then, I have struggled with it since, and I am now come to destroy this great enemy of my country. The perpetual mutiny bill must vanish out of the statute book. The excellent tract of Molyneux was burned — it was not answered; and its flame illumined posterity. This evil paper shall be burned, but burned like a felon, that its execution may be a peace-offering to the people, and that a declaration of right may be planted on its guilty ashes: a new mutiny bill must be formed after the manner of England, and a declaration of right put in the front of it. . . .

9. military assembly.

10. Sir Edward Coke (1552-1634), the politician and constitutional lawyer who had championed the common law against the royal prerogative, had been cited unfavourably by Molyneux and others.

11. Sir William Blackstone (1723-80), the influential British jurist who wrote the first clear description of English law.

12. But see above, the introduction to Molyneux's *The Case of Ireland*.

HENRY FLOOD

(1732-91)

from: RENUNCIATION SPEECH (1782)

[In an attempt to regain his lost popularity and to win favour with the Irish Volunteers, Flood demanded that England should expressly renounce the Declaratory Act of 1720, which gave acts passed in England the power to bind Ireland. The demand was met by a bill hurried through the Westminster parliament on 22 January 1783 on the advice of the new lord lieutenant, Lord Temple. Flood in fact was revealing the limitations of the 'independence' achieved only a month earlier in June 1782, although the enactment of the Westminster parliament was, in the long term, meaningless. Grattan opposed the proposal and from this disagreement grew the outright hostility between the two men, which culminated in Grattan's public attack on Flood and Flood's later defence of his career and character.]

A voice from America shouted to liberty, the echo of it caught your people as it passed along the Atlantic, and they renewed the voice till it reverberated here. What followed? All the propositions that had been separately reprobated were now collectively adopted; the representatives of the people articulated at length the sense of their constituents. The case of Ireland originally stated by the great Molyneux, and burned at the revolution by the Parliament of England,[1] is not now afraid of the fire; it has risen from that phoenix urn, and with the flames of its cradle it illuminates our isle! What is the result? It is now in your power, and I trust it will be in your wisdom to do final justice to the rights and interests of your country; for me, I hope I have not been peculiarly wanting to them.... The first spring of the constitution is the elective power of the people: till that was reinforced by limiting the duration of Parliaments, little could be done.[2] The people wanted constitutional privilege; till the fabric of usurpation, founded on the law of Poynings,[3] had been shaken to its foundation, little could be done; the Parliament wanted conscious dignity till the people were armed; everything could not be done; the nation wanted military power. These were necessary antecedents. The public mind wanted much cultivation. The seed, too, was necessary to be sown, and if I have not been wanting to the preparations of the soil, may I not be permitted to watch over the harvest? To that harvest too, as well as to every other, a prosperous season was necessary, and that season presented itself in the American war. When, therefore, the honourable member [Grattan] in the sunshine of that season, and of his own abilities, brought forward a declaration of rights in Lord Buckingham's government,[4] after that administration had amended his proposition for the purpose of defeating it, I stepped forward, in office as I was, and at the hazard of that office, rescued the principle from the disgrace of a postponement, or from the ruin of rejection. In this session, too, I hope that my humble efforts have not been peculiarly wanting. In ability I will yield to many, in zeal to none; and, if I have not served the public cause more than many men, this at least I may say, I have sacrificed as much to it. Do you repent of that sacrifice? If I am asked, I answer 'No.' Who could repent of a sacrifice to truth and honour, to a country that he loves, and to a country that is grateful? Do you repent of it? No. But I should not rejoice in it, if it were only to be attended with a private deprivation, and not to be accompanied by all its gains to my country. I have a peculiar right, therefore, to be solicitous and ardent about the issue of it, and no man shall stop me in my progress.

Were the voice with which I utter this, the last effort of an expiring nature; were the accent which conveys it to you, the breath that was to waft me to that grave to which we all tend, and to which my footsteps rapidly accelerate, I would go on; I would make my exit by a loud demand of your rights; and

1. Molyneux's *The Case of Ireland's Being Bound by Acts of Parliament in England, Stated* (1698) was probably not burned by the common hangman. See headnote to Molyneux above, p. 871.
2. Flood had long campaigned for parliaments to have a limited duration. The Octennial Act of 1768 was a substantial victory. The Irish parliament usually met in alternate years.
3. Poynings's Law (1494), the ground of English claims to legislate for Ireland.
4. John Hobart, earl of Buckinghamshire, lord lieutenant 1776-80.

I call upon the God of truth and liberty who has often favoured you, and who has of late looked down upon you with such a peculiar grace and glory of protection, to continue to you his inspirings — to crown you with the spirit of his completion, and to assist you against the errors of those that are honest, as well as against the machinations of all that are not so.

I will now move you, That the opinion of all the judges be desired on the following question: 'Does the repeal of the Declaratory Act amount, in legal construction, to a repeal or renunciation of the legal principle on which the Declaratory Act grounded itself?'

Nothing ever was more judicious than the conduct of Great Britain on this occasion. She was so embarrassed abroad, and you were so strong at home, that she could not deny the repeal of the declaratory law. Yet it must ever be her wish to retain the principle of it, because it is the principle of power, which no nation has ever relinquished while it could maintain it.

If there be a pride of England, there is a pride of Ireland too. Now I ask which ought to give way, for one must, and I answer impartially, that which has the worst foundation. Now which is that? The pride of England in this case, is the pride of wrong, and the pride of usurpation. The pride of Ireland is the pride of right, the pride of justice, the pride of constitution. I will not ask you, after that, which ought to give way; but it is wrong to put this question principally upon pride.

But time is not necessary, negotiation alone is sufficient to undo you; you were not born to be negotiators; the negotiator is a dark, austere, inexorable character; you are soft, open, and persuadable; you have not the detailed knowledge, the systematical procrastination, the suspicious reserve, or the frigid perseverance of a negotiator. When have you negotiated that you have not lost? You negotiated at the Restoration, you negotiated at the Revolution, you negotiated at the augmentation of your army, you negotiated your free trade, you negotiated the Mutiny Bill.[5] When have you demanded that you have not succeeded, and when have you negotiated that you have not been deceived?

There never was a time which required more consideration than the present; the national exertion began in the last year of Lord Buckingham's administration,[6] it is now drawing to a period, and whether that shall be glorious or otherwise depends on your wisdom. A short view of what we have done will be a guide to what we should do. We had groaned for a century under an increasing usurpation; the American war broke out, and whilst we were called upon to shed our blood for Great Britain, we were insulted with the application of that principle to Ireland which had revolted America; our feelings were exasperated by the application, and our trade was ruined by the war; we saw ourselves beggars in fact, and slaves in assertion. The merchants flew to a non-importation agreement, the people flew to arms. Amidst this perturbation Parliament assembled, and we amended our address by the demand of a free constitution, that is of an exclusive legislature, on which all freedom of trade must depend — and therefore it was, that I did originally differ with some gentlemen, for I asserted that they had not obtained that freedom of trade of which they had boasted, because they had not obtained that freedom of Parliamentary constitution, without which a freedom of trade could not exist. We received from England a dilatory answer. We shortened our money grants to the crown — we shortened them to the subject. And the Irish public creditors to their immortal honour, embarked so fully with the rights of the nation, as cheerfully to accept of a six months' security. This rapid succession of sober and consistent efforts struck like lightning on the Ministry and Parliament of England; all obstacles gave way; our demand was to be granted in all its plentitude; all the British statutes restrictive of our foreign commerce were to be repealed; and on that constitutional principle on which alone it would be welcome — a principle, which in that early period of this question, I took the first opportunity to lay down in clear, unambiguous, and categorical terms. What was that principle? That, having a Parliament of our own, our foreign trade was necessarily free, and subject to no restrictions as to our ports, but such as our Parliament might impose. This principle, we were told, was admitted by England, as to our foreign trade, and pleaded by her in return, as to her own ports, and those of her own colonies. She admitted

5. Free trade was granted in 1780; a Mutiny Act was passed in 1782; the army was increased after the passage of the Octennial Act in 1768-69.

6. 1780.

the principle which we claimed, and she said she would open to us her colony ports, on equal regulation of trade. The tidings of this emancipation, as it was idly called, landed in Ireland. The Post Office was illuminated by an emissary of the Castle; the College took fire in the next instance by an unhappy contagion, and the city caught the flame in a regular and sympathetic succession.[7] All sober consideration was lost in an ignorant clamour, and the steady pulse of the public yielded to a fever of exultation. What was the consequence? England saw that we were surprized at our success, saw that we had asked more than we expected, concluded that we would accept of infinitely less, and determined that should be as little as she could. First, then, she determined not to repeal all her laws restrictive of our foreign commerce, yet, whilst an atom of such restriction remains, the total impeachment of your Constitution remains; when, therefore, an artful resolution was prepared for this House, on that occasion, expressive of satisfaction in that enlargement of our *foreign* trade, I exclaimed against that word. If you thank the British Parliament, I said, for the enlargement of your foreign trade, you admit she can restrain it, you admit her legislative authority; that is, you gain little in commerce, and you lose everything in constitution. I objected to the word *foreign*, therefore; it belies Ireland, and it deceives Great Britain. The independent gentlemen of the day, however, did not feel, did not take up the principle, yet, though they did not take it up that day, they have felt it since; and though the word was universally admitted then, there is not a man in the nation that would not reject it now. Such was the first of this business. Let us see how much worse we made it in the progress of negotiation. The language of England was the language of common sense. Ireland must have equal regulations of trade, she said, but equal taxes on home consumption she did not say; equal regulations of trade may subsist between a poor country and a rich one, but equal taxes on consumption cannot. Now what has your negotiation made of it? You have made your arrangement a tax-law in part, which ought to have been a trade-law in the whole; that is to say, instead of a regulation in trade, you made it a regulation against trade, and a caustic regulation too. What regulation, indeed, can be much more adversary to trade, than a heavy tax on a raw material imported for the purpose of trade, and for the end of manufacture? So pernicious are such taxes, that the ministers in England, whose profusion has brought them to that country, have endeavoured to extenuate their malignity by two regulations; to console the manufacturer, they tell him that they will open to him the foreign market, by giving him a drawback on his manufactures exported, equal to the tax on the imported material. And they tell him besides, that they will shut up for him the home market, and give him a monopoly of it. How? By laying a prohibitory duty on the manufacture imported from abroad; and what have they done as to manufactured sugars? They have laid a prohibitory duty upon them when imported into England from any other part of the world, Ireland even not excepted. What have we done? We have laid the same prohibitory duty on manufactured sugars imported into Ireland from any other part of the world; but we have excepted England, whereas she did not except Ireland. Now, there was much more reason for our excepting England, than there was for her excepting Ireland, and why? Because Ireland could never, by an possibility, be a rival in sugars to England in the English market, but England is actually a very formidable rival to Ireland in the Irish market. What is the fact? The Irish manufacturer of sugars has but one rival in the world, and that is the English manufacturer of them. And what have we done? We have given him the fullest security against all those that are not his rivals. And we have not given it to him against the only manufacturers that are his rivals; we have given him perfect protection where he is in no danger, and we have not given it to him where he is in all danger. We have done worse by him, we have not only given him as much security against his only rivals, as against those who are not at all his rivals; but we have not left him as much security against his only rivals as he always had before; that is to say, the duty on the imported manufacture now bears a less proportion than ever it did before to the duty on the imported raw materials. By consequence his peril is greater, as his protection is less; and his security being diminished, his danger is enhanced. But this is not all; you have not done for him what England originally pointed out to you in his favour: she proposed equality as the principle of your

7. On 25 May 1782, Dublin was illuminated and celebrations were held on receipt of the news that both houses of the British parliament had unanimously conceded Grattan's demands for independence.

regulation of trade; we adopted it religiously in that part to which it was not applicable, and, where it was pernicious, I mean in the tax part; and we only deserted it in the trade part, where alone it was applicable, and where alone it was beneficial. Such was the spirit in which we negotiated our free trade; let us take care how we negotiate our free Constitution: but the error of that arrangement does not stop here. Its first principle was erroneous; it set out with this maxim: That you were to pay for this as if it were an enlargement, and that you were to pay for it in tax, as if you had not paid it otherwise before. But what is the truth? The sugars of Spain, Portugal, and France, would supply your manufactures, as well as the British West Indian Islands, and generally better; if, whilst you retained those markets, England had opened her colony ports too, this would have been a new market, which is always an advantage to the buyer. But what is the case now? You are suffered to go to the colony market of England, which is the English market in effect, and which is therefore her advantage; but you give up for this all other, and some better markets, which is your advantage. Instead of its being an enlargement, therefore, this is more properly a restriction; and instead of England's granting you a boon in this matter, it is you that gave her a monopoly. Now, a monopoly is so much against the giver, and so much in favour of the obtainer of it, that no nation in its senses ever gives it to another. And if a part of an empire gives it to the head, it cannot be on a principle of trade, because a principle of trade is a principle of gain, whereas this is a principle of loss. On what principle alone can it be given? On a principle of empire. That is to say, in other words, it is a tax or a tribute, and that of the heaviest nature; but, if you were to pay for it in taxes, besides paying for it by monopoly, it would be absurd to pay for it more than it was worth. Now take the whole West Indian commerce, take the utmost proportion of that commerce that could ever fall to your lot, take the utmost proportion of clear profit that can be supposed to accrue from that quantity of trade, and then take the utmost proportion of that clear profit that can be afforded to revenue, and I say it would never amount to that sum which you have agreed to pay on the instant for the contingency of this direct trade, with this additional absurdity, that if you should not be able to establish it, these additional duties will be equally payable upon your old circuitous trade, which before was free from them. Will you trust negotiation again? This arrangement cannot be justified on any commercial principle. Was any constitutional advantage obtained by it? Far from it: the very principle of the arrangement is hostile to the Constitution; it gives to the British Parliament a virtual power of taxing you; for what is the principle of it? That when England taxes a colony produce, you must tax it equally or give up the trade. Thus this arrangement leaves both your trade and your money at the mercy of the Ministry and Parliament of England. Combine this with another law of the same period, the Mutiny Bill, therefore, and see what the result of both is. You complained that the British Parliament should make even a twelve-months law for your army; and what did you do to remedy it? You made an Act, that she should do it for ever. The two greatest powers in the management of human concerns, are the power of the purse, and the power of the sword. You did by these two laws, for so much, delegate away both of these great powers from yourselves to the British Parliament; that is to say, in the very moment that you talked of recovering your own authority, and denying that of the British legislature, you did everything you could to strengthen the power of that Parliament which you meant to overthrow, and to weaken the power of that Parliament which you meant to establish. I do not speak these things in order to say what is disagreeable to any man living, much less to say any thing disagreeable to that body, in defence of whose privileges I have lived these two and twenty years, and in defence of whose privileges I will die. I speak them from a deep conviction of their necessity. You see how you have been negotiated out of every thing, and how dangerous it is to negotiate again. You see how dangerous it is to exult too soon, or to imagine that any thing of this kind is done, while any thing remains undone. You see what a miserable end was made of Lord Buckingham's last session of Parliament, though it began with so much splendour; and as a part of this session has trod the steps of its glory, I would warn the conclusion of it against the steps of its decline. To put a stop, therefore, to the danger of negotiation, and to accelerate the safety of an immediate repeal, and of a final renunciation, I move the resolution I have before stated to you.

THEOBALD WOLFE TONE

(1763-98)

from: AN ARGUMENT ON BEHALF OF THE CATHOLICS OF IRELAND . . . . (1791)

[Tone's pamphlet, written when the author was twenty-eight, now strikes us as remarkable in two contrasting ways. First, it is a measured, constitutional (even 'loyalist') argument in favour of certain reforms, and as such gives no hint of the carnage that would occur seven years later in the United Irishman rebellion, of which Tone was the intellectual sponsor. Second, it is a blunt and steadily unsentimental demythologizing of the revolution of 1782, of Grattan's parliament and of the tradition of parliamentary patriotism. Of course, the carnage of 1798 was largely (but by no means exclusively) the responsibility of government, its troops and informal allies, and Tone was thus its victim rather than its author. In 1791, when he wrote his *Argument*, there were still grounds for hoping that a liberal policy towards Irish catholics could somehow o'erleap the formidable obstacles of a bigoted Irish administration and a self-serving parliamentary majority. The British government under William Pitt sought to move Dublin in this direction at the end of the year, and one notable result was the emergence of protestant ascendancy rhetoric as a bulwark against reform. Later, the very brief tenure of the Earl Fitzwilliam as lord lieutenant in the spring of 1795 ignited similar expectations only to see them quenched within a matter of weeks. Thereafter, Tone and his United Irishmen existed in a wholly changed atmosphere scarcely foreseeable in 1791. The suppression of the United Irishmen, its reorganization as a secret society, repressive use of troops in 1797, and insurrection in 1798 now appear to form a coherent and unbreakable sequence of events.

Tone's pamphlet is fully entitled *An Argument on Behalf of the Catholics of Ireland in which the Present Political State of that Country, and the Necessity of a Parliamentary Reform are Considered. Addressed to the People, and More Particularly to the Protestants of Ireland.* It was published by P. Byrne in Dublin, and later reprinted in Belfast. On the last (p. 54) page of the text, the anonymous author signs off as 'A Northern Whig' and dates his work 'Belfast, August 1, 1791'. In specifically addressing protestants, Tone was of course aiming his argument at that body which controlled political elections and which all but monopolized political life in Ireland. It was partly a tactical mode of address, and partly a matter of realism. Signing himself as he did, he sought to align the pamphlet with the part of Ireland in which protestants were numerous and (to some degree at least) inclined towards democratic ideas; he also sought to link his programme to the Whig innovations of 1688 which had overturned a dynasty. Tone himself came from the middle class, was born into the established Church of Ireland, and cared little for theology of any kind.]

What is our Government? It is a phenomenon in politics, contravening all received and established opinions: It is a Government derived from another country, whose interest, so far from being the same with that of the people, directly crosses it at right angles: Does any man think that our rulers here recommend themselves to their creators in England, by promoting the interests of Ireland, when it can in the most remote degree interfere with the commerce of Great Britain?*[1] But how is this foreign Government maintained? Look to your court calendar, to your pension list, to your concordatum,[2] and you will find the answer written in *letters of gold*: This unnatural influence must be supported by profligate means, and hence corruption is the only medium of Government in Ireland. The people is utterly disregarded and defied: Divided and distracted as they are, and distrustful

* If this be doubted, let the proceedings of last session with regard to the Arigna Iron Works and the Double Loom be remembered, to each of which the smallest parliamentary aid was refused. Why? Because they might interfere with English interests; though the former would have kept 250,000 *l.* annually at home, the greater part of which goes to England; and the latter would at once have doubled the weaving power of the kingdom in the linen, silk, and callico branches. But above all, let the memorable debate on the East India Trade be recalled, when Administration boldly threw off the mask, and told Ireland she should have no such trade, because it might interefere with the interest of England. *They have such a trade in America, and they deserve to have it.*

1. Even after 1782, control of Irish political affairs rested with a small administrative group in Dublin who functioned as the channel through which Britain effectively governed the nominally independent kingdom of Ireland. On 24 January 1791 a petition 'from the proprietors of the Arigna Iron Works praying aid to complete their undertakings' was introduced into the Irish House of Commons. Petitions from various individuals concerning the patenting of new looms were introduced in February and March 1791. The debate on the East India trade opened on 21 February 1791.
2. An order in council for the disposal of funds set apart for particular state purposes.

of each other, they fall an easy prey to English rulers, or their Irish subalterns. The fear of danger is removed from Administration by our internal weakness, and the sense of shame speedily follows it: Hence it is, that we see Peculation[3] protected, Venality[4] avowed, the Peerage[5] prostituted, the Commons[6] corrupted. We see all this at the very hour, when every where but in Ireland reform is going forward, and levelling ancient abuses in the dust.[7] Why are these things so? Because Ireland is struck with a political paralysis, that has withered her strength, and crushed her spirit: She is not half alive, one side is scarce animated, the other is dead; she has by her own law, as it were, amputated her right hand; she has outrun the Gospel precept, and cast her right eye into the fire, even before it has offended her:[8] Religious intolerance and political bigotry, like the tyrant Mezentius,[9] bind the living Protestant to the dead and half corrupted Catholic,[10] and beneath the putrid mass, even the embryo of effort is stifled: When the nation is thus circumstanced, it is not to be wondered at, if even an administration of boobies and blockheads presumed to insult, and pillage, and contemn, and defy her.

Under such an Administration, if God Almighty could in his wrath suffer such an one long to exist, the virtue and the talents of the land would be blasted in the bud. No Irishman of rank could become a member or supporter of Government, without at once renouncing all pretensions to common decency, honesty, or honour: All great endowments of the mind, all lofty sentiments of the soul would be necessarily and eternally excluded; and the Government, when once in such hands, must remain so; political vice, like the principle of fermentation, would propagate itself, and contaminate every succeeding particle, until the fury of an enraged people, or the just anger of offended Heaven should at length, by one blow, destroy or annihilate the whole polluted mass!

But to quit hypothetic speculation, and descend to facts:

I have said, that we have *no National Government*. Before the year 1782,[11] it was not pretended that we had, and it is at least a curious, if not an useful speculation, to examine how we stand in that regard now. And I have little dread of being confused, when I assert, that all we got by what we are pleased to dignify with the name of *Revolution*, was simply, *the means of doing good according to law, without recurring to the great rule of nature, which is above all positive statutes*:[12] Whether we have done good or not, and if not, why we have omitted to do good is a serious question. The pride of the nation, the vanity of individuals concerned, the moderation of some honest men, the corruption of knaves I know may be alarmed, when I assert, that the Revolution of 1782, was the most bungling, imperfect business, that ever threw ridicule on a lofty epithet, by assuming it unworthily: It is not pleasant to any Irishman to make such a confession, but it cannot be helped if truth will have it so: It is much better that we should know and feel our real state, than delude ourselves or be gulled by our enemies with praises, which we do not deserve, or imaginary blessings which we do not enjoy.

I leave to the admirers of that era to vent flowing declamations on its theoretical advantages, and its visionary glories; it is a fine subject, and peculiarly flattering to my countrymen; many of whom were

3. Embezzlement or theft of public funds by those in charge of them.
4. Readiness to sell oneself.
5. The British government frequently used to offer titles in the Irish peerage as a reward for political service often unconnected with Ireland; the practice increased as the eighteenth century came to a close.
6. The Irish House of Commons included many members who were in effect government servants, elected by the influence of great landlords or others.
7. This is as close as Tone comes in the *Argument* to approving of the French Revolution.
8. See Matthew 5. 29: 'And if thy right eye offend thee, pluck it out, and cast it from thee: for it is profitable for thee that one of thy members should perish, and not that thy whole body should be cast into hell.'
9. In Virgil's *Aeneid* (Book VII, lines 647 et seq.), Mezentius is an Etruscan tyrant driven out by his people and obliged to take refuge with Turnus, against whom Aeneas (ancestor of the Romans) is pitted. In earlier versions of the legend, a gift of wine is offered both to Mezentius and the god Jupiter and, since the latter is truly powerful, Mezentius is destroyed.
10. Tone refers to the political rights of protestants and the subjugation of catholics, the energy of the latter being sapped by the legal prohibitions under which they labour; nevertheless, one cannot help but note a degree of anti-catholic prejudice, which is either contrived for its effect on the protestant readership Tone explicitly addressed or is inherent in Tone's own sceptical view of revealed religion.
11. On 16 April 1782, Henry Grattan moved for the third time in the Irish House of Commons a declaration of rights which, on its adoption, came to be regarded as a statement of (limited) Irish parliamentary independence of Britain. (A text of this speech, evidently revised long after the event, is printed above.) The nature of government in Ireland remained unaltered, as did the composition of the House itself.
12. Here Tone argues that the revolution of 1782 did nothing more than assert that laws passed in the Irish parliament were legitimate and not subject to certain vetoes in Britain; the latter part of the matter in italics is a coy reference to doctrines of liberty, as an absolute right, deriving from the French Revolution.

actors, and almost all spectators of it. Be mine the unpleasing task to strip it of its plumage and its tinsel, and shew the naked figure: The operation will be severe; but if properly attended to, may give us a strong and striking lesson of caution and of wisdom.

The Revolution of 1782, was a Revolution which enabled Irishmen to sell at a much higher price their honour, their integrity, and the interests of their country;[13] it was a Revolution, which, while at one stroke it doubled the value of every borough monger in the kingdom, left three-fourths of our countrymen slaves as it found them,[14] and the Government of Ireland in the base and wicked, and contemptible hands, who had spent their lives in degrading and plundering her; nay, some of whom had given their last vote decidedly, though hopelessly, against this our famous Revolution:[15] Who of the veteran enemies of the country lost his place or his pension? who was called forth to station or office from the ranks of opposition? not one! The power remained in the hands of our enemies, again to be exerted for our ruin, with this difference, that formerly we had our distresses, our injuries, and our insults gratis, at the hands of England; but now we pay very dearly to recive the same with aggravation, through the hands of Irishmen; — yet this we boast of, and call a Revolution.

See how much the strength of *the people* has been augmented by the arrangement of 1782! For two successive sessions, we have seen measures of the most undeniable benefit, and the most unqualified necessity to the country, enforced by all the efforts of the most consummate ability, and repelled without even the shadow of argument by Administration; an Administration, consisting numerically of the individuals who had opposed the extension of your commerce in 1779, and the amelioration of your constitution in 1782. You find, or you are utterly senseless, in the loss of the Place Bill,[16] the Responsibility Bill,[17] the Pension Bill;[18] in a word, all the measures of last session, that you have no weight whatsoever, that Administration despise and laugh at you, and that while you remain in your present state of apathy and ignorance, they will continue to insult and to contemn you.

Why do I speak thus of your famous exertions in 1782? Not to depreciate them below their value, for I honour, and I love the spirit that then animated you. I am sure a great majority of those who then conducted you, were actuated by a sincere regard to your interest and your freedom; I am sure that some of your leaders were men of high integrity, and some of consummate wisdom; I do believe that as much, or very nearly as much as could then be done, was done; and though I regret, yet I do not accuse the caution that induced those who acted for you, to stop short in their honourable career: The minds of men were not at that time, perhaps, ripe for exertions, which a thousand circumstances that have since happened, cry aloud for: We are now, I hope, wiser, bolder, and more liberal, and we have the great mistress, dear-bought Experience, to warn us from past errors, and guide us on to future good.

I hope it appears from what I have said, that the Revolution of 1782, is such, as no Irishman of an independent spirit, and who feels for the honour and interest of his country, can acquiesce in *as final*. Much remains to be done, and it is fortunate that the end proposed is so moderate and just, the means so fair, simple, and constitutional, as to leave no ground for accusation with the most profligate of our enemies, or apprehension with the most timid of our friends.

My argument is simply this: That Ireland, as

13. Tone's bitterest comment on Grattan and his followers suggests that the augmented powers of the Irish House of Commons merely resulted in pushing up the price of a bought vote or a bribed member.
14. The population of Ireland at this point is still a matter of discussion among historians; it was common to express the catholic/protestant ratio in simplified fractions. The catholics were not slaves in any literal sense, of course, and the degree of catholic prosperity already evident and politically influential is argued elsewhere in this anthology. 'Borough monger' is a sarcastic designation of politicians who trade in parliamentary seats for boroughs.
15. That the events of 1782 were ostentatiously termed a 'revolution' cannot be doubted, and the objective was to place the declaration of rights in an honourable succession to the Glorious Revolution of 1688. We find Sir Boyle Roche saying in the House of Commons on 27 May 1782, 'that the revolution of 1782, brought as many constitutional blessings to the kingdom, as the revolution of 1688.' Among others who opposed Grattan's declaration was John Fitzgibbon (1749-1802), who became lord chancellor of Ireland in 1789.
16. A Place Bill was introduced for debate in the House of Commons by John Forbes (member for Drogheda) on 10 March 1791; its objective was to bar from membership of the House any man holding an office (a place-holder) under the government.
17. The Responsibility Bill, also introduced by Forbes, on 24 March 1791, sought to make servants of the crown accountable to the department that they served.
18. Forbes's Pension Bill was introduced on 19 March 1791, and sought to bar any holder of a government pension from sitting in the House. The objective of all three of these bills was to purge the House of members who, through various kinds of patronage, were in the pay of the government; all three initiatives were quickly lost.

deriving her government from another country, requires a strength in the people which may enable them, if necessary, to counteract the influence of that government, should it ever be, as it indisputably has been, exerted, to thwart her prosperity: That this strength may be most constitutionally acquired, and safely and peaceably exerted through the medium of a Parliamentary Reform:[19] And finally, that no reform is honourable, practicable, efficacious, or just, which does not include as a fundamental principle, the extension of elective franchise to the Roman Catholics, under modifications hereafter to be mentioned.

I Beg I may not be misunderstood or misrepresented in my first position. When I talk of English influence being predominant in this country, I do not mean to derogate from the due exertion of his Majesty's prerogative: I owe him allegiance, and if occasion should require it, I would be ready chearfully to spill my blood in his service; but the influence I mean, is not as between the King and his subjects, in matter of prerogative, but as between the government and people of England, and the government and people of Ireland, in matter of trade and commerce: I trust in God, we owe the English nation no allegiance; nor is it yet treason to assert, as I do, that she has acquired, and maintains an unjustifiable and dangerous weight and influence over the councils of Ireland, whose interest, wherever it clashes, or appears to clash with hers, must immediately give way: Surely this is no question of loyalty. The King of England is King also of Ireland; he is in theory, and I trust in practice, equally interested in the welfare of both countries; he cannot be offended that each of his kingdoms should by all honourable and just means encrease their own ability, to render him the service due to him; he cannot rejoice, when he hears that his faithful Commons of Ireland by their own law exclude themselves from a commerce with half the known world, in complaisance to a monopolizing English company, though he may, as the common father of both his realms, rejoice, when they vote 200,000 *l.* to secure the very commerce in which they can never bear a part. It is therefore, I repeat it, no question of loyalty: If the King can be interested in the question, it must be on the side of justice, and of Ireland, because his happiness and his pride must be most gratified by the rising prosperity of his people, to which title we have as much claim as the people of England; we love him as well, we are as faithful subjects; and if we render him not as essential services, let our means be considered, and the blighting influence which perpetually visits the harvest of our hopes, and I believe it will be found, that our zeal in his service is only circumscribed by our inability.

It is, therefore, extremely possible for the most truly loyal subject in this kingdom deeply to regret, and conscientiously to oppose the domineering of English influence, without trenching[20] in the smallest degree on the rational loyalty, so long and so justly the boast of Ireland: His loyalty is to the King of Ireland, not to the Honourable United Company of Merchants trading, where he must never trade, to the East Indies: Nor is it to the Clothiers in Yorkshire, nor the Weavers of Manchester, nor yet to the constitutional reforming Blacksmiths of Birmingham, that he owes allegiance:[21] His first duty is to his country, his second to his King, and both are now, and by God's blessing will, I hope, remain united and inseparable.

In England we find a reform in Parliament is always popular, though it is but as a barrier against possible, not actual grievance: The people suffer in theory by the unequal distribution of the elective franchise; but practically, it is perhaps visionary to expect a Government that shall more carefully or steadily follow their real interests. No man can there be a Minister on any other terms. But reform in Ireland is no speculative remedy for possible evils: The Minister and the Government here hold their offices by a tenure very different from that of pursuing the public good. The people here are despised or defied; their will does not weigh a feather in the balance, when English influence, or

19. It was a growing complaint in the years after 1782 that the Declaration of Rights had left the parliament itself utterly unreformed, with rotten boroughs and government patronage returning a substantial number of members. Another level of this complaint stressed the exclusion of catholics. Tone's priority here is an extension of the right to vote (not necessarily the right to sit in parliament) to catholics.

20. encroaching.

21. Here Tone lists several rivals of Irish commercial interests: the East India trade was closed to the Irish; the manufacturers of Yorkshire (wool) and Manchester (linen) blocked the expansion of Irish exports through British legislation, while the populous city of Birmingham was notorious for two features: it was unrepresented in the British parliament and it was a centre of radical thought, especially among dissenters.

the interest of their rulers, is thrown into the opposite scale. We have all the reasons, all the justice that English reformists can advance, and we have a thousand others, that in England never could exist: We have in common with England the royal influence, and the ambition of Ministers to encounter; but we have also the jealous interference of that country to meet in every branch of trade, every department of commerce; and what barriers have we to oppose in our present state of representation? None: Of *four* millions of people, three are actually and confessedly unrepresented; of the remaining fourth, the electors do not exceed 60,000, and the members whom they return, supposing them all, what I wish with truth we could, men of integrity, must remain for ever a minority, for their number amounts but to 82.[22]

22. Tone is underlining the low level of active participation in Commons debates, and the inertia induced by placemen and the members for rotten boroughs. The number of MPs in the House was of course very much higher; allowing for occasional vacancies, it was about three hundred.

JOHN PHILPOT CURRAN

(1750-1817)

from: SPEECH IN FAVOUR OF ARCHIBALD HAMILTON ROWAN (1794)

[Early in 1794, Hamilton Rowan, a member of the Dublin Society of United Irishmen, was charged with distributing a seditious libel, the address of the Dublin Society to the Volunteers, calling them to arms. Since 1793, there had been a concerted campaign on the part of the government to suppress all radical activity, whether by the Volunteers or by the United Irishmen. Public assemblies were declared unlawful and a number of prosecutions were taken out against leading members of both groups. Curran's defence of Rowan took place in January 1794. In this year, he gained great renown for the role he played in defending several United Irishmen, including William Drennan, for whom he secured an acquittal, as he also did for the proprietors of the radical Belfast newspaper, *The Northern Star*. In addition, Curran defended the Rev. William Jackson, who took poison and died in court when he was found guilty of sedition. Rowan, who had been sentenced to two years in Newgate prison on the charge defended by Curran, would have been seriously compromised by his association with Jackson, as was Wolfe Tone. Tone sailed to America and Rowan escaped from prison and fled to France.]

... Gentlemen, you are sitting in a country which has a right to the British constitution, and which is bound by an indissoluble union with the British nation. If you were now even at liberty to debate on that subject; if you were not, by the most solemn compacts, founded upon the authority of your ancestors and of yourselves, bound to that alliance, and had an election now to make; in the present unhappy state of Europe, if you had been heretofore a stranger to Great Britain, you would now say — We will enter into society and union with you:

'Una salus ambobus erit, commune periculum.'[1]

But to accomplish that union let me tell you, you must learn to become like the English people. It is vain to say you will protect their freedom, if you abandon your own. The pillar whose base has no foundation, can give no support to the dome under which its head is placed; and if you profess to give England that assistance which you refuse to yourselves, she will laugh at your folly, and despise your meanness and insincerity. Let us follow this a little further — I know you will interpret what I say with the candour in which it is spoken — England is marked by a natural avarice of freedom, which she is studious to engross and accumulate, but most unwilling to impart; whether from any necessity of her policy, or from her weakness, or from her pride,

1. Virgil, *Aeneid*, II. 710: 'unum et commune periculum, una salus ambobus erit' (we shall have both one common peril, one common salvation).

I will not presume to say, but so is the fact; you need not look to the east nor to the west; you need only look to yourselves.

In order to confirm this observation, I would appeal to what fell from the learned counsel for the crown — 'that notwithstanding the alliance subsisting for two centuries past between the two countries, the date of liberty in one goes no further back than the year 1782.'

If it required additional confirmation, I should state the case of the invaded American, and the subjugated Indian, to prove that the policy of England has ever been, to govern her connexions more as colonies than as allies; and it must be owing to the great spirit indeed of Ireland, if she shall continue free. Rely upon it, she shall ever have to hold her course against an adverse current; rely upon it, if the popular spring does not continue strong and elastic, a short interval of debilitated nerve and broken force will send you down the stream again, and re-consign you to the condition of a province.

... You are living in a country where the Constitution is rightly stated to be only ten years old — where the people have not the ordinary rudiments of education. It is a melancholy story that the lower orders of the people here have less means of being enlightened than the same class of people in any other country. If there be no means left by which public measures can be canvassed, what will be the consequence? Where the Press is free and discussion unrestrained, the mind, by the collision of intercourse, gets rid of its own asperities; a sort of insensible perspiration takes place in the body politic, by which those acrimonies, which would otherwise fester and inflame, are quietly dissolved and dissipated. But now, if any aggregate assembly shall meet, they are censured; if a printer publishes their resolutions, he is punished: rightly, to be sure, in both cases, for it has been lately done. If the people say, let us not create tumult, but meet in delegation, they cannot do it; if they are anxious to promote parliamentary reform in that way, they cannot do it, the law of the last session has for the first time declared such meetings to be a crime.[2]

What then remains? The liberty of the Press *only* — that sacred palladium, which no influence, no power, no minister, no government, which nothing but the depravity, or folly, or corruption of a jury, can ever destroy. And what calamities are the people saved from, by having public communication left open to them? I will tell you, gentleman, what they are saved from, and what the Government is saved from. I will tell you also to what both are exposed by shutting up that communication. In one case sedition speaks aloud and walks abroad: the demagogue goes forth — the public eye is upon him — he frets his busy hour upon the stage:[3] but soon either weariness, or bribe, or punishment, or disappointment, bears him down, or drives him off, and he appears no more. In the other case, how does the work of sedition go forward? Night after night the muffled rebel steals forth in the dark, and casts another and another brand upon the pile, to which, when the hour of fatal maturity shall arrive, he will apply the torch. If you doubt of the horrid consequence of suppressing the effusion even of individual discontent, look to those enslaved countries where the protection of despotism is supposed to be secured by such restraints. Even the person of the despot there is never in safety. Neither the fear of the despot, nor the machinations of the slave, have any slumber — the one anticipating the moment of peril, the other watching the opportunity of aggression. The fatal crisis is equally a surprise upon both, the decisive instant is precipitated without warning — by folly on the one side, or by frenzy on the other; and there is no notice of the treason till the traitor acts. In those unfortunate countries — one cannot read it without horror — there are officers, whose province it is, to have the water which is to be drunk by their rulers, sealed up in bottles, lest some wretched miscreant should throw poison into the draught.

But, gentlemen, if you wish for a nearer and more interesting example, you have it in the history of your own revolution.[4] You have it at that memorable period, when the monarch found a servile acquiescence in the ministers of his folly — when the liberty of the Press was trodden under foot — when venal sheriffs returned packed juries, to carry into effect those fatal conspiracies of the few against the many — when the devoted benches of public

2. The Convention Act of 16 August 1793 declared unlawful assemblies appointed to represent the people or any section of the public. Curran is also referring to various attempts to muzzle the press. In 1793, two United Irishmen, who were printers, had been brought to the bar of the House of Lords for printing 'seditious' political material.

3. Shakespeare, *Macbeth*, V. 5. 25: 'A poor player/That struts and frets his hour upon the stage.'

4. The Glorious Revolution of 1688.

justice were filled by some of those foundlings of fortune who, overwhelmed in the torrent of corruption at an early period, lay at the bottom, like drowned bodies, while soundness or sanity remained in them; but, at length, becoming buoyant by putrefaction, they rose as they rotted, and floated to the surface of the polluted stream, where they were drifted along, the objects of terror, and contagion, and abomination.

In that awful moment of a nation's travail, of the last gasp of tyranny and the first breath of freedom, how pregnant is the example! The Press extinguished, the people enslaved, and the prince undone. As the advocate of society, therefore — of peace — of domestic liberty — and the lasting union of the two countries — I conjure you to guard the liberty of the Press, that great sentinel of the State, that grand detector of public imposture; guard it, because when it sinks, there sinks with it, in one common grave, the liberty of the subject, and the security of the crown.

Gentlemen, I am glad that this question has not been brought forward earlier; I rejoice, for the sake of the court, of the jury, and of the public repose, that this question has not been brought forward till now. In Great Britain analogous circumstances have taken place. At the commencement of that unfortunate war which has deluged Europe with blood, the spirit of the English people was tremblingly alive to the terror of French principles; at that moment of general paroxysm, to accuse was to convict.[5] The danger looked larger to the public eye, from the misty region through which it was surveyed. We measure inaccessible heights by the shadows which they project, where the lowness and the distance of the light form the length of the shade.

There is a sort of aspiring and adventurous credulity, which disdains asserting the obvious truths, and delights in catching at the improbability of circumstances, as its best ground of faith. To what other cause, gentlemen, can you ascribe, that in the wise, the reflecting, and the philosophic nation of Great Britain, a printer has been gravely found guilty of a libel, for publishing those resolutions to which the present minister of the kingdom had actually subscribed his name? — To what other cause can you ascribe, what in my mind is still more astonishing, in such a country as Scotland — a nation cast in the happy medium between the spiritless acquiescence of submissive poverty, and the sturdy credulity of pampered wealth — cool and ardent — adventurous and persevering — winging her eagle flight against the blaze of every science, with an eye that never winks and a wing that never tires — crowned as she is, with the spoils of every art, and decked with the wreath of every muse, from the deep and scrutinizing researches of her Hume,[6] to the sweet and simple, but not less sublime and pathetic, morality of her Burns[7] — how, from the bosom of a country like that, genius, and character, and talents, should be banished to a distant barbarous soil, condemned to pine under the horrid communion of vulgar vice and base-born profligacy, for twice the period that ordinary calculation gives to the continuance of human life?

But I will not further press the idea that is so painful to me, and I am sure must be painful to you. I will only say, you have now an example, of which neither England nor Scotland had the advantage: you have the example of the panic, the infatuation, and the contrition of both. It is now for you to decide, whether you will profit by their experience of idle panic and idle regret; or whether you meanly prefer to palliate a servile imitation of their frailty, by a paltry affectation of their repentance. It is now for you to show, that you are not carried away by the same hectic delusions, to acts, of which no tears can wash away the fatal consequences, or the indelible reproach. . . .[8]

I cannot, however, avoid reverting to a circumstance that distinguished the case of Mr. Rowan from that of the late sacrifice in a neighbouring kingdom.

The severer law of that country, it seems — and happy for them that it should — enables them to remove from their sight the victim of their infatuation. The more merciful spirit of our law deprives you of that consolation; his sufferings must ever remain before our eyes, a continual call upon your shame and your remorse. But those sufferings will do more; they will not rest satisfied

5. Britain had declared war on revolutionary France in 1793. There was a general, partly government-inspired, panic against Jacobinism.

6. David Hume (1711-76), Scottish philosopher, economist and historian.

7. Robert Burns (1759-96), Scottish lyric poet.

8. A reference to the 'Scottish martyrs', Muir and Palmer, sentenced in a Scottish court to fourteen years transportation for their espousal of 'Jacobin' principles.

with your unavailing contrition — they will challenge the great and paramount inquest of society — the man will be weighed against the charge, the witness, and the sentence — and impartial justice will demand, why has an Irish jury done this deed? The moment he ceases to be regarded as a criminal, he becomes of necessity an accuser; and let me ask you, what can your most zealous defenders be prepared to answer to such a charge? When your sentence shall have sent him forth to that stage, which guilt alone can render infamous, let me tell you, he will not be like a little statue upon a mighty pedestal, diminished by elevation; but he will stand a striking and imposing object upon a monument, which, if it does not (and it cannot) record the atrocity of his crime, must record the atrocity of his conviction.

Upon this subject, therefore, credit me when I say, that I am still more anxious for you than I can possibly be for him. I cannot but feel the peculiarity of your situation. Not the jury of his own choice, which the law of England allows, but which ours refuses; collected in that box by a person certainly no friend to Mr. Rowan[9] — certainly not very deeply interested in giving him a very impartial jury. Feeling this, as I am persuaded you do, you cannot be surprised, however you may be distressed, at the mournful presage with which an anxious public is led to fear the worst from your possible determination. But I will not, for the justice and honour of our common country, suffer my mind to be borne away by such melancholy anticipation. I will not relinquish the confidence that this day will be the period of his sufferings; and, however mercilessly he has been hitherto pursued, that your verdict will send him home to the arms of his family, and the wishes of his country. But if, which Heaven forbid! it hath still been unfortunately determined, that because he has not bent to power and authority, because he would not bow down before the golden calf,[10] and worship it, he is to be bound and cast into the furnace; I do trust in God, that there is a redeeming spirit in the constitution, which will be seen to walk with the sufferer through the flames, and to preserve him unhurt from the conflagration.

9. John Gifford, a notorious place-hunter and enemy of the United Irishmen.

10. To discard one's principles for the sake of gain. Aaron made a golden calf idol, when Moses was absent on Mount Sinai, for the Israelites to worship (Exodus 32).

ROBERT EMMET
(1778-1803)

'SPEECH FROM THE DOCK' (1803)

[After the Treaty of Amiens in March 1802, war again broke out between Britain and France in May 1803. This is the larger context in which Robert Emmet's insurrection of 23 July 1803 should be seen. Emmet and his brother Thomas Addis Emmet (1764-1827) were both United Irishmen who had negotiated with Napoleon the previous year with a view to obtaining French assistance for a provisional government of an independent Ireland. An explosion in Emmet's munitions store forced him to launch his insurrection prematurely; allies in Ulster and Wicklow were unable to rally to him, and only about one hundred men supported him in Dublin. After his arrest, he was tried for high treason (19 September). He was found guilty and was executed the following day.

Robert Emmet's concluding speech was quickly circulated in several versions, and the question of what he actually said illustrates vividly the difficulty of authenticating any such oral performance. Late nineteenth-century texts, such as those circulated at the time of the centenary of the 1798 Rebellion, differ markedly from those issued immediately after Emmet's execution. Thus, the speech may be said to have two levels of existence, one incompletely known and probably incomplete, and the second well-known, well-rounded and in part at least more mythical than historical. The fame of the latter, however, is ironically attached to the broadcasting of the former because in the first place it was the government that appears to have exploited the speech for propagandist purposes.

The prisoner's preparations apparently included the

writing of a speech, but whether the speech written was the speech delivered is highly debatable. It seems clear that Emmet was interrupted by the presiding judge, that he was forced to repeat himself in order to make his point, and (perhaps equally importantly) he had already stood throughout a prolonged hearing of a most exhausting case. Nevertheless, as late as 1844, Thomas Moore was informed of a surviving copy in Emmet's own handwriting and that a Mr Marshall (a reading-room superintendent either in Oxford or London) 'is in the possession of that document and . . . can trace it from the hands of the person to whom Emmett [*sic*] gave it.' In the event, Moore appears not to have located the speech. He did, however, interest himself in the last hours of his former friend, and recorded in his journal that

> The person who took down the speech at the trial was, I think, McNally, the son of the barrister, and he had afterwards some conversation with Emmett in the prison. It was during that conversation that Emmett, in speaking of [William Conyngham] Plunket used those expressions ['that viper my father warmed in his bosom'] which McNally introduced subsequently in the speech.

We should note here that Moore accepted without question that words used in the cell after the trial was over found their way into printed versions of the speech from the dock, even if we cannot assume the younger MacNally to be the effective reporter/composer of any one specific text.

The first printed account of Emmet's speech from the dock appeared in the *Dublin Evening Post* of 20 and 22 September 1803, that is, within hours of the execution. This was copied by other newspapers, including *The Times* of London. Given the circumstances, this account does not have the qualities that would render it acceptable as a copy-text for reconstructing what Emmet actually said. One of the prosecuting barristers, William Ridgeway (1765-1817), was a law reporter and editor of many years' experience, and a pamphlet account of the entire trial appeared before the end of the year in at least two states: the first was an account solely of the Emmet trial, and the second a collection of various trials during the months August, September and October 1803. The pages covering Emmet's speech are verbatim identical in each. At least one other edition dated 1803 was published with a Dublin imprint, but with no publisher's name given: this includes a folding frontispiece portrait of the prisoner and a moral quotation in Latin from Sallust. Loyalist agencies also disseminated the speech for propagandist purposes, laying emphasis (by removing other matter) on Emmet's antagonism towards France, the object being to drive a wedge between the United Irishmen and that regime.

Sometime in or after 1807, another version of the speech was circulated in pamphlet form, complete with a quotation from Thomas Moore's 'Oh! blame not the bard', by which the publication can be dated. This is stated to have been issued at the request 'of his friends', although the title-page curiously misdates the trial as 29 September, an error also taken up by some later editions. The friends' text omits part of the attack on France and expands on Britain's tyranny towards Ireland and on the character of Emmet's judges. Even the French contrived to produce a variant text suitable to their political requirements. None of these can be accepted as a verbatim account of Emmet's performance, partly because the notion of strictly verbatim reporting was still in its infancy and partly because none of the parties issuing versions of the speech had any special interest in accuracy per se. The government was anxious to exploit the pathetic failure of the insurrection to deter others with ambitions like Emmet's, and to demoralize the United Irishmen. The French of course were reluctant to reprint anything critical of France that Emmet might have said in his self-justification, while the Dublin friends were keen to emphasize Emmet's nobility of motive and demeanour. But even at a technical level, there were difficulties confronting all but the officially approved reporter: the difficulty of taking notes during a political trial, indeed the difficulty of gaining access to the court in the first place. Ridgeway certainly, and young MacNally probably, were able to overcome this latter difficulty; both also could have drawn on the services of the court's 'chirographer', Thomas Acton.

The differences between these various editions of the speech can be attributed to the objectives of those publishing them at least as easily as to any technical difficulties. There are substantial 'omissions' in almost all texts, as measured against the full accretion of material in the texts all taken together. Sometimes factions of quite opposite views concur in rendering a particular aspect of the speech. For example, both the friends' pamphlet and a loyalist broadsheet version conclude with the now-famous 'let no man write my epitaph' peroration, which occurs in Ridgeway's version only in a staccato form and at a less dramatically effective moment. On the other hand, there is a remarkable indeterminancy as to whether Emmet rebutted charges of being an emissary *to* France, *for* France, or *from* France. One non-separate publication of the speech is worth mentioning in addition to the immediate newspaper report. *Walker's Hibernian Magazine* for September 1803 includes the (now) familiar phrases 'when my country takes her place amongst the nations of the earth. . . .' Although this does not appear in Ridgeway, it does get into the friends' later pamphlet. Finally, this journal gives Emmet's last words as 'I am done', rather than the more familiar and more rhetorically upbeat 'I have done'.

One sinister name occurs at the bottom of the Ridgeway text (see below). It is that of Leonard MacNally (1752-1820), a sworn United Irishman but also a secret agent of the government. If the version issued by Emmet's friends benefited in any way from privileged access to the government's records, then MacNally is a likely candidate for the honour of being the go-between, with his son (according, much later, to Moore) also playing a part. MacNally senior had written to the authorities on 12 September, revealing Emmet's plans (or lack of plans) for his defence. Moreover, he took over with Peter Burrowes (1753-1841) as Emmet's defence counsel from John Philpot Curran. The latter disliked Emmet, though Emmet was in love with his daughter, Sarah Curran (1782-1808). These emotional tensions may or may not have disturbed Emmet's delivery of his speech. One of the prosecuting counsel was William Conyngham Plunket (1764-1854), already referred to in the Moore memoir quoted above, who had been a friend of Christopher Temple Emmet, elder and deceased brother of the accused. According to John Gamble's *Tour Through the North of Ireland*, Emmet in his speech referred to Plunket as 'that viper my father warmed in his bosom.' Personal intimacy perhaps reached its peak when MacNally, the informer/counsel, kissed his client farewell in the courtroom.

The text reproduced here is that of Ridgeway's pamphlet. It has been chosen principally because it has a kind of priority, because its editor had experience of law reporting (though also a part in the trial reported) and because any alternative is faulty in technical details. Ample annotation drawing on other versions is also provided to indicate both similarity and dissimilarity. The subsequent fame of Emmet's 'Speech from the Dock' is a tribute to the power of propaganda generally, even if the government that Emmet sought to overthrow was among the first to exploit the occasion.]

Why the sentence of the law should not be passed upon me, I have nothing to say — why the sentence which in the public mind is usually attached to that of the law, ought to be reversed, I have much to say.[1] —— I stand here a conspirator — as one engaged in a conspiracy for the overthrow of the *British* Government in *Ireland*; — for the fact of which I am to suffer by the law; — for the motives of which I am to answer before God. —— I am ready to do both. —— Was it only the fact of treason — was it that naked fact alone with which I stood charged —— Was I to suffer to other punishment, than the death of the body, I would not obtrude on your attention, but having received the sentence, I would bow my neck in silence to the stroke. But, my Lords, I well know, that when a man enters into a conspiracy, he has not only to combat against the difficulties of fortune, but to contend with the still more insurmountable obstacles of prejudice: — and that if, in the end, fortune abandons him and delivers him over bound into the hands of the law, his character is previously loaded with calumny and misrepresentation. For what purpose, I know not, except, that the Prisoner, thus weighed down both in mind and body, may be delivered over a more unresisting victim to condemnation. —— It is well: — But the victim being once obtained and firmly in your power, let him now unmanacle his reputation. —— Not, my Lords, that I have much to demand from you, — it is a claim on your memory, rather than on your candour, that I am making. I do not ask you to believe implicitly what I say. I do not hope that you will let my vindication ride at anchor in your breasts;[2] — I only ask you, to let it float upon the surface of your recollection, till it comes to some more friendly port to receive it, and give it shelter against the heavy storms with which it is buffetted.

I am charged with being an emissary of *France*, for the purpose of inciting insurrection in the country and then delivering it over to a foreign enemy. — It is false! — I did not wish to join this country with *France*. — I did join — I did not create the rebellion — not for *France*; but for its liberty. It is true, there were communications between the *United Irishmen* and *France*; — it is true, that by that, the war was no surprize upon us. There is a new agent at *Paris*, at this moment, negotiating with the *French Government* to obtain from them an aid sufficient to accomplish the separation of *Ireland* from *England*, and before any expedition sails, it is intended to have a treaty signed, as a guarantee, similiar to that which *Franklin* obtained for *America*.[3] Whether they will do that now, *England*,

1. Court procedure required that the presiding judge ask the convicted man if he had anything to say why sentence should not be passed. The friends' pamphlet version opens, as follows:

   My Lords,
   I am asked what I have to say, why sentence of Death should not be pronounced on me, according to Law! I have nothing to say which can alter your predeterminations, nor that it will become me to [reply?] with any view to the mitigation of that Sentence I must abide by!

2. The friends' pamphlet has 'I have no hopes that I can anchor my character in the breast of a Court, constituted and tramelled as this is.'
3. The friends' pamphlet has a longer passage beginning 'I am charged with being an Emissary to [*sic*] France . . .' which at this point reads 'I wished to procure for my Country, the guarantee which Washington procured for America.' In point of fact, it was Benjamin Franklin who negotiated an American treaty with the French, although George Washington was of course better remembered in the nineteenth century.

you may judge. But the only question with the members of The Provisional Government was: Whether *France* should come to this country, as an enemy? — Whether she should have any pretext for so doing? — Whether the people should look to *France*, as their only deliverer, or through the medium and control of the Provisional Government attain their object? It is not now, that I discovered, or that the rest of the Provisional Government of *Ireland* feel what it is that binds states together. They well know, my Lords, that such a disposition exists only in proportion to its mutuality of interest; and wherever that mutuality does not exist, no written articles can secure the inferior state, nor supply the means of protecting its independence.

In this view, it never was the intention of the Provisional Government of *Ireland* to form a permanent alliance with *France*; well knowing, that if there is between states a permanent mutual interest, more or less, though treaties may be made, yet for the most part, it is not the treaty which binds them together, but a sense of common interest, and where that interest does not exist, treaties are soon represented as unjust — they are qualified and interpreted at pleasure, and violated under any pretext. Under these views, it never was the intention to form a permanent treaty with *France*, and in the treaty which they did make, they had the same guarrantee which *America* had, that an Independent Government should be established in the country, before the *French* should come. — God forbid! that I should see my country under the hands of a foreign power. On the contrary, it is evident from the introductory paragraph of the address of the *Provisional Government* of *Ireland*, that every hazard attending an independent effort was deemed preferable to the more fatal risk of introducing a *French* army into the country. For what? when it has liberty to maintain and independence to keep, may no consideration induce it to submit. If the *French* come as a foreign enemy, Oh, my Countrymen! meet them on the shore with a torch in one hand — a sword in the other — receive them with all the destruction of war — immolate them in their boats before our native soil shall be polluted by a foreign foe.[4] If they succeed in landing, fight them on the strand, burn every blade of grass before them, as they advance; raze every house; and if you are driven to the centre of your country, collect your provisions, your property, your wives and your daughters, form a circle around them — fight while two men are left, and when but one remains, let that man set fire to the pile, and release himself and the families of his fallen countrymen from the tyranny of *France*.

Deliver my country into the hands of *France*! —— Look at the Proclamation. — Where is it stated? — Is it in that part where the people of *Ireland* are called upon to shew the world, that they are competent to take their place among nations? — that they have a right to claim acknowledgment as an *Independent* country, by the satisfactory proof of their capability of maintaining their independence? — by wresting it from *England*, with *their own* hands? Is it in that part, where it is stated, that the system has been organized within the last eight months, *without the hope of foreign assistance*, and which the renewal of hostilities has not accelerated? — Is it in that part, which desires *England* not to create a deadly national antipathy between the two countries? — Look then to another part of the proclamation — look at the military regulations: — is there a word introduced from the *French* nomenclature? — Are not all the terms *English* — all the appellations of the intended constituted authorities — *English*? — Why then say, the system was from *France*? — Yes, there was one argument urged; one quotation from the Proclamation relied upon, to prove, that we must have meant to resort to *France*. 'You are to shew to us, that you have something in reserve wherewith to crush hereafter, not only a greater exertion on the part of the people; but a greater exertion, rendered still greater by *foreign assistance*.' From which an inference is drawn, that foreign assistance is the support of the present system. Because you are called upon to shew, that your strength is such, that you can put down the present attempt without bringing out all your force — to shew, that you have something in *reserve*, wherewith to crush *hereafter*. Therefore, the conclusion drawn is, because a *future* exertion *may be* rendered greater by foreign assistance, that foreign

4. The friends' pamphlet has 'Were the French to come as invaders, or enemies, uninvited by the wishes of the people, I should oppose them to the utmost of my strength! Yes, my Countrymen, I should advise you to meet them upon the beach, with a sword in one hand, and a torch in the other: I would meet them with all the destructive fury of War....' It is thus not the case that the authorities simply inserted anti-French material into their version of the speech, although they certainly highlighted it.

assistance *is* the foundation of the present exertion.

But it is said, we must have had it in view to deliver up the country to *France*, and this is not attempted to be proved upon any ground, but that of assertion. — It is not proved from our declarations or actions; because every circumstance attending the attempt which took place, shews, that our object was to anticipate *France*. — How could we speak of freedom to our countrymen — how assume such an exalted motive and meditate the introduction of a power, which has been the enemy of freedom wherever she appears. — See how she has behaved to other countries. How has she behaved to *Switzerland*, to *Holland*, and to *Italy*? Could we expect better conduct towards us? No! Let not then any man calumniate my memory, by believing that I could have hoped for freedom from the government of *France*, or that I would have betrayed the sacred cause of the liberty of this country, by committing it to the power of her most determined foe.

With regard to this, I have one observation to make: — It has been stated that I came from abroad: — If I had been in *Switzerland*, I would have fought against the *French*; for I believe the Swiss are hostile to the *French*. — In the dignity of freedom, I would have expired on the frontiers of that country, and they should have it entered only by passing over my lifeless corse.[5] — But if I thought the people were favourable to the *French*. — I have seen so much what the consequence of the failure of revolutions are — the oppressions of the higher upon the lower orders of the people. — I say, if I saw them disposed to admit the *French*, I would not join them, but I would put myself between the *French* and the people, not as a victim — but to protect them from subjugation, and endeavour to gain their confidence, by sharing in their danger.

So would I have done with the people of *Ireland*, and so would I do, if I was called upon tomorrow. — Our object was to effect a separation from *England*—.

The Court here interrupted the Prisoner.[6]

Lord NORBURY. At the moment when you are called upon to shew, why sentence of death should not be pronounced against you, according to law, you are making an avowal of dreadful treasons, and of a determined purpose to have persevered in them; which I do believe has astonished your audience. The Court is most anxious to give you the utmost latitude of indulgence to address them, hoping that such indulgence would not be abused by an attempt to vindicate the most criminal measures and principles, through the dangerous, medium of eloquent, but perverted talents. I beseech you therefore to compose your mind, and to recollect, that the patient attention with which you have been listened to is unparalleled in the history of any other country, that did not enjoy the benignant temper of the British Law. You should make some better atonement to expiate your own crimes, and to alleviate the misfortunes you have brought upon your country; with which country, and with your God, I entreat you to make your peace. You must be aware, that a court of justice in endeavouring to control and do away the bad effect of desperate sentiments, which have been thus promulgated, as the effusions of a disturbed and agitated mind, is but fulfilling that duty which it owed to the offended laws of an injured country. You, Sir, had the honour to be a gentleman by birth, and your father filled a respectable situation under the government.[7] You had an eldest brother, whom death snatched away, and who when living was one of the greatest ornaments of the bar.[8] The laws of his country were the study of his youth; and the study of his maturer life was to cultivate and support them. He left you a proud example to follow; and if he had lived, he would have given your talents the same virtuous direction as his own, and have taught you to admire and preserve that constitution, for the destruction of which you have conspired with the most profligate and abandoned, and associated yourself with hostlers, bakers, butchers, and such persons, whom you invited to councils, when you erected your Provisional Government. When you sallied forth at midnight with such a band of assassins, and found yourself implicated in their atrocities, your heart must have lost all recollection of what you were.[9] You had been

5. An archaic word for 'corpse'.
6. This Ridgeway version includes (some, at least, of) the presiding judge's interventions. John Toler (1745-1831) had been made chief justice of the common pleas and baron Norbury in 1800. He was notorious for his reactionary opinions, his harassment of persons in court, and his broad humour. Norbury was made an earl in 1827.
7. Emmet's father had been a physician in the state's employ.
8. Emmet's brother, Christopher Temple Emmet, had died young.
9. The notable victims of Emmet's insurrection were Arthur Wolfe (1739-1803), 1st viscount Kilwarden, and his nephew Richard Wolfe, who were murdered by a mob in Thomas Street, Dublin.

educated at a most virtuous and enlightened seminary of learning,[10] and amidst the ingenuous youth of your country, many of whom now surround you with the conscious pride of having taken up arms to save their country against your attacks upon it; and amongst them there may be a throb of indignant sorrow, which would say — '*Had it been an open enemy, I could have born it; but that it should be my companion and my friend.*'

Mr. EMMET. My Lord ——

Lord NORBURY. If you have any thing to urge in point of law, you will be heard; but what you have hitherto said, confirms and justifies the verdict of the Jury.

Mr. EMMET. My Lord, I did say I had nothing to offer why the sentence of the law should not pass upon me. But if that is all I am asked, that is not all I am to suffer, even from the voice of those who surround me. — But the judge when he pronounces the sentence of the law, does not confine himself to the mere form which is prescribed — he feels it a duty, I am sure from pure motives, to give an exhortation to the Prisoner. —— The judges sometimes think it their duty to dwell upon his motives. — What I claim then is this — to free my character from a foul imputation. Though you, my Lord, sit there as a judge; and I stand here a culprit; yet, you are but a man; — and I am a man also. And when you, or any other judge speak against the motives of a dying man, I do conceive it to be the right of the dying man, — that it is his duty, to vindicate his character and his views from aspersion. — If I say any thing contrary to the law, your Lordship may stop me, and I will submit immediately upon being corrected. — But it is hardly possible, when I am justifying my motives, to avoid mentioning some which must be disagreeable to those I address. — All I can say, is, that they should have been passed over in silence. — If my motives are not to be justified, nothing should be said, but the pronouncing of the sentence. — If I am not permitted to vindicate my character, let no man dare to calumniate my motives. — If I am permitted to go on ——

Lord NORBURY. You have learning and discrimination enough to know, that if a judge were to sit in a court of justice to hear any man proclaim treason, and to proceed to unwarrantable lengths, in order to captivate or delude the unwary, or to circulate opinions or principles of the most dangerous tendency, for the purposes of mischief, it would be an insult to the law, and to the justice of the country, for which those who preside would be responsible; but in every matter relevant to your own case you shall have every indulgence.

Mr. EMMET. Then I have nothing more to say, if I am not permitted to vindicate myself. Vindication[11] rests upon abstract principle, and the views with which that principle is applied. — I did wish to state both — I did wish to state the views which I had, without presuming to make application of them to any body. — I can only say, that my motives, and abhorrence of the spilling of blood, resulted from an ardent attachment to my country, from a sense of public duty, in which I have been brought up from the age of ten years. I had hoped that such a thing as public principle might have existed. But if I go to my grave, with this imputation cast upon me this day, that I wished for personal aggrandizement and dominion, I would go with a heavy weight upon my mind. I appeal to every man who heard it, not to believe it. I would appeal to those who cannot hear what I am not permitted to say, to follow the ATTORNEY-GENERAL, and discharge it altogether from their minds —— Let it remain in silence —— in charitable silence —— I have now done.[12] —— I have burned out my lamp of life. For the public service, I abandoned the worship of another idol I adored in my heart. —— My ministry is now ended. I am now to receive my reward. I am going to my cold grave. — I have one request to make. Let there be no inscription upon my tomb. — Let no man write my epitaph. — No

10. Trinity College, Dublin where Emmet was well-known as a radical. He withdrew from the college in June 1798 in the course of an inquisition conducted against those in sympathy with the United Irishmen.

11. In a letter to the chief secretary, William Wickham (1761-1840), written on the morning of his execution, Emmet began: 'Had I been permitted to proceed with my vindication. . . .' This indicates that Norbury did indeed cut short Emmet's performance, and that the concluding words as given in the Ridgeway version were not intended by Emmet to be the end.

12. It is this passage above all that has gone down in history, although the popular versions are closer to that given in the friends' pamphlet:

> my lamp of life is nearly extinguished — my race is run — the grave opens to receive me and I sink into its bosom. I have but one request to ask at my departure from this world, it is the Charity of its silence — let no man write my epitaph for as no man [who] knows my motives dare he [vindicate] them, let them and me repose in obscurity and peace, and my tomb remain uninscribed, until other times and other men can do justice to my character — when my Country takes her place among the nations of the earth, then, and not till then let my epitaph be written — I have done.

man can write my epitaph. — I am here ready to die. — I am not allowed to vindicate my character. — No man shall dare to vindicate my character, and when I am prevented from vindicating myself, let no man dare to calumniate me. — Let my character and my motives repose in obscurity and peace, till other times and other men can do them justice; *Then* shall my character be vindicated. — Then may my epitaph be written.

Lord NORBURY. I was in hopes that I might have been able to recall you to a more composed state of mind, suitable to the melancholy situation in which you are placed. I lament that it was vain to attempt it. A different conduct would more become a man who had endeavoured to overthrow the laws and the liberties of his country, and who had vainly and wickedly substituted the bloody proscriptions of the Provisional Government, in the room of the most temperate, mild, and impartial justice with which a free country was ever blessed. —— Had you been tried under the system of your own invention, you would not have been listened to for an instant; but your code would have crushed the inventor. And such has been the well-known fate of most of the leaders of modern republicanism, where such talents and dispositions as yours have been resorted to, that the prostituted pen of every revolutionary raver might be put in requisition to madden the multitude, and to give sovereignty to the mob.

Mr EMMET. I beg pardon; — I wish to mention one circumstance, which is, to state expressly, that I did not come from *France*; — I did not create the conspiracy — I found it when I arrived here; — I was solicited to join it, — I took time to consider of it, and I was told expressly, that it was no matter whether I did join it or not — it would go on. I then, finding my principles accord with the measure, did join it, and under the same circumstances would do so again.

Lord NORBURY. The history of your trial, and the circumstances relating to it, are fresh in every man's recollection. Be assured that I have the most sincere affliction in performing the painful duty which devolves upon me, and let me, with the most anxious concern, exhort you, not to depart this life with such sentiments of rooted hostility to your country as those which you have expressed. Be assured that far other sentiments will better contribute to give you comfort at your departure from this life, and to obtain forgiveness and mercy in that which is to come — as well as to give you fortitude to bear that dreadful sentence which at this awful moment I must pronounce.

His Lordship then pronounced the sentence in the usual form, and the prisoner bowed, and retired.

The Prisoner was executed the next day in *Thomas-street.*[13]

Counsel for the Crown	*Counsel for the Prisoner*
Mr Attorney General	Mr Burrowes
Mr Solicitor General	Mr Mac Nally
Mr Plunket	
Mr Mayne	*Agent*
Mr Townsend	Mr L. Mac Nally[14]
Mr Ridgeway	
Mr O'Grady	

Crown Solicitors
T. and W. Kemmis

13. Emmet was hanged and beheaded outside St Catherine's church in Thomas Street, Dublin, close to where the mob in his support had murdered Lord Kilwarden and his nephew. The place of his burial remains unidentified.

14. The names of those listed at the end of the *State Trials* serve to authenticate its version of Emmet's speech. More fully, these persons were:

Standish O'Grady (1766-1840), attorney general 1803; created Viscount Guillamore in 1831.
James McClelland, solicitor general, appointed 12 January 1802.
William Conyngham Plunket (1764-1854).
?Edward Mayne, admitted a barrister in 1781.
Townsend — unknown.
William Ridgeway (1765-1817), prolific law reporter, admitted a barrister in 1790.
?Henry Deane Grady, admitted a barrister 1783.
Thomas Kemmis and William Kemmis (1777-1864) were partners in the firm that acted as crown solicitors.
Peter Burrowes (1753-1841), sometime MP for Enniscorthy in the Irish parliament; opposed the Union; judge of the Insolvent Debtors' Court 1821.
Leonard MacNally (1752-1820), dramatist, barrister and informer.

THE CATHOLIC BOARD

PETITION TO PARLIAMENT (1813)

[The Catholic Committee, founded in 1760, was proscribed under the Convention Act of 1793. In 1812 Daniel O'Connell changed the name of the committee to the Catholic Board, without ever formally challenging the legality of the government's suppression of the committee. The new board was a petitioning body. The following petition is characteristic in its emphasis on loyalty to the crown. Earlier in the year Grattan had carried a resolution in the House of Commons that catholic disabilities be removed, subject to certain conditions. This meant, in effect, that catholics were to swear allegiance to the crown. O'Connell repudiated the resolution, as did the catholic hierarchy; for different reasons, so too did the House of Commons. The petition, humble enough in tone, contains within it an outright rejection by the Irish catholics of the temporal allegiance to the papacy formerly taken for granted. The petition was printed in *The Monthly Museum or Dublin Literary Repertory* (October 1813).]

DUBLIN

On Saturday, Oct. 23d, there was a meeting of the Roman Catholic Board, when the following Petition to Parliament was presented, and unanimously adopted:

WE, the ROMAN CATHOLIC PEOPLE OF IRELAND, again approach the Legislature with a statement of the grievances under which we labour, and of which we most respectfully, but at the same time most firmly solicit the effectual redress. — Our wrongs are so notorious and so numerous, that their minute detail is quite unnecessary, and would indeed be impossible were it deemed expedient. Ages of persecution on the one hand, and of patience on the other, sufficiently attest our sufferings and our submission. Privations have been answered only by Petition — indignities by remonstrances — injuries by forgiveness. It has been a misfortune to have suffered for the sake of our Religion, but it has also been a pride to have borne the best testimony to the purity of our doctrine by the meekness of our endurance.

We have sustained the power which spurned us — we have nerved the arm which smote us — we have lavished our strength, our talent, and our treasures, and buoyed on the prodigal effusion of our young blood, the triumphant Ark of British Liberty.

We approach then with confidence an enlightened Legislature; in the name of Nature, we ask our rights as Men. In the name of the Constitution we ask our privileges as subjects. In the name of God, we ask the sacred protection of unpersecuted piety as Christians.

Are Securities required of us? we offer them — the best securities a throne can have — the affections of a People. We offer faith that was never violated — Hearts that never were corrupted —— Valour that never crouched; every hour of peril has proved our Allegiance, and every Field of Europe exhibits its example.

We abjure all temporal authority, except that of our Sovereign. We acknowledge no civil pre-eminence, save that of our Constitution, and for our lavish and voluntary expenditure, we ask only a reciprocity of benefits.

Separating as we do our Civil Rights, from our Spiritual duties, we humbly desire that they may not be confounded. — We 'render unto Cæsar the things that are Cæsar's,' but we must also 'render unto God, the things that are God's.'[1] — Our Church could not descend to claim a State Authority, nor do we ask for it a State aggrandisement. Its hopes, its powers, and its pretensions, are of another world. And when we raise our hands most humbly to the State, our prayer is not that the fetters may be transferred to the hands which are raised for us to Heaven. We would not erect a splendid shrine even to Liberty, on the ruins of the Temple.

In behalf then of Five Millions of a brave and loyal People, we call upon the Legislature to annihilate the odious bondage, which bows down the mental, phsyical, and moral energies of Ireland, and in the name of that Gospel which breathes

1. Matthew 22.21.

Charity to all we seek freedom of Conscience for all the Inhabitants of the British Empire.

May it therefore please this Honourable House to abolish all penal and disabling Laws, which in any manner infringe Religious Liberty, or restrict the free enjoyment of the sacred Rights of Conscience within these Realms.

And your Petitioners will ever pray.

DANIEL O'CONNELL

(1775-1847)

SPEECH IN DEFENCE OF WILLIAM MAGEE, EDITOR OF THE *DUBLIN EVENING POST* (1813)

[On 5 January 1813, the *Dublin Evening Post* commenced a series of articles analysing the record of the Duke of Richmond (Charles Lennox, 1764-1819, 4th duke) as lord lieutenant of Ireland. The attorney general, William Saurin (*c.*1757-1839), brought a charge of criminal libel against the newspaper's editor, William Magee. Daniel O'Connell was retained to defend him. After some delays, not unconnected with other actions brought against Magee, the case was heard in substance in July 1813, with O'Connell taking the opportunity to transform the defence of an individual newspaper editor and proprietor into a virtuoso display of his own talents as the up-and-coming leader of the catholic community. So total was this exploitation of the occasion that Magee repudiated his own counsel, although the court proceeded to find him guilty of a libel on Richmond. He was fined £500 and sentenced to two years' imprisonment.

O'Connell's principal target was the attorney general himself, and the speech in defence of Magee was the high point of a longer struggle between the two lawyers. If Magee was appalled by his counsel's cheeky assault on the prosecutor in July, O'Connell's uncle and mentor, Maurice 'Hunting Cap' O'Connell (1728-1825), found the later stages of the court-room jousting distasteful and positively dangerous. The old man wrote to this nephew on 14 December 1813:

> However averse and hostile the Attorney-General may be to the Catholics and to their constitutional pursuits to obtain Emancipation, the high situation he enjoys as first law officer of the crown demands a degree of respect and consideration from the bar which should not be lightly forgot or neglected.... I have not only to entreat, but decidedly to insist, that on your part they will be carried on with calmness, discretion and decency....

Yet at the time, O'Connell's scathing attack (on the jury as much as on the attorney general) drew at least one letter of congratulation, which serves to confirm some of the most memorably colourful passages in the speech. 'E.B.' wrote on 28 July 1813:

> Your language I found, I shall not say convincing, but dazzling and overpowering — and as the soul of man is by nature darting into the sublime region of eternity, I beheld with ecstasy the fire of your soul darting through your eyes while addressing the suppressors of vice, the bible distributors....

Although the unknown correspondent enclosed a subscription of a guinea, he ended 'Poor Magee! Alas! poor Yorick!!!'

The authorities were not satisfied. The youthful chief secretary, Robert Peel (1788-1850), was determined to break the liberal press, and Saurin obligingly proposed to sue on the basis that O'Connell's speech (duly reported in the *Dublin Evening Post*) itself contained a libel on him. In the following year the authorities prosecuted the paper for publishing certain resolutions concerning the treatment of Magee passed at a meeting of catholics in Kilkenny, even though Magee had taken his text from a pro-government paper, which was not prosecuted. This was not all: when the paper published (inaccurately it seems) a speech made by O'Connell at a meeting of the Catholic Board, the authorities commenced an action, but the new proprietor of the *Dublin Evening Post*, James Magee (brother to the previous proprietor and editor, now lingering in jail) sought to persuade O'Connell to share the rigours of the trial. O'Connell was prepared to agree, provided he was allowed to supply an accurate statement of what he had actually said, based on shorthand notes taken by a fellow barrister and verified on oath both by O'Connell himself and by the reporting barrister. This the court refused, unless O'Connell stood in fully in Magee's stead. He naturally declined to do this. In such detail one can find more than adequate warning against taking the printed word of newspaper reports as absolutely reliable.

The text below represents about a quarter of that published in *The Select Speeches*, a good deal of the omitted material being devoted to legal technicalities.]

I consented to the adjournment yesterday, gentlemen of the jury, from that impulse of nature which compels us to postpone pain; it is, indeed, painful to me to address you; it is a cheerless, a hopeless task to address you — a task which would require all the animation and interest to be derived from the working of a mind fully fraught with the resentment and disgust created in mine yesterday, by that farrago of helpless absurdity with which Mr. Attorney-General[1] regaled you.

But I am now not sorry for the delay. Whatever I may have lost in vivacity, I trust I shall compensate for in discretion. That which yesterday excited my anger, now appears to me to be an object of pity; and that which then roused my indignation, now only moves to *contempt*. I can now address you with feelings softened, and, I trust, subdued; and I do, from my soul, declare, that I now cherish no other sensations than those which enable me to bestow on the Attorney-General and on his discourse, pure and unmixed compassion.

It was a discourse in which you could not discover either order, or method, or eloquence; it contained very little logic, and no poetry at all; violent and virulent, it was a confused and disjointed tissue of bigotry, amalgamated with congenial vulgarity. He accused my client of using Billingsgate, and he accused him of it in language suited exclusively for that meridian.[2] He descended even to the calling of names: he called this young gentleman a 'malefactor,' a 'Jacobin,'[3] and a 'ruffian,' gentlemen of the jury; he called him 'abominable,' and 'seditious,' and 'revolutionary,' and 'infamous,' and a 'ruffian' again, gentlemen of the jury; he called him a 'brothel keeper,' a 'pander,' 'a kind of bawd in breeches,' and a 'ruffian' a third time, gentlemen of the jury.

I cannot repress my astonishment, how Mr. Attorney-General could have *preserved* this dialect in its native purity; he has been now for nearly thirty years in the class of polished society; he has, for some years, mixed amongst the highest orders in the state; he has had the honour to belong for thirty years to the first profession in the world — to the only profession, with the single exception, perhaps, of the military, to which a high-minded gentleman could condescend to belong — the Irish bar. To that bar, at which he has seen and heard a Burgh and a Duquery; at which he must have listened to a Burston, a Ponsonby, and a Curran; to a bar which still contains a Plunket, a Ball, and despite of politics, I will add, a Bushe.[4] With this galaxy of glory, flinging their light around him, how can he alone have remained in darkness? How has it happened, that the twilight murkiness of his soul, has not been illumined with a single ray shot from their lustre? Devoid of taste and of genius, how can he have had memory enough to preserve this original vulgarity? He is, indeed, an object of compassion, and, from my inmost soul, I bestow on him my forgiveness, and my bounteous pity....

My lord, upon the Catholic subject,[5] I commence with one assertion of the Attorney-General, which I trust I misunderstood. He talked, as I collected him, of the Catholics having imbibed principles of a seditious, treasonable, and revolutionary nature! He seemed to me, most distinctly, to charge us with treason! There is no relying on his words for his meaning — I know there is not. On a former occasion, I took down a repetition of this charge full seventeen times on my brief, and yet, afterwards, it turned out that he never intended to make any such charge; that he forgot he had ever used those words, and he disclaimed the idea they naturally convey. It is clear, therefore, that upon this subject he knows not what he says; and that these phrases are the

1. William Saurin (*c.* 1757-1839), attorney general 1807-22.
2. Billingsgate is the site in London of an old fish market, whose porters were famous for their abusive language.
3. Jacobin, the term O'Connell will later exploit in his attack on Saurin, was the name of the strictest republicans among the French revolutionaries.

4. Walter Hussey Burgh (1742-83), chief baron of the Irish exchequer 1782; barrister and celebrated orator.

Henry Duquery, admitted a barrister 1774, a King's Inns bencher 1779.

Beresford Burston, admitted a barrister 1768, a King's Inns bencher 1784; still alive in 1813.

George Ponsonby (1755-1817), lord chancellor of Ireland 1806; leader of the Whig opposition in the House of Commons from 1808.

John Philpot Curran (1750-1817), reform politician and barrister, who defended many of the United Irishmen in 1798; master of the rolls 1806.

William Conyngham Plunket (1764-1854), attorney general in 1805; lord chancellor of Ireland 1830-41; as a barrister, was one of the team that prosecuted Robert Emmet.

Probably William Ball, barrister, one of the original members of the Royal Irish Academy (1785).

Charles Kendal Bushe (1767-1843), solicitor general for Ireland 1805-22; had a high reputation for uncorruptibility.

5. i.e. on the subject of catholic emancipation.

mere flowers of his rhetoric, but quite innocent of any meaning!

Upon this account I pass him by, I go beyond him, and I content myself with proclaiming those charges, whosoever may make them, to be false and base calumnies! It is impossible to refute such charges in the language of dignity or temper. But if any man dares to charge the Catholic body, or the Catholic Board, or any individuals of that Board with sedition or treason, I do here, I shall always in this court, in the city, in the field, brand him as an infamous and profligate *liar*![6]

Pardon the phrase, but there is no other suitable to the occasion. But he is a profligate liar who so asserts, because he must know that the whole tenor of our conduct confutes the assertion. What is it we seek?

[Chief Justice — What, Mr. O'Connell, can this have to do with the question which the jury are to try?]

Mr. O'Connell. — *You heard the Attorney-General traduce and calumniate us — you heard him with patience and with temper — listen now to our vindication!*[7] ....

The Attorney-General — '*this wisest and best of men,*' as his colleague, the Solicitor-General,[8] called him in his presence — the Attorney-General next boasted of his triumph over Pope and Popery — 'I put down the Catholic Committee; I will put down, at my good time, the Catholic Board.' This boast is partly historical, partly prophetical. He was wrong in his history — he is quite mistaken in his prophecy. He did not put down the Catholic Committee — we gave up that name the moment that it was confessedly avowed, that this sapient Attorney-General's polemical-legal controversy dwindled into a mere dispute about words. He told us that in the English language 'pretence' means 'purpose'; had it been French and not English, we might have been inclined to respect his judgment, but in point of English we venture to differ with him; we told him 'purpose,' good Mr. Attorney-General, is just the reverse of 'pretence.' The quarrel grew warm and animated; we appealed to common sense, to the grammar, and to the dictionary; common sense, grammar, and the dictionary decided in our favour. He brought his appeal to this court, your lordship, and your brethren, unanimously decided that, in point of law — mark, mark, gentlemen of the jury, the sublime wisdom of law — the court decided that, in point of law, *'pretence' does mean 'purpose!'*....

You are all, of course, Protestants;[9] see what a compliment he pays to your religion and his own, when he endeavours thus to procure a verdict on your oaths; when he endeavours to seduce you to what, if you were so seduced, would be perjury, by indulging your prejudices, and flattering you by the coincidence of his sentiments and wishes. Will he succeed, gentlemen? Will you allow him to draw you into a perjury out of zeal for your religion? And will you violate the pledge you have given to your God to do justice, in order to gratify your anxiety for the ascendancy of what you believe to be his church? Gentlemen, reflect on the strange and monstrous inconsistency of this conduct, and do not commit, if you can avoid it, the pious crime of violating your solemn oaths, in aid of the pious designs of the Attorney-General against Popery.

Oh, gentlemen! it is not in any lightness of heart I thus address you — it is rather in bitterness and sorrow; you did not expect flattery from me, and my client was little disposed to offer it to you; besides, of what avail would it be to flatter, if you came here pre-determined, and it is too plain that you are not selected for this jury from any notion of your impartiality?

But when I talk to you of your oaths and of your religion, I would full fain I could impress you with a respect for both the one and the other. I, who do not flatter, tell you, that though I do not join with you in belief, I have the most unfeigned respect for the form of Christian faith which you profess. Would that its substance, not its forms and temporal

6. The Catholic Board (1812-14) was one a sequence of organizations (its name changing frequently) through which emancipation was sought from 1793 to 1829. O'Connell was the leader of its 'democratic' wing, which was at loggerheads with the aristocratic and gentlemanly faction led by Lord Fingall and John Keogh.

7. According to Oliver MacDonagh, no further interruptions from the bench followed this emphatic reply by O'Connell, although one should bear in mind that the text cited has been edited from accounts of the trial as a whole with the intention of recording only O'Connell's performance (O. MacDonagh, *The Hereditary Bondsman; Daniel O'Connell 1775-1829* (London: Weidenfeld and Nicolson, 1988), p. 119.

8. Charles Kendal Bushe, see note 4 above. The epithet 'wise' was constantly applied ironically to Saurin in the *Dublin Evening Post* and elsewhere.

9. Because of the property qualification required of jurymen, there was always likely to be a preponderance of protestants on a Dublin jury; careful selection ensured that the proportion of catholics was minimized where it was not eliminated.

advantages, were deeply impressed on your minds! then should I not address you in the cheerless and hopeless despondency that crowds on my mind, and drives me to taunt you with the air of ridicule I do. Gentlemen, I sincerely respect and venerate your religion, *but* I despise and I now apprehend your prejudices, in the same proportion as the Attorney-General has cultivated them. In plain truth, every religion is good — every religion is true to him who, in his due caution and conscience, believes it. There is but one bad religion, that of a man who professes a faith which he does not believe; but the good religion may be, and often is, corrupted by the wretched and wicked prejudices which admit a difference of opinion as a cause of hatred....

He, indeed, passed on to the next sentence with an air of triumph, with the apparent certainty of its producing a conviction; I meet him upon it — I read it boldly — I will discuss it with you manfully — it is this: —

'They insulted, they oppressed, they murdered, and they deceived.'[10]

The Attorney-General told us, rather ludicrously, that they, meaning the Duke's predecessors, included, of course, himself. How a man could be included amongst his predecessors, it would be difficult to discover. It seems to be that mode of expression which would indicate, that the Attorney-General, notwithstanding his foreign descent, has imbibed some of the language of the native Irish.[11] But our blunders arise not like this, from a confusion of idea; they are generally caused by too great condensation of thought; they are, indeed, frequently of the head, but never — never of the heart. Would I could say so much for the Attorney-General; his blunder is not to be attributed to his cool and cautious head; it sprung, I much fear, from the misguided bitterness of the bigotry of his heart.

Well, gentlemen, this sentence does, in broad and distinct terms, charge the predecessors of the Duke, but not the Duke himself, with insult, oppression, murder, and deceit. But it is history, gentlemen: are you prepared to silence the voice of history? Are you disposed to suppress the recital of facts — the story of the events of former days? Is the historian, and the publisher of history, to be exposed to indictment and punishment?

Let me read for you two passages from Doctor Leland's History of Ireland.[12] I choose a remote period, to avoid shocking your prejudices, by the recital of the more modern crimes of the faction to which most of you belong. Attend to this passage, gentlemen.

> Anno 1574. — A solemn peace and concord was made between the Earl of Essex and Felim O'Nial. However, at a feast, wherein the Earl entertained that chieftain, and at the end of their good cheer, O'Nial, with his wife, were seized; their friends, who attended, were put to the sword before their faces. Felim, together with his wife and brother, were conveyed to Dublin, where they were CUT UP IN QUARTERS.[13]

How would you have this fact described? In what lady-like terms is the future historian to mention this savage and brutal massacre. Yet Essex was an English nobleman — a predecessor of his Grace; he was accomplished, gallant, and gay; the envied paramour of the virgin queen; and, if he afterwards fell on the scaffold, one of the race of the ancient Irish may be permitted to indulge the fond super-

10. Maurice O'Connell, in his edition of the *Correspondence*, states that the libel action was fixed on material in the *Dublin Evening Post* of 23 March 1813. But the sentences that O'Connell begins to quote here are found in the first article of the series, the one that appeared on 5 January:

> If the Administration of the Duke of Richmond had been conducted with more than ordinary talent, its errors might in some degree have been atoned for by its ability, and the People of Ireland, though they might have much to regret, yet would have something to admire; but truly, after the gravest consideration, they must find themselves at a loss to discover any striking feature in his Grace's Administration, that makes it superior to the worst of his predecessors.
>
> They insulted, they oppressed, they murdered and they deceived. The profligate, unprincipled WESTMORLAND — the cold-hearted and cruel CAMDEN — the artful and treacherous CORNWALLIS, left Ireland more depressed and divided than they found her. (p. 2)

It may be that the action cited more than the material of 23 March, or that O'Connell focused on these sentences because they suited his political purposes, rather than constituted the base of the charges against his client. See Maurice J. O'Connell (ed.), *The Correspondence of Daniel O'Connell* Vol. I, 1792-1814 (Dublin: Irish Manuscripts Commission, 1972), p. 336.

11. Saurin was descended from a Huguenot refugee, and so makes a convenient butt for O'Connell's joke about the blunders of language attributed to the native Irish.

12. The Rev. Thomas Leland (1722-85); see his *History of Ireland from the Invasion of Henry II....* (Dublin: Marchbank, 1773).

13. O'Connell quotes accurately from Leland (Vol. 2, p. 257), but does not mention that the passage occurs in a footnote where Leland is in turn quoting from a Gaelic annals source for which he had been given a literal translation by Charles O'Conor of Belnagare. The figure referred to here is usually known as Sir Brian Mac Phelim O Neill (d. 1574); his wife was the daughter of Brian Carragh MacDonnell.

stition that would avenge the royal blood of the O'Nial and of his consort, on their perfidious English murderer.

But my soul fills with bitterness, and I will read of no more Irish murders. I turn, however, to another page, and I will introduce to your notice another predecessor of his Grace the Duke of Richmond. It is Grey, who, after the recal of Essex, commanded the English forces in Munster. The fort of Smerwick, in Kerry, surrendered to Grey at discretion. It contained some Irish troops, and more than 700 Spaniards. The historian shall tell you the rest:

> That mercy for which they sued was rigidly denied them. Wingfield was commissioned to disarm them, and when this service was performed, an English company was sent into the fort.
>
> The Irish rebels found they were reserved for execution by martial law.
>
> The Italian general and some officers were made prisoners of war: but the garrison *was butchered in cold blood*; nor is it without pain, that we find a service so horrid and detestable, committed to Sir Walter Raleigh.[14]

'The garrison was butchered in cold blood,' says the historian. Furnish us, Mr. Attorney-General, with gentle accents and sweet words, to speak of this savage atrocity; or will you indict the author? Alas! he is dead, full of years and respect — as faithful an historian as the prejudices of his day would allow, and a beneficed clergyman of your church.

Gentlemen of the jury, what is the mild language of this paper compared with the indignant language of history? Raleigh — the ill-starred Raleigh — fell a victim to a tyrant master, a corrupt or overawed jury, and a virulent Attorney-General; he was baited at the bar with language more scurrilous and more foul than that you heard yesterday poured upon my client.[15] Yet, what atonement to civilization could his death afford for the horrors I have mentioned?

Decide, now, gentlemen, between those libels — between that defamer's history and my client. He calls those predecessors of his Grace, murderers. History has left the living records of their crimes from the O'Nial, treacherously slaughtered, to the cruel, cold butchery of the defenceless prisoners. Until I shall see the publishers of Leland and of Hume brought to your bar, I defy you to convict my client. . . .[16]

But the times are altered. The Press, the Press, gentlemen, has effectuated a salutary revolution; a commission of defective titles would no longer be tolerated; the judges can no longer be bribed with money, and juries can no longer be —— I must not say it. Yes, they can, you know — we all know they can be still *inquired out*, and 'packed,' as the technical phrase is. But *you*, who are not packed, *you*, who have been *fairly* selected, will see that the language of the publication before us is mildness itself, compared with that which the truth of history requires — compared with that which history has already used.

I proceed with this alleged libel.

The next sentence is this —

'The profligate, unprincipled Westmorland.'[17] I throw down the paper and address myself in particular to some of you. There are, I see, amongst you some of our Bible distributers, 'and of our suppressors of vice.'[18] Distributers of Bibles, suppressors of vice — what call you profligacy? What is it you would call profligacy? Suppose the peerage was exposed for sale — set up at open auction — it was at that time a judicial office — suppose that its price, the exact price of this judicial office, was accurately ascertained by daily experience — would you call that profligacy? If pensions were multiplied beyond bounds and beyond example — if places were augmented until invention was exhausted, and then were subdivided and split into halves, so that two might take the emoluments of each, and no person do the duty — if these acts were resorted to in order to corrupt

14. See Leland, Vol. 2, p. 283; O'Connell's quotation, as given here, is accurate apart from one or two trifles attributable to a transcribing hand.
15. O'Connell probably has Francis Bacon (1561-1626) in mind here; Bacon was subsequently shown to have been guilty of taking bribes.
16. O'Connell does not appear to have used David Hume (1711-76) or his *History of England* (1754-61); his name is cited here to emphasize the 'non partisan' nature of O'Connell's sources.
17. See note 10 above; John Fane (1759-1841), 10th earl of Westmoreland; as lord lieutenant of Ireland (1790-94), he opposed relaxation of the Penal Laws during the 'protestant ascendancy' debates of 1792.
18. This audacious assault upon the jury, fatal of course to his client's slim changes of acquittal, is confirmed by the letter of E. B. cited in the headnote above; the evangelical wing of Irish protestantism was increasingly active in distributing Bibles to the catholic population in an attempt to proselytize, and in condemning alcohol and gambling through societies for 'the suppression of vice'.

your representatives — would you, gentle suppressors of vice, call that profligacy?

If the father of children selected in the open day his adulterous paramour — if the wedded mother of children displayed her crime unblushingly — if the assent of the titled or untitled wittol[19] to his own shame was purchased with the people's money — if this scene — if these were enacted in the open day, would you call that profligacy, sweet distributers of Bibles? The women of Ireland have always been beauteous to a proverb; they were, without an exception, chaste beyond the terseness of a proverb to express; they are still as chaste as in former days, but the depraved example of a depraved court has furnished some exceptions, and the action or criminal conversation, before the time of Westmoreland unknown, has since become more familiar to our courts of justice.

Call you the sad example which produced those exceptions — call you *that* profligacy, suppressors of vice and Bible distributers? The vices of the poor are within the reach of control; to suppress them, you can call in aid the churchwarden and the constable; the justice of the peace will readily aid you, for he is a gentleman — the Court of Sessions will punish those vices for you by fine, by imprisonment, and, if you are urgent, by whipping. But suppressors of vice, who shall aid you to suppress the vices of the great? Are you sincere, or are you, to use your own phraseology, whitewashed tombs — painted charnel-houses? Be ye hypocrites? If you are not — if you be sincere — (and, oh, how I wish that you were) — if you be sincere, I will steadily require to know of you, what aid you expect, to suppress the vices of the rich and great? Who will assist you to suppress those vices? The churchwarden ! — why he, I believe, handed *them* into the best pew in one of your cathedrals, that they might lovingly hear Divine service together. The constable!! — absurd. The justice of the peace! — no, upon his honour. As to the Court of Sessions, you cannot expect it to interfere;[20] and my lords the judges are really so busy at the assizes, in hurrying the grand juries through the presentments, that there is no leisure to look after the scandalous faults of the great. Who, then, sincere and candid suppressors of vice, can aid you? — *The Press*; the Press alone talks of the profligacy of the great; and, at least, shames into decency those whom it may fail to correct. The Press is your, but your only assistant. GO, then, men of conscience, men of religion — go, then, and convict John Magee, because he published that Westmoreland was profligate and unprincipled as a lord lieutenant — do, convict, and then return to your distribution of Bibles and to your attacks upon the recreations of the poor, under the name of vices!

Do, convict the only aid which virtue has, and distribute your Bibles that you may have the name of being religious; upon your sincerity depends my client's prospect of a verdict. *Does* he lean upon a broken reed?[21]

I pass on from the sanctified portion of the jury which I have latterly addressed, and I call the attention of you all to the next member of the sentence —

'The cold-hearted and cruel Camden.'[22]

Here I have your prejudices all armed against me. In the administration of Camden, your faction was cherished and triumphant. Will you prevent him to be called cold and cruel? Alas! today, why have I not men to address who would listen to me for the sake of impartial justice! But even with *you* the case is too powerful to allow me to despair.

Well, *I do* say, the cold and cruel Camden. Why, on *one circuit*, during his administration, there were ONE HUNDRED INDIVIDUALS TRIED BEFORE ONE JUDGE; OF THESE NINETY-EIGHT WERE CAPITALLY CONVICTED, AND NINETY-SEVEN HANGED! I understand *one* escaped; but he was a *soldier* who murdered a *peasant*, or something of that TRIVIAL nature — NINETY-SEVEN victims in one circuit!!!....[23]

In humble and obscure distance, I followed the footsteps of my present adversaries. What their sentiments were then of the authors of the Union, I beg to read to you; I will read them from a newspaper set up for the mere purpose of opposing the Union, and conducted under the control of these gentlemen. If their editor should be gravely denied, I shall only

19. A man who is complaisant about his wife's infidelity; a contented cuckold.
20. Quarter Sessions for the County of Dublin; chairman, John Egan.
21. See II *Kings* 18. 21.
22. See note 10 above; John Jeffries Pratt (1759-1840), 2nd earl and 1st marquis of Camden; as lord lieutenant of Ireland (1794-98) he was responsible for the rigorous military policy that led into, and to a large degree, provoked the insurrection of 1798.
23. This judge has yet to be identified by name.

reply — 'oh cease your funning.'§[24]

The charge of being a Jacobin, was at that time made against the present Attorney-General — him, plain William Saurin — in the very terms, and with just as much truth as he now applies it to my client. His reply shall serve for that of Mr. Magee. I take it from the anti-Union of the 22nd March, 1800.

> To the charge of Jacobin, Mr. Saurin said he knew not what it meant, as applied to him, *except it was an opposition to the will of the British minister.*[25]

So says Mr. Magee; but, gentlemen, my eye lights upon another passage of Mr. Saurin's, in the same speech from which I have quoted the above. It was in these words:

> Mr. Saurin admitted, that debates might sometimes produce *agitations*, but that was the PRICE *necessarily paid for liberty.*[26]

Oh, how I thank this good Jew for the word.[27] Yes, agitation is, as Mr. Saurin well remarked, the price necessarily paid for liberty. We have paid the price, gentlemen, and the honest man refuses to give us the goods. [Much laughing.]

Now, gentlemen, of this Mr. Saurin, then an agitator, I beg leave to read the opinion upon this Union, the author of which we have only called artful and treacherous. From this speech of the 13th March, 1800, I select those passages:

> Mr. Saurin said he felt it his duty to the crown, to the country, and to his family, to warn the minister of the dreadful consequences of persevering in a measure which the people of Ireland *almost unanimously disliked.*

And again—

> He, for one, would assert the principles of the glorious revolution, and boldly declare in the face of the nation, that when the Sovereign power dissolved the compact that existed between the government and the people, that moment the right of resistance accrues.
>
> Whether it would be prudent in the people to avail themselves of that right, would be another question. But if a legislative union were forced on the country, against the will of its inhabitants, it would be a *nullity*, and resistance to it would be a *struggle* against usurpation, and not a *resistance* against law.

May I be permitted just to observe, how much more violent this agitator of the year 1800, than we poor and timid agitators of the year 1813. When did we talk of resistance being a question of prudence! Shame upon the men who call us intemperate, and yet remember their own violence. . . . I have, I hope, shown you the right of my client to discuss the public subjects which he has discussed in the manner they are treated of in the publication before you, yet he is prosecuted. Let me read for you a paragraph which the Attorney-General has not prosecuted — which he has refused to prosecute:

> BALLYBAY, JULY 4, 1813.
>
> A meeting of the Orange Lodges was agreed on, in consequence of the manner in which the Catholics wished to have persecuted the loyalists in this county last year, *when they even murdered some of them for no other reason than their being yeomen and Protestants.*

And, again —

> It was at Ballybay that *the Catholics murdered one Hughes, a yeoman sergeant for being a Protestant, as was given in evidence at the assizes by a Catholic witness.*

I have read this passage from the *Hibernian Journal* of the 7th of this month.[28] I know not whether you can hear, unmoved, a paragraph which makes my blood boil to read; but I shall only tell you, that the Attorney-General refused to prosecute this libeller. Gentlemen, there have been

§A pamphlet under this title was published by the Solicitor-General; it was full of wit and talent.

24. *Cease your Funning; Or, the Rebel Detected* (Dublin: James Moore, 1799, 7th 'edition'). This anonymous and much reprinted pamphlet is usually attributed to Charles Kendal Bushe.
25. *The Constitution, or Anti-Union Post*, 22 March 1800, reporting the House of Commons debate of 19 March 1800:
    > To the charge of Jacobinism, Mr. Saurin said he knew not what it meant as applied to him, except it was an opposition to the will of the British Minister. He remembered when he armed and was sworn to defend the constitution, in the year 1798, against the Jacobins of that day, he and all the Irish gentry co-operating in the same cause were called loyal men, but now that they remain faithful to their principles and their oaths, and defended the constitution against the Minister, they were branded with the appellation of Jacobinism. The agitations in this country, and the discussions that took place in the Irish parlt. [*sic*] were made the pretexts for an Union; but if these arguments were to be admitted, the British parliament could not long survive that of Ireland — If the British Minister wished to get rid of the British Parliament, he would not fail to draw arguments from the Middlesex election, the riots of 1780, and that conspiracy which spread over every corner of the island — and as to the senatorial discussion, which ever there existed a free Parliament, there would exist also free debate. This might sometimes produce agitations, but they were the price necessarily paid for liberty. (p. [2])
26. See previous note.
27. O'Connell echoes Shakespeare's *The Merchant of Venice* here.
28. *Hibernian Journal*, 7 July 1813.

several murders committed in the county of Monaghan, in which Ballybay lies.[29] The persons killed happened to be Roman Catholics; their murderers are Orangemen. Several of the persons accused of these murders are to be tried at the ensuing assizes. The agent applied to me personally, with this newspaper; he stated that the obvious intention was to create a prejudice upon the approaching trials favourable to the murderers, and against the prosecutors. He stated what you — *even you* — will easily believe, that there never was a falsehood more flagitiously[30] destitute of truth than the entire paragraph. I advised him, gentlemen, to wait on the Attorney-General in the most respectful manner possible; to show him this paragraph, then to request to be allowed to satisfy him as to the utter falsehood of the assertions which this paragraph contained, which could be more easily done, as the judges who went that circuit could prove part of it to be false; and I directed him to entreat that the Attorney-General, when fully satisfied of the falsehood, would prosecute the publisher of this, which, I think, I may call an atrocious libel. . . .

No, gentlemen, he does not prosecute this libel. On the contrary, this paper is paid enormous sums of the public money. There are no less than five proclamations in the paper containing this libel; and, it was proved in my presence, in a court of justice, that, besides the proclamations and public advertisements, the two proprietors of the paper had each a pension of £400 per annum, for supporting government, as it was called.[31]

Would I could see the man who pays this proclamation money and these pensions at the Castle. [Here Mr. O'Connell turned round to where Mr. Peele[32] sat.] Would I could see the man who, against the fact, asserted that the proclamations were inserted in all the papers, save in those whose proprietors were convicted of a libel. I would ask him whether this be a paper that ought to receive the money of the Irish people? — whether this be the legitimate use of the public purse? And when you find this calumniator salaried and rewarded, where is the impartiality, the justice, or even the decency of prosecuting Mr. Magee for a libel, merely because he has not praised public men, and has discussed public affairs in the spirit of freedom and of the constitution. Contrast the situation of Mr. Magee with the proprietor of the *Hibernian Journal*; the one is prosecuted with all the weight and influence of the crown, the other pensioned by the ministers of the crown; the one dragged to your bar for the sober discussion of political topics, the other hired to disseminate the most horrid calumnies! . . . .

Is there amongst you any one friend to freedom? Is there amongst you one man, who esteems equal and impartial justice, who values the people's rights as the foundation of private happiness, and who considers life as no boon without liberty? Is there amongst you one friend to the constitution — one man who hates oppression? If there be, Mr. Magee appeals to his kindred mind, and confidently expects an acquittal.

There are amongst you men of great religious zeal — of much public piety. Are you sincere? Do you believe what you profess? With all this zeal — with all this piety, *is* there any conscience amongst you? *Is* there any terror of violating your oaths? Be ye hypocrites, or does genuine religion inspire ye? If you be sincere — if you have conscience — if your oaths can control your interests, then Mr. Magee confidently expects an acquittal.

If amongst you there be cherished one ray of pure religion — if amongst you there glow a single spark of liberty — if I have alarmed religion, or roused the spirit of freedom in one breast amongst you, Mr. Magee is safe, and his country is served; but if there be none — if you be slaves and hypocrites, he will await your verdict, and despise it.

29. Ballybay was at this period notorious for its sectarian clashes, placed as it was on a kind of frontier between protestant and catholic districts.

30. atrociously, villainously.

31. The government effectively subsidized certain newspapers by buying large areas of advertising space in which official notices were printed. In return, it required editorial support for its policy.

32. The name was so spelled at the time; Robert Peel was only twenty-five years of age in 1813 and O'Connell's gesture constituted a patronizing intimidation of the chief secretary. They remained steady enemies, and O'Connell is always reputed to have much later described Peel's smile as resembling 'the brass plate on a coffin'.

RICHARD LALOR SHEIL

(1791-1851)

from: 'A SPEECH MADE IN CORK' (1825)

[Eighteenth-century political rhetoric had been conditioned by the self-conscious rules and conventions of the assemblies in which the orator performed — parliament, court, or theatre. With the coming of the nineteenth century, these arenas were thrown open to wider scrutiny. Daniel O'Connell's court-room practice implicitly acknowledged the presence of a vast audience beyond the physical confines of the court-room itself, in the knowledge that newspaper reports carried his words out into the countryside. O'Connell's development of mass politics, with the passive participation of hundreds of thousands, led to other innovations in rhetorical technique — as at the monster meetings, for example, where auxiliary speakers apparently repeated the great man's words and relayed them to the outlying sections of the crowd who were beyond earshot.

Richard Lalor Sheil assisted O'Connell in the extension of his political tactics in the 1820s, drawing on his experience not only as a barrister but also as a writer for the stage. The speech from which an extract follows illustrates a further dimension to the question of political rhetoric, its sources and audiences. The 1820s were not devoted exclusively to the campaign for (or refusal of) catholic relief from the remaining Penal Laws. In the wake of the Napoleonic wars, Irish agriculture had experienced depressed prices and congested holdings. Agrarian violence rapidly spread with the movement known as 'Captain Rock' and added to these quasi-inarticulate symptoms of social crisis was the impact of evangelical zeal. Protestant evangelists, operating through a score of newly established Bible societies and societies for the enlightenment of the poor (especially the catholic poor), sought to excite an awareness of spiritual crisis in the Irish countryside. There is no doubt that many were engaged in an undeclared campaign to convert catholics to protestantism, and that the distribution of Bibles was more than an end in itself. However, the controversy over these Bibles raised a number of crucial issues in relation to rhetoric and persuasion, which Sheil tackles in the course of the speech excerpted below. Two of these can be noted in advance — issues of propriety (was it proper for a woman to read of violent deeds such as would never be orally discussed in her presence?) — and issues of denominational psychology (is protestant Bible-reading not evidence of a capricious, undisciplined mind?).

But beyond such substantive matters, there lies the brute fact of these prolonged public debates themselves. Confrontations between catholic and protestant clergy were frequently organized as a form of entertainment, lasting several days in some instances. The testimony of converts was lavishly published in pamphlets and an increasingly sectarianized press. Debates on theological topics augmented the regular Sunday sermon. Charles Robert Maturin's novel *Women* (1818) provides an account of the impact of methodist rhetoric on conversation, and there is similar evidence in the court-room speech of O'Connell (above) of the close links between Bible enthusiasm and political discussion in the press.

Sheil's speech, taken from a pamphlet report of the proceedings issued by a Dublin publisher of active protestant sympathies, catches the professional orator, trained for the bar and the stage, attempting to deal both with the dizzying implications of theological dogma and the clammy conditions of the packed lecture hall. It is not surprising that some in Ireland at this time regarded the campaign for catholic emancipation as literally apocalyptic — a sign of the imminent end of the world and Christ's second coming.]

The Chairman said — This, Sir, is a meeting of the members and friends of the Society; if you are a friend to the Society you are entitled to speak.

Mr. Sheil said — Then, Sir, in one sense, I am a friend to the Society, and I shall evince it by an act of substantial friendship, in venturing to give you some honest, though it may possibly be mistaken advice. [*Laughter, and cries of, go on*] Mr. Sheil said, that, when the former meeting was held, to which a gentleman adverted, he was not in Cork, and upon that account he ought not to be considered as an overweening intruder upon their deliberations. They should not shrink from discussion, if it was carried on in a fair and mitigated spirit. The meeting was called a private one; but it exhibited singular evidences of privacy in the numbers by which it was attended.[1] [*Hear, hear*] It concerned the public; a great national question was involved in the proceedings, and it was the right of every individual to remonstrate against a system by which the interests of the whole community were affected. He should studiously avoid giving offence to the

1. In other words, there was a vast crowd in attendance.

religious sensitiveness of the ardent and lovely Theologians whom he saw assembled around him.[2] We should survey the subject, than which, none was more awfully important, with minds pure, unprejudiced, unimpassioned, standing as it were, upon a mighty eminence, in the unclouded atmosphere of heaven, while the mists and storms of the world were passing unheeded beneath us —. [*hear, hear*] He regretted that some observations had fallen from those who preceded him, which reflected upon the creed of the Irish people. At no time were controversial disputations well calculated to promote the real interests of Christianity, and they were peculiarly ill adapted to the fair auditory whom he had risen to address. The religion of a woman ought to be an impassioned meekness, and that sweet spirit which was typified by the dove, should spread its wings upon them. [*Cheering*] While he entreated their forbearance, and that pity for human error that was akin to the love of heaven, he should take care not to abuse their indulgence. He had heard Mr. Noel[3] with pleasure. He had given proof of high intellectual acquirements, and there was in his zeal an internal evidence of sincerity. In one sense only was he an impostor — by practising a delusion upon himself. — [*Hear, hear, hear*] The Honourable Gentleman, and his Caledonian associate, who had manifested so much anxiety for the spiritual welfare of the Irish people, and who was not only a Scotchman but a Captain, [*laughter*] deserved much praise for the motives which had induced their religious excursion. The nautical divine had combined the enthusiasm of his profession with the characteristic sagacity of his country —. [*hear, hear*] Mr. Noel had pathetically lamented the moral degradation and utter wretchedness of the Irish people, and attributed both to the absence of scriptural education. Without comparing him to an empiric,[4] who would fain apply his own favourite remedy to every disease, he should remind him, that the misery of Ireland arose from a vast variety of causes. The Honourable Gentleman had just come from a country whose prosperity was the accumulation of a thousand years. On the other hand, the wretchedness of Ireland was the product of as many centuries of calamity. [*Cheering*] He who was familiar with the luxuries of the English cottage, naturally shrunk from the miseries of the Irish hovel. [The eloquent gentleman here passed the highest encomiums on the English nation, for their *moral tone of feeling as well as their greatness*, and said, that Mr. Noel having come from 'a combination of circumstances the most magnificent that could be imagined,' could not be an adequate judge of what was wretchedness in Ireland.] He would ask whether the vast diffusion of wealth, the extent of commerce, the number of manufactures, and the equality of the people, had produced the riches and the happiness of England — or whether her unparalleled greatness was all owing to the reading of the Scriptures without note or comment? [*Laughter*] Had centuries of iniquitous misrule accomplished nothing in the work of misery, of degradation, and of guilt? If the Honourable Gentleman were better acquainted with Ireland, he would soon perceive, that it is upon the higher classes that his religious labours ought to be bestowed. — This amiable itinerant[5] would, in the course of his sacred peregrinations,[6] soon discover, that it was not in the smoke of the hovel, but in the blaze of the banquet, that the precepts of the Gospel ought to be enforced. — [*hear, hear.*] He would endeavour to impart the practical spirit of Christianity to the barbarous aristocracy of Ireland — to civilize them into pity — to convince them that their wretched serfs are made of the same flesh and blood as themselves, and belong to the great brotherhood of men. With indignation would he behold the system of merciless exaction adopted by the Irish landlord; which is so widely at variance, not only with the principles upon which the English proprietor deals with his tenant, and with the habits of his own great country, but utterly repugnant to the commiserating spirit of those holy writings, the perusal of which he strenuously inculcated. How would his honest nature be excited, when he saw the miserable peasant cast, in a winter's night, with his famished and naked children upon the world? How would his humanity shudder at the scenes of

2. 'lovely Theologians' indicates the prominence of women in the evangelical movement.
3. Baptist Wriothesley Noel (1798-1873), a Scottish evangelist, successful at a very early age.
4. A quack doctor, one who relied on his experience without benefit of training or scientific knowledge.
5. i.e. an itinerant or travelling preacher; a missionary.
6. In the Middle Ages, pilgrims went travelling on peregrinations, journeys through foreign lands undertaken as a form of religious observance and often ending at shrines or other holy places.

desolation which are daily enacted among us? He would then perceive, that his pious adjurations ought to be directed to those very men by whom he has been infected with his opinions of our country; and that he should begin by teaching humanity to the rich, before he taught polemics to the poor. [*Hear, hear*] In the delusion of a benevolent fanaticism, he forgets that the people are less in want of Bibles than of bread. [*Cheering*] God forbid that he [*Mr. Sheil*] should suggest that the lower orders ought not to receive a religious education. He was of opinion that they should be instructed in the established tenets of their forefathers, and of their country, and that they should be taught by means adapted to their capacities, the fixed principles of their ancient and venerable faith. Religion is peculiarly necessary to those who, while the opulent find in the pleasures of actual existence many intense but transitory enjoyments, must look up to heaven for their only consolation. When the poor peasant rises from his bed of misery, he sees in the glories of the morning sun that cheers him to his toil by day, and the infinity of heaven's host that guides him to his home by night, the magnificent attributes of that Being, whom the simple and consoling faith of his fathers teaches him to adore. [*Great cheering*] The Roman Catholic faith contains a body of moral precepts as well calculated to insure salutary results upon society as any modern theory in religion; and although Mr. Noel had said that he was anxious to make Christians of the people, he [Mr. Sheil] hoped that the Honourable Gentleman would not consider him guilty of any very extravagant assumption, when he ventured to insinuate to him, that a Roman Catholic might, peradventure, be a Christian. Mr. S. testified, that he himself was *indeed a Christian*. He also stated, 'that there was one point which he would concede to those whom he opposed. If it were a triumph they might have it, He would confess that reading the BIBLE WAS SUBVERSIVE OF THE ROMAN CATHOLIC CHURCH. Ireland was a Roman Catholic country, and Mr. Noel, if really anxious to diffuse education, would take into account the peculiar cirumstances, the habits, and predispositions of the people in considering the means best adapted to the attainment of that important object. The general perusal of the Bible, without any specific interpretation, was in accordance, perhaps with the desultory and capricious genius of the Protestant religion; but in Ireland there exists a creed utterly incompatible with that wild freedom of opinion, and which is so determined and fixed as to leave no field for the exercise of individual judgment in the construction of the word of GOD. The Roman Catholic faith is built upon the scriptures, as explained by the Church, and if the lower classes were to pursue them without that explanation upon which their religion rests, it is not unlikely that they would contract opinions inconsistent with the meaning invariably annexed by Roman Catholics — by the Church — to the Holy Writings. In one word, it is wholly against the principles of that Church to turn the Bible into a plaything for the fancy, and submit it to all the gross vagaries and monstrous imaginations of every loon.[7] The whole dispute narrows itself into a question of fact. Is it, or is it not, inconsistent with the spirit of Catholicism? If it be, there is an end to the argument; at least it must be admitted, that Roman Catholics are justified in their strenuous opposition to an attempt to subvert their religion. Now who are the persons best qualified to determine that simple fact? One would suppose that the Roman Catholics themselves were as competent to decide the question as those gentlemen who have imported into Ireland a new assortment of curiosities in belief, and seem determined to establish in this country a manufacture of religions. — [*Cheering*] — But, independantly of the objection arising from the essential principles of Catholicism, is it not absurd to make a task book[8] of the Testament,[9] and to convert the Apocalypse into a primer? [*Cheers*] The scriptures have been referred to, in order to shew that it was the will of GOD that they should be universally perused. For this purpose some isolated texts have been tortured into a meaning which they do not rationally bear, while those who have poured out such a torrent of citation, forget that among the Jews, and under the old law, there were many parts of holy writ which women were never permitted to read, and which men were not allowed to peruse until they had attained the age of 30 years. When christianity was first established, it was impossible that the Scriptures could have been generally read, for the art of

7. From 'lunatic', a madman.
8. A task book was one that had to be read (e.g. in school) as a duty or punishment.
9. Since the Book of Revelations (containing an account of the apocalypse to come) is notoriously difficult to interpret, it is singularly inappropriate (Sheil implies) to use it like a primer, a book intended as a *simple* introduction to a topic.

printing was not then known, and by no other means than that great modern discovery could an extensive distribution of the Bible be effected. A manuscript of such bulk as the Old and New Testament, must have cost a sum which a primitive christian cannot be readily supposed to have been capable of procuring, at a period when his poverty was a literal phrase. But let us try the expediency of an indiscriminate perusal of the sacred writings by an appeal to experience. It will scarcely be contended that any great advantage can result from a multifariousness in religion; yet it will not be denied that if each individual is entitled to construe the Scriptures, a great variety of interpretation must be the inevitable consequence. In truth, the inventions of art do not keep pace with the discoveries in religion. [*Hear, hear*] New dogmas are every day propounded to us — they issue with a marvellous facundity from every visionary brain; nor is it to the wise and the learned that the world is indebted for these fantastic revelations. Those mysterious intimations, which have excited the doubts and baffled the sagacity of the most illustrious of mankind, are now simplied from the summit of a sacred beer-barrel, and from the depth of a holy stall —. [*Laughing and cheers*] — Every difficulty vanishes before the inspired interpretation of some illuminated Crispin,[10] and the seamless garment of our Saviour is turned inside-out by some gifted taylor, who alternately cuts out a religion and a coat. [*Cheers*] Of these modern prophets one half are imposters, and the other their own dupes; but whether they be dupes or impostors — Cantwells or Mawworms,[11] or both, (for the union of hypocrisy and fanaticism is not unfrequent,) the consequences to religion, and to common decency, and to common sense are disastrous. The lower classes of the Protestant community are driven into a sort of Biblical insanity by this system of excitation; and madness, now-a-day, almost invariably assumes a religious character. He [Mr. Shiel] would state a singular fact of the lunatics in the asylum in this city, which he had lately visited; there were a vast number whose malady was connected with religion, and amongst those who laboured under that peculiar insanity there was not a single Catholic. [*Hear, hear*] This circumstance was stated by the benevolent Physician who superintended the Hospital, and who seems animated by the philanthropic feelings of a Howard,[12] in his very able work on Insanity, and that gentleman was himself a strenuous Protestant. [*Hear, hear, hear*] Now how could this fact be accounted for, but by refering it to the fanaticism which the unrestrained perusal of the holy writing had produced? An ignorant man, with a heated imagination, sits down to read the Bible; he is told he is its best interpreter, and is illuminated by its special grace — that special madness. [*Hear, hear, hear*] His delirious dreams are taken for the visitation of the spirit, and the images of insanity for the pictures of heaven. [*Loud cheers*] But the Roman Catholic has no field for his invention in belief. — He has a clear, an open, and a long-trodden path to follow, and plods his way to heaven without wandering through that mazy labyrinth in which the Protestant enthusiast is left without a clue. He has an ample scope for the affections of the heart, but has little space for the excursions of the fancy. [*Continued Cheering*] His faith is regulated and certain. He is not cast without a chart or compass upon the vague immensity which religion offers to the mind, but steers his course in a well-known track, by a steady principle, and by a fixed and unrevolving light. The Protestants embark in the Bible upon a voyage of discovery, while the Catholic makes at once for one great haven, and by an ancient and familiar route. He had perhaps pursued this train of illustration too far, and reluctantly compared the advantages of the two religions; but he thought it right to observe, that what he had said was chiefly intended to apply to self-instructed innovators, and not to the Members of the Established Church, whose Hierarchy was as hostile as the Roman Catholic Clergy to the reading of the uninterpreted Scriptures.[13] Before he sat

10. St Crispin (probably a legendary figure) was a missionary to France who maintained himself as a shoemaker. Sheil is evidently pointing to the popularity of evangelicalism among craftsmen (shoemakers, tailors) and his images are devised accordingly.
11. John Cantwell (1792-1866), parish priest of Kilbeggan in 1820 and an enthusiastic supporter of O'Connell; Richard Maw-worm was the title character in Isaac Bickerstaffe's play, *The Hypocrite* (1768).
12. John Howard (*c.* 1726-90), philanthropist and prison reformer.
13. The established Church of Ireland was generally hostile to the more spontaneous activities of the Bible societies and proselytizers, partly because they threatened church discipline and partly because they endangered community relations with the catholic majority. There were, of course, staunch supporters of evangelicalism among the bishops, and the Church of Ireland became noticeably 'lower' in its theology as the century advanced.

down he should beg leave to make one or two observations on what had fallen from Mr. Kenny,[14] who, like the pleader in *Racine's* Comedy,[15] had begun his oration at the commencement of the world, but had afterwards condescendingly passed to the deluge — [*Loud Laughter*] — That Gentleman had discovered in an injunction given to *Abraham*, a felicitous application to Ireland. — [*Shouts of Laughter*] — Providence must have had the Ladies' Auxiliary Bible School[16] in view in the patriarchal times. He would not attempt to pursue him in his progress from Abraham to Moses — from Moses to King David, and from David down to Timothy. But he should follow him from Jerusalem to Wexford, and beg to observe on the animadversions which he had thought proper to pronounce upon a recent and unfortunate transaction. He meant the trial at Wexford, and in which he [Mr Shiel] had been Counsel. — That event was deeply to be deplored, but it had been greatly misrepresented. It was utterly untrue that the parents of the child had beheld its immolation. It was sworn by the father, that the crowd was so great that he was prevented from approaching the Priest, and that he did not even see what was going on. In the next place Mr. Kenny had imputed a belief in the powers of exorcism to the Roman Catholic peasantry, as if it resulted from their religion: but he [Mr Shiel] would state a most important fact, sworn to by a principle witness for the Crown, namely, that Protestants as well as Catholics were present at one of these deplorable instances of human folly, and that a Mrs Winter and her daughter, (both of them Protestants) called, knelt down, and called on God to assist Father Carrol in working the miracle.[17] [*Hear, hear, hear*] Let us not therefore my friends, charge upon this or upon that creed, occurences so monstrous, so revolting; let us rather, in the spirit of humility, grieve while we reflect, that they arise solely from the infirmity of our common nature! To attribute to Roman Catholics an exclusive belief in demoniacal possession was most unjust. A Protestant Bishop, the celebrated Dr. Warburton,[18] had maintained the doctrine, and, it was one for which scriptural authority might be quoted. He would ask Mr. Kenny whether the reading of the Bible by the lower orders was calculated to remove the common superstition, that persons afflicted with epilepsy are possessed by an evil spirit? Do not the Scriptures narrate many instances of exorcism. It is true that it is now held, that the devil has been deprived of this portion of his prerogative; but surely, a peasant, in reading the Scriptures, may readily think that what once was common, is at present not impossible; and besides this very case furnishes an argument to shew that the Scriptures require a comment, for assuredly it is necessary that the cessation of Satanic dominion should be explained to the individual who peruses examples of its former sway. So far from thinking that the Scriptures are calculated to disabuse the people of this frightful infatuation, their perusal of them, without a comment, was calculated to confirm their superstition. He regretted that Mr. Kenny had alluded to this painful incident, because in doing so he had expressed a detestation for the Catholic Religion, which was utterly at variance with the habitual disclaimers of proselytism.[19] If he and those who acted with him, felt so deep an abhorrence for Popery, they could not fail to exert themselves, to preserve the people from so disastrous a belief. It could not be credited, that their execration would not involuntary ooze out. It was not possible that such a metamorphose should take place in Mr. Kenny, as that on one side of the poor man's threshold he should be a strenuous hater of Popery, but the moment he had entered his habitation to administer spiritual relief to his children, he should be *transubstantiated*[20] into an

14. A participant in the dispute.
15. Sheil is surely mistaken here, intending to refer to Molière (1622-73), whose plays (e.g. *Le Bourgeois Gentilhomme*, 1670) often incorporate pedantic figures and bogus scholars.
16. Evangelical organizations made a habit of setting up subcommittees expressly for women, thus channelling their zeal into the cause and away from real control of the movement.
17. Father Carroll, catholic curate of Killinick in County Wexford, was charged with the murder of a young child in 1824. Sheil defended him, and he was found not guilty though insane. The case was widely reported, and became a lurid illustration of the state of public feeling in relation to clerical power; see *Report of the trial of the Rev. John Carroll . . . and five of his parishioners for murder* . . . . Dublin [n.p.], 1824. There was also a London edition, *The particulars of the horrible murder of Catherine Sinnot, a child under four years of age, by the Rev. John Carroll an Irish Catholic priest under pretense of performing a miracle, by casting devils out of the child . . . at Killinick, in . . . Wexford . . . July 8, 1824* (London: Fairburn, 1824).
18. William Warburton (1698-1779), bishop of Gloucester and a friend of Alexander Pope.
19. The organized seeking of converts from one religion to another (usually with an implication of material benefit attached to the conversion).
20. Here Sheil plays on the doctrine of transubstantiation, ironically attributing to the change in Mr Kenny the miraculous proportions of the sacrament itself.

impassioned lover of Catholicity. One advantage had, however, ensued from the honesty of his, [Mr Kenny's] denunciations, and indeed from the whole tone of the proceedings. It was now clear that Proselytism was their substantial object, and that education was only an instrument for the accomplishment of this darling project. He begged pardon of the meeting for having so long trespassed upon them — but he was bound to say, that however great their collision of opinion, he had been heard *with liberality and kindness.* — [*Hear, hear*] He should not abuse it by entering at large into another topic, upon which, before women it might not be delicate to dwell; he alluded to the many passages in Scripture which were written with such force, and he might say with such nakedness of diction, as rendered them unfit for indiscriminate perusal. There were parts of the Old Testament in which images of voluptuousness were presented to the mind on which the imagination of a youthful female ought not to be permitted to repose. To those passages he would not of course refer, or point out the forbidden fruit, but he would venture to assert that the Odes of Anacreon[21] did not display more luxury of imagination or combine more sensual associations than parts of the Old Testament, the perusal of which, by women, was wisely forbidden by the Jewish Church. It was idle to say, in the language of modern cant, that the grace of GOD would prevent the passions from taking fire. Our daily orison contains a prayer, founded upon human frailty, that we should be preserved not only from guilt, but even from temptation,[22] [*Hear*] and if the passages to which he alluded were unfit for an open citation in that assembly, he could not conceive them the appropriate theme of the virgin's meditation. [*Cheers*] The warm fancy of a young and blooming girl could not venture into the sacred bowers of oriental poetry without peril. [*Cheers*] Besides the objection arising to the warm colouring of the Pastoral of Soloman,[23] which was a mystic representation of the conjugal union of the Churches, with which unmarried ladies need not be made prematurely familiar, it should be recollected that the Bible contained details of attrocity at which human nature shuddered. Part of the holy writings consisted of history, and of the narration of facts of a kind that they could not be mentioned in the presence of a virtuous woman without exciting horror. Should a woman be permitted to read in her chamber, what she would tremble to hear at her domestic board? — and shall her eyes be polluted with what her ears shall not be profaned? — Shall she read what she dares not hear? Shall she con over, and revolve, what she would rather die than utter? But these were painful topics. They were forced into debate by those who, in their anxiety to annihilate the religion of the country, forgot the risk to which its morality was exposed. And what good could the atchievement of this object after all effect. In ceasing to be Catholics, were they certain that the people would continue Christians? Let this absurd scheme be abandoned — let the Irish peasant live and die in the religion of his forefathers — let the child rise up from the cradle in the same creed with which the parent descended into the grave — and let the propagators of modern dogmas who send their Missionaries amongst us, remember the denunciation in St. Matthew — '*Woe unto you, ye Scribes, ye Pharisees, ye Hypocrites! ye compass the sea and earth to make a single proselyte, and when you have made him, he is two-fold more a child of hell than before.*'[24] [*Great Cheering*]

21. Thomas Moore (1779-1852) translated the odes of the Greek lyric poet Anacreon in 1800.
22. This refers to the Lord's Prayer: 'Lead us not into temptation ....' Matthew 6. 13.
23. i.e. the Old Testament book known usually as *The Song of Solomon.*
24. The King James version reads: 'Woe unto you, scribes and Pharisees, hypocrites! for ye compass sea and land to make one proselyte, and when he is made, ye make him twofold more the child of hell than yourselves.' (Matthew 23. 15) Such verbatim quoting of scripture was, of course, a characteristic method of Sheil's evangelical adversaries.

Biographies/Bibliographies

William Domville

LIFE. William Domville was a successful lawyer who became attorney general for Ireland on the restoration of Charles II in 1660. He owned a town house in Bride Street and a fine estate at Loughlinstown, south of Dublin: it was at Loughlinstown House that his daughter, Lucy, married William Molyneux in September 1678. Domville was turned out of his office as attorney general by Tyrconnell in 1687; unlike many protestants in a similar position, he refused to flee to England but remained in Dublin, where he died in 1689.

CHIEF WRITINGS. Domville's only significant work is his *A Disquisition touching that great Question concerning an Act in* England *Binding* Ireland .... (1660), the manuscript of which is in Trinity College, Dublin, MS. 890.

BIOGRAPHY AND CRITICISM. J. G. Simms, *William Molyneux of Dublin* (Dublin: Irish Academic Press, 1982) and Patrick Kelly, 'The manuscript of the printer's copy of William Molyneux's *Case of Ireland Stated*, *Long Room*, XVI (1980), 6-13.

William Petty

LIFE. Born Romsey, Hampshire, England in 1623, Petty went to sea, deserted ship and entered the Jesuit College in Caen, Normandy. Thereafter he studied in Utrecht and Amsterdam, matriculated as a student of medicine at Leyden in 1644, studied in Paris and there became a friend of Thomas Hobbes. He received a doctorate in physics from Oxford in 1649 and became a leading member of a scientific and philosophical group that is generally regarded as the forerunner of the Royal Society. Petty became a fellow of Brasenose College and professor of anatomy after a celebrated case in which he 'revived' the corpse of one Anne Green who had been hanged for murder. In 1652 he was appointed physician general to the army in Ireland. In effect he took over the duties of the surveyor general and was effectively in complete control of the forfeiture of Irish lands. He was secretary to Henry Cromwell and was employed in secret despatches between Ireland and England on Cromwell's behalf. His great work, the 'Down Survey' of forfeited Irish lands, was not issued until 1673, in the reign of Charles II. With the fall of the Cromwellian party in 1659, he lost all official appointments and returned to Oxford. Charles II, nevertheless, favoured Petty. He was knighted in 1662, the year the Royal Society was incorporated and the year his cousin John became surveyor general of Ireland. The Act of Settlement and the Act of Explanation secured Petty a large estate in Ireland. His 'Down Survey' was declared the official reference for any disputes. Petty was supported by both the King and the Duke of Ormonde. He favoured administrative and financial reform in Ireland, wished to include the catholics in the political system, which he envisaged as a union of England and Ireland, but which was threatened by dissenters and extremists. He created the science of statistics. His *Political Arithmetic* (1690) traced the source of wealth to labour and land and refuted many current notions about national decay. He died in London in 1687.

CHIEF WRITINGS. *Reflections Upon Some Persons and Things in Ireland* (London, 1660); *Political Arithmetic* (London, 1690); *The Political Anatomy of Ireland* (London, 1691). See also Sir Thomas Larcom (ed.), *History of the Down Survey* (Dublin: Irish Archaeological Society, 1851).

BIOGRAPHY AND CRITICISM. See T. W. Moody, F. X. Martin and F. J. Byrne (eds), *A New History of Ireland* III (Oxford: Clarendon Press, 1976) and T. W. Moody and W. E. Vaughan (eds), *A New History of Ireland* IV (Oxford: Clarendon Press, 1986). See also Volume III of this anthology, p. 1107.

Richard Cox

LIFE. Born in Bandon, Co. Cork in 1650, Cox attended the Inns of Law in London and was called to the Bar in 1673. He returned to Ireland in 1674, married, lived for seven years in Clonakilty, moved to Cork and became the Recorder of Kinsale. Cox was known for his violent anti-catholicism. When James II came to the throne, Cox removed to England and began the writing of *Hibernia Anglicana*, the first part of which appeared in 1689, the second in 1690. On the arrival of William of Orange, Cox went to London and distributed among the members of the convention what he named *A Sheet of Aphorisms*, supporting William's claim to the crown and urging the necessity of his sending speedy relief to Ireland. Cox was appointed secretary to Sir Robert Southwell, crossed over to Ireland with him and was present at the battle of the Boyne. In that year, 1690, he became, successively, second justice of the common pleas and military governor of Cork. He imposed a severe curfew on catholics in the Cork area in 1691. In 1692, he received his knighthood and became a member of the privy council and a member of the commission of forfeitures. He claimed that catholics were entitled to the benefit of the articles of the Treaty of Limerick, but found that this displeased many who were even more bigoted than him. He was chief justice of the Queen's Bench 1711-14. Aodh Buidh MacCruitin (Hugh MacCurtin) criticized him for the anti-Irish slant of his *Hibernia Anglicana* in a satire entitled *Sgiathlúithreach an Choxaigh* (1714), for which Cox is said to have illegally imprisoned him. He died in 1733.

CHIEF WRITINGS. *Hibernia Anglicana: or the History of Ireland from the Conquest thereof by the English to this Present Time* (London, 1689-90; 2nd ed. 1692).

William King

For biography and bibliography, see p. 804.

Robert Molesworth

LIFE. Born in Dublin in 1656, Molesworth was educated at Trinity College, Dublin. His father had supported the parliamentary side in the civil war and young Robert was an ardent supporter of William III in the conflict of 1688-90. James II confiscated his estate in 1689, but William III gave it back and made him a member of the privy council. In 1689-90, Molesworth went to Denmark on a private mission and returned there in 1692 as envoy extraordinary. He gave offence to the Danish court and returned to Ireland in 1694, the year in which he published his famous book on Denmark. The book was well-received by the leading Whig intellectuals because of its anti-clerical and pro-Whig tone, although it also implied hostility to the ruling powers in Ireland. Molesworth was MP for Swords in the Irish parliament 1703-05, and sat in the English parliament from 1705 to 1708. In 1713, Molesworth was discharged as a member of the privy council after a dispute with the convocation of the House of Lords. Steele and Swift joined in the subsequent public debate. Molesworth's reply was a reprint of his preface to Francis Hotoman's *Franco-Gallia* (1713), a book he had translated in 1711. In 1714, he was restored to the privy council and in 1719 was created Baron Molesworth of Phillipstown and Viscount Molesworth of Swords, perhaps on account of his defence of the Peerage Bill of that year. Swift dedicated the fifth *Drapier's Letter* to Molesworth. He died at Brackenstown, Co. Meath in 1725 and was buried at Swords.

CHIEF WRITINGS. *An Account of Denmark as it was in the year 1692*, (London, 1694); *The Principles of a Real Whig*, a reprint of the 1711 preface to Hotoman's *Franco-Gallia* (London, 1775); *Considerations for Promoting Agriculture and Employing the Poor* (Dublin: Grierson, 1723).

BIOGRAPHY AND CRITICISM. See comments in F. Venturi, *Utopia and Reform in the Enlightenment* (Cambridge: Cambridge University Press, 1971); C. Robbins, *The Eighteenth-Century Commonwealth Man* (Cambridge, Mass.: Harvard University Press, 1959); D. Berman, 'The Irish Counter-Enlightenment' in R. Kearney (ed.), *The Irish Mind* (Dublin: Wolfhound Press, 1985), pp. 119-40.

William Molyneux

For biography and bibliography, see p. 804.

Hugh MacCurtin

LIFE. Born in Kilmacreehy, Co. Clare *c.* 1680, MacCurtin learned Irish literature and history from his cousin Andrew, whom he succeeded as titular *ollamh* (chronicler) of the O'Briens of Thomond. About 1707 he went to France under the patronage of Lord Clare and the Dauphin, in whose household he was tutor for seven years. He returned to Ireland in 1714 and wrote two of his best-known poems on the deaths of Donagh O'Loghlen and Lewis O'Brien. His *A Brief Discourse in Vindication of the Antiquity of Ireland* (1717) had 2,338 subscribers, most of them from the old Irish families. Two parts appeared; a third, promised, did not. Most of the material was drawn from *Leabhair na Gceart, Leabhar Gabhala* and

Geoffrey Keating's *History*. Part II contains a full account of the deeds of Brian Boroimhe (Boru). His *The Elements of the Irish Language*, published in Louvain in 1728 in co-operation with a Franciscan priest, Father Murphy, has fourteen chapters of grammar, followed by Bonaventura O'Hussey's catechism in prose and verse. Along with Conor O'Begly, MacCurtin published an important English-Irish dictionary in Paris in 1732 with an introductory poem. His friendship with his cousin Andrew and the poet Tadgh O'Neachtáin provided him with the occasions for some of his best poems. After some years spent as a wandering poet, he kept school in his native parish in the village of Knockin-in-aoird, where he died in 1755.

CHIEF WRITINGS. *A Brief Discourse in Vindication of the Antiquity of Ireland* (Dublin, 1717); *The Elements of the Irish Language* (Louvain, 1728).

BIOGRAPHY AND CRITICISM. See E. O. Reilly, *Transactions of the Iberno-Celtic Society* (Dublin, 1820); J. O'Daly, *Poets and Poetry of Munster* (Dublin: O'Daly, 1849); B. O'Looney (ed.), *A Collection of Poems by the Clare Bards* (Dublin: O'Daly, 1863); Richard Hayes, 'Biographical Dictionary of Irishmen in France', *Studies*, June 1944, 246-47. See also T.W. Moody and W.E. Vaughan (eds), *A New History of Ireland*: Vol IV, *Eighteenth-Century Ireland 1691-1800* (Oxford: Clarendon Press, 1986), pp. 394, 396 and references.

Cornelius Nary

LIFE. Born *c.* 1660 near Naas, Co. Kildare, educated at the Irish College in Paris and the University of Paris (1683-94), Nary became parish priest of St Michan's in Dublin in 1697 or 1698 and continued in this post for almost forty years. He was an eager controversialist and was involved in notable disputes with the protestant rector of St Michan's, John Clayton, and with Archbishop Edward Synge, protestant archbishop of Tuam. His various publications were, in general, poorly received, although Nary retained a considerable reputation as a writer on theological and political matters. He died in 1738.

CHIEF WRITINGS. *A Modest and True Account of the Chief Points of Controversie between Roman Catholics and Protestants ....* (London and Antwerp, 1699; reprinted Antwerp, 1700); *A New History of the World* (Dublin: Edward Waters, 1720); *The Case of the Roman Catholicks of Ireland ....* (Dublin, 1724); *Letter to his Grace, Edward Lord Archbishop of Tuam in answer to his Charitable Address* (Dublin, 1728).

BIOGRAPHY AND CRITICISM. P. Fagan, *The Second City: Portrait of Dublin 1700-1760* (Dublin: Branar, 1986), pp. 134-58.

Francis Hutcheson

For biography and bibliography, see p. 805.

Jonathan Swift

For biography and bibliography, see pp. 393-94.

John Browne

LIFE. John Browne was born *c.* 1700 into a prominent Anglo-Irish family which had settled in County Mayo. He disgraced his name when his conflict with a relative came to the attention of the Irish House of Commons and when he gave evidence in favour of William Wood to the English enquiry into Wood's Halfpence. Swift and others attacked him, and his publications on the Irish economy did little to restore his reputation. He published a number of pamphlets, essays and poems during the 1720s and early 1730s. In 1747, he was involved in disturbances in the Dublin theatre and in 1749 was arrested for killing a Robert Millar in a duel. He was not known as 'Sir' in his lifetime though often referred to as such later. He died in 1762.

CHIEF WRITINGS. *The Case of John Browne Esq.* (London, 1725); *An Essay on Trade in General ....* (Dublin, 1728); *Seasonable Remarks on Trade ....* (Dublin, 1728); *The Benefits which arise to a Trading People from Navigable Rivers ....* (Dublin, 1729); *Reflections upon the Present Unhappy Circumstances of Ireland ....* (Dublin, 1731).

BIOGRAPHY AND CRITICISM. Bryan Coleborne, 'Jonathan Swift and the Dunces of Dublin', PhD thesis, National University of Ireland, 1982.

Thomas Prior

LIFE. Born in Rathdowney, Co. Laois in 1682, educated in the public school in Kilkenny and at Trinity College, Dublin, from which he graduated in 1703. In 1729 he published *A List of the Absentees of Ireland* and in 1730 *Observations on Coin in General*. In 1731, with Samuel Madden and eleven others, he founded the Dublin Society for the Promotion of Agriculture, Manufactures, Arts and Sciences. It was incorporated in 1749 and developed into the Royal Dublin Society. Prior devoted himself to the promotion of material and industrial works among protestants in Ireland. He died in 1751 and was buried in Rathdowney. A monument was erected in Christ Church with an inscription by his former schoolmate, Bishop Berkeley. Thomas Prior House, on Simmonscourt Road in Ballsbridge, Dublin is named after him.

CHIEF WRITINGS. *A List of the Absentees of Ireland ....* (Dublin: R. Gunne, 1729; 3rd ed. 1745; 6th ed. 1783); *Observations on Coin in General* (Dublin: R. Gunne, 1730); *An Authentic Narrative of the Success of Tar-Water in Curing a great Number and Variety of Distempers* (Dublin: M. Rhames, 1746).

BIOGRAPHY AND CRITICISM. D. Clarke, *Thomas Prior, 1681-1751: Founder of the Royal Dublin Society* (Dublin: Three Candles Press, 1951). See also T.W. Moody and W.E. Vaughan (eds), *A New History of Ireland*: Vol IV, *Eighteenth-Century Ireland 1691-1800* (Oxford: Clarendon Press, 1986), pp. 172-73.

Henry Brooke

For biography and bibliography, see p. 759.

Charles Lucas

LIFE. Born in 1713, probably in Ballingaddy, Co. Clare, Lucas became an apothecary. In 1747 he was chosen as representative of his corporation on the common council of Dublin and became convinced that aldermen had usurped the council's power. He published his political addresses in 1748-49 in a bid to win a parliamentary seat and became a popular exponent of the principles of Molyneux and Swift. He was declared an enemy of the state and an order for his imprisonment was issued. Lucas fled to the Isle of Man and thence to Europe. In his absence he was disfranchised. In 1767, having obtained a royal pardon, he returned to Dublin in triumph. Trinity College conferred an honorary degree on him and he was returned to parliament. He wrote regularly for *The Freeman's Journal* and continued his fight against the authorities until his death in 1771.

CHIEF WRITINGS: *A Remonstrance Against Certain Infringements on the Rights & Liberties of the Commons & Citizens of Dublin* (Dublin: J. Esdall, 1743); *Divelina Libera: An Apology for the Civil Rights & Liberties of the Commons and Citizens of Dublin* (Dublin: J. Esdall, 1744); *Lucas Against the World and the World Against Lucas* (Dublin, 1748, 1749; no publisher indicated); *A Second Address to the Free Citizens and Free-Holders of the City of Dublin*, 3rd edition (Dublin: James Kelburn, 1748); *A Letter to the Free Citizens of the city of Dublin* (Dublin: J. Esdall, 1749); *The Political Constitutions of Great Britain and Ireland Asserted and Vindicated ... to which are added the Censor or the Citizens Journal* (London, 1751); *Seasonable Advice to the Electors ... of Ireland in General, to those of Dublin in particular* (Dublin: J. Esdall, 1760); *The Rights & Privileges of Parliament asserted upon Constitutional Principles* (Dublin: T. Ewing, 1770).

BIOGRAPHY AND CRITICISM. Sean Murphy, 'The Lucas Affair: A Study of Municipal and Electoral Politics in Dublin 1742-49', unpublished MA thesis, University College, Dublin, 1981.

George Berkeley

For biography and bibliography, see pp. 804-05.

Charles O'Conor

LIFE. Born near Sligo in 1710 of the O'Conor Don family of Roscommon. They were one of the few catholic families to regain some of the land they had lost in confiscations and were thus able to move to the restored family seat at Belnagare in County Roscommon. O'Conor learned Irish and Latin initially from a local Franciscan, who himself knew no English. He came to Dublin in 1727 to pursue scientific studies, but retained his interest in farming and in the family home. He kept a diary (*dialann*) in Irish and had a considerable correspondence with many of the leading figures of the day, including Edmund Burke. He was a founder member of the Catholic Committee in 1757 and was a hardworking member in the fight to gain relief from the Penal Laws for catholics. O'Conor collected and annotated Irish manuscripts and is one of the founders of the century's interest in Irish culture and antiquarian pursuits. His means were severely reduced when a younger brother, who became protestant, claimed ownership of the family lands. After a long dispute, the matter was resolved when O'Conor paid his brother a large sum of money. O'Conor died in 1791.

CHIEF WRITINGS. *Dissertations on the Antient History of Ireland* (Dublin, 1753); S. Ní Chinnéide, 'Dialann I Chonchúir', *Galvia*, I (1954), pp. 32-41; IV (1957), pp. 4-17; C.C. Ward and R.E. Ward (eds), *The Letters of Charles O'Conor of Belnagare*, Vol. I, 1731-1771; Vol. II, 1772-1790 (Ann Arbor: University Microfilms International, 1980); G. and J. Dunleavy (eds), *The O'Conor Papers* (Madison, Wisconsin: University of Wisconsin Press, 1977).

BIOGRAPHY AND CRITICISM. C.C. and R.E. Ward, 'The Ordeal of Charles O'Conor', *Eire-Ireland*, XIV (1979), pp. 6-14; C.A. Sheehan, 'The Contribution of Charles O'Conor of Belnagare to Gaelic Scholarship in Eighteenth-century Ireland', *Journal of Celtic Studies*, II (1958), pp. 219-37; Ann de Valera, 'Antiquarian and Historical Investigations in Ireland in the Eighteenth Century' (unpublished MA thesis, National University of Ireland, 1978).

Richard Woodward

LIFE. Stepson and pupil of the economist Josiah Tucker, Woodward was born in 1726 and was educated at Wadham College, Oxford (1742-59); dean of Clogher 1764-87; bishop of Cloyne, in County Cork 1781-94. He was the principal founder of the House of Industry in Dublin in 1768 and was influential in the passing of the Poor Relief Act of 1772. Woodward campaigned in the Irish House of Lords for repeal of the penal laws in 1782. In 1787 he was involved in a controversy arising from his pamphlet, *The Present State of the Church in Ireland*, in which he claimed that only members of the established Church of Ireland could be loyal to the state. He also advocated the extinction of the Irish language. The pamphlet went into nine editions and attracted several replies from presbyterians and catholics. Woodward died in 1794.

CHIEF WRITINGS. *An Argument in Support of the Right of the Poor in the Kingdom of Ireland to a National Provision* (Dublin: S. Powell, 1768); *An Address to the Publick on the Expediency of a Regular Plan for the Maintenance & Government of the Poor* (Dublin: E. Lynch, 1775); *The Present State of the Church of Ireland containing a description of it's [sic] precarious situation ... to which are subjoined, some reflections on the impracticability of a proper commutation for tithes and a general account of the origin and progress of the insurrections in Munster* (Dublin: W. Sleater, 1787).

Charles Henry Wilson

LIFE. Born Bailieborough, Co. Cavan, in 1757, the son of the local Church of Ireland rector, Wilson was educated at Trinity College, Dublin and the Middle Temple in London. Instead of practising law, he became a parliamentary reporter, and is remembered only for his substantial compilation — 450 pages — on the Volunteer convention in Dungannon where, we may assume, he acted as a reporter. The title-page announces it as volume one, but no further volume ever appeared. Some of Wilson's Volunteer material was republished in 1938, but his anonymous and posthumously published work has been long forgotten. Nevertheless he was a figure of some significance, acquainted with the Brooke family of Rantavan, and knowledgeable on the literary families and individuals associated with the north midlands — Swift, Goldsmith, the Sheridans and, of course, the Brookes. In his most original work, he anticipated Charlotte Brooke in publishing translations of Gaelic poetry. The collections of material relating to Swift and to Burke contain valuable material. Wilson died in London in May 1808.

CHIEF WRITINGS. *A Compleat Collection of the Resolutions of the Volunteers ... of Ireland which Followed the ... First Dungannon Diet ...*. (Dublin: Hill, 1782); *Select Irish Poems Translated into English* (Dublin: no t-p, 1782); *The Wandering Island; or the History of Mr. Charles North* (London: Ridgway, 1792); *Poverty and Wealth: A Comedy in Five Acts Translated from the Danish of P[eter] A[ndreas] Heiberg* (London: Myers, 1799); *The Irish Valet; or, Whimsical Adventures of Paddy O'Halloran who After Being Servant to Several Masters Became Master of Many Servants* (London: Allen, 1811).

Wilson also edited a number of books, including *Beauties of Edmund Burke* 2 vols (London: Myers, 1798); *The Myrtle and the Vine; or Complete Vocal Library* 4 vols (London: West and Hughes, 1800-01) (also a '3rd edition' 1803); *Swiftiana* (London: Phillips, 1804); *Brookiana* 2 vols (London: Phillips, 1804); *Anecdotes of Eminent Persons* 2 vols (London: Dewick, 1804) was published in several editions, including one entitled *The Polyanthea; or, A Collection of Interesting Fragments ...*.

BIOGRAPHY AND CRITICISM. Seamus O Casaide, 'A Rare Book of Irish and Scottish Verse', *Bibliographical Society of Ireland Publications* Vol. 3, No. 6 (1928) discusses the 1782 anthology. A note by D.J. O'D[onoghue] in *The Irish Book Lover* Vol. 4 (1912), p. 55 draws together details of some other publications, but no comprehensive study of Wilson's output has been published. Part of the writings on the Volunteers was reprinted in *County Louth Archaeological Society Journal* Vol. 9, No. 2 (1938), pp. 162-65.

Henry Grattan

LIFE. Born in Dublin in 1746. His father was recorder of Dublin and MP for the city along with Charles Lucas. Grattan attended Trinity College, Dublin (1763-67) and spent a term at the Middle Temple in London. He cooperated with Flood and others in the publication of a series of political articles in *The Freeman's Journal*, later published as a volume, *Baratariana* (1773). In 1772 he was called to the bar and in 1775 was returned as a member of the Irish parliament. In 1780, Grattan introduced a resolution declaring Irish parliamentary independence, although it was not until 1782 that the motion, at the third moving and with the support of the Volunteers, was passed unanimously in both Houses. Now the acknowledged leader of the independence movement, Grattan was voted a grant of £50,000 by the parliament. In June 1782, Flood put forward the issue of 'simple repeal'; Grattan disagreed and he and Flood, in a bitter collision, ended their former friendship. Grattan continued to attack many aspects of government legislation and supported moves to give catholics relief from the excesses of the penal laws. He was deeply involved in the Fitzwilliam crisis of 1795, and in 1797 vainly protested against the operation of martial law in Ulster. In 1798 his name was struck from the records of the Irish privy council on the trumped-up charge that he was a member of the United Irishmen. In the last session of the Irish parliament on 5 October 1800, Grattan made an impassioned plea against the Act of Union. In 1805 he accepted a seat in the English parliament and spoke there on several occasions on the questions of catholic relief — always unsuccessfully. He died in London in 1820 while on a visit there on behalf of a catholic deputation.

CHIEF WRITINGS. *The Speeches of the Rt. Hon. Henry Grattan, with prefatory observations* (Dublin: Martin, 1811); *The Speeches of the Rt. Hon. Henry Grattan in the Irish and in the Imperial Parliament, edited by his son*, 4 vols (London: Longmans, Hurst and Co.; Dublin: R. Milliken, 1822); *The Speeches of the Rt. Hon. Henry Grattan to which is added his Letter on the Union, with a commentary on his career & character by D.O. Madden* (Dublin: Milliken, 1833; 2nd ed., 1834); *Miscellaneous Works of the Rt. Hon. Henry Grattan* (London: Longman, 1822).

BIOGRAPHY AND CRITICISM. *Memoirs of the Life and Times of the Rt. Hon. Henry Grattan. By his son, H. Grattan*, 5 vols (London: Colburn, 1839-46); R.J. McHugh, *Henry Grattan* (Dublin: The Talbot Press, 1936); S. Gwynn, *Henry Grattan and his Times* (Dublin: Browne and Nolan, 1939); T.W. Moody and W.E. Vaughan (eds), *A New History of Ireland*: Vol. IV, *Eighteenth-Century Ireland 1691-1800* (Oxford: Clarendon Press, 1986). See also Gerard O'Brien, 'The Grattan Mystique', *Eighteenth-Century Ireland* I (1986), 177-94; and W.J. McCormack, 'Vision and Revision in the Study of Eighteenth-Century Irish Parliamentary Rhetoric', *Eighteenth-Century Ireland* II (1987), 7-35.

Henry Flood

LIFE. Flood was born in County Kilkenny in 1732. After spending three years at Trinity College, Dublin, he went to Oxford and the Inner Temple. He pursued the law for a time in England before returning to Ireland and entering parliament as member for Kilkenny in 1759. He helped organize a powerful opposition within the Irish House of Commons against the 'English interest'; among his aims was the independence of the Irish legislature and a limited duration to the life of parliament. This was in part achieved with the passing of the Octennial Act in 1767. Flood killed a political opponent, James Agar, in a duel in 1769. Along with Langrishe and Grattan, he published a series of pseudonymous papers in *The Freeman's Journal* relating to recent political matters; these roused great interest and were published in book form as *Baratariana* (1772). In that year Flood accepted the sinecure of vice-treasurer of Ireland and thereby became a member of the privy council. About this time, Grattan described him as standing 'with a metaphor in his mouth and a bribe in his pocket'. In 1781, he became a colonel of a regiment of the Irish Volunteers and was so hostile to the government that he was relieved of his sinecure and privy council seat. Returning to the opposition benches, he found his popularity gone and Grattan in his place as acknowledged leader. After legislative independence, Flood took up the issue of 'simple repeal', contending that the mere repeal of the Declaratory Act was insufficient and demanding an act of parliament expressly disclaiming the right to legislate for Ireland. Grattan disagreed with him on this issue and, although Flood had regained popularity with the Volunteers, he suffered a savage attack by Grattan on 28 October 1783 in the House of Commons. He vindicated himself on 1 November, giving an account and justification of his whole career. He was the author of a scheme of parliamentary reform which gave no rights to catholics. Flood was willing to grant them religious toleration, but refused to admit them to political life. The scheme was twice rejected. In 1783, Flood was returned to the English House of Commons, but his career there was a failure. In 1790 he failed to be returned to either House and he died the following year.

CHIEF WRITINGS. *Speech of the Right Hon. Henry Flood . . . Feb. 15, 1787, on the Commercial Treaty with France* (Dublin, 1787); *Speech and Proposition of the Right Hon. Henry Flood . . . March 4, 1790, for a Reform in the Representation of Parliament* (London, 1790).

BIOGRAPHY AND CRITICISM. W. Flood, *Memoirs of the Life and Correspondence of the Rt. Hon. Henry Flood, M.P.* (Dublin: John Cumming, 1838); F. Hardy, *Memoirs of the Earl of Charlemont* (London: Cadell and Davies, 1810); W.E.H. Lecky, *Leaders of Public Opinion in Ireland* (Dublin: Saunders, 1861; London: Longman, 1871), pp. 63-103.

Theobald Wolfe Tone

LIFE. Tone was born in Dublin in 1763. He was educated at Trinity College, Dublin, and the King's Inns. He joined the Volunteer movement, and in 1792 became secretary of the Catholic Association. His principal political arena, however, was the Society of United Irishmen, which he helped to found in the weeks following the publication of his *Argument on Behalf of the Catholics* in 1791. His pamphlet had suddenly persuaded key figures among the northern dissenters to adopt the cause of catholic relief, and the new Society was devoted to advancing their combined radical objectives. In 1795, Tone was compromised during the trial of fellow-Unitedman, William Jackson, but was allowed to depart to the United States of America after signing a confession of treason. He maintained his political activities and travelled to France, where he was appointed aide-de-camp for what turned out to be another abortive French naval invasion of Ireland. At the end of the fleet's unsuccessful voyage to the west coast of Ireland, Tone was arrested in Lough Swilly, Co. Donegal, and was court-martialled in Dublin. The circumstances of his death have been debated, but it seems clear that he died on 18 November 1798 as a result of a clumsy attempt at suicide seven days earlier.

CHIEF WRITINGS. Until the final months of his life, Tone was an ebullient, optimistic personality who wrote energetically in his journals, in pamphlets, and in his private correspondence. Together with two friends, Tone also wrote an anonymous novel, incorporating coded views of Irish high society — *Belmont Castle; Or, Suffering Sensibility, Containing the Genuine and Interesting Correspondence of Several Persons of Fashion* (Dublin: P. Byrne, 1790; ed. M. Treacy, MA dissertation, University College, Dublin, 1986). Most of his published works appeared in the early 1790s; all were anonymous. There are references in his journal to short works apparently written but unpublished, and these are now effectively lost. No scholarly edition of his works has been published.

A Review of the Conduct of Administration during the Seventh Session of Parliament . . . [By 'An Independent Whig'] (Dublin: P. Byrne, 1790); *Spanish War! An Enquiry how far Ireland is Bound, Right to Embark in the Impending Contest on the Side of Great-Britain?* (Dublin: P. Byrne, 1790); *An Argument on Behalf of the Catholics of Ireland* . . . . (Dublin: P. Byrne, 1791); *A Vindication of the Conduct and Principles of the Catholics of Ireland . . . To which is added, a Correct Copy of the Petition Presented to his Majesty Jan. 2 1793* The second edition (London: for J. Debrett, 1793); *An Address to the People of Ireland on the Present Important Crisis* [Brest: n.p.], 1796.

BIOGRAPHY AND CRITICISM. Several compilations of Tone's personal writings have appeared, and the most significant of these are: William T. W. Tone (ed.), *The Life of Theobald Wolfe Tone*, 2 vols (Washington, 1826); *The Life and Writings of Theobald Wolfe Tone* (Paris, 1828; Dublin: James Duffy, 1846) (3 vols in the National Library of Ireland); *The Autobiography of Theobald Wolfe Tone, 1763-1798* (ed. with an introd. by R. Barry O'Brien) (London: Fisher Unwin, 1893) (2 vols) (edition in Gaelic 1932); Bulmer Hobson (ed.), *The Letters of Wolfe Tone* (Dublin: Martin Lester, 1921); Seán Ó Faoláin (ed.), *The Autobiography of Theobald Wolfe Tone* (London: Nelson, 1937).

See also J. MacManus, *A Bibliography of Theobald Wolfe Tone* (Dublin: printed by Alex. Thom, 1940).

The now standard, but somewhat ageing, study of Tone is Frank MacDermot, *Theobald Wolfe Tone and His Times* (London: Macmillan, 1939; revised edition Tralee: Anvil Books, 1968). For a broader examination of the period and political context of Tone's life (and a classified bibliography), see Marianne Elliott, *Partners in Revolution; The United Irishmen and France* (New Haven: Yale University Press, 1982). For an up-to-date account of the period more narrowly concerned with events in Ireland, see the final chapter (pp. 170-97) of David Dickson, *New Foundations: Ireland 1660-1800* (Dublin: Helicon, 1987).

Tone has continued to attract commentators. A recent summary biography is Henry Boylan, *Theobald Wolfe Tone* (Dublin: Gill and Macmillan, 1981). A debunking of Tone the republican is essayed in Tom Dunne, *Theobald Wolfe Tone, Colonial Outsider, an Analysis of his Political Philosophy* (Cork: Tower Books, 1982). Tone's continuing appeal to the political liberal is evident in a bicentennial (1963) lecture recently reissued: Hubert Butler, *Wolfe Tone and the Common Name of Irishman* (Gigginstown: Lilliput Press, 1985). Readers who require some further 'angle' on Tone might search for Leo MacCabe, *Wolfe Tone and the United Irishmen. For or Against Christ* (London: Heath Cranton, 1937).

John Philpot Curran

LIFE. Born near Cork in 1750 and educated at Trinity College, Dublin and the Middle Temple in London. He was called to the bar in 1775 and entered the Irish parliament in 1783 as member for Kilbeggan in County Westmeath. Curran resigned from parliament in 1797, despairing of ever reforming the corrupt practices of that body. Before 1793 he had been a popular advocate; afterwards, he became famous as the defender of many of the United Irishmen, including Hamilton Rowan, the Rev. William Jackson, William Drennan and the brothers John and Henry Sheares. He was appointed master of the rolls and member of the privy council in 1806. Curran was renowned for his oratorical gifts and for his conviviality and wit. He retired in 1814 and moved to London, dying at Brompton, Middlesex in 1817.

CHIEF WRITINGS. *Speeches of . . . John Philpot Curran, on the Late Very Interesting State Trials* (Dublin: Stockdale, 1808); T. Davis (ed.), *The Speeches of the Right Hon. J.P. Curran . . . with Memoir and Historical Notices* (Dublin: Duffy, 1845).

BIOGRAPHY AND CRITICISM. W. O'Regan, *Memoirs of Curran* (Dublin: Byrne, 1817); C. Phillips, *Recollections of Curran and Some of his Contemporaries* (London: Hookham and Baldwin; Dublin: Milliken, 1818); W.H. Curran, *Life of the Rt. Hon. John Philpot Curran*, 2 vols (London: Archibald and Constable, 1819); L. Hale, *John Philpot Curran: His Life and Times*, (London: Cape, 1958).

Robert Emmet

LIFE. Emmet was born in Dublin in 1778, and was executed there in 1803, following the collapse of his attempted *coup de état*. While a student at Trinity College, Dublin he took an active part in the debates of the Historical Society, and joined the United Irishmen. When the authorities conducted an inquisition in the college to discover students with radical sympathies, Emmet took his name off the books and so avoided embroilment in the actual events of the 1798 insurrection. Emmet travelled on the Continent where he gained interviews with both Talleyrand and Napoleon, the latter promising (in 1802) to advance Irish independence. Secretly engaged to Sarah Curran (d. 1808), daughter of John Philpot Curran the celebrated lawyer, and drawing on a recent generous legacy, Emmet began to plan a further United Irishman insurrection, but his habits of secrecy, combining with an explosion in his munitions stores, resulted in a premature rising (July 1803) in which his subordinates where unable to join him. The action was largely confined to Dublin, and Emmet retired in despair (caused, it is always said, by his supporters' murder of Lord Kilwarden and his nephew) to the Currans' home at The Hermitage, Rathfarnham, just west of Dublin. There he might have evaded arrest but for his determination to take a suitable farewell of Sarah. He was tried for high treason in September 1803, found guilty and executed on 20 September. The place of his burial remains unidentified.

CHIEF WRITINGS. Emmet published nothing; apart from the proclamations associated with his July insurrection, he is not known to have written anything other than the renowned and problematic 'Speech from the Dock'. Documentation concerning the Emmet conspiracy, its detection, the insurrection, trial and execution, and subsequent reports, is reproduced is *Robert Emmet: The Insurrection of 1803* (London: Her Majesty's Stationery Office for the Public Record Office of Northern Ireland, 1976). This package is part (facsimiles 181-200) of the Public Record Office's educational documentation series, and needs to be used with some caution. A very useful summary of the problems involved in considering the text of Emmet's speech is N.C. Vance, 'Text and Tradition: Robert Emmet's Speech from the Dock' *Studies* (Dublin) Summer 1982, pp. 185-91.

BIOGRAPHY AND CRITICISM. There has been no shortage of *Lives* of Emmet, and imaginative treatments of his romantic last days. Richard R. Madden, *The Life and Times of Robert Emmet, Esq.* (Dublin: James Duffy, 1847) is good by the standards of its time, but avowedly nationalist in its sympathies. Helen Landreth, *The Pursuit of Robert Emmet* (New York: McGraw Hill, 1948; 2nd edition Dublin: Brown & Nolan, 1949) is highly readable. For those who can read Irish, Leon O Broin, *Emmet* (Baile Átha Cliath: Sairseal agus Dill, 1954) is recommended. No modern scholarly study of Emmet has appeared in English. However, Marianne Elliott, *Partners in Revolution: The United Irishmen and France* (New Haven: Yale University Press, 1982) devotes its second last chapter (pp. 282-322) to a valuable reconsideration of Emmet's rebellion, and provides a larger historical context in which to assess him than is usually the case.

Daniel O'Connell

LIFE. Born near Cahirciveen, Co. Kerry, on 6 August 1775. For more than thirty years he was the most formidable figure in Irish public life who never held office, and the heart of his achievement was the assimilation of certain limited objectives (catholic relief) with a broad sense of national development. O'Connell was adopted, in effect, by his uncle Maurice 'Hunting Cap' O'Connell (1728-1825), to whose notions of family pride he was for many years attentive. He was educated first at a catholic secondary school outside Cork, and then at the college of St Omer in northern France. At the latter, he became acquainted with French revolutionary ways and developed a life-long aversion to violence. He read law at Lincoln's Inns, London. Back in Ireland, he was called to the Irish bar in 1798 and a providential bout of illness put him out of commission when the time of decision arose *vis à vis* the United Irishmen's insurrection.

As early as 13 January 1800 O'Connell repudiated in his first public speech the notion that Irish catholics backed the Act of Union, and his emergence as the new and vigorous spokesman for that body was well under way when the Magee case of 1813 indicated the limits under which his vigour had to be exercised. During his early years at the bar, he perfected his rhetorical style, and earned the affectionate nick-name of 'The Counsellor'. In 1823, he founded the Catholic Association to renew agitation for relief; the 'catholic rent' (1824 onwards) brilliantly provided an income for his organization while also binding a mass following to it. In 1825 the Association was suppressed and the House of Lords rejected a relief bill. Following an 1826 election in which a protestant candidate supported by O'Connell's machine was elected in Waterford, O'Connell himself was elected MP for County Clare at a by-election in 1828.

Although he was thus directly responsible for forcing the 1829 Catholic Emancipation Act on the government and its reluctant supporters in the Lords, his own seat in the Commons was not confirmed until his re-election for Clare in 1830. By now he was also known as 'The Liberator'.

Elected unopposed for Dublin in 1832, O'Connell commenced a campaign for an inquiry into the state of the Union in 1834. Though unsuccessful in this, the compromise Lichfield House Compact of the following year brought tangible benefits for Ireland, notably in the administration of Thomas Drummond (1797-1840) as under-secretary (1835-40). O'Connell supported the English Whigs in the 1830s, especially in the matter of municipal reform. As a result of a similar reform in Ireland, he was elected (1841) the first catholic mayor of Dublin since the reign of James II. Though he had founded the Repeal [of the Union] Association in 1840, he avoided controversy during his term of office. By 1842, his cause was augmented by *The Nation* newspaper, although within a few years O'Connell and the paper were to differ markedly on tactical and other issues. In 1843, he cancelled at the last moment a 'monster meeting' for repeal at Clontarf, in keeping with his policy of avoiding violent conflict. Arrested in 1844 on a charge of creating discontent, he eventually succeeded on appeal. Although he lived to draw attention to growing distress in rural Ireland in 1846, O'Connell by 1845 was already rapidly ageing and beset by difficulties, including less than wholly subservient allies in the Young Ireland movement. He last spoke in the House of Commons on 8 February 1847. O'Connell died in Genoa on 15 May 1847 while en route to Rome. His body was buried in Dublin on 5 August, his heart having been earlier interred in Rome.

CHIEF WRITINGS. Although O'Connell's deeds principally consisted in words, he was not a deliberate writer. No modern edition of his speeches, or his incidental writings, has been prepared. But see *A Collection of Speeches by Daniel O'Connell and Richard Lalor Sheil on Subjects Connected with the Catholic Question* (Dublin, 1828.); John O'Connell (ed.), *The Select Speeches of Daniel O'Connell, M.P.*, 2 vols (Dublin: Duffy, 1846); Maurice R. O'Connell's magisterial eight-volume *The Correspondence of Daniel O'Connell* (Dublin: Irish Manuscripts Commission et al., 1972-1980) is indispensable.

BIOGRAPHY AND CRITICISM. The literature here is vast, and what follows is a list of the essential items recently published. Oliver MacDonagh, *The Hereditary Bondsman: Daniel O'Connell 1775-1829* (London: Weidenfeld and Nicolson, 1988) is the first volume of what will surely be the standard biography. The latest study of O'Connell's first major campaign is Fergus O'Ferrall, *Catholic Emancipation; Daniel O'Connell and the Birth of Irish Democracy* (Dublin: Gill and Macmillan, 1985). For the later phase, see the still valuable work by Angus MacIntyre, *The Liberator; Daniel O'Connell and the Irish Party 1830-1847* (London: Hamish Hamilton, 1965).

Richard Lalor Sheil

LIFE. Sheil was born in Drumdowney, Co. Kilkenny in 1791. He was educated first by French émigrés in London, then at Stonyhurst College, and in November 1807 he proceeded to Trinity College, Dublin. His family circumstances were straitened, and after qualifying as a barrister he took to writing for the stage as a means of supplementing his income. His emergence as a political figure was gradual, though by 1825 he was squarely in Daniel O'Connell's confidence, contributing a good deal to the tactics of the Catholic Association. Sheil was one of the first catholics admitted to the inner bar (1830) after the 1829 Emancipation Act. Although his later career was never particularly distinguished, he was appointed master of the mint in 1846 under Lord John Russell's government. Sheil died in Florence in 1851, shortly after being appointed British minister in Tuscany.

Together with W.H. Curran, Sheil contributed 'Sketches Legal and Political' to the *New Monthly Magazine*. As a miscellaneous writer, his dramatic output was quite substantial but uneven in quality. The tragic mode, which he cultivated, was not well served by the demands and tastes of regency England, and even those plays of his that succeeded at the time have not held their place in the canon of English literature. His unpublished plays include several adaptations from the work of others. He has not been the subject of recent research.

CHIEF WRITINGS. *Adelaide; or The Emigrants* (Dublin: for R. Coyne, 1814); *The Apostate* (London: Murray, 1817); *Bellamira; or The Fall of Tunis* (London: Murray, 1818); *Evadne; or The Statue* (London: Murray, 1819); *The Speeches of the Right Honourable Richard Lalor Sheil, M.P. With a Memoir* (Dublin: James Duffy, 1845).

BIOGRAPHY AND CRITICISM. William Torrens McCullagh, *Memoirs of the Right Honourable Richard Lalor Shiel*, 2 vols (London: Hurst and Blackett, 1855).

ANDREW CARPENTER and SEAMUS DEANE, *Editors*

The Shifting Perspective

(1690-1830)

During the period covered in this section — from the battle of the Boyne to catholic emancipation — two civilizations, one Gaelic and one English, existed side by side in Ireland. Neither was secure in its possession of Ireland's land or in its political control of the people; each was trying to come to terms with a world that was in many ways strange and new. After the battle of the Boyne, it was clear that the old Gaelic culture had lost all coherence. Its leaders were gone, the bardic schools dispersed, its lands reduced, its political power extinguished. The English culture, on the other hand, was strengthening daily; but it too had a crisis to overcome. For although this culture was an English transplant, it was profoundly affected by its new environment, even to the point of transformation. Not Gaelic and yet not wholly English, it had to discover either what it was or what it could become. By a remarkable transition, the English living in Ireland in the eighteenth century gradually learned to create a new identity for themselves by recollecting the fragments of the Gaelic tradition and transmuting them into an English that itself was a transmutation of the English civilization from which they derived. In a strange manner, the old Gaelic world was called in to familiarize the new English with the country they had come to, even though it was the defeat of the Gaelic world and its cultural values that had estranged the Irish both from their own and from the settlers' world. However, throughout the eighteenth century there was a long-drawn-out and subtle exercise in acclimatization, which might well have continued into the nineteenth century, had not political conditions throughout Europe in the period between 1789 and 1800 brought any moves towards *rapprochement* to an abrupt end.

If Gaelic civilization was of interest to the English as they became acclimatized to Ireland, the Irish landscape proved an object of equal fascination. With its bogs and its wild, western scenery, it was not only different from England but somehow resistant by its very nature to the systematic improvements and cultivation that were changing the face of England so completely during the eighteenth century. William King's account of the bogs of Ireland vacillates between the expressed wish to make them useful and implicit suspicion that they are somehow, in their implacability and inconvenience, emblematic of all that is troublesome and strange about Ireland. Charles Smith, on the other hand, is early in the field with the notion that such a landscape can best be exploited simply by being looked upon, by being left to its strange beauty and turned into a site for tourists. Both of these accounts show at what a rudimentary level the need to familiarize or domesticate the strange land operated.

On the Continent, the Irish exiles in Louvain, Paris and other centres were still inclined to believe that it was possible to launch a kind of counter-reformation against the onset of the modern world that had dispersed them so widely. Michael Moore, for example, tried to save the world from Cartesianism. Like many exiles, he wished to re-establish what once was and to deny the basic assumptions which legitimized the world that had replaced it. Yet he and his compatriots were fighting an intellectual battle that had long been lost. They could no more heal the Cartesian split than they could restore either the power of catholicism or the prestige of the Gaelic culture. Nevertheless, this continental influence, conservative and nostalgic, largely clerical in its major figures, was to remain a force in Irish life that was to achieve an unexpected access of strength with the founding of the seminary at Maynooth in 1795 — in the decade of the French Revolution. Then the innate conservatism and nostalgia of the Gaelic culture, its repudiation of the 'modern' world, became a politically effective influence that was to endure into the late twentieth century.

Perhaps the most important and symbolic figure of all those represented here is John Toland. Born an Irish-speaking catholic in Donegal, he forsook his faith and entered upon an intellectual career that was to make him notorious as a freethinker and as a founding figure of the Enlightenment. Born into the Gaelic world, he chose the English world; repudiated by it, he turned to Europe and its newly born vision of the rational, secular, human community. Yet towards the end of his life, Toland returned to the culture he had initially forsaken and attempted to reincorporate it, as an object of study and as an early exercise in cultural anthropology, into the Enlightenment's long inquiry into the structure and nature of diverse civilizations. Although this mode of inquiry was ultimately to lead to the encouragement of nationalist feelings, Toland pioneered the attempt to see early Irish history in a detached light, even though his own anti-clerical prejudice made his work, like that of so many Enlightenment historians and scholars, a disguised attack on the malign forces of contemporary history.

With Thomas O'Sullevane, Joseph Cooper Walker, Charlotte Brooke and Edward Bunting, we see the emphatic turn in Irish cultural life that was to lead to the politicizing of antiquarian scholarship by the end of the century. Certain figures, like the blind harpist, Turlogh Carolan, were to become the centre of a cult that had both the worship and the renewal of the past as its primary belief. Those who wrote about Carolan — Oliver Goldsmith, Joseph Cooper Walker, Sir Samuel Ferguson, George Petrie — gave him a symbolic status and a significance that went far beyond anything warranted by his actual musical achievement. He was, above all things, a usable remnant, a figure from the past who was still able to create rather than simply reproduce Irish music. In that respect, he was probably more immediately attractive than the nine harpists who gathered for the harp festival in Belfast in 1792; nevertheless, the music they provided — which Bunting, after his fashion, transcribed — was ultimately to have a more far-reaching influence, particularly through Thomas Moore's *Irish Melodies*, than that of Carolan himself.

Of considerable importance too was the achievement of Charlotte Brooke. Her translations of Gaelic poetry are not in accord with the tone and style of the originals, but, like Moore, she made the Gaelic note available in English. It may be that this note was more akin to the pseudo-Celticism of James Macpherson in Scotland than to the living Gaelic tradition of the 1780s in Ireland, but that is beside the point. Gaelic could survive in English only in a 'Celtic' form. It was that survival which at least created the possibility of the emergence of an Irish cultural identity that would be neither wholly Gaelic nor wholly English. That was the point of the long cultural negotiation between the two cultures that had been undertaken in the eighteenth century.

Yet the recovery of the past in Ireland could not be an innocent scholarly preoccupation. It was one thing to see it as a way of creating an identity that embraced both settlers and natives; it was quite another thing when that movement became allied to the increasingly urgent claims of the Irish catholics for full civic status within the political system. So viewed, antiquarianism was positively revolutionary. It ratified catholic claims and marginalized protestants within the island, first as people who did not belong culturally and, second, it was feared, as people who therefore had no legitimate claim to political power. This anxiety became so widespread that the nineteenth century was to see a counter-attack on 'Gaelic' and especially on pagan Ireland, in which the glamorization of that ancient civilization was derided and characterized as nothing more than a disguised political manoeuvre. It is still the case that any attempt at a 'revival' of anything Irish — from the Irish language to the idea of a historically defined 'Irishness' — is open to the same kind of assault. The incestuous relationship between culture, so conceived, and political power was an inescapable product of the tense conditions of late eighteenth-century Ireland.

In the second part of this selection, we can see, at closer range, aspects of Irish life during this period which register, at a more personal level, some of the strains and tensions already mentioned. John Vesey's account of the treatment of protestants during the reign of James II is a reminder of what his co-religionists feared might recur at any moment throughout this period. It is presented here as typical of the kind of protestant folklore which — supplemented by Sir John Temple's account of the massacres of 1641 or Archbishop King's listing of catholic atrocities during the reign of James II (in *The State of the Protestants* (1691)) — could lead, at any moment during the eighteenth century, to the harsh enforcement of the Penal Laws or to violent anti-catholic agitation. The repression of the catholic faith and of the Irish language led inevitably to a close alliance between the two — as Andrew Donlevy's *Catechism*, typical of much material printed on the Continent in the seventeenth and eighteenth centuries, shows. The link between catholicism and the Irish language was an immensely important one; it was established early in the seventeenth century and directed from continental seminaries, which insisted that priests for the Irish mission be able to minister in the Irish language. If there was an Irish counter-reformation, it had a linguistic as well as a theological aspect and it was much more successful in reawakening the catholic faith of the people than any protestant attempts at weakening it. It was only in the early nineteenth century, under the influence of Daniel O'Connell among others, that catholicism, now directed from Maynooth, forsook the Irish language as one of the badges of its crusade. Of course, the translation of Donlevy's *Catechism* into English must also be seen as an admission of the weakening position of Irish as the spoken language of the people. However, the catholic church intended to retain its teaching functions and its power in both languages, as long as that was necessary.

On the other hand, Swift's letters to Charles Wogan remind us again that there was a ready commerce between gentlemen which the religious division did not prevent. For the impoverished and disenfranchized masses, however, the divide was more real. That *canaille* which Arthur Young and other visitors speak of as thronging the Dublin streets and living in filthy conditions on the edges of the bogs, was socially as well as religiously inferior. In that respect, the masses were unlike their counterparts in England or in any other European country. The long catalogue of visitors to Ireland, which begins to form around mid-century, ensured that for the next 150 years or so there would be a large body of first-hand evidence to show that the plight of the Irish peasantry and urban poor was truly dreadful and not to be compared with that of the underprivileged in other European countries. Their religious affiliation as well as their social class condemned them to horrors only exceeded perhaps by those endured by the peasantry in Poland or Russia. Le Chevalier de la Tocnaye is given here as a representative of a series of travellers, from Arthur Young (1780) to J.B. Kohl, Alexis de Tocqueville and Friedrich Engels in the 1830s and 1840s. Yet nineteenth-century accounts are more harrowing, partly because of the Famine and partly because the Irish were not so dependent in the eighteenth century on the restricted potato diet that was to be theirs in later years. Thus, while in de la Tocnaye's account of Ireland there is contrast between the life of the peasantry and that of the middle and upper classes that seems painful to contemplate, it was not as appalling as it was later to become.

There were Irish as well as foreign tourists. The country had a relatively good road system and some rapidly expanding cities and towns — chiefly Dublin, Cork and Limerick. These towns were, like the social and political systems, clearly divided between the new and elegant and the old and ramshackle sections. The period is well-known for its great achievements in town-planning and in architecture. It is also the case that the increasingly organized patterns of urban life combined with the improving transport system to give a boost to the reputation of tourist spots like Kerry, which offered a pleasing contrast between the wildness of nature and the order of human society, one very dear to eighteenth-century sensibilities. And Dublin, as the second city of the empire and the capital of a country that exercised considerable fascination over the English and the continental Europeans alike, grew and prospered. It boasted fine shops, elegant hotels, magnificent town houses and, during the winter parliamentary season, a social life second only to that of London. Its book trade — able to supply the North American colonies with pirated editions of London-printed books — flourished, and the city gained a well-deserved reputation as a literary centre.

Central to that reputation is the figure of Swift. Mrs Laetitia Pilkington is one among a number of gossips and scribblers who laid the foundations of the great writer's mythological reputation in Ireland. In folklore, he is second only to Daniel O'Connell in popularity and, like Carolan, he became a cult figure who represents, in a sublime form, the crisis of identity that is the hallmark of Anglo-Ireland. If there is a dark side to the busy social life of the Ireland that Mrs Delany describes so chattily and with such valuable detail, there is also a light side to the figure of the formidable, misanthropic dean of St Patrick's. Through such occasional and sometimes casual records, we get some sense, in the interplay between these lights and shades, of the life that was lived by people in Ireland at the time.

Yet there was always a sense of the ephemeral about that life. Its closeted intensity, manifest in Swift, had its opposite in the life of the country gentry, those men and woman, much-beloved of novelists, whose hard drinking and fighting, nerve and brutality, financial recklessness and social style, helped to form one of the many stereotypes of Irish literature. In the end they were doomed to be chastised by a Maria Edgeworth. Although that utilitarian intelligence was brought to bear on their faults and failings, Jonah Barrington, a fine example of their rapscallion culture, redeemed them and himself for posterity by regarding them in the soft lights of a nostalgia for an Ireland that had once been and had forever passed away with the coming of the Act of Union, the decline of Dublin's influence and the rise of nationalist politics. Throughout the nineteenth century, we read of the disappearance of old customs and habits of belief, the fading of ancestral pieties before the march of a uniform progress, the catastrophic effects of the Famine on the freer and wilder life of the Irish of the previous generation. Barrington's value is not only in what he has to say; it is also in the minor genre that he initiated in prose, as had Goldsmith in poetry. The belief that there was once a golden time before the leaden present, the praise of the *ancien régime*, with all its faults and defects, is a powerful one at any time. For the eighteenth century, and for our vision of it, it is especially powerful, partly because its political and social system ended so abruptly in 1800-01, and partly because it left behind, in Dublin, a beautiful city that seemed thereafter to be always in a state of desuetude, matched by a sense of decline in many other aspects of the nation's life. By 1830, as the tithe wars were beginning and in the aftermath of catholic emancipation and the sectarian conflicts of the 1820s, it was possible to believe that life in the eighteenth century had indeed been more gracious, less bitter and, above all, more redolent of promise than it seemed then.

I

In this first section, the selections are designed to give some idea of the cultural and intellectual life of Irish men and women — both in Ireland and abroad — in the eighteenth century. Michael Moore is the sole representative of Irish thought on the Continent, but others — O'Sullevane and Toland, for example — were living and working in England. In addition, so much was happening at home that we can only hint at the richness and variety of eighteenth-century intellectual life in Ireland in the few remaining examples.

MICHAEL MOORE

(1640-1726)

from: DE EXISTENTIA DEI ET HUMANAE MENTIS IMMORTALITATE .... (Of the Existence of God and the Immortality of the Human Mind....) (1692)

[Michael Moore, a catholic from Dublin, was one of the many Irishmen of the seventeenth and eighteenth centuries who had a distinguished career on the Continent. Having studied in France as a young man, Moore returned to Ireland and was ordained into the priesthood. During the reign of James II, he rose to be administrator of the archdiocese of Dublin and was appointed provost of Trinity College, Dublin — the only catholic ever to hold the post. It was due to his influence that the library was not burned by James's soldiers during the military occupation of the college in 1689-90.

Dismissed by James II, Moore went to Italy and France and eventually became rector of the University of Paris. He was a distinguished traditional philosopher, strongly opposed to the new learning that was taking hold in Europe and a particular opponent of the writings of Descartes. Moore dedicated *De Existentia Dei* to the dean and faculty of theology in Paris — as Descartes had dedicated his *Meditations* fifty years earlier — on the grounds that they would be the most fitting judges of such work. It is, in effect, a sustained attack on the fundamental principles of Cartesian philosophy.

The translation, from the work's last chapter, is by Father C. Connellan o.f.m. and Ann Geraghty.]

I. *Real knowledge according to Aristotle*. From all the things that I have been saying up to this point, it is easy to understand correctly the kind and degree of respect Cicero had for Aristotle. He regarded him as the finest intellect of all antiquity, a match indeed for the greatest minds of the Roman Empire. He called Aristotle a man like to God, an outstanding philosopher, easily the leader of philosophers and always to be mentioned after Plato. For almost two thousand years, Aristotle certainly flourished with no less praise among the most learned men of all ages. They regarded him as the prince of philosophers or, at least, the prince of philosophers after Plato. This statement is deserved, for no other philosopher has ever treated more accurately, more fully or more fruitfully of moral or civil law, of the natural discipline of a rational being, of metaphysics itself, of rhetoric or of poetry. All these studies Aristotle either invented or perfected to the highest degree. No one could depart completely from his principles without an obvious danger of being slightly wrong or totally in error. Although, however, some good faithful men, perhaps deservedly, criticised Aristotle and sometimes rejected him because of certain errors — and I would not wish to defend Aristotle on these matters — he was never totally despised by anyone except by someone who totally despised philosophy or, at least, was quite ignorant of it. But as long as the centre-piece of philosophical reasoning flourishes, for the same length of time, men will use a general trust of their senses rather than enthusiastic and mysterious comments.

II. *Real knowledge according to Descartes*. However, men have appeared in our present age who have grown accustomed to despising Aristotle. They have never sufficiently understood Aristotle; perhaps they have never read his works. They are not only unjust to Aristotle but they are also censors of the greatest intellects of many generations which they condemn along with Aristotle. Certainly, they are exposing themselves to accusations of no trivial recklessness and negligence. All posterity will get to know that these changes in philosophy, though plausible, are quite suspect. For these people, it is credible that there should be no commendation of Aristotle from Descartes. I have no doubt but that in due time posterity will be amazed that Descartes should have attained so much fame and have so many followers — a man who never really saw what constituted a genuine philosophical demonstration nor what real 'scientia' or 'knowledge' could be. This was so serious for Descartes that he could not possibly have any genuine concept of rational knowledge. In his assigning of an attribute, in his study of natural science, to the subject knowing or to the object known — this is the very heart of the question of the nature of human knowledge — he erred so seriously that it is certain that he could never have a genuine idea of the true nature of human knowledge. In his defining and determining of the first principles of the subject knowing and of the object known, he had such shameful hallucinations, that it is quite evident that he never understood what constitutes the first principles of philosophy because he was unskilled in and ignorant of metaphysics. Accordingly, he undertook with no less recklessness, a philosophical explanation of material things. He was like a person approaching an interpretation of a Greek code of laws, who, first of all, had not an elementary knowledge of the Greek language and who did not even know the first letters of the Greek alphabet. See chapters 18 and 19 of the first part of the first book where these things are demonstrated by me one by one....

VI. *The novelty, perspicuity and 'easy to grasp' quality of the philosophy of Descartes*. Descartes recommended his own teaching for its apparent novelty and perspicuity. I use the term 'apparent' for both alleged qualities. Most of the things were invented by others and if you examine them in more depth, all of them will appear obscure and false as can easily be seen from what I have said in the book mentioned above. It is indeed very easy for a person to report his own recommendations — in which Descartes almost always excels. To prove the same things is much more difficult; this he was very rarely accustomed to do. Descartes freed himself from this obligation in so far as it was possible; he was a man conscious of his own weakness. You will scarcely ever find a philosopher who reasons in a weaker manner. He tries to indicate sufficiently from his imaginary demonstrations the existence of God and the distinction of the human mind from the body. He scarcely dares to speak of the immortality of the human mind. Nor are his arguments in physics — the philosophical study of ordinary, material things — more valid; they are very rare in his writings and they are much weaker, for the most part, than what he says about the human mind. The suggestion that this philosophy is very easy to learn is what appeals to most people today. It was such that one and a quarter hours was enough to learn the whole system. The disciples of Descartes were not servile in their enthusiasm for his teaching but freely accepted it and, once they had accepted it on molecules, and their shapes and movements, they seemed to think that they knew everything and they neglected all other study. What I say here as a history of the teaching of Descartes is not due to impoliteness or ignorance....

VIII. *The conclusion of this whole work*. That these things taught by Descartes are foolish and false is made sufficiently clear in what I have said in chapter 7 of the first part and chapter I of the third part of the first book, where I have shown that truth in our minds is nothing if not the conformity of the mind with reality itself. This, indeed, comes about through the use of ideas or forms in the mind, which forms are not just similar or like to reality, but are the same as the forms of the object out there in reality. Indeed, if these ideas are not even similar to or like reality outside the mind, as Descartes wished to say, then it is surely necessary to say that the mind has no truth when one has sense experiences, nor is there truth in any appearance or similitude, and so one is always in error. Since this is totally absurd, we must conclude that Descartes had not real 'knowledge' of truth, nor of the mind, nor of ideas, nor of sense experience nor of any type of real knowledge. These things seem certain to me; Descartes was deluded by his own foolish comments, and others were deluded in the same manner. Indeed, wiser people may take care in these matters and their judgement in these subjects will be carefully made. In the first position of importance, however, I state that in all these things said and written by me, I wish to be submissive to the Catholic Apostolic and Roman church which I have always recognised as master of all doctrine and morals and which I have tried to follow; but this has not been without the divine help and grace of Our Lord Jesus Christ to whom, with the Father and the Holy Spirit, let there be praise and glory. Amen.

WILLIAM KING

(1650-1729)

from: OF THE BOGS AND LOUGHS OF IRELAND (1685)

[When the Dublin Philosophical Society was founded in 1683 by William Molyneux and Sir William Petty, it encouraged many of the better-educated Dublin academics and churchmen to turn their minds to experimental or natural philosophy. The Society met weekly to hear papers on all aspects of the 'new learning': the climate, geography and geology of Ireland were considered, as were all the main scientific fields, particularly medicine and botany, as well as navigation, transport, agriculture and a host of miscellaneous subjects.

William King, at this time a fellow of Trinity College, Dublin (later to become dean of St Patrick's, bishop of Derry and archbishop of Dublin) is best known for his philosophical and historical works. This essay, his earliest published work, has been described recently as 'an excellent piece of controlled thinking on a particular problem, ... a good example of seventeenth-century practical research at its best' (K.T. Hoppen, *The Common Scientist in the Seventeenth Century: A Study of the Dublin Philosophical Society 1683-1708* (London: Routledge and Kegan Paul, 1970), p. 153).

The text is taken from *Philosophical Transactions*, XV (London, 1685).]

We live in an island almost infamous for bogs, and yet, I do not remember, that any one has attempted much concerning them; I believe it may be of use to consider their origin; their conveniencies, and inconveniencies; and how they may be remedy'd, or made useful.

I shall give you my thoughts, and observations on each of these; tho' I am satisfy'd, that what I shall be able to say, will be very little, in respect of what would be required, on such an important subject, and so very necessary to the improvement of the kingdom. As to the origin of bogs, it is to be observed, that there are few places, in our northern world, but have been famous for bogs, as well as this; every barbarous ill-inhabited country has them: I take the *loca palustria*, or *paludes*,[1] to be the very same we call bogs: the ancient *Gauls*, *Germans*, and *Britains* retiring, when beaten, to the *paludes*, is the very same that we have experienced in the *Irish*, and one shall find those places in *Italy*, that were barbarous, such as *Liguria*,[2] were infested with them; and therefore I believe the true cause of them is want of industry; at least industry may remove, much more prevent them. There are many bogs of late standing in *Ireland*; when *Odonal* and *Tyrone* came to the relief of *Kinsale*,[3] they wasted the country, especially as they came through *Connaught*, which by the means of earl of *Clanrichard*,[4] was generally loyal; and there is a great tract of ground now a bog, that was then plowed land; and there remains the mansion house of my lord ——— in the midst of it: now if want of industry has in our remembrance made one bog; no wonder if a country, famous for laziness, as *Ireland* is, abound with them. To shew you, how want of industry causes bogs, you must remember, that *Ireland* abounds with springs; that these springs are generally dry, or near dry, in the summer time, and the grass and weeds grow thick about the places where they burst out. In the winter they swell; and run and soften, and loosen all the earth about them; now that swerd or scurf[5] of the earth, that consists of the roots of grass, being lifted up and made fuzzy by the water in the winter, (as I have at the head of some springs seen it lift up a foot or two,) is dried in the spring: and doth not fall together, but wither in a tuft, and new grass springs through it; which, the next winter is again lift up, and so the spring is more and more stopt, the scurf grows thicker and thicker till at first it makes that which we call a quaking bog: and as it grows higher, and dryer, and the grass roots and other vegetables become more putrid together with the mud and slime of the water it acquires a blackness, and grows into that which we

1. marshes, fens.

2. A region in north-west Italy, deriving its name from the ancient Ligurii, who were driven from the Alps by Celtic migrations in the fourth century B.C.

3. The Earl of Tyrone and Hugh O'Donnell marched, with their armies, from Ulster to County Cork in 1601 to try and relieve the Spaniards who were besieged by the English forces in the town of Kinsale.

4. In the wars of the 1640s, Ulick de Burgh, marquis of Clanrickard, used his influence to keep Connacht neutral.

5. swerd = sward: a growth of grass; scurf: a thin layer of turf.

call a turf bog. I believe when the vegetables rot the saline particles are generally washed away with the water, as being apt to be diluted in it; but the oily or sulphureal are those that chiefly remain, and swim on the water, and this is that which gives turf its inflammability. To make this appear, 'tis to be observed that in *Ireland* our highest mountains are covered with bogs, as well as the plains; because our mountains abound more with springs that could be imagined: I remember one high mountain, in the north of *Ireland*, has four loughs[6] on the side of it near the top; now no body living on our mountains; and no care being taken to clear the springs; the whole mountains are over-run with bogs, as I have described.

2. It is to be observed, that *Ireland* doth abound in moss more than, I believe, any kingdom; insomuch that it is very troublesome, being apt to spoil fruit trees, and quicksets;[7] I do not remember, that they, who have written of gardening, or orchards, mention it, which I am sure they would, had they been as much troubled with it, as we are; now this moss is of divers kinds, and that which grows in bogs is remarkable, your light spungy turf is nothing but a congeries[8] of the threads of this moss, as I have frequently observed, before it be sufficiently rotten, (and then the turf looks white and is light,) I have seen it in such quantities and so tough that the turf spades could not cut it: in the north of *Ireland*, they, by way of joke call it *old wives tow*,[9] and curse her that bury'd it, when it hinders them in cutting the turf, it is not much unlike flax:[10] the turf-holes in time grow up with it again, and all the little gutters in bogs are generally filled with it; and truly I chiefly impute the red, or turf bog to it: and from it even the hardened turf when broken, is stringy; tho' there plainly appear in it parts of other vegetables: it is observable that both vegetables and animals have very different forms, when they are kept under and when out of the water; and I am almost (from some observations,) tempted to believe that the seed of this bog-moss, when it falls on dry and parched ground begets the heath: however the moss is so fuzzy and quick growing a vegetable, that it mightily stops the springs, and contributes to thicken the scurf especially in red bogs, where only I remember to have observed it.

3. It is to be observed, that the bottom of bogs is generally a kind of white clay, or rather sandy marl;[11] a little water makes it exceeding soft; and when it is dry it is all dust; and this contributes much to the swelling of the bogs; for the roots of the grass do not stick fast in it; but a little wet loosens them, and the water easily gets in between the surface of the earth and them, and lifts up the surface, as a dropsy[12] doth the skin.

4. 'Tis to be observed, that bogs are generally higher than the land about them, and highest in the middle: the chief springs that cause them being commonly about the middle, from whence they dilate themselves by degrees, as one would blow a bladder;[13] but not always equally, because they sometimes meet with greater obstacles on one side than on the other: whoever has seen bogs, cannot doubt of this; and besides if you cut a deep trench thro' a bog, you will find the original spring, and vast quantities of water will run light, and the bog subside; the bog at *Castle Forbes*,[14] (as I was informed) subsided 30 foot; I could hardly believe that; but found by computation, that it could not be much less than half of it: I believe these, and other observations that might be made being laid together, it is hardly to be doubted, but that I have given the true origin of bogs: those hills, that have no springs, have them not; those that have springs, and want culture,[15] constantly have them: where ever they are, there are great springs: the turf generally discovers[16] a vegetable substance: it is light, and impervious to the water; the ground under it is very pervious: and all these are plainly accountable from the causes I have given.

I must confess there are quaking bogs, caused otherwise; when a stream, or springs runs thro' a flat; if the passage be not tended, it fills with weeds in summer, trees fall a-cross it, and dam it up; then, in winter, the water stagnates farther and farther every year, till the whole flat be covered; then there grows up a co[a]rse kind of grass peculiar to

6. lakes.
7. hedges (usually of thorn bushes).
8. a mass or heap.
9. The unworked (and therefore very tough) fibres of the flax plant.
10. Tough fibres from the flax plant used for making linen.
11. Heavy clay.
12. A disease in which fluid accumulates in various parts of the body.
13. Prepared animal bladders were inflated and used as floats for fishing nets.
14. A famous large estate in County Longford.
15. cultivation.
16. reveals.

these bogs; this grass grows in tufts, and their roots consolidate together, and yearly grow higher, insomuch that I have seen [some] of them to the heighth of a man; the grass rots in winter, and falls on the tufts, and the seed with it, which springs up next year, and so still makes an addition; sometimes the tops of flags[17] and grass are interwoven on the surface of the water, and this becomes by degrees thicker, till it lye like a cover on the water; then herbs take root in it, and by a *plexus*[18] of the roots it becomes very strong, so as to bear a man; I have gone on bogs that would rise before and behind, and sink where I stood to a considerable depth; under was clear water, as some of us experienced by falling in with one leg up to the middle, and that by breaking the surface of the earth where we stood: even these in time will grow red bogs; but may easily be turned into meadow, as I have seen several times, merely by clearing a trench to let the water run away.

The inconveniences of these bogs are very great; a considerable part of the kingdom being rendred useless by them; they keep people at a distance from one another, and consequently hinder them in their affairs, and weaken them; for it is certain, that if suppose 1000 men live on 4 contiguous acres, they can both better assist, and defend one another, than if they lived on 4 not contiguous: and therefore it were good for *Ireland*, the bogs were sunk in the sea, so their good land were all contiguous; but it is further observable here, that generally the land, which should be our meadows, and finest evenest plains, are covered with bogs; this I observed through all *Connaught*, but more especially in *Longford*, and likewise in *West-meath*, and in the north of *Ireland*. These bogs are a great hindrance in passing from place to place; in as much as that you are forced to go far about to avoid them, and on this account the roads are very crooked in *Ireland*; or forc'd (by vast charges[19] to the country) thro' bogs; by these means they are long, and hard to find.

The bogs are a great destruction to cattle, the chief commodity of *Ireland*; in the spring time when the cattle are weak and hungry, the edges of the bogs have commonly grass; and the cattle venturing in to get it, fall into pits or sloughs,[20] and are either drown'd, or (if they are found) spoilt in the pulling out; the number of cattle lost this way is incredible.

They are a shelter and refuge to tories,[21] and thieves, who can hardly live without them.

5. The smell and vapours that are from bogs, are accounted very unwholsome; and the fogs that rise from them are commonly putrid, and stinking: for the rain that falls on them will not sink into them; there being hardly any substance of its softness more impenetrable by water than turf, and therefore rain-water stands on them, and in their pits; it corrupts there, and is exhaled[22] all by the sun, very little of it running away, which must of necessity affect the air.

6. They corrupt our water, both as to its colour and taste; for the colour of the water that stands in the pits, or lies on the surface of the bog, is tinctured by the reddish black colour of the turf; and when a shower comes, that makes these pits overflow, the water that runs over tinctures all it meets, and gives both its colour and stink to a great many of our rivers; as I observed through all the north of *Ireland*.

The natives heretofore had nevertheless some advantage by the woods and bogs; by them they were preserved from the conquest of the *English*; and I believe it is a little remembrance of this, makes them still build near bogs: it was an advantage then to them to have their country unpassable, and the fewer strangers came near them, they lived the easier; for they had no inns, every house where you came was your inn; and you said no more, but put off your brogues[23] and sat down by the fire; and since the natural *Irish* hate to mend highways, and will frequently shut them up, and change them, (being unwilling strangers should come and burthen them;) Tho' they are very inconvenient to us, yet they are of some use; for most of *Ireland* have their firing[24] from them; turf is accounted a tolerable sweet fire, and we having very impolitickly destroyed our wood, and not as yet found stone coal,[25] save in few places, we could hardly live without some bogs: I have seen turf charc'd,[26] it serves to work iron, and as I have been

17. wild irises.
18. network.
19. expense.
20. Deep, boggy holes.
21. Dispossessed Irish who became outlaws.
22. evaporated.
23. Rough leather shoes.
24. fuel.
25. Coal mined from the earth (as distinct from charcoal).
26. turned into charcoal.

inform'd, will serve to make it in a bloomery[27] or iron-work: turf charc'd I reckon the sweetest and wholsomest fire that can be; fitter for a chamber, and consumptive people, than either wood, stone-coal or charcoal.

I know not if it will be worth the observing, that a turf bog preserves things strangely, a corps will lye intire[28] in one for several years; I have seen a piece of leather pretty fresh dug out of a turf bog, that had never in the memory of man been dug before; butter has been found, that had lain above 20 years, and tho' not fit to be eaten yet serv'd well enough to grease wool:[29] trees are found sound and intire in them, and those birch, or alder that are very subject to rot. The trees are supposed by the ignorant vulgar to have lain there ever since the flood,[30] but the truth is, they fell on the surface of the earth; and the bog, as I shewed in the beginning of this discourse, swelling by degrees, at last covered them; and being of an oyly vegetable substance, it, like a balsam,[31] preserves them; the trees burn very well, and serve for torches in the night: I have seen them us'd as lights in catching of salmons....

27. The first forge in an ironworks.
28. uncorrupted.
29. Unusual objects (including caches of butter) are still occasionally found in Irish bogs.
30. i.e. Noah's flood. See Genesis VIII.
31. A preservative ointment.

JOHN TOLAND

(1670-1722)

from: A CRITICAL HISTORY OF THE CELTIC RELIGION, AND LEARNING ... (1718, published 1726)

[John Toland, an intellectual maverick from County Donegal, was one of the few historical writers of the early eighteenth century with a knowledge of the Irish language. This he used in several places, including this eccentric work, often known as *A History of the Druids*. The passages printed below show Toland's well-known anti-clericalism and his discursive style, as well as his awareness of the importance of the systematic collection of Irish manuscripts for the proper study of Irish history.]

... But if in clearing up antient rites and customs, with the origin and institution of certain religious or civil societies (long since extinct,) any communities or orders of men, now in being, should think themselves touched; they ought not to impute it to design in the author, but to the conformity of things, if indeed there be any real resemblance: and, in case there be none at all, they should not make people apt to suspect there is, by crying out tho' they are not hurt. I remember, when complaint was made against an honourable person,[1] that, in treating of the Heathen Priests, he had whipt some Christian Priests on their backs; all the answer he made, was only asking, *What made them get up there?* The benefit of which answer I claim before-hand to myself, without making or needing any other apology. Yet if the correspondence of any Priests with heaven be as slenderly grounded as that of the Druids, if their miracles be as fictitious and fraudulent, if their love of riches be as immoderate, if their thirst after power be as insatiable, and their exercise of it be as partial and tyrannical over the Laity; then, I am not only content they should be touched, whether I thought of them or not; but, that they should be blasted too, without the possibility of ever sprouting up again. For truth will but shine the brighter, the better its counterfeits are shewn: and all that I can do to shew my candour, is to leave the reader to make such applications himself, seldom making any for him; since he that is neither clear-sighted, nor quick enough of conception to do so, may to as good purpose read the *Fairy-tales* as this history.

1. Sir Robert Howard (1626-98), dramatist and wit.

Besides this impartial disposition, the competent knowledge I have of the Northern languages, dead and living (though I shall prove, that no Druids, except such as towards their latter end fled thither for refuge, or that went before with Celtic invaders or colonies, were ever among the Gothic nations) I say, these languages will not a little contribute to the perfection of my work, for a reason that may with more advantage appear in the book itself. But the knowledge of the ancient Irish, which I learnt from my childhood, and of the other Celtic dialects, in all which I have printed books or manuscripts (not to speak of their vulgar Traditions) is absolutely necessary; these having preserved numberless monuments concerning the Druids, that never hitherto have come to the hands of the learned. For as the Institutions of the Druids were formerly better learnt in Britain, by CÆSAR said to be the native seat of this superstitious race, than in Gaule[2] where yet it exceedingly flourished: so their memory is still best preserved in Ireland and the Highlands of Scotland, comprehending the *Hebridæ*, *Hebrides*, or Western Isles, among which is the *Isle of Man*; where they continued long after their extermination in Gaule and South-Britain, mostly by the Romans, but finally by the introduction of Christianity. Besides that much of the Irish Heathen Mythology is still extant in verse, which gives such a lustre to this matter, and of course to the Greek and Roman Fragments concerning the Druids, as could not possibly be had any other way....

XIII. In the mean time 'tis probable your Lordship[3] will be desireous to know, whether, besides the language and traditions of the Irish, or the monuments of stone and other materials which the country affords, there yet remain any Literary records truly antient and unadulterated, whereby the History of the Druids, with such other points of antiquity, may be retriev'd, or at least illustrated? This is a material question, to which I return a clear and direct answer; that not onely there remain very many antient Manuscripts undoubtedly genuine, besides such as are forg'd, and greater numbers interpolated, several whereof are in Ireland itself, some here in England, and others in the Irish Monasteries abroad: but that, notwithstanding the long state of barbarity in which that nation hath lain, and after all the rebellions and wars with which the kingdom has been harrass'd; they have incomparably more antient materials of that kind for their history, to which even their Mythology is not unserviceable, than either the English, or the French, or any other European nation, with whose Manuscripts I have any acquaintance. Of these I shall one day give a catalogue, marking the places where they now ly, as many as I know of them; but not meaning every Transcript of the same Manuscript, which wou'd be endless, if not impossible. In all conditions the Irish have been strangely sollicitous, if not in some degree superstitious, about preserving their books and parchments; even those of them which are so old, as to be now partly or wholly unintelligible. Abundance thro' over care have perished under ground, the concealer not having skill, or wanting searcloth[4] and other proper materials for preserving them. The most valuable pieces, both in verse and prose, were written by their Heathen ancestors; whereof some indeed have been interpolated after the prevailing of Christianity, which additions or alterations are nevertheless easily distinguish'd: and in these books the rites and formularies[5] of the Druids, together with their Divinity and Philosophy; especially their two grand doctrines of the eternity and incorruptibility of the universe, and the incessant Revolution of all beings and forms, are very specially, tho' sometimes very figuratively express'd. Hence their Allanimation and Transmigration.[6] Why none of the natives have hitherto made any better use of these treasures; or why both they, and such others as have written concerning the History of Ireland, have onely entertain'd the world with the fables of it, as no country wants a fabulous account of its original, or the succession of its Princes, why the modern Irish Historians, I say, give us such a medley of relations, unpick'd and unchosen, I had rather any man else shou'd tell. The matter is certainly ready, there wants but will or skill for working of it; separating the Dross from the pure

2. Gaul roughly corresponded to the present France, Belgium, part of Germany, the south Netherlands and north Italy. It was conquered by Julius Caesar 58-51 B.C.
3. The book is cast in the form of a series of letters to Robert, Viscount Molesworth (1656-1725).
4. Treated cloth in which valuable books were wrapped to preserve them.
5. Formulae relating to religious procedures or doctrines.
6. Terms indicating the eternity of the universe and the endless mutations of being. Toland treats these terms as figurative.

Ore, and distinguishing counterfeit from sterling coin. This in the meantime is undeniable, that learned men in other places, perceiving the same dishes to be eternally serv'd up at every meal, are of opinion that there is no better fare in the country; while those things have been conceal'd from them by the ignorant or the lazy, that would have added no small ornament even to their classical studies. . . .

THOMAS O'SULLEVANE

(*c*.1670–*c*.1726)

from: DISSERTATION . . . *PREFIX'D TO THE* MEMOIRS OF THE MARQUIS OF CLANRICARDE (1722)

[This description of an Irish bardic school is the fullest and, apparently, the most accurate to survive. As English cultural influences gradually overcame those of Gaelic Ireland during the seventeenth century, the Irish bardic schools — an essential part of the old structure, given the exalted station of the hereditary bardic families — were forced to close. Amazingly, no full description of a bardic school has survived from the seventeenth century; this passage, written in 1722 by Thomas O'Sullevane, a scholar from County Tipperary living in London, is generally considered to be the most accurate extant account. The main purpose of O'Sullevane's anonymous dissertation was to put into historical context the memoirs of the Marquis of Clanricarde, who had played so important a part in Irish history in the mid-seventeenth century. However, the short passage that follows is a more significant contribution to Irish cultural history than anything else in the book and seems to be based on first- or second-hand information gleaned by O'Sullevane when he was growing up in County Tipperary.]

. . . Concerning the Poetical Seminary, or School . . . it was open only to such as were descended of Poets, and reputed within their Tribes: And so was it with all the Schools of that kind in the Nation, being equal to the Number of Families, that followed the said Calling: But some more or less frequented for the Difference of Professors, Conveniency, with other Reasons, and seldom any come but from remote Parts, to be at a distance from Relations, and other Acquaintance, that might interrupt his Study. The Qualifications first requir'd, were reading well, writing the Mother-tongue, and a strong Memory. It was likewise necessary the Place shou'd be in the solitary Recess of a Garden, or within a Sept[1] or Inclosure, far out of the reach of any Noise, which an Intercourse of People might otherwise occasion. The Structure was a snug, low Hut, and Beds in it at convenient Distances, each within a small Apartment, without much Furniture of any kind, save only a Table, some Seats, and a Conveniency for Cloaths to hang upon. No Windows to let in the Day, nor any Light at all us'd but that of Candles, and these brought in at a proper Season only. The Students upon thorough Examination being first divided into Classes; wherein a regard was had to every ones Age, Genius, and the Schooling had before, if any at all; or otherwise. The Professors, (one or more as there was occasion) gave a Subject suitable to the Capacity of each Class, determining the Number of Rhimes,[2] and clearing what was to be chiefly observ'd therein as to Syllables, Quartans,[3] Concord, Correspondence, Termination, and Union, each of which were restrain'd by peculiar Rules. The said Subject (either one or more as aforesaid) having been given over Night, they work'd it apart each by himself upon his own Bed, the whole next Day in the Dark, till at a certain Hour in the Night, Lights being brought in, they committed it to writing. Being afterwards dress'd, and come together into a large Room, where the Masters waited, each Scholar gave in his Performance,

1. An area marked off for a special purpose.
2. Bardic poetry had strict rules concerning the number of internal and end rhymes in a stanza or poem. See O. Bergin, *Irish Bardic Poetry* (Dublin: Dublin Institute for Advanced Studies, 1970) where this extract is printed.
3. Probably refers to stresses or quantities occurring at intervals of four.

which being corrected, or approv'd of (according as it requir'd) either the same or fresh Subjects were given against the next Day. This Part being over, the Students went to their Meal, which was then serv'd up; and so, after some time spent in Conversation, and other Diversions, each retir'd to his Rest, to be ready for the Business of the next Morning. Every *Saturday*, and on the Eves of Festival Days, they broke up, and dispers'd themselves among the Gentlemen and rich Farmers of the Country, by whom they were very well entertain'd, and much made of, till they thought fit to take their Leaves, in order to reassume their Study. Nor was the People satisfied with affording this Hospitality alone: they sent in by turns every Week from far and near, Liquors, and all manner of Provision towards the Subsistence of the Academy; so that the chief Poet was at little or no Charges, but on the contrary got very well by it, besides the Presents made him by the Students, upon their first coming, which always was at *Michaelmas*;[4] and from thence till the 25th of *March*, during the cold Season of the Year only, did that close Study last. At that time the Scholars broke up, and repair'd each to his own Country, with an Attestation of his Behaviour and Capacity, from the chief Professor, to those that had sent him.

The reason of so long a Vacation was, that being under the hard Duties of the School, the Students could not bear the intense Heat of the other six Months. Nor did they feel much Cold in the very rigour of Winter; whether from the Closeness of the Place, there being but little or no Passage for the cold Air to enter; or so great an Occupation of the Brain, and inward Senses, that the outward were stupefied, or became blunt in their Functions, is matter of Reflection, the Fact it self being very true. But certain it is, that the Imagination, or more immediate working of the Soul, is stronger, and of greater Force, than that which depends upon the ministry of the Organs; as may be seen by lunatic, hair-brain'd People, and Madmen, who tho' tenderly brought up, yet being in the Transports of the said Distempers, undergo many Extremes, which otherwise they could never bear; even so as to lie, and walk naked in bad Weather, without receiving much Harm by it, that can be discern'd. And in *Ireland*, before the Woods were destroyed, and Mountains clear'd of over-grown Heath, Furze, and other Embarassments, nothing was commoner, than to find many of both Sexes, who from too much Melancholy, or some such prevailing Cause, occasioned by Grief, Love, Fright or eminent Danger of Life, being turn'd in their Brains, had ran thither, and there liv'd in Tatters several years, subsisting upon Herbs, Berries, raw Fruit, and the like, as most of the brute Beasts do; which has given Occasion to a Report of the being of wild People in that Country. Wild indeed they were, during the time; and when any of 'em were taken, (which was very difficult to compass, by reason of their great Nimbleness, and Pernicity,[5] exceeding even that of the common Game) it was long and extraordinary Care and Management, that they were brought to their Senses again, but ever remain'd affected or light. And perhaps if *Bedlam*[6] were set open, there would be such living Scarecrows to be soon heard of, and seen, in the Woods and Mountains of *England* also; as in the like case it would be in other Countries.

The Reason of laying the Study aforesaid in the Dark, was doubtless to avoid the Distraction, which Light, and the variety of Objects represented thereby, commonly occasions. This being prevented, the Faculties of the Soul occupied themselves solely upon the Subject in hand, and the Theme given; so that it was soon brought to some Perfection, according to the Notions or Capacities of the Students. Yet the Course was long and tedious, as we find; and it was six or seven Years, before a Mastery, or the last Degree was conferr'd. . . .

4. Michaelmas, the festival of St Michael and all Angels, falls on 29 September.

5. swiftness.

6. A contraction of 'Bethlehem'. The Bethlehem Hospital was the main hospital for lunatics in eighteenth-century London.

CHARLES SMITH

(*c.*1715-62)

from:
THE ANTIENT AND PRESENT STATE OF THE COUNTY OF KERRY (1756)

[Charles Smith, an apothecary from Dungarvan, Co. Waterford and the pioneer of Irish topographical histories, published accurate and readable accounts of the counties of Waterford (1746), Cork (1750) and Kerry (1756). In this passage from his history of Kerry, he is describing — in the manner typical of eighteenth-century topographical writing — the barony of Magunihy and the lake of Killarney. It was descriptions such as these that made Ireland so attractive to travellers seeking 'the sublime'.]

The eastern parts adjoining to the County of Cork, are coarse and mountainous; and besides the mountains of Slievelogher, which in the reign of Queen Elizabeth I, were esteemed impassable, ... it comprehends also the territory called Glanflesk, which has been of late years much improved, enclosed and cultivated; and among others, by Mr Daniel Croneene of Rathmore, near the bounds of the County of Cork, who have planted and well enclosed a considerable parcel of land.

Glanflesk anciently belonged to O'Donoghue; it is now mostly the estate of Lord Kenmare, and is capable of being rendered as well cultivated a tract, as most others in the country. The new turnpike road from Cork to Killarney, has been carried through it, which is of great advantage to all these parts, by rendering the carriage of butter, and other commodities, to and from, that city, infinitely more expeditious, and cheaper than formerly.

This country is watered by the River Flesk for many miles from east to west, which river disembogues itself into Lough Lane, commonly called the Lake of Killarney.

The south side of Glanflesk is bounded by lofty mountains, that divide the counties of Cork and Kerry, and which run in divers ridges to the sea, or rather to the head of Bantry Bay and the River of Kenmare.

The mountain of Mangerton, which stands south-east of Lough Lane, is esteemed one of the highest in this kingdom; by the experiment of the barometer, its altitude was found to be 1020 yards perpendicular above the Lake of Killarney, which is considerably higher than the sea; for that lake in discharging itself, runs a course of some miles, and forms what is called the River Lane, before it joins the ocean.

The mountains called the Reeks which lie to the west of Mangerton, seem, by the eye, to be rather higher than that mountain, but hills which are conical, and terminated in points, appear higher at a distance than those mountains which have a large surface on their tops; as steeples which are terminated by spires, seem to be higher than those covered with domes, the points of the former being as it were more hidden and lost in the atmosphere, than the other.

They are steeper than Mangerton, and have more terrible precipices, and declivities; so that it was in a manner impossible to determine their height by the barometer.

On the west side of that mountain is a large and deep hole, filled with water, which they call the *Devil's Punch-bowl*; it overflows, and makes an agreeable cascade down the side of the mountain in view of Muckross house, the seat of Edward Herbert, Esq. By opening a larger cut on the side of this basin, there would be a broader, more constant and nobler supply of water, which might afford a beautiful cataract, for the greatest part of the year. This water supplies the mills for the iron works, and then falls into Lough Lane, which beautiful lake I am now about [to] describe.

One of the best prospects, which it affords, ... is on a rising ground, near the ruined cathedral of Aghadoe; not but there are many other fine views of it, from every other side, but few of them take in so many particulars, as may be observed from that station. For from hence is to be seen one of the most delicious landscapes in Ireland; and perhaps few countries in Europe afford better. But this is such a masterpiece, that even the Poussins, Salvator Rosa,[1] or the most eminent painter in that way,

1. Nicholas Poussin (1594-1665) and Gaspar Poussin (1600-62), French classical painters; Salvator Rosa (1615-73), Italian landscape painter.

might here furnish himself with sufficient matter, not only to form one, but several entertaining prospects. From this eminence a survey may be taken of the greatest part of this beautiful lake; and likewise of that stupendous amphitheatre of mountains, which are ranged along the opposite shores. Towards the south-east stands the above mentioned mountain called Mangerton, whose feet the lake washes, and whose summit is generally lost in the clouds, it being, from the above recited experiment, justly esteemed one of the highest mountains in Ireland. More towards the centre of the lake, is a high mole,[2] called *Turk*, whose sides down to the verge of the water are beautifully clothed with groves of various kinds of trees. One part of this hill slopes away like a promontory terminating in the lake, forming one side of a canal, which is a passage into the upper lake; as does the point of another mountain called Glenna, the other side of this straight, which is adorned with forest trees. As a fine contrast to this verdure, at the backs of these mountains, stand others, shaped into pyramids, being only naked rocks of a vast height. The grandeur, and magnificence of these mountains not only entertain and surprise the spectator, but he must be also agreeably amused, in contemplating the infinite variety of beautiful colouring they afford. For in one part may be seen the gayest verdure, blended with scarlet fruit, and snowy blossoms, well known properties of the Arbutus;[3] and in other places, the most elegant variety of brown and yellow tints, caused by other kinds of trees and shrubs, appears. All these are intermixed with rock-work, and to soften the whole, a deep, smooth and noble basin of water extends itself beneath this scenary [*sic*]; but to give the reader an adequate idea of this place, would require the pencil of some excellent painter, rather than the pen of any prose writer. All that is proposed by the annexed landscape,[4] is rather to give a likeness, which is what can only be performed in black and white, by lines adorned with light and shade, than to delineate particular beauties, which cannot be effected without the assistance of colours. To the west of Glenna, stands the lofty pike called Tomish, variegated half way to its top, with a wavering forest; and down whose sides, especially after rains, run very considerable cataracts into the great lake. There are many other hills still running more west, as far as the eye can trace for many miles; the nearest and most surprising for their loftiness, are the Reeks already mentioned, whose tops resemble so many pinnacles, or rather spires lost in the clouds. This lower lake is estimated at eight miles in length, and its breadth at four, but it is not so large, as will appear by measuring it on the map, where its true shape is delineated. It is very deep in many parts and the water is sufficiently clear.

The common people hereabouts, have a strange romantic notion, of their seeing in fair weather, what they call a carbuncle,[5] at the bottom of this lake, in a particular part of it, which they say is more than 60 fathoms deep. . . .

2. A great mass of rock.
3. An evergreen tree that grows wild in profusion around the lakes of Killarney.
4. i.e. an engraving in the original edition.
5. A precious stone or gem.

JOSEPH COOPER WALKER

(1761-1810)

from: THE LIFE OF TURLOUGH O'CAROLAN (1786)

[Joseph Cooper Walker, one of the outstanding Irish scholars of the late eighteenth century, wrote valuable works on Irish bards and music, on Irish dress and on the Irish theatre. His life of Carolan — perhaps his best-known work — appears as an appendix to his *Historical Memoirs of the Irish Bards.*]

——————— Thee I revisit safe,
And feel thy sov'reign vital lamp; but thou
Revisit'st not these eyes, that roll in vain
To find thy piercing ray, and find no dawn;
So thick a drop serene hath quench'd their orbs,
Or dim suffusion veil'd. Yet not the more
Cease I to wander, where the Muses haunt.
MILTON's *Address to Light,* Paradise Lost, B. 3.

As several of Carolan's contemporaries are still alive, I thought the present moment the most favourable, for collecting such Anecdotes of him as merit preservation; therefore I seized on it: For 'the incidents which give excellence to biography are of a volatile and evanescent kind, such as soon escape the memory, and are rarely transmitted by tradition.'[1]

Carolan was born in the year 1670, in the village of Nobber, in the county of Westmeath, on the lands of Carolan's-town, which were wrested from his ancestors by the family of the Nugents, on their arrival in this kingdom with Henry the Second. His Father was a poor farmer, the humble proprietor of a few acres, which yielded him a scanty subsistence. Of his Mother, I have not been able to collect any particulars: she was probably the blooming daughter of a neighbouring peasant, in choosing of whom, his father was directed rather by Nature than by Prudence.

The Cabin in which our Bard was born, is still pointed out to the inquisitive traveller. As it is in a ruinous state, it must soon become a prey to all-devouring Time: but the spot on which it stood, will, I predict, be visited at a future day with as much true devotion, by the lovers of natural music, as Stratford-upon-Avon and Binfield are, by the admirers of Shakespeare and of Pope.

He must have been deprived of sight at a very early period of his life; for he remembered no impression of colours.[2] Thus was 'knowledge at one entrance quite shut out,'[3] before he had taken even a cursory view of the creation. From this misfortune he felt no uneasiness: *My eyes,* he used merrily to say, *are transplanted into my ears.*[4]

His musical genius was soon discovered, and his friends determined to cultivate it. About the age of twelve, a proper master was engaged, to instruct him in the practice of the harp; but though fond of that instrument, he never struck it with a master-hand. Genius and diligence are seldom united; and it is practice alone can perfect us in any art. Yet his harp was rarely unstrung: but in general he only used it to assist him in composition; his fingers wandered amongst the strings in quest of the sweets of melody.

Love does not, as Archer teaches Cherry to believe,[5] always enter at the eyes; for Carolan became enamoured of Miss Bridget Cruise (of Cruise-town in the county of Longford) several years after he had lost his sight. His harp now, like the lute of Anacreon,[6] would only sound of love. Though this Lady did not give him her hand, it is imagined she did not deny him her heart. But, like Apollo, when he caught at the nymph, 'he filled his

1. Samuel Johnson, *The Rambler,* No. 60.

2. 'It was to the small-pox, that foe to visual pleasure, he owed the privation of his sight. Such of my Readers as are greedy of anecdote, would not perhaps forgive me if I omitted to mention, that Carolan, though blind, was eminently skilled in the game of Backgammon.' [Walker's note.]
3. cf. John Milton, *Paradise Lost,* III. 50.
4. '"Music, (says Mr. Bew) almost without exception, appears to be the favourite amusement of the blind. There is no other employment of the mind, religious contemplation excepted, that seems so well adapted to soothe the soul, and dissipate the melancholy ideas, which, it may naturally be expected, will sometimes pervade the dispositions of those who are utterly bereft of sight. This, together with the beneficial influence that results from the practice of this delightful art, by quickening and perfecting the sense of hearing, is a matter that deserves the most serious attention." *Observations on Blindness,* in *Memoirs of the Literary and Philosophical Society of Manchester*; a work abounding in curious and elegant Essays.' [Walker's note.]
5. In *The Beaux' Stratagem* by George Farquhar.
6. A Greek poet of the sixth century B.C.

arms with bays.'[7] The song which bears his[8] name is his *chef d'œuvre*: it came warm from his heart, while his genius was in full vigour. 'I have often listened to Carolan (says Mr. O'Conor)[9] singing his ode to Miss Cruise. I thought the stanza's [*sic*] wildly enthusiastic, but neglected to preserve them.'

A very extraordinary instance of the effect of Carolan's passion for this Lady, is related by Mr. O'Connor. He went once on a pilgrimage to St. Patrick's Purgatory, a cave in an island in Lough-Dearg, (in the county of Donegal) of which more wonders are told, than even of the cave of Triphonius [*sic*].[10] On his return to shore, he found several Pilgrims waiting the arrival of the boat which had conveyed him to the object of his devotion. In assisting some of those devout travellers to get on board, he chanced to take a Lady's hand, and instantly exclaimed; *dar lamha mo chardais criost*, (*i.e.* by the hand of my gossip),[11] *this is the hand of Bridget Cruise!* His sense of feeling did not deceive him; it was the hand of her whom he once adored. 'I had the relation from his own mouth, (says Mr. O'Conor) and in terms which gave me a strong impression of the emotions he felt on meeting the object of his early affections.' — Carolan, at the time of this event, was

Nel mezzo del cammin di nostra via.[12]

Our Bard solaced himself for the loss of Miss Cruise, in the arms of Mary Mac Guire, a young lady of a good family in the county of Fermanagh. Miss Mac Guire proved a proud and an extravagant dame: but she was the wife of his choice: he loved her tenderly, and lived harmoniously with her.

It is probable that on his marriage with Miss MacGuire, he fixed his residence on a small farm near Moshill in the county of Leitrim. Here he built a neat little house, in which he gave his friends,

'If not a sumptuous welcome, yet a kind.'[13]

Hospitality consumed the produce of his little farm: he ate, drank and was merry, and improvidently left tomorrow to provide for itself. This sometimes occasioned embarrassments in his domestic affairs; but he had no friend to remind him, 'that nothing will supply the want of prudence, and that negligence and irregularity, long continued, will make knowledge useless, wit ridiculous and genius contemptible.'[14]

At what period of his life, Carolan commenced an itinerant musician, is not known. Nor is it confidently told whether, like Arnaud Daniel, he *n'eût abord d'autre Apollon que le besoin*;[15] or whether his fondness for music induced him to betake himself to that profession; Dr. Campbell indeed seems to attribute his choice of it, to an early disappointment in love.[16] But we will leave the points unsettled, and follow our Bard in his peregrinations. — Methinks I see him mounted on a good horse, and attended by an Harper in the character of a domestic,[17] setting forth on his journey, and directing his course towards Connaught. Wherever he goes, the gates of the nobility and gentry are thrown open to him. Like the Demodocus of Homer,[18] he is received with respect, and a distinguished place assigned him at the table. Near him is seated his Harper, ready to accompany his voice, and supply his want of skill in practical music. — 'Carolan (says Mr. Ritson)[19] seems, from the description we have of him, to be a genuine representative of the ancient Bard.' . . . .

7. The leaves of the bay tree, a small Mediterranean evergreen, also called the laurel.
8. *recte* 'her'.
9. i.e. Charles O'Conor of Belnagare (1710-91).
10. Trophonius was a cunning architect of Greek mythology who was swallowed up by the earth and eventually became the god of an oracle in a deep cave. At this point, Walker has referred the reader to various descriptions of St Patrick's Purgatory in County Donegal and similar places of pilgrimage.
11. This is a mistranslation. It should read: 'by the hand of my godfather' (*cara Chríost*).
12. 'In the middle of the road of our life' — the first line of Dante's *Divine Comedy*.
13. A line from Dryden's translation of Virgil, *Aeneid*, I.
14. Samuel Johnson, *Account of the Life of Mr. Richard Savage* (1744).
15. 'He had at first no other inspiration (Apollo) than need.' Arnaut Daniel was a troubadour who flourished in the late eleventh century.
16. Thomas Campbell, *A Philosophical Survey of the South of Ireland* (London, 1778), p. 450.
17. Walker's note reads: '"He at all times, (says Mr. O'Conor) kept a good pair of horses, and a servant to wait on him." — The Bishop of Dromore informs us, that "in the early times, it was not unusual for a minstrel to have a servant to carry his harp." *Essay on Ancient English Minstrelsy* p. 25.' ['Mr O'Conor' was Charles O'Conor of Belnagare; Thomas Percy, bishop of Dromore, was editor of *Reliques of Ancient English Poetry* (London, 1765). Ed.]
18. Demodocus was a blind bard in Homer's *Odyssey*.
19. Joseph Ritson (1752-1803), the folklore collector. The quotation comes from his *Historical Essay on National Song* (London, 1783).

from:
AN HISTORICAL ESSAY ON THE IRISH STAGE (1788)

[In this essay, Joseph Cooper Walker pioneered the study of Irish drama. As often with his work, the footnotes contain as much information as the text.

The text is taken from *Transactions of the Royal Irish Academy 1788, Antiquities* (Dublin: Royal Irish Academy, 1788).]

In tracing the progress of society we discover the Drama amongst the first amusements of man. Soon as communities were formed, it appeared as well in the bleak regions of the North, as in those countries which feel the genial influence of the sun. Even History, when she first ventured to raise her voice, invoked the aid of the Dramatic muse. It is therefore very extraordinary that we cannot discover any vestiges of the Drama amongst the remains of the Irish Bards, or amongst the amusements of the vulgar Irish of this day,§ though a people so religiously observant of the customs of their ancestors.

It is true that some Irish poems are conducted in a kind of dramatic narrative, and it is probable that these poems were recited at the convivial feasts of the chiefs, and in the public conventions by several bards, each bard assuming and supporting a character in the piece:† but no production in a regular Dramatic form is extant in the Irish language,‡ nor even alluded to by any of our ancient writers. So that if the Stage ever existed in Ireland previous to the middle ages, like the 'baseless fabric of a vision' it has melted into air, leaving not a trace behind.[1]

Yet in the Dances of the vulgar Irish we may discover the features of a rude Ballet, performed in honor of some Pagan deity, and accompanied, it may be presumed, by hymnick verses; and in an ancient description of Tamer Hall, *Druith Righeadh*, or Royal Mimics or Comedians, are expressly mentioned.§§ All this, however, only serves to open a field to conjecture, affording no positive proof of the existence of a Stage amongst the early Irish.

We will then proceed to that period in which Irish history first introduces the Dramatic muse, mingling the waters of Jordan and Helicon.★[2]

That the Irish clergy, as well as their brethren in England, occasionally exhibited Mysteries and Moralities previous to the reign of Henry VIII,§ may be safely inferred from the following record preserved amongst the MSS. of Robert Ware.—

§ It must, however, be observed that the vulgar Irish of the present day exhibit, in many parts of the kingdom, several awkward attempts at Comedy at their weddings and wakes; but these attempts cannot be considered as vestiges of an ancient regular drama. These pieces are called, *The Cottoning of Frize*; *The Marriage Act*; *The Servants serving their Lord at Table*; *The fulling or thickening of Cloth*, and *Sir Sop or Sir Sopin, the Knight of Straw*. The design of the last is evidently to hold up to ridicule the English character, and cannot therefore be a production of high antiquity. I will here give a short analysis of this piece. The principal characters, are an Irish chieftain, who always takes his title from the Irish family of most consequence in the neighbourhood of the place where the play is exhibited; and an English chieftain, denominated Sir Sop or Sir Sopin. Sir Sop is dressed in straw, with a clogad or helmet of the same materials on his head; but the Irish chieftain, who is the favourite hero, is clad in the best clothes that the wardrobes of his rustic audience can afford. When those characters appear on the stage they are separately attended by inferior officers and servants, who, like the ancient Greek chorus, stand at a respectful distance, while the chieftains converse. Sometimes the chief officers are allowed to take a part in the dialogue. With the drift of the plot I am not perfectly acquainted, but know that the catastrophe is brought about by an altercation which arises between our two heroes, and terminates in single combat. In this combat Sir Sopin wounds his adversary, who falls, and a surgeon appears to examine the wound. Regaining his strength the Irish chieftain retires, followed by Sir Sopin. Soon after they enter again, and renewing the combat, Sir Sopin receives a mortal wound, and is borne off the stage. The Irish chieftain having thus gained the field, brandishes his sword and strides exultingly across the stage. Then pausing a while, he addresses himself to heaven, offering thanks for his victory. This done, the curtain falls. — The dialogue is extremely humorous, and interspersed with soliloques [*sic*], songs and dances.

† Some of the Poems to which I allude will be shortly given to the public, translated with elegance, spirit and fidelity, in *The Reliques of Irish Poetry*, now in the press.

‡ Mr. Macpherson has indeed given, as a translation from our Oisin, a little dramatic poem called *Comala*; ... But as the original of this poem has never been produced to the public, we cannot safely number it with the productions of our immortal bard. [James Macpherson's 'Oisin' was, of course, his invention. Ed.]

§§ *Collect. de Reb. Hib.* vol. III. page 531. [The six volumes of *Collectanea de Rebus Hibernicis* (1770-1804) were edited (and partly written) by Colonel Charles Vallancey. Ed.]

★ Perhaps I should have commenced the history of the Irish Stage with the rise of the Mummers in Ireland. 'The Mummers, (says DODSLEY) as bad as they were, seem to be the true original comedians of England.' *Collect. of Old Plays*, vol. i. pref. But the stage rather sprang from, than commenced with the Mummers. Here I will take leave to observe, that, at this day, the dialogue of the Irish Mummers in general (for I have collected it in different parts of the kingdom), bears a strict resemblance, in point of matter, with a specimen of the dialogue of the English Mummers in the reign of Edward III. which Mr. RITSON has happily rescued from oblivion. See *Rem. on the text, and last edit. of Shakespear*. It is also deserving of observation, that our Mummers are always accompanied by a Buffoon, whose dress and antic manners answer the description of the Vice of the old English comedies, the precursor of the modern Punch. This character likewise appears in the pageant with which the Irish rustics celebrate the first of May.

§ Although the classical names of Comedy and Tragedy did not obtain in England till the reign of Henry VIII. (see PERCY's *Reliq. of Anc. Eng. Poet.* vol. i. p. 137.) yet Sir James Ware, speaking of the rejoicings that followed the proclaiming Henry King of Ireland, enumerates comedies with the amusements on that occasion.... But Sir James, little skilled in polite literature, has probably dignified the rude Moralities of our ancestors with the appellation of Comedies.

1. Shakespeare, *The Tempest*, IV. 1. 151.
2. i.e. the Christian and the pagan. The succeeding paragraph is taken from one of Sir James Ware's manuscripts, later printed in Sir John Gilbert, *A History of the City of Dublin* 3 vols (Dublin, 1854-59) III, pp. 3-4.

'Thomas Fitz-Gerald, Earl of Kildare, and Lord Lieutenant of Ireland in the year 1528, was invited to a new play every day in Christmas, Arland Usher being then mayor, and Francis Herbert and John Squire bayliffs, wherein the Taylors acted the part of Adam and Eve; the Shoemakers represented the story of Crispin and Crispianus;[3] the Vintners acted Bachus and his story; the Carpenters that of Joseph and Mary; Vulcan,[4] and what related to him, was acted by the Smiths; and the comedy of Ceres, the goddess of corn, by the Bakers. Their stage was erected on Hoggin-green, (now called College-green,) and on it the priors of St. John of Jerusalem, of the blessed Trinity, and of All-hallows, caused two plays to be acted, the one representing the passion of our Saviour, and the other the several deaths which the apostles suffered.' From this record (which is the first express mention that has occurred to me of the representation of Mysteries and Moralities in Ireland) it should seem, that it was customary with the chief magistrates of Dublin to invite the Lord Lieutenant to a new play every day in Christmas;† and therefore, as I have already observed, it may be inferred, that Dramatic entertainments were exhibited in Ireland before this period. But it was not only to amuse the Chief Governor that Mysteries and Moralities were performed in Dublin: they were got up (to speak in the language of the modern theatre) on every joyful occasion. In a MS. in the library of Trinity College, Dublin, it is related, 'that in an expedition made against James Mac-Connell by the Lord Deputy Sussex in 1557, he was attended by John Usher, Captain, and Patrick Bulkeley, Petty-Captain, with sixty of the city trained-bands;[5] and upon their return THE SIX WORTHIES was played by the city, and the Mayor gave the public a goodly entertainment upon the occasion, found four trumpeters horses for the solemnity, and gave them twenty shillings in money.'

Although it may be presumed, that these exhibitions, as well as those in England at the same period, were conducted by the Church, yet we find, not only from the passages above quoted, but from the following entries in the CHAIN-Book of Dublin,[6] that the corporations usually supplied performers: it also appears from those entries, that the dresses, scenery and machinery, were likewise supplied by the city.

'It was ordered, in maintenance of the Pageant of St. George,[7] that the Mayor of the foregoing year should find[8] the Emperor and Empress with their train and followers, well apparelled and accoutered; that is to say, the Emperor attended with two doctors, and the Empress with two knights, and two maidens richly apparelled to bear up the train of her gown.'

'Item, 2dly. The Mayor for the time being was to find St. George a horse, and the wardens to pay 3s. 4d. for his wages that day: The bailiffs for the time being were to find four horses, with men mounted on them well apparelled, to bear the pole-axe, the standard, and the several swords of the emperor and St. George.'

'Item, 3dly. The elder master of the guild was to find a maiden well attired to lead the dragon, and the clerk of the market was to find a golden line for the dragon.'

'Item, 4thly. The elder warden was to find for St. George four trumpets; but St. George himself was to pay their wages.'

'Item, 5thly. The younger warden was obliged to find the King of Dele and the Queen of Dele, as also two knights to lead the Queen of Dele, and two maidens to bear the train of her gown, all being entirely clad in black apparel. Moreover, he was to cause St. George's Chapel to be well hung in black, and completely apparelled to every purpose, and was to provide it with cushions, rushes, and other necessaries for the festivity of that day.'....

†I have been informed, that it was also formerly customary with the several corporations of Dublin to invite the Chief Governor to a play at St. George's Chapel on the anniversaries of their patron Saints.

3. St Crispin was a shoemaker and became the patron saint of the craft. The (probably) apocryphal tale relates how the brothers Crispin and Crispian went from Rome to Soissons in France in the early fourth century to spread the Christian faith. They maintained themselves by making and mending shoes.
4. The god of fire and the patron saint of metalsmiths.
5. Usually spelt 'train-bands': locally raised bodies of citizen soldiers.
6. Probably the *Treasury Book of the City of Dublin 1541-1612*, kept in the Muniment Room, City Hall, Dublin.
7. The legend of St George (England's patron saint) and the Dragon describes the triumph of a Christian hero over evil. For a fuller account, see W. S. Clarke, *The Early Irish Stage* (Oxford: Clarendon Press, 1955), pp. 10-18.
8. supply.

CHARLOTTE BROOKE

(*c.*1740-93)

from:
RELIQUES OF IRISH POETRY (1789)

[Charlotte Brooke, daughter of the novelist, playwright and pamphleteer Henry Brooke, was encouraged in her interest in Irish literature by Joseph Cooper Walker. Her *Reliques* is the first extended translation of 'polite literature' from Irish into English, and its success shows that her interest in the subject was shared by many in the Ireland of Grattan's parliament. Her enthusiasm about the discovery of Irish literature is shown in the extract from the work's preface.]

PREFACE

... It is really astonishing of what various and comprehensive powers this neglected language [Irish] is possessed. In the pathetic, it breathes the most beautiful and affecting simplicity; and in the bolder species of composition, it is distinguished by a force of expression, a sublime dignity, and rapid energy, which it is scarcely possible for any translation fully to convey; as it sometimes fills the mind with ideas altogether new, and which, perhaps, no modern language is entirely prepared to express. One compound epithet must often be translated by two lines of English verse, and, on such occasions, much of the beauty is necessarily lost; the force and effect of the thought being weakened by too slow an introduction on the mind; just as that light which dazzles, when flashing swiftly on the eye, will be gazed at with indifference, if let in by degrees.

But, though I am conscious of having, in many instances, failed in my attempts to do all the justice I wished to my originals, yet still, some of their beauties are, I hope, preserved; and I trust I am doing an acceptable service to my country, while I endeavour to rescue from oblivion a few of the invaluable reliques of her ancient genius; and while I put it in the power of the public to form some idea of them, by clothing the thoughts of our Irish muse in a language with which they are familiar, at the same time that I give the originals, as vouchers for the fidelity of my translation, as far as two idioms so widely different would allow.

However deficient in the powers requisite to so important a task, I may yet be permitted to point out some of the good consequences which might result from it, if it were but performed to my wishes. The productions of our Irish Bards exhibit a glow of cultivated genius, — a spirit of elevated heroism, — sentiments of pure honor, — instances of disinterested patriotism, — and manners of a degree of refinement, totally astonishing, at a period when the rest of Europe was nearly sunk in barbarism: And is not all this very honorable to our countrymen? Will they not be benefited, — will they not be gratified, at the lustre reflected on them by ancestors so very different from what modern prejudice has been studious to represent them? But this is not all.——

As yet, we are too little known to our noble neighbour of Britain; were we better acquainted, we should be better friends. The British muse is not yet informed that she has an elder sister in this isle; let us then introduce them to each other! together let them walk abroad from their bowers, sweet ambassadresses of cordial union between two countries that seem formed by nature to be joined by every bond of interest, and of amity. Let them entreat of Britain to cultivate a nearer acquaintance with her neighbouring isle. Let them conciliate for us her esteem, and her affection will follow of course. Let them tell her, that the portion of her blood which flows in our veins is rather ennobled than disgraced by the mingling tides that descended from our heroic ancestors. Let them come — but will they answer to a voice like mine? Will they not rather depute some favoured pen, to chide me back to the shade whence I have been allured, and where, perhaps, I ought to have remained, in respect to the memory, and superior genius of a Father[1] — it avails not to say how dear! — But my feeble efforts presume not to emulate, — and they cannot injure his fame.

To guard against criticism I am no way prepared, nor do I suppose I shall escape it; nay, indeed, I do not wish to escape the pen of the *candid* critic: And I would willingly believe that an individual capable

1. i.e. Henry Brooke, who had died in 1783.

of no offence, and pretending to no pre-eminence, cannot possibly meet with any severity of criticism, but what the mistakes, or the deficiencies of this performance, may be justly deemed to merit; and what, indeed, could scarcely be avoided by one unskilled in composition, and now, with extreme diffidence, presenting, for the first time, her literary face to the world....

SONG
For Gracey Nugent§
By Carolan

Of Gracey's charms enraptur'd will I sing!
Fragrant and fair, as blossoms of the spring;
To her sweet manners, and accomplish'd mind,
Each rival Fair the palm of Love resign'd.

How blest her sweet society to share!
To mark the ringlets of her flowing hair;†
Her gentle accents, — her complacent mien!—
Supreme in charms, she looks — she reigns a
Queen!

That alabaster form — that graceful neck,
How do the Cygnet's down and whiteness deck!—
How does that aspect shame the cheer of day,
When summer suns their brightest beams display.

Blest is the youth whom fav'ring fates ordain
The treasure of her love, and charms to gain!
The fragrant branch, with curling tendrils bound,
With breathing odours — blooming beauty
crown'd.

Sweet is the cheer her sprightly wit supplies!
Bright is the sparkling azure of her eyes!
Soft o'er her neck her lovely tresses flow!
Warm in her praise the tongues of rapture glow!

Her's is the voice — tun'd by harmonious Love,
Soft as the Songs that warble through the grove!
Oh! sweeter joys her converse can impart!
Sweet to the *sense*, and grateful to the *heart!*

Gay pleasures dance where'er her foot-steps bend;
And smiles and rapture round the fair attend:
Wit forms her speech, and Wisdom fills her mind,
And *sight* and *soul* in her their object find.

Her pearly teeth, in beauteous order plac'd;
Her neck with bright, and curling tresses grac'd:—
But ah, so fair! — in wit and charms supreme,
Unequal Song must quit its darling theme.

Here break I off: — let sparkling goblets flow,
And my full heart its cordial wishes show:
To her dear health this friendly draught I pour,
Long be her life, and blest its every hour!—

§The fair subject of this Song was sister to the late John Nugent, Esq; of Castle-Nugent, Culambre. She lived with her sister, Mrs. Conmee, near Belanagar, in the county of Roscommon, at the time she inspired our Bard.' *Hist. Mem. of Irish Bards. Append.* p. 78.

†Hair is a favourite object with all the Irish Poets, and endless is the variety of their description: — 'Soft misty curls.' — 'Thick branching tresses of bright redundance.' — 'Locks of fair waving beauty.' — 'Tresses flowing on the wind like the bright waving flame of an inverted torch.' They even affect to inspire it with *expression*: — as 'Locks of *gentle* lustre.' — 'Tresses of *tender* beauty.' — 'The Maid with the *mildly* flowing hair,' &c. &c.

A friend to whom I shewed this Song, observed, that I had omitted a very lively thought in the conclusion, which they had seen in Mr. WALKER's Memoirs. As that version has been much read and admired, it may perhaps be necessary, to vindicate my fidelity, as a translator, that I should here give a *literal* translation of the Song, to shew that the thoughts have suffered very little, either of encrease or diminution from the poetry.

'I will sing with rapture of the Blossom of Whiteness! Gracey, the young and beautiful woman, who bore away the palm of excellence in sweet manners and accomplishments, from all the Fair-ones of the provinces.'

'Whoever enjoys her constant society, no apprehension of any ill can assail him. — The Queen of soft and winning mind and manners, with her fair branching tresses flowing in ringlets.'

'Her side like alabaster, and her neck like the swan, and her countenance like the Sun in summer. How blest is it for him who is promised, as riches, to be united to her, the branch of fair curling tendrils.'

'Sweet and pleasant is your lovely conversation! — bright and sparkling your blue eyes! — and every day do I hear all tongues declare your praises, and how gracefully your bright tresses wave down your neck!'

'I say to the Maid of youthful mildness, that her voice and her converse are sweeter than the songs of the birds! There is no delight or charm that imagination can conceive but what is found ever attendant on Gracey.'

'Her teeth arranged in beautiful order, and her locks flowing in soft waving curls! But though it delights me to sing of thy charms, I must quit my theme! — With a sincere heart I fill to thy health!'

The reader will easily perceive that in this literal translation, I have not sought for elegance of expression, my only object being to put it in his power to judge how closely my version has adhered to my original.

EDWARD BUNTING

(1773-1843)

from: A GENERAL COLLECTION OF THE ANCIENT IRISH MUSIC .... (1796)

[Throughout ascendancy Ireland during the last two decades of the eighteenth century, there was a growing interest in ancient Irish life and in Irish culture. In 1792, the Belfast Society sponsored a gathering of Irish harpers from all over the country and offered prizes for performance in various categories. Edward Bunting was employed to collect, transcribe and publish the airs they played, and his famous collections grew from this time. The airs that Bunting recording are the traditional ones handed down by harpers from generation to generation for a thousand years or more: the old-style Irish harpers were extinct within a few years of Bunting's publications and he can be credited with saving a musical heritage that otherwise would have been lost.]

PREFACE

It is an extraordinary fact, that although Ireland has from a remote antiquity, been celebrated for its cultivation of Music, and admitted to be one of the parent countries of that delightful art, the present is the first General collection of its national airs. Most of them are of such ancient origin, that the names of their authors, and the era in which they were composed, are alike unknown.

The works of some of its latest composers, as Conolan[1] and Carolan, have before been selected; but of these it remained to this day to give accurate copies; while the superior productions of their masters, on whom they had formed their style, and of whose excellence they have fallen short, are now only partially known in the very Country where they once flourished. To rescue them from oblivion, and to open a new source of Musical delight, the public are now presented with the first Volume of such a collection, as has for a long time been eagerly desired.

A brief account of the circumstances which led to this Collection will naturally be expected.

The rapid decrease of the number of itinerant Performers on the Irish Harp, with the consequent decline of that tender and expressive Instrument, gave the first idea of assembling the remaining Harpers dispersed over the different Provinces of Ireland. A meeting of them was accordingly procured at a considerable expense, by the Gentlemen of Belfast on the 12th of July 1792, and liberal Premiums were distributed amongst them, according to their respective merits.

The compiler of this Volume was appointed to attend on that occasion, to take down the various airs played by the different Harpers, and was particularly cautioned against adding a single note to the old melodies, which would seem from inferences, that will afterwards be drawn, to have been preserved pure and handed down unalloyed, through a long succession of ages.

A principal motive to convene this assemblage of the remnant of the Irish Bards, was to procure, while yet attainable, the most approved copies of tunes already in the hands of practitioners, as well as to revive and perpetuate a variety of others extremely ancient of which there were no copies extant and which were therefore likely to become extinct.

This end was, in a great degree, secured by the meeting alluded to; and it has since been perfected by the editor of the present work, who made a tour through a principal portion of the Kingdom for the purpose of comparing the Music already procured, with that in the possession of Harpers in other parts, and of making such additions as would render the work complete.

The work is now before that tribunal, which is the natural Judge of its merits, it may however without presumption, be alleged, that while public taste shall remain sufficiently pure and unadulterated, to be capable of admiring strains which lead directly to the heart, the ancient Music of Ireland will be studied with increasing delight....

1. Thomas Conolan, harper, born in County Sligo, *c.*1640.

II

The remaining passages in this section have been chosen to illustrate the personal side of life in eighteenth-century Ireland. They include diaries and letters, memoirs, travels and a sermon, and are drawn from the world of the Gaelic Irish, the Anglo-Irish, the English in Ireland and the Irish in exile.

JOHN VESEY

(1636-1716)

from: AN ACCOUNT OF SOME OF GOD'S PROVIDENCES TO THE ARCHBISHOP OF TUAM .... (1689-91)

[One of the most interesting of the many vivid accounts of the sufferings of Irish protestants during the reign of James II is that of John Vesey, archbishop of Tuam. Before his enforced departure to England, Vesey maintained one of the largest episcopal households in Ireland, a comfortable palace for his many children and numerous relatives and retainers. Not surprisingly (since Tuam is in a strongly catholic part of Connacht) Vesey had been harassed by his catholic neighbours during the first years of the reign of James II. He was eventually forced to leave and decided to go to England, where he remained until after the battle of the Boyne.

The text is taken from Richard Mant, *The History of the Church of Ireland* (2nd edition, London, 1841), I, pp. 747-50.]

... On the 29th of January 1688[1] I left my home at Tuam, leaving 6 small children, with several of my poor friends & relations, who depended on me, behind, bringing only my wife & 4 of my children with me: the parting was very sorrowful, and the weeping great. I left all my worldly substance, which was considerable, to the value of some thousands of pounds, in stock, furniture, & debts; but my library was to me the most valuable. On the 2nd of Feby following we came safe to Dublin, unmolested in the way, which within a week became impassable by the multitude of skein-men & half-pike-men now called Raparies.[2] On the 6th, (the day 2 years Tyrconill took the government in Ireland[3] & that day 4 years King James the crown in England) I took shipping in Dublin by licence under the great seal of Ireland; & on the 8th, after a most dangerous passage, landed at Hylake road at the point of Worrall in Cheshire,[4] having not in all the world with me above £60 or thereabouts. But Oh God! that wonderful deliverance from the perils of the sea was to me an earnest,[5] that thou wouldst preserve me on the land. Give me grace thankfully to remember it all my days and always employ that life in thy service, which thou didst so very graciously preserve; & grant that I may live to return, & see that Kingdom & Church which I then left in such desolation, in as great peace & happiness as sometimes I have seen it! I stayed at Chester till my servants came over to me, whom I left in Dublin to bring my horses after me: which being of good value, between 3 & 400£, I designed to have sold, & to have lived on the money, hoping it would, being managed with frugality, have maintained any great charge, till the storm that drove over me were passed. But I found the great seal was no protection to my estate that I had left behind: for Tyrconnell ... sent to the stables & took away my set of coach horses, and my pad[6] for his own use, & gave about

1. i.e. 1689.

2. skein-men: 'men with knives', from Ir. *scian* 'a knife'; half-pike-men: 'men with half or short pikes'; Raparies = rapparees: Irish bandits or robbers.
3. Richard Talbot (1630-91), earl Tyrconnell, lord deputy of Ireland at this time, who was replacing protestants with catholics wherever possible and sequestering the property of protestants.
4. Most ships between Dublin and England aimed to land at Chester. Hoylake Road would have been the first sheltered water for a boat heading for Chester. 'Worrall' is The Wirral, a peninsula in north-west Cheshire between the estuaries of the Mersey and the Dee.
5. pledge.
6. A slow riding-horse.

10 other saddle horses to his officers, which they divided among them by lot. On the news of this being done in Dublin, they made a garrison of my house at Tuam in the country, & took & spoiled all they could; driving away my stud,[7] seizing my corn, hay &c, turned out my children out of the house, acting all violences as they pleased, so that they must have perished, had not one person, a roman catholick gentlewoman (one of many of that religion whom I had obliged) been so charitable to take them into her care, which friendship I trust God will enable me to return, in some good office before I die. . . .

As I was coming out of St. Lawrence Jury church[8] on Tuesday May 28th '89 a clergyman pulled me by the gown, and in an entry[9] told me he gave me thanks for my sermon at St. Ann's on Whitsunday, and was sorry for my losses & my countrymens in Ireland; and putting a shilling into my hand desired me to accept it. I asked his name; he said it was not worth enquiring, but bid me thank God. I told him I did so, but desired his name: he said he was one Philips, & lived in Wiltshire. The good man seemed as if he rather wanted my charity. I considered his good will, & was afraid I should have put him out of countenance if I should refuse it, & also that it may be God sent him to try whether I was humble under my affliction; & therefore told him what he gave, I believed, in great kindness, I received with as much thankfulness. It may be it was his mite:[10] & may the cup of cold water given to a prophet, & by a prophet, have the reward of a prophet. I bent the shilling to distinguish it, resolving to keep it to the last if God be pleased to bring me to it: but unfortunately I lost it out of my pocket.

7. A collection of mares kept for breeding.
8. In London.
9. alley or passageway.
10. A coin of very small value. The word is used to echo Mark 12. 42 (in the King James Bible translation): 'And there came a certain poor widow, and she threw in two mites, which make a farthing.'

NAHUM TATE

(1652-1715)

LETTER TO BISHOP WILLIAM KING (1691)

[Nahum Tate, probably the second worst poet laureate ever appointed in England, is notorious as the man who altered Shakespeare's *King Lear* to remove its tragic elements. He was born in Ireland and met Bishop King while they were both at Trinity College, Dublin. He appears to have left Trinity to go to London after collecting his degree. Once there, he earned a precarious living as a hack writer and often seems to have been on the verge of starvation. However we do owe to him (see p. 407) the fine hymn 'While Shepherds Watched their Flocks by Night.' In the letter which follows, Tate hopes, apparently, to keep in contact with a friend from college days who might well be useful to him in the future.

The text is taken from TCD MS. 1995-2008/162.]

London, August the 10th 1691

My Lord,

Understanding that my last came not to your Lordship's Hands, I could not omitt this oppertunity of sending by my brother Simpson. My former was written on his behalf, whom I look upon to be a sincere, honest man. His Necessities and Integrity I know are sufficient Advocates with your Lordship to befriend him with what lies in your Power, and upon the first opportunity. But I am glad to find my Request forestall'd by your own kind Inclination expresst towards him in the Lettr he lately receiv'd from you.

There has nothing of late been more gratefull to mee than to hear of the Honour our Church has receivd by your Lordship's Promotion. The difference of Time and Deluge of Misfortunes that have overwhelm'd mee since I left Ireland have not (I can assure you) had the least Power to deface that Respect and Veneration which I conceiv'd for you upon our first Friendshipp in the Colledge. For to this very minuit I am sensible the same Affection *latet arcana non Enarrabile fibra.*[1]

Now if you should be inquisitive concerning so worthless a Friend as my Self, I can give you but this short unsatisfactory Account. *Vivo equidem vitamque extrema per omnia duco.*[2] For since betwixt the Sickness of my Body and the Vanity of my Mind I was ravished from the University and regular Course of Studdy, I have been forced to drudge for a subsistance by the worst Talent for a troubled nature and Age, — a task that I have now for many years been condemn'd to with more Irksomness and disappointment than I first enterd upon with pleasure and vain expectation. The only advantage that I have receiv'd from my troubles and disasters is an Indifference to this world, a weariness of Mankind, and most of all of my Self. For near twenty years that I have now been condemnd to sojourn in this noisy Town, I have always looked upon it as my Prison and what others call company no other than my Goalers [*sic*]. I have much more to impart, but shall deferr it till I have had the favour of a few Lines from you which I hope you have still so much kindness left as to oblidge mee withall.

I have not altogether so vainly imployed my Pen but that I have written some pieces of poetry which have been, for the sobriety of the matter, so well approvd of by our present Archbishop of Canterbury, that he has of his own accord promised to settle mee in some independent way of living. If I meet not soon with such an opportunity, I have thoughts, upon the Duke of Ormonds[3] return hither from Flanders, of coming back again to Ireland: Bread and silence being all that in this World I have any Ambition left for — beside my being neerer to so good a Friend as your self. I shall trouble you with no more at present but to begg your hearty prayers and continuance of your good will to

Your Lordship's
Most devoted Friend
& humble Servant,
N. Tate

1. Persius, *Saturae*, 5.29: 'latent arcana non enarrabile fibra' (What cannot be expressed lies in the recesses of my heart).
2. Virgil, *Aeneid*, III, 315: 'vivo equidem vitamque extrema per omnia duco' (I live indeed and drag on my life through all extremes).
3. James Butler (1665-1745), 2nd duke of Ormonde, was at this time in the Hague with William of Orange.

ANTHONY DOPPING
(1643-97)

from:
'ON SALVATION . . .'
A SERMON (1680s)

[Anthony Dopping, bishop of Meath 1681-97, was an important figure in the Church of Ireland during the reign of James II and, with William King, ensured its survival when it was under threat from the catholic majority. Dopping, who was married to the sister of William Molyneux, was a lively and entertaining man, much admired by many of his contemporaries. His sermon is included here as an example of the rather old-fashioned and almost metaphysical pulpit oratory of the time.

The text is taken from TCD MS. 1689.]

. . . You have heard that salvacion is difficult to be obtained, that the reason of this difficulty doth proceed from the depravity of our natures, from the rage and Impetuousnesse of our passions, from evill Customs and bad examples, from our busynesse in the world, and the indefinite rules of duty that are prescribed us. Since therefore our happynesse is so glorious, and yet the purchase of it so difficult and laborious, what remains then but that we ridd ourselves of that sloth and lethargy that hath possessed us, and learne to strive the more vigorously, because we have so many difficultys to incounter.

Let us not bee so stupid as to Imagin that religion

will cost us no pains, or the salvacion of our soules no care and endeavours after it: that happynesse should drop into our laps, without any designe or labor on our part, and that after we have done what wee please when wee live, God should snatch us up to heaven immediately when we dye. It would certainly be very unfit that so glorious and excellent a reward as the gospell promiseth should stoop downe like fruit upon a full laden bough, to be pluckd by every idle and wanton hand: that heaven should be prostituted to the lazy desires and faint wishes, to the cheap and ordinary endeavors of slothfull men. Surely God will not so much disparage that happynesse which hee hath prepared for the sons of men as to bestow it upon any who have conceived so low an opinion of it, as to thinke it not worth the labouring for.

And yet if we look into the generality of mens lives, and may be permitted to infer their opinions from their practises, we must be forced to conclude that the greatest number of Christians are of this opinion, because they live and act as if it were the most trifling and inconsiderable concerne they have to mind. Else how comes it to passe that they are more tender of their bodys then their soules, of their temporal then their spiritual concerns? That so many houres are spent at the taverne and so few at their devotions? So much mony lavished away at gaming, and so little expended upon the poore in charity? That they can sit up whole nights in the pursuit of unlawfull pleasures and when God and religion calls for their seirvices, they are not able to watch — no not an houre. Nay, which is worse th[a]n all this, that they continue in an open neglect of most dutys, and an habituall breach of the most Important, and yet thinke themselves in as faire a way for heaven as hee that makes conscience of the most trifling faults. Certainly these men either have no soules or no thoughts, either they are brute beasts, or they never thinke and consider of things; they neither reflect on their present or their future state, or if they doe, it is after so carelesse and transient a way that it leaves no Impressions behinde it. It is like a morning cloud, and as an early dew it passeth away.

Bee perswaded therefore to pawse and consider a little more seriously of things; weigh them in your thoughts, and reflect soberly within yourselves whither[1] the greatest rewards & the most excellent diadems are not worthy of the most active labors and endeavors. Whither a weake man, that wants mony & desires to compasse it, being promised a reward of a thousand pound for the bare portage of it,[2] would not stretch his fingers and tug hard before he would lose it for want of carrying. And shall heaven, which is a glorious and an excellent place, a treasury of content & an ocean of satisfaction be thought not worth the contending for?

Doe not all the usurers and merchants, all the labourers and tradesmen under the sun, toyle and care, labor and contrive, venter and complot[3] for a little mony, which few get, and scarce any man desires so much as to cover five acres of ground with? And is this pitifull scume,[4] this so poore a limited heepe of dirt, the reward of all the labor, and the end of all the care, the designe of all the malice and the recompense of all the wars in the world? And can it bee Imagined that life it selfe, a long, happy, and aeternall one, a perfect and a glorious Kingdome that shall never have an end, nor its joys abated with fears or jealousys, with care and sorrow, — that such a life and such a kingdome, should not be worth a few houres of seriousnesse? That a man that beleives there are such rewards, far more glorious then all his temporall acquisicions: and (I doe hope all that heare me this day, are of this beleife), that they are prepared for him, and that God designs to confer them, should not thinke it worth his while to quit an idle companion or a silly whore, a little drinke or the vitious[5] modes and customs of the world?

Certainly it is, and in the event of things will be found to be the wisest course; and though now in the impetuousnes of our lusts and passions, we doe not thinke so, yet the time will come when we shall find the Contrary, to our sorrow, and find all our opinions baffled and contradicted by the suddenesse of a late and deare bought experience.

Bee wise therefore on this side heaven, and learne to prevent your ruine, before it comes upon you; for the days will come when repentence and Consideracion will be out of date.

1. i.e. whether.
2. i.e. if he would just carry it.
3. take risks and plot together.
4. i.e. scum.
5. i.e. vicious.

JOHN DUNTON

(1659-1733)

from: THE DUBLIN SCUFFLE (1699)

[John Dunton, the eccentric London bookseller, came to Dublin in 1698 partly to hold book auctions and partly to satisfy his urge to travel. He here gives a vivid (if rather unreliable) account of his arrival in Ireland.]

. . . It was in *April* when I came to *Dublin*, and near Eleven a Clock at Night when I landed; so that it was with some difficulty that I got a Lodging for that Night; for which I own my self beholding to Mrs. *Lisle* (the Widow) at the *Dukes-head Tavern in Castle-street*, the first Place I drank at in *Ireland*. I have always *the Unhappiness of being sick at Sea*, which, though it be very irksome to bear, yet I find this good in't, that *it endears the sence of God's Goodness to me when I come to Land*, and makes me the more thankful for my Preservation. Which having perform'd as well as the Fatigue I had been under would permit, I betook my self to my Chamber, and *slept that Night without Rocking*; though in the Morning both my Bed and Chamber seem'd to me to have the same motion that my *fluctuating Cabin* had, the day before. Being got up the next Morning, I again renew'd my Thanks to God, for my Preservation at Sea, and safe arrival at *Dublin*. And now being *drest as it were in Print*, (for my business now was to see and be seen) I marched very *methodically* out of my Lodgings with two (*I can't say a pair of*) Gloves in one hand, and a Cane in t'other; .. . You wou'd smile, Madam,[1] if you had the *Picture of your quondam*[2] *friend at the black Raven*, like an over-grown *Oaf* newly come to Town, staring and gazing at all the Signs, and every thing else in the Streets; pacing out their length, and enquiring ever and anon, *What call ye this Street? Who dwells in yon great House? Whose fine Coach is that?* For thus I rambled through every Street, Alley, and corner of this spacious Town, as you'll find at large in my *Summer Travels*, where 200 Persons will see their Pictures,[3] that at present little expect it; but I leave 'em here, to tell ye the first visit I made in *Dublin*, was to *Nat. Gun*, a Bookseller in *Essex-street*,[4] to whom I was directed by my Friend, Mr. *Richard Wild*, (whom I had left behind me in *London*) 'This *Son of a Gun* gave me a hearty Welcome; and, to do him Justice, *he's as honest a Man as the World affords*; and is so esteemed by all that know him. He is a firm adherer to the established Government, and a declared Enemy to *Popery and Slavery*: So far from dissembling, that he knows not how to go about it; and will speak his Mind, how much soever it may be to his Prejudice. He understands *Stenography as well as Bookbinding*: and he himself is a sort of a Short-hand Character; for he is a *little Fellow*, but one that contains a great deal. And as he is a most incomparable Writer of Short-hand, so he speaks it as well as writes it; and to compleat his Character, He is a *constant shop-keeper*, without earnest Business calls him to the *Drumcondrah*.[5] This *Gun* was a constant and generous bidder at my *Auctions*, where he bought a great quantity of Books, which he as honestly paid for.'

At Mr. *Gun's shop*, I met with Mr. *Bently*, another Bookseller, but his principal Business is Binding; whom I afterwards employed considerably: 'He is a very honest Man, but has met with Misfortunes in the World, by thinking some others as honest as himself, who did not prove so. I ask'd Mr. *Bently*, whether there was not some Eminence in the City, from whence I might survey it? He told me there was; and that from the top of the *Tholsel*,[6] the whole City might be seen: so we went to the *Tholsel*, where we ascended about *half a score Stairs* from the Street, which brought us into a *spacious Room*, supported by great Pillars, and flagg'd (as they term it here) with free Stone,[7] with open

1. This section of the book is cast in the form of a letter to 'an Honourable Lady'.
2. former.
3. Dunton was threatening to write another book about his travels, and indeed did so. His *The Life and Errors of John Dunton Esquire* (1705) contains scores of pen-portraits or 'pictures'.
4. Dunton's is the only eyewitness account of late seventeenth-century Dublin booksellers and their opinions.
5. Drumcondra is now a district of Dublin, north of the Liffey.
6. The city hall.
7. flagg'd: paved; freestone: fine-grained limestone.

Banisters on each side towards the Street; its figure is rather *an oblong than a square*: This is the Place they call the *Change*, where the Merchants meet every day, as on the *Royal Exchange* in *London*. In a corner, at the *South-East* part, is a *Court of Judicature, where they keep their publick Sessions for the City*. Having view'd the lower part, we went up a large pair of Stairs into a publick Room, which had a *large Balconey* looking into *Skinner Row*; and from this Balcony I spoke with my Friend Mr. *Geo. Larkin*, who was then at Mr. *Ray's Printing-house* over-against it. He no sooner saw me, but came over to congratulate my safe arrival, expressing himself very joyful to see me; and I was as glad as he, we having a long time had a kindness for each other, and convers'd by Letter, even when I was in *America*. Having said so much of him, you'll not wonder, Madam, if I send ye an *Epitomy*[8] *of his Character*, (intending to do it more largely in my *Summer Ramble*) 'He is of a midling Stature, somewhat gross, of a Sanguine Complexion, and a hail Constitution both of Body and Mind; and (which I admire where ever I find it) he is of an *even Temper*, not elated when Fortune Smiles, nor cast down with her Frowns; and though his Stars have not been very propitious to him, with respect to his outward Circumstances, (he having had great Losses) yet he has born all with *such a presence of Mind*, as shew'd his Losses to be the effect of his Misfortunes, and not his Faults. His Conversation is extreamly diverting, and what he says is always to the purpose: *He is a particular Votary of the Muses*; and I have seen some of his *Poems* that can't be equall'd: But there is one thing more peculiar to him, which is, That whatever he does, *is upon the Account Civil.*'

I went up with my Friends (Madam) *to the top of the Tholsel*, and there had a View of the whole City; but a Storm that then arose, took from us much of the *Pleasure of the Prospect*: But of that, and the spacious Chambers over the *Change*, where the *Lord Mayor* and *Aldermen* meet, and other *Curiosities* which I saw there, as also of the Government of the City, (*by the Lord Mayor, Aldermen, and Assemblies*) I shall give a more particular[9] Account in my *Summer Ramble*. But this I will say here, (Madam) That of all the Cities in the Kings Dominions, *Dublin* (next to *London*) does justly claim the Precedence.

''Twas at the *Tholsel* I met Mr. *Dell*, a Person whose Understanding and generous Temper, set him above the *common Rate of Men, and shew him to be every way a Gentleman*: I could not but love him for these *qualifications*, but much more as he was an old Acquaintance of my *Honoured Mother-in-law*; and Madam, you can't blame me for this, as she treats me with that Tenderness, that I think her *my own Mother Reviv'd*, and I find shall love her as much. Mr. *Dell* shew'd me a most particular Respect at our *first Meeting*, and continued his Favours to the last Minute I staid in *Ireland*, being one of those that *were so obliging as to see me a Shipboard*.'

From the *Tholsel*, Mr. *Dell*, Mr. *Bently*, and I, were going to the Tavern, but Mr. *Larkin*, by the way, wou'd have me go into *Dick's Coffee-house, where I had been advis'd by* Mr. Wild, *to keep my Auctions*: I readily agreed to his Motion, and went up, saw it, and liked it, as proper for my Purpose; *Dick* shewing me all the Civility I could desire: And I must say this of *Dick*, (notwithstanding our after Quarrel) 'That he is a Witty and Ingenious Man, *makes the best Coffee in* Dublin; and is very Civil and Obliging to all his Customers; of an open and generous Nature; has a peculiar Knack at Bantering, and will *make Rhymes to any thing*: He's of a chearful facetious Temper, and generally speaking fair in his Dealing: And had not *Patrick* assaulted him with the Temptation of a *double Price*, he and I shou'd never have quarrel'd; and yet for all that, I must do him the Justice to say, he carry'd it civilly to me to the very last; and was so kind as to come (with my Friend Mr. *Dell*) to give me a *Farewell* when I left *Ireland*'; thus much for *Dick*: As for his Wife, I shall say this, 'She's an Industrious Woman, handsom enough, one that knows her Duty to her Husband, and how to *respect her Customers*; and in a word, is what a Wife ought to be; and I must own, though her Husband and I scuffled, she treated me always with much Respect.'

From *Dicks* we went to the Tavern, where having drank a Bottle or two (and related the Fatigues of my *Dublin* Voyage) we parted, and went each to our several Lodgings. In my way home I was attackt by an impudent Woman, who desired me to *bestow a Glass of Wine upon her*; I made her no other Answer, than that *the House of Correction stood not far off*; at

8. i.e. epitome: summary.
9. detailed.

which she scower'd away with *all the Heels she could make*, seeming as much scar'd, as if she had been in the most eminent danger of losing her Chastity; when perhaps she could scarce remember the time when she had it. I hope, Madam, you do not esteem any thing I have said here, to be designed *for the magnifying of my own Vertues*; it's practicable enough for a man to make his Reputation clear and not sin; and assure your self, I am not unsensible that *self-Praise is a most odious thing* in any, and I shall ever account it much more so in my self: However it be, Madam, all my Mistakes are entirely submitted to you, who are the best Judge of 'em.

The next day I removed to more convenient Quarters, and deliver'd some Letters which I had brought from *London*. This day Mr. *Dell* gave me a meeting at *Dicks*; from whence we went to the Castle, the *Place of Residence* for the Chief Governors; by Mr. *Dell*'s Interest I had here a view of the Lord *Galway*'s *Bed-Chamber, and other noble Apartments*, but I wave[10] 'em here, designing to speak of 'em in my *Summer Ramble*; however, I'll here attempts *his Lordships Character*, and hope my honest Intention herein will something attone for my great Defects; and the rather still, as his Lordships Merits are above a *Dryden*'s *or a Cowley*'s *Pen*.[11] I own 'tis a bold Undertaking, to offer at the *Character of one of the greatest Men* which our Age has produc'd, especially for one who has not the Honour of being *personally known to him*; however, though I can't perform this Great Task as it ought to be, yet I'll endeavour at *something so like him*, that any one at first glance may say 'twas meant for the Earl of *Galway*, one of the present Lords Justices for the Kingdom of *Ireland*. Then to proceed (tho' with a trembling Hand) to his *Lordships Character*.

The first thing then which is remarkable in him, is, 'He is a Person of *strict Morals, and extraordinary Piety*. His Lordship is advanc'd to the Honours he now enjoys, by his great Humility and Personal Merits. *The Noble Blood that has fill'd his Veins, has not swell'd his Heart*: He is as humble as he is great; he seems set by Heaven on such a conspicuous Place, (as is that of being Lord Justice of *Ireland*) on purpose to guide the People into the Paths of Love and Obedience to their God and King. In a word, he uses such an obliging meen[12] to all, as if he thought *the only thing valuable in Greatness, is the power it gives to oblige*. I wou'd go on with his Lordship's Character, but (as I said before) I find my self unable for this Task; so that (Madam) I shall next proceed (for his Lordship's Character leads me to it) to give some short Account of the *present State of the Kingdom*, according to my best Information, though you may wonder that *Dunton* should trouble his Head with *Politicks*; but since such is the *Custom of Travellers*, Why may not I thrust my self into the Herd? . . .

10. i.e. waive.
11. John Dryden (1631-1700), poet, playwright and critic; Abraham Cowley (1618-67), poet.
12. i.e. mien.

JONATHAN SWIFT
(1667-1745)

from:
TWO LETTERS TO CHARLES WOGAN (1732, 1735)

[In the spring of 1732, Swift received a green velvet bag from an unknown correspondent in Spain. It included an autobiographical history, a commentary on the psalms and some Latin poems. The author, Sir Charles Wogan, was a member of an old Irish family who had made a career for himself serving in continental armies and — among other things — had rescued Clementina Sobieski from Innsbruck so that she could marry the Old Pretender, James Edward Stuart. The letters that Swift sent to Wogan are respectful and friendly and hint at much better relations between protestants and catholics in the 1730s than the traditional view allows.

The texts are taken from Harold Williams (ed.), *The Correspondence of Jonathan Swift*, IV (Oxford: Clarendon Press, 1965), pp. 50-54, 468-700.]

[July-2 Aug. 1732]

Sir,

I received your Packet at least two Months ago, and took all this Time not only to consider it maturely myself, but to show it to the few judicious Friends I have in this Kingdom. We all agreed that the Writer was a Scholar, a Man of Genius and of Honour. We guessed him to have been born in this Country from some Passages, but not from the Style, which we were surprized to find so correct in an Exile, a Soldier, and a Native of *Ireland.* The History of yourself, although part of it be employed in your Praise and Importance, we did not dislike, because your Intention was to be wholly unknown, which Circumstance exempts you from any Charge of Vanity. However, altho' I am utterly ignorant of present Persons and Things, I have made a Shift, by talking in general with some Persons, to find out your Name, your Employments, and some of your Actions, with the Addition of such a Character as would give full Credit to more than you have said (I mean of yourself) in the dedicatory Epistle.

You will pardon a natural Curiosity on this Occasion, especially when I began with so little that I did not so much as untie the Strings of the Bag for five Days after I received it, concluding it must come from some *Irish* Fryar in *Spain,* filled with monastick Speculations, of which I have seen some in my Life, little expecting a History, a Dedication, a poetical Translation of the Penitential Psalms, Latin Poems, and the like, and all from a Soldier. In these Kingdoms you would be a most unfashionable military Man, among Troops where the least Pretension to Learning, or Piety, or common Morals, would endanger the Owner to be cashiered.[1] Although I have no great Regard for your Trade, from the Judgment I make of those who profess it in these Kingdoms, yet I cannot but highly esteem those Gentlemen of *Ireland,* who, with all the Disadvantages of being Exiles and Strangers, have been able to distinguish themselves by their Valour and Conduct in so many Parts of *Europe,* I think above all other Nations, which ought to make the *English* ashamed of the Reproaches they cast on the Ignorance, the Dulness, and the Want of Courage, in the *Irish* Natives; those Defects, wherever they happen, arising only from the Poverty and Slavery they suffer from their inhuman Neighbours,[2] and the base corrupt Spirits of too many of the chief Gentry, &*c*. By such Events as these, the very *Grecians* are grown slavish, ignorant, and superstitious. I do assert that from several Experiments I have made in travelling over both Kingdoms, I have found the poor Cottagers here, who could speak our Language, to have much better natural Taste for good Sense, Humour, and Raillery, than ever I observed among People of the like Sort in *England.* But the Millions of Oppressions they lye under, the Tyranny of their Landlords, the ridiculous Zeal of their Priests, and the general Misery of the whole Nation, have been enough to damp the best Spirits under the Sun.

I return to your Packet. Two or three poetical Friends of mine have read your Poems with very good Approbation, yet we all agree some Corrections may be wanting, and at the same Time we are at a Loss how to venture on such a Work. One Gentleman of your own Country, Name, and Family, who could do it best, is a little too lazy;[3] but, however, something shall be done, and submitted to you. I have been only a Man of Rhimes, and that upon Trifles, never having written serious Couplets in my Life; yet never any without a moral View. However, as an Admirer of *Milton,* I will read yours as a Critick, and make Objections where I find any Thing that should be changed. Your Directions about publishing the Epistle and the Poetry will be a Point of some Difficulty. They cannot be printed here with the least Profit to the Author's Friends in Distress. *Dublin* Booksellers have not the least Notion of paying for a Copy. Sometimes Things are printed here by Subscription, but they go on so heavily, that few or none make it turn to Account. In *London* it is otherwise, but even there the Authors must be in Vogue, or, if not known, be discovered by the Style; or the Work must be something that hits the Taste of the Publick, or what is recommended by the presiding Men of Genius.

When *Milton* first published his famous Poem, the first Edition was very long going off;[4] few either read, liked, or understood it, and it gained Ground merely by its Merit. Nothing but an uncertain State of my Health, (caused by a Disposition to Giddi-

1. dismissed from the army.

2. i.e. the English.

3. It is not clear which member of the Wogan family is referred to here.

4. i.e. sold slowly.

ness which, although less violent, is more constant)[5] could have prevented my passing this Summer into *England* to see my Friends, who hourly have expected me: In that Case I could have managed this Affair myself, and would have readily consented that my Name should have stood at Length before your Epistle, and by the Caprice of the World, that Circumstance might have been of Use to make the Thing known, and consequently better answer the charitable Part of your Design by inciting People's Curiosity. And in such a Case, I would have writ a short Acknowledgment of your Letter, and published it in the next Page after your Epistle; but giving you no Name, nor confessing my Conjecture of it. This Scheme I am still upon, as soon as my Health permits me to return to *England*.

As I am conjectured to have generally dealt in Raillery and Satyr, both in Prose and Verse, if that Conjecture be right, although such an Opinion hath been an absolute Bar to my Rising in the World, yet that very World must suppose that I followed what I thought to be my Talent, and charitable People will suppose I had a Design to laugh the Follies of Mankind out of Countenance, and as often to lash the Vices out of Practice. And then it will be natural to conclude, that I have some Partiality for such Kind of Writing, and favour it in others. I think you acknowledge, that in some Time of your Life, you turned to the rallying Part, but I find at present your Genius runs wholely into the grave and sublime, and therefore I find you less indulgent to my Way by your Dislike of the *Beggar's Opera*, in the Persons particularly of *Polly Peachum* and *Macheath*;[6] whereas we think it a very severe satyr upon the most pernicious Villainies of Mankind. And so you are in Danger of quarrelling with the Sentiments of Mr. *Pope*, Mr. *Gay* the Author, Dr. *Arbuthnot*, myself, Dr. *Young*, and all the Brethren[7] whom we own. Dr. *Young*[8] is the gravest among us, and yet his Satyrs have many Mixtures of sharp Raillery. At the same Time you judge very truly, that the Taste of *England* is infamously corrupted by *Sholes*[9] of Wretches who write for their Bread; and therefore I had reason to put Mr. *Pope* on writing the Poem, called the *Dunciad*, and to hale those Scoundrels out of their Obscurity by telling their Names at length, their Works, their Adventures, sometimes their Lodgings, and their Lineage; not with *A—'s and B—'s* according to the old Way, which would be unknown in a few Years.

As to your Blank-verse, it hath too often fallen into the same vile Hands of late. One *Thomson*, a *Scots*-Man, hath succeeded the best in that Way, in four Poems he hath writ on the four Seasons:[10] yet I am not over-fond of them, because they are all Description, and nothing is doing, whereas *Milton* engages me in Actions of the highest Importance, *modo me Romae, modo ponit Athenis*.[11] And yours on the seven Psalms, &c. have some Advantages that Way.

You see *Pope*, *Gay*, and I, use all our Endeavours to make folks Merry and wise, and profess to have no Enemies, except Knaves and Fools. I confess myself to be exempted from them in one Article, which was engaging with a Ministry to prevent if possible, the Evils that have over-run the Nation, and my foolish Zeal in endeavouring to save this wretched Island. Wherein though I succeeded absolutely in one important Article,[12] yet even there I lost all Hope of Favour from those in Power here, and disobliged the Court of *England*, and have in twenty years drawn above one thousand scurrilous Libels on myself, without any other Recompence than the Love of the *Irish* Vulgar, and two or three Dozen Sign-Posts of the *Drapier* in this City, besides those that are scattered in Country Towns, and even these are half worn out.[13] So that, whatever little Genius God hath given me, I may justly pretend to have been the worst Manager of it to my own Advantage of any Man upon Earth.

Aug. 2] What I have above written hath long lain by me, that I might consider further: But I have

5. Swift suffered from Ménière's syndrome, which caused him periodic giddiness and deafness.
6. John Gay (1685-1732) wrote his ballad opera after Swift had suggested the need for a Newgate prison pastoral. It was first performed on 29 January 1728 and became extremely popular. Polly Peachum and MacHeath are the two principal characters.
7. All members of the Scriblerus Club. This group of London wits and writers (which included Swift) assembled regularly during the early months of 1714 and continued literary contact with each other until at least 1730. *Gulliver's Travels*, Pope's *The Dunciad* and Gay's *The Beggar's Opera* are the major works normally associated with the Scriblerus Club.
8. Edward Young (1683-1765), whose fame as a poet rests on his *The Complaint, or Night Thoughts on Life, Death and Immortality* (1742-44).
9. i.e. shoal (as of fish). The reference is to the writers of Grub Street.
10. James Thomson (1700-48), whose *The Seasons* appeared in book form in 1730.
11. cf. Horace, *Epistles*, II, 1, 213: 'et modo me Thebis, modo ponit Athenis' (That poet puts me now in Thebes and now in Athens).
12. The 'wretched Island' is, of course, Ireland; the article in which Swift succeeded was the withdrawal of the patent for Wood's Halfpence.
13. After the affair of Wood's Halfpence, many pictures of Swift were hung in the streets and used as signs over shops and public houses.

been partly out of Order, and partly plagued with a Lawsuit of ten Years standing, and I doubt very ill closed up, although it concerns two Thirds of my little Fortune. Think whether such Periods of Life are proper to encourage poetical and philosophical Speculations. I shall not therefore tire you any longer, but, with great Acknowledgment for the Distinction you please to shew me, desire to be always thought, with great Truth and a most particular Esteem, Sir, | Your most obedient | and obliged Servant, | J. Swift.

We have sometimes Editions printed here of Books from *England*, which I know not whether you are in a Way of getting. I will name some below, and if you approve of any, I shall willingly increase your library; they are small, consequently more portable in your Marches, and, which is more important, the Present will be cheaper for me.

Dr. YOUNG's Satyrs	GAY's Fables
Mr. GAY's Works	Art of Politicks,[14] and
Mr. POPE's Works	some other Trifles in
POPE's DUNCIAD	Verse, &c.

14. *The Art of Politicks* (1729) by James Bramston.

1735[-6]

Honoured Sir,

I think you are the only person alive who can justly charge me with ingratitude: Because, although I were utterly unknown to you, and become an obscure exile in a most obscure and enslaved country;[1] you were at the pains to find me out, and send me your very agreeable writings, with which I have often entertained some very ingenious friends, as well as myself; I mean not only your poetry, in Latin and English, but your poetical history in prose of your own life and actions, inscribed to me, which I often wished it were safe to print here, or in England, under the madness of universal party now reigning:[2] I mean particularly in this kingdom, to which I would prefer living among the Hottentots, if it were in my power.

I have been often told, that you have a brother,[3] and some near relations in this country, and have oftener employed my friends in vain to learn when any of them came to this town. But, I suppose on account of their religion, they are so prudent as to live in privacy: Although the Court hath thought it better in point of politics, and, to keep the goodwill of Cardinal Fleury,[4] hath thought it proper, to make the Catholics here much more easy than their ill-willers, of no religion, approve of in their hearts. And I can assure you, that those wretches here, who call themselves a parliament, abhor the clergy of our church, more than those of yours, and have made an universal association to defraud us of our undoubted dues.[5]

I have further thanks to give you for your generous present of excellent Spanish wine, whereof I have been so choice, that my butler tells me there are still some bottles left. I did very often ask some merchants here, who trade with Spain, whether this country could not afford something that might be acceptable in Spain, but could not get any satisfaction. The price, I am sure, would be but a trifle. And I am told by one of them, that he heard you were informed of my desire: To which you answered in a disinterested manner, That you only desired my Works. It is true indeed that a printer here, about a year ago, did collect all that was printed in London which passed for mine, as well as several single papers in verse and prose, that he could get from my friends, and desired my leave to publish them in four volumes.[6] He reasoned, That printers here had no property in their copies: That mine would fall into worse hands: That he would submit to me and my friends what to publish or omit. On the whole, I would not concern myself; and so they have appeared abroad, as you will see them in those I make bold to send you. I must now return to mention wine. The last season for it was very bad in France, upon which our merchants have raised the price twenty *per cent*. already, and the present weather is not likely to mend it. Upon this, I have told some merchants my opinion, or perhaps my fancy: That, when the warmth of summer happens to fail in the several winc-countries, Spain and Portugal wines, and those of the South of Italy, will be at least as ripe as those of

1. i.e. Ireland.
2. i.e. the Whigs.
3. Presumably Mr Wogan of Rathcoffey, a relative of Wogan's, who is known to have been living in Ireland.
4. André Hercule de Fleury (1653-1743) was at this time the chief adviser to the young Louis XV and, from 1726 to his death, the effective ruler of France.
5. i.e. tithes.
6. George Faulkner's four-volume edition of Swift's *Works* appeared in 1735.

France in a good year. If there be any truth in this conceit, I would desire our merchants to deal this year in those warmer climates; because I hear that in Spain French vines are often planted, and the wine is more mellow; although, perhaps, the natural Spanish grape may fail for want of its usual share of sun. In this point I would have your opinion; wherein, if you agree, I will make Mr. Hall, an honest Catholic merchant here, who deals in Spanish wine, to bring me over as large a cargo as I can afford, of wines as like French claret as he can get. For my disorders, with the help of years, make wine absolutely necessary to support me. And, if you were not a person of too considerable a rank, (and now become half a Spaniard) I would try to make you descend so low, as to order some merchants there to consign to some of ours, directed to me, some good quantity of wine that you approve of: such as our claret-drinkers here will be content with. For, when I give them a pale wine (called by Mr. Hall *Cassalia*)[7] they say, it will do for one glass, and then (to speak in their language) call for Honest Claret.

7. A wine from Sicily.

LAETITIA PILKINGTON

(*c.*1707-50)

from: MEMOIRS [OF MRS LAETITIA PILKINGTON] (1748)

[When she met Swift — as recounted in the passage which follows — Laetitia Pilkington was only seventeen years old and recently married. Her girlish behaviour and innocence appealed to Swift and he allowed her and her husband Matthew, a poor clergyman with poetic aspirations, to spend a remarkable amount of time with him in his later years. Laetitia herself was of an amorous disposition and her husband eventually divorced her. Swift finally wrote of the Pilkingtons: 'He proved the falsest rogue and she the most profligate whore in either kingdom.']

. . . And now I must confess, as I have talked of ambition, I had a strong one to be known to Dr Swift. As Dr Delany[1] had recommended and introduced Mr Pilkington to him, and the learned lady before-mentioned,[2] I thought it a little hard to be excluded from the delight and instruction I might possibly receive from such conversation; and, having often remonstrated on this head to no purpose, I at last told them (for to give me my due I was pretty pert) 'that truly they were envious, and would not let me see the Dean knowing how much I surpassed them all.' As I spoke this but half serious, I set them all a laughing, and as they were to meet the next day at the Deanery House, to keep the anniversary of his birthday, I enclosed to Dr Delany the following lines:

To the Rev. Dr SWIFT, *on his Birthday*

While I the God-like men of old
In admiration wrapt behold!
Rever'd antiquity explore,
And turn the long-liv'd volumes o'er,
Where Cato, Plutarch, Flaccus shine
In every excellence divine;
I grieve that our degen'rate days
Produce no mighty souls like these;
Patriot, philosopher, and bard
Are names unknown and seldom heard.
Spare your reflection, Phoebus cries,
'Tis as ungrateful as unwise;
Can you complain this sacred day
That virtues or that arts decay?
Behold in SWIFT reviv'd appears
The virtues of unnumber'd years;
Behold in him with new delight,
The patriot, bard, and sage unite;
And Know, Ierne[3] in that name
Shall rival Greece and Rome in fame.

1. Patrick Delany (*c.*1685-1768), dean of Down and a friend of Swift.
2. Constantia Grierson (*c.*1704-32), classical scholar, wife of the printer George Grierson and another friend of Swift.

3. Ireland.

Dr Delany presented these lines to the Dean, and at the same time told him my saucy speech abovementioned. The Dean kindly accepted of my compliment, and said: 'He would see me whenever I pleased.' A most welcome message to me!

A few days after, the Dean sent the Doctor word he would dine with him at Delville,[4] and desired to meet Mr and Mrs Pilkington there. You may be assured I obeyed this welcome summons, and a gentlewoman[5] was so kind as to call on me to go with her. When we arrived, Dr Delany's servant told us his master, the Dean, and Mr Pilkington were walking in the garden; we met them on a noble terrace whose summit was crowned with a magnificent portico, where painting and sculpture displayed their utmost charms. The lady presented me to the Dean, who saluted me, and surprised me by asking her: 'If I was her daughter.' She smiled and said: 'I was Mrs Pilkington.' 'What', says he, 'this poor little child married! God help her, she is early engaged in trouble.' We passed the day in a most elegant and delightful manner; and the Dean, engaging Mr Pilkington to preach for him at the Cathedral[6] the Sunday following, gave me also, with the rest of the company, an invitation to dinner. As the Communion is administered every Sunday in this antique Church, dedicated to St Patrick, the first prelate who taught the Gospel in Ireland, I was charmed to see with what a becoming piety the Dean performed that solemn service; which he had so much at heart that he wanted not the assistance of the Liturgy, but went quite through it without ever looking in the Prayer Book. Indeed, another part of his behaviour on this occasion was censured by some, as favouring of Popery; which was that he bowed to the Holy Table. However, this circumstance may vindicate him from the wicked aspersion of being deemed an unbeliever, since 'tis plain he had the utmost reverence for the Eucharist. Service being over, we met the Dean at the Church door, surrounded by a crowd of poor, to all of whom he gave charity, excepting one old woman, who held out a very dirty hand to him: he told her very gravely: 'That though she was a beggar, water was not so scarce but she might have washed her hands.' And so we marched with the silver verge[7] before us to the Deanery House. When we came into the parlour, the Dean kindly saluted me, and, without allowing me time to sit down, bade me come and see his study; Mr Pilkington was for following us, but the Dean told him merrily: 'He did not desire his company'; and so he ventured to trust me with him into the library. 'Well', says he, 'I have brought you here to show you all the money I got when I was in the Ministry, but do not steal any of it.' 'I will not indeed, Sir', says I; so he opened a cabinet, and showed me a whole parcel of empty drawers. 'Bless me', says he, 'the money is flown!' He then opened his bureau, wherein he had a great number of curious trinkets of various kinds, some of which he told me: 'Were presented to him by the Earl and Countess of Oxford; some by Lady Masham, and some by Lady Betty Germain';[8] at last, coming to a drawer filled with medals, he bade me choose two for myself, but he could not help smiling when I began to poise them in my hands, choosing them by weight rather than antiquity, of which indeed I was not then a judge.

The Dean amused me in this manner till we were summoned to dinner, where his behaviour was so humorous that I cannot avoid relating some part of it. He placed himself at the head of the table, opposite to a great pier-glass[9] under which was a marble sideboard, so that he could see in the glass whatever the servants did at it. He was served entirely in plate,[10] and with great elegance; but, the beef being over-roasted, put us all in confusion: the Dean called for the cook-maid, and ordered her to take it downstairs, and do it less; the maid answered very innocently: 'That she could not.' 'Why, what sort of a creature are you', says he, 'to commit a fault which cannot be amended?' And, turning to me, he said very gravely: 'That he hoped, as the cook was a woman of genius, he should, by this manner of arguing, be able in about a year's time to convince her she had better send up the meat too little than too much done'; charging the men-servants: 'Whenever they imagined the meat was ready, they should take it, spit and all, and bring it up by force, promising to aid them in case the cook resisted.' The Dean then turning his eye on the looking-glass

4. Delany's house near Dublin.
5. Mary Barber (1690-1757), a minor poet and friend of Swift.
6. St Patrick's Cathedral, of which Swift became dean in June 1713.
7. The rod of office carried before a dean.
8. Noble friends from Swift's time in London 1710-14.
9. A tall mirror over the sideboard.
10. i.e. the dishes were all made of silver.

espied the butler opening a bottle of ale, helping himself to the first glass and very kindly jumbling the rest together, that his master and guests might all fare alike. 'Ha! friend', says the Dean, 'sharp's the word, I find; you drank my ale, for which I stop two shillings of your board-wages[11] this week, for I scorn to be outdone in any thing, even in cheating.' Dinner at last was over, to my great joy; for now I had hope of a more agreeable entertainment than what the squabbling with the servants had afforded us.

The Dean thanked Mr Pilkington for his sermon: 'I never', says he, 'preached but twice in my life, and then they were not sermons, but pamphlets.' I asked him: 'What might be the subject of them': he told me: 'They were against Wood's half-pence.' 'Pray, Madam', says he, 'do you smoke?' 'No, indeed, Sir', says I. 'Nor your husband?' 'Neither, Sir.' 'It is a sign', said he, 'you were neither of you bred in the University of Oxford; for drinking and smoking are the first rudiments of learning taught there; and in those two arts no University in Europe can out-do them. Pray Mrs Pilkington tell me your faults.' 'Indeed, Sir, I must beg to be excused, for, if I can help it, you shall never find them out.' 'No', says he, 'then Mr Pilkington shall tell me.' 'I will, Sir', says he, 'when I have discovered them.' 'Pray Mr Dean', says Dr Delany, 'why will you be so unpolite as to suppose Mrs Pilkington has any faults?' 'Why, I will tell you', replied the Dean; 'whenever I see a number of agreeable qualities in any person, I am always sure they have had ones sufficient to poise the scale.' I bowed, and told the Dean: 'He did me great honour.' And in this I copied Bishop Berkeley,[12] whom I have frequently heard declare: 'That when any speech was made to him which might be construed either into a compliment or an affront, or that (to make use of his own word) had two handles, he was so meek and so mild that he always took hold of the best.'

The Dean then asked me: 'If I was a Queen, what I should choose to have after dinner?' I answered: 'His conversation.' 'Pooh!' says he, 'I mean what regale?'[13] 'A dish of coffee, Sir.' 'Why then I will so far make you as happy as a Queen — you shall have some in perfection; for when I was Chaplain to the Earl of Berkeley,[14] who was in the Government here, I was so poor I was obliged to keep a coffee-house, and all the nobility resorted to it to talk treason.' I could not help smiling at this oddity, but I really had such an awe on me that I could not venture to ask him, as I longed to do, what it meant. The bottle and glasses being taken away, the Dean set about making the coffee; but, the fire scorching his hand, he called me to reach him his glove, and changing the coffee-pot to his left hand, held out his right one, ordered me to put his glove on it, which accordingly I did; when, taking up part of his gown to fan himself with, and acting in character of a prudish lady, he said: 'Well, I do not know what to think. Women may be honest that do such things, but, for my part, I never could bear to touch any man's flesh except my husband's, whom perhaps', says he, 'she wished at the Devil.'

'Mr Pilkington', says he, 'you would not tell me your wife's faults. But I have found her out to be a d—ned, insolent, proud, unmannerly slut.' I now looked confounded, not knowing what offence I had committed. ——— Says Mr Pilkington, 'Ay, Sir, I must confess she is a little saucy to me sometimes, but — what has she done now?' 'Done! why nothing but sat there quietly, and never once offered to interrupt me in making the coffee; whereas, had I had a lady of modern good breeding here, she would have struggled with me for the coffee-pot till she had made me scald myself and her, and throw the coffee in the fire — or perhaps at her head, rather than permit me to take so much trouble for her.'

This raised my spirits, and, as I found the Dean always prefaced a compliment with an affront, I never afterwards was startled at the latter (as too many have been, not entering into his peculiarly ironical strain), but was modestly contented with the former, which was more than I deserved, and which the surprise rendered doubly pleasing.

By this time the bell rang for Church; and Dr Delany and Mr Pilkington, who with myself were now all the company (for the rest departed before the coffee was out), were obliged to attend the summons. But, as there is no service in the Cathedral but Evening Prayer at six o'clock, I chose rather to attend the Dean there than go to hear

11. Wages allowed to servants to feed themselves.
12. George Berkeley (1685-1753), philosopher and bishop of Cloyne.
13. Choice article of food or drink.
14. Charles Berkeley (1649-1710), 2nd earl of Berkeley; Swift had been his chaplain when Berkeley was lord justice of Ireland.

another sermon: by this means I had him all to myself for near three hours, during which time he made me read to him the annals of the four last years of the Reign of Queen Anne, written by himself;[15] the intention of which seemed to be a vindication of the then Ministry and himself from having any design of placing the Pretender[16] on the throne of Great Britain. It began with a solemn adjuration that all the facts therein contained were truth, and then proceeded, in the manner of Lord Clarendon,[17] with giving the particular characters of every person whom he should have occasion to mention; amongst whom, I remember, he compared Lord Bolingbroke to Petronius,[18] as one who agreeably mingled business with pleasure. At the conclusion of every period, he demanded of me whether I understood it. 'For I would', says he, 'have it intelligent to the meanest capacity, and, if you comprehend it, 'tis possible everybody may.' I bowed, and assured him I did. And, indeed, it was written with such perspicuity and elegance of style that I must have had no capacity at all if I did not taste what was so exquisitely beautiful....

15. Swift's work was in manuscript at this time; it was published after his death.
16. James Francis Edward Stuart (1688-1766), called the Old Pretender because, as the son of James II, he was a claimant to the thrones of England, Scotland and Ireland.
17. Henry Hyde (1638-1709), 2nd earl of Clarendon, the most famous historian of the day.
18. Henry St John (1678-1751), viscount Bolingbroke, brilliant orator and Tory politician; Gaius Petronius was a Roman satirist of the first century A.D.

MARY DELANY

(1700-88)

LETTER TO MRS ANN GRANVILLE (1731)

[Mrs Delany, born Mary Granville and married to Alexander Pendarves when she was only seventeen or eighteen, was left a widow at the age of twenty-four. She first moved to Ireland in 1731 and sent a stream of letters describing life there to her sister and to other friends in England. Before she returned to England in 1733, she had met Dr Patrick Delany, later to become her second husband, and also Jonathan Swift, who became a friend and correspondent. As Delany's wife, Mary spent many years in Ireland and, after her second husband's death, she returned to London as a highly respected member of the social and cultural elite. At the end of her life, she became a close friend of George III and Queen Charlotte. This letter gives a vivid account of Irish social life in the early 1730s.]

Dublin, Nov. 25, 1731

I must tell you all that has passed since my writing to you last, which was on Thursday. I believe I told you then that we were to spend the evening at Mrs. Butler's.[1] Mrs. Usher, her son and daughter, gave us the meeting. There was a table of quadrille,[2] and one of commerce, of which party was your humble servant. We had a very genteel supper, and were very merry and easy. On Friday we went to the Castle; there was a great deal of company; that day we dined at Dr. Madden's,[3] who always enquires after you. Mr. and Mrs. Wesley[4] were there, they never omit asking how you do, and my good friend Mrs. Wesley joins heartily in wishing you here; Saturday we staid at home the greatest part of the day. I eloped for an hour or two to make a visit to a

1. Mary Pendarves — as she was at this time — was staying with the bishop of Killala, Robert Clayton, and with Mrs Clayton at their magnificent townhouse in St Stephen's Green, Dublin. They introduced her to a wide social circle in the capital and gave her an entrée to 'the Castle', i.e. Dublin Castle, the seat of the vice-regal court. (Only the most important of the social figures mentioned will be identified in the notes that follow.)
2. A card game for four players. 'Commerce' was a card game in which barter was an important feature.
3. Rev. Samuel Madden (1686-1765), clergyman, philanthropist and miscellaneous writer.
4. Mr and Mrs Wesley of Dangan, Co. Meath.

young lady who is just recovered of the small-pox. I think I never saw a prettier creature than she was before that malicious distemper seized her, — a gay, good-humoured, innocent girl, without the least conceit of her beauty; her father has been dead about six months, a worthless man that has left a very uncertain fortune; she paints delightfully. All the men were dying whilst she was *in danger*, but, notwithstanding their admiration of her, not one of them will be generous enough to marry her while the lawsuit is pending; now, indeed, even their adoration will cease, they will not acknowledge her for a divinity since she is divested of those charms that occasioned their devotion. Sunday to church we went — staid at home all the afternoon, Mrs. Percival[5] and Mrs. Usher of the company. Monday being St. Cecilia's Day it was celebrated with great pomp at St. Patrick's Cathedral. We were there in the greatest crowd I ever saw; we went at 10 and staid till 4; there is a very fine organ, which was accompanied by a great many instruments, Dubourg[6] at the head of them; they began with the 1st concerto of Corelli; we had Purcell's Te Deum and Jubilate; then the 5th concerto of Corelli; after that an anthem of Dr. Blow's, and they concluded with the 8th concerto of Corelli. Perhaps you think this was entertainment enough for one day; pardon me, we are not here so easily satisfied as to let one diversion serve for the whole day and we *double and treble* them. Lord Montjoy[7] made a fine ball for the Duke and Duchess of Dorset[8] and their retinue, our house was among the invited people, and Monday was the day fixed on.

After our music we returned home, eat our dinner as expeditiously as we could, and by seven (the hour named) we were all equipped for the ball; Mrs Graham, Miss Granville, and Miss Usher called on us, and we all went away together, nobody was admitted but by tickets. There was four-and-twenty couple, 12 danced at a time, and when they had danced 2 dances, the other 12 took their turn. No lookers on but the Duchess and Mrs. Clayton, who thought it beneath the dignity of a Bishop's wife to dance. The Duke danced with Lady Allen (the Duchess had the headache) Lord Mountjoy with Lady Caroline,[9] Mr. Coot with Lady Lambert, Capt. Pierce with Mrs. Donellan, and Mr. Usher with me; the rest were people you don't know at all.... Before the dancing began, the company were all served with tea and coffee; at 9, every lad took out his lass. At 11, those who were not dancing followed the Duke and Duchess up stairs to a room where was prepared all sorts of cold meats, fruits, sweetmeats, and wines, placed after the same manner as the masquerades. We eat and drank as much as we liked, and then descended to make way for the rest of the company. Mrs. Clayton went away at 12, the Duchess soon after that, and Phil and I staid till 1, and then with much difficulty made our escapes, the rest staid till 4 in the morning. On the whole, the entertainment was more handsome than agreeable, there being too much company.

The next morning we rose at 9 o'clock, put on our genteel dishabille,[10] and went to the Parliament House, at 11, to hear an election determined: the parties were Brigadier Parker the sitting member, and Mr. Ponsonby the petitioner, Mr. Southwell's interest was the first, and the last was Sir R[d] Mead's.[11] I believe we were the most impartial hearers among all the ladies that were there, though rather inclined to Mr. Southwell's side, but the cause was determined in favour of Sir R. M's. I was very well entertained there. Our cousins were also there. About 3 o'clock Mrs. Clayton went home to dinner with her Bishop; we were stout,[12] and staid. Mr. Hamilton, a gentleman I have mentioned to you, brought us up chickens, and ham, and tongue, and everything we could desire. At 4 o'clock the speaker adjourned the House 'till 5. We then were conveyed, by some gentlemen of our acquaintance into the Usher of the Black Rod's[13] room, where we

5. The wife of Robert Percival of Laracor, Co. Meath.
6. Matthew Dubourg (1703-67), 'Master of the State Musick in Ireland'.
7. Thomas Windsor, baron Mountjoy (died 1738).
8. Lionel Sackville (1688-1765), 1st duke of Dorset, lord lieutenant of Ireland 1730-37.
9. Lady Caroline Sackville, younger daughter of the lord lieutenant.
10. i.e. ordinary (not court) clothes.
11. On 23 November 1731, two days before this letter was written, the Irish parliament considered a petition from Richard Ponsonby in which he claimed that Brigadier Gervis Parker had been improperly returned as a member for the borough of Kinsale at a by-election caused by the death of Edward Southwell. After an examination of the poll book and of papers relating to seizures and forfeitures in the revenue for Kinsale, Parker 's election was overturned and Ponsonby declared elected. References to 'Mr Southwell' and 'Sir R. Mead' in Mrs Delany's text are clearly to the borough patrons, and it is interesting to note the way Mrs Delaney reports the outcome as though the candidates themselves were of secondary importance — which, of course, was true. (The editors are grateful to James Maguire for this footnote.)
12. courageous or resolute.
13. Usher to the House of Lords.

had a good fire, &c., and meat, tea, and bread and butter. Were we not well taken care of?

When the House was assembled, we re-assumed our seats and staid till 8; loth was I to go away then, but I thought that my kind companions were tired, and staid out of a compliment to me, so home we came, not a little fatigued with what we had undergone for two days together. Yesterday our assembly, today we shall spend peaceably by our own fireside, and talk over the passed hurries. Miss Forth's two sisters come to town, who are to be introduced to me today, 'tis one of them that paints *so finely*. I believe I did not write you word that Mrs. Foster is parted from her husband. Dean Berkeley[14] and his family are returned to England; they are not at Greenwich. They talk of coming to Dublin early in the spring; I wish they may for I want to be acquainted with him. Mrs. Barber[15] is still in England, she has not yet published her works; I wish she may not spend more money in pursuing this affair than the subscription will answer.

Adieu, my dear sister, — how I long for the packets![16] 'Tis terribly cold, but I wish for an easterly wind, though I would make me ten times colder; I know then I should have my heart warmed by some expressions of yours, without which I could hardly live, or live miserably, like the poor creatures in Greenland, when they lose their sun.

Yours for ever,

ASPASIA[17]

14. George Berkeley, the philosopher, at this time dean of Derry.

15. Mary Barber, the poet and friend of Swift.

16. i.e. the post brought from England in 'packet-boats'.

17. Many correspondents at this time used quasi-classical names for each other.

ANDREW DONLEVY

(*c.*1694-*c.*1761)

from: THE CATECHISM, OR CHRISTIAN DOCTRINE .... (1742)

[Andrew Donlevy's *Catechism* is the most important Irish-English bilingual work published in the eighteenth century; throughout, the Irish text is faced by an English text and the work contains also a long poetic abridgment of the Christian doctrine in Irish verse and a short treatise on the Irish language.

Throughout the eighteenth century, churchmen from curates to archbishops could be found working for the preservation of the Irish language which, by this time, had become closely involved with the catholic faith in Ireland. Catholic priests trained on the Continent for the Irish mission were expected to be able to minister through the medium of Irish, and Andrew Donlevy, prefect of the Irish College in Paris and titular dean of Raphoe, issued this bilingual catechism to help not only the priests but also the people in the transmission of the catholic faith. We print below a section of Donlevy's advertisement or preface and a section from the treatise on the Irish language.]

ADVERTISEMENT

The Bulk of this *Catechism* will probably, at first View, afright such as are used only to little *Abridgments*, *meerly* calculated for *Beginners*, and *chiefly for Children at their Horn-book*,[1] or thereabout. But, in opening it, they will find, it is in *two Languages*, and that, consequently, they have but *Half the Work* on their Hands: They will find by perusing it, that, in this *very Half*, there are several Things, not intended for charging the *Memory*, but for enlightening the *Understanding*, and moving the *Will* to the Practice of Virtue, and Flight of Vice; and that it is interspersed with short *Forms* of Acts of Devotion, and Prayers, to be used on different Occasions, and particularly before and after Confession and Communion, Morning and Evening, and at other Times; so, that it may serve as a Sort of *Prayer-book*, to such as have no better, nor much Time to spare: They will likewise see, that the Print is large, and much Waste occasioned, through the

1. Elementary school text, mounted between thin sheets of transparent horn.

Necessity of placing the Questions and Answers of both Languages, directly opposite to each other; and that some Paper is taken up by Quotations from Scripture, &c. and by Synonymous or Explanatory *Irish* Words: Lastly they will, towards the End, meet with an Abridgment of the *Christian Doctrine* in *Irish* Rhyme, composed upwards of an Age ago by the zealous and learned F. *Bonaventure O Heoghusa*[2] of the Order of *S. Francis*; and also with the Elements of the *Irish* Language, in Favour of such as would fain learn to read it; and thereby be useful to their Neighbour: Where likewise some little Latitude, taken here and there, throughout this Volume, touching the Manner of writing some *Irish* Words and Letters, is accounted for. Yet, notwithstanding this Variety of Subjects, no *one Half* of this Book, is near *half* as long as the Catechism compiled, but in *one Language only*, by Order of the Council of *Trent*,[3] and directed to all those, who have the Cure of Souls, with an Injunction to get it put into the *vulgar Tongue*, and *to teach it the People*; which, it seems, could not hitherto be done in *Ireland*....

It is the great Scarcity of those large *Irish Catechisms*, published upwards of an hundred Years ago, by the laborious and learned *Franciscans* of *Lovain*;[4] and the Consideration of those great Evils, which arise from Ignorance, partly for Want of instructive Books; together with a great Desire of contributing to the Instruction of the poor *Irish* Youth; that gave Birth to the following *Irish Catechism*: Wherein the Commandments, Sacraments, Prayers, &c. are treated more at Large than in any *Irish*, or perhaps, *English Catechism*, that hitherto appeared in Print: And whereby young People, and even those of riper Years may learn, through the Grace of God, to live *Christian-like*; and *be always ready to give some Satisfaction to every one, that asketh them a Reason of that Hope, which is in them.*

Endeavours were made to avoid foreign Expressions, save only such, as Religion had introduced, and are consecrated to it. The plainest and most obvious *Irish* is used therein, preferring, after the Example of S. Augustin, *rather to be censured by Grammarians than misunderstood of the People.* Care also was taken to explain certain Words, which are not used in some Cantons[5] of the Kingdom; ... As to the *English* Part thereof, it was translated, upon a second Thought, perhaps too litterally, from the *Irish*, in Favour of those, who speak only English. It was thought needless to point out, but in one Language, the Places of Scripture &c. from which this Doctrine is drawn; since the Questions and Answers of both Languages do exactly correspond. An Absence of upwards of 31. Years from one's native Country, and the profound Ignorance of the Printer, who understood not one Word of either Language, will be a sufficient Apology, for the Faults of both the Languages, and the Press.

THE ELEMENTS OF THE IRISH LANGUAGE

...*Poets*, not the Ancient and skilful, who took Pains to render their Poems sententious and pithy without much Clipping, but the *Modern Makers* of *Doggrel Rhymes* and *Ballads*; to save Time and Labour, introduced the Custom of clipping and joining Words together, in order to fit them to the Measure of their Verses: Others, who wrote in *Prose*, have, either in Imitation of the *Poets*, or through Ignorance and Want of Judgment, strangely clipped, and spelled, and huddled them together, as they are pronounced; let the Pronunciation be never so irregular and defective; not reflecting, that a *Poetical Licence*, *even* when Justifiable, is not imitable in *Prose*; or that Writing, as People speak or pronounce, is to maim the *Language*, to destroy the *Etymology*, and confound the *Propriety* and *Orthography*: for, not only the several Provinces of *Ireland*, have a different Way of pronouncing, but also the very Counties, and even some Baronies in one and the same County, do differ in the Pronunciation: Nay, some Cantons pronounce so odly, that the natural Sound of both the Vowels and Consonants, whereof, *even* according to themselves, the Words consist, is utterly lost in their Mouths. There are too many Instances of these Suppressions and Jumblings: A few will suffice

2. Bonaventura Ó hEodhasa (*c.*1570-1614), author of the pioneer catechism *An Teagasg Críosduidhe*, printed at Louvain.
3. The Council of Trent (1545-63) was the council of the catholic church that defined the catholic faith in the light of the threat posed by protestantism.
4. e.g. Ó hEodhasa, *An Teagasg Críosduidhe*.
5. regions.

here to shew the Abuse thereof: sgan, sgo, sme, stu, instead of agus gan, agus gur, agus me, or is me, agus tu, or is tu:[1] And all this Mangling and Confusion without so much as an Apostrophe('), to let the Reader see, that some Thing is left out. Again, mac a naṫar, Cuid a nfir, instead of an Aṫar an ḟir. The poor Particle *an* is divided in two, and one Half of it is joined to the subsequent Word, for no other Reason but that in the Pronunciation, the (*n*) comes fast and close upon the following Word, as it frequently happens in all *living Languages*; yet ought not to pervert, or alter the *Orthography*, or Order of Speech in Writing: However from this Fancy of Writing as People speak, chiefly arise not only the Mangling and Jumbling of Words, but also that puzzling Diversity found in the Writings even of those, who know the *Language* in Question, infinitly better than he, who has the Assurance to make these Remarks. But, either they have not reflected, or rather were resolved to imitate their Neighbours, who curtail and confound the different *Parts of Speech*, with far greater Liberty than the *Irish* do; for Instance: I'll, you'll, he'll, &c. cou'dn't, sha'n't, won't, don't, t'other, they're, ne'er, can't, ha'n't, and thousands of that Kind, which, although very fashionable, the judicious *English* Writers look upon as a great *Abuse*, introduced only since the Beginning of *King Charles* the *Second's* Reign; and endeavour to discredit it both by Word and Example.

It is no Wonder then, seeing the *English Tongue*, although in the Opinion of all, it be otherwise much improved, is thus maimed and confounded, *even in Prose*, that a *Language* of neither Court, nor City, nor Bar, nor Business, ever since the Beginning of *King James* the *First's* Reign, should have suffered vast Alterations and Corruptions; and be now on the Brink of utter Decay, as it really is, to the great Dishonour and Shame of the *Natives*, who shall always pass every where for *Irish-Men*: Although *Irish-Men* without *Irish* is an Incongruity, and a great Bull.[2] Besides, the *Irish-Language* is undeniably a very Ancient *Mother-Language*, and one of the smoothest in *Europe*, no Way abounding with Monosyllables, nor clogged with rugged Consonants, which make a harsh Sound, that grates upon the Ear. And there is still extant a great Number of old valuable *Irish Manuscripts* both in publick and private Hands, which would, if translated and published, give great Light into the Antiquities of the Country, and furnish some able Pen with Materials enough, to write a compleat History of the *Kingdom*: What a Discredit then must it be the whole *Nation*, to let such a *Language* go to Wrack, and to give no Encouragement, not *even* the Necessaries of Life, to some of the Few, who still remain, and are capable to rescue those *venerable Monuments of Antiquity* from the profound Obscurity, they are burried in?....

1. The complaint here is against the use of orthography which, although it reflects spoken realizations of the language, ignores the integrity of word forms and the grammatical constructions of Irish.

2. A self-contradictory proposition.

THOMAS CAMPBELL

(1733-95)

from: A PHILOSOPHICAL SURVEY OF THE SOUTH OF IRELAND .... (1778)

[Rev. Thomas Campbell, who was born in County Tyrone and educated at Trinity College, Dublin, was one of the most celebrated preachers of his day. In his *Philosophical Survey*, he adopts the persona of an English visitor to Ireland and describes the country with accuracy and humour. The letter below contains his impressions of Cork. Later, Campbell visited London and became known to Goldsmith, Johnson and Boswell; he makes a number of appearances in Boswell's *Life of Johnson*.]

[A DESCRIPTION OF CORK]

This is a city large and extensive, beyond my expectation. I had been taught to think worse of it, in all respects, than it deserves; it was described as the magazine[1] of nastiness. And as it is the great shambles[2] of the kingdom, I was predisposed to credit these reports; but it is really as clean, in general, as the metropolis. The slaughter-houses are all in the suburbs, and there, indeed, the gale is not untainted; but in the city, properly so called, all is tolerably clean, and consequently sweet. If sufficient care were taken, even the suburbs might be purged of every thing offensive, either to the sight or smell; for they stand upon the declivity of hills, and down each street there is a copious flow of water, perpetually washing down the filth, from the door of each slaughter-house into the river, which surrounds the town. The city is situated, as Spenser graphically describes it, in his marriage of the Thames and Medway.

> The spreading Lee, that like an island fair,
> Encloseth Cork, with his divided flood.[3]

This island is intersected with several canals, either natural or artificial, which, being banked and quayed in, bring up ships almost to every street. The city, however, is mostly composed of lanes, cutting the main-streets at right angles, and so narrow, that one of them, which is but ten feet wide, is called Broad-lane. The houses are old, and far from being elegant in their appearance. On the new quays, indeed, there are some fair looking buildings; which they are obliged to weather slate.[4] And this they do in a manner so neat as to render it, almost, ornamental.

There are two large stone bridges, one to the north, and the other to the south, over the grand branches of the Lee, besides several small ones, and some draw-bridges thrown over the lesser branches or canals. There are seven churches, an exchange, a custom-house, a barrack, several hospitals, and other public structures, yet none of them worth a second look. I have not seen a single monument of antiquity in the whole town, nor heard a bell in any of the churches, too good for the dinner-bell of a country squire. But here is something infinitely better. Here is the busy bustle of prosperous trade, and all its concomitant blessings; here is a most magnificent temple, erected to plenty, in the midst of a marsh. For that it was originally such, if there were no other evidence, the very name imports: the word Cork or Corrach signifying *palus* or fen, as I learn from Lhuid's dictionary.[5]

A bookseller here has put this, and other tracts into my hands, which have been useful to me in my researches. Smith's history of Cork, quoting Stanihurst,[6] reports that 120 years ago, Cork was but the third city in Munster, now it is the second in the kingdom, and therefore called the Bristol of Ireland.

Except in the article of linen, its exports are more considerable than those of Dublin. The balance of Trade, I should conceive, to be against Dublin, the trade of which, chiefly, consists in the importation of luxuries; whereas Cork deals almost entirely in exporting the necessaries of life, beef, pork, butter, hides, tallow, &c.

All the wealth of Munster and Connaught passes through two or three cities, which may be said to have eaten up the surrounding country, where the wretched peasant never tastes the flesh of the cattle which he feeds; but subsists upon potatoes, generally without butter, and sometimes without milk.

What proportion the trade of this city bears to that of Bristol, I have not *data* to form an estimate. If we were to judge from the richness of the shops, there is here a vast inferiority. In some other respects, Cork appears to be the greater city. In 1754 the return of houses in Cork was 7445, in 1766 it was 8113; if we suppose them to have increased at the same rate since, they are now 8614. This is placing them low, for there are great numbers of the poor legally exempted from paying hearth-money;[7] and it is not the interest of the collectors to exceed in their returns. In Bristol, and three miles round it, there are said to be but 9000 houses; if so, the houses in the city alone, are probably not so numerous as those of Cork.

In the reign of Edward IV[8] there were eleven churches in Cork; now there are but seven. Yet it

1. storehouse or district.
2. slaughterhouse.
3. Edmund Spenser, *The Faerie Queene*, IV, ix, 44, 3-4.
4. i.e. fasten slates to the outside walls to shield the houses from the weather.
5. Edward Lhuyd, *Archaeologia Britanica* (1707).
6. Charles Smith, *The Ancient and Present State of the County and City of Cork* (1750); Richard Stanihurst, *The Historie of Irelande* (1577).
7. A tax upon hearths or fireplaces, imposed during the reign of Charles II.
8. Edward IV was king of England 1461-70, 1471-83. The churches are those of the (established) Church of Ireland.

has ever since that time been esteemed a thriving city, and in the memory of man it is said to have been doubled. But we have already seen that the state of population cannot be ascertained from the number of churches; if our ancestors had not more religion than we have, they were certainly more addicted to building religious houses.

To see the reason, why the number of churches has decreased with increasing population, we should recollect, that in the time of Edward IV they had but one religion, that now they have many; and that the catholics outnumber all other denominations, seven to one at least.

As the Romanists adhere religiously to all their old institutions, in the number and division of parishes, and as they have now but seven mass-houses in so large and populous a city, we may fairly suppose that there were no more parishes in Edward's time; though there might have been eleven churches, reckoning in that number the chapels belonging to the four monasteries, which were then in Cork, viz. St. Dominicks's, St. Francis's, the Red Abbey, and the Cill Abbey.

It must too be observed, that though the monasteries are destroyed, the Monks remain to this day, and have regular service in their distinct houses, as in the parish mass-houses. In all of which they have a succession of services, on Sundays and holy-days, from early in the morning, till late at night, for the accommodation of their numerous votaries.

Beside these eleven mass-houses, there are four dissenting meeting-houses, belonging to Presbyterians, Anabaptists, Quakers, and French Protestants. The prevalence of Popish interest in Cork, may be argued from the following trivial circumstance: bidding a fellow whom I had picked up for my *ciceroni*,[9] to conduct me from the cathedral to the bishop's house, he asked me *which bishop?* The same conclusion I drew at Kilkenny, from another trifle; I there heard the titular bishop[10] greeted in the style of his dignity.

On Sunday morning early, I stepped into one of their mass-houses, and a spacious one it was. The priest had just finished the celebration of mass. On the altar stood six candles. A servitor came in, after the priest had withdrawn, and, kneeling before the altar, he entered the rails like those of our chancels; and, after kneeling again, he snuffed out two of the candles; then he kneeled again, and snuffed out two more; he kneeled a fourth time, and extinguished the fifth; the sixth he left burning.

There were several elegant carriages standing before the door when I entered, and a prodigious crowd of people in the street; as motley an assemblage of human creatures as I had ever seen. There was a multitude of beggars imploring alms in the Irish language, some in a high, and some in a low key. Some of them measured out tones as if singing; but in accents the most unmusical that ever wounded the human ear. They were worse than all the tones in Hogarth's *Enraged Musician.*[11] — If this be a bull, consider that I am in Ireland.

Had this Rabelais[12] of the pencil introduced an Irish beggar, he would have set Pasquali[13] mad. In the most perfect of human compositions, there is, you know, something still wanting to render it complete. Pity that the influence of a Cork mendicant should be wanting, to fill up the measure of discord, and thereby render one human production perfect.

Not content with what I saw at mass, I afterwards went to church, the steeple of which exactly answered Shakespear's description in *sloping to its foundation*:[14] which argues the fenny bottom,[15] whereon it stands. I was, however, delighted with the contrast I found here. The service was, throughout, performed with the utmost decency and propriety; they had a good organ, and the singing was remarkably good. The embellishments of the church were neither rich, nor studied; but they were neat and plain; and the audience had, truly, as much the air of opulence and elegance, as most of the congregations in the city of London.

After service they generally betake themselves to a public walk, called the Mall; which is no more than a very ill-paved quay upon one of their canals, with a row of trees on one side, and houses on the other. It is a pleasure, however, to see that they are filling up this canal, and several others, where the water, having no current, must have become noxious to the air in hot weather. On a bridge,

9. guide, someone who escorts sightseers.
10. i.e. the catholic bishop.

11. A satirical engraving by William Hogarth (1697-1764), celebrated caricaturist and social commentator.
12. François Rabelais (*c.*1494-*c.*1553), French humanist and satirist.
13. Niccolo Pasquali (died 1751), Italian composer and violinist, who lived in Dublin in the mid-1740s.
14. *Macbeth*, IV. 1. 58-59.
15. i.e. indicates the boggy valley.

thrown over this canal, is an equestrian statue of his late Majesty,[16] executed in bronze by an artist of Dublin. This with a pedestrian of Lord Chatham,[17] of white marble, and one in plaister of Paris, of king William III. in the Mayoralty-house, are the only statues in this large city.§

If this street were well paved, and the Mall flagged, it would be as ornamental to the town, as agreeable to the ladies. There is another public walk, called the Redhouse walk, west of the city, cut through very low grounds, for a mile in length, planted on each side, where the lower sort walk; and on leaving the Mall, I found it crowded with people, in general, very decently dressed. Farewell.

16. George II (1683-1760), who was on the British throne from 1727 until his death.
17. William Pitt (1708-78), 1st earl of Chatham; Pitt the Elder.

§ A gentleman, whom I heard of in almost every part of Ireland I visited, has this remarkable assertion, relative to the statue of Lord Chatham, marked in Italics, in his *Tour in Ireland*, published since this letter was written, *a house-painter was, at the time I was there, actually at work painting it in oil colours.* What led the *sagacious* and *learned* Writer into an error was this, a house-painter *did* paint in oil colours, the *plaister* statue of King William; which he mistook for the *marble* statue of Lord Chatham. Both of them have high noses and large wigs.

LE CHEVALIER DE LA TOCNAYE

(*c*.1767-?)

from: A FRENCHMAN'S WALK THROUGH IRELAND (1797)

[Jacques Louis de Bougrenet, Chevalier de la Tocnaye, was an officer and a royalist who had fled from France after the French Revolution. Penniless, he decided to walk the roads of England, Scotland and Ireland and to publish an account of his travels. He seems to have survived on the hospitality he received as he travelled. His description of Ireland on the brink of the 1798 rebellion is of great interest; he gives an excellent, and apparently unbiased, idea of ordinary life in Ireland during this time. The translation of his book, *Promenade d'un Français en Irlande*, was made by John Stephenson in 1917.]

... I came to Ardfert,[1] where I presented myself to the Dean, Mr. Grave, and was received as usual with that charming hospitality which always makes me forget, immediately, the fatigues of the road. Ardfert was formerly a bishopric; at present it is united to that of Limerick. In old times there were here many ecclesiastical establishments; the ruins of the old cathedral are the most remarkable remains, although nothing very great. The air of the place is said to be extraordinarily healthy. This has induced a celebrated surgeon to choose it for his place of burying; his tomb is constructed, and his epitaph engraved on it while he is still alive.

In ancient times there stood, in the cemetery of this cathedral, a high round tower with not more than the ordinary appearance of wear. It crushed itself, if the expression may be used, some twelve or fifteen years ago. I say 'crushed' because one would expect that such a building would naturally fall to one side or other, but in this case the stones appeared to tumble straight down, forming a large mass on the spot where the tower had stood. I went a little distance to see the venerable ruins of a Franciscan abbey, and, passing through the scattered debris of remains, I found myself in the presence of the two most beautiful and amiable ladies of Ireland, Lady Glandore and Mrs. Woodcock, who had resolved to be cruel enough to society to absent themselves from it for more than a year. I do not know whether it was their good example which affected me so much at the moment. Certain it is that never in my life did I feel such a desire to become a hermit.

At a little distance there is to be found one of those holy wells round which the inhabitants perform their devotions. This well is very famous, and the people come from afar. They pretend or assert that it can cure all evils, and the devotion consists in going round the well, bare-footed, seven

1. Ardfert, Co. Kerry.

times while reciting prayers, kneeling for a moment at each turn before a black stone, which seems to have been a tombstone, and, while kneeling, they rub the hand over three heads which are cut in the stone, and which are much worn by reason of this hand-rubbing and kissing. Afterwards they pass the hand which has touched the stone over the part of the body which is afflicted, drink a large glass of the water, and wash their feet in the current. Children are sometimes plunged seven times into the cold water, and I have seen people, well clad and having the appearance of being in comfortable circumstances, perform these ceremonies just like the others. I have also seen a very pretty young girl kissing these ugly stones, and I could not help thinking that I would have been a much better restorer if she had paid the reverence to me.

This well is widely renowned in the country, and even the Protestants, who are not very numerous here, when they have tried other remedies in vain, will make up their minds to try the well and go through the usual performances like their Catholic friends. The greater part of these peasants, however, come in a rather careless spirit, seemingly more with a desire to meet their friends than to perform penitences. Speaking to one of the visitors I asked him what was the benefit to be derived from this water. His reply was that he could not tell, and when I asked him why he went through the usual performances, all he could say was 'to do what the others do and to see the women.' In effect, it is at these wells that a great number of marriages are arranged. It is in vain that the priest of the parish has often forbidden his people to go to such places; they have followed this custom so long before the establishment of Christianity that they cannot be broken off it.

In reality, there can hardly be anything more innocent than to go round one of these wells a number of times reciting prayers, and afterwards drinking a glass of water. I will go so far to say that it must be very good for the health of the poor women, since it forces them to take some exercise and to clean themselves. The only thing left to the priest is to see that order is observed in these gatherings, and by his exhortations to warn his people against any impropriety or indecency, and in this the priest of this parish has perfectly succeeded. The good folk come here on Saturday morning and finish their devotions by two o'clock. Then the young fellows make up to their girls and see them safe home to their mothers, chatting the while.

Nearly all the people in this part of the country are Catholics, but Catholic and Protestant agree here very well. The priest performs mass, and the minister preaches, and the two flocks seem not to trouble themselves about each other's religion for the rest of the week. I went on Sunday to the Catholic chapel. The women are always separated from the men here. I suppose this to be to avoid distraction. In the middle of the service the priest made a long discourse in Irish, afterwards translating the principal part into English. He consigned to all the devils (although in highly proper terms) all those infamous enough not to pay his dues.

The priests have great power over their people. They are, in fact, the judges of the country and settle everything connected with morals and manners. They excommunicate a peasant and oblige him to leave a parish. Great care, then, must be taken not to displease them, and especially care must be taken that they get their dues. The Government knows perfectly well that the priests have their people in the hollow of their hand, and, nevertheless, they make enemies of them and treat them badly. Can they make the peasants go whatever way they wish? Well, make them your friends and you have gained the people. I am convinced that a dozen benefices in favour of Catholic priests, at the disposition of the Viceroy, would make them all as flexible and courteous and as desirous to please as their dear brethren in God, the ministers and bishops of the Protestant Church....

JONAH BARRINGTON

(1760-1834)

from: PERSONAL SKETCHES OF HIS OWN TIMES (1827-32)

[Jonah Barrington's famous *Personal Sketches* is a vivid and lively account of life in late eighteenth-century Ireland. The world of which Barrington writes in the extract below (the opening pages of the work) is that also evoked by Maria Edgeworth in *Castle Rackrent* and *The Absentee* — of hard-drinking squires, eccentric landlords and extraordinary mansions. Barrington himself, though a distinguished politician and lawyer was (rightly) accused of misappropriating public funds and had to leave Ireland in 1830. He died in France.]

I was born at Knapton, near Abbeyleix, in the Queen's County,[1] — at that time the seat of my father, but now of Sir George Pigott. I am the third son and fourth child of John Barrington, who had himself neither brother nor sister; and at the period of my birth, my immediate connexions were thus circumstanced.

My family, by ancient patents,[2] by marriages, and by inheritance from their ancestors, possessed very extensive landed estates in Queen's County, and had almost unlimited influence over its population, returning two members to the Irish Parliament for Ballynakill, counties of Kilkenny and Galway.

Cullenaghmore, the mansion where my ancestors had resided from the reign of James the First, was then occupied by my grandfather, Colonel Jonah Barrington. He had adopted me as soon as I was born, brought me to Cullenaghmore, and with him I resided until his death.

That old mansion (the Great House as it was called) exhibited altogether an uncouth mass, warring with every rule of symmetry in architecture. The original castle had been demolished, and its materials converted to a much worse purpose: the edifice which succeeded it was particularly ungraceful; a Saracen's head (our crest) in coloured brick-work being its only ornament. Some of the rooms inside were wainscoted with brown oak, others with red deal, and some not at all. The walls of the large hall were decked (as was customary) with fishing-rods, fire-arms, stags' horns, foxes' brushes, powder-flasks, shot-pouches, nets, and dog-collars; here and there relieved by the extended skin of a kite[3] or a king-fisher, nailed up in the vanity of their destroyers: that of a monstrous eagle, (which impressed itself indelibly on my mind,) surmounted the chimney-piece, accompanied by a card announcing the name of its assassin — 'Alexander Barrington'; — who, not being a *rich* relation, was subsequently entertained in the Great House two years, as a compliment for his present. A large parlour on each side of the hall, the only embellishments of which were some old portraits, and a multiplicity of hunting, shooting, and racing prints, with red tape nailed round them by way of frames, completed the reception rooms; and as I was the only child in the house, and a most inquisitive brat, every different print was explained to me.

I remained here till I was near nine years old; I had no play-fellows to take off my attention from whatever I observed or was taught; and so strongly do those early impressions remain engraven on my memory, (naturally most retentive,) that even at this long distance of time I fancy I can see the entire place as it stood then, with its old inhabitants moving before me: — their faces I most clearly recollect.

The library was a gloomy closet, and rather scantily furnished with every thing but dust and cobwebs: there were neither chairs nor tables; but I cannot avoid recollecting many of the principal books, because I read such of them as I could comprehend, or as were amusing; and looked over all the prints in them a hundred times. While trying to copy these prints, they made an indelible impression upon me; and hence I feel confident of the utility of embellishments in any book intended for the instruction of children. I possessed many of the books long after my grandfather's death, and have some of them still. I had an insatiable passion for

1. Now County Laois.
2. Official grants of land.
3. A bird of prey, belonging to the hawk family.

general reading from my earliest days, and it has occupied the greater proportion of my later life. Gulliver's Travels, Robinson Crusoe, Fairy Tales, and The History of the Bible, all with numerous plates, were my favourite authors and constant amusement: I believed every world of them except the fairies, and was not entirely sceptical as to those 'good people' neither.

I fancy there was then but little variety in the libraries of most country gentlemen; and I mention as a curiosity, the following volumes, several of which, as already stated, I retained many years after my grandfather and grandmother died: — The Journals of the House of Commons; Clarendon's History; The Spectator and Guardian; Killing no Murder; The Patriot King; Bailey's Dictionary; some of Swift's Works; George Falkner's Newspapers; Quintus Curtius in English; Bishop Burnet; A Treatise on Tar-water, by some other bishop; Robinson Crusoe; Hudibras; History of the Bible, in folio; Nelson's Fasts and Feasts; Fairy Tales; The History of Peter Wilkins; Glums and Gouries; somebody's Justice of Peace; and a multiplicity of Farriery, Sporting, and Gardening Books, &c. which I lost piecemeal, when making room for law-books — probably not half so good, but at least much more experimental.[4]

Very few mirrors in those days adorned the houses of the country gentlemen: — a couple or three shaving-glasses for the gentlemen, and a couple of pretty large dressing-glasses, in black frames, for the ladies' use, composed, I believe, nearly the entire stock of reflectors at my grandfather's, except tubs of spring water, which answered for the maid-servants.

A very large and productive, but not dressed-up garden, adjoined the house. The white-washed stone images; the broad flights of steps up and down; the terraces, with the round fish-pond, — rivetted my attention, and gave an impressive variety to this garden, which I shall ever remember, as well as many curious incidents which I witnessed therein.

At the Great House, where the Courts Leet and Baron[5] were duly held, all disputes among the tenants were then settled, — quarrels reconciled, — old debts arbitrated: a kind Irish landlord then reigned despotic in the ardent affections of the tenantry, their pride and pleasure being to obey and to support him.

But there existed a happy reciprocity of interests. The landlord of *that* period protected the tenant by his influence — any wanton injury to a tenant being considered as an insult to the lord; and if the landlord's sons were grown up, no time was lost by them in demanding satisfaction from any gentleman for maltreating even their father's blacksmith.

No gentleman of this degree ever distrained[6] a tenant for rent: indeed the parties appeared to be quite united and knit together. The greatest abhorrence, however, prevailed as to tithe proctors,[7] coupled with no great predilection for the clergy who employed them. These certainly were, in principle and practice, the real country tyrants of that day, and first caused the assembling of the White Boys.[8]

I have heard it often said that, at the time I speak of, every estated gentleman in the Queen's County was *honoured* by the gout. I have since considered that its extraordinary prevalence was not difficult to be accounted for, by the disproportionate quantity of acid contained in their seductive beverage, called rum-shrub[9] — which was then universally drunk in quantities nearly incredible, generally from supper-time till morning, by all country gentlemen — as they said, to keep *down their claret*.

My grandfather could not refrain, and therefore he suffered well: — he piqued[10] himself on procuring, through the interest of Batty Lodge, (a follower of the family who had married a Dublin grocer's widow,) the very first importation of oranges and lemons to the Irish capital every season. Horseloads of these, packed in boxes, were immediately sent to the Great House of Cullenaghmore; and no sooner did they arrive, than the good news of *fresh fruit* was communicated to the Colonel's neighbouring friends, accompanied by the usual invitation for a fortnight.

Night after night the revel afforded uninterrupted pleasure to the joyous gentry; the festivity

4. Barrington's list provides a fascinating insight into the literary taste of country gentry at the time, though several of the titles are impossible to identify. ('Some other bishop' is, of course, Bishop Berkeley.)
5. Regular assemblies of tenants and freeholders in the presence of the landlord.
6. i.e. seized a tenant's chattels if his rent had not been paid.
7. Agents who collected tithes — dues that had to be paid to the local clergy of the established Church of Ireland.
8. Bands of agrarian agitators active in the 1760s.
9. A drink of orange juice and rum.
10. prided.

being subsequently renewed at some other mansion, till the gout thought proper to put the whole party *hors de combat*; having the satisfaction of making cripples for a few months such as he did not kill.

Whilst the convivials bellowed with only toe or finger agonies, it was a mere bagatelle;[11] but when *Mr. Gout* marched up the country, and invaded the head or the stomach, it was then called *no joke*; and Drogheda usquebaugh,[12] the hottest-distilled drinkable liquor ever invented, was applied to for aid, and generally drove the tormentor in a few minutes to his former quarters. It was, indeed, counted a specific;[13] and I allude to it the more particularly, as my poor grandfather was finished by over-doses thereof.

It was his custom to sit under a very large branching bay-tree in his arm-chair, placed in a fine sunny aspect at the entrance of the garden. I particularly remember his cloak, for I kept it twelve years after his death: it was called a *cartouche* cloak, from a famous French robber who, it was said, invented it for his gang for the purposes of evasion. It was made of very fine broad-cloth;[14] of a bright blue colour on one side, and a bright scarlet on the other: so that on being turned, it might deceive even a vigilant pursuer.

There my grandfather used to sit of a hot sunny day, receive any rents he could collect, and settle any accounts which his indifference on that head permitted him to think of.

At one time he suspected a young rogue of having slipped some money off his table when paying rent; afterward, when the tenants began to count out their money, he threw the focus of his large reading-glass upon their hands: — the smart, without any visible cause, astonished the ignorant creatures! — they shook their hands, and thought it must be the *devil* who was scorching them. The priest was let into the secret: he seriously told them all it *was* the devil sure enough, who had mistaken them for the boy that stole the money from the Colonel; but that if he (the priest) was *properly considered*, he would say as many masses as would *bother fifty devils*, were it necessary. The priest got his fee; and another farthing never was taken from my grandfather.

My grandfather was rather a short man, with a large red nose — strong made; and wore an immense white wig, such as the portraits give to Dr. Johnson. He died at eighty-six years of age, of shrub-gout and usquebaugh, beloved and respected. I cried heartily for him; and then became the favourite of my grandmother, the best woman in the world, who went to reside in Dublin, and prepare me for college....

11. trifle.
12. Whiskey from Drogheda.
13. i.e. a specific remedy.
14. plain-woven cloth.

Biographies/Bibliographies

Michael Moore

LIFE. Michael Moore was born in Dublin in 1640. After studying philosophy and divinity in France, he returned to Ireland. In 1684 he was ordained by Luke Wadding, the Roman catholic bishop of Ferns. He became provost of Trinity College, Dublin in 1689, but the Jesuits resented him for persuading James II not to confer the college upon them. Later, the Jesuits procured Moore's deposition after one of his sermons had offended the king. He was ordered to leave the kingdom. Moore achieved distinction in Rome, where he became censor of books. He was highly regarded by Pope Clement XI and was made rector of Barbarigo's newly established college of Montefiascone. He moved to Paris on the death of James II and became rector of the University of Paris on two occasions. He also served as principal of the College de Navarre and was professor of Greek and Latin philosophy at the College de France. Moore went blind in later years and died in 1726.

CHIEF WRITINGS. *De Existentia Dei et Humanae Mentis Immortalitate* .... (Paris, 1692); *Hortatio ad Studium Linguae Grecae et Hebraicae recitata coram eminenti M. Antonio Barbarigo, Card. Archiep. de Montefaliscone* (Montefiascone, 1700); *Vera Sciendi Methodus* (Paris, 1716).

BIOGRAPHY AND CRITICISM. Patrick Boyle, 'Dr Michael Moore', *Archivium Hibernicum*, V (1916), 7-16.

William King

For biography and bibliography, see p. 804.

John Toland

For biography and bibliography, see pp. 803-04.

Thomas O'Sullevane

LIFE. Details about the life of Thomas O'Sullevane are elusive. Born in Tipperary about 1670, he is thought to have obtained a degree in law from the University of Paris about 1690-91. From 1711 he is recorded as being a member of the Middle Temple, London. It is known that he assisted Humfrey Wanley, keeper of the Harleian Library, on Irish manuscripts, from about 1713 until Wanley's death in 1726. Wanley described him as 'the best skilled in the Irish Antiquities of any man I ever knew'. O'Sullevane's chief claim to literary eminence is as the author of the anonymous, 114-page *Dissertation*, prefixed to the *Memoirs of the Marquis of Clanricarde*, which marked the first stage in the controversy over Dermot O'Conor's translation of Keating's *History of Ireland.* He died, probably in a debtor's prison in London, about 1726.

CHIEF WRITINGS. *Dissertation* ... prefix'd to the *Memoirs of the Marquis of Clanricarde* (London, 1722).

BIOGRAPHY AND CRITICISM. Ann de Valera, 'Antiquarian and Historical Investigations in Ireland in the Eighteenth Century' (unpublished MA thesis, National University of Ireland, 1978), pp. 25-28, 49.

Charles Smith

LIFE. Charles Smith was born in Waterford about 1715. He practised as an apothecary at Dungarvan, Co. Waterford, but is best known as the pioneer of Irish topography. He wrote a number of county and city histories. For many years it was believed that he co-wrote, with Walter Harris, *The Antient and Present State of the County of Down* (Dublin, 1744), but recent research suggests otherwise. While two of his books were researched under the auspices of the Physico-Historical Society, he was not a founder-member of that body. Thomas Macaulay praised his writings. He died in Bristol in 1762.

CHIEF WRITINGS. *The Antient and Present State of the County and City of Waterford* (Dublin, 1746); *The Antient and Present State of the County and City of Cork* (Dublin, 1750); *The Antient and Present State of the County of Kerry* (Dublin, 1756).

BIOGRAPHY AND CRITICISM. Ann de Valera, 'Antiquarian and Historical Investigations in Ireland in the Eighteenth Century' (unpublished MA thesis, National University of Ireland, 1978), pp. 62-67.

Joseph Cooper Walker

LIFE. Joseph Cooper Walker was born in 1761, probably in Dublin. Educated at first by Thomas Ball of Dublin, he travelled extensively in his youth, hoping to cure acute asthma. He spent many years in Italy and researched the literature of the country. The study of Irish antiquities was another of his favourite pursuits. On his return to Ireland, Walker stored various art treasures and a valuable library in his elegant residence, 'St Valerie' in Bray, Co. Wicklow. An original member of the Royal Irish Academy, he contributed various papers to its *Transactions*. He died in 1810, leaving behind several works in manuscript, including a journal of his travels.

CHIEF WRITINGS. *Historical Memoirs of the Irish Bards* (London, 1786; new edition, 1818); *Historical Essay on the Dress of the Ancient and Modern Irish*, to which is subjoined a *Memoir on the Armour and Weapons of the Irish* (Dublin, 1788; new edition, London, 1818); *Historical Memoir on Italian Tragedy* (London, 1799); *Historical and Critical Essay on the Revival of the Drama in Italy* (Edinburgh, 1805); 'Anecdotes on Chess in Ireland' in Charles Vallancey, *Collectanea de Rebus Hibernicis*, MDCC XC, Vol. 5, pp. 365-68 (Dublin, 1770-1804); *Memoirs of Alessandro Tassoni* (London, 1815).

BIOGRAPHY AND CRITICISM. R.A. Breathnach, 'Two Eighteenth-Century Irish Scholars: Joseph Cooper Walker and Charlotte Brooke', *Studia Hibernica*, 5 (1965), 88-97; Ann de Valera, 'Antiquarian and Historical Investigations in Ireland in the Eighteenth Century' (unpublished MA thesis, National University of Ireland, 1978), pp. 245-48, 252.

Charlotte Brooke

LIFE. Born about 1740, Charlotte Brooke was the youngest of twenty-two children fathered by Henry Brooke, author of *The Fool of Quality*. He educated her in literature, art and music. She devoted herself to the care of her father, but soon after his death she lost a considerable sum of money in an unsound business investment. Her family failed to obtain her a position in the Royal Irish Academy. Her interest in Irish poetry, signalled early when her translation of a Carolan poem was published anonymously in Joseph Cooper Walker's *Historical Memoirs of the Irish Bards* (1786), was the source of her best-known work. She died at Longford in 1793.

CHIEF WRITINGS. *Reliques of Irish Poetry* (Dublin, 1789; republished, 1818); *Emma; or, the foundling of the wood* (London, 1803); *School for Christians* (Dublin, 1809).

BIOGRAPHY AND CRITICISM. R.A. Breathnach, 'Two Eighteenth-Century Irish Scholars: Joseph Cooper Walker and Charlotte Brooke', *Studia Hibernica*, 5 (1965), 88-97; Ann de Valera, 'Antiquarian and Historical Investigations in Ireland in the Eighteenth Century' (unpublished MA thesis, National University of Ireland, 1978), pp. 246, 250-52; Robert Welch, *A History of Verse Translations from the Irish 1789-1897* (Gerrards Cross, Bucks: Colin Smythe, 1988), especially chapter 3, 'Joseph Cooper Walker and Charlotte Brooke', pp. 28-43.

Edward Bunting

LIFE. Edward Bunting, the son of a Derbyshire engineer, was born in Armagh in 1773. His eldest brother was an organist and music teacher at Drogheda, Co. Louth. Bunting pursued a similar career and went to Belfast in 1784 to be articled to Mr Weir, a local organist. His musical gifts enabled him to earn a living there, but his promise was diminished by a fondness for alcohol and a quick temper. He took a strong interest in old Irish music and travelled to other parts of Ulster, Connacht and Munster to gather material for a book on the subject. After spells in London and Paris, Bunting returned to Ireland via Belgium and Holland and in 1819 married a Miss Chapman. They moved from Belfast to Dublin, where he became a teacher and the organist of St Stephen's. He died in 1843.

CHIEF WRITINGS. *A General Collection of the Ancient Irish Music....* Vol. 1 (London, 1796); (reprinted Dublin: Hodges and Smith, 1851); *The Ancient Music of Ireland, arranged for the Pianoforte.* To which is prefixed a *Dissertation on the Irish Harp and Harpers, including an Account of the Old Melodies of Ireland* (Dublin, 1840); *The Bunting Collection of Irish Folk Music and Songs*, Parts 1-5, edited by Donal J. O'Sullivan, *Irish Folk Song Society Journal*, Vols. 22-27 (1927-36). (See Vol. 22, pp. xxxv-xxxvii, for a bibliography of Bunting's printed collections, compiled by Seamus O'Casaide.)

BIOGRAPHY AND CRITICISM. Charlotte M. Fox, *Annals of the Irish Harpers* (London: Smith, Elder & Co, 1911); Ann de Valera, 'Antiquarian and Historical Investigations in Ireland in the Eighteenth Century' (unpublished MA thesis, National University of Ireland, 1978), p. 252.

John Vesey

LIFE. John Vesey, born in Coleraine in 1636, led a busy life in the Church of Ireland and held a variety of posts. He is famed for his insistence on retaining the fourth part of all tithes collected in his archdiocese of Tuam, thereby seriously impoverishing the clergy and going against recent precedent. His behaviour in the affair was less than admirable. Vesey built a magnificent bishop's palace for himself, his wife and twelve children near Tuam. After the troubles referred to in the passage selected above, Vesey returned to Ireland and became one of the lords justices. He died in 1716.

CHIEF WRITINGS. (ed.), *The Works of ... J. Bramhall....* (London, 1676); *A sermon preached at Windsor before his majesty* (London, 1684); *A sermon preached before the Lord Lieutenant and the two houses of Parliament, in ... Dublin* (London, 1692); *A sermon preach'd to the Protestants of Ireland, in ... London, ... October 23 1689, being the day appointed for an anniversary thanksgiving for the deliverance ... from the bloody massacre of rebellion begun by the Irish papists on the 23d of October 1641* (London, 1689).

Nahum Tate

LIFE. Nahum Tate was born in Dublin in 1652. At the age of sixteen, under the name of Teate, he matriculated at Trinity College, Dublin. After obtaining a BA in 1672, he moved to London and began to write drama and verse. Many of his plays were adapted from earlier productions. His version of *Richard II*, staged in 1681 at the Theatre Royal as *The Sicilian Usurper*, was considered too controversial in the prevailing climate and was suppressed after three performances. Tate's version of *King Lear*, in which Cordelia survives and marries Edgar, superseded the original on the English stage until the 1850s. Tate became poet laureate on the death of Thomas Shadwell in 1692. Reappointed ten years later on Anne's accession to the throne, he also became the historiographer-royal. More an editor, translator or collaborator than an author in his own right, his *New Version of the Psalms* (written in collaboration with Nicholas Brady) contained 'While Shepherds Watched', later a famous Christmas hymn. Shielded from his creditors by the patronage of the Marquis of Dorset, Tate died in debt in London in 1715.

CHIEF WRITINGS. *Brutus of Alba, or, the Enchanted Lovers* (London, 1678); *Loyal General* (London, 1680); *The Sicilian Usurper* (London, 1681); *Lear* (London, 1681); *Ingratitude of a Commonwealth* (London, 1682); the second part of 'Absalom and Achitophel' (London, 1682); *Duke and No Duke* (London, 1685); *New Version of the Psalms*, in collaboration with Nicholas Brady (London, 1696); *Essay on Psalmody* (London, 1710).

BIOGRAPHY AND CRITICISM. Christopher Spencer, *Nahum Tate* (New York: Twayne, 1972); Christopher Spencer, 'A Word for Tate's *Lear*', *Studies in English Literature*, 3 (Spring 1963), 241-52; *The History of King Lear* by Nahum Tate, edited by James Black (London: Arnold, 1976). See Black's introduction (pp. xiii-xxxvii); James Black, 'The Influence of Hobbes on Nahum Tate's *King Lear*', *Studies in English Literature*, 7 (Summer 1967), 377-85; H.F. Scott-Thomas, 'Nahum Tate and the Seventeenth Century', *English Literary History*, 1 (1934), 270.

Anthony Dopping

LIFE. Anthony Dopping, born in Dublin in 1643, was educated at Trinity College, Dublin, of which he became a fellow in 1662. He was appointed, successively, bishop of Kildare and bishop of Meath. During the reign of James II, Dopping was an outspoken opponent of Tyrconnell and voiced the protestant viewpoint in the 'patriot parliament' of 1689. He wrote a number of works against presbyterians and catholics, as well as a preface to the Irish New Testament, and died in 1697.

CHIEF WRITINGS. *Modus tenendi Parliamenta & Consilia in Hibernia* .... (n.p. 1692); *A sermon preached . . . at the funeral of . . . Francis, Lord Archbishop of Dublin* (Dublin, 1694); *Speech of the Right Reverend Anthony, Bishop of Meath, when the Clergy waited on His Majesty at His Camp nigh Dublin, July 7 1690* (Edinburgh, 1690).

John Dunton

LIFE. Hopes that John Dunton, born in 1659, would become the fourth clergyman in the family line proved unfounded. Instead, at the age of fourteen, he was apprenticed to Thomas Parkhurst, a bookseller, and became a publisher in his own right. At first he enjoyed success and he married Elizabeth Annesley in 1682. The depression in trade caused by Monmouth's insurrection forced Dunton to move to New England. He returned to England in 1686 but ran into debt. After travels in Holland and Germany, he settled again in England, where he traded in books for ten years. On the death of his wife in 1697, he married Sarah, daughter of Jane Nicholas of St Albans. The couple soon separated and Dunton quarrelled with his mother-in-law, who accused him of not paying his debts. He arrived in Dublin in 1698 and sold books by auction. His disputes with Patrick Campbell, a bookseller, were typical of his entanglements, which he described in *The Dublin Scuffle* (1699). Subsequent writings showed him to be deranged. Despite publishing political pamphlets in support of the Whigs, Dunton failed to achieve the political recognition he craved. In 1733, twelve or thirteen years after the death of his second wife, he died in obscurity.

CHIEF WRITINGS. *The Athenian Gazette* (London, 1690-96); *The Dublin Scuffle* (London, 1699); *The Case of John Dunton, with respect to Madam Jane Nicholas of St. Albans, his mother-in-law* (London, 1700); *The Life and Errors of John Dunton Esquire* (London, 1705); *Dunton's Whipping-Post; or, a Satire upon Everybody ....* (London, 1706); *Athenianism; or, the New Projects of Mr John Dunton ....* (London, 1710); *Neck or Nothing* (London, 1716); *Mordecai's Memorial; or, There is nothing done for him; a just representation of unrewarded services* (London, 1716); *An Appeal to his Majesty* (London, 1723); *A Cat May Look at a Queen; or, a Satire upon her present Majesty* (n.d.)

BIOGRAPHY AND CRITICISM. Peter Murray Hill, *Two Augustan Booksellers: John Dunton and Edmund Curll* (Kansas: University of Kansas Libraries, 1958); Stephen Parks, *John Dunton and the English Book Trade: A Study of his Career with a Checklist of his Publications* (New York: Garland, 1976).

Jonathan Swift

For biography and bibliography, see pp. 393-94.

Laetitia Pilkington

LIFE. Born in Dublin *c.*1707, Laetitia Van Lewen was the second child of a male midwife of Dutch origin. Indulged by her father, she persuaded him to let her marry Matthew Pilkington, an Irish parson of modest means. She became friendly with Swift and is regarded as a valuable witness to his manners and the personal habits of his later years. Thackeray drew heavily on her anecdotes for his sketch of Swift in *English Humourists*. She separated from Pilkington and settled in London. In 1748 she was sued for debt and was jailed. On her release, she compiled her *Memoirs*. Following an unsuccessful attempt to become a book trader in London, she returned to Dublin, where she died in 1750.

CHIEF WRITINGS. *The Statues; or, the Trial of Constancy* (London, 1739); *Memoirs* 2 vols (Dublin, 1748); 3rd vol. (London, 1754); published subsequently as *Memoirs of Mrs Laetitia Pilkington*, 1712-1750, written by herself; with an introduction by I. Barry (London: G. Routledge & Sons, 1928); 'Poems' included in *Poems by Eminent Ladies* 2 vols (London, 1755); *The Celebrated Mrs Pilkington's Jests; or, the Cabinet of Wit and Humour* (London, 1764).

Mary Delany

LIFE. Mary Granville was born in 1700 in Wiltshire, England. Under pressure from her uncle, Lord Lansdowne, she married Alexander Pendarves about 1717-18. Pendarves, who was nearing his sixtieth birthday at the time of the marriage, died in 1725 without signing a will. His widow moved to Ireland in 1731, where she remained for almost two years. She became friendly with Mrs Grierson and with other literary ladies who followed Swift, and corresponded with the dean on an intermittent basis. She returned to London in 1733 and moved in society circles. The Duchess of Portland became a close friend. In 1743, despite opposition from her brother and her noble friends, she married Patrick Delany. In spite of his poor health and legal difficulties, they remained happy together until his death in 1768. A great favourite with the royal family, her portrait was painted twice by Opie, for George III and for Lady Bute. On the death of the Duchess of Portland in 1784, the king gave Mary Delaney a house at Windsor. Famous for her work with flowers and for her friendship with Fanny Burney, she died in 1788.

CHIEF WRITINGS. *Autobiography and Correspondence of Mary Granville, Mrs Delany*, edited by Lady Llanover, 6 vols (London: Richard Bentley, 1861-62).

BIOGRAPHY AND CRITICISM. Colwyn E. Vullimay, *The Life and Letters of Mary Granville, Mrs Delany, 1700-1788* (London: Geoffrey Bles, 1935); Edward Malins and Knight of Glin, 'Mrs Delany (Mary Granville) and Landscaping in Ireland', *Irish Georgian Society Quarterly Bulletin*, 11, Nos 2-3 (1968), 1-16.

Andrew Donlevy

LIFE. Little is known about the life of Andrew Donlevy. He was born about 1694, probably in Sligo. His early education was gained near Ballymote, Co. Sligo. He arrived in Paris in 1710 and studied in the Irish College, of which he later became prefect. Donlevy took a licentiate of laws in the University of Paris. According to Walter Harris, he became titular dean of Raphoe. Little else has been established about his ecclesiastical career. He is known to have been still alive early in 1761 and is thought to have died later that year.

CHIEF WRITINGS. *An Teagasg Críosduidhe do reir ceasada agus freagartha . . . .* (*The Catechism, or Christian Doctrine, by way of questions and answers . . . .*, Paris, 1742; 2nd edition, Dublin, 1822; 3rd edition, Dublin, 1848); 'The Elements of the Irish Language' (treatise in Paris, 1742 edition of *An Teagasg Críosduidhe*).

Thomas Campbell

LIFE. Born at Glack, Co. Tyrone in 1733, Thomas Campbell studied at Trinity College, Dublin. He was awarded a BA in 1756 and an MA five years later. He took orders and served as curate of Clogher until 1772, when he was collated to the prebend of Tyholland. Highly regarded as a preacher, he became chancellor of St Macartin's, Clogher, in 1773. His *Philosophical Survey of the South of Ireland*, described by Boswell as 'a very entertaining book', contained, for the first time in print, Johnson's epitaph on Goldsmith. Campbell himself wrote part of the memoir of Goldsmith in Bishop Percy's work (1801). He was an advocate of political and commercial union with England. Campbell died in 1795.

CHIEF WRITINGS. *Diary of a Visit to England in 1775* (Sydney: D.N. Welch, 1854); *A Philosophical Survey of the South of Ireland in a series of letters to John Watkinson, M.P.* (Dublin, 1778); *Strictures on the Ecclesiastical and Literary History of Ireland till the Introduction of the Roman Ritual, and the Establishment of Papal Supremacy by Henry II* (Dublin, 1789). (To this was added *Sketch of the Constitution and Government of Ireland down to 1783.*)

BIOGRAPHY AND CRITICISM. Ann de Valera, 'Antiquarian and Historical Investigations in Ireland in the Eighteenth Century' (unpublished MA thesis, National University of Ireland, 1978), pp. 188-92, 206-09.

Le Chevalier de la Tocnaye

LIFE. Jacques Louis de Bougrenet, Chevalier de la Tocnaye, was born a French aristocrat in Brittany about 1767. Forced to flee from France after the French Revolution, he wandered around England and Scotland and published *Promenade autour de la Grande Bretagne* (1795). He then came to Ireland and toured most of the country on foot in 1796 and 1797, with no baggage and no provisions. He had intended to walk the canals and to visit the coalmines of Kilkenny and Leitrim, but the unsettled state of the country forced him to curtail his tour and finish his book quickly. *Promenade d'un Français en Irlande* was published in Dublin in 1797 and its author left the country only a few months before the beginning of the 1798 rebellion.

CHIEF WRITINGS. *Promenade autour de la Grande Bretagne par un officier français emigré* (Edinburgh, 1795); *Promenade d'un Français dans l'Irlande* (Dublin, 1797); *Promenade d'un Français en Suède et en Norvège* (Brunswick, 1801); *A Frenchman's Walk through Ireland 1796-7*, translated by John Stevenson (Belfast: McCaw, Stevenson & Orr, 1917).

BIOGRAPHY AND CRITICISM. See the introduction by John A. Gamble in the reprint of John Stevenson's translation (Belfast: Blackstaff Press, 1985). See also p. 289 of the same edition for conflicting bibliographical information.

Jonah Barrington

LIFE. Jonah Barrington was born near Abbeyleix, Co. Laois in 1760. He studied law at Trinity College, Dublin and was called to the bar. He took silk in 1793 and five years later became a judge in the admiralty. Elected MP for Tuam in 1790, he lost his seat in 1797 but returned to parliament as the member for Clogher the next year. Barrington contested the constituency of Dublin city without success in 1802. He was strongly opposed to union with England, rejecting Lord Clare's offer of the solicitor generalship in 1799. His own stance, however, does not seem to have prevented him bribing other members on the issue. Knighted in 1807, his extravagant lifestyle led him into debt. In 1830 Barrington was found guilty of misappropriating public funds by a commission of inquiry into the Irish courts and was deprived of his office. He went to France, where he died in 1834.

CHIEF WRITINGS. *Personal Sketches of his own Times* 3 vols (London, 1827-32); *Historic Memoirs of Ireland* 2 vols (London, 1832); *The Rise and Fall of the Irish Nation* (Paris, 1833).

W. J. Mc CORMACK, *Editor*

Maria Edgeworth

(1768-1849)

Maria Edgeworth is the central figure in Irish literary history between Swift and the modernist generation of Shaw and Yeats. Her exact place within that history is more difficult to define. Educated by her father in the values of a distinctive English Enlightenment culture, she is remembered today as the instigator of a distinctive Irish regional fiction. Before publishing *Castle Rackrent* in 1800, she had written several works of a didactic kind, many of them for children, and tales of fashionable English and continental society also formed part of her prolific output between 1795 and 1835. Her achievement as an Irish novelist should always be seen in that wider context. It extends that achievement beyond the definitions of the Irish novel that were later to be developed in the nineteenth century.

Her father, Richard Lovell Edgeworth (1744-1817), was descended from an English family which had acquired property in the Irish midlands from the end of the sixteenth century and had added to these holdings since then. Edgeworth was a friend of and collaborator with several prominent English scientists and savants. In 1782, he decided to return to his Irish estates, bringing with him an extensive family, including his daughter Maria, who had been born in Oxfordshire in 1768. The essentially rational and proto-utilitarian interests of Edgeworth and his English associates (Erasmus Darwin, Thomas Day and, later, Sir Humphry Davy) are reflected in his daughter's early writings and contribute to the didactic tone which informs the series of tales that began with *Letters for Literary Ladies* (1795). But her removal to Edgeworthstown, Co. Longford, in the year when Ireland's exclusively protestant parliament gained a measure of independence from Britain, left no real imprint on her writing until 1800, when she published anonymously the novel upon which her fame has since rested. Its full (and highly revealing) title is *Castle Rackrent, an Hibernian Tale: Taken from the Facts, and from the Manners of the Irish Squires, before the year 1782.*

Castle Rackrent is a minor masterpiece in the annals of fiction written in English. In the annals of Irish literary history, it is perhaps too well-known or (more accurately) too much taken for granted. We shall in due course consider some neglected aspects of its highly complex narrative, but for the moment we must observe some of the implications of the novel's title. The setting of the fiction is ostentatiously given as *prior* to 1782, but an examination of the novel's origins reveals many references to and aspects of contemporary politics, mistakenly consigned to the early history of the Rackrent family by several commentators. Moreover, the novel's full title, in juxtaposing the adjectives 'Hibernian' and 'Irish', draws our attention to the distinction between these terms and the effects of having the facts of Irish social life rendered in an Hibernian manner or, more precisely, related by an Hibernian narrator. Finally, it should be said that the short-hand title, *Castle Rackrent*, has the disadvantage of reducing or neglecting the tensions and questions just summarized. Yet it also encapsulates a particular kind of architectural development in the late eighteenth century. Far from being an ancient building of military character, 'Castle Rackrent' may well be thought of as a bourgeois residence, built according to design-book specifications and dignified by the addition of that Gothic inversion, 'Castle . . .'. The reader of the novel should consider the full complexities of this apparently simple tale before espousing any interpretation of it.

The bulk of Maria Edgeworth's remaining fiction is not set in Ireland. Yet, of the first series of *Tales of Fashionable Life* (1809), it is the Irish story 'Ennui' which most deserves attention. The plot turns on that reliable device of folk-tale and romantic narrative — the changeling. When the apparent Earl of Glenthorn reverts to his 'real' place in Irish society, as son of an old nurse, the consequences are disastrous. A previously happy family is destroyed; this is the price exacted for Glenthorn's recovery from *ennui*, neurotic boredom. It is interesting to see how devotedly Edgeworth seeks to re-establish a connection between intrinsic moral worth and social status as she pursues the story of the self-deposed 'earl's' recovery of the estate by marriage to a conveniently available girl. 'Ennui' has a certain attraction as a parable of Anglo-Irish misunderstanding, with its hero who turns out to be — so to speak — his own foster-brother. Its companion tales share with it, however, a concern with the connection between moral and social worth, unusually heightened in the fever of the French Revolutionary period. *The Absentee* has a similar kinship to the other stories in the second series of *Tales of Fashionable Life* (1812), although this second account of a naïve landlord returning to Ireland and to social responsibility is a far more substantial fiction than 'Ennui'. It was *The Absentee* that sent Walter Scott back to the abandoned manuscript of *Waverley* and that, through him, introduced the new genre of historical fiction to Europe. *The Absentee* tells of the return of Lord Colambre to his Irish estates, giving vivid illustrations of the state of society in London, Dublin, fashionable north Wicklow and the desolate Irish midlands. Free from the relentless rationality (and implausibility) of 'Ennui', *The Absentee* impresses with its subtle attempts to convey the contradictions and unspoken reservations of its official theme. The selection of passages from the novel is designed to illustrate the range of these problems and Maria Edgeworth's resource in dealing with them.

Her fourth Irish novel, *Ormond* (1817), is a more orthodox historical fiction of the kind that became familiar throughout the nineteenth century. Despite a certain haste in its composition and, consequently, some hurried attempts to incorporate the example of eighteenth-century English novelists, *Ormond* advances the inner romantic presuppositions that had secretly informed Maria Edgeworth's earlier fiction. In *Ormond*, as in much Romantic literature, personal integrity is discovered in solitude, threatened in civilized society. The remote western landscape of King Corny's Black Islands is more attractive as an ideal than it is useful as a model for emulation. This merely emphasizes how dilute the didactic strain in Maria Edgeworth's fiction had become. It does not lessen the appeal of the landscape nor the romantic longing it represents. From the implicit distinction between 'Hibernian' and 'Irish' in the subtitle of *Castle Rackrent* to the Black Islands of *Ormond*, Maria Edgeworth's fiction posits (rarely presents explicitly) a westward flight. Dublin is preferred to London, the Irish midlands are quickly preferred to Dublin and the wholly imaginary Black Islands of *Ormond* are the ultimate resting place of this progression from metropolitan society towards Nature. Edgeworth's Enlightenment training is never wholly vanquished, but the historical substance of her fiction resides precisely in unresolved tension between resistance to provincialism and longing for an unshakable local reality.

The 'postscript' to *Castle Rackrent*, which is set out below, raises difficult questions about the relationship between culture and politics within the Union inaugurated by the Act of 1800. The fiction that has an English setting (notably *Patronage* of 1814) deserves more attention than it has recently received, for it serves to remind us of the social reality which the United Kingdom of Great Britain and Ireland constituted, as distinct from the hermetic 'Ireland' and 'England' of literary history. Maria Edgeworth has been accused of playing up Irish idiosyncrasy for London publishers and English readers, but an attentive reading of her work will reveal instead a concern with the structural complexities of an English-language culture that sought to incorporate Ireland, a culture which was not simply located within the boundaries of 'old England'. Those boundaries were tacitly accepted by the greatest of her contemporaries, Jane Austen. Only Anthony Trollope, among later nineteenth-century novelists, acknowledged the full extent and imperial range of the society represented in 'English' fiction.

The *Essay on Irish Bulls*[1] (1802, written in col-

1. A bull is an expression involving a ludicrous inconsistency unperceived by the speaker.

laboration with her father) confronts one particular aspect of the relationship between Great Britain and Ireland, that of the English language, which at the same time united and divided them. The various 'voices' in the *Essay* were carefully researched, and this work was to bear fruit in the later novels where there are fine dramatic presentations of Irish characters in non-Irish situations; Sir Terence O'Fay in *The Absentee* is a good example of this. The story of 'Little Dominick', which is set in Wales, comes from the *Essay on Irish Bulls* and shows clearly the extent to which Maria Edgeworth inherited a normative attitude towards language from the Enlightenment, while also demonstrating her ear for various regional accents and dialects. Later, in a letter of 1834, printed below, she showed how sharply and regretfully she perceived her ultimate dilemma as an Irish novelist. Although she lived until 1849, her specific role as the reconciler of modern and antiquarian impulses in Irish literary history had been taken over, as early as 1833, by the founders of *The Dublin University Magazine*.

The transformation, represented by this group, of Enlightenment liberalism (on the issue of political rights for catholics, for example) into the very different mould of Anglo-Irish toryism, has important literary implications. On the surface, it seems that the Young Ireland newspaper, *The Nation*, was the true inheritor of Edgeworth's concerns, rather than *The Dublin University Magazine*. But Edgeworth's profundity had, from the outset, derived from a double structure of ironic distance from the landed gentry and a tacit defence of the landed way of life. This was to be carried on by *The Dublin University Magazine*. *The Absentee* eloquently illustrated the point: initially urging the return of the landlord to his social responsibilities, the novel concluded with a purely ceremonial role for Lord Colambre and his bride-to-be. This incomplete resolution was formulated more exactly in a letter of 1839, in which Edgeworth wrote: 'I begin to think that it is but reasonable that a country should be rendered fit to live in before we complain more of Absentees.'[2] Here is the exculpation of her own class, already begun in *The Absentee* when that novel replaced the notion that morality derives from social function with the very different proposition that intention can in practice support a way of life.

2. M.E. to Fanny Wilson, 4 January 1839, quoted in M. Butler, *Maria Edgeworth* (Oxford: Clarendon Press, 1972), p.453.

Maria Edgeworth has been put on a pedestal as a model of the Anglo-Irish protestant ascendancy 'with its sense of responsibility'.[3] She has been dismissed as merely patronizing in her attitude to the plain people of Ireland. Neither of these judgments does justice to the questions raised by her exemplary fiction.

3. See W. B. Yeats, 'A Commentary on "Parnell's Funeral"'.

from:
CASTLE RACKRENT (1800)

[Thady Quirk is the narrator of the novel, and his ironic mode dominates the work. His narrative is divided into two parts, though there is no indication of this division at the commencement of the first part: this covers the careers of Sir Patrick Rackrent, his son Sir Murtagh and his younger brother, Sir Kit. The second part is introduced as 'Continuation of the Memoirs of the Rackrent Family' and deals solely with the career of Sir Conolly (Condy) Rackrent, who belonged to 'a remote branch' of the family. In the first section of the novel, Thady is, for the most part, a passive recorder of events; in the second section, he is actively implicated in Sir Condy's doings. This new involvement of Thady's arises from the crucial role of his son, Jason Quirk, in ousting the Rackrents from possession. While Thady's narrative is well-known (and the novel is available in several editions), it is not sufficiently acknowledged that his first-person account of the family is surrounded by a number of auxiliary passages, which should not be separated from the two-part narrative. These aspects of the novel deserve particular attention since they indicate the complex attitudes — desires, contradictions, annotations — which surround the brief and familiar narrative. It is only by paying attention to these that we get to grips with the subtle and nefarious nature of Thady's all-too-fluent account of events.]

PREFACE

The prevailing taste of the public for anecdote has been censured and ridiculed by critics who aspire to the character of superior wisdom: but if we consider it in a proper point of view, this taste is an incontestible proof of the good sense and profoundly philosophic temper of the present times. Of the numbers who study, or at least who read history, how few derive any advantage from their labours! The heroes of history are so decked out by the fine fancy of the professed historian; they talk in such measured prose, and act from such sublime or such diabolical motives, that few have sufficient taste, wickedness, or heroism, to sympathise in their fate. Besides, there is much uncertainty even in the best authenticated ancient or modern histories; and that love of truth, which in some minds is innate and immutable, necessarily leads to a love of secret memoirs, and private anecdotes. We cannot judge either of the feelings or of the characters of men with perfect accuracy, from their actions or their appearance in public; it is from their careless conversations, their half-finished sentences, that we may hope with the greatest probability of success to discover their real characters. The life of a great or of a little man written by himself, the familiar letters, the diary of any individual published by his friends or by his enemies, after his decease, are esteemed important literary curiosities. We are surely justified, in this eager desire, to collect the most minute facts relative to the domestic lives, not only of the great and good, but even of the worthless and insignificant, since it is only by a comparison of their actual happiness or misery in the privacy of domestic life that we can form a just estimate of the real reward of virtue, or the real punishment of vice. That the great are not as happy as they seem, that the external circumstances of fortune and rank do not constitute felicity, is asserted by every moralist: the historian can seldom, consistently with his dignity, pause to illustrate this truth; it is therefore to the biographer we must have recourse. After we have beheld splendid characters playing their parts on the great theatre of the world, with all the advantages of stage effect and decoration, we anxiously beg to be admitted behind the scenes, that we may take a nearer view of the actors and actresses.

Some may perhaps imagine, that the value of biography depends upon the judgment and taste of the biographer: but on the contrary it may be maintained, that the merits of a biographer are inversely as the extent of his intellectual powers and of his literary talents. A plain unvarnished tale is preferable to the most highly ornamented narrative. Where we see that a man has the power, we may naturally suspect that he has the will to deceive us; and those who are used to literary manufacture know how much is often sacrificed to the rounding of a period, or the pointing of an antithesis.

That the ignorant may have their prejudices as well as the learned cannot be disputed; but we see and despise vulgar errors; we never bow to the authority of him who has no great name to sanction his absurdities. The partiality which blinds a biographer to the defects of his hero, in proportion as it is gross, ceases to be dangerous; but if it be concealed by the appearance of candour, which men of great abilities best know how to assume, it endangers our judgment sometimes, and sometimes our morals. If her grace the duchess of Newcastle, instead of penning her lord's elaborate eulogium, had undertaken to write the life of Savage, we should not have been in any danger of mistaking an idle, ungrateful libertine for a man of genius and virtue.[1] The talents of a biographer are often fatal to his reader. For these reasons the public often judiciously countenance those, who, without sagacity to discriminate character, without elegance of style to relieve the tediousness of narrative, without enlargement of mind to draw any conclusions from the facts they relate, simply pour forth anecdotes, and retail conversations, with all the minute prolixity of a gossip in a country town.

The author of the following Memoirs has upon these grounds fair claims to the public favour and attention; he was an illiterate old steward, whose partiality to *the family,* in which he was bred and born, must be obvious to the reader. He tells the history of the Rackrent family in his vernacular idiom, and in the full confidence that sir Patrick, sir Murtagh, sir Kit, and sir Condy Rackrent's affairs will be as interesting to all the world as they were to himself. Those who were acquainted with the manners of a certain class of the gentry of Ireland some years ago will want no evidence of the truth of honest Thady's narrative: to those who are totally unacquainted with Ireland, the following Memoirs will perhaps be scarcely intelligible, or probably they may appear perfectly incredible. For the information of the *ignorant* English reader, a few notes have been subjoined by the editor, and he had it once in contemplation to translate the language of Thady in plain English; but Thady's idiom is incapable of translation, and, besides, the authenticity of his story would have been more exposed to doubt if it were not told in his own characteristic manner. Several years ago he related to the editor the history of the Rackrent family, and

1. The references are to *The Life of William Cavendish* (1667), a eulogistic biography by his wife Margaret Cavendish, duchess of Newcastle and to Samuel Johnson's *Account of the Life of Mr. Richard Savage* (1744).

it was with some difficulty that he was persuaded to have it committed to writing; however, his feelings for '*the honour of the family*,' as he expressed himself, prevailed over his habitual laziness, and he at length completed the narrative which is now laid before the public.

The editor hopes his readers will observe that these are "tales of other times:" that the manners depicted in the following pages are not those of the present age: the race of the Rackrents has long since been extinct in Ireland; and the drunken sir Patrick, the litigious sir Murtagh, the fighting sir Kit, and the slovenly sir Condy, are characters which could no more be met with at present in Ireland, than squire Western or parson Trulliber in England.[2] There is a time, when individuals can bear to be rallied for their past follies and absurdities, after they have acquired new habits, and a new consciousness. Nations as well as individuals gradually lose attachment to their identity, and the present generation is amused rather than offended by the ridicule that is thrown upon its ancestors.

Probably we shall soon have it in our power, in a hundred instances, to verify the truth of these observations.

When Ireland loses her identity by an union with Great Britain, she will look back with a smile of good-humoured complacency on the sir Kits and sir Condys of her former existence.

1800.

2. Squire Western and Parson Trulliber are characters in Henry Fielding's *Tom Jones* (1749) and *Joseph Andrews* (1742) respectively.

[The first two paragraphs of Thady's narrative successfully establish the ironic tone that is sustained throughout. However, by means of footnote and glossary, other perspectives are juxtaposed. The opening paragraphs read:]

Monday Morning.[1]

Having, out of friendship for the family, upon whose estate, praised be Heaven! I and mine have lived rent-free, time out of mind, voluntarily undertaken to publish the Memoirs of the Rackrent Family, I think it is my duty to say a few words, in the first place, concerning myself. My real name is Thady Quirk, though in the family I have always been known by no other than '*honest Thady*' — afterwards, in the time of sir Murtagh, deceased, I remember to hear them calling me '*old Thady*,' and now I'm come to 'poor Thady;' for I wear a long great coat* winter and summer, which is very handy, as I never put my arms into the sleeves; they are as good as new, though come Holantide[2] next I've had it these seven years; it holds on by a single button round my neck, cloak fashion. To look at me, you would hardly think 'poor Thady' was the father of attorney Quirk; he is a high gentleman, and never minds what poor Thady says, and having better than fifteen hundred a year, landed estate, looks down upon honest Thady; but I wash my hands of his doings, and as I have lived so will I die, true and loyal to the family. The family of the Rackrents is, I am proud to say, one of the most ancient in the kingdom. Every body knows this is not the old family name, which was O'Shaughlin,

1. For M.E.'s comment on this phrase, see the Glossary, p. 1024.

*The cloak, or mantle, as described by Thady, is of high antiquity. Spencer, in his 'View of the State of Ireland,' proves that it is not, as some have imagined, peculiarly derived from the Scythians, but that 'most nations of the world anciently used the mantle; for the Jews used it, as you may read of Elias's mantle, &c.; the Chaldees also used it, as you may read in Diodorus; the Egyptians likewise used it, as you may read in Herodotus, and may be gathered by the description of Berenice, in the Greek Commentary, upon Callimachus; the Greeks also used it anciently, as appeared by Venus's mantle lined with stars, though afterwards they changed the form thereof into their cloaks, called Pallai, as some of the Irish also use: and the ancient Latins and Romans used it, as you may read in Virgil, who was a very great antiquary, that Evander, when Eneas came to him at his feast, did entertain and feast him sitting on the ground, and lying on mantles: insomuch as he useth the very word mantile for a mantle,

"—— Humi mantilia sternunt:"

so that it seemeth that the mantle was a general habit to most nations, and not proper to the Scythians only.'

Spencer knew the convenience of the said mantle, as housing, bedding, and clothing.

'*Iren.* Because the commodity doth not countervail the discommodity; for the inconveniences which thereby do arise are much more many; for it is a fit house for an outlaw, a meet bed for a rebel, and an apt cloak for a thief. First, the outlaw being for his many crimes and villanies, banished from the towns and houses of honest men, and wandering in waste places, far from danger of law, maketh his mantle his house, and under it covereth himself from the wrath of Heaven, from the offence of the earth, and from the sight of men. When it raineth, it is his pent-house; when it bloweth, it is his tent; when it freezeth, it is his tabernacle. In summer he can wear it loose; in winter he can wrap it close; at all times he can use it; never heavy, never cumbersome. Likewise for a rebel it is as serviceable; for in this war that he maketh (if at least it deserves the name of war), when he still flieth from his foe, and lurketh in the *thick woods (this should be black bogs)* and straight passages waiting for advantages, it is his bed, yea, and almost his household stuff.' [See Edmund Spenser, *A View of the Present State of Ireland,* written in 1596 but not published until 1633 (and then incompletely) by Sir James Ware. The text as it was available to M.E. is reprinted in *Ancient Irish Histories* (2 vols, Kennikat Press, 1970), I, 84-87. The Latin phrase quoted comes from Virgil, *Aeneid,* viii, and means 'They spread napkins on the ground'. The comment *'this should be black bogs'* is M.E.'s addition. Spenser's *View* is cast in the form of a dialogue, and the speaker here is Irenius. Ed.]

2. Hallowe'en.

related to the kings of Ireland — but that was before my time. My grandfather was driver to the great sir Patrick O'Shaughlin, and I heard him, when I was a boy, telling how the Castle Rackrent estate came to sir Patrick; Sir Tallyhoo Rackrent was cousin-german[3] to him, and had a fine estate of his own, only never a gate upon it, it being his maxim that a car[4] was the best gate. Poor gentleman! he lost a fine hunter and his life, at last, by it, all in one day's hunt. But I ought to bless that day, for the estate came straight into *the* family, upon one condition, which Sir Patrick O'Shaughlin at the time took sadly to heart, they say, but thought better of it afterwards, seeing how large a stake depended upon it, that he should by act of parliament, take and bear the surname and arms of Rackrent.

Now it was that the world was to see what was *in* sir Patrick. On coming into the estate, he gave the finest entertainment ever was heard of in the country; not a man could stand after supper but sir Patrick himself, who could sit out the best man in Ireland, let alone the three kingdoms itself.[5] He had his house, from one year's end to another, as full of company as ever it could hold, and fuller; for rather than be left out of the parties at Castle Rackrent, many gentlemen, and those men of the first consequence and landed estates in the country, such as the O'Neils of Ballynagrotty, and the Moneygawls of Mount Juliet's Town, and O'Shannons of New Town Tullyhog, made it their choice, often and often, when there was no moon to be had for love nor money, in long winter nights, to sleep in the chickenhouse, which sir Patrick had fitted up for the purpose of accommodating his friends and the public in general, who honoured him with their company unexpectedly at Castle Rackrent; and this went on, I can't tell you how long — the whole country rang with his praises — Long life to him! I'm sure I love to look upon his picture, now opposite to me; though I never saw him, he must have been a portly gentleman — his neck something short, and remarkable for the largest pimple on his nose, which, by his particular desire, is still extant in his picture, said to be a striking likeness, though taken when young. He is said also to be the inventor of raspberry whiskey, which is very likely, as nobody has ever appeared to dispute it with him, and as there still exists a broken punch-bowl at Castle Rackrent, in the garret, with an inscription to that effect — a great curiosity. A few days before his death he was very merry; it being his honour's birth-day, he called my grandfather in, God bless him! to drink the company's health, and filled a bumper himself, but could not carry it to his head, on account of the great shake in his hand; on this he cast his joke, saying, 'What would my poor father say to me if he was to pop out of the grave, and see me now? I remember when I was a little boy, the first bumper of claret he gave me after dinner, how he praised me for carrying it so steady to my mouth. Here's my thanks to him — a bumper toast.' Then he fell to singing the favourite song he learned from his father — for the last time, poor gentleman — he sung it that night as loud and as hearty as ever with a chorus:

He that goes to bed, and goes to bed sober,
Falls as the leaves do, falls as the leaves do, and
dies in October;
But he that goes to bed, and goes to bed
mellow,
Lives as he ought to do, lives as he ought to do, and
dies an honest fellow.'[6] ...

[Sir Patrick, not surprisingly, died that night, and the rest of the first part of *Castle Rackrent* tells the stories of his successors, Sir Murtagh and Sir Kit. The second part, 'Continuation of the Memoirs of the Rackrent Family', concentrates on the next heir, Sir Conolly or Condy. Extravagant and irresponsible, Sir Condy soon falls into the hands of Jason Quirk, son of Thady, the narrator. At this point in the story, Jason has already gained effective control of the estates and is pressing Sir Condy to yield further.]

So Jason with much ado was brought to agree to a compromise. 'The purchaser that I have ready,' says he, 'will be much displeased, to be sure, at the incumbrance on the land, but I must see and manage him; here's a deed ready drawn up, we have nothing to do but to put in the consideration money and our names to it.' 'And how much as I going to sell? — the lands of O'Shaughlin's town, and the lands of Gruneaghoolaghan, and the lands of Crookagnawaturgh,' says [Sir Condy], just reading to himself, — 'and — Oh, murder, Jason! sure you won't put this in — the castle, stable, and appurtenances of Castle Rackrent.' 'Oh, murder!' says I,

3. i.e. first cousin.
4. cart.
5. i.e. England, Scotland and Ireland, although the first two had been united since 1707. See also the Glossary, p. 1024.
6. This song, of unknown authorship, can be traced back at least to the seventeenth century.

clapping my hands, 'this is too bad, Jason.' 'Why so?' said Jason, 'when it's all, and a great deal more to the back of it, lawfully mine, was I to push for it.' 'Look at him,' says I, pointing to sir Condy, who was just leaning back in his arm-chair, with his arms falling beside him like one stupified; 'is it you, Jason, that can stand in his presence, and recollect all he has been to us, and all we have been to him, and yet use him so at the last?' 'Who will he find to use him better, I ask you?' said Jason; 'if he can get a better purchaser, I'm content; I only offer to purchase, to make things easy and oblige him: though I don't see what compliment I am under, if you come to that; I have never had, asked, or charged more than sixpence in the pound, receiver's fees; and where would he have got an agent for a penny less?' 'Oh, Jason! Jason! how will you stand to this in the face of the county and all who know you?' says I; 'and what will people think and say, when they see you living here in Castle Rackrent, and the lawful owner turned out of the seat of his ancestors, without a cabin to put his head into, or so much as a potatoe to eat?' Jason, whilst I was saying this, and a great deal more, made me signs, and winks, and frowns; but I took no heed, for I was grieved and sick at heart for my poor master, and couldn't but speak.

'Here's the punch,' says Jason, for the door opened; 'here's the punch!' Hearing that, my master starts up in his chair, and recollects himself, and Jason uncorks the whiskey. 'Set down the jug here,' says he, making room for it beside the papers opposite to sir Condy, but still not stirring the deed that was to make over all. Well, I was in great hopes he had some touch of mercy about him when I saw him making the punch, and my master took a glass; but Jason put it back as he was going to fill again, saying, 'No, sir Condy, it sha'n't be said of me, I got your signature to this deed when you were half-seas over: you know, your name and handwriting in that condition would not, if brought before the courts, benefit me a straw; wherefore let us settle all before we go deeper into the punchbowl.' 'Settle all as you will,' said sir Condy, clapping his hands to his ears; 'but let me hear no more; I'm bothered to death this night.' 'You've only to sign,' said Jason, putting the pen to him. 'Take all, and be content,' said my master. So he signed; and the man who brought in the punch witnessed it, for I was not able, but crying like a child; and besides, Jason said, which I was glad of, that I was no fit witness, being so old and doting. It was so bad with me, I could not taste a drop of the punch itself, though my master himself, God bless him! in the midst of his trouble, poured out a glass for me, and brought it up to my lips. 'Not a drop, I thank your honour's honour as much as if I took it though,' and I just set down the glass as it was, and went out; and when I got to the street-door, the neighbours' childer, who were playing at marbles there, seeing me in great trouble, left their play, and gathered about me to know what ailed me; and I told them all, for it was a great relief to me to speak to these poor childer, that seemed to have some natural feeling left in them: and when they were made sensible that sir Condy was going to leave Castle Rackrent for good and all, they set up a whillalu that could be heard to the farthest end of the street; and one fine boy he was, that my master had given an apple to that morning, cried the loudest, but they all were the same sorry, for sir Condy was greatly beloved amongst the childer,[7] for letting them go a nutting in the demesne without saying a word to them, though my lady objected to them. The people in the town, who were the most of them standing at their doors, hearing the childer cry, would know the reason of it; and when the report was made known, the people one and all gathered in great anger against my son Jason, and terror at the notion of his coming to be landlord over them, and they cried, 'No Jason! no Jason! Sir Condy! sir Condy! sir Condy Rackrent for ever!' and the mob grew so great and so loud, I was frightened, and made my way back to the house to warn my son to make his escape, or hide himself for fear of the consequences. Jason would not believe me till they came all round the house and to the windows with great shouts: then he grew quite pale, and asked sir Condy what had he best do? 'I'll tell you what you'd best do,' said sir Condy, who was laughing to see his fright; 'finish your glass first, then let's go to the window and show ourselves, and I'll tell 'em, or you shall, if you please, that I'm going to the Lodge for change of air for my health, and by my own desire, for the rest of my days.' 'Do so,' said Jason, who never meant it should have been so, but could not refuse him the Lodge at this unseasonable time. Accordingly, sir Condy threw up the sash and explained matters, and thanked all

7. The first edition has the following note at this point: 'This is the invariable pronunciation of the lower Irish.' It is interesting that it was omitted in the 1832 edition, which we are using as our copy-text.

his friends, and bid 'em look in at the punch-bowl, and observe that Jason and he had been sitting over it very good friends; so the mob was content, and he sent 'em out some whiskey to drink his health, and that was the last time his honour's health was ever drunk at Castle Rackrent.

The very next day, being too proud, as he said to me, to stay an hour longer in a house that did not belong to him, he sets off to the Lodge, and I along with him not many hours after. And there was great bemoaning through all O'Shaughlin's town, which I stayed to witness, and gave my poor master a full account of when I got to the Lodge. He was very low and in his bed when I got there, and complained of a great pain about his heart, but I guessed it was only trouble, and all the business, let alone vexation, he had gone through of late; and knowing the nature of him from a boy, I took my pipe, and, whilst smoking it by the chimney, began telling him how he was beloved and regretted in the county, and it did him a deal of good to hear it. 'Your honour has a great many friends yet, that you don't know of, rich and poor, in the county,' says I; 'for as I was coming along the road, I met two gentlemen in their own carriages, who asked after you, knowing me, and wanted to know where you was, and all about you, and even how old I was: think of that.' Then he wakened out of his doze, and began questioning me who the gentlemen were. And the next morning it came into my head to go, unknown to any body, with my master's compliments, round to many of the gentlemen's houses, where he and my lady used to visit, and people that I knew were his great friends, and would go to Cork to serve him any day in the year, and I made bold to try to borrow a trifle of cash from them. They all treated me very civil for the most part, and asked a great many questions very kind about my lady, and sir Condy, and all the family, and were greatly surprised to learn from me Castle Rackrent was sold, and my master at the Lodge for health; and they all pitied him greatly, and he had their good wishes, if that would do, but money was a thing they unfortunately had not any of them at this time to spare. I had my journey for my pains, and I, not used to walking, nor supple as formerly, was greatly tired, but had the satisfaction of telling my master, when I got to the Lodge, all the civil things said by high and low.

'Thady,' says he, 'all you've been telling me brings a strange thought into my head; I've a notion I shall not be long for this world any how, and I've a great fancy to see my own funeral afore I die.' I was greatly shocked, at the first speaking, to hear him speak so light about his funeral, and he, to all appearance, in good health, but recollecting myself, answered, 'To be sure it would be as fine sight as one could see, I dared to say, and one I should be proud to witness, and I did not doubt his honour's would be as great a funeral as ever sir Patrick O'Shaughlin's was, and such a one as that had never been known in the county afore or since.' But I never thought he was in earnest about seeing his own funeral himself, till the next day he returns to it again. 'Thady,' says he, 'as far as the wake* goes, sure I might without any great trouble have the satisfaction of seeing a bit of my own funeral.' 'Well, since your honour's so bent upon it,' says I, not willing to cross him, and he in trouble, 'we must see what we can do.' So he fell into a sort of a sham disorder, which was easy done, as he kept his bed and no one to see him; and I got my shister, who was an old woman very handy about the sick, and very skilful, to come up to the Lodge, to nurse him; and we gave out, she knowing no better, that he was just at his latter end, and it answered beyond any thing; and there was a great throng of people, men, women, and childer, and there being only two rooms at the Lodge, except what was locked up full of Jason's furniture and things, the house was soon as full and fuller than it could hold, and the heat, and smoke, and noise wonderful great; and standing amongst them that were near the bed, but not thinking at all of the dead, I was started by the sound of my master's voice from under the great coats that had been thrown all at top, and I went close up, no one noticing. 'Thady,' says he, 'I've had enough of this; I'm smothering, and can't hear a word of all they're saying of the deceased.' 'God bless you, and lie still and quiet,' says I, 'a bit longer, for my shister's afraid of ghosts, and would die on the spot with fright, was she to see you come to life all on a sudden this way without the least preparation.' So he lays him still, though well nigh stifled, and I made all haste to tell the secret of the joke, whispering to one and t'other, and there was a great surprise, but not so great as we had laid out it

* A wake in England is a meeting avowedly for merriment; in Ireland, it is a nocturnal meeting avowedly for the purpose of watching and bewailing the dead; but, in reality, for gossiping and debauchery. [See also the Glossary, p. 1024. Ed.]

would. 'And aren't we to have the pipes and tobacco, after coming so far to-night?' said some; but they were all well enough pleased when his honour got up to drink with them, and sent for more spirits from a shebean-house,* where they very civilly let him have it upon credit. So the night passed off very merrily, but, to my mind, sir Condy was rather upon the sad order in the midst of it all, not finding there had been such a great talk about himself after his death as he had always expected to hear.

The next morning, when the house was cleared of them, and none but my shister and myself left in the kitchen with sir Condy, one opens the door and walks in, and who should it be but Judy M'Quirk[8] herself! I forgot to notice, that she had been married long since, whilst young captain Moneygawl lived at the Lodge, to the captain's huntsman, who after a whilst listed and left her, and was killed in the wars. Poor Judy fell off greatly in her good looks after her being married a year or two; and being smoke-dried in the cabin, and neglecting herself like, it was hard for sir Condy himself to know her again till she spoke; but when she says, 'It's Judy M'Quirk, please your honour, don't you remember her?' 'Oh, Judy, is it you?' says his honour; 'yes, sure, I remember you very well; but you're greatly altered, Judy.' 'Sure it's time for me,' says she; 'and I think your honour, since I *seen* you last, — but that's a great while ago, — is altered too.' 'And with reason, Judy,' says sir Condy, fetching a sort of a sigh; 'but how's this, Judy?' he goes on; 'I take it a little amiss of you, that you were not at my wake last night.' 'Ah, don't be being jealous of that,' says she; 'I didn't hear a sentence of your honour's wake till it was all over, or it would have gone hard with me but I would have been at it sure; but I was forced to go ten miles up the country three days ago to a wedding of a relation of my own's, and didn't get home till after the wake was over; but,' says she, 'it won't be so, I hope, the next time,† please your honour.' 'That we shall see, Judy,' says his honour, 'and may be sooner than you think for, for I've been very unwell this while past, and don't reckon any way I'm long for this world.' At this, Judy takes up the corner of her apron, and puts it first to one eye and then to t'other, being to all appearance in great trouble; and my shister put in her word, and bid his honour have a good heart, for she was sure it was only the gout, that sir Patrick used to have flying about him, and that he ought to drink a glass or a bottle extraordinary to keep it out of his stomach; and he promised to take her advice, and sent out for more spirits immediately; and Judy made a sign to me, and I went over to the door to her, and she said, 'I wonder to see sir Condy so low! has he heard the news?' 'What news?' says I. 'Didn't ye hear it, then?' says she; 'my lady Rackrent that was is kilt[9] and lying for dead, and I don't doubt but it's all over with her by this time.' 'Mercy on us all,' says I; 'how was it?' 'The jaunting car[10] it was that ran away with her,' says Judy. 'I was coming home that same time from Biddy M'Guggin's marriage, and a great crowd of people too upon the road, coming from the fair of Crookaghnawaturgh, and I sees a jaunting car standing in the middle of the road, and with the two wheels off and all tattered. "What's this?" says I. "Didn't ye hear of it?" says they that were looking on; "it's my lady Rackrent's car, that was running away from her husband, and the horse took fright at a carrion[11] that lay across the road, and so ran away with the jaunting car, and my lady Rackrent and her maid screaming, and the horse ran with them against a car that was coming from the fair, with the boy asleep on it, and the lady's petticoat hanging out of the jaunting car caught, and she was dragged I can't tell you how far upon the road, and it all broken up with the stones just going to be pounded, and one of the road-makers, with his sledge-hammer in his hand, stops the horse at the last; but my lady Rackrent was all kilt* and smashed, and they lifted her into a cabin hard by, and the maid was found after, where she had been thrown, in the gripe of the ditch,[12] her cap and bonnet all full of

* *Shebean-house*, a hedge-alehouse. Shebean properly means weak small-beer, taplash. [Taplash = dregs of liquor or very weak beer; *síbín* Ir. = illicit public-house. Ed.]

† At the coronation of one of our monarchs, the King complained of the confusion which happened in the procession. The great officer who presided told his majesty, 'That it should not be so next time.'

8. Earlier in the novel, Sir Condy had nearly married Judy McQuirk, Thady Quirk's niece.

* *Kilt and smashed.* — Our author is not here guilty of an anti-climax. The mere English reader, from a similarity of sound between the words *kilt* and *killed*, might be induced to suppose that their meanings are similar, yet they are not by any means in Ireland synonymous terms. Thus you may hear a man exclaim, 'I'm kilt and murdered!' but he frequently means only that he has received a black eye, or a slight contusion. — *I'm kilt all over* means that he is in a worse state than being simply *kilt*. Thus, *I'm kilt with the cold* is nothing to *I'm kilt all over with the rheumatism*.

9. See the Glossary, p. 1025.

10. A light, two-wheeled horse-drawn vehicle, common in Ireland.

11. A dead animal.

12. i.e. at the bottom of the ditch.

bog water, and they say my lady can't live any way." Thady, pray now is it true what I'm told for sartin, that sir Condy has made over all to your son Jason?' 'All,' says I. 'All entirely?' says she again. 'All entirely,' says I. 'Then,' says she, 'that's a great shame, but don't be telling Jason what I say.' 'And what is it you say?' cries sir Condy, leaning over betwixt us, which made Judy start greatly. 'I know the time when Judy M'Quirk would never have stayed so long talking at the door, and I in the house.' 'Oh!' says Judy, 'for shame, sir Condy; times are altered since then, and it's my lady Rackrent you ought to be thinking of.' 'And why should I be thinking of her, that's not thinking of me now?' says sir Condy. 'No matter for that,' says Judy, very properly; 'it's time you should be thinking of her, if ever you mean to do it all, for don't you know she's lying for death?' 'My lady Rackrent!' says sir Condy, in a surprise; 'why it's but two days since we parted, as you very well know, Thady, in her full health and spirits, and she and her maid along with her going to Mount Juliet's town on her jaunting car.' 'She'll never ride no more on her jaunting car,' said Judy, 'for it has been the death of her, sure enough.' 'And is she dead, then?' says his honour. 'As good as dead, I hear,' says Judy; 'but there's Thady here has just learnt the whole truth of the story as I had it, and it is fitter he or any body else should be telling it you than I, sir Condy: I must be going home to the childer.' But he stops her, but rather from civility in him, as I could see very plainly, than any thing else, for Judy was, as his honour remarked at her first coming in, greatly changed, and little likely, as far as I could see — though she did not seem to be clear of it herself — little likely to be my lady Rackrent now, should there be a second toss-up to be made. But I told him the whole story out of the face, just as Judy had told it to me, and he sent off a messenger with his compliments to Mount Juliet's town that evening, to learn the truth of the report, and Judy bid the boy that was going call in at Tim M'Enerney's shop in O'Shaughlin's town and buy her a new shawl. 'Do so,' said sir Condy, 'and tell Tim to take no money from you, for I must pay him for the shawl myself.' At this my shister throws me over a look, and I says nothing, but turned the tobacco in my mouth, whilst Judy began making a many words about it, and saying how she could not be beholden for shawls to any gentleman. I left her there to consult with my shister, did she think there was any thing in it, and my shister thought I was blind to be asking her the question, and I thought my shister must see more into it than I did; and recollecting all past times and every thing, I changed my mind, and came over to her way of thinking, and we settled it that Judy was very like to be my lady Rackrent after all, if a vacancy should have happened.

The next day, before his honour was up, somebody comes with a double knock at the door, and I was greatly surprised to see it was my son Jason. 'Jason, is it you?' said I; 'what brings you to the Lodge?' says I; 'is it my lady Rackrent? we know that already since yesterday.' 'May be so,' says he, 'but I must see sir Condy about it.' 'You can't see him yet,' says I; 'sure he is not awake.' 'What then,' says he, 'can't he be wakened? and I standing at the door.' 'I'll not be disturbing his honour for you, Jason,' says I; 'many's the hour you've waited in your time, and been proud to do it, till his honour was at leisure to speak to you. His honour,' says I, raising my voice, at which his honour wakens of his own accord, and calls to me from the room to know who it was I was speaking to. Jason made no more ceremony, but follows me into the room. 'How are you, sir Condy?' says he; 'I'm happy to see you looking so well; I came up to know how you did to-day, and to see did you want for any thing at the Lodge.' 'Nothing at all, Mr. Jason, I thank you,' says he; for his honour had his own share of pride, and did not choose, after all that had passed, to be beholden, I suppose, to my son; 'but pray take a chair and be seated, Mr. Jason.' Jason sat him down upon the chest, for chair there was none, and after he had sat there some time, and a silence on all sides, 'What news is there stirring in the country, Mr. Jason M'Quirk?' says sir Condy very easy, yet high like. 'None that's news to you, sir Condy, I hear,' says Jason: 'I am very sorry to hear of my lady Rackrent's accident.' 'I'm much obliged to you, and so is her ladyship, I'm sure,' answered sir Condy, still stiff; and there was another sort of a silence, which seemed to lie the heaviest on my son Jason.

'Sir Condy,' says he at last, seeing sir Condy disposing himself to go to sleep again, 'sir Condy, I dare say you recollect mentioning to me the little memorandum you gave to lady Rackrent about the 500*l*. a-year jointure.' 'Very true,' said sir Condy; 'it is all in my recollection.' 'But if my lady Rackrent dies, there's an end of all jointure,' says Jason. 'Of course,' says sir Condy. 'But it's not a matter of certainty that my lady Rackrent won't recover,' says Jason. 'Very true, sir,' says my master. 'It's a fair speculation, then, for you to consider what the chance of the jointure on those lands, when out of custodiam, will be to you.'[13] 'Just five hundred a-year, I take it, without any speculation at all,' said sir Condy. 'That's supposing the life dropt, and the custodiam off, you know; begging your pardon, sir Condy, who understands business, that is a wrong calculation.' 'Very likely so,' said sir Condy; 'but, Mr. Jason, if you have any thing to say to me this morning about it, I'd be obliged to you to say it, for I had an indifferent night's rest last night, and wouldn't be sorry to sleep a little this morning.' 'I have only three words to say, and those more of consequence to you, sir Condy, than me. You are a little cool, I observe; but I hope you will not be offended at what I have brought here in my pocket,' and he pulls out two long rolls, and showers down golden guineas upon the bed. 'What's this?' said sir Condy; 'it's long since' — but his pride stops him. 'All these are your lawful property this minute, sir Condy, if you please,' said Jason. 'Not for nothing, I'm sure,' said sir Condy, and laughs a little — 'nothing for nothing, or I'm under a mistake with you, Jason.' 'Oh, sir Condy, we'll not be indulging ourselves in any unpleasant retrospects,' says Jason; 'it's my present intention to behave, as I'm sure you will, like a gentleman in this affair. Here's two hundred guineas, and a third I mean to add, if you should think proper to make over to me all your right and title to those lands that you know of.' 'I'll consider of it,' said my master; and a great deal more, that I was tired listening to, was said by Jason, and all that, and the sight of the ready cash upon the bed worked with his honour; and the short and the long of it was, sir Condy gathered up the golden guineas, and tied them up in a handkerchief, and signed some paper Jason brought with him as usual, and there was an end of the business; Jason took himself away, and my master turned himself round and fell asleep again.

I soon found what had put Jason in such a hurry to conclude this business. The little gossoon[14] we had sent off the day before with my master's compliments to Mount Juliet's town, and to know how my lady did after her accident, was stopped early this morning, coming back with his answer through O'Shaughlin's town, at Castle Rackrent, by my son Jason, and questioned of all he knew of my lady from the servant at Mount Juliet's town; and the gossoon told him my lady Rackrent was not expected to live over night; so Jason thought it high time to be moving to the Lodge, to make his bargain with my master about the jointure afore it should be too late, and afore the little gossoon should reach us with the news. My master was greatly vexed, that is, I may say, as much as ever I *seen* him, when he found how he had been taken in; but it was some comfort to have the ready cash for immediate consumption in the house, any way.

And when Judy came up that evening, and brought the childer to see his honour, he unties the handkerchief, and, God bless him! whether it was little or much he had, 'twas all the same with him, he gives 'em all round guineas a-piece. 'Hold up your head,' says my shister to Judy, as sir Condy was busy filling out a glass of punch for her eldest boy — 'Hold up your head, Judy; for who knows but we may live to see you yet at the head of the Castle Rackrent estate?' 'May be so,' says she, 'but not the way you are thinking of.' I did not rightly understand which way Judy was looking when she makes this speech, till a-while after. 'Why, Thady, you were telling me yesterday, that sir Condy had sold all entirely to Jason, and where then does all them guineas in the handkerchief come from?' 'They are the purchase-money of my lady's jointure,' says I. Judy looks a little bit puzzled at this. 'A penny for your thoughts, Judy,' says my shister; 'hark, sure sir Condy is drinking her health.' He was at the table in *the room*,* drinking with the exciseman and the gauger,[15] who came up to see his honour, and we were standing over the fire in the kitchen. 'I don't much care is he drinking my health or not,' says Judy; 'and it is not sir Condy I'm thinking of, with all your jokes, whatever he is of me.' 'Sure you wouldn't refuse to be my lady Rackrent, Judy, if you had the offer?' says I. 'But if

13. jointure = estate held in the joint names of husband and wife, which reverts to the survivor on the death of one; custodiam = a grant under Irish law of crown lands. Jason means that Sir Condy would do well to consider the value to him of lands at present held jointly with his wife if she should die, when the rents would revert to him, rather than to the crown.

* *The room* — the principal room in the house.

14. boy. cf. *garsún* Ir. = boy.

15. An official who checks weights and measures or who generally supervises public works.

I could do better!' says she. 'How better?' says I and my shister both at once. 'How better?' says she; 'why, what signifies it to be my lady Rackrent, and no castle? sure what good is the car, and no horse to draw it?' 'And where will ye get the horse, Judy?' says I. 'Never mind that,' says she, 'may be it is your own son Jason might find that.' 'Jason!' says I; 'don't be trusting to him, Judy. Sir Condy, as I have good reason to know, spoke well of you, when Jason spoke very indifferently of you, Judy.' 'No matter,' says Judy, 'it's often men speak the contrary just to what they think of us.' 'And you the same way of them, no doubt,' answers I. 'Nay, don't be denying it, Judy, for I think the better of ye for it, and shouldn't be proud to call ye the daughter of a shister's son of mine, if I was to hear ye talk ungrateful, and any way disrespectful of his honour.' 'What disrespect,' says she, 'to say I'd rather, if it was my luck, be the wife of another man?' 'You'll have no luck, mind my words, Judy,' says I; and all I remembered about my poor master's goodness in tossing up for her[16] afore he married at all came across me, and I had a choking in my throat that hindered me to say more. 'Better luck, any how, Thady,' says she, 'than to be like some folk, following the fortunes of them that have none left.' 'Oh! King of Glory!' says I, 'hear the pride and ungratitude of her, and he giving his last guineas but a minute ago to her childer, and she with the fine shawl on her he made her a present of but yesterday!' 'Oh, troth, Judy, you're wrong now,' says my shister, looking at the shawl. 'And was not he wrong yesterday, then,' says she, 'to be telling me I was greatly altered, to affront me?' 'But, Judy,' says I, 'what is it brings you here then at all in the mind you are in; is it to make Jason think the better of you?' 'I'll tell you no more of my secrets, Thady,' says she, 'nor would have told you this much, had I taken you for such an unnatural fader as I find you are, not to wish your own son prefarred to another.' 'Oh, troth, *you* are wrong now, Thady,' says my shister. Well, I was never so put to it in my life between these womens, and my son and my master, and all I felt and thought just now, I could not, upon my conscience, tell which was the wrong from the right. So I said not a word more, but was only glad his honour had not the luck to hear all Judy had been saying of him, for I reckoned it would have gone nigh to break his heart; not that I was of opinion he cared for her as much as she and my shister fancied, but the ungratitude of the whole from Judy might not plase him; and he could never stand the notion of not being well spoken of or beloved like behind his back. Fortunately for all parties concerned, he was so much elevated at this time, there was no danger of his understanding any thing, even if it had reached his ears. There was a great horn at the Lodge, ever since my master and captain Moneygawl was in together, that used to belong originally to the celebrated sir Patrick, his ancestor; and his honour was fond often of telling the story that he learned from me when a child, how sir Patrick drank the full of this horn without stopping, and this was what no other man afore or since could without drawing breath. Now sir Condy challenged the gauger, who seemed to think little of the horn, to swallow the contents, and had it filled to the brim with punch; and the gauger said it was what he could not do for nothing, but he'd hold sir Condy a hundred guineas he'd do it. 'Done,' says my master; 'I'll lay you a hundred golden guineas to a tester* you don't.' 'Done,' says the gauger; and done and done's enough between two gentlemen. The gauger was cast,[17] and my master won the bet, and thought he'd won a hundred guineas, but by the wording it was adjudged to be only a tester that was his due by the exciseman. It was all one to him; he was as well pleased, and I was glad to see him in such spirits again.

The gauger, bad luck to him! was the man that next proposed to my master to try himself could he take at a draught the contents of the great horn. 'Sir Patrick's horn!' said his honour; 'hand it to me: I'll hold you your own bet over again I'll swallow it.' 'Done,' says the gauger; 'I'll lay ye any thing at all you do no such thing.' 'A hundred guineas to sixpence I do,' says he: 'bring me the handkerchief.' I was loth, knowing he meant the handkerchief with the gold in it, to bring it out in such company, and his honour not very able to reckon it. 'Bring me the handkerchief, then, Thady,' says he, and stamps with his foot; so with that I pulls it out of my great

16. Earlier in the novel, Sir Condy had decided whether to marry Judy on the toss of a coin.

* *Tester* — sixpence; from the French word tête, a head: a piece of silver stamped with a head, which in old French was called 'un testion,' and which was about the value of an old English sixpence. Tester is used in Shakespeare.

17. i.e. beaten.

coat pocket, where I had put it for safety. Oh, how it grieved me to see the guineas counting upon the table, and they the last my master had! Says sir Condy to me, 'Your hand is steadier than mine to-night, old Thady, and that's a wonder; fill you the horn for me.' And so, wishing his honour success, I did; but I filled it, little thinking of what would befall him. He swallows it down, and drops like one shot. We lifts him up, and he was speechless, and quite black in the face. We put him to bed, and in a short time he wakened, raving with a fever on his brain. He was shocking either to see or hear. 'Judy! Judy! have you no touch of feeling? won't you stay to help us nurse him?' says I to her, and she putting on her shawl to go out of the house. 'I'm frightened to see him,' says she, 'and wouldn't nor couldn't stay in it; and what use? he can't last till the morning.' With that she ran off. There was none but my shister and myself left near him of all the many friends he had. The fever came and went, and came and went, and lasted five days, and the sixth he was sensible for a few minutes, and said to me, knowing me very well, 'I'm in burning pain all withinside of me, Thady.' I could not speak, but my shister asked him would he have this thing or t'other to do him good? 'No,' says he, 'nothing will do me good no more,' and he gave a terrible screech with the torture he was in — then again a minute's ease — 'brought to this by drink,' says he; 'where are all the friends? — where's Judy? — Gone, hey? Ay, sir Condy has been a fool all his days,' said he; and there was the last word he spoke, and died. He had but a very poor funeral, after all.

If you want to know any more, I'm not very well able to tell you; but my lady Rackrent did not die, as was expected of her, but was only disfigured in the face ever after by the fall and bruises she got; and she and Jason, immediately after my poor master's death, set about going to law about that jointure; the memorandum not being on stamped paper, some say it is worth nothing, others again it may do; others say, Jason won't have the lands at any rate. Many wishes it so: for my part, I'm tired wishing for any thing in this world, after all I've seen in it — but I'll say nothing; it would be a folly to be getting myself ill-will in my old age. Jason did not marry, nor think of marrying Judy, as I prophesied, and I am not sorry for it; who is? As for all I have here set down from memory and hearsay of the family, there's nothing but truth in it from beginning to end: that you may depend upon; for where's the use of telling lies about the things which every body knows as well as I do?

The Editor[18] could have readily made the catastrophe of sir Condy's history more dramatic and more pathetic, if he thought it allowable to varnish the plain round tale of faithful Thady. He lays it before an English reader as a specimen of manners and characters, which are, perhaps, unknown in England. Indeed, the domestic habits of no nation in Europe were less known to the English than those of their sister country, till within these few years.

Mr. Young's picture of Ireland, in his tour through that country, was the first faithful portrait of its inhabitants.[19] All the features in the foregoing sketch was taken from the life, and they are characteristic of that mixture of quickness, simplicity, cunning, carelessness, dissipation, disinterestedness, shrewdness, and blunder, which, in different forms, and with various success, has been brought upon the stage, or delineated in novels.

It is a problem of difficult solution to determine, whether an Union will hasten or retard the melioration of this country. The few gentlemen of education, who now reside in this country, will resort to England: they are few, but they are in nothing inferior to men of the same rank in Great Britain. The best that can happen will be the introduction of British manufacturers in their places.

Did the Warwickshire militia, who were chiefly artisans, teach the Irish to drink beer? or did they learn from the Irish to drink whiskey?

1800.

[The Glossary to *Castle Rackrent* ostensibly explains peculiarities of Irish convention to the English reader, but in doing so, often draws attention to the manner in which Irish orthography and idiom preserve, rather than distort, aspects of earlier English linguistic practice. Conceived probably after the initial typesetting had been completed, the Glossary added twenty-nine further notes, some of considerable length. It was printed *after* the narrated text and not in footnote form. The opening sentences of the Glossary are given below, together with

18. i.e. the author, Maria Edgeworth.
19. Arthur Young's *A Tour in Ireland* (1780) was an important source of information on Irish society, in particular on its agricultural economy.

the notes that refer to the passages from the novel provided above.]

GLOSSARY

Some friends, who have seen Thady's history since it has been printed, have suggested to the Editor, that many of the terms and idiomatic phrases, with which it abounds, could not be intelligible to the English reader without further explanation. The Editor has therefore furnished the following Glossary.

Page 1015. *Monday morning.* — Thady begins his memoirs of the Rackrent Family by dating *Monday morning*, because no great undertaking can be auspiciously commenced in Ireland on any morning but *Monday morning*. 'O, please God we live till Monday morning, we'll set the slater to mend the roof of the house. On Monday morning we'll fall to, and cut the turf. On Monday morning we'll see and begin mowing. On Monday morning, please your honour, we'll begin and dig the potatoes,' &c.

All the intermediate days, between the making of such speeches and the ensuing Monday, are wasted: and when Monday morning comes, it is ten to one that the business is deferred to *the next* Monday morning. The Editor knew a gentleman, who, to counteract this prejudice, made his workmen and labourers begin all new pieces of work upon a Saturday.

Page 1016. *Let alone the three kingdoms itself.* — *Let alone*, in this sentence, means *put out of consideration*. This phrase, *let alone*, which is now used as the imperative of a verb, may in time become a conjunction, and may exercise the ingenuity of some future etymologist. The celebrated Horne Tooke[1] has proved most satisfactorily, that the conjunction *but* comes from the imperative of the Anglo-Saxon verb *(beoutan) to be out*; also, that *if* comes from *gif*, the imperative of the Anglo-Saxon verb which signifies *to give*, &c.

Page 1018. *Wake.* — A wake in England means a festival held upon the anniversary of the saint of the parish. At these wakes, rustic games, rustic conviviality, and rustic courtship, are pursued with all the ardour and all the appetite which accompany such pleasures as occur but seldom. In Ireland a wake is a midnight meeting, held professedly for the indulgence of holy sorrow, but usually it is converted into orgies of unholy joy. When an Irish man or woman of the lower order dies, the straw which composed his bed, whether it has been contained in a bag to form a mattress, or simply spread upon the earthen floor, is immediately taken out of the house, and burned before the cabin door, the family at the same time setting up the death howl. The ears and eyes of the neighbours being thus alarmed, they flock to the house of the deceased, and by their vociferous sympathy excite and at the same time soothe the sorrows of the family.

It is curious to observe how good and bad are mingled in human institutions. In countries which were thinly inhabited, this custom prevented private attempts against the lives of individuals, and formed a kind of coroner's inquest upon the body which had recently expired, and burning the straw upon which the sick man lay became a simple preservative against infection. At night the dead body is waked, that is to say, all the friends and neighbours of the deceased collect in a barn or stable, where the corpse is laid upon some boards, or an unhinged door, supported upon stools, the face exposed, the rest of the body covered with a white sheet. Round the body are stuck in brass candlesticks, which have been borrowed perhaps at five miles' distance, as many candles as the poor person can beg or borrow, observing always to have an odd number. Pipes and tobacco are first distributed, and then, according to the *ability* of the deceased, cakes and ale, and sometimes whiskey, are *dealt* to the company:

> Deal on, deal on, my merry men all,
> Deal on your cakes and your wine,
> For whatever is dealt at her funeral to-day
> Shall be dealt to-morrow at mine.

After a fit of universal sorrow, and the comfort of a universal dram, the scandal of the neighbourhood, as in higher circles, occupies the company. The young lads and lasses romp with one another, and when the fathers and mothers are at last overcome with sleep and whiskey (*vino et somno*), the youth become more enterprising, and are frequently successful. It is said, that more matches are made at wakes than at weddings.

1. John Horne Tooke (1736-1812), English political radical and philologist whose *The Diversions of Purley* 2 vols (1786-1805) is famed for its widely speculative etymologies.

Page 1019. *Kilt.* — This word frequently occurs in the preceding pages, where it means not *killed* but much *hurt*. In Ireland, not only cowards, but the brave 'die many times before their death.' — *There killing is no murder*.

from: AN ESSAY ON IRISH BULLS (1802)

[The *Essay* is a series of analyses and semi-fictional sketches on language, behaviour and character. The example that follows shows Maria Edgeworth's interest in the Enlightenment's preoccupation with particular cultures, while also demonstrating her awareness of the comic possibilities offered by the regional theme.]

CHAPTER IV

LITTLE DOMINICK

We have laid down the general law of bulls and blunders; but as there is no rule without an exception, we may perhaps allow an exception in favour of little Dominick.

Little Dominick was born at Fort-Reilly, in Ireland, and bred nowhere until his tenth year, when he was sent to Wales to learn manners and grammar at the school of Mr. Owen ap Davies ap Jenkins ap Jones. This gentleman had reason to think himself the greatest of men; for he had over his chimney-piece a well-smoked genealogy, duly attested, tracing his ancestry in a direct line up to Noah; and moreover he was nearly related to the learned etymologist, who, in the time of Queen Elizabeth wrote a folio to prove that the language of Adam and Eve in Paradise was pure Welsh. With such causes to be proud, Mr. Owen ap Davies ap Jenkins ap Jones was excusable for sometimes seeming to forget that a schoolmaster is but a man. He, however, sometimes entirely forgot that a boy is but a boy; and this happened most frequently with respect to little Dominick.

This unlucky wight[1] was flogged every morning by his master, not for his vices, but for his vicious constructions, and laughed at by his companions every evening for his idiomatic absurdities. They would probably have been inclined to sympathise in his misfortunes, but that he was the only Irish boy at school; and as he was at a distance from all his relations, and without a friend to take his part, he was a just object of obloquy and derision. Every sentence he spoke was a bull; every two words he put together proved a false concord; and every sound he articulated betrayed the brogue. But as he possessed some of the characteristic boldness of those who have been dipped in the Shannon, he showed himself able and willing to fight his own battles with the host of foes by whom he was encompassed. Some of these, it was said, were of nearly twice his stature. This may be exaggerated, but it is certain that our hero sometimes ventured with sly Irish humour to revenge himself upon his most powerful tyrant by mimicking the Welsh accent, in which Mr. Owen ap Jones said to him, 'Cot pless me, you plockit,[2] and shall I never *learn* you Enclish crammer?'

It was whispered in the ear of this Dionysius, that our little hero was a mimick; and he was treated with increased severity.

The midsummer holydays approached; but he feared that they would shine no holydays for him. He had written to his mother to tell her that school would break up the 21st, and to beg an answer, without fail, by return of post; but no answer came.

It was now nearly two months since he had heard from his dear mother or any of his friends in Ireland. His spirits began to sink under the pressure of these accumulated misfortunes: he slept little, ate less, and played not at all; indeed nobody would play with him upon equal terms, because he was nobody's equal; his schoolfellows continued to consider him as a being, if not of a different species, at least of a different *caste* from themselves.

Mr. Owen ap Jones's triumph over the little Irish plockit was nearly complete, for the boy's heart was almost broken, when there came to the school a new scholar — O, how unlike the others! His name was Edwards; he was the son of a neighbouring Welsh gentleman; and he had himself the spirit of a gentleman. When he saw how poor Dominick was persecuted, he took him under his protection, fought his battles with the Welsh boys, and, instead of laughing at him for speaking Irish, he endeavoured to teach him to speak English. In his answers to the first question Edwards ever asked

1. creature.

2. i.e. blockhead. crammer = grammar.

him, little Dominick made two blunders, which set all his other companions in a roar: yet Edwards would not allow them to be genuine bulls.

In answer to the question, 'Who is your father?' Dominick said, with a deep sigh, 'I have no father — I am an orphan* — I have only a mother.'

'Have you any brothers and sisters?'

'No; I wish I had; perhaps they would love me, and not laugh at me,' said Dominick, with tears in his eyes; 'but I have no brothers but myself.'

One day Mr. Jones came into the school-room with an open letter in his hand, saying, 'Here, you little Irish plockit, here's a letter from your mother.'

The little Irish blockhead started from his form, and, throwing his grammar on the floor, leaped up higher than he or any boy in the school had ever been seen to leap before, and, clapping his hands, he exclaimed, 'A letter from my mother! And *will* I hear the letter? And *will* I see her once more? And *will* I go home these holydays? O, then I will be too happy!'

'There's no tanger of that,' said Mr. Owen ap Jones; 'for your mother, like a wise ooman, writes me here, that py the atvice of your cardian, to oom she is coing to be married, she will not pring you home to Ireland till I send her word you are perfect in your Enclish crammer at least.'

'I have my lesson perfect, sir,' said Dominick, taking his grammar up from the floor, '*will* I say it now?'

'*Will* I say it now? No, you plockit, no, and I will write your mother word you have proke Priscian's head[3] four times this tay, since her letter came. You Irish plockit!' continued the relentless grammarian, 'will you never learn the tifference between *shall* and *will*? *Will* I hear the letter, and *will* I see her once more? What Enclish is this, plockit?'

The Welsh boys all grinned, except Edwards, who hummed, loud enough to be heard, two lines of the good old English song,

'And *will* I see him once again?
And *will* I hear him speak?'

Many of the boys were fortunately too ignorant to feel the force of the quotation; but Mr. Owen ap Jones understood it, turned upon his heel, and walked off. Soon afterwards he summoned Dominick to his awful desk; and, pointing with his ruler to the following page in Harris's Hermes,[4] bade him 'reat it, and understant it, if he could.' Little Dominick read, but could not understand.

'Then reat it loud, you plockit.'

Dominick read aloud —

'There is *nothing appears so clearly* an object of the mind or intellect only as *the future* does, since we can find no place for its existence anywhere else: not but the same, if we consider, is *equally true* of the past—.'

'Well, co on — What stops the plockit? Can't you reat Enclish now?'

'Yes, sir; but I was trying to understand it. I was considering, that this is like what they would call an Irish bull, if I had said it.'

Little Dominick could not explain what he meant in English, that Mr. Owen ap Jones *would* understand; and, to punish him for his impertinent observation, the boy was doomed to learn all that Harris and Lowth[5] have written to explain the nature of *shall* and *will*. The reader, if he be desirous of knowing the full extent of the penance enjoined, may consult Lowth's Grammar, p. 52, ed. 1799, and Harris's Hermes, p. 10, 11, and 12, 4th edition. Undismayed at the length of his task, little Dominick only said, 'I hope, if I say it all without missing a word, you will not give my mother a bad account of me and my grammar studies, sir.'

'Say it all first, without missing a word, and then I shall see what I shall say,' replied Mr. Owen ap Jones.

Even the encouragement of this oracular answer excited the boy's fond hopes so keenly, that he lent his little soul to the task, learned it perfectly, said it at night, without missing one word, to his friend Edwards, and said it the next morning, without missing one word, to his master.

'And now, sir,' said the boy, looking up, 'will you write to my mother? And *shall* I see her? And *shall* I go home?'

'Tell me first, whether you understant all this that you have learnt so cliply[6],' said Mr. Owen ap Jones.

That was more than his bond. Our hero's coun-

* Iliad, 6th book, l. 432, Andromache says to Hector, 'You will make your son an orphan, and your wife a widow.'

3. Priscian was a celebrated Roman grammarian. 'To break Priscian's head' means to violate the rules of grammar.

4. James Harris, *Hermes or a Philosophical Inquiry concerning Universal Grammar* (1751 and subsequent editions.)

5. Robert Louth, *A Short Introduction to English Grammar* (1762 and subsequent editions).

6. i.e. glibly.

tenance fell: and he acknowledged that he did not understand it perfectly.

'Then I cannot write a coot account of you and your crammer studies to your mother; my conscience coes against it,' said the conscientious Mr. Owen ap Jones.

No entreaties could move him. Dominick never saw the letter that was written to his mother; but he felt the consequence. She wrote word this time punctually *by return of the post,* that she was sorry that she could not send for him home these holydays, as she heard so bad an account from Mr. Jones, &c. and as she thought it her duty not to interrupt the course of his education, especially his grammar studies. Little Dominick heaved many a sigh when he saw the packings up of all his school-fellows, and dropped a few tears as he looked out of the window, and saw them, one after another, get on their Welsh ponies, and gallop off towards their homes.

'I have no home to go to,' said he.

'Yes, you have,' cried Edwards; 'and *our* horses are at the door to carry us there.'

'To Ireland? me! the horses!' said the poor boy, quite bewildered: 'and will they bring me to Ireland?'

'No; the horses cannot carry you to Ireland,' said Edwards, laughing good-naturedly, 'but you have a home now in England. I asked my father to let me *take* you home with me; and he says "Yes," like a dear good father, and has sent the horses. Come, let's away.'

'But will Mr. Jones let me go?'

'Yes; he dare not refuse; for my father has a living in his gift[7] that Jones wants, and which he will not have, if he do not change his tune to you.'

Little Dominick could not speak one word, his heart was so full. No boy could be happier than he was during these holydays: 'the genial current of his soul,'[8] which had been frozen by unkindness, flowed with all its natural freedom and force.

When Dominick returned to school after these holydays were over, Mr. Owen ap Jones, who now found that the Irish boy had an English protector with a living in his gift, changed his tone. He never more complained unjustly that Dominick broke Priscian's head, seldom called him Irish plockit, and once would have flogged a Welsh boy for taking up this cast-off expression of the master's, but the Irish blockhead begged the culprit off.

Little Dominick sprang forward rapidly in his studies: he soon surpassed every boy in the school, his friend Edwards only excepted. In process of time, his guardian removed him to a higher seminary of education. Edwards had a tutor at home. The friends separated. Afterwards they followed different professions in distant parts of the world; and they neither saw nor heard any more of each other for many years. From boys they grew into men, and Dominick, now no longer little Dominick, went over to India as private secretary to one of our commanders in chief. How he got into this situation, or by what gradations he rose in the world, we are not exactly informed: we know only that he was the reputed author of a much-admired pamphlet on Indian affairs, that the despatches of the general to whom he was secretary were remarkably well written, and that Dominick O'Reilly, esq. returned to England, after several years' absence, not miraculously rich, but with a fortune equal to his wishes. His wishes were not extravagant: his utmost ambition was to return to his native country with a fortune that should enable him to live independently of all the world, especially of some of his relations, who had not used him well. His mother was no more.

Upon his arrival in London, one of the first things he did was to read the Irish newspapers. — To his inexpressible joy, he saw the estate of Fort-Reilly advertised to be sold — the very estate which had formerly belonged to his own family. Away he posted directly to an attorney's, who was empowered to dispose of the land.

When this attorney produced a map of the well-known pleasure-ground, and an elevation of that house in which he had spent the happiest hours of his infancy, his heart was so touched, that he was on the point of paying down more for an old ruin than a good new house would cost. The attorney acted *honestly by his client*, and seized this moment to exhibit a plan of the stabling and offices, which, as sometimes is the case in Ireland, were in a style far superior to the dwelling-house. Our hero surveyed these with transport. He rapidly planned various improvements in imagination, and planted certain favourite spots in the pleasure-ground. During this time the attorney was giving directions to a clerk about some other business: suddenly the name of

7. i.e. could bestow an ecclesiastical benefice.
8. cf. Thomas Gray's *Elegy Written in a Country Churchyard* (1751), line 52.

Owen ap Jones struck his ear — He started.

'Let him wait in the front parlour: his money is not forthcoming,' said the attorney; 'and if he keep Edwards in gaol till he rots —'

'Edwards! Good heavens! — in gaol! What Edwards?' exclaimed our hero.

It was his friend Edwards.

The attorney told him that Mr. Edwards had been involved in great distress by taking upon himself his father's debts, which had been incurred in exploring a mine in Wales; that of all the creditors none had refused to compound, except a Welsh parson, who had been presented to his living by old Edwards; and that this Mr. Owen ap Jones had thrown young Mr. Edwards into gaol for the debt.

'What is the rascal's demand? He shall be paid off this instant,' cried Dominick, throwing down the plan of Fort-Reilly: 'send for him up, and let me pay him off upon the spot.'

'Had not we best finish our business first, about the O'Reilly estate, sir?' said the attorney.

'No, sir; damn the O'Reilly estate,' cried he, huddling the maps together on the desk, and taking up the bank notes, which he had begun to reckon for the purchase money. 'I beg your pardon, sir. If you knew the facts, you would excuse me. Why does not this rascal come up to be paid?'

The attorney, thunderstruck by this Hibernian impetuousity, had not yet found time to take his pen out of his mouth. As he sat transfixed in his armchair, O'Reilly ran to the head of the stairs, and called out in a stentorian voice, 'Here, you Mr. Owen ap Jones; come up and be paid off this instant, or you shall never be paid *at all*.'

Up stairs hobbled the old schoolmaster, as fast as the gout and Welsh ale would let him. 'Cot pless me, that voice,' he began —

'Where's your bond, sir?' said the attorney.

'Safe here, Cot be praised,' said the terrified Owen ap Jones, pulling out of his bosom, first a blue pocket-handkerchief, and then a tattered Welsh grammar, which O'Reilly kicked to the farther end of the room.

'Here is my pond,' said he, 'in the crammer,' which he gathered from the ground; then fumbling over the leaves, he at length unfolded the precious deposit.

O'Reilly saw the bond, seized it, looked at the sum, paid it into the attorney's hands, tore the seal from the bond; then, without looking at old Jones, whom he dared not trust himself to speak to, he clapped his hat upon his head, and rushed out of the room. Arrived at the King's Bench prison, he hurried to the apartment where Edwards was confined. The bolts flew back; for even the turnkeys seemed to catch our hero's enthusiasm.

'Edwards, my dear boy! how do you do? Here's a bond debt, justly due to you for my education. O, never mind asking any unnecessary question; only just make haste out of this undeserved abode: our old rascal is paid off — Owen ap Jones, you know. — Well, how the man stares! Why, now, will you have the assurance to pretend to forget who I am? and must I *spake*,' continued he, assuming the tone of his childhood, 'and must I *spake* to you again in my ould Irish brogue, before you will ricollict your own *little Dominick*?'

When his friend Edwards was out of prison, and when our hero had leisure to look into business, he returned to the attorney, to see that Mr. Owen ap Jones had been legally satisfied.

'Sir,' said the attorney, 'I have paid the plaintiff in this suit; and he is satisfied: but I must say,' added he, with a contemptuous smile, 'that you Irish gentlemen are rather in too great a hurry in doing business: business, sir, is a thing that must be done slowly to be done well.'

'I am ready now to do business as slowly as you please; but when my friend was in prison, I thought the quicker I did his business the better. Now tell me what mistake I have made, and I will rectify it instantly.'

'*Instantly!* 'Tis well, sir, with your promptitude, that you have to deal with what prejudice thinks uncommon — an honest attorney. Here are some bank notes of yours, sir, amounting to a good round sum. You made a little blunder in this business: you left me the penalty, instead of the principal, of the bond — just twice as much as you should have done.'

'Just twice as much as was in the bond, but not twice as much as I should have done, nor half as much as I should have done, in my opinion,' said O'Reilly; 'but whatever I did was with my eyes open: I was persuaded you were an honest man; in which you see I was not mistaken; and as a man of business, I knew you would pay Jones only his due. The remainder of the money I meant, and mean, should lie in your hands for my friend Edward's use. I feared he would not have taken it from my hands: I therefore left it in yours. To have taken my friend out of prison merely to let him go back again to-day, for want of money to keep himself clear with the world, would have been a blunder indeed, but not an Irish blunder: our Irish blunders are never blunders of the heart.'

from: THE ABSENTEE (1812)

[The novel had its origins in a playscript, but the plot was happily adopted as the basis for this, the longest of the *Tales of Fashionable Life*. Nevertheless, the opening chapter's colourful dialogue retains something of the original dramatic form.]

CHAPTER I

'Are you to be at lady Clonbrony's gala next week?' said lady Langdale to Mrs. Dareville, whilst they were waiting for their carriages in the crush-room of the opera-house.[1]

'O yes! every body's to be there, I hear,' replied Mrs. Dareville. 'Your ladyship, of course?'

'Why, I don't know; if I possibly can. Lady Clonbrony makes it such a point with me, that I believe I must look in upon her for a few minutes. They are going to a prodigious expence on this occasion. Soho tells me the reception rooms are all to be new furnished, and in the most magnificent style.'

'At what a famous rate those Clonbronies are dashing on,' said colonel Heathcock. 'Up to any thing.'

'Who are they? — these Clonbronies, that one hears of so much of late?' said her grace of Torcaster. 'Irish absentees, I know. But how do they support all this enormous expence?'

'The son *will* have a prodigiously fine estate when some Mr. Quin dies,' said Mrs. Dareville.

'Yes, every body who comes from Ireland *will* have a fine estate when somebody dies,' said her grace. 'But what have they at present?'

'Ten thousand, I believe,' cried lady Langdale.

'Ten thousand, have they? — possibly,' said her grace. 'I know nothing about them — have no acquaintance among the Irish. Torcaster knows something of lady Clonbrony; she had fastened herself by some means, upon him; but I charge him not to *commit* me. Positively, I could not for any body, and much less for that sort of person, extend the circle of my acquaintance.'

'Now that is so cruel of your grace,' said Mrs. Dareville, laughing, 'when poor lady Clonbrony works so hard, and pays so high, to get into certain circles.'

'If you knew all she endures, to look, speak, move, breathe, like an Englishwoman, you would pity her,' said lady Langdale.

'Yes, and you *cawnt* conceive the *peens* she *teekes* to talk of the *teebles* and *cheers,* and to thank Q, and with so much *teeste* to speak pure English,' said Mrs. Dareville.

'Pure cockney, you mean,' said lady Langdale.

'But does lady Clonbrony expect to pass for English?' said the duchess.

'O yes! because she is not quite Irish *bred and born* — only bred, not born,' said Mrs. Dareville. 'And she could not be five minutes in your grace's company before she would tell you that she was *Henglish,* born in *Hoxfordshire.*'

'She must be a vastly amusing personage — I should like to meet her, if one could see and hear her incog.,' said the duchess. 'And lord Clonbrony, what is he?'

'Nothing, nobody,' said Mrs. Dareville: 'one never even hears of him.'

'A tribe of daughters too, I suppose?'

'No, no,' said lady Langdale; 'daughters would be past all endurance.'

'There's a cousin, though, a miss Nugent,' said Mrs. Dareville, 'that lady Clonbrony has with her.'

'Best part of her, too,' said colonel Heathcock — 'd——d fine girl! — never saw her look better than at the opera to-night!'

'Fine *complexion!* as lady Clonbrony says, when she means a high colour,' said lady Langdale.

'Miss Nugent is not a lady's beauty,' said Mrs. Dareville. 'Has she any fortune, colonel?'

''Pon honour, don't know,' said the colonel.

'There's a son, somewhere, is not there?' said lady Langdale.

'Don't know, 'pon honour,' replied the colonel.

'Yes — at Cambridge — not of age yet,' said Mrs. Dareville. 'Bless me! here is lady Clonbrony come

1. The opening chapter of *The Absentee* provides the names of many characters, great and small. As an indication of the harmful effects of absenteeism (or the alienation of this new nobility), the hero's title is a distortion of a place-name, Colambre instead of Coolamber (Co. Westmeath). To indicate further the significance of names throughout the novel, many minor figures have place-names as surnames. Grace Nugent, ultimately the heroine, bears the name of a famous Irish harp song, composed by the blind musician Turlogh Carolan (see p. 981).

back. I thought she was gone half an hour ago!'

'Mamma,' whispered one of lady Langdale's daughters, leaning between her mother and Mrs. Dareville, 'who is that gentleman that passed us just now?'

'Which way?'

'Towards the door. — There now, mamma, you can see him. He is speaking to lady Clonbrony — to miss Nugent — now lady Clonbrony is introducing him to miss Broadhurst.'

'I see him now,' said lady Langdale, examining him through her glass; 'a very gentlemanlike looking young man, indeed.'

'Not an Irishman, I am sure, by his manner,' said her grace.

'Heathcock!' said lady Langdale, 'who is miss Broadhurst talking to?'

'Eh! now really — 'pon honour — don't know,' replied Heathcock.

'And yet he certainly looks like somebody one should know,' pursued lady Langdale, 'though I don't recollect seeing him any where before.'

'Really now!' was all the satisfaction she could gain from the insensible, immoveable colonel. However, her ladyship, after sending a whisper along the line, gained the desired information, that the young gentleman was lord Colambre, son, only son, of lord and lady Clonbrony — that he was just come from Cambridge — that he was not yet of age — that he would be of age within a year; that he would then, after the death of somebody, come into possession of a fine estate by the mother's side; 'and therefore, Cat'rine, my dear,' said she, turning round to the daughter who had first pointed him out, 'you understand we should never talk about other people's affairs.'

'No, mamma, never. I hope to goodness, mamma, lord Colambre did not hear what you and Mrs. Dareville were saying!'

'How could he, child? — He was quite at the other end of the world.'

'I beg your pardon, ma'am — he was at my elbow, close behind us; but I never thought about him till I heard somebody say "my lord ——"'

'Good heavens! — I hope he didn't hear.'

'But, for my part, I said nothing,' cried lady Langdale.

'And for my part, I said nothing but what every body knows,' cried Mrs. Dareville.

'And for my part, I am guilty only of hearing,' said the duchess. 'Do, pray, colonel Heathcock, have to goodness to see what my people are about, and what chance we have of getting away to-night.'

'The duchess of Torcaster's carriage stops the way!' — a joyful sound to colonel Heathcock and to her grace, and not less agreeable, at this instant, to lady Langdale, who, the moment she was disembarrassed of the duchess, pressed through the crowd to lady Clonbrony, and addressing her with smiles and complacency, was charmed to have a little moment to speak to her — could *not* sooner get through the crowd — would certainly do herself the honour to be at her ladyship's gala. While lady Langdale spoke, she never seemed to see or think of any body but lady Clonbrony, though, all the time, she was intent upon every motion of lord Colambre; and whilst she was obliged to listen with a face of sympathy to a long complaint of lady Clonbrony's, about Mr. Soho's want of taste in ottomans, she was vexed to perceive that his lordship showed no desire to be introduced to her or to her daughters; but, on the contrary, was standing talking to miss Nugent. His mother, at the end of her speech, looked round for 'Colambre' — called him twice before he heard — introduced him to lady Langdale, and to lady Cat'rine, and lady Anne ——, and to Mrs. Dareville; to all of whom he bowed with an air of proud coldness, which gave them reason to regret that their remarks upon his mother and his family had not been made *sotto voce*.

'Lady Langdale's carriage stops the way!' Lord Colambre made no offer of his services, notwithstanding a look from his mother. Incapable of the meanness of voluntarily listening to a conversation not intended for him to hear, he had, however, been compelled, by the pressure of the crowd, to remain a few minutes stationary, where he could not avoid hearing the remarks of the fashionable friends: disdaining dissimulation, he made no attempt to conceal his displeasure. Perhaps his vexation was increased by his consciousness that there was some mixture of truth in their sarcasms. He was sensible that his mother, in some points — her manners, for instance — was obvious to ridicule and satire. In lady Clonbrony's address there was a mixture of constraint, affectation, and indecision, unusual in a person of her birth, rank, and knowledge of the world. A natural and unnatural manner seemed struggling in all her gestures, and in every syllable that she articulated — a naturally free, familiar, good-natured, precipitate, Irish manner, had been schooled, and schooled late in life, into a sober, cold, still, stiff deportment, which she mistook for English. A strong Hibernian accent she had, with infinite difficulty, changed into an English tone. Mistaking reverse of wrong for right, she caricatured the English pronunciation; and the extraordinary precision of her London phraseology betrayed her not to be a Londoner, as the man who strove to pass for an Athenian was detected by his Attic dialect. Not aware of her real danger, lady Clonbrony was, on the opposite side, in continual apprehension every time she opened her lips, lest some treacherous *a* or *e*, some strong *r*, some puzzling aspirate or non-aspirate, some unguarded note, interrogative, or expostulatory, should betray her to be an Irishwoman. Mrs. Dareville had, in her mimicry, perhaps, a little exaggerated, as to the *teebles* and *cheers*, but still the general likeness of the representation of lady Clonbrony was strong enough to strike and vex her son. He had now, for the first time, an opportunity of judging of the estimation in which his mother and his family were held by certain leaders of the ton,[2] of whom, in her letters, she had spoken so much, and into whose society, or rather into whose parties, she had been admitted. He saw that the renegado cowardice with which she denied, abjured, and reviled her own country, gained nothing but ridicule and contempt. He loved his mother; and, whilst he endeavoured to conceal her faults and foibles as much as possible from his own heart, he could not endure those who dragged them to light and ridicule. The next morning, the first thing that occurred to lord Colambre's remembrance, when he awoke, was the sound of the contemptuous emphasis which had been laid on the words Irish Absentees! — This led to recollections of his native country, to comparisons of past and present scenes to future plans of life. Young and careless as he seemed, lord Colambre was capable of serious reflection. Of naturally quick and strong capacity, ardent affections, impetuous temper, the early years of his childhood passed at his father's castle in Ireland, where, from the lowest servant to the well-dressed dependent of the family, every body had conspired to wait upon, to fondle, to flatter, to worship, this darling of their lord. Yet he was not spoiled — not rendered selfish; for in the midst of this flattery and servility, some strokes of genuine generous affection had gone home to his little heart; and though unqualified submission had increased the natural impetuosity of his temper, and though visions of his future grandeur had touched his infant thought, yet, fortunately, before he acquired any fixed habits of insolence or tyranny, he was carried far away from all that were bound or willing to submit to his commands, far away from all signs of hereditary grandeur — plunged into one of our great public schools — into a new world. Forced to struggle, mind and body, with his equals, his rivals, the little lord became a spirited school-boy, and in time, a man. Fortunately for him, science and literature happened to be the fashion among a set of clever young men with whom he was at Cambridge. His ambition for intellectual superiority was raised, his views were enlarged, his tastes and his manners formed. The sobriety of English good sense mixed most advantageously with Irish vivacity: English prudence governed, but did not extinguish, his Irish enthusiasm. But, in fact, England and Irish had not been invidiously contrasted in his mind: he had been so long resident in England, and so intimately connected with Englishmen, that he was not obvious to any of the commonplace ridicule thrown upon Hibernians; and he had lived with men who were too well informed and liberal to misjudge or depreciate a sister country. He had found, from experience, that, however reserved the English may be in manner, they are warm at heart; that, however averse they may be from forming new acquaintance, their esteem and confidence once gained, they make the most solid friends. He had formed friendships in England; he was fully sensible of the superior comforts, refinement, and information, of English society; but his own country was endeared to him by early association, and a sense of duty and patriotism attached him to Ireland. —— 'And shall I too be an absentee?' was a question which resulted from these reflections — a question which he was not yet prepared to answer decidedly.

In the mean time, the first business of the morning was to execute a commission for a Cambridge friend. Mr. Berryl had bought from Mr. Mordicai, a famous London coachmaker, a curricle,[3] *warranted sound*, for which he had paid a sound price, upon express condition that Mr. Mordicai should be answerable for all repairs of the

2. The fashionable world.

3. A light, two-wheeled carriage.

curricle for six months. In three, both the carriage and body were found to be good for nothing — the curricle had been returned to Mordicai — nothing had since been heard of it, or from him; and lord Colambre had undertaken to pay him and it a visit, and to make all proper inquiries. Accordingly, he went to the coachmaker's; and, obtaining no satisfaction from the underlings, desired to see the head of the house. He was answered that Mr. Mordicai was not at home. His lordship had never seen Mr. Mordicai; but just then he saw, walking across the yard, a man who looked something like a Bond-street coxcomb, but not the least like a gentleman, who called, in a tone of a master, for 'Mr. Mordicai's barouche!'[4] —— It appeared; and he was stepping into it, when lord Colambre took the liberty of stopping him; and, pointing to the wreck of Mr. Berryl's curricle, now standing in the yard, began a statement of his friend's grievances, and an appeal to common justice and conscience, which he, unknowing the nature of the man with whom he had to deal, imagined must be irresistible. Mr. Mordicai stood without moving a muscle of his dark wooden face — indeed, in his face there appeared to be no muscles, or none which could move; so that, though he had what are generally called handsome features, there was, altogether, something unnatural and shocking in his countenance. When, at last, his eyes turned and his lips opened, this seemed to be done by machinery, and not by the will of a living creature, or from the impulse of a rational soul. Lord Colambre was so much struck with this strange physiognomy, that he actually forgot much he had to say of springs and wheels — But it was no matter — Whatever he had said, it would have come to the same thing; and Mordicai would have answered as he now did; 'Sir, it was my partner made that bargain, not myself; and I don't hold myself bound by it, for he is the sleeping partner only, and not empowered to act in the way of business. Had Mr. Berryl bargained with me, I should have told him that he should have looked to these things before his carriage went out of our yard.'

The indignation of lord Colambre kindled at these words — but in vain: to all that indignation could by word or look urged against Mordicai, he replied, 'May be so, sir: the law is open to your friend — the law is open to all men, who can pay for it.'

Lord Colambre turned in despair from the callous coachmaker, and listened to one of his more compassionate-looking workmen, who was reviewing the disabled curricle; and, whilst he was waiting to know the sum of his friend's misfortune, a fat, jolly, Falstaff-looking personage came into the yard, and accosted Mordicai with a degree of familiarity which, from a gentleman, appeared to lord Colambre to be almost impossible.

'How are you, Mordicai, my good fellow?' cried he, speaking with a strong Irish accent.

'Who is this?' whispered lord Colambre to the foreman, who was examining the curricle.

'Sir Terence O'Fay, sir —— There must be entire new wheels.'

'Now tell me, my tight fellow,' continued sir Terence, holding Mordicai fast, 'when, in the name of all the saints, good or bad, in the calendar, do you reckon to let us sport the *suicide*?'[5]

'Will you be so good, sir, to finish making out this estimate for me?' interrupted lord Colambre.

Mordicai forcibly drew his mouth into what he meant for a smile, and answered 'As soon as possible, sir Terence.'

Sir Terence, in a tone of jocose, wheedling expostulation entreated him to have the carriage finished *out of hand*: 'Ah now! Mordy, my precious! let us have it by the birthday, and come and dine with us o' Monday at the Hibernian Hotel — there's a rare one — will you?'

Mordicai accepted the invitation, and promised faithfully that the *suicide* should be finished by the birthday. Sir Terence shook hands upon this promise, and, after telling a good story, which made one of the workmen in the yard — an Irishman — grin with delight, walked off. Mordicai, first waiting till the knight was out of hearing, called aloud, 'You grinning rascal! mind, at your peril, and don't let that there carriage be touched, d'ye see, till farther orders.'

One of Mr. Mordicai's clerks, with a huge long feathered pen behind his ear, observed that Mr. Mordicai was right in that caution, for that, to the best of his comprehension, sir Terence O'Fay, and his principal too, were over head and ears in debt.

Mordicai coolly answered, that he was well aware

4. A heavy, four-wheeled carriage.

5. A particularly dangerous type of fast carriage.

of that, but that the estate could afford to dip farther; that, for his part, he was under no apprehension; he knew how to look sharp, and to bite before he was bit: that he knew sir Terence and his principal were leagued together to give the creditors *the go by*; but that, clever as they were both at the work, he trusted he was their match.

'Immediately, sir — Sixty-nine pound four, and the perch[6] —— Let us see —— Mr. Mordicai, ask him, ask Paddy, about sir Terence,' said the foreman, pointing back over his shoulder to the Irish workman, who was at this moment pretending to be wondrous hard at work. However, when Mr. Mordicai defied him to tell him any thing he did not know, Paddy, parting with an untasted bit of tobacco, began and recounted some of sir Terence O'Fay's exploits in evading duns, replevying cattle, fighting sheriffs, bribing *subs*, managing cants, tricking *custodees*,[7] in language so strange, and with a countenance and gestures so full of enjoyment of the jest, that, whilst Mordicai stood for a moment aghast with astonishment, lord Colambre could not help laughing, partly at, and partly with, his countryman. All the yard were in a roar of laughter, though they did not understand half of what they heard; but their risible muscles were acted upon mechanically, or maliciously, merely by the sound of the Irish brogue.

Mordicai, waiting till the laugh was over, dryly observed, that 'the law is executed in another guess sort of way in England from what it is in Ireland;' therefore, for his part, he desired nothing better than to set his wits fairly against such *sharks* — that there was a pleasure in doing up a debtor, which none but a creditor could know.

'In a moment, sir; if you'll have a moment's patience, sir, if you please,' said the slow foreman to lord Colambre; 'I must go down the pounds once more, and then I'll let you have it.'

'I'll tell you what, Smithfield,' continued Mr. Mordicai, coming close beside his foreman, and speaking very low, but with a voice trembling with anger, for he was piqued by his foreman's doubts of his capacity to cope with sir Terence O'Fay; 'I'll tell you what, Smithfield, I'll be cursed if I don't get every inch of them into my power — you know how.'

'You are the best judge, sir,' replied the foreman; 'but I would not undertake sir Terence; and the question is, whether the estate will answer the *tote* of the debts, and whether you know them all for certain ——'

'I do, sir, I tell you: there' Green — there's Blancham — there's Gray — there's Soho' — naming several more — 'and, to my knowledge, lord Clonbrony ——'

'Stop, sir,' cried lord Colambre, in a voice which made Mordicai and every body present start; — 'I am his son ——'

'The devil!' said Mordicai.

'God bless every bone in his body, then, he's an Irishman!' cried Paddy; 'and there was the *ra*son my heart warmed to him from the first minute he come into the yard, though I did not know it till now.'

'What, sir! are you my lord Colambre?' said Mr. Mordicai, recovering, but not clearly recovering, his intellects: 'I beg pardon, but I did not know you *was* lord Colambre — I thought you told me you was the friend of Mr. Berryl.'

'I do not see the incompatibility of the assertion, sir,' replied lord Colambre, taking from the bewildered foreman's unresisting hand the account which he had been so long *furnishing*.

'Give me leave, my lord,' said Mordicai — 'I beg your pardon, my lord; perhaps we can compromise that business for your friend Mr. Berryl; since he is your lordship's friend, perhaps we can contrive to *compromise* and *split the difference*.'

To compromise, and *split the difference*, Mordicai thought were favourite phrases, and approved Hibernian modes of doing business, which would conciliate this young Irish nobleman, and dissipate the proud tempest, which had gathered, and now swelled in his breast.

'No, sir, no!' cried lord Colambre, holding firm the paper: 'I want no favour from you. I will accept of none for my friend or for myself.'

'Favour! No, my lord, I should not presume to offer —— But I should wish, if you'll allow me, to do your friend justice.'

Lord Colambre, recollecting that he had no right, in his pride, to fling away his friend's money, let Mr. Mordicai look at the account; and his impetuous temper in a few moments recovered by good sense, he considered, that, as his person was

6. The driver's seat.
7. Sir Terence had, in effect, avoided those demanding payment for debt (duns); recovered cattle taken from him by giving security to have the matter tried in a court of justice (replevying); bribed appointed proxys or deputies (subs); managed debtors' auctions (cants); tricked custodians (custodees).

utterly unknown to Mr. Mordicai, no offence could have been intended to him, and that, perhaps, in what had been said of his father's debts and distress, there might be more truth than he was aware of. Prudently, therefore, controlling his feelings, and commanding himself, he suffered Mr. Mordicai to show him into a parlour to *settle* his friend's business. In a few minutes the account was reduced to a reasonable form, and, in consideration of the partner's having made the bargain, by which Mr. Mordicai felt himself influenced in honour, though not bound in law, he undertook to have the curricle made better than new again, for Mr. Berryl, for twenty guineas. Then came awkward apologies to lord Colambre, which he ill endured. 'Between ourselves, my lord,' continued Mordicai ——

But the familiarity of the phrase, 'Between ourselves' — this implication of equality — lord Colambre could not admit: he moved hastily towards the door, and departed.

[Chapter VI sees the action move to Dublin from London. Maria Edgeworth's account of the Irish capital corresponds in detail with the accounts given in contemporary travel literature, although the ironic effects are peculiarly her own.

Here, in a resort district south of Dublin, the hero is forcibly reminded of his parents' trivial existence in London. Again, the theatrical substratum of the novel surfaces in brilliantly recorded table-talk.]

CHAPTER VI

The tide did not permit the packet[1] to reach the Pigeon-house, and the impatient lord Colambre stepped into a boat, and was rowed across the Bay of Dublin.[2] It was a fine summer morning. The sun shone bright on the Wicklow mountains. He admired, he exulted in the beauty of the prospect; and all the early associations of his childhood, and the patriotic hopes of his riper years, swelled his heart as he approached the shores of his native land. But scarcely had he touched his mother earth, when the whole course of his ideas was changed; and if his heart swelled, it swelled no more with pleasurable sensations, for instantly he found himself surrounded and attacked by a swarm of beggars and harpies, with strange figures and stranger tones; some craving his charity, some snatching away his luggage, and at the same time bidding him 'never trouble himself,' and 'never fear.' A scramble in the boat and on shore for bags and parcels began, and an amphibious fight betwixt men, who had one foot on sea and one on land, was seen; and long and loud the battle of trunks and portmanteaus raged! The vanquished departed, clinching their empty hands at their opponents, and swearing inextinguishable hatred; while the smiling victors stood at ease, each grasping his booty — bag, basket, parcel, or portmanteau: 'And, your honour, where *will* these go? — Where *will* we carry 'em all to for your honour?" was now the question. Without waiting for an answer, most of the goods were carried at the discretion of the porters to the custom-house, where, to his lordship's astonishment, after this scene of confusion, he found that he had lost nothing but his patience; all his goods were safe, and a few *tinpennies* made his officious porters happy men and boys; blessings were showered upon his honour, and he was left in peace at an excellent hotel, in —— street, Dublin. He rested, refreshed himself, recovered his good-humour, and walked into the coffee-house, where he found several officers, English, Irish, and Scotch. One English officer, a very gentlemanlike, sensible-looking man, of middle age, was sitting reading a little pamphlet, when lord Colambre entered; he looked up from time to time, and in a few minutes rose and joined the conversation; it turned upon the beauties and defects of the city of Dublin. Sir James Brooke (for that was the name of the gentleman) showed one of his brother officers the book which he had been reading, observing that, in his opinion, it contained one of the best views of Dublin which he had ever seen, evidently drawn by the hand of a master, though in a slight, playful, and ironical style: it was 'An intercepted Letter from China.' The conversation extended from Dublin to various parts of Ireland, with all which sir James Brooke showed that he was well acquainted. Observing that this conversation was particularly interesting to

1. i.e. packet-boat, the mail boat between Ireland and Britain.
2. This paragraph brings the absentee back to the land from which he derives his income and his title, and so it is much concerned with establishing the exact topography of his movements. *An Intercepted Letter from China* has been identified as an actual, though anonymous, pamphlet by John Wilson Croker (1780-1857), though M.E. has altered the title and misrepresented the contents for her own purposes. Works relating to Ireland by Spenser and Young are noted above (pp. 1015 and 1023); Sir John Davies (1569-1626) wrote *A Discovery of the True Causes why Ireland was Never Entirely Subdued* (1612). Daniel Augustus Beaufort (died 1821) was related by marriage to the Edgeworths; he published a *Memoir to a Map of Ireland* in 1792. The fictional character's reading list is, thus, largely authentic.

lord Colambre, and quickly perceiving that he was speaking to one not ignorant of books, sir James spoke of different representations and misrepresentations of Ireland. In answer to lord Colambre's inquiries, he named the works which had afforded him the most satisfaction; and with discriminative, not superficial celerity, touched on all ancient and modern authors on this subject, from Spenser and Davies to Young and Beaufort. Lord Colambre became anxious to cultivate the acquaintance of a gentleman who appeared so able and willing to afford him information. Sir James Brooke, on his part, was flattered by this eagerness of attention, and pleased by our hero's manners and conversation; so that, to their mutual satisfaction, they spent much of their time together whilst they were at this hotel; and, meeting frequently in society in Dublin, their acquaintance every day increased and grew into intimacy; an intimacy which was highly advantageous to lord Colambre's views of obtaining a just idea of the state of manners in Ireland. Sir James Brooke had at different periods been quartered in various parts of the country — had resided long enough in each to become familiar with the people, and had varied his residence sufficiently to form comparisons between different counties, their habits, and characteristics. Hence he had it in his power to direct the attention of our young observer at once to the points most worthy of his examination, and to save him from the common error of travellers — the deducing general conclusions from a few particular cases, or arguing from exceptions, as if they were rules. Lord Colambre, from his family connexions, had of course immediate introduction into the best society in Dublin, or rather into all the good society of Dublin. In Dublin there is positively good company, and positively bad; but not, as in London, many degrees of comparison: not innumerable luminaries of the polite world, moving in different orbits of fashion; but all the bright planets of note and name move and revolve in the same narrow limits. Lord Colambre did not find that either his father's or his mother's representations of society resembled the reality which he now beheld. Lady Clonbrony had, in terms of detestation, described Dublin such as it appeared to her soon after the Union; lord Clonbrony had painted it with convivial enthusiasm, such as he saw it long and long before the Union, when *first* he drank claret at the fashionable clubs. This picture, unchanged in his memory, and unchangeable by his imagination, had remained, and ever would remain, the same. The hospitality of which the father boasted, the son found in all its warmth, but meliorated and refined; less convivial, more social; the fashion of hospitality had improved. To make the stranger eat or drink to excess, to set before him old wine and old plate, was no longer the sum of good breeding. The guest now escaped the pomp of grand entertainments; was allowed to enjoy ease and conversation, and to taste some of that feast of reason and that flow of soul so often talked of, and so seldom enjoyed. Lord Colambre found a spirit of improvement, a desire for knowledge, and a taste for science and literature, in most companies, particularly among gentlemen belonging to the Irish bar: nor did he in Dublin society see any of that confusion of ranks or predominance of vulgarity, of which his mother had complained. Lady Clonbrony had assured him, that, the last time she had been at the drawing-room at the castle, a lady, whom she afterwards found to be a grocer's wife, had turned angrily when her ladyship had accidentally trodden on her train, and had exclaimed with a strong brogue, 'I'll thank you, ma'am, for the rest of my tail.'

Sir James Brooke, to whom lord Colambre, without *giving up his authority*, mentioned the fact, declared that he had no doubt the thing had happened precisely as it was stated; but that this was one of the extraordinary cases which ought not to pass into a general rule, — that it was a slight instance of that influence of temporary causes, from which no conclusions, as to national manners, should be drawn.

'I happened,' continued sir James, 'to be quartered in Dublin soon after the Union took place; and I remember the great but transient change that appeared from the removal of both houses of parliament: most of the nobility and many of the principal families among the Irish commoners, either hurried in high hopes to London, or retired disgusted and in despair to their houses in the country. Immediately, in Dublin, commerce rose into the vacated seats of rank; wealth rose into the place of birth. New faces and new equipages appeared: people, who had never been heard of before, started into notice, pushed themselves forward, not scrupling to elbow their way even at the castle; and they were presented to my lord-lieutenant and to my lady-lieutenant; for their excellencies might have played their vice-regal parts to empty benches, had they not admitted such persons for the moment to fill their court. Those of former times, of hereditary pretensions and high-bred minds and manners, were scandalized at all this; and they complained with justice, that the whole *tone* of society was altered; that the decorum, elegance, polish, and charm of society was gone. And I, among the rest,' said sir James, 'felt and deplored their change. But, now it's all over, we may acknowledge, that, perhaps, even those things which we felt most disagreeable at the time were productive of eventual benefit.

'Formerly, a few families had set the fashion. From time immemorial every thing had, in Dublin, been submitted to their hereditary authority; and conversation, though it had been rendered polite by their example, was, at the same time, limited within narrow bounds. Young people, educated upon a more enlarged plan, in time grew up; and no authority or fashion forbidding it, necessarily rose to their just place, and enjoyed their due influence in society. The want of manners, joined to the want of knowledge, in the *nouveaux riches*, created universal disgust: they were compelled, some by ridicule, some by bankruptcies, to fall back into their former places, from which they could never more emerge. In the mean time, some of the Irish nobility and gentry, who had been living at an unusual expence in London — an expence beyond their incomes — were glad to return home to refit; and they brought with them a new stock of ideas, and some taste for science and literature, which, within these latter years, have become fashionable, indeed indispensable, in London. That part of the Irish aristocracy, who, immediately upon the first incursions of the vulgarians, had fled in despair to their fastnesses in the country, hearing of the improvements which had gradually taken place in society, and assured of the final expulsion of the barbarians, ventured from their retreats, and returned to their posts in town. So that now,' concluded sir James, 'you find a society in Dublin composed of a most agreeable and salutary mixture of birth and education, gentility and knowledge, manner and matter; and you see pervading the whole new life and energy, new talent, new ambition, a desire and a determination to improve and be improved — a perception that higher distinction can now be obtained in almost all company, by genius and merit, than by airs and address .... So much for the higher order. Now, among the class of tradesmen and shopkeepers, you may amuse yourself, my lord, with marking the difference between them and persons of the same rank in London.'[3]

Lord Colambre had several commissions to execute for his English friends, and he made it his amusement in every shop to observe the manners and habits of the people. He remarked that there are in Dublin two classes of tradespeople: one, who go into business with intent to make it their occupation for life, and as a slow but sure means of providing for themselves and their families; another class, who take up trade merely as a temporary resource, to which they condescend for a few years; trusting that they shall, in that time, make a fortune, retire, and commence or recommence gentlemen. The Irish regular men of business are like all other men of business — punctual, frugal, careful, and so forth; with the addition of more intelligence, invention, and enterprise, than are usually found in Englishmen of the same rank. But the Dublin tradesmen *pro tempore* are a class by themselves: they begin without capital, buy stock upon credit, in hopes of making large profits, and, in the same hopes, sell upon credit.

Now, if the credit they can obtain is longer than that which they are forced to give, they go on and prosper; if not, they break, turn bankrupts, and sometimes, as bankrupts, thrive. By such men, of course, every *short cut* to fortune is followed: whilst every habit, which requires time to prove its advantage, is disregarded; nor, with such views, can a character for *punctuality* have its just value. In the head of a man, who intends to be a tradesman to-day, and a gentleman to-morrow, the ideas of the honesty and the duties of a tradesman, and of the honour and the accomplishments of a gentleman, are oddly jumbled together, and the characteristics of both are lost in the compound.

He will *oblige* you, but he will not obey you; he will do you a favour, but he will not do you *justice*; he will do *any thing to serve you*, but the particular thing you order he neglects; he asks your pardon, for he would not, for all the goods in his warehouse, *disoblige* you; not for the sake of your custom, but he has a particular regard for your family. Economy, in

3. Brooke's account of Dublin signally does not agree with that expressed in *An Intercepted Letter from J—— T——....* (1804), the original pamphlet by Croker which he is implied to have been reading.

the eyes of such a tradesman, is, if not a mean vice, at least a shabby virtue, of which he is too polite to suspect his customers, and to which he is proud of proving himself superior. Many London tradesmen, after making their thousands and their tens of thousands, feel pride in still continuing to live like plain men of business; but from the moment a Dublin tradesman of this style has made a few hundreds, he sets up his gig,[4] and then his head is in his carriage, and not in his business; and when he has made a few thousands, he buys or builds a country-house — and, then, and thenceforward, his head, heart, and soul, are in his country-house, and only his body in the shop with his customers.

Whilst he is making money, his wife, or rather his lady, is spending twice as much out of town as he makes in it. At the word country-house, let no one figure to himself a snug little box, like that in which a *warm* London citizen, after long years of toil, indulges himself, one day out of seven, in repose — enjoying, from his gazabo, the smell of the dust, and the view of passing coaches on the London road: no, these Hibernian villas are on a much more magnificent scale; some of them formerly belonged to Irish members of parliament, who were at a distance from their country-seats. After the Union these were bought by citizens and tradesmen, who spoiled, by the mixture of their own fancies, what had originally been designed by men of good taste.

Some time after lord Colambre's arrival in Dublin, he had an opportunity of seeing one of these villas, which belong to Mrs. Raffarty, a grocer's lady, and sister to one of lord Clonbrony's agents, Mr. Nicholas Garraghty. Lord Colambre was surprised to find that his father's agent resided in Dublin: he had been used to see agents, or stewards, as they are called in England, live in the country, and usually on the estate of which they have the management. Mr. Nicholas Garraghty, however, had a handsome house in a fashionable part of Dublin. Lord Colambre called several times to see him, but he was out of town, receiving rents for some other gentlemen, as he was agent for more than one property.

Though our hero had not the honour of seeing Mr. Garraghty, he had the pleasure of finding Mrs. Raffarty one day at her brother's house. Just as his lordship came to the door, she was going, on her jaunting-car, to her villa, called Tusculum, situate near Bray. She spoke much of the beauties of the vicinity of Dublin; found his lordship was going with sir James Brooke, and a party of gentlemen, to see the county of Wicklow; and his lordship and party were entreated to do her the honour of taking in their way a little collation at Tusculum.

Our hero was glad to have an opportunity of seeing more of a species of fine lady with which he was unacquainted.

The invitation was verbally made, and verbally accepted; but the lady afterwards thought it necessary to send a written invitation in due form, and the note she sent directed to the *most right honourable* the lord viscount Colambre. On opening it he perceived that it could not have been intended for him. It ran as follows:

'*My Dear Juliana O'Leary,*

'I have got a promise from Colambre, that he will be with us at Tusculum on Friday, the 20th, in his way from the county of Wicklow, for the collation I mentioned; and expect a large party of officers: so pray come early, with your house, or as many as the jaunting-car can bring. And pray, my dear, be *elegant*. You need not let it transpire to Mrs. O'G——; but make my apologies to miss O'G——, if she says any thing, and tell her I'm quite concerned I can't ask her for that day; because, tell her, I'm so crowded, and am to have none that day but *real quality*,

'Yours ever and ever,
'Anastasia Raffarty.

'P.S. And I hope to make the gentlemen stop the night with me: so will not have beds. Excuse haste and compliments, &c.'

Tusculum, Sunday 15.

After a charming tour in the county of Wicklow, where the beauty of the natural scenery, and the taste with which those natural beauties had been cultivated, far surpassed the sanguine expectations lord Colambre had formed, his lordship and his companions arrived at Tusculum, where he found Mrs. Raffarty, and miss Juliana O'Leary, very elegant, with a large party of the ladies and gentlemen of Bray, assembled in a drawing-room, fine with bad pictures and gaudy gilding; the windows were all shut, and the company were playing cards with all their might. This was the fashion of the neighbourhood. In compliment to

4. A light, two-wheeled, one-horse carriage, fashionable at this time.

lord Colambre and the officers, the ladies left the card-tables; and Mrs. Raffarty, observing that his lordship seemed *partial* to walking, took him out, as she said, 'to do the honours of nature and art.'

His lordship was much amused by the mixture, which was now exhibited to him, of taste and incongruity, ingenuity and absurdity, genius and blunder; by the contrast between the finery and vulgarity, the affectation and ignorance of the lady of the villa. We should be obliged to *stop* too long at Tusculum were we to attempt to detail all the odd circumstances of this visit; but we may record an example or two, which may give a sufficient idea of the whole.[5]

In the first place, before they left the drawing-room, miss Juliana O'Leary pointed out to his lordship's attention a picture over the drawing-room chimney-piece. 'Is not it a fine piece, my lord?' said she, naming the price Mrs. Raffarty had lately paid for it at an auction. 'It has a right to be a fine piece, indeed; for it cost a fine price!' Nevertheless this *fine* piece was vile daub; and our hero could only avoid the sin of flattery, or the danger of offending the lady, by protesting that he had no judgment in pictures.

'Indeed! I don't pretend to be a connoisseur or conoscenti myself; but I'm told the style is undeniably modern. And was not I lucky, Juliana, not to let that *Medona* be knocked down to me? I was just going to bid, when I heard such smart bidding; but, fortunately, the auctioneer let out that it was done by a very old master — a hundred years old. Oh! your most obedient, thinks I! — if that's the case, it's not for my money: so I bought this, in lieu of the smoke-dried thing, and had it a bargain.'

In architecture, Mrs. Raffarty had as good a taste and as much skill as in painting. There had been a handsome portico in front of the house: but this interfering with the lady's desire to have a viranda, which she said could not be dispensed with, she had raised the whole portico to the second story, where it stood, or seemed to stand, upon a tarpaulin roof. But Mrs. Raffarty explained, that the pillars, though they looked so properly substantial, were really hollow and as light as feathers, and were supported with cramps, without *disobliging* the front wall of the house at all to signify.[6]

Before she showed the company any farther, she said, she must premise to his lordship, that she had been originally stinted in room for her improvements, so that she could not follow her genius liberally; she had been reduced to have some things on a confined scale, and occasionally to consult her pocket-compass; but she prided herself upon having put as much into a tight pattern as could well be; that had been her whole ambition, study, and problem; for she was determined to have at least the honour of having a little *taste* of every thing at Tusculum.

So she led the way to a little conservatory, and a little pinery, and a little grapery, and a little aviary, and a little pheasantry, and a little dairy for show, and a little cottage for ditto, with a grotto full of shells, and a little hermitage full of earwigs, and a little ruin full of looking-glass, 'to enlarge and multiply the effect of the Gothic.' — 'But you could only put your head in, because it was just fresh painted, and though there had been a fire ordered in the ruin all night, it had only smoked.'

In all Mrs. Raffarty's buildings, whether ancient or modern, there was a studied crookedness.

Yes, she said, she hated every thing straight, it was so formal and *unpicturesque*. 'Uniformity and conformity,' she observed, 'had their day; but now, thank the stars of the present day, irregularity and deformity bear the bell, and have the majority.'

As they proceeded and walked through the grounds, from which Mrs. Raffarty, though she had done her best, could not take that which nature had given, she pointed out to my lord 'a happy moving termination,' consisting of a Chinese bridge, with a fisherman leaning over the rails. On a sudden, the fisherman was seen to tumble over the bridge into the water. The gentlemen ran to extricate the poor fellow, while they heard Mrs. Raffarty bawling to his lordship to beg he would never mind, and not trouble himself.

When they arrived at the bridge, they saw the man hanging from part of the bridge, and apparently struggling in the water; but when they attempted to pull him up, they found it was only a stuffed figure, which had been pulled into the

5. The original Tusculum was a district outside Rome during the late republican period, a fashionable resort associated with such eminent Romans as Cicero and Maecenas. M.E.'s 'Tusculum' is 'fashionable' but wholly untouched by any modern personalities of similar accomplishments. Circumstantial evidence indicates that she had in mind the La Touche house at Bellevue, Co. Wicklow when she described this fictional Tusculum.

6. i.e. significantly.

stream by a real fish, which had seized hold of the bait.

Mrs. Raffarty, vexed by the fisherman's fall, and by the laughter it occasioned, did not recover herself sufficiently to be happily ridiculous during the remainder of the walk, nor till dinner was announced, when she apologised for having changed the collation, at first intended, into a dinner, which she hoped would be found no bad substitute, and which she flattered herself might prevail on my lord and the gentleman to sleep, as there was no moon.

The dinner had two great faults — profusion and pretension. There was, in fact, ten times more on the table than was necessary; and the entertainment was far above the circumstances of the person by whom it was given: for instance, the dish of fish at the head of the table had been brought across the island from Sligo, and had cost five guineas; as the lady of the house failed not to make known. But, after all, things were not a piece; there was a disparity between the entertainment and the attendants; there was no proportion or fitness of things; a painful endeavour at what could not be attained, and a toiling in vain to conceal and repair deficiencies and blunders. Had the mistress of the house been quiet; had she, as Mrs. Broadhurst would say, but let things alone, let things take their course, all would have passed off with well-bred people; but she was incessantly apologising, and fussing, and fretting inwardly and outwardly, and directing and calling to her servants — striving to make a butler who was deaf, and a boy who was harebrained, do the business of five accomplished footmen of *parts and figure*. The mistress of the house called for 'plates, clean plates! —— plates!'

'But none did come, when she did call.'[7]

Mrs. Raffarty called 'Lanty! Lanty! My lord's plate, there! — James! bread to captain Bowles! — James! port wine to the major! — James! James Kenny! James!'

'And panting *James* toiled after her in vain.'[8]

7. A Russian editor of M.E., N. Damurova, compares Shakespeare I *Henry IV*, III. 1. 55: 'But will they come when you do call for them?'

8. cf. 'And panting Time toil'd after him in vain:' Samuel Johnson, 'Prologue spoken by Mr Garrick at the opening the theatre in Drury-Lane, 1747.'

At length one course was fairly got through, and after a torturing half hour, the second course appeared, and James Kenny was intent upon one thing, and Lanty upon another, so that the wine-sauce for the hare was spilt by their collision; but, what was worse, there seemed little chance that the whole of this second course should ever be placed altogether rightly upon the table. Mrs. Raffarty cleared her throat, and nodded, and pointed, and sighed, and sent Lanty after Kenny, and Kenny after Lanty; for what one did, the other undid; and at last the lady's anger kindled, and she spoke: 'Kenny! James Kenny! set the sea-cale at this corner, and put down the grass cross-corners; and match your maccaroni yonder with *them* puddens, set — Ogh! James! the pyramid in the middle, can't ye?'

The pyramid, in changing places, was overturned. Then it was that the mistress of the feast, falling back in her seat, and lifting up her hands and eyes in despair, ejaculated, 'Oh, James! James!'

The pyramid was raised by the assistance of the military engineers, and stood trembling again on its base; but the lady's temper could not be so easily restored to its equilibrium. She vented her ill-humour on her unfortunate husband, who happening not to hear her order to help my lord to some hare, she exclaimed loud, that all the world might hear, 'Corny Raffarty! Corny Raffarty! you're no more *gud* at the *fut* of my table than a stick of celery!'

The comedy of errors, which this day's visit exhibited, amused all the spectators. But lord Colambre, after he had smiled, sometimes sighed. — Similar foibles and follies in persons of different rank, fortune, and manner, appear to common observers so unlike that they laugh without scruples of conscience in one case, at what in another ought to touch themselves most nearly. It was the same desire to appear what they were not, the same vain ambition to vie with superior rank and fortune, or fashion, which actuated lady Clonbrony and Mrs. Raffarty; and whilst this ridiculous grocer's wife made herself the sport of some of her guests, lord Colambre sighed, from the reflection that what she was to them his mother was to persons in a higher rank of fashion. — He sighed still more deeply, when he considered, that, in whatever station or with whatever fortune, extravagance, that is, the living beyond our income, must lead to distress and meanness, and end in shame and ruin. In the morning, as they were riding away from Tusculum and talking over their visit, the officers laughed heartily, and rallying lord Colambre upon his seriousness, accused him of having fallen in love with Mrs. Raffarty, or with the *elegant* miss Juliana. Our hero, who wished never to be nice over much, or serious out of season, laughed with those that laughed, and endeavoured to catch the spirit of the jest. But sir James Brooke, who now was well acquainted with his countenance, and who knew something of the history of his family, understood his real feelings, and, sympathizing in them, endeavoured to give the conversation a new turn.

'Look there, Bowles,' said he, as they were just riding into the town of Bray; 'look at the barouche, standing at that green door, at the farthest end of the town. Is not that lady Dashfort's barouche?'

'It looks like what she sported in Dublin last year,' said Bowles; 'but you don't think she'd give us the same two seasons. Besides, she is not in Ireland, is she? I did not hear of her intending to come over again.'

'I beg your pardon,' said another officer; 'she will come again to so good a market, to marry her other daughter. I hear she said or swore that she will marry the young widow, lady Isabel, to an Irish nobleman.'

'Whatever she says, she swears, and whatever she swears, she'll do,' replied Bowles.

'Have a care, my lord Colambre; if she sets her heart upon you for lady Isabel, she has you. Nothing can save you. Heart she has none, so there you're safe, my lord,' said the other officer; 'but if lady Isabel sets her eye upon you, no basilisk's[9] is surer.'

'But if lady Dashfort had landed I am sure we should have heard of it, for she makes noise enough wherever she goes; especially in Dublin, where all she said and did was echoed and magnified, till one could hear of nothing else. I don't think she has landed.'

'I hope to Heaven they may never land again in Ireland!' cried sir James Brooke: 'one worthless woman, especially one worthless Englishwoman of rank, does incalculable mischief in a country like this, which looks up to the sister country for fashion. For my own part, as a warm friend to Ireland, I would rather see all the toads and serpents, and venomous reptiles, that St. Patrick carrried off in his bag, come back to this island, than these two *dashers*. Why, they would bite half the women and girls in the kingdom with the rage for mischief, before half the husbands and fathers could turn their heads about. And, once bit, there's no cure in nature or art.'

'No horses to this barouche!' cried captain Bowles. — 'Pray, sir, whose carriage is this?' said the captain to a servant, who was standing beside it.

'My lady Dashfort, sir, it belongs to,' answered the servant, in rather a surly English tone; and turning to a boy who was lounging at the door, 'Pat, bid them bring out the horses, for my ladies is in a hurry to get home.'

Captain Bowles stopped to make his servant alter the girths of his horse, and to satisfy his curiosity; and the whole party halted. Captain Bowles beckoned to the landlord of the inn, who was standing at his door.

'So, lady Dashfort is here again? — This is her barouche, is not it?'

'Yes, sir, she is — it is.'

'And has she sold her fine horses?'

'O no, sir — this is not her carriage at all — she is not here. That is, she is here, in Ireland; but down in the county of Wicklow, on a visit. And that is not her own carriage at all; — that is to say, not that which she has with herself, driving; but only just the cast barouche like, as she keeps for the lady's maids.'

'For the lady's maids! that is good! that is new, faith! Sir James, do you hear that?'

'Indeed, then, and it's true, and not a word of a lie!' said the honest landlord. 'And this minute, we've got a directory of five of them abigails,[10] sitting within our house; as fine ladies, as great dashers too, every bit, as their principals; and kicking up as much dust on the road, every grain! — Think of them, now! The likes of them, that must have four horses, and would not stir a foot with one less! — As the gentleman's gentleman there was telling and boasting to me about now, when the barouche was ordered for them there at the lady's house, where lady Dashfort is on a visit — they said they would not get in till they'd get four horses; and their ladies backed them: and so the four horses was got; and they just drove out here to see the points of view for fashion's sake, like their betters; and up with their glasses, like their ladies; and then out

9. A fabulous reptile; its look or even its breath was said to be fatal.

10. An abigail was a lady's maid, named after a character in Beaumont and Fletcher's play *The Scornful Lady* (1610).

with their watches, and "Isn't it time to lunch?" So there they have been lunching within on what they brought with them; for nothing in our house could they touch of course! They brought themselves a *pick-nick* lunch, with madeira and champagne to wash it down. Why, gentlemen, what do you think, but a set of them, as they were bragging to me, turned out of a boarding-house at Cheltenham, last year, because they had not peach pies to their lunch! — But, here they come! shawls, and veils, and all! — streamers flying! But mum is my cue! — Captain, are these girths to your fancy now?' said the landlord, aloud: then, as he stooped to alter a buckle, he said in a voice meant to be heard only by Captain Bowles, 'If there's a tongue, male or female, in the three kingdoms, it's in that foremost woman, Mrs. Petito.'

'Mrs. Petito!' repeated lord Colambre, as the name caught his ear; and, approaching the barouche, in which the five abigails were now seated, he saw the identical Mrs. Petito, who, when he left London, had been in his mother's service.

She recognised his lordship with very gracious intimacy; and, before he had time to ask any questions, she answered all she conceived he was going to ask, and with a volubility which justified the landlord's eulogium of her tongue.

'Yes, my lord! I left my lady Clonbrony some time back — the day after you left town; and both her ladyship and miss Nugent was charmingly, and would have sent their loves to your lordship, I'm sure, if they'd any notion I should have met you, my lord, so soon. And I was very sorry to part with them; but the fact was, my lord,' said Mrs. Petito, laying a detaining hand upon lord Colambre's whip, one end of which he unwittingly trusted within her reach, 'I and my lady had a little difference, which the best friends, you know, sometimes have: so my lady Clonbrony was so condescending to give me up to my lady Dashfort — and I knew no more than the child unborn that her ladyship had it in contemplation to cross the seas. But, to oblige my lady, and as colonel Heathcock, with his regiment of militia, was coming for purtection in the packet at the same time, and we to have the government-yacht, I waived my objections to Ireland. And, indeed, though I was greatly frightened at first, having heard all we've heard, you know, my lord, from lady Clonbrony, of there being no living in Ireland, and expecting to see no trees nor accommodation, nor any thing but bogs all along; yet I declare, I was very agreeably surprised; for, as far as I've seen at Dublin and in the vicinity, the accommodations, and every thing of that nature now, is vastly put-up-able with!'

'My lord,' said sir James Brooke, 'we shall be late.'

Lord Colambre, withdrawing his whip from Mrs. Petito, turned his horse away. She, stretching over the back of the barouche as he rode off, bawled to him, 'My lord, we're at Stephen's Green, when we're at Dublin.' But as he did not choose to hear, she raised her voice to its highest pitch, adding, 'And where are you, my lord, to be found? — as I have a parcel of miss Nugent's for you.'

Lord Colambre instantly turned back, and gave his direction.

'Cleverly done, faith!' said the major.

'I did not hear her say when lady Dashfort is to be in town,' said captain Bowles.

'What, Bowles! have you a mind to lose more of your guineas to lady Dashfort, and to be jockeyed out of another horse by lady Isabel?'

'O, confound it — no! I'll keep out of the way of that — I have had enough,' said captain Bowles; 'it is my lord Colambre's turn now; you hear that lady Dashfort would be very *proud* to see him. His lordship is in for it, and with such an auxiliary as Mrs. Petito, lady Dashfort has him for lady Isabel, as sure as he has a heart or hand.'

'My compliments to the ladies, but my heart is engaged,' said lord Colambre; 'and my hand shall go with my heart, or not at all.'

'Engaged! engaged to a very amiable, charming woman, no doubt,' said sir James Brooke. 'I have an excellent opinion of your taste; and if you can return the compliment to my judgment, take my advice: don't trust to your heart's being engaged, much less plead that engagement; for it would be lady Dashfort's sport, and lady Isabel's joy, to make you break your engagement, and break your mistress's heart; the fairer, the more amiable, the more beloved, the greater the triumph, the greater the delight in giving pain. All the time love would be out of the question; neither mother nor daughter would care if you were hanged, or, as lady Dashfort would herself have expressed it, if you were d—d.'

'With such women I should think a man's heart could be in no great danger,' said lord Colambre.

'There you might be mistaken, my lord; there's a way to every man's heart, which no man, in his own case, is aware of, but which every women knows right well, and none better than these ladies — by his vanity.'

'True,' said captain Bowles.

'I am not so vain as to think myself without vanity,' said lord Colambre; 'but love, I should imagine, is a stronger passion than vanity.'

'You should imagine! Stay till you are tried, my lord. Excuse me,' said captain Bowles, laughing.

Lord Colambre felt the good sense of this, and determined to have nothing to do with these dangerous ladies: indeed, though he had talked, he had scarcely yet thought of them; for his imagination was intent upon that packet from miss Nugent, which Mrs. Petito said she had for him. He heard nothing of it, or of her, for some days. He sent his servant every day to Stephen's Green, to inquire if lady Dashfort had returned to town. Her ladyship at last returned; but Mrs. Petito could not deliver the parcel to any hand but lord Colambre's own, and she would not stir out, because her lady was indisposed. No longer able to restrain his impatience, lord Colambre went himself — knocked at lady Dashfort's door — inquired for Mrs. Petito — was shown into her parlour. The parcel was delivered to him; but, to his utter disappointment, it was a parcel *for*, not *from* miss Nugent. It contained merely an odd volume of some book of miss Nugent's which Mrs. Petito said she had put up along with her things *in a mistake*, and she thought it her duty to return it by the first opportunity of a safe conveyance.

Whilst lord Colambre, to comfort himself for his disappointment, was fixing his eyes upon miss Nugent's name, written by her own hand, in the first leaf of the book, the door opened, and the figure of an interesting-looking lady, in deep mourning, appeared — appeared for one moment, and retired.

'Only my lord Colambre, about a parcel I was bringing for him from England, my lady — my lady Isabel, my lord,' said Mrs. Petito.

Whilst Mrs. Petito was saying this, the entrance and retreat had been made, and made with such dignity, grace, and modesty; with such innocence dove-like eyes had been raised upon him, fixed and withdrawn; with such a gracious bend the lady Isabel had bowed to him as she retired; with such a smile, and with so soft a voice, had repeated 'lord Colambre!' that his lordship, though well aware that all this was mere acting, could not help saying to himself, as he left the house, 'It is a pity it is only acting. There is certainly something very engaging in this woman. It is a pity she is an actress. And so young! A much younger woman than I expected. A widow before most women are wives. So young, surely she cannot be such a fiend as they described her to be!'

A few nights afterwards lord Colambre was with some of his acquaintance at the theatre, when lady Isabel and her mother came into the box, where seats had been reserved for them, and where their appearance instantly made that *sensation*, which is usually created by the entrance of persons of the first notoriety in the fashionable world. Lord Colambre was not a man to be dazzled by fashion, or to mistake notoriety for deference paid to merit, and for the admiration commanded by beauty or talents. Lady Dashfort's coarse person, loud voice, daring manners, and indelicate wit, disgusted him almost past endurance. He saw sir James Brooke in the box opposite to him; and twice determined to go round to him. His lordship had crossed the benches, and once his hand was upon the lock of the door; but, attracted as much by the daughter as repelled by the mother, he could move no farther. The mother's masculine boldness heightened, by contrast, the charms of the daughter's soft sentimentality. The lady Isabel seemed to shrink from the indelicacy of her mother's manners, and appeared peculiarly distressed by the strange efforts lady Dashfort made, from time to time, to drag her forward, and to fix upon her the attention of gentlemen. Colonel Heathcock, who, as Mrs. Petito had informed lord Colambre, had come over with his regiment to Ireland, was beckoned into their box by lady Dashfort, by her squeezed into a seat next to lady Isabel; but lady Isabel seemed to feel sovereign contempt, properly repressed by politeness, for what, in a low whisper to a female friend on the other side of her, she called, 'the self-sufficient inanity of this sad coxcomb.' Other coxcombs, of a more vivacious style, who stationed themselves round her mother, or to whom her mother stretched from box to box to talk, seemed to engage no more of lady Isabel's attention than just what she was compelled to give by lady Dashfort's repeated calls of, 'Isabel! Isabel! colonel G——. Isabel! lord D—— bowing to you. Bell! Bell! Sir Harry B——. Isabel, child, with your eyes on the stage? Did you never see a play before? Novice! major P—— waiting to catch your eye this quarter of an hour; and now her eyes gone down to her play-bill! Sir Harry, do take it from her.

"Were eyes so radiant only made to read?"'[11]

Lady Isabel appeared to suffer so exquisitely and so naturally from this persecution, that lord Colambre said to himself, 'If this be acting, it is the best acting I ever saw. If this be art, it deserves to be nature."

And with this sentiment he did himself the honour of handing lady Isabel to her carriage this night, and with this sentiment he awoke next morning; and by the time he had dressed and breakfasted, he determined that it was impossible all that he had seen could be acting. 'No woman, no young woman, could have such art.' Sir James Brooke had been unwarrantably severe; he would go and tell him so.

But sir James Brooke this day received orders for his regiment to march to quarters in a distant part of Ireland. His head was full of arms, and ammunition, and knapsacks, and billets, and routes; and there was no possibility, even in the present chivalrous disposition of our hero, to enter upon the defence of the lady Isabel. Indeed, in the regret he felt for the approaching and unexpected departure of his friend, lord Colambre forgot the fair lady. But just when sir James had his foot in the stirrup, he stopped.

'By the bye, my dear lord, I saw you at the play last night. You seemed to be much interested. Don't think me impertinent, if I remind you of our conversation when we were riding home from Tusculum; and if I warn you,' said he, mounting his horse, 'to beware of counterfeits — for such are abroad.' Reining in his impatient steed, sir James turned again and added, '*Deeds not words*, is my motto. Remember, we can judge better by the conduct of people towards others than by their manner towards ourselves.'

[A central scene in the novel, Chapter VIII is practically a *tableau vivant* of emblematic references and names, all of which have a particular resonance in Irish cultural history — e.g. O'Halloran, a reference to Sylvester O'Halloran, medical doctor and antiquarian (1728-1807), whose *An Introduction to the Study of the History and Antiquities of Ireland* (1772) was a seminal work for the Gaelic revival of the late eighteenth century. O'Halloran was also one of the founders of the Gaelic Society (1806). The hero is thus forced to stop and consider the larger purpose of his flight from London and of his search for a responsible role in society.]

11. Probably a line from a popular song.

CHAPTER VIII

One morning lady Dashfort had formed an ingenious scheme for leaving lady Isabel and lord Colambre *tête-à-tête*; but the sudden entrance of Heathcock disconcerted her intentions. He came to beg lady Dashfort's interest with count O'Halloran, for permission to hunt and shoot on his grounds next season. — 'Not for myself, 'pon honour, but for two officers who are quartered at the next *town* here, who will indubitably hang or drown themselves if they are debarred from sporting.'

'Who is this count O'Halloran?' said lord Colambre.

Miss White, lady Killpatrick's companion, said, 'he was a great oddity;' lady Dashfort, 'that he was singular;' and the clergyman of the parish, who was at breakfast, declared 'that he was a man of uncommon knowledge, merit, and politeness.'

'All I know of him,' said Heathcock, 'is, that he is a great sportsman, with a long queue,[1] a gold-laced hat, and long skirts to a laced waistcoat.'

Lord Colambre expressed a wish to see this extraordinary personage; and lady Dashfort, to cover her former design, and, perhaps, thinking absence might be as effectual as too much propinquity, immediately offered to call upon the officers in their way, and carry them with Heathcock and lord Colambre to Halloran Castle.

Lady Isabel retired with much mortification, but with becoming grace; and major Benson and captain Williamson were taken to the count's. Major Benson, who was a famous *whip*,[2] took his seat on the box of the barouche; and the rest of the party had the pleasure of her ladyship's conversation for three or four miles: of her ladyship's conversation — for lord Colambre's thoughts were far distant; captain Williamson had not any thing to say; and Heathcock nothing but 'Eh! re'lly now — 'pon honour!'

They arrived at Halloran Castle — a fine old building, part of it in ruins, and part repaired

1. A pig-tail or long plait of hair hanging from the back of the head.
2. A driver of horses.

with great judgment and taste. When the carriage stopped, a respectable looking man-servant appeared on the steps, at the open hall-door.

Count O'Halloran was out fishing; but his servant said that he would be at home immediately, if lady Dashfort and the gentleman would be pleased to walk in.

On one side of the lofty and spacious hall stood the skeleton of an elk; on the other side, the perfect skeleton of a moose-deer, which, as the servant said, his master had made out, with great care, from the different bones of many of this curious species of deer, found in the lakes in the neighbourhood. The leash[3] of officers witnessed their wonder with sundry strange oaths and exclamations. — 'Eh! 'pon honour — re'lly now!' said Heathcock; and, too genteel to wonder at or admire any thing in the creation, dragged out his watch with some difficulty, saying, 'I wonder now whether they are likely to think of giving us any thing to eat in this place?' And, turning his back upon the moose-deer, he straight walked out again upon the steps, called to his groom, and began to make some inquiry about his led horse. Lord Colambre surveyed the prodigious skeletons with rational curiosity, and with that sense of awe and admiration, by which a superior mind is always struck on beholding any of the great works of Providence.

'Come, my dear lord!' said lady Dashfort; 'with our sublime sensations, we are keeping my old friend, Mr. Ulick Brady, this venerable person, waiting to show us into the reception-room.'

The servant bowed respectfully — more respectfully than servants of modern date.

'My lady, the reception-room has been lately painted, — the smell of paint may be disagreeable; with your leave, I will take the liberty of showing you into my master's study.'

He opened the door, went in before her, and stood holding up his finger, as if making a signal of silence to some one within. Her ladyship entered, and found herself in the midst of an odd assembly: an eagle, a goat, a dog, an otter, several gold and silver fish in a glass globe, and a white mouse in a cage. The eagle, quick of eye but quiet of demeanour, was perched upon his stand; the otter lay under a table, perfectly harmless; the Angora goat, a beautiful and remarkably little creature of its kind, with long, curling, silky hair, was walking along the room with the air of a beauty and a favourite; the dog, a tall Irish greyhound — one of the few of that fine race, which is now almost extinct — had been given to count O'Halloran by an Irish nobleman, a relation of lady Dashfort's. This dog, who had formerly known her ladyship, looked at her with ears erect, recognised her, and went to meet her the moment she entered. The servant answered for the peaceable behaviour of all the rest of the company of animals, and retired. Lady Dashfort began to feed the eagle from a silver plate on his stand; lord Colambre examined the inscription on his collar; the other men stood in amaze. Heathcock, who came in last, astonished out of his constant 'Eh! re'lly now!' the moment he put himself in at the door, exclaimed, 'Zounds! what's all this live lumber?' and he stumbled over the goat, who was at that moment crossing the way. The colonel's spur caught in the goat's curly beard; the colonel shook his foot, and entangled the spur worse and worse; the goat struggled and butted; the colonel skated forward on the polished oak floor, balancing himself with outstretched arms.

The indignant eagle screamed, and, passing by, perched on Heathcock's shoulders. Too well bred to have recourse to the terrors of his beak, he scrupled not to scream, and flap his wings about the colonel's ears. Lady Dashfort, the while, threw herself back in her chair, laughing, and begging Heathcock's pardon. 'Oh, take care of the dog, my dear colonel!' cried she; 'for this kind of dog seizes his enemy by the back, and shakes him to death.' The officers, holding their sides, laughed and begged — no pardon; while lord Colambre, the only person who was not absolutely incapacitated, tried to disentangle the spur, and to liberate the colonel from the goat, and the goat from the colonel; an attempt in which he at last succeeded, at the expence of a considerable portion of the goat's beard. The eagle, however, still kept his place; and, yet mindful of the wrongs of his insulted friend the goat, had stretched his wings to give another buffet. Count O'Halloran entered, and the bird, quitting his prey, flew down to greet his master. The count was a fine old military-looking gentleman, fresh from fishing: his fishing accoutrements hanging carelessly about him, he advanced, unembarrassed, to lady Dashfort; and received his other guests with a mixture of military ease and gentlemanlike dignity.

Without adverting to the awkward and

3. The term is normally used for a set of three hounds.

ridiculous situation in which he had found poor Heathcock, he apologised in general for his troublesome favourites. 'For one of them,' said he, patting the head of the dog, which lay quiet at lady Dashfort's feet, 'I see I have no need to apologise; he is where he ought to be. Poor fellow! he has never lost his taste for the good company to which he was early accustomed. As to the rest,' said he, turning to lady Dashfort, 'a mouse, a bird, and a fish, are, you know, tribute from earth, air, and water, to a conqueror ——'

'But from no barbarous Scythian!' said lord Colambre, smiling. The count looked at lord Colambre, as at a person worthy his attention; but his first care was to keep the peace between his loving subjects and his foreign visitors. It was difficult to dislodge the old settlers, to make room for the new comers: but he adjusted these things with admirable facility; and, with a master's hand and master's eye, compelled each favourite to retreat into the back settlements. With becoming attention, he stroked and kept quiet old Victory, his eagle, who eyed colonel Heathcock still, as if he did not like him; and whom the colonel eyed as if he wished his neck fairly wrung off. The little goat had nestled himself close up to his liberator, lord Colambre, and lay perfectly quiet, with his eyes closed, going very wisely to sleep, and submitting philosophically to the loss of one half of his beard. Conversation now commenced, and was carried on by count O'Halloran with much ability and spirit, and with such quickness of discrimination and delicacy of taste, as quite surprised and delighted our hero. To the lady the count's attention was first directed: he listened to her as she spoke, bending with an air of deference and devotion. She made her request for permission for major Benson and captain Williamson to hunt and shoot in his grounds next season: this was instantly granted.[4]

Her ladyship's requests were to him commands, the count said. — His gamekeeper should be instructed to give the gentlemen, her friends, every liberty, and all possible assistance.

4. 'Count' indicates that O'Halloran bears a foreign title and suggests that he has served abroad for regimes hostile to Britain: hence the nervousness of the British officers in his company. Colambre's allusion to the Scythians, together with the strangely emblematic arrangement of the Count's pets, refers to an account in Herodotus (Book IV) of how the Scythians insulted and defeated Darius, king of the invading Persians. The implication is that Colambre declines to see in the Count an adversary or barbarian, despite their very different backgrounds.

Then, turning to the officers, he said, he had just heard that several regiments of English militia had lately landed in Ireland; that one regiment was arrived at Killpatrick's-town. He rejoiced in the advantages Ireland, and he hoped he might be permitted to add, England, would probably derive from the exchange of the militia of both countries: habits would be improved, ideas enlarged. The two countries have the same interest; and, from the inhabitants discovering more of each other's good qualities, and interchanging little good offices in common life, their esteem and affection for each other would increase, and rest upon the firm basis of mutual utility.

To all this major Benson answered only, 'We are not militia officers.'

'The major looks so like a stuffed man of straw,' whispered lady Dashfort to lord Colambre, 'and the captain so like the king of spades, putting forth one manly leg.'

Count O'Halloran now turned the conversation to field sports, and then the captain and major opened at once.

'Pray now, sir,' said the major, 'you fox-hunt in this country, I suppose; and now do you manage the thing here as we do? Over night, you know, before the hunt, when the fox is out, stopping up the earths of the cover we mean to draw, and all the rest for four miles round. Next morning we assemble at the cover's side, and the huntsman throws in the hounds. The gossip here is no small part of the entertainment: but as soon as we hear the hounds give tongue ——'

'The favourite hounds,' interposed Williamson.

'The favourite hounds, to be sure,' continued Benson: 'there is a dead silence till pug[5] is well out of cover, and the whole pack well in: then cheer the hounds with tally-ho! till your lungs crack. Away he goes in gallant style, and the whole field is hard up, till pug takes a stiff country: then they who haven't pluck lag, see no more of him, and, with a fine blazing scent, there are but few of us in at the death.'

'Well, we are fairly in at the death, I hope,' said lady Dashfort: 'I was thrown out sadly at one time in the chase.'

Lord Colambre, with the count's permission, took up a book in which the count's pencil lay, 'Pasley on the Military Policy of Great Britain;' it

5. i.e. the fox.

was marked with many notes of admiration, and with hands pointing to remarkable passages.[6]

'That is a book that leaves a strong impression on the mind,' said the count.

Lord Colambre read one of the marked passages, beginning with 'All that distinguishes a soldier in outward appearance from a citizen is so trifling ——' but at this instant our hero's attention was distracted by seeing in a black-letter book this title of a chapter: 'Burial-place of the Nugents.'[7]

'Pray now, sir,' said captain Williamson, 'if I don't interrupt you, as you are a fisherman too; now in Ireland do you, *Mr.* ——'

A smart pinch on his elbow from his major, who stood behind him, stopped the captain short, as he pronounced the word *Mr.* Like all awkward people, he turned directly to ask, by his looks, what was the matter.

The major took advantage of his discomfiture, and, stepping before him, determined to have the fishing to himself, and went on with, 'Count O'Halloran, I presume you understand fishing, too, as well as hunting?'

The count bowed: 'I do not presume to say that, sir.'

'But pray, count, in this country, do you arm your hook this ways? Give me leave;' taking the whip from Williamson's reluctant hand, 'this ways, laying the outermost part of your feather this fashion next to your hook, and the point next to your shank, this wise, and that wise, and then, sir, — count, you take the hackle of a cock's neck ——'

'A plover's topping's better,' said Williamsom.

'And work your gold and silver thread,' pursued Benson, 'up to your wings, and when your head's made, you fasten all.'

'But you never showed how your head's made,' interrupted Williamson.

'The gentleman knows how a head's made; any man can make a head, I suppose: so, sir, you fasten all.'

'You'll never get your head fast on that way, while the world stands,' cried Williamson.

'Fast enough for all purposes; I'll bet you a rump and dozen,[8] captain: and then sir, — count, you divide your wings with a needle.'

'A pin's point will do,' said Williamson.

The count, to reconcile matters, produced from an Indian cabinet, which he had opened for lady Dashfort's inspection, a little basket containing a variety of artificial flies of curious construction, which, as he spread them on the table, made Williamson and Benson's eyes almost sparkle with delight. There was the *dun-fly*, for the month of March; and the *stone-fly*, much in vogue for April; and the *ruddy-fly*, of red wool, black silk, and red capon's feathers.

Lord Colambre, whose head was in the burial-place of the Nugents, wished them all at the bottom of the sea.

'And the *green-fly*, and the *moorish-fly*!' cried Benson, snatching them up with transport; 'and, chief, the *sad-yellow-fly*, in which the fish delight in June; the *sad-yellow-fly*, made with the buzzard's wings, bound with black braked hemp, and the *shell-fly*, for the middle of July, made of greenish wool, wrapped about with the herle[9] of a peacock's tail, famous for creating excellent sport.' All these and more were spread upon the table before the sportsmen's wondering eyes.

'Capital flies! capital, faith!' cried Williamson.

'Treasures, faith, real treasures, by G—!' cried Benson.

'Eh! 'pon honour! re'lly now,' were the first words which Heathcock had uttered since his battle with the goat.

'My dear Heathcock, are you alive still?' said lady Dashfort: 'I had really forgotten your existence.'

So had count O'Halloran, but he did not say so.

'Your ladyship has the advantage of me there,' said Heathcock, stretching himself; 'I wish I could forget my existence, for, in my mind, existence is a horrible *bore*.'

'I thought you *was* a sportsman,' said Williamson.

'Well, sir?'

'And a fisherman?'

'Well, sir?'

'Why look you there, sir,' pointing to the flies, 'and tell a body life's a bore.'

6. Charles William Pasley's *Military Policy* .... appeared in 1812, the same year as *The Absentee* itself.

7. The Nugents were an important Irish family of Norman extraction, traditionally Jacobite and catholic in their loyalties: thus tension would surround any suggestion of marriage between Grace Nugent and Colambre. The book containing a description of the burial-place of the Nugents has not been identified.

8. An Irish wager, 'A rump of beef and a dozen of claret'.

9. herle = harle: the barb or fibre of a feather. The flies named suggest that the speaker's knowledge of fly-fishing was superficial.

'One can't *always* fish or shoot, I apprehend, sir,' said Heathcock.

'Not always — but sometimes,' said Williamson, laughing; 'for I suspect shrewdly you've forgot some of your sporting in Bond-street.'

'Eh! 'pon honour! re'lly now!' said the colonel, retreating again to his safe entrenchment of affectation, from which he never could venture without imminent danger.

''Pon honour,' cried lady Dashfort, 'I can swear for Heathcock, that I have eaten excellent hares and ducks of his shooting, which, to my knowledge,' added she, in a loud whisper, 'he bought in the market.'

'*Emptum aprum!*'[10] said lord Colambre to the count, without danger of being understood by those whom it concerned.

The count smiled a second time; but politely turning the attention of the company from the unfortunate colonel, by addressing himself to the laughing sportsmen, 'Gentlemen, you seem to value these,' said he, sweeping the artificial flies from the table into the little basket from which they had been taken; 'would you do me the honour to accept of them? They are all of my own making, and consequently of Irish manufacture.' Then, ringing the bell, he asked lady Dashfort's permission to have the basket put into her carriage.

Benson and Williamson followed the servant, to prevent them from being tossed into the boot. Heathcock stood still in the middle of the room, taking snuff.

Count O'Halloran turned from him to lord Colambre, who had just got happily to *the burial-place of the Nugents*, when lady Dashfort, coming between them, and spying the title of the chapter, exclaimed, 'What have you there? — Antiquities! my delight! — but I never look at engravings when I can see realities.'

Lord Colambre was then compelled to follow, as she led the way, into the hall, where the count took down golden ornaments, and brass-headed spears, and jointed horns of curious workmanship, that had been found on his estate; and he told of spermaceti wrapped in carpets,[11] and he showed small urns, enclosing ashes; and from among these urns he selected one, which he put into the hands of lord Colambre, telling him, that it had been lately found in an old abbey-ground in his neighbourhood, which had been the burial-place of some of the Nugent family.

'I was just looking at the account of it, in the book which you saw open on my table. — And as you seem to take an interest in that family, my lord, perhaps,' said the count, 'you may think this urn worth your acceptance.'

Lord Colambre said, 'It would be highly valuable to him — as the Nugents were his near relations.'

Lady Dashfort little expected this blow; she, however, carried him off to the moose-deer, and from moose-deer to round-towers, to various architectural antiquities, and to the real and fabulous history of Ireland, on all which the count spoke with learning and enthusiasm. But now, to colonel Heathcock's great joy and relief, a handsome collation appeared in the dining-room, of which Ulick opened the folding-doors.

'Count, you have made an excellent house of your castle,' said lady Dashfort.

'It will be, when it is finished,' said the count. 'I am afraid,' added he, smiling, 'I live like many other Irish gentlemen, who never are, but always to be, blest[12] with a good house. I began on too large a scale, and can never hope to live to finish it.'

''Pon honour! here's a good thing, which I hope we shall live to finish,' said Heathcock, sitting down before the collation; and heartily did he eat of eel-pie, and of Irish ortolans,* which, as lady Dashfort observed, 'afford him indemnity for the past, and security for the future.'

'Eh! re'lly now! your Irish ortolans are famous good eating,' said Heathcock.

* As it may be satisfactory to a large portion of the public, to all men of taste, the editor subjoins the following account of the Irish ortolan, which will convince the world that this bird is not in the class of fabulous animals:

'There is a small bird, which is said to be peculiar to the Blasquet Islands, called by the Irish Gourder, the English name of which I am at a loss for, nor do I find it mentioned by naturalists. It is somewhat larger than a sparrow; the feathers of the back are dark, and those of the belly are white; the bill is straight, short, and thick; and it is web-footed: they are almost one lump of fat; when roasted, of a most delicious taste, and are reckoned to exceed an ortolan; for which reason the gentry hereabouts call them the *Irish ortolan*. These birds are worthy of being transmitted a great way to market; for ortolans, it is well known, are brought from France to supply the markets of London.' — See Smith's Account of the County of Kerry, p. 186. [The ortolan is a species of bunting. Ed.]

10. i.e. 'Wild boars purchased!'

11. Spermaceti (from the head of the sperm-whale) was anciently used in lamps and to make candles; it was wrapped in order to keep it moist.

12. cf. Alexander Pope, *An Essay on Man*, line 96.

'Worth being quartered in Ireland, faith! to taste 'em,' said Benson.

The count recommended to lady Dashfort some of 'that delicate sweetmeat, the Irish plum.'

'Bless me, sir, — count!' cried Williamson, 'it's by far the best thing of the kind I ever tasted in all my life: where could you get this?'

'In Dublin, at my dear Mrs. Godey's; where *only*, in his majesty's dominions, it is to be had,' said the count.

The whole vanished in a few seconds.

''Pon honour! I do believe this is the thing the queen's so fond of,' said Heathcock.

Then heartily did he drink of the count's excellent Hungarian wines; and, by the common bond of sympathy between those who have no other tastes but eating and drinking, the colonel, the major, and the captain, were now all the best companions possible for one another.

Whilst 'they prolonged the rich repast,'[13] lady Dashfort and lord Colambre went to the window to admire the prospect: lady Dashfort asked the count the name of some distant hill.

'Ah!' said the count, 'that hill was once covered with fine wood; but it was all cut down two years ago.'

'Who could have been so cruel?' said her ladyship.

'I forget the present proprietor's name,' said the count; 'but he is one of those who, according to *the clause of distress* in their leases, *lead, drive, and carry away*, but never *enter* their lands; one of those enemies to Ireland — those cruel absentees!'

Lady Dashfort looked through her glass at the mountain: — lord Colambre sighed, and, endeavouring to pass it off with a smile, said frankly to the count, 'You are not aware, I am sure, count, that you are speaking to the son of an Irish absentee family. Nay, do not be shocked, my dear sir; I tell you only because I thought it fair to do so: but let me assure you, that nothing you could say on that subject could hurt me personally, because I feel that I am not, that I never can be, an enemy to Ireland. An absentee, voluntarily, I never yet have been; and as to the future, I declare ——'

'I declare you know nothing of the future,' interrupted lady Dashfort, in a half peremptory, half playful tone — 'you know nothing: make no rash vows, and you will break none.'

13. Alexander Pope, *The Rape of the Lock*, III, 112.

The undaunted assurance of lady Dashfort's genius for intrigue gave her an air of frank imprudence, which prevented lord Colambre from suspecting that more was meant than met the ear. The count and he took leave of one another with mutual regard; and lady Dashfort rejoiced to have got our hero out of Halloran Castle.

[Though the novel is evidently heading towards 'a happy ending' in Colambre's marriage with Grace Nugent, the conclusion actually takes the form of a letter. This distances the reader from a sentimental interpretation while drawing in broader social perspectives.]

LETTER FROM LARRY TO HIS BROTHER, PAT BRADY, AT MR. MORDICAI'S, COACHMAKER, LONDON.[1]

'My dear brother,

'Yours of the 16th, enclosing the five pound note for my father, came safe to hand Monday last; and with his thanks and blessing to you, he commends it to you herewith enclosed back again, on account of his being in no immediate necessity, nor likelihood to want in future, as you shall hear forthwith; but wants you over with all speed, and the note will answer for travelling charges; for we can't enjoy the luck it has pleased God to give us, without *yees*;[2] put the rest in your pocket, and read it when you've time.

'Old Nick's[3] gone, and St. Dennis along with him, to the place he come from — praise be to God! The *ould* lord has found him out in his tricks; and I helped him to that, through the young lord that I driv, as I informed you in my last, when he was a Welshman, which was the best turn ever I did, though I did not know it no more than Adam that time. So *ould* Nick's turned out of the agency clean and clear; and the day after it was known, there was surprising great joy through the whole country;

1. This concluding letter from Larry Brady to his brother in England constitutes the earliest fictional treatment of emigrant Irish workers in Britain, even if the treatment is highly indirect. The topic was not one that caught even Charles Dickens's attention. That Larry Brady's brother works for Mordicai, the coachmaker of the opening chapter, sets up a neat circularity while also indicating that the abandonment of absenteeism is not a course open to all grades of Irishmen.
2. i.e. you (plural).
3. 'Old Nick' and 'St. Dennis' are Mr Nicholas and Mr Dennis Garraghty, the unscrupulous and unjust agents who had managed the Clonbrony and Colambre estates and whose villainy has been exposed by Lord Colambre, who had visited the estates *incognito*.

not surprising, either, but just what you might, knowing him, *ra*sonably expect. He (that is, old Nick and St. Dennis) would have been burnt that night — I *mane*, in *effigy*, through the town of Clonbrony, but that the new man, Mr. Burke,[4] came down that day too soon to stop it, and said, "it was not becoming to trample on the fallen," or something that way, that put an end to it; and though it was a great disappointment to many, and to me in particular, I could not but like the jantleman the better for it any how. They say, he is a very good jantleman, and as unlike old Nick or the saint as can be; and takes no duty fowl, nor glove, nor sealing money;[5] nor asks duty work nor duty turf. Well, when I was disappointed of the *effigy*, I comforted myself by making a bonfire of old Nick's big rick of duty turf, which, by great luck, was out in the road, away from all dwelling-house, or thatch, or yards, to take fire: so no danger in life or objection. And such another blaze! I wished you'd seed it — and all the men, women, and children, in the town and country, far and near, gathered round it shouting and dancing like mad! — and it was light as day quite across the bog, as far as Bartley Finnigan's house. And I heard after, they seen it from all parts of the three counties, and they thought it was St. John's Eve[6] in a mistake — or couldn't make out what it was; but all took it in good part, for a good sign, and were in great joy. As for St. Dennis and *ould* Nick, an attorney had his foot upon 'em with an habere a latitat,[7] and three executions hanging over 'em: and there's the end of rogues! and a great example in the country. And — no more about it; for I can't be wasting more ink upon them that don't deserve it at my hands, when I want it for them that do, as you shall see. So some weeks past, and there was great cleaning at Clonbrony Castle, and in the town of Clonbrony; and the new agent's smart and clever: and he had the glaziers, and the painters, and the slaters, up and down in the town wherever wanted; and you wouldn't know it again. Thinks I, this is no bad sign! Now, cock up your ears, Pat! for the great news is coming, and the good. The master's come home, long life to him! and family come home yesterday, all entirely! The *ould* lord and the young lord, (ay, there's the man, Paddy!) and my lady, and miss Nugent. And I driv miss Nugent's maid and another; so I had the luck to be in it along *wid* 'em, and see all, from first to last. And first, I must tell you, my young Lord Colambre remembered and noticed me the minute he lit at our inn, and condescended to beckon me out of the yard to him, and axed me — "Friend Larry," says he, "did you keep your promise?" —— "My oath again[8] the whiskey, is it?" says I. "My lord, I surely did," said I; which was true, as all the country knows I never tasted a drop since. "And I'm proud to see your honour, my lord, as good as your word, too, and back again among us." So then there was a call for the horses; and no more at that time passed betwix' my young lord and me, but that he pointed me out to the *ould* one, as I went off. I noticed and thanked him for it in my heart, though I did not know all the good was to come of it. Well no more of myself, for the present.

'Ogh, it's I driv 'em well; and we all got to the great gate of the park before sunset, and as fine an evening as ever you see; with the sun shining on the tops of the trees, as the ladies noticed; the leaves changed, but not dropped, though so late in the season. I believe the leaves knew what they were about, and kept on, on purpose to welcome them; and the birds were singing, and I stopped whistling, that they might hear them; but sorrow bit could they hear when they got to the park gate, for there was such a crowd, and such a shout, as you never see — and they had the horses off every carriage entirely, and drew 'em home, with blessings, through the park. And, God bless 'em! when they got out, they didn't go shut themselves up in the great drawing-room, but went straight out to the *tir*rass,[9] to satisfy the eyes and hearts that followed them. My lady *laning* on my young lord, and miss Grace Nugent that was, the beautifullest angel that ever you set eyes on, with the finest complexion, and sweetest of smiles, *laning* upon the *ould* lord's arm, who had his hat off, bowing to all, and noticing the old tenants as he passed by name. O, there was great gladness and tears in the midst; for joy I could scarce keep from myself.

'After a turn or two upon the *tir*rass, my lord Colambre *quit* his mother's arm for a minute, and

4. Mr Burke is a just estate manager who had been wrongfully dismissed by Lord Clonbrony and is now replacing the Garraghty brothers.
5. Money that had to be paid to the land agent when contracts were signed and sealed.
6. Midsummer's night when bonfires were lit.
7. i.e. enforcement of court judgments.
8. i.e. against.
9. i.e. terrace.

he come to the edge of the slope, and looked down and through all the crowd for some one.

'"Is it the widow O'Neil,[10] my lord?" says I; "she's yonder, with the white kerchief, betwixt her son and daughter, as usual."

'Then my lord beckoned, and they did not know which of the *tree*[11] would stir; and then he gave *tree* beckons with his own finger, and they all *tree* came fast enough to the bottom of the slope forenent[12] my lord: and he went down and helped the widow up (O, he's the true jantleman), and brought 'em all *tree* up on the *tir*rass, to my lady and miss Nugent; and I was up close after, that I might hear, which wasn't manners, but I couldn't help it. So what he said I don't well know, for I could not get near enough, after all. But I saw my lady smile very kind, and take the widow O'Neil by the hand, and then my lord Colambre *'troduced* Grace to miss Nugent, and there was the word *namesake*, and something about a check curtain; but, whatever it was, they was all greatly pleased: then my lord Colambre turned and looked for Brian, who had fell back, and took him with some commendation, to my lord his father. And my lord the master said, which I didn't know till after, that they should have their house and farm at the *ould* rent; and at the surprise, the widow dropped down dead; and there was a cry as for ten *berrings*.[13] "Be qui'te," says I, 'she's only kilt for joy;" and I went and lift her up, for her son had no more strength that minute than the child new born; and Grace trembled like a leaf, as white as the sheet, but not long, for the mother came to, and was as well as ever when I brought some water, which miss Nugent handed to her with her own hand.

'"That was always pretty and good," said the widow, laying her hand upon miss Nugent, "and kind and good to me and mine."

'That minute there was music from below. The blind harper, O'Neill, with his harp, that struck up "Gracey Nugent."

'And that finished, and my lord Colambre smiling, with the tears standing in his eyes too, and the *ould* lord quite wiping his, I ran to the *tir*rass brink to bid O'Neil play it again; but as I run, I thought I heard a voice call "Larry!"

'"Who calls Larry?" says I.

'"My lord Colambre calls you, Larry," says all at once; and four takes me by the shoulders and spins me round. "There's my young lord calling you, Larry — run for your life."

'So I run back for my life, and walked respectful, with my hat in my hand, when I got near.

"Put on your hat, my father desires it," says my lord Colambre. The *ould* lord made a sign to that purpose, but was too full to speak. "Where's your father?" continues my young lord. "He's very *ould*, my lord," says I. — "I didn't *ax* you how *ould* he was," says he; "but where is he?" — "He's behind the crowd below, on account of his infirmities; he couldn't walk so fast as the rest, my lord," says I; "but his heart is with you, if not his body." — "I must have his body too: so bring him bodily before us; and this shall be your warrant for so doing," said my lord, joking: for he knows the *natur* of us, Paddy, and how we love a joke in our hearts, as well as if he had lived all his life in Ireland; and by the same token will, for that *rason*, do what he pleases with us, and more may be than a man twice as good, that never would smile on us.

'But I'm telling you of my father. "I've a warrant for you, father," says I; "and must have you bodily before the justice, and my lord chief justice." So he changed colour a bit at first; but he saw me smile. "And I've done no sin," said he; "and, Larry, you may lead me now, as you led me all my life."

'And up the slope he went with me as light as fifteen; and, when we got up, my lord Clonbrony said, "I am sorry an old tenant, and a good old tenant, as I hear you were, should have been turned out of your farm."

'"Don't fret, it's no great matter, my lord," said my father. "I shall be soon out of the way; but if you would be so kind to speak a word for my boy here, and that I could afford, while the life is in me, to bring my other boy back out of banishment."

'"Then," says my lord Clonbrony, "I'll give you and your sons three lives,[14] or thirty-one years, from this day, of your former farm. Return to it when you please. And," added my lord Colambre, "the flaggers,[15] I hope, will be soon banished." O, how could I thank him — not a word could I proffer — but I know I clasped my two hands, and prayed for him inwardly. And my father was dropping down

10. A kind and hospitable widow who had given Lord Colambre lodging when he was travelling *incognito* and who, with her daughter Grace, had been unjustly evicted from her cottage by Nicholas Garraghty.
11. i.e. three.
12. opposite.
13. i.e. buryings.
14. i.e. life-time leases.
15. i.e. feeble or useless tenants.

on his knees, but the master would not let him; and *obsarved*, that posture should only be for his God. And, sure enough, in that posture, when he was out of sight, we did pray for him that night, and will all our days.

'But, before we quit his presence, he called me back, and bid me write to my brother, and bring you back, if you've no objections, to your own country.

'So come, my dear Pat, and make no delay, for joy's not joy comp*la*te till you're in it — my father sends his blessing, and Peggy her love. The family entirely is to settle for good in Ireland, and there was in the castle yard last night a bonfire made by my lord's orders of the *ould* yellow damask furniture, to please my lady, my lord says. And the drawing-room, the butler was telling me, is new hung; and the chairs with velvet as white as snow, and shaded over with natural flowers by miss Nugent. Oh! how I hope what I guess will come true, and I've *rason* to believe it will, for I dreamt in my bed last night it did. But keep yourself to yourself — that miss Nugent (who is no more miss Nugent, they say, but miss Reynolds, and has a new found grandfather, and is a big heiress, which she did not want in my eyes, nor in my young lord's), I've a notion, will be sometime, and may be sooner than is expected, my lady viscountess Colambre — so haste to the wedding. And there's another thing: they say the rich *ould* grandfather's coming over; — and another thing, Pat, you would not be out of the fashion — and you see it's growing the fashion not to be an Absentee.

'Your loving brother,
'Larry Brady.'

LETTER TO MICHAEL PAKENHAM EDGEWORTH (19 February 1834)

[In this famous letter to a distant kinsman, Maria Edgeworth takes a formal farewell of Irish fiction, though her last Irish novel, *Ormond*, had appeared seventeen years earlier. The Ireland of the 1830s was troubled by sectarian bitterness and strife. The belated and reluctant passage of the Catholic Emancipation Act (1829) and the Tithe War of 1830-31 were indications of the increasing friction between the new catholic Ireland of Daniel O'Connell and the protestant Ireland, which had lost its political leadership with the Act of Union (1800).]

... Sophy despatched a letter for you last week, in which I am sure she told you all domestic occurrences. Barry has bought Annaghmore in the King's County:[1] an excellent house; and Sophy and Barry and all the children are to stay with us till Sophy's health — very delicate — is strengthened, and till they have furnished what rooms they mean to inhabit at Annamore; this looks better than with the *gh*, but Sophy stickles for the old Irish spelling.

Molly and Hetty, and Crofton and child, are all flourishing; poor old George is declining as gently and comfortably as can be. When we go to see him, his eyes light up and his mouth crinkles into smiles, and he, as well as Molly, never fails to ask for Master Pakenham. Though *Helen*[2] cannot reach you for a year, Fanny has desired Bentley to send you a copy before it is published. I should tell you beforehand that there is no humour in it, and no Irish character. It is impossible to draw Ireland as she now is in a book of fiction — realities are too strong, party passions too violent to bear to see, or care to look at their faces in the looking-glass. The people would only break the glass, and curse the fool who held the mirror up to nature[3] — distorted nature, in a fever. We are in too perilous a case to laugh, humour would be out of season, worse than bad taste. Whenever the danger is past, as the man in the sonnet says,

> We may look back on the hardest part and laugh.

Then I shall be ready to join in the laugh. Sir Walter Scott once said to me, 'Do explain to the public why Pat, who gets forward so well in other countries, is so miserable in his own.' A very difficult question: I fear above my power. But I shall think of it continually, and listen, and look, and read....

1. Now County Offaly.
2. A novel by M.E. published in 3 volumes in 1834.
3. *Hamlet*, III. 2. 25.

Biography/Bibliography

LIFE. Born Black Bourton, Oxfordshire in January 1768 (or perhaps 1767). Her father had inherited an estate of modest size in the Irish midlands, and in 1782 the family returned permanently to live in

Edgeworthstown, Co. Longford. Began her writing career in 1787; in 1795 published anonymously *Letters for Literary Ladies.* The family were forced to flee their home in autumn 1798 in consequence of the French invasion of the west of Ireland. The following year she visited (with her father) her imprisoned publisher in London. In January 1800, *Castle Rackrent* was published anonymously, and later that year the Act of Union between Britain and Ireland was passed. During a lull in the wars with France, M. E. and her father visited Paris and Brussels in October 1802, and in Paris she was wooed by Abraham Edelcrantz, a Swedish diplomat, whose offer of marriage she rejected. In the wake of *Tales of Fashionable Life* (2nd series 1812) she visited London and was fêted by Lord Byron, Sir Humphry Davy and others. Her correspondence with Walter Scott commenced in 1814, though the two did not meet until 1823. In June 1817 her father died, and *Ormond* (pub. July 1817) was in effect her farewell to Irish fiction. The deteriorating condition of Irish affairs in the 1820s led to an increased conservative tone in her view of society, and after *Helen* (1834) she published no more fiction. She died in Edgeworthstown on 22 May 1849.

CHIEF WRITINGS. No standard edition of Maria Edgeworth's works has been published. For the fiction, the text of *Tales and Novels* 18 vols (London: Baldwin & Crodock, 1832-33) has been preferred. Consult also George Watson's annotated ed. of *Castle Rackrent* (Oxford: World's Classics, 1980). *The Absentee* has been edited and annotated by W. J. Mc Cormack and Kim Walker (Oxford: World's Classics, 1987). *Belinda* and *Patronage* (both with introductions by Eva Figes) were republished by Pandora Books in 1986. For the bibliography proper, see B.C. Slade, *Maria Edgeworth 1767-1849; a Bibliographical Tribute* (privately published, 1937).

BIOGRAPHY AND CRITICISM. The standard 'life' is Marilyn Butler, *Maria Edgeworth: a Literary Biography* (Oxford: Clarendon Press, 1972). To this add four collections of letter: Augustus J. C. Hare (ed.), *The Life and Letters of Maria Edgeworth* 2 vols (London: Arnold, 1894); Christina Colvin (ed.), *Maria Edgeworth: Letters From England 1813-1814* (Oxford: Clarendon Press, 1971); Edgar E. Mac Donald (ed.), *The Education of the Heart: the Correspondence of Rachel Mordecai Lazarus and Maria Edgeworth* (Chapel Hill: University of North Carolina Press, 1977); Christina Colvin (ed.), *Maria Edgeworth in France and Switzerland; Selections from the Edgeworth Family Letters* (Oxford: Clarendon Press, 1979).

A broader, yet essential, background appears in Harriet Jessie Butler and Harold Edgeworth Butler (eds), *The Black Book of Edgeworthstown and Other Edgeworth Memoirs 1595-1817* (London: Faber & Gwyer, 1927); Desmond Clarke (ed.), *Memoirs of Richard Lovell Edgeworth Begun by Himself and Concluded by his Daughter Maria Edgeworth* 2 vols (Shannon: Irish University Press, 1969). Michael Hurst's *Maria Edgeworth and the Public Scene; Intellect, Fine Feeling and Landlordism in the Age of Reform* (London: Macmillan, 1969) is a valuably concentrated study of M.E.'s views in the 1820s.

Chapter 6 of Donald Davie's *The Heyday of Sir Walter Scott* (London: Routledge, 1961) and Chapters 3 and 4 of W. J. Mc Cormack's *Ascendancy and Tradition in Anglo-Irish Literary History from 1789 to 1939* (Oxford: Clarendon Press, 1985) discuss the fiction in detail. Thomas Flanagan's *The Irish Novelists 1800-1850* (New York, London: Columbia University Press, 1959), though uncritically romantic at times, is still highly readable; chapter 2 is on M.E. Tom Dunne's *Maria Edgeworth and the Colonial Mind* (Cork: Cork University Press, 1984) is the best of the many brief monographs.

SEAMUS DEANE, *Editor*

Thomas Moore

(1779-1852)

Moore is still, in terms of popular appeal, Ireland's national poet. His fame rivalled that of his friend Byron in England and it reached further afield with the publication in 1817 of *Lallah Rookh*, an oriental romance of abnormal length, languor and *longueurs*. But it is as the author of the *Irish Melodies*, published in ten numbers between 1808 and 1834, that he is most enduringly remembered. The airs for which he wrote the words came to him from Edward Bunting's *A General Collection of the Ancient Irish Music* (1796), the harvest of the Belfast Harp Festival of 1792, at which nine Irish harpers revealed to him the wealth of Irish traditional music. Bunting did not in fact understand 'the essential structures of the music, fashioned on a system of modes rather than major and minor keys.'[1] He could not, therefore, record what he had heard. The first act of translation, even of transmogrification, had taken place even before Moore asked Bunting to cooperate with him in joining his words to the native airs. Bunting refused, but when William Power, a Dublin music-seller, proposed that Sir John Stevenson should 'arrange' the music to fit Moore's words, the offer was taken up. It is not, therefore, entirely to the point to say that Moore violated the old music to make it accommodate his own purposes. He too was involved in an act of translation. 'Had I not', he claimed, 'ventured on these very allowable liberties, many of the songs now most known and popular would have been still sleeping, with all their authentic dross about them, in Mr. Bunting's first volume.' Bunting himself had the magnanimity to admit that 'The beauty of Mr. Moore's words in a great degree atones for the violence done by the musical arranger to many of the airs which he has adopted.'

The astonishing popularity of Moore's *Irish Melodies* is part of the history of Irish nationalism. The eighteenth-century background helps to explain this. In an earlier section, the growth of antiquarianism has been detailed and the connections between that and a growing national and cultural consciousness indicated. Moore took some of the fruits of antiquarian labour and processed them for general consumption. He made a version of ancient Ireland accessible and acceptable to a contemporary Irish and English audience. In doing so, he no doubt sinned against the doctrine of authenticity, but in doing that he simply focussed on an issue that was to remain central in Irish culture for more than a century afterwards. That issue was translation. In the passage from an Irish- to an English-speaking culture, something was inevitably going to be lost. Perfect authenticity to the original could not possibly be achieved; it became routine to dismiss various attempts to effect the changeover as spurious, fake, reductive. Many such attempts were. Harsh things can be said of Sir Samuel Ferguson or Standish O'Grady in this regard, but their historical importance is undeniable. The same is true of Moore. However one may rail against some of the more sugared of his confections, their popularity ensured that they would become as integral a part of the Irish culture as the airs and songs that they replaced or displaced. It is difficult to exaggerate the scale and intensity of the public welcome for his *Irish Melodies*. Moore was feted wherever he went, in London and in Dublin. The Ireland his works popularized became part of the English consciousness too. This had its

1. Seán O'Boyle, *The Irish Song Tradition* (Skerries: Gilbert Dalton, 1976); D. Hammond (ed.), *A Centenary Selection from Moore's Melodies* (Skerries: Gilbert Dalton, 1979).

political as well as its cultural effects. Without the accompanying music, the artificiality of his words appears more pronounced. Yet their charm, although faded, is as undeniable as their effect. Irish national feeling was slumbering until Moore awoke it. 'I was only the wind to the sleeping harp, and "all the wild sweetness I waked was its own."'

Moore's contemporary popularity is less remarkable than it first appears when we remember that volumes like *The Pleasures of Hope* (1799) by Thomas Campbell (1777-1844) and *The Pleasures of Memory* (1792) by Samuel Rogers (1763-1855) were among the most admired of the time. Their easy sentiment and banal rhythms were apparently irresistible to a large readership. This infantile romanticism was more effectively exploited by Moore than by any other writer. Campbell's laments over the fate of Scotland and Scottish heroes, or over Red Indian braves, did not have the power of Moore's laments over Erin and her long litany of heroes, partly because the state of Erin was a matter of considerable anxiety in England at that time, and partly because Moore was technically superior in his handling of rhyme, rhythm and the cliché. He appeals to his reader in soft imperatives: 'Go where glory waits thee', 'Remember the glories', 'Oh! breathe not his name', 'Say wilt thou weep'. The reader adds his or her own intensity to such appeals, and the music dwells on them in a mixture of rapture and pathos. Yet most appealing of all is the heroic-sentimental refusal to allow any force to conquer the undying spirit — be it the spirit of love or of Erin, or of any other threatened entity. Moore's settings are dark, but his themes are honour-bright. His heroics are all the choicer because they are those of the sweet-natured against oppression, relentlessly confident that their spiritualized goodness will prevail.

The long history of Irish catholic petitions to England, pleading for justice, relief from penal legislation, admission to citizenship, recognition of the petitioners' humanity and tradition, reaches an unexpected culmination in Moore's melodies. He was politically aware of his country's misfortunes and maltreatment, but still, in eighteenth-century fashion, he thought that this could be alleviated if the request were sufficiently persuasive. He looked askance at the actual heroics of his Trinity College friend, Robert Emmet, who led a rebellion in Dublin in 1803 and was hanged and beheaded for his pains. He frankly hated the brilliant, aggressive demagoguery and jibing of his contemporary Daniel O'Connell, the great lawyer and politician who organized the Irish catholics into a political force. Moore was a constitutional poet in that he admired rebellion in his verse and steered clear of it in his actions and in most of his prose. The past is a safer territory than the present, and Moore explores it in eccentric fashion with the help of historians like Sylvester O'Halloran or Ferdinando Warner or antiquarians like Charles Vallancey. In that light, he too is a user of antiquarian research on behalf of the catholic cause. His satirical poems about Orange bigotry, English Tory politicians and idiot prejudice make his feelings clear. Like many people of a Whig disposition and an apologetic state of mind, numerously represented in the Irish catholic commercial community from which he sprang, Moore believed that catholic emancipation would finally relieve his fellow-countrymen of their distress by lifting away forever the shadow of the Penal Laws. After that, there would be a sunshine relationship between England and Ireland. He used all the resources of the pianoforte and of his popularity to bring this about. In his 'Letter on Music, to the Marchioness Dowager of Donegal', which was prefixed to the third number of the *Melodies* (1810), Moore went to some lengths to explain how Irish music reproduced 'the features of our history and our character' by its variations of 'turbulence' and 'softness', 'mirth and sadness', and claims that he has endeavoured to regain, from the 'tasteless decorations' of 'our own itinerant musicians' what he calls 'the pure gold of the melody'. He continues: 'With respect to the verses which I have written for these Melodies, as they are intended to be sung rather than read, I can answer for their sound with somewhat more confidence than for their sense. Yet it would be affectation to deny that I have given much attention to the task, and that it is not through want of zeal or industry, if I unfortunately disgrace the sweet airs of my country, by poetry altogether unworthy of their taste, their energy, and their tenderness.' Having exempted himself from 'the rigours of literary criticism', he then goes on to attack those commentators in English newspapers who had claimed that the tendency of the *Irish Melodies* was politically 'mischievous'. Moore refuses to give serious attention to those who 'identify nationality with treason, and who see, in every effort for Ireland, a system of hostility to England.' A work of this nature, he claims, is directed, not at the lower and more inflammatory classes of people. 'It looks much higher for its audience and readers; it is found upon the pianofortes of the rich and educated.' He could not have been more specific about the 'respectable', bourgeois nature of Irish nationalism and its wish to achieve a homologous relationship with the England from which it seemed so eager to distinguish itself.

On that basis, Moore was quickly recruited by Irish nationalism as its most representative poet. Not until the songs of *The Nation* newspaper were published in 1843, under the title of *The Spirit of the Nation*, did he have any rival. Even then, the later publication was confirming only what Moore's songs had already achieved. The sentimental song and the political ballad became the primary popular forms for nationalistic fervour. They were the popular music of the century in Ireland and it is as difficult to exaggerate as it is to measure their effect. Moore made the cause of Ireland and the dream of perfect love sacred causes, spiritualizing each as an enterprise for the sake of which life itself was not too great a price. In fact, it was the only price worth paying. So even his evocations of Irish landscape, of the remembered valley or home of the exile, are evocations of place that the spirit never leaves, of an Ireland that persists through all changes and catastrophes as the beloved place. This charismatic rendering of traditional affections was perfectly suited to the ardent, exclusive spirit of nationalism. The songs had a quality of feeling that catholic emancipation could not appease. *The Spirit of the Nation* gave an added militancy to Moore's elegance, but each aided and abetted the popularity of the other.

It is right to speak of Moore's elegance because no one was more conscious of it than he, especially in the writing of the *Irish Melodies*. On several occasions he refers, in prefaces and footnotes, to the 'wildness' and intricacy of the original air and the reduced version of this that he is obliged to provide. The dispute between wildness and elegance was a hackneyed one by the turn of the nineteenth century. The rediscovery of the popular ballad, the various 'translations' and redactions of old Celtic or medieval English verse, had inclined many to believe that the polished language of modern England was far removed from the intensities of 'natural' poetry. This quarrel is part of the history of romanticism, but Moore's minor role in it is a curious one. He had begun as a translator of Anacreon, and he maintained, throughout his writing life, a fidelity to the ideal of polished excellence and finish, which was central to the long tradition of classical translation in eighteenth-century England. The standard poeticisms of his language and the intricate turns of his stanzas bear witness to this. Moore wanted to 'civilize' the Gaelic tradition in the sense that he wanted to modernize it and make it acceptable to the dominant taste of the reading public of the time in England. By making Gaelic poetry and song agreeably elegant, he was making them available to contemporary taste. What he did to the airs that Bunting collected was an anticipation of the next great dispute over the relationship between authenticity and artificiality. In Ireland especially, this was always a political dispute in scholarly disguise, never more effectively manifested than in Sir Samuel Ferguson's review of James Hardiman's *Irish Minstrelsy* (1831) in *The Dublin University Magazine*. Hardiman's volumes were claiming in effect that authenticity was a peculiarly catholic business, although the translations he provided for his collection of songs were woefully lacking in any of the characteristics usually associated with that quality. Ferguson attacked him on this ground, and in doing so returned to Moore to help him point up the distinction between the modern Irish gentlemen and what he dubbed the *Merus Hibernicus*, an ambiguous term that means 'pure' or 'mere' Irishman, depending on what stress the writer wishes to choose in the authenticity debate:

> The contrast between the native songs and [the] lyrics of Moore, is indeed strangely striking — as strange as uncouthness can present in juxtaposition with politeness, but still no more than that which may be admitted to have distinguished the Merus Hibernicus from the modern Irish gentleman. We will look in vain for the chasteness, the appositeness, the antithetical and epigrammatic point, and the measured propriety of prosody ... among the rude rhymes which accompanied the same notes two centuries ago....

Ferguson strikes to the heart of the matter here, although he may have done so unwittingly. The translation of Gaelic into English was an action that had profound political implications. When read as the translation of something wild and savage into something regulated and polished, it becomes a metaphor of the translation of catholic into protestant, of native and antique authenticity into modern and equally native civility. Moore was the most outstanding figure in the long process of transformation that had begun in the eighteenth century and was to be carried on into the twentieth — the transformation of one culture into the idiom of another while attempting to preserve in the new idiom as much as possible of the old culture. It was a pitting of the foreign against the native, so that the foreign thereby would become Hibernicized and the native Anglicized. In other words, what had been a political problem for centuries was now becoming, self-consciously, a cultural issue. We may say that Moore's elegance was frequently reduced to enervation; we may say that his words do not live without their accompanying music, or that the music is violated by the artificiality of the words; we may laud or regret his influence on Irish nationalism. Yet, ultimately, the kind of issue raised by Moore's poetry, or, more particularly by the *Irish Melodies* and some of the *National Airs*, lies at the heart of Irish writing for more than a century afterwards. The endless attempt to achieve a self-conscious virtuoso modernism in the English language, as evident in Moore or Ferguson as in Joyce or O'Casey, as it is equally evident in O'Connell (the devoutly catholic Benthamite), is one of the classic features of a culture in which translation plays a central role. Moore's popularity is perhaps the strongest indication of the general realization that his work contains within itself these large questions and also, remarkably, provides a memorable answer to at least some of them. What he did with incomparable smoothness and ease, James Clarence Mangan was later to do in torment, irony and with an integrity and force very far removed from anything we meet with in Moore. Yet between them, as poets who were essentially translators and transmogrifiers, they display the mixture of dependence and independence that is such a persistent and apparently incongruous feature of Irish poetry in the nineteenth century.

from:
INTOLERANCE, A SATIRE (1808)

[The Appendix to this work appeared in the volume *Corruption and Intolerance*, published anonymously.]

To the foregoing Poem, as first published, were subjoined, in the shape of a Note, or Appendix, the following remarks on the History and Music of Ireland. This fragment was originally intended to form part of a Preface to the Irish Melodies; but afterwards, for some reason which I do not now recollect, was thrown aside.

Our history, for many centuries past, is creditable neither to our neighbours nor ourselves, and ought not to be read by any Irishman who wishes either to love England or to feel proud of Ireland. The loss of independence very early debased our character; and our feuds and rebellions, though frequent and ferocious, but seldom displayed that generous spirit of enterprise with which the pride of an independent monarchy so long dignified the struggles of Scotland. It is true this island has given birth to heroes who, under more favourable circumstances, might have left in the hearts of their countrymen recollections as dear as those of a Bruce or a Wallace;[1] but success was wanting to consecrate resistance, their cause was branded with the disheartening name of treason, and their oppressed country was such a blank among nations, that, like the adventures of those woods which Rinaldo wished to explore,[2] the fame of their actions was lost in the obscurity of the place where they achieved them.

——— Errando in quelli boschi
Trovar potria strane avventure e molte,
Ma come i luoghi i fatti ancor son foschi,
Che non se n' ha notizia le più volte.[3]

1. Robert Bruce (1274-1329) was king of Scotland 1306-29. In 1297 he joined Sir William Wallace (*c.*1270-1305) in armed resistance to the English and the campaign for national independence.
2. Rinaldo is the cousin of Orlando and brother of Bradamante, the maiden-warrior. The woods are the site of Orlando's madness and many adventures.
3. Ariosto, *Orlando Furioso*, canto iv, stanza 56:
'They said that in the wood and forest find
Adventures strange and feats of arms he might,
But as the place, so are the actions blind,
That oft their doings never come to light'
(trans. Sir John Harington, 1591).

Hence is it that the annals of Ireland, through a lapse of six hundred years, exhibit not one of those shining names, not one of those themes of national pride, from which poetry borrows her noblest inspiration; and that history, which ought to be the richest garden of the Muse, yields no growth to her in this hapless island but cypress and weeds. In truth, the poet who would embellish his song with allusions to Irish names and events, must be contented to seek them in those early periods when our character was yet unalloyed and original, before the impolitic craft of our conquerors had divided, weakened, and disgraced us. The sole traits of heroism, indeed, which he can venture at this day to commemorate, either with safety to himself, or honour to his country, are to be looked for in those ancient times when the native monarchs of Ireland displayed and fostered virtues worthy of a better age; when our Malachies wore around their necks collars of gold which they had won in single combat from the invader, and our Briens deserved and won the warm affections of a people by exhibiting all the most estimable qualities of a king. It may be said that the magic of tradition has shed a charm over this remote period, to which it is in reality but little entitled, and that most of the pictures, which we dwell on so fondly, of days when this island was distinguished amidst the gloom of Europe, by the sanctity of her morals, the spirit of her knighthood, and the polish of her schools, are little more than the inventions of national partiality, — that bright but spurious offspring which vanity engenders upon ignorance, and with which the first records of every people abound. But the sceptic is scarcely to be envied who would pause for stronger proofs than we already possess of the early glories of Ireland; and were even the veracity of all these proofs surrendered, yet who would not fly to such flattering fictions from the sad degrading truths which the history of later times presents to us?

The language of sorrow, however, is, in general, best suited to our Music, and with themes of this nature the poet may be amply supplied. There is scarcely a page of our annals that will not furnish him a subject, and while the national Muse of other countries adorns her temple proudly with trophies of the past, in Ireland her melancholy altar, like the shrine of Pity at Athens, is to be known only by the tears that are shed upon it; '*lacrymis altaria sudant*.'[4]

4. Statius, *Thebaid*, xii, line 488, 'the altars are soaked in tears.'

There is a well-known story, related of the Antiochians under the reign of Theodosius, which is not only honourable to the powers of music in general, but which applies so peculiarly to the mournful melodies of Ireland, that I cannot resist the temptation of introducing it here. — The piety of Theodosius, would have been admirable, had it not been stained with intolerance; but under his reign was, I believe, first set the example of a disqualifying penal code enacted by Christians against Christians.[5] Whether his interference with the religion of the Antiochians had any share in the alienation of their loyalty is not expressly ascertained by historians; but severe edicts, heavy taxation, and the rapacity and insolence of the men whom he sent to govern them, sufficiently account for the discontents of a warm and susceptible people. Repentance soon followed the crimes into which their impatience had hurried them; but the vengeance of the Emperor was implacable, and punishments of the most dreadful nature hung over the city of Antioch, whose devoted inhabitants, totally resigned to despondence, wandered through the streets and public assemblies, giving utterance to their grief in dirges of the most touching lamentation. At length, Flavianus, their bishop, whom they had sent to intercede with Theodosius, finding all his entreaties coldly rejected, adopted the expedient of teaching these songs of sorrow which he had heard from the lips of his unfortunate countrymen to the minstrels who performed for the Emperor at table. The heart of Theodosius could not resist this appeal; tears fell fast into his cup while he listened, and the Antiochians were forgiven. — Surely, if music ever spoke the misfortunes of a people, or could ever conciliate forgiveness for their errors, the music of Ireland ought to possess those powers.

5. The Emperor Theodosius the Great (*c.* 346-395) was a strict Athanasian and imposed orthodoxy throughout the Eastern and Western Empires.

IRISH MELODIES (1808-34)

PREFACE

[This is the Preface to the 1840-42 edition of Moore's poems.]

Though an edition of the Poetry of the Irish Melodies, separate from the Music, has long been called for, yet having, for many reasons, a strong objection to this sort of divorce, I should with difficulty have consented to a disunion of the words from the airs, had it solely depended upon me to keep them quietly and indissolubly together. But, besides the various shapes in which these, as well as my other lyrical writings, have been published throughout America they are included, of course, in all the editions of my works printed on the Continent, and have also appeared, in a volume full of typographical errors, in Dublin. I have therefore readily acceded to the wish expressed by the Proprietor of the Irish Melodies, for a revised and complete edition of the poetry of the Work, though well aware that my verses must lose even more than the 'animae dimidium',[1] in being detached from the beautiful airs to which it was their good fortune to be associated.

1. half of its life. Horace, *Odes*, iii, 8.

from:
IRISH MELODIES

Go where glory waits thee

Go where glory waits thee,
But, while fame elates thee,
  Oh! still remember me.
When the praise thou meetest
To thine ear is sweetest,
  Oh! then remember me.
Other arms may press thee,
Dearer friends caress thee,
All the joys that bless thee,
  Sweeter far may be;
But when friends are nearest,
And when joys are dearest,
  Oh! then remember me!

When, at eve, thou rovest
By the star thou lovest,
  Oh! then remember me.
Think, when home returning,
Bright we've seen it burning,
  Oh! thus remember me.
Oft as summer closes,
When thine eye reposes
On its ling'ring roses,
  Once so lov'd by thee,
Think of her who wove them,
Her who made thee love them,
  Oh! then remember me.

When, around thee dying,
Autumn leaves are lying,
  Oh! then remember me.
And, at night, when gazing
On the gay hearth blazing,
  Oh! still remember me.
Then should music, stealing
All the soul of feeling,
To thy heart appealing,
  Draw one tear from thee;
Then let memory bring thee
Strains I us'd to sing thee, —
  Oh! then remember me.

Remember the glories of Brian the brave

Remember the glories of Brian the brave,[1]
  Tho' the days of the hero are o'er;
Tho' lost to Mononia,[2] and cold in the grave,
  He returns to Kinkora[3] no more.
That star of the field, which so often hath pour'd
  Its beam on the battle, is set;
But enough of its glory remains on each sword,
  To light us to victory yet.

Mononia! when Nature embellish'd the tint
  Of thy fields, and thy mountains so fair,
Did she ever intend that a tyrant should print
  The footstep of slavery there?
No! Freedom, whose smile we shall never resign,
  Go, tell our invaders, the Danes,
That 'tis sweeter to bleed for an age at thy shrine,
  Than to sleep but a moment in chains.

Forget not our wounded companions, who stood[4]
  In the day of distress by our side;
While the moss of the valley grew red with their blood,
  They stirr'd not, but conquer'd and died.

1. Brian Boru, an Irish king, who died fighting the Danes at the battle of Clontarf in 1014. He is credited with breaking Danish power in Ireland.
2. Munster.
3. Brian Boru's royal residence in County Limerick.
4. Moore refers to a passage from Sylvester O'Halloran's *General History of Ireland* (1778), in which he tells how Brian Boru's crack troops, the Dalgeis, attacked on their way back from Clontarf and fought alongside their wounded, who demanded that they be tied to stakes so that they too could participate in the battle.

That sun which now blesses our arms with his light,
  Saw them fall upon Ossory's[5] plain; —
Oh! let him not blush, when he leaves us tonight,
  To find that they fell there in vain.

5. Ossory was an ancient kingdom of Ireland, the borders of which are now traced by those of the catholic episcopal see, including Counties Kilkenny and Laois and parts of County Offaly.

Erin! The tear and the smile in thine eyes

Erin, the tear and the smile in thine eyes,
Blend like the rainbow that hangs in thy skies!
  Shining through sorrow's stream,
  Saddening through pleasure's beam,
  Thy suns with doubtful gleam,
    Weep while they rise.

Erin, thy silent tear never shall cease,
Erin, thy languid smile ne'er shall increase,
  Till, like the rainbow's light,
  Thy various tints unite,
  And form in heaven's sight
    One arch of peace!

Oh! breathe not his name

[In his story of Emmet's reaction to the tune 'The Red Fox' (see p. 1061), Moore continues: 'How little did I then think in one of the most touching of the sweet airs I used to play to him, his own dying words would find an interpreter so worthy of their sad but proud feeling; or that another of those mournful strains would long be associated, in the hearts of his countrymen, with the memory of her who shared with Ireland his last blessing and prayer.' He is referring here to 'Oh! breathe not his name' and 'She is far from the land' respectively. The first of these is Moore's response to the reported last words of Emmet's famous speech from the dock at his trial for high treason in September 1803: 'I have but one request to ask at my departure from this world: it is — *the charity of its silence*. Let no man write my epitaph; for as no man who knows my motives dare now vindicate them, let not prejudice or ignorance asperse them. Let them and me rest in obscurity and peace, and my tomb remain uninscribed, and my memory in oblivion, until other times and other men can do justice to my character. When my country takes her place among the nations of the earth, *then, and not till then*, let my epitaph be written. I have done.']

Oh! breathe not his name, let it sleep in the shade,
Where cold and unhonour'd his relics are laid:
Sad, silent, and dark, be the tears that we shed,
As the night-dew that falls on the grass o'er his head.

But the night-dew that falls, though in silence it
  weeps,
Shall brighten with verdure the grave where he
  sleeps;
And the tear that we shed, though in secret it rolls,
Shall long keep his memory green in our souls.

She is far from the land

She is far from the land[1] where her young hero sleeps,
  And lovers are round her, sighing:
But coldly she turns from their gaze, and weeps,
  For her heart in his grave is lying.

She sings the wild song of her dear native plains,
  Every note which he lov'd awaking; —
Ah! little they think who delight in her strains,
  How the heart of the Minstrel is breaking.

He had liv'd for his love, for his country he died,
  They were all that to life had entwin'd him;
Nor soon shall the tears of his country be dried,
  Nor long will his love stay behind him.

Oh! make her a grave where the sunbeams rest,
  When they promise a glorious morrow;
They'll shine o'er her sleep, like a smile from the West,
  From her own lov'd island of sorrow.

1. 'She' is Sarah Curran, the beloved of Robert Emmet, executed in 1803. When her father, John Philpot Curran, discovered her secret engagement to Emmet, he behaved so severely that she took refuge with friends in Cork. There she married a Captain Sturgeon in 1805. She died in England three years afterwards.

When he, who adores thee

When he, who adores thee, has left but the name
  Of his fault and his sorrows behind,
Oh! say wilt thou weep, when they darken the fame
  Of a life that for thee was resign'd?
Yes, weep, and however my foes may condemn,
  They tears shall efface their decree;
For Heaven can witness, though guilty to them,
  I have been but too faithful to thee.

The harp that once through Tara's halls

The harp that once through Tara's halls[1]
The soul of music shed,
Now hangs as mute on Tara's walls,
As if that soul were fled. —
So sleeps the pride of former days,
So glory's thrill is o'er,
And hearts, that once beat high for praise,
Now feel that pulse no more.

No more to chiefs and ladies bright
The harp of Tara swells;
The chord alone, that breaks at night,
Its tale of ruin tells.
Thus Freedom now so seldom wakes,
The only throb she gives,
Is when some heart indignant breaks,
To show that still she lives.

1. Tara, near Navan, Co. Meath, was the seat of the high kings of Ireland until the sixth century.

Rich and rare were the gems she wore[1]

Rich and rare were the gems she wore,
And a bright gold ring on her wand she bore;
But oh! her beauty was far beyond
Her sparkling gems, or snow-white wand.

'Lady! dost thou not fear to stray,
So lone and lovely through this bleak way?
Are Erin's sons so good or so cold,
As not to be tempted by woman or gold?'

'Sir Knight! I feel not the least alarm,
No son of Erin will offer me harm: —
For though they love woman and golden store,
Sir Knight! they love honour and virtue more!'

On she went, and her maiden smile
In safety lighted her round the Green Isle;
And blest for ever is she who relied
Upon Erin's honour and Erin's pride.

1. Moore claims that this ballad was founded on an anecdote related in Ferdinando Warner's *History of Ireland* (1763), about a beautiful young woman, adorned with jewels and a costly dress, carrying a wand topped by a valuable ring, who walked safely throughout the length of Ireland. Warner was an English clergyman and writer on miscellaneous subjects. On the strength of his *Ecclesiastical History of the 18th Century*, he decided to attempt a history of Ireland. He was in touch with Charles O'Conor of Belnagare, who hoped that Warner would write a justificatory history of the Irish. He visited Ireland about 1761 and met with some success in tracking down documents.

The meeting of the waters[1]

There is not in the wide world a valley so sweet
As that vale in whose bosom the bright waters meet;[2]
Oh! the last rays of feeling and life must depart,
Ere the bloom of that valley shall fade from my heart.

Yet it *was* not that Nature had shed o'er the scene
Her purest of crystal and brightest of green;
'Twas *not* her soft magic of streamlet or hill,
Oh! no, — it was something more exquisite still.

'Twas that friends, the belov'd of my bosom, were near,
Who made every dear scene of enchantment more dear,
And who felt how the best charms of nature improve,
When we see them reflected from looks that we love.

Sweet vale of Avoca! how calm could I rest
In thy bosom of shade, with the friends I love best,
Where the storms that we feel in this cold world should cease,
And our hearts, like thy waters, be mingled in peace.

1. Moore visited Avoca, between Rathdrum and Arklow in County Wicklow, in 1807.
2. The waters of the rivers Avonmore and Avonbeg.

How dear to me the hour

How dear to me the hour when daylight dies,
And sunbeams melt along the silent sea;
For then sweet dreams of other days arise,
And memory breathes her vesper sigh to thee.

And, as I watch the line of light, that plays
Along the smooth wave tow'rd the burning west,
I long to tread that golden path of rays,
And think 'twould lead to some bright isle of rest.

Let Erin remember the days of old

[In the Preface to the fourth volume of his *Poetical Works* (1841), Moore related how he used to play airs from Bunting's collection on the piano. 'Robert Emmet used sometimes to sit by me, when I was thus engaged; and I remember one day his starting up as from a reverie, when

I had just finished playing that spirited tune called The Red Fox. "Oh that I were at the head of twenty thousand men, marching to that air!"' Moore indicates in a footnote that this song is to that tune.]

Let Erin remember the days of old,
  Ere her faithless sons betray'd her;
When Malachi wore the collar of gold,[1]
  Which he won from her proud invader,
When her kings, with standard of green unfurl'd,
  Led the Red-Branch Knights[2] to danger; —
Ere the emerald gem of the western world
  Was set in the crown of a stranger.

On Lough Neagh's[3] bank, as the fisherman strays,
  When the clear cold eve's declining,
He sees the round towers of other days
  In the wave beneath him shining;
Thus shall memory often, in dreams sublime,
  Catch a glimpse of the days that are over;
Thus, sighing, look through the waves of time
  For the long faded glories they cover.

1. Moore cites Warner's *History of Ireland* to support this reference to Malachi, the tenth-century king of Ireland, who took a collar of gold from a Danish champion he defeated in single combat.
2. The Ulster warriors of pre-Christian times. Moore's source here is Sylvester O'Halloran's *An Introduction to the Study of the History and Antiquities of Ireland* (1772).
3. The source of the legend of Lough Neagh's inundation of the countryside is in Giraldus Cambrensis, *Topographia Hibernica* (*c.*1187).

The song of Fionnuala[1]

Silent, oh Moyle,[2] be the roar of thy water,
  Break not, ye breezes, your chain of repose,
While, murmuring mournfully, Lir's lonely daughter
  Tells to the night-star her tale of woes.
When shall the swan, her death-note singing,
  Sleep, with wings in darkness furl'd?
When will heaven, its sweet bell ringing,
  Call my spirit from this stormy world?

Sadly, oh Moyle, to thy winter-wave weeping,
  Fate bids me languish long ages away;
Yet still in her darkness doth Erin lie sleeping,
  Still doth the pure light its dawning delay.

1. Fionnuala was the daughter of Lir in Irish legend. She and her sisters were transformed into swans and condemned to fly over the waters and lakes of Ireland until the ringing of the Mass-bell, signifying the arrival of Christianity, would give them release.
2. The Moyle is the stretch of water between the Mull of Kintyre in Scotland and the Antrim coast near Cushendall.

When will that day-star, mildly springing,
  Warm our isle with peace and love?
When will heaven, its sweet bell ringing,
  Call my spirit to the fields above?

Believe me, if all those endearing young charms

Believe me, if all those endearing young charms,
  Which I gaze on so fondly today,
Were to change by tomorrow, and fleet in my arms,
  Like fairy-gifts fading away,
Thou wouldst still be ador'd, as this moment thou art,
  Let thy loveliness fade as it will,
And around the dear ruin each wish of my heart
  Would entwine itself verdantly still.

It is not while beauty and youth are thine own,
  And thy cheeks unprofan'd by a tear
That the fervour and faith of a soul can be known,
  To which time will but make thee more dear;
No, the heart that has truly lov'd never forgets,
  But as truly loves on to the close,
As the sun-flower turns on her god, when he sets,
  The same look which she turn'd when he rose.

Erin, oh Erin

Like the bright lamp, that shone in Kildare's holy
    fane,[1]
  And burn'd thro' long ages of darkness and storm,
Is the heart that sorrows have frown'd on in vain,
  Whose spirit outlives them, unfading and warm.
Erin, oh Erin, thus bright thro' the tears
Of a long night of bondage, thy spirit appears.

The nations have fallen, and thou still art young,
  Thy sun is but rising, when others are set;
And tho' slavery's cloud o'er thy morning hath
    hung
  The full noon of freedom shall beam round thee
    yet.
Erin, oh Erin, tho' long in the shade,
Thy star will shine out when the proudest shall fade.

Unchill'd by the rain, and unwak'd by the wind,
  The lily lies sleeping thro' winter's cold hour,

1. The legendary inextinguishable fire associated with St Bridget at Kildare. fane = temple or cathedral church.

Till Spring's light touch her fetters unbind,
And daylight and liberty bless the young flower.
Thus Erin, oh Erin, *thy* winter is past,
And the hope that liv'd thro' it shall blossom at last.

Oh! blame not the bard

Oh! blame not the bard,[1] if he fly to the bowers,
Where Pleasure lies, carelessly smiling at Fame;
He was born for much more, and in happier hours
His soul might have burn'd with a holier flame.
The string, that now languishes loose o'er the lyre,
Might have bent a proud bow to the warrior's dart;
And the lip, which now breathes but the song of desire,
Might have pour'd the full tide of a patriot's heart.

But alas for his country! — her pride is gone by,
And that spirit is broken, which never would bend;
O'er the ruin her children in secret must sigh,
For 'tis treason to love her, and death to defend.
Unpriz'd are her sons, till they've learn'd to betray;
Undistinguish'd they live, if they shame not their sires;
And the torch, that would light them thro' dignity's way,
Must be caught from the pile, where their country expires.

Then blame not the bard, if in pleasure's soft dream,
He should try to forget, what he never can heal:
Oh! give but a hope — let a vista but gleam
Through the gloom of his country, and mark how he'll feel!
That instant, his heart at her shrine would lay down
Every passion it nurs'd, every bliss it ador'd;
While the myrtle, now idly entwin'd with his crown,
Like the wreath of Harmodius, should cover his sword.[2]

1. Moore supplies the following note: 'We may suppose this apology to have been uttered by one of those wandering bards, whom Spenser so severely, and, perhaps, truly, describes in his State of Ireland, and whose poems, he tells us, "were sprinkled with some pretty flowers of their natural device, which have good grace and comeliness unto them, the which it is a great pity to see abused to the gracing of wickedness and vice, which, with good usage, would serve to adorn and beautify virtue."'
2. Harmodius (6th century B.C.) and his companion Aristogiton tried to kill the tyrant Hippias and his brother Hipparchus. They were said to have shielded their swords in myrtle leaves. Both were killed and later were known as the Liberators of Athens. Moore claims that Alcaeus wrote a poem in their honour, but it was in fact Simonides.

But tho' glory be gone, and tho' hope fade away,
Thy name, lov'd Erin, shall live in his songs;
Not ev'n in the hour, when his heart is most gay,
Will he lose the remembrance of thee and thy wrongs.
The stranger shall hear thy lament on his plains;
The sigh of thy harp shall be sent o'er the deep,
Till thy masters themselves, as they rivet thy chains,
Shall pause at the song of their captive, and weep.

Avenging and bright

Avenging and bright fall the swift sword of Erin[1]
On him who the brave sons of Usna betray'd! —
For every fond eye he hath waken'd a tear in,
A drop from his heart-wounds shall weep o'er her blade.

By the red cloud that hung over Conor's dark dwelling,
When Ulad's[2] three champions lay sleeping in gore —
By the billows of war, which so often, high swelling,
Have wafted these heroes to victory's shore —

We swear to revenge them! — no joy shall be tasted,
The harp shall be silent, the maiden unwed,
Our halls shall be mute, and our fields shall lie wasted,
Till vengeance is wreak'd on the murderer's head.

Yes, monarch! tho' sweet are our home recollections,
Though sweet are the tears that from tenderness fall;
Though sweet are our friendships, our hopes, our affections,
Revenge on a tyrant is sweetest of all!

1. One of the earliest celebrations in English of the legend of Deirdre and the sons of Usna, who were betrayed and killed by King Conor. This was later to be treated by other writers, including Synge and Yeats.
2. Ulster's.

At the mid hour of night

At the mid hour of night, when stars are weeping, I fly
To the lone vale we lov'd, when life shone warm in thine eye;

And I think oft, if spirits can steal from the regions of air,
To revisit past scenes of delight, thou wilt come to me there,
And tell me our love is remember'd, even in the sky.

Then I sing the wild song 'twas once such pleasure to hear!
When our voices commingling breath'd, like one, on the ear;
And, as Echo far off through the vale my sad orison rolls,
I think, oh my love! 'tis thy voice from the Kingdom of Souls,
Faintly answering still the notes that once were so dear.

One bumper at parting

One bumper[1] at parting! — though many
Have circled the board since we met,
The fullest, the saddest of any,
Remains to be crown'd by us yet.
The sweetness that pleasure hath in it,
Is always so slow to come forth,
That seldom, alas, till the minute
It dies, do we know half its worth.
But come, — may our life's happy measure
Be all of such moments made up;
They're born on the bosom of Pleasure,
They die 'midst the tears of the cup.

As onward we journey, how pleasant
To pause and inhabit awhile
Those few sunny spots, like the present,
That 'mid the dull wilderness smile!
But Time, like a pitiless master,
Cries 'Onward!' and spurs the gay hours —
Ah, never doth Time travel faster,
Than when his way lies among flowers.
But come, — may our life's happy measure
Be all of such moments made up;
They're born on the bosom of Pleasure,
They die 'midst the tears of the cup.

We saw how the sun look'd in sinking,
The waters beneath him how bright;
And now, let our farewell of drinking
Resemble that farewell of light.
You saw how he finish'd, by darting
His beam o'er a deep billow's brim —
So, fill up, let's shine at our parting,
In full liquid glory, like him.
And oh! may our life's happy measure
Of moments like this be made up,
'Twas born on the bosom of Pleasure,
It dies 'mid the tears of the cup.

1. A glass filled to the brim, usually for a toast.

'Tis the last rose of summer

'Tis the last rose of summer
Left blooming alone;
All her lovely companions
Are faded and gone;
No flower of her kindred,
No rose-bud is nigh,
To reflect back her blushes,
Or give sigh for sigh.

I'll not leave thee, thou lone one!
To pine on the stem;
Since the lovely are sleeping,
Go, sleep thou with them.
Thus kindly I scatter
Thy leaves o'er the bed,
Where thy mates of the garden
Lie scentless and dead.

So soon may *I* follow,
When friendships decay,
And from Love's shining circle
The gems drop away.
When true hearts lie wither'd,
And fond ones are flown,
Oh! who would inhabit
This bleak world alone?

The Minstrel Boy

The Minstrel Boy to the war is gone,
In the ranks of death you'll find him;
His father's sword he has girded on,
And his wild harp slung behind him. —
'Land of song!' said the warrior-bard,
'Though all the word betrays thee,
One sword, at least, thy rights shall guard,
One faithful harp shall praise thee!'

The Minstrel fell! — but the foeman's chain
  Could not bring his proud soul under;
The harp he lov'd ne'er spoke again,
  For he tore its chords asunder;
And said, 'No chains shall sully thee,
  Thou soul of love and bravery!
Thy songs were made for the pure and free,
  They shall never sound in slavery.'

Dear Harp of my Country

Dear Harp of my Country! in darkness I found thee,
  The cold chain of silence had hung o'er thee long,
When proudly, my own Island Harp, I unbound thee,
  And gave all thy chords to light, freedom, and song!
The warm lay of love and the light note of gladness
  Have waken'd thy fondest, thy liveliest thrill;
But, so oft hast thou echo'd the deep sigh of sadness,
  That ev'n in thy mirth it will steal from thee still.

Dear Harp of my Country! farewell to thy numbers,
  This sweet wreath of song is the last we shall twine!
Go, sleep with the sunshine of Fame on thy slumbers,
  Till touch'd by some hand less unworthy than mine;
If the pulse of the patriot, soldier, or lover,
  Have throbb'd at our lay, 'tis thy glory alone;
I was *but* as the wind, passing heedlessly over,
  And all the wild sweetness I wak'd was thy own.

In the morning of life

In the morning of life, when its cares are unknown,
  And its pleasures in all their new lustre begin,
When we live in a bright-beaming world of our own,
  And the light that surrounds us is all from within;
Oh 'tis not, believe me, in that happy time
  We can love, as in hours of less transport we may; —
Of our smiles, of our hopes, 'tis the gay sunny prime,
  But affection is truest when these fade away.

When we see the first glory of youth pass us by,
  Like a leaf on the stream that will never return;
When our cup, which had sparkled with pleasure so high,
  First tastes of the *other*, the dark-flowing urn;
Then, then is the time when affection holds sway
  With a depth and a tenderness joy never knew;
Love, nurs'd among pleasures, is faithless as they,
  But the love born of Sorrow, like Sorrow, is true.

In climes full of sunshine, though splendid the flowers,
  Their sighs have no freshness, their odour no worth;
'Tis the cloud and the mist of our own Isle of showers,
  That call the rich spirit of fragrancy forth.
So it is not mid splendour, prosperity, mirth,
  That the depth of Love's generous spirit appears;
To the sunshine of smiles it may first owe its birth,
  But the soul of its sweetness is drawn out by tears.

As slow our ship

As slow our ship her foamy track
  Against the wind was cleaving,
Her trembling pennant still look'd back
  To that dear Isle 'twas leaving.
So loath we part from all we love,
  From all the links that bind us;
So turn our hearts as on we rove,
  To those we've left behind us.

When, round the bowl, of vanish'd years
  We talk, with joyous seeming, —
With smiles that might as well be tears,
  So faint, so sad their beaming;
While mem'ry brings us back again
  Each early tie that twined us,
Oh, sweet's the cup that circles then
  To those we've left behind us.

And when, in other climes, we meet
  Some isle, or vale enchanting,
Where all looks flow'ry, wild, and sweet,
  And nought but love is wanting;
We think how great had been our bliss,
  If Heav'n had but assign'd us
To live and die in scenes like this,
  With some we've left behind us!

As trav'llers oft look back at eve,
  When eastward darkly going,
To gaze up on that light they leave
  Still faint behind them glowing, —
So, when the close of pleasure's day
  To gloom hath near consign'd us,
We turn to catch one fading ray
  Of joy that's left behind us.

When cold in the earth

When cold in the earth lies the friend thou hast lov'd,
Be his faults and his follies forgot by thee then;
Or, if from their slumber the veil be remov'd,
Weep o'er them in silence, and close it again.
And oh! if 'tis pain to remember how far
From the pathways of light he was tempted to roam,
Be it bliss to remember that thou wert the star
That arose on his darkness, and guided him home.

From thee and thy innocent beauty first came
The revealings, that taught him true love to adore,
To feel the bright presence, and turn him with shame
From the idols he blindly had knelt to before.
O'er the waves of a life, long benighted and wild,
Thou camest, like a soft golden calm o'er the sea;
And if happiness purely and glowingly smil'd
On his ev'ning horizon, the light was from thee.

And though, sometimes, the shades of past folly might rise,
And though falsehood again would allure him to stray,
He but turn'd to the glory that dwelt in those eyes,
And the folly, the falsehood, soon vanish'd away.
As the Priests of the Sun, when their altar grew dim,
At the day-beam alone could its lustre repair,
So, if virtue a moment grew languid in him,
He but flew to that smile, and rekindled it there.

Remember thee

Remember thee? yes, while there's life in this heart,
It shall never forget thee, all lorn[1] as thou art;
More dear in thy sorrow, thy gloom, and thy showers,
Than the rest of the world in their sunniest hours.

Wert thou all that I wish thee, great, glorious, and free,
First flower of the earth, and first gem of the sea,
I might hail thee with prouder, with happier brow,
But oh! could I love thee more deeply than now?

No, thy chains as they rankle, thy blood as it runs,
But make thee more painfully dear to thy sons —
Whose hearts, like the young of the desert-bird's nest,
Drink love in each life-drop that flows from thy breast.

1. forsaken, forlorn.

Whene'er I see those smiling eyes

Whene'er I see those smiling eyes,
So full of hope, and joy, and light,
As if no cloud could ever rise,
To dim a heav'n so purely bright —
I sigh to think how soon that brow
In grief may lose its every ray,
And that light heart, so joyous now,
Almost forget it once was gay.

For time will come with all its blights,
The ruin'd hope, the friend unkind,
And love, that leaves, where'er it lights,
A chill'd or burning heart behind: —
While youth, that now like snow appears,
Ere sullied by the dark'ning rain,
When once 'tis touch'd by sorrow's tears
Can never shine so bright again.

Sweet Innisfallen

Sweet Innisfallen, fare thee well,
May calm and sunshine long be thine!
How fair thou art let others tell, —
To *feel* how fair shall long be mine.

Sweet Innisfallen, long shall dwell
In memory's dream that sunny smile,
Which o'er thee on that evening fell,
When first I saw thy fairy isle.

'Twas light, indeed, too blest for one,
Who had to turn to paths of care —
Through crowded haunts again to run,
And leave thee bright and silent there;

No more unto thy shores to come,
But, on the world's rude ocean tost,
Dream of thee sometimes, as a home
Of sunshine he had seen and lost.

Far better in thy weeping hours
To part from thee, as I do now,
When mist is o'er thy blooming bowers,
Like sorrow's veil on beauty's brow.

For, though unrivall'd still thy grace,
Thou dost not look, as then, *too* blest,
But thus in shadow, seem'st a place
Where erring man might hope to rest —

Might hope to rest, and find in thee
  A gloom like Eden's, on the day
He left its shade, when every tree,
  Like thine, hung weeping o'er his way.

Weeping or smiling, lovely isle!
  And all the lovelier for thy tears —
For though but rare thy sunny smile,
  'Tis heav'n's own glance when it appears.

Like feeling hearts, whose joys are few,
  But, when *indeed* they come, divine —
The brightest light the sun e'er threw
  Is lifeless to one gleam of thine!

As vanquish'd Erin

As vanquish'd Erin wept beside
  The Boyne's ill-fated river,[1]
She saw where Discord, in the tide,
  Had dropp'd his loaded quiver.
'Lie hid,' she cried, 'ye venom'd darts,
  Where mortal eye may shun you;
Lie hid — the stain of manly hearts,
  That bled for me, is on you.'

But vain her wish, her weeping vain, —
  As Time too well hath taught her —
Each year the Fiend returns again,
  And dives into that water;
And brings, triumphant, from beneath
  His shafts of desolation,
And sends them, wing'd with worse than death,
  Through all her madd'ning nation.

Alas for her who sits and mourns,
  Ev'n now, beside that river —
Unwearied still the Fiend returns,
  And stor'd is still his quiver.
'When will this end, ye Powers of Good?'
  She weeping asks for ever;
But only hears, from out that flood,
  The Demon answer, 'Never!'

1. William III defeated the deposed James II in a battle on the banks of the Boyne in 1690.

They know not my heart

They know not my heart, who believe there can be
One stain of this earth in its feelings for thee;
Who think, while I see thee in beauty's young
  hour,
As pure as the morning's first dew on the flow'r,
I could harm what I love, — as the sun's wanton ray
But smiles on the dew-drop to waste it away.

No — beaming with light as those young features are,
There's a light round thy heart which is lovelier far:
It *is* not that cheek — 'tis the soul dawning clear
Thro' its innocent blush makes thy beauty so
  dear;
As the sky we look up to, though glorious and
  fair,
Is look'd up to the more, because Heaven lies
  there!

I wish I was by that dim Lake

I wish I was by that dim Lake,[1]
Where sinful souls their farewell take
Of this vain world, and half-way lie
In death's cold shadow, ere they die.
There, there, far from thee,
Deceitful world, my home should be;
Where, come what might of gloom and pain,
False hope should ne'er deceive again.

The lifeless sky, the mournful sound
Of unseen waters falling round;
The dry leaves, quiv'ring o'er my head,
Like man, unquiet ev'n when dead!
These, ay, these shall wean,
My soul from life's deluding scene,
And turn each thought, o'ercharg'd with gloom,
Like willows, downward tow'rds the tomb.

As they, who to their couch at night
Would win repose, first quench the light,
So must the hopes, that keep this breast
Awake, be quench'd, ere it can rest.
Cold, cold, this heart must grow,
Unmov'd by either joy or woe,
Like freezing founts, where all that's thrown
Within their current turns to stone.

1. Glendalough, the monastic site in County Wicklow. The monastic remains stand beside one of the two lakes.

from: NATIONAL AIRS (1818)

Oft, in the stilly night
(Scotch Air)

Oft, in the stilly night,
Ere Slumber's chain has bound me,
Fond Memory brings the light
Of other days around me;
The smiles, the tears,
Of boyhood's years,
The words of love then spoken;
The eyes that shone,
Now dimm'd and gone,
The cheerful hearts now broken!
Thus, in the stilly night,
Ere Slumber's chain hath bound me,
Sad Memory brings the light
Of other days around me.

When I remember all
The friends, so link'd together,
I've seen around me fall,
Like leaves in wintry weather;
I feel like one,
Who treads alone
Some banquet-hall deserted,
Whose lights are fled,
Whose garlands dead,
And all but he departed!
Thus, in the stilly night,
Ere Slumber's chain has bound me,
Sad Memory brings the light
Of other days around me.

from: SONGS, BALLADS AND SACRED SONGS (1849)

The dream of home

Who has not felt how sadly sweet
The dream of home, the dream of home,
Steals o'er the heart, too soon to fleet,
When far o'er sea or land we roam?
Sunlight more soft may o'er us fall,
To greener shores our bark may come;
But far more bright, more dear than all,
That dream of home, that dream of home.

Ask of the sailor youth when far
His light bark bounds o'er ocean's foam,
What charms him most, when ev'ning's star
Smiles o'er the wave? to dream of home.
Fond thoughts of absent friends and loves
At that sweet hour around him come;
His heart's best joy where'er he roves,
That dream of home, that dream of home.

The homeward march

Be still, my heart: I hear them come:
Those sounds announce my lover near:
The march that brings our warriors home
Proclaims he'll soon be here.

Hark, the distant tread,
O'er the mountain's head,
While hills and dales repeat the sound;
And the forest deer
Stand still to hear,
As those echoing steps ring round.

Be still, my heart, I hear them come,
Those sounds that speak my soldier near;
Those joyous steps seem wing'd for home, —
Rest, rest, he'll soon be here.

But hark, more faint the footsteps grow,
And now they wind to distant glades;
Not here their home, — alas, they go
To gladden happier maids!

Like sounds in a dream,
The footsteps seem,
As down the hills they die away;
And the march, whose song
So peal'd along,
Now fades like a funeral lay.

'Tis past, 'tis o'er, — hush, heart, thy pain!
And though not here, alas, they come,
Rejoice for those, to whom that strain
Brings sons and lovers home.

Calm be thy sleep

Calm be thy sleep as infants' slumbers!
Pure as angel thoughts thy dreams!
May ev'ry joy this bright world numbers
Shed o'er thee their mingled beams!

Or if, where Pleasure's wing hath glided,
There ever must some pang remain,
Still be thy lot with me divided, —
Thine all the bliss, and mine the pain!

Day and night my thoughts shall hover
Round thy steps where'er they stray;
As, ev'n when clouds his idol cover,
Fondly the Persian tracks its ray.
If this be wrong, if Heav'n offended
By worship to its creature be,
Then let my vows to both be blended,
Half breath'd to Heav'n and half to thee.

The exile

Night waneth fast, the morning star
Saddens with light the glimm'ring sea,
Whose waves shall soon to realms afar
Waft me from hope, from love, and thee.
Coldly the beam from yonder sky
Looks o'er the waves that onward stray;
But colder still the stranger's eye
To him whose home is far away.

Oh, not at hour so chill and bleak,
Let thoughts of me come o'er thy breast;
But of the lost one think and speak,
When summer suns sink calm to rest.
So, as I wander, Fancy's dream
Shall bring me o'er the sunset seas,
Thy look, in ev'ry melting beam,
Thy whisper, in each dying breeze.

Love thee, dearest? love thee?

Love thee, dearest? love thee?
Yes, by yonder star I swear,
Which through tears above thee
Shines so sadly fair;
Though often dim,
With tears, like him,
Like him my truth will shine,
And — love thee, dearest? love thee?
Yes, till death I'm thine.

Leave thee, dearest? leave thee?
No, that star is not more true;
When my vows deceive thee,
He will wander too.
A cloud of night
May veil his light,
And death shall darken mine —
But — leave thee, dearest? leave thee?
No, till death I'm thine.

My heart and lute

I give thee all — I can no more —
Though poor the off'ring be;
My heart and lute are all the store
That I can bring to thee.
A lute whose gentle song reveals
The soul of love full well;
And, better far, a heart that feels
Much more than lute could tell.

Though love and song may fail, alas!
To keep life's clouds away,
At least 'twill make them lighter pass
Or gild them if they stay.
And ev'n if Care, at moments, flings
A discord o'er life's happy strain,
Let love but gently touch the strings,
'Twill all be sweet again!

'Tis all for thee

If life for me hath joy or light,
'Tis all from thee,
My thoughts by day, my dreams by night,
Are but of thee, of only thee.
Whate'er of hope or peace I know,
My zest in joy, my balm in woe,
To those dear eyes of thine I owe,
'Tis all from thee.

My heart, ev'n ere I saw those eyes,
Seem'd doom'd to thee;
Kept pure till then from other ties,
'Twas all for thee, for only thee.
Like plants that sleep, till sunny May
Calls forth their life, my spirit lay,
Till, touch'd by Love's awak'ning ray,
It liv'd for thee, it liv'd for thee.

When Fame would call me to her heights,
She speaks by thee;
And dim would shine her proudest lights,
Unshar'd by thee, unshar'd by thee.

Whene'er I seek the Muse's shrine,
Where Bards have hung their wreaths divine,
And wish those wreaths of glory mine,
   'Tis all for thee, for only thee.

Oh, call it by some better name

Oh, call it by some better name,
   For Friendship sounds too cold,
While Love is now a worldly flame,
   Whose shrine must be of gold;
And Passion, like the sun at noon,
   That burns o'er all he sees,
Awhile as warm, will set as soon —
   Then, call it none of these.

Imagine something purer far,
   More free from stain of clay
Than Friendship, Love, or Passion are,
   Yet human still as they:
And if thy lip, for love like this,
   No mortal word can frame,
Go, ask of angels what it is,
   And call it by that name!

Biography/Bibliography

LIFE. Born in 1779 in Aungier Street, Dublin, the son of a grocer and of an adoring mother, Moore was one of those to benefit from Trinity College's recent change of policy in admitting catholics. He graduated from Trinity in 1800, the same year as his first publication, *The Odes of Anacreon*. He remembered being taken upon the knee of the United Irishman, Napper Tandy, in 1792 and hearing patriotic toasts to the onset of Irish freedom. The great rebellion of 1798 made a deep impression, particularly the brutality of the government forces in extinguishing it. At Trinity, he knew Robert Emmet, the rebel who was to lead an abortive rising in Dublin in 1803. Emmet made no attempt to recruit Moore.

Moore went to London in late 1799 and was an immediate success in aristocratic circles. Lord Moira, the Duke of Bedford and the Marquis of Lansdowne befriended him, as did Byron, Lord John Russell, Walter Scott and many others. His conversation, his singing, his spendthrift conviviality endeared him to many. He gained an Admiralty post at Bermuda in 1803, reached there in 1804, delegated his duties to a deputy and, after a few months, went on a tour of the United States. This episode was to rebound on him when his deputy in Bermuda absconded and left him with a debt of £6,000 to pay. Moore was forced to live abroad in Paris from 1819 to 1822. His satiric verse, never so popular as his other work, was much more politically open in its hostility to Tory politicians and the ill-treatment of Ireland, particularly over the issue of catholic emancipation. It was also popular at the time. His *Intercepted Letters* (1813), aimed at the Prince Regent and his ministers, went into fourteen editions in one year. But it was the *Irish Melodies* that won Moore his most enduring fame, just as his Persian tale in verse, *Lallah Rookh* (1817), gained him most money and contemporary fame. Although happily married in 1811 to Bessie Dyke from Kilkenny, Moore's life was overshadowed by the deaths of his five children. After the death of his close friend Lord Byron, Moore became involved in a lawsuit that led to his acquiescience in the burning of Byron's memoirs. After 1819, he lived in Sloperton Cottage, Wiltshire, on Lord Lansdowne's estate. After 1822, he made very favourable financial arrangements with his publishers, although from the mid-1820s most of his work was in prose and was much less popular than his verse. He wrote little after 1835, the year of a particularly successful and triumphant return to Dublin. Moore became seriously ill in 1847 and gradually declined into an early and distressing senility. He died in 1852 at Sloperton. His mother, who had been so dominant in his life, outlived him by thirteen years. She presented his library to the Royal Irish Academy.

CHIEF WRITINGS. *Irish Melodies* 2 vols (Dublin and London, 1808); vol. 3 (London and Dublin, 1810); vol. 4 (London and Dublin, 1811); vol. 5 (London and Dublin, 1813); vol. 6 (London and Dublin, 1815); vol. 7 (London, 1818); vol. 8 (London, 1821); vol. 9 (London, 1824); vol. 10 (London, 1834). (The first collection of the *Melodies* was published in Dublin by W. Power in 1820.) *Corruption and Intolerance* (London, 1808); *Intercepted Letters; or the Two-Penny Post-Bag* by 'Thomas Brown the Younger' (London, 1813); *Sacred Songs* vol. 1 (London and Dublin, 1816); vol. 2 (London, 1824); *Lallah Rookh; An Oriental Romance* (London, 1817); *The Fudge Family in Paris*, by 'Thomas Brown the Younger' (London, 1818); *National Airs* vol. 1 (London and Dublin, 1818); vol. 2 (London and Dublin, 1820); vols 3 & 4 (London, 1822); vol. 5 (London, 1826); vol. 6 (London, 1827); *The Loves of the Angels* (London, 1823); *Memoirs of Captain Rock, the Celebrated Irish Chieftain, with Some Account of his Ancestors* (London, 1824); *Memoirs of the Life of the Right Honourable Richard Brinsley Sheridan* (London, 1825); *The Epicurean; A Tale* (London, 1827); *The Life and Death of Lord Edward Fitzgerald* (London, 1831); *Travels of an Irish Gentleman in Search of Religion* (London, 1833).

Collections and Editions: *The Poetical Works of Thomas Moore* Collected by Himself, 10 vols (London: Longmans, 1841); Lord John Russell (ed.), *The Memoirs, Journal and Correspondence of Thomas Moore*, 8 vols (London: Longmans, 1853-56); A.D. Godley (ed.), *The Poetical Works of Thomas Moore* (London: Henry Frowde, 1910); W.S. Dowden (ed.), *The Letters of Thomas Moore*, 2 vols (Oxford: Clarendon Press, 1964); P. Quennell (ed.), *The Journal of Thomas Moore* (London: Collins, 1964).

BIOGRAPHY AND CRITICISM. H.M. Jones, *The Harp That Once* (New York: Henry Holt, 1937); L.A.G. Strong, *The Minstrel Boy: A Portrait of Tom Moore* (New York: Knopf, 1937); M.A. de Ford, *Thomas Moore* (New York: Twayne, 1967); T. de Vere White, *Tom Moore, The Irish Poet* (London: Hamish Hamilton, 1977); H.H. Jordan, *Bolt Upright: The Life of Thomas Moore* 2 vols (Salzburg, 1975); R. Welch, *Irish Poetry from Moore to Yeats* (Gerrards Cross: Colin Smythe, 1980); P.C. Power, *The Story of Anglo-Irish Poetry, 1800-1922* (Cork: Mercier Press, 1967); T. Tessier, *The Bard of Erin. A Study of Thomas Moore's 'Irish Melodies' 1808-1834* (Atlantic Highlands, New Jersey: Humanities Press, 1981); T. Brown, 'Thomas Moore: A Reputation' in *Ireland's Literature: Selected Essays* (Mullingar, Co. Westmeath: The Lilliput Press, 1988).

W.J. Mc CORMACK, *Editor*

Language, Class and Genre

(1780-1830)

I. A NEW MIDDLE CLASS?

One of the few generalizations about literature in English that has gained a wide degree of acceptance is the interconnection of the novel as a literary form and the middle class as a social formation. This is a dynamic interconnection: Ian Watt's pioneering study of Defoe, Fielding and Richardson, first published in 1957, is entitled *The Rise of the Novel*, and historians are similarly concerned with the rise or emergence of the middle class or even of successive middle classes, for it is a characteristic of this historical phenomenon that newness is stressed. The link with the novel is emphasized even in that genre's name.

Historians of England have written of the Henrician middle classes, of the mid-seventeenth-century middle classes, and so on up to our own day, in each case stressing the emergence of a *new* middle class. In Ireland, the issue is (as you would expect) both more complicated and more simplified. Until very recently, it was not uncommon to find literary critics declaring that, in whatever period of Irish literary history they were concerned with (the 1720s, the Romantic, or the Victorian period), no middle class existed! Thus, while English historians produced new middle classes apparently at will, critics of Irish literature denied that the species had ever been introduced into Ireland. The position has been modified by developments in the study of both history and literature. In the context of an Irish literary history, attention has gradually focused on the emergence of a catholic middle-class culture in the 1820s and afterwards. The political event central to this argument is, of course, the achievement of catholic emancipation in 1829; the longer context is the Victorian age, which culminated in Ireland with the jettisoning of the landowner, Charles Stewart Parnell, as leader of an essentially bourgeois Irish Party. Thus, in the annals of Irish fiction, John Banim (1798-1842) is a pioneer of this emergent catholic intelligentsia, Patrick (Canon) Sheehan (1852-1913) a significant post-Parnellite figure, and James Joyce (1882-1941) the problematic heretic-cum-hero of the entire historical movement. However, this general paralleling of political events with the growth of a catholic middle-class canon of fiction distorts many important details. Among these, one might point to the quantity of fiction written in or about Ireland in the eighteenth century, the work of nineteenth-century novelists whose origins and/or values are fundamentally bourgeois but whose denominational affiliation is not catholic, and (in the field of non-literary history) the existence and indeed prosperity of a middle class (including catholics) before 1800.

So the field of discussion has to be restricted, lest it stretch back to pre-reformation days and forward to those of Seamus Heaney (born in 1939) and John Hume (born in 1937) whose careers (in poetry and politics) are often intelligently discussed in not dissimilar terms. In effect, the present section pivots around the date of the Act of Union (1800), with historical commentary drawn predominantly from the last two decades of the eighteenth century, and literary material from the first three of the nineteenth. No exclusive attention is given to the novel, or even to fiction, although the novel is increasingly prominent as we move towards the latter end of the period.

Historians have recently drawn our attention to

the limited (though still real) extent of catholic losses in the various 'settlements' of the seventeenth century. In so far as these relate to landed estate, one should note that not every stage in the process had involved loss: following the restoration of the monarchy in 1660, a court of claims 'more than doubled the share of catholic-owned land, with catholic ownership in Leinster counties such as Meath and Dublin recovering sharply.'[1] Although the defeat of King James II ensured that no such pattern was sustained, the Williamite settlement (completed by 1703) reduced the pre-war landholding of the catholic gentry by less than a third. Nevertheless, by the end of the first decade of the eighteenth century, about 14 per cent of Ireland remained in their hands. If this figure has seemed small in the eyes of more recent generations, we should remember that the vast majority of the population owned no land whatever, and this by reason of their *social* status within the prevailing economic system.

Two consequences of this situation are immediately relevant here. First, the Penal Laws did not proceed to dispossess catholics but rather to circumscribe their relationship with land by measures resulting in a degree of nominal conformity, by which some individual members of catholic families protected their interests by subscribing publicly to the tenets of the established church. In *The Conformists* (1829), John Banim wrote a fiction based on one (prevalent) interpretation of such practice: the view of the conformer as renegade. The 1713 election had seen the return of about a dozen Tory MPs who were recent converts from catholicism, and there was a strong Tory showing in districts where catholic voters survived in some strength. Edmund Burke's father had been born a catholic, but his becoming a lawyer required affiliation to the established church. Burke's wife, Jane Nugent, remained a catholic all her life, and it is not surprising that Burke himself was sometimes accused (wrongly) of being a secret catholic.

Apart from the limited durability of catholic landholding and of catholic (indirect) political influence, a further consequence of the penal restrictions *vis-à-vis* landed estate was the redirection of catholic energy and the growth of catholic prosperity in the commercial realm. It is possible that this shift also contributed to the weakening of the Irish language, which never succeeded in transforming its traditional and pastoral character into an urban or managerial idiom. However that imponderable may be judged, this second feature of the Irish eighteenth century acquires a more urgent political significance in its last two decades. By 1792, the vexed question of the relaxation of the Penal Laws controlling catholic participation in the country's political life was already on the agenda, at least in London if not in Dublin.

It has been recognized for some time that these conditions resulted in the growth of a new middle class in Ireland. Maureen Wall, who pioneered this reassessment, identified two reasons why the situation had not been acknowledged for what it was.[2] First, the pursuit of trade was held in some contempt in Ireland, where a country estate was regarded as the symbol of worldly success and refinement. Some indication of this can be gauged from Maria Edgeworth's *Castle Rackrent* (1800), where both Sir Conolly Rackrent and Jason Quirk have trained as lawyers, and Sir Conolly has preferred the indolent life to that of a legal practice like Jason's. Indeed, what little of Jason's professional activities are admitted to the novel relate as much to business as to law. Law is shown clearly to be an instrument of class change, at least as far as the possession of landed estate is concerned. Second, catholics tended to keep quiet about their commercial success — Jason Quirk is for the most part an absent character in *Castle Rackrent* — especially in the first half of the century, a tactic that did not prevent protestant rivals from complaining about the proportion of the country's wealth controlled by the allegedly disloyal 'papists'. The corporation of Galway petitioned parliament in 1762 because only 350 of the city's 14,000 inhabitants were protestant and because the catholic majority possessed 'the wealth of the town, or by much the greater part of it. . . .' In Limerick, the reality differed from the law in much the same way. Whereas the early part of the century had seen catholic merchants live unostentatiously in the unfashionable parts of the town (and catholic tradesmen in fact were confined to a district outside the

1. David Dickson, *New Foundations: Ireland 1660-1800* (Dublin: Helicon, 1987), p. 7.

2. Maureen Wall [née MacGeehin], 'The Rise of a Catholic Middle Class in Eighteenth-Century Ireland', *Irish Historical Studies*, Vol. 9, No. 42 (September 1958), 91-115.

city proper), later one finds the richest catholic merchant families — the Roches and the Arthurs — engaged in extensive building programmes, with Patrick Arthur effectively defining the fashionable part of the town after 1770 by his building of Arthur's Quay and adjacent streets. Yet even at this date, by which time catholic prosperity was evident, many factors (including the Penal Laws themselves) protected catholics from conspicuous spending and ostentation. In some respects Irish catholics in the eighteenth century epitomized the economic law of delayed gratification that Max Weber was much later to associate with 'the spirit of protestantism'. By a neat corollary, the tendency of those favoured by the regime to treat landed estate as the emblem of their success resulted in land becoming a veritable albatross, a badge of social if not economic inertia, and this precisely in the late nineteenth and early twentieth century — Weber's period.

II. THE EMERGENCE OF PROTESTANT ASCENDANCY

These two factors, pride and discretion, combined to generate an opacity of language when the question of social class was analysed. In looking at the literary aspect of this historical process, the role of language is crucial. Edmund Burke found it so at the time. Commentators on eighteenth-century society were frequently distracted from the task of describing the wealth and commerce of the nation into discussions of nomenclature. The English agriculturalist Arthur Young (1741-1820) published *A Tour in Ireland* in 1780, and it remains a major source of information on economic affairs. In 1793 Samuel Crumpe (1766-96), an Irish physician, won a prize from the Royal Irish Academy for *An Essay on the Best Means of Providing Employment for the People of Ireland*. These and other witnesses to late eighteenth-century conditions emphasize the anomalous position of the middling ranks of society in Ireland. In introducing such material, we shall find it helpful to look also at the more spontaneous discussions of class that arose in the course of pamphlet disputes. For example, within the society that Young and Crumpe describe, a lawyer such as Dominick Trant could refer in a pamphlet to

> that middle race of men from which the bar, the pulpit, and the public offices are supplied with their most distinguished ornaments: from this order the army and navy usually received their officers. — This class (the gentlemen farmers of this country and of England) and the substantial yeomanry, constitute the pride and security of every free state not absolutely commercial.[3]

The pamphlet in question was published on 30 January 1787, and events later in the year were to prove to its author the volatile state of Irish class relations. It is not too much to say that the distinctive *change* in Irish literary culture signalled by the publication of *Castle Rackrent* arose in part at least from the subterranean (and, later, the obvious) turmoil of the social classes in Ireland and elsewhere.

These were to be revolutionary years. The *Freeman's Journal* of 4-6 January 1787 noted that 'the order of Monks is in a tottering state in France at this moment.' In the 1790s the uncertainty became positively dangerous as the impact of the French Revolution was felt in protestant Belfast as well as in the areas of the far south traditionally linked with the Continent by trade and family connection. Anxiety in relation to Jacobin influence in Cork was undoubtedly in excess of the evidence, but the authorities keenly felt the coming together of catholic demands for relief from the most vexatious of the Penal Laws and dissenter enthusiasm for some of the democratic principles of Jacobinism. Even before the French Revolution, Munster was in a state of grave disorder, with the army being dispatched to quell what was regarded as a veritable insurrection by the Whiteboys in protest at the collection of tithes.

Although this agrarian organization had been assimilated into a larger history of secret societies whose social base was assumed to be the deprived and desperate elements in the population, the Munster disturbances were coordinated by individuals from the upper ranks of society, among them Sir John Colthurst and Lady Jeffereyes. Indeed Dominick Trant killed Colthurst in a duel arising from the pamphlet just quoted, and the position of Lady Jeffereyes as a fellow patron (with Colthurst) of the Whiteboys was rendered more anomalous in that her brother was John Fitzgibbon, then attorney general in the Irish government.

The basis for Trant's confident definition of

3. Dominick Trant, *Considerations on the Present Disturbances in the Province of Munster. . . .* (Dublin: P. Byrne, 1787), p. 17.

middle-class independence in civil society underwent a severe testing in the course of the fifteen years to come. In this context it is worth recalling Karl Marx's argument in the 1840s that 'if *one* class is to stand for the whole of society, then ... one particular sphere of society must appear as the *notorious crime* of the whole of society, so that the liberation of this sphere appears as universal self-liberation.'[4] In the 1790s, Ireland was not to have a class capable of acting in this revolutionary fashion, and it is not frivolous to argue that this condition arose in part at least because Irish society had too many spheres playing the part — not of the victim, but of the notorious criminal. However that may be, a series of reversals and experiments in the language of class division got under way during this period.

Late in 1786 Richard Woodward, the bishop of Cloyne, Co. Cork, had issued a pugnacious tract entitled *The Present State of the Church of Ireland*, in which he pointed the finger at the two foes of religious and political establishment: the catholics and the presbyterians. In the course of this, he used the term protestant ascendancy, declaring:

> I need not tell the Protestant proprietor of land, that the security of his title depends very much (if not entirely) on the Protestant ascendancy; or that the preservation of that ascendancy depends entirely on an indissoluble connection between the Sister Kingdoms.[5]

At first glance, this appears to refer simply enough to the upper stratum of Irish society, so frequently mentioned in (later) history books under the same title, the protestant ascendancy. However, it is vitally important to observe precisely how Woodward did use the phrase. He used it to stress the ascendancy of protestantism in the arrangements of the state and its governance, and the word 'ascendancy' might equally well have been replaced by 'predominance', 'supremacy' or some such term. As evidence of this, we need only look elsewhere in Woodward's pamphlet, where he refers to the 'ascendency' of the clergy in 'Italy, Spain, Portugal, Germany, Denmark, Sweden, Hungary and Poland ... [and] the commercial States of France and England'.[6] Ascendancy (however one spells it) does not here name any distinctive Irish class; the word is applied to a very broad range of countries and the church-state relations pertaining there. It is true that Woodward also uses the (now) familiar phrase 'protestant ascendancy' on four or five occasions in the course of his pamphlet, and uses it in connection with the particular Irish problems that are his major concern. On the last of these occasions, he argues that a commutation of tithes

> by shutting up many Churches ... must rapidly diminish the number of Clergymen; and at the same time, by raising in the like proportion the number and influence of the Romish Priests, must cause the Protestant interest to decline in a Ratio Compounded of both: Which increased by depression of spirits on one side, and by animation of hope and foreign assistance on the other, must soon overthrow the Protestant Ascendency.[7]

It is easy to see how the last six words, later, could be read as referring to the destruction of a social class (an elite). However, one should not read back into the 1780s a subsequent interpretation or application of the phrase "protestant ascendancy'. To do so would be to make even cloudier the terminology employed to identify particular elements in Irish society.

The Present State of the Church of Ireland did not comment on the particular linguistic usage that later became so familiar. It did, however, emphasize the importance of language in a different sphere of social relations. In rural areas, the clergy

4. Karl Marx, 'A Contribution to the Critique of Hegel's Philosophy of Right. Introduction' in *Marx, Early Writings* (Harmondsworth: Penguin, 1975), p. 254.
5. Richard Woodward, *The Present State of the Church of Ireland: Containing a Description of it's* [sic] *Precarious Situation; and the Consequent Danger to the Public. Recommended to the Serious Consideration of the Friends of the Protestant Interest. To which are Subjoined, Some Reflections on the Impracticability of a Proper Commutation for Tithes; and a General Account of the Origin and Progress of the Insurrections in Munster* (Dublin: W. Sleater, 1787, [recte December 1786]), p. 17.

   'The protestant interest' was a phrase used in the late seventeenth century and throughout the eighteenth, to indicate without ambiguity the connection between economic interest and social formation. Its definition can be traced back at least to William Petty (1623-87), and its displacement now by 'the protestant ascendancy' enacts the process of concealment inherent in all ideological constructs.
6. ibid., pp. 59, 58; see also a footnote on p. 33 of the 1792 pamphlet cited in note 20 below, which reports Edward Sweetman referring to 'presbyterian ascendancy' in Scotland and 'catholic ascendancy' in Canada.
7. Woodward, p. 77.

of the Church of Ireland 'cannot prevail against a Priest always at hand, and master of the Irish language'. Far from encouraging his colleagues to learn the language of the rural majority, Woodward declared that 'it should be the object of Government, rather to take measures to bring it into entire disuse' and noted complacently that 'the English language is becoming more general.' Nevertheless

> the want of an universal use of the English Tongue ... is a matter of infinite moment; and in every point of view extremely to be regretted. The difference of Language is a bar of Separation between Descendants of the Irish and English, which too much pains cannot be employed to remove. It obstructs Religion; it embarrasses Civil intercourse; it prevents cordial Union.[8]

These sentiments were widely shared by those in authority, and the altering proportions and tensions existing between the English and Irish languages form a background to the emergence of such new terms as 'the protestant ascendancy'.

Among the many pamphlets that flew from the printing presses in reply to or support of *The Present State*, that entitled *A Critical Review of the B[ishop] of Cloyne's Publication* was distinguished for its attention to the role of language in the political realm. The author, signing himself 'An Unbiassed Irishman', was in fact Edward Sheridan, a doctor by profession. Arguing that 'Language is so often abused in this unhappy country,' he proceeded to conclude (rather unexpectedly) 'that we may readily distinguish between the title and nature of a thing....'[9] And quoting the last of Woodward's 'protestant ascendancy' passages, Sheridan observed: 'The expressions, "by raising in the like proportion the number and influence of the Romish Priests" are not clear to me.'[10] What is noteworthy in Sheridan's reply to Woodward is his non-use of the term protestant ascendancy, and his attention to the way in which language necessarily conditions the political, social or theological messages it transmits.

8. ibid., pp. 53-54, 90.
9. [Edward Sheridan], *A Critical Review of the B. of Cloyne's Publication; With Occasional Remarks on the Productions of Some Other Writers, Particularly Those of Trinity College, and on the Conduct of the Present Ministry. Addressed to his Lordship. By an Unbiassed Irishman* (Dublin: John Chambers, 1787), pp. 92-93.
10. ibid., p. 50.

A lengthy pamphlet war was sustained throughout 1787, subsiding towards the end of the year. In all, nine editions of *The Present State* were published by the end of the year, and a tenth was issued in 1788. The general issues raised were once again rendered urgent by the events in Paris in 1789 and after. In 1791 the British government sought to modify the penal code in Ireland so as to wean catholics away from any devil's alliance with the revolution; powerful interests in Dublin resisted these reforms, and in the course of a heady rhetorical conflict the term 'protestant ascendancy' was applied for the first time to signify (vaguely) a social group.[11] But while the term came in the nineteenth century to label the estate-owning class in the Irish countryside, in 1792 protestant ascendancy emerged from the guild representatives in Dublin Corporation, and membership of the guilds was limited to protestants. While many catholics still postponed any public claim to be recognized as middle-class, protestants coined a new vocabulary to elevate them above the threat to their monopoly in decisive matters of trade and commerce. By silence and neologism, the title of 'bourgeois' effectively was allowed to remain unclaimed.

There soon emerged an echo-coinage 'catholic ascendancy', although it never achieved anything like the lexical stability of 'protestant ascendancy'. The process may be observed in one of its stages of development in a speech by Lord Minto in the House of Lords in April 1799, and in an anonymous pamphlet published the following year in Dublin.

> MINTO: The dilemma, there, has hitherto consisted in this. The Protestants could not be supported in that ascendancy which seems necessary even for their protection, without derogating from what may appear to be a natural right of the Catholics. The Catholics could not be supported in their claim of equality, without transferring to them that ascendancy which equality of rights must draw to the larger body.... An Irish Parliament, in which the ascendancy is either Protestant or Catholic, and it cannot choose

11. Evidence of this new usage is cited at length in W.J. Mc Cormack, 'Vision and Revision in the Study of Eighteenth-Century Irish Parliamentary Rhetoric', *Eighteenth-Century Ireland: Iris an Dá Chultúr* No. 2 (1987), 7-35.

> but lie on one side or the other, may be expected still, I fear, to gore and lacerate their country, by one or other of the horns of this dilemma.[12]

The pamphlet from which the next extract is taken refers a little later to Minto's arguments, but first it declares:

> If in the year 1798 Ireland had been left to the exercise of her boasted independence, or if Great Britain were either now, or at any future period, to leave her to settle her contending interests and religious divisions, and to decline interfering in her domestic differences, the contest would, indeed, be of short duration, and must infallibly be terminated by the overthrow of the present establishment in church and state. Protestant Ascendancy, which can only be supported by British connection, must expect to be thrown aside as an insolent usurpation; and Catholic Emancipation might be expected, by the law of retaliation, founded on the passions of the human heart, to be transformed into Catholic tyranny, instead of stopping short at Catholic ascendancy.[13]

The author of this anonymous publication, who explicitly relates the behaviour of Wexford ultra-protestants (such as Gowan and Beaumont, whom Myles Byrne accuses of brutality, though no names are given in the 1800 pamphlet) to the emergence of protestant ascendancy, was a Scotsman, William Ogilvie (1736-1819), sometime tutor of Lord Edward Fitzgerald and a confidant of the Leinster family.

Although 'catholic ascendancy' is never taken up as the name of any social group, nor is it ever cited as a condition (either actual or positively desired), it does have a certain limited currency as the term for a future or potential state of affairs that is either feared (by protestants, for instance) or abjured in advance (by catholics). In the changing balance of power within the Catholic Committee in the years before 1812, the unease felt by John Keogh (1740-1817) in relation to the relentless genius of the young Daniel O'Connell (1775-1847) was focused at least once on the risk that O'Connell's greater aggression might result either in the unfortunate achievement of catholic ascendancy or (more likely) in inflaming the more than adequate fears of protestants. Thus, inside the committee in January 1811, Dr Thomas Drumgoole (*c.*1750-*c.*1826) begged 'leave to inform Mr Keogh that the committee disclaimed any such ascendancy'.[14] And in the course of the great agitation for catholic emancipation in 1812, O'Connell explicitly utters this abjuration and simultaneously locates the source from which the phrase 'catholic ascendancy' was being transmitted, that is, from the opponents of emancipation who were, all but unanimously, ultra-protestant themselves:

> They accuse us of a wish for Catholic ascendency. Their inconsistency in the accusation is glaring and ridiculous. They first blame us for asking Emancipation as a right; and they then say that we are desirous of a Catholic ascendency. Does not the demanding Emancipation as a right imply that an equality of privileges is the right of every citizen, be his religion what it may? ... there is no event which I should consider more fatal to the liberties of Ireland than what they have called a Catholic ascendency....[15]

Much later in O'Connell's career, in 1840 when he campaigned for reform of the franchise in Dublin Corporation elections, one of his principal opponents, Isaac Butt (1813-79) repeatedly warned of 'popish ascendancy'.[16] Thus, just as protestant ascendancy was backdated so as to appear to be an eighteenth-century phenomenon, so catholic ascendancy was projected forward to loom in spectral reality as an imminent catastrophe. That, however, brings us beyond the period under discussion, and we should return to the issue of class in the 1790s and after.

III. TOWN AND COUNTRY

The terms 'middle-class' and 'bourgeois' are not in fact synonymous. The classic French notion of the

12. *The Speech of Lord Minto in the House of Peers, April 11, 1799, on ... an union....* (Cork: George Cherry, 1799), pp. 62-63. The speech was widely reprinted during the Union debates, and cited extensively in the controversy.
13. *Protestant Ascendancy and Catholic Emancipation Reconciled by a Legislative Union; with a view of the transactions in 1782....* (Dublin: for J. Milliken, 1800), pp. 55-56.
14. *The Life and Speeches of Daniel O'Connell, edited by his son John O'Connell* (Dublin: Duffy, 1846), p. 69.
15. ibid., p. 263.
16. See Isaac Butt, *Irish Municipal Reform....* (Dublin: Curry, 1840), passim.

bourgeois as the enfranchised citizen of a chartered town has its own precision, for which 'middle-class' substitutes a typically English blur. In Ireland, the older towns (Dublin, Galway, Waterford, Drogheda) had had prosperous merchant communities which were disrupted by the political and military consequences of the Reformation. In the eighteenth century, an exclusively protestant franchise rendered municipal politics a highly lucrative area of monopoly to which the ambitious apprentice of sound protestant loyalties might aspire. After the Williamite settlement, Dublin had seen many families emerge into civic life. The city fathers were, to a degree, a new protestant elite, which in some instances augmented itself through the conforming of individual catholics. Although their regime was impregnable throughout the eighteenth century, the very newness and lack of pedigree of these families generated an element of insecurity and overcompensation. After the Union and the disappearance of the all-protestant Irish parliament, these corporate towns became a network of resisting points of protestant strength, while the countryside developed political and cultural patterns of a somewhat less absolute kind. Thomas Moore distinguished carefully between the anxieties of catholics living in the Ulster countryside 'surrounded by armed Orangemen' and the anxieties of 'the Catholic inhabitants of towns and cities, whom the spirit of Corporation Ascendancy haunts through all the details of life.'[17] This was written in the early 1820s during the agrarian disturbances conducted across the south of Ireland in the name of 'Captain Rock'.

The rise of Belfast as an important commercial centre towards the end of the eighteenth century produced a different psychological reaction, in which the very newness of the city provided an opportunity for a generous convergence of interests, at least in the short term. Belfast developed its own intellectual life, well supplied with newspapers, with educational and other institutions — the Linenhall library, founded in 1788, for example. No strong literary movement emerged there in the Romantic period, however, and Northern politics was perhaps less coloured by the theatrical and literary fashions that undoubtedly affected the behaviour of a parliamentarian like Henry Grattan (1746-1820) and an insurrectionist like Robert Emmet (1778-1803). While Dublin Corporation assimilated so colourful a personality as John Giffard (1746-1819), whose alleged catholic childhood did not impair his adult talents as anti-catholic bigot — he was known familiarly as 'The Dog in Office' — more substantial citizens organized their political life through bodies such as the Catholic Committee. Theobald Wolfe Tone (1763-98) was appointed agent and assistant secretary to the committee in 1792, and through him Northern dissent, French democracy and Dublin middle-class lobbying may be seen in combination.

The rebellion of 1798, with its catholic peasant armies in Mayo and Wexford, resulted both from this combination and from the brutal and provocative measures government adopted in response. It had distinctly urban origins in so far as its ideology was concerned, and an equally distinctive and contrasting rural area of occurrence. The disconnected theatres of the rebellion — add east Ulster to Wexford and Mayo — serve to emphasize the regional variations that have to be acknowledged as qualifying any single account of Irish society. It is possible to distinguish several areas for consideration here: the city of Dublin and its political debates, Munster (especially the rich farming areas in Counties Cork and Limerick), and the province of Ulster, where the events of 1798 had such repercussions for catholic and protestant alike. It cannot be assumed that other regions resembled any of these three in the way class divisions operated. There are distinct advantages to be gained from reading tours as different as those of Young and John Gamble on the one hand, and novels like Edgeworth's *The Absentee* and Gerald Griffin's *The Collegians* on the other. Regional diversity is an actuality even in so small a country as Ireland; yet fiction, even regional fiction, necessarily involves a degree of generalization that can obscure those divergences. Louis Cullen has analysed the background to communal conflict in north Wexford before 1798, and suggested that new land possessors such as John Hunter Gowan overstretched their investments and pursued a style of life they could not afford to maintain in changing economic circumstances. Gowan was an active and violent Orangeman, and he provoked bitter resentment in Myles Byrne (1780-1862), a catholic neighbour who regarded his own claim to gentry status as infinitely superior to Gowan's.

17. [Thomas Moore], *Memoirs of Captain Rock, the Celebrated Irish Chieftain, With Some Account of his Ancestors, Written by Himself.* (London: Longman, 1824), pp. 348-49.

Byrne's *Memoirs* should be read in two contexts beyond the autobiographical: first, it has a place among the nineteenth-century novels dealing with 1798, not because it is in some damaging sense fictitious but because *they* are so preoccupied with memory and with memories of rebellion in particular: second, it aligns itself with other memoirs and histories of the period, often answering the charges or assumptions of other writers even without naming them. This subliminal reading required by some of the literature accords with other techniques of decoding. Contrary to the popular image of marauding peasant bands assailing ancient castles, Wexford in 1798 is better understood as the consequence of a contest between insufficiently stabilized elements — 'upwardly mobile' protestants of relatively humble origins and the middle-class catholic leadership of the United Irishmen.[18] Apart perhaps from the remote islands, the Yeatsian dream 'of the noble and the beggarman' resembles no actual state of Irish society in the period under discussion.[19]

The county of Cork had seen a great deal of Whiteboy activity in the 1780s, and several prominent landowners had participated in encouraging Whiteboy resistance to ecclesiastical authority. Yet in 1798, Cork was comparatively peaceful, despite the earlier attempts of the French to land at Bantry Bay. The attitude of Cork city's commercial sector can be observed through its response to the agitations about reform in 1792 and 1793. Whereas very few pamphlets on the Whiteboy controversy were originally published in Cork, or reprinted there from Dublin editions, the discussions of the Dublin-based catholic lobby were republished in Cork. One participant, Charles Ryan, declared that 'the words "*Protestant Ascendancy*", like the Cabala, are used as a magic term to keep back the reason, to suppress the justice, and to alarm the fears of our Protestant countrymen', while another (Mr Sweetman from Wexford) emphasized the combination of alchemical fantasy and the technology of the printing press in the dissemination of the new terminology as a bulwark against catholic claims:

> The Letter containing the Plan is analysed in the Castle alembic, and nothing is heard throughout the land but Sedition, Treason, Rebellion, Byrne! The types are again made to sweat for it; and the effulgence of ascendancy erudition deigns once more to illuminate the political horizon.[20]

Edmund Burke's 'Letter to Richard Burke', written earlier in 1792, speaks of 'the mischiefs that vex the world' which arise from words: 'The word Protestant is the charm that locks up in the dungeon of servitude three millions of your people. It is not amiss to consider this spell of potency, this abracadabra....' Later, Edward Sheridan, in revising his 'Unbiassed Irishman' pamphlet, also stressed this seemingly magical aspect of protestant ascendancy ideology. But here, language plays on the side of reform. The punning reference to Edward Byrne (chairman of the Catholic Committee) was taken up later in the discussion when John Keogh reminded his audience of their economic power in the land — 'My respectable friend near me [i.e. Byrne] pays the revenues of this country 80,000 l. a year.'[21] Keogh was himself a merchant of very considerable wealth, a model Dublin bourgeois (though highly radicalized) but for the laws that excluded him, as a catholic, from participation in the councils of the city.

The presence of the clergy in the Irish countryside and towns should not be neglected in considering the emergence of a middle class. The eighteenth century, by and large, had not been a period of religious fervour. Relations between the denominations were undoubtedly strained, but they were rarely inflamed. The growth of evangelical zeal in the various strands of protestantism was one contributing factor to the deterioration of this grudging tolerance. John Wesley first visited Ireland in 1747 and in the next forty-four years he returned many times to

18. L.M. Cullen, *The Emergence of Modern Ireland 1600-1900* (London: Batsford, 1981), pp. 214-15, 227.
19. See W.B. Yeats, 'The Municipal Gallery Revisited', in *The Poems: A New Edition*, ed. Richard J. Finneran (London: Macmillan, 1983), p. 321. Of course Yeats here does not *claim* that Irish society was composed solely of noblemen and beggars, but indicates a preference that is silent as to other levels of society.
20. *Proceedings at the Catholic Meeting of Dublin duly Convened on Wednesday, October 31, 1792, at the Exhibition-Room, Exchequer-Street....* (Dublin: H. Fitzpatrick, 1792), pp. 10, 27. The 'Letter' referred to in the last of these quotations was the proposal circulated by Edward Byrne in relation to the reform of the Penal Laws.
21. ibid., p. 48.

tour and preach, spending in all several years in the country.[22] Among those influenced by his preaching was the Brooke family of County Cavan, notably the novelist Henry Brooke (*c.*1703-83) whose daughter Charlotte Brooke (*c.*1740-93) pioneered the rendering of Irish poetry into English. Wesleyan methodism, which appealed principally to the middle classes in the bigger towns but nevertheless remained the preserve of a small minority in the overall denominational patchwork, was frequently the object of scorn both from catholic and established church sources. The behaviour of, and reception given to, Lorenzo Dow (an American evangelist known as 'Crazy Dow') indicates a number of significant divisions in Irish society. Arriving in the immediate aftermath of the 1798 rebellion, and intent on opposing Irish catholicism practically unaided, Dow was nonetheless a republican in politics and he earned himself a spell in Belfast jail. Irish methodists were split between the respectable men in Dublin, who wanted nothing to do with Dow, and those in the countryside who admired his style and his success.[23] C.R. Maturin's *Women* (1818) is one of the few works of fiction to touch on this aspect of change in Irish society; its subtitle, *Pour et Contre*, encapsulates a sense of antagonism and systemic opposition. Moreover, Maturin's highlighting of women in the title of his novel does more than emphasize the importance of females in evangelical circles; it helps to draw attention to the increasing importance of women writers (Charlotte Brooke, Maria Edgeworth, Lady Morgan) and of the social position of women during the period. William Thompson (*c.*1785-1833) wrote an *Appeal* on their behalf, which had its impact on Karl Marx and on the larger world of socialist thought; its origins in Thompson's Cork should not be forgotten. Similarly Gerald Griffin (1803-40) in his *The Christian Physiologist* (1830), by means of its (admittedly somewhat mechanical or simplified) concentration on each of the five senses in turn, acknowledges the psychological dimension that had been more fulsomely embraced by Maturin.

Political factors also contributed to deteriorating relations between the different denominations. Largely because of Edmund Burke's effort, a seminary for the training of catholic priests was established at St Patrick's College, Maynooth in 1795. (The Orange Order was founded later in the same year, and spread not only in Ulster but also into southern counties like Wicklow, Wexford and Cork, with a resulting increase in anti-catholic activity.) Maynooth replaced a system whereby aspirant priests travelled to the Continent for their education, a system that had practically confined the priestly vocation to relatively well-to-do families. As Maynooth-trained priests began to take up parishes in the early years of the new century, their social inferiority *vis-à-vis* their predecessors did not go unnoticed. Meanwhile, popular resistance to the payment of tithes to the established clergy had led increasingly to an identification of them with the landlords — tithe being regarded as an additional form of rent. The changing social background from which the catholic clergy was being recruited, linked to the growing isolation of their Church of Ireland counterparts, underlined the belief that middle-class ways were synonymous with catholicism and that protestants belonged to that ill-defined but influential group, 'the Anglo-Irish protestant ascendancy'.

The experience of the Le Fanu family in County Limerick in the 1820s and 1830s illustrates several aspects of the pattern while also qualifying the stereotype.[24] Dean Le Fanu, the novelist's father, was frequently short of ready cash, while the neighbouring parish priest, Thomas O'Brien Costello, lived in considerable ease in a house aptly named Castle Comfort. The Le Fanus also felt a considerable degree of animosity towards Thomas Moore (1779-1852), whom they regarded as a social upstart. Yet the facts of the matter are that Moore, the son of a catholic grocer, won greater access to high society in London than the diligently conformist, such as Sheridan Le Fanu (1814-73), ever did. Of course, their individual personalities must be credited with affecting the general contrast, but the runaway success of Moore's *Irish Melodies* in the drawing-rooms of Regency England illustrates one of the ways in which cultural material from the old

22. See Elizabeth Jay (ed.), *The Journal of John Wesley: A Selection* (Oxford: Oxford University Press, 1987), pp. 101-04.

23. See David Hempton, *Methodism and Politics in British Society 1750-1850* (London: Hutchinson, 1984), p. 94.

24. W.J. Mc Cormack, *Sheridan Le Fanu and Victorian Ireland* (Oxford: Clarendon Press, 1980), pp. 1-71 passim.

Gaelic domain could be accommodated in a new and distinctly 'genteel' aesthetic. Moore's work is extensively represented elsewhere (p. 1053) in this anthology, and the present section is not the place to discuss its great variety. Yet, in connection with his *Melodies*, it should be noted that the drawing-room song was not Moore's invention. His mastery of this kind of writing, however, signalled the convergence of a defeated Gaelic past and a metropolitan audience that was intellectually curious but not intellectually demanding. *Drawing room* might be emphasized to indicate the abandonment of political rhetoric with the extinction of the Irish parliament, and the elevation in its stead of the family as a collective image of Irish ambition. The close association of the *Melodies* with the pianoforte further underlines the domestication of this heritage, and much later in Joyce's fiction the piano is ironically placed to sound a note of familial dissolution — providing the accompaniment to the Miss Morkans's party in 'The Dead', and the approaching death of Stephen's mother, recalled in *Ulysses*.

IV. AFTER THE UNION

The Act of Union (1800) had important consequences that must be acknowledged. Within the United Kingdom of Great Britain and Ireland, conditions on the smaller island came under the direct scrutiny of the Westminster parliament, where the majority of members had little or no first-hand knowledge of the country. Sectarian animosity persisted, and in 1808 Woodward's *The Present State of the Church of Ireland* was republished. (John Wilson Croker's *A Sketch of the State of Ireland* is part of this controversy.) Edward Sheridan once again answered the (now-deceased) bishop, but the 1808 edition of his *Critical Review* possesses features that vividly illustrate the alterations of terminology in the years since 1787. Even in the preface to a so-called 'second edition' of his pamphlet, Sheridan had already underlined the importance of linguistic change:

> if men are not on their guard against the abuse of language, the perversion of terms, the tricks and artifices of speech-jugglers, they will no longer distinguish between truth and falsehood, virtue and vice.[25]

By June 1808, however, Sheridan himself had assimilated the new term that his old foe, Richard Woodward, had launched into circulation twenty years earlier. In a new introduction to his 'Unbiassed Irishman' pamphlet, he bitterly attacked William Pitt (1759-1806, prime minister of Britain at the time of the Union) for his failure to keep faith with Ireland and the catholics, and partly exonerated Trinity College, Dublin from the accusations he had levelled against it in 1787. But, in addition, Sheridan now employs the term 'ascendancy' on a dozen occasions within thirty pages to characterize a class or group in Ireland whose activities he deplores. There are 'ascendancy calumniators', and 'an ascendancy bigot'; the 'magic of ascendancy' is generally condemned. In the revision of his original pamphlet, Sheridan (who had never used Woodward's 'protestant ascendancy' except to quote a sentence and find its expressions unclear) has come to accept the term as a recognizable social description. The pamphleteer who warned of the dangers in failure to recognize an abuse of terms is not immune to the widespread introduction of undefined terms into the language of political debate.

Since promises of catholic emancipation were not kept, and because the recession that followed the end of the Napoleonic wars brought hardship to the agricultural sector, the 'state of Ireland' was frequently discussed in parliament. Or rather, parliamentary inquiries were established to gather data on social conditions in Ireland. The resulting reports cover the period of renewed agrarian violence associated with the eponymous 'Captain Rock' and of political agitation led by Daniel O'Connell. In particular, the wave of outrages that spread out from south County Limerick in the early 1820s and afterwards resulted from the economic jeopardy suffered by a 'middleman' stratum of landholders in the wake of post-war recession, although the traditional imagery of oath-bound secret societies continued to be employed.[26] It was from this area of Limerick that Gerald Griffin drew his knowledge of farming society. The paradoxical effect of the Union, however, was that Ireland, instead of being more intimately united with Britain, became the remote subject of statistical

25. [Edward Sheridan], *The Third Edition of the Unbiassed Irishman....* (Dublin: H. Fitzpatrick, 1808), p. xxi.

26. W.J. Mc Cormack, *Ascendancy and Tradition in Anglo-Irish Literary History from 1789 to 1939* (Oxford: Clarendon Press, 1985), pp. 170, 405-06.

questionnaires. The growth of an impersonal state bureaucracy in Ireland was in many respects more rapid and experimental than in Britain and, by way of a Newtonian reaction, Irish society increasingly came to emphasize the distinctiveness, even the uniqueness, of its class relations.

The term 'bureaucracy' was coined by Sydney Owenson (*c*.1783-1859), better known as a novelist under her married title, Lady Morgan. In 1818, she wrote of 'Beaucratie or office tyranny, by which Ireland had been so long governed.' Her fiction, though often thought excessive in its romantic gestures, frequently analyses the psychological condition of a society torn between faith in its uniqueness on the one hand and, on the other, experience of an impersonal administrative system that was simultaneously advancing round the entire globe through the operations of an explicit colonialism. Insight into this dilemma, and (less certainly) imaginative release from it, were increasingly sought through the writing of fiction, often fiction set in the past. Morgan's *The O'Briens and the O'Flahertys* (1827) is one of several novels written about the political and military crisis of the 1790s. In it, she advances a very doubtful interpretation of economic history, interwoven with a perceptive commentary on class tensions which has not yet succumbed to the new terminology emerging since 1786:

> Down to the middle of the last century, a feeling of insecurity in all classes prevailed through this anomalous condition of things; which, while it kept capital out of the country, paralyzed industry, and, misdirecting the restless energy of the people, awoke a spirit of litigation, that has long been a ridicule and a reproach to the national character. The small but ascendant party of protestants, scarcely less harassed than the victims of their own oppression, suffered through their fears of the disabilities they had themselves imposed; and largely participated in the insecurity of property, which they had inflicted on their catholic opponents. An agitating though suppressed emotion pervaded the whole population; and whatever brought the question of property into debate, was sure to throw the community into fermentation. . . .[27]

27. Sydney, Lady Morgan, *The O'Briens and the O'Flahertys, a National Tale* (London: Colburn, 1827) Vol. 1, pp. 106-07.

The struggle for catholic emancipation in the 1820s was not simply an attempt to right the wrongs of the past. It took place, and was resisted, in the context of Britain's colonial expansion in the wake of the empire's success against Napoleonic France. John Banim in *The Anglo-Irish of the Nineteenth Century* (1828) deals not only with the plot — familiar since Maria Edgeworth's *The Absentee* (1812) — of a landlord gradually discovering his role in life by returning to his Irish estates, but casts this paradigmatic story among such central figures of British politics as Lord Castlereagh (1769-1822, foreign secretary 1812-22) and John Wilson Croker (1780-1857, secretary to the Admiralty, and coiner of the party term 'the Conservatives'). That Castlereagh and Croker — like George Canning (1770-1827, prime minister at the time of his death), and Arthur Wellesley, the duke of Wellington (1769-1852, prime minister 1828-30) — were Irish by birth (or in Canning's case, by immediate background) in no way diminishes the force of this collocation of provincial Irish setting, political crisis and linguistic innovation. Years after the close of the period surveyed here, the Famine of 1845-47 will provide eloquent testimony to the consequences of this drastically divided socio-political focus, the provincial and the imperial, together with the consequences of the mutual incomprehension within Ireland, produced through rival terminologies, opposing ideologies of the past. The upheaval in the ownership of landed estate that followed the Famine inaugurated yet another wave of emerging middle-class values, leading after the fall of Parnell in 1890 to the triumph of tenant proprietorship at the beginning of the twentieth century.

V. UNSTABLE STYLE?

Even though there had been a considerable bourgeois prosperity before 1800, it is still true that the novelists of the early nineteenth century display many of the characteristics of pioneers. If this does inadequate justice to the confidence of Maria Edgeworth's fiction, we should recall that the formative intellectual background of her upbringing had been her father's circle in the English midlands, a circle in which scientific and progressive educational values were eagerly pursued. Nevertheless, the elaborate structure of framing devices employed in *Castle Rackrent* served a purpose beyond that of irony; it supported with lavish evidence of apparent editorial stability and glossarial conventionality a fiction of dangerous innovation, fiction in which land is lost and family advances only through the zig-zag of an essentially impotent genealogy. The Edgeworths' 'utilitarianism before its time', as one might call it, differs drastically from the values to be inculcated in a society where land offered the principal definition of identity and prosperity. In the nineteenth century, Edgeworth was to count among her correspondents such people as the chemist Sir Humphry Davy (1778-1829) and the economist David Ricardo (1772-1823). Such bourgeois rationalism may be contrasted with a greater curiosity about psychological matters than one finds in Morgan and Maturin, even if these last-named writers are too often led by their emotional commitments into a blurring of social categories that Edgeworth would only rarely sanction.

Of the writings represented in the present section, we note in Charles Robert Maturin's *Women* (1818), a novel set for the most part in middle-class methodist and suburban Dublin, a reliance on a variety of techniques, including some borrowed from Gothicism. In John Banim's novel, the very term enshrined in the title, 'The Anglo-Irish', is rivalled, debated, and earned in the course of dinner-party conversations where characters seek names for their hyphenated relation to Ireland and to Britain. The opening of Gerald Griffin's *The Collegians* (1829) is marked by a grim, perhaps excessive, determination to establish a literary style that will convincingly authenticate a hitherto neglected social milieu. One can see in Griffin repeated and overdetermined exercises in what stylists would call *foregrounding*: successive layers of social reality, successive items in the survey of a domestic scene are brought to the fore, each as much jeopardizing as complementing the prominence of the other. The business of establishing the solidity of his Limerick farmers' economic position in the 1780s evidently called for such techniques.

Other novelists, including Edgeworth, Morgan and the Banim brothers, introduced or annotated their fiction with what amount to flying buttresses of factual documentation. John Gamble (*c.*1770-1831), however, illustrates a different side to this phenomenon: born an Ulsterman, he silently adopts the persona of a nondescript traveller in describing the social landscape of his native province. While it appears to be yet another tour (like Arthur Young's), his *Sketches of Dublin and the North of Ireland* possesses a modicum of fictional narrative. Apart from the travel writing represented here, Gamble wrote three novels and a collection of tales. His name can serve to remind us of how relatively unexplored the mass of Irish fictional writing still remains, and the combination of tentative experiment and tendentious editorializing in some other novelists similarly can signal the extent to which these early nineteenth-century writers felt cut off from a literary heritage. This in itself does not prove the absence of such a heritage, but illustrates the profound sense of disruption and discontinuity that generally characterized the romantic period. Yet to overemphasize instability as a fault in the style of Irish writing in these years would be a mistake, based on a too-ready acceptance of the contemporary English reading of Jane Austen, William Wordsworth and others as the faithful recreators of stable property relations in Britain.

The relationship between politics and song or verse underwent a major transformation in the 1840s with the sudden proliferation of patriotic ballads through *The Nation*. Previous to this, Moore is the only poet of real achievement, and his reputation is more European than British. Four comparatively isolated examples of popular poems are given here. Richard Milliken (1767-1815) is not remembered for anything other than 'The Groves of Blarney'. On the surface it appears to be a precocious squib, preserved solely for its outrageous rhymes, for its distant relationship to the Irish song 'Preab san-Ol' (translated by John Philpot Curran (1750-1817)) and its more direct relationship with F.S. Mahony's 'The Bells of Shandon'. Yet its reference to 'Lady Jeffreys that owns this station' in the second stanza puts us in touch with the volatile politics of Munster in the 1780s and Lady Jeffereyes's sponsorship of Whiteboy insurrection. In Milliken's comic poem, she is anachronistically defeated by Oliver Cromwell, a retrospective ambition typical of much Irish Tory literature in this period. 'The Liberty Tree' possesses a different kind of Janus-perspective on political affairs, for the tree was a symbol of French revolutionary endeavour and was venerated as such by the United Irishmen: here, an Orange song, apparently with a

Dublin provenance, invokes both the name of Hibernia and the liberty tree in a rousing defence of the Williamite revolution in 1689 and, thus, of the status quo in Ireland. 'The Lass of Richmond Hill', by comparison, will strike readers as a return to the period sensibility we associate with Thomas Moore. Yet the author of this still-popular song was Leonard MacNally (1752-1820), simultaneously the barrister who defended his many friends among the United Irishmen and the secret agent who betrayed them to the government. Among his many literary productions was a stage version of Laurence Sterne's *Tristram Shandy* (1783). Through MacNally's 'schizoid' relating of politics to literary sentiment, one gains access to a hidden dimension of the cultural inheritance Moore exonerates in such poems as 'Oh! blame not the bard'.[28]

If Maria Edgeworth was the most accomplished novelist, and Tom Moore the dominant poet of the period, Daniel O'Connell was unchallenged as the most forceful personality in Irish public affairs. For politics thrived after the Union. It was, however, a politics very different from the uniformed gallantry of the Volunteer corps and the mannered hall of mirrors that had been the Irish House of Commons. O'Connell was usually described as a very powerful orator; his power lay in the ability to sway large audiences of the disenfranchised, or jurymen with little previous experience of rhetorical technique. Fellow-members of the imperial parliament were less impressed. He perfected the first mass movement in British politics, and in so doing he willingly allowed himself to be portrayed as a rough diamond, an interloper, a parvenu. He also acquired near-mythic status in the popular imagination, which accorded him a wholly undeserved reputation for extra-marital fertility. His letters show him to be a far more representative figure, a professional man concerned to have the good opinion of his wife. At the centre of James Joyce's 'The Dead', Gabriel Conroy, who is similarly concerned, worries inwardly about a speech. Later he returns from his aunts' party in the family home to spend the night in a darkened city hotel. On the journey through the sleeping streets, he cheerfully salutes the inert statue of Daniel O'Connell. Even as a self-mocking self-portrait of the estranged author, Gabriel is bidding farewell to a century of middle-class change and decay.

28. For a further discussion of MacNally's symptomatic place in cultural debate in this period, see the Introduction to Maria Edgeworth's *The Absentee* edited by W.J. Mc Cormack and Kim Walker (Oxford: Oxford University Press, 1988).

29. James Joyce, *Dubliners* (London: Jonathan Cape, 1967), p. 203.

[The Editor acknowledges the help of Eve Patten for her research on Gerald Griffin and Charles Maturin.]

ARTHUR YOUNG

(1741-1820)

from: A TOUR IN IRELAND: WITH GENERAL OBSERVATIONS ON THE PRESENT STATE OF THE KINGDOM; MADE IN THE YEARS 1776, 1777, AND 1778, AND BROUGHT DOWN TO THE END OF 1779 (1780)

[Young had begun to write about agricultural matters in the mid-1760s, and his Tours to England, Ireland and France form an important stage in the development of writing on economic affairs, especially in relation to Ireland. The three extracts here date from the months, respectively, of July, August and September 1776 when Young moved from County Fermanagh southwards through Longford, and then further south into Munster. His matter-of-fact style is of course artificial, at least in part, preserving a tone of immediate observation even after the passage of several years. Young's informants were the local resident gentry and nobility, and these were augmented by his own observations. His implicit diagnoses harmonized well with the optimistic climate associated with the 1780s and early 1790s, the period of what is called 'Grattan's Parliament' (Henry Grattan was perpetually in opposition); Young is cited more than once in Maria Edgeworth's fiction. Essentially he was laying the basis for an analysis of Irish conditions that would encourage a more intensive exploitation of natural resources, even at the price of relaxing political control of that large portion of the population who were still bound by various anti-catholic laws. A classic liberal, in fact, for whose prescriptions the drastic reversals in Anglo-Irish politics from 1795 onwards proved highly damaging, Young approved of industry, regularity, and the development of capital generally.]

It was with regret I heard that the rent of a man who had been so spirited an improver, should be raised so exceedingly. He merited for his life the returns of his industry. But the cruel laws against the Roman Catholics of this country, remain the marks of illiberal barbarism. Why should not the industrious man have a spur to his industry whatever be his religion; and what industry is to be expected from them in a country where leases for lives are universal, if they are secluded from terms common to every one else? What mischief could flow from letting them have leases for life? None; but much good in animating their industry. It is impossible that the prosperity of a nation should have its natural progress, where four fifths of the people are cut off from those advantages which are heaped upon the domineering aristocracy of the small remainder.[1]

In conversation with Lord Longford[2] I made many enquiries concerning the state of the lower classes, and found that in some respects they were in good circumstances, in others indifferent; they have, generally speaking, such plenty of potatoes, as always to command a bellyful; they have flax enough for all their linen, most of them have a cow and some two, and spin wool enough for their cloaths; all a pig, and numbers of poultry, and in general the complete family of cows, calves, hogs, poultry, and children, pig together in the cabbin; fuel they have in the utmost plenty; great numbers of families are also supported by the neighbouring lakes; which abound prodigiously with fish; a child with a packthread and a crooked pin, will catch perch enough in an hour for the family to live on the whole day, and his Lordship has seen 500 children fishing at the same time, their [*sic*] being no tenaciousness in the proprietors of the lands about a right to the fish; besides perch, there is pike upwards of five feet long, bream, tench, trout of 10lb. and as red as a salmon, and fine eels; all these are favourable circumstances, and are very conspicuous in the numerous and healthy families among them.

Reverse the medal: they are ill cloathed, and make a wretched appearance, and what is worse, are much oppressed by many who make them pay too dear for keeping a cow, horse, &c. They have a practice also of keeping accounts with the labourers, contriving by that means, to let the poor wretches have very little cash for their year's work. This is a great oppression, farmers and gentlemen keeping accounts with the poor is a cruel abuse: so many days work for a cabbin — so many for a potatoe garden — so many for keeping a horse — and so many for a cow, are clear accounts which a poor man can understand well; but farther it ought never to go; and when he has worked out what he has of this sort, the rest of his work ought punctually to be paid him every Saturday night. Another circumstance mentioned was the excessive practice they have in general of pilfering. They steal every thing they can lay their hands on — and I should remark, that this is an account which has been very generally given me: all sorts of iron, hinges, chains, locks, keys, &c. — gates will be cut in pieces, and conveyed away in many places as fast as built; trees as big as a man's body, and that would require ten men to move, gone in a night. Lord Longford has had the new wheels of a car stolen as soon as made. Good stones out of a wall will be taken for a fire-hearth, &c. though a breach is made to get at them. In short, every thing, and even such as are apparently of no use to them — nor is it easy to catch them, for they never carry their stolen goods home, but to some bog-hole. Turneps are stolen by car loads; and two acres of wheat pluckt off in a night. In short, their pilfering and stealing is a perfect nuisance! How far it is owing to the oppression of laws aimed solely at the religion of

1. Young discusses the effects of the penal laws at several other places in his *Tour*. Between 1776, the time of his travels, and the passing of the Act of Union in 1801, these laws had been mitigated in many regards; however, failure to deliver a more comprehensive emancipation for catholics (as envisaged during the Union negotiations) led to an increasingly frustrated Irish catholic mood in the thirty years before the Emancipation Act of 1829.
2. Edward Michael Pakenham (1743-92), 2nd baron Pakenham.

these people, how far to the conduct of the gentlemen and farmers, and how far to the mischievous disposition of the people themselves, it is impossible for a passing traveller to ascertain. I am apt to believe that a better system of law and management would have good effects. They are much worse treated than the poor in England, are talked to in more opprobrious terms, and otherwise very much oppressed.

Left Packenham-hall.[3]

Land sells, at rack rent,[4] at 20 to 24 years purchase: has not fallen. Rents are fallen in 5 or 6 years 2*s*.[5] an acre. There is a great deal of letting lands in the gross to middle men, who re-let it to others; these middle men are called *terney begs*,[6] or *little landlords*, which prevail very much at present. These men make a great profit by this practice. The people in all the neighbourhood increase very fast. They are all in general much more industrious, and in better circumstances than they were some years ago. Their food, for three-fourths of the year, chiefly potatoes and milk, and the other quarter oatmeal: in the winter they have herrings. They have all a bellyful of food whatever it is, as they told me themselves; and their children eat potatoes all day long, even those of a year old will be roasting them. All keep cows, and some cocks and hens, but no turkeys or geese. Six people, a man, his wife and 4 children, will eat 18 stone of potatoes a week, or 252 lb., but 40 lb. of oatmeal will serve them. Rent of a cabbin, garden, and one acre, 20*s*. a cow's grass 30*s*. a cow requires one acre and a half for summer; and they buy a little hay for winter, and give the cow small potatoes and cabbage-leaves, &c.

The common people are remarkably given to thieving, particularly grass, timber, and turf; and they bring up their children to *hoking* potatoes, that is, artfully raising them, taking out the best roots, and then replanting them, so that the owner is perfectly deceived when he takes up the crop. A poor man's turf from 15*s*. to 20*s*. Living is exceedingly cheap here; besides the common provisions, which I have every where registered, wild ducks are only 3*d*.[7] and powder and shot: Plover, 1½*d*. and ditto: woodcocks, 1*d*. and ditto: Snipes, 1½*d*. and ditto; teal, 2*d*. and ditto, and widgeon the same; salmon, 1½*d*. a lb. trout, perch, pike, and bream, so plentiful as to have no price. Sir James Caldwell[8] has taken 17 cwt. of fish, bream and pike, in one day: cod, 3*s*. a dozen: whiting, from 8*d*. to 1*s*. a dozen: herrings, from 3*d*. to 9*d*. per 100: lobsters, from 3*s*. 6*d*. to 4*s*. a dozen: oysters, 6*d*. to 20*d*. a 100: eels, 2*s*. a dozen: crabs, 1*s*. to 2*s*. a dozen: wages, £6 dairy-maids, and others, £4. There is very little weaving in this country, except what is for their own use, but spinning is universal in all the cabbins. They receive for spinning spangle yarn, or four hanks, 1*s*. 2*d*. a spangle, and they will spin it in four days. Country servants are hired at £3 a year, who engage to do the work of the house, and spin a hank, that is a dozen a day, there are 12 cuts to the dozen.

* * *

September 15th, to Blarney Castle,[9] S.J. Jefferys,[10] Esq; of whose great works in building a town at Blarney, I cannot give so particular an account as I wish to do; for I got there just as he and his family were on the point of setting out for France.[11] I did not however let slip the time I had for making some enquiries, and found that in 1765, when Mr. Jefferys began to build this town, it consisted only of two or three mud cabbins; there are now 90 houses. He first established the linen manufactory, building a bleach-mill, and houses for weavers, &c. and letting them to manufacturers from Cork, who have been so successful in their works, as to find it necessary to have larger and more numerous edifices, such as a large stamping

3. The residence of the barons Longford. Note how Young preserves the businesslike brevity of the traveller's notes, even though the *Tour* was published four years later.
4. A 'rack rent' was not necessarily exorbitant, but simply one that rose (from a supposedly low) initial level through increasing stages. The pejorative tone of the term results to some extent from its incorporation into the title of Maria Edgeworth's first novel, *Castle Rackrent*.
5. two shillings.
6. From two Irish words, *tiarna* = (land)lord; *beag* = small, petty.
7. three (old) pence.
8. Author of *Enquiry into the Restrictions on the Trade of Ireland* (Dublin, 1766) and other publications.
9. Blarney Castle, at Blarney in County Cork, had been the seat of the MacCarthys until it was forfeited by Lord Cloncarty in 1689, after which it passed into the possession of St John Jefferys's family.
10. James St John Jefferys (the name is spelled in several different ways) was sometime Member of Parliament for the borough of Midleton, Co. Cork. Sometime before 1773, he had married Arabella, daughter of Counsellor John FitzGibbon, and thus had become brother-in-law to the future earl of Clare, John FitzGibbon (the younger.)
11. In the 1780s, the Jeffreys had a reputation for political extravagance, with Arabella Jefferys's alleged involvement with the Whiteboys, who were, in turn, often thought (wrongly) to be in league with France. For more in this connection, see notes to R.A. Milliken's 'The Groves of Blarney' below (p. 1102).

mill for printing linens and cottons, to which is annexed another bleach-mill, and since [then] there has been a third erected; the work carried on is that of buying yarn, and weaving it into linens, ten pence to thirty pence white; also diapers, sheeting, ticking, and linens and cottons of all sorts printed here, for common use and furniture. These several branches of the linen, employ 130 looms, and above 300 hands.

Another of Mr. Jefferys's objects has been the stocking manufacture, which employs 20 frames, and 30 hands, in buildings erected by him; the manager employing, by covenant, a certain number of apprentices, in order by their being instructed, to diffuse the manufactory. Likewise a woollen manufactory, a mill for milling, tucking, &c. broad cloths; a gigg mill for glossing, smoothing, and laying the grain; and a mill for knapping, which will dress above 500 pieces a year, but will be more, when some alterations now making are finished. A leather mill for dressing shamoy,[12] buck, or skins, fully employed. A large bolting mill, just finished, and let for £32 a year. A mill, annexed to the same, just finishing, for plating; and a blade mill for grinding edged tools. A large paper mill, which will be finished this year. He has been able to erect this multiplicity of mills, thirteen in all, by an uncommon command of water.

The town is built in a square, composed of a large handsome inn, and manufacturers' houses, all built of excellent stone, lime, and slate. A church, by the first fruits,[13] and liberal addition of above £300 from Mr. Jefferys. A market-house, in which are sold a hundred pounds worth of knit stockings per week. Four bridges, which he obtained from the county, and another (the flat arch) to which he contributed a considerable sum. Much has been done, yet is not the design near finished.

12. A phonetic spelling of chamois.
13. A fund peculiar to the established Church of Ireland.

SAMUEL CRUMPE

(1766-96)

from:
AN ESSAY ON THE BEST MEANS OF PROVIDING EMPLOYMENT FOR THE PEOPLE OF IRELAND.
TO WHICH WAS ADJUDGED THE PRIZE PROPOSED BY THE ROYAL IRISH ACADEMY FOR THE BEST DISSERTATION ON THAT SUBJECT
(1793)

[Crumpe may be less well-known that Arthur Young, but he has the added interest of being Irish by birth, and of writing at the outset of the 1790s, a decade that was to see dramatic reversals of prediction and political loyalty. His swift passing over of the upper classes in a disquisition of ways of providing employment is an indirect indicator of changes to come, and his emphasis on the grades of middle-class pretension provide a striking parallel to the kind of social analysis behind Maria Edgeworth's *Castle Rackrent*.]

... The people of Ireland may be divided into three classes; the high, the middle, and the commonalty. The first there is no necessity of noticing; they differ little from their neighbours in England, and their vices or virtues can but slightly affect the employment of the other inferior ranks of community.

By the middle rank of Irishmen, I do not understand a wealthy and respectable yeomanry. So valuable a division of citizens we are yet, alas! unacquainted with. Neither do I, in this class, include the mercantile part of the community, although they properly belong thereto. — They do not, it is true, possess the spirit of industry, and application to business, which those of the same description do in England and Holland; but they are not so addicted to dissipation and extravagance as the middle rank of country gentlemen. They hold, it may be said, an intermediate rank with respect to industry; possessing neither the scrupulously attentive spirit of business and industry, which distinguishes the English merchant, nor the unthinking spirit of extravagance which ruins the Irish *gentleman*. The class I speak of is principally composed of men of small estates, who generally live beyond their income; and those landholders known by the name of *middle-men*, who take large districts of the country from those possessed of extensive estates, and either cover them with black cattle and sheep, or re-let them at extravagant rents to wretched and indigent cottagers. The injuries this description of people occasion to the agriculture of the kingdom we shall hereafter have occasion to explain; their character, so far as respects the industry and employment of the people, is here only to be examined. Let me premise, that I shall delineate in this, as in every other instance, merely a *general* one; many exceptions to it exist, and I am happy to see such are daily increasing. Still, however, it will be found the predominant character, and one which must considerably obstruct the general employment and industry of any society wherein it prevails.

The general characteristics of the class of society I speak of, are dissipation, idleness, and vanity. Every man with a few acres of land, and a moderate revenue, is dignified, as a matter of course, with the title of *Esquire*;[1] and, be his family ever so numerous, the incumbrances on his little patrimony ever so considerable, he must support a pack of hounds, entertain with claret, or if not able, with whiskey; keep a chaise and livery servants,[2] and ape, in short, his superiors in every respect. Meanwhile his debts are increasing, his creditors growing clamorous, and every industrious occupation, which might relieve his distresses, neglected, as utterly beneath the dignity of a *gentleman*.

The numerous instances of this nature which occur cannot but possess a very serious, extensive, and powerful influence in the obstruction and depression of national industry and employment. The bad debts of men of business are more numerous in Ireland than can well be imagined: such must considerably injure and obstruct the industrious. Those sums which should be saved for the younger children of the family, and laid out in the establishment of some industrious occupation, that would enable them to afford employment to thousands of their countrymen, are either squandered in idle extravagance, or, if collected from the fortune which the hopeful heir apparent may obtain in matrimony, are employed by those on whom they are bestowed, in pursuing the laudable example they have been accustomed to from infancy. But the influence of such example is still more extensive: its ruinous contagion extends to the most inferior ranks. The labouring hind[3] quits his spade, to pursue his landlord's pack of beagles on foot, and at night intoxicates himself with whiskey, while his master enjoys a similar pleasure with liquors more refined and palatable.

To the same source are we to trace those nuisances to every rank of society, denominated *bucks* and *buckeens*.[4] Such, in general, are either the eldest sons of the gentlemen of small property we have described; or the younger children of those possessed of larger, who have received their scanty pittance, of which the augmentation by industrious means is never once attempted, and the final dissipation, one would imagine, deemed impossible. To stand behind a counter, superintend a farm, or calculate in a compting-house,[5] would be beneath the dignity of such exalted beings, and disgrace the memory of their *gentlemen* ancestors. But would not such pursuits be finally more useful to their country, and more grateful to their own feelings, than a mode of life which dissipates the funds that should be employed in industry, corrupts the manners of the people, ruins the health and annihilates the fortune of the individual, and, in general, finally leads them to subsist as mendicants on the charity of some more opulent relation. 'Tis disgusting to see such beings gaming at a hazard table,[6] bustling at a horse race, quarrelling over their claret, or hallooing after a fox, arrayed, perhaps, in an equipage they have neither inclination nor ability to pay for. Let us turn from the picture — the only satisfaction attendant on its examination is, that the species are daily diminishing. May they speedily be extinct.[7]

1. An esquire was a young man of noble or gentle birth who accompanied a knight; more recently, it was used after the name of one deemed to be a gentleman.
2. A chaise was a pleasure- or travelling-carriage; livery was a distinctive uniform worn by menservants or chauffeurs.
3. A (farm) servant, married perhaps and with a cottage provided for him. The term is largely Scottish in use.
4. Buck (a male deer) becomes 'a dashing fellow'; the suffix is taken over from Irish, and is a diminutive. The *OED* dates 'buckeen' from 1793, the date of Crumpe's *Essay*.
5. A counting-house, an office or building where commercial book-keeping and correspondence are carried on.
6. At which the dice-game, hazard, is played.
7. This paragraph may be echoed in the Edgeworthian observation that the habits of the Irish squires depicted in *Castle Rackrent* date from before 1782 and are less and less evident.

To the same general aversion to industry, and tendency to dissipation, and to a considerable share of family vanity, are we to ascribe the silly, but more excusable, propensity of *gentlemen*, to educate their children in *gentlemanly* professions. Hence arise the daily increasing numbers of curates[8] with scanty salaries, or none, attornies[9] preying on the public, ensigns[10] without the means of rising higher, physicians without patients, and lawyers without briefs. More advantageous would it be, as well to the individuals immediately concerned, as to the general employment of the people, if they had been bred to industrious occupations, wherein success, with prudence, is almost certain; and wherein the capital expended in their education would be laid out with greater advantage to themselves, and the inevitable increase of employment to the people.

The character of the inferior class of the community comes next to be considered; and, as more intimately connected with the question respecting the best means of providing employment for the people, demands attentive examination. I shall, as in the preceding instance, chiefly consider those traits which have obvious reference to the subject before us.

8. Deputies to the parish clergy, for whom they performed the practical offices in return for a lesser payment.
9. The profession of attorney was not, by 1793, closed to catholics. To judge from comments made by one member of the Irish parliament, Michael Smyth, there may have been an overcrowding of the profession in the early 1790s (see *Parliamentary Register* for 18 February 1792).
10. Low-ranking officers in an infantry regiment.

EDMUND BURKE

(1729-97)

LETTER TO THOMAS HUSSEY (1796)

[The letter is undated, but from internal evidence it can be assigned to the period between 9 December 1796 and the end of that month. Thomas Hussey (1741-1803) had undertaken a confidential mission to Madrid, and worked to check discontent among catholics in the public service in Ireland. When the seminary at Maynooth was established in 1795, he became its first president and in the next year was elevated to the rank of bishop (of Waterford and Lismore). Thus, in addition to being a trusted agent of the British crown, he had become a leader of catholic opinion in Ireland. The conflict occasioned by these divergent roles is elaborated by Burke to the point where he presents it as a choice between equally (or nearly equal) unacceptable alternatives: the letter proceeds to describe Napoleon and the Irish 'powers that be', and concludes with advice to Irish middle-class catholics as to how they should conduct themselves.]

My dear Sir

This morning I received your letter of the 30th of November from Maynooth.[1] I dictate my answer from my Couch, on which I am obliged to lie for a good part of the Day. I cannot conceal from you, much less can I conceal from myself, that, in all probability I am not long for this world. Indeed things are in such a Situation independantly of the Domestic wound[2] that I never could have less reason for regret in quitting the world than at this moment; and my End will be, by several, as little regretted.

I have no difficulty at all in communicating to you or, if it were of any use to mankind at large, my sentiments and feelings on the dismal state of things in Ireland; but I find it difficult indeed to give you the advice you are pleased to ask, as to your own conduct in your very critical Situation.

You state, what has long been but too obvious, that it seems the unfortunate policy of the Hour, to put to the far largest portion of the Kings Subjects in Ireland, the desperate alternative, between a

1. A town in County Kildare, once a stronghold of the Fitzgerald family, at which St Patrick's College had been established in 1795 as the first catholic seminary to have been sanctioned since the Reformation. Burke had been influential in this development, intended to wean Irish catholics away from France, where candidates for the priesthood had been educated throughout the seventeenth and eighteenth centuries.
2. Burke's beloved son, Richard, had died in August 1794.

thankless acquiescence under grievous Oppression, or a refuge in Jacobinism[3] with all its horrors and all its crimes. You prefer the former dismal part of the choice. There is no doubt but that you would have reasons if the election of one of these Evils was at all a security against the other. But they are things very alliable[4] and as closely connected as cause and effect. That Jacobinism, which is Speculative in its Origin, and which arises from Wantonness and fullness of bread, may possibly be kept under by firmness and prudence. The very levity of character which produces it may extinguish it; but the Jacobinism which arises from Penury and irritation, from scorned loyalty, and rejected Allegiance, has much deeper roots. They take their nourishment from the bottom of human Nature and the unalterable constitution of things, and not from humour and caprice or the opinions of the Day about privileges and Liberties. These roots will be shot into the Depths of Hell, and will at last raise up their proud Tops to Heaven itself. This radical evil may baffle the attempts of Heads much wiser than those are, who in the petulance and riot of their drunken power are neither ashamed nor afraid to insult and provoke those whom it is their duty and ought to be their glory to cherish and protect.

So then the little wise men of the West,[5] with every hazard of this Evil, are resolved to persevere in their manly and well timed resolution of a War, against Popery. In the principle and in all the proceedings it is perfectly suitable to their character. They begin this last series of their Offensive Operations by laying traps for the consciences of poor Foot-Soldiers.[6] They call these wretches to their Church (empty of a Volonteer congregation) not by the Bell, but by the whip. This Ecclesiastic military discipline is happily taken up, in order to form an Army of well scourged Papists into a firm Phalanx for the support of the Protestant Religion. I wish them Joy of this their valuable discovery in Theology, Politicks and the Art military. Fashion governs the World; and it is the fashion in the great French Empire of Pure and perfect Protestantism,[7] as well as in the little busy medling Province of servile imitators that apes, at an humble distance, the Tone of its Capital, to make a Crusade against you poor Catholicks. But whatever may be thought in Ireland of its share of a War against the Pope in that outlying part of Europe, the Zealous Protestant Buonoparté[8] has given his late Holiness far more deadly blows in the center of his own power and in the nearest seats of his influence, than the Irish Directory[9] can arrogate to itself within its own Jurisdiction from the utmost efforts of its political and military skill. I have my doubts, (they may perhaps arise from my ignorance) whether the Glories of the Night expeditions in surprizing the Cabin fortresses in Louth and Meathe or whether the Slaughter and expulsion of the Catholic Weavers by another set of Zealots in Armagh, or even the proud trophies of the late potatoe Field in that County,[10] are quite to be compared to the Protestant Victories on the Plains of Lombardy; or to the possession of the Fiat of Bologna, or to the approaching Sack of Rome where even now the Protestant Commissaries give the Law.[11] In all this Business great Britain, to us merely Secular politicians, makes no great figure; but let the glory of great Britain shift for itself as it may. All is well, provided Popery is crushed.

This War against Popery furnishes me with a Clue that leads me out of a *Maze* of perplexed politicks, which without it I could not in the least understand. I now can account for the whole. Lord Malmsbury[12] is sent to prostrate the dignity of the English Monarchy at Paris, that an Irish Popish common Soldier may be whipt in to give an appearance of habitation to a deserted protestant Church in Ireland. Thus we balance the account. Defeat and dishonor abroad; Oppression at Home

3. The radical principles of the Jacobins, the dominant party in the French revolutionary assembly.
4. Able to enter into an alliance or union.
5. A mocking allusion to the wise men from the east who paid homage to the infant Jesus.
6. Burke had recently concerned himself with the victimization of catholics serving in the army.
7. From the time of the debates concerning the new term 'protestant ascendancy' (1792), Burke had ironically inverted the terms protestant (in Irish contexts) and directory (in France) to suggest that the former were unwittingly assisting the latter.
8. Napoleon Bonaparte (1769-1821), synonymous with French revolutionary zeal.
9. By this Burke means the group who effectively controlled Irish affairs; of course, no such formal body existed.
10. In 1795 and the autumn of 1796, disturbances had occurred in Connacht and Ulster, and the Orange Order had been founded as a result of sectarian conflict in County Armagh in September 1795. It was Burke's view that some of these incidents were deliberately exploited by the Irish authorities for their own ends.
11. Napoleon's victories in Italy. Bologna had been declared a republic along French lines.
12. James Harris (1746-1820), 1st earl of Malmesbury, conducted negotiations in Paris and Lille in 1796-97.

— We sneak to the Regicides,[13] but we boldly trample upon our poor fellow Citizens. But all is for the Protestant Cause.

The same ruling principle explains the Rest. We have abdicated the Crown of Corsica,[14] which had been newly soldered to the Crown of Great Britain and to the Crown of Ireland, lest the British Diadem should look too like the Popes triple Crown. We have ran away from the People of Corsica, and abandonned them without Capitulation of any kind; in favour of those of them who might be our friends. But then, it was for their having capitulated with us, for Popery, as a part of their Constitution. We make amends for our Sins by our Repentance, and for our Apostacy from Protestantism by a breach of faith with popery. We have fled, overspread with dirt and ashes but with hardly enough of Sack Cloath to cover our nakedness.[15] We recollected that this Island, (together with its Yews and its other salubrious productions) had given birth to the illustrious Champion of the Protestant World Buonoparté — It was therefore not fit (to use the favorite French expression) that the Cradle of this religious Hero should be polluted by the feet of the British Renegade Slaves, who had stipulated to support Popery in that Island whilst his friends and fellow Missionaries are so gloriously employed in extirpating it in another — Our policy is growing every day into more and more consistency. We have shewed our broad back to the Meditterrenian. We have abandoned too the very hope of an alliance in Italy. We have relinquished the Levant[16] to the Jacobins. We have considered our Trade as nothing — Our policy and our honor went along with it; but all these objects were well sacrificed to remove the very suspicion of giving any assistance to that Abomination, the Pope, in his insolent attempts to resist a truly protestant power resolved to humble the Papal Tiara, and to prevent his pardons and his dispensations from being any longer the standing terror of the wise and virtuous Directory of Ireland; who cannot sit down with any tolerable comfort to an innocent little Job, whilst his Bulls[17] are thundering thro' the world. I ought to suppose that the arrival of General Hoche[18] is eagerly expected in Ireland; for He, too, is a most zealous Protestant; and he has given proof of it by the studied cruelties and insults by which He put to death the old Bishop of Dol;[19] whom, (but from the mortal fear I am in lest the suspicion of Popery should attach upon me) I should call a glorious martyr and should class him among the most venerable prelates that have appeared in this Century. It is to be feared however, that the Zealots will be disappointed in their pious hopes by the Season of the Year,[20] and the bad condition of the Jacobin Navy, which may hinder him this Winter from giving his Brother Protestants in Ireland his kind assistance in accomplishing with you what the other friend of the cause, Buonoparté, is doing in Italy; and what the Masters of these two pious Men the Protestant Directory of France, have so thoroughly accomplished in that the most Popish, but unluckily whilst popish the [most] cultivated, the most populous and the most flourishing of all Countries the austrian Netherlands.

When I consider the narrowness of the views and the total want of human wisdom displayed in our Western Crusade against Popery, it is impossible to speak of it but with every mark of contempt and scorn — yet one cannot help shuddering with horror when one contemplates the terrible consequences that are frequently the results of craft united with Folly — placed in an unnatural elevation. Such ever will be the issue of things, when the mean vices attempt to mimick the grand passions. — Great men will never do great mischief but for some great End. For this they must be in a state of inflammation and in a manner out of themselves — Among the nobler Animals whose blood is hot, the bite is never poisonous, except when the Creature is mad; but in the cold blooded reptile race, whose poison is exalted by the Chemistry of their icy complexion, their venom is the result of their health, and of the perfection of their Nature — Woe to the County in which such snakes, whose primum Mobile[21] is their Belly, obtain wings and from Serpents become dragons. It is not that these

13. Burke is referring to the execution of Louis XVI of France in 1793, but uses the emotive term associated with the killing of Charles I of England in 1649.
14. The British were withdrawing from the Mediterranean island of Corsica, a process completed in 1797.
15. Sackcloth and ashes were the biblical emblems of mourning; see Jonah 3. 6.
16. The former name for the area of the east Mediterranean now occupied by Lebanon, Syria, and Israel.
17. papal edicts.
18. Louis-Lasare Hoche (1768-97), French general in the revolutionary wars.
19. Urbain-René de Hercé (1726-95), executed on 28 July 1795.
20. i.e. Christmas.
21. Primary motive power, or first cause.

people want natural Talents and even a good cultivation; on the contrary, they are the sharpest and most sagacious of mankind in the things to which they apply — But having wasted their faculties upon base and unworthy objects, in any thing of a higher order, they are far below the common rate of two legged animals.

I have nothing more to say, just now, upon the Directory in Ireland which indeed is alone worth any mention at all. As to the Half Dozen, (or half score as it may be) of Gentlemen, who, under various names of authority, are sent from hence to be the subordinate agents of that low order of beings, I consider them as wholely out of the question — Their virtues or their vices; their ability or their Weakness, are matters of no sort of consideration. You feel the thing very rightly — all the evils of Ireland originate within itself. That unwise body, the United Irishmen,[22] have had the folly to represent those Evils as owing to this Country, when in truth its chief guilt is in its total neglect, its utter oblivion, its shameful indifference and its entire ignorance, of Ireland and of every thing that relates to it, and not in any oppressive disposition towards that unknown region. No such disposition exists. English Government has farmed out Ireland, without the reservation of a pepper Corn rent[23] in Power or influence, publick or individual, to the little narrow Faction that Domineers there. Thro' that alone they see, feel, hear, or understand, any thing relative to that Kingdom; nor do they any way interfere that I know of, except in giving their countenance and the sanction of their Names to whatever is done by that *Junto*.[24]

Ireland has derived some advantage from its independance on the Parliament of this Kingdom; or rather it did derive advantage from the arrangements that were made at the time of the establishment of that Independance. But human blessings are mixed; and I cannot but think, that even these great blessings were bought dearly enough, when along with the weight of the authority, they have totally lost all Benefit from the superintendancy of the British Parliament. Our Pride is succeded by fear. It is little less than a breach of Order, even to mention Ireland in the House of Commons of Great Britain. If the people of Ireland were to be flayed alive by the predominant faction it would be the most critical of all attempts so much as to discuss the Subject in any public Assembly upon this side of the Water. If such a faction should by its folly or inquiry or both, provoke disturbances in Ireland, the force paid by this Kingdom would infallibly be employed to repress them. This would be right enough, if our public Councils here at the same time possessed and employed the means of enquiry into the merits of that cause in which their blood and treasure were so laid out. By a strange inversion of the order of things not only the largest part of the Natives of Ireland are thus annihilated; but the Parliament of Great Britain itself is rendered no better than an instrument in the hands of an Irish faction — This is ascendancy with a Witness! In what all this will end it is not impossible to conjecture; tho' the exact time of the accomplishment cannot be [fixed] with the same certainty as you may calculate an Eclipse.

As to your particular conduct it has undoubtedly been that of a good and faithful Subject, and of a man of integrity and honour — You went to Ireland this last time, as you did the first time, at the express desire of the English Minister of that Department, and at the request of the Lord Lieutenant himself.[25] You were fully aware of the Difficulties that would attend your Mission; and I was equally sensible of them — Yet you consented, and I advised, that you should obey the voice of what we considered as indispensible duty. We regarded as the great Evil of the time the growth of Jacobinism, and we were very well assured that from a variety of causes no part of these Countries were more favorable to the growth and progress of that Evil than our unfortunate Country. I considered it as a tolerably good omen, that Government would do nothing further to foment and provoke the Jacobin malady, that they called upon you, a strenuous and steady Royalist, and an enlightened and exemplary Clergyman; A man of birth and respectable connexions in the Country; a man well informed and conversant in State Affairs, and in the general

22. Founded in October 1791, the Society of United Irishmen was the principal expression of French-style democracy and republicanism in Ireland. After official moves to suppress it in 1794, it was reconstituted as a secret oath-bound organization in 1795. In name at least, the United Irishmen led the insurrection of 1798.
23. A nominal payment.
24. A variant of *junta* — a cabal or faction.
25. Hussey had spent the summer of 1796 in England; the lord lieutenant of Ireland at the time of Hussey's mission there (September 1796) was John Jeffreys Pratt (1759-1840), 2nd earl of Camden.

Politicks of the several Courts of Europe, and intimately and personnally habituated in some of those Courts. I regretted indeed that the Ministry which had my most earnest good wishes declined to make any sort of use of the reiterated information you had given them of the designs of their Enemies, and had taken no notice of the noble and disinterested Offers, which thro' me, were made for employing you to save Italy and Spain to the British Alliance. But this being past and Spain and Italy lost I was in hopes, that they were resolved to put themselves in the right at home by calling upon you that they would leave on their part no cause or pretext for Jacobinism except in the seditious disposition of Individuals; but I now see that instead of profiting by your advice and services, they will not so much as take the least notice of your written representations or permit you to have access to them on the part of those whom it was your Business to reconcile to Government as well as to conciliate Government towards them. Having rejected your services as a friend of Government, and in some sort in its employment, they will not even permit to you the natural expression of those sentiments which every man of sense and honesty must feel, and which every plain and sincere man must speak upon this vile plan of abusing Military discipline and perverting it into an instrument of religious persecution. You remember with what indignation I heard of the scourging of the Soldier at Carrick[26] for adhering to his religious Opinions — It was at the time when Lord FitzWilliam[27] went to take possession of a short lived Government in Ireland — Breves et infaustos populi Hiberni amores.[28] He could not live long in power because he was a true Patriot, a true friend of both Countries a steady resister of Jacobinism in every part of the World. On this occasion he was not of my Opinion. He thought, indeed that the Sufferer ought to be relieved and discharged and I think he was so: But as to punishments to be inflicted on the Offender, he thought more lenient measures comprehended in a general plan to prevent such Evils in future, would be the better course. My Judgement, such as it was, had been, that punishment ought to attach so far as the Laws permitted, upon every evil action of subordinate power as it arose. That such acts ought at least to be marked with the displeasure of Government because general remedies are uncertain in their Operation when obtained, and that it is a matter of great uncertainty whether they can be obtained at all. For a time *his* appeared to be the better Opinion. Even after He was cruelly torn from the embraces of the people of Ireland, when the Militia and other Troops were encamped, (if I recollect rightly, at Loughlinstown)[29] you yourself with the knowledge and acquiescence of the suceeding Government publickly performed your function to the Catholicks then in Service. I believe too that all the Irish who had composed the foreign Corps taken into British pay had their regular Chaplains. But we see that things are returning fast to their old corrupted Channels. There they will continue to flow.

If any material Evil had been stated to have arisen from this Liberty that is, if Sedition Mutiny, or disobedience of any kind to Command, had been taught in their Chappels, there might have been a reason for not only forcing the Soldiers into Churches where better doctrines were taught, but for punishing the Teachers of disobedience and Sedition, — But I have never heard of any such Complaint. It is a part therefore of the Systematic illtreatment of Catholicks — This System never will be abandonned as long as it brings advantage to those who adopt it — If the Country enjoys a momentary quiet it is pleaded as an argument in favour of the good effect of wholesome rigours — If, on the Contrary, the Country [grows] more discontented; and if riots and disorders multiply, new Arguments are furnished for giving a vigorous support to the authority of the Directory on account of the rebellious disposition of the people. So long therefore as disorders in the Country become pretexts for adding to the power and emolument of an odious Junto, means will be found to keep one part of it or other in a perpetual state of confusion and disorder. This is the old traditionary policy of

26. The soldier was James Hyland, of the 14th Light Dragoons, based at Carrick-on-Suir, Co. Leitrim. He was given two hundred lashes in December 1794 for refusing to attend service in the parish church on the grounds that he was a conscientious catholic.
27. William Wentworth Fitzwilliam (1748-1833), 2nd earl of Fitzwilliam, in his very short term as lord lieutenant, early in 1795 indirectly encouraged hope that catholic emancipation would come quickly. He was recalled abruptly by William Pitt for allegedly exceeding his instructions.
28. 'Brief and unblessed are the loves of the Irish people'; based on Tacitus, *Annals* II, 41.
29. Loughlinstown is south of Dublin; during the summer of 1795 several regiments were encamped there, and Hussey had urged the appointment of catholic chaplains.

that sort of men. The discontents which under them break out among the people become tenure by which they hold their situation.

I do not deny, that in these Contests the people however oppressed are frequently much to blame, whether provoked to their excesses or not, undoubtedly the Law ought to look to nothing but the Offence and to punish it. The redress of grievances is not less necessary than the punishment of disorders; but it is of another resort. In punishing however, the Law ought to be the only rule — If it is not of sufficient force, a force, consistent with its general principles, ought to be added to it. The first duty of a State is to provide for its own conservation. Until that point is secured it can preserve and protect nothing else; but, if possible, it has a greater interest in acting according to strict Law, than even the Subject himself. For if the people see, that the Law is violated to crush them they will certainly despise the Law. They on their part will be easily Led to violate it whenever they can, by all the means in their power. Except in cases of direct War, whenever Government abandons Law, it proclaims Anarchy.

I am well aware, (if I cared one farthing for the few Days I have to live, whether the vain breath of men blow hot or cold about me) that they who censure any Oppressive proceeding of Government are exciting the people to Sedition and revolt. If there be no oppression it is very true or if there be nothing more than the lapses, which will happen to human infirmity at all times and in the exercise of all power, such complaints would be wicked indeed — These lapses are exceptions implied: an allowance for which is a part of the understood covenant by which Power is delegated by fallible men to other men that are not infallible; but whenever a hostile spirit on the part of Government is shewn the Question assumes another form. — This is no casual Errour, no lapse, no sudden surprise. Nor [is] it a question of civil or political Liberty. What contemptible stuff it is to say, that a Man who is lashed to Church against his conscience would not discover that the whip is painful, or that He had a conscience to be violated, unless I told him so? Would not a penitent Offender confessing his Offence, lamenting it, and expiating it by his blood, when denyed the consolation of Religion at his last moments, feel it as no injury to himself or that the rest of the world would feel so horrible and impious an oppression with no indignation, unless I happened to say it ought to be reckoned amongst the most barbarous acts of our barbarous time. Would the people consider their being taken out of their beds and transported from their family and friends to be an equitable and legal and charitable proceeding, unless I should say that it was a violation of Justice, and a dissolution, 'pro tanto,'[30] of the very compact of human Society? If a House of Parliament whose Essence it is to be the Guardian of the Laws, and a Simpathetic protector of the rights of the people (and eminently so of the most defenceless) should not only countenance but applaud this very violation of all Law, and refuse even to examine into the Grounds of the necessity upon the allegation of which Law was so violated, would this be taken for a tender Solicitude for the welfare of the poor, and a true proof of the representative Capacity of the House of Commons, unless I should happen to say (what I do say) that the House had not done its duty either in preserving the sacred rules of Law or in justifying the woeful and humiliating privilege of necessity. They may indemnify and reward others. They might contrive, if I was within their grasp, to punish me, or if they thought it worth while to stigmatize me by their censures; but who will indemnify them for the disgrace of such an Act? Who will save them from the censures of Posterity? What act of Oblivion will cover them from the wakeful memory, from the Notices and issues of the Grand remembrancer, the God *within*? Would it pass with the people, who suffer from the abuse of lawful power when at the same time they suffer from the use of lawless violence of Jacobins amongst themselves that Government had done its duty and acted leniently in not animadverting on one of those Acts of violence? If I did not tell them, that the lenity with which Government passes by the Crimes and oppressions of a favourite faction, was itself guilty of the most atrocious of all Cruelties. If a Parliament should hear a declamation, attributing the Sufferings of those who are destroyed by these riotous proceedings to their misconduct and then to make them self-felonious, and should en effet refuse an enquiry into the fact, is no inference to be drawn from thence, unless I tell men in high places, that these proceedings taken together form not only an encouragement to the abuse of Power, but to riot, sedition, and a rebellious Spirit which sooner

30. to that extent.

or later will turn upon those that encourage it?

I say little of the business of the Potatoe field,[31] because I am not yet acquainted with the particulars. If any persons were found in arms against the King, whether in a field of Potatoes, or of Flax, or of Turnips, they ought to be attacked by a military Power, and brought to condign Punishment by course of Law — If the County in which the Rebellion was raised, was not in a temper fit for the execution of Justice, a Law ought to be made, such as was made with regard to Scotland[32] on the Suppression of the rebellion of 45 to hang the Delinquents. There could be no difficulty in convicting men who were found 'flagrante delicto'.[33] But I hear nothing of all this. No Law, no tryal, no punishment commensurate to Rebellion; nor of a known proportion to any lesser delinquency, nor any discrimination of the more or the less guilty. Shall you and I find fault with the proceedings of France, and be totally indifferent to the proceedings of Directories at home. You and I hate Jacobinism as we hate the Gate of Hell — Why? Because it is a System of oppression. What can make us in love with oppression because the Syllables Jacobin are not put before the *ism*. When the very same things are done under the *ism* preceded by any other Name in the Directory of Ireland.

I have told you, at a great length for a Letter, very shortly for the Subject and for my feelings on it, my sentiments of the scene in which you have been called to act, — on being consulted you advized Sufferers to quiet and submission; and giving Government full credit for an attention to its duties you held out, as an inducement to that submission, some sort of hope of redress. You tryed what your reasons and your credit could do to effect it. In consequence of this piece of Service to Government you have been excluded from all communication with the Castle;[34] and perhaps you may thank yourself that you are not in Newgate.[35] You have done a little more than in your circumstances I should have done. You are indeed very excusable from your motive; but it is very dangerous to hold out to an irritated people Any hopes that we are not pretty sure of being able to realize. The Doctrine of Passive obedience, as a Doctrine, it is unquestionably right to teach; but to go beyond that, is a sort of deceit; and the people who are provoked by their Oppressors do not readily forgive their friends, if whilst the first persecutes and the others appear to deceive them. These friends lose all power of being serviceable to that Government in whose favor they have taken an illconsidered Step. Therefore my Opinion is, that untill the Castle shall shew a greater disposition to listen to its true friends than hitherto it has done, it would not be right in you any further to obtrude your services. In the mean time upon any new Application from the Catholics you ought to let them know simply and candidly how you stand.

The Duke of P——d[36] sent you to Ireland from a situation in this Country of advantage, and comfort to yourself and of no small utility to others. You explained to him in the clearest manner the conduct you were resolved to hold. I do not know that your writing to him will be of the least advantage — I rather think not; yet I am far from sure, that you do not Owe it to him, and to yourself to represent to his Grace the matters which, in substance, you have stated to me.

If any thing else should occur to me I shall, as you wish it, communicate my thoughts to you. In the mean time, I shall be happy to hear from you as often as you find it convenient. You never can neglect the great object of which you are so justly fond; and let me beg of you not to let slip out of your mind the Idea of the auxiliary studies and acquirements, which I recommended to you to add to the merely professional pursuits of your young Clergy; and above all, I hope that you will use the whole of your influence among the Catholics to persuade them to a greater indifference about the Political Objects which at present they have in view. It is not but that I am aware of their importance; or wish them to be abandond. But that they would follow opportunities and not to attempt to force any thing. I doubt whether the priveleges they now seek or have lately sought are compassable. The Struggle

31. The disturbances in Ulster, referred to in note 10 above, had commenced when potatoes had been dug out of a field in defiance of the owner.
32. 'An Act for the more easy and speedy trial of such persons as have levied, or shall levy war against his majesty' (19 Geo. III c. 9), 1746.
33. in the act.
34. Dublin Castle, the seat of English government in Ireland.
35. Synonymous with prison. Newgate had been a London prison since the Middle Ages.
36. William Henry Cavendish Bentinck (1738-1809), 3rd duke of Portland, was home secretary 1794-1801.

would, I am afraid only lead to some of Those very disorders which are made pretexts for further Oppression of the oppressed. I wish the leading people amongst them would give the most Systematic attention to prevent a frequent communication with their adversaries. There are a part of them proud, insulting, capricious, and tyrannical. These of Course will keep them at a distance. There are others of a seditious Temper who would make them at first the instruments and in the End the Victims of their factious Temper and purposes. Those that steer a middle course are truly respectable but they are very few. Your friends ought to avoid all imitation of the Vices of their proud Lords. To many of these they are themselves sufficiently disposed. I should therefore recommend to the middle ranks of that description in which I include not only all merchants but all farmers and tradesmen, that they would change as much as possible those expensive modes of living and that dissipation to which our Countrymen in general are so much addicted. It does not at all become men in a State of persecution. They ought to conform themselves to the circumstances of a people whom Government is resolved not to consider as upon a par with their fellow Subjects. Favour they will have none. They must aim at other rescources to make themselves independent in fact before they aim at a nominal independence. Depend upon it, that with half the privileges of the others, joined to a different System of manners they would grow to a degree of importance to which, without it, no privileges could raise them; much less any intrigues or factious practices. I know very well, that such a discipline among so numerous a people is not easily introduced; but I am sure it is not impossible — If I had youth and strength, I would go myself over to Ireland to work on that plan, so certain I am, that the well being of all descriptions in the Kingdom, as well as of themselves depends upon a reformation among the Catholicks. The work will be very slow in its operation but it is certain in its effect. There is nothing which will not yield to perseverance and method. Adieu! My dear Sir — you have full liberty to shew this Letter to all those (and they are but very few) who may be disposed to think well of my Opinions. I did not care, so far as regards myself, whether it was read on the change; but with regard to you more reserve may be proper — But that you will best judge.

MYLES BYRNE

(1780-1862)

from: MEMOIRS (1863)

[Myles Byrne was one of the Wexford rebel leaders during the 1798 insurrection, better connected than other catholic leaders but still the social inferior of Bagenal Harvey, the protestant gentleman whom the rebels chose as their principal commander. His *Memoirs*, written many years after the event and edited by his widow, devote only the first of three volumes to the Wexford insurrection, and it is from this volume that the following extracts are selected. Byrne's recollections are remarkable for two features: first, his emphasis on the substance and dignity of the network of catholic families that constituted his milieu; second, his (perhaps part-unconscious) casting of his material as a narrative of conflict between this surviving catholic world and an upstart class of petty magistrates, insecure landowners and yeoman captains whom he repeatedly epitomizes in the figure of John Hunter Gowan. Behind both of these procedures lies an evident intention to answer (explicitly for the most part) accounts of the Wexford rebellion offered by earlier writers, participants, apologists and historians alike.

Byrne spent ten years in Napoleon's army, and the *Memoirs* generally reflect the straightforward character of an uncomplicated soldier. The style is often painfully sentimental (the adjective 'poor' is much overworked), and the substance is contradictory here and there. At the same time, Byrne is advancing a specific interpretation of the events of 1798, one in which 'the people' play a significant rhetorical part; he may be read, in other words, as a precursor of the Fenians of the 1860s. Given the passing of many years between his early life and the time of writing, details concerning servants' names, precise locations and so on are sometimes impossible to identify completely.]

The first united irishman's funeral that took place being attended by vast crowds, and put into sections and marching order, by a young man of the name of Toole (of Anagh), who wished to imitate one he had seen in Dublin, attracted the notice of Hunter Gowan and of course made him suspect that something extraordinary was going on in the country. — As I shall have often to allude to the cruelties and cold-blooded murders committed by this monster, it is necessary to mention what he was.[1]

He had for many year distinguished himself by his activity in apprehending robbers, for which he had been rewarded by a pension from government. He was a low fellow, but this pension enabled him to hold some rank in the country. He called his place 'Mont Nebo' and planted his land with trees of different kinds. He kept a pack of hounds, and wished to be looked upon as a great sportsman; he felt much mortified when the neighbouring gentlemen refused to hunt with him.[2]

He happened one day to be led by the chase some miles from his own place, and fell in with old Garrett Byrne of Ballymanus, who, with his hounds, was in full chase.[3] The latter enraged at being crossed in his sport by an 'upstart', as he called Hunter Gowan, gave him a horse whipping and told him never to presume to come in his way again. Gowan took the law of Garrett Byrne and ran him into great expense. This occurence (of the horse whipping) took place many years previous to 1798, but it would appear, that, from that moment, Gowan swore eternal hatred to catholics in general, but most particularly against the Byrnes.

A brother of Hunter Gowan lived in Gory[4] and kept a saddler's shop there; he was considered a good sort of man, without any pretence of being above what he was.

Garrett Byrne was a descendant of one of the oldest and most distinguished branches of the Byrnes of the county of Wicklow; he inherited the small estate of Ballimanus and lived in great style, associating with men of the highest rank in the county, all of whom esteemed and feared him: he was a perfect gentleman; he was dexterous in the use of arms, particularly the small sword and pistol. My father often saw him shoot swallows from his hall door with a pistol ball. He brought up his family with high notions of what they owed to their ancestors. He had five sons, all splendid men, Garrett, John, Coclough, Edward, and poor Billy or William, who was executed at Wicklow,[5] and two daughters, Nelly and Fanny, both fine women, and very well educated.

. . .

Many of the low-bred magistrates availed themselves of the martial law, to prove their vast devotion to government, by persecuting, and often torturing the inoffensive country people. Archibald Hamilton Jacob and the Enniscorthy yeomen cavalry never marched out of the town without being accompanied by a regular executioner, with his ropes, cat o'nine tails, etc.[6]

1. This funeral took place some time before the general outbreak of insurrection. Annagh was described by Father John Kavanagh (who was born there in 1749) as a pleasant vale near Gorey. Byrne himself came from Monaseed in the same northern part of County Wexford. He was thus a neighbour of John Hunter Gowan, who held land near Gorey and built a residence for himself. Earlier, Gowan had been employed by the public authorities to apprehend malefactors, and it was only in 1798 that he became a magistrate and a yeoman captain. Gowan was present at a meeting of the National Grand Orange Lodge in Dublin on 9 April 1798, and so may be regarded as crucial to the introduction of Orangeism into County Wexford. Louis Cullen has interpreted the break-up of the Gowan holdings in the years after 1798 as evidence of 'the underlying difficulties which middlemen faced in keeping together the small lease-held estates which were essential to attaining — and preserving — economic and social status.' (*The Emergence of Modern Ireland 1600-1900*, pp. 231-32). For Gowan's belated incorporation into the 'demonology' of Irish literature, see the poem 'Mount Nebo', and the title-poem, in Hugh Maxton, *At the Protestant Museum* (Mountrath: Dolmen Press, 1986), pp. 9-11, 39-42.
2. Mount Nebo, in the Bible, is one of the points from which Moses is permitted to glimpse the Promised Land he shall never enter; see Deuteronomy 32. 49:

    Get thee up into this mountain Abarim, unto mount Nebo, which is in the land of Moab, that is over against Jericho; and behold the land of Canaan, which I give unto the children of Israel for a possession.

   This choice of name might even be read as an anticipation of Gowan's failure to gain acceptance by the longer-established Wexford gentry.
3. Garrett Byrne (senior), a kinsman of Myles Byrne, and father of Garrett and William Byrne, who both participated in the rebellion. Ballymanus is an isolated mountain area to the south-west of Aughrim in County Wicklow, close to the Wexford border.
4. Generally spelled Gorey, a substantial town in north Wexford, serving much of the Wicklow border district.
5. William Michael Byrne (to give him his full name) was executed on 26 September 1799.
6. Archibald Hamilton Jacob, an Enniscorthy magistrate, had been listed in a rebel proclamation of 9 June 1798 with others who had particularly offended the United Irishmen. Contemporary accounts of his wanton cruelty have been accepted by the most recent historian of 1798, Thomas Pakenham. Byrne, however, cannot be justified in regarding him as 'low born': several other members of the family held office, and one was mayor of Wexford town.

Hawtry White, Solomon Richards, and a protestant minister of the name of Owens were all notorious for their cruelty and persecuting spirit; the latter particularly so, putting on pitch caps and exercising other torments.[7] To the credit of some of his victims, when the vile fellow himself was in their power, and was brought a prisoner to the insurgent camp at Gory, they sought no other revenge than that of putting a pitch cap on him. I had often difficulty in preventing the others, who had suffered so much at his hands, from tearing him to pieces. He, in the end, escaped, with many other prisoners, being escorted and guarded by men who did not consider that revenge, or retaliation of any kind, would forward the sacred cause they were embarked in: particularly, as they were desirous it should not be thought that it was a religious war they were engaged in. Although several of the principal chiefs of the united irishmen were protestants, the Orange magistrates did all they could to spread the belief, that the Catholics had no other object in view, but to kill their protestant fellow subjects, and to give weight to this opinion, they did what they could to provoke the unfortunate people to commit outrages and reprisals, by killing some and burning their houses.

In short, the state of the country, previous to the insurrection, is not to be imagined; except by those who witnessed the atrocities of every description committed by the military and the Orangemen, who were let loose on the unfortunate, defenceless and unarmed population.

The infamous Hunter Gowan now sighed for an opportunity to vent his ferocious propensity of murdering his catholic neighbours in cold blood. When the yeomanry corps were first formed, he was not considered sufficiently respectable to be charged with the command of one; but in consequence of the proclamation of martial law, he soon obtained a commission of the peace and was created a captain and was commissioned to raise a cavalry corps: in a short time he succeeded in getting about thirty or forty low Orangemen, badly mounted; but they soon procured better horses, at the expense of the unfortunate farmers, who were plundered without redress. This corps went by the name of the black mob; their first campaign was, to arrest all the Catholic blacksmiths and to burn their houses. Poor William Butter, James Haydon and Dalton, smiths whom we employed to shoe our horses and do other work, for many years before, were condemned to be transported, according to the recent law enacted, that magistrates upon their own authority could sentence to transportation. But the monster Hunter Gowan, thinking this kind of punishment too slight, wished to give his young men an opportunity to prove they were staunch blood-hounds. Poor Garrett Fennell who had just landed from England, and was on his way to see his father and family, was met by this corps, and tied by his two hands up to a tree; they then stood at a certain distance and each man lodged the contents of his carabine in the body of poor Fennell, at their captain's command[8].

. . .

I feel this long digression necessary at this epoch of my narrative, on account of the great pains taken by the enemies of the independence of Ireland, to make it appear, that the catholic united Irishmen had no other object in view than retaliation and revenge on their protestant fellow countrymen during the war. If none but the slanderer sir Richard Musgrave[9] had propagated such a calumny, I would not deign to refute it, but the book-making bigot, the protestant minister Gordon,[10] whilst he allows that the greatest

7. White was captain of the Ballaghkeene yeomen cavalry, and his name appeared in the proclamation of 9 June 1798. A tenant of Lord Mountnorris, he held landed property in a manner similar to that of Hunter Gowan, and Louis Cullen has surmised that White was involved in the spread of Orangeism in the east of County Wexford.

Solomon Richards (of Solsborough, Co. Wexford) led the Enniscorthy cavalry; he was sometime justice of the peace, and high sheriff for the county; a namesake-ancestor had been governor of Wexford town in Cromwell's time.

The Rev. Roger Carmichael Owen (graduated Trinity College, Dublin 1777; died in 1844) was brother of Mrs Jane Adams whose memoir testifies to his temporary insanity (before and?) during his imprisonment by the rebels. He had loudly declared himself an Orangeman and had led a 500-strong band of his parishioners. Mrs Adams's description of his condition tallies closely with Byrne's, while Sir Jonah Barrington confirms Byrne's accusations of barbarity; the rebels released Owen into his sister's custody and he lived to be rector of Kiltennel 1804-35, having presumably recovered his wits.

8. None of these men can be traced further: blacksmiths were strategic figures for the secret manufacture of weapons, and so were particularly vulnerable.

9. Richard Musgrave (*c*.1757-1818), first baronet. In the second edition of his *Memoirs of the Different Rebellions in Ireland* (Dublin: printed by Marchbank, 1801), he claimed that 1,250 copies of the first edition had been sold in two months.

10. Rev. James Bentley Gordon (1750-1819) published a *History of Ireland to the Union* (Dublin, 1805), *History of the Rebellion in Ireland in the Year 1798* (Dublin, 1801), and a work on the history and geography of North America.

atrocities and murders were committed by the protestant yeomanry on the unarmed and innocent catholics, previous to the rising, still condemns father John Murphy, as a vulgar, ferocious fanatic, because he had the courage to take the field and give battle to those blood-thirsty troops in which Gordon's son was an officer. Is this impartial history?[11]

On the other hand, honest Edward Hay,[12] one of the catholic aristocracy, who had his brother executed in Wexford as an united Irish man, and chief of insurgents, wishes to make it appear, in his narrative, that there were very few united Irish men in his country, the county of Wexford; because, the reports found at Oliver Bonds scarcely made mention of the county of Wexford.[13] The reason is simple. The county Delegate, Robert Graham, had the good fortune to arrive too late at Bonds, and escaped. Therefore, his report of men and arms, to the provincial meeting could not be ascertained.[14]

In an other page Edward Hay tells, that from the exhortations and exertions of the priests in every parish, the pikes were surrendered, and generally lodged in the chapels at night. He also mentions that Bagnel Harvey[15] had brought all from his district the day he was arrested. Thus, as none but united Irishmen would risk having pikes, and they were discovered every where, it proves that the great mass of the people were united Irishmen. The government knew it perfectly. Therefore it is useless to strive to maintain, that the county of Wexford people were less desirous than those of other counties to shake off the yoke of England.

What a misfortune for Ireland not to be able to produce one historian who could boast, that he was neither a place hunter, placeman[16] or pensioner of the English government! To such a man, the most valuable materials could be furnished. — What a pity and misfortune, that the author of 'captain Rock'[17] did not possess a thousand a year, or at least an independence which might have enabled him to live out of England! He could have brought his history of Ireland down to the union, and even later, instead of leaving it off at the reign of Henry VIII; thereby he would have had an opportunity of doing justice to father John, and to all those brave patriots of 1798 who sacrificed every thing dear to them, life, fortune, all the enjoyments on earth, to see Ireland free and governed by Irishmen, and as she ought to be, in place of being the last and most unfortunate country on the face of the globe.

...

No pen can describe the dreadful state of my unfortunate aunt and her four daughters at this awful moment. To add to their misery, one of the assassins had the brutality to tell the eldest daughter Mrs Kinsla,[18] who had been married but a year or two before, that she would find something else to weep over when she returned home. She had come but half an hour before to visit her family; her own place being but a short mile from her father's house. As the monster told her, when she went home, she found her husband lying dead in the court yard, and a young child of a few months old in his arms. The unfortunate man had taken it out of its cradle, thinking that the sight of the poor infant might soften Beaumont's heart, and incline him to mercy. But this staunch supporter of the protestant ascendency, could not let so good an opportunity pass of proving his loyalty to his king, by thus exterminating a catholic neighbour. Yet strange to say, his own three sisters were very strict roman catholics, and respectable ladies, holding a certain

11. Gordon's only son, Richard Bentley, was entered on the books of Trinity College, Dublin on 1 April 1799 'aged 18', and thus would have been no older at the time. It is possible that Byrne confused him with a Major Gordon in the Dumfries regiment.
12. Edward Hay (*c*.1761-1826) published his *History of the Insurrection in the County of Wexford in the Year of 1798* in Dublin in 1801; it is still regarded as a useful source.
13. Oliver Bond (1760-98), a Dublin wool merchant and an original member of the 1791 Society of the United Irishmen; tried and found guilty of high treason following the raid on his premises, he died in prison.
14. Robert Graham came from Coolgreaney, north of Gorey, and was a cousin of Byrne's on Byrne's mother's side.
15. Beauchamp Bagenal Harvey (1762-98), barrister, presided at United Irishmen meetings in 1793. Appointed to command the Wexford rebels in May 1798; generally acknowledged as a humane but mediocre leader; counter-martialled and executed by crown forces at the collapse of the rebellion.
16. Both 'place hunter' and 'placeman' — people who persistently sought a post in the public service — have pejorative connotations.
17. The allusion here to Thomas Moore's *Memoirs of Captain Rock* (1824) exemplifies Byrne's determination to eschew any kind of subtle apology for rebellion and to prefer a bold declaration of the Wexford United Irishmen's organized resistance; this, nonetheless, leads him into a rhetorical flourish in the next paragraph where, despite the dignities of the Byrnes and other notable catholic families, he speaks of England's driving 'even slaves to desperation'.
18. Byrne's uncle was named Breen and he lived at Castletown, Co. Wexford. Captain Beaumont (of Hyde Park, Co. Wexford), previously on friendly terms with Breen, shot him and one of his sons in front of the Breen womenfolk; Kinsella (in the usual spelling) is a common Wexford name.

station amongst the catholic gentry of the country; they were, Mrs William Talbot of Castle Talbot, Mrs Barry Lawless of Shank hill, and miss Mary Beaumont.[19]

I have met all these ladies in company, at Paris, after the restoration of the Bourbons. Of course I had no conversation with them on the cold blooded murders perpetrated in our unfortunate country; I presume they lamented the active part their brother took in these horrible deeds.

I met also in Paris, Mrs Butler, a daughter of that notorious monster Hunter Gowan. It was well known, that neither this lady, nor any of her 'thirteen' sisters[20] (all of whom were unmarried at the time of the insurrection), ever took the least pains to mollify their father, or turn him from his cruel propensity to spilling blood: on the contrary, they seemed to take delight, and to be amused preparing the poor 'croppies'[21] heads for receiving the pitch caps, cutting the hair and making what they called asses crosses on them, previous to the application of this infernal blistering invention of torture, which was introduced into the county of Wexford by the colonel of the North Cork militia, lord Kingsborough and his vile Orange associates.[22] — After all this, and the piqueting, half-hanging and flogging which the magistrates had recourse to, are our poor people to be blamed for the reprisals they were goaded on to inflict? — No doubt cold-blooded murders must ever disgrace the most sacred cause, and the perpetrators of them should be held up to everlasting execration by all brave men, and nothing can excuse the burning of the barn at Scullabogue with the prisoners it contained; yet it never appeared that it was a premeditated action; it could only have been the act of some cowardly ruffians, escaping from the battle of Ross, and never could be attributed to any one above the meanest vulgar wretch; and the cowardly Dixon who got the prisoners put to death on the bridge of Wexford, was a seafaring 'cannibal', who took advantage of the chiefs being away at the camp, to commit this atrocious crime: these brave leaders would have saved liberty this lamentable disgrace; not one of them ever suffered or countenanced such reprisals.[23] — On the side of the english army, the cold-blooded murders were perpetrated at the instigation of the generals in command, who not only presided at the executions, but allowed their undisciplined soldier to enter the houses and violate the unfortunate women, who had no means of escaping from these brutal monsters. To the honour of our army, there was not a single instance of a female belonging to the enemy, ever being molested during the war; and no place of worship of any religion was ever desecrated; whilst thirty three roman catholic chapels were burned to the ground. The protestant church of Old Ross was burned on the second of june 1798; it was said to have been burned by accident; at all events it was the only one.[24]

19. Two observations may be made on this last paragraph; first, that 'protestant ascendancy' is associated with Beaumont's criminal violence; second that Beaumont's female relatives were catholic, it being conventional that children of a 'mixed' marriage between protestant and catholic followed the denominational affiliation of the parent of the same sex (girls with mother, boys with father). Barry Lawless of Shankhill is referred to in the traditional ballad 'Come all you warriors'.
20. John Hunter Gowan had a large family and an unconventional sex-life, the number and consanguinity of his many children being imprecisely known; after his death the estate was disputed, and a son, Ogle Gowan, departed for Canada, where he founded the Orange Order of British America. The sceptical quotation marks around 'thirteen' may indicate Byrne's belief in an even larger progeny or may be a French typesetter's transfer of the same marks that originally had qualified 'sisters'.
21. The rebels of 1798 wore their hair cut very short as a sign of their sympathy for the French Revolution.
22. Robert King (1754-99), viscount Kingsborough and 2nd earl of Kingstown, colonel of the North Cork Militia, which were introduced into Wexford in April 1798. Byrne's view of Kingsborough's attitude towards women in Wexford is confirmed even in the letters of the viscount's patron, the Earl of Shannon; in 1797 he had shot dead the illegitimate son of his wife's brother with whom his daughter had eloped.
23. For an account of 'captain' Dixon's supervision of the massacre (and his subsequent flight), see Thomas Pakenham, *The Year of Liberty* (London: Panther, 1978), pp. 291-96.
24. Byrne's emphasis on the violation of women by crown forces and the honouring of both women and churches by the rebels may be read as the conclusion of a prolonged and intricate interrelating in his narrative of sexual energies, with Gowan and his family providing the focal point.

FOUR POPULAR SONGS

1789-1815

[The period of the French Revolution saw a sudden transformation of the traditional ballad into popular, politically aware song. Although ballads of love, misfortune (comic or otherwise) and death continued to be composed, the Revolution brought a new force into articulation: *the people* in an ideologically positive and dynamic sense. In Ireland, both the United Irishmen's rebellion of 1798, and the counter movement of protestant loyalism, gave birth to a mass of popular songs. The Wexford rising, in particular, has been well commemorated in song, and the first example given here is a narrative of the progress of the rebels — incomplete because, of course, the rising has not yet (in the singer's terms) achieved its objectives.

The second example is an Orange song, closer to a call to action than to narrative of actions already commenced; its origins are not in Ulster, however, but in Dublin.

'The Groves of Blarney' is thought to have been written in 1797 or 1798, and it is said that additional verses were composed during the rebellion to provide a commentary on contemporary events. Finally, in 'The Lass of Richmond Hill' we encounter a more socially elevated song, originally published in the London *Public Advertiser* in August 1789, a month after the fall of the Bastille in Paris; the author of the anonymous song is now known to be Leonard MacNally, a Dublin barrister and United Irishman who (it emerged after his death in 1820) had also been a government informer and the betrayer of the men whom he defended in court as fellow-Unitedmen.

In the context of this section of the anthology, a feature that these songs share is a certain imitation in genre or imagery, the exploitation of an earlier form or style, which is recalled and transformed in the course of the new song. Each of the four examples employs this technique in a distinctive way. And, since it should be admitted that 'The Lass of Richmond Hill' does not so much embody the technique of imitation or mimicry as help to extend and disguise the pervasive doubleness of its author, detailed commentary is reserved for the biographical note on MacNally. Notes are added on a stanza-by-stanza basis, with a lengthier commentary on the background to 'The Groves of Blarney'.

'Come All You Warriors' borrows the language of ancient conflict, and buttresses this with the names of 'renowned nobles', such as Julius Caesar, in order to lend both dignity and hope to the more immediate cause of John Murphy facing 'one hundred Corkmen'. While 'Come All You Warriors' seeks to assimilate these later combatants into the high register of noble conflict, 'The Groves of Blarney' emphasizes this gulf between commonplace Irish names and a ludicrously mixed list of antique names — 'Neptune, Plutarch, and Nicodemus' — and does so for comic and deflationary effect.

The liberty tree was a symbol used in both the American and French revolutions, signifying the planting of a new society that will expand in future years. The song was written by 'J.B.' of Orange Lodge No. 471. The appropriation of this image by the Orangemen may at first sight seem paradoxical, but Orangeism emphasized its loyalty to 'British liberty' as distinct from the more abstract 'rights of man' invoked by radicals from Tom Paine (1735-1809) onwards. All four songs use place-names or the names of historical personages to evoke the immediacy of their inspiration.]

ANON.

'Come All You Warriors'

Come all you warriors, and renowned nobles,
Who once commanded brave warlike bands;
Lay down your plumes, and your golden trophies,
Give up your arms with a trembling hand,
Since Father Murphy, of the County Wexford,
Lately roused from his sleepy dream,
To cut down cruel Saxon persecution
And wash it away in a crimson stream.

Sure Julius Caesar, nor Alexander,
Nor renowned King Arthur e'er could equal him;
For armies formidable he has conquered,
Though with two gunmen he did begin.
Camolin cavalry he did unhorse them,
Their first lieutenant he cut him down;
With shattered ranks and with broken columns
They retreated home to Camolin town.

On the Hill of Oulart he displayed his valour,
Where one hundred Corkmen lay on the plain,
And at Enniscorthy, his sword he wielded,
And I hope he'll do it once more again.
The loyal townsmen gave their assistance,
We'll die or conquer, they all did say,
The yeomen's cavalry made no resistance,
While on the pavement their corpses lay.

When Enniscorthy became subject to him,
'Twas then to Wexford we marched our men,

And on the Three Rocks took up our quarters,
  Waiting for daylight the town to win.
With drums a-beating the town did echo,
  And acclamations from door to door;
On the Windmill Hill we pitched our tents,
  And we drank like heroes, tho' paid no score.

On Carrig-ruadh for some time we waited,
  Then next for Gorey we did repair,
In Tubberneering we thought no harm,
  The bloody army was waiting there.
The issue of it was a close engagement,
  While on the soldiers we played warlike pranks,
Thro' sheepwalks, hedgerows, and shady thickets,
  There were mangled boddies and broken ranks.

The shudd'ring cavalry, I can't forget them,
  We raised the brushes on their helmets straight,
They turned about, and they scud for Dublin
  As if they ran for a ten-pound plate;
Some got to Donnybrook, and some to Blackrock,
  And some up Shankhill without wound or flaw;
And if Barry Lawless be not a liar,
  There's more went grousing up Luggelaw.

With flying colours we marched on to Limerick,
  And to Kilcavan we did repair;
'Twas on Mount-Pleasant we called the county,
  And pointed cannons at the army there.
When we thought fit, we marched on to Gorey;
  The next was Arklow we did surround.
The night being coming, we regretted sorely,
  Tho' one hundred soldiers lay on the ground.

The towns of England were left quite naked
  Of all its army, both foot and horse;
The Highlands of Scotland were left unguarded,
  Likewise the Hessians, the sea they crossed.
To the Windmill Hill of Enniscorthy
  Their British fencibles they fled like deers;
And our ranks were tattered, and sorely scattered
  For the loss of Kyan and the Shelmaliers.

But if the Frenchmen they had reinforced us —
  Landed their transports in Baggenbunn,
Father John Murphy he would be their seconder,
  And sixty thousand along with him come;
Success attend the sweet County Wexford,
  Threw off its yoke and to battle run.
Let them not think we gave up our arms,
  For every man has a pike or gun.

Stanza 1: Essentially displays the vocabulary of chivalric combat (plumes, golden trophies), the notion of the hero who has been subject to some spell, seeming-death, or other condition, which has led to the crisis he now rises to resolve.

Stanza 2: Heroic names are juxtaposed with the locality of Camolin; the inhabitants of nearby Boulavogue, led by their parish priest Father John Murphy (*c*.1753-98), routed a corps of the Camolin cavalry on 26 May 1798.

Stanza 3: On the same day, at Oulart, Murphy's men defeated the North Cork Militia.

Stanza 4: Enniscorthy is a town (with castle) on the river Slaney in the centre of County Wexford; just outside the town is Vinegar Hill (or Windmill Hill) where the rebels ultimately suffered a fatal reverse on 21 June 1798.

Stanza 5: The Wexford and Wicklow rebels developed guerilla methods of fighting, tempting the cavalry to attack them through hedges filled with thorny bushes; when ridden into these traps, the horses threw their riders.

Stanza 6: The place-names near Dublin, listed to plot the retreat, are of course highly misleading as far as historical evidence is concerned, but bolster the heroic achievement that the singer is celebrating.

Stanza 7: Limerick here is actually a tiny river in north Wexford, and not the city on the Shannon; Kilcavan is in the same area of the county. The rebels' failure to capture the town of Arklow (just across the county border in Wicklow), in an attack led personally by Father Murphy, effectively limited the rising to the confines of Wexford and prevented the insurgents joining with the United Irishmen in Dublin or the midlands.

Stanza 8: Here the introduction into Wexford of huge numbers of troops stationed elsewhere in the British dominions is presented not so much as the signal of imminent defeat for the rebels but of the desolation wreaked on the British possessions elsewhere; it is a deflection of the listener's attention. Esmond Kyan (executed 1798 by the crown; a catholic gentleman holding the rank of colonel) failed to lead his men of Shelmalier into position in readiness for the battle of Vinegar Hill-

Stanza 9: Hope of substantial military support from revolutionary France had been the basis of the United Irishmen's plan for a rising. Baginbun (standard spelling) is a headland on the south coast of the county.

'J.B.'

'The Tree of Liberty'

Sons of Hibernia, attend to my song,
Of a tree call'd th'Orange, it's beauteous and strong;
'Twas planted by William, immortal is he!
May all Orange brothers live loyal and free.
    Derry down, down, traitors bow down.

Around this fair trunk we like ivy will cling,
And fight for our honour, our country, and king;
In the shade of this Orange none e'er shall recline
Who with murd'rous Frenchmen have dar'd to
  combine.
    Derry down, down, Frenchmen bow down.

Hordes of barbarians, Lord Ned in the van,
This tree to destroy laid an infamous plan;
Their schemes prov'd abortive, tho' written in blood,
Nor their pikes, nor their scythes could pierce
  Orange wood.
    Derry down, down, rebels bow down.

While our brave Irish tars protect us by sea,
From false perjur'd traitors this island we'll free;
Priest Murphy's war-vestment they'll find of no use,
Whenever we meet them they're sure to get goose,
Derry down, down, priestcraft bow down.

Hundreds they've burned of each sex, young and old,
From Heaven the order — by priests they were told;
No longer we'll trust them, no more to betray,
But chase from our bosoms those vipers away.
Derry down, down, serpents bow down.

Rouse them, my brothers, and heed not their swearing,
Absolv'd they have been for deeds past all bearing;
Mercy's misplac'd, when to murderers granted,
For our lands and our lives those wretches long panted.
Derry down, down, reptiles bow down.

Then charge high your glasses, and drink our Great Cause,
Our blest Constitution, our King, and our Laws;
May all lurking traitors, wherever they be
Make the exit of Sheares, and Erin be free.
Derry down, down, traitors bow down.

Stanza 1: The use of Hibernia (and Erin in the last stanza) indicates the extent to which Orangeism was able to draw on the romantic vocabulary of the late eighteenth century when evoking Ireland. The notion that the Orange Order (its members sometimes referred to each other as 'brother') is named after the orange tree is of course without any basis in fact. The Order is named after William (1650-1702), prince of the house of Orange and later William III of England, Scotland and Ireland; Orange being originally a town on the Rhone in France. The last line of each stanza refers back to another ballad of the period, 'Croppies Lie Down'.
Stanza 3: Lord Edward Fitzgerald (1763-98) was son of the 1st Duke of Leinster and a principal United Irishman negotiator with the French. Pikes were manufactured by the blacksmiths for the rebels; scythes were used by the aroused peasantry as improvised weapons.
Stanza 4: tar = sailor; for Father Murphy, see notes to the previous song.
Stanza 5: It was a belief of loyalists that catholic rebels had been absolved by their priests from the spiritual consequences of their actions, however sinful.
Stanza 7: i.e. fill your glasses and drink a toast to the protestant cause, the constitution of 1688, and so on. The brothers Henry and John Sheares (1753-98; 1766-98) were protestant United Irishmen, executed in Dublin.

RICHARD ALFRED MILLIKEN (1767-1815)

The Groves of Blarney (1797/98)

The groves of Blarney they are so charming,
All by the purling of sweet silent streams;
Being banked with posies that spontaneous grow there,
Planted in order by the sweet rock close.
'Tis there the daisy, and the sweet carnation,
The blooming pink, and the rose so fair;
The daffodowndilly, besides the lily, —
Flowers that scent the sweet fragrant air.
Oh, ullagoane, &c.

'Tis Lady Jeffreys that owns this station,
Like Alexander, or Queen Helen fair;
There's no commander throughout the nation
For emulation can with her compare.
She has castles round her, that no nine-pounder
Could dare to plunder her place of strength;
But Oliver Cromwell he did her pummell,
And made a breach in her battlement.
Oh, ullagoane, &c.

There's gravel walks there for speculation,
And conversation in sweet solitude;
'Tis there the lover may hear the dove, or
The gentle plover, in the afternoon.
And if a young lady should be so engaging
As to walk alone in those shady bowers,
'Tis there her courtier he may transport her
In some dark fort, or underground.
Oh, ullagoane, &c.

For 'tis there's the cave where no daylight enters,
But bats and badgers are forever bred;
Being moss'd by natur', that makes it sweeter
Than a coach and six, or a feather bed.
'Tis there's the lake that is stored with perches,
And comely eels in the verdant mud;
Besides the leeches, and the groves of beeches,
All standing in order for to guard the flood.
Oh, ullagoane &c.

'Tis there's the kitchen hangs many a flitch in,
With the maids a stitching upon the stair;
The bread and biske', the beer and whisky,
Would make you frisky if you were there.
'Tis there you'd see Peg Murphy's daughter
A washing *praties* forenent the door,
With Roger Cleary, and Father Healy,
All blood relations to my lord Donoughmore.
Oh, ullagoane, &c.

There's statues gracing this noble place in,
All heathen goddesses so fair, —

Bold Neptune, Plutarch, and Nicodemus,
All standing naked in the open air.
So now to finish this brave narration,
Which my poor geni' could not entwine;
But were I Homer, or Nebuchadnezzar,
'Tis in every feature I would make it shine.
Oh, ullagoane, &c.

Stanza 1: For Blarney, see General Note below; purling = (of water) flowing with a whirling motion; 'ullagoane' is an attempt to render the conventional Irish expression of regret, grief (from *olc* = bad, unfortunate).
Stanza 2: For 'Lady Jeffreys', see General Note below; note the conjunction of Alexander (historical figure of the ancient world), Helen of Troy (Homeric legend), and Oliver Cromwell (1599-1658), lord protector of the Commonwealth 1653-58.
Stanza 4: Note the recurrent sexual or erotic theme developed from the concluding lines of the previous stanza.
Stanza 5: A flitch is a salted and cured side of pork; biske' = biscuit; praties = potatoes; forenen(s)t = facing towards; Richard Hely-Hutchinson (1756-1825) became 1st earl of Donoughmore in 1800; consequently the assertion made in the memoir cited below, that this stanza was added during the 1798 rebellion, cannot stand. Hely-Hutchinson's family were long connected with Cork politics, and had a reputation for ambitious social climbing.
Stanza 6: Here the traditional Irish ballad convention of listing classical names is exploited to comic effect by ludicrous juxtaposition: Neptune is the Roman god of the sea; Plutarch (*c*.50-120) an ancient historian and biographer; Nicodemus a Pharisee mentioned in St John's gospel as a supporter of Jesus; Homer is the legendary (?) founder of Greek epic verse; and Nebuchadnezzar an Old Testament conqueror of the Jews.

General Note: This is one of the best known, and yet most elusive, of popular poems. Some comment on its evolution seems appropriate. Evidently written in 1797 or 1798, it was not included in *Poetical Fragments of the late Richard Alfred Milliken, with an Authentic Memoir of his Life* (1823), although the memoir recorded the following details of its composition:

> An itinerant poet, with a view of being paid for his trouble, composed a song in praise (as he doubtless intended) of Castle Hyde, the beautiful seat of the Hyde family, on the river Blackwater; but instead of the expected remuneration, the poor poet was driven from the gate, by order of the then proprietor, who, from the absurdity of the thing, conceived that it could be only meant as mockery; and in fact a more nonsensical composition could scarcely escape the pen of a maniac. The author however, well satisfied of its merits, and stung with indignation and disappointment, vented his rage in an additional verse, against the owner, and sung it wherever he had an opportunity of raising his angry voice. As satire, however gross, is but too generally well received, the song first became a favourite with the lower orders, then found its way into ballads, and at length into the convivial meetings of gentlemen. It was in one of those that Mr Millikin undertook in the gaiety of the moment, to produce a song, that if not superior, should be at least equal in absurdity to Castle Hyde, and accordingly, adopting the tune, and taking Blarney for his subject, he soon made good his promise. The Groves of Blarney, which was received by the company with a burst of applause, soon rivalled its predecessor Castle Hyde, and continued long the favourite of every laughter-loving party: — of late it has been introduced on the stage, by Mathews the Comedian, and is very well received by the London audience. During the rebellion, several verses were, in the heat of party, added to this song, particularly those alluding to the mean descent of a certain noble lord; but they were *not* the production of the original author, who, incapable alike of scurrility, or personal enmity to those with whom he differed in opinion, scorned such puerile malice. (pp. xxiv-xxvi)

The text is taken from *The Popular Songs of Ireland, Collected and Edited by T[homas]* Crofton Croker (London: Colburn, 1839), pp. 147-49. Croker 'copied from the author's manuscript', and included the stanza (no. 5) which touches on Lord Donoughmore's blood relations. Although he conceded that other stanzas had been added by other hands, and did not expressly claim the fifth as Milliken's, Croker rightly concluded that the poem would be incomplete without it. 'The Groves of Blarney' thus exemplifies a number of features more usually thought of as characteristic of anonymous- or folk-poetry: an original occasion linked to rivalry or poetic competition, uncertainty as to a precise date of composition, the use of a traditional tune or preordained form, the addition of late material and so on. Yet despite all these factors, the poem was omitted from Milliken's posthumous collection, and the question should be asked — why?

Blarney is a town in County Cork, about three miles from Cork city, extensively developed in the latter half of the eighteenth century by James St John Jeffereyes (died 1796). Arthur Young, in his *A Tour in Ireland* (1780), described improvements to the town, adding:

> Mr Jefferys, besides the above establishments, has very much improved Blarney Castle and its environs; he has formed an extensive ornamented ground, which is laid out with considerable taste; an extensive plantation surrounds a large piece of water, and walks lead through the whole; there are several very pretty sequestered spots where covered benches are placed. (Vol. I, p. 315; see the first item in this section for details of Young's *Tour*.)

We may take it that the poem takes off from an actual site, one associated with the enterprise of the husband of 'Lady Jeffreys' (as Milliken spells the name). The castle, however, had been the property of the MacCarthy family until they forfeited it through their Jacobitism; in 1703 it was purchased by Lord Chief Justice Pyne, who sold it to General Sir James Jeffereys. Robert MacCarthy (died 1769), titular earl of Clancarty, unsuccessfully attempted to recover the family estates. These historical details at first might seem superfluous in annotating what seems a non-sensical poem (with its heroic listing of oddly assorted flowers, fish) written in imitation of an absurd one. However, the remarkable political reputation of 'Lady Jeffreys' in the 1780s and after suggests that Milliken was using nonsense as a mask for a historical perspective of his own. We therefore must look to the lady.

Mrs Arabella Jeffereyes was the eldest sister of John Fitzgibbon (1749-1802), 1st earl of Clare, the most powerful Irish architect of the Union with Britain. Her sister, Eleanor, was married to Dominick Trant, who in 1787 killed Sir John Conway Colthurst in a duel. (For Trant's 1787 pamphlet, see the Introduction to this section, above.) Mrs Jeffereyes and Sir John (a neighbour at Blarney and, like James St John Jeffereyes, an ardent developer of local industry) were particularly regarded as being 'gentry Whiteboys', that is, the wealthy patrons of agrarian resistance to tithes and clerical payments generally. In such incidents as that in which Mrs Jeffereyes employed several thousand Whiteboys to drain the lake at Blarney, she drew down the wrath of her brother (in 1787, he was attorney general) who evidently put an end to her radical exploits. However, Mrs Jeffereyes remained something of a local character; she and her son George Charles Jeffereyes went to law with mutual accusations of libel (with less precise allegations laid against her of murdering three patients in Simpson's Hospital, Dublin) in 1809. In the only published record of this apparently abandoned lawsuit, Arabella Jeffereyes is named as 'Lady Arabella Jeffries Groves' (see *A Full and Accurate Report . . . the Prosecution of the Countess Dowager Annesley and Lady Arabella Jeffries Groves against George Charles Jeffries Esq., and David Foley. . . .* (Dublin: Cox, 1811)). In evidence cited therein (p. 9), one man is reported to have declared 'I am not one of Mrs Jeffries "blackguard relations".'

It seems clear that Milliken's 'Lady Jeffreys' is more than a comic figure in a nonsensical song, and that any stanza added to ridicule the Earl of Donoughmore was facilitated by the poem's half-concealed political codes. The song's omission from a Cork collection of Milliken's work also indicates that these codes still had a power to give offence as late as 1823.

LEONARD MacNALLY

(1752-1820)

The Lass of Richmond Hill (1789)

On Richmond hill there lives a lass
More bright than May day morn,
Whose charms all other maids surpass
A rose without a thorn.
This lass so neat with smiles so sweet
Has won my right good will,
I'd crowns resign to call her mine,
Sweet lass of Richmond hill.
Sweet lass of Richmond hill,
Sweet lass of Richmond hill.
I'd crowns resign to call her mine,
Sweet lass of Richmond hill.

Ye zephyrs gay that fan the air
And wanton thro' the grove,
Oh! whisper to my charming fair
'I die for her and love'.
This lass so neat . . . etc.

How happy will the shepherd be
Who calls this nymph his own.
Oh! may her choice be fix'd on me,
Mine's fix'd on her alone.
This lass so neat . . . etc.

Stanza 1: Richmond is on the Thames, about eight miles south-west of London. MacNally's first wife, a Miss I'Anson, lived there, although the poem is also associated with gallantries addressed to a daughter of the Duke of Richmond. See the biographical note on MacNally at the end of this section.

JOHN WILSON CROKER

(1780-1857)

[John Wilson Croker will be remembered mainly for his acidic criticism written for the *Quarterly Review* and for his incomparable knowledge of the course of the French Revolution. However, his youthful exercises in anonymous pamphleteering deserve attention.

In the first series of extracts printed below, Croker is employing the long tradition of 'the oriental traveller' whose reports on European civilization are mock-naive and deeply satirical. Although the tradition dates back to Montesquieu's *Lettres persanes* (1721) and earlier, it was the Irishman, Oliver Goldsmith, who most suavely exploited the technique for a satire of British manners. Croker, by comparison, is less urbane. However, the city on which he turned his youthful yet already chilling eye was post-Union Dublin, where local literary endeavour was in a temporary decline.

The year 1808, when the second pamphlet by Croker excerpted here was published, saw the beginning of a new phase in the campaigns for catholic emancipation. The Irish whigs, led by Henry Grattan, presented catholic petitions in the united House of Commons; these were rejected, despite a proposal (voiced by George Ponsonby (1755-1817) MP) that an accommodation between the British government and the Vatican allowing the former in effect to veto episcopal appointments. Later in the year, the Irish catholic bishops also rejected the proposal. Croker's pamphlet, discussing emancipation, appeared amid an upsurge of publications on the topic. It is said that Spencer Perceval (1762-1812), then chancellor of the exchequer, was so impressed by Croker's presentation of his case (which Perceval actually rejected) that he arranged for the young man's advancement in the civil service.]

from: AN INTERCEPTED LETTER FROM J——T——ESQ., WRITER AT CANTON, TO HIS FRIEND IN DUBLIN, IRELAND (1804)

All their public buildings are, what we should call, ill placed; some, for instance, stand so close to the river side, that one should get into a boat to see them, and there is no boat to be had. Others are stuffed into such wretched alleys, that in order to get any view of them, you must ascend into the opposite houses, and the owners of the opposite houses are not always willing to admit you.

Some are built obliquely to the streets which lead to them, and in other cases the streets are laid out at angles with the buildings.

Of their principal temples one is surrounded by slaughter houses and butcher's stalls, and the other is the chief ornament of a trunk-maker's back yard.[1]

The palace of the Great Counsel, called §*Li-pou*, which is now held in *Pe-kin*, is considered as the finest piece of architecture in China, and indeed it is scarcely possible to behold it, without the liveliest feelings of admiration, but unluckily the *Money-brokers* have purchased it as a chamber of commerce, and have set about altering it to their *own fancies*, by pulling down a magnificent colonade, which not long since cost the Li-pou near †60,000 *ta-hels* to erect. I thought at first, that the money-brokers expected the colonade to refund in the pulling down, the prodigious sums which had been expended in building it, but I am informed that they have no such mercenary motives, and that this lamentable destruction is a pure effort of their *taste*. Confess, my Friend, that though we must not dispute about tastes, it is a pity that money-brokers should meddle with the fine arts.[2]

The annual revenues paid by this city to the Imperial treasury, amount to nearly three million *ta-hels*,‡ yet the harbour is so bad, that scarcely a winter passes without the loss of many valuable lives, and (what the Chinese *feel* more) many valuable ships. Some enlightened mandarines have indeed proposed plans for making an artificial port, where vessels may take refuge in stormy weather; but it is feared, that the great expense will deter the Government from this desirable undertaking; I cannot, however, be of this opinion, as I am told, that as much money as would have completed a considerable portion of this object, has been within the last year expended in building fortified towers, to defend a shore, which as some *military* mandarines assert, it is impossible that an enemy could approach.[3] Of this I can be no competent judge, but I *can* see, that it will be very *satisfactory*, if the Malays and Cochin-Chinese, (with whom we are at present at war,) will have the *generosity* to come up the river of Quang-tcheu, to be blown to pieces, when the greater part of the coast of the province is perfectly at their service.

If we are to form our judgments from the number of their shops, the Quang-tcheuese are some of the richest people in the world; if we argue from what these shops profess to contain, they would appear to be the most elegant and tasteful, but the truth is, they are neither one nor the other; few of these shops are rich or well assorted; some of them have indeed a striking appearance at first from the profusion of fine things exhibited at their windows, but when you find that this show is always the same, that the identical articles are exposed to day that were exposed this day twelve months, you are inclined to fear, that this stationary splendour is not a certain proof of great riches or refined taste, and in truth the best of their warehouses are these which sell you, at second hand and at double price, the fineries and luxuries of Pekin.[4] I am even afraid that the first principles of trade are not here generally understood, for instead of that decent civility which so often forces you to buy what you do not want, you are too frequently received with a sullen surliness; nor do all the tradesmen seem to have discovered the secret that enriches our Irish shopkeepers, that small profits and quick returns are better than extortion and stagnation. — But however inferior to us they may be in business they most wonderfully excel us in dignity; and it is not uncommon to see a shopkeeper sitting behind his counter in all the solemn state of a mandarine, and this indeed is but the *lex talionis*,[5] for you can hardly

§"The Chief Council of Mandarines which superintends laws and customs is called *Li-pou*."
† About £18,000 sterling.
‡ About £900,000 sterling.

1. Christ Church cathedral, Dublin.
2. The *Li-pou* is the Irish parliament, which, by the Union of 1801, was moved to London. Irish members thereafter sat in the united imperial parliament. The parliament building had been erected in 1729-32, and despite the post-1800 alterations upon which Croker dwells here, it remains perhaps Dublin's finest eighteenth-century building. After the Union, it was sold to the Bank of Ireland (Croker's 'money-brokers'), who were obliged by the terms of the sale to alter the façade.
3. These are the Martello towers which form a linking series around Dublin bay, their purpose being the rapid transmission of signals, rather than a substantive defence of the city. (The name derives from Cape Mortello in Corsica.)
4. Dublin as a deposed capital, forced to follow London's fashions, was a recurrent theme in the nineteenth century.
5. the law of retaliation.

imagine how many of the mandarines look like shopkeepers.

It is a custom here to give names to their warehouses as gentlemen in Europe do to their country seats, and those names are always of strict propriety, as you shall judge. One of them is named the Temple of Fortune, and in this a man sells you small scraps of paper inscribed with certain talismanic characters, and this paper, as the vender promises, will produce you a prodigious fortune.[6]

6. i.e. lottery tickets.

from:
A SKETCH OF THE STATE OF IRELAND, PAST AND PRESENT (1808)

XXXVI. 4. On the subject of catholic emancipation all men speak and write, but few candidly — its supporters and its opponents are equally injudicious or unjust; the reason is, that the parties of the state have divided the question between them; and contest it, not for its sake, but their own: it is the means, not the object of the war.

The Roman empire was divided into two factions, and the green and the blue distracted the civilized world.[1] Did the civilized world bleed for the colour of an actor's coat, when they seemed to do so? No. They bled for their party, not for its Symbol. Catholic emancipation is the green and blue of Ireland, the colour of the division, not the cause. This, Emmett[2] and Mc. Nevin,[3] liberal, sagacious, and well informed, have admitted: though Keogh,[4] Newport,[5] and Parnel,[6] furious, shallow, and bigotted, deny it.

How else could half a nation so pertinaciously seek, and the other half refuse an almost empty privilege? How else can it have happened that every concession has produced commotion, and complaint encreased as the grievance disappeared? Twenty years ago there was much to desire, and to refuse, and the catholic code was scarcely thought of: there now remains, unconceded, nothing in which the *people* are concerned. Yet to the catholic code is attributed all our misfortunes. The truth is, the parties have made the question, not the question the parties.

XXXVII. Let us review and refute the sophisms of both; and the first of the emancipators. 1. 'The merits of the catholics.' — What merits? They have been loyal in 1745 and 1797; perhaps in 1798 and 1803;[7] but if they were — as they were not — unexceptionably loyal, what is the merit? Is it a virtue not to be criminal; is, not to rebel, supererrogation? Admit, however, the merit; has it not been already rewarded? A century of penalties remitted in half a score of years, is it no boon? Admit, still, that the reward was inadequate; We then ask, was the catholic so much *more* loyal than the protestant, that the latter should be stripped of his ascendancy to clothe the former. The conclusion is, that he, who vaunts his loyalty as a merit, has little merit in his loyalty, and that when catholic merit is pleaded against the ascendancy, protestant merit should be pleaded for it, and a balance struck. 2. The emancipators allege 'the force and power of the catholic body,' and apply the argument doubly; offering assistance — or threatening opposition. What new assistance can we have? Two-thirds of our military are already catholics; because two-thirds of our population are so. If the proportion of catholic soldiers and sailors be greater, it is and will be so, because they are the poorer sect; poverty, in all countries, takes refuge in the armies; nor would catholic emancipation make one man in Ireland a soldier, who had wealth enough to remain a citizen. Thus vanishes their promised aid. Their hostility I do not fear. The catholic force can never be united against the present establishments of law and property; and, if it should, it would find that physical strength is not the best part of power. 3. It has been alleged that 'all our disturbances have

1. Green and blue were the colours used by opposing parties in the ancient Roman circuses.
2. Robert Emmet (1778-1803), United Irishman, leader of the abortive 1803 insurrection in Dublin. Or his brother Thomas Addis Emmet (1764-1827), United Irishman, emigrated to the United States of America.
3. William James MacNeven (1763-1841), United Irishman; arrested in 1798; subsequently emigrated to the United States of America.
4. John Keogh (1740-1817), wealthy Dublin catholic leader.
5. Sir John Newport (1756-1843), MP for Waterford 1803-32.
6. William Parnell (later Parnell-Hayes; died 1821); his *Historical Apology for the Irish Catholics* had been published in Dublin in 1807.

7. These are the dates of crises for the British government; in 1745, Charles Edward Stuart, the Young Pretender, landed in Scotland and raised a rebellion, though catholic Ireland made no effort to follow suit; 1797 saw disturbances in (mainly protestant) Ulster; 1798 and 1803 brought outright rebellion, but the first of these was by no means exclusively catholic, and the leadership of the second (much smaller) affair was protestant.

sprung from the hardships under which the catholics labour'; What is this, but to say, that they are *not* patient and loyal — that the rebellions and massacres, which we hoped were political, have all been *catholic*; the works of a perverse and pestilent sect, incapable of gratitude, unworthy of indulgence, unfit for toleration. Such is the false and detestable allegation of the partizan, espousing the catholic cause without affection, and calumniating his friend to dupe his opponents. But let *us* not charge upon the catholic as a crime, the frenzy of his advocate. 4. 'The moral unjustice of the catholic laws' is vehemently urged but not easily proved. The papists, when able, proscribed the protestant: the victorious protestant copied the papist statute against its enacters. We may doubt that this was wise, but not that it was just. Who pities the inventor and victim of the brazen bull?[8] 'But it is unjust,' the catholics add, 'that the minority of a people should restrict the majority, which majority we are.' True, numerically, as two exceed one. But if rank, property, education, industry, skill, manners, intelligence — the essences of a nation — be estimated, they are, of Ireland even, a weak minority; as, both numerically and morally, they are of the empire at large.

8. Perillus the Athenian made a bull of brass for the tyrant Phalaris as an instrument for executing criminals. Phalaris, much impressed by its ingenious cruelty, tested it on the inventor himself, who was shut in the machine and baked to death by means of fires lit under it.

Finally, their plea should be, not of their force, nor of their numbers, but of their moderation, liberality, and innocuous tenets; if they prove the former, without the latter, they prove against themselves.

XXXVIII. Their adversaries have but little advantage over them in the argument. The fear of the protestant, like the complaint of the papist, comes too late. It strains at the gnat, having swallowed the camel.

I can well conceive why Lord Clare[9] would have strangled papist privilege in its birth; why he feared to make the first plunge down the declivity of concession; why he refused power to the numerous and dangerous. But I cannot conceive, why, we should now feel this after-alarm; why having rushed down precipes, we stop short at a slope; why we indulge the populace, and restrict the few, the rich, the noble, and the loyal.

If we fear the revengeful bigotry of the papist, let us not exasperate, without disarming him. The influence of the gentry and priesthood, let us conciliate or unnerve; we are in a practical dilemma. We must resume all that we have granted, or grant all that we retain.

I, confidently, advise the latter course.

9. John Fitzgibbon (1749-1802), 1st earl of Clare and lord chancellor of Ireland from 1789; implacable opponent of concession to catholics, and architect of the Union.

JOHN GAMBLE

(*c.*1770-1831)

from: SKETCHES OF DUBLIN AND THE NORTH OF IRELAND (1811, 1826)

[Little is known of John Gamble, and most of his published work took the form of travel literature and historical fiction. The example that follows illustrates some of the powers of observation and inclination to categorize that inform both kinds of writing. Gamble was a northern supporter of the United Irishmen, or at least, a supporter of their general policies. His presentation of Dublin, in the first of the chapters reprinted below, genuinely possesses a degree of external impartiality without the presumption of superiority that vitiated many contemporary British travellers' accounts of the Irish capital. His view of Ulster, on the other hand, is really that of a native, despite the maintenance of a traveller's perspective. Gamble's characterization of Ulster presbyterians and catholics is worthy of note, not simply because it contributes to the growing body of comment cast in terms of psychological types or even quasi-racial distinctions, but because it is the work of someone whose political commitments were to secular radicalism.

The historical novel, as Walter Scott was shortly to demonstrate, thrived on antagonistic divisions, rival camps and irreconcilable differences, and the world Scott depicted was very different from the complexities of class society as it was gradually unfolding in the wake of the Industrial Revolution. For Scott, the English Middle Ages, the seventeenth century in Scotland, and even the Jacobite rising of 1745, provided ample evidence of a hierarchical society in a state of crisis. The thrust of his imagination, however, emphasized the redundancy of these past conflicts for the generation who read his novels. Irish writers such as John Banim (*The Boyne Water*, 1826), Gerald Griffin (*The Invasion*, 1832), and Sheridan Le Fanu (*The Cock and Anchor*, 1845) adopted the Scott model, but found that the survival of such conflicts into the Irish present sabotaged attempts to produce an Olympian perspective on history. In addition, and by an ironic compensatory mechanism, their efforts to imagine an Ireland that predated middle-class tensions sometimes led them to disguise (or even deny) the existence of those tensions in the present. In the case of Le Fanu, there is ample evidence of a subjective, even personal, stratum of allusion running through fictions allegedly set in the seventeenth or eighteenth centuries. Gamble's writings form a significant prelude to these exercises in historical fiction partly because he is more attentive to the existence of a middle-class dimension to Irish society, and partly because he is himself caught up in the categorizing of religious denominations as contrasting mental attitudes. In the last pages of Gamble's *Sketches*, a curious anonymity is imposed on certain figures, as if they were to be treated not so much as particular people whose careers might be verified but as if they were references in a manifest fiction masquerading as real human beings. Reading these passages is like having a bird's eye view of certain isolated, strategic stages — preliminary stages, no doubt, but important ones — in the making of a genre, the Irish historical novel.

For reasons explained in note 11 to Chapter XXVIII below, the first edition (1811) of this work is very scarce and the passages that follow are taken from the second edition of 1826.]

CHAPTER IX

Style of living in Dublin — Society — Professional men — Barristers — Progress of luxury — Hospitality — Inference from the number of beggars.

Dublin

I am come here at an unlucky period — visiting Dublin in August is as bad as going to the country at Christmas — the town is as bare of company now as the trees are then of leaves, or the earth is of verdure. Fashion has prodigious influence in this metropolis; and the gentry, merchants, and tradesmen, think it incumbent on them to pass the summer out of town, because the fashionables of London go at that season to watering places. Notwithstanding the gaiety of Dublin, I do not think a stranger would find it a pleasant residence after its novelty has subsided; — there is, no doubt, much hospitality, and, on slight introduction, he may get many dinners;[1] but, as ostentation mingles in its full proportion with kindness of heart in these invitations, this hospitality is rather a holiday suit (if I may so speak) than a plain jacket; it is drawn forth on state occasions, but is too costly for every day's wear. The usages of Dublin make it necessary to give dinners, often beyond the income of the entertainer; who, in his ordinary mode of living, probably pays the penalty of his occasional profusion. He never wishes, therefore, to be taken unawares, or to expose himself to the chance of being caught at his humble meal of mutton and whiskey punch by the man who a few days before had feasted with him on venison and claret: a stranger, therefore, does not find his hospitality a resource at the time he wants it most — in the hour of languor and lassitude, when it would be so agreeable to have a house to step into on the footing of unreserved intercourse.

Nor does the public life perform what the private denies: the *savoir vivre*[2] is but moderately advanced in Dublin: there are none of those comfortable eating-houses in which London so much abounds, where one often meets rational and agreeable society, and has a good dinner at a reasonable price; without being obliged to swallow a quantity of sloe-juice, which the courtesy of England denominates wine. The taverns in Dublin are either so miserably low that a respectable person cannot be seen going into them, or are equally extravagant with the most expensive London ones. The lodging-houses, with some exceptions, and I have been lucky enough to get into one, are liable to the same objection: they are either barracks, which the mop seems never to

1. The visitor was often invited home to dinner by people willing to display their own prosperity or keen to listen to his views. Note how this chapter opens, not only with a list of topics which summarize its contents, but also with a 'date-line', Dublin, to convey the impression that the author was writing as he travelled. These lists of topics did not appear in the 1811 edition.
2. Good breeding, relaxed and elegant conduct.

have visited, or beyond all reason extravagant. In all these and various other conveniences, London abounds to a degree that makes it, of all other places, the most agreeable residence for a man of small fortune: nor is there, perhaps, a town in the world, where a man, who hangs loosely by society, can glide more gently down the stream of time, or where, if he cannot greatly enjoy, he can *endure* life better. Dublin has another great disadvantage: paradoxical as it may appear, it is too small for retirement; a stranger can never long remain so; curiosity busies itself about his profession, his fortune, and manner of living, until every thing about him becomes known: he may be said, therefore, to be too much on his good behaviour. This, as far as morality is concerned, is perhaps an advantage; but in various minor matters of economy it is attended with many evils: a man, watched by eyes more numerous and wakeful than those of Argus,[3] can neither eat, drink, nor dress, as he likes; he cannot live for himself, but for the world. Places of amusement are not numerous here — until lately there was but one theatre; and even that resource will not continue many days longer, as it shortly closes for the summer: drinking will then be the only amusement; and it is not half so good a summer as a winter one. The weather just now is insufferably warm, and wine is by no means so agreeable a beverage as water: I shall, therefore, leave this in a day or two, to breathe the cooler air of the northern mountains, where excessive heat is as rare as adultery. A traveller can no more quit a town, however, than he can turn off a servant, without giving it a character — like an epilogue, after a new play, it is always expected of him. — In conformity, therefore, to immemorial usage, I shall say a few words of the general state of society and manners in Dublin; though, when I speak, I had better perhaps remain silent; when I seem to move, I may make little progress; and when I flatter myself with giving a group, I may only sketch a few individuals.

There are few resident nobility in Dublin. Irish Nobility is a sickly and delicate plant: like the myrtle, it does not do in this northern climate: it thrives only in the sunshine of court favour: it is not a noun-substantive kind of greatness; it cannot stand by itself; it leans for support on the minister, who often finds the propping-up of this tender vine an embarrassing and expensive species of gardening. People of large landed property are equally rare: these gentry, like swallows, take an annual flight to England, where they hop about from London to Weymouth, from Bath to Cheltenham,[4] till their purses are as empty as their heads; when they return to wring further sums from the hard hands of their wretched tenants, who seldom see them but on such occasions. The learned professions may be therefore said to form the aristocracy of Dublin — law, physic, and gospel, take the lead here, and give the ton[5] in manners, as well as in morals and literature. These three professions go hand-in-hand; though haud passibus æquis:[6] law is always the foremost. A physician can be but a knight, or, at the best, physician to the Lord Lieutenant: a lawyer may be Lord Chancellor, and rule the Lord Lieutenant himself: — the wool-sack is a very comfortable seat, far softer than the bench of a bishop, and therefore much higher in public estimation.

The Irish bar contains many men of shining abilities: the eloquence of Mr. Curran is well known and generally admired; Mr. Bushe, the Solicitor-general, is considered an able reasoner and sound lawyer; and Mr. Plunkett, the late Attorney-general, is an admirable public speaker, either at the bar or in parliament.[7] The style of the Irish bar is different from that of the English. It is less solemn and decorous, but more lively and animated, more glowing and figurative, more witty and sarcastic; it reasons less, it instructs less, it convinces less, but it amuses more; it is more ornamented, more dramatic; it rises to the sublime, it sinks to the

3. Argus was a king in Greek legend who had a hundred eyes, only two of which closed when he slept.

4. Weymouth, Bath and Cheltenham were fashionable resort towns in England.

5. the tone, the fashionable style.

6. not with equal steps.

7. John Philpot Curran (1750-1817), Charles Kendal Bushe (1767-1843), William Conyngham Plunket (1764-1854). In the 1811 edition, reference to Plunket is followed immediately by the following (omitted from the 1826 edition):

> This gentleman, however, was severely reprobated for his conduct on the trial of Mr. Emmet, for high treason, about seven years ago. Mr. Plunkett [*sic*], who was then only King's Counsel, conducted the prosecution against this unfortunate young man, with a rancour and virulence which shocked and surprised every person acquainted with his obligations to his father and family. Mr. Plunkett's reasons for this conduct have never been made known, though it injured him very much in public estimation. Crown lawyers have at all times been of the blood-hound tribe; they seldom lose scent of their prey, either from considerations of gratitude or humanity. . . .

humorous, it attempts the pathetic — but in all this there is too much of the tricks of a juggler. I do not say that an Irish advocate thinks less of his client than an English one, but he appears to think less; he appears to think most of himself — of his own reputation, of the approbation of his brethren, the applause of the spectators, and the admiration of the court. I dare say I should be most gratified by specimens of eloquence taken at the Irish bar, but were either my life or my fortune at stake, I should like to be defended at an English one.

In society the Irish lawyer is equally amusing; there is a mixture of gentlemanly manners and professional acuteness; of gay repartee and classic allusion, which makes him often an instructive, and always an agreeable companion. Yet even here it is easy to remark the traces of the defects I have mentioned: a rage to shine, and disposition to dazzle; his wit cloys by repetition, and his allusions are often forced and far-fetched — difficultly found, and not worth the trouble of seeking: he is too fond of antithesis, likewise, and says smart, rather than sensible things; specious rather than solid things. This disposition, however, to be witty rather than wise, is not confined to the gentlemen of the bar, but is universal through the city. In every party I have been in, talkers were many, and listeners were few; and wit, or what was meant to be such, was bandied about with the bottle, or the cards. As many of these would-be wits had little pretensions to it, we had often to laugh when there was no joke, and much merriment when there was little reason for it. They are great punners, and to do them justice, I heard some excellent ones. I should recommend the editor of a fashionable print, who seems so partial to this species of humour, to import a quantity for the use of his paper, as the stock on hand is of the vilest kind. I am not clear, however, but that this constant effort after wit produces beneficial effects in Dublin society. It animates the man and sharpens his faculties, and makes him alive to the approbation of those about him; — he is the complete reverse, therefore, of the lazy, lounging man of fashion in London; who holds it the essence of ton to be haughty, silent, supercilious, and indifferent; who, unlike Falstaff, is not only not witty himself, but a damper of it in others; who sits by the side of genius without a wish to be instructed by it, by the side of venerable old age without a desire to contribute to its comforts, and by the side of beauty, which he surveys with the scrutinising look of a jockey at a horse-fair, without the smallest effort to make himself agreeable.

The lower classes of the inhabitants of this city have afforded abundant materials to the dramatist, as well as to the tourist. They are represented as a wrong-headed and a warm-hearted, a whimsical and eccentric kind of people who get drunk and make bulls,[8] and who cannot open their mouths that something funny and witty does not come tumbling out, like pearls, every time she spoke, from the lips of the fair princess Parizade, in the Arabian Nights' Entertainments.[9] I do not deny that there may be some foundation for this character; but if I am to judge from what I have seen myself, it is greatly exaggerated. A Dublin shoeblack,[10] like a London one, may sometimes utter a quaint or witty saying, which the uncouthness of his appearance, and the singularity of his accent, may render more striking; but I should suppose most of the stories told of him are without any foundation; and that their authors give as recollection, what is only invention.

Luxury has made as great progress among people in business here, as in any other place I have ever visited. A shopkeeper gives splendid entertainments, and his wife elegant routs,[11] in which her own manner and appearance, that of the females she invites, and the costliness and embellishments of her furniture, would bear comparison with persons of a much higher rank; nor does her husband acquit himself with less propriety at the foot of his table, or in the drawing-room. In this respect the Dublin shopkeeper has infinite advantage over the London one: in morals he is not, I believe, inferior, but in manners he is decidedly superior; he is cheerful and easy, frank and unembarrassed; in conversation he is lively and pleasing — he may not have much to say, but the manner is excellent; his ideas, from the nature of his profession, are not numerous; but, like the goods in his shop, he possesses the art of showing them off to advantage. The universal prevalence of good-

8. A bull is a verbal error unperceived by the speaker, who conveys a meaning (often ludicrous) that he or she did not intend.
9. *The Arabian Nights* was still relatively unknown in the English-speaking world in 1811, the standard European editions deriving from Antoine Galland's *La mille et une Nuits* (1704-12). Lane's (expurgated) English edition did not arrive until 1840.
10. Someone, usually a boy, who cleaned shoes in the street or in hotels.
11. Large evening parties or receptions, much in vogue in the eighteenth and nineteenth centuries.

breeding, among all descriptions of respectable people in Dublin, must strike the most unobservant spectator: to assign a plausible reason for it would not be easy. I should attribute it in a great measure to vanity; to a slavish imitation, and servile admiration of fashion and rank, which lead them to adopt their prejudices, to echo their opinions, to copy their manners, and to boast of their acquaintance. Vanity, indeed, seems the prominent feature of every inhabitant of Dublin: he is vain of himself, vain of his city, of its beauty, of the splendour of its public buildings, and of its vast superiority over London. In this respect, doubtless, he is deserving of praise, which he would get more readily, if he did not demand it so imperiously. The difference between a citizen of London and Dublin seems to be this: the latter is vain, and the former is proud; he has a lofty opinion of his country and of himself; he never dreams that this can be disputed; and, satisfied with it himself, is indifferent even if it should: the latter is not so assured of a ready acquiescence to his claims, either for his city or for himself; perhaps he is not so well assured of them himself; nor if he were, could he exist so well on his own resources. His advantages and superiority must be reflected from the eyes, the tongue, and consideration of others, to make them truly valuable to himself. In this observation, however, I do not deny but that I may be refining too much, and that Dublin vanity only strikes me more, because I am accustomed to it less. In the account I have just been giving, I beg leave to be understood I only comprise the Protestants; I have not seen a sufficient number of Catholics to form a decided opinion of their character; though I have seen enough to be convinced that there is a considerable difference between them and the Protestants.[12] — In their air and manner, in their ready acquiescence, and smiling civility, I think I perceive the traces of the thraldom in which they have so long been held; while in the erect and upright step of the Protestant we recognize the freeman. We recognize something more — we perceive the lofty bearing of an individual of a cherished caste, situated in the midst of a rejected one. We may imagine an Englishman in the East Indies, or a Creole in the West; or if we wish to be further fanciful, we may try to imagine a Norman knight about two centuries after the Conquest, when he was beginning to regard those around him as his countrymen.[13]

The citizens of Dublin (Catholics I believe as well as Protestants) are hospitable: how much of this is benevolence, how much ostentation, is an ungracious point for a man who has benefited by it to decide; nor does it admit of easy decision. I shall be tempted, however, to give them credit for a considerable portion of the former: if some alloy mixes with the gold, if the statue is partly brass, and partly clay, it is the same, perhaps, with most of our virtues, and most of our actions. This hospitality, however, compared to what it was in former times, is much on the decline: — writers like me, who cheerfully eat their dinners, and allow them no credit for giving them, may have some share in this; but the increasing pressure of the times, which makes it every year more difficult to support a family, is probably the great reason: along with this, hospitality is seldom to be met in excess in any town, when it comes to a certain magnitude, or in any community, at a certain point of civilization. But if hospitality has diminished, charity remains: were the faults of the inhabitant of Dublin ten times greater than I have described his foibles, he has charity enough to cover them all; his foibles he has in common with others, his charity is peculiarly his own. I know of no spot in existence, of the size of the city of Dublin, where there is such unbounded munificence: in London, no doubt, there are many valuable institutions for the relief of distress, — and God forbid I should undervalue them, — but still it must be remembered, that much is compulsory, and not meritorious; much the mere consequence of boundless wealth: the man who rolls on guineas may well bestow farthings on the poor. But the charity of Dublin is not strained:[14] it is not founded on acts of parliament; it is not weighed and measured by the standard of law; nor is it the gilded offering, the filleted and garlanded sacrifice of

12. It is hard to believe that Gamble encountered any difficulty in making contact with catholics living in Dublin, and his comment should be read either as a reflection of the official status credited to protestants (in relation to the city corporation), or as a means of contributing to a kind of narrative persona, or (least likely) as evidence of his personal choice in seeking company.

13. Here the quasi-racial characterization is explicit, though not without unexpected details — for example, the citing of a Creole as a superior figure in the West Indies. 'Creole' was used to indicate the descendant of Europeans in central America, but was more often used of someone of 'mixed' origins.

14. cf. Portia's speech in Shakespeare's *The Merchant of Venice*, IV. 1. 184: 'The quality of mercy is not strain'd....'

wealth. It gives not on compulsion, it gives not from a hoard. The waters of the Liffey do not bear, like the waves of the Thames, the riches of the two hemispheres; the inhabitants of its banks have no Eastern mines of gold; but they have what is better still — they have humane and benevolent hearts.

The number of beggars in Dublin is remarked by all travellers, and is said to prove its poverty. Admirable reasoners, who see nothing but on one side! — Does it not prove its charity likewise? There are few beggars in London: what is the reason? — there is little poverty, perhaps, will be the answer: — Is that so? — is that indeed so? — is there really little poverty in London? — Alas! there is much; much suffering, much sorrow, much want in every quarter, in every lane, and in every street — but there are few beggars — if there were many they would *starve*....

CHAPTER XXVIII

Society in the north of Ireland — Character of the Northerns — Instances of their success in life — Colonel T——— Lord Moira's commendation of Ulster — Female manners — Conclusion.

A———.

Since writing my last I have met with a slight accident. I must confine myself for a few weeks to my chamber, and forego the pleasure I proposed to myself, in visiting the Giant's Causeway.[1] I hope to enjoy it, however, on some future occasion. As it is probable, therefore, I may again resume this subject, I shall only make (in addition to those I have already made) a few general remarks on the inhabitants of the north of Ireland.

In other parts of Ireland, it is to be lamented that there are only two classes in society, and that the third, which is the best, is wanting — it is not wanting here. But there are not only three classes, but it may likewise be said, three nations. The gentry, who are the English Irish. The merchants, shopkeepers, and manufacturers, who are the Scotch Irish, and the servants, small farmers, and labourers, who are mostly composed of the native Irish. The second class is the most rational, the most enlightened, and by far the most industrious body; equally removed from the extremes of want and wealth, it is in the middle state, between poverty and riches, in which the royal preacher wished to be placed.[2] It must be admitted, however, that profusion on the one hand, and the exactions of landlords on the other, are inclining it to the side of poverty. In most other countries the gentry give the tone to society; it is the middle class (in a great degree, at least,) that gives it here — it is the link which unites the other two: to a certain degree, correcting their errors and softening their hatreds. In consequence of this, the gentry of the north are milder in their manner, 'and bear their faculties more meekly,'[3] than in the west and south of Ireland.

It is, therefore, among the Presbyterians of Ulster that the provincial character is to be sought; and I am happy to be able to remark that, after attentive examination, I find their virtues far more numerous than their defects. In general they are great readers of the Bible. It is the first book that is put into their hands, and all their ideas take a tinge from it, and often their phrases; they are accustomed to reflect, and to talk on the doctrines it contains, and are, therefore, great reasoners on theological, as well as on other subjects. A simple countryman has been known to stand up in the meeting-house, and address the preacher, on what he called false doctrine.

There are few great farmers; the country people are mostly weavers, and have a few acres of land only. This is the ancient, and almost patriarchal mode of life, more favourable to happiness and morality, to national prosperity, though not perhaps to bloated national greatness, than any other. The character and appearance of the English people have been materially injured by crowding such immense numbers of men and women into vast manufactories in large towns. The children of such people are weak, ricketty, and generally as deformed in mind as in body. I have remarked that ricketty people are almost always malevolent. Envy, perhaps, may have some share in this.

1. The Giant's Causeway is a large and striking formation of exposed basalt columns on the coast in County Antrim, popularly believed to reach under the sea to Scotland, and used by giants in their journeys to and fro. Note that at the beginning of this chapter, Gamble is much more guarded about his exact location in Ulster; he has *not* visited the Causeway, and thus the A———., standing for the place from which he ostensibly writes, may not be Antrim.

2. 'Give me neither poverty nor riches.' Proverbs 30.8.
3. cf. Shakespeare *Macbeth*, I. 7. 17: 'Hath borne his faculties so meek....'

The better class of country people[4] live in great abundance; wine is not much used, but they have great plenty of what they like better, and what is, perhaps, better adapted to the climate, which is whiskey punch. They are slovenly in their habits, and an Englishman would often feel disgust at the state in which their houses are kept. These are in general large unhewn masses of stone, with little ornament without, and little cleanliness within. Only what is necessary is attended to, utility alone is thought of, rarely beauty. A northern farm-house, therefore, is an accurate resemblance of the northern character; it is a picture without a frame, a bed without a curtain, a drawing-room without a carpet. It is astonishing how little idea Presbyterians have of pastoral beauty; the Catholic has ten times more fancy — but a Presbyterian minds only the main chance. If he builds a cottage, it is a prison in miniature; if he has a lawn, it is only grass; the fence of his grounds is a stone wall, seldom a hedge; his garden has kale,[5] but rarely has flowers; nature may give him the honeysuckle, but he seldom plants the rose.

The truth is, that a Presbyterian has a sluggish imagination: it may be awakened by the gloomy or terrific, but seldom revels in the beautiful. The sweet delusions, therefore, with which fancy loves to deck poor, weak, naked human nature, he is a stranger to. For this reason works of poetry are little relished by the Northerns. I know of only one instance of a poet of any eminence being born here: Farquhar, the author of the Beaux Stratagem, and other esteemed dramatic works,[6] and I should suppose from the name that he was of an ancient Irish family. This latter remark may appear fanciful, but it is just. The ancient Irish retain, with the names, much of the ancient expression of feature, and much of the ancient character. When a descendant of one of them marries a woman of Scottish blood, we see, in the children, the varied predominance of Scottish steadiness and frugality, or Irish thoughtlessness and impetuosity, as their features resemble either of the parents. This is a most curious circumstance, and a man of observation, who resided long enough here to collect a sufficient number of facts, might throw much light on a very dark subject. The natives of the place never attend to this, and would, probably, laugh at it if it was proposed to them. Men never think strange what they are long accustomed to, but they think strange, probably silly, the man who thinks it so. The peasant, perched on some alpine cliff which overlooks the precipice, does not admire the wisdom of the Englishman, who forsakes his verdant meads to climb those perilous rocks, and shiver in that boundless snow. The fisherman, whose hut is on the strand, sees no grandeur in the ocean, feels no terror from the tempest's roar.

In the Northern character there is much probity, much integrity and friendliness; but it has few of the lighter virtues which grace many other nations. It is estimable, therefore, rather than amiable; it is desirable more as a friend than acquaintance; it is a piece of massy[7] plate, valued for its weight and solidity, but not for its fashion. Man is, here, more as he came from the hands of nature: rough and headlong, boiling and bubbling from the rock, he is like one of his own mountain torrents, which dashes against immense stones, rude projections, and has not yet formed to itself a passage and bed; he has not the mild and mitigated tones, the gentle manners, which now characterise English society; he is more peremptory in contradiction, more familiar in his address, and louder in his laugh. I do verily believe, paradoxical as it may appear, that Irish morals (I mean northern Irish) are preferable to English, but in manners they are far short of them. But this, perhaps, is unavoidable; we cannot have the graces of perfect civilization with the manly virtues of a less advanced state. We cannot at once smell the blossoms of spring, and gather the fruit of autumn. Nor, perhaps, is this very high polish of civilization desirable. Time, which mellows the colours of the picture, destroys likewise the canvas on which they are laid.

Though the Northerns possess so little suavity of manners at home, I know no people who acquire it sooner abroad, or who sooner get rid of their provincial features and accent. They have been very successful in making their way in England, by regular and combined effort. Their conduct is orderly and proper; but as their original accent is Scotch, and they soon acquire an English one, they are seldom taken for natives of Ireland: nor, when

4. The term 'country people' covered all those who lived in the countryside (as opposed to towns) excluding the gentry and clergy; in other words, the common people.

5. cabbage.

6. George Farquhar (1678-1707) was born in Derry. *The Beaux' Stratagem* (1707) was his last play.

7. A literary word for 'massive'.

the prejudice against that country is considered, is it very wonderful that they should not be in a hurry to claim connexion with it? Ireland is therefore in a great measure deprived of the advantage of their good character. Several most respectable physicians in London are natives of this part of the county, but hardly any of them are known there to be such. Lord Castlereagh[8] is another strong instance of the facility with which they acquire the manners of Englishmen. When Lord Melville,[9] and other Scotchmen, were high in office, even at the time their conduct was most approved of, they were viewed with some jealousy by the people; but Lord Castlereagh blended more naturally with them; his politics might not be approved of, but there was no feeling of national distinctness either in him to them, or in them to him. Little as I approve of some parts of the public conduct of this noble lord, I am happy to bear testimony to the many estimable qualities he displays in private life. I know from unquestionable authority, that on more than one occasion during the late rebellion, his *humanity* saved those whom justice would have condemned. A poor lad, the son of a blind harper, wandered barefooted and barelegged a few years ago from the town of Strabane: he returned some time afterwards, a reverend Dean of the church, and is now a Bishop.[10]

Colonel T———, chief secretary to the commander-in-chief, is another fortunate Northern. He went into the army at a very early period of life, unknown and unfriended.[11] The polish of his manners, the elegance of his address, and the integrity of his conduct, soon procured him patrons. The Duke of York, in a particular manner, took an active share in promoting his interest. He sent him as military secretary along with General Whitelock, to South America.[12] After the unsuccessful termination of that expedition, he took him into his own office at the Horse-Guards. In the discharge of its duties, Colonel T——— has given universal satisfaction; he presents a fair picture of the Northern character, modified no doubt, by early association with the army and people of rank. He is not deficient in that judicious *assentation*,[13] without which it is impossible long to please any great man; yet with none of the servility of which the Scotch have been accused. The native Irish, from their want of this assentation, seldom make their way well in life: not that they are incapable of flattery, but their habitual flightiness makes it liable to many interruptions. The folly or passion of an hour, oftentimes destroys the labour of years.

Long before the abolition of the slave-trade in the West Indies, it was put a stop to in the island of St. Helena by the indefatigable exertions of the governor, who is a native of the county of Cavan, in

8. Robert Stewart (1769-1822), 2nd marquis of Londonderry, but better known as Viscount Castlereagh; foreign secretary 1812-22.
9. Robert Melville (1527-1621), 1st baron Melville, a Scottish diplomat who served during the reigns of Elizabeth I and James I, and who was prominent in the Scottish monarch's retinue after James's accession to the English throne in 1603. Note how Gamble parallels Castlereagh in London with figures from the period of England and Scotland's first constitutional convergence.
10. Gamble, as a native of Strabane, Co. Tyrone, may have privileged information here. However, among the bishops of the Church of Ireland living in 1811, I have been unable to identify one who fits this description.
11. It is difficult to make out what is going on in this passage. 'Colonel T———' might be presumed to be Sir Henry Torrens (1779-1828), who was born in Derry, was military secretary to Whitelocke (see note 12) in 1807 and (later that year) was appointed assistant military secretary to the commander of the forces, the Duke of York, being promoted secretary in October 1809. However, it seems that Torrens was only promoted a colonel in the army in February 1812, i.e. later than the period of which and in which Gamble originally wrote. The 1811 edition has a distinctly unfriendly simile at the conclusion of this passage:

    destroys the labour of years, *like a good cow which gives plenty of milk, but has a careless heel*.

The italicized material does not appear in the 1826 edition, but indicates the narrator's attitude towards 'Colonel T———' in an unmistakeable manner.

Another candidate for the distinction of being 'Colonel T———' is Sir Herbert Taylor (1775-1839), who certainly fits *some* aspects of the description: he was private secretary to the Duke of York when the latter was commander-in-chief; moreover, he served in Ireland (1798-99) as secretary to Lord Cornwallis when he was lord lieutenant. However, Taylor was English and not Northern Irish, and he was far from humble by birth.

The problem may not essentially be one of tracing factual data. Gamble's attitude to Colonel T———'s personality is ambiguous (see note 13), and his emphasis on the colonel's talents for pleasing the great may relate to Taylor's career not only as secretary to the Duke of York, but subsequently to George III, and the queen. It may be relevant to note here that Gamble got into trouble with William Conyngham Plunket (1764-1854), sometime attorney general, by including in the first edition of the *Sketches* the gist of a remark attributed to Robert Emmet concerning Plunket — 'that viper my father warmed in his bosom'. (See note 7 to Chapter IX above; by commencing legal proceedings, Plunket forced the publishers to withdraw unsold copies.) In other words, Gamble had some appetite for verbal in-fighting, and he may well be settling personal scores both here in relation to 'Colonel T———' and in relation to the Strabane-born bishop. On the face of it, there is no reason why two individuals who are apparently being lauded for their successful overcoming of humble origins should not be named in what purports to be a factual tour, more or less after the manner of Arthur Young.
12. John Whitelocke (1757-1833), lieutenant-general; failed to recapture Buenos Aires in 1807, cashiered in 1808 following a court-martial in which his military secretary, Torrens, was required to give evidence.
13. Obsequious gesture or act of assenting.

this province.[14] He had much misrepresentation, obloquy, and even danger to encounter; but his philanthropy made him regardless of them all. On such conduct comments are unnecessary. To the virtuous belongs a reward superior to the praises of men — the approbation of their own hearts; yet I cannot forego the gratification of inscribing on those pages the name of Colonel Robert Brooke.

Lord Moira,[15] in one of his speeches in the House of Lords, said, that there was more information in the province of Ulster, than in any other country in the universe of equal extent. This, I think, is exaggerated praise; they are (as far as my observation extends) a rational and thinking, rather than a reading people; their natural good sense, however, enables them to talk with great propriety on most subjects of conversation. They are, if I may so express myself, workmen who do much with few tools; they are musicians who ring many changes on few bells. I know of but one periodical publication in the whole province; a magazine printed in Belfast; a work replete with sound sense and just observation, delivered in plain and perspicuous language. In these respects, it is a striking contrast to the general run of Dublin compositions; the authors of which, from their eager solicitude to please, often fail to do it: they substitute tinsel for gold, and shadow for substance; the matter is overwhelmed with its ornaments; the man is smothered in his armour. I have often, on reading a page of fine writing in a Dublin newspaper, exclaimed, with the Greeks of old, 'what is all this to Hercules!'[16] If my advice had any weight with these gentlemen, I should recommend them 'more matter with less art.'[17] The desire to be brilliant, and to dazzle, is too obvious, and is almost universal. The judge on the bench, and the bishop in the pulpit, are equally guilty of it. They write and speak of a subject, but they think of themselves. They resemble a handsome servant-maid, who appears busy in putting the flowers in her mistress's head, but is all the time adjusting herself in the mirror before her.

It would be unpardonable in a sketch of this kind, not to say a few words of the ladies. In general they are fair and well-looking. They are not unsuccessful copyists of English fashions, and have a good deal the appearance of English women. If there is a shade of difference, it is that their features are larger, and their persons rather more masculine. They are very fond of dancing; in which they display more vivacity and rapidity of movement than elegance or grace. This, perhaps, may be no evil. Young women who are taught the steps of opera-dancers, are often apt (if I may be allowed the pun) to make *false steps*. — They are chaste in a degree that hardly any country this day can boast of. Adultery, or an intrigue even, is unknown among females in the middle class. A married woman may be violent, may be a termagant;[18] an unmarried one may be pert, may be ignorant, may be flippant, but they are

> Chaste as the icicle
> That hangs on Dian's temple.[19]

To an Englishman, as may be easily conceived, the plainness of their accent would at first be unpleasant. But his ear would soon accommodate itself to it, perhaps even find beauty in it; a great beauty in a female, an apparent freedom from affectation and assumption.

The northern Irish accent, as I have elsewhere remarked, is neither a Scotch nor an Irish one, but a mixture of both, as the people are. Their pronunciation is broad, with a considerable degree of asperity in some places, and with some degree of it in all. In common with the inhabitants of every other part of Ireland, they give the letter *a* the open sound in almost all those words in which the English give it the long and slender one. In the course of this work I have marked the very general substitution of *i* for *e*. Another peculiarity of their pronunciation, is an unpleasant thickening or doubling of the letter *r*; thereby rendering this rough and jarring consonant still rougher and harsher.

14. Robert Brooke (died 1802), a member of the Brooke family of Rantavan, Co. Cavan, and thus a relative of the novelist Henry Brooke (*c*.1703-83) and his daughter Charlotte Brooke (*c*.1740-93), the translator; he was attached to the East India company, tried unsuccessfully to develop a model industrial village at Prosperous, Co. Kildare; afterwards he was appointed governor of St Helena.
15. Francis Rawdon-Hastings (1754-1826), 1st marquis of Hastings and 2nd earl of Moira, opposition politician and soldier. In March 1799 he made a notable speech against the Union.
16. cf. Seneca, *Hercules Furens*, line 1262.
17. Shakespeare, *Hamlet*, II. 2. 95.
18. A termagant was originally a violent and unreasonable deity, often introduced into morality plays, and whose name was attached to women of a similar disposition.
19. cf. Shakespeare, *Coriolanus*, V. 3. 65:

> Chaste as the icicle
> That's curdied by the frost from purest snow,
> And hangs on Dian's temple.

As I have already mentioned that the native Irish in this province are mostly servants, small farmers (cotters, in Irish phrase), and labourers, it would be unfair to judge the general character by men in their situation. They appear to me to have many of the good qualities, and many of the bad ones, which have been attributed to them. They are warm-hearted, friendly, cheerful, and affectionate; but they are regarded with distrust: they are, therefore, cunning; they are drunken, and in that condition, turbulent and quarrelsome; long trampled on too and oppressed, they are subservient when they are not turbulent, and thoughtless of remote consequences, and fondly attached to the country, to the soil, which they deem their own, they eagerly take land at any rent, and bow down before greatness, or its representation, in all that lowliness of prostration which delegated greatness in a particular manner so loves. In a contest for land, therefore, they are as sure to outbid, as, of late years at least, they are to be preferred to their more unbending Presbyterian antagonists; and scarcely are they settled when they take wives, and beget children to inherit their miseries, and possibly to avenge them.

The Presbyterians of Ulster will, I have no doubt, be found by every traveller who views them without prejudice, to be what I have described them, a sedate and orderly people. Whether they are so because they are Presbyterians, or are Presbyterians because they are sedate and orderly, I shall not positively determine; but I should suspect the latter. Men at length settle into the religion the best suited to their temperaments, as every man after forty is said to be his own best doctor. Modes of religion are modified by disposition and climate, and those which are adopted by one people, would be rejected, and with reason, by another. The cold and unadorned religion of Scotchmen would little suit the warm and glowing imaginations of Italians or Greeks. Religion is uniform and universal; the modes of it partial, and as varied as our countenances and complexions, — of no more importance (could men be brought to think so) than the garment of the preacher. The pure and benevolent heart is the only offering worthy of the Deity, and equally acceptable, I trust, whether it ascends from the Catholic chapel, or the Protestant cathedral; the Turkish mosque or the Pagan temple; the gorgeous dome of civilization, the clay-built altar of the savage, or the barbarous hut of the Esquimaux.

CHARLES ROBERT MATURIN

(1782-1824)

from: WOMEN; OR, POUR ET CONTRE (1818)

[As a novelist, Maturin is remembered primarily for his Gothic masterpiece *Melmoth the Wanderer*, published in 1820. At a lower level he is acknowledged as the author of some 'Irish' novels of wild incident, but *Women* is rarely accorded more than a passing word of comment. It is true that it is an oddity in its author's literary production, being concerned with urban middle-class life, with methodism, and with female central characters. But, as the subtitle declares, this novel is also an investigation of powerful oppositions, written when Irish society was undergoing complex realignments in the wake of the 1798 rebellion, the Union, and the Tory hegemony of the Napoleonic era. The story tells of two women's love for the same man, and in the end these women (or one of them at any rate) learn that they are mother and daughter. Two men love the younger of the women, and in addition to these over-abundant romantic entanglements there is the rivalry of protestant and catholic attitudes: the elder women (named Zaira) is a singer by profession, closely associated with continental values, and passionate by nature; the younger (Eva Wentworth) is repressed and pious. By the time that Zaira learns (from her own mother, a colourful hag with a gift for ringing phrases even on her death-bed) that her long-lost child is Eva Wentworth, Eva herself is expiring. The man whom they have both loved, De Courcy, does not long survive her, dying at the age of nineteen.

Intelligent interest in *Women* can be restricted to two very different matters: (a) certain events that predate the official action and that are summarily related only in the closing pages; and (b) fictional dialogue, its absorption of evangelical idiom, and its display of rival temperaments. The latter can be observed in the early chapters; the first chapter records how De Courcy meets Eva in a strange encounter involving screams, carriages and rustic cottages; the second (printed below) brings the two together again in church, their hands jointly holding a tiny hymn book, a scene that recurs throughout nineteenth-century English fiction with insipid regularity. The third (also printed in its entirety) shows us De Courcy among the evangelicals who have adopted the waif-like Eva. The plot is too prolix for summary, and it seems preferable to treat the later stages of the novel through analysis here rather than through a further extensive selection from Maturin's uneven and meandering prose. Some details of the ultimate dénouement are helpful, for they illustrate how the apparently trite or uncontrolled incidents of Maturin's novel relate to larger patterns in modern Irish culture. The exotic Zaira finally goes to her dying mother, and learns that her own child had been a girl who is still alive. The old hag (Eva's grandmother, that is) tells how Zaira's father had been given the infant at birth, and also tells how he died.

It is this proto-history that is significant:

> 'There was a child, that the foreign villain you married took from you the minute it was born, and sent to your father; he did not care whether it lived or died. Your father gave it to a woman he knew nothing about, except that she went about helping the poor, and teaching them her own religion, (but it was not the true one,) on the condition that he never saw or heard more of it or you.'
>
> 'My father!' said Zaira ... 'But he is dead.'
>
> 'He is!' said the hag.... 'He brought all his bastards into the house, after you left him to marry that foreign rogue, (he was of the true church, however, more's the pity.) Well, where was I — oh! — they lived together like the devils in hell — they drank, and cursed, and fought by the hour — and one night they quarrelled in their drink, and one of the boys, his favourite, struck him, and the devil was strong in him; he knocked his old father down, and dragged him by his grey hair to the head of the stairs; and when he was a-dragging of him, (your father,) along by the hair, the old man cried out, and he said, "Oh, drag me no further than the stairs, for there *I dragged my own father*, but no further." The cry of the father sobered the boy; he saw what he had done and his father lying at the feet of him, and he ran back to the room, where there was a loaded piece ... and he shot himself through the head....' (Vol. III, pp. 394-96)

Two patterns are discernible here, and the link between them constitutes one of the central though submerged themes of Anglo-Irish literature. Quite openly, the old woman indicates the difference in denomination between those to whom the infant was born ('the true church', as she regards catholicism) and those to whom she was entrusted ('not the true' religion, that is, methodism). But, in a far less open way, another pattern is at work in the relatively brief précis of the hag's narration, with crucial events following upon each other in rapid and suggestive succession. Zaira's foreign husband is instantly replaced by her father at the infant's birth; that father then distances himself from the infant and its mother, and is violently assaulted by a bastard son who shoots himself at the shouted recollection of an earlier patricidal attack. The novel makes it clear that the recent attack both symbolically and actually results in the father's death as well as his son's:

> 'He was the father's *darlint* (after you) — he heard the shot — and he never spoke a word more, but to say, "that shot went through my heart, though he [only] struck me." He never spoke more than that till he died. That was his end....' (Vol. III, p. 396)

In the first pattern, shame attaches to the transfer of a child from one denomination to another; in the second, a kind of mimed incest (father replaces husband) and all-but explicit parricide results from drunken debauchery. With James Clarence Mangan's translation of Zacharias Werner's *The Twenty-Fourth of February* acting as a go-between (see p. 1212), similar dual patterns surface again in W.B. Yeats's play *Purgatory* (1938). However, in Yeats's dramatic scheme of things, offence against class — the Old Man is the son of an alliance between a stable groom and a lady of the 'Big House' — has replaced denominational treason.

The larger significance of Maturin's *Women*, then, lies in its treatment of the interaction of class, denomination, and altering codes of taboo. The novelist's penchant for the Gothic and the wild undoubtedly has damaged his attempt to portray the mores and the conversational style of his drawing-room Dubliners. His very lack of masterly control — the male term is deliberate — appears to admit evidence of historic changes all too frequently denied in Irish literary discussion. These include the growth of a middle class and the disguise of this in relation to protestantism. But, more particularly, the now polarized catholic/protestant relationship is seen increasingly as a paradigm of exclusivist difference rather than of resemblance and comparison. The growth of methodism and of evangelicalism generally in Dublin can be traced earlier than 1818 — John Wesley began his Irish tours in the 1740s — and the link between proselytism and the treatment of orphans, foundlings and abandoned children also reaches well back into the eighteenth century. The date that Maturin chose for his fictional setting — 1813 — was important both in relation to the campaign for catholic emancipation and for altering attitudes towards catholicism among protestant groups who (like the catholics) lay outside the Establishment. The date is aptly chosen, even if the exact political manoeuvres cannot be traced on the pages of the novel. But, in a broader sense, it was in the three decades between the Union and the granting of catholic emancipation that the infinitely tighter link between sexual taboo and denominational exclusivity was forged under the ideological auspices of protestant ascendancy; indeed the knots were drawn so tight as to become practically invisible, except in such instances as the lumpy prose of Maturin's fiction. The role of methodism (the term is used fairly loosely by Maturin) in *Women* is important not for any chronological priority it may have in the annals of Irish fiction, but in its tense conjunction of emergent forms of social control within the conventions of an emergent genre, the nineteenth-century Irish novel. Gerald Griffin's *The Collegians* (1829) in some respects offers an antithetical view of denominational relations in the context of property, class and sexual liaison.]

CHAPTER II

Te captam somniis teneo.[1]

This constant uneasy contemplation retarded his recovery. In the evenings he was particularly lonely and depressed; and one evening in particular saw Montgomery going to leave him with a reluctance which he was ashamed to avow.

'Where are you going, Montgomery?'

'To Bethesda Chapel,[2] to the evening lecture.'

'They say you are a Methodist,' said De Courcy, laughing.

'If I minded what fools said of me, I should have a fine time of it,' said Montgomery, bluntly.

'Take me with you, provided always you do not convert me,' said De Courcy, hiding his unwillingness to be alone under a forced laugh.

'If God does not convert you, man never can,' said Montgomery. So they went both of them together.

Bethesda Chapel was crowded; the pressure in the aisle soon separated De Courcy and Montgomery; and the former continued standing till he was almost exhausted. An elderly lady, towards the close of the sermon, opened a pew-door, and, by a courteous motion, invited him to enter; his figure and appearance, unlike any in the place, had struck her; and when she saw him often remove the thick hair from his pale forehead, on which the drops of weakness were every moment bursting out, she felt affected by this contrast of youth, gigantic height, and apparent debility. He accepted her offer; but still continued to stand in fixed attention to the preacher, and this circumstance pleased the old lady. She turned her eyes often towards him, and wished him well. The sermon ended; and the hymn, in which many of the congregation joined, began.

Close to De Courcy, the tones of a voice more soft, more rich, more plaintive, and more pure, than it seemed possible for human organs to utter, 'rose like a stream of rich distilled perfumes.'[3] Ignorant of music as a science, but 'tremblingly alive'[4] to its influence, he listened; — the voice, strengthening with the joining voices of the congregation, and aided by the swell of the organ, sounded so distinctly, that De Courcy, starting, for the first time perceived a young female standing beside him, whose simple dress, low stature, and slight figure, had hitherto escaped his observation. Her face was completely concealed by her large bonnet, and her figure lost in a dark pelisse, and her whole appearance was so petite and obscure, that De Courcy bent to listen whether those delicious sounds were indeed uttered by her.

As he leaned near her, the young female, with that liberty which seems to inspire confidence, but not to express it, offered him her hymn-book, and pointing with her white finger to the page, pursued her sacred song with as little emotion as if her sister held the other leaf. De Courcy bent over the book, which was so small that their hands almost touched each other; his eyes, fixed on the white fairy fingers so near, wandered over the lines without distinguishing them; — that thrilling voice so close to him, those tones that seemed to turn the very air into music, gave him sensations of delight, such as Milton felt when he said, '*Intremuit læto florea terra sono*.'[5] He did not wish for some moments to catch a

1. *Recte* 'ego somniis iam captum teneo' (Each night in my dreams I hold you captive): Horace, *Odes IV*, I, 37-38.
2. In Biblical times, Bethesda was an intermittent spring near the sheep-gate of Jerusalem (see John 5. 2) where Christ performed miracles. The name (meaning 'house of mercy') was adopted widely for non-conformist chapels and meeting-halls. Dorset Street in the north of the city was the site of the Dublin establishment of this name. It was closely linked with evangelically minded students and fellows in Trinity College, Dublin. At one point, the college provost forbade his students from attending services at the chapel.
3. John Milton, *Comus*, line 555.
4. Fanny Burney, *Early Diary 1768-1778*, speaks of 'the agonising sensibility which is tremblingly alive to each emotion of sorrow' (3 July 1771).
5. John Milton, 'Elegia tertia. In Obitum Praesulis Wintoniensis' [Elegy III. On the Death of the Bishop of Winchester], line 58. An English

glimpse of her face — he felt as if the present moment were to last for ever — as if the sounds which he then heard were never to cease. It was only at the conclusion of the hymn (when the lady attempting to withdraw the book, which he still held unconsciously, looked up with a slight expression of surprise) that he beheld a countenance which gleamed on him like a vision of the past. The ringlets of pale gold, curling like the untortured locks of childhood, falling over her cheek, like the shade of brilliant foliage over a bed of blossoms; the eyes of Heaven's own blue, in which every feeling of the pure heart was written, and not a feeling that might not be avowed to men and angels; the lips, over whose young roses no breath but of devotion had ever sighed; her whole aspect reflecting the mild glory of that holy harmony, whose last notes trembled on her half-open lips, and her glance so suddenly raised, so suddenly withdrawn, — he recognised all — it was herself — the very female he had saved — she evidently did not know him, — he was much altered by his illness, and this was the first time he thought or felt he was. He still continued to gaze on her, as we watch the sleep of a beautiful infant, delighted with its calm unconscious beauty, and feeling that when it awakes it will turn to us with looks of love.

The congregation were dispersing; the elderly lady and her young companion made several unassisted attempts to open the pew-door; at length De Courcy recollected himself, and attempted to assist them, but his trembling hands only increased the difficulty, and Montgomery, who was in the aisle, was obliged to release the party. As they went out, the young lady, with a motion that seemed rather the result of religious benignity than of worldly courtesy, turned and slightly bowed to De Courcy. He saw once more those eyes that breathed of heaven; and the unuttered sound that trembled on her lip had more of sweetness than any that courtly politeness ever breathed or dictated; and the grace of her fairy form, as it glided down the aisle, left him without power to follow her but with his eyes.

'I am much altered,' said he to himself, 'yet *she* might have known me'; and a feeling like pride mingled in his determination not to claim her notice. He watched her; — she turned and looked steadily at him; — a smile of bright and timid pleasure trembled over her beautiful features for a moment, the next she appeared to grow very weak, and caught the arm of the elderly lady for support, while she feebly extended one hand towards De Courcy. He rushed forward and caught it; the elderly lady appeared alarmed, and Montgomery looked on in silent amazement; for some moments he thought that De Courcy's delirium had returned, and a considerable time elapsed before a short and hurried explanation introduced them to each other. There was much embarrassment in the manner of the elderly lady as she indistinctly alluded to the eventful night of Eva's danger, and pressed De Courcy to allow her family an opportunity of expressing their gratitude to him under their own roof. Charles bowed in silent delight, and they then separated.

De Courcy wandered away alone; he wished to be far from the city, from its inhabitants, from all mankind if possible. At length he felt himself in the country; the cold clear splendour of a winter night was around him; he was at last alone with his own heart, and its new-born inmate, passion in its first purity and brightness. He communed with himself and was still. Oh, what gleams of heaven burst on the soul in such a moment, when creation seems renewed, and we awake to an existence so new, so bright, so delicious, that the very elements seem to harmonize with our feelings; and the stars, and heaven itself, appear to hold a silent alliance with the thoughts that are burning within us! He looked round him, and the earth, though in darkness, appeared lovelier to him than in the brightest noon of a summer's day. He looked upward, and wondered that the stars had never appeared so resplendent to him before. He sighed, and felt respiration itself a delight. He tried a thousand times to utter some name that seemed at the bottom of his heart, but knew not what name to call on; — his whole mind seemed but one idea — his whole existence but one feeling; — a glow like that of summer pervaded his whole frame, and he trembled with a grateful consciousness of life he had never known before. It was so late when he awoke from his delirium, that he found on his arrival at the College[6] the gates were shut. One

translation might read, 'The flowery earth quivered with a joyful sound.'

6. i.e. Trinity College, the sole college of the University of Dublin. The gates were closed at a certain hour, and resident students had to report late.

might have supposed his situation comfortless enough as he leaned against the iron railing till the gates were opened; but those moments were perhaps the most delicious of his existence. What dreams were his? — The dreams that passion sheds but once on the heart before its purity has received a tinge from the senses, or its ardour can anticipate the possibility of disappointment or infelicity!

CHAPTER III

πικρου δ' ερωτος ησσηθησομαι[1]

EURIPIDES

The next day, at an early hour, De Courcy was in Dominick Street;[2] he easily discovered the house — it was a handsome, but a very grave-looking one. The name of 'Wentworth,' was on the door. There are some houses that seem to bespeak their inhabitants, and De Courcy had a kind of feeling that this was one of them, at the moment he touched the knocker. He was shewn into a room furnished plainly, but in a manner that shewed if luxuries were wanting, wealth certainly was not, and in a few minutes Mrs Wentworth entered the room. He had not leisure to observe her, and the bare circumstance of her being an inmate in the same house with that object, gave an indescribable interest to the observation. She appeared about fifty years of age; her person was plain; but her clear commanding eye, the severe simplicity of her manners, and a consciousness of perfect sincerity accompanying every word she uttered, and communicating itself irresistibly to her hearers, made one respect her the moment they beheld her, and love her a very few moments afterwards. Withdrawn and recollected from the embarrassment of the preceding night, her manner appeared comparatively cold, but it was rather the coldness of habit than of character; there was more, too, of the measured and limited phraseology of the evangelical people in her conversation; but when she continued to speak for any time, one easily saw that the range of her mind was far more extensive than that of the objects to which it was confined. She herself appeared to feel this self-imposed constraint, and to escape from it from time to time, but soon returned again; and the final impression which she left was that of strong sense, rigid rectitude of principle and conduct, and a temper and heart naturally warm, but subdued by the power of religion.

She expressed herself with earnest gratitude to De Courcy for the preservation of her niece, and then made the most minute and searching enquiries into the events of that strange night. During the detail which De Courcy gave, she was so much agitated, that he would have paused had she not urged him to go on, with an earnestness very remote from curiosity.

'And can you possibly, madam,' said De Courcy, 'guess at the authors or the motives of this outrage?' Mrs Wentworth was silent. — 'It is a most mysterious proceeding,' said De Courcy, anxious to relieve himself from this embarrassing silence.

'There is a mystery'; said Mrs Wentworth, speaking almost involuntarily, and while she spoke she shewed so much agitation, that the subject was dropped as if by mutual and tacit consent.

The silence that followed was broke by the entrance of Mr Wentworth, in whom De Courcy recognized the uncle. The appearance of this man almost dissolved the spell which appears to us to hang over every object dwelling under the roof of those we love, and attracts the heart irresistibly, even to inanimate things, which they have consecrated by a touch or a look. His manners were repulsive, his understanding narrow, and his principles inflexibly rigid; his mind was rather tenacious than strong; what little he knew, he knew thoroughly, and what he once acquired he retained for ever. Early in life he had made a large fortune with a spotless character, and having retired from business, found his mind utterly vacant; by the persuasion of his wife, he was induced to listen to the evangelical preachers, and (as is often the case with converts either in early youth or in advanced life,) in a short time he far outwent his preceptors. Calvinism, Calvinism was every thing with him; his expertness in the five points would have foiled even their redoubtable refuter, Dr Whitby[3] himself; but his theology having obtained full possession of his head, seemed so satisfied with its conquest, that it never ventured to invade his heart. His mind was completely filled with a system of doctrines, and his

1. 'I shall be vanquished by a bitter love', *Hippolytus*, line 727. Phaedra is speaking.
2. A fashionable Georgian residential area in north Dublin.
3. Daniel Whitby (1638-1726) published his *Defence of the Nicene Faith* in 1718.

conversation with a connexion of phrases, which he often uttered mechanically, but sometimes with a force that imposed not only on others, but on himself. In this state he was perhaps as happy as he could be, for he had a gratifying sense of his own importance, and his conscience was kept tranquil by listening to or repeating sounds, which to him had all the effect of things. Never was Mirabeau's acute remark, that 'words are things,'[4] more strongly verified than in the case of Mr Wentworth's religion.

Mrs Wentworth introduced them to each other, and, hoping to warm her husband's coldness, was loud in her praises of De Courcy's courage and humanity. Mr Wentworth listened with the impatient air of a man who is waiting to speak himself; and then turning to De Courcy, exhorted him to consider himself under every dispensation, whether or providence or grace, as the humble and worthless instrument of Divine Power.

'I trust, young man, that you consider yourself (though the preserver of my niece,) as not a jot higher in the divine eye than those who were probably leagued against her life. They may yet be as brands snatched from the burning, and so, through Divine Power, may you.'

De Courcy, unused to this language, could only answer by silent blushes and bows; but these bows and blushes became him much, and Wentworth at once set him down as a convert. Mrs Wentworth, who felt as much for her husband as for him, was beginning to express her regret that her niece could not thank him in person, and her surprise that so long an interval had elapsed previous to his introduction, when Montgomery entered the room, and enquired after Eva with all the familiarity of *l'ami du famille*.[5]

De Courcy felt thunderstruck. By a tenacity as strong as it was unaccountable, he had never mentioned to Montgomery the events of that extraordinary night. It floated in his imagination like a vision; and Montgomery, occupied by his attention to his patient, had never believed that any intercourse existed between him and the Wentworth family, till their brief and singular introduction at the Bethesda Chapel, the preceding evening. Mrs Wentworth answered his enquiries after Eva, and then, apparently forcing herself to give some account of De Courcy being present, said, in a low voice and hesitating manner, that the family owed him unspeakable obligations for the services he had rendered Eva. Montgomery instantly extended his hand in frank and cordial gratitude, though he was totally unconscious of the nature of the services alluded to. De Courcy gave his in return, but it was with a coldness he could not account for; the ardour of Montgomery's enquiries had infused a chillness into him, which, while he disdained himself for, he could not resist. At this moment they would have been delighted to have exchanged situations; Montgomery would have wished to be her preserver, and De Courcy to be her friend. He soon after retired, not without a warm invitation from Mrs Wentworth to dine with them on the following day; it was as sincerely, though not as warmly repeated by Mr Wentworth, and De Courcy accepted it with a delight he dared not express.

'We do not live in the world,' said Mrs Wentworth, in a qualifying manner; 'there are only grave quiet people to be with us; but at your age I trust you are rather governed by your feelings than by the world in your choice of society.'

'I trust,' said Wentworth, 'he is governed by neither, but by grace.' And so they parted.

The next day he dined at Dominick-Street, and found that Mrs Wentworth's qualifying manner was not without a meaning, for he was introduced to a class of society whom he had never before met with. A large evangelical party dined at the house, (for the evangelical people remunerate themselves for renouncing the mixed assemblies of the world by frequent meetings among themselves,) and the men and women were unlike any men and women De Courcy had ever encountered before. The women all dressed with the utmost simplicity, with absolute plainness, arms covered to the wrists, and necks to the ears; no distinction of appearance between maid and matron, except that the former wore their hair very simply arranged; and the latter, however young, had their heads invariably covered. The men — they neither paid the general attention to women that is usual in mixed companies, nor separated in groups to talk of politics; they sat apart 'on their chairs sublime, in thought more elevate,

4. Mirabeau, Honoré-Gabriel Riqueti (1749-91), was an orator and politician prominent in the early stages of the French Revolution. The quoted phrase can be found, however, in Byron:

But words are things; and a small drop of ink,
Falling, like dew, upon a thought, produces
That which makes thousands, perhaps millions, think.

Don Juan, III, 88.

5. Correctly, *l'ami de la famille*, the friend of the family.

and reasoned high.'[6] De Courcy heard terms used by them, some of which he did not understand, and others which he did, he thought quite unfit for loose and general discussion. He felt himself quite disconsolate; and approaching a gentleman who stood leaning against one of the windows, he ventured a few observations on the position of the allied armies, then sufficiently interesting and critical, for *it was in the close of the eventful year* 1813.[7]

'Very true, sir,' said the gentleman, with a contraction of countenance that appeared to De Courcy quite pantomimic, 'very true; you are speaking of the downfall of the power of Buonaparte, but have you ever thought of the means of overthrowing the power of Satan, and extending the kingdom of Christ?'

Dinner was announced at the end of this triumphant sentence, — the party mixed, — the dinner was excellent, but without parade; the first course contained the substance of two or three more splendid but less substantial. De Courcy remarked particularly the man who had rebutted him just as they went down to dinner. He was tall, but very ungraceful; a strange consciousness of importance mingled itself most uncouthly with his coarse figure and awkward manners; his hair was red; his eye small, but keen and piercing; his voice powerful, but not melodious; most repulsively softened when he addressed females, to whom, however, he paid obvious attention. He never spoke but on one subject; and on that his eloquence was over-powering, and his information profound, but it was only on one side; he was a sturdy orthodox Calvinist, skilful in argument, vehement in declamation, and amply equipped with weapons from the old armoury of Geneva, well furbished by modern artists, which he wielded with equal force and dexterity. But his manners, his habits of disputation, and even his pulpit oratory, powerful as it was, were strongly tinged with the original vulgarity of his origin and nature.

He was the son of a poor labourer, the tenant of a wealthy gentleman in Cork, whose wife was evangelical; she instructed the children of her husband's tenants in her own system; her husband gave her no disturbance; he followed his fox-hounds all day, and damned his wife's Methodism over his claret all night. The good lady went her own way, and discovering in this lad, maugre[8] his fierce red hair and bare broad feet, evident marks of his being 'a growing and gracious character';[9] and astonished at the fluency and eloquence with which he repeated his acquired creed, and gave the word of exhortation to his ragged family, wondering round the mud-walls of his native cabin, and exhorted the old women (who gossipping, squabbling, and even drinking forty yards distant from the chapel door, fell on their knees in the mire at the tinkling of the bell which announced the elevation of the Host) to turn from the error of their ways, and seek the Lord. — She proposed a subscription[10] among her friends to enable him to enter the university, and be qualified 'to minister at the altar.'

The subscription went on zealously, and young Macowen entered college; but when once there, *his views*, as they were called, expanded so rapidly, that no Church Episcopalian, Presbyterian, or Independent,[11] had the good fortune precisely to suit his sentiments in orthodoxy of system, or purity of discipline. Thus he moved a splendid and erratick meteor, shedding his light on the churches as he passed, but defying them all to calculate his orbit, or ascertain his direction. In the mean time, it had been suggested to him that many evangelical females, of large fortune, would not be unwilling to share his fate. This hint, often repeated and readily believed, threw a most odious suavity into his manner; his overblown vulgar courtesy was like the flowers of the poppy, all glare and stench. Under

6. The last seven words are found as line 558 of Milton, *Paradise Lost*, Book II. The inclusion of the first three within quotation marks may be a printer's error.
7. In this year, Wellington's army entered France, and thus signalled the approaching end of the Napoleonic empire. Eighteen thirteen was a crucial year in the dispute concerning the terms on which catholic emancipation might be linked to a government veto over the appointment of catholic bishops by the Vatican.
8. From the French *malgré*, in spite of.
9. It seems likely than this and other phrases in quotation marks are thus indicated to stress that they are fossil-phrases, that is, the conversational stock-in-trade of persons like those in the novel. They frequently have the effect of conveying the sanctimonious tone of the implied speaker.
10. A subscription was a fund (or contribution to a fund) raised from a number of people to finance a specific project or publication: subscribers underwrote the project by promising funds in advance.
11. Three divisions of the reformed church, differing mainly on issues of church government. The first was ruled by bishops; the second favoured rule by the presbyters of individual churches within a framework of sessions under the general assembly; the third originally stressed the autonomy of congregations and gave rise to several different sects and sub-groups.

these circumstances, he had become the intimate of the Wentworth family; and from the moment he beheld Eva, his feelings were what he could not describe, and would not account for even to himself, but what he was determined implicitly to follow. His system took part with his inclinations, and in a short time he believed it a duty to impress her with the conviction that her salvation must depend on her being united with him. When a perverted conscience is in league with the passions, their joint influence is irresistible.

There is, among the evangelical people, an establishment something like the Court of Wards, abolished under James the First;[12] a determination to dispose of wealthy unmarried females to distinguished professors or preachers, who are not equally favoured by fortune, and the families of the former conceive themselves not only honoured, but benefited by the exchange. Thus the evangelical system is rapidly assuming the aspect of the papal, and, by the union of intellectual influence with actual wealth, bids fair to rival it in power as well as in pretensions. On this Macowen relied much, and, strange to say, on his personal advantages still more. He had been strongly recommended to the Wentworths, and held in the family something like the office of director[13] in a Catholic continental family; but from the moment he beheld De Courcy, he felt his influence shaken. His beauty, his youth, his distinguished services, — the enthusiasm of feeling that trembled in his slight and graceful form, — the broken music of his firm mellow voice, as he addressed even the relatives of Eva, — the deep but vanishing crimson of his cheek, as for a moment, at the end of his hurried enquiry after her, his eye fell on herself, — and the sudden dropping of his white eyelids, with their rich, dark, humid fringe, through which the eye spoke more than words could utter — all this Macowen saw, and looked at him askance, 'with jealous leer malign.'[14] The dinner went on; the men and women, seated alternately, spoke of their popular preachers, and of popular works of evangelical divinity, and of eloquent speeches made at the meetings of the Bible Society,[15] and of the diffusion of the gospel throughout Ireland; and they uttered sundry strictures on the parochial clergy who opposed the circulation of evangelical tracts, with many a by-blow at the contrast between the Calvinistic articles of the Church of England, and the Arminian creed[16] of her modern sons.

Such was the conversation; and when the women retired, it was not a whit more enlarged. One man talked incessantly of the 'election of grace,' his mind literally seemed not to have room for another idea; every sentence, if it did not begin, ended with the same phrase, and ever subject only furnished matter for its introduction. Dr Thorpe's last sermon at Bethesda was spoken of in terms of high and merited panegyric.[17]

'Very true,' said he; 'but — a — a — Did you think there was enough of election in it?'

A late work of the same author (his clever pamphlet on the Catholic petition) was mentioned.

'But does he say any thing of election in it?'

'There was no opportunity,' said Mr Wentworth.

'Then he should have made one — Ah, I would give very little for a book that did not assert the election of grace!'

Once seated in his election-saddle, he posted on with alarming speed, and ended with declaring, that Elisha Coles, on God's Sovereignty,[18] was worth all the divinity that ever was written. 'I have a large collection of the works of godly writers,' said he, turning to De Courcy, 'but not one work that ever was, would I resign for that of Elisha Coles.'

'Won't you except the Bible?' said De Courcy, smiling.

'Oh, yes — the Bible — ay, to be sure, the Bible,' said the discomfited champion of election; 'but still

12. Intended to foster English habits and protestant beliefs in those committed to its care, the Court of Wards was abolished in 1662 under Charles II, not under James I.
13. A priest acting as spiritual adviser to a powerful individual, family or institution. Not a confessor.
14. John Milton, *Paradise Lost*, IV. 503.
15. Probably the Hibernian Bible Society, founded by the clergyman attached to the Bethesda Chapel.
16. Views attributed to Jacobus Arminius (1560-1609), a Dutch protestant theologian who opposed Calvin, especially on predestination, refusing to hold God responsible for evil.
17. Maturin may be blending factuality and anachronism here: Rev. William Thorpe (born *c*.1780) did preach a farewell sermon at the Bethesda Chapel, but his *Address to the protestants of Great Britain and Ireland, on the subject of catholic emancipation* (Dublin: Graisberry and Campbell, 1814) did not appear until the year after that in which the action of the novel is set (1813). Thorpe's earliest traceable publication, a *Sermon* of 1806, was published in Dublin by William Watson, who also issued a great deal of Hannah More's work in chapbook form between the years 1796 and 1803. For More, see note 24 below.
18. Elisha Coles (*c*.1608-88) was a Calvinist and the author of *A Practical Discourse of God's Sovereignty* (1673).

you know' — and he continued to mutter something about Elisha Coles, on God's Sovereignty.

Another, who never stopped talking, appeared to De Courcy a complete evangelical *time-keeper*; — the same ceaseless ticking sound; — the same vacillating motion of the head and body; and his whole conversation turning on the various lengths of the sermons he had heard, of which, it appeared, he was in the habit of listening to four every Sunday.

'Mr Matthias preached exactly forty-eight minutes. I was at Mr Cooper's[19] exhortation at Plunket-street in the evening, and it was precisely fifty-three minutes.'

'And how many seconds?' said Mrs Wentworth, smiling, for she felt the ridicule of this.

Close to De Courcy were two very young men, who were comparing the respective progress they had made in the conversion of some of their relations. They spoke on this subject with a familiarity that certainly made De Courcy start.

'My aunt is almost entirely converted,' said one. 'She never goes to church now, though she never missed early prayers at St Thomas's for forty years before. Now,' with a strange tone of triumph, 'now, is your sister converted as much as that?'

'Yes — yes — she is,' answered the other, eagerly; 'for § she burned her week's preparation[20] yesterday, and my mother's too along with it.'

The other was dumb at this incontrovertible mark of conversion. De Courcy felt shocked; for he thought, however opposite to their sentiments might be the contents of the book in question, this *auto da fe*[21] of its pages might have been spared; and he recollected the decent superstition of the Turks, who collect and preserve with the greatest care every scrap of paper on which the name of God has been accidentally written. At last, De Courcy tried to ingratiate himself with the party, by attempting to speak on the only subject discussed among them; and, in answer to some observation of Macowen's, he tasked his memory to cite some passages from Fletcher's eloquent 'Appeal.'[22] Macowen at once silenced him, by telling him, with a chilling look, that Fletcher was an Arminian; and as little as he understood of the phrase, it was enough to signify that he was *hors de combat*[23] in the present engagement. He made one more faint attempt to rally by quoting a passage, which he imagined to possess resplendent beauty and truth, from 'Cœlebs in search of a Wife.'[24] It was that fine speech of Lucilla's father, where he speaks of the internal evidence a believer has of his own conversion; and concludes with the utmost felicity of allusion, 'One thing the Christian knows, that whereas he was blind he now seeth.'[25]

De Courcy spoke with eloquent animation; but the dubious shake of the head, the sign of stifled reprehension, the 'damning of faint praise,'[26] made him feel that heterodoxy was not confined to Arminianism alone in the opinion of the party; and that Hannah More herself, in spite of her ample strides to the evangelical side of the question, was still regarded by rigid Calvinists as 'little better than she should be.'[27] All he had now to do, was to cover his retreat by 'joining the ladies';[28] and never was retreat effected with less glory and more satisfaction. But when he arrived in the drawing-room, the same monotonous and repulsive stillness; the same dry circle (in whose verge no spirit could be raised) reduced him to the same petrifying medium with all around. The females were collected round the tea-

§ Fact; me ipso teste. [i.e. the author testifies that this detail is factual. Ed.]

19. Benjamin Williams Matthias (or Mathias) (1772-1841) was chaplain at the Bethesda 1805-35. His family remained prominent in Dublin protestant clerical life until the middle of the twentieth century.
19. The Rev. William Cooper was minister at the Sion Chapel in Whitechapel, London. He appears (from the title-page of Edward Sheppard's *A Letter to William Cooper, of Dublin*. . . . 1806) to have been Irish by either birth or residence. In 1799 he published *The Flying Angel: a Sermon delivered in . . . Armagh* (London: Chapman, 1799). His connection with Plunket Street is established through *The Funeral Sermon of the late Head of the Roman Church, Pope Pius VII; preached in Plunket-street Meeting-house, on Thursday evening, Sept. 13, 1823. By William Cooper*. (Dublin: R.M. Tims, 1823).
20. Prayers used (in written form) by catholics preparing to take the sacrament of holy communion.
21. (Portuguese) act of faith; often used of an act of inquisition — for example, the burning of a heretic.
22. Probably John William Fletcher (1729-85), who defined the essential methodist position in *Checks to Antinomianism* (1771).
23. out of action.
24. Written by Hannah More (1745-1833), *Coelebs in Search of a Wife* (1809) is a string of social sketches and moral precepts linked by the hero's search for a young woman possessing all the qualities stipulated by his departed parents.
25. This is the kind of thing Mr Stanley says, repeatedly; but he does not say these precise words. cf. Chapter XXXVIII.
26. cf. Alexander Pope, 'Epistle to Dr Arbuthnot', line 201: 'Damn with faint praise. . . .'
27. Another fossil-phrase. As a proverbial phrase, it can be traced back at least to *Pasquil's Jests* (1604), after which it appears in many authors as a standard idiom.
28. In shape, a fossil-phrase. It was customary for ladies to leave the dinner-table before the men drank port or smoked cigars. A man's early departure during the latter stage could be excused by his expressing a wish to join the ladies.

table; the conversation was carried on in pensive whispers; a large table near them was spread with evangelical tracts, &c. The room was hung with dark-brown paper; and the four unsnuffed candles burning dimly (the light of two of them almost absorbed in the dark bays[29] that covered the table on which they stood,) gave just the light that Young might have written by, when the Duke of Grafton sent him a human skull, with a taper in it, as an appropriate candelabrum for his tragedy writing-desk.[30] The ladies sometimes took up these tracts, shook a head of deep conviction over their contents, laid them down, and the same stillness recurred. The very hissing of the tea-urn, and the crackling of the coals, was a relief to De Courcy's ears.

The fact was, his presence was a constraint on them; for religious people never feel themselves quite at ease, except in the presence of those whose opinions are similar to their own, or so opposite as to justify a challenge to open a controversy. De Courcy felt this, and also felt that the constraint he imposed was doubled on himself; still he lingered, for he had a hope to support him — the hope that brought him there; and, though not yet realized, it seemed to grow stronger every moment its indulgence was suspended. He might yet obtain one glance from Eva, one conscious look, any thing that intimated they had met before, met even in terror and distress; for any thing allied to strong emotion, seems to us allied to love, and we can hardly see those who have participated with us in strong emergencies without feeling a tie of the heart to them. A stranger, with whom we have suffered shipwreck, appears ever after to us as a friend. For a look he had come, and for a look he still waited. When he appeared before dinner, she had recognized him only by a slight bow, and afterwards appeared engaged among the females of the party; and now, though nearer to her than before, her down-cast eyes were fixed on some netting, and though silent, she appeared deeply attentive to the few words that were uttered near her. It was only at a moment when all eyes happened to be withdrawn from her, (except De Courcy's,) that she raised hers, and their smile, for hers were eyes that could smile, made him feel more than all the eloquence that gratitude or passion ever poured forth. Oh! how a smile can repay love, even for the sacrifice of life; how hearts can understand each other, when the eyes alone are the interpreters between them; and language, in all its infinite variety, affords nothing so expressive as a look! Yet, in the look of Eva, there was nothing for presumption, or even for hope to dream of; in her beautiful eyes nothing could be read but the timid thanks of a helpless terrified girl for protection from danger, — thanks which she had not the courage to convey in words, and which she felt it almost a crime to express by a look. For months after he fed on that look; it came to him like a beam of light, and he forgot whether it was day or night when it glanced before his eyes.

The whispers of the party were now faintly rising into articulate murmurs, and De Courcy caught some singular sentences. Mrs Wentworth asked a drooping consumptive girl next to De Courcy, how far she had got in the Pilgrim's Progress.

'I have got no further than the *Slough of Despond*,[31] ma'am,' said the poor girl, with a phthysicky[32] querulousness of accent almost ludicrous.

On his other hand sat a lady, whose life was divided between the kitchen and the conventicle;[33] and a singular tinge, from her divided pursuits, pervaded her conversation. She was giving a history of her converting her cook, but made perpetual digressions to a fillet of veal that had been overdone the day before. 'And Mary, after my reading to you, says I, three sermons of Romaine's[34] this very day, and leaving Burder's Village Sermons[35] on your dresser, I did not expect, Mary, you would have spoiled that veal — you should think of your duty, Mary, at your spit, and not have spoiled that veal, — but indeed,' in a lowered, confidential voice, 'the jack[36] is not so good as it ought to be.'

29. i.e. baize, a woollen fabric resembling felt and used to cover tables.
30. Edward Young (1683-1765), best known as a poet whose *Night Thoughts* (1742) was immensely popular; his two tragedies were *Busiris* (1719) and *The Revenge* (1721). Augustus Henry Fitzroy, (1735-1811), 3rd duke of Grafton, was a patron of the arts.

31. A miry place in the early pages of *The Pilgrim's Progress* (1678), a religious allegory by John Bunyan (1628-88):

> As the sinner is awakened about his lost condition, there arise in his soul many fears and doubts, and discouraging apprehensions, which all of them get together, and settle in this place.

32. Usually spelled phthisicky, and deriving from the name of a disease, phthisis; wheezy, consumptive-like.
33. A meeting house or chapel for religious assembly.
34. William Romaine (1714-95); his *Twelve Sermons on the Law and the Gospel* appeared in 1806.
35. George Burder (1752-1832), English congregationalist who preached extensively throughout the British Isles; founded the Religious Tract Society in 1799. His *Village Sermons* appeared in eight volumes between 1798 and 1816, and were much reprinted.
36. A device for turning a spit upon which meat is roasted.

In a few moments the rest of the party came up, and then Charles witnessed a new scene. The evenings of religious people are necessarily monotonous; they do not dance, they do not play cards, and music (except sacred music) is rarely admitted. When tea was over, and it was a long operation, (for men who drink little wine are much attached to the milder excitement of the tea-table) a table was placed in the centre of the room, with a Bible and a Hymn-Book; a layman of distinguished gifts was requested to 'give a word of exhortation,'[37] and some clerical members of the party were urgent in the request. He complied, and opening the Bible, selected a verse from the Epistle to the Romans, and addressed the audience in an *extempore* discourse. The language was excellent, and the matter equally so, to those who relish Calvinistic divinity. At the conclusion, another of the party gave a long *extempore* prayer, in which he petitioned the Deity that the eyes of *one*, who was yet in darkness, might be enlightened to behold the glory of the truth; and Charles, who felt that he was the only one to whom the petition was applicable, blushed, even on his knees, at the application.

The service concluded with a hymn, in which most of the company joined, some with science, but all with devotion. The harmony was good, for there were many voices; yet Charles could hear but one. — Her angel figure, as it bent over the harp, — her white slender arms, — her clustering locks, thrown back by a motion of the head, so graceful, yet so infantine, — and her upcast eyes, as their pale-blue lustre broke from beneath the shade of her ringlets, might have made a poet or a painter think of a young Cecilia[38] in her first moments of inspiration, but could make a lover only think of herself.

The party separated early; and Charles, though surprised, was pleased to find that no allusion was made to the adventure of the preceding evening, nor did it even appear to be known to the rest of the party. He could not bear the thought of standing like a mark for congratulation to be discharged at by strangers; but even the fear of it was spared him. In fact, Mr and Mrs Wentworth wished the subject to be never known, or soon forgot; the latter from strong and just reasons, and the former because he had the sense, in all important matters, to be governed by his wife.

37. A fossil-phrase.

38. The patron saint of music, especially church music. She was blind and is supposed to have been martyred. Both Pope and Dryden wrote odes in her honour.

WILLIAM THOMPSON

(*c*.1785-1833)

from: AN APPEAL OF ONE HALF THE HUMAN RACE, WOMEN, AGAINST THE PRETENSIONS OF THE OTHER HALF, MEN.... (1825)

[William Thompson was early impressed by Jeremy Bentham's theories, supported Robert Owen's co-operativism, and anticipated Karl Marx's notion of surplus value. His best remembered work, however, is the feminist tract from which the following passages are taken. They appear in Part II.]

Political rights are necessary to women as a check on the almost inveterate habits of exclusion of men. It is in vain to sanction by law a civil right, or to remove an exclusion, if the law affords no means to those whom it designs to benefit of causing the right or permission to be enforced. Women may be eligible by law to the situation of professors; the law may protect them when married from the personal violence or constraint of any kind of their husbands, as fully as it protects husbands against them; but if none but men are to be the electors, if none but men are to be jurors or judges when women complain against men of partiality and injustice, is it in human nature that a sympathy from old habit, from similarity of organization and trains of thought, from love of domination, should not have a tendency to make men swerve from the line of justice and strict impartiality, should not make them underrate the pretensions of women, and be lenient to the errors of men? When to this are joined the superior strength, the *secrecy* of domestic wrongs, and thence the means of transgression and impunity, who can doubt the necessity of an equally mixed, as resulting from equal political laws, in order to be an impartial, tribunal, in all cases where women are the parties as against men, or men as against women? True that under the shield of equal laws and equal morals, such cases would bear but a small proportion to the whole number of cases brought into judgement, the greater proportion of them being unconnected with sexual concerns; in all which cases men or women, as found most convenient, would naturally discharge the duties: but why, in cases where men are necessarily interested parties, give them a monopoly of judging? Though the present exclusions of women, particularly in marriage, from most of the rights of property, as well as from almost all other rights, were removed, it is very probable that, partly from want of inclination, partly from motives of convenience, numbers of women qualified would not offer themselves for offices, and would not exercise their political rights; yet would the consciousness in the minds of men of such powers of control existing amongst women cause them so to regulate their conduct, as to render for the most part unnecessary any party display of their power. In all cases where partiality was only suspected, women would of course exercise their rights. If but few women were themselves elected as representatives, their influence would cause such men to be elected as would enact equal laws between the two great portions of the race, or would cause such men as showed an inclination to revive the old reign of brutality and injustice to be replaced by other men or by women. Now is it possible to conceive that any set of legislators, male or female, particularly men, would not be more inclined to make and preserve laws of entire reciprocity and equal justice between women and men, when they knew that their constituents were equally balanced, and that injustice on their part would necessarily enlist a few of either party amongst the injured half, and thus create a majority of the whole constituents against them? Under the system of exclusive political rights, though nearly one half of men joined with the whole of women in reprobation of unequal laws, those laws, as long as there was a majority of one of the whole males in favor of injustice, could persevere in injustice, in contempt of the wishes of three fourths, wanting one, of the whole race. Under the system of non-exclusion, *all men* but one could not effect injustice against women. The one just man giving his casting vote to the equal votes of women, would wipe away from men the opprobrium of the meditated wrong. Who can doubt then of the necessity of the enjoyment of equal political rights by women as a preservative against the possibility of the monstrous evil of three fourths, *wanting one*, of every community being every day liable to be oppressed by one fourth, *plus one*? Nothing less than giving equal rights to all, men and women, can guard against such evils, can promote the equal happiness of all. . . .

Sleeps there an infant on your bosom, to the level of whose intellect the systematic despotism and pitiful jealousy of man have not sought, and for the most part successfully sought, to chain down yours? Does no blush rise amongst you — swells no breast with indignation, at the enormous wrong? Simple as ye are, have ye become enamoured of folly? do you indeed believe it to be a source of power and of happiness? Look to your masters: does knowledge in their hands remain idle? is it with them no source of power and happiness? Think ye then indeed that it is of the use of what are called your personal charms alone that man is jealous? There is not a quality of mind which his animal propensities do not grudge you: not one, those only excepted which, like high-seasoned or far-fetched sauces, render you, as objects of sense, more stimulating to his purely selfish desires. Do ye pretend to enjoy with him, at this banquet of *bought* or *commanded* sensuality, the sensuality of prostitution or of marriage? He has a system of domineering hypocrisy, which he calls morals, which brands with the name of vice your enjoyment, while it lauds with the name of virtue, or gilds with that of innocent gratification, his. What quality, worth the possession, and capable of being applied to useful purposes for your own independence and happiness, do you possess, of which ignorant man is not jealous? Strength is his peculiar prerogative; it is *unfeminine* to possess it: hence every expedient is used in what is called your education, to enervate your bodies, by proscribing that activity which is as necessary to health as to preservation from inevitable casualties. Muscular weakness, what is called delicacy of health approaching to disease, helplessness, are by a strange perversion of language denominated rather perfections than defects in women, in order to increase their dependence, even their *physical* dependence on man; gratifying by one operation his two ruling animal propensities, sexual desire and love of domination. Hectic delicacy of health — though to yourselves accompanied by torment and followed by death — excites man's appetite; and utter weakness, no matter what personal evils it may entail on the possessor, gratifies his love of domination, by rendering his aid on every trivial occasion indispensable for your protection or for your most trifling exertions. Not satisfied with the inferiority of strength which your comparative size and structure, under the name of nature, give you, his poor jealousy increases it a hundredfold by all the resources of a vicious and partial physical training: and for this weakness and helplessness you are subsequently reproached, as a mark of your natural physical inferiority! Of strength of mind in you the ignorant amongst men, that is to say, the bulk of men, are still more jealous than of strength of body. Cowardice, that is to say, dread without reason, and in consequence of that dread, incapacity of using the means of preservation in your power against the most trifling attacks of the most contemptible animals or even insects or petty accidents, is by the sexual system of morality rather a virtue than a vice in you. No matter what inconveniences you personally suffer from this pernicious quality, no matter how your minds through life are tormented by it; it is of much more importance that man's vanity should be perfumed with his comparative hardihood than that you should be happy. Not on benevolence, but on antipathy, or malignant jealousy of your good, is the cursed system of sexual morality founded. Strength, without which there can be no health, both of body and mind, would cause you to approach too nearly to those high prerogatives in your masters, with whom to aim at an equality is the summit of female audacity, if not of wickedness. Prudence for the management of your affairs, wisdom for the guidance of your voluntary actions, the same unrelenting jealousy of ignorance proscribes. An education of baby-clothes, and sounds, and postures, you are given, instead of real knowledge; the *incidents*[1] are withheld from you, by which you could learn, as man does, the management of affairs and the prudential guidance of your own actions; and thus factitiously incapacitated, man interposes, seizes on your property, leaves you none to manage, and assumes the despotic guidance of your actions, as the right of his superior wisdom and prudence! Every moral and intellectual quality of which you might be possessed, is thus deliberately and systematically sacrificed at the shrine of man's all-devouring jealousy, of his most immoral love of superiority, deriving pleasure where if benevolent he could not avoid feeling pain, from the contemplation of the weaknesses, vices, or privations, thus entailed upon you his fellow-creatures. That no intellectual faculties may be by you developed, it is *immoral* that you should exercise even the faculty of speech (though it is a quality at times of the highest virtue, exciting the utmost admiration in *man*), to address in public, that is to say, to address any where, numbers of your fellow-creatures; this high and exciting source of influence and intellectual improvement, man's universal jealousy having also monopolized. On the stage, as servants, as *despised* servants, you may act and receive his payment to flatter his eye and ear; but for your own interest in life, to turn to any serious use those powers of graceful and reasoning eloquence, which these illicit occasions have shown you to possess, and with which they have enabled you to thrill man's overpowered faculties, his cowardly and malignant jealousy forbids the exercise. An excluding law would be in this case superfluous. Though superhuman wisdom were to be gleaned by woman, as grains from the well reaped fields of men, and in spite of their exclusions, your lips, the vehicle of such wisdom, would be closed, in spite of the vain permissions of law, by the superior strength of men, even by open force! ....

Under such arrangements, women may have equal improvement and use of all their faculties with men: under these circumstances, they may derive as much of happiness from every source — of the senses, of intelligence, and sympathy — as men, according to the peculiarities of organization of each: under these circumstances, all may be perfectly equal in rights, duties, and enjoyments, according to their capabilities of acting, suffering, and enjoying. If men from an average superiority of strength, be able to add more to general happiness in the way of increasing the products of labor, where would happiness, where would men be

1. Privileges, burdens, customs commonly or invariably attaching to an office, estate, or the like.

found, were it not for the peculiar pains, privations and cares which women suffer in nourishing and rearing the infancy of the whole race? Against the almost doubtful advantage, in the present state of improved chemical and mechanical science and art, of mere superiority of animal strength on the part of men, in increasing their utility or contributions to the common happiness, may not the unquestionable usefulness of the employment of that part of the time of women which is consumed in preserving the race be opposed? Which more indispensable for human happiness, that a few more broadcloths or cottons should be every year produced, or that the race itself should be every year increased and kindly and skilfully nurtured? Wherever the principle of Association prevailed, justice would prevail, and these mutual compensations — as nurturing infants against strength — would be fully admitted; no person cheerfully exerting his or her means, whatever they might be, for the common benefit, would be punished for the scantiness of those means, still less for the pains or privations attending their developement. In this, as in all the other arrangements of Mutual Co-operation, the punishments of nature, whether arising from decrease of enjoyments or from positive pain, would not only perhaps be found sufficient for all useful purposes, but would rather demand compensation than factitious increase.

But in a state of society where these compensations are not allowed, where man's advantage of superior strength is heightened by every possible means, rendered more effective by a monopoly of knowledge and fenced round by exclusive privileges; where woman's peculiar efforts and powers for the common benefit of the race are looked upon as an additional badge of inferiority and disgrace; where, instead of *compensation* for physical suffering and care useful to the whole race, such inconveniences, joined to those of inferior strength, are aggravated by every possible brutal contrivance of forced ignorance and exclusion from almost all the means of wealth and influence, pleasure and improvement; where man, for the exercise of his peculiar talent, strength, attended naturally in its developement with pleasure, rewards himself with every factitious benefit within the reach of his strength, and, amongst other apparent benefits, with the subjection of one half his species; while woman for the exercise of her peculiar faculty or talent, the bearing and nurture of infants, equally the independent gift of nature, but attended in its developement with pain, privation, and care, instead of being rewarded, as man is for his natural advantage of strength, is punished, the helplessness of suffering being made the basis of still further degradation; where the generality of men, educated in brutal ignorance of the art of social happiness, seek for no higher pleasures from their intercourse with women than the gratification of the mere animal feeling of selfish appetite, and the still viler pleasure of mere despotic control over the objects of that appetite, and the children which it may be instrumental in producing; — in such a state of things you may well doubt that the mere removal of partial sexual restraints would raise woman to an equality with man. Many as are the years during which the Catholics of Ireland have been eligible to some few corporation and other offices, but very few of them have been so elected, because *the keys of admission were absurdly or perfidiously left in the hands of the exclusionists.*[2] So must it in some measure be with the removal of the partial legislation and partial morals affecting women. Men, from their acquired advantages, must be every where the executors and judges — for a long time at least — under the new regulations, themselves parties or sympathizing with the parties in every cause.

In the mean time, however, until the association of men and women in large numbers for mutual benefit shall supersede the present isolated mode of exertion by individual competition, assert every where your right as human beings to equal individual liberty, to equal laws, political, civil, and criminal, to equal morals, to equal education, — and, as the result of the whole, to equal chances, according to the extent and improvement of your faculties and exertions, of acquiring the means of happiness, with men. Immense would be the accession of happiness to both men and women by such a change, though it should still leave uncompensated those casualties, attended with pain and privation to you individually, but of the very highest order of utility to the whole race, to which you are exclusively subjected. The removal of all *partial* existing restraints of law or custom, and the unfolding of the career of equal exertion to women

2. The exclusion from municipal life, imposed on catholics after the defeat of James II in 1690, had relaxed to some degree even by the 1760s, although important prohibitions remained in force until 1840.

and men, instead of being any obstacle to your further advancement under the system of Mutual Co-operation, would be the most certain step in the progress towards it, would prepare you to perceive its benefits, and render you anxious on the first opportunity to embrace them. No wretches ever passed from a state of slavery to a state of freedom without more or less of mental excitement, without more or less of alarm to the timid amongst their masters. These are partial and necessary evils, swelling almost into blessings from the immensity of preponderant good by which they are followed. Regard them not. Truth, benevolence, the interest of the whole human race, are on your side. Persevere, and you must be free. If to your intelligence and efforts this mighty change in human affairs shall be indebted, you will lay men under an obligation of gratitude to you, in comparison with which the past use of your mere animal charms would be like the fretful dream of the morning....

DANIEL O'CONNELL

(1775-1847)

SEVEN LETTERS (1817-43)

[Daniel O'Connell's stature as the leading figure of Irish public life in the first half of the nineteenth century is unchallengeable. He was not a prolific writer and, as far as the verbal arts are concerned, his enduring reputation has rested largely on his speeches. However, the eight-volume edition of his *Correspondence* brings to life another side of The Liberator. Here we find the thoughtful, affectionate husband, the proud family man, the busy man of the world scribbling letters en route to election meetings, or musing on Irish history.

The texts of the letters are taken from the edition cited in the bibliography, together with the notes provided in that edition (here indicated by 'a', 'b' etc.) Further details have been provided in the usual sequence of numbered notes.]

To Charles Phillips[1]

Bath [Somerset], 16 October 1817

My dear Charles,

I got letters from both the Currans yesterday, containing the melancholy intelligence of their father's death.[a] I will go up to the funeral the moment I hear from you or them. William,[b] in his letter, promises to write again this day. What a man has Ireland lost! His utility, to be sure, was in his *very* latter days neutralized by illness and absence; but what a man was he! Of *all* — the *only* incorrupted and faithful....

There is a loneliness and heaviness over me when I think of this great man whom we have lost. Charles, there never was *so* honest an Irishman. His very soul was Republican Irish. Look to his history in 1778, in '82, in 1798 — at the Union — at all times — in all places. Look to it, my dear friend — even for your own sake, but, above all, for his: you must erect a monument to both.

Write to me the moment you receive this letter and just say how long I can remain here and be *in full* time for the funeral. All the Irish in London, of all classes, must be invited. The upper ranks by cards — the lower, thus: — A printed bill must be sent to all the public houses resorted to by the working Irish to mention the hour when the funeral will commence and to request that all persons will fall in, two by two, as they arrive, at the remote end of the procession. I think it would be as well that all persons were required to wear a shamrock. Perhaps this may be said to be too fantastical, but I think it would be well. On *his* coffin should be laid a broken harp and a wreath of shamrock. I rather think there should be a committee formed to make arrangements.[c] Whether I go to town or not on Saturday or

a. John Philpot Curran. John B. H. Curran (1784-1832), second son of John P. Curran, and his brother, William, were both present at their father's death (*Dublin Historical Record*, XV, no. 2 [April 1959], p. 57).

b. William Henry Curran (1789-1858), son of John Philpot Curran. Called to the bar, 1816; author of *Life of John Philpot Curran* and *Sketches of the Irish Bar*. See *Boase*....

1. Of Cheltenham, England.

c. Despite O'Connell's suggestion of a public funeral for Curran, he was buried quietly at Paddington. In 1834 his remains were transferred to Glasnevin, Dublin, where a monument was raised to him designed by Thomas Moore (Leslie Hale, *John Philpot Curran: His Life and Times* [London 1958], pp. 273-4; also *DNB*).

wait until Monday will depend on young Curran's letter of this date. It would affect you to see how sensibly my little girls feel *his* death. There have been some wet eyes, I promise you. Remember me most kindly to both the Currans.

To his wife,[1] *Merrion Square*

Limerick, 15 March 1820

My darling Heart,

... This is a *good* assizes. You will, however, be surprised to hear that I had a client convicted yesterday for a murder for whom I fought a hard battle, and yet I do not feel any the most slight regret at his conviction. It is very unusual with me to be *so* satisfied, but he is a horrid villain. In the first place he got a creature, a lovely creature of fifteen, to elope with him from her uncle who brought her up an orphan and to rob him of his all, 100 guineas, and in three weeks after he contrived to get her into a boat on the Shannon with his servant, said when he returned to Glin that he left her at Kilrush, then reported she had gone off with a sea captain, and she was not heard of afterwards for near two months when a mutilated carcase floated on shore, or rather was thrown, which was identified to be hers from some extremely remarkable teeth. He will be hanged tomorrow unless being a gentlemen prevents him.[a]

I have agreed to go to the Mallow election for Becher Wrixon.[b] I leave this late on Friday or early on Saturday if the contest goes on. There are but 300 freeholders so that I shall be in Tralee to Breakfast on Wednesday....

I got last night Hall's pamphlet.[c] I have not had time to read it yet....

a. John Scanlan, hanged in Limerick on 16 March 1820 for the murder of Ellen Hanley, his body being given for dissection (*Ennis Chronicle*, 18 Mar. 1820). It was on this case that Gerald Griffin based his classic, *The Collegians: A Tale of Garryowen* (1829), which in turn provided Dion Boucicault with his material for *The Colleen Bawn* (first performed 27 Mar. 1860).

b. O'Connell was to assist as election agent William Wrixon Becher, a Whig-Liberal candidate for the Mallow seat in the general election. Born 1780, died 1850, he assumed the additional name of Becher, his mother's name. Created baronet, 1831; married 18 December 1819 Eliza O'Neill, the celebrated actress.

c. A pamphlet by Col. Francis Hall entitled *An Appeal to the Irish Nation on the Character and Conduct of General Devereux* (Dublin 1820).

1. O'Connell married his cousin, Mary O'Connell (1778-1836) in 1802.

To his wife at Tours[1]

Merrion Square, 26 [27 and 31
December 182

My own darling Love,

... On Tuesday the 24th my last letter went of to you. On that day we assembled at the Mayor's an went up in great procession at about two o'clock t the Castle.[2] I was in Court dress but with a unpowdered wig. There were at least from twent to thirty in Court dresses, the rest in plain clothes The Duke of Leinster and Lord Meath were of th party. Dr. Troy and Dr. Murray were in the dresse in which the King received them.[3] The scene a the Castle begin with a great scramble fo refreshments. It was quite a bear garden. Of cours I kept free of that scene. There was a quantity o wine and cakes demolished in high style and college lad, tall and strong in his cap and gown, go his share of the wine and distinguished himsel afterwards by translating his Connaught dialect o broken English into worse Latin to everybody h could get to listen to him. The Lord-Lieutenan arrived about three o'clock.[4] We were then usherec into a large room called St. Patrick's Hall. It ha rising seats at the sides, three rows one above th other, a canopy and throne at the end. The seat were crowded. The committee[a] filled the centre o the room. The Lord-Lieutenant ordered a chair fo Dr. Troy. My worthy collegian fell in with th Committee and got talking his bad Latin. I neve saw a more vulgar hound. The Lord-Lieutenan was surrounded by a suite in superb uniforms. Th address was badly read by the Mayor, the answe admirably delivered by the Marquis and there wer bursts of applause which I believe to be very mucl out of rule. Then there was a levée at which a those in Court dress were admitted. My friend th

a. The presentation of the loyal address to the lord-lieutenant was in th hands of an *ad hoc* committee of twenty-one, set up at the Royal Exchang meeting of 20 December.

1. Mrs O'Connell and some of the children were holidaying at Tours in France.
2. The group assembled at the lord mayor's residence, and proceeded to Dublin Castle.
3. The 3rd duke of Leinster was Augustus Frederick Fitzgerald (1791-1874); the 10th earl of Meath was John Chamber Brabazon (1772-1851); neither was a political figure. John Thomas Troy (1739-1823), a Dominican, was made catholic archbishop of Dublin in 1784. He was succeeded by Daniel Murray (1768-1852).
4. The lord lieutenant was Richard Colley Wellesley (1760-1842), marquis Wellesley, and brother of the Duke of Wellington.

collegian got in by means of his cap and gown and notwithstanding his thick shoes, and I believe, worsted stockings. As the Lord-Lieutenant went round the circle bowing to each of us, the collegian followed with his nose occasionally almost in the Marquis' face. It was provoking and ludicrous. At last he fastened on Dr. Troy who could not get rid of him until I interfered and took him off. Then an aide-de-camp came and got a beefeater or battle-axe guard man to take my worthy collegian into custody and turn him out.[5] If I had my children at home I would make them laugh for an hour at the grotesque and impudent conduct of the fellow. It has not been noticed in any newspapers but it was not the less laughable and provoking. I do not think I shall soon forget the figure of *the animal*. The Lord-Lieutenant received us most kindly. His answer was admirable. In short, every thing in this respect is going on as well as possible. Maurice[6] made his first appearance at the Castle and drank a couple of glasses of *royal* wine. Yesterday in the evening Maurice and I rode out to Glencullen[7] where we dined and slept. Oh, darling, it is beautifully cold. There never was such weather in Ireland. The wind is south-east, cold, clear, sharp and delightful. I walked in this morning from Glencullen and let O'Mara's messenger ride the horse. I take it to be full nine miles for it cost me two hours and a half to walk it and I ran a great deal of the first two miles. I afterwards refreshed myself with a warm bath, the first bath by the by which I have taken since I returned to Ireland. My legs are battered, I mean my feet, from the walk. I dined on a brace of wild ducks that I got from Kerry.... I fear I will not be able to go to Kerry for a full week yet, and I am beginning to be impatient for another letter from you. Darling heart, good night.

Friday, 27 December.

I spent my day at home working for you and my children. Mrs. Blaquiere[b] called here this day but I did not see her. Her husband who used to ride about on a white horse (you remember he and his former wife were visitors of ours in Westland Row) is confined in a madhouse.... We have a strong report that the King is married or going to marry a daughter of Marquis Conyngham and for my part I believe that there is some truth in the report. It would be a delightful thing to keep the Duke of York from all chance of the throne.... This evening there came a letter for him [Maurice] from Morgan[8] which I opened and read. I could not for the life of me avoid reading a letter from Tours, from Tours in which my heart is wrapt. Tell my own own Danny that I will write to him the moment I hear that he can read.... I do not think I shall be able to leave this for Kerry before the 6th of January and I must be back again in one fortnight. I wish I could avoid going down at all.... Tell Ellen that Moore's *Loves of the Angels*[c] is come out. I got it a while ago and read it in half an hour. It is only an account of three angels that fell in love with three ladies and although the subject is not very promising it is really an exquisitely beautiful little poem. A separated husband and wife are described and the evils of separation,

> All this they bear but not the less
> Have moments rich in happiness
> Blest meetings after many a day
> Of widowhood past far away
> When the loved fair again is seen.

This is what your husband looks to as the recompense of this his solitary widowhood.[9] Oh, how I long to see again the loved face of my Mary and those of my loved girls and boys. How I wish I was reading this poem for them. It is short, a mere trifle for such a poet, but exquisitely sweet and not stained with a single indelicate thought. The poetry is full of Moore's magic. In spite of the *Edinburgh Review* Moore is the very prince of poets. There is more melody and harmony in his versification than in any other poet I ever read.

b. Eliza, second daughter of William Roper, Rathfarnham Castle, Co. Dublin. Married 1818 Peter Boyle de Blaquiere, son of first Baron de Blaquiere.

c. Published on 23 December and attacked in the leading journals on religious grounds. See Wilfred S. Dowden, ed., *The Letters of Thomas Moore*, 2 vols. (Oxford 1964), II, 512 n.

5. The aide-de-camp was an officer who accompanied the lord lieutenant or represented him at social functions; beefeaters are yeomen warders of the Tower of London. O'Connell here mocks the elaborate regalia of the lord lieutenant's guards. Note his use of the term 'collegian' (cf. Gerald Griffin's novel) for a student or recent graduate.
6. Maurice O'Connell (1803-53), O'Connell's eldest son.
7. Glencullen in south County Dublin, home of the O'Mara family.
8. Morgan O'Connell (1804-85), O'Connell's second son, who had accompanied the family to Tours.
9. O'Connell exaggerates affectionately here.

All our accounts are warlike. You will certainly have war.[10] Stock-jobbing is endeavouring to keep the fact out of sight but depend upon it you will have war....

31 December

... Maurice and I have a round of invitations. We dine this day at Alderman McKenny's, tomorrow with Mr. Milliken,[d] the day after at Mr. Somers', the day after at Mr. Roose's, the lottery office keeper. I am also tomorrow to go up to the Park[e] on the occasion of presenting a Catholic address from Derry[f].... Tell my own Dan that I cannot write to him until I get a certificate in due form from Ellen that he can read, for it would be very idle to write directly to a boy who could not read. I submit that to his own good sense and delicacy. I got also this day a letter from poor Devereux[g] from Santa Fé de Bogota dated in July last. He is coming home to 'his idol'. He writes in his usual strain. He is to bring home £100,000, no less I assure you. They say in Kerry that '*half would not be bad*'. There is also a letter for Morgan in which Devereux promises to bring Morgan home his pay and prize money. I believe Morgan will not buy many cakes with the remittance. What you will be glad of is to hear that little Maurice[h] is well and has a company in Sandes' Regiment. Colonel Hall however is no more. Poor fellow! He was not, however, so attentive to Morgan as I think he might have been. There is also some Featherstone dead.[i] I do not know who he was. I believe I will not be able to go at all to Kerry....

d. Richard Milliken, 104 Grafton Street, Dublin; bookseller to the king and to Dublin University.

e. Phoenix Park, where the vice-regal residence was situated.

f. Unidentified, but possibly in support of the lord-lieutenant as was the Kerry address.

g. John Devereux was at this time endeavouring to collect the cost of his expedition from the government of Gran Colombia.

h. Maurice O'Connell of the Irish Legion.

i. This information seems to be inaccurate. Col. Francis Hall was assassinated in Quito, Ecuador, in 1833. There is no Featherstone listed among the legion. There is, however, a George Featherstonhaugh who was killed at the battle of Bompona on 7 April 1822. O'Connell seems to have confused Hall with Featherstonhaugh, who sailed with Wilson's Hussars to Venezuela in 1818 as an artillery officer and later joined the Rifles. The mistake about his death arises from Devereux's letter of 16 July 1822 to Morgan O'Connell which was included in a letter of the same date to O'Connell. The letter reads: 'Poor Featherstone Hall is gone. Col. Hall still remains at Caraccas at the head of the Topographical Department of the Republic' (Fitz-Simon Papers).

10. O'Connell predicts a European war, resulting from a crisis in Spain.

To his wife, Merrion Square, Dublin

'Cookes', Albermarle Street
[London, 7 March 1825]

My own darling,

Only think that I *this day only* got your letter of the 3d of March. Darling, you *ought* to write to me every day. While I am here I implore of you to do so.

Yesterday we dined at the Duke of Norfolk's.[1] We had four Dukes — Sussex, Norfolk, Devonshire and Leinster — four Earls, Fitzwilliam, Grey, Shrewsbury and Donoughmore, four barons, Clifford, Stourton, Arundel and Nugent,[a] two lords by courtesy, Killeen and Duncannon, two baronets, Burdett and Esmonde. I was placed between the Duke of Devonshire and Earl Grey. I had no notion of such splendour. There were from two to three thousand pounds worth of new plate purchased for the occasion besides all the old family gold and silver plate. The house[b] is magnificant [*sic*]. Splendid suite of rooms, splendidly furnished, and one of the dining-rooms, that in which we dined, is said to be as handsome as any in England. It was the house in which George the 3d was born. It was impossible to have everything more *majestic* altogether but your husband is lost *by flattery*. You cannot think how everybody says that it is *I* who am carrying emancipation, that it will be carried this sessions I look on as nearly certain.

Tomorrow, darling, I will write to the General,[c] please God. Depend on my making an arrangement complete with Col. Fitzsimon. Every day I like his nephew[d] more and more. The bracelets will, I understand, cost upwards of £50, that is, sixteen guineas each for the setting and about seven guineas for the drawing the miniature. That makes *close* on fifty pounds Irish, but, darling, if I possibly can I

a. Charles (Clifford), sixth Baron Clifford of Chudleigh (1759-1831); educated at Douai, St. Omer, Bruges and Liège. James Everard (Arundell), tenth Baron Arundell (1785-1834), married 1811 Mary Anne, only daughter of first marquess of Buckingham. The only Catholic peer who voted against the 1832 Reform Bill. George (Nugent-Grenville), second Baron Nugent of Carlanstown (I) (1789-1850). M.P. for Buckingham, 1810-12; Aylesbury, 1812-32, 1847-50. Lord of the treasury, 1830-32.

b. Norfolk House, St James Square, London.

c. His uncle, Count O'Connell.

d. Christopher Fitz-Simon.

1. The 12th duke of Norfolk was Bernard Edward Howard (1765-1842), a catholic, who had been made earl marshal by the Westminster parliament in 1824.

will do what you wish about them. Perhaps if I could get my picture painted here we could get them set cheaper in Ireland. I have, darling, no political news to give you this day. The Duke of Sussex was particularly attentive to me yesterday, and I liked him better perhaps on that account than I did the first dinner. Earl Grey is a cold man in his manner but of high principle. To descend from him to Jack Lawless, we have your friend Jack Lawless foaming upon two things, first that there is nothing really to *complain* of about securities in point of religion and secondly that the 40s freeholders are likely to be extinct. Jack affects great patriotism on this subject, and although Sir Francis Burdett's opinion is against him, he would hardly allow Sir Francis to speak on the subject.[2] You cannot well conceive any thing so rude as his manner was to Sir Francis. . . .

2. Sir Francis Burdett (1770-1844), a radical of sorts until the Reform Act of 1832, after which he leaned towards the conservatives. The Jack Lawless referred to appears to have been John Lawless (1773-1837), who had been a friend of the United Irishman leadership, was a staunch supporter of catholic emancipation but an opponent of O'Connell; he was known as 'honest Jack' for the blunt expression of his views.

To his wife

Dromana [Co. Waterford], 19 June 1826

My own sweet Love,

Here I am at this lovely spot.[a] I believe it is that which Lady Morgan makes the scene of many of the incidents in *Florence McCarthy*.[b] It is really a beautiful situation. As to yesterday, *first*, I wrote to you from Waterford and enclosed you a cheque for £35; next, sweetest, we heard an early mass at Waterford and then started for Dungarvan. We breakfasted at Kilmacthomas, a town belonging to the Beresfords but the people belong to us.[1] They came out to meet us with green boughs and such shouting you can have no idea of. I harangued them from the window of the inn, and we had a good deal of laughing at the bloody Beresfords. Judge what the popular feeling must be when in this, a Beresford town, every man their tenant, we had such a reception. A few miles farther on we found a chapel with the congregation assembled before mass. The Priest made me come out and I addressed his flock, being my second speech. The freeholders here were the tenants of a Mr. Palliser,[c] who is on the adverse interest, but almost all of them will vote for us. We then proceeded to Dungarvan on the coast. There are here about four hundred voters *belonging* to the Duke of Devonshire. His agents have acted a most treacherous part by us, and our Committee at Waterford were afraid openly to attack these voters lest the Duke should complain of our violating what he calls his neutrality.[2] But I deemed that all sheer nonsense, and to work we went. We had a most tremendous meeting here; we harangued the people from a platform erected by the walls of a new chapel. I never could form a notion of the great effect of popular declamation before yesterday. The clergy of the town most zealously assisted us. We have, I believe, completely triumphed, and I at present am convinced we shall poll to the last man of these voters. We then had a public dinner and great speeching. We broke up about nine, and Wyse and I came here with Mr. Stuart in his carriage.[3] We arrived about half after ten, and are going this day to Lismore on another mission.

I cannot tell you what a sweet spot this is. The tide rises to a considerable distance away and gives this noble river a most majestic appearance. Darling, I must give up poetic ideas and tell you in plain prose that I do doat on you and your children.

a. Dromana, Cappoquin, Co. Waterford. Residence of Villiers Stuart, successful pro-Catholic candidate in the Waterford election.

b. *Florence McCarthy: An Irish Tale*, by Sydney Owenson, Lady Morgan (1818).

c. Wray Palliser (1789-1862), Kilcomragh Lodge, near Kilmacthomas, Co. Waterford. Son of John Palliser, Derrylusken, Co. Tipperary. Lt. Col. in Waterford Militia, 1810-62.

1. The Beresfords were a powerful aristocratic family, Tory in politics, who had wielded immense power in the Irish parliament. In 1826 Lord John George de la Poer Beresford (1773-1862) was Church of Ireland archbishop of Armagh and primate of Ireland. The family's territorial base was County Waterford, which O'Connell was at this moment subverting.

2. The dukes of Devonshire have an Irish residence in Lismore Castle, Co. Waterford.

3. Sir Thomas Wyse (1791-1862), politician and diplomat; campaigned actively for emancipation in 1825, later sat in parliament as the member for Waterford. Henry Villiers Stuart (1803-74), the pro-emancipation candidate in the election, was duly elected in 1826.

To John Hill Burton[a]

Derrynane, 3 December 1835

My dear Sir,

Such a history of Ireland as you speak of would

a. John Hill Burton (1809-1881), Scottish historian and lawyer; born in Aberdeen; wrote elementary histories under the name of 'White'; contributor to *Edinburgh Review*; edited the works of Jeremy Bentham in conjunction with Sir John Bowring. See *DNB*.

be of incalculable advantage to the cause of justice and truth but are there readers for it? You are aware that Moore is publishing *a history*.[b] Taylor of the *Morning Herald* has published *a history*.[c] Lawless has published a thing he calls a history.[d] There are others.

But this is not what I most fear. The ancient story of Ireland is principally fabulous and the fable is one devoid of interest. I rely on the fragment of Gildus and on Bede for my notions of Ireland in the Dark Ages.[1] That there was *all* the learning of the times, a high spirit of religious devotion, much ascetism [*sic*], is perfectly true but what must be the state of civil policy when the lands were held not by individuals but by the clan, when the succession to the chief power and property was governed by no rule of descent but belonged to the nearest relation who was also the *bravest* man. That ingredient in the right had all its natural effects.

I am not writing an essay on Irish history but we will throw ancient history nearly overboard. From the time of the 2nd Henry till the wars of 1641 little of interest — barbaric feuds, barbaric manners. I have dwelt on these periods until I have been sickened with disgust. The hellish spirit of Queen Elizabeth alone throws a species of 'funereal glare' over part of that interval. From the reign of Elizabeth you *prepare* for 1641. Thence to the present hour Irish history is of interest.

I am running from your questions. Let me put my reply thus:

1st. I am ready to give you all the assistance in my power but that aid can be effectual I fear only in Dublin.

2d. That there is no person possessed of sufficient leisure and ability to be useful, at least, I know of no such person.

3d. That the principal aid you could get in Dublin would be the facility to examine state papers and the files of Irish newspapers for the last sixty or eighty years.

4th. You must not rely in the least on Mr. Wyse's history of the Catholic Association[e] even for dates or facts. It is full of all kinds of errors.

In short the only clue to the modern history of Ireland is the volume of Irish newspapers. They give dates and facts but of course are not to be relied on for motives or speculations.

I will hopelessly try to get you aid in Dublin but if you could come there while I was in that town I would procure for you the documents I mention. I got the copy of Queen Mary's letters you were kind enough to leave me. Many thanks. Poor murdered Mary![2] But I owe you infinitely more for the pamphlets. They are indeed most kind.

Do you know anything of the writers of a publication in Edinburgh called the *Christian Instructor*? They have played one of the most shabby tricks that ever was perpetrated upon me, and have published a letter of mine manifestly not intended for publication and have added one of the most consummate pieces of ignorance and impudence I ever witnessed — as a reply to a letter intended to close a *private* correspondence.[f]

b. Thomas Moore, *The History of Ireland*, 4 vols., London, 1835-46.
c. Unidentified. John S. Taylor was a prolific writer of newspaper articles.
d. John Lawless, *A Compendium of the history of Ireland, from the earliest period, to the reign of George I, Dublin*, (1814).
e. Thomas Wyse, *Historical Sketch of the Late Catholic Association of Ireland*, 2 vols., London, 1829.
f. The letter to which O'Connell refers was one dated 28 October 1835 which he addressed to 'Philo Liberal' and which was apparently published by the recipient in the *Edinburgh Christian Instructor*. In the letter he makes some hostile references to Protestant theological beliefs such as he would probably have refrained from making in a public letter.

1. Usually spelled Gildas, a 6th-century British historian who wrote in Latin. In his history of Britain, the Venerable Bede (673-735) relates the early inhabitants of Ireland to the Scythians.
2. Mary Queen of Scots (1542-87) was executed, although Elizabeth I later maintained that she had not intended the sentence of death to be carried out. It seems a little late for O'Connell's burst of sympathy in 1835.

To Richard Barrett[a]

Merrion Square, 23 March 1843

My dear Barrett,

I saw with great surprise in the last *Pilot* a paragraph which you certainly took from some other newspaper, headed 'O'Connell and Dickens,' and purporting to be a quotation from an alleged letter of mine to the editor of a Maryland Newspaper, published at Baltimore, and called the *Hibernian Advocate*. The thing is from beginning to end a gross lie. I never wrote a letter to that newspaper, nor am I in the habit of corresponding with the editors of American papers.

I have seen, indeed, with great contempt, but without much surprise, in several American newspapers, letters deliberately published under my signature, given to the American public as genuine documents — all of course being forgeries, but published by the editors as if perfectly genuine.

a. Its text suggests that this letter may have been written as a private one, even though Barrett published it in his *Pilot*. . . .

This is a species of outrageous rascality which has been seldom attempted in this country, and seems reserved for the vileness of a great portion of the newspaper press in the United States — that portion of it which seems to exceed in every species of infamy even the basest of the base, the London *Times*.

I am surprised that you did not take notice that this forgery was published in a slave-holding state — a state in which there is that moral contamination about the press which, I think you ought to know, would preclude me from having any communication with it. *Hibernian Advocate!* Oh, miserable wretch, you are, indeed, fit to circulate fictitious documents, for even your very name must be a forgery.

Few people admire more the writings of Dickens, or read them with deeper interest, than I do. I am greatly pleased with his 'American Notes.'[b] They give me, I think, a clearer idea of every-day life in America than I ever entertained before. And his chapter containing the advertisement respecting negro slavery is more calculated to augment the fixed detestation of slavery than the most brilliant declamation or the most splendid eloquence. That chapter shews out the hideous features of the system far better than any dissertation on its evil could possibly produce them, odious and disgusting to the public eye.

But I cannot help deploring one paragraph in the work. It is one full of the ignorant and insolent spirit of infidelity respecting the rigid Order of Benedictine Monks — I say, *of infidelity*, because surely no *Christian* man could place upon an equality the duellist murderer with the ascetic servant of the Cross of Christ![c]

b. Charles Dickens, *American Notes*, written and published in 1842.

c. In Chapter XIII of his *American Notes* Dickens describes Trappist monks, who had formerly had a monastery at St Louis, Missouri, as 'fanatics' and 'gloomy madmen.' He sees their departure, and the death of some duellists who had more recently killed each other in the vicinity, as 'no great loss to the community.' The edition of *American Notes* herewith consulted is that of Chapman & Hall Limited, London, 1891 (pp. 146-7).

THREE CLERGYMEN GIVE EVIDENCE TO A COMMITTEE OF THE HOUSE OF COMMONS (1825)

[From 1822 onwards, the decade that effectively ended with catholic emancipation (1829) saw the establishment of parliamentary committees charged with investigating the state of affairs existing in Ireland. Agrarian violence, the heightened pitch of the campaign for emancipation, and agricultural depression combined to suggest forcibly to the authorities in London that Irish conditions required special investigation. Committees of inquiry, established by the House of Commons, were empowered to conduct interviews with legal and local government officials and with knowledgeable individuals such as landlords and the clergy of the various churches. Transcripts of these interviews (which were conducted in London, and involved a vast expenditure of time by all concerned) were published, and these in turn fed the public (or at least the official) appetite for further inquiries. The question-and-answer format ensured that the topic and the tone of an interview were constantly under the control of the committee chairman or of the individual committee member charged with conducting a particular interview. While the published 'blue book' reports contained a vast amount of information on social conditions in Ireland, the determination of the inquiry was to a degree established in advance, with definitions of normality adopted from the English background of the House of Commons majority. This categorical distance between actual Irish conditions and ideal English ones of course would be minimized if one were to read similar reports on the condition of the English poor and so forth, but the formality of the question-and-answer session underlined the unfamiliarity of the Irish (and frequently catholic) modes of thought revealed by the interviewees.

One particular feature of Irish society intrigued the English inquiring mind — its secret societies. In the 1820s, a violent agitation organized under the name 'Captain Rock' spread out from west Limerick into the rest of Munster, the flash-point having been the behaviour of a new agent (an Englishman, Alexander Hoskins) on the estate of the Courtenay family at Newcastle West. 'Captain Rock' had many predecessors in the business of leading oath-bound secret societies that administered rough justice to those who offended their notions of what was right in relation to rents, tithes, leases, and so forth. The enclosed and yet pervasive nature of these societies gave them the eloquently simple title of 'the system', while the eighteenth-century term 'Whiteboy' was also applied to any participant in 'the system'. The parliamentary inquiry, in its anonymous assumption of moral absolutes, was a curiously appropriate forum for eliciting information about the impact of these societies.

Clergy formed a substantial proportion of the interviewees. The established church drew a tithe (a notional ten per cent levy) on most kinds of agricultural production in its parishes; in a country where the Establishment was a minority church, the catholic felt this to be a grievance. Reciprocally, any withholding of tithes by the larger population was promptly felt as a serious reduction of income in the Church of Ireland rectory or glebehouse. Thus, Church of Ireland clergymen found themselves in the dual position of semi-official spokesmen and interested private parties to the tithe disputes of the 1820s and 1830s. Their catholic counterparts were also valued sources of information because they frequently were the most articulate members of a community whose numerical strength lay among the poorest and less literate elements in society. Catholic priests frequently deplored the careless opulence of the local rector, while spokesmen for the Church of Ireland tended to look down on the level of culture evinced by the parish priest. Both were often wrong: rectors (such as Thomas Philip Le Fanu, father of the novelist Sheridan Le Fanu) were sometimes strapped for cash (he borrowed from his wine-merchant to attend his sister's funeral); parish priests (such as Thomas O'Brien Costello, Le Fanu's counterpart in Abington, Co. Limerick) were sometimes men of high refinement, broad culture and inherited substance.

It was an increasing habit among supporters of the Establishment in the 1820s to blame the seminary at Maynooth (founded in 1795) for an alleged decline in the conduct of catholic priests, and an associated increase in their political commitments. Both of the catholic priests quoted below (Kiely and Costello) were educated at St Patrick's College, Maynooth. Neither matched these stereotyped images. Kiely had discouraged the collection of Daniel O'Connell's 'catholic rent' in his County Cork parish of Mitchelstown. Costello, a friend and supporter of O'Connell's, had built for himself an impressive residence which he named Castle Comfort. The third cleric, Mortimer O'Sullivan, had been born into a catholic family; like his brother Samuel, he converted to the established church and became a doughty protestant controversialist and a popular contributor to the theological entertainments of the period. (One of these, in April 1827, lasted six days!) The topics upon which Kiely was questioned were fairly typical: priestly income, the confidentiality of the confessional, local landlords and their attitudes, the status of freeholders (i.e. certain voters), the impact of the campaign for catholic emancipation, crime, secret societies and their oaths.

In contrast, O'Sullivan was questioned about the influence of differences between catholic and protestant theology, though in recognition of his talents as a debater it has to be said that he managed to turn the interview into matters of his own choosing at the price of provoking hostility and even incredulity in the committee members. Whereas Kiely spoke of financially desperate middlemen evading the law and resorting to crime, O'Sullivan blamed survivors of the 1798 rebellion for the current agrarian violence or at least persons influenced by fugitives of a quarter of a century earlier. Immediately before O'Sullivan's comments printed here, the interviewer drew his attention to the *loyalty* of English catholics during the crisis of the Spanish armada in 1588. To a later comment by O'Sullivan on a papal declaration about oaths, the interviewer responded:

> How long ago did this take place? — In the beginning of the 15th century, but it is in consequence of that decree, a doctrine of the church.
> That is now four hundred years ago? — It is.
> Have you any more modern instances.... — No....

In this way was O'Sullivan's penchant for a long view of historical conspiracies openly mocked by the committee. Moreover, recent politics and religion were also frequently blurred in his view of the socio-economic distress of the period, while Costello emphasized that no reference to religious affiliation was reflected in the oaths of those secret societies through whom the agitation against tithes was conducted. In O'Sullivan's usage, 'class' was a term applied all but exclusively to the catholic population, while the difference between catholics and protestants was explicitly that between different religions rather than differing denominations within the Christian religion. These strategies effectively insulated protestant privilege from the kinds of assault he feared most.]

1. From the Evidence of Rev. James Kiely
15 April 1825

I was appointed to the parish of Mitchelstown about the time that Mr. Baker, of Lismacue, was murdered, and I found, at that time, there were a few in my parish tainted with the spirit of Caravatism that prevailed in the county of Tipperary; and I reasoned with the people, and one morning a number, I believe ten or eleven, of young lusty fellows came to my house, and declared to me that they were initiated in the system, and declared their sorrow for it, and that they would detach themselves from it.[1] As soon as I heard of any disturbances in the county of Limerick, immediately after Mr. Hoskins' business, I was on my guard; and I appointed, in the different villages in my parish, two or three individuals, unknown to one another, to apprise me of any encroachment upon the good feeling of the people; and through the exertions of those people, and through the good disposition of the parishioners generally, tranquillity was preserved.[2] ...

If it were an object to the Committee I would enter into more detail, because I have made it my particular study, and I published two letters in the Southern Reporter, addressed to Mr. Hyde, and signed a *Well Wisher*. I found, by some means or other, I was known to be the author, and I thought it right to stop; but the fact was, that the disturbances originated in the western part of the county of Limerick, through the conduct of Mr. Hoskins, the times were very bad for the farmers, and there was a peculiar kind of gentry, a kind of middle order between the rich gentry of the country and the peasantry; persons who were generated by the excessive rise of the agricultural produce during the war, and got the education of persons above their rank; by the fall of the times these were reduced to their original level, without the habit of labour, they associated with the lowest description, and in order to keep themselves in the possession of their lands, and so forth, they deferred to the system, and hence, I believe, arose the organization in the system itself, that could not have been devised by the lowest order of the peasantry. In many instances, the persons alluded to had the cunning to keep themselves a good deal out of view, but when the system began to explode they fled the country, and they carried the feeling with them in their course ...[3]

1. During this period it was common to date events by referring to the murder of some local figure. The violence associated with Whiteboyism and with 'Captain Right' (to use another of these eponymous terms) was augmented by clashes between factions often with a merely familial or regional identity. The 'caravats' were one such faction, who distinguished themselves by wearing a scarf (in Irish *carabhat*).
2. Alexander Hoskins became agent on the Courtenay estate at Newcastle West, Co. Limerick, in 1818 or shortly afterwards. He attempted to force the payment of rents in arrears, and refused reductions of current rents, even when such were common elsewhere. After a failed attempt to attack Hoskins in the castle at Newcastle West, his assailants intercepted his son, Thomas Hoskins, who was returning from field sports; young Hoskins died of his wounds on 1 August 1821. His father resigned on 10 October 1821. Local authorities date the commencement of the Captain Rock agitation from this period.
3. By fleeing 'the country', Kiely means moving out of the district, to a neighbouring county perhaps.

2. From the Evidence of Rev. Thomas O'Brien Costello 18 April 1825

From the history of the disturbance, as it has now been found by experience, it appears that it originated in the conduct of a gentleman on the Courtenay estate; he was very severe towards the tenants, and the people who were in wealth previous to that were reduced to poverty, and they thought proper to retaliate upon him and his family, and upon those who took their lands, and this was the origin of it, and the same spirit so spread all over the country, that if a person made an offer for another man's farm, a party was made up to attack him; if the landlord was considered severe there were notices served, and his house attacked, and from this general principle private parties were formed who began robbing in the country; they demanded at every house a sovereign, as they said, to procure powder and ball for the general cause of redressing wrongs, but in fact they were only private robbers.

Was there anything in their oaths connected with the subject of religion? — Not as far as ever I heard....

You mentioned, that the present Bishop of Limerick was the Protestant clergyman of your parish? — He was at that time.[1]

Did you and he live upon good terms? — Upon the most cordial terms at all times, and to this day.

Did you derive advantage from that friendly communication? — Very much advantage from his advice, and from his countenance to the measures that I adopted.

Did it contribute generally, in other respects, to enable you to exercise your functions among your people with advantage? — While in the country, as much as he possibly could he assisted me.

Who has succeeded the Bishop? — He is succeeded by a Mr. Lefanu.[2]

1. John Jebb (1775-1833), sometime rector of the parish of Abington in County Limerick, and later (1822-27) bishop of Limerick; a reformer and liberal who published a number of learned works.
2. Thomas Philip Le Fanu, rector of Abington from 1822 until his death in 1845, but an absentee during the early years of his tenure.

Is he resident? — No.

Do the people feel a loss from the want of the residence of the Protestant clergyman in the parish? — They do conceive that if he resided in the parish he would either give them some employment, or, at least, that his revenue would in some measure revert to them, or a part of it; but, residing at a distance, they conceive that they pay their money and get no sort of return in the way of worldly profit or advantage.[3]

Then his residence would reconcile them, in some degree, to the payment of the tithes? — Nothing in truth would reconcile them to the payment of tithes; but it would in some degree.

Do you know why Mr. Lefanu is not resident? — He holds some situation in the park in Dubin, as chaplain to some schools, and he is obliged to reside there.[4]

Are the tithes collected with any degree of severity in your part of the country? — The people in my parish feel as all people do in Ireland, the tithes a very great burden; but the burden is increased in general by the conduct of the proctor.[5]

What is his course of proceeding, with regard to the valuing and collecting of the tithes? — At a certain season of the year, he and an assistant or two go over the lands and value the tithes; when this is concluded, he sits every Sunday at a public-house near the chapel, and there he gives audience to the different farmers, when they come to propose terms for their tithes, during this conference they are generally drinking, for which drink the farmer must pay; they may agree on that Sunday, or they may not, and if not there will be a second sitting, at which the same transaction will take place; after they agree, the time of payment arrives, and the proctor comes to this house again to receive the tithes, and if the farmer is not ready to pay he will apply to him for time, and on this application there will be more drink, for which the farmer must pay; hence I have heard many of the farmers say, that they have expended a sum nearly equal to the tithes for drink, before they commenced paying any portion of the tithe.

3. A resident clergyman would contribute to the local economy in many diverse ways — by purchasing goods, hiring servants, sponsoring public works, and of course through charity.
4. Le Fanu had been appointed chaplain to the Royal Hibernian Military School in the Phoenix Park, Dublin, in 1815. His successor, on his ultimate taking up residence in Abington, was the Rev. Samuel O'Sullivan whose brother Mortimer (*c.*1791-1859) published a response to Thomas Moore's satirical *Memoirs of Captain Rock* (1824), and (with William Phelan) a *Digest of Evidence on the State of Ireland* (1826).
5. A tithe proctor was employed by the clergyman each year to assess the value of the crops upon which farmers were levied; a great deal of corruption and casual brutality was associated with the position, and the extraction of drink in the way described by Costello was both a means of increasing the proctor's 'income' and of humiliating the farmers. It is not surprising that the temperance movement, led by Father Theobald Mathew (1790-1856), was regarded with suspicion by some protestants; it struck at a valuable part of the system of patronage and control upon which tithe income depended.

3. From the Evidence of Rev. Mortimer O'Sullivan 26 April 1825

You state, that there is a distinction between the opinions entertained by the Roman Catholic laity and those entertained by the Roman Catholic clergy? — Oh, yes; the respectable class of the Roman Catholic laity are, generally speaking, quite untinged with that political feeling which their religion might infuse in them, and the very lowest classes would be led by the priest of the parish, perhaps with as much effect as they would be led by the Pope; but at present there is between the higher classes and those which are very low, a class of persons becoming influential in the Roman Catholic body, who did not at all apply themselves to political concerns before; and this middle class is that to which I look with most apprehension, for what is to be the future fate of Ireland. They are persons who are influenced by radical principles, and by that which is most rancorous in the Roman Catholic system, this is a class which had very little authority in former times; but I think from the formation of committees latterly, the committees branching out from the Roman Catholic Association,[1] and held in little country towns and country villages, those men acquired an importance in their own eyes, which they had not before, and the gentry I think in some instances contributed to increase it, finding them serviceable for their party purposes; and now that class of men, the class below the gentry of the Roman Catholics and above the mere plebeians, is the class which I think will be most dangerous.

1. By 'Roman Catholic Association', O'Sullivan means the Catholic Association of Ireland, founded by Daniel O'Connell and Richard Lalor Sheil in 1823.

JOHN BANIM

(1798-1842)

from: THE ANGLO-IRISH OF THE NINETEENTH CENTURY (1828)

[John Banim, assisted by his brother Michael Banim (1796-1874), published *Tales by the O'Hara Family* in 1825 and 1826. John, though he was younger and lived a much shorter life, was the more prolific in writing novels under his own name, and *The Anglo-Irish of the Nineteenth Century* is remarkable among these in attempting a (more-or-less) contemporary setting. The title itself reflects two nervous emphases: an uncertainty as to how social groups in (or from) Ireland should be named, and the challenging newness of the nineteenth century. In the first chapter, the question of naming those in Ireland who adopt English ways is raised by Sir Robert Flood, while throughout the novel there are tensely incompatible allusions to a 'contemporary' setting. Several of the characters are said to be based on real-life figures (see note 1 below), and much of the novel's value lies in the debates that occur across the dinner-table (the example of Thomas Love Peacock may be evident here). Chapter II deals with such a gathering in London, while Chapter X (of Volume II) is set in Dublin after the hero (Gerald Blount, younger son of a peer) has travelled over from England. (Mr Gunning, a cynical yet perceptive Scotsman, provides a further perspective on the Irish/English tension.) If the first of these chapters deals with the uncertainties of policy and nomenclature, the second of them emphasizes the excessive certainty of the landlords and their associates (including, note, a brewer-cum-banker) in anticipating treacherous rebellion by the Irish catholics. Subsequent developments in the plot depend on melodrama and coincidence, though *The Anglo-Irish of the Nineteenth Century* has also been commended for the way in which it concludes — in what resembles a brusque parody of Maria Edgeworth's optimistic endings. Banim combines a strain of political radicalism with a more immediately evident fatalism, and the locus for these conflicting reactions is the language of social description.]

VOLUME I

CHAPTER II

Of the persons of this scene the schoolboy is my hero, and I shall therefore transcribe his impressions of it.

Gerald, then, at the mere appearance of his third-named guardian, painfully felt the contrast between his unfashionable, though respectable dress and mien, and the tall figure of the Minister,[1] clad in a silken and richly-flowered morning-gown, as, advancing a step, he gracefully returned the loose, abrupt bow of Mr. Knightly.[2] The frank military politeness of Sir Robert Flood, and the air of his straight person, neatly expressed in a blue undress frock,[3] braided and buttoned up to his chin, produced another contrast, as he and Knightly greeted each other, equally unfavourable to the Irish squire. In turn, the visitor was named to Lord Clangore, and Gerald noticed the bare civility of his brother's recognition. In some surprise, however, he remarked the final issue of their meeting.

Knightly, after his second butting bow to the General, turned quickly, with outstretched hand, and some modification of his set smile, to his titled ward; the young nobleman all but stepped back, and not withdrawing his eyes from the other's face, as if to form a reason for not seeing his hand, just inclined his chin towards his breast, whereat Mr. Knightly checked himself, looked askance, tried to imitate the polite nod, new-fashioned to him, with which he was received, — and, during the attempt, Gerald thought that a slight but bitter smile darted out of the corners of his mouth and of his half-closed lids. Could this uncouth gentleman feel, or rather affect to feel, any unbecoming sentiment towards Gerald's brother? But he was not able to conclude his mental question, when the subject of it suddenly wheeled round upon himself, and, not waiting for formal presentation to the schoolboy, or giving him time to stand on his guard, plunged on both his hands, and, with strong and overcharged language, expressed his joy at seeing him.

1. Based on the character of Robert Stewart (1769-1822), 2nd marquis of Londonderry, but better known by his earlier title, Viscount Castlereagh: chief secretary for Ireland 1799-1801, during which period he was the main architect of the policies that pushed the Union through the Irish parliament (1800); war secretary in the imperial government (1805 and 1807); foreign secretary 1812-22.
2. Banim may have intended this name to echo (distantly) the judicious and retiring Mr Knightley in Jane Austen's *Emma* (1816).
3. An informal frock-coat.

All proceeded to the breakfast parlour, Mr. Knightly still keeping firm hold of his new hat; and, ere he would occupy the chair pointed out to him, he bethought himself of walking quickly across the room, and depositing it on a side-table. As he returned to his chair, a servant, removing it to the hall, called from him a questioning glance; and though, at length, he seated himself quietly, and with somewhat of the self-possession of a gentleman, Gerald smiled to observe the grave scrutiny with which he peered at (so Gerald thought) the flame lighted under a richly-embossed chocolate-pot.[4]

'Peter Bell,'[5] whispered Lord Clangore to his brother, who sat close by him; 'he carries all the out-of-doors character of Peter in his face; and has he tied his ass to the railings?'

'Caliban,'[6] answered Gerald, 'the marks of his talons are on my hands.'

'Observe him now, Gerald,' as Mr. Knightly took a steady survey of the dishes round the table; 'attend, and you may see

The longings of the Cannibal arise,
Although he speaks not, in his wolfish eyes.'[7]

And allowing for some poetical license, the quotation seemed not misapplied. After declining, but not till he caused his host to repeat its name, to be helped to Perigord-pie,[8] Mr. Knightly demanded what was a round, encrusted, disguised something, in the middle of the board. At the answer 'smoked tongue,' his countenance brightened, and he zealously put in his claim for some to the General, and at the same time plied Lord Clangore, who presided over a pair of cold fowls. And over and over again he would be helped to both together; and between his pauses, having tea to his hand, cup after cup slaked his insatiate thirst — it was prodigious. Once he seemed to relax, and an attendant motioned to change his plate; but the sudden way in which Mr. Knightly seized, and, with an earnest 'beg your pardon,' — detained it, smiling to himself all the time, startled and amused, at once, the two junior spectators.

Catching Gerald's eye during his serious occupation, Mr. Knightly smiled more expressively than ever, and seemed to think there might exist some slight necessity for palliation. 'Ay, my honourable young cousin,' he said, 'when you come to see us in Ireland, this is the way we'll teach you to breakfast: first teaching you that a couple of hours' walk before hand is indispensable in the case: I have just been rambling over Primrose Hill as far as Highgate.'[9]

'My brother thanks you, Sir,' said Lord Clangore, after exchanging a glance with Gerald, 'and *when* he goes to see you in Ireland, will most gladly become your pupil.'

Gerald, not quite so fully possessed with a feeling of equality towards men of matured years as was his Lordship, feared this irony might prove too strong; he comforted himself, however, with the hope that it would not be understood; and, indeed, the quiet 'You are very good, my Lord,' with which Mr. Knightly replied, set him at ease.

'Over Primrose-hill, and on to Highgate!' said the Minister, smiling: 'indeed, Mr. Knightly, you astound us poor cockneys.'[10]

'I fear so, my Lord; but Irish mountaineers[11] will follow their old habits.'

'No doubt,' said Sir Robert. 'Are they getting any quieter, Mr. Knightly?'

It was a quick turn of the conversation, yet Mr. Knightly's 'No, indeed, General,' showed that he accepted it quite in course.

'Unhappy, misguided creatures,' continued Sir Robert.

4. A utensil in which drinking chocolate was served.
5. The simple potter in William Wordsworth's poem (1819) of the same name. There is more than Clangore's contempt in Banim's use of the analogy for Knightly. The poem, which tells how Peter is spiritually reformed by riding an ass back to the home of its dead owner, evoked great hilarity and ridicule on publication. One verse in the first two editions (suppressed in later versions) has an awkward aptness for the scene in which Knightly here finds himself. Peter is staring at the floating, drowned figure of the ass's owner:

Is it a party in a parlour?
Cramm'd just as they on earth are cramm'd —
Some sipping punch, some sipping tea,
But as you by their faces see,
All silent and all damn'd!

6. The monster in Shakespeare's *The Tempest* and previous lord of the island recently come under the civilized sway of Prospero.
7. This quotation cannot be identified.
8. A meat pie flavoured with truffles.
9. Highgate is a neighbour of Hampstead in London and stands upon rising ground to the east of Hampstead Heath.
10. The Minister's application to himself of the term traditionally used for (humble) Londoners, those born within the sound of the bells of St Mary-le-Bow in Cheapside, is doubly ironic in that his 'original' (Castlereagh) was Irish and he himself is far from humble by birth or character.
11. Originally those who lived in mountains, rather than people who climbed mountains for exercise or in exploration. 'Irish mountaineers' carries implications of uncouthness or lawlessness associated with remote districts. In Irish argot, 'the mountainy men' were irreconcilable or intransigent backwoodsmen.

'Unhappy, misguided creatures,' assented Mr. Knightly, much in earnest.

'And when *will* they grow quiet, Sir?'

'When, indeed, General?'

'What with White-boys and Right-boys, United-men, Shanavests, Caravats, Threshers, Carders, and now, Rockites,[12] I believe, all I have heard or read of them since I left the country, shows that the old people of Ireland never can be peaceable so long as they remain what they are.'

'Plainly shows it, Sir Robert.'

'The mass of our half-countrymen are certainly difficult to govern,' said the Minister; 'I fear, they may be said to give His Majesty's Councils as much continued, though petty trouble, as any people who are, or have been, our declared enemies.'

'And I fear so, too, my Lord.'

'And 'tis a problem they should, Mr. Knightly; — for whether we consider their long experience of the Government and of the laws of England; or their necessitous knowledge of their own level in the scale of nations; or their constant opportunities to grow wiser, by observing the course pursued by other people, and especially by their neighbours, towards happiness and prosperity; in fact, in whatever way we balance the question, we are unable to forge it into any tangible solution capable of being comprehended according to the rules of cause and effect.'

Here may be detected instances of the rather infelicitous clash of imagery that occasionally marked his Lordship's language; without depriving it, however, of the power of persuading or convincing, which it is well known to have possessed, and in which few were his rivals.

'One is sometimes thrown,' said Mr. Knightly, 'upon the unphilosophical supposition that would attribute to an ill-organized nature, their restlessness — to use no harder word, my Lord.'

'Their turbulence, their ferocity, Sir,' resumed Sir Robert Flood: 'their thirst of human life; — and there, Sir, I *have* used your harder word, though you will not call it too hard, after all.'

'Not a bit too hard, Sir Robert.'

'And in Heaven's name, Mr. Knightly, resuming my former question, when are we to witness any abatement of excesses, which refuse peace, nay, even personal security, to such English capitalists, or English gentlemen, or Irish gentlemen of English descent, as may think of settling in the country?'[13]

'I suppose you to ask, General, if atrocities are becoming less frequent, and I answer, no. It was but a few nights before I began my journey to England, that, only three miles from my own house, an industrious Scotchman, who had recently taken a large farm, fell a victim, along with two of his servants, to the savage vengeance of Captain Rock's desperadoes.'[14]

'And yet you live in Ireland, Sir!'

'Why, Sir Robert,' smiling apologetically, 'one must live where one can. Perhaps if I lived in your affluent and luxurious England, along with my half-dozen of raw-boned sons, and my seven or eight gadding daughters, I could not well manage my small means for living at all; and so, as in the hope of advantage, the East-Indiaman braves the Cape, and the caravan the Desert,[15] I must brave — no — not brave — that wouldn't do — but I must take my chance against Captain Rock.'

'It is, however, to be hoped,' resumed the Minister, 'that when the important measure of Union, as yet but nominally effected between the two countries, shall have fully come into operation, there will begin, in Ireland, a change of character, which must speedily repay us for the season of turmoil we now endure, and which will show itself as much the result of a well-squared dove-tailing with England, taking root during a necessary previous time, as the present sad state of things may be said to flow from a want of that close and kindly interweaving between the two people.'[16]

'If your Lordship means that Ireland will never

12. These are the names (chronologically) of various agrarian secret societies active from the 1760s onwards, but especially in the 1780s and 1820s. The 'United-men' (The Society of United Irishmen, founded in 1791) commenced as an open organization devoted to non-sectarian democratic politics on the French revolutionary model, but in 1795 it was forced by government pressure to reorganize clandestinely: the rebellion of 1798 was prompted (if not everywhere led) by the United Irishmen.

13. It was a common complaint in the 1820s that investment in Ireland had been frightened off by agrarian violence.

14. Captain Rock was the name under which agrarian unrest was organized in Munster in the 1820s, commencing in west Limerick in 1821. Previous agrarian campaigns had been led by 'Captain Right'.

15. Ships of the East India Company sailed around the Cape of Good Hope on voyages to the Pacific. The 'caravan' was originally a company of pilgrims and/or merchants travelling together for security in east or north Africa.

16. The paragraph finely illustrates the Minister's mixed metaphors: 'well-squared dove-tailing . . . taking root . . . may be said to flow from a want of . . . interweaving.'

be quiet, or prosperous, or worth living in, until English views, interests, industry — English character, in fact — take place of the views, interests, and indolence, instead of industry — which confer *its* present character — then I agree with your Lordship,' said the General.

'In detail, Sir Robert, I meant that.'

'In a word, until the great majority of the population cease to be merely Irish,[17] and become, like the only portion of it who are now respectable, intelligent — ay, or civilized, — English-Irish,'[18] continued Sir Robert.

'Well, and my meaning allows of that construction too,' assented the Minister. 'Yes; I like your word, Sir Robert; it defines almost to a point what I might admit to have been my own previous opinion: yes, *my* first cure for the evils of Ireland, certainly would be to make all her people English-Irish.'

'And it would be *my* first cure too,' observed Mr. Knightly, as if rather speaking to himself, than to those around him.

'Begin then, my Lord, we pray you,' said the young Viscount.

'Or, my Lord,' added Gerald, upon whom little of the conversation had been lost, 'Walter, here, or I, shall scarce live long enough to pay our Irish tenantry a visit; don't you think so, Walter?'

'Indeed I do.'

'But why, my good young friends?' asked the Minister with a condescending smile.

'Explain as well as you can, Gerald,' said Lord Clangore.

'Thus then, my Lord'; and in a little embarassment [*sic*] the schoolboy addressed the Minister — 'until one can sleep soundly in one's bed in Ireland, one can hardly think of going there; and Sir Robert, and Mr. Knightly, and even your Lordship, seem to say, that this must not be expected for a great many years.'

'Fairly argued, Gerald,' laughed Sir Robert.

'My dear young Lord Clangore,' resumed the Minister, assuming one of those full, manly expressions of face and manner which often distinguished him; 'it is due to your ripening years, to remind you that, as has already been noticed, his Majesty's Government *have* made the beginning you so properly wish for. The legislative Union of Great Britain and Ireland may, indeed, be said to be the first link of that great chain which, in intellect, civilization, happiness, and glory, and at the same time, in habits, pursuits, and morals, is destined to interfuse into one national current, the people of England and Ireland.'

'I thank your Lordship for your explanation,' said Lord Clangore, 'and I fully accept it; and yet it is grievous to think that our young logician here is still right, when he supposes that many, many years must elapse before an Irish nobleman or gentleman, or, as I admit the propriety of the epithet, an English-Irish one, can reckon upon residing comfortably and happily amongst his mere Irish dependants.'

'Before that, many, many years must pass away, indeed,' remarked Knightly.

'Meantime,' resumed Lord Clangore, 'while the purely Irish of the present day, in different ranks of society, utter the language of disaffection to England, or frightfully outrage her laws, what shall we call their conduct with reference to the expected change?'

'Call it, if your Lordship pleases, the yeasty workings, which denote a decomposing process in the moral elements of the people, and which, pursuant to the theory, must leave behind a settled and purer state of society,' answered — not the Minister, nor the General, but Mr. Knightly, out of his turn and place.

'And are we merely to look on at the fermentation?' continued Lord Clangore, glancing round to his more important friends.

'I suppose so,' again put in Knightly; 'fiddling'[19] with his spoon.

'But can you not also suppose, Sir, a moment, during which we *could* not merely look on?'

'I had rather not, my Lord': Knightly smiled and bowed.

'Tut, my good young Lord,' said the General, rising; 'you only contemplate circumstances as

17. Although the term is regarded as contemptuous (mere = nothing more than), its original associations were non-prejudicial in themselves (as, even, in Edmund Spenser, for whom mere = pure, unmixed). Of course, this unbroken pureness in the Irish represented a threat to Spenser's policy, and so the negative tonality of 'mere Irish' began to emerge.

18. It is noticeable that this suggested compound term differs from that in the novel's title; this, together with Sir Robert's emphasis on *his* term, indicates the uncertain search for a descriptive vocabulary.

19. The quotation marks are either a printer's error, or they may suggest that Banim still regarded the meaning 'playing aimlessly, toying' as non-standard English, although the word occurs in Swift and earlier authors.

likely as any that could occur to facilitate the change we all think desirable. And so, indeed, says our distinguished countryman, now immortalizing himself on the Peninsula.[20] One of the chief causes of Ireland's turbulence is her self-flattering conviction, that, as yet, she has been but half conquered. Whenever she deserves it, then, he argues, conquer her to her heart's content, and she will be quieter. And I think it a fair syllogism; and, for my own part, can imagine no state of things better calculated to let us remodel the old Celtic character — to make it, in fact, English-Irish — that's still my word — that one offered by the salutary humiliation, perhaps diminution, of a newly-conquered people!'

'Faith! and it might be as good a way as any, General,' assented Mr. Knightly.

'I agree,' said Lord Clangore.

'And I,' said Gerald.

All now arose, and as a hint for furthering the real business of the morning, the Minister showed the way back to his library.

It often happens that, when men meet about some specific matter of importance, the accidental conversation which precedes its discussion, proves tenfold the extent of that which arranges it. And such was the case in the present instance. Little could be suggested for the future advantage of their wards by the three guardians, or by one of the wards, Lord Clangore, in behalf of his brother, or his sister, or himself, which all did not seem to have previously, though tacitly, agreed in. Lady Augusta could not yet be removed from Devonshire, nor invited to resume her literary and other studies, notwithstanding a manifest improvement in her health, reported by Lord Clangore, who, since their common calamity, had been to visit her. The young Viscount would return to Cambridge, complete his terms, and at one and twenty inherit his considerable estates in England and Ireland: then, if state ambition swayed his mind, no young nobleman could have better prospects. And, almost upon the same plan, Gerald was to go back to Westminster, afterwards to the University,[21] and against the time when he must be called upon to consider it, make up his mind in the choice of a profession, — the portion of patrimony lying in Ireland, to which his father's will entitled him, not seeming to dispense with his own exertions in the world. At present, he could not say what profession he might ultimately select.

During the conversation on these points Mr. Knightly scarce spoke a word, except when he assented. As the meeting was about to dissolve, however, he asked,

'When Lord Clangore shall have attained his twenty-first year, I presume we may reckon upon seeing him amongst us in Ireland?'

'That requires consideration,' said the Minister.

'The late Lord Clangore often objected to any son of his residing in Ireland,' said Sir Robert, 'or even temporarily mixing in the anomalous crowd called Irish Society, at least till an advanced period of life.'

'Then you will be one of the true English-Irish, my Lord?' pursued Mr. Knightly, good-humouredly.

'I will, Sir,' answered his noble ward.

'And so will I,' echoed Gerald.

'Like all of us who — to speak modestly — do not put Ireland to the blush,'[22] resumed Sir Robert Flood.

'We shall regret your absence, even while we admire the motive for it, my Lord'; and Mr. Knightly was bowing himself out of the room.

'Do you leave town soon, Sir?' asked Sir Robert.

'Today, General, for Devonshire, in the three-o'-clock coach, that starts from Lad-lane;[23] and thence, with little delay, home to Captain Rock'; and continuing his bows, Mr. Knightly withdrew.

20. Sir Arthur Wellesley (1769-1852), who became duke of Wellington in 1814. His campaign in the Iberian Peninsula lasted from 1808 to 1813, and the implication that the novel's action is set at some point during this period cannot be reconciled with earlier references to Captain Rock (1821). However, in 1828, when Banim published the novel, Wellington was prime minister.

21. The Westminster alluded to here is the public school in London, not the parliament buildings. 'The University' may be read as either Oxford or Cambridge, the ancient universities of England.

22. 'To put to the blush' is to make someone blush with shame or confusion.

23. Now incorporated into Gresham Street in London EC2.

VOLUME II

CHAPTER X

Gerald would not own to himself that his continued spleen arose chiefly from being deprived of the honour of occupying a chair at Miss Maria Gore's right-hand. He rather accounted for his silent and grave face, amid the clatter of (except his companion, Gunning) every one around him, while all arranged themselves at table, by dwelling upon the repeated offences offered to his private sentiments, as to the pretensions of 'Knightly's eldest son' to an alliance with his family. It was very officious, and strange, and Irish, in Gerald's mind. Miss Flint he scarcely condescended to be angry with; flippancy and impertinence were in the way of her vocation. But Mr. Gore could not so readily be passed by. Upon what grounds was a gentleman, so very slightly acquainted with Gerald, at liberty to question him concerning a matter of such peculiar delicacy? Granted, these Knightlies, particularly the old lady, had rendered important services to Augusta and her brothers, by nursing her through very doubtful symptoms of a very dangerous complaint; but could their sense of obligation conferred, stop at nothing short of the appropriation of the high-born individual they had thus merely nursed, and of her considerable fortune, into the bargain? And must Lord Clangore and the Honourable Gerald Blount, be compelled to evince their gratitude of obligation received, by assenting to a remuneration so unsuitable and extortionate, and by no other means? Who were the best judges of the question? They themselves, or Miss Flint, and such as she, with her comments upon Gerald's want of heart; and Mr. Gore, and such as he, with his most unwarrantable freedoms? As to Miss Maria Gore, and her pretty indignation at, no doubt, his lack of generosity and common feeling in not agreeing with her and her sentimental correspondent, Augusta, upon the propriety of his sister 'paying' the Knightlies, 'with herself' and her sixty thousand pounds, (thus Gerald accounted for the little scene between him and the young lady,) why, he could find in his heart, (bad as she was pleased to think it,) to excuse *her*, upon the score of exalted notions of things, and of heroic friendship for, of course, her much-wronged Augusta.

These thoughts passed rapidly through Gerald's mind, as he seated himself by his agreeable friend Gunning, and were now interrupted by a young clergyman pronouncing grace, to which there was appended an impromptu prayer, as follows: — 'And shield and interpose to save us, O Lord, ever, and now, and most especially this coming night, from the blind hatred and fury of our cruel enemies!'

The faces which an instant before had been cheerful, darkened, and were cast down, while the young cleric sonorously and slowly uttered these words; the festive clatter of more than twenty tongues subsided in deep silence; and when he had ended, an impressive 'amen!' arose from all, — three of the party only excepted. One was Gerald, who, in consequence of Flood's badinage about the fleet of turf-boats during the day, strongly inclined to treat the whole matter lightly, and would not therefore lightly 'worry Heaven with prayers';[1] another was Gunning, who, his napkin seriously adjusted, had been glancing, half-critically, half-hungrily, at the soup, and now cried 'stuff!' instead of 'amen,' ('amen stuck in his throat,')[2] loud enough to be heard beyond Gerald's ear, into which the expressive monosyllable had, by a quick turn of his head, been directed; and the third was Miss Maria Gore, who just demurely held her tongue, until an ostentatious 'amen!' from the gallant officer at her side, caused her to exchange a glance with him, and then she distinctly smiled.

'Maria?' remonstrated Miss Gore severely, though in an undertone, as she fixed her almost flashing eyes on her sister.

'Well, Selina?' responded Maria quietly. It was evident to Gerald that the sisters might love each other better. But the independent, though, as has been said, quiet look of the one, was a match for the dictatorial regard of the other; and with a shrug on the part of Miss Gore, the matter ended.

Sighing, from the effects of the termination of the grace, and, for the first time since Gerald had known them, their smiles faded, if not quite withered, Mr. and Mrs. Gore began to do the honours of their table.

Gunning, having been at last helped to soup, just tasted it, and then abruptly took leave of his spoon.

'Don't touch it,' he said to Gerald, 'it will freeze you; they have iced it, and it will poison you with bay-salt[3] and cayenne.'

Gerald had, however, already entitled himself to form his own opinion; and he now thought Gunning's censure too harsh, and told him so.

'Nonsense! you're as bad as they; the thing is as plain as my stick: it might have been tolerable vermicelli, if it had not been left to grow cold in their mismanaged Irish kitchen; and then they tried to make it hot with seasoning instead of fire, (the fire was boiling or roasting some of the great joints

1. i.e. disturb the Almighty with requests.
2. cf. Shakespeare, *Macbeth*, II. 2. 31-32: '"Amen" stuck in my throat.'
3. sea salt.

we are yet to see,)[4] and they succeeded.'

So, Mr. Gunning, all but groaning with impatience, would for the present only chew a morsel of crust, and along with it 'the cud of sweet and bitter fancy.'[5]

By and by, however, he ventured on fish, which, excepting that he called it also 'cold and spoiled,' seemed to please him better.

He proposed a glass of Madeira with Gerald, and had scarce raised it to his lips, when, not going to the trouble of hiding a horrid grimace, he put it down again. Mr. Gore caught both the grimace, the action, and also the glance, but with a conscious dropping of his eye, took no notice. Gerald sipped the wine, and observed it in his glass, and felt, indeed, assured, that, whatever might have been its original merit, it was now out of order, — hot, and discoloured from recent shaking. Nor, recollecting Mr. Gore's futile visit, a few hours before, to the office of the disobliging wine-merchant, did he see much difficulty in assigning a reason why.

Gerald, really feeling for his old friend, thus disappointed of the pleasant stimulant reckoned upon by palate and stomach, advised him to try the Sherry. Gunning did, and pronounced it worse than the Maderia. The Moselle, and the light French wines, he would not touch: he hated them — hated every French potation except La Fitte, and that — even could one hope for it under the name of Claret *here*,[6] — he must not expect to see till the dessert appeared.

As a desperate resource he called for beer. The servant handed it, and he sent it back to the sideboard, in the hearing of the identical brewer, Mr. Blake, whose manufacture it was, and who sat almost opposite to him; — malt liquor is certainly not found as good in Dublin as in London. He asked for soda-water. There was none: but ginger-beer[7] was at his service.

'No. Whoever liked that stuff,' he muttered to Gerald, 'might go seek it, in a rural visit to the heights of Primrose-hill, of a sunny Sunday.'

Meantime, dinner went on, through its removes and courses, each abundant, and, it might generally be admitted, well-cooked and nicely arranged, if not neatly served. But Mr. Gunning, though he condescended to offer substantial proofs of his good opinion of a saddle of mutton, of different kinds of wild-fowl, and of the pastry, still contended, in his asides to Gerald, that he had never got through so uncomfortable a dinner.

'It quite agrees,' he continued, 'with all I have heard of every thing in Ireland, where every thing just comes near to what it ought to be — manner, mind, dress, house, furniture, equipage, dinner — and yet always wants a certain something to make it as perfect as we have it at home.'

But Gerald, from his slight insight into the hurry and doubt which had presided over the first needful arrangements for this particular dinner, argued that Mr. Gunning was not quite at liberty to take it as a fair specimen of all the other dinners given by individuals of wealth, as well as of fashion, throughout the Emerald Island.

'Champagne?' queried Mr. Gunning, in mixed satisfaction, doubt, and surprise, as an attendant proffered it, while he devoured some preserved-fruit pie — 'Well!' he turned round to be ready for the glass, saying to Gerald, 'in the fuss this makes, one can swallow it, whatever it is like': and when he had caused the foaming liquor to disappear — 'Gooseberry,' he added; 'but good gooseberry, however'; and he seemed slightly conciliated.

'Mr. Blount, my esteemed young friend, you will agree with us, poor English-Irish, that our lot *is* a sad one, in this wretched country,' began Mr. Gore, adverting to a conversation which for some time had been going on between almost all the guests except Gunning and Gerald, who did not even attend to it; 'and so will your excellent friend at your right.'

'I don't know that,' said Gunning.

'But, my worthy Mr. Gunning,' resumed Mr. Gore, in almost the full re-bloom of his smiles, which reminded Gerald of an old air of his country, 'a rose tree in full bearing':[8] — 'Before we accept your dissent, you will allow us to remind you upon what grounds we have all agreed to reckon on the great pleasure of your vote: you surely are aware in

4. The parenthesis is not of course spoken by Gunning, but with it the narrator directs the reader forward.
5. 'To chew the cud' is a proverbial expression meaning to think over, to consider slowly.
6. Sherry and Madeira are fortified wines, Moselle is a dry white wine, La Fitte the name of a chateau/vineyard in the Bordeaux region. Claret is a general term for the red wines of Bordeaux, and one used indiscriminately in eighteenth- and nineteenth-century Ireland where claret-drinking was regarded as an excessive habit of the land-owning and professional classes.
7. An effervescent, slightly alcoholic drink made by fermenting a mixture of syrup, root ginger and yeast.
8. This quotation cannot be identified.

what a situation we are this evening placed; scarce able to enjoy the happiness of each other's society; scarce able to celebrate, convivially, the domestic event that brings us together.'

'I certainly was not aware that you were all placed in any such situation,' answered Gunning.

'Indeed! — not that we sit here expecting, in the course of a few hours, an attempt to destroy us, and every person of our religious and political opinions in Dublin?'

'No. What kind of an attempt? by whom? — what the deuce does he mean?' turning to Gerald.

'By the Popish Rockites, my dear friend, who rush up from their native wilds for the purpose, and who are to be joined by the old Popish rebels of the liberty,[9] my dear Sir — the discontented weavers.'

'With their shuttles,[10] positively,' lisped Flood. Gunning looked hard from Mr. Gore to him; and after a moment's scrutiny, seemed to comprehend.

'How has this been found out?' he inquired dubiously.

'We are not, perhaps, precisely in possession of the information necessary to answer your question, my good Sir; or, perhaps,' — assuming official mystery — 'it would not be considered prudent at the Cawstle[11] if we did answer it; but found out the thing has been.'

'And you are so positive that it must happen?'

'Providence — who, since the first planting of English interests in this miserable country, has wonderfully upheld those interests, against an immense numerical odds of the Papist people — may, indeed, be pleased to avert our danger. But so nearly positive are we of what we have to encounter, that, before twilight, the guards were doubled at the Cawstle, and at every other point through Dublin; our garrison, of many thousand men, received orders to be in readiness for instant action; horse-police, (the great Duke's excellent institution when he was Secretary[12] at the Cawstle,) assisted by squadrons of the —th dragoons, began to patrol our streets, — hush! there some of them go by; — and you could not find one loyal Protestant house, in our whole city, unbarricaded, this moment, or the male inmates of one unprepared to defend to the last, their hearths, their families, their religion, and all that is dear to them.'

'Then, I suppose, I sit in a fortified hold?'[13]

'Indeed, my dear friend, you do. I took every precaution, to be sure, against unnecessarily alarming, by my measures, such of our guests as the affair might prove new to, or might jar too much'; bowing, and now sadly smiling from one lady to another round the table.

'But we knew we could depend on you, Mr. Gore; indeed, we did,' said Miss Flint.

'Thank you, my dear Miss Flint; I hope still to be found worthy of your good opinion. But, my dear Mr. Gunning, I trust I was not, therefore, deficient in energy and foresight, in arranging every means of defence; and so well secured are our doors and windows, so watchful my servants, and so well armed too, together with many who hear me, that, even supposing our patrols surprised abroad in the city, it will require a large and determined body of rebels to overpower us.'

'Oh, we need have little fear, after all,' resumed Miss Flint; 'the savages will get what they deserve — only I don't know what in the living world I shall do with myself when I hear the shots, and hear them roaring for us!' It seemed that Miss Flint enjoyed her panic in a strange kind of way, and anticipated the commotion in as much glee as anxiety.

'Then, from all you tell me, Mr. Gore, you must excuse my saying — notwithstanding your excellent soups, wines, and every thing else — that I wish I was safe at home, in No. 13, —— street, Grosvenor-square, instead of sitting here, this night.'

'Ah, my kind friend, well may you be excused; Ireland is, indeed, the country to wish to get out of.'

'Well; and 'tis the country *to* get out of, if we survive this bloody night; — and there's my comfort; and yours, too, should you only be inclined to follow my example.'

'But how? when — to live — we *cannot*, my dear friend; — when here, fortune has cast our lot, for good or ill — you surely will not at last decline to admit that lot to be, as I have said, a very sad one.'

9. One of the districts of Dublin known (even today) as 'the Liberties'. In the late eighteenth and early nineteenth centuries, inhabitants of these areas (especially craftsmen and their apprentices) were thought of as incorrigibly riotous. The description of them as 'popish rebels' reflects the speaker's tendency to read all social unrest as an omen of political catastrophe.
10. Bobbin-like devices used in weaving.
11. Spelled to indicate an affected accent. Dublin Castle was the centre of British administration in Ireland.
12. The 'great Duke' is Wellington, who was chief secretary for Ireland 1807-09.
13. A place of refuge, which could be held against attackers; a stronghold.

'Yes, indeed, since you cannot enjoy yourselves, in your houses, after dinner, in the metropolis of Ireland, watched over by your garrison of so many thousand men, without expecting to have yourselves put to death in cold blood. But to me, an Englishman, it seems rather strange that you cannot. Is there nothing to be done to get you and the people of the country to live better friends?'

'Nothing, my dear Mr. Gunning. They are a half-savage race who hate us, our religion, our superior station, and our English descent, just as the Caffers and Hottentots hate the members and subjects of our paternal Colonial Government at the Cape,[14] and —'

'If you give them the same cause for hatred, as that Colonial Government, which you call paternal, gives to the Caffers and Hottentots, I love *them* for hating *you* with all their hearts and souls,' interrupted Gunning.

'And I,' said Gerald.

'But of course you do not?' continued this plain-speaker, half-willing to relieve the profound blank of countenance his comment had produced.

'Indeed we do not. On the contrary, we strain every nerve to benefit them, and they won't let us.'

'How, twice over?'

'In the first place, we establish for them, all over the country, at great expense, our funds derived from individual donations and subscriptions, and from parliamentary grants; and into these schools they will not send their wild little children, merely because their bigoted priests object to our Bible without note or comment.'

'Nay,' said Mr. Priestly, 'we open that Bible to them, and on the authority of its Word, we prove to them that their priests are the teachers of an idolatrous and blasphemous superstition, in the mire of which they and their children wallow, and —'

'They won't believe you, I suppose?' asked Gunning.

'Before the rescinding, within the last forty years, of the principal penal statutes, they were inclined to be quieter, though they never could have grown to like us,' said the Judge's son, who was 'going to the bar'[15] — a great 'go,' (as he would himself have said,) amongst all classes of young English-Irish, from the tradesman's son to the Earl's; — 'Since, then, however, according as Papist-attornies, and barristers, and merchants, and farmers, have sprung up, and have been permitted to brawl their way on, in the Four-Courts, and to make demagogue speeches at taverns, and to engage in all kinds of traffic, and to take, nay, to become absolute proprietors of land, — while nothing can be more injurious to English ascendancy[16] in this country, than their thus engrossing much professional and social influence, which ought to be limited to the King's loyal subjects, the sturdiness, and the presumption, generated, at the same time, amongst the lower orders of their countrymen, in consequence of their petty elevation, is intolerable, Mr. Gunning, and may be said to be the chief cause of our uncomfortable situation in Mr. Gore's house, Sir, this very night.'

'If they spare us, this very night, I have no quarrel with them about the "sturdiness" however,' said Gunning; 'I hope they'll grow as sturdy as they can, it will be all the better for them — the peasants of my country are sturdy rascals, and I think well of them for it — I am sturdy myself, and I like myself because I am. But, concerning the presumption?'

'Perhaps Mr. Gunning will allow me to explain that,' said old Sir John Lumley, bowing graciously; 'I ought to know something of it; I have been dealing with those people these — that is, since I came of age; and about the time mentioned by my learned young friend opposite to me — or rather some years afterwards — I found them tractable, and respectful, and obedient, almost to the extent one could expect from beings of their caste; but, as my learned young friend also has said, ever since persons of their religion, and sprung almost from their own class, began to figure away as counsellors, forsooth, and demagogues, and gentlemen farmers, ay, and landed gentlemen too, and rich merchants —'

'And would-be bank-directors[17] — I beg your pardon, Sir John, but my hint may add to the

14. The Cape Colony in southern Africa finally became British in 1814, and was thereafter harassed by Kaffir (Caffer) tribes. As early as 1726 the term 'Hottentot' (another tribe of this region) had become pejorative in English, and the drift here is to identify the Irish with these despised African peoples. Barry Sloan (*The Pioneers of Anglo-Irish Fiction*, pp. 99, 102-03) comments on Banim's awareness of racialist assumptions.

15. Studying law before being called to the bar (as a barrister).

16. The noun is now familiar all but exclusively through the phrase 'the protestant ascendancy' (see Introduction to this section for an account of its emergence), but here the noun's availability for other compounds is still evident.

17. A crisis had occurred in Irish banking in 1820.

information you are conveying to our English friend,' said the brewer of the beer Mr. Gunning had sent back to the sideboard, who, by the way, *was* a bank-director.

'Yes, Mr.—a—a—Blake — thank you; — yes, Mr. Gunning, some of those mushroom, purse-proud Papists, thought to foist themselves in also amongst the respectable persons who manage the important concerns of our national bank; but they met the repulse they merited. And to continue — ever since the common people of this country saw their fellow-papists making way in the different pursuits I have described, nothing can equal the remarkable change that has taken place in their demeanour towards the Protestant noblemen and gentry, who, generally speaking, are, thank God! yet their landlords.'

'For instance, Sir John?'

'Why, my good Sir, these fellows absolutely begin to threaten you, upon the slightest provocation, with summoning you, and processing you, and going to law with you.'

'The deuce they do,' sneered Gunning.

'Think of that!' cried Miss Flint.

'Yes, Sir,' resumed Sir John; 'I assure you, Mr. Gunning — I assure you, Mr. Blount — that the son of a fellow whom, thirty or forty years ago, you might have paid with a horse-whipping, or with setting your dogs at his heels, if he presumed to teaze you with a complaint of high rent, or a complaint against your land-steward, or for breaking his fence, or for treading down a few of his potatoe-stalks, or a few blades of his corn, or what not, out hunting — the son of that same fellow will now threaten to indict you for a common assault at the quarter-sessions, when you only lay your whip across his shoulders, upon any such annoying occasion.'

'The slave! Does he not knock you clean down?' asked Gunning, suddenly thumping the table, as he gave way to the indignation of a man born, and, almost to the present moment, living amongst a free and independent people.

The ladies started. The gentlemen looked at each other. During a short pause — 'This is quite too bad,' said he to Gerald; 'come away.'

'Stay, for Heaven's sake!' said Gerald, as he prepared to rise upon his stick: 'I share your feelings; but let us recollect ourselves, — our fair friends; see, they are frightened.'

'Are they? I beg your pardon, Mrs. Gore,' grunted Gunning, quietly re-seating himself.

'Besides,' added Gerald, 'you know we cannot well force our way out of this fortified house; and even if we did, it were but to face the Rockites and disaffected weavers.'

'Stuff! — if there really were such a mob in the streets, I could find in my heart to go out and head them in upon these people.'

'But the main question,' said Mr. Gore, softening over the late little explosion with a muster of all his best graces, 'and, indeed, the most useful one, is, how are we to take millions of wretched and ferocious peasantry of Ireland, out of the hands of those who so inflame them against us, in order, as you so properly have remarked, my dear Mr. Gunning, to live at peace with them, and to guard against the recurrence of such nights as we now sit exposed to?'

'Educate them,' said Lady Offally.

'Your Ladyship knows they won't be educated on our plan.'

'Couldn't noblemen and gentlemen get a law passed to take their children from them by force, and send them to school?' asked Miss Gore regally, with a slight glance upon Sir John.

'If indeed, by any good and lawful means, we could get the poor infants under our care, at the very earliest age, and allow them to develope the "determination which God has given to their nature," and "the germ of his everlasting Word, by which the whole universe was created, and upon which all existence, spiritual as well as material, depends," resumed Lady Offally, quoting from a mystic little book,[18] 'then, indeed, we might hope to see the natives of this country improved in the rising generation. A few of such infant schools, on the principle of Pestalozzi,[19] established by myself, I have great hopes of, as you know, Miss Flint.'

18. Spiritual handbooks proliferated as the capacity of the printing presses increased with successive technical advances.
19. Johann Heinrich Pestalozzi (1746-1827), Swiss educational reformer. His theories, which laid the foundation for modern elementary education, were adopted in Ireland by John Synge (1788-1845), grandfather of the playwright John Millington Synge (1871-1909). John 'Pestalozzi' Synge (as he became known) was responsible for publishing educational primers at Roundwood, Co. Wicklow; for example, *The Relations and Description of Forms, According to the Principles of Pestalozzi* (1817). However, Synge was also an active evangelical, and in 1827 he moved to Devonshire to join a group of 'Brethren', followers of a movement launched in Dublin in 1825 but later better known as The Plymouth Brethren. In Banim's novel, Lady Offally combines Synge's evangelicalism and his Pestalozzian educational theories.

'Ah, no wonder!' assented Miss Flint; 'those your Ladyship showed me, last month, in the country! Lots of the poor little dears, Mrs. Gore, sitting on mats, to keep the damp of the clay floor from their poor little — bodies,' hesitating, 'and none of them more than three or four years old; and they so comfortable there, the day long, out of harm's way, and fretted with nothing in the world wide, but just allowed to "develope the consciousness of the divine germ within their own hearts!' Think of that! So, educate them after dear, delightful Pestalozzi, I say too.'

'Educate them, but not so vaguely,' observed Mr. Priestly: 'educate them in the letter as well as in the spirit of the Word: that, and that only, will allow you to be friends with them, and avert recurrences of such a night as this.'

'That is, convert them,' said Lord Harmer.

'Keep them down,' recommended Sir John Lumley.

'And begin with the demagogues,' added the Judge's son, 'and the "counsellors,"' with a sneer.

'Make them tidy,' exhorted Miss Flint; 'support our society, teach them to go neat, and to turn small loans, and to whitewash.'

At the last word Mr. Gore slightly started.

'Set them to drain all the bogs,' said Lord Offally.

'And to improve the fisheries,' hinted Lord Friar.

'Thin them,'[20] advised a young Fellow of Dublin College.

'That's the way,' agreed the Militia lieutenant.

'Yes, ship them off, in fleets, to our colonies,' recommended Mr. Blake.

'And afterwards, — indeed, immediately, — make marriage amongst those who stay at home, except under prescribed circumstances, and at a certain age, penal,' said the young clergyman who had pronounced grace, a deep student in Malthus.[21]

'Think of that!' cried Miss Flint, looking very much pleased at him, (though astonished and puzzled,) in gratitude for his confining matrimony to 'a certain age.'

'Mine is a shorter way,' resumed the young Fellow of College; 'they and their demagogues threaten us with their numbers — *let* them rebel.'

'Ay, and thin them then,' echoed the lieutenant.

'What say you, Mr. Gunning?' asked Mr. Gore.

'Oh, nothing like leather,' answered the cynic.

Mrs. Gore arose to lead her fair battalion to the drawing-room, ere Mr. Gunning gave his reply; as if, indeed, she and they were not to sit and listen to the opinions of so uncouth a person.

The moment they had retired, Lord Friar raised his glass, and while his common, vacant, and disagreeable features betrayed a peculiar excitement — 'Come, Gore,' he said boisterously, 'you shall have *my* remedy in my old toast at the "Beef-steak," and here it is — "The Pope in the pillory, the pillory in h-ll, pelted with priests by the d——l!"'

Amid the cheer which followed, Gunning arose, and said, 'I decline that toast.'

'And so do I,' said Gerald, standing by his side, and offering him his unhurt arm.

Glances were interchanged round the table, and Lord Friar began to swell. A shout in the street, as if in answer to the cheer that had just been given, diverted the rising storm. Every face now looked more seriously occupied; the next instant, while the shouts abroad continued, a kind of clashing was heard. The next, screams echoed from the drawing-room; a rush of light and small feet came downstairs; two servants, pale and agitated, stumbled into the dining-room, both faltering — 'Oh, Sir! — Oh, gentlemen!' and as Mrs. Gore and all of her fair party, Miss Maria Gore excepted, rushed in, still more pale and frightened, some yet shrieking, (Miss Flint the loudest,) and some prepared to swoon in the first pair of strong arms they could encounter — 'Up, gentlemen, and arm! — Spike! throw open the lockers of that sideboard![22] It is the bloodthirsty yell of the Papists, by Heavens!' cried Mr. Gore.

20. i.e. reduce their numbers.
21. Rev. Thomas Robert Malthus (1766-1834), the English economist who put forward the theory that human resources grow at a crucially slower rate that human population, and who therefore argued for 'checks' on population growth; his *The Nature and Progress of Rent* was published in 1815.
22. During periods of agrarian unrest, weapons were kept in the sideboards of larger houses as a precaution against sudden attacks; hence they were locked until the emergency arose. In this case, the emergency is a false alarm.

GERALD GRIFFIN

(1803-40)

from: THE COLLEGIANS: A TALE OF GARRYOWEN (1829)

[Gerald Griffin's life was short and his writing career produced a patchwork fictional description of Ireland to which both the historical novel and the shorter tale contributed. *The Collegians* is unchallengeably his greatest achievement, and indeed it possesses a unique position in the canon of Irish fiction for its detailed social description and its fictionalized plot, which it suggests as together symbolic of an Irish catholic middle-class milieu. The story is based on an actual incident that occurred in Griffin's native County Limerick, a callous killing of a young woman (Ellen Hanley) whose body was washed up on the Shannon estuary at Kilrush, Co. Clare at the end of July 1819. John Scanlon, of one of Limerick's leading families, was arrested and charged; Daniel O'Connell defended Scanlon, but he was convicted and executed. (A humbler accomplice, Stephen Sullivan, had been arrested somewhat later, and he too was convicted and executed.) The common belief that Griffin acted as a court-room reporter during the trial cannot be supported by the available evidence.

The four opening chapters of the novel are rich in details, stylistic and allusive, which establish an urbane relation between the narrator and the reader. Quotation acts as a form of mutual understanding, and the deliberate elaboration of the physical scene moves very gradually to relate aspects of social history that give the as yet delayed theme of emotional dichotomy a deeper significance. First, there is the distance in time between County Limerick in the 1770s or 1780s and in the 1820s, a distance that the narrative relates explicitly to the status of 'middlemen' epitomized here in Mr Daly, Kyrle Daly's father. Second, there is the intervention, so to speak, of Scanlon's actual crime between the historical setting and the narrator's present-day perspective; if the reader recognizes this impingement of recent events upon the fiction, then the contrast between conditions in the 1780s and the 1820s is modified, if not indeed compromised. Commentators have pointed to what they regard as 'incongruities' in the decor of the Daly household, and one critic has sought to explain them by differentiating between rural Irish society and a normal, stable society. It seems more profitable to concentrate on the manner in which Griffin establishes a detailed yet unobtrusive domestic interior in which the Dalys take their breakfast. While the lower-class characters (Eily O'Connor, her father, and her uncle, who is a priest) are explicitly catholic, Griffin maintains a more generalized depiction of the middle-class household. In terms of verisimilitude, the principal male characters cannot be depicted as having trained to be barristers and yet also be depicted as catholics, unless the claim of setting the novel in the early 1780s is abandoned. But Griffin is far from presenting the Daly family as conformists to the established church. What his technique achieves is a more subtle *indeterminacy* on the question of denomination.

On this score, a contrast with Maturin's *Women* is obvious. Yet both novels focus upon emotional dichotomy, and it is worth adding that both novels are concerned with *fatal* passion, with kinds of extreme *mésalliance*, emphasized in each case by the presence of a more cautious attendant (anti-) hero. In part the fictional hero's conflict is treated through a contrast between him (Hardress Cregan) and his friend Kyrle Daly, the contrast of sensibility (or passion) and sense (or caution). It is possible to read this not simply as an Irish exercise in themes well established by Jane Austen more than a decade earlier, but also as an inquiry into the historical substance of desire, of hope, of ambition. Here the complex relationship between the time of the setting (imprecise and even inconsistent though it may be) and the time of Griffin's writing of *The Collegians* gains further interest. For the past and present may also be interpreted in terms of passion and caution, and the narrator's occasional observations on changing fortunes (among the cottiers, for example) are one way in which the past is implicitly censured for the ambition or complacency of the characters who lived then. The opening chapters of *The Collegians* succeed as fiction in a way that little else written in the period under review succeeds. One can look ahead as far as the middle of the nineteenth century and say with confidence that Griffin comes closer to accomplishment in this genre than any Irish novelist apart from Maria Edgeworth. And yet he abandoned literature in favour of the religious life, and then died at the age of thirty-six.]

CHAPTER I

HOW GARRYOWEN ROSE, AND HOW IT FELL

The little ruined outlet, which gives its name to one of the most popular national songs of Erin,[1] is

1. A poetical name for Ireland, used in the romantic period. In grammatical form it is actually the genitive of the Irish name Eire.

situate on the acclivity of a hill near the city of Limerick, commanding a not uninteresting view of that fine old town, with the noble stream that washes its battered towers, and a richly cultivated surrounding country. Tradition has preserved the occasion of its celebrity, and the origin of its name, which appears to be compounded of two Irish words signifying 'Owen's garden.' — A person so called was the owner, about half a century since, of a cottage and plot of ground on this spot, which from its contiguity to the town, became a favourite holiday resort with the young citizens of both sexes — a lounge presenting accommodations somewhat similar to those which are offered to the London mechanic by the Battersea tea-gardens.[2] Owen's garden was the general rendezvous for those who sought for simple amusement or for dissipation. The old people drank together under the shade of trees — the young played at ball, goal, or other athletic exercises on the green; while a few lingering by the hedge-rows with their fair acquaintances, cheated the time with sounds less boisterous, indeed, but yet possessing their fascination also.

The festivities of our fathers, however, were frequently distinguished by so fierce a character of mirth, that, for any difference in the result of their convivial meetings, they might as well have been pitched encounters. Owen's garden was soon as famous for scenes of strife, as it was for mirth and humour; and broken heads became a staple article of manufacture in the neighbourhood.

This new feature in the diversions of the place, was encouraged by a number of young persons of a rank somewhat superior to that of the usual frequenters of the garden. They were the sons of the more respectable citizens, the merchants and wholesale traders of the city, just turned loose from school with a greater supply of animal spirits than they had wisdom to govern. Those young gentlemen being fond of wit, amused themselves by forming parties at night, to wring the heads off all the geese, and the knockers off all the hall doors in the neighbourhood. They sometimes suffered their genius to soar as high as the breaking a lamp, and even the demolition of a watchman; but, perhaps, this species of joking was found a little too serious to be repeated over frequently, for few achievements of so daring a violence are found amongst their records. They were obliged to content themselves with the less ambitious distinction of destroying the knockers and store-locks, annoying the peaceable inmates of the neighbouring houses, with long continued assaults on the front doors, terrifying the quiet passengers with every species of insult and provocation, and indulging their fratricidal propensities against all the geese in Garryowen.

The fame of the 'Garryowen boys' soon spread far and wide. Their deeds were celebrated by some inglorious minstrel of the day in that air which has since resounded over every quarter of the world; and even disputed the palm of national popularity with 'Patrick's day.'[3] A string of jolly verses were appended to the tune which soon enjoyed a notoriety similar to that of the famous 'Lilliburlero, bullen-a-la' which sung King James out of his three kingdoms.[4] The name of Garryowen was as well known as that of the Irish Numantium, Limerick, itself,[5] and Owen's little garden became almost a synonime for Ireland.

But that principle of existence which assigns to the life of man its periods of youth, maturity, and decay, has its analogy in the fate of villages, as in that of empires. Assyria fell, and so did Garryowen! Rome had its decline, and Garryowen was not immortal. Both are now an idle sound, with nothing but the recollections of old tradition to invest them with an interest. The still notorious suburb is little better than a heap of rubbish, where a number of smoked and mouldering walls, standing out from the masses of stone and mortar, indicate the position of a once populous row of dwelling houses. A few roofs yet remain unshaken, under which some impoverished families endeavour to work out a wretched subsistence by maintaining a species of huxter trade,[6] by cobbling old shoes, and manufacturing ropes. A small rookery wearies the ears of the inhabitants at one end of the outlet, and a rope-

2. A fashionable recreational area in south London.

3. The song 'Garryowen' tells how, in the 1770s, two young squireens of Limerick, Johnny Connell and Darby O'Brien, ran riot in the district, defying all authority. 'Patrick's Day in the Morning' was another song particularly popular in Limerick.

4. A vigorously anti-Jacobite song which in the 1680s and 1690s became a rallying anthem for those who deposed King James II and fought against him in Ulster. The orange lily was the symbol of the supporters of William of Orange, and the words 'Lilliburlero, bullenala' seemingly are a corruption of *An lile ba léir é ba linn an lá* (The lily was triumphant and we won the day).

5. Numantia was a Celtic site in Spain. It withstood Rome until 133 B.C.; with its fall, organized resistance to Rome came to an end in Spain. Limerick endured a prolonged siege in 1691 by the forces of William III, Irish Jacobite resistance generally coming to an end with the Treaty of Limerick.

6. i.e. huckster: a pedlar, a hawker.

walk[7] which extends along the adjacent slope of Gallows-green, (so called for certain reasons) brings to the mind of the conscious spectator, associations that are not calculated to enliven the prospect. Neither is he thrown into a more jocular frame of mind as he picks his steps over the insulated paving stones that appear amid the green slough with which the street is deluged, and encounters at the other end, an alley of coffin-makers' shops, with a fever hospital on one side, and a church-yard on the other. A person who was bent on a journey to the other world, could not desire a more expeditious outfit than Garryowen could now afford him: nor a more commodious choice of conveyances, from the machine on the slope above glanced at, to the pest-house[8] at the farther end.

But it is ill talking lightly on a serious subject. The days of Garryowen are gone, like those of ancient Erin; and the feats of her once formidable heroes are nothing more than a winter's evening tale. Owen is in his grave, and his garden looks dreary as a ruined church-yard. The greater number of his merry customers have followed him to a narrower play-ground, which, though not less crowded, affords less room for fun, and less opportunity for contention. The worm is here the reveller, the owl whoops out his defiance without an answer, save the echo's, the best whiskey in Munster would not now 'drive the cold out of their hearts';[9] and the withered old sexton is able to knock the bravest of them over the pate with impunity. A few perhaps may still remain to look back with a fond shame to the scene of their early follies, and to smile at the page in which those follies are recorded.

Still, however, there is something to keep the memory alive of those unruly days, and to preserve the name of Garryowen from utter extinction. The annual fair which is held on the spot presents a spectacle of gaiety and uproar which might rival its most boisterous days; and strangers still enquire for the place with a curiosity which its appearance seldom fails to disappoint. Our national lyrist[10] has immortalized the air by adapting to it one of the liveliest of his melodies; — the adventures, of which it was once the scene, constitute a fund of standing joke and anecdote which are not neglected by the neighbouring story-tellers; — and a rough voice may still occasionally be heard by the traveller who passes near its ruined dwellings at evening, to chaunt a stanza of the chorus which was once in the mouth of every individual in the kingdom:

'Tis there we'll drink the nut-brown ale
An pay the reck'nin' on the nail
No man for debt shall go to jail
From Garryowen a gloria.[11]

7. A long stretch of ground used for twisting ropes in manufacture. In the novel, it is an early omen of fatal events to come, since ropes were associated with hanging and execution.
8. A refuge, or place of detention, for those suffering from the plague or other contagious disease.
9. A traditional and well-attested claim for the liquid in question.
10. Thomas Moore (1779-1852).
11. A verse from 'Garryowen'; see note 3 above.

CHAPTER II

HOW EILY O'CONNOR PUZZLED ALL THE INHABITANTS OF GARRYOWEN

But while Owen lived,[1] and while his garden flourished, he and his neighbours were as merry together, as if death could never reach the one, nor desolation waste the other. Among those frequenters of his little retreat whom he distinguished with an especial favour and attention, the foremost was the handsome daughter of an old man who conducted the business of a rope-walk in his neighbourhood, and who was accustomed on a fine Saturday evening to sit under the shade of a yellow osier that stood by his door, and discourse of the politics of the day — of Lord Halifax's administration — of the promising young patriot Mr. Henry Grattan — and of the famous Catholic concession of 1773.[2] Owen, like all Irishmen, even of

1. Griffin here is generating what purports to be an actual, historical figure from the place-name Garryowen. The effect of course is to underline the pastness of this period.
2. George Montague Dunk (1716-71), 2nd earl of Halifax, was viceroy of Ireland 1761-63. This was the period when Whiteboy insurrection originally began in Munster, a fact ostentatiously not alluded to in sketching this historical background. Henry Grattan (1746-1820) did not enter parliament until 1775, making his maiden speech in December 1775. The catholic concessions of 1773 — here listed *after* reference to Grattan, as if he were somehow a participant in their implementation — were nothing substantial or distinctive, although there were minor concessions in statutes of 1772 and 1774. In all, this sentence presents a very loose historical summary, in which the nineteenth-century veneration of Henry Grattan is central but implausible.

Note, however, that this is the period about which Mihil O'Connor discourses, and so this may lie some years earlier than the central

the humblest rank, was an acute critic in female proportions, and although time had blown away the thatching from his head, and by far the greater portion of blood that remained in his frame had colonized about his nose, yet the manner in which he held forth on the praises of his old friend's daughter was such as put to shame her younger and less eloquent admirers. It is true, indeed, that the origin of the suburban beauty was one which, in a troubled country like Ireland, had little of agreeable association to recommend it;[3] but few even of those to whom twisted hemp was an object of secret terror, could look on the exquisitely beautiful face of Eily O'Connor, and remember that she was a rope-maker's daughter; few could detect beneath the timid, hesitating, downcast gentleness of manner, which shed an interest over all her motions, the traces of a harsh and vulgar education. It was true that she sometimes purloined a final letter from the King's adjectives, and prolonged the utterance of a vowel beyond the term of prosodaical orthodoxy,[4] but the tongue that did so seemed to move on silver wires, and the lip on which the sound delayed

'long murmuring, loth to part'[5]

imparted to its own accents an association of sweetness and grace, that made the defect an additional allurement. Her education in the outskirts of a city had not impaired the natural tenderness of her character; for her father, who all rude as he was, knew how to value his daughter's softness of mind, endeavoured to foster it by every indulgence in his power. Her uncle, too, who was now a country parish priest, was well qualified to draw forth any natural talent with which she had been originally endowed. He had completed his theological education in the famous university of Salamanca,[6] where he was distinguished as a youth of much quietness of temper and literary application, rather than as one of those furious gesticulators, those *'figures Hibernoises,'* amongst whom Gil Blas, in his fit of logical lunacy, could meet his only equals.[7] At his little lodging, while he was yet a curate at St. John's,[8] Eily O'Connor was accustomed to spend a considerable portion of her time, and in return for her kindness in presiding at his simple tea-table, father Edward undertook to bestow a degree of attention on her education, which rendered her, in a little time, as superior in knowledge, as she was in beauty, to her female associates. She was remarked likewise at this time, as a little devotee, very regular in her attendance at chapel, constant in all the observances of her religion, and grave in her attire and discourse. On the coldest and dreariest morning in winter, she might be seen gliding along by the unopened shop-windows to the nearest chapel, where she was accustomed to hear an early mass, and return in time to set every thing in order for her father's breakfast. During the day she superintended his household affairs, while he was employed upon the adjacent rope-walk; and, in the evening, she usually slipped on her bonnet, and went across the street to father Edward's, where she chatted away until tea was over; if he happened to be engaged in reading his daily office, she amused herself with a volume of moral entertainment, such as Rasselas Prince of Abyssinia, or Mr. Addison's Spectator,[9] until he was at leisure to hear her lessons. An attachment of the purest and tenderest nature was the consequence of those mutual attentions between the uncle and niece, and it might be said that if the former loved her not as well, he knew and valued her character still better than her father.

Father Edward however was appointed to a parish, and Eily lost her instructor. It was for her a severe loss, and most severe in reality when its effect upon her own spirits began to wear away. For some

---

action involving his daughter. Or it may be contemporary. The date remains indeterminate.

3. 'suburban' in the sense that Eily lives on the outskirts of the city, though Griffin's awareness of the growth of English cities and living patterns cannot be discounted.
4. In other words, Eily omitted pronunciation of the final 'g' in present infinitives (givin' etc.) and she drawled.
5. 'Loath to Depart' is the name of a tune, and the phrase has become fossilized in the language.
6. Salamanca is an ancient Spanish university (founded 1227, chartered 1243) in which an Irish college was established in 1592; it was closely associated with the training of priests for Ireland in the eighteenth century.
7. Gil Blas is the comic hero of a novel of the same name by Alan-René Lesage (1668-1747), translated into English by Tobias Smollett in 1749.
8. Catholic parish in the city of Limerick; the post-emancipation St John's Cathedral dates from 1856.
9. Samuel Johnson (1709-84) published his fictional allegory *Rasselas* in 1759. *The Spectator* was a periodical conducted by Sir Richard Steele (1672-1729) and Joseph Addison (1672-1719) in 1711-12, and revived by Addison in 1714. The papers published in it were presented as if written by 'Mr Spectator', a much travelled observer of human life. Note here the distinctly English and literary reading that Eily absorbs in her uncle, the priest's house.

months after his departure, she continued to lead the same retired and unobtrusive life, and no eye, save that of a consummate observer, could detect the slightest alteration in her sentiments, the least increase of toleration for the world and worldly amusements. That change however had been silently effected in her heart. She was now a woman — a lovely, intelligent, full grown woman — and circumstances obliged her to take a part in the little social circle which moved around her. Her spirits were naturally light, and, though long repressed, became readily assimilated to the buoyant tone of the society in which she happened to be placed. Her father, who, with a father's venial vanity, was fond of showing his beautiful child among his neighbours, took her with him one evening to Owen's garden, at a time when it was unusually gay and crowded, and from that evening might be dated the commencement of a decided and visible change in the lovely Eily's character.

As gradual as the approach of a spring morning, was the change from grave to gay in the costume of this flower of the suburbs. It dawned at first in a handsome bow-knot upon her head-dress, and ended in the full noontide splendor of flowered muslins, silks, and sashes. It was like the opening of the rose-bud, which gathers around it the winged wooers of the summer meadow. 'Lads, as brisk as bees,'[10] came thronging in her train, with proffers of 'honourable love and rites of marriage';[11] and even among the youths of a higher rank, whom the wild levity of Irish blood and high spirits, sent to mingle in the festivities of Owen's garden, a jealousy prevailed respecting the favour of the handsome rope-maker's daughter. It was no wonder that attentions paid by individuals so much superior to her ordinary admirers, should render Eily indifferent to the sighs of those plebeian suitors. Dunat O'Leary, the hair-cutter, or Foxy Dunat, as he was named in allusion to his red head, was cut to the heart by her utter coldness. Myles Murphy, likewise, a good natured farmer from Killarney, who travelled through the country selling Kerry ponies, and claiming relationship with every one he met, claimed kindred in vain with Eily, for his claim was not allowed. Lowry Looby too, the servant of Mr. Daly, a wealthy middleman[12] who lived in the neighbourhood, was suspected by many to entertain delusive hopes of Eily O'Connor's favour — but this report was improbable enough, for Lowry could not but know that he was a very ugly man; and if he were as beautiful as Narcissus,[13] Mihil O'Connor would still have shut the door in his face for being as poor as Timon.[14] So that though there was no lack of admirers, the lovely Eily, like many celebrated beauties in a higher rank, ran, after all, a fair chance of becoming what Lady Mary Montague has elegantly termed 'a lay nun.'[15] Even so a bookworm, who will pore over a single volume from morning till night, if turned loose into a library, wanders from shelf to shelf, bewildered amid a host of temptations, and unable to make any election until he is surprised by twilight, and chagrined to find, that with so much happiness within his grasp, he has spent, nevertheless, an unprofitable day.

But accident saved Eily from a destiny so deeply dreaded and so often lamented as that above alluded to, — a condition which people generally agree to look upon as one of utter desolation, and which, notwithstanding, is frequently a state of greater happiness than its opposite. On the eve of the seventeenth of March, a day distinguished in the rope-maker's household, not only as the festival of the national Saint, but as the birth-day of the young mistress of the establishment;[16] on this

10. 'As brisk as bees' is a standard simile; a quotable instance occurs in James Boswell's *Life of Johnson* (1791).

11. Given the humble station of these poor suitors, these phrases are to be read as hopelessly unreal or insincere.

12. 'In districts where grain cultivation expanded after the 1750s or where sub-tenants' own cattle herds had grown, the chief tenantry increasingly released land to smallholders until eventually they became dependent on rent rather than agricultural sales for the greater part of their income. In this way, such tenants earned the new label that [Arthur] Young ungraciously bestowed on them in the 1770s: middlemen.' David Dickson, *New Foundations: Ireland 1660-1800* (Dublin: Helicon, 1987), pp. 109-10.

But if we recall not only the period of which Griffin writes (with some liberty as to historical fact), but also the period in which he wrote (the 1820s as described by the three clergymen on pp. 1135-38), then the benign and secure position of the middleman has to be read at several levels.

13. In Greek myth, Narcissus was a figure who so admired his own beauty gazing at his reflection in a pool, that he was changed into the flower that nods its head downwards towards water.

14. In Shakespeare's *Timon of Athens*, Timon, once immensely wealthy and vainly generous, comes to a position of absolute poverty.

15. Lady Mary Wortley Montague (1689-1762), English writer, who famously quarrelled with Alexander Pope.

16. The coincidence of Eily's birthday with Ireland's patron saint's day suggests a kind of national allegory running beneath the romantic narrative of Eily and Hardress; but if this is so, the allegory is deeply inauspicious of national ambitions in that Eily's fate is already sealed, as the ominous symbolism of her father's profession indicates. This pessimistic parallel between Ireland's patron and the doomed heroine

evening, Eily and her father were enjoying their customary relaxation at Owen's garden. The jolly proprietor was seated as usual, with his rope-twisting friend, under the yellow osier, while Myles Murphy, who had brought a number of his wild ponies to be disposed of at the neighbouring fairs, had taken his place at the end of the table, and was endeavouring to insinuate a distant relationship between the Owens of Kilteery, connections of the person whom he addressed, and the Murphys of Knockfodhra, connections of his own. A party of young men were playing fives at a ball alley,[17] on the other side of the green; and another, more numerous, and graced with many female figures, were capering away to the tune of the fox-hunter's jig, on the short grass.[18] Some poor old women, with baskets on their arms, were endeavouring to sell off some *Patrick's crosses* for children, at the low rate of one halfpenny a piece, gilding, paint, and all.[19] Others, fatigued with exertion, were walking under the still leafless trees, some with their hats, some with their coats off, jesting, laughing, and chatting familiarly with their female acquaintances.

Mihil O'Connor, happening to see Lowry Looby among the promenaders, glancing now and then at the dance, and whistling Patrick's day,[20] requested him to call his daughter out of the group, and tell her that he was waiting for her to go home. Lowry went, and returned to say, that Eily was dancing with a strange young gentleman in a boating dress, and that he would not let her go until she had finished the slip jig.[21]

It continued a sufficient time to tire the old man's patience. When Eily did at last make her appearance, he observed there was a flush of mingled weariness and pleasure on her cheek, which showed that the delay was not quite in opposition to her own inclinations. This circumstance might have tempted him to receive her with a little displeasure, but that honest Owen at that moment laid hold on both father and daughter, insisting that they should come in and take supper with his wife and himself.

This narrative of Eily's girlhood being merely introductory, we shall forbear to furnish any detail of the minor incidents of the evening, or the quality of Mrs. Owen's entertainment. They were very merry and happy; so much so, that the Patrick's eve approached its termination, before they arose to bid their host and hostess a good night. Owen advised them to walk on rapidly in order to avoid the 'Pathrick's boys' who would promenade the streets after twelve, to welcome in the mighty festival with music and uproar of all kinds. Some of the lads he said, 'might be playen' their thricks upon Miss Eily.'[22]

The night was rather dark, and the dim glimmer of the oil-lamps which were suspended at long intervals over the street doors tended only in a very feeble degree to qualify the gloom. Mihil O'Connor and his daughter had already performed more than half their journey, and were turning from a narrow lane at the head of Mungret-street,[23] when a loud and tumultuous sound broke with sudden violence upon their hearing. It proceeded from a multitude of people who were moving in confused and noisy procession along the street. An ancient and still honoured custom summons the youthful inhabitants of the city on the night of this anniversary to celebrate the approaching holiday of the patron Saint and apostle of the island, by promenading all the streets in succession, playing national airs, and filling up the pauses in the music with shouts of exultation. Such was the procession which the two companions now beheld approaching.

The appearance which it presented was not altogether destitute of interest and amusement. In the midst were a band of musicians who played

is contrasted in the optimistic, though inconsistent, citations of political reform in the 1770s.

If one turns from the fiction to the actual crime upon which Griffin based the central plot of *The Collegians*, the date takes on a further significance. John Scanlon, despite Daniel O'Connell's advocacy, was hanged on 16 March 1820, i.e. St. Patrick's Eve, for the murder of Ellen Hanley. (See O'Connell's letter of 15 March 1820, above.) Griffin is not entirely clear as to whether his fated heroine was born on the 16th or the 17th, and so her birthday may fall on the patron saint's day or on the date on which the real-life murderer of her near-namesake (Eily O'Connor) was executed. Thus she is perilously balanced between honour and contumely.

17. Hand-ball was a popular game in the late eighteenth century, and survived into the twentieth.
18. 'The short grass' is trimmed, what we would today call a lawn, though this latter term in the seventeenth and eighteenth centuries was usually applied to open grass-land, as in a park.
19. Probably made of woven and decorated straw, as in the case of the still familiar St Bridget's Cross.
20. 'St. Patrick's Day' was a popular song, and its echo in these early chapters sustains the mordant parallelism discussed in note 16 above.
21. A type of folk dance with a more subtle rhythm than the more familiar jig.
22. The phrases in quotation marks are used to indicate idiom and accent, and thus to remind the reader of the social milieu. 'thricks' = tricks.
23. Named after an early Christian monastic site, three miles south-west of Limerick.

alternately 'Patrick's day,' and 'Garryowen,' while a rabble of men and boys pressed round them, thronging the whole breadth and a considerable portion of the length of the street. The men had got sprigs of shamrock in their hats, and several carried in their hands lighted candles protected from the wasting night-blast by a simple lamp of whited brown paper. The fickle and unequal light which those small torches threw over the faces of the individuals who held them, afforded a lively contrast to the prevailing darkness.

The crowd hurried forward singing, playing, shouting, laughing, and indulging, to its full extent, all the excitement which was occasioned by the tumult and the motion. Bedroom windows were thrown up as they passed, and the half dressed inmates thrust their heads into the night air to gaze upon the mob of enthusiasts. All the respectable persons who appeared in the street as they advanced, turned short into the neighbouring byways to avoid the importunities which they would be likely to incur by a contact with the multitude.

But it was too late for our party to adopt this precaution. Before it had entered their minds, the procession (if we may dignify it by a name so sounding) was nearer to them than they were to any turn in the street, and the appearance of flight with a rabble of men, as with dogs, in a provocation of pursuit. Of this they were aware — and accordingly instead of attempting a vain retreat, they turned into a recess formed by one of the shop doors, and quietly awaited the passing away of this noisy torrent. For some moments they were unnoticed; the fellows who moved foremost being too busy in talking, laughing, and shouting, to pay any attention to objects, nor directly in their way. But they were no sooner espied than the wags assailed them with that species of wit, which distinguishes the inhabitants of the back lanes of a city, and forms the terror of all country visitors. These expressions were lavished upon the rope-maker and his daughter, until the former, who was as irritable an old fellow as Irishmen generally are, was almost put out of patience.

At length, a young man observing the lamp shine for a moment on Eily's handsome face, made a chirp with his lips as he passed by, as if he had a mind to kiss her. Not Papirius[24] himself, when vindicating his senatorial dignity against the insulting Gaul, could be more prompt in action than Mihil O'Connor. The young gentleman received in return for his affectionate greeting a blow over the temple which was worth five hundred kisses. An uproar immediately commenced, which was likely to end in some serious injury to the old man and his daughter. A number of ferocious faces gathered round them uttering sounds of harsh rancour and defiance; which Mihil met with equal loudness and energy. Indeed all that seemed to delay his fate and hinder him from sharing in the prostration of his victim was the conduct of Eily, who flinging herself in bare armed beauty before her father defended him for a time against the upraised weapons of his assailants. No one would incur the danger of harming, by an accidental blow, a creature so young, so beautiful, and so affectionate.

They were at length rescued from this precarious condition by the interposition of two young men in the dress of boatmen who appeared to possess some influence with the crowd, and who used it for the advantage of the sufferers. Not satisfied with having brought them safely out of all immediate danger, the taller of the two conducted them to their door, saying little on the way and taking his leave as soon as they were once in perfect safety. All that Mihil could learn from his appearance was, that he was a gentleman, and very young — perhaps not more than nineteen years of age. The old man talked much and loudly in praise of his gallantry, but Eily was altogether silent on the subject.

A few days after, Mihil O'Connor was at work upon the ropewalk, going slowly backward in the sunshine, with a bundle of hemp between his knees, and singing '*Maureen Thierna*.'§ A hunch-backed little fellow in a boatman's dress, came up, and saluting him in a sharp city brogue,[25] reminded the old rope-maker that he had done him a service a few evenings before. Mihil professed his acknowledgements, and with true Irish warmth of heart, assured the little boatman that all he had in the world was at his service. The hunch-back however only wanted a few ropes and blocks for his boat and even for those he was resolute in paying honourably. Neither did he seem anxious to satisfy the curiosity of old Mihil with respect to the name and quality of his com-

§ Little Mary Tierney.

24. A Roman patrician, Lucius Papirius Cursor is described by Livy (Books 8 and 9) as strict and severe.

25. Brogue is the term generally given to the Irish accent as spoken in England by emigrants; a strong regional or dialectal accent.

panion; for he was inexorable in maintaining that he was a turf boatman from Scagh who had come up to town with him to dispose of a cargo of fuel at Charlotte's Quay.[26] Mihil O'Connor referred him to his daughter for the ropes, about which he said she could bargain as well as himself, and he was unable to leave his work until the rope he had in hand should be finished. The little deformed, no way displeased at this intelligence, went to find Eily at the shop, where he spent a longer time than Mihil thought necessary for his purpose.

From this time forward the character of Eily O'Connor seemed to have undergone a second change. Her former gravity returned, but it did not re-appear under the same circumstances as before. In her days of religious retirement, it appeared only in her dress, and in her choice of amusements. Now, both her recreations and her attire were much gayer than ever, so much so as almost to approach a degree of dissipation, but her cheerfulness of mind was gone, and the sadness which had settled on her heart, like a black reef under sunny waters, was plainly visible through all her gaiety. Her father was too much occupied in his eternal rope-twisting to take particular notice of this change, and, besides, it is notorious that one's constant companions are the last to observe any alteration in one's manner or appearance.

One morning, when Mihil O'Connor left his room, he was surprized to find that the breakfast table was not laid as usual, and that his daughter was not in the house. She made her appearance, however, while he was himself making the necessary arrangements. They exchanged a greeting somewhat colder on the one side, and more embarrassed on the other, than was usual at the morning meetings of the father and daughter. But when she told him, that she had been only to the chapel, the old man was perfectly satisfied, for he knew that Eily would as readily think of telling a falsehood to the priest, as she would to her father. And when Mihil O'Connor heard that people were at the chapel, he generally concluded (poor old man!) that it was only to pray they went there.

In the meantime Myles Murphy renewed his proposals to Eily, and succeeded in gaining over the father to his interests. The latter was annoyed at his daughter's obstinate rejection of a fine fellow like Myles, with a very comfortable property, and pressed her either to give consent to the match or a good reason for her refusal. But this request, though reasonable, was not complied with: and the rope-maker, though not so hot as Capulet,[27] was as much displeased at the contumacy of his daughter. Eily, on her part, was so much afflicted at the anger of her only parent, that it is probable her grief would have made away with her if she had not prevented that catastrophe by making away with herself.

On the fair day of Garryowen, after sustaining a long and distressing altercation with her father and her mountain suitor, Eily O'Connor threw her blue cloak over her shoulders and walked into the air. She did not return to dinner, and her father felt angry at what he thought a token of resentful feeling. Night came, and she did not make her appearance. The poor old man in an agony of terror reproached himself for his vehemence, and spent the whole night in recalling with a feeling of remorse every intemperate word which he had used in the violence of dispute. In the morning, more like a ghost than a living being, he went from the house of one acquaintance to another to enquire after his child. No one however had seen her, except Foxy Dunat, the haircutter, and he had only caught a glimpse of her as she passed his door on the previous evening. It was evident that she was not to return. Her father was distracted. Her young admirers feared that she had got privately married, and run away with some shabby fellow. Her female friends insinuated that the case might be still worse, and some pious old people shook their heads when the report reached them, and said they knew what was likely to come of it, when Eily O'Connor left off attending her daily mass in the morning, and went to the dance at Garryowen.

26. Limerick was a prosperous port, serving the poorer areas of County Clare as well as its own more prosperous hinterland to the east.

27. In Shakespeare's *Romeo and Juliet*, two Veronese families, the Montagues and the Capulets, are bitter rivals, and the young lovers Juliet (a Capulet) and Romeo (a Montague) tragically attempt to cross these battle lines in their passion for each other.

CHAPTER III

HOW MR. DALY THE MIDDLEMAN SAT DOWN TO BREAKFAST

The Dalys (a very respectable family in middle life) occupied, at the time of which we write, a handsome cottage on the Shannon side, a few miles from the suburban district above-mentioned.

They had assembled, on the morning of Eily's disappearance, a healthy and blooming household of all sizes, in the principal sitting room for a purpose no less important than that of dispatching breakfast. It was a favourable moment for any one who might be desirous of sketching a family picture. The windows of the room, which were thrown up for the purpose of admitting the fresh morning air, opened upon a trim and sloping meadow that looked sunny and cheerful with the bright green aftergrass[1] of the season. The broad and sheety river washed the very margin of the little field, and bore upon its quiet bosom, (which was only ruffled by the circling eddies that encountered the advancing tide,) a variety of craft, such as might be supposed to indicate the approach to a large commerical city. Majestic vessels, floating idly on the basined flood, with sails half furled, in keeping with the languid beauty of the scene; lighters burthened to the water's edge with bricks or sand; large rafts of timber, borne onward towards the neighbouring quays under the guidance of a shipman's boat-hook; pleasure-boats, with gaudy pennons hanging at peak and topmast; or turf boats with their unpicturesque and ungraceful lading, moving sluggishly forward, while their black sails seemed gasping for a breath to fill them; such were the *incidents* that gave a gentle animation to the prospect immediately before the eyes of the cottage-dwellers. On the farther side of the river arose the Cratloe hills,[2] shadowed in various places by a broken cloud, and rendered beautiful by the chequered appearance of the ripening tillage, and the variety of hues that were observable along their wooded sides. At intervals, the front of a handsome mansion brightened up in a passing gleam of sunshine, while the wreaths of blue smoke, ascending at various distances from amongst the trees, tended to relieve the idea of extreme solitude which it would otherwise have presented.

The interior of the cottage was not less interesting to contemplate than the landscape which lay before it. The principal breakfast table (for there were two spread in the room) was placed before the window, the neat and snow white damask cloth covered with fare that spoke satisfactorily for the circumstances of the proprietor, and for the housewifery of his helpmate. The former, a fair, pleasant faced old gentleman in a huge buckled cravat and square-toed shoes, somewhat distrustful of the meagre beverage which fumed out of Mrs. Daly's lofty and shining coffee-pot, had taken his position before a cold ham and fowl which decorated the lower end of the table. His lady, a courteous old personage, with a face no less fair and happy than her husband's, and with eyes sparkling with good nature and intelligence, did the honours of the board at the farther end. On the opposite side, leaning over the back of his chair with clasped hands in an attitude which had a mixture of abstraction and anxiety, sat Mr. Kyrle Daly, the first pledge of connubial affection that was born to this comely pair.[3] He was a young man already initiated in the rudiments of the legal profession; of a handsome figure; and in manner —— but something now pressed upon his spirits which rendered this an unfavourable occasion for describing it.

A second table was laid in a more retired portion of the room, for the accommodation of the younger part of the family. Several well burnished goblets, or *porringers*,[4] of *thick* milk flanked the sides of this board, while a large dish of smooth-coated potatoes reeked up[5] in the centre. A number of blooming boys and girls, between the ages of four and twelve, were seated at this simple repast, eating and drinking away with all the happy eagerness of youthful appetite. Not, however, that this employment occupied their exclusive attention, for the prattle which circulated round the table frequently became so boisterous as to drown the conversation of the older people, and to call forth the angry rebuke of the master of the family.

The furniture of the apartment was in accordance with the appearance and manners of its inhabitants. The floor was handsomely carpetted, a lofty green fender fortified the fire-place, and supplied Mr. Daly in his facetious moments with occasions for the frequent repetition of a favorite

1. The fresh growth that springs up after a crop of hay has been harvested.
2. Barren hills on the south coast of County Clare, across the river from west Limerick.
3. Kyrle is an unusual Christian name in modern Ireland, a late eighteenth- and early nineteenth-century version of Cyril; it appears to have been used more in Munster than in the other provinces.
4. Strictly speaking, a porringer is a small basin (in rural parts sometimes called a crock) in which milk is kept, or from which porridge might be eaten.
5. piled up.

conundrum —— 'Why is that fender like Westminster Abbey?' a problem with which he never failed to try the wit of any stranger who happened to spend a night beneath his roof. The wainscoated walls were ornamented with several of the popular prints of the day, such as Hogarth's Roast Beef — Prince Eugene — Schomberg at the Boyne — Mr. Betterton playing Cato in all the glory of

'Full wig, flower'd gown, and lacker'd chair'

or the royal Mandane, in the person of Mrs. Mountain, strutting among the arbours of her Persian palace in a lofty tête and hooped petticoat.[6] There were also some family drawings, done by Mrs. Daly in her school-days, of which we feel no inclination to say more than that they were very prettily framed. In justice to the fair artist it should also be mentioned that, contrary to the established practice, her sketches were never re-touched by the hand of her master; a fact which Mr. Daly was fond of insinuating, and which no one, who saw the pictures, was tempted to call in question. A small book case, with the edges of the shelves handsomely gilded, was suspended in one corner of the room, and on examination might be found to contain a considerable number of works on Irish History — for which study Mr. Daly had a national predilection, a circumstance much deplored by all the impatient listeners in his neighbourhood, and (some people hinted) in his own household; some religious books; and a few volumes on cookery and farming. The space over the lofty chimney piece was assigned to some ornaments of a more startling description. A gun rack, on which were suspended a long shore gun, a brass barrelled blunderbuss, a cutlass, and a case of horse pistols, manifested Mr. Daly's determination to maintain, if necessary, by force of arms, his claim to the fair possessions which his honest industry had acquired.[7]

'Kyrle' said Mr. Daly, putting his fork into a breast of cold goose, and looking at his son — 'you had better let me put a little *goose*' [with an emphasis] 'on your plate. You know you are going a wooing today.'

The young gentleman appeared not to hear him. Mrs. Daly, who understood more intimately the nature of her son's reflections, deprecated, by a significant look at her husband, the continuance of any raillery upon so delicate a subject.

'Kyrle, some coffee?' said the lady of the house; but without being more successful in awakening the attention of the young gentleman.

Mr. Daly winked at his wife.

'Kyrle!' he called aloud, in a tone against which even a lover's absence was not proof — 'Do you hear what your mother says?'

'I ask pardon sir — I was absent, I — what were you saying, mother?'

'She was saying' continued Mr. Daly with a smile 'that you were manufacturing a fine speech for Anne Chute, and that you were just meditating whether you should deliver it on your knees, or out of brief, as if you were addressing the Bench in the Four Courts.'[8]

'For shame, my dear! — Never mind him, Kyrle, I said no such thing. I wonder how you can say that, my dear, and the children listening.'

6. This is an important piece of verbal iconography and serves to establish a certain level of indeterminateness in the social and denominational background of the Daly family. All the subjects in these prints are conventional enough in themselves, but the presence of both Prince Eugene (1663-1736) of Savoy and Frederick Herman Schomberg (1615-90) generates either historical tension or symbolic reconciliation. Prince Eugene, though an ally of the Duke of Marlborough, was also one of catholic Europe's great military heroes (especially against the Turks); moreover, his mother was a niece of Cardinal Mazarin (1602-61). Schomberg was the Dutch general to whom protestant William of Orange entrusted his army in Ireland. Commentators have tended to regard these decorations in the Dalys' room as 'wildly inappropriate', or to defend their 'incongruities' on the ground that Irish society was in turmoil. Leaving aside these attempts to measure the verisimilitude or probability of the scene, we can see that Griffin is leaving room for the reader to be happily agnostic as to the credal affiliation of the Dalys.

William Hogarth (1697-1764) was an English painter and engraver. Thomas Betterton (1635-1710) was the greatest actor of the Restoration theatre. Joseph Addison's *Cato* was produced in 1713. Mrs Rosoman Mountain (*c.* 1768-1841) was an English actress and singer whose husband (James Kelly) was Irish by birth; she was the subject of more than one portrait. The royal Mandane may be *Mandane, Drama per musica*, published in Italian and English in London in 1742, and revived, but the part-name is common in eighteenth-century opera. In Beaumont and Fletcher's *A King and No King* (1611) a waiting woman is called Mandane.

Note that Betterton was dead before Addison's *Cato* was produced and so can never have acted in it. The effect here is another instance of Griffin's use of composite (and anachronistic) name-clusters to suggest harmony in the Daly household. The play succeeded in pleasing all shades of political opinion in England, and at the stylistic level it also succeeded (on the page, if not on the stage) in incorporating the formal devices of French drama. The line quoted is also based on an anachronism — the trappings of Restoration and Augustan dress transposed to ancient Rome and the 'harmony' of past and present.

7. The display of guns is prominent because it alludes to the long-retained penal law prohibiting the bearing of arms by catholics; the presence of guns does not establish Daly as a protestant, however, because the date of the novel's setting is also rendered indeterminate by such irreconcilable details as those discussed in note 2 to Chapter II.

8. In other words, as if he were a lawyer in the Dublin courts. (Catholics were admitted to the bar in 1792.)

'Pooh! the little angels are too busy and too innocent to pay us any attention,' said Mr. Daly, lowering his voice however. 'But speaking seriously, my boy, you take this affair too deeply to heart; and whether it be in our pursuit of wealth — or fame — or even in love itself, an extreme solicitude to be successful is the surest means of defeating its own object. Besides, it argues an unquiet and unresigned condition. I have had a little experience, you know, in affairs of this kind,' he added, smiling and glancing at his fair helpmate, who blushed with the simplicity of a young girl.

'Ah, sir,' said Kyrle, as he drew nearer to the breakfast table with a magnanimous affectation of cheerfulness. 'I fear I have not so good a ground for hope as you may have had. It is very easy, sir, for one to be resigned to disappointment when he is certain of success.'

'Why, I was not bidden to despair, indeed,' said Mr. Daly, extending his hand to his wife, while they exchanged a quiet smile, which had in it an expression of tenderness and of melancholy remembrance. 'I have, I believe, been more fortunate than more deserving persons. I have never been vexed with useless fears in my wooing days, nor with vain regrets when those days were ended. I do not know, my dear lad, what hopes you have formed, or what prospects you may have shaped out of the future, but I will not wish you a better fortune than that you may as nearly approach to their accomplishment as I have done, and that Time may deal as fairly with you as he has done with your father.' After saying this, Mr. Daly leaned forward on the table with his temple supported by one finger, and glanced alternately from his children to his wife; while he sang in a low tone the following verse of a popular song:

'How should I love the pretty creatures,
    While round my knees they fondly clung,
To see them look their mother's features,
    To hear them lisp their mother's tongue!
And when with envy Time transported
    Shall think to rob us of our joys —
You'll in your girls again be courted,
    And I ——

with a glance at Kyrle —

And I go wooing with the boys.[9]

9. An unidentified popular song.

And this, thought young Kyrle, in the affectionate pause that ensued, this is the question which I go to decide upon this morning; whether my old age shall resemble the picture which I see before me, or whether I shall be doomed to creep into the winter of my life, a lonely, selfish, cheerless, money-hunting old bachelor. Is not this enough to make a little solicitude excusable, or pardonable at least?

'It is a long time now,' resumed Mr. Daly 'since I have had the pleasure of meeting Mrs. Chute. She was a very beautiful but a very wild girl when I knew her. Nothing has ever been more inexplicable to me than the choice she made of a second husband. You never saw Anne's step-father, Tom Chute, or you would be equally astonished. *You* saw him, my love, did you not?'

Mrs. Daly laughed and answered in the affirmative.

'It shewed indeed a singular taste' said Mr. Daly. 'They tell a curious story too, about the manner of their courtship.'

'What was that sir?' asked Kyrle, who felt a strong sympathetic interest in all stories connected with wooers and wooing.

'I have it, I confess, upon questionable authority — but you shall hear it, such as it is — Now, look at that young thief!' he added laughing, and directing Kyrle's attention to one of the children, a chubby young fellow, who, having deserted the potato-eating corps at the side-table, was taking advantage of the deep interest excited by the conversation, to make a sudden descent upon the contents of the jappaned[10] bread basket. Perceiving that he was detected, the little fellow relaxed his fingers, and drew back a little, glancing, from beneath his eye-lashes, a half dismayed and bashful look at the laughing countenance of his parent.

'Charles is not well today' said the mother, in a compassionate tone, and cutting him a large wedge of her best home-made bread, which the lad began to demolish with a degree of rapidity that scarcely corroborated the assertion.

'But the story sir?' said Kyrle.

'But the story — Well, little Tom Chute, (he might have been better called little Tom-tit, only that he was not half so sprightly) was a very extraordinary man, for although he was small and fat, he was not merry, nor talkative. You would have pitied him to see him walking about a ball

10. Varnished with a hard substance (imported from Japan).

room with ruffles that looked like small buckles, and a queue[11] half as long as himself, reminding one of the handle of a pump when the sucker is up — with the most forlorn aspect in the world, as if he were looking for a runaway wife. It was a curious anomaly in his character that although he — (Silence, there! my dear, will you speak to those children) — that although he always *looked* miserable in the midst of society, he really *was* so when out of it, as if the continued embarrassment and mortification which he experienced were a stimulus which he could not do without. Round, fat, shy, awkward, and oily, as he was, however, he tumbled his little rotund figure into the heart of Mrs. Trenchard, who was at that time, though a widow, one of the leading belles in Munster. A fair friend was the first to disclose this rapturous secret to poor Tom, for he might have known Mrs. Trenchard for a century without being able to make it out himself. He did not know whether he should be most frightened or pleased at the intelligence — but certain it is that in the warmth of his first feelings, he made a tender of his hand to the lady, and was instantly accepted. A dashing, handsome fellow who had been rejected by her some time before, and who knew Chute's irresolute temper, resolved to indemnify himself for the mortification he had received by throwing some embarrassment in the way of the nuptials, and effected it simply enough. It seems the lady's accomplishments were of a very general description, for besides playing the harpsichord to admiration, she could manage a horse with any hero of the County Club,[12] and was known to join their hunting parties, and even to ride a steeple chase with eclat. Indeed it was generally admitted that she possessed more spirit than might have answered her purposes, or her husband's either. What fancy she could have taken to Tom Chute, I cannot for my life conceive. Well, this fellow met Tom going to her house one evening, as spruce as a water wagtail, with his queue poking up behind like the flag staff in the stern of a privateer. They got into conversation about the widow. "Beautiful creature, isn't she?" simpered Tom, blushing up to the eyes, for it was another funny foible of Tom's, to redden up like a rose whenever there was any discourse of ladies; even when nobody dreamed of any thing like raillery. "Beautiful creature, isn't she?" says Tom. "Beautiful indeed" replied the other. And Tom stood on his toes, threw out his right elbow and took snuff. "And accomplished, I think?" "And very sensible" says the other. "And lively" says Tom. "And high spirited" says the other. "So they say, her late husband found, poor man, to his cost." Tom dropped his jaw a little, and looked inquisitive. But the other, who saw that his business was done, declined all explanation, and hurried off with a concluding remark, that "the lady was unquestionably a capital *whip*."[13] Well, Tom got a sudden attack of — I don't know what complaint, went home that night, and sent an apology to the widow. He was not seen near her house for a fortnight after, and a report reached her ears that he had some notion of quitting the country. But if he had, she put a stop to it. One morning when Tom was looking over his books, he was startled by the apparition of a tall woman in a riding dress, with a horsewhip in one hand, and a case of duelling pistols in the other. She nodded to Tom. "I understand" said she ——'

At this moment, a potatoe peel, flung from the side-table, whisked past Mr. Daly's nose, and with happier aim, lighted on that of Prince Eugene in the print before mentioned. The venerable, but too little venerated, story teller, who had been for the last few minutes endeavouring to raise his voice, so as to make it audible above the encreasing uproar of the young people, now turned round, at this unparalleled and violent aggression, and confronted the daring group in awful silence. Satisfied, however, with the sudden hush of terror which this action occasioned, and willing to reserve the burst of wrath for a future transgression, he turned again in silence; and directing the servant girl who was in the room, to take the potatoe peel off Prince Eugene's nose, he resumed the thread of his narrative.

'"I understand," said Mrs. Trenchard — for it was no other than the widow — "that you intend leaving Ireland?" Tom stammered and hesitated. — "If my brother were living," continued the lady, "he would horsewhip you — but although he is not,

11. pigtail.
12. About this time, County Clubs, or clubs for gentlemen farmers and so forth, began to spring up in Ireland; the Cork Farmers' Club was associated in the mid-1780s with political discontent, but the general association was one of social advancement and self-esteem.
13. In this sense, a person who can use a whip (e.g. to keep hounds under control).

Hetty Trenchard is able to fight her own way. Come, sir, my carriage is at the door below; either step into it with me this minute, or take one of those pistols, and stand at the other end of the room." Well, Tom looked as like a fool as any man in Ireland. He would'nt fight, and he would'nt be horsewhipped; so that the business ended in his going into the carriage and marrying the lady. Some persons indeed insinuated that Tom was observed in the course of the day to chafe his shoulders two or three times with an expression of pain, as if his change of condition had been the result of a still harsher mode of reasoning than I have mentioned; but this part of the story is without foundation.'

'What a bold creature!' said the gentle Mrs. Daly.

'And is it possible, sir,' asked Kyrle, 'that this amazon is the kind old lady whom Anne Chute attends with so much affection and tenderness in her infirmity?'

'Ah, ha! Kyrle, I see the nature of the bolt that has wounded you, and I like you the better for it, my boy. A good face is a pippin that grows on every hedge, but a good heart, that is to say, a well regulated one, is the apple of the Hesperides,[14] worth even the risk of ease and life itself.'

Kyrle assented to this sagacious aphorism with a deep sigh.

'Are the Cregans and they on terms now?' asked Mrs. Daly.

'As much on terms as two families of such opposite habits can be. The Chutes invite the Cregans to a family dinner once or twice in the year, and the Cregans ask the Chutes to their Killarney cottage; both of which invitations are taken as *French compliments*,[15] and never accepted. Cregan himself hates going to Castle Chute, because he has nobody there to make the jovial night with him, and young Hardress, (your friend, Kyrle), is too wild a lad to confine himself to mere drawing room society. Apropos, talk of ——, 'tis a vulgar proverb, and let it pass; but there goes his trim pleasure boat, the Nora Creina, flying down the river, and there sits the youth himself, tiller in hand, as usual. Patcy, bring me the telescope; I think I see a female dress on board.'

The telescope was brought, and adjusted to the proper focus, while a dozen eager faces were collected about the small window, one over another, in the manner of those groups in painting called 'Studies of Heads.'

'That is he, indeed,' continued Mr. Daly, resting the glass on the window-frame, and directing it towards the object of their attention — 'there is no mistaking that dark and handsome face, buried up as it is in his huge oiled penthouse hat, and there is his hunch-backed boatman, Danny Mann, or Danny the Lord,[16] as the people call him since his misfortune, tending the foresheet in the bow. But that female — there is a female there, unquestionably, in a blue mantle, with the hood brought low over her eyes, sitting on the ballast. Who can she be?'

'Perhaps, Danny Mann's cousin, Cotch Coonerty?' said Mrs. Daly.

'Or some western dealing woman[17] who has come up to Limerick to purchase a reinforcement[18] of pins, needles, whiskey, and Reading-made-easys,[19] for her village counter, and is getting a free passage home from young master Hardress.'

'Like enough, like enough; it is just his way. — Hillo! the fellow is going to run down that fishing cot, I believe!'

A hoarse cry of 'Bear away! Hold up your hand!' was heard from the water, and reiterated with the addition of a few expletives, which those who know the energy of a boatman's dialect will understand without our transcribing them here. The pleasure-boat, however, heedless of those rough remonstrances, and apparently indisposed to yield any portion of her way, still held her bowsprit close to the wind, and sailed on, paying no more regard to the peril of the plebeian craft, than a French aristocrat of the *vielle cour* might be supposed to exhibit for that of a *sans culottes* about to be trodden down by his leaders in the Rue St. Honoré.[20] The

14. The Hesperides were nymphs, the daughters of Hesperus.
15. False or insincere compliments, scarcely intended to convince in the first place.
16. There is a folk tradition associating those who are disabled or disfigured with God, though here an ominous note is also sounded, since Danny will be implicated in Eily's death.
17. A woman who trades, or deals in goods; the structure of the phrase suggests the grammar of the Irish language spoken in the districts lying to the west of Limerick city.
18. i.e. to reorder pins for her to sell; again, the idiom suggests the vocabulary of an Irish speaker using English as a second language.
19. Elementary reading primers.
20. Griffin's French is faulty here; he evidently wants to allude to an aristocrat of the *ancien régime*, or of 'the old court' (*vielle cour*) in distinction from a *sans culottes* (literally 'one with no breeches') in the Parisian district of St Honoré. But these are ostentatiously terms made familiar by the French Revolution, an event that falls between

fishermen, with many curses, backed water, and put about as rapidly as possible; but without being able to avoid the shock of the Nora Creina, who just touched their stern with sufficient force to make the cot dart forward nearly an oar's length through the water, and to lay the rowers sprawling on their backs in the bottom. Fortunately the wind, which had sprung up with the returning tide, was not sufficiently strong to render the concussion more dangerous.

'Like his proud mother in every feature,' said Mr. Daly — 'Is it not singular that while we were speaking of the characters of the family, he could not pass our window without furnishing us with a slight specimen of his own. See how statelily the fellow turns round and contemplates the confusion he has occasioned. There is his mother's grandeur blended with the hair-brained wildness and idle spirit of his father.'

'Hardress Cregan's is the handsomest boat in the river,' said Patcy, a stout sunburnt boy — 'She beat all the Galway hookers[21] from this to Beale. What a nice green hull! — and white sails and beautiful green colours flying over her peak and gaff-topsail! Oh! how I'd like to be steering her!'

Mr. Daly winked at his wife, and whispered her that he had known Rear-Admirals come of smaller beginnings. Mrs. Daly, with a little shudder, replied that she should not wish to see him a Rear-Admiral, the navy was so dangerous a service. Her husband, in order to sooth her, observed that the danger was not very near at hand.

In the meantime, Hardress Cregan became a subject of vehement debate at the side-table, to which the juvenile squadron had returned. One fair haired little girl declared that she was his 'pet.' A second claimed that distinction for herself.

'He gave me an O'Dell cake[22] when he was last here,' said one.

'And me a stick of peppermint.'

'He gave me a ——' in a whisper — 'a kiss.'

'And me two.'

'He did'nt—'

'He did.'

'I'll tell dadda it was you threw the potatoe peel while ago.'

'Ah ha, tattler-tell-tale!'

'Silence there! fie! fie! what words are these?' said Mrs. Daly, 'come, kiss and be friends, now, both of you and let me hear no more.'

The young combatants complied with her injunctions, and, as the duelling paragraphs say, 'the affair terminated amicably.'

'But I was speaking,' Mr. Daly resumed, 'of the family pride of the Cregans. It was once manifested by Hardress's father in a manner that might make an Englishman smile. When their little Killarney property was left to the Cregans, amongst many other additional pieces of display that were made on the occasion, it behoved Mr. Barny Cregan to erect a family vault and monument in his parish churchyard. He had scarcely however given directions for its construction when he fell ill of a fever, and was very near enjoying the honour of *hanselling*[23] the new cemetery himself. But he got over the fit, and made it one of his first cares to saunter out as far as the church, and inspect the mansion which had been prepared for his reception. It was a handsome Gothic monument ocupying a retired corner of the churchyard, and shadowed over by a fine old sycamore. But Barny, who had no taste for the picturesque, was deeply mortified at finding his piece of sepulchral finery thrown so much into the shade. "What did I or my people do," he said to the architect, "that we should be sent skulking into that corner? I paid my money and I'll have my own value for it." The monument was accordingly got rid of, and a sporting, flashy one erected opposite the gateway with the Cregan crest and shield, (in what herald's office it was picked up I cannot take upon me to say,)[24] emblazoned on the frontispiece. Here, it is to be hoped, the aspiring Barnaby and his posterity may one day rest in peace.

'That would be a vain hope, I fear' said Kyrle, 'at least so far as Mr. Cregan is concerned, if it were true, as our peasantry believe, that the churchyard is frequently made a scene of midnight mirth and revel, by those whose earthly carousals are long concluded. But what relationship is there between that family and Mrs. Chute?'

'She is step sister to Mrs. Cregan.'

the period about which Griffin is writing and that in which he writes. Once again, the tension between the time of the novel's action and its composition becomes evident.

21. A commercial fishing boat using hooks and lines in place of nets.
22. A small, bun-like sweetmeat.
23. To handsel is to inaugurate, to be the first to try, something.
24. Socially ambitious families of little 'breeding' were anxious to acquire coats of arms, crest and the trappings of heraldry; the theme recurs in fiction by Maria Edgeworth, Lady Morgan, Lady Clarke, and in the satirical observations of the more radical newspapers from the 1780s onwards.

'Indeed? So near?'

'Most veritable, therefore look to it. They tell a story —'

But the talkative old gentleman was interrupted in his anecdotical career by the entrance of a new actor on the scene.

CHAPTER IV

HOW MR. DALY THE MIDDLEMAN ROSE UP FROM BREAKFAST

But what pen less gifted than his of Chios, or his of Avon, the delineator of Vulcan or of Grumio,[1] can suffice to convey to the reader any idea of the mental and bodily proportions of this new comer, who thrust his small and shining head in upon the family party, to awaken their curiosity, and to rob Mr. Daly of so many attentive listeners as he numbered around him at this moment!

The person who opened the door acted as a kind of herdsman or out-door servant to the family, and was a man of a rather singular appearance. The nether parts of his frame were of a size considerably out of proportion with the trunk and head which they supported. His feet were broad and flat like those of a duck; his legs long and clumsy, with knees and ancles [*sic*] like the knobs on one of those grotesque walking-sticks, which were in fashion among the fine gentlemen of our own day, some time since; his joints hung loosely, like those of a paste-board merry-andrew;[2] his body was very small; his chest narrow; and his head so diminutive, as to be even too little for his herring shoulders.[3] It seemed as if nature, like an extravagant projector, had laid the foundation of a giant, but running short of material, as the structure proceeded, had been compelled to terminate her undertaking within the dimensions of a dwarf. So far was this economy pursued, that the head, small as it was, was very scantily furnished with hair; and the nose, with which the face was garnished, might be compared for its flatness to that of a young kid. 'It looked' as the owner of this mournful piece of journeywork himself facetiously observed, 'as if his head were not thought worth a roof, nor his countenance worth a handle.' His hands and arms were likewise of a smallness that was much to be admired, when contrasted with the hugeness of the lower members, and brought to mind the fore-paws of a Kangaroo, or the fins of a seal, the latter similitude prevailing when the body was put in motion, on which occasions they dabbled about in a very extraordinary manner. But there was one feature in which a corresponding prodigality had been manifested, namely the ears, which were as long as those of Riquet with the Tuft,[4] or of any ass in the Barony.

The costume which enveloped this singular frame, was no less anomalous than was the nature of its own construction. A huge *riding coat* of grey frieze hung lazily from his shoulders, and gave to view in front a waistcoat of calf-skin with the hairy side outwards; a shirt, of a texture almost as coarse as sail-cloth, made from the refuse of flax; and a pair of corduroy nether garments, with two bright new patches upon the knees. Grey worsted stockings, with dog-skin brogues well paved in the sole, and greased until they shone again, completed the personal adornments of his unaspiring personage. On the whole, his appearance might have brought to the recollection of a modern beholder one of those architectural edifices, so fashionable in our time, in which the artist, with an admirable ambition, seeks to unite all that is excellent in the Tuscan, Doric, Corinthian, and Ionic order,[5] in one coup d'oeil.[6]

The expression of the figure though it varied with circumstances, was for the most part thoughtful and deliberative; the effect in a great measure of habitual penury and dependance. At the time of Lord Halifax's administration,[7] Lowry Looby, then a very young man, held a *spot of ground* in the neighbourhood of Limerick, and was *well to do* in the world, but the scarcity which prevailed in

1. Chios was reputedly the birthplace of Homer, who delineated Vulcan (in Greek, Hephaestus) in the *Iliad*. Avon is the river which flows through Stratford-on-Avon where Shakespeare (the Bard of Avon) was born. Gumio is one of Petruchio's servants in Shakespeare's *The Taming of the Shrew*.
2. One who entertains by means of antics and buffoonery.
3. Sloping or slight shoulders, from the proverb 'as lean as a shotten herring'.
4. An English translation of the title of one of Charles Perrault's fairy-tales, 'Riquet à la houppe', a story of the beauty-and-the-beast type.
5. Styles of classical architecture, Tuscan being a Roman modification of Greek.
6. at a glance; with a single look.
7. i.e. *c.*1761-63; the difficulties that resulted in Looby's loss of his holding might be more closely related to social disturbance than simply to economic hardship. Note the comparison with conditions of the 1820s (next note) and the absence of any reference to agrarian violence either in the 1760s or in the 1820s.

England at the time, and which occasioned a sudden rise in the price of beef, butter, and other produce of grazing land in Ireland, threw all the agriculturists out of their little holdings, and occasioned a general destitution, similar to that produced by the anti-cottier system in the present day.[8] Lowry was among the sufferers. He was saved, however, from the necessity of adopting one of the three ultimata of Irish misery, begging, listing,[9] or emigrating, by the kindness of Mr. Daly, who took him into his service as a kind of runner between his farms, an office for which Lowry, by his long and muscular legs, and the lightness of the body that encumbered them, was qualified in an eminent degree. His excelling honesty, one of the characteristics of his country, which he was known to possess, rendered him a still more valuable acquisition to the family than had been first anticipated. He had moreover the national talent for adroit flattery, a quality which made him more acceptable to his patron than the latter would willingly admit, and every emulsion of this kind was applied under the disguise of a simpleness, which gave it a wonderful efficacy.

'Ha! Lowry—' said Mr. Daly 'Well, have you made your fortune since you have agreed with the Post-master?'

Lowry put his hands behind his back, looked successively at the four corners of the room, then round the cornice, then cast his eyes down at his feet, turned up the soles a little, and finally straightening his person, and gazing on his master replied, 'To lose it I did, Sir, for a place.'

'To lose what?'

'The place as postman, sir, through the country westwards. Sure there I was a gentleman for life if it was'n't my luck.'

'I do not understand you Lowry.'

'I'll tell you how it was, masther. Afther the last postman died, sir, I took your ricommendation to the Post-masther, an' axed him for the place. "I'm used to thravelling, sir," says I, "for Misther Daly, over, and—." "Aye," says he, takin' me up short, "an' you have a good long pair o' legs I see." "Middling, sir," says I, (he's a very pleasant gentleman) its equal to me any day, winther or summer, whether I go ten miles or twenty, so as I have the nourishment. "'Twould be hard if you didn't get that any way," says he, "Well, I think I may as well give you the place, for I do'n' know any gentleman that I'd sooner take his ricommendation then Misther Daly's, or one that I'd sooner pay him a compliment, if I could."'

'Well, and what was your agreement?'

'Ten pounds a year, sir,' answered Lowry, opening his eyes, as if he announced something of wonderful importance, and speaking in a loud voice, to suit the magnitude of the sum, 'besides my clothing and shoes throughout the year.'

''Twas very handsome, Lowry.'

'Handsome, masther? 'Twas wages for a prince, sir. Sure there I was a made gentleman all my days, if it was'n't my luck, as I said before.'

'Well, and how did you lose it?'

'I'll tell you, sir,' answered Lowry, 'I was going over to the Post-masther yestherday, to get the Thralee[10] mail from him, and to start off with myself, on my first journey. Well an' good, of all the world, who should I meet, above upon the road, just at the turn down to the Post-office, but that red-headed woman that sells the free-stone,[11] in the sthreets? So I turned back.'

'Turned back, for what?'

'Sure the world knows, masther, that it is'nt lucky to meet a red-haired woman an' you going of a journey.'[12]

'And you never went for the mail-bags!'

'Faiks,[13] I'm sure I did'nt that day.'

'Well, and the next morning?'

'The next morning, that's this morning, when I went, I found they had engaged another boy in my place.'

'And you lost the situation!'

'For this turn, sir, any way. 'Tis luck that does it all. Sure I thought I was cock sure of it, an' I having the Post-masther's word. But indeed, if I meet that free-stone crathur[14] again, I'll knock her red head against the wall.'

'Well, Lowry, this ought to show you the folly of your superstition. If you had not minded that

8. In the 1820s, extensive evictions were employed to reduce the large number of uneconomical smallholdings and subdivisions of these, with consequent dreadful hardship for the cottiers. County Limerick was particularly disturbed during the period.
9. i.e. enlisting in the army.
10. Tralee, Co. Kerry.
11. Possibly whetstone, i.e. a kind of sandstone used for sharpening knives.
12. A widespread superstition.
13. A short form of 'faykins', meaning 'Faith' (as an interjection).
14. i.e. creature.

woman when you met her, you might have had your situation now.'

''Twas she was in fault still, begging your pardon, sir,' said Lowry, 'for sure if I did'nt meet her at all this would'nt have happened me.'

'Oh,' said Mr. Daly, laughing, 'I see that you are well provided against all argument. I have no more to say, Lowry.'

The man now walked slowly towards Kyrle, and bending down with a look of solemn importance, as if he had some weighty intelligence to communicate, he said — 'The horse, sir, is ready, this way, at the doore abroad.'[15]

'Very well, Lowry. I shall set out this instant.'

Lowry raised himself erect again, turned slowly round and walked to the door with his eyes on the ground, and his hand raised to his temple, as if endeavouring to recollect something farther which he had intended to say.

'Lowry!' said Mr. Daly as the handle of the door was turned a second time. Lowry looked round.

'Lowry, tell me — did you see Eily O'Connor, the rope-maker's daughter, at the fair of Garryowen yesterday?'

'Ah, you're welcome to your game, Masther.'

''Pon my word, then, Eily is a very pretty girl, Lowry, and I'm told the old father can give her something besides her pretty face.'

Lowry opened his huge mouth, (we forgot to mention that it *was* a huge one,) and gave vent to a few explosions of laughter which much more nearly resembled the braying of an ass. 'You are welcome to your game, masther,' he repeated; — 'long life to your honour.'

'But is it true, Lowry, as I have heard it insinuated, that old Mihil O'Connor used, and still does, twist ropes for the use of the County Gaol?'

Lowry closed his lips hard, while the blood rushed into his face at this unworthy allegation. Treating it however as a new piece of 'the masther's game,' he laughed and tossed his head.

'Folly† on — sir — folly on.'

'Because, if there were the case, Lowry, I should expect to find you a fellow of too much spirit to become connected, even by affinity, with such a calling. A rope-maker! a manufacturer of rogue's last neckcloths — an understrapper to the gallows — a species of collateral hangman!'

'A' then, Missiz, do you hear this? And all rising out of a little ould fable of a story that happened as good as five year ago, because Moriarty the crooked hangman, (the thief!) stepped into Mihil's little place of a night, and nobody knowen of him, an bought a couple o' pen'orth o' whip-cord for some vagary or other of his own. And there's all the call Mihil O'Connor had ever to gallowses or hangmen in his life. That's the whole tote o' their *insiniwaytions*.'

'Never mind your master, Lowry,' said Mrs. Daly, 'he is only amusing himself with you.'

'Oh, ha! I'm sure I know it ma'am; long life to him, and 'tis he that's welcome to his joke.'

'But Lowry ——'

'A' heavens bless you, now masther, an let me alone. I'll say nothing to you.'

'Nay, nay, I only wanted to ask you what sort of a fair it was at Garryowen yesterday.'

'Middling, sir, like the small *piatees*,[16] they tell me,' said Lowry, suddenly changing his manner to an appearance of serious occupation, 'but 'tis hard to make out what sort a fair is when one has nothing to sell himself. I met a huxter an she told me 'twas a bad fair because she could not sell her piggins, an I met a pig-jobber, an he told me 'twas a dear fair, pork ran so high, an I met another little meagre creatur, a neighbour that has a cabin on the road above, an he said 'twas the best fair that ever come out o' the sky, because he got a power[17] for his pig. But Mr. Hardress Cregan was there, and if he did'nt make it a dear fair to some of 'em, you may call me an honest man.'

'A very notable undertaking that would be, Lowry. But how was it?'

'Some o' them boys, them Garryowen lads, sir, to get about Danny Mann, the Lord, Mr. Hardress's boatman, as he was comen down from Mihil's with a new rope for some part o' the boat, and to begin *reflecting*[18] on him in regard o' the hump on his back, poor creatur! Well, if they did, Masther Hardress heerd 'em, and he having a stout blackthorn in his hand, this way, and he made up[19] to the foremost of 'em, "What's that you're saying, you scoundrel?" says he, "What would you give to

† Follow.

15. The spelling of 'door' is to indicate pronunciation (long vowel); 'abroad' is an Irish idiom meaning 'outside' or 'out and about'.

16. potatoes; the dialect pronunciation is strongly influenced by Gaelic.
17. A lot (of money).
18. casting ridicule.
19. advanced.

know?" says the other, mighty impudent. Master Hardress made no more, only up with the stick, and without saying this or that, or by your leave, or how do you do, he stretched him. Well, such a scuffle as began among 'em was never seen. They all fell upon Master Hardress, but faix[20] they had only the half of it, for he made his way through the thick of 'em without as much as a mark. Aw, indeed, it is'nt a goose or a duck they had to do with when they came across Mr. Cregan, for all.'

'And where were you all this while, Lowry?'

'Above, in Mihil's door, standen an looken about the fair for myself.'

'And Eily?'

'Ah, hear to this again, now! I'll run away out o' the place entirely from you, master, that's what I'll do.' And, suiting the action to the phrase, exit Lowry Looby.

'Well, Kyrle,' said Mr. Daly, as the latter rose and laid aside his chair, 'I suppose we are not to expect you back tonight?'

'Likely not, sir. If I have any good news to tell, I shall send an answer by Lowry, who goes with me; and if——' something seemed to stick in his throat, and he tried to laugh it out —— 'if I should be unsuccessful, I will ride on to the dairy-farm at Gurtenaspig,[21] where Hardress Cregan promised to meet me.'

Mr. Daly wished him better fortune than he seemed to hope for, and repeated an old proverb about a faint heart and a fair lady.[22] The affectionate mother, who felt the feverishness of the young lover's hand as he placed it in her's, and probably in secret participated in his apprehensions, followed him to the steps of the hall-door. He was already on horseback.

'Kyrle,' said Mrs. Daly smiling while she looked up in his face and shaded her own with her hand, 'Remember, Kyrle, if Anne Chute should play the tyrant with you, that there is many a prettier girl in Munster.'

Kyrle seemed about to reply, but his young horse became restive, and as the gentleman felt rather at a loss, he made the impatience of the animal an apology for his silence. He waved his hand to the kind old lady, and rode away.

'And if she *should* play the tyrant with you, Kyrle,' Mrs. Daly continued in soliloquy, while she saw his handsome and graceful figure diminish in the distance, 'Anne Chute is not of my mind.'

So said the mother as she returned to the parlour, and so would many younger ladies have said, had they known Kyrle Daly as well as she did.

While Mrs. Daly, who was the empress of all housekeepers, superintended the removal of the breakfast table, not disdaining, with her own fair hands, to restore the plate and china to their former neatness, the old gentleman called all his children around him, to undergo a customary examination. They came flocking to his knees, the boys with their satchels thrown over their shoulders, and the girls with their gloves and bonnets on, ready for school. Occasionally, as they stood before the patriarchal sire, their eyes wandered from his face toward a lofty pile of sliced bread and butter, and a bowl of white sugar which stood near his elbow.

'North-East!' Mr. Daly began, addressing the eldest.—

It should be premised that this singular name was given to the child in compliance with a popular superstition; for sensible as the Dalys were accounted in their daily affairs, they were not wholly exempt from the prevailing weakness of their countrymen. Mrs. Daly's three first children died at nurse, and it was suggested to the unhappy parents that if the next little stranger were baptized by the name of North-East, the curse would be removed from their household.[23] Mrs. Daly acceded to the proposition, adding to it at the same time the slight precaution of changing her nurses. With what success this ingenious remedy was attended, the flourishing state of Mr. Daly's nursery thenceforward sufficiently testified.

'North-east,' said the old gentleman, 'When was Ireland first peopled?'

'By Partholanus,[24] sir, in anno mundi 1956, the great, great, great, great, great, great grandson of Noah.'

'Six greats. Right my boy. Although the Cluan Mac Noisk[25] makes it 1969. But a difference of a few

20. See note 13 above.
21. An anglicized form of a Gaelic place-name meaning 'The Bishop's Field.'
22. 'Faint heart ne'er won fair lady.'
23. Proverbially north = health; east = wealth.
24. This is the origin myth preserved in *Leabhar Gabhála Éireann* (The Book of Invasions of Ireland).
25. i.e. The Annals of Clonmacnois, a source surviving only in an English translation made by Conall MacGeoghegan in 1627. Griffin would have used some intermediary source, such as the work of Sylvester O'Halloran (1728-1807), the distinguished Limerick antiquarian.

years at a distance of nearly four thousand, is not a matter to be quarrelled with. Stay, I have not done with you yet. Mr. Tickleback tells me you are a great Latinist. What part of Ovid are you reading now?'

'The Metamorphoses, sir, book the thirteenth.'

'Ah, poor Ajax! He's an example and a warning for all Irishmen.[26] Well, North-east, Ulysses ought to supply you with Latin enough to answer me one question. Give me the construction of this, *Mater mea sus est mala*.'

The boy hesitated a moment, laughed, reddened a little and looked at his mother. 'That's a queer thing, sir,' he said at last.

'Come, construe, construe.'

'*My mother is a bad sow*,' said Northeast, laughing, 'that's the only English I can find for it.'

'Ah, Northeast! Do you call me names, my lad?' said Mrs. Daly, while she laid aside the china in a cup-board.

''Tis dadda you should blame, ma'am, 'twas he said it. I only told him the English of it.'

This affair produced much more laughter and merriment than it was worth. At length Mr. Daly condescended to explain.

'You gave me one construction of it,' said he, 'but not the right one. However, these things cannot be learned all in a day, and your translation was correct, North-East, in point of grammar, at all events. But, (he continued, with a look of learned wisdom,) 'the true meaning of the sentence is this, *Mater*, mother, *mea*, hasten, *sus*, the sow, *est*, eats up, (*edere*, my boy, not *esse*,) *mala*, the apples.'

'Oh, its a *cran*[27] I see,' said the boy with some indignation of tone. 'One isn't obliged to know *crans*. I'd soon puzzle you if I was to put you all the *crans* I know.'

'Not so easily as you suppose perhaps,' said his father in dignified alarm, lest his reputation should suffer in the eyes of his wife, who really thought him a profound linguist. 'But you are a good boy. Go to school, North-East. Here, open your satchel.'

The satchel was opened, a huge slice of bread from the top of the pile above mentioned was dropt into it, and North-East set off south-south-west out of the house.

'Charles, who is the finest fellow in Ireland?'

'Henry Grattan, sir.'

'Why so, Sir?'

'Because he says we must have a free trade, sir.'[28]

'You shall have a lump of sugar with your bread for that. Open your satchel. There. Run away now to school. Patcy!'

'Sir?'

'Patcy, tell me, who was the first Lord Lieutenant of Ireland in the present reign?'[29]

Patcy, an idle young rogue, stood glancing alternately at the pile of bread, and at his father's face, and shifting from one foot to another like a foundered nag.[30] At last he said stoutly —

'Julius Caesar, sir.'

'That's a good boy. Ah, you young villain, if I had asked you who won the last boat-race, or how many hookers went by this morning, you'd give me a better answer than that. Was it Julius Caesar sailed round the revenue Cutter, near Tarbert,[31] the other day?'

'No, sir, it was Larry Kett.'

'I'll engage you know that. Well, tell me this, and I'll forgive you — Who was the bravest seaman you ever heard of? always excepting Hardress Cregan.'

'Brown, sir, the man that brought the Bilboa ship into Youghal, after making prisoners of nine Frenchmen — the fellows, dadda,' the boy continued warming with his subject — 'that were sent to take the vessel into France, and Brown had only three men and a boy with him, and they retook the ship and brought her into Youghal. But sure one Irishman was more than a match for two Frenchmen.'

'Well, I perceive you have some knowledge in physics, and comparative physiology. There's some hope of you. Go to school.' And the pile of bread appeared a few inches lower.

The remainder was distributed amongst the girls, to whom the happy father put questions, in

26. In Ovid's telling of the story of the Homeric hero, Ajax competes with Ulysses for the armour of Achilles, loses, and kills himself in his mad frenzy. The moral for Irishmen, evidently, is that allies should not fall out over trifles.
27. From 'crank', a verbal trick or conceit.
28. In 1779, Henry Grattan made a formal demand for the removal of certain restrictions on Irish commerce. This was accepted by parliament, and during the following year the appropriate legislation was passed to permit exportation to British settlements in Africa and America.
29. The correct answer is Lord Halifax.
30. A lame horse (from 'founder', an inflammation in the laminar structure of a horse's foot, but, exploiting the verb 'to founder' meaning 'to sink' (like a ship)).
31. Small port on the coast of north Kerry, near the border with County Limerick.

history, geography, catechism, &c. proportioned to the capacity of each. At length, he descended to the youngest, a little cherub with roses of three years' growth in her cheeks.

'Well, Sally, my pet, what stands for sugar?'

'I, dadda.'

'Ah, Sally's a wag I see. You do stand for it indeed, and you shall get it. We must not expect to force nature' he added, looking at his wife and tossing his head. 'Every beginning is weak — and Sam Johnson[32] himself was as indifferent a philologist once in his day. And now, to school at once, darlings, and bring home good judgments. Nelly will go for you at three o'clock.'

The little flock of innocents, who were matched in size like the reeds of a pandean pipe, 'each under each[33] having left the scene, Mr. Daly proceeded to dispatch his own affairs, and possessed himself of his hat and cane.

'I'll step over to the meadow, my dear — and see how the hay gets on. And give me that pamphlet of Hutchinson's — Commercial Restraints[34] — I promised to lend it to father Malachy. And let the stranger's room be got ready, my love, and the sheets aired, for I expect Mr. Windfall the tax-gatherer to sleep here tonight. And, Sally, if Ready should come about his pigs that I put in pound[35] last night, let him have them free of cost, but not without giving the fellow a fright about them; and above all, insist upon having rings in their noses before night. My little lawn is like a fallow field with them. I'll be back at five.'

Saying this, and often turning his head as some new commission arose to his memory, the Munster 'Middleman'[36] sallied out of his house, and walked along the gravelled avenue humming, as he went, a verse of the popular old song —

'And when I at last must throw off this frail
covering
Which I've worn for three score years and
ten,
On the brink of the grave I'll not seek to
keep hovering,
Nor my thread wish to spin o'er again.
My face in the glass I'll serenely survey,
And with smiles count each wrinkle and
furrow,
For this old worn out stuff that is thread
today,
May become everlasting tomorrow.
Tomorrow! Tomorrow!
May become everlasting tomorrow!'

Such, in happier days than ours, was the life of a Munster farmer. Indeed, the word is ill adapted to convey to an English reader an idea of the class of persons whom it is intended to designate, for they were and are, in mind and education, far superior to the persons who occupy that rank in most other countries. Opprobrious as the term 'middleman' has been rendered in our own time, it is certain that the original formation of the sept[37] was both natural and beneficial. When the country was deserted by its gentry, a general promotion of one grade took place amongst those who remained at home. The farmers became gentlemen, and the labourers became farmers, the former assuming, together with the station and influence, the quick and honourable spirit, the love of pleasure, and the feudal authority which distinguished their aristocratic archetypes — while the humbler classes looked up to them for advice and assistance, with the same feeling of respect and of dependance which they had once entertained for the actual proprietors of the soil. The covetousness of landlords themselves, in selling leases to the highest bidder, without any enquiry into his character or fortunes, first tended to throw imputations on this respectable and useful body of men, which in progress of time, swelled into a popular outcry, and ended in an act of the legislature for their gradual extirpation.[38] There are few now in that class as prosperous, many as intelligent and high-principled, as Mr. Daly.

32. Samuel Johnson (1709-84), whose *Dictionary* was published in 1755.
33. Shakespeare, *A Midsummer Night's Dream*, III. 2. 239.
34. *The Commercial Restraints of Ireland Considered. In a Series of Letters to a Noble Lord. Containing a Historical Account of the Affairs of that Kingdom, so far as They Relate to this Subject* (Dublin: Hallhead, 1779). The anonymous pamphlet (240 pages) was written by John Hely-Hutchinson (1724-94), an important and ambitious politician of the day.
35. An enclosure maintained by the authorities for straying animals or for animals seized as security for unpaid debts.
36. See note 12 to Chapter II above (p. 1154). But note also the manner in which Mr Daly's stature is confirmed as he makes his exit; his role in the novel subsequently is limited, and interest focuses on his son, Kyrle, and on Kyrle's friend, Hardress Cregan.
37. The term properly relates to a subdivision of traditional Irish society, and is introduced here to dignify the uncertain status of middlemen. Note that the explanation Griffin offers for the rise of middlemen emphasizes gentry absenteeism, in contrast to that provided by the professional historian (see note 12 to Chapter II above).
38. In the 1820s, various attempts were made by legislation to limit sub-leasing in the manner that had led to the growth of a middleman class.

Biographies/Bibliographies

Arthur Young

LIFE. Born at Whitehall in London on 11 September 1741, Young was the son of a Suffolk clergyman. At an early age he met David Garrick and John Wilkes, and was precociously talented as a boy. In 1758 he left school to become an apprentice in a commercial firm, and in 1765 he entered into what proved to be an unhappy marriage. Unsuccessful as a practical farmer *c*. 1768, he contemplated emigrating to the American colonies. Young's writings, commencing in the 1760s, gradually established him as an authority on the economic base of farming, although his economic thinking is far from original. (He also wrote four novels in his early years.) In 1776 he made his first visit to Ireland; the following year he became land agent on the Kingsborough estates in County Cork. William Pitt consulted Young about his Irish policies in 1785. From 1784 to 1809, Young edited the *Annals of Agriculture* and contributed extensively to its columns. In 1793 he became secretary to the Board of Agriculture. Young continued to extend his interest in society, especially rural society, visiting France from May to November 1787. In 1789 he witnessed some of the inaugurating events of the French Revolution at Versailles and Paris. Blind by 1811, and devastated by the death of a beloved daughter, he passed into a melancholy old age before dying in 1820.

CHIEF WRITINGS. Young is now remembered for his tours. *A Six Weeks' Tour through the Southern Counties* (London, 1768); *A Six Months' Tour through the North of England* (London, 1771); *Political Arithmetic* (London, 1774); *A Tour in Ireland* (London, 1780); *Travels in France* (London, 1792-1794). An *Autobiography* appeared in 1898, edited by M. Betham-Edwards.

BIOGRAPHY AND CRITICISM. John G. Gazley, *The Life of Arthur Young 1741-1820* (Philadelphia: American Philosophical Society, 1973). There is an amusing depiction of Young in Fanny Burney's novel *Camilla* (1796).

Samuel Crumpe

LIFE. Born in Limerick in 1766, educated as a physician in Edinburgh. His *Essay on the Best Means of Providing Employment for the People* secured him membership of the Royal Irish Academy. Crumpe died in 1796.

CHIEF WRITINGS. *An Inquiry into the Nature and Properties of Opium* (1793); *An Essay on the Best Means of Providing Employment for the People of Ireland* (1793).

Edmund Burke

For biography and bibliography, see pp. 853-854.

Myles Byrne

LIFE. Born in Monaseed, Co. Wexford in 1780, the son of a farmer. Participated in preparations for the United Irishman insurrection, and saw action at Vinegar Hill and elsewhere in 1798. He later assisted Robert Emmet, escaped to France and joined Napoleon's army. Byrne was invested in the Légion d'Honneur in 1813 and was appointed *chef de bataillon* in 1830. He died in Paris in 1862, and is buried in Montmartre cemetery. His memoirs were prepared for publication by his widow.

Richard Alfred Milliken

LIFE. Milliken (or Millikin) was born in Castle Martyr, Co. Cork, in 1767, of Scottish and Quaker background. Encouraged by Henry Boyle (later earl of Shannon), he qualified in Dublin as an attorney; however, his life was bounded by his native county, and despite enlistment in the Royal Cork Volunteers during the rebellion of 1798, his career was uneventful. In 1797-98, Milliken ran a magazine, *The Casket*, with his sister. He wrote a little for the stage, did some painting, and now is remembered solely for the (supposedly) nonsensical poem reprinted above. He died in 1815, and is buried in Douglas, Co. Cork.

CHIEF WRITINGS. *The River-side, a Poem in Three Books* (Cork: J. Connor, 1807); *The Slave of Surinam; or, Innocent Victim of Cruelty* (Cork: Mathews, 1810); *Poetical Fragments of the late Richard Alfred Milliken, with an Authentic Memoir of his Life* (London: Longman, 1823).

Leonard MacNally

LIFE. MacNally was born in Dublin in 1752. He lived in Bordeaux as a young man, opened a grocery shop in Dublin's St Mary's Lane in 1771, and was called to the bar in 1776. Although he spent time in London in the 1780s — he was there during the Gordon Riots of June 1780, and wrote plays, comic operas and adaptations for the stage — his career is inextricably bound up with the fate of Irish radicalism in the 1790s and the early years of the new century. A sworn member of the United Irishmen, MacNally represented many fellow-members in court when they faced charges of high treason. From 1794 onwards he was simultaneously working for the government as a spy inside the radical movement. He is alleged to have sold Robert Emmet for £200 in 1803, and yet to have devised the prisoner's defence. His double-life became known only after his death in Dublin in 1820.

MacNally's adaptations and parodies, in drama and fiction, of Laurence Sterne indicate something of his cast of mind. Like Richard Brinsley Sheridan and Richard Lalor Sheil, MacNally combined active politics with writing for the theatre. His secret betrayals of men whom he continued apparently to defend and befriend suggest a far more morbid involvement in the dualities of theatrical spectacle than anything attempted by Sheridan in the impeachment of Warren Hastings, or by Sheil in his far less momentous appearances in the Irish courts. No modern, or indeed even Victorian, study of MacNally has been attempted.

CHIEF WRITINGS. 1. Published Plays: *The Apotheosis of Punch* (London: Wenman, 1779); *Retaliation* (London: Blyth, 1782); *Tristram Shandy* (after Sterne's novel) (London: Bladon, 1783); *Robin Hood* (London: Alman, 1784); *Fashionable Levities* (London: Robinson, 1785); *Richard Coeur de Lion* (London: Debrett, 1786); *Critic Upon Critic* (London: Brand, 1788); *Cottage Festival* (London: Brand, 1796).

2. Fiction/Prose Sketches: *Sentimental Excursions to Windsor* (London: Walker, 1781).

3. Political and Legal Writings: *The Claims of Ireland and the Resolutions of the Volunteers Vindicated* .... (London: Johnson, 1782); *Abstract of Acts Passed in Parliament* (1786); *An Address to the Whig Club* (Dublin, 1790); *Rules of Evidence on Pleas of the Crown* (Dublin, 1802; London: Butterworth, 1802); *The Justice of the Peace for Ireland* (Dublin, 1808; also 1812, 1820).

John Wilson Croker

LIFE. Born in Galway in 1780, educated at Trinity College, Dublin and at Lincoln's Inn, London. Entered parliament as MP for Downpatrick in 1807, and was briefly chief secretary for Ireland the following year; became secretary to the Admiralty in 1809, a post he held until 1830. An opponent of parliamentary reform, Croker retired from the House of Commons on the passing of the Reform Act in 1832. As a literary figure, he is best remembered as a contributor to the *Quarterly Review*, John Keats's 'Endymion' being the most renowned victim of his trenchant criticism. Credited with the introduction of the term 'Conservatives' into the political vocabulary (*Quarterly Review*, January 1830), he supported Sir Robert Peel until 1845. Benjamin Disraeli caricatured Croker as Rigby in his novel *Coningsby*. He died in Hampton, Middlesex in 1857.

CHIEF WRITINGS. Croker was a prolific writer on many subjects. Those dealing with Ireland are *Familiar Epistles to Frederick Jones Esq., on the State of the Irish Stage* (Dublin: Barlow, 1804); *An Intercepted Letter from J—T—Esq. Writer at Canton, to his Friend in Dublin, Ireland* (Dublin: Mahon, 1804); *A Sketch of the State of Ireland, Past and Present* (Dublin: Mahon, 1808).

Other notable works include his edition of James Boswell's *Life of Samuel Johnson* (London: John Murray, 1831); *Military Events of the French Revolution of 1830* (1831); *Essays on the Early Period of the French Revolution* (London: Murray, 1857). See also the posthumously published 3-volume collection edited by Louis J. Jennings, *The Croker Papers ... 1809 to 1830* (London: John Murray, 1884). A modern and abridged edition by Bernard Pool is also valuable, *The Croker Papers, 1808-1857* (London: Batsford, 1967).

BIOGRAPHY AND CRITICISM. M. F. Brightfield, *John Wilson Croker* (Berkeley: University of California Press, 1940).

John Gamble

LIFE. Born in Strabane, Co. Tyrone, about 1770, Gamble was educated as a surgeon in Edinburgh. He joined the army as a surgeon, and served in the Low Countries in 1798. Sympathetic to the protestant radical aspect of the United Irishmen, he returned to Ireland, and travelled much of the country on foot as a preparation for his various travel writings. His life remains obscure and he has not been the subject of recent research. He died in 1831.

BIOGRAPHY AND CRITICISM. A brief bibliography by A. Albert Campbell can be found in *The Irish Book Lover* Vol. 1 (1909), pp. 20-21.

Charles Robert Maturin

LIFE. Born in Dublin, of Huguenot stock, in 1782, and educated at Trinity College, Dublin. Entered the Church of Ireland, and was first appointed to Loughrea in County Galway, a parish with earlier evangelical associations; later appointed to St Peter's, Dublin. Throughout his life, Maturin's clerical income remained small, and he acquired considerable debts through the misfortunes of his father. These difficulties were augmented by his own personal eccentricity and a talent for being misunderstood by his ecclesiastical superiors. A tragedy, *Bertram* (1816), was successfully produced by Edmund Kean at Drury Lane, London, but his attempts to make a living in the theatre were frustrated by S. T. Coleridge's devastating criticism in *Biographia Literaria* (1817). He first wrote novels as a means of meeting his financial responsibilities, but despite Sir Walter Scott's guarded encouragement, Maturin never disciplined his work, which is remarkable for its Gothic complications and emotional extravagance. Several of his novels are set in Ireland, although he also used continental locations. Maturin's influence in France was considerable, and Balzac wrote a continuation of *Melmoth the Wanterer*. Maturin died in York Street, Dublin in October 1824.

CHIEF WRITINGS. *The Fatal Revenge; or The Family of Montorio* (London: Hurst, 1807); *The Wild Irish Boy* (London: Longman, 1808); *The Milesian Chief* (London: Colburn, 1812); *Bertram; or the Castle of St. Aldobrand: A Tragedy* (London: Murray, 1816; French trans. 1821); *Manuel: A Tragedy* (London: Murray, 1817); *Women; or, Pour et Contre* (London: Longman; Edinburgh: Constable, 1818); *Fredolfo: A Tragedy* (London: Hurst; Edinburgh: Constable, 1819); *Sermons* (London: Hurst; Edinburgh: Constable, 1819); *Melmoth, the Wanderer* (London: Bentley, 1820; French trans. by Eugenie Fournier-Pescay Begin, Paris, 1821); *The Albigenses: A Romance* (London: Hurst; Edinburgh: Constable, 1824); *Five Sermons on the Errors of the Roman Catholic Church* (Dublin: Folds, 1824).

BIOGRAPHY AND CRITICISM. Niilo Idman, *Charles Robert Maturin, His Life and Works* (Helsingfors, 1923); W. Scholten, *Charles Robert Maturin, The Terror Novelist* (Amsterdam, 1933); Fannie Elizabeth Ratchford and William Henry McCarthy (eds), *The Correspondence of Sir Walter Scott and Charles Robert Maturin, with a Few Other Allied Letters* (Austin: University of Texas Press, 1937).

William Thompson

LIFE. Born in Roscarbery in County Cork about 1785, and inheriting a substantial estate, Thompson spent his life studying and implementing schemes of radical democracy and socialist economics. His friends included Jeremy Bentham and David Ricardo, and his economic writings are cited in the first volume of Karl Marx's *Das Kapital*. The passage directly quoted by Marx relates specifically to the drastic separation of the man of intellect from 'the productive labourer', and knowledge becomes 'an instrument, capable of being detached from labour and opposed to it.'

Thompson's commitment to feminist emancipation resulted from his relationship with Anna Wheeler, the married daughter of an Irish archbishop and the god-daughter of Henry Grattan. In this sphere he placed more trust in the ameliorating power of legislation than one might expect from a proto-Marxist theoretician of surplus value, but Mrs Wheeler's legal difficulties with her vexatious husband deeply affected Thompson's thought in relation to the status of women. Under the pseudonym Vlasta, she contributed to Robert Owen's *Crisis*.

Thompson established a co-operative on his estate in Cork, and at his death (28 March 1833) bequeathed it to the co-operative in a will that was contested by relatives, to the great loss of all concerned.

CHIEF WRITINGS. *Practical Education for the South of Ireland* (Cork, 1818); *An Inquiry into the Principles of Distribution of Wealth Most Conducive to Human Happiness* (London, 1824); *Practical Considerations for the Speedy and Economic Establishment of Communities on the Principle of Co-operation* (London, 1825); *An Appeal of One Half the Human Race, Women, against the Pretensions of the Other Half, Men, to Retain them in Political, and thence in Civil and Domestic, Slavery* (London, 1825); *Labour Rewarded — the Claims of Labour and Capital Conciliated; Or, How to Secure to Labour the Whole Products of its Exertions* (London, 1827).

There have been several republications of the *Appeal* (notably London: Virago Press, 1983). An Italian translation, *Appello di meta del genere umano* (trans. Silvia Franchini) was published in Rimini and Florence in 1974.

BIOGRAPHY AND CRITICISM. Richard Pankhurst, *William Thompson: Britain's Pioneer Socialist, Feminist and Co-Operator* (London: Watts, 1954).

Daniel O'Connell

For biography and bibliography, see pp. 959-60.

BIOGRAPHY AND CRITICISM. In connection with the themes of the letters reproduced in this section, an additional study worth examination is Charles Chevenix Trench, *The Great Dan; a Biography of Daniel O'Connell* (London: Cape, 1984).

John Banim

LIFE. Born in Kilkenny in 1798, Banim first devoted himself to the study of art at the Royal Dublin Society, then wrote for the London stage before commencing his career as novelist. *Tales by the O'Hara Family* were written in collaboration with his elder brother Michael (1796-1874). John Banim's last years were overshadowed by ill health. He died in Kilkenny in 1842.

CHIEF WRITINGS. *The Celt's Paradise* [a poem] (London: John Warren, 1821); *Damon and Pythias: A Five Act Tragedy in Verse* (revised by R.L. Shiel, London, 1821); *A Letter to the Committee Appointed to Appropriate a Fund for a National Testimonial Commemorative of His Majesty's First Visit to Ireland* (Dublin: Milliken, 1822); *Revelations of the*

Dead-Alive (London, 1824); *The Boyne Water* (London: Simpkin and Marshall, 1826; French trans. by M.A.J.B. Defauconpret, Paris, 1829; English text reprinted Lille, 1976); *The Anglo-Irish of the Nineteenth Century* (London: Colburn, 1828); *The Denounced* (London: Colburn and Bentley, 1830); *The Smuggler* (London, 1831); *Chaunt of the Cholera, Songs for Ireland* (London, 1831).

(With Michael Banim) *Tales by the O'Hara Family* (2 series, London: Simpkin and Marshall, 1825; London: Colborn, 1826); *The Bit o' Writing* (London: Saunders and Otley, 1838).

BIOGRAPHY AND CRITICISM. Patrick J. Murray, *The Life of John Banim* (London, 1857); Thomas Flanagan, *The Irish Novelists 1800-1850* (New York/London: Columbia University Press, 1959); Mark D. Hawthorne, *John and Michael Banim (The 'O'Hara Brothers'): A Study in the Early Development of the Anglo-Irish Novel* (Salzburg: Institut für Englische Sprache und Literatur, Universitat Salzburg, 1975); Barry Sloan, *The Pioneers of Anglo-Irish Fiction 1800-1850* (Gerrards Cross: Colin Smythe; Totowa, New Jersey: Barnes & Noble, 1986); J.M. Cahalan, *Great Hatred, Little Room: The Irish Historical Novel* (Syracuse: Syracuse University Press; Dublin: Gill and Macmillan, 1984); J.M. Cahalan, *The Irish Novel: A Critical History* (Dublin: Gill and Macmillan, 1989).

Gerald Griffin

LIFE. Born in 1803 in Limerick and educated there. In 1820 Griffin moved to London and wrote first for the stage. His career as novelist commenced with *Holland Tide*, and reached its peak with *The Collegians* (1829), which was later transferred to the stage by Dion Boucicault (*c*.1820-90) as *The Colleen Bawn* (1860). Disappointed with fame, Griffin destroyed many of his manuscripts on entering the Christian Brothers order. He died in the North Monastery, Cork in June 1840. On the strength of *The Collegians* alone, he can be regarded as the finest literary delineator of the life of the Irish middle class before the Famine.

CHIEF WRITINGS. *Holland Tide* (London: Simpkin and Marshall, 1827); *Tales of the Munster Festivals* (London: Saunders and Otley, 1827); *The Collegians: A Tale of Garryowen* (London: Saunders and Otley, 1829); *The Rivals* [*and*] *Tracy's Ambition* (London: Saunders and Otley, 1830; reprinted Lille, 1978); *The Christian Physiologist; Tales Illustrative of the Five Senses* (1830); *The Invasion* (London: Saunders and Otley, 1832); *Tales of My Neighbourhood* (London: Saunders and Otley, 1835); *The Duke of Monmouth* (London: Bentley, 1836); *Talis Qualis; or, Tales of the Jury Room* (London: Maxwell, 1842); *Poetical Works* (London: Simpkin and Marshall, 1842-43).

BIOGRAPHY AND CRITICISM. Daniel Griffin, *The Life of Gerald Griffin* (1843); Ethel Mannin, *Two Studies in Integrity: Gerald Griffin and the Revd Francis Mahony ('Father Prout')* (London: Jarrold's, [n.d.]; John Cronin, *Gerald Griffin 1803-1840: A Critical Biography* (Cambridge: Cambridge University Press, 1978). See also works by Flanagan, Cahalan and Sloan listed under Banim above.

W.J. Mc CORMACK, *Editor*

The Intellectual Revival

(1830-50)

After the end of the Napoleonic Wars (1815), Ireland experienced a series of powerful traumas. The fall in agricultural prices was not peculiar to Ireland, but it combined with other factors to create a highly disturbed mood in the Irish countryside from 1820 onwards. The failure of the British government to deliver catholic emancipation (as promised with the Act of Union in 1800) added a distinctive ideological flavour to the agrarian conflict of the 1820s, a decade in which Daniel O'Connell's long campaign for emancipation finally reached its zenith. The disturbances associated with the name 'Captain Rock' had begun in County Limerick in late 1821 and 1822, and these merged in the minds of many conservative (a word then emerging) Irishmen with the campaign for catholic emancipation. That measure, followed by the first great Reform Act (1832), seemed to announce the disappearance of the secure prestige and power that Irish protestants felt themselves to have possessed since early in the previous century. Union with Britain in effect had bound the Irish middle classes to a government in Westminster that was as likely to be Whig and reformist as Tory and reactionary.

Such, at least, is the background usually presented to the emergence in the 1830s of an articulate and talented movement among Irish intellectual protestants, a movement that is best exemplified in *The Dublin University Magazine*, founded in 1833. However, there is evidence to suggest that some of the causes of this intellectual ferment lie somewhat earlier and in less local areas.

First of all, changes in the Irish economy after the Union inevitably affected the social and cultural outlook of the population as a whole. Two developments preoccupied the public mind of the day: the impact of the railways, and the controversy over Poor Law provisions for Ireland. Neither of these issues appears on the surface to have cultural significance, although they monopolized a good deal of space in the newspapers and journals of the day. The railway reached Ireland early (1831), just four years after the inauguration of the British system; and, although its development was uneven, it gradually and relentlessly altered the relationship between the regions of Ireland, between the provincial towns and the major cities. The related growth of the west of Ireland as an area of recreation was facilitated by improved transport, and so the earlier 'romantic' West became accessible to middle-class families such as the Wildes and the Bewleys. Simultaneously, the Synge family was losing interest in its western holdings and would soon begin to develop commercially its valuable land in Dublin city. In literary terms, one also should note the delayed admission of the railway into Irish fiction: the Irish novel, for the most part, sought to ignore these mundane but important changes. The legal provision of some relief for the poor was the subject of a heated and extended debate in Ireland, posing questions about the Irish landlords' ability to support a Poor Law, the comparability of conditions in the different parts of the newly *United* Kingdom, and the ethical issue of providing sustenance with or without labour in return. Here, too, the cultural significance of the debate is not immediately evident. But if one considers how many of the Irish writers of the 1830s and 1840s had their roots in the rural middle class, then the impact of an issue that drew attention to divergences between British and Irish attitudes cannot be overlooked.

More particularly relevant to the cultural revival,

however, were the improvements in printing technology, which not only altered the possibilities of publication but opened up wholly new areas of society to literacy and the communication of ideas. Concern about the developments was by no means expressed exclusively by the Irish: Coleridge manifested unease as early as 1817 in the *Biographia Literaria*, and he is one of the intellectual patrons of the early Victorian revival in Ireland. Technical innovations were slow to reach Ireland, and the ideologues of *The Dublin University Magazine* were not of one mind about the advantage of improved communications. On the one hand the (mainly catholic) masses might avail of cheaply produced Bibles and similar reading: on the other, the limited and hence valorized domain of High Literature was in danger of being flooded by pamphlets, papers and penny-dreadfuls.

The second matter requiring careful attention is the thorny problem of sectarianism. It is of course true that *The Dublin University Magazine* was founded by a group of men exclusively protestant, and true also that some of the leading figures associated with *The Nation* (founded in 1842) were protestants. But it does not follow that the immediate aims or underlying objectives of Samuel Ferguson (1810-86) and Thomas Davis (1814-45) have to be interpreted in the light of protestantism — and this irrespective of whether one defines that term theologically or culturally. The work of James Clarence Mangan (1803-49) can be fully appreciated only if one acknowledges the influence upon him, not only of his own impoverished urban existence in Dublin, but of the 'devotional revolution' that was then re-energizing catholicism throughout the island (Mangan was a leading contributor to *The Dublin University Magazine* and *The Nation*). This devotional revolution not only resulted in the growth of parish organization in the catholic church but, through a renewed interest in the liturgy, it raised profound questions about the relationship between language and public life, between poetic form and multilingualism (the liturgy was Latin, the congregations English-speaking in Dublin, Irish-speaking in Galway).

Samuel Ferguson was born in Belfast, to a middle-class family of Scottish descent, and so might seem remote from these considerations. Yet one of his earliest and most influential publications in *The Dublin University Magazine* (in 1834) was a four-part review of James Hardiman's *Irish Minstrelsy*. Here, in a different context, is the same problem that later preoccupied Mangan: the relationship between languages and forms of social action. Much has been made of the fact that Ferguson seeks to liberate the songs recorded by Hardiman from what he takes to be a peculiarly Irish catholic piety; less has been said, less *could* be said of any sectarian cause on whose behalf Ferguson was allegedly conducting the rescue mission. The Gaelic literature translated by Hardiman (and also, in the course of his review, by Ferguson) was a source to which Irish intellectuals turned in this decade of inquiry, unease and experiment. There were other sources — continental ones, for example — a fact that should not be overshadowed by the mighty impact of the larger movement towards a revival of Gaelic. More important still, the Gaelic past was not just a source *from* which strength, direction and inspiration (those quintessentially romantic needs) might be acquired, but an objective or target *towards* which the colonizing forces of the intelligentsia might be concentrated.

If Thomas Davis is the best remembered of *The Nation* group, this may have as much to do with his early death, the popularity of his ballads, and the much-commented-upon sweetness of his character, as with his father having been an Englishman. His partner on *The Nation*, Charles Gavan Duffy (1816-1903), had previously been editor of the Belfast *Vindicator*, a vigorous organ of the city's catholic minority. Two names alone, Mangan's and Duffy's, should be enough to rebut the notion that the intellectual and political revival of the 1830s and 1840s was, in any intrinsic way, protestant in philosophy or character. But if a third name of equal stature will help to dissolve the tendency to see the period as a specifically *protestant* revival, then Denis Florence McCarthy's (1817-82) is the one to cite. That a large number of those engaged in the revival were protestants, not only by background but by religious practice, is hardly surprising, given the very recent emancipation of catholics under the law and the generally inferior place that they were seen to possess in polite society. Undoubtedly, the tension between Irish protestants, who were for the most part supporters of the Union with Britain, and Irish catholics, who were dissatisfied with that Union, looms large in the controversies of the day.

However, to see the period in terms of a rigid

division and conflict between two politicized denominations would be a gross oversimplification. There was a body of opinion among catholics who favoured their own advancement within Britain, and whose intellectual energies were directed into such channels as *The Dublin Review* (founded in 1836). The *Review* could hardly be described as impartial, but it was not a flagship of aggressive nationalism. The many weekly magazines associated with the publisher James Duffy (1809-71) were undoubtedly national in sentiment; but in many other, equally important, respects — the balance of 'romantic' fiction, household hints, news, direful verse, and so on — they conformed to a broad Victorian pattern. This is especially true towards the end of the 1840s, when such journalism was proliferating.

On the protestant side, there were of course notable figures who deviated (some would say revolted) from the norm of protestant content with the terms of 1800. But, as against the famous rebel names of John Mitchel (1815-75) and William Smith O'Brien (1803-64), one should list also Lord Rossmore (a County Monaghan landowner), Sir David Roose (stockbroker), and Thomas Steele (political functionary), to go no further than Daniel O'Connell's associates in the 1820s. In the succeeding decade, anxiety concerning religious truth marked many of the writers of fiction who came from protestant stock. This is only in keeping with a broader pattern of Victorian doubt evident throughout the kingdom, and might be best related to the spiritual experience of their catholic colleagues by reference to that confident revival of devotion current in the catholic church. Finally, there are those figures such as William Carleton (1794-1869), Charles Lever (1806-72), Isaac Butt (1813-79), and William Maziere Brady (1825-94), the variety of whose changes of allegiance, political and denominational, constitutes a veritable Heisenbergian 'uncertainty principle' of Irish ideology.

This latter point is not flippant, for readers in Irish literary history have been too prone to accept a kind of physical solidity in the structure of society. What is important in the emergence of Isaac Butt, the leader of the Home Rule party in the 1870s, from the Isaac Butt who in the 1840s thundered in the private cabals of the Metropolitan Conservative Society, is not the uncertainty or unpredictability of that change. Rather, it is the manifest inadequacy of any rigid binary scheme (catholic/protestant; nationalist/unionist; radical/conservative, or whatever) to account for the full complexity of a culture deeply embedded in the half-articulated exchanges, the half-observed nudges, and the largely unnoticed common assumptions that link and bind and relate more than they separate or set off the realities behind the slogans. Even in so qualifying the conventional stereotype, I have not adequately treated of the altering social and cultural existence of Irish presbyterians (mainly in Ulster), although in my own defence I can argue that such changes became significant rather later than the period examined in this section.

If the literature is innovatory, tentative and discontinuous, the political background appears in contrast almost adamantine. Daniel O'Connell's prolonged campaign for catholic emancipation had brought into being a new kind of political organization and method, based on the mobilization of large masses of people under a leadership that still retained centralized control. Thirty years earlier, in the 1790s, the potent phrase *protestant ascendancy* had been launched from fairly inauspicious origins, to become (in time) resonant with Yeatsian dignity, the ancient name (it seemed) of a noble caste. Crucial to the propagation of that slogan in the first instance was a new efficiency of journalism at the disposal of those propagating it. *Catholic emancipation* acquired a rival distinction, especially in the 1820s; *Repeal of the Union* likewise in the 1840s. Each of these slogans, in its turn, demonstrated the manner in which new techniques of propaganda and political mobilization came to pervade the life of Irish society. They were also powerful, sudden and disruptive instances of the way language could be compacted and dispatched throughout society, with enormous cultural and political effect. The novelists and poets of the 1830s and 1840s were intensely aware of such effects, and they devoted much of their creative energies to investigating the larger meanings that lay behind such clichés, even when they frequently preferred a more oblique approach to the inexorable realities of Irish life. These inquiries form an important stratum in the material assembled in this section. Related to them is a sense of caution, the value recognized in *indirect* modes: this forms a second, equally important, stratum. Add to these the impact of changing economic and technological conditions, and the crucial place of the intellectual revival that occurred in Ireland between (roughly) 1833 and 1848 will be evident.

Although the 1840s are remembered for *The Nation* in Ireland, and for Chartism and a host of important novels in England — for example, W.M. Thackeray's *Vanity Fair* (1847-48) and Emily Brontë's *Wuthering Heights* (1848) — the commencement and consolidation of intellectual revival in Ireland took place in the previous decade. In archaeology, Celtic studies, fiction, poetry, new ideas and voices had already been well established by 1840. The best way to inspect this process lies in an examination of Irish periodicals in which much of the work was either published or reviewed.

The Dublin University Magazine appeared monthly between 1833 and 1877, and is the supreme archive of Irish Victorian experience, especially that of the protestant (and, oddly, protestant *southern*) middle classes. The founders, who included the translator John Anster (1793-1867), the lawyer and politician Isaac Butt, and the newspaper proprietor and versifier John Francis Waller (1810-94), were all connected with Trinity College (the sole college of Dublin University), although the magazine never had any official connection with it. Information on its inner organization is scarce because research has been frustrated by the absence or disappearance of editorial records.[1] The most significant editors were Isaac Butt in the mid-1830s, Charles Lever in the early 1840s, and Joseph Sheridan Le Fanu (1814-73) for most of the 1860s.

The Nation was founded in 1842, but its origins may be traced a little earlier and in a milieu that brings it into contact with *The Dublin University Magazine*. Of its three founders, Thomas Davis, Charles Gavan Duffy, and John Blake Dillon (1816-66), only Davis had been educated at Trinity College. While an undergraduate, he was elected auditor of the College Historical Society (the leading debating club), and among the contributions to *The Nation* that are printed below is included Davis's inaugural address to the Society, even though the text dates from several years earlier than the magazine. Davis and Le Fanu had served together on at least one undergraduate committee, and their common background in the rural middle class deserves attention. Gavan Duffy had been brought south from Belfast by Daniel O'Connell; born in County Monaghan, he shared the rural (if not the protestant) background of Davis. Dillon was a catholic from County Mayo in the far west and, like Le Fanu and Davis, he studied for the bar in Dublin. It has not been sufficiently noted that these founding figures in *The Nation* were all provincial young men come up to Dublin in pursuit of professional careers.

The Nation had a motto: 'To create and foster public opinion, and make it racy of the soil.' The phrase and concept 'public opinion' was just coming into circulation in the 1840s, and the motto unites the founders' up-to-date outlook with their concern for Irish identity in the past as well as the present — 'the soil' of Ireland is its timeless symbol. And as its name unambiguously declared, *The Nation* devoted itself to the propagation of a nationalist ideology. This distinguished it to some extent from Daniel O'Connell's campaigns, which many saw as being closely identified with a catholic cause. But, whereas *The Dublin University Magazine* regarded the renaissance of catholic energies with hostility, the founders of *The Nation* hoped for an ecumenical partnership between catholic, protestant, and dissenter: in this sense they maintained some of the principles of 1790's republicanism. Like the contributors to *The Dublin University Magazine*, Davis and his colleagues placed great emphasis on literature as a means of stimulating national pride, and encouraged the literary exploration of Irish history and topography. However, *The Nation* was aimed at a more popular audience than its 'rival'; it appeared weekly rather than monthly, and adopted the format of a small newspaper, as distinct from a magazine or journal. Its literary contributions were for the most part poems (including translations) and regular reviews of Irish publications.

Whereas *The Dublin University Magazine* has undoubted links with conservative politics, its appearance of lofty elevation, above the events of the day, stands in contrast to the nexus of campaigns, causes and caucuses in which *The Nation* thrived. The latter was the organ of Young Ireland, a grouping of O'Connell's supporters in the campaign for Repeal of the Union, emphasizing the need for national regeneration, for a practical programme of cultural renewal (involving the establishment of reading rooms) and for a tolerant admission of all creeds and denominations to the 'common name of Irishman'.Through Duffy and

1. See bibliography (pp. 1297-98, *sub* Isaac Butt).

Mitchel they had links with the reality of northern politics, while through Smith O'Brien they were in touch with liberal feeling among the old land-owning class. O'Connell remained the dominant figure, but Young Ireland offered a kind of loyal opposition within the larger movement, seeking to reduce the element of the Liberator's personal infallibility, while also pointing to his occasional overreliance on the catholic clergy. Ultimately, a breach with O'Connell became inevitable, but by then he was in any case an old and exhausted man.

The Nation has had a long and confused history, the name being revived periodically as a tribute to the original paper of 1842. Throughout the 1840s, the editors conducted a vigorous campaign to declare their independence of O'Connell and of the catholic bishops, while also being confronted by the suspicion of Irish conservative opinion. Thomas Davis was the chief editor from 1842 to his death in 1845, when he was succeeded by John Mitchel, who himself seceded in 1847. The disaster of the Famine, and the *laissez faire* response of the British government, persuaded some supporters of Young Ireland that rebellion was inevitable. With 1848, the first 'existence' of *The Nation* came to an end. By then, O'Connell and Davis were both dead: Mitchel and Smith O'Brien had been transported to Australia; and Gavan Duffy was shortly to quit Ireland, ultimately to build a new career in Australian politics. Thus, the selection that follows (pp. 1248-92) is representative of a relatively self-contained episode in Irish history. While it is easy to see this in terms of the lives (and deaths) of the principal participants, *The Nation* should be recognized also as part of a broader movement in European liberalism. Young Ireland had its model or counterpart in several continental countries, including Italy and Germany, and the paper represented a bold attempt to write into existence an Irish liberal philosophy.

SAMUEL FERGUSON

(1810-86)

A DIALOGUE BETWEEN THE HEAD AND HEART OF AN IRISH PROTESTANT (1833)

[Samuel Ferguson (knighted in 1878) was one of *The Dublin Magazine*'s most prolific and influential contributors, his wide range of interests (Gaelic culture, public administration, archaeology) providing a base for a broad survey of the state of middle-class morale in the first half of the Victorian period. 'A Dialogue between the Head and Heart of an Irish Protestant' appeared towards the end of the magazine's first year of publication. The dialogue form, though it has an obvious romantic aspect in the juxtapositioning of thought and feeling, self-interest and self-abandonment, also draws on an older tradition of writing, which in Ireland includes Edmund Spenser's *A View of the Present State of Ireland* (1596), the several dialogues on various subjects political, linguistic and moral by Jonathan Swift, and George Berkeley's more strictly philosophical 'Three Dialogues between Hylas and Philonous' (1713). The reader should take care not to identify either of the speakers with Ferguson, nor rush to assume that one of the opinions uttered is privileged by the author over and above the other. Although a distinct strain of anti-catholic animus appears to be a common property of both Heart and Head, one should not deduce this to be a constant in the elaborate transactions of the Dialogue. (Conventionally a protestant, Ferguson was less prone to religious concerns than many of his fellow contributors.) At the same time, the piece's two-part structure imposes its own limitations, tending towards a preference for the formulation of problems as much as towards solutions in the shape of 'either/or'.]

HEAD: You are in an unreasonably bad temper.

HEART: I am in a bad temper, and somewhat dangerous, but not unreasonable. Have I not good cause to be in a bad temper? Here are we, the loyal protestant gentry of Ireland, by whose attachment to the law, and the church, and the crown, this Island has for two hundred and fifty years (ever since its actual conquest) been preserved to the British Empire. We, by whom three dangerous rebellions have already been put down in this realm, and who would be ready to put down an other *in the same cause*, were it to burst out tomorrow.[1] Here are we, I say, who are the controllers of popery; the safeguards of British connection; the guarantees of the empire's integrity; the most respectable body of men for our members, in all Europe, whether we be considered with regard to wealth, industry, intellect, position, or absolute power; here are we, I say again, who in a word, are the arbiters of Britain's fate, deceived, insulted, spoiled, and set at defiance.

HEAD: Softly; softly. The whigs still love our church, though they have been her involuntary spoliators. They cannot be such fools, as not to value our friendship, though they have much against their design, estranged our affections. See, now of late, when they perceived to what a miserable state we are reduced, through their mismanagement, have they not sacrificed their pride of principle, and exposed themselves to the charges of hypocrisy, and tyranny, for our sake?[2]

HEART: They have sacrificed no principle who never had any. They have done nothing for our sake, who never had an aim beyond the gratification of their own political conceits. Is it for our sake, that we are exposed to as much of the indignity of their bill, as the vilest clamours of the Arena?[3] Is it for our sake, that we dare no more meet than a mob? Is it for our sake, that we are denied even the use of their bill's authority, for the collection of our rightful property?

HEAD: Surely it is something in our favour, to be able to lie down without the fear of having our houses burned, or our throats cut before morning. It is something for a man to be able to walk from his own door to his place of worship, without risk of being shot at from behind his father's tombstone. It is something for a man to get his rents, too; and the privilege of setting one's lands to tenants of one's own choosing, is also something. The bill was unconstitutional, and galling: but it has had the effect desired. It has tranquillized the country.

HEART: Tranquillity; do you call it? The tranquillity of fear for an unjust power, is more than open violence. It is either manhood prostrated, or deeper malice concealed. Yet you will never cease taunting me with our tranquillity. Go, taunt the plundered traveller, with the quiet comforts of his gag![4]

HEAD: There you go! bouncing, and puffing in the face of reason. The only act ever done by the whigs, that can be called a boon to the Irish Protestant, you rebel against as hotly as if it had been catholic emancipation,[5] or an Irish church bill. True; I can see very plainly the illegality of that act, and can be well aware, that while it continues in force, we are *de jure*[6] deprived of magna charta;[7] but I rest the most secure confidence; the most fearless assurance in my knowledge, that the application of that bill, can never *de facto* place us beyond the pale of the constitution. It is a rod that we care not to see laid on the shoulders of the turbulent, and lawless. *Our backs are at Lord Brougham's defiance.*[8]

HEART: Though the necessity, and the benefits of that bill, were demonstrated to me a hundred times in the day, I could not think of its framers, without abhorrence and disgust. They, who for twenty years did nothing but irritate the sore, which proper treatment had cicatrized[9] within a single month; it well becomes them now, to call out for the knife, and the searing iron! They, whose whole talk has been of liberty, and the blessings of the constitution; of the rights of man; the unalienable rights of man, and the hatefulness of arbitrary power — it well becomes them to be the first to propound an edict like a Russian ukase![10] Hypocrites and tyrants! may they live to reap — Oh! God forbid that the seed which they have sown, should ever come to maturity; but if it do, then may they be the first to reap a harvest of abundant punishment! May they be the first to see their spurs of privilege chopped off by the cleaver of a hangman mob! May they be the first to see the ruffian soldier stable his horses in their cabinets! — Infamy eternal cling to their memories, who, when one salutary summer shower of the law, would have quenched for ever, the

1. i.e. the rebellions of 1641, 1798 and 1803; 'in the same cause' echoes the protestant notion of the great cause (of Whiggish liberty).
2. The Reform Act (1832) and the Church Temporalities (Ireland) Act (1833) greatly alarmed the Irish gentry.
3. The central area of an amphitheatre where combatants meet; hence, a battlefield.
4. i.e. one who is bound and gagged may be reminded of the blissful silence thus obtained.
5. Catholic emancipation was conceded in 1829.
6. in law. *de facto* (below) means in practice.
7. A great charter, recognizing certain rights and privileges.
8. Henry Peter Brougham (1778-1868), baron Brougham and Vaux, was lord chancellor, the chief minister responsible for law in the British government, from 1830 to 1833. He played an important part in the debates over the parliamentary reform bill.
9. healed (of a wound).
10. The edict of a tsar, having governmental authority in itself; any arbitrary declaration.

smouldering causes of sedition, did, for their own base purpose, rake them together, and fan them into flames, and who, when that conflagration had burned the barriers, and overleaped the rampart, and was bursting at last into the very sanctuary of the capitol, did, for the suppression of that, their own incendiarism, pull down our transept of the triple temple, where Irish honour still lies prostrate and suffocating among the blackened ruins.

HEAD: Rather say that Irish honour shines brighter for the sacrifice she has made to Irish safety. For they who truly checked the flame, were not the whigs, but the Irish protestants, without whose assent, their bill had never passed into law. That their honour is either blackened or tarnished, I deny. Nay, that these bold and virtuous men, by controlling the very feelings which you have now expressed, (*and which they universally have felt rebelling within them, against their better reason*) and by thus submitting their private indignation to their sense of the public good, have gained themselves a civil glory, far more honorable than the most romantic pride of partial patriotism could bestow — that they have won such an honour, I say, is clear to the eyes of every man in the Empire, who can value the goods of peace, and the protection of the laws.

HEART: What do you mean by protection of the laws, when the very extension of the so called protection, is itself the utter annihilation of that law?

HEAD: 'Salus populi, suprema lex.'

HEART: 'Fiat justitia, ruat cœlum!'[11]

HEAD: And if the sky did fall, let me ask who would be the 'larks?'[12] But away with the idleness of childish metaphor. If revolution had, in Ireland, a successful issue, what would become of our estates, our liberties of conscience; our personal liberties; our lives? Oh, we would respect the rights of property, says the Popish plotter,[13] and we would never deprive another of his religious liberty, after struggling so long, and so devotedly for our own — all we would ask would be your co-operation in carrying into effect the decrees of our parliament, or to speak more clearly, we would only insist on your subjection and obedience (the necessary consequences, mark you, of minority in numbers, when universal suffrage and ballot voting, shall have cast all the power of the nation, be it republic or what you will, into the hands of our own people). Then as to your church; if the whigs leave her anything, we would of course apply that to national purposes; and you surely could not object to a like appropriation of lands confiscated by their owners levying war against their country.' But if I ask, what is meant by national purposes? 'Why' replies our jesuit, 'the march of mind must be directed by an authority, competent to so high an office; and what authority, save that of the Church, has moral power qualifying it for the intellectual command of a whole people? The Church, my friend, must be re-established. The spirit of heresy must be eradicated — *You Protestants, my excellent fellow, must either conform or quit.* This may seem hard, yet it is no more than the *lex talionis*.[14] Times, Sir, are altered; you have had your day. 'Tis our turn now.

HEART: This talk of the nation, the republic, the levying of war, the forfeiture of estates, and seizure of church lands, alarms me. You do not seem to consider a repeal of the union,[15] but to speculate on a violent separation.

HEAD: *It is a separation on which I speculate.* A repeal of the union, as the phrase is generally understood, I take to be a sham, a pretence, the mere shadow of a stalking horse; a thing that has existence only in theory, like a whig's doctrine of the three estates.[16]

HEART: And can you for a moment bear the contemplation of such an event as the first, without dread and abhorrence?

HEAD: Horror and shrinking are for you. I can contemplate, unmoved, any state of affairs that may await us. If changes go on as they have for some time proceeded, I can, without either fear or wonder, contemplate the enactment of laws for the British Empire, by the lowest demagogues, (by delegated tinkers, if you please) and I can consider the enforcement of these laws entrusted to the pikes

11. 'The well-being of the people is the highest law' (Cicero, *De Legibus* III, iii, 8). The second quote is 'Fiat justitia, et ruant coeli' (William Watson, *Quodlibets of Religion and State* (1602)): 'May justice prevail even though the sky should fall' (as a consequence).
12. Meaning either 'those who would stay airborne, survive' or 'those who would frolic, benefit, lark about'.
13. The Popish Plot (1678) was the invention of Titus Oates, who sought to incriminate catholics in a largely non-existent conspiracy against Charles II.
14. The law of retribution.
15. A return by constitutional means to the quasi-independent state Ireland was in before the Act of Union of 1800.
16. The Lords Spiritual (bishops), the Lords Temporal (peers), and the Commons.

of sans-culottes.[17] If then I can look on such a state of things unmoved, I need not shrink from the consideration of that which seems, at all events, not more improbable; for, if Catholic emancipation produce repeal, so surely will repeal produce ultimate separation; and so sure as we have a separation, so surely will there be war levied, estates confiscated, and the Popish church established.

HEART: In such a crisis we would be in a sad case — between the devil and the deep sea.

HEAD: Our duty and line of conduct would be plain, supposing England still to be the Old England that she has not yet ceased to be. Yet why do I say so? for while England is as now, Repeal can not take place.

HEART: I boasted but now of our strength, and yet I see how our strength would be weakness, in the event of that which you hint must accompany Repeal.

HEAD: I do not hesitate to avow it. *Repeal can never take place until the Protestants of Ireland are disgusted by, and alienated from, the English Government*.

HEART: In such a crisis, which God in his mercies avert, I do feel that our present available power would be almost useless; for, at present we stand midway upon the balance, and by leaning to either side can make the opposite scale kick the beam; but in circumstances such as another Revolution might produce, our position would be altered in proportion to the change of those we deal with; and in truth, I fear, unless we qualify ourselves for some new mode of action, we should hardly be able to touch the beam at all.

HEAD: It *is* much to be lamented that the Protestant gentry of Ireland have not sooner begun their apprenticeship to the craft and mystery of self-defence. Yet even on that account we must admire them the more; for it has been their frank and manly confidence in the honor of the British Government that has hitherto prevented them from seeking or using the arms in which others, less scrupulous and more selfish, have been disciplining themselves for the last ten years. But it is time now to lay aside all romantic punctilios, all weak forbearances; to gather together, and, seeing that concession has begot concession, like the draughts of a drunkard, to make known our determination that we will concede no more; that, if further abandonment of our rights be wrung from us by violence, we also will take up the game that has been played to such advantage by the rest.

HEART: We are not yet enough initiated in the arts of agitation to play it with the same success.

HEAD: I am aware that we are, individually, too much gentlemen to cope, in the excitement of a rabble's sympathy, with such persons as the brawlers of the Corn-Exchange. And I am, besides, conscious that the subjects with which we must have to deal, will always present to our adversaries an aspect much more easily reconcilable to the views of the mob, than that in which we must contemplate them. Tell a man that, by the changes you desire, he will have his whiskey at half-a-crown the gallon, his tea at one and six-pence by the pound, his claret, if he be a wine-drinker, at eight-pence a-bottle, and his loaf, if he have a family of many mouths, at double size and less than half price, and you will experience little difficulty in persuading him to lend you his assistance in carrying these changes into effect. But, if by close reasoning and a complicated chain of nice conclusions, you endeavour to demonstrate to the same man, that by gaining these benefits, he must inevitably lose others of much more vital importance, such as the comforts of an orderly state of society, constant employment, sure markets, high wages — or if you attempt to show him the likelihood of such events compromising his personal or moral liberty, or sinking his country in the scale of nations — if you attempt this, I say, you will find that his perceptions, which were keen and perspicuous in the apprehension of positive good, are dull and incredulous where contingent evils are sought to be exhibited.

HEART: Another disadvantage we labour under is the opinion, which we have never with sufficient vigour contradicted, that our opponents have, in their Irish blood, a stronger claim to credit for disinterested nationality than we who are, generally speaking, comparatively 'strangers.'

HEAD: This is a mistake which must not be allowed to mislead us longer. Supposing (which I do not for a moment admit) that we are universally strangers by blood, as the Normans were in England, yet have the newest comers amongst us, as good a claim, now, to the name of Irishmen, as had these Norman invaders to that of Englishmen in the time of the Edwards. Between the battle of

17. Literally, 'trouserless ones', the have-nots; in the French Revolution a name for a mob who brandished pikestaffs.

Hastings and the days of Cressy and Poictiers, [*sic*][18] they had scarcely a longer time or better opportunity of making themselves a national nobility than we have had from the Battle of the Boyne[19] to the present day. Yet what a difference!

HEART: And why?

HEAD: Because, forsooth, we live in an age too far advanced in intellect to suffer our imitation of these founders of British greatness. But why waste time in lamenting the loss of that which is irrevocable? Protestant ascendancy, which promised to make us another England, is by the fraud and violence of traitors rendered ineffectual for good or evil, and come after it what may, whether a Popish Establishment, a tolerating French philosophical morality, or Deism at large, Ireland never can be that which Protestant ascendancy might have made her. Yet stripped as we are of power and privilege, neither Whig tyranny nor Popish malice can deprive us of our birthright, which is the love of Ireland.

HEART: I know not whence my blood may have been drawn, but it circulates with a swifter liveliness at the name of this country, and I feel and know that I am the heart of an Irishman.

HEAD: And ten to one the chances that your blood has been drawn from a source as purely Irish as that of O'Connor or O'Brien. The Scot, returning to the land that sent him forth, need not be ashamed to recognise his cousins of the South, — but away, again, with the idleness of country, kindreds, and invasions. The Celt may have been expelled by the Nemedian, the Nemedian by the Firbolg, the Firbolg by the Tuatha de Danaan,[20] the Tuatha de Danaan by the Scot, the Scot by the Anglo-Norman — but what of that? *They were all Irishmen in turn, and* WE *are Irishmen now.* Would that this were our only difference: but, alas! what are those curious distinctions of the genealogist, to the contending principles of Popery and Protestantism, that have made a thousand men murderers in one night!

HEART: Aye, I could burst at the thought of *that*.

HEAD: A difference, too, which time, in many respects, has made only more inveterate.

HEART: And worse than all, an evil, resignation to which is crime.

HEAD: That the conversion of the Irish Romanists will yet be effected by a reformation as sudden as that in England, I am still fondly willing to expect. Meanwhile, the mere neighbourhood of Protestantism is gradually liberalizing them. They are already disclaiming juggleries of which, fifty years ago, they would have boasted. The common sense of the times, too, is an active auxiliary among their better sort.

HEART: Common sense alone does not know where to stop: I would not have Ireland like France.

HEAD: I make a wide distinction between common sense and the march of mind: Yet doubtless, we may have reasonable fears of an ultra-reformation here, some day, if Protestantism be not pushed with greater vigour in time.

HEART: On the heads of those who have crippled the Irish Church, be the shame and punishment, if she do not overtake the spoiler, and that quickly.

HEAD: Of that, unless by a providential revolution of opinion, I now see no reasonable prospect. We will drive Popery by degrees from lie to lie, each one contested with the obstinacy of despair; but between the outworks of trick and legerdemain, and the citadel of church supremacy what a wilderness of error inexplicable — what pitfalls, traps, and labyrinths — what sloughs and stenches of superstition! But, above all, and beyond all, what a rampart in the deluded people's love? For the Irish priesthood hold the hearts of their seduced victims in even firmer bondage than their minds.

HEART: I confess, were I myself the heart of an Irish Roman Catholic (and many thousands good as I beat in the hearts of Popish Irishmen,) it would claim all your influence to make me withdraw that support, however evidently misapplied. They have fasted for it, fought for it, suffered confiscation, exile, and death for it; through good and ill they have been constant and true to this; and the human heart cannot deny some charity to such devotedness.

HEAD: *And were I the sympathizing counsellor of such a will, I would conceive another rebellion of* 1641.[21] If you and I, then, can in speculation accord

18. At the battle of Hastings (1066) the Normans established themselves in England; the other names are of later battles in which the English were victorious in France — Crécy (1346), Poitiers (1356).

19. The battle, fought in July 1690, that established William III's control over Ireland. The protestant forces overcame the Jacobite army of James II.

20. Successive waves of invaders in early Irish mythology and proto-history.

21. The events of the year 1641 remain a matter of dispute among historians, but to Irish protestants the date was synonymous with treacherous catholic rebellion.

charity to priestcraft and humane motives to massacre and treason, think what a danger we are in, who are as one to five among those who feel in passionate reality what we have here confessed in cool imagination. You are, in this, culpably charitable.

HEART: And in this are not you culpably the reverse?

HEAD: What! in affirming that, were I on the shoulders of a priest-led Irishman, I would project rebellion? It would claim two hundred years' experience of their acts reversed to shake my certainty of that axiom.

HEART: Alas! what a chance of success could they have?

HEAD: If their present scheme succeed, they will have every chance of success.

HEART: And their present scheme?

HEAD: Is *to revolutionize England, that we, being disgusted, may join them in rebelling here.*

HEART: What then?

HEAD: *To put down Protestantism and proclaim the most catholic republic.*

HEART: Surely, surely, they would spare the rights of conscience.

HEAD: Mark you; when we passed the Six Acts[22] we were as far advanced in civilization as the Papists of Ireland are at this day. *What we did then, they would do now.*

HEART: Then let us never join them.

HEAD: If their designs come to maturity in England, it will matter little which side we take. If we save our lands from the Romish claimant here today, we lose them to the Deist confiscator there tomorrow; for Hume, Cobbett, and the rest would emulate Cromwell to the last.[23] Here is a sentiment by no means uncommon among the English radicals. 'When we assume the reins of government,' say they, 'we will deal out that meed[24] of justice to Ireland which her peculiar exigencies may seem most to demand. Having so done, should the Irish, either through the levity of the Papists, or the pride of the Protestants, evince dissatisfaction with our arrangements, and proceed to cast any impediment in the way of the march of mind, it will then become our duty, as men earnestly bent on benefitting the community, to coerce the Irish.'

HEART: Insufferable rogues!

HEAD: Say rather blind and overweening braggarts; for, if England were revolutionised, her nobility and prime gentry dispersed, her yeomanry disaffected, her manufacturing towns thrown out of employment, her redundant population clamouring for Irish provisions and Irish absentees, and she herself, stripped of her colonies and reduced to her poor twelve millions of hungry citizens; then I would ask the authors of this tremendous gasconade,[25] what would be their chance, although still two to one against an indignant, and for the first time united people? 'So far from having to dread the youthful energies of this new France,' I have heard a Popish gentleman well argue, 'it would seem that all the chances of defensive success were on our side. We have no manufacturing population to be thrown into starvation and rebellion on every check in the progress of society: *England has five* millions. We have no exports not available at home. Should our Cork, our Waterford, our Dublin, or Belfast traders be blown back to port by the stormy denunciations of those long-minded orators, their beef, butter, and pork, are the very things we want, and best know how to use; but the English penknives, needles, pots, pans, and gaudy calicoes, will neither encrease themselves, nor feed others without a market. Again, *the Protestants secured*, we are to a man unanimous in any project anti-English; while the ghosts of those who fell at Marston Moor or Naseby,[26] can prophecy what bloody discord would be the portion of our liberal coercers. Nay more, we have, under any circumstances, the old good will of France and America, while England is, as she ever was, hated and feared by both.' Such are the speculations of those men from whom the British democrats expect co-operation. So far as it conduces to the good of the Romish Church and the glory of rebellion they will receive it, but no further. *Popery and Infidelity will hunt together so long as a Protestant Church and Aristocracy are to be run down, but let them once dip their muzzles in the blood of the last Bishop, and, with tusks sharper than wolves', they will turn and tear each other's throats.*

22. i.e. the principal Penal Laws against catholics, passed immediately after William III's victory in 1691.
23. David Hume (1711-76) and William Cobbett (1763-1835) are cited here as prophets of religious indifference whose followers might confiscate, as Oliver Cromwell's did in the seventeenth century.
24. recompense, reward.
25. (French) boast.
26. Battles (Marston Moor 1644; Naseby 1645) of the English Civil War in which Cromwell routed the royalist armies of Charles I.

HEART: But I cannot endure so closely the thought of our contending with Englishmen.

HEAD: It is a revolting prospect, a hideous thing to contemplate on either side; and, now that we have used it, I gladly say, away with the abominable thought for ever.

HEART: But for what purpose conjure up so monstrous an apparition?

HEAD: *To teach you to repress your apologetic, compromising, prurient, rebellious, sympathies.* And that by exhibiting to you the consequences of their indulgence. We will require all the painful severity of self-denial, and the fearless adoption of all most strict and rigid principles of political and religious loyalty to be enabled to avert that portentous crisis, with the prospect of which you have been so wholesomely alarmed. Were I near enough to be governed by your perverse suggestions, we would be precipitated into the very midst of it tomorrow.

HEART: You do me injustice. Had I not been loyal as yourself, you might feast the carrion crows today from a gibbet — but I am tormented and enraged by the condition to which our loyalty has brought us. — Deserted by the Tories, insulted by the Whigs, threatened by the Radicals, hated by the Papists, and envied by the Dissenters, plundered in our country-seats, robbed in our town houses, driven abroad by violence, called back by humanity, and, after all, told that we are neither English nor Irish, fish nor flesh, but a peddling colony, a forlorn advanced guard that must conform to every mutinous movement of the pretorian[27] rabble — all this, too, while we are the acknowledged possessors of nine tenths of the property of a great country, and wielders of the preponderating influence between two parties; on whose relative position depend the greatest interests in the empire. — I love this land better than any other. I cannot believe it a hostile country. I love the people of it, in spite of themselves, and cannot feel towards them as enemies.

HEAD: Yet it is one of the necessities of your existence that they should feel as enemies towards you.

HEART: Well, well, I would not call them my countrymen if they could not remember and resent an injury.

HEAD: We did them no injury. If there be any country on earth which should thank another for having rescued it from bloodshed and barbarism, it is Ireland, and that other is Great Britain. Is it injury to establish peace where, for a thousand years preceding, there had been unabated war?

Is it injury to fix the rights of society where, from time immemorial, no man could call a single acre his own? Is it injury to extend the mild influence of just laws over men who else could hardly separate right from wrong? or is it injury to introduce the religion of the Bible for the fictions and traditions of designing man?

HEART: I cannot argue. I only feel that, in the heart of a mere Irishman, I would have rebelled against the forced favour.

HEAD: It is fair and natural that all gallant spirits should sympathize with one another; nor can I blame the brave man who recognizes as admirable a courage in Shane O'Neill[28] as in Harry Percy[29] — they both were very valiant rebels — so was Hugh Tyrone;[30] perhaps as good a captain as Claverhouse or Montrose.[31] Owen Roe was a famous general, and a brave gentleman;[32] but remember, I beseech you, *had they succeeded, we had not been here.* Had they succeeded, the Irish today would have been fit rivals of the Greeks or Portuguese — as it is, they are a great part of a great empire. So much for the injustice of English interference.

HEART: It is not of English interference they complain. Their great outcry is against English *misgovernment.*

27. (from Latin, praetor) of the imperial bodyguard; thus 'pretorian rabble' is a contradiction in terms.

28. Shane O'Neill (1530-67) was an Ulster chieftain. He destroyed the Scottish settlements of the McDonnells in Antrim, invaded the Pale and burnt Armagh.

29. The Sir Henry Percy (1364-1402), nicknamed Hotspur because of his daring and impetuosity, depicted in the first part of Shakespeare's *Henry IV*. In 1403 he joined his father's rebellion against Henry but was killed at the battle of Shrewsbury.

30. Hugh O'Neill (*c.* 1550-1616), 2nd earl of Tyrone, known as the Great O'Neill. He served the English government in Ireland during the 1580s but rebelled in 1594. Although he inflicted a heavy defeat on the English at the battle of the Yellow Ford (1598), the Irish were routed while trying to join a Spanish force that arrived in Kinsale in 1601. He sailed from Lough Foyle with other chiefs in 1607 and settled in Rome, where he died.

31. John Graham of Claverhouse (1648-89), lord Dundee, led a highland rising for James II in Scotland in 1689; James Graham Montrose (1612-50) was the leading supporter of Charles I in Scotland during the Civil War. Both men figure prominently in novels (*Old Mortality* (1816) and *A Legend of Old Montrose* (1819) by Sir Walter Scott (1771-1832)). Scott had died the year before the publication of this article. His influence on Irish literature was enormous. It is worth noting that 'Head' cites historical figures who have been transformed into literary heroes.

32. Owen Roe is Eoghan Rua O'Neill (*c.* 1590-1649), Irish military leader against the Scots and the parliamentarians, whom he defeated at the battle of Benburb (1646).

HEAD: That is because they have not the candour or the courage to declare the true cause of their indignation. They talk of seven centuries of misgovernment: now, for more than four out of those seven hundred years this is absolutely false. Up to the time of Elizabeth there was in reality *no government to mismanage*. Till then, the English could scarce govern themselves, much less a turbulent and angry neighbour; and, *had the Irish been formed of the stuff to make a nation*, they had, every year of that time, an opportunity on more than equal terms of asserting their right to govern themselves — nay, of actually becoming the dominant island of the two. Could they have done so, had they possessed elements of a nation, then the English would have been, indeed, the dog in the manger, and the charge of misgovernment, or rather of government prevented, might stand; but let any man of common discretion look at any district either within or without the pale,[33] to enquire whether or no, during all that time, it needed, or could spare protection, and whether he directs his attention to the stone castle of the Hibernicized Baron, who lived by Coign and Livery,[34] or to the timber Dun[35] of the native Chieftains, supported by Bonaghts and Cuttings,[36] or to the forest, or the mountain cavern of the freebooter, subsisting by the plunder of his neighbour's cattle, he will find in all ranks and classes, and among all varieties of men, the same selfish clanship, the same contracted tyranny and blind savage levity, which, from Castle Dun and Cave will give him full assurance over all the island, that till the time of Elizabeth Ireland possessed no where either the will or the power of governing herself. After Elizabeth's time, indeed, that question may admit of argument; but much or little as they may have had, the English have always had more. Whether that power has been too laxly or too strictly exercised since Ireland's actual government began, I leave any reasonable man to gather from the fact, that, during its most vigorous operation we prospered exactly in proportion to our late decay under its relaxing influence.

HEART: Protestant ascendancy was indeed a noble scheme and worthy a great politician; yet, as in the misfortunes of our best friends, there is still something pleasing to us, I can extract even from its overthrow some comfortable solace in the thought that, while we escape our own responsibility, others undergo the risk of an experiment which, if it fail, will justify us to the world, and if it succeed will benefit our country. For the sake of the latter event, I could well submit to the substantiation of all their charges against us.

HEAD: God grant that it may have such an issue. But I cannot say that I submit to a consequence of it, which never can take place: Irish prosperity under the new system, would in no way fix an imputation on the old. Our modern theorists have sprung into existence with the steam-engine and the rail-road. Whatever these effect, they will lay claim to, and whatever good be the consequence of their joint influence, they must share its reputation together.

HEART: After all, they are neither steam-engines, rail-roads, nor canals, that make a great people. They are the effect, not the cause. The Romans were the nation of the gown before a stone was laid in the via Appia. Magna Charta will outlast the reform bill, although Watling-street[37] was the only paved road that rung to the tramp of the assembling barons. Our own volunteers are not altogether eclipsed by the trades' union, even though, in these unenlightened times, no empty truck-boat, crossed once a week the utilized Bog of Allen.[38] *The men and the cause make the great people, and no instrument so worthy as the strong hand.*

HEAD: If the question were to be so arbitrated, come two to one, and welcome: but our enemy's boast is, that that day's gone by. We must fight our battle now with a handful of types and a composing-stick, pages like this our field, and the reading public our arbiter of war. Yet even here, although the odds are so fearfully against us, we will take our stand upon the sacred mount whence Luther and Calvin thrust down the baffled thunders of Rome, and at the foot of which the traitor and the treason lay crushed, and once

33. An extensive area surrounding Dublin in which government had been fully effective during the medieval period, so named because it was once marked out by a paling.
34. A general term for the various fees exacted by Gaelic chieftains by quartering and billeting their dependents on the countryside.
35. (Irish) hill-fort, fortress.
36. Forms of Gaelic tribute and entail in relation to property in the mid-sixteenth century: 'bonaght' recently had been described by the English historian Henry Hallam (1777-1859) as a barbarous practice; 'cutting' was essentially the same as tailage.
37. The great Roman road across Britain from Dover to the Severn.
38. A great bog, covering much of the central plain of Ireland, some 370 square miles in area.

despairing under the virtuous energies of Burke.[39]

HEART: Well said! You enlarge and gratify me. I burn with an ardour as holy as that which might have filled me on the embattled banks of Boyne. Let us go up together, and unfurl the old flag from the summit: and assail it who may, be he Papist or Protestant, Whig, Tory, or Radical, you shall have courage, and fortitude, and hope unfailing in its defence, while I have a drop of blood from which to gather them. Nay (for the mere defence of our assaulted principles is far from satisfying my enlarged desires,) — advance your standard into the very middle of the enemy's camp, plant it on every hill in Ireland, and I will inspire and support you to the last.

HEAD: Where now are your Popish sympathies?

HEART: Here; warm as ever. I cannot give up the nature of humanity, but I were unworthy the heart of a Christian could I not submit to some self-sacrifice for the Lord's sake. I still love my Popish countrymen. I love them so much, that I would bear the pain of seeming their error's persecutor, (and they and error are so closely linked, that such a character were little different from what the world calls an oppressor), for the sake of being able to love them absolutely as free, loyal, and united Protestants.

HEAD: Yet these have been the feelings of all the men who have been called Ireland's misgovernors, and these are now the feelings of all us whom the Irish Papists hate as their priests hate truth, *and whom, until both priest and people know and love the truth of Protestantism, they will continue to hate, if it were till doomsday*.

39. Edmund Burke (1729-97), Irish politician and writer. His *Reflections on the Revolution in France* (1790) was a major statement of conservative thought.

from:
HIBERNIAN NIGHTS' ENTERTAINMENT (1833)

[Ferguson began publication of a long-running series of 'Hibernian Nights' Entertainment' in December 1833. Like the 'Dialogue', indeed like the vast majority of prose contributions to the magazine, this was anonymous. Drawing on the well-known Arabian Nights' tales, he was able to bring together material of a highly disparate nature, some of it historical, some mythic, some fictional. Although the example of the Arabian Nights seems an obvious one, there are less evident implications. Like several other cycles of fairy tales, the Arabian tales had their putative origin in a sentence of death. A sultan's wife, king's son, or some such personage, is to be executed, but, because of his status, he is allowed to tell a story before the sentence is carried out. The story he tells, of course, is the neverending or interlocking narrative, which so impresses his hearers that his life is spared, indeed the success (or duration) of his narrative is itself the postponement of death.

In the context of *The Dublin University Magazine*, such a model has a powerful political and cultural significance. The anonymous author necessarily appears as the representive of a larger authority, the anxious yet privileged Irish protestant middle classes, embarked on the project of defining and/or discovering a cultural identity in the face of democratic upheaval in Ireland and reformist hostility in Westminster. The parallels with traditional story-telling are clear — the life, not so much of a privileged individual, but of a social elite, is endangered, and the elaboration of a cultural narrative is seen as a means of postponing, perhaps preventing the threatened end. The magazine itself, at a level above that of the individual contribution, effects a postponement, perhaps even a transvaluation, of extinction. In this sense, Ferguson's choice of material takes on an additional resonance, and his use of the story of Deirdre and the sons of Usnach is highly (but positively) ironic. *Their* deaths, as narrated in the first instalment of the 'Hibernian Nights' Entertainment', stand in for the anticipated extinction of the elite for which the anonymous author speaks. Moreover, the fictive context in which the tale of Deirdre is related also has its point: Dublin Castle in the winter of 1592 imprisoned young Irish princes, enemies of the crown, and *their* telling of the story of ancient slaughter is a means of hastening the optimum moment for escape. (The reader is assumed to know that the escape plan succeeded, that rebellion followed, and that by the beginning of the next decade the cause of Gaelic Ireland was absolutely lost.) Thus Ferguson brings three layers of Irish history into relation: the mythic past of Deirdre, the Elizabethan past of Hugh O'Donnell and his fellow captives, and the nineteenth-century present of Ferguson and his readers. All three layers share, one should note, an Ulster background, though *The Dublin University Magazine* was not to prove particularly attentive to Ulster perspectives on Anglo-Irish affairs. Finally, note how there is a further box-within-box aspect to the writing, a feature that has suggestive affinities with Shakespeare's *Hamlet*. The story begins with the guards on duty, who allude to the princes unwillingly housed within: then follows the older tale of the sons of Usnach and their deaths, and within that there is a further core of the poems — Ferguson was to be Yeats's most distinguished predecessor in rendering ancient Irish mythic material in verse.]

THE FIRST NIGHT

It was the close of a bleak and stormy day, in the winter of 1592. The mists rising from the marshy banks and bare bed of the Liffey, met the descending gloom of twilight, and thickened into palpable darkness the obscurity that hung around the old castle of Dublin. Birmingham Tower alone stood out, dim and huge, against the dusky sky, like a great rock from amid the sea of vapours that filled the wet ditches, and lay in dense volume on the Castle-yard.

The sentinel, pacing his narrow stripe [*sic*] of platform, cast a glance at the dim outline frowning above him; and, as he strode to and fro more rapidly, to drive the increasing chillness from his limbs, solaced the tedious dreariness of his watch with the reflection that, cheerless as was his walk upon the bare battlements, still more miserable was the plight of those he guarded. 'By my troth, Miles Dymock,' he muttered, 'cold as is thy watch upon these old walls, yonder young bloods, I trow, have colder quarters in the Deputy's dungeon: little space for any exercise to keep their limbs from freezing on the length of a traverse bar and a sliding fetter. Poor gentlemen! 'tis cruel usage for youths of their noble blood; unworthy usage, by my head, if I dare say it; for it is reported that they are princes by birth among their own people. Well! what hath Miles Dymock to do with either chief or tanist?[1] Harry Moulton will shortly be coming hither to relieve my post; and then for a flagon of ale and a sleep on the guard-house bench, with thanks to Heaven that I am neither prince of Tyrconnell,[2] nor tanist of Tyrone; but a plain English yeoman of Kent, and a poor halbardier[3] in the service of our good Queen Elizabeth. Ho! who goes there?' The sentry's soliloquy was broken by the sound of advancing footsteps. ''Tis I, Raymond Fitz Walter, warden of the tower.' The countersign was given, and the warden, with his men, passed on to the postern of the keep. 'So, friend, Nicholas,' said the sentry, detaining one of the keeper's attendants as they passed, 'bear you a good supper to the Irish nobles? By the rood,[4] they had need of hearty entertainment to qualify the discomfort of their lodging! What new face is that I see among the warden's men?' 'A new comrade sent hither in the place of Pierre Waldron, who lieth sick in Kilmainham hospital[5] — an old serving man of the Earl of Ormonde[6] — an Irishman himself, but of English blood, and a loyal subject of the pale.' 'How like you the new comer?' 'Not over much, in truth. He is a grave man, and taketh little part in our merriment over the can; but, as I hear, a shrewd scholar, knowing in both tongues, and a man of discreet counsel. Wherefore, he hath been chosen by the Deputy to be private guard over the princes, that he may, perchance, discover from their conversation something to the advantage of the Queen's government.' 'Foul fall the spying traitor!' cried the sentinel, 'what can the poor gentlemen have to say in their confinement, that it importeth any but themselves to know?' 'Be that the affair of my Lord Deputy, my friend, who hath appointed them to be watched,' replied the other; 'there may be reasons, I'll warrant, for what is done which we know not: certain it is, however, and I have it on good authority, that the North is again unquiet, where the great Earl of Tyrone[7] still hatches mischief with Maguire;[8] Kavanagh,[9] too, is daily plundering Kildare, and here upon the southern border of the pale, 'tis but a month since Feagh Mac Hugh, the great O'Byrne,[10] burned and pillaged the country, from Rathfarnham[11] to the city wall: five of mine own bullocks, which his kerns drove from the pastures of Rathgar,[12] are even now grazing in the fastnesses of Luggelaw, or Glenmalaur,[13] if they

1. (from Gaelic, *tanáiste*) successor-designate, heir, second-in-command.
2. Hugh Roe O'Donnell (*c.*1571-1602), known as Red Hugh, was imprisoned in Dublin Castle, but escaped on Christmas night in 1591. Tir Conaill was essentially the lands of present-day County Donegal.
3. A soldier who carried a halberd — a spear fitted with an axe head.
4. The rood is the cross of the crucifixion. 'By the rood' is an expletive indicating an emphatic declaration.
5. A priory of the Knights Hospitallers had been built in Kilmainham, to the west of Dublin city *c.* 1174; a more recent hospital for veteran soldiers was built in the late seventeenth century when the great Duke of Ormonde was lord lieutenant.
6. Thomas (Dubh) Butler (1532-1614), 10th earl of Ormonde.
7. Hugh O'Neill (*c.* 1550-1616), 2nd earl of Tyrone and principal Irish leader against the Elizabethans.
8. Hugh Maguire (died 1600), lord of Fermanagh.
9. The Kavanaghs of Wicklow had been intermittently in rebellion since 1581.
10. Fiachaidh mac Aodha O Broin (*c.* 1544-97), chief of the O'Byrnes of Wicklow, who made frequent raids on the Pale.
11. A district south-west of Dublin where the archbishop had a palace; by 1833 it was really a suburban village.
12. The kerne was an unarmoured Gaelic footsoldier. Rathgar is a district between Dublin and Rathfarnham, distinctly within suburban consciousness by 1833.
13. A mountain and a concealed glen in the heart of County Wicklow.

be not already eaten by his hungry galloglasses.'[14] 'But what have O'Donnell and O'Neill to do with thy five bullocks?' said the soldier. 'They may have helped to eat them, for aught I know,' replied the attendant, 'while abroad with O'Toole; but that is not to the point: the reason of this strictness is to gather from them whatever they may have heard of their friends' intentions, while lurking among the mere Irish[15] of the mountains during the six days of their last escape. Knowest thou not that they are but newly recaptured, after breaking out of the Castle as never man broke before?' 'Something I have heard since my return,' replied the soldier, 'of their needing a stricter watch; but little of the reason.' 'Why, sir,' said Nicholas, 'they broke out while it was still day; and after getting over the wall, and passing the ditch, had the hardihood to come back upon the drawbridge, and thrust a log of wood through the links of the great staple chain, so that when the alarm was given, and we ran to throw open the gates, we could not draw the bolts, nor get out in pursuit, until we had procured the help of those without to remove the bar, and let the chain be drawn.' 'By St. Anthony, a shrewd device!' exclaimed the soldier; 'a shrewd device, and boldly practised: and how caged ye the flown birds again?' 'O'Toole,[16] to whom they fled, after harbouring them for the space of a week, returned them to us; but whether through treachery, or because he could no longer protect them, I cannot aver.' 'But how came they at first into our hands?' questioned the soldier. 'That is a longer story,' replied Nicholas, 'but as the warden has no need of me till after settling his accounts with the keeper of the stores, I shall take a turn along the battlements, for the sake of old friendship, cold as it is, and tell thee. The O'Neills have been kept close prisoners here, since Tyrone made his first peace with the deputy. They are the sons of Shane a Diomas, that is, Shane the Proud,[17] of whose wild exploits thou hast so often heard; and it is feared that if they got abroad among their northern kindred, we would have all Shane's old retainers in arms again. As for O'Donnell, his capture was both strange and wonderful; and as I was present at the exploit, I shall tell thee how it was brought about. It is now almost four years since, but I well remember the morning, when being ordered with my comrades to embark ourselves in a ship then lying in the bay, we went on board, not knowing what expedition might be destined for us, or whither we might be about to sail. Neither knew the crew, nor any on board, save the captain of the bark, and one or two of his chief friends. Having laid in good store of French and Spanish wine, we set sail, and steering southward, held along by the coast of Wicklow, and Wexford, so that many thought we might, perhaps, be bound for Bristol haven, or the narrow seas; but after passing the point of Toskar,[18] our captain altering his course, turned our vessel's head towards the west, and for three days bore onward towards the ocean; so that many surmised that we might be on our voyage to the new countries, whence they bring the gold and silver of the Indians;[19] but, anon, altering our course once more, we began to sail northward, having many mountains and islands on our right hand, by which we judged that we had gone the circuit of the whole southern parts of this realm of Ireland, and were destined to land upon its western side, as we at length did, after passing innumerable rivers, rocks, and headlands. So steering landward, we sailed up the mouth of a great river, with fair green meadows, and high hills on either hand, until we came in sight of a strong castle, built on a green mound by the shore. Here having cast out our anchor, and furled our sails, we awaited in some amaze what we might be ordered to do; for it seemed to us that we were about to lay siege to the castle, and much we marvelled that such an enterprise should be undertaken with so small a number; but instead of arms or armour, our captain now commanded us to take forth five casks of Spanish wine, and place them in our boat. We did so; and rowing on shore, where the wild Irishmen now stood in great crowds, wondering at the strange sight of a ship, such as ours, upon their river, we set the casks upon the land, and by an interpreter invited all who wished to come and

14. Mercenary soldiers or retainers maintained by Irish chieftains from the fourteenth to the sixteenth centuries.
15. Strictly the 'pure Irish', but the phrase had accumulated pejorative overtones by the nineteenth century.
16. The O'Toole territory lay in a mountainous district of central and west Wicklow, including the Glen of Imaal.
17. Shane O'Neill (1530-67), the Ulster chieftain.
18. Tuscar (or Tuskar) Rock off the County Wexford coast, an important navigation point; a lighthouse was erected in 1815.
19. Voyages to the New World, prompted by stories of fabulous wealth in legendary 'El Dorado', were sponsored by prominent Elizabethans, including Sir Walter Raleigh, who had served in Ireland in 1580. The 'Indians' therefore were to be preferred as victims of colonialism over the 'mere Irish'.

purchase. The wine was so excellent, and cheap withal, for he asked but ten cows' skins for a cask, that in a short space all our store was purchased up, and from the castle to the shore was nothing to be seen but dancing and jollity thenceforth till evening. We meanwhile returning to our ship, remained awaiting the issue of this strange adventure, uncertain what might be our captain's design, but marvelling much that such a voyage should be undertaken for the sake of so poor a return. Next morning came a kern, in a small boat, from the castle, who bore a message from the great Mac Swiney,[20] desiring that more wine should be sent on shore, as he wished to purchase provision for a feast to be given to the young tanist of Tyrconnell, O'Donnell, sirnamed Hugh the Red, who was then staying at his castle, with others of the young Irish nobility. Then our captain commanded one to go with his messenger to the castle of Mac Sweeney, and to say that all his merchantable stock had been already sold; but that, if the young princes of Donegal would come on board our ship, they should be freely entertained from his own store, with whatever of the choicest wines of Spain and France, he kept for his private pleasure. When our messenger reached the castle — they call that pile, if I remember right, Dundonald — there were about the young princes only their servants and gallo-glasses, and, having none to restrain them, they, with one accord, leaped into their skiff, and came laughing and jesting towards us. Our captain, doffing his cap, received them cordially on his vessel's side; and, dismissing all but O'Donnell, Mac Sweeny Oge[21] and another, placed before them the most savoury meats and the most delicious wines. Then the young princes continued feasting, till being warmed with wine and strong aqua vitæ[22] of France, they forgot their desire to return to the shore, and sat singing and jesting till sleep overpowered their senses. Whereupon our captain taking their swords from their sides, and their daggers from their belts, called upon us to carry them into the small cabin. We there shut them down under hatches, and set sail. An eastern breeze carried us safely out of the river, for the mere Irish had no vessels in which to pursue us, although many thousands hearing of their princes' capture, thronged the shore on either side eager for our destruction. And thus we bore away the young heir of Tyrconnell, who now lies with a chain round each ankle in yonder tower, where, save the week of his escape, he has lain for three twelvemonths, and where the Deputy hath I think, decreed that he shall lie till the day of his death.' 'By the mass, it was an unworthy and a churlish snare to lay for any noble gentleman!' cried the soldier, 'and if we can conquer the island by no manlier means than treachery and ambuscading,[23] I care not how soon I give up my chance of the five hundred acres promised me in the forfeited lands of Sir Brian Mac Walter of the Rore.'[24] 'Nay,' cried Nicholas, 'thou art over nice in judging of the devices of our governors. I'll warrant thee it was not without authority from them we dare not blame that our captain did the exploit I have told thee of, — but there, I see the warden's light in the loophole of the tower stair: I must go — farewell, honest soldier — keep thine own counsel and a strict watch — adieu.' 'Farewell, comrade,' said the soldier, resuming his walk, while the other joining his companions and master ascended the winding stone stair that led through the thickness of the wall from the postern of the tower to the upper chambers.

The warden turning his huge key in an iron-bolted door, led the way into a stone-floored and vaulted apartment of confined dimensions, for the thickness of the walls was so great that their bulk left little room within. In this chamber were the captives. They sat on an oaken bench before the embers of a decayed fire; and the clank of iron, as they moved on their keeper's entrance, told that they were fettered. Two were young men fully grown and large sized, but sickly from long imprisonment: these were the sons of John the Proud,[25] Art and Henry. The third was, by his auburn head, taller than either of the others, although a youth of little more than nineteen. His ruddy cheek showed no symptom of ill health, and his eye was bright and quick as that of a free mountaineer. Large boned and sinewy, although perfectly proportioned, the noble young man seemed formed by nature for equal excellence in action and endurance. He was dressed in the British

20. One of the long-established Scottish family of professional soldiers who were sub-chiefs to the O'Donnells of Tirconnell. (The spelling varies in succeeding paragraphs.)
21. Gaelic *óg*, 'young'.
22. An archaic name for brandy.
23. ambushing.
24. Sir Brian Mac Walter of the Rore (Roe), a Gaelic chieftain of County Derry.
25. See note 17 above.

costume, but the long hair curling to his shoulders, and the unshaven upper lip, proclaimed his nation — this was Hugh Roe O'Donnell. He seemed scarcely conscious of his keeper's entrance; but kept his eye fixed on the dark wall before him, as if on its dingy plain he were, in imagination, marshalling those warriors whom he afterwards led to victory, through the broken battalions of Elizabeth's bravest armies.

'Sirs,' said the warden, as his attendants placed upon a rude table their evening repast, 'be pleased to conclude your supper with what dispatch you may, as my orders are to remove the instruments by which you might do mischief to your attendants, or to one another, with the greatest convenient speed.' So saying, he took his seat near the door, while the two O'Neills turning with indignant glances, addressed themselves to the viands before them; but perceiving that O'Donnell took no notice of their preparation, one of them addressed him. 'Fair cousin, wilt thou not eat? The keeper fears to leave his knives among us, lest we cut a breach in the castle wall, and stab the guards, or make our way to the chamber of the Deputy himself, and avenge our wrongs with one shrewd thrust of a carving knife.' 'Ha!' cried Hugh, awakening from his reverie, 'does the Saxon dog dare to impose his presence at our meals!' and starting up, forgetful of his chains, strode towards the door to expel the unwelcome overseer; but the fetter checked him, and he had almost fallen from the sudden shock; he recovered himself, and returning to his bench, sat down without a word, and relapsed into a similar fit of abstraction to that from which he had so ineffectually roused himself. 'Sirs,' said the keeper, 'it grieves me to intrude upon your privacy, or to limit your enjoyment of your repasts; but my orders are too strict to be infringed, and I must need remain with you for a little longer. When I shall retire, I also leave, by the lord chamberlain's commands, an attendant to continue with you during the night. He is well armed, and instructed to oppose any violence that may be shown him. Sir Hugh O'Donnell, time presses; if thou wouldst sup, I pray thee fall to.' A deep imprecation in Gaelic burst from the lips of the young chief; but he remained where he sat, with his back to the table, gazing as before at the blackened wall over the low and ashy hearthstone. Equally unavailing were the solicitations of his companions — he answered them in their native tongue, briefly and with kindness, but emphatically, and they pressed him no farther. Presently, having washed down their slender fare with a draught of water, the young men withdrew from the table, their chains clanking as they moved, to their original seats upon the bench, beside their fellow captive. The warden then having seen the table cleared, retired with his men, and closing the door, left their new attendant, who had hitherto remained unnoticed in the back ground, seated in the farther corner of the chill and gloomy apartment.

The three youths spoke not for some time, for Hugh's superior energy of character had gained him an ascendancy over the others, which forbade their interrupting his meditations whenever they took that fierce earnestness that marked his present manner. They sat in silence, without bestowing a look on their attendant, and he had not moved from his seat since the warden's departure. He was a man of advanced age, yet still of unimpaired vigour. Locks of pale yellow fell from his partly bald head down upon his shoulders, and a close beard of grizzled red curled round a well-formed and expressive mouth: his dress was that of a yeoman of the guard, but the sharp features and light-limbed figure marked the Irishman. O'Donnell at last, drawing a hard breath through the distended nostril, and casting himself back on his seat, exclaimed to his companions — 'So cousins! we are not to be permitted even the poor privilege of unnoticed conversation. This spying villain, I'll warrant, is to report all our words to the bastard Deputy — a knife in the churlish hound's throat! I would to God and Saint Columb Kill,[26] I had him and his ten best men-at-arms before myself and my three foster brothers for one short hour in the gap of Barransmore.[27] — Ha! Henry, if we ever get back to the Black Valley,[28] we will make a bright bonfire of Ardmullen castle for this!' 'I would rather see Glenwhirry,' answered Henry, 'and the blue mountains of Dalaradia[29] — ah, Art! if we were once in merry Antrim, we would soon drive the black strangers from the country of Hugh Buy!'[30]

26. Colum Cille (521-97), the saint who founded a monastery at Derry, hence associated with the north-west generally.
27. A mountain mass in Donegal.
28. The Black Valley and Ardmullen Castle are both in County Donegal.
29. (Irish, *Dal Araighe*) a kingdom in north-eastern Ireland from which Scotland was originally Gaelicized.
30. 'Buy' here is a corruption of Irish *buidhe*, meaning fair or yellow-haired. Hugh Buidhe was the founder of a branch of the O'Neills at Clanaboy, which literally means the clan of Aodh Buidhe.

'I'd give the best year of my life,' cried Art, 'to hear the war-cry of our house once more upon the hills of Killultagh[31] — Mother of God! for one note of the gathering of Claneboy!'

'Lamh dearg aboo!'[32]

Cried a voice, low but tremulously earnest, at their backs. The three young men leaped to their feet with a simultaneous cry that drowned the clash of iron, and, standing before them, beheld in their attendant the well-known features of their fosterer and clansman Turlogh Buy O'Hogan, the Bard of Tulloghoge.

For a moment the old man stood gazing with inexpressible love on the three noble youths so long and hopelessly denied to the longing eyes of their people; then rushing forward cast himself on his knees before them, and clasping their hands successively in his, pressed them to his lips and to his heart, in silent but adoring affection. 'My son, my prince, my king!' he at last articulated, 'my joy, my glory, my hope and promise! — branches of the old tree of nobleness! lights of valour and generosity! do I again behold your fair faces, and the gleam of your bright heads like waving gold? Long, long have I planned and pondered, long have I done and suffered what no price but the hope of seeing you again before I die, could have bribed me to endure. I have been the servant of the Saxon, and the slave of the Saxon's servant for your sakes, and if need were, I had been the menial of the slave's slave, that I might at last put my old eyes to rest upon the faces of your royal father's sons! — News for you, my princely masters, I have brave news from the north! Maguire and O'Rourk are stirring like stout gentlemen in Roscommon and the Brenny,[33] and the earl is drawing his country to a noble head at the Blackwater:[34] Donell Spaniagh holds Idrone[35] by strong hand; and the bold O'Byrnes overhang the very city walls from the Three Rocks to the gap of Glencree.[36] Mac Carthy More and Desmond are ready to take up the game in Munster, and it wants but O'Donnell in Ballyshannon and O'Neill in Castlereagh to raise such a storm about the head of this cruel queen, as shall ere long beat the rifled crown from her withered brows, and blow across the seas those robbers of our lands and snarers of our chieftains' children, never to trample on our blessed soil again!' 'Ah Turlogh,' cried O'Donnell, 'thou tellest us a tale we have already heard in the castle of O'Toole ten days back — alas, we were then at liberty, and thy hopes had ere long been verified, but that mischance befel us as thou hast heard, and here we stand today with fetters on our feet in Dublin Castle, while others play the noble game over green woods and broad mountains; but our friends and people, languishing for their lost leaders, stay idly in their duns and castles, and strike no stroke for liberty or honor! I vow a stone chapel and two bells of silver to Saint Columb Kill, if he will but release me out of this bondage before New Year's day!' 'Noble prince,' cried the bard, 'thou shalt be feasting again in the castle of Dundonald before that day, if there be truth in man! I have not come hither only to gaze on thy face and tell thee to despair — no — we fly together on next Christmas night: till then, dear sons of my heart, be patient and discreet, nor let your jailors suspect that you have aught of new hope since my appointment to your charge. Blessed Mother! it wrings my heart to see the sons of your kingly fathers perishing for cold in the dark dungeon of their enemies. Here, let me pile these faggots on the embers and trim our wretched lamp. Dear Saviour! that my eyes should ever see Saxon fetters on the limbs of my heart's children! Alas, alas, I cannot now undo them, but while you sit I can relieve you somewhat of their weight.' While he spoke he renewed the sinking fire, and supporting the chains upon the footrail of the rude bench, in some measure relieved the sitting captives of their weight; then placing himself on a low seat at one side, forgot for a time the danger and discomforts of his and their situation in mutual inquiries and fond recollections.

At length O'Donnell, recurring to the subject nearest his heart, broke in on the conversation by demanding — 'How many days till Christmas?' 'One-and-twenty,' replied Turlogh. 'And before Christmas we may not make the attempt?' continued O'Donnell. 'Not till then, prince; for, until Christmas, that company of halbardiers in

31. A site in east Ulster associated with this branch of the O'Neills.
32. (Irish) 'Red Hand Triumphant', a war cry based on the red-hand emblem of Ulster.
33. Two counties, the latter being modern Cavan, once known as Breifne.
34. The river Blackwater rises in County Tyrone, flows generally east and north and enters the south-west end of Lough Neagh. It served as a boundary between Ulster and the South.
35. Donall Spaineach Mac Murrough (died 1631), the last nominal king of Leinster, who rose in rebellion with Hugh O'Neill but made a separate peace with the government. (He gained his nickname 'the Spanish' through years spent in Spain as pupil to Thomas Stukely.) Idrone was a district in what is now County Carlow.
36. Places in County Wicklow.

whom I have my trust, take not the guard of the wall next the city, over which I would, with God's and Columb Kill's permission, purpose our escape.' 'Enough,' replied O'Donnell; 'until then, as well as we may, let us forget our hopes and fears; and as thou art to be with us every night, let us sleep during the day, if watched by any other, and while away our hours till morning in thy company, with some pleasant occupation of making rhymes or story-telling, as is the wont, when not employed in any enterprize of moment, at the castles of our chieftains and knights. Alas, 'tis now four years since Owen Ward last sung his verses in my father's honor, to the music of the harp, in Ballyshannon hall. Ah, when shall I hear again the sweet sound of strings, and melody of ladies' voices? When shall I sit again by the great hall fire, wandering in fancy with Finn and his old warriors, through enchanted castles and over magic seas? When shall I stand with the three sons of Usnach, holding the castle of the Red Branch against Conor Mac Nessa and his Ulster legions, with Deirdre by my side, still fearlessly bending over the chess-table on which she plays against her lover, lest he should catch alarm from her desertion of the game? Ho! Turlogh, do but tell us this story of clan Usnach, without slip or blunder, and I will yet make thee bard of Tirconnell, if Saint Columb do but hear my vow, and grant me life and liberty to perform my promise.' 'Noble prince,' said Turlogh, 'it hath long been my use and occupation to be a bard, as well to the clan O'Neill as to those of my own name. I will tell the tale of clan Usnach, or any other that may be most pleasing to your noblenesses, without desire of fee or hope of reward, beyond doing what may please your fathers' sons in their captivity.' 'Thanks, true and faithful clansman!' said O'Donnell: 'let my noble kinsmen name the tale; and do thou, while these fagots throw unaccustomed warmth through our chill chamber, try whether thy skill can make us for one night forget that we are captives.' 'Let it be the "Sons of Usnach",' said Art; 'I ever loved to hear of the three waves roaring round the blue border of Connor's shield.' 'I would I had my harp here,' said Turlogh, 'that I might sing the songs of Deirdre as they ought to sound from the string: but, alas! I had forgotten; the notes of a harp were dangerous to be heard from a prisoner's dungeon; so I shall chant the strains as best I may, and abstain from singing, lest we should be overheard.' So saying, Turlogh drew his seat nearer the cheerful blaze now flickering on the red hearth-stone, and with half-closed eyes began the tale of

THE DEATH OF THE CHILDREN OF USNACH

The nobles of Ulster were feasting in the house of Felimy, the son of Dall, the rymer of king Conor. Then was the wife of Felimy busied in attendance on her guests, though shortly to become a mother. Cups and jests go round, and the house resounded with the revel. Suddenly the infant screamed in the womb of its mother, and the bitter pains of child-birth fell upon her. Then arose Cathbad the Druid, and prophesied, as she was borne away — 'Under thy girdle, O woman, screamed a woman child, fair-haired, bright-eyed, beautiful — a virgin who will bring sorrow on Ulster — a birth fatal for princes — a child of disaster: let her name be Deirdre.' Then sat they all in amaze till the infant was brought in; and it was a female child; and Cathbad looked upon it, and again prophesied—

'Child of sorrow, sin, and shame,
Deirdre be thy dreaded name!
Child of doom! thy fatal charms
Soon shall work us deadly harms.

Long shall Ulster mourn the night
Gave thine eyes their blasting light—
Long shall Usnach rue the day
Showed his sons their fatal ray.

Wo, Emania,[37] to thy wall —
Wo to Ulster's palace hall —
Wo to Fergus — wo to Yeon[38] —
Fourfold wo to Usna's son!

Bitter wo and black dishonour,
Fall upon the foul clean Connor!
Good has lost, and evil won her,
Deirdre be the name upon her.

When Cathbad ceased, the nobles present with one voice cried out that the child should not live; but Connor would not permit them to slay the child, for he believed not the words of Cathbad, and

37. Latinized form of the Irish, Emain Macha, locus of the Red-branch tales; the modern name is Navan Fort, in County Armagh.
38. Rendering of the Irish personal name, Eoghan.

he already longed to have the infant to himself. So, taking the child from Felimy, the king commanded that she should be cared for by his own people; and when the baby was nursed, he sent her to be brought up in a lonely fort, where she should never see man till he might make her his own wife. Here Deirdre dwelt till she had grown to be the most beautiful maiden in all Ireland; and never yet had seen a man, save one aged and morose tutor. But on a certain day in winter, when her tutor was slaying a calf before the gate of the fort, to prepare food for her, she saw a raven drinking the blood upon the snow. Then said she to her nurse, 'Lovely, in truth, were the man marked with these colours — body like the snow, cheeks like the ruddy blood, and hair black as the wing of the raven — ah, Lewara, are there such men in the world without?' 'Many such,' said Lewara, 'but the fairest of all is in the king's house — Naisi, the son of Usnach.' 'Alas!' cried Deirdre, 'if I get not sight of that man I shall die!' Then her nurse plotted how she should bring Naisi and Deirdre together.

Now, on a certain day, Naisi was sitting in the midst of the plain of Eman, playing on a harp. Sweet, in truth, was the music of the sons of Usnach. The cattle listening to it, milked ever two-thirds more than was their wont; and all pain and sorrow failed not to depart from whatsoever man or woman heard the strains of that melody. Great also was their prowess. When each set his back to the other, all Connor's province had been unable to overcome them. They were fleet as hounds in the chase: they slew deer with their speed.

Now, then, as Naisi sat singing on the plain of Eman, he perceived a maiden approaching him. She held down her head as she came near him, but passed without speaking. 'Gentle is the damsel who passeth by,' said Naisi. Then the maiden looking up, replied, 'Damsels may well be gentle where there are no youths.' Then Naisi knew that it was Deirdre, and great dread fell upon him. 'The king of the province is bethrothed to thee, oh damsel,' he said. 'I love him not,' she replied, 'he is an aged man; I would rather love a youth like thee.' 'Say not so, oh, damsel,' said Naisi; 'the king is a better spouse than the king's servant.' 'Thou sayest so,' replied Deirdre, 'that thou mayest avoid me.' Then plucking a rose from a briar, she flung the flower to him, and said, 'Now art thou ever disgraced if thou rejectest me.' 'Depart from me, I pray thee, damsel,' said Naisi. 'Nay,' replied Deirdre, 'if thou dost not take me to be thy wife, thou art dishonoured before all the men of thy country: and this I know from my nurse Lewara.' Then Naisi said no more; and Deirdre took his harp, and sat beside him, playing sweetly. When the men of Ulster heard the delightful sound, they were enchanted. But the sons of Usnach rushed forth, and came running to where their brother sat, and Deirdre with him. 'Alas,' they cried, 'what hast thou done, O brother? Is not this the damsel fated to ruin Ulster?' 'Ah, me!' said Naisi, 'I am disgraced before the men of Erin for ever, if I take her not after that which she hath done.' Then he told them the tale of what had happened. 'Evil will come of it,' said the brothers. 'I care not,' said Naisi, 'I had rather be in misfortune than in dishonour. We will fly with her to another country. There is no country of Erin in which we will not have welcome and protection.'

They then took counsel together, and for the love they bore to Naisi, resolved to accompany him wheresoever he might go. So that night they departed, taking with them three times fifty men of might, and three times fifty women, and three times fifty greyhounds, and three times fifty attendants; and Naisi took Deirdre to be his wife. Then being pursued by Connor, who was greatly enraged at the loss of his betrothed spouse, they wandered hither and thither over Erin, in constant danger from their enemies, from Esro to Benedar, and from Dundelgan to Almain.[39] At length, weary of wandering through Erin, they sailed by Ulster into the realm of Alba,[40] and made their home in the midst of a wild therein.

Here, when the chase of the mountain failed them, they fell upon the herds and cattle of the men of Alba; and the fame of their exploits reaching the ears of the king of that country, they were received into friendship and allegiance by him. But upon a certain day, when the king's steward made a circuit of the palace, early in the morning, he saw Naisi and Deirdre asleep in their tent. Then said he to the king, 'O king, we have at length found a meet wife for you. There is in the bed of Naisi, son of Usnach, a woman worthy of the sovereign of the west of the

39. Esro is a corruption of Ess Ruaid, modern Assaroe, near Ballyshannon, Co. Donegal; Benedar is modern Howth, Co. Dublin; Dundelgan is a corruption of Dun Dealgain, modern Dundalk, Co. Louth; Almain may be a misprint for Emain, for Emain Macha was frequently known simply by the first element in the place-name.
40. Scotland.

world: let Naisi be slain, O king, and marry thou the maiden thyself.' 'Nay,' said the king, 'do thou first solicit her in private.' It is done so. Deirdre informs Naisi of all this; and, moreover, how the son of Usnach would be put forward into danger till he should be slain, that the king might wed her being left without her husband. 'Away, therefore,' she said, 'for if you depart not tonight, you will be slain tomorrow.' Then the sons of Usnach departed from the palace of the king of Alba, and went into a distant island of the ocean.

Upon a certain day, King Conor was feasting with his nobles in the mansion of Emania, and there was sweet music and delight among all present. And after the bards had sung, in delightful measures, their branches of kindred and boughs of genealogy, King Conor raised his royal voice and said: 'I would know of you, princes and nobles, whether you have ever seen a feast better than this, or a mansion better than the mansion of Emania?' 'We have seen none,' they replied. 'And again,' said Conor, 'I would fain know of you, if there be anything whatsoever here wanting.' 'Nothing,' they replied. 'Say not so,' said Conor, 'I well know what is here wanting; the presence of the three renowned youths, the martial lights of the Gael, the three noble sons of Usnach, Naisi, Aini, and Ardan. Alas, that they should be absent from us for the sake of any woman in the world! Hard bested they are, and outlawed in an island of the ocean, fighting with the men of the king of Alba. Sons of a king indeed they are, and well could they defend the sovereignty of Ulster — I would that they were with us.' Then the nobles replied and said: 'Had we dared to speak our thoughts, this is what we would ourselves have said; and moreover that had we but the three sons of Usnach in the country, Ulster alone would not be inferior to all the rest of Erin: for, men of might they are, and lions for valour and prowess.' 'Let us then,' said Conor, 'dispatch messengers to Alba, to the island of Loch Etive, to the fastness of the clan Usnach, to solicit their return.' 'Who can give sufficient surety of safety to induce the sons of Usnach to come into thy kingdom?' asked they. 'There are three only of all my nobles,' said Conor, 'on whose guaranty against my anger, the sons of Usnach will trust themselves; and they are, Fergus, Cuchullan, and Conell Carnach: one of these will I send upon this message.'

Then taking Conell Carnach into a place apart, Conor asked him what he would do if he should send him for the sons of Usnach, and that they should come to harm while under his pledge of safe conduct. 'Whomsoever I might find injuring them,' said Conell Carnach, 'on him would I straightway inflict the bitter pain of death.' 'Then can I perceive,' said Conor, 'that dear to you I myself am not.' A like question asked Conor of Cuchullan, and of him received a like answer. Then called he apart Fergus the son of Roy, and in like manner questioned him; this said Fergus in answer. 'Thine own blood I shed not; but whomsoever else I should find doing injury to those in my safe conduct him would I not permit to live.'

'Then,' said Conor, 'I perceive thou lovest me. Go thou to the clan Usnach, and bring them to me on thy guaranty; and return thou by the way of Dun Barach, but let not the sons of Usnach tarry to eat meat with any till they come to the feast I shall have prepared for their welcome in Emania. Give me thy pledge to do this.' Then Fergus bound himself by solemn vow to do the king's commands, and so returning together, they joined the other nobles and bore away that night in feasting and delight. The king, however, called Barach, the son of Cainti, into a place apart, and asked him had he a feast prepared at his mansion? 'I have a feast prepared in Dun Barach,' said Barach, 'to which thou and thy nobles are ever welcome.' 'Let not Fergus then depart from thy mansion,' said Conor, 'without partaking of that feast on his return from Alba.' 'He shall feast with me for three days,' replied Barach, 'for we are brothers of the Red Branch, and he is under vow not to refuse my hospitality.' Next morning Fergus, with his two sons, Buini Borb, and Illan Finn, and Callon the shield-bearer, bearing his shield, departed from Emania for pleasant Alba. They sailed across the sea until they came to Loch Etive, to the island of the sons of Usnach. Here dwelt the clan Usnach in green hunting booths along the shore. And Deirdre and Naisi sat together in their tent, and Conor's polished chessboard between them, and they played at chess. Now when Fergus came into the harbour, he sent forth the loud cry of a mighty man of chase. And Naisi hearing the cry, said, 'I hear the call of a man of Erin.' 'That was not the call of a man of Erin,' replied Deirdre, 'but the call of a man of Alba.' Then again Fergus shouted a second time: 'That was surely the cry of a man of Erin,' said Naisi. 'Nay, 'twas not, indeed,' replied Deirdre, 'let us play on.' Then, again, Fergus shouted a third time, and Naisi knew that it was the cry of Fergus, and he said, 'If the son of Roy be in existence, I hear his hunting shout from the loch: go forth Ardan, my brother, and give our kinsman welcome.' 'Alas,' said Deirdre, 'I knew the call of Fergus from the first.' 'Why didst thou then conceal it, my queen?' said Naisi. Then Deirdre answered, 'Last night I had a dream. Three birds came to us from the plains of Emania, having each a drop of honey in its beak; and they departed from us, having each a drop of our blood in place of the drop of honey.' 'And how dost thou read that dream, O princess?' said Naisi. 'That Fergus cometh with false messages of peace from Conor,' she replied, 'for sweeter is not honey than the message of peace of the false man.' 'Nay, think not so,' said Naisi; 'Fergus is long in the port: go Ardan, meet him quickly, and guide him to our tent.' Then Ardan went and welcomed Fergus, and embraced him and his sons, and kissed them and demanded of them the news from Erin. Then they told him, and thereafter came to the tent of Naisi, where he and Ainli, and Deirdre were together. Then with many kisses to Fergus and his sons, they asked what news from Erin. 'Good news,' said Fergus, 'Conor hath sent us to be your warranty of safe-conduct, if you will return to Emania.' 'There is no need for them to go thither,' said Deirdre, 'greater is their own sway in Alba than the sway of Conor in Erin.' 'To be in one's native land is better than all else,' said Fergus, 'for of little worth are power or prosperity to a man if he seeth not each day the land that gave him birth.' 'True, it is,' said Naisi, 'dearer to me is Erin than Alba, though in Alba I should enjoy more fortunate estate than in Erin.' 'Put your trust in me,' said Fergus, 'I pledge myself for your safe-conduct.' 'Let us go then,' said Naisi, 'we will go under Fergus's safe-conduct to our native land.'

They whiled away that night until the dawning of next day; then went they down to their ships and set sail across the sea. And Deirdre looked back upon the land of Alba, and as it sunk over the waters, raised the mournful song of her farewell.

Farewell to fair Alba, high house of
  the sun,
Farewell to the mountain, the cliff,
  and the dun:
Dun Sweeny adieu! for my love
  cannot stay,
And tarry I may not when love cries
  away.

Glen Vashan! Glen Vashan! where
  roe bucks run free,
Where my love used to feast on the
  red deer with me,
Where, rocked on thy waters while
  stormy winds blew,
My love used to slumber,
  Glen Vashan! adieu!

Glendaro! Glendaro! where birchen
  boughs weep
Honey dew at high noon o'er the
  nightingale's sleep,
Where my love used to lead me to
  hear the cuckoo
'Mong the high hazel bushes,
  Glendaro! adieu!

Glen Urchy! Glen Urchy! where
  loudly and long
My love used to wake up the woods
  with his song,
While the son of the rock, from the
  depths of the dell,
Laughed sweetly in answer,
  Glen Urchy! farewell!

Glen Etive! Glen Etive! where
  dappled does roam,
Where I leave the green sheeling
  I first called a home;
Where with me and my true love
  delighted to dwell
The sun made his mansion —
  Glen Etive! farewell!

Farewell to Inch Draynach, adieu to
  the roar
Of blue billows bursting in light on
  the shore;
Dun Fiagh! farewell, for my love
  cannot stay,
And tarry I may not when love cries
  away.[41]

By this they had reached the port of Dun Barach; and Barach himself meeting them upon the shore, welcomed Fergus and his sons, and the sons of Usnach, and Deirdre also, with kisses eager and

41. The places named in the song are in modern Argyll and Inverness.

affectionate. Then Barach said to Fergus — 'Tarry, and partake of my feast; for I will not let thee part from me for three days without breaking thy vow of brotherhood and hospitality.' When Fergus heard this, he became crimson red, for anger, from head to foot, and thus he said — 'Thou hast done ill, O Barach, to ask me to thy feast, knowing, as thou dost, that I am bounden to Conor not to let the sons of Usnach, who are under my safe-conduct, tarry night or day for entertainment from another, till they reach Emania, where he hath his banquet prepared to welcome them.' 'I care not,' said Barach, 'I lay thee under the ban of our order if thou rejectest my hospitality.' Then Fergus asked of Naisi what he should do? and Deirdre answered — 'Thou must either forsake Barach or the sons of Usnach: it were truly more meet to forsake thy feast than thy friends who are under thy protection.' 'Neither Barach nor the sons of Usnach will I forsake,' said Fergus; 'for I will remain with Barach, and my two sons, Illan Finn and red Buini Borb, shall be your escort and pledge of safe-conduct, in my stead, to Emania.' 'We care not for thy safe-conduct,' said Naisi; 'our own hands have ever been our pledge of protection'; and he departed from Fergus in great wrath; and Ardan, and Ainli, and Deirdre, and the two sons of Fergus followed him, and they left Fergus sad and gloomy behind them.

Then said Deirdre — 'I would counsel that we go to the isle of Rathlin,[42] and abide there till Fergus shall be free to accompany us; for I fear this safe-conduct will not long protect us.' Then did Naisi and the sons of Fergus reproach her, and they said they would not take that counsel, but go forward to Emania even as they were. 'Alas!' said Deirdre; 'would that I had never left the long-grassed Alba!' But when they had come to Fincairn watch-tower, on the mountain of Fuadh,[43] Naisi perceived that Deirdre did not accompany them, for sleep had fallen upon her; and on returning he found her in a deep slumber in the valley; and when she was awakened, she arose in grief and fear. 'Alas!' she said, 'I dread treachery: I had a dream, and in my vision I beheld Illan Finn fighting for us, and Buini Borb idle, and his head on Buini Borb, and Illan Finn's trunk headless.' 'Thy lips are lovely, but thy prophesy, nought save evil,' said Naisi. 'Let the vengeance of thy lips fall on the stranger. I fear not treachery. Let us on.' And so they went on till they came to Ardsallagh; and then Deirdre said to Naisi — 'I see a cloud over Emania, and it is a cloud of blood. I counsel you, O sons of Usnach, go not to Emania without Fergus; but let us go to Dundalgan, to our cousin Cuchullan, till Fergus shall have fulfilled his obligation to Barach.' 'I fear not,' said Naisi; 'let us proceed.' Then again Deirdre cried — 'O! Naisi, look at the cloud over Emania: it is a cloud of blood; gore drops fall from its red edges. Ah me! go not to Emania tonight; let us go to Dundalgan — let us take shelter with Cuchullan.' 'I fear not,' said Naisi; 'I will not hear thy counsel; let us proceed.' 'Grandson of Roy,' said Deirdre, 'seldom have we not been of one accord before — I and thou, Naisi! This had not been so that day when Lewara led me to your seat upon the plain of Emania.' 'I fear not,' said Naisi; 'let us on!' 'Sons of Usnach,' again said Deirdre, 'I have a signal by which to know if Conor designs treachery against us. If we be admitted into the mansions of Emania, Conor designs not harm towards us; if we be lodged apart, in the mansion of the Red Branch, then doth Conor surely meditate us evil.' By this they were arrived before the gates of Emania. Then Naisi knocked at the gate, and the door-keeper demanded who was without? 'Clan Usnach and Deirdre,' replied Naisi. Then were they conducted towards the house of the Red Branch, by Conor's orders. ''Twere better to take my counsel even yet,' said Deirdre, 'for evil is surely now designed for us.' 'We will not do so,' said Illan Finn, the son of Fergus; 'cowardliness hath never been known of the sons of my father. I and Buini Borb shall go with you to the Red Branch.' Then moved they on to the house and entered it; and attendants brought them rich viands and sweet wines, until all were satisfied and cheerful, save only Deirdre and the sons of Usnach; for they partook not of much food or drink, being weary from their journey, and in dread of their lives. Then said Naisi, 'bring hither the chessboard, that we may play'; and he and Deirdre played upon the polished chess-board.

And now when Conor knew that Deirdre was in the Red Branch, he could not rest at the feast, but said — 'Whom shall I find that will do my errand to the Red Branch, to tell me whether her beauty lives upon Deirdre; for, if her own face and figure live upon her, there is not in the world a woman more

42. An island off the north coast of County Antrim.

43. i.e. Sliabh Fuaid, a mountain in County Armagh.

beautiful than she.' Then said Lewara, the nurse, 'I will do thine errand.' For she dearly loved both Naisi and Deirdre, whom she, at first, had brought together. Then Lewara, coming to the Red Branch, found Naisi and Deirdre with the polished board between them, playing at chess; and she gave them kisses eager and affectionate, and said, 'Alas! my children, you do not well to spend your time in games and pleasure, while Conor cannot rest for the thoughts of the treachery he designs you. Wo is me, this night will be a black night for the clan Usnach, if ye bar not fast your doors and windows, and fight not courageously O sons of Fergus, and manfully defend your charge till Fergus himself cometh.' Then shed she bitter tears, and returned to the mansion of Emania; and Conor asked what tidings. 'Tidings of good and of evil,' replied Lewara; 'and my good tidings are, that the sons of Usnach are three of the most valiant and noble; of the most excellent form and aspect of all the men in the world; and that, with their help, thou mayest henceforth sway all Erin if thou wilt; and my evil tidings are, that she, who at her departure from Erin was the fairest of women, is now bereft of her own form and aspect, and is lovely and desirable no longer.' Then Conor's wrath and jealously abated, and he went on feasting until a second time he thought of Deirdre, and he said, 'whom shall I find to bring me true tidings from the Red Branch? is there any here will do my errand truly?' Then none of the nobles answered; for they feared to abet the king, in violating the pledge of Fergus, as they dreaded he now meditated to do. Then said Conor to one of his people, 'knowest thou who slew thy father, O Trendorn?' 'Naisi Mac Usnach slew my father, and my three brothers,' replied Trendorn. 'Go thy way, then,' said Conor, 'and bring me true tidings of Deirdre, whether her beauty still live upon her; for, if it doth, there is not on the ridge of earth a woman lovelier than she.' Then Trendorn went to the Red Branch, and found one window unfastened, and looked through it, and saw Naisi and Deirdre within, and the polished board between them, and they playing. And Deirdre said to Naisi, 'I see one looking at us through the window.' Then Naisi flung the chessman he held in his hand, at the spy, and dashed his eye out of the head of Trendorn. And Trendorn went to Conor, and told him, and Conor cried aloud, 'This man who hath maimed my servant would himself be king!' Then asked he, what tidings of Deirdre? 'Such beauty liveth upon her,' said Trendorn, 'that there is not, on the ridge of earth a woman so beautiful.' As Conor heard this his jealousy and hatred were renewed, and he rose from the table in great wrath, and cried that the sons of Usnach had sought to slay his servant, and called upon his people to go and assault the Red Branch, and bring them forth, that they might be punished.

Then came the troops of Ulster to the Red Branch, and sent forth three dreadful shouts about it, and set fire and flames to the doors and windows. And the sons of Usnach, when they heard the shouts, demanded who were without. 'Conor and Ulster,' cried the troops, and shouted fearfully. 'Villains,' cried Illan Finn, 'would ye break my father's pledge?' 'Ravishers and villains,' cried Conor, 'would ye abet the seducer of my wife?' 'Ah me,' said Deirdre, 'we are betrayed, and Fergus is a traitor.' 'If Fergus hath betrayed you,' said Red Buini Borb, 'yet will not I betray you'; and he threw open the gates, and went forth with his men, and slew thrice fifty men of might abroad, and made dreadful confusion among the troops. Then Conor demanded who made that havock of his people, and Buini answered, 'I, Red Buini Borb, the son of Fergus.' 'Hold thy hand,' said Conor, 'and I will bestow upon thee the territory of Slieve Fuadh.' Then Buini Borb held back his hand from the carnage, and demanded, 'Wilt thou aught else?' 'I will make thee mine own prime councillor,' replied Conor; and Buini Borb desisted from the slaughter, and went his way. But his territory was made that night a desert; and it is called Dalwhinny to this day, a wild moor on the mountains of Fuadh. When Deirdre saw that Buini Borb had deserted them, she said, 'Traitor father, traitor son: well knew I that Fergus was a traitor!' 'If Fergus was a traitor,' said Illan Finn, 'yet will not I be a traitor: while liveth this small straight sword in my hand, I will not forsake the sons of Usnach!' Then Illan Finn went forth with his men and they made three swift onslaughts round about the mansion, and slew thrice an hundred men of might abroad, and came in again where Naisi sat playing at chess with his brother Ainli, for the sons of Usnach would not let their calm hearts be troubled by that alarm. Then taking torches, Illan Finn and his men went forth a second time, and slew their men of might abroad, and drove the bearers of flame and fire from around the mansion. Then it was that Conor cried, 'Where is my own son Fiara Finn?' 'I am here my king,' cried Fiara. 'As I live,' said Conor, 'it was on the same night that thou and Illan Finn were born; go then and do battle with him manfully. And as he is clad in his father's arms, clothe thou thyself in mine. Take Ocean, Flight, and Victory — my shield, my spear, and my claymore,[44] and do good battle for your father with this son of Fergus.' Fiara then arrayed himself in his father's noble and bright armour, and went to the Red Branch, and did good battle with Illan Finn. They fought a fair fight, stout and manly, bitter and bloody, savage and hot, and vehement, and terrible, till Illan Finn beat down Fiara, so that he forced him to crouch beneath the shelter of his shield. Then the waves round the blue rim of Ocean roared, for it was the nature of Conor's shield that it ever resounded as with the noise of stormy waves when he who bore it was in danger. And the three chief seas of Erin roared with all their waves responsive to the shout of Ocean. The wave of Tuath, and the wave of Cliona, and the fishy-streaming wave of Inver-Rory roared around Erin for the danger of Fiara. Conall Carnach sitting on the rock of Dunseverick heard the tumult from Loch Rory and the sea, and taking his arms and calling his men of might, came towards Emania, where he knew that Conor, his sovereign, was in peril. There, on the open field before the mansion of Red Branch, he found Fiara Finn sore pressed by his adversary, and, coming behind him, he thrust his sword through the heart of Illan Finn, whom he knew not, for he had not yet beheld his face. 'Who hath pierced me at my back?' asked Illan Finn, 'when he might have had fair battle, face to face, had he sought it?' 'Nay, rather, who art thou?' said Conall. 'Illan, the son of Fergus,' replied Illan Finn; 'and art thou Conall Carnach? — Alas, it is even so. Evil is the deed thou hast done, Conall, to slay me while defending the clan Usnach, who are in the Red Branch under my father's pledge of safe-conduct from Alba.' 'By my hand of valour,' cried Conall, 'this shall not be unavenged,' and he struck Fiara Finn a sharp stroke where he stood, and lopped away his head from his body, and went thence in great wrath and sorrow. The weakness of death then fell darkly upon Illan, and he threw his arms into the mansion, and called to Naisi to fight manfully, and expired.

And now the men of Ulster came again to assault the Red Branch, and to set fire and faggots to the doors. Then forth came Ardan and his men and put out the fires, and slew three hundred men of might abroad, and scattered the troops. And Ainli, with his men, went forth the other third of the night, and slew six hundred abroad, and made sore havoc of Conor's people. Naisi himself came forth with his men the last third of the night, and ere day dawn had slain two hundred and driven all the troops from around the mansion. And at dawn, Conor brought all the men of Ulster, and he and the clan Usnach, with their men, joined battle on the plain and fought a fierce fight till broad day. And the battle went against the men of Ulster; and till the sands of the sea, the leaves of the forest, the dew-drops of the meadow, or the stars of heaven be counted, it is not possible to tell the number of heads, and hands, and lopped limbs of heroes, that then lay bare and red from the hands of Naisi and his brothers and their people on that plain. Then Naisi came again into the Red Branch to Deirdre, and she encouraged him and said: 'We will yet escape: fight manfully and fear not.' Then the sons of Usnach made a phalanx of their shields, and spread the links of their joined bucklers around Deirdre, and bounding forth like three eagles, swept down upon the troops of Conor, making sore havoc of his people in that onslaught. Now when Cuthbad the Druid saw that the sons of Usnach were bent on the destruction of Conor himself, he had recourse to his acts of magic; and he cast an enchantment over them, so that their arms fell from their hands, and they were taken by the men of Ulster, for the spell was like a sea of thick gums about them, and their limbs were clogged in it that they could not move.

Then was there no man in the host of Ulster, that could be found who would put the sons of Usnach to death, so loved were they of the people and nobles. But, in the house of Conor was one called Maini Rough Hand, son of the king of Lochlin; and Naisi had slain his father and two brothers; and he undertook to be their executioner. So the sons of Usnach were there slain; and the men of Ulster, when they beheld their death, sent forth three heavy shouts of sorrow and lamentation. Then Deirdre fell down beside their bodies, wailing and weeping, and she tore her hair and garments, and bestowed kisses on their lifeless lips, and bitterly bemoaned them. And a grave was opened for them, and Deirdre, standing by it, with her hair

44. A large two-edged broadsword.

dishevelled, and shedding tears abundantly, chanted their funeral song.

The lions of the hill are gone,
And I am left alone — alone —
Dig the grave both wide and deep,
For I am sick, and fain would sleep.

The falcons of the wood are flown,
And I am left alone — alone —
Dig the grave both deep and wide,
And let us slumber side by side.

The dragons of the rock are sleeping
Sleep that wakes not for our weeping,
Dig the grave, and make it ready,
Lay me on my true love's body!

Lay their spears and bucklers bright
By the warrior's sides aright;
Many a day the three before me
On their linked bucklers bore me.

Lay upon the low grave floor
'Neath each head, the blue claymore;
Many a time the noble three
Reddened these blue blades for me.

Lay the collars, as is meet,
Of their greyhounds at their feet,
Many a time for me have they
Brought the tall red deer to bay.

In the falcon's jesses[45] throw,
Hook and arrow, line and bow;
Never again, by streain or plain,
Shall the gentle woodsmen go!

Sweet companions ye were ever,
Harsh to me, your sister, never,
Woods and wilds and misty vallies
Were with you as good's a palace.

Oh! to hear my true love singing
Sweet as sound of trumpets ringing!
Like the sway of ocean swelling
Rolled his deep voice round our dwelling.

45. Short leather straps attached to the legs of hawks and falcons to hold them on the wrist.

Oh! to hear the echoes pealing
Round our green and fairy sheeling,
When the three with soaring chorus,
Passed the silent sky-lark o'er us!

Echo now, sleep, morn and even—
Lark, alone enchant the heaven!
Ardan's lips are scant of breath,
Naisi's tongue is cold in death.

Stag, exult on glen and mountain,
Salmon, leap from loch to fountain,
Heron, in the free air warm ye—
Usnach's sons no more will harm ye!

Erin's stay no more you are,
Rulers of the ridge of war!
Never more 'twill be your fate
To keep the beam of battle straight.

Wo is me! by fraud and wrong,
Traitors false, and tyrants strong,
Fell clan Usnach, bought and sold,
For Barach's feast and Conor's gold!

Wo to Eman roof and wall!
Wo to Red Branch, hearth and hall!
Tenfold wo and black dishonor
To the foul and false clan Conor!

Dig the grave both wide and deep
Sick I am, and fain would sleep!
Dig the grave, and make it ready—
Lay me on my true-love's body!

Whereupon Deirdre fell down and expired beside the grave. And they laid her in the grave with the sons of Usnach, and piled their cairn, and their names were written on the stone above them. Then fell the curse upon clan Conor; for Fergus, the son of Roy, slew Conor, and burned Emania and the Red Branch to the ground, and no man hath inhabited them from that day to this. So ends the history of the three sons of Usnach.

'Had I been Fergus,' said Henry O'Neill, when Turlogh concluded, 'I would never have deserted my charge for Barach's banquet.' 'Ah,' said Turlogh, 'thou takest no thought of the strange usages of different times and nations. I might readily have made Barach detain Fergus, by claiming his aid in some expedition against an enemy, undertaken for that purpose, and impossible to be avoided by a friend and brother in arms; or I might have detained Fergus on an assembly at Dun Barach, of his order, whereof he was a high dignitary, and being so, could not refuse attendance; or I might have invented any more likely excuse that I had thought fit: but what I have told you is according to the ancient account, which hath never been varied during many hundred years of constant tradition, and which hath delighted more princes, and nobles, and honourable audiences than any other story of Milesian times; and this obligation of hospitality, although it be not now practised, yet hath its old existence never been doubted by any bard or story-teller of ancient or modern day. Truly it was a strange and ungracious observance to detain a man against his will, and already angry with his host, at a banquet which neither could enjoy while that anger of the guest continued; and, doubtless, Fergus was in high wrath all the time of his reluctant stay at Dun Barach: yet such is the tale our ancestors have told us, and it becomes not us to alter or corrupt it.' 'Neither can I understand,' said Henry, 'how it was that the nobles of Ulster, who had such love to the sons of Usnach, could permit Conor, on a pretence so trifling as the maiming of his servant, to violate both his own pledge and that of Fergus, by slaying their friends and fellow-nobles before their faces, without either remonstrance or resistance.' 'Such is the history as we have heard it,' said Turlogh, 'the power of the king was supreme; the nobles were at a distance from their own provinces and troops; and all the violence committed was done by the army of the enraged monarch.'

'Again,' said Henry; but he was interrupted by Art — 'What matter, brother, how the thing was brought about, so that the generosity, and valour, and fortitude, and true love which make the true delight of the tale be not hindered in their operation and display? With the clang of the magic shield ringing in my ears, and the picture of the brother's heroic composure and the damsel's serene constancy before my eyes, I can think of nothing but noble deeds and generous affections: my eyes are dazzled with the glorious flashing of swords and battle-axes; my ears drink in the exulting din of battered armour, while my heart melts within me for pity and compassion, and sweet thoughts of those who love me, and who would do and suffer as much for my sake in a like extremity.' 'Far different thoughts have been mine,' said O'Donnell, withdrawing his eyes from an intense contemplation of some scene in the vacancy before him, 'not that my breast hath not been stirred with many and strong emotions of indignation, sympathy, or tender remembrance; but truth to tell, I have thought far less of private wrong, or personal affections, than of my country's miserable condition which hath ever been caused and continued by even such feuds and tyrannies among ourselves, as those related to us by Turlogh. And I think, with my cousin Art in this, that it matters little for the nature of those small hinges whereon the mechanical operation of the story turns, so that we be not prevented from seeing clearly the chief truth that the tale at large teacheth. Here, behold what strife and weakness arose for Ulster, from making private wrongs and jealousies the causes of public commotion: behold the nobles disgusted with the king, the king sacrificing the best and bravest of his own subjects; and, in the end, inviting, by the weakness he had himself occasioned, the invasion of another potentate, and the final subjection of his own people to the rule of strangers. Alas, it hath been ever thus; and Conors, and Dermots, and Teige Caoluisces[46] have never been wanting to perpetuate the curse of division and weakness. In God's name, my cousins, let not the old quarrels of our houses, hinder our hearty union now! If injury be done by either to the other, let the brehon[47] settle who is the offender, and who the sufferer, while we employ our common arms in upholding the means and power of reparation in both. What though Hugh Calvagh, my own near kinsman, was robbed of wife and lands, by your father, Shane? think you I have better chance of recovering my right from Elizabeth, than from you? No; let us first join in keeping the country, and let us settle its division after. Before God, and Columb Kill, it is my firm belief that we are strong enough, if united, to hold the three provinces against the world! Where could the Claneboys, and men of O'Nelan, and the Fews, most readily muster on the other side of Blackwater?' 'We would join you,' replied Art, 'with Claneboy, anywhere, either in Turlogh Lynach's country, or O'Cahan's; the fort newly built on the Blackwater, would check our

46. Caol Uisce is literally translated in the place-name Narrow Water (County Down) between Warrenpoint and Newry. In 1258 Tadg Ó Briain offered the kingship of Ireland to Brian Ó Néil at Caol Uisce.
47. judge (from Irish *breathamh*).

march south of Loch Neagh.' 'At Tulloghoge, then, be it'; said Hugh, 'we will draw down our forces by the earl's country, and assault the fort together; then raise the Mac Kennas and Mac Mahons, drive the Bagnalls into Newry; and narrow the northern pale to Eash Oriall;[48] by my father's bones, a fair exploit! The earl would, beyond doubt, join us, for he hateth Bagnall, as well on his sister's account, whom the marshall hath married against his will, as from his close and dangerous neighbourhood to Dungannon. Ha! we will have another blow for land and liberty, before we see the strangers stable their steeds in our castle halls, and send their ploughs through our raths and hunting grounds! Bagnall and Clifford, Bingham and Fitzwilliam, ye shall yet rue the day you first saw Irish land! — Ho! Art and Henry, let us go and fix the levies.' He rose, unconscious of his captivity, as if to take his seat at a council table; but the fetter again checked him, and he again sat down with a bitter sigh. 'I had forgotten,' he cried, 'while meditating English overthrow, that I am still a captive in the chains of England. Yet, why repine? Let me rather thank Heaven that hath sent thee, Turlogh, to lighten my captivity and give me these dreams of glory which are so sweet while they last, that I would freely suffer ten such awakings for the forgetfulness of one such hour as this thou hast afforded me.' 'Praise be to Him who hath given me the power,' replied Turlogh: 'with his permission you shall yet enjoy many such hours. Meanwhile, 'tis time for you, my noble masters, to retire for the night, lest our voices, heard longer, excite the apprehensions of the guard.'

48. Oriel was a lordship in County Armagh.

ISAAC BUTT
(1813-79)

PAST AND PRESENT STATE OF LITERATURE IN IRELAND (1837)

[Isaac Butt's authorship of 'Past and Present State of Literature in Ireland' cannot be proven absolutely, but the editorial tone adopted throughout argues strongly in favour of an attribution to him. Moreover, there were at the time few other known contributors to *The Dublin University Magazine* capable of formulating such an argument. The essay constitutes, in effect, the first attempt at a theory of Anglo-Irish literature. Although Butt is best remembered as the leader of the Home Rule party, his early career deserves careful attention. Born in County Donegal and educated at Trinity College and the King's Inns (Dublin), he threw himself energetically into a host of youthful projects of which the *Magazine* was only one. He founded a newspaper called the *Protestant Guardian*, practiced successfully at the Bar, intrigued in the Metropolitan Conservative Society, and even found time in the 1840s to write an anonymous novel, *The Gap of Barnesmore*, set in his native county. His defence of William Smith O'Brien in the political trials of 1848, and later his defence of Fenian prisoners in the 1860s, lead into his more renowned political phase as a nationalist. But in 1837, he was a stout champion of protestant privilege and the connection with Britain. His analysis of the literary situation of Ireland, *vis-à-vis* the London publishers, the development of print technology, and the expansion of literacy show him already alert to the anomalies of the Union. His greatest debt is undoubtedly to Coleridge, and the passage beginning 'It is one of the most important distinctions ....' follows closely the literary genealogy advanced in the second chapter of the *Biographia Literaria*. Readers today may find the argument a trifle long-winded, the digressions excessive. The piece is republished complete, however, in order to allow Butt's conservative-radical analysis to emerge intact, with all its hestitations, regrets and recognitions.]

Often as we have desired to summon the attention of our readers to the interesting subject of the literary prospects and intellectual state of this country, we have been deterred by the consideration of the varied topics, with which a full and accurate view of this subject must be complicated. Of these, some are difficult to pronounce upon with accuracy or precision; some entangled in dispute, some involved in party feeling. It is easy to conceive, how any question that affects the nation's mind must comprehend views from which the literary essayist would gladly extricate the train of his reasoning, did a just regard to truth allow. But the literature of a nation, and of this nation in particular, is affected by its political state and influential upon it. And this double dependance becomes more important, either as effect or cause, in proportion as the stage of civilization is lower, and the operation of the conservative principles of society less developed.

Though we shall endeavour to keep on the surface of common interest, yet we must bespeak some intelligent attention, while we attempt a brief statement of the general causes by which the country is, in this respect, retarded or advanced.

Of these general causes, three claim especial notice. The state of the time, the state of Ireland as affected by it, and the state of literature at this period. From these heads a correct and comprehensive view of the difficulties before us will be obtained. From this, we can more clearly ascertain the advantages to be looked for in the promotion of our home literature. And lastly, estimate satisfactorily, our capabilities, advantages, and the progress we have actually gained. Such, we trust, will be felt to offer no uninteresting train of inquiry and reflection, to any one who feels an interest in the real honor and improvement of his country. The most standard perfection of legislative institutions would be an inadequate substitute for the *blessing of civilization*; *without this*, mild laws can afford no shelter, equal rights would be an injustice, and freedom but an abuse.

In taking a compass, which, to some, may at first appear more wide than is necessary for the purpose of considering the literary prospects of this country, we can only say that our view requires it, and request a patient hearing. To consider the objects of literature, otherwise than in its bearing on the more permanent interests, and more vital and essential elements of national progress, would be to narrow a most extensive subject into one of little moment. In this tempestuous crisis, when the elements of the social state appear to be involved in a preternatural rapidity of progression, either for good or evil, we should be ashamed to sit gravely engaged in speculating on the progress of the tenth-rate poetry, or third-rate scholarship of the day. We care little how the souvenirs and forget-me-nots might best multiply their insect existence, or the twopenny ballad-mongers find favor with Curry and Co.[1] All this, though harmless in itself, and even desirable as a portion of more important changes, may well lie over for future consideration. When the hopes of the year are secured, and the bladed fields set our hearts at rest for the future harvest, we may find leisure to watch the humble-bee in his honied range, or to be amused by the butterfly as its painted wing glances from flower to flower amidst the gay profusion of the spring. Not that we are deficient in the cordial goodwill which rises in our breast, when we behold the teeming, but not superfluous, trifles of modern literary journey-work piled in all their elegance of external ornament on the publisher's table; or that we are insensible enough not to feel a more intense and lively satisfaction, when, by the inestimable kindness of the worthy authors, these valuable specimens of typography and binding, appear on our own table, and awaken our hearts to silent gladness — *tacitum pretentant gaudia pectus.*[2] But it is not with these, or even with the productions of a higher form, that we feel ourselves engaged in entering on a topic, which, according to our social theory, embraces the most important principles of national welfare.

It is one of the most important distinctions between us and England, that its literature and civilization have begun in distant ages. When the morasses and forests of Ireland were yet under the domination of the 'ragged royal race of Tara', as they are not inaptly described by our *national* lyrist Moore,[3] and our fine peasantry were the oppressed slaves of chieftains as unlettered as themselves: the fathers of English poetry, the Chaucers, and the Gowers, and the Surreys, and the Spensers had long bequeathed their deathless names and writings to the mind of time. The literature of England appeared as a star 'in the forehead of the morning sky'[4] from the very twilight of the cloistered superstitions of the middle ages, and shed its early light on the foundations of the British constitution. It has grown with its growth, into a splendor and stability, which changes and political concussions

1. William Curry Junior and Company published *The Dublin University Magazine* in which this article appeared.

2. A version of Virgil's 'Tacitum vivit sub pectore vulnus', i.e. 'The secret wound still lives within his breast'.

3. Thomas Moore (1779-1852), the Irish poet whose *Irish Melodies* became extremely popular as drawing-room songs. Catholic by upbringing and mildly radical in politics, he was actively disliked by the conservative Irish gentry, partly no doubt because of his social success in England.

4. Shakespeare, *Coriolanus*, II.1. 57.

have had no power to lessen. And what is more to our purpose, it has slowly and efficiently, in the course of ages, produced all its varied effects upon the nation's mind. It is desirable that the reader should conceive these effects — a sentence will point them out. It is well known that there is in every educated nation (though in different degrees) a process whereby opinion, as it becomes accumulated and matured, becomes expanded, simplified, and reduced to practice; passing in this progress from the student in his closet to the artizan in his warehouse, and the peasant in his hamlet. Thus it has often been noticed, that the abstruse learning of one time tends to become the popular opinion of the following. And what is at least equally important, though less observable, an imperceptible moral growth, which may be regarded as the effect of this, is also taking place with more constancy. This can only indeed be measured, by the means which we have of comparing man in distant intervals, or in distinct stages of civilization. Now, in Ireland, the case is widely different; our literature, or rather our literary cultivation, has been recently engrafted; and under circumstances which must have controlled its influences most unfavorably. There was here nothing of that expanding downward of mind — that slow communication of opinion — that incorporation of knowledge with the mind — that subduing and correcting or altering of old manners, prejudices, and associations, which is the actual progress of civilization. This can be but the result of time: its very first causes cannot be said to have existed here. The civilization of our higher orders was but a light across the waters from another shore — too feeble in its expansion to shed influence on the crowd. It was isolated refinement, seated on the verge of primitive rudeness. The line between the educated and uneducated classes was too broad — a dark, impassable gulph, from the depths of which national animosities, barbaric prejudices and superstitions, and the resisting powers of a domineering hierarchy, exhaled their anti-civilizing influences. But we must pass to the present, before we see the accumulated effect of these. To appreciate our present state, we must take one short glance upon the present position of British literature.

In England, literature is at the present moment retrogressive. This, with regard to that country is an occasional recurrence of small importance; but as it nearly affects the question as to our own progress, it behoves us to give it some attention. Two causes quite opposite in their nature and tendencies, have affected the literature of the day; one, the influence of political excitement which has absorbed the public attention, and diminished the power of all the milder sources of excitement. The other, more curious and less understood, will require a few more words.

A spirit, unfavorable to literature, has been aided by the corruption of literature. This requires a few remarks. The exigencies of multiplied political business have lowered the tone of political oratory and writing into a style more adapted to detail, and employing a far inferior class of faculties. In addition to this fact may be noticed another, perhaps more effective in the same way: the causes which have brought the popular mind more largely into the discussion of public questions, have necessarily called for a more superficial method and style. Profound and general views may preside in the cabinet of the statesman, but when he stands up in his place he must keep to the level of the hustings if he would be heard or read. The graceful and persuasive, or impressive appeal to the principles of an enlightened audience, or to the inborn feelings of humanity, or the venerable conventions of time, would be out of place, and listened to with just impatience by modern men of business and detail, wisely economical of time. As for wit, and the tasteful embellishment of style, their day has long gone by; they would hang upon the slipshod newspaper prose of a modern debate, as Gibbons's flowered carvings, on the rough but useful masonry of Kingstown pier.[5] We are not here speaking the language of critical censure, which would be misplaced and ridiculous. We state the fact, as it is and ought to be. It is only with its bearing on our peculiar topic we are concerned.

The second of our proposed principles is more difficult to deal with, as it is itself an opposite principle, and in a great measure to be regarded as the existing progress of the intellect of the age. But we claim candid and discriminating attention. The modern advance of discovery and invention has been rapid beyond any known rate of human progress; and in this, there can be but one concurring sentiment of admiration and thankfulness.*

* It has redeemed, and perhaps mitigated, probably, too, governed and beneficially modified the evil workings of a revolutionary age. It would be

5. Grindling Gibbons (1648-1720) was a woodcarver in the baroque style. Kingstown is the present Dún Laoghaire, Co. Dublin.

But we have nothing to do with this. In this vast movement the public mind has received a proportionate impulse; and the effect on taste, style, and language, and on the cultivation of all arts not immediately connected with it, has been marked and great. The old conventions of the human mind soon began to dissolve before the ascendency of change: the ancient forms of thought and the barriers of style were broken down to let in a deluge of opinion, and to enlarge the bounds of speech to the measure of these new and vast accessions to the stock of knowledge. Of this, two consequences arose, the effects on the *manner* and on the *matter* of English composition. In the first, the nice, subtle and refined rules, which result from the very constitution of the mind, and which are exemplified in all those standard writings which have ever survived the *fashion* of their hour, were abandoned and forgotten. A style, expanded beyond all due bounds, swoln with a new language, the result of new theories, and stripped of the old harmony and the terse idiom of a style that had gradually arisen from the study of the classic models, came into vogue, and obtained possession of the rising generation. By this poetry and prose were alike affected; and the whole body of English literature passed into a *state of transition*, the less perceivable as the critic partook of the spirit of the time. It became an object to attain facility, abundance and simplicity; but the progress was forced beyond the natural rate of the mind. The facility became slipshod laxity — the abundance, indiscriminate and torrent verbosity — and the simplicity, incomposite vulgarity. Now, although this revolutionary stage of literature may be, and, in our opinion is, the needful preliminary to a happier stage, in which the dregs of change shall have cleared away and the crude materials become combined into a harmonious form: yet in the meantime, literature has lost its enchantment with its chaste and cultivated grace. A feeble luxuriance of new-coined words, phrases only striking as innovations, metaphors profuse and inappropriate, illustrations by obscure conceit, are the overflowing ornaments of the large class of writers who occupy the London press. This was for a time concealed and moderated by the happy concurrence of half a dozen illustrious writers — amongst whom Scott and Byron may be named — equal to those of any period or nation. After these, with their distinguished peers, *all referable to the previous period*, had left the stage, a cloud of clever writers, whom their fame concealed, began to occupy their places in public notice, and to overflow the press with glittering inanity and florid poverty. New leaders, in the dearth of better, rose to eminence: and distinguished themselves as inferiors can alone be distinguished, by exaggeration and monstrosities of every sort. Bombast; fantastic niceties; gallicisms; paradoxes involving silly truism, and affected violations of English idiom — *At magnum fecit, quod verbis Græca Latinis miscuit.*[6] For the truth of these remarks we refer the critical reader to the novels and poetry of the last ten years; to the great mass of public speeches, and to the London fashionable periodicals, monthly and annual; with, however, this qualifying remark, that by far the most sterling portion of the talent of the day has, of late years, found its way into our periodical literature. Such being the state of the time, there is nothing in literature apart from its distortions and unnatural stimuli, to occupy the attention of the better portion of the public intellect. They who have taste and leisure find it necessary to go back to the period of a more sterling nature. But the exigencies of business, or the love of artificial excitement, such as may be satisfied by the dregs of the circulating libraries, supply the whole of the demand for the multifarious, but corrupt and surface literature of the day. This vicious state of things is much aggravated by reaction, from the tone of intercourse it has caused. The conversation of eminent men has no attraction, no refined sparkle of wit, no profound remark, no play of comment and criticism, no attic[7] repose; their speaking, nothing of standard eloquence. This, to be sure, is as it should be; we are not the fools to censure. In the stirring strife of the age, no leading mind can stay to puzzle about the humanities: we claim no proud exemption from the taint of the time, or the infirmities of human nature. We frankly plead guilty to these charges, if such they can be called: in our composition we are not always too fastidious in

a digression to prove, what we cannot pass without affirming, that this advance is in no way connected with the political spirit of the times, which has yet dexterously contrived to derive respectability from its alliance. Nothing, however, can be more widely separate in principle than the practical science of modern discovery and the speculative politics which have encumbered it with a *pretended* patronage.

6. 'It was a great feat, however, to blend Latin with Greek.' Horace, *Satires*, I.10.20-21.

7. Classically elegant, simple and pure.

language, or over nice in harmony: we cannot always resist the temptation of glitter without appropriateness and the noble desire to emancipate poetry from those severe laws which were once supposed to constitute its peculiar character and charm: and we feel, like our brother bards, that the composition of verse is much facilitated by adopting the loose periods of a fustian[8] prose. We would not be thought fastidious in these days of literary license, and trust for our excuse to the frankness of our confession. But the truth must be told; literature is for the present, like many better things, broken up and deprived of its higher influences. We are in one of those dull cycles which have often come round to damp the spirit of every age; we have revolved to the days of Hayley, and the della Cruscan school.[9] We are not, like that emasculated school, devoid of matter, and prolix without sense. Our error is in the other extreme; instead of style without sense, our fault is circumstantial dullness without attention to style. But the result is, there is no public feeling in favor of literature,* and there is nothing in literature to merit such a feeling. We do not, however, wish to derive strength from exaggeration; and on this point, there is one remark which we cannot pass in silence. It is very usual to refer the whole of the ill success of literary speculations to the apathy of the public. — This we believe to be an overstatement. Nothing worthy of success in any eminent degree, has now, or at any time, failed to attract the degree of attention to which it has been entitled by its merits. On the contrary, in the dullest of times, the public has its favourites — in the absence of higher names, the writers of the cockney school[10] are read; and there is a stir and bustle among the publishers which, for a moment, appears opposed to our theory. But there is a solution for this difficulty. The vast increase of the middle order has brought with it a proportional influx of minds and interests into the field of intellectual and commercial action; a vast increase both of readers and writers is the consequence, and with it an increase of trade, which indicates nothing but the merely *numerical increment* which has caused it. Every one reads more or less — tracts, compilations, abstracts, abridgments, and elementary treatises, altogether unconnected with literature (in its idiomatic sense) forms the better part of this reading. The ornamental publications, which owe their chief attractions to embellishment, and which swell their bulk with prose and verse that no one thinks of reading, occupy a large share of this trade, and hold to literature the place which the modern puppet-shows of the stage obtain with respect to the legitimate drama. A vast multiplicity of readers, has created a demand for books; but even this is magnified to observation, by another consequence, distinct from any we have mentioned: the vast production of works which have no circulation and no readers. These are published at the expense of their authors, and afford no measure of the public market. We have stated these facts with sparing moderation, and with the consciousness of treading on delicate ground. There is a partizanship in the time, that affects all subjects which are open to the discussions of opinion: and we write in fear of giving offence to the fanaticism of schools, the admirers and idolaters of the vices of great men.

All changes find their period. The time cannot be far remote for the restoration of literature to its legitimate form and influence. There are heads and hearts enough, which have not bowed the knee to Baal;[11] and a few leading writers, in the seasonable moment will suffice to bring back a more regulated and principled tone, to the public taste. It only requires that the attention of the more solid intellects as yet absorbed in more vital operations, should be turned to the cultivation of letters and the arts of peace; to redeem them from the hands of the old women and children, who have the field to themselves. The undigested mass of new thoughts and words will become digested and assimilated by skill and labour — and other Popes and Addisons will arise to chasten, harmonize, and simplify, to clear and purify the well of 'English undefiled.'[12]

But we must return to our intent. It was, so far,

* Considered simply as a matter of taste; and distinct from the desire of knowledge.

8. pompous, bombastic.
9. William Hayley (1745-1820) was a minor poet and biographer; *della Crusca* is Italian for 'of the chaff', signifying here a poetic movement of little substance that began in England in the late eighteenth century.
10. London-born writers of lower middle-class origins, such as John Keats and Leigh Hunt.
11. A pagan god whom the Israelites encountered when they reached Canaan.
12. Edmund Spenser, *The Faerie Queene*, IV. 2. 32: 'Dan Chaucer, well of English undefiled.'

our object to fix the general state of literature, from which alone all particular views can be justly comprehended; and we were also desirous to make it appear that we do not lay too much stress on causes exclusively local. Our literature *is that of England*— we are substantially English in name, laws, and prospects. We have had the full benefit of the literature of England, and must partake of its changes. The effects we have been noticing can be traced here also. Not among our publishers or book marts — for these we have not had — but in our social circles and public institutions. Like our intellectual nurse, our social and forensic tones are changed from what they were. An apathy of taste reigns, attributable to the same causes, which lay like a leaden spell upon the British world. A spirit of utilities governs the tongue and pen with its untrimmed and feeble, though full and useful style — its naked details, and diffuse but *unprincipled* reasonings. Wit and classic allusion have long ceased to throw their graceful and fascinating lustre over the intercourse and conduct of public men. The time has passed when a moral axiom was thought important enough to be gravely bandied between the bench and the bar; but when wit was carried to perfection; when deep and leading truths were expressed with the strength and power of dignified simplicity, and when a chaste and pointed precision of style gave evidence to the reigning spirit from which they came. Though, properly speaking, we have had no literature; yet such was the pervading influence of the day of Flood and Grattan, and their cotemporaries, which not only ruled the listening senate, or gave attraction to the popular pamphlet, but pervaded domestic life.[13]

No literature had yet taken root in Ireland, except a trifling and occasional appearance of pamphlets, which, from their uniformly specific purpose, were confined to shed their glow-worm radiance on trivial points of local or ephemeral interest. The spirit of the time did not favour the colonization of literature into Ireland; it was not in such a state of circumstances that it might be expected *to begin*; for such is the consideration important to be kept in view.

But there was another very peculiar process going on in Ireland to corrupt the taste and partially to obscure our national reputation. — The public speaker, as will ever be the case, found it necessary to accommodate his style to its purposes: — and the peculiar state of the country called forth a style of rhetoric, adapted to please the most uncultivated ear and understanding. Clouds of sublimated nonsense, — 'the melancholy madness of poetry' — drew thunders of applause from listening streets. The miserable cant of a barbaric patriotism was tricked out in the waste of poetical commonplaces, and adorned with the meretricious tinsel of extravagant conceits and metaphors, which seemed to have sense and propriety, because they were not understood: — real talent set off, and occasionally redeemed this sad degeneracy — Sheil and O'Connell[14] could not be without meaning; but their followers and admirers made sad work. — For a moment popular admiration was made an argument in behalf of the extravagances by which it was won. But this could not last; the Edinburgh Review[15] broke the spell, and Irish eloquence fell in the market. Such demonstrations could do little to excite the better portion of our mind.

Let us now briefly notice the operation of this state of things on the populace of Ireland. It is not more important with reference to the subject, than it is itself strange and anomalous; presenting to the observer, a singular combination of barbarism and civilization, affecting the same class, and involving the self-same intellects, in the strong glare of contrasted light and darkness.

Over by far the larger districts of the country, if an intelligent stranger were to have full means to observe the manners, the moral principles and training, the opinions of knowledge of the peasantry, he might well feel as one transported some two centuries backward in the scale of progress. If, on the other hand, the same observer were to introduce among these seemingly simple and undisciplined barbarians, questions of national theology and politics, and really contrive to draw them into the sincere exertion of their understandings, he would be equally astonished to observe a niceness of logical tact — an intelligence

13. Dublin had been a great centre of political pamphleteering in the late eighteenth century. Henry Grattan and Henry Flood were the most distinguished orators of the Irish parliament.

14. Richard Lalor Sheil (1791-1851), politician and dramatist; Daniel O'Connell (1775-1847), 'the Liberator', architect of catholic emancipation (1829) and later leader of the unsuccessful movement to repeal the Union with Britain. Both were regarded as skilled orators in their day.

15. A major British literary and political journal of the nineteenth century, founded in 1802.

in the politics of the day — and generally a progress in that casuistry, which depends exclusively on the native power or the habitual use of the mere intellect — such as might do no discredit to Maynooth.[16] Such is the anomalous inequality, which, whether we have exaggerated it or not, exists to obscure the question as to our real state of advance. While we must be allowed to stand below the level of English and Scottish civilization, in all its more momentous elements, we stand at the lowest on a level with them in the mere development of intellectual power. To shew the little value, or indeed serious disadvantage of this condition, would be to digress widely from the purpose we have in view.* But we may advantageously notice its obvious cause.

While a dominant superstition, of which it is the vital principle to depress the advances of the mind in every direction, has with other familiar causes of a historical and political kind, conspired to foster ignorance and retard civilization, a violent political fermentation, with the causes of which our discussion is not involved, has operated as a powerful stimulant on the national mind, and awakened all the faculties of a people — by nature, shrewd and observant — into their intensest action. These dispositions have found a school in the political arena, only inferior in power and mischievous efficiency to the mob-oratory which produced very similar effects in the 'fierce democracy'[17] of Ancient Greece. The ear for oratorical effects — the logical sense — the expansive tact that brings the mind into contact with events, have been fostered and matured at the public hustings and at the agitation meetings. But the sole food which has been thus imbibed, has been from the misstatements of faction — partial views of fact — fallacious principles and all the prejudices and ignorances which have ever formed the material and ammunition of party warfare. Thus trained, developed and furnished with a system of specious fallacies, cunningly interwoven with the grievous realities of their condition, the bulk of the Irish peasantry exhibit a singular mixture of cultivation and barbarism — of shrewdness and ignorance — of sensitiveness and brutality — of meanness and moral elevation.

These considerations are capable of an application far more extensive than it is our desire to give them. For while a highly educated class is also to be found throughout the country, existing rather within itself, than in contact with the public mind, the body of the Irish gentry is also in no small measure affected by causes arising out of the same state of things. The close propinquity and personal nature of the causes of political excitement, seem to have given them an exclusive possession of the mind. Men are classed by their party feelings, and rather to be characterised by the colour of their creed, than by any personal attribute. The gentry of Ireland are Whigs and Tories. And while the civilization of the 19th century sits in the twilight of the darker ages, a fierce conflict, fiercely carried on, suppresses, obstructs, and confines the diffusion of the mental element of civilization. There is thus on every side, broadly and plainly visible, a diffusion of moral and intellectual action, quite distinct from the humanizing principles of knowledge or education — a spurious vitality in the nature of disease, in which faction only derives growth: — by which thought and talent, sentiment and opinion, abundantly called forth, are shaped as they rise to the narrow views of the day, and moulded to the blind expediencies of either party. Every thing is looked on by public feeling through this misty medium, and nothing is rightly appreciated that does not in some way connect itself with public events and party notions; while, to the convulsions of party are added the noise of theological contentions, and the struggles of ecclesiastical defence.

It should indeed be noticed before we leave this topic, that the obstacles to progress, which we have here been explaining, were the more likely to be protracted, that there has been no very decided

*Even among the gifted writers of this teeming age, this distinction can be followed up to its consequences. It will uniformly appear, how much more the value of all reasoning depends on the just principles — the disciplined feeling and rightly directed moral sense which begins and governs its course, than the most brilliant subtlety of mere intellect. No degree of acuteness or ratiocinative ingenuity has been known to guard its possessors from every extreme of error and fatuity. The one true security is right knowledge and sincere intent. In this all will agree — that while truth is but on one side, exceeding ability is often found on both; but the great evil of ignorant cleverness is really the self-confidence in error; and the added power it places in the grasp of the sophist. Intellectual perception, it must be observed, does not extend further than the apprehension of the intellectual art itself. The false premise passes with ignorance, and the dexterous logic amuses and satisfies the subtle and ingenious.

16. The town in County Kildare where, in 1795, a seminary was established for training men for the catholic priesthood.
17. In Milton's *Paradise Regained* (IV. 269), the phrase actually is 'fierce democraty'.

principle of counteraction. In former times, as still, the mind of Ireland received its impulses from the maturer action of that of England; but England has itself been, for the same period, the stage of a complex revolution, of very varied and of opposite effects as regards this subject. — If we consider this with a view to her political influences on Ireland, one sentence must here express our opinion: — she has made this country, itself convulsed from end to end, the arena of a revolutionary contest. But the same contest, though it has been far from shaking in the same degree the mature structure of the social system in England, has there, as here, long since arrested and withered the germs from which literature derives its growth; the public ear is there almost as dull as here, to all that concerns not the feelings of party. This is, however, not an abiding condition: political excitement itself wears out, or with its causes, subsides. And there is in the vast accession of knowledge — of principles — of language and of educated minds, a powerful reaction preparing in favor of an advance more exclusively moral and intellectual. There is in educated man, in proportion as he rises in the scale of mind, a tendency to strive after permanent principles and results; and though public virtue, or self-interest, or vanity, may draw men wholly into the collisions of ephemeral questions, and parties — yet these having subsided, the calmer and more abiding interests, and the more profound and elevated realms of truth, excellence and beauty, obtain the preference of the intellectual part of our nature.

Having now taken as large a compass as we think necessary for a superficial and popular view of the prospects and advantages of Irish literature, other topics of more immediate connexion with the subject present themselves: — our actual capabilities; the obstacles that exist to retard us; the efforts which have failed; the progress we have made; the objects to be gained by success; the necessary conditions of that success; and the means we have to pursue.

Our actual capabilities are, we are inclined to believe, much undervalued. Every one who is practically conversant with the opinions of Ireland and the Irish, abroad, must be aware that the general estimate of our moral and intellectual condition is of the lowest. In Germany, France, Italy, in fact, through Europe, and still more in America, our island may be said to represent the ancient *ultima Thule*[17] of civilization.

The vast capabilities of this country for literary pursuit, are in fact concealed by the overpowering demand of the English marts. Whatever is produced here is consumed there. The better portion of our mind is absorbed into the sphere of the ascendant genius of England, and thus our *real progress* is concealed from the eyes of the world. Neither is it only America, which has but a fortuitous knowledge of our existence, or France, which all but excludes us from the scale of literary existence; but indeed England, our sister, with whom we have so long taken sweet counsel — in England, while there is an exaggerated notion of our wit and imagination, nothing can be more observable than the very low opinion which there exists as to our state of civilization, and of our literary pretensions.

The causes of this impression are not foreign from our purpose. The bitterness and ferocious personality of our party conflicts — seen by our neighbours apart from its circumstancial causes — is attributed by them to our backward state of progress in civilization. Again, this impression is much confirmed by the fact that it is also widely felt by the better classes of Irish society. We think it right to observe, by the way, that we consider the notion to be a very monstrous exaggeration, unhappily too well supported by appearances. A confirmatory impression is, however, propagated by the very fact, that there is not, and has never been, any native mart for the productions of Irish talent; and while the business of the English press and book-market is as largely carried on as the paving of London, by Irish labourers — thus fully demonstrating the real productive power and industry of the country — Ireland not only has no publishing mart — no literary centre — but in fact the name of Dublin on the title-page has hitherto been a strong objection against a new book. We pass lightly over minor facts — the uniform resort of our Irish writers to the London press — the want of co-operation among the Dublin publishers, which affords the writer but too just a cause for this desertion — and many other facts of minute detail, which operate to increase the vast apparent disproportion when (in the loose way in which all such

18. The phrase is Virgil's (*Georgics* I.30) and means the last extremity, the end of the world. It refers to the furthest island of Europe, sometimes identified with Iceland.

comparisons are made) we are compared with our neighbours.

When our lifeless streets and dull marts are contrasted with those of London: — the bustling and crowded commerce — the enormous real, and vaster nominal wealth — the teeming overflow of projects and speculations, and all the produce of every class and form of mind — the brilliant galleries of modern art — the daily, monthly, quarterly, annual press — the glare, glitter, and magnificent ostentation of the central city of the civilized world, the resort of every tongue, and the theatre of the talent and intrigue of every land — populous, refined, powerful, wealthy — sending its report far and wide on all the winds, and stretching its arm judicially and authoritatively over all the nations under heaven. Such is a faint reflection of the impression (no matter as to its truth) through which the Englishman and the foreigner are compelled to look on our condition, and to estimate our advance as a country. It is little to the purpose, that we can with truth affirm our splendid capabilities — moral, intellectual, physical, and local; nor is it of any weight in our present statement to maintain accusation and impute injustice. Such is the state of fact and opinion which affects us in relation with other countries. Local evils are, we know, exaggerated by distance; but so it is, that while the sound of strife is heard from our shores, with uniform and increasing fierceness, there is no softening indication of taste, enlightened opinion, learning, genius, or of any feature of civilized and cultivated humanity — nothing that testifies our actual advance, to countries which are far behind us in all the essential elements of national progress. Such is a very summary and inadequate view of the common impression which drains wealth, knowledge, and commercial enterprise from our shore — which makes the emigration of our talent a necessary thing, and justifies the absentee.

But not to weary attention, we pass to a more enlivening aspect of this discussion. Notwithstanding all we have said, Ireland has advanced and is advancing. We do not despair of her fortunes — rich, abundant, and beautiful has been, and is the vegetation of her mind. No negligence can fail to see the overflow of natural material — we need not speak of the native humour, shrewdness, and vivacity of imagination — and it is as unnecessary to point out the splendid results where the soil has been tested by education. We might take the occasion to speak of Burke, the comprehensive in views — the profound and searching in reason — the consummate in elocution — the high-souled and chivalric in feeling.[19] We might launch out freely and truly on the host of lesser, yet still first-rate names — Sheridan, Grattan, Curran, and others, not inferior in their department.[20] We might dwell with no small satisfaction on our Goldsmith, with whom England has not, in his own walk, one other name to compare — who first and last brought to perfection the verse of Dryden and Pope — the natural, the simple, the graceful, the pathetic, the sublime without inflation, the flowing without redundance — 'qui omnes fere scribendi genus tetigit, et nullum tetigit, quod non ornavit,'[21] as his great cotemporary and friend has written in the truth of that judgment which is uttered over the tomb, where flattery finds no echoes. We shall not name the living, but assuredly there are names among us not soon to be blotted out from the record of after days. We challenge no ridiculous comparison with our maternal soil — the land of Newton, Shakespeare, Milton, Bacon, the unrivalled minds of Europe: — such master-spirits are not the common produce of their time. We simply affirm our claim to no small catalogue of illustrious men; and we may add, that there is a constant though concealed stream of Irish talent flowing to swell the mass of English and Scottish literature. We might, indeed, on this head, point to the public arena of party strife, and ask who are the foremost on either side, the most effective in appeal, the most allowed in power, either for good or evil, all Irish, nearly to a man. It is an easy transition to imagine this overflow reduced within its channel, and spreading the light of civilization at home. We have said to imagine, because, in truth, many obstacles must be overcome, and time must have brought forth many changes before this desirable consummation is to be reached. But it lies within the fair scope of exertion, and, therefore, it is no vain or useless object to fix upon. It is to be looked for from enlightened effort; and we are disposed further to

19. Yet another indication of Edmund Burke's pre-eminence among the influences at work in early Victorian Irish conservatism.

20. Richard Brinsley Sheridan (1751-1816), playwright and politician; Henry Grattan (1746-1820), politician and orator; John Philpot Curran (1750-1817), barrister, judge and minor writer.

21. Samuel Johnson composed the Latin epigraph for Oliver Goldsmith's (1728-74) tomb in Westminster Abbey, London; this part of it may be translated, 'There was no kind of writing which he did not touch on, and he enhanced everything he touched.'

point it out as a result in the course of a progress which has actually set in.

Already there is a change upon the spirit of the time. In the wildest burst of the storm there is a still small voice among the elements of wrath, and fury, and popular madness. A slow but growing sense of their delusion is stealing from rank to rank among the people so long abused — the false pledge, redeemed by accumulated lies, has grown almost too broad and black for infatuation's self to mistake for any thing divine or good. The language of truth and right have acquired an expansive and still expanding influence and authority; and there is among the higher and nobler class of spirits a trustful expectation of more congenial times, when the winter shall be past, the rain over and gone, and the flowers shall appear on the earth. Even amid the din of party there is a growing desire to revert to more permanent and standard thoughts and things; and in the waste of a depraved literature, a strong spirit of just and true criticism is beginning to indicate the approach of that spirit of refinement and severe good taste which is now wanting to correct, reduce, chasten, and harmonize the tumultuous and turbid exuberance of our unprincipled and random literature.

There is a tendency in civilization, when it has reached a certain point, to advance onwards towards perfection. This may not be reached, because the distance is infinite, and the course interrupted. In observing this important principle, we must always make allowance for small indications, such as must seem trifling to unphilosophical understandings. This must be our apology for noticing the continued efforts and failures of the Dublin press for some years back, to produce periodical works. The vast and rapid increase of intellectual excitement, the spread of knowledge, and the coarse stimulus of political feeling and action among the middle classes, had the natural consequence of bringing more mind into action. The pressure of intellectual effort soon began to find or make channels for itself. As we have noticed already, England, and in a lesser degree Scotland afforded rapid outlets, and by absorbing, concealed the abundance of the production; but at the same time numerous literary productions of a more youthful, untrained, and therefore transient and obscure character, also began to spring up season after season, into an existence scarcely known beyond the writers themselves, who paid the cost, and with juvenile admiration exulted in their unfledged authorship; for they were for the most part boys, receiving their first bent from a spirit that was in the time. To these we have ground for adding, there was no small accession from the humblest walks of handicraft occupation. The books had no sale, and the writers no payment; it was a labour of love, and all seemed willing to contribute their share. The tinker's well-trained ear betrayed itself in the harmonious jingle of his rhyme; the tailor vindicated his goose by swan-like notes; printers' devils were evoked by most unheard-of incantations, and uttered strange responses. All Castle-street chimed together in 'Kidderminster stuff', and Thomas-street answered 'from its misty shroud.'[22] Thus one gay swarm followed another, and was swept into the stream of oblivion. Experience pronounced their epitaph as they disappeared — tinker and tailor became sadder and wiser men[23] — and it became perceptible that essays and poems were not altogether to be compassed by plain stitch and solder; and that even Lilly and Voster, Euclid and Murray[24] must undergo some important transmutations in the mind, before they were likely to effloresce in the form of readable literature. The county of Kerry itself, famous time out of mind for its Latinity, could not support a literary effort which wanted the essential principle by which all successful effort thrives, the sinews of war and commerce, money. Nothing, in truth, had the effect of repressing for a single season, the laudable efforts thus begun; and as the youthful writers grew more ripe, they now and then exhibited transient gleams of higher pretension and even occasionally brought out flashes of very considerable power; but it was absolutely impossible they could have in the bulk a material success, beyond that we have described.

22. Castle Street, to the north of Dublin Castle, had been a centre of the book trade in the eighteenth century; Kidderminster is an English town famous for its carpets (stuff); Thomas Street lay west of Dublin Castle and Christ Church in a poor district.

23. cf. Samuel T. Coleridge, *The Rime of the Ancient Mariner*, VII, stanza 25.

24. William Lilly (*c.*1468-1522), grammarian; Elias Voster, mathematical textbook author; Euclid, ancient geometer; Lindley Murray (1745-1826), an American grammarian. Each of these oddly assembled names exemplifies a kind of popularizing knowledge or simplified wisdom. Euclid was of course adapted for schoolboy use, as were Lilly's writings on language. Murray's *English Grammar* (1795), the first standard English grammar, sold one-and-a-half million copies within 40 years of publication. Voster, the most obscure, was published in Limerick (1803) and in Cork (1829).

Patriotism itself could not find heroism to read, still less pay for such callow literature. The mere desire of public good never has, or ought to retain the efforts of any marketable mind; and as it sprung up to maturity the effective talent of the country found its level and its price. It obtained from the profitable wisdom of our neighbours that value which all should seek who have any thing which they have the power and right to dispose of. The talent of the successful writer, is the result of much labour, and that of the severest kind — it is the mature fruit of many trials, and often the result of a waste of the better years of life, and of many of the happier sensibilities of our nature — melted down into that crucible over which the student broods in the fever of ambition, and the sorrow of hope deferred, for the visionary prize of some surviving fame, so hardly won, and so invidiously allowed.

It was, therefore, an indispensable preliminary to the desirable object of calling home our scattered forces, and concentrating those lights which were so long losing themselves in the full-orbed day of England and Scotland, into a native and home existence, that this operation should commence, where alone all that is permanent or effective can commence, with the public-spirited and enterprizing trade. But the obstacles to be encountered were seemingly insurmountable. The name of Dublin on a title-page was a sufficient reason for neglect, and, in the case of periodical literature, it was too truly the indication of youthful incompetence, while many of the English periodicals had no unprofitable possession of the tables of the Irish gentry. A strong prepossession of this nature, combined with the usual caprice of fashion to exclude every thing of home growth. Capital, enterprize, patience and no small portion of experience, were necessary to obtain even a chance of fair trial. A combination of accepted writers, who had already secured the voice of criticism and public notice, was to be secured at considerable cost; the loss attendant on such undertakings, under such circumstances, was to be sustained; and the risk of the more serious loss consequent on failure, where all had failed, to be dared.

How *we* have entered upon and triumphed over these disadvantages needs not to be dwelt on. We trust that the bold experiment may be felt to be so far successful. Of this the public may rest secure; and this upon the strength of an obvious commercial principle, of which nothing but the most extreme infatuation can lose sight; that we have not one permanent contributor, who has not been received in the pages of our most successful cotemporary periodicals, and who has not met the undoubted testimony of public applause, or the approval of authorized criticism. To vouch for the merit of every article, or even of every monthly number, would be absurd; to such praise no periodical is entitled. Having taken the best steps to ensure the cooperation of mature and able men, we must abide by their inequalities and trust to the common sense of our readers. Let it be felt that, if indulgence were to be claimed in any case, it is in ours. Yet we ask no indulgence, though we are grateful for the justice which we cordially acknowledge to have received from the public. It is in truth among the best indications of these distracted times, that our country should have produced her first successful attempt at native literature, and that a decided and uncompromising political tone has not had the effect of eliciting any respectable reproof among our radical contemporaries.

We must conclude our summary, and we fear too meagre notice, by a brief enumeration of the public advantages to be hoped for from this undertaking. To appreciate them by the mere success of a magazine, would be unjust. To retain at home, a large portion of our native genius and learning is a first and obvious advantage; to give encouragement and hope to more; to awaken that literary tone which humanizes, polishes and adorns private life; to shed a civilized grace over the name of Ireland in foreign countries; to give a home direction to the sympathies of the better mind of our countrymen who spend fortune and talent abroad; to attract capital and enterprize to our shore; and, by shewing the way, awaken that life in the Irish publishing trade, which alone is wanting to raise us to the level of our neighbours. One successful adventure is but the step to another; and there is no reason, but those which arise from long-clinging prejudices, why Dublin should not be the centre of Irish cultivation, in all that improves and humanizes. An Irish press may, we trust, well supply the place which a native legislature once held — a focus of talent, and a nursery for the production of eminent men. It would be absurd to suppose, that the tone of society, that taste, knowledge and every sentiment which belongs to cultivated society, does not gain power and influence by the intermixture of minds professedly devoted to polite literature. In the Scottish metropolis society, through all its circles, takes its impulses from a few individual centres; and these impulses are, by an insensible but sure process, communicated from rank to rank through many a widening circle, until they embrace the land. Such, as far as we can express it in a few words, is the benefit we propose, and the principle on which we depend.

In throwing these reflections before our readers, we have studiously endeavoured to keep within the level of ordinary experience and observation, and to avoid tasking attention by any elaborate analysis of social causes or workings; nor have we aimed to lead the reader into detail, further than the distinct statement of our view absolutely required. The time is not yet arrived when we may securely launch into the depths of our moral and intellectual history; topics of more immediate interest engross the public ear, and the sense to which we would appeal, is yet but a 'consummation devoutly to be wished for'.[25] Yet, having begun and continued our labors, under a solemn sense of their importance to this country, we entertain a sanguine assurance of their success, and it is our settled conviction, that when calmer and more prosperous days shall allow the public mind to look back on this troubled period, with a view undisturbed by party strife, that these efforts will be recollected as among the first favorable gleams of national amelioration, and that it will be deemed no trivial incident of an eventful time, that has brought so far towards maturity the first literary journal on the settled principles of commerce.

Our valuable, extensive, and still extending circulation, with the unanimous voice of the public press, which has every where laid aside party feeling to cheer us on, may sufficiently attest that we do not overrate our success. Difference of opinion has not withheld the impartial approbation of our opponents; and they who from their position are most likely to appreciate the influence of public causes cannot be supposed to have erred, in thus setting their friendly stamp on our pretensions.

Of our contributors we have already dropped some words. The well-known convention, which throws a transparent veil over the names of periodical writers, makes it impossible to allude to these gentlemen otherwise than collectively. But we cannot allow ourselves to speak doubtfully or equivocally of persons whose talents do honour to their country, and whose names are for the greater part to be recorded in their historic wreath. We would not exchange our contributors for those of any other periodical in the empire; though the public may feel assured, that, in proportion as our means increase with our circulation, no effort shall be wanting to secure whatever power of talent, or weight of name, the best mind of the day affords. This is but the natural operation of that commercial process which is the basis of every rational undertaking. One fact, connected with this topic, may be stated as serving to exhibit, in part, the natural underworking of a literary establishment of this description. The enormous mass of clever manuscripts of every kind — poetry, essays, reviews, tales, critical dissertations, without measure or respite — which flow monthly on our hands, so as to make the task of selection impossible to ordinary diligence; and insertion — had we a number for every day in the year — quite out of the question: from this, we say, it will at once appear to what an extent the faculties of the national mind are set to work. Thus, on a moment's reflection, will it be seen how we humanize the land. However inflamed by local discontent or party feeling — however maddened by agitation, or exasperated by religious animosity — the moment we appear in the remotest village, where there is half-a-crown to purchase, or a tongue to read us, a new spirit falls over the minds of men. The village orator leaps from his tub, and tunes his genius to romance and song; the blacksmith stops swallowing the tailor's news, and commits his glowing inspiration to the post; the apothecary and the gauger make up their recent coolness, and an able treatise on things in general finds its way to our desk. — Every public road, that converges to our dwelling, from every quarter of the land, sends in its daily torrent of wit and inspiration, to testify our influence, and the extent of our fame, and to give solid assurance that Ireland is at her humanities, and that our circulation is a mission of light and power. Our numerous extern contributors have indeed reason to be grateful to us, both for what we have done for them, and for what we have left undone; the gentle excitement of their talent, and the discreet concealment of their dulness; — some we have encouraged — some we have laughed at — some advised to try some other amusement — but all with paternal

25. Shakespeare, *Hamlet*, III.1. 4-5.

tenderness, and in the confidential secrecy of office. Petulant remonstrances we have received with dignified forbearance; appeals to our patriotism, with a bland smile of compassion; offers of canvass for readers, on the score of some prosaic ineptitude, or dribbling commonplace of rhyme, we have heard in silent scorn. But this indeed is a subject in itself.

We have made no allusion to our political functions. These, amongst our own peculiar friends and supporters, need no praise, and can convey no recommendation to those who differ from us. Yet, even on this topic there are some general observations of much importance to be observed in the conduct of a periodical like this. One of the general advantages which we have at least in our power, and within the scope of our plan, is the more general and historic aspect with which political events may be invested in the more deliberate retrospect of the month. We do not desire to be misunderstood into the absurd notion, that we would shut ourselves out from a fair and manly use of the weapons of party controversy, which are flashing and circling round our ears wherever we turn. Such dastardly discretion never gains its cowardly object; it cannot serve our friends, or gain the respect of our honourable adversaries; 'to be weak is miserable, doing or suffering'.[26] We are conservative; and no feeble vacillation shall dishonor our steady and upright strength. We cannot assent to the suspicious friendship that would counsel an impotent moderation, where vigor and intrepid activity prompt to rough collision; we laugh to scorn the silly reproach of newspaper politics. We assert and shall not relinquish our right to fling aside our literary tiara — our jewelled wand, with which we sit pointing oracularly to the destinies of the nation, and leaping down into the thronged arena, to lay about us among our friends of the press, as long and as stoutly as our spirit impels. Our friends of the daily press are, we contend, excellent companions, and we do not shrink from the comparison. But, this point being saved, there is another consideration of much importance, which we shall keep in view, so far as our purposes and duties admit, '*exceptis excipiendis*', as the worthy prior of Jorvaulx Abbey is recorded to have said upon a very similar occasion.[27] In our column the inflammatory topics of the month will mostly be found to appear through the softening medium of afterthought, and when they have already in some degree undergone the sifting of public opinion. They may thus be expected, so far as may be, to appear comparatively divested of the rancorous tone, and of the irritating, degrading and disgusting personality which is offensive to the mind of a gentleman, to whatever party he may be attached. So far as the topic before our notice shall admit of it, we shall endeavour to take our stand on the high ground of principle, and to enlarge the compass of political discussion by historical and philosophical views. Thus may we hope to supply a momentous desideratum in the state-craft of the day, which is not less remarkable for its ability in the labyrinth of small details and expediencies which fill our eyes and ears on every side, than for its near-sightedness, as to directions and results, the natural effect of superficial and narrow views.

26. Milton, *Paradise Lost*, I, lines 157-58.

27. 'exceptis excipiendis' is a legal maxim; 'those things being excepted which it is requisite should be excepted'. Jervaulx Abbey is in Yorkshire.

JAMES CLARENCE MANGAN

(1803-49)

THE TWENTY-FOURTH OF FEBRUARY (1837)

[James Clarence Mangan was the most versatile and prolific writer of verse of the period, and the full extent of his periodical publications is still unknown. His original poetry displays great technical skill, and an emotional register heavily biased towards melancholy; but many of the poems destabilize themselves, turning into self-parody or burlesque. It is principally as a translator that he is now remembered, though here too there is disagreement among scholars as to the authenticity of the 'originals' that Mangan translated. To *The Dublin*

University Magazine he contributed several series of translations, notably from the German, and the text that follows appeared in such a series.

There is no doubt about the authenticity of the original German play translated here, and Mangan was not the first to bring it to the attention of an English-speaking audience. Its author, Zacharias Werner (1768-1823), was a minor dramatist of the Storm-and-Stress movement, and his *Der Vierundzwanzigste Februar* dates from 1809. Mangan often used his exotic sources as an obliquely placed mirror to the realities of Ireland, often indeed invented such sources so as to ensure that they fitted his requirements. In *The Twenty-Fourth of February*, he faithfully renders Werner's melodrama of inexorable and murderous Fate, while also providing an intriguing forerunner to W. B. Yeats's late play *Purgatory*, in which the pattern of murder is explicitly related to Irish class conflict. Given Werner's ecstatic religious personality, and his changes of denominational loyalty, Mangan's choice of play indicates a shrewd perception of the relevance of Werner's drama to Irish culture.]

A TRAGEDY, IN ONE ACT

Translated from the German of Friedrich Ludwig Zacharias Werner.

By the author of the Anthologia Germanica.

'Lead us not into temptation.' — *Luke* ix, 4.

Who made the heart, 'tis He alone
Decisively can try us;
He knows each chord, its various tone,
Each spring its various bias.
Then at the balance let's be mute—
We ne'er can well adjust it;
What's done *we partly may compute-*
We know not what's resisted.[1]

BURNS

DRAMATIS PERSONAE

WALTER KRUTH, *a Swiss Landmann*
KATHERINE, *his wife*
KURT, *their son, in disguise and unknown*

The scene is laid in Schwarrbach House, a lonely inn on the summit of the Ghemmi Alps, in Switzerland, between Kanderstag and Leuk.

1. The last stanza of 'Address to the Unco Guid, or the Rigidly Righteous' by Robert Burns (1759-96).

SCENE I

An inner and an outer room in WALTER'S *house, divided by a partition wall, against which a scythe and a large knife are seen hanging. In the background a straw bed and an old arm-chair. Time, night. A lamp is burning on a table in the outer room. A small kitchen-clock strikes the hour of eleven.*

KATHERINE (*alone at her spinning-wheel*):
Eleven o'clock, and Walter not come back yet!
He set out hence for Leuk at break of day this morn.
God send him home in safety! What a racket
The wind keeps up without! The demon blows his horn
Of storms as though he'd rent it with each gust,
Or fling it at the Ghemmi's summit, just
As Walter flung the knife! What darkening thought flits o'er
My mind? Ha! yes — 'tis even so. Once more
Returns to us the avenging time and tide —
In *February* Walter's father died.
Long years have rolled since then, and still that ghastly sight
Haunts me with preternatural vividness.
But Walter — God! — he may be lying tonight
Crushed underneath some avalanche's tower,
And we in this deplorable distress!
For now we are breadless, fireless, woodless — our
Stone-hearted creditors have all but torn
The last rug from our bed! Have we not cause to mourn?
Awfully is the curse fulfilled — a dread
Commandment is the fourth!* — And then our son who fled
From home and us, while yet a stripling — red
With his young sister's blood — he, too, we have heard, is dead!
O, were his mother so! — the grave is now her wished-for bed.
But let me chase these dismal thoughts. My head
Is full of them. I'll sing. A merry lay, 'tis said,
Is med'cine to the heart that Grief weighs down like lead.

* *Honor thy father and thy mother,* the fifth commandment is reckoned as the fourth in Germany, both by the Lutherans and Roman Catholics. (Asterisked notes are Mangan's.)

(*Sings*) — *O! why is thy sword so red, so red,*
Edward, Edward?
Because I have slain my falcon dead,
Therefore my sword is so red, so red.
*O, woe is me!**
A hateful song, and ends so foolishly!
(*A noise is heard at the window*)
Brr! — what a rustling! Surely that can be
None other than my husband. Let me see.
(*See goes to the window*)
It is an owl! The storm hath driven him hither.
How he gloats on me with his goggle eyes!
Avaunt, foul thing! *Come who, come will*, he cries,
He calls me to the grave — and I am hasting thither.
The owl, men say, hath scent of corpses ere
Death come, and I am half a corpse even now,
I feel so desolate here in my despair;
This lone, lost house upon the Ghemmi brow
Is such a dreary pile! — for miles around
Nought but wild rocks and glaciers meet the sight.
Now, too, 'tis Winter — we are doubly bound
By the rude spirits of this Alpine height;
I, at least, am. How shall I baffle care?
I'll try some other song — some sprightlier air.
(*Sings*)—*The boor he is poor; the boor is a boor;*
Then let him follow his plough;
In his flat hat and his smock frock
He has clothing enow, I trow, I trow,
I trow he has clothing enow.
With his hat a-cock,
And his belted frock,
He's one of the old, the good old stock.
The boor he is not a noble;
The boor he is only a boor;
His life it is loaded with trouble——
Christ save us! Was it not this blithe
Song Walter sang when he took down the scythe?

*The original of the old song of which these garbled lines misrepresent the first verse, is Scottish, and may be found in *Percy's Reliques*, vol. i. p. 59.[2] Several versions and perversions of it have appeared in Germany, where it is regarded as a lyrical curiosity. The verse corresponding with the above runs thus:

Quhy dois zour brand sae drap wi' bluid,
Edward, Edward?
Quhy dois zour brand sae drap wi' bluid,
And quhy sae sad gang zee, O?
O, I hae killed my hauke sae guid,
Mither, mither;
O, I hae killed my hauke sae guid,
And I had nae mair bot hee, O.

2. Thomas Percy (1729-1811) published *Reliques of Ancient English Poetry* in 1765.

(*A knocking is heard at the door*)
A knocking at the door!—and louder!—this
Must surely be my husband. Ha! it is.
(*She hastens to the door and opens it*)

SCENE II

Enter WALTER, *covered from head to foot with flakes of snow; in one hand he carries a staff, and in the other a lantern, in which the light is expiring.*

KATHERINE: (*while she brushes away the snow from his clothes*) Thou heedless loiterer, thou! A pretty hour to come home at!

WALTER: I am drenched through shirt and shoon. Quick, light a fire!

KATHERINE: With what?

WALTER: Ah, true! — Our wood is out — but come, ne'er fret for that! Sing! Shout!

KATHERINE: Shout?

WALTER: Ay! — all's over — our life's rudder
Is lost — the Bailie[3] gave me this, while yet in Leuk a claimant
For mercy at his feet I knelt, and begged a month for payment. (*Gives her a slip of paper*)

KATHERINE: He granted it?

WALTER: Read, woman!

KATHERINE: Man! thou mak'st me shudder. (*reads*) — WHEREAS Walter Kruth, sometime soldier in the Army of the Confederates, and afterwards keeper of that auberge or inn on the Ghemmi Alps, commonly called and known by the name of Schwarrbach, is justly and fairly indebted unto Johann Jugger of Leuk, in the Canton of Valais, farmer, in the sum of three hundred florins, good and lawful money of the Republic; as by a copy of the bill of exchange passed by the said Walter Kruth to the said Johann Jugger hereunto annexed doth appear: AND WHEREAS the said Walter Kruth, though often requested to make payment of the said sum to the said Johann Jugger, hath hitherto refused and still doth refuse to pay the same or any part thereof: WE therefore authorise and command you, the bailies of our bailiwick, or any three of you, to proceed on the morning of tomorrow, the twenty-fifth of February instant, to the said house called Schwarrbach, so that you be there by eight of the clock, and in default of payment of the said sum of three hundred florins, to

3. A dialect spelling of 'bailiff'.

enter the said house and distrain[4] the goods and chattels thereof, and also to take possession of the fields and grounds, and other the rights, members and appurtenances, of what nature or kind soever, to the said house belonging, or in anywise appertaining, for satisfaction of the said debt and such costs as may have been incurred in the recovering of the same: AND, inasmuch as it hath been notified to us that the proceeds of the sale of said house and lands will not be sufficient to cover the said debt and costs, WE further command you, or any three of you, to take into custody the person of the said Walter Kruth, before the hour of nine of the clock on the morning of the said day, and him, the said Walter Kruth, forthwith to lodge in the House of Correction at Leuk, to the end that by manual labour he may satisfy such portion of the said debt of three hundred florins, and the costs attendant thereupon, as shall remain unpaid after the said sale of the house and premises aforesaid. For all which this writ shall be your sufficient warrant and discharge. And herein fail not at your peril.

Given at our Manor-court of Leuk, this
24th day of February, 1804.
WILHELM GOTTFRIED SPERLING,
Deputy Magistrate and Sub-sheriff of Leuk,
in the Canton of Valais.

O, God! didst thou not go to Jugger, and beseech
Him to allow thee time?
WALTER: Did I not go? The leech!
Did I leave aught unsaid that might induce him
To grant the paltry respite I desired?
No block of stone is harder than his bosom!
'Away!' he cried; 'I have nought to grant;
I am tired
Of beggars.—Ere tomorrow's sun be risen
Pay me my cash, or else march into prison!'
KATHERINE: Didst thou go round to our kinsfolk — to our aunts and cousins?
WALTER: Bah, wife! they slammed their house-doors in my face by dozens.
KATHERINE: Yet these are blood-relations!
WALTER: And a faithful sample
Of such — the last to help one, and the first to
trample!
KATHERINE: The ingrates! — in our better days they feasted at our table.
WALTER: Pooh! eaten bread is soon forgotten.
KATHERINE: Then thou wert not able
To bring aught with thee?
WALTER: Nought, excepting this (*laying half a loaf on the table*)
Given me by poor Lame Klaus, who knows what
hunger is.
Tonight 'twill keep us both from starving.
KATHERINE: And
Tomorrow?
WALTER: When the serjeants come I have one
Resource: — let slaves bear on their fronts the
brand
Of infamy, and trail existence on,
Begirt with scorn and ignominy — *I*
Know how to balk Dishonour — and to die!
KATHERINE: O, misery! Hast thou tried all
means, then?
WALTER: All!
And all in vain — the once Accurst remains
Accurst for ever!
KATHERINE: Thy fierce eyes appal
My soul! Yet, hear me. On the Kander Plains
Dwells Hubert Meckler — he is rich — is old —
He owns innumerable herds — has cheese
Enough to plaster the whole Alps, and gold
Like chaff! — he lives alone, in sottish ease
And sordid luxury — the brutish wight
Is also generally drunk at night,
And sleeps with doors unbarred. Thou might'st,
unknown
To mortal, glide into the chamber where
His well-crammed coffers lie, and — Nay, forbear
Those frowns! thou surely couldst repay the loan
When God should bless us.
WALTER: *Us*, the Accursèd?
KATHERINE: This
Were not a robbery. Canst thou see the Abyss
Of Ruin yawn below thy feet, nor feel
A wish to escape it? Would I have thee *steal*?
No! thou need'st merely *borrow* — merely *take*.
Thy liberty, life, honor are at stake;
And now to rescue all, by borrowing from thy
neighbour
A handful of his golden rubbish — what
We could restore in time by dint of labour,
Can that be criminal? O, surely not!
WALTER:
Degraded woman, hide thy head, ashamed!
I — an old soldier of the Helvetic Brotherhood—
I, who have sat beside the men that framed

4. seize (personal property).

Those laws which I defended with my blood—
I, who have read the Chronicles — who know
Of Winkelried and Tell,[5] and share the zeal
Which led our lowliest peasants centuries ago
To expend their lives and labors for the
Commonweal—
I, to whom thirty years back was given by
Berne Council a certificate that I
Had single-handed borne a standard from the foe—
I steal! — Wife, wife, thou art indeed sunk low!

KATHERINE:
For God's sake be but calm! — be but less wild!

WALTER:
Thy father was a preacher. Can *his* child
Counsel to theft?

KATHERINE: Thine anguish kills me! Would
To Heaven I could but save thee with my bosom's
blood!

WALTER:
Look to thyself! — For me, my course is plain—
No Kruth was ever yet the inmate of a gaol;
And shall *I* be the first to cast a stain
Upon my father's honor? Never! Quail
Not, therefore, when I tell thee my determination:
Tomorrow, when the hirelings come to take
Me hence to the stone den of my incarceration,
I go unmurmuring along with them
To where the Lemmer Glacier fronts the
Dauben Lake,
And then — let Heaven absolve me or condemn,
For this most pardonable of self-slaughters—
As there's a Power above, I plunge into the waters!

KATHERINE: Great God!

WALTER: 'Tis better perish thus,
Hard though a death like this may be,
Than live to loathe my life, and see
My fair name stigmatised as infamous!

KATHERINE:
Oh, live, and I will beg for thee! — I'll roam
With thee through all the distant cantons round!
For thee, for thy sake, I'll renounce my home,
Where such cold, glacier-hearted men are found!
Where these bleak winds are never heard to blow
Man may be merciful. Oh, let us go!
We'll leave this cursèd mansion to itself—
Nought in't belongs to us — thou knowest we owe
All, to the last, least cup upon the shelf—
We'll beg our bread from strangers — they are
human!

WALTER:
Beg? Strangers? Hast thou lost thy senses, woman?
What! wouldst thou have me be thy murderer?—as
I should be, doubtless, if I dragged thee hence
In this remorseless Winter, when the dense
And overwhelming avalanche's mass
Sweeps down in thunder upon all beneath,
And, like my father's curse, rethreatens thee with
death.
My father's curse! thou wonnest that for me—
I have shared it eight-and-twenty years with thee—
'Tis time I were forgiven, and thou wert free!
Wert thou but disencumbered of mine aid,
Thou might'st earn better bread, and lead a
happier life—
Earn better bread, I say — for never must the wife
Of Walter Kruth make beggary her trade!

KATHERINE: And thou, then?

WALTER: I will dare to go before
My God, exonerated from the curse.

KATHERINE:
And laden with a weightier and a worse—
The guilt of self-destruction, and the sore
Disgrace thou heapest on thy father's fame—
While I, thy dear-bought burden, live but to
deplore
My lot, until the grave shall shroud my shame!

WALTER: Is self-destruction, then, dishonor?

KATHERINE: Flee
The dark temptation, Satan's deadly snare!
The blood of the Redeemer flowed for thee.
Take up thy Bible. We will join in prayer
And penitential tears. Drear though our prospect
be,
God's goodness still forbids us to despair.

WALTER:
It *is* a desperate step. I own I am half dismayed.

KATHERINE:
Prayer is thy best resource — pray fervently!

WALTER:
In eight-and-twenty years I have not prayed—
Not since my father died. Pray thou for me!

KATHERINE:
Get me the Bible, then. Oh God! the agony
Of my torn heart!

WALTER: I'll reach it down to thee. (*He takes down the Bible from a shelf. A loose leaf falls out of it*)
What's that?

5. Arnold von Winkelried (died 1386) and Wilhelm Tell (early fourteenth century) were legendary Swiss heroes, associated with resistance to tyranny. Tell refused to salute Gessler, Albert I's tyrannical bailiff and, when he was forced to shoot an apple off his son's head as a punishment, he did so.

KATHERINE: A leaf has fallen out.
WALTER: (*picking it up*) Ay, and
There's somewhat written on it. Let us see.
Just hold the light a moment in thy hand. (*Reads*)
On the 24th of February, 1776,
At the hour of Twelve at night,
Died
My father, Conrad Kruth,
Aged 74.
✠
With a large cross below the record. (*Wildly*) Is the
Cross large enough to hide the curse, think'st thou?
KATHERINE:
O woe! Death's ice-cold hand seems on me now!
WALTER:
What day o' the month is this?
KATHERINE: Alas! dismiss the
Thought from thy mind!
WALTER: Shew me the Sheriff's writ.
KATHERINE: (*giving it to him*)
Oh! kneel and pray to him who can remit
All sins!
WALTER: (*reading*) *Leuk, 24th of February*. This
Day is the anniversary of his
Death! All is clear to me.
KATHERINE: Alas! it is.
WALTER:
Thou knowest not what I allude to. Mark me now!
Today I came from Leuk. As twilight fell I clomb
that brow
Of the Alpine heights, which wheels and winds
and twines
Along, slippery and steep, in snake-shaped,
zig-zag lines.
Thou knowest I am a man unfearing human wrath,
Unfearing aught save shame. I had gone this path
A thousand times before, by night, by day;
Yet now — I wist not how it happed — the way
Seemed still extending, never-ending, and the
gaunt
Rock-wall stretched out, out, out, through
limitless wastes of distance!
What wonder if all this should somewhat damp
and daunt
My spirit? It appeared as though my entire
existence
Were grown one tortuous labyrinth of rocks,
pools, and chasms,
An Alpine Pass of agony and convulsive spasms,
From which I sought an outlet evermore in vain!
'Twas as a feverish dream, wherein thou mountest
Interminable steps on steps with pain,
And panic, and sickheartedness, and countest
More and still more and more beyond, yet liest
Moveless the while. That passed. I reached
the highest
Point of the Alps. The spectral depths below
Lay gloomy as my conscience! Thence I took
The westward path. Here, casting a chance look
Moonward, through clouds plethoric with
stacked snow,
The Lemmer Glacier suddenly rose out
Before me in relief against the skies,
With its vast hoary head and glassy eyes—
The image of my father when — about
To gasp his life's last breath from that old chair,
(*pointing to the arm-chair*) — he
Sank backwards paralysed and blue! *The
twenty-fourth of February*
Flashed on my soul. I felt that strong thought shake
Me, brain and body. Wife! I felt it take
Me by the throat, as with Death's giant pains,
Or as the headman's axe. Flames bubbled in
my veins.
I rushed in frenzy o'er the frozen Dauben Lake—
When lo! — my light was flickering down —
there flew
Full up against my lantern, one of those huge daws[6]
That nestle by the lake-side. With his claws
He clung to it, croaking, as I heard my father do,
While yet a struggler between Death and Life,
And whetted, rubbed, and rasped his yellow
beak—
So like the haft of that accursed knife — (*pointing
towards the knife that hangs against the wall*)—
Against the lantern's bars. I may have been
o'erweak,
But, wife! I trembled like an infant. Hear, nor start.
The sound was as the sharpening of a scythe!
KATHERINE:
Hold! hold! Thou slayest me! Thou mak'st me
writhe
In torment!
WALTER: (*wildly*) Then through all the caverns of
my heart
Rang and resounded the enormous cry
Of *Murderer!* — and the pullet that had made
A murderer of our son, came fluttering by
Blackly before my fancy!
KATHERINE: Kneel, and pray for aid!

6. i.e. jackdaws.

WALTER:
No! no! Heaven's gates are barred against me for my crime.
Despair has filled this dwelling since the time,
The night, the incancellable night that father
Exhausted on't the vial of his curse.

(*A knocking is heard at the door*)

KATHERINE: Somebody knocks!
WALTER: It is his ghost!
KATHERINE: Say, rather,
Some wanderer who has haply lost his way.
WALTER:
Were he the devil himself, he scarce can make us worse
Than we are now. Admit him, come what may!

(KATHERINE *opens the door*)

SCENE III

Enter KURT, *in a foreign travelling garb, somewhat fantastically put on; a hunter's wallet is slung across his shoulders; by his side hangs a short sword; a huge money-bag, from which protrude the butt-ends of a brace of pistols, is attached to a girdle that encircles his waist; in one hand he carries a lantern; in the other a long and crooked Alpine staff, shod with iron.*

KURT: (*on the threshold*) God save all here!
WALTER: Come in.
KURT: Perhaps I might—
(*Aside*) How irrepressible is my delight!
I scarcely can forbear to clasp them in my arms.
WALTER: Might *what*, friend?
KURT: Beg a lodging for the night.
WALTER:
Why, if a truss of straw have any charms
For your tired limbs, you are welcome to it freely.
KURT:
Thanks! A snug room and cheerful chat are really
Rich luxuries to the weary wanderer.
WALTER: Chat
Is a cheap article; you shan't want[7] that:
And a small room is ready to receive you;
But as to food and fire — these, I believe, you
Must do without, for wood we have none, nor more
Than this half-loaf to keep the Wolf of Famine from the door.
KURT: (*Aside*)
How my heart bleeds to find them suffering so!
Gladly would I reveal myself — but no!
I dare not till I sound them — I must first
Learn if they still abhor the wretched boy they cursed.
KATHERINE: (*in an under tone to* WALTER)
He seems a good youth.
WALTER: (*in the same tone*): *Seems?* — humph!
KATHERINE: (*to* KURT) You may thank your God
You escaped the avalanches, and your lantern blown
Out. Did you climb the Alps thus lightless and alone?
KURT:
The snow gave light enough — besides, I have often trod,
In my camp-cloak, these heights. I know my Fatherland.
WALTER:
A Swiss Confederate — so? — then welcome, brother!

(*He extends his hand to* KURT, *but again suddenly draws it back*)

KURT:
Your hand — oh! let me kiss that dearest hand!
WALTER:
Beware! forbear! There is a withering blight
On it! If you be yet uncursed, shun it beyond another!
KURT: (*Aside*)
I am tongue-tied by his wild words of despair!
WALTER:
Come, you are weary. Stretch yourself down there,
And we will freeze and hunger through the night!
KURT:
I don't see why we should — I've in my knapsack what will stand t'ye;
Roast-meats and baked, a flask of cherry-brandy,
And two old bottles of Sicilian wine.

(*Taking, as he speaks, a variety of provisions out of his wallet, and placing them on the table*)

WALTER: (*looking alternately at* KURT *and the provisions*)
You seem a jolly fellow in your line.
KURT:
Each for himself, and God for all. I eat
And drink the best I can. Come, Gammar Kitty,[8] take a seat. (*They seat themselves at the table*)

7. be lacking.

8. Gammar is a rustic variant of 'grandmother', used to mean 'old woman' (cf. the sixteenth-century play *Gammer Gurton's Needle*).

KATHERINE:
How is't you know my name?
KURT: Tut! where is't one won't meet
Kitties in scores?
WALTER: (*Aside*) An odd fish this, I guess!
KURT: (*Aside*)
How shall I e'er be able to repress
The tumult of my feelings? What a dense
Load lies upon my heart! (*Aloud to* WALTER) Come, worthy master mine —
Your health!
WALTER: Folk say it is an ugly sign
When the host banquets at his guest's expense.
KATHERINE:
The gentleman is good. Oh! could thy heart drink peace
In with each drop of this delicious wine!
WALTER:
Well, here's to a happy death! (*drinks*)
KURT: And may revengeful feeling cease
'Mong kindred henceforth! Place your hands in mine.
(*He takes* WALTER'*s hands between his own*)
May none curse more!
KATHERINE: May none curse more!
WALTER: (*slowly*) Curse . . . more!
KATHERINE:
This glorious beverage! how it can restore
The drooping soul, and where Grief raves, can lull it!
KURT:
You don't eat. Here are sausages, roast-meat,
Some good black puddings and a dainty pullet.
KATHERINE:
That last's a dish of which I dare not eat.
KURT: Nor I.
KATHERINE: Why not?
KURT: No matter. Come, fall to!
WALTER:
I'd rather, if 'twere all the same to you,
Stick to the wine — it warms my heart.
KURT: (*to* KATHERINE) Good mother,
Oblige me with a knife. I dropped my own upon the way.
WALTER: Take down our knife.
(KATHERINE *takes down the large knife from the wall, and reaches it to* KURT, *who takes it from her hand slowly and hesitatingly*)
KURT: That! Have you got no other?
KATHERINE: No other.
KURT: (*Aside*) There it stays, and evermore will stay,
The blood-gout! Would I had died within my mother's womb!
WALTER: What are you looking at?
KURT: The blood!
WALTER: The blood? From whom,
Pray, did you learn that that was blood?
KURT: Alas!
I know the hue too well!
WALTER: Come, brother, fill your glass—
Bygones are bygones to the end. To think
Too much upon the Post betrays the ass.
KURT:
I am glad to hear you tell me that. I drink
To your son's health, if — if — you have a son. (*drinks*)
KATHERINE: Oh!
KURT: Mother!
WALTER: Truce to your groans; his day is done;
'Tis long since he departed to his goal.
May *we* soon reach our own!
KATHERINE: But not the one we merit.
KURT: Then here's to a happy death, which brings peace to the accursèd spirit!
WALTER: I'll pledge you there! (*drinks*) You seem a devilish droll
Chap, with your hunting-pouch and robber-pistols —quite
Like a Wild Yager![9] Pray, why came you here by night?
KURT: I walked from Kanderstag today, and cannot borrow
More than a few short hours for sleep, for I must be in Leuk tomorrow.
WALTER: (*giving his hands to* KURT)
Then we'll set out together, countryman!
KURT: Odso![10]
Your hand is cold as Death!
WALTER: And do you fear Death?
KURT: No!
Where hot shot showered like hail I have faced him o'er and o'er.
I have been a soldier.
WALTER: Good! Here's to the brave Swiss Corps! (*drinks*)
Tell me some stirring story of your soldier-life.

9. i.e. *Jaeger*, the German word for huntsman.
10. An exclamation of surprise.

I, too, must gird my loins tomorrow for the strife!
KURT: (*hesitatingly*)
You — had a son —
WALTER: Forbear!
KURT: Who left you at
A juvenile age.
WALTER: Come, come; no more of that!
KURT: Perhaps, then *you* had better first begin
Your tale. The fact is that I know this inn
Much longer than you think. In all Leuk town
There was none like it ere its name went down.
WALTER: Damn it! who told you that?
KURT: Now all seems wretchedness;
You speak, in chilling tones, of hunger and distress.
WALTER: What's that to you? Drink! Here's to
Freedom's war (*drinks*)
KURT: How isn't you seem to have lost yourself
so far?
WALTER: Well — since you know so much, hear
more. You are
Or were a soldier, comrade — and so must
Be aware how a man will sink when once the abyss
Yawns a yard under him.
(KURT *betrays great restlessness in his motions, and changes his position repeatedly*)
But how is this?
You seem yourself a half-curst kind of dust—
Shifting your bob so,[11] every now and then,
And wriggling this and that way like a hen
On a hot griddle!
KATHERINE: (*to* KURT) Pardon him; I think
His brain is somewhat addled by the drink.
WALTER: I am grey before my time,
But still as green in soul as ere I passed my prime!
A soldier in the wars,
I have had mine own fair share of honorable scars,
And on the battle-plain
Have cloven many a morion,[12] many a scull in twain.
Thc Council Berne at large
Certified these my services in my discharge.
My father, Conrad Kruth—
God give us grace! — he was a passionate man from youth—
Then kept this inn, you mind;
But psha! 'tis nonsense talking — pitch the topic to the wind!
KURT: This glass to your father's soul!
WALTER: No, no, friend!
KATHERINE: O! despair not
Of reconciliation! — Drink!
WALTER: I cannot, wife! — I dare not!
Each poison-drop were as an arrow
Cancering my blood and bones and marrow.
Young man! I loved my father well—
I have stood my desperate ground, defiance in my heart and face,
While the red battle blazed like Hell,
But when the curse — the curse, you know, — thrills through me as a spell
I shiver!
KURT: Well — we'll change the theme.
WALTER: Not so! — yourself shall judge my case.
I'll treat you to a sketch of facts, precisely as they were and are.
When I left the ranks of War,
Fixed in mind no more to roam,
Father chose to take me home,
As his cares and guests were many.
I, a carl[13] of thirty, stout,
Bold and warm of blood as any,
Thought 'twas time to seek me out
One whose heart my heart might treasure,
As its mate in pain and pleasure.
Numbers came, but in my sight
None the peer of Katherine here;
She was fair, could read and write,
And we loved with love sincere.
In the Canton Berne her father
Died a priest* Of all they gather
Such good folk bequeath us only
Books and children when they leave us.
Could I, say, desert the lonely
Girl, mein Herr? The sin were grievous!
I had gone for good or ill
Now too far: the knot was tied.
KATHERINE: Ah! but 'gainst his father's will —
Oft I've thought on that and sighed.
WALTER: Ay — our marriage was without his
Knowledge. When he found it out his
Wrath boiled o'er, for he was not
Tame of temperament, but hot

11. i.e. moving your head abruptly.
12. A protective helmet used in the sixteenth and seventeenth centuries.

**Ein Pfarrherr*, a Protestant Rector.

13. Variant of churl: farm labourer.

As his own hot brandy-barrels.
Kate and I long bore his quarrels,
Till one night, just twenty-eight
Years ago today — the date
TWENTY-FOURTH OF FEBRUARY,
I had been to Leuk that day,
And came home halfcocked and gay,
Mischievous perhaps, and merry.
Twelve, the midnight hour, had tolled—
Yellow shone the moon as gold
All athwart the mottled gloom,
As I entered this my room.
Kate was sitting yonder, knitting.
Father then resumed his old
Trick of railing, nothing loth.
I was wicked. For a while
Patiently I took each vile
Epithet he showered on both,
Till at last he called Kate a bastard — a parson's bastard!
Then, then my religion and reason and patience were mastered—
Mein Herr! — who asperses your wife
Touches your honor, your more than life!
'Twas a javelin in my flesh. The blood all madly began
To sing and seethe and revel
In rills of flame through my veins. I clenched my fist at the man.
Kate wept. She — I — I — Damn the devil!
I know that what I did was evil—
But — but to stand and hear a coarse tongue stigmatise
Your wife, while she, beloved as helpless, flies
Into your arms for help — What ails you, friend? Your eyes
Drop tears.

KURT: Oh! Man should guard his bosom well
'Gainst thoughts whose birthplace is the gulf of Hell.

WALTER: You are a wise young man!
For me I always wanted worldly craft.
That night my rage outran
My reason: — father belled away — *I laughed.*
This made him wild — he raved — he swore—
I, boiling at my bosom's core,
Still laughed as if in quiet scorn — I eyed
Him grinningly, and, taking down my scythe—
That yonder — I began to chant a blithe
Old air — *The grass is growing — must whet my scythe for mowing;*
Daddy may bluster, clapperclaw[14] *and chide;*
I'll set his oaths to music— hiss, hiss, hiss!
And while I sharped the scythe I trolled some lay like this—
The boor he is poor; the boor is a boor—
Then let him go follow his plough;
In a flat hat and a smock frock
He has clothing enough, I trow.
Then father began to foam like the breakers upon a leeshore,
To yell, to dance like a madman, to stamp, to storm, to roar—
'Thou strumpet!' he cried to the weeping girl—
Mein Herr! I felt the chamber whirl—
I — flesh and blood couldn't stand it longer—
The devil, the Prince of Devils, is stronger
Than I — I hurled my knife — ay, that in your hand — the knife
I had used in whetting the scythe — I was drunk!— I hurled it full
At his face — my father's face! — it might have laid open his scull—
But — glory to God! — it missed him — missed him! Didn't it, wife?

KATHERINE: It did.

WALTER: He fell back in his chair, and his visage
grew lilac and blue
And stony. — 'Accursed,' he exclaimed, still foaming — 'Accursed be you,
And accursed be your wife and your offspring!' Kate then was three months gone
In her first and perilous pregnancy. Well — he hadn't yet done.
He sat up stiff in his chair. His eyes were glazed in their last eclipse,
And the curdled froth sat stagnant upon his collapsèd lips.
'Accursed,' he half-croaked, half-howled, 'Accursed be you and your brood!
On you and on them through life be the guilt of your father's blood!
May you yet be the murderer's murderer, as you are mine this night!'
He said no more. He dropped back. A fresh paralytic shaft had shot
Like lightning through his veins. All Hell's roaring surges of fire

14. To claw with the open hand and nails; hence, figuratively, to revile, to drub (someone).

Billowed up in my breast and brain. He died
 upon the spot.
 KATHERINE: (*to* KURT)
What ails you? You grow pale.
 KURT: O, nothing; I am quite
Well. 'Tis perhaps the wine. Drink, neighbour!—
 in a higher
World Mercy has annulled that curse!
 KATHERINE: There, Walter! — hearest thou?
 WALTER: (*to* KURT)
A man learns much from such as you — somehow
I, too, occasionally think the same.
Father's own youth was not exempt from blame.
He told us once in's winecups that he had
Dragged *his own* father — who, it seems, was mad
As he himself — by the grey locks about
The room and dashed him on the floor. Now *I*
But flung a knife at *mine*. He died, no doubt,
But he was old — 'twas time for him to die.
I did not kill him — did I? People say
That if you kill your father the same hand
With which you killed him grows up from the
 clay
Above his grave. Now I have often scanned
The spot all round, and yet saw nothing save
Green grass, which grows, you know, on every
 grave
 KURT: Of course — of course. You haven't told
me, though,
How the sad change in your affairs took place.
 WALTER:
'Twas rather strange — but from that night of woe
And frenzy I had neither luck nor grace.
We set out, Kate and I, resolved on helping
 one another,
But still it seemed as if at each hand's turn
A devil stepped between us. She became a mother
In three months more, for which we had cause
 to mourn
Her first child bore the accursèd mark of Cain—[15]
A blood-red scythe was printed on his arm.
The image had been floating in her brain
During her pregnancy. But of the harm
And ill and misery wrought us by that boy
I had best say nothing now. I pardon him.
 KURT: (*eagerly*) You do?
 WALTER: Yes. God be praised, he is dead; and
that's one source of joy.

15. Genesis 4.15.

Well — in five years we had a daughter too.
The girl was like an angel.
 (KURT *immediately rises from his chair*)
 WALTER: What d'ye want?
 KURT: Nothing. It is a way I have. I can't
Rest for a minute in one spot.
 (*He walks to and fro*)
 WALTER: So like our Kurt! The devil
Drove him for ever up and down. In most
Respects the lad was sharp above the level
Of boys in general — but seemed tempest-tossed
By a dark spirit within. Was that the curse?
 KURT: How should I know? You are getting
worse and worse.
 WALTER: Enough. One day — the fatal day
Of *February twenty-four*,
The children were engaged at play
Together near the door.
The damnèd knife lay on the floor.
The boy was seven years old, the girl but two—
Kate had just killed a pullet — eh, Kate?
 KATHERINE: Oh, 'tis true!
I never think on that without a chilly trembling;
It vexed me by its *cluck, cluck, cluck*, — the note
Struck my distempered fancy as resembling
Old Kruth's croak when the rattles took his throat.
 WALTER: The boy had seen my wife
Sticking the pullet. 'Come,' he said — and took
His sister's arm — 'we'll play at Kitchen: I will be
 the cook
And you the pullet. Stand!' I saw him seize the
 knife.
I bounded forward. All too late. The child
Lay weltering in her blood — her throat one
 gaping gash.
You weep! You are good. *I* wept not — I was
 wild!
 KURT: And thereupon you — cursed him?
 WALTER: It was rash—
But he was but a child and therefore could not be
Amenable to justice then; and as
I did not wish him to escape scot-free
I cursed him!
 KURT: But your better judgment has
Revoked the curse?
 WALTER: Long since. The grave, you know,
Must bound all mortal maledictions.
 KURT: (*aside*) Oh,
Father! (*Aloud*) But if he were alive, and should
Return repentent to his parents, would
You not receive him and embrace him?

WALTER: No!
I NEVER could behold him!
KURT: (*aside*) Woe! O, Woe!
(*Aloud*) And what became of him?
KATHERINE: His father in his first
Frenzy had nearly murdered him. To guard against the worst
I sent him to an uncle resident at Thun—
A learned man — who wrote me thus: 'Your son
Is talented and spirited and quick
To learn — but there's a something adverse in his star.
He chases but the Phantomy and Far—
Is hurried and perturbed — half lunatic
And quite intractable — and when I have gone
So far as to admonish him, though in a quiet way,
He weeps and tells me that the scythe upon
His arm prevents his resting night or day.'
So my good uncle wrote. To him the history
Of his mark — as to all — remained a mystery.
KURT:
You wept much when your son absconded?
KATHERINE: Oh!
WALTER: (*in a low tone to* KATHERINE)
Katherine, beware! This Yager seems to know
All that has happened. Is he a magician?
I fear I have been much freer than I ought.
KATHERINE: But how d'ye know he absconded?
KURT: Why, — I — thought —
I guessed he might have tired of his condition.
WALTER: Guessed?
KATHERINE: He grew up, we heard, a froward[16] lad:
He had run away from school — my uncle had
Bound him apprentice to an artist, but
He had run away from him, too, o'er and o'er;
So uncle, finding he could do no more
And thinking he could do no less, too, shut—
Him up within the Work-house.* Here he didn't tarry,
However, long, before he escaped — and 'twas, as we were told,
Precisely on the fatal day, THE TWENTY-FOURTH OF FEBRUARY,
He being barely then fourteen years old,
That he enlisted as a soldier in
The hosts of Revolutionary France.
This we discovered afterwards by chance,
A letter having reached my uncle which
Mentioned the fact.
KURT: And neither kith nor kin
Have learned about him since?
KATHERINE: Who — save a few odd rich—
Were left survivors of the Revolution?
WALTER: (*to* KURT)
You are the devil's pick-thought! I begin
To think you are hoaxing us. What is't you mean
By pumping people so? Death and confusion!
I tell you he is dead.
KURT: But how you have been
Reduced to this sad state of destitution
You have *not* told me.
WALTER: Friend! your every look and query
And your odd pacings to and fro are very
Peculiar! I'm not fond of spinning yarns.
Distempers killed my cattle — fire consumed my barns—
And avalanches crushed my fields. No toil
Availed me. As you came from Kanderstag
You marked a barren tract of blasted soil
Lying half-buried underneath snow-crag
And Alpine-granite. Twelve years back it was
The terrible invader swept in thunder
Down from the Rinderhorn, o'erwhelming as
It rolled man, beast, crops, meadows, vineyards. Under
Those mighty frozen masses which you passed
Lay once luxuriant orchards and rich pasture-ground.
All were left desolate for miles around.
And now the unhappy failure of our last
Year's harvest — this has been the finishing stroke.
We are now in debt — in wretchedness — the yoke
Of beggary presses on us. One by one
Loured[17] our disasters, and withal 'twas very
Remarkable that each came always on
The ominous TWENTY-FOURTH OF FEBRUARY.
KURT: (*reseating himself*)
Can I do nought to ameliorate your lot?
WALTER:
Why, between you and me, then, if you have got
Any loose cash to lend—
KURT: Loose cash to lend?
Ay! that I have — enough! — and gladly would

*House of Correction, or Penitentiary.

16. contrary, obstinate.

17. lurked.

Do more than lend it you. But patience! — God is good.
Bear with your ills tonight — tomorrow He will end
Them all!

WALTER: Tomorrow? God will, eh? Or p'rhaps you mean the devil?

KATHERINE:
O, self-tormentor!

WALTER: Friend! you are many cuts above my level.
You seem a something 'twixt a conjuror and a priest—
Gentry with whom, d'ye know, I don't much care to chaffer.*[18]

KURT: Ah, Father Walter!

WALTER: That's my name — Well, well — your wine's the thing, at least (*drinks*)
But why d'ye chamber crags by night?

KURT: Ah, Gaffer![19]
My life's page, like your own, is overdarked and sad.

WALTER: Hail fellow, then, well met! You are just *my* man, egad!

KURT: I, also, like the son you spoke of, had
Once the misfortune to commit — a murther!

WALTER: Oho! How happened that?

KURT: Enquire no further.
The history would but make my scarred wounds bleed
Afresh. Enough, that for the fatal deed
I was compelled to fly from home. It happed in
The town of Berne that a compatriot took
A fancy to me, purely from my look,
And hired me as his valet. He was Captain
In the Swiss Guards, those heroes whom the *Sans Culottes* of Paris tore from limb to limb.[20]
Difficult was it, doubtlessly, for him
To leave his country — but poor Louis' wrongs
Spake trumpetmouthed — he had no resource
Besides. He went. I also went, of course.

WALTER: Wild work in Paris then?

KURT: Fancy you see by some concussion
The whole tremendous range of the Alpine Glaciers
Wrenched from their beds — fancy you see them rush on,
Gigantical and crashing, through the embrasures
Of the cleft mountains, down the vales — while groupes
Below, beholding the Destroyers advance,
Sing, clap their hands, laugh, reel about, and dance,
The savage portion uttering yells and whoops
Of welcome — fancy this, and then you gaze
On a dim sketch of Paris in those monstrous days.

WALTER: You saw our comrades murdered? — saw them as they fell
Butchered within the Tuileries?[21]

KURT: I saw
The sweltering night descend, moonless and dun as Hell,
As though revolted Nature willed to draw
A pall of blackness over that infernal
Harvest of carnage. But let *me* — accurst myself— refrain
From picturing scenes enough to bring the eternal
Wrath of Heaven's God on France.

WALTER: Yet pray explain—

KURT: When we thus saw them perish — saw them piked and shot,
Far from their own loved hearths and ancient land,
In contest for a king whose lieges they were not,
A king to whom Affection's, Honor's band
But knitted them — a king who, near the spot
That saw him sceptred, suffered at the hand
Of his own children death—

WALTER: Ay, ay — such things
Have come to pass, through Satan's help, where parents were *not* kings.

KURT: My master then, whom I was fortunate
Enough to save through a portico, perceiving
He could no longer tamely tolerate
The rabble's ruffianism, resolved on leaving
The country. Suffering and our common land
Cemented us. How far o'er Earth and Ocean
We roamed, I recked not — even to Death's dark strand
Would I have followed him with fond devotion.
We sailed for St. Domingo[22] his (my master's)

*This tragedy, it may be not amiss to observe, was written before the author became a Roman Catholic priest.

18. bargain, bandy words.
19. A variant of godfather; hence 'old man'.
20. Sans culottes (French) literally means 'without knee breeches', i.e. the ragged classes who were thought of as a major disruptive force during the French Revolution of 1789.
21. A royal residence in Paris, so named from the tile-yards on the site
22. Santo Domingo, capital of Hispaniola (now the Dominican Republic), the oldest surviving city founded by Europeans in the western hemisphere.

Exchequer furnishing the charges, and
After the usual maritime disasters
Landed, not caring much for sea or land.

WALTER:
You've been to the New World! You're a great traveller, then!

KATHERINE:
Ah! there you found the blest and happy men!

KURT:
Yes, among those untainted *here*, and *there*;
(*pointing to his heart and his head*)
The rest were like the folk we meet elsewhere.
My patron here became a planter. Daily
He seemed to like me better. Time passed gaily,
And Europe was forgotten. Now and then
He joked and chatted with me. Best of men!
He had still perhaps been living but for me.
A curse is like a pestilence — 'tis catching.
I fell ill of the Yellow Fever. He
Nursed me, until, exhausted by his watching,
He imbibed the poison. He expired at last.

WALTER: Did he turn yellow?

KURT: Yes.

WALTER: A man at whom *I* cast
A knife grew blue. 'Tis evident that Death is
Himself a dyer now-a-days.

KURT: Alas!
Why was not I too doomed to fall beneath his
(Death's) shaft? Red Murder, like a wall of brass,
Had severed me from Mankind long before.—
Why was I spared to — But of this no more.
I was now rich — my master had bequeathed
All his plantations, goods and gold to me—
Yet was I poor — as poor a wretch as breathed!
Alas! when Conscience burns in vain would we
By all Earth's wealth and luxuries try to win us
One half-hour's respite from the Hell within us!

WALTER: (*to* KATHERINE)
Ha! hear'st thou that! Now must I not —
(KATHERINE *goes into the inner room to prepare the bed for* KURT)

KURT: But Angel Hope for ever hovers
O'er even the dreariest dwelling of Despair;
And as the hen outspreads her wings and covers
Her clutch when wheels the vulture in the air,
So Mercy lifts her shield o'er Man, and the sharp shafts of Vengeance
Whirr ever towards, but strike him not, from Hell's unresting engines.
And Hope and Mercy whispered me that in my native clime
I should not pray to Heaven in vain to assoil me of my crime.
The waterfalls, the woods, the mountains rang
With the one note all day and night — 'Come home!'
The Glaciers, as if conscious of each pang
I suffered, cried — 'We melt — Come home! Come home!'
The little Alpine bells tinklingly sang—
'Rest for the wanderer and a happy home!'
Methought the very planets as they rolled
Bade me exchange the New World for the Old.
So, home I have come at last, laden with gold,
After an absence of near twenty years,
To glad my parents' hearts. My biggest money-bag
Rests with my mule to night at Kanderstag—
Tomorrow all will reach me. Then will I with tears
Cast myself on my father's — on my mother's breast;
Then shall the wanderer find the promised rest,
And the once Curst will prove the trebly Blest.
(KATHERINE *again enters*)

WALTER: (*rising up*) Where do your parents live?

KURT: They live — about — three miles
From this.

WALTER: Indeed? Three miles from this? that's queer!
I thought we had nought for nine miles round, but piles
Of naked rocks. No matter — one thing's clear—
You're a sharp lad; you have conned your parts of speech;
Have mixed in life, and have your tale to tell;
Have heard the Glaciers sing and planets preach,
And know which way the cat jumps pretty well.

KATHERINE: (*to* KURT) Did you hear any thing about our son
In Paris?

KURT: Your son Kurt?

WALTER: (*aside*) He knows his name!*

KATHERINE: Yes. We had news that he was killed in one
Of those fierce popular outbursts.

KURT: (*aside*) I must frame
A tale to try them. (*Aloud*) 'Twas too true. I saw him vainly strive
Against the butchers. I beheld him fall—
His blood gushed out upon my clothes.

* Werner appears to forget that Walter had already mentioned the name of his son.

KATHERINE: O! were he but alive,
How freely would I now forgive him all!
KURT: (*stretching out his arms, as though he would embrace his mother*) Oh!
WALTER: Drop those clap-trap tricks. We are not to be
Played on like children. Go to bed. Good night!
Your room is ready yonder, as you see.
KATHERINE:
You'll find I have made your little straw-bed right.
KURT: Will you awaken me by eight o'clock?
WALTER:
If *I* should not, the Sheriff's men will. They'll
Be here betimes to hale[23] me off to gaol.
KURT: Just God!
WALTER: Does that, then, give you such a shock?
KURT: When will they come?
WALTER: At eight, or thereabouts.
KURT: Then call me up at seven.
WALTER: At any hour
You please. You seem to fight shy of the scouts
Of Justice. Were you ever in their power?
KURT: (*aside*)
Oh, my fond heart! how long have I repressed
Thy struggling throbs!
WALTER: Come — go to bed — 'tis time.
KURT: Good night!
WALTER: Good night!
KURT: All — all — both curse and crime—
Will soon be cancelled!
KATHERINE: Take a good night's rest.
(*She puts a light in the lantern, and gives it to him*)
WALTER: And cross yourself against the Evil One.
(KURT *retires*)
KATHERINE: He is gone.
WALTER: Kate, take these flasks and plates away;
Our last, our hangman's midnight meal* is done—
Tomorrow ends our agonies for aye.
(*He seats himself in the arm-chair*)
KATHERINE: (*as she hangs the large knife against the wall*)
Well, that's a strange young man, I can't but say.
KURT: (*in soliloquy in his room*)
Here, where I first beheld the light, where first mine infant words were spoken,
Here, in the house, below the roof, with her, the cherished one, who gave
Me this unblest and vagrant life — here let my pilgrim's staff be broken—
And here, too, let the vengeful curse be buried in Forgiveness' grave!
(KATHERINE *applies her ear and eye alternately to an aperture in the partition*)
WALTER:
Listening? For shame, Kate! Listeners never hear
Good of themselves.
KATHERINE: He unbinds his girdle. Dear!
But that bag round his waist is really vast!
WALTER:
His head don't ache, I trow, from whom our guest untied it last.
KATHERINE: What meanest thou?
WALTER: Don't mind me. Go to bed.
KURT: (*in soliloquy*)
In this small stilly room, times without number,
The Alpine horn has lulled me into slumber.
O! that my golden dreams had never fled!
KATHERINE:
He is speaking to himself, about his gold!
WALTER: Wilt thou
Not go to bed?
KATHERINE: Be calm — I am going now.
Art not thou coming too?
WALTER: Not yet.
KATHERINE: He spoke so much about our son!
WALTER: (*passionately*)
'Our son,' 'our son,' for ever. Thunderbolts! have done,
Or I'll run off this night!
KATHERINE: O, Walter — God of Heaven!
If this should be *himself* — he whom for years
We have fancied dead. Oh, long, long since he was forgiven
By me — do thou forgive a mother's tears!
WALTER:
Now, by my troth, wife, this is past endurance!
Thou mockest, bravest me! I say he *is* dead.
Didst thou not long ago receive assurance,
That of the brave Swiss corps in which he enlisted,
Not one survived? That on that bloody night
Whereof our lodger lied, all, *all*, to a man,
Were mercilessly massacred? And can,
Or will, think'st thou, the tomb forego its right?
Shall our long-buried son forsake his grave?
As well might'st thou expect my father would walk in

* *Henkersmahl*, the phrase in the original, means the supper which in some parts of Germany is given to a condemned criminal the night before his execution, and at which he is privileged to eat and drink *ad libitum*.

23. haul, drag.

Even now — again begin to rage and rave—
And again curse us. No! Death is the penalty of Sin.
The grave's precipitous bridge-path once gone o'er,
The pilgrim's foot recrosses it no more.

KURT: (*in soliloquy*)
What was't withheld me from at once revealing
Myself? We spoke together, I and they,
So cordially! I could have wept away
My life upon their bosoms then! But still some hell-engendered feeling
O'ermastered me, oppressed my spirit, froze
The fountains of affection as they rose,
And bound me in chains of trembling to the close.

KATHERINE: (*who has seated herself on the straw-bed in the back-ground*)
Who can he be, our guest?

WALTER: Whoe'er he be, he is
No better than he should be, trust me.

KATHERINE: He
Said that his parents lived a league from this.

WALTER:
Humbug — all humbug! Save the owls and we,
None dwell upon these heights.

KATHERINE: He seems so kind—
So gentle.

WALTER: Gentle? Pr'ythee, wert thou blind?
Didst thou not mark his eye-balls' lurid glow
As he glared on us, pacing to and fro?
I have been a soldier, wife! I know these kind of men—
None braver — fronting Death even in his deadliest den;
But the eye, wife! — the flashing eye — the gaze
That cannot fix — the wandering glance — betrays
The Devil! These be demoniacs — hell-possessed—
For whom Earth, save the grave, harbours no place of rest.

KATHERINE:
He has left his wine there still. Drink yet one cup— thou'lt feel
The better for the draught.

WALTER: Then here I drink to his weal. (*drinks*)

KATHERINE:
And God assoil his soul, and grant it rest and light!
(*She lies down, and falls asleep*)

WALTER: (*filling out another glass*)
Fain would I say Amen! but since the accursèd night,
I cannot pray forgiveness. Would to Heaven I might!

KURT: (*in soliloquy*)
O, God of mercy! quell the gloomy
And ghastly thoughts that shake me here.
Let not my sister's blood pursue me,
Nor let me sink through groundless fear!
Be she mine intercessor, kneeling
Before thy Throne of Grace above,
And let the frozen founts of Feeling
Be melted by the breath of Love!
Yes! thanks, Almighty God, to thee!
My tears even now are flowing free.

WALTER: (*replenishing his cup*)
'Tis nearly twelve. Ere twelve tomorrow
I shall have shaken off this load of sorrow,
For then — Hark! how the screech-owls rave!
Methinks they scream. 'Down wretch, into thy watery grave!'
And must it be so? Is there nought can save?

KATHERINE: (*groaning in her sleep*) Oh!

WALTER: She is suffering. 'Tis a den of woe,
This old curse-rotted house, where each accursed
Sire curses his recursing son, and no
Feelings but those of pain and gloom are nursed.
The Yager there may sleep — he has his gold—
Well! if he has his gold, I have his wine — (*drinks*)
I have the Yager's wine — and wine, I opine,
Will keep me out of water; so, I hold,
Will gold; — I'll have his gold! — eh? — how?— avaunt, vile Enemy!
What thrice-damn'd devil bred that thought in me?

KATHERINE: (*singing in her sleep*)
O, why is thy sword so red, so red,
Edward, Edward?

WALTER: Poor creature! she is singing in her sleep.

KATHERINE: (*singing*)
Because I have slain my falcon dead.

WALTER: She seems to breathe uneasily and deep.
Some dream disturbs her. I must rouse her.
(*He approaches the bed and stirs her*)
Kate!

KATHERINE: (*starting up*) Wha — what?

WALTER: What ails thee?

KATHERINE: Oh! there's such a weight
On my poor heart!

WALTER: Thou sangest in thy sleep.

KATHERINE:
Sang in my sleep?

WALTER: Of slaying a falcon dead!

KATHERINE: Ah, yes! I don't know why that song should keep
Running perpetually in my head.

WALTER: Is that the song that ends with some such trash
As this—

Because I have slain my father dead,
Therefore my sword is so red, so red,
And on you be the guilt of it, mother.

KATHERINE: The same.

WALTER: What maudlin balderdash!

KATHERINE: Art coming soon to bed? I feel so chill!

WALTER: By' nd by.

KATHERINE: Then I'll get up. I can't lie still.
O God! what weary burdens are our sins!

(*She rises weeping from her straw bed*)

WALTER: Souls, Kate, *will* gamble, and the devil wins.

KURT: (*in prayer*)

Overcome with anguish,
To thee I cry!
Here I pine and languish,
But thou art nigh,
O! beyond this Vale of Dole,
Shew me where Life's waters roll—
Raise the eyes of my sick soul
To thee on high!

WALTER: That song of the Red Sword is so — so silly!
But, wife! I am burning inly, yet I am chilly—

KATHERINE: And so am I.

WALTER: I am taken with a dizziness.
That — robber! — has he drugged us, thinkest thou?
If I supposed so, I'd soon do his business.
I have left some stout trunks headless before now.
I see thee shudder — are thy thoughts upon
The curse?

(*His eye wanders wildly around the room, and at length rests upon the clock*)

Ha! How the minute-hand runs on!
I am frozen. Light a fire! —

KATHERINE: Where is the wood?

WALTER: Take down that hated scythe. This many a year it
Has hung there rusting, doing us no good.

KATHERINE: I ever tremble when I go too near it.

(*She takes down the scythe, chops the handle in pieces, and kindles a fire*)

KURT: (*in soliloquy*)

I am absolved. Again my breast grows cheery.
'Peace!' like an Alpine bell, tones from above.
Descend, oh, soothing Sleep, and fold a weary
Wanderer of Earth in thine embrace of love!
How oft I have hung my horn on this dear wall!
Here still I see the nail that bore it. All
My early boyhood's treasured recollections
Crowd on my mind. Again my sister's hand
Wreathes garlands for me. Oh, my fatherland!
With thee are twined my holiest affections.

(*He hangs his clothes, as he undresses, on a large nail protruding from the partition wall. Shortly afterwards the nail gives way, and the clothes fall on the floor*)

WALTER: What was't that fell?

KATHERINE: I know not.

WALTER: Some strange fear
Creeps through my blood. Reach me the Bible here.

(KATHERINE *brings him the Bible, and then takes her place again by the fire*)

KURT: (*in soliloquy*) The nail has given way. No matter: I
Can soon refasten it; at least I'll try.

WALTER: (*reading in the Bible*)
*Des Caters Sergen baut den Kindern Hæuser, aber der Mutter fluch reisit sie wieder nieder.**[24]
The *father's* blessing? No! — not so: — the *father*
Has curses only, and *his* curse o'erthrows
The house that through the *mother's* blessing rose.
That is the eligible reading rather.

(KURT, *in endeavouring to fix the nail in the wall, displaces the knife hanging on the other side, which falls at* KATHERINE'*s feet*)

KATHERINE: (*starting up*) Oh!

WALTER: (*regarding her with a wild and absent look*) Where? What?

KATHERINE: 'Twas the knife — it fell, I know not how.

WALTER: Is not our guest a murderer?

KATHERINE: Heavens! what meanest thou?

KURT: (*in soliloquy*)
Thank God! I have gained the goal at last:
Tomorrow morn will see
My mule brought here triumphantly;
And ere the noon be past
I well may hope
My gold will ope

*The passage, I believe, is *Ecclesiasticus* iii. 11.

24. *Ecclesiasticus*, III. 11 reads: 'For the glory of a man is from the honou of his father; and a mother in dishonour is a reproach to the children.

The gates of Peace and Paradise for me.
(He takes the money-bag from the table)
Come then, beloved gold,
I crossed the ocean by thine aid:
By thee are honest hearts and bold
Exertions late or soon repaid.
I have brought thee from the New World to the Old,
To place thee in my parents' hand.
Let God direct the rest
As unto Him seems best.
(He places the bag under the head of the straw mattress)
All hail, once more, my fatherland!
(He stretches himself in bed and falls asleep. The light in the lantern gradually expires)

WALTER:
He called himself a murderer in my recollection—
He is an outlaw therefore — any man
May strip and plunder him that will or can.
The law affords him not the least protection.

KATHERINE: For God's sake!—

WALTER: I might slay him, wer't my whim;
No power could punish me for killing him.

KATHERINE: O, for the love of Christ!

WALTER: Be not alarmed:
I have no such bloody thoughts: he shan't be harmed;
Only, considering our position,
And knowing well this outlawed stranger
To be a robber, and — perhaps — magician,
At all events a carl that threatens danger
To the Confederacy, I would fain
Go shares with him in what he has.

KATHERINE: O, man, refrain
From heaping sin on sin!

WALTER: And plunge into the tide
Tomorrow, a crime-laden suicide?
So be it then! — although to fleece a thief
To save one's life were anything but guilt—
But be it so! — the pain of death is brief.

KATHERINE: *(distractedly)* God! — gracious God!——

WALTER: Shall I?

KATHERINE: Do — what — thou — wilt.

WALTER: Then light me!

KATHERINE: Death and Hell!
(She takes the lamp and precedes him)

WALTER: The midnight falls — it is
Fit hour for darker deeds — and I'll accomplish this,
Even though my father fronted me anew
To blast me with his looks of livid blue.
Thou tremblest, wife?

KATHERINE: With cold!

WALTER: *(seeing the knife at his feet)* Ah! there thou art!
Thou'lt come with me! *(Takes it up)*

KATHERINE: Thou — would'st not — shed his blood?

WALTER: *(as he enters the inner room)*
No, foolish woman, no! — no need to start.
But caution in a case like this is good.
There are a thousand uses for a knife;
It is so — sharp an instrument, and — Wife!
I scent a corpse — there is a charnel-smell
Here! ——

KATHERINE: O, come back!

WALTER: He is sleeping. Where, I wonder,
Can he have put his gold? — Ah! ah! I see it under
The bolster. Come have at it!

KATHERINE: Never!

WALTER: O, 'tis well!
I see thou hast no fancy for the job.
But — *'tis* a dirty business — thus to rob
A stranger. We'll abandon it. *(He puts the knife up in his bosom)*

KATHERINE: O, some
Angel inspires thee!

WALTER: Yes — if death must come,
Let us die guiltless. Ha! but *are* we guiltless, then?
(The clock strikes twelve. WALTER *counts the strokes)*
One, Two, Three, Four, Five, Six, Seven, Eight, Nine, Ten,
Eleven, Twelve. Old man! thou need'st not storm again.

KATHERINE: *(endeavouring to draw him towards the door)* O, come!
*(*WALTER *opens the door softly, and re-enters the outer-room, but staggers back again in a moment, aghast and quivering)*

WALTER: *(between his teeth)* Brr!

KATHERINE: God! what ails thee?

WALTER: I — I — dare not — enter.

KATHERINE: Why?

WALTER: *He* sits there — blue, stiff — the old tormentor—
Dids't thou not mark how horribly he eyed me?

KATHERINE: *(looking in)* Thou dreamest?

WALTER: *(drawing* KATHERINE *nearer to him)*
Stay — stay here — stay close beside me.

There! — Pray! — help *me* to pray!
(*He lifts up his hands in a supplicatory attitude*)
KATHERINE: O, could I win thee grace by prayer!
WALTER:
Our father, who . . . hast cursed me! — Ha! see there!
See how the sleeper laughs derisively
At me! He laughs that I am curst, and he
Is not!
KATHERINE: (*still drawing him towards the door*)
O, come, lest Satan conquer thee!
WALTER:
Our father . . . . Hark! I hear his gold — it cries aloud to me,
Come who come will. How it disturbs the lonely
Midnight! Thou hearest it?
KATHERINE: I hear the screech-owls only.
WALTER:
No! no! 'tis his gold! — and his gold, his gold will free me for ever,
Will free me from this hell-vulture that gnaws day and night my liver.
See his audacious red cheeks! — how they laugh!— while I stand here, and shiver.
He, forsooth, shall exult in his gold, the sneaking deceiver!
He shall be rich and uncurst, and a stranger to famine and fever,
While I, after years of toil and bitter heart-breaking endeavour,
Find myself driven to the grave for a shelter. Yet am I less clever?
Am not I also a man, and as stalwart in doublet and beaver?
Shall he, the poltroon, by night steal forth as a robber and reaver,
While I am to plunge for a bed in the depths of the rushing river,
Only because I am poor, and the shafts of Misfortune's quiver
Have been exhausted on me? Shall I brook such injustice? Never!
No! I will rescue myself, though the deed should eternally sever
My soul from its last hope of Heaven! So, sorcerer, stand and deliver!
(*He stoops down and endeavours to detach the bag of gold from its position under the mattress.* KURT *is disturbed by the effort and awakes*)
KURT: (*half unconsciously*)
Ha! — robbers! — murderers!——

WALTER: Murderer in thy teeth! (*He takes the knife from his bosom, and stabs* KURT *twice*)
KURT: (*faintly*)
By — *your* — hand, then, — my father — I — meet Death!
(WALTER *staggers back, horror stricken*)
KATHERINE: (*wildly*) My son! — my son! ——
KURT: I — am — that — ill-starred — youth.
Read — this — and — see.
(*He half raises himself up with a last effort, and takes from beneath the pillow a paper which he hands to* WALTER. WALTER *hurries to the camp*)[25]
WALTER: (*reading*)
THE PASSPORT OF KURT KRUTH OF SCHWARRBACH.
(*The paper drops from his hands*)
O, Accurst! what hast thou done?
KATHERINE: (*supporting* KURT *in her arms*)
I see the scythe on's arm. My son! — my son!
Destroy me, too, inhuman murderer, as
Thou hast destroyed thy child!
KURT: (*to* WALTER *and* KATHERINE)
The — father* — has
Forgiven — you — both. The — curse — is cancelled. Live!
WALTER: (*kneeling down before* KURT)
And thou — dost thou forgive?
KURT: I do.
WALTER: And God — doth *He* forgive?
KURT: (*after a pause*) May He! (*He dies*)
KATHERINE: He dies!
WALTER: (*rising up*)
In Heaven's name, then, to appease
God's wrath as best I may, and drain the cup
Of Punishment and Penance to the lees,
Tomorrow I surrender myself up
To Justice. When the axe hath done its task,
'Twill be for God to weigh and judge. To His
Eye the bared heart lies naked without mask.
This is indeed a day of days — it is
An awful FEBRUARY TWENTY-FOUR.
Enough — God's mercy is for evermore.
(*The curtain falls*)

**Der Vater*, that is, *Walter's* father. The definite article is frequently used in German poetry instead of the possessive pronoun, especially where the employing of the latter would interfere with the metre. Thus Gellert writes, *Ein kranker Vater rief den Sohn* — a sick father called *the* son. In the present instance the transference of this idiom into English becomes unavoidable; for as Conrad was not the father of Katherine, to whom, as much as to Walter, Kurt speaks, the pronoun would be inappropriate and absurd.

25. i.e. camp bed.

SHERIDAN LE FANU

(1814-73)

STRANGE EVENT IN THE LIFE OF SCHALKEN THE PAINTER (1839)

[Sheridan Le Fanu, though not among the founders of *The Dublin University Magazine*, was foremost among its contributors of fiction, commencing in January 1838 with the first of the 'Purcell Papers'. Ten of the twelve instalments exploit an eighteenth-century Irish setting, the exceptions being a selection of ballads and the story that follows (it being set exclusively on the Continent). Hand in hand with this feature is the extreme representation of the supernatural — it will be a constant correlation in Le Fanu's later fiction that continental Europe stands for explicit evil and ideological betrayal.

As a narrative persona, Father Purcell is a highly ironic figure in Le Fanu's stories. Throughout the 1830s, the Irish countryside was deeply disturbed by a campaign withholding tithe payments that the established church clerics levied on the (largely) catholic peasantry. The Le Fanu family endured a kind of besiegement in a County Limerick glebe house (the author's father was dean of Emly), while their income and morale were severely depleted. Thus, Le Fanu's use of a catholic priest as narrator ironically links the historical setting of the stories (the time of penal repression of catholicism) and the time of their composition when the protestant clergy were under considerable pressure from a resurgent catholic majority. This correlation of past and present had an additional point for Le Fanu, whose ancestors had reached Ireland from France at the time of the Williamite wars. The close correlation of a continental setting and evil incarnate suggests a deeply rooted sense of guilt on Le Fanu's part concerning his heritage.

The two painters whom Le Fanu deals with in the story, Gottfried Schalken and Gerard Dou, were important contributors to the 'genre' school of Dutch art in the seventeenth century. Schalken was in fact a pupil of Dou's, but there is no reason to believe that any other details of the story are based on historical fact. The picture described does not resemble any known canvas of Schalken's, although the description of its style and composition fits the painter's usual practice. Two aspects of Le Fanu's particular choice of artist should be noted: first, Schalken's Dutch background specifies the origin (with William, prince of Orange) of the Irish eighteenth century in which the Le Fanus had prospered; second, as a *genre* painter, Schalken depicted scenes from middle-class life and had a fondness for domestic incidents of minor wickedness — flirtation, petty theft, fornication — or moments of pathetic distress. While the 'Purcell Papers' generally present a vaguely aristocratic cast of Jacobite characters, it in this isolated story of a Dutch middle-class painter that Le Fanu comes closest, though obliquely, to his own social being.]

BEING A SEVENTH EXTRACT FROM THE LEGACY OF THE LATE FRANCIS PURCELL, P.P.[1] OF DRUMCOOLAGH

You will, no doubt, be surprised, my dear friend, at the subject of the following narrative. What had I to do with Schalken, or Schalken with me?[2] He had returned to his native land, and was probably dead and buried before I was born; I never visited Holland nor spoke with a native of that country. So much I believe you already know. I must, then, give you my authority, and state to you frankly the ground upon which rests the credibility of the strange story which I am about to lay before you. I was acquainted, in my early days, with a Captain Vandael, whose father had served King William in the Low Countries, and also in my own unhappy land during the Irish campaigns.[3] I know not how it happened that I liked this man's society spite of [4]his politics and religion: but so it was; and it was by means of the free intercourse to which our intimacy gave rise that I became possessed of the curious tale which you are about to hear. I had often been struck, while visiting Vandael, by a remarkable picture, in which, though no *connoisseur* myself, I could not fail to discern some very strong peculiarities, particularly in the distribution of light and shade, as also a certain oddity in the design itself,

1. parish priest.
2. The central figure in the story is not fictional. Gottfried Schalken (as it is usually spelled) was an actual historical figures. He lived from 1643 to 1706 and was a minor but gifted Dutch painter whose apprenticeship with Gerard Dou (or Douw) is well attested. The story is taken from a series written by Le Fanu, ostensibly based on the papers of an Irish catholic priest. It is the only story in the series set outside Ireland.
3. The wars between King James II of England and his Dutch son-in-law, William, prince of Orange, which were decided in a series of battles fought in Ireland between 1689 and 1691.
4. despite.

which interested my curiosity. It represented the interior of what might be a chamber in some antique religious building — the foreground was occupied by a female figure, arrayed in a species of white robe, part of which is arranged so as to form a veil. The dress, however, is not strictly that of any religious order. In its hand the figure bears a lamp, by whose light alone the form and face are illuminated; the features are marked by an arch smile, such as pretty women wear when engaged in successfully practising some roguish trick; in the back ground, and excepting where the dim red light of an expiring fire serves to define the form, totally in the shade, stands the figure of a man equipped in the old fashion, with doublet and so forth, in an attitude of alarm, his hand being placed upon the hilt of his sword, which he appears to be in the act of drawing.

'There are some pictures,' said I to my friend, 'which impress one, I know not how, with a conviction that they represent not the mere ideal shapes and combinations which have floated through the imagination of the artist, but scenes, faces, and situations which have actually existed. When I look upon that picture, something assures me that I behold the representation of a reality.'

Vandael smiled, and, fixing his eyes upon the painting musingly, he said—

'Your fancy has not deceived you, my good friend, for that picture is the record, and I believe a faithful one, of a remarkable and mysterious occurrence. It was painted by Schalken, and contains, in the face of the female figure, which occupies the most prominent place in the design, an accurate portrait of Rose Velderkaust, the niece of Gerard Douw,[5] the first, and, I believe, the only love of Godfrey Schalken. My father knew the painter well, and from Schalken himself he learned the story of the mysterious drama, one scene of which the picture has embodied. This painting, which is accounted a fine specimen of Schalken's style, was bequeathed to my father by the artist's will, and, as you have observed, is a very striking and interesting production.'

I had only to request Vandael to tell the story of the painting in order to be gratified; and thus it is that I am enabled to submit to you a faithful recital of what I heard myself, leaving you to reject or to allow the evidence upon which the truth of the tradition depends, with this one assurance, that Schalken was an honest, blunt Dutchman, and, I believe, wholly incapable of committing a flight of imagination; and further, that Vandael, from whom I heard the story, appeared firmly convinced of its truth.

There are few forms upon which the mantle of mystery and romance could seem to hang more ungracefully than upon that of the uncouth and clownish Schalken — the Dutch boor — the rude and dogged, but most cunning worker of oils, whose pieces delight the initiated of the present day almost as much as his manners disgusted the refined of his own; and yet this man, so rude, so dogged, so slovenly, I had almost said so savage, in mien and manner, during his after successes, had been selected by the capricious goddess, in his early life, to figure as the hero of a romance by no means devoid of interest or of mystery. Who can tell how meet he may have been in his young days to play the part of the lover or of the hero — who can say that in early life he had been the same harsh, *unlicked*, and rugged boor which, in his maturer age, he proved — or how far the neglected rudeness which afterwards marked his air, and garb, and manners, may not have been the growth of that reckless apathy not unfrequently produced by bitter misfortunes and disappointments in early life? These questions can never now be answered. We must content ourselves then, with a plain statement of facts, or what have been received and transmitted as such, leaving matters of speculation to those who like them.

When Schalken studied under the immortal Gerard Douw, he was a young man; and in spite of the phlegmatic constitution and unexcitable manner which he shared (we believe) with his countrymen, he was not incapable of deep and vivid impressions, for it is an established fact that the young painter looked with considerable interest upon the beautiful niece of his wealthy master. Rose Velderkaust was very young, having, at the period of which we speak, not yet attained her seventeenth year, and, if tradition speaks truth, possessed all the soft dimpling charms of the fair, light-haired Flemish maidens. Schalken had not studied long in the school of Gerard Douw, when he felt this interest deepening into something of a keener and intenser feeling than was quite consistent with the

5. Gerard Dou or Douw (1613-75), a portrait and genre painter of Leyden, was himself a pupil of the young Rembrandt. His depictions of settled, middle-class life were extremely popular.

tranquillity of his honest Dutch heart; and at the same time he perceived, or thought he perceived, flattering symptoms of a reciprocity of liking, and this was quite sufficient to determine whatever indecision he might have heretofore experienced, and to lead him to devote exclusively to her every hope and feeling of his heart. In short, he was as much in love as a Dutchman could be. He was not long in making his passion known to the pretty maiden herself, and his declaration was followed by a corresponding confession upon her part. Schalken, however, was a poor man, and he possessed no counterbalancing advantages of birth or otherwise to induce the old man to consent to a union which must involve his niece and ward in the strugglings and difficulties of a young and nearly friendless artist. He was, therefore, to wait until time had furnished him with opportunity and accident with success; and then, if his labours were found sufficiently lucrative, it was to be hoped that his proposals might at least be listened to by her jealous guardian. Months passed away, and, cheered by the smiles of the little Rose, Schalken's labours were redoubled, and with such effect and improvement as reasonably to promise the realization of his hopes, and no contemptible eminence in his art, before many years should have elapsed.

The even course of this cheering prosperity was, however, destined to experience a sudden and formidable interruption, and that, too, in a manner so strange and mysterious as to baffle all investigation, and throw upon the events themselves a shadow of almost supernatural horror.

Schalken had one evening remained in the master's *studio* considerably longer than his more volatile companions, who had gladly availed themselves of the excuse which the dusk of evening afforded, to withdraw from their several tasks, in order to finish a day of labour in the jollity and conviviality of the tavern. But Schalken worked for improvement, or rather for love. Besides, he was now engaged merely in sketching a design, an operation which, unlike that of colouring, might be continued as long as there was light sufficient to distinguish between canvas and charcoal. He had not then, nor, indeed, until long after, discovered the peculiar powers of his pencil, and he was engaged in composing a group of extremely roguish-looking and grotesque imps and demons, who were inflicting various ingenious torments upon a perspiring and pot-bellied St. Anthony, who reclined in the midst of them, apparently in the last stage of drunkenness. The young artist, however, though incapable of executing, or even of appreciating, any thing of true sublimity, had, nevertheless, discernment enough to prevent his being by any means satisfied with his work; and many were the patient erasures and corrections which the limbs and features of saint and devil underwent, yet all without producing in their new arrangement any thing of improvement or increased effect: The large, old-fashioned room was silent, and, with the exception of himself, quite deserted by its usual inmates. An hour had passed — nearly two — without any improved result. Daylight had already declined, and twilight was fast giving way to the darkness of night. The patience of the young man was exhausted, and he stood before his unfinished production, absorbed in no very pleasing ruminations, one hand buried in the folds of his dark hair, and the other holding the piece of charcoal which had so ill executed its office, and which he now rubbed, without much regard to the sable streaks which it produced, with irritable pressure upon his ample Flemish inexpressibles.—[6] 'Pshaw!' said the young man aloud, 'would that picture, devils, saint, and all, were where they should be — in hell!' A short, sudden laugh, uttered startlingly close to his ear, instantly responded to the ejaculation. The artist turned sharply round, and now for the first time became aware that his labours had been overlooked by a stranger. Within about a yard and half, and rather behind him, there stood what was, or appeared to be, the figure of an elderly man: he wore a short cloak, and broad-brimmed hat, with a conical crown, and in his hand, which was protected with a heavy, gauntlet-shaped glove, he carried a long ebony walking-stick, surmounted with what appeared, as it glittered dimly in the twilight, to be a massive head of gold, and upon the breast, through the folds of the cloak, there shone what appeared to be the links of a rich chain of the same metal. The room was so obscure that nothing further of the appearance of the figure could be ascertained, and the face was altogether overshadowed by the heavy flap of the beaver[7] which overhung it, so that not a feature could be discerned. A quantity of dark hair escaped from

6. A prudish word for 'trousers'.
7. The lower part of the face-guard of a helmet.

beneath this sombre hat, a circumstance which, connected with the firm, upright carriage of the intruder, proved that his years could not yet exceed three-score or thereabouts. There was an air of gravity and importance about the garb of this person, and something indescribably odd, I might say awful, in the perfect, stone-like movelessness of the figure, that effectually checked the testy comment which had at once risen to the lips of the irritated artist. He, therefore, as soon as he had sufficiently recovered the surprise, asked the stranger, civilly, to be seated, and desired to know if he had any message to leave for his master.

'Tell Gerard Douw,' said the unknown, without altering his attitude in the smallest degree, 'that Minheer Vanderhausen, of Rotterdam, desires to speak with him on tomorrow evening at this hour, and, if he please, in this room, upon matters of weight — that is all — good night.'

The stranger, having finished this message, turned abruptly, and, with a quick but silent step quitted the room, before Schalken had time to say a word in reply. The young man felt a curiosity to see in what direction the burgher of Rotterdam would turn on quitting the *studio*, and for that purpose he went directly to the window which commanded the door. A lobby of considerable extent intervened between the inner door of the painter's room and the street entrance, so that Schalken occupied the post of observation before the old man could possibly have reached the street. He watched in vain, however. There was no other mode of exit. Had the old man vanished, or was he lurking about the recesses of the lobby for some bad purpose? This last suggestion filled the mind of Schalken with a vague horror, which was so unaccountably intense as to make him alike afraid to remain in the room alone and reluctant to pass through the lobby. However, with an effort which appeared very disproportioned to the occasion, he summoned resolution to leave the room, and, having double-locked the door and thrust the key in his pocket, without looking to the right or left, he traversed the passage which had so recently, perhaps still, contained the person of his mysterious visitant, scarcely venturing to breathe till he had arrived in the open street.

'Minheer Vanderhausen,' said Gerard Douw within himself, as the appointed hour approached, 'Minheer Vanderhausen of Rotterdam! I never heard of the man till yesterday. What can he want of me? A portrait, perhaps, to be painted; or a younger son or a poor relation to be apprenticed; or a collection to be valued; or — pshaw, there's no one in Rotterdam to leave me a legacy. Well, whatever the business may be, we shall soon know it all.'

It was now the close of day, and every easel, except that of Schalken, was deserted. Gerard Douw was pacing the apartment with the restless step of impatient expectation, every now and then humming a passage from a piece of music which he was himself composing; for, though no great proficient, he admired the art; sometimes pausing to glance over the work of one of his absent pupils, but more frequently placing himself at the window from whence he might observe the passengers who threaded the obscure by-street in which his studio was placed.

'Said you not, Godfrey,' exclaimed Douw, after a long and fruitless gaze from his post of observation, and turning to Schalken — 'said you not the hour of appointment was at about seven by the clock of the Stadhouse?'

'It had just told [*sic*] seven when I first saw him, sir,' answered the student.

'The hour is close at hand, then,' said the master, consulting a horolage as large and as round as a full-grown orange. 'Minheer Vanderhausen from Rotterdam — is it not so?'

'Such was the name.'

'And an elderly man, richly clad?' continued Douw.

'As well as I might see,' replied his pupil; 'he could not be young, nor yet very old neither, and his dress was rich and grave, as might become a citizen of wealth and consideration.'

At this moment the sonorous boom of the Stadhouse clock told, stroke after stroke, the hour of seven; the eyes of both master and student were directed to the door; and it was not until the last peal of the old bell had ceased to vibrate, that Douw exclaimed—

'So, so; we shall have his worship presently — that is, if he means to keep his hour; if not, thou may'st wait for him, Godfrey, if you court the acquaintance of a capricious burgomaster; as for me, I think our old Leyden contains a sufficiency of such commodities, without an importation from Rotterdam.'

Schalken laughed, as in duty bound; and after a pause of some minutes, Douw suddenly exclaimed—

'What if it should all prove a jest, a piece of mummery got up by Vankarp, or some such worthy. I wish you had run all risks, and cudgelled the old burgomaster, stadholder, or whatever else he may be, soundly. I would wager a dozen of Rhenish,[8] his worship would have pleaded old acquaintance before the third application.'

'Here he comes, sir,' said Schalken, in a low admonitory tone; and instantly upon turning towards the door, Gerard Douw observed the same figure which had, on the day before, so unexpectedly greeted the vision of his pupil Schalken.

There was something in the air and mien of the figure which at once satisfied the painter that there was no *mummery* in the case, and that he really stood in the presence of a man of worship; and so, without hesitation, he doffed his cap, and, courteously saluting the stranger, requested him to be seated. The visitor waved his hand slightly, as if in acknowledgment of the courtesy, but remained standing.

'I have the honour to see Minheer Vanderhausen of Rotterdam?' said Gerard Douw.

'The same,' was the laconic reply of his visitant.

'I understand your worship desires to speak with me,' continued Douw, 'and I am here by appointment to suit your commands.'

'Is that a man of trust?' said Vanderhausen, turning towards Schalken, who stood at a little distance behind his master.

'Certainly,' replied Gerard.

'Then let him take this box and get the nearest jeweller or goldsmith to value its contents, and let him return hither with a certificate of the valuation.'

At the same time, he placed a small case about nine inches square in the hands of Gerard Douw, who was as much amazed at its weight as at the strange abruptness with which it was handed to him. In accordance with the wishes of the stranger, he delivered it into the hands of Schalken, and repeating *his* directions, despatched him upon the mission.

Schalken disposed his precious charge securely beneath the folds of his cloak, and rapidly traversing two or three narrow streets, he stopped at a corner house, the lower part of which was then occupied by the shop of a Jewish goldsmith. Schalken entered the shop, and calling the little Hebrew into the obscurity of its back recesses, he proceeded to lay before him Vanderhausen's packet. On being examined by the light of a lamp, it appeared entirely cased with lead, the outer surface of which was much scraped and soiled, and nearly white with age. This was with difficulty partially removed, and disclosed beneath a box of some dark and singularly hard wood; this, too was forced, and after the removal of two or three folds of linen, its contents proved to be a mass of golden ingots, closely packed, and, as the Jew declared, of the most perfect quality. Every ingot underwent the scrutiny of the little Jew, who seemed to feel an epicurean delight in touching and testing these morsels of the glorious metal; and each one of them was replaced in its birth with the exclamation: '*Mein Gott*, how very perfect!! not one grain of alloy — beautiful, beautiful.' The task was at length finished, and the Jew certified under his hand the value of the ingots submitted to his examination, to amount to many thousand rix-dollars.[9] With the desired document in his bosom, and the rich box of gold carefully pressed under his arm, and concealed by his cloak, he retraced his way, and entering the studio, found his master and the stranger in close conference. Schalken had no sooner left the room, in order to execute the commission he had taken in charge, than Vanderhausen addressed Gerard Douw in the following terms—

'I may not tarry with you tonight more than a few minutes, and so I shall briefly tell you the matter upon which I come. You visited the town of Rotterdam some four months ago, and then I saw in the church of St. Lawrence your niece, Rose Velderkaust. I desire to marry her, and if I satisfy you as to the fact that I am very wealthy, more wealthy than any husband you could dream of for her, I expect that you will forward my views to the utmost of your authority. If you approve my proposal, you must close with it at once, for I cannot command time enough to wait for calculations and delays.'

Gerard Douw was, perhaps, as much astonished as any one could be, by the very unexpected nature of Minheer Vanderhausen's communication, but he did not give vent to any unseemly expression of surprise, for besides the motives supplied by prudence and politeness, the painter experienced a kind of chill and oppressive sensation, something like that which is supposed to affect a man who is placed unconsciously in immediate contact with

8. wine.

9. Currency used for trade with the East.

something to which he has a natural antipathy — an undefined horror and dread while standing in the presence of the eccentric stranger, which made him very unwilling to say any thing which might reasonably prove offensive.

'I have no doubt,' said Gerard, after two or three prefatory hems, 'that the connection which you propose would prove alike advantageous and honourable to my niece; but you must be aware that she has a will of her own, and may not acquiesce in what *we* may design for her advantage.'

'Do not seek to deceive me, sir painter,' said Vanderhausen; 'you are her guardian — she is your ward — she is mine if *you* like to make her so.'

The man of Rotterdam moved forward a little as he spoke, and Gerard Douw, he scarce knew why, inwardly prayed for the speedy return of Schalken.

'I desire,' said the mysterious gentleman, 'to place in your hands at once an evidence of my wealth, and a security for my liberal dealing with your niece. The lad will return in a minute or two with a sum in value five times the fortune which she has a right to expect from a husband. This shall lie in your hands, together with her dowry, and you may apply the united sum as suits her interest best; it shall be all exclusively hers while she lives — is that liberal?'

Douw assented, and inwardly thought that fortune had been extraordinarily kind to his niece; the stranger, he thought, must be both wealthy and generous, and such an offer was not to be despised, though made by a humourist, and one of no very prepossessing presence. Rose had no very high pretensions, for she was almost without dowry; indeed altogether so, excepting so far as the deficiency had been supplied by the generosity of her uncle; neither had she any right to raise any scruples against the match on the score of birth, for her own origin was by no means elevated, and as to other objections, Gerard resolved, and, indeed, by the usages of the time, was warranted in resolving not to listen to them for a moment.

'Sir,' said he, addressing the stranger, 'your offer is most liberal, and whatever hesitation I may feel in closing with it immediately, arises solely from my not having the honour of knowing any thing of your family or station. Upon these points you can, of course, satisfy me without difficulty?'

'As to my respectability,' said the stranger, drily, 'you must take that for granted at present; pester me with no inquiries; you can discover nothing more about me than I choose to make known. You shall have sufficient security for my respectability — my word, if you are honourable: if you are sordid, my gold.'

'A testy old gentleman,' thought Douw, 'he must have his own way; but, all things considered, I am justified in giving my niece to him; were she my own daughter, I would do the like by her. I will not pledge myself unnecessarily however.'

'You will not pledge yourself unnecessarily,' said Vanderhausen, strangely uttering the very words which had just floated through the mind of his companion; 'but you will do so if it is necessary, I presume; and I will show you that I consider it indispensable. If the gold I mean to leave in your hands satisfy [*sic*] you, and if you desire that my proposal shall not be at once withdrawn, you must, before I leave this room, write your name to this engagement.'

Having thus spoken, he placed a paper in the hands of Gerard, the contents of which expressed an engagement entered into by Gerard Douw, to give to Wilken Vanderhausen of Rotterdam, in marriage, Rose Velderkaust, and so forth, within one week of the date hereof. While the painter was employed in reading this covenant, Schalken, as we have stated, entered the studio, and having delivered the box and the valuation of the Jew, into the hands of the stranger, he was about to retire, when Vanderhausen called to him to wait; and, presenting the case and the certificate to Gerard Douw, he waited in silence until he had satisfied himself by an inspection of both as to the value of the pledge left in his hands. At length he said—

'Are you content?'

The painter said he would fain have another day to consider.

'Not an hour,' said the suitor coolly.

'Well then,' said Douw, 'I am content — it is a bargain.'

'Then sign at once,' said Vanderhausen, 'I am weary.'

At the same time he produced a small case of writing materials, and Gerard signed the important document.

'Let this youth witness the covenant,' said the old man; and Godfrey Schalken unconsciously signed the instrument which bestowed upon another that hand which he had so long regarded as the object and reward of all his labours. The compact being thus completed, the strange visitor folded up the paper, and stowed it safely in an inner pocket.

'I will visit you tomorrow night at nine of the clock, at your house, Gerard Douw, and will see the subject of our contract — farewell'; and so saying, Wilken Vanderhausen moved stiffly, but rapidly out of the room.

Schalken, eager to resolve his doubts, had placed himself by the window, in order to watch the street entrance; but the experiment served only to support his suspicions, for the old man did not issue from the door. This was very strange, very odd, very fearful; he and his master returned together, and talked but little on the way, for each had his own subjects of reflection, of anxiety, and of hope. Schalken, however, did not know the ruin which threatened his cherished schemes.

Gerard Douw knew nothing of the attachment which had sprung up between his pupil and his niece; and even if he had, it is doubtful whether he would have regarded its existence as any serious obstruction to the wishes of Minheer Vanderhausen. Marriages were then and there matters of traffic and calculation; and it would have appeared as absurd in the eyes of the guardian to make a mutual attachment an essential element in a contract of marriage, as it would have been to draw up his bonds and receipts in the language of chivalrous romance. The painter, however, did not communicate to his niece the important step which he had taken in her behalf, and his resolution arose not from any anticipation of opposition on her part, but solely from a ludicrous consciousness that if his ward were, as she very naturally might do, to ask him to describe the appearance of the bridegroom whom he destined for her, he would be forced to confess that he had not seen his face, and if called upon, would find it impossible to identify him. Upon the next day, Gerard Douw having dined, called his niece to him, and having scanned her person with an air of satisfaction, he took her hand, and looking upon her pretty, innocent face with a smile of kindness, he said—

'Rose, my girl, that face of yours will make your fortune.' Rose blushed and smiled. 'Such faces and such tempers seldom go together, and when they do, the compound is a love potion, which few heads or hearts can resist; trust me, thou wilt soon be a bride, girl; but this is trifling, and I am pressed for time, so make ready the large room by eight o'clock tonight, and give directions for supper at nine. I expect a friend tonight; and observe me, child, do thou trick thyself out handsomely. I would not have him think us poor or sluttish.'

With these words he left the chamber, and took his way to the room to which we have already had occasion to introduce our readers — that in which his pupils worked.

When the evening closed in, Gerard called Schalken, who was about to take his departure to his obscure and comfortless lodgings, and asked him to come home and sup with Rose and Vanderhausen. The invitation was, of course, accepted, and Gerard Douw and his pupil soon found themselves in the handsome and somewhat antique-looking room which had been prepared for the reception of the stranger. A cheerful wood fire blazed in the capacious hearth; a little at one side an old-fashioned table, with richly carved legs, was placed — destined, no doubt, to receive the supper, for which preparations were going forward; and ranged with exact regularity, stood the tall-backed chairs, whose ungracefulness was more than counterbalanced by their comfort. The little party, consisting of Rose, her uncle, and the artist, awaited the arrival of the expected visitor with considerable impatience. Nine o'clock at length came, and with it a summons at the street door, which being speedily answered, was followed by a slow and emphatic tread upon the staircase; the steps moved heavily across the lobby, the door of the room in which the party which we have described were assembled slowly opened, and there entered a figure which startled, almost appalled, the phlegmatic Dutchmen, and nearly made Rose scream with affright; it was the form, and arrayed in the garb of Minheer Vanderhausen; the air, the gait, the height was the same, but the features had never been seen by any of the party before. The stranger stopped at the door of the room, and displayed his form and face completely. He wore a dark-coloured cloth cloak, which was short and full, not falling quite to the knees; his legs were cased in dark purple silk stockings, and his shoes were adorned with roses of the same colour. The opening of the cloak in front showed the under-suit to consist of some very dark, perhaps sable material, and his hands were enclosed in a pair of heavy leather gloves, which ran up considerably above the wrist, in the manner of a gauntlet. In one hand he carried his walking-stick and his hat, which he had removed, and the other hung heavily by his side. A quantity of grizzled hair descended in long tresses from his head, and its folds rested upon the plaits of a stiff ruff, which effectually concealed his neck. So far all was well; but the face! — all the flesh of the face was coloured with the bluish leaden hue, which is sometimes produced by the operation of metallic medicines, administered in excessive quantities; the eyes were enormous, and the white appeared both above and below the iris, which gave to them an expression of insanity, which was heightened by their glassy fixedness; the nose was well enough, but the mouth was writhed considerably to one side, where it opened in order to give egress to two long, discoloured fangs, which projected from the upper jaw, far below the lower lip — the hue of the lips themselves bore the usual relation to that of the face, and was, consequently, nearly black; the character of the face was malignant, even satanic, to the last degree; and, indeed, such a combination of horror could hardly be accounted for, except by supposing the corpse of some atrocious malefactor which had long hung blackening upon the gibbet to have at length become the habitation of a demon — the frightful sport of satanic possession. It was remarkable that the worshipful stranger suffered as little as possible of his flesh to appear, and that during his visit he did not once remove his gloves. Having stood for some moments at the door, Gerard Douw at length found breath and collectedness to bid him welcome, and with a mute inclination of the head, the stranger stepped forward into the room. There was something indescribably odd, even horrible, about all his motions, something undefinable, that was unnatural, unhuman — it was as if the limbs were guided and directed by a spirit unused to the management of bodily machinery. The stranger said hardly any thing during his visit, which did not exceed half an hour; and the host himself could scarcely muster courage enough to utter the few necessary salutations and courtesies; and, indeed, such was the nervous terror which the presence of Vanderhausen inspired, that very little would have made all his entertainers fly bellowing from the room. They had not so far lost all self-possession, however, as to fail to observe two strange peculiarities of their visitor. During his stay he did not once suffer his eyelids to close, nor even to move in the slightest degree; and farther, there was a death-like stillness in his whole person, owing to the total absence of the heaving motion of the chest, caused by the process of respiration. These two peculiarities, though when told they may appear trifling, produced a very striking and unpleasant effect when seen and observed. Vanderhausen at length relieved the painter of Leyden of his inauspicious presence; and with no small gratification the little party heard the street door close after him.

'Dear uncle,' said Rose, 'what a frightful man! I would not see him again for the wealth of the States.'

'Tush, foolish girl,' said Douw, whose sensations were any thing but comfortable. 'A man may be as ugly as the devil, and yet if his heart and actions are good, he is worth all the pretty-faced, perfumed puppies that walk the Mall. Rose, my girl, it is very true he has not thy pretty face, but I know him to be wealthy and liberal; and were he ten times more ugly' — ('which is inconceivable,' observed Rose) — 'these two virtues would be sufficient,' continued her uncle, 'to counterbalance all his deformity, and if not of power sufficient actually to alter the shape of the features, at least of efficacy enough to prevent one thinking them amiss.'

'Do you know uncle,' said Rose, 'when I saw him standing at the door, I could not get it out of my head that I saw the old, painted, wooden figure that used to frighten me so much in the church of St. Laurence of Rotterdam.'

Gerard laughed, though he could not help inwardly acknowledging the justness of the comparison. He was resolved, however, as far as he could, to check his niece's inclination to ridicule the ugliness of her intended bridegroom, although he was not a little pleased to observe that she appeared totally exempt from that mysterious dread of the stranger, which he could not disguise it from himself, considerably affected him, as also his pupil Godfrey Schalken.

Early on the next day there arrived from various quarters of the town, rich presents of silks, velvets, jewellery, and so forth, for Rose; and also a packet directed to Gerard Douw, which, on being opened, was found to contain a contract of marriage, formally drawn up, between Wilken Vanderhausen of the *Boom-quay*, in Rotterdam, and Rose Velderkaust of Leyden, niece to Gerard Douw, master in the art of painting, also of the same city; and containing engagements on the part of Vanderhausen to make settlements upon his bride, far more splendid than he had before led her guardian to believe likely, and which were to be secured to her use in the most unexceptionable manner possible

— the money being placed in the hands of Gerard Douw himself.

I have no sentimental scenes to describe, no cruelty of guardians, or magnanimity of wards, or agonies of lovers. The record I have to make is one of sordidness, levity, and interest. In less than a week after the first interview which we have just described, the contract of marriage was fulfilled, and Schalken saw the prize which he would have risked any thing to secure, carried off triumphantly by his attractive rival. For two or three days he absented himself from the school; he then returned and worked, if with less cheerfulness, with far more dogged resolution than before — the slumbers of love had given place to that of ambition. Months passed away, and, contrary to his expectation, and, indeed, to the direct promise of the parties, Gerard Douw heard nothing of his niece or her worshipful spouse. The interest of the money which was to have been demanded in quarterly sums, lay unclaimed in his hands. He began to grow extremely uneasy. Minheer Vanderhausen's direction in Rotterdam he was fully possessed of; after some irresolution he finally determined to journey thither — a trifling undertaking, and easily accomplished — and thus to satisfy himself of the safety and comfort of his ward, for whom he entertained an honest and strong affection. His search was in vain, however; no one in Rotterdam had ever heard of Minheer Vanderhausen. Gerard Douw left not a house in the Boom-quay untried; but all in vain — no one could give him any information whatever touching the object of his inquiry; and he was obliged to return to Leyden nothing wiser than when he had left it. On his arrival he hastened to the establishment from which Vanderhausen had hired the lumbering, though, considering the times, most luxurious vehicle, which the bridal party had employed to convey them to Rotterdam. From the driver of this machine he learned, that having proceeded by slow stages, they had late in the evening approached Rotterdam; but that before they entered the city, and while yet nearly a mile from it, a small party of men, soberly clad, and after the old fashion, with peaked beards and mustaches, standing in the centre of the road, obstructed the further progress of the carriage. The driver reined in his horses, much fearing, from the obscurity of the hour, and the loneliness of the road, that some mischief was intended. His fears were, however, somewhat allayed by his observing that these strange men carried a large litter, of an antique shape, and which they immediately set down upon the pavement, whereupon the bridegroom, having opened the coach-door from within, descended, and having assisted his bride to do likewise, led her, weeping bitterly and wringing her hands, to the litter, which they both entered. It was then raised by the men who surrounded it, and speedily carried towards the city, and before it had proceeded many yards, the darkness concealed it from the view of the Dutch charioteer. In the inside of the vehicle he found a purse, whose contents more than thrice paid the hire of the carriage and man. He saw and could tell nothing more of Minheer Vanderhausen and his beautiful lady. This mystery was a source of deep anxiety and almost of grief to Gerard Douw. There was evidently fraud in the dealing of Vanderhausen with him, though for what purpose committed he could not imagine. He greatly doubted how far it was possible for a man possessing in his countenance so strong an evidence of the presence of the most demoniac feelings, to be in reality any thing but a villain, and every day that passed without his hearing from or of his niece, instead of inducing him to forget his fears, on the contrary tended more and more to exasperate them. The loss of his niece's cheerful society tended also to depress his spirits; and in order to dispel this despondency, which often crept upon his mind after his daily employment was over, he was wont frequently to prevail upon Schalken to accompany him home, and by his presence to dispel, in some degree, the gloom of his otherwise solitary supper. One evening, the painter and his pupil were sitting by the fire, having accomplished a comfortable supper, and had yielded to that silent pensiveness sometimes induced by the process of digestion, when their reflections were disturbed by a loud sound at the street door, as if occasioned by some person rushing forcibly and repeatedly against it. A domestic had run without delay to ascertain the cause of the disturbance, and they heard him twice or thrice interrogate the applicant for admission, but without producing an answer or any cessation of the sounds. They heard him then open the hall-door, and immediately there followed a light and rapid tread upon the staircase. Schalken laid his hand on his sword, and advanced towards the door. It opened before he reached it, and Rose rushed into the room. She looked wild and haggard, and pale with exhaustion and terror, but her dress surprised them as much even as her unexpected appearance. It consisted of a kind of white woollen wrapper, made close about the neck, and descending to the very ground. It was much deranged and travel-soiled. The poor creature had hardly entered the chamber when she fell senseless on the floor. With some difficulty they succeeded in reviving her, and on recovering her senses, she instantly exclaimed, in a tone of eager, terrified impatience—

'Wine, wine, quickly, or I'm lost.'

Much alarmed at the strange agitation in which the call was made, they at once administered to her wishes, and she drank some wine with a haste and eagerness which surprised them. She had hardly swallowed it, when she exclaimed, with the same urgency.

'Food, food, at once, or I perish.'

A considerable fragment of a roast joint was upon the table, and Schalken immediately proceeded to cut some, but he was anticipated, for no sooner had she become aware of its presence, than she darted at it with the rapacity of a vulture, and, seizing it in her hands, she tore off the flesh with her teeth, and swallowed it. When the paroxysm of hunger had been a little appeased, she appeared suddenly to become aware how strange her conduct had been, or it may have been that other more agitating thoughts recurred to her mind, for she began to weep bitterly and to wring her hands.

'Oh send for a minister of God,' said she; 'I am not safe till he comes; send for him speedily.'

Gerard Douw despatched a messenger instantly, and prevailed on his niece to allow him to surrender his bedchamber to her use; he also persuaded her to retire to it at once and to rest; her consent was extorted upon the condition that they would not leave her for a moment.

'Oh that the holy man were here,' she said; 'he can deliver me — the dead and the living can never be one — God has forbidden it.'

With these mysterious words she surrendered herself to their guidance, and they proceeded to the chamber which Gerard Douw had assigned to her use.

'Do not, do not leave me for a moment,' said she; 'I am lost for ever if you do.'

Gerard Douw's chamber was approached through a spacious apartment, which they were now about to enter. Gerard Douw and Schalken each carried a wax candle, so that a sufficient degree of light was cast upon all surrounding objects. They were now entering the large chamber, which, as I have said, communicated with Douw's apartment, when Rose suddenly stopped, and, in a whisper which semed to thrill with horror, she said—

'Oh, God! he is here, he is here; see, see, there he goes.'

She pointed towards the door of the inner room, and Schalken thought he saw a shadowy and ill-defined form gliding into that apartment. He drew his sword, and, raising the candle so as to throw its light with increased distinctness upon the objects in the room, he entered the chamber into which the shadow had glided. No figure was there — nothing but the furniture which belonged to the room, and yet he could not be deceived as to the fact that something had moved before them into the chamber. A sickening dread came upon him, and the cold perspiration broke out in heavy drops upon his forehead; nor was he more composed, when he heard the increased urgency, the agony of entreaty, with which Rose implored them not to leave her for a moment.

'I saw him,' said she; 'he's here. I cannot be deceived — I know him — he's by me — he is with me — he's in the room; then, for God's sake, as you would save me, do not stir from beside me.'

They at length prevailed upon her to lie down upon the bed, where she continued to urge them to stay by her. She frequently uttered incoherent sentences, repeating, again and again, 'the dead and the living cannot be one — God has forbidden it'; and then again, 'rest to the wakeful — sleep to the sleep-walkers.' These and such mysterious and broken sentences, she continued to utter until the clergyman arrived. Gerard Douw began to fear, naturally enough, that the poor girl, owing to terror or ill-treatment, had become deranged, and he half suspected, by the suddenness of her appearance, and the unseasonableness of the hour, and, above all, from the wildness and terror of her manner, that she had made her escape from some place of confinement for lunatics, and was in immediate fear of pursuit. He resolved to summon medical advice, as soon as the mind of his niece had been in some measure set at rest by the offices of the clergyman whose attendance she had so earnestly desired; and until this object had been attained, he did not venture to put any questions to her, which might possibly, by reviving painful or horrible recollections, increase her agitation. The clergyman soon arrived — a man of ascetic countenance and venerable age — one whom Gerard Douw respected much, forasmuch as he was a veteran polemic,[10] though one, perhaps, more dreaded as a combatant than beloved as a Christian — of pure morality, subtle brain, and frozen heart. He entered the chamber which communicated with that in which Rose reclined, and immediately on his arrival, she requested him to pray for her, as for one who lay in the hands of Satan, and who could hope for deliverance — only from heaven.

That our readers may distinctly understand all the circumstances of the event which we are about imperfectly to describe, it is necessary to state the relative position of the parties who were engaged in it. The old clergyman and Schalken were in the anti-room of which we have already spoken; Rose lay in the inner chamber, the door of which was open; and by the side of the bed, at her urgent desire, stood her guardian; a candle burned in the bedchamber, and three were lighted in the outer apartment. The old man now cleared his voice, as if about to commence, but before he had time to begin, a sudden gust of air blew out the candle which served to illuminate the room in which the poor girl lay, and she, with hurried alarm, exclaimed—

'Godfrey, bring in another candle; the darkness is unsafe.'

Gerard Douw, forgetting for the moment her repeated injunctions, in the immediate impulse, stepped from the bedchamber into the other, in order to supply what she desired.

'Oh God! do not go, dear uncle,' shrieked the unhappy girl — and at the same time she sprung from the bed, and darted after him, in order, by her grasp, to detain him. But the warning came too late, for scarcely had he passed the threshold, and hardly had his niece had time to utter the startling exclamation, when the door which divided the two rooms closed violently after him, as if swung to by a strong blast of wind. Schalken and he both rushed to the door, but their united and desperate efforts could not avail so much as to shake it. Shriek after shriek burst from the inner chamber, with all the piercing loudness of despairing terror. Schalken and Douw applied every energy and strained every nerve to force open the door; but all in vain. There was no sound of struggling from within, but the screams seemed to increase in loudness, and at the same time they heard the bolts of the latticed window withdrawn, and the window itself grated upon the sill as if thrown open. One *last* shriek, so long and piercing and agonised as to be scarcely human, swelled from the room, and suddenly there followed a death-like silence. A light step was heard crossing the floor, as if from the bed to the window; and almost at the same instant the door gave way, and, yielding to the pressure of the external applicants, they were nearly precipitated into the room. It was empty. The window was open, and Schalken sprung to a chair and gazed out upon the street and canal below. He saw no form, but he beheld, or thought he beheld, the waters of the broad canal beneath settling ring after ring in heavy circular ripples, as if a moment before disturbed by the immersion of some large and heavy mass.

No trace of Rose was ever after discovered, nor was any thing certain respecting her mysterious wooer detected or even suspected — no clue whereby to trace the intricacies of the labyrinth and to arrive at a distinct conclusion was to be found. But an incident occurred, which, though it will not be received by our rational readers as at all approaching to evidence upon the matter, nevertheless produced a strong and a lasting impression upon the mind of Schalken. Many years after the events which we have detailed, Schalken, then remotely situated, received an intimation of his father's death, and of his intended burial upon a fixed day in the church of Rotterdam. It was necessary that a very considerable journey should be performed by the funeral procession, which, as it will readily be believed, was not very numerously attended. Schalken with difficulty arrived in Rotterdam late in the day upon which the funeral was appointed to take place. It had not then arrived. Evening closed in, and still it did not appear.

Schalken strolled down to the church — he found it open — notice of the arrival of the funeral had been given, and the vault in which the body was to be laid had been opened. The officer, who is analogous to our sexton, on seeing a well-dressed gentleman, whose object was to attend the expected funeral, pacing the aisle of the church, hospitably invited him to share with him the comforts of a blazing wood fire, which, as was his custom in winter time upon such occasions, he had kindled in the hearth of a chamber which communicated, by a flight of steps, with the vault below. In this

10. A controversialist, especially in theological matters.

chamber Schalken and his entertainer seated themselves, and the sexton, after some fruitless attempts to engage his guest in conversation, was obliged to apply himself to his tobacco-pipe and can, to solace his solitude. In spite of his grief and cares, the fatigues of a rapid journey of nearly forty hours gradually overcame the mind and body of Godfrey Schalken, and he sank into a deep sleep, from which he was awakened by some one's shaking him gently by the shoulder. He first thought that the old sexton had called him, but *he* was no longer in the room. He roused himself, and as soon as he could clearly see what was around him, he perceived a female form, clothed in a kind of light robe of muslin, part of which was so disposed as to act as a veil, and in her hand she carried a lamp. She was moving rather away from him, and towards the flight of steps which conducted towards the vaults. Schalken felt a vague alarm at the sight of this figure, and at the same time an irresistible impulse to follow its guidance. He followed it towards the vaults, but when it reached the head of the stairs, he paused — the figure paused also, and, turning gently round, displayed, by the light of the lamp it carried, the face and features of his first love, Rose Velderkaust. There was nothing horrible, or even sad, in the countenance. On the contrary, it wore the same arch smile which used to enchant the artist long before in his happy days. A feeling of awe and of interest, too intense to be resisted, prompted him to follow the spectre, if spectre it were. She descended the stairs — he followed — and, turning to the left, through a narrow passage, she led him, to his infinite surprise, into what appeared to be an old-fashioned Dutch apartment, such as the pictures of Gerard Douw have served to immortalize. Abundance of costly antique furniture was disposed about the room, and in one corner stood a four-post bed, with heavy black cloth curtains around it; the figure frequently turned towards him with the same arch smile; and when she came to the side of the bed, she drew the curtains, and, by the light of the lamp, which she held towards its contents, she disclosed to the horror-stricken painter, sitting bolt upright in the bed, the livid and demoniac form of Vanderhausen. Schalken had hardly seen him, when he fell senseless upon the floor, where he lay until discovered, on the next morning, by persons employed in closing the passages into the vaults. He was lying in a cell of considerable size, which had not been disturbed for a long time, and he had fallen beside a large coffin, which was supported upon small stone pillars, a security against the attacks of vermin.

To his dying day Schalken was satisfied of the reality of the vision which he had witnessed, and he has left behind him a curious evidence of the impression which it wrought upon his fancy, in a painting executed shortly after the event we have narrated, and which is valuable as exhibiting not only the peculiarities which have made Schalken's pictures sought after, but even more so as presenting a portrait as close and faithful as one taken from memory can be, of his early love, Rose Velderkaust, whose mysterious fate must ever remain matter of speculation. The picture represents a chamber of antique masonry, such as might be found in most old cathedrals, and is lighted faintly by a lamp carried in the hand of a female figure, such as we have above attempted to describe; and in the back-ground, and to the left of him who examines the painting, there stands the form of a man apparently aroused from sleep, and by his attitude, his hand being laid upon his sword, exhibiting considerable alarm: this last figure is illuminated only by the expiring glare of a wood or charcoal fire. The whole production exhibits a beautiful specimen of that artful and singular distribution of light and shade which has rendered the name of Schalken immortal among the artists of his country. This tale is traditionary, and the reader will easily perceive, by our studiously omitting to heighten many points of the narrative, when a little additional colouring might have added effect to the recital, that we have desired to lay before him, not a figment of the brain, but a curious tradition connected with, and belonging to, the biography of a famous artist.

CHARLES LEVER
(1806-72)

from:
JACK HINTON, THE GUARDSMAN (1842)

[Charles Lever enjoyed greater popular success in his day than did Sheridan Le Fanu, though Lever's fiction has not retained its appeal in the twentieth century. His early novels were serialized in *The Dublin University Magazine* (the one below appeared in March 1842), and a standard feature of the plots was the plight of an intelligent young man (sometimes English) adrift in the comic backwaters of post-Union Ireland. *Jack Hinton, the Guardsman* follows this pattern faithfully, and while readers of a nationalist tendency have in the past deprecated Lever's patronizing attitude to the ordinary Irishman, there are already present in this relatively early novel signs of the more serious concerns of Lever's later work. The chapter that follows is set in the Phoenix Park, outside Dublin, the headquarters of the British military presence. The sham battle is fought between two units of the imperial army, but the real passions that emerge in the heat of the exercise are those of the Insurrection of 1798 when catholic rebels in Wexford were defeated by the army at Vinegar Hill. Amid the highly moral version of picaresque adventure, which is Lever's forte as a Victorian novelist, this acknowledgment of the unresolved conflicts of the past is dexterously introduced: the imitation of battle, presented in a novel which (as Aristotle would have it) is the 'imitation of an action', threatens to turn all too real.]

CHAPTER VI — THE SHAM BATTLE

I have mentioned in my last chapter how very rapidly I forgot my troubles in the excitement of the scene around me. Indeed, they must have been much more important, much deeper woes, to have occupied any place in a head so addled and confused as mine was. The manoeuvres of the day included a sham battle; and scarcely had his excellency passed down the line, when preparations for the engagement began. The heavy artillery was seen to limber up, and move slowly across the field, accompanied by a strong detachment of cavalry: columns of infantry were marched hither and thither with the most pressing and eager haste; orderly dragoons and staff officers galloped too and fro like madman; red-faced plethoric[1] little colonels bawled out the word of command, till one feared they might burst a blood vessel; and already two companions of light infantry might be seen stealing cautiously along the skirts of the wood, with the apparently insidious design of attacking a brigade of guns. As for me, I was at one moment employed carrying despatches to Sir Charles Asgill, at another conveying intelligence to Lord Harrington — these, be it known, being the rival commanders, whose powers of strategy were now to be tested before the assembled and discriminating citizens of Dublin. Not to speak of the eminent personal hazard of a service which required me constantly to ride between the lines of contending armies, the fatigue alone had nigh killed me. Scarcely did I appear breathless at head quarters on my return from one mission, when I was despatched on another. Tired and panting, I more than once bungled my directions, and communicated to Sir Charles the secret intentions of his lordship, while with a laudable impartiality I disarranged the former's plans by a total misconception of the orders. Fatigue, noise, chagrin, and incessant worry, had so completely turned my head, that I became perfectly incapable of the commonest exercise of reason. Part of the artillery I ordered into a hollow, where I was told to station a party of riflemen. Three squadrons of cavalry I desired to charge up a hill, which the seventy-first highlanders were to have scrambled up, if they were able. Light dragoons I posted in situations so beset with brushwood and firs, that all movement became impossible; and, in a word, when the signal-gun announced the commencement of the action, my mistakes had introduced such a new feature into tactics, that neither party knew what his adversary was at, nor indeed had any accurate notion of which were his own troops. The duke, who had watched with the most eager satisfaction the whole of my proceedings, sat laughing upon his horse till the very tears coursed down his cheeks; and as all the

1. Plethora is a condition caused by dilation of superficial blood vessels, especially characterized by a reddish face.

staff were more or less participators in the secret, I found myself once more the centre of a grinning audience, perfectly convulsed at my exploits. Meanwhile, the guns thundered, the cavalry charged, the infantry poured in a rattling roar of small arms; while the luckless commanders, unable to discover any semblance of a plan, and still worse, not knowing where one half of their forces were concealed, dared not adventure upon a movement, and preferred trusting to the smoke of the battle as a cover for their blunders. The fusilade, therefore, was hotly sustained — all the heavy pieces brought to the front; and while the spectators were anxiously looking for the manoeuvres of a fight, the ammunition was waxing low, and the day wearing apace. Dissatisfaction at length began to show itself on every side; and the duke assuming, as well as he was able, somewhat of a disappointed look, the unhappy generals made a final effort to retrieve their mishaps, and aides-de-camp were despatched through all the highways and by-ways, to bring up whoever they could find as quickly as possible. Now then began such a scene as few even of the oldest campaigners ever witnessed the equal of. From every dell and hollow, from every brake and thicket, burst forth some party or other, who up to this moment believed themselves lying in ambush. Horse, foot, and dragoons, artillery, sappers, light infantry, and grenadiers, rushed forward wherever chance or their bewildered officer led them. Here might be seen one half of a regiment blazing away at a stray company of their own people, running like devils for shelter, — here some squadrons of horse, who, indignant at their fruitless charges and unmeaning movements, now doggedly dismounted, were standing right before a brigade of twelve-pounders, thundering mercilessly amongst them. Never was witnessed such a scene of riot, confusion, and disorder. Colonels lost their regiments, regiments their colonels. The fusileers captured the band of the Royal Irish, and made them play through the heat of the engagement. Those who at first expressed *ennui* and fatigue at the sameness and monotony of the scene, were now gratified to the utmost by its life, bustle, and animation. Elderly citizens in drab shorts and buff waistcoats, explained to their listening wives and urchins the plans and intentions of the rival heroes, pronouncing the whole thing the while the very best field-day that was ever seen in the Phoenix.

In the midst of all this confusion, a new element of discord suddenly displayed itself. That loyal corps, the Cork militia, who were ordered up to attack close to where the duke and his staff were standing, deemed that no better moment could be chosen to exhibit their attachment to church and state than when marching on to glory, struck up, with all the discord of their band, the redoubted air of 'Protestant Boys'. The cheer burst from the ranks as the loyal strains filled the air; but scarcely had the loud burst subsided, when the Louth militia advanced with a quick step, their fifes playing 'Vinegar-hill'.

For a moment or two the rivalry created a perfect roar of laughter; but this very soon gave way, as the two regiments, instead of drawing up at a reasonable distance for the interchange of an amicable blank cartridge, rushed down upon each other with the fury of madmen. So sudden, so impetuous was the encounter, all effort to prevent it was impracticable. Muskets were clubbed or bayonets fixed, and in a moment really serious battle was engaged; the musicians on each side encouraging their party, as they racked their brains for party-tunes of the most bitter and taunting character; while cries of 'Down with King William!' 'To hell with the Pope!' rose alternately from either side.

How far this spirit might have extended, it is difficult to say, when the duke gave orders for some squadrons of cavalry to charge down upon them, and separate the contending forces. This order was fortunately in time; for scarcely was it issued, when a west country yeomanry corps came galloping up to the assistance of the brave Louth.

'Here we are, boys!' cried Mike Westropp, their colonel. 'Here we are: lave the way! lave the way for us! and we'll ride down the murthering Orange villains, every man of them!'

The Louth fell back, and the yeomen came forward at a charge — Westropp standing high in his stirrups, and flourishing his sabre above his head. It was just then that a heavy brigade of artillery, unconscious of the hot work going forward, was ordered to open their fire upon the Louth militia. One of the guns, by some accident, contained an undue proportion of wadding, and to this casual circumstance may, in a great degree, be attributed the happy issue of what threatened to be a serious disturbance; for, as Westropp advanced cheering and encouraging his men, he received this wadding slap in his face. Down he tumbled at once, rolling over and over with the shock; while, believing that he had got his death-wound, he bellowed out—

'Oh, blessed Virgin! there's threason in the camp! hit in the face by a four-pounder, by Jove. Oh, duke darling! Oh, your grace! Oh, holy Joseph, look at this! Oh, bad luck to the arthillery for spoiling a fair fight. Peter' — this was the major of the regiment — 'Peter Darcy, gallop into town and lodge informations against the brigade of guns. I'll be dead before you come back.'

A perfect burst of laughter broke from the opposing ranks, and while his friends crowded round the discomfited leader, the rival bands united in a roar of merriment that for a moment caused a suspension of hostilities. For a moment, I say; for scarcely had the gallant Westropp been conveyed to the rear, when once more the bands struck up their irritating strains, and preparations for a still more deadly encounter were made on every side. The matter now assumed so serious an aspect that the duke was obliged himself to interfere, and order both parties off the ground; the Cork deploying towards the lodge, while the brave Louth marched off with banners flying and drums beating in the direction of Knockmaroon.

These movements were conducted with a serio-comic solemnity of the most ludicrous kind, and although the respect for viceregal authority was great, and the military devotion of each party strong, yet neither one nor the other was sufficient to prevent the more violent on both sides from occasionally turning, as they went, to give expression to some taunting allusion or some galling sarcasm, well calculated, did the opportunity permit, to renew the conflict.

A hearty burst of laughter from the duke indicated pretty clearly how he regarded the matter; and, however the grave and significant looks of others might seem to imply that there was more in the circumstance than mere food for mirth, he shook his sides merrily: and, as his bright eye glistened with satisfaction, and his cheek glowed, he could not help whispering his regret that his station compelled him to check the very best joke he ever witnessed in his life.

'This is hot work, Sir Charles,' said he, wiping his forehead as he spoke; 'and, as it is now past three o'clock, and we have a privy council at four, I fear I must leave you.'

'The troops will move past in marching order,' replied Sir Charles pompously: 'will your grace receive the salute at this point?'

'Wherever you like, Sir Charles; wherever you like. Would to heaven that some good Samaritan could afford me a little brandy and water from his canteen. I say, Hinton, they seem at luncheon yonder in that carriage: do you think your diplomacy could negotiate a glass of sherry for me?'

'If you'll permit me, my lord, I'll try,' said I, as disengaging myself from the crowd, I set off in the direction he pointed.

As I drew near the carriage — from which the horses having been taken, was drawn up beside a clump of beech trees for the sake of shelter — I was not long in perceiving that it was the same equipage I had so gallantly rescued in the morning from the sabres of the horse-police. Had I entertained any fears for the effects of the nervous shock upon the tender sensibilities of Mrs. Paul Rooney, the scene before me must completely have dispelled my uneasiness. Never did a merrier peal of laughter ring from female lungs than hers as I rode forward. Seated in the back of the carriage, the front cushion of which served as a kind of table, sat the lady in question. One hand, resting upon her knee, held a formidable carving-fork, on the summit of which vibrated the short leg of a chicken; in the other she grasped a silver vessel which, were I to predicate from the froth, I fear I should pronounce to be porter.[2] A luncheon on the most liberal scale, displayed, in all the confusion and disorder inseparable from such a situation, a veal pie, cold lamb, tongue, chickens, and sandwiches; drinking vessels of every shape and material; a smelling bottle full of mustard, and a newspaper paragraph full of salt. Abundant as were the viands, the guests were not wanting: crowds of infantry officers, flushed with victory or undismayed by defeat, hobnobbed from the rumble[3] to the box; the steps, the springs, the very splinterbar had its occupant; and truly a merrier party, or a more convivial, it were very difficult to conceive.

So environed was Mrs. Rooney by her friends, that I was enabled to observe them some time, myself unseen.

'Captain Mitchell, another wing? Well, the least taste in life of the breast? Bob Dwyer, will you never have done drawing that cork?'

2. A dark sweet ale brewed from black malt.
3. A folding outside seat at the back of certain carriages.

Now this I must aver was an unjust reproach, inasmuch as to my own certain knowledge, he had accomplished three feats of that nature in about as many minutes; and, had the aforesaid Bob been reared from his infancy in drawing corks, instead of declarations, his practice could not have been more expert. Pop, pop, they went; glug, glug, glug, flowed the bubbling liquor, as sherry, shrub,[4] cold punch, and bottled porter succeeded each other in rapid order. Simpering ensigns, with elevated eyebrows, insinuated nonsense, soft, vapid, and unmeaning as their own brains, as they helped themselves to ham or dived into the pastry; while a young dragoon, who seemed to devote his attention to Mrs. Rooney's companion, amused himself by constant endeavours to stroke down a growing mustache, whose downy whiteness resembled nothing that I know of, save the ill-omened fur one sees on an antiquated apple-pie.

As I looked on every side to catch a glance at him whom I should suppose to be Mr. Rooney, I was myself detected by the watchful eye of Bob Dwyer, who, at that moment, having his mouth full of three hard eggs, was nearly asphyxiated in his endeavours to telegraph my approach to Mrs. Paul.

'The edge-du-cong, by the mortial!'[5] said he, sputtering out the words, as his bloodshot eyes nearly bolted out of his head.

Had I been a Bengal tiger, my advent might have caused less alarm. The officers not knowing if the duke himself were coming, wiped their lips, resumed their caps and shakos,[6] and sprang to the ground in dismay and confusion: as Mrs. Rooney herself, with an adroitness an Indian juggler might have envied, plunged the fork, drumstick and all into the recesses of her muff; while with a back hand she decanted the XX upon a bald major of infantry, who was brushing the crumbs from his facings.[7] One individual alone seemed to relish and enjoy the discomfiture of the others: this was the young lady whom I before remarked, and whose whole air and appearance seemed strangely at variance with every thing around her. She gave free current to her mirth; while Mrs. Paul, now suddenly restored to a sense of her nervous constitution, fell back in the carriage, and appeared bent upon a scene.

'You caught us enjoying ourselves, Mr. Stilton?'

'Hinton, if you'll allow me, madam.'

'Ay, to be sure — Mr. Hinton. Taking a little snack, which I am sure you'd be the better of after the fatigues of the day.'

'Eh, au, au! a devilish good luncheon,' chimed in a pale sub,[8] the first who ventured to pluck up his courage.

'Would a sandwich tempt you, with a glass of champagne?' said Mrs. Paul, with the blandest of smiles.

'I can recommend the lamb, sir,' said a voice behind.

'Begad, I'll vouch for the porter,' said the major. 'I only hope it is a good cosmetic.'

'It is a beautiful thing for the hair,' said Mrs. Rooney, half venturing upon a joke.

'No more on that head, ma'am,' said the little major, bowing pompously.

By this time, thanks to the assiduous attentions of Bob Dwyer, I was presented with a plate, which had I been an anaconda, instead of an aide-de-camp, might have satisfied my appetite. A place was made for me in the carriage; and the faithful Bob, converting the skirt of his principal blue into a glass-cloth, polished a wine-glass for my private use.

'Let me introduce my young friend, Mr. Hinton,' said Mrs. Paul, with a graceful wave of her jewelled hand towards her companion. 'Miss Louisa Bellew, only daughter of Sir Simon Bellew, of ——' what the place was I could not well hear, but it sounded confoundedly like Killhimansmotherum, 'a beautiful place in the county Mayo. Bob, is it punch you are giving?'

'Most excellent, I assure you, Mrs. Rooney.'

'And how is the duke, sir? I hope his grace enjoys good health. He is a darling of a man.'

By-the-by, it is perfectly absurd the sympathy your third or fourth-rate people feel in the health and habits of those above them in station, pleased as they are to learn the most commonplace and worthless trifles concerning them, and happy when, by any chance, some accidental similitude would seem to exist, even between their misfortunes.

'And the dear duchess,' resumed Mrs. Rooney, 'she's troubled with the nerves like myself. Ah! Mr.

4. A drink made with orange or lemon juice, sugar, spices and rum.
5. Aide de camp (French), an officer who attends a commander on the field of battle. 'mortial' = 'mortal'; 'by the mortal' was a common invocation.
6. A shako was a tall, usually cylindrical military headdress, with a plume and often a peak, very popular in the nineteenth century.
7. The jacket collar and cuffs of a military uniform.
8. subaltern.

Hinton, what an affliction it is to have a sensitive nature; that's what I often say to my sweet young friend here. It's better for her to be the gay, giddy, thoughtless, happy thing she is than ——' Here the lady sighed, wiped her eyes, flourished her cambric, and tried to look like Agnes in the Bleeding Nun.[9] 'But here they come. You don't know Mr. Rooney? Allow me to introduce him to you.'

As she spoke, O'Grady cantered up to the carriage, accompanied by a short, pursy,[10] round-faced little man, who, with his hat set knowingly on one side, and his top-boots scarce reaching to the middle of the leg, bestrode a sharp, strong-boned hackney,[11] with cropped ears and short tail. He carried in his hand a hunting-whip, and seemed, by his seat in the saddle and the easy finger upon the bridle, no indifferent horseman.

'Mr. Rooney,' said the lady, drawing herself up with a certain austerity of manner, 'I wish you to make the acquaintance of Mr. Hinton, the aide-de-camp to his grace.'

Mr. Rooney lifted his hat straight above his head, and replaced it a little more obliquely than before over his right eye.

'Delighted, upon my honour — faith, quite charmed — hope you got something to eat — there never was such a murthering hot day — Bob Dwyer open a bottle of port — the captain is famished.'

'I say, Hinton,' called out O'Grady, 'you forgot the duke it seems; he told me you'd gone in search of some sherry, or something of the kind; but I can readily conceive how easily a man may forget himself in such a position as yours.'

Here Mrs. Paul dropped her head in deep confusion, Miss Bellew looked saucy, and I, for the first time remembering what brought me there, was perfectly overwhelmed with shame at my carelessness.

'Never mind, boy; don't fret about it; his grace is the most forgiving man in the world; and when he knows where you were ——'

'Ah! captain,' sighed Mrs. Rooney.

'Master Phil, it's yourself can do it,' murmured Paul, who perfectly appreciated O'Grady's powers of blarney, when exercised on the susceptible temperament of his fair spouse.

'I'll take a sandwich,' continued the captain. 'Do you know, Mrs. Rooney, I've been riding about this half-hour to catch my young friend, and introduce him to you; and here I find him comfortably installed, without my aid or assistance. The fact is, these English fellows have a flattering, insinuating way of their own, there's no coming up to. Isn't that so, Miss Bellew?'

'Very likely,' said the young lady, who now spoke for the first time; 'but it is so very well concealed, that I for one could never detect it.'

This speech, uttered with a certain pert and saucy air, nettled me for the moment; but as no reply occurred to me, I could only look at the speaker a tacit ackowledgment of her sarcasm; while I remembered, for the first time, that, although seated opposite my very attractive neighbour, I had hitherto not addressed to her a single phrase of even common-place attention.

'I suppose you put up in the Castle, sir,' said Mr. Rooney.

'Yes; two doors lower down than Mount O'Grady,' replied the captain for me. 'But come, Hinton, the carriages are moving; we must get back as quick as we can. Good-bye, Paul. Adieu! Mrs. Rooney. Miss Bellew, good morning.'

It was just at the moment when I had summoned up my courage to address Miss Bellew, that O'Grady called me away: there was nothing for it, however, but to make my adieus while extricating myself from the *débris* of the luncheon. I once more mounted my horse, and joined the viceregal party as they drove from the ground.

'I'm delighted you know the Rooneys,' said O'Grady, as we drove along: 'they are by far the best fun going. Paul good, but his wife superb.'

'And the young lady?' said I.

'Oh, a different kind of thing altogether. By-the-by, Hinton, you took my hint, I hope, about your English manner?'

'Eh? why? how? what did you mean?'

'Simply, my boy, that your Coppermine-river kind of courtesy[12] may be a devilish fine thing in Hyde-park or St. James's, but will never do with us poor people here. Put more warmth into it, man. Dash the lemonade with a little maraschino; you'll feel twice as comfortable yourself, and the girls like you all the better. You take the suggestion in good part, I'm sure.'

9. See Anon., *The Bleeding Nun; or, Raymond and Agnes, A Romance* (London: Kemmish, 1820).
10. short-winded; fat.
11. A breed of harness horse with a high-stepping trot.
12. i.e. very cold, icy. The Coppermine river is in the far north of Canada's North West Territories.

'Oh, of course,' said I, somewhat stung that I should get a lesson in manner, where I had meant to be a model for imitation, 'if they like that kind of thing, I must only conform.'

from: THE NATION

CHARLES GAVAN DUFFY
(1816-1903)

[*The Nation* sold for sixpence (today's 2½ pence), and had a sales figure of about 10,000, resulting in a readership of close on a quarter of a million. Given the popular audience to which it was addressed, together with its 'tabloid' format, *The Nation* rarely produced lengthy analytical articles comparable to Butt's 'Past and Present State of Literature in Ireland'. On the other hand, the weekly paper carried news items which would have been dated in *The Dublin University Magazine*. No simple contrast between the two publications can be encouraged. Apart from Davis's early address, all the contributions printed below appeared anonymously.

The central role of Charles Gavan Duffy in *The Nation*'s development can be detected very early. In the first issue, he anonymously contributed what amounts to the paper's manifesto.]

'To create and to foster public opinion in Ireland— to make it racy of the soil.' — Chief Baron Woulfe.[1]

DUBLIN, SATURDAY, OCTOBER 15, 1842

With all the nicknames that serve to delude and divide us — with all their Orangemen and Ribbonmen, Torymen and Whigmen, Ultras and Moderados, and Heaven knows what rubbish besides, there are, in truth, but two parties in Ireland: those who suffer from her National degradation, and those who profit by it.[2] To a country like ours, all other distinctions are unimportant. This is the first article of our political creed; and as we desire to be known for what we are, we make it our earliest task to announce that the object of the writers of this journal is to organise the greater and better part of those parties, and to strive, with all our soul and with all our strength, for the diffusion and establishment of its principles. This will be the beginning, middle, and end of our labours.

And we come to the task with a strong conviction that there never was a moment more favorable for such a purpose than the present. The old parties are broken, or breaking up, both in England and Ireland — Whiggery, which never had a soul, has now no body; and the simplest partisan, or the most selfish expectant — who is generally a creature quite as unreasonable — cannot ask us to fix the hopes of our country on the fortunes of a party so weak and fallen.[3] Far less can we expect anything from Toryism, which could only serve us by ceasing to *be* Toryism; even in its new and modified form it means the identical reverse of all we require to make the masses in this country happier and better. But this shifting of parties — this loosening of belief in old distinctions and dogmas, has prepared men's minds for new and greater efforts. Out of the contempt for mere party politics will naturally grow a desire to throw aside small and temporary remedies — to refuse to listen any longer to those who would plaster a cut finger, or burn an old wart, and call this doctoring the body politic — and to combine for great and permanent changes. The point of honor which restrained multitudes from abandoning Whiggery, while their service could sustain it in its old accustomed place, can operate no more. The idiot hope, that Toryism might for once

1. Arthur Wolfe (1739-1803), first viscount Kilwarden, lord chief justice of Ireland from 1798; killed during the insurrection led by Robert Emmet.
2. The Orange Order was founded in 1795, to protect protestant privilege. Ribbonism was a less formally organized secret society, overwhelmingly of catholics. Tories and Whigs were the two dominant English political parties, though Tory derives from an Irish Gaelic term and Whig from a Scottish usage. Of the less official terms, Ultras (from the Latin) were extremists, Moderados weren't.
3. The Whigs had just lost a general election, in July 1841, and Robert Peel had become prime minister for the second time.

produce something good, has been pretty well disappointed; and, after an unexampled lull in politics, the popular party are ready, and willing, and anxious once again to be up and doing.

On this new spirit our hope for Ireland depends — and it will be our frequent duty hereafter to impress our views in detail on our readers, and to indicate all the ways and means of their accomplishment. We believe we will have the advice and co-operation of many of the wisest and best of our countrymen; and as our pages will be always open to fair discussion, we hope to reflect the popular mind, and gather the popular suffrage, within our columns upon this and all other questions of national politics.

But let us guard ourselves, from the very beginning, against being understood, when we speak of politics, to mean the thing which the phrase expresses in the vulgar tongue of journalism. By politics we mean the science of government, and all the facts and circumstances with which it must naturally deal. We do not mean, and never by any accident will mean, the calculation of chances on Mr. EDWARD LITTON's remaining for life a deputy in the Court of Chancery, or the comparative merits or demerits of Messrs. BREWSTER and Sergeant GREENE, or any other matter or thing which has not some direct leaning on the condition of our country; not that we by any means debar ourselves from laughing with SYDNEY SMITH, or at TRASHEM GREGG,[4] upon all proper occasions; but we will call this badinage, or pleasantry, or anything but politics.

For this National party in Ireland we believe it indispensable to its usefulness to claim, now and always, the right to stand at the head of all combined movements of Reformers in this country. They have too long forgotten or mistaken their true position. Is it not a lamentable absurdity — a blunder almost too ludicrous for an English commander in Affghanistan — to have the officers of an army less resolute and courageous than the soldiers? NAPOLEON, we believe, did not choose the Generals who led his legions to victory from the most timid and hesitating of the aristocracy, but from bold and sagacious men, whether in the ranks or on the staff. Those who go farthest ought naturally to lead the way. 'Come with us as far as we go together,' say the Moderate or Non-National party. 'Certainly,' we are prepared on all occasions to reply; 'but as we go farthest, just permit us, for convenience sake, to go foremost.' This is the tone which naturally belongs to a National party, and wanting which they must always want the dignity and solidity necessary to accomplish great effects.

But the first duty of men who desire to foster Nationality, is to teach the People not only the elevating influence but the intrinsic advantage of the principle and the thing. You cannot kindle a fire with damp faggots; and every man in the country who has not an interest in the existing system ought to be shown, as clearly as an abstract truth can be demonstrated, that National feelings, National habits, and National government, are indispensable to individual prosperity. This will be our task; and we venture to think we will perform it indifferently well.

But no National feeling can co-exist with the mean and mendicant spirit which esteems everything English as greater and better than if it belonged to our own country, and which looks at all the rest of the world through the spectacles of Anglican prejudice. There is no doubt at all that the chief source of the contempt with which we are treated by England is our own sycophancy. We abandon our self-respect, and we are treated with contempt; nothing can be more natural — nothing, in fact, can be more just. But we must open our eyes and look our domineering neighbour in the face — we must inspect him, and endeavour to discover what kind of a fellow he is. Not that we ought to do him injustice — not that we ought to run into opposite extremes — not, above all, that we ought to take universal England to be fairly represented by the disagreeable person who sometimes condescends to visit *H*ireland — a fat man, with his head in the clouds and his brains in his belly, looking the incarnation of self-importance, and saying, as plainly as plum-pudding countenance can speak — 'I am a Great Briton.' JOHN BULL is as much a better fellow than this animal, as he is worse than what our shameful sycophancy would make him. We must learn to think sensibly and candidly about him; and we do not doubt that THE NATION will tend materially to this end.

We may be told that we expect to effect too much

4. Edward Litton, a barrister, in 1839 had led a small band of Irish protestants who resisted government plans to liberalize municipal government in Ireland. Abraham Brewster (1796-1874) was an Irish barrister. By his title 'Sergeant', Greene was also a lawyer. The Rev. Tresham James Gregg (nicknamed Trashem by Daniel O'Connell) was a violently anti-catholic publicist.

through the means of a newspaper, but nobody who knows this country thoroughly will say this. A newspaper is the only conductor to the mind of Ireland. Periodicals or books make no considerable impression because they have no considerable circulation. Speeches are more effective; but we include them among the materials of journalism. O'CONNELL the orator, is as much the food of the Press as O'CONNELL the writer.[5] And it is undeniable that the journals, with all their means and appliances, were, and are, and are to be for many a day, the stimulating power in Ireland. Their work may not be apparent, but it is not the less sure; its slow and silent operation acts on the masses as the wind, which we do not see, moves the dust, which we do see — and in both cases the invisible giant is sometimes forgotten.

But, in addition to all that journalism has been, we shall add a new element to its strength. Men who have hitherto only written books, will now take this shorter and surer road to the popular mind. Already the ablest writers in the country are banded together to do this work; but we shall, besides, rally round us the young intellect of the country. Many a student, pent among books, has his mind full of benevolent and useful thoughts for his country, which the habits of a student's life would prevent him for ever from pouring out in the hot arena of politics. Such men will find a fitting vehicle in THE NATION; and our kindred love of letters will often induce them to turn with us from the study of mankind in books, to the service of mankind in politics. Such a legion will be more formidable than 'a thousand men all clad in steel'; each of them may fairly represent the multitude whom his intellect can set in motion; and the weapons which they will lay to the root of corruption will not be less keen or trenchant because they may cover them with the flowers of literature.

5. Daniel O'Connell (1775-1847), the Liberator.

'THOMAS MOORE' (1842)

[Duffy was also intensely interested in literature, and indeed at one point he read the manuscript of Sheridan Le Fanu's first attempt at a novel, advising the author on the treatment of Irish historical episodes. Literature, for *The Nation*, was not only the embodiment of Ireland's soul but also a field for propagandist colonization. The 'National Gallery' series included accounts of many Irish writers, and Gavan Duffy's essay on Thomas Moore points to the paper's commitment to the formulation of a coherent national culture in which recent catholic achievement would exist side by side with such figures as Jonathan Swift, Oliver Goldsmith and Laurence Sterne.]

> 'But half the effect would be lost, unless I could print his face with his joke.'
>
> (*Captain Rock*, p.245)

'There's Moore,' said we, handing this print to Ulick Burke; 'the best portrait painter in France, and the best wood-engraver out of it, have prepared that likeness for *The Nation*.'

'Surely,' he answered, 'Moore must look older; he is sixty-two, and heard the Volunteer's drums in his cradle.'[1]

'No matter,' we replied, 'that is as like him as possible; the last time we saw him was two days before the Whig dinner to Lord Morpeth[2] (at which he refused to attend). Moreover, 'twas near that corner of Trinity-street next King William's statue[3] — he was eyeing it as he went along, with a half-comical, half-serious look, just as he looks there now. He cannot have changed much since then.' 'At all events,' said Ulick, who is something of an artist, and has painted Connaught girls in his day, ''tis better than Lawrence's[4] comic daub prefixed to Moore's new edition — 'The gold and green edition,' as O'C[onnell?] calls it.'[5]

'There,' we continued, 'are the round contradictory eyes, projecting so as to tell you (even if you do not see him swinging his eye-glass') — 'A fashion for which,' interrupted our friend, 'the Queen is said to have fallen out with Lord Kitehill's daughter'[6] — 'that he is,' we went on, not minding the scandal, 'near-sighted; and yet they look as if they saw, and meddled with everything.

1. The Volunteer movement was highly influential in Irish politics between 1778 and 1792. Originally created to defend the country during the absence of regular troops in America (and so military in style), it came to demand reform and a degree of independence.
2. George William Frederick Howard (1802-64), sometime viscount Morpeth and later 7th earl of Carlisle, was chief secretary in Ireland 1835-41. Much later he was viceroy in Ireland.
3. King William III's statue was a major landmark and a cause of controversy in Dublin. Its site, in College Green near the junction with Trinity Street, is by a pleasing irony now occupied by a monument to Thomas Davis.
4. Sir Thomas Lawrence (1769-1830), English portrait painter; in 1820, he succeeded Benjamin West as president of the Royal Academy of Arts.
5. An annotated set of *The Nation* (in the Royal Irish Academy) specified Daniel O'Connell as the author of this comment.
6. On 23 October 1830, Moore sang at a private function when the Princess Victoria was present, and noted her appreciation of music in his journal.

But the wrinkled and clutched-up under eye-lid, and something like a groping movement of the head and neck, confirm one's first impression.'

'How much of the clever, petted, self-possessed wit of the "pet of the petticoats,"[7] there is in his nose and upper-lip; yet no one would expect that smooth, firm cheek and chin in so wild a boy as Moore is said to have been in his young days, and one who has talked, thought, studied, and lived so much. That full, almost swelling look about the head is very characteristic of him; and so is the single sweep round his temple and jaw; yet somehow and somewhere there ought to be a wrinkle more.' —

'But,' said our friend, who appeared to agree with the criticism, 'why, in the devil's name, did you put the little Whig into *The Nation* at all?' 'Because he is an Irishman, of whose genius Ireland is proud, and for whose services she is grateful; and we showed him where we had written, on a proof of the portrait, Byron's lines from the "Avatar of Brunswick" his revenge,' as he says, 'for Moore having attacked *his* Neapolitan Carbonari.'

If aught save oblivion could quench for an hour
My contempt for a people, so servile, yet sore —
Which, tho' trod like the worm, will not turn upon power;
'Tis the glory of Grattan and genius of Moore.[8]

'And what of that?' rejoined our friend; 'Byron himself said that, "Tommy loves a lord."[9] No doubt he praised the lord, and the lord, as in gratitude bound, praised Tommy,' and forthwith he jumped up and ran out, unwilling to listen to eulogy or defence of Moore.

'And can this,' thought we, taking up the "Melodies" — 'can this be forgotten?' No; these songs are no longer as they were, popular only in the drawing-rooms of Europe and America; they are gradually becoming known to the middle classes in Ireland, and the Irish translation bids fair to reach the mind of our peasantry. It may be fault or excellence in them; but Moore's songs bear translation. They not only have appeared in every European language, but they supplied the Poles with their most popular revolutionary and national songs during the last war — the highest honor ever shown to a lyrist — for Tyrtoeus, the Athenian schoolmaster, composed his Spartan songs in the Spartan camp.[10]

Why have the critics taken to disparaging Moore? Partly because he was over-praised. Even the latest favorable review of him is an extravagant and vulgar eulogy — a barrel-organ hymn to his praise. Men are tired of hearing him called the bard; and though we can trace the same mind (if not the same pen) from Bolster's 'Cork Quarterly,'[11] through the jibes of 'Fraser,'[12] and the solemner censure of 'Blackwood,'[13] yet we every day meet men uninfluenced by these writings, who question Moore's claims to genius.

Not only disgust at this coarse and exclusive praise, but excessive familiarity with a few, and those not the best of his songs, has helped out this scepticism as to his power in humbler circles. Moore's purse may have been served, but his fame has suffered from the law of copyright. There is no edition accessible to the people of any part of Moore's works except a few of the 'Melodies.' Again — the 'Melodies' were meant to be sung, and yet the music is out of print and enormously dear. Yet, we believe, with all this, no book (except the short lives of Lord Edward and Emmett)[14] has had such circulation here as the miserable edition of the earlier 'Melodies.'[15] When the rest of Moore's poems and the music of the 'Melodies' are to be had, his fame will be as great as ever.

Our patriots, too, are intolerant with Moore, because he is not all-out Irish; and seem to think they have some right to complain of him.

7. Untraced.
8. cf. the final stanza of Byron's 'The Irish Avatar'.
9. Apparently first observed in a letter to Leigh Hunt, but later publicly announced; Byron admired Moore, in fact.

10. Properly Tyrtaeus, Greek elegaic poet of the 7th century B.C. An Athenian legend has it that Athens sent him, a lame schoolmaster, to Sparta when Sparta needed help in a war.
11. *Bolster's Quarterly Magazine* was published in Cork between 1826 and 1831, Bolster being the publisher's name.
12. *Fraser's Magazine* was one of Victorian England's most successful magazines.
13. *Blackwood's Magazine*, a Scottish journal issued from 1817 by the firm that later published George Eliot's *Middlemarch*; a sternly sensible organ.
14. Moore's biography of Lord Edward Fitzgerald, *The Life and Death of Lord Edward Fitzgerald*, was published in 1831. He wrote no life of Emmet. Davis may be confusing this with Moore's *Memoirs of the Life of the Right Honourable Brinsley Sheridan*.
15. Moore's *Irish Melodies* is not a single volume, but a series of publications commencing in 1807. The reference is probably to the first collection, *Irish Melodies* (Dublin, 1820).

Now, fair play is a jewel. Let us remember what Moore was, and what he has done.

He was the son of a shopkeeper in Aungier-street — was unfortunate enough to write verses as soon as he could scribble without 'a copy' — shared in private theatricals at ten years' old — entered College at thirteen (when the bill of '93[16] first admitted Catholics to the University); and, in the same year, sent amorous rhymes to the *Anthologia Hibernica*,[17] and gave in his College exercises in English verse, instead of prose Latin like his neighbours. Thus he went through all the hazards of precocious talent, and, no doubt, suffered for it.

Talked of and spoiled of course he was. With great social talents, of a luxurious nature, and received, through the Moiras[18] (as a boy), into the best society of dissipated Dublin — might not a life frittered away in indulgence, and a genius exercised only in boudoir pedantry, have been looked for? But Moore had also known better things.

'*I remember*,' he said, 'being taken by my father (in 1792) to one of the dinners given in honor of the Revolution, and sitting on the knee of the Chairman, while the following toast went enthusiastically round — 'May the breezes from France fan the Irish oak into verdure!' He was in the junior and senior Historical Societies with Robert Emmett [*sic*] — heard his eloquence, and possessed his intimacy, if not his friendship. Emmett's mind must have greatly influenced him. He 'used sometimes,' says Moore, 'sit by me,' when playing the Irish airs from Bunting;[19] 'and I remember one day his starting up as from a reverie when I had just finished playing that spirited tune called the 'Red Fox,' and exclaiming, 'Oh, that I were at the head of twenty thousand men marching to that air!'

Edward Hudson,[20] Moore's dearest friend, was imprisoned as a United Irishman, and from a sketch on the walls of his cell the poet took the thought of his song, ''Tis believed that this harp.'

Moore was cross-questioned by Clare at the famous College visitation of '97,[21] and he held his own manfully against the imperious inquisitor.

Among the passions of the rebellion — an incipient contributor to the press — the auditor of Grattan, and the intimate of Emmett — he learned a lesson of patriotism which time may have unsettled, but which misfortune increased, and prosperity could not destroy.

'The child is father of the man:'[22] and of these elements here poured into his boyhood, Moore's cup of life has been composed. Luxury, aristocratic elegance, and wit, curl round a solid and aspiring patriotism like light clouds round a mountain, or a lady's pledge in a knight's helmet. Fancy and folly dip their branches and their brambles into the stream of his strongest passions. In the background of many of his triumphs, his faults are seen flying — flying, but seen!

But we must write about Moore, not mimic him. He early commenced a translation of 'Anacreon,'[23] and, in search of materials, used to frequent Marsh's Library (at St. Patrick's Cathedral).[24] He was often shut in there after the library hours, and there laid the foundation of his varied and 'out-of-the-way' learning.

He entered the Middle Temple in 1799, being in his nineteenth year, and immediately published the 'Anacreon.' In consequence of this, and of Lord Moira's introduction, he received some slight civilities (and no more) from that selfish vagabond, George Prince of Wales; and this promised to ruin him, by the attractive and dissipated society to which it gave him a passport. Yet there (as in his Dublin circle) he met men whose wildest indulgence were full of thought and fancy — the madness of fallen angels — the revels of Olympian gods. Sheridan and Fox[25] were among the revellers.

Yet, in another way it seriously injured him,

16. The Catholic Relief Act of 1793 was arguably the single most important measure of its kind before emancipation in 1829.
17. *Anthologia Hibernica* was subtitled a 'monthly collection of science, belles lettres, Irish history, antiquities, topography etc.'. Four volumes appeared in 1793-94, each being about 500 pages in length. It was thus a major contribution to intellectual life in Ireland.
18. Francis Rawdon-Hastings (1754-1826), 2nd earl of Moira, who, with his wife, acted as one of Moore's most influential patrons.
19. Edward Bunting (1773-1843), musicologist; his first collection of Irish music appeared in 1796.
20. Imprisoned in 1798, later emigrated to the United States of America where he became a pioneer in dentistry.
21. The authorities suspected the existence of a United Irishman 'cell' in Trinity College, Dublin. The vice-chancellor of the college (John FitzGibbon, the earl of Clare), and one of the fellows (Patrick Duigenan) conducted a visitation in April 1797, interrogating undergraduates and fellows alike.
22. From William Wordsworth's 'Ode: Intimations of Immortality from Recollections of Early Childhood'.
23. Moore's *Odes of Anacreon* was published in 1800.
24. The library founded by Archbishop Narcissus Marsh (1638-1713) stands to the south of Saint Patrick's Cathedral in Dublin.
25. Richard Brinsley Sheridan (1751-1816) and Charles James Fox (1749-1806) were the principal leaders of the Whig party.

by connecting him so much with England. Living in the land of the oppressor and the company of aristocrats, Moore weakened the fire of his passions and corrupted his taste. Lansdowne House[26] lured him from the people, and Slopperton Cottage, Somersetshire,[27] was an odd abode for the national bard. We never think of the author of the 'Melodies' — the passionate and fanciful Irishman, caged in by the adulation and formality of his present life — without recalling the wild starling shut up, and calling out in taught words, but real feeling — 'I can't get out,' 'I can't get out,' said the starling.

This grieves us; but let us be just.

Look at Moore's life — 'tis that of a literary man — his works. His prose, with but one considerable exception (his 'Life of Byron') belong to the Irish people — the 'Lives of Sheridan and Fitzgerald,' his 'Captain Rock,' his 'Travels of an Irish Gentleman,' and his 'History of Ireland.'[28]

The 'Life of Sheridan' may be weak; and the history *is* cold, feeble, and English — a grief to *his* friends — a gratification to the haters of Ireland; but the 'Life of Fitzgerald' is a patriot's offering on a native shrine; and 'Captain Rock' is the wisest, wittiest, and most successful attempt ever made to interest the honor, humanity, the imagination, and good humour of the oppressor, in the cause of the wronged, without in the least compromising the pride and honor of the oppressed.

Moore's first poems sung no sentiment save love. Nor let anyone make light of this; for on verses far inferior and much less decorous, Catullus,[29] Anacreon, and others have floated down to us. Yet we confess that, among the clustering loveliness, the grace, and the unrivalled playfulness of the poems to Julia and Nea, we lack the hearty, passionate love of Burns, and of that race of Scottish bards of whom Burns is the most known. Indeed, in all his poems, there is too much chiselling and polish, and too little rough vigour and plain words. Most of his latest have ability without passion; but the ability is of the highest order — full of jest and true sparkling epigram — a humour which never hesitates and rarely repeats itself; and if his irony be not as terrible as Swift's, his sarcasm is as keen as Voltaire's.[30]

But to the intermediate period which produced the 'Melodies,' 'Lalla Rookh,'[31] the 'National Songs,'[32] Moore will owe his future fame as a poet. It is of this time Sheridan's words are true — 'No man puts so much of his heart in his fancy as Tom Moore — his soul seems as if it were a particle of fire separated from the sun, and was always fluttering to get back to the source of light and heat.'[33]

No man has hazarded severer criticisms on himself than Moore. For instance, the prose of 'Lalla Rookh' has the most plausible and cutting strictures on the verse; yet 'tis a glorious book — 'tis a long, wild, sweet, barbarous, and fascinating melody. Malcolm, Elphinstone, Burns[34] — no bad judges — speak of its accuracy in history, manners, scenery, and costume, as perfect; and that it truly represents Oriental character and feeling, the intense admiration with which it is viewed by all Persians and Indians acquainted with it (and they are not a few), is the best proof. 'The Vale of Cashmere,' in 'The light of the Harem,' and the 'Gardens in Mokanna,' are hardly inferior to Spenser. 'The Guebre's Mount' might have been painted by Salvator Rosa;[35] and if ever there was a pure lover, a gallant, faithful, and devoted chief, a patriot to glorify defeat, and shed an example from the light of his funeral pile, it is Hafed the Persian. And, reader, if you doubt that Moore is a poet, and of the highest order, take up that scene where the prayer is prayed that redeems the Peri.[36]

26. London home of the Petty-FitzMaurice family, marquises of Lansdowne.
27. Properly spelled Sloperton, Moore's permanent English home.
28. *The Works of Lord Byron; with his Letters and Journals, and his Life* (1835); *Memoirs of the Life of the Right Hon. R. B. Sheridan* (1825); *The Life and Death of Lord Edward Fitzgerald* (1831); *Memoirs of Captain Rock, the Celebrated Irish Chieftain* (1824); *Travels of an Irish Gentleman in Search of a Religion* (1833); *The History of Ireland* (1833-46).
29. Catullus (*c.* 84-54 B.C.), Roman poet noted for his erotic themes.
30. Jonathan Swift (1667-1745) and Voltaire (1694-1778) are regarded as the supreme masters of satire, in English and French respectively, of the eighteenth century.
31. Moore published his long 'oriental romance' in 1817.
32. Moore's *National Airs* appeared in several volumes between 1818 and 1827.
33. Untraced.
34. Sir John Malcolm (1769-1833), diplomat, historian, and administrator of India; George Keith Elphinstone (1746-1823), viscount Keith, an admiral who in his younger days had sailed in the Far East, notably to China and Ceylon; Burns is either Sir Alexander Burnes (1805-41), traveller in Asia, and linguist, or James Burnes (1801-62), physician in India.
35. Salvator Rosa (1615-73), Italian painter, immensely popular in England for his wild landscapes, thought to be prime examples of 'The Sublime'.
36. The second tale in Moore's *Lallah Rookh*, 'Paradise and the Peri', tell how this sprite, expelled from heaven, is readmitted when she brings the 'gift most dear to the Almighty'. It is a repentant tear prompted by the sight of an old man kneeling to pray.

We recollect seeing an eccentric sign of enthusiasm for Moore — it was a sketch, (in which, if there were vulgarity, the Greeks, who hung a balance in the sky, and Milton, who weighed the fate of Jehovah's foe in it, were vulgar), where the 'Epicurean'[37] was pictured weighing down all Byron's works — an extravagant and undeserved praise; and yet the 'Epicurean' is a sweet story, full of indulgence and religion, faith, and self-will, the characteristics of generous minds. The publication of 'Alciphron,'[38] a bad versification of it, injured the 'Epicurean,' and gave occasion to the ablest critique ever written on Moore, that in the *Citizen*.[39]

As a lyrist, Moore belongs to the classical school; Archilochus,[40] Horace,[41] and Catullus, influenced his taste and restrained his powers. He is among the first of his school, and, at least, equal to his models. It may be that he and they are inferior to the narrative lyrists, the old ballad writers; and it is certain that he has not habitually equalled Burns and Beranger.[42] But is it nothing to have written some songs equal to their best, and even, in the bulk of his melodies, to be inferior only to them? Where does joy sparkle more wildly-daring than in his 'To Ladies' eyes a round, boy,' or 'Wreath the Bowl,' or 'The song for the Pococurante Society'? What gayer courtship is there than 'Nora Creina'? — what tenderer woe than in 'Love's Dream,' 'I saw from the beach,' 'As a beam on the face of the waters may flow,' and that song which we just this minute heard a well-looking fellow whistling under the window, 'As slow our ship its foamy track,' to say nothing of the ever-heart-dwelling 'Oft in the stilly night'? What more passionate love than in 'I saw thy form in youthful prime,' or 'Come rest in this bosom'? And where — except in Beranger, and in one rare instance in Burns, and in four or five scattered poems — will you meet more truthful and inspiring patriotism than in the 'Songs of Innisfallen,' the too much quoted 'Remember thee,' or 'Oh, where's the slave so lowly?' Enough these; we could name others not inferior, enough to make immortal the fame of the bard, and the gratitude and love of his country. Even the coldest critics may take them in ransom for his coldly-glittering imagery in many songs, and the patriot accept them as peace offerings for the so-called 'History of Ireland.'

Of one of these songs, 'While History's Muse,' Moore tells us he remarked, when the Emancipation Bill was passed by Wellington, 'that he never suspected he was a prophet till then'; for in it the great warrior is bidden to consummate his glory by emancipating his countrymen.

Moore is an orator, too. Besides many admirable speeches at literary dinners in Dublin, Paris, and London, he has been successful more than once in replying to the congratulations of frieze-coated men in Wexford and elsewhere; and a few years ago we heard him — certainly under the compulsion of as intolerant enthusiasm as we ever witnessed — address a full theatre in Dublin, on a night when he patronised the performance, and nothing could be in better taste than his short, plain, earnest thanks. And on the 15th of September, 1830, at a meeting held at Home's mart[43] in Dublin, where Sheil[44] made one of his most brilliant speeches, and where the proprietor of the *Evening Mail*, Mr. Sheehan, and Mr. George Alexander Hamilton,[45] vied with each other in fiery democracy, Moore spoke, and far excelled them all. His delivery that day was hearty and impressive, his voice was distinct through the huge room, and his thoughts (worded like a veteran orator's) came with more instruction, relevancy, and feeling, and were received with more tear-filled eyes and soul-filled voices, than any we heard on that (in Ireland) memorablest day of a believing time. We did not think we had much to say of Moore when we sat down — we know not how to stop writing about him.

37. Moore's *The Epicurean, a Tale* was published in 1827.
38. In 1839, Moore published *Alciphron: a poem*, a versified rendering of *The Epicurean*; the edition was illustrated by J. M. W. Turner.
39. Published in Dublin, *The Citizen* was 'a monthly journal of politics, literature, and art' which ran to two substantial volumes in 1839-40.
40. Archilochus (7th century B.C.) was a Greek poet with a taste for anti-romantic and satirical topics.
41. Horace, properly Quintus Horatius Flaccus (65-8 B.C.), Rome's greatest non-epic poet.
42. Pierre Jean de Béranger (1780-1857), French lyric poet, who, like Burns, fitted his verse to popular melodies. Since he used his poems to express republican and Bonapartist ideas, his popularity and influence were considerable.
43. Home's mart in Dublin, in fact the National Mart. The meeting was held to celebrate the 1830 French Revolution, Charles X having abdicated on 2 August.
44. Richard Lalor Sheil (1791-1851), dramatist, orator and politician; an associate of Daniel O'Connell. After catholic emancipation in 1829, he became MP for Milborne Port, Somerset.
45. *The Dublin Evening Mail* was a staunchly conservative paper, so that the idea of its proprietor vying with anyone in fiery democracy is laughable. Thomas Sheehan was its proprietor. George Alexander Hamilton (1802-71) became Conservative MP for Dublin University in 1843. Moore's own account of the meeting in his diary suggests that Sheil was less impressive, and Moore himself less confident than the present article claims. There were about 2,000 people present.

'MR. LEVER'S "IRISH" NOVELS' (1843)

[The difference of attitude, both in literary and political terms, between *The Dublin University Magazine* and *The Nation* was rarely clearer than in their estimate of Charles Lever's merits as a novelist. The analysis that follows constitutes one of the longest articles on a literary topic published in *The Nation*, and its close scrutiny of Lever's text indicates Gavan Duffy's concern with the treatment of Irish life in fiction. Lever's biographers aver that the novelist was deeply wounded by the criticism, which contributed to his decision shortly afterwards to leave Ireland. Lever's later fiction displays a growing sympathy with Irish national feeling, and it is ironic that Gavan Duffy had by then abandoned Ireland for a career in Australian politics.]

The time is long gone by when the Quack and the Clown carried on a prosperous partnership in the sale of nostrums — the one collecting a crowd with his antics, and the other, by his indomitable effrontery, persuading them into the purchase of the rubbish. In this enlightened and sceptical century we might be inclined to doubt that there ever existed a people who could be cheated by such naked Charlatanism, if we had not their legitimate successors in our own day, in the patrons of Mr. Lever, who has revived the boisterous merriment of the Clown in his style, and the intrepid ignorance of the Quack in his plots. We are a patient and long-enduring people, we Irish; and there is truth in the national imputation, that when one of us is put upon a spit, half-a-dozen others will cheerfully help to turn him, till he is roasted to a cinder. But we are less tolerant of injury from the stranger; and when the son of an English artisan — which it is no discredit to Mr. Lever to be — issues, month after month, a series of grotesque portraits, begotten between the prejudice of his country and the ignorance of his class, and entitles them the Irish people, it is fully time to call out for 'Justice to Ireland.'

The character of our countrymen is an enigma to those who know them best: their habitual gaiety, their wild grief, their piety, their ferocity, their hospitality, and all the changeable phases of their disposition, require years of observation and study to understand; and there is, perhaps, but one writer, after all, who has reduced the phenomena to order, and mastered the philosophy of Irish life. To attain a glimmering of this knowledge, education and opportunity (not to speak of natural capacity for the task) must be united even in one born and bred among the people. To an Englishman it is altogether unattainable. If 'none but a poet can understand a poet,'[1] we may be excused for maintaining that none but an Irishman can understand an Irishman. The ablest stranger would find the investigation surrounded by insurmountable difficulties, for nearly a similar reason that Newton or Nelson[2] would make at best a contemptible critic upon Shakespeare.

But Mr. Lever has not been daunted by any of these difficulties — he has found a shorter road to his object than any of his predecessors, as a poacher finds it a shorter and more convenient way to go through the hedge than round by the gate. Taking the common stage-Irishman, who figures in farces and never existed anywhere else in the universe, he has borrowed wholesale from contemporary writers incidents in which to exhibit him, and sprinkling in the dialogue a few jokes to be found in every jest-book, the result has been, the works which are called Irish novels. Let us not be supposed to exaggerate — we know nothing of the gentleman except through his writings, and have no wish to make him worse than he is; but as counsel for Ireland against her libeller, we must not shrink from our duty, and we are prepared to show that a large proportion of Mr. Lever's writings are not new (to use a mild periphrasis), and that what is new is marked by the most incredible ignorance of the country about which he writes.

We are not unaware that he has a long list of admirers, and that his works have been lauded in the newspapers almost as immeasurably as Holloway's Ointment.[3] We perceive, indeed, by the advertisement on the cover of a number of *Charles O'Malley*,[4] that 'his productions, compared with the recent writings of Mr. Dickens, bear the same analogy as does the sun to a taper';* and the same authority pronounces his portraitures 'most natural, and characteristic of the natives of the Green Isle.' Indeed, their wonderful truth was universally proclaimed by the English journalists —

* *Worcester Journal.*

1. Untraced.
2. Sir Isaac Newton (1642-1727), English scientist; Horatio, Viscount Nelson (1758-1805), English vice-admiral.
3. Thomas Holloway (1800-83), English inventor and vendor of a famous patent medicine.
4. Charles Lever's novel was first published in monthly instalments, quite a normal procedure at the time.

who were such competent judges of the matter — and moreover, by not a few at home. We do not blame Englishmen for admiring them; nothing could be more reasonable or in course, as they formed their taste and acquired their notions of Irish life in the exact schools from which they were borrowed — the stage and the caricature-shop. A fellow who wears a pipe in his hat-band — thinks a crow-bar a 'nate article' and 'mighty convanient to crack a skull with' — swears by 'my showl', and addresses everyone as 'honey' and 'joy', is what these people have in their mind when they think of an Irishman; and the nearer the portraiture comes to this standard, the more correct and characteristic they esteem it. Even at home this criterion is by no means an unusual one. Many resort to plays or novels for notions of their countrymen, instead of looking into the streets and fields; and in verification of the old fable, the actor who plays the pig is generally pronounced more natural and piggish than the pig himself. We have recently read all Mr. Lever's completed works with great attention, and we seriously and deliberately declare that there is not one national character in the entire series to which we have ever met a corresponding man or woman in real life; while the majority have exactly the same relation to the actual people among whom we live that the scarecrow, intended to represent an Irishman on the cover of *Charles O'Malley*, bears to a Meath or Tipperary peasant, as you find him at his labour or in his sports. The same spirit of exaggeration is at work everywhere, engrafted upon a monotony of character which argues, not merely a poverty of invention, but an utter ignorance of human nature. There is no anatomy — no contrast — no shade — no repose. A peasant is *all* brogue and blunder — a country gentleman an *eternal* fighter and eater — and the life of an officer a perennial succession of dining, supping, drinking, and joking, not only impossible to any man made up of nerves, sinews, muscles, and a complicated system of digestive organs, but which would infallibly exhaust a convivial steam-engine. It would be quite as reasonable, and more charitable of our English neighbours, to fall back upon their ancient notions, that we had tails and horns, than to believe these other physical impossibilities of us.

However, our present business is not to convict Mr. Lever of misrepresenting us. It is difficult to uproot favourite prejudices, and we might fail to convince our English friends that we are not the drunken, rioting, lunatic race he chooses to picture us. We will accordingly content ourselves at present with demonstrating that the incidents, which he has been exhibiting as his experience of Irish life, are stolen from as many sources as the contents of a gipsy's wallet; and that he is more ignorant of the leading events of the history, social and political, of the periods which he attempts to describe, than Mr. Morrison,[5] the other quack, of the principles of medicine. Having established these facts beyond dispute, perhaps there will be less difficulty hereafter in proving that he is not the most competent person, morally or intellectually, to paint the national character of a people.

Mr. Lever's first novel, *Harry Lorrequer*, unlike the first work of a man of genius, which, if sometimes immature and diffuse, is always fresh and racy, was a mere imitation, borrowed by wholesale from the writings of Mr. Maxwell — chiefly *My Life*.[6] To read them together is like comparing the two best parodies in the *Rejected Addresses* with Byron and Scott.[7] The resemblance is quite as close, and the enjoyment would be as great if it were not that a plagiarism suggests very different feelings from a parody. The resemblance of style (which it would occupy too much time to illustrate), will suggest itself to any reader familiar with the books; and the incidents it will not be difficult to recall.

In both novels the hero, who is a military man, happens to have a namesake who is also a cousin, and for whom he is mistaken, and thereby gets into incredible scrapes — in both novels the hero is a moderate, temperate gentlemen, whereas his cousin is a harum-scarum-extravagant person — in both there is an unfriendly relative, upon whose favor the plot turns, and who in each case relents at the end, and endows the hero with a large estate. In *My Life*, Captain Blake's uncle sends a challenge to the uncle of his nephew's betrothed, a fine melodramatic incident of which there is no trace in *Harry*

5. Probably Thomas Morrison (died 1835?), an English medical writer who moved to Dublin in 1806. He analysed the Brunonian theory according to which all disease is caused by an excess or deficiency of excitement. *The Nation* took particular pride in refusing to accept classified advertisements from what it regarded as 'quack' doctors.
6. William Hamilton Maxwell (1792-1850), Irish novelist and popular historian. *Adventures of Captain Blake; or, My Life* was published in three volumes in 1835; a second edition in 1838.
7. The title of a book by James and Horatio Smith (1775-1839; 1779-1849) first published in 1812 and subsequently running to many editions: it contained literary parodies, the best being of Byron and Scott.

Lorrequer; but we find it very effectively reproduced in *Charles O'Malley*, whose uncle (a copy of Manus Blake, by the way) does exactly the same thing by the father of Lucy Dashwood. There is a duel in *My Life*, and, of course, there is a duel in *Harry Lorrequer*. In Mr. Maxwell's novel the parties go to the ground without the hero's having ascertained the name of his adversary — Ditto, in Mr. Lever's. In both cases the second of this unknown adversary is an Irishman, who loves fighting above all things, and who is famous for his skill in managing such affairs. This personage picks a 'sweet spot' for placing the parties in *My Life*, and in *Lorrequer* he does precisely the same thing. In both novels there is joking upon the way in which the ground was stepped — upon the discussion whether the distance should be ten paces or twelve — upon the politeness with which the seconds saluted each other, and the sociality with which they chatted while they were arranging the details for sending a couple of gentlemen out of the world. So far, so well; but Maxwell's hero fights with 'saw-handled pistols', whereas it is his opponent uses these weapons in *Lorrequer* — a bold and broad departure from the original. In both novels there is the identical adventure of one of the subordinate characters mistaking a strange chaise for his own, and driving off in it to the great detriment of a third party. In *My Life*, one of the characters ran away with the wrong lady — an accident which we were disappointed in not finding in *Harry Lorrequer*, as its probability suited so exactly for transplanting to that soil; but we were consoled by its consequent appearance in *Charles O'Malley*. Mr. Maxwell paints a lady who attempts to decoy an inexperienced young officer into matrimony, and Mr. Lever does the same. Both ladies spout poetry — the former quotes —

'In peace love tunes the shepherd's reed.'

The latter —

'There are hearts that live and love alone.'

There are a number of letters from Connaught in *My Life*, of which we have no account in *Harry Lorrequer*; but again *Charles O'Malley* comes to the rescue. We beg the reader to compare them himself — to quote them at length would be intolerable — and he will find such gentle metamorphoses as the following:

'Biddy Macan, the girl with the black eyes, that you sent the cloak and bonnet to from Dublin, has gone for change of air to her aunt's in Roscommon. The devils in the neighbourhood wanted to make some story about you, &c.' — *Letter from Connaught* in *'My Life'*.

'Peggy Maher left this on Tuesday — she was complaining of a weakness; she's gone to consult the doctors. I am sorry for poor Peggy' — *Letter from Connaught* in *'Charles O'Malley'*.

Elsewhere he will find such pleasant parallels as this:

'Well, I think,' said the surgeon, 'A SICK CERTIFICATE WILL DO: but the disease?' 'Consumption,' said Jack the Devil; 'I had a *fourth cousin* that died of it.' 'It won't do,' said his counsellor; 'they will expect you to drink milk, eat fish and wear flannel.'

'D—n fish and flannel,' replied the invalid; 'What do you think of blood to the head?' 'Won't answer,' was the reply; 'they would put you on the muzzle, interdict port, and prohibit hunting. Come, I have it — you have overgrown your strength, require country air, gentle exercise, and a generous diet. COULD YOU MANAGE A SHORT COUGH?' The doctor hemmed — the patient imitated it. 'Very good — try again — excellent. I have seen a man in phthisis that could not cough as well.'

— *My Life*, page 185.

'A SICK CERTIFICATE!' said I, in some surprise. 'The only thing for you,' said Fitzgerald, taking a long pinch of snuff; 'and I grieve to say you have a most villanous look of good health about you.' 'I must acknowledge I never felt better.' 'So much the worse — so much the worse,' said Fitzgerald, despondingly; 'is there no *family complaint* — no respectable heirloom of infirmity, you can lay claim to from *your kindred*?' 'None that I know of, unless a very active performance on the several occasions of breakfast, dinner, and supper.'

★ ★ ★

Fitz proceeded to strike my chest several times, with his finger tips. 'TRY A SHORT COUGH now,' said he. 'Ah! that will never do.'

— *Harry Lorrequer*.

Of general 'conveyancing', there is more than one reader can pretend to point out; for, though our acquaintance with English literature is reasonably extensive, Mr. Lever may have poached on a hundred preserves of which we have never even heard. No poverty or obscurity is a protection against his rapacity. Unlike the chivalrous robbers of whom we used to read in the nursery (while Mr. Ainsworth[8] yet was not), who plundered the rich and protected the poor, all pay tribute who fall into his hands. He is as indiscriminate in his pilferings as *Filch* in the *Beggar's Opera*[9] — now tugging at the gold watch of Mr. Maxwell, anon delving his fingers among the rags and filth of Watty Cox's[10] literary unmentionables, to draw forth a handful of coppers. In fact, in assiduity and expertness he is entitled to be considered a genuine *Chevalier d'Industrie*.

Examples are as plenty as blackberries. In *Charles O'Malley* his uncle escapes from his creditors on a sudden dissolution of parliament, by feigning death and going off in a hearse. The same incident, in all its details, may be found in one of the stories called *To-day in Ireland*.[11] In *Jack Hinton* the rescue of Louisa Bellew at St. Lerran's Well is taken from *The Antiquary*,[12] and bears the same resemblance to the original that the woodcuts after Raphael in the *Penny Magazine*[13] do to the actual Cartoons. *Harry Lorrequer* forges autographs to astonish his female acquaintances; but *Vivian Grey* did exactly the same, though a great while before.[14] In *O'Malley*, old Dalrymple talks to his young friend of the blessings of matrimony, of the happiness of marrying a kindred spirit — instances his own wife and himself, and all but offers him his daughter, every feature of which may be found in the scene in *Gilbert Gurney*,[15] where he is stimulated to propose for Miss Wells by her father. Again, in *O'Malley* an old cavalry horse, under the influence of former habits, obeys the sound of a trumpet and carried his rider among a troop of dragoons, an incident made so familiar by the poetry and illustrations of 'Dr. Syntax,'[16] that it is not easy understanding how Mr. Lever could venture to bring it again before the public.

But these are mostly single incidents; let us take a few scenes. In the fifteenth number of *Charles O'Malley*, Colonel O'Shaughnessy tells the story of his father's arrest by an ingenious bailiff. He was on his keeping, and guarded himself so well there was no reaching him; but one day, observing from his window a duel which he thought was managed unfairly, he rushed out to give his services to the party, and was arrested notwithstanding a desperate resistance, in which he gave the bailiff some tremendous blows. So says Mr. Lever; but Watty Cox, some two dozen years before, told the same story:

'The Reillys had a warrant about two years since, against a gentleman of the name of O'Hara, who lived in Blessington-street. It was found hopeless to obtain an interview with Mr. O'Hara, as he kept the key of the hall-door, and a constant fire in all his chimnies, which precluded an exercise of Mr. Neil's ingenuity. However, it was made known by Mr. Reilly's chief attorney, Mr.——, who usually dines at Mr. Reilly's table, that Mr. O'Hara was a Connaught gentleman, and consequently an admirer of pistol exercise — a man who would rather fight twenty battles, or spend ten pipes of port on his visitors, than pay ten pounds. Reillys taking advantage of their legal friend's hint, prepared to hook their game by a bait exactly suited to his taste. They appeared next morning about four o'clock, dressed in proper character, attended by one gentleman, on a piece of waste ground, exactly under Mr. O'Hara's windows, their horses were made fast to a stump of a tree, their pistol cases were laid on the grass, while they proceeded to measure ground, as if they were preparing an affair of honor; the cabal and argument was so continued that it should reach the ears of Mr. O'Hara, who was not deaf to the noise. He got up, and perceiving two gentlemen on a serious affair, struck with the awkward novelty of a duel with only one second, ran downstairs, and most cordially offered his friendly assistance to make up the deficiency in point of numbers. The gentlemen bowed, and one of them stepping up, told him very politely he had a writ against him. Nothing can describe O'Hara's

8. William Harrison Ainsworth (1805-82), popular author of historical and adventure novels, twenty-nine of them.
9. John Gay (1685-1832), English poet and dramatist, best known for *The Beggar's Opera* (1728).
10. Walter Cox (1770-1837), Irish gunsmith and journalist.
11. *Today in Ireland* was the work of Eyre Evans Crowe (1799-1868).
12. Sir Walter Scott (1771-1832) published *The Antiquary* in 1815.
13. There were several journals with names of this kind, generally a cheap medium for the dissemination of culture to the lower middle classes, e.g. *The Irish Penny Magazine* (1833) and *The Irish Penny Journal* (1840-41).
14. *Vivian Grey* was Benjamin Disraeli's first novel, published with great success in 1826-27.
15. *Gilbert Gurney* was an anonymous novel (1836) by Theodore Edward Hook (1788-1841), English writer, wit and (possibly) embezzler, who founded and edited *John Bull*, a Tory periodical.
16. A fictional character invented by William Combe (1741-1823) for verses to accompany comic illustrations by Thomas Rowlandson (1756-1827). *The Tour of Dr. Syntax in Search of the Picturesque* (1812) was a great success.

confusion at losing his liberty, and the amusement he promised himself by the combat. He recovered from the surprise in a second or two, and so enraged was he while they were leading him off the ground, that he snapped a large stick from one of his guards, and in a twinkling gave the elder Reilly three or four blows which had nearly dispatched the gripper,[17] and eventually would have caused his death, had not the united skill of Surgeons Redmond and Drury poised him above the grasp of death with great difficulty and success.' — *Watty Cox's Magazine, vol. 8, page 27.*

The following parallel will speak for itself:

They had never seen a Scotch regiment before, and were consequently somewhat puzzled at the costume, till at last one more cunning than the rest explained it by saying 'they are in such a hurry to kill the poor black man, they came away without their breeches!' — *Charles O'Malley, page* 189.	Pat, who in all the varieties of life, had never seen the Highland costume before, gazed in surprise on his fallen enemy, addressing him in his native language — 'Take that, and much good may it do you; you were in a divil of a hurry after me this morning when you did not wait to put on your breeches!' — *Teeling's Narrative of the Irish Rebellion, page* 221.[18]

In *Jack Hinton* (No. VII), there is a story of Major Mahon's arrest, while keeping his house to avoid bailiffs. He fell in love with a widow across the way, made tender signals to her at the window, and finally, one day seeing her (as he thought) fall opposite his door, rushed out to assist her, and was captured by a pair of bailiffs, disguised as the widow and her servant. It is unnecessary to quote both stories after the proofs we have already exhibited; but the same anecdote will be found in Watty Cox's *Magazine* for 1815, page 82. So much for the incidents which English criticism has pronounced natural, genuine, original, and racy, and the main charm of the *Lorrequer* novels.

A still larger proportion of Mr. Lever's materials are borrowed from that very ill-used personage, Joe Miller.[19] If jokes become classical by antiquity, many of those in the volumes before us may be traced back to Hierocles, and most of the others his friends may insist upon enjoying on the same principles that the butler in Goldsmith's comedy, relishes old *Hardcastle's* favourite story, 'Ecod, master, if I'm not to laugh, you must not tell the story of old grouse in the gun room, for I have been laughing at that *these thirty years*.'[20] Let us take a few examples here and there out of a couple of his earliest volumes. We have Dr. Quill enlisting in the 33d regiment, to be near his brother in the 34th — a joke that has seen more service than the Commander of the Forces. We have Micky Free objecting to a French prisoner being liberated from his grasp on the old grounds — 'If you had as much trouble in catching him as I had, you'd think twice before letting him out.' We have a gentleman described as 'the father of the poor, and uncle to Lord Donoughmore,' *vice* the old story of Boyle, the celebrated scholar, who was presented to a country meeting as 'the father of chemistry, and brother of the Earl of Cork'. Elsewhere, we have our ancient acquaintance, the anecdote of the Irishman (of course an Irishman must be the scape-goat) mistaking a pompous and pedantic direction to *lave* a slovenly soldier in the river for one to *leave* him there; the popular story of Curran dumb-founding a fishwoman by calling her an adjective (with, however, the material difference that Mr. Lever's man calls his antagonist a pronoun!); the venerable joke of a regiment being first mustered and then peppered; the familiar caution to a duellist who could break a glass at twelve paces, that he must not reckon upon the same skill in an actual encounter, as the glass had no pistol in hand; the famous story of Father O'Leary meeting a countryman exhibiting in a show in France as a wild Indian (served up in *Harry Lorrequer* as 'Billy M'Cabe and the Knight of Kerry'); and the ancestral joke of the pilot, who, when questioned whether he knew the rocks along the coast he was steering by, replied, 'By Gor, I do, and there's one of them,' metamorphosed into a car driver on the Rock-road who warns his 'fare' of a rut, and being asked if he knew its whereabouts, of

17. In Irish usage, a sheriff's officer, a bailiff.
18. Charles Hamilton Teeling (1778-1850), United Irishman and journalist; his *Personal Narrative of the Rebellion of 1798* was published in 1828.
19. *Joe Miller's Jest-Book* was published in 1739, the year following the death of the comedian Joseph Miller (born 1684) after whom it was named — without authority. Thus a 'Joe Miller' is a tired joke, a chestnut.
20. Hardcastle is a character in Oliver Goldsmith's comedy, *She Stoops to Conquer*.

course replies, 'By Gor, you're in it.' These grave and reverend seignors are really entitled to be put on the peace establishment;[21] and unless Mr. Lever intend them, like the skeleton at an Egyptian banquet, as an antidote to unbecoming merriment, their presence among modern men is inexcusable. Cardinal Wolsey's Hall at Hampton Court,[22] with its arms and banners of the sixteenth century, does not throw us back more completely among the forgotten dead.

But Mr. Lever's songs are greatly admired; and if we left him bare of reputation for prose, he might still, we may be told, rest securely upon them. We shall see. The most admired, and, in fact, the best of his songs, is 'Widow Malone' in *Charles O'Malley*, which we insert for the sake of those who may not have seen it before:

THE WIDOW MALONE

Did ye hear of the Widow Malone,
Ohone!
Who lived in the town of Athlone
Alone?
Oh! she melted the hearts
Of the swains in them parts,
So lovely the Widow Malone,
Ohone!
So lovely the Widow Malone.

Of lovers she had a full score,
Or more:
And fortunes they all had galore,
In store;
From the minister down
To the clerk of the crown,
All were courting the Widow Malone,
Ohone!
All were courting the Widow Malone.

But so modest was Mrs. Malone,
'Twas known
No one ever could see her alone,
Ohone!
Let them ogle and sigh,
They could ne'er catch her eye
So bashful the Widow Malone,
Ohone!
So bashful the Widow Malone,

Till one Mister O'Brien from Clare,
How quare!
It's little for blushin' they care
Down there;
Put his arm round her waist,
Gave ten kisses at laste,
'Oh,' says he, 'you're my Molly Malone,
My own;'
'Oh,' says he, 'you're my Molly Malone.'

And the Widow they all thought so shy,
My eye!
Ne'er thought of a simper or sigh,
For why?
But 'Lucius,' said she,
'Since you've made now so free,
You may marry your Mary Malone,
Ohone!
You may marry your Mary Malone.'

There's a moral contained in my song,
Not wrong;
And one comfort it's not very long,
But strong;
If for widows you die,
Larn to *kiss*; *not* to *sigh*;
For they're all like sweet Mistress Malone,
Ohone!
Oh! they're all like sweet Mistress Malone.

There is not certainly a more shameless plagiarism on record than the imitation of this song — words, air, name, and spirit — from a still better one, which set our grandfathers in a roar:

THE ATHLONE LANDLADY

'Twas in the sweet town of Athlone
Liv'd the beautiful Widow Malone;
She kept the Black Boy,
Was an armful of joy,
And had plenty of lovers, och hone, och hone;
O the world for you, Widow Malone.

There was Bolus the medical drone,
And Latitat all skin and bone;
But physic and law
Both stuck in her craw,

21. cf. *Othello*, I. 3.76: 'most potent, grave and reverend signiors'. An officer unable to continue to bear arms actively was 'put on the peace establishment', i.e. he still received an income.
22. A magnificent (now royal) house outside London, famous for its gardens and other luxuries. Thomas, Cardinal Wolsey (*c.* 1475-1530), was lord chancellor of England during the reign of Henry VIII.

And she couldn't digest them, och hone, och hone,
O success to sweet Mistress Malone.

But Cupid, who's the devil's own,
Sent a lad who soon altered her tone;
'Twas brave Serjeant Mac Whack,
With long sword and broad back,
And his roguish black eyes at her thrown, och hone;
O they bothered poor Widow Malone.

The love-sick sweet Mistress Malone,
So fond of the soldier was grown,
That in secret she'd sigh,
'For the Serjeant I die,
Oh! I'm tired of lying alone, och hone.'
More of that to you, Mistress Malone.

Still the lawyer and doctor will groan,
And each tease the poor Widow, och hone!
Till one day Pat Mac Whack
Kick'd them out in a crack,
And a smack gave sweet Katty Malone, och hone;
'O you've won me,' cried Widow Malone.

Soon they wedded and bedded, och hone,
While with fun sure the stocking was thrown,
And he's the man of the house,
And his beautiful spouse
Is sweet Mistress Mac Whack, late Malone, Malone;
So more luck to you Mac Whack and Malone.

We believe the next in reputation of Mr. Lever's songs — if we may venture to call them his — is one entitled 'The Pope', which we subjoin:

THE POPE

I

The Pope he leads a happy life,
He fears not married care nor strife,
He drinks the best of Rhenish wine,
I would the Pope's gay lot were mine.

Chorus

He drinks the best of Rhenish wine,
I would the Pope's gay lot were mine.

II

But, then, all happy's not his life —
He has not maid, nor blooming wife,
Nor child has he to raise his hope —
I would not wish to be the Pope.

III

The Sultan better pleases me,
His is a life of jollity;
His wives are many as he will —
I would the Sultan's throne then fill.

IV

But even he's a wretched man,
He must obey his Alcoran;[23]
And dares not drink one drop of wine —
I would not change his lot for mine.

V

So then I'll hold my lowly stand,
And live in German Vaterland;
I'll kiss my maiden fair and fine,
And drink the best of Rhenish wine.

VI

Whene'er my maiden kisses me
I'll think that I the Sultan be;
And when my cheery glass I tope,
I'll fancy then I am the Pope.

Before we got rid of our schoolboy jacket, and when Mr. Lever was still unknown to fame, we had listened a hundred times to a better version of the same song, which we beg to hand into the court of criticism, duly authenticated:

THE POPE AND THE SULTAN

I

The Pope sits in St. Peter's chair,
And many a well-fed monk is there;
He quaffs at will the choicest wine —
I would St. Peter's keys were mine!

II

But, no! 'tis never his to prove
The melting kiss of woman's love;
And who, to spend his hours alone,
Would choose to sway the world's own throne?

III

The Sultan hath his harem fair,
And many a sweet Circassian's[24] there;
No curtain lecture gives his wife —
Gods! but that were a merry life!

23. Another name for the Koran, the sacred book of Islam.
24. An inhabitant of a region on the Black Sea, north of the Caucasus Mountains.

IV

But, stop! 'tis never his to know
Of rosy wine, the inspiring glow:
His Alcoran forbids the bowl —
Such lot would suit but ill my soul!

V

But could I mix the tulip's bloom
With the red rose's sweet perfume;
Could I but mingle Pope with Turk —
Methinks that were a glorious work!

VI

I'd think whene'er I stole a kiss,
What Sultan could do more than this?
And, when laid senseless on the floor,
I'll cry, 'the Pope could drink no more!'

— *Copied from the 'Dublin Observer' upwards of a dozen years ago.*

But out of all comparison with the rest stands the song 'The Monks of the Screw'. It is full of humour, like the veins of a vigorous man with blood, and sparkles, if not quite like a diamond, at least like an Irish diamond. Here it is:

When St. Patrick our order created,
  And called us the Monks of the Screw,
Good rules he revealed to our abbot,
  To guide us in what we should do.

But first he replenished his fountain
  With liquor the best in the sky,
And he swore by the word of his saintship
  That fountain should never run dry.

My children, be chaste, till you're tempted;
  While sober be wise and discreet;
And humble your bodies with fasting
  Whene'er you have nothing to eat.

Then be not a glass in the convent,
  Except on a festival, found;
And this rule to enforce, I ordain it
  A festival all the year round.

Mr. Lever did not imitate this from anybody. It has the evidence of an original conception about it, and was obviously cast in one mind and at one heat. He did not imitate it, but he stole it, 'woof and warp', as they say in the north, without one word of alteration, from Charles Phillips's *Recollections of Curran*, one of the least known, but most delightful books of biography in the world.[25] It was, in fact, the production of John Philpot Curran.[26]

To turn for a minute, for variety's sake, to a song which undoubtedly is Mr Lever's own, we find the following verse put into the mouth of Mickey Free, in *Charles O'Malley*:

'The picquets are fast retreating, boys;
The last tattoo is beating, boys:
  So let every man
  Finish his can,
And drink to our next merry meeting, boys!'

If any Irishmen committed the bull of making a private soldier in the Peninsular war[27] sing a parody upon one of Moore's melodies, we fancy he would have more *gumption*[28] than to exhibit him squeezing such syllables through his teeth as '*re-treeting*' and '*beeting*' rhyming to meeting; whereas any Mickey of the genuine growth of Galway would have talked of 'retrayting' and 'bating' rhyming to slating. But we beg pardon; it is like making a charge of petty larceny against a man convicted of a capital offence, to criticise errors of style in such a writer as we have in hands. The punishment of the minor offence necessarily merges in the greater; as it is not according to judicial etiquette to whip a man *after* he has been hanged.

So much for his materials — now for the knowledge of the gentry and the people, with which they are worked up. If he is not original in his incidents, he is certainly perfectly original in his facts. Of Irish history and Irish gossip — that traditionary chit-chat which renders Scott's historical novels so racy and delightful — he is in a state of the most comical ignorance. When, in his supreme contempt of mere Irish education, he makes Mrs. Paul Rooney[29] talk of her family coming in with 'Oliver Cromwell and the Danes',

25. Charles Phillips (*c.*1787-1859) Irish lawyer who made his name in London when he defended the reputation of Queen Caroline (1820). His *Recollections of Curran and Some of his Contemporaries* appeared in 1818.
26. John Philpot Curran (1750-1817), parliamentarian, a strong advocate of catholic emancipation. The father of Sarah, he treated her harshly when he learned of her engagement to Robert Emmet.
27. A term used for the campaigns in Spain and Portugal against Napoleon, especially those involving Arthur Wellesley, duke of Wellington (1769-1852). W. H. Maxwell (see note 6 above) had been among the first to exploit the setting for rollicking stories of military and romantic adventure.
28. gumption = common sense; more technically, it is a substance which carries colours in the mixing of paints.
29. Character in Lever's *Jack Hinton* (1843), who bears a resemblance to Mrs Anastasia Raffarty in Maria Edgeworth's *The Absentee* (1812).

her anacronism [*sic*] is a trifle to the incessant confusion of dates and eras which Mr Lever himself commits. There is actually nothing in Mrs. Malaprop's[30] or Mrs. Ramsbottom's[31] blunders to equal it. We are profoundly convinced that, if you stood upon Carlisle-bridge,[32] and stopped every grown man that passed for half an hour, nine-tenths of them would be better acquainted with the periods in which Mr. Lever's scenes are laid than he is. We expect no credit for exposing his blunders — they are open and palpable as day, and must have suggested themselves to the majority of his readers in this country. In England, of course, they are gospel.

To 'example you' in blunders, he has the Attorney's Corps in full operation a dozen years after the Union; Moore a judge, while Curran is a practising barrister;[33] a priest offering up six masses in one day, and some of them after dinner;[34] a delegate from Orange Lodge, No. 13,476, visiting Connaught during the lifetime of Hussey Burgh,[35] who died before the institution was in existence; and who, had he lived to the present day, would not have seen as many hundred lodges in operation as Mr. Lever gives us thousands; a man calling for the police while Curran is on circuit — who, however, very properly do not come at the call, as they were not in existence for a score of years after![36] — an Irish boy of that era performing the Cockney[37] blackguardism of putting his extended fingers to his nose to express derision; Ballinasloe located in the Home Circuit;[38] a denunciation of Daniel O'Connell, and a laudation of Sir Harcourt Lees, during the viceroyalty of the Duke of Rutland, while the one was probably in St. Omer's and the other in Trinity College making acquaintance with the classics;[39] and a conversation on the controversial powers of Father Tom Maguire,[40] before the battle of Waterloo.

Harry Lorrequer fortunately does not meddle with our national annals, and we only find such evidence of general ignorance as talking of the present premier as *Sir* Robert Peel, and joking upon schedule A of the reform bill during the Peninsular war;[41] with which we have at present nothing to do. But in *O'Malley* and *Hinton* he revels like a Vandal in the destruction of all the land-marks of history and civilization. It was with genuine surprise that we found *Jack Hinton* coming to Dublin, between thirty and forty years ago, by a packet-boat and a jarvey,[42] as it would have been perfectly characteristic of the book to convey him by a steam-packet and the Kingstown railway. Nothing daunts — nothing impedes him. Time and space fall before him, and men meet their distant posterity at his command. He mounts the breach, mixes in the council, and lifts the veil from the orgies of the spirits of the age with equal confidence. Alas, that 'fools should rush where angels fear to tread!'[43]

Charles O'Malley opens in Daly's Club-house,[44] at a date fixed neither before nor after the Union, but which could not possibly be more than a year and a half after it, as we have a story told in the first chapter which is stated to have happened *two years before* in the Irish House of Commons — nay, presently after, we have Sir Harry Boyle talking of bringing a question before 'the House' as if it still sat in College-green; yet before a year from that time our hero is fighting the French in Portugal, and ultimately witnesses the fall of Napoleon. And all this, which time, in her old slow and sure way, took fifteen years to accomplish, Mr. Lever gets through in as many months.

But *Jack Hinton* is the very perfection of

30. Character in Richard Brinsley Sheridan's comedy, *The Rivals*.
31. Another stock character in the dramatic repertoire.
32. Carlisle-bridge (now known as O'Connell Bridge) was built in 1790 and quickly became a new centre point for Dublin.
33. See *Timon of Athens*, I. 2.47: 'I'll example you with thievery'. These are impossible anachronisms. For example, John Philpot Curran had been forced to abandon his practice as a barrister in 1789, though he later became master of the Irish rolls.
34. It was improper for a priest to serve mass after dinner.
35. Walter Hussey Burgh (1742-83) died twelve years before the Orange Order was founded (1795).
36. The Irish Constabulary was formed in 1830, although the Peace Preservation Force had been set up earlier, in 1814.
37. A native of London, speaking a characteristic dialect of English. Traditionally a Cockney is someone born within the sound of the bells of St. Mary-le-Bow Church.
38. Ballinasloe (Co. Galway) is on the Western Circuit in the court system.
39. Daniel O'Connell (1775-1847) was twelve, and Sir Harcourt Lees (1776-1852) eleven, in the year of Rutland's death, 1787. St Omer's was a Jesuit college in northern France which O'Connell, like many Irish catholics, attended.
40. Rev. Thomas Maguire (1792-1847) was twenty-three in the year of the battle of Waterloo; he came to prominence in the mid-1820s as a catholic controversialist.
41. Robert Peel (1788-1850) succeeded to his father's baronetcy only in 1830, and the Reform Bill was debated in 1832; thus both references in the context of the peninsular campaigns are anachronistic.
42. A hackney coachman.
43. cf. Alexander Pope, *Essay on Criticism*: 'For Fools rush in where Angels fear to tread' (line 625).
44. The leading club for gentlemen of fashion in Dublin; it stood in College Green.

blundering. It opens in 181-, or sometime between 1810 and 1813, which is the date of several of the concluding events. In this era he makes the Duke of Rutland[45] Lord Lieutenant of Ireland, though the duke was in his grave more than twenty years before. In the course of the work the hero is invited to meet Hussey Burgh (blundered into Harry Burgh), who had supped with the gods while he was still in his swaddling clothes; and, by-and-bye, just before he sets out for the Peninsula to fight under Sir Arthur Wellesley, he spends an evening with 'The Monks of the Screw', a convivial and political society which had expired eighteen years before. In this body — which, we need scarcely observe, was almost as thoroughly a free trade association as the Anti-Corn Law League is today, and nearly as obnoxious to government — he meets the English Secretary of State, the Attorney-General Toler (Lord Norbury),[46] and the Chief Baron of the Exchequer. And here the blundering actually becomes threefold. He specifies Yelverton[47] and the Chief Baron as two of the monks, though Yelverton was obviously the Chief Baron whom he had in his mind, and Toler and the Attorney-General as two more, though it is equally clear that Toler, and the Attorney-General in question were one. After this, it is not strange that Wellesley Pole[48] is the English secretary who shares the festivity, though, of course, he might with equal propriety be represented as a guest at one of Sallust's suppers.[49] On the same occasion Curran and Parsons are present, and spoken of by their sirnames, though at the date of the scene in *Hinton* the one was a judge and the other an earl. A little further on in 1813, we find Curran labouring at an assizes town as counsel in one of those unhappy cases of outrage in which his services were so often engaged when he was at the bar; but which there was considerable objection to employing him in at that date, as he had not only been half-a-dozen years on the bench, but was actually negotiating his retirement with the government.

Some of these mistakes, we may be told, are trifles. Perhaps so; but they are trifles which no Irish gentleman would be guilty of even in casual conversation, and which, in the works of a writer assuming to be a national novelist, are unpardonable. But the majority are not only not trifles, but argue a profound and unaccountable ignorance of the most common incidents of history. We are inclined to doubt whether Mr. Lever knows that there ever was a union with England — certainly he must be unacquainted with the date and history of it, for it is just as ridiculous a blunder to make the existence of 'The Monks of the Screw' after, instead of before, that event, as to date the peace of Paris[50] before the battle of Waterloo, or the Catholic Association after the concession of the relief bill.[51] If some future 'National Novelist' describe William Pitt resisting O'Connell and the Repeal agitation, and Lord Charles Campbell dismissing Lord Ffrench[52] from the magistracy, he will not outrage the letter and spirit of history more thoroughly than Mr. Lever does when he makes the merry Duke of Rutland and Hussey Burgh contemporaries with the conqueror at Waterloo.

We trust we have fulfilled our pledge of proving this writer to be altogether unworthy of credit as a witness against the character of the Irish people. An artist who caricatured a background from Claude,[53] a group from Wilkie,[54] and a design from Hogarth,[55] and called it painting from nature, would be as well entitled to have his claim allowed. Of the morality of the proceeding we say nothing — neither will we venture to assign the position in the Republic of Letters to which it will reduce him — our sole object being to protect the country from the consequences of his grotesque libels. Against the writer personally — whom we have often read with

45. Charles Manners (1754-87), 4th duke of Rutland; lord lieutenant in Ireland from 1784 until his death.
46. John Toler (1745-1831) became Irish attorney general in 1798; he was created 1st earl of Norbury in 1827.
47. Barry Yelverton (1736-1805) became chief baron of the exchequer in 1783.
48. William Wellesley-Pole (1763-1845) was chief secretary for Ireland 1809-12.
49. Gaius Sallustius Crispus (86-34 B.C.), Roman historian, sometime governor of Numidia, notorious for his accumulation of luxury.
50. By the Peace of Paris, 30 May 1814, the French recognized the boundaries of their neighbours. After Waterloo, a Second Peace of Paris (20 November 1815) was signed, by which the French made far greater concessions.
51. The Catholic Association (founded May 1823) achieved its principal objectives with the passage of the Emancipation Act of April 1829.
52. Together with twenty-three other magistrates (including Daniel O'Connell), Charles Austin Ffrench (3rd baron Ffrench) was dismissed at the end of May 1843, i.e. in the month immediately before the appearance of this article. Campbell appears to be an error (deliberate, by switching a Christian name?) for John Campbell (1779-1861, created 1st baron Campbell in 1841), who was a prominent reformer in the Law Lords.
53. Claude Lorrain (1600-82), French landscape painter, known as 'Claude'.
54. Sir David Wilkie (1785-1841), Scottish *genre* painter.
55. William Hogarth (1697-1764), English painter of social scenes.

great amusement, partly created by his liveliness, and partly, to be sure, by his blunders — we have not a particle of ill-will. We wish him all manner of success in any other department of literature, but we trust his career as an Irish novelist is at an end. We interdict, him, then, from the same conscientious motive that a trader nails a base sovereign to his counter — Mr. Lever who is a kind of Birmingham Boz,[56] falls naturally into this category — and certainly with the same object — to prevent his further circulation among an honest and credulous community.

56. 'Boz' was Charles Dickens's original pseudonym. As Duffy started out by quoting a comparison between Lever and Dickens, so he concludes with a contemptuous echo, the 'Birmingham' added perhaps to draw attention to Lever's father, an English builder settled in Dublin.

ANONYMOUS
OUR PERIODICAL LITERATURE

[The title 'Our Periodical Literature' was one frequently used for casual reviews of current magazines. The example that follows, however, goes beyond this routine business, to compare book — and periodical — writing, and to assess the pressures at work upon the writer in Ireland in the late 1840s. The article deserves comparison with Isaac Butt's longer piece in *The Dublin University Magazine* — see above — and with the first editorial of *Duffy's Irish Catholic Magazine* — see below. The three pieces provide contrasting perspectives on the relation of politics and literature. The authorship of this article is unknown.]

I. — *The Dublin University Magazine.* M'Glashan, D'Olier-street.
II. — *Duffy's Irish Catholic Magazine.* J. Duffy, 10, Wellington-quay.
III. — *The People's Magazine.* Belfast: Arthur Lewis, 14, Rosemary-street.

Good reader! withdraw your eyes and heart for a little while from the awful stories of inquests and relief reports — from the perusal of Whig speeches, and the consideration of the prospects of next year's harvest — for a little while — a very little — until we examine whether the new soul that sometime came into Ireland still exists, and whether it is energetic enough still to live, to outlast 'Irish distress',[1] and to outlive 'English sympathy'.

This soul reveals itself most clearly in our literature. Since 1840 we have done more to lay down the basis of a true national literature than any people ever did in the same time, against the same obstacles. We have had more nationality dragged to light, in one way or another — more of the ancient, the monastic, and military records of our predecessors in this island, deciphered and explained, than any province, in the time, ever had. But this has mostly been book-work. The heavy quartos of the Archaeological Society, the publications of Messrs. Hodges and Smith, and Mr. McGlashan, the more compact monthly series of Mr Duffy — now drawing to a close — have done this work.[2] They have fixed many facts on their right basis, and dispersed the theoretic clouds that concealed from us the summits of others. They have taught us to know the peculiarities of our ancestors and their works. They have exhumed the mutilated remains of many heroes, and re-erected them before our wondering eyes. Very much, indeed, of what a preliminary book literature ought to do, has been done.

But there is work of this kind, which cannot be done in books, but in periodicals. The bookmaker, who has to dispatch a generation in a page, or a century in a chapter, cannot descend — without ruin to his subject and his own fame — to recognise the present wants of literature, or to suggest temporary remedies. A text which treats of a thousand years back, with notes full of what Germans might call 'todayisms', is a barbarous anomaly. Moreover, a book is never considered to be a prospectus, or an argument. It is the result of study, and not the process, which the author is bound to give. It ought to possess, as far as any human work can, fulness and finish, with all its facts facing one point, and marching harmoniously together. Periodicals, on the contrary, can be precisely what books cannot be. The writers of periodicals are a sort of Ordnance Survey in the country of the arch-enemy, Ignorance.[3] Their light

1. The article appeared during the Great Famine, with its endless reports from coroners' inquests and relief committees. At Westminster the Whigs had been in power since June 1846.
2. James M'Glashan, a Scotsman, had been active in Dublin publishing since the 1830s. He had become publisher of *The Dublin University Magazine* in 1846. James Duffy (1809-71) was the leading publisher of the Young Ireland group, and of various periodicals designed to meet the needs of the catholic masses.
3. The Ordnance Survey of Ireland had begun in 1830, had published its first report in 1839, and was the subject of a government commission

equipments at once proclaim them neither horse nor foot, but pioneers. It is for them to map the road, and to erect their signal flags from height to height. If any among them desires more conclusive work, he can fall back into the regular ranks; but he must then cease to be a periodic. The cause of the failure of many books has been that they had too much of the periodical; and, on the other hand, the cause of the decay of some famous periodicals was that they became too bookish, and were sunk to the depths by the leaden weight of seven learned articles.

Keeping this in view, we come to consider the present state of our own periodical literature, the obstacles its writers have to surmount, and the good they might effect to themselves and the country by the adoption of one or two general principles of action.

Our oldest and ablest magazine is the *University*. It is not too much to say that its two last volumes contain more good writing than the cotemporary volumes of any other monthly periodical in the language. They are enriched with the inimitable translations of Mangan and the epic ballads of Ferguson; Carleton's unwearied pen seems in each number but to exceed its former triumphs; others, whose names are hidden from the public, but who are scarce less entitled to fame, have contributed their quotas of memoir, *miscellanea*, and antiquarianism, with a skill and a learning most creditable to the fame of our chief city.[4] But the *University* has two very serious faults. Some who write in it are for ever thrusting their religion between their subjects and their readers. It would seem as if they knew no other way to honor it but to puff it. Now, this, to say the least of it, is very bad taste. Religion is not to be written up between the covers of any miscellaneous publication. It is a subject for the privacy of an inner closet, or of the still lonelier closet of the heart. It is not to be exhibited on the first day of a month or the last day of a week, as a headpiece to a political argument or a tailpiece to an historical review. It is a sacred and sequestered thing which good men hide in their hearts, which hypocrites only affect on their faces. The only place where it may be meetly exhibited is in those temples of revelation where, like the Jewish publican, men should go to pray and not to display. In books and publications especially dedicated to religion the sacred names of God and Saviour may sound well; but in publications with a homily on one side and a satire on the other — with a sermon here and a drama leering at it from the other page — bah! What we object primarily, then, to the *University Magazine* is, that religion, that is, doctrine, should be mixed up with mere worldly literature as part of the whole. Our second fault to the *Magazine* is, that its tone is politically West-British! Perhaps we should say *was* such. The two or three last numbers are greatly improved from some we remember to have read not very long ago. The notion of an Irishman of any of the four provinces talking of 'the march of *our* army on Cabul', '*our* left wing charging at Sobraon', '*our* flag being insulted at Tahiti', was, the very sight of it, so emetic in its nature, that we never swallowed a morsel of the *University*'s delicious literature without the fear of its being immediately dislodged by the effects of its politics. This political stain is gradually disappearing, and the sectarian blotch will follow. The literature will live in spite of the bigotry. The black spots can never wholly deface the sun.

Our second magazine, in point of time, and as yet of reputation, is the *Irish Catholic Magazine* of Mr. James Duffy. It is often ungracious, and always unwise, to pronounce summarily for or against a new serial. But, from the two numbers before us, we have every anticipation that this magazine, if well edited, may rival or even excel the *University*. The proportion of scholarly and able Irishmen who would prefer its pages, as a theatre, to those of the elder periodical, is greater than our Conservative friends imagine. Besides, these can consistently display a further Irish past, both national and religious, than the other — they can more consistently chronicle the holidays, the games, and the superstitions of the people. If the editor of the magazine makes a selection of a dozen or twenty contributors of this class — who know something of each other, in order to work cordially — and who are anxious to serve letters and their country in purity and tolerance of spirit, this magazine, we think, is destined to take and keep a high, if not the

---

in 1843, whose favourable report was rejected by the authorities. The Survey constituted by far the most thorough attempt by an administration to get to grips with the topography and social life of Ireland, an undertaking open to conflicting interpretations.

4. The February issue of *The Dublin University Magazine* had seen the commencement of James Clarence Mangan's 'Anthologia Hibernica' and — significantly for a reviewer in *The Nation* — a biographical piece on Thomas Davis by Samuel Ferguson. The March issue carried a short story by William Carleton, 'O'Sullivan's Love: a Legend of Edenmore'.

very highest place, in our periodical literature. But if, on the contrary, chance or untrained contributors serve up hashed Vallancy[5] or pilfered Petrie,[6] the character of the publication will be utterly ruined with the sensible part of the community; and the unreasoning crowd, after three or four issues, will suffer it to die out.

The *Belfast People's Magazine* is a little periodical, very well printed, and very earnest about reading-rooms and public wash-houses. It is adorned with a frontispiece, representing steamships and other commercial craft, in the foreground of a town — Belfast. It is said to be intended for the working-classes. But it must go a little further, or it will fail. It must have the marks of being written by *Irish*men for the *Irish* working-classes. It will not do to have an Irish town on the vignette — it must *seem* Irish and *be* Irish, if it would live long and be honored in the land.

This, then, is our whole force in periodical literature — two Dublin magazines and one at Belfast. The *Dublin Review* we do not count.[7] It is owned and printed, and managed in England. It should be called an 'English Review, in which Irish articles are permitted to be inserted to satisfy Irish subscribers.' This name may be too long, and it would be too true. No magazine is now published at Cork, Limerick, or Galway, nor, indeed, is it necessary. Two, or at most three, good monthlies are quite enough for one kingdom like ours.

We now come to consider those general principles of action indispensable to the usefulness of our periodical literature — they are in number three: I. To regard controversy as in itself a thing highly undesirable in current literature. II. Never to quote a thought, or use a fact, discovered by another without acknowledgment. III. To take every opportunity of quoting Irishmen who have written on any subject successfully, in preference to any other authority.

On the matter of controversy, we think the genius for argument so long exhibited in this nation most unsuited to our present wants. This genius, in the first instance, comes of the mixture of races and bloods. Even the faculties of a single man of mixed race contend with each other for mastery. He is for ever on a rack of cross purposes, now tugged this way, and now that. But if he possess sense, wisdom, judgment, or whatever you call it — a faculty confined exclusively to no race-temperament — he will be able to govern these opposite tendencies, and to turn them all one way. The penal struggles encouraged the cultivation of argument. Every Catholic of any education was obliged to be prepared at all points for polemical controversy; but now they have got the substance of restitution, they can well dispense with the verbiage of retort and defence. The parliamentary struggles of the last century, and the popular agitations of this, all helped to perpetuate this unhappy predilection for controversy. What we wanted in reality was a *creative* spirit — a spirit that could discover power in its elemental fragments, and fuse them into form. A spirit rather like Roger O'Moore's and Tone's, than Swift's or O'Connell's. We wanted this spirit in politics — one such appeared, alas! only to be snatched away. We still want such a man for our literature.[8]

The Literary organizer would find in this country materials of a great dramatic history, 'full of emotions', to quote a phrase of Gerald Griffin's.[9] He would find materials for a Ballad Poetry which would ensure European reputation, if thoroughly Irish and isolated in sentiment and character. He would find materials for Romance which would link our history with that of every distinguished Christian people so clearly that Ireland would have friends in all the closets and in most of the cabinets of the civilised world. Not to speak now of the capacity or advantages he would find existing for the cultivation of exact science and of art, these achievements of themselves would do more to raise

5. Charles Vallancey (1721-1812), military engineer, surveyor and eccentric antiquarian, who claimed an affinity between the Irish and the ancient Carthaginians in *An essay on the antiquity of the Irish language* (1772), published in *Collectanea de Rebus Hibernices* (1770-90).
6. George Petrie (1789-1866), painter, musicologist and antiquarian. From 1833 to 1839 he was attached to the Ordnance Survey.
7. *The Dublin Review* was a catholic quarterly magazine founded in 1836 and surviving well into the twentieth century. Though essentially English in its origins, it owed its name in part at least to the prestige of Daniel O'Connell in catholic intellectual circles.
8. Roger O'Moore, or more usually Rory O'More (*c.* 1620-52), participated in the 1641 Rising but later tried to make terms between Owen Roe O'Neill and the Marquis of Ormonde. Theobald Wolfe Tone (1763-98), leader of the United Irishmen, renowned for his belief in substituting 'the common name of Irishman' for the various sectarian identities of the day. Jonathan Swift (1667-1745) and Daniel O'Connell (1775-1847) are here presented as spokesmen for their different denominational identities, protestant and catholic respectively. This presentation of the four men lacks depth, to say the least. The spirit who appeared in politics and was snatched away was Thomas Osborne Davis (1814-45).
9. Gerald Griffin (1803-40), novelist.

fame and friends for Ireland than all the patronage of England or the sympathy of America. Shakespeare has been worth more to England, in foreign service, than Nelson or Wellington. Shakespeare's genius was essentially creative. Look at his historical plays, and then at the old chronicles from which he took the dry bones. He was not beneath searching for a fact in any quantity of rubbish. Even to the personal appearance, peculiarities of complexion or expression, he studied his originals. Even he, the *author* of *Falstaff*, pored, until his eyes grew dim, over Caxton, Hollingshed [*sic*], and Buchanan.[10]

We do not contend that controversy, polemical or literary, is bad; only that its cultivation is incompatible with the foundation of an Irish literature. In cases of great consequence, affecting primary facts in history, or primary doctrines, men should always be prepared to defend their convictions of truth. Such, for instance, was Mr. Petrie's undertaking about the Round Towers.[11] It was to be decided whether the only peculiar edifices we possessed were of Pagan or Christian origin, what was [*sic*] their uses, and their history. It has been decided. But the controversy we deprecate is that which, unarmed with facts, lies ever on the watch to assail a proposition. The empty and egotistical parade of dialectics, which, while it would demolish everything erected by others is totally incapable of creating anything of itself. This is the troubled and restless spirit which the *Catholic Magazine* and the *University* have alike to keep under, and discountenance, and purge from Ireland.

The second general principle is one that no right-thinking man will ever violate — that is, quoting or using the words of another without acknowledgment.[12] Literary society, too, always vindicates itself against such assailants. If the culprits do not feel they are outlawed, they are so, in fact. They are regarded as the Gypsies of letters, who are to be trusted just as long as you have your eyes on them.

The third general principle is, that Irish writers should guard, and otherwise serve in all consistent ways, the fame of one another. This is, and has been, our own principle. The danger to be guarded against in this is, that it does not degenerate into mutual puffery. We must not make our geese swans if they are geese. But when, on the other hand, this country has produced — as we all know it has — many men of great ability, research, and labour, it is due to them and to the common parent to be generous in our appreciation of their efforts. When we consider what our literature has to struggle with, this will appear still more necessary. We have to labour against the *prestige* of England in vindicating our history and our heroes. We have to create an Irish literature in English tongue [*sic*], without the marked advantage of a dialect, or a *patois* like the Scotch. And, speaking of the Scotch, it reminds us that this principle of mutual assistance has eminently distinguished the *literati* of that sage nation. Mackenzie and Brown helped the unknown Waverley into its first success. Scott himself bestowed as much reputation upon Leyden and Hogg as they earned for themselves. The Messrs. Chambers, the Edinburgh publishers, following in Sir Walter's steps, have helped more than one Scotsman to distinction in our own generation.[13] When will we learn to fraternise in this way? The work, thank Heaven, has begun for some time. Hear, on this very subject, the last *University Magazine*:

> While we write, a new literary periodical has started into existence — 'Duffy's Catholic Magazine', with the general literature of which we will not at present find fault. In an article, however, on Druids and Druidism, it has published, and thus endeavoured to revive, the nonsensical fancies of Vallancey and his school of imaginary antiquarians, which we had hoped the labours of Petrie, O'Donovan, Hardiman, Todd, and Eugene O'Curry,[14] the Irish scribe and interpreter of the nineteenth century, and other investigators, had long since dispelled.

10. William Caxton (*c.* 1422-91), England's first printer; Raphael Hollinshed (*c.* 1520-*c.* 1580), chronicler; George Buchanan (1506-82), Scottish historian.
11. Petrie's *Essay on the Round Towers of Ireland* appeared in 1833, and firmly established the Christian origin of the towers.
12. This reflects *The Nation*'s hostility to Charles Lever, whom it had ably demonstrated to have been a plagiarist — see pp. 1255-1265 above.
13. George Mackenzie (1669-1725), Scottish biographer; William Brown (1766-1835), Scottish historical writer. *Waverley* (1814) was Walter Scott's first novel. John Leyden (1775-1811) and James Hogg (1770-1835) were lesser Scottish writers. The Edinburgh publishing firm of W. & R. Chambers was founded in the 1820s.
14. John O'Donovan (1809-61), genealogist and translator of the *Annals of the Four Masters* (1848-51); James Hardiman (*c.* 1790-1855), historian and author of *Irish Minstrelsy, or Bardic Remains of Ireland*; James Henthorn Todd (1805-69), one of the founders of the Irish Archaeological Society; Eugene O'Curry (1796-1862), editor and translator of Irish texts and professor of Irish history and archaeology in the Catholic University of Ireland from 1854.

Among the recent labourers in the field of Irish history we must not omit our brother 'Young Irelanders', for if by that appellation are to be included those who, irrespective of politics or creed, have toiled for nationality, who have manfully stood forward for the honor of our common country, who have endeavoured to advance her science and her arts, to preserve her monuments and antiquities, and to elevate and spread abroad a knowledge of her history, there have been, and there are, 'Young Irelanders', good men and true, who are neither Repealers in politics, nor Roman Catholics in religion. We are not frenzied by the retrospective poetry which has emanated from many of those talented, enthusiastic, and warm-hearted sons of Ireland, no more than we would be by songs, which told again the wars of York and Lancaster, or the bloody massacre of Glencoe;[15] nor are we ready to 'flesh every sword to the hilt'[16] in a Saxon, when we read those reprints of some of the old and sad tales of English misgovernment, and English treachery &c, which they have published; but we thank them cordially for using the great powers, which undoubtedly they possess, and that among a class of the community hitherto inaccessible to such teaching, not only in the cause of liberty and nationality, but in that of Irish history, literature, and antiquities.[17]

This is the closing paragraph of an article on the scenery and history of the Boyne — a good ground from which to preach union among Irishmen!

15. The killing in February 1692 of thirty or forty MacDonalds of Glencoe by forces led by Captain Robert Campbell. The victims seem to have been slaughtered because of their alleged catholicism (in fact they were probably episcopalians) and for their Jacobite sympathies.
16. Thomas Moore, 'The Song of O'Ruark, Prince of Breffni'.
17. From the final paragraphs of an article on the river Boyne by William Wilde (1815-76) in *The Dublin University Magazine*, Vol. 29 (March 1847), p. 358. It is possible that the sentences quoted here were not Wilde's but were interpolated by the editors.

THOMAS DAVIS (1814-45)

[Thomas Davis died in 1845, just at the onset of the Famine. He quickly acquired the status of hero among his colleagues, and several commemorations followed on his death. The publication, in three instalments, of his address to the College Historical Society in 1839, was *The Nation*'s longest retrospective tribute.]

THE YOUNG IRISHMAN OF THE MIDDLE CLASSES (published 1848)

This lecture was delivered by Davis just before the commencement of his public career, to a students' club called the Historical Society, of which he was president. We now present it as his legacy to the Confederate Club.

[PART I]

GENTLEMEN — You consist of members and students of the learned professions; many of you cherish a literary ambition — most of you hope for success in public life; you thus, though coming here with different powers and various qualities, are yet all under circumstances which will make the acquisition of the orator's powers an object of ambition. Your country and your times offer opportunities for a generous, — temptations to a selfish — ambition. I trust, I am sure, your impulses are not ungenerous. Methinks I know the elements at work within you. You aspire to political power, and you must be up and doing. You will, ere you reach the goal, need an amount of labour which you little thought of at the starting.

'Tis no light thing to move the mind of man. 'Tis no child's play to wield the passions. The recruit must not seek to lead an army, nor the student to instruct a nation. Look back on those who have been the mind-chieftains in the civil strifes of Ireland — Swift, Lucas, Grattan.[1] Did all the boasted precocity of Irish genius abridge their toils? No; a youth of hardest study — a manhood of unceasing labour, are the facts common to the lives of them all; and yet they lived under favorable auspices for individual eminence. Though the Irish leaders have not seldom been unblessed with ancestral wealth or dignity, yet the body of competitors for political power were of the aristocracy; for they inherited a monopoly of education — that which summons men to distinction. You also belong to what are called the upper classes in Ireland. But you will have competitors from whom your ancestors were free.

The college in which you and your fathers were *educated*, from whose offices seven-eighths of the Irish people are excluded by religion — from whose

1. Jonathan Swift (1667-1745); Charles Lucas (1713-71); Henry Grattan (1746-1820), often regarded as a succession of 'patriot' figures in Irish public life.

porch many, not disqualified by religion, are repelled by the comparative dearness, the reputed bigotry and pervading dullness of the consecrated spot — that institution seems no longer to monopolise the education-funds of Ireland. Trinity College seems to have lost the office for which it was so long and so well paid, of preventing the education of the Irish. The people think it better not to devote all their spare cash to a university, so many of whose favorite alumni are distinguished by their adroit and malignant calumnies on the character, and inveterate hostility to the good of that people with whose land and money they are endowed. The self-denying virtues are, 'passing away, passing away'.[2]

Do you weep their departure? or are you consoled by the number of people-wrongs still endured? But away with this insulting jest — your hearts are with your countrymen, yours is a generous ambition to lead them, not their foes.

But then, I repeat, you must strip for the race; you will have competitors from among the people. The middle classes of Ireland are now seeking in spite of the most perverse opposition chronicled in the annals of even Anglo-Irish bigotry, to establish provincial colleges; schools for their own education. When the men of the middle class once come into the field, if I do not greatly overrate the stuff of which they are made, they will compel the men of the upper classes at home — nay, with humility be it said, the men of every country, to fight a hard battle for their literary laurels and political renown. Prepare for that time. If you would rule your countrymen, you must be greater than they. But even now the National Schools, the first bold attempt to regenerate Ireland, are working — aye, and, with all their faults, working well. The lower classes, for whom they are suited and designed, are beginning to add the acquisitions of science and literature to that facile apprehension, ingenuity, and comprehensive genius, with which even their enemies credit them. I tell, you, gentlemen of Trinity College, the peasant boys will soon put to the proof your title to lead them; and the only title likely to be acknowledged in the people-court, is that which our countryman, himself once a peasant boy, ascribes to Pericles:

He waved the sceptre o'er his kind,
By nature's first great title mind.[3]

2. From 'Passing Away' (1825) by Mrs F. Hemans.
3. George Croly (1780-1860), 'Pericles and Aspasia' in *Poems* (1831).

Gentlemen, I have not come here to flatter you. That many of you possess the highest natural abilities I feel convinced, but that is probably true of many who preceded you. And when I compare the cotemporary literature of Ireland with the gifted nature of the Irish, I am forced to think there are some gross errors in the education of the only class which hitherto has received any education. Many of you acknowledge this, and professedly join this society, less for its peculiar advantages than to correct such errors. I think you do wisely: these errors may be lessened by exertions here, and that belief has determined the nature of this address. This is no professor's chair. My opinions have no weight save from the truth they may bear, and the proofs with which they are combined. Chosen from among yourselves to advise you touching your intellectual pursuits, it is my plain duty to tell you your defects: thus alone can I convince you of the necessity for a remedy, and not until then can we be prepared to discover it.

You are all, I believe, connected with the Dublin University. Of how many of its graduates may I say, that to prepare for college occupies their boyhood, to pass through college occupies the time between boyhood and manhood; and having, loaded with cautions like Swift, or with honors like many a dunce I know, got to their degrees, they are by their parents supposed to have received *a good general education*, and to be fitted to devote the rest of their lives to spending or making a fortune, as they are endowed with an estate or a profession. If, as assuredly is the case, you, born under propitious stars, have been preserved from such a destiny, do you owe your superiority over the multitude of A.B.'s, T.C.D. to the system of the college? No; they are the result of the system — you of a generous nature too strong for it.

Yet Trinity College has a fine bill of fare. First you have mathematics, in which, to make the best of it, you are taught to follow out subtle trains of reasoning without reference to the principles of investigation, which few students will study voluntarily; and further, whole years are thus spent on subjects admitting of demonstration, with anything like to which you will seldom have to do for the rest of your lives.

Then comes that amphibious thing called natural philosophy, consisting (as taught in Dublin College) of some application of mathematics to the general properties of matter, and to the simpler physical phenomena. But so far as these sciences illustrate the human mind in the history of their improvement, and in the relations which physical science bears to human progress, they are ill-taught. Perhaps it is not the business of a college to teach, nor is it important to comprise, in a general education, the practical part of natural philosophy or mathematics. Indeed the fault of the French system is, that it does so, largely. But then they are equally ill-taught if you regard them fitted to supply illustrations of mind, or a guide to nature. As branches of natural history — astronomy, mechanics, and such subjects, are so *ill-taught*, that I verily believe the twelve months members of the Mechanics' Institute[4] could teach them to half the medal men in college. Indeed, to the professors of medical or mechanics' institutes, all that geology, physiology, and chemistry contain, is handed over. Natural history could not be tortured into a scholastic form; it could only be taught in the way it was investigated, and as alone all subjects can be well taught, by analysis. But be that as it may, external nature supplies inexhaustible materials for thought and illustration to the philosopher, the poet, and the orator; though some of the greatest of them never studied it in the schools, yet all were familiar to its face. You have facilities for the study of it outside the university, and you may lay up a hive of such materials, useful and agreeable for both public and private life, without once fluttering a wing in the collegiate parterre. Ireland offered temptations to such pursuits, of which we are at length beginning to avail ourselves.[a]

The cumbrous state of our literature renders a formal study of metaphysical and moral philosophy essential. Indeed, without an early acquaintance with the abstruser philosophy, few minds will be able to force their way through the thicket of subjects and authors which surround them in modern society. And not only will the critical and comprehensive temper resulting from such inquiries marshal your way and pioneer your path in all your studies and pursuits; but many subjects, as the foundations of government, the rationale of reward and punishment and the leading truths of political[b] economy, rest on facts common to all minds, and learned in metaphysical schools. If I mistake not, Butler's, Cicero's, and Hume's[5] philosophical works, are the proper horn-books[6] for the lawyer, the statesmen, and the divine. May I suggest to you, that contemporaneously with the process of getting definitions by rote, which is essential to collegiate distinction, some efforts might be made by students to compare the different systems of philosophy and the relative merits of these systems, when tested by their own or their neighbours' minds. Such a society as ours is plainly unfit for the purpose; but whether a metaphysical society, meeting to inquire, not to dispute, could be established within the walls of college, I leave you, who are personally interested in its formation, to determine: I am content to have suggested it to you.

The classics, even as languages, are shafts into the richest mines of thought which time has deposited. The fossils of Greek and Latin mind prove races like enough in opinions to enable us to understand and sympathise with them, were they now, for the first time, discovered by the moderns. But in sooth we have been, through every faculty of mind, and every member of society, through our literature, our languages, our laws, our arts of war and peace, galvanised, as it were, by the minds of Greece and Rome, though the force of our life may be of Gothic or Celtic origin. And this great and original difference between us and the ancients makes their literature, in some respects, the more valuable for that unlikeness. Who that has thought for himself, or been taught to think in Lord Bacon's school, cannot feel this advantage? Classic literature, though tinctured with its own doctrinal cavils, its own prejudices and superstitions, is free from cavils and prejudices and superstitions like to ours; and from these last is the only danger to us. The contrast

a. I refer to the increase of societies for the study of natural history. This is owing mainly to the exertions of the medical profession, so often, as here, in advance of their life.

4. The system of Mechanics' Institutes, providing self-education for the lower classes, was founded in 1823.

b. Dr. Bailie (in his Essays on Value) and Archbishop Whately have sufficiently shown that metaphysical philosophy is the real remedy for the word-squabbles and confusion of the Political Economists. [Samuel Bailey (1791-1870), author of *A Critical Dissertation on . . . Value* (1825); Richard Whately (1787-1863), protestant archbishop of Dublin from 1831, and sometime professor of economics at Dublin University. Ed.]

5. Joseph Butler (1692-1752), English bishop, theologian and moralist; Marcus Tullius Cicero (106-43 B.C.), Roman orator, philosopher and consul; David Hume (1711-76), Scottish philosopher, economist and historian.

6. elementary primers.

of our idolatries and theirs (to use Bacon's metaphor) is the most instructive of criticisms, while the standard truths which we find there, undisguised by such errors as could deceive us, mete our growth, or discover our degeneracy. Many a mind have they saved from doubt and dogmatism. No language of mine shall underrate the value of such a possession. Injured though they be, still are they a mighty mass of the picked thoughts of two most renowned nations — nations, too, the very death of whose states of society has stamped on their works immortal freshness and originality.

But, gentlemen, these are benefits which can only be derived from classic studies by a powerful and already disciplined mind, and which are supposed to require a very close knowledge of two difficult languages; but in my judgment the last requisite is overstated, for it is preferable to read well a good translation than to stumble through the original; and any fair man, considering how much of the spirit of classic lore can be translated, will confess the folly of expecting one man out of a hundred, to learn so much from the originals as from good translations. We do not hesitate as to this in the comparatively easy modern, why then do so in the more difficult ancient languages?

I may shortly state here, that my objections to the classical system of the Dublin College are, that even if well pursued, it takes from a young man the best years of his life to inform him on the languages, poetry, politics, religion, manners, and conditions of nations which have perished from the earth many centuries ago; and that having so employed the spare years between boyhood and business, you insure, as far as in you lies, his ignorance of all the facts that have happened, all the knowledge that has been discovered, all that imagination has produced for some seventeen hundred years. He is ignorant of modern history, including that of his own country, whose facts would, if stored in his memory, be of direct use and application, unlike those of any remote time or unconnected country, which are of use only by analogy. He knows not of what materials the people around him are composed; he knows not the origin of their thoughts and feelings; he therefore knows not themselves. The condition of cotemporary nations is surely more valuable to be known than that of extinct people. He is equally ignorant of modern languages; of French, essential to him if he visit any foreign nations other than Britain or America; of German, the root of that English language which it is more important for him to speak and write with critical fluency, than to command every dialect of the Greeks or Italians from the Attic to the Oscan.[7] Finally, for English literature, he is left to the accidents of a circulating library, or a taste beyond that of his instructors.

I venture to assert, and could prove that numerous works, English, French, and German, are intrinsically superior to the corresponding Greek, and still more above the parallel Roman works. But even though the ancient writers were of more value to their countrymen than the modern writers to theirs, yet lay aside the philosophical, and, so to speak, the esoteric use of the classics which I have mentioned, and fling the old writers among modern people, and instantly the superiority is lost. I do not say all their value is gone, but the living men and women teach us more of strength and beauty than the mummies or the statues of a dead race.[c] But this is an inadequate condemnation of the system. If the student knew the politics and philosophy, and felt the poetry, or even appreciated the facts to be found in the Greek and Roman writers, I might forgive the error of selecting such studies in preference to native and modern; but still he would leave college, if not well instructed, yet possessed of much valuable thought, and prepared to master the more important subjects which he would want in his professional, literary, or political career. But no, his memory is crammed with phrases and rules of prosody, and what is called literal, that is to say, erroneous translation of words, or correct translation if you will; familiarizing him, I may remark, with a foreign idiom ere he has learned his own, and, therefore, almost precluding him from ever writing good English. Seriously, what does the student learn besides the words of the classics?[d] The thoughts are obscured not merely by the foreign language, but by allusions and opinions which he begins to guess at towards the close of his career. How strange would it be if a young man could benefit by such an occupation!

c. There is a story told of Benjamin West, which pleases more than his paintings do: When unexpectedly shown the Apollo Belvidere, 'My God!' he exclaimed, 'a young mohawk warrior.' A brilliant and sagacious criticism, and worth analysing.

d. Does he generally learn as much?

7. Attic was the dialect of classical Greek adopted as the model of excellence; the Oscans (or Opici) were one of the south Italic tribes whose language (akin to Latin) is extinct.

Men cannot master *all* knowledge. If you believe this conclude with me that a knowledge of his own nature and duties, of the circumstances, growth, and prospects of that society in which he dwells, and of the pursuits and tastes of those around him, accompanied too, by the running comment of experience, is what every man should first learn; if he does learn this he has learned enough for life and goodness; and if he finds this not enough he is prepared in the only feasible way to profit by studying the works and thoughts of ancient Italy, or Greece, or France, modern Italy or Germany. If the student take more interest in the history, and feel more admiration for the literature, or even derive more profit from the contemplation of those moderns than of these ancients, let us not condemn his taste or doubt his wisdom. The varieties of feeling, interest, and opportunity make these differences, and a preference for the study of the modern continental nations is fostered and vindicated by the greater analogy of the people of these islands to them than to the men of old Greece or old Italy.

I do not mean to say that some knowledge is not picked up by all the students, and much knowledge by some; and yet college may be an inferior school to the few, and is mischievous to the many, by leading them into a five years specious idleness. Even for a knowledge of the classics the plan of beginning with them is bad. To a man of genius they cannot be mischievous or useless; he has thought or read up to them. But I believe that if no one foreign literature were preferred, a much larger number of men would be apt and good classical scholars than are so now; and, therefore, as it is only to those who succeed that the present system can be called good, that such would be a better means of encouraging classic studies than the present.

I ask you again, how can the student profit by the study of the difficult literature of any foreigners, ancient or modern, till he learns to think and feel; and these he learns easiest from world or home life, refined and invigorated by his native literature; and even if by chance the young student, fresh from a bad school,[e] has got some ideas of the picturesque, the generous, the true, into his head, he is neither encouraged nor expected to apply them to his classic studies. Classics! good sooth, he had better read with the hedge-school boys the History of the Rogues, Tories, and Rapparees, or Moll Flanders,[f][8] than study Homer and Horace in Trinity College. I therefore protest, and ask you to struggle against the cultivation of Greek, or Latin, or Hebrew, while French or German are excluded;[g] and still more strongly should we oppose the cultivation of any, or all of these, to the neglect of English and, I should add, Irish literature.

I may as well say something here on the study of that language which is spoken by the majority of our countrymen, and by the people of the countries immediately east and west of this kingdom. English philological studies are, to say the least, useful in the formation of style. I do not say they are essential, but they certainly give an accuracy and aptness to the writing of him who is familiar with them. There are so few English works on the philosophy of words, that I may enumerate them. Tooke's Diversions of Purley[9] is the most valuable for acquiring a critical habit in etymology and grammatical analysis; for the common use of words, Webster's Dictionary[10] is the best; Todd's Johnson,[11] as an authority and illustration for the modern variations; but Richardson is the hand-book for him who would cultivate a pure English style.[12] Horne Tooke, to be sure, was of opinion that each word had

e. That is to say, from any school in which he is likely to be prepared for college. Our private schools are absolutely contemptible. One hardly knows which to condemn most, the stupid ignorance of the teachers or the niggardliness of the parents, whose stinginess has produced and endures such schools; yet there are men of learning and genius pining and annually dying away even within Trinity College. But they are so unfortunate, as far as this life is concerned, as to have generous tastes, and independent characters. These men should 'rage, not drop' for as a ——— says, ''tis for woman to lament, man to remember.'

f. These were some of the standard authors in the hedge-school library, so says the Report of the Education Commissioners. See some more of this *Catalogue Raisonné* in Moore's *Captain Rock*, p. 187 etc.

g. There are professors of French, German, and Italian, and medals are given once a year to promote such studies; but they form no part of the graduate course, or even the fellowship, and the provisions for teaching them are notorious mockeries.

8. Daniel Defoe published *Moll Flanders* in 1722. On the hedge-schools, see P. J. Dowling, *The Hedge Schools of Ireland* (London, 1935, rev. ed. Cork: Mercier Press, 1968). Rapparees were Irish irregular soldiers of the late seventeeth century, although the term was used of plunderers and robbers.

9. John Horne Tooke (1736-1812) established his reputation as a philologist with this work, from 1786 onwards.

10. Noah Webster (1758-1843) published his *American Dictionary of the English Language* in 1828.

11. Henry John Todd (1763-1845), a chaplain to the British royal family, published his edition of Samuel Johnson's *English Dictionary* (1755) in 1818.

12. Charles Richardson (1775-1865), English lexicographer; his chief work, a *New English Dictionary*, was published 1835-37.

but one and an unalterable meaning in language. Richardson has pressed this error still further, and has thereby enfeebled the otherwise admirable essay prefixed to his larger Dictionary, but his errors (if so they be) only give a sterner purity and force to the language he teaches. His faults are on the right side, for one whose native language is English, though inconvenient enough to a foreigner. Cobbett's Grammar,[13] the book on words in Locke's Essay,[14] some chapters in the first volume of Mill's Treatise on the Mind,[15] are the only other books of consequence; at least, if I add a few articles in the Magazines, the list is complete. When you have examined these books — and they are well worth reading — you must trust to the effect of your other literary studies, to the eager and full mind, to *supply* you with words and varieties of style, and to your metaphysical studies, to a patient taste, and habits of revision to *correct* them.

The standard authors, especially the older writers — the writers who preceded Lord Bacon, contain the best vocabulary. These books, in common with their successors to Queen's [*sic*] Anne's time,[16] are rather affluent in words than critical in the application of them. Shakespeare is more exact and felicitous, and equally copious. The fault of most writers since Shakespeare's time has been the neglect of Saxon words for Latin, and the employment of a Latin, and more lately a French idiom. I may mention that Spenser[17] was the favorite leisure book of that word-wielder, William Pitt,[18] and of his grandfather, Chatham.[19] Erskine and Fox[20] are said to have known Milton and Shakespeare almost by heart. Curran's[21] inspiration, next to the popular legends of Ireland, was the English translation of the Bible.[h] Coleridge, indeed, says that a man familiar with it can never write in a vulgar style; but this, like many of Coleridge's show-sayings, is an exaggeration.[22] I could add many other authorities for my liking for the language of the early English poets and chroniclers; but their fault, a profusion of imagery, more often fitted to obscure than illustrate, to confuse than make plain, went on increasing. For ordinary use, therefore, Bolingbroke,[23] Swift, Hume, and even Cobbett, with all his coarseness, and the common letters and narratives of the last century, are safer though not so splendid models. Amongst the orators, whom you will, and perhaps, ought to copy more than other writers, you can study the speeches of Pitt, for a splendid plausibility; Fox,[24] for an easy diction and fluent logic; Sheridan,[25] for wit; Curran for wit and pathos; Burke and Grattan,[i26] for grandeur and sublimity of thought, language, and illustration. Erskine[27] possesses most of these qualities, but with a chaster, and, methinks, less racy manner; but perhaps surpassing all, by combining the best qualities

h. 'The style of this translation is, in general, so enthusiastically praised, that no one is permitted either to qualify, or even explain the grounds of his approbation. It is held to be the perfection of the English language. I shall not dispute this proposition; but one remark, as to a matter of fact, which cannot be reasonably censured, that in consequence of the principle of adherence to the original version which had been kept up ever since the time of Henry VIII, it is not the language of the reign of James I. It may in the eyes of many, be better English, but it is not the English of Daniel, or Raleigh, or Bacon, as any one may easily perceive. It abounds in part, especially in the Old Testament, with obsolete Phraseology and with single words, long since abandoned, or retained only in provincial use.' *Hallam's Literature of Europe*, vol. 3, page 131.

i. In wealth of imagination and in expressive power, Grattan is next to Shakespeare: his speeches are full of the most valuable information on Irish politics, and are the fit hand book for an Irishman. But his style is not for imitation; let no subject assume the purple.

13. William Cobbett (1762-1835), English journalist and miscellaneous writer; became a radical, and in 1832 an MP. He published his *English Grammar for the Use of Schools* in 1817.
14. John Locke (1632-1704), English philosopher; his *Essay Concerning Human Understanding* was published in 1690.
15. James Mill (1773-1836); his *Analysis of the Phenomena of the Human Mind* appeared in 1829.
16. Anne (1665-1714), queen of England, Scotland and Ireland from 1702 to her death. The notable authors of her age were Alexander Pope (1688-1744) and Jonathan Swift.
17. Edmund Spenser (*c.*1552-99), English poet, author of *The Faerie Queene*.
18. William Pitt (1759-1806) (Pitt the Younger), British prime minister at the time of the Union (1801); reviled in Ireland for his failure to deliver catholic emancipation as promised.
19. The first earl of Chatham, William Pitt the Elder (1708-78), was father, and not grandfather, of the architect of the Union.
20. Thomas, first baron Erskine (1750-1823), a lawyer and advocate who defended Thomas Paine, lord chancellor 1806-07; Charles James Fox (1749-1806), a leader of the Whig party and champion of liberal causes.
21. John Philpot Curran (1750-1817), Irish barrister, judge, and songwriter.
22. Samuel Taylor Coleridge (1772-1834), English romantic poet. He discusses the influence of bible-reading on style in Chapter XVII of *Biographia Literaria* (1817).
23. Henry St John (1678-1751), 1st viscount Bolingbroke, brilliant orator and Tory politician.
24. Charles James Fox was noted for his oratory and scholarship as well as for his statesmanship.
25. Richard Brinsley Sheridan (1751-1816), Irish dramatist and English parliamentarian.
26. Edmund Burke (1729-97), politician and writer. For Grattan, see note 1 above.
27. Thomas Erskine was especially renowned for some of his 'Defences', e.g. *Defence of William Stone* (1796).

of all, are the speeches so valuable, and so little known of Lord Plunket.[j28] His precise vigour marks him the Demosthenes[29] of the English language. But I am coming to our cotemporaries. Criticism on them *could not* be unprejudiced. I shall hazard but one piece of advice: keep to the plainer styles. However you may dislike their opinions, or question their depth of judgment, the style of Southey,[30] Smith,[31] and some few more of the older reviewers is excellent. Coleridge, Carlyle[k32] and the rest of the Germanic set[33] are damaging English nearly as much as the Latinists did; their writings are eloquent, lively, and vigorous, to those who understand them; curry and muligatawney[34] to the literary world, but 'caviare to the multitude'.[35] Just as the dish possesses a high cooked and epicurean flavour, is it unfit for the people or the men of the people. The literary style most in fashion is corrupt, and corrupting; the patois of the coteries, it is full of meaning and sensibility to them. But as your horoscope tells not of coterie fame, shun that jargon. The orator should avoid using it as one would a pestilence; for the people own not its power — it belongs not to the nations.

I have mentioned and illustrated the vices of the university system. I need not say that it is with its system I quarrel. Some of its members are my very good friends, and many pleasant hours[l] have I spent within the walls of the merry monastery. I have not, personally, one sad or angry reminiscence of old Trinity; and it is, therefore, with pain I sum up its defects; which are, that the subjects of its studies are not adapted to the different tastes, interests, and capacities of the students; that this evil is aggravated by the peculiar direction of this exclusive system, shutting out the literature of modern nations, especially the English, which should be the first and principal study, and the Irish, which should, at least, be in the second rank; lastly, that the studies, of what kind soever, are pursued in a dogmatical and shallow spirit, loading the memory with the words of the ancient literators, and the definitions and conclusions of the modern philosophers; but neglecting, making indeed no effort, to cultivate the reason, imagination, or sentiments of the students. Is my reasoning fallacious? I pray you to look around your different circles, and you will see the native abilities of hundreds of young men ruined in our college. 'By their fruits ye shall know them.'[36]

Gentlemen, the Dublin university is the laughing-stock of the literary world, and an obstacle to the nation's march; its inaccessible library, 'the mausoleum of literature', and effete[m] system of instruction, render it ridiculous abroad; add its unaccounted funds, and its bigot laws, and know why it is hated at home.

I have already pointed out to you how some faults of the collegiate system may be remedied by voluntary association. I shall presently show you that many of its defects may be compensated by this society. But then comes the question, Would not an academic reform accomplish all these objects at once? I doubt it. Material improvements could be made, but that university education should be continued at all seems questionable, and this doubt extends to the collegiate system generally, metropolitan and provincial, though to the latter in a less

j. Dudley writes: 'I wish you had heard Plunket. He had made great speeches before, but in this he has surpassed them all. I have not for many years heard such an astonishing display of talent. His style is quite peculiar; for its gravity I prefer it to all others of which I have ever heard a specimen. If he had been bred to parliament, I am inclined to think he would have been the greatest speaker that ever appeared in it.' *Lord Dudley's Letters to the Bishop of Llandaff*, page 280. [John William Ward (1781-1833), 1st earl of Dudley; British foreign secretary 1827-28. Ed.]

k. I speak of their style merely, which is like that of the Puritans; but it was natural in the latter; it is imitative in the others. Carlyle is a more honest, but less learned thinker than Coleridge. Their opinions are unsafe, but their works are of the greatest use in tempting men by their enthusiasm, or forcing them by their paradoxes, to think.

l. Alas for such hours, few can, fewer will return; alas for the companions of the past!

'Some are dead, and some are gone,
And some are changed I wist not why.'

m. I should make an exception in favor of the medical and surgical school, but that is a thing apart. The alterations of the divinity course have made it more laborious, but more bigot-fostering than ever.

28. William Conyngham Plunket (1764-1854), 1st baron Plunket, lord chancellor of Ireland 1830-41.
29. Demosthenes (*c.* 384-322 B.C.), the greatest of the ancient Greek orators.
30. Robert Southey (1774-1843), English poet and man of letters. He was a principal contributor and reviewer in the *Quarterly Review*.
31. Sydney Smith (1771-1845), English clergyman, lecturer and wit. The Smith of Smiths.
32. Thomas Carlyle (1795-1881), Scottish historian and essayist.
33. Carlyle and Coleridge were both much influenced by German idealism, and helped to disseminate similar philosophical notions in England. William Taylor (1765-1836) was the most influential translator of the 'Germanic set'.
34. Curry and muligatawney are both highly spiced oriental dishes, the latter a soup of Anglo-Indian origin.
35. A version of Shakespeare's phrase 'caviare to the general' in *Hamlet*, II. 2. 465, meaning something above the taste of ordinary people.
36. cf. Matthew 7. 20.

degree. I might rely on their being in this dilemma that, if they do not enforce residence, they are intellectually useless; and, if they do, they are morally pernicious, by destroying family ties, and, too often, purity of character.

But I do not rest on this. I contend that theory and experience show the superiority of the lyceum to the university system; that during childhood, the mind requires to be guided, though not schooled, as it commonly is, and that the affections do then most deserve and repay cultivation, form conclusive reasons for the *domestic* education of children. But in more educated years, I believe that a young man, whether, a hermit, he seclude himself with nature and his own breast to instruct him, or more wisely combine for mutual instruction with his fellows, will by either way grow into an eager, thorough-thinking man; and become better informed, and of more vigorous faculties, than had he been dry-nursed by a candidate bishop, or tied to the apron-string of even such an *alma mater* as Trinity College.

Gentlemen, the lyceum system was that of Greece in its best days — of Greece, when it produced in two hundred years more eminent men than did all Europe with all its universities in twice that period.

Universities, at best, can only store the memory which wants no aid; they are not fit to develop the other powers of head and heart. I entreat of you to bear this *assertion* of mine in mind, when I come to speak of the working of this society on its members. I cannot now discuss the question at length; suffice it, in support of the truth and relevancy of my opinion, that such societies as this are strictly lyceums, bearing a close resemblance in their mode of operation to the famous schools of Athens; and, furthermore, such societies have existed among the students of Italy, Spain, France, England, and Germany, indeed of all Europe, to *compensate* the evils of the *universities*. Indeed, I at first intended to have traced out what would be a good education, and then to have shown the fitness of the lyceum system to teach it; but I remembered that my reasoning would be met, in the mind of every good easy man, with the question, was not Trinity College, after all, a very good thing? Therefore, I have gone to the trouble of showing it to be a bad thing in theory. I appeal to the experience of every *disinterested* man of sense in proof of its positive inefficacy; and if I be told that the general idleness or dullness of the students would make any higher system so much too good as to be good for nothing, I shall then appeal to the history of the lyceum system, to the minute experience of every man on mind-formation, and lastly, to poor calumniated human nature itself.[n]

But be the university education good or bad, with it, and such knowledge as they have smuggled from novels, newspapers, and experience, the students are flung out to spend, as chance may lead, the years till business compel them to industry. How is this interval generally past? You recollect the song:

> Now I'm of age and come into my property
> Devil a ha'p'orth I'll think of but fun.

Gentlemen, let the Purists and Calvinists pour out their gloomy and often hypocritical invectives against the weakness of man, I have no sympathy with their declarations; the path of reasonable virtue may be narrow; they make it a sword-bridge — God made it wider.[o] He made man, and the path of his pilgrimage or triumph. He limits our aberrations as he steers the courses of the suns — to no unvarying road — employing our errors to instruct us, justifying his attributes to himself, and ultimately to us; and he has so made man, that 'to step aside is human'.[37] Do not, therefore, suppose me a 'pedant in morals', when I tell you that to spend the noon of life in trifles or indulgences, is for a feeble and degenerate mind. God forbid that we should so sin against human nature as to become cold, gloomy, and ambitious men. No! I rejoice *that* is not the side we err to.

> O life, how pleasant is thy morning,
> Young fancy's rays the hills adorning,
> Cold pausing caution's lesson scorning,
> We frisk away,
> Like schoolboys at the expected warning
> To joy and play.

n. I would suggest the propriety of forming an Irish Lyceum, with sections for the study of the different branches of philosophy, history, and literature. Sections should be specially devoted to the cultivation of the IRISH language, and to promoting a knowledge of Ireland's natural history, its statistic and civil history, and its native literature. I have spoken to many persons about it, and all thought the plan feasible.

o. There is no such thing as philosophical misanthropy — *Taylor*, Preface to Philip Van Artevelde. [Sir Henry Taylor (1800-86), English author; his play of this name was a great success in the mid-1830s.]

37. Robert Burns, *Address to the Unco Guid*, line 10.

We wander here, we wander there,
We eye the rose upon the briar,
Unmindful that the thorn is near
Among the leaves,
And though the puny wound appear,
Short while it grieves.[p]

p. Burns, 'The Vision'.

[PART II]

But, gentlemen, a manhood of mere pleasure preludes an old age of care, a death of contempt. In that dangerous time, therefore, ere professional business, like a Mentor, comes to our aid, how useful such societies as this must be in leading the mind from frivolous thoughts to grave studies, and preparing the spirit for stirring scenes; even then, as an occupation of so much time otherwise likely to be fooled away, a membership of our society is useful. But it does much more; and first, it is a noble, indeed the only effective institute of the social sciences. It is perhaps more valuable in this way than as a school of oratory; whether it shall be a school for eloquence or loquacity depends more on the management of it, but whether well or ill used, *it teaches things which a citizen should know*. If a member prepare himself for your debates, and listen to, or engage in them, how many valuable subjects must he learn. In politics, the various questions relating to local and central governments, the host of disputes of doctrines of representation, its proper extent and restrictions, and the plans for its improvement. How far, if at all, monarchy and aristocracy should be imposed on democracy, the undoubted basis of free government; and whether a social equality should or indeed could be added to the political; and when, in addition to these, you discuss such details as the influence of a free press, of the jury system and penal code, you lay a broad and deep foundation for political knowledge.

Again, in political economy, there are the disputes, whether, of the agricultural or manufacturing systems, one should be encouraged to the exclusion of the other; ending generally in the conviction, that all classes in the country should be left to their own natural development; only taking care that no matter how connected with, or dependent on each other, they shall, if possible, be independent of the stranger. Then the question on poor and corn laws,[1] on absenteeism, colonies, and finance, afford opportunities for acquiring a knowledge not only of these particular topics, but of fixing in the memory, and applying the doctrines of supply and demand, wages, capital, rent, and taxation, so hard to learn, indeed so ill learned by systematic reading, but which, always of importance, have become still more so in our day. The production, accumulation, distribution, and consumption of wealth occupy much, indeed too much regard. You must, and here you can learn these things. The people are pressing on in a career certain of sweeping away every law and custom which impedes their physical comfort, though in doing so they may overthrow some of the barriers which protect their morals, and therefore guard their happiness.

Gentlemen, if we stopped here, if only these subjects I have named were earnestly studied (and voluntary studies are always earnest), would you not have learned more of the things which you would want in life, more of what goes to make a wise and influential citizen, than from the demonstrations and 'dead vocables'[2] of the whole college course[?] But we do not stop here. I shall not mention your discussions on literary subjects; for except when such a society contains a number of men practised in debate, and of vast information, it is vain to think of debating them; and even then they do not excite a sufficiently warm interest. Yet familiarity with the standard writers is an essential preparation for your political debates; and the critical habits which grow up naturally from competition, render this as a mere literary society of some value. But, gentlemen, this is a Historical Society and ample means does it afford for studying history; not as a record of facts, but with that philosophy which first examines these facts as parts of political and social institutions, as manifestations of human nature on great occasions; and having done so, and *not before*, applies them to the circumstances occurring around it, to the institutions and men of its own time.

Without knowing the history of a time, we cannot accurately comprehend its philosophy.

1. The Poor Law Amendment Act of 1834 created unions of parishes, managed by boards of guardians who were elected by ratepayers. Outdoor relief stopped, and paupers were forced into workhouses where conditions were deliberately harsh. The corn laws, by which duties were charged on grain imported into Britain, became a major political issue after 1815. Peel eventually secured the partial repeal of the corn laws in June 1846.
2. i.e. empty words.

Taste and politics alike receive from history correctives which prevent over-refinement. I would especially point to the opinions of the middle ages, when an ingenuity in speculation quite unequalled, led to profitless refinement, from the want or neglect of the touchstone of experience, which history combined with personal observation (that is, past and cotemporary history) could, and could alone supply.

But it is not more than this? What! will you tell me that history is no teacher of the head and heart? it is — it is example that gives impulse and vitality to principles. I might tell you of the faults from which a knowledge of history shields us. Is it nothing to warn us against the brilliant vices of an aristocracy? Is it nothing that its beacons gleam to keep people from *beginning* to shed blood.

Philosophy may account for the danger, and may on its principles forewarn the people; but without the garnered thoughts of history, would philosophy have discovered those truths? or will a man, or a senate, or a people, be more influenced by a string of metaphysical truths, or by the portrait taken from life of the blood-stained and jewelled despot, or the picture of a scaffold-applauding mob? History well read is a series of pictures of great men, and great scenes, and great acts. It impresses the principles and despair, the hopes and powers of the Titan's [*sic*] of our race. Every high hill and calm lake, every rich plain and rolling sea in the time-world is depictured in history's pages. With rare exceptions, *national history* does dramatic justice, alien history is the inspiration of a traitor.[a]

In home-history, the best is generally the greatest; though the clatter of cotemporary fame may have concealed the good by the celebrity of the great, yet Washington is more dear to history than Frederic, Brutus than Caesar.[3] Historic writing begins now to be improved, or rather regenerated, restored to what it was in Greece. 'Tis a glorious world, historic memory. As we gaze, we long to resemble. Our mental bulk extends, as each shade passes in visioned pomp or purity. From the grave, the sage warns: from the mound, the hero, from the temple, the orator-patriot, inspire: and the poet sings in his shroud.

The field of fame, the forum of power, the death-bed or scaffold of patriots, 'who died in righteousness'[4] — you look — you pause — you 'swear like them to live, like them to die'.[5] You have a list of questions not long, which I defy any man to study, with the view of making really sound speeches in this room, without learning much, and that well too. Men (I speak, having known its working) learn history in this society with a rapidity and an ease, a profundity in research, and sagacity in application, not approached by any other mode of study. Suppose a man to prepare a defence of what most histories condemn, or to censure some favorite act, or man, or institution, or policy: he makes use of all the generalities of criticism, he shakes the authority of popular writers, or shows our reasoning inapplicable from the different state of society on which we reason from that in which we live, and by which alone we are apt to judge. In his eagerness to persuade, he becomes more sensitive of the times of which he speaks than could the solitary student, and we half follow him to the scene over which his spirit stalks.

In aught that could be called a good speech on a historical subject, there is not merely a laborious selection of such facts as have an argumentative or illustrative value, and of those alone; they must be united, not by crude generalities or tiresome details, but by practical intermediate principles. Familiar command of such principles justly confers a character for maturity in thought, and they are more readily suggested by close thinking on historical analogies, than by refinements on general principles. Gentlemen, you will find that the employment of facts by the lawyer and senator is exactly similar to this which I have described as ours; and if so, a practice of speaking here would

a. I mean the histories of a country, by hostile strangers. They should be refuted and then forgotten. Such are most histories of Ireland, and yet Irishmen neglect the original documents and such compilations as Carey's Vindiciae; and they sin not by omission only — too many of them receive and propagate on Irish affairs, 'quicquid Anglia mendax in historia audet'. [Matthew Carey (1760-1839), bookseller and pamphleteer in Dublin, Paris and Philadelphia; published *Vindiciae Hibernicae* in 1819 to refute accepted views of the Irish rebellion of 1641. Ed.]

3. George Washington (1732-99), general and first president of the United States of America; Friedrich II (1712-86), king of Prussia, known in English as Frederick the Great; Marcus Junius Brutus (85-42 B.C.), a Roman who led the conspiracy to assassinate the great general Gaius Julius Caesar (*c.* 100-44 B.C.) whom he suspected of imperial ambition.

4. cf. *Revelations* 14. 13: 'Blessed are the dead which die in the Lord.' This phrase is used in the service for the burial of the dead in the Book of Common Prayer as used by the Church of Ireland.

5. An adaptation of Thomas Moore's line, 'That ye like him may live, like him may die', from 'Lines on the Death of Joseph Atkinson, Esq. of Dublin', in *The Poetical Works* (London, 1840-41).

seem no bad discipline for the bar or senate.[b] I would suggest to you that your questions might be so systematically chosen, as, without diminishing the interest, to take in the more important changes and conditions of ancient and modern states. For example, are there not questions which open up the nature, both theoretical and working, of the constitutions of the leading states of Greece, separately, and also as a confederation, bearing *some* likeness to those of the Netherlands, Lombardy, and America? The effects of the conquest of Asia by Alexander, give a question not unlike that of India by the English — alien civilisation — native ruin. It were easy to name many questions from Grecian history, affording ample and accessible materials, *which we do not sufficiently use*.

Rome fares better from our hands. We have its whole early constitution displayed in the question on the tribunician power; the feuds of the aristocracy, first of race, then of wealth, with the plebeians; the institutions which so long remedied these disorders, and at last failed, and *why* they perished. The wisdom of adopting the imperial constitution, if well discussed, would develope [*sic*] the circumstance, which defeated the policy of Cicero and Pompey, the patriotism of Sulpicius and Brutus.[6] Then comes the time when 'Rome imperial bowed her to the storm,'[7] and by the deluge of rushing war, the seeds of renascent freedom were spread over southern Europe; and though the trees which sprung from the diluvium wore a rude form, yet tough was the fibre, deep the root, and healthy the sap. The autumns of war, the winters of superstition have come and gone, and yet are many of them sound at the core; and even were they dead, they have leaved and fruited, and their kind has been transplanted to far lands. But as yet we are in the vestibule: let us pass in this temple of history from the antique periods; and as we advance through the aisles of time, we stop to gaze on, perchance we open, the tomb of the crusader, and demand the hopes that maddened him, the state and circumstances of his peers and vassals. We glance in anger at the brutal conqueror of the Saxons, or with more interest eye the trophies of Agincourt,[8] or the standards so often lost and won in the wars of the Roses;[9] and we question the gain, motives, and effects of this civil fray, or that foreign conquest; or we turn with holier emotions to the banners which waved over the peasants of Sempach and Dalecarlia,[10] or the civic emblems which led on the leaguers of Lombardy and Holland to victory and Confederate freedom.[11] But hastily, too hastily, we move to the altar of modern civilisation, and yet it is a glorious show; glorious in the names of its saints, more glorious in those of its martyrs; splendid, if not always free from idolatrous rites, is the sacrifice of its priests; yet more noble is the occasional, the interrupted worship of the laity and the democracy; sublime are the hymns of rejoicing for the past; melting its songs of sorrow over the departed great; divine its thanksgivings for the blessings present; yet more sublime, yet more pathetic, divine are the anticipations of the future which its prophets sing. Who can discuss the nature of each revolution which reformed England, convulsed France, and liberated America, without becoming a wiser man: who can speculate on their destinies, and not warm with hope?

I shall not now reprove your neglect of Irish history. I shall say nothing of it but this, that I never heard of any famous nation which did not honor the names of its departed great, study the fasti,[12] and the misfortunes — the annals of the land, and cherish the associations of its history and theirs. The national mind should be filled to overflowing with such thoughts. They are more enriching than mines of gold, or ten thousand fields of corn, or the

b. The style of speaking acquired in a good Historical Society is certainly best suited to political assemblies; yet, even for the bar, a Historical Society is preferable to what is called a Law Debating Society, in which popular law and crabbed rhetoric struggle for mastery with a heavy perseverance. And I may add, that a few campaigns in a debating society might give the pulpit oratory of the deacons a flexibility and fairness, contrasting it favorably with that of the priests. Three out of four of the orators of the last eighty years (the oratorical period in these kingdoms) were trained in debating societies, as were all the great orators of Greece and Rome.

6. There were several notable Romans of this name who were distinguished for their admirable politics. For Brutus, see note 3 above.
7. Byron, *Childe Harolde's Pilgrimage*, Canto IV, xlvi.
8. A battle between England and France, fought on 25 October 1415. Henry V's notable victory against superior numbers revived England's military standing.
9. Dynastic wars fought between the houses of Lancaster (red rose) and York (white rose) for the English throne 1455-85.
10. Sempach, a town in Switzerland at which Arnold von Winkelried gained Swiss freedom in 1386: for von Winkelried, see note 5 to J.C. Mangan's translation of 'The Twenty-fourth of February' above. Dalecarlia is an ancient province of Sweden, whose peasant inhabitants revolted against Danish occupation in 1521.
11. The struggles of these states against their imperial conquerors were taken as models of national resistance in the nineteenth century.
12. Roman calendars or records of events.

cattle of a thousand hills; more ennobling than palaced cities stored with the triumphs of war or art; more supporting in danger's hour than colonies, or fleets, or armies. The history of a nation is the birthright of her sons — who strips them of that, 'takes that which not enriches him but makes them poor indeed'.[13]

Such is a partial and feebly-drawn sketch of the information which may be learned here; and incomplete as is any account of it, it still is so extensive, that I may seem to exaggerate; but the wonder ceases when we look to the advantages inherent in our mode of study. Gentlemen, we hear frequent invectives against what is clumsily called universalism in education; and certainly, if this refer to authors, or even languages, no invective seems necessary; it will be sufficient to send the bold aspirant into any public library, even of Trinity College, and after a week's rumaging he will come out convinced of the utter hopelessness of any attempt at universalism. Authors are a cannibal race, they devour each other's carcasses, and the death of one set supports the lives of another. There is a certain set of books which any man mixing in literary circles must read to please the world; there is another set which he ought to read for his own sake, and they are the few master-pieces of his own, and, if convenient, of foreign literature. Perhaps about twenty writers in English, a dozen in Greek and French, and half of that number in each of the other popular languages, will comprise this class.

With these exceptions, which may be reduced still further, every prudent man will study *subjects, not authors*. Thus alone can you go through the wilderness of writers, *and it is only by requiring ourselves to master subjects that we render this society what it is — a means of sound general education.* When once this is acquired, you can get that sort of knowledge of writers which enables you to refer to them on occasion. Learning, as such, is the baggage of the orator: without it, he may suffer exhaustion or defeat from an inferior foe; with it, his speed and agility are diminished. Those are best off who have it in magazines, to be drawn on leisurely occasion. That which should be carried by the memory should be borne after the expedite fashion, leaving the other faculties free; but borne some of it must be. Learning is necessary to orator, and poet, and statesman. Book-learning when well digested, and vivified by meditation, may suffice, as in Burke and Coleridge; but otherwise it is apt to produce confusion and inconsistency of mind, as it *sometimes* did in both these men. Far better is *the learning of previous observation*, the learning of past emotions and ideas, the learning caught by conversation, invented or dug up by meditation in the closet or the field; impressions of scenery, whether natural or artificial, in the human, animal, or material world. Such learning is used by every great poet, philosopher, and orator; perhaps it requires propitious training or nascent genius to be able to acquire it, but ability to acquire ensures ability to use.

When Grattan paced his garden, or Burns trod his hillside, were they less students than the print-dizzy denizens of a library? No; that pale form of the Irish regenerator is trembling with the rush of ideas; and the murmuring stream, and the gently-rich landscape, and the fresh wind converse with him through keen interpreting senses, and tell mysteries to his expectant soul, and he is as one inspired; arguments in original profusion, illustrations competing for his favor, memories of years long past, in which he had read philosophy, history, poetry, awake at his call. That man entered the senate-house, no written words in his hand, and poured out the seemingly spontaneous,[c] but really learned and prepared lullaby over Ireland's cradle, or keen over Ireland's corse.

Read, too, Burn's [*sic*] own account of the birth and growth of some of his greatest lyrics. Read, and learn to labour, if you would be great. There is no more common error than that great works are usually the result of extemporaneous power. You have all read an article on Sheridan by Lord Brougham,[14] full of depreciating criticism, founded on the evidences, the chisel marks of composition, which Sheridan left, and so many others (Brougham among the number) concealed. Henry

13. cf. Shakespeare, *Othello*, III. 3. 157-61:
Who steals my purse steals trash; 'tis something, nothing;
'Twas mine, 'tis his, and has been slave to thousands;
But he that filches from me my good name
Robs me of that which not enriches him,
And makes me poor indeed.

c. After repeated experience and after he had filled his mind with knowledge, Grattan, or such a man could, when greatly roused, compose his speeches in the house, or make the design and execution of them simultaneous.

14. Henry Peter Brougham (1778-1868), baron Brougham and Vaux, lord chancellor 1830-33, and founder of London University in 1828. Richard Brinsley Sheridan (1751-1816), Irish dramatist and English parliamentarian.

Brougham is a *metaphysician*; he made no *mistake* on this; but Lord Brougham is an egotist, and he *misrepresented*.

You are familiar to weariness with the talk about inspirations and sudden efforts of genius, in novelists and the daily press. The outbursts of most minds, until highly educated are frothy or ashes-laden. The instances adduced to the contrary will be found fallacious. The continuous and enthusiastic labours of men brimful of knowledge, proved the energy of the men, not the inutility of learning. But then, as I have told, or rather described to you, experience[d] is even a greater well of knowledge than books. Without experience, book-learning makes the pedant, and spoils the man.

The common fault of all education, public and private, is that memory, which requires less care, receives an exclusive attention. No crop is sought from the other faculties, reason, fancy, imagination; and accordingly, the business of life finds too many unschooled in thinking, unprepared to act.

The best way of teaching others things we know, and of analysing or discovering things unappreciated or unknown is this: On the very threshold of every art, and science, and subject of thought, men, either from its known uses and applications, from some knowledge of a particular detail of its exterior, or working, or the materials used in constructing it; or from knowing the history of its formation; or from any or all of these; or from the analogy of some combinations of them, should try to judge of other parts, and their origin; or, if you will, guess at the whole from any part of it. Analogy is the first law of thought, and therefore we may do thus, naturally and without presumption, 'worms in the cabinet drawer' though we be and proceeding as I have described, and testing and correcting our guesses and fancies by learning; these particular facts, acquired by deliberate study, become mixed with our other information or familiar knowledge, and we arrive always at *characteristic*, if not actual truths, and ultimately acquire that power of general analysis which is the main force of a great mind. If our memory or information be deficient, our reason is exercised in the highest and most inventive way. Thus only can the inventive faculties, reason, fancy, imagination, be trained. Once they have been so trained, once the mind can readily anticipate, combine, and compare information, the acquisition and use of knowledge has no imaginable limit.[e] *Here*, fortunately, invention and judgment are as *much demanded* and are *therefore as well supplied* as mere information. And this forms the distinctive superiority of Lyceum teaching over every other kind.

Gentlemen, do not, however, suppose that information and matured powers, such as I have named, can be produced by an occasional or idle attendance at our meetings, or by chattering speeches without preparation; no, to borrow an expression, you must 'read yourselves full, and think yourselves hungry',[15] on the society's questions for *at least* two or three years. I entreat of you to abandon the notion that you will speak well merely from speaking often. Of a surety, all your faculties grow with use, but this very quality of mind behoves you to be judicious as well as earnest in the exercise of your powers. A bad style grows worse by repetition, as much as a good style improves; or, more generally, bad habits grow as rapidly as good ones. Give up the idea of being great orators *without preparation*, till you are so *with it*. When you are, with your utmost labour, able to make one really great speech, you will be above me, my criticism, and my advice, but will, perchance, agree with my opinion.[f]

d. That is, the deliberate noticing and treasuring for use, of our experience our treating every scene and group as a book to read, as materials for every variety of thought or sentiment. Ariosto's father one day rebuked him sharply, charging him with some great fault, but all the while he returned no answer. Soon after his brother began the same subject, but he easily refuted him, and with a strong argument justified his own behaviour. 'Why then,' said his brother, 'did you not satisfy my father?' 'In truth,' said Ludovico, 'I was thinking of part of my comedy and methought my father's words so suited to the part of an old man chiding his son, that I forgot I was concerned in it myself, and thought only of making it part of my play.' Shakespeare must have lived doing thus.

e. Most writers underrate the power of improving or forming faculties. When I see a man who knows or foreknows his powers, and plans his own faculty-formation, I think of Napoleon, who, when someone said it was impossible to do a certain thing, replied, 'do not let me hear that foolish word again.' This is the creed of a man of action, rather than of a spectator. Edmond [*sic*] Burke's 'presiding principle and prolific energy' seems the finest, indeed a perfect rule of action for self-government, and all government. See the Reflections on the French Revolution, p. 220 to 225 of the Dublin edition.

f. The printed addresses of which I spoke at the beginning of this paper, are full of analysis and rules of application, connected with this part of my subject. The writers on metaphysics and rhetoric, from Aristotle to Mill, and Quinctilian to Whateley, also contain plenty of good truths on the principles of persuasion and the tactics of debate. Their advice being general is easier understood than acted on. I have sought to batter down the more salient errors which I saw and felt; to deal with what is now here and what might be; and rather to offer a few careful, than many loose commendations. My fellow-students can follow out this as well as I could, but their attention wanted some urgency. They have at their head one much better able to advise them than I am, and one who can enforce advice by example.

15. A version of the Latin proverb, 'Multa docet fames', or 'Hunger teaches many things'.

The advantage of speaking *generally* with a *complete* preparation, both of matter and style, is that when occasionally you speak (voluntarily or otherwise) with *incomplete* preparation, your *usual* arrangement and style will present a good and, what is more, an *easily-imitated* model; and thus, not only will your manner of speaking be kept accurate and forcible, but you will acquire that quality useful to all men of business, and *essential* to the orator and the public man, *presence of mind*. I think there is scarcely a finer expression in the language. It conveys, in picturesque words, a vigorous thought. Great orators have not only great but present minds. They are self-possessed, and have all their resources at command. The memory, the knowledge must be prodigious, that can carry a man through the common business of life without the position strange, and the occasion sudden opening in his path, to trip or pit-fall the star-gazer. But, in the great contests of public life, no day but demands the presence of a mind unembarrassed by prejudice, unimpeded by knowledge obsolete, or wisdom inapplicable; a mind whereby a man can think on his legs, and act discreetly even when he acts from his intuitions, steering his course by the same power that impels him. But the men who, by often extemporizing as the spirit moved them, have got unabashed brows and flippant tongues, are as far from this noble attainment, as the pertness of the sparrow differs from the valour of the eagle.

But let me reiterate that a prudent and industrious use of this society can alone make it a means of improvement. To the idle and the vain your membership may be a probation in folly. I have known men of some capacity come here, professedly with the design of learning oratory. I have watched them till their patriotism cooled, their sagacity lessened, their courtesy not improved, all from a reckless misuse of the society.

There is another danger I would warn you against. Eloquence is contained in words, and, therefore, some men would turn an oratorical society into a word-school. There are worse employments than inventing smart sentences, though some men would quarrel with a friend for the sake of uttering one. There are worse pastimes than spinning periods, though some men prefer the display of such fabrics, to character for sense, or the cause of justice. I do not object to the study of language; I commend it to your early and learned care, but do not suppose that a court of justice, that a political assembly, that a senate, or even a vestry, that a mob of peers or peasants, will care for fine words, unless there be strong thoughts within them.

The successful orator must be *prepared* in a *good style*, *ready* with a *fluent* one; but he must *also* be learned in the sympathies and the prejudices *of all* his audiences, but *especially* of their influential men; he must have a thorough knowledge of the *materials* on which, and with which he is to work. Common industry will inform him on the *immediate* subject of discourse, and his task is done. Some will tell you not to rouse the animosity of a judge, or the suspicions of a jury, with shewy words, or weary a mob with cold words. No, gentlemen, but thoughts, thoughts; the wise man against the wordy man all the world over. And even for style sake, study thoughts *before* words. The style suggested by long meditation on the subject is mostly apt to it, forcible and consistent. A style *formed* by verbal studies or imitation is generally inflated, unequal, and obscure. In fine, then, the order of your noviciate should be, much research and more meditation preceding, combining with, and following the research. When you have acquired a facility in discovering information, and inventing and combining thoughts, it remains for you to *make opportunities*[g] for *gradually* learning to *speak well* without *particular* preparation. Act thus with eagerness, enterprise, and with much reflection, and you will succeed.

Gentlemen, I have detained you very long; bear with me yet a little while. I would give you my parting advice.

If you suppose it possible to be great orators, great statesmen, greatly known, without having expanded hearts, and mighty imaginations, without being great men, you sadly deceive yourselves. Hear the second poet of Scotland, (for Burns is the first) hear how Scott murmurs his requiem over the tomb of Charles Fox —

> Mourn genius and love profound,
> And wit that loved to play not wound;
> And all the reasoning powers divine,
> To penetrate, resolve, combine,
> And feelings keen, and fancy's glow —
> They sleep with him, who sleeps below.[h]

g. The strong man never waits for, he makes opportunities.
h. Marmion, Introduction to the first Canto.

If you want to be great orators, you must not set about learning the mountebank juggles — the phrase-spinning tricks of little men attempting great parts. I shall not wrong you by supposing that any petty vanities or selfish hopes brought you here. No; I believe that the bold aspirations of your boyhood (for the foundation of greatness is laid in childhood), those pure and dazzling visions which have flashed upon you in dreams, and caught the steadier glance of your young waking eye, have not yet faded wholly away. What, though many a glorious expectation has failed? What, though even you have learned that toil and danger guard the avenue to success? What, though disappointment and suffering have somewhat touched you, and made you less sanguine; yet, has not time rewarded your sorrows — has it not refined — has it not purified — has it not strengthened, even when it humbled you? This world is called hard; 'tis the *outside* of each little circle of feelings and ties that is so, and who is not within the bounds of at least one such? None here, I trust; and yet if there be one so wounded and desolate — one who longs for that solitude which it has been said is 'fit only for a demon or an angel', or for the equally dubious quiet of the tomb — such a soul must, under the benign influence of early feelings, and propitious circumstances and the teaching nobler than that of manhood, which is given to us then, have felt the generous resolve to serve a world which might not thank him. Oh, if I had the power to 'bid the happy thought of innocent days play at his heart-strings',[16] and in enthusiastic strains to melodise the conviction, that nor prosperity, nor content, nor the blessings of friendship or love (which are dearest to the minds) can lift to the same sublimity, or should warm with the same proud joy, as the consciousness of him who is a benefactor of mankind. Let not gentleness or virtue shrink from the boisterous elements of publicity; such a spirit makes a calm around; nor let want or rank or wealth awe him into silence,

> For service comes of gentleness
> And lealest hearts of low degree.[17]

To each has God given a career of possible improvement; it may exceed, it may fall short of that in other ages. The march during the daylight of *our* age may be limited by the time and training; but we have it in our power to accelerate that march.

The time is past when the omnipotence of the sword might excuse the sentimental or learned, or melancholy retirement. The man who now avoids his citizenship has no defence but imbecility; for if he have sagacity and learning he has *power*, and sins in folding up his talent from want of zeal to use it. He lacks not means, but a virtuous will.

I would especially desire the diffusion of civic zeal, because in it I see the means, the only means of human improvement. The effect of modern civilisation up to a certain point has been good; it has tended to free man from the dominion of an armed minority, who stupified and worked the human race as if they were so many machines which they had made, and could make, and had no reason to abstain from abusing, save the prudence of perpetuating them. This step has been taken in some countries, and seems likely to be taken in all. But on the shore of democracy is a monstrous danger; no phantasm, is it, but alas! too real — the violence and frowardness of selfish men, regardful only of physical comfort, ready to sacrifice to it all sentiments — the generous, the pious, the just (victims in their order), till general corruption, anarchy, despotism, and moral darkness shall re-barbarise the earth. A great man[i] has said, if you would qualify Democracy for power, you must 'purify their morals, and warm their faith, if that be possible'. How awful a doubt. But it is not the morality of laws, not the religion of sects, that will do this. It is the habit of rejoicing in high aspirations and holy emotions; it is charity in thought, word, and act; it is generous faith, and the practice of self-sacrificing virtue. To educate the heart and strengthen the intellect of man, are the means of ennobling him. To strain every nerve to this end, is the duty from which no one aware of it can shrink. A sphere of *influence* belongs to every man and every age, and over every man, and every nation, and every succeeding age: but that of *action* is more confined. The influence of moral power extends but gradually and indirectly over cotemporary foreign nations. Those whose acts can directly influence the republic of nations are few, and at so lonely an elevation above common habit, that they

16. Untraced.
17. Untraced.

i. De Tocqueville, preface to *La Democratie en Amérique*. What might not the clergy do if they would devote themselves in a charitable and liberal spirit to the work of moral civilisation? [Charles Alexis de Tocqueville (1805-59) published his classical study of American society between 1835 and 1840. Ed.]

usually lose our common sympathies, and their power is a curse. But no man is without a sufficient sphere of action, and of direct influence. I speak not of private life, in it, blessed be God! our people are tender, generous, and true-hearted. But, gentlemen, you have a country. The people among whom we were born, with whom we live, for whom, if our minds are in health, we have most sympathy, are those over whom we have power — power to make them wise, great, good. Reason points out our native land as the field for our exertions, and tells us that without patriotism a profession of benevolence is the cloak of the selfish man; and does not sentiment confirm the decree of reason? The country of our birth, our education, of our recollections, ancestral, personal, national; the country of our loves, our friendships, our hopes; *our* country — the cosmopolite is unnatural, base — I would fain say, impossible. To act on a world is for those *above* it, not *of* it. *Patriotism is human philanthropy*.

[PART III]

Gentlemen, many of you possess, more of you are growing into the possession of great powers, powers which were given for good, which you may use for evil. I trust that not as adventurers, or rash medlers, will you enter on public life. But to enter on it in some way or other the state of mind in Ireland will compel you. You must act as citizens, and it is well, 'non nobis solum nati sumus, ortusque nostri partem patria vindicat'.[1] Patriotism once *felt* to be a duty, *becomes* so. To act in politics is a matter of duty everywhere; here, of necessity. To make that action honorable to yourselves, and serviceable to your country, is a matter of choice. In your public career you will be solicited by a thousand temptations to sully your souls with the gold and place of a foreign court, or the transient breath of a dishonest popularity; dishonest, when adverse to the good, though flattering to the prejudice, of the people. You now abound in patriotism, and are sceptical of public corruption; yet, most assuredly, if you be eloquent and strong-thinking, threats and bribes will be held out to you. You will be solicited to become the barking misleaders of a faction, or the gazehounds of a minister — dogs who can tell a patriot afar off. Be jealous of your virtue *then*; yield not. Bid back the tempter. Do not grasp remorse. Nay, if it be not a vain thought, in such hours of mortal doubt, when the tempted spirit rocks to and fro, pause, and recall one of your youthful evenings, and remember the warning voice of your old companion, who felt as a friend, and used a friend's liberty. Let the voice of his warning rise upon your ear; think he stands before you as he does now, telling you in such moments, when pride, or luxury, or wrath make you waver, to return to communings with nature's priests,§ the Burns, the Wordsworths, the Shakespeares, but above all, to nature's self. She waits with a mother's longings for the wanderer; fling yourself into her arms, and as your heart beats upon her bosom, your native nobility will return, and thoughts divine as the divinest you ever felt will bear you unscathed through the furnace. Pardon the presumption, pardon the hope ('tis one of my dearest now,) 'forsan et *haec* olim meminisse juvabit'.[2]

And I do not fear that any of you will be found among Ireland's foes. To her every energy should be consecrated. Were she prosperous, she would have many to serve her, though their hearts were cold in her cause. But it is because her people lieth down in misery and riseth to suffer, it is therefore you should be more deeply devoted. Your country will, I fear, need all your devotion. She has no foreign friend. Beyond the limits of green Erin there is none to aid her. She may gain by the feuds of the stranger; she cannot hope for his peaceful help, be he distant, be he near; her trust is in her sons. You are Irishmen. She relies on your devotion. She solicits it by her present distraction and misery. No! her past distraction — her present woe. We have no more war-bills: we have a mendicant bill for Ireland. The poor and the pest house are full, yet the valleys of her country, and the streets of her metropolis swarm, with the starving. The poet has described her

§ Poetry is the instructor of the heart and fancy. As man is a moral and imaginative being, beyond 'the reasoning self-sufficing thing,' his heart is the virgin soil wherein poetic feeling, that is, lofty sentiment, the sense of beauty, the desire of perfection, the joy of goodness, may be sown with a certainty of a rich crop. I rejoice at the early cultivation of poetic taste nowadays, not as a means of fame, nor for ostentation; but to accustom the young to look abroad, with the eye pure and undefiled, thence to fill his soul with what may nourish it, and give it immortal longings.

1. Cicero, *De Officiis* I.vii. 22: 'We are not born for ourselves alone, but our country claims a share of our being.'

2. Virgil, *Aeneid* I, 203: 'Perhaps some day it may be a pleasure to recall these sufferings.'

More dear in her sorrow, her gloom and her showers,
Than the rest of the world in its sunniest hours.[3]

And if she be miserable, if 'homely age hath the allurin[g] beauty took from her poor cheek, then who hath wasted it?'[4] The stranger from without, by means of the traitor within. Perchance 'tis a fanciful thing, yet in the misfortunes of Ireland, in her laurelled martyrs, in those who died 'persecuted men for a persecuted country',[5] in the necessity she was under of bearing the palms to deck her best to the scaffold-foot and the lost battle-field, she has seemed to be chastened for some great future. I have thought I saw her spirit from her dwelling, her sorrowing place among the tombs, rising, not without melancholy, yet with a purity and brightness beyond other nations, and I thought that God had made her purpose firm and her heart just; and I knew that if he had, small though she were, his angels would have charge over her, 'lest at any time she should dash her foot against a stone'.[6] And I have prayed that I might live to see the day when, amid the reverence of those, once her foes, her sons would

Like the leaves of the shamrock unite,
A partition of sects from one foot-stalk of right:
Give each his full share of the earth and the sky,
Nor fatten the slave where the serpent would die.'†

But not only by her sufferings does Ireland call upon you: her past history furnishes something to awake proud recollections. I speak not of that remote and mysterious time when the men of Tyre traded to her well-known shores, and every art of peace found a home on her soil; and her armies, not unused to conquest, traversed Britain and Gaul. Nor yet of that time, when her colleges offered a hospitable asylum to the learned and the learning of every land, and her missions bore knowledge and piety through savage Europe; nor yet of her gallant and romantic struggles against Dane, and Saxon, and Norman;‡ still less of her hardy wars, in which her interest was sacrificed to a too-devoted loyalty in many a successful, many a disastrous battle. Not of these. *I speak of sixty years ago. The memory is fresh, the example pure, the success inspiring*. I speak of 'THE LIFETIME OF IRELAND!'§

But if neither the present nor the past can rouse you, let the sun of hope, the beams of the future, awake you to exertion in the cause of patriotism. Seek, oh! seek to make your country not behind at least in the progress of the nations. Education, the apostle of progress, hath gone forth. Knowledge is not virtue, but may be rendered its precursor. Virtue is not alone enjoyment — is not all happiness; but be sure, when the annunciation of virtue comes, the advent of happiness is at hand. Seek to make your country forward in her progress to that goal, where she, in common with the other nations, may hear that annunciation of virtue, and share the advent of happiness, holiness, and peace.

Gentlemen, I have done. You have been disappointed: you expected, your partiality expected from me, prescriptions to make the best of good speeches at the bar, pulpit, and senate — all in a brilliant address. Yet, though to hear them has given you little pleasure, and to write them has cost me little time, the *thoughts* are not rash or inconsiderate: they were *the best I had*. It would have been easier, much easier, for me to have written rhetorical precepts, and the distinctions of a shallow metaphysics, and to have conveyed such thoughts in a showy diction and with pointed periods. I should have avoided the trouble of combining my scattered thoughts on the subject of our education, but I should have violated my conscious duty. I should have won a louder and more frequent cheer.† You would have cheered, and have

† 'Beauties of the Poets', p. 38.

‡ Ireland was then a confederation with local governments, and her stubborn and protracted resistance may be added to the many such instances collected by Sismondi, to show the greater stability and greater defensive force of countries with a minute local organisation and self-government over the largest centralised powers. See the admirable 'Etudes sur les Constitutions des Peuples Libres', p. 290 (Brussels edition) to the end. See also, Lord Caernarvon on the Basques. 'Sketches', vol. 2.

§ Curran.

† I was in no sanguine mood when I penned that paragraph. I perhaps misjudged the expectations; I much underrated the generosity of my friends. They heard my lay sermon kindly, attentively, and with no cold or critic minds.

3. Thomas Moore, 'Remember me', in *Irish Melodies*.
4. Shakespeare, *The Comedy of Errors*, II. 1. 89: 'Hath homely age the alluring beauty took/From my poor cheek?'
5. Untraced.
6. The source, modified above, is the Gospel of Saint Matthew 4. 6: 'And saith unto him, If thou be the Son of God, cast thyself down: for it is written, He shall give his angels charge concerning thee: and in *their* hands they shall bear thee up, lest at any time thou dash thy foot against a stone.'

   Given that the speaker is Satan, tempting Christ in the wilderness, Davis's use of the phrase is noteworthy.

forgotten me. I shall heartily wish you, gentlemen, what each of you will, I know, wish me in return: that you may struggle and succeed in a career, honorable and useful to yourselves and those who are dear to you, in time, and which — I say it in the sincerest solemnity of my heart — may render you better fitted for eternity.

Now, tell me, candidly, do you think it can be any pleasure to me, to advance opinions, which, differing as they do from those of most of my co-temporaries, must have been taken up with much hesitation? Think you I have many temptations to advance opinions, which so many of you, my friends and companions, will censure. *You* will respect, for you know my motives. There are some, not of you, who are likely enough to read this paper, who will condemn me, as well as it, harshly, uncharitably, ignorantly — I shall not mind them. But let *you* fairly weigh my opinions, and if you approve of them, do not suffer *what will then be your opinions* to be sneered down — do not be swindled or bullied out of them; and trust me, you will find that your *interest as well as your duty* is to avow and act on them. You have much to learn, much to dare. Look on our class in Ireland; are they worthy of their nature or their country? Are they like the young men of Germany; as students, laborious; as thinkers, profound and acute? like the young men of France, independent, fearless, patriotic? like the young men of England, Scotland, and America, energetic, patient, successful? (I speak of the virtues of these foreigners). And if not, if the young men of Ireland are careless, prejudiced, unhonored — if their pupilage never ends — if no manhood of mind, no mastery in action comes to most of them — if preparation, thought, action, wisdom, the order of development in successful men, is not for them; if so, are their misleaders, the duped or duping apostles of present systems, alone to blame? No; you, young Irishmen, must blame yourselves. The power of self-education, self-conduct is yours.

Are you ambitious of honorable success? — you must become learned, determined, just, pious. There is no short-cut to greatness. You who are called the upper classes in Ireland, possess no institutions for any sort of instruction, worthy of you. Nay, more; so strong are bigotry, interest, and laziness, that you will get none. *You must found your own institutes — you must conduct your own affairs.* I have discussed some, and hinted at other parts of the subjects which I thought most useful for you to reflect on. If you will discuss them fearlessly and unshrinkingly, 'tis well. I care little for the fate of any opinions, but much for the fate of free discussion. Accept no opinion or set of opinions without examination, no matter whether they be enrobed in pomp, or holiness, or power; admire the pomp, respect the power, venerate the holiness; but for the opinions, strip them; if they bear the image of truth, for its sake cherish them; if false, condemn them. That faith or philosophy, which proclaims the unlimited right and innocence of free inquiry and self-government of mind, is moving among you. Are there none to bear its standards? Will you linger when such powers are in motion? Do you pay no worship to plain unritual virtue? Owe you no allegiance to truth? Or are places on one hand, and prejudices on the other, to keep you apart from each other, and from the common highway to your country's prosperity? You have capacities; will you use them or will you not? Will you use them for free thought — for virtue — for Ireland? Intellect has its duties as well as its rights; the rights of power, fame, and authority, cannot be withheld from it; human nature cannot refuse them; but the duties to yourselves — your fellows — your country, have you not neglected? Are you now compromising them? How long will you sin against patriotism? Let no one dare to call me factious, for bidding you act in union with any men, be they of what party they may, for our common country.

I shall not apologise for taking the same freedom with you collectively, that (you know) I should take with each one of you in private.

I leave these things with you. I feel my own weakness, but am equally conscious of, and ready to assert my right of free thought and expression; but you, some of you at least, possess powers as well as rights. I, therefore, have done my duty in pointing out, though with feeble arm, the path I believe you ought to pursue.

ANONYMOUS

DREADFUL LOSS OF LIFE IN THE CATHOLIC CHAPEL, GALWAY (1842)

[Much of the news coverage in *The Nation* was given over to lengthy accounts of debates in parliament, in Dublin corporation and other local bodies, and in the Repeal Association. Nevertheless, the paper attempted to act as a disseminator of news as well as opinion, frequently adopting the nineteenth-century practice of quoting (with acknowledgments) from other papers. The incident reported below has several points of interest. First, despite emancipation in 1829 and the resulting boom in church building, many catholic churches were very old, and structurally unsound because they were never designed for public use by a congregation. (Many were, in fact, converted lofts, this recalling the penal period of covert celebration of the mass.) *The Nation*'s coverage of the Galway accident is a good instance of its ability both to report news indirectly and to work towards a sense of communal identity by listing the dead, citing alternative accounts, and quoting personal testimonies. The piece cannot be ascribed to any one author or compiler.]

With unmixed regret we lay the following particulars before our readers. We take them from the Freeman *and* Mail:

GALWAY, DECEMBER 25 — It is with feelings of the deepest anxiety and anguish I have to communicate to you the dreadful catastrophe which has occurred this morning, in the parochial chapel of this town, whereby upwards of thirty lives have been lost, and several persons maimed and wounded, many of whom are not likely to recover. This melancholy event, which throws a gloom over the festivities of this holy season, occurred, I understand, in a manner somewhat similar to the affair in Francis-street chapel, Dublin, this time two years. Early mass, and an Irish sermon, having been announced, the congregation collected in great numbers, and between six and seven o'clock the chapel was densely crowded. Divine service had not commenced when an alarm was given that the gallery was giving way. The pressure of the crowd caused a rung or two of the front railing to break, and the noise of the broken timber increased the alarm to such an extent that the whole congregation, particularly those on the gallery, were thrown into a state of the utmost consternation and confusion, each person making the best possible exertion to escape the danger. Many jumped from the gallery amongst the crowd in the body of the chapels [*sic*] while others broke the front windows, and threw themselves into the street. The consequences are appalling — the screams and lamentations of the numerous friends most afflicting — every countenance denotes grief and distraction. Thus the joy of the natal day of our Divine Redeemer has been changed into mourning and woe. If I can procure the names of the unfortunate sufferers ere I close this letter, I shall send them.

(FROM ANOTHER CORRESPONDENT)

GALWAY, DEC. 25. — As a constant reader of your paper, I write to give you the earliest information of a very sad catastrophe which occurred in this town this morning at the Parish Chapel, whereby from forty to fifty persons were killed, under the following awful circumstances:

As is usual here on every Christmas morning, the first Mass is read at the Parish Chapel at six o'clock, A.M. The doors opened at five o'clock. There is always an Irish sermon at first, which is attended almost exclusively by the country people, the inhabitants of the Liberties of the town, and the working classes. Before six o'clock the chapel was so densely crowded that there was no getting into it, either by the aisle or gallery. In the centre of the aisle, and under a large chandelier, is a high step-ladder, which opens out in form of the letter A. On this some persons were crowding up, and, by some means or other broke one or two of the steps. The noise of the crash or break being heard plainly on the gallery, the persons there thought that *it* was giving way, whereupon a simultaneous rush was made to the stair-case (which is not very wide); some of the first getting down, from the great pressure, fell, and those immediately behind them fell over them, and thus, from the constant pressure from above, there was no time to extricate them, until, melancholy to relate, from forty to fifty have been taken up quite dead!

Never was a more distressing scene witnessed than the multitudes coming in from the surrounding districts, looking out for some friend or other amongst the dead, and then the screams and shouts, as each discovers a father, mother, sister, or brother! While I write seven dead bodies lie at the Commercial News-room; the Town Dispensary is also full, as is the watch-house, and Temperance Rooms, and the sacristy of the chapel. One of the doctors in attendance tells me he never heard of so many cases without one recovery. In short, any one that fell, did so to rise no more!

Not the smallest break or damage was done to the chapel, with the exception of some of the windows, which the crowd broke, when throwing themselves out into the street, so dreadful was the alarm —

others threw themselves into the aisle of the chapel. If all had remained quiet, no damage would have been done, as there was no ground for the alarm.

JOHN KELLS INGRAM (1823-1907)

[*The Nation* inaugurated a new style of Irish political ballad, blending the narrative and heroic features of the traditional form with a sentimental strain and regularized pattern of rhyme and metre that reflected its middle-class preoccupations. Of the many ballads published in the paper, none became more popular, and *instantly* popular, than John Kells Ingram's 'The Memory of the Dead', often referred to simply by its first line. It was published anonymously in *The Nation* in April 1843. Ingram was born in County Donegal but, like John Mitchel, was educated in Newry, Co. Down. Unlike Mitchel, he quickly conformed to the expectations of his protestant background and, having given Young Ireland its anthem, devoted himself to an exemplary career as a scholar in Trinity College, Dublin. A prolific writer on philosophical, historical and economic topics, Ingram became president of the Royal Irish Academy and vice-provost of Trinity College.

'The Memory of the Dead' points to Young Ireland's descent from the United Irishmen, but also distances the earlier republicans by its easy rhymes and avoidance of concrete detail. It compares badly with contemporary ballads of the 1790s, such as 'Father Murphy' and 'The Croppy Boy', though the last-named also acquired a euphuistic Victorian text in the course of time.]

The Memory of the Dead

Who fears to speak of Ninety-Eight?
  Who blushes at the name?
When cowards mock the patriots' fate,
  Who hangs his head for shame?
He's all a knave, or half a slave,
  Who slights his country thus;
But a *true* man, like you, man,
  Will fill your glass with us.

II

We drink the memory of the brave,
  The faithful and the few —
Some lie far off beyond the wave,
  Some sleep in Ireland, too;
All — all are gone — but still lives on
  The fame of those who died;
All true men, like you, men,
  Remember them with pride.

III

Some on the shores of distant lands
  Their weary hearts have laid,
And by the stranger's heedless hands
  Their lonely graves were made.
But, though their clay be far away
  Beyond the Atlantic foam —
In true men, like you, men,
  Their spirit's still at home.

IV

The dust of some is Irish earth;
  Among their own they rest;
And the same land that gave them birth
  Has caught them to her breast;
And we will pray that from their clay
  Full many a race may start
Of true men, like you, men,
  To act as brave a part.

V

They rose in dark and evil days
  To right their native land;
They kindled here a living blaze
  That nothing shall withstand,
Alas! that Might can vanquish Right —
  They fell and pass'd away;
But true men, like you, men,
  Are plenty here to-day.

VI

Then here's their memory — may it be
  For us a guiding light.
To cheer our strife for liberty,
  And teach us to unite.
Through good and ill, be Ireland's still,
  Though sad as theirs your fate;
And true men be you, men,
  Like those of Ninety-Eight.

ANONYMOUS

'IRISH'

[*The Nation* did not publish material in Irish, although it frequently referred approvingly to efforts to foster the language. The two pieces that follow were printed together in the news-section of the paper.]

In everything that concerns the language and history of Ireland we feel interested. We are glad to have further signs that a sound taste is growing up in the country. We learn from booksellers that the demand for Irish books has so increased that they bring double the price they did three years ago; but this cannot lead to the exclusion of them from the middle classes, as we have every now and then some fresh work, as superior in value as in cheapness to the older books, on our native country and literature.

We have before us the prospectus of a work of the highest excellence and lowest price — a Translation of the Annals of the Four Masters by OWEN CONNELLAN[1] — to be published by B. GERAGHTY, of 8, Anglesea-street, in twenty-four fortnightly parts, at 1s. each. A *portion* of these Annals are given in *Irish and Latin* in DR. O'CONNOR'S Rerum Hibernicarum Scriptores[2] — a work which sells for 18 guineas at the lowest. Messrs. HODGES and SMITH have procured subscribers for an edition, price five guineas, in Irish and English, to be edited by JOHN O'DONOVAN.[3] In permanent value to the History and Language of Ireland, we cannot compare the work before us with these.

But, on the other hand, this translation, announced by MR. GERAGHTY, is of far more popular interest. Its price and its English (alas! that we should be forced to say so) will put it within reach of the middle classes. In it they will find genuine Irish history, unadulterated by creed, unbiassed by politics — simple, strong, and native. We give an extract from the Prospectus, and wish the work success:

> It may be necessary, in as brief a space as possible, to inform the reader of the great care which the learned antiquaries, who preserved and compiled these faithful records, took in arranging and digesting in proper order what was to be handed down to posterity, as a land-mark whereby they were to be guided through that portion of Irish history which these annals comprehend. It may be necessary also to state that the O'Clerys were hereditary historians to the O'Donnells, princes of Tyrconnell, now the county of Donegal, and that Michael O'Clery, of this respectable family, was the chief or most prominent among the compilers of these annals. He was assisted by Cucogry or Peregrine O'Clery, and Conary O'Clery; these with Peregrine O'Duigenan of Kilronan, in the county of Roscommon, were the four principal compilers — hence the work was called '*The Annals of the Four Masters*.' But there were two others, who rendered most important service in the compilation — namely Fearfeasa O'Muleconaire or O'Conry, and Maurice O'Conry, both of the county of Roscommon.
>
> Michael O'Clery was a native of Donegal, and born about the year 1580. He was distinguished for his great abilities, application and piety, and retired to the Irish Franciscan Monastery at Louvain, where his great knowledge of the Irish language attracted the notice of his countryman, the learned Hugh Ward,[4] then lecturer at Louvain, and guardian of its monastery. Ward, fully appreciating the character of O'Clery, determined to avail himself of his assistance and abilities, to put into execution a project he had long formed of rescuing from oblivion the annals and antiquities of his native land. Actuated by a spirit of patriotism and love of literature, O'Clery eagerly embraced the proposal, returned to Ireland, commenced his labours, and collected a vast number of ancient documents which he transmitted to his friend at Louvain; but the lamented death of Ward put a stop for a time to those noble intentions. However, the learned John Colgan, also a native of Donegal, then at Louvain, afterwards made ample use of these manuscripts when compiling his '*Acta Sanctorum Hiberniæ*' and 'Trias

1. Owen Connellan (1800-69), Irish scholar and translator; his edition of the *Annals of the Four Masters* duly appeared in 1846.
2. Charles O'Conor (1764-1828), Irish scholar and antiquarian; his *Rerum Hibernicarum Scriptores Veteres* appeared between 1814 and 1826.
3. John O'Donovan (1809-61), one of the leading Irish scholars of the century; his edition of the Four Masters appeared between 1848 and 1851.
4. Hugh Boy Macanward (Mac an Bhaird, or Ward) (*c.*1508-1635), historian.

Thaumaturga,' those great works on the Irish saints. O'Clery continued his collections in Ireland for a period of *fifteen years*, travelled through all parts of the country, and amassed all the ancient records, civil and ecclesiastical, that could be obtained, and then spent years in arranging for publication this vast mass of materials. Amongst the collection enumerated as being used in the compilation of The Annals of the Four Masters are mentioned the Annals of Tigernach, the Annals of Innisfallen, the Book of Clonmacnoise, the Annals of Ulster, the Book of Conquests, the Book of the Mac Firbises of Leacan, of the O'Duigenans of Kilronan, of the MacBruodins, of the O'Conrys, the Book of the Island of All Saints in Lough Rea, and many others.[5] After a life spent in the service of literature and of his country, O'Clery died at the convent of Donegal, in the year 1643, and left to posterity the reputation of a truly great and learned man.

This is an apt place to introduce a report of the Rev. Mr. Coney's introductory lecture on Irish. That Trinity College has neglected its duties towards our native language should make its present managers the more eager to forward Irish literature and compensate for the sins of their predecessors. Why then do we find so heavy an item in the Archaeological Society's[6] account for Irish printing, when that is done in the College Printing-office, and ought, on no account, to be charged for? — and why does not the University Press support a periodical devoted to Irish literature and antiquities?

5. For an account of the *Annals*, see Douglas Hyde, *A Literary History of Ireland from the Earliest Times to the Present Day* (first published in 1899; London: Benn, 1967), pp. 573-82.
6. The Irish Archaeological Society had been founded in 1840, and it merged with The Celtic Society in 1853 to become The Irish Archaeological and Celtic Society; this latter became a major force in the Celtic Revival movement.

LECTURE ON THE IRISH LANGUAGE

A 'prelection'[1] was delivered on Wednesday in the Divinity School, Trinity College, by the Rev. Mr. Coneys,[2] Professor of Irish, as an introduction to the study of that language for the academic year that has just commenced. The learned professor divided the subject under two heads; first, the interest and importance of the study of the Irish language as a branch of comparative philology; and secondly, its utility, or rather necessity, as a substantive portion of the education of a clergyman to enable him to fulfil the duties of the mission in Ireland. With the religious branch of the subject, which occupied by much too great a proportion of the lecture, considering that it was a public one, and therefore partly addressed to a lay audience, we have nothing to do. Of the other head we proceed to give a brief abstract.

The importance of the Celtic in the study of the origin and affinity of languages has been lately understood and acknowledged by European writers. The science of Comparative Philology — for it has now assumed all the dignity of a science — is itself but very modern. The ancients had no idea of it, and it dates, properly speaking, no farther back than the close of the last century; but new as it is, it has been, until a much later period, very imperfect, from the ignorance in which its great continental professors, especially the Germans, have been, of the Celtic dialects, which form so important a link in the great chain or family of the Indo-European languages. This defect has been ably pointed out, and, to some extent, repaired by the learned Adolphus Pictet[3] of Geneva, whose work on the affinity of the Celtic with the Sanscript [*sic*] was, a few years since, crowned by the French Academy of Inscriptions and Belles-Lettres. That learned writer has distinctly shown that the Celtic belong to the group of Indo-European or Indo-Germanic languages, which, we may observe, comprise, besides the Indian, the Persian, the Greek, the Roman, the Teutonic or German, and the Slavonian, all of which exhibit, in different degrees, unequivocal marks of their relationship; the Celtic being, as Pictet remarks, the most western member of the family. The Celtic he divided into two distinct

1. public lecture, or discourse.

2. The Reverend Thomas de Vere Coneys, who had conducted a mission among the poor Irish of St Giles in London before being appointed professor of Irish at Trinity College. There was a formal link between the Divinity School and the teaching of Irish in the college.
3. Adolphe Pictet (1799-1875), Swiss philologist, published *De l'Affinité des langues celtiques avec le sanscrit* . . . . (Paris) in 1837.

branches — the Gaelic and the Cymric; and those are subdivided, the former into Irish and Erse, or the Highland dialect; the latter into the Welsh, the Cornish, and the Armoric, or language of Brittany. The two principal branches are sufficiently distinct to constitute them different languages, and the idioms of the Gaelic have a much more intimate affinity with each other than have those of the Cymric branch. 'The Irish,' he observes, 'is by far the more important of the Gaelic dialects, and its written monuments,' he continues, 'which embrace history, philology, legislation, and poetry, are very numerous, and ascend to a very remote antiquity.' M. Pictet concludes from his researches that there is an intimate affinity between the entire framework of the Celtic and that of the Sanscrit; and that a knowledge of the Celtic is of the greatest importance for the solution of questions that relate to a period prior to the light of history, the application of language to this latter species of study, or comparative philology, resembling in fact that of comparative anatomy to the study of physiology and natural history. The smallest fragment of art, the most scanty remnant of a crumbling monument has given rise to the profoundest investigations into the origin and manners of the primitive races in the various countries of Europe; but by far the most prolific source of information on that subject has been found in language itself; and this is the chasm which so long prevailed in that interesting science, from an ignorance of the Celtic, the more to be lamented. Thus does Dr. Pritchard [*sic*], in his late important work on the Races of Mankind,[4] deeply regret that ignorance on the part of the German savans [*sic*] who made comparative philology the subject of their labors. The learned professor then proceeded to quote various passages from Archbishop Usher,[5] the German philosopher, Leibnitz[6] and Dr. Johnson,[7] to show the interest and importance attributed by those illustrious scholars to the study of the Irish, or rather of the Celtic language. Writing to Dr. O'Connor,[8] in the year 1757, Dr. Johnson thus mentioned the subject: 'I have long wished that the Irish literature were cultivated. Ireland is known by tradition to have been the seat of piety and learning, and surely it would be very acceptable to those who are curious, either in the original of nations, or the affinity of languages, to be further informed of the revolutions of a people so ancient, and once so illustrious. I hope you will continue to cultivate this kind of learning, which has lain so long neglected, and which, if it be suffered to remain in oblivion for another century, may, perhaps, never be retrieved.'[9] And again, in twenty years, writing to the same distinguished person on the same subject, he observed — 'What the Irish language is in itself, and to what language it has affinity, are very interesting questions, which every man wishes to see resolved that has any philological or historical curiosity. Dr. Leland[10] begins his history too late; the ages which deserve an exact inquiry are those times, for such there were, when Ireland was the school of the west, the quiet habitation of sanctity and literature. If you could give a history, though imperfect, of the Irish nation from its conversion to Christianity to the invasion from England, you would amplify knowledge with the new views and new objects.'[11] The learned professor mentioned some of the few efforts that had been made to revive the Irish language, the principal being that of the celebrated Mr. Flood,[12] who bequeathed to that university a large property, valued then at 5,000*l.* but since at 7,000*l.* a year, to support an Irish professorship to encourage works on Irish literature, and to purchase books and manuscripts in the Irish language; but as the university could not sustain its claim to the bequest by law, that means of promoting the Irish language

4. Evidently James Cowles Prichard, M.D., F.R.S.; the title of one of his works closely parallels Pictet's — *The Eastern Origin of the Celtic Nations Proved by a Comparison of their Dialects with the Sanskrit* . . . . (Oxford, 1831). No title of Prichard's comes closer to that reported in the above article than *The Natural History of Man* (London, 1843).
5. James Ussher (1581-1656), archbishop of Armagh, patristic scholar and churchman, who devoted much of his energies to the cause of a distinctive Irish (reformed) church; his collected works were published between 1847 and 1864.
6. Gottfried Wilhelm Leibnitz (1646-1715), German philosopher; for his interest in Gaelic, see Erich Poppe, 'Leibniz and Eckhart on the Irish Language', *Eighteenth-Century Ireland/Iris an dá Chultúr* I (1986), 65-84.
7. Samuel Johnson (1709-84), English poet, critic, and man of letters.
8. Charles O'Conor (1710-91), the scholar through whom a tradition of Gaelic culture was transmitted from the age of Queen Anne to the romantic period. Known as 'O'Conor of Belnagare'.
9. Johnson to O'Conor, 9 April 1757: see James Boswell, *Life of Samuel Johnson* (ed. G. B. Hill; rev.) Oxford: Clarendon Press, 1971 I, pp. 321-22.
10. Thomas Leland (1722-85) published his *History of Ireland from the Invasion of Henry II* in 1773.
11. Johnson to O'Conor, 19 May 1777: loc. cit. III, pp. 111-12.
12. Henry Flood (1732-91), Irish statesman, accounted the finest orator of his day.

was lost. The learned professor then proceeded to the second or religious branch of his subject, through which it is unnecessary for us to follow him; in the above outline we have done no more than mention the points on which, in the first part of his prelection, he addressed his audience.

JAMES DUFFY

(1808-71)

A CATHOLIC LITERATURE FOR IRELAND (1847)

[Twenty-two monthly numbers of *Duffy's Irish Catholic Magazine* appeared from February 1847 onwards, but the journal never succeeded in establishing itself on the market. Its purpose, as is explained in the opening editorial article which follows, was to foster a catholic literature that would be national too and even, to some degree, liberal in its ethos. James Duffy had prospered as a bookseller and publisher of anthologies; his repeated efforts to establish a journal were less successful. One can detect a certain reservation about intellectual innovation even in this editorial manifesto (of February 1847), and the events of 1848 were to emphasize the extent to which the larger intellectual revival more properly associated with the 1830s and very early 1840s had run out of steam. Nevertheless, *Duffy's Irish Catholic Magazine* anticipates later cultural developments and concerns, the fiction of Charles Kickham and Patrick Sheehan, and the more cohesive blend of national and catholic values that was to flourish subsequently.]

The very highest aspiration we can make for our infant Periodical is, that it may be the forerunner of a Catholic literature in Ireland. If its humble labours can in any degree conduce to that great end, then, whatever be in other respects its failure or success, its mission will be more than amply fulfilled. For such a literature does seem to us, almost beyond any other thing, the essential want of this country. Civil freedom and national prosperity may, and we trust shall be won before this generation of Irishmen has passed away — but we have only to cast our eyes abroad to see that even freedom and prosperity may come on terms far too dear.[1] If here, as elsewhere, the day that looks on the active development of our energies should also behold the intellect of the nation hopelessly divorced from the only spirit that can guide or purify; should see our Youth wasting mind and golden years in the uneasy chase of half truths, of which the end is but error and evil; should see a People hungering and thirsting after knowledge, and finding no fruit to satisfy them save what is deadly to their spiritual life; and should thus see sown, even in the midst of apparent blessings, the certain seeds of future crime and anarchy; would we not — even in this terrible year of famine — revolt at the exchange?

These apprehensions, we trust, will be belied; but who, looking to the condition of mankind, will say they are imaginary? Of late ages, the Church has had to do battle with the spirit of the world, embodied in a mightier and subtler form than in all previous time. From the corruption of nature, from human passions, and the persecution of kings and emperors, she has always suffered, and always must. But in former centuries there was, at least, no distracting dissonance between the secular learning that informed, and the Divine authority which claimed to direct the mind. There breathed throughout even secular works a spirit of religious reverence which harmonized with, and fortified the belief of the people. Pitfalls there were for pride and wilfulness, but at least, no galaxy of false lights for the deception of the earnest and sincere. But now, for a century and more, the learning of the world, the basis of systems of philosophy and polity, all that has been crowned with the high names of Genius and Intelligence, has been (why should we conceal it?) in by far the greater measure, hostile to, or estranged from Catholicity. The wisdom of man has been but too manifestly at variance with the wisdom of God. There has been a literature of Protestantism which obtained its chief development in

1. The 1840s was a decade of radical discontent in western Europe, as the Chartists in England exemplified. Eighteen forty-eight was 'the year of revolutions'.

England, and whose day is now almost gone by: a literature of French philosophy, and lastly, a literature of German philosophy, which again acted on France and England, and which is now the most progressive principle opposed to Catholicism in the world. There has been indeed, of late years, a strong Catholic reaction, as numbers of profound works produced on the Continent, and the Anglo-Catholic movement in England, may testify; but still, the surface of the current continues to run in the other direction.[2]

The condition of a young mind in France or Germany, in our days, is unhappy and perilous in the extreme. It is girt by a circle of infidelity, from which it is wonderful if it escape. In every branch of knowledge which the craving intellect turns to, from history and political science down to the lightest works of fiction, the poison of scepticism prevails. The student drinks it in from the authoritative lips of teachers and professors. In society as in books, he finds it the reigning spirit. Between such a philosophy, so taught and sanctioned, clothed with all that dazzles and captivates the natural man, appealing both to the passionate desire of novelty, and the passionate admiration of favourite authors which are so characteristic of youth, between this and the submissive belief and exacting practice of the Church, how unequal a conflict. Who can wonder that the faith, even of those who from association and religious instinct cling to it the longest, is at length sapped and displaced.

In Ireland, we have been educated for the most part, by the Protestant literature of England — a literature, anti-Catholic, no doubt, but not to be named either for power or malice, in comparison with the modern literature of the Continent. As to the ignorant sneers and violence against Catholicity with which it abounds, it is one of our earliest lessons to learn to steel ourselves against them, so that after a time they cease to wound us. And there is in the body of English literature, if not a religious spirit, yet a full recognition of the truths of revelation; and so far as the influence of Christianity on our social and secular ideas is concerned, there is so much in common between Catholics and Protestants, that the citadel of our faith has not been much injured by it. Still it has been mischievous in more ways than one. The very fact of our being obliged, as we said, to become hardened to insults and mockeries against the peculiar doctrines of Catholicity, is itself an evil — so much of religion depends upon awe and reverence for things unseen, that it is no light mischief to be familiarized with contempt for sacred mysteries. We become callous where we should be most sensitive, and swallow as matter of course what should instinctively revolt us as blasphemy against the Holy of Holies.§[3] But besides this, the Protestant tone of our literature has undoubtedly had a tendency, if not to undermine the citadel, yet to shatter some of the outworks of Catholic belief. If it has not had much effect in making Catholics infidels, or Protestants, yet it has in a great measure stripped us of whatever is striking and peculiar in the tone of Catholicity. It diminishes reverence for Catholic rites and ceremonies, chills the love of Catholic institutions and usages, and generates a contempt for pious traditions, not absolutely of faith, and an indolent unenquiring scepticism as to everything miraculous in church history; and if the bent of thought which it produces does not absolutely refuse to coexist with Catholic belief, yet it tends to deprive the latter of the pervading and overarching influence which it ought to exercise upon all our ideas and habits, to drive it, as it were, into a corner of our mind. In brief, its effect is to make Catholics intrench themselves within the *minimum* of Catholic faith, believing just what they must believe on pain of heresy, and no more; and priding themselves upon having their Catholicity as little unlike Protestantism as possible.

All these results are sad enough, and of themselves loudly call for counteraction. But the literatures of religious Protestantism — Protestantism itself, as a religious system, are in their

§What a striking example of this are Peter Plymley's Letters? — a book written in favour of the political rights of Catholics, and whose advocacy was hailed by them with delight, yet stuffed with the most insolent and unseemly ribaldry against their religion. One passage, from the very beginning of the book, we thought of quoting, but forbear from positive disgust.

2. Anglo-Catholicism was a movement (first) within the established Church of England associated with John Henry Newman (1801-90) and others at Oxford. Newman's *Romanism and Popular Protestantism* (1837) was an early statement of this position.

3. Sydney Smith published the fictitious *Letters of Peter Plymley* in 1807-08. In these Rev. Abraham Plymley's arguments in favour of continuing the disabilities imposed on catholics are demolished by his brother Peter, who nevertheless mocks the 'nonsense' he regards catholicism to be.

decline. The right of private judgment has given birth to younger and more daring progeny. The English sceptical writers, though the earliest, did not produce their deepest effect in their own country, but transmitted their influence to France, where there sprang up an organized and aggressive army of unbelief. Their mode of attack was conducted with consummate art. They did not, like the English freethinkers, confine themselves to heavy philosophical treatises scarce opened by the multitude; but through tale, and essay, and epigram — in dictionaries and encyclopaedias, with the keenness of a matchless wit, and all the graces of style, they sought but too successfully to taint the very atmosphere of letters with their principles.[4] So artfully, too, did they blend their covert assaults against religion with attacks on real abuses in church and state, that they at length succeeded in confounding these two things; and one party came to hate the church the more, as the antagonist of freedom, the other to dread liberty as the handmaid of irreligion. Nor was it on the Christian dispensation alone that they made war — they ridiculed and scoffed at any sense of dignity or mystery in the nature and life of man. No solemn social bond, no depth of awe or reverence, no obedience or holy fear was recognised by them; everything was mean, superficial, and intelligible. How far this fatal philosophy extended, and what have been its results on the world are manifest to all. But other doctrines have since gained ground, doctrines which had their root in Germany, and which agree with the French in rejecting revelation, but in almost nothing else. These Germans were revolted at the mean and false portrait of human nature drawn by the school of Voltaire. They felt that there were heights and depths in man which no plummet of French philosophism had sounded. They acknowledged the mysteriousness of life, the greatness of enthusiasm and devotion, the majesty of duty, the sacredness of law. They are full of lofty and unworldly speculation; of Christianity they speak respectfully, reverentially even, as being one, and hitherto the best, of the transitory forms in which great truths took shape: Mahometanism being another of those forms.[5] But what belief they propose to substitute for old Christianity — what resting place their doctrines yield for the wearied spirit — what curb for the rebellious passions, let no man ask, for no man we are sure will be able to answer. They cheat us with an array of imposing words — faith, and truth,* and reverence and annihilation of self — ideas which, in the heart of a Christian, have a relation and significance, but which with them present no tangible conception, but at best are a poetic exaltation of the brain — with some a half belief, with others an utter cant. Thus the German philosophy though better, because less earthy and sensual, and because it at least excites the desire of celestial truth which it cannot gratify, is yet less consistent than the French. The one lays plainly before you a barren desert as the sum of man's hopes here and hereafter, the other deludes you with the fugitive semblance of the living waters. We will be pardoned these considerations for the sake of the sad fact, that these doctrines — a bland materialism or a shadowy, unmeaning spiritualism — are diffused through every vein of the present mind of Europe.

As to the results of all this. No one will ask us, at this day, to prove the effects of literature upon the ideas and actions of mankind, or to show to how large a degree men in this age are what books make them. We would not refer to so trite a theme as the French Revolution, were it not for the sort of opinion that has grown current of late, that that portent, with all its diabolic crimes, was the natural and necessary consequence of the previous oppression of the government and aristocracy; that it is a lesson to kings and rulers, and to no others. That there was gross oppression, and scandalous neglect on the part of both civil and ecclesiastical authorities, no one can deny; and further, we may admit, that the ferocities of an excited mob are things incident to every violent change. But it should never be lost sight of that the extreme wickedness of the French revolution — the wholesale judicial murders — the establishment of Atheism by law — the destruction of all holy ties, were the work not of the multitude, but of the middle classes who rose to power. And it seems to us the grossest absurdity to conceive that such

4. This is a late instance of the classic case against Voltaire, Diderot and Rousseau as the instigators of the French Revolution and modern infidelism.

5. For example, Novalis (1772-1801), German poet.

*Et dicebant: veritas et veritas; et multi eam dicebant mihi, et nusquam erat in eis. — *S. Aug. Confes.*, LIII. ['And they said: there is truth and truth; and many said this to me, but it was never to be found in them.' Ed.]

things would have been done or tolerated, if every spark of religious principle, or restraint, had not been long extinguished in the minds of those classes by the influence of Voltaire and his confederates. — And further, if any one ask for the effects of this literature, we tell them to look abroad over Europe at this day. What principles and rules of action are predominant in the cabinets and councils of kings and statesmen? Principles of justice, of deference to the Church, and a horror of intrenching upon its privileges or province? No: but incessant schemes to have the Church gagged, and bound at their feet, subservient to their worldly policy, and winking at their wickedness. Utilitarianism, Benthanism [*sic*], modern enlightenment — call it what you will, the seed was sown by Hume and Voltaire.[6] Again, we say, cast your eyes over Europe. In France, Prussia, Spain, England, even Austria, the endeavour is to make the Church the creature and slave of the civil power. Religion has to battle for its clearest and most sacred rights. Surveying these things, let us acknowledge the influence which the sceptical philosophy has exercised upon the modern world.

The modern literature of England, by which we mean the productions of the last twenty years or so, is next to worthless — with few exceptions, most trashy and emasculate. Still such as it is, it reflects and helps to shape its time, and to those who look a little below the surface, who watch indications rather than expressions, and regard colour as well as matter, it is manifest that here too, whatever vital principle there is, is not fixed faith of any kind, but the floating uncertainties of Germanism.

But Ireland, how is she to be made proof against all these influences? This problem, the most momentous of the many that surround us, is one that must be solved under worse penalties than any political disaster. The heart of the country, thank God, is sound; no people in Europe more deeply religious. But in our gratitude and just pride for this, let us not lose sight of the auxiliary causes that contributed to it, nor presume too much on the grace that has been bestowed us. Let us remember that it was one consequence of the Penal Laws, to burn into the heart of the Irish Catholic an intense devotion to his persecuted religion — that the forbidden education which the gentleman received abroad and the peasant at home, made religion a vital part of knowledge. The latter looked up to his priest as the fountain of all information, sacred or profane, that man could need. The hedge-schoolmasters, with all their pedantry and absurdity — even with all their vices — never ceased to inculcate a love of their own religion, blended, perhaps, with too fierce a hatred of its oppressors.[7] Let us remember that, during the long struggle against religious tyranny, the idea of Catholicity became knit with that of liberty; that theological controversy was almost a part of that battle, and that it was necessary for politicians to become familiar with and explain the doctrines of the Church, in order to answer the aspersions of their antagonists.

Nearly all this has changed, or is changing. No longer bound by the bond of persecution — no longer in the heat of a semi-religious struggle — no longer unaffected by the current of opinion elsewhere, and with an irrespressible tendency towards education of all kinds, the intellectual and spiritual future of Ireland is a theme of the deepest anxiety and moment. Her condition may be likened to that of an individual mind, naturally vigorous and inquisitive, but, long cramped and restrained, possessing deep instincts and affections, but no regulated structure of opinion, and which, when released from bondage and springing forth to seize the fruit of knowledge, is open to influences from every quarter of Heaven. How this plastic mind shall be moulded; whether the soul of thought that is about to enter into Ireland shall be the harmonious counterpart of that soul of faith which has guided and upheld her through the furnace of the past; whether her mature reason shall be pregnant with the conviction now living unspoken in the heart of her millions — that in true religion is found the cycle of all duty and all moral truth — whether the wise among her sons shall be wise enough to know that whatsoever is not subordinate to this is foolishness; whether the character of Ireland among the nations shall be one of lofty Christian zeal, as well as lofty nationality — these considerations may well have an interest for us. But to expect

6. Utilitarianism — the theory that actions are right if they are useful; Benthamism — a form of utilitarianism according to which one should seek the greatest happiness of the greatest number (named after Jeremy Bentham); David Hume (1711-76), Scottish philosopher; Voltaire (1694-1778), French writer and thinker.

7. Hedge-schools, or unauthorized schools meeting in whatever accommodation was available, survived into the nineteenth century. Their masters were renowned for classical erudition, prodigious feats of indiscriminate memory, and other excesses.

that these great results will come spontaneously; that the mind of Ireland, with no pains taken to guide it aright, and buffeted by all the winds of temptation, will tread securely and directly in the true path, seems to us a confidence against reason and nature.

Such a Catholic literature as we long for, and could shape an ideal of — a literature religious to the core, which should reflect the majesty and eternal truth of our Faith, and its beauty and poetry as well; Irish, too, to the core — thrilling with our Celtic nature, and coloured by our wonderful history; such a literature, and its glorious associate, a high Catholic and national art, may be of slow formation, and wait long for their maturity. And, indeed, they demand something beyond the ordinary labours of genius. Still, a beginning may be made. A beginning has been made in the works of our dear Gerald Griffin; the tone and spirit of which, whatever be his theme, leave nothing to be desired.[8] And we scarce know how much a little effort in their right direction may effect. For when the heart and sympathies of a people are with you, it is easy to influence their minds. Let what has been done of late, in infusing a spirit of nationality into our literature, be a lesson to us. Formerly, that spirit was as rare in current books as a tone of Catholic religion is now. But once a few zealous men set themselves to preach the principles of national feeling, what a bound was made by the popular mind in that direction. How eagerly did they imbibe everything that was said and sung of the wrongs and hopes of Ireland, and of her forgotten heroes. Because these things were but the expression of what they themselves had dumbly felt — but the touching of a chord with which their own pulses beat in unison.

And of this national literature, a word may be said in relation to our own design. Of the deep sincerity as well as ability of the men whose work it is, and of the good they have achieved in arousing our sense of national dignity and affection, no one can say too much. Still we think they committed a mistake in not basing their labours more on the religious feelings of the mass of the people whom they addressed. The reason of this was, no doubt, the desire to find a way to the hearts of Irishmen of all religions. Yet it was, in a great degree, an error, and one which, we believe, they will come more and more to recognise. At all events, it has left one-half, and the more necessary half, of the teaching required by the majority of our countrymen to be yet laboured at.

If there were but a few zealous sowers, how quickly would a little seed produce a harvest in such a soil. And what materials for the undertaking — what a well is our history from whence to draw the beneficent waters that we seek. Those distant ages to which Alfred and Bede have borne testimony, when our doctors instructed and our saints converted Europe, and the hymns of an Irishman were adopted as the chants of the whole Western Church — that proud time is not a fiction, or the hyperbole of national vanity — it rests upon evidence as sound as any fact in history.[9] To reproduce this age, and the acts and words of its holy men and women, for the Irish people at this day — to give them therein a genuine and high source of national pride, from that alone what fruits might not spring? Have we not — but this work has been already commenced, and we trust will be carried out by the same zealous hand — have we not to become familiar with the men of the seventeenth century, with their Spanish fervour and loftiness, and intensity of Catholic nationality? And from our worst days of suffering, what lessons may be drawn? Is not our history for ages one martyrdom? There is a halo of true glory resting on our sad annals if we had but eyes to read them right — a truer glory than is found in our protracted resistance on the field, or the occasional victories that flash through the long night of disaster. Of these, the bitter result after all is, that we were conquered; but there was another, and a far higher field of battle, in which the victory was wholly ours, and the ignominy our conqueror's. Lord of land and life, and not sparing either, he sought to be lord of conscience too, and was uniformly and utterly baffled. A race, taunted with their fickleness, and too often divided, too often in other things unstable as water, were in this, in the struggle for an unseen good, the very type of resolute tenacity, of unity and

8. Note that Griffin (1803-40), who is cited favourably in *The Nation*'s article on periodical literature, is the only Irish author explicitly approved of here.

9. Alfred (849-99), king of the west Saxons at the time of the Danish invasion of England, also a writer on religious topics and the patron of Johannes Scottus Ériugena. The venerable Bede (673-735) was a historian and scholar. *The Ecclesiastical History of the English People*, which Bede completed in 731, is the most important history written in England before the sixteenth century. King Alfred supervised its translation into Old English.

unconquerable will. We know not if a time will ever come when men will recognise, in Christian fortitude and fidelity, a higher thing than the bravest fighting — if they do this country will assuredly stand high. But, at least, *we* should impress this truth upon ourselves. We long to see a sense of these things entering deeply into the minds of our educated young men; to see their character and opinions formed by that part of our history too; to see our future politicians and statesmen distinguished for Christian wisdom as well as for a noble courage, that when the liberty of this land is won, she may be a light to modern as she was to ancient nations, not the imitator of their madness and injustice. And if, as a fond imagination might at times believe, that independence which she has ever longed for with more than Hebrew longing, be delayed till she can embrace it and use it in this spirit, can we feel otherwise than deeply thankful to that Providence which 'shapes our ends, rough-hew them how we will.[10]

To descend from these high hopes to this Periodical of ours, which presumes to be the pioneer of so great a work. There are many difficulties in our path, but we cannot conceal from ourselves that the greatest lies in our own deficiencies. Would that our qualifications for the task bore any proportion to our conviction of its necessity. Still, as we said, a beginning may be made, in the hope that as we proceed we shall acquire both clearer views as to our path, and more assured strength to tread it.

10. cf. *Hamlet*, V. 2. 10-11:
'There's a divinity that shapes our ends,
Rough-hew them how we will.'

Biographies/Bibliographies

Samuel Ferguson

LIFE. Ferguson was born in 1810 in High Street, Belfast, to a family of Scottish origins recently reduced in circumstances. He wrote journalism at an early age, graduated from Trinity College, Dublin in 1832, and was called to the Irish bar in 1838. Although he travelled extensively, Dublin remained his home for the rest of his life. He contributed prolifically to *Blackwood's Magazine* and *The Dublin University Magazine*, and to the publications of the Royal Irish Academy.

Ferguson combined an interest in poetry, in Gaelic culture, archaeology, science, and public administration. His four-part review of James Hardiman's *Irish Minstrelsy* appeared in *The D.U.M.* between April and November 1834: it represents a turning point in the translation and interpretation of Gaelic poetry, and fuelled the romantic nationalism of Young Ireland. Ferguson was on friendly terms with Thomas Davis and Gavan Duffy, and associated himself with a protestant repeal movement in the 1840s, though his political instincts remained conservative. His 'Lament for Thomas Davis', a fine example of Young Ireland poetic sentiment, did not appear in *The D.U.M.* until February 1847, nearly two years after its composition.

Ferguson pursued an active career at the bar, with which he combined an energetic commitment to the study of Irish antiquities. In 1867, he was appointed to the new post of deputy-keeper (the chief executive office) of the public records of Ireland, and thoroughly reorganized the dispersed records placed under his control. He was knighted in 1878, and in 1881 was elected president of the Royal Irish Academy. In 1848, he married Mary Catherine Guinness, of the well-known Dublin brewing family. Ferguson died in Howth, Co. Dublin in August 1886.

CHIEF WRITINGS. *Lays of the Western Gael* (London: Bell & Daldy, 1867; 2nd ed. Dublin: Sealy, Bryers & Walker, 1880); *The Cromlech on Howth* (London: Day, 1864); *Congal: An Epic Poem* (London: Bell, 1872), 2nd ed. (Dublin: Sealy, Bryers & Walker, 1893); *Poems* (London: Bell; Dublin: M' Gee, 1880); *Shakespearian Breviates* (Dublin: Hodges Figgis, 1882); *The Forging of the Anchor* (London: Cassell, 1883); *Ogham Inscriptions in Ireland, Wales, and Scotland* (Edinburgh: Douglas, 1887); *Hibernian Night's Entertainment* (Dublin: Sealy, Bryers & Walker, 1887); *The Remains of Saint Patrick* (Dublin: Sealy, Bryers & Walker, 1888). Padraic Colum (ed.), *The Poems of Samuel Ferguson* (Dublin: Allen Figgis, 1963).

BIOGRAPHY AND CRITICISM. The essential work is his wife's *Sir Samuel Ferguson in the Ireland of his Day* 2 vols (Edinburgh: Blackwood, 1896). This contains long excerpts from letters and poems, and includes a checklist of his publications in periodicals and elsewhere. Malcolm Brown, *Sir Samuel Ferguson* (Lewisberg: Bucknell University Press, 1973) is a useful short study. A recent commentary is provided by Robert O'Driscoll, *An Ascendancy of the Heart; Ferguson and the Beginnings of Irish Literature in English* (Dublin: Dolmen Press, 1976); T. Brown and B. Hayley (eds), *Samuel Ferguson — A Centenary Tribute* (Dublin: Royal Irish Academy, 1987); G.J. Doyle, 'Sir Samuel Ferguson. A Critical Biography', Unpublished PhD thesis, National University of Ireland, 1989.

Isaac Butt

LIFE. Born in Stranorlar, Co. Donegal in 1813, the son of a protestant rector. Butt was educated at Trinity College, Dublin and the King's Inns. He was called to the bar in 1838, but had already achieved a reputation as a political journalist through joint-editorship of *The Dublin University Magazine* (1834-38). Initially, his involvement in conservative politics centred on the Metropolitan Conservative Association, through which he expressed a vigorous opposition to Daniel O'Connell and the Whigs, though some in the Association nervously considered favouring Repeal of the Union to save Ireland from Whiggish reform. In 1848 he defended some of the Irish rebels before departing as MP for Harwich in 1852. Although he was subsequently elected for Youghal, Co. Cork, Butt passed most of the next ten years in England. In 1859, he was called to the English bar. Between 1865 and 1869 he defended many Fenian prisoners, and in 1870 was instrumental in the founding of the Home Government Association. As leader of the Irish Party in the Westminster parliament, he put the notion of Home Rule for Ireland on the political agenda, though only after his deposition and the election of Charles Stewart Parnell did the idea achieve its full expression.

Butt lectured and wrote prolifically. The items marked with an asterisk in the list below are fiction. He was slovenly in appearance and occasionally bohemian in his behaviour, on one occasion being gaoled for debt. Before he died, he had taken an interest in catholic religious practices, but no evidence of conversion exists. He died in Dundrum, Co. Dublin in 1879. His wife, Elizabeth (née Swanzy) outlived him, dying in 1897 in her eighty-ninth year.

CHIEF WRITINGS. Apart from lectures and speeches, Butt's principal publications are *Ovid's Fasti* (trans.) (Dublin: Milliken, 1833); *The Georgics of Virgil* (trans.) (Dublin: Milliken, 1834); **Irish Life in the Castle,* *the Courts and the Country* 3 vols (London: How & Parsons, 1840); *A Voice for Ireland. The Famine in the Land* (Dublin: M' Glashan, 1847); *Zoology and Civilization* (Dublin: M' Glashan, 1847); **The Gap of Barnesmore* (London: Smith, Elder, 1848); *The Transfer of Land* (Dublin: Smith, 1857); *History of Italy from the Abdication of Napoleon I* 2 vols (London: Chapman and Hall, 1860); **Chapters of College Romance* (London: Skeet, 1863); 'Bishop Berkeley and his Writings' in *Afternoon Readings in the Museum, St. Stephen's Green, Dublin* (London: Bell & Daldy, 1865), pp. 185-224; *The Liberty of Teaching Vindicated* (Dublin: Kelly; London: Simpkin, Marshall, 1865); *Land Tenure in Ireland: A Plea for the Celtic Race* (Dublin: Falconer, 1866); *The Irish Querist* (Dublin: Falconer, 1867); *The Irish People and the Irish Land* (Dublin: Falconer; London: Ridgeway, 1867); *A Practical Treatise on the New Law of Compensation* (Dublin: Falconer; London: Butterworth, 1871); *Home Government for Ireland* (Dublin: Irish Home Rule League, 1874); *The Problem of Irish Education* (London: Longman, 1875). The fourth volume of *The Wellesley Index to Victorian Periodicals* (Toronto: University of Toronto Press, 1987), in analysing *The Dublin University Magazine*, attributes 'Past and Present State of Literature in Ireland' to Samuel O'Sullivan (1790-1851) on evidence that does not include resemblance between the article and Butt's notes to his edition of Virgil's *Georgics*. Stylistically, the article lacks O'Sullivan's maturity.

BIOGRAPHY AND CRITICISM. Terence de Vere White, *The Road of Excess* (Dublin: Browne and Nolan, 1946); David Thornley, *Isaac Butt and Home Rule* (London: MacGibbon & Kee, 1964); W.J. McCormack, 'Isaac Butt and the Inner Failure of Protestant Home Rule' in Ciaran Brady (ed.), *Worsted in the Game: Losers in Irish History* (Dublin: The Lilliput Press, 1989), pp. 121-31.

James Clarence Mangan

LIFE. Born in Fishamble Street, Dublin in 1803, Mangan remains something of a biographical enigma. His sustained emphasis on his own poverty and misfortune is not satisfactorily documented in many respects. He worked as a clerk, became a contributor to the *Dublin Weekly Satirist* in the early 1830s, was taken up by the editors of *The Dublin University Magazine*, to which he contributed both prose and poetry, and later by *The Nation*. He was employed by the Ordnance Survey and by the librarian of Trinity College, Dublin, but seems never to have had a steady income or stable life. Disappointed in love, he had recourse to narcotics. He died of cholera in 1849. Through the use of anonymity and pseudonymity, the extent of his writing still remains unsettled, and manuscript sources are extremely rare. Editions of the poems published after his death are unsatisfactory in many respects, and Mangan's bibliography awaits its codifier. The list that follows is limited to works published during his lifetime, though D. J. O'Donoghue's *Life and Writings of James Clarence Mangan* (Edinburgh: Geddis; Dublin: Gill, 1897) should be consulted.

CHIEF WRITINGS. *Anthologia Hibernica: German Anthology*. (translations) 2 vols (Dublin: Curry, 1845); *The Poets and Poetry of Munster* (Dublin: O'Daly, 1849); *Poems by James Clarence Mangan* intro. by John Mitchel (New York: P.M. Haverty, 1859); *Essays in Prose and Verse*, ed. C.P. Heehan (Dublin: Duffy, 1884); *Poems of James Clarence Mangan*, Centenary Edition, ed. D.J. O'Donoghue (Dublin: M. H. Gill, 1903); *Prose Writings of James Clarence Mangan*, ed. D. J. O'Donoghue (Dublin: M. H. Gill, 1904).

BIOGRAPHY AND CRITICISM. An unfinished *Autobiography* has been newly edited by James Kilroy (Dublin: Dolmen Press, 1968), but it is unreliable as a source for factual information. Rudi Holzapfel's *James Clarence Mangan: A Checklist of Printed and Other Sources* (priv. pub., 1969) is useful for students of the life and the work. Two major Irish writers have discussed Mangan: W. B Yeats, 'Clarence Mangan' (1886); 'Clarence Mangan's Love Affair' (1891) reprinted in Yeats, *Uncollected Prose 1* (London: Macmillan, 1970). pp. 114-19, 194-198; James Joyce, 'James Clarence Mangan' (1902) reprinted in Joyce, *Critical Writings* (New York: Viking, 1959), pp. 74-83. James Kilroy, *James Clarence Mangan* (Lewisberg: Bucknell University Press, 1970) is a serviceable account of our present knowledge of and response to Mangan. Jacques Chuto, 'Mangan's "Antique Deposit" in TCD Library' (*Long Room*, No. 2 (1970), 38-39 deals painstakingly with a detail in Mangan's career. Also see David Lloyd, *Nationalism and Minor Literature: James Clarence Mangan and the Emergence of Irish Cultural Nationalism* (Berkeley: University of California Press, 1987).

Joseph Thomas Sheridan Le Fanu

LIFE. Born in Dublin in 1814 and brought up first in the Phoenix Park and at Abington, Co. Limerick, Le Fanu was the eldest son of a church of Ireland clergyman whose Huguenot father's rectitude had been tempered by marriage with Sheridan flair. Sustained unrest in the Irish countryside throughout the 1820s and 1830s prefaced Le Fanu's education at Trinity College, where he met Isaac Butt and the *Dublin University Magazine* contributors; his own first publication appeared in the issue of January 1838. Called to the bar in 1839, he rarely practiced, but pursued a career as a writer of journalism and fiction. Though, by affiliation to the Metropolitan Conservative Association and by temperament, Le Fanu was a Tory, he joined with several Young Irelanders in efforts to mitigate the effects of the Great Famine. He married Susannah Bennett in 1844; they had four children. After the embarrassment of the 1848 Rising (in which several of his erstwhile associates were involved), a feeble attempt to get a Conservative nomination for the parliamentary elections in 1852, and the death of his wife in 1858, Le Fanu became increasingly withdrawn. He grew learned in, but not necessarily convinced by, the mystical doctrines of Emanuel Swedenborg and these are employed structurally in his best novel, *Uncle Silas*. Newspaper proprietorship (*The Warder* and *The Dublin Evening Mail*) provided an adequate but limited income, which he supplemented through the acquisition and editorship of *The Dublin University Magazine* from 1861 to 1869. For the last decade of his life he was known to Dublin society as the 'Invisible Prince'. He travelled little, apart from brief annual holidays in north Wales where some of his later novels are set. Le Fanu died in 1873 at his home in Merrion Square, Dublin.

CHIEF WRITINGS. *The Cock and Anchor, being A Chronicle of Old Dublin.* Anon. 3 vols (Dublin: Curry, 1845); *The Fortunes of Colonel Torlogh O'Brien; A Tale of the Wars of King James* Anon. (Dublin: M' Glashan; London: Orr, 1847); *Ghost Stories and Tales of Mystery* Anon. (Dublin: M' Glashan; London: Orr, 1851); *The House by the Church-yard* 3 vols (London: Tinsley, 1863); *Wylder's Hand: A Novel* 3 vols (London: Bentley, 1864); *Uncle Silas: A Tale of Bartram-Haugh* 3 vols (London: Bentley, 1864); *The Prelude, Being a Contribution towards a History of the Election for the University* by John Figwood (pseud.) (Dublin: Herbert, 1865); *Guy Deverell* 3 vols (London: Bentley, 1865); *All in the Dark* 2 vols (London: Bentley, 1866); *The Tenants of Malory: A Novel* 3 vols (London: Tinsley, 1867); *A Lost Name* 3 vols (London: Bentley, 1868); *Haunted Lives: A Novel* 3 vols (London: Tinsley, 1868); *The Wyvern Mystery* 3 vols (London: Tinsley, 1869); *Checkmate* 3 vols (London: Hurst and Blackett, 1871); *The Rose and the Key* 3 vols (London: Chapman and Hall, 1871); *Chronicles of Golden Friars* 3 vols (London: Bentley, 1871); *In a Glass Darkly* 3 vols (London: Bentley, 1872).

Posthumously: *The Purcell Papers* 3 vols (London: Bentley, 1880); *The Poems of Joseph Sheridan Le Fanu* (London: Downey, 1896); *Madam Crowl's Ghost and Other Tales of Mystery*, ed. M.R. James (London: Bell, 1923); *Borrhomeo the Astrologer*, ed. W.J. McCormack (Edinburgh: Tragara Press, 1985).

Recent editions: *Best Ghost Stories of J.S. Le Fanu*, ed. E.F. Bleiler (New York: Dover, 1964); *The House by the Church-yard* introduction by Elizabeth Bowen (London: Blond, 1968); *Ghost Stories and Mysteries*, ed. E.F. Bleiler (New York: Dover, 1975); *Uncle Silas; A Tale of Bartram Haugh*, ed. W.J. McCormack (Oxford: World's Classics, 1980).

BIOGRAPHY AND CRITICISM. 'Fragment d'un journal intimes de J.S. Le Fanu ... 18 Mai 1858' (ed. Jean Lozes) *Caliban* (Toulouse) n.s.

Vol. 10, No. 1 (1974), pp. 153-64; William Le Fanu, *Seventy Years of Irish Life* (London: Arnold, 1893); T.P. Le Fanu, *Memoir of the Le Fanu Family* (Manchester: priv. pub., 1924); Elizabeth Bowen, 'Uncle Silas' (1946), reprinted in Bowen, *Collected Impressions* (London: Longman, 1950), pp. 3-17; Nelson Brown, *Sheridan Le Fanu,* a short survey of life and works (London: Barker, 1951); Ken Scott, 'Le Fanu's "The Room in the Dragon Volant"', *Lock Haven Review* No. 10 (1968), 25-32; Kevin Sullivan, 'The House by the Churchyard: James Joyce and Sheridan Le Fanu' in R.J. Porter and J.D. Brophy (eds), *Modern Irish Literature* (Syracuse: Syracuse University Press, 1972), pp. 315-34; Kevin Sullivan, 'Sheridan Le Fanu: The Purcell Papers 1838-40', *Irish University Review* Vol. 2, No. 1 (1972), 5-19; W.J. Mc Cormack, *Sheridan Le Fanu and Victorian Ireland* (Oxford: Clarendon Press, 1980).

Charles James Lever

LIFE. Born in Dublin in 1806, and educated at Trinity College there, Lever was by professional training a medical doctor. However, after extensive travel on the Continent and in Canada, and a spell of duty during a cholera epidemic in Ulster, he began his career as novelist with *Harry Lorrequer* (1837) which was serialized in *The Dublin University Magazine*. Its harmless version of picaresque adventures became immediately popular and for a decade Lever was Charles Dickens's rival as a popular novelist. Between 1842 and 1845 he was editor of the *D.U.M.,* but he fell foul of the increasingly confident and articulate cultural nationalism of *The Nation*, and left Ireland for Italy. The best of his emigré novels is *The Dodd Family Abroad* (1853-4), but his later work is gradually characterized by a more serious engagement with the historical pressures that contributed to the intractable realities of Irish life. In 1857, Lever was appointed British consul at Spezzia, and acted in the same capacity at Trieste from 1867 until his death there in 1872. His irrepressible humour was severely tested in his last years by the conduct of his son.

CHIEF WRITINGS. Lever was an extremely prolific novelist (with in excess of thirty titles to his credit), but little of his work has survived the more astringent criticism of Irish literature introduced by W.B. Yeats. The collected edition of 1897-99 in 37 volumes, published by Downey, was prepared by the novelist's daughter and contains memoranda and bibliographical notes.

BIOGRAPHY AND CRITICISM. W.J. Fitzpatrick, *The Life of Charles Lever* (London: Downey, 1901; new edition, Lionel Stevenson); *Dr. Quicksilver; the Life of Charles Lever* (London: Chapman and Hall, 1939). The charge of plagiarism advanced by Charles Gavan Duffy in the article printed above has been augmented by John Hemming in 'Charles Lever and Rodolphe Toepffer', *Modern Language Review* 1948, 88-92.

Charles Gavan Duffy

LIFE. Born in Monaghan town in 1816 and trained as a journalist in Belfast. Became joint-editor of *The Nation* in 1842, with Thomas Davis and John Blake Dillon. Established 'The Library of Ireland', and developed a highly popular brand of liberal nationalism. Though he was Daniel O'Connell's co-accused (the charge, sedition) in 1843-44, he opposed O'Connell's federalist ideas in the same year. He established good relations with Sheridan Le Fanu and Isaac Butt, despite divergences of political opinion. In 1847 Gavan Duffy formed the Irish Confederation, and advocated an independent Irish party at Westminster. Arrested in connection with the rising of 1848 but acquitted, he avoided transportation to Australia. He accompanied Thomas Carlyle on the latter's tour of famine-stricken Ireland, and did his best to mitigate the Scotsman's reaction against poverty. In 1850, Duffy became joint leader of the Irish Tenant League with Frederick Lucas, and two years later was elected MP for New Ross. By the mid-1850s he was disillusioned by the Irish party's failure at Westminster, and in November 1855 he emigrated to Australia, where he succeeded brilliantly as a politician and land reformer. In the state of Victoria, he became a member of the House of Assembly in 1856; minister of land and works 1857-59 and 1862-65; prime minister 1871-72, and speaker of the House 1876-80. He was knighted in 1873. Duffy spent his final years back in Europe, writing his memoirs and a life of Thomas Davis, among other things. In seeking to advance the cause of Irish literature, he collided with an aspiring writer called W. B. Yeats. He died in Nice, France in 1903, and is buried in Glasnevin cemetery, Dublin. No biography has appeared.

CHIEF WRITINGS. ed. *The Ballad Poetry of Ireland* (Dublin: Duffy, 1845); *The League of North and South: An Episode in Irish History 1850-54* (London: Chapman and Hall, 1886); *Thomas Davis: The Memoirs of an Irish Patriot 1840-46* (London: Kegan Paul, 1890); *Conversations with Carlyle* (London: Sampson Low, 1892); *Young Ireland: A Fragment of Irish History 1840-1850 . . . Final revision* (London: Fisher Unwin, 1896); *My Life in Two Hemispheres* 2 vols (London: Fisher Unwin, 1898).

Thomas Osborne Davis

LIFE. Born in Mallow, Co. Cork in 1814 to a family of English extraction, Davis graduated from Trinity College, Dublin in 1836. At Trinity, he came under the influence of the shadowy Thomas Wallis (a tutor of advanced political views) and established himself as a persuasive thinker in the College Historical Society. Together with Charles Gavan Duffy and John Blake Dillon, he founded *The Nation* in 1842. Within Young Ireland, his task was to win the support of the protestant middle classes, and friction with Daniel O'Connell's predominantly catholic following inevitably resulted. Higher education figured crucially on the list of issues upon which the two men differed — Davis was for the government's new 'godless' colleges — and it is a measure of Davis's junior position that he was never even a candidate for parliamentary election. His facile poetry, eloquent journalism, and early death enhanced a personal reputation for integrity and disinterested patriotism. Before his death in 1845, he was engaged to marry Miss Ann Hutton. Apart from his journalism, Davis was not a prolific writer, though innumerable selections from his work appeared in the century after his death. No modern biography has been attempted.

CHIEF WRITINGS. *Speeches of ... John Philpot Curran* (Dublin: Duffy, 1843, new ed., expanded 1845); *Literary and Historical Essays*, ed. Charles Gavan Duffy (Dublin: Duffy, 1846); *The Poems of Thomas Davis*, ed. Thomas Wallis (Dublin: Duffy, 1846); *The Life of J.P. Curran* (Dublin: Duffy, 1846); *Letters of a Protestant, on Repeal* (Dublin: Irish Confederation, 1847); T.W. Rolleston (ed.), *Prose Writings of Thomas Davis* (London, 1890).

BIOGRAPHY AND CRITICISM. Charles Gavan Duffy, *Thomas Davis: The Memoirs of an Irish Patriot, 1840-1846* (London: Fisher Unwin, 1892); J.M. Hone, *Thomas Davis* (London: Duckworth, 1934); W.B. Yeats, *A Tribute to Thomas Davis* (Oxford: Blackwell, 1947); Denis Gwynn, *O'Connell, Davis, and the Colleges Bill* (Cork: Cork University Press; Oxford: Blackwell, 1948); Malcolm Brown, *The Politics of Irish Literature from Thomas Davis to W.B. Yeats* (London: Allen & Unwin, 1972).

John Kells Ingram

LIFE. Born in Temple Carne, Co. Donegal in 1823 and educated first at a school in Newry, Co. Down, Ingram became a scholar in Trinity College, Dublin in 1840 and thereafter lived an academic existence; appointed professor of oratory and English literature, 1852; regius professor of Greek, 1866; librarian, 1879. Ingram was a scholar of European standing who met Thomas Carlyle in 1849, and travelled to France to visit the philosopher Auguste Comte in 1855. He subsequently edited a selection of Comte's letters (1901), having earlier declared himself a Comtean positivist. A founder member of the Statistical Society of Ireland, and sometime president of the Royal Irish Academy, he wrote a number of important articles for the 9th edition of *Encyclopaedia Britannica* and for

Palgrave's *Dictionary of Political Economy*. In 1892, he edited (from manuscripts in Cambridge) the first English translation of Thomas à Kempis's *De Imitatione Christi*. In 1862 he married Madeline Clarke of Derry; they had two sons and two daughters. Ingram died in Dublin in 1907.

CHIEF WRITINGS. A 46-page bibliography of Ingram's publications, prepared by T. W. Lyster, appeared in *An Leabharlann* Vol. III, No. 1, 1909. The following list is selected from his book-length productions: *Considerations on the State of Ireland* (Dublin: Ponsonby, 1864); *A History of Political Economy* (Edinburgh: Black, 1888) (trans. into ten languages including Japanese); *A History of Slavery and Serfdom* (London: Black, 1895); *Love and Sorrow* (sonnets) (Dublin: priv. pub., 1897); *Sonnets and Other Poems* (London: Black, 1900); *Outlines of the History of Religion* (London: Black, 1900); *Human Nature and Morals According to Auguste Comte* (London: Black, 1901); *Practical Morals, A Treatise on Universal Education* (London: Black, 1904); *The Final Transition: A Sociological Study* (London: Black, 1905).

BIOGRAPHY AND CRITICISM. C.L. Falkiner, *Memoir of John Kells Ingram* (Dublin: Sealy, Bryers, 1907); *Who Was Who 1897-1916* (London: Black, 1920), p. 368.

James Duffy

LIFE. Born in Monaghan in 1809, Duffy established himself in Dublin as a leading bookseller and publisher, serving the interests (not always compatible) of the Young Ireland party and the catholic middle classes. He published important works of fiction, both originally and in reprint series, by John Banim, William Carleton and Gerald Griffin. He died in Dublin in 1871.

INDEX OF FIRST LINES OF POEMS

VOLUME I

The first lines of excerpts are indicated by an ellipsis.

GENERAL INDEX

VOLUME I

This index includes only those names that have particular importance for the texts in this volume. Names that occur only in annotations and in fleeting references have been excluded.

Bold numerals indicate text selections; italic numerals indicate biographical and bibliographical listings; roman numerals indicate other references.

THE FIELD DAY ANTHOLOGY OF IRISH WRITING

THE FIELD DAY ANTHOLOGY OF IRISH WRITING

VOLUME II

General Editor: Seamus Deane
Associate Editors: Andrew Carpenter, Jonathan Williams

Derry
Field Day Publications
Distributed by Faber & Faber Limited

First published in 1991
by Field Day Publications, Foyle Arts Centre,
Old Foyle College, Lawrence Hill, Derry,
Northern Ireland BT48 7NJ

Distributed by Faber & Faber Limited
3 Queen Square
London WC1N 3AU

For the Set of Three Volumes ISBN 0 946755 20 5

Typeset in Ireland by Phototype-Set Ltd, Drumcondra, Dublin.
Printed in the United States by Kingsport Press

1 2 3 4 5 6 7 8 9 0

Contents

POLITICAL WRITINGS AND SPEECHES 1850-1918

SEAMUS DEANE

IRISH GOTHIC AND AFTER 1820-1945

W.J. Mc CORMACK

CONSTRUCTING THE CANON: VERSIONS OF NATIONAL IDENTITY

LUKE GIBBONS, *Faculty of Communications, Dublin City University, Dublin*

PROSE FICTION 1880-1945

AUGUSTINE MARTIN, *Department of English, University College, Dublin*

SEAMUS DEANE, *Editor*

Poetry and Song 1800-1890

I Poetry 1800-1890

Any selection of poems from Irish writers of the nineteenth century is bound to be bedevilled by the discrepancy between the quality of some of the poems and their representative status. More bluntly, it may be said that some of the best-known poems are, to present-day taste, among the worst. By 'worst', most readers now would mean those that are propagandistic, full of standard clichés and rhythmic vulgarities. Thomas Davis is probably among the most important and worst of Irish poets, from that point of view. But it is not necessary or wise to replace hostility to a political ideology with an aesthetic ideology. The poetry of this period manifests a series of individual and sometimes group attempts to come to terms with the implications of a doctrine which was understood to provide a solution to the Irish political-cultural problem but which, at the same time, also revealed the profound contradictions which that solution was supposed to overcome. The doctrine stated that there was an organic relationship between language, culture and national destiny. The rediscovery or revival of that relationship was, therefore, a cultural as well as a political project. One fed into the other. All European nationalisms — German, Italian, English, French and others — shared this notion, although with varying degrees of intensity. For it was natural that the so-called satellite cultures — that is, those that were not imperial, as the French or the English were — would find the appeal of such a doctrine especially strong. Germany found it irresistible and the Germanic influence on Irish nationalism was important, as Davis, Charles Gavan Duffy and, in a characteristically more oblique way, James Clarence Mangan, all testify.

The contradictions were obvious from the start, but it was the effort to suppress them that produced the particular forms of the literature and of the political movements — Repeal, Young Ireland, the Fenians. All these movements threatened revolutionary violence. In all three cases — in 1843 at the proposed mass-meeting at Clontarf, in 1848 at Ballingarry, and in the one-day rebellion of 1867 — the violence was almost phantasmal. The inglorious separation between the grand designs and the pathetic actions is as much a feature of the cultural as of the political enterprise. A devastating contradiction paralyzed both and it shows very clearly in the poetry and ballads of the time. It continued to show itself for a century thereafter.

The political rhetoric could not be translated into action because it bespoke a unity of purpose that did not exist. The militancy of the language of O'Connell and the Repeal movement, the sham military organization of the monster meetings, the endless call to arms of Young Ireland's poetry and the fierce invective of the Fenians, especially of John Mitchel's *United Irishman*, all ended in farce and indecision. There were too many internal divisions to permit concerted action. Some wanted rebellion, others revolution; some wanted catholic, some wanted secular, some wanted protestant nationalism; some wanted separation from Britain, others wanted legislative independence under the crown; some feared violence, others longed for it, many believed the threat of it would be substitute enough for the fact of it. All wanted to lay claim to an essential Irishness, but none could agree on what its identifying marks were — catholicism, the Gaelic culture, the protestant tradition, the national character as reconstituted by the temperance movement and education. Yet it was impossible to find an agreed solution even to the educational problem, as the disputes over the setting up of the new university colleges made clear. Incoherence of purpose was disguised in the language of utopian possibility.

The limitations of the political situation were mirrored in the circumstances in which many of the poets lived and wrote. Most of them were in poverty or exile for long stretches. They survived by clinging on to an organized grouping, like Young Ireland, or Irish unionism, both of which had publications — *The Nation* and *The Dublin University Magazine* — in which their work could appear, but to the policies of which it would also have to conform. This extreme limitation produced in many of the poets feckless, despairing or depressed behaviour; yet their verse is, by contrast, full of grandiose gesture and assertions of an untrammelled freedom, even though the freedom is often understood to be accessible only through undying loyalty to a noble cause — Ireland, or love, or the vocation of poetry itself. Poets, then, tended either to be members of a consolidated grouping or, failing that, to be loners condemned to a vaporous subjectivity, just as the group members were condemned to the production of standardized clichés.

This structural organization of Irish writing was to persist into the twentieth century, with the Irish Revival and the northern poets as the dominant groups and the consequent marginalization of those who did not wholly or properly belong. But within these groupings, certain writers emerged as leading figures, able to modulate between the demands of the group and of the individual self. Samuel Ferguson, James Clarence Mangan and W.B. Yeats are the obvious examples from the nineteenth century. As for the loners, George Darley and William Allingham would be equally exemplary figures. But, in general, the situation of most of the writers here did not allow for the possibility of their producing much more than the most occasional verse. It is appropriate that those who published in *The Nation* should have used pseudonyms. They actually sought a kind of anonymity, the fame that would belong, not to themselves, but to their poems. The model for that anonymity was in the ballad tradition. So many of the poems selected here gravitate towards it and some of them actually achieved that degree of fame for a time. In his *Short Life of Thomas Davis 1840-1846* (1895), Charles Gavan Duffy tells us that Davis's aims 'were far away from literary success. All his labours tended only to stimulate and discipline the people.' Davis produced nearly fifty ballads in three years, all published in *The Nation* and, according to Duffy, he 'used to say that, if he had his will, the songs of the *Nation* would be remembered in after times, and the authors quite forgotten . . . .' In many ways, Davis's wish was granted. Some of the most politically effective ballads are, to all intents and purposes, anonymous. But those that aimed at or achieved 'literary success' have had a different fate.

For the difference between the anonymous and the pseudonymous is crucial and large. Most of these writers survived in that zone in which the poet has, at one extreme, no name, and at the other, a fake name. They were neither balladeers nor poets, but some hybrid and usually unhappy combination of the two.

In addition, we find that early death and sometimes an even earlier extinction of reputation was the lot of most of the poets in the period between catholic emancipation (1829) and the death of Parnell (1891). Gerald Griffin died at thirty-six, after imposing upon himself the severest monastic fasts during his final two-year retreat from the world. Thomas Furlong was thirty-three when he died of consumption. James (or Jeremiah) Joseph Callanan, at the end of a rather miserable life, died in Lisbon at the age of thirty-four, after a despairing effort to board ship so that he might die in Ireland. Edward Walsh was so unhappy as a schoolmaster to convicts on Spike Island in Cork Harbour that he envied the lot of the Fenian leader John Mitchel, who was waiting there to be transported as a felon to Australia. Walsh died when he was forty-five. The much better-known Thomas Davis died at the age of thirty. The best-known of all, James Clarence Mangan, died of cholera, aged forty-six, after a life of obscurity and five years of extreme poverty. Thomas D'Arcy McGee was assassinated at the age of forty-three. Two years' imprisonment probably hastened the end of John Keegan Casey, who died aged twenty-four and is said to have had 50,000 people at his funeral. John Francis O'Donnell finally got an official appointment with a steady salary after twenty-five years of punishing hackwork for more than a dozen journals and newspapers; but in four months he was dead, aged thirty-seven. Although many poets lived a respectably long time and, even though some of them were distressingly productive throughout their lives, it is nevertheless remarkable that so many died so young and that so few ever achieved any kind of notice. Death often did no more than put the final seal on obscurity.

Perhaps only four or five poets of the nineteenth century in Ireland achieved a body of distinctive and coherent work — Thomas Moore, Ferguson, Mangan, Allingham and, with some reservations, Darley. It would not be difficult to include in a selection of this kind as many as one hundred poets, most of whom are remembered for only one lyric, or for one translation or ballad. Lady Dufferin wrote 'The Irish Emigrant'; William Pembroke Mulchinock wrote 'The Rose of Tralee', Sylvester Mahony 'The Bells of Shandon'; John Kells Ingram is remembered for 'The Memory of the Dead' and John Keegan Casey for 'The Rising of the Moon'. Most of the lyrics so remembered are songs, and that is a fact of some importance. Yet any sustained reading in this literature would do no more than affirm the sense that a general malaise afflicted the poetry as well as the poets.

It was difficult for most of these writers to gain recognition. A considerable number tried to win the attention of successful men-of-letters, many of whom were editors of magazines. William Maginn, for instance, tried to promote the career of Callanan by having his poems published in *Blackwood's Magazine*. Others attained the small fame of being known by a soubriquet — John D. Fraser (1809-49), another early casualty, was called the 'poet of the workshop' because he was a cabinet-maker by trade; John Keegan, his exact contemporary, was known as the 'peasant poet', John Francis O'Donnell as the 'poet of the Fenian movement'. As with the use of pseudonyms, this is another instance of hidden naming, identifying a writer as having value because he belonged to a group. The individual poet is merely the producer who belongs to a particular social or economic territory and from whom a specific kind of verse is to be expected. All that was needed to make this species of production available was the appropriate organization or factory. In the nineteenth century, that was almost always the journal or magazine. Book publication was secondary to that and many writers published few or even no books in their lifetimes. Their work was, by definition, occasional: piece-work of a kind and piecemeal in its effects.

When John Banim went to London with a tragedy under his arm, Gerald Griffin advised him (wisely) to forgo the stage and send poems to the periodical press. This provides at least one explanation for the proliferation of poets and for the tenuous fame that attached to so many for one remembered effort. Most of them were occasional poets because the system of periodical publishing encouraged occasional verse. Never before had there been so many magazines and journals. Never before had there been so many writers. Yet that was by no means the whole story.

Although there was a periodical press with an insatiable hunger for material, there was also an audience to which that press deferred in matters of taste and opinion. To write for such an audience (or audiences), the poet had to take as his subject-matter that which was widely considered to be properly poetical or politically acceptable. Frequently, a poem had to be both these things to have any chance of publication. The situation was further complicated by the fact that the English periodical press generally expected from its Irish contributors something quite different from the kind of material sought by the Irish periodicals. In England, the Irishman had been discovered to be, at his best, witty, sentimental, enthusiastic, impervious to practical considerations and much inclined to drinking and wastefulness. This was part of the heritage of the new form of what we may call instant antiquarianism, the discovery of the age-old patterns of Irish folk-life miraculously preserved in the amber of poverty and illiteracy. Irish writers hastened to cater to and further stimulate this historicized version of the Irish national character. Thomas Crofton Croker's *Fairy Legends and Traditions of the South of Ireland*, Eyre Evans Crowe's *Today in Ireland*, both published in 1825, were characteristic specimens of the kind of material that was to be incorporated into the fiction of novelists like Gerald Griffin and John and

Michael Banim. Maria Edgeworth's Irish novels had inaugurated this vogue in fiction long before, but it extended from there to the journalism of writers like William Maginn, contributor to *Blackwood's* and one of the founders of *Fraser's Magazine* in 1830, to which Francis Sylvester Mahony prolifically contributed under the pseudonym Father Prout.

Irish folklore material did not establish itself as successfully in poetry as it did in fiction. Stories from Irish sagas and legends were another matter, as Ferguson proved, but his translations and adaptations, although profoundly influential, were not popular in the sense that Moore's poems or the poems and songs of the writers for *The Nation* were. The audience for Irish poetry was in Ireland, not in England. In the prevailing conditions, especially after the Famine and the collapse of the Young Ireland movement in 1848, it was inevitable that much of the verse would be dominated by the question of Ireland — her tragic past, her beautiful landscape, her fight against the oppressing Saxon foe, her re-emergence as the object of the poet's ultimate fidelity to those affections and endearments that the world would otherwise ignore or reduce. Seen in this light, much of the poetry of the time is no more than a reflection of the counter-revolutionary emphasis on local attachment and childhood feeling, which had been transformed by Burke into the basis for the defence of traditional society and pieties. In Ireland, this essential traditionalism, which owed something also to the Jacobite longings of the eighteenth-century Gaelic poetry — much of which was being translated into English at the time — took on a rebellious, nationalistic coloration. When combined with a militant programme of propaganda against the English, the distinction between poetry and national feeling was rewritten. In effect, the cultural renovation of Ireland became, for unionists and nationalists alike, a political project.

The unionist view, dominated by Samuel Ferguson, was that the ancient poetry of the Irish could be brought into line with the requirements of civilized modern forms, enacting on the level of literature what was, for him, desirable on the level of politics. The nationalist view, dominated by Thomas Davis and the Young Ireland movement, was that Ireland could, through literature, rediscover an ancient cultural identity that would differentiate her markedly from England, even though this would have to be done through the medium of the English language. Both views assumed a spiritual essence that was definitive of the nation and expressible in literature rather than elsewhere. Such a literature demanded, therefore, that the poet manifest some contact with or aspect of that essence. This was both a characteristic of and a criterion for worthwhile poetry. In practice, this meant that idealized versions of Ireland, frequently drawn from the past, were proffered as zones of reconciliation, in which Ireland would have overcome its internal distresses and joined fully in the human community. The local and the marginal would have become the universal and the central community. This was a variation of German idealism. Longing for the unattainable, the absorption of the self in the communal, were literary equivalents of the emergent nationalism in both countries.

With the founding of *The Nation* newspaper, and the subsequent separate publication of the volume *The Spirit of the Nation* (1843), comprising what it called 'Political Songs and Ballads', poetry finally achieved popularity by allying itself with music and disengaging itself from any serious attempt to deal with Irish experience outside the conventions imposed by the powerful, if callow, demands of the Young Ireland movement. Thus, three kinds of music influenced the development of poetry throughout the century. Moore's *Irish Melodies* provided nationalist sentiment with a degree of respectability that was guaranteed by the possession of a drawing-room and a pianoforte. When the sentiment prevailed over the nationalist feeling, these melodies, which were for their audience in Ireland like arias from an extended national operetta, had to compete with songs from the three genuine operettas that became such an integral part of Dublin musical life by the turn of the century: *The Bohemian Girl* (1843) by Michael Balfe (1803-70), *The Lily of Killarney* (1862) by Julius Benedict (1804-85), and *Maritana* (1845) by William Vincent Wallace (1814-65). Balfe's 'I dreamt I dwelt in marble halls', Benedict's 'The Moon has raised her lamp above' and Wallace's 'Yes, let me like a soldier fall' and 'There is a flower that bloometh' became, with Moore's songs, part of the standard repertoire of those ubiquitous Irish tenors whose most renowned members include James Joyce's father, Joyce himself and John McCormack (1884-1945). This was a specifically middle-class musical world.

On the other hand, *The Nation*'s poets used many old Irish airs and some of their own making to further the militant tradition of rebellion against English, or, as they put it, 'Saxon' rule and oppression. These songs, often execrable as poetry, had an enormous appeal to all of a national cast of mind, but few of them were deemed to be as 'respectable' as the melodies and arias of Moore and the operettas. Finally, the translators and collectors, from James Hardiman and George Petrie to John O'Daly, D. F. MacCarthy, Edward Walsh and Douglas Hyde, were anxious to preserve in English as much as possible of the original spirit of the Irish songs and poems they translated, seeking thereby some ultimate reconciliation between the English language and that essential spirit, although in some cases believing, as Hyde did, that only the revival of the Irish language would guarantee either the survival or the reconciliation so variously and ambivalently sought. This more scholarly tradition was, oddly, closer to the mass of popular songs that had remained in the common possession of the people at least since the eighteenth century and often from a much earlier period. In all these instances, there was a mobilization of poetry to the national purpose of reawakening and recovering the sense of Ireland's uniquely tragic and heroic history. As a result, poetry as popular song became an important weapon in the long war against colonialism. Since it was then widely assumed throughout Europe that the ballad was the original poetry of the people, nationalist movements tended to give it an unprecedented political prominence. It was assumed, therefore, that when the old Irish music was put to new English lyrics, the native spirit would hibernicize the English language rather than be anglicized by it. Although this pious hope was to be repudiated by Hyde, Pearse and others in the later years of the century, it was retained and nurtured by compilers like D.F. MacCarthy who, in the introduction to his *Book of Irish Ballads* (1846), claimed that the contents of his volume proved that 'we can be thoroughly Irish in our writings without ceasing to be English.' Further, such ballads would constitute the beginning of a national literature, which would then go on to develop through successive, increasingly native, stages.

Charles Gavan Duffy's *The Ballad Poetry of Ireland* (1845) was more popular than MacCarthy's collection and rivalled *The Spirit of the Nation* in popular esteem. It reached 39 editions in twenty-one years. Duffy's introduction could hardly have been the reason for its popularity, but it does explain some features of the prevailing conceptions of the function of Irish poetry at that time. Its first function, of course, was to be Irish. Most of Gavan Duffy's material is taken from what he calls 'Anglo-Irish Ballads', which were 'the production of educated men, with English tongues but Irish hearts.' For 'no stranger ever did or can write the popular poetry of any people.' He writes at length of authors being '*essentially* [Irish] in character and spirit'; of 'distinct and intrinsic nationality'; of infusing 'the ancient and hereditary spirit of the country into all that is genuine in our modern poetry'; of 'the ordinary effect of native poetry' as cherishing 'love of home and homely associations, which, elevated and spiritualized, becomes love of country.' This is a language that derives from Burke and looks forward to Daniel Corkery. Yet, Duffy stresses, as do all the Young Irelanders, that all this Irish essence has to be re-expressed in the English language. He is conscious that success in this line requires that Irish-English become, through all the mutilations of language that had been experienced over three centuries, a literary language in its own right:

> The soul of the country, stammering its passionate grief and hatred in a strange tongue, loved still to utter them in its old familiar idioms and cadences. Uttering them, perhaps, with more piercing earnestness, because of the impediment; and winning, out of the very difficulty, an unconscious grace and triumph.

Gavan Duffy admits that Germany and England gave him the stimulus to produce a collection of native ballads, hoping that in Ireland also, the ballads 'will herald the happy coming of a native literature.' Mangan, especially, seemed to him the first portent of that new dawn. Moore had world-wide fame, but 'there were still tracks in his native country that had never fallen under his sway.' Mangan, in contrast, had been robbed of fame by the 'systematic seclusion' of his life as a writer. Yet he had the respect of his fellow poets. He was pure in a sense that Moore was not. He was also of the nation, of that spiritual essence, to a degree that Moore could not hope to emulate.

Given this background, we can see why Joyce thought Mangan to be the one important poet of the century, in whom 'an hysterical nationalism received its final justification.' Joyce not only believed in the Mangan myth; he was, after John Mitchel and some of Mangan's editors and colleagues, one of its most ardent supporters. The myth was in part that of the poet as romantic outsider, but, more importantly, Mangan's tragic alienation was interpreted as a manifestation of Ireland's own pitiful position. He was more than a propagandist; he was the embodiment of the nationalist view of the country's position. To that degree, in his poetry Mangan achieved a presence and a force that Joyce admired.

Mangan was one of the chief contributors to *The Nation*, but some of his most important early connections were made as a contributor to the *Dublin Penny Journal* (1832-33), founded by Caesar Otway and George Petrie, to the anti-tithe weekly *The Comet* (1831-35), to *The Dublin University Magazine* (1833-77) and to Petrie's *Irish Penny Journal*, founded in 1840. In addition, for almost four years (early 1838 to late 1841) Mangan was employed as copyist in the office of the historical branch of the Irish Ordnance Survey. There he renewed his acquaintance with scholars like George Petrie (1790-1866), John O'Donovan (1809-61) and Eugene O'Curry (1796-1862). With their help he began to learn Irish and produced some of his best-known pieces from literal translations of Gaelic poems supplied by them, particularly by O'Curry. Although Mangan's knowledge of Irish was never secure, not comparable to his proficiency in German, for instance, this did not inhibit his reputation as the greatest of the Irish national poets and the one most capable of carrying into English some of the force and grandeur of the originals. It is characteristic of him and of the period that this should be so. Irish was dying as a living language and simultaneously gaining strength as the object of academic study and political investment. Mangan's poetry catches that transitional moment. The fidelity to the Irish original is questionable and the effect on his English is disturbing. He is between two languages. In fact, in most of his poems, he assumes a persona, deflecting the responsibility for the poem to some putative original, Irish, German, 'Coptic', Arabic. No poet more consistently exploited the issue of translation; all his original work is, in some sense, translated. In Irish poetry, he availed of the translations of Ferguson, O'Curry, John O'Daly and many others to recompose his own versions; in other respects, the cavalier freedom with which he treated his original sources reveals the same strange combination of parasitism and originality. He was a poet of the periodical press, he was a translator, he was a member of the Ordnance Survey office, which translated the Irish landscape and its place-names into English equivalents, he was an amateur scholar in the company of professionals and, most of all, he was the poet with a myth — a man of startling appearance and tragic life who, in his poverty and obscurity, remained faithful to his inspiration in the midst of the fragmentation of a culture and society. More than anyone else, Mangan negotiated successfully between the positions of seclusion and anonymity on the one hand and identification with a group and fame on the other. It was entirely apt that he should die as the Great Famine ended. He was one of its ancillary victims and, thereby, one of the most perfectly pedigreed of the Irish literary heroes.

Yet this representation of Mangan depends on the nationalist recruitment of him as a heroic failure whose life was blighted by the appalling conditions of Ireland under British rule. Perhaps his central importance, like that of Moore and of Ferguson, is bound up with the series of problems that attends upon the issue of translation. Mangan's translations stand in a delicate and ambiguous relationship to their 'originals', when those originals exist. By making the possibility of translation problematic, he questions the very basis of Irish cultural nationalism, which, after all, assumes the translatability of Irish spirit into English words. The connection between the self and national essence is ironically questioned in his work; but the further irony is that it was his work which was most readily annexed by the nationalist movement in its desire to create the conditions for a national, bourgeois state.

George Darley, too, had all the qualifications necessary for failure, although he had not Mangan's capacity to mythologize them. He had great ambitions, but no matching talent. Darley was unfortunate in love, had to earn his money by hack reviewing, was plagued by a paralyzing stammer he could not cure, by rheumatism and by what he quaintly called 'a tertian headache'. His first volume of poems, *The Errors of Ecstasie* (1822) lost him money; his second work, *The Labours of Idleness* (1826), a collection of prose tales into which twenty-seven poems are set, was published under a pseudonym (Guy Penseval) and promptly disappeared from public view; in 1827, he had his only minor success with the publication of his verse-drama, *Sylvia, or The May Queen: A Lyrical Drama*. The poem for which he is now most remembered, *Nepenthe* (1835), was privately printed for distribution among his friends. Two other verse dramas and five mathematical textbooks were the sum total of his remaining publications. Even though from 1822 he wrote regularly for John Scott's famous journal, the *London Magazine*, and got to know fellow contributors like Charles Lamb, John Clare and H.F. Cary, the translator of Dante, his name rarely appears in the correspondence and memoirs of the time. No letters between him and Lamb have survived. Writing in 1840, Darley wondered why *Sylvia* had not placed him among the major poets: 'It ranked me among the *small* poets. I had as soon be ranked among the piping bullfinches.'

Nevertheless, that is where he remains. He is one of those Irish writers whose development and career is comprehensible in the English, rather than the Irish, context. It is no surprise that Darley was interested in painting, for his work has some of the fake grandeur of contemporary historical paintings, like those of his compatriot James Barry and of Benjamin Robert Haydon. The synoptic view of human history and the drum-roll of great names and events, particularly attractive if they are exotic and foreign, has its attractions, but they are reduced by the nerveless monotony of the verse. In effect, Darley had no audience. He was a gifted writer who faded for want of a governing theme. In that respect, he is one of the many casualties of nineteenth-century Romanticism.

Darley could hardly make a stronger contrast with Samuel Ferguson. Ferguson, a Belfast unionist, had a cultural and political programme that he expounded in the pages of *The Dublin University Magazine*. He wanted the Irish people to 'live back in the country they live in' and to that end, besides his numerous essays, he produced a long series of translations from the Irish in his pursuit of a cultural renovation that would link together catholic and protestant in a single, shared identity. Some of his translations are famous; some were taken up and improved by Mangan. Many of his longer poems, like *Congal* (1872), are wearisome efforts. But he did bring to his translations an energy and a crusading spirit that attracted the young Yeats and stimulated him into further investigation of his country's poetic heritage. Although Ferguson is a figure of great historical importance, as a poet he is very much among the 'piping bullfinches' of whom Darley wrote. Nevertheless, he did have an audience and he did have a background out of which he could appeal to that audience. As a result, his work does not suffer from the occasionalism of many others. It is governed by a purpose and, in remarkable fashion, manages to achieve it. For him, translation was not an action that generated crisis in his writing. It liberated him as a poet and helped him to attain his best effects. The 'transparency' of his translations contrasts strongly with the difficulties of Mangan's texts. This is not simply a matter of 'poetic' quality. Ferguson's theory of cultural politics was predicated on the notion that union between the Irish and English civilizations was possible and desirable. He comes as close to the original as he possibly can, whereas Mangan interferes with it, intruding upon its autonomy and thereby questioning it. Ferguson's practice is quite other. He seeks union between two languages and two cultures; his translations are his proof that the search is justified.

William Allingham was, for a time, editor of *Fraser's Magazine* and a friend of many of the best-known English writers of the period. An ardent admirer of Tennyson, to whom he was introduced by Coventry Patmore, Allingham visited the great man when he could and frequented Pre-Raphaelite literary circles on his regular visits to London. London was his capital, not Dublin, although he wished to be recognized as an Irish poet. His position as a customs officer in Ballyshannon, Co. Donegal (and in various other places, including Belfast) did not provide him with many opportunities to nourish his gifts. Allingham's reputation, until recently, has tended to categorize him as a regional poet whose lyrics about Ballyshannon and fairies sufficiently attested to his essential quality. This is unjust. His achievement and importance are greater than has been generally recognized, although in the last twenty years John Hewitt has helped to establish Allingham's position more securely. In his *Diary*, Allingham records that

> I came early to the consciousness that I was living in a discontented and disloyal country; it seemed the natural state of things that the

> humbler class — which was almost synonymous with Roman Catholic, should hate those above them in the world, and lie in wait for a chance of despoiling them.

Ballyshannon was a garrison town, but once, when the soldiers had been withdrawn, Allingham saw a troupe of Whiteboys, agrarian rebels, march through the town, armed with scythes and pikes. It was Allingham's awareness of the political divisions in Ireland, combined with his love for the ancient Irish world and its culture, which had 'come down from times long before any English existed', that gives his best work its particular force and importance. He used to compose anonymous ballads that he had made into broadsheets and sold at fairs and markets, enjoying hearing his own songs sung by his neighbours. In fact Allingham was one of the many who recognized the influence of the ballad tradition on poetry and wrote a useful essay on the subject, 'Irish Ballad Singers and Street Ballads' in 1851. Yet this anonymous success was not matched by the reception of his published work. His *Fifty Modern Poems* (1865) sold very few copies and no subsequent volume ever won general acclaim. Anonymity was a more potent title to an audience than was his own name. Allingham, lacking Mangan's subtle awareness of this phenomenon, was unable to exploit it. It was Mangan, after all, who wrote the poem called 'The Nameless One', a characteristically Mangan poem about having no name, no presence. Only he learned how to use anonymity and pseudonymity as a mode of identification.

Yet Allingham produced one of the best narrative poems of the time, *Laurence Bloomfield in Ireland* (1864). Its subject is the land, and the battle for it between landlords and tenants. It is the only poem of sustained quality to treat this central theme of nineteenth-century Irish life. The story of the improving landlord, Laurence Bloomfield, had been told before in Irish literature, although it had never been treated in verse. It is true that the idealized peasantry, the savage Ribbonmen, the Orange bigots, the landlords and their heartless agent, Pigot, are all stereotypes. Yet Allingham is able to give some sense of the political alienation that lay at the heart of the Irish situation, partly because the hostile positions were so calcified that the stereotype was both unavoidable and a true reflection of the congealed attitudes about which he writes. The poem is weakly conventional in many respects; the octosyllabic couplet, effective in satirical verse, has not the impetus that narrative verse requires. Yet it remains one of the most noteworthy achievements in verse narrative before Yeats and the subsequent flowering of the long poem in Irish writing thereafter.

While in his long poem Allingham blended what we may call the political and the picturesque elements prevailing in Irish poetry at the time, John Francis O'Donnell kept them separate in a manner that is a telling comment on the division of labour to which the Irish poet, split between two audiences, was condemned. O'Donnell's political poetry is fiercely nationalistic. He competed with John Keegan Casey for the position of the 'Fenian poet'. Yet all his nationalist poetry was published in Ireland, in journals like *The Nation*, *Duffy's Hibernian Magazine*, *The Shamrock* and the London-based *The Irish People*, a Fenian newspaper. His love poems and poems of exile appeared in English journals, including Dickens's *All the Year Round*. O'Donnell was improvident and feckless in his ways. He held many journalistic positions, but none for long. Yet he is a phenomenon that deserves notice. He was one of those poets whose work changes in relation to his two audiences, English and Irish. The change is so pronounced that he represents, better than anyone else, the plight of the writer who, forced to subsist on the pathetic fees paid by the periodical press, managed to combine brief fame at home as a political writer and total obscurity in England as a writer of occasional, sentimental verse. O'Donnell published only one volume in his lifetime; by 1891, when an edition of his poems was brought out by the Southwark Literary Society, his reputation had almost disappeared. In him the split between strident patriotic propaganda and a more personal, self-consciously 'private' preoccupation is perfectly embodied. He was trapped in a prison-house of language in which two audiences, English and Irish, were his warders. Despite this, he managed to liberate part of his experience into poetry.

The peculiar blend of politeness and sentimentality that Moore had brought to Irish verse, persisted in the poetry of later writers like Oscar Wilde and James Joyce, enhanced in their cases by the preciousness and local intensities favoured by the aesthetic movement. Indeed Yeats, too, is drawn to that form of elegant insipidity. These writers are dealt with later, but it is right to acknowledge the debt they owed to the native tradition in English (or Englished) verse. As the idea of Ireland changes from the winsome land of legend and fairy to the turbulent and threatening land of mass starvation and Fenian revolutionaries, the literary culture also begins to alter. In effect, literature found a way of combining these two disparate elements. Helped by Standish O'Grady and ably seconded by the writings of Ernest Renan and Matthew Arnold on the Celtic spirit, a heroic vision of Ireland emerged, evoking the legendary past, the contemporary folk-culture and the militant revolutionary spirit. Ireland was now, more definitively than ever, pitted against, not just England, but a version of England that served as the emblem of the modern world. To the extent that England was philistine, urban, industrial, commercial, full of ugly cities and lonely, alienated people, it was the modern world in its most advanced state of development. To all that, Ireland was opposed; further, to those in Ireland who tried to reproduce that version of English life, the Irish were doubly opposed. This led to some internecine war, fought at first with the mock training weapons of cultural discrimination. Various classes were attacked. The catholic middle class and the protestant landed class were favourite targets, often of each other as well as of others. But the breakthrough that heralded the Irish Revival had been achieved. Ireland was now the heroic culture, defiantly confronting the modern world and finally beginning to express its sense of its own destiny in an English that had come to absorb its Gaelic inheritance rather than be disturbed by it. The colonized culture was turning into a colonizing culture, a place with a missionary future in the drear modern age.

The image of the Revival is so strong that almost everyone who precedes it is read as one of its precursors, or is ignored if no proleptic echo is to be found in the work. Yet it remains true that it was Yeats who reconceived an essentially uncertain, hesitant poetic tradition as a unique contribution to the formation of a new world literature. Moore, Mangan and Ferguson were all recruited to ratify a version of Ireland which was very far removed from the country that had emerged in shock from the last years of the eighteenth century. The act of translation, so central to the literary enterprise in Ireland, could go no further.

JOHN O'KEEFFE

(1747-1833)

from: THE AGREEABLE SURPRISE (1781)

[This nonsense lyric occurs in O'Keeffe's play *The Agreeable Surprise*, staged at the Haymarket in 1781. It anticipates the playful drollery of writers like William Maginn and Father Prout (see below). It is usually printed as a lyric in its own right.]

Jingle

Amo, amas,
I love a lass,
As cedar tall and slender;
Sweet cowslip's face
Is her nominative case,
And she's of the feminine gender.
Horum quorum,
Sunt divorum,
Harum, scarum, Divo,
Tag rag, merry derry, periwig and bobtail
Hic, hoc, harum, genitivo.

MARY BALFOUR

(1780-1819)

from:
HOPE: A POETICAL ESSAY
(1810)

[Mary Balfour's are among the earliest translations from the Irish. In the first of these poems, there is no serious attempt to come to terms with the original. The second confirms that her idiom is as conventional as that of Thomas Campbell, the Scottish poet, of whom she is an imitator. Nevertheless, Balfour's stanzas are more intricate then her mentor's.]

In Ringlets Curl'd Thy Tresses Flow

In ringlets curl'd thy tresses flow,
  And bright and sparkling are thine eyes,
Time in thy absence lingers slow,
  When measur'd by a lover's sighs.
Had sacred rites once crown'd my love,
  With bounding steps the fields I'd tread,
Oh, grief! that we no longer rove
  Where Truigha's lonely green woods spread.

Oh! would that on thy bosom laid,
  While Erin's sons are hush'd to rest,
I might beneath the green-wood shade
  Breathe the pure raptures of thy breast!
Sweet blooming flower! thy sex's pride,
  To me a guiding star thou art,
And Heaven itself will sure preside
  O'er love that fills a virtuous heart.

My charmer! let us haste away
  To Truigha's woods our footsteps bend,
Where streams through water-cresses play,
  And Uchais lovely plains extend;[1]
There holly berries glowing red,
  With nuts and apples sweet abound,
Green rushes there shall strew our bed,
  And warblers chaunt their lov'd notes round.

1. Truigha and Uchais possibly are debased versions of the names of areas in County Sligo and County Mayo.

The Dew each Trembling Leaf Inwreath'd

The dew each trembling leaf inwreath'd,
  The red-breast sweetly sung,
The balmy air with fragrance breath'd
  From bow'rs with roses hung:
The setting sun still faintly gleam'd,
  And swift and sweet the moments flew
With her, whose smile too artless seem'd,
  To hide a heart untrue.

But now o'er dreary scenes I range,
  Where once such beauties shone,
Yet blooming nature knows no change,
  Alas! 'tis all my own.
The rose still holds its lovely form,
  The dew still sparkles on the tree,
But, oh! the smile that gave the charm
  No longer beams for me!

JAMES STUART

(1764-1842)

from:
POEMS ON VARIOUS SUBJECTS (1811)

[Stuart is chiefly remembered for his researches in the history of the Armagh-Newry area. His *Historical Memoirs of the City of Armagh, for a period of 1373 years* (1819) is a useful contribution to antiquarian scholarship, notable also for its attack on Edward Ledwich's *The Antiquities of Ireland* (1790), in which Ledwich had disputed the historical basis of the stories concerning St Patrick. Stuart's single volume of verse is undistinguished, save for the topographical poem 'Morna's Hill', from which the following extract is taken. Various historical sites and landscapes associated with Armagh are described in the poem. Part of its interest now is the antiquarian theme; but it also a poem in which the conventions of eighteenth-century narrative verse are employed with a degree of assurance. These conventions remain alive in the work of Henry Luttrell and, above all, in that of William Allingham.]

from: MORNA'S HILL

... Behold that monument of former times,
Yon mouldering abbey.[1] O'er the roofless walls,
Green ivy creeps; and through the grass-grown aile,
Sepulchral monuments, with sculpture rude,
Tell to the passengers the simple tale
Of sorrow and of death. There Science once,
Amid the splendid fabrick reigned supreme.
Her, the rude turbulence of lawless pow'r
Had exiled from the venerable seats
Of philosophick lore. Yet here escaped
From the fierce tumult of vindictive war,
Secure the nymph with calm Religion dwelled,
Sequestered from the world. Around her thronged
Her sacred sons, a pure and holy train,
Who, from the heaven-descended virgin caught
Celestial inspiration. Wide around
They spread the living flame; and Europe saw
The torch of learning, which barbarian hands
Had quenched in Gothick night, illume once more
Th' astonished nations. Now the lonely pow'r
Of silence broods amid the ruined scene,
Where once soul-moving strains of joy divine,
With halleluiahs filled the lofty dome;
And the deep-pealing organ poured around
Celestial tones that raised the raptured soul,
Borne on a flood of harmony sublime,
Ev'n to the heav'n of heav'ns. Ah whither now
Is fled the sacred choir, whose silver notes
Blending concordant, floated on the gale
In tides of solemn musick: or again,
Melting in gentle cadence died away,
'Till scarce the list'ning ear in rapture lost,
Could catch the doubtful sound? Sweet was the strain,
As the soft breathings of Eolian harp,
When Zephyr, ling'ring on the trembling strings,
Prolongs the murm'ring thrill that seems to float
High over head, amid the realms of air.
And whither now is fled the meek-eyed sage,
Who scorning all the tinsel pomp of life,
Retired with virtue to the peaceful cell,
And lived to God alone? No longer moves,
In grand procession to the sacred shrine,
The awe-struck train, or bows the humble knee
With contrite heart, before the king of kings.
Time with his iron grasp, resistless tears
The massy fabrick. To the earth descends
The lofty roof, and round the naked walls,
Grim Ruin stalks. The gothick arches bend
In awful desolation. There the owl
Hides moping[2] from the glaring face of day;
Or when the moon-beam, through the parted wall,
Tinges the prostrate tombs with silver light,
Shrieks forth his sorrows; and the sombrous bat,
On wandering wing, flits o'er the solemn scene,
With hideous aspect and uncertain flight.
Meet emblem this of all the joys of man,
And all his earthly glories. High he builds,
Elate and confident, his airy hopes,
Nor dreads the latent storm, that lurks to blast.
The unsubstantial vision. Pleasure's spell,
The blaze of pomp, the gaudy crown of power,
And all the splendours of this transient life,
Before the wand of time dissolve away,
Ev'n like the meteor's glance, whose lucid form
Sinks in the gulf of darkness. Ah behold,
What mighty empires fall to rise no more!
Prone in the dust, what gorgeous cities lie
In shapeless ruin! Queen of eastern realms,
O Babylon! where are thy lofty walls,
Thy warlike battlements, thy temples vast,
Thy marble streets, thy palaces and towers,
Thy pendent gardens, and thy silver baths?
Go Luxury, and view that awful scene!
Behold the viper and the scaly snake
Twine through the prostrate walls, where jocund Mirth
And Revelry and noisy Riot shared
With kings the splendid banquet. Look at Thebes!
Where are her high-arched porticoes, her domes
Of solid granite, and her hundred gates,
Through whose expanding valves, in bright array
And glowing panoply refulgent clad,
Issued embattled hosts? Ev'n thus shall fall

1. Stuart identifies this as: 'The ruins of an abbey in the neighbourhood of Armagh, founded by St. Patrick, A.D. 457, one of the most celebrated ecclesiastical universities in the world.'

2. cf. Thomas Gray, *Elegy Written in a Country Churchyard*, stanza 3: 'The moping owl does to the moon complain.'

Those lofty cities, that in later days
Lift their aspiring heads; and future bards
Shall ask where Pekin was, or search in vain,
Constantinople, for thy solemn mosques
And ruined battlements! And thus at last,
When circling Time hath run his ages o'er,
Merged in eternity, shall earth itself
And all those splendid worlds that roll above,
Melt into empty space; and angels show
To heav'n's new denizens, in wonder rapt,
The vacant spot, where once their glowing orbs,
Enrobed in light, had wheeled their glorious course.

HENRY LUTTRELL

(*c.*1765-1851)

from: ADVICE TO JULIA: A LETTER IN RHYME (1820)

[Luttrell was once a well-known and much-admired member of the Holland House circle in London. He was renowned for his wit and for the elegance of his verse. Byron admired *Advice to Julia*; although almost forgotten now, it is a fine example of the polished *vers de société* which the older members of the circle, particularly Luttrell's close friend Samuel Rogers, practised and which Byron was to transform and burlesque. Luttrell described the poem as a picture 'of modern habits and manners, and of the amusements and lighter occupations of the higher classes in English society.' The story, such as it is, concerns Julia's coquettish behaviour towards Charles, her betrothed, in the interval between their engagement and their marriage. This allows Luttrell to survey London's changing social scene and particularly to satirize the leisure activities of the increasingly prosperous commercial classes, who ape those of their social superiors.]

. . . Once would he[1] loiter, ere 'twas dark,
'Mongst Nymphs and Satyrs in the Park:
The Park! that magnet of the town,
That idol to which all bow down.
See how the universal throng,
Borne in one swelling tide along,
Crowds to its turf-clad altars, there
To beg the blessing of fresh air!
Throughout the week, but most on one day
Enjoyed beyond all others — Sunday,
With many a mutual punch and shove,
To Hyde Park Corner on they move.
Like bees, that, when the weather's warm,
Grow weary of their hives and swarm,
All active on that day of rest,
Pressing on every side, and pressed
In 'Phœbus eye' from east to west
With a fair chance, while thus they busy 'em,
To 'sleep' that evening 'in Elysium.'[2]

Perchance, a truant from his desk,
Some lover of the picturesque,
Whose soul is far above his shop,
Hints to his charmer where to stop;
And the proud landscape, from the hill, eye
Which crowns thy terrace — Piccadilly!
Whispering, 'My dear, while others hurry,
Let us look over into Surry.'[3]
There, as the summer-sun declines,
Yet still in full-orbed beauty shines,
As, all on fire beneath his beams,
The fret-work of the Abbey[4] gleams;
While on its towers a golden flood
Is poured, above the tufted wood,
His charmer (kindred spirits, see
The blest effects of sympathy!)
Is busied in a tasteful trial
To spell the hour upon the dial!

1. Charles, Julia's betrothed, who once used to lead the life of a man about town.

2. *Henry V*, IV. 1. 290-92:
'... from the rise to set
Sweats in the eye of Phoebus and all night
Sleeps in Elysium.'

3. Surrey, a county in south-east England, bounded on the north by the river Thames.

4. Westminster Abbey.

Mark how the mighty snow-ball gathers!
Lads, lasses, mothers, children, fathers,
All equal here, as if the pavement
To level them were like the grave meant,
As if one will informed the whole,
And uged them to a common goal.
See, in the living mass confounded,
All shapes, all sizes, slim, and rounded;
Every variety of features
That e'er distinguished human creatures!
Nor less their *habits* disagree:
Some have, at sunset, risen from tea;
Some linger on till Dusk at nine
Bids them retire to dress and dine.
The same pursuits together jumble
The rich and poor, the proud and humble.
Th' enfranchised tradesman, if he stirs,
Here, jostles half his customers.
Here, in a rage, the Bond-street spark
Is bearded by his father's clerk;
While yon proud dame (O sad event!) is
Out-elbowed by her own apprentice.

What goads them on? — The influence
Of Nature and of Common sense.
Thus they shake off the weekly yoke
Of business and its weekly smoke,
With verdure thus refresh their eyes,
And purchase health by exercise;
Giving their gasping lungs fair play,
And their cramped limbs a holiday:
And since, like others less polite,
Fine folks have lungs, and limbs, and sight,
All destined to the same employment,
All eager for the same enjoyment;
Here Sense and Nature have it hollow,
And Fashion is constrained to follow,
To join the vulgar happy crew,
And fairly do as others do.

Of this thy progeny be proud,
O England! though a motley crowd.
Can Europe or the world produce,
Alike for ornament or use,
Such models of stout active trim men,
Or samples of such lovely women?
Such specimens of order, dress,
Health, comfort, inbred cleanliness,
As here displayed, the summer-sun
Lingering seems proud to shine upon?

But, O! the treachery of our weather,
When Sunday folks are met together!
Its tempting brightness scarce matured,
How suddenly the day's obscured!
Bless me, how dark! — Thou threatening cloud,
Pity the *un-umbrella'd* crowd.
The cloud rolls onward with the breeze —
First, pattering on the distant trees
The rain drops fall — then quicker, denser,
On many a Parasol and Spencer;[5]
Soon drenching, with no mercy on it,
The straw and silk of many a bonnet.
Think on their hapless owners fretting,
While feathers, crape and gauze are wetting!
The fruits of all their weekly toil
Given to the element for spoil!
Think of the pang to well-dressed girls,
When, pinched in vain, their hair uncurls!
When ringlets from each lovely pate
Hang mathematically straight!
As off, on every side, they scour,
Still beats the persecuting shower,
Till, on the thirsty gravel smoking,
It fairly earns the name of *soaking*.
Fiercer and fiercer blows the gust,
Burthened at once with rain and dust:
Breathless they scud, some helter skelter
To carriages, and some for shelter;
Lisping to coachmen drunk or dumb
In *numbers* — while no numbers come.
Nor sheds are near, nor open shops
Protect them from the big round drops:
Their sarsenets[6] spoiled, their stockings splashed,
Their muslins prematurely washed;
Some in their clinging clothes so lank,
Others so bouncing, *all* so blank,
Enraged, resigned, in tears or frowning,
Look as if just escaped from drowning;
While anxious thoughts pursue them home,
Whence their next Sunday's dress must come....

5. A short, double-breasted overcoat without tails, worn by men.
6. Dresses of very fine silk material.

[Luttrell heard that Lord Lauderdale had learned by heart Samuel Rogers's poem, 'Human Life'. Thomas Moore's oriental romance, *Lalla Rookh* (1817), set in Persia, had won him a reputation that rivalled Byron's. The poem was said to be popular in Persia itself. Luttrell wrote this squib, as from Rogers, to comment ironically on his countryman's recent fame. Never one to take offence where he could take advantage, Moore reprinted the poem in his *Diary*.]

Luttrell to Moore (1818)

I'm told, dear Moore, your lays are sung
(Can it be true, you lucky man?)
By moonlight in the Persian tongue,
Along the streets of Ispahan.

'Tis hard, but one reflexion cures,
At once, a jealous poet's smart:
The Persians have translated yours,
But Lauderdale has mine by heart.

GEORGE DARLEY

(1795-1846)

from: NEPENTHE (1835)

[Darley described the 'general object or mythos of the poem' as showing 'the folly of discontent with the natural tone of human life. Canto I attempts to paint the ill-effects of over-joy, Canto II, those of excessive melancholy.' In each canto, a magic elixir stimulates the poet to ecstasy and sends him on his fantastic journeys. Nepenthe is a nectar that flows from the ashes of the Phoenix. In Canto II the magic potion comes from the source of the White Nile in the mountains of the Moon. By the close of Canto II, the poet is longing for a return to Ireland, to a state in which extreme desires or feelings are modified into a harmony.]

Canto I

. . . O blest unfabled Incense Tree,
That burns in glorious Araby,
With red scent chalicing the air,
Till earth-life grow Elysian there!

Half buried to her flaming breast
In this bright tree, she makes her nest,
Hundred-sunned Phenix! When she must
Crumble at length to hoary dust!

Her gorgeous deathbed! her rich pyre
Burnt up with aromatic fire!
Her urn, sight high from spoiler men!
Her birthplace when self-born again!

The mountainless green wilds among,
Here ends she her unechoing song!
With amber tears and odorous sighs
Mourned by the desert where she dies!

Laid like the young fawn mossily
In sun-green vales of Araby,
I woke, hard by the Phenix tree
That with shadeless boughs flamed over me;
And upward called by a dumb cry
With moonbroad orbs of wonder, I
Beheld the immortal Bird on high
Glassing the great sun in her eye;
Steadfast she gazed upon his fire,
Still her destroyer and her sire!
As if to his her soul of flame
Had flown already, whence it came;
Like those that sit and glare so still
Intense with their death struggle, till
We touch, and curdle at their chill! —
But breathing yet while she doth burn,
The deathless Daughter of the sun!
Slowly to crimson embers turn
The beauties of the brightsome one;
O'er the broad nest her silver wings
Shook down their wastful glitterings;
Her brinded neck high-arched in air
Like a small rainbow faded there;
But brighter glowed her plumy crown
Mouldering to golden ashes down:
With fume of sweet woods, to the skies,
Pure as a Saint's adoring sighs,
Warm as a prayer in Paradise,
Her life-breath rose in sacrifice!
The while with shrill triumphant tone
Sounding aloud, aloft, alone,

Ceaseless her joyful deathwail she
Sang to departing Araby!

Deep melancholy wonder drew
Tears from my heartspring, at that view;
Like cresset shedding its last flare
Upon some wistful mariner,
The Bird, fast blending with the sky,
Turned on me her dead-gazing eye
Once, — and as surge to shallow spray,
Sank down to vapoury dust away!

O fast her amber blood doth flow
From the heart-wounded Incense Tree,
Fast as earth's deep-embosomed woe
In silent rivulets to the sea!

Beauty may weep her fair first-born,
Perchance in as resplendent tears,
Such golden dewdrops bow the corn
When the stern sickleman appears;

But oh! such perfume to a bower
Never allured sweet-seeking bee,
As to sip fast that nectarous shower
A thirstier minstrel drew in me!

My burning soul one drop did quaff —
Heaven reeled and gave a thunder-laugh!
Earth reeled, as if with pendulous swing
She rose each side through half her ring,
That I, head downward, twice uphurled,
Saw twice the deep blue underworld.
Twice, at one glance, beneath me lie
The bottomless, boundless, void sky!
Tho' inland far, me seemed around
Ocean came on with swallowing sound
Like moving mountains serried high! —
Methought a thousand daystars burned
By their mere fury as they turned,
Bewildering heaven with too much bright,
Till day looked like a daylight night.
Brief chaos, only of the brain!
Heaven settled on its poles again,
And all stood still, but dizzily....

Canto II

. . . Still at thy works in mute amaze,
Sorrow and envy and awe, we gaze!
Enlarge our little eyeballs still
To grasp in these degenerate days,
Marvels that shewed a mighty will
Huge power and hundred-handed skill,
That seek prostration, and not praise
Too faint such lofty ears to fill! —
From Ind to Egypt thou are one,
Pyramidal Memphis to Tanjore,
From Ipsambul to Babylon
Reddening the waste suburban o'er;
From sand-locked Thebes to old Ellore,[1]
Her caverned roof on columns high
Pitched, like a Giant brood that bore
Headstrong the mountain to the sky:
That one same Power, enorm, sublime,
Thou art, from antique clime to clime,
Eternal stumbling block of Time!
Whose fragmentary limbs do stay,
Stones of offence, his difficult way,
And turn it o'er our works of clay.
Lo! where thy strength colossal lay
Dormant, within the deep-sunk halls
Of cities labyrinthian
'Mid sandy Afric, and the walls
Of sunburnt Syria or Deccan,[2]
Up from the bilging globe he calls
Sea to surprise thee! or enthralls
Earth to deluginous ocean,
So far he may; with foamy van
Whelming her shores where thou bedreamed
Heard'st not the tide that o'er thee teemed
Mountains of water! — Ay in vain!
O'ersailing vessels see below
Clear, through the glass-green undulous plain,
Like emerald cliffs unmoved glow
Thy towering forms stretched far a-main:
By Coromandel,[3] or that side
Neptunian Ganges rolls the tide
Of his swoln sire; by Moab's Lake[4]
Whose purulent flood dry land doth slake
With bittern ooze, where that salt Wife

1. Memphis was the second greatest city of ancient Egypt, after Alexandria, until the Roman conquest and the fortification of the camp of Babylon, across the river Nile. Tanjore was one of the great religious centres of ancient India. Ipsambul is a version of Istanbul. Babylon, capital of Mesopotamia, on the river Euphrates, was one of the greatest cities of the ancient world. Its walls were of burnt brick, hence 'reddening'. The Thebes referred to here was the former capital city of Egypt. Ellore or Ellora in India is, in Darley's description, a temple in which the 'pillars are cut out of the mountain forming its roof.'
2. The Deccan sultanate, comprising the greater part of the Indian continent, flourished in the sixteenth century.
3. The Coromandel Coast is on the Bay of Bengal in India.
4. The Dead Sea.

Drinks her own tears she weeps as rife,
Empillared there, as when she turned
Back tow'rds her liquorish[5] late-spent life
Where Shame's sulphureous cities burned;[6]
By Dorian Sicily and Misene[7]
Upon whose strand thou oft didst lean
Thy temple-crowned head; and where
Antium[8] with opposite Carthage were;
By green Juvernia's[9] giant road
Paved from her headlong slope and broad
Sands down to Rachlin's[10] columned isle,
And dim Finn Gael's[11] huge-antred pile
Where his vast orgue, high fluted, stands
Basaltic, swept with billowy hands
Oft, till the mystic chancel mourn
To weltering biers around it borne
Hoarse ritual o'er the wreckt forlorn;
There did the scythed Demon hew
Sheer, the cyclopian causeway through
Letting the steep Icelandic Sea
In on the Ibernian and on Thee! — ....

... Till I found me once again
By the ever-murmuring main,
Listening across the distant foam
My native church-bells ring me home; —
Alas! why leave I not this toil
Through stranger lands, from mine own soil?
Far from ambition's worthless coil,
From all this wide world's weary moil, —
Why leave I not this busy broil,
For mine own clime, for mine own soil,
My calm, dear, humble, native soil!
There to lay me down at peace
In my own first nothingness.

5. licentious.
6. Lot's wife, who looked back to the cities of the plain, Sodom and Gomorrah, infamous for their sin and corruption. She was turned into a pillar of salt (Genesis 19.26).
7. Sicily was a Greek (Dorian) colony. Misene or Misenum was a town on the northern headland of the Bay of Naples.
8. Antium, modern Anzio, in ancient times the principal Volscian city, later a seaside resort. It looked across to Carthage in North Africa. Both cities were for a time centres of resistance to Rome.
9. Ireland.
10. The reference seems to be to Rathlin island, off County Antrim, and to the Giant's Causeway, also on the Antrim coast.
11. Fingal's Cave on the Isle of Staffa in Scotland's Inner Hebrides. Darnley says that it 'has a range of basalt pillars denominated the Organ'.

THOMAS FURLONG

(1794-1827)

[In his review of James Hardiman's *Irish Minstrelsy* (1831), Samuel Ferguson has this to say of Furlong: 'Mr. Furlong was a man of strong poetic feeling, but of slender poetic art. He had but little fancy, less imagination, and, we had almost said, no judgment. In raciness, in naivete, in quaint characteristic expression, his versions fall immeasurably short of the original; and were not their mawkish poverty in this respect relieved by the genuine glow of sentiment with which his good feeling often redeems his bad taste, would deservedly fall under unmitigated censure. Furlong is now no more, and as he left behind him nothing worthy to live, so must his name also soon pass from the precincts of an obscure fame, to which it has been fondly elevated to the admiration of sanguine but incompetent admirers.'

In the anonymous introduction to the second edition of *The Misanthrope*, the writer gives a brief account of Furlong's withdrawal from the world. He lived in London from about 1819, 'excluded from all society; reviling and abusing his species and shunning their company and conversation; he never stirred out but when he went to the office of a Newspaper, of which he was assistant editor; he admitted neither man nor woman servant into his apartments; he would listen to no physician in his illness; nor would he allow any minister of religion to come near him — and to sum up his character, he died as he had lived! — Yet this man was once chearful and open-hearted, but early disappointments had soured his temper and altered his disposition.' Furlong is an exemplary case of a writer entrapped within a dark and inexpressible subjectivity. He was one of the chief translators of the songs in Hardiman's *Irish Minstrelsy* (1831). This poem is a salute to that enterprise. As is often the case, the Irish music is identified with 'nature'; all else is 'art'.]

The Spirit of Irish Song (1829)

Lov'd land of the bards and saints! to me
There's nought so dear as thy minstrelsy;
Bright is Nature in every dress,
Rich in unborrowed loveliness;
Winning is every shape she wears;
Winning she is in thine own sweet airs;
What to the spirit more cheering can be
Than the lay whose ling'ring notes recall
The thoughts of the holy, the fair, the free,
Belov'd in life, or deplor'd in their fall!
Fling, fling the forms of art aside —
Dull is the ear that these forms enthrall;
Let the simple songs of our sires be tried —
They go to the heart, and the heart is all.

from:
IRISH MINSTRELSY (1831)

[This famous song was to be translated by Ferguson and, in a canonical form, by Mangan. Furlong published it in Hardiman's *Irish Minstrelsy.* It is included here as a point of comparison with the later translations. Roisin Dubh means Little Black Rose. Hardiman says that it 'is an allegorical ballad in which strong political feelings are conveyed as a personal address from a lover to his fair one. The allegorical meaning has been long since forgotten, and the verses are now remembered and sung as a plaintive love ditty. It was composed in the reign of Elizabeth of England to celebrate our Irish hero *Hugh Ruadh O'Donnell* of Tirconnell. By *Roisin Dubh,* supposed to be a beloved female, is meant Ireland.' Mangan was to restore the political meaning so emphatically that the song became a central one in the Irish nationalist repertoire and provided one of the most haunting themes in Seán Ó Riada's *Mise Eire* of 1966.]

Roisin Dubh

Oh! my sweet little rose, cease to pine for the past,
For the friends that came eastward shall see thee at last;
They bring blessings and favours the past never knew
To pour forth in gladness on my Roisin Dubh.

Long, long, with my dearest, through strange scenes I've gone,
O'er mountains and broad valleys I still have toiled on;
O'er the Erne I have sailed as the rough gales blew,
While the harp poured its music for my Roisin Dubh.

Though wearied, oh! my fair one! do not slight my song,
For my heart dearly loves thee, and hath loved thee long;
In sadness and in sorrow I still shall be true,
And cling with wild fondness round my Roisin Dubh.

There's no flower that e'er bloomed can my rose excel,
There's no tongue that e'er moved half my love can tell,
Had I strength, had I skill the wide world to subdue,
Oh! the queen of that wide world should be Roisin Dubh.

Had I power, oh! my loved one, but to plead thy right,
I should speak out in boldness for my heart's delight;
I would tell to all round me how my fondness grew,
And bid them bless the beauty of my Roisin Dubh.

The mountains, high and misty, through the moors must go,
The rivers shall run backward, and the lakes overflow,
And the wild waves of old ocean wear a crimson hue,
Ere the world sees the ruin of my Roisin Dubh.

WILLIAM MAGINN

(1794-1842)

from: THE O'DOHERTY PAPERS (1855)

[This poem was first published in *Blackwood's Magazine* (January 1822) and later was included in *The O'Doherty Papers.* Maginn and his friend Sylvester Mahony played various literary games in several languages. One of Maginn's pen-names was 'Pandemus Polyglot'. This is one of the best-known examples of a humorous aspect of the translation problem.]

The Wine-Bibber's Glory: A New Song

Tune — 'The Jolly Miller.'

Quo me Bacche rapis tui plenum? — HOR.[1]

If Horatius Flaccus made jolly old Bacchus
So often his favourite theme;
If in him it was classic to praise his old Massic
And Falernian[2] to gulp in a stream;
If Falstaff's vagaries 'bout Sack and Canaries[3]
Have pleased us again and again;
Shall we not make merry on Port, Claret, or Sherry,
Madeira, and sparkling Champagne?

First Port, that potation preferred by our nation
To all the small drink of the French;
'Tis the best standing liquor for layman or vicar,
The army, the navy, the bench;
'Tis strong and substantial, believe me, no man shall
Good Port from my dining-room send;
In your soup — after cheese — every way it will please,
But most, tête-à-tête with a friend.

Fair Sherry, Port's sister, for years they dismissed her
To the kitchen to flavour the jellies —
There long she was banish'd, and well nigh had vanished

1. 'Where are you taking me, Bacchus, full of wine?' Horace, *Odes* XXV, 3, line 1.
2. Italian wines mentioned in Horace.
3. Shakespeare's Falstaff praised the virtues of sack (sherry) and Canaries (Spanish wine).

Toporis Gloria: A Latin Melody

To a tune for itself, lately discovered in Herculaneum — being an ancient Roman air — or, if not, quite as good.

Cum jollificatione boisterosâ, *i.e.* with boisterous jollification.

Si Horatio Flacco de hilari Baccho
Mos carmina esset cantare,
Si Massica vina vocaret divina,
Falernaque sciret potare;
Si nos juvat mirè Falstaffium audire
Laudentum Hispanicum merum,
Cor nostrum sit lætum, ob Portum Claretum,
Xerense, Campanum, Maderum.

Est Portum potatio quam Anglica natio
Vinis Galliæ prætulit lautis: —
Sacerdote amatur — et laicis potatur
Consultis, militibus, nautis.
Si meum conclave hoc forte et suave
Vitaverit, essem iniquus,
Post caseum — in jure — placebit secure
Præsertim cum adsit amicus.

Huic quamvis cognatum, Xerense damnatum,
Gelatâ culinâ tingebat,
Vinum exul ibique dum coquo cuique
Generosum liquorem præbebat.

To comfort the kitchen maids' bellies;
Till his Majesty fixt, he thought Sherry when sixty
Years old like himself quite the thing;
So I think it but proper, to fill a tip-topper
Of Sherry to drink to the king.

Sed a rege probatum est valdè pergratum
Cum (ut ipse) sexagenarium —
Largè ergo implendum, regique bibendum
Opinor est nunc necessarium.

Though your delicate Claret, by no means goes far, it
Is famed for its exquisite flavour;
'Tis a nice provocation to *wise* conversation,
Queer blarney, or harmless palaver;
'Tis the bond of society — no inebriety
Follows a swig of the Blue;
One may drink a whole ocean, but ne'er feel commotion
Or headache from Chateau Margoux.

Claretum, oh! quamvis haud forte (deest nam vis)
Divina sapore notatur;
Hinc dulcia dicuntur — faceta nascuntur —
Leniterque philiosophizatur.
Socialis potatio! te haud fregit ratio
Purpureo decoram colore!
Tui maximum mare liceret potare
Sine mentis frontisvé dolore.

But though Claret is pleasant, to taste for the present
On the stomach it sometimes feels cold:
So to keep it all clever, and comfort your liver,
Take a glass of Madeira that's old;
When 't has sailed for the Indies, a cure for all wind 'tis,
And cholic 'twill put to the rout;
All doctors declare a good glass of Madeira
The best of all things for the gout.

Etsi vero in præsenti Claretum bibenti
Videatur imprimis jucundum.
Cito venter frigescat — quod ut statim decrescat
Vetum vinum Maderum adeundum.
Indos si navigârit, vento corpus levârit,
Coliccamque fugârit hoc merum;
Podagrâ cruciato 'Vinum optimum dato
Clamant medici docti Maderum.'

Then Champagne! dear Champagne! ah! how gladly I drain a
Whole bottle of Oeil de Perdrix;
To the eye of my charmer, to make my love warmer,
If cool that love ever could be.
I could toast her for ever — but never, oh, never
Would I her dear name so profane;
So, if e'er when I'm tipsy, it slips to my lips, I
Wash it back to my heart with Champagne!

Campanum! Campanum! quo gaudio lagenam
Ocelli Perdricis sorberem!
Ad dominæ oculum exhauriam poculum
Tali philtro si unquam egerem —
Propinarem divinam — sed peream si sinam
Nomen carum ut sic profanatur,
Et si cum Bacchus urget, ad labia surgit
Campano ad cor revoletur.

'Tis the Last Glass of Claret

[One of a short sequence called 'Moore-ish Melodies', this comic version of Thomas Moore's 'The Last Rose of Summer' was first published in the *Literary Gazette* of 1821. Maginn was as famous for his drinking as for his eccentric learning.]

'Tis the last glass of Claret,
Left sparkling alone,
All its rosy companions
Are *clean'd out* and gone.
No wine of her kindred,
No Red Port is nigh,
To reflect back her blushes
And gladden my eye.

I'll not leave thee, thou lone one,
This desert to crown:
As the bowls are all empty,
Thou too shalt float down.
Thus kindly I drink up
Each drop of pure red,
And fling the bright goblet
Clean over my head.

So soon may dame Fortune
Fling me o'er her head,
When I quit brimming glasses
And bundle to bed.

When Champaigne is exhausted,
And Burgundy's gone,
Who would leave even Claret
To perish alone.

JAMES (JEREMIAH) JOSEPH CALLANAN

(1795-1829)

from: THE POEMS OF J. J. CALLANAN (1847)

[Callanan is often said to have been one of the first translators from the Irish to have achieved something like a natural fluency in English. Both 'The Convict of Clonmel' and 'The Outlaw of Loch Lene' show a marked advance on anything Furlong could achieve.]

Dirge of O'Sullivan Bear

[Charles Gavan Duffy, in *The Ballad Poetry of Ireland* (1843), reproduces the note Callanan appended to the 'Dirge of O'Sullivan Bear'. Murty Oge (Young Murty) O'Sullivan of Berehaven in County Cork was an eighteenth-century soldier and recruiter of men for the continental Irish Brigade. He was informed on by a Mr Puxley whom, in return, he shot dead. The military surrounded O'Sullivan's well-fortified house and persuaded his servant Scully to wet the powder in O'Sullivan's guns. O'Sullivan was fatally wounded while trying to escape. His body was tied to a boat and dragged through the sea from Berehaven to Cork (Murty, Muircheartach in Irish, means 'expert at sea'). There his head was cut off and fixed on the county jail, where it remained for several years. The dirge for him, translated by Callanan, was said to have been composed by his nurse. In another version, O'Sullivan had just returned from the battle of Fontenoy (1745) in which the Irish brigade had broken the English defences. Puxley was a military officer who burned down O'Sullivan's house and murdered his father-in-law.]

The sun upon Ivera
  No longer shines brightly;
The voice of her music
  No longer is sprightly;
No more to her maidens
  The light dance is dear,
Since the death of our darling,
  O'SULLIVAN Bear.

SCULLY! thou false one,
  You basely betray'd him;
In his strong hour of need
  When thy right hand should aid him;
He fed thee; — he clad thee; —
  You had all could delight thee;
You left him; — you sold him; —
  May Heaven requite thee!

SCULLY! may all kinds
  Of evil attend thee;
On thy dark road of life
  May no kind one befriend thee;
May fevers long burn thee,
  And agues long freeze thee;
May the strong hand of God
  In his red anger seize thee.

Had he died calmly,
  I would not deplore him,
Or if the wild strife
  Of the sea-war closed o'er him;
But with ropes round his white limbs,
  Through ocean to trail him,
Like a fish after slaughter! —
  'Tis therefore I wail him.

Long may the curse
  Of his people pursue them;
SCULLY that sold him,
  And soldier that slew him,
One glimpse of Heaven's light
  May they see never;

May the hearth-stone of hell
  Be their best bed for ever!

In the hole which the vile hands
  Of soldiers had made thee,
Unhonoured, unshrouded,
  And headless they laid thee;
No sigh to regret thee,
  No eye to rain o'er thee,
No dirge to lament thee,
  No friend to deplore thee.

Dear head of my darling,
  How gory and pale,
These aged eyes saw thee
  High spiked on their gaol;
That cheek in the summer sun
  Ne'er shall grow warm,
Nor that eye e'er catch light,
  But the flash of the storm.

A curse, blessed ocean,
  Is on thy green water,
From the haven of Cork
  To Ivera of slaughter,
Since the billows were dyed
  With the red wounds of fear,
Of Muiertach Oge,
  Our O'SULLIVAN Bear.

The Convict of Clonmel
(from the Irish)

How hard is my fortune
  And vain my repining;
The strong rope of fate
  For this young neck is twining!
My strength is departed,
  My cheeks sunk and sallow,
While I languish in chains
  In the gaol of Clonmala.

No boy of the village
  Was ever yet milder;
I'd play with a child
  And my sport would be wilder;
I'd dance without tiring
  From morning 'till even,
And the goal-ball I'd strike
  To the light'ning of Heaven.

At my bed foot decaying
  My hurl-bat is lying;
Through the boys of the village
  My goal-ball is flying;
My horse 'mong the neighbours
  Neglected may fallow,
While I pine in my chains
  In the gaol of Clonmala.

Next Sunday the patron
  At home will be keeping,
And the young active hurlers
  The field will be sweeping;
With the dance of fair maidens
  The evening they'll hallow,
While this heart once so gay
  Shall be cold in Clonmala.

The Outlaw of Loch Lene
(from the Irish)

O many a day have I made good ale in the glen,
That came not of stream, or malt, like the brewing of men,
My bed was the ground, my roof, the greenwood above,
And the wealth that I sought — one far kind glance from my love.

Alas! on that night when the horses I drove from the field,
That I was not near from terror my angel to shield.
She stretched forth her arms, — her mantle she flung to the wind,
And swam o'er Loch Lene, her outlawed lover to find.

O would that a freezing sleet-winged tempest did sweep,
And I and my love were alone far off on the deep!
I'd ask not a ship, or a bark, or pinnace to save, —
With her hand round my waist, I'd fear not the wind or the wave.

'Tis down by the lake where the wild tree fringes its sides,
The maid of my heart, the fair one of Heaven resides —
I think as at eve she wanders its mazes along,
The birds go to sleep by the sweet wild twist of her song.

GERALD GRIFFIN
(1803-40)

from:
THE POETICAL WORKS
(1842-43)

[Although primarily a novelist, Griffin won some reputation as a poet. Of the two poems printed here, the song 'Aileen Aroon' is much the more famous. It has had many renderings into English, but Griffin's version remains the most popular. The Irish original is reprinted in Volume I, 'Literature in Irish 1600-1800', pp. 307-08.]

Ancient Lullaby

Darkness o'er the world is creeping,
Slumber while the heavens are weeping,
While the kerns[1] their watch are keeping,
And all eyes beside are sleeping.

Heaven's dark curtains now are closing,
The wild winds in peace reposing;
Now the harper old is prosing,
While his chieftain's eyes are dozing.

Heavy is the humming number;
Let the witch that scatters slumber,
In her passage halt and murmur,
Till her dews thy lids encumber.

Dull and dim the moon is gleaming,
Drowsy is the owlet's screaming,
Sullen sounds and gloomy seeming
Soon shall mingle in thy dreaming.

1. Foot soldiers in medieval Ireland.

Aileen Aroon

When like the early rose,
Aileen aroon!
Beauty in childhood blows,
Aileen aroon!
When like a diadem
Buds blush around the stem,
Which is the fairest gem?
Aileen aroon!

Is it the laughing eye?
Aileen aroon!
Is it the timid sigh?
Aileen aroon!
Is it the tender tone,
Soft as the string'd harp's moan?
Oh, it is truth alone,
Aileen aroon!

When, like the rising day,
Aileen aroon!
Love sends his early ray,
Aileen aroon!
What makes his dawning glow,
Changeless through joy or woe?
Only the constant know,
Aileen aroon!

I know a valley fair,
Aileen aroon!
I knew a cottage there,
Aileen aroon!
Far in that valley's shade
I knew a gentle maid,
Flower of the hazel glade,
Aileen aroon!

Who in the song so sweet?
Aileen aroon!
Who in the dance so neat?
Aileen aroon!
Dear were her charms to me,
Dearer her laughter free,
Dearest her constancy,
Aileen aroon!

Were she no longer true,
Aileen aroon!
What should her lover do?
Aileen aroon!
Fly with his broken chain
Far o'er the sounding main,
Never to love again,
Aileen aroon!

Youth must with time decay,
Aileen aroon!
Beauty must fade away,
Aileen aroon!
Castles are sacked in war,
Chieftains are scattered far,
Truth is a fixed star,
Aileen aroon!

JAMES CLARENCE MANGAN
(1803-49)

from:
THE COMET (1832)

To my Native Land

Awake! arise! shake off thy dreams!
  Thou art not what thou wert of yore:
Of all those rich, those dazzling beams,
  That once illum'd thine aspect o'er,
Show me a solitary one
Whose glory is not quenched and gone.

The harp remaineth where it fell,
  With mouldering frame and broken chord;
Around the song there hangs no spell —
  No laurel wreath entwines the sword;
And startlingly the footstep falls
Along thy dim and dreary halls.

When other men, in future years,
  In wonder ask, how this could be?
Then answer only by thy tears,
  That ruin fell on thine and thee,
Because thyself wouldst have it so —
Because thou welcomedst the blow!

To stamp dishonour on thy brow
  Was not within the power of earth;
And art thou agonised, when now
  The hour that lost thee all thy worth,
And turned thee to the thing thou art,
Rushes upon thy bleeding heart?

Weep, weep, degraded one — the deed,
  The desperate deed was all thine own:
Thou madest more than maniac speed
  To hurl thine honours from their throne.
Thine honours fell, and when they fell
The nations rang thy funeral knell.

Well may thy sons be seared in soul,
  Their groans be deep by night and day;
Till day and night forget to roll,
  Their noblest hopes shall mourn decay —
Their freshest flowers shall die by blight —
Their brightest suns shall set in night.

The stranger, as he treads thy sod,
  And views thy universal wreck,
May execrate the foot that trod
  Triumphant on a prostrate neck.
But what is that to thee? Thy woes
May hope in vain for pause or close.

Awake! arise! shake off thy dreams!
  'Tis idle all to talk of power,
And fame, and glory — these are themes
  Befitting ill so dark an hour;
Till miracles be wrought for thee,
Nor fame nor glory shalt thou see.

Thou art forsaken by the earth,
  Which makes a by-word of thy name —
Nations, and thrones, and powers, whose birth
  As yet is not, shall rise to fame,
Shall flourish, and may fall — but thou
Shalt linger as thou lingerest now.

And till all earthly power shall wane,
  And Time's grey pillars, groaning, fall;
Thus shall it be, and still in vain
  Thou shalt essay to burst the thrall
Which binds, in fetters forged by fate,
The wreck and ruin of WHAT ONCE WAS GREAT!

from:
THE VINDICATOR (1839)

A Despairing Sonnet

For once I dreamed that mutual love was more
Than a bright phantom-thought; and when mankind
Mocked mine illusion, then did I deplore
Their ignorance, and deem them cold and blind.
And years rolled on, and still I did adore
The unreal image loftily enshrined
In the recesses of mine own sick mind.
Enough; — the spell is broke — the dream is o'er,
The enchantment is dissolved — the world appears
The thing it is — a theatre — a mart.
Genius illumines, and the wand of art
Renews the wonders of our childhood's years;
Power awes, — wealth shines, — wit sparkles; — but the heart,
The heart is lost, for love no more endears.

from:
THE DUBLIN UNIVERSITY MAGAZINE (1840)

[Published in the sequence *Litterae Orientales, IV, Arabian, Persian and Turkish Poetry* in April 1840, this is not a translation at all, but an original creation by Mangan. The Barmecides were a princely family of Baghdad, one of whom put a succession of empty dishes before a beggar, pretending that they contained rich food. A Barmecide is, then, one who offers imaginary food or illusory benefits. Mangan adapts this story to his own purposes.]

The Time of the Barmecides

(From the Arabic)

My eyes are filmed, my beard is grey,
I am bowed with the weight of years;
I would I were stretched in my bed of clay,
With my long-lost youth's compeers:
For back to the Past, though the thought brings woe,
My memory ever glides —
To the old, old Time, long, long ago,
The Time of the Barmecides.
To the old, old time, long, long ago,
The Time of the Barmecides.

Then Youth was mine, and a fierce wild will,
And an iron arm in war,
And a fleet foot high upon ISHKAR's hill,
When the watch-lights glimmered afar,
And a barb as fiery as any I know,
That Khoord or Beddaween rides,
Ere my friends lay low — long, long ago,
In the Time of the Barmecides;
Ere my friends lay low — long, long ago,
In the Time of the Barmecides.

One golden djann† illumed my board,
One silver zhaun* was there;
At hand my tried Karamanian sword,
Lay always bright and bare,
For those were days when the angry blow
Supplanted the word that chides, —
When hearts could glow — long, long ago,
In the Time of the Barmecides;
When hearts could glow — long, long ago,
In the Time of the Barmecides.

Through city and desert my mates and I
Were free to rove and roam,
Our diapered canopy the deep of the sky,
Or the roof of the palace-dome —
O! ours was that vivid life to and fro
Which only Sloth derides: —
Men spent Life so, long, long ago,
In the Time of the Barmecides,
Men spent Life so, long, long ago,
In the Time of the Barmecides.

I see rich Bagdad once agen,
With its turrets of Moorish mould,
And the Khalif's twice five hundred men,
Whose binishes[1] flamed with gold;
I call up many a gorgeous show —
Which the Pall of Oblivion hides —
All passed like snow, long, long ago,
With the Time of the Barmecides;
All passed like snow, long, long ago,
With the Time of the Barmecides!

But mine eye is dim, and my beard is grey,
And I bend with the weight of years; —
May I soon go down to the House of Clay
Where slumber my Youth's compeers!

†goblet.
*dish.

1. Cavalry cloaks.

For with them and the Past, though the thought
wakes woe,
My memory ever abides;
And I mourn for the times gone long ago,
For the Times of the Barmecides!
I mourn for the Times gone long ago,
For the Times of the Barmecides!

from:
THE DUBLIN UNIVERSITY MAGAZINE (1844)

[First published in the fifth section of *Litterae Orientales*, this poem too is Mangan's own, not a translation. Mangan had shown interest in the Caramanian struggle against the Ottoman empire. The exile is kidnapped as a youth to become a soldier for those who tyrannize his own people.]

The Caramanian Exile

(From the Turkish)

I see thee ever in my dreams,
Karaman!
Thy hundred hills, thy thousand streams,
Karaman! O, Karaman!
As when thy gold-bright morning gleams,
As when the deepening sunset seams
With lines of light thy hills and streams,
Karaman!
So thou loomest on my dreams,
Karaman!
Nightly loomest on my dreams,
Karaman! O, Karaman!

The hot bright plains, the sun, the skies,
Karaman!
Seem deathblack marble to mine eyes,
Karaman! O, Karaman!
I turn from Summer's blooms and dyes;
Yet in my dreams Thou dost arise
In welcome glory to my eyes,
Karaman!
In thee my life of life yet lies,
Karaman!
Thou still art holy in mine eyes,
Karaman! O, Karaman!

Ere my fighting years were come,
Karaman!
Troops were few in Erzerome,
Karaman! O, Karaman!
Their fiercest came from Erzerome;
They came from Ukhbar's palace-dome;
They dragged me forth from thee, my home,
Karaman!
Thee, my own, my mountain-home,
Karaman!
In life and death, my spirit's home,
Karaman! O, Karaman!

O, none of all my sisters ten,
Karaman!
Loved like me my fellow-men,
Karaman! O, Karaman!
I was mild as milk till then,
I was soft as silk till then;
Now my breast is as a den,
Karaman!
Foul with blood and bones of men,
Karaman!
With blood and bones of slaughtered men,
Karaman! O, Karaman!

My boyhood's feelings, newly born,
Karaman!
Withered, like young flowers uptorn,
Karaman! O, Karaman!
And in their stead sprang weed and thorn:
What once I loved now moves my scorn;
My burning eyes are dried to horn,
Karaman!
I hate the blessèd light of morn,
Karaman!
It maddens me the face of Morn,
Karaman! O, Karaman!

The Spahi wears a tyrant's chains,
Karaman!
But bondage worse than this remains,
Karaman! O, Karaman!
His heart is black with million stains:
Thereon, as on Kaf's blasted plains,
Shall never more fall dews and rains,
Karaman!
Save poison-dews and bloody rains,
Karaman!
Hell's poison-dews and bloody rains,
Karaman! O, Karaman!

But Life at worst must end ere long,
Karaman!
Azreel[1] avengeth every wrong,
Karaman! O, Karaman!
Of late my thoughts rove more among
Thy fields; — o'ershadowing fancies throng
My mind, and texts of bodeful song,
Karaman!
Azreel is terrible and strong,
Karaman!
His lightning-sword smites all ere long,
Karaman! O, Karaman!

There's care tonight in Ukhbar's halls,
Karaman!
There's hope, too, for his trodden thralls,
Karaman! O, Karaman!
What lights flash red along yon walls?
Hark! hark! — the muster-trumpet calls! —
I see the sheen of spears and shawls,
Karaman!
The foe! the foe! — they scale the walls,
Karaman!
Tonight Murád or Ukhbar falls,
Karaman! O, Karaman!

1. The angel of death.

from:
THE IRISH MONTHLY MAGAZINE (1845)

[This is a translation or adaptation from the German orientalist and poet Friedrich Rückert (1788-1866), one of a number gathered together under the title *Loose leaves from an Odd Volume.*]

The Night is Falling

The night is falling in chill December,
The frost is mantling the silent stream,
Dark mists are shrouding the mountain's brow;
My soul is weary: I now
Remember
The days of roses but as a dream.

The icy hand of the Old Benumber,
The hand of Winter, is on my brain;
I try to smile, while I inly grieve;
I dare not hope or believe
That Summer
Will ever brighten the earth again.

So, gazing gravewards, albeit immortal,
Man cannot pierce through the girdling Night
That sunders Time from Eternity,
Nor feel this Death-vale to be
The portal
To realms of Glory and Living Light.

from:
THE NATION (30 May 1846)

[The source that Mangan used for *Roisin Dubh* (1849) and *Dark Rosaleen* (1846) was probably Hardiman's *Irish Minstrelsy* (1831) and Sir Samuel Ferguson's review of it in *The Dublin University Magazine*, where Ferguson gave a literal translation of the original, by a Father Costello of County Clare. Mangan wrote two poems entitled *Roisin Dubh* (Little Black Rose), but it is in *Dark Rosaleen*, the most famous version, that he fuses two readings of the original. Hardiman claimed that the poem was an allegory of a man's love for Ireland; Ferguson countered that it was a poem by a priest for his beloved. Mangan gradually brings the elements of the love poem and the patriotic ballad together to give the definitive version. It is believed that *Roisin Dubh*, although published later, was written earlier. See also the version by Thomas Furlong, p. 17 above.]

Dark Rosaleen

O, my Dark Rosaleen,
Do not sigh, do not weep!
The priests are on the ocean green,
They march along the Deep.
There's wine . . . from the royal Pope
Upon the ocean green;
And Spanish ale shall give you hope,
My Dark Rosaleen!
My own Rosaleen!
Shall glad your heart, shall give you hope,
Shall give you health, and help, and hope,
My Dark Rosaleen.

Over hills, and through dales,
Have I roamed for your sake;
All yesterday I sailed with sails
On river and on lake.

The Erne, ... at its highest flood,
  I dashed across unseen,
For there was lightning in my blood,
  My Dark Rosaleen!
  My own Rosaleen!
Oh! there was lightning in my blood,
Red lightning lightened through my blood,
  My Dark Rosaleen!

All day long, in unrest,
  To and fro, do I move.
The very soul within my breast
  Is wasted for you, love!
The heart ... in my bosom faints
  To think of you, my Queen,
My life of life, my saint of saints,
  My Dark Rosaleen!
  My own Rosaleen!
To hear your sweet and sad complaints,
My life, my love, my saint of saints,
  My Dark Rosaleen!

Woe and pain, pain and woe,
  Are my lot, night and noon,
To see your bright face clouded so,
  Like to the mournful moon.
But yet ... will I rear your throne
  Again in golden sheen;
'Tis you shall reign, shall reign alone,
  My Dark Rosaleen!
  My own Rosaleen!
'Tis you shall have the golden throne,
'Tis you shall reign, and reign alone,
  My Dark Rosaleen!

Over dews, over sands
  Will I fly, for your weal:
Your holy delicate white hands
  Shall girdle me with steel.
At home ... in your emerald bowers,
  From morning's dawn till e'en,
You'll pray for me, my flower of flowers,
  My Dark Rosaleen!
  My fond Rosaleen!
You'll think of me through Daylight's hours,
My virgin flower, my flower of flowers,
  My Dark Rosaleen!

I could scale the blue air,
  I could plough the high hills,
Oh, I could kneel all night in prayer,
  To heal your many ills!

And one ... beamy smile from you
  Would float like light between
My toils and me, my own, my true,
  My Dark Rosaleen!
  My fond Rosaleen!
Would give me life and soul anew,
A second life, a soul anew,
  My Dark Rosaleen!

O! the Erne shall run red
  With redundance of blood,
The earth shall rock beneath our tread,
  And flames wrap hill and wood,
And gun-peal, and slogan cry,
  Wake many a glen serene,
Ere you shall fade, ere you shall die,
  My Dark Rosaleen!
  My own Rosaleen!
The Judgment Hour must first be nigh,
Ere you can fade, ere you can die,
  My Dark Rosaleen!

from:
THE POETS AND POETRY OF MUNSTER (1849)

Roisin Dubh (Black-Haired Fair Rose)

Since last night's star, afar, afar
  Heaven saw my speed,
I seem'd to fly o'er mountains high,
  On magic steed,
I dashed though Erne! the world may learn
  The cause from Love
For, light or sun shone on me none,
  But *Roisin Dubh*!

O, Roisin mine! droop not nor pine;
  Look not so dull!
The Pope from Rome hath sent thee home
  A pardon full;
The priests are near: O! never fear!
  From Heaven above
They come to thee — they come to free
  My *Roisin Dubh*!

Thee have I loved — for thee have roved
  O'er land and sea:

My heart was sore — it evermore
  Beat but for thee;
I could but weep — I could not sleep —
  I could not move;
For, night or day, I dreamt alway
  Of *Roisin Dubh*!

Through Munsters lands, by shores and strands,
  Far could I roam,
If I might get my loved one yet,
  And bring her home.
O, sweetest flower, that blooms in bower,
  Or dell, or grove,
Thou lovest me, and I love thee,
  My *Roisin Dubh*!

The sea shall burn, the earth shall mourn,
  The skies rain blood —
The world shall rise in dread surprise
  And warful mood —
And hill and lake in Eirè shake,
  And hawk turn dove —
Ere you shall pine, ere you decline,
  My *Roisin Dubh*!

from: SPECIMENS OF THE EARLY NATIVE POETRY OF IRELAND (1846)

[Eochaidh Ó hEodhasa (O'Hussey), one of the greatest of the bardic poets, had as his master Hugh Maguire, lord of Fermanagh and a leading opponent of the English in the Elizabethan wars. In the winter of 1600, Maguire accompanied Hugh O'Neill in the long march to Kinsale, where a Spanish fleet was to land troops. O'Hussey remained at home in Fermanagh, composing this lament for his chief. It is full of premonitions of the ultimate disaster that was to overtake the Irish forces at Kinsale. Maguire was killed outside Cork. In his review of Hardiman's *Irish Minstrelsy*, Samuel Ferguson translated part of the poem and praised O'Hussey's powers as a poet.

The Irish original is printed in Volume I, 'Literature in Irish 1600-1800', pp. 278-79.]

O'Hussey's Ode to the Maguire

Where is my Chief, my Master, this bleak night,
  mavrone?[1]

1. Irish, *mo bhrón* (my sorrow).

O, cold, cold, miserably cold is this bleak night for
  Hugh,
It's showery, arrowy, speary sleet pierceth one
  through and through,
Pierceth one to the very bone!

Rolls real thunder? Or, was that red livid light
Only a meteor? I scarce know; but through the
  midnight dim
The pitiless ice-wind streams. Except the hate that
  persecutes *him*,
Nothing hath crueller venomy might.

An awful, a tremendous night is this, me-seems!
The floodgates of the rivers of heaven, I think,
  have been burst wide —
Down from the overcharged clouds, like unto
  headlong ocean's tide,
Descends grey rain in roaring streams.

Though he were even a wolf ranging the round
  green woods,
Though he were even a pleasant salmon in the
  unchainable sea,
Though he were a wild mountain eagle, he could
  scarce bear, he,
This sharp sore sleet, these howling floods.

O, mournful is my soul this night for Hugh
  Maguire!
Darkly, as in a dream, he strays! Before him and
  behind,
Triumphs the tyrannous anger of the wounding
  wind,
The wounding wind, that burns as fire!

It is my bitter grief — it cuts me to the heart —
That in the country of Clan Darry this should be
  his fate!
O, woe is me, where is he? Wandering, houseless,
  desolate,
Alone, without or guide or chart!

Medreams I see just now his face, the strawberry-
  bright,
Uplifted to the blackened heavens, while the
  tempestuous winds
Blow fiercely over and round him, and the smiting
  sleet-shower blinds
The hero of Galang tonight!

Large, large affliction unto me and mine it is,
That one of his majestic bearing, his fair, stately form,
Should thus be tortured and o'erborne — that this unsparing storm
Should wreak its wrath on head like his!

That his great hand, so oft the avenger of the oppressed,
Should this chill, churlish night, perchance, be paralysed by frost,
While through some icicle-hung thicket — as one lorn and lost —
He walks and wanders without rest.

The tempest-driven torrent deluges the mead,
It overflows the low banks of the rivulets and ponds —
The lawns and pasture-grounds lie locked in icy bonds,
So that the cattle cannot feed.

The pale bright margins of the streams are seen by none.
Rushes and sweeps along the untameable flood on every side —
It penetrates and fills the cottagers' dwellings far and wide —
Water and land are blent in one.

Through some dark woods, 'mid bones of monsters, Hugh now strays,
As he confronts the storm with anguished heart, but manly brow —
Oh! what a sword-wound to that tender heart of his were now
A backward glance at peaceful days!

But other thoughts are his — thoughts that can still inspire
With joy and an onward-bounding hope the bosom of MacNee —
Thoughts of his warriors charging like bright billows of the sea,
Borne on the wind's wings, flashing fire!

And though frost glaze tonight the clear dew of his eyes,
And white ice-gauntlets glove his noble fine fair fingers o'er,
A warm dress is to him that lightning-garb he ever wore,
The lightning of the soul, not skies.

AVRAN[2]

Hugh marched forth to the fight — I grieved to see him so depart;
And lo! tonight he wanders frozen, rain-drenched, sad, betrayed —
But the memory of the limewhite mansions his right hand hath laid
In ashes warms the hero's heart!

2. Irish, *amhrán* (song). A final stanza that recapitulates the entire poem.

from: THE NATION (1846)

[Originally published in *The Nation* (11 July 1846), with an epigraph: '"Et moi, j'ai été aussi en Arcadie." — And I, I too have been a dreamer. — Inscription on a painting by Poussin.' In fact, in Poussin's famous painting, the inscription is in Latin, 'Et in Arcadia ego', and Mangan's French and English renderings of it identify the dreamer with death — death as the gateway to vision. There is no specific source for the poem.]

A Vision of Connaught in the Thirteenth Century

I walked entranced
Through a land of Morn;
The sun, with wondrous excess of light,
Shone down and glanced
Over seas of corn
And lustrous gardens aleft and right.
Even in the clime
Of resplendent Spain,
Beams no such sun upon such a land;
But it was the time,
'Twas in the reign,
Of Cáhal Mór of the Wine-red Hand.[1]

Anon stood nigh
By my side a man
Of princely aspect and port sublime.
Him queried I —
'O, my Lord and Khan,[2]

1. Mangan claims that Irish and Oriental poets agree in attributing aspects of weather and harvest to the qualities of the reigning monarch.
2. The Irish *ceann* means 'head' or chief, but Mangan uses the Oriental title 'as *really fancying* myself in one of the regions of Araby the Blest.'

What clime is this, and what golden time?'
When he — 'The clime
Is a clime to praise,
The clime is Erin's, the green and bland;
And it is the time,
These be the days,
Of Cáhal Mór of the Wine-red Hand!'

Then saw I thrones,
And circling fires,
And a Dome rose near me, as by a spell,
Whence flowed the tones
Of silver lyres,
And many voices in wreathèd swell;
And their thrilling chime
Fell on mine ears
As the heavenly hymn of an angel-band —
'It is now the time,
These be the years,
Of Cáhal Mór of the Wine-red Hand!'

I sought the hall,
And, behold! . . . a change
From light to darkness, from joy to woe!
King, nobles, all,
Looked aghast and strange;
The minstrel-group sate in dumbest show!
Had some great crime
Wrought this dread amaze,
This terror? None seemed to understand!
'Twas then the time,
We were in the days,
Of Cáhal Mór of the Wine-red Hand.

I again walked forth;
But lo! the sky
Showed fleckt with blood, and an alien sun
Glared from the north,
And there stood on high,
Amid his shorn beams, A SKELETON!
It was by the stream
Of the castled Maine,
One Autumn eve, in the Teuton's land,
That I dreamed this dream
Of the time and reign
Of Cáhal Mór of the Wine-red Hand!

[This Irish poem by John Collins (Seán Ó Coileáin) had already been translated by Thomas Furlong in Hardiman's *Irish Minstrelsy* and by Samuel Ferguson in his *Dublin University Magazine* review of Hardiman. Teach (or Tigh) Molaga, the House of St Molaga, a disciple of St David of Wales, was an early Christian foundation, later a Franciscan friary, which was burned 'with all the towne' by an English force in 1642. The name of the village of Timoleague in County Cork is an anglicized version of the monastic name. Mangan notes this in a footnote on the first publication of the poem in *The Nation* (8 August 1846), thereby obeying Thomas Davis's advice to look to the new Ordnance Survey maps of Ireland to identify the territories referred to in the Irish poems. Mangan worked for the Ordnance Survey, itself an enormous work of renaming, translation and anglicization.]

Lament Over the Ruins of the Abbey of Teach Molaga

I wandered forth at night alone,
Along the dreary, shingly, billow-beaten shore.
Sadness that night was in my bosom's core,
My soul and strength lay prone.

The thin wan moon, half overveiled
By clouds, shed her funéreal beams upon the scene;
While in low tones, with many a pause between,
The mournful night-wind wailed.

Musing of Life, and Death, and Fate,
I slowly paced along, heedless of aught around,
Till on the hill, now, alas! ruin-crowned,
Lo! the old Abbey-gate!

Dim in the pallid moonlight stood,
Crumbling to slow decay, the remnant of that pile
Within which dwelt so many saints erewhile
In loving brotherhood!

The memory of the men who slept
Under those desolate walls — the solitude —
the hour —
Mine own lorn mood of mind — all joined to
o'erpower
My spirit — and I wept!

In yonder Goshen[1] once — I thought —
Reigned Piety and Peace: Virtue and Truth were
there;

1. A region of ancient Egypt, granted to Jacob and his descendants by the kind of Egypt and inhabited by them until the Exodus (see Genesis 45.10).

With Charity and the blessed spirit of Prayer
  Was each fleet moment fraught!

  There, unity of Work and Will
Blent hundreds into one: no jealousies or jars
Troubled their placid lives: their fortunate stars
  Had triumphed o'er all Ill!

  There, knolled each morn and even
The Bell for Matin and Vesper: Mass was said
    or sung —
From the bright silver censer, as it swung,
  Rose balsamy clouds to Heaven.

  Through the round cloistered corridors
A many a midnight hour, bareheaded and unshod,
Walked the Grey Friars, beseeching from their God
  Peace for these western shores!

  The weary pilgrim, bowed by Age,
Oft found asylum there — found welcome, and
    found wine.
Oft rested in its halls the Paladine,
  The Poet and the Sage!

  Alas! alas! how dark the change!
Now round its mouldering walls, over its pillars low,
The grass grows rank, the yellow gowans[2] blow,
  Looking so sad and strange!

  Unsightly stones choke up its wells;
The owl hoots all night long under the altar-stairs;
The fox and badger make their darksome lairs
  In its deserted cells!

  Tempest and Time — the drifting sands —
The lightning and the rains — the seas that sweep
    around
These hills in winter-nights, have awfully crowned
  The work of impious hands!

  The sheltering, smooth-stoned massive wall —
The noble figured roof — the glossy marble piers —
The monumental shapes of elder years —
  Where are they? Vanished all!

  Rite, incense, chant, prayer, mass, have ceased —
All, all have ceased! Only the whitening bones half
    sunk
In the earth now tell that ever here dwelt monk,
  Friar, acolyte, or priest,

  Oh! woe, that Wrong should triumph thus!
Woe that the olden right, the rule and the renown
Of the Pure-souled and Meek should thus go down
  Before the Tyrannous!

  Where wert thou, Justice, in that hour?
Where was thy smiting sword? What had those
    good men done,
That thou shouldst tamely see them trampled on
  By brutal England's Power?

  Alas! I rave! ... If Change is here,
Is it not o'er the land? Is it not too in me?
Yes! I am changed even more than what I see.
  Now is my last goal near!

  My worn limbs fail — my blood moves cold —
Dimness is on mine eyes — I have seen my children
    die —
They lie where I too in brief space shall lie —
  Under the grassy mould!

§ § §

  I turned away, as toward my grave,
And, all my dark way homeward by the Atlantic's
    verge,
Resounded in mine ears like to a dirge
  The roaring of the wave.

2. Field flowers, probably daisies.

[The poem below creates three landscapes — Siberia, Ireland in the midst of the Famine, and Mangan's own inner desolation.]

Siberia

In Siberia's wastes
  The Ice-wind's breath
Woundeth like the toothèd steel.
Lost Siberia doth reveal
  Only blight and death.

Blight and death alone.
  No Summer shines.
Night is interblent with Day.
In Siberia's wastes alway
  The blood blackens, the heart pines.

In Siberia's wastes
  No tears are shed,
For they freeze within the brain.
Nought is felt but dullest pain,
  Pain acute, yet dead;

Pain as in a dream,
  When years go by
Funeral-paced, yet fugitive,
When man lives, and doth not live,
  Doth not live — nor die.

In Siberia's wastes
  Are sands and rocks.
Nothing blooms of green or soft,
But the snowpeaks rise aloft
  And the gaunt ice-blocks.

And the exile there
  Is one with those;
They are part, and he is part,
For the sands are in his heart,
  And the killing snows.

Therefore, in those wastes
  None curse the Czar.
Each man's tongue is cloven by
The North Blast, who heweth nigh
  With sharp scymitar.

And such doom each drees,[1]
  Till, hunger-gnawn,
And cold-slain, he at length sinks there,
Yet scarce more a corpse than ere
  His last breath was drawn.

1. endures.

['The Warning Voice' appeared as the Famine intensified in 1846. An epigraph from Balzac translates: 'It seems to me we are on the eve of a great battle. The armies are there, but I see no general.']

The Warning Voice

Ye Faithful! — ye noble!
  A day is at hand
Of trial and trouble,
  And woe in the land!
O'er a once greenest path,
  Now blasted and sterile,
    Its dusk shadows loom —
It cometh with Wrath,
  With Conflict and Peril,
    With Judgment and Doom!

False bands shall be broken,
  Dead systems shall crumble,
    And the haughty shall hear
Truths yet never spoken,
  Though smouldering like flame
    Through many a lost year
In the hearts of the Humble;
For, hope will expire
As the Terror draws nigher,
    And, with it, the Shame
Which so long overawed
  Men's minds by its might —
And the Powers abroad
  Will be Panic and Blight,
And phrenetic Sorrow —
  Black Pest all the night,
And Death on the morrow!

Now, therefore, ye True,
Gird your loins up anew!
By the good you have wrought!
By all you have thought,
  And suffered, and done!
    By your souls! I implore you,
      Be leal to your mission —
  Remembering that *one*
    Of the *two* paths before you
      Slopes down to Perdition!
To you have been given,
  Not granaries and gold,
But the Love that lives long,
  And waxes not cold;
And the Zeal that has striven
  Against Error and Wrong,
And in fragments hath riven
  The chains of the Strong!
Bide now, by your sternest
Conceptions of earnest
Endurance for others,
Your weaker-souled brothers!
Your true faith and worth
  Will be History soon,
And their stature stand forth
  In the unsparing Noon!

You have dreamed of an era
  Of Knowledge, and Truth,
    And Peace — the *true* glory!
Was this a chimera?
  Not so! — but the childhood and youth
    Of our days will grow hoary,
Before such a marvel shall burst on their sight!
  On *you* its beams glow not —
  For *you* its flowers blow not,
You cannot rejoice in its light,
  But in darkness and suffering instead,
  You go down to the place of the Dead!
  To *this* generation
  The sore tribulation,
  The stormy commotion,
  And foam of the Popular Ocean,
    The struggle of class against class;
  The Dearth and the Sadness,
    The Sword and the War-vest;
  To the *next*, the Repose and the Gladness,
      'The Sea of clear glass,'
    And the rich Golden Harvest!

Know, then, your true lot,
  Ye faithful, though Few!
    Understand your position,
    Remember your mission,
And vacillate not,
  Whatsoever ensue!
Alter not! Falter not!
    Palter[1] not now with your own living souls,
    When each moment that rolls
  May see Death lay his hand
On some new victim's brow!
Oh! let not your vow
  Have been written in sand!
  Leave cold calculations,
  Of Danger and Plague,
To the slaves and the traitors
Who cannot dissemble
  The dastard sensations
That now make them tremble
  With phantasies vague! —
The men without ruth —
  The hypocrite haters
Of Goodness and Truth,
Who at heart curse the race
  Of the sun through the skies;

1. haggle, prevaricate.

And would look in God's face
  With a lie in their eyes!
To the last do your duty,
  Still mindful of this —
That Virtue is Beauty,
  And Wisdom, and Bliss;
So, howe'er, as frail men, you have erred on
  Your way along Life's throngèd road,
Shall your consciences prove a sure guerdon[2]
    And tower of defence,
    Until Destiny summon you hence
  To the Better Abode!

2. reward.

[This is said to be a translation from the Irish of Peadar Ó Doirnín (1682-1768). In *Essays in Prose and Verse* (Dublin, 1906), Mangan's editor, C. P. Meehan, cites this comment of Mangan's: 'The following song which I have translated from the Irish of O'Doran, refers to a singular *atmospherical* phenomenon said to be observed sometimes at Blackrock, near Dundalk, at daybreak, by the fishermen of that locality. Many similar narratives are to be met with in the poetry of almost all countries; but O'Doran has endeavoured to give the legend a political colouring, of which, I apprehend, readers in general will hardly deem it susceptible.' A brief inspection of the Irish original shows that Mangan has adopted nothing more than the title and the first line. Edward Walsh has a faithful translation in *Irish Popular Songs* (1847).]

The Dawning of the Day

'Maidin chiuin dham cois bruach na traga'

'Twas a balmy summer morning,
    Warm and early,
  Such as only June bestows;
Everywhere the earth adorning
    Dews lay pearly
  In the lily-bell and rose.
Up from each green-leafy bosk and hollow
  Rose the blackbird's pleasant lay,
And the soft cuckoo was sure to follow.
  'Twas the Dawning of the Day!

Through the perfumed air the golden
    Bees flew round me;
  Bright fish dazzled from the sea,
'Till medreamt some fairy olden-
    Worldspell bound me
  In a trance of witcherie.

Steeds pranced round anon with stateliest housings,
  Bearing riders prankt[1] in rich array,
Like flushed revellers after wine-carousings —
  'Twas the Dawning of the Day!

Then a strain of song was chanted,
    And the lightly-
  Floating sea-nymphs drew anear.
Then again the shore seemed haunted
    By hosts brightly
  Clad, and wielding shield and spear!
Then came battle-shouts — and onward rushing —
  Swords, and chariots, and a phantom-fray.
Then all vanish'd; the warm skies were blushing
  In the Dawning of the Day!

Cities girt with glorious gardens,
    Whose immortal
  Habitants in robes of light
Stood, methought, as angel-wardens
    Nigh each portal,
  Now arose to daze my sight.
Eden spread around, revived and blooming;
  When . . . lo! as I gazed, all passed away —
. . . I saw but black rocks and billows looming
  In the dim chill Dawn of Day!

1. bedecked.

from:
THE POETS AND POETRY OF MUNSTER (1849)

[This is a typical adaptation by Mangan of the conventional *aisling* poem of eighteenth-century Ireland, of which Aogán Ó Rathaille (Egan O'Rahilly, *c.*1670-1726) was the foremost practitioner.

The Geraldines were an old Irish family, dispossessed after the Williamite wars, as were all the families mentioned here. It was standard practice to claim for such families descent from the Milesians, the first inhabitants of Ireland, themselves supposed to have a Phoenician or Middle-Eastern origin. The girl celebrated here has both beauty and noble ancestry. She is easily seen as a figure representing Ireland. More than most, O'Rahilly was able to give his love poems a political resonance.]

The Geraldine's Daughter

Epigraph: By EGAN O'RAHILLY
Air: 'Sea and Shore'

A Beauty all stainless, a pearl of a maiden,
  Has plunged me in trouble, and wounded my
    heart.
With sorrow and gloom are my soul overladen;
  An anguish is there, that will never depart.
I could voyage to Egypt across the deep water,
  Nor care about bidding dear Eire farewell,
So I only might gaze on the Geraldine's Daughter,
  And sit by her side in some green, pleasant dell.

Her curling locks wave round her figure of lightness,
  All dazzling and long, like the purest of gold;
Her blue eyes resemble twin stars in their brightness,
  And her brow is like marble or wax to behold!
The radiance of Heaven illumines her features,
  Where the Snows and the Rose have erected their
    throne;
It would seem that the sun had forgotten all
    creatures
  To shine on the Geraldine's daughter alone!

Her bosom is swan-white, her waist smooth and
    slender,
  Her speech is like music, so sweet and so free;
The feelings that glow in her noble heart lend her
  A mien and a majesty lovely to see.
Her lips, red as berries, but riper than any,
  Would kiss away even a sorrow like mine.
No wonder such heroes and noblemen many
  Should cross the blue ocean to kneel at her shrine!

She is sprung from the Geraldine race — the
    great Grecians,
  Niece of Mileadh's sons of the Valorous Bands,
Those heroes, the sons of the olden Phenicians,
  Though now trodden down, without fame,
    without lands!
Of her ancestors flourished the Barrys and Powers,
  To the Lords of Bunratty she, too, is allied;
And not a proud noble near Cashel's high towers
  But is kin to this maiden — the Geraldine's Pride!

Of Saxon or Gael there are none to excel in
  Her wisdom, her features, her figure, this fair;
In all she surpasses the far-famous Helen,
  Whose beauty drove thousands to death and
    despair.
Whoe'er could but gaze on her aspect so noble
  Would feel from thenceforward all anguish
    depart,
Yet for me 'tis, alas! my worst woe and my trouble,
  That her image must always abide in my heart!

from:
THE IRISHMAN (1849)

[In this poem Mangan attributes his wretchedness to alcoholism. It is an important poem in the canon, for it establishes the notion of his obscurity and misery and, even while attributing it to drink, mystifies it. There is some deeper woe, of which alcoholism is the symptom.]

The Nameless One

Roll forth, my song, like the rushing river
That sweeps along to the mighty sea;
GOD will inspire me while I deliver
My soul of thee!

Tell thou the world, when my bones lie whitening
Amid the last homes of youth and eld,[1]
That there was once one whose veins ran lightning
No eye beheld.

Tell how his boyhood was one drear night-hour,
How shone for *him*, through his griefs and gloom,
No star of all Heaven sends to light our
Path to the tomb.

Roll on, my song, and to after ages
Tell how, disdaining all earth can give,
He would have taught Men, from Wisdom's pages,
The way to live.

And tell how, trampled, derided, hated,
And worn by Weakness, Disease, and Wrong,
He fled for shelter to GOD, who mated
His soul with song —

With song which alway, sublime or vapid,
Flowed like a rill in the morning-beam,
Perchance not deep, but intense and rapid —
A mountain-stream.

Tell how this Nameless, condemned for years long
To herd with demons from Hell beneath,
Saw things that made him, with groans and tears, long
For even Death.

1. old age.

Go on to tell how, with genius wasted,
Betrayed in Friendship, befooled in Love,
With spirit shipwrecked, and young hopes blasted,
He still, still strove —

Till, spent with Toil, dreeing[2] Death for others,
And some whose hands should have wrought for *him*
(If children live not for sires and mothers),
His mind grew dim;

And he fell far through that pit abysmal,
The gulf and grave of Maginn and Burns,[3]
And pawned his soul for the Devil's dismal
Stock of returns —

But yet redeemed it in days of darkness,
And shapes and signs of the Final Wrath,
When Death, in hideous and ghastly starkness,
Stood on his path.

And tell how now, amid Wreck and Sorrow,
And Want, and Sickness, and houseless nights,
He bides in calmness the Silent Morrow
That no ray lights.

And lives he still, then? Yes! Old and hoary
At thirty-nine, from Despair and Woe,
He lives, enduring what future Story
Will never know.

Him grant a grave to, ye pitying Noble,
Deep in your bosoms! There let him dwell!
He, too, had tears for all souls in trouble,
Here and in Hell.

2. enduring.
3. William Maginn and Robert Burns were both victims of alcoholism.

from:
THE POETS AND POETRY OF MUNSTER (1849)

[This is a very free adaptation of Donogh Mac Conmara's original. Sir Samuel Ferguson gave another version in his review of Hardiman's *Minstrelsy*, where he envisages the poem as representing 'a green spot of neutral ground where all parties may meet in kindness, and depart in peace.' Mangan, typically, transforms this reading of the poem into a lament for the desolated and beloved place. John O'Daly, who identifies the air for this song as *Uileachan Dubh*, dates the melody in the early seventeenth century and explains the meaning of *Uileachan Dubh* as 'a black-haired head of a round shape or form'. He mentions that some think the phrase 'allegorically means Ireland', but says it is evidently a love expression, 'of which the political coloration has entirely faded from the minds of the people'.]

The Fair Hills of Eire O!

Take a blessing from my heart to the land of my birth,
And the fair Hills of Eire, O!
And to all that yet survive of Eibhear's[1] tribe on earth,
On the fair Hills of Eire, O!
In that land so delightful the wild thrush's lay
Seems to pour a lament forth for Eirè's decay —
Alas! alas! why pine I a thousand miles away
From the fair Hills of Eire, O!

The soil is rich and soft — the air is mild and bland,
O the fair Hills of Eire, O!
Her barest rock is greener to me than this rude land;
O the fair Hills of Eire, O!
Her woods are tall and straight, grove rising over grove;
Trees flourish in her glens below, and on her heights above;
O! in heart and in soul, I shall ever, ever love
The fair Hills of Eire, O!

A noble tribe, moreover, are the now hapless Gael,
On the fair Hills of Eire, O!
A tribe in Battle's hour unused to shrink or fail,
On the fair Hills of Eire, O!
For this is my lament in bitterness outpoured,
To see them slain or scattered by the Saxon sword.
Oh, woe of woes to see a foreign spoiler horde,
On the fair Hills of Eire, O!

Broad and tall rise the *Cruachs*[2] in the golden morning's glow
On the fair Hills of Eire, O!
O'er her smooth grass for ever sweet cream and honey flow
On the fair Hills of Eire, O!
O, I long, I am pining, again to behold
The land that belongs to the brave Gael of old;
Far dearer to my heart than a gift of gems or gold
Are the fair Hills of Eire, O!

The dewdrops lie bright 'mid the grass and yellow corn
On the fair Hills of Eire, O!
The sweet-scented apples blush redly in the morn
On the fair Hills of Eire, O!
The water-cress and sorrel fill the vales below;
The streamlets are hushed, till the evening breezes blow;
While the waves of the Suir, noble river! ever flow
'Near the fair Hills of Eire, O!

A fruitful clime is Eire's, through valley, meadow, plain,
And the fair land of Eire, O!
The very 'Bread of life' is in the yellow grain
On the fair Hills of Eire, O!
Far dearer unto me than the tones music yields,
Is the lowing of the kine and the calves in her fields,
And the sunlight that shone long ago on the shields
Of the Gaels, on the fair hills of Eire, O!

1. Eibhear is a poetic name for the parent of the Gaels.
2. Either mountains or cairns on top of a mountain.

from: DUBLIN UNIVERSITY MAGAZINE (1840)

Twenty Golden Years Ago

O, the rain, the weary, dreary rain,
How it plashes on the window-sill!
Night, I guess too, must be on the wane,
Strass and Gass[1] around are grown so still.
Here I sit, with coffee in my cup —
Ah! 'twas rarely I beheld it flow
In the taverns where I loved to sup
Twenty golden years ago!

Twenty years ago, alas! — but stay —
On my life 'tis half-past twelve o'clock!
After all, the hours *do* slip away —
Come, here goes to burn another block!
For the night, or morn, is wet and cold,
And my fire is dwindling rather low:—
I had fire enough, when young and bold,
Twenty golden years ago!

1. Street and lane.

Dear! I don't feel well at all, somehow:
  Few in Weimar dream how bad I am;
Floods of tears grow common with me now,
  High-Dutch floods, that Reason cannot dam.
Doctors think I'll neither live nor thrive
  If I mope at home so — I don't know —
Am I living *now*? I *was* alive
    Twenty golden years ago.

Wifeless, friendless, flagonless, alone,
  Not quite bookless, though, unless I chuse,
Left with nought to do, except to groan,
  Not a soul to woo, except the Muse —
O! this, this is hard for *me* to bear,
  Me, who whilome[2] lived so much *en haut*,
Me, who broke all hearts like chinaware
    Twenty golden years ago!

P'rhaps 'tis better; — Time's defacing waves
  Long have quenched the radiance of my brow —
They who curse me nightly from their graves
  Scarce could love me were they living now;
But my loneliness hath darker ills —
  Such dun-duns[3] as Conscience, Thought and Co.,
Awful Gorgons! worse than tailors' bills
    Twenty golden years ago!

Did I paint a fifth of what I feel,
  O, how plaintive you would ween I was!
But I won't, albeit I have a deal
  More to wail about than Kerner[4] has!
Kerner's tears are wept for withered flowers,
  Mine for withered hopes; my Scroll of Woe
Dates, alas! from Youth's deserted bowers,
    Twenty golden years ago!

Yet, may Deutschland's bardlings flourish long!
  Me, I tweak no beak among them; — hawks
Must not pounce on hawks; besides, in song
  I could once beat all of them by chalks.
Though you find me, as I near my goal,
  Sentimentalizing like Rousseau,
O! I had a grand Byronian soul
    Twenty golden years ago!

Tick-tick, tick-tick! — Not a sound save Time's,
  And the windgust, as it drives the rain —
Tortured torturer of reluctant rhymes,
  Go to bed, and rest thine aching brain!
Sleep! — no more the dupe of hopes or schemes;
  Soon thou sleepest where the thistles blow —
Curious anticlimax to thy dreams
  Twenty golden years ago!

2. once.
3. Dun meaning 'dull' and duns meaning 'those who pursue one for a debt'.
4. Andreas Justinus Kerner (1786-1862), a German poet whose melancholy Mangan much favoured.

from: THE NATION (1849)

[The subtitle of 'The Lovely Land' refers to an unspecified painting by the Irish artist Daniel Maclise (1806-70) of Cork, famous for his historical paintings, especially *The Marriage of Strongbow and Aoife* (1854). Maclise was interested in Irish antiquities and made a number of sketches of architectural remains, one of which may be the occasion of this poem.]

The Lovely Land

(On a Landscape, Painted by M******)

Glorious birth of Mind and Color,
  Gazing on thy radiant face
  The most lorn of Adam's race
Might forget all dolor!

What divinest light is beaming
  Over mountain, mead, and grove!
  That blue noontide sky above
Seems asleep and dreaming.

Rich Italia's wild-birds warble
  In the foliage of those trees,
  I can trace thee, Veronese,[1]
In these rocks of marble!

Yet no! Mark I not where quiver
  The sun's rays on yonder stream?
  Only a Poussin[2] could dream
Such a sun and river!

What bold imaging! Stony valley,
  And fair bower of eglantine!
  Here I see the black ravine,
There the lilied alley!

1. Paolo Veronese (*c.* 1528-88), Venetian painter, famous for his ceilings and frescoes.
2. Nicolas Poussin (1594-1665), French landscape painter.

This is some rare clime so olden,
  Peopled, not by men, but fays;[3]
  Some lone land of genii days,
Storyful and golden!

Oh, for magic power to wander
  One bright year through such a land!
  Might I even one hour stand
On the blest hills yonder!

But — what spy I? . . . O, by noonlight!
  'Tis the same! — the pillar-tower

3. fairies.

  I have oft passed thrice an hour,
Twilight, sunlight, moonlight!

Shame to me, my own, my sire-land,
  Not to know thy soil and skies!
  Shame, that through Maclise's eyes
I first see thee, IRELAND!

No! no land doth rank above thee
  Or for loveliness or worth!
  So shall I, from this day forth,
Ever sing and love thee!

FRANCIS SYLVESTER MAHONY

(1804-66)

from: THE RELIQUES OF FATHER PROUT . . . . (1836)

[Mahony is better known by his pseudonym, Father Prout. His miscellaneous collection of essays and poems, *The Reliques of Father Prout*, provides the setting for the poems presented here. Taken out of context, they lose some of the charm of his various invented personae and of the glee with which he turned several languages — English, French, Latin, Italian and Greek — to comic purposes. The 'Bells of Shandon' occurs in an essay called 'The Rogueries of Thomas Moore', in which Mahony-Prout invents sources in various languages from which he claimed Moore plagiarized. This is a novel turn to the question of translation. In effect, Moore is accused of translating from originals that were created after he had written. In this particular instance, Prout claims that the poem 'The Bells of Shandon', which he had written years before when he was a student at the Irish College in Rome, was stolen by Moore and republished as his own 'Evening Bells: A Petersburg Air': 'But any one can see that he only rings a few changes on my Roman ballad, cunningly shifting the scene as far north as he could, to avoid detection. He deserves richly to be sent on a hurdle to Siberia.']

The Bells of Shandon

'Sabbata pango,
Funera plango,
Solemnia clango'[1]
Inscrip. on an old Bell

With deep affection
And recollection
I often think of
  Those Shandon bells,
Whose sounds so wild would
In the days of childhood
Fling round my cradle
  Their magic spells.
On this I ponder
Where'er I wander,
And thus grow fonder
  Sweet Cork, of thee;
With thy bells of Shandon,
That sound so grand on
The pleasant waters
  Of the river Lee.

1. Bog Latin, which can be rendered:
'I record the Sabbath, I lament at funerals, I resound on solemn occasions.'

I've heard bells chiming
Full many a clime in,
Tolling sublime in
  Cathedral shrine,
While at a glib rate
Brass tongues would vibrate —
But all their music
  Spoke naught like thine;
For memory dwelling
On each proud swelling
Of the belfry knelling
  Its bold notes free,
Made the bells of Shandon
Sound far more grand on
The pleasant waters
  Of the river Lee.

I've heard bells tolling
Old 'Adrian's Mole' in,
Their thunder rolling
  From the Vatican,
And cymbals glorious
Swinging uproarious
In the gorgeous turrets
  Of Notre Dame;
But thy sounds were sweeter
Than the dome of Peter
Flings o'er the Tiber,
  Pealing solemnly; —
O! the bells of Shandon
Sound far more grand on
The pleasant waters
  Of the river Lee.

There's a bell in Moscow,
While on tower and kiosk, O!
In Saint Sophia
  The Turkman gets,
And loud in air
Calls men to prayer
From the tapering summit
  Of tall minarets.
Such empty phantom
I freely grant them;
But there is an anthem
  More dear to me, —
'Tis the bells of Shandon
That sound so grand on
The pleasant waters
  Of the river Lee.

The Attractions of a Fashionable Irish Watering-Place

The town of Passage[1]
Is both large and spacious,
And situated
  Upon the say.
'Tis nate and dacent
And quite adjacent
To come from Cork
  On a summer's day:
There you may slip in
To take a dipping,
Fornent the shipping
  That at anchor ride.
Or in a wherry[2]
Come o'er the ferry,
To Carrigaloe,
  On the other side.

Mud cabins swarm in
This place so charming,
With sailor garments
  Hung out to dry;
And each abode is
Snug and commodious.
With pigs melodious
  In their straw-built sty.
It's there the turf is,
And lots of murphies,
Dead sprats and herrings
  And oyster-shells;
Nor any lack, O!
Of good tobacco —
Though what is smuggled
  By far excels.

There are ships from Cadiz,
And from Barbadoes,
But the leading trade is
  In whisky-punch;
And you may go in
Where one Molly Bowen
Keeps a nate hotel
  For a quiet lunch.
But land or deck on,
You may safely reckon,
Whatever country

1. Passage and Carrigaloe are villages in County Cork.
2. A light rowing boat.

You came hither from,
On an invitation
To a jollification,
With a parish priest
That's called 'Father Tom.'

Of ships there's one fixed
For lodging convicts
A floating 'stone jug'
Of amazing bulk;
The hake and salmon,
Playing at backgammon,
Swim for divarsion
All round this 'hulk';
There 'Saxon' jailors
Keep brave repailors
Who soon with sailors
Must anchor weigh
From the em'rald island
Ne'er to see dry land
Until they spy land
In sweet Bot'ny Bay.

EDWARD WALSH
(1805-50)

from: RELIQUES OF JACOBITE POETRY (1844)

[This poem by Seaghan Claragh or John McDonnell of Cork (1691-*c.* 1750) is one of several by this poet, chosen by John O'Daly and translated by Walsh in the *Reliques.* The volume was originally published in several numbers of eight pages each, costing one penny, since O'Daly thought that Hardiman's *Irish Minstrelsy* had been out of reach of those 'for whom such a work should be intended ... the *Irish peasantry.*' Each of the songs or poems was given in Irish, then in interlinear literal translation, and finally in Walsh's 'metrical versions'. The first number was devoted to an introduction to the Irish language. This was, in itself, an admission that the language had receded to an alarming degree by 1844. The emphasis on Jacobite poetry was also significant. What O'Daly and Walsh were doing in this collection amounted to an attempt to revive the language and to associate it with a political project, the vaguely powerful wish to relieve Ireland of English rule through alliance with a foreign power.

The strength of the Munster literary tradition in Irish, asserted here, was to remain an important feature of the attempt to revive Irish, particularly in the development of the Gaelic League, founded in 1893, and in the later writings of Daniel Corkery, Frank O'Connor and others. (See T. Garvin, *Nationalist Revolutionaries in Ireland 1858-1928* (Oxford: Clarendon Press, 1987), pp. 91-102.)]

An Bonnaire Fiadha-Phuic (The Cruel Base-Born Tyrant)

(A Jacobite Relic)
Closely translated from the Irish

What withered the pride of my vigour?
The lowly-sprung tyrant train
That rule all our border with rigour,
And ravage the fruitful plain —
Yet once when the war-trumpet's rattle
Arous'd the wild clansman's wrath,
They, heartless, abandon'd the battle,
And fled the fierce foeman's path.

The loved ones my life would have nourish'd
Are foodless, and bare, and cold —
My flocks by their fountains that flourish'd,
Decay on the mountain wold —
Misfortune my temper is trying;
This raiment no shelter yields —
And chief o'er my evils undying,
The tyrant that rules my fields!

Alas! on the red hill where perish'd
The offspring of heroes proud,
The virtues our forefathers cherish'd,
Lie pall'd in their blood-stain'd shroud!

And O! for one hero avenger,
With aid o'er the heaving main,
To sweep from *Clar-Fodhla*[1] the stranger,
And sever his bondage chain!

1. One of the traditional poetic names for Ireland.

from: IRISH POPULAR SONGS (1847)

[In the *Introductory Remarks* to this volume, Walsh, like John O'Daly in the preface to the *Reliques*, laments the fading of Irish, blaming the hedge-schoolmasters, the village teachers and parents, especially those parents with no English who force their children to speak it, thereby creating ludicrous and tragic failures of communication. He praises Irish as being particularly suited to lyric poetry and objects to the efforts of Charlotte Brooke and James Hardiman, both of whom forced the words of the song from the tune with which it is naturally allied. Both O'Daly and Walsh praised Thomas Moore in this regard. His marriage of words and music seemed to them admirable. A second edition of this volume appeared in 1883, with a preface by one 'J.S.S.'. He resumes the lament over the dying language, saying that 'the march of intellect has only taught us to be ashamed of our nationality', deploring the effect on Irish music of the free supply of harmoniums by the Board of National Education and noting how it had become a mark of social status to leave Irish music and the Irish language behind. Arias from Italian operas rather than traditional songs were now 'echoing from the parlour of some comfortable shopkeeper of Killybegs or Westport ... and shopkeepers' daughters who had perforce to speak Irish in Berehaven, did not know a word of the language when they came to fashionable Cork.' Nevertheless, the wildness and recklessness of Owen Roe O'Sullivan is deprecated by his translator. Walsh assures his audience that nothing offensive was ever produced in Irish poetry — that is nothing that would offend a Victorian-catholic sensibility. This was not true, but is of a piece with the development of the notion that Irish represented tradition, purity, fidelity, and a whole combination of sterling values that the modern world had lost.]

Owen Roe O'Sullivan's Drinking Song

This cup's flowing measure
I toast to that treasure,
The brave man whose pleasure
   Is quaffing rich wine,
Who deep flagons draining,
From quarrels abstaining,
The morn finds remaining
   All joyous divine —
   It ne'er shall be mine
   To gather vile coin,
To clowns at life's waning,
   For aye to resign!

Some churls will come slinking
To practise cheap drinking,
Where the generous are linking
   New joys to the old —
Vile starveling! what matter
If curses should shatter
Your land-marks, and scatter
   To strangers your gold!
   When laid in the mould,
   All naked and cold,
Your dames thus may patter
   Your death-song, behold: —

'Let heroes strike under
At Paris, why wonder,
Or Jason, who plunder
   From dragons did rive?
The red-branched hero
May sink down to zero
And Caesar and Nero
   In vain with him strive.
   Let the rich herds arrive
   That in Munster survive,
And I'll yield them, my dear, oh!
   To clasp thee alive!

My soul! how grief's arrow
Hath fix'd in my marrow!
O'er that cold coffin narrow
   I'll weep evermore —
By the hand of my father
This moment I'd rather
From the grave thee to gather,
   Than gold's yellow store!
   All feasts I'll give o'er;
   I'm stricken and frore[1] —
Oh, grave at Kilmather
   Be my roof-tree and floor!

1. frozen.

'My bosom friends inner
Gather round your poor sinner;
My kerchief and pinner[2]
To pieces shall go.
In the Lee wildly springing,
I'll end this beginning,
His death-song still singing
Who valued me so' —
While round tears thus flow,
And wailing and woe,
To a youth near her clinging,
She beckons alow!

2. Either a pinafore or a cap with two long flaps pinned on.

[Charles Gavan Duffy, in *The Ballad Poetry of Ireland* (1845), provides the background to this poem: 'This ballad is founded on the story of Daniel O'Keefe, an outlaw famous in the traditions of the County of Cork, where his name is still associated with several localities. It is related that O'Keefe's beautiful mistress, Margaret Kelly, tempted by a large reward, undertook to deliver him into the hands of the English soldiers; but O'Keefe, having discovered in her possession a document revealing her perfidy, in a frenzy of indignation stabbed her to the heart with his *skian*. He lived in the time of William III, and is represented to have been a gentleman and a poet.']

Mairgread ní Chealleadh

At the dance in the village
Thy white foot was fleetest;
Thy voice 'mid the concert
Of maidens was sweetest;
The swell of thy white breast
Made rich lovers follow;
And thy raven hair bound them,
Young Mairgread ní Chealleadh.

Thy neck was, lost maid,
Than the *ceanabhan*[1] whiter;
And the glow of thy cheek
Than the *monadan*[2] brighter;
But death's chain hath bound thee,
Thine eyes glazed and hollow,
That shone like a sunburst,
Young Mairgread ní Chealleadh.

No more shall mine ear drink
Thy melody swelling;
Nor thy beamy eye brighten
The outlaw's dark dwelling;
Or thy soft heaving bosom
My destiny hallow,
When thine arms twine around me,
Young Mairgread ní Chealleadh.

The moss couch I brought thee
Today from the mountain,
Has drank the last drop
Of thy young heart's red fountain —
For this good *skian*[3] beside me
Struck deep and rung hollow
In thy bosom of treason,
Young Mairgread ní Chealleadh.

With strings of rich pearls
Thy white neck was laden,
And thy fingers with spoils
Of the Sassenach maiden;
Such rich silks enrob'd not
The proud dames of Mallow —
Such pure gold they wore not
As Mairgread ní Chealleadh.

Alas! that my loved one
Her outlaw would injure —
Alas! that he e'er proved
Her treason's avenger!
That this right hand should make thee
A bed cold and hollow,
When in Death's sleep it laid thee
Young Mairgread ní Chealleadh!

And while to this lone cave
My deep grief I'm venting,
The Saxon's keen bandog[4]
My footsteps is scenting;
But true men await me
Afar in Duhallow.[5]
Farewell, cave of slaughter,
And Mairgread ní Chealleadh.

1. bog-cotton.
2. A red berry, found on wild marshy mountains.

3. knife.
4. bloodhound.
5. A townland in County Cork.

Mo Craoibhin Cno

My heart is far from Liffey's tide
And Dublin town;
It strays beyond the southern side
Of Knockmealdown,

Where Cappoquin hath woodlands screen,
  Where Avonmore's waters flow,
Where dwells unsung, unsought, unseen,
  Mo craoibhin cno,[1]
Low clustering in her leafy green
  Mo craoibhin cno!

The high-bred dames of Dublin town
  Are rich and fair,
With wavy plume and silken gown,
  And stately air;
Can plumes compare thy dark brown hair?
  Can silks thy neck of snow?
Or measur'd pace thine artless grace,
  Mo craoibhin cno,
When harebells scarcely show thy trace,
  Mo craoibhin cno?

I've heard the songs by Liffey's wave
  That maidens sung —
They sung their land the Saxon's slave,
  In Saxon tongue —
Oh! bring me here that Gaelic dear
  Which cursed the Saxon foe,
When thou didst charm my raptured ear,
  Mo craoibhin cno!
And none but God's good angels near,
  Mo craoibhin cno!

I've wandered by the rolling Lee!
  And Lene's[2] green bowers —
I've seen the Shannon's wide-spread sea,
  And Limerick's towers —
And Liffey's tide, where halls of pride
  Frown o'er the flood below;
My wild heart strays to Avonmore's side,
  Mo craoibhin cno!
With love and thee for aye to bide,
  Mo craoibhin cno!

1. My little nut-tree branch.

2. Loch Lene in County Kerry.

SAMUEL FERGUSON
(1810-86)

from:
LAYS OF THE WESTERN GAEL (1867)

The Burial of King Cormac

Introductory Note

Cormac, son of Art, son of Con Cead-Catha,[1] enjoyed the sovereignty of Ireland through the prolonged period of forty years, commencing from A.D. 213. During the latter part of his reign, he resided at Sletty on the Boyne, being, it is said, disqualified for the occupation of Tara by the personal blemish he had sustained in the loss of an eye, by the hand of Angus 'Dread-Spear,' chief of the Desi, a tribe whose original seats were in the barony of Deece, in the county of Meath. It was in the time of Cormac and his son Carbre, if we are to credit the Irish annals, that Fin, son of Comhal, and the Fenian heroes, celebrated by Ossian, flourished. Cormac has obtained the reputation of wisdom and learning, and appears justly entitled to the honour of having provoked the enmity of the Pagan priesthood, by declaring his faith in a God not made by hands of men.

'Crom Cruach and his sub-gods twelve,'[2]
  Said Cormac, 'are but carven treene;[3]
The axe that made them, haft or helve,
  Had worthier of our worship been.

But he who made the tree to grow,
  And hid in earth the iron-stone,

1. Con or Conn of the hundred battles.

2. Crom Cruach was the god of winter and patron of agriculture who stood on May Slaught in County Cavan and was worshipped at Samhain, the Celtic New Year. The twelve sub-gods are held to represent the twelve months of the year.

3. trees.

And made the man with mind to know
  The axe's use, is God alone.'

Anon to priests of Crom was brought —
  Where, girded in their service dread,
They minister'd on red Moy Slaught —[4]
  Word of the words King Cormac said.

They loosed their curse against the king;
  They cursed him in his flesh and bones;
And daily in their mystic ring
  They turn'd the maledictive stones,[5]

Till, where at meat the monarch sate,
  Amid the revel and the wine,
He choked upon the food he ate,
  At Sletty, southward of the Boyne.

High vaunted then the priestly throng,
  And far and wide they noised abroad
With trump and loud liturgic song
  The praise of their avenging God.

But ere the voice was wholly spent
  That priest and prince should still obey,
To awed attendants o'er him bent
  Great Cormac gather'd breath to say, —

'Spread not the beds of Brugh for me[6]
  When restless death-bed's use is done:
But bury me at Rossnaree[7]
  And face me to the rising sun.

'For all the kings who lie in Brugh
  Put trust in gods of wood and stone;
And 'twas at Ross that first I knew
  One, Unseen, who is God alone.

4. Where the priests of Crom ministered.
5. Ferguson cites John O'Donovan's comment on the *clocha breca* or speckled stones of Cashel, Co. Tipperary: 'They are round stones of various sizes and arranged in such order as that they cannot easily be reckoned, and, if you believe the natives, they cannot be reckoned at all. These stones are turned, and ... their order changed by the inhabitants on certain occasions, when they visit this shrine to wish good or evil to their neighbours.'
6. Bruigh na Boinne, the supernatural dwelling of the pagan gods and cemetery of the Irish pagan kings. Brugh seems to have been situated on the north bank of the Boyne. In this area are to be found the great megalithic tombs of Newgrange and Dowth.
7. The Christian burial place of the Irish kings in County Cavan.

His glory lightens from the east;
  His message soon shall reach our shore;
And idol-god, and cursing priest
  Shall plague us from Moy Slaught no more.'

Dead Cormac on his bier they laid:—
  'He reign'd a king for forty years,
And shame it were,' his captains said,
  'He lay not with his royal peers.

His grandsire, Hundred-Battle, sleeps
  Serene in Brugh: and, all around,
Dead kings in stone sepulchral keeps
  Protect the sacred burial ground.

What though a dying man should rave
  Of changes o'er the eastern sea?
In Brugh of Boyne shall be his grave,
  And not in noteless Rossnaree.'

Then northward forth they bore the bier,
  And down from Sletty side they drew,
With horseman and with charioteer,
  To cross the fords of Boyne to Brugh.

There came a breath of finer air
  That touch'd the Boyne with ruffling wings,
It stirr'd him in his sedgy lair
  And in his mossy moorland springs.

And as the burial train came down
  With dirge and savage dolorous shows,
Across their pathway, broad and brown
  The deep, full-hearted river rose;

From bank to bank through all his fords,
  'Neath blackening squalls he swell'd and boil'd;
And thrice the wondering gentile lords
  Essay'd to cross, and thrice recoil'd.

Then forth stepp'd grey-hair'd warriors four:
  They said, 'Through angrier floods than these,
On link'd shields once our king we bore
  From Dread-Spear and the hosts of Deece.[8]

And long as loyal will holds good,
  And limbs respond with helpful thews,
Nor flood, nor fiend within the flood,
  Shall bar him of his burial dues.'

8. See Ferguson's introductory note to the poem (p. 43).

With slanted necks they stoop'd to lift;
  They heaved him up to neck and chin;
And, pair and pair, with footsteps swift,
  Lock'd arm and shoulder, bore him in.

'Twas brave to see them leave the shore;
  To mark the deep'ning surges rise,
And fall subdued in foam before
  The tension of their striding thighs.

'Twas brave, when now a spear-cast out,
  Breast-high the battling surges ran;
For weight was great, and limbs were stout,
  And loyal man put trust in man.

But ere they reach'd the middle deep,
  Nor steadying weight of clay they bore,
Nor strain of sinewy limbs could keep
  Their feet beneath the swerving four.

And now they slide and now they swim,
  And now, amid the blackening squall,
Grey locks afloat, with clutchings grim,
  They plunge around the floating pall.

While, as a youth with practised spear
  Through justling crowds bears off the ring,
Boyne from their shoulders caught the bier
  And proudly bore away the king.

At morning, on the grassy marge
  Of Rossnaree, the corpse was found,
And shepherds at their early charge
  Entomb'd it in the peaceful ground.

A tranquil spot: a hopeful sound
  Comes from the ever youthful stream,
And still on daisied mead and mound
  The dawn delays with tenderer beam.

Round Cormac Spring renews her buds:
  In march perpetual by his side,
Down come the earth-fresh April floods,
  And up the sea-fresh salmon glide;

And life and time rejoicing run
  From age to age their wonted way;
But still he waits the risen Sun,
  For still 'tis only dawning Day.

['Lament over the Ruins of the Abbey of Timoleague' is an important poem because of the background to its three translations — one by Thomas Furlong in Hardiman's *Irish Minstrelsy*, this one in Ferguson's review of Hardiman in *The Dublin University Magazine* and one by Mangan (see p. 30). Ferguson objects to Hardiman's emphasis on the guilt of the first protestant reformers for the destruction of the abbey. He attempts to characterize this as a sectarian animus, totally unnecessary after the passage of catholic emancipation in 1829. Even though he acknowledges that Hardiman had written his notes and commentary before 1829, Ferguson sees no reason for their being kept intact in the published version of 1831: 'He does not bate a jot of his most indignant obstinacy, he does not expunge an expression of his most inveterate and unchangeable hatred for Clan Luther, and the Saxon, but disfigures his book and disgraces himself by flinging in the teeth of his manumission, the whole miserly hoardings of his hatred when a slave.' Ferguson's rendering disguises the specific religious element in the destruction of the abbey and transmutes it into a version of the romantic ruin. Immediately thereafter, he gives a translation of 'The Fair Hills of Holy Ireland', citing this as an instance of that 'neutral ground' on which all Irish people might meet without animosity.]

Lament over the Ruins of the Abbey of Timoleague

JOHN COLLINS, died, 1816

Lone and weary as I wander'd
  By the bleak shore of the sea,
Meditating and reflecting
  On the world's hard destiny;

Forth the moon and stars 'gan glimmer,
  In the quiet tide beneath, —
For on slumbering spray and blossom
  Breathed not out of heaven a breath.

On I went in sad dejection,
  Careless where my footsteps bore,
Till a ruin'd church before me
  Open'd wide its ancient door, —

Till I stood before the portals,
  Where of old were wont to be,
For the blind, the halt, and leper,
  Alms and hospitality.

Still the ancient seat was standing,
Built against the buttress grey,
Where the clergy used to welcome
Weary travellers on their way.

There I sat me down in sadness,
'Neath my cheek I placed my hand,
Till the tears fell hot and briny
Down upon the grassy land.

There, I said in woeful sorrow,
Weeping bitterly the while,
Was a time when joy and gladness
Reign'd within this ruin'd pile; —

Was a time when bells were tinkling,
Clergy preaching peace abroad,
Psalms a-singing, music ringing
Praises to the mighty God.

Empty aisle, deserted chancel,
Tower tottering to your fall,
Many a storm since then has beaten
On the grey head of your wall!

Many a bitter storm and tempest
Has your roof-tree turn'd away,
Since you first were form'd a temple
To the Lord of night and day.

Holy house of ivied gables,
That wert once the country's pride,
Houseless now in weary wandering
Roam your inmates far and wide.

Lone you are today, and dismal, —
Joyful psalms no more are heard
Where, within your choir, her vesper
Screeches the cat-headed bird.

Ivy from your eaves is growing,
Nettles round your green hearth-stone,
Foxes howl, where, in your corners,
Dropping waters make their moan.

Where the lark to early matins
Used your clergy forth to call,
There, alas! no tongue is stirring,
Save the daw's[1] upon the wall.

1. i.e. jackdaw's.

Refectory cold and empty,
Dormitory bleak and bare,
Where are now your pious uses,
Simple bed and frugal fare?

Gone your abbot, rule and order,
Broken down your altar stones;
Nought see I beneath your shelter,
Save a heap of clayey bones.

Oh! the hardship, oh! the hatred,
Tyranny, and cruel war,
Persecution and oppression,
That have left you as you are!

I myself once also prosper'd; —
Mine is, too, an alter'd plight;
Trouble, care, and age have left me
Good for nought but grief tonight.

Gone, my motion and my vigour, —
Gone, the use of eye and ear;
At my feet lie friends and children,
Powerless and corrupting here:

Woe is written on my visage,
In a nut my heart would lie —
Death's deliverance were welcome —
Father, let the old man die.

Pastheen Finn

(Irish Rustic Song)

Oh, my fair Pastheen is my heart's delight,
Her gay heart laughs in her blue eye bright;
Like the apple blossom her bosom white,
And her neck like the swan's, on a March morn bright!
Then, Oro, come with me! come with me! come with me!
Oro, come with me! brown girl, sweet!
And, oh! I would go through snow and sleet,
If you would come with me, brown girl, sweet!

Love of my heart, my fair Pastheen!
Her cheeks are red as the rose's sheen,
But my lips have tasted no more, I ween,
Then the glass I drank to the health of my queen!
Then, Oro, come with me! come with me! come with me!
Oro, come with me! brown girl, sweet!

And, oh! I would go through snow and sleet,
If you would come with me, brown girl, sweet!

Were I in the town, where's mirth and glee,
Or 'twixt two barrels of barley bree[1],
With my fair Pastheen upon my knee,
'Tis I would drink to her pleasantly!
Then, Oro, come with me! come with me! come with me!
Oro, come with me! brown girl, sweet!
And, oh! I would go through snow and sleet,
If you would come with me, brown girl, sweet!

Nine nights I lay in longing and pain,
Betwixt two bushes, beneath the rain,
Thinking to see you, love, once again;
But whistle and call were all in vain!
Then, Oro, come with me! come with me! come with me!
Oro, come with me! brown girl, sweet!
And, oh! I would go through snow and sleet,
If you would come with me, brown girl, sweet!

I'll leave my people, both friend and foe;
From all the girls in the world I'll go;
But from you, sweetheart, oh, never! oh, no!
'Till I lie in the coffin, stretch'd cold and low!
Then, Oro, come with me! come with me! come with me!
Oro, come with me! brown girl, sweet!
And, oh! I would go through snow and sleet,
If you would come with me, brown girl, sweet!

1. malt whiskey.

Ceann Dubh Deelish[1]

(Irish Song)

Put your head, darling, darling, darling,
Your darling black head my heart above;
Oh, mouth of honey, with the thyme for fragrance,
Who, with heart in breast, could deny you love?
Oh, many and many a young girl for me is pining
Letting her locks of gold to the cold wind free,
For me, the foremost of our gay young fellows;
But I'd leave a hundred, pure love, for thee!
Then put your head, darling, darling, darling,
Your darling black head my heart above;
Oh, mouth of honey, with the thyme for fragrance,
Who, with heart in breast, could deny you love?

1. Dear dark head.

Cashel of Munster

(Irish Rustic Ballad)

I'd wed you without herds, without money, or rich array,
And I'd wed you on a dewy morning at day-dawn grey;
My bitter woe it is, love, that we are not far away
In Cashel town, though the bare deal board were our marriage-bed this day!

Oh, fair maid, remember the green hill side,
Remember how I hunted about the valleys wide;
Time now has worn me; my locks are turn'd to grey,
The year is scarce and I am poor, but send me not, love, away!

Oh, deem not my blood is of base strain, my girl,
Oh, deem not my birth was as the birth of the churl;
Marry me, and prove me, and say soon you will,
That noble blood is written on my rightside still!

My purse holds no red gold, no coin of the silver white,
No herds are mine to drive through the long twilight!
But the pretty girl that would take me, all bare though I be and lone,
Oh, I'd take her with me kindly to the county Tyrone.

Oh, my girl, I can see 'tis in trouble you are,
And, oh, my girl, I see 'tis your people's reproach you bear:
'I am a girl in trouble for his sake with whom I fly,
And, oh, may no other maiden know such reproach as I!'

The Coolun

(Irish Rustic Ballad)

Oh, had you see the Coolun,[1]
Walking down by the cuckoo's street,
With the dew of the meadow shining
On her milk-white twinkling feet.

1. Maiden of the flowing locks.

My love she is, and my *coleen oge*,[2]
  And she dwells in Bal'nagar;
And she bears the palm of beauty bright
  From the fairest that in Erin are.

In Bal'nagar is the Coolun,
  Like the berry on the bough her cheek;
Bright beauty dwells for ever
  On her fair neck and ringlets sleek:
Oh, sweeter is her mouth's soft music
  Than the lark or thrush at dawn,
Or the blackbird in the greenwood singing
  Farewell to the setting sun.

Rise up, my boy! make ready
  My horse, for I forth would ride,
To follow the modest damsel,
  Where she walks on the green hill side:
For, ever since our youth were we plighted,
  In faith, troth, and wedlock true —
She is sweeter to me nine times over
  Than organ or cuckoo!

For, ever since my childhood
  I loved the fair and darling child;
But our people came between us,
  And with lucre our pure love defiled:
Oh, my woe it is, and my bitter pain,
  And I weep it night and day,
That the *coleen bawn*[3] of my early love
  Is torn from my heart away.

Sweetheart and faithful treasure,
  Be constant still, and true;
Nor for want of herds and houses
  Leave one who would ne'er leave you:
I'll pledge you the blessed Bible,
  Without and eke within,
That the faithful God will provide for us,
  Without thanks to kith or kin.

Oh, love, do you remember
  When we lay all night alone,
Beneath the ash in the winter-storm,
  When the oak wood round did groan?
No shelter then from the blast had we,
  The bitter blast or sleet,
But your gown to wrap about our heads,
  And my coat round our feet.

2. Irish, *cailín óg* (young girl).
3. Irish, *cailín bán* (fair-haired girl).

THE DEATH OF DERMID

[This tale is taken from the Fionn cycle, a series of stories centred on the legendary warrior Fionn mac Cumhaill and his companions. Like the tale of Deirdre in the Ulster cycle, it concerns the loss of a wife by an elderly husband to a young rival. According to Proinsias MacCana, the story is a proximate source for the Tristram and Iseult legend.

Gráinne is betrothed to the widowed Fionn but, on her wedding night, lays Diarmaid (Dermid) ua Duibhne under a spell and persuades him to elope with her. They wander all over Ireland, pursued by Fionn's warriors. The places where they sleep, usually associated in folklore with the dolmens that are scattered throughout the Irish countryside, are known as 'The Bed of Diarmaid and Gráinne'. Finally peace is made and the lovers settle down and have children. However, during the chase for a magic boar, Diarmaid, as had been prophesied, suffers a wound from which only a draught of water from the hands of Fionn can cure him. Fionn is persuaded to go for the water, but on each of the three times he brings it, he remembers his love for Gráinne and his betrayal and lets the water flow through his fingers. On the third occasion, he finds Diarmaid dead. The variations on this story, which are incorporated into Ferguson's version, are based on the account given by Standish O'Grady and are reprinted in the volume *Finn and his Companions* (1892).]

Finn on the mountain found the mangled man,
The slain boar by him. 'Dermid,' said the king,
'It likes me well at last to see thee thus.
This only grieves me, that the womankind
Of Erin are not also looking on:
Such sight were wholesome for the wanton eyes
So oft enamour'd of that specious form:
Beauty to foulness, strength to weakness turn'd.'
'Yet in thy power, if only in thy will,
Lies it, oh Finn, even yet to heal me.'

'How?'

'Feign not the show of ignorance, nor deem
I know not of the virtues which thy hand
Drew from that fairy's half-discover'd hall,
Who bore her silver tankard from the fount,
So closely follow'd, that ere yet the door
Could close upon her steps, one arm was in;
Wherewith, though seeing nought, yet touching all,
Thou grasped'st half the spiritual world;
Withdrawing a heap'd handful of its gifts, —
Healing, and sight prophetic, and the power
Divine of poesy: but healing most

Abides within its hollow: — virtue such
That but so much of water as might wet
These lips, in that hand brought, would make me whole.
Finn, from the fountain fetch me in thy palms
A draught of water, and I yet shall live.'

'How at these hands canst thou demand thy life,
Who took'st my joy of life?'

'She loved thee not:
Me she did love and doth; and were she here
She would so plead with thee, that, for her sake,
Thou wouldst forgive us both, and bid me live.'

'I was a man had spent my prime of years
In war and council, little bless'd with love;
Though poesy was mine, and, in my hour,
The seer's burthen not desirable;
And now at last had thought to have a man's share
Of marriage blessings; and the King supreme,
Cormac, had pledged his only daughter mine;
When thou, with those pernicious beauty-gifts,
The flashing white tusk there hath somewhat spoil'd,
Didst win her to desert her father's house,
And roam the wilds with thee.'

'It was herself,
Grania, the Princess, put me in the bonds
Of holy chivalry to share her flight.
"Behold," she said, "he is an aged man,
(And so thou art, for years will come to all;)
And I, so young; and at the Beltane[1] games,
When Carbry Liffacher[2] did play the men
Of Brea, I, unseen, saw thee snatch a hurl,
And thrice on Tara's[3] champions win the goal;
And gave thee love that day, and still will give."
So she herself avow'd. Resolve me, Finn,
For thou art just, could youthful warrior, sworn
To maiden's service, have done else than I?
No: hate me not — restore me — give me drink.'

'I will not.'

'Nay, but, Finn, thou hadst not said
"I will not," though I'd ask'd a greater boon,
That night we supp'd in Breendacoga's lodge.
Remember: we were faint and hunger-starved
From three days' flight; and even as on the board
They played the viands, and my hand went forth
To raise the wine-cup, thou, more quick of ear,
O'erheardst the stealthy leaguer set without;
And yet should'st eat or perish. Then 'twas I,
Fasting, that made the sally; and 'twas I,
Fasting, that made the circuit of the court;
Three times I cours'd it, darkling, round and round;
From whence returning, when I brought thee in
The three lopp'd heads of them that lurk'd without —
Thou hadst not then, refresh'd and grateful, said
"I will not," had I ask'd thee, "Give me drink."'

'There springs no water on this summit bald.'

'Nine paces from the spot thou standest on,
The well-eye — well thou knowest it — bubbles clear.'

Abash'd, reluctant, to the bubbling well
Went Finn, and scoop'd the water in his palms;
Wherewith returning, half-way, came the thought
Of Grania, and he let the water spill.

'Ah me,' said Dermid, 'hast thou then forgot
Thy warrior-art that oft, when helms were split,
And buckler-bosses shatter'd by the spear,
Has satisfied the thirst of wounded men?
Ah, Finn, these hands of thine were not so slack
That night, when, captured by the king of Thule,[4]
Thou sayest in bonds within the temple gate
Waiting for morning, till the observant king
Should to his sun-god make thee sacrifice.
Close-pack'd thy fingers then, thong-drawn and squeezed,
The blood-drops oozing under every nail,
When, like a shadow, through the sleeping priests
Came I, and loos'd thee: and the hierophant
At day-dawn coming, on the altar-step,
Instead of victim straighten'd to his knife,
Two warriors found, erect, for battle arm'd.'

Again abash'd, reluctant to the well
Went Finn, and scoop'd the water in his palms,

1. The May games. There is no reference in the literature to such an occasion.
2. Cairbre Lifeachair, the son of King Cormac mac Airt, the high king of Ireland in the Finn literature. Cairbre is an important, though secondary, figure in the Finn cycle.
3. The hill in County Meath, site of the palace of the high king.
4. The source here is probably the story in *An Bruidhean Chaorthainn* where Finn is captured by the King of Scandinavia and freed.

Wherewith returning, half-way, came the thought
That wrench'd him; and the shaken water spill'd.

'False one, thou didst it purposely! I swear
I saw thee, though mine eyes do fast grow dim.
Ah me, how much imperfect still is man!
Yet such were not the act of Him, whom once
On this same mountain, as we sat at eve —
Thou yet mayst see the knoll that was our couch,
A stone's throw from the spot where now I lie —
Thou showedst me, shuddering, when the seer's fit,
Sudden and cold as hail, assail'd thy soul
In vision of that Just One crucified
For all men's pardoning, which, once again,
Thou sawest, with Cormac, struck in Rossnaree.'[5]

Finn trembled; and a third time to the well
Went straight, and scoop'd the water in his palms;
Wherewith in haste half-way return'd, he saw
A smile on Dermid's face relax'd in death.

5. This motif does not belong to the Finn cycle but to the Ulster Cú Chulainn cycle.

from: THE DUBLIN UNIVERSITY MAGAZINE (1847)

Lament for the Death of Thomas Davis

I walked through Ballinderry in the springtime,
When the bud was on the tree,
And I said, in every fresh-ploughed field beholding
The sowers striding free,
Scattering broadcast for the corn in golden plenty,
On the quick, seed-clasping soil,
Even such this day among the fresh-stirred hearts of Erin
Thomas Davis, is thy toil!

I sat by Ballyshannon in the summer,
And saw the salmon leap,
And I said, as I beheld the gallant creatures
Spring glittering from the deep,
Through the spray and through the prone heaps striving onward
To the calm, clear streams above,
So seekest thou thy native founts of freedom, Thomas Davis,
In thy brightness of strength and love!

I stood on Derrybawn in the autumn,
I heard the eagle call,
With a clangorous cry of wrath and lamentation
That filled the wide mountain hall,
O'er the bare, deserted place of his plundered eyrie,
And I said, as he screamed and soared,
So callest thou, thou wrathful-soaring Thomas Davis,
For a nation's rights restored.

Young husbandman of Erin's fruitful seed-time,
In the fresh track of danger's plough!
Who will walk the heavy, toilsome, perilous furrow,
Girt with freedom's seed-sheets now?
Who will banish with the wholesome crop of knowledge
The flaunting weed and the bitter thorn,
Now that thou thyself art but a seed for hopeful planting
Against the resurrection morn?

Young salmon of the flood-time of freedom
That swells round Erin's shore,
Thou wilt leap against their loud, oppressive torrents
Of bigotry and hate no more!
Drawn downward by their prone material instinct,
Let them thunder on their rocks, and foam;
Thou hast leaped, aspiring soul, to founts beyond their raging,
Where troubled waters never come.

But I grieve not, eagle of the empty eyrie,
That thy wrathful cry is still,
And that the songs alone of peaceful mourners
Are heard today on Erin's hill.
Better far if brothers' wars are destined for us —
God avert that horrid day, I pray! —
That ere our hands be stained with slaughter fratricidal,
Thy warm heart should be cold in clay.

But my trust is strong in God who made us brothers,
That He will not suffer these right hands,
Which thou hast joined in holier rites than wedlock,
To draw opposing brands.
O many a tuneful tongue that thou madest vocal,
Would lie cold and silent then,
And songless long once more should often-widowed Erin
Mourn the loss of her brave young men.

O brave young men, my love, my pride, my promise,
'Tis on you my hopes are set,
In manliness, in kindliness, in justice,
To make Erin a nation yet;
Self-respecting, self-relying, self-advancing,
In union or in severance, free and strong,
And if God grant this, then, under God, to Thomas Davis
Let the greater praise belong!

THOMAS DAVIS
(1814-45)

from:
THE SPIRIT OF THE NATION (1845, 1882)

[All these ballads were first published in *The Nation* newspaper, beginning with the sixth number ('Lament for the Death of Owen Roe O'Neill'). The first edition of *The Spirit of the Nation,* the original title, appeared in March 1843, as a sixpenny booklet, containing the poems that had appeared in the newspaper up to that date. In autumn 1844, a second part appeared. The work went through several editions and dozens of reprintings. A new edition appeared in January 1845, much expanded, with accompanying music and in a much larger format. A second edition of this appeared in September 1882. The text of Davis's poems is taken from that edition. 'The West's Asleep' has as accompanying air, the old tune 'Brink of the White Rocks'. 'Song of the Volunteers of 1782' is sung to the air of the 'Boyne Water'.]

Lament for the Death of Owen Roe O'Neill

TIME. — *10th November* 1649. SCENE. — *Ormond's Camp, County Waterford.* SPEAKERS. — *A veteran of Owen O'Neill's clan, and one of the horsemen, just arrived with an account of his death.*[1]

'Did they dare, did they dare, to slay Owen Roe O'Neill?'
'Yes, they slew with poison him, they feared to meet with steel.'
May God wither up their hearts! May their blood cease to flow!
May they walk in living death, who poisoned Owen Roe!

'Though it break my heart to hear, say again the bitter words.'
'From Derry, against Cromwell, he marched to measure swords:
But the weapon of the Sasanach[2] met him on his way,
And he died at Clough Oughter, upon St. Leonard's day.[3]

'Wail, wail ye for the Mighty One! Wail, wail ye for the Dead!
Quench the hearth, and hold the breath — with ashes strew the head.
How tenderly we loved him! How deeply we deplore!
Holy Saviour! but to think we shall never see him more.

'Sagest in the council was he, kindest in the hall!
Sure we never won a battle — 'twas Owen won them all.
Had he lived — had he lived — our dear country had been free;
But he's dead, but he's dead, and 'tis slaves we'll ever be.

1. Owen Roe O'Neill arrived in Ulster in 1642 to rally the Ulster insurgents and the Catholic Confederacy against the forces of the English crown. His greatest victory was at Benburb, Co. Armagh in 1646, over the Scots army of Major-general Robert Monro. James Butler, the duke of Ormond, was leader of the confederate army and a supporter of the English crown. He resisted Cromwell's siege of Waterford in November 1649.

2. Sassenach is an Irish and Scottish term for an English person, a Saxon.

3. O'Neill died on 6 November (St Leonard's Day) after an illness that was rumoured to have been brought on by poison. Clough Oughter is in County Cavan.

'O'Farrell and Clanrickarde, Preston and Red Hugh,
Audley, and MacMahon,[4] ye are valiant, wise, and true;
But — what, what are ye all to our darling who is gone?
The Rudder of our Ship was he, our Castle's corner stone!

'Wail, wail him through the Island! Weep, weep for our pride!
Would that on the battle-field our gallant chief had died!
Weep the victor of Benburb — weep him, young men and old;
Weep for him, ye women — Your Beautiful lies cold!

'We thought you would not die — we were sure you would not go,
And leave us in our utmost need to Cromwell's cruel blow —
Sheep without a shepherd, when the snow shuts out the sky —
Oh! why did you leave us, Owen? Why did you die?

'Soft as woman's was your voice, O'Neill! bright was your eye,
Oh! why did you leave us, Owen? Why did you die?
Your troubles are all over, you're at rest with God on high,
But we're slaves, and we're orphans, Owen! — why didst thou die?'

4. O'Farrell, Clanrickarde, Preston and Audley were all members of the Catholic Confederacy in the wars of 1641-49. Hugh Roe McMahon was executed as a rebel in 1591 and Red O'Donnell fled to Spain after the defeat at Kinsale in 1601. He too is alleged to have been poisoned.

['Song of the Volunteers of 1782' is Davis's tribute to the Irish Volunteers of the late eighteenth century, whose concerted campaign helped win legislative independence for Ireland in 1782. Led by Lord Charlemont, the Volunteers assembled at Dungannon in February 1782 and passed a number of revolutionary proposals. Henry Grattan and Henry Flood were the leading parliamentary orators of the day and strongly supported the Volunteer movement. Charles Lucas had been a leading spokesman for Irish rights in the 1760s; and William Molyneux had stated Ireland's case for an independent parliament in 1698.]

Song of the Volunteers of 1782

Hurrah! — 'tis done — our freedom's won,
Hurrah for the Volunteers!
No laws we own, but those alone
Of our Commons, King, and Peers.
The chain is broke — the Saxon yoke
From off our neck is taken;
Ireland awoke — Dungannon spoke —
With fear was England shaken.

When Grattan rose, none dar'd oppose
The claim he made for freedom;
They knew our swords, to back his words,
Were ready, did he need them.
Then let us raise, to Grattan's praise,
A proud and joyous anthem;
And wealth, and grace, and length of days,
May God in mercy grant him!

Bless Harry Flood, who nobly stood
By us, through gloomy years,
Bless Charlemont, the brave and good,
The Chief of the Volunteers!
The North began; the North held on
The strife for native land!
Till Ireland rose, and cow'd her foes —
God bless the Northern land!

And bless the men of patriot pen —
Swift, Molyneux, and Lucas;
Bless sword and gun, which 'Free Trade' won —
Bless God! who ne'er forsook us!
And long may last the friendship fast,
Which binds us all together;
While we agree, our foes shall flee
Like clouds in stormy weather.

Remember still, through good and ill,
How vain were prayers and tears —
How vain were words, till flashed the swords
Of the Irish Volunteers.
By arms we've got the rights we sought
Through long and wretched years —
Hurrah! tis done, our freedom's won —
Hurrah for the Volunteers!

My Grave

Shall they bury me in the deep
Where wind-forgetting waters sleep?

Shall they dig a grave for me,
Under the green-wood tree?
Or on the wild heath,
Where the wilder breath
Of the storm doth blow?
Oh, no! oh, no!

Shall they bury me in the Palace Tombs,
Or under the shade of Cathedral domes?
Sweet 'twere to lie on Italy's shore;
Yet not there — nor in Greece, though I love it
more.
In the wolf or the vulture my grave shall I find?
Shall my ashes career on the world-seeing wind?
Shall they fling my corpse in the battle mound,
Where coffinless thousands lie under the ground?
Just as they fall they are buried so —
Oh, no! oh, no!

No! on an Irish green hill-side,
On an opening lawn — but not too wide;
For I love the drip of the wetted trees —
On me blow no gales, but a gentle breeze,
To freshen the turf: put no tombstone there,
But green sods deck'd with daisies fair.

Nor sods too deep: but so that the dew,
The matted grass-roots may trickle through —
Be my epitaph writ on my country's mind,
'He serv'd his country, and lov'd his kind' —
Oh! 'twere merry unto the grave to go,
If one were sure to be buried so.

Nationality

A nation's voice, a nation's voice —
It is a solemn thing,
It bids the bondage-sick rejoice —
'Tis stronger than a king.
'Tis like the light of many stars,
The sound of many waves;
Which brightly look through prison bars;
And sweetly sound in caves.
Yet is it noblest, godliest known,
When righteous triumph swells its tone.

A nation's flag, a nation's flag —
If wickedly unrolled,
May foes in adverse battle drag
Its every fold from fold.
But in the cause of Liberty,
Guard it 'gainst Earth and Hell;
Guard it till Death or Victory —
Look you, you guard it well!
No saint or king has tomb so proud,
As he whose flag becomes his shroud.

A nation's right — a nation's right —
God gave it, and gave, too,
A nation's sword, a nation's might,
Danger to guard it through.
'Tis freedom from a foreign yoke,
'Tis just and equal laws,
Which deal unto the humblest folk,
As in a noble's cause.
On nations fixed in right and truth,
God would bestow eternal youth.

May Ireland's voice be ever heard,
Amid the world's applause!
And never be her flag-staff stirred,
But in an honest cause!
May freedom be her very breath,
Be Justice ever dear;
And never an ennobled death
May son of Ireland fear!
So the Lord God will ever smile,
With guardian grace, upon our isle.

Celts and Saxons

We hate the Saxon and the Dane,
We hate the Norman men —
We curs'd their greed for blood and gain,
We curse them now again.
Yet start not, Irish born man,
If you're to Ireland true,
We heed not blood, nor creed, nor clan —
We have no curse for you.

We have no curse for you or yours,
But Friendship's ready grasp,
And Faith to stand by you and yours,
Unto our latest gasp —
To stand by you against all foes,
Howe'er or whence they come,
With traitor arts, or bribes, or blows,
From England, France, or Rome.

What matter that at diff'rent shrines
  We pray unto one God —
What matter that at diff'rent times
  Our fathers won this sod —
In fortune and in name we're bound.
  By stronger links than steel,
And neither can be safe nor sound
  But in the other's weal.

As Nubian rocks, and Ethiop sand
  Long drifting down the Nile,
Built up old Egypt's fertile land
  For many a hundred mile;
So Pagan clans to Ireland came,
  And clans of Christendom,
Yet joined their wisdom and their fame
  To build a nation from.

Here came the brown Phœnician,
  The man of trade and toil —
Here came the proud Milesian,[1]
  Ahungering for spoil;
And the Firbolg and the Cymry,[2]
  And the hard, enduring Dane,
And the iron Lords of Normandy,
  With the Saxons in their train.

And oh! it were a gallant deed
  To show before mankind,
How every race and every creed
  Might be by love combined —
Might be combined, yet not forget
  The fountains whence they rose,
As, filled by many a rivulet
  The stately Sionainn[3] flows.

Nor would we wreak our ancient feud
  On Belgian or on Dane,
Nor visit in a hostile mood
  The hearths of Gaul or Spain;
But long as on our country lies
  The Anglo-Norman yoke,
Their tyranny we'll signalize,
  And God's revenge invoke.

We do not hate, we never curs'd,
  Nor spoke a foeman's word
Against a man in Ireland nurs'd,
  Howe'er we thought he err'd;
So start not, Irish born man,
  If you're to Ireland true,
We heed not race, nor creed, nor clan,
  We've hearts and hands for you.

1. Irish Milesius was a fictitious king of Spain whose sons were supposed to have conquered Ireland.
2. Welsh.
3. The river Shannon.

The West's Asleep

When all beside a vigil keep,
The West's asleep, the West's asleep —
Alas! and well may Erin weep,
When Connaught lies in slumber deep.
There lake and plain smile fair and free,
'Mid rocks — their guardian chivalry —
Sing oh! let man learn liberty
From crashing wind and lashing sea.

That chainless wave and lovely land
Freedom and Nationhood demand —
Be sure, the great God never plann'd,
For slumbering slaves, a home so grand.
And, long, a brave and haughty race
Honoured and sentinelled the place —
Sing oh! not even their sons' disgrace
Can quite destroy their glory's trace.

For often, in O'Connor's van,
To triumph dash'd each Connaught clan —
And fleet as deer the Normans ran
Through Coirrslabh Pass and Ard Rathain.
And later times saw deeds as brave;
And glory guards Clanricarde's grave —
Sing, oh! they died their land to save,
At Aughrim's slopes and Shannon's wave.[1]

And if, when all a vigil keep,
The West's asleep, the West's asleep —
Alas! and well may Erin weep,
That Connaught lies in slumber deep.
But — hark! — some voice like thunder spake:
'The West's awake, the West's awake' —.
Sing, oh! hurra! let England quake,
We'll watch till death for Erin's sake!

1. The Coirrslabh (recte, Coirrshliabh) Pass is in the Curlew Hills, north of Boyle, Co. Roscommon. It was the site of a battle between Irish and Norman forces in 1230; Ardrathan, Co. Galway was also the site of a Norman-Irish battle in 1225. In both cases the Normans were defeated. The Clanricarde family fought against English arms at Aughrim, Co. Galway in 1691.

AUBREY THOMAS DE VERE
(1814-1902)

from: THE SISTERS, INISFAIL AND OTHER POEMS (1861)

[Aubrey de Vere's poetry manifests his lifelong wish to see reconciliation between the opposing racial and religious groupings in Ireland. Where his politics failed, his piety took over. In the second section of the volume *The Sisters, Inisfail,* he attempted to give the crucial events in Irish history in a sequence of poems. 'Its aim', he said, 'is to embody the *essence* of a nation's history. . . . Looking back upon history, as from a vantage ground, its general proportions become palpable; and the themes to which poetry attaches herself are either these critical junctures upon which the fortunes of a nation turn, or such accidents of a lighter sort as illustrate the character of a race. A historic series of poems thus becomes possible, the interest of which is continuous, and the course of which reveals an increasing significance.' This project, although not notably realized as poetry, indicates the kinship between de Vere and other creators of the conditions for the Revival like Ferguson, Moore and O'Grady.]

In Ruin Reconciled

I heard a woman's voice that wailed
  Between the sandhills and the sea:
The famished sea-bird past me sailed
  Into the dim infinity.

I stood on boundless, rainy moors:
  Far off I saw a great Rock loom;
The grey dawn smote its iron doors;
  And then I knew it was a Tomb.

Two queenly shapes before the grate
  Watched, couchant on the barren ground;
Two regal shades in ruined state,
  One Gael, one Norman; both discrowned.

Song

The little Black Rose shall be red at last!
  What made it black but the East wind dry,
And the tear of the widow that fell on it fast?
  It shall redden the hills when June is nigh!

The Silk of the Kine shall rest at last!
  What drave her forth but the dragon-fly?
In the golden vale she shall feed full fast
  With her mild gold horn, and her slow dark eye.

The wounded wood-dove lies dead at last:
  The pine long-bleeding, it shall not die!
— This song is secret. Mine ear it pass'd
  In a wind o'er the stone plain of Athenry.

The Year of Sorrow

Ireland — 1849

(Spring)

Once more, through God's high will and grace
  Of hours that each its task fulfils,
  Heart-healing Spring resumes its place; —
  The valley throngs and scales the hills,

In vain. From earth's deep heart o'ercharged,
  The exulting life runs o'er in flowers; —
The slave unfed is unenlarged:
  In darkness sleep a Nation's powers.

Who knows not Spring? Who doubts, when blows?
  Her breath, that Spring is come indeed?
The swallow doubts not; nor the rose
  That stirs, but wakes not; nor the weed.

I feel her near, but see her not;
  For these with pain uplifted eyes
Fall back repulsed; and vapours blot
  The vision of the earth and skies.

I see her not — I feel her near,
  As, charioted in mildest airs,
She sails through yon empyreal sphere,
  And in her arms and bosom bears

That urn of flowers and lustral dews,
  Whose sacred balm, o'er all things shed,
Revives the weak, the old renews,
  And crowns with votive wreaths the dead.

Once more the cuckoo's call I hear;
  I know in many a glen profound

The earliest violets of the year
  Rise up like water from the ground.

The thorn I know once more is white;
  And far down many a forest dale
The anemones in dubious light
  Are trembling like a bridal veil.

By streams released that singing flow
  From craggy shelf, through sylvan glades,
The pale narcissus, well I know.
  Smiles hour by hour on greener shades.

The honeyed cowslip tufts once more
  The golden slopes; with gradual ray
The primrose stars the rock, and o'er
  The wood-path strews its milky way.

From ruined huts and holes come forth
  Old men, and look on yonder sky!
The Power Divine is on the earth:
  Give thanks to God before ye die!

And ye, O children worn and weak,
  Who care no more with flowers to play,
Lean on the grass your cold, thin cheek,
  And those slight hands, and whispering, say,

'Stern mother of a race unblest,
  In promise kindly, cold in deed! —
Take back, O Earth, into thy breast,
  The children whom thou wilt not feed.'

(Winter)

Fall, snow, and cease not! Flake by flake
  The decent winding-sheet compose;
Thy task is just and pious; make
  An end of blasphemies and woes.

Fall flake by flake! by thee alone,
  Last friend, the sleeping draught is given;
Kind nurse, by thee the couch is strown —
  The couch whose covering is from heaven.

Descend and clasp the mountain's crest;
  Inherit plain and valley deep;
This night, in thy maternal breast.
  A vanquished nation dies in sleep.

Lo! from the starry Temple gates
  Death rides, and bears the flag of peace;
The combatants he separates;
  He bids the wrath of ages cease.

Descend, benignant Power! But O,
  Ye torrents, shake no more the vale;
Dark streams, in silence seaward flow;
  Thou rising storm, remit thy wail.

Shake not, tonight, the cliffs of Moher,
  Nor Brandon's base, rough sea! Thou Isle,
The rite proceeds! From shore to shore,
  Hold in thy gathered breath the while.

Fall, snow! in stillness fall, like dew.
  On temple's roof and cedar's fan;
And mould thyself on pine and yew,
  And on the awful face of man.

Without a sound, without a stir,
  In streets and wolds, on rock and mound,
O omnipresent Comforter,
  By thee, this night, the lost are found!

On quaking moor, and mountain moss,
  With eyes upstaring at the sky,
And arms extended like a cross,
  The long-expectant sufferers lie.

Bend o'er them, white-robed Acolyte!
  Put forth thine hand from cloud and mist
And minister the last sad rite,
  Where altar there is none, nor priest.

Touch thou the gates of soul and sense;
  Touch darkening eyes and dying ears;
Touch stiffening hands and feet, and thence
  Remove the trace of sin and tears:

And ere thou seal those filmed eyes,
  Into God's urn thy fingers dip,
And lay, 'mid eucharistic sighs,
  The sacred wafer on the lip.

from:
THE DUBLIN UNIVERSITY MAGAZINE (1849)

Irish Colonization: 1848

England, thy sinful past hath found thee out!
  Washed was the blood-stain from the perfumed
    hand:

O'er lips self-righteous smiles demure and bland
Flickered, though still thine eye betrayed a doubt,
When round thy palace rose a People's shout —
'Famine makes lean the Helots' helpless land.'
What made them Helots? Gibbet, scourge, and brand,
Plaguing with futile rage a faith devout.
England! six hundred tyrannous years and more
Trampling a prostrate realm, that strength out-trod,
Which twenty years availed not to restore.
Thou *wert* thy brother's keeper — from the sod
His lifeblood crieth. Expiate thou that crime,
Or bear a branded brow throughout all time.

Fell the tall pines! — thou nobler Argo, leap
Wide winged deliverer, on the ocean's floods;
And westward waft the astonished multitudes
That rot inert, and hideous Sabbath keep:
Or, stung to madness, guiltier ruins heap
On their own heads. No longer fabled Gods
Subdue vext waves with tridents and pearl rods;
Yet round that bark heroic Gods shall sweep,
And guard an infant Nation. Hope shall flush
With far Hesperean welcome billows hoary:
Valor and virtue, love and joy, and glory,
A storm-borne Iris, shall before you rush;
And there descending, where your towers shall stand
Look back, full faced, and shout, 'Britannia, land!'

I heard, in deep prophetic trance immersed,
The wave, keel-cut, kissing the ship's dark side —
Anon men shouted, and the cliffs replied:
O what a vision from the darkness burst!
Europe so fair a city never nursed
As met me there! It clasped in crescent wide
The gulf, it crowned the isles, the subject tide
O'er-strode with bridges, and with quays coerced.
In marble from unnumbered mountains robed,
With altar-shaped acropolis and crest,
There sat the queenly City, throned and globed:
Full well that beaming countenance expressed
The soul of a great people. From its eye
Shone forth a second Britain's empery.

How looks a mother on her babe, a bard
On some life-laboured song? With humble pride,
And selfless love, and joy to awe allied: —
So should a state that severed self regard,
Her child beyond the waves. Great Nature's ward,
And Time's, that child one day, with God for guide,
Shall waft its parent's image far and wide;
Yea, and its Maker's, if by sin unmarked.
Conquest I deem a vulgar pastime: trade
Shifts like the winds; and power but comes to go:
But this is glorious, o'er the earth to sow
The seed of Nations: darkness to invade
With light: to plant, where silence reigned and death,
The thrones of British law and towers of Christian faith.

England, magnanimous are thou in name:
Magnanimous in nature once thou wert;
But that which oftimes lags behind desert,
And Crowns the dead, as oft survives it — fame.
Can she whose hand a merchant's pen makes tame,
Or sneer of nameless scribe; can she whose heart
In camp or senate still is at the mart;
A Nation's toils, a Nation's honours claim?
Thy shield of old torn Poland twice and thrice
Invoked; thy help as vainly Ireland asks,
Pointing with stark, lean finger, from the crest
Of western cliffs plague-stricken, to the West —
Grey-haired though young. When heat is sucked from ice,
Then shall a Firm discharge a Nation's tasks.

THOMAS CAULFIELD IRWIN

(1823-92)

from: VERSICLES (1856)

[Irwin was one of the most highly educated of the Irish poets of this period. His knowledge of classical and modern European literature is evident in his prose, but it left little impress on his poetry, save for the mingled influences of Tennyson and Keats.]

Angelo

I sit at eve within the curtain's fold,
Where shone thy gentle face in the full moon
So many an eve; and sing some antique tune
We sung together oftentimes of old:
In that dear nook the lonely moonbeams fall,
And touch thy empty chair with mournful light:
Thy picture gazes on me from the wall;
I hear thy footsteps in old rooms at night.

On lonely roads beneath the darksome dawn,
When broods upon the broad dead land the wind,
I wander sadly, looking oft' behind,
Maychance that I may see thy sceptre wan;
For still I deem thou followest me, and still
Believe that love departs not with the clay:
Thy face looks on me from the morning hill,
Thy smile comes sadly from the close of day.

Oft, oft by sandy ridges o'er the sea,
Or over distant famished fields at night,
Where sheds some low blue star its slenderest[1] light,
I seek in earth's dim solitudes for thee:
Proud of the everlasting love I bear,
Still mix with nature, drawing thence relief;
While, from the void of sunset's empty air,
The stars look on the glory of my grief.

1. Later editions have 'pale' instead of 'blue', 'thinnest' instead of 'slenderest'.

from: SONGS AND ROMANCES (1878)

Summer Wanderings

Lo! down the smoothes of water now
Slides on some old barge travel-worn,
And heavily heaped with yellow corn,
From the valley's harvest lands;
Beside the helm the steersman stands;
While 'mid the heaps of harvest wealth,
Girls with cheeks as red as morn,
All autumn-bronzed on neck and brow,
Buxom with the gun and wind
Lie in tumbles: — faint behind
The sleeky ripple gurgles slow
Back to its level calm of glass;
Onward as they swiftly pass,
The ripples stutter round the prow;
And as the wearied horses pause
Beside the hedge of crimson'd haws,
The veined water-lights waver and gleam
The boat rope whisps, and drippingly slacks
In lisping plashes into the stream.
Blue insects, in the large-leaved cool,
By starts jet o'er the quiet pool:
Around the stalk of the hollyhock,
The yellow, long, thin-waisted wasp,
Emitting sounds, now like a lisp
In the dry glare, now like a rasp,
Climbs slowly with stealthy clasp,
And vicious, intermittent hum;
Nosed awhile each sickly bloom
Withered round the edges crisp —
Then headlong vanishing grows dumb.

from: SONNETS ON THE POETRY AND PROBLEMS OF LIFE (1881)

I

The rough green wealth of wheaten fields that sway
In the low wind of midsummer all day;
The morning valley's warm perfumed breeze
Floating from southern sycamore shadowed rills,
The singing forest on the dawn-topped hills,
The living depth of azure spacing seas:
Still, brooding shadows upon mossy walls,
Aërial vapours crumbling down the heights,
Silence of woods amid green mellow lights,
And sighs of distant drizzling waterfalls:

The sweet faint breath of the short moonlit nights
From misty meadows where the quaint crake[1] calls;
Rare pageants in the western day withdrawn,
And fleets of rich light-laden clouds at dawn.

IV

Remote from smoky cities, aged and grey,
I pass the long-drawn Summer sea-side day:
Now reading in the garden arbour where
In light and silence comes the freckled morn
When dews are on the leaf, and cool the air;
The faint wave wash is heard the beach along,
Whence a warm wind waves languidly the corn;
And poised in haze the lark shakes out her song;
Now hearing in deep grass the sweeping scythe,
And, in the sultry stillness voices blythe,
'Till day is done. Blue coolness comes once more:
The reapers bind in twilight the last sheaf,
And the fresh spring-tide foams the sloaky[2] reef
As floats the white moon up the lonely land.

V

Into the wood at close of rainy day
I walk, dim cloud above, green leaves around;
Upon the humid air only the sound
Of drop on drop stirring the stillness grey:
Almost I hear the rose leaves fall away
Too heavily weighed with damp to cling o'er-blown
To their wet branches straggling o'er the copse;
Until the faint waved twilight airs entone
Tide-like along the blossom'd beech tree-tops;
And amid showers and flowers scattering, alone
Pass from the fresh dusk solitude among
Meadows in clouded moonlight, glimmeringly
Seen like the low blue hills; and hear the song
Of the last bird, and wash of the cool sea.

VIII

The apples ripen under yellowing leaves,
And in the farm yards by the little bay
The shadows come and go amid the sheaves,
And on the long dry inland winding way:
Where, in the thinning boughs each air bereaves,
Faint sunlights golden, and the spider weaves.
Grey are the low-laid sleepy hills, and grey
The autumn solitude of the sea day,
Where from the deep 'mid-channel, less and less
You hear along the pale east afternoon
A sound, uncertain as the silence, swoon —
The tide's sad voice ebbing towards loneliness:
And past the sands and seas' blue level line,
Ceaseless, the faint far murmur of the brine.

1. corncrake.
2. i.e. covered with slawk, a sea-weed.

DENIS FLORENCE MacCARTHY

(1817-82)

from: BALLADS, POEMS AND LYRICS, ORIGINAL AND TRANSLATED (1850)

[This is the best known of a number of poems written about the round towers of early Christian Ireland. As was usual at the time, their great antiquity is stressed and their endurance as symbols of the early Irish civilization.]

The Pillar Towers of Ireland

The pillar towers of Ireland, how wondrously they stand
By the lakes and rushing rivers through the valleys of our land;
In mystic file, through the isle, they lift their heads sublime,
These gray old pillar temples, these conquerors of time!

Beside these gray old pillars, how perishing and weak
The Roman's arch of triumph, and the temple of the Greek,
And the gold domes of Byzantium, and the pointed Gothic spires,
All are gone, one by one, but the temples of our sires.

The column, with its capital, is level with the dust,
And the proud halls of the mighty and the calm homes of the just;
For the proudest works of man, as certainly, but slower,
Pass like the grass at the sharp scythe of the mower!

But the grass grows again when in majesty and mirth,
On the wing of the spring, comes the Goddess of the Earth;
But for man in this world no springtide e'er returns
To the labours of his hands or the ashes of his urns!

Two favourites hath Time — the pyramids of Nile,
And the old mystic temples of our own dear isle;
As the breeze o'er the seas, where the halcyon[1] has its nest,
Thus Time o'er Egypt's tombs and the temples of the West!

The names of their founders have vanished in the gloom,
Like the dry branch in the fire or the body in the tomb;
But today, in the ray, their shadows still they cast —
These temples of forgotten gods — these relics of the past!

Around these walls have wandered the Briton and the Dane —
The captives of Armorica,[2] the cavaliers of Spain —
Phœnician and Milesian, and the plundering Norman Peers —
And the swordsmen of brave Brian,[3] and the chiefs of later years!

How many different rites have these gray old temples known!
To the mind what dreams are written in these chronicles of stone!
What terror and what error, what gleams of love and truth,
Have flashed from these walls since the world was in its youth?

Here blazed the sacred fire, and, when the sun was gone,
As a star from afar to the traveller it shone;
And the warm blood of the victim have these gray old temples drunk,
And the death-song of the druid and the matin of the monk.

Here was placed the holy chalice that held the sacred wine,
And the gold cross from the altar, and the relics from the shrine,
And the mitre shining brighter with its diamonds than the East,
And the crosier of the pontiff and the vestments of the priest.

Where blazed the sacred fire, rung out the vesper bell,
Where the fugitive found shelter, became the hermit's cell;
And hope hung out its symbol to the innocent and good,
For the cross o'er the moss of the pointed summit stood.

There may it stand for ever, while that symbol doth impart
To the mind one glorious vision, or one proud throb to the heart;
While the breast needeth rest may these gray old temples last,
Bright prophets of the future, as preachers of the past!

1. A poetic name for the kingfisher.
2. An ancient name for Brittany.
3. Brian Boru (*c*.941-1014), king of Ireland from 976 until he was slain by Norsemen at the battle of Clontarf.

WILLIAM ALLINGHAM
(1824-89)

from:
LAURENCE BLOOMFIELD IN IRELAND, A MODERN POEM (1864)

[This poem is in twelve sections or, as Allingham calls them, chapters. It tells the story of young Laurence Bloomfield, 'Irish born and English bred', returning to his native place and encountering there the harsh divisions of the Irish agrarian system. The peasant Doran family is caught between the heartless landlords, led by their agent Pigot, and the brutal Ribbonmen, the outlaw organization that their son joins. Pigot is assassinated after Bloomfield fires him and Bloomfield then takes charge of the situation and, by the exercise of justice and forgiveness, restores Ballytullagh to peace and prosperity. Allingham contributed the following Preface to the first edition.]

PREFACE

In this poem on every-day Irish affairs (a new and difficult, and for more than one reason a ticklish literary experiment), all readers who know Ireland will certainly see a good deal of truth, not taken up at second-hand; though on many points of opinion they are sure to differ from the writer, and from each other. It is free from personalities, and neither of an orange nor a green complexion; but it is Irish in phraseology, character and local colour, — with as little use as might be of a corrupt dialect, and with no deference at all to the stage traditions of Paddyism. It first appeared in *Fraser's Magazine* and is now presented much revised and partly re-arranged.

The scene is a district in Ireland, of extent such as might be seen in panorama from a moderate eminence; inland, but not far from the coast, with mountain-range, hills, moors, and bogs, wide rich plain, a river, and a lake. The persons are Sir Ulick Harvey, an old landed proprietor; his nephew, Mr. Bloomfield, a young one; Mr. Pigot, agent to both; tenants upon each estate; with so much as seemed proportionate respecting their wives, families, and friends, neighbouring landlords, clergy, Ribbonmen, politicians, &c. The parish is named Kilmoylan; the hamlet, Ballytullagh, on Tullagh Hill; the town, Lisnamoy; Sir Ulick's mansion, Lisnamoy House; Mr. Bloomfield's, Croghan Hall, under Croghan Mountain, and near Lough Braccan. In an Irish whirlwind of contending interests and opinions, Bloomfield finds his own way to a central spot of peace in the heart of the storm.

Ireland, be it remembered, with two thousand miles of coastline, inclosing thirty-two counties, is not a very small country, and is far from a homogeneous one. To be *doctrinaire* on so large and complex a subject is the furthest possible thing from the present writer's intention.

V

BALLYTULLAGH

The hamlet Ballytullagh, small and old,
Lay negligently cluster'd in a fold
Of Tullagh Hill, among the crags and moor;
A windy dwelling-place, rough, lonesome, poor;
So low and weather-stain'd the walls, the thatch
So dusk of hue, or spread with mossy patch,
A stranger journeying on the distant road
Might hardly guess that human hearts abode
In those wild fields, save when a smoky wreath
Distinguish'd from huge rocks, above, beneath,
Its huddled roofs. A lane goes up the hill,
Cross'd, at one elbow, by a crystal rill,
Between the stepping-stones gay tripping o'er
In shallow brightness on its gravelly floor,
From crags above, with falls and rocky urns,
Through sward below, in deep deliberate turns,
Where each fine evening brought the boys to play
At football, or with *camuns* drive away
The whizzing *nagg*;[1] a crooked lane and steep,
Older than broad highways, you find it creep,
Fenced in with stooping thorn-trees, bramble-brakes,
Tall edge-stones, gleaming, gay as spotted snakes,
With gold and silver lichen; till it bends
Between two rock-based rough-built gable ends,
To form the street, if one may call it street,
Where ducks and pigs in filthy forum meet;

1. A camun is a hurling stick; the nagg is the ball.

A scrambling, careless, tatter'd place, no doubt;
Each cottage rude within-doors as without;
All rude and poor; some wretched, — black and bare
And doleful as the cavern of Despair.
And yet, when crops were good, nor oatmeal high,
A famine or a fever-time gone by,
The touch of simple pleasures, even here,
In rustic sight and sound the heart could cheer.
With voice of breezes moving o'er the hills,
Wild birds and four-foot creatures, falling rills,
Mingled the hum of huswife's wheel, cock-crow,
The whetted scythe, or cattle's evening low,
Or laugh of children. Herding went the boy,
The sturdy diggers with spade and *loy*,[2]
The tether'd she-goat browsed the rock's green ledge,
The clothes were spread to dry on sloping hedge,
The *colleens*[3] did their broidery in the shade
Of leafy bush, or gown-skirt overhead,
Or wash'd and *beetled*[4] by the shallow brook,
Or sung their ballads round the chimney-nook
To speed a winter night, when song and jest
And dance and talk and social game are best:
For daily life's material good enough
Such trivial incidents and homely stuff.
Here also could those miracles befall
Of wedding, new-born babe, and funeral;
Here, every thought and mood and fancy rise
From common earth, and soar to mystic skies....

A day was fixed, arrears must then be paid,
For more police a tax on all was laid, —
New little barracks dropt in lonely spots
Where moping constables bewail'd their lots, —
For now the Ribbon-Snake was known to glide
With secret venom round the country-side;
Till Tullagh Hill became a place accurst,
And Ballytullagh stood for blot the worst
On Magisterial map. In two years' time
The tranquil nook was grown a nest of crime,
A den of were-wolves to a landlord's sight;
And Pigot only ask'd for legal right.

Rich neighbouring farmers, no way ill-disposed,
Their cautious lips, if not their eyes, keep closed;
They dread revenge, they dread the public shame
That clings and reeks around th' *informer's* name;
For Ireland's long tradition, lingering yet,
Hath in two scales the Law, the People set.
Nay, Ribbonism keeps Landlordism in check.
They blame, they fear, but will not break its neck;
To them belongs no sense of commonweal,
Authority as alien still they feel,
Ruled, without partnership or wholesome pride,
By Government that governs from outside.
Their native Church, where peasant sons might rise,
The rulers first despoil'd, and now despise.
Trade, wealth, flow elsewhere, why they cannot guess,
Save by constraint of ruling selfishness.
In their own narrow bound, the constant fight
For land goes on, with little ruth or right,
So far as they can see; but every man
Takes all advantage that he safely can.
And so, as in the chamber of a mist
Moving as they move, sadly they persist,
And let the puzzling world be as it list.

2. A turf spade.
3. girls.
4. Pounded with a beetle, a heavy hand tool, usually made of wood.

from: SONGS, BALLADS AND STORIES (1877)

The Girls' Lamentation

With grief and mourning I sit to spin;
My Love passed by, and he didn't come in;
He passes by me, both day and night,
And carries off my poor heart's delight.

There is a tavern in yonder town,
My Love goes there and he spends a crown;
He takes a strange girl upon his knee,
And never more gives a thought to me.

Says he, 'We'll wed without loss of time,
And sure our love's but a little crime'; —
My apron-string now it's wearing short,
And my Love he seeks other girls to court.

O with him I'd go if I had my will,
I'd follow him barefoot o'er rock and hill;
I'd never once speak of all my grief
If he'd give me a smile for my heart's relief.

In our wee garden the rose unfolds,
With bachelor's-buttons and marigolds;
I'll tie no posies for dance or fair,
A willow-twig is for me to wear.

For a maid again I can never be,
Till the red rose blooms on the willow tree.
Of such a trouble I've heard them tell,
And now I know what it means full well.

As through the long lonesome night I lie,
I'd give the world if I might but cry;
But I mus'n't moan there or raise my voice,
And the tears run down without any noise.

And what, O what will my mother say?
She'll wish her daughter was in the clay.
My father will curse me to my face;
The neighbours will know of my black disgrace.

My sister's buried three years, come Lent;
But sure we made far too much lament.
Beside her grave they still say a prayer —
I wish to God 'twas myself was there!

The Candlemas crosses[1] hang near my bed;
To look at them puts me much in dread,
They mark the good time that's gone and past:
It's like this year's one will prove the last.

The oldest cross it's a dusty brown,
But the winter winds didn't shake it down;
The newest cross keeps the colour bright;
When the straw was reaping my heart was light.

The reapers rose with the blink of morn,
And gaily stook'd up the yellow corn;
To call them home to the field I'd run,
Through the blowing breeze and the summer sun.

When the straw was weaving my heart was glad,
For neither sin nor shame I had,
In the barn where oat-chaff was flying round,
And the thumping flails made a pleasant sound.

Now summer or winter to me it's one;
But oh! for a day like the time that's gone.
I'd little care was it storm or shine,
If I had but peace in this heart of mine.

1. Little crosses woven of straw. A new cross is added each year, and the old ones are left until they fall to pieces.

Oh! light and false is a young man's kiss,
And a foolish girl gives her soul for this.
Oh! light and short is the young man's blame,
And a helpless girl has the grief and shame.

To the river-bank once I thought to go,
And cast myself in the stream below;
I thought 'twould carry us far out to sea,
Where they'd never find my poor babe and me.

Sweet Lord, forgive me that wicked mind!
You know I used to be well-inclined.
Oh, take compassion upon my state,
Because my trouble is so very great.

My head turns round with the spinning-wheel,
And a heavy cloud on my eyes I feel.
But the worst of all is at my heart's core;
For my innocent days will come back no more.

The Ruined Chapel

By the shore, a plot of ground
Clips a ruin'd chapel round,
Buttress'd with a grassy mound;
  Where Day and Night and Day go by,
And bring no touch of human sound.

Washing of the lonely seas,
Shaking of the guardian trees,
Piping of the salted breeze;
  Day and Night and Day go by
To the endless tune of these.

Or when, as winds and waters keep
A hush more dead than any sleep,
Still morns to stiller evenings creep,
  And Day and Night and Day go by;
Here the silence is most deep.

The empty ruins, lapsed again
Into Nature's wide domain,
Sow themselves with seed and grain
  As Day and Night and Day go by;
And hoard June's sun and April's rain.

Here fresh funeral tears were shed;
Now the graves are also dead;
And suckers from the ash-tree spread,
  While Day and Night and Day go by;
And stars move calmly overhead.

The Fairies

Up the airy mountain,
Down the rushy glen,
We daren't go a-hunting
For fear of little men;
Wee folk, good folk,
Trooping all together;
Green jacket, red cap,
And white owl's feather!

Down along the rocky shore
Some make their home,
They live on crispy pancakes
Of yellow tide-foam;
Some in the reeds
Of the black mountain lake,
With frogs for their watch-dogs,
All night awake.

High on the hill-top
The old King sits;
He is now so old and gray
He's nigh lost his wits.
With a bridge of white mist
Columbkill[1] he crosses,
On his stately journeys
From Slieveleague to Rosses;
Or going up with music
On cold starry nights,
To sup with the Queen
Of the gay Northern Lights.

They stole little Bridget
For seven years long;
When she came down again
Her friends were all gone.
They took her lightly back,
Between the night and morrow,
They thought that she was fast asleep,
But she was dead with sorrow.
They have kept her ever since
Deep within the lake,
On a bed of flag-leaves,
Watching till she wake.

By the craggy hill-side,
Through the mosses bare,
They have planted thorn-trees
For pleasure here and there.
Is any man so daring
As dig them up in spite,
He shall find their sharpest thorns
In his bed at night.

Up the airy mountain,
Down the rushy glen,
We daren't go a-hunting
For fear of little men;
Wee folk, good folk,
Trooping all together;
Green jacket, red cap,
And white owl's feather!

1. Glencolumbkille is in the south of County Donegal.

The Winding Banks of Erne:

Or, The Emigrant's Adieu to Ballyshannon (A Local Ballad)

Adieu to Ballyshannon! where I was bred and born;
Go where I may, I'll think of you, as sure as night and morn,
The kindly spot, the friendly town, where everyone is known,
And not a face in all the place but partly seems my own;
There's not a house or window, there's not a field or hill,
But, east or west, in foreign lands, I'll recollect them still.
I leave my warm heart with you, though my back I'm forced to turn —
So adieu to Ballyshannon, and the winding banks of Erne!

No more on pleasant evenings we'll saunter down the Mall,
When the trout is rising to the fly, the salmon to the fall.
The boat comes straining on her net, and heavily she creeps,
Cast off, cast off! — she feels the oars, and to her berth she sweeps;
Now fore and aft keep hauling, and gathering up the clue,
Till a silver wave of salmon rolls in among the crew.
Then they may sit, with pipes a-lit, and many a joke and 'yarn'; —
Adieu to Ballyshannon, and the winding banks of Erne!

The music of the waterfall, the mirror of the tide,
When all the green-hill'd harbour is full from side to side —
From Portnasun to Bulliebawns, and round the Abbey Bay,
From rocky Inis Saimer to Coolnargit sandhills grey;
While far upon the southern line, to guard it like a wall,
The Leitrim mountains, clothed in blue, gaze calmly over all,
And watch the ship sail up or down, the red flag at her stern; —
Adieu to these, adieu to all the winding banks of Erne!

Farewell to you, Kildoney lads, and them that pull an oar,
A lug-sail set, or haul a net, from the Point to Mullaghmore;
From Killybegs to bold Slieve-League, that ocean-mountain steep,
Six hundred yards in air aloft, six hundred in the deep;
From Dooran to the Fairy Bridge, and round by Tullen strand,
Level and long, and white with waves, where gull and curlew stand; —
Head out to sea when on your lee the breakers you discern! —
Adieu to all the billowy coast, and winding banks of Erne!

Farewell Coolmore, — Bundoran! and your summer crowds that run
From inland homes to see with joy th' Atlantic-setting sun;
To breathe the buoyant salted air, and sport among the waves;
To gather shells on sandy beach, and tempt the gloomy caves;
To watch the flowing, ebbing tide, the boats, the crabs, the fish;
Young men and maids to meet and smile, and form a tender wish;
The sick and old in search of health, for all things have their turn —
And I must quit my native shore, and the winding banks of Erne!

Farewell to every white cascade from the Harbour to Belleek,
And every pool where fins may rest, and ivy-shaded creek;
The sloping fields, the lofty rocks, where ash and holly grow,
The one split yew-tree gazing on the curving flood below;
The Lough, that winds through islands under Turaw mountain green;
And Castle Caldwell's stretching woods, with tranquil bays between;
And Breesie Hill, and many a pond among the heath and fern, —
For I must say adieu — adieu to the winding banks of Erne!

The thrush will call through Camlin groves the live-long summer day;
The waters run by mossy cliff, and bank with wild flowers gay;
The girls will bring their work and sing beneath a twisted thorn,
Or stray with sweethearts down the path among the growing corn;
Along the river side they go, where I have often been, —
O, never shall I see again the days that I have seen!
A thousand chances are to one I never may return, —
Adieu to Ballyshannon, and the winding banks of Erne!

Adieu to evening dances, when merry neighbours meet,
And the fiddle says to boys and girls, 'Get up and shake your feet!'
To 'shanachus'[1] and wise old talk of Erin's days gone by —
Who trench'd the rath[2] on such a hill, and where the bones may lie
Of saint, or king, or warrior chief; with tales of fairy power,
And tender ditties sweetly sung to pass the twilight hour.
The mournful song of exile is now for me to learn —
Adieu, my dear companions on the winding banks of Erne!

1. old stories, histories, genealogies.
2. earthen fort, enclosure.

Now measure from the Commons down to each end of the Purt,
Round the Abbey, Moy, and Knather, — I wish no one any hurt;
The Main Street, Back Street, College Lane, the Mall, and Portnasun,
If any foes of mine are there, I pardon every one.
I hope that man and womankind will do the same by me;
For my heart is sore and heavy at voyaging the sea.
My loving friends I'll bear in mind, and often fondly turn
To think of Ballyshannon, and the winding banks of Erne.

If ever I'm a money'd man, I mean, please God, to cast
My golden anchor in the place where youthful years were pass'd;
Though heads that now are black and brown must meanwhile gather grey,
New faces rise by every hearth, and old ones drop away —
Yet dearer still that Irish hill than all the world beside;
It's home, sweet home, wher'er I roam, through lands and waters wide.
And if the Lord allows me, I surely will return
To my native Ballyshannon, and the winding banks of Erne.

THOMAS D'ARCY McGEE

(1825-68)

from: THE POEMS OF THOMAS D'ARCY McGEE (1869)

[This poem was at one time as well-known as McGee's 'The Famine in the Land'. It is one of many poems on the subject. See C. Morash, *The Hungry Voice: The Poetry of the Irish Famine* (Dublin: Irish Academic Press, 1989). The editor acknowledges Dr Morash's generosity in allowing him to see page-proofs of his anthology before publication.]

The Woeful Winter: Suggested by Accounts of Ireland, in December 1848

They are flying, like northern birds over the sea for fear,
They cannot abide in their own green land, they seek a resting here;
Oh! wherefore are they flying, it is from the front of war,
Or have they smelt the Asian plague the winds waft from afar?

No! they are flying, flying, from a land where men are sheep,
Where sworded shepherds herd and slay the silly crew they keep;
Where so much iron hath pass'd into the souls of the long enslaved,
That none was found by fort or field, or in Champion's right hand waved.

Yea! they are flying hither, breathless and pale with fear,
And it not the sailing time for ships, but winter, dark and drear;
They had rather face the waters, dark as the frown of God,
Than make a stand for race and land on their own elastic sod.

Oh! blood of Brian, forgive them! oh, bones of Owen, rest![1]
Oh, spirits of our brave fathers, turn away your eyes from the West!
Look back on the track of the galleys that with the soldiers came —
Look! look to the ships of Tyre, moor'd in the ports of Spain.

1. Brian Boru (*c.*941-1014) and Owen Roe O'Neill (*c.*1590-1649) were Irish warrior chieftains who fought and defeated the Norse and the English respectively.

But look not on, dread fathers! look not on the shore
Where valour's spear and victory's horn were sacred signs of yore.
Look not toward the hill of Tara, or Iveagh, or Ailech high!
Look toward the East and blind your sight for they fly at last, they fly!

And ye who met the Romans behind the double wall,
And ye who smote the Saxons as mallet striketh ball,
And ye who shelter'd Harold and Bruce[2] — fittest hosts for the brave —
Why do you not join your spirit-strength, and bury her in the waves?

Alas! alas! for Ireland, so many tears were shed,
That the Celtic blood runs palely, that once was winy red!
They are flying, flying from her, the holy and the old,
Oh, the land has alter'd little, but the men are cowed and cold.

Yea! they are flying hither, breathless and pale with fear,
And it not the sailing-time for ships, but winter dark and drear;
They had rather face the waters, dark as the frown of God,
Than make a stand for race and land, on their own elastic sod.

2. The Celts who sheltered King Harold of England and Robert Bruce of Scotland are no longer the warriors of Tara, Iveagh or Aileach, all royal and ancient forts.

JOHN FRANCIS O'DONNELL

(1837-74)

from: POEMS (1891)

[Although he was sometimes known as the 'Fenian poet', O'Donnell's non-patriotic verse is of more interest and wears a good deal better. When he is represented in anthologies, his poems are seldom given in complete form, no doubt because he can vary wildly in quality even within a single poem. But that is itself part of the interest of his work. His instability is characteristic of the tradition, such as it was, that he inherited. Few Irish writers before him dealt with the life of the exile in the metropolis without falling into a stylized sentimentality of the kind that made songs like Lady Dufferin's 'The Irish Exile' so popular.]

The Return

Once more the red familiar streets
Are round me; and the Irish sky,
Filled with its myriad cloudy feats,
Bends deep above. The sea is nigh:
I fancy that its music comes
Between the triply-breasted ships,
Where Dublin quay clasps close the tide,
Palace and hovel reared beside,
And the salt wind upon my lips.

Dear City of the days long dead,
Where hopeless Hope o'erlooks the seas,
Thy very life with Death is wed —
Where are thy dazzling pageantries?
Where is the pride that nerved thee once —
The glory of secure renown?
Thou seated here, provincialised,
Beggared and utterly despised —
Queen with rent robe and shattered crown.

The beauty of the sunrise smites,
With fire of heaven, thy temple walls;
The splendour of the sweet lights
The pillared porches of thy halls;
Glory, and grace, and colour fill
Thy measure to its wide extent;
But thou art torpid as the kings
Who sleep in the imprisoning rings,
That make their grave and monument.

What man could know and love thee not,
Even in the garments of thy shame —
Even in thy bitter, bitter lot —
Thou stainless lady, free from blame?
Thy very pavements ring with song,
For there the Irish heart took voice —
There struck the high heroic chord —
There uttered the inspiring word
That bade the Celtic world rejoice.

If ashes be thy meed today,
The Crown awaits thee with the Cross,
And heaven, that is thy hope and stay,
Keeps record of each tear and loss.
The nations totter in the dust,
Their might, their power, as shadows flee,
But thou keep'st in those earnest eyes,
Blue as thy radiant, sapphire skies,
The Springtide of Eternity.

Drifting

Float, little bark, down yonder stream,
By many a margin fringed with bloom
Of lilies, amber-leaved and wan,
And poplars fair with silver gleam;
Float round yon island in the sun,
Slide slowly through the winking gloom
Of many an immemorial wood,
Whose trunks make cloisters for the flood.

Blow southern wind, and fill her wake
With creamy swirlings, faint and sweet —
Go, break the sunlight on her sail;
Loosen the blossom in the brake,
And waft, from primrose plot and vale,
Their odours rich and exquisite
Go, little bark, the shining west.
Shall find thy prow a nook of rest.

Speed, happy lovers, stream and breeze
Glide with ye towards the peaceful night
O babble softly in her ear,
Dark-violet river, till she sees
The golden-hornèd star appear,
Suspent in azure mist and light,
And hears, across the sobbing foam,
Bell-voices and the songs of home.

Float on, float on! The heavens are fair,
The last flame burns amid the leaves,
The last bird pipes on yonder bough,
The last crow blackens the rich air,
The cistus[1] drowses on the eaves,
The lustrous freshet trickles slow;
The earth has lost the sun, and lo!
Around the oaks the brown bats go.

1. Yellow-white or reddish roselike flowers.

My Jack

Along the roof-line, sharp and red,
The black crows stand against the sky,
And windy clamourings are bred
Within the elm trees standing nigh.
Hard clinks the chapel's evening bell,
The mill-wheel answers dreamily;
Whilst from the deep carnation sky
A glory rolls down field and fell:
It smites the mountain to the north,
It burns upon the window free,
Where Jack stands up, with eyes of mirth
And clapping hands, to welcome me.

Dear lads, again, the wild gold hair
Makes ringlets in the autumn wind,
And in those eyes, so blue and fair,
The sweet, fresh soul has grown more kind
How quaintly, too, those arms are set —
In indolent, and frank repose,
Upon the long green box, where grows
The wild thyme mixed with mignonette![1]
O happy shout! the choiring lark,
Caged coyly by the glinting pane,
Ne'er uttered, between light and dark,
A blither, a more natural strain.

Come down, and dance into my arms,
My heart shall have full holiday;
Come, let us range by smoking farms,
And poppied girths of wheat and hay.
The scythe is glittering in the grass,
The weeds are burning on the hill,
The blackbird's voice is scarcely still —
He keeps a song for Candlemas.

1. A plant cultivated for the fragrance of its blossoms.

O hasten, ere the stars are up,
  And bring the moonrise in their wake;
Haste ere the lily folds its cup,
  And vanishes into the lake.

Your hand in mine, your mouth to mine,
  The perfect, pure-lipped rosy shell
That on the feast of Valentine,
  Seven months ago, bade me farewell!
Ah, Jack, that voice was in my ear
  When in the night-time by the Main[2]
  The German house-tops hissed with rain,
The chimneys shuddered far and near.
Against the clouds the old house rose,
  Behind it spread the rolling wolds,
And you stood in the privet close
  Among the yellow marigolds.

That dream is fact; we too again
  By long belovèd hedges walk,
And separation's bitter pain
  Dies in the music of your talk.
The stifled pang, the injured sense,
  The shame of doubt, the wrong of sin,
  Turn into benedictions in
Your clear sun-lighted innocence.
Look, there's the sun behind the wood,
  The clouds one puff of golden gloom;
Now for the night's divinest mood —
  Low laughters and the lamp-lit room.

2. The German river that flows through Frankfurt to join the Rhine just above Mainz.

A July Dawn

We left the city, street and square,
  With lamplights glimmering through and
    through,
And turned us toward the suburb, where —
  Full from the east — the fresh wind blew.

One cloud stood overhead the sun —
  A glorious trail of dome and spire —
The last star flickered, and was gone;
  The first lark led the matin choir.

Wet was the grass beneath our tread,
  Thick-dewed the bramble by the way;
The lichen had a lovelier red,
  The elder-flower a fairer grey.

And there was silence on the land,
  Save when, from out the city's fold,
Stricken by Time's remorseless wand,
  A bell across the morning tolled.

The beeches sighed through all their boughs;
  The gutsy pennons of the pine
Swayed in a melancholy drowse,
  But with a motion sternly fine.

One gable, full against the sun,
  Flooded the garden-space beneath
With spices, sweet as cinnamon,
  From all its honeysuckled breadth.

Then crew the cocks from echoing farms,
  The chimney-tops were plumed with smoke,
The windmill shook its slanted arms,
  The sun was up, the country woke!

And voices sounded 'mid the trees
  Of orchards red with burning leaves,
By thick hives, sentinelled by bees —
  From fields which promised tented sheaves;

Until the day waxed to excess,
  And on the misty, rounding grey —
One vast, fantastic wilderness,
  The glowing roofs of London lay.

Reminiscences of a Day

(Wicklow)

O dim delicious heaven of dreams —
  The land of boyhood's dewy glow —
Again I hear your torrent streams
  Through purple gorge and valley flow,
  Whilst fresh the mountain breezes blow.
Above the air smites sharp and clear —
  The silent lucent spring it chills —
But underneath, moves warm amidst
    The bases of the hills.

With scalps fire-charged, or violet,
  The grim peaks pierce the open sky;
There may the storm at midnight fret
  Its strength in moans of agony,
  Whilst tempest-shaped the clouds roll by

Pale lightnings leap from scar to scar,
Between the hurtlings of the rains,
And four-fold thunders peal throughout
The loud rejoicing glens.

But not tonight, O lovely land,
Bear'st thou the colour of the storm;
The wind that fans my cheek is bland
And delicate, and sweet, and warm.
No wracks portending ill deform
The starry azure of those skies,
Where Dian flames a fiery crest,
Bernice's hair across the north —
Orion down the west.

The cloud that helms the mountain's brow,
The cataract that leaps and cries,
Have long-lost meanings — voices — now
For manhood's wakened ears and eyes.
Forbid it God I should despise
The other meanings, long since lost
'Mid the thronged cities' smoking fold —
Vague intimations that made time
A very time of Gold.

Here, 'mid the mountains and the mists,
I as a child, with hair grown grey,
Tired of the ever widening lists —
Sick of unresting fray and fray,
Yet without that obscure decay
Which chills the sources of the heart,
And blasts the flowers of simple joy,
Come, in the rainbow lights to dance,
And feel I'm still a boy.

I know the years have wrought me wrong,
And I have wronged myself beside;
Degenerate speech, degenerate song,
Dinned in my ears from morningtide —
The shame I shun, yet must abide —
Have smitten me; yet here I am
'Midst mountains lately white with snows:
They nurse the storm upon their tops,
And in their heart, the rose.

The violet is at my feet —
The slender flower of glorious blue;
The daisy, parti-coloured, sweet,
Gives the hill grass a richer hue,
The rough furze lights its fires anew.
Here hurled the rain, here rolled the storm;
Each did its worst — each wrought its part —
'Twas Nature's share — shall I not have
Also a fresh, new heart?

Far from the cities, far from streets —
Far from the cries of suffering wrongs,
Away from scenes where Commerce beats
Its praises upon iron gongs,
How sweet to listen to the songs
Which tell me, spite of all despairs,
The Holy Land that gave me birth
Shall yet rise up, and reign and rule
O'er her own seas and earth.

Shout out that hope, you mountain spires —
Shout it, deep gorge and lake profound;
Shout it, you pine slopes, red with fires —
Return me no uncertain sound.
Give — were it my heart's latest bound —
That hope to breathe upon the wave
Which soon shall carry me away,
Far from the sharp-contrasted lights
Of Irish night and day.

O friend of radiant, lucent mind,
And boundless charity of heart,[1]
As through the hills we climb and wind —
See the red deer leap up and start
Out in the sun — that we must part
Flings sadness on this tender morn —
A lengthening shadow on the path,
That flows in curious maze between
The wild wood and the rath.

I see the stars above the Alp
Of Bendhu's mighty presence rise;
They scale his chest — they crown his scalp —
They clothe him with a pale sunrise:
I gaze — and tears are in my eyes.
The morning flows across the wild,
The free bird down the valley slips —
I listen to its shrill, sweet cry,
And songs are on my lips.

But lo, once more the evening comes,
And shadows deepen down the wold,
The distant peaks take purpler glooms,
And through Imaile's entangled fold

1. O'Donnell identifies this friend as Rev. C. P. Meehan.

Blazes the sun — a disk of gold.
O God of Peace, the heavens are near
The stars in shining millions brood;
Thy calm has fallen on my soul,
And on this solitude!

An Interview

And you've just come from Ireland; that's your plea
For all those sickening substances of thought,
Steeped in your brain, a jelly-fish at sea
Or with the limpets blue in rock-craft caught,
You left us when your brain was overwrought
By the slow processes of decimals,
And piling on interminable nought,
Soul rises, but sense wavers, staggers, falls,

Down to a wholly terminable degree,
Well, not of meannness; for, I like you yet,
Spite of your office and its pageantry,
And your poor goose-quill, never dry, nor wet.
That quill which time, experience, will not whet,
But go on jargoning from base to top,
Letting who will be waiting on who'll let,
With here and there the dumb official stop.

You colour! Oh, don't mind it; you've come back
From Limerick, and watched the Shannon pour
Its salmon-threaded waters, track on track
Round many a bending pause of weir and shore,
And trodden beach, that raves for evermore;
By castled ruins, red with leaves, like wine,
And lakes that simmer in the moonlight frore;[1]
And here you come and babble of the Rhine.

You tell me, and I laugh, of Lurlie's rock —[2]
That emerald mountain stooping to the wave —
What of Doonass — the hurrying rush, the shock,
Like hosts embattled — tangled shield and glaive?[3]
The tost plume sinking, and not one to save.
All this is vulgar to your alien ears,
You like a finer music — something new —
A ghastly catalogue of precious tears,
A moon half rising, and a world of blue.

1. very cold, frosty.
2. The Lorelei is the name of a steep rock on the right bank of the Rhine, renowned for its echo. It is the traditional haunt of a siren who lures boatmen to their end.
3. An archaic word for sword.

Well, have it; and still curl your lip august
At Dublin, Dublin people, Dublin ways;
Of course you've worn off all the ancient rust
Of poverty, and sad declining days,
When first a shilling set your eyes ablaze.
I love the Providence which keeping time —
Change after change, as waters keep their hue,
And, meditating one Supreme Sublime,
Consummated its final task in you.

You don't love Ireland; all the Race is coarse,
You, with your toothpick, sitting where you are
(From last night's orgie rather bleared and hoarse)
Loom like a fog that clings to some still star
Apparent; when the fen and mist's at war.
'And, oh! she had such well-bred English ways!'
You idiot! It does your sneak's heart good,
Half sofa-wise to sit, and leer, and gaze,
And dream comparisons of rival blood.

And Limerick, and Dublin, as you think,
Are vulgar, prejudiced — you don't see there,
Betwixt the social class the social link,
The pure maids mixing with the syren's stare,
Nor that astute development of hair
Shorn off some convict. Ah, your taste is fine —
A rolling meteor tost by fouler wind,
London, as you praise it, is divine,
And the loved city of my heart behind.

Well, go, and babble; there are fools to hear;
But give me back that sweet, calm, Limerick maid,
Who passed the phantom of a lovely fear,
By our old casement, bright but still decayed,
Whilst my pure mother knitted in the shade
Of the bow-ivy. There is London town,
Glutted with light and *** but you know.
Here, you purveyor of that King and Crown,
Glasses for two — a cab for Pimlico.[4]

4. A district in London, on the north bank of the Thames.

Happy Christmases

I

In the December weather, grey and grim,
In the December twilight, keen and cold,
Stood the farmhouse on the green-reached hill
Piled with thatched roofs, mellowed into gold;

Under the dark eaves trailed the famished vines,
  Blood-ribbed skeletons of autumn days,
And the quaint windows, looking to the downs,
  Flickered and darkened in the ruddy blaze.

Three leagues around, the meadows to the moon
  Yearned like a silver dreamland, faint and white,
Below the deep-ploughed road a little pool
  Glimmered breezily in the tender light.
The great ash caught the glory as it dropped
  From bough to bough fantastically fair,
And the stars looked into its leafless heart,
  Through shifting vapours and translucent air.

Wild looked the gardens round the drowsy house,
  The laurel sparkled in the sifting frost;
But the white gables, where the roses grew,
  In the dank atmosphere of fog, were lost;
The wicket swang with a perturbèd cry,
  The mighty watch-dog crossed the dial floor;
My heart beat as I stroked his shaggy head —
  My heart throbbed as I stood beside the door.

In the sweet Christmas light that filled the porch,
  As with a glory round a saint she stood,
Welcomes innumerable were on her lips,
  And her cheeks reddened with tumultuous blood.
My own, my darling one, my life, my love,
  That made the common ways of earth divine;
'Twas sweet to stand beneath the balmy roof,
  Three fingers of thy gloveless hand in mine.

But dearer, sweeter, richer still to know
  That thou wert mine, and that thy gentle heart,
Won by long sufferance — won in hope and doubt —
  For me preserved a sanctuary apart;
Some sweet spot in a maiden's nature, where
  Her thoughts flower loveliest with unconscious
    growth
The Eden of her soul where passion lives,
  As if the guest to go or stay were loth.

In the old chairs before the household fire
  We sat and gossiped; we had histories,
Dear nooks beside the winding river banks,
  Dear names carved deep upon the cherry trees.
Old quarrels that the fresh love consecrates
  As with some richer and diviner charm,
Old theories we wove as oft we went
  Through the soft evening pastures, arm in arm.

And oft I raised my head, when the tall urn
  Bubbled between us, and I caught your eyes,
Dear, holy love, fixed sad upon my brows,
  And full of dim, delicious mysteries;
Our hands upon the cloth one moment met,
  A rough hand, and five fingers cool and white,
And the whole chamber vanished in the mist
  Of an unknown and exquisite delight.

Do you remember how your father looked —
  Stared me with pity, stared at me in wrath;
Well, he was old, and sorrowing shadows lie
  On the thick hedges of a downward path.
He did not love me; I was strange to him;
  His mind had measure of the ancient score;
He liked a man whom the king's herald knew
  And nailed his pedigree above his door.

Those were poor times (you did not love me less)
  And weary toil fetched slender recompense;
Silent and sad the grey past hung behind,
  Before the future loomèd dark and dense.
I saw the sneer that writhèd on his lips,
  And the white pallor of his feudal blood;
I rose, and stood, and trembled on the floor,
  Passion, and love, and misery at feud.

And then I went, but when I reached the path,
  Slid straight between the alder trees, I turned,
The moon looked yellowly across the downs,
  The moon upon the broken dial mourned;
The moon looked full into your yearning face,
  And touched the raven ripples of your hair;
But the old saint-like atmosphere was lost
  To the fierce vision blended with despair.

Forgive me, oh, forgive me, patient one,
  I blamed you for my sorrow and my shame;
Once — thrice I turned and stood to say good-bye,
  But with the message wild reproaches came.
Out on the night, a-past the wicket step,
  Out in the dark, disconsolate and poor,
Sad as the wind that, blown from the low hills,
  Fainted in monodies from moor to moor.

II

The year lay dying in the east,
The Christmas chimes had swung and ceast,
The Christmas light died at the feast.

Down looked the moon, but looked no more
Upon the silent river shore,
Or on the hilltops faint and hoar.

Down into London's struggling gloom,
Down on the city of the Doom,
A scarf of cloud around her bloom.

Below the bridge the black ships lay,
The thin lamps gleamed from quay to quay,
The thin masts trembled in the grey.

At times a voice was heard to cry
Some sudden warning; by-and-by
A swift plunge told its mystery.

And deep and grim the river went
Past arch, and tower, and monument,
As with a wail of discontent.

The clocks tolled two, and near and far
Rung in a fierce prophetic war,
The chimes roared back with brazen jar.

And as they ceased to clang and stir,
The foggy night grew silenter,
As nearer day the moments were.

Upon the bridge I stood alone,
Listening to the slow waves' moan,
Lapping the weedy buttress stone.

Friendless and homeless, 'twas to me
A sort of Christmas company
To watch the swirls glide to the sea,

To see the starlight glimmer grim,
Across the currents vague and dim,
And wish that I could go with them.

I touched my breast and trembled — there —
'Twas chiller than the morning air —
Close lay a cherished lock of hair.

And then, dear heart, my eyes grew wet;
I saw, in vision desolate,
The hill — the house where first we met.

The sweet old landscapes that we knew,
When nights were fair and skies were blue,
And every wind in odour flew.

I said: 'Tonight, beside the hearth,
The light of the sweet household mirth;
Old days to her are little worth.

Or if they come they scarcely raise
A tear to dim her laughing gaze,
And glitter in the Christmas blaze.

Buried and dead am I to her;
The sighs of some new worshipper,
Make all her selfish pulses stir.

Some neat, new suitor, in disguise
Of hollow laughs and tempting lies,
And fine sense of proprieties.'

Behind her chair I see him sit,
Filling her ear with borrowed wit,
Which she pronounces exquisite.

And the soft fingers and the palm,
That were to me earth's precious balm,
She gives him with untroubled calm.

And by-and-by, for his reward,
She rises to the harpsichord,
And crucifies my darling bard.

O, heartless havoc! when such ears
Suck in the whispers of the spheres,
Nor utter thoughts in silent tears!

O, shameless barter of a faith,
Sworn to exist unto her death:
Trifled away in one short breath!

I clenched my hands in bitter woe,
I felt my brain in tears could flow,
But my ill-angel answered — No!

The sun came up, the cloud went down,
And the sick daylight, dank and brown,
Struggled across the mighty town.

And I went — whither, ask me not —
Mine own, that morning is forgot;
Hidden in one blind mercy blot.

III

'Twas summer time, the radiant world of June
  Fell on the dreamful earth,

Within — 'twas coolest shadow; the red broom
Lay piled upon the hearth.

Through the slim spaces in the lattice breadth
The sun sloped from the eaves;
The very atmosphere waxed tremulous
With the green stir of leaves,

With airy whispers from the distant woods,
Around the moorland reach —
The whisper of the fainting lilac boughs,
The low voice of the beech.

The subtle melodies the hot gusts sucked
From the quaint woodland bridge,
That shone a perfect circle in the brook,
Beyond the last wold ridge.

And when the birds sang and the echoes blew,
And beat upon the blind,
That shook, a purple languor, in the sun,
And rose with the sweet wind,

Again for me the old world charm revived;
It seemed as after death
One woke from sleep upon a fairer earth —
The dreamland of our faith.

Beside each other in the porch we sat,
The quaint old-fashioned place,
Built up of knotted boughs and peakèd roofs,
And rich in country grace.

Between us and the roadway stretched the lawn;
The wicket was not seen,
For the laburnums raised their slender trunks
And branching firs between.

Long on the grass the gable shadows stretched,
And then the chimneys threw
Their grim phantasmal shadows on the sward,
That dim and dimmer grew.

'At last, at last,' I dare not see her face,
I dare not catch her eyes;
But my heart yearned with a sudden pain,
My breath was choked in sighs.

'Can you love me?' I asked, 'Dear, answer me.'
The purple curtain shook;
I heard the ripple of sweet moans that mocked
The murmur of a brook,

Of a pure brook that glides in summer time,
Through fields and pleasant air,
Stealing the beauty of the golden moss
And lilies white and fair.

So it was all confest; my own was mine,
And I in peace was blest;
A tender hand upon my shoulder lay,
A face was on my breast.

And ere the holy lights of Christmas threw
Their glory on our life,
Under one roof, beside one household fire,
I sat beside my wife.

Dark grew the dial, but we little recked
How the sweet minutes ran;
Or how the dusk was posting up the east,
A faint star caravan.

For we were happy though my love was sick —
Sick with protracted doubt
That digs the heart in sepulchres, and blows
The flame of patience out.

I had returned to her, and conquered much —
Conquered the goods of life;
And dragged a conscience and a victor's spoil
Out of the seething strife.

I had returned to her. In the whole world
Else whither could I go?
I knew the path as if my feet had left
Their prints within the snow.

And she — the light came back in her sick eyes,
The light of the rich past —
She caught my hand in silence and in tears,
And then she said, 'At last.'

Dear love, God's sweetest sweetness comes in woe,
His balm is given in pain;
The Angel of the Promise wakes and smiles
Above the cloud and rain.

By the Turnstile

There's light in the west, o'er the rims of the walnut,
Low croons the stream, in the meadows below,
Shrill sings the robin, a-top of the briar,

Black, through the golden dusk, darkens the crow.
O love, from the hamlet, that gleams in the sallows,
Come up through the pastures — come upwards and smile,
That your dear face may shine twenty roods through the twilight,
And sprinkle with starbeams the stones of the stile.
Come hither, come hither,
'Tis midsummer weather;
Airy-paced, violet-eyed, dainty-lipped lisper,
For into your pink ear, sweetheart, if you let me,
If but for a moment, I'd hurriedly whisper.

O daisies that glitter in long tangled grasses,
White wastes of delight that stream fair to the moon,
Unprison your lids, though the dank dew is falling,
And catch the sweet footsteps that hasten here soon.

To Spring

From the grey wicket of the morn,
Under the shadow-braided skies,
With violet twilights in thine eyes,
Thou walkest across the fresh, green corn.

I see thy pathway in the dark,
Thy sweet feet print the fields with light
With primroses and snowdrops white,
And silver on the larch tree's bark.

I know thy coming. Underneath
The black and leafless lattices,
There comes the moan of blowing trees,
The wallflower's faint ascetic breath.

I know thy coming — for the air
Blows soft upon the sleeted pane,
And drips the eaves with amber rain,
And scatters odours everywhere.

Far down, amid the shallows dank
Of the cold freshets, mallow-blooms
Are broadening in the willow glooms,
And cowslips flame on brae and bank.

O peace, O rest! Thou wintry jar
Of piping nights and mornings cold,
With fogs upon the sunless wold,
And thunders in the west afar;

Leave us a while, that we may rise,
With bright hands on the happy latch,
That we may go abroad and catch
The season's passion from the eyes

Of fringèd daisies that espy
The sun's return, before the furze
Turns golden; or the swallow stirs
His dusk wing in our faithless sky.

On many a sandy river shore,
And emerald lawn, the chestnut stands,
And shines along the pasture lands,
The gleam of blossomed sycamore.

And in the hours of sunshine brief,
But barred with shadows every one,
On gables looking to the sun,
The honeysuckle gathers leaf.

Blessed be thou, sweet time of spring,
And not alone that thou dost come,
Thy white arms piled with freshened bloom,
And songs that make the woodland ring.

No more amid the myrrhs and palms,
Of highest heaven, dost thou repose,
And feel upon thy crownless brows
The light of ever-crimson calms.

Thine aim is higher. Thou are the type
Of resurrection — of the spring
That yet shall wake the sleeping thing,
When God is pleased, and time is ripe.

II Popular Songs

This brief selection of popular songs is included to indicate the intimacy between poetry, whether in Irish or English, and music in the culture of nineteenth- and twentieth-century Ireland. The emphasis is on the nineteenth century because it was then that the collection and preservation of Irish music was undertaken in a characteristically antiquarian spirit. From Bunting to Petrie and Joyce, the explicit purpose of the great enterprise was to rescue material that had been almost entirely lost and to find some way, through the transcription of the original Irish into English, of making the riches of the folk tradition available to an audience to which that tradition was foreign and/or unknown.

The standard description of the music as 'ancient' is not only an indication of its great age but also of its vestigial existence in the present. Yet there was nothing peculiarly 'ancient' about Irish music, nor was it the case that it was near extinction. These presuppositions were integral to the belief that Gaelic culture must be transposed, both in its music and in its language, into a modern idiom so that its spirit might survive. That belief underlay Thomas Moore's *Irish Melodies*, Edward Walsh's *Irish Popular Songs* (1847), George Petrie's *Ancient Music of Ireland* (1855) and Patrick Weston Joyce's *Ancient Music of Ireland* (1873). Inevitably, disputes arose about the effect of these attempted transpositions. The relationship between the music and the Gaelic words was often misunderstood; the music itself, since Bunting's time, had been transcribed into major and minor keys, although it was, as Seán O'Boyle and Donal O'Sullivan have pointed out, a modal music; moreover, the English translations, even when supplied by the people who sang the songs, were often 'improved' to accommodate the prevailing conceptions of what was proper or acceptable. As a consequence, the folk tradition and the traditional modes of singing in the old style (*sean-nós*) were transmuted into a peculiar variant of Victorian sentimentality. Such music became very popular. The drawing-room song had little to recommend it musically, but its sentimental appeal was rooted in the belief, enhanced by disasters like the Famine and the mass emigration of the 1840s and 50s, that the music was the lingering remains of a vanishing culture. The antiquarian spirit both exploited and was exploited by cultural nostalgia, the more pronounced in an age that was inclined to believe that modern industrialization had been achieved at the expense of traditional rural values and pieties. This was true for the urban masses both in England and the United States; even more so, it was true for the large Irish exile population that formed part of them. Exile was both geographic and historical. The Irish were removed in space and in time from their heritage and, on that account, were more spectacularly than others the victims of the iron age of political economy and the factory system.

The sentimentalizing and bowdlerizing process might have continued unchecked, aided by those who, like Alfred Perceval Graves, sincerely believed that they were still involved in a rescue mission, had not Carl Hardebeck and the Gaelic League arrived on the scene. Hardebeck recorded words and music together and based his work on the assumption, shared by the Gaelic League, that Irish was still a living language, not a historical remnant. He tried to create a notation that would do justice to the intricacies of traditional singing. This marked an advance. But it was the arrival of the recording machine that more effectively reproduced and then broadcast the traditional music of the expert singers of the countryside. This in turn led to a revitalization of the music in the twentieth century. Ironically, it was modern technology, not antiquarian scholarship, that showed what the musical tradition actually was.

Nevertheless, the antiquarian enterprise and the sentimentalizing process that was its accompaniment cannot be ignored, for by now they are themselves part of the musical tradition and, with their translations and adaptations, part of the poetic tradition as well. This selection gives them prominence and does no more than insinuate a contrast between their work and that of some twentieth-century counterparts, like Donal O'Sullivan and Brian O'Rourke. For the songs of the traditional practitioners and the songs of

Thomas Moore, Lady Dufferin and many others are together part of a repertoire that is one of many cultural manifestations of the tortuous negotiations between Gaelic and English modes of civilization that remain central to the island's history.

In a more obvious fashion, political ballads, some of them adapted to traditional airs, exerted a considerable influence in a country where music held such sway and at a time when illiteracy was common. *The Nation*, more than any other publication, exploited this opportunity both under Young Ireland leadership and later under the editorship of the Sullivan brothers. The popularity of the ballad-sheet and the broadsheet, the replacement of the wandering poet by the itinerant ballad singers at fairs and markets, the formation, established since the eighteenth century, of political and music clubs, helped to nurture *The Nation*'s deliberate attempt to make the political ballad instrumental in the raising of national consciousness. The political ballad established its own line of heroic figures, either from the distant past (Granuaile, Owen Roe O'Neill, Red Hugh O'Donnell) or from the present (Emmet, Tone, O'Connell, Parnell, the Manchester Martyrs). It also adapted motifs from the eighteenth-century *aisling*, anticipating help from overseas in Ireland's fight against England, or making a love poem a disguised declaration of faith to Ireland. There is nothing intrinsically original in these ballads. They are different from their eighteenth-century predecessors in the degree to which their dissemination was organized as a political practice. In them, as in the eighteenth century, we see the importance of Dublin as the centre in which English musical conventions are adapted to Irish national purposes and, conversely, traditional Irish airs are converted to English-language songs. The relationship between music and language remains, especially in English, a troublesome one. One set of words can be adapted to a variety of tunes. This is much less true of songs in the Irish language. But it was this endless mobility, these transpositions and transformations, that gave the political ballad its popularity in local areas. As with folk songs, to find the 'true' original is often impossible. A song wanders; it is smoke in the wind. Yet the proximity of words to music, songs to poems and translations, to political heroes and to political events, is so close that some indication, however slight, of this important feature of the Irish tradition in writing, is worth having.

(a) Traditional Folk Songs

THE LAMENT OF RICHARD CANTILLON

[George Petrie's headnote to this song in the *Ancient Music of Ireland* reads as follows:

> This simple air, consisting of four phrases, and which I have but little doubt is very ancient, was noted last year [1854] from the singing of the blind Limerick woman, Mary Madden. Of the words sung to it, and which have given to it the above name, Mr. Curry has supplied me with the following copy, transcribed from a MS. in his possession. This song, as Mr. Curry tells me, was written about the year 1750, by Richard *Mor* (or the big) Cantillon, of *Rath Fraoich* — now Marland — between *Ceann-a-Tochair*, or, the Causeway, and Ballyheigue, in the county of Kerry; and it was addressed to the beautiful Bridget O'Halloran, daughter of Maurice *Mor* O'Halloran and Catherine MacCarthy, of the Marsud family. I should observe that, as the melody has no second strain, or part, it must be sung twice to each stanza of the song; and from this circumstance I am strongly inclined to believe that it is not the air to which the song was originally adapted.]

Slán leat a shiúr.
Ní fuláir dham 'beith ar síubhal,
Le h-eagla do mhasladh, 's go ghcaillfeá do chlú;
'Sgo n-déarfaidhe go h-árd
Gur liúm 'bhí do pháirt,
A mhodhail-bhean, do gheall dam, 'sdo mheall mé mar chách.

Ar mo luighe 'dham aréir,
Do smaoineas trém 'néal
Gur síobhra 'chaith saighead leam, 'sdo mhill mé go h-aéibh;
Cé gheaobhainn sínte rem' thaobh,
Go caoin is go faon,
Acht bríghdeach na rinn rosg, ó thaoibh Locha Léin.

Do sgríobhasa chughat,
Go caoin is go ciúin,
Leitir faoi shéala, chum éalaighthe liúm;
A phéarla na lúb,
Mana ndéanair-si súd.
Béad am'shíobhra 'ngleannta, nó a dteampall fá'n úir.

Mo chreach is mo dhíth,
Nach i Máire 'tá na luighe,

Agus Bríghid an chúil chraobhaigh 'beith taobh linn na súidhe;
Gur le guth binn a cinn
Thig na róinte dho linn,
An fiadh-phoc ó'n gceó-chnoc, 'san smólach do'n chraoibh.

Nách dúbach bocht an cás,
'Bheith ag tuitim a ngrádh
Le gile, le finne, 'sle buige na mná;
A chraobh úr gan cháim,
Ná'r thréig riamh a bláth,
'Sgur ar Ghaoidhilge do léighfinn do thréighibh, a bháb.

'Seo beannacht dhuit uaim,
Gan stad, siar ó thuaigh,
O fhágann sí Raith Fraoigh, go dtéidh do'n Chill Mhuair;
A laegh ghil, 'sa uain,
Léad' théacht chúgham go luath
'Sgheóbhair lán an tighe d'fhailtíbh, is lán mhí chum suain.

Croidhe cráidhte ar gach aon
'Thabharfadh náire dhúinn araon,
Is déarfadh gur bheárnasa bán-chnis na gcraobh;
'Sgur lán-fhios dho'n tsaoghal
Ná deárnas riamh lé
Acht súgradh gan tábhacht, nó gáire gan chlaon.

TRANSLATION

Farewell, my friend,
I must be away,
Lest you be defamed, or your character lost;
And that it might be said aloud
That you were partial to me,
O modest woman, who favoured, but deceived, like all others.

As I lay me down last night,
I thought in my sleep
That a fairy had shot me, and destroyed my soul;
And that I found at my side,
In her beauty reclined,
Bridget of the star-eyes, from the banks of Loch Lein!

I have written to you,
Gently and timidly,
A letter well sealed, that you'd elope with me;
And if this you won't do,
Thou pearl of the ringlets,
I shall be a sprite of the valleys, or in the church's deep mould.

It's my loss and my ruin,
That 'tis not Mary that's laid low,
And Bridget of the flowing hair to be placed by my side;
At whose musical voice
Come the seals from the deep,
The stag from the mist-crag, and the thrush from the tree.

What a sad and poor case,
To be dying of love
For the whiteness, the fairness, and the softness of the dame;
O faultless fresh branch,
Which never lost its blossom,
It is in Gaelic I could trace all your graces, O maid!

Here is a blessing to you from me,
Without delay, to the north-west,
From its starting at Rathfree till it reaches Killmore;
My bright fawn, and my lamb,
That you might come soon
To a houseful of welcomes, and a month for repose.

Sore hearts be to those
Who would slander us both,
And say that I sullied the white-sided maid;
While the world well knows
That I've done to her no more
Than sport without meaning, or laugh without guile.

THE CURRAGH OF KILDARE
or
THE WINTER IT IS PAST

[In his *Ancient Music of Ireland* (1855), George Petrie considers the competing claims of Irish or Scottish origins for this song. He decides in favour of the Irish. It was collected in 1780 from a singer called Betty Skillin, who sang the latter half of each stanza twice.]

The winter it is past,
And the summer's come at last,
    And the blackbirds sing on every tree;
The hearts of these are glad,

But mine is very sad,
  Since my true love is absent from me.

The rose upon the brier,
By the water running clear,
  Gives joy to the linnet and the bee;
Their little hearts are blest,
But mine is not at rest,
  While my true love is absent from me.

A livery I'll wear,
And I'll comb down my hair,
  And in velvet so green I'll appear;
And straight I will repair
To the Curragh of Kildare,
  For it's there I'll find tidings of my dear.

I'll wear a cap of black,
With a frill around my neck;
  Gold rings on my fingers I'll wear;
It is this I'll undertake
For my true lover's sake;
  He resides at the Curragh of Kildare.

I would not think it strange
Thus the world for to range,
  If I only got tidings of my dear;
But here in Cupid's chain,
If I'm bound to remain,
  I would spend my whole life in despair.

My love is like the sun,
That in the firmament does run,
  And always proves constant and true;
But his is like the moon,
That wanders up and down,
  And every month it is new.

All you that are in love,
And cannot it remove,
  I pity the pains you endure;
For experience lets me know
That your hearts are full of woe,
  And a woe that no mortal can cure.

AN RABH TÚ AG AN GCARRAIG?
(Have you been at Carrick?)

[These lyrics were printed in Edward Walsh's *Irish Popular Songs* (1847) and again in John O'Daly's *Poets and Poetry of Munster* (1849) in a translation by Mangan. O'Daly says the song is the masterpiece of Dominic O'Mongan (or Mungan) and that it was composed early in the eighteenth century 'for a celebrated beauty of her day, Eliza Blacker, of Carrick, County of Armagh, who became afterwards Lady Dunkin, of Upper Cloher Court, Bushmills, County of Antrim, now called Dunderave Castle ....' In his note to the song, Walsh says: 'This is a song of the South, but there are so many places of the name of Carrick ... that I cannot fix its precise locality.' In this song, 'when the pining swain learns that his absent mistress is not love-sick like himself, he praises the beauty of her copious hair, throws off a glass to her health, enumerates his sufferings, and swears to forego the sex for ever; but she suddenly bursts upon his view, and his resolves vanish into thin air ....']

An raibh tú ag an gCarraig, nó bhfaca tú féin mo
  ghrádh,
Nó a bhfaca tú gile, finne, agus sgéimh na mná,
Nó a bhfaca tú an tubhal ba cúbhartha is ba
  mhillse bláth,
Nó a bhfaca tú mo bhalantíne nó a bhfuil sí d'a
  claoidh mar táim?

Do bhíosa ag an gCarraig, is do chonairc mé féin
  do ghrádh,
Do chonairc mé gile, finne, agus sgéimh na mná,
Do chonairc mé an tubhal ba cúbhartha is ba
  mhillse bláth,
Do chonairc mé do bhalantín agus ní'l sí d'a claoidh
  mar táir!

Is fiú cúig ghuinea gach ribe da gruaig mar ór,
Is fiú oiread eile a cuideachta úair roimh ló;
A cúilín trom triopallach a tuitim léi síos go feóir
'Sa chuaichin na finne, ar mhiste do shláinte d'ól?

'Núair bhím-se am chodla bian osnadh gan
  bhrígh am chliabh,
Is mé am luidh eadar cnocaibh go dtigidh an dúach
  aníar;
A rúin dhil s'a chogair ní'l fortacht mo chúis acht
  Dia,
Is go ndearnadh loch fola do sholus mo shúl ad
  dhiaidh!

Is go dtigidh an cháisg air lár an fhoghmhair
  bhuidhe,
Is lá fhéil Pátruig lá nó dhó na dhiaigh,
Go bhfása an bláth bán tre lár mo chomhra chaol,
Páirt da grádh go brath ní thabharfad do mhnaoi!

Siúd i síos an Ríogh-bhean áluin óg,
A bhfuil a grúaig léi sgaoilte síos go béal a bróg,
Sí an eala i mar an lítis do shíolraigh ón tsár fuil mhór,
Charaid gheal mo chroidhe, céad míle fáilte romhat!

TRANSLATION

Have you been at Carrick, and saw you my true-love there?
And saw you her features, all beautiful, bright, and fair?
Saw you the most fragrant, flowering, sweet apple-tree? —
O! saw you my lov'd one, and pines she in grief like me?

I have been at Carrick, and saw thy own true-love there;
And saw, too, her features, all beautiful, bright, and fair;
And saw the most fragrant, flowering, sweet apple-tree —
I saw thy lov'd one — she pines not in grief, like thee!

Five guineas would price every tress of her golden hair —
Then think what a treasure her pillow at night to share,
These tresses thick-clustering and curling around her brow —
O, Ringlet of Fairness! I'll drink to thy beauty now!

When seeking to slumber, my bosom is rent with sighs —
I toss on my pillow till morning's blest beams arise;
No aid, bright Beloved! can reach me save GOD above,
For a blood-lake is form'd of the light of my eyes with love!

Until yellow Autumn shall usher the Paschal[1] day,
And Patrick's gay festival come in its train alway —
Until through my coffin the blossoming boughs shall grow,
My love on another I'll in life bestow!

Lo! yonder the maiden illustrious, queen-like, high,
With long-flowing tresses adown to her sandal-tie —
Swan, fair as the lily, descended of high degree,
A myriad of welcomes, dear maid of my heart, to thee!

1. Passover, Easter.

CASADH AN TSUGÁIN
(The Twisting of the Rope)

[In *Irish Popular Songs*, Walsh provides the following note to this song: 'This is said to be the original song composed to that delightful tune, "The Twisting of the Rope". Tradition thus speaks of its origin. A Connaught harper having once put up at the residence of a rich farmer, began to pay such attentions to the young woman of the house, as greatly displeased her mother, who instantly conceived a plan for the summary ejectment of the minstrel. She provided some hay, and requested the harper to twist the rope which she set about making. As the work progressed and the rope lengthened, the harper, of course, retired backward, till he went beyond the door of the dwelling, when the crafty matron suddenly shut the door in his face, and then threw his harp out of the window. The version sung in the south of Ireland has some additional stanzas, but I give the song as it is found in Hardiman's *Minstrelsy*, vol. I., where it is left untranslated.']

Nach é an cat marbh chas ann na h-áitesi mé,
'S a liacht cailín deas do fhágasa mo dhiaigh;
Tháinic me steach's an teach raibh grádh geal mo cléibh,
'S chuir an chailleach amach air chasadh an t-súgáin mé!

Má bhidheann tú liom, bidh liom do ló a's d'oidhche;
Má bhidheann tú liom, bidh liom ós comhair an t-saoghail;
Má bhidheann tú liom, bidh liom gach órdlach ann do chróidhe;
'S é má leun nach liom trathnóna thú mar mhnaoi!

Ar shíos a Sligeach chur mé eolus air mo ghrádh,
Ar shuas a n-Gaillibh d'ól mé léi mo sháith;
Dar brigh mo bhasa muna léigfidh dhamhsa mar a táim
Déanfaidh mé cleas a bhainfeas siubhal as na mnáibh!

TRANSLATION

What mortal conflict drove me here to roam,
Though many a maid I've left behind at home;

Forth from the house where dwelt my heart's dear
  hope,
I was turned by the hag at the twisting of the rope!

If thou be mine, be mine both day and night,
If thou be mine, be mine in all men's sight,
If thou be mine, be mine o'er all beside —
And oh, that thou wert now my wedded bride!

In Sligo first I did my love behold,
In Galway town I spent with her my gold —
But by this hand, if thus they me pursue,
I'll teach these dames to dance a measure new!

TÁIM SÍNTE AR DO THUAMA (From the Cold Sod that's O'er You)

[Walsh included this song in his own translation in *Irish Popular Songs.*]

Táim sínte ar do thuama,
  Is do gheóir ann do shíor me;
Dá mbeadh barr do dhá lámh agam
  Ní sgarfainn leat choíche.
A úilín is a annsacht,
  Is am domh-sa luí leat,
Tá bola fuar na cré orm,
  Dath na gréine 's na gaoithe!

Tá cló ar mo chroí-se
  'Tá líonta le grá dhuit,
Lionndubh ar thaobh thíos de
  Chomh cíordhubh le h-áirne.
Is má bhaineann aon ní dhom
  'S go gclaoifeadh an bás me,
Bead-sa im shí gaoithe
  Romhat thíos ar na bánta!

Nuair is dó le mo mhuinntir
  Go mbím-se ar mo leaba,
Ar do thuama 'sea bhím sínte
  Ó oíche go maidin:
A' cur síos mo chruatan
  'S a' crua-ghol go daingean.
Tré mo chailín ciúin stuama
  Do luadh liom 'n-a leanbh!

An cuimhin leatsa an oidhche,
  Do bhíosa 'gus tusa;
Fá bhun an chrainn draighnigh,
  'S an oidhche ag cur cuisne;
Céad moladh le h-Íosa,
  Nach dheárnamar an milleadh.
'S go bhfuil do choróin mhaighdeanuis,
  Na crann soillse ar do choinne!

Tá an Sagairt 's na Bráithre,
  Gach lá liom a bhfearg;
Do chionn bheith an ngrádh leat,
  A óigbhean is tú marbh;
Dhéanfain fosgadh air an ngaoith dhuit
  'S díon duit ó'n bhfearthain:
Agus cúmhadh ghéar mo chroidesi
  Thú bheith shíos ansa talamh!

Tabhair do mhallacht dod mháthairín.
  'S áirmhidhsi t-athair;
'S a mairion dod cháirde,
  Go léireach na seasamh:
Nár léig dam thú phósadh
  'S tu beó 'gam ad bheatha,
Agus nach n-iarrfainn mar spréid leat,
  Ach lúidhe liom air leaba!

TRANSLATION

From the cold sod that's o'er you
  I never shall sever —
Were my hands twin'd in your's, love,
  I'd hold them for ever —
My fondest, my fairest,
  We may now sleep together,
I've the cold earth's damp odour,
  And I'm worn from the weather!

This heart, fill'd with fondness,
  Is wounded and weary;
A dark gulf beneath it
  Yawns jet-black and dreary —
When death comes, a victor,
  In mercy to greet me,
On the wings of the whirlwind,
  In the wild wastes you'll meet me!

When the folk of my household
  Suppose I am sleeping,
On your cold grave, till morning,
  The lone watch I'm keeping;
My grief to the night wind,
  For the mild maid to render,
Who was my betrothed
  Since infancy tender!

Remember the lone night
  I last spent with you, love,
Beneath the dark sloe-tree,
  When the icy wind blew, love —
High praise to the Saviour
  No sin-stain had found you,
That your virginal glory
  Shines brightly around you!

The priests and the friars
  Are ceaselessly chiding,
That I love a young maiden,
  In life not abiding —
O! I'd shelter and shield you,
  If wild storms were swelling,
And O! my wreck'd hope,
  That the cold earth's your dwelling!

Alas, for your father,
  And also your mother,
And all your relations,
  Your sister and brother,
Who gave you to sorrow,
  And the grave 'neath the willow,
While I crav'd, as your portion,
  But to share your chaste pillow!

PÉARLA AN BHROLLAIGH BHÁIN
(The Pearl of the White Breast)

[George Petrie acknowledges Eugene O'Curry as his source for this song in the introductory note to the music and words in *Ancient Music of Ireland*. O'Curry sang it to Petrie in Irish as he had himself learnt it from his father. The words are not, Petrie guesses, as old as the melody, which O'Curry placed in the early seventeenth century. Petrie considered the song 'as not unworthy of preservation, as well in its original language, as in a nearly literal verified translation, which I have attempted with a view to convey to the reader some idea of a very usual metrical structure in Irish lyrical composition.' The song is now more commonly called 'The Snowy-Breasted Pearl'.]

Tá cailín deas am chrá
Le bliain agus le lá,
  Is ní fhéadaim a fáil le bréaga;
Níl aiste chlis le rá
Dá gcanaid fir le mná
  Nár chaitheamar gan tábhacht lé-si.
Don Fhrainnc nó don Spáinn
Dá dtéadh mo ghrá,
  Go raghainn-se gach lá dá féachain;
'S maran dúinn atá i ndán
An ainnir chiúin seo d'fháil,
  Och! Mac Muire na ngrás dár saora!

Is a chailín chailce bhláith,
Dá dtugas searc is grá,
  Ná túir-se gach tráth dhom éara;
'S a liacht ainnir mhín im dheáidh
Le buaibh is maoin 'n-a láimh,
  Dá ngabhaimís it áit-se céile.
Póg is míle fáilte
Is barra geal do lámh
  'Sé 'n-iarrfainn-se go bráth mar spré leat;
'S maran domh-sa taoi tú i ndán,
A phéarla an bhrollaigh bháin,
  Nár thí mise slán ón aonach!

TRANSLATION

There's a colleen fair as May,
For a year and for a day
I have sought by ev'ry way, — Her heart to gain.
There's no art of tongue or eye,
Fond youths with maidens try,
But I've tried with ceaseless sigh, — Yet tried in
  vain.
If to France or far-off Spain,
She'd cross the wat'ry main,
To see her face again, — The seas I'd brave.
And if 'tis heav'n's decree,
That mine she may not be,
May the Son of Mary me — In mercy save.

Oh, thou blooming milk-white dove,
To whom I've given true love,
Do not ever thus reprove — My constancy.
There are maidens would be mine,
With wealth in hand and kine,
If my heart would but incline — To turn from thee.
But a kiss, with welcome bland,
And touch of thy fair hand,
Are all that I'd demand, — Wouldst thou not spurn;
For if not mine, dear girl,
Oh, Snowy-breasted Pearl!
May I never from the Fair — With life return!

AN CLÁR BOG DÉIL
(The Soft Deal Board)

[Also known as 'Cashel of Munster', especially in Sir Samuel Ferguson's translation, the song is given here in Edward Walsh's version from *Irish Popular Songs*.]

Do ghlacfainn tú gan ba, gan púint,
gan áireamh spré,
A chuid 'en tsaol, le toil do mhuínntre,
dá mb'ail leat mé.
'Sé mo ghalar dúch gan mé 'gus tú,
a dhian-ghrá mo chléibh,
I gCaiseal Mumhan's gan do leabaidh fúinn
ach an clár bog déil!

Siúil, a chogair, is tar a chodla
liom féin don ghleann,
Gheó tú fosca, leabaidh fhlocais
is aer cois abhann;
Beidh na srotha a' gabháil thorainn
faoi ghéagaibh crann,
Beidh an londubh i n-ár bhfochair
is an chéirseach ann.

Searc mo chléibh do thug mé féin duit,
agus grá tré rún,
Dá dtigeadh sé do chor sa' tsaol
go mbéinn féin is tú,
Ceangal cléireach eadrainn araon,
's an fáinne dlúth —
Is dá bhfeicinn féin mo shearc ag aon fhear
gheóinn bás le cumha!

Dia Domhnaigh nuair a chinn
ag an dteampoll í,
Fallaing riabhach is ribín uaithne uirthi
anún mar ghnaoi,
Agus gúna do sguabfadh
na gleannta fraoich:
Och! 'sé mo bhuaire mar do luadh liom
'n-a maighdin í!

Tá úr-phíob ag mo mhúirnín,
is a bráid mar aol,
A cúilín casta búclaidheach
a' fás go féar;
'Sé mo chumha nimhe nách san úir síos
do fágadh mé
Sara stiúiríodh mé i gcúigibh
is mo ghrá thar m'éis!

TRANSLATION

I would wed you, dear, without gold or gear
or counted kine,
My wealth you'd be, would your friends agree,
and you be mine.
My grief, my gloom! that you do not come,
my heart's dear hoard!
To Cashel fair, though our coach were there
but a soft deal board!

Oh, come, my bride, o'er the wild hills' side,
to the valley low,
A downy bed for my love I'll spread,
where waters flow;
And we shall stray where streamlets play,
the groves among,
Where echo tells to the listening dells
the blackbirds' song.

Love tender, true I gave to you,
and secret sighs,
In hope to see, upon you and me,
one hour arise
When the priest's blest voice would confirm my
choice, and the ring's strict tie:
If wife you be, love, to one but me, love,
in grief I'll die!

In church at prayer first I saw the fair
in glorious sheen,
In mantle flowing, with jewels glowing,
and frontlet green,
And robe of whiteness whose fold of lightness
might sweep the lea,
Oh, my heart is broken since tongues have spoken
that maid for me!

A neck of white has my heart's delight,
and breast like snow,
And flowing hair whose ringlets fair
to the green grass flow —
Alas! that I did not early die
before the day
That saw me here, from my bosom's dear
far, far away!

BEAN AN FHIR RUAIDH
(The Red-haired Man's Wife)

[The English translation is by Douglas Hyde, from *Love Songs of Connacht* (1893), with modifications by Donal O'Sullivan, *Songs of the Irish* (1960).]

Tá siad dá rá
  Gur tú sáilín socair i mbróig,
Tá siad dá rá
  Gur tú béilín tana na bpóg.
Tá said dá rá,
  'Mhíle grá dhil, go dtug tú dham cúl,
Cé go bhfuil fear le fáil,
  'S leis an táilliúirín bean an fhir ruaidh.

Do thugas naoi mí
  I bpríosún ceangailte cruaidh,
Boltaí ar mo chaolaibh
  Is míle glas as súd suas.
Thúrfainn-se sidhe
  Mar thúrfadh eala cois cuain,
Le fonn do bheith sínte
  Síos le bean an fhir ruaidh.

Shaoil mise, a chéad-shearc,
  Go mbeadh aon-tigheas idir mé 's tú,
Shaoil mé 'n-a dhéidh sin
  Go mbréagfá mo leanbh ar do ghlúin.
Mallacht Righ Neimhe
  Ar an té sin bhain dhíom-sa mo chlú,
Sin, agus uile go léir
  Lucht bréige chuir idir mé 's tú.

Tá crann ins an ngáirdín
  Ar a bhfásann duilliúr is bláth buí,
An uair leagaim mo lámh air
  Is láidir nach mbriseann mo chroí.
'Sé mo shólás go bás,
  Is é d'fháil ó fhlaitheas anuas,
Aon phóigín amháin,
  Is é d'fháil ó bhean an fhir ruaidh.

Ach go dtig lá an tsaoghail
  'N-a réabfar cnuic agus cuain,
Tiocfaidh smúit ar an ngréin
  'S beidh na néalta chomh dubh leis an ngual.
Beidh an fhairrge tirim,
  Is tiocfaidh na brónta 's na truaighe.
'S beidh an táilliúr a' sgreadach
  An lá sin faoi bhean an fhir ruaidh.

TRANSLATION

'Tis what they say,
  Thy little heel fits in a shoe,
'Tis what they say,
  Thy little mouth kisses well too.
'Tis what they say,
  Thousand loves, that you left me to rue;
That the tailor went the way
  That the wife of the red-haired man knew.

Nine months did I spend
  In a prison closed tightly and bound;
Bolts on my smalls
  And a thousand locks frowning around.
But o'er the tide
  I would leap with the leap of a swan,
Could I once set my side
  By the bride of the red-haired man.

I thought, O my life,
  That one house between us would be,
And I thought I would find
  You coaxing my child on your knee.
But a curse from on high
  For ever on him let it be,
And the bands of the liars
  Who put silence between you and me.

There's a tree in the garden
  With blossoms that tremble and shake,
With my hand on its bark,
  I feel that my heart it must break.
On one wish alone
  My soul through the long months ran,
One little kiss
  From the wife of the red-haired man.

But the day of doom shall come.
  And the hills and the harbours be rent;
Mist shall fall on the sun
  From the thunder-clouds heavily sent;
The sea shall be dry,
  And the earth under mourning and ban;
Then loud shall he cry
  For the wife of the red-haired man.

AN DRAIGHNEÁN DONN
(The Blackthorn Tree)

[The translation is by Donal O'Sullivan, *Songs of the Irish.*]

Fuaireas féirín lá aonaigh
ó bhuachaill deas,
Agus céad rud nach é sin
ó rogha na bhfear.
Sgala cléibh ar an té adéarfadh
nach tú mo shearc,
A bhuachaill ghléigil is breáth' i n-Éirinn,
's go n-éalóinn leat!

Síleann céad fear gur leó féin mé
nuair ólaim lionn,
Ní airím iad nuair a smaoiním
ar a chómhrá liom.
Cúm is míne ná an síoda
tá'r Shliabh na mBan Fionn,
'S tá mo ghrá mar bhláth na n-áirne
ar an draighneán donn.

Is glaise súil é ná féar is drúcht air
's ná duilliúr na gcrann,
Is gile taobh é ná sneachta séite
ar Shliabh Uí Fhloinn —
Sneachta séite is é dhá shíor-chur
nó 'tuitim go mall,
'S go bhfuil mo ghrá-sa mar bhláth na n-áirne
ar an draighneán donn.

A ógánaigh an chúil dualaigh
agus é cas ó n-a bharr,
Níl spuaic air ón tsluasaid
ná mairg ón rámhan.
A Dhia tá thuas, cuireas fuacht
agus teas ins a' lá,
Gan mé i n-uaigneas na coille dualgaí,
go nguilfinn mo sháith!

Is fear gan chéill bhíos a' dréim leis
an gcrann a bhíos árd,
Is go bhfuíodh crann beag le n-a thaobh
dhéanas réidh ar a láimh.
Cé gur árd é an crann caorthainn
bíonn sé searbh i n-a bharr,
'S go bhfásann sméir is subha craobh ar
a' gcrann is ísle bláth.

Shaoil mé féin nach 'ceasacht spré orm
a bheadh grá mo chroí,
'S nach bhfáigfeadh sé 'n-a dhéigh mé
mar gheall ar mhaoin;
Fó-ríor géar nach bhfuilim féin is
an té úd a chráidh mo chroí

I ngleanntán sléibhe i bhfad ó éinneach
is an drúcht 'n-a luí!

Cebé arab oth leis é, molfa mise
grá mo chroí,
Cebé arab oth leis é, suífe mise
le n-a thaoibh;
An té lerab oth leis é, míle osna
tré lár a chroí —
A réalt a' tsoluis, i mbéal gach phobail
is tú chráidh mo chroí!

A Dhé dhílis! goid é dhéanas mé
má imíonn tú uaim?
Níl eólas 'un do thighe agam,
'un do theine nó 'un do chúil.
Tá m'athair faoi leatruim'
is mo mháthair go dúch,
Fir a' bhaile seo go mór i bhfeirg liom,
is mo ghrá i bhfad uaim!

A chéad shearc, ná tréig mise
ar airgead nó ar ór,
'S a chéad shearc, ná tréig mise
ar mhóran stóir,
A chéad shearc, ná tréig mise
ar mhacha breá bó,
'S gur tú an chéad fhear dar léig mé leis
mo rún go h-óg!

Beir leat me — 's níl airgead
ná ór agam,
Beir leat me — 's níl ba boga
ar mhóin agam,
Beir leat me — 's níl bábáinín
óg faoim chrios,
Nó muna mbeirir ní mhairim-se
bliain ó 'niu!

TRANSLATION

I got a fairing last fair-day
from a handsome boy,
And plenty I don't mention
from my true love and joy.
My bitter curse be on the first
who denies we are one,
My hope of heaven! my heart is given
to thee alone!

There's many thinking when I'm drinking
 that I'm surely theirs,
But to their pleading I'm unheeding
 with his whisper in my ears.
His dear face has all the graces
 of mountain and of lea,
And his bosom is like the blossom
 of the blackthorn tree.

His eye is far brighter
 than the dew at e'en,
His side is far whiter
 than the snow on Slieve Flynn,
Snow that's pelting or softly melting
 or falling free,
And his bosom is like the blossom
 of the blackthorn tree.

His curling hair is as fair as
 the leaves' sun and shade,
His white hands are unbranded
 by rough shovel or spade.
O Creator who makest
 windy weather and still,
Lead O lead me where none will heed me,
 to weep my fill!

'Tis but folly to scan holly
 or more lofty trees,
When in the bushes where water rushes
 we find heart's ease.
Though the rowan so high is growing,
 its berry is tart,
While near the ground fruit sweet and sound
 will charm the heart.

Do not neglect me or reject me
 because I'm poor,
Take O take me and ne'er forsake me
 for lack of store!
Would to heaven I were at even
 with him who broke my heart,
With him only, in a valley lonely,
 ne'er, ne'er to part!

Whoso resents it will not prevent it,
 my love's my pride,
Whoso resents it will not prevent it,
 I'll sit by his side.
May who resents it be demented
 and nevermore thrive!
O my dearest, 'tis thou who tearest
 my heart alive!

Son of Mary! without my dearie
 what shall I do?
I cannot meet him, I may not greet him,
 I'm left to rue.
Father, mother, each worse than other,
 sit down and sigh,
Men who'd woo me now look through me,
 and pass me by.

O first love and best love,
 don't look for kine,
O first love and best love,
 though poor I'm thine.
O first love and best love,
 thy love I crave,
O best love, my first love
 to thee I gave!

I'm thine, love, be mine, love,
 and heed not gold,
I'm thine, love, be mine, love,
 nor sheep in fold.
Take me — I've no baby
 as yet unborn,
Take me — shouldst thou forsake me
 I'll die forlorn!

A BHUACHAILL AN CHÚIL DUALAIGH
(O Youth of the Flowing Hair)

[Petrie includes this in his *Ancient Music of Ireland.* The setting he provides was noted from the singing of Patrick Coneely of Galway in 1839. Part of his commentary on the song reads: 'I am, as usual, indebted to my friend Mr. Curry for a copy of this song, which he believes to be a very ancient one; for it was considered as such by his father and other old people, by whom he often heard it sung. He further believes it to be a Munster song; but it is certainly also known in Connaught, where it is commonly called *Oganach an chúil dualaigh,* — the word *Oganach* being a synonymous term with *Buachaill* — "a youth, a boy" . . . .'

The second stanza of the Irish is not given in Petrie's translation.]

A bhuachaill an chúil dualaigh,
 Cár chodail mé 'réir?

Ag colú do leapan,
  'S níor airigh tú mé.
Dá mbeadh fios mo cháis agat,
  Ní chodlófá néal.
'S gurab é do chómhrá binn blasta
  D'fhág an osna so im thaobh.

Nuair luim ar mo leabain
  'Sí m'aisling ochón,
'S ar m'éirghe dham ar maidin
  'Sí mo phaidir mo dheór,
Mo ghruaig bhí 'n-a dualaibh
  Is d'imigh 'n-a ceó,
'Chionn grá 'thúirt don bhuachaill
  Nach bhfuighead-sa go deó!

A bhuachaill an chúil dualaigh,
  Nár fheice mé Dia
Go bhfeicim-se do sgáile
  'Teacht 'dir mé is an ghrian!
Ní thuigeann tú mo mhearú,
  'S ní airíonn tú mo phian,
Is mar bharr ar gach aindeis
  Is leat do chailleas mo chiall!

A bhuachaill an chúil dualaigh,
  An bhfuil ár sonas le fáil,
Nó a' mbeimid 'n-ár gcomhnuí
  In aon lóisdín amháin?
Sinn araon pósda,
  A stóir 's a dhian-ghrá,
Ár naimhdíbh fá bhrón,
  Is ár gcómhgas go sámh

TRANSLATION

Oh! youth of the flowing hair,
  Where slept I last night?
At the side of your bed,
  And you felt me not there:
Had you known my sad case,
  Not a wink would you have slept;
Since it was your sweet converse
  That caused this pain in my side.

. . . . . .

Oh! youth of the flowing hair,
  May I never see God,
If I do not see your shadow ever
  Between me and the sun!
You understand not my ravings,
  And you feel not my pain;
And to end my sad fortune,
  I have lost by you my reason.

Oh! youth of the flowing hair,
  Shall we find our good luck,
Or shall we ever together
  In the one dwelling be?
You and I married —
  Dear store of my heart!
Our foes in deep sorrow,
  And full happy our friends!

AN CHUIMHIN LEAT AN OÍCHE ÚD?
(Do You Remember That Night?)

[In the *Ancient Music of Ireland*, Petrie comments: 'The song which has given a popular name to this melody has been committed to writing for me by Mr. Curry; and as it is not a composition of recent date, nor wanting in interest as the love-song of a peasant girl, it has appeared to me to be not unworthy of preservation, in connexion with the air to which it had been adapted.']

An cuimhin leat an oíche úd
  Do bhí tú ag an bhfuinneóg,
Gan hata, gan laimhnne
  Dhod dhíon, gan chasóg?
Do shín mé mo lámh chút,
  'S do rug tú uirthi barróg,
Is d'fhan mé id chomhluadar
  Nó gur labhair an fhuiseóg!

An cuimhin leat an oíche úd
  Do bhí tú agus mise
Ag bun an chrainn chaorthainn
  'S an oíche a' cur chuisne?
Do cheann ar mo chíochaibh,
  Is do phíob gheal dhá seinm,
Is beag do shaoileas an oíche úd
  Go sgaoilfeadh ár gcumann!

A chumainn mo chroí 'stigh,
  Tar oíche ghar éigin,
Nuair luífid mo mhuinntir,
  Chun cainte le chéile.
Beidh mo dhá láimh ad thímcheall,
  Is mé ag innsint mo sgéil dhuit,
'S gurab é do chómhra suairc mín tais
  Do bhain radharc fhlaithis Dé dhíom!

Tá an teine gan choigilt
  Is an solus gan mhúcha,
Tá an eochair faoi an ndorus,
  Is tarraing go ciúin í.
Tá mo mháthair 'n-a codla
  Agus mise im dhúiseacht,
Tá m'fhoirtiún im dhorn,
  Is mé ullamh chun siúil leat!

TRANSLATION

Do you remember that night
  That you were at the window,
  With neither hat, nor gloves,
  Nor coat to shelter you;
  I reached out my hand to you,
  And you ardently grasped it,
  And I remained to converse with you
  Until the lark began to sing?

Do you remember that night
  That you and I were
  At the foot of the rowan-tree,
  And the night drifting snow;
  Your head on my breast,
  And your pipe sweetly playing?
  I little thought that night
  Our ties of love would ever loosen.

O beloved of my inmost heart,
  Come some night, and soon,
  When my people are at rest,
  That we may talk together;
  My arms shall encircle you
  While I relate my sad tale
  That it is your pleasant soft converse
  That has deprived me of heaven.

The fire is unraked,
  The light unextinguished,
  The key under the door,
  And do you softly draw it.
  My mother is asleep,
  And I am quite awake;
  My fortune is in my hand,
  And I am ready to go with you.

MY LAGAN LOVE

[The poet Joseph Campbell collected this song in Fanad, north Donegal about 1903-04. It was first published in *Songs of Uladh* (Belfast and Dublin, 1904) in an arrangement by Herbert Hughes. This version has five stanzas; but when Campbell published it again, possibly a year later in *Three Traditional Ulster Airs* (London, n.d.), in an arrangement by Hamilton Harty, only two stanzas survived. It is this arrangement that has become most popular and the two-stanza form is reprinted here. The additional stanzas in *Songs of Uladh* are inferior in quality.

Campbell's introductory note to the first version is as follows: 'I got this from Proinsias mac Suibhne, who played it to me on the fidil. He had it from his father, Seaghan mac Suibhne, who learned it from a sapper working on the Ordnance Survey in Tearmann about fifty years ago. It was then sung to a ballad called "The Belfast Maid", now forgotten in Cill-mac nEnain.'

The Ordnance Survey had in fact taken place about seventy years before. The townland of Tearmann is close to the village of Kilmacrennan (Cill-mac nEnain), not far from Letterkenny.]

Where Lagan stream sings lullaby,
There blows a lily fair;
The twilight gleam is in her eye,
The night is on her hair.
But like a love-sick leanannsidhe,[1]
She has my heart in thrall.
No life I own nor liberty,
For love is lord of all.

And often when the beetle's horn
Has lulled the eve to sleep;
I steal up to her sheiling lorn
And through the dooring peep;
There by the cricket's[2] singing-stone
She spares[3] the bogwood fire,
And sings in sad sweet undertone,
The song of heart's desire.

1. *Leanann sidhe* is a fairy mistress, one whose love consumed the man who was the object of it. The only escape from the thrall of this love was to find someone else acceptable to her.
2. The cricket was traditionally associated with good fortune and its chirping by the fireside presaged good fortune.
3. Campbell prints 'spares' in both versions, although it is now usually rendered as 'stirs'.

'ÓGÁNAIGH ÓIG
(Young Lad)

[This song is included in Donal O'Sullivan's *Songs of the Irish* in his own translation.]

'Ógánaigh óig a bhfuil ór in do phéarlaibh,
Is iomdha cailín óg do phógadh do bhéilín!

Is trua gan mé bheith ag ól leat ar bórd i mBinn Éadair,
Agus ór bheith in ár bpócaíbh is sinn pósta le chéile!

'Sé shaoil mise féin (mar bhí mé gan eólas)
Gurbh ionann domh do lámh-sa agus fáinne pósta;
Do shaoil mé 'n-a dhéigh sin gur tú an réalt eólais,
Nó mar bhláth na subh-chraobh ar gach taobh do na bóithribh!

Is trua Dé gan mise is an giolla dubh ar iarraidh
Naoi n-oíche, naoi lá 'gus ceithre ráithe na bliana,
I seómra bheith druidthe le fuinneógaibh iarainn,
Glas ar a' dorus is an eochair ar iarraidh!

Is trua géar nach bhfuil mise agus óigfhear na súl glas
A' súgra 's ag éisteacht le cléireach ár bpóstaí;
Is cinnte dá mbeadh déannach go mbeinn féin is m'óigfhear
A' siúl ar fud coillte le soillse an tráthnóna!

Bhí mé seacht seachtaine ar leabaidh na fuinneóige
Ag éisteacht le n-a aisling is a' féachaint tráth chodlódh sé.
Tá dhá bhinn m'fhallainn a' falach gach aon phóige,
'S gurab é grá an radaire tharraing mé 'un trioblóide!

'Ógánaigh óig is míne ná an síoda,
Agus d'anál níos cumhrtha ná bola na time,
Do lochta go deó deo ní chuirfinn-se síos duit
Ach amháin mar fheabhas agus chodlann tú an oíche!

TRANSLATION

Young lad with the curls and the lips made for kissing,
Would to God you and I from our people were missing,
In a tavern at Howth or abroad in the heather,
With gold in our purse, and we wedded together!

I thought, O my love, (I was young and not clever)
That your troth, like a ring, meant you'd part from me never:
You seemed after that like the star in my heaven,
Or the raspberry blossom on the roadside at even!

Would the dark lad and I were where no one could enter,
For nine days and nine nights and from spring until winter,
With iron-bound shutters to fasten our chamber,
And the key in a place not a soul could remember!

How I wish that the dark lad and I were both kneeling
At the altar in church, with the wedding-bells pealing!
If the clergy were late, be sure I and my dearest
Would roam in the sun through the depths of the forest!

Seven weeks by the window a vigil I'm keeping,
As I list to his dreaming and watch him while sleeping;
I'm hiding each kiss with my mantle bent double,
And 'tis love for the rascal has brought me to trouble!

Young lad in whose face the shy sunbeam reposes,
Whose breath is far sweeter than thyme or wild roses,
I never could blame you, your faults I pass over,
Excepting you sleep far too sound for a lover!

INGHEAN AN PHAILITÍNIGH
(The Palatine's Daughter)

[Donal O'Sullivan, in *Songs of the Irish*, provides the background to this song: 'This is a County Kerry song, Ballyseedy being a short distance south-east of Tralee and Currans about half-way being Castleisland and Farranfore. "Mr. Oliver" was doubtless a land-agent ... the English version is the production of some countryman, roughly translating the Irish.

'The settlement of the Palatines in Munster forms an interesting story. The inhabitants of the Palatinate were reduced to penury by the War of the Spanish Succession, and the English Government of the day decided to plant some of them in Ireland with the idea of increasing the numerical strength of Protestantism in this country. The project was carried through at a cost of £20,000, borne by the Irish Exchequer, and in 1711 about three hundred families reached Dublin. Many of them remained there and quickly became absorbed in the general population. The rest settled on the land, mostly in Limerick and North Kerry, where the landlords leased holdings to them at a half or a third of the rent current in the district. "The poor Irish", says Arthur Young in his *Tour of Ireland*, "are seldom treated in this way. When they are, they work much greater improvements than is common among these Germans." About 1770 large numbers of them went to America, their departure being attributed by John Wesley to the selfish folly of the landlords, who exacted the full rent of the land as the leases fell in. Many of the remainder intermarried with the native Irish and became Catholics, like *The Palatine's Daughter*.']

Ó! lá breá aoibhinn maragaidh
  's mé a' gabháil thrí Bhail' Ó Síoda,
Cé casfaí ins a' tslí orm ach
  inghean a' Phailitínigh?
Ó! d'fhiosaruigh sí fios m'ainime,
  'nó goidé an baile ó go mbíonn tú?
A' dtiocfá féin abhaile liom
  seal i dtigh mo mhuinntre?'
'Sé dubhart, 'Is buachaill greanta mé
  do chomhnuíonn i gCoirínibh.'

'Má thréigeann tú an t-aifreann
  do gheó tú mé le pósa.
Mar a dhein mo cháirde féinig is
  a maireann eile beó aca.
Ghéo tú ór is airgead
  is talamh gan aon chíos liom,
Agus litir ó *Mhister Oliver*
  go bhfuil m'athair caithte, críonna,
Is cailín deas chun taistil leat,
  más meón leat Pailitíneach.'

Do dhruideas-sa 'n-a h-aice siúd
  is do thugas dí cúpla póigín:
'Is má théim-se féin abhaile leat
  an bhfagha mé tú le pósa?'
'Sé dubhairt sí, 'Ná bíodh eagal ort,
  tair liom is míle fáilte,
Is gheó tú le toil m'athar mé,
  's gan dearmad mo mháithrín,
Gheó tú stoc ar thalamh liom
  is mairfimíd go sásta.'

Is anois tá mo dhuainín críochnuithe
  's gan peann ná dubh im dhearnain,
Do thug sí an t-óigfhear barrfhionn lé
  abhaile go dtí n-a máthair.
Do chríochnuíodar an maraga
  is bhí sé annsan 'n-a mháistir,
Fuair sé tigh is talamh lé
  'gus iothala chluthmhar shásta,
Is annsan do dhein sé Caitliceach
  den ainnir mhilis mhánla.

TRANSLATION

As I roved out one evening through
  the groves of Ballyseedy,
Whom should I meet on a cool retreat
  but an Irish Palatine's[1] daughter?
She asked my name and station O!
  or where was my dwelling arbour?
Or would I come along with her
  to see her own dear father?
I said I was a rakish lad,
  In Currans I was in sarvice.

'If you forsake the Mass and sacraments
  you'll get me and my portion,
As I have done in person and
  my forefathers before me.
You'll get gold and silver O!
  and land without tax or charges,
And a letter from Mister Oliver
  my father's unfit for sarvice,
And a pretty lass to wed with you,
  if you choose a Palatine's daughter.'

I courteously saluted her
  And twice I kissed my darling:
'And if I go home along with you
  shall I get you as my partner?'
She said, 'A thousand welcomes O!
  and be not the least alarmèd,
You'll have my mother's blessing and
  best wishes of my father,
You'll get stock and property,
  and we'll be happy ever after.'

And now my song is ended and
  my pen is out of order,
She brought this handsome young man
  in presence of her father.
They agreed and soon get married O!
  and then he became master,
He got his landed property,
  his haggard[2] and his barn,
And then he made a Catholic
  Of the Irish Palatine's daughter.

1. Prince's.
2. A stockyard for hay.

SNAIDHM AN GHRÁ
(The True Lovers' Knot)

[In *Songs of the Irish*, Donal O'Sullivan appends the following comment: 'My friend Mr. A. Martin Freeman, who noted this touching song in County Cork, published with it his translation of an explanatory note given in connection with another version, obtained in Kerry. I reproduce it here with his permission.

'According to this note, the girl's parents married her to a rich man, her lover being poor. The rich fiancé knew nothing of the girl's love for another. When the poor man heard that his sweetheart was to be married, "the weakness of death came upon him, and he lay down to wait for the parting of his soul and body. Well, the engaged couple were married one morning, and that same morning the young woman was told that her best-beloved was on his death-bed. So she said to her husband, 'Oh,' said she, 'a great friend of mine is very sick to-day, and I should like to go and see him.' 'Very well,' said he, 'go along,' thinking it was a good sign in his wife to be going to see a sick person on the very day of her marriage. She went to the house where the sick man lay, and went up to the bed and threw herself on her knees, and looked lovingly at him, speaking as follows:

[*Here follows the dialogue in verse.*]

For he had died while she was saying this last verse. Then she lay down by his side and died too. The neighbours said they ought to be buried in one grave; but when her husband heard the whole story he would not agree to this. Indeed, he buried his wife as far away from the body of her lover as was possible in that churchyard. But soon two trees sprung up, one out of his grave and one out of hers. They grew upwards and bent towards each other, till there came five fingers, as it were, on the top of each tree, and these fingers interlocked."']

(Cailín)
'Is mo ghrá go léir tú, agus Dé do bheatha chúm!
Mo ghrá do shúile, agus t'éadan leathan geal,
Mo ghrá do chroí, nár smaoing ar mh'atharrach,
Mo ghrá mh'fhear óg, 's is é mo bhrón bheith
sgartha leat!'

(Fear)
'Níl id ghrá-sa ach mar a bheadh mám 'en tsneachta
'muigh,
Nú cúr lae Márta, 'chaithfeadh caise dhe,
Nú puis den ghaoith thig do dhruím na fairrge,
Nú tuile shléi bheadh t'réis lae fearthanna!'

(Cailín)
''S cá bhfeacaís mo ghrá-sa ná mo pháirt let
atharrach?
Ná dul ag ól leó ar bhórd go ceanasach?
Mar nár smaoingeas im chroí ná im aigne
Luí 'n-a gclúid, agus gan tú bheith ceangailthe.'

(Fear)
''S go deimhin, a mhianaigh, níor smaoingeas
masla dhuit,
Ná tú bhreith liúm gan cead ód bhantharlain,
'Dtaobh gan amhras gur bh'fhearr liom agam tu
Ná'n dá asbal déag, is ná maor an anama.'

(Cailín)
'Glaéidh ar Dhia go dian chun t'anama,
'S ar a' Maighdean Naomhtha, 'sí céile is fearra
dhuit,
'Sí thúrfaidh saor tú lá dhaortha an anama;
Séan mo ghrá-sa 'gus mo pháirt 'n fhaid a mhairfe
tú!

(Fear)
'Ní shéanfad do ghrá-sa ná do pháirt 'n fhaid a
mhairfe mé,
Ná go ceann seacht mbliain t'réis dul 'on talamh
dom;
Mar níor shín do chéile riamh fós ar leabaidh leat,
'S go deimhin, nuair a shínfidh, sínfead-sa
eadaraibh!'

(Cailín)
''S nách gránda an fuath é, t'réis muarán ceanais
duit,
Cuir mh'fhir phósda go deó i n-earraid liom,
A'troid 's a' coimheascar, a'bruíon 's ag acharann,
'S gan tusa beò 'gam chun mo sgéal duit 'aithris!'

TRANSLATION

(She)
'You are my heart's love, and how I welcome you!
I love your eyes, and your bright open countenance,
I love your heart, that ne'er thought of another,
My beloved young man, 'tis my grief we are parted!'

(He)
'There's nought in your love but of snow just a
handful,
Or the spray cast in March at the foot of a waterfall,
Or a catspaw of wind that the smooth sea is ruffling,
Or a mountainy stream that the rain makes a
torrent!'

(She)
'And when did you see me show love for another?
Or sit with them drinking at table so merrily?
For never in life did I wish for their company,
E'en though you and I had not yet been betrothèd!'

(He)
'Indeed then, my darling, I never thought ill of you,
Nor would claim you for mine without leave from your mother,
Though truly I swear I would rather possess you
Than God's chosen twelve or my soul's Angel Guardian.'

(She)
'Pray to the Lord that your soul may gain heaven,
And the Blessed Virgin, the spouse that is best for you;
'Tis she is your shield on the dread Day of Judgement;
As long as you live, you must shun my affection!'

(He)
'As long as I live, I'll ne'er shun your affection,
Nor for seven long years when the grave has received me.
For your newly wed husband has never yet lain with you,
And I swear, when he does, that you'll find me between you!'

(She)
'How wicked and hateful, when I was so fond of you,
To come between me and my husband for ever,
Making him jealous and angry and quarrelsome.
When you're no longer alive for me to confide in!'

AN BEINNSÍN LUACHRA
(The Little Bunch of Rushes)

[Donal O'Sullivan's note explains something about the traditional translations of such songs: 'This is one of the best-known of Irish Gaelic songs, and numerous versions exist of both words and air. The beautiful tune here given may well be thought to be worthy of a better theme; at the same time, the excellent assonance of the original makes the poem a melodious one.

'The girl was presumably gathering rushes for thatch or for carpet-making, but her bundle has the same symbolical meaning as thyme in English folk song, such as the familiar verse in 'The Seeds of Love':

I once had a sprig of thyme,
It prospered night and day,
By chance there came a false young man
And he stole my thyme away.

A popular Irish song was sometimes given an English dress and issued as a broadsheet; and in this case I gave the broadsheet version in place of a strict metrical translation of the original. The humble and unknown translators of such pieces knew Irish well, but their knowledge of English prosody was far to seek; and so, probably quite unconsciously, they imitated the assonance of their originals. To realise this to the full, one must bear in mind that the pronunciation is that of the Irish countryside — 'daycent' for 'decent', 'crayture' for 'creature', 'plaising' for 'pleasing', 'aisy' for 'easy', and so on. The internal assonance then becomes obvious. To take the third verse as an example:

I said, 'My charming cr*ay*ture,
Be pl*ai*sing to me and kind,
This moment is the s*ai*son
That eng*a*ges my tender mind.
These rushes cost some l*a*bour,
'Tis pl*ai*n that the like do grow;
Then grant me your kind f*a*vour,
Embr*a*ce me and *ai*se my woe'.]

Ó! maidin aoibhinn uaibhreach
Ar bhruach na coille is glaise bláth,
Bhí mo ghadhairín liom a' gluaiseacht
Go h-uasal is mo ghunna im láimh.
Casadh orm stua-bhean
Ba ruaidhe ghile dheise bhreá,
Agus birtín léithi buailte
Dhen luachair ba dheise bláth.

Is d'fhéachas ar na cuantaibh,
'S do bhí an t-uaigneas againn um neóin,
Do dhruideas leis an stuaire
Is d'fhuaduíos uaithi cúpla póg.
'Sé dúirt sí liom go h-uaibhreach,
'Fan uaim is ná cuir orm stró,
'S ná sgaip mo bheinnsín luachra
Is a bhfuaireas dá thrioblóid.'

'A chailín bhig na luachra,
A' leigfeá-sa do bheart ar lár?
Nó a' dtiocfá liom i n-uaigneas
Faoi bhruach na coille is glaise bláth?
Sagairt ní bhfuíodh sgéal air,
Nó éinneach dá bhfuil le fáil,
Go dtiocfaidh caint don chéirseach
Nó béarla don londubh bhreá.'

'A chailín bhig na luachra,
  Glac suaineas is fan go réidh;
Ní cáll duit a bheith uaibhreach
  I n-uaigneas is tú leat féin.
Má sgaip mé do chuid luachra,
  Is dual go bhfuil cuid tar h'éis;
Bainfead beinnse muar dhuit,
  Is ualach mar thuille léi.'

TRANSLATION

As I roved out one morning
  Down by a clear river side,
With dogs and gun commanding
  In decent and becoming pride,
I spied a lovely creature
  Whose fair locks I chanced to view,
With a bunch of rushes making,
  As pleasing as ever grew.

I looked about most careful,
  The place being free and clear,
I used some kind endeavours
  With this fair mind I loved so dear.
She said, 'Kind sir, be easy,
  I am a maid, you needs must know,
These rushes cost some labour,
  So spare them and let me go.'

I said, 'My charming creature,
  Be pleasing to me and kind,
This moment is the season
  That engages my tender mind.
These rushes cost some labour,
  'Tis plain that the like do grow;
Then grant me your kind favour,
  Embrace me and ease my woe.'

I gently did embrace her,
  In my arms I did her entwine:
'If your parents they are pleased now,
  In wedlock's bands we will join.
My heart you've captivated
  On this place where the rushes grow,
And for ever I'll embrace you,
  And your bonny bincheen luachara O!'

PREAB SAN ÓL!
(Another Round!)

[The author of this song, Riocard Bairéad (Richard Barrett), was born in Belmullet, Co. Mayo in 1739 and died there in 1819. He was a contemporary of John Philpot Curran, whose poem 'The Deserter's Meditation' (see Volume I, p. 485) resembles this in many ways. The metre is also employed by Richard Milliken in 'The Groves of Blarney' (see Volume I, p. 1101). In fact, metrically, 'Preab San Ól' is a song like *An Cailín Bán* (The Fair-Haired Girl) which corresponds more exactly to Milliken's and Curran's verses.

Petrie gives a detailed description of this mode of versification in his *Ancient Music of Ireland*, pp. 46-47. The verses, when printed with the music, are written in eight long lines, although, without the music they would or could be written in sixteen short lines, divided into four sections. In each section there are three lines of five and one of four syllables, with the five-syllable lines ending in rhyming disyllables. The fourth and eighth, and the twelfth and sixteenth lines rhyme with one another respectively. This mode of verse is called *Ocht-fhoclach Bec* in Irish, corresponding in general terms with the French *rime couée*. The following song retains the double stanzas of eight lines each to correspond to the two parts of the melody and employs, in the Irish, a complicated pattern of consonantal and assonantal rhymes which cannot be carried over into English. The text and translation are from Donal O'Sullivan's *Songs of the Irish.*]

Is iomdha slí do bhíos ag daoine
  A' cruinniú píosaí 's a déanamh stóir,
'S a luíod a smaoiníos ar ghiorra an tsaoil seo,
  'S go mbéidh siad sínte faoi leac go fóill.
Má's tighearna tíre, diúic nó rí thú,
  Ní cuirfíor pinn leat a' dul faoi'n bhfód:
Mar sin 's dá bhrí sin níl beart níos críonna
  Ná bheith go síorruí 'cur preab san ól!

An ceannuí craosach níl meón ná slí ar bith
  Le ór a dhéanamh nach bhfeicthear dhó,
An ráta is daoire ar an earra is saoire,
  Is ar luach shé bpine go gcuirfeadh cróin.
Do réir chaint Chríosta is ní do-dhéanta
  An cámhall cíocrach a thabhairt thríd a' gcró:
Mar sin 's dá bhrí sin níl beart níos críonna
  Ná bheith go síorruí 'cur preab san ól!

An long ar sáile níl clúid ná ceárd
  I nach gcaithfeadh cáirde ar feadh an domhain mhóir,
Ó ríocht na Spáinne suas Gibráltar,
  Agus ansan áit a mbíonn an Grand Seigniór.
Le gach cárgo líonfadh málaí
  Ní choinneódh an bás uaidh uair ná ló:
Mar sin, a cháirde, níl beart níos fearr dhúinn
  Ná bheith mar tá sin, 'cur preab san ól!

Is gearr a' saol tá ag a' lili sgiamhach,
  Cé gur buí agus gur geal a góil,
Agus Solamh críonna ina chulaí ríoghmhail
  Nach bhfuil baol air i n-áille dhó.
Níl sa' tsaol seo ach mar sionán gaoithe,
  Gath a sgaoiltear nó slám dho cheó:
Mar sin 's dá bhrí sin níl beart níos críonna
  Ná bheith go síorruí 'cur preab san ól!

TRANSLATION

Why spend your leisure bereft of pleasure
  Amassing treasure? Why scrape and save?
Why look so canny at every penny?
  You'll take no money within the grave!
Landlords and gentry, for all their plenty,
  Must still go empty — where'er they're bound:
So to my thinking we'd best be drinking,
  Our bumpers clinking in round on round!

The huxter greedy will grind the needy,
  Their straits unheeding, shouts 'Money down!'
His special vice is his fancy prices,
  For a florin's value he'll charge a crown.
With hump for trammel the scripture's camel
  Missed the needle's eye and so came to ground:
Why pine for riches while still we've stitches
  To hold our breeches? — Another round!

The shipman trading to Spain or Aden
  Returns well laden with oil and corn,
Or from Gibraltar his course he'll alter
  And steer for Malta and the Golden Horn.
With easy motion he sails life's ocean,
  And ne'er a notion he'll soon go aground:
So, lads and lasses, because life passes,
  Let's fill our glasses for another round!

King Solomon's glory, so famed in story,
  Was far outshone by the lily's guise;
But hard winds harden both field and garden,
  Pleading for pardon the lily dies.
Life's but a bubble of toil and trouble,
  A feathered arrow — once shot, ne'er found:
It's nought but miming — so ends my rhyming,
  But still we've time for just one last round!

MÁIRÍN DE BARRA

[In *Blas Meala*, Brian O'Rourke describes this as a 'typical man's love-song' in which standard ideas are expressed — the young man is sick with love, would give anything to obtain the girl, and is weeping in grief at not being able to have her. The song is generally regarded as anonymous, although O'Rourke mentions an attribution to Seán O Coileáin (1754-1817). The text is that given in *Blas Meala/A Sip from the Honey-Pot* (1985).]

A Mháirín de Barra, do mharaigh tú m'intinn,
Is d'fhág tú dubhach dealbh mé i nganfhios dom
  mhuintir;
Ar mo luí ar mo leaba dhom is ortsa bhímse a'
  cuimhneamh,
Is ar m'éirí dhom ar maidin, mar do chealg tú an
  croí ionam.

Do thugas is do thugas is do thugas óm chroí
  greann duit,
Ar Dhomhnach Fhéile Muire na gCoinneal sa
  teampall,
Dod shúilín ba ghlaise ná uisce na ngeamhartha,
Is dod bhéilín ba bhinne ná an druid nuair a
  labhrann.

Do shíl mé tú a mhealladh le briathra is le póga,
Do shíl mé tú a mhealladh le leabhair is le móide;
Is do shíl mé tú a mhealladh ar bhreacadh ha
  heornan,
Ach d'fhág tu dubhach dealbh ar theacht don
  bhliain nódh mé.

Is aoibhinn don talamh a siúlann tú féin air,
Is aoibhinn don trealamh ar a seineann tú véarsaí;
Is aoibhinn don leaba ina luíonn tú fé éadach,
'S is ró-aoibhinn don óigfhear a gheobhaidh tú mar
  chéile.

A Mháirín, glac mo chomhairle, is ná seoltar tú ar
  t'aimhleas;
Seachain an stróinse, fear séidte na hadhairce.
Gaibh leis an óigfhear a nglaonn siad Ó Floinn air;
Pós é de ghrá réitigh, ós é is toil le do mhuintir.

Do shiúlfainn is do shiúlfainn is do shiúlfainn an
  saol leat;
Do raghainnse thar sáile gan dhá phingin spré leat;
Mo mhuintir 's mo chairde go brách do thréigfinn,
Is go leigheasfá ón mbás mé ach a rá gur leat féin
  mé.

D'ólfainn agus d'ólfainn agus d'ólfainn do shláinte,
Is dá mbeinn ar bord loinge d'ólfainn ní b'fhearr í;

Dá mbeinnse im bhanaltra do bhréagfainn do bhábán;
Siúd ort is ól deoch is Dé do bheatha i do shláinte.

TRANSLATION

Oh, Máirín de Barra, you have made my mind feeble,
And you've left me sad and lonely, all unknown to my people;
As I lie on my pillow, it's of you I'm always dreaming,
And when I rise in the morning, my heart is still bleeding.

Oh, Máirín, you swept away my sense without warning,
As you knelt in the chapel on Candlemas morning;
Your eyes were far purer than the dewdrops on the barley,
And your voice was far sweeter than the linnet or starling.

I thought I would win you with kisses and coaxing,
I thought you'd be conquered by my promises and boasting;
I was sure that I could charm you as the barley turned golden,
But you left me broken-hearted when the harvest was over.

Oh, happy are the pathways where you stray and you saunter,
And happy are the blackbirds with the melodies you've taught them;
Oh, happy and thankful are the blankets that warm you,
And how happy for the bridegroom who'll stand beside you at the altar.

Oh, Máirín, take my warning, don't let any man cheat you,
Stay away from the tailor and beware of his scheming;
As O'Flynn is my name, I swear I'd never ill-treat you,
Oh, clasp me to your heart, love, you'll have your people's agreement.

Oh, Máirín, if you'd have me, I would walk the world proudly,
I'd take you over the water with no thought of a dowry;
I'd leave my friends and my own people, I'd have no fear of drowning,
For you'd save me from the grave, love, if you placed your arms round me.

Now I'll drink to your health, love, I'll drink it late and early,
And if we were on the sea, love, I'd drink deep as we were sailing;
If you'd meet me on the quay, love, there's no fear I'd keep you waiting,
And, please God, in a year, love, you could be feeding our baby.

LIAM Ó RAGHALLAIGH
(Liam O'Reilly)

[According to Brian O'Rourke, this song, which originated in north-west Mayo, was written by a man called Micheál Mag Raith: 'It appears that Liam O'Reilly was drowned — some time before 1800 — in Sruwaddacon Bay, where the Glenamoy river enters the sea. The accident happened when he was rowing home to his bride, Neilí Nic Siúrtáin, having delivered the eighty-year-old officiating priest back to the village of Kilcommon after the wedding ceremony.'

The air used in O'Rourke's accompanying tape to the song is 'a slowed-down version of the one generally known as "The Star of the County Down" . . . .']

I mo bhaintreach 's i mo mhaighdean 'sea fágadh mé go hóg,
'S ó ar chuala sibh, a chairde, gur báthadh mo mhíle stór?
Dá mbeinnse sa mbád an lá sin agus mo dhá láimh a bheith ar an scód,
Dar m'fhocal dhuit, a Liam Uí Raghallaigh, gur deas mar leigheasfainn do bhrón.

An cuimhneach libhse an lá úd a bhí an tsráid seo lán de mharcaigh,
Ag sagairt is ag bráithre is iad ag trácht ar ár mbainis?
Bhí an fhidil ar clár ann is an chláirseach á freagairt,
Is bhí triúr de na mná bána ann le mo ghrá geal a chur ar a leaba.

Níor mhór liom dhuit, a Liam Uí Raghallaigh, tú bheith i do chliamhain ag an rí,
Agus cuirtíní geala gléigeala a bheith ar gach taobh díot is tú in do luí,

Maighdeán chiúin chéillí a bheith ag réiteach do chinn,
Is ó luadh muid go hóg le chéile, 's é an trua mar d'éag tú le mo linn.

Níorbh ionadh liom scéal cráite a bheith amárach ag t'athair,
Ná ag banaltra na gcíocha bána a bhíodh a' tál ort is tú in do leanbh;
Ní áirím do bhean phósta nár chóirigh ariamh do leaba,
Is nuair a shíl mé a bheith ad phógadh is ar do thórramh a bhí an bhainis.

Bhí tú ar an triúr úd a chuaigh go Cill Chomáin,
Ag tíolacadh an Athar Píotar a bhí in aois a cheithre fichid;
Dá dtiocfá faoi cheann míosa, ach mo léan choíche, ní thiocfaidh,
'S nach trua sin bean san oíche is a caoifeach i mbarr toinne.

Tá do shúile ag na péiste is tá do bhéilin ag na portáin,
Tá do dhá láimhín gheala ghléigheala faoi ghéarsmacht na mbradán;
Ó, cúig phunt is ea a bhéarfainn don té a thóigfeadh mo dhianghrá,
Is 'sé mo léan thú a bheith i t'aonraic, a Neilí ghléigheal Nic Siúrtáin.

Mo mhallacht do na saoir a rinne an bád,
'S nár aithris dhom fhéin go raibh an t-éag ins na cláir;
Dá dtéitheá go Coillte Eochaill agus an t-adhmad a cheannach daor,
Ní báifí mo mhíle stóirín ar chóstaí Mhal Bay.

TRANSLATION

Will ye not weep for my great sorrow? for I'm a widow and still a maid,
And my husband of a morning is tossed and rolling upon the waves;
Had I been in the boat that evening holding fiercely on to the sail,
I swear on the Bible, Liam O'Reilly, I'd have saved you from your fate.

Do you remember that summer morning when the horsemen rode down our street,
And the friars and the clergy made their way to our wedding feast?
Oh, the fiddler played his heart out, the harper's answer was strong and sweet,
And there were fair maids there in plenty to place my darling between the sheets.

'Twould not surprise me, Liam O'Reilly, if you had royalty for your bride,
And if curtains of finest purple were shining round you on every side,
With a train of gracious ladies to arrange your hair with pride;
But you were mine, and the day you claimed me, you were taken by the tide.

'Tis no wonder they say of your father the heart inside him has turned to lead,
And likewise your white-haired mother on whose white milk you once were fed,
Not to mention the girl you married, who never managed to share your bed,
For when my arms should have been around you, oh, you were drowned and lying dead.

'Tis the cause of all my grieving you went that evening to Kilcommon;
When Father Peter asked for oarsmen, why did you answer that fateful summons?
As I lie alone in the night-time, I cry and hope for your homecoming,
For when her lover floats on the ocean, oh, life is lonesome for a woman.

Oh, the crabs have devoured your mouth, love, the eels have feasted upon your eyes,
And your white hands so strong and tender are now the salmon's proudest prize;
I'd pay a fortune to any boatman who'd show me where your body lies,
And ease the burden of Nellie Jordan, who'll get no rest till the day she dies.

There is a boatbuilder in this village, the curse of widows on him I lay;
He gave no warning that my darling would perish on our wedding day;
If he'd gone to Derryinver, for decent timber prepared to pay,
My only love would not be floating off the coast of Mal Bay.

AN CHÚILFHIONN
(The Coolun)

['An Chúilfhionn' means 'the maiden of the flowing locks'. Bunting includes it in his *Ancient Music of Ireland* in a four-stanza version. Thomas Furlong gives a six-stanza version in Hardiman's *Irish Minstrelsy* and John O'Daly a three-stanza version in *Poets and Poetry of Munster*. Hardiman attributed the song to Carolan, under the title 'Molly St George'. Samuel Ferguson also included a translation in *Lays of the Western Gael*. The version presented by Carl Hardebeck in *Ceatha Ceóil* V (1902) differs in many important ways from earlier nineteenth-century versions. The original version, if any true original exists, has been attributed to Muiris Ua Duagain (Maurice O'Dugan), a Tyrone poet of the seventeenth century, but the poem is thought by several commentators to be a good deal older.

It is almost impossible to find an English translation that adheres to any of the Irish versions. They seem to be renderings of different conflations of the Irish. The English version printed here does not appear to exist in any printed version, but is widely attributed to Dominic Behan, a brother of Brendan Behan. Its relation to the chosen Irish text — from P. O. Canainn (ed.), *Filidheacht na nGaedheal* (1940) — is sometimes close, sometimes distant, but it does capture something of the spirit of this old love-song about the tragic separation of the lover and his fair-haired beloved.]

An bhfaca tú an chúilfhionn is í ag siubhal ar na bhóithribh,
Ag ionnsáidhe na h-úrchoille is an drúcht ar a bróga,
'Sí mo shearc í 'sí mo rún í, is níl tnúth aici le h-óige,
Agus rug sí barr áilne ar mhnáibh breághtha na Fodhla.

I mBeal-Áth-na-Gár atá an stáid-bhean bhreágh mhódhamhail,
'Bhfuil a gruadh nar na caorthainn agus sgéimh in a clódh geal,
Budh bhinne guth a bhéilsan na an chéirseach 's ná an smólach,
'S ná an londubh ar na coilltibh le soillse tráthnóna.

Éirigh id shuidhe, a bhuachall, agus gléas damh mo ghearrán,
Nó go leanfaidh mé an stuaidh-bhean úd suas ar na cnocáin,
Tá sí dá síor-luadhadh liom ó bhí sí na leanbhán,
'S go mbudh bhinne liom naoi n-uaire í na an chuach 's na h-orgáin.

Ma thug mo chroidhe grádh dhuit 's gur tú áilne gach solais,
'S gan mo mhuintir sár-shásda leat, a ghrádh dhil na gcomann,
Páirt mhór de 'm chruadhtan is mé ag cruadh-ghul go daingean,
Faoi 'm leannán breágh uasal do luadhadh liom im leanbh.

A stór dhil mo chroidhe! bí díleas agus daingean damh,
Ná tréig rún do chléibh i ngeall air é bheith dealbh,
Bhéarfainn duit-se an Bíobla a bhfuil faoi agus thairis,
Go dtiubhradh Dia díleas ár sáith dhúinn le caitheamh.

An cuimhin leat-sa an oidche bhí tusa agus mise
Fá bhun an chrann chaorthainn is an oidhche ag cur chuisneadh,
Ní raibh fascadh ón ngaoith againn ná dídean on bhfearthainn,
Act mo chota chur fúinn agus do ghúna chur tharainn.

TRANSLATION

O say did you see her, by the gloaming or the sunrise,
As she stepped, like a faun in a vale of nacre,[1]
Or sang far sweeter than the lark or thrush
At eventide.

Red ripened her cheeks, like the berry upon the tree,
And her neck, more graceful than the swan's is,
Her lips like petals from the red rose
Smiled on me.

When she was a little girl and I a tender child
I loved her. But our parents' money placed between us,
So farewell my chailín dheas mo chroidhe,[2] fair flower
Of Balnagar.

Wait for me forever, by the place where we lay alone
Through the night, while the elfin storm-wind rustled,

1. mother-of-pearl.
2. Irish, 'dear girl of my heart'.

And the old ash trembled in the dark with loud and
Fearful moan.

I will come to my coolun,[3] ere the life of my corpse
shall wander,
And we'll hold, as we did when in our childhood,
My little jewelled flower of Erin, sweet flower
Of Balnagar.

3. Girl of the flowing locks.

SELECT BIBLIOGRAPHY

Collections: B. Breathnac, *Ceol Rinnce na hÉireann* (Dublin: Oifig an tSólathair, 1963); Part 2 (Dublin: Oifig an tSólathair, 1976; new edition, 1982); Edward Bunting, *A General Collection of the Ancient Irish Music* (London: W. Power, 1796); *A General Collection of the Ancient Music of Ireland* (London: Clementi, 1809); *The Ancient Music of Ireland, Arranged for the Pianoforte* (Dublin: Hodges Smith, 1840) — all three collections are available in the facsimile reprint (Dublin: Waltons, 1969); D. O'Sullivan (ed.), *The Bunting Collection of Irish Folk Music and Songs* Parts I-VI, 1927-39. Issued as Vols XXII-XXIX of the *Journal of the Irish Folk Song Society*, reissued as Vol. V of the 1967 edition (below); D. O'Sullivan (ed.), with M. O Suilleabháin, *Bunting's Ancient Music of Ireland* (Cork: Cork University Press, 1983); C.G. Hardebeck, *Ceatha Ceóil* Parts I-VII (Dublin: Connradh na Gaeilige, 1902-03); D. Hyde, *Abhráin Gradha Chúige Chonnacht or, The Love Songs of Connacht* (Dublin: Gill and Co.; London: T. Fisher Unwin, 1893); *Journal of the Irish Folk Song Society* Vols I-XXIX (1904-37), republished in 6 vols (London: 1967); *Journal of the Folk Song Society* Vols I-VIII (London: 1899-1931); P.W. Joyce, *Ancient Music of Ireland* (Dublin: McGlashan, 1873); *Irish Music and Song* (Dublin: Gill, 1888); *Old Irish Folk Music and Songs* (London: Longmans Green & Co.; Dublin: Hodges, Figgis & Co., 1909); R. M. Levey, *The First Collection of the Dance Music of Ireland* Vol. I (London: T. Fisher Unwin, 1858), Vol. II (London: T. Fisher Unwin, 1873; facsimile reprint 1858 (Dublin: Waltons, 1965); M. Mulcahy and M. Fitzgibbon, *The Voice of the People. Songs and History of Ireland* (Dublin: O'Brien Press, 1982); S. O'Boyle, *The Irish Song Tradition* (Dublin: Gilbert Dalton, 1976); J. O'Daly, *The Poets and Poetry of Munster* First Series (Dublin: J. O'Daly, 1849; 2nd ed., 1850; 3rd ed., 1884; 4th ed., 1925); C. O Lochlainn (ed.), *Irish Street Ballads* 2 vols (Dublin: The Three Candles Ltd., 1939); *More Irish Street Ballads* (Dublin: Three Candles Press, 1965); B. O'Rourke, *Blas Meala/A Sip from the Honey-Pot: Gaelic Folksongs with English Translations* (Dublin: Irish Academic Press, 1985); D. O'Sullivan, *Songs of the Irish. An Anthology of Irish Folk Music and Poetry with English Verse Translations* (Dublin: Browne and Nolan; New York: Crown Publishers Inc., 1960; reprinted Dublin and New York, 1967); George Petrie, *Ancient Music of Ireland* (1855); *Music of Ireland* (1882); *The Petrie Collection of the Ancient Music of Ireland* 2 vols (Dublin: Dublin University Press, 1855-82); Sir C. Stanford (ed.), *The Complete Collection of Irish Music as Noted by George Petrie* (1902-05); F. Roche, *The Roche Collection of Traditional Irish Music* (Cork: Ossian Publications, 1983); H. Shields (introd.), *Popular Music in Eighteenth-Century Dublin* (Dublin: Folk Music Society of Ireland and Na Píobairí Uilleann, 1985); H. Shields, *Narrative Songs in Ireland: Lays, Ballads and Come-all-yes* (Dublin: Irish Academic Press, 1990); *The Spirit of the Nation* (Dublin: Duffy, 1846; 2nd revised edition 1882); E. Walsh, *Irish Popular Songs* (Dublin: J. McGlashan; London: W.S. Orr & Co., 1847); G.-D. Zimmermann, *Songs of Irish Rebellion. Political Street Ballads and Rebel Songs* (Dublin: Allen Figgis, 1967).

(b) Anglo-Irish Songs and Ballads

ANONYMOUS

CASTLE HYDE

As I roved out on a summer's morning
Down by the banks of Blackwater side,
To view the groves and the meadows charming,
The pleasant gardens of Castle Hyde;
'Tis there I heard the thrushes warbling,
The dove and partridge I now describe;
The lambkins sporting on ev'ry morning,
All to adorn sweet Castle Hyde.

The richest groves throughout this nation
And fine plantations you will see there;
The rose, the tulip, the rich carnation,
All vying with the lily fair.
The buck, the doe, the fox, the eagle,
They skip and play by the river side;
The trout and salmon are always sporting
In the clear streams of sweet Castle Hyde.

There are fine walks in these pleasant gardens,
And seats most charming in shady bowers.

The gladiators both bold and darling
  Each night and morning do watch the flowers.
There's a church for service in this fine arbour
  Where nobles often in coaches ride
To view the groves and the meadow charming,
  The pleasant gardens of Castle Hyde.

There are fine horses and stall-fed oxes,
  And dens for foxes to play and hide;
Fine mares for breeding and foreign sheep there
  With snowy fleeces in Castle Hyde.
The grand improvements they would amuse you,
  The trees are drooping with fruit of all kind;
The bees perfuming the fields with music,
  Which yields more beauty to Castle Hyde.

If noble princes from foreign nations
  Should chance to sail to this Irish shore,
'Tis in this valley they would be feasted
  As often heroes have been before.
The wholesome air of this habitation
  Would recreate your heart with pride.
There is no valley throughout this nation
  In beauty equal to Castle Hyde.

I rose from Blarney to Castlebarnet,
  To Thomastown, and sweet Doneraile,
To Kilshannick that joins Rathcormack,
  Besides Killarney and Abbeyfeale;
The flowing Nore and the rapid Boyne,
  The river Shannon and pleasant Clyde;
In all my ranging and serenading
  I met no equal to Castle Hyde.

I KNOW WHERE I'M GOING

I know where I'm going, she said,
  And I know who's going with me;
I know who I love —
  But the dear knows who I'll marry.

Feather beds are soft,
  And painted rooms are bonny,
But I'll forsake them all
  To go with my love Johny;

Leave my dresses of silk,
  My shoes of bright green leather,
Combs to buckle my hair,
  And rings for every finger.

O some say he's black,
  But I say he's bonny —
The fairest of them all,
  My winsome handsome Johny.

I know where I'm going, she said,
  And I know who's going with me;
I know who I love —
  But the dear knows who I'll marry.

THE NIGHT BEFORE LARRY WAS STRETCHED

The night before Larry was stretched
  The boys they all paid him a visit;
A bait in their sacks, too, they fetched;
  They sweated their duds till they riz it:
For Larry was ever the lad,
  When a boy was condemned to the squeezer,[1]
Would fence all the duds[2] that he had
  To help a poor friend to a sneezer,[3]
    And warm his gob 'fore he died.

The boys they came crowding in fast,
  They drew all their stools round about him,
Six glims[4] round his trap-case[5] were placed,
  He coudn't be well waked without 'em.
When one of us asked could he die
  Without having duly repented,
Says Larry, 'That's all in my eye,
  And first by the clergy invented,
    To get a fat bit for themselves.'

'I'm sorry, dear Larry,' says I,
  'To see you in this situation;
And, blister my limbs if I lie,
  I'd as lieve it had been my own station.'
'Ochone! it's all over,' says he,
  'For the neckcloth I'll be forced to put on,
And by this time tomorrow you'll see
  Your poor Larry as dead as a mutton,
    Because, why, his courage was good.

'And I'll be cut up like a pie,
  And my nob from my body be parted.'

1. hangman.
2. pawn all the clothes.
3. A consoling drink or drinks.
4. candles.
5. cell.

'You're in the wrong box, then,' says I,
'For blast me if they're so hard-hearted:
A chalk on the back of your neck
Is all that Jack Ketch dares to give you;
Then mind not such trifles a feck,[6]
For why should the likes of them grieve you?
And now boys come tip us the deck.'

The cards being called for, they played,
Till Larry found one of them cheated;
A dart at his napper[7] he made
(The boy being easily heated):
'Oh, by the hokey, you thief,
I'll skuttle your nob with my daddle![8]
You cheat me because I'm in grief,
But soon I'll demolish your noddle,
And leave you your claret to drink.'

Then the clergy came in with his book,
He spoke him so smooth and so civil;
Larry tipped him a Kilmainham look,
And pitched his bag wig to the devil;
Then sighing, he threw back his head
To get a sweet drop of the bottle,
And pitiful sighing, he said:
'Oh, the hemp will be soon round my throttle,
And choke my poor windpipe to death.

'Though sure it's the best way to die,
Oh, the devil a better a-livin',
For sure when the gallows is high
Your journey is shorter to Heaven;
But what harasses Larry the most,
And makes his poor soul melancholy,
Is to think of the time when his ghost
Will come in a sheet to sweet Molly —
Oh, sure it will kill her alive.'

So moving these last words he spoke,
We all vented our tears in a shower;
For my part I thought my heart broke,
To see him cut down like a flower.
On his travels we watched him next day;
Oh, the throttler! I thought I could kill him;
But Larry not one word did say,
Nor changed till he came to 'King William'[9]
Then, musha![10] his colour grew white.

When he came to the nubbling chit,[11]
He was tucked up so neat and so pretty,
The rumbler[12] jogged off from his feet,
And he died with his face to the city;
He kicked, too — but that was all pride,
For soon you might see twas all over;
Soon after, the noose was untied;
And at darky we waked him in clover,
And sent him to take a ground sweat.

6. a damn.
7. head.
8. fist.
9. i.e. to the statue of King William, formerly in College Green in the centre of Dublin.
10. An abbreviated form of the Irish exclamation *mo samhael* (my soul).
11. The site of the hanging.
12. trapdoor.

THE RAKES OF MALLOW

Beauing, belling, dancing, drinking,
Breaking windows, damning, sinking,
Ever raking, never thinking,
Live the rakes of Mallow.

Spending faster than it comes,
Beating waiters, bailiffs, duns,
Bacchus' true-begotten sons,
Live the rakes of Mallow.

One time naught but claret drinking,
Then like politicians thinking
To raise the sinking-funds when sinking,
Live the rakes of Mallow.

When at home with dada dying
Still for Mallow water crying;
But where there's good claret plying,
Live the rakes of Mallow.

Living short but merry lives;
Going where the devil drives;
Having sweethearts but no wives,
Live the rakes of Mallow.

Racking tenants, stewards teasing,
Swiftly spending, slowly raising,
Wishing to spend all their lives in
Raking as in Mallow.

Then to end this raking life,
They get sober, take a wife,
Ever after live in strife,
And wish again for Mallow.

FINNEGAN'S WAKE

Tim Finnegan lived in Walkin Street,
A gentleman Irish mighty odd,
He had a tongue both rich and sweet,
An' to rise in the world he carried a hod.[1]
Now Tim had a sort of a tipplin' way,
With the love of the liquor he was born,
An' to help him on with his work each day,
He'd a drop of the craythur ev'ry morn.

Whack fol the dah, dance to your partner,
Welt the flure, yer trotters shake,
Wasn't it the truth I told you,
Lots of fun at Finnegan's Wake.

One morning Tim was rather full,
His head felt heavy which make him shake,
He fell from the ladder and broke his skull,
So they carried him home his corpse to wake,
They rolled him up in a nice clean sheet,
And laid him out upon the bed,
With a gallon of whiskey at his feet,
And a barrel of porter at his head.

His friends assembled at the wake,
And Mrs. Finnegan called for lunch,
First they brought in tay and cake,
Then pipes, tobacco, and whiskey punch.
Miss Biddy O'Brien began to cry,
'Such a neat clean corpse, did you ever see,
Arrah, Tim avourneen,[2] why did you die?'
'Ah, hould your gab,' said Paddy McGee.

Then Biddy O'Connor took up the job,
'Biddy,' says she, 'you're wrong, I'm sure,'
But Biddy gave her a belt in the gob,
And left her sprawling on the floor;
Oh, then the war did soon enrage;
'Twas woman to woman and man to man,
Shillelagh law did all engage,
And a row and a ruction soon began.

1. An open wooden box attached to a pole, for carrying bricks.
2. (Irish) darling.

Then Micky Maloney raised his head,
When a noggin of whiskey flew at him,
It missed and falling on the bed,
The liquor scattered over Tim;
Bedad he revives, see how he rises,
And Timothy rising from the bed,
Says, 'Whirl your liquor round like blazes,
Thanam o'n dhoul,[3] do ye think I'm dead!'

3. My soul to the devil.

THE LAMBS ON THE GREEN HILLS

The lambs on the green hills, they sport and they
play,
And many strawberries grow round the salt sea,
And many strawberries grow round the salt sea,
And many's the ship sails the ocean.

The bride and bride's party to church they did go,
The bride she rode foremost, she bears the best
show,
But I followed after with my heart full of woe,
To see my love wed to another.

The first place I saw her 'twas in the church stand,
Gold rings on her finger and her love by the hand,
Says I, 'My wee lassie, I will be the man
Although you are wed to another.'

The next place I seen her was on the way home,
I ran on before her, not knowing where to roam,
Says I, 'My wee lassie, I'll be by your side
Although you are wed to another.'

'Stop, stop,' said the groomsman, ''till I speak a word,
Will you venture your life on the point of my sword?
For courting so slowly you've lost this fair maid,
So begone, for you'll never enjoy her.'

Oh, make now my grave both large, wide and deep,
And sprinkle it over with flowers so sweet,
And lay me down in it to take my last sleep,
For that's the best way to forget her.

THE PARTING GLASS

O, all the money e'er I had,
I spent it in good company.

And all the harm I've ever done,
Alas! it was to none but me.
And all I've done for want of wit
To mem'ry now I can't recall,
So fill to me the parting glass,
Goodnight and joy be with you all.

Oh, all the comrades e'er I had,
They're sorry for my going away,
And all the sweethearts e'er I had,
They'd wish me one day more to stay,
But since it falls unto my lot,
That I should rise and you should not,
I gently rise and softly call,
Good night and joy be with you all.

If I had money enough to spend,
And leisure time to sit awhile,
There is a fair maid in this town,
That sorely has my heart beguiled.
Her rosy cheeks and ruby lips,
I own she has my heart in thrall,
Then fill me the parting glass,
Good night and joy be with you all.

IF I WAS A BLACKBIRD

If I was a blackbird, I'd whistle and sing
And I'd follow the ship that my true love sails in,
And on the top riggings I'd there build my nest.
And I'd pillow my head on his lily-white breast.

I am a young maiden and my story is sad
For once I was courted by a brave sailor lad.
He courted me strongly by night and by day,
But now my dear sailor is gone far away.
(Chorus)

He promised to take me to Donnybrook fair
To buy me red ribbons to bind up my hair.
And when he'd return from the ocean so wide,
He'd take me and make me his own loving bride.
(Chorus)

His parents they slight me and will not agree
That I and my sailor boy married should be.
But when he comes home I will greet him with joy
And I'll take to my bosom my dear sailor boy.
(Chorus)

WILLIAM PEMBROKE MULCHINOCK

(*c.*1820-64)

from: BALLADS AND SONGS (1851)

The Rose of Tralee

The pale moon was rising above the green mountain,
The sun was declining beneath the blue sea,
When I stray'd with my love to the pure crystal fountain
That stands in the beautiful vale of Tralee.

She was lovely and fair as the rose of the summer,
Yet 'twas not her beauty alone that won me,
Oh, no, 'twas the truth in her eyes ever beaming
That made me love Mary, the Rose of Tralee.

The cool shades of evening their mantle were spreading,
And Mary, all smiling, was list'ning to me,
The moon through the valley her pale rays was shedding
When I won the heart of the Rose of Tralee.

Tho' lovely and fair as the rose of the summer,
Yet 'twas not her beauty alone that won me,
Oh, no, 'twas the truth in her eyes ever beaming
That made me love Mary, the Rose of Tralee.

LADY DUFFERIN

(1807-67)

from: SONGS, POEMS AND VERSES (1894)

[This song is usually printed in five stanzas, but the original version has eight. It is for this and for 'Terence's Farewell' that Lady Dufferin is chiefly remembered.]

The Irish Emigrant

I'm sitting on the stile, Mary,
  Where we sat side by side,
On a bright May morning long ago,
  When first you were my bride.
The corn was springing fresh and green,
  The lark sang loud and high,
The red was on your lip, Mary,
  And the love light in your eye.

The place is little changed, Mary,
  The day is bright as then;
The lark's loud song is in my ear,
  And the corn is green again;
But I miss the soft clasp of your hand,
  Your breath warm on my cheek,
And I still keep list'ning for the words
  You never more may speak.

'Tis but a step down yonder lane,
  The little church stands near;
The church where we were wed, Mary —
  I see the spire from here.
But the graveyard lies between, Mary, —
  My step might break your rest,
Where you, my darling, lie asleep
  With your baby on your breast.

I'm very lonely now, Mary,
  For the poor make no new friends;
But oh! they love the better far
  The few our Father sends!
And you are all I had, Mary,
  My blessing and my pride;
There's nothing left to care for now
  Since my poor Mary died.

Yours was the good brave heart, Mary,
  That still kept hoping on,
When trust in God had left my soul,
  And half my strength was gone.
There was comfort ever on your lip,
  And the kind look on your brow.
I bless you, Mary, for that same,
  Though you can't hear me now.

I thank you for the patient smile
  When your heart was fit to break;
When the hunger pain was gnawing there
  You hid it for my sake.
I bless you for the pleasant word
  When your heart was sad and sore.
Oh! I'm thankful you are gone, Mary,
  Where grief can't reach you more!

I'm bidding you a long farewell,
  My Mary kind and true!
But I'll not forget you, darling,
  In the land I'm going to!
They say there's bread and work for all,
  And the sun shines always there;
But I'll not forget old Ireland,
  Were it fifty times as fair!

And when amid those grand old woods
  I sit and shut my eyes,
My heart will travel back again
  To where my Mary lies;
I'll think I see the little stile
  Where we sat side by side, —
And the springing corn and bright May morn,
  When first you were my bride.

PERCY FRENCH

(1854-1920)

from:
CHRONICLES AND POEMS OF PERCY FRENCH (1922)

[French's work as a civil engineer took him to some of the most remote and beautiful districts of late Victorian and Edwardian Ireland, where he saw the consequences of emigration and impoverishment. Originally written for a middle-class audience, his light verse and songs have become genuinely popular in the years since his death.]

The Mountains of Mourne[1]

Oh, Mary, this London's a wonderful sight,
Wid the people here workin' by day and by night:
They don't sow potatoes, nor barley, nor wheat,
But there's gangs o' them diggin' for gold in the street —
At least, when I axed them, that's what I was told,
So I just took a hand at this diggin' for gold,
But for all that I found there, I might as well be
Where the Mountains o' Mourne sweep down to the sea.

I believe that, when writin', a wish you expressed
As to how the fine ladies in London were dressed.
Well, if you'll believe me, when axed to a ball,
They don't wear a top to their dresses at all!
Oh, I've seen them meself, and you could not, in thrath,
Say if they were bound for a ball or a bath —
Don't be startin' them fashions now, Mary Machree,[2]
Where the Mountains o' Mourne sweep down to the sea.

I seen England's King from the top of a 'bus —
I never knew him, though he means to know us:[3]
And though by the Saxon we once were oppressed,
Still, I cheered — God forgive me — I cheered wid the rest.
And now that he's visited Erin's green shore,
We'll be much better friends than we've been heretofore,
When we've got all we want, we're as quiet as can be
Where the Mountains o' Mourne sweep down to the sea.

You remember young Peter O'Loughlin, of course —
Well, here he is now at the head o' the Force.[4]
I met him today, I was crossin' the Strand,
And he stopped the whole street wid wan wave of his hand:
And there we stood talking of days that are gone,
While the whole population of London looked on;
But for all these great powers, he's wishful like me,
To be back where dark Mourne sweeps down to the sea.

There's beautiful girls here — oh, never mind!
With beautiful shapes Nature never designed,
And lovely complexions, all roses and crame,
But O'Loughlin remarked wid regard to them same:
'That if at those roses you venture to sip,
The colour might all come away on your lip,'
So I'll wait for the wild rose that's waitin' for me —
Where the Mountains o' Mourne sweep down to the sea.

1. A mountain range in County Down.
2. Machree = *Mo Chroi* (my heart), a term of endearment in Irish.
3. King Edward VII visited Ireland twice.
4. 'Force' in Ireland meant the police force.

from:
PROSE, POEMS AND PARODIES (1925)

'Are Ye Right There, Michael?'

A Lay of the Wild West Clare[1]

You may talk of Columbus's sailing
Across the Atlantical sea

1. A play on 'lay' as a term of heroic literature, 'wild west' as an American region of violence and danger, and 'west Clare' as part of the name of the railway company — The West Clare Railway.

But he never tried to go railing
  From Ennis as far as Kilkee.[2]
You run for the train in the mornin',
  The excursion train starting at eight,
You're there when the clock gives the warnin',
  And there for an hour you'll wait.

(Spoken):
  And as you're waiting in the train,
  You'll hear the guard sing this refrain:

'Are ye right there, Michael? are ye right?
Do you think that we'll be there before the night?
  Ye've been so long in startin',
  That ye couldn't say for sartin'[3] —
Still ye might now, Michael, so ye might!'

They find out where the engine's been hiding,
  And it drags you to sweet Corofin;
Say the guard, 'Back her down on the siding,
  There's the goods from Kilrush comin' in.'
Perhaps it comes in in two hours,
  Perhaps it breaks down on the way;
'If it does,' says the guard, 'be the powers,
  We're here for the rest of the day!'

(Spoken):
  And while you sit and curse your luck,
  The train backs down into a truck!

'Are ye right there, Michael, are ye right?
Have ye got the parcel there for Mrs. White?
  Ye haven't! Oh, begorra!
  Say it's comin' down tomorra —
And it might now, Michael, so it might!'

At Lahinch the sea shines like a jewel,
  With joy you are ready to shout,
When the stoker cries out, 'There's no fuel,
  And the fire's taytotally out.[4]
But hand up that bit of a log there —
  I'll soon have ye out of the fix;
There's a fine clamp of turf in the bog there;'[5]
  And the rest go a-gatherin' sticks.

2. Ennis is the county town of Clare; Kilkee is a seaside resort. Other place-names are equally authentic.
3. 'for certain'.
4. 'totally extinguished'.
5. A clamp is a neat pile of cut peat, stored as fuel.

(Spoken):
  And while you're breakin' bits of trees,
  You hear some wise remarks like these:

'Are ye right there, Michael? are ye right?
Do ye think that ye can get the fire to light?'
  'Oh, an hour you'll require,
  For the turf it might be drier —'
  'Well, it might now, Michael, so it might!'

Kilkee! Oh, you never get near it!
  You're in luck if the train brings you back,
For the permanent way is so queer, it
  Spends most of its time off the track.
Uphill the ould engin' is climbin',
  While the passengers push with a will;
You're in luck when you reach Ennistymon,
  For all the way home is down-hill.

(Spoken):
  And as you're wobbling through the dark,
  You hear the guard make this remark:

'Are ye right there, Michael? are ye right?
Do you think that ye'll be home before it's light?'
  ''Tis all dependin' whether
  The ould engin' howlds[6] together —'
'And it might now, Michael, so it might!'

6. holds.

(c) Political Ballads

BOULAVOGUE

[The author of this ballad was P. J. McCall (1861-1919), a founder-member of the Irish National Literary Society (1892) along with Yeats, Douglas Hyde and others. It was first printed in the *Irish Weekly Independent* (18 June 1898) under the title 'Father Murphy of The County Wexford', as a contribution to the centenary of the 1798 rebellion. G.-D. Zimmermann has shown that it was based on the 1798 songs, 'Come All You Warriors . . . ., 'Some Treat of David' and 'Father Murphy, or the Wexford Men of '98' (although there is another, related, song called simply 'Father Murphy'). It was originally set to the tune of 'Father Murphy', but is now sung to the tune of 'Youghal Harbour' and, since 1922, has been known as 'Boulavogue'. The text used here is McCall's, as printed by Zimmermann in *Songs of Irish Rebellion*, although there is another, more popular version in P. Walsh's *Songs of the Gael* 4th Series (1922).

Father John Murphy was the parish priest of Kilcormack, near Boulavogue, Co. Wexford. In May 1798 he led his parishioners against the British militia in a series of successful encounters at Camolin, Enniscorthy and other places named in the song. He was killed in battle by the British yeomanry.]

At Boulavogue, as the sun was setting
  O'er the green May meadows of Shelmalier,
A rebel band set the heather blazing,
  And brought the neighbours from far and near.
Then Father Murphy, of old Kilcormack,
  Spurred up the rocks with a warring cry —
'Arm! Arm!' he cried, 'for I've come to lead you —
  Now priest and people must fight or die!'

He led us on 'gainst the coming soldiers,
  And the cowardly Yeomen we put to flight;
Down at the Harrow, the Boys of Wexford
  Showed Bookey's regiment how men could fight!
Look out for hirelings, King George of England,
  Search every kingdom that breeds a slave!
For Father Murphy, of the County Wexford,
  Sweeps o'er the earth like a mighty wave!

We took Camolin and Enniscorthy,
  And Wexford storming, drove out our foes;
'Twas at Slieve Kiltha our pikes were reeking
  With the crimson stream of the beaten Yeos.
At Tubberneering and Ballyellis
  Full many a Hessian[1] lay in his gore!
Ah, Father Murphy, had aid come over,
  A green flag floated from shore to shore!

At Vinegar Hill, o'er the pleasant Slaney,
  Our heroes vainly stood back to back,
And the Yeos at Tullow took Father Murphy,
  And burned his body upon the rack.
God give you glory, brave Father Murphy,
  And open heaven to all your men;
The cause that called you may call tomorrow
  In another war for the Green again.

1. German mercenaries in the British army.

GOD SAVE IRELAND

[On 23 November 1867, three Fenians, William Philip Allen, Michael Larkin and Michael O'Brien, were executed for the murder of Sergeant Charles Brett during the rescue of the Fenian leaders, Thomas J. Kelly and Timothy Deasy, from a police van in Manchester. The incident created a wave of anti-Irish feeling in England. The evidence that led to the conviction of the three men was flimsy and the witnesses called against them were disreputable. The 'Manchester Martyrs' were given a public funeral in Dublin attended by over sixty thousand people. The incident confirmed Irish disbelief in British justice and aided recruitment into the Irish Republican Brotherhood, an alternative name for the Fenians. One of the accused who was acquitted, Edward O'Meagher Condon, said at the close of his speech from the dock: 'I have nothing to regret, or to retract, or take back. I can only say, "God Save Ireland".' His co-defendants took up the phrase and repeated it.

Timothy Daniel Sullivan (1827-1914), the journalist, politician and brother of Alexander Martin Sullivan, the owner of *The Nation* from 1855, wrote this ballad and published it in *The Nation* on 7 December 1867. He fitted the words to the American military air, 'Tramp, tramp, tramp, the boys are marching', then popular in Ireland. The song was an immediate success and became, in effect, the national anthem of the Fenians and of Irish nationalism in general until 1916.]

  High upon the gallows tree
  Swung the noble-hearted Three,
By the vengeful tyrant stricken in their bloom;
  But they met him face to face,
  With the courage of their race,
And they went with souls undaunted to their doom.
  'God save Ireland!' said the heroes;
  'God save Ireland!' said they all:
  'Whether on the scaffold high
  Or the battle-field we die,
Oh, what matter, when for Erin dear we fall!'

  Girt around with cruel foes,
  Still their spirit proudly rose,
For they thought of hearts that loved them, far and near;
  Of the millions true and brave
  O'er the ocean's swelling wave,
And the friends in holy Ireland ever dear.
    'God save Ireland!' said they proudly;...
(*Chorus*)

  Climbed they up the rugged stair,
  Rung their voices out in prayer,
Then with England's fatal cord around them cast,
  Close beneath the gallows tree,
  Kissed like brothers lovingly,
True to home and faith and freedom to the last.
    'God save Ireland!' prayed they loudly; ...
(*Chorus*)

Never till the latest day
Shall the memory pass away
Of the gallant lives thus given for our land;
But on the cause must go,
Amidst joy, or weal, or woe,
Till we've made our isle a nation free and grand.
'God save Ireland!' say we proudly;
'God save Ireland!' say we all:
(*Chorus*)

THE OLD ORANGE FLUTE

In the County Tyrone, in the town of Dungannon,
Where many a ruction myself had a han' in,
Bob Williamson lived, a weaver by trade,
And all of us thought him a stout Orange blade.
On the Twelfth of July as around it would come,
Bob played on the flute to the sound of the drum,
You may talk of your harp, your piano or lute
But there's nothing compared with the ould Orange flute.

But Bob the deceiver he took us all in,
For he married a Papish called Brigid McGinn,
Turned Papish himself, and forsook the old cause
That gave us our freedom, religion, and laws.
Now the boys of the place made some comment upon it,
And Bob had to fly to the Province of Connacht
He fled with his wife and his fixings to boot,
And along with the latter his old Orange flute.

At the chapel on Sundays, to atone for past deeds,
He said *Paters* and *Aves* and counted his beads,
Till after some time, at the priest's own desire,
He went with his old flute to play in the choir.
He went with his old flute to play for the Mass,
And the instrument shivered, and sighed: 'Oh, alas!'
And blow as he would, though it made a great noise,
The flute would play only 'The Protestant Boys.'

Bob jumped, and he started, and got in a flutter,
And threw his old flute in the blest Holy Water;
He thought that this charm would bring some other sound
When he blew it again, it played 'Croppies lie down';
And for all he could whistle, and finger, and blow,
To play Papish music he found it no go;
'Kick the Pope,' 'The Boyne Water,' it freely would sound,
But one Papish squeak in it couldn't be found.

At a council of priests that was held the next day,
They decided to banish the old flute away
For they couldn't knock heresy out of its head
And they bought Bob a new one to play in its stead.
So the old flute was doomed and its fate was pathetic,
'Twas fastened and burned at the stake as heretic,
While the flames roared around it they heard a strange noise —
'Twas the old flute still whistling 'The Protestant Boys.'[1]

1. All the tunes played by the loyal flute are, of course, standard items in the Orange-protestant repertoire.

THE CROPPY BOY

[The tune to which this famous song of the 1798 Rebellion is most often sung is the traditional air *Cailín ó chois tSiúre*, a variant of which, 'The Robber' or 'Charley Reilly', was recorded by Bunting in his *Ancient Music of Ireland* (1840). There are several broadside versions and at least seven different versions in collections. 'The Croppy Boy' is so called because it was a French revolutionary fashion to crop the hair short at the back; this was taken to be a sign of revolutionary sympathies. The song in all its versions refers to the 1798 Rebellion in Wexford. In some the Croppy Boy escapes, vowing to return to his beloved and to continue the fight against English tyranny; in others, he is arrested by a militia man who, dressed as a priest, hears the Croppy's confession before he goes to fight on Vinegar Hill, the site of the rebels' ultimate defeat.]

It was early, early in the spring,
The birds did whistle and sweetly sing,
Changing their notes from tree to tree
And the song they sang was 'Old Ireland Free'.

It was early, early in the night,
The Yeoman cavalry gave me a fright,
The Yeoman cavalry was my downfall
And I was taken by Lord Cornwall.

It was in the coach house that I was laid
And in the parlour that I was tried.
My sentence passed and my courage low
As to Duncannon I was forced to go.

As I was going up Wexford Street
My own first cousin I chanced to meet.
My own first cousin did me betray
And for one bare guinea swore my life away.

As I was passing my father's door
My brother William stood in the door,
My aged father stood there before
And my own dear mother her hair she tore.

As I was going up Wexford Hill
Oh who would blame me to cry my fill?
I looked behind and I looked before
And my own dear mother I shall ne'er see more.

As I was standing on the scaffold high
My own dear father was standing nigh.
My own dear father did me deny
And the name he gave me was 'The Croppy Boy'.

It was in Duncannon this young man died
And in Duncannon his body was laid.
Now all good people that do pass by
O spare a tear for 'The Croppy Boy'.

CROPPIES LIE DOWN

[This popular Orange song dates from about 1798. It was attributed then to 'the late gallant Captain Ryan' — whom G.-D. Zimmermann guesses may have been the man who was killed at the arrest of the United Irish leader, Lord Edward Fitzgerald. Zimmermann cites evidence that the tune had a partisan meaning several months before the rebellion and was much sung by the militia and yeomanry. This is not surprising, since they were, in effect, engaged on a campaign of indisciplined provocation and terror under the command of General Lake, the incompetent who had replaced the more intelligent and tolerant commander-in-chief, Sir Ralph Abercromby. There were then and have been since many texts written to the tune. Zimmermann counted seventeen in one collection of 1798; since then there have been several adaptations, created to apply the theme of the song to different political conditions.]

We soldiers of Erin, so proud of the name,
Will raise upon Rebels and Frenchmen our fame;
We'll fight to the last in the honest old cause,
And guard our religion, our freedom, and laws;
We'll fight for our country, our king, and his crown,
And make all the traitors and croppies lie down.

Chorus:
Down, down, croppies lie down.

The rebels so bold — when they've none to oppose —
To houses and hay-stacks are terrible foes;
They murder poor parsons, and also their wives,
But soldiers at once make them run for their lives;
And wherever we march, thro' the country or town,
In ditches or cellars, the croppies lie down.

United in blood, to their country's disgrace,
They secretly shoot whom they dare not to face;
But when we can catch the sly rogues in the field,
A handful of soldiers make hundreds to yield,
And the cowards collect but to raise our renown,
For as soon as we fire the croppies lie down.

While they, in the war that unmanly they wage
On woman herself turn their blood-thirsty rage,
We'll fly to protect the dear creatures from harms,
And shelter them safely when clasp'd in our arms:
On love in a soldier no maiden will frown,
But bless the dear boys that made croppies lie down.

Should France e'er attempt, or by fraud or by guile,
Her forces to land on our emerald isle,
We'll shew that they ne'er can make free soldiers slaves,
And only possess our green fields for their graves;
Our country's applauses our triumph will crown,
While low with the French, brother, croppies lie down.

When wars and when dangers again shall be o'er,
And peace with her blessings revisit our shore;
When arms we relinquish, no longer to roam,
With pride will our families welcome us home,
And drink, as in bumpers past troubles we drown,
A health to the lads that made croppies lie down.

THE WEARING OF THE GREEN

[The song dates from about 1800; several versions were printed in the nineteenth century. The best-known version is that written by Dion Boucicault for his play *Arrah-na-Pogue* (1864), although traces of the others are frequently found in the renderings of Boucicault's version. Green was the colour for revolution in Ireland, since the United Irishmen and numerous songs ('The Suit of Green', 'The Green Above the Red', 'The Jacket

Green', 'The Green Cockade') were composed and distributed in broadsheets to promote national feeling.

The song is sung by Shaun the Post in Act One, Scene IV of *Arrah-na-Pogue*.]

O Paddy dear and did you hear the news that's going round?
The shamrock is forbid by law to grow on Irish ground;
St. Patrick's Day no more we'll keep, his colours can't be seen,
For there's a bloody law agin the wearing of the green.
I met with Napper Tandy,[1] and he took me by the hand,
And he said, 'How's poor old Ireland, and how does she stand?'
She's the most distressful country that ever yet was seen,
They are hanging men and women for the wearing of the green.

Then since the colour we must wear is England's cruel red,
Sure Ireland's sons will ne'er forget the blood that they have shed.
You may take the shamrock from your hat and cast it on the sod,
But 'twill take root and flourish there, though under foot 'tis trod.
When law can stop the blades of grass from growing as they grow,
And when the leaves in summer-time their verdure dare not show,
Then I will change the colour that I wear in my caubeen,[2]
But till that day, please God, I'll stick to wearing of the green.

But if at last our colour should be torn from Ireland's heart,
Her sons with shame and sorrow from the dear old isle will part;
I've heard a whisper of a country that lies beyond the sea
Where rich and poor stand equal in the light of freedom's day.
O Erin, must we leave you, driven by a tyrant's hand?
Must we ask a mother's blessing from a strange and distant land?
Where the cruel cross of England shall nevermore be seen,
And where, please God, we'll live and die still wearing of the green.

1. James Napper Tandy (1740-1803), United Irishman.
2. pipe.

THE SHAN VAN VOCHT

[The most popular version of this song dates from 1797, although the first printed version occurs in *The Nation* (29 October 1842) and an entirely different one was published in *The Spirit of the Nation*, with words by Michael Doheny, in 1882. The song originally is said to have been apolitical, dealing with the theme of a young man married to an old woman. The phonetic rendering of the Irish, *An tSeanbhean Bhoct* (The Poor Old Woman), has always been used, in its many variants, as the title of the political ballad. M. J. Barry's version in *The Songs of Ireland* (Dublin, 1845) has stanzas that are often incorporated into the most popular version, given here.]

Oh! the French are on the sea,
Says the *Shan Van vocht*;
The French are on the sea,
Says the *Shan Van vocht*;
Oh! the French are in the bay,
They'll be here without delay,
And the Orange will decay,
Says the *Shan Van vocht*.

Chorus

Oh! the French are in the bay,
They'll be here by break of day,
And the Orange will decay,
Says the *Shan Van vocht*.

And where will they have their camp?
Says the *Shan Van vocht*;
Where will they have their camp?
Says the *Shan Van vocht*;
On the Currach of Kildare,
The boys they will be there
With their pikes in good repair,
Says the *Shan Van vocht*.

To the Currach of Kildare
The boys they will repair,

And Lord Edward will be there,
   Says the *Shan Van vocht*.

Then what will the yeomen do?
   Says the *Shan Van vocht*;
What *will* the yeomen do?
   Says the *Shan Van vocht*;
What *should* the yeomen do,
But throw off the red and blue,
And swear that they'll be true
   To the *Shan Van vocht*.

What *should* the yeomen do
But throw off the red and blue,
And swear that they'll be true
   To the *Shan van vocht*.

And what colour will they wear?
   Says the *Shan Van vocht*;
What colour will they wear?
   Says the *Shan Van vocht*;
What colour should be seen
Where our fathers' homes have been,
But their own immortal Green?
   Says the *Shan Van vocht*.

What colour should be seen
Where our fathers' homes have been,
But their own immortal Green?
   Says the *Shan Van vocht*.

And will Ireland then be free?
   Says the *Shan Van vocht*;
Will Ireland then be free?
   Says the *Shan Van vocht*;
Yes! Ireland SHALL be free,
From the centre to the sea;
Then hurra for Liberty!
   Says the *Shan Van vocht*.

Yes! Ireland SHALL be free,
From the centre to the sea;
Then hurra for Liberty!
   Says the *Shan Van vocht*.

JOHN KEEGAN CASEY
(1846-70)

from:
A WREATH OF SHAMROCKS
(1866)

[This song was written about 1865 by John Keegan Casey, who published regularly in *The Nation* under the pseudonym 'Leo'. In *The Reliques of John K. Casey ('Leo')* (1878), his biographer, Eugene Davis, estimates that over one thousand copies of this ballad circulated in broadsheet form in Longford, Cavan and Westmeath before Casey even came to Dublin. Casey was arrested for his association with the Fenian movement in 1867 and his prison sentence hastened his death three years later. Fifty thousand people attended his funeral.

The text below is taken from the first edition of Casey's *A Wreath of Shamrocks: Ballads, Songs and Legends* (Dublin: McGee, 1866). In later reprintings, the attempt to reproduce dialect is generally ignored.]

The Rising of the Moon

A.D. 1798

'Oh! then tell me, Shawn O'Ferrall,
   Tell me why you hurry so?'
'Hush, ma bouchal,[1] hush and listen,'
   And his cheeks were all a-glow.
'I bear ordhers from the captain,
   Get you ready quick and soon,
For the pikes must be together
   At the risin' of the moon.'

'Oh! then tell me, Shawn O'Ferrall
   Where the gatherin' is to be?'
'In the ould spot by the river,
   Right well known to you and me.
One word more — for signal token
   Whistle up the marching tune,
With your pike upon your shoulder
   By the risin' of the moon.'

Out from many a mud-wall cabin
   Eyes were watching thro' that night,
Many a manly chest was throbbing
   For the blessed warning light.

1. my boy.

Murmurs passed along the valleys
  Like the banshee's lonely croon,
And a thousand blades were flashing
  At the risin' of the moon.

There beside the singing river
  That dark mass of men was seen,
Far above the shining weapons
  Hung their own beloved green.
'Death to every foe and traitor!
  Forward! strike the marchin' tune,
And hurrah, my boys, for freedom!
  'Tis the risin' of the moon.'

Well they fought for poor old Ireland
  And full bitter was their fate
(Oh, what glorious pride and sorrow
  Fill the name of Ninety-Eight.)
Yet, thank God, e'en still are beating
  Hearts in manhood's burning noon,
Who would follow in their footsteps
  At the risin' of the moon!

Biographies/Bibliographies

John O'Keeffe

For biography and bibliography, see Volume I, p. 657.

Mary Balfour

LIFE. Mary Balfour was born in Derry in 1780, the daughter of a protestant minister. She was a schoolteacher at Limavady and in Belfast. She died in 1819.

CHIEF WRITINGS. *Hope: A Poetical Essay: with Various Other Poems* (Belfast: Smith and Lyons, 1810); *Kathleen O'Neil, a grand national melodrama, in 3 acts* (Belfast: Archbold & Duncan, 1814).

James Stuart

LIFE. Born in Armagh in 1764, Stuart was educated at Armagh Royal School and Trinity College, Dublin, from which he graduated in 1789. In 1812, he became the first editor of the *Newry Telegraph* and from 1815 to 1819 edited the *Newry Magazine.* He moved to Belfast in 1821 and became editor of the *News Letter*, in which he published a series of theological letters, later collected into a volume entitled *The Protestant Layman* (1825). He died in Belfast in 1842.

CHIEF WRITINGS. *Poems on Various Subjects* (Belfast: Smyth, 1811); *Historical Memoirs of the City of Armagh, for a period of 1373 years* (Newry: Wilkinson; London: Longman, 1819); *The Protestant Layman; or, the challenge issued by D. O'Connell . . . accepted* (Belfast: Smyth, 1825; 2nd edition London: Hurst, 1828).

Henry Luttrell

LIFE. Born in Ireland about 1765, a natural son of Lord Carhampton, Luttrell represented Clonmines, Co. Wexford in the last Irish parliament (1798). He commuted his post in the Irish government for a pension. In 1802 he was sent to the West Indies to manage his father's estates, but soon returned to London and became a close friend of Samuel Rogers and other members of the Holland House circle, including Byron, Mackintosh, Sheridan and Moore. Renowned as a wit, and admired within that circle as a poet, he survives now as a minor figure in the memoirs and letters of the period. He died in London in 1851.

CHIEF WRITINGS. *Advice to Julia: A Letter in Rhyme* (London: Murray, 1820; 3rd revised edition 1822); *Crockford House* (London: Murray, 1827).

BIOGRAPHY AND CRITICISM. Mrs A. Crosse, 'An Old Society Wit', *Temple Bar* (January 1895); A. Dobson, 'Luttrell's Letters to Julia' in *A Paladin of Philanthropy and Other Papers* (London: Chatto and Windus, 1899), pp. 216-32.

George Darley

LIFE. Born in Dublin in 1795, Darley studied classics and mathematics at Trinity College, Dublin, graduating in 1820. He went to London the following year and began to write for the *London Magazine* on a regular basis in 1822. Plagued by ill-health, an appalling stammer and, apparently, a broken love affair, Darley failed to win an audience for his work and had success only with his mathematical textbooks. Although he was admired by Thomas Carlyle and H. F. Cary, he was despondent at his lack of a wider success. He died in London in 1846.

CHIEF WRITINGS. *The Errors of Ecstasie: A Dramatic Poem. With Other Pieces* (London: G. and B. Whittaker, 1822); *The Labours of Idleness, or, Seven Nights' Entertainments* by Guy Penseval (London: John Taylor, 1826); *Sylvia, or, The May Queen. A Lyrical Drama* (London: for John Taylor by James Duncan, 1827); *Nepenthe* (London: privately printed, 1835); *Thomas A Becket. A Dramatic Chronicle* (London: Edward Moxon, 1840); *Ethelstan; or, the Battle of Brunanburgh. A Dramatic Chronicle* (London: Edward Moxon, 1841); R.A. Streatfeild (ed.), *Selections from the Poems of George Darley* (London: Methuen, 1904); R. Colles (ed.), *The Complete Poetical Works of George Darley* (London: Routledge, 1908); A. Ridler (ed.), *Selected Poems of George Darley* (London: The Merrion Press, 1979).

BIOGRAPHY AND CRITICISM. C.C. Abbott, *The Life and Letters of George Darley* (London: Humphry Milford, 1928); A.J. Leventhal, *George Darley (1795-1846)* (Dublin: Dublin University Press, 1950); J. Heath-Stubbs, *The Darkling Plain: A Study of the Later Fortunes of Romanticism in English Poetry from George Darley to W.B. Yeats* (London: Eyre and Spottiswoode, 1950); G. Greene, 'George Darley' in *The Lost Childhood and Other Essays* (London: Jonathan Cape, 1951).

Thomas Furlong

LIFE. Furlong was born near Ferns, Co. Wexford in 1794, the son of a small farmer. He was apprenticed to a Dublin grocer and later was given a comfortable position in Jameson's whiskey distillery to enable him to cultivate his talents. Tom Moore and Lady Morgan befriended him after his first volume of poems appeared in 1819. He contributed to *The New Monthly Magazine* and in 1821 was a founding member of and thereafter a contributor to *The New Irish Magazine.* Furlong was an enthusiastic supporter of the campaign for catholic emancipation and a close friend of Daniel O'Connell. Besides the translations for Hardiman's *Irish Minstrelsy*, which he completed about 1825, Furlong devoted a great deal of effort to the translation of some of the songs of the great Irish harpist, Turlogh Carolan. His long poem, *The Doom of Derenzie*, was published in

London in 1829, the year of emancipation, two years after his early death from consumption.

CHIEF WRITINGS. *The Misanthrope and Other Poems* (London: H. Colburn, 1819; Dublin: Underwood, 1821); *The Plagues of Ireland* (Dublin: privately printed, 1824); *The Doom of Derenzie* (London: J. Robins, 1829); James Hardiman (ed.), *Irish Minstrelsy* 2 vols (London: J. Robins, 1831).

BIOGRAPHY AND CRITICISM. A. de Blacam, 'Two Poets Who Discovered Their Country', *Irish Monthly* 74 (1946), 357-65; J. Hardiman, 'Memoir of Thomas Furlong' in *Irish Minstrelsy* Vol. I, pp. lxix-lxxx; M. Russell, 'Our Poets, no. 17: Thomas Furlong', *Irish Monthly* 18 (1888), 421-26; P. C. Power, *The Story of Anglo-Irish Poetry 1800-1922* (Cork: Mercier Press, 1967); C. O'Hainle, 'Towards the Revival: Some Translations of Irish Poetry, 1789-1897' in P. Connolly (ed.), *Literature and the Changing Ireland* (Gerrards Cross: Colin Smythe; New Jersey: Humanities Press, 1982), pp. 37-57.

William Maginn

LIFE. Maginn was born in Cork in 1794, the son of a schoolteacher. He graduated from Trinity College, Dublin in 1811 and, on his father's death, took over as principal of the Marlborough Street School, Cork. He contributed sketches to *Blackwood's Magazine* and, in 1823, married and went to London to devote himself entirely to writing. After various employments with different magazines, he and Hugh Fraser founded *Fraser's Magazine* in 1830; some of his best work, including *Homeric Ballads* and *A Gallery of Literary Portraits*, appeared in this journal. He was joint editor of the *Evening Standard* and a regular contributor to *Punch* and the *Literary Gazette*. Maginn was one of the most important contributors to the *Noctes Ambrosianae* which ran in *Blackwood's* from 1822 to 1835. His prolific output was weakened by his drinking and the subsequent debts, which were so serious that he was several times imprisoned. His health broke down and he died of tuberculosis at Walton-on-Thames in 1842, shortly after his release from prison. Maginn was widely known and admired in London literary circles. He knew Greek, Latin, German, Italian, French and Spanish, but practically no Irish.

CHIEF WRITINGS. R. Skelton MacKenzie (ed.), *Miscellaneous Writings of the Late Dr. Maginn* 5 vols (New York: Redfield, 1855-57) Vols I and II contain *The O'Doherty Papers*, III *The Shakespeare Papers*, IV *The Homeric Ballads*, V *The Fraserian Papers*; R. S. MacKenzie (ed.), *Noctes Ambrosianae*, 5 vols (New York: Middleton, 1863-65): this contains Maginn's various contributions to the famous series of dialogues between J. G. Lockhart, J. Wilson, J. Hogg and others; R.W. Montagu (ed.), *Miscellanies: Prose and Verse* 2 vols (London: Sampson Low, 1885); *Ten Tales* (London: Partridge, 1933). Maginn also wrote a political novel, never reprinted: *Whitehall, or the Days of George the Fourth* (London, 1827).

BIOGRAPHY AND CRITICISM. E.V.H. Kenealy, 'Our Portrait Gallery, no. 34: William Maginn LL.D.', *Dublin University Magazine* 23 (1844), 72-101.

James Joseph Callanan

LIFE. James (or Jeremiah) Callanan was born in Cork in 1795. He entered the ecclesiastical college of St Patrick's, Maynooth in 1818, but left after two years, attended Trinity College, Dublin as an outpensioner and left two years later, without graduating. He became a school tutor and taught at William Maginn's school in Cork. Maginn helped him to have some of his poems published in *Blackwood's Magazine* in 1823. Callanan left teaching and spent most of his time in Counties Cork and Kerry, collecting ballads and legends of the Irish-speaking people. He contracted tuberculosis and went to Lisbon to recover, but died there in 1829.

CHIEF WRITINGS. *The Recluse of Inchidony and Other Poems* (London: Hurst, Chance, 1839); *The Poems of J.J. Callanan* (Cork: Bolster, 1847), especially valuable for the biographical introduction by M.F. McCarthy; *The Poems of J.J. Callanan* (Cork: Daniel Mulcahy, 1861).

BIOGRAPHY AND CRITICISM. Bridget G. McCarthy, 'Jeremiah J. Callanan, Part I. His Life; Part II: His Poetry', *Studies* 35 (1946), 215-29, 387-99; D. O. Crowley, *Irish Poets and Novelists* (San Francisco: Bannerman, 1893).

Gerald Griffin

For biography and bibliography, see Volume I, p. 1172.

James Clarence Mangan

For biography and bibliography, see Volume I, p. 1298.

Francis Sylvester Mahony

LIFE. Born in Cork in 1804, Mahony was educated by the Jesuits at Clongowes Wood College, Co. Kildare, and later trained as a priest at Amiens, Paris and Rome. In 1830 he returned to Clongowes as prefect of studies, but his participation in a riotous escapade had him sent back to Rome, where he was ordained as a priest, but not as a Jesuit, in 1832. Two years later, he went to London to work as a journalist, after a disagreement with his local bishop. Thereafter, he was a defrocked priest. Mahony wrote for *Fraser's Magazine* until 1837, taking the pen-name Father Prout, and later for *Bentley's Miscellany*. He spent nine years on the Continent as correspondent for various newspapers and died in Paris in 1866. He is buried in the vaults of Shandon Church, Cork.

CHIEF WRITINGS. *The Reliques of Fr. Prout late P.P. of Watergrasshill in the County of Cork, Ireland* (London: James Fraser, 1836); *The Final Reliques of Father Prout (the Rev. Francis Mahony)* collected and edited by B. Jerrold (London: Chatto and Windus, 1876); C. Kent (ed.), *The Works of Father Prout* (London: G. Routledge & Sons, 1881).

BIOGRAPHY AND CRITICISM. C. Clemen, 'A Neglected Humorist: Father Prout', *Catholic World* CXXXVII (1933), 706-10; E. Mannin, *Two Studies in Integrity: Gerald Griffin and the Rev. Francis Mahony ('Father Prout')* (London: Jarrolds; New York: Putnam, 1954).

Edward Walsh

LIFE. Born in Derry of a Cork father in 1805, Walsh was taught in the hedge-schools. He was imprisoned for taking part in the tithe war, and was schoolteacher to the convicts on Spike Island in Cork Harbour and to the inmates of the Cork Union workhouse. He contributed regularly to *The Nation*, *Irish Penny Journal*, *Science and Literature*, and the *Dublin Journal of Temperance*. Walsh is one of the best and most influential translators of Irish in the nineteenth century. He died in 1850.

CHIEF WRITINGS. *Reliques of Irish Jacobite Poetry; with biographical sketches of the authors, interlineal literal translations and historical illustrative notes by John Daly; together with metrical versions by E. Walsh* (Dublin: S. Machen, 1844) 2nd edition Dublin: M. H. Gill, 1883; *Irish Popular Songs; with English metrical translations and introductory remarks and notes by E. Walsh* (Dublin: J. McGlashan; London: W. S. Orr & Co., 1847).

BIOGRAPHY AND CRITICISM. C. J. Kickham, 'E. Walsh, a memoir' in J. Maher (ed.), *The Valley Near Slievnamon, A Kickham Anthology* (Kilkenny: Kilkenny People, 1942); R. Farren, *The Course of Irish Verse in English* (London: Sheed and Ward, 1948); R. Welch, *A History of Verse Translation from the Irish 1789-1897* (Gerrards Cross: Colin Smythe, 1987).

Samuel Ferguson

For biography and bibliography, see Volume I, p. 1297.

Thomas Davis

For biography and bibliography, see Volume I, p. 1299.

Aubrey Thomas de Vere

LIFE. Aubrey de Vere was born in 1814, the third son of the poet and dramatist Sir Aubrey de Vere (1788-1846), in Curragh Chase, the family mansion in Adare, Co. Limerick. de Vere was educated at Trinity College, Dublin. He worked hard to relieve the sufferings in his neighbourhood during the Famine and published his book on the general situation, *English Misrule and Irish Misdeeds*, in 1848. He was a friend of many of the Victorian writers and sages, dedicating his first book of poems to John Henry Newman and championing the cause of Tennyson. de Vere left the anglican faith in 1851 and became a catholic. He never married and died in the family home in 1902.

CHIEF WRITINGS: *English Misrule and Irish Misdeeds* (London: J. Murray, 1848); *Poems* (London: Burns & Lambert, 1855); *The Sisters, Inisfail and Other Poems* (London: Longman; Dublin: McGlashan and Gill, 1861); *The Infant Bridal* (London: Macmillan, 1864); *Irish Odes and Other Poems* (New York: The Catholic Publications Society, 1869); *The Legends of St. Patrick* (London: H. S. King; Dublin: McGlashan & Gill, 1872); *The Foray of Queen Maeve and Other Legends of Ireland's Heroic Age* (London: Kegan Paul, 1882); *The Poetical Works of Aubrey de Vere* Vols 1-3 (London: Kegan Paul), Vols 4-6 (London: Macmillan, 1898); *Medieval Records and Sonnets* (London: Macmillan, 1893).

BIOGRAPHY AND CRITICISM. Anonymous, 'The Poems of the de Veres', *Dublin University Magazine* XXI (February 1843), 190-204; J. P. Gunning, *Aubrey de Vere: A Memoir* (Limerick: Guy; London: Simpkin and Marshall, 1902); M. P. Reilly, *Aubrey de Vere, Victorian Observer* (Lincoln: University of Nebraska Press, 1953); W. Ward, *Aubrey de Vere: A Memoir* (London: Longmans, Green, 1904); P.A. Winckler and W. V. Stone, 'Aubrey Thomas de Vere 1814-1902: A Bibliography', *Victorian Newsletter* no. 10, Supplement (1956), 1-4.

Thomas Caulfield Irwin

LIFE. Irwin was born in 1823 in Warrenpoint, Co. Down. His father was a doctor and the family was well-off. His education was at the hands of private tutors. In 1848 he began to write for magazines and by the mid-1850s had become a regular contributor to *The Nation* and *The Dublin University Magazine*. Irwin was a prolific writer of tales and stories, some 130 in all, only a few of which have been published in book form. His novel, *From Caesar to Christ*, appeared in 1853 and various translations from classical and modern European writers were published in subsequent years. Irwin became wildly eccentric in his old age. He died in 1892.

CHIEF WRITINGS. *Versicles* (Dublin: W.M. Hennessy, 1856); *Poems* (Dublin: McGlashan and Gill, 1866); *Irish Historical and Legendary Poems* (Glasgow: Cameron and Ferguson, 1868); *Songs and Romances* (Dublin: Gill, 1878); *Pictures and Songs* (Dublin: Gill; London: Simpkin, Marshall and Co, 1880); *Sonnets on the Poetry and Problems of Life* (Dublin: Gill, 1881); *Poems, Sketches, and Songs* (Dublin: Gill, 1889); *Winter and Summer Stories, and Slides of Fancy's Lantern* (Dublin: Gill, 1879); ed., *The Irish Monthly Illustrated Journal*, Nos. 1-3 (January-March 1873).

BIOGRAPHY AND CRITICISM. W. Rooney, 'Thomas Caulfield Irwin', *New Ireland Review* 7 (1897), 86-100; G. Taylor, 'A Neglected Irish Poet', *The Bell* 3 (1942), 308-12; L. H. Victory, 'Thomas Caulfield Irwin', *The United Irishman* (30 November 1901), 6.

Denis Florence MacCarthy

LIFE. Born in Dublin in 1817, MacCarthy began publishing in the Dublin periodical press in 1834. He contributed to most of the important journals of the day, including *The Dublin University Magazine* and *The Nation*. For a time he was considered to be a successor to Thomas Moore and was much sought after by various centenary committees to write odes in celebration of their heroes, including Moore and Daniel O'Connell. He was a distinguished translator of Spanish verse and drama, especially of Calderón. In 1855 he delivered a series of lectures on poetry for Cardinal Newman at the Catholic University of Dublin; later he gave other series on the poets of Spain and on sixteenth-century drama. In 1864 MacCarthy lived for a time on the Continent and thereafter for some years in London. He returned to Ireland a few years before his death in Blackrock, Co. Dublin, in 1882.

CHIEF WRITINGS. (ed.) *The Book of Irish Ballads* (Dublin: James Duffy, 1846); *The Poets and Dramatists of Ireland* (Dublin: James Duffy, 1846); *Ballads, Poems and Lyrics, Original and Translated* (Dublin: J. McGlashan, 1850); *Underglimpses and Other Poems* (London: David Bogue, 1857); *The Bell-Founder and Other Poems* (London: David Bogue, 1857); *Mysteries of Corpus Christi by Calderón de la Barca* (Dublin: Duffy, 1857); *Poems* (Dublin: M. H. Gill and Son, 1882; 2nd ed. 1884).

William Allingham

LIFE. Allingham was born in 1824 in Ballyshannon, Co. Donegal. He spent most of his working life as a customs official, although from an early date he lived for regular periods in London and eventually came to know most of the important Victorian writers. Tennyson was his idol and he cultivated the laureate's friendship with a relentless assiduity. Dante Gabriel Rossetti, Browning and Carlyle were also good friends and Allingham further widened his acquaintances when he became editor of *Fraser's Magazine* in 1872, nine years after he had settled in England. He died in Hampstead in 1889.

CHIEF WRITINGS. *Poems* (London: Chapman and Hall, 1850); *Day and Night Songs* (London: Routledge, 1854); *Laurence Bloomfield in Ireland, A Modern Poem* (London: Macmillan, 1864; reprinted New York: AMS, 1972); *Fifty Modern Poems* (London: Bell & Daldy, 1865); *Songs, Ballads and Stories* (London: Bell, 1877; reprinted New York: AMS Press, 1972); *Varieties in Prose* (London: Longmans Green, 1893); *Sixteen Poems*, selected and edited by W.B. Yeats (Dundrum: Dun Emer, 1905); J. Hewitt (ed.), *The Poems of William Allingham* (Dublin: Dolmen Press, 1967); H. Allingham and D. Radford (eds), *William Allingham: A Diary* (London: Macmillan, 1907; revised ed. by G. Grigson (London: Centaur, 1967).

BIOGRAPHY AND CRITICISM. H. Allingham and E.B. Williams (eds), *Letters to William Allingham* (London: Longmans, 1911); G.B. Hill (ed.), *Letters of Dante Gabriel Rossetti to William Allingham, 1854-1870* (London, Fisher Unwin, 1897); P.S. O'Hegarty, *A Bibliography of William Allingham* (Dublin: Thom, 1945); A. Warner, *William Allingham: An Introduction* (Dublin: Dolmen Press, 1971); *William Allingham* (Lewisburg, Pennsylvania: Bucknell University Press, 1975); 'William Allingham: Bibliographical Survey', *Irish Book Lore* 2 (1976), 303-07.

Thomas D'Arcy McGee

LIFE. McGee was born in Carlingford, Co. Louth in 1825. In 1842 he emigrated to the United States and became editor of the Boston newspaper *The Pilot*. On his return to Ireland, he became a leading figure in the Young Ireland movement and worked with Gavan Duffy on *The Nation* newspaper, becoming co-editor and contributor under the name of 'Amergin'. He escaped to America after the 1848 rising and ten years later moved to Canada where he became a prominent politician. McGee became strongly critical of the Fenian movement and denounced its physical force campaign. He was assassinated by a Fenian sympathizer near the parliament buildings in Ottawa in 1868.

CHIEF WRITINGS. *Historical Sketches of O'Connell and His Friends* (Boston: Donahoe & Rohan, 1844); *Gallery of Irish Writers: The Irish Writers of the XVIIth Century* (Dublin: Duffy, 1846); *A Memoir of the Life and Conquest of Art McMurrough* (Dublin: Duffy, 1847); *Memoir of Charles Gavan Duffy* (Dublin: W. Hogan, 1849); *Poems* (Dublin: The Nation, 1852); *Canadian Ballads and Occasional Verses* (Montreal: Lovel, 1858); *A Popular History of Ireland* (Glasgow: Cameron & Ferguson, 1862); *The Poems of Thomas D'Arcy McGee* (London, New York, Montreal: Sadleir, 1869).

BIOGRAPHY AND CRITICISM. A. Brady, *Thomas D'Arcy McGee* (Toronto: Macmillan, 1925); I. M. Skelton, *The Life of Thomas D'Arcy McGee* (Gardenvale, Canada: Garden City Press, 1925); J. Phelan, *The Ardent Exile: The Life and Times of Thomas D'Arcy McGee* (Toronto: Macmillan, 1951); N. Vance, *Irish Literature: A Social History* (Oxford: Blackwell, 1990).

John Francis O'Donnell

LIFE. O'Donnell was born in Limerick in 1837. At the age of fourteen, he contributed verses and prose sketches to the *Kilkenny Journal*. He later became a reporter on the *Munster News* and sub-editor on the *Tipperary Examiner*. He left for London soon after he married a Miss Jones from Tipperary and was briefly editor of the catholic newspaper, *Universal News*, before returning to Dublin to work for *The Nation* under A. M. Sullivan. As editor of the catholic periodical *The Lamp*, he published a serial novel, *Evictions and Evicted*, wrote nationalist poems for *The Irish People, The Shamrock* and *The Irishman* and published love poems in the *Dublin Review, Chambers's Journal* and Dickens's *All The Year Round*. Charles Dickens was a good friend to him. In 1862 O'Donnell was editor of *Duffy's Hibernian Magazine*, in 1863-64 he edited the *Irish People* in London, a 'mouthpiece of the Fenians', but he was never a member of the Irish Republican Brotherhood. From 1865 to 1868, he was editor of *The Tablet* in London, and in 1870 began to contribute to *Zozimus*, a comic illustrated paper edited by Richard Dowling, who edited O'Donnell's poems in 1891. In 1872-73, O'Donnell published many poems in *The Nation* and, anonymously, his second serial novel, *Sadlier, the Banker; or, the Laceys of Rathcore*. He died in London in 1874 and is buried at Kensal Green.

CHIEF WRITINGS. *The Emerald Wreath: A Fireside Treasury of Legends, Stories, &c.* by Caviare (pseud. J. F. O'Donnell), with illustrations by the Brothers Dalziel (Dublin: James Duffy, 1864); *Memoirs of the Irish Franciscans* (Dublin: James Duffy, 1871); *Poems* with an introduction by Richard Dowling (London: Ward and Downey, 1891).

BIOGRAPHY AND CRITICISM. Apart from Dowling's introduction to the *Poems*, the best source is M. MacDonagh, 'John Francis O'Donnell' in the 'Irish Graves in England' series, *Evening Telegraph* (Dublin, 1891).

William Pembroke Mulchinock

LIFE. W.P. Mulchinock was born in Tralee, Co. Kerry about 1820, of a prosperous merchant family. His life was without notable incident until 1841 when he met and fell in love with the young catholic governess of his sister's family, Mary O'Connor. Yet such was the opposition to their relationship that Mulchinock was tricked into running away, for fear of arrest. He became a war correspondent on the North-West frontier in 1843, during the British war on Afghanistan. He returned home in 1849 to hear that Mary had just died. Soon after, he married Alicia Keogh and they went to America, where Mulchinock became literary editor of *The Irish Advocate*. He met a number of American writers, including Longfellow, to whom he dedicated his poems in 1851. His wife became deeply involved in the anti-slavery movement. In 1855, after a period of estrangement, he left America for Ireland, leaving behind his wife and two daughters. Mulchinock spent his remaining years seeking solace in drink and, apparently, grieving for Mary O'Connor. He died in Tralee in 1864 and was buried in Clogherbrien, beside Mary O'Connor, in accordance with his last wish.

CHIEF WRITINGS. *Ballads and Songs of William Pembroke Mulchinock* (New York: T. W. Strong, 1851).

BIOGRAPHY AND CRITICISM. J. T. Caball, *The Rose of Tralee: The Story of a Tradition* (Tralee: The Kerryman, 1964).

Lady Dufferin

LIFE. Lady Dufferin was born in England in 1807. She was the grand-daughter of Richard Brinsley Sheridan and sister of the writer Caroline Norton. In 1925 she married Captain Price Blackwood, heir to the Marquess of Dufferin and Ava. They lived in Italy, England and Ireland. Her husband died in 1841; she remarried in 1867 but was widowed within a few months. Lady Dufferin died in London in 1867.

CHIEF WRITINGS. *Lispings from Low Latitudes* (London: Murray, 1893); *Songs, Poems and Verses by Helen, Lady Dufferin*, edited with a Memoir and Some Account of the Sheridan Family by her Son the Marquess of Dufferin and Ava (London: Murray, 1894); Marquess of Dufferin and Ava (ed.), *A Selection of the Songs of Lady Dufferin* (London: Murray, 1895).

Percy French

LIFE. Born in Cloonyquin, Co. Roscommon in 1854, William Percy French was educated at Trinity College, Dublin, where he qualified as a civil engineer. He joined the Board of Works as a surveyor of drains in County Cavan. He became known as a humorist and entertainer in prose and verse. Many of his songs are still popular. He died in Formby, Lancashire in 1920.

CHIEF WRITINGS. *The First Lord Liftinant and Other Tales* (Dublin: Mecredy and Kyle, 1890); *The Irish Girl, Comedy Opera* (London: Boosey, 1918); Mrs de Burgh Daly (ed.), *Chronicles and Poems of Percy French* (Dublin: The Talbot Press, 1922); also *Prose, Poems and Parodies* (Dublin: The Talbot Press; London: Simpkin, Marshall, 1925).

BIOGRAPHY AND CRITICISM. J. N. Healy, *Percy French and His Songs* (Cork: Mercier Press; London: Herbert Jenkins, 1966, reprinted as *The Songs of Percy French* (Cork, Dublin: Mercier Press, 1983); B. O'Dowda, *The World of Percy French* (Belfast: Blackstaff Press, 1981).

John Keegan Casey

LIFE. John Keegan Casey was born at Mount Dalton, near Mullingar, Co. Westmeath in 1846, the son of a peasant farmer. Despite the poverty and hardship of his situation, he studied hard to become a writer. His first poem was published in *The Nation* in 1862, under the pseudonym 'Leo'. In 1867, the year after publication of his first collection of poetry, he was arrested and imprisoned for his connections with Fenianism. He spent almost two years in jail and his health was irretrievably damaged. Casey died in 1870. Fifty thousand people attended his funeral. He was widely known through the pages of *The Nation* for his patriotic verse; it was only after his death that the title the 'Fenian poet' passed on to John Francis O'Donnell.

CHIEF WRITINGS. *A Wreath of Shamrocks: Ballads, Songs and Legends* (Dublin: McGee, 1866); *The Rising of the Moon, and Other Ballads* (Glasgow: Cameron & Ferguson, 1869).

BIOGRAPHY AND CRITICISM. E. Davis (ed.), *Reliques of John K. Casey ('Leo')* (Dublin: Pigott, 1878).

SEAMUS DEANE, *Editor*

The Famine and Young Ireland

The Irish Famine was the last disaster of its kind in Western Europe, although it was by no means the first in Ireland. In the century before 1845 there had been several serious shortages, with the years 1740, 1817 and 1822 probably being the most lethal. Between 1816 and 1842 there were fourteen partial or complete failures of the potato crop. However, the scale and duration of the Great Famine were such that generally it has been believed that Ireland was thereby irrevocably changed in its political, social and economic structures and attitudes. Although there is no evidence that the Famine was a deliberate act of genocide, there is no doubt either that, had Britain exerted its will and its might in a sustained manner, Ireland could have been saved from the worst effects of the catastrophe. The British treasury spent £9.5 million pounds on relief, some of it on loan. In the Crimean War, several years later, it spent £69.3 million.

Political hostility towards Ireland reduced the British commitment to saving the country from the consequences of its long-term poverty and sudden misfortune. There was a widespread belief that the Irish either liked being poor or were too delinquent to be anything else; equally, it was believed by some that the Famine was an act of providence that would rid the United Kingdom of its most intractable problem. The Irish themselves often expressed the view that they had been deserted by God as well as by man. The depth of their demoralization was in accord with this feeling of almost total abandonment. Hundreds of thousands of people starved to death or fell prey to the accompanying diseases in a country where food was plentiful. It seemed to be beyond the ingenuity or will of man to 'bring the people and the food together'. In addition, the collapse was so total that the reasons for it go beyond the actual potato blight that precipitated it. As in the twentieth century, the repetition of famine in the midst of plenty poses fundamental problems about the economic and political order, which are avoided rather than answered by the exercise of belated charity, no matter what its motive, scale or provenance.

The immediate political issue was raised, not by the Famine itself, but by the British response to it. Under Sir Robert Peel, the British prime minister, that response had been sharp and effective. The purchase of Indian meal and the setting up of relief schemes to provide employment were effective in dealing with the partial failure of the potato crop in 1845-46; but its total failure in the following year posed more severe problems for the quite different, less flexible policies of the Whigs, under Lord John Russell, who had come into power in the summer of 1846. Russell's administration was devoted to the prevailing doctrines of political economy. In effect, that meant that there should be as little state interference as possible in dealing with the distress, that private enterprise should take the initiative, and that the cost of Irish poverty should be paid for by the Irish themselves. This policy was pursued with such determined rigour that the widespread distress became wholesale catastrophe, and no belated modifications of its application were sufficient to do more than provide slow-motion alleviation to the headlong progress of hunger and disease. Even the measures that were taken had their impact reduced by incompetence and corruption in their administration.

It is not difficult to see why the failure of the potato crop had such devastating consequences. It was merely the bursting of the economic aneurysm that had threatened the Irish system for fifty years or more. It is much more difficult to determine why the Irish economy was in such a poor state. This is not the purpose of a brief introduction. It may be said, in a summary of the received wisdom on the subject, that the effect of the Union of 1800, the collapse of agricultural prices after 1815, the ruin of the cottage industries, the integration of Ireland into the British common market in 1824, the long-term effects of the land tenure system in Ireland, the lack of capital accumulation, of a managerial class, of the 'protestant' work-ethic and of natural resources, combined with the consequences of increased emigration in the 1815-45 period, the growth of the Irish population with a high dependency ratio and the over-reliance on one crop that could not be stored easily, together with a number of other subsidiary factors, all helped to make Ireland poor and the potato blight more catastrophic there than in Scotland, England or any other part of Europe.

Yet, as early as 1847, Isaac Butt, the first professor of political economy at Trinity College, Dublin and a fervent supporter of the Union, pointed out the central political flaw in the British response to the Irish crisis. If the Union meant anything at all, it should be able to provide, for any one stricken part of the United Kingdom, the consolidated support of the whole of that kingdom. Yet Ireland was being treated as though it was a separate political entity, not an integral part of that Union that was determinedly supported as a constitutional arrangement and so puzzlingly ignored as an economic reality. It was this recognition that led Butt finally to sponsor the idea of a federal system as a modification of the Union. His pamphlet of 1847, *The Famine in the Land*, is one of the first signs of the immense repercussions of the Famine on the ways in which Irish people regarded the constitutional relationship between the two islands. Later to be the founder of the Home Rule League, Butt was already taking the first steps towards a conclusion that Parnell and Davitt were to govern. His adherence to the principles of political economy was not as evangelical as was that of the British treasury. He realized that, in the Irish situation, such doctrinaire thinking was incompatible with the political implications of Unionism. Perhaps, too, it may be said that his increasing conviction that Ireland should have its own legislature was stimulated by the recognition that the treasury's version of political economy would not have been applied with that degree of rigour in England, Wales or Scotland.

The long O'Connellite campaign to repeal the Union had been effective to this extent — the Irish were not regarded as part of the British political community. They wanted to be treated differently from the other constituent parts. During the Famine, they were. For a Unionist, this was a distressing revelation. It should also be said that for economists like John Stuart Mill and others, Ireland challenged *laissez-faire* orthodoxy to such an extent that it was finally modified to the point that state intervention, as a deliberate policy, replaced the old theory. The various revisions to which he subjected his *Principles of Political Economy* (1848) are an index of the difficulties faced by those officials at the treasury who regarded *laissez-faire* individualism as one of the unalterable laws of the universe.[1]

Laissez-faire was a doctrine that could be pursued in English circumstances without disastrous consequences. This was not the case in Ireland. In his 1848 essay, *What is to be done with Ireland?*, Mill argued that the problem there was not demagogism of the O'Connell or of the Mitchel variety; nor was it the fecklessness of the Irish. The problem was the land system itself. It had to be

1. Mill refers to the connection between his *Political Economy* and the Famine in his *Autobiography* (1873), Chapter VII: 'The work was commenced in the autumn of 1845, and was ready for the press before the end of 1847. In this period of little more than two years there was an interval of six months during which the work was laid aside, while I was writing articles in the *Morning Chronicle* . . . urging the formation of peasant properties on the waste lands of Ireland. This was during the period of the Famine, the winter of 1846-47, when the stern necessities of the time seemed to afford a chance of gaining attention for what appeared to me the only mode of combining relief to immediate destitution with permanent improvement of the social and economical condition of the Irish people. But the idea was new and strange; there was no English precedent for such a proceeding: and the profound ignorance of English politicians and the English public concerning all social phenomena not generally met with in England (however common elsewhere), made my endeavours an entire failure. Instead of a great operation on the waste lands, and the conversion of cottiers into proprietors, Parliament passed a Poor Law for maintaining them as paupers: and if the nation has not since found itself in inextricable difficulties from the joint operation of the old evils and the quack remedy, it is indebted for its delivery to that most unexpected and surprising fact, the depopulation of Ireland, commenced by famine, and continued by emigration.'

For a detailed account of Cairnes's influence on and correspondence with Mill, see Appendix H to *Principles of Political Economy* Vol. III, Book III, pp. 1038-95, in J.M. Robson (ed.), *Collected Works of John Stuart Mill* (Toronto: University of Toronto Press; London: Routledge and Kegan Paul, 1965). For Mill's essays on Ireland, see *Collected Works* VI (1982), especially pp. 497-532.

extinguished. The social condition of Ireland, Mill declared, 'once for all, cannot be tolerated; it is an abomination in the sight of mankind.' Those who argued that it was impossible were ratifying the intentions of what he called 'the Irish revolutionary party.' By the time Mill came to write his better-known *England and Ireland* (1868), the Fenian bombing campaign in Britain was in full career and he horrified his English audience by expanding on his earlier suggestion that it was the 'superstitious' English notion of property that lay at the heart of the matter in Ireland.

In making his distinction between the Irish and English ideas of property, between the rights of the cultivators of the soil and those of the owners of the land, Mill was influenced by the writings of Ireland's most distinguished economist John Elliot Cairnes (1823-75), whom he had met in 1859 and with whom he maintained a friendship and correspondence thereafter. Cairnes was the first economist to expose the fact that *laissez-faire* was a doctrine that had arisen out of specific social and industrial conditions in England and that it was, therefore, neither applicable to Ireland nor anything like a scientific law in itself. His views on this matter were fully formulated by 1870 and it is obvious, even from the extracts from his writings given below, that it was the Irish experience in the period from the Famine to the first Land Act that provided the proof for his quite revolutionary views. Cairnes was anxious to defend political economy itself, as well as to effect improvements in the Irish land system. It was precisely the kind of rigorous adherence to doctrinal economic belief, so characteristic of British politicians and treasury officials, that had given political economy a bad name and had also contributed so much to Irish misery. It is appropriate that an Irish economist should be foremost in exploding the malign myth of *laissez-faire* and in advocating the necessity of state intervention to control and resolve the economic disorder generated by the system in Ireland.

Although Butt's intervention was important in the 1840s and Cairnes's contribution more enduringly significant, they attracted less attention than the reaction to the crisis of the Young Ireland movement. Thomas Davis died in 1845. The Young Ireland that he had done so much to create was already going through the trauma of separation from O'Connell's Repeal Movement and its subsequent reconstitution into the Irish Confederation of 1847 under the leadership of William Smith O'Brien and Charles Gavan Duffy. In his memoir, *Young Ireland: A Fragment of Irish History 1840-45* (1880), Duffy declared that, whatever contemporary history associated with Young Ireland,

> ... nearly all that will be permanently remembered of the labours and sufferings of the men who composed it were events accomplished after the death of Davis and the apparent rout and dispersion of his friends.

Thomas Francis Meagher, Thomas D'Arcy McGee, Devin Reilly, John Mitchel and James Fintan Lalor had not known Davis at all. Yet it was these men, particularly the last two and, in Duffy's opinion, Lalor most of all, who came 'to modify the action of the party more than any one then living.' It is this 'left-wing' of Young Ireland that came to prominence as a result of its interpretation of the political and economic consequences of the Famine.

This is not to deny Davis's own influence. John O'Leary, Yeats and others confirm it. But the nationalism of Davis was peculiarly, even weirdly, ineffective in Famine conditions. All his heartfelt propaganda for the preservation of what remained of the Irish language, for the reformulation of the Irish national identity, for the fusion of the mixed strains of the Irish race into a cultural unity, almost vaporized in the heat of the crisis that struck just as he died. If Irish cultural identity was to be preserved or created by an initial repudiation of British industrialism and utilitarianism, then the kind of state intervention needed to meet the requirements of the Irish people during the Famine was, in theory at least, not to be welcomed. It seems not to have occurred to Davis, as it did to Isaac Butt, that the problems of the Irish economy and the problems of Irish cultural identity were intertwined. Ireland was neighbour to the most powerful economy in the world. During the Famine, what it needed more than anything else was to have the resources of that economy put at its disposal. As Butt pointed out, the cess levied on Irish landlords for the relief schemes should, in all consistency, have been levied on the whole of the United Kingdom. That, in economic terms, is what Union should have meant. The fostering of home-bred industries behind protective barriers, advocated by Davis and by later twentieth-century Irish governments, was a naive extension into economics of a theory of cultural independence. If Ireland were to become independent of the English-speaking economies of Britian and the United States, it would have to undergo a social as well as a cultural revolution. Emigration before, during and after the Famine merely emphasized its degree of dependence and put paid to any hope of making the Irish language a distinctive badge of Irish nationality.

In fact, the language revival movement, after Davis, but partly because of him, could only become a badge of provincialism, not because its aims were not noble or worthy, but because the conditions under which the revival was envisaged were economically unattainable or politically unimaginable. The weight of O'Connell and the catholic church, particularly the latter, was always on the side of an English-speaking polity, although the church was willing, even eager, to assert the language as a specifically Irish catholic possession in order to emphasize the unique catholicism of the English-speaking Irish in a predominantly protestant Anglo-Saxon world. Davisite cultural nationalism might have been successful had it be allied to a revolutionary politics; but its closest allegiance was to a species of cultural insularity that could be maintained only by economic dependence on the Anglo-Saxon world, against which the insularity was defined and represented as independence. Of those who could speak Irish after the Famine, many would not. One witness, speaking of the 1870s, said:

> In my young days at home in Ballinamona near Mallow every one over forty knew Irish. No one spoke it. It wasn't lucky.[2]

The Famine was a disaster for the Irish language but so too was the coincidence of the Famine and a theory of cultural nationalism that wanted to preserve the language in the amber of nostalgia and economic ignorance. When the realities of the situation were confronted in the hungry 1840s, it was the Irish speakers who had to face them. They did so either by dying or by forsaking Ireland and the Irish language. The young Irish left the island that Young Ireland, in its initial phase, had tried to create in response to the peculiar conditions obtaining in a part of the United Kingdom that was, simultaneously, a colony of the United Kingdom.

Although Davis's version of cultural nationalism was to be restored and developed within forty or fifty years of his death, the immediate reaction to what was happening during the Famine concentrated on the revelation of Ireland's colonial status within the constitutional framework of the Union. There is remarkable unanimity on this theme, even though the conclusions derived from it are often divergent. Archbishop John MacHale, well-known for his militantly catholic view of current political issues — like that of the proposed new university system, on which his and O'Connell's views had clashed with those of the non-sectarian Davis — wrote to Lord John Russell on 15 December 1846 with a heightened version of the argument for repeal, now buttressed by his account of the spectacular distress of the country. In this letter, he indicated what was to become the widely shared view of left- and right-wing commentators:

> Such is now the frightful state of this country, brought on, as it were, by a systematic collusion between the Irish landlords and the English legislature, and to which Ireland never would have been reduced, had she the protection of a native parliament. The famine has not, it is true, directly sprung from the Union. But severe as it is, it would not be so fatal, if Ireland had not been rendered too feeble to cope with the calamity, by the emaciating process to which it had been previously subjected.

According to MacHale, Ireland had been feeding England for forty-six years with the choicest beef and wheat, while coming to depend itself on the potato. This was the result of an at least tacit agreement between the landed classes and the English government. Friedrich Engels, who made notes towards a history of Ireland in 1869-70, came to the same conclusion. In a letter of 1856 to Karl Marx, after returning from a visit to Ireland, Engels wrote:

> Gendarmes, priests, lawyers, bureaucrats, squires in pleasant profusion and a total absence of any and every industry, so that it would be difficult to understand what all these parasitic growths found to live on if the misery of the peasants did not supply the other half of the picture . . . of so-called self-government there is not a trace. Ireland may be regarded as the first

2. Department of Irish Folklore, University College, Dublin: Famine MS 1069. 140.

> English colony and as one which because of its proximity is still governed exactly in the old way, and here one can already observe that the so-called liberty of English citizens is based on the oppression of the colonies.

In his incomplete *History of Ireland*, Engels repeats what MacHale had said:

> Today England needs grain quickly and dependably — Ireland is only fit for cattle pastures.

Common to both texts is the belief that the Irish colony had been exploited by collusion between the landlords and the government, and that this, more than anything else, had weakened and demoralized the Irish people to the point at which they had become hopelessly vulnerable to a stroke of fate like the potato blight. Although both would have supported Davis's questionable idea that protective tariffs would have saved Ireland from the worst effects of free trade, their ultimate emphasis is different. Ireland needs independence in order to survive and this independence must have, as its first priority, the reconsideration of the land question and the breaking of the conspiratorial connection between the English government and Irish landlords against the welfare of the mass of the Irish people.

This is the breaking point between Davis's Young Ireland cultural nationalism and Lalor's transformation of the issue into an analysis of the relationship between nationalism and the land. Lalor made the land question the central social question in Ireland and he made it a national issue, thereby creating the possibility of a nationalism that would involve a social and economic, as well as a political, revolution. In this he was mentor to Michael Davitt and James Connolly and those who drafted the Democratic Programme of the First Dáil in 1919. If landlordism was to be permitted to survive, it would be at the behest of the Irish people and on condition that it broke its nefariously anti-national alliance with the British government. Lalor, like Davitt, did not envisage the replacement of landlordism by peasant proprietorship. He was, in effect, enunciating a socialist theory of ownership, as did Davitt, although neither was to see this bear fruit. However, the immediate point is that the Famine had persuaded Lalor that the national questions of repeal of the Union and cultural identity were meaningless unless the question of the land was given priority. In 1847 and afterwards, that was a question of life or death.

John Mitchel was persuaded by Lalor's thesis and took it one step further. His interpretation of the Famine is in many ways the most important because it was the most influential. For Mitchel, the Famine was the ultimate step in the conquest of Ireland. The country was to be converted into a cattle and wheat farm to feed the industrial population of England, but only after the deliberate extermination of the people by a policy, executed by both Peel and Russell, designed to seize the opportunity presented by the potato blight, to finally get rid of the 'Celt', to depopulate Ireland and dissolve the political problem of that island while solving Britain's own economic problem. This view of the matter led him inevitably to consider again the question of violence, on which Young Ireland had broken with O'Connell after Meagher's famous 'Sword Speech' in 1846. If the Irish people were to be exterminated, it would be better that they should at least die fighting than co-operate in demoralized humiliation in their own extinction. Mitchel's sponsorship of violence was both a repudiation of O'Connell's constitutional policies and, in a sense, a counsel of despair. Since Ireland would never receive justice from England, because it was in the nature of the colonial relationship that it could not and would not, then at least it should resist as fiercely as possible its mighty imperialist foe. In so doing, it should also use all possible cultural aids to sustain its sense of difference, separation and will to survive.

Mitchel's ferocious rhetoric is, like much of *The Nation*'s verse and prose propaganda, locked within a narrow range of feeling. Like Davis and Meagher, and even Lalor, he conducts his arguments on the terms dictated by the forces by which he feels oppressed. It is not that they want to subvert those forces as such. Instead, they want to be on a par with them; they want the 'Celt' to be equivalent to, if also different from, the 'Saxon'. They do not oppose the racism by which they are humiliated. They want to extend its imperatives to include the Irish, not to exclude them. James Connolly is the first Irish nationalist to make a serious attempt to break out of this automatic trap. To make the distinction between Celt and Saxon something akin to a gender difference involves the acceptance of the old colonial distinction between national characters. Mitchel reveals this most blatantly in various scattered remarks in his writings about the supremacy of the white over the coloured races, in his support for the institution of slavery and, in general, in his adherence to the notion that social and political formations are inscribed in some predestined national fate, which the Irish, by a series of misfortunes, have failed to realize for themselves. Enslavement, in Mitchel's view, is not for the white races. Yet to demonstrate this in the case of Ireland, he, like Davis, had to create for the Irish a unique Celtic destiny which the English, in order to complete their preordained mission in the world, had to abort. As this kind of argument disappears into a metaphysical distance, the writing of the Young Irelanders becomes ever more overstrained in the effort to cross that forever vanishing interval.

Still, in bleak fact, it did not seem extravagant or melodramatic to those who survived the Famine that a policy of genocide had been in operation. British rule had always been harsh and unforgiving in Ireland; in this instance, it seemed that the failure to provide food in a country well-stocked with it, the penal regime of the workhouses, the passage and enforcement of coercion acts, the eager defence of private property, the clearances of starving people from the land, evictions, subsidized emigration in the notorious 'coffin-ships', the various instances of proselytizing in which conversion to protestantism was made the condition of receiving food, and innumerable acts of tyranny and cruelty to the sick and starving by government agents and landlords all confirmed the Mitchel thesis. Close to a million died; a million and a half emigrated. In ten years Ireland's population decreased by 20 per cent. The genocide theory was especially believed by the emigrants to America, and their numbers and their bitterness were to provide essential support for the formation of the Fenian movement in 1858. But the belief outlived that too. It became part of the traditional knowledge of the countryside, so that when, on the centenary of the Famine, the Irish Folklore Commission sent out a questionnaire, to discover what memories of and beliefs about it survived, a high percentage of the replies cited a belief in the conspiracy between the Irish landlords and the British government to break the spirit of the Irish people and, if possible, to exterminate them during those terrible years. Some accounts from this questionnaire are included here to demonstrate the endurance of this belief but, more simply, to give a glimpse of the little-known descriptions of the conditions in which people then lived. Along with these are some of the slightly better-known written records of those who saw the effects of the Famine at first hand. The Famine about which William Carleton wrote had occurred earlier, but the Great Famine was raging as his novel appeared and he took the opportunity to press upon his audience the dreadful relevance of what he had written to the Ireland of 1847.

Lalor's warning to the Irish landlords went unheeded by the landowners themselves, but was more closely attended to and acted upon by the British governments of succeeding decades. Although they emerged from the Famine with consolidated power (all the greater because so many insolvent landlords had been swept away by the Encumbered Estates Act), they remained transfixed on the most barbed of Lalor's accusations — that the relationship between landlord and tenant had to be revised or dismantled. In the end, it was dismantled, although it took many decades, a good deal of violence and an enormous mass of complex legislation to effect this. The alliance between the forces of political nationalism and the agrarian protest survived until the fall of Parnell. It was Michael Davitt who sustained that alliance and who extended Lalor's ideas about land nationalization, although he was also able, with Parnell's aid, to link that to the Home Rule question, the political issue that had replaced the repeal of the Union. Davitt's view of Young Ireland and the effects of the Famine on its organization gives Lalor a centrality that the cultural nationalists were later to reassign to Davis.

It was only then, in the last decade of the century, that the original cultural nationalism of Young Ireland re-emerged in its Davisite form, to make its contribution to the Irish Literary Revival. Yet, even then, one of its most powerful exponents, Standish O'Grady, himself a member of the landlord class, directed the cultural nationalist doctrine primarily at the landlords and fumed at their incapacity to receive it and thereby to reassume their traditional leadership. Although Yeats was to carry this crusade to unexpected lengths in his poetry, it was, in the end, the tenantry who finally took over the land and the political power that went with it. Landlordism was abolished in the Free State in 1923 and in Northern Ireland in 1925. The Famine took its toll over a long period. It was a crisis that changed the fate of every class and creed in Ireland, but most especially that of the tenantry and the landlords, the two groups most profoundly involved in the catastrophe.

Since then, a favourite theme of writers and historians has been the difference between pre- and post-Famine Ireland, the change in attitude that came over a community and the cataloguing of the effects it had on the fortunes of the Irish language, on marriage patterns and fertility rates, the nationalist interpretation of history, the land-hunger which was gratified only by peasant proprietorship, on the musical and literary tradition and, above all, on the demographic history of an island that ever since has lost a considerable percentage of its most gifted people to other countries in an apparently endless and by now traditional continuation of the panic emigration of those years from 1845 to 1850. By now, the Famine may not appear quite so apocalyptic; it seems to be the culmination of a process that had been evolving over thirty years, since the end of the Napoleonic wars. But the view of it taken by those who had lived through it governed later responses to a remarkable degree. Young Ireland's twin contribution — the genocide theory of Mitchel and the plea for a revolution in the land-tenure system made by Lalor — had political consequences that reverberated well into the twentieth century.

THOMAS FRANCIS MEAGHER

(1823-67)

from:
THE SWORD (28 July 1846)

[Meagher's famous speech against the Peace Resolutions, brought forward by Daniel O'Connell in Conciliation Hall, Dublin, led to the secession of the Young Irelanders from the Repeal Association. Since the death of Thomas Davis, with whom O'Connell had had a public quarrel the previous year, Young Ireland had become more and more militant in the pages of *The Nation*. O'Connell had decided to challenge the movement directly on the issue of violence and to force all its members to forswear violent action in all circumstances.

Meagher's reply snapped the remaining links between the O'Connells and Young Ireland. The speech was interrupted by John O'Connell, and Meagher thereupon left the hall with his Young Ireland comrades. Although the French uprising of 1848 was to bring them close again to the Repeal Movement, the alliance was only temporary; the breach that Meagher formally made here proved to be final. It should be said that he, like the rest of his Young Ireland colleagues, was better at praising soldierly violence than in performing it. The discrepancy between his rhetoric and the bathos of the 1848 insurrection is almost comic.]

... I was speaking of the true sentiments which should animate the people. Inspired by such sentiments, the people of this country will look beyond the mere redress of existing wrongs, and strive for the attainment of future power. A good government may, indeed, redress the grievances of an injured people; but a strong people alone can build up a great nation. To be strong a people must be self-reliant, self-ruled, self-sustained. The dependency of one people upon another, even for the benefits of legislation, is the deepest source of national weakness. By an unnatural law it exempts a people from their first duties — their first responsibilities. When you exempt a people from these duties, from these responsibilities, you generate in them a distrust in their own powers — thus you enervate, if you do not utterly destroy, that bold spirit which a sense of these responsibilities is sure to inspire, and which the exercise of these duties never fails to invigorate. Where this spirit does not actuate, the country may be tranquil — it will not be prosperous. It may exist — it will not thrive. It may hold together — it will not advance. Peace it may enjoy, for peace and serfdom are compatible. But, my lord, it will neither accumulate wealth nor win a character. It will neither benefit mankind by the enterprise of its merchants, nor instruct mankind by the examples of its statesmen. I make these observations, for it is the custom of some moderate politicians to say, that when the Whigs have accomplished the 'pacification' of the country, there will be little or no necessity for Repeal. My lord, there is something else, there is everything else, to be done when the work of 'pacification' has been accomplished — and here I will observe, that the prosperity of a country is, perhaps, the sole guarantee for its tranquillity, and that the more universal the prosperity, the more permanent will be the repose. But the Whigs will enrich as well as pacify! Grant it, my lord. Then do I conceive that the necessity for Repeal will augment. Great interests demand great safeguards, and the prosperity of a nation requires the protection of a national senate. Hereafter a national senate may require the protection of a national army. So much for the prosperity with which we are threatened; and which, it is said by gentlemen on the opposite shore of the Irish Sea, will crush this Association, and bury the enthusiasts, who clamour for Irish nationality in a sepulchre of gold. And yet, I must say, that this prediction is feebly sustained by the ministerial programme that has lately appeared. On the evening of the 16th, the Whig premier[1] ... is reported to have made this consolatory announcement: 'We consider that the social grievances of Ireland are those which are most prominent — and to which it is most likely to be in our power to afford, not a complete and immediate remedy, but some remedy, some kind of improvement, so that some kind of hope may be entertained that some ten or twelve years hence the country will, by the measures we undertake, be in a far better state with respect to the frightful destitution and misery which now prevails in that country. We have that practical object in view.' After that most consolatory announcement, my lord, let those who have the patience of Job and the poverty of Lazarus, continue in good faith 'to wait on Providence and the Whigs' — continue to entertain 'some kind of hope' that if not 'a complete and immediate remedy,' at least 'some remedy,' 'some improvement,' will place this country in 'a far better state' than it is at present, 'some ten or twelve years hence.'....

But we, my lord, who are assembled in this Hall, and in whose hearts the Union has not bred the slave's disease — we have not been imperialised — we are here to undo that work, which, forty-six years ago, dishonoured the ancient peerage, and subjugated the people of our country. My lord, to assist the people of Ireland to undo that work I came to this Hall. I came here to repeal the Act of Union — I came here for nothing else. Upon every other question I feel myself at perfect liberty to differ from each and every one of you. Upon questions of finance; questions of a religious character; questions of an educational character; questions of municipal policy; questions that may arise from the proceedings of the legislature: upon all these questions I feel myself at perfect liberty to differ from each and every one of you. Yet more, my lord, I maintain that it is my right to express my opinion upon each of these questions, if necessary. The right of free opinion I have here upheld: in the exercise of that right I have differed, sometimes, from the leader of this Association,[2] and would do so again. That right I will not abandon; I will maintain it to the last. In doing so, let me not be told that I seek to undermine the influence of the leader of this Association, and am insensible to his services. My lord, I will uphold his just influence, and I am grateful for his services. This is the first time I have spoken in these terms of that illustrious Irishman, in this Hall. I did not do so before — I felt it was unnecessary. I hate unnecessary praise: I scorn to receive it — I scorn to bestow it. No, my lord, I am not ungrateful to the man who struck the fetters off my arms, whilst I was yet a child; and by whose influence my father — the first Catholic who did so for two hundred years — sat, for the last two years, in the civic chair of an ancient city.[3] But, my lord, the same God who gave to that great man the power to strike down an odious ascendancy in this country, and enabled him to institute, in this land, the glorious law of religious equality — the same God gave to me a mind that is my own — a mind that has not been mortgaged to the opinions of any man or any set of men; a mind that I was to use, and not surrender. My lord, in the exercise of that right, which I have here endeavoured to uphold — a right which this Association should preserve inviolate, if it desires not to become a despotism — in the exercise of that right I have differed from Mr. O'Connell on previous occasions, and differ from him now. I do not agree with him in the opinion he

1. Lord John Russell (1792-1878) had become prime minister in July 1846. Peel had resigned because his repeal of the corn laws had split the Conservatives.

2. Daniel O'Connell.

3. Waterford. Meagher's father was lord mayor of the city 1844-46, and, later, its MP 1847-57.

entertains of my friend, Charles Gavan Duffy — that man whom I am proud indeed to call my friend, though he is a 'convicted conspirator,' and suffered for you in Richmond Prison. I do not think he is a 'maligner'; I do not think he has lost, or deserves to lose, the public favour. I have no more connection with the *Nation* than I have with the *Times*. I, therefore, feel no delicacy in appearing here this day in defence of its principles, with which I avow myself identified. My lord, it is to me a source of true delight and honest pride to speak this day in defence of that great journal. I do not fear to assume the position. Exalted as it be, it is easy to maintain it. The character of that journal is above reproach; and the ability that sustains it has won a European fame. The genius of which it is the offspring, the truth of which it is the oracle, have been recognised, my lord, by friends and foes. I care not how it may be assailed; I care not howsoever great may be the talent, howsoever high may be the position of those who now consider it their duty to impeach its writings: I do think that it has won too splendid a reputation to lose the influence it has acquired. The people, whose enthusiasm has been kindled by the impetuous fire of its verse, and whose sentiments have been ennobled by the earnest purity of its teaching, will not ratify the censure that has been pronounced upon it in this Hall. Truth will have its day of triumph, as well as its day of trial; and I do believe that the fearless patriotism which, in those pages, has braved the prejudices of the day, to enunciate new truths, will triumph in the end. My lord, such do I believe to be the character, such do I anticipate will be the fate of the principles that are now impeached. This brings me to what may be called the 'question of the day.' Before I enter upon that question, however, I will allude to one observation which fell from the honourable member for Kilkenny, and which may be said to refer to those who have expressed an opinion that has been construed into a declaration of war. The honourable gentleman said, in reference, I presume, to those who dissented from the resolutions of Monday, that those who were loudest in their declaration of war, were usually the most backward in acting up to those declarations. My lord, I do not find fault with the honourable gentleman for giving expression to a very ordinary saying; but this I will say, that I did not volunteer the opinion he condemns: to the declaration of that opinion I was forced. You left me no alternative — I should compromise my opinion, or avow it. To be honest I avowed it. I did not do so to brag, as they say. We have had too much of that 'bragging' in Ireland — I would be the last to imitate the custom. Well, I dissented from those 'peace resolutions,' as they are called. Why so? In the first place, my lord, I conceive there was not the least necessity for them. No member of this Association advised it. No member of this Association, I believe, would be so infatuate as to do so. In the existing circumstances of the country an incitement to arms would be senseless, and, therefore, wicked. To talk, now-a-days, of repealing the Act of Union by the force of arms, would be to rhapsodise. If the attempt were made, it would be a decided failure. There might be riot in the street — there would be no revolution in the country. Our esteemed under-secretary, Mr. Crean, will more effectively promote the cause of Repeal by registering votes in Green Street, than registering fire-arms in the Head-Police Office. Conciliation Hall on Burgh Quay is more impregnable than a rebel camp on Vinegar Hill;[4] and the hustings at Dundalk will be more successfully stormed than the magazine in the park. The registry club, the reading-room, the hustings, these are the only positions in the country we can occupy. Voters' certificates, books, reports, these are the only weapons we can employ. Therefore, my lord, I do advocate the peaceful policy of this Association. It is the only policy we can adopt. If that policy be pursued with truth, with courage, with fixed determination of purpose, I firmly believe it will succeed. But, my lord, I dissented from the resolutions before us, for other reasons. I stated the first — now I come to the second. I dissented from them, for I felt that, by assenting to them, I should have pledged myself to the unqualified repudiation of physical force in all countries, at all times, and in every circumstance. This I could not do; for, my lord, I do not abhor the use of arms in the vindication of national rights. There are times when arms will alone suffice, and when political ameliorations call for a drop of blood, and many thousand drops of blood. Opinion, I admit, will operate against opinion. But . . . force must be used against force. The soldier is proof against an argument, but he is not proof against a bullet. The

4. Vinegar Hill was the last stronghold of the Wexford rebels in 1798. Conciliation Hall, alongside the river Liffey at Burgh Quay in Dublin, was the headquarters of O'Connell's Repeal Association.

man that will listen to reason, let him be reasoned with; but it is the weaponed arm of the patriot that can alone avail against battalioned despotism. Then, my lord, I do not disclaim the use of arms as immoral, nor do I believe it is the truth to say, that the God of heaven withholds his sanction from the use of arms. From that night in which, in the valley of Bethulia, He nerved the arm of the Jewish girl to smite the drunken tyrant in his tent,[5] down to the hour in which He blessed the insurgent chivalry of the Belgian priests,[6] His Almighty hand hath ever been stretched forth from His throne of light, to consecrate the flag of freedom — to bless the patriot sword. Be it for the defence, or be it for the assertion of a nation's liberty, I look upon the sword as a sacred weapon. And if, my lord, it has sometimes reddened the shroud of the oppressor — like the anointed rod of the high priest, it has, as often, blossomed into flowers to deck the freeman's brow. Abhor the sword? Stigmatise the sword? No, my lord, for in the passes of the Tyrol it cut to pieces the banner of the Bavarian, and through those cragged passes cut a path to fame for the peasant insurrectionist of Innsbruck.[7] Abhor the sword? Stigmatise the sword? No, my lord, for at its blow, and in the quivering of its crimson light a giant nation sprang up from the waters of the Atlantic, and by its redeeming magic the fettered colony became a daring, free Republic. Abhor the sword? Stigmatise the sword? No, my lord, for it swept the Dutch marauders out of the fine old towns of Belgium — swept them back to their phlegmatic swamps, and knocked their flag and sceptre, their laws and bayonets, into the sluggish waters of the Scheldt.[8] My lord, I learned that it was the right of a nation to govern itself — not in this Hall, but upon the ramparts of Antwerp. This, the first article of a nation's creed, I learned upon those ramparts, where freedom was justly estimated, and where the possession of the precious gift was purchased by the effusion of generous blood. My lord, I honour the Belgians, I admire the Belgians, I love the Belgians for their enthusiasm, their courage, their success, and I, for one, will not stigmatise, for I do not abhor, the means by which they obtained a Citizen King, a Chamber of Deputies.

[Here John O'Connell interposed to prevent Meagher being further heard, and the Young Irelanders in a body quitted Conciliation Hall for ever.]

5. Judith beheaded Holofernes in his tent in the valley of Bethulia: Judith 13. 1-18.
6. As a result of the revolution of 1830, Belgium was separated from the Netherlands and became an independent kingdom. The political divisions between the Belgians and the Dutch corresponded with religious divisions between catholic and protestant.
7. Andreas Hofer (1767-1810), the son of an innkeeper, led the Tyrolean peasants in a revolt against Bavaria and the French in 1809. After several military successes, the Austrians made him governor of the Tyrol. The Treaty of Schönbrunn (October 1809) obliged Austria to abandon the Tyrol, but Hofer resisted. He was betrayed, was court-martialled by the French and was shot.
8. After the Belgian revolution of 1830, the river Scheldt formed the critical line of division between the new state and Holland.

WILLIAM CARLETON

(1794-1869)

from: THE BLACK PROPHET (1847)

[This novel first appeared in *The Dublin University Magazine* between May and December 1846. When it was published in book form the following year, Carleton dedicated it to Lord John Russell, Britain's prime minister because 'I cannot help thinking that the man who, in his ministerial capacity, must be looked upon as a public exponent of those principles of Government which have brought our country to her present calamitous condition, by a long course of illiberal legislation and unjustifiable neglect, ought to have his name placed before a story which details with truth the sufferings which such legislation and neglect have entailed upon our people.'

In his Preface, Carleton makes clear that the sufferings he describes are those he witnessed in the years 1817 and 1822. Now that the Great Famine has struck, he can only say that this proves 'how far the strongest imagery of Fiction is frequently transcended by the terrible realities of Truth.' The novel attacks various groups — money-lenders, extortionists, landlords, middlemen and government — for the dire state of the country before the disaster of 1845-50.

The first excerpt is from Chapter XVII, the second from Chapter XX.]

... At this precise period,[1] the state of the country was frightful beyond belief; for it is well known that the mortality of the season we are describing was considerably greater than that which even cholera occasioned in its worst and most malignant ravages. Indeed, the latter was not attended by such a tedious and lingering train of miseries as that which, in so many woful shapes, surrounded typhus fever. The appearance of cholera was sudden, and its operations quick, and although, on that account, it was looked upon with tenfold terror, yet for this very reason the consequences which it produced were by no means so full of affliction and distress, nor presented such strong and pitiable claims on human aid and sympathy as did those of typhus. In the one case, the victim was cut down by a sudden stroke, which occasioned a shock or moral paralysis both to himself and the survivors — especially to the latter — that might be almost said to neutralize its own inflictions. In the other, the approach was comparatively so slow and gradual, that all the sympathies and afflictions were allowed full and painful time to reach the utmost limits of human suffering, and to endure the wasting series of these struggles and details which long illness, surrounded by destitution and affliction, never fails to inflict. In the cholera, there was no time left to feel — the passions were wrenched and stunned by the blow, which was over, one may say, before it could be perceived; whilst, in the wide-spread but more tedious desolation of typhus, the heart was left to brood over the thousand phases of love and misery which the terrible realities of the one, joined to the alarming exaggerations of the other, never failed to present. In cholera, a few hours, and all was over; — but in the awful fever which then prevailed, there was the gradual approach — the protracted illness — the long nights of racking pain — day after day of raging torture — and that dark period of uncertainty when the balance of human life hangs in the terrible equilibrium of suspense — all requiring the exhibition of constant attention — of the eye whose affection never sleeps — the ear that is deaf only to every sound but the moan of pain — the touch whose tenderness is felt as a solace, so long as suffering itself is conscious — the pressure of the aching head — the moistening of the parched and burning lips — and the numerous and indescribable offices of love and devotedness, which always encompass, or should encompass, the bed of sickness and of death. There was, we say, all this, and much more than the imagination itself, unaided by a severe acquaintance with the truth, could embody in its gloomiest conceptions.

In fact, Ireland, during the season, or rather the year we are describing, might be compared to one vast lazar-house[2] filled with famine, disease, and death. The very skies of heaven were hung with the black drapery of the grave, for never since, nor within the memory of man before it, did the clouds present shapes of such gloomy and funereal import. Hearses, coffins, long funeral processions, and all the dark emblems of mortality were reflected, as it were, on the sky, from the terrible works of pestilence and famine which were going forward on the earth beneath it. To all this the thunder was constantly adding its angry peals, and the lightning flashing, as if uttering the indignation of heaven against our devoted people; and what rendered such fearful manifestations ominous and alarming to the superstitious was the fact of their occurrence in the evening and at night — circumstances which are always looked upon with unusual terror and dismay.

To any person passing through the country such a combination of startling and awful appearances was presented as has probably never been witnessed since. Go where you might, every object reminded you of the fearful desolation that was progressing around you. The features of the people were gaunt, their eyes wild and hollow, and their gait feeble and tottering. Pass through the fields, and you were met by little groups bearing home on their shoulders, and that with difficulty, a coffin, or perhaps two of them. The roads were literally black with funerals; and, as you passed along from parish to parish, the death-bells were pealing forth, in slow but dismal tones, the gloomy triumph which pestilence was achieving over the face of our devoted country — a country that each successive

1. The year is 1817.

2. 'Lazar' is an archaic word for leper.

day filled with darker desolation and deeper mourning.

Nor was this all. The people had an alarmed and unsettled aspect, and whether you met them as individuals or crowds, they seemed, when closely observed, to labour under some strong and insatiable want that rendered them almost reckless. The number of those who were reduced to mendicancy was incredible, and if it had not been for the extraordinary and unparalleled exertions of the clergy of all creeds, medical men, and local committees, thousands upon thousands would have perished of disease or hunger on the very highways. Many, indeed, did so perish; and it was no unusual sight to meet the father and mother, accompanied by their children, going, they knew not whither, and to witness one or other of them lying down on the roadside; and well were they off who could succeed in obtaining a sheaf of straw on which, as a luxury, to lay down their aching head, that was never more to rise from it, until borne, in a parish shell, to a shallow and hasty grave.

Temporary sheds were also erected on the roadsides, or near them, containing fever-stricken patients, who had no other home; and when they were released at last from their sorrows, nothing was more common than to place the coffin on the roadside also, with a plate on the lid of it, in order to solicit, from those who passed, such aid as they could afford to the sick or starving survivors.

That, indeed, was the trying and melancholy period in which all the lingering traces of self-respect — all recollection of former independence — all sense of modesty was cast to the winds. Under the terrible pressure of the complex destitution which prevailed, everything like shame was forgotten, and it was well known that whole families, who had hitherto been respectable and independent, were precipitated, almost at once, into all the common cant of importunity and clamour during this frightful struggle between life and death. Of the truth of this, the scenes which took place at the public soup shops, and other appointed places of relief, afforded melancholy proof. Here were wild crowds, ragged, sickly, and wasted away to skin and bone, struggling for the dole of charity like so many hungry vultures about the remnant of some carcase which they were tearing, amid noise, and screams, and strife, into very shreds; for, as we have said, all sense of becoming restraint or shame was now abandoned, and the timid girl, or modest mother of a family, or decent farmer, goaded by the same wild and tyrannical cravings, urged their claims with as much turbulent solicitation and outcry as if they had been trained since their very infancy to all the forms of impudent cant and imposture.

This, our readers will admit, was a most deplorable state of things; but, unfortunately, we cannot limit the truth of our descriptions to the scenes we have just attempted to pourtray [*sic*]. The misery which prevailed, as it had more than one source, so had it more than one aspect. There were, in the first place, studded over the country, a vast number of strong farmers, with bursting granaries and immense haggards,[3] who, without coming under the odious denomination of misers or meal-mongers, are in the habit of keeping up their provisions in large quantities, because they can afford to do so, until a year of scarcity arrives, when they draw upon their stock precisely when famine and prices are both at the highest. In addition to these there was another still viler class; we mean the hard-hearted and well-known misers — men who at every time, and in every season, prey upon the distress and destitution of the poor, and who can never look upon a promising spring or an abundant harvest without an inward sense of ingratitude against God for His goodness, or upon a season of drought, or a failing crop, unless with a thankful feeling of devotion for the approaching calamity.

During such periods, and under such circumstances, these men — including those of both classes — and the famished people, in general, live and act under antagonist principles. Hunger, they say, will break through stone walls; and when we reflect that, in addition to this irresistible stimulus, we may add a spirit of strong prejudice and resentment against these heartless persons, it is not surprising that the starving multitudes should, in the ravening madness of famine, follow up its outrageous impulses, and forget those legal restraints, or moral principles, that protect property under ordinary or different circumstances. It was just at this precise period, therefore, that the people, impelled by hunger and general misery, began to burst out into that excited stupefaction which is, we believe, peculiar to famine riots. And what rendered them still more exasperated than they probably would have been was, the long lines of provision carts which met or intermingled with the

3. Yards where corn was stacked.

funerals on the public thoroughfares whilst on their way to the neighbouring harbours for exportation. Such, indeed, was the extraordinary fact! Day after day vessels laden with Irish provisions, drawn from a population perishing with actual hunger, as well as with the pestilence which it occasioned, were passing out of our ports, whilst, singular as it may seem, other vessels came in freighted with our own provisions, sent back, through the charity of England, to our relief.

It is not our business, any more than it is our inclination, to dwell here upon the state of those sumptuary enactments which reflected such honour upon the legislative wisdom that permitted our country to arrive at the lamentable condition we have attempted to describe. We merely mention the facts, and leave to those who possess position and ability the task of giving to this extraordinary state of things a more effectual attention. Without the least disposition, however, to defend or justify any violation of the laws, we may be permitted to observe that the very witnessing of such facts as these by destitute and starving multitudes, was in itself such a temptation to break in upon the provisions thus transmitted as it was scarcely within the strength of men, furious with famine, to resist. Be this as it may, however, it is our duty, as a faithful historian, to state that at the present period of our narrative the famine riots had begun to assume something of an alarming aspect. Several carts had been attacked and pillaged, some strong farmers had been visited, and two or three misers were obliged to become benevolent with rather a bad grace. At the head of these parties were two persons mentioned in these pages — to wit, Thomas Dalton and Red Roddy Duncan, together with several others of various estimation and character, some of them, as might be naturally expected, the most daring and turbulent spirits in the neighbourhood.

Such, then, was the miserable state of things in the country at that particular period. The dreadful typhus was now abroad in all its deadly power, accompanied, on this occasion, as it always is among the Irish, by a panic, which invested it with tenfold terrors. The moment fever was ascertained, or even supposed, to visit a family, that moment the infected persons were avoided by their neighbours and friends as if they carried death, as they often did, about them, so that its presence occasioned all the usual interchanges of civility and good-neighbourhood to be discontinued. Nor should this excite our wonder, inasmuch as this terrific scourge, though unquestionably an epidemic, was also ascertained to be dangerously and fatally contagious. None, then, but persons of extraordinary moral strength, or possessing powerful impressions of religious duty, had courage to enter the houses of the sick or dead for the purpose of rendering to the afflicted those offices of humanity which their circumstances required, if we except only their nearest relatives, or those who lived in the same family. . . .

. . . The climate of Ireland is so unsettled, its soil so various in quality, and the potato so liable to injury from excess of either drought or moisture, that we have no hesitation in stating the startling fact of this annual famine as one we can vouch for, upon our own personal knowledge, and against the truth of which we challenge contradiction. Neither does an autumn pass without a complaint peculiar to those who feed solely upon the new and unripe potato, and which, ever since the year '32, is known by the people as the 'potato cholera.' With these circumstances the legislature ought to be acquainted, inasmuch as they are calamities that will desolate and afflict the country, so long as the potato is permitted to be, as it unfortunately is, the staple food of the people. That we are subject, in consequence of that fact, to periodical recurrences of dearth and disease, is well known and admitted; but that every season brings its partial scourge of both these evils to various remote and neglected districts in Ireland, has not been, what it ought long since to have been, an acknowledged and established fact in the sanitary statistics of the country. Indeed, one would imagine, that after the many terrible visitations which we have had from destitution and pestilence, a legislature sincerely anxious for the health and comfort of the people, would have devoted itself, in some reasonable measure, to the humane consideration of such proper sumptuary and sanitary enactments, as would have provided not only against the recurrence of these evils, but for a more enlightened system of public health and cleanliness, and a better and more comfortable provision of food for the indigent and poor. As it is at present, provision-dealers of all kinds, mealmongers, forestallers,[1]

1. People who bought goods before they had reached the public market.

butchers, bakers, and huxters, combine together, and sustain such a general monopoly in food, as is at variance with the spirit of all law and humanity, and constitutes a kind of artificial famine in the country; and surely these circumstances ought not to be permitted, so long as we have a deliberative legislature, whose duty it is to watch and guard the health and morals of the people.

At the present period of our narrative ... the popular outrages had risen to an alarming height. Up to the present time occasional outbreaks, by small and detached groups of individuals, had taken place at night or before dawn, and rather in a timid or furtive manner, than with the recklessness of men who assemble in large crowds, and set both law and all consequences at open defiance. Now, however, destitution and disease had wrought such woful work among the general population, that it was difficult to know where or how to prescribe bounds to the impetuous resentment with which they expressed themselves against those who held over large quantities of food in order to procure high prices. At this moment the country, with its waste, unreaped crops, lying in a state of plashy[2] and fermenting ruin, and its desolate and wintry aspect, was in frightful keeping with the appearance of the people when thus congregated together. We can only say, that the famine crowds of that awful year should have been seen in order to be understood and felt. The whole country was in a state of dull but frantic tumult, and the wild crowds, as they came and went in the perpetration of their melancholy outrages, were worn down by such startling evidences of general poverty and suffering, as were enough to fill the heart with fear as well as pity, even to look upon. Their cadaverous and emaciated aspects had something in them so wild and wolfish, and the fire of famine blazed so savagely in their hollow eyes, that many of them looked like creatures changed from their very humanity by some judicial plague, that had been sent down from heaven to punish and desolate the land. And in truth there is no doubt whatsoever, that the intensity of their sufferings, and the natural panic which was occasioned by the united ravages of disease and famine, had weakened the powers of their understanding, and impressed upon their bearing and features an expression which seemed partly the wild excitement of temporary frenzy, and partly the dull, hopeless apathy of fatuity — a state to which it is well known that misery, sickness, and hunger, all together, had brought down the strong intellect and reason of the wretched and famishing multitudes. Nor was this state of feeling confined to those who were goaded by the frightful sufferings that prevailed. On the contrary, thousands became victims of a quick and powerful contagion which spread the insane spirit of violence at a rapid rate, affecting many during the course of the day, who in the early part of the morning had not partaken of its influence. To no other principle than this can we attribute the wanton and irrational outrages of many of the people. Every one acquainted with such awful visitations must know that their terrific realities cause them, by wild influences that run through whole masses, to forget all the decencies and restraints of ordinary life, until fear and shame, and the becoming respect for order, all of which constitute the moral safety of society, are thrown aside or resolved into the great tyrannical instinct of self preservation, which, when thus stimulated, becomes what may be termed the insanity of desolation. We know that the most savage animals, as well as the most timid, will, when impelled by its ravenous clamours, alike forget every other appetite but that which is necessary for the sustainment of life. Urged by it alone, they will sometimes approach and assail the habitations of man, and, in the fury of the moment, expose themselves to his power, and dare his resentment — just as a famine mob will do, when urged by the same instinct, in a year of scarcity.

There is no beast, however, in the deepest jungle of Africa itself, so wild, savage, and ferocious, as a human mob, when left to its own blind and headlong impulses. On the morning in question, the whole country was pouring forth its famished hordes to intercept meal-carts and provision vehicles of all descriptions, on their way to market, or to the next seaport for shipment; or to attack the granaries of contractors or provision-dealers, and all who, having food in large quantities, refused to give it *gratis*, or at a nominal price, to the poor. Carts and cars, therefore, mostly the property of unoffending persons, were stopped on the highways, there broken, and the food which they carried openly taken away, and, in case of resistance, those who had charge of them were severely beaten. Mills were also attacked and pillaged, and in many instances large quantities of flour and grain not only

2. wet, marshy.

carried off, but wantonly and wickedly strown about the streets and destroyed.

In all these acts of violence there was very little shouting; the fact being, that the wretched people were not able to shout, unless on rare occasions; and sooth to say, their vociferations were then but a faint and feeble echo of the noisy tumults which in general characterize the proceedings of excited and angry crowds. Truly, these pitiable gatherings had their own peculiarities of misery. During the progress of the pillage, individuals of every age, sex, and condition — so far as condition can be applied to the lower classes — might be seen behind ditches, in remote nooks — in porches of houses, and many on the open highways and streets, eating, or rather gobbling up raw flour or oatmeal; others, more fortunate, were tearing and devouring bread, with a fury, to which only the unnatural appetites of so many famished maniacs could be compared. As might be expected, most of these inconsiderate acts of license were punished by the consequences which followed them. Sickness of various descriptions, giddiness, retchings, fainting-fits, convulsions, and, in some cases, death itself, were induced by this wolfish and frightful gluttony on the part of the starving people. Others, however, who possessed more sense, and maintained a greater restraint over their individual sufferings, might be seen in all directions hurrying home, loaded with provisions of the most portable description, under which they tottered and panted, and sometimes fell utterly prostrate from recent illness, or the mere exhaustion of want. Aged people, grey-haired old men, and old women bent with age, exhibited a wild and excited alacrity that was grevious [*sic*] to witness, whilst hirpling[3] homewards — if they had a home, or if not, to the first friendly shelter they could get — a kind of dim exulting joy feebly blazing in their heavy eyes, and a wild sense of unexpected good fortune working in unnatural play upon the muscles of their wrinkled and miserable faces. The ghastly impressions of famine, however, were not confined to those who composed the crowds. Even the children were little living skeletons, wan and yellow, with a spirit of pain and suffering legible upon their fleshless but innocent features; whilst the very dogs, as was well observed, were not able to bark, for, indeed, such of them as survived, were nothing but ribs and skins. At all events, they assisted in making up the terrible picture of general misery which the country at large presented. Both day and night, but at night especially, their hungry howlings could be heard over the country, or mingling with the wailings which the people were in the habit of pouring over those whom the terrible typhus was sweeping away with such wide and indiscriminating fatality. . . .

3. walking lamely, hobbling.

PEADAR Ó LAOGHAIRE

(1839-1920)

from: MO SGÉAL FÉIN (My Own Story) (1915)

[An tAthair Peadar Ó Laoghaire (Father Peter O'Leary) was only six when the Famine struck. It was nearly seventy years later that he wrote his famous autobiography, *Mo Sgéal Féin,* in which is preserved, along with the horrifying stories of starvation, the bitterness felt for the English treatment of the Irish during 'The Hunger'. The starvation of the people in the midst of plenty was seen as the culmination of the English policy towards Ireland, and the land system as the structure in which this catastrophe was permitted to happen. It is no surprise that Ó Laoghaire and his people regarded the Fenians as the most admirable of all Irish revolutionary groups.

This is chapter six of the autobiography in Cyril T. Ó Céirin's translation. The places named are all in County Cork.]

As soon as understanding comes to a child, it is usual for people to be asking him what would his vocation in life be, when he would be big. I well recall that question being put to me very often. I don't recall having any other answer to give to it but the one, solitary answer: that I would be a priest. From the beginning that much was settled in my mind and I don't recall that there was ever anything other than that. Neither do I recall when my mind first settled on my becoming a priest when I would be grown up.

I know well that people used to be making fun of the story, for it was clear to everyone that my father had nowhere near the necessary capital to set about such an undertaking. As soon as I got any sense, I also knew that he hadn't got the capital, but that did not prevent me from being steadfast in my mind about becoming a priest, whatever way this would come about. If it were not for the blight coming on the potatoes and the bad times that came afterwards, I don't say that he would not have been able to give me the necessary amount of schooling. But the bad times turned everything upside down.

A strange thing — it was the big, strong farmers who were the first to fall! The man who had only a small farm, the grass of six or seven cows, kept his hold; the man with the big, broad, spacious farm was soon broken when the changed times came. He, who had only a little, lost only a little. Before this, there was no big rent or big demands on him. He was accustomed to living without much extravagance. It wasn't too difficult for him to tighten his belt a little bit more, and to answer the small demands on him without too much hardship. But he, who had a big farm, was accustomed to the expensive way of life. He was independent as long as his farm responded. When the change came, the returns from the farm came to a sudden stop. The loss, the extravagance, the demands were too great. It was impossible to meet them and they swept him off his feet. I well recall how I would hear the latest news and how it caused amazement: 'Oh! Did you hear? Such a person is burst! His land is up for sale. He's gone. He slipped away. His land is up!'

You would often hear 'His land is up!' — but you wouldn't hear at all that time 'His land has been taken by another person'. Nobody had any wish to take land. Things used to be very bad for those who had lost their land. They'd have neither food nor credit and there was nothing they could do but go looking for alms. They would not be long begging when they used to go into a decline and they'd die. As they were not accustomed to hunger or hardship, they couldn't stand it long when the hunger and hardship would come on them. Often, when the hunger was very severe, they'd have to rise and move out and head for the house of some neighbour (who, perhaps, would be as needy as themselves, or close to it) to see if they could get a mouthful of something to eat, which might take the frenzy of hunger off them.

One day, when I was eight years of age (I seem to remember that I was standing at the corner of the haggard), I saw a woman coming towards me up the hill. She was barefoot, walking very slowly and panting, as if she had been running. She was blowing so much, her mouth was wide open, so that I had a sight of her teeth. But the thing that amazed me altogether was her feet. Each foot was swollen so that, from the knee down, it was as big and as fat as a gallon-can. That sight took such a firm grip on my mind that it is before my eyes now, every bit as clear-cut as it was that day, although it is around three score years and five since I saw it. That woman had been fairly independent and free from adversity until the blackness had come upon the potatoes.

Another day — I can't tell if it was before or after that — I was inside in our house, standing on the hearthstone, when a boy came in the door. I saw the face that was on him and the terror that was in his two eyes, the terror of hunger. That face and those two eyes are before my mind now, as clear and as unclouded as the day I gave them the one and only look. Somebody gave him a lump of bread. He snatched the bread and turned his back to us and his face to the wall and he started right into eating it so ravenously that you would think he would choke himself. At the time I did not realize that I was so amazed by him or by his voracity, but that sight has stayed in my mind, and will stay as long as I live.

I remember one evening during the period, when the people were running in and out and they talking away. In the winter, it was. The night was after falling. I heard someone saying, 'It was down by Carriginanassey I heard the shout!' 'There it is again!' said another, and they all ran out. A while afterwards, they came back in with a poor, old fellow between them. They put him standing on the floor — he was hardly able to stand. I was facing him and I had a view of his features. His mouth was wide open and his lips, upper and lower both, were drawn back, so that his teeth — the amount he had of them — were exposed. I saw the two, big, long, yellow eye-teeth in his mouth, the terror in his eyes and the confusion in his face. I can see them now as well as I could see them then. He was a neighbour. It is how the hunger drove him out to see if he could find anything to eat and the poor man went astray in the bog that was below Carriginanassey. When he found himself going astray, he became afraid that he would fall into a hole and be drowned. He stopped then and began to shout. That was a custom — there was a certain shout for the purpose — for anyone going astray. Each one knew how to send up that *liúgh*,[1] so that, when they heard it, everybody would know the meaning of it, and the people would gather and seek the person who was going astray.

There was a little stable at the head of the house. A poor person by the name of Patrick Buckley came and shelter was given to himself, his wife and two children in the stable. They stayed for some weeks there, but they had a small cabin for themselves after that. Sheila was the name of the elder of the two children. We had a serving-boy — Conor was his name — and I overheard Sheila talking to him one day.

'Con,' she said, in Gaelic.

'Coming, Sheila,' Con said.

'I have no speech now,' she said.

'*Airiú*,[2] what else have you got, Sheila?' Con said.

'English,' says she.

'*Airiú*, what English could you have?' Con said.

'Peter's English and Seáinin-Philib's English.' (Seáinin-Philib was another poor person, who lived in a cabin beside the place.)

'But surely English is speech, Sheila?'

'English speech?' she said in amazement. 'If it was, surely people would understand it!'

One day, Sheila's mother had a handful of gravel in the little broad-bottomed pot, the griddle-oven they used to call it, as she was going to bake a cake; she was scouring and scraping the inside of the griddle-oven with the gravel.

'Oh, Mam!' Sheila said, 'is it how you'll put gravel in the cake?' 'It is,' said her mother.

Out went Sheila. She saw Con.

'Oh, Con,' says she, 'What'll we do? What'll we do at all?'

'What's on you now, Sheila?' Con said.

'The grey-green gravel my mother's putting in the cake for us and I don't know how in the world we'll be able to eat it. All our teeth'll be broken. Some of the stones in the gravel are very big. Not one of us will have a tooth left in his head. It's all right for Little Jeremiah he hasn't got any teeth at all yet.'

Little Jeremiah was Sheila's small, young brother. In with Con until he'd see what Sheila's mother was doing. When he saw what the gravel was being used for, they had a great laugh.

The famine came. Sheila and her father and mother and little Jeremiah had to go down to Macroom into the poorhouse. No sooner were they inside than they were all separated from each other. The father was put among the men. The mother was put among the women. Sheila was put among the small girls. And Jeremiah was put among the very young children. The whole house, and all the poor people in it, was smothered in every kind of evil sickness, the people, almost as fast as they'd come in, falling down with a malady and — God bless the hearers! — dying as fast as the fever came on them. There used not be room for half of them in the house. The amount that would not be able to get in could only go and lay themselves on the bank of the river, on the lower side of the bridge. You would see them there every morning, after the night was over, stretched out in rows, some stirring, some quiet enough without any stir at all out of them. In a while, certain men would come and they would take those, who were not stirring, and they would put them into trucks. They would take them to a place beside Carrigastyra, where a great, wide, deep hole had been opened for them, and they would put them altogether down into the hole. They would do the same with all who had died in the house after the night.

It was not too long, after their going in and after his separation from his mother, that death came to little Jeremiah. The small body was thrown up on the truck and taken to the big hole, and it was thrown in along with the other bodies. But it was all the same to the child: long before his body was thrown in the hole, his soul was in the presence of God, in the joys of the heavens. It was not long until Sheila followed little Jeremiah. Her young body went into the hole, but her soul went up to where little Jeremiah was, in the presence of God, in the joy of the heavens, where she had solace and the company of the saints and angels, and the company of the Virgin Mary, and speech that was better by far than 'Peter's English and Seáinin-Philib's English'.

1. shout, noise.
2. Come now.

The father and mother were asking and questioning as often as they were able about Sheila and little Jeremiah. The children were not long dead when they heard about it. All the poor people had Gaelic. The superiors hadn't got it, or else they spoke it poorly. The poor people could often get word about each other without the superiors knowing it. As soon as the father and mother found out that the pair of children had died, such a grief and a brooding came over them that they could not stay in the place. They were separated from each other, but they found the opportunity of sending word to each other. They decided to steal away from the place. The wife's name was Kit. Patrick first slipped out of the house. He waited for Kit at the top of the Road of the Whisps. In a while, he saw her coming, but she was walking very slowly. The sickness was on her. They pushed on towards Carrigastyra. They came to the place where the big hole was. They knew that the two children were down in the hole with the hundreds of other bodies. They stood beside the hole and they wept their fill. Up on Derryleigh to the east of the Caharin was the cabin in which they had been living before they went into the poorhouse. They left the big hole and they headed north-west for Derryleigh, where the cabin was. The place was six miles of a journey from them, and the night was coming, but they pushed on. The hunger was on them and the sickness on Kit. They had to walk very slowly. When they had put a couple of miles of the journey past them, Kit was forced to stop. She was not able to walk any farther. A neighbour came across them. Drink and some little bit of food was given to them, but fear would not allow anyone to give them shelter since they were only just after coming out of the poorhouse and the evil sickness was on the woman. Patrick only lifted the woman onto his back and pushed on north-westwards for the cabin.

The poor man himself was weak enough. It would have been hard on him to put the journey by him without having any load. With the load, he was often forced to stop and to leave his load down on the ditch of the road for a while. But whatever weariness was on him, he continued to put that journey by him. He did not part with his load. He reached the cabin. The cabin was cold and empty before him, without fire nor heat.

The morning after, some neighbour came to the cabin. He went inside. He saw the pair there and they both dead, and the feet of the woman in Patrick's bosom, as if he had been trying to warm them. It would seem that he had felt the weakness of death coming over Kit and her feet cold, and he put the feet into his own bosom to take the cold from them.

'He was a good, loyal, noble man!' some person might say, perhaps, 'and the deed he did was a noble one!'

It is true. But I will tell you this much. Thousands of deeds of the same kind were done in Ireland during that period, and nobody was one whit amazed at the excellence of the deeds. According to everyone, Patrick Buckley had only done a thing that any man, who was worth calling a Christian, would have done.

That little man-een, whose name was Michael O'Leary, was living in a cabin not far from that in which Patrick Buckley and his wife died. Black Michael was a nick-name they had on him. Cathleen Purcell was his wife's name. They had the full of the house of children. There wasn't as much as one word of English in themselves or in the children. The famine came hard on them. Tadhg was the name of their eldest son. He saw his father and mother growing weak with the hunger, and the youngest member of the family stretched dead in a corner of the cabin. At nightfall, he took an axe and a knife with him and out he went. He went into the cowhouse of one of the neighbours and he killed a beast. He took some of the skin from it, stripping the amount of meat he wanted to bring with him. He took away the two hind quarters and came home. They all had a good meal that night. When the hunger had been taken from them, Tadhg took out the body that was in the corner, and he made a hole out in the garden and put the body in it.

When the morning came, the people who owned the cow rose and found the cow dead out in the shed, with its two hind quarters gone. The owner went to Macroom and got a search warrant. He had an idea where the meat was brought. He and whatever law-officer he had with him came to Black Michael's cabin. The bones and some of the meat was found. Tadhg was taken prisoner and brought to Macroom and put into prison. When the time came for it, he was tried. He was sentenced without much hesitation and transported. I never heard any report since then of what happened him afterwards nor of what end befell him.

Michael and Cathleen and those of the family who still lived left the cabin and took to the roads.

Some days after they had gone away, a neighbour was going past the cabin. He saw a hound, with something in his mouth, in the garden; the hound threw down the thing he had in his mouth and ran away. The neighbour came over and he nearly fell with the shock and the horror when he saw that it was a person's hand that the dog had in his mouth! Tadhg hadn't made the hole deep enough before he had put the body down into it.

The neighbour found a box or something of the sort. He took the rest of the body from the hole, and brought the box to the nearest graveyard and buried it. It was not cause for wonder at that time to see a person going by himself to a graveyard and a coffin with him in his cart, or on the back of two cattle if he hadn't got a horse nor a cart.

That was the way things were then, ugly and hateful and loathsome, round about the area in which I was reared. I understand that the story was exactly the same all about the whole of Ireland. And, to make matters altogether worse, it was not really by the will of God that things were so. It was that way because of the will of people. There was sent out from Ireland that year as much — no! twice as much — corn as would have nourished every person living in the country. The harbours of Ireland were full of ships and the ships full of Irish corn: they were leaving the harbours while the people were dying with the hunger throughout the land.

'Why wasn't the corn kept here?' someone will say, perhaps.

It was not kept because it had to be sold to pay the rent, it and the butter and the meat, and every other bit of produce from the land, excepting the potatoes. The blackness took away the potatoes and then there was no food left for people to eat.

Someone will say, perhaps: 'Why wasn't a law made to protect the people from the injustice that forced the people to sell the corn and not to keep anything for themselves to eat?'

I'm sorry for your want of knowledge! 'A law to protect the people,' you say? *Airiú*, if you had spoken to the gentlemen of England at that time of a law to protect the people, they would have said you were mad.

It was not at all for the protection of the people that the English made laws that time. To crush the people down and to plunder them, to put them to death by famine and by every other kind of injustice — that's why the English made laws in those days. It is a strange story, but the English had a sort of proverb then. Here's the proverb: 'To give the tenant his rights is an injustice to the landlord'.

ASENATH NICHOLSON

(*c.* 1794–*c.* 1858)

from:
LIGHTS AND SHADES OF IRELAND (1850)

[This book is Mrs Nicholson's second account of a visit to Ireland. Her first book, *Ireland's Welcome to the Stranger* (1847), is more generally known under the title of its abridged version, *The Bible in Ireland*, published in 1926. The subtitle explains in part what the author sought to do: 'Excursions through Ireland, in 1844 and 1845, for the purpose of personally investigating the condition of the poor.' Mrs Nicholson also wanted to introduce the catholic Irish to the Bible, although she did this in the mildest way. She praises the courtesy with which she was received, although at times it was subtler and more delicate than she perceived. Her quixotic enterprise provided a useful account of Ireland just before the Famine began. The poverty she describes is so extreme that it takes little to imagine the effect of the potato failure of 1845 and 1846 on the people she met. During the Famine she returned again to Ireland and, in the third part of this volume (the first two were 'Early History' and 'Saints, Kings and Poets of the Early Ages') she described what she saw of 'The Famine of 1847, '48 and '49'.

The titles to these extracts are editorial.]

THE INDIAN MEAL

. . . And the yaller Indian[1] was called by all manner of epithets, and went through all manner of ordeals but the right one. The Indian meal by some was stirred in cold water with a stick, then put quite dry upon a gridle [*sic*], it consequently crumbled apart, there was no turning it; and one desponding woman came to me, saying, 'That the last bit of turf had died on her, and not a ha'porth of the yaller Indian would stop with its comrade.' Others made what they called 'stirabout'; this was done, too, by first steeping in cold water, then pouring it into a pot, and immediately after swelling, it became so thick that it could not be stirred, neither would it cook in the least. The 'stirabout' then became a 'standabout,' and the effect of eating this was all but favourable to those who had seldom taken farinaceous food. They actually were afraid to take it in many cases, the *government* meal in particular, fearing that the 'Inglish intinded to kill them' with the 'tarin and scrapin'; but when hunger had progressed a little, these fears subsided, and they cared neither what they ate, or who sent it to them.

Had the women of the higher classes known how to prepare these articles in a proper manner, much money might have been saved, and many lives rescued, which are now lost.

When the first clamour had a little subsided, there followed the recipes for cooking Indian meal. One of these, highly celebrated for a while, was from Italy, and called 'Polentia';[2] whether spelt correctly the learned must decide; but this same Polentia would do for *gentlemen* and *ladies* too. The recipe cannot precisely be given; but enough to know that it was turned and overturned — covered and uncovered — boiled and steamed in a pot — and then came out genteelly, in a becoming shape, according to the form of the pot used. Now this was often on the tables of the gentry, for the recipe and meal were from Italy; the poor would only hear of this at a distance — the cooking they could never attain. Next came American recipes: these, with all due credence, were accepted as the one thing needful, for they possessed these redeeming qualities: — first, they were from *America*, the land which they loved, for many of their 'kin' were there; next, that though they thought that nobody but negroes ate it — yet negroes *lived* on that food; and 'sure the Americans wouldn't hurt em.'

These recipes were prepared in due form, and made up with suets, fats, sweets, and spices, so that the Laird John Russell himself could 'ate em.' A great and grand meeting of lords and nobility was held, called by the poor, the 'yaller Indin maitin'; and a *bona fide* sanction put on to the Indian meal cake. Here again was a difficulty — the meal was for the hungry; Where could they procure spices, sweets, and fats for such delicacies? — and as they thought that these were necessary to make it safe to eat, then their fears were awakened anew. But a few weeks adjusted all these difficulties, for when the number of the slain had increased in every parish, all murmuring of the quality of food ceased — they suffered in uncomplaining silence.

It was on the evening of December 7th, when about stepping into the train, at Kingstown,[3] for Dublin, I heard a policeman relating to a bystander a case of famine at the south. The potatoe, I knew, was partly destroyed; but never thought that actual famine would be the result. The facts were so appalling, that had they not come from a policeman, who, it should be said, are in general men of veracity, my mind would have doubted; and when he added that 'I got this information from a friend who was present in the court, and who wrote the circumstances to me,' all queries were removed.

A man had died from hunger, and his widow had gone into the ploughed field of her landlord to try to pick a few potatoes in the ridges which might be remaining since the harvest; she found a few — the landlord saw her — sent a magistrate to the cabin, who found three children in a state of starvation, and nothing in the cabin but the pot, which was over the fire. He demanded of her to show him the potatoes — she hesitated; he inquired what she had in the pot — she was silent; he looked in, and saw a dog, with the handful of potatoes she had gathered from the field. The sight of the wretched cabin, and still more, the despairing looks of the poor silent mother and the famished children, crouched in fear in a dark corner, so touched the heart of the magistrate, that he took the pot from the fire, bade the woman to follow him, and they went to the

1. The British prime minister, Sir Robert Peel, acted swiftly in late 1845 to purchase Indian meal to prevent starvation. The meal was stored in food depots and distribution began in the spring of 1846. The yellow (yaller) meal was known by various names, including 'yaller Indian'.
2. The Italian cornmeal dish is Polenta.
3. Now Dún Laoghaire, Co. Dublin.

court-room together. He presented the pot, containing the dog and the handful of potatoes, to the astonished judge. He called the woman — interrogated her kindly. She told him they sat in their desolate cabin two entire days, without eating, before she killed the half-famished dog; that she did not think she was stealing, to glean after the harvest was gathered. The judge gave her three pounds from his own purse; told her when she had used that to come again to him.

This was a compassionate judge, — and would to God Ireland could boast of many such.

I heard that story, heart-rending as it was, and soon found that it was but a prelude to facts of *daily*, yes, *hourly* occurrence, still more appalling. The work of death now commenced; the volcano, over which I felt that Ireland was walking, had burst, though its appearance was wholly different from anything I had ever conceived; a famine was always in Ireland, in a certain degree; and so common were beggars, and so many were always but just struggling for life, that not until thousands were reduced to the like condition of the woman last mentioned, did those, who had never begged, make their wants known. They picked over and picked out their blackened potatoes, and even ate the decayed ones, till many were made sick, before the real state of the country was known; and when it fell, it fell like an avalanche, sweeping at once the entire land. No parish need be anxious for neighbouring ones — each had enough under his own eye, and at his own door, to drain all resources, and keep alive his sympathy. It was some months before the rich really believed that the poor were not making false pretences; for at such a distance had they ever kept themselves from the 'lower order,' who were all 'dirty and lazy'; that many of them had never *realized* that four millions of people were subsisting entirely on the potatoe, and that another million ate them six days out of seven, entirely; they did not *realize* that these 'lazy ones' had worked six or eight months in the year for eight-pence and ten-pence, but more for sixpence, and even three-pence in the southern parts, and the other four months been 'idle' because 'no man had hired them'; they did not *realize* that the disgusting rags with which these 'lazy' ones disgraced their very gates, and shocked all decency, were the *rags* which they had contributed to provide; and such were often heard to say that this judgment was what they might expect, as a reward for their 'religion and idleness.' But the wave rolled on; the slain were multiplied; the dead by the way-side, and the more revolting sights of families found in the darkest corner of a cabin, in one putrid mass, where, in many cases, the cabin was tumbled down upon them to give them a burial, was somewhat convincing, even to those who had doubted much from the beginning.

There were some peculiarities in this famine which history has not recorded in any other. It may be scrupled whether any were heard to say that they did not deserve it — that they had not been such sinners above all others, that they must suffer so much — and so little plundering was never known in any famine as this, scarcely ever was a bread shop disturbed, though the poor creatures have been found dead under its window, in sight of it; the old proverb, that 'hunger will break through a stone wall,' was never exemplified during the famine; some carts, laden with meal, have been pillaged, and some boats have been robbed, but these were not common occurrences; occasionally, in the cities, would a man throw a stone at a street lamp, or do some other trifling mischief, always in presence of a policeman, that he might be put in jail, where the law must feed him. This was certainly an alternative for a starving man not so much to be censured as admired. Let it be stated that these men had applied for work in vain. I will descend to particulars; and state what my eyes have seen and my ears heard, and be answerable for what shall be stated.

The first starving person that I saw was a few days after the story of the woman and dog had been related. A servant in the house where I was stopping, at Kingstown, said that the milk woman wished me to see a man near by, that was in a state of actual starvation; and he was going out to attempt to work on the Queen's highway; a little labour was beginning opposite the house, and fifteen-pence-a-day stimulated this poor man, who had seven to support, his rent to pay, and fuel to buy. He had been sick with fever; the clothes of his family, that would fetch any price, had been pawned or sold, and all were starving together. He staggered with his spade to the work; the overseer objected; but he entreated to be allowed to try. The servant went out and asked him to step into the kitchen; and, reader, if you never have seen a starving human being, *may you never!* In my childhood I had been frighted with the stories of ghosts, and had seen actual skeletons; but imagination had come short of the sight of this man. And here, to those who have never watched the progress of protracted hunger, it might be proper to say, that persons will live for months, and pass through different stages, and life will struggle on to maintain her lawful hold, if occasional scanty supplies are given, till the walking skeleton becomes in a state of inanity — he sees you not, he heeds you not, neither does he beg. The first stage is somewhat clamorous — will not easily be put off; the next is patient, passive stupidity; and the last is idiocy. In the second stage, they will stand at a window for hours, without asking charity, giving a vacant stare, and not until peremptorily driven away will they move. In the last state, the head bends forward, and they walk with long strides, and pass you unheedingly. The man before-mentioned was emaciated to the last degree; he was tall, his eyes prominent, his skin shrivelled, his manner cringing and childlike; and the impression *then* and *there* made never *has* nor ever *can* be effaced; it was the *first*, and the beginning of these dreadful days yet in reserve. He had a breakfast, and was told to come in at four and get his dinner. The family were from home; the servant had an Irish heart, consequently my endeavours were all seconded. Often has she taken the loaf allowed for her board-wages, (that, is so much allowed weekly for food,) and sliced nearly the whole away — denying herself, for the suffering around her. It must be mentioned that labourers for the public, on roads, seldom or never ate more than twice a day, at ten and four; their food *was* the potatoe and oatmeal stirabout, and buttermilk, the *luxury* which was seldom enjoyed. This man was fed on Indian meal, gruel, buttermilk or new milk and bread in the morning; stirabout, buttermilk and bread, at four. Workmen are not paid at night on the public works, they must wait a week; and if they commence labour in a state of hunger, they often die before the week expires; many have been carried home to their wretched cabins, some dead and others dying, who had fallen down with the spade in their hands. The next day after this wretched man was fed, another, in like condition, at work in the same place, was called in and fed; he afterwards died, when the labour was finished, and he could get no more work. The first man gradually gained strength, and all for him was encouraging; when my purse became low — so many had been fed at the door that a pot was kept continually boiling, from seven in the morning till seven at night; Indian meal was then dear; the Americans had not sent their supplies; and much did my heart shrink at the thought that my means must be exhausted.

Let me here speak of the virtues of Indian meal; though always having been accustomed to it, more or less, not till December, 1846, in the famine of Ireland, did I know its value. It was made into gruel, boiled till it became a jelly; and once a day from twenty-five to thirty were fed — some who walked miles to get it; and every one who had this privilege recovered, without tasting anything but that, once a day — they always took it till they wanted no more; and this too without bread. One old man daily walked three miles, on his staff, for this, and he grew cheerful; always most courteously thanking me, saying, 'It nourishes my ould heart, so that it keeps me warm all the night.'

I had told these two labourers that when they found the gate locked they must know that I had no more to give them, and they must go home. The sad hour arrived; the overseer sent me word that he thanked me for feeding them so long; they must otherwise have died at their work. The gate was shut, and long and tedious were the two next days. One child of the poor man died, and he buried it in the morning before light, because if he took an hour from labour he would be dismissed. When the poor creatures that had daily been fed with the gruel came, and were told there was no more for them, I felt that I had sealed their doom. They turned away, blessing me again and again, but 'we must die of the hunger, God be praised.'

I would not say that I actually murmured, but the question did arise, 'Why was I brought to see a famine, and be the humble instrument of saving some few alive, and then see these few die, because I had no more to give them?'

Two days and nights dragged on. News were constantly arriving of the fearful state of the people, and the spectres that had been before my eyes constantly haunted me. My bedroom overlooked the burying-ground. I could fancy, as I often arose to look into it, that some haggard father was bringing a dead child, lashed to his back, and laying him on some tombstone as had been done, and leaving it to the mercy of whoever might find it a grave!

I was sitting in solitude, alone, at eleven o'clock, when the man of the house unexpectedly arrived. He had a parcel; in that parcel there was money from New York, and that money was for *me*!

No being, either christian or pagan, if he never

saw a famine, nor possesses a feeling heart, can understand what I then felt. I adored that watchful Hand that had so strangely led and upheld me in Ireland; and now, *above all* and *over all*, when my heart was sinking in the deepest despondency, when no way of escape appeared, this heavenly boon was sent! The night was spent in adoration and praise, longing for the day, when I might again hang over the 'blessed pot,' as the Irish called it. I lay below on a sofa, and saw no tombstones that night.

The morning came — the pot was over the fire. As soon as shops were opened, meal, bread, and milk were purchased. The man of the house went early to his business in Dublin. The gate was unlocked — the breakfast was prepared. The quantity was well nigh doubled, though enough had always been provided before. The sight of the man was more than I wished to abide; he was again sinking — had taken nothing but a 'sup,' as he termed it, of some meagre slop but once in the day, because his children would *all* die if he took it from them. The other soon followed; and while they were taking their breakfast, I was reading from New York the result of a meeting there in behalf of the Irish. This awakened gratitude towards my country unknown before; and now should I not be unmindful of the Hand that had led me through this wilderness thus far, and in every emergency carried me almost miraculously through, what I am about to record of the few following months, so far as self is concerned, should be withheld....

DONEGAL

... He had struggled hard during the famine to keep his tenantry from suffering, without much foreign aid, had sacrificed much, and difficulties were increasing.

This man[1] has proved to a demonstration what can be done even with the most hopeless, and under the most discouraging circumstances; for if Lord George Hill could transform those wild mountain goats, even to common civilized *bullocks*, what could not be done with any and *all* of the wild game of Ireland? Pity, great pity, that so few have applied the right key to the Irish heart! Still greater pity that so few believe there *is* a key that can find a right entrance; give Lord George Hill a patent right, and let all who will improve it, and Ireland will arise.

Now, in 1850, he writes, 'Say that *no person* died of famine at Gweedore, though many of the aged and infants, from being scantily fed, died earlier than otherwise they would, as well as from change of diet; also that the people are reviving in a great degree, from the potatoe having held out this year.'

Lord George Hill is an Irishman, of the Hillsborough family, in the county Down, brother to the *late* and uncle to the present Marquis of Downshire, a *true Irishman*, who lives and acts for his country.

Two miles from Gweedore an English gentleman had fixed a residence on the woody side of a hill, with a fine lake at a little distance, who was attracted there by the beauty of the scenery, and a desire to enjoy the evening of his days in a romantic peaceful retirement among a peasantry which pleased him; and his wife and daughters were quite an acquisition to the scattered intelligent class, which dotted the wild scenery there. His family were then in England, and when I met him a few weeks after in Derry, he said, 'I waited all day to see you, but when you come again we shall not be disappointed.' He died a few weeks after, and left a sad breach in the hearts of many.

This little incident is named to show how much the English, who go to Ireland because they admire the country, and justly appreciate the people, are beloved. They are always mentioned with the greatest admiration where they have behaved with a proper condescension and kindness to the people.

My next excursion was from Gweedore to Dungloe, with Mr. Forster, who conducted me to his pretty cottage and lovely family, in the parish of Templecrone. It was a wild and dreary waste which led us to it — here and there a cluster of miserable cabins, and still more miserable inmates, met the eye; now and then a hungry being would crawl out and make some sorrowful complaint of neglect by the relieving officer, which could not be remedied; but when we reached the cottage of my guide, all bespoke plenty and comfort. Here, in the midst of desolation and death, this isolated bright spot said, 'Mercy is not clean gone for ever.' Here was the minister of Templecrone, who had come to dine, for he heard that a stranger who pitied Ireland was to be there, and his heart was made of tenderness

1. Lord George Hill (1801-79) was a model landowner whose benevolent paternalism made his estates in Gweedore, Co. Donegal, famous in the Famine years. The book from which Mrs Nicholson later quotes was *Facts from Gweedore* (1845; 2nd edition 1846).

and love. Seldom can be met a being where such amiable, tender, and sympathetic kindness, are united with energy and perseverance, as were in this man. He was alive to every tale of woe, and active to surmount all difficulties; with his own hands, he laboured to assist the poor — they have laid their dead around his gate in the night, knowing that the 'blessed minister would not let them be buried without a board on 'em.' We spent a painful-pleasant evening at this hospitable house, talking of the dreadful scenes of death in their midst, and then the kind man rode eight miles on horseback to his home. The next day we were to visit Arranmore, a pretty sunny island, where peace and comfort had ever reigned. The peasantry here were about 1500 in number, occupying a green spot three miles in length, and had always maintained a good character for morality and industry. They kept cows, which supplied them with milk, sheep with wool, geese with beds, fowls with eggs; and grew oats, potatoes, and barley; they wore shoes and stockings, which none of the female peasantry can do in the country places; they likewise spun and made their own wearing apparel, and as the difficulty of crossing the channel of the sea, which was three miles, was considerable, they seldom visited the mainland. When they saw the potatoe was gone, they ate their fowls, sheep, and cows, and then began to cross the sea to Templecrone for relief. What could they find there? One man could do but little to stay the desolation. Hundreds had died before this, and though I know that painful scenes were in waiting, yet, if possible, the half was not told me. Six men, beside Mr. Griffith, crossed with me in an open boat, and we landed, not buoyantly, upon the once pretty island. The first that called my attention was the death-like stillness — nothing of life was seen or heard, excepting occasionally a dog. These looked so unlike all others I had seen among the poor — I unwittingly said — 'How can the dogs look so fat and shining here, where there is no food for the people?' 'Shall I tell her?' said the pilot to Mr. Griffith, not supposing that I heard him.

This was enough: if anything were wanting to make the horrors of a famine complete, this supplied the deficiency. Reader, I leave you to your thoughts, and only add that the sleek dogs of Arranmore were my horror, if not my *hatred*, and have stamped on my mind images which can never be effaced.

We made our first call at the door of the chapel; the fat surly-looking priest was standing there; and, saying to him, 'Your people, sir, are in a bad state.' 'Bad enough, they give *me* nothing.' 'Why should they? — you cannot expect or *ask* anything of the poor starving creatures.' The curate withdrew, leaving the battle to be decided by the priest, pilot, and myself, for he had known him before. 'Ah,' said the pilot, softly, 'he's a hard one; *there's* the christian for you,' pointing to the curate, 'he's the man that has the pitiful heart, — not a cratur on the island but would lay down the life for him.' This pilot was a Roman catholic, but that characteristic impartiality, peculiar to the Irish, where justice and mercy are concerned, belonged to him likewise. We went from cabin to cabin, till I begged the curate to show me no more. Not in a solitary instance did one beg. When we entered their dark, smoky, floorless abodes, made darker by the glaring of a bright sun, which had been shining upon us, they stood up before us in a speechless, vacant, staring, stupid, yet most eloquent posture, mutely *graphically* saying, 'Here we are, your bone and your flesh, made in God's image, like you. *Look at us!* What brought us here?' May God forgive me, and I believe He will, or I would not say it. With Job, I said, 'Let darkness and the shadow of death stain that day when first the potatoe was planted in this green isle of the sea,[2] to oppress the poor labourer, and at last bring him to a valley of death — *deep, dark, intricate* — where slimy serpents, poison lizards, and gnawing vultures creep and wind about his wasted limbs, and gnaw into the deepest recesses of his vitals.'

In every cabin we visited, *some* were so weak that they could never stand nor sit, and when we entered they saluted us, by crawling on all fours toward us, and trying to give some token of welcome. *Never, never* was the ruling passion stronger in death. That *heart-felt* greeting which they give the stranger, had not in the least died within them; it was not asking charity, for the curate answered my inquiries afterwards, concerning the self-control, which was the wonder of all, that he had sent a man previously through the island, to say that a stranger, from across the sea, was coming to visit them, but she had no money or food to give, and they must not trouble her. I gave a little boy a biscuit, and a thousand times since have I wished that it had been thrown into the sea; it could not save him: he took it between his bony hands, clasped it tight, and half-

2. Adapted from Job 3.5.

bent as he was, lifted them up, looked with his glaring eyes upon me, and gave a laughing grin that was truly horrible. The curate turned aside, and beckoned me away. 'Did you see that horrid attempt to laugh?' 'I cannot stay longer,' was my answer. We hurried away. The noble-minded pilot said, 'Will you step into my little place, and I will show you the boiler where I made the soup and stirabout, while the grants lasted.' These grants were mostly sent by the churches in England, and some poor deserving persons selected to give them out, and a very small compensation granted them, from the food they were distributing; and it should be here remarked, that when mention is made of the difference between 'hirelings' and 'volunteers,' I mean those 'hirelings' who were paid by government great salaries, and like the slave-overseers, could order *this* flogging, and withhold *that*, according to his own caprices. This does not in the *least* apply to such distributors as these.

The house of this man was a step in advance of the common cabins, and every part as clean as cabin or cottage could be; his young despairing wife sat, with a clean cap and apron on, for she knew we were coming, and uncomplainingly answered our inquiries respecting food, that they had not eaten that day, and the husband led us into the next room, opened a chest, took out a small bowl, partly filled with some kind of meal, and solemnly declared that they had not another morsel *in* the cabin or *out*, nor a sixpence to buy any. The curate said, 'I know him well, he is a deserving man, and tells us the truth.'

When we left this cabin we passed a contiguous one, and a decently clad woman, with shoes and stockings, and blue petticoat, (that was the kind the peasants always wore in their days of comfort,) very pleasantly offered me a bowl of milk. Astonished at the sight of such a luxury, I refused, from the principle that it would be robbing the starving. 'I regret,' said the curate, as we turned away, 'that you did not take it, her feelings were deeply injured; a shadow of disappointment,' he said, 'came over her face, as she answered in Irish: "The stranger looks wairy and her heart is drooping for the nourishment."' O, my Heavenly Father! *my 'heart drooping for nourishment,'*[3] after having taken a wholesome breakfast, and with the prospect of a good dinner at our return. A second kind woman was about making the same offering, when I begged Mr. Griffith, who spoke Irish, to say how much I thanked her; but that I never drank milk, and was not in the least hungry. Enquiring how we came to find milk, the pilot answered, that scattered here and there, a comfortable farmer, who had milked some three or four cows, had saved one from the wreck; but that would soon go, and then all music die together. We hurried away. And now for the burying-ground. 'You have seen the living and must now see the place of the dead.'

A famine burying-ground on the sea-coast has some peculiarities belonging to itself. First, it often lies on the borders of the sea, without any wall, and the dead are put into the earth without a coffin, so many piles on piles that the top one often can be seen through the thin covering; loose stones are placed over, but the dogs can easily put these aside, and tear away the loose dirt. This burial-place was on a cliff, whose sides were covered with rough stones, and the ascent in some parts very difficult. We ascended, sometimes keeping erect, and sometimes being obliged to stoop and use our hands. When we reached the top, the painful novelty repaid all our labour. It was an uneven surface of a few perches,[4] with new-made graves and loose stones covering them. A straw rope was lying near a fresh-dug grave, which the pilot said belonged to an old man, who two days before he saw climbing the cliff, with a son of fifteen lashed to his back by that cord, bringing in his feeble hand a spade. 'I untied the cord, took the corpse from the father's back, and with the spade, as well as I could, made a grave and put in the boy'; adding, 'Here you see so many have been buried, that I could not cover him well.'

This was the burial-place of Arranmore, and here, at the foot, was the old roaring ocean, dashing its proud waves, embracing in its broad arms this trembling green gem, while the spray was continually sprinkling its salt tears upon its once fair cheek, as if weeping over a desolation that it could not repair. At a little distance was a smooth green field, rearing its pretty crop of young barley, whose heads were full and fast ripening for the sickle. 'This,' said Mr. Griffith, 'is the growth of seed which was presented by William Bennet, last March; the poor creatures have sowed it, and if the hands that planted it live to reap the crop, they will have a little bread. Take a few heads of it, and send them to him as a specimen of its fine growth, and of

3. cf. Psalms 119.81.

4. A perch is a unit of length equal to 5½ yards.

their care in cultivating it.' 'Had these industrious people,' he added, 'been supplied in the spring with seed of barley and turnips, they would not need charity from the public. The government sent a supply around the coast, the delighted people looked up with hope, when to their sad disappointment, this expected gift was offered at a price considerably higher than the market one, and we saw the ships sailing away, without leaving its contents; for not one was able to purchase a pound. And we have since been told, that the "lazy dogs" were offered seed, but refused, not willing to take the trouble to sow it.'

We left without doing *one* favour, and without being asked to do one, except to drink a basin of milk. We found two little meagre, almost naked girls, sitting upon the beach picking shells and grinding them in their clean teeth; they gave a vacant look as we spoke, but answered not.

I gave the six boatmen a shilling each, who had not eaten one mouthful that day, and Mr. G. added sixpence each. Their grateful acknowledgments were doubly affecting, when they said, 'This is more than we have had at one time since the famine,' and they hastened to the meal-shop to purchase a little for their starving families. We went to a full dinner, prepared in that style which the gentry of Ireland are accustomed to prepare for guests; but what was food to me? The sights at Arranmore were food sufficient. What could be done? Mrs. Forster said, she had written to England, till she was ashamed to tire their generosity again; not once had she been refused from the churches there, and she felt that their patience must be exhausted. She gave the names of some of her donors. A letter was written in the desperation of feeling to an Independent minister there; and God for ever bless him and his people, for the ready response. Arranmore was relieved a little. . . .

MAYO

. . . A cabin was seen closed one day a little out of the town, when a man had the curiosity to open it, and in a dark corner he found a family of the father, mother, and two children, lying in close compact. The father was considerably decomposed; the mother, it appeared, had died last, and probably fastened the door, which was always the custom when all hope was extinguished, to get into the darkest corner and die, where passers-by could not see them. Such *family* scenes were quite common, and the cabin was generally pulled down upon them for a grave. The man called, begging me to look in. *I did not*, and *could not* endure, as the famine progressed, sights, as well as at the first, they were too *real*, and these realities became a dread. In all my former walks over the island, by day or night, no shrinking or fear of danger ever retarded in the least my progress; but now, the horror of meeting living walking ghosts, or stumbling upon the dead in my path at night, inclined me to keep within when necessity did not call. The entire face of the country was changed, for though poverty always was brooding her dismal wings over that island, yet *now* she had sharpened her teeth, and in many parts desperation was driving the people to deeds which had long slept, or which never before had been transacted. A class of persons, driven to madness by idleness and hunger, were prowling at night through some parts of the country, calling themselves 'Molly Maguires.' These go from house to house, in disguise, demanding money, and if denied, they card the refuser till the skin becomes lacerated; this scratching is performed sometimes with a card and sometimes with the whin-bush, which is full of small thorns, but these thorns, when applied to the skin, take leave of the bush, and remain there, so that the sufferer must often continue days before he can rid himself of these troublesome comrades. Many of these marauders have been apprehended, yet the practice did not cease, because they were encouraged by the country people, who had cattle in the pounds which had been seized for taxes, and these expert gentry, for a small reward, liberated and restored the animals to the original owners. A good supper of the best bread, butter, milk, and fowls, which the farmer could supply, ended the evening's jollity. Whiteboys, Peep-o'-day boys, Lady Clares, and Molly Maguires,[1] are hereditary entailments, having existed ever since parcelling out the land so

1. These were all agrarian secret societies. There were at least a dozen such societies in the late eighteenth and in the nineteenth centuries. The Molly Maguires date from 1835; they were so-called because they wore women's clothes to disguise themselves during their operations. The Whiteboys, a Munster organization, date from 1761. Lady Clares operated in Connacht and West Munster in the early decades of the nineteenth century. Peep-o'-Day boys is the only organization named here that was confined to protestants. It was founded in Ulster in the 1780s and its defeat of the catholic Defenders in 1795 led to the formation of the Orange Order.

unjustly, as a reward of plunder, was done to a few. Uncultivated as the mind of the Irish peasantry may be it is not *inactive* — the pool is not stagnant — life of *some* kind will sparkle up; and truly, if ever oppression was justifiable in making wise men 'mad,' it is in Ireland. When the cup is full it will flow over; — and the saying, that Ireland '*must* have a rebellion every forty or fifty years,' has a law of nature for its foundation. The *grand* river that supplies the mighty 'Niagara,' flows quietly on for many a mile, till it reaches a certain point, when it takes a rapidity, gathering force as it proceeds, till it meets the fearful precipice down which it has roared and tumbled for ages, and down which it *will* roar and tumble till *nature* herself shall be dissolved.

The so-called 'Rebellion' of 1848,[2] which sadly sealed the fate of Mitchell and O'Brien, was *precisely* this law. They had *waited* and *suffered, suffered* and *waited*, till they reached the awful chasm — the famine. They had seen it swallow its thousands, and they saw and *felt* that this chasm *might* have been closed; they looked on, they agitated, till their philanthropic love of country and deep sense of justice rushed into a temporary *madness*, *rashness*, and an *insanity* which hurled them headlong into their present abyss. The Tipperary men,[3] who congregated on that hill, with their flocks and herds, gave a rational reply to the priest, who exhorted them to disperse, *rational* — for uncultivated barbarians, as their enemies call them.

The priest pointed them to the absurdity, the *rashness*, of rising against so formidable an enemy as England and her soldiers stationed in the country. 'Better suffer than fight, and fight for *nothing, too*.' They added, 'It isn't the likes of us, yer riverence, that looks for the right, or the Repale,[4] but the long winter of the famine will be on us, and we shall die with the hunger; the blackguard taxes will take all the cattle, and we took 'em here, plaise yer riverence, to ate, and let the soldiers shoot us, and that will be the quick death for us; better than the long hunger, yer riverence — better than the hunger.' Now, that was certainly, for '*barbarians*,' quite a *civilized*, if not *philosophical* answer, and quite in keeping with Irish coolness in difficulty and danger. It was something like a company from a district in the south of Ireland, in the time of the first winter of the famine. They had given up all hope of life, and consulted to go in company to the poor-house, and die there, that they might be buried in coffins. Such a haggard array of misery had never been seen before in *one body*, and the soldiers were ordered to be on the spot at the workhouse to keep all in safety. These despairing creatures paused before the red coats and guns, and implored them to shoot them down, and end their long misery at once. This was no false bravado. They were sincere, and not one among them, it is believed, would have shrunk in face of that death.

This rebellion, it should be told, was not that ungrateful affair as has been represented. It was not agitated, or scarcely *known*, among the thousands who had been charitably fed in the famine. It originated among the higher classes of well-fed politicians, who were too *enlightened* not to know the causes of their country's sufferings, and too *humane* to look on with indifference. They were seconded by a lower class of men, who had not as yet felt the whole force of the famine in their own stomachs, but knew it must speedily come upon them. 'Give us death by the bullet,' they said, 'and not the starvation.' All this should be taken into consideration; and beside, this rebellion had nothing to do with the *sectarian* spirit of the country. Protestants were at the head of it, and many of the catholics chimed in, but the priests, as a body, stood aloof, and expostulated with their people to do the same. The O'Connells[5] were loud against it, in word and action; and had the catholics as a body united their forces, Ireland would have been one vast field of blood.

2. The 1848 rebellion of Young Ireland was an inglorious and futile affair. John Mitchel (1815-75) was in fact transported to Australia before the rebellion; William Smith O'Brien (1803-64) took part in the affair and was transported to Van Diemen's Land. He was released in 1854.
3. In the last days of July 1848, a small group under Smith O'Brien fought with policemen in the widow McCormack's cabbage patch in Ballingarry, Co. Tipperary. The local priest was a Father Fitzgerald.
4. i.e. the Repeal of the Union.
5. Daniel O'Connell died in 1847. He had indeed made his opposition to violence clear and had forced a break with the Young Irelanders over this issue in 1846. In this he was supported by his son, John O'Connell, although the French uprising of 1848 had led to some rapprochement between the different parties on this issue. Mrs Nicholson's historical and political references are often slightly askew.

CHRISTIAN CHARITY

. . . 'The bare-foot or the poor parson don't cross that gate, only the gentry ma'am,' implied that the poor well understood, that these christian gentry had a bridge over which none but the *respectable* must pass, and this they really supposed was a *part* and *parcel* of the religion which the bible taught, for, to the honour of the catholics, this was not their practice, at least towards me, even in the highest stations of life. And among the dissenters, there were noble exceptions; whenever a bible-reader was found — with but solitary specimens here and there — they were accessible, hospitable, and many of them deeply imbued with the principles of the gospel. Accommodating themselves as they must and do to the lowest classes, they reach the main-spring of the heart, and when they take spiritual weapons *exclusively*, they find a soil where good seed can be sown, and where it has sprung up to everlasting life. Here emphatically was exemplified the difference between a true and living faith, which works by *love*, and a *dead* one which works by party — 'Come,' said a humble poor catholic, 'and I'll shew ye the man: there is not a cabin in the parish, but his blessed feet have crawsed, and it's he that gives the plain raidin', and discourses us so kindly, and I'll go in with ye to his cottage, and shew ye the mistress.' They were never afraid to go in with me to one of these houses, and it would be very difficult to make many of these peasants believe that the bible, which these 'blessed men was tachin',' was the same translation as that of the upper classes. These men do what the superficial age would call the *dog-work* of the church — the work which some, who hold a higher station in it, would not stoop to do, but it is the *very work*, the work which, as an individual, from individual observation, I venture to say is the *best* work done in Ireland, and at the last account, when the 'pearls' are made up, 'Well done good and faithful servant,' will be said to many who now are scantily rewarded either by money or honours of those who have sent them there.

They are doing Christ's work, to the same class of people, and in the same that He did it.

The old hackneyed story of popery in Ireland has been so turned and twisted that every side has been seen — nothing new can be said about it. There it stands, its principles are well known, its superstitions and persecuting character, its idolatries, and all its trimming and trappings are the same in essence, as when Queen Elizabeth put her anathemas forth against its creeds and practice; and with all her errors she maintains a few principles and practices which would be well for her more bible neighbours to imitate. Her great ones are more accessible; the poor of their own class, or of any other, are not kept at such an awful distance; the stranger is seldom frowned coolly from their door; to *them* there appears to be a sacredness in the very word with which they would not trifle; the question is not, is he or she 'respectable,' but a *stranger*; if so then hospitality must be used without grudging. In the mountains, and sea-coast parts, it has ever been the custom to set the cabin door open at night, and keep up a fire on the hearth, that the way-faring man, and the lone stranger, should he be benighted, could see by the light that there is a welcome for him, and if they have but one bed, the family get up and give it to the stranger, sitting up, and having the fire kept bright through the night. This has been done for me, without knowing or asking whether I was Turk or Christian; and were I again to walk over that country, and be out at nightfall in storm and peril, as has been my lot, and come in sight of two castle-towers, one a Roman and the other a protestant owner; and were the former a mile beyond, my difficult way would be made to *that*, knowing that when the porter should tell the master a *stranger* was at the gate, he would say, 'Welcome the stranger in for the night, or from the storm.' The protestant *might* do the same, but there would be a *doubt*. His answer would probably be, 'A stranger! — How comes a stranger here at this late hour, tell him we do not admit persons into our house unless we *know* them.' Christian reader, this is one *strong* reason why you should admit them, because you do *not* know them. The catholics are much more humble in their demeanour, and certainly much more hospitable and obliging in all respects, as a *people*. They are more self-denying, will sacrifice their own comforts for the afflicted, more readily they will attend their places of worship, clothed or unclothed, and beggars take as high a place often in the chapel, as the rich man; the 'gold ring and costly apparel,'[1] is not honoured here, as in the protestant and dissenting churches; and it is remarked that when any turn to the protestant faith, they never lose that condescension, nor put on those pretences of wordly respectability, as their protestant brethren do.

This is the impartial candid *last* look that I take of the *outward* manifestations of religion in that miserable country, and any and *all* are challenged to contradict its reality as a whole, until the test has

1. II Samuel 1.23.

been made as *long*, and in the *same* way, in a famine and out of one, walking and riding, with money and without, in castle and cabin, in bog and in glen, by land and by water, in church and in chapel, with rector, curate, and priest, in markets and fairs, cattle-shows and flower-shows, in every position that they have been placed for the last six years, not excepting O'Connell's agitation, and Smith O'Brien's rebellion, O'Connell's imprisonment, and O'Brien's banishment, and can only say, if wrong deductions have been made, may they be forgiven and corrected.

A little for the Relief Officers at parting. To those who have been entrusted with money for the poor, and have been *bountifully* paid for the care of the loan put in your hands, if you have done by the starving poor, as you would that they should do unto you in like circumstances — if you have given the same quality and quantity of bread, that you should be willing to receive and eat — if you have never sent a starving one empty away, when you had it by you, because ease would be disturbed — if dinners and toasts have not drained any money that belonged to the poor, then 'well done good and faithful servant'; and if you *have* may you be forgiven, and never be left 'to feel the hunger.' My lot was to be once in a house where a sumptuous feast was held among this class of labourers, and that was in the midst of desolation and death. They 'tarried, to speak most modestly, a little too long at the wine'[2] *that* night, and drank toasts, which if they honoured the Queen, did little credit to men in their station, and in their responsible work. But I have seen and handled the 'black bread' for months, and have told the story. I have seen many sent from the relief, on days of giving it out, without a mouthful, and have not a doubt but many died in consequence of this, when they should and *might* have been fed. Time will not allow of dwelling on these cases; but one which was vividly impressed, and particularly marked at the time, may serve as a specimen. Going out one cold day in a bleak waste on the coast, I met a pitiful old man in hunger and tatters, with a child on his back, almost entirely naked, and to appearance in the last stages of starvation; whether his naked legs had been scratched, or whether the cold had affected them I knew not, but the blood was in small streams in different places, and the sight was a horrid one. The old man was interrogated, why he took such an object into sight, upon the street, when he answered that he lived seven miles off, and was afraid the child would die in the cabin, with two little children he had left starving, and he had come to get the bit of meal, as it was the day he heard that the relief was giving out. The officer told him he had not time to enter his name on the book, and he was sent away in that condition; a penny or two was given him, for which he expressed the greatest gratitude; this was on Wednesday or Thursday. The case was mentioned to the officer, and he [was] entreated not to send such objects away, especially when the distance was so great.

The next Saturday, on my way from the house where the relieving-officer was stationed, we saw an old man creeping slowly in a bending posture upon the road, and the boy was requested to stop the car. The old man looked up and recognised me. It was he who had the child upon his back in the dreadful state. I did not know him, but his overwhelming thanks for the little that was given him that day, called to mind the circumstances; and, inquiring where the child was, he said the three were left in the cabin, and had not taken a 'sup nor a bit' since yesterday morning, and he was afraid some of them would be dead upon the hearth when he returned. The relieving-officer had told him to come on Saturday, and his name should be on the book, he had waited without scarcely eating a mouthful till then, and was so weak he could not carry the child, and had crept the seven miles to get the meal, and was sent away with a promise to wait till the next Tuesday, and come and have his name on the books. This poor man had not a penny nor a mouthful of food, and he said tremulously, 'I must go home and die on the hairth with the hungry ones.' The mother had starved to death. He was given money to purchase seven pounds of meal; he clasped his old emaciated hands, first fell upon his knees, looked up to heaven and thanked the good God, then me, when the boy was so struck with his glaring eyes, and painful looks, that he turned aside, and said, 'let us get away.' The old man kept on his knees, walking on them, pausing and looking up to heaven; and thinking myself that seven pounds would not keep four scarcely in existence till Tuesday, we stopped till he came upon his knees to the car; he was given money enough to purchase seven pounds more; when, for a few moments, I feared that he would die on the path. His age, exhaustion by hunger, and the feelings of a father,

2. Proverbs 20.1.

together with the sudden change, from despair to hope, all were so powerful, that with his hands clasped, clinching the pennies, and standing upon his knees, he fell upon his face, and for some time remained there; he was finally restored to his knees, and the last glimpse we had of this picture of *living death*, he was behind us on the path, descending a hill upon his knees. What his future destiny was I never knew; but the Relieving Officer expressed no feelings of compunction when told of it some time after, nor did he know whether he had applied again. If he died, what then? was the answer. This solitary case is only a specimen of, to say the least, *hundreds*, who might have been saved, had these stewards applied the funds where *most* needed. Those who were obliged to walk miles, and lie out over night often upon the highway-side, were sent back to come again, while those who lived nearest, had the most strength, and could clamour the loudest for their rights, were soonest supplied. This Relieving Officer was an Irishman, and though among some of these there was great compassion and long continued, yet as a whole the English were much *more so*; and had they, without being advised or influenced in the least by the Irish landlords and Irish Relieving Officers, taken their own course, much better management of funds and better management for the suffering would have followed. The English were unused to such sights as Ireland in her *best* times presents, besides they never had oppressed these poor ones, while the rich powerful Irish, like our slaveholders in the United States, had long held them writhing in their grasp, some of them beside had been too lavish, their means for sporting and pleasure were lessening, and why not take their share of what they wanted, while it was in their hands? The English officers, entirely unacquainted even with the location of distressed districts, till, for the first time, their eyes were saluted with these frightful sights, would certainly be led to apply means, *when* and *where* more experienced ones should direct. The Irish landlords too, had another strong temptation. They had many comfortable farmers, who, till the famine, had not only paid them *good* rent, but had turned the worst soil into beautiful fields. They must either abide on the land and pay less rent, or none at all, till the famine ceased, or they must emigrate. Now a few hundred pounds would keep these tenants on their feet, and pay the landlord. And if these landlords had not before been influenced by the grace of God to do justice, it cannot be expected in this peculiar crisis they should suddenly be transformed to act so against their own worldly good. Who would trust a dog with his dinner if the dog be hungry? These are not random strokes made to finish a book, nor to gratify a splenetic sour spirit; particular prejudices have not been the spring of motion in this work; but being flung into *all* and *every* position how could I but see *all* and *every* thing that fell in my way? In the *worst* districts my tarry was generally the longest, and in some cases I literally carried out the precept 'Into whatever house ye enter there abide and thence depart,'[3] where the most information could be gained, and the family who invited me were able to supply all needful things, and had urged the visit, however protracted it might be; and in the face and eyes of all sincerity on *their* part, they had been taken at their word, and though the blarney grew thinner and weaker, yet I had long since accustomed my palate to bread without butter or honey, and potatoes without gravy or salt. This was not always done with the best grace, but it was a part of the self-denying work allotted me when my means for giving to the dying had been nearly exhausted? Why should I take what was actually *mine* and pay for lodgings when invited to accept them, where there was 'straw and provender' sufficient, and when too, it was offered so kindly, and this money could advance a better interest.

In saying farewell to all I have seen and done, I am not expecting to be fully understood; party politicians, sectarian professors of religion, pleasure-seeking worldlings, and such as love to be called by men, 'Rabbi,' cannot *understand*, and how can they be lenient even if they forgive; and my only request is, that the Master who sent me may not at last frown upon my puny endeavours for the good of suffering Ireland, and of that country I candidly and fearlessly give my *firm unwavering* testimony, that with all her *imperfections*, she deserves more pity than blame, and that in despite of all her strugglings, for centuries, barely to breathe, there yet remains in her enough valuable material, if brought out, and rightly manufactured, to make her, if not the brightest gem, yet *as* bright as any that sparkles in the ocean. She possesses an ingredient in her composition, beyond all other nations — an elasticity of such strength, that however weighty the depressing power may be, she

3. Mark 6.10.

returns to her level with greater velocity than any people whatever, when the force is removed.

Then arise to her help; let every protestant and dissenter put on the *whole* armour; let them together cast their tithes and *regium donums*[4] 'to the moles and to the bats,'[5] and stand out in the whole panoply of the gospel; then indeed will they appear 'terrible as an army with banners,'[6] let their wordly respectability be laid aside for the 'honour that comes from God,'[7] and let them do as Christ did, 'condescend to men of low estate.'[8] Who can tell if the professed church of Christ of all denominations should do her *first* work there, but that a loophole would be made, through which government might look beyond the dark cloud that has covered her reign over that island, and joyfully say *'Live, for I have found a ransom!'* For though government *now* holds the church in her hands, could she do so if the church was moved by an Almighty power? God now *suffers*, but does he *propel*? Is not the machinery of the church there one of the 'sought-out inventions,'[9] which never emanated from the uprightness of God? *See to it, see to it*, and then talk with success of the idolatries of popery....

4. A sum payable to the presbyterian church in Ireland; from 1802 to 1869 it was a charge on the exchequer of the United Kingdom.
5. Leviticus 11.19.
6. The Song of Solomon 6.10.
7. II Peter 1.17.
8. The Epistle of Paul to the Romans 12.16.
9. Ecclesiastes 2.29.

WILLIAM STEUART TRENCH

(1808-72)

from: REALITIES OF IRISH LIFE (1868)

[Trench's account of the Famine is especially valuable because, as a land agent who knew his business thoroughly, he brought professional skill to bear in describing and dealing with it. From the first appearance of the blight to the panic-stricken emigration to America, Trench remains loyal to his training and to his admirable sense of social responsibility. There is no more graphic record of the incompetent administration of the government relief schemes and the contrasting local successes of the unofficial work of dedicated individuals in dealing with the catastrophe. The absence of a managerial class and of the rudiments of any social or economic infrastructure, so painfully evident in this account, meant that only a benign and efficient paternalism could even begin to deal with the plight of the demoralized peasantry.]

CHAPTER VII

THE POTATO ROT

None of those who witnessed the scenes which took place in Ireland during the 'potato rot' and the 'famine years' are likely ever to forget them. These scenes came to pass within a year or two after I had resigned my post as agent to the Shirley estates in the county of Monaghan.

On leaving Carrickmacross I went to reside at Cardtown, my place in the Queen's County.[1] It adjoins an extensive mountain tract of land which I had purchased, and which I had for some years previously been engaged in reclaiming. Having resigned Mr. Shirley's agency, I was able to devote my time and energies more exclusively to this work, and the mode of reclaiming being chiefly through the means of the potato, as the only green crop which grows luxuriantly in rough ground with previously imperfect tilth, I planted each year larger and larger quantities of that root. Guano having been at that time (1845) recently brought into use as a manure, was found to be particularly suited to the production of the potato; I accordingly applied a liberal quantity to the crop, which was most luxuriant, and well repaid the labor, money, and attention necessarily bestowed upon it.

My plan of reclaiming was very simple. The land to be acted on consisted generally of rough

1. Now County Laois.

mountain pasture covered with heather. There were no stones, or few of sufficient size, to impede the course of the plough. The land was first limed with eighty barrels of lime to the Irish acre (about fifty to the statute acre), spread broadcast upon the surface. The land was then ploughed down into what were termed 'lazy beds,' that is, narrow ridges about five feet in width, with a furrow between each ridge. Into these ridges the seed of the potato was put by merely sticking the spade into the rough ground, and dropping in the seed or 'set' at the back of the spade; the spade being then withdrawn, the seed remained two or three inches under the surface. Guano, six hundred weight to the acre, was then scattered over the ridges, care being taken that the guano should not come into immediate contact either with the seed or with the lime. And this being done, the furrows were dug, the clay shovelled over the ridges, and the whole made up into 'lazy beds,' — rough underneath where heather and sods lay rudely massed together, but when covered up with the fresh dug soil from the furrows, presenting a neat and finished appearance above. The potato grew to perfection in this rude description of tillage; and whilst it was growing, the heather rotted under the influence of the lime, and, together with the other superabundant vegetable matter, was turned by the action of the lime into a most valuable manure. The guano stimulated an enormous and luxuriant growth, and when the potatoes were in course of being dug out, the act of digging mixed the lime, manure, and the several soils together into an even texture, leaving the land which had hitherto been scarcely worth one shilling per acre, in excellent order for sowing corn crops or grass seeds, and permanently worth at least one pound per acre.

I had taken much pains for some years previously in ascertaining, through repeated experiments, the success of this system of cultivation; and having found that in every case the process of reclamation was repaid, or nearly so, in the first year by the sale of the potato crop alone, leaving behind it land, increased from ten to twenty-fold in value, I planted in the year 1846 about one hundred Irish acres* of mountain land under potatoes, counting, as surely as any farmer can count on reaping any crop, upon a produce worth at least 30*l.* per acre. I was living at this time at Cardtown, where I had been engaged in building large additions to my dwelling-house, in fact a new house as it stands at present. My reclamation had succeeded beyond my most sanguine expectations, and in the month of July, 1846, my potato crop, for its extent and luxuriance, was the wonder of every one who saw it; and at the very moderate price of threepence per stone, — a price potatoes could always then command, — I felt certain, humanly speaking, of realizing by their sale at least 3,000*l.*

The reclamation of my mountain property had been a subject of considerable interest to many of the most intelligent agriculturists in Ireland. In the first instance, a silver medal, and afterwards a gold medal, had been offered by the Royal Agricultural Society of Ireland, 'For the best report on the largest quantity of waste land reclaimed in Ireland,' and in both cases I succeeded in obtaining this honorary distinction. The whole details of the plan, and the cost attendant thereon, were published in the Transactions of the Society, and many people thought, and I was myself amongst the number, that at last one of the great difficulties of Ireland at that day, — namely, the reclamation of her waste lands, and the profitable employment of her superabundant labor, — was about to be solved by this hitherto successful experiment. For some years I had not less than two hundred laborers, employed constantly at those works, draining, levelling, liming, and the heavy work of sowing and digging out again enormous quantities of potatoes. A more cheering sight it was scarcely possible to conceive than to witness these numerous laborers, employed at good wages themselves, collected from all quarters where labor was abundant, producing food for thousands of people whilst reclaiming one of the wastes of Ireland. But all this passed away like a dream on the sudden failure of the potato, and 'the happy valley,' as the sloping sides of my mountain property of Baureigh, with a clear trout stream running in the hollow, was frequently called by those who visited the works, was by that fearful calamity turned into a valley of woe.

On August 1st of that calamitous year, 1846, I was startled by hearing a sudden and strange rumor that all the potato fields in the district were blighted; and that a stench had arisen, emanating from their decaying stalks. I immediately rode up to visit my crop, and test the truth of this report; but I found it as luxuriant as ever, in full blossom, the stalks matted across each other with richness, and promising a splendid produce, without any

*Equal to 162 English or statute acres.

unpleasant smell whatever. On coming down from the mountain, I rode into the lowland country, and there I found the report to be but too true. The leaves of the potatoes on many fields I passed were quite withered, and a strange stench, such as I had never smelt before, but which became a well-known feature in 'the blight' for years after, filled the atmosphere adjoining each field of potatoes.

The next day I made further inquiries, and I found the disease was fast extending, and on rooting up some of the potato bulbs under the withered stalks, I found that decay had set in, and that the potato was rapidly blackening and melting away. In fields having a luxuriant crop, the stench was generally the first indication of disease, and the withered leaf followed in a day or two afterwards. Much alarm now prevailed in the country; people looked blank enough, as they asked each other if they had seen this new and formidable disease. Those, like me, who had staked a large amount of capital on the crop, hitherto almost a certainty, and at least as sure as the crop of wheat or turnips or any other agricultural produce, became extremely uneasy; whilst the poorer farmers looked on helplessly and with feelings of dire dismay at the total disappearance of all they had counted on for food.

Each day, from the time I first heard of the disease, I went regularly to visit my splendid mountain crop, and each day saw it apparently further advanced in course of arriving at a healthy and abundant maturity.

On August 6, 1846, — I shall not readily forget the day, — I rode up, as usual, to my mountain property, and my feelings may be imagined when, before I saw the crop, I smelt the fearful stench, now so well known and recognized as the death-sign of each field of potatoes. I was dismayed indeed, but I rode on: and, as I wound down the newly engineered road, running through the heart of the farm, and which forms the regular approach to the steward's house. I could scarcely bear the fearful and strange smell, which came up so rank from the luxuriant crop then growing all around; no perceptible change, except the smell, had as yet come upon the apparent prosperity of the deceitfully luxuriant stalks, but the experience of the past few days taught me that all was gone, and the crop was utterly worthless.

I need not tell how bitterly I was disappointed, overthrown as all my anticipations of profitable results were by this great calamity. Not only did I foresee the loss of my 3,000*l.* — no small sum to a man who had just surrendered an agency of 1,000*l.* per annum; but I felt, also, that the hopes of future success, on which I had expended a large capital, and much time and thought for years, were gone, — that it would be madness ever to venture on the trial of such a crop again; and that all my labor, and patient experiments, which had hitherto turned out so completely successful were, — by this new and fearful calamity, sent by the special hand of God, and the like of which had never appeared in nature before, — utterly blasted....

But my own losses and disappointments, deeply as I felt them, were soon merged in the general desolation, misery, and starvation which now rapidly affected the poorer classes around me and throughout Ireland. It is true that in the more cultivated districts of the Queen's County and the midland counties generally, not many deaths occurred from actual starvation. I mean, that people were not found dead on the roads or in the fields from sudden deprivation of food; but they sank gradually from impure and insufficient diet; and fever, dysentery, the crowding in the workhouse, or hardship on the relief works, carried thousands to a premature grave. The crop of all crops, on which they depended for food, had suddenly melted away, and no adequate arrangements had been made to meet this calamity, — the extent of which was so sudden and so terrible that no one had appreciated it in time, — and thus thousands perished almost without an effort to save themselves.

Public relief works were soon set on foot by the Government. Presentment sessions were held, relief committies organized, and the roads were tortured and cut up; hills were lowered, and hollows filled, and wages were paid for half or quarter work, — but still the people died. Soup kitchens and 'stirabout houses' were resorted to. Free trade was partially adopted. Indian meal poured into Ireland; individual exertions and charity abounded to an enormous extent, — but still the people died. Many of the highest and noblest in the land, both men and women, lost their lives, or contracted diseases from which they never afterwards recovered, in their endeavors to stay this fearful calamity, — but still the people died. We did what we could at Cardtown; but, though the distress there was far less than in most other places, yet our efforts seemed a mere drop of oil let fall upon the ocean of misery around us, — and still the people died!

Before the close of this year, being wholly unable from private sources to grapple with the vast extent of misery around us, and seeing also that there was no hope of the recovery of the potato, and that my occupation as an extensive reclaimer of land through its medium was suddenly brought to a close, I resolved to adapt myself as well as I could to this new condition of affairs. By this time an outcry had arisen against the public road relief works, and every one demanded some more useful and '*reproductive*' employment for the masses, now dependent on public charity. The Government thus was much in want of some one to set on foot a practicable plan to meet this public demand, and to organize a system of reproductive works, such as draining, subsoiling, liming, etc., and thus, as it were, draw the people from the roads into the fields. Acting, therefore, on the experience I had already acquired in the reclamation of land, I drew up a complete plan, embracing forms and specifications, etc., for draining, subsoiling, and the like. I then went to Dublin, and laid the whole project before the Board of Public Works....

Such was my first practical acquaintance with the fearful 'Potato Rot' of 1846, — the effects of which have produced a social revolution in Ireland. It hurried on the introduction of free trade. It indirectly brought about the arterial drainage of many of the main rivers of Ireland. It created the Land Improvement Act.[2] It brought into existence the Incumbered Estates Court,[3] one of the most important Acts ever passed in Ireland. It drove some millions of people to the other side of the Atlantic, and sent many thousands to an untimely grave. It broke up, to a great extent, the small farms of Ireland. It relieved the plethora of the labor market. It removed the needy country gentlemen, and forced them to sell their estates into the hands of capitalists. It unlocked millions of capital, since then laid out on the improved cultivation of the land. It brought over hundreds of Scotchmen and Englishmen, who have farmed on an extended and more scientific system than had before then been the practice in Ireland; and, in short, it has produced a revolution in the country which has lasted ever since. Its immediate effects were so appalling, and its final results so remarkable, that these few notes descriptive of its first appearance, as it came under my own immediate observation, may not prove wholly without interest.

But I must record some features of the potato rot as it appeared in other districts less favored than the Queen's County. The population of that country was never very excessive, the farms were moderate in size, and, valuable as the potato was as an esculent,[4] and most useful as I had proved it to be in the reclamation of waste lands, yet it rarely formed, as in other districts, the sole food of the people. During the period whilst I was engaged in organizing the system of drainage for the Board of Works, fearful scenes were being enacted in other parts, and especially in the south and west of Ireland. There the cottier system prevailed to its fullest extent; and, in the mountain districts where but little corn was grown, and where the people lived almost exclusively upon the potato, the most dire distress arose. Dark whisperings and rumors of famine in its most appalling form began to reach us, but still we could scarcely believe that men, women and children were actually dying of starvation in thousands. *Yet so it was.* They died in their mountain glens, they died along the sea-coast, they died on the roads, and they died in the fields; they wandered into the towns, and died in the streets; they closed their cabin doors and lay down upon their beds, and died of actual starvation in their houses.

To us, even at the time, it appeared almost incredible that such things should be. But a cry soon arose from the west, and especially from the district of Skibbereen and Schull in the county of Cork, which left no further doubt as to the real position of affairs; hundreds, nay thousands, of people had died, and were dying, in those districts, of absolute, direct starvation.

It is not my object or intention here to enter into any description of the arrangements which were made by Government to meet this dire calamity.... My present intention is merely to state what occurred under my own observation, or that of my immediate friends. When first this dreadful cry resounded through the land, the question which occurred to every thinking and practical mind was, '*Why should these things be?*' Ireland was not like

2. One of the Land Acts of 1860.

3. The Encumbered Estates Act of 1849 established a court that had powers to transfer debt-burdened land from insolvent to solvent owners. As a result, many landlords were replaced by new and sometimes highly predatory owners.

4. Any edible substance.

any part of India, cut off from extraneous supplies. It was true the potatoes had rotted, and it was true the people had depended on the potato almost alone for food. But there was abundance of corn, abundance of flour, and abundance of meal in the country, not to speak of herds of sheep and cattle innumerable; and, in the midst of such plenty, *why should the people die?* There was also abundance of money to purchase food: money was freely offered from many quarters, and was ready to flow forth in a mighty stream from the charitable people of England, to almost any extent. If so, I may again ask, *Why should the people die?*

To solve this problem some friends and relatives of mine proposed to visit the then notoriously distressed district of Schull, in the west of the county of Cork, and endeavor to ascertain for themselves the cause of this extraordinary position of affairs. Accordingly the Rev. Frederick F. Trench, a gentleman well-known for his philanthropy, and the Rev. Richard C. Trench, then rector of Itchenstoke in Hampshire, — now Archbishop of Dublin,[5] — agreed to visit the district in person. The result of their inquiries was very simple. There was, as I have stated, abundance of corn and abundance of meal within some few miles of the district, and no lack of funds to purchase these provisions; and yet in near proximity to this plenty, the people were dying by hundreds, of actual dire starvation, merely for want of some one with sufficient energy and powers of organization *to bring the food and the people together*. This was the apparently simple problem to be solved, and to effect it they set themselves vigorously to work. In one place they found a most benevolent clergyman, who having obtained large funds from England to mitigate the famine, appeared in the morning at his own hall door, and threw handfuls of shillings and sixpences amongst the crowd who had collected to receive the charity. Amiable gentleman no doubt he was, and most honorable in the distribution of all he had received; but he forgot that starving people could not eat sixpences or shillings, and the food was some ten miles off. The people had no strength nor energy to seek, purchase, or cook meal or flour, and with the silver in their hands, they died. In another place they found the priest of the parish utterly paralyzed by the magnitude of the desolation around him. He had given all he had to the people, there was no food whatever in his house, and he stood really in danger of being starved himself, with money in his pocket, and abundance of corn near at hand.† Such was the position of affairs, — the people dying, plenty of food within reach, plenty of money to purchase it, plenty of fish in the sea adjoining, — but no one with forethought and arrangement enough to cook the victuals, catch the fish, draw the corn across the mountains, and bring the food and the people together!

The plan adopted by these energetic philanthropists was very plain and simple. They first sought for funds; and the appeal was immediately and most generously responded to. They then engaged active earnest men, as temporary agents, over a district containing some sixty-seven townlands. And having selected the places most suitable for their operations, they opened what they then termed 'soup kitchens,' but what were really *depôts of boiled meal*, made into a thick nutritious food which in Ireland is called '*stirabout*.' It is perhaps the simplest and most palatable form in which a wholesome well-cooked food can be obtained cheaply in half an hour. These depôts, of which there were nineteen in the district, were placed within two or three miles of each other, sufficiently near to enable all those who wanted food, and who were willing and able to walk a short distance, to obtain at least one good meal each day, the only condition or stipulation being that they should come as clean as their case admitted, to the food depôt.

I will not venture to describe the harrowing scenes which presented themselves to these gentlemen and their assistants. I will not dilate upon the 'sliding coffin,'†† through which so many bodies were passed into the same open grave, it being impossible to procure coffins for all; nor upon the emaciated forms which crawled for food to the newly-established depôts. Suffice it to say, that in a very brief period, namely, from April 1, until May 10, 1847, they distributed, free, to the starving population, 102,129 meals within a district comprising sixty-seven townlands; in other words, they fed with one good meal per diem 2,553 persons for

5. Rev. Richard Trench (1807-86) was archbishop of Dublin 1864-84.

†The sea along the coast abounded with fish, but there were no nets, no boats, and no one to organize the simplest fishing operations.

††A coffin made with a sliding bottom, so that, by drawing out the bottom, the body fell into the grave, and the coffin could be used again for the same purpose.

forty consecutive days at the wonderfully moderate cost of 2*d.* per meal, inclusive of all expenses....

I have purposely avoided giving any details of individual suffering in the harrowing forms in which they presented themselves to myself during that fearful period. A book could be written on this subject; but of what avail would it be now? It is generally admitted that about 200,000 persons died of the famine in Ireland;[6] and my object is to show that if proper precautions had been taken in time, — by energetic men capable of undertaking the task, — to feed those who were unable to work, the famine would have been stayed, and most of the people saved.

6. The actual figure is now agreed to be about 800,000.

CHAPTER VIII

THE EXODUS. KENMARE

... The district of Kenmare[1] at that period, — January, 1850, — was not in a desirable condition. 'The famine,' in the strict acceptation of the term, was then nearly over, but it had left a trail behind it, almost as formidable as its presence. The mountain district around Kenmare had not escaped its effects. The circumstances of that country were peculiar. The Union[2] of Kenmare consists of a vast valley, with an arm of the sea, usually called the 'Kenmare River,' running up the centre for the distance of about six-and-twenty miles. On either side of this estuary, the mountains rise continuously to a distance of seven or eight miles from the shore, thus making an enormous valley about thirty miles long and sixteen wide. Within this district but little corn is grown. The portions of land reclaimed from the rocky mountains, on which alone corn could be raised, are so small, that they are barely sufficient to grow potatoes and turnips enough for the consumption of the people, and their cattle, throughout the winter. The exports of the district may be said to consist exclusively of butter, young cattle, and sheep, — whilst the inhabitants subsisted on potatoes, milk, and butter, together with cured fish, bacon, and a very small supply of oats, grown upon the reclaimed portion of land amongst the rocks. There is no access nearer than Killarney, which is twenty miles distant, to any corn-growing country.

1. A market town in County Kerry.
2. A Union was the unit of administration adapted for the purposes of the Poor Law Amendment Act (1834), revised in 1847 to increase the number of Unions and to permit direct outdoor relief.

The estate of the Marquis of Lansdowne in the Union of Kenmare had at this time been much neglected by its local manager. It consists of about sixty thousand acres, and comprises nearly one-third of the whole union. No restraint whatever had been put upon the system of subdivision of land. Boys and girls intermarried unchecked, each at the age of seventeen or eighteen, without thinking it necessary to make any provision whatever for their future subsistence, beyond a shed to lie down in, and a small plot of land whereon to grow potatoes. Innumerable squatters had settled themselves, unquestioned, in huts on the mountain sides and in the valleys, without any sufficient provision for their maintenance during the year. They sowed their patches of potatoes early in spring, using seaweed alone as a manure. Then as the scarce seasons of spring and summer came on, they nailed up the doors of their huts, took all their children along with them, together with a few tin cans, and started on a migratory and piratical expedition over the counties of Kerry and Cork, trusting to their adroitness and good luck in begging, to keep the family alive till the potato crop again came in. And thus, in consequence of the neglect or supineness of the agent, who, — in direct violation of his lordship's instructions, and without his knowledge, — allowed numbers of strangers and young married couples to settle on his estate, paying no rent, and almost without any visible means of subsistence, not only the finances, but the character and condition of the property, were at a very low ebb indeed. The estate, in fact, was swamped with paupers.

The desolation which a sudden failure of the staple food of the people, in a remote valley like this, must necessarily bring along with it, may be imagined. The scenes in Schull and Skibbereen were here enacted over again. As the potato melted away before the eyes of the people, they looked on in dismay and terror; but there was no one with energy enough to import corn to supply its place. Half Ireland was stunned by the suddenness of the calamity, and Kenmare was completely paralyzed. Begging, as of old, was now out of the question, as all were nearly equally poor; and many of the wretched people succumbed to their fate almost without a struggle.

The agent of the estate, who on my first arrival

was my chief informant, did not seem to consider that any one in particular was to blame for this. He talked of it as 'the hand of God.' The whole thing had come so suddenly, and all those residing at Kenmare were so entirely unprepared, and incapable of meeting it, that an efficient remedy was utterly out of the question.

In the midst of this most dire distress, Lord Lansdowne[3] came forward in the most generous manner, and offered money to any extent, — in fact a *carte blanche*, — to save the lives of the people. But there was no one in the country capable of undertaking the task. The magnitude of the suffering seemed to paralyze all local efforts to avert it, and his lordship's unbounded liberality was but little tested or applied. And thus almost in the midst of plenty, — for there was abundance of corn within a few miles distant, — famine stalked unmolested through the glens and mountains of Glanerought.*

It was indeed admitted to me by many intelligent men, that if there had been one man of firmness and energy in the district, he might have saved thousands of lives by the adoption of the same kind of plan as that so successfully organized by the Messrs. Trench in the west of the neighboring county of Cork, and which had turned out so effective even in a quarter with which they were wholly unconnected. But the local gentry were paralyzed, the tradesmen were paralyzed, the people were paralyzed, and the cottiers and squatters and small holders, who now saw the consequences of their previous folly in unlimited subdivision, unable from hunger to work, and hopeless of any sufficient relief from extraneous sources, sank quietly down, some in their houses, some at the 'relief works,' and died almost without a struggle.†

Such were the scenes which had taken place in that then secluded valley, not long previous to my arrival.

When I first reached Kenmare in the winter of 1849-50, the form of destitution had changed in some degree; but it was still very great. It was true that people no longer died of starvation; but they were dying nearly as fast of fever, dysentery, and scurvy within the walls of the work-house. Food there was now in abundance; but to entitle the people to obtain it, they were compelled to go into the work-house and 'auxiliary sheds,'†† until these were crowded almost to suffocation. And although out-door relief had also been resorted to in consequence of the impossibility of finding room for the paupers in the houses, yet the quantity of food given was so small, and *the previous destitution through which they had passed was so severe*, that nearly as many died now under the hands of the guardians, as had perished before by actual starvation.

In illustration of this state of things, I may mention an event which occurred to myself, soon after my arrival in the district.

I was in the habit, at this time, of attending the meetings of the Poor Law Board of Guardians, of which I had not yet become a member.

The numbers at that time receiving relief in the whole union of Kenmare were somewhat about ten thousand. In June, 1849, six months previous to my coming, they had reached the highest point, about ten thousand four hundred persons being then in receipt of relief. They had diminished slightly at the time to which I allude.

After a day of painful toil in the duty of admitting paupers, I was obliged to leave before the board broke up, as I had important business in Killarney, and I started on horseback to ride across the mountains. I had not gone far, when a messenger came posting after me to say, that the government officer, then in attendance at the board, was very desirous to see me. I asked if the case was urgent, and was told that it was very urgent indeed.

I returned of course, and found the members of the board looking certainly blank enough. The officer immediately informed me that the contractor, to whom a very large amount of money was due, had positively refused to give another sack of meal unless he received an instalment in cash that day. No one could well blame him. The board was bankrupt; repeated promises had been made to him of payments, which had not been fulfilled, and

*The name of the barony in which Lord Lansdowne's Kerry estate is situated.

†Several of the respectable shop-keepers in the town of Kenmare informed me that at this period four or five dead bodies were frequently found in the streets, or on the flags, in the morning, the remains of poor people who had wandered in from the country in search of food; and that they dreaded to open their doors lest a corpse should be found leaning against it.

3. Henry Petty-Fitzmaurice (1780-1863), 3rd marquess of Lansdowne, spoke on Irish distress in the House of Lords in 1847. He opposed the attempt to place the burden of financing relief on landowners.

††The work-houses being at this time quite unable to hold the numbers who crowded in, large auxiliary timber sheds were erected in convenient places, and in these were housed immense numbers of paupers, for whom room could not be found in the main building.

credit was utterly gone. At length I proposed that we should all put our hands in our pockets, and offered, on my own account, to double whatever total the rest of the board would subscribe amongst them, and take chance for the union refunding the money afterwards. The board however declined, and I could not get a 10*l.* note subscribed. I called the government officer aside into another room, and said, 'Will you tell me exactly what you think will be the consequence if the contractor refuses to let us have another load of meal?'

'I have thought over this,' he replied, 'and considering the numbers who are depending exclusively on this food and who are already in the last stage of destitution, on out-door relief, in distant parts of the union where this meal should now be sent, I feel confident that not less than from twelve to fifteen hundred persons will be dead before twenty-four hours are over.'

'Is it possible?' said I, — 'Can this really be true?'

'I think, sir,' said he, 'I am rather under than over the estimate.'

I could no longer hesitate. I fortunately happened to have some private funds in bank. I made the necessary arrangements for the payment of a portion of the debt, and the contractor forwarded the meal. Even now I tremble to think what might have occurred, either if I had gone too far towards Killarney to be recalled, or if I had not happened, at the time, to be in a position to make the necessary arrangements.

It may readily be supposed that this was a very serious state of things for a stranger to enter upon as the agent of Lord Lansdowne's estate in this union, and consequently, as such, the most responsible person in the district. I can hardly describe my anxiety of mind, as day after day the increasing responsibilities of the post I had assumed developed themselves before me. No one else would now stir. They had not done much before; and now that I took a prominent part amongst them, they held back and would do nothing. All, indeed, cried aloud that 'something ought to be done,' but few were able or willing to subscribe, and none had energy enough to attempt to grapple with the difficulty. Thus, by degrees, I felt myself placed almost alone, to meet, as I could, this fearful mass of pauperism.

The position was a most anxious one; but I endeavored to meet it steadily. Lord Lansdowne had kindly intimated to me that funds on the most liberal scale, — in fact to any amount required, — would be at my disposal for anything which would be for the advantage of the district; and the development of my plans was looked forward to with much anxiety. I remember a curious scene which took place about this time.

I was sitting one evening in my study, — I think it was in the month of May, 1850, — when I heard rather a strange humming noise, as of the suppressed voices of many hundred people. It came from the direction of the 'Brewery,' a short distance from Lansdowne Lodge. The noise was a very peculiar one, and unlike anything I had ever heard before. I was on the point of rising to ascertain the cause, when the servant rushed into the room, exclaiming, 'Oh, sir, the Brewery is on fire!' This brewery was an enormous building, formerly used for the purpose designated by its name, but now converted into an auxiliary poor-house, in which about three hundred pauper children were lodged. I went down without a moment's delay; and, just as I entered the premises, I met the school-master, who had charge of the building and all the children in it. I found him in great alarm.

'What is the matter?' I asked.

'I don't know, sir,' he replied. 'I believe the brewery is on fire; but I dare not open the door to see, as the children have got the alarm inside, and have become actually mad with fright; they would surely rush down the high stone steps, and half of them be killed in the panic.'

'Is there only one way out for the whole three hundred children?' I asked.

'That is all,' replied he.

'Give me the key'; and I went up the stairs to the door. A set of stone steps, with a stone parapet along them, led to a small, square-flagged platform immediately outside the door of the building. I saw at once that the man was so far right, that if the door were suddenly opened, a rush from the inside would inevitably be made, which must drive numbers over the parapet, and many would probably be killed by the fall, or smothered by the others passing over them, before such a number of children, in the wild state of panic in which they then were, could emerge from the building.

Seeing all this at a glance, I nevertheless opened the door, and pressing my foot against the low stone parapet on the opposite side of the platform, so as to retain firm possession of the door-way, I looked into the building. The sight which presented itself was strange and wild. Inside was a large room, in which as many children as it could possibly hold were crammed. The panic of the fire had seized them, and they were fast losing their senses with terror. The eyes of some were already staring wide, almost idiotic in expression. Others clenched their little fists, and ground their teeth, and threatened me in the most furious manner. And, in some cases, grown-up women, — nurses they appeared to be, — with infants in their arms, cursed and swore at me, insisting that I was there to prevent their getting out, and that I was determined to burn them all together in the house. It was a dreadful scene of terror and despair, and the panic was evidently increasing.

I immediately entered the room, closing the door behind me, and raising my hand, I said, in a loud voice, —

'I will let you all out this moment. There is no danger whatever. Be quiet and you shall all get out.'

But I might as well have spoken to maniacs in Bedlam.[4] They raised a panic-stricken shriek in reply, and struggled to get at the door. There was nothing now to be done but to let them out as carefully as I could. So I got outside the door again, and opened a few inches to prevent a rush of the children over the parapet; and thus, letting them out one by one, kicking, screaming, and some of them actually biting at my legs, they all got safely down the stone steps, and not a single one of them was hurt. I then went inside to examine the house for the fire. There was none: it was altogether a false alarm!

On my return to the door, the scene in the courtyard below was a very curious one. About eighteen or twenty children, chiefly boys of about twelve years of age, were lying on the gravel, some with their eyes staring and their bodies working in hideous contortions, completely idiotic from the fright. Some were quite motionless, but doubled back as if under the influence of cramp or tetanus. Some were apparently dead. So strange a scene of killed and wounded I never saw in my life. The excellent doctor of the union soon afterwards arrived, and I handed over the patients to him. To my surprise, he seemed to think but little of the matter, and assured me they would soon recover. But he admitted that had I opened the door suddenly, without insisting as I stood by that each should have time to reach the bottom of the steps in safety, vast numbers must inevitably have been killed.

In an hour or two most of them had recovered, and, with some difficulty, we got them all again into the building and to bed. I walked all through the wards just as the children were going to rest, and it was curious to watch the starts, and mutterings, and convulsive sobs which numbers exhibited as they gradually dropped asleep. It was evident that the panic had greatly affected the entire mass of children. I had never seen a panic, though I had often heard of one, before. It is not, by any means, a pleasant thing to witness.

Such was the state of things in Kenmare at the time to which I allude.

My first step was to endeavor to relieve, in some degree, the plethora of the poor-house; and for this purpose I offered employment, outside, to all those who had entered it chargeable to Lord Lansdowne's estate. I promised them reasonable wages in draining, subsoiling, removing rocks and stones, and such-like out-of-door labor. No sooner had I made this proposal, than about three hundred gaunt, half-famished men, and nearly as many boys and women, appeared in my field the next morning, all of them claiming my promise, but none of them having any tools wherewith to labor! Here was a new dilemma. The offer of employment had been accepted with only too great avidity; but the creatures had not a spade, nor a pick-axe, nor a working tool amongst them. Fortunately, a large depôt of these articles had lain stored in a tool-house hard by, — remnants of the public works. These I immediately appropriated, and, before noon, about one-half the people were employed. The remainder I sent again to the poor-house, telling them, to return the next day and I would endeavor to procure implements to lend them. They did so. And, partly by buying, partly by borrowing, and by making some of them work with their hands alone, I managed to keep most of them employed.

But although at first this system met with great approbation in the district, yet I found it quite impossible to continue it. In the first place, not much more than one-fourth of a reasonable value in labor could be obtained from those who proposed to work; and in the next, being now in employment, they had of course to leave the workhouse. Where

4. Bedlam became a common name for a lunatic asylum, after the Hospital of St Mary of Bethlehem in London.

then were they to lodge at night? Every lane, every alley, every cabin in the town was crowded to excess with these unhappy work-people, and they slept by threes and fours together wherever they could get a pallet of straw to lie upon. But I plainly saw that this could not go on. The towns-people began to complain of the scenes in the town at night; and when a wet day came and the people could not work, nearly one-half of them were obliged to return for the day to the poor-house, creating immense confusion by the sudden influx of such a body of famished newcomers, and the remainder wandered about, objects of the utmost compassion.

Accordingly, after the most anxious deliberation, I arrived at the final conclusion that this system could not be carried on. I felt it would be madness in me to assume the responsibility of keeping three hundred paupers in employment, most of them removed only one step from the grave, as, if any accident should happen to prevent them from obtaining *daily pay*, whether they had work or not, which I had hitherto managed at great inconvenience to give them, many lives might be lost in a night; a result for which I, — not in law, but perhaps in public opinion, — might immediately be called to account.

I therefore resolved to put into practice a scheme which I had meditated for a long time previously, namely, to go myself to Lord Lansdowne at Bowood, to state to him the whole circumstances of the case, and to recommend him to adopt an extensive system of voluntary emigration as the only practicable and effective means of relieving this frightful destitution.

This plan, accordingly, I carried into effect. And in the month of November, 1850, I went over to England; and having been invited to visit his lordship at Bowood, I remained there five days.

During my stay I had frequent and lengthened interviews with that most enlightened and liberal statesman. The broad sketch of the plan I laid before him was as follows: I showed him by the poor-house returns, that the number of paupers off his estate and receiving relief in the workhouse amounted to about three thousand. That I was wholly unable to undertake the employment of these people in their present condition, on reproductive works; and that if left in the workhouse, the smallest amount they could possibly cost would be 5*l.* per head per annum, and thus that the poor-rates must necessarily amount, for some years to come, to 15,000*l.* per annum, unless these people died or left, — and the latter was not probable. I stated also, that hitherto the people had been kept alive in the workhouse by grants from the rates in aid and other public money; but that this could not always go on. That the valuation of his estate in that district scarcely reached 10,000*l.* per annum; and thus, that the poor-rates necessary to be raised in the future off the estate to support this number of people, would amount to at least thirty shillings in the pound. I explained further to him, that under these circumstances, inasmuch as the poor-rates were a charge prior to the rent, it would be impossible for his lordship to expect any rent whatever out of his estate for many years to come.

The remedy I proposed was as follows: That he should forthwith offer *free emigration* to every man, woman, and child now in the poor-house and *chargeable to his estate.* That I had been in communication with an emigration agent, who had offered to contract to take them to whatever port in America each pleased, at a reasonable rate per head. That even supposing they all accepted this offer, the total, together with a small sum per head for outfit and a few shillings on landing, would not exceed from 13,000*l.* to 14,000*l.*, a sum less than it would cost to support them in the workhouse for a single year. That in the one case he would not only free his estate of this mass of pauperism which had been allowed to accumulate upon it, but would put the people themselves in a far better way of earning their bread hereafter; whereas by feeding and retaining them where they were, they must remain as a millstone around the neck of his estate, and prevent its rise for many years to come; and I plainly proved that it would be cheaper to him, and *better for them*, to pay for their emigration at once, than to continue to support them at home.

His lordship discussed the matter very fully, and with that kindness, good sense, and liberality which characterized all his acts; and on my leaving Bowood he gave me an order for 8,000*l.* wherewith to commence the system of emigration, with a full understanding that more should be forthcoming if required.

I shall not readily forget the scenes that occurred in Kenmare when I returned, and announced that I was prepared at Lord Lansdowne's expense to send to America every one now in the poor-house who was chargeable to his lordship's estate, and who desired to go; leaving each to select what port in

America he pleased, — whether Boston, New York, New Orleans, or Quebec.

The announcement at first was scarcely credited; it was considered by the paupers to be too good news to be true. But when it began to be believed and appreciated, a rush was made to get away at once.

The organization of the system required, however, much care and thought.

The mode adopted was as follows: Two hundred each week were selected of those apparently most suited for emigration; and having arranged their slender outfit, a steady man, on whom I could depend, Mr. Jeremiah O'Shea, was employed to take charge of them on their journey to Cork, and not to leave them nor allow them to scatter, until he saw them safely on board the emigrant ship. This plan succeeded admirably; and week after week, to the astonishment of the good people of Cork, and sometimes not a little to their dismay, a batch of two hundred paupers appeared on the quays of Cork, bound for the Far West.

A cry was now raised that I was exterminating the people. But the people knew well that those who now cried loudest had given them no help when in the extremity of their distress, and they rushed from the country like a panic-stricken throng, each only fearing that the funds at my disposal might fail before he and his family could get their passage.

So great was the rush from the poor-house to emigrate, and so great was the influx into the house to qualify (as I generally required the application of that sure test of abject poverty before I gave an order for emigration), that the guardians became uneasy, and said the poor-house would be filled with those seeking emigration, even faster than it could be emptied. But I told them not to be alarmed, — that all demands should be met. And thus, two hundred after two hundred, week after week, departed for Cork, until the poor-house was nearly emptied of paupers chargeable to the Lansdowne estate; and in little more than a year 3,500 paupers had left Kenmare for America, all free emigrants, without any ejectments having been brought against them to enforce it, or the slightest pressure put upon them to go.

Matters now began to right themselves; only some fifty or sixty paupers remained in the house, chargeable to the property over which I had the care, and Lord Lansdowne's estate at length breathed freely.

It must be admitted that the paupers despatched to America on such a sudden pressure as this, were of a very motley type; and a strange figure these wild batches of two hundred each, — most of them speaking only the Irish language, — made in the streets of Cork, as well as on the quays of Liverpool and America. There was great difficulty in keeping them from breaking loose from the ship, not only in Cork, but in Liverpool, where the ships touched before they left for the West. Their chief device was to escape out of the ships almost naked, to hide all their good clothes which had been furnished them as an outfit, and to appear only in their worst rags. In this costume they took delight in rushing through the streets of Cork and Liverpool in large bodies, to the real terror of the inhabitants. In short, I do believe that so strange, unmanageable, and wild a crew had never before left the shores of Ireland. But notwithstanding their apparent poverty, they were all in the most uproarious spirits; there was no crying nor lamentation, as is usual on such occasions; all was delight at having escaped the deadly workhouse.

I need hardly dilate upon the abuse and vituperation which the adoption of such an extensive system of emigration brought down upon me from many well-known quarters. The whole thing had been done so quickly, that no efforts of opponents could in the least prevail against it; but no sooner was it completed than I became the object of the vilest and most bitter abuse. I was accused of an extensive system of 'clearing the land *by eviction*', though I had not evicted a single tenant for the purpose, nor sent one person away, except by the earnest entreaty of the emigrant himself. But I pass over the system of falsehood and misrepresentation which then prevailed and which has since then prevailed, even in a more virulent degree. When necessary, I explained my conduct to my noble employer, Lord Lansdowne; and his lordship in every case thoroughly approved of what I had done. By degrees this abuse subsided, and the most sensible people in the district admitted that an inestimable benefit had been rendered to Kenmare.

I am happy to say that the most favorable accounts have been received, — and are to this day coming back, — from every quarter to which the emigrants were despatched. Money in large quantities has been sent home by them to their friends. Happily no accident ever occurred to a single ship which carried out the Kenmare emigrants. Almost all, down even to the widows and children, found employment soon after landing, and escaped the pestilence of the work-house; and to this hour I can never experience any other feelings but those of pleasure and gratification at having been the means of sending so many miserable beings to a land far richer and more prosperous than Ireland. The condition of the estate outside the poor-house was also vastly improved. Great numbers of the smaller class of tenantry, men whose holdings amounted in value to five shillings, ten shillings, or one pound per annum, and who could scarcely be expected to find the means of decent support on such a holding, — even though they paid no rent at all, — now voluntarily gave up their plots of land, and most gladly emigrated to the Far West. These plots were added to the adjoining tenants' farms; and thus the number of tenants on the rent-roll were considerably reduced. Vast numbers of cottiers, or under-tenants, also, as well as the small farmers, left; and at last a fair equilibrium was established between the demand and supply of labor. In short, the famine was over, and Lord Lansdowne's estate was righted.

I will here mention an anecdote of a newspaper reporter, which occurred to me about that time.

I was walking one day in company with some other guardians, from the poor-house to Lansdowne Lodge, after a meeting of the Board, when a man dressed in thread-bare black, but with a jaunty and impudent air, came up to me and said, —

'Are you Mr. Trench, sir?'

'I am,' replied I.

'A few words with you apart, if you please,' said he.

I dropped a little behind with him, and asked him what he wanted.

'A nice country this, sir,' he remarked.

'Yes,' said I, — 'tolerably so.'

'Strange doings down here, I believe!'

'Really, sir,' I replied. 'I am at a loss to understand your meaning, or what you can want with me, — will you be good enough to state your business?'

'I will, sir. I am the reporter of the ——; we have heard strange accounts at our office of your conduct, and the people where we publish our paper are anxious to know the truth of them. I am come down to examine into these matters myself, — to go over the ground myself, — you know, sir, it is the only way; and to report the facts to the public.'

'Well, sir,' replied I, 'as that is your mission, I wish you every happiness and fine weather. I have no doubt you will meet many who will tell you a great deal which it may suit your views to publish, and you will probably be able to make out a very interesting story. I wish you a good-morning.'

'Good-morning, sir,' returned he; and we parted.

In about five minutes after, I heard his step behind me again; and turning round, he once more addressed me, and asked me still more mysteriously for a few moments' private talk. I fell back with him again behind my friends.

'*You don't happen at present to have any money about you, sir?*' he asked in a confidential manner. 'I have just been at the post-office, and to my *great surprise*, I find that the remittances I expected have not come, and you know I can't travel over the country without money.'

'Really, sir,' I replied, 'your position is no doubt perplexing; but in the first place, I have very little money about me, and in the next, you could hardly expect me to lend it to you if I had much.'

'Oh, sir, that is no doubt very natural in you, but, — *you haven't got even five shillings about you at present, — have you?*'

'Sir,' said I, 'this is a most extraordinary application upon your part. I have just five shillings about me, neither more nor less; but surely you, the reporter to a public journal, cannot be in want of five shillings!'

'Look at me, sir,' he replied, assuming at once and in reality an air of the most abject poverty, casting suddenly off his jaunty air, and relaxing every muscle of his frame as he stood before me the picture of hungry want. 'Look at me, sir, — I want food. Do I look like a man who had broken his fast today? Not want five shillings? Give me *one* shilling, sir, to get something to eat, and I will give you my heart-felt blessing.'

I was much shocked; I saw that truth was stamped upon his face.

'Oh, sir,' said I, 'this really quite alters the case between us. I cannot bear to see a man of your probable education in want of so trifling a sum. Here is the only money I have about me, and if I had more, I assure you it should be yours'; and I handed him the only five shillings in my pocket.

'God bless you, sir,' he returned, with a look of deep thankfulness; 'you may depend on it I will never forget it.'

He left, and I saw him no more; but in a short time afterwards my attention was called to an article setting forth the vast improvements which had taken place under my 'enlightened superintendence' on Lord Lansdowne's estate in Kerry, and describing it as a Garden of Eden.

I can never think of this little incident without reflecting what a strange amount of good or evil, usefulness or mischief, truth or falsehood, — nay, even the making or the blasting of a man's character in the eyes of a large portion of the world, — may be thus placed in the hands of one who was so pressed by want as to be influenced in the whole tone of his remarks, — which go forth to thousands on the wings of the daily press, — by the gift of a five-shilling piece! By me I can truly say it was given in sheer pity for his hungry and wretched state, but if given with the basest motives, it is possible the effect might in this case have been the same.

It may here be asked what was the cause of all this misery, and all this after-cost upon the estate of a kind-hearted and generous nobleman? I answer at once, *the pernicious system of subdivision and subletting of land.* No one who has not tried it can conceive the difficulty in which an Irish landlord or agent is placed with regard to this matter. I can truly say *its prevention has been the great difficulty of my life as a land agent.* The collection of rent is almost always easy on a well-managed estate; but the prevention of subdivision is almost always difficult. The desire to subdivide is by no means confined to the larger tenants, nor even to those who hold land to the moderate value of 30*l.*, or 20*l.*, or even 10*l.* per annum; but tenants possessed of holdings valued at only 1*l.* or 2*l.* per annum frequently endeavor, openly or by stealth, to subdivide these little plots of land, and erect huts or sheds upon them for their young people to marry and settle in, utterly regardless of the certain poverty which must necessarily await them where there are no other means of support. And yet if any landlord or agent is determined to resist this system, and to evict those who in spite of all remonstrances and entreaties persist in this pernicious course, — though the plot of land be scarcely sufficient to feed a goat, and the hut be of the most degraded class, — he is attacked with a virulence and bitterness of hostility which none who do not live in Ireland can imagine; sometimes by the local press, sometimes by local agitators both lay and clerical, who hold him up to public odium and indignation as an exterminator, and sometimes (though not in Kerry) by the blunderbuss or bludgeon of the assassin, that really it requires no little moral as well as physical courage to face the storm which is certain to be raised against him!

I am convinced that Lord Lansdowne's former agent, — an amiable and kind-hearted gentleman, who had presided over the estate for more than thirty years, — would have resisted this system if he dared; but he dreaded to meet the storm of abuse which he knew awaited him from so many quarters, if he attempted it. He therefore quietly shut his eyes to the state of things which he must have known was going on, in the vain hope, I presume, of 'making things pleasant' to his noble employer in England; and thus, when the potato suddenly failed, the whole system collapsed, spreading death and misery around.

The extent to which subdivision and subletting to squatters had been carried may be estimated from the fact, that notwithstanding the vast number, — 4,600 people, — that were sent to America at Lord Lansdowne's expense, off this estate alone, *within a period of three or four years from the commencement of the system;* and although little or no subdivision has taken place since then, yet at this moment the average rent of each farm is only 11*l.* per annum; an average far too small to enable tenants to support and educate their families in tolerable comfort and respectability.

Ever since that terrible period, however, Lord Lansdowne's estate has, in general, advanced rapidly in prosperity. The numerous consolidations which were then effected have invariably been attended with advantage; and although it is still very far from what one would wish it to be, yet no one who knew the estate before, and who visits it now, can be otherwise than struck with the extraordinary change which has taken place upon it for the better. His lordship did not confine his expenditure to emigration; he entered largely upon the improvement of the dwellings of the people and the better cultivation of the land. And after a period of eighteen years I was enabled during the last session of Parliament to give a statement before the Select Committee of the House of Lords on the Irish Tenure of Land Bill, — of the improvements carried out by Lord Lansdowne on this property, such as I question if many of the most liberal landlords have exceeded on their estates in England.

MEMORIES OF THE FAMINE

(a) SOUTH KERRY

[In 1945, on the centenary of the beginning of the Famine, the Irish Folklore Commission sent a questionnaire to all parts of the country, asking for information on the traditions and memories relating to the Famine in various localities. The several volumes of manuscript replies that were gathered are now part of the holdings of the Department of Irish Folklore in University College, Dublin.

The following excerpt is of particular interest because it deals with the traditions about the famine in the Lansdowne estates in County Kerry, where William Steuart Trench was land agent. His account, on the preceding pages, gives a much more benign view of the measures taken by Lansdowne and himself to alleviate the distress. It is notable, in this as in many of the other replies to the questionnaire, that the belief that the landlords and the government were ultimately responsible for the failure of relief schemes and that a policy of genocide was not at all unlikely, remains explicit or implicit. Mitchel's citing of *The Times* newspaper on the extinction of the Celt (see p. 178) is reproduced, showing the closeness between the oral and the written views of the Famine and indicating the extent of Mitchel's influence. Moreover, just as the British government and landlords were seen as exploiters of the opportunity presented by the Famine, so the shopkeepers were universally praised for having stood by the people and were given what goods they had on extended credit. Not one of the responses to the questionnaire says anything critical about the shopkeepers. They are seen much more prominently and more favourably than the priests.

This account, gathered from local farmers, was recorded by Donnchadh Sheáin Uí Shúillíobháin from Kenmare on 30 April 1945. The text is excerpted from MS 1068, 102-106. The Irish is rendered in Roman script and a few variant spellings have been made uniform. It is otherwise reproduced as recorded. The translation is by Marion Treacy.]

Bhí Gortaí in Érin roimh an Gorta Dubh. Bhí an ceann ba mheasa díobh sa bhliain 1822. . . . Is í an chúis a bhí le gach gorta sa tír seo an dubh nú duíbheachán ar ghasaibh na prátaí. . . . Ní raibh aon léigheas ag na daoine ar an dubh in 1822, 1845-52, ná sa bhliain 1879, bliain an-fhliuch. Is ar éigin a bhí leath bharra an bhliain sin. Ní raibh eolas ar léigheas cloch gorm go dtí 1900 A.D. . . .

Ní raibh an galar ró olc in 1845, ach bhí sé ag dul i measa go dtí 1848. Bhí na daoine bochta ag dul i laige ó 1845 anuas go dtí gur tháinig an lug ar an lag ortha ins na blianta 1847-8. (Na blianta dubha.) Ní raibh an síol phrátaí ag mórán aca, agus dá mbeadh féin, ní raibh dar láidir a dóthain chun iad do chur; ach bhí cruithneacht, eórna, coirce, agus seagal ag na féirmeoiribh ba shaidhbhire. Ní raibh easba arbhair ortha san chun bídh. Bhí na hAchta Arbhair [Corn Laws] ar siúbhal an uair úd; agus do b-éigean leis na féirmeoirí an t-arbhar do dhíol chun an cíos do ghlana. Gidh go raibh eólas cruinn ag rialtas Shasana mar bhí an scéal annso, ní chuireadar stop le h-imirce an choirce; agus ní raibh na tiarnaí talmhan díomhain, ach chó beag. Bhíodar ag caitheamh amach na daoine bochta ar thaobh an bhóthair chun bás dfhághail le gorta agus pláig. Fuaireadar bás sa tigh, sa pháirc, le h-ais chlaidhe, agus ar thaobh an bhóthair. Chuala go raibh leanbh ag ól bainne cích a mháthair, agus iad araon marbh!! . . . . D'iarr O'Conaill ar an bhFeis i Sasanna an gorta do stop, nú mar a ndeunfhadaois go bhfaghadh leath mhilliún daoine bás in Érin; agus fóroír bfíor dho, mar do thuit sé amach mar a dubhairt sé. D'éisteadar leis mar dheadh, agus leigeadar amach an coirce. Fuair na daoine bás, nuair a bhí an biadh imighithe. Is chuir an London *Times* liúgh mór amach annsan le h-áthas mór 'go raibh an Celt gone with a vengeance'. Is mór an iongnadh ná dubhradar buídheacas le Dia!!

Bhí cómhra giúise gur bhfuraiste an bun dfoscailt agus do dhúnadh lán le marbh go minic ar trucaillibh ag dul go reiligí ag cur fé chré. Chuir san stop leis an pláig. . . .

Thosnuigheadar ar bhóthairí do dheunamh, ar dhraineáil, ar cladhthacha etc. Thugadar airgead do na tiarnaí talmhana chun fallaí móra do chur suas timcheall a náruis chun ná feiceadh na daoine bochta iad i nao'char, agus tá siad ann fós le feiscint.

Do chuir an Tiarna Lansdowne — 4adh Marcus — milte daoine bochta as a eastát i gCiarraí Theas go dtí Nua Eabhroch, USA san bhliain 1848 A.D. Tháinig an long mhór isteach go Dúnchiaráin san Abhainn Chinnmara. Chuadar ar bhórd annsan. Cailleadh cuid aca le galar sa long, agus fuaireadar uaig uisciúil; shrois an cuid eile go galarach Nua Eabhroc, cuireadh isteach na galaraig in óispidéal ann — sa 'Lansdowne Ward' — agus fuair mórán aca bás ann. Na dhiaigh sin, do chuireadh iad fan bannc na h-abhann Hudson chun leasú don talmhain!!!

I rith an Gorta, bhí súp ag tabhairt amach do na daoine ba ghátaraí, boithre ag deunamh annso agus annsúd, agus droicidí a bhí an-ghátarach chó maith.... San am úd, cuireadh suas óspidéal maith in áit folláin aorach i dtaobh thiar thuaidh de Neidín leis, mar bhí gádh mór leis. San am san, do réir dlíghe, bhí ar na tiarnaí talaimh leath na sraithe do dhíol san óispideál agus as an eastát; agus ba shaoráideach iad do chur ag leasú an Hudson ná díol asta abhus. Ní h-aon bhréag a rádh go raibh 'itching palm' ag an tiarna úd....

Dhein Lansdowne aon rud amháin go maith an uair úd — do mhaith sé cíos bliana dhóibh. Bé an sean-scéal ag rialtas Shasanna é — bhíodar riamh ró-mhall. Mar a deir an sean-fhocal — An sean-scéal i gcómhniú, agus ní beag linn a bhrónuí.

Bhí sclábhuí nú dhó in gach feirm mhór an uair úd, agus páircín nú dhá cheann, nú trí cinn ag gach aon acu. Is iad do dhein obair na feirme do'n feirmeoir mór. Chuiridís prátaí ins na páirciní ó bhliain go bliain. Ar a shon san bhí an talamh ró lag ar fad, agus tháinig an duibheachán nú dubh níos troime ortha súd ná ar thalmhain na feirmeoirí móra, mar bhí acraí díomhaoin aca súd. Is olc an curadóireacht an síol ceudna do chur sa talamhain ceudna ó bhliain go bliain, mar tógann sé an biadh ceudna as; agus marbhíon easba bhídh gach ní saolta. Ní raibh leigheas ná tuigsint aca ar sin go raibh sé ró dheánach. Thuit an lug ar an lag ortha annsan. Bhí cíos dhá uair níos troime fé na tíarnaí beaga na fé Lansdowne, mar gur tiarna saibhir a beadh é, gidh gur Shylock amuigh agus amach a beadh an 4adh Marcuis.... Níor chuala go raibh na siopadóirí cruaidh in aimsir an Gorta mór 1845-52 A.D....

TRANSLATION

There were famines in Ireland before the Black Famine and the worst of them was in 1822.... The cause of every famine in this country was blight on the stems of the potatoes.... People had no remedy for the blight in 1822, in 1845-52 or in 1879, which was a very wet year. They had hardly half a crop that year. They didn't know of the blue-stone cure[1] until 1900.

The disease was not too bad in 1845, but it was worsening steadily up to 1848. The poor people had been getting weaker since 1845 until, in 1847 and 1848, they were finally smitten. (These were known as the black years.) Most of them had not potato seed, but even if they had some, they had scarcely enough strength to plant it. The richest farmers had wheat, barley, oats, rye and corn. They had plenty of cereal to eat. The Corn Laws were in force at the time and the farmers had to sell the cereal crops to pay the rent. Even though the British government knew very well how things were, they didn't stop the export of corn, and the landlords had no conscience. They used to throw the poor people out on the roads to die from famine and plague. They died at home, in the field, beside the ditch and at the side of the road. There was a story of a child found still on its mother's breast, as though drinking her milk, and both of them dead! ...[2] O'Connell asked the English parliament to stop the Famine, for, if they didn't, half a million people would die in Ireland. And, alas, he was right, for it happened just as he said. The government listened to him and distributed the meal. Yet the people died when the food had gone and the London *Times* announced with joy 'that the Celt had gone with a vengeance'. It's a wonder they didn't say thank God![3]

There were coffins with bottoms that could easily open and close; they were full of corpses and they were regularly going to the graveyards for burial. This stopped the plague....

They started making roads, draining, building bridges.... The landlords were given money to erect high walls so that the poor people would not see them [the landlords] at all — and the walls are still to be seen.

Lord Lansdowne, the 4th Marquess, sent thousands of people from his estate in south Kerry to New York, USA in 1848. The ship came into Dunkeerin on the Kenmare river. They boarded there. Some of them died of disease on the ship and got a watery grave. The others reached New York. The fever-ridden and the diseased were hospitalized there in the 'Lansdowne Ward' and many of them died there. After that they were buried on the banks of the river Hudson to fertilize the land!!![4]

1. A copper compound, the most common form of which was known as Bordeaux mixture, first used in France in 1885.

2. This incident is reported in many places in Famine tradition.

3. See Letter X of Mitchel's *The Last Conquest of Ireland (Perhaps)* below, p. 178.

4. Compare this with Trench's account in 'The Exodus' chapter above. It was, in fact, the 3rd Marquess of Lansdowne who was responsible.

Throughout the Famine the most needy people were given soup, roads were made here and there, and badly needed bridges. . . . At that time, a much-needed hospital was built in a healthy, open spot north-west of Kenmare. According to the law then, the landlords had to sell half the produce from their estates to the hospital and it was cheaper for them to send the people to fertilize the banks of the Hudson than to pay for them at home. It's the plain truth — that Lord Lansdowne had an 'itching palm'.

Lansdowne did one good thing at that time. He remitted a year's rent. But it was the same old English story — they were always too late, as the proverb says, and there's nothing we can do about it.

Every large farm had one or two labourers then and each of them had one or two or three little fields. It was they who did the work for the big farmers. Year after year they planted potatoes in their little fields. As a result, the soil was exhausted and the blight fell heavier on their land than on the land of the big farmers — for they had rich acreage and fallow land. It's bad farming to sow the same crop in the same soil year after year since it uses up the same nourishment, and lack of food kills every living thing. There was no cure for or understanding of this until it was too late. It went from bad to worse for the labourers. Rent was twice as heavy under the tenant farmers than under Lansdowne for he was a rich lord, although he was an out-and-out Shylock, that same 4th Marquess. . . . No one ever heard of shopkeepers being harsh during the great Famine of 1845-52. . . .

GEORGE PETRIE

(1789-1866)

from: THE PETRIE COLLECTION OF THE ANCIENT MUSIC OF IRELAND (1855)

[In his introduction to *The Ancient Music of Ireland*, Petrie gives an account of the effect of the Famine on the 'land of song'. This passage has often been cited under the title 'The Great Silence'. His anxiety to record the songs that he included in his great work is all the sharper because Petrie recognized that the old Ireland had begun to disappear and that neither its music nor its language could survive, except through the efforts of collectors like himself. Since the 1830s, Petrie had been a key figure in the attempt to recover and record Ireland's past and to invest this recovery with a powerful political idealism. The Famine made that enterprise even more crucial.]

The inevitable result of the changes in the character of the Irish race which had long been in operation, and which had already almost entirely denationalized its higher classes, had been suddenly effected, as by a lightning flash, by the calamities which, in the year 1846-7, had struck down and wellnigh annihilated the Irish remnant of the great Celtic family. Of the old, who had still preserved as household gods the language, the songs and traditions of their race and localities, but few survived. Of the middle-aged and energetic whom death had yet spared, and who might for a time, to some extent, have preserved such relics, but a few remained that had the power to fly from the plague and panic-stricken land; and of the young, who had come into existence, and become orphaned, during those years of desolation, they, for the most part, were reared where no mother's eyes could make them feel the mysteries of human affections — no mother's voice could soothe their youthful sorrows, and implant within the memories of their hearts her songs of tenderness and love — and where no father's instructions could impart to them the traditions and characteristic peculiarities of feeling that would link them to their remotest ancestors. The green pastoral plains, the fruitful valleys, as well as the wild hillsides and the dreary bogs had equally ceased to be animate with human life. 'The land of song' was no longer tuneful; or, if a human sound met the traveller's ear, it was only that of the feeble and despairing wail for the dead. This awful, unwonted silence, which during the famine and subsequent years, almost everywhere prevailed, struck more fearfully upon their imaginations, as many Irish gentlemen informed me, and gave them a deeper feeling of the desolation with which the country had been visited, than any other circumstances which forced themselves upon their attention; and I confess that it was a consideration of the circumstances of which this fact gave so striking an indication, that, more than any other, overpowered all my objections, and influenced me in coming to a determination to accept the proposal of the Irish-Music Society.

In this resolution, however, I was actuated no less by a desire to secure to the public, by publication, the large store of melodies which I had already collected, than by the hope of increasing that store, during the progress of my work, by a more exhaustive devotion of mind and time to this object than I had ever previously given to it. I felt assured that it was still possible, by a zealous exertion, to gather from amongst the survivors of the old Celtic race, innumerable melodies that would soon pass away for ever; but that such exertion should be immediate. For, though I have no fear that this first swarm from the parent hive of the Indo-Germanic race would perish in this their last western asylum; or that they would not again increase, and, as heretofore, continue to supply the empire with their contribution of fiery bravery, lively sensibility, and genius in all the aesthetic arts, — yet I felt that the new generations, unlinked as they must be with those of the past, and subjected to influences and examples scarcely known to their fathers, will necessarily have lost very many of those peculiar characteristics which so long had given them a marked individuality; and, more particularly, that among the changes sure to follow, the total extinction of their ancient language would be, inevitably, accompanied by the loss of all that as yet unsaved portion of their ancient music which has been identified with it.

ISAAC BUTT

(1813-79)

from: A VOICE FOR IRELAND. THE FAMINE IN THE LAND (1847)

[The Famine, and British government policy towards Ireland during the critical years, brought about a change in the opinions of the staunchly unionist and conservative lawyer and journalist, Isaac Butt. He spoke and wrote intelligently on economic affairs, but his central contribution at this time was to point out the paradox of the British government's position. If Ireland was part of the United Kingdom, then it was wrong and absurd to treat it now, in the midst of calamity, as a separate nation which was a charge on the British treasury. If Ireland were so treated, then what meaning did the Union have? By 1870 the answer to this question was to lead Butt to federalism and Home Rule.]

. . . The refusal or neglect to suspend the navigation laws, was the climax of infatuation. While food was deficient in the country, and the freight of corn from America had risen to three times its ordinary rate, not a vessel of any foreign nation would have been permitted to unload a cargo of grain in any one of our ports.

If ministers resolved to trust the lives of the Irish people to private enterprize, was it not common sense and common justice to them that private enterprize should be unencumbered by any restrictions in the execution of the task of supplying, at the notice of a few months, provisions to five millions of people; yet, during the months in which food might have been imported into the country, the ministry left the importation of corn impeded by the restrictions of the navigation laws, and subject to a duty on importation which an order in council might have removed.

It is difficult to trace this history without indignation. We can understand the verdict of the coroner's jury, who, in days when inquests were held in Ireland upon the bodies of men found dead upon the highway, returned upon the body of a man who died of starvation while toiling at the public works, and fell dead of exhaustion with the implements of labour in his hand, a verdict of murder against the ministers who had neglected the first responsibility of government. Can we wonder if the Irish people believe — *and believe it they do* — that the lives of those who have perished, and who will perish, have been sacrificed by a deliberate compact to the gains of English merchants, and if this belief has created among all classes a feeling of deep dissatisfaction, not only with the ministry but with English rule.

Let us not be misunderstood. Of any such compact we acquit the ministers. In the resolution they originally formed, they were actuated by a sincere, but most mistaken belief, that they could best secure a supply of food to Ireland by declaring their determination to leave all to be done by the ordinary operations of trade. But these must be excused, who, while they witness the scenes of horror that too many in Ireland are daily seeing, believe that the subsequent deliberations of the cabinet were too much influenced by the fear of offending powerful British interests — that the omission to remove the duty from the importation on corn — to suspend the navigation laws — and to import provisions into Ireland at government expense, when it became manifest that by no other means could the emergency be met, indicated a tender regard for the interests that might have been affected by a change in their policy, which gave too much weight to those interests, and too little to the safety of the Irish people, and which, in all probability, would not long have delayed remedial measures, had the interests to be sacrificed been Irish ones.

The folly of relying on private enterprize to supply the deficiency, is proved incontestably by the result. Private enterprize has not saved us from the horrors of the famine. With Indian corn at the price of 15s. 4d. a quarter on the other side of the Atlantic, and 60s. in London! with wheat 32s. and 73s.! private enterprize has failed to import it. The applications of the best established principles of political economy would have enabled any man of ordinary sagacity to have foreseen this result. All the ordinary demands of civilized life are, doubtless, best met by those spontaneous processes in which the self-interest of man directs his activity and energy in the channels best adapted to supply these demands; but sudden and extraordinary emergencies must be met by other means. These are the occasions upon which it is of value to all that great resources should be wielded by the governing power to effect rapidly great ends.

If ever there was an occasion upon which practical proof could be given of the value to every member of the state of that association of men into states, that permits the government to wield mighty powers for the common good — if ever there were a time when men in the remotest corners of Ireland might have been taught the lesson that they have a deep interest in the strength and greatness of the United Empire, this famine presented that occasion. Tell us not that it was beyond the power of the combinations which the strength of the British empire could have wielded, to have brought to the ports of Ireland subsistence for all her people. Who is there that will say, that in such an empire all that strength should not have been put forth? What nobler triumph of British greatness could be imagined, than to have collected in the ports of famine-stricken Ireland, vessels of all nations laden with food? This would have been an exhibition of British power and British greatness, compared with which the most glorious of her fleets, or the vastest of her arsenals, would bring to the mind but a poor idea of majesty and strength. Six months ago it was possible to have done all this. The opportunity was lost; and Britain is now branded as the only civilized nation which would permit her subjects to perish of famine, without making a national effort to supply them with food.

In what parallel case do we find statesmen willing to trust to the ordinary operations of commerce, to supply in any country a sudden and unexpected demand for human subsistence? If England had occasion to send an army into some country destitute of food, would her statesmen content themselves with seeing that the soldiers were provided regularly with their pay, and trust to the speculations of private enterprize to follow them with the necessary articles of food? Multiply that army to four millions, and you have exactly the case of the starving Irish in this year, so far as to allow presentments to be made for works of profitable cultivation of the land; and a letter from the Chief Secretary stated the terms and conditions upon which this departure from the enactments of the statute would be allowed.[1]

Great praise is, beyond all question, due to the wisdom and the boldness of this measure — one, for the benefit of which Ireland is, we believe, altogether indebted to the strong representations of Lord Besborough [*sic*]. But we cannot help thinking its effect has been ridiculously exaggerated by the apologists of government. It was, perhaps, making the best of the Labour Rate Act that could be made of it, without a total contravention of its principle; but this could neither supply its deficiencies nor obviate its mischiefs. The employment of the labour was still to be impeded by the cumbrous machinery of presentment sessions, and its remuneration loaded with the enormous expense of pay-clerks and officials. It could not neutralize the evil effects of the indolent habits fostered by employment which the people felt to be eleemosynary.[2] To say that this latter would have enabled the gentry, by cordial co-operation with the government, to mitigate entirely the evils of the former act, as has been said by advocates of the government, whose opinions we respect, strikes us as utterly wild. To remedy these evils required measures very different from those which any Lord Lieutenant could venture to carry, on his own authority, into effect. Far be it from us, however, to detract from the praise and gratitude that Lord Besborough has received for even this slight approximation to a better order of things. We cannot but believe that if the suggestions of the men who dictated this policy, had received more attention in Downing-street, Ireland would not now complain of the utter neglect of her interests manifested in the imperial councils for so many months.

Condemning, as we do, the Labour Rate Act, it would be unjust to deny the good that it has effected. Whatever evils have been attendant on its train, it has been the means of preserving the lives of thousands of Irishmen. God forbid that any man should have raised, should even now raise, his hand to stop its operations, until some substitute is put in its place. By its operation, masses of the people have been fed, who, but for its existence, would, in all probability, have perished. We must never forget that this has been effected by its means. We may complain, — indeed, we do complain, that this has been done with a mixture of danger and evil from which more comprehensive measures would have saved us, while they did this more efficiently; but to the positive good it has accomplished we cannot shut our eyes.

Nor can we help observing, that those who look upon the state of Ireland as only to be remedied by a poor law that will fully recognize the right of every man to earn his bread by his labour, saw with satisfaction, not unmingled with surprise, that this principle, from which modern legislation appeared to be departing, was now, in the pressure of this calamity, embodied for the first time in an enactment relating to Ireland. What was the principle of the Labour Rate Act? That it was the duty of each locality to give to every man within it, who was willing to work, the means of livelihood. This is just the principle of the much misunderstood and maligned poor law of Queen Elizabeth. If it be just and expedient in time of famine, it cannot be wrong or inexpedient in a country in which a great portion of the population are always bordering upon famine. We confess we were among the number of those who saw with satisfaction this great principle for the first time even partially acknowledged in Irish legislation. We are perfectly convinced that until it be fully and honestly carried out, Ireland can never become prosperous. We cannot hope to lay the foundation of any solid Irish prosperity upon the hopeless slough of misery and despair that forms the substratum of our social state. Even the imperfect recognition of this principle were worth to the country a great price. But the man badly reads the signs, and ill understands the policy of legislation, who can be surprised that the ministry, who proposed to feed the people in time of famine by a Labour Rate Act, were prepared to follow it at no distant day by extending to Ireland's habitual destitution the remedy of outdoor relief.

The new year opened gloomily on Ireland. By this time the appalling extent of the calamity, and the inefficiency of the measures adopted to meet it, were, at least, partially understood. A vague sense of alarm possessed men's minds. The terror was perhaps, exaggerated, because the evils apprehended were indefinite. The public eye was

1. Henry Labouchere (1789-1869), chief secretary for Ireland 1846-47, under the lord lieutenant, the 4th Earl of Bessborough, effectively repealed the Labour Rate Act of Sir Charles Trevelyan, head of the treasury, in the 'Labouchere Letter' of 1846. That act had made relief work, a local, not a government, charge. Bessborough ordered the change in policy.
2. Given as an act of charity.

shocked by whole columns of the daily newspapers occupied exclusively with deaths by starvation. Men's hearts failed them with fear, for looking for the things which should come. The landlords saw ruin in the enormous imposts which the Labour Rate Act placed upon their estates — the merchant and the trader feared it in the general stagnation which they anticipated as the consequence of general distress. Rents were, in many parts of the country, withheld, and alarmists stated they were so universally. It is impossible to conceive a more gloomy picture than that presented by Irish society at the close of the disastrous year '46, yet all men looked forward to the meeting of Parliament with something like hope. The Irish people looked with confidence to Sir Robert Peel, in office or out of office; they calculated that his practised sagacity and comprehensive mind would have pointed out the inadequacy of what had been done, and suggest what ought to be done; and one fortnight before the meeting of Parliament, had the choice of premier depended on the suffrages of the Irish nation, Sir Robert Peel would have commanded their almost unanimous votes.

These expectations, perhaps unreasonable, have been disappointed. The Queen's speech, and the debate on the address, spread through Ireland the conviction that Parliament was as supine as the ministry. Nor ought it to be disguised that the part of the session which is past has shaken the attachment of many to the Imperial and British constitution. Men have asked themselves, to what is to be attributed the apparent acquiescence in a policy which, right or wrong, has resulted in the sacrifice of such multitudes of our fellow Christians by the most horrible of all deaths? They have asked if the house in which this sacrifice has called forth so little inquiry, represent indeed the commons of the empire. How is it that the GRAND INQUEST of the nation has made no inquiry as to the death of thousands of the people? Men who have hated democracy all their lives, began seriously to reflect whether the people had influence enough upon a Parliament in which their sufferings were so little heeded. Irishmen, too, began to feel that they were legislated for by men ignorant of the condition and circumstances of their country. From this feeling arose the meeting of the landed proprietors in January last, which for one day assumed the form of an Irish convention; from this emanated the resolutions of many of the grand juries of Ireland, in which were propounded sentiments bordering very closely upon those of Federalism, if not of Repeal.

This unfortunate state of feeling has been aggravated by the rejection of the measure known as Lord George Bentinck's[3] bill — it has been exasperated, as well as aggravated, by the manner in which senators, not, perhaps, of much character or influence in either house, have spoken of the Irish nation — language, of which we scarcely know whether we should most wonder that Englishmen were found base enough to speak it, or that, when it was spoken, Irishmen were not found adequately to resent.

We know that in the feelings of these spiteful malignants, the English nation do not participate; it is among the few blessings of the crisis that Irishmen have been taught how deeply the better heart of England sympathizes with their affliction. The aid which Englishmen have generously sent to Ireland has produced this counteracting effect: but Irishmen do still believe that in these feelings of good will, the parliament does not represent the people of England, and contrasts are drawn in the mind of many of the warmest advocates of British connexion, between the manner in which a British parliament have met, and an Irish parliament would have met, the calamity that has befallen us.

What can be more absurd — what can be more wicked, than for men professing attachment to an imperial Constitution to answer claims now put forward for state assistance to the unprecedented necessities of Ireland, by talking of Ireland being a drain upon the *English* treasury? By such declamation as this some English senators opposed the proposition of Lord George Bentinck, not to advance the money, but to pledge the credit of the empire to facilitate undertakings in this country, which, in enriching Ireland, would have increased the strength of the empire at large. If the Union be not a mockery, there exists no such thing as an English treasury. The exchequer is the exchequer of the United Kingdom. Its separation into provincial departments is never thought of when imperial resources are to be spent, or imperial credit pledged, for objects principally or exclusively of interest to the English people. Ireland has been deprived, by the Union with England, of all separate power of action. She cannot do now, as in

3. In 1847 William George Bentinck (1802-48) proposed a scheme for a loan of £16 million for the construction of Irish railways.

the days of her parliament she might have done — draw upon her own resources, or pledge her own credit, for objects of national importance. Irishmen were told, indeed, that in consenting to a Union which would make them partners with a great and opulent nation, like England, they would have all the advantages that might be expected to flow from such a Union. How are these expectations to be realized, how are these pledges to be fulfilled, if the partnership is only to be one of loss, and never of profit to us? If, bearing our share of all imperial burdens — when calamity falls upon us we are to be told that we then recover our separate existence as a nation, just so far as to disentitle us to the state assistance which any portion of a nation, visited with such a calamity, had a right to expect from the governing power? If Cornwall had been visited with the scenes that have desolated Cork, would similar arguments have been used? Would men have stood up and denied that Cornwall was entitled to have the whole country share the extraordinary loss?

JAMES FINTAN LALOR

(1807-49)

from: THE NATION (24 April 1847)

[In this letter to Gavan Duffy, editor of *The Nation*, Lalor addresses the Irish landlords in the midst of the Famine crisis with the warning that they must join with the people or be flung aside by them. This is the first notable occasion on which the land question is given priority over the political question. It was Lalor's achievement to link the nationalism of Young Ireland with the idea of a social revolution. In this he made a number of converts, John Mitchel and Michael Davitt among them. The force of his arguments created a left wing in Young Ireland which finally would separate from the central group led by Smith O'Brien and Gavan Duffy, neither of whom had any revolutionary aspirations beyond the question of the Anglo-Irish constitutional relationship.]

A NEW NATION

Proposal for an Agricultural Association between the Landowners and Occupiers

TO THE LANDOWNERS OF IRELAND

TINAKILL, ABBEYLEIX,
April 19

I address you, my lords and gentlemen, from a great distance — the distance that separates you from the people — for I am one of the people. This is a disadvantage of some account, and might be discouraging at a season more settled. But I know that in periods of peril, when distress and disaster are present, and danger and dread are in the future, men are allowed to assume rights which must lie in abeyance during ordinary times. This is my reason and right in addressing you — that I am excited and authorised by the feelings and emergencies of the occasion. This is my claim to a hearing. Not that I ask it in my own cause or in that of the class I belong to; not that I urge it for sake of the masses of men who are unable to ask it for themselves; but that I claim a hearing and crave to be heard on your own behalf — on behalf of your own interest, and honour, and existence, as owners of that soil on which thousands now are famishing to death for want of food.

My general object in addressing you is that of calling public notice, if I can, to the full extent of the effects which I think must inevitably follow fast on present events, if the course of those events be not checked or changed. All the facts I possess I have considered and counted in one view together, in their connexion and consequence, and inferred the result. This is a task which few others, I fear, have undertaken, nor is it any matter of surprise. Within sight and sound of this dismal calamity, amid the actual horrors of every passing hour, it is scarcely possible to look far into the future, or take thought and care for remote results. In the presence of famine men are blind to its effects. It is doing its work in the dark, and no watch is set or warning raised. From every house and every voice throughout this land there is but one cry now — the cry for food. Food for today and for tomorrow — for this year and the next. But not all the clamour and outcry that has been raised throughout Ireland during the last few months has added a single pound to the supply of food either for this year or the next. What men were unable to do, they set about doing; what they were able to do, they left and are leaving undone. For something else is wanting, and requires to be provided, besides food for today or tomorrow — else a revolution is at hand. A revolution of the worst type and character — not such as when a nation breaks up under armed violence, to reunite and rise on structure as strong as before; but such as when it falls in pieces, rotting to a final and fætid ruin.

Beside the general object mentioned, I have a particular and more definite purpose, which will develop itself as I proceed. It would be useless to state it formally before it can be fully understood. Though I write more especially for you, my lords and gentlemen, landowners of Ireland, yet I write also for the public; and shall address myself to either, as occasion may seem to demand.

The failure of the potato, and consequent famine, is one of those events which come now and then to do the work of ages in a day, and change the very nature of an entire nation at once. It has even already produced a deeper social disorganisation than did the French revolution — greater waste of life — wider loss of property — more than the horrors, with none of the hopes. For its direction still seems dragging downwards, while her revolution took France to the sun — gave her wealth, and victory, and renown — a free people and a firm peasantry, lords of their own land. It has unsettled society to the foundation; deranged every interest, every class, every household. Every man's place and relation is altered; labour has left its track, and life lost its form. One entire class, the most numerous and important in Ireland, has already begun to give way; and is about being displaced. The tenant-farmer of ten acres or under is being converted into an 'independent labourer.' But it is accomplishing something more than mere social derangement, or a dislocation of classes. It has come as if commissioned to produce, at length and not too soon, a dissolution of that state and order of existence in which we have heretofore been living. The constitution of society that has prevailed in this island can no longer maintain itself, or be maintained. It has been tried for generations; it has now, at least, been fully and finally tested; and the test has proved fatal. It was ever unsound and infirm; and is now breaking to pieces under the first severe experiment, an experiment which that of any other country would have easily withstood. Nor heaven nor human nature will suffer it to be re-established or continue. If the earth, indeed, with all things therein was made wholly for the few and none of it for the many, then it may continue; if they be bound to submit in patience to perish of famine and famine-fever, then it may continue. But if all have a right to live, and to live in their own land among their own people; if they have a right to live in freedom and comfort on their own labour; if the humblest among them has a right to a full, secure and honest subsistence, not the knavish and beggarly subsistence of the poorhouse, then that constitution cannot and it shall not be re-established again. When society fails to perform its duty and fulfil its office of providing for its people; it must take another and more effective form, or it must cease to exist. When its members begin to die out under destitution — when they begin to perish in thousands under famine and the effects of famine — when they begin to desert and fly from the land in hundreds of thousands under the force and fear of deadly famine — then it is time to see it is God's will that society should stand dissolved, and assume another shape and action; and he works his will by human hands and natural agencies. This case has arisen even now in Ireland, and the effect has already followed in part. Society stands dissolved. In effect, as well as of right, it stands dissolved, and another requires to be constituted. To the past we can never return, even if we would. The potato was our sole and only capital, to live and work on, to make much or little of; and on it the entire social economy of this country was founded, formed and supported. That system and state of things can never again be resumed or restored; not even should the potato return. A new adjustment is now to be formed, is to form and develop itself; a new social order to be arranged; a new people to be organised. Or otherwise that people itself is about to become extinct. Either of these is inevitable; and either is desirable. In condition and character and conduct, a stain to earth, a scandal among the nations, a shame to nature, a grievance to Heaven, this people has been for ages past — a dark spot in the path of the sun. Nature and Heaven can bear it no longer. To any one who either looks to an immediate directing Providence, or trusts to a settled course of natural causes, it is clear that this island is about to take existence under a new tenure; or else that Nature has issued her decree — often issued heretofore against nations and races, and ever for the same crime — that one other imbecile and cowardly people shall cease to exist, and no longer cumber the earth.

The power of framing a new order of arrangement is in your hands, my lords and gentlemen, if you choose to exercise it. The work of reconstruction belongs of right to you, if you have the wisdom and the will to do it. It is in emergencies and occasions like the present, rather than in ordinary and settled times, that a national aristocracy is required; and if they be not worthy of such occasions, they are worthless altogether. It is a time like this that tries and tests the worth of a class, as it tests the worth of individual men. Not to time should the task be committed, nor to chance; not to the government of England, which is incompetent to the case; not to the parliament of England where you are made a mark for pelting at; nor to the desperate remedies of men whom you have, yourselves, made desperate. Ireland demands from you now something more than her present dole of daily food — a mode and system of procuring full food for herself. She looks to you for this — that she be not condemned to live as a beggar on public alms, nor as a pauper on public works and poorhouse rations; but aided and enabled to find or form a mode of making her own bread in all future time by free, unforced, and honest labour. She has lost her means of living; she requires some other, more sufficient and secure than those she has lost. Her demand, in full and fine, is for what is of more effective worth and weight than all the political constitutions that were ever fashioned; for what senates or sovereigns cannot make or unmake, but men must make for themselves — her demand is for a new SOCIAL CONSTITUTION under which to live. This is the task you are called on to undertake — the work you are wanted to do, or forfeit your footing in this island of ours — a work to which political constitution is little in comparison and light in importance. Political rights are but paper and parchment. It is the social constitution that determines the condition and character of a people, that makes and moulds the life of man.

We are now living in the midst of a social anarchy, in which no man knows with certainty what he is, or what he can call his own. Never was government or guidance more necessary to a people; but government or guidance there is none, for the one great purpose needed. An extreme and extraordinary case has arisen — one that seldom arises in modern times — and not to be treated by any ordinary law. A new structure of society has to be created; and the country has a right to require of you to counsel, and conduct, and lead her; because you own her soil; because your own worth and value are in question — your own interest and position involved and committed; because the work cannot so speedily and safely be done without your aid; because in some respects and in some degree you are considered chargeable with the calamitous crisis that has occurred; because your rights of ownership are thought by numbers to be the main or only obstacle to the creation at once of a sound system of social prosperity and happiness, which would be formed by the natural energies and social instincts of mankind, if those energies were left free to act, and not fettered or interfered with by your claims of dominion; and finally because you ought of right to be where you have never chosen to be — at the head of this people. And at their head or at their side you must now stand, or your aid will not be taken. On other terms it will not now be accepted; and the work will be done by other hands than yours. You are far less important to the people than the people are to you. You cannot stand or act alone, but they can. In the case that has arisen the main power is in their hands, the little in yours. Your power of position has departed. You cannot reform and reorganise a whole people without their consent and co-operation. You cannot act against them — you cannot act without them. They can do what is wanted of themselves and without your assistance. They have the will and may learn the way. A dissolution of the social system has taken place. The failure of the potato was the *immediate exciting* cause. Into the *predisposing* causes it is needless for the present to enquire. There was no outrise or revolt against it. It was not broken up by violence. It was borne for ages in beggarly patience, until it perished by the visitation of God in the order of nature. A clear original right returns and reverts to the people — the right of establishing, and entering into a new social arrangement. The right is in them because the power is in them. The right lodges where the power lodges. It is not a case to which governments or parliaments are competent. The sole office and duty of government under the circumstances is that of supporting the destitute, and maintaining public order during the period of transition, and re-organisation. Should it attempt doing more than this, it will be assuming a power which it does not possess, and cannot even make an effort to exercise witout committing injustice, doing injury, and suffering defeat. With the great body and mass of the people, in their original character and capacity, resides of necessity the power, in its full plentitude, of framing or falling into a new form of organisation — a new mode of living and labour. Your aid, my lords and gentlemen, is most desirable, if accorded on terms, and in a mode which would be thought likely to contribute to general benefit and happiness. On other terms or for other objects — with a view to your own personal interests alone, and on terms to assert and secure your own position at any cost to the country and community — if offered on such views and terms, your service and aid will not be accepted; and the present condition of anarchy will be protracted by strife and struggle, terminating possibly in violent convulsion, from which you, at least, would come out the losers, whoever might be the winners. To ensure against such a contingency it is necessary that you should now combine and co-operate with that people from whom, for long ages, you have stood apart, aliens and enemies to them as they to you. They count more in millions than you count in thousands. If you desire that they and you should now join hands to carry the boat over the rapids, it must be on terms which they will accept; on terms of advantage to them as well as to you — and the first condition and very basis of a union must be the distinct acknowledgment and assertion, in its widest extent, in its fullest force, power, and plenitude, of the principle of ALLEGIANCE TO COUNTRY. On any other basis no federation can form or be formed to take effect or be of force in Ireland now. To save mistake I ought to mention, and mark what it is I do not mean, as well as what my meaning is. I do not mean that you should declare for Repeal. I scarcely know that I can call myself a Repealer, further than this — that I would not say aye to the question if it were put to me to decide. The results of Repeal would depend on the means and men by whom it should have been accomplished. It might give to Ireland all that Ireland wants, and withering in want of — equal liberty, and equal laws, science and art, manufacture and trade, respect and renown; wealth to the merchant, security and comfort to the cottage; its pride of power and place to the castle, fame and fortune to genius and talent, all of that which ennobles and endears to man the land he lives in — this it might do. It might subject us to an odious and ignoble tyranny. I am far from wishing you to take any course that would pledge you to Repeal, or to any other political measure. I do not write with a view to Repeal, or any other political object whatever. My meaning is far more general, and states itself in more general terms. Nothing is requisite or required that would commit you in particulars, to any political party, cause, or course of conduct.

But a full act and avowal of attachment and allegiance to this island, in priority and preference to any and every other country — this is required, and will be strictly required; not in mere idle form of protest and profession, but in full efficient proof and practice. That Ireland is your own mother-country — and her people your people — that her interest and honour, her gain and her glory, are counted as your own — that her rights and liberties you still defend as part of your inheritance — that in peace you will lead her progress, and carry her banner in battle — that your labour shall be in her service, and your lives laid down at her need — that henceforth you will be not a foreign garrison but a national guard; this you must declare and adopt, as the principle of your proceeding, and the spirit of your action, and the rule of your order; for these are the duties of nobility. Adopt this principle, and you are armed; on it is your safety and your strength; the future is fettered at your feet, and your name and race shall flourish and not fail. Ireland is yours for ages, yet on the condition that you will be Irishmen, in name, in faith, in fact. Refuse it, and you commit yourselves, in the position of paupers, to the mercy of English ministers and English members; you throw your very existence on English support, which England soon may find too costly to afford; you lie at the feet of events, you lie in the way of a people, and the movement of events and the march of a people shall be over you. Allegiance to this fair island; it is your title of tenure to the lands you hold, and in right of it you hold them. If you deny and disown it you assert another title, and must determine to hold your inheritance by force, at your own will and to our injury, in despite and defiance of us and ours for ever. This would be a bootless and feeble insult, and dangerous withal, for your title is worth little indeed under the law you would appeal to: that while from Ireland you take rank and revenue, blood and birth and name — everything that makes home, and binds to country — you yet look not to her, but to another land, for home and country; that you desert and disown, if not hate her old native people; that in England are your hearts and hopes, and that all your household gods are English. This crime is charged to you: unjustly charged I trust it is — for a worse crime, and more infamous than disloyalty or treason to kings or crowns is disloyalty or treason to country. It is a crime not made by lawyers, but made by God; a crime against nature itself — against all its laws, affections, interests, and instincts. Yet the charge is not made against you without colour of truth and show of reason. On every question that arises, in every contest and collision, whether of honour or interest, you take side and cause with England. All blame for this does not rest on you; but some of it does. Much and most of it rests on a class of men whose claim to attention, however strong, I must defer to a future letter. All such ground of charge must be removed and renounced. For ever, henceforth, the owners of our soil must be Irish. To all who own land or living in Ireland, Ireland henceforth must be the Queen-island. She holds in her hands the hostages for their fealty, and will not longer put up with TREASON. On no other common ground or general principle can a federation take place between the nobles of the land and the nation at large, than that of common faith and fealty to this their common country.

The formation of the Irish Party was hailed at the time by many as one step of a movement in the direction of Ireland.[1] It may, perhaps, indicate a change of ideas, if not of feelings. You have probably begun to find out that if your feelings are English, yet your fortunes are Irish; that Ireland's peril is perilous to yourselves; that in renouncing your country and adopting another, you renounce and revolt from the laws of nature; and that nature herself is strong enough to punish the treason. You have, moreover, got some slight cause to doubt whether England esteems your attachment as of any value, your interest as of much importance, or your very existence as worth the expense and peril of supporting. But we recognise nothing Irish in this party except its name; nothing that can entitle it to command or call round it the hearts or hopes of this people; or raise it to any higher position than that of a mere club and a petty club, formed by a class for the single object of saving its own little interests from injury, at any cost to the country. Whether for its professed or its private objects, shelter as an Irish party or as a landowners' club, it is equally and utterly inefficient, and can do nothing for the salvation of the country or for yours. It excludes the people. It embraces no great public principles, passions, purpose, or policy. It bears no banner, and shows no motto. It rallies no support, and inspires no confidence; proposes nothing, and promises nothing. To resist the minister, should his measures of relief or improvement be deemed injurious to the landowners — this appears the sole object of the Irish Party. But your claims as landowners are no longer maintainable or defensible on their own merits and means. To maintain, you must connect them with those of your country. A union between parties of the same class — a union of landowners with each other is adequate to no purpose now. The union required is a union between all classes of whom the people is composed. You are powerless without a people beside or behind you. You must call the commons into your council; and make their private interests and public objects — nay even perhaps their public passions — a part of your policy. The Irish Party must expand and enlarge into the Irish people; or another, and more effective Association be framed.

To organise a new mode and condition of labour — a new industrial system; to frame and fix a new order of society; in a word, to give to Ireland a new social constitution under which the natural capacity of this country would be put into effective action; the resources of its land, labour, and capital developed and made available; its slumbering and decaying energies of mind and muscle excited, directed, and employed; and the condition and character of its people reconstructed, improved, and elevated; this I have already stated is the general object which now calls for the united action of the landowners and people of Ireland in association assembled. The energies of nature and action of time, working together in their wonted course and current, will indeed, in long or short, be

1. The Irish Council, formed in 1847, was representative of all classes and religious groups. It failed in its attempt to alleviate famine distress and collapsed as the landlord elements within the group sought coercion to reduce the increasing chaos.

adequate, without aid or effort of ours, to form a new and effective settlement of society; but the fabric thus formed will be raised out of the relics, and rest on the ruins of the present existing people in all classes. For their own safety and preservation it is necessary that all those classes should now combine to take the direction of that revolution which will otherwise effect itself, and which indeed is in actual process of being effected without their consent, control, or guidance. That position has become too perilous to maintain. Your path of safety, as well as of honour, is now the public highway. No bye-way of your own will carry you through the perils that beset, and the greater perils that are before you. There are many and important questions at issue between you and the landholders, between you and the labourers, between you and the people, between you and other classes of the people, between those classes among themselves. No government, no legislation, no general statutes, no special statutes, no power on earth but the parties concerned, no mode on earth, save that of voluntary agreement, can settle those questions. Why should we not meet and settle them amicably? Leave them not to be settled by time, or to be settled by strength.

What to create a complete and efficient industrial economy; to form and give force to a new state and mode of existence; to organise and animate, and put into healthy vigorous action that complex living machine, a social system; to frame and adjust the fabric of society in its mightiest proportions and minutest parts with all its vast and various interests, arrangements, orders and conditions, independent, yet involved, conflicting, yet co-operating — what to do all this? A work impossible to man; and which, in extent, or detail, he never yet undertook or attempted to perform. A work of which the theory and principles are beyond his knowledge or discovery, and the practical execution beyond his utmost power. Nature has reserved it to herself, to effect by a process of her own, for which no artificial process was or can be substituted with success. A work we cannot do, God's hand alone, not man's, can do it. True — and neither can you form in all its parts the smallest plant that grows. But sow the seed and the plant forms. The powers of vitality but require to be set in movement, and the contrivances of nature left free to act. Even so it is in the case we consider. That work may be done, and *you* must do it or others will; and you must do it at once for it cannot be waited for. Nor is it, when examined, an undertaking that need dazzle or daunt by its magnitude or multiplicity, the meanest mind of all amongst us. It includes no such complication of difficult questions as it may seem to; and the only question actually involved is one easy of settlement, when put into comparison with its apparent mass. Its theory contains itself in a single principle; its practical solution is comprised and completed in a single operation. Lay but the foundation and the work is done. Lay the foundation; nature effects the rest; society forms and fits itself, even as the plant grows when the seed is sown. Lay deep and strong the only foundation that is firm under the foot of a nation — a secure and independent agricultural peasantry. A secure and independent agricultural peasantry is the only base on which a people ever rises, or ever can be raised; or on which a nation can safely rest.

A productive and prosperous husbandry is the sole groundwork of a solid social economy. On it and out of it springs the mechanic, and artisan, and trading dealer; fed and fostered by it these swell into the manufacturer and merchant, who multiply into merchants and manufacturers; sustained by it still, these enlarge, and gather, and solidify into companies, corporations, classes — into great manufacturing and mercantile systems and interests, which often, like unnatural children, disown and desert the mother that bore and the nurse that fed them; without it there is neither manufacture or trade — nor means to make them, for it is agriculture alone that furnishes those means. Food is our first want — to procure it our first work. The agricultural class, therefore, must precede and provide for every other. It is first in order of nature, necessity, and time. It is an abundant agriculture alone that creates and sustains manufactures, and arts, and traffic. It is an increasing agriculture alone that extends them. For it is the surplus of food it accumulates, after providing ordinary subsistence, that forms new wants and demands, and the modes and means to meet and satisfy them. Such is the actual process; a process that never yet was reversed, or carried out in any other course or order; so it was at first, and so will it be for ever — in every time, in every clime, in every country. Adopt this process; create what has never yet existed in Ireland an active and affluent husbandry, a secure and independent agricultural peasantry, able to accumulate as well as to produce

— do this, and you raise a thriving and happy community, a solid social economy, a prosperous people, an effective nation. Create the husbandman, and you create the mechanic, the artisan, the manufacturer, the merchant. Thus you will work on the ordinance of God, in the order and with the powers of nature. All the natural motives and means with which man is endowed will come then to your relief and assistance, and do the rest. Any further interference with the course and process of natural laws would be useless and mischievous. Neither monarchs nor mobs ever yet were able to manage or modify that natural process with success; or ever attempted to enforce interference without doing grievous injury and gross injustice. The abortive and mischievous legislation of both old and recent times affords lessons enough of this, if we choose to learn them.

There seems to be a vague impression on a large portion of the public mind of this country that national attention and exertion, as well as individual effort, should be directed into a course the reverse in its steps and stages of that natural order which I have pointed out. We are in the habit of hearing it asserted that a large development of manufacturing industry is what Ireland needs, and that to establish it should be her chief objects. It is even assumed, not unfrequently, that a manufacturing system must precede, and is the only mode of promoting, the improvement and prosperity of agriculture itself. This is an error I could wish to see abandoned. It distracts effort and attention from the point on which both ought to be directed, and on which they could act with effect. I am prepared to prove — what, indeed, any man may prove to himself — that neither by the private enterprise of individuals or companies, neither by the force of national feeling anyhow exerted, neither by public association or public action of any kind or extent nor by government aid, if such aid could be expected — neither by these or by any other means and appliances can a manufacturing system be established in Ireland, nor so much as a factory built on firm ground, until the support of a numerous and efficient agricultural yeomanry be first secured. Good friends, you that are recommending us to encourage native manufacture and to form manufacturing associations; tradesmen and townsfolk of Ireland will you cease to follow a phantom, and give hand and help to create such a yeomanry?

My general object, the formation of a new social economy thus resolves itself into the formation of a new agricultural system. The principles on which that new system is to be founded must either be settled by agreement between the landowners and the people, or they must be settled by a struggle. What I think those principles ought to be, if they be made articles of agreement, as well as the practical mode of arriving at and arranging such agreement, I shall take another opportunity of stating.

You, however, my lords and gentlemen, it would appear from your present proceedings, have already settled among yourselves the entire future economy of your country — determined the fortunes and fate of this entire island — disposed of the existence of this little people of eight millions. The small landholdings are to be 'consolidated' into large farms, the small landholders 'converted' into 'independent labourers'; those labourers are, of course, to be paupers — those paupers to be supported by a poor law — that poor law is to be in your hands to manage and administer. Thus is to be got rid of the surplus of population beyond what the landowners require. Meantime, by forcible ejectments, forced surrender, and forced emigration, you are effecting the process of 'conversion' a little too rapidly, perhaps for steady and safe working.

And so, it seems, you have doomed a people to extinction and decreed to abolish Ireland? The undertaking is a large one. Are you sure your strength will not be tested? The settlement you have made requires nothing to give it efficacy, except the assent or acquiescence of eight millions of people. Will they assent or acquiesce? Will Ireland, at last, perish like a lamb and let her blood sink in the ground, or will she turn as turns the baited lion? For my own part I can pronounce no opinion; and for you, my lords and gentlemen, if you have any doubts on the question, I think it would be wisdom to pause in your present course of proceeding until steps can be taken and measures adopted for effecting an accommodation and arrangement between you and the present occupiers of the soil, on terms that would preserve the rights and promote the interests of each party. If you persevere in enforcing a clearance of your lands you will force men to weigh your existence, as landowners, against the existence of the Irish people. The result of the struggle which that question might produce ought, at best, to be a matter of doubt in your minds; even though you should be aided, as you doubtless would be, by the unanimous and cordial support of the people of England, whose respect and esteem for you are so well known and so loudly attested. . . .

from:
THE IRISH FELON
(24 June 1848)

[John Martin (1812-75), John Mitchel's brother-in-law, founded *The Irish Felon* to replace Mitchel's *United Irishman* after Mitchel had been transported to Van Diemen's Land. Lalor was co-editor. In the first number, Lalor puts forward what is in effect to be the programme of the Fenian Brotherhood, finally making the break with O'Connell's moral force tactics and deriding the limited form of constitutional independence he sought and which had been briefly won earlier in 1782. Instead of Grattan, the architect of 1782, the nationalist hero now becomes Wolfe Tone, the republican martyr of 1798. In this article, Lalor anticipates the militant spirit of Pearse and the Irish Republican Brotherhood.]

. . . Without agreement as to our objects we cannot agree on the course we should follow. It is requisite the paper should have but one object and that the public should understand what that object is. Mine is not to repeal the Union, nor restore Eighty-two. This is not the year '82; this is the year '48. For Repeal I never went into 'Agitation' and will not go into insurrection. On that question I refuse to arm, or to act in any mode — and the country refuses. O'Connell made no mistake when he pronounced it to be not worth the price of one drop of blood; and for myself, I regret it was not left in the hands of Conciliation Hall whose lawful property it was and is. Moral force, and Repeal, the means and the purpose, were just fitted to each other, *Arcades ambo*, balmy Arcadians both. When the means were limited it was only proper and necessary to limit the purpose. When the means were enlarged, the purpose ought to have been enlarged also. Repeal in its vulgar meaning, I look on as utterly impracticable by any mode of action whatever, and the constitution of '82 as absurd, worthless, and worse than worthless. The English government will never concede or surrender to any species of moral force whatsoever; and the country-peasantry will never arm and fight for it — neither will I. If I am to stake life and fame it must assuredly be for something better and greater, more likely to last, more likely to succeed, and better worth success. And a stronger passion, a higher purpose, a nobler and more needful enterprise is fermenting in the hearts of the people. A mightier question moves Ireland today than that of merely repealing the Act of Union. Not the constitution that Tone died to abolish, but the constitution that Tone died to obtain, independence, full and absolute independence, for this island, and for every man within this island. Into no movement that would leave an enemy's garrison in possession of all our lands, masters of our liberties, our lives and all our means of life and happiness — into no such movement will a single man of the greycoats enter with an armed band, whatever the town population may do. On a wider fighting field, with stronger positions and greater resources than are afforded by the paltry question of Repeal, must we close for our final struggle with England, or sink and surrender. Ireland her own — Ireland her own, and all therein, from the sod to the sky. The soil of Ireland for the people of Ireland, to have and to hold from God alone who gave it — to have and to hold to them and their heirs for ever, without suit or service, faith or fealty, rent or render, to any power under Heaven. From a worse bondage than the bondage of any foreign government, from a dominion more grievous and grinding than the dominion of England in its worst days — from the cruellest tyranny that ever yet laid its vulture clutch on the body and soul of a country, from the robber rights and robber rule that have turned us into slaves and beggars in the land that God gave us for ours. — Deliverance, oh Lord; Deliverance or Death — Deliverance, or this island a desert! This is the one prayer, and terrible need, and real passion of Ireland today, as it has been for ages. Now, at last it begins to shape into defined and desperate purpose; and into it all smaller and meaner purposes must settle and merge. It might have been kept in abeyance, and away from the sight of the sun — aye, till this old native race had been finally conquered out and extinguished *sub silentio*, without noise or notice. But once propounded and proclaimed as a principle, not in the dusk of remote country districts, but loudly and proudly, in the tribunes of the capital, it must now be accepted and declared, as the first great Article of Association in the National Covenant of organised defence and armed resistance; as the principle to take ground, and stand and fight upon. When a greater and more ennobling enterprise is on foot, every inferior and feebler project or proceeding will soon be left in the hands of old women, of dastards, impostors, swindlers, and imbeciles. All the strength and manhood of the island — all the courage, energies, and ambition — all the passions, heroism, and chivalry — all the strong men, and strong minds — all those things that make revolutions will quickly desert it, and throw themselves into the greater movement, throng into the larger and loftier undertaking and flock round the banner that flies nearest the sky. There go the young and the gallant, the gifted, and the daring, and there too go the wise. For wisdom knows that in national action *littleness* is more fatal than the wildest rashness; that greatness of object is essential to greatness of effort, strength, and success; that a revolution ought never to take its stand on low or narrow ground, but seize on the broadest and highest ground it can lay hands on; and that a petty enterprise seldom succeeds. Had America aimed or declared for less than independence she would probably have failed, and been a fettered slave today.

Not to repeal the Union, then, but to repeal the Conquest — not to disturb or dismantle the empire, but to abolish it forever — not to fall back on '82 but act up to '48 — not to resume or restore an old constitution, but to found a new nation, and raise up a free people, and strong as well as free, and secure as well as strong, based on a peasantry rooted like rocks in the soil of the land — this is my object, as I hope it is yours; and this, you may be assured, is the easier, as it is the nobler and more pressing enterprise. For Repeal, all the moral means at our disposal have been used, abused, and abandoned. All the military means it can command will fail as utterly. Compare the two questions. Repeal would require a national organization; a central representative authority, formally convened, formally elected; a regular army, a regulated war of concerted action, and combined movement. When shall we have them? Where is your National Council of Three Hundred? Where is your National Guard of Three Hundred Thousand? On Repeal, Ireland, of necessity, should resolve and act *by the kingdom*, all together, linked and led; and if beaten in the kingdom there would be nothing to fall back upon. She could not possibly act by parishes. To club and arm would not be enough, or rather it would be nothing; and for Repeal alone Ireland will neither club nor arm. The towns only will do so. A Repeal-war would probably be the fight and defeat of a single field-day; or if protracted, it would be a mere game of chess — and England, be assured, would beat you in the game of chess. On the other question all circumstances differ, as I could easily show you. But I have gone into this portion of the subject prematurely and unawares, and here I stop — being reluctant besides to trespass too long on the time of her Majesty's legal and military advisers.

I would regret much to have my meaning, in any degree, misconceived. I do not desire, by any means, to depreciate the value and importance of Repeal, in the valid and vigorous sense of the term, but only in its vulgar acceptation. I do not want to make the tenure question the sole or main topic or purpose of the *Felon*, or to make Repeal only secondary and subservient. I do not wish — far from it — to consider the two questions as antagonistic or distinct. My wish is to combine and cement the two into one; and so, perfect, and reinforce, and carry both. I, too, want to bring about an alliance and 'combination of classes' — an alliance more wanted and better worth, more feasible effective and honourable, than any treasonable alliance with the enemy's garrison, based on the surrender and sacrifice of the rights and lives of the Irish people. I want to ally the town and country. Repeal is the question of the town population; the land tenure question is that of the country peasantry; both combined, taking each in its full extent and efficacy, form the question of Ireland — her question for the battle-day.

The principle I state, and mean to stand upon, is this, that the entire ownership of Ireland, moral and material, up to the sun, and down to the centre, is vested of right in the people of Ireland; that they, and none but they, are the land-owners and law-makers of this island; that all laws are null and void not made by them; and all titles to land invalid not conferred and confirmed by them; and that this full right of ownership may and ought to be asserted and enforced by any and all means which God has put in the power of man. In other, if not plainer words, I hold and maintain that the entire soil of a country belongs of right to the people of that country, and is the rightful property not of any one class, but of the nation at large, in full effective possession, to let to whom they will on whatever tenures, terms, rents, services, and conditions they will; one condition, however, being unavoidable, and essential, the condition that the tenant shall bear full, true, and undivided fealty, and allegiance to the nation, and the laws of the nation whose lands he holds, and own no allegiance whatsoever to any other prince, power, or people, or any obligation of obedience or respect to their will, orders, or laws. I hold further, and firmly believe, that the enjoyment by the people of this right, of first ownership of the soil, is essential to the vigour and vitality of all other rights; to their validity, efficacy, and value; to their secure possession and safe exercise. For let no people deceive themselves, or be deceived by the words, and colours, and phrases, and forms, of a mock freedom, by constitutions, and charters and articles, and franchises. These things are paper and parchment, waste and worthless. Let laws and institutions say what they will, this fact will be stronger than all laws, and prevail against them — the fact that those who own your land will make your laws, and command your liberties, and your lives. But this is tyranny and slavery — tyranny in its wildest scope, and worst shape; slavery of body and soul from the cradle to the coffin — slavery, with all its horrors, and with none of its physical comforts and security; even as it is in Ireland, where the whole community is made up of tyrants, slaves, and slave-drivers. A people whose lands and lives are thus in the keeping and custody of others, instead of in their own, are not in a position of common safety. The Irish famine of '46 is example and proof. The corn crops were sufficient to feed the island. But the landlords *would* have their rents in spite of famine, and in defiance of fever. They took the whole harvest and left hunger to those who raised it. Had the people of Ireland been the landlords of Ireland, not a single human creature would have died of hunger, nor the failure of the potato been considered a matter of any consequence.

This principle, then, that the property and possession of land, as well as the powers of legislation, belong of right to people who live in the land and under the law — do you assent to it in its full integrity, and to the present necessity of enforcing it? Your *reason* may assent, yet your *feelings* refuse and revolt — or those of others at least may do so. Mercy is for the merciful; and you may think it pity to oust and abolish the present noble race of landowners, who have ever been pitiful and compassionate themselves.

What! is your sympathy for a class so great, and your sympathy for a whole people so small? For those same land-owners are now treading out the very life and existence of an entire people, and trampling down the liberties and hopes of this island for ever. It is a mere question between a people and a class — between a people of eight millions and a class of eight thousand. They or we must quit this island. It is a people to be saved or lost — it is the island to be kept or surrendered. They have served us with a general writ of ejectment. Wherefore, I say, let them get a notice to quit at once; or we shall oust possession under the law of nature. There are men who claim protection for them, and for all their tyrannous rights and powers, being as 'one class of the Irish people.' I deny the claim. They form no class of the Irish people, or of any other people. Strangers they are in this land they call theirs — strangers here and strangers everywhere, owning no country and owned by none; rejecting Ireland, and rejected by England; tyrants to this island, and slaves to another; here they stand hating and hated — their hand ever against us, as ours against them, an outcast and ruffianly horde, alone in the world, and alone in its history, a class by themselves. They do not know, and never did belong to this island. Tyrants and traitors have they ever been to us and ours since first they set foot on our soil. Their crime it is and not England's that Ireland stands where she does today — or rather it is our own that have borne them so long. Were they a class of the Irish people the Union could be repealed without a life lost. Had they been a class of the Irish people that Union would have never been. But for them we would now be free, prosperous and happy. Until they be removed no people can ever take root, grow up and flourish here. The question between them and us must sooner or later have been brought to a deadly issue. For heaven's sake, and for Ireland's, let us settle it now, and not leave it to our children to settle. Indeed it *must* be settled now — for it is plain to any ordinary sight that they or we are doomed. A cry has gone up to heaven for the living and the dead — to save the living, and avenge the dead.

There are, however, many landlords perhaps, and certainly a few, not fairly chargeable with the crimes of their order; and you may think it hard they should lose their lands. But recollect, the principle I assert would make Ireland *in fact* as she is of *right*, the mistress and queen of all those lands; that she, poor lady, had ever a soft and grateful disposition; and that she may, if she please, in reward of allegiance, confer new titles, or confirm the old. Let us crown her a queen; and then let her do with her lands as a queen may do.

In the case of any existing interest, of what nature soever, I feel assured that no question but one would need to be answered. Does the owner of that interest assent to swear allegiance to the people of Ireland, and to hold in fee from the Irish nation? If the assent may be assured he will suffer no loss. No eventual or permanent loss, I mean; for some temporary loss he must assuredly suffer. But such loss would be incidental and inevitable to any armed insurrection whatever, no matter on what principle the right of resistance would be resorted to. If he refuse — then I say away with him — out of this land with him — himself and all his robber rights, and all the things himself and his rights have brought into our island — blood, and tears, and famine, and the fever that goes with famine. Between the relative merits and importance of the two rights, the people's right to the land, and their right to legislation, I do not mean or wish to institute any comparison. I am far indeed from desirous to put the two rights in competition, or contrast, for I consider each alike as the natural complement of the other, necessary to its theoretical completeness, and practical efficacy. But, considering them for a moment as distinct, I do mean to asset this — that the land question contains, and the legislative question does *not* contain, the materials from which victory is manufactured; and that, therefore, if we be truly in earnest and determined on success, it is on the former question, and not on the latter that we must take our stand, fling out our banner, and hurl down to England our gage[1] of battle. Victory follows that banner alone, that and no other. This island is ours, and have it we will, if the leaders be true to the people, and the people be true to themselves.

The rights of property may be pleaded. No one has more respect for the real rights of property than I have; but I do not class among them the robber's right by which the lands of this country are now held in fee for the British crown. I acknowledge no right of property in a small class which goes to abrogate the rights of a numerous people. I acknowledge no right of property in eight thousand persons, be they noble or ignoble, which takes away all rights of property, security, independence, and existence itself, from a population of eight millions, and stands in bar to all the political rights of the island, and all the social rights of its inhabitants. I acknowledge no right of property which takes away the food of millions, and gives them a famine — which denies to the peasant the right of a home, and concedes, in exchange, the right of a workhouse. I deny and challenge all such rights, howsoever founded or enforced. I challenge them, as founded only on the code of the brigand, and enforced only by the sanction of the hangman. Against them I assert the true and indefeasible right of property — the right of our people to live in this land and possess it — to live in it in security, comfort and independence, and to live in it by their own labour, on their own land, as God and nature intended them to do. Against them I shall array, if I can, all the forces that yet remain in this island. And against them I am determined to make war — to their destruction or my own.

These are my principles and views. I shall have other opportunities to develop and defend them. I have some few other requisitions to make, but I choose to defer them for other reasons besides want of time and space. Our first business, before we can advance a step, is to fix our own footing and make good our position. That once done, this contest must, if possible, be brought to a speedy close.

1. A glove or other object flung down to indicate a challenge to fight.

JOHN MITCHEL

(1815-75)

from: JAIL JOURNAL (1854)

[Mitchel's belief that the British government used the Famine as an instrument of genocide became an integral part of the Irish nationalist crusade against British rule. Those who were most convinced and therefore most bitter were the emigrants who had been forced to flee the country and were congregated in large numbers in the United States. It is important to remember, then, that *Jail Journal* was originally published in Mitchel's New York newspaper *The Citizen* (January to August 1854). The resentment that Mitchel articulated for the American-Irish had its political manifestation later in the Fenian movement.]

INTRODUCTORY

. . . In 1846 came the Famine, and the 'Relief Acts' advancing money from the Treasury, to be repaid by local assessment; and of course there was an aggravated and intolerable Poor-rate to meet this claim. Of which Relief Acts, only one fact needs to be recorded here — that the Public Works done under them were strictly ordered to be of an unproductive sort — that is, such as would create no fund to repay their own expenses.[1] Accordingly, many hundreds of thousands of feeble and starving men were kept digging holes, and breaking up roads — doing not only no service, but much harm. Well, then, to meet these Parliamentary advances there was nothing but *rates*: and, *therefore*, there was the higher premium to landlords on the extermination, that is the slaughter, of their tenantry. If the clearing business had been active before, now there was a rage and passion for it; and as if the Cheap Ejectment Acts were not a speedy enough machinery, there was a new Poor-law enacted containing amongst other clauses, the 'Quarter Acre clause,' which provided that if a farmer, having sold all his produce to pay the rent duties, rates and taxes, should be reduced, as many thousands of men were, to apply for public out-door relief, he should not get it until he had first delivered up all his land to the landlord.[2] Under that law it is the able-bodied idler only who is to be fed — if he attempt to till but one rood of ground, he dies. This simple method of ejectment was called 'passing paupers through the workhouse' — a man went in, a pauper came out.

Under these various Poor-laws and Relief Acts, there were at least 10,000 government offices, small and great; looking and canvassing for these were 100,000 men; a great army in the interest of England.

At the end of six years, I can set down these things calmly; but to see them might have driven a wise man mad. There is no need to recount how the Assistant Barristers and Sheriffs, aided by the Police, tore down the roof-trees and ploughed up the hearths of village after village — how the Quarter Acre clause laid waste the parishes, how the farmers and their wives and little ones in wild dismay, trooped along the highways — how in some hamlets by the seaside, most of the inhabitants being already dead, an adventurous traveller would come upon some family eating a famished ass — how maniac mothers stowed away their dead children to be devoured at midnight — how Mr. Darcy of Clifden, describes a humane gentleman going to a village near that place with some crackers, and standing at the door of a house; 'and when he threw the crackers to the children (for he was afraid to enter), the mother attempted to take them from them' — how husband and wife fought like wolves for the last morsel of food in the

1. Peel introduced relief schemes in 1846 to provide work and money with which to buy food. These included various improvements to piers and harbours and, chiefly, to roads. The Whig government under Lord John Russell reorganized the works scheme and laid itself open to the charge that the work to be done was of a largely unproductive nature. It was the Whig administration too that imposed the cost of the schemes on property owners in the distressed areas. The relief works were phased out midway through 1847 and were replaced by a direct relief programme.

2. A Poor Law Amendment Act was passed in 1846 to reorganize the administration of the workhouse system. Part of its aim was to make the Irish landlords, rather than the treasury, pay the cost of relief. It was in the financial interest of the landlords to evict smallholders; this led to the 'Famine clearances'. The act also contained a clause, known as the 'Gregory' or 'Quarter-Acre Clause', which excluded from relief anyone with a holding of more than a quarter of an acre. As a consequence, many smallholders were forced to sell and emigrate or to take workhouse relief.

house; how families, when all was eaten and no hope left, took their last look at the Sun, built up their cottage doors, that none might see them die nor hear their groans, and were found weeks afterwards, skeletons on their own hearth; how the 'law' was vindicated all this while; how the Arms Bills were diligently put in force, and many examples were made; how starving wretches were transported for stealing vegetables by night;[3] how overworked coroners declared they would hold no more inquests; how Americans sent corn, and the very Turks, yea, negro slaves, sent money for alms; which the British Government was not ashamed to administer to the 'sister country'; and how, in every one of these years, '46, '47 and '48, Ireland was exporting to England, food to the value of fifteen million pounds sterling, and had on her own soil at each harvest, good and ample provision for double her own population, notwithstanding the potato blight.

To this condition had forty years of 'moral and peaceful agitation' brought Ireland. The high aspirations after a national Senate and a national flag had sunk to a mere craving for food. And for food Ireland craved in vain. She was to be taught that the Nation which parts with her nationhood, or suffers it to be wrestled or swindled from her, thereby loses all. O'Connell died heart-broken in 1847 — heart-broken not by a mean vexation at seeing the power departing from him; the man was too great for that; but by the sight of his People sinking every day into death under their inevitable, inexorable doom. His physicians ordered him to a warmer climate: in vain: amidst the reverent acclamations of Paris, through the sunny valleys of France, as he journeyed southward, that *Banshee* wail followed him and found him, and rung in his dying ear. At Genoa he died: ordering that the heart should be taken out of his dead body, and sent, not to Ireland, but to *Rome*; a disposition which proves how miserably broken and debilitated was that once potent nature.

Politics, by this time, was a chaos in Ireland. 'Conciliation Hall'[4] was sending forth weekly an abject howl for *food! food!* The 'Irish Confederation'[5] (of which the present writer was a member) had no much clearer view through the gloom; though it had more energy and honesty. Two or three vain efforts were made by its leaders to put a good man into the representation (Meagher at Waterford),[6] or to keep a bad man out (Monahan at Galway)[7] — both efforts in vain. The representation and the franchise were too cunningly calculated for British interests.

Every week was deepening the desolation and despair throughout the country; until at last the French Revolution of February, '48, burst upon Europe. Ireland, it is true, did not then possess the physical resources or the high spirit which had 'threatened the integrity of the Empire' in '43; but even as she was, depopulated, starved, cowed and corrupted, it seemed better that she should attempt resistance, however heavy the odds against success, than lie prostrate and moaning as she was. Better that men should perish by the bayonets of the enemy than by their laws.

3. In a footnote, Mitchel cites a case at Bantry Sessions in which a couple was transported for seven years for stealing turnips and parsnips.
4. Conciliation Hall, on Burgh Quay, Dublin, was the home of O'Connell's Repeal Association. The Young Irelanders were scornful of O'Connell's plea for food to the Whig government with which he had been in alliance.
5. Mitchel was a founding member of the Irish Confederation, formed in 1847 after Young Ireland's split with O'Connell's Repeal Association. Mitchel resigned from the Confederation in 1848 after a disagreement on the issues of passive resistance and guerilla warfare — both advocated by Mitchel himself.
6. Thomas Francis Meagher, one of the most charismatic of the Confederates, was defeated in a by-election in Waterford in early 1848. Mitchel had opposed Gavan Duffy's attempt to get Meagher elected on the grounds that it was a concession to the constitutional politics by which Ireland had been ruined.
7. In February 1847, the Confederates combined with the Repeal Association in a by-election in Galway against James Monaghan, the solicitor general. Monaghan won by four votes. A petition against personation for Monaghan failed. This was another moment in Mitchel's increasing disgust with the constitutional methods advocated by his Confederate friends.

from:
THE LAST CONQUEST OF IRELAND (PERHAPS) (1861)

[This book was first published in serial form in the United States in 1858. Mitchel's aim was to inform the Americans of recent Irish affairs and to counteract the propaganda of the British press. It is a gloomy and angry account of what seemed to Mitchel to be the triumph of a deliberate policy of extermination and suppression by the British in Ireland. His title is taken from the French poet Béranger's 'Ma dernière chanson, Peut-être', the implication being, as Mitchel sees it, that the last history or poem written may be final but may, equally, be followed by another.

The extracts below are from Letters X, XII, XIII and XIV.]

X

Before the grave had yet closed on Thomas Davis[1] [there] began to spread awful rumours of approaching famine. Within the next month from all the counties of Ireland came one cry of mortal terror. Blight had fallen on the crop of potatoes — the food on which five millions of the Irish people had been reduced to depend for subsistence; three millions of them wholly and exclusively. We are at the beginning of the first year of the six years' *Famine*.

To Sir Robert Peel it would have seemed an impious tempting of Providence to neglect this weapon thus graciously placed in his hand for the consummation of the conquest on which he was bent.[2] If the 'Repeal' could not be crushed out by coercion, nor bought out by corruption, it might now be starved out by Famine. The thing was done by a process of 'relieving' and 'ameliorating';[3] — for in the nineteenth century civilized governments always proceed upon the most benevolent motives; — but it was done; and so effectually done for that time, that, a few years afterwards, the London *Times* (perhaps prematurely) thought it might announce 'The Celts are *gone* — gone *with a vengeance*. The Lord be praised.'[4]

1. Thomas Davis died on 16 September 1845.
2. Sir Robert Peel had opposed Daniel O'Connell's movement for the Repeal of the Union (The Repeal Association) by banning mass meetings — like that at Clontarf in 1845, by reactivating the Convention Act of 1793 and, in 1846, during the Famine, bringing in the Irish Coercion Bill, on which he was defeated.
3. Various famine relief measures were introduced by the governments of Peel and Lord John Russell. The Young Irelanders, Mitchel among them, regarded these as half-hearted and insufficient. They wanted, not treasury aid, but repatriation of monies extorted from Ireland to relieve the Famine.
4. This remark was quoted several times in later comments on the Famine — e.g. Michael Davitt's *The Fall of Feudalism in Ireland* (1904) and in several traditional accounts, as in the extract from south Kerry quoted above, pp. 158-60.

XII

... From all this you may begin to appreciate the feeling that then prevailed in the two islands — in Ireland a vague and dim sense that they were somehow robbed — in England a still more vague and blundering idea that an impudent beggar was demanding their money with a scowl in his eye and a threat upon his tongue.

In truth, only a few either in England or in Ireland, fully understood the bloody game on the board. The two cardinal principles of the British policy in this business seem to have been these two:—*first*, strict adherence to the principles of 'political economy' — and, *second*, making the whole administration of the Famine a government concern. 'Political Economy,' became about the time of the Repeal of the Corn Laws a favourite study, or rather, indeed, the creed and gospel of England. Women and young boys were learned in its saving doctrines; one of the most fundamental of which was — 'there must be no interference with the natural course of trade.' It was seen that this maxim would ensure the transfer of the Irish wheat and beef to England; for that was what they called the natural course of trade. Moreover this maxim would forbid the government, or relief committees, to sell provisions in Ireland any lower than the market price, — for this is an interference with the enterprize of private speculators; it would forbid the employment of government ships, — for this troubles individual ship owners; and further, and lastly, it was found, (this invaluable maxim) to require that the public works to be executed by labourers employed with borrowed public money, should be unproductive works; that is works which would create no fund to pay their own expenses. There were many railroad companies at that time in Ireland that had got their charters; their roads have been made since; but it was in vain they asked then for government advances, which they could have well secured and soon paid off; the thing could not be done. Lending money to Irish railroad companies would be a discrimination against English companies — flat interference with private enterprize.

The other great leading idea completed Sir Robert's policy. It was to make the Famine a strictly government concern. The Famine was to be administered strictly through officers of the government, from High Commissioners down to policemen. Even the Irish General Relief Committee, and other local Committees of charitable persons who were exerting themselves to raise funds to give employment, were either induced to act in subordination to a Government Relief Committee which sat in Dublin Castle — or else were deterred from importation of food by the announcement in Parliament that the *Government* had given orders somewhere for the purchase of foreign corn. For instance, the Mayor of Cork and some principal inhabitants of that city, hurried to Dublin and waited on the Lord Lieutenant, representing that the local committee had applied for some portion of the parliamentary loans, but 'were refused assistance on some points of official form — that the people of that county were already famishing, and both food and labour were urgently needed. Lord Heytesbury simply recommended that they should communicate at once with the *Government* Relief Committee' — as for the rest, that they should consult the Board of Works. Thus every possible delay and official difficulty was interposed against the efforts of local bodies — Government was to do all. These things, together with the new measure for an increase in the police force (who were their main administrative agents throughout the country) led many persons to the conclusion that the enemy had resolved to avail themselves of the famine in order to increase governmental supervision and espionage; so that every man, woman, and child in Ireland, with all their goings out and comings in, might be thoroughly known and registered — that when the mass of the people began to starve, their sole resource might be the police-barracks — that Government might be all in all; omnipotent to give food or to withhold it, to relieve or to starve, according to their own ideas of policy and of good behaviour in the people.

It is needless to point out that Government patronage also was much extended by this system; and by the middle of the next year, 1847, there were 10,000 men salaried out of the Parliamentary loans and grants for relief of the poor — as Commissioners, Inspectors, Clerks, and so forth; and some of them with salaries equal to an American Secretary of State. So many of the middle classes had been dragged down almost to insolvency by the ruin of the country, that they began to be eager for the smaller places as Clerks and Inspectors; for those 10,000 offices, then, it was estimated there were 100,000 applicants and canvassers — so much clear gain from 'Repeal.'

The Repeal Association continued its regular meetings, and never ceased to represent that the true remedies for Irish Famine were Tenant-Right — the stoppage of export — and Repeal of the Union; — and as those were really the true and only remedies, it was clear they were the only expedient which an English parliament would *not* try. The Repeal members gained a kind of Parliamentary victory, however, this spring: — they caused the defeat of the Coercion Bill with the aid of the Whigs. Sir Robert Peel had very cunningly, as he thought, made this Bill precede the Corn Law Repeal Bill; and as the English Public was all now most eager for the cheapening of bread, he believed that all parties would make haste to pass his favourite measure first. The Irish members went to London, and knowing they could not influence legislation otherwise, organized a sort of mere mechanical resistance against the Coercion Bill: that is, they opposed first reading, second reading, third reading, opposed its being referred to Committee, moved endless amendments, made endless speeches, and insisted upon dividing the house on every clause. In vain it was represented to them that this was only delaying the Corn Law Repeal, which would 'cheapen bread.' O'Brien replied that it would only cheapen bread to Englishmen, and enable them to devour more and more of the Irish bread and give less for it. In vain ministers told them they were stopping public business — they answered that English business was no business of theirs. In vain their courtesy was invoked. They could not afford to be courteous in such a case, and their sole errand in London was to resist an atrocious and torturing tyranny threatened against their poor countrymen.

Just before this famous debate there had been very extensive clearing of tenantry in Connaught; and, in particular one case, in which a Mrs. Gerrard had, with the aid of the troops and police, destroyed a whole village, and thrown out two hundred and seventy persons on the high road. The *Nation* thus improved the circumstance with reference to the 'Coercion Bill':

> Some Irish Member, for instance, may point to the two hundred and seventy persons thrown out of house and home the other day in Galway, and in due form of law (for it was all perfectly legal) turned adrift in their desperation upon the wide world — and may ask the Minister, if any of these two hundred and seventy commit a robbery on the highway — if any of them murder the bailiff who (in exercise of his duty) flung out their naked children to perish in the winter's sleet — if any of them, maddened by wolfish famine, break into a dwelling-house, and forcibly take food to keep body and soul together, or arms for vengeance

— what will you do? How will you treat that district? Will you indeed *proclaim* it? Will you mulct the house-holders (not yet ejected) in a heavy fine to compound for the crimes of those miserable outcasts, to afford food and shelter to whom they wrong their own children in this hard season? Besides sharing with those wretches his last potato, is the poor cottier to be told that he is to *pay* for policemen to watch them day and night — that he is to make atonement in money (though his spade and poor bedding should be auctioned to make it up) for any outrage that may be done in the neighbourhood? — but that these GERRARDS are not to pay one farthing for all this — for, perhaps, their property is encumbered, and, it may be, they find it hard enough to pay their interest, and keep up such establishments in town and country as befit their rank? And will you, indeed, issue your commands that those houseless and famishing two hundred and seventy — after their roof trees were torn down, and the ploughshare run through the foundations of their miserable hovels — are to be *at home* from sunset to sunrise? — that if found straying, the gaols and the penal colonies are ready for their reception?

It was precisely with a view to meet such cases that the Coercion Bill had been devised; and, were not our representatives well justified, sir, in resisting such a measure courteously or otherwise? The English Whigs, and, at length, the indignant Protectionists, too, joined the Repealers in this resistance — not to spare Ireland, but to defeat Sir Robert Peel, and get into his place. And they did defeat Sir Robert Peel, and get into his place. Whereupon, it was not long before Lord John Russell and his Whigs devised a new and more murderous Coercion Bill for Ireland themselves. . . .

XIII

. . . In the meantime the Famine and the Fever raged: many landlords regained possession without so much as an ejectment, because the tenants died of hunger; and the county coroners, before the end of this year, were beginning to strike work — they were so often called to sit upon famine-slain corpses. The verdict, — 'Death by Starvation,' — became so familiar that the county newspapers sometimes omitted to record it; and travellers were often appalled when they came upon some lonely village by the western coast, with the people all skeletons upon their own hearths. Irish landlords, sir, are not all monsters of cruelty. Thousands of them, indeed, kept far away from the scene, collected their rents through agents and bailiffs, and spent them in England or in Paris. But the resident landlords and their families did, in many cases, devote themselves to the task of saving their poor people alive. Many remitted their rents, or half their rents; and ladies kept their servants busy and their kitchens smoking with continual preparation of food for the poor. Local Committees soon purchased all the corn in the government depots (at market price, however,) and distributed it gratuitously. Clergymen, both Protestant and Catholic, I am glad to testify, generally did their duty; except those absentee clergymen, bishops and wealthy rectors, who usually reside in England, their services being not needed in the places from whence they draw their wealth. But many a poor rector and his curate shared their crust with their suffering neighbours; and priests, after going round all day administering extreme unction to whole villages at once, all dying of mere starvation, often themselves went supperless to bed.

The Western and South-Western coast, from Derry round to Cork, is surely the most varied and beautiful coast in all the world. Great harbours, backed by noble ranges of mountains, open all around the Western coast of Munster, till you come to the Shannon mouth; there is a fine navigable river opening up the most bounteously fertile land in the island — Limerick and Tipperary. North of the Shannon, huge cliff-walls, rising eight hundred feet sheer out of deep water, broken by chasms and pierced by sea-caves, 'with high embowed roof,'[1] like the choir of a cathedral; then the Bay of Galway, once thronged with Spanish and Irish ships, carrying wine and gold, — but now [1858], it appears, dangerous and fatal (*statio male fida carinis*)[2] to steam-ships bound for America. Westward from Galway, and round the circuit of Connaught, the scene becomes savage and wild, with innumerable rocky islands, — deep inlets, narrow and gloomy, like Norwegian *fiords*, — and grim steep mountains hanging over them. But the

1. John Milton, *Il Penseroso*, line 157.
2. Virgil, *Aeneid* II. 23: 'an unsafe anchorage for ships'.

most desolate region of all is found in Ulster. As you travel northwards from Killybegs, by way of Ardara, Glenties and Dunglow, you pass for nearly forty miles through the dreariest region of moor and mountain that is to be found within the five ends of Ireland. Wide tracts of quaking bog, interspersed with countless dismal lakes, intersected by rocky ridges, and traversed by mountain rivers roaring in tawny foam to the sea. The two or three wretched villages that lie along this road give to a traveller an impression of even more dreariness and desolation than the intervening country: a cluster of ragged-looking, windowless hovels, whose inhabitants seem to have gathered themselves from the wastes, and huddled together to keep some life and heat in them; a few patches of oats and potatoes surrounding the huts, and looking such a miserable provision for human beings against hunger in the midst of those great brown moors; hardly a slated building to be seen, save one or two constabulary and revenue police-stations, and a court-house in Glenties, for dealing out 'justice,' and close by that a certain new building — the grandest by far that those Rosses people ever saw — rearing its accursed gables and pinnacles of Tudor barbarism, and staring boldly with its detestible [*sic*] mullioned windows, as if to mock those wretches who still cling to liberty and mud cabins — seeming to them, in their perennial half-starvation, like a Temple erected to the Fates, or like the fortress of Giant Despair, whereinto he draws them one by one and devours them there — the Poorhouse.

This is the estate of a certain Marquis of Conyngham:[3] and for him those desolate people, while health lasts, and they may still keep body and soul together, outside the Poorhouse, are for ever employed in making up a *subsidy*, called rent; which that district sends half-yearly to be consumed in England, or wherever else it may please their noble proprietor to devour their hearts' blood and the marrow of their bones.

So it is; and so it was, even before Famine, with almost the whole of that coast region. The landlords were all absentees. All the grain and cattle the people could raise were never enough to make up the rent: it all went away, of course; it was all consumed in England; but Ireland received in exchange stamped rent receipts. Of course there were no improvements, — because *they* would have only raised the rent; and in ordinary years many thousands of those poor people lived mainly on sea-weed some months of every year. But this was trespass and robbery; for the sea-weed belonged to the lord of the manor, who frequently made examples of the depredators.*

Can you picture in your mind a race of white men reduced to this condition? White men! Yes of the highest and purest blood and breed of men.[4] The very region I have described to you was once — before British civilization overtook us — the abode of the strongest and richest clans in Ireland ....

After a struggle of six or seven centuries, after many bloody wars and sweeping confiscations, English 'civilization' prevailed, — and had brought the clans to the condition I have related. The ultimate idea of English civilization being that 'the sole *nexus* between man and man is cash payment,' — and the 'Union' having finally determined the course and current of that payment, out of Ireland into England, — it had come to pass that the chiefs were exchanged for landlords, and the clansman had sunk into able-bodied paupers.

The details of this frightful famine, as it ravaged those Western districts, I need not narrate; — they are sufficiently known. It is enough to say that in this year, 1846, not less than 300,000 perished, either of mere hunger, or of typhus-fever caused by hunger. But as it has ever since been a main object of the British Government to conceal the amount of the carnage (which, indeed, they ought to do if they can) I find that the Census Commissioners, in their report for 1851, admit only 2,041 'registered' deaths by famine alone.

A Whig Ministry, however, was now in power; and the people were led to expect great efforts on the part of government to stay the progress of ruin. And I am bound to say that O'Connell used all his power to make the people depend upon that expectation. In August it became manifest that the potato-crop of '46 was also a total failure; but the products otherwise were most abundant, — much

* I have defended poor devils on charges of trespass by gathering sea-weed below high-water mark, and remember one case in which a large number of farmers near the sea were indicted *for robbery*, on the charge of taking limestone from a rock uncovered at low water only — to burn it for spreading on their fields.

3. Francis Nathaniel Conyngham was later notorious in Connacht for his treatment of the people of Kilkee. See Sylvester Malone, *Tenant-Wrong Illustrated in a Nutshell* (Dublin: Kelly, 1867).

4. Mitchel supported the South in the American Civil War and defended the institution of slavery.

more than sufficient to feed all the people. Again, therefore, it became the urgent business of British policy to promise large 'relief,' so as to ensure that the splendid harvest should be allowed peacefully to be shipped to England as before; and the first important measure of the Whigs was to propose a renewal of the *Disarming Act*, and a further increase in the Police-force.[5] Apparently the outcry raised against this had the effect of shaming ministers, for they suddenly dropped the Bill for this time. But the Famine could not be correctly administered without a Coercion Bill of some sort; so the next year they devised a machinery of this kind, the most stringent and destructive that had yet been prescribed for Ireland. In the meantime, for 'Relief' of the Famine, — they brought forward their famous *Labour-Rate Act*.[6]

This was, in few words, an additional poor rate payable by the same persons liable to the other poor rates; the proceeds to be applied to the execution of such public works as *the government* might choose; the control and superintendance to be entrusted to *government officers*. Money was to be in the meantime advanced from the Treasury, in order to set the people immediately to work; and that advanced was to be repaid in ten years by means of the increased rate. There was to be an *appearance* of local control, inasmuch as barony sessions of landlords and justices were to have power to meet, (under the Lord Lieutenant's order,) and suggest any works they might think needful, provided they were strictly unproductive works; but the control of all was to be in the government alone.

Now the class which suffered most from the potato-blight consisted of those small farmers who were barely able, in ordinary years to keep themselves above starvation after paying their rents. These people, by the Labour-rate Act, had an additional tax laid on them; and not being able to pay it, could but quit their holdings, sink to the class of able-bodied paupers, and enrol themselves in a gang of government *navvys*, — thus throwing themselves for support upon those who still strove to maintain themselves by their own labour on their own land.

In addition to the proceeds of the new Poor Rate, Parliament appropriated a further sum of £50,000 to be applied in giving work in some absolutely pauper districts, where there was no hope of ever raising rates to repay it. £50,000 was just the sum which was that same year voted out of the English and Irish revenue, to improve the buildings of the British Museum.

So there was to be *more* Poor Law, more Commissioners, (this time under the title of Additional Public Works Commissioners); innumerable officials in the Public Works, Commissariat and constabulary departments; and no end of stationary [*sic*] and red tape; — *all* to be paid out of the rates. On the whole, it was hoped that provision was made for stopping the 'Irish howl' this one season.

You have already been told that Irishmen of all classes had almost universally condemned the Poor Law at first; so, as they did not like Poor Law, they were to have *more* Poor Law. Society in Ireland was to be re-constructed on the basis of Poor Rates, and a broad foundation of able-bodied pauperism. It did not occur to the English — and it never will occur to them — that the way to stop Irish destitution is to Repeal the Union, so that Irishmen might make their own laws, use their own resources, regulate their own industry. It was in vain, however, that anybody in Ireland remonstrated. In vain that such journals as were of the popular party condemned the whole scheme....

It may seem astonishing that the gentry of Ireland did not rouse themselves at this frightful prospect, and universally demand the Repeal of the Union. They were the same class, sons of the same men, who had in 1782 wrested the independence of Ireland from an English Government, and enjoyed the fruits of that independence in honour, wealth, and prosperity, for eighteen years! Why not now? It is because, in 1782 the Catholics of Ireland counted as nothing, now they are numerous, enfranchised, exasperated; and the Irish landlords dare not trust themselves in Ireland without British support. They looked on tamely, therefore, and saw this deliberate scheme for the pauperization of a nation. They knew it would injure themselves; but they took the injury, took insult along with it, and submitted to be reproached for begging *alms*, when they demanded restitution of a part of their own means.

5. The Whig government introduced a Coercion Bill in 1847 to deal with increasing violence in Ireland. The police force was strengthened and its close knowledge of the country's affairs is evident in its statistical collections, especially the agricultural statistics of Ireland, published annually from 1847.

6. The Whig ministry under Russell passed the Labour Rate Act in 1847. It replaced Peel's treasury grant with a loan, repayable with interest by the landed property of Ireland. This was an example of the Whigs' doctrinaire application of 'political economy'.

Over the whole island, for the next few months, was a scene of confused and wasteful attempts at relief: bewildered barony sessions striving to understand the voluminous directions, schedules and specifications, under which alone they could vote their own money to relieve the poor at their own doors; but generally making mistakes, for the unassisted human faculties never could comprehend those ten thousand books and fourteen tons of paper; insolent commissioners and inspectors, and clerks snubbing them at every turn, and ordering them to study the documents; efforts on the part of the proprietors to expend some of the rates at least on useful works, reclaiming land or the like, which efforts were always met with flat refusal and a lecture on political economy; (for political economy, it seems, declared that the works must be strictly useless, — as cutting down a road where there was no hill, or building a bridge where there was no water, — until many good roads became impassable on account of pits and trenches;) plenty of jobbing and peculation all this while; and the labourers, having the example of a great public fraud before their eyes, themselves defrauding their fraudulent employers, — quitting agricultural pursuits and crowding to the public works, where they pretended to be cutting down hills and filling up hollows, and with tongue in cheek received half wages for doing nothing. So the labour was wasted; the labourers were demoralized; and the *next* year's famine was ensured.

Now began to be a rage for extermination beyond any former time; and many thousands of the peasants who could still scrape up the means fled to the sea, as if pursued by wild beasts, and betook themselves to America. The British army also received numberless recruits this year (for it is sound English policy to keep our people so low that a shilling a day would tempt them to fight for the Devil, not to say the Queen), and insane mothers began to eat their young children who died of famine before them, — and still fleets of ships were sailing with every tide, carrying Irish cattle and corn to England. There was also a large importation of grain from England into Ireland, especially of Indian corn; and the speculators and shipowners had a good time. Much of the grain thus brought to Ireland had been previously exported *from* Ireland, and came back laden with merchants' profits and double freights and insurance to the helpless people who had sowed and reaped it. This is what Commerce and Free Trade did for Ireland those days.

Two facts, however, are essential to be borne in mind — *first*, that the nett result of all this importation, exportation, and re-importation (though many a ship-load was carried four times across the Irish Sea, as prices 'invited' it,) was, that England finally received the harvests to the same amount as before; and *second*, that she gave Ireland — under free-trade in corn — less for it than ever. In other words, it took more of the Irish produce to buy a piece of cloth from a Leeds manufacturer, or buy a rent-receipt from an absentee proprietor.

They could do without much of the cloth, but as for the rent-receipts, these they must absolutely buy; for the bailiff, with his police, was usually at the door, even before the fields were reaped; and he, and the Poor-rate Collector, and the Additional Poor-rate Collector, and the County-cess[7] Collector, and the Processor-server with Decrees, were all to be paid out of the first proceeds. If it took the farmer's whole crop to pay them, which it usually did, he had, at least, a pocketfull of receipts, and might see lying in the next harbour the very ship that was to carry his entire harvest and his last cow to England.

What wonder that so many farmers gave up the effort in despair, and sunk to paupers? Many Celts were cleared off this year, and the campaign was, so far, successful.

7. A 'cess' was a tax or levy; now known as 'rates'.

XIV

. . . And the people perished more rapidly than ever. The Famine of '47 was far more terrible and universal than that of the previous year. The Whig Government, bound by political economy, absolutely refused to interfere with market-prices, and the merchants and speculators were never so busy on both sides of the Channel. In this year it was that the Irish Famine began to be a world's wonder; and men's hearts were moved in the uttermost ends of the earth by the recital of its horrors. The London *Illustrated News* began to be adorned with engravings of tottering, windowless hovels in Skibbereen and elsewhere, with naked wretches dying on a truss of wet straw; and the constant language of English ministers and members in Parliament created the impression abroad that Ireland was in need of *alms*, and nothing but alms:

whereas Irishmen themselves uniformly protested that what they required was Repeal of the Union, so that the English might cease to devour their substance.

It may be interesting to you to know how the English people were faring all this while; and whether 'that portion of the United kingdom,' as it is called, suffered much by the Famine in Ireland and in Europe. Authentic *data* upon this point are to be found in the financial statement of Sir Charles Wood, Chancellor of the Exchequer, in February, 1847. In that statement he declares — and he tells it, he says, with great satisfaction — that 'the English people and working classes' are steadily growing more comfortable, nay, more luxurious in their style of living. He goes into particulars even to show how rapidly a taste for good things spreads amongst English labourers, and bids his hearers 'recollect that consumption could not be accounted for by attributing it to the higher and wealthier classes, but must have arisen from the consumption of the large body of the people and the working classes.'

And what do you think constituted the regimen of the 'body of the people and working classes' in that part of the world? And in what proportion had its consumption increased? Why, in the matter of *coffee*, they had used nearly seven million pounds of it more than they did in 1843; of *butter* and *cheese* they devoured double as much within the year as they had done three years before within the same period. 'I will next,' says the Chancellor of the Exchequer, 'take *currants*,' (for currants are one of the necessaries of life to an English labourer, who must have his pudding on Sunday at least); and we find that the quantity of currants used by the 'body of the people and working classes' had increased in three years from 254,000 cwt. to 359,000 cwt. by the year. Omitting other things, we come to the Chancellor's statement, that since 1843 the consumption of *tea* had increased by 5,400,000 lbs. It is unnecessary to say they had as much beef and bacon as they could eat, and bread *à discretion*, — and as for beer! —

So they live in merry England. . . .

JOHN ELLIOT CAIRNES

(1823-75)

from: ESSAYS IN POLITICAL ECONOMY . . . . (1873)

[This essay was first published in the *Fortnightly Review* (January 1870). It is important because it demonstrates how the Irish Famine and subsequent disorders arose from a radically defective and unjust system, which was upheld for what seemed to many people to be perfectly sound economic reasons. Cairnes explains that economic beliefs are culturally derived and that therefore they should not be clung to in the face of circumstances that contradict them. In saying this, he undermines the position of those who advocated *laissez-faire* as though it were a law of nature and anticipates the policies of state intervention which were increasingly applied in Ireland and were later, with J. M. Keynes, to become the governing feature of British economic theory in the mid-twentieth century. It is at times difficult to see how Cairnes can reconcile his view of political economy's independence of the systems it deals with and his admission that is is also derived from these. But that is such a large question that it cannot be dealt with here. Cairnes sees the Famine and the land question in a context so different from most other contemporary commentators that this in itself merits his inclusion in this anthology.]

POLITICAL ECONOMY AND LAND

Various as have been the schemes recently offered to public notice for the settlement of the Irish land question, one feature is noticeable as more or less prominently characterizing them all — a profound distrust of Political Economy. Just in proportion as a plan gives promise of being effective, does the author feel it necessary to assume an attitude, if not of hostility, then of apology, towards this science. It is either sneered at as unpractical and perverse, or its authority is respectfully put aside as of no account 'in a country so exceptionally situated as Ireland.' This state of opinion is perfectly intelligible. In its earlier applications to practical affairs Political Economy found itself inevitably in collision with numerous regulative codes, partly the remnants of feudalism, partly the products of the commercial doctrines of a later age, but all founded on the principle of substituting for individual discretion the control of those in power. It thus came naturally to be identified with the opposite principle; and was known to the general public mainly as a scientific development of the doctrine of *laissez-faire*. The Free-trade controversy of course gave great prominence to this side of the system, and of late the idea that all Political Economy is summed up in *laissez-faire* has been much fostered by the utterances of some public men and writers, who have acquired a certain reputation as political economists, chiefly, it would seem, through the pertinacity with which they have enforced this formula, insisting on its sufficiency, not merely in the domain of material interest, but over the whole range of human life. If *laissez-faire* is to be taken as the sum and substance of economic teaching, it follows evidently enough that intervention by the State to determine the relative status of those holding interests in the soil involves an economic heresy of the deepest dye; and it is not strange, therefore, that those who accept or defer to this idea of the science should, in attempting to deal with the Irish problem, evince some susceptibility in reference to Political Economy. In effect, it is very evident that two courses only are open to economists of this hue. Either they must hold by their maxims, and, doing so, remit the solution of the Irish difficulty to civil war and the arbitrament of armed force; or, accepting the plea of Ireland's exceptional condition, they must be content to put aside their science for the nonce, and legislate as if it were not. The latter is the course that fortunately has for the most part been taken. Economic laws — so it seems now to be agreed upon by thinkers of this school — do not act except where circumstances are favourable, and have no business in a country so unfortunately situated as Ireland. This is one view of the relation of Political Economy to such questions as that presented by the present state of Ireland. In my opinion, it is a radically false, and practically a most mischievous view; one, therefore, against which, alike in the interest of the peace of Ireland and for the credit of economic science, I am anxious with all my energy to protest. I deny that economic doctrine is summed up in *laissez-faire*; I contend that it has positive resources, and is efficacious to build up as well as to pull down. Sustained by some of the greatest names — I will say by every name of the first rank in Political Economy, from Turgot and Adam Smith to Mill[1] — I hold that the land of a country presents conditions which separate it economically from the great mass of the other objects of wealth, — conditions which, if they do not absolutely and under all circumstances impose upon the State the obligation of controlling private enterprise in dealing with land, at least explain why this control is in certain stages of social progress indispensable, and why in fact it has been constantly put in force, wherever public opinion or custom has not been strong enough to do without it. And not merely does economic science, as expounded by its ablest teachers, dispose of *à priori* objections to a policy of intervention with regard to land, it even furnishes principles fitted to inform and guide such a policy in a positive sense. Far from being the irreconcilable foe, it is the natural ally of those who engage in this course, at once justifying the principle of their undertaking, and lending itself as a minister to the elaboration of the constructive design.

As regards the main ground on which the distinction between land and other forms of wealth depends, little more needs be done than unfold the argument contained in a few weighty sentences in which Mr. Mill has summed up the case: — 'Moveable property can be produced in indefinite quantity, and he who disposes as he likes of anything which, it can be fairly argued, would not have existed but for him, does no wrong to anyone. It is otherwise with regard to land, a thing which no man made, which exists in limited quantity, which was the original inheritance of all mankind, and which whoever appropriates keeps others out of its possession. Such appropriation, when there is not enough left for all, is, at the first aspect, an usurpation on the rights of other people.'[2] Where

1. J. Turgot (1727-81), controller general of France before the Revolution and an expert financier; Adam Smith (1723-90), author of the classic work *An Inquiry into the Nature and Causes of the Wealth of Nations* (1776); John Stuart Mill (1806-73), the leading political economist of the day, upon the later editions of whose *Principles of Political Economy* Cairnes had a considerable influence. Cairnes firmly rejected attempts to claim that Adam Smith would have opposed his suggestions for land reform: 'This does Smith flagrant injustice .... The ruling thought of all that he has said on this subject is the supreme importance of security of tenure for the tenant, as the essential foundation and mainspring of all agricultural progress.'
2. *Principles of Political Economy*, Chapter 2.

wealth is provided by human industry, its having value is the indispensable condition to its existence — to its existence at least in greater quantity than suffices for the producer's own requirements; and the most obvious means of rendering this condition efficacious as a stimulus to industry is to recognize in the producer a right of property in the thing he has produced. This, I take it, is, economically speaking, the foundation on which private property rests, and is, if I mistake not, the most solid and important of all the reasons for the institution. It is one which applies to all the products of human industry — a category comprising (with some unimportant exceptions) moveable wealth in every form, as well as some forms of immoveable wealth, but which obviously can have no application to a commodity which 'no man has made.'[3] It has been urged, indeed, that this reasoning is not rigorous, and that strict logic would require us to extend the description given of land to every form of wealth, moveable as well as immoveable, elaborated by the hand of industry or still lying crude in the earth, since, in the last resort, all is traceable alike to materials furnished by nature — which 'no man has made.' But this is to fall into the error of the Physiocrates,[4] and to confound wealth with matter. The street and palace, the corn and cotton, the goods that fill our warehouses, whatever be the form imparted to them by industry, all, no doubt, derive their material existence in the last resort from things which no man has made: no man has made the matter of which they are composed; but, as *wealth*, as things possessing exchange value, they exist, not through the liberality of nature, but through the labour and enterprise of man. . . .

There may be good reasons for the institution of property in land — on that I am not for the moment concerned to express an opinion — but they are not the reasons which support the institution in its other forms; in particular, landed property is wanting in that foundation — in the judgment of most people, I apprehend, the strongest of all those on which property rests — the expediency of securing the labourer in the fruit of his toil.

The argument, as thus far conducted, carries me, I admit, no further than to this negative conclusion. It rebuts an *à priori* objection to legislative action in such cases as Ireland presents, founded upon an assumed analogy between land and other kinds of wealth. To exhibit the positive reasons which explain and vindicate a policy in the direction contemplated we must go a step further, and bring into view the causes which determine the existence and growth of agricultural rent, and, in relation to these causes, the position occupied by the owners of land on the one hand, and by the general community on the other.

The phenomenon of agricultural rent, let me briefly explain, is economically considered, of this nature: — it consists of the existence in the returns to agricultural industry of a value over and above what is sufficient to replace the capital employed in agriculture with the profit customary in the country. This surplus value arises in this way. The qualities of different soils being different, and the capital applied even to an area of uniform fertility not being all equally productive — farms differing besides in respect of their situation, proximity to market, and other circumstances — it happens that agricultural produce is raised at varying costs; but it is evident that when brought to common markets it will, quality for quality, command the same price. Hence arises, or rather hence would arise in the absence of rent, a vast difference in the profits upon agricultural industry. The produce raised on the best soils, or under other circumstances of exceptional advantage, will bear a much larger proportion to the outlay than that raised under less favourable circumstances; but as it is clear that, in a community where people engage in agriculture with a view to profit, even this latter portion would need to carry such a price as would give the producer the same profits which he might obtain in other occupations (for otherwise he would not engage in its production), it follows that all the produce except this, sold as it is, quality for quality, at the same price, must yield a profit over and above the customary profit of the country. This surplus profit is known to political economists as 'rent,' and

3. Cairnes has a long footnote to this which reads in part: 'To guard against misapprehension, it may be as well to state that I do not recognise in this argument any proof of a "natural right" to property in anything, even in that which our hands have just made. If it is right it should belong to us, it is not . . . because we have made it, but because it is expedient that property so acquired should belong to him who so acquires it . . . . The distinction, then, between landed property and property in the products of industry is not that in the latter case there is a "natural right" to property which does not exist in the former, but that there are grounds of expediency for recognizing the right in the one case which have no place in the other.'

4. The Physiocrats, dominated by François Quesnay (1694-1774) and Turgot, developed economic theories founded on the notion that all wealth derived from land.

we may henceforth conveniently distinguish it from the rent actually paid by cultivators as 'economic rent.' Arising in the manner described, 'economic rent' cannot properly be said to owe its existence to either labourer, capitalist, or landlord. It is rather a factitious value incident to the progress of society under external physical conditions which necessitate the raising of raw produce at different costs. This being its essential nature, it is plain that, so long as the rent paid by the cultivator of a farm does not exceed what the amount of 'economic rent' would be, so long those engaged in agricultural industry will be on neither a better nor a worse footing than those engaged in other occupations. The labourer will have the ordinary wages, the capitalist the ordinary profit of the country. On the other hand, it is evident that if the cultivator be required to pay more than this — if the rent exacted from him encroach upon the domain of wages and profits — he is so far placed at a disadvantage as compared with other producers, and is deprived of the ordinary inducements to industry. It thus becomes a question of capital importance, what provision exists in the conditions of an industrial community to prevent this result; what security we have that — the land of a country being once given up to private speculation — the limits set by 'economic rent' shall, in the main, be observed in the actual rent which landlords obtain. Does the principle of *laissez-faire* — that play of interests developed by competition which in manufacturing and trading operations maintains the harmony of individual with general interests — does this suffice to secure, under ordinary circumstances, the same harmony in the transactions of which land is the subject? If it shall appear that it does not, then, I think, a case will have been made out for the interposition of some other agency — public opinion, custom, or, failing these, direct State action — to supply that which the principle of unrestricted competition has failed to supply — to secure an end which cannot but be regarded as among the legitimate ends of government — the coincidence in an important field of human activity of the individual with the general well-being....

The discussions on the Irish question, whatever differences of opinion they may have disclosed, have at least made one point clear: no settlement of Irish land can be effectual which still leaves with landlords the power of indefinitely raising rent. I think it may be said that amongst those who know the country, and have seriously grappled with the problem, there is a very general agreement upon this point. The end may be approached by different paths and realized in different forms. Compulsory leases, recognition and extension of tenant-right, simple fixity of tenure, are amongst the modes; arbitration courts, the opinion of official experts, the prices of produce, have been suggested as the methods of procedure; but in whatever manner, through whatever machinery, the plans that really promise to be effectual involve at bottom the principle of depriving landlords of the power of raising rent — the principle, therefore, of imposing on the State the obligation of saying what a 'fair rent' is. It is very evident that this must be so — that the landlord, with the power still left him of raising his rent at will, could easily defeat the most stringent provisions of the most apparently drastic land code. Of what avail to the cultivator would be a right of occupancy if the landlord can attach to that right impossible conditions? Of what advantage the right of selling the good-will of his farm, if the rent can be raised at the landlord's discretion against the incoming tenant? Where would be the gain from leases if the limits of the rent are not known? The regulation of rent is thus of the very essence of the case; it is felt to be so by all who have really grasped the problem; and yet it will be found that this topic has in general been kept rather carefully in the background. The reason for this hesitancy it is not difficult to guess. Few Englishmen can hear without something of a cold tremor a proposal to fix rent by law. And yet the consequences are perhaps unfortunate. For all the reserve, it is felt that the efficacy of the several competing schemes really depends in the last resort upon this condition. *Omne ignotum pro mirifico.*[5] Imagination magnifies the difficulty which is kept so carefully out of sight. Conscious that it lies behind, people hesitate to venture into what they expect will prove an economic *cul-de-sac*; or, if they must choose, the danger is they will choose the scheme, not which is most efficacious, nor even which is least revolutionary, but which best contrives to veil this terrible bugbear. Now, if the fixing of rent by State authority be really indispensable to an effective settlement of this question, it is surely well that the

5. *Recte* 'omne ignotum pro magnifico est' (for wonder grows where knowledge fails) — Tacitus, *Agricola* 30, 13.

fact be frankly accepted. I have already shown that Political Economy furnishes no presumption against the propriety of this course. Let us now see if it cannot practically help the solution.*

According to some who pass for authorities, Political Economy has very little to say upon this subject. The worth of land is so much money as it will bring; and to seek a criterion for rent — nay, to attempt to conceive rent at all — otherwise than as it is determined by the market, is in the opinion of these wise persons a hopeless, if not an absurd undertaking. Had they reflected that what they pronounce to be an impossibility is, in point of fact, performed by not a few landlords in Ireland — by every landlord there who does not let his lands on the admittedly ruinous principle of competition — they might have seen reason to distrust the accuracy of scientific knowledge which led to conclusions so flagrantly at variance with fact. Unless, however, in what I have said above on the doctrine of rent I have very grossly misrepresented economic teaching, Political Economy is involved in no such conflict with fact as the view in question would imply. On the contrary, it recognizes in the returns from land the existence of an element — that which I have designated 'economic rent' — which is no other than the 'fair valuation rent' of good landlords. It not only recognizes this element, but can state the conditions determining its amount and the laws of its growth. The 'fair valuation rent' of the popular platform admits, in short, of being reduced to strictly scientific expression. The only point really debatable is as to the means of practically determining the entity in question in given cases. But, as I have just said, the thing is in fact done every day, with sufficient accuracy for practical purposes, by those who manage Irish estates; and that can scarcely be an insoluble problem which scores of landlords and land-agents solve every year.

In approaching the practical problem, there are two parts that will need to be kept distinct — the first starting of the new system, and the keeping it going after it has been started. Over and above the determination of a fair rent, the former will involve the much more serious practical difficulty of appraising tenants' past improvements. Some able writers have expressed themselves as if this latter difficulty might be evaded by permitting to occupiers the sale of their good-will. This would no doubt be so, were the question of rent once settled; but with this still open, the value of the occupation right would be uncertain, while the settlement of the rent plainly cannot take place till the abatement in consideration of tenants' improvements is known. Thus the necessity of an independent valuation of tenants' improvements, wherever landlord and tenant cannot themselves come to an agreement, is inherent in the case. Questions of this kind, involving, as they often will, disputes about minute details, can obviously only be satisfactorily dealt with by authorities adjudicating in the localities, and taking evidence in disputed cases from competent persons who have inspected the farms. Complicated and delicate questions no doubt they will be, demanding from those to whom the settlement is entrusted no small amount of patience, sagacity, and firmness; but questions not less complicated and delicate have already been unravelled by Englishmen in India; and it is hard to see why the same qualities of mind which have threaded their way through the mazes of Hindu customary law to results of order and substantial justice should not be equal to dealing with the problem, analogous, but less complicated, and less remote from English modes of thought, presented by Irish land.

These will be the initiatory difficulties; but these once surmounted, past improvements once ascertained, existing rents once adjusted to existing circumstances, there is no reason that the future working of the status principle should not be brought under general rules, and reduced to a system. Confining our attention to rent, with which alone I am at present concerned, the problem, as I conceive it, will then lie in such an adjustment of this element from time to time as shall satisfy and reconcile the two following conditions:— (1) to secure to the cultivators, so long as they fulfil the conditions of their tenure, the due reward of their industry; and (2) to do substantial justice to the reasonable expectations of those who, on the faith of Acts of Parliament and the past policy of the country, have embarked their fortunes in Irish land....

*Throughout the discussions on the Irish Land Act the Government again and again denied their intention to interfere with the landlord's power of raising his rent; but nothing is more certain than that the Act does interfere, though in a circuitous and indirect way, with this power; and further, that it owes whatever success it has achieved to the knowledge shared alike by tenants and landlords that this power resides in the new law.

[A quarter of a century after the Famine, Cairnes was still obliged to attack the claims of economic orthodoxy to the status of a science. 'Political Economy and Laissez-Faire' was an introductory lecture, delivered in University College, London in November 1870. Cairnes had become professor of political economy there in 1866 — while still professor of jurisprudence and political economy at Queen's College, Galway. It is his most damaging attack on the weakness of the *laissez-faire* doctrine.]

POLITICAL ECONOMY AND LAISSEZ-FAIRE

... Looking around us on the social needs of the time, we are bound, I think, to confess that we do not find much work of a merely negative sort to do; and we must therefore acknowledge that, if Political Economy be merely what a widely prevalent opinion supposes it to be, if the sum and outcome of its teaching be *laissez-faire*, the field for its activity, in this country at least, must henceforth be a narrow one. Under these circumstances, it is not strange if the interest felt in the study is of a languid sort. Where the opinion prevails that *laissez-faire* marks the limit of industrial reform, that when we have set individual enterprise free we have done all that in such matters can be done, Political Economy will naturally be regarded with a good-natured tolerance in consideration of its past services, combined with a profound indifference, based on the conviction that it has become in the course of events a practically obsolete scheme of thought. Such, it seems to me, is in point of fact the state of feeling on this subject amongst a large number of educated people in this country at the present time.

Amongst a large number, but not universally; for there are those whose faith in *laissez-faire* is not quite so absolute as that of the majority; who hold that there are ends to be compassed in social and industrial life which can only be reached through the action of society as an organized whole; and that, while the mere negative and destructive part of industrial reform has been well-nigh completed, a work of positive and reconstructive reform still lies before us. What will be the attitude of this section of thinkers towards a speculation putting itself forward as a scientific vindication of the principle of 'letting things alone'? Inevitably one of hostility. When people think they see before them a field for useful action, in which good may be done by measures of a positive kind, they naturally feel impatient of a system propounding *laissez-faire* as the last word of human wisdom. Thus, if I have correctly seized the current impression respecting this branch of speculation, we have found at least a partial explanation of the phenomenon which I have proposed for consideration. People neglect Political Economy because they regard it as practically obsolete, as out of relation to the actual work of the time; or they oppose it because they think it has begun to be obstructive; and the view taken by depreciators and opponents is in each case the nature result of the conception they have formed of the study. And here it is that I join issue with both classes. I altogether deny the correctness of their view of the science; and, as the most effectual means of exploding it, I shall now endeavour to shown that the maxim of *laissez-faire* has no scientific basis whatever, but is at best a mere handy rule of practice, useful, perhaps, as a reminder to statesmen on which side the presumption lies in questions of industrial legislation, but totally destitute of all scientific authority.

In proceeding to argue this point, I must ask you, in the first place, to note what this doctrine of *laissez-faire*, if it is to be taken as a scientific principle, really means. The implied assertion, as I understand it, is this: that, taking human beings as they are, in the actual state of moral and intellectual development they have reached; taking account, further, of the physical conditions with which they are surrounded in the world; lastly, accepting the institution of private property as understood and maintained in most modern states, — the promptings of self-interest will lead individuals, in all that range of their conduct which has to do with their material well-being, spontaneously to follow that course which is most for their own good and for the good of all. Such is the assertion with which we have now to deal; and you will at once see that it involves the two following assumptions: first, that the interests of human beings are fundamentally the same — that what is most for my interest is also most for the interest of other people; and, secondly, that individuals know their interests in the sense in which they are coincident with the interests of others, and that, in the absence of coercion, they will, in this sense, follow them. If these two propositions be made out, the policy of *laissez-faire* — the policy, that is to say, of absolute abstention on the part of the State in all that concerns material well-being — follows with scientific rigour. But can they be made out? For my part I am disposed to accept the first one; I am disposed to believe that human interests, well understood, are fundamentally at one; only let me in passing suggest a caution. Let us not confound the statement that *human* interests are at one with the statement that *class* interests are at one. The latter I believe to be as false as the former is true, and, moreover, to be one of those plausible optimist falsities against which it especially behoves us in the present day to be on our guard. But accepting the major premiss of the syllogism, that the interests of human beings are fundamentally the same, how as to the minor? — how as to the assumption that people know their interests in the sense in which they are identical with the interests of others, and that they spontaneously follow them *in this sense*? . . . . Nothing is easier than to show that people follow their interest, in the sense in which they understand their interest. But between this and following their interest in the sense in which it is coincident with that of other people, a chasm yawns. This chasm in the argument of the *laissez-faire* school has never been bridged. The advocates of the doctrine shut their eyes and leap over it.

For, to examine the question more nearly, and to come at once to the important point — granting that people may, in a certain sense, be trusted to see most clearly their own interest, and to pursue with avidity what they so regard, what is it that people understand to be their interest? What did landlords, as a class, understand to be their interest down to 1846, when they maintained the Corn Laws as indispensable to their rents, and the prop of their political power? What do the same class now understand as their interest, when they avail themselves of the power given them by the law to put their estates in settlement, create life-interests, entails, collateral charges, interposing endless artificial obstacles between the land of the country and the living people who inhabit it, to the practical exclusion from the possession of land of the enormous majority of Englishmen? What do Irish landlords understand to be their interest when they are only withheld by fear of assassination, or by law, from evicting their tenants in order to consolidate their estates? What did employers in former days understand to be their interest when they enacted statutes of labourers? or, in more recent times, when a ten hours' Act has become necessary to protect women and children against the consequences of an unscrupulous pursuit of gain? What is the notion those farmers form of their interest who employ the gang system as described in recent parliamentary reports? or, again, those members of trades-unions, who pass rules against task-work and in favour of uniform wages for the skilful and the inept, the idle and the industrious, rules against machinery and in favour of inefficient methods of manual labour, rules against the admission of their fellows to sharing with themselves the opportunities of a livelihood offered by the market, rules, in a word, against the most efficacious use of man's power over nature, and the fair distribution of the proceeds of toil — what, in the idea of these trades-unionists, is their interest? To give one instance more, what was the notion of their interest entertained by the slaveholding aristocracy in the Southern States of the American Union, who, seeing with their own eyes the exhausting and ruinous effects of the system they upheld; seeing its influence in preventing the rise of a skilled industrial class, and in thus almost wholly excluding manufacturing industry from the States where it prevailed; seeing its effects in consigning to lawless barbarism more than a half of the entire rural population, — nevertheless rose in arms to maintain it, and not merely to maintain, but to extend it far and wide over the continent of America? Or, turning from particular examples to broad results, can any one seriously consider the present condition of the inhabitants of these islands — these islands where industrial freedom has for nearly half a century had greater scope than in any previous age or in any other country, but where also the extremes of wealth and poverty are found in harsher contrast than they have been ever found elsewhere; where one man consumes more value in a single meal than goes to feed and clothe the family of another for a month; where the entire land of the country is owned by less than a hundred thousand persons out of a population of thirty millions; where one in every twenty persons is a pauper; where the great bulk of the agricultural population look forward with calm resignation to spending their old age in a workhouse; while the artisan population of the towns find themselves about once in ten years in the midst of a frightful commercial catastrophe, which consigns hundreds of thousands to ruin — I ask if any one can seriously consider this state of things, and yet repose in absolute satisfaction and confidence on his maxim of *laissez-faire*? Nor is it merely the co-existence of this state of things with an unparalleled freedom in all directions of industrial and commercial enterprise that we have to consider. The truly significant circumstance is that the policy in question, the policy expressed by *laissez-faire*, has been steadily progressive for nearly half a century, and yet we have no sign of mitigation in the harshest features of our social state. I beg of you to consider the lesson taught by the repeal of the Corn Laws. That was one of the most important steps ever taken in carrying out the policy of *laissez-faire* — as all economists believe a thoroughly sound and wise step. Well, now, observe what the repeal of the Corn Laws has done for us, and also what it has not done for us. It has given an immense impulse to our general trade; our exports and imports have, since the passing of the measure, enormously increased; our wealth and population have advanced with unexampled rapidity. But the able men who led the agitation for the repeal of the Corn Laws promised much more than this. They told us that the Poor Laws were to follow the Corn Laws; that pauperism would disappear with the restrictions upon trade, and the workhouses ere long become obselete institutions. I fear this part of the programme has scarcely been fulfilled. Those ugly social features, those violent contrasts of poverty and wealth, that strike so unpleasantly the eye of every foreign observer in this country, are still painfully prominent. The signs of the extinction of pauperism are not yet very apparent ....

There is then no evidence, either in what we know of the conduct of men in the present stage of their development, or yet in the large experience we have had of the working of *laissez-faire*, to warrant the assumption that lies at the root of this doctrine. Human beings know and follow their interests according to their lights and dispositions; but not necessarily, nor in practice always, in that sense in which the interest of the individual is coincident with that of others and of the whole. It follows that there is no security that the economic phenomena of society, as at present constituted, will always arrange themselves spontaneously in the way which is most for the common good. In other words, *laissez-faire* falls to the ground as a scientific doctrine. I say as a scientific doctrine; for let us be careful not to overstep the limits of our argument. It is one thing to repudiate the scientific authority of *laissez-faire*, freedom of contract, and so forth; it is a totally different thing to set up the opposite principle of State control, the doctrine of paternal government. For my part I accept neither one doctrine nor the other; and, as a practical rule, I hold *laissez-faire* to be incomparably the safer guide. Only let us remember that it is a *practical rule*, and not a doctrine of science; a rule in the main sound, but like most other sound practical rules, liable to numerous exceptions; above all, a rule which must never for a moment be allowed to stand in the way of the candid consideration of any promising proposal of social or industrial reform. It is from this point of view that the argument I have been urging assumes a practical aspect. *Laissez-faire*, freedom of contract, and phrases of like import, have of late become somewhat of bugbears with a large number of people. It is enough to mention them, to discredit by anticipation the most useful practical scheme. What did we hear during the discussions on the Irish Land Bill? Political Economy again and again appealed to as having pronounced against that measure. Now, what did this mean? Simply that the Bill interfered with freedom of contract, violated the rule of *laissez-faire* — charges perfectly true, and which would have been decisive against the Bill had these phrases really possessed the scientific authority which members of Parliament supposed them to possess. Now, it is against this understanding of the doctrine that my argument is directed. So understood, I hold it to be a pretentious sophism, destitute of foundation in nature and fact, and rapidly becoming an obstruction and nuisance in public affairs....

Alike in the case of the physical and of the economic world, the facts we find existing are the results of causes, between which and them the connection is constant and invariable. It is, then, the constant relations exhibited in economic phenomena that we have in view, when we speak of the laws of the phenomena of wealth; and in the exposition of these laws consists the science of Political Economy. If you ask me wherein lies the utility of such an exposition of economic laws, I answer, in precisely the same circumstance which constitutes the utility of all scientific knowledge. It teaches us the conditions of our power in relation to the facts of economic existence, the means by which, in the domain of material well-being, to attain our ends. It is by such knowledge that man becomes the minister and interpreter of Nature, and learns to control Nature by obeying her.

And now I beg you to observe what follows from this mode of conceiving our study. In the first place, then, you will remark that, as thus conceived, Political Economy stands apart from all particular systems of social or industrial existence. It has nothing to do with *laissez-faire* any more than with communism; with freedom of contract any more than with paternal government, or with systems of *status*. It stands apart from all particular systems, and is moreover absolutely neutral as between all. Not, of course, that the knowledge which it gives may not be employed to recommend some and to discredit others. This is inevitable, and is only the proper and legitimate use of economic knowledge. But this notwithstanding, the science is neutral, as between social schemes, in this important sense. It pronounces no judgment on the worthiness or desirableness of the ends aimed at in such systems. It tells us what their effects will be as regards a specific class of facts, thus contributing data towards the formation of a sound opinion respecting them. But here its function ends. The data thus furnished may indeed go far to determine our judgment, but they do not necessarily, and should not in practice always, do so. For there are few practical problems which do not present other aspects than the purely economical — political, moral, educational, artistic aspects — and these may involve consequences so weighty as to turn the scale against purely economic solutions....

Now I desire to call particular attention to this characteristic of economic science, because I do not think it is at all generally appreciated, and because some serious and indeed lamentable consequences have arisen from overlooking it. For example, it is sometimes supposed that, because Political Economy comprises its expositions theories of wages, profits, and rent, the science is *therefore* committed to the approval of our present mode of industrial life, under which three distinct classes, labourers, capitalists, and landlords, receive remuneration in those forms. Under this impression, some social reformers, whose ideal of industrial life involves a modification of our existing system, have thought themselves called upon to denounce and deride economic science, as forsooth seeking to stereotype the existing forms of industrial life, and of course therefore opposed to their views. But this is a complete mistake. Economic science has no more connection with our present industrial system than the science of mechanics has with our present system of railways. Our existing railway lines have been laid down according to the best extant mechanical knowledge; but we do not think it necessary on this account, as a preliminary to improving our railways, to denounce mechanical science. If wages, profits, and rent find a place in economic theories, this is simply because these *are* the forms which the distribution of wealth assumes as society is now constituted....

ALEXANDER MARTIN SULLIVAN

(1830-84)

from: NEW IRELAND (1877)

[Sullivan's influence was great because he was the sole proprietor and editor of *The Nation* from 1855 to 1876. Renowned for his hostility to the Fenians and to the left-wing element in Young Ireland, he provides a counter-balance to the genocidal view of the Famine. Looking back over thirty years of public life, Sullivan is able to give an interesting account of the changes that the Famine had brought about. His fulsome sentiment and political mildness is characteristic of the particular species of constitutional Irish nationalism of which he is an important, although never well-loved, representative.]

CHAPTER VI

'THE BLACK FORTY-SEVEN'

There is probably no subject on which such painful misunderstanding and bitter recrimination have prevailed between the peoples of England and Ireland as the Irish famine. The enmities and antagonisms arising out of other historical events were at all events comprehensible. The havoc and devastation which ensued upon the Royalist-Cromwellian war of 1641-1650, the confiscations and proscriptions which followed the Stuart struggle in 1690, the insurrection of 1798, and the overthrow of the Irish constitution in 1800, were causes of ire, on the one side or the other, as to the reality of which there was at least no controversy. But it was not so in this case. The English people, remembering only the sympathy and compassion which they felt, the splendid contributions which they freely bestowed in that sad time, are shocked and angered beyond endurance when they hear Irishmen refer to the famine as a 'slaughter.' In Ireland, on the other hand, the burning memory of horrors which more prompt and competent action on the part of the ruling authorities might have considerably averted, seems to overwhelm all other recollection, and the noble generosity of the English people appears to be forgotten in a frenzy of reproach against the English Government of that day.

I know not whether the time has even yet arrived when that theme can be fairly treated, and when a calm and just apportionment of blame and merit may be attempted. Today, full thirty years after the event, I tremble to contemplate it.

In 1841 the population of Ireland was 8,175,124 souls. By 1845 it had probably reached to nearly nine millions. The increase had been fairly continuous for at least a century, and had become rapid between 1820 and 1840. To any one looking beneath the surface the condition of the country was painfully precarious. Nine millions of a population living at best in a light-hearted and hopeful hand-to-mouth contentment, totally dependent on the hazards of one crop, destitute of manufacturing industries, and utterly without reserve or resource to fall back upon in time of reverse; what did all this mean but a state of things critical and alarming in the extreme? Yet no one seemed conscious of danger. The potato crop had been abundant for four or five years, and respite from dearth and distress was comparative happiness and prosperity. Moreover, the temperance movement had come to make the 'good times' still better. Everything looked bright. No one concerned himself to discover how slender and treacherous was the foundation for this general hopefulness and confidence.

Yet signs of the coming storm had been given. Partial famine caused by failing harvests had indeed been intermittent in Ireland, and quite recently warnings that ought not to have been mistaken or neglected had given notice that the esculent which formed the sole dependence of the peasant millions was subject to some mysterious blight. In 1844 it was stricken in America, but in Ireland the yield was healthy and plentiful as ever. The harvest of 1845 promised to be the richest gathered for many years. Suddenly, in one short month, in one week it might be said, the withering breath of a simoom[1] seemed to sweep the land, blasting all in its path. I myself saw whole tracts of potato growth changed *in one night* from smiling luxuriance to a shrivelled and blackened waste. A shout of alarm arose. But the buoyant nature of the Celtic peasant did not yet give way. The crop was so profuse that it was expected the healthy portion would reach an average result. Winter revealed the alarming fact that the tubers had rotted in pit and store-house. Nevertheless the farmers, like hapless men who double their stakes to recover losses, made only the more strenuous exertions to till a larger breadth in 1846. Although already feeling the pinch of sore distress, if not actual famine, they worked as if for dear life; they begged and borrowed on any terms the means whereby to crop the land once more. The pawn-offices were choked with the humble finery that had shone at the village dance or christening feast; the banks and local money-lenders were besieged with appeals for credit. Meals were stinted, backs were bared. Anything, anything to tide over the interval to the harvest of 'Forty-six.'

O God, it is a dreadful thought that all this effort was but more surely leading them to ruin! It was this harvest of Forty-six that sealed their doom. Not partially but completely, utterly, hopelessly it perished. As in the previous year, all promised brightly up to the close of July. Then, suddenly, in a night, whole areas were blighted; and this time, alas! no portion of the crop escaped. A cry of agony and despair went up all over the land. The last desperate stake for life had been played, and all was lost.

The doomed people realised but too well what was before them. Last year's premonitory sufferings had exhausted them; and now? — they must die!

My native district figures largely in the gloomy

1. A suffocating sand-laden wind of North Africa.

record of that dreadful time. I saw the horrible phantasmagoria — would God it were but that! — pass before my eyes. Blank stolid dismay, a sort of stupor, fell upon the people, contrasting remarkably with the fierce energy put forth a year before. It was no uncommon sight to see the cottier and his little family seated on the garden fence gazing all day long in moody silence at the blighted plot that had been their last hope. Nothing could arouse them. You spoke; they answered not. You tried to cheer them; they shook their heads. I never saw so sudden and so terrible a transformation.

When first in the autumn of 1845 the partial blight appeared, wise voices were raised in warning to the Government that a frightful catastrophe was at hand; yet even then began that fatal circumlocution and inaptness when it maddens one to think of. It would be utter injustice to deny that the Government made exertions which judged by ordinary emergencies would be prompt and considerable. But judged by the awful magnitude of the evil then at hand or actually befallen, they were fatally tardy and inadequate. When at length the executive did hurry, the blunders of precipitancy outdid the disasters of excessive deliberation.

In truth the Irish famine was one of those stupendous calamities which the rules and formulæ or ordinary constitutional administration were unable to cope with, and which could be efficiently encountered only by the concentration of plenary powers and resources in some competent 'despotism' located in the scene of disaster. It was easy to foresee the result of an attempt to deal 'at long range' with such an evil — to manage it from Downing Street, London, according to orthodox routine. Again and again the Government were warned, not by heedless orators or popular leaders, but by men of the highest position and soundest repute in Ireland, that even with the very best intentions on their part, mistake and failure must abound in any attempt to grapple with the famine by the ordinary machinery of Government. Many efforts, bold and able efforts, were made by the Government and by Parliament eighteen months subsequently — I refer especially to the measures taken in the session of 1847. But, unfortunately, everything seemed to come too late. Delay made all the difference. In October 1845 the Irish Mansion House Relief Committee implored the Government to call Parliament together and throw open the ports. The Government refused. Again and again the terrible urgency of the case, the magnitude of the disaster at hand, was pressed on the executive. It was the obstinate refusal of the Government to listen to such remonstrances and entreaties, and the sad verification subsequently of such apprehensions, that implanted in the Irish mind the bitter memories which still occasionally find vent in passionate accusation of 'England.'

Not but the Government had many and weighty arguments in behalf of the course they took. Firstly, they feared exaggeration, and waited for official investigation and report. Even when official testimony was forthcoming, the Cabinet in London erred as the Irish peasantry did, in trusting somewhat that the harvest of 1846 would change gloom to joy. When the worst came in 1846-47, much precious time was lost through misunderstanding and recrimination between the Irish landlords and the executive; charges of neglect of duties on one hand, and of incapacity on the other, passing freely to and fro. No doubt the Government feared waste, prodigality, and abuse if it placed absolute power and unlimited supplies in the hands of an Irish board; and one must allow that, to a commerical-minded people, the violations of the doctrines of political economy involved in every suggestion and demand shouted across the Channel from Ireland were very alarming. Yet in the end it was found — all too late, unfortunately — that those doctrines were inapplicable in such a case. They had to be flung aside in 1847. Had they been discarded a year or two sooner a million of lives might have been saved.

The situation bristled with difficulties. 'Do not demoralise the people by pauper doles, but give them employment,' said one counsellor. 'Beware how you interfere with the labour market,' answered another. 'It is no use voting millions to be paid away on relief works while you allow the price of food to be run up four hundred per cent.; set up Government depôts for sale of food at reasonable price,' cried many wise and far-seeing men. 'Utterly opposed to the teachings of Adam Smith,' responded Lord John Russell.

At first the establishment of public soup-kitchens under local relief committees, subsidised by Government, was relied upon to arrest the famine. I doubt if the world ever saw so huge a demoralisation, so great a degradation, visited upon a once high-spirited and sensitive people. All over the country large iron boilers were set up in which what was called 'soup' was concocted; later on Indian-meal stirabout was boiled. Around these boilers on the roadside there daily moaned and shrieked and fought and scuffled crowds of gaunt, cadaverous creatures that once had been men and women made in the image of God. The feeding of dogs in a kennel was far more decent and orderly. I once thought — ay, and often bitterly said, in public and in private — that never, never would our people recover the shameful humiliation of that brutal public soup-boiler scheme. I frequently stood and watched the scene till tears blinded me and I almost choked with grief and passion. It was heart-breaking, almost maddening, to see; but help for it there was none.

The Irish poor-law system early broke down under the strain which the famine imposed. Until 1846 the workhouses were shunned and detested by the Irish poor. Relief of destitution had always been regarded by the Irish as a sort of religious duty or fraternal succour. Poverty was a misfortune, not a crime. When, however, relief was offered, on the penal condition of an imprisonment that sundered the family tie, and which, by destroying home, howsoever humble, shut out all hope of future recovery, it was indignantly spurned. Scores of times I have seen some poor widow before the workhouse board clasp her little children tightly to her heart and sob aloud, 'No, no, your honour. If they are to be parted from me I'll not come in. I'll beg the wide world with them.'

But soon beneath the devouring pangs of starvation even this holy affection had to give way, and the famishing people poured into the workhouses, which quickly choked with the dying and the dead. Such privations had been endured in every case before this hated ordeal was faced, that the people entered the Bastile merely to die. The parting scenes of husband and wife, father and mother and children, at the board-room door would melt a heart of stone. Too well they felt it was to be an eternal severance, and that this loving embrace was to be their last on earth. The warders tore them asunder — the husband from the wife, the mother from the child — for 'discipline' required that it should be so. But, with the famine fever in every ward, and the air around them laden with disease and death, they knew their fate, and parted like victims at the foot of the guillotine.

It was not long until the workhouses overflowed and could admit no more. Rapidly as the death-rate made vacancies, the pressure of applicants overpowered all resources. Worse still, bankruptcy came on many a union. In some the poor-rate rose to twenty-two shillings on the pound, and very nearly the entire rural population of several were needing relief. In a few cases, I am sorry to say, the horrible idea seemed to seize the landowners on the boards that all rates would be ineffectual, and that, as their imposition would result only in ruining 'property,' it was as well to 'let things take their course.' Happily an act of Parliament was passed in 1846 which gave the poor-law commissioners in Dublin power to deal with cases of delay or refusal to make adequate provision for maintenance of the workhouse. All such boards were abolished by sealed order, and paid vice-guardians were appointed in their place. To these, as well as to elected boards willing to face their duty, the commissioners were empowered to advance, by way of loan, secured on the lands within the union, funds sufficient to carry on the poor-law system. Had it not been for this arrangement, the workhouses would have closed altogether in many parts of the country.

The conduct of the Irish landlords throughout the famine period has been variously described, and has been, I believe, generally condemned. I consider the censure visited on them too sweeping. I hold it to be in some respects cruelly unjust. On many of them no blame too heavy could possibly fall. A large number were permanent absentees; their ranks were swelled by several who early fled the post of duty at home — cowardly and selfish deserters of a brave and faithful people. Of those who remained, some may have grown callous; it is impossible to contest authentic instances of brutal heartlessness here and there. But granting all that has to be entered on the dark debtor side, the overwhelming balance is the other way. The bulk of the resident Irish landlords manfully did their best in that dread hour.* If they did too little compared

*No adequate tribute has ever been paid to the memory of those Irish landlords — and they were men of every party and creed — who perished martyrs to duty in that awful time; who did not fly the plague-reeking workhouse or fever-tainted court. Their names would make a goodly roll of honour. The people of Bantry still mourn for Mr. Richard White of Inchiclogh, cousin of Lord Bantry, who early fell in this way. Mr. Martin, M.P. — 'Dick Martin,' Prince of Connemara — caught fever while acting as a magistrate, and was swept away. One of the most touching stories I ever heard was that told me by an eye-witness of how Mr. Nolan of Ballinderry (father of Captain J. P. Nolan, M.P.), braving the deadly typhus in Tuam workhouse, was struck down, amidst the grief of a people who mourn him to this day.

with what the landlord class in England would have done in similar case, it was because little was in their power. The famine found most of the resident landed gentry of Ireland on the brink of ruin. They were heritors of estates heavily overweighted with the debts of a bygone generation. Broad lands and lordly mansions were held by them on settlements and conditions that allowed small scope for the exercise of individual liberality. To these landowners the failure of one year's rental receipts meant mortgage foreclosure and hopeless ruin. Yet cases might be named by the score in which such men scorned to avert by pressure on their suffering tenantry the fate they saw impending over them. They 'went down with the ship.'

In the autumn of 1846 relief works were set on foot, the Government having received parliamentary authority to grant baronial loans for such undertakings. There might have been found many ways of applying these funds in reproductive employment, but the modes decided on were draining and road-making. Of course it was not possible to provide very rapidly the engineering staff requisite for surveying and laying out so many thousands of new roads all over the country; but eventually the scheme was somehow hurried into operation. The result was in every sense deplorable failure. The wretched people were by this time too wasted and emaciated to work. The endeavour to do so under an inclement winter sky only hastened death. They tottered at daybreak to the roll-call; vainly tried to wheel the barrow or ply the pick, but fainted away on the 'cutting,' or lay down on the wayside to rise no more. As for the 'roads' on which so much money was wasted, and on which so many lives were sacrificed, hardly any of them were finished. Miles of grass-grown earthworks throughout the country now mark their course and commemorate for posterity one of the gigantic blunders of the famine time.

The first remarkable sign of the havoc which death was making was the decline and disappearance of funerals. Amongst the Irish people a funeral was always a great display, and participation in the procession was for all neighbours and friends a sacred duty. A 'poor' funeral — that is, one thinly attended — was considered disrespectful to the deceased and reproachful to the living. The humblest peasant was borne to the grave by a parochial *cortège*. But one could observe in the summer of '46 that, as funerals became more frequent, there was a rapid decline in the number of attendants, until at length persons were stopped on the road and requested to assist in conveying the coffin a little way further. Soon, alas! neither coffin nor shroud could be supplied. Daily in the street and on the footway some poor creature lay down as if to sleep, and presently was stiff and stark. In our district it was a common occurrence to find on opening the front door in early morning, leaning against it, the corpse of some victim who in the night-time had 'rested' in its shelter. We raised a public subscription, and employed two men with horse and cart to go around each day and gather up the dead. One by one they were taken to a great pit at Ardnabrahair Abbey[2] and dropped through the hinged bottom of a 'trap-coffin' into a common grave below. In the remoter rural districts even this rude sepulture was impossible. In the field and by the ditch side the victims lay as they fell, till some charitable hand was found to cover them with the adjacent soil.

It was the fever which supervened on the famine that wrought the greatest slaughter and spread the greatest terror. For this destroyer when it came spared no class, rich or poor. As long as it was 'the hunger' alone that raged, it was no deadly peril to visit the sufferers; but not so now. To come within the reach of this contagion was certain death. Whole families perished unvisited and unassisted. By levelling above their corpses the sheeling[3] in which they died, the neighbours gave them a grave.

No pen can trace nor tongue relate the countless deeds of heroism and self-sacrifice which this dreadful visitation called forth on the part, preeminently, of two classes in the community — the Catholic clergy and the dispensary doctors of Ireland. I have named the Catholic clergy, not that those of the Protestant denominations did not furnish many instances of devotion fully as striking,† but because on the former obviously fell

†The Protestant curate of my native parish in 1847 was the Rev. Alexander Ben Hallowell, subsequently rector of Clonakilty. There were comparatively few of his own flock in a way to suffer from the famine; but he dared death daily in his desperate efforts to save the perishing creatures around him. A poor hunchback named Richard O'Brien lay dying of the plague in a deserted hovel at a place called 'the Custom Gap.' Mr. Hallowell passing by, heard the moans and went in. A shocking sight met his view. On some rotten straw in a dark corner lay poor 'Dick' naked, except for a few rags across his body. Mr. Hallowell rushed to the door and saw a young friend on the road: 'Run, run with this shilling and buy me

2. In County Cork.
3. Usually spelt shieling: a hut.

the brunt of the trial. For them there was no flinching. A call to administer the last rites of religion to the inmate of a plague-ward or fever-shed *must* be, and is, obeyed by the Catholic priest, though death to himself be the well-known consequence. The fatality amongst the two classes I have mentioned, clergymen and doctors, was lamentable. Christian heroes, martyrs for humanity, their names are blazoned on no courtly roll; yet shall they shine upon an eternal page, brighter than the stars!

But even this dark cloud of the Irish famine had its silver lining. If it is painful to recall the disastrous errors of irresolution and panic, one can linger gratefully over memories of Samaritan philanthropy, of efficacious generosity, of tenderest sympathy. The people of England behaved nobly; and assuredly not less munificent were the citizens of the great American Republic, which had already become the home of thousands of the Irish race. From every considerable town in England there poured subscriptions, amounting in the aggregate to hundreds of thousands of pounds. From America came a truly touching demonstration of national sympathy. Some citizens of the States contributed two shiploads of breadstuffs, and the American Government decided to furnish the ships which should bring the offering to the Irish shore. Accordingly two war-vessels, the *Macedonian* and the *Jamestown* frigates, having had their armaments removed, their 'gun-decks' displaced and cargo bulk-heads put up, were filled to the gunwale with best American flour and biscuits, and despatched on their errand of mercy. It happened that just previously the British naval authorities had rather strictly refused the loan of a ship for a like purpose, as being quite opposed to all departmental regulations (which, to be sure, it was), and a good deal of angry feeling was called forth by the refusal. Yet had it a requiting contrast in the despatch from England, by voluntary associations there, of several deputations or embassies of succour, charged to visit personally the districts in Ireland most severely afflicted, and to distribute with their own hands the benefactions they brought.

Foremost in this blessed work were the Society of Friends, the English members of that body co-operating with its central committee in Dublin. Amongst the most active and fearless of their representatives was a young Yorkshire Quaker, whose name, I doubt not, is still warmly remembered by Connemara peasants. He drove from village to village, he walked bog and moor, rowed the lake and climbed the mountain, fought death, as it were, hand to hand, in brave resolution to save the people. His correspondence from the scene of his labours would constitute in itself a graphic memorial of the Irish famine. That young 'Yorkshire Quaker' of 1847 was destined a quarter of a century later to be known to the empire as a minister of the Crown — the Right Hon. W. E. Forster, M.P.[4]. . . .

It is a remarkable fact that the traveller who now visits the west and south of Ireland, and seeks to gather from the people reminiscences of the famine time, will find praise and blame a good deal mingled as to nearly every other relief agency of the period; but naught save grateful recollection of the unostentatious, kindly, prompt, generous, and efficacious action of the Friends' committee. Fondly as the Catholic Irish revere the memory of their own priests who suffered with and died for them in that fearful time, they give a place in their prayers to the 'good Quakers, God bless them,' Jonathan Pim, Richard Allen, Richard Webb, and William Edward Forster.

The Irish famine of 1847 had results, social and political, that constitute it one of the most important events in Irish history for more than two hundred years. It is impossible for any one who knew the country previous to that period, and who has thoughtfully studied it since, to avoid the conclusion that so much has been destroyed, or so greatly changed, that the Ireland of old times will be seen no more.

The losses will, I would fain hope, be in a great degree repaired; the gains entirely retained. Yet much that was precious was engulfed, I fear,

some wine,' he cried. Then he re-entered the hovel, stripped off his own clothes, and with own hands put upon the plague-stricken hunchback the flannel vest and drawers and the shirt of which he had just divested himself. I know this to be true. *I* was the 'young friend' who went for and brought the wine.

4. William Edward Forster (1818-86) visited Connemara on a relief mission in 1845-49. He was under-secretary for the colonies in 1865. Sullivan was writing before Forster's appointment as chief secretary for Ireland, during the Land War (1880-82). In that role, he became hated throughout Ireland for his coercion measures, under which he imprisoned Parnell, Michael Davitt and many hundreds of others. He was nicknamed 'Buckshot' Forster because he had buckshot substituted for bullets for the Royal Irish Constabulary. He resigned because of a disagreement with Gladstone over the Kilmainham 'Treaty' with Parnell. His successor was Lord Frederick Cavendish, who was assassinated by the Invincibles.

beyond recovery. 'Here are twenty miles of country, sir,' said a dispensary doctor to me, 'and before the famine there was not a padlock from end to end of it.'

Under the pressure of hunger, ravenous creatures prowled around barn and storehouse, stealing corn, potatoes, cabbage, turnips — anything, in a word, that might be eaten. Later on the fields had to be watched, gun in hand, or the seed was rooted up and devoured raw. This state of things struck a fatal blow at some of the most beautiful traits of Irish rural life. It destroyed the simple confidence that bolted no door; it banished for ever a custom which throughout the island was of almost universal obligation — the housing for the night, with cheerful welcome, of any poor wayfarer who claimed hospitality. Fear of 'the fever,' even where no apprehension of robbery was entertained, closed every door, and the custom, once killed off, has not revived. A thousand kindly usages and neighbourly courtesies were swept away. When *sauve qui peut* had resounded throughout a country for three years of alarm and disaster, human nature becomes contracted in its sympathies, and 'every one for himself' becomes a maxim of life and conduct long after. The open-handed, open-hearted ways of the rural population have been visibly affected by the 'Forty-seven' ordeal. Their ancient sports and pastimes everywhere disappeared, and in many parts of Ireland have never returned. The outdoor games, the hurling-match, and the village dance are seen no more.

With the greater seriousness of character which the famine period has imprinted on the Irish people, some notable changes for the better must be recognised. Providence, forethought, economy are studied and valued as they never were before. There is more method, strictness, and punctuality in business transactions. There is a graver sense of responsibility on all hands. For the first time the future seems to be earnestly thought of, and its possible vicissitudes kept in view. More steadiness of purpose, more firmness and determination of character, mark the Irish peasantry of the new era. God has willed that in the midst of such awful sufferings some share of blessings should fall on the sorely shattered nation.

MICHAEL DAVITT

(1846-1906)

from: THE FALL OF FEUDALISM IN IRELAND (1904)

[In this excerpt from his famous book, Davitt repeats Mitchel's attack on the collusion during the Famine between the British government and the Irish landlords at the expense of the people. He goes further than Mitchel by including within this conspiratorial circle the Irish catholic clergy who, once the tithe war was over and the Maynooth grant increased, were willing collaborators with the British government in preaching the virtues of law and order to a starving people. Even the alignment of these forces is not a sufficiently satisfactory explanation, in Davitt's view, for the meekness and helplessness with which the Irish went to their doom. The development of the genocide theory had always had, implicit within it, the justification for a countering violence which, however hopeless, would be at least better than abject surrender. This version of Fenian doctrine was to reappear in even more intense form in the writings of Patrick Pearse. But Davitt still saw the land question as central to the solution of the national question, tending to argue that repeal of the Union was for the inhabitants of the towns what settlement of the land question was for the rural inhabitants. In this, he repeated what Lalor had already said. The problem of linking the land question and the constitutional question was to be solved for him later in his alliance with Parnell.]

CHAPTER V

I. — THE GREAT FAMINE AND THE YOUNG IRELANDERS

It is related that Mr. John O'Connell, M.P., eldest son of the Liberator, read aloud in Conciliation

Hall, Dublin, a letter he had received from a Catholic bishop in West Cork, in 1847, in which this sentence occurred, 'The famine is spreading with fearful rapidity, and scores of persons are dying of starvation and fever, but the tenants are bravely paying their rents.' Whereupon John O'Connell exclaimed, in proud tones, 'I thank God I live among a people who would rather die of hunger than defraud their landlords of the rent!' It is not, unfortunately, on record that the author of this atrocious sentiment was forthwith kicked from the hall into the sink of the Liffey. He was not even hissed by his audience; so dead to every sense and right of manhood were the Irish people reduced in these black years of hopeless life and of a fetid pestilence of perverted morality.

There is possibly no chapter in the wide records of human suffering and wrong so full of shame — measureless, unadulterated, sickening shame — as that which tells us of (it is estimted) a million of people — including, presumably, two hundred thousand adult men — lying down to die in a land out of which forty-five millions' worth of food was being exported, in one year alone, for rent — the product of their own toil — and making no effort, combined or otherwise, to assert even the animal's right of existence — the right to live by the necessities of its nature. It stands unparalleled in human history, with nothing approaching to it in the complete surrender of all the ordinary attributes of manhood by almost a whole nation, in the face of an artificial famine.

England's callous action has been pleaded: Smith O'Brien's warnings, in 1845, to Sir Robert Peel, and this minister's answer by a coercion bill, in 1846; the dilatory and heartless policy of Lord John Russell; and the lupine conduct of the Irish landlords, in pressing for money grants from public funds to relieve distress, out of which rents might be extracted. All this, and everything else that stands in the records of this awful epoch against this class, may be urged, in truth and in reprobation, but it neither explains nor extenuates nor excuses in any way the wholesale cowardice of the men who saw food leave the country in ship-loads, and turned and saw their wives and little ones sicken and die, and who 'bravely paid their rent' before dying themselves.

What was the explanation of this inhuman spirit of social suicide?

It is a serious question to answer, but I firmly believe the answer to be this: During the tithe war of the thirties the peasantry were organized to resist the payment of these penal levies upon Catholics. Tithes were a combined injustice upon both priests and people, and there was a tacit, if unacknowledged, co-operation between the spirit of Whiteboyism and of the anti-tithe combinations in the conflict against the laws responsible alike for the wrongs inflicted on the peasantry both as Catholics and tenants. The great Dr. Doyle[1] preached an endless and unrelenting war against tithes. O'Connell hurled all his powers of invective, and all the might of his great following, against this 'Protestant tyranny' of the Established Church. And it is on record that it was in an attempt to seize upon the cow of a priest, on the demand of tithes from a Protestant parson, that the fight ensued at Carrigshock[2] in which a dozen police and soldiers were killed, and the hands of the English Parliament were forced in the passing of the Tithe Commutation Act of 1838.[3]

No sooner was an end put to the tithe war than the usual denunciations of secret societies, of Whiteboyism, of Ribbonism,[4] and of every combination of an illegal kind or character, was recommenced in pastoral letters, from altars, and from the O'Connell platforms. To war against tithes was righteous and legitimate. To continue the combat against landlordism and unjust rent would do injury to Catholic as well as to Protestant interests, and this was a moral abomination, 'a violation of Catholic doctrine', and all the rest.

All this moral and loyal toadyism to the law and

1. James Warren Doyle (1786-1834), catholic bishop of Kildare and Leighlin 1819-34. He was the first member of the hierarchy to give support to Daniel O'Connell and the Catholic Association in the struggle for catholic emancipation. He was a prolific writer to the press, under the initials J.K.L. (James, Kildare and Leighlin). His best known pamphlets were *A Vindication of the Religious and Civic Principles of the Irish Catholics* (1822) and *On the Origin, Nature and Destination of Church Property* (1831).
2. The tithe war lasted from 1830 to 1838. It was a protest against the payment of tithes by catholics to the protestant established church, most especially by those among them who could least afford it. It began on the Carlow-Kilkenny border when a catholic priest organized resistance against the distraining of his cattle. His bishop, James Warren Doyle, supported him. One of the most notorious incidents in the tithe war occurred at Doon, near Carrigshock, in County Limerick, where the Church of Ireland rector seized a cow belonging to a catholic priest in lieu of tithe payment. In the ensuing confrontation between police, soldiers and people, the military opened fire and nineteen people were killed.
3. The Tithe Commutation Act of 1838 converted the tithe into a rent charge and abolished the hated tithe-proctors and tithe-farmers.
4. The Ribbon Society was a secret agrarian catholic society.

order of the time did not placate the enemy of Repeal. Nothing of the kind. O'Connell and some of his chief supporters were prosecuted and imprisoned, and the great moral-force movement, led by the Liberator and the Catholic clergy, was put down by a not very formidable show of force; not, however, before the government of Sir Robert Peel had taken the precaution to increase the Maynooth grant.[5]

The collapse of O'Connell — in his old age and with impaired powers — the rivalry of the Young Irelanders with the movement cursed by John O'Connell's leadership, and the teachings of *The Nation* newspaper, though dividing the educated national opinion of the cities and towns into factions, left the mass of the people — the peasantry of the country — under the all but absolute leadership of the bishops and priests.

The year 1845 saw the dread herald of the coming calamity in the failure of the potato crop, and in the efforts of Sir Robert Peel in the next session, with true British spirit, to safeguard in time the menaced interests of the landlord garrison by an attempt to pass a coercion act to enforce the payment of rents. These were warnings to the people's leaders as to what the callous English and landlord spirit would stand for in any great national peril that might arise. But the altars thundered against the wickedness of Ribbonism just the same. The pastorals of the bishops smote the Whiteboys, and proclaimed the general obligation of obeying magistrates and masters, as carrying authority from a divine source; and it was in this mood, and in a kindred one of begging for alms from the Parliament of a nation that would sink Celtic Ireland beneath the waves of the Atlantic if she could, that the awful crisis of the great famine was faced by the popular and moral guides of the peasantry of Ireland. The position and policy of these leaders, the backbone of the Repeal Association, was to proclaim, in the month of July, 1846 — with the dread famine fiend already waving its wings of death over the country — the following slavish political profession:

'First. Most dutiful and ever-inviolate loyalty to our most gracious and ever-beloved sovereign, Queen Victoria, and her heirs and successors forever.

'Secondly. The total disclaimer of, and the total absence from, all physical force, violence, or breach of the law; or, in short, any violation of the laws of man, or the ordinances of the Eternal God, whose holy name be ever blessed!

'Thirdly. The only means to be used are those of peaceable, legal, and constitutional combinations of all classes, sects, and persuasions of her Majesty's most loyal subjects, and by always legal means and objects.'[6]

Even in the meeting in Dublin at which this crawling political creed was reaffirmed — even there only one voice — that of Thomas Francis Meagher — was raised in protest against the impotency and disgrace of this policy in face of the greatest calamity that had befallen Ireland since the Cromwellian extermination.

The government and the Church had put down Whiteboyism, Ribbonism, and all illegal combinations, and the responsibility for what followed — for the holocaust of humanity which landlordism and English rule exacted from Ireland in a pagan homage to an inhuman system — must be shared between the political and spiritual governors of the Irish people in those years of a measureless national shame. One power ruled the material interests of the people, the other their religious and moral convictions. Both authorities preached law and order — one by coercion, soldiers, police, and evictions; the other in homilies, sermons, and denunciation.

Both, too, agreed in fathering upon the Almighty the cause of the famine. It was the visitation of God! Hundreds of thousands of women, children, and men were, on this hideous theory, murdered by starvation because of some inscrutable decree of the God of the poor, who, two thousand years before, had died to rescue them from the actual slavery of the Roman Empire, and of other pagan powers, by His Gospel teaching, and life among the working-people. No more horrible creed of atheistic blasphemy was ever preached to a Christian people than this; and looking back with a shudder upon that time one can well understand now how and why it was that myriads of human beings, into

5. The original (1795) grant of £9,000 to St Patrick's College, Maynooth was increased by Sir Robert Peel to £26,000 in 1845. This was discontinued in 1871 and was replaced by a capital sum. The increase was part of Peel's policy of conciliation combined with 'firmness' — coercion acts.

6. Quoted from Father J. O'Rourke's *The History of the Great Irish Famine of 1847 with Notices of Earlier Irish Famines* 3rd ed. (1902), p. 138. Davitt drew quite heavily on this source in his account of the Great Famine and references to earlier famines.

whose souls this moral poison had been instilled, should have lain down and died, 'in obedience to the will of God,' after having 'bravely paid their rent'....

The facts of this unparalleled famine are matters of history, and do not require reproduction in this story.... There were a few disturbances at Westport, in Mayo, Dungarvan, Mallow, Skibbereen, Killarney, and other places, in most of which clergymen distinguished themselves by 'restraining the people,' thereby earning the special thanks of the Lord Lieutenant of the time for their services to 'law and order.'

Had the people been encouraged to stop the exportation of food when O'Connell's demand for a measure of this kind had been refused in 1845 (a measure resorted to by the Irish executive of the period in the famine of 1740-41), the hands of the government would have been forced in time, and the horrors of 'Black 47' would have been greatly mitigated. He was not backed up as he ought to have been by those who differed with him on other questions. . . . The friction between O'Connell and the Young Irelanders followed; the split of 1847 eventuated. O'Connell died in the same year at Genoa, on his way to Rome, it is said, broken-hearted, and the people were left to the consolation that they were victims of God's famine, and not of landlordism or of English rule.

A dozen repetitions of Carrigshock in the three southern provinces, in the early part of 1846 — in reply to Peel's proposed coercion — would have largely saved the situation. O'Connell's proposal ought to have been the minimum demand of Ireland that year, and on its refusal the whole country should have been thrown into social revolt, against the payment of all rent to landlords, with vigilance committees in every seaport to stop all exportation of food. Lives would, of course, be lost, but had five thousand men died then for the right to live on the products of their labor, they would have redeemed the race of the period from the stigma of national pusillanimity, and have saved three-fourths of the slaves who subsequently died like sheep, without leaving on record one single redeeming trait of courageous manhood to the credit of their memories.

The conduct of the Irish landlords before, during, and after the famine was only in keeping with and worthy of their record. Nothing more inhumanly selfish and base is found to the disgrace of any class in any crisis in the history of civilized society. They urged the government to pass coercion; they pressed for more stringent laws for the better payment of rents; they carried out evictions, and did everything else that their antecedents and character generally would incite so morally corrupt a privileged order to commit. There were a few exceptions to the general conduct of the mercenary horde, but these only bring into greater contrast the vulture propensities of the mass of Irish land-owners of the time....

II.—JAMES FINTAN LALOR

It is no part of my task to deal at any length with the birth, teaching, and influence of *The Nation*, the poetry and power of Thomas Davis, or the great impetus which Gavan Duffy's and Mitchel's propaganda gave to the cause of nationalism from 1842 to the famine years. All this belongs to the domain of popular history, and the ample records of the progress thus made, left to us in the writings of Duffy and Mitchel, render any such task altogether unnecessary.

Both Duffy and John Blake Dillon made *The Nation* a powerful advocate of land reform. They raised no uncertain voice in behalf of a fundamental change in the tenure of land, such as would offer greater security to the cultivators. Not in one but in scores of numbers of the great organ Duffy, Davis, and Dillon had founded were the doctrines of 'the land for the people' advanced, almost as radically as in the later times when John Blake Dillon's son preached his father's evangel of land emancipation in every county of Ireland. But *The Nation* was read chiefly in the cities and towns, and not so generally among the common people. Its supporters were far more interested in the fortunes of the national movement than in the changes of tenure urged upon Parliament in the interests of the tenant farmer.

The Young Irelanders were no more 'agrarians' than O'Connell's following. Smith O'Brien, their leader, was himself a landlord. While he was in every sense a chivalrous Irishman and a moderate land reformer, as a Parliamentarian he could not shake off all the social influences of the class to which he belonged, and anticipate the action of Mr. Parnell by becoming the leader of a revolt against the system upheld by England for the advantages of his own order. Herein lay another reason why the history of the famine years will ever be a record of Celtic humiliation.

John Mitchel's fiery spirit went into revolt against the whole Repeal movement when it had nothing more to offer to the people menaced with a dire calamity than moral-force arguments and professions of loyalty. He felt that the crisis cried out for some revolutionary media as the only desperate remedy which equally desperate evils require. He had no fixed ideas of how such a revolution should be organized or carried on. He only saw the need, and he boldly proclaimed it.

Up to 1847 Mitchel, like all the Young Irelanders, hoped for a coming-over of the landlords to the people's side, as did smaller men than Mitchel in later years. The landlords had encouraged this view until they saw all danger of a no-rent movement pass, when they threw off the mask and clamored as ever for repression. This conduct enraged Mitchel, and he commenced to change his views in their regard. Before this change had made any marked headway in his opinion he had proposed an extraordinary scheme — a strike against the payment of poor rates, half of which were chargeable to the landlords. The object was, of course, to force the hands of the government in this manner into the adoption of exceptional measures of state assistance; but the way in which this was proposed to be done condemned the plan as utterly impracticable, and as possessing no real revolutionary impulse or impelling power.

In the mean time — that is, early in 1847 — a series of letters commenced to appear in *The Nation* over the signature of an otherwise unknown person, 'James F. Lalor,' residing in a village in Queen's County.[7] They at once riveted the attention of Duffy and Mitchel by their powerful style, direct force, concentrated passion, and revolutionary fire. The writer called for action, not debate. The time for discussion had gone by. Repeal was not the issue then. It was the agony question of the people's lives. The cause and culprit for the condition of the country were not so much the English government as the Irish landlords, and the remedy lay in a strike against rent and not in any paltry scheme for the withholding of rates. The incurable and calculated treason of the landlord class to country and people was demonstrated in language of burning invective, and the Confederation and Repeal clubs were called upon, in terms of commanding dignity and force, to drop their parleying with the territorial traitors and strike at the main source, not alone of the present but of past and, unless destroyed, of future calamities to the nation — landlordism.

This programme captured Mitchel's combative mind. It was the plan which could alone rouse the country into most general action, cause the government most embarrassment, and give more punishment to the class who had betrayed Smith O'Brien into the expectation of their adhesion to the national cause, only to persuade the English government in the autumn session of 1847 to give Ireland coercion instead of a national administration. This perfidy won Mitchel over, more or less, to Lalor's plans and principles....

There was no real Irish revolutionary mind in the '48 period except Lalor's. There were brilliant writers, ardent patriots, eloquent orators, and nationalist poets; a galaxy of talent, of fine characters, of noble idealists, and of splendidly earnest men. But it was only in the head and heart of a little, deformed gentleman-farmer's son — a descendant of an outlawed 'Tory' of the early confiscations — that the spirit and fire and purpose of a true Celtic revolutionist were found. Lalor's plan was suited to the race, the time, and the calamity it was intended to cope with. It was exactly what the occasion demanded. It combined the national sentiment with the agrarian interest and passion, and would have rallied the aggressive Whiteboy and Ribbon spirit, and entire peasant feeling of the country, behind a movement that would have given Lord Clarendon[8] a social insurrection, as well as a revolutionary nationalist uprising, to deal with before that revolutionary year of 1848.

To avert all the horrors of the situation would probably have been impossible even if Lalor's plans had been acted upon when first proposed. For even he had been dilatory in dealing with the spirit of social disease that crept into the life of Ireland in 1846. But there would have been less loss of life, less national shame to lament over in after years, while there would have been a far speedier settlement of the land and national questions....

7. Now County Laois.

8. George Villiers (1800-70), 4th earl of Clarendon, was lord lieutenant of Ireland 1847-52.

MEMORIES OF THE FAMINE

(b) RANNAFAST, CO. DONEGAL

[Rannafast is still an Irish-speaking area in north-west Donegal. It was not among the most severely affected areas, yet, as the following account shows, the misery and hardship were extreme enough. Most of all, this extract demonstrates the traditional belief that the Famine destroyed the old communal spirit that previously had characterized Irish rural life.

The extract is from MS 1074, Serial no. 360B. It was recorded by Aodh Ó Duibheanaigh on 9 August 1945, from the narrative of the years 1845-52 by Máire Ní Grianna of Rannafast, The Rosses, Co. Donegal. She was eighty-one at the time.

The translation is by Emer Deane.]

Tháinig blianta an ghorta agus an droch shaoghal agus an t-ocras agus bhris sin neart agus spiorad na ndaoiní. Ní rabh ann ach achan nduine ag iarraidh bheith beo. Chaill siad a' dáimh le chéile. Ba chuma cé a bhí gaolmhar duit, ba do charaid an t-é a bhéarfadh greim duit le chur in do bhéal. D'imthigh an spórt agus a' caitheamh aimsire. Stad an fhilidheacht agus a' ceol agus damhsa. Chaill siad agus rinne siad dearmad den iomlán agus nuair a bhisigh an saoghal ar dhóigheannaí eile ní tháinig na rudaí seo ariamh arais mar a bhí siad. Mharbh an gorta achan rud.

Dheireadh na seandaoiní gur ins a'tsamhradh 1846 a thuit an aicid dhubh ar na preátaí annseo a' chead uair. Chuaidh na daoiní a luighe san oidhche agus na cuibhrinn phréataí uilig deas glas agus iad ag amharc galanta. Ach nuair a d'éirigh siad ar maidin ní rabh oiread agus gas amhain fághta ins na cuibhrinn nach rabh doighte go talamh ag an aicid. Bhí sé ró-luath sa tseasúr le preátaí ar bith a bheith deánta aca agus nuair a tháinig an aicid ní tháinig siad a dhath níos fuide ar aghaidh. Ní rabh na daoiní ábalta a dhath a dheánamh leis na preátaí, dóigheadh go talamh iad in a'n oidhche amháin agus ní rabh aca ach seasamh agus amharc ortha no ní rabh maith goide an giollacht a dheanfaidh ortha na dhiaidh sin ní thiocfadh siad. Deirtear nar thuit an aicid dhubh ariamh aroimhe go dtí sin, ach achan bhliadhain na dhiaidh ar feadh sé no seacht de bhliadhna i dtratha an ama cheadna thuit sí arais ach nach rabh sí comh h-olc ariamh ó shoin agus bhí sí an bhliadhain sin, agus tá sí tughtha de bheith tuitim corr uair go fóill annseo. Is beag duine a rabh preátaí ar bith curtha acu 1847. De thairbhe an dóigh ar mheath na preátaí an bhliadhain roimhe sin ní raibh aon preátaí aca le cur i dtalamh ina an Earraoch '47. Sin a 't-am a dtáinig a' t-ocras i gceart agus cibe fuair bás leis an ochras an t-am sin agus na dhiaidh sin a fuair siad bás.

Ní fuair cuid mor daoiní bás leis an ocras annseo. Bhí bliadhanta mhaithe choirce annseo bliadhanta an ghorta agus duine ar bith a shábhail é agus a bhfuair min deánta de bhí siad-san ceart go leor, ach a mhuinntir a bhí i muinghin na bhpreátaí bhí siad-san caillte agus fuair a mbunadhas bás. Shíl na creatúir go mbéadh siad ábalta a bheith beo ar bhiadh cladaigh ach ní rabh, chaithfeadh siad beagan de shugh an talaimh a ithe le na gcoinneail beo. Bhíodh siad 'na luighe istuigh ins na toighte agus gan iad ábalta siubhal, bheadh siad comh lag sin leis an ocras. Agus rachadh siad amach fríd na cuibhrinn ar a gceithre boinn agus d'íosfadh siad a sáith de fhéar agus de lustan agus bhéadh siad in innimh siubhal 'un toighe. Bhí mathaireachaí páistí ina luighe ins na leabhthacha agus na páistí thart fá dtaobh daobhtha agus iad comh lag agus nach rabh siad ábalta éirighe agus luighfeadh siad annsin go bhfaghadh duine indiaidh an duine eile aca bás leis an ocras. Seandaoiní agus páistí is mo a fuair bás de'n ocras. An áit a rabh daoiní laidire bhí siad ábalta an cruadhtan a sheasamh níos fearr.

Coire an Bhrot

Nuair a thoisigh na daoiní 'fhághail bháis leis an ocras cuireadh coire mór suas i Rann-na-Feirste a dheanamh brot no sugh, fá choinne na daoiní a choinneail beo. Ní rabh seanchus ar bith ag na sean-daoiní ca h-áit a dtáinig a 'coire as no cé a thug ann é. Cnámha a bhithear a bhruith ann leis an bhrot a dheánamh agus níl cuntas ar bith ach oiread cá rabh na cnámha sin a teacht as. Duine ar bith a rabh a dhath le h-ithe aige no gléas air a dhath 'fhághail le h-ithe ar dhóigh ar bith ní bhfuigheadh sé a dhath de'n bhrot. Ach ní rabh móran de'n cineal sin annseo. Gugan amháin brot sa lá a gheobhadh achan duine. Bhíodh na sloighte cruinn annsin nuair a bheithfidh a' tabhairt amach a'bhrot agus iad a' brúgh agus a' marbhadh a chéile ag iarraidh fághail isteach fhad leis a 'choire achan duine ag iarraidh a bheith roimh an duine eile ar mhéad agus bhéadh de ocras ortha. Bhí an t-ocras comh mór sin agus nach rabh trócaire in aon duine leis a'duine eile. Mar sin féin eadar a'brot agus cibe seibhte eile a bhí na daoiní a dhéanamh le biadh trágha agus luibheannaí an talamh choinnigh se beo iad ach níl ann ach gur choinnigh. Bhí an coire sin i Rann-na-feirste, 'Coire-na-Gorta', go dtí tá tamall bliadhanta ó shoin. . . .

An Fiabhras
Ní bhfuair mórán uilig bás annseo leis an ocras le taoibh a méid a fuair bás leis an fhiabhras. Bhí na daoiní comh lag agus comh caitte ag an ocras agus ag an ampla nuair a tháinig an fiabhras agus nach rabh siab ábalta an aicid a sheasamh agus mar sin de fuair na céadtaí aca bás. Ní rabh ospuideal ar bith annseo no doctúir ach oiread. . . .

TRANSLATION

The years of the Famine, of the bad life and of the hunger, arrived and broke the spirit and strength of the community. People simply wanted to survive. Their spirit of comradeship was lost. It didn't matter what ties or relations you had; you considered that person to be your friend who gave you food to put in your mouth. Recreation and leisure ceased. Poetry, music and dancing died. These things were lost and completely forgotten. When life improved in other ways, these pursuits never returned as they had been. The Famine killed everything.

The old people said that in the summer of 1846 the potato blight struck for the first time. People went to sleep at night with the potato fields looking green and healthy; when they got up the next day, every stem in the fields was ruined by the disease. It was too early in the season for the potatoes to be ready and when the blight came they developed no further. Nothing could be done with the potatoes. In one night they were scorched and the people could do nothing but stand and watch them. No matter how hard they worked after that, the potatoes didn't grow. It is said that the blight had never struck before then, but every year after that for the next six or seven years, it happened again but never so disastrously as in that first year. Even now the same thing is happening; it's liable to break out now and then. Hardly anyone planted potatoes in 1847. Because of the ruin of the year before, they didn't have one potato to sow in the ground in the spring of '47. That's when the hunger struck and it was from that point on that the deaths began.

Not many people died from hunger here. There were good years for oats here, and during the Famine anyone who saved the oats made meal from it. Those people were alright. But those who were dependent on the potatoes were lost. Their families died. The poor creatures, they thought they would be able to live on seafood, but they weren't. They needed a little of the produce of the soil to stay alive. They used to stay inside in their cabins, not able to walk, so weak were they with hunger. They would go out in the fields on all fours and eat their fill of grass and weeds and then they'd be able to walk home. Mothers lay in their beds with the children beside them and they were so weak they were not able to get up. They used to lie there until one after another they died of hunger. The hunger killed the old and the children for the most part. Stronger people were able to survive the hardship.

The Gruel Cauldron
When the people began to die of hunger, a big cauldron was set up in Rannafast to make broth or gruel to keep people alive. No-one knew where it came from or who had sent it. Bones were boiled to make the broth and there's no record of where those bones came from. Anyone who had anything at all to eat or any way of getting it would get no broth at all. But there weren't many here who could do that. Every one got one serving of broth per day. Crowds would be milling around as they gave out the broth and they'd be pushing and shoving, nearly killing one another to get up to the cauldron. Everyone was trying to get in before others, so great was the hunger. No one had mercy for anyone else. At any rate, between broth and whatever the soil produced and seafood or weeds, they were kept alive, but barely so. That cauldron was in Rannafast until a few years ago. . . .

The Fever
Far more died of fever than of hunger. The people were so wasted and weak with hunger and starvation that, when the fever came, they could not withstand the disease and therefore hundreds of them died. There were no hospital or doctor in this area either. . . .

Biographies/Bibliographies

GENERAL WORKS

(a) YOUNG IRELAND
Thomas Davis and Young Ireland (a selected bibliography) (Dublin: Stationery Office, 1945); T.F. O'Sullivan, *The Young Irelanders* (Tralee: The Kerryman, 1944); D. Gwynn, *Young Ireland and 1848* (Cork: Cork University Press; Oxford: Basil Blackwell, 1948); R. Davis, *The Young Ireland Movement* (Dublin: Gill and Macmillan; Totowa, New Jersey: Barnes and Noble, 1987); J. Hutchinson, *The Dynamics of Cultural Nationalism* (London: Allen and Unwin, 1987); D. Lloyd, *Nationalism and Minor Literature* (Berkeley: University of California Press, 1987).

(b) THE FAMINE
W. P. O'Brien, *The Great Famine in Ireland* (London: Downey, 1896); J. O'Rourke, *The History of the Great Irish Famine of 1847 with Notices of Earlier Irish Famines* 3rd ed. (Dublin: Duffy, 1902, reprinted Dublin: Irish Academic Press, 1988); G.A.P. O'Brien, *The Economic History of Ireland from the Union to the Famine* (London: Longmans, Green, 1921); R. D. Edwards and T. D. Williams (eds), *The Great Famine. Studies in Irish History 1845-1852* (Dublin: Browne and Nolan, 1956; New York: New York University Press, 1957); R.D. Collison Black, *Economic Thought and the Irish Question, 1817-70* (Cambridge: Cambridge University Press, 1960); C. Woodham-Smith, *The Great Hunger: Ireland 1845-49* (London: Hamish Hamilton, 1962); R. D. Crotty, *Irish Agricultural Production: Its Volume and Structure* (Cork: Cork University Press, 1966), pp. 35-83; G. O Tuathaigh, *Ireland Before the Famine 1798-1848* (Dublin: Gill and Macmillan, 1972); I. A. Glazier and M. Tepper (eds), *the Famine Immigrants: Lists of Irish Immigrants Arriving at the Port of New York 1846-1851* 7 vols (Baltimore: Genealogical Publishing Company Inc, 1983-86); J. Mokyr, *Why Ireland Starved: A Quantitative and Analytical History of the Irish Economy, 1800-1850* (London, Allen and Unwin, 1985); M. E. Daly, *The Famine in Ireland* (Dublin: Dublin Historical Association, 1987); C. Ó Grada, *Ireland Before and After the Famine: Explorations in Economic History 1800-1925* (Manchester: Manchester University Press, 1988); C. Morash (ed.), *The Hungry Voice. The Poetry of the Irish Famine* (Dublin: Irish Academic Press, 1989).

Thomas Francis Meagher

LIFE. Born in Waterford in 1823. His father was lord mayor of the city 1844-46 and its MP 1847-57. Meagher was educated by the Jesuits at Clongowes Wood, Co. Kildare and at Stonyhurst, Lancashire. In 1844, he went to Dublin to study law, but became involved in politics. He was a powerful speaker at Repeal Association meetings in Conciliation Hall and won fame for his 'Sword' speech against the Peace Resolutions on 28 July 1846. This led to the secession of the Young Irelanders from the Repeal Association. Because of this speech, Thackeray dubbed him 'Meagher of the Sword'.

Meagher was a founder member of the Irish Confederation in 1847. He failed to win an important by-election in Waterford in February 1848 and a month later was arrested on a charge of sedition, following a speech at a Confederation meeting in which he threatened the use of force. While out on bail, he was sent as an emissary from Young Ireland to Paris to congratulate the provisional government after the uprising there. He returned with the gift of the tricolor flag for the citizens of Dublin — later adapted as the Irish national flag. Meagher was acquitted of the sedition charge and became a member of the Confederate war directory. With William Smith O'Brien he toured the country trying to organize an insurrection. After the failure of 1848, he was arrested and sentenced to death, commuted to penal servitude for life to Van Diemen's Land (now Tasmania).

Meagher escaped in 1852 and went to New York where he became a popular lecturer and helped Mitchel to found the *Citizen* newspaper. He also founded his own paper, *Irish News*, which ran from 1856-60. After a number of exploring expeditions in Central and North America, he joined the Union army in the American Civil War and became brigadier general of the 'Irish Brigade' which fought in most of the most important battles of the war and was almost annihilated. After the war he was appointed territorial secretary (1865) and acting governor of Montana territory (1865-66). He died in mysterious circumstances, allegedly falling overboard from a steamer and drowning in the river Missouri in 1867.

CHIEF WRITINGS. *The Orations of Thomas F. Meagher. (Revised by himself)*. First Series; Second Series Supplements to *The Nation*, 5 June 1852; 3 July 1852; *Speeches on the Legislative Independence of Ireland* (New York: Redford, 1870; with a memorial oration by R. O'Gorman, New York: Haverty, 1870); A. Griffith (ed.), *Meagher of the Sword. Speeches of Thomas Francis Meagher in Ireland, 1846-1848. His Narrative of Events in Ireland in July 1848, Personal Reminiscences ....* (Dublin: Gill, 1916).

BIOGRAPHY AND CRITICISM. M. Cavanagh, *Memoirs of Gen. Thomas Francis Meagher ... with selections from his speeches, lectures and miscellaneous writings....* (Worcester, Mass.: The Messenger Press, 1892); W. F. Lyons, *Brigadier-General Thomas Francis Meagher: His Political and Military Career; with selections from his speeches and writings* (New York: Sadleir, 1870; Glasgow: Cameron, Ferguson, 1870; 2nd ed., London: Burns, Oates, 1870); A. Downey, *The Complete Young Irelander: Thomas Francis Meagher* (Waterford: Carthage Press, 1945); R. G. Athearn, *Thomas Francis Meagher: An Irish Revolutionary in America* (Boulder, Colorado: University of Colorado Press, 1949); D. Gwynn, *Thomas Francis Meagher* (Dublin: National University of Ireland, 1962).

William Carleton

LIFE. Born in Prillisk, Co. Tyrone, in 1794, Carleton's only education was at a hedge-school. When his family was evicted in 1813, he joined the outlawed Ribbonmen for a time. He went to Maynooth with the intention of becoming a priest, but soon turned from that, married and became a protestant. He began to write sketches of Irish country life for the *Christian Examiner*, edited by Caesar Otway, a fervent anti-catholic propagandist. Carleton contributed also to *The Dublin University Magazine*, *The Nation*, *The Irish Penny Journal* and many other periodicals. His *Christian Examiner* sketches became *Traits and Stories of the Irish Peasantry* (1830-33) which established his fame. Thereafter he turned to the novel. He died in Dublin in 1869, leaving his *Autobiography* unfinished.

CHIEF WRITINGS. *Father Butler; The Lough Dearg Pilgrim* (Dublin: W. Curry, 1829); *Traits and Stories of the Irish Peasantry* 2 vols (Dublin: Curry, 1830); *Traits and Stories of the Irish Peasantry* 2nd Series, 3 vols (Dublin: W.F. Wakeman, 1833); *Tales of Ireland* (Dublin: Curry, 1834); *Fardorougha the Miser; or, The Convicts of Lishnamona* (Dublin: Curry, 1839); *The Fawn of Springvale, The Clarionet and Other Tales* (Dublin: Curry, 1841); *Art Maguire; or, The Broken Pledge* (Dublin: J. Duffy, 1845); *Parra Sastha; or, The History of Paddy-Go-Easy and His Wife Nancy* (Dublin: J. Duffy, 1845); *Rody the Rover; or, The Ribbonman* (Dublin: J. Duffy, 1845); *Tales and Sketches* (later published as *Tales and Stories of the Irish Peasantry*) (Dublin: J. Duffy, 1845); *Valentine McClutchy, The Irish Agent; or, Chronicles of the Castle Cumber Property* 3 vols (Dublin: J. Duffy, 1845); *The Black Prophet, A Tale of Irish Famine* (London and Belfast: Simms & McIntyre, 1847); *The Emigrants of Ahadarra, A Tale of Irish Life* (London and Belfast: Simms & McIntyre, 1848); *The Tithe Proctor, a Novel. Being a Tale of the Tithe Rebellion in Ireland* (London: Simms and McIntrye, 1848); *Red Hall; or, The Baronet's Daughter* 3 vols (London: Saunders and Otley, 1852); *The Squanders of Castle Squander* 2 vols (London: Illustrated London Library, 1852); *Willie Reilly and His Dear Colleen Bawn* 3 vols (London: Hope, 1855); *The Silver Acre and Other Tales* (London: Ward Lock, 1862).

BIOGRAPHY AND CRITICISM. W. B. Yeats, *Stories from Carleton, with an introduction* (London: W. Scott, 1889); D. J. O'Donohue, *The Life of William Carleton* 2 vols (London: Downey & Co., 1896); B. Kiely, *Poor Scholar. A Study of the Works and Days of William Carleton* (London:

Sheed and Ward, 1947); *The Autobiography of William Carleton* with Preface by Patrick Kavanagh (London: MacGibbon & Kee, 1968); A. Boué, *William Carleton, Romancier Irlandais (1794-1869)* (Paris, 1978); B. Hayley, *Carleton's Traits and Stories and the Nineteenth-Century Anglo-Irish Tradition* (Gerrards Cross: Colin Smythe, 1983).

Peadar Ó Laoghaire

LIFE. Peadar Ó Laoghaire was born in 1839 at Clondrohid, Co. Cork, and educated at the National School, Macroom, St Colman's College, Fermoy, and Maynooth, where he was ordained in 1867. His life as a priest was spent in west Cork; in 1891 he became parish priest of Castlelyons. He supported the Land League and was a founder-member of the Gaelic League in 1893. He had a disputatious career in the League, quarrelling with its leaders over matters of spelling and speech. His prolific writing career began when he was in his mid-fifties and his famous autobiography, *Mo Sgéal Féin*, was written when he was sixty-six. Ó Laoghaire was the first writer to have a collection of stories published in Irish, *Ar nDóithín Araon* (1894) and the first to have a play produced in the Irish language, *Tadgh Saor* in Macroom, Co. Cork, in 1900. His best-known work, *Séadna* (1904), was later adopted as a school text. He adapted many of the Irish sagas and translated several European classics into Irish. He died at Castlelyons in 1920.

CHIEF WRITINGS. *Séadna* (Dublin: Irish Book Company, 1904); *Mo Sgéal Féin* (Dublin: Irish Book Company, 1915), trans. C. T. Ó Céirin, *My Own Story* (Cork: Mercier Press, 1970). (See also Volume III, p. 932.)

Asenath Nicholson

LIFE. Born in Vermont in the late eighteenth century, possibly in 1794, Asenath Hatch went to New York in the early 1830s and married Norman Nicholson in 1833. Ten years later he died. In 1842 she opened a temperance boarding house in New York. The year after her husband's death, she sailed on the steamer *Brooklyn* from New York to Ireland. After some time there, she obtained from the Hibernian Bible Society a stock of Bibles, some in Irish, some in English, for distribution among the people. She returned to Ireland after the outbreak of the Famine. Little is known of her thereafter.

CHIEF WRITINGS. *Ireland's Welcome to the Stranger; or, Excursions through Ireland, in 1844 & 1845, for the purpose of personally investigating the condition of the poor* (London: Gilpin, 1847); *The Bible in Ireland* ed. with an introduction by A. T. Sheppard (abridged version of *Ireland's Welcome*) (London: Hodder and Stoughton, 1926); *Lights and Shades of Ireland* (London: Houlston and Stoneman, 1850); *Annals of the Famine in Ireland, in 1847, 1848 and 1849* [ed. by J. L.] (New York: Haverty, 1851).

William Steuart Trench

LIFE. Born in 1808, near Portarlington, Co. Laois, the fourth son of Thomas Trench, dean of Kildare. He was educated at the Royal School, Armagh and at Trinity College, Dublin. He chose and trained for the career of land agent. In 1849, Trench was appointed agent to the estates of the Marquis of Lansdowne in Kerry; in 1851 he became, in addition, agent to the property of the Marquis of Bath in Monaghan and of Lord Digby in Offaly in 1856. His *Realities of Irish Life* (1868) had five editions in a year and was widely praised in the reviews and magazines. In 1871, he published a novel, *Ierne: A Tale,* based on the same material, but it was not a success. He died in Carrickmacross, Co. Monaghan in 1872.

CHIEF WRITINGS. *Realities of Irish Life* (London: Longmans, 1868); reprinted with a Preface by Patrick Kavanagh (London: MacGibbon and Kee, 1966); *Ierne; A Tale* 2 vols (London: Longmans, Green, 1871).

George Petrie

LIFE. Born in Dublin in 1789, Petrie was educated at Samuel Whyte's School in Dublin and the arts school of the Royal Dublin Society. In 1808 he travelled throughout Dublin and Wicklow, collecting music and sketching ancient ecclesiastical architecture. He was the leading figure in the topographical section of the Ordnance Survey, employing John O'Donovan, Eugene O'Curry and James Clarence Mangan. Although the Survey was discontinued in 1840, Petrie continued the work he had begun through his membership of the Irish Archaeological Society (1840), the Ossianic Society (1853) and the Royal Irish Academy, which he reorganized. He exhibited regularly at the Royal Hibernian Academy, of which he became a member in 1828. His watercolours and sketches became famous, particularly 'The Last Round of the Pilgrims at Clonmacnoise' and 'Gougane Barra'. He co-edited the *Dublin Penny Journal* (1832-33) and edited the *Irish Penny Journal* (1842). The Royal Irish Academy awarded him gold medals for his famous *Essay on the Round Towers of Ireland* (1833) and *On the History and Antiquities of Tara Hill* (1839). His collections of Irish music were key works in the early Celtic revival. Petrie is one of the most important figures in the history of nineteenth-century Ireland. He died in Dublin in 1866.

CHIEF WRITINGS. *On the History and Antiquities of Tara Hill* (Dublin: R. Graisberry, 1839); *The Ecclesiastical Architecture of Ireland, Anterior to the Norman Invasion; Comprising an Essay on the Origin and Uses of the Round Towers of Ireland. . . .* (Dublin: Hodges and Smith, 1845); *The Petrie Collection of the Ancient Music of Ireland* 2 vols (Dublin: Dublin University Press, 1855-82).

BIOGRAPHY AND CRITICISM. W. Stokes, *The Life and Labours in Art and Archaeology of G. Petrie* (London: Longmans, 1868); M. Dillon, 'George Petrie (1789-1866)', *Studies* (Autumn 1967), 266-76; G. J. Calder, *George Petrie and the Ancient Music of Ireland* (Dublin: Dolmen Press, 1968); J. Sheehy, *The Rediscovery of Ireland's Past; The Celtic Revival 1830-1930* (London: Thames and Hudson, 1980), pp. 22-45, 58-61; J. Hutchinson, *The Dynamics of Cultural Nationalism: The Gaelic Revival and the Creation of the Irish Nation State* (London: Allen and Unwin, 1987), pp. 80-90.

Isaac Butt

For biography and bibliography, see Volume I, p. 1297.

James Fintan Lalor

LIFE. Lalor was born in 1807 at Tenakill in Queen's Country (Laois). His father took a prominent part in the anti-tithe movement of the 1830s and was MP for the county 1832-35. Lalor suffered from a congenital spinal disease which left him deaf, near-sighted and deformed. He broke with his father, who supported Daniel O'Connell and believed that the achievement of Repeal of the Union would lead to land reform. He and his father were reconciled in 1846, the year Lalor began a detailed analysis of the land problem. He supported Young Ireland's break with O'Connell in 1846 and began publishing a series of letters in *The Nation* in January 1847, advocating land confiscation, a new theory of land ownership and a struggle for national independence. He attracted the more militant members of Young Ireland or, as it had been renamed, the Irish Confederation, including John Mitchel, Thomas Devin Reilly and Michael Doheny. His attempts to found a land league and to start a rent strike in 1847-48 both failed.

After Mitchel's transportation, John Martin started *The Irish Felon* newspaper as a successor to Mitchel's *United Irishman.* When Martin was arrested, Lalor, who had been a chief contributor, ran the newspaper almost single-handedly. It lasted only five numbers, from June to July 1848. After the 1848 insurrection, Lalor was arrested and imprisoned under the Suspension of Habeas Corpus Act. His health deteriorated in jail and he was released some months later. He became friendly with men who would later be members of the Fenian Brotherhood — Thomas Clarke Luby, Charles Kickham and John O'Leary. In 1849 he tried to organize another insurrection. The attempt was a failure and Lalor returned to Dublin, where he died two days later, in December 1849.

CHIEF WRITINGS. *The Writings of James Fintan Lalor, With an Introduction Embodying Personal Recollections by John O'Leary, and a Brief Memoir by O'D(onoghue?)* (Dublin: T. G. O'Donoghue, 1895); N. Marlowe (ed.), *James Fintan Lalor: Collected Writings* (Dublin and London: Maunsel, 1916): *James Fintan Lalor, Patriot and Political Essayist: Collected Writings; with a biographical note by L. Fogarty* (Dublin: Talbot Press, 1947); *The Rights of Ireland and The Faith of a Felon . . . with an introduction by James Connolly* (Dublin: Socialist Party of Ireland, n.d.).

BIOGRAPHY AND CRITICISM. L. M. Fogarty, *James Fintan Lalor, Patriot and Political Essayist (1807-1849). With a preface by Arthur Griffith* (Dublin: Maunsel, 1918); T. P. O'Neill, 'Fintan Lalor and the 1849 Movement', *An Cosantóir, The Irish Defence Journal* X, No. 4 (April 1950), 173-79; *Fintán Ó Leathlobhair* (Dublin: Cló Morainn, 1962); David N. Buckley, *James Fintan Lalor: Radical* (Cork: Cork University Press, 1990).

John Mitchel

LIFE. Born near Dungiven, Co. Derry in 1815, the son of a presbyterian minister. Mitchel was educated at Trinity College, Dublin, worked for a time in Newry and Banbridge, eloped with the seventeen-year-old Jenny Verner and married her in 1837. Gavan Duffy successfully proposed him as a member of the Repeal Association in 1843. He became a writer for *The Nation* in 1845; in 1848, he founded his own newspaper, the *United Irishman*, in which he advocated armed insurrection against British rule. He was arrested and after a scandalous trial was sentenced to fourteen years transportation, on the charge of treason felony. After a time in Bermuda, Mitchel finally arrived in Van Diemen's Land (now Tasmania), where he lived until 1853.

In that year he escaped to America, became a journalist and supported the South in the Civil War. He helped the Fenian movement in America, but quarrelled with its leader, James Stephens. In 1875 he returned to Ireland as an undischarged felon, was elected MP for Tipperary, was disqualified and then re-elected. Within a few days of this triumph, he died in Newry.

CHIEF WRITINGS. *The Life and Times of Aodh O'Neill, Prince of Ulster* (Dublin: Duffy, 1846); *Jail Journal; or, Five Years in British Prisons* (New York: *The Citizen*, 1854; Haverty, 1868; Thomas Flanagan (ed.), Dublin: University Press of Ireland, 1982); *The Last Conquest of Ireland (Perhaps)* (Dublin: The Irishman Office, 1861); *The History of Ireland from the Treaty of Limerick to the Present Time* (Glasgow: Cameron and Ferguson; London: C. Griffin and Co.; Dublin Duffy, 1869); *An Ulsterman for Ireland, being letters to the Protestant farmers, labourers and artisans of the North of Ireland*, with a foreword by Eóin MacNeill (Dublin: Candle Press, 1917); *An Apology for the British Government in Ireland* (Dublin: M.H. Gill and Son, 1920).

BIOGRAPHY AND CRITICISM. J. G. Hodges, *Report of the Trial of John Mitchell* [*sic*] for *Felony at the Commission Court, Dublin, May 1848* (Dublin: Thom, 1848); W. Dillon, *Life of John Mitchel* 2 vols (London: Kegan Paul, Trench & Co., 1888); S. MacCall, *Irish Mitchel, A Biography* (London: Nelson, 1938). See also R. Davis, *The Young Ireland Movement* (Dublin: Gill and Macmillan; Totowa, New Jersey: Barnes and Noble, 1987).

John Elliot Cairnes

LIFE. Born in Castlebellingham, Co. Louth in 1823, Cairnes was educated at Trinity College, Dublin, graduating in 1848. He gained his MA in 1854. While working in Galway, Cairnes befriended William Nesbitt, professor of Latin at Queen's College. He coaxed Cairnes to take up the study of political economy. Cairnes won the Whately Chair at Trinity College, Dublin, which he held from 1856-61. In 1859 he was appointed to the chair of jurisprudence and political economy at Queen's College, Galway. He retained this position until 1870, even though he was made professor of political economy at University College, London in 1866. He resigned from the London chair in 1872 because of poor health and died in London in 1875.

CHIEF WRITINGS. *The Character and Logical Method of Political Economy* (London: Longman & Co., 1857; 2nd rev. ed. Macmillan, 1875); *The Slave Power; Its Character, Career & Possible Designs: Being an Attempt to Explain the Real Issue in the American Contest* (London: Parker, Son & Bourn, 1862; 2nd enl. ed., Macmillan, 1863); *Essays in Political Economy. Theoretical and Applied* (London: Macmillan, 1873); *Political Essays* (London: Macmillan, 1873); *Some Leading Principles of Political Economy Newly Expounded* (London: Macmillan, 1874; reprinted New York: Augustus Kelley, 1967).

BIOGRAPHY AND CRITICISM. W. Bagehot, 'Professor Cairnes' in R. H. Hutton (ed.), *Biographical Studies* (London and New York: Longmans, Green and Co., 1895); A. Weinberg, *John Elliot Cairnes and the American Civil War: A Study in Anglo-American Relations* (London: Kingswood Press, 1969); T. A. Boylan and T. P. Foley, 'John Elliot Cairnes, John Stuart Mill and Ireland: Some Problems for Political Economy' in A. E. Murphy (ed.), *Economists and the Irish Economy from the Eighteenth Century to the Present Day* (Dublin: Irish Academic Press/Hermathena, 1984), pp. 96-119; 'Cairnes, Hearn and Bastable: The Contribution of Queen's College, Galway, to Economic Thought' in D. O Cearbhaill (ed.), *Galway: Town and Gown 1484-1984* (Dublin: Gill and Macmillan, 1984).

Alexander Martin Sullivan

LIFE. Sullivan was born in 1830 in Bantry, Co. Cork, brother to Timothy Daniel Sullivan. He became the uncle of Tim Healy. Sullivan was a member of Young Ireland, worked as a journalist in Liverpool and Dublin and in 1855 became proprietor and editor of *The Nation*. He was a bitter opponent of the Fenians and was the first man to be called (by James Stephens) a 'felon-setter', ever since a term of deep opprobrium in Ireland. Sullivan was imprisoned in 1868 for supporting the Manchester Martyrs; was a founder member of the Home Rule League and was MP for Louth 1874-80. In 1876, he passed *The Nation* over to his brother, T. D. Sullivan. He had the statue to Henry Grattan on College Green erected out of monies collected on his own behalf while in prison. He died in Beckenham, Kent in 1884.

CHIEF WRITINGS. *Brilliant Chapters from Modern Irish History* (Glasgow: Cameron and Ferguson, n.d.); *Ireland at the Bar! The State Trials — 1881* (Dublin: J. J. Lalor, 1881); *The History of Ireland from the Rebellion of Robert Emmet to the Fenian Insurrection* (Boston: Murphy and McCarthy, n.d.); *New Ireland* 2 vols (London: Low, Marston, Searle and Rivington, 1877).

BIOGRAPHY AND CRITICISM. T. D. Sullivan, *A.M. Sullivan. A Memoir* (Dublin: T. D. Sullivan, 1885).

Michael Davitt

LIFE. Davitt was born in Straide, Co. Mayo in 1846. His family was evicted in 1850 and emigrated to Lancashire where Davitt worked as a child labourer in a cotton mill. When he was ten years old, his right arm was severed in an industrial accident at the mill. Davitt joined the Irish Republican Brotherhood, was involved in a famous, if abortive, raid on Chester Castle in 1867, and was chief arms purchaser for the organization until 1870 when he was arrested and sentenced to fifteen years' imprisonment on a dubious charge of incitement to murder.

After seven years of harsh treatment in jail, he was released and went to the USA, where he met John Devoy. In 1879 he returned to Mayo and took part in the land agitation that led to the foundation of the Land League of Mayo. He persuaded Parnell to participate in the land agitation. This 'New Departure', which included Fenian support mobilized by Devoy, helped to produce the Land Act of 1881. It was ended by the Kilmainham 'Treaty' of 1882, in which Parnell promised to co-operate with Gladstone in return for modifications of the Land Act and an end to the coercion acts. Davitt thought this a crucial mistake on Parnell's part.

During the Land War Davitt was imprisoned on several occasions. He became familiar with the ideas of English socialism and began to incorporate these into his interpretation of the Irish land and the Irish national questions. Elected MP for Meath in 1882, Davitt was unseated by special writ of the House of Commons; this happened again in 1892 when he was elected for North Meath. Finally allowed to take his seat as representative for East Cork later in 1892, he was forced to resign in 1893 on being declared a bankrupt.

During the Parnell divorce crisis, Davitt was one of the fiercest critics of Parnell's leadership. He supported the foundation of the British Labour Party, but remained committed to the Liberal Party for the sake of Home Rule. He withdrew from parliament in protest against the Boer War and visited South Africa to lend support to the Boer cause. His advocacy of land nationalization and of undenominational education aroused a good deal of hostility and incomprehension, the former from the catholic hierarchy, the latter from the tenantry. He died in Dublin in 1906.

CHIEF WRITINGS. *Leaves from a Prison Diary; or, Lectures to a Solitary Audience* 2 vols (London: Chapman and Hall, 1885); reprinted with an Introduction by T. W. Moody (Shannon: Irish University Press, 1972); *Life and Progress in Australasia* (London: Methuen & Co., 1898); *The Boer Fight for Freedom* (New York: Funk and Wagnall, 1902); *Some Suggestions for a Final Settlement of the Land Question* (Dublin: Gill and Son, 1902); *Within the Pale, The True Story of Anti-Semitic Persecutions in Russia* (London: Hurst and Blackett, 1903); *The Fall of Feudalism in Ireland* (London: Chapman and Hall, 1904).

BIOGRAPHY AND CRITICISM. D. B. Cashman, *The Life of Michael Davitt, Founder of the National Land League. To which is added, the secret history of the land league, by Michael Davitt* (London: Washbourne, 1923); F. Sheehy-Skeffington, *Michael Davitt, Revolutionary, Agitator and Labour Leader* (London: Fisher Unwin, 1908); J. W. Good, *Michael Davitt* (Dublin: Cumann Leigheacht an Phobail, 1921-22); B. E. Kunina, *Maikl Davitt* (transliterated title) (Moscow: Mysl, 1973): T. W. Moody, *Davitt and Irish Revolution, 1846-82* (Oxford: Oxford University Press, 1983).

SEAMUS DEANE, *Editor*

Political Writings and Speeches 1850-1918

In the period from the end of the Famine to the Easter rebellion of 1916, Irish political life was dominated by three organized groups: the Irish Republican Brotherhood (the executive council of the Fenian organization), the Irish Parliamentary Party, and the Land League. The Fenians, as they were commonly called, derived, in their personnel and in their ideas, from the militant wing of Young Ireland and from the after-effects of the Famine. Influenced by John Mitchel and James Fintan Lalor, they determined, under the leadership of James Stephens, to organize and to wait for the opportune moment to break the connection with England by the use of force. Fenianism was an American as well as an Irish phenomenon: the post-Famine emigration had created an Irish community in the United States which found in John Devoy one of the most effective and enduring of revolutionary organizers. The Irish Parliamentary Party also, though less directly, owed its policies and cohesion to the consequences of Ireland's treatment during the Famine. Isaac Butt's conversion from extreme unionism to the policy of Irish federalism, and thence to Home Rule, gave the party a defined policy that Charles Stewart Parnell put into effect by manipulation of the parliamentary system and exploitation of the balance of power in the British party system at Westminster. The Land League, too, had its origin in the campaign against the Irish landlords which was part of the Famine's political heritage, although it owed some of its methods to the techniques of sabotage and assassination which had been practised since the eighteenth century by various, less organized, groups of rural outlaws who created the agrarian disturbances that were a favourite topic of British newspapers in their reports on the situation in Ireland. Michael Davitt's solution to the land problem in Ireland was never realized; Parnell's attempt to win Home Rule for Ireland failed. Only the IRB-Fenian conspiracy can be said to have had a measure of success, fortuitous though that was in the aftermath of 1916. A fourth organization, the Ulster Unionist Council, was not formed until 1904, in response to the Home Rule crises of the 1880s and 1890s. Its activities had an immediate effect on the nationalists, inspiring them to form the Irish Volunteers, but not inspiring them to take with sufficient seriousness the threat of secession, which was to have such unexpected consequences for Britain and Ireland between 1912 and 1922.

In Stephens, Devoy, Parnell, Davitt and, later, Edward Carson, Ireland produced a group of leaders who, for all their heroic and often brilliant campaigns, were defeated in their ultimate aims of achieving either an Irish republic, a socialist system of land tenure, Home Rule, or No Home Rule. The favourite tactic of both nationalists and unionists was to combine violence or the threat of it with parliamentary or constitutional methods. It was then and still is conventional to say that the history of Ireland since the 1780s could be understood as a series of variations between the impulse to violent rebellion and the countering impulse towards constitutional agitation. Davitt and Patrick Pearse both favoured this mode of interpretation and it is an implicit theme in the writings of Mitchel and in the anti-Union campaigns of Daniel O'Connell. But these are not alternating impulses. They are coexistent and, at times, when they combined, as in the New Departure of 1879 and in the Ulster Unionist Council campaign of 1911-12, their power was formidable. In this period, the leader who most effectively made that combination work was Parnell and his downfall was so traumatic in its consequences that none of the nationalist-republican organizations, which had been temporarily co-operating under his direction, escaped the ensuing internecine feuds. A cold war, as intense in some respects at the later Civil War, exacerbated the country's political divisions. The schism reproduced itself over and over again in Irish political, social and cultural life for the next forty years. The earlier split between O'Connell and the Young Irelanders was its prelude, the Civil War its aftermath, but the Parnell crisis itself took the central position and became a symbol of the country's interpretation of its struggle to represent itself as unified in the midst of division.

Parnell was almost triumphant; it is in the gap between the actual achievement and the almost actual achievement that the myth of Parnell took root and that the sense of betrayal, well nourished in earlier Irish history by the contributions of traitors and informers, was finally internalized as a sense of self-betrayal. Ireland was divided; its aspiration towards unity was subverted by the dread of achieving it. Yeats made his Cú Chulainn into a version of Parnell, and Joyce made his Parnell into a version of Ireland itself. Parnell became a legend in literature because he had been destroyed by the hidden hatred of the autonomy and independence that he embodied in himself and was about to realize for others. Like Synge's *Playboy*, Parnell had to be repudiated; acceptance of him would mean forsaking dependence on the very system of oppression that he had threatened to overthrow.

Part of the problem for a revolutionary organization like the Fenians was the fact that Ireland was stabilizing and its economy improving because of the success of constitutional pressure in seeking reforms. Although the usual spate of coercion acts did not abate and, despite the fact that the idea of justice in the British legal system was a bad joke played time and again on those unfortunates who were hauled before it, important concessions were won. The land problem was eventually solved or dissolved between 1870 and 1903, although even after that date it reappeared in a different form, with large grazier farmers assuming the role formerly occupied by landlords. The educational system was improved, despite the largely successful efforts of the catholic church to control it; the Church of Ireland was disestablished; agricultural production increased, local government was made more democratic. The process of modernization, while subject to periodic setbacks, transformed the country and made it a much more tolerable place to live in than it had been before the Famine. It is arguable that, to the degree that Ireland was incorporated within the British Victorian scheme of things, the transformation was not inspiring, but it did reduce the revolutionary impetus towards separation. The land problem, the overtaxation of Ireland since the Union in 1800, the corrupt legal system — all were targets of various parliamentary and revolutionary groups in this period, but the concessions and reforms offered to alleviate these made it difficult to make any one or any combination of them a firm basis for a separatist programme. Ultimately, the separatist idea had to find its justification in a theory of cultural, even racial, difference. In the aftermath of the Parnell crisis, the Gaelic League and the Irish Literary Revival — distinct but interwoven movements — were able to make this a dominant theme. Patrick Pearse is a crucial figure in this regard because it is he who finally links this declaration of cultural difference with the claim for political separatism, exploiting thereby the failure of parliamentarianism and incorporating within it the increasingly emphatic identification of catholicism with nationalism.

Pearse's programme had two immediate implications. The first was that nationalism, in its separatist, revolutionary form, became far more exclusive than it had been either with the Fenians or with the Parnellites. The consequence of that was a complete failure to recognize the reality of the Ulster situation and the inapplicability to it of the theory of Gaelic or Celtic culture in its contemporary (as opposed to its earlier) formulation. The second implication was that Ireland's difference with England was now basing itself on an anti-modernist attitude. As England became more democratic and more radical, Ireland looked to nostalgic versions of conservative politics and culture — supplied by the clergy and by writers — for projections of its own destiny. Thus, radical movements in England and the radical demand of the Irish for separation, ostensibly akin to one another, were in fact opposed. One looked to democratic reform and modernization for the achievement of its aims; the other, Irish nationalism, looked to separation and the repudiation of difference. The position is complex, for it would be wrong to say that Irish nationalism was therefore anti-democratic. It was opposed to that kind of democratic reform which England was undergoing, more on the ground that it was English than that it was democratic. James Larkin and, more importantly, James Connolly were to attempt to overcome this intramural contradiction in Irish nationalism, but it could be argued that they were themselves overcome by it. Nationalism was a liberation movement in so far as it was opposed to English imperialism, but it was an incarcerating movement in so far as its opposition to imperialism extended to hostility towards even those forces in England itself that were anti-imperialistic.

For a time, there were alternatives to separatist, cultural nationalism. One was Fenianism, the other was Parnellism. Fenianism had a long battle, which it finally won and lost simultaneously, with a problem that may be expressed in this way: it could organize funerals but it could not organize an insurrection. In other words, it could rely on mass support for gestures of defiance but not for acts of rebellion. Only a few people would turn up for an insurrection; hundreds of thousands would turn up for a funeral. It was easier to admire than to imitate a John O'Leary or an O'Donovan Rossa. James Stephens, much criticized for his endless deferral of the day of revolution, at least recognized the scale of organization required if farce-rebellions like 1848 and, as it turned out, 1867, were to be avoided. The marshalling of the funerals of Terence Bellew MacManus and of the Manchester Martyrs was impressive; so too was the stand taken against the catholic clergy's interference in politics, ratified by the role of the church in the Parnell crisis. Further, John Devoy in America was another believer in the need for organization and the priority of propaganda victories over ramshackle military adventures. The rescue of Stephens and of Fenian prisoners from Australia were far more effective blows against the establishment than an abortive uprising. Fenianism took as gospel John Mitchel's, and later Davitt's, explanation for the failure of 1848 during the Famine. The people were demoralized and therefore chose to die of starvation rather than in rebellion. Fenianism was a movement aimed to overcome that demoralization by the exercise of a steely determination embodied in a well-drilled militant secret society. It helped to create that climate of opinion which finally prevailed after 1916. Then there had been a funeral (O'Donovan Rossa's) followed by an insurrection. As usual, the crowds turned out for the funeral and only a tiny number for the insurrection. But the executions that followed brought out the Fenian constituency, which had been created, with the help of the Land League and the somewhat unwitting help of the Irish Parliamentary Party, over almost sixty years.

The military chivalry, and the fierce determination of the Fenians, made such a startling contrast with the squalid bickerings of the Parliamentary Party after Parnell, that this too aided their cause. They served long and brutal prison sentences and spent extended periods in exile; but many of them also managed to live to a great age and therefore became — O'Leary is the prime example — emblematic figures for the younger generation, as noble as Parnell, but not humiliated as he was. The sequence of mass funerals followed by minority insurrection finally made its impact in the one place where propaganda is usually most effective — in the polls. Yet even as it won the war, Fenianism, now calling itself Sinn Féin, lost a crucial battle. It managed a radical separation; it broke British rule in most of Ireland, but it did so with a brand of nationalism that was far more conservative and catholic, far less republican, than it had originally conceived. Through Pearse, catholicism and nationalism formed an alliance which peripheralized secular republicanism. In important respects, the catholic church reaped the harvest that Fenianism had sown — a bitter irony, given the mutual hostility between them. On top of that, the problem of Ulster and the nature of unionism (as distinct from Orangeism) was not only ignored; it was more profoundly misunderstood and underestimated.

Parnellites misunderstood unionism too, but seemed to believe that their tactic of conciliation — practiced chiefly by Parnell himself, John Redmond and William O'Brien — would be successful in winning it over to the Home Rule cause. Parnell and Redmond, especially, thought that the conversion of the southern landed gentry to that cause would be sufficient to make the necessary amalgamation. Home Rule could be won by all the Irish wanting it; it could not be lost simply because of British reluctance. Just as it came within sight, the Great War began and Redmond, following the logic of his own and his former leader's position, urged the Irish and the Ulster Volunteers to fight together in one cause and thereby solder the unity that would make the legislation effective. It was not only Easter 1916 and its aftermath that made this a futile hope. At the heart of the matter was a difference between southern and northern unionism which no-one in the Parliamentary Party seems to have seen clearly. Ulster would get the Home Rule she did not want, but only because that was the price that had to be paid for the maintenance of the union with Britain. The possibility of seeing the Ulster situation more clearly was reduced by the after-effects of Parnell's fall, the continuing disputes between Parnellites and anti-Parnellites, the intransigence of John Dillon, and John Redmond's lack of political realism. Redmond was unlike Parnell in his readiness to rely on British politicians to deliver Home Rule. Moreover, the United Party that he led from 1900 to his death was united in name only. He could not reconcile the various factions or control the dominant ex-lieutenants of the great leader — Dillon, Tim Healy and William O'Brien. Redmond's policy of conciliation and toleration culminated in his Woodenbridge speech, but all that led to was the joint destruction of many thousands of both Irish and Ulster Volunteers — and for no political gain. He appeared to have inverted the situation that Parnell had created and exploited with such skill. Instead of having Britain's Liberal Party dependent on the Irish Party, he let it be seen that the Irish Party was dependent on it. It was more and more widely believed that Parnell had been destroyed at the behest of the Liberals; now Home Rule was being withheld in a similar fashion. Parliamentary methods seemed futile unless there was force behind them.

Davitt's Land League had, for a time, supplied that element of force and threat. It took all Parnell's skill to mould the militancy of the movement to his own purposes. So effective was he in this that, by 1903, it seemed to his successor, John Redmond, that the land issue had finally been solved. It did not appear so to either Michael Davitt or William O'Brien. Both of them, in their very different ways, had the perception to recognize that the movement for independence was linked with the form that the settlement of the land question would ultimately take. Davitt, in particular, wanted the solution to stimulate in the Irish a sense of the land as a communal possession. Without that sense, land reform would change only the nature of the problem. It would bring in an inefficient system of peasant proprietorship that would still leave the plight of the landless unchanged and would weaken that generosity of spirit which his increasingly pronounced vision of socialism required as the basis for a truly revolutionary conclusion to the long struggle. He shared with the Fenians (and with anti-Parnellites like John Dillon) the fear that the various land acts, by appeasing large numbers of farmers, would rob the revolutionary movement of its impetus. His book *The Fall of Feudalism in Ireland* (1904) is important because it completes what Lalor and Mitchel had begun — the campaign against the garrison ascendancy of landed proprietors and against the spirit of helpless subservience in the people who had lived and died in such miserable conditions under it. Yet Davitt had to acknowledge the limitations of these achievements. The sense of national brotherhood and community was insufficient to overcome the hunger for individual ownership of the land. Neither the spirit of the people nor their agricultural productivity were sufficiently improved by land reform. In that sense it did reduce the commitment to Home Rule. It placated an important constituency without transforming the community.

On the other hand, William O'Brien, in founding his United Irish League (UIL) in 1898, seemed to believe that the basis of a new community could be formed by the creation of an alliance between the outgoing landed gentry and the incoming peasant proprietors. In effect, this would be a union between catholic and protestant elements which, if successful, would have an emollient effect upon sectarian feeling throughout the island. Although the UIL had its successes, not the least of which was the reunification of the Irish Parliamentary Party, in the end it too failed to make mutually supportive the connection between land reform and the movement for self-government. It was Arthur Griffith, the founder of Sinn Féin, who was able to preach a doctrine of economic self-sufficiency that would be allied to a national purpose — but only on the condition that the Irish withdraw from Westminster and cease the pursuit of the elusive and meaningless Home Rule, which Grattan and Flood had already won in 1782-83. The question of the form of the connection between the two islands was not, in Griffith's account, centred on the issue of executive power; it was a formal connection, soluble by accepting that the islands were under one crown.

Griffith's *The Resurrection of Hungary* (1904) draws a rather quaint parallel between the respective positions of Hungary and Ireland within the Austrian and British Empires. The pertinence or otherwise of the analogy does not matter in the least now and did not matter a great deal then. The comparison was a rhetorical device to stimulate the public into thinking of an alternative to Home Rule and to make economic sufficiency a priority of this new departure. According to Griffith, the legitimacy of the Irish claim to self-government had been conceded in the Renunciation Act of 1783. Since then, Britain had denied that legitimacy and had promoted futile rebellion in the cause of separatism in order to provide an excuse for reducing Ireland to economic servitude and incorporating its independent parliament within the walls of Westminster. Thus, the tradition of violent rebellion, from the United Irishmen down to the Fenians, was in effect nothing more than an instrument of British policy, inaugurated by Pitt. The Sinn Féin idea was novel in that it offered an alternative to both the constitutional and the physical force movements as they were then. It by no means reconciled them, but it provided a concept of legitimacy that Pearse and his colleagues were able to mobilize on behalf of the physical force movement and that made the efforts of the Irish Party at Westminster appear redundant. Sinn Féin weakened the Irish Party and strengthened the physical force movement. Yet it simultaneously cast doubt on the republican claim to a revolutionary ancestry, and reproduced, in a different form, the old conflict between constitutionalism and rebellion. Where Pearse derived legitimacy from Tone and 1798, Griffith claimed it from Grattan and Flood and 1782-83. The distinction, which did not seem so crucial at the turn of the century, became so after the Anglo-Irish Treaty of 1921. It must be said, though, that Griffith, no more than any other politician of the period, envisaged the possibility of a partitioned island. He assumed that what had been won in the eighteenth century could be resumed in the twentieth century, with the achievement of economic self-sufficiency as the enabling factor. Ulster's political opposition at first did not seem to him a formidable reality.

So, in the light of Sinn Féin policy, there was no need to worry, like the Fenians and Dillon, that the reforms from Westminster might rob the movement towards self-government of its rationale. Nor was there need to hope — with Redmond and O'Brien — that the success of such reforms might lead to a conciliation of all the parties affected by them in Ireland. Griffith simply postulated the notion that nothing at all need come from Westminster; the vital legitimacy already had been conceded, was on the statute book and only had to be made effective. Ireland's claim to self-government effectively was already established.

After 1916, Sinn Féin was merely the umbrella movement for the descendants of the Fenians and the Irish Republican Brotherhood. By then, the republic had been proclaimed, legitimacy had been reformulated as the tradition of the physical force movement and the withdrawal from Westminster and the setting up of separate Irish institutions of government, as advocated by Griffith, followed. The outstanding issues of the land and the Ulster question could not alter the amazing fact that the IRB-Fenian movement, dressed in Sinn Féin colours, finally won the support of the majority of the Irish people in 1918. Riven by dissension, wooed by elusive promises, without a great leader and without a defined policy, the Irish Party broke under the strain of the world war and the insurrection. Nothing legitimized the violence of the Irish revolutionaries more effectively than the violence of the British authorities. Constitutionalism collapsed. The new Sinn Féin had exposed the pharisaic face of British rule in Ireland. The trouble was that, through Griffith's influence, the Irish claim to the legitimacy of their own constitutional existence could thereafter be challenged by the opposing Irish claim to the legitimacy of violence against any constitutional arrangement that seemed unsatisfactory or incomplete. But in this old debate, rehearsed in totally different circumstances, the Irish Party had no part to play.

But perhaps the worst blow to the Irish Party had been self-inflicted long before in Committee Room 15 of the House of Commons, by the overthrow and subsequent death of Parnell. His shade haunted the Irish Party thereafter. At key moments — in 1898, for example — its ignoble divisions and squabbles seemed to invoke in the people at large a longing for that solitary presence. Even William O'Brien's UIL of 1898 could not make the party look particularly inspiring in the centenary year of 1798. In

1916, the party could not stop the executions of the leaders of the rebellion. Parnell, in his austerity and in his disdain, was the only leader who seemed capable of making the ambiguity of his policies part of the cryptic nature of his personality. He served both the idea of constitutional politics and of physical force. Most of all, he never seemed to plead. Parnell was recruited into the literature, the memoirs, the popular press of the period — journalism was a strong profession among the members of his party — as the individual embodiment of the autonomy to which the country aspired. The British had tried to destroy him and had failed; success came only when the Irish decided to destroy him themselves.

Parnell's fate was a parable. Independence could be won from the British but only the Irish could lose it themselves, through internecine fighting. All the crises and issues of those years had plainly shown how severe and multiple were the sources of mutually ruinous strife. Most importantly, the relationship between the proponents of constitutional and violent methods, itself a source of endless division and comment, seemed to have been resolved by Parnell before it was resolved by the community he led.

Finally, this strange man had given up his authority and his achievements for a woman's love. That added both to his glamour and to the scandal he represented. Against the opposition of church and state, he demanded from his party fidelity to himself as a person. Although it was not given, the refusal was felt as a betrayal. Once the uncrowned king was dead, the only possible successor was his myth. His career belonged to history; his fall became a legend. Then the legend itself became part of the historical consciousness of the people again. As such, it remained a parable of self-creation and self-mutilation, tragically appropriate for the decades after his death.

I. UNIONISM TO HOME RULE

W.E.H. LECKY

(1838-1903)

from:
LEADERS OF PUBLIC OPINION IN IRELAND (1861)

[This essay was published in the first edition of Lecky's first important work, *Leaders of Public Opinion in Ireland* (1861). It was not reprinted in the later editions. Lecky's title is simply 'Clerical Influences'; the subtitle given here was supplied by W.E.G. Loyd and F. Cruise O'Brien, who published this essay, with a introduction, for the Irish Self-Government Alliance in 1911. The editors hoped to show that 'National Self-Government' was the surest means of 'destroying sectarian ill-feelings' and would, when achieved, 'obliterate the line upon which politics and religion coincide in Ireland.' In reprinting Lecky's essay of fifty years before, they hoped to show that the lack of patriotism and public spirit lamented by Lecky had been repaired by the Home Rule movement. This was a view of the matter shared by Isaac Butt (see following excerpt), although Lecky himself was never so sanguine. He disliked democracy, he favoured the Union and therefore he was bound to seek some system of government in Ireland that would be oligarchic, benign and civilizing in its effects. His vision of the Irish eighteenth century is an embodiment of this political dream. The last five volumes of his eight-volume *A History of England in the Eighteenth Century* are devoted to Ireland and to a description of the culture that might have emerged from the eighteenth-century experience.

In this essay, Lecky demonstrates what seemed to him to be governing conditions for the disabling divisions of

Irish public life. The premise of his argument throughout is that a failure in the public spirit of a nation leads to the withering of all aspects of its cultural, social and political existence. Burke's influence is patent in the distinction between 'organic' and 'mechanical' governments and in Lecky's insistence on the need to find a consensual basis, deriving from the traditions and character of the people, for the operation of effective government.]

CLERICAL INFLUENCES. AN ESSAY ON IRISH SECTARIANISM AND ENGLISH GOVERNMENT

... 'Government,' to adopt a fine saying of Kossuth,[1] 'is an organism and not a mechanism.' It should grow out of the character and the traditions of the people. It should present a continuous, though ever-developing, existence, connecting the present of the nation with its past. The statesman should be merely the representative of his age, accomplishing those changes which time and public opinion had prepared. The mechanical system, which regards only the intrinsic excellence of a political arrangement, irrespectively of the antecedents and the public opinion of the people, proves the invariable source of national calamity. Sometimes it produces vast and heterogeneous empires, disunited in feeling in proportion as they are centralised in government; exhibiting a legislative system almost perfect in compactness, symmetry, and harmony, and a people smouldering in continual half-suppressed rebellion. Sometimes, as in Ireland, it exhibits the strange spectacle of a free Government almost neutralised in its action by the discontent of the people, and failing in the most glaring manner to discharge its functions as the organ of their feelings and of their opinions.

There is, perhaps, no Government in the world that succeeds so admirably in eliciting, sustaining, and directing public opinion, as that of England. It does not, it is true, escape much adverse criticism among the people. A system so complex, and, in some respects, so anomalous, presents numerous points of attack, and the transparent element of publicity that invests all political matters in England, renders its defects peculiarly apparent.... But in one respect its excellence is indisputable. No intelligent foreigner, we believe, could land upon the English coast without being struck with the intensity of the political life pervading every class of the community. It permeates every pore; it thrills and vibrates along every fibre of the political body; it diffuses its action through the remotest village; it differs equally from the dull torpor of most continental nations in time of calm, and from their feverish and spasmodic excitement in time of commotion. Everywhere is exhibited a steady, habitual interest and confidence in the proceedings of Government. The decision of Parliament, if not instantly accepted, is never without its influence on the public mind. The ill-feeling, the suspicions, the apprehensions, the peccant humours that agitate the people, find there their vent, their resolution, and their end.

Little or nothing of this kind is to be found in Ireland. Severed from their ancient traditions, and ruled by a Legislature imposed on them contrary to their will; differing essentially in character and in temperament from the nation with whom they are thus associated; humiliated by the circumstances of their defeat and by the ceaseless ridicule poured on them through every organ of the press, and through every channel of literature, the Irish people seem to have lost all interest in English politics. Parliament can make their laws, but it cannot control or influence their feelings. It can revolutionise the whole system of government, but it cannot allay one discontent, or quell one passion. Public opinion is diseased — diseased to the very core. Instead of circulating in healthy action through the land, it stagnates, it coagulates, it corrupts. The disease manifests itself in sullen discontent, in class warfare, in secret societies, in almost puerile paroxysms of hatred against England, in a perpetual vacillation on all points but one — antipathy to the existing system.... The mass of the people seem to have no intelligible principles and no settled sympathies. Two-thirds of the population — the portion that is most distinctively and characteristically Irish — the classes who form the foundation of the political system, and who must ever rise in wealth and importance, seem to follow implicitly the guidance of the priests, and, like them, to be thoroughly alienated from England....

The gravity of the facts we have mentioned is sufficiently evident, yet, if these were all, the evil would most probably be but temporary — a discontent which was purely retrospective would hardly prove permanent. Ill feeling would grow fainter every year, as the memory of the past faded

1. Lajos Kossuth (1802-94), Hungarian nationalist leader in the revolution of 1848.

from the minds of the people, and the existence of a free press necessitating *some* public opinion would gradually identify the public mind with that of England. Unfortunately, however, there exists in Ireland a topic that effectually prevents discontent from languishing, or the sentiments of the two nations from coalescing. Sectarian animosity has completely taken the place of purely political feeling, and paralyses all the energies of the people. This is indeed the master curse of Ireland — the canker that corrodes all that is noble and patriotic in the country, and, we maintain, the direct and inevitable consequence of the Union. Much has been said of the terrific force with which it would rage were the Irish Parliament restored. We maintain, on the other hand, that no truth is more clearly stamped upon the page of history, and more distinctly deducible from the constitution of the human mind, than that a national feeling is the only effectual check to sectarian passions. Nothing can be more clear than that the logical consequences of many of the doctrines of the Church of Rome would be fatal to an independent and patriotic policy in any land — nothing is more clear than that in every land, where a healthy national feeling exists, Roman Catholic politicians are both independent and patriotic.

But, putting this case for a moment aside, consider that of an evangelical Protestant. If the power of government be placed in the hands of a man who has a vivid, realising, and ever-present conviction that every idolater who dies in his belief is doomed to a future of wretchedness, compared with which the greatest earthly calamity is absolutely inappreciable; that the doctrinal differences between the members of a church whose patronage he administers really influence the eternal welfare of mankind; that this visible world, with all its pomp and power, with all its intellectual and political greatness, is but as a gilded cloud floating across the unchanging soul, and that the political advantages of the acquisition of an empire would be dearly purchased by the death of a single soldier who died unrepentant, and who would have repented had he lived; — we ask any candid man to consider what sort of a governor such a person would prove himself. Is it not self-evident that anyone who was thoroughly penetrated with a belief in these doctrines, who habitually and systematically observed in his actions and his feelings the proportion of religious to temporal things which he recognises in his creed, would govern almost exclusively with a view to the former? Possessing enormous power that might be employed in the service of his church, he would sacrifice every other consideration — the dignity, the stability, the traditional alliances, the future greatness, of the nation — to this single object. His policy would dislocate the whole mechanism of government. It would at least place an insuperable barrier to the future prosperity of his country. And if men who believe these doctrines do not act in the manner we have described, the reason is very obvious. Just as in everyday life, the man who has persuaded himself of the nothingness of human things finds his conviction so diluted and dimmed by other feelings that he takes an interest in common business, such as he could not take if he realised what he believed; so the politician finds the national and patriotic spirit that pervades the atmosphere in which he moves a sufficient corrective of his theological views. These latter give a tincture and bias to his political feeling, but they do not supplant it. They blend with it, and form an amalgam, not perhaps quite defensible in theory, but exceedingly excellent in practice. The nation which is actuated by the same mixed motives always selects for power men who are thus moderate and unimpassioned in their views, and it is deeply sensible of the fact that no greater political calamity can befall a land than to be governed by religious enthusiasts.

Now the application of what we have said to the case of the Irish Roman Catholics is evident. The Roman Catholic doctrines concerning the nature of heresy, the duty of combating it, and the authority of the Pope in every land can be easily shown to be in many conceivable cases incompatible with a patriotic discharge of the duties of a representative, especially in a Protestant country. The opponents of emancipation dilated continually on this fact, and they argued that the Roman Catholic members would never assimilate with the Protestants, that they would never really seek the welfare of the country, that they would remain an isolated and, in some respects, a hostile body, drawing their real inspiration from the Vatican. The advocates of the measure replied by pointing to the numerous instances in which Roman Catholic politicians in other countries discharged their duties as patriots, in defiance of the exertions of the priests and of the wishes of the Pope.... But at the same time most persons, we think, will allow that the predicted assimilation of the Roman Catholic with the Protestant members has not taken place, that the sectarian feelings of the former have not been neutralised or materially modified by other sentiments, and that their chief interests are attached to Rome and to the priests. The explanation of this fact seems to be that the tenets we have adverted to have these dangerous tendencies when their force is undiluted and unimpaired. In most countries a purely political and patriotic feeling exists to counteract them — in Ireland it does not exist. The people of Ireland do not sympathise in the proceedings of the Imperial Parliament, and they have no national legislature to foster and to reflect the national sentiment. If purely political feeling be eliminated from a people who possess a representative system, and who are separated by rival creeds, the result is inevitable. The people and their representatives will be divided into those who are actuated by personal and those who are actuated by sectarian motives. We greatly doubt whether any conceivable alteration of religious endowments or of the other semi-religious matters so much complained of would effectually check the sectarian character of Irish politics. The evil has a deeper source, and must be met by a deeper remedy.

If the characteristic mark of a healthy Christianity be to unite its members by a bond of fraternity and love, there is no country in the world in which Christianity has more completely failed than in Ireland, and the failure is distinctly and directly attributable to the exertions of the clergy. With the religious aspect of this subject we have now no concern, but its political importance is of the most overwhelming and appalling magnitude.

It is a lamentable but, we fear, an undoubted fact that if the whole people of Ireland were converted to Mohammedanism nine-tenths of the present obstacles to the prosperity of the country would be removed. The great evil that meets us on every side, that palsies every political effort, and dwarfs the growth of every secular movement, is — that the repulsion of sectarianism is stronger than the attraction of patriotism. The nation is divided into two classes who are engaged in virulent, unceasing, and uncompromising strife. Differences of race, that would otherwise have long since been effaced, are stereotyped by being associated with differences of belief. Rancour, that would naturally have passed into the domain of history, exhibits a perpetual and undiminished energy; for of all methods of making hatred permanent and virulent, perhaps the most effectual is to infuse a little theology into it. The representatives of the Protestants scarcely disguise their anti-national feelings. They have cut themselves off from all the traditions of Swift, of Grattan, and of Curran. They have adopted a system of theology the most extreme, the most aggressive, and the most unattractive. They have made opposition to the Roman Catholics the grand object of their policy, and denunciation of the Maynooth Grant[2] (which they stigmatise as sinful) the most prominent exhibition of that policy. There is scarcely an article that appears in *The Times* newspaper, ridiculing Ireland and the Irish, that is not reproduced with applause by a large section of the Protestant journals.

It is an observation of Burke's that 'when the clergy say their church is in danger they speak broad, and mean that their emoluments are in danger';[3] and perhaps upon this principle the policy of the Protestant clergy may be considered advantageous to Protestantism in Ireland. In every other respect there can be little question that it is merely detrimental — that it is absolutely ruinous to it. Religion is the empire of the sympathies, and a Church that is in habitual opposition to the sympathies, the wishes, and the hopes of the mass of the people — a Church which is identified in their minds only with a recollection of bygone persecutions and of the defeat of a great popular movement — a Church which has cast aside its nationality, and associated itself with all that is unpatriotic, will never progress among the people. Persecution has sometimes caused such a church to triumph; by argument and eloquence it never can. The experience of three hundred years has sufficiently demonstrated the fallacy of the old theory of the 'expansive character' of Protestantism, and of the irresistible force of truth. Simple, unmingled reasoning never converts a people. When the taint of selfishness is on a preacher, his arguments are as empty wind. It would be impossible to conceive a more invidious position than that which the Protestant Church now occupies in Ireland, in spite of the numerous and the immense

2. The British government grant to the Roman catholic seminary at Maynooth, Co. Kildare was increased from £9,000 to £26,000 in 1845, to the dismay of many Irish protestants.
3. These words have not been traced in Burke's writings.

advantages it possesses. Historically the Protestant can show that in the time of her national independence Ireland was unconnected with Rome — that it was England that introduced and fostered the Roman Church in Ireland; that most of those illustrious men whose eloquence furnishes even now the precepts and the expositions of patriotism were Protestants and were Liberals; and that even when the Protestants as a body were opposed to the national cause there were never wanting men of intellect and of energy who left the ranks to join it, and who not unfrequently proved that 'the gleaning of the grapes of Ephraim is better than the vintage of Abiezer.'[4] He can show that the landlords, who are chiefly Protestants, are obviously the natural leaders of the people. He can prove that Protestantism is eminently adapted, from its character, to coalesce with every form of Liberalism; that 'the Reformation was the dawn of the government of public opinion';[5] that every subsequent step towards the emancipation of mankind may be distinctly traced to its influence; and that the Church of Rome has associated herself indissolubly with the despotic theory of government....

Yet notwithstanding all these advantages — notwithstanding the zeal, the piety, and the learning to be found among the Protestant clergy — notwithstanding the eloquence which they exhibit to a greater extent than any other class of their fellow-countrymen, the Protestant Church seems doomed to a hopeless unpopularity in Ireland. Its position is so obviously a false one — its estrangement from the people is so patent that mere arguments avail little in its behalf. Its opposition to the national cause reacts fatally upon itself. The Church that has sold the birthright will never receive the blessing.

Of the political attitude of the Roman Catholic priests it is not necessary to say much. No generous mind can withhold a tribute of admiration from the fidelity, the zeal, and the disinterestedness they have manifested as religious teachers under obstacles of almost unparalleled magnitude. No sincere Liberal can deny that their political leadership has been ruinous to nationality in Ireland. Since the death of O'Connell their continual object has been to make the political strength of their country a weapon in the service of the Vatican. They have exerted their whole influence to prevent that harmony and assimilation of classes which is the only hope of their country. They have laboured most constantly and most effectively to widen every breach, to increase every cause of division, and to prevent in every way in their power the Roman Catholics from mingling with the Protestants. No one, we think, can deny this who has followed their policy on the educational question,[6] who has observed the tone of their organs in the press, or who has perused those dreary semi-political pastorals which their prelates are continually publishing.... But they have gone further than this. The very essence of the policy of O'Connell and of his predecessors was, that the public opinion of a nation should determine its form of government. Of this principle — the only principle upon which the policy of O'Connell was defensible — the Irish Roman Catholics, guided by their priests, are now the bitterest opponents. They have come forward more prominently than any other people as the supporters of the Papal Government at a time when that Government is maintained only by foreign power, and when it has avowedly identified itself with the cause of despotism in Italy.[7]

They have in their hostility to this principle in a great measure abandoned the Liberal party, to which they owe almost every privilege they possess, to identify themselves with the party which has been the unwavering opponent of all religious equality. In other words, they have connected themselves with those who, according to their own principles, have ever been the curse of Ireland, in hopes of thus making themselves the curse of Italy. The only two possible solutions of the present discontents of Ireland are the complete fusion of the people of Ireland with the people of England, or

4. Judges 8.2.
5. John Stuart Mill, *On Liberty* (1859).

6. Sir Robert Peel introduced the Provincial Colleges Act in 1845 to meet the catholic demand for a catholic system of higher education. Three colleges, in Belfast, Cork and Galway, were linked in 1850 to form the Queen's University in Ireland. Queen's University, Belfast was, as a consequence, the first state-built university in the British Isles. The non-denominational nature of the colleges earned them the title the 'godless colleges' and the scheme was fiercely opposed by O'Connell and by Archbishop MacHale of Tuam, although it was welcomed by the Young Irelanders. Under MacHale's influence, papal rescripts were issued in 1847 and 1848 condemning the colleges. Dr Paul Cullen, an agent in Rome for the Irish bishops, was also hostile; the Synod of Thurles (1850), under his leadership, issued a condemnation, followed a year later by another from Pope Pius IX.
7. In 1860 about a thousand Irishmen answered the appeal of Pope Pius IX to fight for the papacy against the forces of Italian nationalism. On their return in 1861 they became known as the Irish Brigade.

else the creation of a healthy national feeling in Ireland, uniting its various classes, and giving a definite character to its policy. Since the death of O'Connell the Roman Catholic priests have been an insuperable obstacle to either solution.

Among the Roman Catholics the priests seem almost omnipotent. Among the Protestants, though the clergy do not exercise by any means the same sway, they have nevertheless succeeded in giving a completely sectarian character to politics. The Protestant press is thoroughly sectarian in its tone. The great questions on the hustings are semi-religious, the Maynooth Grant, the Educational system, the proportion of Protestants and Roman Catholics appointed to office by the Government.

It is thus that Ireland, being deprived of that legislature which has hitherto proved the only effectual organ of national feeling, has come completely under the influence of sectarian passions: class against class, creed against creed, nation against nation; a spectacle of perpetual disunion, of virulent and unabating rancour. All the various elements of dissension of the present and of the past are flung into the alembic of sectarianism, and there fused and blended into an intense, a relentless, and, as it would seem, an increasing hatred. During the lifetime of O'Connell there was a kind of reversionary loyalty among the people. They looked forward to the restoration of the Irish Parliament as the termination of all agitation. Their leader endeavoured earnestly to conciliate the different sections of the people. He placed patriotism before sectarianism, and adopted intelligible principles of policy. While he held the reins of power we should never have heard a eulogy of the Sepoys,[8] or seen the people identifying themselves with foreign despotism; but since he has passed away national feeling seems to have almost perished in the land, and sectarianism to have become more unmitigated and undiluted than in any former period. With the exception of the upper orders, who are in every country somewhat cosmopolitan in their sympathies, and who always readily adapt themselves to any political arrangement, the alienation of the people from English politics seems as absolute and as fixed as ever....

8. The Indian troops who mutinied in 1857-58 were supported by many Irish people. See John O'Leary, in the excerpt from *Recollections of Fenians and Fenianism* (p. 255 below).

The best reason for entrusting political power chiefly to the upper orders, in a constitution like that of England, is not because they are better educated or more thoroughly patriotic than others, or because they have a greater stake in the country, or pay a larger proportion of the taxation, but because they, of all classes, are most skilled in compromise. The refinements of good society, which mould and form their entire natures, are all but an education in compromises. They teach how to conceal disagreeable thoughts — how to yield with grace — how to avoid every jar, and control every passion — how to acquire a pliant and acquiescent manner. The lower classes feel more intensely in political matters — they express their feelings more emphatically — they pursue their course with a more absorbing vehemence. A democratical assembly may govern with energy and wisdom, but it is scarcely possible that it can continue to govern in harmony with another assembly of a different shade of politics. Should further reforms render the House of Commons thoroughly democratical in feeling, the present constitution of England would, doubtless, be much endangered, and the evil of a party whose primary wishes are not attached to the interests of the empire proportionately increased.

And, under any circumstances, dissension between two nations that are so nearly associated must be in itself an evil. Seven hundred years, if they have multiplied causes of dissension, have also multiplied ties of connection. The two nations seem naturally designed for each other, and each without the other is imperfect. Each possesses many of the attributes of greatness, but each is deficient in some qualities for which the other is distinguished. In both nations we find an almost perfect courage and an almost boundless spirit of enterprise; but Englishmen exhibit that steady perseverance, that uniform ascendency of reason over passion, which we so seldom find in Ireland; while Irishmen possess the popularity of manners and the versatility of disposition in which Englishmen are lamentably deficient. Ireland, if contented, would be the complement of England; while hostile, it continues a constant source of danger.

Is this state of things likely to continue? We confess we are not as sanguine as some persons seem to be about the effect of time in assimilating the character of the two nations, and banishing the existing animosity. The discontent in Ireland differs, we think, in kind from that of the twenty years preceding the Union. Then it arose from the imperfections of the national organ of public opinion, now it arises from the want of any such organ; then it diminished every year, while at present political feeling seems to fade more and more into sectarianism. The evil at present is not a torpor of the public mind, but a substitution of a semi-religious for a purely political public opinion. We see few symptoms of this evil abating. The Government, indeed, labours with evident earnestness and considerable success to steer evenly between the two creeds, but the super-abundant theological energies of the English people are constantly welling over upon Ireland. England is consequently but a synonym for Protestantism with the people, and is therefore the object of an undiminishing sectarian antipathy. The very attachment of a large section of the Irish Protestants to England is sufficient to repel the Roman Catholics, for that attachment is more sectarian than political. It is as the Bible-loving land, the bulwark of Protestantism, the terror of Popery. The Established Church serves alsc to foster the sectarian spirit, which, under all these circumstances, possesses an astonishing vitality. It has been observed, too, that the Roman Catholic system being essentially traditional, has a tendency to petrify and to preserve all traditional feelings. We sometimes find Roman Catholic nations changing greatly, but it is generally when their Church has lost its hold upon their characters. The difference between the two religions is much more than a difference of doctrines. The Roman Catholic system forms a type of character wholly different from that of the Protestants, with different virtues and vices, with different modes of thought and feeling. There is so little affinity between the two types, that the Roman Catholics can go on year by year within their own sphere, thinking, acting, writing, speaking, and progressing without being in any very great degree affected by Protestant thought, without losing their distinctive tendencies or sentiments. Much has been said of the effect of the spread of education in destroying sectarianism. A system of education that would attack the religious policy of the Roman Catholics would be, of course, absolutely out of the question; and, in a country like Ireland, where the people are intensely religious in their feelings, we believe the education of the priest must ever prove stronger than the education of the schoolmaster. Nor should we forget that there seems at present a strong probability of national education becoming separate, and consequently thoroughly sectarian. While the bulk of the clergy of both religions denounce the only system of mixed education that appears practicable, it becomes a grave question how long such a system can be maintained.

One thing, however, seems certain — that no system of education that directs the attention of the people to the history of their own land can fail to quicken the national feeling among them. The great obstacle to every liberal party in Ireland, has been the prevailing ignorance of Irish history. The great engine by which the Repeal movement progressed was the diffusion of historical treatises and of the speeches of the leading orators of the past. There are, perhaps, few better means of conjecturing the future of a nation, than to examine in what direction its enthusiasm is likely to act. In Ireland there can scarcely be a question upon the subject. Ever since the dawn of public opinion, there has been a party which has maintained that the goal to which Irish patriots should tend, is the recognition of their country as a distinct and independent nationality, connected with England by the Crown; that in such a condition alone it could retain a healthy political life, and could act in cordial co-operation with England; that every other system would be transient in its duration, and humiliating and disastrous while it lasted. To this party all the genius of Ireland has ever belonged. It is scarcely possible to cite two Irish politicians of real eminence who have not, more or less, assisted it. Swift and Molyneux originated the conception; Burke aided it when he wrote in approval of the movement of '82, and denounced the Penal Laws and the trade restrictions that shackled the energies of Ireland; Sheridan, when he exerted all his eloquence to oppose the Union; Flood, when he formed the national Party in Parliament; Grattan, when he led that party in its triumph and in its fall. The enthusiasm which springs from the memory of the past will ever sustain it; the patriotic passion, which makes the independence of the land its primary object, will foster and inspire it. This passion is too deeply imbedded in human nature to be eradicated by any material considerations. Like the domestic affection, it is one of the first instincts of humanity. As long as the nation retains its distinct character and its history, the enthusiasts of the land will ever struggle against a form of government which was tyrannically imposed, and which has destroyed the national feeling among the people. Statesmen may regard that enthusiasm as irrational, but they must acknowledge its existence as a fact. He who eliminates from his calculations the opinions of fools, proves that he is himself worthy of being enrolled under that denomination.

Another important element of dissension is the tone habitually adopted by English writers towards Ireland. Reasoning *a priori* we might have imagined that common decency would have rendered that tone guarded and conciliatory; for, if England has sometimes had cause to complain of Ireland, Ireland has had incomparably more cause to complain of England. For seven hundred years England has ruled over a nation which has exhibited more than average intellect at home, and far more than average success abroad — a nation which, though its faults are doubtless many and serious, is certainly neither unamiable, ungrateful, nor intractable — and she has left it one of the most discontented and degraded in Europe. She has ruled over a country which seemed designed by Providence to be one of the most flourishing in the world: indented with the noblest harbours — placed between two continents as if to reap the advantage of both — possessing a temperate and salubrious climate and a soil of more than common fertility — and she has left it one of the poorest, one of the most wretched on earth. A fatal blast seems to rest upon it and to counteract all the advantages of Nature. The most superficial traveller is struck with the anomaly. His first inquiry is: What tyranny has so thwarted the designs of Providence? He finds that, according to the confessions of English writers for the six hundred and fifty years that elapsed between the Conquest and the emancipation of the Catholics, the English government of Ireland was one long series of oppressions — that massacres and banishments, confiscations and disqualifications, compulsory ignorance and trade restrictions, were all resorted to; that the industry of the country was so paralysed that it has never recovered its elasticity; that the various classes of the people were so divided that they have never regained their unity; that the character of the nation was so formed and moulded in the die of sorrow, that almost every prominent vice ingrained in the national character may be distinctly traced to the influences of bygone tyranny; and that, when the age of disqualifications had passed, a legislative system was still retained in defiance of the wish of the people, by the nation which proclaims itself the most emphatic asserter of the rights of nationalities.

Such is the past of English government of Ireland — a tissue of brutality and hypocrisy, scarcely surpassed in history. Who would not have imagined that in a more enlightened age the tone of the British press towards Ireland would have been at least moderate, friendly, and conciliatory? Let any candid man judge whether it is so. Let him observe the prominence given to every crime that is committed in Ireland, to every absurdity that can be culled from the Irish press, to every failure of an Irish movement. Let him observe the ceaseless ridicule, the unwavering contempt, the studied depreciation of the Irish character and intellect habitual in the English newpapers. Let him observe their persistent refusal to regard Irish affairs in any light but the ridiculous, and then answer the question for himself. We believe impartial Englishmen will scarcely deny what foreign observers unanimously declare, that the object of the most influential section of the English press is to discredit the Irish intellect and the Irish character before England and before Europe.... As long as Englishmen adopt a tone of habitual depreciation in speaking of the present of Ireland, Irishmen would betray their country were they to suffer the curtain to fall upon its past.

In considering the future of public opinion in Ireland, there is one measure which may some day be carried into effect that would probably have a very great influence, though in what direction it is exceedingly difficult to determine — I mean the disendowment of the Established Church.[9] I waive altogether the discussion of the justice of such a measure, and confine myself to the results that might follow it.... If we regard the question in the light of the past, it seems evident that the Establishment has hitherto been the strongest bulwark of the Union. O'Connell could scarcely have failed if the bulk of the Protestants had not held aloof from him. A very large section at least of those Protestants opposed him simply through love of the Establishment, which they argued could not continue to exist under an Irish Parliament. To the present day we believe that a considerable proportion of the Protestants are attached to the Union on this

9. Achieved in 1869.

ground alone. Whether, in the event of a disendowment of the Establishment, their alienation would be compensated for by any permanent attachment of the Roman Catholics, is a matter of opinion on which it is impossible to pronounce with any certainty.

While, however, I regard the pictures drawn by some writers of the future content of Ireland as absurdly overcharged, I am far from wishing to paint the prospects of the country in colours of unmingled gloom. I do not believe that mere material prosperity or the increase of education will necessarily reclaim public opinion, but I do not overlook the fact that the general tone of thought and feeling in England and on the Continent must modify it greatly. One of the most prominent characteristics of the spirit of the age is its tendency to disassociate politics from religion, and to diminish the extraordinary stress once laid upon dogmatic theology.... The liberality of sentiment pervading the literature of the century will sooner or later do its work, and should any man of transcendent intellect arise in Ireland, he will find that the public mind has been gradually preparing to receive him. There is, perhaps, no country in the world that would respond to the touch of genius so readily as Ireland in the present day. All the elements of a great movement exist among the people — a restless, nervous consciousness of the evil of their present condition, a deep disgust at the cant and the imbecility that are dominant, a keen and intense perception of the charm of genius. Irishmen sometimes forget their great men when they are dead, but they never fail to recognise them when they are living. That acute sense of the power of intellect, and especially of eloquence, which sectarianism has never been able to destroy, which has again and again caused assemblies of the most violent Roman Catholics to hang with breathless admiration on the lips of the most violent Orangemen, is, we think, the most encouraging symptom of recovery. Should a political leader arise whose character was above suspicion, and whose intellect was above cavil, who was neither a lawyer nor a lay preacher, who could read the signs of the times, and make his eloquence a power in Europe, his influence with the people would be unbounded. The selfishness, and bigotry, and imbecility, that have so long reigned, would make the resplendency of his genius but the more conspicuous; the waves of sectarian strife would sink to silence at his voice; the aspirations and the patriotism of Ireland would recognise him as the prophet of the future.

We look forward with unshaken confidence to the advent of such a leader. The mantle of Grattan is not destined to be for ever unclaimed. The soil of Ireland has ever proved fertile in genius, and in no other country in Europe has genius so uniformly taken the direction of politics. Meantime the task of Irish writers is a simple, if not a very hopeful one. It is to defend the character of the nation, aspersed and ridiculed as it is by the writers of England, and still more injured by the vulgarity, the inconsistencies, and the virulence of a large section of those of Ireland. It is to endeavour to lead back public opinion to those liberal and progressive principles from which, under priestly guidance, it has so lamentably aberrated. It is, above all, to labour with unwearied zeal to allay that theological fever which is raging through the land; to pursue this work courageously and unflinchingly amid unpopularity and clamour and reproach; 'to sit by the sick bed of their delirious country, and for the love they bear that honoured name to endure all the insults and all the rebuffs they receive from their frantic mother.'[10] A thankless but not an ignoble task! The Irishman who makes a friend of a fellow-countryman of a different religion to his own is a benefactor to Ireland. As long as the frenzy of sectarianism continues; as long as blind hatred is the actuating principle of the people, Ireland never can rise to a position of dignity or prosperity. She never can act in harmony with other sections of the empire; she never can find content at home or become respected and honoured abroad. Her power would be at once an evil to herself and to England. Her independence would be the dismemberment of the empire. The greatest of all our wants is a lay public opinion. When a healthy national feeling shall have been produced, uniting the different sections of the people by the bond of patriotism and shattering the political ascendency of the clergy, the prosperity of Ireland will have been secured. Whether the public mind may then tend to the ideal of Grattan or the ideal of Pitt,[11] to

10. The actual quotation from Burke's *Letter to a Member of the National Assembly* (1791) reads: '... of those who watch day and night by the bedside of their delirious country, who, for their love to that dear and venerable name, bear all the disgusts and all the buffets they receive from their frantic mother.'

11. William Pitt the Younger (1759-1806), Britain's prime minister 1783-1801, 1804-06, secured the passage of the bill for the Union, but resigned in 1801 when George III denied catholic emancipation.

a distinct Parliament or to a complete fusion with England, I do not venture to predict; but I doubt not that, in whatever direction it may act, it will eventually triumph....

ISAAC BUTT

(1813-79)

from: THE PARLIAMENTARY POLICY OF HOME RULE (1875)

[This is a printed version of the speech Butt delivered to the electors of Limerick on 23 September 1875. On 30 June 1874, he had made the first formal introduction of the Home Rule demand in parliament, after the general election of that year had seen the arrival of 59 Irish members with at least a nominal commitment to the new cause. The Home Rule League had been established in November 1873. It first met in January 1874; two weeks later the general election was held. Butt scarcely had time to formulate the new policy, either to the liberal unionists or to the recently extended electorate. This speech is an important moment in his articulation of the meaning of the Home Rule policy. In it, he claims that Home Rule in fact would provide the anti-sectarian public opinion that Lecky had claimed was sorely lacking in Ireland. In the 1876 session of parliament, Parnell stated that 'home rule would necessarily entail the repeal of the Union'. Butt did not agree; for him it was vital that liberal unionism be won to the cause precisely on the ground that it would be beneficial to Ireland without being detrimental to the Union.]

UNION OF IRISHMEN

... And may I not add to these two results another equal in its importance to either of them. In the Home Rule movement we have taught men of different creeds to meet together in the brotherhood of being fellow-workers in a struggle for the freedom and greatness of their native land. We have done much to break down the animosities falsely called religious which have been so long the curse of our country. We have succeeded to an extent never before realised in accomplishing that union between Catholic and Protestant which was the cherished object of O'Connell's great heart. I have been present at many meetings of our Home Rule Council, at which matters of deep interest to Ireland have been freely and unreservedly discussed, but at which no stranger could have told the religious profession of any one man who took part in the discussion; when he could not tell, except it might be by some difference in dress, whether he was a Catholic or Protestant clergyman who spoke; and I have hailed in this the omen and earnest of the day that will yet come when a voice will come from a united Ireland, demanding equal rights for all, and liberty and Self-Government for the common country of us all....

GENERAL POLICY

In fulfilling the task I have undertaken this evening I am afraid I must trespass for some time on your patience by a statement that may be tedious. It will be necessary for me briefly to refer to most of the subjects which have engaged, or which ought to have engaged, the attention of Irish politicians. Upon all of these I am quite sure the Irish party in the House of Commons ought to take action. It is of the utmost importance to the national cause that upon all those questions the demands of the Irish people should be placed clearly and distinctly before the British Parliament. You know that from the day you elected me I have always stated that this should be the course of your representatives. I have always said that every measure we could succeed in obtaining was a help to Home Rule. If Ireland be in earnest in her demand for Self-Government everything that gives vigour to her national life adds strength to that demand. Every measure of justice that is refused supplies another argument for Home Rule. But I never entertained a doubt that in the position in which we are placed it is the duty of the Irish representatives to press in earnestness and sincerity on Parliament the measures which Ireland needs. It is their duty to themselves, to the great cause they represent — their duty to their country, and, I will say it, to the assembly of which they are members — that they should, to the utmost of their power, protest against each and every part of the system of mis-government which is crushing and degrading their country; that they should demand redress for every grievance which Ireland endures, whether it be the evils of our land system, which are still unredressed, or the attempt to force upon us a system of education of which the nation disapproves. In the denial of equal rights and privileges with England — in all the various forms in which the mischief of anti-national rule shows itself — upon every grievance, I repeat, we ought to demand redress and justice, and leave to the Parliament that does so all the responsibility of rejecting our demand. Wherever we saw the chance of carrying a good measure, I believe we ought to use every effort for its success.

HOME RULE — FIRST OBJECT

But in saying this I must not be misunderstood. Every day's experience of the Imperial Parliament but deepens my conviction of the absolute incompetency of that Parliament to manage Irish affairs, and my conviction that Ireland never can enjoy good government, contentment, or prosperity until those affairs are managed by a Parliament of our own. But more than this. Every hour increases my confidence that the restoration of that Parliament rests with ourselves — that if the Irish people show themselves resolute and determined to obtain it, it must be conceded....

CONFIDENCE IN THE FUTURE

I end as I began by saying my confidence in the triumph of our cause is unshaken. The plans we have formed may fail, England may be deaf to all the appeals of reason. I have explained to you the plans on which I propose to work; they may fail, but if they do my confidence in our cause is unshaken.[1] I confide in the unconquered and unconquerable determination of the Irish people to be free. I confide, I say it reverently, in that God who has preserved that people mysteriously and miraculously from the persecution of seven hundred years; from the attempt to drive them from their native land, from the sword of Cromwell, from the confiscations of Elizabeth, from the famine of 1846; has guided them miraculously against persecution unparalleled in the history of the world, and has kept them true to their ancient faith. I believe in that God that He intends great destinies for the Irish race, and I trust in Him that those destinies will be accomplished. Men may laugh at this as fanaticism. There are those who, if they dared, would not believe in the coming of tomorrow's sun. As the shades of night have closed around us, in many a place where unholy trades are plied, in the dens where deeds of plunder and violence are done, in the haunts of infamy and crime, in the abodes of impurity and vice — there are those who hate the coming of tomorrow's sun that will pour the blessed light of day on their dishonest or unholy avocations; but just as well might these men stamp on the earth, and bid that sun not rise again but leave their darkness undisturbed, as all the men who have profited by the long night of Ireland's darkness think to stay that sun of freedom that will yet rise and invigorate and flood with light every nook and corner of our land.

1. This was the heart of the matter. If his plans failed, Butt had no alternative in view. It was his refusal to go farther, to admit, in his own phrase, that 'we have no common interest with England' which deprived him of the leadership and left the way open to Parnell, Joseph Biggar, T.P. O'Connor and John Dillon.

from:
LAND TENURE IN IRELAND; A PLEA FOR THE CELTIC RACE (1866)

[This is one of the pamphlets by Butt that Michael Davitt claimed 'became text-books for Land League speakers and writers.' The excerpt is from the Preface to the third edition (all three editions came out in 1866). Part of its interest now is Butt's concern with the Fenians and his recognition that they, with their emigrant support abroad, posed a threat to the relationship between England and Ireland, which was underestimated by the British government. Equally underestimated, of course, was the sense of radical injustice that created militant organizations like the Fenians. Butt finds the roots of this feeling in the system of landlordism. This tract is therefore one of the many that made the evils of landlordism central to the critique of the Irish national situation. Yet the success of this attack upon landlordism in the end did not lead to the solution of the national question. It was overtaken by the drive for separation from the United Kingdom, a consequence that would have horrified Butt.]

. . . I knew and felt how hard it is to expect men to give to the great problem of Ireland's social condition the calm, the patient, the laborious investigation without which the difficulties of that problem can never be understood. Yet, confident in the power of truth, I did hope that even such words as I could use might not be without their influence in inducing men of intellect and thought to consider the Irish question in a point of view in which possibly it had never been presented to them before.

In this hope I wrote — not to appeal to the passions of the people — not flattering the prejudices of any class — but endeavouring, calmly and patiently, to reason out the conclusions which long and careful reflection had established as convictions in my own mind.

In this hope I have not been disappointed. Apart from public criticism, I have received the far more valuable testimony of many private communications. I am perfectly convinced that the views expressed in these pages are gradually but surely making their way. It is among the most gratifying of these instances that I have received assurances from many persons allied with territorial interests in Ireland — persons holding strongly the opinions generally described as conservative, that reading this tract, with the strongest prejudices against it, they became convinced of the justice and expediency of the proposal it contains.

One argument has been used against me, which I confess I have never read, either in public or private comments, without shame and indignation. It is said by many that my proposal is right, that my arguments are unanswerable, but *that it is impracticable, because there is no hope of the British Parliament ever acceding to it*.

Now, in the first place, I must say that this is no answer to the tract. I did not undertake to prove that any particular Parliament or government would accede to the proposal I made. I did undertake to prove, and I have proved, that the measure I advocate is essential to the very existence of the Irish people.

If it be said that this is true, but that, nevertheless, we have a form of government under which it can never be passed — what is this but to say that our present constitution is one wholly unfit for the Irish nation? It is one that fails in the very first duty of government to that nation. This is a question, be it remembered, affecting the homes of the Irish people, the very existence of the tenant farmer — the lives of his children. Upon this question I am told that no matter how conclusively I prove that a certain measure is essential to the preservation of the Irish people — to the well-being of all classes in the Irish community — I am wrong in urging it, because there is no chance of the English Government ever letting it become law. *Non meus hic sermo.*[1] The argument is one that ought not to be used by any friend to English connexion — by any person friendly to the existing order of things. To what does it inevitably lead? To this. The form of government to which such an argument can apply is one that ought not to exist for one hour, if it be possible for any exertion or sacrifice on the part of Irishmen to destroy it. . . .

I for one must reiterate the expression of my belief that throughout the great mass of the Irish people there exists not merely disaffection to, but hatred of, British rule. The Irish peasant regards the Law and the Government as his natural enemies. I have traced, I believe, clearly and satisfactorily, this spirit of disloyalty to that system of land tenure which makes the law of landlord and tenant a code of conquest and enmity to his home. But whatever be the cause, no one who really knows the country will deny the fact. Throughout the greater part of Ireland the mass of the people are entirely disaffected to English institutions, English power, and English law. They are not the true friends of England who would vainly endeavour to conceal this.

No man will deliberately say that this is a state of things which ought to be permitted to continue. It is not safe for the country; it is not safe for the Irish gentry; it is not — I say it emphatically — it is not safe for the British Crown. The terror of British arms may repress that disaffection into sullen discontent. It is easy to tell us of the hopelessness of insurrection, of the crushing power that would trample down, in a few hours, the desultory rising of an undisciplined peasantry. All! all may be true!

1. *Recte* 'nec meus hic sermo est' (this is no talk of mine): Horace, *Satires* II, ii, 2.

but there is a lesson in all history which tells us that no empire ever yet was safe which nurtured in its bosom a whole community of rebels to its sway.

But far more formidable than our domestic disaffection is the startling fact which recent events have revealed to us, that wherever the Irish race have found a home in distant lands, they have carried with them their hatred of England — a hatred no longer muffled by the deadening influences which depressed them at home. How often, in years not long gone by, were British statesmen warned that in driving Irishmen from Ireland they were only creating a more formidable community of enemies abroad? Who will say that the warning is not now realized?

Time was — not many years ago — when the great American continent was really to us another world. In the memory of the present generation those who had emigrated to it were separated for their lives from home politics and home concerns. To the 'Exile of Erin' who had made his home in Maryland or New York, except in vain and fond regrets, Ireland was nothing. He was nothing to Ireland. The far-seeing sagacity of genius might discern that there were links which still bound a severed race in a common fortune, which one day or other they would assert in common; but, forty or even twenty years ago, the British statesman who thought only of the present might safely have disregarded the fiercest passions which then agitated the Irish emigrants in the United States.

This is not so now. The increased intercourse between nations, the freer interchange of thought, the physical discoveries which have shortened the passage over the Atlantic — those more marvellous ones which are now enabling us to transmit the instantaneous message — all these things have brought the great Western Republic close to our shores. The Irish race on each side of the Atlantic are not now as entirely separated as they were. The millions of Irishmen who are dispersed over the continent of America are every day more identified with the Irish at home. In feeling, in sympathy, in political sentiment, they are become one people as well as one race.

I have no wish to exaggerate the importance or the danger of that Fenian conspiracy, of which the great characteristic is that it has combined into common action the disaffection of Irishmen in Ireland and of those in the United States. Those who formed that organization may, in a more literal sense, repeat the boast of Canning[2] — they saw the weakness of Irish disaffection as compared with the tremendous force to which, at home, it is opposed. They have called in the resources of the New World to redress the inequality of the balance of power in the Old.

But surely there is no one whom official or professional duty has led to trace the course of that organization, however imperfectly revealed, who has not felt the enormous power of Irish disaffection. The name of James Stephens[3] is now familiar in every district of the great continent of North America — in every hamlet in the United Kingdom. It is known in every country in Europe. A few years ago he was an obscure individual — without wealth, or station, or distinction. If he is now formidable — surely he is so, even to British power — it is to be traced to nothing but this, that alone, unaided, without friends, or influence, or money, he dared to rely on the disaffection of Irishmen, wherever they were to be found, and with dauntless energy and an unwearying perseverance, set himself to appeal to it. If that disaffection had not existed in a character and with a fanaticism of which we can only form a faint idea from indications such as this, he would have only been beating the air.

In what I have written as to the existence of Irish disaffection, I have expressed, and meant to express, no opinion whatever upon the question — how far the people have attached themselves to the conspiracy which is evidently causing so much uneasiness to the government. The two things are perfectly distinct. There are thousands, and tens of thousands, of Irishmen who have stood aloof from that movement because they would not take the responsibility of engaging their countrymen in a hopeless insurrection. There are thousands and tens of thousands more who have actively discountenanced and opposed it, either from the same motive, or because they regarded it as associated with views hostile to religion; many more because they credited the statements which represented the whole plan as one of communism or plunder. But these men are not therefore loyal to the British crown. No mistake could be greater than to suppose

2. George Canning (1770-1827), British foreign secretary 1822-27 and briefly prime minister in 1827, used this phrase in a speech in 1826.
3. James Stephens (1824-1901), one of the founders and chief organizer of the Fenians.

that all even of those who are determinedly opposed to Fenianism are, therefore, well affected to the government under which they live. The real extent of Irish disaffection will never be revealed until an opportunity arises when men can join the standard of revolt with a rational prospect of success, and under circumstances which would ensure them a regular government if they succeeded in subverting that which is established.

We have no means of judging of the actual strength in enrolled numbers of the secret confederation which unquestionably exists — still less of forming an opinion how many of these could be relied on when the occasion for their services had actually arisen. It is not a little remarkable, that among all the revelations which were made at the state trials of last Winter,[4] no information was given as to the numbers of the confederacy.... No informer could even say that he had ever heard of such an estimate. For anything that was proved at these trials, the strength of the conspiracy may be estimated at anything from 5,000 to 100,000 men. We can only conjecture its strength from the preparations made by Government to meet it, and from the evidences that are supplied by the occasional discoveries that occur. We may assume that our rulers do not move troops and gunboats, and agitate and alarm the whole country, without reliable information of the existence of a really dangerous organization. We may also suppose that men would not import quantities of elaborately finished rifles, unless they had some persons ready to use them. In the inferences which may be drawn from these and some few similar facts, consists nearly the whole knowledge possessed by the Irish public on the subject.

They are, however, sufficient to establish that the Fenian organization has, at all events, acquired considerable strength. When we recollect all the influences by which it was opposed — all the obloquy by which it was borne down — and call to mind, at the same time, the apparent weakness of the agencies by which it was created — it astonishes us to find that it ever could have attained to a strength sufficient to give one hour's uneasiness to the Government of a country like this.

I enter on no discussion as to the motives or the criminality of those who have taken part in this confederation. There are obvious reasons why I should not do so. But dealing with the existence of that organization as a fact, I ask of any one who has been compelled to consider it — whether it does not suggest subjects of the gravest reflection. Owing its origin to the individual energy of a young man destitute of all the advantages which might mark him out as a leader of a movement — encountered by influences whose opposition any man would have pronounced fatal — without leaders — without any apparent popular enthusiasm — it has, beyond all question, combined a large number of Irishmen, both here and in America, in a confederation hostile to British power, and important enough to demand preparations of no ordinary character to resist it. The fact is not altered by all the abuse that can be heaped upon Stephens and his associates. The more you can disparage the agents who have accomplished these results, the stronger is the evidence of the intensity of the disaffection which answered to their appeal.

It is in that intense deep-rooted and fanatical disaffection, and not in any particular organization or leader that the danger consists. Trample out the Fenian conspiracy tomorrow, and the disaffection remains — in all probability, made more intense in its nature by the very means employed for its suppression. You can put down rebellion by force — you can destroy disaffection only by doing justice. If I am right in tracing that spirit of disaffection to the oppression of our system of land tenure — a system which admits of those accursed clearances which, in one year, desolated 50,000 Irish homes — so long as this system is continued, you have the Irish as enemies both at home and abroad. Even the extermination of the people but increases the danger to English power. The emigrant vessel that carried away the evicted tenant, may have freed the Irish landlord of an incumbrance and a danger. It did not rid English power of a foe. It transferred one to a sphere in which his enmity became more dangerous and more active. Eight millions of the Irish people hostile to British power, whether they be in Ireland or America, are a standing menace to England more formidable than fleets and fortresses in sight of her shores. Ireland is her weakness in the eyes of Europe and America — her weakness in the secret

4. Many of the Fenian leaders were arrested and tried in the winter of 1865. Butt is writing this in December 1866. Stephens was among those arrested, but he escaped from Richmond Prison in an episode that made him more famous and emphasized the importance of the American connection, represented by John Devoy, who engineered the escape.

councils of her cabinet. IS NO EFFORT TO BE MADE TO REMOVE ALL THIS? It is in no spirit of hostility to England that I write the words which, if unheeded now, will be remembered and quoted when it is too late. If means be not devised to conciliate the Irish race, England will one day or other trace her sorest humiliations to the deep and deadly enmity of that race.

If there be any truth in the reasonings contained in this tract, the first, the vital step in that conciliation, must be to enfranchize the Irish serf — to give to the Irish occupier a hold upon his country and his home. Once effect this great measure of wisdom and justice and it will be easy to settle all other matters which can give occasion for discontent. We would adjust them, not with a hostile population doing battle for their lives, but with a people to whom we would have given an interest in the soil of their native country, and, therefore, in its tranquillity — a people whom we would have reconciled to our institutions and our laws.

I cannot help thinking, that even in the narrowest sense of the word, and in reference to Irish questions, he is the true Conservative who would, even at the expense of depriving landlords of an arbitrary power of eviction, accomplish this result.

from:
IRISH FEDERALISM (1875)

[This statement of his federal scheme demonstrates Butt's belief that the Union could be preserved only by the creation of a separate parliament in Ireland to deal with Irish domestic affairs. At all times he is aware of the implicit threat of separation and of the violence that extreme disaffection threatens to generate. As always, the weakness of his position is not in the enunciation of it, but in the helplessness consequent upon a repudiation of it. In his parliamentary tactics and in his writings, Butt found it hard to convince people that he was wholly devoted to the federal scheme, partly because rejection of it would lead inevitably to a demand for the repeal of the Union. This is a step he would not and could not take. It is in this year that he finally loses leadership of the Home Rule movement to Parnell.]

CHAPTER I

THE QUESTION STATED

I venture in the following pages to submit to the people both of England and Ireland, a clear and distinct proposal for a new arrangement of the relations of the two countries, as a substitute for that entered into at the commencement of the present century.

I do so under a deep conviction that the time is come when it is essential to the interests of both countries that there should be a readjustment or modification of the Union arrangements. I believe that a very large proportion of the Irish people are willing to accept such a Federal Union between the countries as would give an Irish Parliament control over all the domestic affairs of Ireland, while an Imperial Parliament still preserved the unity and integrity of the United Kingdom as a great power among the nations of the world. The present state of feeling in Ireland offers to Irish patriots at least a hope of uniting all classes and creeds of Irishmen in a national effort to win self-government for their country. It offers to England an opportunity of conciliating the Irish people without making concessions which would involve revolutionary changes or endanger the stability of the Empire. It may be that these hopes are to be disappointed. That opportunity may be neglected. If it be so, I will not, therefore, despair of the cause of Ireland or Ireland's nationality — a cause as indestructible as the mountains of her land, or as the ocean which surrounds it. But I am persuaded that never again will there be such an open[ing] for the peaceful solution of questions which will one day or other find their settlement, no matter by what means.

It is in the earnest hope that these pages may contribute something to effect a union of Irishmen in seeking for a moderate and peaceful settlement of our relations with England that I venture on a task from which every personal consideration would keep me aloof. In undertaking to sketch out the outline of a Federal Constitution between the two countries, I know well the difficulties that must be encountered. Experience has, even in my own case, abundantly verified to me the wisdom of Edmund Burke's warning against the rashness of those who propose legislative measures except from the seat of authority. It is difficult for any private individual to frame details which very often require information which unaided individual resources can rarely command. Upon such a question as that of the relations between England and Ireland, any person who proposes anything like a detailed settlement is sure to arouse prejudices and to offend crotchets;[1]

1. peverse notions, bigotries.

he exposes his plans to criticism which of necessity descends into cavils, and he runs the additional risk of wounding feelings of national honour and pride if he suggests a settlement which falls short of the expectation of those who have cherished — it may be exaggerated — notions of Ireland's position.

Nevertheless I believe it is essential to the cause of 'Federalism' that some practical design of a Federal Constitution should be offered for the consideration of the public. If I attempt to sketch that design, it is not from the vain imagination that I can offer it in the precise shape which it is likely ultimately to assume. The outline I suggest is intended rather as a framework for suggestion and deliberation than as a complete plan. With all the difficulties that attend such proposals, I am quite sure that there are many questions upon which it is of importance that some one should take the risk of placing before the public a distinct and definite proposal, so as to bring them from the range of mere speculative discussion into that of real and practical deliberation. The question of a Federal Constitution for Ireland is pre-eminently one of these. I do not hope or indeed desire that a universal acquiescence should be given to all the details of the proposals which I make, but I believe that I may do an essential service to the cause of Irish nationality by submitting a plan sufficiently detailed to be a practical one, and which may, at all events, accustom men to reflect and reason upon the principles which I attempt to embody in that plan.

It is in this spirit, and this spirit only, that I take on myself to present an outline of a Federal Constitution, which I believe would have a chance of securing the support of large classes of the Irish nation, and to which we can reasonably ask the assent of the English people. I cannot too distinctly say that for the proposals I make no one is responsible but myself. I should be very sorry to be supposed even to bind myself to them as the best that can be devised even for the immediate object which they have in view. If we can accomplish a peaceful settlement of the great international question between England and Ireland, room must be left for mutual concessions after consultation with many interests and deliberations upon many things. If the present opportunity for such an adjustment is let pass we may soon, in the rapid progress of modern events, be carried far beyond the reach of proposals like those which I now make.

Upon the general principles of a Federal Constitution I cannot do better than quote resolutions which three months ago were unanimously adopted at a meeting of gentlemen representing very different shades of political opinions.[2] These resolutions have since been submitted to a large number of persons throughout the country, and it is not too much to say that they have received an amount of approval and adhesion from men of all creeds and classes, such as never was accorded to any proposal for securing home government. A large number of gentlemen (more I believe than 400), including landed proprietors and mercantile men of high standing — Protestant and Roman Catholic clergymen, and men of political opinions generally supposed to be irreconcilable, have formed themselves into a committee, hitherto a private one, of which they have declared the following to be the objects:

> To obtain for our country the right and privilege of managing our own affairs, by a Parliament assembled in Ireland, composed of her Majesty the Sovereign, or her successors, and the Lords and Commons of Ireland.
>
> To secure for that Parliament, under a Federal arrangement, the right of legislating for and regulating all matters relating to the internal affairs of Ireland, and control over Irish resources and revenues, subject to the obligation of contributing our just proportion of the Imperial expenditure.
>
> To leave to an Imperial Parliament the power of dealing with all questions affecting the Imperial Crown and Government, legislation regarding the Colonies and other dependencies of the Crown, the relations of the United Empire with foreign states, and all matters appertaining to the defence and the stability of the Empire at large.
>
> To attain such an adjustment of the relations between the two countries, without any interference with the prerogatives of the Crown, or any disturbance of the principles of the constitution.

The committee which has adopted these resolutions includes within it a sufficient number of men representing various sections of political opinions to give fair ground for the belief that all classes of Irishmen are prepared to unite in a demand for a

2. The Home Rule League meeting of July 1877.

Federal arrangement, based upon the general principles contained in them — or, perhaps, to speak more accurately, that Irishmen generally would be willing to place their own peculiar views as to the future of their country in abeyance, in order honestly and fairly to try the great experiment involved in the proposal of such an arrangement.

Beyond these resolutions no one has authority to commit any of those who have concurred in them. I can only take on myself to suggest a plan by which I believe the spirit of these resolutions can be carried out, at least in all essential elements. It is one in which in substance I would counsel all who are sincerely desirous for the establishment of Irish nationality to ask the concurrence of all classes of their countrymen.

The arrangement proposed is, I have said, that which is popularly known as a Federal Union between the countries. It is not worthwhile to consider whether the word Federalism, in its proper sense, be the most appropriate term to express what is proposed. I will not even stop to inquire whether the Union I suggest belongs to that class of arrangements which Lord Brougham[3] calls Federal Unions proper, or to those which he designates as improper or imperfect, or, as is more probable, is one partaking of the character of both. It is enough to say that I intend to propose a system under which England, Scotland, and Ireland, united as they are under one sovereign, should have a common executive and a common national council for all purposes necessary to constitute them, to other nations, as one state, while each of them should have its own domestic administration and its own domestic Parliament for its internal affairs. I say each of them, because, although my immediate concern is only with Ireland, I do not suppose that if Irishmen obtain the separate management of Irish affairs it is at all likely that Englishmen or Scotchmen would consent to the management of their domestic concerns by a Parliament in which Irish members had still a voice. Whether England and Scotland would still desire to have the internal affairs of Great Britain managed by one common Parliament is a matter entirely for themselves to decide.

History, it need scarcely be said, records many instances of Federal Unions existing in all ages of the world. The principle has been at all times recognized by mankind that there may be countries so united by circumstances and positions as to make it their common interest to be joined in one common state — yet so separate as to make it necessary for the domestic affairs of each of them to be managed by an administration of its own. Federalism is, indeed, only an application of the great principle of freedom which maintains local privileges against the despotism of central power. From the formation of the Achæan League[4] to the incorporation of the North American Provinces into one dominion of Canada,[5] the principle has forced itself upon nations. The Germanic Confederation, established at the Congress of Vienna,[6] recognized it. For centuries each of the Swiss Cantons has preserved its perfect independence — while differing as they do in religion, in language, and in race, they have found unity and security in one general confederation, and one general diet[7] of them all. The great confederation of the States of the Western Republic is only another illustration of the universality of the instinct which teaches men that nations as well as individuals may combine, and that there is no inconsistency between the existence of a legislature regulating the internal affairs of each portion of the confederation and a central legislature, directing with efficiency and unity the combined power of all.

But, perhaps, the most remarkable tribute to the principle of Federalism is to be found in the course taken by the British Parliament in the year 1867, when it was thought wise to incorporate into one dominion all the North American provinces of the British Crown. Each of these provinces had its separate legislature and separate administration. When the English Parliament combined them into one dominion, each of them was left with that separate administration and separate legislature for its own domestic affairs. A common Parliament and a common Administration were provided for the concerns of the dominion. The contiguity of

3. Henry Peter Brougham (1778-1868), baron Brougham and Vaux, one of the founders of the *Edinburgh Review* (1802), a political orator and a prolific writer. He had sponsored the idea of federal union for Canada.

4. A confederation of cities on the Gulf of Corinth. There were two Archaeon Leagues, but the second was more important and is probably what Butt had in mind. It was founded in 280 B.C.

5. The British North America Act (1867) established the dominion of Canada, comprising a federation of the former Upper Canada and Lower Canada, New Brunswick and Nova Scotia.

6. The Germanic Confederation was constituted at the Congress of Vienna in June 1815. It comprised, among other territories, Austria, Prussia, Bavaria, Saxony, Hanover, Würtemberg and Baden.

7. legislative assembly.

these provinces to each other necessitated some details which would be inapplicable to the case of England and Ireland. The control of railways was, for instance, reserved to the Parliament of the dominion lest a central State might interfere to prevent the best and most direct communication between its neighbours. There is no reason why Ireland should not have exclusive control over its own railway communication. A similar observation applies to the Post Office and to some other things. The insular situation of Ireland fits us for a larger share of government than may be given to a country separated from another by an imaginary line. The limits of the central and the local power must depend in each Federal Union upon the circumstances and position of the countries comprising it, and in no small degree upon their constitution. We have, at all events, the remarkable fact that when the North American provinces were united in 1867, this was done upon a Federal principle preserving for each province its distinct Parliament. Well would it be for both England and Ireland if the same principle had been thought of when the attempt was made to make of England and Ireland one country instead of the natural and reasonable plan of uniting the two countries into one state.

It is obvious that in carrying out the plans of such a Federal arrangement, so far as Ireland is concerned there are three general questions practically to be settled.

1st. What is to be the constitution of the Imperial Parliament?

2nd. What is to be the constitution of the Irish Parliament?

3rd. What are to be the functions and powers of each?

Before proceeding to offer suggestions upon each of these questions there are subjects to which it is necessary briefly to refer.

This tract is not intended as a general discussion of the question of the maintenance of the Union in its present form. It is designed rather to show by practical suggestions how that Union may be safely modified than to argue a question upon which the minds of the great majority of Irishmen are made up. It were easy to show that the necessity of a re-adjustment of the Union arrangements rests upon the plainest practical grounds. The attempt made by the Union to give Parliamentary government to Ireland, through the medium of the English Parliament, increased by the addition of some Irish representatives, has wholly failed. It has failed in producing the results which were sought for by its promoters. It has failed in giving consolidation and security to the Empire at large. The chief argument used by Mr. Pitt in favour of the Union was that the French descent upon Ireland proved that Ireland was the vulnerable part of the Empire. If England were driven or drawn into war tomorrow, Ireland would present a far stronger temptation to an invader than it did in 1798. It has failed in bringing about any identity of interest or feeling between the two countries. There never was a period in the history of Ireland when there was greater dissatisfaction with English rule. No Irishman need be told that it has failed in giving to Ireland either prosperity or peace. At the end of seventy years of Union we are the most discontented, the most distracted, and, with all our great advantages, the poorest country in Europe....

CHAPTER VII

GENERAL CONSIDERATIONS

Failure of the Union Scheme

I have said that I do not intend this tract as an argument against our present system of Union. I have assumed that the great majority of the Irish nation wish that system to be changed. I have occupied myself, not in proving that wish to be reasonable, but in showing how it can be safely and practically carried out. There are, however, considerations which lie on the surface of this question to which I venture earnestly to invite the attention of all persons interested in its solution.

I may ask of any rational man, Englishman or Irishman, or Scotchman, whether it be not true that the system of government established at the Union has failed? It is useless in answering this question to tell me of great measures of wisdom and liberality passed by the Imperial Parliament. Every government is to be tested by its results; and the system of rule which at the end of seventy years has not succeeded in giving peace or contentment or prosperity to a country has failed. In attaching Ireland to England — the great and primary object of the Union — it has miserably broken down. It is enough to condemn it to say that it has not yet made us one country — one in interest and feeling. None of the Imperial objects sought by it have been gained. I have already referred to the remarkable statement of Mr. Pitt, that he urged the union of the countries, because the French attempts upon Ireland had proved Ireland to be the weak point of the empire in time of war. I have said that if England were drawn or driven into war tomorrow, Ireland would offer incomparably more temptations to an invader than it did in 1798. There is now [in the 1870s] far less real union and sympathy between the two countries than there was in 1790. There is in the minds of a large portion of our people a hatred of English government to an extent and of an intensity which never existed before. In all the Imperial purposes of the Union it is impossible to conceive a more complete disappointment of every expectation that was entertained. Instead of uniting Ireland in bonds of common interest and feeling with England, it has more than ever alienated the Irish people. Under the Union there has grown up all over the world a race of Irish emigrants hostile to England, and forming, it might almost be said, one vast conspiracy — a conspiracy of thought and feeling, if not of action — against her power. Ireland is every year becoming more and more the weakness and the reproach of the Crown of Great Britain.

In all Irish purposes the failure is, if possible, still more complete. The social history of Ireland since the Union is a record of poverty and suffering such as could not be supplied by the annals of any other country upon earth. Hundreds of thousands of Irishmen have literally died of starvation in their own land. Millions have been ruthlessly driven from their native soil. The wealth and the prosperity which were promised us have never reached our shores. At the end of seventy years of union with the richest country in Europe, Ireland is still the poorest and the most wretched. I know of no more melancholy or humiliating record than that contained in the annals of Irish legislation since the Union. It is even more humiliating than the gloomy roll of persecuting laws which fill up the seventy years which followed the final conquest of Catholic Ireland at the Boyne — because it records good intentions frustrated, designs apparently conceived in a spirit of wisdom and liberality mysteriously baffled.... The best of our political history presents nothing but a series of blunders and failures. Measures of conciliation have invariably failed to conciliate. Measures of coercion have not yet succeeded in crushing disaffection. They have never had more than a temporary and partial effort in repressing crime. A lavish system of corruption has succeeded in demoralizing a portion of Irish society, but it has failed in purchasing for our rulers any real influence or support. The most ignoble system of police despotism in Europe has irritated and fretted and lowered the spirit of our people, but it has not given us that peace for which some persons would endure a well-administered police tyranny. Our statute book is a melancholy record of arms acts! insurrection acts! acts for suspending the habeas corpus! for suppressing party processions! for prohibiting public meetings! as if brute force was the one expedient of Irish Government, and the highest object of Irish Statesmanship was to crush down the spirit of the nation.

At the end of seventy years an administration the most liberal in profession that England has ever seen, is ruling Ireland by enactments more arbitrary than any previous ministry ever ventured to propose. A general disarmament of the nation is the only plan that can be devised for keeping the public peace....

And all the while there is — I cannot say in spite of, but rather cherished and fostered by, all these measures of repression, deep in the hearts of the people themselves — a sullen but fiery hatred of English rule, which most assuredly only needs a favourable opportunity to assume the form of a determination to get rid of it.

Disgrace and Danger to England in the Present State of Things

I need scarcely say no Irishman ought to be satisfied with the present condition of affairs — *Ought any Englishman?* I am quite sure that the interests of England are more concerned than those of Ireland in a peaceful and equitable adjustment of the relations between the countries. To Ireland the day of deliverance, sooner or later, must come. The system of government which is now crushing down Ireland cannot last. It may be after years of suffering and struggle — it may be with the sacrifice of many a patriot life — it may be with more endurance in dungeons, more victims on the scaffold — it may be when all the present generations are sleeping in their graves, but the emancipation of Ireland is certain one day or other to come. For England the question is a very different one. If Irish rights be won by a revolution the days of British power are numbered. I know the scorn and contempt with which men will receive or pretend to receive this language. But he is not a wise minister for England who defies the hostility of the Irish race. He is no wise statesman who dreams that an empire is safe which holds in its bosom one-third of its people as its foes. This is a subject upon which, for obvious reasons I do not care to dwell. But the man, no matter in what seat of authority he sits, is a short-sighted fool who makes light of the danger with which Irish disaffection menaces English power....

I am quite sure that if England will aid our efforts by giving us the right of self-government in our own affairs, those who think thus have power and influence enough to control the passions of that section of our people whom long misgovernment has driven to believe in a separation from England as the only remedy for Irish wrong. The concession of a domestic Parliament would make the cry for separation powerless, even if it were ever raised. In a few years the wish would be forgotten. Under an Irish Government we would in seven years become more identified with England than we have in seven centuries of oppression. As the terrible barriers of separation which are raised by the exercise of tyranny and the sense of wrong disappeared, all the influences of union which are to be found in our near neighbourhood — our common language — our common institutions — our thousand ties of kindred, of interest, and of trade, would have their fair and full operation in making us not in name but in reality, in interest, and affection, one united state.

But while I thus point to the fact that all the powerful elements of Irish opinion are on the side of the English connexion — while I say, unhesitatingly, that with the concession of an Irish Parliament we may safely trust to these influences to maintain the connexion, and more than the connexion, the friendship, of the two countries — I would not speak the whole truth if I did not add, that if Ireland is to pass through troublous times without any concession to her nationality, then, indeed, events may arise which no man can attempt to control. Among the warmest friends of British connexion there are many, very many, who believe that their first and highest allegiance is due to their native land — who would follow the banner of their country wherever it might lead, and who would prefer almost any future for that country to the prospect of the eternal continuance of things as they are.

Every right-minded man will earnestly hope and pray that means may yet be found of averting from the human race the evils which must follow a general war among nations. But if this hope be realized this will not diminish the importance, although it may remove the pressure, of the Irish question. Wars will come again. 'England's difficulty' will be, one day or other, 'Ireland's opportunity'[1]....

Effect of the Union on England

If I have written strongly, and it may be boldly, on the subject of the danger that attends the continuance of Irish disaffection, I have certainly done so in no spirit of menace. Still more remote from my thoughts is anything like hostility to England. I know that it is ungracious to speak of danger from Ireland, even if it be in the language of warning. But accidental circumstances gave me an insight into the extent and intensity — perhaps I might add into the resources — of Irish disaffection, and with the strong convictions I have formed, I could not honestly conceal the belief I entertain. I turn with pleasure to a view of the question on which I can write in a manner more congenial to my own feelings, and, I admit at once, more calculated to make way with the English people.

The best argument that I can address to any high-minded Englishman in favour of the concession of a native Parliament to Ireland, is that Irish affairs would be better managed by an Irish Parliament, and that under such a Parliament Ireland would be happier and more contented than she is now. I may, however, without wounding any of his national susceptibility, use the argument that the present condition of Ireland is before the civilized world a reproach to the English nation. When in an evil hour England took upon herself the Parliamentary government of Ireland, she took upon herself a task which she could not possibly perform. A popular representative assembly at one with the people is the essential necessity of Parliamentary government. The Irish people can never find such an assembly in a representative assembly which is really and essentially an English — which at all events is certainly not an Irish — one. The failure was inherent in the very nature of the attempt; but of that failure England has all the responsibility, and incurs all the odium and reproach.

1. The phrase is Daniel O'Connell's.

II FENIANISM 1858-1916

DION BOUCICAULT

(*c.*1820-90)

from: ARRAH-NA-POGUE (1864)

[Although Boucicault has often been misrepresented as purveying the worst kind of Irish stereotypes, his declared intention was to *abolish* stage-Irishry. The underlying political rationale in his work is confirmed by his strong nationalist sentiments. His play *The Shaughran* (1874) had a contemporary Fenian setting and in 1876 Boucicault wrote an open letter to the British prime minister, Benjamin Disraeli, demanding, in the name of the thousands who had seen the play, that all Fenian prisoners be released. In the same year he arranged a reception in New York for escaped Fenian prisoners and contributed proceeds from his plays for the relief of prisoners' families.

Boucicault's Irish plays were characterized by spectacular stage-settings which allowed him to exploit the dramatic — and subversive — potential of Irish scenery with its many historical and political associations. Since the eighteenth century, the Irish landscape had been alternately treated as the site of uncultivated barbarism or picturesque wildness. In this play, which has the 1798 Rebellion as its setting, the landscape is in effect politicized. The scenery itself, not just the Irish character, is shown to be resistant to colonial occupation — 'civilization'. The Fenian dynamite campaign that culminated in the explosions at Clerkenwell Prison in London in 1867, in which twelve people were killed, created such a reaction that *Arrah-na-Pogue* was banned throughout the British Empire.

In the opening scene of the play, the daring rebel Beamish Mac Coul accosts the obsequious process-server Michael Feeny in the wild surroundings of the ancient monastic site of Glendalough in County Wicklow. This lonely glen, with its round tower and monastic remains, serves as a characteristic, even stereotyped, emblem of Ireland for the English and, indeed, for Irish audiences of the nineteenth century. Yet Boucicault's humorous treatment of the episode reveals an underlying irony. He exploits the stereotype for comic purposes but also with a political intent. Ireland is an alien place in which the landscape contains a threat; yet it is also a familiar place in that the threat is dismissible as unreal, as nothing more than a joke. Boucicault uses the humorous treatment of the Irish as a quaint or strange people in order to make the point that this is itself a tactic of oppression disguised as condescension.]

ACT I, SCENE 1

Glendalough; Moonlight. The Ruins of St. Kevin's Abbey, the Round Tower, the Ruined Cemetery, the Lake and Mountains beyond; Music. BEAMISH MAC COUL *discovered.*

Enter OINY

OINY: All right, sir; the car from Hollywood is in sight.

BEAMISH: How many passengers?

OINY: There's only one, sir.

BEAMISH: That is our man. Hark ye, boys!

Enter LANTY, LANIGAN, REGAN, *and* MORAN

Take your stations so that you may give me timely warning of any alarm in the barracks yonder, or the approach of the patrol.

REGAN: More power, sir.

OINY: We'll be as 'cute as crows, yer honour.

ALL: Never fear, sir.

BEAMISH: Away with you!

(They retire. LANTY, REGAN, MORAN, LANIGAN, OINY *and two others.* BEAMISH *stands behind a part of the ruin)*

Enter FEENY

FEENY: When a man thravels wid a big lump of money in his pocket, he is offering a reward for his own murdher. Why am I afeard? Sure this district is proclaimed,[1] so divil a one dare set fut outside his cabin-dure afther night-fall widout a pass. And

1. During times of serious agrarian disorder, entire districts were proclaimed by being placed under military alert.

there below is the barrack, full of soldiers, widin the cast of my voice. (BEAMISH *appears*) I'd like to see the skulkin' rebel that would show his nose on Derrybawn. (*Going as he speaks, finds* BEAMISH *opposed to him*) Oh, Lord!

BEAMISH: It is a fine night, Mr. Michael Feeny.

FEENY: So-o it is, long li-life to it; good night, sir. (*Trying to pass*)

BEAMISH: Stop. You have just come from Hollywood, where you have collected the rents of an estate.

FEENY: Is it me? I'd be on me oath ——

BEAMISH: Silence. The estates of the rebel Beamish Mac Coul were confiscated — your employer collects the rent for the Government, now I collect for the Mac Coul; so, hand over the amount.

FEENY: Is this robbery? and widin call of the barracks!

BEAMISH: If you lift your voice over a whisper to alarm the patrol, it will be murder as well as robbery. Not a word!

FEENY: (*Whispering*) I wouldn't wake a weazel.

BEAMISH: Quick, the money!

FEENY: Whisht, you'll rise the soldiers, an' I'll be kilt. (*Drops on his knees*) There's the money.

BEAMISH: Right. A bag of gold and a roll of notes. (*Receives the money from* FEENY)

FEENY: (*While* BEAMISH *examines it, aside*) Oh, wait a bit, me fine fellow, you can't move very far widout a pass; and only let me get safe out of this, and widin half an hour I will set a pack of redcoats on yer scent that will scour these hills and hunt the life out of ye.

BEAMISH: Good! Now your pass. (*Approaching* FEENY)

FEENY: Me what?

BEAMISH: Your pass — out with it — I want it to secure my free passage across the mountains.

FEENY: (*Giving* BEAMISH *papers*) But how am I to get home widout it?

BEAMISH: There's your road. (*Pointing and putting him across*) At every fifty paces there's a man stationed behind either a rock or a bush — he will see you straight to your door; and take a friendly advice, don't turn from the path, nor speak a word till you are safe in bed. Now be off!

FEENY: Oh, tare an' ages![2] Captain, dear, don't ax me to go alone. Oh, murdher! is it pass them file of divils? Are they armed, Colonel?

BEAMISH: Each man has two blunderbusses on full cock, and a bayonet pointed straight at you.

FEENY: I'm a corpse! Oh, Captain, Colonel, darlin', don't lave me! Two blunderbushes lookin' at me, and a bagginet on full cock. How will I get home at all? I've got a canal running down the middle of my back. I'm as wake[3] as a wet rag this minit.

BEAMISH: Come, off with you!

FEENY: I'm goin', sir. Where's my legs at all? Captain, jewel, may I run?

BEAMISH: No, that would alarm the patrols, and seal your fate.

FEENY: Oh, murdher, don't sale my fate, sir, and I'll creep on my hands and knees; pass the word, Colonel, to kape them quiet. Oh do, sir, give them the office. Oh, blessed day, my inside is all fiddle-strings, and my blood is turnin' into buttermilk.

Exit

BEAMISH: Hush!

(*Re-enter the men as before. They all run, looking after* FEENY; *then group. When* BEAMISH *throws bag of money, it is caught by* OINY) There he goes; we need fear no alarm from him. I have turned every stone and every bush on his road into a sentinel, ha, ha! Now, boys, divide this gold among ye. (*Throws them the gold*) You need not hesitate to take it, for the money is my own — I leave Ireland tomorrow, and for ever. I could not part from you without giving you some token of my gratitude for the fidelity and love you have shown towards me.

OINY: Ah, sir, wouldn't we pour out our blood, dhrop by dhrop, any day for the Mac Coul?

BEAMISH: I know it. For six weeks past I have found shelter on these hills under the noses of the military, while a reward of £500 offered for the capture of the rebel Beamish Mac Coul has not tempted your starvation to betray me.

ALL: Long life t'ye, sir; bless you always!

BEAMISH: See, the morning is beginning to tip the heights of Mullacor; we must part. In a few hours I shall be on the sea, bound for a foreign land; perhaps never again shall I hear your voices nor see my native hills. Oh, my own land! my own land! Bless every blade of grass upon your green cheeks! The clouds that hang over ye are the sighs of your exiled children, and your face is always wet with their tears. *Eirne meelish, Shlawn loth!*[4] Fare ye

2. Derived from 'tear and aches (of Christ).'

3. weak.

4. Sweet Ireland, goodbye.

well! And you, dear Abbey of St. Kevin, around which the bones of my forefathers are laid.

OINY: Long life to them!

ALL: The Mac Coul! the Mac Coul!

They crowd round him....

[In this scene, Boucicault turns a stereotype on its head, using the 'brogue' and whimsy associated with Irish character to obstruct the legal rational basis of colonial administration. Shaun the post (a man of letters in more ways than one, and later to be reincarnated in *Finnegans Wake* as Shaun the Post) is arraigned in court for helping the rebel Beamish Mac Coul and the faithful Arrah-na-Pogue. He is questioned by a British major and the Irish-born Colonel O'Grady. Boucicault distinguishes very carefully between their reactions. The Englishman cannot administer his form of justice when the prisoner will not even concede that he can be categorized as an individual by his name. The Anglo-Irishman is taken by the loquacity and the subversive humour of Shaun's refusal to cooperate. Boucicault is reminding his audience that in Ireland it is possible to be convicted just by being named. The various acts of special legislation, like the Treason Felony Act, which had John Mitchel and many after him transported or imprisoned, was designed to give the name of traitor to an individual who had done no more than say or write things that the government found disagreeable. To admit to anything, even one's name, in such a system was to leave oneself open to incrimination. Yet Boucicault, in making this point, pleases his English audience by appearing to be characteristically 'Irish' in his humour.]

ACT II, SCENE 5

SERGEANT *brings in* ARRAH

MAJOR: Has the article of war constituting this court-martial been duly read? (SERGEANT *bows*) I think then, Colonel, we may proceed.

ARRAH: (*Among the mob*) Now mind what you are saying, darlin'.

SHAUN: Never fear, dear, never fear — divil a ha'porth they'll get out of me.

MAJOR: Your name?

SHAUN: Is it my name, sir? Ah, you're jokin'! Sure there's his honour beside ye can answer for me, long life to him!

MAJOR: Will you give the Court your name, fellow?

SHAUN: Well, I'm not ashamed of it.

O'GRADY: Come, Shaun, my man.

SHAUN: There, didn't I tell ye! he knows me well enough.

MAJOR: Shaun (*writing*), that's the Irish for John, I suppose.

SHAUN: No, sir; John is the English for Shaun.

MAJOR: What is your other name?

SHAUN: My mother's name?

MAJOR: Your other name.

SHAUN: My other name? D'ye think I've taken anybody else's name? Did ye ever know me, boys, only as Shaun?

ALL: That's thrue. You may put that down agin him, Major.

SERGEANT: Order!

REGAN: What do *you* know about it?

O'GRADY: He is called Shaun the Post.

SHAUN: In regard of me carrying the letter-bag by the car, yer honour.

MAJOR: Now, prisoner, are you guilty or not guilty?

SHAUN: Sure, Major, I thought that was what we'd all come here to find out.

ARRAH: Don't confess, Shaun.

SHAUN: (*Aside*) Never fear; I'm not such a fool as they think.

MAJOR: (*Impatiently*) Are you guilty or not guilty?

SHAUN: How would I know till I hear the evidence?

O'GRADY: Well, Shaun, you *have* pleaded *guilty* to this charge of robbery and violence.

SHAUN: Well, O'Grady ——

MAJOR: Prisoner, you must not presume to address the Court with curt insolence, calling this gentleman 'O'Grady', in that familiar manner.

O'GRADY: Your pardon, Major. You are not aware of our Irish ways. I am the O'Grady, the head of the sept. This man belongs to the sept of the Mac Coul, and as your kings are called without offence by their Christian names, 'George', or 'William', our chiefs are called 'O'Grady', or 'Mac Coul'. Pardon the digression — but the man gives me my title and no more. (MAJOR *bows*)

SHAUN: Ah, the ignorance of thim Inglish!

O'GRADY: Go on, my good man.

SHAUN: I did plade guilty last night, and so I was thin,[1] your worship; but I want to say that I am as innocent as a fish this morning.

MAJOR: You wish to withdraw your plea?

SHAUN: My what?

MAJOR: Your plea.

1. then.

SHAUN: No — what would I? (*Turning to crowd*) Will I do that? (*They shake their heads*) No, I couldn't, sir. (*The* SERGEANT *leans over and whispers in* SHAUN's *ear*) Oh, ah! Well — I see. I don't know, sir, but I want to do whatever will get me off.

MAJOR: Withdraw his plea. The prisoner pleads 'Not Guilty'. (*Crowd shout*)

SHAUN: Thank ye kindly, Major. It is all over, Arrah. (*Jumps over dock —* SERGEANT *expostulates with him*)

MAJOR: What is the fellow doing?

SHAUN: Oh, Major, sure you wouldn't go back of your word. Didn't his honour say fair and plain — 'He is not guilty', ses he.

ALL: Oh, Major, ye did. Long life to the Major, boys.

SERGEANT: Order there. (*The* SERGEANT *forces* SHAUN *back into the dock*)

SHAUN: You can't thry a man twice over for the same offinse.

MAJOR: Really this must be stopped; the dignity of the Court must be preserved.

SHAUN: (*To the crowd*) D'ye hear that, boys? Preserve your dignity, you blackguards, till ye get outside.

MAJOR: Now, Mr. Feeny, state your charge.

FEENY: (*Rising*) Plase your worships. (*Advances to end of table*) (*Jeers from crowd*)

O'GRADY: Stop. What's your name?

FEENY: Michael Feeny.

O'GRADY: Your business?

FEENY: Well, your worship ——

O'GRADY: Don't worship me, man, and confound me in your mind with the devil. Speak straight, if you can. What's your dirty trade?

FEENY: Sure ye know well enough, sir. I am an officer of the law, sir.

O'GRADY: I *do* know you well enough, but these gentlemen do not, and I mean they shall. Are you a process-server?

FEENY: Well?

O'GRADY: Yes or no?

FEENY: Y-e-e-es.

O'GRADY: An informer on occasions?

FEENY: I did ——

O'GRADY: Out with it! — yes or no.

FEENY: Y — yes.

O'GRADY: How many times have you been committed to gaol?

FEENY: Is it me that's on my thrial, Colonel, or Shaun the Post?

O'GRADY: Don't question me, sir. I want an answer. Come, how often were you in prison?

FEENY: I disremember.

CROWD: (*Jeering*) He disremembers!

O'GRADY: No doubt, but I don't. (*Takes up a paper and reads*) Three times for perjury, once for theft, and three times for petty offences. (*Looks up*) Will I name the prisons and the length of your periods of incarceration?

FEENY: I wouldn't ax ——

O'GRADY: Yes or no?

FEENY: (*Quickly*) No. (*A laugh in the Court*)

O'GRADY: Now, go on; the Court has your name and trade; you may proceed.

FEENY: (*Whimpering*) It's mighty hard, so it is, to be put upon this way, and me only doing my duty. Sure your worships knows well all I've got to say. It's tuk down in the impositions agin the prisoner. Is it my fault if Shaun confessed to the robbery? Did I put the idays in his head or the notes in his pocket? Then why am I to be schraped[2] down to bethray my misfortunes underneath? It's mighty hard upon me entirely, so it is.

O'GRADY: You come here to accuse the prisoner; stop snivelling over yourself, and thry your hand on him.

FEENY: Sure, Colonel, dear, Shaun has accused himself.

MAJOR: Do you swear that the notes produced were part of the property of which you were robbed?

OINY: Now isn't that a quare question for the Major to ask? — a fellow that would swear the bark out of an old dog! (*Jeers and menaces*)

FEENY: I do, sir.

MAJOR: Prisoner, do you wish to ask this witness any questions?

SHAUN: I wouldn't bemane[3] myself by bein' seen talkin' to him.

ALL: Long life to you, Shaun!

MAJOR: Stand down.

FEENY *retires*

KATTY: Oh! look at him, sitting on the size of a sixpence!

OINY: Look at his whisker! — like a dirty ha'porth of tobacco!

MAJOR: You hear what he says — if these notes were his, how came they in your possession?

2. scraped.
3. bemean — a less common word for 'demean'.

SHAUN: Sure, Major, that's what he didn't prove — he broke down there entirely, sir.

MAJOR: But this is for you to establish.

SHAUN: Sure, Major that would be accusing myself.

MAJOR: Have you heard the evidence?

SHAUN: Do you call that evidence? Yes, I did — I heard all of it; and if I am to be found guilty on that chap's swearin', it will be a wrong bill. The Recordher knows him well, and wouldn't sintence a flay[4] for backbitin' on that fellow's oath. Come out of that, Michael Feeny, and hear me. When St. Pathrick drove all the crapin' things out of Ireland, he left one sarpint behind, and that was your great grandfather.

MAJOR: This is not to the point.

O'GRADY: It is a mighty fine outburst of natural eloquence; go on, my man, crush that reptile if you can.

4. flea.

SHAUN: Crush him. I'd ax no betther. I've had him under my fist; but he is like some vermin ye can't crush, they stick so flat in the dirt.

MAJOR: This is very irrelevant.

O'GRADY: That's prejudice, Major. I never listened to anything more compact in the way of vituperation.

MAJOR: But abuse is not evidence. (*To* SHAUN) Have you any witnesses to call?

SHAUN: Devil a one, Major, barrin' you'd like to stand up for a poor boy in throuble yourself, and say a good word for me.

MAJOR: Then this case is closed. I think, gentlemen the facts are plain. We have but one duty to perform.

O'GRADY: I'm for letting him off.

MAJOR: On what grounds?

O'GRADY: The eloquence of the defence.

MAJOR: I regret to say that we cannot admit so Irish a consideration. . . .

GEORGE SIGERSON

(1836-1925)

from: MODERN IRELAND . . . . (1868)

[Sigerson's volume of essays is a valuable commentary on the rise of Fenianism as seen by a man who understood its importance but wished to see measures adopted that would reduce its power. In the first essay reprinted here, he derides the current distinction between Celt and Anglo-Saxon — something he was also to do in relation to Irish poetry — and replaces it with his own account of the traditional influences that moulded Irish habits and, as a consequence, provided an explanation for the appeal of Fenianism.

In the second extract, he observes the difference between the rank and file membership of the Fenians and that of Young Ireland and the O'Connellite party. The importance of the American connection, especially during the American Civil War, is as evident and important to him as it was to many of the Fenian leaders.

In the third extract, he considers the significance of the execution and funerals of the Manchester Martyrs of 1867. He points out the futility of repression and advocates instead a policy of amelioration that will help develop the sense of a national life in Ireland. The similarity between Sigerson's views and those of an English radical, like John Stuart Mill, whose essay *England and Ireland* appeared in the same year, is striking. Mill makes vigorously explicit the point that Sigerson more gently insinuates — that the Fenian rebellion 'is not one of grievance or suffering; it is a rebellion for an idea — the idea of nationality.' Mill was as anxious as Sigerson to bring forward concessions that might rob Fenianism of its appeal. Modern commentary on the Fenian movement tends to argue that the Fenians were increasingly worried by the success of reforming policies in reducing their appeal and robbing them of a focussed grievance. But Mill made the point that Sigerson also begins to perceive: 'Revolt against practical ill-usage may be quelled by concessions; but wait till all practical grievances have merged in the demand for independence, and there is no knowing that any concession, short of independence, will appease the quarrel.' Sigerson's essays, like Mill's, are warnings against the underestimation of Fenianism and the misreading of the political situation in Ireland because of the stereotyped views of national character, English and Irish, which played such a role in the contemporary estimates of the political realities of the situation.

The text is taken from the second edition of 1869. The work's full title is *Modern Ireland: Its Vital Questions, Secret Societies, and Government*.]

IRISH REPUBLICANISM

No theory is more popular with a certain class of writers than that which asserts a total difference of character to exist between the inhabitants of Ireland and of England. Whenever a question of Irish political life arises, this theory is sure to be produced at the same time, and paraded as the solution of the problem. On one side of St. George's Channel[1] there is the Anglo-Saxon, of a character essentially self-reliant, self-asserting, stubborn, and tenacious, caring nothing for titles, nothing for leaders, and very little for princes. These qualities he shares with all Teutonic races, as was so plainly seen in Germany, before Count Bismarck's swoop,[2] and may even yet be discerned by any student of the proceedings of the North German Parliament. If further proof were requisite, a backward glance at the history of England would be sufficient to furnish it. Beyond the Irish Channel, however, all is different. There dwell the Celts, a fickle race, easily moved, and loving to be patronized and noticed by great people. They are gregarious, fond of organizing, and devoted to their leaders with blind submissiveness. They do not care for political progress, but they have a very keen ear for music. Fenianism is not really popular amongst them; it is merely a sickly exotic. All the tenant farmer wants is to be allowed to sit happy under the shelter of his own landlord's 'great house.' To speak of Republicanism in connection with such a race shows how little is known of their real character. Plainly, their ancient system of government was an iron feudalism, and the descendants of the vassals still cast a yearning look back to their lost despotic masters, and would fain even now twine their affections round their landlords, if the latter, not seeing this, did not rather, generally, prefer to be absentees. The simple remedy, therefore, for all the ills and discontent of the Irish people is to disregard the clamour of demagogues for rights and redress, and to send back the absentee landlords to the bosom of their anxious tenantry.

This theory is based on a misconception of the old organization of the island, and on a curious ignorance of the actual state of the country. It follows, that statesmen who employ it for the solution of Irish problems, are obliged to make frequent use of it; for, in spite of the most satisfactory explanations, the questions come up again and again, as fresh as ever. Whatever influence the ancient clan-system may have had in moulding the character of the people, it will certainly not be made clear by confusing such a mode of organization with the feudal system. The clansman was a very different person from the feudal vassal or retainer. In many respects he was the equal of his chief, bound to him, in frequent instances, by the ties of kinship, and possessing a voice in his election. Both were ruled by well-defined laws of rights and privileges. 'There are four dignitaries of a territory who can be degraded,' says the *Senchus Mor*,[3] 'a false-judging king, a stumbling bishop, a fraudulent poet, and an unworthy chieftain who does not fulfil his duties.' Thus these ancient Celts were acquainted with the art of deposing their great men, to whom they are usually supposed to have been so submissive. Furthermore, this ancient law, which no Brehon could abrogate, goes on to explain that by 'a false-judging king' is meant, in particular, 'one who pronounces a false sentence on his tenants,' and that, 'whether it be concerning a small thing or a large, it makes him equally unworthy.' If the Irish tenant of the present day preserves so much of the traditions of the past as to regard his landlord with the same feelings that his ancestors cherished towards their petty kings, it is to be feared that he may entertain ideas with reference to him totally undreamed of by English journalists. Should he fancy, for instance, that a landlord who raises the rent because of improvements made by his tenant, or a landlord who ejects without giving any compensation for tenant improvements, resembles 'a king who pronounces a false sentence on his tenants,' he might also imagine that he is a 'dignitary of a territory' who should be degraded. Applying the same rule to the case of an absentee

1. The body of water that separates Ireland from England and Wales.
2. Otto von Bismarck (1815-98), chief minister of Prussia, whose goal was the unification of Germany, fought wars with Denmark over Schleswig-Holstein in 1864 and with Austria and the other German states in 1866.
3. *Recte* Senchas Már, the prime manuscript source for the study of the Brehon Laws.

landlord, would he not also be tempted to regard him, not as the father of the prodigal regarded his son, but as 'an unworthy chieftain who does not fulfil his duties?' These and other laws of a similar character moulded the Irish nation; and there cannot be a doubt that they influence yet, to some extent, the popular mind. The Brehon laws remained in full force throughout the larger portion of Ireland long after Henry II's time. Two centuries ago, there were regularly established Brehons or judges; and many of the 'agrarian outrages' of later days may perhaps be explained by a reference to the old laws of the country. The abolition of the native laws and native judges was followed by the establishment of secret societies, which enforced the sentences of their own tribunals....

With laws such as these to guide us in discriminating the groundwork of the Irish national character, it is impossible not to regard the theory we have referred to as an exceedingly shallow one. If we proceed to examine what influences have in later times been likely to act upon and mould the Irish mind, we shall not find them such as are adapted to counteract the ancient ideas. The superstructure is of a piece with the groundwork. Whilst a new system has been given to the country, little trouble has been taken to naturalize it. The new dignitaries have not sought to make themselves popular; on the contrary, they have frequently estranged themselves even bodily. Of course there are exceptions — many and great; but, on the other hand, the highest and most influential dignitary of all has constantly avoided the country. Royalty has been the chief absentee. The negative effect of all this would be sufficiently great, even were there no other causes tending in the same direction. Not only, however, have there been such causes, but other influences also have arisen adverse to the new order of things, and not contrary to, though more advanced than, the older views. The formation of a great, prosperous, and hospitable Republic as a neighbour, although a distant one, was calculated powerfully to influence the Irish mind. Had the national character been framed on the feudal mould, it would not have been naturally in harmony with the new views that came upon it from the west; but to a people who had once made laws for the election and deposition of their kings and chiefs, Republicanism appeared natural and not unfamiliar. Subsequent events were not calculated to counteract such a view among Irishmen. In America the ministers of their religion were put on a footing of exact equality with all others; their political martyrs were canonized; and their refugees were warmly welcomed. Food was shipped to them from the great Republic in the time of their grievous want; and those of their kindred who had crossed the Atlantic never wearied of sending home flattering reports and golden enclosures. To crown all, their military aptitudes found there a ready outlet and a fitting reward. They were placed in a position of perfect equality before the law, and they esteemed nothing more dearly.

But it has been too much the custom to speak of the Irish as altogether Celts, and then to construct the usual theory. Even in the days of the native chiefs there were Norse and Anglo-Saxon settlers amicably established in various parts of Ireland. Then, again, the Danes forced themselves upon its ports, and surely bequeathed some portion of their characteristics to the inhabitants, after they had lost sovereign rule. In the restricted sense in which some writers use the word, Dublin could not be spoken of as an Irish city; there, as elsewhere, the Normans succeeded the Danes. What remnant of these races was not absorbed by the native population — becoming in the process 'more Irish than the Irish themselves'[4] — was collected into the mass of the Cromwellian colony; difference of religion here intervening to prevent the subsidence and absorption of the latest settlers. We have seen how the native Irish population stood with respect to republican ideas: were the traditions of the followers of Cromwell such as to make them differ from the others on this subject? On the contrary, though starting from different points, they arrived at the same result.... They had a reason of their own, too, for regarding the Americans with favour. They sympathised with them as with fellow-colonists. Both had had differences with the central authority; and when the American colony pressed on against restrictive laws, and broke them, the Norman-English colony in Ireland passed votes of sympathy, and carried their imitation so far as to obtain an acknowledgment of the independence of the Irish Parliament. The nobles of the colony did not wish to go farther.

It is desirable to ascertain what actually caused

4. A much-quoted remark, originally referring to the assimilation of the Normans into Irish society in the twelfth century.

the formation of an avowedly Republican society at that period, as the fact may throw some light on the origin of the so-called 'Irish Republican Society' of the present day. A Committee of the Irish House of Commons declared its opinion that 'the Rebellion of 1798 originated in a system framed, not with a view of obtaining either Catholic emancipation or any reform compatible with the existence of the Constitution, but for the purpose of subverting the Government, separating Ireland from Great Britain, and forming a Democratic Republic, founded on the destruction of all Church establishment, the abolition of ranks, and the confiscation of property.' The description doubtless was found officially useful, but it is not altogether in harmony with facts. The Irish Parliament was exceedingly corrupt. A great majority of the House of Commons were mere nominees of the Peers, who were themselves to a very considerable extent the slaves as well as the creatures of the Viceroy. The Volunteers, when they had achieved legislative independence, wished to give that independence some security by achieving a reform of the Legislature itself. They presented their plan of reform to Parliament; but the latter body refused to receive it, on the ground that they would not seem to be intimidated by an armed force. Then Reform was pressed upon them by petitions from all the civil organizations, but with no effect; whereupon an association was formed in the colony for 'a complete and radical reform of the representation of the people in Parliament.' In order to fuse the whole nation together, the Association declared also 'that no reform is practicable, efficacious, or just, which shall not include Irishmen of every religious persuasion.' The 'United Irishmen' were at first simply Reformers; they asked for manhood suffrage, annual parliaments, the payment of representatives, and the abolition of a property qualification. It was not until they found that Parliamentary action made no progress that they betook themselves to Republicanism. The extreme party then prevailed, as is usual in such cases.

Change but a few names, and here is the history of the causes which have produced the Irish Republicanism of the present day. Some years ago the whole country pressed the Legislature with petitions for a reform of the land-laws. It made no progress. One of the leaders of the movement died, as some say, of a broken heart; another left his country in despair, and went to Australia, where he became a minister and introduced a land law.[5] The rank and file of the agitation streamed out hopelessly to America, where they now appear as 'Fenians.' Those who remained at home nourished a sullen discontent, and in due time organized themselves, to some extent, into a Republican society, having sympathizers even in Great Britain, just as in the last century there were 'United Englishmen' and 'United Scotchmen' as well as 'United Irishmen.'

5. The reference is to the leaders of the Tenant League of 1850, Frederick Lucas (1812-55) and Charles Gavan Duffy (1816-1903), who emigrated to Australia in 1855 and became prime minister of Victoria.

THE VITALITY OF FENIANISM

False appreciations of the character, origin, and aims of what is now known as Fenianism have betrayed most of our public writers into the utterance of false prophecies. The forces which combined to constitute the Fenian movement have not been analyzed with that calm impartiality which would give soundness to the judgment, and an instinctive perception of the meaning and power of the conspiracy. Its strongest elements have thus been quoted as the clearest evidences of its weakness. Our attention has been repeatedly invited to the fact that the social position of Irish insurgents has greatly fallen since Lord Edward Fitzgerald's time, and even since the less brilliant period of Smith O'Brien and his companions.[1] This the public has been asked to accept as an argument that Fenianism is more vulgar, and therefore less formidable, than former insurrectionary movements. Were the men of 1793, however, inferior in vigour to the leaders of 1789 in France, because they were more plebeian? The argument, so long and largely insisted upon, will not stand a moment's thoughtful investigation. Had the promoters of Fenianism believed that the addition to their ranks of those who had much property to lose would have strengthened their power, they would have striven to conciliate them, following the tactics of 1848. They did nothing of the sort. Almost the first symptom of their presence in the country was the expression of opinions depreciatory of so-called popular leaders, and sarcastically severe on the

1. The aristocratic leaders of, respectively, the United Irishmen and of the inglorious Young Ireland rebellion of 1848.

prominent personages of 'Young Ireland.' Such persons, it was said, might join the Brotherhood if they pleased; but they must be content to accept a subordinate place, and work their way up, if found worthy of promotion. The projectors of the association did not want men of position, scrupulous with respect to risk; what they wanted was the rank and file of an Irish army. A peasant could pull a trigger quite as easily as a gentleman, could undergo fatigue better, and would be less likely to display a want of trust in his self-confident superiors.

To provide these raw levies with competent officers was not a difficulty, but the reverse. The American war was accepted as a military training school by tens of thousands of the more ardent Irish emigrants in the United States. Before that, indeed, the American division of the society had been organizing and drilling a few incomplete regiments; and the amount of pains taken in this process of self-instruction may be judged from the fact, that many of their privates were at once appointed officers in the new levies on the out-break of the war. This gave them an opportunity, by which they were not slow to profit, of spreading Fenian views, and of increasing the numerical power of the Brotherhood. So great became their influence, that in some Irish regiments no man had a chance of promotion who was not a member of the Brotherhood, as a correspondent in one of the Irish-American papers complained. Here, then, was a nursery of commanders, men peculiarly adapted for the purposed work, because they had risen, generally, from the position occupied by the masses in Ireland, shared their sympathies, and understood their feelings. That, here as elsewhere, the Irish did not fail to distinguish themselves by deeds of desperate valour, the generous testimony of Confederate writers amply proves. Their gallant onsets turned the beam of victory on more than one American battle-field, as the charge of the *Brigade Irlandaise* had done before, for France, at Fontenoy.[2] Their fame, somewhat exaggerated no doubt, penetrated every peasant's cot in Ireland, both by newspapers which republished the special reports of the vigilant Irish-American press, and by private letters recording the promotion of the writers to ranks hitherto regarded in Ireland as the exclusive perquisites of the ascendancy party, and therefore hedged with a certain divinity. The natural results followed. Young men poured out from the old country to share in their glory, and became initiated in the Republican principles of their comrades: a revolution was accomplished in their minds, giving them self-confidence, and inducing them, as veterans who had bought their commissions with their blood, to think of the home-forces without alarm. At the same time, the rout of raw levies at Bull's Run[3] taught them what, in the commencement of operations in their native country, they might expect; whilst the subsequent successes gave them a hope of ultimate triumph. They drew from their experience in the American campaign the lesson that, in Ireland, their best plan would be to shun the example of the United Irish of 1798, to avoid pitched battles, and compel the British commander to disperse his troops in order to keep in check their guerilla bands. By adopting and persevering in this strategy, they hoped both to inure their men to arms and to keep their flag flying in the country until they could claim for Ireland recognition as a belligerent power.

The influence of the Irish element in the United States is not to be despised. When it chooses it can give the casting vote in several States; and there is no doubt that the Fenian chiefs were correct in their anticipation that a real rising in Ireland would band together its most widely-separated ranks. The American people, they argued, would not withhold their sympathy, nor be chary of their gold; and they counted confidently on the American merchants, who suffered so much from privateers fitted out in English ports, to enforce the law of retaliation to its fullest extent. Proofs of sympathy on the part of Americans of high standing they had in abundance.... In fact, the only voices raised against them were those of some of the Catholic clergy and their organs in the press. This, however, rather tended to make the non-Catholics regard them with favour, as proving them to be truly independent republicans, not to be cowed by clerical dictation. The American laity are peculiarly proud of being 'free citizens,' and jealous of anything resembling

2. Irish troops were part of a large French army that resisted a combined force of English, Hanoverian, Austrian and Dutch soldiers advancing to relieve the town of Tournai in France. The great battle took place at the village of Fontenoy, in what is now Belgium, in May 1745.

3. In the first and second battles of Bull Run of 1861 and 1862, the Confederate forces were successful. The New York Irish Brigade, led by Francis Meagher, former Young Irelander, fought bravely at the second of these battles and in all the major engagements of the war thereafter.

interference with their privileges. Distrustful of the Irish as over-submissive to their clergy, they accepted the Brotherhood as showing, in their own words, that they were assuming the stature and mien of freemen, beneath the sun of Washington. . . .

It was not until exactly ten years ago that the germ of the actual Brotherhood was planted by John O'Mahony, originally a 'gentleman farmer' of Tipperary. Having been compromised in the abortive movement of 1848, he fled to Paris, where he lived for some time with a younger and suppler refugee, James Stephens, the son of a Kilkenny clerk. Here Stephens, whilst translating a novel of Dickens for the *feuilleton*[4] of the *Moniteur*, got acquainted with some unquiet spirits of the Continental revolutionary societies. O'Mahony and he became enrolled members, and studiously made themselves acquainted with the best methods of secret organization for ulterior purposes. When their plans were matured they consulted some French officers, veteran Irish rebels of 1798, and some American officers, who had been leaders of 'Young Ireland.' The scheme did not win encouragement. The American fund was not given; and the two refugees had to depend upon themselves. Stephens went to Ireland, forming first the Phœnix Society, which exploded, whilst from its ashes emerged the greater 'I.R.B.,' which signifies the 'Irish Republican Brotherhood.' O'Mahony proceeded to the United States to organize the Transatlantic Irish nation. In 1857, aided by another refugee, Colonel Doheny, he founded the 'E.M.A.' or 'Emmet Monument Association,' the allusion being to that passage of Robert Emmet's speech in the dock, in which he requests that his epitaph may remain unwritten till full justice can be done to his memory. The first attempt was a failure. But the explosion of the Phœnix Society, trifling as it was, sufficed to stir the interest of the Transatlantic Irish, and induce some of them to become members of O'Mahony's new organization, the Fenian Brotherhood. What suggested the word 'Fenian' was, no doubt, Keating's Gaedhlic History of Ireland, which O'Mahony published with a translation.[5]

Now, it is easy to perceive that there is but a half truth in the statement so frequently heard, that Fenianism is of American origin, and has no source in Irish grievances. Technically, indeed, there have not been any Fenians in Ireland except those who came from over the Atlantic; but then there has existed a society of 'Irish Republicans' in Ireland specifically identical with them, and even anterior in date of formation. How the two societies appeared to each other, magnified by the sea-mists through which they were viewed, should not be forgotten; for it has greatly helped to give them both vitality. If the 'Irish Republic' were alone to be dealt with, it would now be a matter of history. But American Fenianism is not directly to be met; and it knows its strength and its value as a base of supply. 'Fenianism,' says the New York *Irish People* (a paper at present confiscated in the Irish Post Office), 'contemplates the organization of the Irish elements in America in one great national association for the purpose of combining all the vast resources at its command, moral, national, and political, and directing them intelligently, systematically, and determinedly towards the liberation of Ireland. It contemplates, secondly, the formation of allied associations in Ireland, Great Britain, the British Provinces, and wherever else any branch of the Irish nation may be found in sufficient force.' The element to be operated on in Ireland is not badly described by a sober witness, the Bishop of Kerry, in a recent pamphlet. Having stated that the upper and upper-middle class are loyal, 'because for them Emancipation has been a reality; it has given them the rights and privileges which follow rank and wealth,' he adds: 'It is not so with the millions for whom Emancipation has had no practical or appreciable result. For them,' as a consequence, 'the past still lives in the present; they think they are an oppressed race. Men live in the hope of what they call a deliverance of their native land. Hence a dreamy, unreal, discontented existence. Like the Athenians asking in their streets, "What news? Is Philip dead?"[6] we have a people

4. That part of a European newspaper carrying reviews and serialized fiction.

5. John O'Mahony (1815-77) went to New York in 1853 and, along with Michael Doheny (1805-63), founded the Emmet Monument Association in 1857. The Phoenix Societies were founded by Jeremiah O'Donovan Rossa in Skibbereen, Co. Cork in 1856. O'Mahony supported himself in America by making a translation of Geoffrey Keating's *Foras Feasa ar Éirinn* in 1857. He helped Stephens to found the Irish Republican Brotherhood in Ireland in 1858; simultaneously he founded its American counterpart, known as the Fenians.

6. Philip of Macedonia (382-36 B.C.), father of Alexander the Great, threatened and finally conquered the Athenians. Only the news of his death could relieve them of their fear.

expecting good fortune from some unforeseen chance, or from the possible ruin of the power which they consider the cause of their miseries.' Dr. Moriarty[7] thinks that this state of affairs is due to the existence of the Irish Church Establishment; but it is not due to this alone. A study of the popular press in America, as well as in Ireland, will show how much the many abortive efforts made in Parliament to deal with the land question have caused confidence in the good intentions of the Legislature to give place to despair, and even to suspicion of an irreconcilable hostility. Expectations have been raised only to be disappointed; and thus it has come to pass that a Presbyterian Clergyman, prominent in the agitation for tenant-right, has become one of the Executive Council of the 'Irish Republic.' Hope deferred makes a nation desperate.

7. David Moriarty (1814-77), Roman catholic bishop of Kerry 1856-77, notorious for the ferocity of his condemnation of the Fenians. The pamphlet referred to here is *Letter on the Disendowment of the Established Church* (Dublin, 1867).

HOW TO DEAL WITH FENIANISM

The surprise occasioned by the recent Fenian outbreak at Manchester is not a hopeful symptom. It indicates a want of acquaintance with the actual position of affairs, which promises ill for the immediate future. It is a repetition, on a small scale, of the mistake which was made by so many of the Northern politicians during the American civil war, and which gives their speeches such a ludicrous appearance, when they are read by the light of events. At every capture of a prominent Fenian, at every attempt at revolt which has been put down, at every trial where a batch of political prisoners has been consigned to penal servitude, the same story has been repeated. The 'neck of the rebellion' has been broken several times; 'the bubble has burst' more than once. The thought has been merely the offspring of the wish. Men have been anxious to accept any view that could plausibly relieve them from the duty of studying what might reveal painful objects, and make action necessary. But the oftener the neck of the rebellion has been broken, the more clearly it has been shown to be hydra-headed; and the more frequently the bubble has burst, the more palpable it has become that those causes remain which can send other like bubbles to the surface from the fermenting elements beneath. . . .

It is evident that if the masses in Ireland were at any time given up to agitation — that is, devoted to seeking from parliamentary action the redress of the evils they complain of — there would be no room amongst them for Fenianism, since the latter is essentially hostile to appeals to what it considers an alien and inimical Legislature. It is not to agitation, but to the death of agitation, that Fenianism owes its being. If the millions sought for redress from the Legislature for grievances which the Legislature admitted to be such, and if after seeing Parliament admit these grievances they found that, in spite of many fervent professions, nothing practical was done, is it to be wondered at that they despaired of parliamentary redress? Despair of legislative action gives the death-blow to agitation which is fed by a hope of it; and despair of peaceful petitioning opens the way for the contemplation of the last resource of peoples. The Tenant League agitation had been extinguished; its chiefs had retired into private life, exiled themselves in despair, or died with disappointed hopes; the nation had fallen into an apparent apathy, upon which the dominant party triumphantly congratulated themselves. And then Fenianism began. A little leaven — a few years — and the material so well prepared by hands which kneaded for other ends has been leavened throughout. Those who abhor agitation for fear it should wrest some privilege from themselves, or conquer some long-lost right for the majority of their countrymen, should learn that its suppression must be followed by conspiracy, so long as the grievances it springs from remain, and a people remains to feel them. Despair is not contentment. When a wound is no longer complained of, it is often because gangrene has set in.

The same superficial spirit which has misapprehended the origin of Fenianism has likewise misunderstood its powers of existence, and made men unable to conceive a wise or efficient method of dealing with it. Judging it by what they have seen of other movements, those who are under the influence of this spirit, have fancied that the vitality of Fenianism depended upon the influential action of one or two persons. They have argued falsely, but after a popular method, that the Irish are such hero-worshippers and so devoted to their leaders that the life of the movement would last only so long as the chiefs were at liberty to act. These chiefs have been regarded, also, as actuated only by base and selfish motives; and it has been held that if the eyes of their dupes could be once opened to their iniquity, the whole affair would collapse. Yet we have seen leader after leader discarded, and the two founders whose assistance was supposed absolutely essential — Stephens and O'Mahony — excommunicated and disgraced; whilst the association still survives, and even flourishes. Manifest mistakes have been made by the chiefs, and detected by the rank and file; accusations of dishonesty have been bandied about against prominent officials; informers have cropped up as plentifully as could have been expected; but none of these things, nor all of them combined, have been sufficient to annihilate the association.[1] One reason for this may doubtless be found in the republican and democratic form assumed by the brotherhood. Its mode of government is not from above downwards, but from beneath upwards. Its root cannot be severed at a single stroke, for it does not spring from one or two principal men, but arises by some thousands of inconspicuous rootlets. We must bear in mind that it has been fully organized; and that by the organization given it, the vitality of the association has not been centralized in one part, but developed around innumerable local centres, carefully linked together. Some of the chiefs may be captured, few or many; but that does not disorganise the Society; the 'circles' can elect new 'centres'; and new 'head-centres' can be chosen to replace the old. So long as the broad basis of the rank and file exists, so long can it raise up the pyramid of officers. To sweep off the most prominent men, therefore, is not to destroy the association; to have been misled into thinking the contrary, shows that the reality of things has not been understood.

It has been remarked that the Irish Republican Society is not equal, as far as regards social status, with certain organizations which preceded it; and here is another reason why Fenianism is so hard to kill. One of the higher animals, where the nerve-material is gathered into one chief centre, is easily stricken dead by a blow upon it; but how is it with a polyp? A thousand individuals or centres of vitality are combined together in a common polypdom; the mass may be cut and severed into many pieces, but life endures none the less, and with it the power of retrieving losses. Thus it is vain to dream that the detention of some of its chiefs, and the flight of others, have had any greater effect than to mar somewhat the working of the Society, to decapitate some circles, to isolate others, and to disorganize a few of the weakest. These things are not irretrievable. They are such as to cause delay, but not despair. And it must also be borne in mind that the half of the Society beyond the Atlantic has all along remained fully organized and hopeful.

These are facts which must be faced when the question how to deal with Fenianism is considered. There are people who appear to fancy that rigorous measures have not yet been tried, and who exclaim that no further hope of obtaining the Queen's mercy must be allowed to exist. If they think that any exercise of mercy heretofore has helped to stave off the dissolution of the Society in Ireland, they err. It is a fact that the Irish Tories did not more desire the execution of some of the political prisoners than did many of the Fenians themselves.... If the association were on the point of expiring, an execution of political prisoners, so far from hastening its death, would make every ramification of it tingle and glow with renewed life and vigour. The Irish are not cowards; nor when their feelings are once engaged do they stop to calculate the cost. Long years of experience should at least have taught us this — that by a system of penal rule we gain nothing but undying resistance and perpetual hostility. There is indeed no need to theorize on this subject. It is a fact that the Irish State Trials, so far from awing the population, won for the prisoners an amount of sympathy which they never received when they were free to act. And it is no less the fact that deaths — the deaths of those who were killed in affrays with the military and constabulary — have had by no means that deterrent effect which the advocates of rigorous measures think they ought to have. Men who have served through the American campaign are less repelled by fear of death than by dread of prison life; and the same rule holds with those of their kith and kin who have joined the republican ranks in Ireland.

Besides, a severe policy, useless at home because of the democratic form of the organization, would be worse than useless when considered with regard to foreign affairs. It would at once raise Fenianism in America and elsewhere to a pitch of prosperity which it has not hitherto attained, and give it,

1. After the failure of the 1867 rising, John O'Mahony's Fenian brotherhood was replaced by the new Clan-na-Gael organization. Stephens was deposed as 'head-centre' before the rising, largely because he wished to postpone it.

together with a new lease of life, a more favourable position in the eyes of the Americans. As it is, things go well with it in the United States, as far as popularity is concerned. It has done good service to the dominant Republican party, and several of the leaders of that party have openly avowed themselves well disposed to it. Moreover, the Fenians themselves are working to effect a union of the two sections into which they are divided, and have appointed delegates to confer with each other....

In all the great centres of England, Wales, and Scotland the association is much stronger than would be readily supposed. The Irish support it in larger proportion than at home; and there is also an English Republican Brotherhood to countenance and assist it.

The true way of dealing with Fenianism is to detach the popular sympathies from it; and this can only be done by effecting a complete change in the condition and government of Ireland.

THE EFFECT OF THE FENIAN EXECUTIONS

When a funeral procession was organized in London the day after the executions at Manchester,[1] a consoling comparison was immediately instituted between the activity of the Irish in England and the apathy of the Irish at home. Fenian sympathies manifested themselves, it was said, where their presence was least to be dreaded; they were quiet where they had been thought most formidable. The history of the next fortnight showed the amount of reliance to be placed on this optimist conclusion. The streets of Dublin have been thronged with a procession largely recruited from the respectable ranks, and composed of persons of various creeds, contented to sink the differences by which Irishmen are so often divided in a common homage to national sentiment. The number of those who actually took part in it was very large — the most competent judges fixing it at 25,000, while other authorities, not all friendly, estimate it at from 30,000 to 40,000. Even the highest of these figures by no means represents the amount of interest called forth in the city. An immense proportion of the spectators wore the funeral colours, and many persons were seen with them at the windows even of houses of the better class. Much of this feeling would probably have led to a more active participation in the ceremony if the weather had not been cold and wet to a degree unusual even in December. One remarkable feature was the presence of about 2,000 children of both sexes, so young that they must have been sent there by, or at any rate with the consent of, their parents. This is a proof that the sympathy, instead of being confined to men who are very young or very reckless, extends to fathers of families, to men who in sacrificing the comfort and risking the health of their children by sending them to stand for hours in the mud in preparation for a walk of six miles through driving sleet, could have had no motive except the desire to identify them with the cause to which they are themselves attached. Perhaps this fact is even more significant than the numbers, or the military bearing, of well-dressed young men who attended....

Clearly then the strange belief that the executions would have a deterrent effect on the Irish people has not been justified by the result. Those who held it can scarcely have made sufficient allowance for difference of circumstances and character. To the prosperous, well-to-do man, with no very strong religious convictions death is doubtless a thing to shudder at. He prefers, naturally enough, the comfortable realities of the present to the cold uncertainty of an unknown future. It does not follow that the poor man, to whom life is a hard struggle, and the glories of the future a vivid reality, will equally shrink from the portal of that brighter existence. The ordinary teaching of the Catholic Church has given to the world beyond the grave a distinctness of which the mass of Protestants have little conception; and the outlines thus drawn have been filled up yet more minutely by popular tradition. On a nation at once Catholic and unprosperous this fact is calculated to have an effect which may easily be overlooked by those who are strangers to both conditions. The argument for a vigorous policy of repression in the case of Fenianism, sometimes deduced from the success of the O'Connell prosecutions, shows an equal misconception of Irish affairs. The conditions of the two movements are wholly antagonistic. O'Connell's weapon was 'moral force'; his agitation was orderly or it was nothing. An adverse verdict cut the ground from under him. A party

1. Three young Irishmen were hanged in November 1867 for killing a policeman in Manchester while attempting to rescue two Fenian prisoners from a prison van.

which professed respect for the Constitution and the law had no *locus standi* left it when the highest legal authorities had pronounced its policy unconstitutional. And the result of the O'Connell trial was as much a triumph for the party of action as for the party of order. After Mr. Mitchel had been convicted,[2] he reminded the Government of his previous declaration that he would compel them to treat Ireland as a conquered country. The Young Ireland policy of that day expressly aimed at provoking an evident collision between the Government and the people, in order that the latter might unlearn all that O'Connell had taught them, might abandon Constitutional action in despair of Parliamentary redress, and might brood in secret over the counsel: 'una salus victis nullam sperare salutem.'[3] It took longer than Mr. Mitchel expected for the mass of the people, whom his journal did not reach, to forget the living lesson of O'Connell's presence; but in a new generation, educated by schools, by the Temperance movement,[4] by the famine, by emigration, and above all by foreign military service, the seed found a congenial soil, and bore its natural fruit in Fenianism.

In this connection the view of the recent executions taken in the French and American press is not without importance. On the Continent Fenianism has until lately been regarded merely as a curiosity. After the Manchester executions, however, a new tone has been adopted by journalists; and two powerful motives will probably prevent its being speedily changed. The reactionists, so often troubled by English censure and by the contrast, pointed by domestic opponents, between foreign absolutism and English Constitutionalism, eagerly catch at the opportunity of silencing their Liberal adversaries with the argument that even in England the scaffold has been found necessary to the maintenance of authority. A large part of the Liberal party, recognizing the advantage thus gained by its foes, is angry because it can no longer refer with undiminished confidence to the example of England. And the more advanced Democrats, who insist on separating the English people from their Government, declaim with increased severity against the aristocracy as an enemy to freedom....

In itself this expression of hostile opinion may be a small matter. These utterances of the foreign press, however, must be taken into account in estimating the force of Irish feeling. Extracts, embodying all the strongest passages, are sure to be circulated throughout Ireland; and the belief, exaggerated though it may be, in French and American sympathy, can hardly fail to exert a powerful influence on an impassioned and excited people. Even without this stimulus the change of opinion in Ireland during the last two years has been remarkable enough to arrest the attention of every thoughtful politician. In 1865 the attitude of the great mass of the population towards the Fenians was one of incredulous impatience. They were anathematized from the altars: they were absolutely without influence in the country. Two years of repression without any redress of the grievances acknowledged by every Liberal statesman have disarmed the bulk of indigenous opposition to Fenianism, and gone far to identify the movement in popular estimation with the cause of the nation at large. And most momentous of all has been the change during the weeks which followed the executions at Manchester.

Men who had hitherto been firm believers in the sufficiency of those measures of remedial legislation, which have been so long discussed and evaded, have now lost faith in their effect; and it has become a question no longer merely whether the Church Establishment must be abolished and the position of the tenant class secured,[5] but whether even these concessions of justice will bring healing in their train, unless they are combined with some positive step towards organization and development of the national life of Ireland.

2. John Mitchel (1815-75) was arrested in 1848, tried for treason-felony, convicted and sentenced to fourteen years' transportation.
3. 'There is but one safety to the vanquished — to hope for no safety.' Virgil, *Aeneid* II, 354.
4. Rev. Theobald Mathew (1790-1856), a Capuchin priest, led a temperance crusade in Ireland and Britain between 1839 and 1844 and extended it to Irish America in 1849. The movement was outstandingly successful.
5. The Church of Ireland was disestablished in 1869 and the first Land Act was passed in 1870.

CHARLES J. KICKHAM

(1828-82)

from:
KNOCKNAGOW,
or The Homes of Tipperary (1873)

[*Knocknagow* has probably been reprinted more often than any other Irish novel. It is usually cited as having been first published in 1879, but A.M. Sullivan published the first edition, now very rare, in 1873. The first 36 chapters were published serially in *The Emerald*, New York, and in *The Shamrock*, Dublin. It is a long unwieldy novel, concerned above all to show how the village of the title, in County Tipperary, is depopulated through the operation of the Land Laws and through the greed of those who benefited from them. The plot is so ramshackle as to be beyond summary, but the novel made its impact through the depiction of aspects of the catholic peasant life in the years between the Famine and the Land Wars. It follows the stereotypes of much Victorian fiction, but when it breaks free of these — which is seldom — it registers with some authenticity the system under which the people lived and the effects it had on them. In the following excerpt, from Chapter 32, we have rehearsed the well-known dispute between the priests and the militants. Kickham, like all the Fenians, believed that violence was justified against the oppressors who used the law to retain their privilege. If the law was an enemy to the people, the people should be enemies of the law. The priest tries to rebut this argument, but is surprised that the visiting Englishman, Mr Lowe, does not come to his aid. Finally, the political dispute is surrendered for the love interest, the story of the relationship between Mat Donovan, better known as Mat the Thrasher, and Bessy Morris. The combination of political anger and kitsch sentiment is characteristic of Kickham and of the novel.]

Father Hannigan and Maurice Kearney, with old Phil Morris and Phil Lahy, and a few more choice spirits, drew close together round the social board, and enjoyed themselves in their own way.

'I gave my daughter to Ned Brophy,' said old Larry Clancy, in reply to a question of Father Hannigan's — 'I gave my daughter to Ned Brophy, because he has a good lase.'[1]

'A good landlord is as good as a good lease,' said Maurice Kearney.

'I do not know that,' returned Larry Clancy, slowly and emphatically. 'For my own part, I'd rather have a good lase wud the worst landlord, than no lase wud the best landlord that ever broke bread. Security is the only thing to give a man courage.'

'He's right,' exclaimed old Phil Morris, striking his stick against the ground. 'Security is the only thing. But if every man was of my mind he'd have security or know for what.'

'Hold your tongue, you old sinner,' said Father Hannigan, who had often combated Phil Morris's views, as to how the land question could be brought to a speedy settlement.

'I have my old pike yet — an' maybe I'd *want* id yet!' he exclaimed, with a look of defiance at the priest. 'An the man that'd come to turn *me* out on the road, as I see others turned out on the road, I'd give him the length uv id, as sure as God made Moses.'

'And swing for it,' said Father Hannigan.

'Ay, an' swing for it,' shouted the old Croppy;[2] for it was a musket bullet that shattered Phil Morris's knee in '98. 'Ay, an' swing for it.'

'And be damned,' added the priest. 'Don't you know 'tis murder — wilful murder?'

'I don't know that,' he replied. 'But the prayers of the congregation would carry the man's sowl to heaven, that'd do a manly act, an' put a tyrant out uv the country, and keep other tyrants from following his example. 'Tis self-defence,' he added, striking his stick against the ground; ''tis justice.'

''Tis bad work,' said Father Hannigan. 'And take my word, luck or grace will never come of it.'

'I agree with you,' Hugh Kearney observed, who had joined them during the latter part of the discussion.

'You do!' exclaimed old Phil, turning upon him with a scowl. 'An' who the divil cares what you or

1. lease. Ned Brophy, although in love with another woman, Norah Hogan, marries Larry Clancy's daughter because Clancy has money. The subsequent wedding celebrations form one of the novel's most famous set pieces. Kickham was anxious to repudiate what he saw as the contemporary inclination to put money and status before love in the making of a marriage.

2. A croppy was the popular name for someone who had fought in the rebellion of 1798. Hair cropped close at the back was taken to be a sign of French Jacobin sympathies.

the likes of you agree with? You're well off as you are, and little trouble id gives you to see the people hunted like dogs.'

'You're wrong there, Phil,' replied Hugh. 'I'd like to see that old pike of yours taken from the thatch for a manly fight like that you fought in '98. But that's a different thing.'[3]

'Well, I know that,' returned Phil Morris, letting his chin drop upon his chest, and seeming to brood over the subject for a minute or two. 'But five years ago,' he added, 'I could count three-an'-twenty houses, big an' little, between the cross uv Liscorrig an' Shanbally-bridge; an' today you couldn't light your pipe along that whole piece uv a road, barrin' at wan house — and that's my own. An' why am I left there? Because they *knew* I'd do id,'[4] he muttered through his clenched teeth, as if he were speaking to himself.

'Let him alone,' said the priest. 'There's no use in talking to him.'

'There's raison in what he says,' said old Larry Clancy, in his slow, emphatic way. 'I say,' he added, looking at the priest, 'there's raison in what he says.'

'Don't be talking foolish' returned Father Hannigan, who saw that the eyes of three or four small farmers were fixed inquiringly on his face. 'Good never came of it.'

'Do you hear him?' exclaimed old Phil Morris, turning to Hugh Kearney.

'Well, to a great extent,' said Hugh, after a short silence — for he saw they all expected he would speak — 'to a great extent I agree with Father Hannigan. But there is no use in denying that the dread of assassination is the only protection the people have against extermination in this part of Ireland.'

'I say 'tis justice in the eye uv God,' exclaimed old Phil Morris, 'to punish the bloody tyrants — the robbers and murdherers that rob the people uv their little spots, an' turn 'em out to perish. 'Tis justice to punish the bloody robbers!' And as old Phil struck his stick against the ground and looked around, there was a murmur of applause from the bystanders, who by this time were pretty numerous.

3. Kearney is a big farmer and therefore less inclined to support violence than the old rebel and small tenant, Phil Morris. He says that the rebellion of 1798 was more 'manly' than the contemporary practice of assassinating landlords.

4. He was left because the landlords knew that he would take to assassination if they dispossessed him, as they had done his neighbours.

'The man that believes he is robbed or persecuted,' said the priest, 'cannot be an impartial judge. If every one was to take the law in his own hands, there would be nothing but violence and bloodshed.'

'Well, what do you say to giving the exterminators a fair trial before judge an' jury?'

'What judge and jury?'

''Tisn't the judge an' jury in the coort-house,' returned Phil Morris, 'because they're all for the tyrants, an' some uv 'em tyrants themselves; but a fair jury uv the people, an' a fair judge.'

'I know what you mean,' said Father Hannigan. 'But if the judge and jury in the court-house be all for the tyrant, don't you think your judge and jury would be as much for the victim?'

'No; they'd never condemn a man that didn't desarve id,' replied Phil.

'Ignorant men,' rejoined the priest, 'blinded by passion — perhaps smarting under wrong themselves, or dreading that their own turn might come next — couldn't be a fair judge and jury, Phil, even if what you speak of were lawful or just in the sight of God. So hold your tongue.'

'Ay, that's the way always. "Howld your tongue" settles id.'

'There is Mr. Lloyd,' continued Father Hannigan, as that gentleman returned to his seat; 'and if he put out a tenant would you shoot him?'

'The divil a hair uv his head would be touched,' replied Phil. 'He gives good lases at a fair rent; and the man that does that won't turn out a tenant unless he desarves to be turned out. Answer me this wan question. Did you ever know uv a good landlord to be shot, or a good agent? Answer me that.'

'Well, no,' replied the priest, 'I never did.'

'There it is,' observed Larry Clancy, as if that settled the question, and Father Hannigan had thrown up the sponge.

'Well, now, Mr. Lowe,' said Father Hannigan, 'what's your opinion of this matter?'

'I am almost entirely ignorant of it,' he replied. 'But I confess I came over to Ireland under the impression that the people were lawless and revengeful, particularly in your county.'

'You only saw the dark side of the picture,' returned Father Hannigan. 'We are not so black as we are painted.'

'I believe that. And a remark made by an Irish judge, with whom I had the honour of dining a few weeks ago, made a great impression on me, I confess.'

'What did he say?'

'He had sentenced several men to be hanged a short time before, and a gentleman present made some severe remarks, while discussing the subject of agrarian outrages, when Judge —— said: "I never met an instance of a landlord being killed, who did not deserve — I won't say to be hanged, as I am a judge — but I do say, a case of the kind never came before me that the landlord did not deserve to be *damned!*"'

Old Phil Morris looked with astonishment at the speaker.

'Put id there,' he exclaimed, reaching his horny hand across the table. 'If you were the divil you're an honest man.'

'I don't despair of old Ireland yet,' said the priest. 'The people are good if they only get fair play.'

'Ireland will never do any good till we have trade and manufactures of our own,' observed Phil Lahy. And a certain thickness of utterance indicated that Phil had forgotten his resolution respecting the cordial long ago.

'Our rulers crushed our trade and manufactures,' said Father Hannigan.

'Yes,' returned Phil Lahy, 'but the people are too much given to farming. A beggarly sky farmer[5] that's stuck in the mud from mornin' to night, an' don't know beef from mutton — no, nor the taste of an egg; for if he dare look at a hen's tail, his wife would fling the dish-cloth at him. An' that poor crawler, with his head bald from the rain droppin' on it from the eave from standin' outside his honour's window, waitin' till his honour condescended to talk to him — that beggar would despise the tradesman an' look down on him. Tom Hogan comes in to me this mornin' to know was there any news in the paper. "There is," says I. "I'll read one uv the best articles ever you heard for you," says I. "Look at the markets," says Tom Hogan. Ha! ha! ha!' And Phil Lahy laughed quite sardonically. '"Look at the markets." Ha! ha! ha!'[6]

'There's some truth in what you say,' said Father Hannigan.

'Ay,' continued Phil, 'an' the big farmer will make doctors an' attorneys of his sons, instead of setting 'em up in business.'

'I'm going to bind my youngest son to his uncle,' said Mr. Kearney.

'For a wonder,' returned Phil Lahy, tasting his punch; and, not considering it up to the mark, adding another glass of whiskey.

'That's what I call a *double entendre*,[7] Phil,' said Father Hannigan.

'I fear you are forgetting your promise,' Hugh observed.

'What promise?' Phil asked.

'Not to drink anything stronger than cordial.'

Phil Lahy stared at the speaker for half a minute; and then stared at the *double entendre* for half a minute more.

In fact, Phil Lahy left himself in a dilemma. Making a sudden dive, however, at the ginger cordial decanter, he filled his glass and carefully added the glass of cordial to the two glasses of whiskey in his tumbler.

'Will that please you?' he asked, turning to Hugh, as if *that* didn't satisfy him nothing could.

Hugh rubbed his hand over his face, and did his best to keep from laughing.

'Would you doubt Phil for getting out of a promise?' observed Father Hannigan. 'He'd drive a coach-and-six through any promise that ever was made — as old Dan[8] used to say of an Act of Parliament.'

'Old Dan said many a good thing,' rejoined Phil Lahy, not choosing to notice the reference to the 'promise.' 'But the best thing ever he said,' he continued, casting about for something that would turn the conversation away from promises and cordial altogether — 'the best thing ever he said was: "England's difficulty is Ireland's opportunity,"'[9] exclaimed Phil Lahy, as the happy apothegm suddenly flashed into his mind at the very moment that he was about taking refuge in a severe fit of sneezing. 'An' you'll see Ireland yet ——' Here Phil stopped short, as if he had lost the thread of his discourse; but after a good pull at the tumbler, he seemed to find it again, and added —

5. hill farmer. All his produce would go towards paying the rent.
6. It seems absurd to Lahy that a small farmer like Hogan would show interest in the market news.
7. A double pun(ch)?
8. Daniel O'Connell, who used the phrase about driving 'a coach and six' through the obnoxious clauses of the Catholic Emancipation bill in a letter to his wife in March 1829.
9. See the letter from James Stephens to Jeremiah O'Donovan Rossa on this famous phrase (p. 263 below).

'when a redcoat will be as great a curiosity as a white blackbird. There's a storm brewin',' he continued, with a portentous scowl. 'Columbkill's words is comin' to pass.[10] An' the day will come when we can drive the invader out of Ireland — wud square-bottles, as Mat the Thrasher said the other day.'

'But I don't like to hear you running down the farmers,' observed Father Hannigan.

'I don't run down the farmers — except when they deserve id.'

'Manufactures are good,' continued Father Hannigan; 'and we'll have enough of them when our fine harbours are crowded with the shipping of America — and of the whole world. But for all that I'd be sorry to see the homes of the peasantry disappearing from our hills and our plains, and the people crowded into factories.'

'You're right,' exclaimed Phil Lahy, almost with a shout.

'Princes or lords may flourish or may fade.[11]

Mat Donovan has a new song that touches upon that.'

'Come, Mat, give us the new song,' said Father Hannigan.

'I'm afeard I haven't id be heart right yet, sir,' replied Mat.

'Oh, we'll excuse you; we'll excuse all mistakes,' rejoined the priest. 'Come, Mr. Hanly,' he called out to Lory — who with a dozen others was battering the floor to the tune of 'O'Connell's Trip to Parliament'[12] — 'We're going to get a song. Give the poor pipers and fiddlers a rest. Come, Mat, up with it!'

There was a general movement towards the table, and all waited anxiously for Mat the Thrasher's new song, of which many of the company had heard.

Mat Donovan leant back in his chair, and with a huge hand resting on the table, and clutching one of the gilt buttons on the front of the blue body-coat with the other, he turned his eyes to the collar-beams, and sang in a fine mellow voice

10. The so-called 'Prophecies' of St Columbcille, in which the final defeat of the English and their expulsion from Ireland was foretold, had been part of peasant lore at least since the millenarian crusades of the 1820s.
11. Oliver Goldsmith, *The Deserted Village*, line 53, although Phil should have said 'Princes and lords'. It is appropriate that this poem should be cited, since Kickham's theme resembles that of Goldsmith's poem.
12. A popular reel. Numerous songs were written in the nineteenth century about O'Connell and his achievements.

THE PEASANT-FARMER'S SONG —
FOR THE TIME TO COME

I've a pound for to lend, and a pound for to spend —
And *cead mille failte*[13] my word for a friend;
No mortal I envy, no master I own —
Nor lord in his castle, nor king on his throne.
Come, fill up your glasses, the first cup we'll drain
To the comrades we lost on the red battle plain!
Oh, we'll cherish their fame, boys, who died long ago —
And what's that to any man whether or no?

The spinning-wheels stop, and my girls grow pale,
While their mother is telling some sorrowful tale,
Of old cabins levelled, and coffinless graves,
And ships swallowed up in the salt ocean waves.
But, girls, that's over — for each of you now
I'll have twenty-five pounds and three-year-old cow;
And we'll have *lan na mhala*[14] at your weddings I trow —
And what's that to any man whether or no?

Come here, *bhean na tigha*[15] sit beside me a while,
And the price of your heart let me read in your smile.
Would you give your old home for the lordliest hall?
Ha! — you glance at my rifle that hangs on the wall.
And your two gallant boys on parade-day are seen
In the ranks of the brave 'neath the banner of green;
Oh! I've taught them to guard it 'gainst traitor and foe —
And what's that to any man whether or no?

But the youngest of all is the 'white-headed boy'[16]
The pulse of your heart, and our pride and our joy:
From the dance and the hurling he'll steal off to pray,
And will wander alone by the river all day.

13. A standard phrase of welcome in Irish: 'A hundred thousand welcomes.'
14. Literally, 'the full of a bag' — i.e. an abundance.
15. 'The woman of the house.'
16. Traditional phrase, translated from the Irish, for the favourite son.

He's as good as the priest at his Latin I hear,
And to college, please God, we'll send him next
year.
Oh, he'll offer the Mass for our souls when we
go —
And what's that to any man whether or no?

Your hands, then, old neighbours! one more
glass we'll drain;
And *cead mille failte* again and again!
May discord and treason keep far from our shore,
And freedom and peace light our homes
evermore.
He's the king of good fellows, the poor, honest
man;
So we'll live and be merry as long as we can,
And we'll cling to old Ireland through weal and
through woe —
And what's that to any man whether or no?

There was a shout of applause at the conclusion of Mat Donovan's song; and some of the women were seen to wipe the tears from their cheeks with their aprons. Bessy Morris raised her eyes to his; and as she laid her hand upon his arm while turning away her head to reply to a question of Hugh Kearney's, Mat Donovan pressed his hand over his eyes, and caught his breath, as if he had been shot through the body.

Bessy Morris resumed her coquettish ways as she went on talking to Hugh Kearney, who was evidently captivated by her. If he had proposed for her on the spot, with or without his father's consent, and if it were arranged that they were to be married that day week, or any day before Ash-Wednesday,[17] it would not have surprised Mat Donovan in the least. But while she talked and laughed with Hugh Kearney, her hand remained resting on the sleeve of the blue body-coat. Perhaps this little incident did not mean much. Mat Donovan never for a moment thought it meant anything. But he kept his arm quite still, and would not have frightened away that little hand for a trifle.

'That's a right good song, Mat,' said Father Hannigan.

'The chorus,' observed Phil Lahy, who seemed in a mood for contradiction, 'is as ould as the hills.'

'So much the better,' replied the priest. 'Are we going to get a song from anyone else?'....

17. Ash Wednesday is the opening of Lent, during which marriages were not celebrated.

JOHN O'LEARY

(1830-1907)

from: RECOLLECTIONS OF FENIANS AND FENIANISM (1896)

[O'Leary's *Recollections* demonstrate the connection between Young Ireland and the Fenian movement. He traces the linking influences — from Davis to Mitchel and John Martin to James Stephens — which governed his own development and, further, bears witness to the hostility of the Irish catholic clergy to the Fenian movement. By the time the book was published, O'Leary had himself become, for Yeats and others, a noble and representative figure from the previous generation, just as Martin, Mitchel and others had been potent symbols for the young O'Leary himself. Although a powerful figure in the Fenian movement in his last days, he did not seem to be aware of the resurgence that was secretly taking place within the movement and he could hardly have been enamoured of the manner in which Patrick Pearse was to re-establish a close relationship between Fenian revolutionary ideals and catholicism.

The first excerpt is from the book's opening chapter.]

... I commence my story, then ... by telling how I became a Young Irelander — for here was certainly the root of the matter to me. I have said something of this elsewhere more than once, but here I must go more fully into it.

Sometime in the year 1846, while recovering from a fever, I came across the poems and essays of

Thomas Davis, then recently dead. What Davis has been to more than a generation of Irishmen since his death is well kown in his own country, and may in a measure be understood by Englishmen now, since the publication of his prose writings (edited by T.W. Rolleston, in the Camelot series), and of his life, written by his co-labourer and friend, Sir C.G. Duffy.[1] What he was then to me I feel as if I can only faintly shadow forth at this distance of time. Perhaps it may give some notion of the effect produced on me to say that I then went through a process analogous to what certain classes of Christians call 'conversion.' I can but vaguely remember my unregenerate state. Doubtless (from my surroundings) I was not anti-Irish or West-British:[2] but then I am confident I was not strongly Irish, and I am sure I was strongly ambitious, and can easily conceive that my ambition, stimulated by much reading of English literature, necessarily either directly or indirectly anti-Irish in spirit, might have led me where it has unfortunately led so many of my countrymen before and since. Now, however, everything was changed. The world was an altered world to me. I felt in quite a new sense that I was an Irishman, and that for weal or woe my fate must be linked with that of my country. I do not think that either then or since I ever had much of that spurious Irishism of Moore's song, which associates Ireland with virtue and England with guilt;[3] but Irish in a higher and better sense I think I may claim to have at least struggled to be, and, in so far as I have fought the good fight, to Thomas Davis more than to any other, or, indeed more than to all others, is the credit due. I do not like to exaggerate, and do not think I am doing so. I do not, of course, mean in the least to convey that the largest part of my intellectual and moral training does not necessarily come from other and wider regions, but for all that is Irish in me, and, above all, for the inspiration that made me Irish, the fountain and the origin must always be sought in Davis.

But what came out of all this? Little, perhaps, at once — or at least little in the shape of action. What must have followed very soon was the close study of the leading columns, and indeed of many other columns, of the *Nation* newspaper. For what I found there I was, of course, perfectly prepared by the previous reading of Davis; and what was to be found in that paper I must leave the reader to gather from another pen than mine. Something, however, I must say even at this stage as to how the *Nation* affected me; later I shall have more to tell. In leading article, essay, and poem we read, from week to week, the story of Ireland's sufferings under English rule; and now and then we heard of other countries groaning under alien domination, and of their efforts, successful or unsuccessful, to shake it off. At first, perhaps, the teaching of the *Nation* was not directly unconstitutional, though, indirectly, it certainly was so from the beginning. From ceasing to 'fear to speak of '98'[4] to wishing to imitate the men of that time the transition was very easy indeed to the youthful mind. Many, if not most, of the younger amongst us were Mitchelites before Mitchel, or rather before Mitchel had put forth his programme. We were told much about the doings of Hugh O'Neill and Owen Roe and Sarsfield, and led to seek what more we could gather about them elsewhere. But as to the men of '98 there was no difficulty where to search and what to find. We had the fascinating 'Memoirs of Wolfe Tone,'[5] and the very laborious and full, if somewhat dull and chaotic, book of Madden,[6] and many a biography and history beside. I may perhaps be mixing up some things in my memory here; but the impression I mean to convey is certainly correct. I may be attributing to the *Nation* other things than I got from it; but that matters little, for Davis was the *Nation* and the *Nation* was Davis; and in saying this I most surely do not in the least mean to detract from the merit of the many able men who with Davis, and without him, made the *Nation*. Anyway, the feeling and sentiment upon which I acted then, and have mainly acted ever since, came from Davis; and what the *Nation* no doubt gave me, or taught

1. T.W. Rolleston (ed.), *Prose Writings of Thomas Davis* (London, 1890); C. Gavan Duffy, *Thomas Davis: The Memoirs of an Irish Patriot 1840-1846* (London: Fisher Unwin, 1892).
2. A term coined by the journalist D. P. Moran (1872-1936) to describe members of the Irish Parliamentary Party. The term describes the pro-British attitudes and sympathies of some Irish people.
3. The reference is to Thomas Moore's 'The Song of O'Ruark, Prince of Breffni' which has the closing lines:
   'On *our* side is Virtue and Erin!
   On *theirs* is the Saxon and Guilt.'
4. 'Who fears to speak of Ninety-Eight?' is the first line of John Kells Ingram's ballad 'The Memory of the Dead', first published anonymously in *The Nation* in April 1843.
5. O'Leary must be referring to W.T. Wolfe Tone (ed.), *Life of Theobald Wolfe Tone ... Written by Himself, and Continued by his Son* (Washington D.C., 1826; London, 1827).
6. R.R. Madden, *The United Irishmen: Their Lives and Times*, 4 vols (Dublin, 1842-46).

me where to get, were such additional facts and fancies as my opinions sought by way of justification of the faith that was in me.

While all this commotion was going on in the internal man, many external events were occurring which need some notice here, for their bearing upon my future actions if not my future thoughts. In the year '47, when I was about 17 years of age, I left Carlow School, and towards the close of the same year I entered Trinity College. This was the time when the Irish Confederation — the Young Ireland seceding body — and its associated clubs were in full swing. I at once joined the Grattan Club, presided over by 'Meagher of the Sword,' and of course was assiduous in my attendance not only upon its meetings but upon the more important ones of the parent association. At these assemblages I necessarily heard much explosive oratory, notably from the aforesaid Meagher, but also from O'Gorman, Doheny, M'Gee, and many others more or less known to fame at the time, who have mostly slipped out of the memory of the present generation . . . .

[O'Leary resumes his narrative in the aftermath of the sequence of events that began with the founding of the Tenant League in 1850, the Irish Brigade in 1851 and the new Independent Irish Party which fought the 1852 general election. All these were preceded by the Young Ireland movement in its first phase, under the leadership of Thomas Davis. O'Leary now comes into contact with the more militant remnants of the movement, particularly John Martin, Mitchel's friend.]

CHAPTER VII

I have come here to a natural halting-place in my narrative, when I left the Queen's Colleges in the summer of 1853; and it seems to me as if this were the place to say something of the effect produced on the more youthful minds, and indeed upon many older ones, too, by the new agitation to which I have alluded before. I need not go at any length into the business itself. All that needs to be known about it can be found in Sir C.G. Duffy's 'North and South'; as all about Young Ireland can be gathered from his first and far more interesting book.[1] In the earlier stages of the agitation — the Pope's Brass Band part of the performance, with Keogh and Sadlier as the chief players[2] — I personally felt no interest whatever, save of the negative sort. It was, of course, more or less discouraging and depressing to see the people so easily deceived by such patent pretenders to patriotism, as they ought to have appeared from the beginning, and such shameless scoundrels, as these agitators proved themselves to be before very long. The emphatically, if not exclusively, Catholic nature of the agitation, and the support given it and its leaders even to the shameful end, by such a large section of the priesthood, with the Pope's Legate at their head, did not fail to increase a slight anti-clerical feeling left in me as a result of the opposition of the priests to the Young Ireland movement. Nor has anything that has occurred since that now distant time made me any way more in love with 'priests in politics.' The Irish priests, as priests, and in the ordinary discharge of parochial and pastoral functions, are mostly very much to be commended, if not admired; but when they step out of the sanctuary into the street, or, still worse, profane the sanctuary itself with their violent denunciations of men and things, then indeed our feeling becomes very different from one of admiration, and the result is that our clerical agitators, while gaining little as politicians, mostly lose much as priests.

In what I may call the second stage of the agitation, when it became nearly, if not entirely, agrarian, and certainly unsectarian, under the leadership of Lucas, Duffy, G.H. Moore,[3] and others, then indeed the thing wore a somewhat

1. Charles Gavan Duffy's book on the Tenant League (see note 7 to Chapter IX below) was *The League of North and South: An Episode in Irish History 1850-1854* (London, 1886); his other book, referred to here, was *Young Ireland: A Fragment of Irish History, 1840-1850* (London and New York, 1880).

2. The Pope's Brass Band was a popular title for the Irish Brigade, a group of Liberal MPs at Westminster who banded together to oppose the Ecclesiastical Titles Bill in 1851. Supported by Archbishop Cullen, they founded an extra-parliamentary movement known as the Catholic Defence Association. The group's leader was George Henry Moore (1811-70), father of the novelist George Moore, and it included the notorious Sadleir (misspelled by O'Leary) and Keogh (see note 5, Chapter IX). The Brigade formed the Independent Irish Party in union with the Tenant League.

3. Frederick Lucas (1812-55), journalist and politician, founded *The Tablet* in 1840, after his conversion to catholicism in the previous year. He became involved with Gavan Duffy and G.H. Moore in the Tenant League and the Independent Irish Party. He appealed to Rome over Archbishop Cullen's intervention in a by-election in 1854, went to Rome, had two interviews with the pope and yet, despite support from Dr John MacHale, archbishop of Tuam, got nowhere. His ill-advised journey created a clerical and lay reaction which damaged the Independent Party. He died from a heart attack while awaiting the result of his appeal to Rome. He too is a figure whose fate confirmed the Fenians' dislike of the church's interventions in political matters.

altered aspect to me and others. Of Lucas, from what I read in his paper, I thought very well personally, and what I have read of him since, in his life by his brother, and elsewhere, has only increased my admiration of his character; but I had some natural prejudice against him as an Englishman, who could not well feel with us in our national aspirations. Of Duffy we, of course, all thought well, though we were not without a certain feeling that, if he had not abandoned the National programme, he was at least inclined to put it somewhat into the background for the time being. G.H. Moore, whose antecedents were not altogether good, from the National point of view, we were still beginning to like, and grew to like better as years went on. So that from the side of the leaders there was nothing to divert sympathy from the movement, while there was one thing about their following very much calculated to attract us. This was what seemed — and, alas! only seemed — the union of North and South, Presbyterian and Catholic joined heart and soul together. But notwithstanding all these favourable circumstances this movement left the youthful heart and mind of the country very much untouched. It might be that we did not feel the agrarian grievance as strongly as we ought; but I think it was mainly because we felt confident that the English Parliament did not care to remove that grievance, or indeed any grievance. And surely all experience previous to Fenianism, and even to a great extent all subsequent experience, tends to prove that England, in the case of Ireland, never yields to any other argument save that of force, in some of its varying forms. It is quite unnecessary for my purpose to go over the oft-told tale of Emancipation, the Abolition of Tithes, the Disestablishment of the Church, and the first Land Bill.[4] I might, too, if I were inclined to be polemical, which I am not here and now, give very substantial reasons to show that the element of force in many different shapes was anything but foreign from the passing of the second Land Act too.[5] But however these things were, are, or are to be, it was at the time to which I have now come in my narrative a rooted conviction in my mind, and, I believe, in the minds of most Nationalists of my generation, that we could get from England nothing but what we could wring from her. We also felt, or at least I felt fully, that we were not then in any position to act, nor likely to be for a good while to come; and that so we had little to do under the circumstances but to try to possess our souls in peace, watching and waiting for that better day which we had little doubt would some time come.

And so the years passed on, leaving Ireland where she was, disgusted, disheartened, and, to all outward appearance, entirely apathetic. The period between the collapse of the Tenant League and the rise of Fenianism was the 'deadest' time in Irish politics within my memory, and perhaps within the memory of any man now living. We were not indeed without our excitements during this period; but they were none of our making, and so left us very much where we were. There was the Crimean War, for instance, which stirred England to the very depths, but which only touched the outer fringe, or, perhaps, I had better call it, the upper crust of Irish Society. The masses were interested, if not moved, but in an adverse sense from that of England. The Czar Nicholas, who, to the prejudiced and stupid English mind of the time, was simply the incarnation of evil, was to the equally prejudiced, but by no means stupid, Irish mind not in any way a saint or hero, but a being who, whatever might be his nature, must necessarily be beneficent to Ireland in proportion as he was maleficent to England. That was rather a simple way of looking at things, but it has always been our way, is our way still — all pretence of 'union of hearts' notwithstanding — and can only cease to be our way when our relations with England cease to be what they are.

Our feelings during the Crimean War were somewhat complicated by the fact that the French were on the side of England. We did not, any of us, wish them any ill, though many of us wished no good to their scoundrel of an Emperor.[6] But in the next difficulty of England there was no such complication of feeling. Our feelings — that is the feelings of the great mass of Irishmen — were entirely on the side of India during the mutiny.[7] We were altogether untouched by the thrilling stories of

4. Catholic Emancipation (1829), the Tithe Commutation Act (1837), the Disestablishment of the Church of Ireland (1869), the Landlord and Tenant Act of 1870 (although O'Leary could be referring to the 1860 Landlord and Tenant Law Amendment Act) were all wrested from the British government after great political pressure and considerable violence.
5. The Land Law (Ireland) Act of 1881 was drawn up at the height of the Land War.
6. Napoleon III, emperor of the French 1852-70.
7. The Indian Mutiny took place in 1857-58; the Crimean War in 1853-56.

Indian cruelty, knowing but too well, from our own history, that England was quite sure to give as good as she got; and all subsequent and authentic accounts of the suppression of the mutiny show that we were quite right in preserving our equanimity, and that England in every sense showed herself quite worthy of her ancient fame, on this occasion.

The Crimean War and the Indian Mutiny came and went, but left us quite as we were before. England's difficulty is proverbially said to be Ireland's opportunity, but opportunities may present themselves to nations, as to individuals, to little effect. Here were opportunities — especially in the case of the Indian Mutiny, when Ireland was nearly entirely denuded of troops — if only we could avail ourselves of them. But, alas! we could not. The country had not yet recovered from the physical collapse of '48, or what may be called the moral collapse of '55.[8] She was without organization, or even the thought of organization, and so such an opportunity as we had not had for long before, have not had since, nor are likely to have soon again, passed away, leaving us no nearer freedom. If Fenianism had been then, things might have been far different now; but the idea still lay more or less dormant in the brain of James Stephens, to wake up into activity, however, very soon after.

But I must go back for a short while to my small personal concerns, which will, however, soon bring me face to face with the subject proper of this book. The session of '53-'54 I spent in Dublin, moving on to London for that of '54-'55; but in neither of these periods or places can I remember anything to have occurred which had any particular bearing upon my political future. The next year, however, things were somewhat different, and I was in some small measure cast into the political current again. I then changed the scene of my studies, or at least operations, which I fear were growing, or at least tending to grow, less and less medical, to Paris. There I was again, or perhaps rather for the first time, brought into intimate contact with the men as well as the things of the '48 movement. . . . Here for the first time I met John Martin;[9] and this I have ever considered as a sort of era, if not in my intellectual, at least in my moral existence. Martin was a man of fair ability, but without any particularly prominent or brilliant mental gift; well educated, and rather well read, but without any claim to anything like learning in any branch of human inquiry. He was, however, something far better than clever or learned; he was simply, *me judice*,[10] the best man I have ever met in this world, and I have but little hope of meeting a better, however long I may remain in it. Then there was to me the all-important consideration, at that time as it is still, that Martin's goodness and nobility, if no doubt theoretically and in a degree taking the whole world into some sort of consideration, were still, and ever remained, practically and profoundly devoted to the land that bore him. He had, too, then an adventitious importance in my eyes, as in those of most of the young men, in that he was the oldest, most intimate, and presumably best-beloved of all the friends of John Mitchel. Of Martin I shall probably have more to say before I have done; but the name of Mitchel reminds me here that in death as in life the two friends were united, and that both may fairly be said to enjoy that euthanasia which the ancients so much desiderated. Mitchel had returned to Ireland in the year 1875, and been elected by the county Tipperary to the English Parliament, in which he neither would nor could sit. But before he could take any very definite step in the matter he was seized by an acute attack of that bronchitis from which both he and Martin had long suffered, and sank down, like the old war-horse he was, literally worn out with the toil and moil of the fray. Martin, who was then attending to his Parliamentary duties in London, hastened over to Newry to the funeral, took cold on his passage, and followed his friend, with only a week's interval, to the grave.

8. Presumably O'Leary is referring to the collapse of the Independent Irish Party with Lucas's appeal to Rome, his death in that year and Gavan Duffy's emigration in 1856.

9. John Martin (1812-75), a schoolfriend of John Mitchel's in Newry, Co. Down, later married Mitchel's sister, Henrietta. A Young Irelander, later a member of the Irish Confederation, he helped Mitchel to edit the *United Irishman* and James Fintan Lalor to bring out *The Irish Felon*. He was transported to Van Diemen's Land (now Tasmania) for five years on the newly invented charge of 'treason-felony'. Martin was a founder member of the Home Government Association in 1871. He died nine days after Mitchel's funeral. His seat, as MP for Meath, was won by Parnell.

10. in my judgment.

CHAPTER IX

In the thirty-ninth issue of the paper[1] Kickham deals with what he calls 'a furlong or two of

1. The Fenian newspaper, *The Irish People* (1865). O'Leary, it seems, was writing this chapter in 1893.

Pastoral' from Dr. Cullen,[2] who was nearly as long-winded as some of his successors. I quote a passage from the pastoral, which will show clearly that ecclesiastical tactics have not changed since Dr. Cullen's time. Then, as now, if you differ from a priest in politics, you must necessarily be for subverting the faith and corrupting the morals of his congregation. 'As publications, hostile to religion and morality, perverting the judgment by the falsest, but not unfrequently the most specious sophistry, while pretending to enlighten it, or influencing the passions by the most dangerous incentives to vice, while affecting to give a faithful picture of life and nature — form one of the most fatal and widely diffused means employed by the demon for the destruction of souls, it will be the imperative duty both of parents and pastors to prevent, so far as their influence extends, the reading and circulation of such pernicious books, novels, romances, several cheap English publications, which appear in weekly numbers, *and some newspapers lately established in Ireland, which, whilst pretending to be the organs of the Irish people, seem to have no other object but to vilify the Catholic Church, and to withdraw our people from its pale* — all such publications offending against faith and morals, are calculated to do the greatest mischief, and ought to be cautiously avoided and severely condemned by all good Christians. The only protection against the poison they contain, is to banish them from every house, and to destroy them when they fall into your hands.' I need scarcely say that the italics are mine, not the Archbishop's. But let us now listen to Kickham. After defying the Archbishop to 'produce one ungarbled passage in support of his assertion,' he proceeds to carry the war into the enemy's camp. 'If faith and morals have been subverted in his diocese, let him charge it to his own imprudence, or attribute it to his own neglect. The doctrines which subverted the faith or debauched the morals of his flock were not taught in the columns of the *Irish People*. What we have taught, and what we shall continue to teach, is, that Dr. Cullen or any other ecclesiastic is not to be followed as a guide in political matters.' Here is the horrible heresy, here is the perversion of faith and corruption of morals. We declined to consider the Archbishop of Dublin infallible in politics, much less the next parish priest or the first curate. 'We have yet to hear,' continues the article, 'what Dr. Cullen did previous to the establishment of those journals pretending to be the organs of the Irish people to limit the circulation in Ireland of journals really subversive of faith and morals. What steps did he take with reference to Reynolds' publications, *Family Heralds, Penny Dispatches*, and other cheap periodicals. We leave *Harlots' Progresses* and horrible suicides to cheap English publications.[3] We have no need of such heroes as those that disgrace these publications, and demoralize their readers. We find *heroes* enough, both lay and clerical, among the traitors to Ireland. Those we have unsparingly condemned. Is it by working on the extravagant fears of the people, and putting forth a farrago of folly and misrepresentation: defending one slander by another, that Dr. Cullen expects to crush the cause of Ireland? Appeals to people's feelings and prejudices are the last resort of a man who finds arguments fail him. Dr. Cullen knows that, though the *Irish People* should find no difficulty in refuting his statement, the poison of his pastoral is diffused through a thousand channels through which the refutation can never enter.' This is strong language, but reading it calmly now, some twenty-eight years after it was written, I cannot feel that it was too strong for the circumstances or the occasion.

In the concluding paragraph of the article, Kickham puts the case, as between us and Archbishop Cullen and the clergy generally, in a plain and naked form.... 'To crush the *Irish People* no means are unjust or ungentlemanly. In several instances the clergy have used intimidation[4] with our agents, where they found argument fail them. When have the clergy been known to do this, or where, with regard to English cheap literature? None of those English publications are so described

2. Cardinal Paul Cullen (1803-78), was archbishop of Dublin 1852-78 and the first Irish cardinal (1866). He was a bitter opponent of the Fenians, a vigorous supporter of the papacy and the predominant influence in the reorganization of the catholic church in Ireland in the later nineteenth century.

3. The Reynolds brothers, John Russell and Henry Robert, were, like Charles Edward Mudie and W.H. Smith, congregationalists who provided popular novels and cheap magazines and newspapers for the general public. William Hogarth's *The Harlot's Progress* (1732) provided a cautionary tale of the sort of doom that awaited the sinner; O'Leary uses it here as a model of the lurid depictions of vice much favoured by the popular Victorian press.

4. O'Leary's own note to this reads, in part: 'The paper, week after week, was crowded with letters, describing all sorts of misrepresentations of us and intimidation of our readers by priests in all parts of the country.' He specifies examples in a later chapter.

in the last pastoral of Dr. Cullen as to point them out to the public. They are merely used as a pretext, while the most stupid of his flock must see that he meant the *Irish People*, by "some newspapers lately established in Ireland. . . ." So Dr. Cullen knows in his heart that his policy is hostile to the liberty of Ireland. He knows that plain statements setting that policy before the public in its true light must carry the conviction to the heart of every Irishman, that Dr. Cullen may be the friend of religion, but that he is the deadly foe of *Irish Liberty*.'

'Tis hard to know what is in the heart of any one. Cardinal Cullen and Charles Kickham have long since gone where what we think of them matters probably little to them. *There* their motives and actions will be weighed and judged unerringly, whereas our judgment must be of necessity most fallible. But how stands it here below with the memories of the cardinal and the convict? Dr. Cullen's name is seldom mentioned, or, when mentioned, is generally associated with the infamous ones of Sadlier [*sic*] and Keogh,[5] while the man himself, with his strong will and, I believe, undoubted piety, is little respected, save within a very limited region, and not particularly loved or liked in any. The name of Charles Kickham, on the contrary, though perhaps less known to his countrymen than it ought to be, is never mentioned save with respect and love, a respect and love which will, I think, go on increasing as the ages go by, and the thoughts and feelings and passions and prejudices of the present pass away. Even as regards religion, which is ever the burthen of the song of all these bishops and priests, I doubt whether any candid priest or layman could say now that Cardinal Cullen was a better Catholic than Charles Kickham, and those who would consider him a better Christian must, I think, have very different notions of Christianity from what its founder had.

But to come back to our story, and the year '64 and the forty-fourth number of the paper, where we find a long article, by Kickham, entitled 'Pulpit Denunciation — Priests in Politics.' The text for Kickham's sermon was supplied this time by a certain Rev. Mr. Cooke, of the order of Mary Immaculate, who, from what I have heard, I believe to have been a very holy man, and a clever one too, but neither his holiness nor his cleverness prevented him from saying the most foolish thing that had been yet said by any of our clerical adversaries. This reverend gentleman declared from the pulpit that it was a mortal sin to read the *Irish People*. Of course Kickham had no difficulty with the Rev. Mr. Cooke, and little quarrel with him. The mere mention of what he said was enough for all men not idiots. But Kickham went on to show where our sin lay, and how it was 'mortal' in the literal, not the theological sense. We meant to kill clerical dictation, and we did kill it. If it has come to life again in another generation, the fault is not ours.

The article, while allowing that many priests were good Nationalists, dwells at length on the utter unfitness of priests as political leaders for the one reason, if for no other, that they were not free agents. 'If we knew a priest whom nature had marked as a leader of men, ready and willing to take his stand at the head of the people, we should ask him to pause. We should dread the consequence. Every priest believes he is bound to bow humbly to the decrees of his ecclesiastical superiors. And the censure might come at some critical moment when the eyes of the people would be turned to him,[6] and then the people should be left distracted, bewildered, and disheartened. This is why we think it our duty to teach the people not to hope or wish for ecclesiastical leadership; and we wonder every national priest in Ireland does not do the same.'

As usual, Kickham utilizes the Tenant Right movement[7] to show the uselessness or worse of

5. John Sadleir (1815-56), a nationalist businessman and politician, and William Keogh (1817-78), a judge, were both members of the Independent Irish Party, which they helped to destroy by breaking their pledge not to take office in Lord Aberdeen's coalition government 1852-55. In 1852 Sadleir became lord of the treasury and Keogh became solicitor general. Keogh was notorious for the ferocity of his remarks and sentences against the Fenians when he was special commissioner at their trials in 1865. Sadleir embezzled on a large scale. He committed suicide. So too did Keogh, after showing signs of mental instability in his last years. Both men were bywords among the nationalists for unsavoury behaviour and treachery.

6. In a note, O'Leary cites as an example Rev. John Kenyon (1812-69), parish priest of Templederry, Co. Tipperary, a militant supporter of John Mitchel and John Martin. However, under episcopal pressure, he opposed the rising of 1848. O'Leary claims that there were several recent cases among the priests who supported the Tenant Right movement.

7. The Tenant League, founded by Gavan Duffy in 1850, aimed to secure the famous three Fs — Fair Rent, Fixity of Tenure and Free Sale. In association with the Irish Brigade, it led to the formation of the Independent Irish Party in 1852. The party was pledged not to support any government that refused to grant the three Fs. Sadleir and Keogh (see note 5 above) defected and weakened the party. It was finally destroyed by the withdrawal of clerical support after complaints about Archbishop Cullen were brought to Rome. These events confirmed the Fenian suspicion of 'priests in politics'.

'priests in politics.' 'Well might one of the best and ablest priests of the League, on finding his effort to save the people from extermination baffled by members of his own order, exclaim — 'Tis not the people who are rotten. 'Tis the priests are rotten, aye and the bishops are rotten!' Such was the lesson the collapse of the Tenant Right movement taught one of its prominent clerical supporters. What wonder if the Fenians learned the same lesson, and many other lessons too.

[In this extract, O'Leary gives examples of Kickham's, Thomas Luby's and his own contributions to *The Irish People*. Thomas Clarke Luby (1822-1902) was a Young Irelander, a close colleague of James Fintan Lalor, a member of the IRB and one of the chief contributors to *The Irish People* from 1863 to 1865 when he, along with the other Fenians, was arrested. Later, in the United States, he worked closely with O'Donovan Rossa. The Rev. Mr Dixon referred to is probably Joseph Dixon (1806-66), archbishop of Armagh 1852-66. Dixon was a close friend of Cardinal Cullen and shared his hostility towards the Fenians.]

CHAPTER X

... The major part of Kickham's article was devoted to a Rev. Mr. Dixon who, at a 'Mission' in Clonmel, denounced the Fenians after the usual fashion, promising at the same time to open the eyes of the people of Clonmel 'about these Fenians.' 'What must be the thought,' says Kickham, 'in the heart of the young man who burns to strike a blow for his trampled motherland, while he listens to a minister of his religion slandering the men whose lives are devoted to the holy old cause for which our fathers so often bled?'.... Men have seemed, and may seem again, *for a time*, to be serving God and Ireland when they were really only serving themselves and England. Kickham goes on to quote from Father Luke Wadding[1] that 'time was when we had wooden chalices and golden priests, but now we have golden chalices and wooden priests.' Kickham asks if we have again come round to this state of things, and *that* is a question which, I fear, will have to be asked over and over again.

The last article in the paper, headed 'Mr. Hankey[2] on Ireland,' was mine. As I have said before, my *rôle* was generally quite different from Luby's or Kickham's. I was mostly critical, whether of our native doubters, shams, and other disagreeable entities, or of foreign critics and calumniators. The opening paragraph will serve fairly well as a specimen of the sort of thing I was in the habit of writing. 'If we are seldom edified we are almost always sure to be amused by an Englishman's notions about Ireland. Your typical Englishman cannot spend two weeks in Ireland without thinking he has seen everything and knows everything, though, from the nature of things, he can see very little and knows next to nothing at all. As a general rule he knows little about any country but his own, chiefly because he cares little. All knowledge of man or nature, to be worth much, must be based on sympathy; and, if the mind's eye do not look lovingly on the landscape (or the land), there is little chance the bodily eye will find much beauty in it.' This Hankey, by the way, was a splendid specimen of the *serious* (we are chiefly favoured by the comic) travelling Englishman. He was strong in statistics, and had been a member of a Committee of the House of Commons on Irish taxation. He feels bound then, to tell us, as the result of a journey from Clifden to Cork, that 'he could see no evidence in any part which he visited that taxation has any appreciable effect in preventing the cultivation of the land, or arresting the ordinary satisfactory progress of reproductive labour.' This is funny enough, but it is nothing to what he has to say about the way the taxes, of which it was complained that 'the expenditure by the Government was niggardly,' were spent. Hankey 'could see no evidence, however, that such was the case. Police or constabulary, paid by Government, and whose wages are necessarily spent on the spot, are to be met with in groups in almost every village.' This enlightened Englishman acknowledges that we had one grievance; that was, that we still had a Lord Lieutenant, and that the Queen, or even the Prince of Wales, seldom came among us. Mr. Hankey thought that, if only we were favoured with occasional visits from the Queen, 'the whole mass of one of the most impulsive people in the civilized

1. Luke Wadding (1588-1657), a Franciscan priest and scholar, founder of St Isidore's College in Rome. He strongly supported the catholic rebellion of 1641. His best-known work, from which the quotation is taken, is his history of the Franciscan order, *Annales Ordinis Minorum* 8 vols (1625-54).

2. Thomson Hankey (1805-93), Liberal MP, director of the Bank of England and author of a number of works on political economy. The work referred to here is *Irish Grievances* (London, 1881).

world would be ready to fall down and almost worship her.' It seems idle to comment, however briefly, upon such stupid gush as this. It seems an elderly, statistical, dry-as-dust gentleman can at times be as foolishly sentimental as the most silly school-girl. To be sure, this Mr. Hankey was not alone in his craze about his Queen, and what she might do if she looked in upon us poor Irish from time to time. It never occurs to your Hankeys in what a moral position they place their Queen. She will not put herself even a little out in order to link two nations together in amity. If there were even a grain of truth in these bushels of loyalistic chaff, the Queen of England, instead of being the model she is supposed to be, would be a monster she certainly is not. But her Majesty, though she had never, I believe, been even a fortnight in Ireland, knows us far better than her Hankeys do. I had the felicity, for the first and last time, of seeing her Britannic Majesty on her first visit to this country, in the year 1849, and I can certify that on that occasion she was received with considerable curiosity, and, as far as one could judge, a total absence of all other feelings. She passed down the broadest street in Dublin, or perhaps in Europe, amid a gaping crowd, but, as far as I could at all see or hear, without a single cheer or other sign of sympathetic interest. And her Majesty did not like her position, if one were to judge by her looks, and no wonder either. I saw a very similar scene some twenty years after in Paris, at the reception of the Shah of Persia, who was gazed upon by vast crowds, which made not the slightest pretence of regarding him in any other light than that of a mere curiosity, the big diamond in his hat attracting quite as much attention as its wearer, and, no doubt, a great deal more regard. But the Shah, unlike the other potentate, was apparently sublimely indifferent as to how he was regarded by any such mere *profanum vulgus*.[3] I am perhaps diverging somewhat from Fenianism, but scarcely so far as I seem. Royal visits and lying descriptions of them, and sentimental gush over their possible and impossible effects, may help Britishers and West Britishers to throw dust in each other's eyes, but they most certainly do not make, or tend to make, the 'mere Irish,' or the Irish 'fall down and almost worship,' but rather stand up, and scoff or scowl, as their special temperaments or moods at the time being may urge them. I was young when I saw the Queen, and certainly enthusiastic, but enthusiastic about everything she did not represent. And as it was with me then, so presumably, bating perhaps some of the enthusiasm, was it with the vast crowd who gazed on her that day in Sackville Street. I am now old, but if *per impossibili* or *per improbabili*, I were to look upon that Queen again, I cannot imagine that my feelings would be essentially other than what they were then. Times have changed much since, and doubtless I have changed with them. But in some things, and especially in the region of the emotions, I have not changed, or changed but little. My feeling towards England was then quite the reverse of loving, and so is it still; and my feeling towards England's Queen was then, as it is now, one of complete indifference.

3. '[I despise the] uninitiated mob', Horace, *Odes*, Book III, 1, 1.

JEREMIAH O'DONOVAN ROSSA

(1831-1915)

from: O'DONOVAN ROSSA'S PRISON LIFE (1874)

[Rossa, like many of the Fenians, was anxious to explain why the aims of Irish catholicism and those of Irish republicanism had diverged by the late nineteenth century. The reorganized catholic church was, in his view, part of the British establishment in Ireland. The fight for Ireland was, therefore, no longer the fight for 'catholicity'. Like O'Leary, O'Donovan Rossa sought a union between Irish people of different creeds and faiths rather than the so-called 'union of hearts' between Ireland and England. The first had to precede the latter. Reversing these priorities simply ensured division in Ireland under the guise of amity between the two islands.]

CHAPTER I

... Then came the Reformation, and [England] commenced to persecute the Irish Catholics and root out the whole race, because they would not become Protestant, for she thought that, by becoming Protestant, they may become less Irish or more English. For a time the words Protestant and English were synonymous; also the words Irish and Catholic, and hence arose that curse of religious antagonism which, for three centuries, blighted the prospects of our people for independence. The English interest was represented by Protestantism principally, and the interest of nationality by Catholicism — so much so that Catholic Irishmen came to feel that, in fighting against Protestantism, they were fighting against England, and, in fighting for Catholicity, they were fighting for Ireland. The priest was the person most sought after, most persecuted by the English, and the most loved, most looked to, and most protected by the Irish. He became the guide and the controller of their action, and he was ever faithful in defending and leading the people to defend the interests of the Church. The faith and the spirit of liberty in the people were not crushed, and, in the growing enlightenment of the present century, England — for the purpose of maintaining her dominion — has thought proper to change her policy. She now patronises the Church, hugs to her bosom its dignitaries, and trusts that they — having influence over the people — will keep them from rebellion. Some of those dignitaries have labored hard to do this in the movement for which I was imprisoned. It is in times of peace that the Church flourishes, and, in the interest of the Church, many will not blame the clergy. Few will blame them, too, for opposing a rebellion where the necessary means of success would not be forecalculated; but, where I could be at issue with them would be in the matter of their opposition to us while providing the means, and few will deny that we had that opposition in Ireland during the past thirteen years. There was no diocese in Ireland where the men who were organizing means to fight England, were not denounced from the altars and sent away from the confessionals unshriven. It is right also to add that there was no diocese in which there were not many priests to bless the laborers and wish God-speed to the work; but the tongues and hands of these clergymen 'were tied' as they themselves would say, by the higher ecclesiastics, while the 'bad priests,' as we called them, were allowed full scope to denounce us and brand us as infidels before we were any way unfaithful.

In making these observations wholly regarding the action of Catholics towards the independence of Ireland, I must not be understood as excluding the efforts of other religious people in that direction. During the last century many Protestants and Presbyterians were sent to the scaffold and the convict-ship for daring to maintain that they, as Irish-born men, should have an independent Ireland; and in the late revolutionary movement we had a blending of all the sects for liberty. This was as disagreeable to the bigots as to the English enemy. A union of creeds does not seem desirable to Church or State, and both united in assailing those who were bringing it about as traitorous and disreputable. The State had some reason to attack them, but the Church had very little; for those who were banded together to fight for civil and religious liberty would be the first to stand in defence of their faith if any foe threatened their altars. The Catholic members of the organization found themselves, at the outset, denounced by Catholic priests; and this gave birth to a strange feeling in the breasts of young men who grew up looking upon a priest as the embodiment of hostility to England. They considered that in resolving to battle for the rights of their native land, they had taken a noble resolution, and, in swearing to do so they did not feel, between themselves and their God, that they had committed a sin. But finding themselves condemned, nay damned, for this act, afforded them food for reflection, and what wonder if some of them disregarded the denunciations and labored on? I did. I saw that the time was gone when the priest and the people were as one persecuted. I saw that the priest was free and comparatively happy, while the people were still enslaved, and decidedly miserable. The tradition that my boyhood received of fighting for my religion in fighting for my country, and in fighting for my country I was fighting for my religion, was broken; for here I had sworn to fight for Ireland, and I was set upon as an enemy of Catholicity. The calumny is kept up; but I can afford to live it down. The politico-religious faith of my fathers is taken to pieces, and as the Irish head of the Church believes that in fighting for Ireland now I am not fighting for Catholicity, I must presume, on the other hand, to believe that in fighting for Catholicity I am not at all fighting for

Ireland. I don't put my country before my God; but I put it before religious ascendency of any denomination. The Church has many defenders, and needs my aid as little as she need fear my hostility; Ireland has few, and I am beginning to fear they will not be able, unless aided more earnestly than they have been, to work out her immediate salvation.

I do not write my book as a champion of religion, or as one who would assail it. I write neither as a Catholic nor as a Protestant. I come before the public merely as an Irishman, wishing to see my country free for all religious denominations; and wishing to see, for the purpose of overcoming them, all the obstacles that stand in the way of its freedom. If I speak of the interference of religious people in its political concerns, it is not from choice but from necessity. I hold it absolutely impossible for any one to speak truly of the movements of the people towards independence if he ignores the religious elements that are set in motion to sway the people to one side or the other. Religion and politics are as yet in Ireland inseparable. I should like to see the man who could give a history of the one without touching on the other. I could not do so; and as I am going to tell the whole truth, and nothing but the truth, I am not going to attempt such a story; but I will 'nothing extenuate or aught set down in malice.'[1] . . .

1. *Othello*, V.2.341-42: 'nothing extenuate,/Nor set down aught in malice . . . .'

[There follows Rossa's well-known account of the formation of the Irish Republican Brotherhood centre in Skibbereen, Co. Cork. The importance of the emigrant American connection is particularly appropriate for the region that had suffered most from death and emigration during the Famine.]

CHAPTER II

. . . After the English government had crushed the movement in '48, Ireland appeared spiritless and politically dead. Charles Gavan Duffy left the country in '54,[1] saying he left the cause of freedom a corpse on the dissecting table. But, like the seed put into the ground, it must only have been rotting to produce new life; for a few years after we find it in vigorous existence again, and the authorities putting forth all their strength to overcome it. My own experiences now commence, and, like all writers who have anything to say of movements in which they took part, I must become a bit of an egotist. . . .

1. Duffy in fact had emigrated in 1856.

In the month of May, 1858, one of my companions called into my residence in Skibbereen and asked me to take a walk with him, as he had something of importance to communicate to me. I went out, and during our ramble up the Steam-mill road he informed me that on the preceding evening he had received a note of introduction from a stranger, given to him by a mutual friend in Bandon. The stranger told him that the Irishmen in America had resolved to aid us at home in achieving the independence of Ireland, and the aid was to consist of arms and of men. If we had a certain number of men sworn to fight, there would be an equal number of arms in Ireland for these men when enrolled, and an invading force of from five to ten thousand before the start. The arms were to be in the country before the men would be asked to stir; they would not be given into their hands, but they were to be kept in hiding-places until the appointed time, when every Centre[2] could take his men to the spot and get the weapons. As soon as we had enrolled the men willing to fight we were to get military instructors to teach us how to do so as soldiers. I jumped at the proposition of 'joining'; and next day I inoculated a few others whom I told to go and do likewise. The stranger who came to the town that May evening was Mr. Stephens, and I was promised an introduction to him in a short time if I would work well. We had a society in Skibbereen at this time called the Phœnix National and Literary Society.[3] It was a revolutionary one, though not oathbound, and we were contemplating affiliations in connection with it in the neighboring towns around at the time I speak of. We gave it the name Phœnix to signify that the nation was to rise again from its ashes. We had about one hundred members, and before a month had elapsed from the day of Mr. Stephens' visit we had over ninety of them enrolled in the new movement.

Before the autumn months had passed away we

2. The Centre was the key organizer of a local Fenian unit.
3. The society, founded by Rossa in 1856, ostensibly was literary but in fact was political. The original society had a number of branches. Raided in 1858 on the word of an informer, and condemned by the local catholic clergy, nevertheless by 1859 it was fully integrated with the IRB through the efforts of James Stephens.

had the whole district of country in a blaze, and in October we had a drill-master sent to us from Dublin. He had served a period in the American army, and well and truly he did his work amongst us, despite all the police watchings and huntings. . . .

from:
ROSSA'S RECOLLECTIONS 1838 to 1898 (1898)

[The week after the Terence MacManus funeral in Dublin (see Devoy selection below), James Stephens, under the pseudonym J. Kelly, wrote to Rossa about the impending conflict, as then seemed likely, between Britain and the United States at the outbreak of the American Civil War. The letter is a typical example of Stephens's dictatorial attitudes and his reasoned ingenuity in delaying the call to insurrection. Rossa, like most of the other Fenians, was impressed, although John O'Mahony and other American Fenians were less so. It seemed to them, and to men like Kickham, that Irish soldiers fighting in the Civil War should be used as soon as possible for fighting in Ireland. This anxiety did not help them to foresee how bitter and long-drawn out the war would be, although the near-extinction of Meagher's sixty-ninth regiment in several of the war's bloodiest battles was to give some of them pause.]

CHAPTER XXII

A LETTER OF MUCH IMPORT, WRITTEN BY JAMES STEPHENS, IN THE YEAR 1861

Though I spoke of the McManus funeral before, I have now to speak of it again. I find among my papers a letter written by James Stephens to John O'Mahony, the week after the funeral took place in Dublin. It deals trenchantly with the milk-and-water Irish patriots of that time and even of this time who are ever telling us that 'England's difficulty is Ireland's opportunity,' and ever calling upon us to 'bide our time,' and do nothing until that time comes.

This is that letter:

BROTHER — Your last letter (30th Nov.) was placed in my hand yesterday by Lieut. O'Connor. On the whole it is the healthiest, and consequently the most pleasant communication I have had from you for years. This is owing to its freedom from what looked like a chronic disease in you — fault-finding in general and a proneness to advice, and even lecturing, men of ripe years who have proved themselves the only practical workmen this country has produced in our time. I say this without the most remote intention to hurt you in any way, and solely that you may henceforth avoid what has been not alone irritating to me, but calculated to lower you in the estimation of men who would otherwise think highly of you. Now, if ever, there should be a thorough understanding and union between us, and to this end it is incumbent on us to cut as little as possible against the grain. . . . And here, I may as well say a few words about the American Deputation. The Brothers, without exception, have given thorough satisfaction; Jeremiah Kavanagh, especially, has been of important service to us, owning not only to his zeal and subordination, but also to his natural talents as a ready and effective speaker. But I wish it to be distinctly understood that I am thoroughly satisfied with all the Brothers. On their return, they can be of much service to us here, not only in the fulfilment of their usual duties, but in holding up to just scorn and reprobation the vile press and sham patriots we have to deal with — the brood who have so long passed as the 'Trusted Leaders' of the people. By Demas,[1] we have scared and routed them somewhat here; but the *coup de grace* can be given them yonder by the Deputation. As you are wise and true — to yourself, to us, and to your country — do not neglect to favor all willing hearts in this great duty.

Crisis or no Crisis?[2] — *that* is the question. Another question, of far more importance to us, is this: If a *real* crisis, what will be its consequences to us? I shall offer a few observations on these two points. If there be one thing, in connection with the cause of Ireland, I more cordially detest than any other, it is what scribblers or spouters call 'a Crisis.' It has been the chronic bane of Ireland — a more

1. An appropriate quotation from The Second Epistle of Paul to Timothy 4.10: 'For Demas hath forsaken me, having loved this present world. . . .'
2. When a US warship boarded the English mail steamer, the *Trent*, in 1861 and seized four Confederate envoys en route to Europe, public opinion in Britain, orchestrated by Lord Palmerston, was outraged. Washington received a peremptory demand from London for the release of the envoys, British troops were ordered to British North America (Canada), and American public opinion was moved in support of the American action. On 1 February 1862, the envoys were given up and the crisis was resolved.

fatal bane than famine or any other the enemy have had, to perpetuate their rule. A bane — a scourge — a disease — a devil's scourge it has been to us. Its best known formula has resolved itself into this: 'England's difficulty is Ireland's opportunity.' Blind, base and deplorable motto — rallying-cry — motive of action — what you will. May it be accursed, it, its aiders and abettors. Owing to it, and them, the work that should *never* have stood still, has been taken up in feverish fits and starts, and always out of time, to fall into collapse when the 'opportunity,' predestined to escape them, had slipped through their hands. Ireland's trained and marshalled manhood alone can *ever* make — could ever have made — Ireland's opportunity. And this opportunity, the manhood of Ireland alone, without the aid of any foreign power — without the aid of even our exiled brothers, could have been *made* any time these thirty years; and, whether England was at peace or war, with this manhood alone we could have won our own. But our duped and victimized countrymen, giving ear to the imbecile or knavish cry of 'English difficulty,' stood, with mouth agape, and over and over again, waiting — 'biding their time' — till the opportunity came, and left them as before. Accursed, I say, be the barren, lunatic or knavish clods who raised this dog souled cry — a cry to be heard even *now*, in the mouths of the slanderous brood who, as you say, 'first misled and then abandoned a brave and devoted people.' They are, I say, raising the cry once more — this cry of — a crisis — 'England's difficulty.' By the time this reaches you — before it reaches you — you shall have heard of the 'Mass Meeting' at the Rotundo.[3] I shall speak of it myself by and by; but for the present, I pass on to the — crisis! *Is* it to be a *real* crisis after all? I am far from convinced of it. Nothing, far as I can see, has taken place to preclude an arrangement — a compromise of some sort. It seems to me that the reasons for this, especially on the side of America, are very cogent.... Are the men at Washington so ignorant of human nature as to hope, even in the face of a foreign foe, for a fusion with the South? Then look to Europe. There, the feeling, and what is of far greater weight in human action, the interests of all are decidedly with England. It is by no means impossible — even improbable — that France will be thoroughly with England. America cannot possibly be blind to this; if blind now, her eyes will be opened, probably, in time to stave off a collision. Granted, however, that human passions, human blindness — shall hurry the States into this war with England, and that we shall have a bona fide crisis. Granted, too, that Europe shall rise above mere interest, stand aloof from the fray, and leave England to fight it out single-handed. What will then be the consequences to us? Do you hope for good results? I am not by any means sanguine; or, to be thoroughly outspoken, it seems to me — I apprehend — that, in the case in question, far more evil than good shall accrue to us. Once engaged with England, our communications with America are at an end; at least, no men can come home, and even money, only in an indirect and roundabout way. Then, the cry will be on your side, 'let us settle our own difficulties first — let us drive the enemy from our shores, and then we shall do your business for you.' How long will this state of things last? How many of the best of our race shall be sacrificed in this way? And they, poor dupes and victims, shall be all the while dreaming that they are serving their native land! Then, again, some popular soldier, gifted with more heart than brain, or without much of either, may get it into his head to prepare an expedition, 'homeward bound.' Let us suppose he has forced the double blockade — yonder and here — and that he has actually set foot on Irish soil. He landed where he could; but, for the sake of argument, I suppose he landed on some point where we are strong. To suppose the contrary would be to talk of utter ruin to us and the cause of Ireland forevermore. For we have but this one chance. Any man who holds the contrary, is incapable of making up the sum — two and two are four. There he is, then, on some favorable point. How many men could he bring to us under the circumstances? Granted — again for the sake of argument — that the number is considerable. As we have had no understanding with him — as he takes us as much by surprise as the enemy — we have only to make the most of the — shall I call it Godsend? Then again — but I will not go on in this strain of conjecture. I shall merely say that I augur no good for us from this war, so much desired by certain Irish patriots. The consummation most

3. Stephens arranged a number of meetings in the round room of the Rotunda (Rotundo) in Dublin between 1861 and 1865, in which organized groups of Fenians dominated the representatives of constitutional parties. The meeting referred to took place in November 1861.

devoutly to be wished[4] for by us is this: An arrangement or compromise of some kind between North and South, and the consequent disbandment of the army. Then, as well as meantime, our communications would be open with you; money and men might be coming over to us, and we would choose our own time for the first blow. Indeed, the advantages to us appear to me so manifest, in this latter case — that of England keeping out of the struggle — that it would be boresome to you to point them out. Were we in the field, it would be clearly an advantage to us to have England in a death-struggle with America; but I am more than doubtful of the advantages to be gained by us should this struggle begin before we rise. But of course — or is it so? — we can do nothing to bring about or prevent this war. You say that, should it take place, 'your purpose is to offer your own services and those of your friends to the United States government to serve against England, in Ireland if possible, but if not, anywhere.' I look upon this as wise, and fully approve of it.... Now, in case of a war with England, all the Irish race on the American continent will be into it; so that you could not stand aloof without the utter loss of your influence. Clearly you must to the field, and the more prominent your position, the better for Ireland. Granted, then, that you are in the field, and in a foremost position, I would not allow myself, even then, to be too hasty in urging on an expedition. I should keep up my correspondence with home, and be sure that everything was right there, convinced that, without a vast power of trained men at home, armed already, or to be provided with arms by me, the expedition — if not far beyond anything that has ever in that way steered for the Irish shore — could only compromise the last chance like every preceding one. I would not, like so many ignorant or silly men, fancy that 10,000 or 20,000, or even 30,000 Irish-Americans, could if landed on our shores, give freedom to my country, unless, as already said, a vast power of trained men, armed already, or to be armed by me, were ready to fly to my standard. I would not allow myself to be deluded by the lunatic dream, that a mob, however numerous or numberless, could make victory a certain or even a probable thing. I would believe, on the other hand, that a trained power at home — say of 100,000 men — already armed, or for whom I bought arms, could — nay would — be sure to do more with the aid of so small a number as 1,000, than an auxiliary force of even 30,000 could ever effect, if backed by a mere mob, whatever its number. I would therefore and as already said, be sure that there was at home a strong power of trained men to cooperate with the force brought by me, and till I was sure of this, nothing could force me to undertake a descent on the Irish shores, convinced that such descent, so far from serving my country, would only deprive her of the last chance of freedom. These are amongst the many things sure to be suggested to me, should I ever find myself in the position I supposed you in *toute a l'heure*.[5] Let us be provided against all contingencies.

In haste, yours faithfully

J. KELLY, (JAMES STEPHENS)....

4. cf. *Hamlet*, III. 1. 63-64.

5. (Fr.) a while ago.

JOHN DEVOY

(1842-1928)

from: RECOLLECTIONS OF AN IRISH REBEL . . . . (1929)

[Devoy was chief organizer of the Fenians in the 1860s, controller of Clan-na-Gael in America in the 1880s, supporter of Davitt and Parnell, of Thomas Clarke and of Pearse and the Irish Volunteers in the preparations for 1916, the man who arranged Roger Casement's meeting with the German ambassador in 1914, supporter of the Treaty in 1921 and ally, then enemy, of de Valera. His long life as revolutionary organizer is a testimony to the interlocking movements, constitutional and military, that dominated the Irish scene for over sixty years. The funeral of Terence Bellew MacManus (1823-60) is important as one of the great propaganda successes of Fenianism in its early stages, won at the expense of both the British government and the catholic church. The archbishop of Dublin, Dr Paul Cullen, refused permission for lying-in-state at the Pro-Cathedral and banned the participation of catholic clergy in the ceremonies. This ban was broken by Father Patrick Lavelle (1825-86), who delivered the graveside oration. The funeral was later to be echoed in that of O'Donovan Rossa, organized by Devoy and the IRB in 1915 (see below, p. 274).

MacManus had escaped from Van Diemen's Land (Tasmania), to which he had been transported for his participation in the 1848 rising, with Thomas Francis Meagher. He died, impoverished, in the United States. In the following year, Lavelle gave further support to the Fenian philosophy of revolution in a Dublin lecture, 'The Catholic Doctrine of the Right of Revolution'. He was supported against Cullen by the nationalist archbishop, John MacHale. The Fenians were opposed to the clerical influence in politics, but the clergy was itself divided on the issue. The MacManus funeral was one of the early events that helped crystallize this conflict, although it also led to dissensions among the different 'wings' of the Fenian organization itself.]

CHAPTER III

BURIAL OF TERENCE BELLEW McMANUS

The organization was well on its way to success in the Summer of 1861 when Terence Bellew McManus died in California, and the Nationalists there decided to send his body to Ireland for burial in Dublin.

He was a Monaghan man, and was in business in Liverpool when the Young Irelanders seceded from the Repeal Association and started on their propaganda. The Clubs of the Irish Confederation (which was the name of their organization) held meetings in Dublin, at which insurrection was openly advocated and many of the members bought rifles and practised target shooting, but the leaders did nothing but make speeches. William Smith O'Brien (a descendant of Brian Boru) was the leader, but, though a fairly good Parliamentary speaker, he was not a popular orator. Charles Gavan Duffy was a pretty good speaker, but wrote better. John Mitchel spoke well, and his articles in the *United Irishman* were revolutionary propaganda of the highest order. Thomas Francis Meagher was the star orator of the Young Irelanders; he prepared his speeches carefully, committed them to memory and delivered them with fine elocutionary effect. Thousands thronged to the Music Hall in Lower Abbey Street when the meetings were held, to hear him, and he made many converts among the younger members of the Repeal Association, which had no good speaker in Conciliation Hall[1] after Daniel O'Connell had left for Italy, broken in health.

McManus was not an orator, but he was a clear-headed, practical man. He came over from Liverpool to take part in Smith O'Brien's projected insurrection in Tipperary and after its failure was convicted and transported to Van Dieman's [*sic*] Land, where all the Young Ireland leaders were confined. He was the first of them to escape, in 1853, and got to California, where he settled down and subsequently died. There was not much of an organization in San Francisco at the time, but a meeting of Irish citizens appointed a committee to escort his remains to Ireland and secure burial in Glasnevin. There were demonstrations in every city along the route to New York. The body was held in New York for a few days before shipment to Ireland and honored by the Irish people here, the Fenian Brotherhood taking charge.

There was no Atlantic cable in those days and the news of the death of McManus only reached Ireland a few days before the arrival of the body, so there was little time for preparation. But the time was well utilized. Stephens and Denieffe[2] were the only Fenian leaders then in Dublin, and the general Irish public knew little or nothing about them. There were a few veterans of 1848, and some new men like the Sullivans of the *Nation* who thought it was their prerogative to take charge of all Nationalist demonstrations, so when a committee was formed, there was a contest for control of it.

The body of McManus was received in Cork by a hastily organized committee and large crowds attended the funeral procession there. At every station where the train bearing the remains stopped, there were great crowds which stood silently with bared heads until the train left, but there was no organization. The word had reached the people that the body of the Rebel of 1848 was on the train and they turned out spontaneously to honor it.

1. Conciliation Hall in Dublin was the meeting place of O'Connell's Repeal Association.
2. Joseph Denieffe (1833-1910), former Young Irelander, emigrated to the United States and helped James Stephens found the IRB. His memoir, *A Personal Narrative of the Irish Revolutionary Brotherhood* (New York, 1906), is a valuable document.

In Dublin, the two elements on the committee were unanimous in seeking to have a mass said at the Cathedral in Marlborough Street and to have the body lie in state in it, but Archbishop Cullen positively refused. The committee then decided to hold the wake in the Mechanics' Institute on Lower Abbey Street,[3] a few blocks away from the Cathedral. Instead of throwing a damper on the demonstration of respect for the dead, the Archbishop's action only intensified popular feeling and vast crowds stood for many blocks in the contiguous streets waiting for their turn to view the remains. Among them were many priests, including the famous Father Kenyon of Templederry, County Tipperary, and Father Meehan of Dublin, both friends of John Mitchel.[4]

There were rather warm debates at the committee meetings over the arrangements for the funeral, and the selection of the speakers, but the Fenians won complete control. Father Kenyon, who was a fine speaker, but spoke with a strong brogue, knew nothing of the Fenians, but he was as strong a Nationalist as any of them. The sister of McManus had written to him, asking him to take charge of the funeral, as she knew no more of the new movement than he.

He was satisfied with the explanations given and the funeral went off according to program. John O'Clohessy, who had recently returned from India, where he served in the Bombay Horse Artillery, was selected as Marshal of the procession. He was a handsome man with a fine figure, and he had a talent for managing processions. He had handled the crowds which greeted the Irish Papal Brigade at the Kingsbridge station on their return from Italy a few months previously, and speedily brought order out of chaos, so the men of Dublin knew his capacity for such things.[5] He had joined the organization very early, was one of the Dublin 'Centres', and was later sentenced to a term of imprisonment. His brother Michael (later well known in New York) was also an active member and had a hand in the arrangements for the funeral. They were sons of a Dublin policeman from Clare.

The arrangements for the funeral were perfect and were carried out with precision. It was much bigger than the funeral of O'Connell. Dublin had never seen anything like it before. All the trade societies took part in it and it seemed as if every man in Dublin was in line, or on the streets as an onlooker. The trains that morning brought great crowds from all parts of the country, practically all of whom fell into line. O'Clohessy selected a number of ex-British soldiers and Papal Brigade men as his assistants and gave them instructions the night before. The handling of the procession, which was several miles long, was faultless, and the demeanor of the vast crowd which lined the sidewalks along the route was most respectful. All heads were bared as the cortege passed, and women prayed aloud.

As the procession passed the spot in Thomas Street where Robert Emmet was hanged in 1803, and the house on the same street where Lord Edward Fitzgerald was stabbed to death with a cane sword by Capt. Ryan in 1798, each contingent stood for a moment and the men took off their hats. At every historic spot on the way to Glasnevin, there were appropriate demonstrations. The men in line were of fine physique and their splendid bearing greatly impressed the English newspapermen. The latter thought they had all been drilled, but Irishmen are born soldiers and fall into military step naturally.

In the cemetery a dense mass of people stood near the grave and speeches were made by Jeremiah Cavanagh and Captain Smith of San Francisco, which were heartily cheered. After the funeral services the immense crowd disbanded in an orderly manner.

Several thousand country people remained for a few days after the funeral to see the city and hundreds of them were sworn into the organization by friends and relatives resident in the Capital, and they started it going in their home districts after their return.

The funeral was a test, not of the strength of Fenianism, but of the revival of the fighting National spirit, which had been thought dead after the great Famine of 1847 and the failure of the Young Ireland Movement in 1848. Dublin itself

3. Later this building housed the Abbey Theatre.
4. Rev. John Kenyon (1812-69) supported Young Ireland after the split with O'Connell's Repeal Association in 1846. Rev C.P. Meehan (1812-90) was a contributor of verse to *The Nation*, edited the poems of Thomas Davis and James Clarence Mangan and was known for his strong nationalist sympathies.
5. About 1,000 Irishmen answered the appeal of Pope Pius IX in 1860 to defend the papal states against the forces of Italian nationalism. They went out as individuals but returned as a brigade, to warm welcomes, even from Fenians, who saw no contradiction between fighting against Italian national self-determination and for the same self-determination in Ireland. They provide one more instance of the complicated relationships between Fenianism and catholicism.

was surprised at the magnificent demonstration, and the countrymen returned to their homes inspired with new hope.

The English Government was also surprised and greatly disappointed and the London press voiced its feelings. The Ireland they thought incapable of giving them further trouble of a serious nature, they now realized was filled with the old militant National Spirit. The population was still over 6,000,000, which was 2,000,000 less than in 1847 when emigration began on a large scale after havoc had been wrought by hunger and typhus, but the people were still numerous enough to give the Alien Government food for thought. But that only awakened their fears. It did not make them dream of conciliation, and their minds were occupied only with plans for further repression. A habit that had lasted for nearly seven centuries was hard to change, and it required much more than processions marching through the streets of Dublin to bring about the alteration. The determination to keep Ireland suppressed, in population and in industry, remained as strong as ever. Every concession had to be wrung from England and all of them were halting, incomplete and evasive, including the last one in 1921.

The significance of the popular outpouring in Dublin on November 10, 1861, lay in the fact that McManus was wholly unknown in Ireland before his conviction in 1848. All the great body of the people knew was that he had suffered imprisonment for Ireland and had escaped from prison in Tasmania.

The effect of the McManus funeral demonstration in the country was very marked. It gave a strong impetus to the Fenian Movement and made recruiting easy. The contest with the 'Moderates' for control of the demonstration, resulting, as it did, in complete success, inspired the young men with great confidence, but it also had some bad effect. It developed a spirit of intolerance which prevented union with the 'Moderates' on reasonable terms and turned their sympathy away. This produced evil results in later years, but for the moment it made Fenianism strong and aggressive.

I missed the McManus funeral, much to my regret (as I was then serving in the French Foreign Legion),[6] and could only read the reports of it in a tent in Algeria. But when I returned to Dublin in 1862 and heard the inside story from the men who had taken part in it, I was amazed at the extraordinary change which had taken place in the spirit of the country. It marked a turning point in the history of the movement, and Fenianism made rapid progress thereafter.

6. Devoy enlisted in the French Foreign Legion in 1861 to gain military experience for the fight for an Irish republic. He returned to Ireland in 1862.

[James Stephens, the founder of the Irish Republican Brotherhood, the executive body of the Fenian organization, was arrested in November 1865. Devoy masterminded his escape from Richmond Prison, another one of the propaganda successes of the early Fenians, although one badly needed after the many arrests and severe sentences of 1865.]

CHAPTER XIII

THE RESCUE OF STEPHENS

Stephens' defiant speech when arraigned before the magistrate to be committed for trial led the public to believe that he had strong resources at his back. A week later most people felt that on the day of his arraignment he knew all about the arrangements for the rescue from prison, which afterwards took place on November 24, 1865, and that this knowledge justified his attitude of defiance. He ever after encouraged this belief, but the simple truth is it was utterly without foundation. Stephens at that time knew nothing whatever of the possibility of escape and the idea had not yet entered the mind of the man who afterwards conceived and executed the plan which restored the Chief Organizer to liberty.

Strictly speaking, it was not an escape, but a rescue. The accounts published in the newspapers at the time were all wrong and references to it in books since then are equally misleading.

A.M. Sullivan, although corrected in a public letter by the principal actor in restoring the captive to freedom, says, even in the last edition of his 'New Ireland', that Stephens made his exit through the front door of the prison.[1] The British Government has never done justice to the Portuguese Governor, Marquess, whom the Castle officials dismissed for alleged criminal negligence in connection with the escape. And there were thousands of Irishmen who

1. A.M. Sullivan's *New Ireland* (1887). Various accounts of Stephens's escape were popular for a time. An apocryphal version of the escape is given in Joyce's *Ulysses*, in the 'Proteus' episode.

believed for many years after that the Fenian Chief was released with the connivance of the British Government.

The story of the Rescue from Richmond Prison is as follows:

Among the officers of the prison were John J. Breslin,[2] hospital steward, and Daniel Byrne, one of the two night watchmen. Byrne was a member of the Fenian organization, having been sworn in by Captain John Kirwan, the ex-Papal Zouave,[3] but Breslin, although a man of strong Nationalist opinions, did not belong to the I.R.B. Neither was his brother Michael a Fenian, who just then was a clerk in the Police Superintendent's office, a station which enabled him to render most important service to the conspirators.

John Breslin had a conversation with Stephens in the prison the day after the arrest and made up his mind at once that he was a superior man. He had a day off a little later and found that his brother Niall, who was an active worker in the movement, was full of some idea about getting Stephens out. He asked Niall: 'Is this man necessary to the organization?' Niall assured him that he was and John replied that it couldn't amount to much if the loss of one man could hurt it so badly. However, he added that it would be easy enough to take him out, but, with the airs common to Irish elder brothers to their juniors added: 'I'd like to hear it from someone of more importance than you.' Niall put him in communication with Colonel Thomas J. Kelly[4] and the work of preparation for the rescue was at once begun. All the communications between Kelly and the prison, whether verbal or written, were carried on through Michael Breslin, who went there in his police uniform, and his visits never aroused the faintest suspicion. He even brought in the false keys with which the doors were opened.

John Breslin's daily tour through the prison with the doctor gave him many opportunities for communicating with the prisoners. He not only accompanied the doctor and took down his directions about medicine, but went back and delivered it, retaining the keys until his work was done. He had ample opportunity for personal interviews with Stephens and kept him fully informed.

The plan was very simple and effective, and was Breslin's in every detail. Stephens occupied one of the hospital cells in a small corridor on the third floor. The only other occupants of the corridor were his colleague, Charles J. Kickham,[5] and a regular jailbird named McLeod. The Governor, to provide against any possibility of escape, had a police sentinel placed on the other side of the door leading to that portion of the prison where O'Leary, Luby, Mulcahy, Roantree[6] and the other Fenian prisoners were quartered, while the other entrance to the corridor was secured by two doors, one of wood and the other of iron. McLeod was in a cell between those of Stephens and Kickham, and had orders from the Governor to ring his gong on the first sound of anything unusual in the neighboring cells. This would have at once given the alarm and have effectually prevented escape. The policeman could not unlock the door between him and the corridor, and the iron door at the other end could only be opened by the pass key, which was locked in the Governor's safe. The Governor's office, where all the keys were deposited at a certain hour every evening, was effectually protected from all attempts from the inside by a heavy iron gate, locked on the side facing the main entrance.

Breslin had a latch key which opened the door of the hospital, where he slept, and that leading to the portion of the prison where Stephens was confined. To enable him to enter the corridor he must have a pass key, and to open the cell door another key. He took impressions in beeswax of the regular keys in use in the daytime, and new ones were filed down to fit the impressions by Michael Lambert, an optician who was an active Fenian. Even at this

2. John J. Breslin (*c.*1836-88) was a member of the IRB. He emigrated to the United States and became a prominent member of Clan na Gael. Devoy used him again to supervise the rescue of Fenian prisoners from Freemantle, Australia, on the whaling ship, *Catalpa*, in April 1876.
3. A Papal Zouave was one of a French corps organized at Rome in 1860 for the defence of the pope.
4. Colonel Thomas J. Kelly (1833-1908), born in Galway, emigrated to the United States, fought in the American civil war and became chief of staff within the IRB. In 1867 he planned a raid on the arsenal at Chester Castle in England, in preparation for a rising. The plan misfired, Kelly was arrested and he in turn was rescued from a police van in Manchester in the incident that led to the hanging of the rescuers, the Manchester Martyrs, for the killing of a policeman during the escape.
5. Charles J. Kickham (1828-82), prominent Fenian and author of *Knocknagow*. He was imprisoned 1865-69.
6. O'Leary and Luby, well-known Fenians and joint editors of *The Irish People*, are dealt with earlier in this section. Mulcahy was a minor figure. William Francis Roantree (1829-1918) was one of the most effective Fenian recruiters. Like the others, he was arrested in 1865 and was sentenced to ten years, reduced later to exile. He went to the United States with Devoy and Rossa and returned to Ireland in 1900.

early stage of the affair a hitch occurred which showed the lack of precision and promptness characterizing the whole Fenian movement. The beeswax was not forthcoming at the time appointed. After waiting several days Breslin was obliged to go out and buy it himself, thus running the risk of giving a clue to the police that might be the means of convicting him if brought to trial. The keys were finally in Breslin's hands, but even at the last moment he was obliged to do some filing on one of them, and to run some extra risk by fitting it to the lock of a door that Byrne, his colleague in the enterprise, could not open.

The keys having been fitted, Colonel Kelly was notified and arrangements were made to receive Stephens on the outside of the prison walls. Byrne was on watch every second night.

So sure were the authorities of the safety of the captives that no military guard was placed in the prison, but a regiment of cavalry and a battery of artillery were quartered at Portobello Barracks, within fifteen minutes' walk. The only guard was a detachment of Metropolitan Police, four of whom were stationed inside the main entrance and others at various points in the prison. That night care was taken that they were given plenty of porter and they were in a heavy sleep on their chairs when the event came off.

At the inception of the plot, Colonel Kelly sent for me and told me the duty I was to perform. For various reasons, I happened to be better acquainted with the local officers and rank and file of the Dublin organization than any man then within Kelly's reach. He told me he wanted me to pick out from ten to twelve of the very best men I knew in Dublin for a special work, requiring courage, coolness, and self-control. They all ought to know how to use revolvers, but were not to use their arms even if fired upon, unless ordered to do so. They were to be capable of making a desperate fight if necessary. I was to avoid as much as possible selecting Centres, American officers or men filling other positions demanding constant attention. Kelly did not then tell me the exact nature of the work, but I had no doubt it was to rescue 'The Captain'.

A few days later, when I reported for his approval the men I had selected, he told me it was to act as a bodyguard for Stephens on his release by men inside the prison; that there would probably be no need for us, but we were to be on hand in case any accident should interrupt the escape. A dozen men, he said, would be quite enough, including himself and two others. These two were John Ryan, the son of a Liverpool dry goods merchant, a splendid type of man, mentally and physically, and Michael Lambert, the optician. He told me I was to have charge of the party under his directions, and I was to conceal them in small squads in positions covering every avenue of approach to the prison.

I selected nine men, whom I considered to be the best fitted for all the possibilities involved in the attempt. Nearly all of them were wanted by the police, and many afterwards suffered imprisonment. Most of them had seen some kind of service. All knew how to handle both rifle and revolver. Paddy Kearney was of exceptional courage and decisive character. Michael Cody possessed great strength and determination. He was an ex-Dublin-militia man and had a weakness for punching peelers[7] occasionally. John Harrison was a corn porter of magnificent proportions, who had spent some time in the English navy and seen service at Bomarsund under Admiral Napier.[8] He had never had any difficulty with the police, but had knocked out the best men among the Dublin coal porters who were at that time mostly anti-Fenians. Denis Duggan was a young coach builder, who had served in the English Volunteers, and was noted for his courage and coolness. Jack Mullen was the son of a Dublin shopkeeper and had led a roving life. When a boy he had enlisted in the English, and had later on served in the American navy, participating in some of the principal naval fights of the Civil War. Matthew O'Neill was a Dublin stonecutter, who had never seen any service. He was Centre of one of the most important Circles in the City, and was a man of fine physique. Jack Lawler had never been a soldier, and was rather small, but was recommended as a man of great pluck. William Brophy was a carpenter and a strong man. Pat Flood, a Dublin cork cutter, was a powerful man, and an old member of the organization. These, with Kelly and the two men chosen by him, and myself, were the only persons outside the walls of Richmond prison that night.

Colonel Kelly informed me that a supply of revolvers would be ready, so that each man would be

7. policemen. The term was applied first to the Irish constabulary, founded by Sir Robert Peel when he was chief secretary for Ireland 1812-18.

8. Bomarsund was a strong fortress on one of the Aland islands in the Baltic, taken by Sir Charles Napier in August 1854.

fully armed and prepared. None of these men was informed of the nature of the work on hand, but Colonel Kelly confided the secret to some of those around him, and they in turn revealed it to a 'few friends'. I learned after the rescue, that in this way the news spread until at least 200 men in Dublin knew of it. The subject had become a pretty general topic of conversation among the officers of the organization. This led to a serious embarrassment. Scores of men, especially the recently arrived Irish-American officers, felt hurt because they were not chosen to take part in the affair, and they angrily remonstrated. One man, a civilian, who heard the rumor just as he was leaving for the south, was so overjoyed at the prospect that on the very night of the escape he confided the knowledge to a soldier of the Fourth Royal Irish Dragoon Guards, then stationed at Ballincollig, County Cork, whom he wanted to swear in. The trooper refused to be sworn in, and immediately gave information to the authorities, who sent it to the Castle. It reached Cork Hill about the time the news of the escape was spreading dismay among the officials. Had the dragoon's story reached Dublin a few hours earlier, Stephens would have been sent to break stones in Portland[9] with O'Leary, Luby, and his other lieutenants. Another version of this incident at Cork was published many years ago, but, apart from the details, it is certain that the ill-advised remark of the man who conveyed the rumor from Dublin might well have resulted in bringing to naught the plans for Stephens' rescue.

When the night set for the rescue arrived, the plans were ready inside the prison, and the authorities had not the faintest suspicion of anything wrong. The same police guard did duty, no soldier was any nearer than Portobello Barracks, and the Governor retired as usual in full serenity and without a shadow of suspicion. I had reports from the barracks up to a late hour in the evening and knew that no movement either of troops or police indicated the taking of any precautionary measures, or the existence of the slightest misgivings for the safety of the caged Fenian Chief. The Crown lawyers and the Sheriff were busily preparing for the trials, and every partisan of British rule in Ireland looked hopefully forward to the speedy collapse of the conspiracy. A few striking examples were to be made, the prisoners of lesser note were to be let off with short terms of imprisonment, and panic and demoralization could be trusted to do the rest. Ireland would relapse into the calm of despair, and the crowbar brigade and the emigrant ship would soon effect a final solution of the Irish problem. Dublin Castle slept tranquilly that night, with no warning of the panic and consternation that was to overtake it on the morrow.

Towards midnight the little squad of men told off[10] for a bodyguard dropped one by one into Lynch's public house in Camden Street, a short distance from the prison, where Ned Waydick was in charge, and quietly awaited the word to move. But the promised revolvers were not forthcoming, and much disgust was expressed. Kearney, who had a hot temper, flew into a violent rage, and berated the leaders for their seeming neglect. He was a born soldier, and expected soldierly precision and promptitude in such matters. 'If they mismanage a little thing like this,' he said, 'how is it going to be when the real work comes?'

The fault, however, was not that of Colonel Kelly, but of the man to whom he assigned that duty. Had those selected for the rescue any idea in advance that the revolvers would not be available at the appointed time, they could have supplied themselves during the day. The situation had to be remedied immediately, and at a late hour that evening John Ryan and I had to hire an outside car and apply to friends living in different parts of the city, and by midnight all but four of the men had revolvers. Two were brought to the spot where Colonel Kelly and a few of the men were stationed in a field opposite the prison, about an hour before the escape, by Nick Walsh. Eleven men only had revolvers; one had a large knife, and a thirteenth man had no weapon whatever, and was sent home early in the night. Not a man refused to go to the ground, although some were unarmed when they started out. Yet they fully expected a fight with police, warders or soldiers before the work was finished.

The night was dark and wet, and the few policemen on duty in the lonely neighborhood of the prison kept as much as possible under shelter. A thorough search was made of the Circular Road, on which the prison fronts, Love Lane, the bank of the Grand Canal, which runs at the rear of the prison,

9. Isle of Portland, a rocky peninsula on the coast of Dorset, England, on which there was a convict prison.

10. i.e. counted and dismissed (of soldiers).

and a little lane running from the Circular Road to Dolly's Bridge, which crosses the canal close to the prison grounds. One policeman was met sheltering himself under an elm tree on the canal bank and another peeped out of a hallway on the Circular Road, near Clanbrassil Street, but a little conversation enlivened by a swig from a flask of whiskey, revealed the fact that not a single extra man was out and that nothing startling was expected.

The men arrived on the ground by different routes in small groups, and quietly took up positions previously assigned them. Kelly, Ryan, Lambert and Brophy were at a point opposite the prison wall, in a field on the other side of the Circular Road, keeping in the shadow of a high wall running diagonally inward from the road. Kearney, Cody, Mullen and Lawler were placed under the shadow of a hedge at the gate of the same field, directly opposite the prison gate. Harrison, Duggan and O'Neill were in a little dark nook at the western end of the prison wall between the latter and the wall of a cabbage garden that lay between the Circular Road and the canal. Flood had been sent home because we had no revolver for him. He offered to stay, but Kelly wanted no man without a weapon. The nook was partly overhung by the branches of trees. My instructions were to move from post to post, reporting at intervals to Colonel Kelly till the time fixed for the escape, when I was to take my place with him. A low mud wall separated the field from the Circular Road, and in a hole on the inside of this wall John Ryan had, earlier in the night, deposited a coil of stout rope with knots arranged at about every two feet of its length, so as to make it easier for Stephens to climb by when it was flung over the wall.

Here the men waited expectantly in the drizzling rain for the signal which was to tell them that Stephens had been let out of the prison and was waiting inside the outer wall for the rope to be thrown over. He was to throw gravel over the wall as a signal that the rope was wanted, and the 'quack, quack!' of a duck repeated by Ryan was to announce that the moment was at hand. But there was a genuine duck in a neighboring garden that raised a false alarm once.

When the prison clock struck one Breslin left his quarters in the hospital and quietly opened the door leading to the corridor where Stephens' cell was situated. No one else was up but Byrne, and Stephens who was waiting in his cell dressed and ready to move. Ascending the stairs noiselessly, Breslin opened the two doors leading into the corridor as quietly as he could, but it was impossible to do so without making a slight noise. The policeman on the other side of the door at the other end might hear if he was listening, and if McLeod was awake, there would be trouble. Stephens heard Breslin turn the key in the cell door. He slid from the hammock where he had been lying dressed. No superfluous words were spoken. Stephens, after receiving a loaded revolver from Breslin, followed the latter as noiselessly as possible out of the corridor and down the stairs. Here an anxious pause of a few moments was made. If McLeod, the jail-bird, rang his gong, all was over; but no sound came from his cell. He afterwards explained his silence by saying that the key which let Stephens out of his cell would also open his, and that had he given the alarm his throat would have been cut. Hearing no alarm, Breslin opened the door leading out into the prison yard. Between this yard and the Governor's garden was a very high wall, which had to be crossed before the outer wall could be reached. Breslin had been told by Byrne that the ladder used in lighting the lamps in the yard was long enough to enable a man to cross the wall, but on making the experiment now he found that a tall man standing on the top rung of the ladder could not reach within several feet of the top of the wall. Byrne had not tried the ladder, as he had promised to do. This was a serious hitch. McLeod might have rung his gong and alarmed the prison without Breslin being able to hear it, and not a moment could be spared. After a hurried consultation he decided to return to the prison, and, with Byrne's help, bring out two long tables from the lunatics' dining room, on which to place the ladder. There was an unoccupied sentry box close to where they stood, and inside this he placed Stephens. For all he knew, there might be a policeman stationed in the Governor's garden; so, assuring Stephens that Byrne and he would take care of anything between the sentry box and the prison door, he told him to shoot any man coming from the other direction.

The two tables were carried out as quickly as possible, and placed one on top of the other against the wall at a point where Breslin knew there was a tool shed on the other side, which would facilitate the descent. The ladder was then placed on the upper table and held by Byrne and Breslin, while Stephens ascended.

As Stephens stepped on the ladder he turned round and handed Breslin the revolver. This left an unfavorable impression on Breslin which nothing could efface. If there should be a policeman in the Governor's garden he could easily stop the further progress of the fugitive, and the men outside the wall could do nothing to aid him. Stephens climbed up the ladder, and, although there was some glass on the top of the wall, easily got over it, and dropped down to a shed on the other side and thence to the ground. He walked over to a pear tree indicated by Breslin, which grew close to the outer wall, and which would aid him in climbing it. Hearing no footsteps outside, he took a handful of gravel and flung it on to the Circular Road.

This signal was at once recognized. It was only the work of a minute for the little party with Kelly to cross the road and fling one end of the rope over the wall. Four of us held it, and in a second there was a strong tug at the other end of the rope and we felt him struggling upward, till at last we saw his head and shoulders at the top of the wall, which was about eighteen feet high. The whole party, as well as I can remember, had by this time rushed to the spot, and 'The Captain' was greeted good-naturedly, but in subdued tones. He peered down as if gauging the distance to the ground, and was quite out of breath. After he had vainly tried to hitch the rope between two stones on the top of the wall so that he might use it in descending, John Ryan told him to drop down with his back to the wall, and we would catch him. He did so and Ryan caught his feet on his chest, the sand on the soles leaving the imprint of the shoes on Ryan's buttoned coat. It staggered Ryan, and as Stephens was coming down I caught him about the knees and let him slide to the ground. I felt him tremble as I let him down, a fact probably caused as much by his physical exertion as by the reaction to the nerve-wracking strain of his enforced wait in the sentry box in the inner yard. At all events, it gave the first shock to the belief I had previously entertained in his coolness and self-possession.

Stephens and Kelly at once crossed the Circular Road and turned into Love Lane, a long winding street, running through market gardens and having few houses. From Love Land they turned into Brown Street. In this street was the house where the C.O.I.R.[11] was to be concealed. Mrs. Boland, a sister of James O'Connor, later Member of Parliament for West Wicklow, had undertaken to shelter him, and John O'Connor, her brother, then a bright boy of fifteen, who had acted as messenger between Kelly and Stephens before his arrest, was on the lookout. Here he remained in safety, and ever afterwards we used to call Mrs. Boland 'the best man of the O'Connor family'. She was one of the most devoted of the many good women of the Fenian movement.

I had been ordered by Kelly to see that anything that might give a clue to the nature of the escape should be removed from outside the wall. The only thing of that kind was the rope, and I found unexpected difficulty with that. Every man present wanted to get a piece of it, and a few succeeded.

We started off in small groups, and the state of elation in which the men all were was indicated by a remark by John Ryan, who was walking with me. 'John,' he said, 'we have tonight witnessed the greatest event in history.' 'Well,' I replied, 'I suppose it is the greatest in our little movement up to the present, but I hope we'll best it soon.'

As we got to a point on the Circular Road opposite the prison gate we heard the loud bang of a door, and we thought the alarm must have been given and expected momentarily to see the gate open and the policemen rush out. Lest such event might result in the recapture of Stephens, the men all ran up, every man pulled his revolver, and we waited expectantly, but there was not another sound or a sign. We then separated and went our various ways. Breslin and Byrne said later that they had neither banged a door nor heard any noise, but twelve of us outside heard it so distinctly that there could be no mistake about it.

A few minutes later I learned how much the matter had become practically public property. As Ryan and I turned into Camden Street he said to me, 'I promised Sam Clampett that I would call and let him know the thing has come off all right. He lives just here.' I new Sam, who was a Protestant and a member of James O'Connor's Circle. He was a bright, handsome little fellow. Sure enough, his wife and he were waiting up to hear the news. She too was, of course, a Protestant, and a great Fenian. They welcomed us effusively and a bottle of whiskey was produced. The three men drank 'The Captain's' health in a bumper. Ryan and I were wet from long exposure to the drizzle and the draught was timely.

11. Chief Organizer of the Irish Republicans.

Breslin left the tables and the ladder as they stood when Stephens crossed the inner wall, and the false keys in the door, so that there might be no mistake about the manner of the escape, and returned to his room in the hospital, which he reached a little after 2 o'clock. He wore a pair of patent leather shoes, so that his ordinary ones might not be soiled, and after carefully wiping the sand and dust from them he put them away, and brushing his clothes, got into bed and pretended to be 'fast asleep' immediately. Byrne continued to make his usual rounds, but not until 4 o'clock did he raise the alarm and report finding the tables and ladder against the prison wall.

A scene of wild confusion ensued. The whole prison staff was aroused, and every nook and corner of the building and the grounds was searched for the fugitive. The Castle authorities were at once notified, and in a few hours the police were scouring the city, searching houses and watching trains and outgoing vessels of all kinds. The garrison was placed under arms. Similar precautions were taken elsewhere and an utter panic prevailed among the Loyalists. Landlords and magistrates were paralyzed with dismay, and fully expected the outbreak of a formidable insurrection.

I stopped that morning at the house of my aunt in Mabbot Street. Her husband, William Delaney, was in the building business in a small way, and the yard, which was full of building material, had a door opening on a lane which ran into Talbot Street. I had the key of this door buried in sand so that I could reach it from the outside and the back door of the house had been left open for me. Here I had arranged that O'Neill should also sleep that morning and he was waiting for me in the lane when I got over. Thinking that we might have been followed, he insisted on sleeping in his clothes, and he presented a curious spectacle as he slept. He had a portion of the rope coiled around his body and four loaded revolvers — he had collected three besides his own — in his belt. I had two others, but, though I slept in my clothes, I kept the firearms within reach.

We were anxious to learn how the people felt about the news, so we were up early, got the papers, reported for orders to Colonel Kelly, returned the borrowed revolvers and visited several places frequented by our men. We found them all in high spirits and everyone talking of the event. At Lynch's in Camden Street, the place we had started from, there was a large party of our friends and several men who were not Fenians, but all were equally enthusiastic.

Had Stephens been ready to give the word then he could have got five followers for the one that would have answered his call at any previous time.

The people were wild with delight. Men who had till then looked with open hostility or cold indifference on Fenianism were seized with a sudden enthusiasm. They shook hands with their Fenian acquaintances in the streets, and congratulated them on the victory. It was the one proud day of the Fenian movement. The Government had been beaten in their own stronghold, and not a man ever suffered the loss of a hair.

Byrne was arrested next day and committed for trial, but two successive juries disagreed, and he was finally released and allowed to leave the country. Not a shadow of suspicion rested on Breslin, and he remained at his post for a whole year, when, finding that he was likely to be arrested, he quietly slipped on board the Holyhead boat at 'Kingstown', and was in Paris the following night. Neither Breslin nor Byrne contracted for or ever received a single penny for the work. It was a labor of love.

[Rossa died at St Vincent's Hospital, Staten Island, New York on 29 June 1915 after a long illness. There was a funeral in New York and then, after a struggle for control of the funeral in Ireland among members of Clan-na-Gael, Thomas Clarke, one of the 1916 leaders, and John Devoy, took over. This famous occasion rightly reminds Devoy of the MacManus funeral, fifty-four years earlier. The difference was that, in this instance, the occasion was a prelude to rebellion.]

CHAPTER XLVI

O'DONOVAN ROSSA

. . . A cablegram from Tom[1] to me asked the Clan to send the body to Ireland and telegrams from the members of the Executive throughout the country

1. Thomas Clarke (1857-1916), imprisoned in harsh conditions in English jails 1883-98. He worked with Devoy in Clan-na-Gael in the USA, returned to Dublin in 1907 and helped set up a military council to examine the possibilities for an armed insurrection. He was the senior member of the provisional government of the Irish Republic proclaimed in 1916 and the first signatory to the Proclamation of Independence. He was executed on 3 May 1916 for his part in the Easter Rising.

authorized me to take charge. I kept my grip on the arrangements, doing nothing without the consent of Mrs. O'Donovan Rossa, until the body was placed on board the steamer, accompanied by his wife and daughter Eileen (now Mrs. McGowan) on July 17.

On the arrival of the *St. Paul* in Cobh[2] the body was received by a committee of the I.R.B. and taken to Dublin.

Unlike his predecessor Cardinal Cullen, Archbishop Walsh[3] was a Nationalist, and there was a High Mass at the Cathedral in Marlborough Street. The remains then lay in state in the City Hall, where many thousands of people from all parts of Ireland viewed them. There was a constant stream of visitors and there were many touching scenes as old friends gave vent to their sorrow. Irish Volunteers mounted guard.

The funeral took place on Sunday, August 1st, and was the most imposing demonstration ever held in Ireland, exceeding even the great McManus funeral in 1861. Thousands of uniformed Irish Volunteers marched behind the bier and the civilian procession was several miles long, while a dense mass of people lined the sidewalks all the way from the City Hall to Glasnevin Cemetery. Padraic Pearse delivered the funeral oration at the graveside; it was a historic speech.[4]

The military display marked the wonderful progress of the National Movement since the funeral of Terence Bellew McManus, and the *Irish Times* noted the fact by estimating the number of trained men in line who were fit for service (*for England*) at the front in France. The Irish Tory mind is a curious compound of absurdities and seems incapable of thinking straight.[5]

The demonstration was a great success from every point of view. It was splendidly managed, perfect order and discipline prevailed from start to finish and it had a great effect on the country. It was the most significant demonstration against English Rule that had taken place before Easter Week, 1916, and it had considerable effect in preparing the way for it. . . .

2. Cobh, a port to the south-east of Cork city, was called Queenstown from 1849 to 1922, but Rossa would not have used this name.
3. William Joseph Walsh (1841-1921), catholic archbishop of Dublin 1885-1921. A fervent nationalist, he supported Sinn Féin and spoke against the Government of Ireland Act of 1920. The British government opposed his appointment as archbishop because of his support for the Land League, Parnell and the Irish Parliamentary Party.
4. See below p. 293.
5. *The Irish Times* was then the organ of unionist opinion.

III. FENIANISM, THE LAND LEAGUE AND HOME RULE

MICHAEL DAVITT

(1846-1906)

from: THE FALL OF FEUDALISM IN IRELAND (1904)

[In the chapter 'Home Rule and Land Reform', Davitt gives a succinct account of the developments that brought about the combination of forces behind the Home Rule movement which were to be so expertly marshalled by Parnell. Davitt joined the IRB and was involved in the raid on Chester Castle in 1867; as arms purchaser for the Fenians, in 1870 he was arrested and sentenced, on a dubious charge, to fifteen years' imprisonment. Released into exile after seven years, he went to the United States, met John devoy, and in 1879 returned to his native Mayo where he helped to found the Land League. He persuaded Parnell to become involved in the land agitation. Through him, the militant spirit of Fenianism, the social grievances of the Land League and the parliamentary methods of Parnell were reconciled and moulded into a formidable movement.]

CHAPTER VII

HOME RULE AND LAND REFORM: ISAAC BUTT

... The genesis of the Home-Rule agitation was the twofold influence of the amnesty movement,[1] led by Mr. Butt, for the release of the Fenian prisoners, and the resentment of a section of the Irish loyalists against the imperial Parliament for the disestablishment of the Irish State Church.[2] It was an instance of two extremes being encouraged by circumstances to create a medium party. The spirit of Fenianism, acting through the agitation for amnesty, and the revolt of Irish Toryism, occasioned by an act of English justice, selected, as it were, in the person of Isaac Butt, a compendium of honest compromise, and enabled the one-time Irish Conservative, now a converted nationalist, to think out and project a programme which was to seek a solution of the Anglo-Irish question by the means of a Federal Home Rule Parliament in Dublin. Both extremes fell away from this middle programme in a few years. The union of antagonizing Irish elements was too sudden to be enduring. A new force was soon to be created which was to carry Home Rule forward by the momentum of a land war, to be actively renewed more upon the lines of James Fintan Lalor's principles than on those of Duffy's Tenant League or Butt's programme of the three F's — fixity of tenure, fair rents, and free sale.[3] It was to be a joint evolution of Fenianism and Home Rule....

1. The Amnesty Association was founded by John 'Amnesty' Nolan (died 1887) in 1868 to campaign for the release of imprisoned members of the Irish Republican Brotherhood. Nolan was its secretary and Isaac Butt its president. The Association was active until 1872 and was successful in gaining the release of a number of important Fenians.
2. The Church of Ireland was disestablished in 1869 despite strong Tory opposition in Ireland and England.
3. Lalor's principles were much more radical than those of Gavan Duffy's Tenant League (1850) or Butt's federalism as embodied in the Home Government Association (1870) and the Home Rule League (1873). Butt disapproved of the tactics of the Fenian wing of the Home Rule party.

[In this chapter Davitt explains his view of the 'New Departure' in Irish politics, by which he meant a policy of co-operation between Fenians and the Irish Parliamentary Party. His reading of Irish history, briefly given here, had persuaded him that the division between militant and 'moral-force' movements in Irish politics was a weakness which only something like the New Departure could overcome. Davitt initiated the idea, it was taken up by John Devoy, who gave it the name by which it is now known, and communicated to Parnell by cable. Despite opposition from Fenians like Kickham, it was agreed at a meeting in Paris in 1879 that the enterprise should proceed. The Fenians in America financed the campaign; Davitt led the land agitation in Ireland; Parnell represented and supported the demands for land reform at Westminster. The gains of the New Departure were embodied in Gladstone's Land Act of 1881. Davitt's version of the interchange between militant and moral-force movements in Irish history was modified and adapted by Pearse. It remains one of the most popular interpretations of Irish political developments.]

CHAPTER XI

THE NEW DEPARTURE

... What was wanted was to link the land or social question to that of Home Rule, by making the ownership of the soil the basis of the fight for self-government. Tactically it would mean an attack upon the weakest point in the English hold on Ireland, in the form of a national crusade against landlordism, while such a movement would possess the additional advantage of being calculated to win a maximum of auxiliary help from those whom the system had driven out of the country. An organized agitation of this character and purpose, aiming at a unity of combative forces in Ireland in a combined attack upon landlordism and English rule, and directly inviting the active aid of Irishmen abroad, needed a leader of aggressive qualities, and such a man had at this opportune juncture appeared in the person of Mr. Parnell....

Movements of national importance against English power in Ireland have had this special peculiarity: they have regularly alternated between attempts at insurrection and moral-force agitations. One has succeeded the other in uniform sequence for the past one hundred and fifty years. The result has been that a claim for constitutional reform by the argument of a previous attempt at rebellion has always possessed the convincing force of actuality. This, in turn, enabled the advocates of extreme measures to palliate rebellion by pointing to the concessions which were made through its agency to the demands of moral-force agitation. The landlord Parliament of the Pale threatened England with the Volunteers, and won from fear what would not be granted to prayer or debate.[1] The '98 rebellion was precipitated by government agency the better to crush the Parliament and leaders who might possibly call an armed body of Irishmen into existence in a darker hour of England's peril.[2] But the attempts of Tone and Fitzgerald, and later of Emmet, to overthrow English rule were powerful arguments in favor of granting emancipation to the Catholic; and John Keogh[3] and O'Connell reaped to some extent the fruits of Emmet's, Fitzgerald's, and Tone's sacrifices.

Next, the organized policy of violence by which the odious tithe system was attacked and put down gave point and force to the Liberator's claims for Repeal.[4] Though a hater of revolutions, O'Connell was aware of the potency of reasoning which lay in the existence of extremer men and movements than those he controlled, and the 'Litchfield [*sic*] House plot'[5] was within an ace of registering on the page of history the concession of a federal form of self-government for Ireland that would have forestalled Home Rule by more than the length of Mr. Parnell's lifetime.

On the collapse of Repeal the revolutionists of '48, as already related, who had decried the methods of O'Connell as worse than useless, put their own panacea in evidence, and produced Ballingarry and state trials.[6] Moral force follows physical force again in the movement of the Tenant-League and independent opposition, only to fail because the '48 'rebellion' had frightened nobody, while treachery and Archbishop Cullen had killed the hopes of Duffy and Lucas in the fifties.[7] Next Fenianism emerges, and the failure of the insurrectionary attempt of 1867 called for a recourse once more to the alternative of action within the law. Mr. Butt's Home-Rule agitation had, however, grown out of the amnesty organization, and this fact, together with the labors of the Home-Rule leader on the land question, offered a field and an opportunity for calling for a new departure, in a movement that might enlist the spirit and purpose of revolution, in co-operation with open agitation, and possibly equalize alike the fruits of concession or the penalties of failure.

Heretofore the extreme nationalists had only been able to serve the ends of the constitutionalists in efforts at revolution which purchased penal servitude for themselves. Their part in the struggle of Ireland was to fail and to face punishment, in order that moral-force leaders should find strong arguments in their dangerous undertakings and look for concessions as the certain fruits of their sufferings and sacrifices. The division of penalty and of concession was too one-sided to be always encouraging to the men of action, and the time had come when greater gains might hopefully be counted upon from a rational policy of making the open movement more revolutionary in aim and purpose, if not in method, and without antagonizing the most earnest and reliable of the believers in parliamentary action. It would also be worthwhile trying to interrupt the order which had hitherto obtained in alternate Irish movements by combining both, as far as practicable, and for such a common-sense plan of semi-revolutionary action to enlist the active help of the fifteen or twenty million of Irish located beyond the seas. . . .

I have already dwelt upon the change which the

1. The reference is to 'Grattan's parliament' and the legislative independence achieved in 1782 after the foundation of the Irish Volunteers during the American War of Independence.
2. The rebellion of 1798 was felt by England to be especially threatening because of the success of the French revolutionary armies and the fear of an invasion of Ireland.
3. John Keogh (1740-1817), leader of the Irish catholics, through his chairmanship of the Catholic Committee 1791-1817. He sympathized with the aims of the United Irishmen, like Tone, Fitzgerald and Emmet, but feared that their revolutionary violence would compromise the catholic claims, for which he had campaigned by constitutional means.
4. The tithe war of 1830-38 surprised the authorities by its violence.
5. The Lichfield House Compact of March 1835 was an informal agreement, reached at the home of the Earl of Lichfield, between Daniel O'Connell and Lord Melbourne. In effect it placed O'Connell on the side of the Whigs against Sir Robert Peel's government. In return, Melbourne promised to settle the tithes question and to introduce municipal reform to help catholics. It is an exaggeration on Davitt's part to say that any form of federal self-government was implied by such an agreement.
6. The rising of 1848 and the arrest and imprisonment or transportation of the Young Ireland leaders.
7. The reference is to the collapse of the Independent Irish Party in which Gavan Duffy and Frederick Lucas were prominent. The treachery of Sadleir and Keogh and the opposition of Archbishop Cullen put an end to it.

influences of American citizenship had worked in the minds of extreme Irishmen in the direction of wider and wiser methods of revolutionary action. It was a change of view akin to a corresponding tendency among many moral-force men, who had promoted Mr. Parnell's leadership through the machinery of the Home-Rule Confederation of Great Britain[8] — an auxiliary branch of the Home-Rule League of Ireland. Some of the prominent men in this confederation were Fenians. They, too, were anxious to move on other lines more conformable to a rational conception of what the work should be that could promise a hope of better things for Ireland. These moderate Fenians were active partisans of Mr. Parnell's, and this is how Mr. John Devoy alluded to them and their anticipation of a 'new departure' in the very year of 1877....

Mr. Parnell was president of this branch of the Home-Rule movement in Great Britain and was the leader of the obstructionist policy.[9] The ruling spirits of the confederation were his stanchest [*sic*] supporters, and it was their election of him in place of Mr. Butt as president of this body, at a convention in Liverpool, which virtually placed Mr. Parnell at the head of the Home-Rule movement. . . .

An 'alliance' between the revolutionary or Fenian organization and Mr. Parnell was neither directly nor indirectly urged or advised in any way, at any of such meetings,[10] or otherwise by me. What was proposed was an open participation in public movements in Ireland by extreme men, not in opposition to Mr. Parnell or moral-force supporters, but with the view of bringing an advanced nationalist spirit and revolutionary purpose into Irish public life, in a friendly rivalry with moderate nationalists, in the work of making English rule more difficult or impossible, and for such a line of action I appealed both for Clan-na-Gael[11] and general Irish-American approval and support.

A tentative programme put forward at these meetings embraced: (1) A declaration that the want of national government was the chief want of Ireland; (2) a policy of independent action by an Irish party in Parliament; (3) an agitation for the settlement of the land question, with planks for the betterment of laborers' dwellings, the nationalizing of education and of public bodies, and the right of Irishmen to carry arms. At one of these meetings, held in the Park Theatre, Brooklyn, on October 13, Mr. John Devoy made an impromptu speech, having been called for by the audience. It was the speech of the evening, and dealt almost entirely with my proposal to turn nationalist energies upon a solution of the land question. In the *Irish World*[12] of October 26th Mr. Devoy's speech was fully reported, and his opening sentences contained this statement:

> I will say that I endorse the views set forth in the able lecture you have just heard from Mr. Davitt, and that I fully approve of the public policy he proposes for the national — that is, the revolutionary-party....

8. The Home Rule Confederation of Great Britain was founded in 1873 by Isaac Butt to gain the support of Irish people in Britain for Home Rule. Parnell replaced Butt as president in 1877. The organization was heavily infiltrated by the IRB.
9. The obstructionist policy or what is now known as 'filibustering' was pioneered by Joseph G. Biggar (1828-90), MP for Cavan and a member of the IRB. He was also a strong supporter of the Land League.
10. Davitt is referring to a series of meetings addressed by Davitt in various American cities in 1878. He is opposing the version of the genesis of the New Departure given by Barry O'Brien, a biographer of Parnell.
11. Clan-na-Gael was an Irish-American republican revolutionary organization founded in 1867. It was a secret society. John Devoy become one of its most powerful figures and persuaded Clan-na-Gael to agree to the New Departure. The Clan survived until 1940.
12. In fact *The Irish Nation*, one of Devoy's newspapers in the United States.

[In this, the final chapter of his book, Davitt appeals to the British working-classes to support the Irish struggle against British imperialism. While in jail (on several occasions) he had read a number of English socialist works and these helped to broaden his vision of the Irish struggle. These ideas were to survive in the writings of James Connolly and left-wing republicanism in Ireland in the twentieth century. Davitt still holds on to the notion of the distinctive nature of the 'Celtic' race, although this dangerously protean idea could be used as easily to defend as to attack imperialism.]

CHAPTER LX

A FUTURE RACIAL PROGRAMME

. . . The rational solution of the whole Irish question lies in the complete severance of the parliamentary connection between Great Britain and Ireland. I have shown, I hope, clearly and convincingly, how the complete autonomy of Ireland would be no injury, wrong, or menace to the people of Great

Britain. On the other hand, we have either to continue to see our country slowly dying from the poison of imperialism, and have it identified with or incorporated in a system which is the very negation of Celtic nationality, or we must resolutely demand and strenuously labor to obtain the full freedom of Irish rule which will alone avert the complete ruin of the fatherland of the race.

The Irish race have a place in the world's affairs of today that is incompatible with the position which Ireland occupies as a kind of vegetable-patch for selfish imperial purposes. We are fully twenty millions of the world's population, and though four-fifths of these reside out of Ireland, they are potential factors, nevertheless, in the political fate and fortunes of the country from which a rule of stupidity and race-hatred drove their progenitors away. Moreover, Ireland and its race have a mission in the world, have national characteristics, a distinctive individuality and ideas, greatly differing from Anglo-Saxonism, with its purely materialistic spirit and aims. These alone entitle our country to a recognized and separate place in the ranks of civilized states.

British imperialism has done its utmost to deny us the means of making these facts known to other nations. It has poisoned the ears of the civilized world against us for centuries. The part played by Ireland in the early Christian civilization of Europe, in the nurture of learning, and in the scholastic labors of her students and missionaries after the break-up of the Roman Empire; the settled forms of government which were in force in our country, even anterior to the Christian era — all these records of great humanizing service rendered to society by the Celtic people of Ireland in the childhood period of European civilization have been obscured or denied by the agencies of English prejudice, in order to keep from the Irish the recognition which these services frequently obtained from continental states and powers in the Middle Ages.

Ireland is not without allies in other lands, thanks to the power of our race beyond the seas; and she has never yet initiated a movement which was not in line with true progress and liberty. A free Canada and a free Australia are as certain in the future as that tomorrow will follow today; and a continued denial of national self-government to Ireland may see not alone an Irish, but an Australian, a Canadian, and a South-African movement, in our time, with the same end and aim — namely, independent nationhood.

This book has a serious, reforming purpose beyond the telling of the life-story of a great Irish movement. It aspires to point out to the thinkers and leaders of the industrial millions of Great Britain how the poorest of workers — the tillers of the soil in Ireland — succeeded by combination in overthrowing an all-powerful territorial aristocracy, entrenched in the ownership of the chief means of employment in Ireland and in one of the legislative chambers of the Imperial Parliament; and how it induced the two great British parties conjointly, as governments, to loan £150,000,000 in state credit, towards curing some of the evils of class misrule.

The lessons of political organization, and of a practical reforming spirit shown in a voluntary payment of members of Parliament by means of popular subscription; the intelligent and combative uses of the great weapon of passive resistance employed in a national combination; the complete elimination of class and of moneyed leadership in that combination; the great triumph for labor won in the ownership of the land for industry as against monopoly; and the local government of counties and of districts by the people, and not by landlords, capitalists, squires, or parsons — these lessons, if rightly learned by the industrial democracy of England, Scotland, and Wales, and if applied in the manner of this Irish movement, would soon give to the toiling millions of Great Britain a programme with a better prospect of substantial results than any proposed taxation of food can possibly offer to the wealth-producers across the Irish Sea.

What we wanted in Ireland was protection against those who had a monopoly of the chief sources of employment — the landlords. We have broken the bonds of that monopoly and completely crushed its political power.

What English, Welsh, and Scotch workers, traders, and taxpayers need in competition with the producers of other countries, is, not less, but more, free trade — free trade in the growing of food, in a legal protection against a private tax called rent upon its industry; free trade in the building of houses for the people, by protection against ground-rents levied upon the progress of industrial centres by landlordism; free trade in the production of coal and iron ore, by the application to public purposes of the private taxes called mineral royalties, now imposed by landlords upon every workshop, manufacturer, artisan, trader, and domestic fireplace in the three countries by the class who are in legislative possession of the House of Lords and largely of the House of Commons.

It is to progress in this direction that the Irish movement tends. It seeks no reforms in the betterment of the economic and social conditions of our population, or in the democratic government of Ireland by its own people, that are not in harmonious line and in sympathetic co-operation with the industrial and political enfranchisement of the working-classes in Great Britain from the burden of landlordism in field, workshop, coal-mine, factory, city office, and domestic hearthstone — and in the making of laws in the Imperial Parliament....

from: SOME SUGGESTIONS FOR A FINAL SETTLEMENT OF THE LAND QUESTION (1902)

[In this pamphlet, Davitt acknowledges that his scheme to nationalize the land of Ireland had failed because of the hunger of the tenantry for individual proprietorship.]

I must, I deeply regret, admit that a plan of Land Nationalisation such as I hoped amidst the many pleasing dreams of Portland Prison might for ever solve the Irish agrarian problem will not recommend itself to the people of Ireland. I tried in four or five years of patient and uphill propaganda in the early eighties to recommend such a settlement to the country. The feeling of our race in America and Australia was also tested by me in the same direction in later years, but with the same result. The plan was either disliked, or misunderstood, or the principle on which it rested — national, as against individual, lordship of the soil — did not appeal to the strong human desire or passion to hold the land as 'owner' which is so inherent in Celtic nature. In addition to all this, the preponderating political force in Ireland resides in the tenant-farmer class, and most public men, naturally enough, advocate such changes and reforms as the predominant feeling and desires of the constituencies most strongly favour. Popular sentiment was undoubtedly behind Mr. Parnell when he virtually contested this issue with me in 1883 and 1884, and though, singularly enough, he came round almost completely to my views after the unhappy split of 1890, the country has remained, as far as I can judge, overwhelmingly for an 'occupier ownership' of the land as against the 'national ownership' which Fintan Lalor[1] passionately pleaded for after the great Famine, and which I have urged almost in vain upon the acceptance of the Nationalists of my time.

I still hold fondly and firmly to this great principle, and I believe a National ownership to be the only true meaning of the battle cry of the Land League — The Land for the People — but there are some faiths which cannot move Irish mountains, and I have to confess that mine has proved to be one of them.

1. James Fintan Lalor (1807-49), the most militant and penetrating critic of the land system in the Young Ireland movement. He preached the doctrine that the ownership of Ireland 'is vested in the people of Ireland'.

THOMAS CLARKE

(1857-1916)

from: GLIMPSES OF AN IRISH FELON'S PRISON LIFE (1912-13)

[In May 1883, Clarke was sentenced to penal servitude for life for his involvement in a Clan-na-Gael dynamiting campaign in Britain. He served over fifteen years of his sentence. Clarke wrote this account of his experiences in prison in the IRB newspaper *Irish Freedom*, founded in 1910 by Bulmer Hobson and suppressed by the British government in 1914. The articles were collected into a book, under the title given above, by P.S. O'Hegarty; it was published in 1922.

Fenian prison literature is almost a genre in itself. From the Treason Felony Act of 1848 to the Crimes Act of 1877, the category of political prisoner was gradually abolished. Fenians were treated as common criminals, as far as status was concerned, although they were subjected to much harsher and more degrading treatment than any common criminal. O'Leary, Rossa, Kickham, Clarke and many others recorded the brutalities of the penal system and thereby won the sympathy and admiration of many who did not otherwise support their political aims. The history of the changes in the penal system for political offenders was detailed by E. Dwyer Gray, editor of *The Freeman's Journal*, in *The Treatment of Political Prisoners in Ireland* (1889) and by George Sigerson in *Political Prisoners at Home and Abroad* (1890). Sigerson gave details on the number of prisoners who died or were driven insane by the treatment meted out to them and described the administrative and other changes that gave jailers, rather than legislators, the power to govern the penal regime within British prisons. Wilfrid Scawen Blunt, the English diplomat who supported the Irish nationalist cause, was the first to refuse to wear prison clothes when imprisoned in 1887. His example was later followed by the Irish Parliamentary Party members, William O'Brien and Timothy Harrington.

The issue has remained a contentious one to the present day. Clarke's description of body searches, being not allowed to sleep and other tortures is strikingly similar to the accounts of the brutalities of the prison regime in Northern Ireland in recent years. There the issue of political status was contested by the refusal to wear clothes, by the 'dirty protest' and by the hunger strike. The criminalization process was a determined effort on the part of the British government to deny the existence of political prisoners in the British system. Political prisoners were, as Sigerson pointed out, a category of people to be found in Russia, Naples and the Balkans — not in Britain. Prison literature contributed a great deal to the general repudiation of a legal system that was blatantly corrupt in its mode of appointments to the bench, in its practice of jury-packing and, as ultimately was the case, in the conduct of the police who put the law into effect. The history of protest against the legal system includes not only the Fenians who were most savagely punished by it, but also constitutional politicians, like Isaac Butt and John Redmond.]

I

EARLY PRISON THOUGHTS

... We treason-felony prisoners were known in Chatham as 'The Special Men,'[1] and some twelve or fourteen of us were kept, not in the ordinary prison halls, but in the penal cells — kept there so that we could be the more conveniently persecuted, for the authorities aimed at making life unbearable for us. The ordinary rules regulating the treatment of prisoners, which, to some extent, shield them from foul play and the caprice of petty officers, these rules, as far as they did that, were, in our case, set aside, in order to give place to a system devised by the governor of the prison, Captain Harris. This was a scientific system of perpetual and persistent harassing, which gave the officers in charge of us a free hand to persecute us just as they pleased. It was made part of their duty to worry and harass us all the time. Harassing morning, noon, and night, and on through the night, harassing always and at all times, harassing with bread and water punishments, and other punishments, with 'no sleep' torture and other tortures. This system was applied to the Irish prisoners, and to them only, and was specially devised to destroy us mentally and physically — to kill or drive insane. It was worked to its utmost against us for six or seven years, and it was during that time that all the men who succumbed went mad. One feature of this system was the 'no sleep' torture, and for about four of these years I was kept at the most laborious work in the prison, as moulder in the iron foundry on heavy castings. In addition, I was under special surveillance, and the officers had to pay special attention to me, or, in other words, they must annoy me by every means in their power. At night, jaded in body and mind with the heavy labour of the day and the incessant nagging of the officers, I would return to my cell, and when once inside the door would fling myself on the floor and not move until supper-time. If I went to bed before the bell rang it meant a bread and water punishment, and I was already getting enough of their systematic starvation. When the bell rang I would turn into bed, sometimes to sleep, sometimes to lie awake for hours, with body too weary and nerves too shattered for any refreshing sleep to come. If sleep came I was wakened within an hour by a noise something like the report of a small cannon being fired close beside me. The officer was inspecting us, and had merely banged the heavy iron trapdoor after him. With the same loud noise the trap would be banged all through the night at hour intervals. The prisoner might get a few short snatches of sleep between the inspections, or perhaps his nervous system was so shattered with

1. 'Special Men' was a category applied only to Irish political prisoners in the 1880s. Most of them were imprisoned under the Treason-Felony Act of 1848, hurried through Westminster to secure the imprisonment and transportation of Young Ireland leaders. Chatham is a town in Kent, some thirty miles from London.

this and other ingenious tortures that he would not be able to sleep at all. This went on night after night, week after week, month after month, for years. Think of the effects of this upon a man's system, and no one will wonder that so many were driven insane by such tactics. The horror of those nights and days will never leave my memory. One by one I saw my fellow-prisoners break down and go mad under the terrible strain — some slowly and by degrees, others suddenly and without warning. 'Who next' was the terrible question that haunted us day and night — and the ever-recurring thought that it might be myself added to the agony.

Can I ever forget the night that poor Whitehead[2] realised that he was going mad. There in the stillness between two of the hourly inspections, I heard the poor fellow fight against insanity, cursing England and English brutality from the bottom of his heart, and beseeching God to strike him dead sooner than allow him to lose his reason. Such episodes are ineffaceable in the memory, they burn their impress into a man's soul.

2. Albert Whitehead, a Fenian, sentenced with Clarke in 1883.

II

THE INHUMAN TREATMENT OF DR. GALLAGHER

John Daly, James F. Egan, and myself during all those dark and hopeless years had each other's confidence and gave each other support and encouragement. The utmost endeavour of the authorities to crush us failed because we met it in a spirit of defiance, and stood loyally by each other with friendship — aye, with love and sympathy. Every precaution that the prison officers could think of was taken to prevent us 'special men' from communicating with each other. The closest surveillance, the utmost vigilance, and savagely severe punishments were awarded us if we were detected. Yet all their vigilance was set at nought, Daly, Egan, and myself right along were in constant communication with each other. We had our code of signals for communicating to each other by sight — these we owed to Egan; we had our post office,[1] authorised, not by the Postmaster-General, but by John Daly. Through our post office thousands of notes passed. We had our telephones and our cell telegraph, which latter was introduced by myself very early in our imprisonment.

1. Clarke and his comrades had developed a system of passing signs and notes; the notes were written in lead on brown toilet-paper.

A couple of months after Gallagher, Whitehead, Curtin and I arrived in Chatham, sitting in my cell one day racking my brains to find a way to defeat the gaoler's sleepless vigilance the idea of telegraphing suggested itself. All that I could remember about the subject was that the Morse system was based upon two sounds — which were represented on paper by a dot and a dash. The problem was to produce two different kinds of knocks on the wall of the cell and to combine the two sounds into a workable alphabet. After trying different kinds of knocks on my cell table I was satisfied that the dull knock made by the knuckles could not be mistaken for the sharp knock made by a button or slate pencil. I got my slate, and soon had an alphabet worked out. . . .

Being thus closely in touch with Gallagher and Whitehead, as time went on I noticed them change and get queer, and I knew that step by step their reason was giving way. When they were released they were pronounced by the experts who examined them to be hopelessly insane, yet they were no worse then than they had been for the last seven or eight years of their imprisonment. Everyone inside the prison walls — officers and prisoners — priest, parson, and doctor knew right along that they were insane. The English Home Office knew it, but their vengeance had to be sated whether the victims went mad under the torture or not. For seven or eight years, knowing well that they were insane, the authorities continued to punish them in the most cruel manner for their little irrational acts, for which they were in no sense accountable.

Daly, Egan and myself, although getting it as hard as, and perhaps harder than, our companions, did all we could to have attention drawn to the monstrous inhumanity of their treatment. Governor Harris and his warders simply laughed at us. Many and many a letter that we got to write to our friends outside was filled with denunciations of the way these insane prisoners were treated. Gallagher, Whitehead, Duff, McCabe, Devany, Flanagan, and Casey were all out of their minds at this time. Our letters were, of course, suppressed, and never got farther than the Governor of the prison. I still have a copy of a letter I wrote to Mr. John E. Redmond,[2]

2. Redmond's attack on the legal system is printed below (p. 342).

who paid me many a visit in prison, and whose kindness on those occasions I can never forget. When this letter was written I managed to make a shorthand copy of it, and this copy, with some other documents, I managed to smuggle out of prison when I was released. The letter was dated June 18th, 1895, but was, of course, suppressed, and never reached its destination. I will quote one part of this letter in order to show the pitiable condition of the insane prisoners and the brutality of the Government in keeping men in such a condition in penal servitude:

> It is nothing directly concerning myself or my case that causes me to take the unusual course of sending you a letter. What I wish to bring under your notice has reference to one of my fellow-prisoners here, J 463, Albert Whitehead.... Whitehead is, as you are doubtless aware, one of the unfortunate Irish prisoners whose mind has been shattered by the villainous treatment to which we have been subject. It is now some seven or eight years since he first broke down, and at no time since has he recovered.... His fellow-prisoners — or those of them that are not so far gone as himself — are to a man convinced of his insanity, convinced many times over, and you will find all the lately-released Irish prisoners, without a single exception, are of the same opinion.... It is true he is not what is called outrageous — the nearest approach to that are the times when he has kept us awake all night long raving at the top of his voice. But although so far not dangerous to others, he certainly is dangerous to himself, and it is upon this point what I am about to narrate bears.
>
> One day, a couple of weeks ago, while at work in the carpenters's shop, where he and I are employed, happening to glance round in his direction (the officer was away at the other end of the shop) I saw Whitehead kneeling on the floor gathering something like salt off a board and putting the stuff into his mouth. The stuff was crushed glass. I went over to him, and dropping on my knee beside him caught him by the shoulder and asked him what he was eating glass for. He looked at me with the pitiful, dazed stare that is habitual to him now, and said, 'What, what!' I picked up some of the fragments that he had dropped, and again asked him, 'What do you mean by eating this glass; don't you know it will kill you?' He replied in a dull, listless way, 'A pound of it would do you no harm,' and then kept repeating in answer to all my questions, 'A pound of it would do you no harm.' With my handkerchief I dusted away the fragments before him and searched round his bench for more glass. Finding some more I threw it out of the window. All this only occupied a few minutes, and, luckily for me, my 'flagrant violation of the prison rules' was unobserved by the officer. Had I been seen I would have been visited with a term of bread and water punishment. Just think of it — a whispered word of sympathy to this poor fellow — a single word spoken with a view to prevent him killing himself, and I would receive as severe a punishment as the authorities here inflict on habitual criminals for thieving. And yet here in England they go into hysterics over the horrors and brutality of Siberia and ring the changes on the humanity of the English prison system.... The truth is that as far as a refined system of cruelty is concerned there is nothing on God's earth today to compare with the treatment which we Irish prisoners have been receiving at the hands of the English Government.

I then went on to ask Mr. Redmond to endeavour to have an impartial and competent man sent down to examine into Whitehead's mental state and put a stop to the monstrous cruelty that had been carried on for so many years. As I said before, the letter was suppressed, and is now in the English Home Office, preserved along with my prison record and dozens of other letters I wrote that were likewise never delivered by the authorities....

I was expecting a visit from Mr. Redmond about this time, and he came to see me soon after. I told him all about the Whitehead affair, and about the letter I had written to himself which had been suppressed. I asked him on his return to London to see the Home Secretary if possible and put the facts before him concerning Whitehead, and suggest to the Home Secretary to have that suppressed letter of mine sent for, and by every means urge him to have an independent alienist[3] sent down to examine Whitehead's mental condition. I have every reason to believe that Mr. Redmond did this. At all events, very shortly after Mr. Redmond's visit a couple of experts came to Portland Prison and examined Whitehead and Gallagher, and in the course of

3. A person who treats mental diseases, a psychiatrist.

some weeks after they and some others of the Irish prisoners were released.

The prison officials tried to make out that Whitehead was feigning insanity all along. In fact, up to the time he and Gallagher were released the doctors maintained that both of them, as well as the others, were perfectly sane, and merely shamming insanity, and they kept on punishing these poor lunatics for shamming insanity. I have a copy of a prison report on Gallagher's case submitted to the Home Secretary by the prison's visitors. Such documents are painful reading, but the truth about English methods has got to be told, and so I will give their own official report, taken from their Blue Book, and let it speak for itself:

> As to Gallagher's treatment, we find in September 1887 he, according to the report of the medical inspector and medical officer, commenced feigning insanity, and since that time he has been constantly under medical observation, and he has also incurred 16 punishments for refusing to go out to labour and using improper language to officers. In October 1888 he commenced vomiting his food, and continued to do so until February 1889, *and thus managed to reduce himself into a very low state*. He was admitted to the infirmary, and the vomiting ceased, and shortly afterwards — in March 1889 — was discharged from the infirmary.... He was re-admitted in September 1889, and has continued under medical treatment till the present time (*that is, 19th April, 1890, when the report was sent in*) for debility caused by persistent vomiting, which the medical officer believes to be voluntary, and pretended insanity. Dr. Blandford describes him as subdued and reticent in manner, with a downcast eye full of suspicion, and said that his manner appeared to indicate that he felt that he had been foiled in his attempt to deceive, but that he was still playing a part, and he thinks he is a dangerous man, who will require very careful watching and management.

This was the sort of reports [*sic*] the English Home Office wanted, and they got them, and meanwhile the torture of the insane prisoners went on.

When Dr. Gallagher was finally released Dr. Ferris, the New York specialist who examined him, pronounced his recovery hopeless, and attributed his insanity solely to the treatment he had received in prison. Dr. Ferris said in his report:

> I see his companion, Whitehead, is also demented. The prison officials must have treated these men cruelly. Gallagher's condition is worse than death. The torture we are told he received during the first five years — now that we know he is insane for eight years — must have been very severe. The punishing of this man for shamming was cruel in the extreme. No one who sees Gallagher two or three times could for a moment doubt the reality of his insanity. To mistake his acts for shamming is inexplicable.
>
> (*Signed*),
>
> ARTHUR WARREN FERRIS.

Savoy Hotel, New York City,
September 7th, 1896.

Dr. Gallagher is still living. He has been in a lunatic asylum on Long Island, New York, since his release in 1896. Whitehead, on his arrival in America, was also examined by experts, and likewise pronounced to be hopelessly insane and placed in an asylum.[4] Such is the 'humanity' of England's prison system where Irish political prisoners are concerned!

4. Dr Thomas Gallagher (1851-1925) was released, after a public outcry, in 1896. He died in a New York sanatorium without recovering his sanity.

VII

BOBBY BURNS OF CHATHAM

... England might force me to associate with the dregs raked in from the gutters, might shave my head like theirs, and stamp the Government broad arrow all over me; humiliation might be heaped on to me with an unsparing hand, and punishments — diabolically brutal — measured out for years, but never for one moment did I forget I was an Irish Political Prisoner, and, in spite of it all, never felt any degradation. On the contrary, I wore that convict garb with a certain amount of pride, and took satisfaction in the thought that with all her laws and with all her power this great England could not force me — one of the mere units of the Irish rank and file — to regard myself as one of the criminal class any more than I could ever be forced to regard myself as English.

The struggle for Irish freedom has gone on for

centuries, and in the course of it a well-trodden path has been made that leads to the scaffold and the prison. Many of our revered dead have trod that path, and it was these memories that inspired me with sufficient courage to walk part of the way along that path with an upright head....

VIII

THE GOLDEN RULE OF LIFE FOR A LONG SENTENCE PRISONER

In the course of these articles I have referred at length to the brutal severity of the prison treatment of the Irish political prisoners, but in this connection, up to the present, I have only dealt with what might be termed the crude brutality of our jailers — such as the long periods of starvation punishment, the no sleep torture, the perpetual harassing, etc. But besides punishment of this class there was another and more refined kind that seemed inspired by a spirit of devilry and aimed at galling the finer feelings of a man's nature and was calculated to blur and deaden the moral sense. As an instance of this class I will mention the 'Special Search' which occurred frequently — about twice a month through all the years. On these occasions we would be stripped stark naked and subjected to the most minute examination of our person — so minute that often the bull's eye lamp was used. Had this search stopped short at a minute examination of the hands and between the fingers, of the soles of the feet and between the toes, of the mouth and inside the jaws and under the tongue, it would be disagreeable enough; but it went further and to such a disgustingly indecent extent that I must not here do more than imply the nature of it. This search would sometimes be carried out to the officers' accompaniment of a running fire of comments in keeping with the nature of the work they were engaged on.

Besides this search we were subject to the ordinary 'rub down' search at least four times a day. In this the prisoner merely unbuttoned all his clothing without removing it, and the officer carefully felt him all over. I have been obliged to complain to the prison authorities of the indecent and hurtful way some of the officers mauled me while subjecting me to this search. That complaint will be found entered up in the official 'Complaint Sheet' with my other records.

When the English Government, in 1848, decided to degrade the Irish political prisoner to the level of the ordinary criminal and passed the Treason Felony Act, they did not tell the world it would be part and parcel of the game to try and debase his mind and sap his self-respect. Nevertheless, such undoubtedly seemed to be the spirit and design of the authorities in their attitude towards the political prisoners during my time.

EÓIN Mac NEILL

(1867-1945)

THE NORTH BEGAN (1913)

[Mac Neill, professor of early Irish history in University College, Dublin, wrote this article for *An Claidheamh Soluis* (*The Sword of Light*), the journal of the Gaelic League which he had helped to found in 1893. It is generally regarded as the crucial document that led to the founding of the Irish Volunteers, formally established at a meeting in the Rotunda in Dublin on 25 November 1913. The article appeared on 1 November.

In January 1913, the Ulster Unionist Council, founded in 1905 to oppose Home Rule for Ireland, decided to unite the scattered groups of Ulster unionist militants into the Ulster Volunteer Force. Led by Edward Carson (1854-1935) and James Craig (1871-1940), the unionists proclaimed their readiness to resist Home Rule and, if necessary, to set up their own government in Ulster. Mac Neill saw this threatened revolt against the British government as an example to the rest of Ireland, even though he believed the idea of Ulster separatism to be impractical and absurd. What the North had begun, the rest of the country should follow. The article persuaded the IRB, most especially one of its leading figures, Bulmer Hobson (1883-1969), that Mac Neill would be the ideal figure to attract support for the idea of a Volunteer force. Following Davitt's policy in relation to the New Departure with Parnell, the IRB wanted to embrace, within the leadership of the Volunteers, a number of moderate figures who would command the sympathy of many supporters of the Irish Parliamentary Party and Gaelic League enthusiasts and who would, in addition, modify the catholic church's disapproval of anything associated with the Fenians or with the idea of revolutionary action. At first the IRB had twelve members in the provisional committee of thirty which led the Volunteer movement. By the autumn of 1914, however, by which time three of the future leaders of the 1916 Rebellion — Patrick Pearse, Thomas MacDonagh and Joseph Mary Plunkett — had joined the IRB, the Brotherhood was in a position to take over the leadership of the Volunteers.

The title of the article is taken from Thomas Davis's poem 'The Song of the Volunteers of 1782' which contains the phrase 'The North began'. The parallel with the Volunteers of the eighteenth century was widely canvassed, although the fact that there were two distinct Volunteer forces in Ireland in 1913 made, or should have made, the analogy suspect to those who were willing to be seduced by it into believing that an all-Ireland movement of resistance had emerged. Along with Home Rule, there also had emerged the shadow of rebellion and partition.]

A wonderful state of things has come to pass in Ulster. Three distinct parties, each too weak to be of much force in politics, have ranged themselves against home rule. These are the Orange industrial workers, mainly Church of Ireland Protestants; the Presbyterian rural community; and the remnant of the feudal aristocracy. The first two elements have been drawn together by what is called the 'No-Popery' sentiment. This fact has been turned to account by the third element, and, when dual ownership, land purchase, and the abolition of grand jury government had apparently consigned feudalism to the incurable ward, a combination of landlords, land-agents, land-lawyers, and their adherents, in return for conferring the stamp of 'respectability' on the 'No-Popery' sentiment, has managed to secure the control of an alliance of wage-earners and rent-payers. That this is literally true may be verified by anyone who consults the newspaper files for (1) the names of those who took the initiative in the organization of the Ulster 'Unionist Clubs',[1] and (2) the names of the numerous *personnel* of the Ulster 'Provisional Government'.[2] To attain such an ascendancy seems almost a miracle of political adroitness, but there is another side of the picture.

The Parliament Act[3] deprived Irish feudalism of what hitherto had been its chief resource, the effective support of British feudalism in the legislature. Then the masters of the Ulster triple alliance decided on an extraordinary step, the enrolment of a Volunteer force[4] manned by their 'allies', the 'Unionist' wage-earners and rent-payers. Of the three 'allied' forces, one only, the managing element, is really 'Unionist'. Intermarriage, social intercourse, and self-interest unite the decaying feudal aristocracy of Ireland to the still opulent feudal aristocracy of Great Britain; but history shows and observation confirms that the Orange democracy and the Presbyterian rural party are home rulers in principle and in essence. The loyalty of Orangemen to the 'Crown', the 'Constitution', the 'Empire', and the 'Union' arise[s] out of the notion that these entities secure them in possession of home rule and a little more. But whenever any abatement of that little more seems likely to come from constitutional developments, loyalty and affection instantaneously put on a different face. The Presbyterian country party, as history shows, though slower to move and understand, is not less radically attached to home rule than the Orange party.

The skill of the feudal element in obtaining the lead is more than counterbalanced by their fatuity in starting among the essential home rulers of their present following the most decisive move towards Irish autonomy that has been made since O'Connell invented constitutional agitation. The Ulster Volunteer movement is essentially and obviously a home rule movement. It claims, no doubt, to hold Ireland 'for the Empire'; but really it is no matter whether Ireland is to be held for the

1. The Unionist Clubs Council, formed after the introduction of the second Home Rule bill in 1893, was encouraged by the British prime minister, Lord Salisbury, and was dominated by landowners and businessmen.

2. The Ulster Unionist Council, formed in 1905, was the co-ordinating body of unionist resistance to Home Rule. Besides Craig and Carson, the Council had the leadership and support of Andrew Bonar Law, leader of the Conservative opposition in the House of Commons, Lady Londonderry and her husband, the sixth marquess, president of the UUC and its chairman in 1913. In September 1913, the UUC delegated its powers to a provisional government of seventy-seven members, with Carson as chairman of the Central Authority.

3. The Parliament Act of 1911 modified the powers of the House of Lords, making it impossible for the Lords to kill measures sent to it from the Commons.

4. The Ulster Volunteer Force enrolled about 90,000 men; they drilled in Orange Halls and in the grounds of sympathetic landowners.

empire or for the empyrean, against the pope, against John Redmond, or against the man in the moon. What matters is *by whom Ireland is to be held.* Lord Lansdowne,[5] speaking recently against home rule, spoke fine old medieval words, 'We have Ireland and we mean to keep her.' The Ulster Volunteers reply, '*We* are going to hold Ireland — of course for your lordships.'

The true meaning of this extraordinary development is dawning painfully on English Unionists. They are beginning to understand that Sir Edward Carson has knocked the bottom out of Unionism.[6] To add to their comfort, a Mr Arnold White has been proving in elaborate detail that the present available resources of the British army are not sufficient to put down the Volunteer movement in four of the thirty-two Irish counties. In any case, it appears that the British army cannot now be used to prevent the enrolment, drilling, and reviewing of Volunteers in Ireland. There is nothing to prevent the other twenty-eight counties from calling into existence citizen forces to hold Ireland 'for the Empire'. It was precisely with this object that the Volunteers of 1782 were enrolled, and they became the instrument of establishing self-government and Irish prosperity.[7] Their disbanding led to the destruction alike of self-government and of prosperity, and the opportunity of rectifying a capital error of this sort does not always come back again to nations.

The more responsible section of English Unionist opinion has taken alarm and is tentatively drawing away from the two-edged sword of 'Ulster'. But even the rashest English Unionists are clearly in great uneasiness; and while they threaten with Ulster, they are openly beseeching the other side to find them a way out of their mess. Dick Steele's[8] creditors once sent him a deputation, as they said, 'to discuss his difficulties with him'. 'Pardon me, gentlemen,' was his remark, 'your difficulties, not mine.' Sir Edward Carson proclaimed that, in launching his new Ulster policy, he had not counted the cost. It looks like it.

The moral of the story is that, in public movements, every element of sham and insincerity is a mortgage given to destiny. I do not say that Sir Edward Carson is insincere. Probably he, too, like the Orangemen and Presbyterians, is at heart a home ruler, and thinks that the sort of home rule that he wants is best guaranteed by the semblance of government from outside. His English allies, however, hoped that his master-move would do effective electioneering work for them, and the fact that since he 'drew the sword' in Ulster he has devoted most of his energies to a political tour in Great Britain shows that he has lent himself to the game.[9] That does not pay. In Ulster, too, the local managers, the feudal remnant, who have good reason not to be in earnest when they make a military array of wage-earners and rent-payers, thus mounting and loading a machine gun whose mechanism they cannot hope to control, have shown their hand and have been found evidently bluffing. Their 'Provisional Government', with its pompous detail of phantom departments, put on paper in secret session at a Belfast club, is the most ridiculous piece of political histrionics ever staged.[10] A parcel of schoolboys would be ashamed to own it. In order to pretend strength they arranged to hold reviews in such overwhelming nationalist districts as Omagh, Raphoe, Armagh, Newry and Kilkeel, but perhaps the crowning sham was the announcement of an insurance fund of £1,000,000.[11] The real insurance fund for real war is fighting material, men, arms, ammunition, transport, ships, fortifications; and those who are in earnest about war will not devote a penny to any other sort of insurance. All this shows that feudalism in Ireland

5. Henry Charles Keith Petty-Fitzmaurice, 5th marquess of Lansdowne, was unionist leader in the House of Lords. His predecessor, the 3rd marquess, is referred to in the section 'The Famine and Young Ireland' (see p. 151 above).
6. Mac Neill's point is that Carson's threat of rebellion against the Home Rule bill amounted to a declaration of Ulster independence. After 1922, the point had more force.
7. The belief that self-government and prosperity were naturally allied was even more important to the unionists than to the Irish nationalists. The Ulster Solemn League and Covenant had, as its first priority, 'the material well-being of Ulster as well as the whole of Ireland'.
8. A story often told of the improvident Irish dramatist Richard Steele (1672-1729).
9. The Unionist Associations of Ireland, founded in 1907, organized a propaganda campaign on behalf of the unionist cause throughout Britain. It was most effective in the 1911-24 period and Carson participated in a series of meetings arranged by the UAI.
10. The scheme for a provisional government, should Home Rule become law, included military and civil committees to which departmental matters would be entrusted. Approval for this scheme was given on 24 September 1913 by the UUC, during the week in which MacNeill wrote this article.
11. Carson proposed that an indemnity guarantee fund to compensate members of the UVF for loss or disability in resisting Home Rule should have a target of £1,000,000. He personally guaranteed £10,000. At the meeting on 24 September, £250,000 had been guaranteed and the target was reached soon after.

is doating[12] as well as decaying, and the cheap cuteness that can play successfully upon religious fanaticism is no proof of any higher form of intelligence.

English Unionists realize, explicitly or instinctively, that the Ulster Volunteers have scuttled the ship; some of them, sooner than admit their discomfiture, are hankering after the separation from Ireland of what they are pleased to call 'homogeneous Ulster',[13] namely, the four eastern counties. Not a single responsible man and no assembly of men in Ireland has authorized this proposal. All nationalist opinion and any Unionist opinion that has been expressed is strongly hostile to it. And for a very good reason.

There is no 'homogeneous Ulster'. It is impossible to separate from Ireland the city that Saint Patrick founded,[14] the city that Saint Columba founded,[15] or the tombs of Patrick, Brigid and Columba. They would defy and nullify the attempt. It is impossible to separate from Ireland the 'frontier town' of Newry, the men of south Down, Norman and Gael, the Gaelic stock of the Fews that hold 'the Gap of the North',[16] the glensmen of south Derry, or north Antrim. If there were any possibility of civil war, if civil war were assured, not to speak of its being insured, these districts alone would hold immovable all the resources of General — I believe — Richardson.[17] There are besides the 100,000 nationalist home rulers of Belfast, and others, Protestants, Catholic, Orange and Presbyterian, in every corner of the four counties, who under any change of government are certain to 'revert to type'. With what facility they have fallen in with the idea of holding Ireland — for the empire!

It is evident that the only solution now possible is for the empire either to make terms with Ireland or to let Ireland go her own way. In any case, it is manifest that all Irish people, Unionist as well as nationalist, are determined to have their own way in Ireland. On that point, and it is the main point, Ireland is united. It is not to follow, and it will not follow, that any part of Ireland, majority or minority, is to interfere with the liberty of any other part. Sir Edward Carson may yet, at the head of his Volunteers, 'march to Cork'.[18] If so, their progress will probably be accompanied by the greetings of ten times their number of National Volunteers, and Cork will give them a hospitable and a memorable reception. Some years ago, speaking at the Toome Feis,[19] in the heart of 'homogeneous Ulster', I said that the day would come when men of every creed and party would join in celebrating the defence of Derry and the battle of Benburb.[20] That day is nearer than I then expected.

12. deranged, weak-minded.
13. This concept was prominent in the discussions at the Buckingham Palace Conference of 1914.
14. Armagh.
15. Derry.
16. An area in south Armagh.
17. Sir George Richardson, a retired lieutenant-general in the British army, assumed command of the Ulster Volunteer Force in July 1913.
18. Carson spoke of marching on Cork with the UVF in 1913.
19. Toome is a nationalist town in County Antrim. A *feis* is a celebration of Gaelic culture, chiefly featuring dance and song. The Gaelic League had introduced this sort of thing as a way of reviving the Gaelic spirit.
20. The siege of Derry in 1689 was a protestant triumph; the battle of Benburb (1646) was one of the great successes of Owen Roe O'Neill. Both were Ulster triumphs of major significance for all Ireland.

PATRICK H. PEARSE

(1879-1916)

from: THE MURDER MACHINE (1916)

[Pearse's pamphlet, published under this title, was a selection from articles on Irish education; it appeared in 1913 in *Irish Freedom* and the *Irish Review*. As founder of St Enda's school in Rathfarnham, Co. Dublin, Pearse had more experience in education than in anything else. He wanted to supplant the examinations and cramming of the existing educational system with something much more free and liberal, the model for which he believed was to be found in the old Irish fosterage-system. The

Intermediate Education Act of 1878 not only organized an Education Board and an examination system, it allocated money to school managers on the basis of results obtained in the intermediate examinations. Pearse opposed this as a deadening and as an anglicizing force in Irish life. His return to a version of pagan and Christian Ireland was not merely a schoolteacher's alternative to the dull, official programme. It was an attempt to recover nationality through education. Indeed, it was part of the revolution that he had planned for that year.]

V

AN IDEAL IN EDUCATION

... The modern child is coming to regard his teacher as an official paid by the State to render him certain services; services which it is in his interest to avail of, since by doing so he will increase his earning capacity later on; but services the rendering and acceptance of which no more imply a sacred relationship than do the rendering and acceptance of the services of a dentist or a chiropodist. There is thus coming about a complete reversal of the relative positions of master and disciple, a tendency which is increased by every statute that is placed on the statute book, by every rule that is added to the education code of modern countries.

Against this trend I would oppose the ideal of those who shaped the Gaelic polity nearly two thousand years ago. It is not merely that the old Irish had a good education system; they had the best and noblest that has ever been known among men. There has never been any human institution more adequate to its purpose than that which, in pagan times, produced Cuchulainn and the Boy-Corps of Eamhain Macha and, in Christian times, produced Enda and the companions of his solitude in Aran.[1] The old Irish system, pagan and Christian, possessed in pre-eminent degree the thing most needful in education: an adequate inspiration. Colmcille[2] suggested what that inspiration was when he said, 'If I die it shall be from the excess of the love that I bear the Gael.' A love and a service so excessive as to annihilate all thought of self, a recognition that one must give all, must be willing always to make the ultimate sacrifice — this is the inspiration alike of the story of Cuchulainn and of the story of Colmcille, the inspiration that made the one a hero and the other a saint.

1. Cuchulainn first made his name as a hero when he went to Emain Macha (Navan Fort, Co. Armagh) and routed the youths who had been reared there under the king's protection. St Enda, according to tradition, had as his disciples and students the early founders of monasteries in Ireland: Finnian, Ciaran, Brendan and Colmcille. Enda was the first of the Irish monks to retire into solitude, on the Aran Islands, off the coast of County Galway.
2. St Columba or Colmcille emigrated to Iona in 563 or 565. Many poems and laments for this exile have been attributed to him.

VI

MASTER AND DISCIPLES

In the Middle Ages there were everywhere little groups of persons clustering round some beloved teacher, and thus it was that men learned not only the humanities but all gracious and useful crafts. There were no State art schools, no State technical schools: as I have said, men became artists in the studio of some master-artist, men learned crafts in the workshop of some master-craftsman. It was always the individual inspiring, guiding, fostering other individuals; never the State usurping the place of father or fosterer, dispensing education like a universal provider of readymades, aiming at turning out all men and women according to regulation patterns.

In Ireland the older and truer conception was never lost sight of. It persisted into Christian times when a Kieran[1] or an Enda or a Colmcille gathered his little group of foster-children (the old word was still used) around him; they were collectively his family, his household, his *clann* — many sweet and endearing words were used to mark the intimacy of that relationship. It seems to me that there has been nothing nobler in the history of education than this development of the old Irish plan of fosterage under a Christian rule, when to the pagan ideals of strength and truth there were added the Christian ideals of love and humility. And this, remember, was not the education system of an aristocracy, but the education system of a people. It was more democratic than any education system in the world today. Our very divisions into primary, secondary, and university crystallize a snobbishness partly intellectual and partly social. At Clonard Kieran, the son of a carpenter, sat in the same class as Colmcille, the son of a king. To Clonard or to Aran

1. Ciaran or Kieran was the founder of the great monastic centre of Clonmacnoise on the river Shannon in the sixth century. Clonard, in the Irish midlands, was founded by St Finnian.

or to Clonmacnois went every man, rich or poor, prince or peasant, who wanted to sit at Finnian's or at Enda's or at Kieran's feet and to learn of his wisdom.

Always it was the personality of the teacher that drew them there. And so it was all through Irish history. A great poet or a great scholar had his foster-children who lived at his house or fared with him through the country. Even long after Kinsale[2] the Munster poets had their little groups of pupils; and the hedge schoolmasters of the nineteenth century were the last repositories of a high tradition.

I dwell on the importance of the personal element in education. I would have every child not merely a unit in a school attendance, but in some intimate personal way the pupil of a teacher, or, to use more expressive words, the disciple of a master. And here I nowise contradict another position of mine, that the main object in education is to help the child to be his own true and best self. What the teacher should bring to his pupil is not a set of readymade opinions, or a stock of cut-and-dry information, but an inspiration and an example; and his main qualification should be, not such an overmastering will as shall impose itself at all hazards upon all weaker wills that come under its influence, but rather so infectious an enthusiasm as shall kindle new enthusiasm. . . .

2. The battle of Kinsale (1601) marked the defeat of the Gaelic order in Ireland.

VII

OF FREEDOM IN EDUCATION

I have claimed elsewhere that the native Irish education system possessed pre-eminently two characteristics: first, freedom for the individual, and, secondly, an adequate inspiration. Without these two things you cannot have education, no matter how you may elaborate educational machinery, no matter how you may multiply educational programmes. And because those two things are pre-eminently lacking in what passes for education in Ireland, we have in Ireland strictly no education system at all; nothing that by any extension of the meaning of words can be called an education system. We have an elaborate machinery for teaching persons certain subjects, and the teaching is done more or less efficiently; more efficiently, I imagine, than such teaching is done in England or in America. We have three universities and four boards of education. We have some thousands of buildings, large and small. We have an army of inspectors, mostly overpaid. We have a host of teachers, mostly underpaid. We have a Compulsory Education Act. We have the grave and bulky code of the Commissioners of National Education, and the slim impertinent pamphlet which enshrines the wisdom of the Commissioners of Intermediate Education.[1] We have a vast deal more in the shape of educational machinery and stage properties. But we have, I repeat, no education system; and only in isolated places have we any education. The essentials are lacking.

And first of freedom. The word freedom is no longer understood in Ireland. We have no experience of the thing, and we have almost lost our conception of the idea. So completely is this true that the very organisations which exist in Ireland to champion freedom show no disposition themselves to accord freedom: they challenge a great tyranny, but they erect their little tyrannies. 'Thou shalt not' is half the law of Ireland, and the other half is 'Thou must.'

Now, nowhere has the law of 'Thou shalt not' and 'Thou must' been so rigorous as in the schoolroom. Surely the first essential of healthy life there was freedom. But there has been and there is no freedom in Irish education; no freedom for the child, no freedom for the teacher, no freedom for the school. Where young souls, young minds, young bodies, demanded the largest measure of individual freedom consistent with the common good, freedom to move and grow on their natural lines, freedom to live their own lives — for what is natural life but natural growth? — freedom to bring themselves, as I have put it elsewhere, to their own perfection, there was a sheer denial of the right of the individual to grow in his own natural way, that is, in God's way. He had to develop not in God's way, but in the Board's way. The Board, National or Intermediate as the case might be, bound him hand and foot, chained him mind and soul, constricted him morally, mentally, and physically with

1. The Commissioners of National Education dealt with primary school (national school) education, a system established in 1831. The Intermediate Board of Education for Ireland, established in 1878, dealt with secondary schooling. The three universities in 1916 were the Queen's University of Belfast, the National University of Ireland and Trinity College (Dublin University).

the involuted folds of its rules and regulations, its programmes, its minutes, its reports and special reports, its pains and penalties. I have often thought that the type of English education in Ireland was the Laocoon:[2] that agonising father and his sons seem to me like the teacher and the pupils of an Irish school, the strong limbs of the man and the slender limbs of the boys caught together and crushed together in the grip of an awful fate. And English education in Ireland has seemed to some like the bed of Procustes [*sic*], the bed on which all men that passed that way must lie, be it never so big for them, be it never so small for them: the traveller for whom it was too large had his limbs stretched until he filled it; the traveller for whom it was too small had his limbs chopped off until he fitted into it — comfortably.[3] It was a grim jest to play upon travellers. The English have done it to Irish children not by way of jest, but with a purpose. Our English-Irish systems took, and take, absolutely no cognisance of the differences between individuals, of the differences between localities, of the differences between urban and rural communities, of the differences springing from a different ancestry, Gaelic or Anglo-Saxon. Every school must conform to a type — and what a type! Every individual must conform to a type — and what a type! The teacher has not been at liberty, and in practice is not yet at liberty, to seek to discover the individual bents of his pupils, the hidden talent that is in every normal soul, to discover which and to cherish which, that it may in the fullness of time be put to some precious use, is the primary duty of the teacher. I knew one boy who passed through several schools a dunce and a laughing-stock; the National Board and the Intermediate Board had sat in judgment upon him and had damned him as a failure before men and angels. Yet a friend and fellow-worker of mine discovered that he was gifted with a wondrous sympathy for nature, that he loved and understood the ways of plants, that he had a strange minuteness and subtlety of observation — that, in short, he was the sort of boy likely to become an accomplished botanist....

The idea of a compulsory programme imposed by an external authority upon every child in every school in a country is the direct contrary of the root idea involved in education. Yet this is what we have in Ireland. In theory the primary schools have a certain amount of freedom; in practice they have none. Neither in theory nor in practice is such a thing as freedom dreamt of in the gloomy limbo whose presiding demon is the Board of Intermediate Education for Ireland. Education, indeed, reaches its nadir in the Irish Intermediate system. At the present moment there are 15,000 boys and girls pounding at a programme drawn up for them by certain persons sitting round a table in Hume Street. Precisely the same textbooks are being read tonight in every secondary school and college in Ireland. Two of Hawthorne's *Tanglewood Tales*,[4] with a few poems in English, will constitute the whole literary pabulum of three-quarters of the pupils of the Irish secondary schools during this twelvemonths. The teacher who seeks to give his pupils a wider horizon in literature does so at his peril. He will, no doubt, benefit his pupils, but he will infallibly reduce his results fees. As an intermediate teacher said to me, 'Culture is all very well in its way, but if you don't stick to your programme your boys won't pass.' 'Stick to your programme' is the strange device on the banner of the Irish Intermediate system; and the programme bulks so large that there is no room for education.

The first thing I plead for, therefore, is freedom: freedom for each school to shape its own programme in conformity with the circumstances of the school as to place, size, personnel, and so on; freedom again for the individual teacher to impart something of his own personality to his work, to bring his own peculiar gifts to the service of his pupils, to be, in short, a teacher, a master, one having an intimate and permanent relationship with his pupils, and not a mere part of the educational machine, a mere cog in the wheel; freedom finally for the individual pupil and scope for his development within the school and within the system. And I would promote this idea of freedom by the very organisation of the school itself, giving a certain autonomy not only to the school, but to the particular parts of the school: to the staff, of course, but also to the pupils, and, in a large school, to the various sub-divisions of the pupils. I do not plead

2. Laocoon, a Trojan priest, tried to save his two sons from sea-serpents, but they wreathed themselves about him and crushed him.
3. Procrustes, a thief from Attica, tied travellers on a bed. If their length exceeded that of the bed, he cut their limbs short; if they were too short for the bed, he stretched them until their length equalled that of the bed.
4. Nathaniel Hawthorne's *Tanglewood Tales for Girls and Boys* (1853) is a book of stories adapted from Greek myths.

for anarchy. I plead for freedom within the law, for liberty, not licence, for that true freedom which can exist only where there is discipline, which exists in fact because each, valuing his own freedom, respects also the freedom of others.

VIII

BACK TO THE SAGAS

That freedom may be availed of to the noble ends of education there must be, within the school system and within the school, an adequate inspiration. The school must make such an appeal to the pupil as shall resound throughout his after life, urging him always to be his best self, never his second-best self. Such an inspiration will come most adequately of all from religion. I do not think that there can be any education of which spiritual religion does not form an integral part; as it is the most important part of life, so it should be the most important part of education, which some have defined as a preparation for complete life. And inspiration will come also from the hero-stories of the world, and especially of our own people; from science and art if taught by people who are really scientists and artists, and not merely persons with certificates from Mr. T.W. Russell;[1] from literature enjoyed as literature and not studied as 'texts'; from the associations of the school place; finally and chiefly from the humanity and great-heartedness of the teacher.

A heroic tale is more essentially a factor in education than a proposition in Euclid. The story of Joan of Arc or the story of the young Napoleon means more for boys and girls than all the algebra in all the books. What the modern world wants more than anything else, what Ireland wants beyond all other modern countries, is a new birth of the heroic spirit. If our schools would set themselves that task, the task of fostering once again knightly courage and strength and truth — that type of efficiency rather than the peculiar type of efficiency demanded by the English Civil Service — we should have at least the beginning of an educational system. And what an appeal an Irish school system might have! What a rallying cry an Irish Minister of Education might give to young Ireland! When we were starting St. Enda's I said to my boys: 'We must re-create and perpetuate in Ireland the knightly tradition of Cuchulainn, "better is short life with honour than long life with dishonour"; "I care not though I were to live but one day and one night, if only my fame and my deeds live after me"; the noble tradition of the Fianna, "we, the Fianna, never told a lie, falsehood was never imputed to us"; "strength in our hands, truth on our lips, and cleanness in our hearts"; the Christ-like tradition of Colmcille, "if I die it shall be from the excess of the love I bear the Gael."' And to that antique evangel should be added the evangels of later days: the stories of Red Hugh and Wolfe Tone and Robert Emmet and John Mitchel and O'Donovan Rossa and Eoghan O'Growney.[2] I have seen Irish boys and girls moved inexpressibly by the story of Emmet or the story of Anne Devlin,[3] and I have always felt it to be legitimate to make use for educational purposes of an exaltation so produced.

The value of the national factor in education would appear to rest chiefly in this, that it addresses itself to the most generous side of the child's nature, urging him to live up to his finest self. If the true work of the teacher be, as I have said, to help the child to realise himself at his best and worthiest, the factor of nationality is of prime importance, apart from any ulterior propagandist views the teacher may cherish. The school system which neglects it commits, even from the purely pedagogic point of view, a primary blunder. It neglects one of the most powerful of educational resources.

It is because the English education system in Ireland has deliberately eliminated the national factor that it has so terrifically succeeded. For it has succeeded — succeeded in making slaves of us. And it has succeeded so well that we no longer realise that we are slaves. Some of us even think our chains ornamental, and are a little doubtful as to whether we shall be quite as comfortable and quite as respectable when they are hacked off.

It remains the crowning achievement of the 'National' and Intermediate systems that they have wrought such a change in this people that once loved freedom so passionately. Three-quarters of

1. Thomas Wallace Russell (1841-1920) was vice-president of the Department of Agriculture and Technical Instruction 1907-18. The department dealt with the secondary technical schools.

2. These well-known Irish heroes cover the period from the Gaelic world to the Fenians and the contemporary Gaelic revival, in which Rev. Eugene O'Growney (1863-99) was a prominent figure.

3. Anne Devlin, housekeeper to Robert Emmet, protected him after his abortive rising and, despite imprisonment and threats, refused to divulge any information about him.

a century ago there still remained in Ireland a stubborn Irish thing which Cromwell had not trampled out, which the Penal Laws had not crushed, which the horrors of '98 had not daunted, which Pitt had not purchased: a national consciousness enshrined mainly in a national language. After three-quarters of a century's education that thing is nearly lost.

A new education system in Ireland has to do more than restore a national culture. It has to restore manhood to a race that has been deprived of it. Along with its inspiration it must, therefore, bring a certain hardening. It must lead Ireland back to her sagas.

Finally, I say, inspiration must come from the teacher. If we can no longer send the children to the heroes and seers and scholars to be fostered, we can at least bring some of the heroes and seers and scholars to the schools. We can rise up against the system which tolerates as teachers the rejected of all other professions rather than demanding for so priest-like an office the highest souls and noblest intellects of the race. . . .

The fact is that, with rare exceptions, the men and women who are willing to work under the conditions as to personal dignity, freedom, tenure, and emolument which obtain in Irish schools are not the sort of men and women likely to make good educators. This part of the subject has been so much discussed in public that one need not dwell upon it. We are all alive to the truth that a teacher ought to be paid better than a policeman, and to the scandal of the fact that many an able and cultured man is working in Irish secondary schools at a salary less than that of the Viceroy's chauffeur.

O'DONOVAN ROSSA: GRAVESIDE PANEGYRIC (1915)

[In this famous oration, Pearse calls up, in the person of O'Donovan Rossa, the Fenian tradition of militancy and then links that with the United Irishmen of Tone and the Young Irelanders of John Mitchel. All the Irish revolutionary organizations — the IRB, the Irish Volunteers and the Irish Citizen Army — were at Glasnevin cemetery, as well as a huge crowd of onlookers. After the speech, there was a moment's silence, then a great wave of applause and cheering. Of all the Fenian funerals, this was the most successful and the most menacing.]

A Ġaeḋeala

Do hiarraḋ orm-sa laḃairt indiu ar son a ḃfuil cruinniġṫe ar an láṫair so agus ar son a ḃfuil beo de Ċlannaiḃ Gaeḋeal, ag molaḋ an leoṁain do leagamar i gcré annso agus ag griosaḋ meanman na gcarad atá go brónaċ ina ḋiaiḋ.

A ċáirde, ná bíoḋ brón éinne atá ina ṡeasaṁ ag an uaiġ so, aċt bíoḋ buiḋeaċas againn inar gcroiḋṫiḃ do Ḋia na ngrás do ċruṫuiġ anam uasal áluinn Ḋiarmuda Uí Ḋonnaḃáin Rosa agus ṫug sé ḟada ḋó ar an saoġal so.

Ba ċalma an fear ṫu, a Ḋiarmuid. Is tréan d'ḟearais caṫ ar son cirt do ċine, is ní beag ar ḟuilingis; agus ní ḋéanfaiḋ Gaeḋil dearmad ort go bráṫ na breiṫe.

Aċt, a ċáirde, ná bíoḋ brón orainn, aċt bíoḋ misneaċ inar gcroiḋṫiḃ agus bíoḋ neart inar gcuisleannaiḃ, óir cuiṁniġimís naċ mbíonn aon ḃás ann naċ mbíonn aiséirġe ina ḋiaiḋ, agus gurab as an uaiġ so agus as na huaġannaiḃ atá inar dtimċeall éireoċas saoirse Ġaeḋeal.

It has seemed right, before we turn away from this place in which we have laid the mortal remains of O'Donovan Rossa, that one among us should, in the name of all, speak the praise of that valiant man, and endeavour to formulate the thought and the hope that are in us as we stand around his grave. And if there is anything that makes it fitting that I, rather than some other, I rather than one of the grey-haired men who were young with him and shared in his labour and in his suffering, should speak here, it is perhaps that I may be taken as speaking on behalf of a new generation that has been re-baptised in the Fenian faith, and that has accepted the responsibility of carrying out the Fenian programme. I propose to you then that, here by the grave of this unrepentant Fenian, we renew our baptismal vows; that, here by the grave of this unconquered and unconquerable man, we ask of God, each one for himself, such unshakable purpose, such high and gallant courage, such unbreakable strength of soul as belonged to O'Donovan Rossa.

Deliberately here we avow ourselves, as he avowed himself in the dock, Irishmen of one allegiance only. We of the Irish Volunteers, and you others who are associated with us in today's task and duty, are bound together and must stand together henceforth in brotherly union for the achievement of the freedom of Ireland. And we know only one definition of freedom: it is Tone's definition, it is Mitchel's definition, it is Rossa's definition. Let no man blaspheme the cause that the dead generations of Ireland served by giving it any other name and definition than their name and their definition.

We stand at Rossa's grave not in sadness but rather in exaltation of spirit that it has been given to us to come thus into so close a communion with that brave and splendid Gael. Splendid and holy causes are served by men who are themselves splendid and holy. O'Donovan Rossa was splendid in the proud manhood of him, splendid in the heroic grace of him, splendid in the Gaelic strength and clarity and truth of him. And all that splendour and pride and strength was compatible with a humility and a simplicity of devotion to Ireland, to all that was olden and beautiful and Gaelic in Ireland, the holiness and simplicity of patriotism of a Michael O'Clery or of an Eoghan O'Growney.[1] The clear true eyes of this man almost alone in his day visioned Ireland as we of today would surely have her: not free merely, but Gaelic as well; not Gaelic merely, but free as well.

In a closer spiritual communion with him now than ever before or perhaps ever again, in a spiritual communion with those of his day, living and dead, who suffered with him in English prisons, in communion of spirit too with our own dear comrades who suffer in English prisons today, and speaking on their behalf as well as our own, we pledge to Ireland our love, and we pledge to English rule in Ireland our hate. This is a place of peace, sacred to the dead, where men should speak with all charity and with all restraint; but I hold it a Christian thing, as O'Donovan Rossa held it, to hate evil, to hate untruth, to hate oppression, and, hating them, to strive to overthrow them. Our foes are strong and wise and wary; but, strong and wise and wary as they are, they cannot undo the miracles of God who ripens in the hearts of young men the seeds sown by the young men of a former generation. And the seeds sown by the young men of '65 and '67 are coming to their miraculous ripening today. Rulers and Defenders of Realms had need to be wary if they would guard against such processes. Life springs from death; and from the graves of patriot men and women spring living nations. The Defenders of this Realm have worked well in secret and in the open. They think that they have pacified Ireland. They think that they have purchased half of us and intimidated the other half. They think that they have foreseen everything, think that they have provided against everything; but the fools, the fools, the fools! — they have left us our Fenian dead, and while Ireland holds these graves, Ireland unfree shall never be at peace.

1. Michael O'Clery (1575-1643), a Franciscan friar, was the compiler, with three others, of *The Annals of the Four Masters* (*c.*1636). O'Growney's *Simple Lessons in Irish* (1897-1900) and his role in the Gaelic League revival, linked him, in Pearse's mind, with O'Clery's attempt to retrieve the fortunes of the Gaelic culture.

from: THE SOVEREIGN PEOPLE (1916)

[In this pamphlet, written in March 1916, Pearse defines the genealogy of Irish revolution and describes its spiritual dynamic. He plainly admits that it is he who is making 'the necessary synthesis' of all the elements that have preceded him. Although very much in the Fenian tradition, Pearse is unlike all the predecessors he mentions, in his religious emotionalism and in his conviction that religion and revolution can be co-ordinated in such a way as to produce, as a political reality, an Irish nationhood.]

... This denunciation of woe against the enemy of Irish freedom is as necessary a part of the religion of Irish nationality as are Davis's pleas for love and concord between brother Irishmen. The Church that preaches peace and goodwill launches her anathemas against the enemies of peace and goodwill. Mitchel's gospel is part of the testament, even as Davis's is; it but reveals a different facet of the truth. A man must accept the whole testament; but a man may prefer Davis to Mitchel, just as a man may prefer the gospel according to St. Luke, the kindliest and most human of the gospels, to the gospel of St. John.

Mitchel's teaching contains nothing that is definitely new and his. He accepted Tone; he accepted Davis; he accepted in particular Lalor; and he summed up and expressed all their teaching in a language transfigured by wrath and vision. Tone is the intellectual ancestor of the whole modern movement of Irish nationalism, of Davis, and Lalor, and Mitchel, and all their followers; Davis is the immediate ancestor of the spiritual and imaginative part of that movement, embodied in our day in the Gaelic League; Lalor is the immediate ancestor of the specifically democratic part of that movement, embodied today in the more virile labour organisations; Mitchel is the immediate ancestor of Fenianism, the noblest and most terrible manifestation of this unconquered nation.

And just as all of the four have reached, in different terms, the same gospel, making plain in turn different facets of the same truth, so the movements I have indicated are but facets of a whole, different expressions, and each one a necessary expression, of the august, though denied, truth of Irish Nationhood; nationhood in virtue of an old spiritual tradition of nationality, nationhood involving Separation and Sovereignty, nationhood resting on and guaranteeing the freedom of all the men and women of the nation and placing them in effective possession of the physical conditions necessary to the reality and to the perpetuation of their freedom, nationhood declaring and establishing and defending itself by the good smiting sword. I who have been in and of each of these movements make here the necessary synthesis, and in the name of all of them I assert the forgotten truth, and ask all who accept it to testify to it with me, here in our day and, if need be, with our blood.

At the end of a former essay[1] I set that prophecy of Mitchel's as to the coming of a time when the kindred and tongues and nations of the earth should give their banners to the wind; and his prayer that he, John Mitchel, might live to see it, and that on that great day of the Lord he might have breath and strength enough to stand under Ireland's immortal Green.[2] John Mitchel did not live to see it. He died, an old man, forty years before its dawning. But the day of the Lord is here, and you and I have lived to see it.

And we are young. And God has given us strength and courage and counsel. May He give us victory.

1. 'Ghosts' (1915).
2. Mitchel's words in *Jail Journal* are: 'God! let me live to see it. On that great day of the Lord, when the kindreds and tongues and nations of the old earth shall give their banners to the wind, let this poor carcase have but breath enough and strength enough to stand under Ireland's immortal Green!'

ROGER CASEMENT
(1864-1916)

from: SPEECH FROM THE DOCK (1916)

[The attorney general who led the prosecution against Casement was F.E. Smith, later 1st earl of Birkenhead. Smith was aide-de-camp to Sir Edward Carson in the Ulster Volunteer Force (hence his nickname 'Galloper Smith'). Casement was charged under an Act of Edward III (25 Edward III, Cap 2) passed in 1351; that declared it treasonable 'If a man be adherent to the King's enemies in his realm giving to them aid and comfort in the realm or elsewhere. . . .' Smith argued that there should be a comma in each case after the word 'realm'; this apparently made a sufficient difference in law to convict Casement. Smith was himself, through his participation in the Ulster rebellion, open to conviction on the same grounds, with or without commas.

A.M. Sullivan, who conducted Casement's defence, argued against the inclusion of commas in the hope of proving that Casement could not be tried for treason if the act had been committed outside the king's realm, i.e. in Germany. Sullivan intended to make a contrast between the treasonable utterances of the unionists, particularly Smith, before the Great War and those of Casement after it had begun. But he failed to do so, being reluctant to alienate the authorities. Smith later became lord chancellor and was a member of the British delegation that negotiated the Treaty of December 1921.

It was Casement's trial and execution which made him important to the Irish nationalist cause. The British cabinet's decision to circulate the 'Black Diaries', showing Casement to be a homosexual, was a skilful piece of character assassination which recalled the cruder efforts of *The Times*'s forgeries against Parnell. In a similar fashion, Smith, as prosecutor of Casement and henchman of Carson, recalled Oscar Wilde's trial, at which Carson had been prosecutor. The Parnell, Wilde and Casement trials had in common the sexual element and the consequent exploitation of feelings of revenge and outrage at the perpetrators. The transition, in the cases of Parnell and Casement, from the sexual to the political 'treason' is linked up with accusations of forgery, deceit and black propaganda. All three cases contributed, in later years, to that favourite species of memoir, 'Famous Trials'.

The political repercussions of the Casement trial were complex. One element of the defence strategy, discussed at George Bernard Shaw's house during the trial, but not used by the inert and careful Alexander Sullivan, counsel for the defence, was the suggestion that Casement should demand to be treated as a prisoner of war. With Casement's burial in quicklime in Pentonville prison, the indignity habitual in the case of a murderer, the issue was further complicated. The British government's policy of criminalization of Irish political offenders had been carried so far in this instance, with the publication of the diaries, the burial, the charge of treason under an antiquated act, the prosecution led by a man notoriously guilty of rebellion against the crown, that it brought to what Irish people considered a scandalous cumulation the process that had begun with the Treason-Felony Act in 1848. The execution of Roger Casement and the accompanying distortions and propaganda were remembered with bitterness for several decades.]

... I may say at once, my lord, that I protest against the jurisdiction of this court in my case on this charge ... and the argument that I am now going to read is addressed not to this court, but to my own countrymen. There is an objection, possibly not good in law, but surely good on moral grounds, against the application to me here of this old English statute, 565 years old, that seeks to deprive an Irishman today of life and honour, not for 'adhering to the king's enemies', but for adhering to his own people. When this statute was passed in 1351, what was the state of men's minds on the question of a far higher allegiance — that of a man to God and His kingdom? The law of that day did not permit a man to forsake his Church, or deny his God, save with his life. The 'heretic' then had the same doom as the 'traitor'. Today, a man may forswear God and His heavenly kingdom without fear or penalty — all earlier statutes having gone the way of Nero's edicts against the Christians; but that Constitutional phantom, 'the King', can still dig up from the dungeons and torture-chambers of the Dark Ages a law that takes a man's life and limb for an exercise of conscience....

Judicial assassination today is reserved only for one race of the king's subjects — for Irishmen, for those who cannot forget their allegiance to the realm of Ireland.... With all respect, I assert this court is to me, an Irishman, not a jury of my peers to try me in this vital issue; for it is patent to every man of conscience that I have an indefeasible right, if tried at all under this statute of high treason, to be tried in Ireland, before an Irish Court and by an Irish Jury. This court, this jury, the public opinion of this country, England, cannot but be prejudiced in varying degrees against me, most of all in time of war. I did not land in England. I landed in Ireland. It was to Ireland I came; to Ireland I wanted to come; and the last place I desired to land in was England.

But for the Attorney-General of England there is only England; there is no Ireland; there is only the law of England, no right of Ireland; the liberty of Ireland and of Irishmen is to be judged by the power of England. Yet for me, the Irish outlaw, there is a land of Ireland, a right of Ireland, and a charter for all Irishmen to appeal to, in the last resort, a charter that the very statutes of England itself cannot deprive us of — nay, more, a charter that Englishmen themselves assert as the fundamental bond of law that connects the two kingdoms. This charge of high treason involves a moral responsibility, as the very terms of the indictment against myself recite, inasmuch as I committed the acts I am charged with to 'the evil example of others in the like case'. What was the evil example I set to others in the like case, and who were these others? The 'evil example' charged is that I asserted the right of my own country, and 'the others' to whom I appealed to aid my endeavour were my own countrymen. The example was given not to Englishmen, but to Irishmen, and 'the like case' can never arise in England, but only in Ireland. To Englishmen, I set no evil example, for I made no appeal to them. I asked no Englishman to help me. I asked Irishmen to fight for their rights. The 'evil example' was only to other Irishmen, who might come after me and in 'like case' seek to do as I did. How, then, since neither my example nor my appeal was addressed to Englishmen, can I be rightly tried by them?

If I did wrong in making that appeal to Irishmen to join with me in an effort to fight for Ireland, it is by Irishmen, and by them alone, I can be rightfully judged. From this court and its jurisdiction I appeal to those I am alleged to have wronged and injured by my 'evil example', and claim that they alone are competent to decide my guilt or innocence. If they find me guilty, the statute may affix the penalty; but the statute does not override or annul my right to seek judgment at their hands. This is so fundamental a right, so natural, so obvious, that it is clear the Crown were aware of it when they brought me by force and by stealth from Ireland to this country. It was not I who landed in England, but the Crown that dragged me here, away from my own country, to which I had returned with a price upon my head; away from my own countrymen, whose loyalty is not in doubt, and safe from the judgment of my peers, whose judgment I do not shrink from. I admit no other judgment but theirs. I accept no verdict save at their hands.

I assert from this dock that I am being tried here, not because it is just, but because it is unjust. Place me before a jury of my countrymen, be it Protestant or Catholic, Unionist or Nationalist, Sinn Feinach or Orange, and I shall accept the verdict, and bow to the statute and all its penalties. But I shall accept no meaner finding against me than that of those whose loyalty I endangered by my example and to whom alone I made appeal. If they adjudge me guilty, then guilty I am. It is not I who am afraid of their verdict — it is the Crown. If this is not so, why fear the test? I fear it not. I demand it as my right. This is the condemnation of English rule, of English-made law, of English government in Ireland, that it dare not rest on the will of the Irish people, but exists in defiance of their will: that it is a rule derived not from right, but from conquest. But conquest, my lord, gives no title; and, if it exists over the body, it fails over the mind. It can exert no empire over men's reason and judgment and affections; and it is from this law of conquest that I appeal. I would add that the generous expressions of sympathy extended to me from many quarters, particularly from America, have touched me very much. In that country, as in my own, I am sure my motives are understood, and not misjudged — for the achievement of their liberty has been an abiding inspiration to Irishmen, and to all men elsewhere, rightly struggling to be free. . . .

My counsel has referred to the Ulster Volunteer movement, and I will not touch at length upon that ground, save only to say this: that neither I nor any of the leaders of the Irish Volunteers, who were founded in Dublin in November, 1913, had any quarrel with the Ulster Volunteers as such, who were born a year earlier. Our movement was not directed against them, but against the men who misused and misdirected the courage, the sincerity and the local patriotism of the men of the north of Ireland. On the contrary, we welcomed the coming of the Ulster Volunteers, even while we deprecated the aims and intentions of those Englishmen who sought to pervert to an English party use — to the mean purposes of their own bid for place and power in England — the armed activity of simple Irishmen. We aimed at winning the Ulster Volunteers to the cause of a United Ireland. We aimed at uniting all Irishmen in a natural and national bond of cohesion based on mutual self-respect. Our hope was a natural one and, were we left to ourselves, not hard to accomplish. If external influences of disintegration would but leave us alone, we were sure that nature itself must bring us together. It was not we, the Irish Volunteers, who broke the law, but a British party. The Government had permitted the Ulster Volunteers to be armed by Englishmen, to threaten not merely an English party in its hold on office, but to threaten that party through the lives and blood of Irishmen.

The battle was to be fought in Ireland in order that the political 'outs' of today should be the 'ins' of tomorrow in Great Britain. A law designed for the benefit of Ireland was to be met, not on the floor of Parliament, where the fight had indeed been won, but on the field of battle much nearer home, where the armies would be composed of Irishmen slaying each other for some English party gain; and the British Navy would be the chartered 'transports' that were to bring to our shores a numerous assemblage of military and ex-military experts in the congenial and profitable business of holding down subject populations abroad. Our choice lay in submitting to foreign lawlessness or resisting it, and we did not hesitate to choose. But while the law-breakers had armed their would-be agents openly, and had been permitted to arm them openly, we were met within a few days of the founding of our movement — that aimed at a United Ireland from within — by Government action from without, directed against our obtaining any arms at all.

The manifesto of the Irish Volunteers, promulgated at a public meeting in Dublin, November 25th, 1913, stated with certainty the aims of the organisation, as I have outlined them. If the aims set out in that manifesto were a threat to the unity of the British Empire, then so much the worse for the Empire. An Empire that can only be held together by one section of its governing population perpetually holding down and sowing dissension among a smaller but none the less governing section, must have some canker at its heart, some ruin at its root. The Government that permitted the arming of those whose leaders declared that Irish national unity was a thing that should be opposed by force of arms, within nine days of the issue of our manifesto of goodwill to Irishmen of every creed and class, took steps to nullify our efforts by prohibiting the import of all arms into Ireland as if it had been a hostile and blockaded coast. And this Proclamation of the 4th December, 1913, known as the Arms Proclamation, was itself based on an illegal interpretation of the law, as the Chief Secretary[1] has now publicly confessed. This Proclamation was met by the loyalists of Great Britain with an act of still more lawless defiance — an act of widespread gun-running into Ulster, that was denounced by the Lord Chancellor of England as 'grossly illegal and utterly unconstitutional'. How did the Irish Volunteers meet the incitements to civil war that were uttered by the party of law and order in England?[2]

I can answer for my own acts and speeches. While one English party was responsible for preaching a doctrine of hatred, designed to bring about civil war in Ireland, the other — and that the party in power — took no active steps to restrain a propaganda that found its advocates in the Army, Navy and Privy Council — in the Houses of Parliament and in the State Church — a propaganda the methods of whose expression were so 'grossly illegal and utterly unconstitutional' that even the Lord Chancellor of England could find only words and no repressive action to apply to them. Since lawlessness sat in high places in England, and laughed at the law as at the custodians of the law, what wonder was it that Irishmen should refuse to accept the verbal protestations of an English Lord Chancellor as a sufficient safeguard for their liberties? I know not how all my colleagues on the Volunteer Committee in Dublin received the growing menace, but those with whom I was in closest co-operation redoubled, in face of all these threats from without, our efforts to unite all Irishmen from within. Our appeals were made to Protestant and Unionist as much almost as to Catholic and Nationalist Irishmen. We hoped that by the exhibition of affection and goodwill on our part towards our political opponents in Ireland, we should yet succeed in winning them from the side of an English party, whose sole interest in our country lay in its oppression in the past, and in the present in its degradation to the mean and narrow needs of their political animosities.

It is true that they based their actions — so they averred — on 'fears for the Empire' and on a very diffuse loyalty that took in all the peoples of the Empire, save only the Irish. That blessed *Empire* that bears so paradoxical resemblance to charity! For if charity begins at home, *Empire* begins in other men's homes, and both may cover a multitude of sins. I, for one, was determined that Ireland was much more to me than *Empire*, and that, if charity begins at home, so must loyalty. Since arms were so necessary to make our organisation a reality, and to give to the minds of Irishmen, menaced with the most outrageous threats, a sense of security, it was our bounden duty to get arms before all else. I decided, with this end in view, to go to America, with surely a better right to appeal to Irishmen there for help in an hour of great national trial than those envoys of *Empire* could assert for their week-end descents on Ireland, or their appeals to Germany. If, as the right honourable gentleman, the present Attorney-General,[3] asserted in a speech at Manchester, Nationalists would neither fight for Home Rule nor pay for it, it was our duty to show him that *we* knew how to do both. Within a few weeks of my arrival in the United States, the fund that had been opened to secure arms for the Volunteers of Ireland amounted to many thousands of pounds. In every case the money subscribed, whether it came from the purse of the wealthy man or the still readier pocket of the poor man, was Irish gold.

Then came the war! — which, as Mr. Birrell said, 'upset all calculations'. It upset mine no less than Mr. Birrell's, and put an end to my peaceful effort in America. A constitutional movement in Ireland is never very far from a breach of the constitution, as the loyalists of Ulster have been so eager to show us. A constitution, to be maintained intact, must be

1. Augustine Birrell (1850-1933), chief secretary for Ireland 1907-16. The Arms Embargo was a reimposition of an earlier Arms Act.
2. In April 1914, the Ulster Volunteer Force landed a consignment of arms and ammunition at Larne, Co. Antrim. Although condemned as unconstitutional, the action was ignored by the police and the army.
3. F.E. Smith (1872-1930), the prosecutor, served as attorney general 1915-18.

the achievement and the pride of the people themselves, must rest on their own free will and on their own determination to maintain it, instead of being something resident in another land, whose chief representative is an armed force — armed not to protect the population, but to hold it down. We had seen the workings of 'the Irish Constitution' in the refusal of the Army of Occupation at the Curragh to obey the orders of the Crown.[4] And now that we were told the first duty of an Irishman was to enter that army, in return for a promissory note, payable after death — a scrap of paper that might or might not be redeemed — I felt, over there in America, that my first duty was to keep Irishmen at home in the only army that could safeguard our national existence. If small nationalities were to be the pawn in this game of embattled giants, I saw no reason why Ireland should shed her blood in any cause but her own, and, if that be treason beyond the seas, I am not ashamed to avow it, or to answer for it here with my life. And when we had the doctrine of Unionist loyalty at last — 'Mausers[5] and Kaisers, and any King you like', and I have heard that at Hamburg, not far from Limburg on the Lahn — I felt that I needed no other warrant than that these words conveyed, to go forth and do likewise.[6]

The difference between us was that the Unionist champions chose a path which they felt would lead to the woolsack, while I went a road I knew must lead to the dock and the event proved we were both right. The difference between us was that my 'treason' was based on a ruthless sincerity that forced me to attempt in time and season to carry out in action what I said in words, whereas their treason lay in verbal incitements that they knew need never be made good in their bodies. And so I am prouder to stand here today, in the traitor's dock, to answer to this impeachment, than to fill the place of my right honourable accusers.

We have been told, have been asked to hope, that after this war Ireland will get Home Rule as a reward for the life-blood shed in a cause which, whoever else its success may benefit, can surely not benefit Ireland. And what will Home Rule be in return for what its vague promise has taken, and still hopes to take, from Ireland? It is not necessary to climb the painful stairs of Irish history — to review the long list of British promises, made only to be broken; of Irish hopes, raised only to be dashed to the ground. Home Rule, when it comes, if come it does, will find Ireland drained of all that is vital to its very existence, unless it be that unquenchable hope that we build on the graves of the dead. We are told that if Irishmen go by the thousands to die *not* for Ireland, but for Flanders, for Belgium, for a patch of sand on the deserts of Mesopotamia, or a rocky trench on the heights of Gallipoli,[7] they were winning self-government for Ireland. But if they dare to lay down their lives on their native soil, if they dare to dream even that freedom can be won only at home by men resolved to fight for it there, then they are traitors to their country.

But history is not so recorded in other lands. In Ireland alone, in this twentieth century, is loyalty held to be a crime. If loyalty be something less than love and more than law, then we have had enough of such loyalty for Ireland or Irishmen. Self-government is our right, a thing born in us at birth, a thing no more to be doled out to us or withheld from us by another people than the right to life itself — the right to feel the sun or smell the flowers, or love our kind. It is only from the convict these things are withheld, for crime committed and proven — and Ireland, that has wronged no man, that has injured no land, that has sought no dominion over others — Ireland is being treated today among the nations of the world as if she were a convicted criminal. If it be treason to fight against such an unnatural fate as this, then I am proud to be a rebel, and shall cling to my 'rebellion' with the last drop of my blood. If there be no right of rebellion against a state of things that no savage tribe would endure without resistance, then I am sure that it is better for men to fight and die without right than to live in such a state of right as this. Where all your rights have become only an accumulated wrong, where men must beg with bated breath for leave to subsist in their own land, to think their own

4. The Curragh Incident or Mutiny, as it is called, occurred in March 1914. Led by Major-General Hubert Gough, fifty-six officers at the Curragh Military Camp in County Kildare decided to offer their resignations rather than move against the Ulster opponents of Home Rule.
5. A Mauser was a high-velocity magazine rifle named after P.P. von Mauser (1838-1914), a German firearms inventor.
6. Casement is referring to the fact that Ulster unionists had attempted to get arms from Germany and is reminding the court of their dubious loyalty to the English crown, given their earlier actions and pronouncements. He himself had tried to form an Irish brigade from Irish prisoners of war. A number of them had been assembled at Limburg on the river Lahn, north-west of Frankfurt, in December 1915.

7. All sites of bloody battles in World War I.

thoughts, to sing their own songs, to garner the fruits of their own labours, and, even while they beg, to see things inexorably withdrawn from them — then, surely, it is a braver, a saner and a truer thing to be a rebel in act and deed against such circumstances as these than tamely to accept it as the natural lot of men.

AMENDED CONSTITUTION OF THE IRISH REPUBLICAN BROTHERHOOD (1873)

[Bulmer Hobson reprinted this as an appendix to his memoirs, *Ireland Yesterday and Tomorrow* (1968). This is the Constitution adopted when the IRB was reorganized in 1873. It remained in place until at least after 1916, perhaps until 1921. Hobson writes: 'This copy was made by me from a copy printed for the Supreme Council about 1910 which in turn was taken from older copies. Only a few copies were ever in existence at any one time.' He signed this statement and dated it 29.4.1947.

For Hobson, and one would guess for James Stephens, whose impress remained on the constitution after he had been removed from office, one of the crucial features of the document is clause 3, in which the IRB declares itself to be subject to the decision of the Irish nation on the question of starting a war with England. This is the clause ignored by the caucus of IRB men within the Irish Volunteers in 1916.]

Whereas the Irish People have never ceased to struggle for the recovery of their independence since the date of its destruction and *whereas* it has on this 17th Day of March, the day of our Patron Saint, St. Patrick, 1873, been resolved by a convention of Irish Patriots, held in Dublin and representing associations of Irishmen existing in various parts of Ireland, England and Scotland to amend the Constitution of the present Irish Revolutionary Organisation for the purpose of overthrowing English power in Ireland, and of establishing an independent Irish Republic. Said organisation being known as The Irish Republican Brotherhood and governed by a Council entitled 'The Supreme Council of the Irish Republican Brotherhood and Government of the Irish Republic.' The following is declared to be and promulgated as the Amended Constitution of the Irish Republican Brotherhood and of the Supreme Council of the Irish Republican Brotherhood and Government of the Irish Republic.

CONSTITUTION OF THE IRISH REPUBLICAN BROTHERHOOD

1. The I.R.B. is and shall be composed of Irishmen, irrespective of class or creed resident in Ireland, England, Scotland, America, Australia, and in all other lands where Irishmen live, who are willing to labour for the establishment of a free and independent Republican Government in Ireland.
2. The I.R.B. whilst labouring to prepare Ireland for the task of recovering her independence by force of arms shall confine itself in time of peace to the exercise of moral influences — the cultivation of union and brotherly love amongst Irishmen — the propagation of Republican Principles and the spreading of a knowledge of the national rights of Ireland.
3. The I.R.B. shall await the decision of the Irish Nation as expressed by a majority of the Irish people as to the fit hour of inaugurating a war against England and shall, pending such an emergency, lend its support to every movement calculated to advance the cause of Irish independence, consistently with the preservation of its own integrity.
4. The mode of initiating members into the I.R.B. shall be the rendering of the following Oath of Allegiance to its Government:

   'In the presence of God. I .... do solemnly swear that I will do my utmost to establish the national independence of Ireland, and that I will bear true allegiance to the Supreme Council of the Irish Republican Brotherhood and Government of the Irish Republic and implicitly obey the Constitution of the Irish Republican Brotherhood and all my superior officers and that I will preserve inviolable the secrets of the organisation.'

5. No one shall be inducted into the I.R.B. whose character for sobriety, truth, valour and obedience to Authority cannot bear scrutiny.
6. Each member of the I.R.B. shall contribute according to his means for the production of war materials and also towards the expense of keeping up communication in the different divisions of the I.R.B. and for maintaining the efficiency of the Supreme Council.
7. In every case where arms are lost through negligence the department through the neglect of which the loss has occurred shall be responsible for the value of the arms.
8. The members of the I.R.B. resident in towns or parishes shall be directed and governed by an officer to be entitled a centre and to be elected by the members of the I.R.B. each body of members electing the centre for their own town or parish.
9. The members and centres of the I.R.B. shall be directed and governed by an officer to be entitled a County Centre and to be elected by the centres of the respective counties, and in England and Scotland the towns shall be grouped into districts corresponding in population to the counties in Ireland and each district shall be directed and governed by a District Centre who shall be elected by the Centres of his district.
10. The I.R.B. shall be divided into seven electoral divisions — to wit — Leinster, Ulster, Munster, Connaught, North of England, South of England and Scotland and in each division one Civil and one Military Secretary shall be elected by the County or District Centres and the duty of the Civil Secretary shall be to act in all respects as deputy of the member of the Supreme Council of his division and in the event of the removal of said member by the act of the enemy, disability or death the Civil Secretary shall exercise authority in the division until a new member of the Supreme Council shall have been elected in the manner provided for in the Constitution of the Supreme Council; and the duties of the Military Secretary shall be to execute all orders received by him in relation to the procuring, distribution and safe keeping of arms and ammunition.
11. The term of office of all members of the I.R.B. shall be subject to removal at any time by a two-thirds vote of the electoral body.
12. The divisional officers shall have power to make all bye-laws framed in accordance with the spirit of the Constitution — which they may deem necessary for the purpose of local organisation.
13. Each County or District Centre shall on or before the last day in each month send in a report of the position and progress of affairs to the Civil Secretary of his division who shall forthwith send it to the member of the Supreme Council for the Division, by whom it shall be forwarded to the Secretary of the Supreme Council.
14. In each of the large cities, to wit — Dublin, Cork, Limerick, Belfast, London and Glasgow — a committee of five shall be elected by the centres whose duty shall consist in directing local organisation subject to the supervision and control of the County or District Centres.
15. No member of the I.R.B. shall receive any information respecting the organisation, except what shall be necessary for the performance of his duty, and no member of the I.R.B. shall be at liberty to make use of any such information he may accidentally acquire.

AMENDED CONSTITUTION OF THE SUPREME COUNCIL OF THE I.R.B. AND GOVERNMENT OF THE IRISH REPUBLIC

1. The Supreme Council of the Irish Republican Brotherhood and Government of the Irish Republic is and shall be composed of eleven members; seven of said members shall be elected by the seven electoral divisions as marked out in the Constitution of the Irish Republican Brotherhood, and the remaining four shall be honorary members and shall be elected by the seven, to whom alone their names shall be known and enactments of the Government so constituted shall be the laws of the Irish Republic until the territory thereof shall have been recovered from the English Enemy and a permanent Government established.
2. The manner of the election of the before-mentioned seven members of the Supreme Council shall be as follows:

The County or District Centres shall be assembled in convention and shall elect a Committee of five of their number, who under seal of an oath of secrecy, shall elect the member of the Supreme Council for the division whereunto they belong.

3. The term of office of the Supreme Council shall be two years but any member may be removed at any time by a two-thirds vote of his constituents or a two-thirds vote of the Supreme Council and any member of the S.C. wishing to resign will give one month's notice to his constituents and to the S.C.
4. There shall be an Executive of the Supreme Council, composed of the President, Secretary and Treasurer of that body, the decision of any two of whom shall be binding on all.
5. The duty of the President of the Supreme Council shall be to direct the working of the Irish Republican Brotherhood in all its departments, subject to the control of the Supreme Council.
6. The appointment, suspension and removal of all departmental officers shall be vested in the Executive subject to the approval of the Supreme Council.
7. No member of the Supreme Council or officers in the employment thereof shall be in receipt of any salary from the funds of the Supreme Council of the Irish Republican Brotherhood.
8. The authority of the Supreme Council shall be unquestioned by those who have become, or may hereafter become members of the I.R.B. and the Supreme Council is hereby declared in fact as well as by right the sole Government of the Irish Republic and has authority to levy taxes, negotiate loans, make war and peace and do all other acts necessary for the protection of the Irish Republic and members of the Supreme Council shall be bound to this constitution and to one another by an oath of fidelity and inviolable secrecy and every act or attempted act of any member of the I.R.B. to subvert the authority of the Supreme Council shall in time of peace be a grave misdemeanour and punishable accordingly and in time of war every such act or attempted act shall be treason and punishable with death.
9. The Supreme Council reserves to itself the right of dealing with all friendly powers on all matters concerning the welfare of Ireland and the advancement of the cause of Irish Independence.
10. Executive power shall never be vested in one man, but shall be vested in the President, Secretary and Treasurer of the Supreme Council.
11. Every member of the I.R.B. and every member of the Supreme Council owes Civil and Military obedience to the Executive of the Supreme Council and the President thereof is in fact as well as by right, President of the Irish Republic.
12. In the event of the Supreme Council being unavoidably reduced in number, the member or remaining members shall exercise the authority of the Supreme Council until such time as the vacancies shall have been filled up which shall be done as soon as possible and the same for the Executive.
13. The military authority shall at all times be and remain subject to the Civil Government and shall never be permitted to arrogate to itself the power of legislating or of restraining in any way the Constitution of the Irish Republic as promulgated by the Supreme Council.
14. At each meeting of the Supreme Council the members thereof shall hand in a summarised statement of the receipts and expenditure of the respective divisions.
15. The Supreme Council shall have power to award Capital Punishment only in cases of treason and the crime of treason is hereby defined as any wilful act or word on the part of any member of the I.R.B. or of the Supreme Council calculated to betray the cause of Irish Independence and subserve the interest of the British or any other foreign Government in Ireland to the detriment of Irish Independence.
16. The Supreme Council shall appoint a secret court in each of the seven divisions of the I.R.B. for the trial of all members charged with the commission of treason or grave misdemeanours.
17. The Supreme Council shall undertake the punishment of all minor offences committed by members of the I.R.B. once the offending members have removed from the division whereunto they belong and in cases where members unlawfully appropriate moneys entrusted to them for national purposes, such

members shall be expelled [from] the I.R.B. and the Supreme Council shall draw up a list of the names of such members, and circulate it through all parts of the I.R.B. and forward copies of it to representative Irishmen in every part of the world in order that those who rob the treasury of their country may be held up to the execration of all honest men.

18. In the Irish Republic there shall be no state Religion but every citizen shall be free to worship God according to his conscience, and perfect freedom of worship shall be guaranteed as a right and not granted as a privilege.
19. The Supreme Council shall have power to alter or revise the foregoing constitution of the Irish Republican Brotherhood and of the Supreme Council of the Irish Republican Brotherhood and Government of the Irish Republic but whenever it is contemplated to make any alterations it shall be necessary to give one month's notice of the meeting of the Supreme Council at which such alteration is proposed to be effected; and it shall require a two-thirds vote of the Supreme Council to make the proposed change.

By Order of
THE SUPREME COUNCIL

IV PARNELL AND PARLIAMENTARIANISM 1891-1918

CHARLES STEWART PARNELL

(1846-91)

from: WORDS OF THE DEAD CHIEF (1892)

[Between the death of Daniel O'Connell in 1847 and the Easter Rising of 1916, C. S. Parnell was the dominant figure in Irish politics — for all the brevity of that dominance. He became leader of the Irish Party in the Westminster parliament in 1877, and died (embattled) fourteen years later in October 1891. Although he was at the head of the New Departure — an alliance of parliamentary and extra-parliamentary forces, including the Land League and the American Fenian exiles — his sphere of operation was almost exclusively the parliamentary party. He had no effective role in municipal or civic life in Ireland; and his aloof personality both protected him from, and made him ultimately vulnerable to, the machinations of committees and lobbies. Finally, as a protestant landlord (of no strong religious convictions), he had little contact with the ecclesiastical or parochial aspects of Irish politics.

Parnell made his mark initially by his trenchant disregard of parliamentary manners, declaring on 30 June 1876 in the House of Commons: 'I wish to say as publicly and directly as I can that I do not believe, and never shall believe, that any murder was committed at Manchester.' This reference to an incident in the Fenians' campaign, in which a police sergeant had been killed, won him the admiration of the 'advanced section' of Irish public opinion, but scarcely displays any great rhetorical ability. At the height of his career, Parnell managed a campaign of parliamentary obstruction that involved marathon speeches rather than persuasive talent. Even in his last days, after he had been rejected by many in his old party and had been denounced by English liberals and Irish bishops, his performances on the hustings (see below) do not dazzle or impress, either intellectually or emotionally. In policy, Parnell was highly flexible, while giving the appearance of heroic dedication to a cause. In intellect, he was not distinguished; and in breadth of cultural reference he was, frankly, very narrow indeed.

It remains undeniable that Parnell dominated the imagination of at least two generations: those born (like himself) after O'Connell's achievement of catholic emancipation, and those (like James Joyce) born when Parnell himself already had stepped onto the public stage of politics. His personal presence has been much assessed as an influence; his ability to unite (however temporarily) diverse sectors of Irish public opinion may explain his reputation in life, but scarcely can explain the Christmas dinner scene in Joyce's *A Portrait* or the vehement and self-wounding attachment of so late a poem of W. B. Yeats's as 'Parnell's Funeral' (1934).

One clue to the enigma of Parnell may be found in the extracts printed below. Although these were not chosen with the intention of proving the point, they do record

Parnell's reiterated acknowledgment of *public opinion*. His was the first Irish political movement ably served (both at home in Ireland, in the United States, and even in Britain) by a commercially vigorous newspaper press. In the former two countries, there was a sympathetic section of the press; in the last named, Parnell's vindication in the inquiry concerning letters published by *The Times* constituted a triumph over a public opinion he had often scorned. While the parliamentary record duly preserved the tedious exercises in filibustering by which he manipulated the English parties, his loyal press in Dublin and New York took up the texts of his extra-parliamentary utterances. These were occasionally notable for a single phrase but, as *Words of the Dead Chief* indicates, such phrases were easily isolable. Even Parnell's notorious fall can be attributed to the power of public opinion at least as plausibly as it can be explained in terms of substantive politics. Journalists were prominent among both his lieutenants and his ultimate opponents.

The texts given below are, in every case, from the 1892 anthology edited by Jennie Wyse-Power of the speech in question — no further reduction has been implemented. The date of the anthology, together with its title, clearly declares its pro-Parnellite loyalties in the ferocious recriminative atmosphere of that decade. Finally, one should note that no scholar has thought it worthwhile to compile a complete edition of Parnell's speeches; he was not in the company of Henry Grattan (whom he repeatedly invokes).

The text, headnote and annotations for Parnell's writings have been prepared by W. J. Mc Cormack.]

AT LIMERICK

August 31st 1879

I firmly believe that, bad as are the prospects of this country, out of that we will obtain good for Ireland.... It is the duty of the Irish tenant farmers to combine amongst themselves and ask for a reduction of rent, and if they get no reduction where a reduction is necessary, then I say that it is the duty of the tenant to pay no rent until he gets it. And if they combined in that way, if they stood together, and if being refused a reasonable and just reduction, they kept a firm grip of their homesteads, I can tell them that no power on earth could prevail against the hundreds of thousands of the tenant farmers of this country. Do not fear. You are not to be exterminated as you were in 1847, and take my word for it it will not be attempted. You should ask for concessions that are just. Ask for them in a proper manner, and good landlords will give these conditions. But for the men who had always shown themselves regardless of right and justice in their dealings with these questions, I say it is necessary for you to maintain a firm and determined attitude. If you maintain that attitude victory must be yours. If when a farm was tenantless, owing to any cause, you refuse to take it, and the present most foolish competition amongst farmers came to an end, as undoubtedly it now must, these men who are forgetful of reason and of common sense must come to reconsider their position. I believe that the land of a country ought to be owned by the people of the country. And I think we should centre our exertions upon attaining that end.... When we have the people of this country prosperous, self-reliant, and confident of the future, we will have an Irish nation which will be able to hold its own amongst the nations of the world. We will have a country which will be able to speak with the enemy in the gate — we will have a people who will understand their rights, and, knowing those rights, will be resolved to maintain them. We must all have this without injustice to any individual.

AT ENNIS

September 19th 1880

I have seen that the more independence the Irish Party showed, the more respect it gained for itself and for Ireland.... Now what are you to do to a tenant who bids for a farm from which another tenant has been evicted? [Several voices — 'Shoot him.'] I think I heard somebody say, 'Shoot him.' I wish to point out to you a very much better way, a more Christian and charitable way, which will give the lost man an opportunity of repenting. When a man takes a farm from which another man has been evicted you must shun him on the roadside when you meet him; you must shun him in the streets of the town; you must shun him in the shop; you must shun him in the fairgreen, and in the marketplace, and even in the place of worship by leaving him alone, by putting him into a moral Coventry,[1] by isolating him from the rest of his country as if he were the leper of old — you must show him your detestation of the crime he has committed. If you

1. To be sent to Coventry is to be shunned or ostracized. In his *History of the Great Rebellion*, Clarendon says that royalist prisoners captured in Birmingham were sent to Coventry, a stronghold of the parliamentary forces.

do this you may depend on it there will be no man so full of avarice, so lost to shame, as to dare the public opinion of all right-thinking men in the country and transgress your unwritten code of laws.... I would strongly recommend public men not to waste their breath too much in discussing how the land question is to be settled, but rather to help and encourage the people in making it, as I just said, ripe for settlement. When it is ripe for settlement you will probably have your choice as to how it shall be settled, and I said a year ago that the land question would never be settled until the Irish landlords were just as anxious to have it settled as the Irish tenants.... But I stand here today to express my opinion that no settlement can be satisfactory or permanent which does not ensure the uprooting of that system of landlordism which has brought the country three times in a century to famine.... We have been accused of preaching Communistic doctrines when we told the people not to pay an unjust rent, and the following out of that advice in a few of the Irish counties had shown the English Government the necessity for a radical alteration in the land laws. But how would they like it if we told the people some day or other not to pay any rent until this question is settled.... If the 500,000 tenant farmers of Ireland struck against the 10,000 landlords, I should like to see where they would get police and soldiers enough to make them pay.[2]

2. This is the speech from which the practice of 'boycotting' (named after Charles Cunningham Boycott (1832-97), the landlord concerned) arose.

AT WEXFORD

October 9th 1881

You have gained something by your exertions during the last twelve months, but I am here today to tell you that you have gained but a fraction of that to which you are entitled. And the Irishman who thinks that he can now throw away his arms, just as Grattan disbanded the Volunteers in 1782,[1] will find to his sorrow and destruction when too late that he has placed himself in the power of a perfidious and cruel and unrelenting English enemy.

1. The Volunteers were not disbanded in 1782, by Henry Grattan or by anyone else; Parnell's knowledge of Irish history was feeble.

[Referring to Mr. Gladstone's recent Guildhall speech he said:]

Not content with maligning you, he maligns your bishops, he maligns John Dillon.[2] He endeavours to misrepresent the Young Ireland party of 1848. No misrepresentation is too patent, too mean, or too low for him to stoop to. And it is a good sign that this masquerading knight-errant, this pretended champion of the rights of every other nation except those of the Irish nation, should be obliged to throw off the mask today, and to stand revealed as the man who by his own utterances is prepared to carry fire and sword into your homesteads unless you humbly abase yourselves before him, and before the landlords of the country. But I had forgotten. I said that he maligned everybody. Oh, no. He has a good word for one or two people. He says the late Isaac Butt was a most estimable man, and a true patriot.[3] When we in Ireland were following Isaac Butt into the lobbies, endeavouring to obtain the very Act which William Ewart Gladstone[4] — having stolen the idea from Isaac Butt — passed last Session, William Ewart Gladstone and his ex-Government officials were following Sir Stafford Northcote and Benjamin Disraeli[5] into the other lobby. No man is good in Ireland until he is dead and unable to do anything more for his country. In the opinion of an English statesman no man is good in Ireland until he is dead and buried, and unable to strike a blow for Ireland. Perhaps the day may come when I may get a good word from English statesmen, as being a moderate man, after I am dead and buried.... When people talk of public plunder they should first ask themselves, and recall to mind who were the first plunderers in Ireland. The land of Ireland has been confiscated three times over by the men

2. John Dillon (1851-1927), one of Parnell's supporters in the Land League, was Member of Parliament first for Tipperary and then for Mayo.
3. Isaac Butt (1813-79), lawyer, man of letters, and politician. Initially a supporter of a strongly protestant and conservative line in politics, he defended nationalist prisoners in 1848 and again after the Fenian events of the 1860s. He founded the Home Government Association in 1870, and subsequently became the first leader of an Irish Party at Westminster committed to Home Rule.
4. William Ewart Gladstone (1809-98), the leader of the Liberal Party, was architect of an intended Home Rule solution to the Irish problem; prime minister of Britain four times: 1868-74; 1880-85; 1886 and 1892-94.
5. Sir Stanford Henry Northcote (1818-87), later 1st earl of Iddlesleigh; Benjamin Disraeli (1804-1891), 1st earl of Beaconsfield, prime minister of Britain 1868, 1874-1880. Both men were Tories or Conservatives, though Northcote had also been a friend of Gladstone's during the latter's early and Tory phase.

whose descendants Mr. Gladstone is supporting in the enjoyment of the fruits of their plunder by his bayonets and his buckshot. And when we are spoken to about plunder, we are entitled to ask who were the first and the biggest plunderers.... This doctrine of public plunder is only a question of degree.... In one last despairing wail he says — 'And the Government are expected to preserve peace with no moral force behind it.' The Government has no moral force behind it in Ireland, the whole Irish people are against them. They have to depend for their support upon a self-interested and a very small minority of the people of this country, and therefore they have no moral force behind them; and Mr. Gladstone in those few short words admits that English government has failed in Ireland. He admits the contention that Grattan and the Volunteers of 1782 fought for; he admits the contention that the men of '98 died for; he admits the contention that O'Connell argued for; he admits the contention that the men of '48 staked their all for; he admits the contention that the men of '65, after a long period of depression, and apparent death of National life in Ireland, cheerfully faced the dungeon and the horrors of penal servitude for, and he admits the contention that today you in your overpowering multitudes have established, and please God will bring to a successful issue, namely — that England's mission in Ireland has been a failure, and that Irishmen have established their right to govern Ireland by laws made by themselves on Irish soil. And he wound up with a threat — this man who has no moral force behind him — he wound up with a threat — 'No fear of force, and no fear of ruin through force shall prevail, as far as we are concerned, and it is in our power.' I say it is not in his power to trample on the aspirations and the rights of the Irish nation with no moral force behind him. These are very brave words that he uses, but it strikes me that they have a ring about them like the whistle of a schoolboy on his way through a churchyard at night to keep up his courage. He would have you to believe that he is not afraid of you, because he has disarmed you, because he has attempted to disorganize you, because he knows that the Irish nation is today disarmed as far as physical weapons go, but he does not hold this kind of language with the Boers.[6] At the beginning of the session he said something of this kind with regard to the Boers. He said that he was going to put them down, and as soon as he had discovered that they were able to shoot straighter than his own soldiers he allowed these few men to put him and his government down... I trust that as the result of this great movement we shall see that, just as Gladstone by the Act of 1881 has eaten all his old words, has departed from all his formerly declared principles, now we shall see that these brave words of this English Prime Minister will be scattered as chaff before the united and advancing determination of the Irish people to regain for themselves their lost land, and their legislative independence.

6. The Boers were descendants of the Dutch colonists who had settled in Africa. The first Boer War took place in 1880-81 when the Transvaal under Paul Kruger rebelled against the British government and won a convincing victory at Majuba Hill in February 1881. The Boers enjoyed considerable support in Ireland.

DEBATE ON THE ADDRESS

HOUSE OF COMMONS,
February 23rd 1883

... I can assure the House that it is not my belief that anything I can say, or wish to say at this time, will have the slightest effect on the public opinion of the House, or upon the public opinion of this country. I have been accustomed during my political life to rely upon the public opinion of those whom I have desired to help, and with whose aid I have worked for the cause of prosperity and freedom in Ireland: and the utmost that I desire to do in the very few words which I shall address to this House, is to make my position clear to the Irish people at home and abroad from the unjust aspersions which have been cast upon me by a man who ought to be ashamed to devote his high ability to the task of traducing them. I don't wish to reply to the questions of the right hon. gentleman.[1] I consider he has no right to question me, standing as he does in a position very little better than an informer with regard to the secrets of the men with whom he was associated, and he has not even the pretext of that remarkable informer [James Carey][2]

1. i.e. William Edward Forster (1818-86), chief secretary for Ireland 1880-82. Forster had assailed Parnell ferociously at the beginning of the 1883 parliamentary session. The present extract is taken from Parnell's reply.
2. James Carey (1845-83), a member of the Invincibles (the terrorist group that assassinated the chief secretary and under-secretary in the

whose proceedings we have lately heard of. He had not even the pretext of that miserable man that he was attempting to save his own life. No, sir: other motives of less importance seem to have weighed with the right hon. gentleman in the extraordinary course which he has adopted on the present occasion of going out of his way to collect together a series of extracts, perhaps nine or ten in number, out of a number of speeches — many hundreds and thousands — delivered during the Land League movement by other people and not by me, upon which to found an accusation against me for what has been said and done by others. . . . The right hon. gentleman has asked me to defend myself. Sir, I have nothing to defend myself for. The right hon. gentleman has confessed that he attempted to obtain a declaration or public promise from me which would have the effect of discrediting me with the Irish people. He has admitted that he failed in that attempt, and failing in that attempt, he lost his own reputation. He boasted last night that he had deposed me from some imaginary position which he was pleased to assign to me; but, at least, I have this consolation — that he also deposed himself. . . . I have taken very little part in Irish politics since my release from Kilmainham.[3] I expressed my reason for that upon the passing of the Crimes Act. I said that, in my judgment, the Crimes Act would result in such a state of affairs that between the Government and secret societies it would be impossible for constitutional agitation to exist in Ireland. I believe so still. . . . It would have been far better if you were going to pass an Act of this kind and to administer an Act of this kind as you are going to administer it, and as you are obliged to administer it — up to the hilt — that it should be done by the seasoned politician who is now in disgrace. Call him back to his post! Send him to help Lord Spencer in his congenial work of the gallows in Ireland![4] Send him to look after the Secret Inquisitions of Dublin Castle! Send him to superintend the payment of blood money! Send him to distribute the taxes which an unfortunate and starving peasantry have to pay for crimes not committed by them! All this would be congenial work. We invite you to man your ranks, and send your ablest and best men. Push forward the task of misgoverning Ireland! For my part I am confident as to the future of Ireland. Although her horizon may appear at this moment clouded, I believe that our people will survive the present oppression as we have survived many and worse ones. And although our progress may be slow it will be sure, and the time will come when this House and the people of this country will admit once again that they have been mistaken; that they have been deceived by those who ought to be ashamed of deceiving them; that they have been led astray as to the method of governing a noble, a generous, and an impulsive people; that they will reject their present leaders who are conducting them into the terrible course, which, I am sorry to say, the Government appears to be determined to enter; that they will reject these guides and leaders with just as much determination as they rejected the services of the right hon. gentleman the member for Bradford.[5]

Phoenix Park, Dublin in May 1882). After his arrest, Carey turned Queen's evidence. He was sent to South Africa by the British authorities, but one of the Invincibles, Patrick O'Donnell, shot him dead on board ship between Cape Town and Natal.

3. Parnell was imprisoned in Kilmainham Jail from October 1881 to 2 May 1882.

4. John Poyntz (1835-1910), 5th earl Spencer, was lord lieutenant of Ireland for the second time 1882-85.

5. Forster (see note 1 above) was MP for Bradford in Yorkshire.

AT CORK

January 21st, 1885

I hold that it is better even to encourage you to do what is beyond your strength, even should you fail sometimes in the attempt, than to teach you to be subservient and unreliant. . . . We consider that whatever class tries to obstruct the labourer in the possession of those fair and just rights to which he is entitled that class shall be put down — and coerced if you will — into doing justice to the labourer. . . . It is given to none of us to forecast the future, and just as it is impossible for us to say in what way or by what means the National question may be settled — in what way full justice may be done to Ireland — so it is impossible for us to say to what extent that justice should be done. We cannot ask for less than the restitution of Grattan's Parliament, with its important privileges, and wide and far-reaching constitution. We cannot, under the British Constitution, ask for more than the restitution of Grattan's Parliament, but no man has a right to fix the boundary of the march of a nation. No man has a right to say 'Thus far shalt thou go, and no further'; and we have never attempted to fix the *ne plus ultra*[1] to the progress of Ireland's nationhood, and we never shall. But, gentlemen, while we leave these things to time, circumstances, and the future, we must each one of us resolve in our own hearts that we shall at all times do everything that within us lies to obtain for Ireland the fullest measure of her rights. In this way we shall avoid difficulties and contentions amongst each other. In this way we shall not give up anything which the future may put in favour of our country: and while we struggle today for that which may seem possible for us without combination, we must struggle for it with the proud consciousness that we shall not do anything to hinder or prevent better men who may come after us from gaining better things than those for which we now contend.

1. 'no further beyond'; in other words, 'limit', 'boundary'.

AT GALWAY

February 10th 1886

I have told you that I did not know of Mr. Lynch's claims, and having recommended him [Captain O'Shea] in my position, I was bound not to recede one hair's breadth, one jot, but carry through that recommendation to the bitter end, and to test whether the people of Galway and the people of Ireland had confidence in me, which I believe they have, and which the result of this election will show that they have renewed.[1] I have never led during eleven long years, since my entry into public life, I have never led the Irish people astray. I have never led them into any crooked path. I have never led the Irish party astray. When courage was required, when it was necessary for the interests of the nation, I have shown it; and when moderation was required, when moderation was necessary, and temperate judgment for the interests of the nation, I had courage to show it, and I never will lead the party or the nation astray until we have gained for you the right to lead and govern yourselves.

1. In 1885-86 a by-election arose for the Galway constituency, and Parnell supported the candidature of Captain William Henry O'Shea (1840-1905) with whose wife he was already conducting an affair. Michael Aloysius Lynch stood as a rival nationalist candidate, but in a constituency with 2,265 electors O'Shea won by 942 votes to 54. O'Shea in effect was blackmailing Parnell, as the divorce crisis of 1890 was to demonstrate.

AT PORTSMOUTH, AFTER THE DEFEAT OF MR. GLADSTONE'S HOME RULE BILL

June 25th 1886

It is, I believe, about the first time I have had the honour of addressing a mainly English audience. And I have been induced to do so now because I rely greatly upon the spirit of fair play among the English masses, and because the issues for my country are so great and so vital at the present moment — the issues which underlie this present struggle — that the Irishman who remains silent when it might be possible to do something to help his country would be more unworthy than tongue could describe.... I have, in my career as a member of Parliament, never wittingly injured the cause of the English working man. I have done something to show my sympathy for the masses of the people of this country.... Some years ago it was my privilege to strike with English members a successful blow in favour of the abolition of flogging in the army and navy. We were met then by the very same arguments as we are met with today, and from the same class of persons. It was said by the late Lord Beaconsfield[1] that the integrity of the British Empire would be endangered if flogging were abolished, and he called a great meeting at one of the Ministerial offices in London, a great meeting of his supporters both in the Lords and Commons, for the purpose of exhorting them to stand shoulder to shoulder in defence of the British Empire against the abolition of flogging in the army .... I have shown you that in some respects the Irish settlement proposed by Mr. Gladstone does not give a Parliament, a Legislature with the powers possessed by Grattan's Parliament; but I have shown you on the other hand that as regards our own exclusively domestic business it gives larger powers, more important powers, more valuable powers for Ireland itself than was possessed by Grattan's, and therefore we think that this settlement proposed by Mr. Gladstone will prove a more durable settlement than the restitution of the Grattan Parliament or the Repeal of the Union would prove.... Imperial unity does not require or necessitate unity of Parliaments. Will you carry that away with you and remember it, because it is the keystone of our whole proceedings.... I should say that Ireland

1. Benjamin Disraeli, 1st earl of Beaconsfield, died in 1881.

would justly deserve to lose her privilege if she passed laws oppressive of the minority.... So far as coercion was concerned it has not brought you any nearer to the end of the Irish question.... One great fault in English coercion has been that no matter what your intentions have been when you have commenced coercion, you have never discriminated between political agitators and breakers of the law.... Lord Carnarvon[2] will not deny that he was as strong a Home Ruler as I was last August, and that when he went over to Ireland he became stronger and stronger every day he lived in that country. There is another thing he has not denied: he has not denied that he sought an interview with me in order to speak to me and consult with me about a Constitution for Ireland.... Untold is the guilt of that man who, for party purposes, does not take advantage of the spirit which is abroad amongst the English to put the hand of the Irish into that of the English to close the strife of centuries — a strife that has been of no advantage to the people of either country; a strife that has only been for the benefit of the money-grabbing landlords; a strife that has impeded popular progress in England as well as in Ireland, and that must continue to impede it; a strife which is fanned for the purpose of cheating you out of your rights, and to divert the energies of the newly enfranchised masses of Great Britain from the redress of their grievances to the odious task of oppressing and keeping down the small sister country.

2. Henry Howard Molyneux Herbert (1831-90), 4th earl of Carnarvon, lord lieutenant of Ireland 1885.

PRESENTATION OF ADDRESSES FROM THE MUNICIPAL BODIES OF IRELAND TO MR. PARNELL AT THE WESTMINSTER PALACE HOTEL, LONDON, CONGRATULATING HIM ON THE COLLAPSE OF THE PIGOTT CONSPIRACY

1890

I should have preferred to have gone to my grave with the stigma of these letters upon me — cowardly, mean, and contemptible as these letters were — rather than submit my country and my countrymen to the humiliating ordeal that was forced upon us as the accompaniment of the inquiry into the authenticity of these letters.... We did not accept this Commission.[1] We do not — we never have acknowledged the justice of the reference. We did not admit, we never have admitted, by any word or act of ours that this tribunal was a fair tribunal, or one of a character and constitution competent to inquire into the issues laid before it. For these issues, as they have been put before the commission of judges, are not issues which can ever be decided by any earthly tribunal.... I believe the verdict of history will be on our side; but there are questions which, from their very nature, must be left to history to settle, and no tribunal of judges, ignorant of the history of Ireland, knowing nothing of the character of her people without information as to the surrounding circumstances — by education, birth, feeling and habits of thought, political conviction, and training averse to the aspirations of Ireland — no such tribunal is fitted or able to decide the grave issues that have been laid before this Commission for decision.... I believe that our cause is so good and so strong, and that our position today stands so clear before the public opinion of the world, that even under all these disadvantages which I have recited to you, even with the dice loaded against us, and with the cards — with the trump card, as they had hoped — up their sleeves, we shall come out of this far-reaching inquiry untouched and unharmed, but brightened by the trial, and that our country will stand clearer and prouder than when she entered upon this ordeal.... If our constitutional movement were to fail I would not continue twenty-four hours at Westminster. The most advanced section of Irishmen, as well as the least advanced, have always thoroughly understood that the Parliamentary policy was to be a trial, and that we did not ourselves believe in any possibility of maintaining for all time or for any lengthened period an incorrupt and independent Irish representation at Westminster.

1. When *The Times* newspaper published a series of articles on 'Parnellism and Crime' in 1887-88, Lord Carnarvon proposed a special commission to investigate the allegations; this eventually established that the letters attributed to Parnell were forgeries, the work of Richard Pigott (1828-89). Pigott's court-room mispelling of 'hesitancy' as 'hesitency' confirmed the forgeries. This minute detail of Parnell's career makes its way into Joyce's *Finnegans Wake* (1939).

MR. PARNELL'S SPEECH IN COMMITTEE ROOM No. 15

[6] *December 1890*

The men whose ability is now so conspicuously

exercised as that of Mr. Healy and Mr. Sexton,[1] will have to bear their responsibility for this. . . . Why did you encourage me to come forward and maintain my leadership in the face of the world if you were not going to stand by me? . . . I want to ask you before you vote my deposition to be sure you are getting value for it. . . . I know what Mr. Gladstone will do for you; I know what Mr. Morley[2] will do for you; and I know there is not a single one of the lot to be trusted unless you trust yourselves. Be to your own selves true and hence it follows, as the day the night, thou can'st not be false to any man. . . .[3] If I am to leave you tonight I should like to leave you in security. I should like, and it is not an unfair thing for me to ask, that I should come within sight of the Promised Land; that I should come with you, having come so far, if not to the end of this course, that I should at least come with you as far as you will allow and permit me to come with you, at least until it is absolutely sure that Ireland and I can go no further.

1. Timothy Michael Healy (1855-1931), a Parnellite MP for various constituencies; he had already broken with his leader on the issue of O'Shea's role in the Galway election of 1886. His biting sarcasm made him Parnell's most dangerous critic in 1890-91, and subsequently Healy attempted to lead a clericalist party and succeeded in legally representing the employers during the 1913 Dublin lock-out. He was rewarded for his efforts by being appointed first (1922-28) governor general of the Irish Free State. Thomas Sexton (1848-1932) was successively MP for various Irish constituencies, and a brilliant parliamentary orator. He first supported and then abandoned Parnell during the party crisis arising from the latter's involvement in the O'Shea divorce case.
2. John Morley (1838-1923), 1st viscount Morley; twice chief secretary for Ireland; a notable author, he published a study of Edmund Burke in 1879.
3. cf. *Hamlet*, I.3.78.

AT LONGFORD

February 22nd 1891

I took off my coat for the purpose of obtaining and consummating the future of Irish nationality. That position was accepted by the men of Ireland, and upon that position I have stood during these long years. . . . I shall stand upon this constitutional platform until they have torn away the last plank from under our feet. I desire to say here tonight that I believe we can win on the constitutional platform. But if we cannot win upon it, well, I shall be prepared to give way to better and stronger men, and it can never be said of us that by anything that we have done we have prevented better or abler men than ourselves from dealing with the future of our race.

AT LIMERICK

May 24th 1891

I was confident from the first moment when these troubles commenced that it was my duty to do one of two things — either to fight the battle out to the end or to obtain such securities from the English party which asked Ireland to surrender her independence and freedom of judgment, and independence should be attended with as little ill and mischief to our country as possible. . . . If I were driven from my position as leader of the nation, I should still continue to battle on behalf of independent Ireland, of freedom of action and thought for my countrymen. As citizen of Ireland, it would be still my duty to go on with this fight. I tell you, fellow-countrymen, that once you allow your members to break the ranks, to lose their independence, to take their orders from an English political party or English statesman, then you may bid good bye to hopes of benefits and reform for Ireland by political action and that powerful constitutional weapon which I forged for you, and which I put into your hands and taught you to use with advantage to yourselves, will break and be shattered in your hands, and that proud position which Ireland has attained will be lost for ever if our countrymen once forget the teachings of history and are forgetful of the means by which they have won their proud position of strength and independence.

AT LISTOWEL

September 13th 1891

But what I conceive we are striving for is this — they say that because they happen to constitute the majority of the Irish members that therefore they are entitled to bind the minority not only of the Irish members, but also of the Irish people — to compel the minority to obey their orders. That might have been so had it happened that these orders were not given by Mr. Gladstone. But we strive not for leadership. We strive to preserve our own independence and the independence of our country, which these men say we are to give up to them because they contend they are in the majority.

What would you say to the consistency and judgment of a man who announces today that it was a ridiculous thing to go to Mr. Gladstone and ask for pledges, and who, six or seven months before at Boulogne,[1] was a party to an arrangement by which Mr. Gladstone was asked for pledges. He [John Dillon] was quite willing to do a ridiculous thing, and agree to a ridiculous thing, so long as he saw any chance of keeping me out of public life, and getting me to retire. A very curious thing in connection with these Boulogne negotiations, when talking of judgment and common-sense — I will not say statesmanship — that the only portions of them that Mr. O'Brien begged me not to publish, in case during his imprisonment I found it necessary to publish any portion of them, were the proposals composed by Mr. O'Brien, with the help of Mr. Dillon, in America, before he left, accepted by Mr. M'Carthy[2] and Mr. Sexton when he arrived in France, and actually proposed to me as a solution of the question, and which I found so absurd and ridiculous, and so traitorous to the Liberal allies of these men that they were obliged to admit that they were utterly untenable and unsuitable. Mr. O'Brien can publish these proposals if he chooses, and also the counter proposals I made afterwards if he wishes, not because I think that the counter proposals that I made were suitable or sufficient, and had not many faults in them, but because it was the best thing that I could advise at the moment for the purpose of satisfying the desire which existed in the country, that the peril in some way or other should be got over, and a settlement of this dispute should be arrived at.

If I were dead and gone tomorrow, the men who are fighting against English influence in Irish public life would fight on still; they would still be Independent Nationalists; they would still believe in the future of Ireland a Nation; and they would still protest that it was not by taking orders from an English Minister that Ireland's future could be saved, protected, or secured.

I will not be a party to setting up the power of the Liberal party which it is sought to put over us in England, and the power of another sort sought to be put over us in Ireland. I trust that the coming Local Government Bill of the present Government may contain these provisions which will be of the utmost good to the labouring classes of the country. If it does not contain these provisions, it will be our duty to leave no stone unturned to see that before that measure leaves the House of Commons it shall have such provisions added to it, and certainly, if we can manage it in any way we will put into that measure provisions that will enable many a poor labouring man who has to emigrate at the present moment to stay at home, to bring up his family at home, and be one of the future mainstays and strength of Ireland a nation. Now, fellow-countrymen, of amnesty. I should have gladly welcomed the presence of Mr. O'Brien and Mr. Dillon on the platform at the Phoenix Park. But if they did not like to come on our platform, let them get one of their own and advocate the cause of the captives from that platform. They cannot consistently maintain the attitude of silence, and of neutrality upon this question, merely because their new leader, Sir William Harcourt[3] thinks political prisoners have not been sufficiently punished for the offences they committed so many years ago. They must shake themselves loose from their English allies upon this question if they are going to maintain a single shred of their title as Irish Nationalists.... It is idle, then, to seek to persuade you that this is merely a question of leadership. It is a question of a grave difference of opinion as to the means by which the future of our country can be secured. I agree to the fullest extent that Ireland's cause is independent of any man. Ireland's cause would live as it has lived, and we believe will live, despite the efforts of traitorous and cowardly seceders; and if the seceders swept us all out of public life tomorrow, Ireland's cause would still survive. This struggle is not continued for the purpose of supporting the claim of any man, but for the purpose of declaring that the conduct of the chosen representatives of Ireland who elected their leader on the morning of one day, and on the afternoon of that same day, because an English leader ordered them to do so, reversed their decision, was conduct unworthy of Irish Nationalists, and most

1. Negotiations between Parnell and his critics were conducted at this French port before the final split in the Irish Party (see note 1, p. 315).
2. William O'Brien (1852-1928), journalist and politician, was repeatedly imprisoned for his support of tenant causes; he became an anti-Parnellite after the split of 1890-91.

Justin McCarthy (1830-1912), journalist and politician, the first (1-6 November 1890) leader of the anti-Parnellites.

3. Sir William George Granville Venables Vernon Harcourt (1827-1904), the politician who persuaded Gladstone to repudiate Parnell's leadership of the Irish Party following the divorce case of 1890.

unworthy of men who put themselves forward as representatives of the Irish nation. . . . What are we fighting for? We assert today in this town of Listowel what we asserted in 1885 and the years before it, that no man has a right to fix the boundary of a nation — that no man has a right to limit the aspirations of our people.[4]

4. Note that Parnell repeats here the famous theme of an earlier speech (see the Cork speech of January 1885 above): his resources were almost exhausted, and he died on 6 October 1891.

TO THE PEOPLE OF IRELAND (1890)

[By the end of November 1890, the question of Captain William O'Shea's suit for divorce — with Parnell as the guilty correspondent — was nearly a year old. As leader of the Irish Parliamentary Party at Westminster, Parnell was placed between two forces, neither of which could lightly tolerate his implication in divorce proceedings. One of these was English public opinion, or rather the non-conformist aspect of English opinion upon which the Liberal Party under William Ewart Gladstone depended for electoral support. The second was catholic opinion in Ireland. Naturally, debate had raged inside the Irish Party about the best line of conduct for the leader to follow, but Parnell was not greatly accustomed to heeding advice on political, let alone personal, matters. His career had been a series of apparent (and in many cases, actual) triumphs over major difficulties. His experience did not prepare him for the decisions he was called upon to make.

On 28 November 1890, Parnell read a manifesto to a number of his loyal followers at a London apartment. Justin McCarthy, whom Parnell had expressly invited to the meeting, objected as soon as the document had been read. Challenged by Parnell to specify what exactly made it 'all objectionable . . . offensive to our English allies' in McCarthy's eyes, the latter instanced the phrase 'English wolves'. According to R. Barry O'Brien, from whose work the text of the manifesto is taken, Parnell was equally insistent that these words were not removable.

On Saturday morning, 29 November 1890, the text appeared in the newspapers. Although it was interpreted as a response to Gladstone's effective ultimatum to the Irish Party (that Parnell be removed), internal warfare resulted inside the party. Monday, 1 December, saw the gathering of Irish members in Westminster's Committee Room 15, which led to Parnell's fall and the split in Irish political representation. He died on 6 October 1891, having married Mrs Katharine O'Shea on the previous 25 June.

Without this sudden conclusion to the career of a man still only forty-five years of age, it is unlikely that Parnell could have been incorporated into the martyrology of Anglo-Irish literature. For W. B. Yeats, as for others, the party had thrown Parnell to the wolves. The manifesto that wrecked Parnell as politician contained the phrase that saved him for literature.]

The integrity and independence of a section of the Irish parliamentary party having been sapped and destroyed[1] by the wirepullers of the English Liberal party, it has become necessary for me, as the leader of the Irish nation, to take counsel with you, and, having given you the knowledge which is in my possession, to ask your judgment upon a matter which now solely devolves upon you to decide.

The letter of Mr. Gladstone to Mr. Morley,[2] written for the purpose of influencing the decision of the Irish party in the choice of their leader, and claiming for the Liberal party and their leaders the right of veto upon that choice, is the immediate cause of this address to you, to remind you and your parliamentary representatives that Ireland considers the independence of her party as her only safeguard within the constitution, and above and beyond all other considerations whatever. The threat in that letter, repeated so insolently on many English platforms and in numerous British newspapers, that unless Ireland concedes this right of veto to England she will indefinitely postpone her chances of obtaining Home Rule, compels me, while not for one moment admitting the slightest probability of such loss, to put before you information which until now, so far as my colleagues are concerned, has been solely in my possession, and which will enable you to understand the measure of the loss with which you are threatened unless you consent to throw me to the English wolves now howling for my destruction.

In November of last year, in response to a repeated and long-standing request, I visited Mr. Gladstone at Hawarden,[3] and received the details of the intended proposals of himself and his colleagues of the late Liberal Cabinet with regard to Home Rule, in the event of the next general election favouring the Liberal party.

It is unnecessary for me to do more at present

1. According to R. Barry O'Brien (*The Life of Charles Stewart Parnell* (London: Smith, Elder, 1899) 2nd ed. Vol. 2, pp. 258-65), at the meeting on 3 December 1890 Parnell maintained that this sentence should have read 'apparently sapped and undermined. . . .'
2. William Ewart Gladstone (1809-1898) Liberal leader at this date; John Morley (1838-1923) member of parliament and man of letters.
3. Hawarden Castle in north Wales was Gladstone's residence.

than to direct your attention to certain points of these details, which will be generally recognised as embracing elements vital for your information and the formation of your judgment. These vital points of difficulty may be suitably arranged and considered under the following heads:

(1) The retention of the Irish members in the Imperial Parliament.

(2) The settlement of the land or agrarian difficulty in Ireland.

(3) The control of the Irish constabulary.

(4) The appointment of the judiciary (including judges of the supreme court, county court judges, and resident magistrates).

Upon the subject of the retention of the Irish members in the Imperial Parliament Mr. Gladstone told me that the opinion, and the unanimous opinion, of his colleagues and himself, recently arrived at after most mature consideration of alternative proposals, was that, in order to conciliate English public opinion, it would be necessary to reduce the Irish representation from 103 to 32.

Upon the settlement of the land it was held that this was one of the questions which must be regarded as questions reserved from the control of the Irish Legislature, but, at the same time, Mr. Gladstone intimated that, while he would renew his attempt to settle the matter by Imperial legislation on the lines of the Land Purchase Bill of 1886, he would not undertake to put any pressure upon his own side or insist upon their adopting his views — in other and shorter words, that the Irish Legislature was not to be given the power of solving the agrarian difficulty, and that the Imperial Parliament would not.

With regard to the control of the Irish constabulary, it was stated by Mr. Gladstone that, having regard to the necessity for conciliating English public opinion, he and his colleagues felt that it would be necessary to leave this force and the appointment of its officers under the control of the Imperial authority for an indefinite period, while the funds for its maintenance, payment, and equipment would be compulsorily provided out of Irish resources.[4]

The period of ten or twelve years was suggested as the limit of time during which the appointment of judges, resident magistrates, &c., should be retained in the hands of the Imperial authority.

I have now given a short account of what I gathered of Mr. Gladstone's views and those of his colleagues during two hours' conversation at Hawarden — a conversation which, I am bound to admit, was mainly monopolised by Mr. Gladstone — and pass to my own expressions of opinion upon these communications, which represent my views then and now.

And, first, with regard to the retention of the Irish members, the position I have always adopted, and then represented, is that, with the concession of full powers to the Irish Legislature equivalent to those enjoyed by a State of the American Union, the number and position of the members so retained would become a question of Imperial concern, and not of pressing or immediate importance for the interests of Ireland. But that with the important and all-engrossing subjects of agrarian reform, constabulary control, and judiciary appointments left either under Imperial control or totally unprovided for, it would be the height of madness for any Irish leader to imitate Grattan's example and consent to disband the army which had cleared the way to victory.[5]

I further undertook to use every legitimate influence to reconcile Irish public opinion to a gradual coming into force of the new privileges, and to the postponements necessary for English opinion with regard to constabulary control and judicial appointments, but strongly dissented from the proposed reduction of members during the interval of probation. I pointed to the absence of any suitable prospect of land settlement by either Parliament as constituting an overwhelming drag upon the prospects of permanent peace and prosperity in Ireland.

At the conclusion of the interview I was informed that Mr. Gladstone and all his colleagues were entirely agreed that, pending the General Election, silence should be absolutely preserved with regard to any points of difference on the question of the retention of the Irish members.

I have dwelt at some length upon these subjects, but not, I think, disproportionately to their importance. Let me say, in addition, that, if and when

4. The transitional arrangements involved in any Home Rule government's being established in Ireland would (in English eyes at least) have required only a gradual handing over of police powers to local authorities, the background to the entire proposal having been one of sustained opposition to law implementation in Ireland.

5. Parnell's citation of Henry Grattan is designed to invoke a warm rather than an accurate recollection of the Volunteers of 1782.

full powers are conceded to Ireland over her own domestic affairs, the integrity, number, and independence of the Irish party will be a matter of no importance; but until this ideal is reached it is your duty and mine to hold fast every safeguard.

I need not say that the questions — the vital and important questions — of the retention of the Irish members, on the one hand, and the indefinite delay of full powers to the Irish Legislature on the other, gave me great concern. The absence of any provision for the settlement of the agrarian question, of any policy on the part of the Liberal leaders, filled me with concern and apprehension. On the introduction of the Land Purchase Bill by the Government at the commencement of last session, Mr. Morley communicated with me as to the course to be adopted. Having regard to the avowed absence of any policy on the part of the Liberal leaders and party with regard to the matter of the land, I strongly advised Mr. Morley against any direct challenge of the principle of State-aided land purchase, and, finding that the fears and alarms of the English taxpayer to State aid by the hypothecation[6] of grants for local purposes in Ireland as a counter-guarantee had been assuaged, that a hopeless struggle should not be maintained, and that we should direct our sole efforts on the second reading of the Bill to the assertion of the principle of local control. In this I am bound to say Mr. Morley entirely agreed with me, but he was at the same time much hampered — and expressed his sense of his position — in that direction by the attitude of the extreme section of his party, led by Mr. Labouchere.[7] And in a subsequent interview he impressed me with the necessity of meeting the second reading of the Bill with a direct negative, and asked me to undertake the motion. I agreed to this, but only on the condition that I was not to attack the principle of the measure, but to confine myself to a criticism of its details. I think this was false strategy, but it was strategy adopted out of regard to English prejudices and Radical peculiarities. I did the best that was possible under the circumstances, and the several days' debate on the second reading contrasts favourably with Mr. Labouchere's recent and abortive attempt to interpose a direct negative to the first reading of a similar Bill yesterday.

Time went on. The Government allowed their attention to be distracted from the question of land purchase by the Bill for compensating English publicans, and the agrarian difficulty in Ireland was again relegated to the future of another session. Just before the commencement of this session I was again favoured with another interview with Mr. Morley. I impressed upon him the policy of the oblique method of procedure in reference to land purchase, and the necessity and importance of providing for the question of local control and of a limitation in the application of the funds. He agreed with me, and I offered to move, on the first reading of the Bill, an amendment in favour of this local control, advising that, if this were rejected, it might be left to the Radicals on the second reading to oppose the principle of the measure. This appeared to be a proper course, and I left Mr. Morley under the impression that this would fall to my duty.

But in addition he made me a remarkable proposal, referring to the probable approaching victory of the Liberal party at the polls. He suggested some consideration as to the future of the Irish party. He asked me whether I would be willing to assume the office of Chief Secretary to the Lord Lieutenant of Ireland, or to allow another member of my party to take the position. He also put before me the desirability of filling one of the law offices of the Crown in Ireland by a legal member of my party. I told him, amazed as I was at the proposal, that I could not agree to forfeit in any way the independence of the party or any of its members; that the Irish people had trusted me in this movement because they believed that the declaration I had made to them at Cork in 1880 was a true one and represented my convictions, and that I would on no account depart from it. I considered that, after the declarations we have repeatedly made, the proposal of Mr. Morley, that we should allow ourselves to be absorbed into English politics, was one based upon an entire misconception of our position with regard to the Irish constituencies and of the pledges which we had given.

In conclusion, he directed my attention to the Plan of Campaign estates.[8] He said that it would be

6. 'Hypothecation' is not a word admitted to the *Oxford English Dictionary*, but it means 'assumption on the basis of a hypothesis'.

7. Henry du Pré Labouchère (1831-1912), journalist and radical politician.

8. The Plan of Campaign (1886-91) was a scheme (of which Parnell was critical) according to which Irish tenants sought a reduction of rent by threatening to withhold all rent. Many tenants on estates where the

impossible for the Liberal party when they attained power to do anything for these evicted tenants by direct action; that it would be also impossible for the Irish Parliament, under the powers conferred, to do anything for them, and, flinging up his hands with a gesture of despair, he exclaimed: 'Having been to Tipperary, I do not know what to propose in regard to the matter.'[9] I told him that this question was a limited one, and that I did not see that he need allow himself to be hampered by its future consideration; that, being limited, funds would be available from America and elsewhere for the support of those tenants as long as might be necessary; that, of course, I understood it was a difficulty, but that it was a limited one, and should not be allowed to interfere with the general interests of the country.

I allude to this matter only because within the last few days a strong argument in many minds for my expulsion has been that, unless the Liberals come into power at the next general election, the Plan of Campaign tenants will suffer. As I have shown, the Liberals propose to do nothing for the Plan of Campaign tenants by direct action when they do come into power, but I am entitled to ask that the existence of these tenants, whom I have supported in every way in the past, and whom I shall continue to support in the future, shall not constitute a reason for my expulsion from Irish politics. I have repeatedly pledged myself to stand by these evicted tenants and that they shall not be allowed to suffer, and I believe that the Irish people throughout the world will support me in this policy.

Sixteen years ago I conceived the idea of an Irish parliamentary party independent of all English parties. Ten years ago I was elected the leader of an independent Irish parliamentary party. During these ten years that party has remained independent, and because of its independence it has forced upon the English people the necessity of granting Home Rule to Ireland. I believe that party will obtain Home Rule only provided it remains independent of any English party.

I do not believe that any action of the Irish people in supporting me will endanger the Home Rule cause, or postpone the establishment of an Irish Parliament; but even if the danger with which we are threatened by the Liberal party of today were to be realised, I believe that the Irish people throughout the world would agree with me that postponement would be preferable to a compromise of our national rights by the acceptance of a measure which would not realise the aspirations of our race.[10]

campaign was implemented were evicted and suffered considerable hardship. Parnell, aware that the Campaign was really criminal from the outset, persuaded the organizers not to extend it beyond those estates that had been implicated first.

9. The county of Tipperary had a long history of agrarian disturbance, and its name was synonymous with Irish land problems.

10. R. Barry O'Brien's footnote here reads 'Mr. Gladstone and Mr. Morley denied the accuracy of Parnell['s] account of the interviews with them.'

R. BARRY O'BRIEN

(1847-1918)

from:
THE LIFE OF CHARLES STEWART PARNELL (1898)

[O'Brien had many conversations with Parnell in 1890-91. In this account, we hear something of Parnell's sense of betrayal and of his determination, of his attitude towards constitutional agitation and its relation to physical force movements, and of his wary attitude towards English politicians. In retrospect, it is evident that he was right to distrust Gladstone's successors in the Liberal Party. Parnell's confidence that only he could carry Home Rule does not seem misplaced, although, as always, he failed to take into account the political repercussions of the divorce case.]

CHAPTER XXVI

NEARING THE END

While the Boulogne negotiations[1] were proceeding

1. Parnell met William O'Brien at Boulogne on 30 December 1890 and on 6 and 7 January 1891, to discuss the crisis. On 3 February, he met

Parnell continued to carry on the war in Ireland; he rested not a day, not an hour. Every Saturday night he left London for Dublin. On Sunday he addressed a meeting in some part of the country. On Monday he was back in Dublin again to confer with his followers there, and to direct operations. On Tuesday he returned to London, attended occasionally at the House of Commons, crossed when necessary to Boulogne, sometimes addressed meetings in England, and on Saturday started afresh to Ireland.

'You are over-doing it,' I said to him one night when he looked fatigued and harassed. 'Yes,' he rejoined, 'I am doing the work of ten men; but (suddenly) I feel right well. It does me good.' There was nothing that displeased him more than the least suggestion that he could not stand this constant strain.

In April there was an election in North Sligo. Parnell put up a candidate; but he was beaten, after a fierce fight, though not by so large a majority as the Anti-Parnellites had commanded in Kilkenny. In July there was another election in Carlow. Parnell again put up a candidate, and he was again beaten. But these defeats did not relax his efforts. After the Carlow election he delivered a stirring speech, bidding his followers to be of good cheer and never to despair.[2]

'If,' he said, 'we should happen to be beaten at the next general election, we will form a solid rallying square of the 1,500 good men who voted for Ireland's nationhood in the County Carlow, of the 2,500 heroes who voted for the same cause in North Sligo, and of the 1,400 voters in North Kilkenny who stood by the flag of Irish independence.'

I saw him often in London during his flying visits, when he received reports and gave directions about the Parnellite organisation in England. Sometimes he was little disposed to talk, on other occasions he was unusually conversational.

One evening we sat together in the Smoking-room of the House of Commons. He smoked a cigar, sipped a cup of tea or coffee, and looked restful and almost genial. When the business which I had come to talk about was disposed of, he said suddenly and *à propos* of nothing, 'What do you think of English alliances?' I said I thought an Irish alliance with an English party was a mistake, for the English party and for the Irish. I referred to the case of O'Connell's alliance with the Melbourne Ministry.[3] He said, 'I know nothing about that. I am very ignorant.' I smiled. 'Yes,' he said, 'I mean what I say. I am very ignorant of these things. I have read very little, but I am smart, and can pick up information quickly. Whatever you tell me about O'Connell you will find I will remember.' I then told him the story of the Melbourne alliance, so far as I was able; pointing out how it had ended in O'Connell's plunging into repeal, and in the Liberals afterwards fighting shy of Irish questions until the Fenian outbreak. The upshot of the alliance, I said, was that O'Connell lost faith in the British Parliament, and the Liberals felt that they had burned their fingers over Ireland, and accordingly tried to keep clear of the subject in the future. 'I agree,' he said; 'an English alliance is no use. It is a mistake to negotiate with an Englishman. He knows the business better than you do. He has had better training, and he is sure, sooner or later, to get you on a bit of toast.[4] You must keep within your own lines and be always ready to fight until you get what you want. I gained nothing by meeting Mr. Gladstone. I was no match for him. He got more out of me than I ever got out of him.' 'Why,' I asked, 'did you make a close alliance with the Liberals in 1886?'[5] 'Some change had to be made,' he answered. 'You see, they had come round to Home Rule. We could not go on fighting them as we did before their surrender.' 'But then, a close alliance was a mistake,' I said; 'even a Liberal said to me that it would have been better for the Irish and the Liberals to have moved on parallel lines than on

O'Brien and John Dillon at Calais. This stormy meeting put an end to the negotiations. Neither O'Brien nor Dillon could go to England or Ireland, since they had skipped bail. When they did return, they were arrested and jailed.

2. In December 1890, the savagely fought North Kilkenny election was won by the anti-Parnellite candidate by just over 1,000 votes. Although the by-elections in April and July 1891 were lost by a narrower margin, Parnell's position was almost hopeless by the summer of that year.

3. The Lichfield House Compact of 1835 committed O'Connell to supporting the administration of Lord Melbourne, prime minister 1834 and 1835-41. Although Melbourne's administration introduced a number of reforms, he himself refused to consider Repeal or Home Rule, the issue on which O'Connell had fought the general election of 1835. O'Connell was heavily criticized for his alliance with the Whigs. Like Parnell's with the Liberals, it brought reforms but never achieved the central aim — Repeal.

4. i.e. cornered. 'To be had on toast' means to be swindled.

5. The product of that alliance, after the general election of 1885, was the first Home Rule Bill of 1886, introduced in April and defeated in June.

the same line.' 'I did not,' he answered, 'want a close alliance. I did not make a close alliance. I kept away from the Liberals as much as I could. You do not know how much they tried to get at me, how much I was worried. But I tried to keep away from them as much as I had ever done. I knew the danger of getting mixed up with English statesmen. They only make you give way, and I give way a great deal too much.' 'Your people made a close alliance with the Liberals,' I said. 'I could not help that,' he answered. 'They ought to have known my wishes. They knew all the time I had been in public life I avoided Englishmen. I did not want them to rush into English clubs, or into English Society, as it is called. You talk of O'Connell. What would O'Connell have done in my position?' I answered: 'The difference between you and O'Connell is, that he always remained at the wheel,[6] you often let others run the ship.' 'Ah!' he replied with energy, 'that was my mistake, I admit it. I have not denied my faults. I committed many mistakes; that was the greatest. They call me a dictator. I was not dictator enough. I allowed them to do too much. But (clenching his fist and placing it quietly on the table) that will not happen again. It is called my party. It is everybody's party more than mine. I suppose you think that I have nominated every member of the party. I have not; other people nominated them. Look at —— (nodding his head towards an Irish member who sat some distance from us). How did he get into Parliament? I will tell you. C—— (nodding his head in the direction of another Irish member), C—— came to me and said, "Mr. —— (I had never heard of him before) would make a useful member. He is a Protestant, he is a landlord, he is an Oxford man, and he is a good speaker. He would be useful in the English constituencies." "Well," I said, "take him," and that was how Mr. —— came into Parliament. I dare say he makes pretty speeches, and I suppose he thinks himself a great Irish representative. I could give you other cases of the same kind. Most of those men got in in this way.' I said: 'Still you are responsible. All these men owe their political existence to you.' 'I admit my responsibility. I am telling you what was the practice. I did not build up a party of personal adherents. I took the nominees of others,' he rejoined. 'I do not say I was blameless. I have never said it. But was I to have no rest, was I to be always on the watch?' I broke in: 'A dictator can have no rest, he must be always on the watch.' Without heeding the interruption, he went on, as was his wont, to finish his own train of thought: 'Was no allowance to be made for me? I can assure you I am a man always ready to make allowances for everyone.' He then shook the ashes from his cigar, stood up, and without another word walked out on the Terrace.

Parnell was right. There was no man more ready to make allowances, no man more ready to forgive and to forget. A member of the party had (in the days before the split) grossly insulted him. This individual was subsequently driven out of the National ranks, though not for this reason, but for his Whig leanings. Afterwards it was suggested that he should be brought back. Parnell at once accepted the suggestion. 'Parnell was quite willing,' this ex-M.P. said to me, 'to take me back, but Healy and Dillon objected, and the matter was let drop.' During the Special Commission it was suggested that Mr. Healy (for whom Parnell could have had no love after the Galway election)[7] should hold a brief. Parnell consented at once. But Davitt strongly objected, and the suggestion was not, therefore, carried out. 'Healy,' said an old Fenian to Parnell, 'seems to have the best political head of all these people.' 'He has the only political head among them,' rejoined Parnell.

In some of his speeches Parnell had made personal attacks on Mr. Gladstone. I thought these attacks undeserved and told him so. He said: 'What have I said?' I replied, 'You remember as well as I.' 'I called him an old gentleman,' he said. 'Well, he is an old gentleman; there is no harm in that.' I said: 'I wish you would take this matter seriously.' 'Well, but,' he repeated, 'what have I said? What have I called him? Tell me.' 'Well,' I rejoined — 'you will probably smile, but it is not, after all, a smiling matter — you called him "a grand old spider." I met Morley[8] (who is not unfriendly to you) in the Lobby and he said, "Do you think I can have any-

6. Tim Healy's phrase for Parnell, 'the man at the wheel', was coined at a meeting in Dublin in November 1890.

7. In the Galway by-election of 1886, Parnell recommended for the seat Captain O'Shea, the husband of Katharine O'Shea, the woman whose lover he had been for several years. Tim Healy and Joseph Biggar led a furious campaign against this recommendation. Healy publicly referred to Katharine O'Shea as Parnell's mistress. Parnell forced O'Shea on the party, but the rancour remained.

8. John, Viscount Morley (1838-1923), British Liberal statesman and writer.

thing to do with a man who called Mr. Gladstone 'a grand old spider'?"' Parnell smiled and answered: 'I think that is complimentary — spinning all kinds of webs and devices, that's just what he does.' I said: 'I wish you would take this matter seriously. It is really unworthy of you. No man has avoided personalities all these years more than you. Why should you descend to them now?' Parnell (angrily): 'You all come to me to complain. I am fighting with my back to the wall, and every blow I hit is criticised by my friends. You all forget how I am attacked. You only come to find fault with me. You are all against me.' I said: 'I do not think you ought to say that. If I were against you I would not be here. I do not come as Mr. Gladstone's friend; I come as yours, because I feel it is unworthy of you.' 'You are right,' he said, suddenly placing his hand on my shoulder; 'personal abuse is wrong. I have said these things and forgotten them as soon as I have said them. But you are right in talking about it.'

Upon another occasion I said that Mr. Gladstone deserved well of Ireland, adding, 'Almost all that has been done for Ireland in my time has been done by Mr. Gladstone — Gladstone *plus* Fenianism, and *plus* you.' We then talked about the Fenians and separation. I said: 'Every Irish Nationalist would go for separation if he thought he could get it; we are all Home Rulers because we do not believe separation is possible.' After a pause he said, showing no disposition to continue the subject: 'I have never gone for separation. I never said I would. The physical force men understand my position very well. I made it clear to them that I would be satisfied with a Parliament, and that I believed in our constitutional movement; but I also said that if our constitutional movement failed, I could not then stand in the way of any man who wished to go further and to try other means. That was the position I always took up. I have never changed, and I still believe in our constitutional movement. I believe that with our own Parliament, if England does not meddle, we can build up our country.' I said: '——,' naming an old Fenian, 'says that there has been too much land and too little nationality in your movement all the time.' 'Does he suggest,' rejoined Parnell, with a slight touch of sarcasm, 'that the land should have been neglected?' No,' I rejoined, 'but he thinks that you allowed it to overshadow the National movement.'

Parnell. 'That could not have been helped. Remember the crisis of 1879.[9] There was distress and famine; the tenants rushed [to] the movement. Besides, the claims of the tenants were just in themselves, and ought to have been taken up.' 'The Fenians,' I said, 'are the real Nationalist force in Ireland.' 'That is true,' he rejoined.

One of our last talks was about the Liberal leaders and the progress of Home Rule in England. He spoke of the seceders. 'What do they expect?' he said. 'Do they think that Home Rule is so near that anyone may carry it through now?' I replied: 'That is what they do think. I heard that one of them said: "The ship has crossed the ocean. She is coming into port. Anyone can do the rest."' A faint smile was the only response. 'Do they think,' he continued, 'that the Liberal leaders will carry Home Rule? I say nothing about Mr. Gladstone now, but remember Mr. Gladstone is an old man. He cannot live for ever. I agree that he means to establish some kind of Irish Parliament. What kind? That is the question I have always raised. He will be satisfied if he gives us any kind of Parliament. He is an old man, and he cannot wait. I am a young man, and I can afford to wait. I want a Parliament that we shall be able to keep and to work for our country, and if we do not get it this year or next I can wait for half a dozen years; but it must be a real Parliament when it comes. I grant you all you say about Mr. Gladstone's power and intentions to establish a Parliament of some kind, but Home Rule will not come in his time. We have to look to his successors. Depend upon it I am saying what is true. Who will be his successors? Who are the gentlemen whom the seceders trust? Name them to me, and I will tell you what I think.'

I named Mr. Morley. 'Yes,' said Parnell, 'Mr. Morley has a good record. I have always said that. But has Mr. Morley any influence in England? Do you think that Mr. Morley has the power to carry Home Rule? Will England follow him? Will the Liberal party follow him? I do not think that Morley has any following in the country.'

I said: 'Well, there is Asquith.[10] He is a coming man. Some people say he may be the Liberal leader of the future.'

9. Famine in 1879 led to the formation of the Land League by Michael Davitt. Parnell supported the League and, with John Dillon, introduced the boycott as its chief weapon.

10. Herbert Asquith (1852-1928) was Britain's prime minister 1908-16. He introduced the Third Home Rule Bill in 1912 and had it suspended for the duration of World War I.

Parnell. 'Yes, Mr. Asquith is a coming man, a very clever man; but (looking me straight in the face) do you think Mr. Asquith is very keen about Home Rule? Do you think that he will risk anything for Home Rule? Mr. Asquith won't trouble about Home Rule, take my word for that.'

I said: 'There is Campbell-Bannerman.[11] I hear that he is a very good fellow, and he made about as good an Irish Secretary as any of them.' 'Yes,' he replied, 'I dare say he is a very good fellow, and as an Irish Secretary he left things alone (with a droll smile) — a sensible thing for an Irish Secretary. If they do not know anything they had better do nothing.' I said: 'The most objectionable Englishman is the Englishman who suddenly wakes up and imagines he has discovered Ireland — the man who comes to you and says: "You know I was a Home Ruler before Mr. Gladstone."'....

Parnell ... said: 'But do you think that Campbell-Bannerman has any influence? He is not going to lead the Liberal party. I think he has no influence.'

I said: 'Lord Rosebury.[12] He has influence.'

Parnell. 'I know nothing about Lord Rosebery. Probably he has influence. But do you think he is going to use it for Home Rule? Do you think he knows anything about Home Rule or cares anything about it?

I said: 'Sir William Harcourt.'[13]

Parnell. 'Ah, now you have come to the point. I have been waiting for that.' Then, turning fully round and facing me, he continued: 'What do you think of Sir William Harcourt? He will be the Liberal leader when Mr. Gladstone goes. Do you think he will trouble himself about Home Rule? He will think only of getting his party together, and he will take up any question that will best help him to do that. Mark what I say. Sir William Harcourt will have to be fought again.'

'Do you think,' I asked, 'that the Home Rule movement, the movement for an Irish Parliament, has made any real progress in England?'

'It has taken no root,' he answered, 'but our movement has made some progress.'

'The land question,' I said, 'has made progress. The labour movement here has helped it; the cry against coercion has told. But has the demand for an Irish Parliament made way? Do the English electors understand it? Do they really know the difference between Home Rule and Local Government? I doubt it.'

He said: 'I think we are hammering it into them by degrees. You must never expect the English to be enthusiastic about Home Rule. I have always said that. But they are beginning to see the difficulties of governing Ireland. They find they cannot do it, and Home Rule must come out of that.'

'Well,' I said, 'I do not know that. If Mr. Gladstone were to say tomorrow that Local Government would do after all, they would turn round at once and say that Home Rule and Local Government were the same thing.'

'Yes,' he said, 'that is true; but we have only to keep pounding away and to take care that they do not go back. They will not work it out in the way you think. They will find Ireland impossible to govern, and then they will give us what we want. That is what will happen. We must show them our power. They will bow to nothing but power, I assure you. If we hold together there is nothing that we cannot do in that House.'

I said: 'Hold together! There is an end to that for a long time. It will take you ten years to pull the country together again.'

'No,' he rejoined very quietly; 'I will do it in five years — that is what I calculate.'

'Well, Gladstone will be dead then,' I said. 'The whole question to me is, you and Mr. Gladstone. If you both go, Home Rule will go with you for this generation.'

'But I will not go,' he answered angrily; 'I am a young man, and I will not go.' And there was a fierce flash in his eyes which was not pleasant to look at.

The fight went on, and not a ray of hope shone upon Parnell's path. In Ireland the Fenians rallied everywhere to his standard, but the whole power of the Church was used to crush him. In June he married Mrs. O'Shea, and a few weeks later 'young' Mr. Gray,[14] of the 'Freeman's Journal,' seized upon

11. Sir Henry Campbell-Bannerman (1836-1908) was chief secretary for Ireland 1884-85 and prime minister 1905-08. He attempted to introduce a measure of devolved government in place of Home Rule.

12. Lord Rosebery (1847-1929) succeeded Gladstone as prime minister in 1894 but was in office for only about fifteen months. On assuming office, he immediately gave an indication that his commitment to Home Rule was, to say the least, qualified.

13. Sir William Harcourt (1827-1904) persuaded Gladstone to repudiate Parnell's leadership after the divorce proceedings. He was chancellor of the exchequer 1886, 1892-94, and 1894-95. He was leader of the Liberal Party 1896-98.

14. Edward Dwyer Gray, editor of the newspaper in succession to his father. *The Freeman's Journal* deserted Parnell at the last moment, under clerical pressure. Thereafter it was amalgamated with Tim

the marriage as a pretext for going over to the enemy, because it was against the law of the Catholic Church to marry a divorced woman. But Parnell, amid all reverses, never lost heart. On the defection of the 'Freeman's Journal' he set immediately to work to found a new morning paper — 'The Irish Daily Independent.'[15] He still continued to traverse the country, cheering his followers, and showing a bold front to his foes. At moments he had fits of depression and melancholy. He did not wish to be alone. He would often — a most unusual thing for him — talk for talking's sake. He would walk the streets of Dublin with a follower far into the night, rather than sit in his hotel by himself. . . .

Healy's *National Press*, the leading anti-Parnellite newspaper. The reorganization of the board of the reconstituted paper was one more squalid and bitter affair that lasted until 1893.

15. The first issue appeared on 18 December 1891, two months after Parnell's death. At first the paper employed many members of the IRB; then it was taken over by John Redmond and finally was bought by William Martin Murphy and renamed the *Irish Independent* (1905).

MICHAEL DAVITT

from: THE FALL OF FEUDALISM IN IRELAND (1904)

[This excerpt from Davitt's account of the Parnell split and the famous meeting in Committee Room 15 of the House of Commons is given to provide further background to the great myth of the tragic leader. Davitt does not hesitate to condemn Parnell; but he is aware of the disastrous consequences of the sequence of events that began with the divorce case and culminated in Parnell's ruin and death. In Davitt's view, the Irish Parliamentary Party's first mistake was to re-elect Parnell as its sessional chairman on 25 November 1890, eight days after the jury in the divorce case had found a verdict against him. Parnell ignored the advice of John Morley, one of Gladstone's colleagues, to withdraw from the leadership for a time until the storm had blown over.]

CHAPTER LII

SAMSON AGONISTES

. . . The subsequent action of the Irish party was an instance of wisdom coming too late. They attempted to correct the first mistake by committing another. Two blunders were to amend that of the initial election, and for eight or ten days the newspaper readers of the political world perused the debates in 'Committee-room 15' with a relish which an Irish faction fight can alone provide for the keen appetite of Ireland's enemies. It was a debate over the coffin of Home Rule by the men who had been parties to the deed which Mr. Parnell was permitted to commit, unrestrained, in their presence.

Many good things were well said during the discussion — which could have been more appropriately spoken on November 25th. Mr. McCarthy[1] quoted Grattan in his fine expression, 'No man can be lavish with his honour, or woman with her virtue, or country with its liberty.'[2] Mr. Sexton[3] told Mr. Parnell that, 'no service rendered by any leader to any cause entitled him to effect its ruin.' Mr. Parnell's contemptuous rejoinder was: 'You elected me unanimously. You now want to throw me over at Mr. Gladstone's dictation. You all have said, again and again, that I am indispensable to the Irish cause. For these and other reasons I shall remain.' These were not his exact words, but they represent the spirit and purpose of his defiance to all the arguments and influences that had been used on the other side.

1. Justin McCarthy (1830-1912), one of Parnell's chief lieutenants. Gladstone informed McCarthy that Parnell was no longer acceptable to the Liberal Party as leader of the Irish Party. McCarthy could not persuade Parnell of this and when Gladstone published an account of his position, McCarthy became the leader of the anti-Parnellites. On 6 November 1890 he led the withdrawal of members of the party from Committee Room 15.
2. Grattan's speech of 1 April 1780 on Ireland's right to independence. The actual quotation in the revised version of the speech is: 'A nation's liberty cannot, like her treasures, be meted and parcelled out in gratitude: no man can be grateful or liberal of his conscience, nor woman of her honour, nor nation of her liberty.' The 'fine expression' does of course insinuate a reference to Mrs O'Shea, the divorce proceedings and Parnell's sacrifice of his nation's welfare.
3. Thomas Sexton (1848-1932), chief spokesman on finance for the Irish Parliamentary Party, known as 'silver-tongued Sexton' for his brilliance in public speaking. At first he had proposed Parnell for the sessional chairmanship, but he withdrew his support when it became clear to him that this would cause the ruin of the party.

He had presided over his own trial by his colleagues. They were treated by him with studied contempt during the whole proceedings, and never once did he admit, by word or sign or action that he had done any wrong or that the party had any right to go back upon its first decision. At one time during the discussion it looked as if the appeals that had been addressed to him had weakened his resolution. He asked for forty-eight hours' time for reflection. This was hopefully given. He sought the direction of whatever hidden influence had completely usurped his personal power and will, and returned obdurate and unrelenting. He would risk all and concede nothing. Neither Ireland, nor Home Rule, nor his party, nor his own political salvation had weighed against whatever counsels had urged him — knowingly, no doubt — to a ruin which might, thereby, be that of the cause that Pigott's forgeries,[4] sworn to by O'Shea,[5] had failed, through Pigott's confession and suicide, to destroy. The die was cast. The Irish party was split in two, and with it the entire league movement throughout the world. The Irish Samson had pulled the pillars from beneath the temple of a great cause in his own downfall.

No blunder of his party, or weakness of his chief lieutenants, or consideration for man or woman, offered even the shadow of a rational excuse for Mr. Parnell's action. He had been treated in the most indulgent manner and spirit by his colleagues, even after the facts about the Gladstone letter had leaked out. It was proposed to him, in their behalf, that he could appoint a committee of his party — men of his own preference and selection — to conduct its affairs during a six months' absence. He could offer to resign his seat in Cork — an offer which would not be accepted. The chair of the party would be left vacant; no one would occupy it, if the offer were made; no offer of the kind would come from his colleagues. He could withdraw from his position until the storm blew over, marry the lady for whom, or from whom, all this disaster had been brought upon a movement with which she as an Englishwoman had no friendly concern, and then come back and resume his old position. More generous terms had never been offered to a man whose own act had brought him face to face with the threatened ruin of himself and his party. It was in a deliberate refusal to accept of this way of escaping from a position of his own making, and not on the grounds of his moral misconduct, that Mr. Parnell made himself impossible as a leader, and which compelled the men who had built up the Irish movement with him to declare themselves his antagonists in his efforts to undo his and their work.

The most noted and influential of his lieutenants pronounced against him after all attempts to reason him into a sane line of action had failed. Those who took his side were the men of least prestige and experience in the party. These were likewise in a marked minority. Division in Ireland followed on similar lines. Mr. Parnell's former clerical and episcopal supporters went with the majority. The minority in the country, however, included a majority of the most active of local leaders. Friends were driven asunder. Families even became divided. Some town or village in a county would be found practically of one way of thinking, while another hamlet or town, a few miles away, would hold to the opposite side. This was what happened in Ireland. In the United States the whole league organization toppled over like a house of cards. 'Committee-room 15' undid, in ten days, the work of as many missions from Ireland and the labors of ten years in building up a great auxiliary organization beyond the Atlantic. The friends in Great Britain and Australasia remained more or less with ranks unbroken, only dispirited, and on the side of the majority.

In the Kilkenny, Sligo, and Carlow elections, which followed the 'split,' the popular verdicts upheld the action of the majority, and condemned that of the Parnellite factionists. The people had been appealed to, and their judgment was emphatic. Still, Mr. Parnell resolutely refused to listen to any decision against him, or to adopt any alternative course to one of dogged, ruthless desperation. Former implacable opponents espoused his cause, without opening his eyes to the significance of this sinister sympathy, and without any protest from those who were conducting his

4. Richard Pigott (1828-89), who forged letters for *The Irish Times* newspaper implicating the Parnellites in crime. In a subsequent inquiry he condemned himself by his misspelling of the word 'hesitancy' as 'hesitency' — an item commemorated by Joyce. He fled to Madrid where he committed suicide.

5. Captain William O'Shea (1840-1905), husband of Parnell's mistress, Katharine O'Shea, and a member of the Irish Parliamentary Party. He told the Special Commission on the Pigott forgeries that he believed that Parnell's signature on a letter to *The Times*, condemning the Phoenix Park murders, was genuine. O'Shea was in Madrid when Pigott committed suicide there. He sued for divorce in late 1889, citing Parnell as co-respondent, and was granted a decree nisi on 18 November 1890.

campaign. Every enemy of Home Rule in Ireland and England wished him success, and every land-grabber in Ireland insulted his former record by taking his side. Men and bodies formerly against him, when he stood for a united Ireland and a mighty race movement, now ranged themselves against his opponents, and lent him a help which was only offered in the hope of thereby destroying the great organization of which he had been the trusted leader. And in this disastrous course a great personality was driven by the impulse of a fatal pride and the backing of a reckless factionism [*sic*] to rush headlong to ruin.

It would be a useless and sorrowful task to inflict upon the reader the story of the internecine conflict forced upon his own movement by Mr. Parnell. No good or even historic end would be served in such a narrative. It would tell only of a heart-breaking conflict between men who were separated by no principle of political faith, and no aim of public duty, in a country which had almost reached the goal of its long-deferred national hopes. It was a most hateful and senseless struggle, and earned for our cause some pity and much contempt from former supporters who were not of our race. It rendered the work of political life in Ireland a pathway strewn with thorns for those whose duty it was to defend the land movement and the cause of Home Rule against the revolt of Mr. Parnell and his followers. One can only hope that the recording angel in the paradise, or purgatory, reserved for Irish patriots in the fabled regions of Hy-Brazil[6] will charitably obliterate from his tablets the words spoken and written in these years of humiliating sectional strife. . . .

6. 'The Elysium of the Celtic legends' [Davitt's note].

T. P. O'CONNOR

(1848-1929)

from: MEMOIRS OF AN OLD PARLIAMENTARIAN (1929)

[Almost forty years after the event, Thomas Power O'Connor's recreation of the famous meetings in Committee Room 15 in the House of Commons between 26 November and 6 December 1890 was still vivid in its particulars, even though he was not present. 'Tay Pay', as he was known, was a fine gossip columnist.

Gladstone wrote to John Morley on 24 November, after the verdict had gone against Parnell in the uncontested divorce case brought by Captain O'Shea, asking that it be shown to Justin McCarthy, vice-chairman of the Irish Parliamentary Party, who was to make known its contents to Parnell. In effect, Gladstone stated that Parnell could not remain head of his party and retain the Liberal alliance. McCarthy failed to convince Parnell that this was indeed the case. The Parliamentary Party, not knowing of Gladstone's letter, re-elected Parnell its chairman for the next parliamentary session. In response, Gladstone published his letter to Morley. Parnell refused to reconsider his position as chairman. The catholic hierarchy then announced a meeting for 3 December. On 29 November Parnell published a *Manifesto to the Irish People*, attacking Gladstone and the Liberals and a section of his own party. Thereafter, the disputes in Committee Room 15 dragged on until, on 6 December, Justin McCarthy led out 44 members, leaving Parnell with 27 followers. The party had split and would not reunite again until 1900.]

Committee-Room 15: The First Day, November 26, 1890

When on that dreadful night after the Party meeting, the Irish members heard Gladstone's letter read to them, Parnell had left the House, but a requisition was drawn up, signed by thirty-one members, asking the Whips to call the Party together again on the following afternoon. The meeting-place again was Room No. 15, and Parnell, on taking the chair, would not accept the plea of some of his supporters that the meeting was not in order: he said that on a requisition so widely signed it was the duty of the Whips to call the meeting. . . .

Mr. Sexton[1] appealed to Parnell, in view of the danger of Home Rule candidates being defeated at

1. Thomas Sexton (1848-1932), at that time MP for West Belfast, was known as a brilliant public speaker and was nicknamed 'silver-tongued Sexton'.

the General Election, to reconsider his position as Chairman of the Party, and to retire temporarily. He suggested that after Parnell's retirement the chairmanship should not be filled, but that the affairs of the Party should be managed by a committee of members to be nominated by Parnell himself, until they could safely recall him. Mr. M'Carthy and other members added their appeal. Parnell still said nothing. After an adjournment to enable certain members to bring in private Bills, there were speeches on the other side insisting that Parnell should not retire. Mr. Sexton thought that the views of every member of the Party should be obtained, and, as there were many members absent, the meeting adjourned till the following Monday.

In the meantime Parnell had issued his 'Manifesto' to the Irish People....

The 'Manifesto' was a very long document, purporting in the main to give a report of private *pourparlers*[2] between Gladstone and Parnell at Hawarden a year before, with regard to the Home Rule Bill which the Liberals would introduce in the event of being returned to power....

There was also the matter of the evicted tenants, so many of whom had lost their lands owing to their obedience to the instructions of the Land League.[3] Their fate was a burning question in Ireland at this time, and there was expectation that a Liberal Government would restore them. They were another factor that helped to embarrass the issue in Committee Room No. 15; and in his 'Manifesto' Parnell quoted Morley as saying to him with a gesture of despair that the Liberals, if returned to power, could not do anything for these evicted tenants by direct action. In its purely rhetorical passages the 'Manifesto' crossed the Rubicon;[4] such references as that to 'English wolves now howling for my destruction' could not possibly help the situation, though it might rally old Fenians to his side.[5] M'Carthy asked him to take it out, and Parnell answered promptly that, whatever went out, that phrase must remain.

The Second Day, December 1, 1890

On Monday, December 1, the Irish Party reassembled in Room No. 15, with Parnell in the chair....

It was in the debate on this amendment[6] that the first of the many scenes between Mr. Healy and Parnell occurred. I have told what ill-feeling there had been between the two men for some years. In one of the letters read in the Divorce Court Mrs. O'Shea quoted Parnell as saying of Mr. Healy that it was ill fighting with a chimney-sweep, for, whether you were in the right or the wrong, you would get soiled.

Curiously, at a meeting held in the Leinster Hall, Dublin, three days after the decree *nisi*, Mr. Healy had made an impassioned defence of Parnell's leadership, ending up with a phrase that was to become a slogan of the Parnellites: 'Don't speak to the man at the wheel!' That, however, was before Gladstone's letter. Now in Committee-Room 15 Mr. Healy boldly contested the truth of Parnell's account of the secret conversations at Hawarden. 'You will have the difficulty of summing up to this jury, you being at the same time the judge and the defendant,' said Mr. Healy. He accused Parnell of using 'false words' at a meeting at Liverpool, whereupon Parnell sprang to his feet and cried, 'I will not stand an accusation of falsehood from Timothy Healy, and I call upon him to withdraw his expressions'. Mr. Healy said he would do so 'out of respect for the authority of the chair', and, directly

2. i.e. informal or preliminary conferences. Hawarden Castle in Flintshire, north Wales, was Gladstone's home for sixty years.
3. The Land War had been renewed with the Plan of Campaign (1886-91) organized by Tim Healy, William O'Brien, John Dillon, Tim Harrington and others. The aim was to secure a reduction in rent for the tenant. When evictions followed, there was great turmoil, much of it caused by the operation of A.J. ('Bloody') Balfour's Perpetual Coercion Act of 1887. By 1891, the Plan was failing for want of funds and for want of support from Parnell, who had always held aloof from it.
4. i.e. took an irrevocable step. When Julius Caesar crossed the small river Rubicon in 49 B.C. and marched on Rome, he went beyond the limits of his province and became an invader in Italy, precipitating a war with Pompey and the senatorial party.
5. A phrase that is re-echoed by Joyce and many others. His countrymen, Joyce wrote in *The Shade of Parnell* (1912), 'did not throw him to the English wolves; they tore him to pieces themselves.' In fact, Parnell's *Manifesto* was a bad political error and alienated many potential supporters (see pp. 312-15 above).
6. William Abraham, a protestant member of the Irish Parliamentary Party, had moved: 'That, acting upon the imperative sense of duty to our country, we, the members of the Irish Party, do declare that Mr. Parnell's tenure of the chairmanship of this Party is hereby terminated.' Parnell, employing delaying tactics, ruled this out of order until a previous motion by John Barry, suggesting an adjournment until Friday to enable Parnell to reconsider his position, be debated, even though the Friday had already gone by, this being Monday. Barry was an associate of Tim Healy. Then another MP, Colonel Nolan, proposed an amendment to Barry's motion, stating 'That the question touching the chairmanship of the Irish Parliamentary Party be postponed until the members have had an opportunity of personally ascertaining the views of their constituents, and until the Party can meet in Dublin.' This amendment led to the scene between Parnell and Healy.

addressing Parnell, he continued, 'I say to Mr. Parnell his power has gone. He derived that power from the people. We are the representatives of the people. Place an iron bar in a coil and electrolize that coil, and the iron bar becomes magnetic. The Party was that electric action. There [pointing to Mr. Parnell] stood the iron bar. The electricity is gone, and the magnetism with it, when our support has passed away. I then say and declare that my vote shall be for the deposition of the chairman of this Party.'

In his reply Parnell said: 'Mr. Healy has been trained in this warfare. Who trained him? Who saw his genius first? Who telegraphed to him from America? Who gave him his first opportunity and chance? Who got him his seat in Parliament? That Mr. Healy should be here today to destroy me is due to myself.' It was at the close of this speech that he made the emotional appeal to his Party not to leave him when they were in sight of the Promised Land. When Mr. Justin M'Carthy was pointing out the strangeness of Parnell's conduct in concealing the Hawarden conversations from all his colleagues, and spoke of the whole transaction as betraying 'a vital error of judgment', Parnell interjected 'Hear, hear'.

In the course of the subsequent speeches during that long sitting there were many passage-at-arms between the more hotly tempered members on both sides, and at every stage the breach was becoming more irrevocable. Just at midnight the adjournment of the debate was moved, and Parnell declared that the 'Ayes' had it. Mr. Healy pointed out that the chairman had not put it to the 'Noes'. When Mr. Parnell rose as if to move away, Mr. Healy moved that Mr. M'Carthy take the chair, which brought from Parnell the angry retort that he had not left it yet. Challenged by Mr. Healy to put the question, Parnell said angrily, 'I am not going to have my ruling challenged by Mr. Timothy Healy'.

Parnell was striving to avoid a division so soon. The vote would inevitably have followed the line of cleavage in the Party, whereas Parnell hoped by delay and the wandering nature of the debate to detach some opponents from the majority before the parties had been stereotyped in a division. Thus, after all, he declared that the 'Noes' had it, and his followers did not dare to challenge a division. Having thus insisted on their right, the majority soon afterwards consented to the adjournment.

The Third Day, December 2, 1890

The next day's debate opened at noon on Tuesday. Parnell again called upon his secretary to read a new batch of letters and resolutions in his favour....

At length Mr. Healy demanded what was the question before the meeting. 'A discussion', said Parnell, 'has been opened by Mr. Barry on the question of communication with the delegates in America, and the discussion will have to proceed to its end.' To this Mr. Healy retorted: 'Another piece of pure obstruction'; whereupon Parnell said, 'I think that is a most insolent and impertinent observation — a most insolent and impertinent observation'. Mr. Healy appealed to his friends not to continue the discussion.... So the wearisome business went on, lifted out of its monotony now and then by sharp-tempered recrimination. Old Fenians like James O'Kelly and J. F. X. O'Brien found themselves on opposite sides, while one of the Parnellites had actually supported Butt and Shaw against Parnell in the far-away days when the movement began.[7] Every supporter of Parnell in the room had his say, according to instructions, for Parnell believed that time and delay would be on his side. During one of the last speeches Parnell bent over to Mr. Sexton and said with pleasant humour, 'I say, Sexton, are you fellows going to keep this thing up all night?' The joke was that the majority had been forced to listen for the greater part of two days to speeches from the minority.

The division was taken after midnight. Parnell knew he would lose on the vote, but still he betrayed no sign of excitement, but stood with a list of the Party in his hand. The room was lit by lamps and candles placed on the tables, and as Parnell put the amendment his pale face was in shadow.

He read the amendment in a low, unfaltering voice, and, looking up at his colleagues, said, 'All who are in favour of it will say "Aye"'. His friends shouted for all they were worth. But a moment later came the remorseless 'Noes'. The irrevocable moment had come, when unity and discipline were no longer to bind that Party like a band of brothers.

7. James O'Kelly (1845-1916), former member of the IRB, active in the Land League and the New Departure, MP for North Roscommon and a Parnellite. He introduced Parnell to the spy, Henri Le Caron. James Francis Xavier O'Brien (1828-1905) took part in the 1867 Rising, was imprisoned, and later became MP for Mayo 1885-95. He joined the anti-Parnellite faction. William Shaw (1823-95) succeeded Isaac Butt as chairman of the Home Rule Party in 1879, but was narrowly defeated for the leadership of the party in 1880.

'I think the "Ayes" have it,' said Parnell quietly, fighting for his hand to the last.

A vote being demanded, he did not longer resist, but called out the names alphabetically. The first two — Abraham and Barry — were against him; the next two — Blane and Byrne — were for him. But soon numbers began to tell against him, as eager partisans kept count. Some answered their names quietly, others with emphasis. When Parnell called out his own name and responded 'Aye', there was a loud cheer from his supporters. At the end he totted up the numbers and said without emotion, 'I find that the Noes are 44 and the Ayes 29, so I declare that the Noes have it by a majority of 15'. There was no demonstration, and the meeting, on Parnell's suggestion, adjourned until the next day. As he left the room, Parnell told some waiting journalists that he was 'more than satisfied with the result'. To his supporters he used to say, 'We have only to get back eight men to have a majority'.

The Fourth Day, December 3, 1890

... When the Party assembled on the next day (Wednesday), Mr. Clancy, one of Parnell's supporters, put forward an amendment: 'That in view of the difference of opinion that has arisen between Mr. Gladstone and Mr. Parnell as to the accuracy of Mr. Parnell's recollection of the suggestions offered at Hawarden in reference to suggested changes in and departures from the Home Rule Bill of 1886 on the subject of the control of the Constabulary and the settlement of the land question, the Whips of the Party be instructed to obtain from Mr. Gladstone, Mr. John Morley,[8] and Sir William Harcourt[9] for the information of the Party, before any further consideration of the question, what their views are with regard to these vital points'.

Parnell was not in the room when Mr. Clancy concluded his speech, and Mr. Sexton asked would Parnell resign if the Party considered that the Liberal guarantees were satisfactory? Mr. Redmond said Parnell would in that contingency resign. Parnell was sent for. It seemed that there would be a way out after all. As Parnell entered the room Mr. Healy rose, and speaking with great emotion said, 'I wish to make a personal declaration in your regard, Mr. Parnell. I wish to say that if you feel able to meet the Party on these points my voice will be the first at the very earliest moment possible consistent with the liberties of my country to call you back to the leadership of the Irish race.' Then Mr. Healy wept.

Mr. Sexton sought an assurance from Parnell that he would allow the Party as a whole to determine whether the Liberal leaders' reply was satisfactory, and, if they so decided, that he would then voluntarily retire from the leadership. Parnell asked for time to consider his reply, and the meeting was accordingly adjourned until the next day....

The Fifth Day, December 4, 1890

When the Party assembled at noon on Thursday, Parnell declared, in answer to Mr. Sexton's question of the day before, that he 'could not agree to surrender his responsibility or any part of his responsibility'. He then read a resolution declaring that no Home Rule Bill which did not confer immediate control of the police and power to deal with the land question on the Irish Parliament would be regarded as satisfactory by the Party. He intimated his intention, if that resolution were adopted, of proposing a further one by which the Whips and five members from each side in the Party should meet and select from themselves a deputation of six to seek an interview with Gladstone, Harcourt, and Morley, 'for the purpose of ascertaining whether their views are in accordance with the views of the Party on those points as above expressed, and whether they will agree to embody those views in their Home Rule Bill and make them vital to the measure'.

It was in answering these proposals that Mr. Healy made a very vehement speech, during which he had many heated passages with the chairman. 'We shall sit here,' he said, 'or a sufficient number of us shall sit here, and when you have your speeches delivered we will return and we will vote your deposition, be it today, or tomorrow, or Saturday, or Sunday — aye, the better the day the better the deed.' He went on to read a speech which Parnell had delivered six months before.

MR. HEALY: On that occasion he said he 'undertook to hold aloof from all English parties until an English party would concede to Ireland the just rights of the Irish people'.

8. John, 1st Viscount Morley (1838-1923), a powerful figure in English politics and later (1892-95) chief secretary for Ireland, had acted as adviser and intermediary to Gladstone and Parnell.

9. Sir William Harcourt (1827-1904), home secretary in Gladstone's second ministry 1880-85, later several times chancellor of the exchequer and Liberal Party leader 1896-98.

MR. PARNELL: Hear, hear.

MR. HEALY: Will he cheer what follows?

MR. PARNELL: Every word of it. Read it.

MR. HEALY: Every precious word. (*Reading*) 'That time has since come'. Where is the cheer for that?

MR. PARNELL: Hear, hear.

MR. HEALY: I have extracted it at last, rather feebly, I suggest. (*Reading*) 'That time has since come about when an English party — a great English party, under the distinguished leadership of Mr. Gladstone — has conceded to Ireland those rights, and has enabled us to enter into an honourable alliance, honourable and hopeful for our country'. With a 'garrulous old man'. [A previous gibe by Parnell.]

MR. PARNELL: That is interpolation.

MR. HEALY: (*Reading*) 'Honourable for that great English party: an alliance which I venture to believe will last.' What broke it off?

Mr. Parnell, Colonel Nolan, and Dr. Fitzgerald each replied: 'Gladstone's letter.'

MR. HEALY: It perished in the stench of the Divorce Court.

Having read further from Parnell's speech, Mr. Healy came to the sentence: 'I am confident that Mr. Gladstone's genius will be equal to the task, that he will be powerful enough to reconcile and assuage the prejudices which still unhappily prevail to some extent.'

MR. PARNELL: Hear, hear.

MR. HEALY: I wonder he never succeeded in assuaging Mr. Parnell's prejudice.

MR. PARNELL: He never has, and never will.

MR. HEALY: Then he never assuaged your prejudice, and you hoped he would assuage those of your countrymen.

MR. PARNELL: Hear, hear.

MR. HEALY: 'Physician, heal thyself'. You recommend the Gladstone prescription to the Irish nation, and you declare in advance that their prejudices may safely be allayed and they may safely accept the aid of Mr. Gladstone's genius; but he cannot allay your prejudices. I retain my hillside opinion of the whole transaction.

In his peroration Mr. Healy said: 'Whatever be the insults hurled at me by any section of my countrymen, whatever taunts may be addressed to me in the course of this feud, I will endure them as we have endured ten years of slavery in this House, ten years of labour, ten years of self-suppression, ten years of sacrifice; yet we will go to our people and we will tell them what are the real issues in this matter, for though hitherto some of them have been covered up and enclosed, we shall not shirk, and I shall not shirk, stating them broadly and openly to the people — and with the people be the verdict. If you, sir, should go down, you are only one man gone. Heads of greater leaders have been stricken on the block before now for Ireland, and the Irish cause remained. The Irish people can put us down, but the Irish cause will remain always. For the future I have no fear. Instead of being distressed, I am confident and buoyant. Instead of wishing myself dead, as I have heard some men do, I am glad to be alive for Ireland. I am glad in this hour of her sorrowful destiny to be able to stand with her, and stand with her we shall, be the issue what it may.'

Mr. John Redmond, who continued to support Parnell, was speaking, when an incident charged with dramatic irony occurred. Mr. Redmond described Parnell as the one man who was capable of saving the nation, and of discussing Home Rule on an equality with the leaders of the English parties. There was no other man, said Mr. Redmond. Mr. Healy here interjected; 'Suppose Mr. Parnell died?' At which Parnell exclaimed, with emphasis, amid the cheers of his colleagues: 'I don't intend to die.' In ten months Parnell was dead.

Mr. Redmond concluded his speech with the ominous words: 'I assert my belief that the dethronement of Mr. Parnell will be the signal for kindling the fires of dissension in every land where the Irish race has found a home. Let no man accuse me of wishing to kindle those fires; but they will be lighted if this act is done, and in them will be burned to ashes the last hopes of the Irish people in this generation for the freedom of their country.'

Mr. Sexton, who followed, pointed out that they had offered, if Parnell retired temporarily, to place the leadership in commission, and that Parnell could himself nominate the committee. He described the situation through which Ireland was passing as being like living on the crater of a live volcano. As a result of Mr. Sexton's appeal, Parnell gave an assurance that, if the majority of the Party decided by vote that the reply which was being sought from the Liberal leaders was satisfactory, he would resign the leadership, and he added: 'You might have had that at the beginning of the meeting if you had not Mr. Healy's speech.' 'No, sir,' Mr. Healy retorted, 'if we had not your speech.'....

The Seventh Day, December 6, 1890

This was to be the last day of the Party meeting together in one body as Parnell had himself created it. It was Saturday, December 6, 1890. Before the Party met at noon, the majority had come together and determined that the issue would have to be decided that day. The session was to be prorogued for Christmas on the following Monday or Tuesday, and it was now a race between the will of the majority and Parnell's artful tactics to delay a decision until the Party would have to meet elsewhere....

The last meeting of the Party began in Committee-Room 15 at noon, and, as Saturday is not a Parliamentary day, they met by favour of the Serjeant-at-Arms, who had granted the use of the room until six o'clock. It was the twelfth day since the proceedings opened, and the sixth successive day of debate.

Parnell immediately began his astute tactics for delaying a direct motion for his deposition. Soon he had the meeting wrangling over the Gladstone negotiations.... When nearly three hours had been spent in discussion, Mr. Sexton delivered the ultimatum of the majority that the proceedings would have to be brought to a close that day; and that if a motion to determine the final question were not put from the chair, they would have to 'take such other measure as may be open to them'.

After the majority had cheered this statement of policy, Parnell blandly suggested adjournment for lunch....

When the Party reassembled — the very last time they were all to meet together — the sub-committee's report was read by Mr. John Redmond. At its close Mr. Abraham and one of Parnell's supporters, Mr. John O'Connor,[10] rose. Parnell called on his man. Members of the majority shouted for Abraham. For the first time in these long and trying debates the meeting seemed to lose control of itself. Apart from individual outbursts of temper inevitable to the circumstances, the members had conducted themselves with patience and self-command. But now pent-up feelings broke loose, and Mr. Abraham came close to Parnell and proceeded to shout his resolution, which could not, however, be heard in the uproar. Mr. Abraham handed his resolution to Mr. Justin M'Carthy, from whose hand Parnell snatched the paper, and seemed to be about to tear it up, but instead placed it in his pocket. 'Give us back our document!' cried Mr. Healy. Mr. Arthur O'Connor,[11] one of the majority, appealed to his colleagues to manifest to 'the chairman, our late leader', every respect. Mr. Healy said that the chairman had called on Mr. John O'Connor, although Mr. Abraham had been the first to rise. 'Healy, you will have to answer for this!' cried one of the Parnellites. 'So will you, too!' retorted Mr. Healy. The chairman again called on Mr. John O'Connor. 'Abraham, Abraham!' cried Mr. Healy. 'I am your chairman until you depose me,' said Parnell, and Mr. Healy replied: 'Allow me to depose you'. Mr. M'Carthy complained that Parnell had struck the letter out of his hand. 'You were about to put some resolution, thereby usurping my functions', said Parnell. Mr. Healy moved that Mr. Abraham be heard, but was ruled out of order by the chair.

These unpleasant scenes lasted half an hour. Then it was arranged that Mr. Abraham would be allowed to move his resolution after Mr. John O'Connor had spoken. Mr. O'Connor brought in a resolution expressing dissatisfaction that Gladstone had refused to give Home Rule guarantees unless Parnell were deposed. He went on to point the moral that while the Irish members were contesting Parnell's leadership, the Liberal leaders had placed themselves unreservedly under Gladstone, showing a united front. Sir William Harcourt, when invited to meet the sub-committee, had replied, 'Treat with Mr. Gladstone'. Here Mr. Arthur O'Connor interjected: 'He is not a member of the Party'. At this Mr. John Redmond said: 'He is the master of the Party'. Then Mr. Healy cried: 'Who is to be mistress of the Party?'

At that terrible interjection passion froze. Parnell rose, with that blazing light in his eyes, and members thought he would strike Mr. Healy. Mr. Sexton felt the gravity of the remark so much that he confessed he hoped that Parnell would do so. Mr. Arthur O'Connor said: 'I appeal to my friend the chairman'. 'Better appeal to your own friends',

10. John O'Connor (1850-1928), former member of the IRB Supreme Council and MP for Tipperary 1885-90, lost his seat because of his loyalty to Parnell.

11. Arthur O'Connor MP, former Fenian and a close associate of Tim Healy.

said Parnell, 'better appeal to that cowardly little scoundrel there, that in an assembly of Irishmen dares to insult a woman.'

The moment came at length when Mr. Abraham moved: 'That we, the members of the Irish Parliamentary Party, declare that Mr. Parnell's tenure of the chairmanship of the Party is hereby terminated.' When Parnell ruled that this was not an amendment to the motion proposed by Mr. John O'Connor, Mr. Healy cried: 'Bravo, bravo!' 'Mr. Healy,' said Parnell, 'I will not stand very much more from you.'

The Split, December 6, 1890

There was further futile discussion: Parnell would not allow the Abraham amendment to be brought in — throughout the sittings he had wielded the powers of the chair most arbitrarily. At last the final moment had come, and Mr. Justin M'Carthy undertook the grave duty of declaring the breach. He performed his task in a few sentences with courage, but with a sort of sad gentleness which must have found an echo in most hearts in the shattered Party. 'I therefore feel', he concluded, 'that the longer we debate, the more we may possibly grow in passion, the more we may become unkindly, the more bitter things we may say. I see no further use carrying on a discussion which must be barren of all but reproach, ill-temper, controversy, and indignity, and I therefore suggest that all who think with me at this grave crisis should withdraw with me from this room.' Forty-five members went out in silence, twenty-seven remaining behind. Parnell called out to one of the departing members for whom he had a particular liking, but the member would not come back. A minor drama of the departure was when Mr. M'Carthy's son, Mr. Justin Huntly M'Carthy, who had hitherto supported Parnell, declared that, as a member of a constitutional party, he would go with the majority.[12]

Downstairs in the Conference Room the majority, with one of the Party Whips in the chair, appended their signatures to the following resolution: 'That, acting under an imperative sense of duty to our country, we, the undersigned, being an absolute majority of the whole number of the Irish Parliamentary Party, declare that Mr. Parnell's term of chairmanship of this Party is hereby terminated.' Mr. Justin M'Carthy was elected chairman of the Party, with a committee of eight — including three of us who were at that time in America — 'to exercise jointly with the chairman the powers and discharge the functions hitherto attached to the chairmanship of the Party'. The meeting declared the Party's independence of other parties, and that no measure of Home Rule could be entertained that did not satisfy the aspirations of the Irish people.

The 'split' had begun. Three days afterwards Parnell started for Ireland to begin the relentless fight which he was to wage in defence of his own leadership until ten months later, when death claimed him.

12. Justin Huntly McCarthy (1861-1936) surprised many members by this sudden switch to the group of anti-Parnellites led by his father, Justin McCarthy (1830-1912), at this time MP for Derry City.

TIMOTHY MICHAEL HEALY

(1855-1931)

from: LETTERS AND LEADERS OF MY DAY (1928)

[Healy is not the most reliable but is certainly the most entertaining of the many witnesses to what happened in Committee Room 15. His reminiscences are in part a defence of his actions and of his remarks — usually more memorable than the actions — which made him feared and, to a degree, despised by the very gentlemanly set, best represented by the endlessly civil and boring Justin McCarthy. Healy represents himself as less conniving than he was, although his attitude towards Parnell is more complex than is usually allowed. His letters to his wife are a great resource; she kept his, but he did not keep her's, so, after thirty-eight years he can resort to a version of what she must have asked to elicit his replies. Nevertheless, his explanations are an indication of the bitterness and recrimination that was to come in the next decade. The parliamentary movement lost its hard-won respectability and support. Healy, like William O'Brien (see below p. 346), understood this even while they contributed to the process.]

CHAPTER XXIV

PARNELL' S TRIUMPH (1889)

. . . O'Shea's divorce proceedings against Parnell were launched in December, 1889. They were regarded in Ireland as a fresh persecution by *The Times*. Anyone who turns to the *Freeman*[1] of that period will find resolutions from hundreds of branches of the National League expressing scorn at and disbelief in, them. One of the *Freeman* staff, Edward Ennis, called on me. (He became Registrar to the Lord Chancellor, and later Under-Secretary for Ireland.) I asked him why the *Freeman* encouraged a campaign of incredulity when every one knew of the scandal. Gloomily he answered, 'Oh, we have to keep up the pretence.' So notorious were the facts that David Plunket (Lord Rathmore),[2] on returning to the Commons Lobby from the Lords one day, said to Justin MacCarthy [*sic*], 'Well, Justin, how is your great Chief?' 'Oh,' MacCarthy replied, 'We don't see much of him.' 'No?' smiled Plunket, with the stammer which enhanced his raillery, 'I suppose he prefers taking his 'O'She-um cum dignitate'!'[3] . . . .

Though he had not been in Ireland for five years, his dictatorship seemed secure, despite his neglect, and he thought his position impregnable. In his last session of Parliament as leader (1890) he never attended the House until the day of prorogation.[4] Then he strolled into the smoke-room, which was empty save for the laborious and watchful Sexton, who for a score of years was a vigilant sentinel at Westminster, and never missed a chance to advance Irish interests. Parnell took out a cigar, and with his back to the empty fire-grate (it was August) said in a critical tone, 'Sexton, never before have I known a session in which the Irish estimates were so perfunctorily discussed!'

When Sexton told me this I asked, 'Did you retort that this may have been due to his absence?' 'No,' said Sexton, disdainfully, 'I felt too disgusted.' . . . .

We remitted his philanderings to moralists. We were politicians, who wished to keep the movement on an even keel, and preserve its unity. David's sins were not allowed to dethrone him in Israel. Parnell, however, would make no sign of remorse or acknowledgment of the existence of a public conscience. He declared in Dublin a few days after his deposition, 'My fault, if it has been a fault, has not been a fault against Ireland.' This, despite the fact that Gladstone had declared his own leadership of Liberalism would become a 'nullity' if Parnell remained at our head.

Parliament met on the 25th of November, 1890, and that day the Irish Party assembled in Room 15 to the number of 65 to elect a Sessional Chairman. John Morley . . . handed a letter to Justin McCarthy from Gladstone, to read to the Party. That letter . . . was unhappily phrased. It declared that Parnell's continued leadership 'would be productive of consequences disastrous in the highest degree to the Cause of Ireland, and would render Gladstone's retention of the leadership of the Liberal Party almost a nullity.' An impression had been disseminated by Parnell that his re-election would be followed by his resignation, and was only to be regarded as a 'parting salute to the Chief.' McCarthy, believing this, wished to avoid unpleasantness. In other words, he supposed Parnell was a patriot, who would not bring sorrow and strife on Ireland. Parnell knew McCarthy better than McCarthy knew Parnell.

Gladstone, under the impression that McCarthy had read his letter to the Party, published its text that evening. This haste was deplorable. Dismay became universal, for it was mistakenly assumed that the Party knew of the letter and flouted Gladstone. When Parnell's devices to secure re-election were seen through, the feeling of the Party veered round. McCarthy told his alarmed friends that he had informed Parnell of the letter before the meeting, and thought he would retire after re-election. It was not just of John Morley to pick out McCarthy, an amiable and kindly personality, and make him Parnell's headsman. He should have addressed himself officially to the secretaries of the Party, who would quickly have bruited about Gladstone's intentions. When they learnt them,

1. The *Freeman's Journal*, founded in Dublin in 1763, was strongly in favour of Home Rule and the Land League. The National League referred to here was founded by Parnell in 1882 as the constituency organization of the Irish Parliamentary Party.
2. David Plunket (1838-1919), 1st baron Rathmore, was MP for Dublin University 1870-95 and held several posts in different conservative administrations.
3. Pun on 'Otium cum dignitate' (*recte* 'cum dignitate otium', 'a peaceful life with honour'), Cicero, *Pro Sestio*, XLV, 98.
4. This is untrue.

they saw they had been tricked, and Parnell was pressed to call another meeting to consider the letter. He refused. McCarthy and Sexton waited on him, but he was not even civil. Sexton then suggested that a requisition should be signed to force the calling of a fresh meeting, and this was done. Thirty-one signatories within an hour came forward.

On the requisition being delivered to Parnell he muttered, 'I don't intend to allow myself to be dictated to by a parcel of boys,' and vowed he would not attend the meeting. Warned that with him, or without him, it would be held, he readvised himself. Next day his colleagues to the number of 64 assembled in Committee Room 15. Parnell on taking the chair inquired what the meeting was called for. Then breaking into a smile, he confessed, 'Well, of course, we all know the reason.'

John Barry then moved that a further meeting be held two days later to give the Chairman an opportunity of reconsidering his position. Parnell retorted that his mind was made up, and that it was useless to ask him to retire, as he had been unanimously elected.

One of his henchmen moved an adjournment until Monday 'in order to ascertain the views of the delegates in America.' This was agreed to.

On the Thursday several colleagues telegraphed me to Dublin to come to London, and, despite poor health, I went. At Holyhead I received a message from Dr. Kenny, M.P., begging me to go back, but I kept on my journey. On Friday (three days after the debate on the leadership began) I reached Westminster. Yet I was denounced later as the author of Parnell's downfall, although before I arrived he had lost the support of the best elements in the Party.

Looking back over thirty-eight years I bear witness that the majority which took sides against him (before I came) were men with a single eye to the interests of Ireland, and that he had not the support of half a dozen independent M.P.s. His other backers had financial reasons for upholding him.

When I reached the House of Commons, Parnell cut me stonily. I had not then said a word unfriendly to him, beyond wiring McCarthy: 'Think Parnell should defer to Gladstone.' Still I deplored Gladstone's letter, and was anxious to smooth over difficulties and find a way out. Years later I obtained the clue to his rudeness from his secretary, Henry Campbell, whom I had helped to make Town Clerk of Dublin. He explained that D.J. Hishon, an official of the Dublin National League, telegraphed Parnell: 'Healy is going tonight to London as your deadly enemy.'

This brutality from an ignorant underling helped to shape and warp the destiny of Ireland for twenty years.

I did not conceal before leaving Dublin my view that Parnell's buoyancy was ended and that he could not be refloated in the political storm unless he resigned and got re-elected for Cork. His re-election would not have been challenged, and but for Hishon's message, I might have brought Parnell round to this view. But in his sorest hour he leant on the advice of dependents instead of independents. Their counsels led to his ruin and death. Though from ill-health and other causes he had become an empty shell, yet, if well backed, his shrouded personality might have been retained as a figure-head. The colleagues who withdrew from him only did so when he became a menace to Irish interests.

CHAPTER XXV

PARNELL'S FALL (1890)

... On Saturday, 29th November, he [Parnell] put forth a manifesto asserting that, on his visit to Gladstone at Hawarden the year before, he received details of the Home Rule plans of the next Liberal Cabinet. He alleged that the integrity of a section of the Irish Party had been 'apparently sapped and destroyed' by the wire-pullers of Liberalism, who claimed the right to veto their choice of a leader, and appealed to the Irish people 'not to consent to throw me to the English wolves now howling for my destruction.' He complained that in any future Home Rule Bill the Irish Legislature would not be given power to settle the Land question, control the Constabulary, or appoint judges or magistrates.

These lies were baited to catch gudgeons.[1] In private he told his friends that the Manifesto was 'the greatest political coup of the century.' Every one else saw that it was framed to bunker down the Divorce issue, and draw a red herring across the scent. It delighted the Tories, for after Parnell visited Gladstone at Hawarden he expressed the utmost confidence in and admiration for him. At

1. A small slender fish. Slang usage for persons who are easy to trick or cheat.

Edinburgh his speech in praise of Gladstone was fulsome. It is true that at Hawarden he displayed aloofness. Breakfast there was the favourite meal for holding conversation, and Parnell would not come down for it. At dinner he came late, without tendering an apology. It may have been the acme of statesmanship, but it was barbarously un-Irish....

When the adjourned debate in Room 15 opened, Parnell called on his secretary (Campbell) to read messages in his support. These were all faked. The most offensive was one against Sexton from a secondhand bookseller of ill-repute in Dublin, the late William Hickey. So coarse was it that I protested. Parnell blandly apologized, and said he was not aware of its contents. This finished him in my estimation....

Gladstone refused (not being in power) to give any pledges as to the next Home Rule Bill, and on the 6th December, 1890, Parnell presided for the last time over the Party.

The debates had wearied on more than a week. Mr. Goschen characterized them as 'the greatest he ever read.' They banished interest from the House of Commons, but enthralled and hurt Ireland.

Parnell's plan was to bring about the collapse of the session so that the struggle would end on the prorogation of Parliament. He was in collusion with the Tory Whips and his policy dovetailed into theirs. On the night before the final sitting he muttered to J.M. Tuohy, the *Freeman's* London correspondent, 'Biggar[2] appeared to me last night.' Said Tuohy, 'You mean you dreamt about him?' 'Oh, no,' answered Parnell, 'he appeared to me.' Tuohy, who was fiercely on his side, told me this.

On the morning of our last meeting we called on Parnell at the Westminster Palace Hotel and told him that at 6 p.m. that evening the majority would leave Room 15 and take no further part in its futilities. As we went towards the door he drew me aside to one of the pillars in the hall, saying, 'Healy, let us shake hands for, it may be, the last time. I am told you believed yesterday that I had a revolver in my pocket and was about to use it. I assure you that this was not so. I should never dream of bringing a weapon into any meeting of my countrymen, especially into one where excitement was likely to be kindled.' I replied, 'Thank you, Parnell.' We shook hands, and so parted for ever.

2. Joseph G. Biggar (1828-90), MP for Cavan, who specialized in the parliamentary technique of obstruction. He supported Parnell's leadership, but died before the crisis.

At five o'clock that evening I wrote my wife:

HOUSE OF COMMONS,
6th December, 1890.

We are within a few minutes of disruption. We cannot get the Liberals to say anything while Parnell remains chairman, and he refuses to allow any resolution to be moved requiring him to resign. We had a row today as he called upon John O'Connor to move a resolution, when we wished William Abraham to be heard. We shouted for him, and there was slight disorder. Abraham handed his resolution to McCarthy, and we called on McCarthy to put it. Parnell roared that he would not allow him to act as chairman, and snatched the paper out of his hand. McCarthy did not know what was in the paper. Sexton appealed to the meeting to hear O'Connor for a short time, as we did not intend to remain listening to obstructive speeches. McCarthy rose and dignifiedly explained that he had risen to a point of order when Parnell snapped a paper out of his hand. Parnell made a kind of apology, and O'Connor was heard to move a resolution against Gladstone.

In the midst of his speech John Redmond shouted that Gladstone would be 'the master of the Party.' I asked, 'Who would be the mistress of the Party?' Whereupon Parnell called me 'a dirty little scoundrel who insulted a woman.' I made no reply, being content with the thrust, which will stick as long as his cry about Gladstone's 'dictation' continues. I knew compromise would be impossible.

I did not approve of the negotiations, but feel we did not do wrong in trying. Sexton insists on my writing a manifesto to our people. I must leave myself in the hands of men like him, who have done so well.

At six o'clock, Parnell having refused to put any question touching his deposition, Justin McCarthy rose to announce our withdrawal. Forty-four colleagues followed him out. Many of us shook hands with those from whom we were separating. It was a friendly break-off, and dignity was preserved throughout....

CHAPTER XXVIII

PARNELL DIES AT BRIGHTON (1891)

... Parnell feared Fridays, and dreaded Octobers.

His personality has been often limned. The mischief he wrought after the Split cannot dim admiration for his powers. During the debates in Room 15 he tried twice to be a patriot, and promised to reconsider his position. Then he retreated to Brighton, and returned to Westminster after a night there, adamant in his determination to hold fast. A steelly [*sic*] gaze shone from his eyes, but till the last day of the debates, when rough epithets were hurtling, one could always (as the French say) 'discern the gentleman at a league.' His old skill, energy, unscrupulousness and resource reburned in his frame. Genius shone like the upcast flame from an expiring candle.

In conflict with his Party he achieved his earlier stature, and displayed an astuteness, resolution and courage greater than he had ever shown against the British.

His funeral was a great affair. The crowd looked so resolute that Sir Garnet Wolseley (the Irish Commander-in-Chief)[1] declared it was 'the only crowd he was ever afraid of.'

The emotion caused by Parnell's death was deep. The invention that his last words were, 'Give my love to my colleagues and the Irish people,' was mere 'propaganda.' Irish-Americans subscribed to erect a statue in Dublin to him.

He had long before his death ceased to be an effective force, and during the debates on his deposition every expedient was exhausted by opponents to retain him as a figure-head.

Handsome, dignified, and emotionless, he never unduly pressed his view against that of his colleagues. I travelled with him in America, and afterwards worked beside him in Parliament for ten years. Nothing in his personal dealings savoured of arrogance.

His range of knowledge — outside engineering and, perhaps, astronomy — was small. He knew no history, and no theology. He confided to me, as we walked after a late sitting past the Seven Dials,[2] in 1878, that his religious views tended towards those of an uncle who was a 'Plymouth Brother.'[3] Ignorant as I was of the tenets of that creed, I asked him to enlighten me, but he could not do so. He said Paley's *Evidences of Christianity*[4] upset his faith....

1. Field Marshal Viscount Wolseley (1833-1913), commander-in-chief of the British Forces in Ireland 1890-55. He was born in Dublin.

2. An area of London, near Westminster.
3. A protestant group formed in Dublin in 1827, opposed to anything High Church; strictly Calvinistic and millenarian.
4. William Paley (1743-1805), whose *Evidences of Christianity* (1794) upset the faith of many Christians, even though the book was written as a defence of revealed religion.

FRANK HUGH O'DONNELL

(1848-1916)

from:
A HISTORY OF THE IRISH PARLIAMENTARY PARTY (1910)

[O'Donnell was irascible and volatile. He left the Irish Parliamentary Party in 1885, feeling that he, not Parnell, should have been its leader. His bitterness towards Parnell increased as time wore on. He blamed him for having split the party, for having lost the opportunity of gaining true Home Rule for Ireland, for his 'confederacy' with the American Fenians and the British treasury, and for destroying the 'influence of Ireland as a Catholic Power in the Empire' (*The Lost Hat* (1914)). Most of all he blamed the catholic clergy for having organized a national testimonial for Parnell, to finance the 'London Life', as he called it, of 'a sordid charlatan and debauchee'. His scorn for 'our Political Clergy', for Parnell and for what he called 'Ribbon Fenians' was emphatic.

Yet O'Donnell also disliked what he saw as Gladstone's interference in Irish affairs, a point of view that William O'Brien was also to express as late as 1918 when he too decided, on later evidence, that the Irish Party had betrayed Parnell at the behest of the English government. O'Donnell is interesting because his attack on all and every side is an indication of the hopelessness felt by many people after the fall of Parnell. No organization or movement seemed capable of bringing about any substantial change. Ireland had, in O'Donnell's view, lost all self-respect, although he is fairly sure that this would not have been the case had Frank Hugh O'Donnell been elected leader of the Irish Parliamentary Party. The

Gaelic League and the new Sinn Féin party also come under his lash, although, as in his other assaults, O'Donnell never loses an acute perception of the weaknesses and flaws of the various nationalist movements.]

CHAPTER X

... While Ireland, desperately clinging to unity — that elusive phantom of Irish effort — made light of a spot on the sun of its long idolatry, Mr. Gladstone, theoretically ambuscaded behind the Nonconformist conscience, was aiming an explosive bullet into the least protected flank of the Parnellite party, soon to be known, for the most part, as the Gladstonian Home Rulers, anti-Parnellites, or McCarthyites. Mr. Gladstone sent for the most single-minded of the Gladstonians in the Irish party, Mr. Justin McCarthy, a Liberal to the backbone, whom his lifelong friend, Lady St. Helier, said 'was totally unfit to be member of the Home Rule party' — an English writer of considerable ability as a novelist and populariser of English history, formerly editor of the *Morning Star*, meek and mild, and affable in all companies, a literary Liberal of literary Liberals.[1] Principally from his connexion through his wife with the then leader of the Home Rule party, Mr. Shaw, he had been brought into Parliament. Parnell was charmed by his gentleness and popular reputation, and made him vice-chairman on his own accession to power. He lent his name to several of Parnell's least tranquillising ventures, such as the co-directorship of the *United Irishman*; but, of course, if Mr. Justin McCarthy had been discovered with Guy Fawkes's mask and lantern,[2] nobody would have thought the worse of him. The Gladstonian Home Rulers were soon to name him their leader! Mr. Gladstone sent for this amiable gentleman, and told him that if the wicked chief of the Parnellites did not retire, Mr. Gladstone could have nothing more to do with Home Rule and would decline the premiership. He added most carefully and considerately, as Lord Morley notes, that he would on no account put any pressure on the Irish party — who were entirely free to come to any conclusion — but, if they did not hunt Parnell, then he, Gladstone, would dish[3] Home Rule, or words to that effect. Poor Mr. Justin McCarthy almost sank into the earth at the dispiriting prospect of an Ireland without a Gladstone. Mr. Justin McCarthy only saw Mr. Parnell just before Parnell was elected unanimously chairman again; and on his mentioning the awful communication from Mr. Gladstone, was profoundly hurt by Parnell's curt remark that 'he was going to stand to his guns and would only consult Ireland.' Mr. Justin McCarthy felt this very much; and so also, but gradually, did an enlarging number of the Gladstonised Parnellites who had voted unanimously for a political adherence to a political leader. 'Ireland without Gladstone!' Appalling thought.

As soon as the dollar-collecting delegates in America heard that Gladstone wanted the retirement of Parnell, they felt, like Mr. Justin McCarthy, that an Ireland without a Gladstone was simply unthinkable.[4]... With tears in their telegrams, Messrs. T. P. O'Connor, William O'Brien, and John Dillon — the three who did *not* keep the bridge[5] — wired home that 'Mr. Gladstone must be obeyed.' Yet the devil was in it, that a couple of years later, after Parnell had been hunted to his grave, the omnipotent Gladstone was not able to pass his second Gladstonian Home Rule Bill after all! Parnell might just as well have been left to live a little longer.

There followed a hideous and dishonourable time. At first it was not devoid of comic elements, the clowning which accompanied the tragedy, as in a Shakesperian play. All lobbies and corridors at Westminster were filled with Gladstonised Parnellites declaring with stifled sobs that 'they would never have put Parnell again in the chair if

1. Justin McCarthy was a prolific writer and very much involved in the literary life of London, but he was not an Englishman. One of his autobiographical works is *An Irishman's Story* (1905); his *A History of Our Own Times* 6 vols (1877-1905) has some interesting information. The fifth volume deals with the Parnell crisis, as do parts of his *Reminiscences* (1899) and *Our Book of Memories* (1912). He wrote several popular histories on English historical figures, including Gladstone, Queen Anne and the four Georges. McCarthy, while not a subtle politician, acted in good faith throughout the crisis and maintained his friendship with Parnell to the end.
2. Guy Fawkes (1570-1606) was executed for his part in the Gunpowder Plot to blow up James I and the Houses of Parliament in 1605.
3. Slang for to 'ruin' or 'spoil'.
4. John Dillon, T. P. O'Connor and William O'Brien, with others, were on a fund-raising tour in the United States when the crisis came. They telegrammed their support for Parnell on 20 November; after Gladstone's letter was published, they began to change their minds. A cable of 28 November to Parnell urged him to retire. Then, after Parnell's Manifesto of 29 November, they cabled to say that it had convinced them that 'Mr. Parnell's continued leadership is impossible.' O'Donnell is simplifying the account and placing the American delegates in the worst possible light.
5. The reference is to Thomas Macaulay's poem 'Horatius' from *Lays of Ancient Rome* (1842) in which Horatius, Laertius and Herminius keep the bridge leading into Rome against the invading Tuscans.

they thought it would make Mr. Gladstone retire.' They were lachrymose. They were in wrath and despair.... The Continent was immensely interested. From Vienna to Paris, and further, the ladies were Parnellite; and with woman's common sense wanted to know what the flirtations of a statesman had to do with the Board of Works, or the Budget, or even the Railways. Everybody was hugely amused at Mr. Gladstone's morality. People had wondered at his taking 'le parti des dynamiteurs' to his arms; and now they noted gleefully that he was far more severe towards 'l'adultère' than 'l'assassinat.' When the Irish bishops came out with their belated endorsement of *Gladstonius de Matrimonio*,[6] it was the turn of the Catholic clergy in half a dozen Catholic States to shake and roll with laughter. The Continental clergy are Conservative or semi-Conservative to a man. The complicity of notorious Irish ecclesiastics in the propagandism of the Land League had brought the Irish churchmen into evil odour with all the wearers of violet and cardinal red from Westphalia to the toe of Italy. But when the bishops who had never boggled at the plan of campaign now made such a holy fuss about an *amourette*[7] that to them was at least a half-dozen years old, and when the absurdity was done to help Sir Gladstone, who always protested above all things against the priest in politics, the hilarity around episcopal tables threatened to become uproarious. 'Volià le Vaticanisme for ever!' When, in addition, it was announced in all the French, and German, and Italian newspapers, that the two lost souls of the new Paolo and Francesca[8] were stout Protestant, for whose spiritual condition the most reverends of Maynooth had no responsibility whatever, neither on earth nor in heaven, nor under the earth, the joke bordered on bad theology. Some priests of the Irish colleges tried to explain that the Maynooth hierarchy were concerned to preserve the spotless purity of Ireland from the contamination of bad example, and the last remnants of ecclesiastical gravity collapsed! The spotless purity of Ireland appeared to be a fragile investment according to this explanation.

Unhappily it was no laughing matter among ignorant and ductile classes or masses in Ireland. I remembered the Reform Act of 1884 and the 500,000 peasant voters who had swamped the constituencies. That crude multitude had followed the churchmen and the Leaguers to elect Parnell's candidates a couple of years ago; being practically told also that Gladstone had promised Parnell to divide the rest of the Irish estates among the virtuous tenantry. When now the churchmen and the great Gladstone told them together that 'Parnell had betrayed Ireland for an Englishwoman,' how would all these incompetents behave? I felt certain that some strategy was necessary. My just resentment at a hundred things ill done by my old comrade yielded to the gravity of his present misfortune, which threatened public calamity to all Ireland. And he had been such a bonny fighter!.... I am not sure that I would have felt so much sympathy with Parnell in his fall, notwithstanding my instinctive detestation of foreign intervention in Irish affairs, if I had not known from the commencement, what is tolerably patent to all the world now, that the popular idol had been all through the very reverse of the strong and far-seeing statesman which popular legend and party calculation combined to invent. Long after his death, Lord Morley has admitted that Parnell never possessed a shred of constructive ability. I knew from the commencement that my gallant and pertinacious comrade through so many years of guerrilla fighting in the House of Commons, never could be anything but a hero of a battlefield without the slightest capacity for becoming a planner of campaigns. His courage, his distinction, his Anglo-Irish lineage, connected with some of the best patriotic traditions, had all pointed him out to the undistinguished leaders of the vast hosts of national discontent, who, without prestige themselves, all the more eagerly desired a figurehead who should possess that quality at least. Parnell's family pride and personal vanity did the rest. He was literally incapable of rejecting the tinsel crown, even on the terms of the Land League. If we consider it, it was a tremendous bribe. Unlimited wealth for political purposes, considerable wealth for private enjoyment, where there had been nothing but privation before, oceans of enthusiasm, fierce denunciation by Ireland's enemies, answering applause from the Irish Nationalists, the violence of British ministers, the submission and adulation of British ministers — surely all these formed a mass of temptation more than enough to overheat the fancy of a stronger and

6. A parody of the title of a papal bull, 'Gladstone on Marriage'.
7. trifling love affair.
8. Francesca da Rimini and her husband's brother, Paolo, fell in love. When their relationship was discovered, they were put to death in 1289. Dante relates his conversation with Francesca at the end of the fifth canto of the *Inferno*.

more unselfish man.... I knew that with all his weakness and all his shutting fast the eyes to hideous facts, Parnell loathed his Land League surroundings. His contempt for his members of Parliament passed the limits of common courtesy, and far exceeded the limits of common prudence. The revolting pack that turned and rent him at Mr. Gladstone's whistle had many a kick and cuff to avenge. The measureless bitterness of his latest scorn for the 'sweeps' and for the 'gutter-sparrows'[9] was a revelation to those alone who did not know some previous history. There was inherent weakness and manifest deficiency of character in all this. It largely explained, no doubt, why some of those who knew him most intimiately, such as Biggar,[10] his closest ally, and Healy, his private secretary, turned against him with a special and unsparing animus. I never doubted, and I do not doubt now, that if Parnell had remained in the Home Rule party, and had never met the infinite temptations from an unworthy quarter, he would have risen to marked distinction as an Irish patriot, and would have powerfully contributed to the consolidation of that national unity which was to be shattered in his name. I could not have stood upon his platform even against Mr. Gladstone, but I felt that I could give my most earnest counsels to Parnell's defence against dictation from the side of English politicians.

In referring to the action of the churchmen against Parnell, it would be unjust to deny that they had some reasons as Catholic churchmen for their special animosity, and for their violent revelation of that animosity as soon as the Divorce Court on the one side, and Mr. Gladstone's action on the other, had given them their opportunity. For nearly twenty years the political influence of Maynooth had seen itself, if not thrust aside, sorely diminished by the Home Rule laity. Isaac Butt, Mr. Shaw, Parnell, were three lay chiefs of Ireland who all represented, in varying degrees, the revolt of Ireland from the ecclesiastical tutelage which was incarnate in the traditions of O'Connellism. The Home Rulers were religious, and full of respect for religion. They were reverential towards the clergy. Home Rule was a thoroughly lay movement, embracing Protestant and Catholic patriots alike, and the most honoured of priests and bishops appeared upon its platforms, not as masters but as citizens. In addition to the discontent of the Irish clergy at this position was added, first the suspicion and then the conviction that Parnell was profoundly hostile to Catholicism. Parnell possessed no learning, but his family and class traditions had made him unfavourable to the Catholic creed, his American blood had intensified this tendency, and his patriotic sentiments, early awake to the frequent alliances between Maynooth and Whitehall, had confirmed and aggravated his dislikes. There must have been many among his intimates or followers who were aware of this disposition.... The most direct, the most vigorous, the most uncompromising adversary of Lord Rosebery and his programme was Mr. J. E. Redmond, M.P., at that time leading the little band who still upheld the name of the dead Parnell.[11] Today Lord Rosebery's discarded programme, which Mr. Redmond rejected in 1894 as evidently tantamount to the permanent shelving of the Home Rule question, is now formally and enthusiastically supported by Mr. J. E. Redmond, M.P., and the entire body of the post-Parnellite party. Why? The answer is obvious, if we remember that the Irish Catholic Church welcomes, without saying so, every plausible pretext for putting off Home Rule until 'Latter Lammas';[12] and that the post-Parnellite party, being the absolute creation and the permanent dependant of the clergy, is loyally bound to postpone Home Rule to any distant season for which a pretext can be found. During the coming years of Radical agitation which are now promised to us, and during the British struggle for fundamental alterations of the British Constitution, the Irish clergy and their parliamentary puppets will continue to entrance the hearts of patriots by the eloquence of their wishes for Home Rule, and will also be able to guarantee the undisturbed maintenance of the British connexion in which alone they trust — by the facile expedient of waiting for the termination of the interminable discussion on

9. Specific references to Tim Healy. T. P. O'Connor mentions Parnell's reference to Healy as a 'chimney-sweep'. Healy published a pamphlet in 1890, *Under Which Flag? or Is Parnell to be the Leader of the Irish People? By a Gutter Sparrow.*

10. Joseph Biggar (1828-90) was MP for County Cavan from 1874 until his death. He joined the IRB in 1875, but was expelled two years later because he refused to relinquish his parliamentary activities.

11. In 1894, Lord Rosebery, who succeeded Gladstone as prime minister in March of that year, said in the House of Lords that, before Home Rule could be granted to Ireland, 'England, as the predominant partner in the Three Kingdoms, will have to be convinced of its justice and equity.' This caused a political storm and strained relations with the Irish Party.

12. Another way of saying 'Never'.

Houses of Lords and Elective Senates and Secondary Chambers, which will be going on at Westminster and elsewhere — perhaps for the full period of Lord Rosebery's century.

An indispensable qualification of this statement must be added here. Though the Irish churchmen applaud the chase after the House of Lords, or any other quarry which may serve to divert their public from the pursuit of Home Rule, it must be understood well that the first moment that there is danger of the real creation of a single-chamber convention at Westminster, to be supplemented by a single-chamber convention at Dublin, the alarm and terror of the entire ecclesiastical world interested in Irish affairs, from the Shannon to the Tiber, would at once approach a degree of tragedy quite unparalleled since the coming of Cromwell or the Battle of the Boyne. A single-chamber parliament at Westminster would — to the Catholic churchmen — be synonymous with the ascendancy of the most Calvinistic section of the Protestant religion, aggravated by the alliance of the most free-thinking section of the English democracy. The single-chamber convention at Dublin, established and commissioned by the similar body at Westminster, would inevitably involve principles of representation and legislation fatal to the most moderate claims of the political hierarchy of Ireland, and seriously menacing many of the most justifiable requirements of the Catholic religion. The chase after the House of Lords may then be expected only to endure so long as there is little danger of the noble quarry being broken up by the strangely assorted pack. The most elementary sense of justice obliges me to add that there is not a single move in the game which the priests are playing with such subtlety and determination that cannot be paralleled, at least in changefulness and variety, by a hundred combinations and recombinations in the history of government by party at Westminster since the Act of Union alone. We need not refer to preceding times. To espouse one cause in order to avoid another, to make a tremendous show of public anxiety on one account merely in order to divert public attention from a different matter, to demand advance in one direction in order to disguise the abandonment of former positions — these are tricks of the trade, familiar not only to veterans of parliamentarianism, but to every tyro who seeks to qualify himself for the smiles of the Treasury bench.

Two movements, operating in different spheres, but possessing a connected significance, have developed during the post-Parnellite period, and will be found to deserve the most serious attention of those who love and those who hate the nationhood of Ireland. The first of these manifestations of sentiment was the league for the revival of the ancient Irish language, the originating genius of which was Dr. Douglas Hyde, a Protestant clergyman from the west of Ireland, whom the beauty of Irish myths and folksongs, on the lips of peasants innocent of the English language, had first filled with personal delight, and next inspired with the ambition to revive the neglected tongue enshrining such gems. It was apparently a forlorn hope which this Irish minister of a creed unpopular in Ireland had dared to undertake. All classes of the Irish population, including most of the most ardent Nationalists, had despaired of the old tongue. Worse than despair, they ignored it. The poets of Young Ireland wrote their songs of the nation in the speech of the Englishman's nation. But Catholic churchmen had practically abandoned it for generations before it had ceased to be spoken currently by the masses of the rural population. Few students for the sacerdotal ministry were required to study Gaelic at Maynooth, and hundreds of Gaelic congregations were obliged to take on trust the sermons of their spiritual fathers, who could not for the life of them say the Lord's Prayer in Irish. The consequences to the Catholic religion of the Irish race were calamitous. When the great emigrations began, and when literally millions of the Gaelic peasantry found themselves transplanted to the fields and cities of a new country, and when they and their children found themselves asked to give a reason for their faith in answer to the arguments or gibes of new fellow-citizens, the absence of pastoral instruction in the dogmas of their religion proved fatal in hundreds of thousands of cases to the retention of the formal traditions of Catholic usage which they had brought with them across the ocean. As for the world of politicians at home, they were content to demolish the Englishmen with an English volubility which the English could rarely imitate.

It was into this unpromising condition of affairs that Dr. Douglas Hyde, some dozen years ago, brought his enthusiastic advocacy and his untiring resolution. The Gaelic League was founded, the hearts and imaginations of the young men and young women were inflamed with a generous ardour. The study of the ancient speech has long since risen to a national and political fact of distinct importance. It still met with little welcome either from Church or State, but popular demonstrations and enlarging studies continued to demonstrate with increasing fervour that a new object of interest had arisen in Ireland. Of course it was inevitable that the influence of the clergy should be sought on behalf of such a movement. The question still remains today whether the churchmen will ever seriously put their shoulders to the wheel in order to give national supremacy to the resuscitated language. Undoubtedly, there are inconsiderate zealots among the apostles of Gaelic who would leave very little of a world of letters beyond copies or imitations of the Gaelic relics, which have more or less survived the accidents of centuries and the hostility of Norman and Saxon lords and Roman prelates. There is certainly more than a danger of anti-clerical tendencies resulting from over-meditation on the centuries long previous to Tudors and Cromwells, when the enemies of Ireland were not Lutheran innovators, and when the swords and spears of invaders were blessed with crusading privileges by popes of Rome. In the present stage of the movement, it is still premature to assert whether the bishops will do all that the Gaelic League demands, or whether the Gaelic League will have to do without the bishops. In either event, the action of the churchmen will be dictated by conscientious convictions deserving of the utmost respect, even when deserving of the utmost opposition.

The unenthusiastic attitude of the hierarchy in face of the Gaelic League has been naturally reflected in the aloofness of the Parliamentarians, which has been bitterly deplored by official organs of Dr. Douglas Hyde's association. Mr. John Dillon, M.P., has come forward quite significantly to warn the Gaels that their pretension to make the Irish language a compulsory subject of matriculation in the new university, which has been called National, cannot be supported.[13] When I used to defend the study of Gaelic forty years ago, it was as a patriotic complement of a general education. It cannot be concealed that there are many zealots of Gaelic today who would wipe out for young Irishmen the records of European culture, and confine their study to the fragments of an undeveloped form of speech with no practical connexion with modern or ancient civilisation, and with less numerical influence and range than some of the dialects of the Upper Amazon and many of the dialects of the lesser races of India. . . .

If the Irish churchmen were all the obscurantists which some hostile critics have described, they could not achieve the ideal of reaction more thoroughly than by confining 'the youthful mind of Ireland' within such a Gaelic wigwam, in order to learn nothing but the primeval tongue of the tribe as reproduced by the help of O'Growney's lectures on Irish pronunciation.[14] The post-Parnellite party may be congratulated on their aloofness from patriotic exaggerations of this description. No movement, however, is to be judged by its eccentricities, and we may hope that the proposed diet on 'the classics of the Gael instead of the classics of the Greek' has not yet been adopted as the exclusive nourishment of the Gaelic League.

The Sinn Féin movement, as it is called, has come with the professed mission to realise in politics and society the ideal in letters of the forementioned braves of the Gaelic wigwam. In some respects it would not be incompletely fitted by the old criticism that what was true in it was not new, and that what was new was decidedly not true. It professes to be based on one patent absurdity, the allegation that the Hungarians obtained the restoration of their constitution after Magenta and Sadowa, without reference to these crushing blows to Austria's power, by simple abstention from the consumption of Austrian commodities![15] By producing everything which she consumes, Ireland is to emancipate herself from dependence on England, and the millennium of Irish liberty and prosperity will have arrived when we shall have burned everything that comes from England except coals, as Dean Swift's irony suggested two centuries

13. Dillon attacked the compulsory Irish issue in a speech to the National Convention of the United Irish League in February 1909. (See F. S. L. Lyons, *John Dillon: A Biography* (London: Routledge, 1968), pp. 305-06.)

14. Rev. Eugene O'Growney (1863-99), a founder-member of the Gaelic League, professor of Celtic literature and language at St Patrick's College, Maynooth 1891-94, wrote a column of Irish lessons for a weekly newspaper. They were collected and published in four parts as *Simple Lessons in Irish* (1897-1901).

15. Austria was defeated by France at the battle of Magenta in 1859 and by Prussia at Sadowa in 1866. O'Donnell is referring directly to Arthur Griffith's *The Resurrection of Hungary* (1904), the basic text of the Sinn Féin movement, founded by Griffith and espousing withdrawal from Westminster as one of its policies (see below, p. 354).

ago. At the same time, a foreign demand for the superabundant crops and manufactures of the country is to be stimulated by the appointment of Irish consuls accredited to foreign governments by the Irish nation — not yet recognised as an Independent State — with instructions to persuade the said foreigners of the superior merits of Irish goods and chattels.... This simple — decidedly simple — short-cut to commercial affluence is 'perhaps the most novel feature of the Sinn Féin programme.' It is perhaps not the most valuable. A theory of strict abstention from representation in the Imperial Parliament is a leading feature of Sinn Féin. Sinn Féin, I should observe, is the Gaelic expression for 'Our own selves' — a somewhat unlovely subject of inspiration — and is intended to rivet the attention of Sinn Féiners on Ireland and Irish interests as the sole object of their concern at all times. It is, in fact, a selfish-sounding and undignified equivalent for patriotism or nationalism, and can accordingly be described as novel in appearance and antiquated in fact. The young men who are bound in the movement call themselves Sinn Féiners instead of Nationalists. That is all.

Behind and beneath the empty frivolities of the first theorists of the movement there remains the fact that large numbers of Irishmen and Irishwomen, mostly belonging to the younger generation, are taking a pride in Irish nationality and language, and are devoting themselves to a propaganda on behalf of the cultivation of Irish industry and the improvement of Irish agriculture, which, however they may turn out, produce a delightful sense of honesty that has been long dissociated from parliamentarian politics. There may be nothing new in Sinn Féin beyond its name, which is neither lofty nor lovely, but the reality of a great reaction on behalf of higher and purer ideals of national life and national pride cannot be overlooked by any intelligent observer. There is a truer manliness and womanliness about the young adherents of Sinn Féin which, if no catastrophe occur to check the generous enterprise, must introduce a cleaner spirit and a purer air into Dublin society. In conjunction with the Gaelic League, Sinn Féin devotes itself to the encouragement of reading and the promotion of pastimes connected with the nationality of Ireland. No words can describe adequately the appalling barrenness and dullness which have fallen upon intelligence and amusement alike in the capital and throughout the provinces. Until the Gaelic League and Sinn Féin appeared, the monotonous brutality of the agrarian passions roused by the Land League, and the monotonous trickery of the parliamentary intrigues which followed the degradation of Home Rule, had spread throughout town and village an apparent incapacity for any higher form of human activity than cheering a politician or boycotting a neighbour. The emigration from Ireland has been immensely stimulated by the inexpressible aridity and stagnation of all Irish life. The nearest approach to a social gathering was the celebration of some semi-religious occasion. The local bookshop even had nothing better than a stock of 'penny dreadfuls'[16] from London and mawkish productions of a tractarian kind. Of course, it may be difficult for the taste for higher and better recreation to flourish along with such hideous parodies of popular education as are afforded by the ignorance-ridden primary schools and the money-making machines that are called secondary schools. The Gaelic League and the Sinn Féin movement may be unable to supply the want of the system of public education possessed by all the progressive nations of Europe, but the Gaelic League and the Sinn Féin movement are already spreading that deep and noble detestation of existing evils and their causes, which may well change the social and intellectual atmosphere of rural Ireland itself. It has to be deplored, indeed, that some of the most prominent Sinn Féiners have shown themselves singularly unequal to the obligations of a movement which ought to appeal to all Irishmen who love their country. The absurd and offensive denunciation of Irish recruits for the military service must jar most offensively upon that immense class of Irish Conservatives whose contributions to the warlike glory of the Empire form the proudest element in the story of a thousand families. On the commonest grounds of mere matter of fact it should be needless to demonstrate the futility of urging a spirited young Irishman, who cannot find a civil trade to nourish him, on no account to accept a becoming uniform, a good bed and breakfast, and a shilling a day in his pocket as the price of volunteering to fight the enemies of Ireland's constitutional king. The ardent and oratorical Sinn Féiner, who appeals to Duffy and Murphy 'never to take the Saxon shilling,' might be seriously embarrassed if Duffy

16. Cheap and lurid books or magazines.

or Murphy asked him if he would contribute an Irish penny instead.

It may or may not be a good omen of their success that the Sinn Féiners are strong in the city of Dublin. It is a drawback to the affections of that fallen capital that it changes them with methodical velocity. Dublin prides itself upon its pellucid patriotism, and the knights of the Red Branch probably faded from history because they omitted to be inscribed upon the Roll of Freemen of the Dublin City Hall. A number of eminent Nationalists, notwithstanding, have expressed singularly depreciatory opinions upon Dublin from the Nationalist point of view. Even Wolfe Tone has written in his diary that 'a corporal's guard would drive the mob of Dublin,' and ill-fated Emmet found that mob quite as worthless supporters as Wolfe Tone opined. When John Mitchell [*sic*], the rebel editor of 1848, was carried away into transportation without the thousands of Dublin patriots lifting a finger, he spake thuswise: 'Adieu, Dublin! Adieu, city of bellowing slaves and genteel villas!'[17] Dublin is the city of facile admiration and ineffective fidelities. The whole of the Nationalist glory of Dublin — by descent it is only an Anglo-Danish emporium — comes from the Irish Protestant Parliament and the monuments of their hands, the palace of the Legislature and the deserted Customs House. But for a generation the Dublin corporation has meanly excluded every Irish Conservative from its civic chair! The Lord Mayor's salary of £3000 a year is reserved for occupation by seniority confined to the one side of the Chamber alone. Nor is the boycott unknown to Sinn Féin policy. Alas! The more Dublin changes, the more it is the same as before. . . .

17. The actual quotation from Mitchel's *Jail Journal* (1854), chapter 1, is: 'Dublin City, with its bay and pleasant villas — city of bellowing slaves — villas of genteel dastards — lies now behind us. . . .' Tone, in the entry in his diary for 22 February 1796, wrote of his dealings with the French, who had offered 2,000 men for an invasion of Ireland, 'That with regard to myself, I would go if they would send but a corporal's guard. . . .'

JOHN REDMOND

(1856-1918)

from: SPEECHES OF JOHN REDMOND MP (1910)

[The Boer War (1899-1902) was universally condemned by the Irish Parliamentary Party, most vociferously by John Dillon. The parallels with Ireland were too tempting to be dismissed, and the fact that Joseph Chamberlain, who had killed the Home Rule Bill in 1886 and the attempt to reintroduce it in 1893, was the architect of the war, made the hostility even more pronounced. Redmond had just been elected, the day before, as chairman of the newly united Irish Parliamentary Party. This was, therefore, his first speech in that capacity. Moreover, the heroism of the Boers in their fight against the British Empire made a painful contrast with the squabbles of the Irish Party; the centenary celebrations of the great Rebellion of 1798 brought the point home even more sharply. Redmond was to follow the logic of the South African parallel in 1914, when he claimed that both South Africa and Ireland would readily fight on behalf of Britain, now that their justified grievances had been dealt with.]

IRELAND AND THE BOER WAR

Amendment to the Address
House of Commons, 7th February 1900

Mr. Redmond moved the following Amendment to the Address

> But we humbly represent to your Majesty that the time has come when the war at present being waged in South Africa should be brought to a close, on the basis of recognising the independence of the Transvaal and the Orange Free State.

Mr. Speaker, I do not rise for the purpose of endeavouring to renew discussion about topics which have been the subject of the debate for the last week. I have no intention of perpetuating the wearisome and shameful story of the inefficiency and insincerity of the diplomacy which has led this country into a war for an ostensible object which could easily have been obtained by a little patience and goodwill, and a little conciliation. Still less do I desire to enter into any criticism of the political and military blunders which have brought disaster on your arms since the commencement of the war. My object is entirely different. I desire as far as possible to leave the past alone. I may say I have no particular sympathy with the recriminations which have passed between both the front benches as to the responsibility for this war. In my view both are responsible, though in different degrees, for its initiation, and both are equally responsible for its prosecution. My object is to explain and justify the feeling of Ireland upon this subject, and that will be evidenced by the votes of eighty Members of this House, who think and will act as one man. The sympathy of Ireland is with the two South African Republics. We abhor this war; we call for its stoppage, and we declare our intention to do all that in us lies to maintain the independence of these two little Republics, which was won by untold sacrifices, and defended by a heroism which is without a parallel in the history of the world. I know, of course, that putting this view forward in this assembly must be unpalatable to many Members on both sides, but every sober-minded man must agree with me, that if a large body of Members hold this view it is well that the view should be expressed; and I trust the expression of opinion of eighty Members of this House, representing the majority of the people of Ireland, will be listened to, if not with respect, at any rate with patience. The sympathy of Ireland is with the Boers. Why is this? On what foundation is it based? What is the explanation of it? I propose to answer shortly those questions. We in Ireland have been accused of being indiscriminate in our sympathies and our views of this war; we are told we know nothing of the merits of the quarrel, and that our sympathies with the Boers have one real and only motive, which is antagonism to England; that we should be against England, right or wrong; and I have even heard it said that if it was Germany who was fighting, and England was defending the Boers, we should turn right round. And it was alleged that if England had gone to war, as she undoubtedly ought to have done, three years ago to avenge the massacre of the Armenian Christians, our sympathies would have been on the side of the Great Assassin.[1] I want to be perfectly frank and candid. There is both truth and untruth in that charge. It is true that wherever the Empire is involved in a difficulty of complication which diminishes its great strength, a feeling of hope and satisfaction stirs through the veins of men of the Irish race both at home and abroad. This is a fact which stares you in the face, and it is folly to conceal it. It is one of those facts which statesmen should study and observe and try to understand. It is not our fault that it is a fact, but yours. It is the fault of the history which you and your predecessors have made. You thought you had got rid of the Irish question when in 1895 you overwhelmed Home Rule by a majority of 150.[2] You thought you had got rid of it in 1800 when you abolished the Irish Parliament,[3] because, twenty years before, when you were engaged in your wicked American war, a war which particularly compares with the present war, you were confronted with this same phenomenon of the Irish seeking to take advantage of your difficulties and sympathising with your foe. Why was Ireland prone to these views then as it is now? It does not lie in the cussedness of the Irish, it is due to the simple fact that Ireland one hundred years ago felt she was treated with systematic injustice and deprived of her true rights. She had the same feeling before, and the same cause will at all times produce the same result in the history of nations. Some day, not perhaps far off, in that Ireland which you are about to create for yourselves in South Africa, you may find white people rejoicing in the Empire's difficulties and sending messages of sympathy to your foes. I would urge this country, before it is involved more deeply in this ill-fated war, to endeavour to learn something from the history of your own experience in Ireland and the American colonies, and from contrasting the history of other great portions of the Empire, and to beware of pursuing to the bitter end the chapter which, whatever way the military operations may go, whether you succeed in this war or not, can only be a story of misfortune and disgrace.

1. Under the Ottoman Empire, Armenians in Turkey were discriminated against as non-Muslim. Abdul Hamid II, the Turkish sultan, instigated a series of massacres in the mid-1890s in which thousands of Armenians were killed. The atrocities alienated most of the Great Powers, but Kaiser Wilhelm II maintained friendly relations with the sultan.
2. In June 1895 a unionist government, headed by Lord Salisbury, was returned to office. In fact, the Home Rule Bill of 1893 was rejected by the Lords by a majority of 419 to 41.
3. The reference is to the Act of Union (1800).

I admit, in the frankest manner, that the feeling of the mass of the Irish people is hostile to the Empire. At this moment it would be hypocrisy for me to attempt to deny it, and it would be the utmost folly for you to attempt to minimise it.... But having said so much I entirely deny that the attitude of the Irish people towards this war is governed wholly or even mainly by that sentiment. Irishmen are just as capable as anyone else of judging the policy and the merits of the conflicts in which this Empire chooses to embroil itself, more especially when, as in the present instance, an impoverished and overtaxed country is called upon to pay so heavy a proportion of the cost, and when so many thousands of Irish families, rich and poor alike, are called upon to pour forth the still more precious treasure of their children's blood. Do not imagine that this war does not come home to us in Ireland. It is scarcely an exaggeration to say that there is scarcely a family in Ireland, from the poor people who live in Dublin slums to the highest in the land, that is not represented, in one shape or other, upon one side or other at the front. This is more the case with regard to Ireland than it is here, because in proportion to the population a larger number of our people take to soldiering for the mere love of the calling than with you, and when they do get to the front a far larger proportion of them are thrust into dangerous posts. I candidly admit that in one sense I cannot but rejoice that so many Irishmen are fighting in this cause. I recognise the duties and obligations of the soldier's calling — 'His not to reason why; his but to do or die'[4] — and recognising that, I, as an Irishman, cannot help feeling a thrill of pride at the record of the heroism of the Irish lads from Mayo and Roscommon, who have suffered so terribly in this war. I could not help noticing that, while those brave and devoted press correspondents who have sent accounts of the operations to this country have paid generous tributes to the gallantry of these Irish regiments, in the official reports from General Buller[5] and other officers in command no such mention has been made....

It is not only that Irishmen are entitled to judge of this war, and the merits and policy of this enterprise, but as a rule their judgment is more likely to be sound than yours. For one thing, Irishmen are not subject to those passions of Imperial greed and pride and arrogance which habitually obscure the judgment of large classes of Englishmen on these occasions. They are not as materialistic in their aims, and they have, moreover — and it has often been accounted one of their weaknesses that they have — what is called a sympathetic temperament. They have a faculty for understanding other races, and so long as it is true that no Imperial policy can be wise or sound which is not morally right, so long I maintain that these instincts are more likely to lead the nation to a sound conclusion than, say, the instincts of the average modern Jingo in this country. By this means the Irish people, by a perfectly natural and, as I think, unerring process, have come to entertain a genuine abhorrence of this war, and a genuine admiration for the little heroic Republics that are facing and thwarting your effort to destroy their independence. I assert emphatically that the sympathies of the Irish people would be in precisely the same direction if England were not concerned in the matter at all. Our sympathies would be on the side of the independence of these Republics, no matter what was the Power that was attempting to act as the bully and the oppressor in South Africa. If you look back over your own history you will see that in every war of this kind in which the Empire has been engaged the sympathies of Irishmen have always gone in the right direction, and not their sympathies only but their counsel and advice, and their counsel and advice have invariably been disregarded and rejected. Go back for a moment to the conflict which lost you America, and the memory of which is the real reason why today you cannot win the friendship and alliance of the United States. Go back to the history of that war. Who led the Opposition; who inspired, who planned, who worked through steadfast years in opposition to that luckless war? An Irishman, and in doing so he poured forth a wealth of political wisdom which has been the nourishment of your wiser statesmen ever since, and which if it could be only understood, and acted upon by your statesmen of today, would induce you even now to retrace your steps, and by an early peace to retrieve to some extent what I believe is the worst mistake of your Imperialism. Yes, Burke and Sheridan and Grattan and the mighty Irishmen of that day took precisely the same stand in that eventful controversy that we

4. Alfred, Lord Tennyson, 'The Charge of the Light Brigade':
'Theirs not to reason why,
Theirs but to do and die.'
5. Sir Redvers Buller (1839-1908) took command of troops in the Boer War in 1899, but he was soon superseded by Lord Roberts.

their humbler countrymen take today upon the question of this war. They had to face the self-same abuse, the same unstinted criticism that we have to do. But who in the world of politics dares to say now that they were not absolutely in the right? No; the organised and obstinate pride of the rulers of that day would not accept advice from the treacherous Irish Members, and America was lost. In crises like this your best advisers have always been Irish statesmen and Irish soldiers. But you have always distrusted their advice, whether in the case of the present war or in other struggles.... I say, therefore, that we arrive by quite a natural process at our sympathies with these Republics. How could it be otherwise? We would be stocks or stones if our admiration were not aroused by one of the finest spectacles that the world has witnessed since Thermopylæ — the resistance of these two little Republics to the most powerful Empire of modern times. I think I am speaking the sentiments of all generous-minded men in this House — no matter what view they take of the war — when I say that we admire the pluck and heroism of the old grey-bearded Boer side by side with the dauntless courage of the Boer of sixteen in the stand they have already made against this mighty Empire in defence of what they believe to be right. Do they surrender their independence without a struggle? Do the Free Staters, thinking only of their crops, abandon their brothers in the Transvaal? Had they done so we should all, without distinction of creed or party, have heartily despised them; and it seems to me that but for this bloody struggle the world would have been robbed of one of its most stirring episodes. I think the world at large owes a deep debt to these two little Republics for showing, in this degraded age, that there are other things to fight for than gold, and for which they are prepared to lay down their lives....

[There follows an excerpt from a speech delivered at Birr on 10 November 1907. Redmond points to the appalling record of the Irish legal system in the nineteenth century as further proof of the necessity of Home Rule for Ireland. After citing a recent case in which innocent men were imprisoned for a crime committed and known to have been committed by a policeman, he asserts 'that there is a deep-rooted and widespread distrust in, and suspicion of, the law and the administration of it in Ireland.']

THE ADMINISTRATION OF JUSTICE IN IRELAND (1907)

... What is the origin of this distrust? That is the important question. It springs, no doubt, to some extent from the fact that the laws under which we live in Ireland are foreign laws, made by a foreign Parliament. It springs also largely from the fact that many of these criminal laws are not only tyrannical and oppressive, but are special laws for Ireland, that could not be passed for England. But most of all this distrust springs from the manner in which the criminal laws are administered in Ireland, and from the character of the tribunals which administer them. Foreign laws coming to Ireland, as Gladstone said, 'in foreign garb,' can never command the respect of the people. It is the same all over the world. Do you think Englishmen would respect laws made in France by a French Parliament, in which the Englishmen were only as one to six? Do you think the Australians or Canadians would respect laws made in London? But these laws of ours are not only foreign-made laws, but many of the criminal laws are tyrannical, oppressive and exceptional, enacted specially for Ireland, which were not, and never could have been, enacted for England. To prove that, I need not go far back. It would be easy to show how in past times the Law of Treason was far more oppressive in Ireland than in England. It would be easy to refer to the code of the Whiteboy Acts, one of the most oppressive codes ever enacted, and unknown in Great Britain.[1]

But it is unnecessary to go to the past; it is sufficient for us to know that there has been a Coercion Act for Ireland for every year since the Union, and at this very moment, although there is a Liberal Government in power, pledged to govern Ireland, according to Irish ideas, and according to democratic ideas, there is in existence a perpetual, a permanent Coercion Act,[2] under which tomorrow, at the will of a single individual, all our most cherished rights and liberties could be suppressed. Tomorrow, by a scratch of the pen, the Lord Lieutenant could deprive you of the right of public

1. In 1765, the Irish Parliament passed an act to prevent tumultuous uprisings. Many people were executed by hanging, drawing and quartering. Many more were convicted on trumped-up charges in a hysterical anti-poverty atmosphere.
2. One-hundred-and-five coercion acts were passed between 1800 and 1921. The Perpetual Coercion Bill was passed in 1887.

meeting, of your right of trial by jury, call into existence as a tribunal to try you two Removables,[3] paid servants of his, who most either obey his orders or lose their office. I think I need say no more to show you that these criminal laws are not only foreign, but exceptional, and oppressive and made specially for Ireland.

But the real reason, after all, for distrust of the law is to be found in the fact that the whole criminal law of Ireland is administered on a different system and in a different spirit from that which prevails, and is administered, in England. From the days of the trial of O'Connell, trial by jury in the case of political offences has been little better than what Lord Denman [*sic*] described it: 'A mockery, a delusion, and a snare.'[4] In political or semi-political cases trial by jury is rendered a ghastly farce by the deliberate packing of juries by the Crown, and has been turned into that by successive Governments, Tory or Liberal. This practice poisons the very fountains of justice, and is unknown in England.... One Government may pack more than another; but the mischief is done, and the distrust of administration of justice is universal and deep-rooted.

One other point: those who are called on to administer the law ought to be above suspicion. They are in England.

In England men are appointed to the Bench for their professional fitness and qualities; in Ireland, as we know, under successive Governments, men are appointed to the Bench simply for political services; and the more bitter partisan a man is — the more outspoken an enemy he is to the rights of the people — the more certain he has been, in the past, to find his way to the Bench. In England, when a politician is promoted to the Bench, except in the rarest cases, he leaves his politics behind him; but in Ireland, all through the century, and down to this very moment, the Irish people are familiar with the political judge, the partisan on the Bench, with the inevitable result that the mass of the people have no confidence whatever in the impartiality of the tribunal. Now I need not go back to the past for an illustration. Only the other day the Lord Chief Justice of Ireland, in open court, attacked the Attorney-General because he did not prosecute certain prominent politicians. I exceedingly regret that the Attorney-General did not respectfully ask his lordship to mind his own business. It was no business of his. The duty and the grave responsibility of deciding who shall be prosecuted for political offences, and who shall not, rests on the Attorney-General and the Executive Government of the day; and for a judge on the Bench to attempt to influence, or, as it might be said, to intimidate the Attorney-General and the Executive Government in the discharge of this delicate and responsible duty, is a scandal which, in my opinion, could take place nowhere in the civilised world except in Ireland. Just think for a moment what a serious matter this might be. Suppose tomorrow that the Lord Chief Justice goes down to his Court and orders the Attorney-General to prosecute me; and suppose the Attorney-General takes his orders, and does prosecute me; then I am to be sent for trial before the very judge who has ordered my indictment; — and the Irish people, in the face of such things, are blamed because they have no confidence in the administration of justice. You would think that of all men living the present Lord Chief Justice of Ireland would be the last to be guilty of this indiscretion. It is not the first time that he has afforded an argument to us. It is not the first time he has given us an example of the demoralising effects of the absence of National Self-government....

Now, have I established my point? Let me briefly sum it up. I say there is today a widespread distrust of the administration of justice in Ireland. This I say is the natural and inevitable result, first of foreign-made laws, then of exceptional and oppressive laws; then of the vital difference in the system, principle and practice in the administration of the laws in England and in Ireland; then, further, there is the practice of exhuming old and obsolete laws like that of Edward III for the purpose of punishing political opponents; then that distrust is due to the difference in the mode of appointing judges, and finally, and above all else, to the system of jury-packing unknown in England, which poisons the fountains of justice. These things cannot be contradicted; and if so, I have made an unanswerable argument in favour of Home Rule, of condemnation of British rule, under which such enormities are possible.

3. Resident magistrates in Ireland.
4. Thomas, Lord Denham (1779-1854), in his judgment in *O'Connell* v. *the Queen* on 4 September 1844, said: 'Trial by jury itself, instead of being a security to persons who are accused, will be a delusion, a mockery, and a snare.'

from: IRELAND AND THE WAR (1915)

[The text is from the Dublin edition of 1915, subtitled *Extracts from Speeches made in the House of Commons and in Ireland since the Outbreak of the War*. In committing Ireland to the War, Redmond was assuming that Home Rule had been effectively gained and that the relations between Britain and Ireland could henceforth be conducted on a new and friendlier footing. He first offered the Irish Volunteers as an internal defence force, but this was rejected by Herbert Asquith, the British prime minister. Redmond then encouraged the Volunteers to join the British army in his speech at Woodenbridge, Co. Wicklow. In calling for Volunteer support for Britain, Redmond hoped that the Ulster and the Irish Volunteers, by fighting on the same side, would create the conditions in which could be found 'the most inestimable treasure ... in creating a free and united Ireland — united, North and South, Catholic and Protestant.' This wholehearted commitment, seen in the retrospect of the 1916 executions and the collapse of the Home Rule movement, with the extinction of the Irish Parliamentary Party in the 1918 elections, now seems to have been a glaring error of political judgment on Redmond's part. Nevertheless, he took the bulk of the Irish Volunteers with him into the National Volunteers. The remainder stayed with the IRB and a section was to join with the Irish Citizen Army to fight in the Easter Rising.]

HOUSE OF COMMONS — *August 3rd, 1914*

I hope the House will not consider it improper on my part, in the grave circumstances in which we are assembled, if I intervene for a very few moments. I was moved a great deal by that sentence in the speech of the Secretary of State for Foreign Affairs in which he said that the one bright spot in the situation was the changed feeling in Ireland. In past times, when this Empire had been engaged in these terrible enterprises, it is true — it would be the utmost affectation and folly on my part to deny it — the sympathy of the Nationalists of Ireland, for reasons to be found deep down in centuries of history, has been estranged from this country. Allow me to say, Sir, that what has occurred in recent years has altered the situation completely. I must not touch, and I may be trusted not to touch, on any controversial topic; but this I may be allowed to say, that a wider knowledge of the real facts of Irish history has, I think, altered the views of the democracy of this country towards the Irish question, and today I honestly believe that the democracy of Ireland will turn with the utmost anxiety and sympathy to this country in every trial and every danger that may overtake it. There is a possibility, at any rate, of history repeating itself. The House will remember that in 1778, at the end of the disastrous American War, when it might, I think, truly be said that the military power of this country was almost at its lowest ebb, and when the shores of Ireland were threatened with foreign invasion, a body of 100,000 Irish Volunteers sprang into existence for the purpose of defending her shores. At first, no Catholic — ah! how sad the reading of the history of those days is! — was allowed to be enrolled in that body of Volunteers, and yet, from the very first day, the Catholics of the South and West subscribed money and sent it towards the arming of their Protestant fellow-countrymen. Ideas widened as time went on, and finally the Catholics in the South were armed and enrolled with their fellow-countrymen of a different creed in the North. May history repeat itself today. There are in Ireland two large bodies of Volunteers.[1] One of them sprang into existence in the South. I say to the Government that they may tomorrow withdraw every one of their troops from Ireland. I say that the coast of Ireland will be defended from foreign invasion by her armed sons, and for this purpose armed Nationalist Catholics in the South will be only too glad to join arms with the armed Protestant Ulstermen in the North. Is it too much to hope that out of this situation there may spring a result which will be good, not merely for the Empire, but good for the future welfare and integrity of the Irish nation? I ought to apologise for having intervened, but while Irishmen generally are in favour of peace, and would desire to save the democracy of this country from all the horrors of war; while we would make every possible sacrifice for that purpose, still, if the dire necessity is forced upon this country, we offer to the Government of the day that they may take their troops away, and that if it is allowed to us, in comradeship with our brethren in the North, we will ourselves defend the coasts of our country.

1. The Ulster Volunteer Force, founded in 1912, and the Irish Volunteers, founded in 1913. The parallel between these forces and the Volunteers of 1788 was almost obligatory for members of the Irish Parliamentary Party. The achievement of legislative independence in 1782, however, was regarded by many leading figures outside the party — including Arthur Griffith — as a sham.

DECLARATION ISSUED BY MR. REDMOND ON BEHALF OF THE IRISH PARTY — *September 17th, 1914*

The whole-hearted endorsement by the Irish people and the Irish Volunteers of the spirit of my declaration, made on the impulse of the moment, and without seeking for any conditions whatever, that the defence of Ireland might safely be left to the sons of Ireland themselves, shows the profound change which has been brought about in the relations of Ireland to the Empire by the events of the past three years.

The Irish people know, and appreciate the fact fully, that at long last, after centuries of misunderstanding, the democracy of Great Britain has finally and irrevocably decided to trust them, and to give them back their national liberties.

By overwhelming British majorities, a Charter of Liberty for Ireland has been three times passed by the House of Commons, and in a few hours will be the law of the land. A new era has opened in the history of the two nations.

During the long discussion of the Irish problem, in Parliament and on the platform, we promised the British people that the concession of liberty would have the same effect in Ireland as in every other part of the Empire, and notably, in recent years, in South Africa, that disaffection would give way to friendship and goodwill, and that Ireland would become a strength, instead of a weakness, to the Empire.

The democracy of Great Britain listened to our appeal, and have kept faith with Ireland. It is now a duty of honour for Ireland to keep faith with them.

A test to search men's souls has arisen. The Empire is engaged in the most serious war in history. It is a just war, provoked by the intolerable military despotism of Germany. It is a war for the defence of the sacred rights and liberties of small nations, and the respect and enlargement of the great principle of nationality. Involved in it is the fate of France, our kindred country, the chief nation of that powerful Celtic race to which we belong; the fate of Belgium, to whom we are attached by the same great ties of race, and by the common desire of a small nation to assert its freedom; and the fate of Poland, whose sufferings and whose struggles bear so marked a resemblance to our own.

It is a war for high ideals of human government and international relations, and Ireland would be false to her history, and to every consideration of honour, good faith, and self-interest, did she not willingly bear her share in its burdens and its sacrifices.

We have, even when no ties of sympathy bound our country to Great Britain, always given our quota, and more than our quota, to the firing-line, and we shall do so now.

We have a right, however, to claim that Irish recruits for the Expeditionary Force should be kept together as a unit, officered as far as possible by Irishmen, composed, if possible, of county battalions, to form, in fact, an 'Irish Brigade,' so that Ireland may gain national credit for their deeds, and feel, like other communities of the Empire, that she, too, has contributed an army bearing her name in this historic struggle.

Simultaneously with the formation of this Irish Brigade, for service abroad, our Volunteers must be put in a state of efficiency as speedily as practicable, for the defence of the country.

In this way, by the time the war ends, Ireland will possess an army of which she may be proud.

I feel certain that the young men of our country will respond to this appeal with the gallantry of their race.

In conclusion, I would appeal to our countrymen of a different creed, and of opposite political opinions, to accept the friendship we have so consistently offered them, to allow this great war, as to which their opinions and ours are the same, and our action will also be the same, to swallow up all the small issues in the domestic government of Ireland which now divide us; that, as our soldiers are going to fight, to shed their blood, and to die at each other's side, in the same army, against the same enemy, and for the same high purpose, their union in the field may lead to a union in their home, and that their blood may be the seal that will bring all Ireland together in one nation, and in liberties equal and common to all.

SPEECH AT WOODENBRIDGE, CO. WICKLOW, VOLUNTEER REVIEW — *September 21st, 1914*

Fellow-countrymen, it was a fortunate chance that enabled me to be present here today. I was motoring past, and I did not know until I arrived here that this gathering of the Volunteers was to take place at Woodenbridge. I could not deny myself the pleasure and the honour of waiting to meet you, to meet so many of those whom I have personally known for many long years, and to see them fulfilling a high duty to their country. I have no intention of making a speech. All I desire to say to you is that I congratulate you upon the favourable beginning of the work which you have made. You have only barely made a beginning. You will yet have hard work before you can call yourselves efficient soldiers, and you will have to have in your hands — every man — as efficient weapons as I am glad to see in the hands of some, at any rate, of your number. Looking back, as I naturally do, upon the history of Wicklow, I know that you will make efficient soldiers. Efficient soldiers for what? Wicklow Volunteers, in spite of the peaceful happiness and beauty of the scene in which we stand, remember this country at this moment is in a state of war, and your duty is a twofold duty. The duty of the manhood of Ireland is twofold. Its duty is, at all costs, to defend the shores of Ireland against foreign invasion. It is a duty more than that of taking care that Irish valour proves itself; on the field of war it has always proved itself in the past. The interests of Ireland — of the whole of Ireland — are at stake in this war. This war is undertaken in defence of the highest principles of religion and morality and right, and it would be a disgrace for ever to our country, and a reproach to her manhood, and a denial of the lessons of her history, if young Ireland confined their efforts to remaining at home to defend the shores of Ireland from an unlikely invasion, and shrunk from the duty of proving on the field of battle that gallantry and courage which has distinguished our race all through its history. I say to you, therefore, your duty is twofold. I am glad to see such magnificent material for soldiers around me, and I say to you — Go on drilling and make yourselves efficient for the work, and then account yourselves as men, not only in Ireland itself, but wherever the firing line extends, in defence of right, of freedom, and of religion in this war.

WILLIAM O'BRIEN

(1852-1928)

from: THE DOWNFALL OF PARLIAMENTARIANISM (1918)

[William O'Brien was one of the most volatile and eccentric of the leading members of the Irish Parliamentary Party. His natural propensity to disillusion was greatly encouraged by the chain of events from the downfall of Parnell to the rise of Sinn Féin. In this sometimes bitter, sometimes melancholy and generally perceptive retrospect, O'Brien charts the collapse of the constitutional movement for Home Rule.]

I

THE INEVITABLENESS OF FORMER DEFEATS

... The choice of Ireland in 1890 was not that Sunday-school choice between vice and virtue, between the all black and the all white, between shining angel and darkest devil which would make human judgments in great affairs an enviably easy process. There were faults — and, still worse, unpardonable misunderstandings — among both sets of protagonists. The Parnell divorce suit has long assumed an aspect which the Puritans of the first outraged weeks little conceived of. Lord Morley's Autobiography makes the astounding revelation that Gladstone himself would fain have dropped out of his letter the famous threat of throwing up the leadership, and that it was only forced upon him at the last under the pressure of the Party hacks — the threat which alone could have reconciled any considerable section of the Irish race to parting with Parnell.[1] Gladstone's own part in the transaction grows more and more consonant with the breadth

1. John Morley, *Recollections* (1917). O'Brien was convinced that Gladstone had been forced to demand Parnell's expulsion by other members of the Liberal Party. This made it all the more clear to him that the betrayal of Parnell had been part of British political strategy.

as well as suppleness of his statesmanship. His judgment was overborne by the Party politicians, who made him the victim of their own ineffable failure to establish confidential negotiations either with Parnell or with his Party before the blue sky grew black with thunder. On the other hand, the course of events has graven in Irish memory in characters that never can be erased the warnings on which Parnell founded his refusal to be expelled from the leadership by dictation from England. One was his conviction of the danger of any blind dependence upon the Liberal Party — unjustified, indeed, in the unique case of Gladstone himself, but bitterly confirmed throughout the succeeding quarter of a century by a hundred tricks of wily opportunism on the part of his Liberal lieutenants and of their successors. In his other motive for refusing to desert the Irish leadership — his conviction which was unquestionably inspired by knowledge and not by vanity that he was the only Irishman of the moment who could have held the manœuvres of English party politicians in effective check, and, above all, who could hold together an Irish Party who, without him, would be half-a-dozen able sub-leaders without a leader — time has vindicated his foresight with a deadly accuracy which the heart of Ireland still aches to recall.

The tragedy of 1890, however, was the work of black Erinys[2] rather than a mischance of practical politics. If nobody could have foreseen it, probably nobody could have remedied it until the poison had worked itself out by slow and agonizing degrees. The two magnificent hosts that must have carried Home Rule to victory fell to hacking one another to pieces. The shivering Home Rule majority of 40 which came back in 1893 could only serve as a tantalising proof of what the majority must have been had the banners of Gladstone and Parnell gone into the battle side by side. It served also as a monument to the genius of the marvellous old man who, with Parnell in his grave, with an Irish Party rent into three sections half mad with disappointments and recriminations, and with a powerful section of his own Liberal Party already thinking above all else how they were to be ridded of this Irish *damnosa hereditas*[3] nevertheless with his single arm fought the way of his Home Rule Bill to its last stage in the House of Commons and might quite possibly have rechallenged the opinion of Britain with a better heart, were not his Liberal lieutenants in a scarcely more decent haste to execute Gladstone than they had been to execute Parnell. Lord Morley's amazing autobiography shifts three-fourths of the responsibility from Parnell and Ireland to the shoulders of Gladstone's untrusty subordinates. But, divide the guilt how we may, Destiny decreed the thing was not to be done and there was an end.

2. The Furies of Greek mythology.
3. 'ruinous inheritance', Gaius, *Institutes*, ii.163.

II

THE INEXCUSABLENESS OF THE PRESENT DISASTER

Far otherwise was it with the *dégringolade*[1] of the Home Rule coalition which the Liberal reaction of 1906 brought into irresistible power.[2] This time the catastrophe was the product of human feebleness and of the shifty morals of the politicians, reducing to nothingness such a concentration of happy conditions as seemed to defy the power of incapacity, or even perfidy, to forbid success. The joint Liberal-Irish majority was an overwhelming one. The dregs of the old Unionist Party of the Boer War did not seriously count, either in debate or in the voting lobby. Better still, the ancient intransigeant [*sic*] solidarity of the Unionists against Home Rule was broken once for all by Mr. George Wyndham's adventurous policy in Ireland. Landlordism, which furnished England with the mainguard of her 'garrison' in Ireland, and for whose pay the worst of England's governmental crimes against Ireland had to be committed, had miraculously vanished from the scene amidst universal rejoicings, and not the least in the camp of the disbanded 'garrison' themselves.[3] The revolution had been planned across a friendly council-table in the Dublin Mansion House by the most authentic Unionist and Nationalist

1. crash, tumble.
2. With a sufficient majority to avoid dependence on the Irish Parliamentary Party, the Liberal government, after 1905, was not disposed to treat Home Rule as an urgent issue. The session of 1906 was barren for the Irish Party. Arthur Griffith's advice that it should withdraw from Westminster began to attract attention at this time.
3. George Wyndham (1863-1913), the Conservative government's chief secretary for Ireland 1900-05. The Wyndham Land Act of 1903 effectively transferred ownership of the land to the Irish tenantry. He aroused unionist hostility in 1902 when organizing the Land Conference, on the recommendation of which the Land Act was based.

leaders.[4] Nothing on the Irish Unionist side hindered the happy accord on the most intractable of all Irish disorders — the agrarian one — from widening into a concordat of Protestant and Catholic for a Home Rule settlement in the same spirit of sunny toleration among Irishmen which was the glory of Grattan's Parliament and of Wolfe Tone's United Irishmen. It is no longer doubtful that Wyndham himself, in whose veins coursed the generous blood of Lord Edward Fitzgerald, was an active sympathiser with Lord Dunraven's first tentative essays towards Home Rule.[5] That their joint efforts have not long ago reached their efflorescence in a blissful Irish settlement by consent must, unhappily, be laid to the account, not of 'Ulster,' which, as a fortress of resistance to Home Rule, was non-existent in the Irish life of the time, but of the same knot of narrow Nationalist politicians who were subsequently to emasculate and nullify Liberal Home Rule, and who then conceived they were doing a deed of far-seeing patriotism by blocking every approach to Unionist Home Rule and routing Wyndham out of the Irish Government and into his grave.[6] But from the point of advance reached by Wyndham and his Lord Lieutenant and his Under Secretary in their hardy adventure, the thin remnants of the Unionist Party in the House of Commons could never recede again....

Given two men of the stature of Gladstone and Parnell in control of such a situation, nothing could have hindered them from passing a great, a conciliatory, and a satisfying Home Rule Statute with a measure of general consent which nobody in his senses would think of withstanding. They would have been free to put it into force without any danger to the public peace which the police could not adequately cope with. There was unluckily no such Liberal leader and there was no such Irish leader. The years of omnipotence of the Coalition passed in certain beggarly measures of almost purely Party interest for the Liberal Party. They passed without any legislative fruit at all for Ireland except the utter bedevilment of Home Rule by a Parliament specially commissioned by the country to make Home Rule complete and effectual. An Irish Party, united and disciplined to the point at which unity became a disease — a unity which their few critics in the House of Commons consistently refused to ruffle while the Home Rule Bill was in gestation — an Irish Party to which the whole daily Press of Nationalist Ireland paid humble homage, and which commanded unlimited funds and a pathetic allegiance from the Irish race in every quarter of the globe — not only failed to achieve the object for which their omnipotence was entrusted to them. They failed to suggest a generous scheme of Home Rule, failed to amend a line of it in Committee, and failed to extract from the farcical measure 'placed on the Statute-Book' any actual result whatsoever except a half-yearly Order in Council postponing its operation to the Greek Kalends.[7] This would have been a sorry account enough of their stewardship of their tremendous powers. But worse remained behind. They consented twice over, after a long interval for reflection, to a partition of their country, which would have erected six of Ireland's most opulent counties, with one-fourth of her entire population, into a separate State specially delimited with a view of eternising religious and racial antagonisms. Darkest error of all, because the source of all the rest, the representatives of Ireland abdicated their independence, and abdicated it into the hands of the English Party which all the hopes of their country depended upon their being able to keep sternly up to the pledge of 'full self-government for Ireland' on which they had come into office, and on the smallest departure from which they could be turned out of office, had not the Irish representatives becomes their stipendiaries instead of their freeborn equals.

4. The Lord Mayor's official residence in Dublin, the Mansion House was the venue for the meeting of the Land Conference 1902-03. The nominated unionists turned down the invitation to the conference and were replaced by Lord Dunraven. It is an exaggeration, therefore, to claim that the conference was quite so ecumenical as O'Brien claims.
5. Lord Dunraven (1841-1926), a model landlord, who sought to bring about a peaceful settlement to the land problem and the Home Rule issue.
6. Unionist pressure forced Wyndham to resign in 1905. His health was permanently impaired by the stresses of his position in Ireland.
7. In other words, to postpone it for ever. There were no calends in the Greek months.

III

IRISH PATRIOTS AND THE ENGLISH TREASURY

The acceptance of salaries from the British Treasury, after a faint show of reluctance, will be found to be the *fons et origo*[1] of a catalogue of blunders, indecisions and futilities which, without the explanation of that one capital mistake, would seem to betray in the Irish leaders an incurable incapacity, not to speak of explanations still more uncomplimentary.... The Party of Parnell was the emanation of the Irish people. From them it derived all its powers, all its resources, and all such poor rewards as an unemancipated people can bestow upon their soldiers; and from its absolute independence of any power whatever outside the shores of Ireland, it derived all its terrors in the eyes of English Party managers, and all its opportunities of tempting them, instead of being tempted. For a quarter of a century the Irish people never failed to contribute munificently to the war-chest of their representatives. But that was because they had done well, and only so long as they did well. The moment symptoms of lethargy or demoralization set in the Irish people possessed the remedy in which the Parliament of the Stuarts found salvation — the stoppage of supplies — a power they had exercised with effect in recent years. That power was now gone. Contributions from Ireland, or from America or Australia were no longer indispensable. A cheque from the British Treasurey enabled an Irish member to make light of Irish opinion for a whole Parliament, and an expert electioneering machine made him sure of re-election. When Butt and Parnell began their work the acceptance of an office of profit by a solitary Irish member was enough to work the country into a fever of indignation. Now the whole body of Irish representatives, eighty-four strong, became the pensioner of Mr. Lloyd George,[2] by an arrangement which a change of Ministry, or even a change of mind of the existing Minister, might any year put an end to. It was not wilful corruption, but it opened the door to a feebleness of *moral* that, in poor human nature, is too often apt to eventuate in corruption.

It was an astounding change, and all the more dangerous because it was over and done with before the country had any real understanding of what was on foot. . . .

Political intolerance was aggravated by a new form of religious intolerance which, on the Nationalist side, had never been heard of before, and which supplied 'Ulster' with its only rational argument by exhibiting in the actual public life of Ireland those very sectarian tests and disabilities which the Orange reactionaries affected to apprehend from a Home Ruled Ireland. Union and affection between Irishmen of all creeds and racial origins was the breath of life of that Irish nationality which was worshipped generation after generation by Grattan's Protestant Volunteers, by Wolfe Tone's United Irishmen, by the heroes of the Young Ireland cycle, and by the Fenian men. The first words of the charter of Wolfe Tone's United Men: 'This society is constituted for the purpose of forwarding a brotherhood of affection, a communion of right, and a union of power among Irishmen,' were also adopted as the first words of the Constitution of the United Irish League,[3] before that organisation became the prey of the secret Hibernian Lodges. For that healing doctrine — the one safeguard against disintegration in a country with such a history of ethnic and sectarian divisions there was substituted, without the slightest notice to the Irish people, the ascendancy of an occult order, the first condition of admission to whose ranks was that the postulant must be a Catholic and must subject himself to a rigid Catholic test before initiation. Here were two new standards of Irish nationality and of the most pernicious character — secrecy and religious exclusivism — standards fatal to the creation of a United Ireland — specially planned indeed to prevent it, since the object in view was not freedom for all Irishmen but a monopoly of place and patronage for one particular category of them.

1. source.
2. David Lloyd George (1863-1945) was British prime minister 1916-22.
3. An agrarian organization founded by O'Brien in 1898 under the slogan 'The Land for the People'.

V

THE NEW ORDER OF PSEUDO CATHOLIC PLACEHUNTERS

The new Hibernian Order was the revival for placehunting purposes of a body of Catholic Defenders who, with perfect justice in their day, rose up against a detestable Orange combination for the extermination of the Catholic tenantry of the County of Armagh. There was now no shadow of justification for re-opening that dark and bloodstained chapter. There was not even the excuse of Catholic fanaticism, for 'The Board of Erin

Hibernians,' as they called themselves (whenever they were not glorying in the nick-name of 'The Mollies,' inherited from an old shebeen-keeper in whose house the leaders of some of the old Ribbon Societies used to meet),[1] were more than once laid under interdict by the Catholic Church for the evil practices of their Organisation and the blasphemous form of their original ceremony of initiation. The object of the present recrudescence and amazing spread of 'The Board of Erin' Hibernians was only too mournfully obvious. It was to establish a secret machinery for the distribution of the gigantic patronage, Imperial and local, which the Liberal alliance placed at the disposal of the political leaders, and to repay the political leaders by enrolling in every parish in the country a closely-knit brotherhood, powerful enough to make the electoral interests of the politicians secure, and to stifle any public criticism of their proceedings. Worst of all, the sinister transformation of the historic principles of Irish Nationality had been effected, like the enrolment of the members of Parliament on the Treasury paysheet, before the common people had any real inkling of what had happened. The new Order, with its battalions of office-holders and office-seekers at its beck, had assumed supreme control of the public organization, of its officials and its funds, and during the years while the Home Rule Bill was following its course, the honest Irish citizen was hushed into an almost religious silence by the solemn assurance, from every platform and in every newspaper, that 'the last obstacle to Home Rule was gone,' if the Irish people would only give an unquestioning allegiance to their leaders, Liberal and Irish. Freedom of opinion, which was crushed by open violence on the platform, was suppressed or garbled by much more dangerous weapons in the Press. The Hibernian propaganda, through the channel of correspondents in the offices of their organs in Dublin, Cork and Belfast, not only gave them a daily monopoly of the Liberal Press of Great Britain as well as Ireland, but enabled them, with an extraordinary success, to permeate the public opinion of America and Australia with their own version of events. There is the simple explanation of the atrophy of Irish public opinion, while the old ideals of Nationality were being exchanged for the greed of the place-hunter, and a far more formidable obstacle to Home Rule than the House of Lords raised up in Ulster by trading the interests of one set of bigots, real or sham, and one description of selfish ascendancy, against another. Without the explanation, freemen might well form a withering verdict as to Ireland's capacity for self-government in face of her silence and helplessness while her liberties and ideals were being thus dishonoured under her eyes. It was a miracle of popular trustfulness, but a miracle only saved from being a crime by the pathos of the poor people's belief that their abject self-effacement was a great deed of Unity for the sake of the National Freedom, which, they were assured, nothing but criticism of the Party could now delay.

VI

THE CASE OF MR. REDMOND

The carefully-organized ignorance which can be pleaded for the people cannot with equal truthfulness be pleaded for their titular leader. Mr. Redmond was an Irish gentleman of high personal honour, as well as of uncommon oratorical graces. It would be unjust to his capacity, as well as to his character, to attribute to a mere 'easy optimism of incompetence,' the extraordinary persistence with which, for five years, he went on repeating with the assuredness of a divine revelation that the battle was over and won — that 'there was no longer an Ulster Difficulty' — that the miserable Measure whose passage to the Statute Book was celebrated at the time with Hibernian bonfires and is now spoken of only with the contempt of universal Ireland, was 'a better Act than the Bill of 1886 which Mr. Parnell accepted as a settlement and a far better and freer Constitution than Grattan and the Volunteers won in 1782'§ and that the actual opening of the Irish Parliament, thus grandiloquently described, was 'as certain as the rising of the morrow's sun.' His self-

1. The Board of Erin was the executive of the Ancient Order of Hibernians, a catholic body formed in reaction to the Orange Order. The Board was created to heal a split between the American and Irish branches of the organization in 1902. It raised money for the Irish Parliamentary Party. The Ribbon Societies were part of the underground system of agrarian secret societies. They first appeared in 1826. The Molly Maguires (Mollies) was another such society, active in Ireland from 1835 to 1855, after which it spread to the United States as an offshoot of the Ancient Order of Hibernians and became powerful in the Pennsylvanian coalfields 1875-77. O'Brien's source for the name seems to be his own. The members disguised themselves by dressing in women's clothing.

§Mr. Redmond to the Dublin Corporation, July 20, 1915.

deception seemed to betray an incredible want of prescience in a leader of men. But the best defence of Mr. Redmond's leadership really is that he never was the leader. If in the last years he managed to persuade himself that his optimism was not insincere, the true explanation of the almost uninterrupted series of blunders which characterised the course of his nominal leadership is, that he found himself compelled to pursue a programme in which he profoundly disbelieved, carried out by men in whose wisdom he never even pretended to be a believer. Of this, there can be no rational dispute. He himself publicly avowed that he was in substantial agreement on all points with the present writer up to the moment when the latter severed his connection with the Irish Party in November, 1903, and that severance would never have taken place except as a protest against the plot to wreck the Policy of Conciliation in the hour of its most splendid promise.... For every development of Irish Party policy from that date was in the direction of reversing the settlement of 1903, of obstructing the progress of Land Purchase, and eventually killing it, of reviving the bitterness between classes and religious denominations, of rousing the alarms and flouting the resistance of 'Ulster,' and trusting all the hopes of Ireland to the generosity of the Liberal Alliance and the Act which paralysed the veto of the House of Lords. Practically every blunder of which Mr. Redmond's memory bears the heavy reproach was the blunder of advisers (not to say masters), whose English Radical and anti-Conciliationist tenets he, in his inner forum, mistrusted. Nevertheless he enfeoffed himself to men who could detect nothing in the policy and the Act which have made Ireland one of the most prosperous nations in Europe, except 'a landlord swindle,' which, in their wise eyes, was bound to lead straight to 'National Bankruptcy.' He deserted the authorised National Unity, and took sides with the Disunionists who had just launched 'a determined campaign' against the Policy to which not only he but every Nationalist organization and representative authority in the country stood solemnly committed. And he aided for years in duping the unfortunate country into the belief that it was the Disunionists who represented 'Unity and Majority Rule.' The impudent 'Unity' cry of the Disunionists coerced the country and ruined it.

Feebleness of character, it may be said, if it be not dishonesty? Feebleness, no doubt, was the secret of the initial blunder of his surrender in 1903 from which all the subsequent tide of follies flowed. It was due in large part to private circumstances which need not now be dwelt upon, but which at the moment shook the confidence of the people of Ireland in his own transactions under the Purchase Act; but his capitulation to the wreckers of the settlement of 1903 must above all else be set down to his honest and abiding horror of the danger of a renewal of the Parnell Split, if he persisted in the policy to which the immense majority of the people had given their allegiance in every constitutional form. He took meekly the threats of 'rending the National ranks asunder' with which he was plied, and allowed the will of the country to be overridden by 'the determined campaign' launched against the policy of which he was the standard-bearer by three men of enormous influence who had persuaded themselves that the Land Conference settlement was 'a mortgage of the future of the country in a moment of weakness,' and that Wyndham's overtures to Home Rule covered some dark treason to Ireland. Mr. Redmond himself crystallised his defence in the bewildering apophthegm: 'Better be united in the pursuit of a short-sighted and foolish policy than divided in pursuit of a far-seeing and wise one.' With the ethics of this extraordinary proposition this is not the place to deal. But its essential unwisdom was to confound the National Unity of which the Policy of Conciliation was the assured begetter with the Party Unity, which was indeed achieved with an iron discipline never attempted before, but with the tragic result for the country that the 'far-seeing and wise policy' was untimely finished with, and 'the short-sighted and foolish one' has led the Irish Cause into the welter of defeats, disappointments, betrayals and despair in which it is at the present moment immersed. He possibly averted the Party Split with which he was threatened by the three men from whom alone a Split could come; but by his capitulation he quite certainly gave the signal for the policy of United Unwisdom which shipwrecked Home Rule and himself.

VII

THE REAL MASTERS AND THEIR WORK

The tragedy was that Mr. Redmond, as his famous 'war speech' proved, possessed the affability and personal charm which would have made him an incomparable leader if the purpose was to conciliate English or Irish Unionist opponents, while he was acting against all his own natural instincts in pursuing the policy of exasperation forced upon him by the threat of rending the country asunder unless he submitted to the Liberal alliance and the bear-baiting of 'Ulster.' His long succession of failures was in reality a succession of reluctant testimonies to the wisdom of the policy he felt himself coerced to throw over. The real directing force lay elsewhere. Of the three powerful Irishmen who reduced the glorious opportunity of 1903 to a nullity only one now survives as an actual living force, but Mr. Dillon's word was made thenceforth supreme by the adhesion of a younger man of an audacious ambition, supported by a certain trick of flashy Socialist rhetoric which fascinated the unreflecting and by extraordinary gifts as an organiser. Since his uprise in the double capacity of Secretary of the open organisation and of National President of the secret one, Mr. Dillon's new lieutenant had enlisted the active fighting forces of the country in the service of a political machine popular alike with pseudo-Catholic place-hunters and with the believers in the English Democracy, and made none the less formidable by the secret signs and passwords with which the initiated were bound together.[1] A third force in the combination was the genial Mr. T. P. O'Connor — consistently throughout his life an English Radical first of all — who as President for twenty years of the Irish Nationalist Organisation of Great Britain, had gradually diverted that vast fabric of Irish opinion from its original function under Butt and Parnell as an electoral force to be thrown either on the Liberal or the Conservative side according to the shifting interests of Ireland, and had turned it into a reliable Hiberno-Radical chapel-of-ease of the Liberal Party. The only change hinted at for the future would seem to be that Mr. T. P. O'Connor's chattel interest in the Irish vote in Great Britain is to be made over to the English Labour Party on the usual loose terms — that is to say, on no terms at all, so far as Ireland is concerned. These three gentlemen, the guests of Mr. Lloyd George at a certain historic breakfast party in Downing street, are those to whom the glory, or the guilt, of the Liberal Home Rule policy properly belongs....

1. O'Brien is referring to Tim Healy and the sequence of events beginning with the Land Conference of 1903 and the founding by Healy of the constituency organizations, the Irish National Federation (1891-1900) and the People's Rights Association (1897-1901).

XVIII

WHY SINN FEIN WON THE COUNTRY

Sinn Fein has captured the best elements of Nationalist opinion for three substantial reasons which no railing of the politicians can rebut. Sinn Fein has saved the country from the three plagues of Partition, Conscription, and Corruption, and, be the fault whose it may, there was no other force left which could have saved her from any of the three. These are claims upon the national gratitude which will not easily be forgotten. The Sinn Feiners have yet to develop qualities of statesmanlike insight and breadth of toleration for all their countrymen before they can hope to inspire unconditional confidence for Sinn Fein's own sake. But castle-building for the future is not what the country is for the moment concerned with. 'The first thing first,' and the first thing is to deliver the National Cause from the men for whom incorrigible incompetence is the most merciful plea that can be invented to palliate their failure to turn to account the most colossal powers and opportunities that ever fell to the lot of Irishmen. It is proved to the satisfaction of nearly all their own disinterested adherents that they failed, not for want of being trusted, but because they were trusted too blindly and too long — not for want of Unity, but owing to the excess of a diseased Party Unity which has grown into a gangrene to the destruction of the true National Unity that might long ago have accomplished its healing work. The first condition of any safety for the future must be the removal from the helm of leaders who to this hour stand committed to the Partition of the country — be the same more or less — as the indispensable price for ever setting their precious 'Act on the Statute Book' going. Sinn Fein alone possesses the material forces and the high purposes which can unhorse the Board of Erin tyranny on the electoral field. The men whom the General Election will place in power may or may not do much better; they cannot by any conceivable possibility do worse. That is, I think, the fixed conviction of a people driven to desperation by the deceit of petty leaders, Irish and English....

The downfall of Parliamentarianism does not in the least import the dying down of the Irish Difficulty. It does not even necessarily involve the abandonment of Parliamentarianism; be it only conducted with the old elasticity and fearlessness, according to the shifting conditions of the Irish battle-front. It is the Parliamentarianism of the present that must die the death — the Parliamentarianism that eats the bread of English Party managers, and ends by setting the two countries at more bitter variance than ever. Truly the most daring thing in the sorry story of 'I and my Party,' is the impudence with which they request the country, not only to forgive their past, not only to give them a new lease of omnipotence, but to clear from their path every Irish Nationalist who helped to save the country from their unspeakable follies. In nothing is their hardihood more amusing than in the pretence that it is they who are the sole guardians of 'the Constitutional movement.' It is they, on the contrary, and not Sinn Fein, who have brought 'the constitutional movement' to its present state of decomposition.

'Constitutionalism' in a country whose grievance is that she possesses no constitution is an historical humbug. Parnell built up his movement, not by railing at Fenianism in the spirit of a professor of Constitutional history, but by incorporating its tremendous forces in his ranks and acknowledging no criterium[1] of the rectitude of his political action, be it 'constitutional' or 'unconstitutional,' except whether it was, in the circumstances, the best thing to be done for Ireland. Nationalists with a memory will smile at denunciations of 'unconstitutional action' from the John Dillon of the Mitchel Election in Tipperary and of the early Land League manner, and will find a woeful falling off, rather than a richer wisdom in the John Dillon of the Hardinge Commission Report.[2] When he claims the apostolic succession from Parnell's notions of 'constitutionalism,' it is quite certain he would have been hooted off any platform of the Land League or the Plan of Campaign if he attempted to air any of his latter-day speeches there. And for the claim that 'the Party' represent the intellect as well as the patriotism of our Nation, it can only be observed that if 'the Party' did indeed exhaust her supply of capacity for public action, Ireland were a lost land. In any future Parliament, such men could only be, in a more abject sense than ever, so much clay in the hands of English Ministerial potters.

Will Sinn Fein, if they get from the country the same mandate she gave to Parnell in the 'Eighties, exhibit Parnell's skill in the use of 'constitutional' weapons, as well as his daring in utilising 'unconstitutional' ones? I do not know, but, unless they do, I think I know that they will not long retain the confidence which will, doubtless, be accorded them in a generous measure at the General Election. As yet they have given no ground for a condemnation beforehand. In an hour of National shame, they gave an example of spotless personal character. The Lord Lieutenant, in his evidence before the Hardinge Commission, confessed with a groan that the Sinn Fein movement had not furnished Dublin Castle with a single informer — that leprous growth which was never before absent from Irish secret organisations. Their plans for their apparently maniacal raid upon Dublin elicited the admiration of their bitterest enemies. Heaven send their good qualities may not fail them on a larger field and for a less bloody purpose!

The point on which all genuine 'Constitutionalists' except the bankrupt politicians are at one is, that a General Election, at the earliest possible moment must be first step towards the allaying of the present 'putrid fever' which rages in Ireland. The usurpation of Mr. Lloyd George's Long Parliament of placemen, defensible enough perhaps for war reasons in England, is without a rag of justification in Ireland. It deprives a country, throttled by Martial Law, of any rational method of self-expression. It deprives English Ministers of any means of getting into touch with Irish opinion, except through members of Parliament who are in notorious disaccord with their constituents — who represent the realities of the Irish demands little more than the Derby dog represents the Epsom crowd that chevvy him off the course. Until the representatives of Ireland be men who come authentically back from the electorate, instead of men trembling at the thought of meeting them, nothing can be done to give an Irish settlement a new start; much may be done to destroy the last chance of it....

1. criterion.
2. A royal commission of inquiry into the causes of the Easter Rising was announced by Herbert Asquith, the British prime minister, on 10 May 1916. Lord Hardinge of Penshurst was chairman. The report was published on 3 July 1916.

V. SINN FÉIN 1904-18

ARTHUR GRIFFITH

(1871-1922)

from: THE RESURRECTION OF HUNGARY (1904)

[The text is that of the third edition of 1918, which Griffith oversaw and for which he wrote a new preface. By that time, the cause of parliamentarianism was in a sorry plight. Griffith pushed home his advantage as strongly as possible in the new preface, reiterating his view that the Act of Union of 1800 was the incorporative act that had generated the worse of Ireland's ills. The acceptance of that Act and its consequences leads, in his view, to parliamentarianism — that is, the tactics of the Irish Parliamentary Party, at this stage only months away from destruction at the polls. The assertion of the Renunciation Act of 1783, in which Britain yielded its so-called right to legislate for Ireland, led to constitutionalism. This was, in short, parliamentarianism in Dublin, not in London. Griffith disengages himself from the physical force tradition. He is carefully insinuating his policy of passive resistance between the outgoing parliamentarianism and the incoming Sinn Féin, the party that was to take the name but only part of the policies of Griffith's own organization.

The Hungarian analogy can be briefly indicated. Count Beust was the author of the Austro-Hungarian *Ausgleich* of 1867 that established the Austro-Hungarian dual monarchy. This was the culmination of the policy of passive resistance organized by Ferenc (Francis) Deák against Austrian rule and in the aftermath of Lajos Kossuth's abortive 1848 revolution. Griffith's parallel with Ireland is sometimes illuminating, sometimes not. In essence, what he wants to establish is the idea that the independence won in the eighteenth century was the foundation of the movement towards self-government. All British legislation since then had been invalid; further, the effects of British policy had been psychologically as well as economically devastating for Ireland. *The Resurrection of Hungary* is a therapeutic programme for a dismayed and shocked country. Of course the worst was still to come, but in January 1918 it may have appeared, for a moment, that the worst had passed.]

PREFACE TO THE FIRST EDITION (1904)

The series of articles on the 'Resurrection of Hungary' originally appeared in 'The United Irishman'[1] during the first six months of the present year [1904]. The object of the writer was to point out to his compatriots that the alternative of armed resistance to the foreign government of this country is not acquiescence in usurpation, tyranny, and fraud. . . .

Sixty years ago, and more, Ireland was Hungary's exemplar. Ireland's heroic and long-enduring resistances to the destruction of her independent nationality were themes the writers of Young Hungary dwelt upon to enkindle and make resolute the Magyar people. . . . Times have changed, and Hungary is now Ireland's exemplar.

It is in the memory of men still living when Hungary had not five journals in which a word of the Hungarian language was permitted to appear, when she had no modern literature save a few patriotic songs; when she had no manufactures of moment, and no commerce, save with her enemy, Austria; when she was cursed with an atrocious land-system and ruled by foreign bureaucrats; when her whole revenue did not reach £6,000,000 yearly, and her finances were robbed to perpetuate her oppression.

Today the revenue of Hungary is £42,000,000 — 800 newspapers and journals are printed in the Hungarian language. She possesses a great modern literature, an equitable land-system, a world-embracing commerce, a thriving and multiplying people, and a National Government. Hungary is a Nation.

1. Griffith's weekly paper appeared from 1899 to 1906. The title was taken from John Mitchel's newspaper of 1847. In 1906, the paper was replaced by Griffith's new publication, *Sinn Féin*.

She has become so because she turned her back on Vienna. Sixty years ago Hungary realised that the political centre of the nation must be within the nation. When Ireland realises this obvious truth and turns her back on London the parallel may be completed. It failed only when, two generations back, Hungary took the road of principle and Ireland the path of compromise and expediency.

PREFACE TO THE THIRD EDITION (1918)

In the fourteen years that have passed since 'The Resurrection of Hungary' was written, Ireland, continuing to pursue the policy rejected by Hungary in its conflict with Austria, has had its population further reduced by eighty thousand souls and its taxation trebled.

In the British Parliament, whither it sent its representatives, those representatives during that period supported in office four successive English Governments; associated Ireland with England's declaration of war upon Germany; aided England's Government to impose English war taxes upon this country; declared that Irish manhood must subserve the war aims of England; announced willingness to aid England to conscript Irish youth should it be necessary to English victory; and agreed with England to partition Ireland in the twentieth century as Russia, Prussia and Austria partitioned Poland in the eighteenth.

In the same space of time sixteen Irishmen were executed and two thousand five hundred Irishmen deported and imprisoned on proof or suspicion of seeking that measure of independence for Ireland which England claims for nations that lie within the dominion of the Powers upon whom she declared war.

In the past year the British Premier[1] stated in the British House of Commons (a) that Ireland is still as unreconciled to England as it was in the days of Oliver Cromwell; (b) that the Irish representatives in England's Parliament had never claimed for Ireland that sovereign independence England claims for Belgium, Serbia, Rumania and Poland; and (c) that England would never yield Ireland back her sovereign independence.

These are the evil fruits of Parliamentarianism masquerading as Constitutionalism — physical and economic decay, moral debasement, and national denial.

The constitutional leader of Hungary — Francis Deak — refused to associate his country with Austria's war against Prussia even when Austria bid the restoration of Hungary's independence as the price. None but the Government of a free Hungary might pledge the lives and property of the people of Hungary. The pseudo-constitutional leaders of Ireland pledged Ireland's blood and treasure to England's war upon Germany and Austria-Hungary without even offer of the bribe of Irish independence, and without reference to the Irish people. The Irish people have disowned their false leaders, but the sin was less in the men than in the system. Irish Parliamentarianism, born of the Act of Union and based upon admission of English right over Ireland, was inherently vicious. It constituted not a national expression, but a national surrender. It was the acceptance of moral and constitutional right in another country to shape our destinies; and whither it led the Irish people — to the attempted renunciation of their national past and their national future — to provincialism, partition, and foreign conscription — was whither it tended by the law of its being.

When Mr. Pitt, having struck down an organised and centred Ireland, induced the Irish to send their representatives to a foreign Senate to discuss with a foreign majority the affairs of this country, and to accept the vote of the foreign majority as the deciding factor — Mr. Pitt came nearer to conquering Ireland than came Mountjoy,[2] who handed over Ireland to Elizabeth 'carcases and ashes,' or than came Cromwell when, with fire, sword, and slaveship, he 'settled Ireland for all time.' For Mr. Pitt achieved by fraud what the warriors failed to gain by force. He confused the moral standards of the nation. He caused Ireland to revolve on an axis not its own. He made Irish nationality a doubter of its own existence, and in Irish politics he made a chaos.

Thus most Irishmen lost the instinct of thinking nationally, and came to think of Ireland in terms of English Toryism or English Whiggery, English Radicalism or English Socialism. They grew to look upon this English party or class as a friend, and that

1. David Lloyd George (1863-1945) was Britain's prime minister 1916-22.

2. Charles Blount (1563-1606), 8th baron Mountjoy, was lord deputy (1601-03) and lord lieutenant (1603) in Ireland and suppressed the revolt of the Great O'Neill.

English party or class as an enemy. Hence they ceased to recognise in all English parties and classes the same England in different garments. Mesmerised by London — whither its eyes were turned away — Ireland permitted, one by one, the attributes of nationhood to be filched, and in the end the Irish Nation, dwindling from the earth, listened to the spellbinders who half-persuaded it that duty and allegiance lay outside itself, and were in fact due to that country which had erased its name from the list of independent nations.

Ireland was sick — mind-drugged by Parliamentarianism — but Ireland is convalescing. The memory of what she was and the realisation of what she is are restoring her to national health. She sees herself as Hungary came to see herself — through eyes no longer fitted to foreign spectacles. She sees Finland stand up a free Republic, Poland arise a sovereign Kingdom. She asks shall she, their elder sister, be less in the world's account, and she demands today an equal independence. It is the story of the Sibylline Books.[3]

Fifty-seven years ago the London 'Times,' writing of the struggle then waging, said of the Hungarians —

> They wish to be Hungarians, and not Germans, and they have no desire to be dragged by Austria into German politics and be compelled to spend their money and lives in pursuit of objects in which they have no interest.

That is today the position of the people of Ireland. They wish to be Irish, and not English, and they have no desire to be dragged by England into British politics and be compelled to spend their money and their lives in pursuit of objects in which they have no interest.

3. A collection of oracular statements preserved in ancient Rome and consulted by the Senate in times of emergency. According to Livy, originally there were nine books offered to Tarquin by the Sibyl of Cumae, but the offer was rejected and she burnt three of them. She offered the other six at the same price. Again they were rejected, so she burnt three more. The remaining three were eventually bought for the original sum.

CHAPTER II

... We need not call in question the validity of the 'Act' of Union on the ground that it was carried by corruption and intimidation of the vilest type, or on the ground that what were declared to be fundamental provisions have since been violated by the English Government. The 'Act' of Union was never valid. It does not and cannot exist as a law under the Constitution. The members of the Irish Parliament had no legal power to terminate the existence of that Parliament. They were, in law, simply trustees for the time being of a power proceeding from the people, and they were bound in law to deliver that trust back into the hands of its owners. Instead they sold it.... No legal authority exists or can exist in the English Parliament to legislate for Ireland. If Ireland had adopted in 1800 towards the illegal Act of Union with England the attitude Hungary adopted in 1849 towards the illegal Union with Austria, England could not have sustained the 'Act' of Union for ten years. Had Henry Flood lived she might have done so.[1] Grattan was incompetent. He was an excellent orator, sincerely patriotic, but he was neither a statesman nor a leader of men. Plainly enough, like Saurin and Plunkett and Bushe[2] and the other Irish legists he saw that the 'Act' of Union was unconstitutional, but having salved his conscience by saying so, he considered he had done his duty to his country and returned to his favourite occupation of making eloquent speeches. All of the miscalled 'constitutional' leaders who followed him worked on the assumption that the Act of Union was legal and binding. O'Connell asked for an impossibility when he asked for Repeal of the Union — there can be no legal repeal of an illegality....

Gladstone's Bill[3] proposed to erect a legislature in Dublin, subordinate to the Parliament of London — a legislature whose existence could be terminated in forty-eight hours if a majority of the British members of the British Parliament so desired, and this legislature was to be excluded from having any voice in questions of war and

1. It was Henry Flood who forced the Renunciation Act on Britain, claiming that Grattan's declaration of Irish independence was, in constitutional terms, a sham.
2. William Saurin (*c.* 1757-1839), a lawyer and conservative politician, who prosecuted prominent United Irishmen in 1798 and led members of the Irish Bar in opposition to the Act of Union. He was savagely attacked by O'Connell in the seditious libel case against John Magee in 1813. (For this and for the quarrel between Grattan and Flood, see the section 'Political Prose: Cromwell to O'Connell' in Volume I, pp. 922-25, 941-48.)

   William Conyngham Plunkett (1764-1854), a lawyer and conservative politician, defended the United Irishmen in the trials of 1798 and strongly opposed the Union.

   Charles Kendal Bushe (1767-1843), nicknamed the 'Incorruptible', was solicitor general and then chief justice 1822-41 and an opponent of the Union.
3. The Second Home Rule Bill of 1893.

peace, foreign affairs, the army and navy, international treaties, customs dues, matters of currency, indirect taxation, etc. In return, Ireland was to resign for ever her status as a separate nationality and become a province of the Empire. There was scarce a province of the Austrian Empire whose petty Diet did not possess greater powers than Gladstone proposed to give his 'Irish Legislature,' and the proposal in 1861 of the Austrians to give Hungary a Legislature with absolute power over the internal affairs of Hungary, but yet terminable in certain circumstances by the Act of the Viennese Parliament, was unanimously and contemptuously rejected by the Hungarian people....

Count Beust[4] admitted that the geographical position of Ireland was more favourable than the geographical position of Hungary, but he argued it as a serious weakness of her claim, that, unlike Hungary, Ireland had not a separate language and literature, and that she had, unlike Hungary, *given her case away by sending members to the British Parliament, thus recognising its authority*. The first of Beust's objections was made in ignorance of Ireland, and would not, of course, be urged by him if he lived today. Ireland has a distinct language and literature of its own. The second is more serious, but not fatal. From the inception of 'The United Irishman' we have opposed the sending of Irishmen to sit in the British Parliament on two grounds (1) That it is a recognition of the usurped authority of a foreign assembly to make laws to bind the people of Ireland, and (2) That the policy of Parliamentarianism has been materially and morally disastrous to the country. We need not labour the latter point. No measure of a beneficial nature for this country has ever been passed by the British Parliament as a result of the presence, speeches, and action of the delegation from Ireland. The five measures which are usually accepted as beneficial, passed for Ireland by that Parliament — the Catholic Emancipation Act, the Tithes Act, the Church Disestablishment Act, the Land Act of 1881 — with the supplementary Ashbourne Act — and the Local Government Act, were passed as a result of the unconscious carrying out by the people of the Hungarian policy — the policy of Passive Resistance — with occasional excursions into the domain of Active Resistance at strategic points. In one sentence the impotence of the Irish Parliamentary Party in Westminster can be exhibited. It has been there for thirty-three years — a generation — to keep it there Ireland has expended over £600,000 — and during the period of its existence the population of Ireland has decreased by 20 per cent., and the taxation of Ireland for British purposes has increased by 70 per cent. No condemnation is further needed than these figures. A man who runs his business on such lines ends in the Bankruptcy Court. A nation which persists in running its business on such lines must inevitably go smash.

The recognition of the competency of a British Parliament to make laws to bind this country, which the attendance of the Parliamentary Party at Westminster implies, is, of course, a great political mistake; but Count Beust's contention that Ireland surrendered her case when she returned men to sit in the British Parliament, goes too far. The Act of Union is illegal and unconstitutional. Acceptance of seats in the British Parliament by Irishmen cannot render this illegal enactment legal. The temporary acceptance of the Act of Union as binding has had the unfortunate result of misrepresenting the position of Ireland to the world, and of confusing the minds of her people. It has led them into a cul-de-sac, and ignorance, vanity, and selfishness on the part of their leaders prevented them admitting the truth, and retracing their steps.

O'Connell had one statesmanlike idea in his latter life. It flashed across his mind to summon the Irish Parliament to meet in Dublin, and, ignoring the illegal 'Act' of Union, proceed to legislate for the country. There then existed a law known as the Convention Act, which forbade the assembly of delegates in Ireland, and the British Government attempted to counter O'Connell by its use. O'Connell sought to evade the provisions of the Act by calling his assembly the Council of Three Hundred,[5] and the Young Irelanders, recognising the political wisdom of the move, enthusiastically supported O'Connell — they even for the moment thought they had misjudged the Tribune in holding

4. Friedrich Ferdinant Beust (1809-86) helped to negotiate the *Ausgleich* (compromise) of 1867 that led to the establishment of the Austro-Hungarian monarchy. He was created a count in 1868.

5. The proposal, first made by *The Nation* newspaper, was then taken up by O'Connell. The Council never came into existence. There had been three hundred members in the Irish parliament before the Union.

him to be no statesman. 'If the members be wise and brave,' said John Mitchel, 'Ireland will be saved.' The British Government was alarmed as it had not been alarmed since 1798. 'In six months,' said Lord John Russell,[6] 'the power and functions of government will be wrested from our hands, and the Lord Lieutenant will sit powerless in Dublin Castle.' The preparations for the meeting of the Council of Three Hundred proceeded apace. Thomas Davis was selected to sit for the County Down, John Mitchel for the town of Banbridge: then O'Connell discarded his own proposal. The Council of Three Hundred never met — the 'Arbitration Courts,' which had been formed throughout the land to supersede the English Law Courts, were abandoned, and the English Government breathed freely again. Had Ireland been led by a statesman then, the end of the English government of Ireland was at hand. It is sixty years since, and our population has decreased by one-half. Our rights remain. The withdrawal of the Irish Parliamentary Party from the British Parliament and the summoning of the Council of Three Hundred to meet in Dublin are the initial steps for Ireland to take in the application of a National Policy.

The Council of Three Hundred should meet in Dublin during a period of the year, and initiate, discuss, and pass measures calculated to benefit the country. These measures once passed, the County Councils, Urban Councils, Poor Law Boards, and other representative bodies should, so far as they have legal powers — and the powers of the Irish County Councils and Poor Law Boards are more extensive than most Irishmen wot of[7] — enforce them. For instance, the County Councils have power to make monetary grants and levy rates for desirable purposes. If the Council of Three Hundred pass a measure affecting the industries or agriculture of Ireland, the County Councils can by united action give the measure much of the legal force of an Act passed by the British Parliament. Let it be recollected that even under the Coercion Act, there is no violation of the law committed by 300 gentlemen meeting in Dublin and recommending the adoption of measures to the Irish people calculated to improve their condition, and that there is nothing illegal in the Irish representative bodies using their full powers to give force to these recommendations.... A sum of £25,000 is raised annually for the upkeep of an impotent Irish Parliamentary Party in the British Parliament. This sum should continue to be raised, but be devoted to quite a different object, to the upkeep in all the great European capitals and important commercial centres of capable and patriotic Irish men of business, whose duties would be (1) to keep Europe acquainted with the truth about the struggle in Ireland, and (2) to secure a profitable market for Irish goods and produce abroad....

The institution of a system of Protection for Irish industries would be one of the principal duties of the Council of Three Hundred, and one that, by the co-operation of the Irish public bodies, could be made effective. The Hungarians inaugurated and carried out such a system by means of the 'Vedegylet'[8] association. The supersession of the English civil courts in this island, by the institution of 'Arbitration Courts,' such as the Young Irelanders projected and the Hungarians established, would be a matter of no difficulty and great profit to the nation. Voluntary Arbitration Courts are legal, and their decisions have all the binding force of law when the litigants sign an agreement to abide by them. The Irish abroad, especially in America, could form a valuable auxiliary, both by rendering aid to Irish industrial enterprises and obstructing and thwarting the designs of English foreign policy, as the Hungarian exiles did from 1849 to 1867 in the case of Austria — although far less in number than the Irish abroad. It would, of course, be a principal duty of the Council of Three Hundred to keep Irishmen out of the ranks of the English armed forces. In Hungary the County Councils saw so effectively to this that the Austrian army was rendered ineffective, and went to pieces in seven days before the Prussians.

We have but roughly indicated how the policy which made Hungary what it is today may be applied to Ireland; where the circumstances of the countries differ, it is a work of detail to adapt the policy. For its successful working clear-thinking, uncompromising men are required to lead. There is no doubt of the readiness of the people to follow. The people of Ireland are not less patriotic and not less intelligent than the people of Hungary —

6. Lord John Russell (1792-1878), Whig prime minister 1846-52, 1865-66.

7. are aware of.

8. An association founded to promote home industries and discourage imports.

three-fourths of their misfortunes are traceable to their pusillanimous, incompetent, and sometimes corrupt leaders. An Irish Deak[9] would have found in Ireland a support as loyal and as strong as Deak found in Hungary. But the Irish Deak never appeared, and shallow rhetoricians imposed themselves upon the people in his stead. Thus for a hundred years, with brief interruptions, Ireland has been consistently misled, and has paid for her weakness with the lives of half her people, and the loss of her fortune.

In the latter part of the eighteenth century, Ireland, by the determination and wisdom of her sons, was raised from the position of an insignificant and poverty-stricken province to the status of a nation and to a prosperity as great as that of any civilised country of her extent and population then existent. What Irishmen did in the eighteenth century, Irishmen are competent to do in the twentieth — what the Hungarians did for Hungary Irishmen can do for Ireland. None who reflect can doubt that, carried out with the same determination, the policy which resurrected Hungary from the tomb that Austria built for her in 1849 at Vilagos[10] can end the usurped authority of England to rule our country.

9. Ferenc Deák (1803-76) became the recognized leader of the Hungarian nation after 1849. In 1867 his negotiations with the Austrian Chancellor, F. F. Beust, led to the *Ausgleich*, by which Hungary received a form of Home Rule.

10. A town in what is now Romania where the Hungarian revolutionary army under General Gorgey surrendered to the Russians, who had intervened in favour of the Austrians. The surrender marked the end of Kossuth's independent republic.

WILLIAM P. RYAN

(1867-1942)

from: THE POPE'S GREEN ISLAND (1912)

[Ryan's career as a journalist was a series of battles against clerical and social oppressions in Ireland. His first newspaper, the *Irish Peasant*, fought for the rights of laymen and nation; in his second newspaper, the *Irish Nation*, he concentrated on labour, housing, land-purchase and other questions. 'What the *Irish Nation* called applied Christianity', he wrote in the Introduction to *The Pope's Green Island*, 'was described by the anti-social as "Socialism", and that was assumed to be diabolical. Others, especially those who accepted one or other official political party policy, would have the consideration of social ills and sores put away pending the triumph of the policy in the unveiled and idealised future. Meanwhile more and more of the nation might decay or emigrate.'

Ryan wanted to make the policy of what was known as 'Irish-Ireland' free of provincialism and sectarianism. He was, like the Fenians, opposed to clerical interference in politics and attacked their covert hostility to the aims of the Irish independence movement. These involved not only separation from England, but the birth of a new spirit of self-esteem and self-sufficiency in the people. He had no time for the myth of the Celt, no patience with the autocratic and arthritic power of an ill-educated and fearful clergy, and he anticipated many of the drearier aspects of Irish social developments that were to emerge more fully after 1922. Much of what he wrote in 1912 was still perfectly applicable ten and even twenty years later.]

CHAPTER II

THE ISLE OF EXTREMES

[Ryan explains how the anglicizing influence of Maynooth created confusion in the minds of the Irish-speaking laity. Because of the alliance between the priests and people in penal times, this new alienation had contrastingly disturbing effects. The position of the priest was transmogrified in the popular imagination.]

. . . Eventually in rural places the priest in the folk conception had become a wonder-worker, a sacred magician. He could work miracles at will, he could turn obstreperous sinners into animals, to quarrel with him was unlucky in the gravest degree. Such beliefs were common in my youthful days in the country; those who had come to doubt them were regarded as daring sceptics. They are held still in various places, but the scepticism is now more general. I have never known of a case in which a priest spoke out publicly against them. Indeed, the notion of mysterious priestly power is tacitly encouraged by a number of the Catholic clergy. Apparently they would fain have the people regard them as potent local successors to that magical St. Patrick — the hero of the great Irish clerical epic — with whom I deal in other pages. Some Irish Catholic laymen whose reason rebels against this whole folk-lore conception of the priesthood have yet a curious feeling, when they come into opposition to priests over social, educational, or intellectual issues, that they contend in a sense with the occult and the unknown. There is a touch of weirdness in the air.

Again, a great deal of the theology, history, &c., propounded by many Irish priests is crude, old-fashioned, or materialistic. It has stern, sombre, barbaric phases. It has much more relation to the Old Testament than the New. Indeed, not a little of what was hardest and grimmest in Judaism has been turned to their purpose and is preached with a vengeance. Their material Hell is horrible melodrama; they have done much to make of us a Devil-obsessed people. They take Genesis with bald literalness, their world is just 6000 years old; to them everything before the Christian era, except more or less of Judaism, was heathenism wild or foul. Of any philosophy of involution and evolution they reck nothing or accept nothing. Catholic philosophy generally seems a sealed or an unused book to them; their sermons and their avowedly religious books or booklets are innocent thereof. Progressive priests voice their feelings on the want with great candour. The general sermons and magazine articles are pietistic, emotional, rhetorical, verbose, controversial, or boastful in turn, but few that I have ever heard or read — a very large number indeed — breathe the finer spirit of Catholicity. Numerous Irish priests, who in themselves are earnest and zealous personalities, do not seem to try or care to put their better selves into their addresses. They often appear to have a rather indifferent opinion of the mentality of their congregations. Furthermore, a considerable proportion of them apparently cannot use language, in public at all events, with any sense of mastery, responsibility or style. It would often be exceedingly unkind to judge an Irish priest by his language. It misrepresents, even parodies, rather than typifies, himself. He is more human and more natural than his speech or his writing.

Another great trouble is that so much of the priesthood has now no particular apostolic or evangelical sense; it is largely professional, highly formalistic, afraid of new ideas, hazy in its notions of the outer world, even of the progressive Catholic elements thereof; alarmed, above all things, over any and every development of 'Socialism': it has lost the old collectivist Catholic ideal. Above the priesthood reigns the episcopacy, which, as a whole, is still more formalistic, more fearful of human nature, more remote from social and intellectual realities, more inimical to nearly all things distinctively Irish; an alien institution for the most part, but one that in this century is steadily losing its prestige. A few members, mostly later appointments, recognise and sympathise with vital Irish ideas, and so possess some living influence. But, generally speaking, the episcopacy is regarded by progressive priests and active laymen as the obedient servant of the Vatican and its diplomatic and political policy, on the one hand, and a check, so far as circumstances allow, on the development of a distinctive and cultured Irish nation, on the other. Apparently it does not want thought or overmuch culture and native spirit at home, and it desires more and more of the Irish race to go abroad as missionaries of one kind or another. Its policy and predilections at all events are regarded with suspicion, and its personalities as a rule are not rated high by the young generation. An able young priest summed up the matter rather mordantly for me one day in Dublin: 'Every man of individuality makes mistakes. No man who makes mistakes is made a bishop. Consequently. . . .' Over the capable and advanced young priests the bishops are apt to exercise their power autocratically and in present circumstances the young clerics themselves can only endure and hope. The knowledge of such autocratic action, however, has sharpened and intensified the freer lay criticism of recent years.

There is a further most interesting factor, new if superficially regarded, but really the recovery, remanifestation, and development of a long-dormant or neglected force. This is represented by the Gaelic League, and already we can see that not only has it consciously affected the national outlook and inlook, but that unconsciously it has affected the religious or theological position in more ways than one. In the national order it has given effect to truths that many forgot in the eighteenth century, and that most Irish people, especially leaders, never dreamt of in the nineteenth century. As to the other order, it need only be noted at this point that old Gaelic ideas about man and woman and life show much that is markedly different from the general Roman view. Even in the mediæval Gael's philosophy, while there was a decided Roman element, a very human Gael remained withal. Gradually the Gael receded or shrank, or seemed to do so; from an early part of the eighteenth century conventional 'Irish history' pays little attention to him; Swift, the Volunteers, Grattan's Parliament, &c., occupy the stage. He was there withal; he was strong in some respects and had his own distinctive inner life, if a lowly outer one, till the Famine of 1846-7. Even in the succeeding five decades, though still less regarded and reckoned with, he kept a certain vitality, as we shall see. The Gaelic continuity was never broken. And to the terms 'Gael' and 'Gaelic' we are not necessarily to attach a particular racial significance. I mean by the Gael a unit or type of the age-old civilisation that expressed itself through Irish, ancient, middle, or modern. This civilisation, when it was strong, absorbed Normans and others. Dr. Geoffrey Keating himself, the early modern Irish classic, was of the type known as 'Sean-Ghall,' the old or early-settling foreigner. Now, for a decade and a half, with the Gaelic League and its developments, direct and indirect, we have the Gael again, very much alive in places. Thousands have been given a new vision and impulse. The Church itself — as the 'Church' is popularly understood — is not easy in its mind about it all, and we shall see the why and the wherefore. It is a many-sided case. For one thing we have come to hear declarations of a self-realisation, a recovery of the romance of life, a sense of the hero in man — ancestral man and the man of today — that ring like heresy on the ears of our older ecclesiastics, and of some who are not old....

While such extremes meet in our island there are other extremes which do not meet, and know nothing of one another. There is extraordinary diversity in the social and intellectual conditions, and there are strata which cannot really be said to have any 'social' or 'intellectual' life at all. In these the housing and living conditions are simply abominable: I refer, amongst other haunts, to city slum stretches and wretched cabins of the west and elsewhere which I have seen myself. But all is not wretchedness in apparently forlorn cabins by any means. The Irish speaker will be able to draw out a store of traditional song and story and legend again and again. I shall give at a later stage a remarkable instance of what has come to us from one of the humblest of Connemara homes. A curious point about many of their tenants is their shadowy and unreal conception of Dublin and everything east of the Shannon, while of American centres like Portland and Boston, to which so many of their kindred go, sometimes to return with their savings and settle at home, they speak as familiarly as if they were but a few parishes away. America is in a sense their metropolis and market town, while some of them have seriously asked if Dublin is a part of Ireland. In dealing with Ireland, even Catholic Ireland, we must not forget her variety, her unconnected strata, her unrelated psychologies. I have seen a heroic Ireland, a mediæval Ireland, an intensely modern Ireland, and some Irelands I would find it hard to classify approximately. And often I have felt that creed, philosophy, race-mind, nation, and all such systematisation and generalisation are, when all is said, incidental. They but deal, so to say, with social, psychic, and other 'soil' and environment. The arresting importance and mystery is the 'seed' set in this soil — the individual soul in this transient but doubtless immensely significant part of its experience and destiny.

CHAPTER III

POPE, PRIESTS, AND PROTESTANTS

So far as my experience goes, Englishmen of most kinds, and Irish Protestants of some kinds, are rather obsessed by the Pope, while Irish Catholics are not. In Catholic Ireland most of the time the Pope seems remote; a venerable personality to be sure to the simple-hearted masses, but a little vague; to the intellectual an occasional problem; to the spiritual or the philosophical a factor sometimes delicately explained and sometimes almost explained away, often not recked of at all. Save on rare occasions his Holiness gives no appreciable trouble to the minds of Irish Catholics. But plenty of them, priests as well as laity, sometimes speak with severity of his advisers and of himself in so far as they and he are parts and pillars of Vaticanism, or the diplomatic and political side of Rome. The general Irish Catholic makes a clear distinction between Rome as a spiritual centre and Rome as a worldly centre. The Vatican in its human and worldly capacity is not regarded in a friendly light in Ireland; quite the contrary. It is popularly understood to be hostile to Irish aspirations; and it is also believed that its aid is often sought against Ireland or Irishmen by English statesmen or diplomats, acting, of course, indirectly or semi-officially. . . .

Irish candour on the subject of the machinery of Rome, and the sharp distinction drawn by Irish Catholics between essential Catholicity and Vaticanism, are no new story, though the rising generation has still clearer thoughts on the subject than the old. At the same time it is interested in numerous new activities, and Rome the greater part of the time is quite apart from its consciousness; it only declares itself on the matter of Roman unfriendliness to Ireland, or troubles particularly about it when in one way or another it is brought specially under notice. And then in all candid discussions it is taken for granted by Irish Catholic laymen and Irish-minded priests that no matter what changes or evolution may take place in the country the Pope and the Vatican will be pro-English always, never pro-Irish, and that if any clash or trouble should happen to come they would take the part of England against Ireland. Rome, for one thing, illusive as the dream may appear, expects that England will yet become Catholic — prayers for 'the conversion of England' are said regularly in English Catholic churches. But taking facts as they are it is natural enough that the Vatican should desire to conciliate England in every possible way, thereby tending to make matters easier for the Church round the empire. As against a world-power like the British empire Ireland in herself counts for little or nothing at Rome; at least that is the general Irish Catholic view, shared by those Irish priests and laymen who ought to know something particular about Roman policy. Rome looks on Ireland as a small 'safe' place, mainly important as a training-ground and jumping-off board for missionaries who will 'spread the faith' abroad. Which brings us to another crucial point. All the interesting things that have happened in Ireland in this century have been inspired by the ideal of making Ireland more fruitful and attractive in and for herself, socially, industrially, artistically, intellectually. We might call it native intensive culture. This home concentration and creativeness does not please Rome, as far as Rome understands what is happening, and it certainly does not please the great majority of the Catholic bishops — though they cannot very well oppose it directly and ostensibly — who are the agents and pillars of Rome and its policy. An educated Ireland, alive with eager ideals, and primarily and mainly interested in Ireland, would not suit them at all. It would not be a submissive Ireland — it would not say with the ironical Irish Catholic friend who re-wrote the Nicene Creed, 'I believe in one submissive Catholic flock of sheep' — and a prime article of its faith would be, as we can see already, that the real missionary work for Irishmen is in Ireland, it would leave other lands to provide their own apostles for the most part. The Irish home zest and intensive culture already in being explain a great deal that is superficially puzzling. The positive work, however, is more interesting in itself than in its bearing upon any controversy or side-issue.

In earlier years when Gaelic Leaguers began to come into clash here and there with ecclesiastics over issues that ecclesiastics alone had long decided — English sermons in Aran first brought trouble in an acute degree — progressive young priests as well as laymen were exceedingly anxious that the laity should be clear on the whole question of the relation of priests and people, and furthermore on the relation of Ireland and Rome. They saw that we were passing out of a semi-patriarchal and also somewhat serf-like age, that much of the new generation had schemes and purposes of its own and would not endure the leading-strings of the old. Hence, without a thorough understanding of their relative rights and positions, a dangerous if not disastrous division between clergy and laity would almost inevitably come to pass. That the laity had very decided rights in the Church, and that Churchmen had very definite duties, long neglected, to the nation, were basic facts emphasised from the first, and they were enunciated in connection with current happenings and discussions, during our whole Boyne Valley year, in the *Irish Peasant*.[1] . . .

When all is said, however, it is mainly bishops

1. The Meath newspaper edited by Ryan 1905-06.

and priests, not the Pope, that the Irish Catholic has to take into practical account, and his later relations towards these ecclesiastics, in national and theological matters, are revealed in subsequent pages.

Curiously enough, the issues of the 'Ne Temere'[2] decree attracted scarcely any attention in the country.... When the new pronouncement came to be looked into more particularly it was variously regarded. Many remained indifferent; mixed marriages were outside their experience, and the question did not interest them; they would speak more strongly on the official order in Irish dioceses that a Catholic who entered a Protestant Church for any purpose, even to act as 'best man' at the wedding of a Protestant friend, committed a 'sin' so great that pardon was 'reserved' for the bishop, not a lowly priest....

Yet all the time the question that most deeply concerned, and concerns, a certain Irish Catholic element is not that of the denomination of the clergyman who performs the marriage ceremony, but the far deeper matter of the mental and spiritual attitude of the contracting parties. This has long been with us, especially in connection with a peculiar Irish situation. Though not Catholic theology in theory, it is more than suggested in practice that rite and minister really make the marriage, and sanctify certain unions which many regard as odious — those that are the result of the sheer commercial system of 'match-making,' described in other pages, and in later years criticised severely. It is another instance of the rising spiritual view in opposition to the formalistic view, the assumption that the clergyman is all-important rather than incidental. Some who wonder why Irish Catholics are not much moved by matters like the 'Ne Temere' decree overlook the fact that a great many of them are preoccupied with problems like the above and others arising directly out of their own peculiar conditions and transitional circumstances.

One question which has caused immeasurably more feeling and discussion than any Papal pronouncement made directly or indirectly to Ireland is that of the clerical control of our primary education, not only religious but secular. It was exhaustively discussed, as already noted, in the *Irish Peasant*. The laity in scores of places had become keenly interested in matters of education. Apart from school concerns, the work done in Gaelic League branches, Coisde Ceanntair,[3] Feis Committees, Irish Training Colleges, Industrial Development Associations, and other bodies, showed a very practical zeal for what was in the broad sense education. Yet the conservative clergy stood sternly for undivided managerial control and what was described as in practice the keeping of a rope round the neck of the teachers. They insisted that the interests of faith and morality demanded this dominance, and that opposition was inspired by 'secularism' and hostility to religion. Broad-minded men like the Rev. Dr. McDonald,[4] senior Professor of Theology in Maynooth, admitted the untenable and preposterous nature of this claim. At last it came to be more widely understood that the clerics were not managers in their priestly capacity, as many had innocently imagined, but were there by virtue of English legislation. England in theory objects to Rome rule and the 'priest in the schools', but rules indirectly through Rome and sets the priest in complete managerial control of the vast majority of primary schools in Ireland. And a truly piquant irony is that if a bill to institute even partial popular control were introduced at Westminster, the clerical managers would certainly endeavour to rouse an agitation against it, and — judging by numerous remarks of theirs — would passionately declare to their flocks: 'The wicked English Government [whose representatives we are] wants to drive the priests and religion [which we personally seldom or never teach the pupils] out of the schools of Ireland, and substitute secularists and infidels [people whose religious training has been, or might have been, imparted by us]. Rally to your faithful priests who have been always the champions of Faith and Fatherland.'

Whether the Britons or the clergy have the more reason to laugh to themselves I cannot determine. It has been said that the most brilliant thing ever done by the Irish priests was the invention of the legend that they have been always on the side of the people.

2. The papal decree *Ne temere* took effect from 19 April 1908. It meant that catholics were thereafter bound in all circumstances by the catholic form of marriage, even when the other partner was not catholic.

3. Irish for 'District Section or Branch.'

4. Dr Walter McDonald (1854-1920), professor of dogmatic theology at St Patrick's College, Maynooth from 1881, a noted controversialist who engaged with the catholic hierarchy over many disputatious issues.

And I sometimes think the most brilliant and mordant touch of English irony is not in English literature but in English government and life — getting Rome to try to 'keep us good' on the one hand, and on the other, putting the priest in pride of place over our schools and the teachers of our youth, and then inveighing against Rome rule, and calling us a priest-ridden people.

In Ireland itself an incidental little irony is that some of the Protestants who co-operate heartily in the new movements grow alarmed on occasion over Catholic lay criticism of bishops and priests, deeming it dangerously strong or indiscreet. They endeavour from time to time to put on the brake, so to say, and ensure gentler going and mellowness of temper....

CHAPTER VII

ECCLESIASTICS, EVE AND LITERATURE

[Ryan's account of the clerical attacks on dangerous and corrupting literature, and its accompanying concentration on sexual matters, anticipates the oppressive atmosphere that the Censorship of Publications Act of 1929 was to intensify. The position of women in Irish society was further reduced by the prevailing sexual ethic.]

... The priest who has by far the most commanding place in the Irish popular imagination is Canon Peter O'Leary,[1] of Castlelyons, Co. Cork, and *his* philosophy of woman in life, and his view of woman as she is often reflected in literature, are somewhat naïve and peculiar. Canon O'Leary suggests a man who came out of an old saga, but after sixty years or more of rural Munster experience, has grown homely and racy without losing anything of the saga spirit, while at the same time he has acquired a veneer of conservative Irish ecclesiasticism. He does not seem at all the same individuality when he speaks or writes as the old hero, the fireside philosopher or story-teller, and the defender or revealer of clerical interests or preferences. He does all these things with great energy just as the spirit moves him. He is the most popular of our home authors, and appeals to foreign students just as much as to our own; thus Zimmer[2] considered him to be the raciest and most idiomatic writer of modern Irish. He was born sixty-six years ago, when there was still a great deal of culture in rural Munster; Irish, English, and Latin were known in his native parish — schoolmasters of the older style were often keen Latinists. During his whole career as a priest, Father Peter (or 'An tAthair Peadar'), as he is familiarly called, has worked hard for the education of the people. At one time he conducted a classical school, and in other parishes he established night schools and reading-rooms, and attended to them regularly himself. He believes, however, that only at the starting of the Gaelic League did he really begin to live in the worthy sense. He liked it because it was democratic, and he is a literary democrat....

With his stories, dialogues, modernisations of mediæval Irish tales, and other things, Father Peter is quite a literature to a large democracy. Thousands of people who do not or cannot actually read him themselves listen delightedly while younger folk give them the benefit of his narrative or his shrewd philosophy. He is the favourite fireside author.... In his work for this natural rural realm, particularly in the south—work which, of course, also reaches school and college and other students — Father Peter is unique, an enlivening figure and force to contemplate. When he bursts into controversy, especially in English, he is seldom felicitous, least of all when he tries to uphold a clerical tradition or pretension. One of his greatest literary raids in the last few years was that in 1908 against all English fiction without exception. He asked, 'Is the English Language Poisonous?' and decided in the affirmative — which must have been bad news for our bishops — English fiction had absolutely poisoned it. He recalled a country boy's description of what the youth called a 'navvil': a boy and a girl to fall in love with each other and somebody to make mischief between them. And then in the innocence of his troubled heart he unloaded much like this upon an alarmed people:

1. Canon Peter O'Leary (1839-1920), more generally known as An tAthair Peadar, was parish priest of Castlelyons, Co. Cork from 1891. He was dedicated to the language revival and was a founder-member of the Gaelic League. It was in Ryan's newspaper, the *Irish Peasant* (July 1906) that he declared, 'It was not till the start of the Gaelic League that I really began to live in a worthy sense.' O'Leary was famous for his clear, colloquial style and was a prolific author, adapting many of the ancient sagas and medieval tales. His most famous works were his autobiography *Mo Sgéal Féin* (*My Story*), published in 1915, and his novel *Séadna*, serialised in 1894 and published in book form in 1904. O'Leary's bibliography runs to 487 items (see Volume III, p. 817).

2. Heinrich Zimmer (1851-1910), German linguist and philologist.

Look over the whole range of English fiction. What is it all but that country boy's 'navvil'? No change. No new thought. Not a single new idea. All the talk we hear about 'plot' and 'art' and 'originality' — save the mark!— is only talk about some new jingle rung on the very same three strings! In order to ring those new jingles, all the lowest and most degrading phases of the lowest and most degrading of human passions are searched for and exhibited to the mind of the reader. Then, and here is the point that answers the above question: the most polished refinement of diction is used for the purpose of covering but not hiding the vilest matter. That refined diction is poisonous language. It is rotten language, as rotten as anything which is corrupt. It is unwholesome. It ruins the mental health of those who read those English 'navvils,' just as rotten food would ruin their bodily health.

I made the obvious remark at the time that Father Peter's English reading must have been peculiarly unfortunate, for his 'judgment' of English fiction, whether we took the old or the new writers, was preposterous. True, a good deal of stuff we would not take as a gift in London was thrust under our eyes at the bookstalls in Ireland and solemnly reviewed in the *Freeman's Journal*, but Canon O'Leary, our Irish literary lawgiver, ought to have been more careful in his preferences.

The ensuing discussion was lively and profitable. As in others of its kind we had that sharp clash and candid expression of opinion from which those whose minds were capable of moving were brought to a clearer understanding not only of the issue and things bound up with it but also of themselves. Such intellectual combats also did something to clear away a share of those merely misty or moonshiny notions, 'spooks' or wraith-like semblances of opinions, that had been passing for truths in hundreds of Irish minds for a long time. We had a little legion of people still who dwelt in a very cloudy cloudland between an idealised Ireland and a phantom England. More and more of them came to learn a little of Irish and English reality, objective and subjective. In the rotten-novel-and-poisoned-language discussion the speech was very frank indeed. It was admitted, of course, that a good deal of the fiction which came from England was trash, and clerics were ironically reprimanded for (on their own showing) their liberal acquaintance with it. But there was other fiction, and their criticism of it was really that criticism of human nature to which they were ever prone. They wanted to take the life-blood out of literature, to destroy its value as a record of human experience and spiritual biography. . . .

But the conservative clerics and their friends are slow to recognise realities. They talk on occasion as strongly as Canon O'Leary in his controversies, but unlike him they do nothing serious for reform and progress in Irish education and the natural development and cultivation of the Irish mind. Yet they are astonished if neglected or suppressed mind grows weedy and frivolous, or vicious in its quasi-literary preferences. Periodically they became alarmed over the reading-matter of large sections of the people. For some years sermons and the little pietistic productions of the Irish Catholic Truth Society[3] were expected to prevail against it. Of course the hope was vain. The next 'remedy' was wilder. In 1911 'Vigilance Committees' were established in several cities, at first ostensibly to deal with English Sunday newspapers, but it soon became evident from the declarations of certain bishops and other ecclesiastics that there was a desire to bar 'Socialistic' and general publications unwelcome to the powers that be. It was quickly recognised by thoughtful Irish observers that this outburst of 'Vigilance', crude in itself, and in some degree humiliating, would be almost certain to develop, if leaders and their friends had their way, into an intolerable intellectual censorship. It was subjected to candid criticism in *An Claidheamh Soluis*, *An tEireannach*, and the *Irish Review*, the most thoughtful and independent of our later Irish publications.[4]

The tragi-comedy of the Irish conservative clerical attitude to woman and literature, and the efforts to keep both in the way it is imagined in episcopal 'palaces' and priests' houses that they ought to go, are beyond telling. The censors strive with a certain sadness in their hearts, for they feel that whatever they do the trouble cannot really be

3. The Catholic Truth Society of Ireland was founded at a meeting of the Maynooth Union in 1899. It published penny pamphlets in response to the halfpenny newspaper, launched by Harmsworth's *Daily Mail* in 1896. There have been many versions of the Vigilance Committees since 1911, most of them committed to the censorship of 'trashy' literature emanating from England or Ireland.

4. *An Claidheamh Soluis* (*The Sword of Light*) was the official organ of the Gaelic League from 1899. *An tEireannach (The Irishman)* and the *Irish Review* were independent journals in the early years of the twentieth century.

removed, only 'regulated' in a haphazard way. Woman cannot be abolished, and literature, which finds her so dangerously interesting, cannot be suppressed. The trouble did not originate in Ireland; it really began with 'Eve,' on whom Irish ecclesiastics preach with extraordinary feeling and emphasis. If Adam could have sufficed at the morning-time of the manifestation of the world! Had there been no Eve and no womanhood there would probably have been no trouble with literature; nothing in its pages would have shocked a curate or brought a blush to the brow of the most sensitive bishop. Eve is the eternal shadow on the Irish ecclesiastical landscape.

Biographies/Bibliographies

Fenianism and the Land League

In addition to the items listed in the individual bio-bibliographies, the following select bibliography may be consulted.

T. W. Moody (ed.), *The Fenian Movement* (Cork: Mercier Press, 1968); J. Lee, *The Modernisation of Irish Society 1848-1918* (Dublin: Gill and Macmillan, 1973); W. S. Neidhart, *Fenianism in North America* (London: Pennsylvania State University Press, 1975); L. O Broin, *Revolutionary Underground: The Story of the Irish Republican Brotherhood 1858-1924* (Dublin: Gill and Macmillan, 1976); P. Bew, *Land and the National Question in Ireland 1858-82* (Dublin: Gill and Macmillan; Atlantic Highlands, New Jersey: Humanities Press, 1978); H. Senior, *The Fenians and Canada* (Toronto: Macmillan, 1978); S. Clarke, *Social Origins of the Irish Land War* (Princeton: Princeton University Press, 1979); K. R. M. Short, *The Dynamite War: Irish-American Bombers in Victorian Britain* (Dublin: Gill and Macmillan, 1979); P. Jalland, *The Liberals and Ireland* (Brighton: Harvester Press, 1980); L. Cullen, *The Emergence of Modern Ireland* (Dublin: Gill and Macmillan, 1981); T. Garvin, *The Evolution of Irish Nationalist Politics* (Dublin: Gill and Macmillan; New York: Macmillan, 1981); B. M. Touhill, *William Smith O'Brien and his Irish Revolutionary Companions in Penal Exile* (Columbia: University of Missouri Press, 1981); P. Quinlivan and P. Rose, *The Fenians in England 1865-1872: A Sense of Insecurity* (London: John Calder; New York: Riverrun, 1982); D. Keenan, *The Catholic Church in Nineteenth-century Ireland* (Dublin: Gill and Macmillan, 1983); J. O'Shea, *Priests, Politics and Society in Post-Famine Ireland* (Dublin: Wolfhound Press, 1983); C. Townshend, *Political Violence in Ireland: Government and Resistance since 1848* (Oxford: University Press, 1983); M. Winstanley, *Ireland and the Land Question 1800-1922* (London: Methuen, 1984); K. T. Hoppen, *Elections, Politics and Society in Ireland 1832-1885* (Oxford: Clarendon Press, 1984); J. A. Cole, *Prince of Spies: Henri Le Caron* (London: Faber and Faber, 1984); R. V. Comerford, *The Fenians in Context: Irish Politics and Society 1848-82* (Dublin: Gill and Macmillan; Atlantic Highlands, New Jersey: Humanities Press, 1985); T. Garvin, *Nationalist Revolutionaries in Ireland 1858-1928* (Oxford: Clarendon Press, 1987).

Parnellism

This select general bibliography is meant to supplement the items given in the individual bibliographies.

C. C. O'Brien, *Parnell and His Party 1880-90* (Oxford: Clarendon Press, 1957); H. Howarth, *The Irish Writers 1880-1940: Literature Under Parnell's Star* (London: Rockliff, 1958); F. S. L. Lyons, *The Fall of Parnell 1890-91* (London: Routledge and Kegan Paul, 1960); M. Hurst, *Parnell and Irish Nationalism* (London: Routledge and Kegan Paul, 1968); M. Brown, *The Politics of Irish Literature: From Thomas Davis to W. B. Yeats* (Seattle: University of Washington Press, 1972); D. W. Miller, *Church, State and Nation in Ireland 1898-1921* (Dublin: Gill and Macmillan; Pittsburgh, University of Pittsburgh Press, 1973); F. S. L. Lyons, *Charles Stewart Parnell* (New York: Oxford University Press, 1977); A. O'Day, *The English Face of Irish Nationalism: Parnellite Involvement in British Politics 1880-1886* (Dublin: Gill and Macmillan, 1977); P. Bew, *C. S. Parnell* (Dublin: Gill and Macmillan, 1980); M. Steinman, *Yeats's Heroic Figures: Wilde, Parnell, Swift, Casement* (London: Macmillan, 1983); W. M. Murphy, *The Parnell Myth and Irish Politics 1891-1956* (New York: Peter Lang, 1986); P. Bew, *Conflict and Conciliation in Ireland 1890-1910: Parnellites and Radical Agrarians* (Oxford: Clarendon Press, 1987).

W. E. H. Lecky

LIFE. Born in Newtown Park, Co. Dublin in 1838, William Edward Hartpole Lecky was educated at Cheltenham and Trinity College, Dublin. He taught at Trinity and represented the university in Westminster from 1895 to 1903. He opposed Home Rule and supported the co-operative movement begun by Sir Horace Plunkett. His reputation as an historian was established by 1870, but he declined the chair of history at Oxford in 1892. His liberal unionist position is developed in his rebuttal of J. A. Froude's *History of Ireland*, the rancour of which is effectively exposed by Lecky's more temperate and measured approach. He died in Dublin in 1903.

CHIEF WRITINGS. *Leaders of Public Opinion in Ireland* (London: Saunders, 1861; revised edition Longmans, Green and Co., 1871); *History of the Rise and Influence of Rationalism in Europe* 2 vols (London: Longmans, Green and Co., 1865); *History of European Morals from Augustus to Charlemagne* 2 vols (London: Longmans, 1869); *A History of England in the Eighteenth Century* 8 vols (London: Longmans, 1878-90); *A History of Ireland in the Eighteenth Century* 4 vols (London: Longmans, 1892-96; 1902-03); abridged, with an introduction by L. P. Curtis Jnr. (Chicago and London: Chicago University Press, 1972); *The Political Value of History* (London: E. Arnold, 1892); *Democracy and Liberty* 2 vols (London: Longmans, 1896); *The Map of Life: Conduct and Character* (London: Longmans, 1899); E. Lecky (ed.), *Historical and Political Essays* (London: Longmans, 1908).

BIOGRAPHY AND CRITICISM. E. Lecky, *A Memoir of the Right Hon. William Edward Hartpole Lecky, by his wife* (London: Longmans, 1909); J. Morley, 'Lecky on Democracy' in *Miscellanies* 4th Series (London: Longmans, 1908); J. J. Auchmuty, *Lecky, A Biographical and Critical Essay* (Dublin: Hodges, Figgis; London: Longmans, 1946); H. Montgomery Hyde (ed.), *A Victorian Historian, Private Letters of W. E. H. Lecky, 1859-1878* (London: Home and Van Thal, 1947); H. F. Mulvey, 'The Historian Lecky: Opponent of Irish Home Rule', *Victorian Studies* (June 1958), 337-52; D. McCartney, 'Lecky's *Leaders of Public Opinion in Ireland*', *Irish Historical Studies* XIV, No. 54 (September 1964), 119-41; D. McCartney, 'Lecky and the Irish University Question', *Irish Ecclesiastical Record* (August 1967), 102-12; Donal McCartney, 'W. E. H. Lecky', *Carloviana* I, No. 15 n.s. (December 1966), 8-13; Donal McCartney 'W. E. H. Lecky: Lost Leader of Public Opinion in Ireland', PhD thesis, National University of Ireland 1970.

Isaac Butt

For biography and bibliography, see Volume I, p. 1297.

Dion Boucicault

LIFE. Born Dionysius Lardner Boursiquot in Dublin in 1820 (or possibly in 1822), he worked for a short time in Guinness's brewery before emigrating to London to pursue a stage career. He had his first great stage success in 1841 with *London Assurance*; thereafter he established a remarkable international reputation as playwright, actor, stage-director and impresario. He wrote over 150 plays, but it was not until the success in 1861 of *The Colleen Bawn* (The Fair-Haired Girl), based on Gerald Griffin's novel *The Collegians* (1829), that the Irish material in his plays became predominant. *Arrah-na-Pogue* (Arrah of the Kiss) was produced in Dublin and London in 1864-65; *The Shaughran* (The Wanderer) opened in New York in 1874. All three were enormously successful, partly because of his wife's portrayal of the heroines. He rewrote the nationalist song 'The Wearing of the Green' and sang it provocatively in front of London audiences in 1865. He was nominated for a parliamentary seat in County Clare (thus prefiguring Eamon de Valera!) and was even moved to write a popular nationalist history, *The Fireside Story of Ireland* in 1881. After an amazing career, in which he had made and lost three fortunes and become an international celebrity, he died in New York in 1890.

CHIEF WRITINGS. *The Colleen Bawn; or, The Brides of Garryowen* (New York, 1860); *Arrah-na-Pogue; or, The Wicklow Wedding* (New York: French's Standard Drama, 1868?); *The Shaughran* (published in acting editions, 1873); all three are in D. Krause (ed.), *The Dolmen Boucicault* (Dublin: Dolmen Press; New York: Oxford University Press, 1964); P. Thomson (ed.), *Plays by Dion Boucicault* (Cambridge: Cambridge University Press, 1984); A. Parkin (ed.), *Dion Boucicault: Selected Plays* (Gerrards Cross: Colin Smythe, 1985). For a full bibliography, see S. E. Molin, 'Dion Boucicault' in R. Hogan (ed.), *Dictionary of Irish Literature* (Dublin: Gill and Macmillan, 1980), pp. 117-18.

BIOGRAPHY AND CRITICISM. T. Walsh, *The Career of Dion Boucicault* (New York: Dunlop Society, 1915); R. Hogan, *Dion Boucicault* (Boston: Twayne, 1969); S. E. Molin and R. Goodfellowe, 'Dion Boucicault, The Shaughran, a Documentary Biography. Part One, the Early Years' in *George Spelvin's Theatre Book* II (1979); J. M. Nelson, 'From Rory and Paddy to Boucicault's Myles, Shawn and Conn: The Irishman on the London Stage 1830-1880', *Eire-Ireland* 13, No. 3 (Fall 1978), 79-105; R. Pine (ed.), *Dion Boucicault and the Irish Melodrama Tradition*, a special edition of *Prompts* (Bulletin of the Irish Theatre Archive), No. 6 (September 1983); S. M. Watt, 'Boucicault and Whitbread: The Dublin Stage at the End of the Nineteenth Century', *Eire-Ireland* 18, No. 3 (Fall 1983), 23-53; S. E. Molin and R. Goodfellowe, 'Nationalism on the Dublin Stage', *Eire-Ireland* 21, No. 1 (Spring 1986), 135-38.

George Sigerson

LIFE. Born near Strabane, Co. Tyrone in 1836, Sigerson was educated at Letterkenny Academy, at Paris and at Queen's Coollege, Cork. He translated and edited the work of Charcot on diseases of the nervous system, became a fellow of the Royal University, professor of biology at University College, Dublin and president of the National Library Society in 1893. He was also a member of the Irish Literary Society and in 1884 was appointed a member of the Royal Commission on Prisons. Sigerson's essays and poems, the latter mostly translations from the Irish, had a considerable impact; his influence is evident in the writings of W. P. Ryan and is acknowledged in the dedication of Thomas MacDonagh's *Literature in Ireland* (1916). His daughter, Dora Sigerson Shorter, became a well-known poet. Sigerson was appointed a senator of the Irish Free State in 1922. He died in Dublin in 1925.

CHIEF WRITINGS. *The Poets and Poetry of Munster* 2nd Series, (Dublin: John O'Daly, 1860); *Modern Ireland: Its Vital Questions, Secret Societies, and Government* (London: Longmans, Green, Reader and Dyer, 1868; 2nd ed., 1869); *Political Prisoners at Home and Abroad* (London: Kegan Paul, Trench, Trubner & Co., 1890); *Bards of the Gael and Gall* (London: T. Fisher Unwin, 1897; 2nd enlarged edition, 1907); *The Last Independent Parliament of Ireland* (Dublin: Gill, 1919); *The Easter Song of Sedulius* (Dublin: The Talbot Press, 1922); *Songs and Poems*, introduction by P. Colum (Dublin: Duffy, 1927).

Charles J. Kickham

LIFE. Charles Kickham was born in Mullinahone, Co. Tipperary in 1828. At thirteen, an accident with gunpowder left him deaf and damaged his sight. He was a fervent supporter of Young Ireland and had to go into hiding after the 1848 rebellion. In 1860 he joined the Irish Republican Brotherhood and in 1865 became editor of the Fenian newspaper *The Irish People*. He was arrested and sentenced to fourteen years' imprisonment in 1865, but was released in 1869 in poor health. He became chairman of the IRB in 1872, a position he held until his death at Blackrock, Co. Dublin ten years later.

CHIEF WRITINGS. *Sally Cavanagh; or, The Untenanted Graves* (Dublin: W. B. Kelly; London: Simpkin, Marshall, 1869); *Knocknagow, or The Homes of Tipperary* (Dublin: Duffy, 1873, 1879); *For the Old Land: A Tale of Twenty Years Ago* (Dublin: Gill, 1886); *The Eagle of Garryroe* (Dublin: Martin Lester, 1920); *Tales of Tipperary* (Dublin: The Talbot Press, 1926); H. L. Doak (ed.), *Poems of Charles Joseph Kickham with a life and notes* (Dublin: Educational Company, 1931); J. Maher (ed.), *The Valley near Slievenamon: A Kickham Anthology* (Kilkenny: Kilkenny People, 1942); *Sing a Song of Kickham: Songs of Charles J. Kickham with Gaelic Versions and Musical Notations* (Dublin: Duffy, 1965).

BIOGRAPHY AND CRITICISM. R. J. Kelly, *Charles Joseph Kickham: Patriot and Poet* (Dublin: Duffy, 1914); J. J. Healy, *Life and Times of Charles J. Kickham* (Dublin: Duffy, 1915); P. S. O'Hegarty, 'Kickham's Novels', *Irish Booklover* XXVI (1938), 41-43; R. V. Comerford, *Charles J. Kickham: A Study in Irish Nationalism and Literature* (Dublin: Wolfhound Press, 1979).

John O'Leary

LIFE. Born in Tipperary in 1830, O'Leary was educated at Carlow, the Queen's Colleges of Cork and Galway and Trinity College, Dublin. Deeply influenced by Thomas Davis and the Young Ireland movement, he took part in the 1848 rising, for which he was arrested and imprisoned. He was one of the more radical members of the movement and was a vigorous supporter of James Fintan Lalor. O'Leary was recruited into the Fenian movement by James Stephens and acted as his go-between with John O'Mahony in the United States. He worked for the Fenian newspaper *The Irish People* and was arrested and sentenced to twenty years' imprisonment when the paper was suppressed in 1865. He spent nine years in prison and was released on condition that he spend the rest of his sentence in exile. He lived in Paris for most of these years, and consulted there with Parnell and Devoy on the issue of the New Departure. He was opposed to parliamentary politics in the struggle against British rule and also was against extreme terrorist violence. In 1885 he returned to Dublin. After the Parnell split in 1890, he supported Parnell. From 1887 he edited the Gaelic Athletic Association newspaper, *The Gael*, in which he published Yeats, Douglas Hyde, Katharine Tynan and others. O'Leary became a symbolic figure for the new literary generation and was especially influential upon and helpful to Yeats. From 1885 to 1907 he was president of the Supreme Council of the Irish Republican Brotherhood and in 1898 was president of the committee to organize the centenary celebrations of the United Irishmen. In 1900 he became first president of Cumann na nGaedhal. He died in Dublin in 1907.

CHIEF WRITINGS. *Young Ireland: The Old and the New. Being the inaugural address of the Young Ireland Society, delivered in the Round Room, Rotundo, 19 January 1885* (Dublin, 1885); *What Irishmen Should Know: What Irishmen Should Feel* (Dublin: Cahill, 1886); *Recollections of Fenians and Fenianism* (London: Downey, 1896; facsimile reprint with introduction by M. Bourke, 2 vols, Shannon: Irish University Press, 1969).

BIOGRAPHY AND CRITICISM. M. Bourke, *John O'Leary: A Study in Irish Separatism* (Tralee: Anvil Books, 1967).

Jeremiah O'Donovan Rossa

LIFE. Born in Rosscarbery, Co. Cork in 1831, O'Donovan Rossa was educated locally in an Irish-speaking area that was badly hit by the Famine, during which he worked at distributing relief. He founded the Phoenix National and Literary Societies at Skibbereen which became part of the Irish Republican Brotherhood in 1858 at the invitation of James Stephens. He emigrated to the United States, returned in 1863 to become business manager of *The Irish People*, was arrested in 1865 with the other Fenian leaders and was sentenced to life imprisonment after attacking the judge in a speech lasting eight hours. He was treated with great cruelty in prison. The Amnesty Association led a campaign on his behalf and he was released in 1871. With John Devoy and other Fenians, he went to New York and received an address of welcome from the House of Representatives. O'Donovan Rossa contributed to *The Irishman* newspaper, became head centre of the Fenians and helped organize for a dynamiting campaign in Ireland. He returned to Ireland in 1894 and again in 1904-06. After his death in New York in 1915, his remains were removed to Ireland. It was at his graveside in Glasnevin Cemetery that Patrick Pearse made his famous oration.

CHIEF WRITINGS. *Irish Rebels in English Prisons: A Record of Prison Life* (New York: Kenedy, 1882; originally published in 1874 as *O'Donovan Rossa's Prison Life: Six Years in English Prisons*); Abridged version, S. Ua Cearnaigh (ed.), *My Years in English Jails* (Tralee: Anvil Books, 1967); *Edward O'Donnell: A Story of Ireland of Our Day* (New York: Green's, 1884); *Rossa's Recollections 1838 to 1898* (New York: O'Donovan Rossa, 1898).

John Devoy

LIFE. Born in Johnstown, Co. Kildare in 1842. He joined the Fenians in his early teens, enlisted in the French Foreign Legion to gain military experience, spent a year in Algeria and returned to Ireland in 1862 to become an organizer for the Irish Republican Brotherhood. He recruited many Irish soldiers serving in the British army. Devoy became chief organizer of the IRB in 1865 and arranged the escape of James Stephens from Richmond Prison. Arrested in 1866 and sentenced to fifteen years imprisonment, he was released in 1871 on condition that he left the British Isles. In the United States, he worked as a journalist, joined Clan-na-Gael and organized the escape of Fenian prisoners from Australia. He supported Davitt and Parnell in the New Departure, took control of Clan-na-Gael and kept up a propaganda barrage against the British in his newspapers, the *Irish Nation* and *The Gaelic American*. He supported Patrick Pearse's school and helped raise funds for the Irish Volunteers in 1914. During World War I, he tried to interest Germany in supporting the Irish cause and arranged Roger Casement's contact with the German ambassador in Washington. He supported the Treaty of 1921, broke with de Valera and regarded the Treaty as the first step towards the republican Ireland for which he had struggled for so long. He died in Atlantic City, New Jersey in 1928.

CHIEF WRITINGS. *Recollections of an Irish Rebel. The Fenian Movement . . . Personalities of the Organisation* (New York: Young, 1929); S. O Luing (ed.), facsimile reprint (Shannon: Irish University Press, 1969); *The Irish Land League, Its Origin, Progress and Consequences* (New York: Patterson and Neilson, 1882).

BIOGRAPHY AND CRITICISM. D. Ryan, *The Phoenix Flame, A Study of Fenianism and John Devoy* (London: Arthur Barker, 1937); W. D'Arcy, *The Fenian Movement in the United States 1858-1886* (Washington D.C.: Catholic University of America Press, 1947); W. O'Brien and D. Ryan (eds), *Devoy's Post Bag*, 2 vols (Dublin: Fallon, 1948-53); D. Lynch and F. O'Donoghue, *The I.R.B. and the 1916 Insurrection* (Cork: Mercier Press, 1957); S. O Luing, *John Devoy* (Dublin: Cló Morainn, 1961); T. N. Brown, *Irish-American Nationalism 1870-1890* (Philadelphia and New York: Lippincott, 1966); A. J. Ward, *Ireland and Anglo-American Relations 1899-1921* (London: Weidenfeld & Nicolson, 1969); L. O Broin, *Fenian Fever, An Anglo-American Dilemma* (London: Chatto and Windus, 1971); T. D. Williams, 'The Irish Republican Brotherhood' in T. D. Williams (ed.), *Secret Societies in Ireland* (Dublin: Gill and Macmillan; New York, Barnes and Noble, 1973).

Michael Davitt

For biography and bibliography, see p. 208.

Thomas Clarke

LIFE. Thomas Clarke was born in 1857 on the Isle of Wight where his father was serving in the British army. He emigrated to the USA in 1880, joined Clan-na-Gael and met Dr Thomas Gallagher, with whom he joined in a dynamiting campaign in Britain. He and Gallagher were arrested in 1883 and were sentenced to life imprisonment under the Treason-Felony Act. Clarke spent fifteen years in jail; the experience undermined his health. Gallagher was driven insane. On his release, Clarke returned to the United States and worked on *The Gaelic American* newspaper with John Devoy. In 1907 he returned to Dublin and set up a tobacconist's shop at the corner of Parnell Square. This became a centre of revolutionary discussion and intrigue. He was elected to the Supreme Council of the IRB, encouraged the setting up of a military council to determine the chances of an insurrection and established the Dublin Central Branch of the Wolfe Tone Clubs Committee. With the help of Clan-na-Gael funds, he and his colleagues, Bulmer Hobson and Denis McCullough, gained control of the *Irish Freedom* newspaper and used it to further their republican aims. He was the senior member of the Provisional Government declared on Easter Monday 1916. Thomas Clarke was executed for his part in the Rising on 3 May 1916.

CHIEF WRITINGS. *Glimpses of an Irish Felon's Prison Life* (Dublin and London: Maunsel and Roberts, 1922).

Eóin Mac Neill

LIFE. Born in Glenarm, Co. Antrim in 1867, educated at St Malachy's College, Belfast and the Royal University of Ireland. He was a leading figure in the foundation of the Gaelic League in 1893, became editor of the *Gaelic Journal* in 1894, of *Fainne an Lae* in 1898, of *An Claidheamh Soluis* in 1899. In 1909 he was appointed professor of early Irish history in University College, Dublin. In 1913, after the publication of 'The North began', he was elected president of the Irish Volunteers. He countermanded the plans for the 1916 Rising on learning that Pearse and others had planned the rebellion without informing him. In 1916 he was court-martialled and sentenced to life imprisonment, but was released the following year. In the 1918 election he was elected MP for Derry City and the National University of Ireland. From January to April 1919, he was minister for finance in the First Dáil and later minister for industries. Mac Neill was the Free State representative on the Boundary Commission in 1924, but resigned from it and refused to accept the Commission's report. After retiring from political life in 1927, he founded the Irish Manuscripts Commission, and was president of the Royal Society of Antiquaries of Ireland 1937-40 and president of the Royal Irish Academy 1940-43. He died in Dublin in 1945.

CHIEF WRITINGS. *Phases of Irish History* (Dublin: Gill, 1919; reprinted Dublin-Sydney: Gill, 1968); *Celtic Ireland* (Dublin: Martin Lester, 1921).

BIOGRAPHY AND CRITICISM. J. Ryan, 'Eoin Mac Neill, 1867-1945', *Studies* 34 (1945), 433-48; F. X. Martin (ed.), *The Irish Volunteers*

(Dublin: Duffy, 1963); M. Tierney, 'Eoin Mac Neill: A Biographical Study, in J. Ryan (ed.), *Eoin Mac Neill, Saint Patrick* (Dublin: Sign of the Three Candles, 1964), pp. 9-34; F.X. Martin and F.J. Byrne (eds), *The Scholar Revolutionary: Eoin Mac Neill 1867-1945 and the Making of the New Ireland* (Shannon: Irish University Press, 1973). This volume contains a full bibliography of Mac Neill's writings.

Patrick Pearse

For biography and bibliography, see p. 561.

Roger Casement

LIFE. Born in Sandycove, Co. Dublin in 1864, but brought up in County Antrim. In 1892 he entered the British colonial service and was awarded a knighthood in 1911, two years before his retirement. In the interval he had become internationally known for his reports on the atrocities committed by Europeans in the Belgian Congo and in South America. Casement became involved with Irish nationalist politics, joined the Gaelic League and befriended Bulmer Hobson, Alice Stopford Green, Joseph Biggar and others. In 1913, he became a member of the provisional committee of the Irish Volunteers. In the following year, on a visit to the United States, he made contact through John Devoy with the German Embassy and later travelled to Berlin. He vainly attempted to raise an Irish brigade among Irish prisoners of war in Germany and was frustrated in his efforts to obtain for the Volunteers an adequate supply of arms from the German authorities. He sailed for Ireland on a U-Boat to try to prevent the Easter Rising, which in his view needed more arms if it was to have any chance of success. On landing at Banna Strand in County Kerry, he was arrested, taken to Dublin and then London, where he was being interrogated when the Easter Rising began. Charged with high treason, Casement was sentenced to death. While movements to win a reprieve were being organized and supported by influential people, George Bernard Shaw for one, the government unofficially circulated copies of his diaries to indicate that he was homosexual and to undermine the campaign for his reprieve. The Black Diaries, as they were called, were successful in their effects. Casement was hanged at Pentonville Prison on 3 August 1916. In 1965, the British Labour government gave permission for his remains to be returned to Ireland and he was reinterred in Glasnevin cemetery, Dublin after a state funeral.

CHIEF WRITINGS: H. O. Mackey (ed.), *The Crime Against Europe. The Writings and Poetry of Roger Casement* (Dublin: C. J. Fallon Ltd., 1958).

BIOGRAPHY AND CRITICISM: G. H. Knott (ed.), *Trial of Sir Roger Casement* (Edinburgh and London: Hodge, 1917); D. Gwynn, *The Life and Death of Roger Casement* (London: Cape, 1930); M. Borsa, *La tragica impresa di Sir Roger Casement* (Verona: Mondadori, 1932); W. J. Maloney, *The Forged Casement Diaries* (Dublin and Cork: n.p., 1936); H. O. Mackey, *The Life and Times of Roger Casement* (Dublin: Fallon, 1954); R. McColl, *Roger Casement: A New Judgement* (London: Hamish Hamilton, 1956); A. Noyes, *The Accusing Ghost of Roger Casement* (London: Gollancz; New York: Citadel Press, 1957); P. Singleton Gates and M. Girodias, *Casement: The Black Diaries. An Account of Roger Casement's Life and Times* (Paris: Olympia Press, 1959); H. Montgomery Hyde, *Trial of Sir Roger Casement* (London: Hodge, 1960); H. O. Mackey, *Roger Casement: A Guide to the Forged Diaries* (Dublin: Apollo Press, 1962); B. Inglis, *Roger Casement* (London: Hodder and Stoughton, 1973); B. L. Reid, *The Lives of Roger Casement* (New Haven: Yale University Press, 1976); S. O'Cleirigh, *Casement and the Irish Language* (Dublin: Clódhanna Teoranta, 1977); R. Sawyer, *Casement, The Flawed Hero* (London: Routledge and Kegan Paul, 1984).

Charles Stewart Parnell

LIFE. Born in Avondale, outside Rathdrum, Co. Wicklow in 1846, Parnell was educated in England. When his father died in 1859, Parnell inherited the Avondale estate. The family lived in Dublin throughout the 1860s. He went to Magdalene College, Cambridge, from which he was sent down in 1869. His parliamentary career began in 1875 when he contested and won the seat for Meath for the Home Rule League. In 1876 he attracted the attention of the Irish Republican Brotherhood when he declared that no murder had been committed at Manchester in 1867 in the Manchester Martyrs affair. In 1877 Parnell was elected president of the Home Rule Confederation of Great Britain. In 1878 he participated in the 'New Departure', a policy of co-operation between constitutionalists and Fenians. Within a year, he was the leader of the new policy and President of the Land League. Accompanied by John Dillon and, later, by Tim Healy, he went to North America in 1879-80 to win support for Home Rule. The trip was an outstanding success. Parnell was so well received in Toronto that Healy dubbed him the 'uncrowned king of Ireland'. In the 1880 election, the Home Rule party was successful; among those returned was Captain William H. O'Shea, with whose wife, Katharine, Parnell began an affair that year. Agrarian violence and the British policy of coercion led Parnell to promote the policy of boycotting and a No Rent manifesto. While in jail at Kilmainham, he and Gladstone concluded the so-called 'Kilmainham Treaty' of 1882 in an effort to defuse the Land War. The Phoenix Park murders of that year put an end to their efforts. Thereafter, Parnell devoted himself to the policy of Home Rule. His tactic was to hold the balance of power between the main English parties in parliament and to bargain for Home Rule as the price of his support. Gladstone's conversion to Home Rule in late 1885 led to the introduction of the first Home Rule Bill in 1886. Its defeat was followed by a Conservative victory, but Parnell and his party remained committed to the Liberals. In 1886 he took up residence with Katharine O'Shea and began to become more remote from his supporters and to pay less attention to parliamentary business. In 1887, *The Times* published a series of damaging articles, 'Parnellism and Crime', based on forged letters. A Special Parliamentary Commission investigation followed, but the forgery was exposed and Parnell was vindicated. On Christmas Eve 1889, Captain O'Shea filed for divorce, citing Parnell as co-respondent. This led to his downfall; Gladstone withdrew his support, the Irish Party split on the question of Parnell's leadership and the catholic hierarchy issued a condemnation of his conduct on the day of his marriage to Katharine O'Shea in June 1891. Exhausted by campaigning in the bitter byelections of 1890-91, Parnell died on 6 October 1891 in Brighton, in the arms of his wife.

CHIEF WRITINGS. J. Wyse-Power (ed.), *Words of the Dead Chief: being extracts from the public speeches and other pronouncements of C. S. Parnell . . . with an introduction by Miss Anna Parnell, and a facsimile of portion of Mr. Parnell's famous manifesto to the Irish people* (Dublin: Sealy, Bryers & Walker, 1892).

BIOGRAPHY AND CRITICISM. See the listings under 'Parnellism' (p. 366).

R. Barry O'Brien

LIFE. Born in Kilrush, Co. Clare in 1847, O'Brien was educated privately and at the Catholic University, Dublin. Called to the bar in 1874, he also worked as a journalist and edited *The Speaker*. He was chairman of the London Gaelic League 1892-1906 and its president 1906-11. O'Brien was a loyal follower of Parnell and was for a time his unofficial private secretary. He died in London in 1918.

CHIEF WRITINGS: *The Parliamentary History of the Irish Land Question from 1829 to 1869, and the Origin and Results of the Ulster Custom* (London: Sampson, Low, Marston, Searle and Co., 1880); *Fifty Years of Concessions to Ireland, 1831-1881* (London: Sampson, Low, 1883): *Irish Wrongs and English Remedies, with other Essays* (London: Kegan Paul, Trench and Co., 1887); *Thomas Drummond, Under-Secretary in Ireland 1835-1840: Life and Letters* (London: Kegan Paul, Trench and Co., 1889); *The Life of Charles Stewart Parnell, 1846-1891* 2 vols (London: Smith, Elder and Co., 1898): *A Hundred Years of Irish History* (London:

Isbister, 1902); *Irish Memories* (London: T. Fisher Unwin, 1904); *England's Title in Ireland* (London: T. Fisher Unwin, 1905); *Dublin Castle and the Irish People* (Dublin and Waterford: Gill, 1909); as editor, *The Autobiography of Wolfe Tone* 2 vols (London: T. Fisher Unwin, 1893); *Speeches of John Redmond, M.P.* (London: T. Fisher Unwin, 1910).

T. P. O'Connor

LIFE. Born in Athlone in 1848, Thomas Power O'Connor was educated at the Queen's College, Galway. In 1870 he moved to England and became a journalist; he had good political contacts in the Liberal Party. He was MP for the Scotland Division of Liverpool 1885-1929. An early supporter of the Home Rule Confederation of Great Britain, he also supported the Land League and Parnell. He helped in the drawing up of the famous *Manifesto to the Irish in England* (1885) in which Parnell asked Irish voters to oppose the Liberals. He supported Parnell during the split. He was known as 'Tay Pay' after his most popular newspaper, *T.P.'s Weekly,* which he established in 1902. In 1917 he became the first film censor. He died in London in 1929.

CHIEF WRITINGS: *Life of Lord Beaconsfield* (London and Belfast: William Mullan and Son, 1879); *Gladstone's House of Commons* (London: Ward and Downey, 1885); *The Parnell Movement: With a Sketch of Irish Parties from 1843* (London: Kegan Paul & Co., 1886); *Sketches in the House. The Story of a Memorable Session* (London: Ward, Lock, 1893); *Parnell and Home Rule: The Man and the Measure. Being a re-issue of two books. 'The Life of Charles Stewart Parnell' and 'Sketches in the House'* (London: Ward, Lock, n.d.); *Charles Stewart Parnell: A Memory* (London: Ward, Lock, Bowden & Co., 1891); *Memoirs of an Old Parliamentarian* 2 vols (London: Ernest Benn, 1929).

Timothy Healy

LIFE. Born in Bantry, Co. Cork in 1855. After schooling at the Christian Brothers' School in Fermoy, he emigrated to England. As parliamentary reporter for *The Nation,* Healy played an important part in charting the rise of Parnell. Acting as Parnell's secretary during the North American tour in 1880, he dubbed Parnell 'the uncrowned king of Ireland'. He was elected to Westminster in 1880 as MP for Wexford and was called to the bar in 1884. His expertise in agrarian law made him an important figure in the debates on the Land Act of 1881. Healy broke with Parnell over the nomination of Captain O'Shea at the Galway by-election of 1886 and publicly referred to Katharine O'Shea as Parnell's mistress in the course of that campaign. In 1886 he conceived the idea of the Plan of Campaign in support of tenants who could not pay their rents. When the split in the Irish Parliamentary Party came, he was a leading figure in the attack on Parnell and was head of the anti-Parnellite Irish National Federation from 1891 to 1895. He represented the employers during the inquiry into the Lockout of 1913. He lost his parliamentary seat to Sinn Féin in the election of 1918. After the establishment of the Free State in 1922, Healy was made governor general 1922-28. He died in Dublin in 1931.

CHIEF WRITINGS: *Why There is an Irish Land Question and an Irish Land League* (Dublin: Gill, 1881); *A Record of Coercion. Votes of Irish Members for the Enlightenment of Irish Electors* (Dublin: Webb, 1881); *Loyalty Plus Murder* (Dublin: Gill, 1884); *Under Which Flag? or Is Parnell to be the Leader of the Irish People? By a Gutter Sparrow* (Dublin: J.J. Lalor, 1890); *Why Ireland is Not Free. A Study of Twenty Years in Politics. History of the Irish Nationalist Party 1875-1898* (Dublin: Nation Office, 1898); *Stolen Waters. A Page in the Conquest of Ulster* (London: Longmans, 1913); in a shorter version, *The Great Fraud of Ulster* (Dublin: The Talbot Press, 1917); *Letters and Leaders of My Day* 2 vols (London: Thornton, Butterworth, 1928).

BIOGRAPHY AND CRITICISM: L. O'Flaherty, *The Life of Tim Healy* (London: Cape, 1937); M. Sullivan, *No Man's Man* (Dublin: Browne and Nolan, 1943).

Frank Hugh O'Donnell

LIFE. Born in 1848 in County Donegal, educated at Queen's College, Galway. He worked as a journalist in London before becoming MP for Galway in 1874 and for Dungarvan in 1877. O'Donnell was one of the most noted of the Irish Parliamentary Party's obstructionist speakers. He was defeated by Parnell for the leadership of the party in succession to Isaac Butt and thereafter never accepted Parnell as leader. He was also hostile to the Land League. In 1885 he resigned his seat and concentrated on journalism. His bitterness against Parnell and the failure to attain Home Rule was relentless. Tim Healy christened him 'Crank Hugh'. He died in London in 1916.

CHIEF WRITINGS. *The Ruin of Education in Ireland and the Irish Fanar* (Dublin: Nutt, 1902); *The Stage Irishman of the Pseudo-Celtic Drama* (London: Longmans, 1904); *Paraguay on the Shannon. The Price of a Political Priesthood* (London: King; Dublin: Hodges, Figgis, 1908); *A History of the Irish Parliamentary Party* 2 vols (London: Longmans, Green & Co., 1910); *The Lost Hat: The Clergy, the Collection, the Hidden Life* (London: Murray and Co., 1914).

John Redmond

LIFE. Born in 1856 in Ballytrant, Co. Wexford. He was educated at Clongowes Wood College and Trinity College, Dublin. Redmond was returned as MP for New Ross 1881-85 and for North Wexford 1885-91. He read law at Gray's Inn, was called to the English bar in 1885 and to the Irish bar in 1887, but never practised. He became one of Parnell's chief lieutenants and remained loyal to him throughout the crisis of 1890-91. He was elected MP for Wexford in 1891 and held the seat until his death. When the Irish Parliamentary Party was reunited in 1900, he became its leader, although he could not control prominent figures like William O'Brien and Tim Healy. He gave Asquith support in 1911 and in return gained the Home Rule Bill of 1912. Unionist opposition was by now consolidated, but Redmond refused anything more than temporary exclusion of Ulster from the Bill. He demanded half the seats on the ruling committee of the Irish Volunteers in an attempt to control their activities. With the outbreak of war, the Home Rule Bill was suspended, although it was believed that Redmond had finally won what his party had so long sought. His speech at Woodenbridge, urging the Volunteers to join the British army, angered the IRB, but most Volunteers, henceforth known as the National Volunteers, answered Redmond's call. After 1916, which Redmond called 'A German intrigue', his pleas for leniency towards the leaders went unheeded. In 1917, he suggested that an Irish convention be called to discuss the problems of Home Rule. He died during the convention in March 1918 and did not see the extinction of his party in the election of the following year.

CHIEF WRITINGS. *Historical and Political Addresses 1883-1897* (Dublin: Sealy, Bryers and Walker; London: Simpkin, Marshall, Hamilton, 1898); R. B. O'Brien (ed.), *Speeches of John Redmond, M.P.* (London: Fisher Unwin, 1910); *Ireland and the War; Extracts from Speeches made in the House of Commons and in Ireland since the Outbreak of the War* (Dublin: Sealy, Bryers and Walker, 1915).

BIOGRAPHY AND CRITICISM. L. G. Redmond-Howard, *John Redmond* (London: 1910); W. B. Wells, *John Redmond* (London: Longmans, 1919); D. R. Gwynn, *The Life of John Redmond* (London: Harrap, 1932).

William O'Brien

LIFE. Born in 1852 at Mallow, Co. Cork, O'Brien was educated at Cloyne Diocesan School and at Queen's College, Cork. In 1868 he began his career as a journalist and was invited by Parnell to edit the Parnellite newspaper *United Ireland*, which he did from 1881 to 1890. He was imprisoned with Parnell in 1881 and became one of his chief lieutenants. As founder member of the Plan of Campaign, he was subject to a series of arrests, imprisonments and charges. With John Dillon, he skipped bail in 1890 and went to the United States. As a consequence, he was out of the country when the divorce crisis broke. He met Parnell at Boulogne in December 1890, but could not be persuaded to take over the leadership of the party from Justin McCarthy. After 1892, O'Brien lived in Mayo and founded the United Irish League in 1898 to improve the lot of the people on the land. The success of this movement led to the reunification of the Irish Parliamentary Party under John Redmond's leadership. From 1899 to 1908, O'Brien made his own newspaper, *The Irish People*, the forum for his views. These were largely based on the belief in the necessity of reconciliation between all Irish factions. O'Brien broke with his party in 1903, attempted to negotiate with Sinn Féin, rejoined the party in 1908 and resigned in 1909. He returned to politics as MP for Cork and as editor of *The Cork Accent* and the *Cork Free Press*. He voted against the Third Home Rule Bill of 1914, spoke in favour of recruitment in 1914-15, but after the Rising of 1916 recognized that Sinn Féin had won the sympathy of the people and did not contest the 1918 election, in which the Irish Parliamentary Party was annihilated. He retired to Mallow and declined to be nominated a senator in the new Free State. He died in London in 1928.

CHIEF WRITINGS. *The Influence of the Irish Language on Irish National Literature and Character* (Cork: Gay & Co., 1892); *Irish Ideas* (London and New York: Longmans, Green and Co., 1893); *The Irish National Question and the Land Acts. Speeches delivered at Cork . . . 1903* (Dublin: Irish People Office, 1903); *Recollections* (London: Macmillan, 1905); *An Olive Branch in Ireland and Its History* (London: Macmillan, 1910); *Sinn Fein and its Enemies* (Dublin: Maunsel, 1917); *The Downfall of Parliamentarianism: A Retrospect for the Accounting Day* (Dublin: Maunsel, 1918); *Evening Memories; being a continuation of 'Recollections'* (Dublin and London: Maunsel, 1920); *The Responsibility for Partition Considered with an Eye to Ireland's Future* (Dublin: Maunsel and Roberts, 1921); *The Irish Revolution and How it Came About* (Dublin: Maunsel and Roberts, 1923); *Edmund Burke as an Irishman* (Dublin: Gill, 1924); *The Parnell of Real Life* (London: Fisher Unwin, 1926).

BIOGRAPHY AND CRITICISM. P. J. Meehan, *Life of John Dillon, M.P., and William O'Brien, M.P., Ireland's Patriots* (New York: Law and Trade Printing Co., n.d.); J. V. O'Brien, *William O'Brien and the Course of Irish Politics 1881-1918* (Berkeley: University of California Press, 1976).

Arthur Griffith

LIFE. Born in Dublin in 1871, Griffith was educated at the Christian Brothers School, Strand Street. As an apprentice printer, he worked on the *Irish Independent* and *The Nation*. He was a founder member of the Celtic Literary Society (1893) along with William Rooney, a journalist friend who influenced him deeply. He was a member of the Gaelic League and of the Irish Republican Brotherhood. In 1897-99 he was in South Africa and supported the Boers. Returning to Ireland, he became editor of the *United Irishman* and founded Cumann na nGaedheal with Rooney in 1900. His *The Resurrection of Hungary* (1904) sold over 30,000 copies. In it he advocated a dual monarchy for Ireland and the rest of the United Kingdom, based on the system adopted in Austria and Hungary in 1867. His economic doctrine was one of self-sufficiency, reflected in the title of his newspaper *Sinn Féin*, which replaced the *United Irishman* in 1906 and survived until it was suppressed by the government in 1914. Griffith repudiated the Home Rule Bill of 1912, joined the Irish Volunteers in 1913 and participated in the Howth gun-running incident of 1914. Although he did not take part in the Easter Rising of 1916, he was arrested and imprisoned for almost a year.

After the Rising, Sin Féin became the political wing and name of the republican movement. Griffith stood aside to allow Eamon de Valera to become president; he became vice-president. While de Valera was in America, Griffith became acting president of Dáil Eireann, was arrested and imprisoned 1920-21, until his release under the terms of the Truce. He headed the Irish delegation to London (October-December 1921), but was outwitted by Lloyd George in the Treaty negotiations, primarily over the question of Ulster and partition. He defeated de Valera in the election for presidency of the Dail and in 1922 agreed to the bombardment of the Four Courts, the action that began the Civil War. He died in Dublin in 1922 and was the first Irish leader to be buried as Head of State.

CHIEF WRITINGS. *The Resurrection of Hungary: A Parallel for Ireland* (Dublin: James Duffy, 1904; Dublin: Duffy, 1918); *The 'Sinn Fein' Policy* (Dublin: Duffy and Gill, 1906); *How Ireland is Taxed* (Dublin: National Council Pamphlets, no. 6, 1907); *How Ireland has 'Prospered' under English Rule* and *The Slave Mind* (New York: Irish Progressive League, 1911); *The Nature of Sinn Fein* (Dublin: Sinn Fein, Tract no. 4, 1917); *To Rebuild the Nation* (Dublin: Mahon, 1919?); *Ireland's Economic Situation: England's Irish Philanthropy* (Washington D.C.: Friends of Irish Freedom, 1920); *Arguments for the Treaty* (Dublin: Martin Lester, 1922?); S. Whelan (ed.), *Economic Salvation and the Means to Attain It* by Arthur Griffith (Dublin, Whelan, n.d.); *A Study of the Originator of the Sinn Fein Movement* (Dublin, Cahill, n.d.). Griffith also edited John Mitchel's *Jail Journal* (1913), *Thomas Davis: The Thinker and Teacher. The Essence of his Writings in Poetry and Prose* (1914), Michael Doheny, *The Felon's Track* (1914) and wrote the preface to L. M. Fogarty's *James Fintan Lalor* (1918).

BIOGRAPHY AND CRITICISM. R. M. Henry, *The Evolution of Sinn Fein* (Dublin: The Talbot Press, 1920); G. A. Lyons, *Some Recollections of Griffith and His Times* (Dublin: The Talbot Press, 1923); D. Shaw, *The Drama of Sinn Fein* (London: Collins, 1923); P. S. O'Hegarty, *The Victory of Sinn Fein* (Dublin: The Talbot Press, 1924); P. Colum, *Ourselves Alone; The Story of Arthur Griffith and the Origin of the Irish Free State* (New York: Crown Publishers, 1959) published under the title *Arthur Griffith* (London and Dublin: Browne and Nolan, 1959); D. McCartney, 'The Sinn Fein Movement' in K. B. Nowlan (ed.), *The Making of 1916* (Dublin: Gill and Macmillan, 1969), pp. 31-50; R. Davis, *Arthur Griffith and Non-violent Sinn Fein* (Dublin: Anvil Books, 1974); C. Younger, *Arthur Griffith* (Dublin: Gill and Macmillan, 1981); V. E. Glandon, *Arthur Griffith and the Advanced Nationalist Press: Ireland, 1900-1922* (New York: Lang, 1985).

William P. Ryan

LIFE. Born near Templemore, Co. Tipperary, in 1867. Ryan moved to London and worked as a journalist on *The Catholic Times*, *The Sun*, *The Weekly Sun*, *The Morning Leader* and *The Daily Chronicle*. He was active in Irish societies in London, particularly the Gaelic League, the Southwark Literary Society and the Irish Literary Society. In 1905, Ryan returned to Ireland to take up the editorship of the *Irish Peasant*, a County Meath weekly that he transformed into one of the leading Irish newspapers. He supported the Gaelic League and the whole Irish-Ireland philosophy and attacked the attitude of the catholic hierarchy towards these movements. Cardinal Logue condemned the newspaper and forced its closure in 1906. Ryan told the story of the paper and its closure in *The Plough and the Cross* (1910). His socialist views made him unpopular with the clerical establishment. He edited the *Irish Nation* 1908-10 and, when that failed, returned to London where he continued his journalistic career. His son, Desmond Ryan, became a distinguished journalist and historian of the republican movement. William P. Ryan died in London in 1942.

CHIEF WRITINGS. *The Heart of Tipperary* (London: Ward and Downey, 1893); *The Irish Literary Revival* (London: Ward and Downey, 1894); *Starlight through the Thatch* (London: Downey, 1895); *Sidheoga ag Obair* (Dublin: Conradh na Gaeilge, 1904); *The Plough and the Cross* (Dublin: The Irish Nation, 1910); *The Pope's Green Island* (London: James Nisbet & Co., 1912); *The Labour Revolt and Larkinism* (London: Daily Herald Office, 1913); *Caomhin O Cearnaigh* (Dublin: Dublin Gaelic League, 1913); *The Celt and the Cosmos* (London: Nutt, 1914); *The Irish Labour Movement* (Dublin: The Talbot Press, 1918); *Gaelachas i gCein* (Dublin: Oifig Díolta Foillseacháin Rialtas, 1933).

DECLAN KIBERD, *Editor*

The London Exiles: Wilde and Shaw

It is customary to describe Oscar Wilde and George Bernard Shaw as artists who abandoned the depressed Dublin of their youth for the cosmopolitan glamour of a career in London. Both men, after all, so described themselves. Yet such an analysis takes no account of the success with which they challenged, by personal behaviour as well as by artistic skill, the prevailing stereotypes of the Irish in Britain. The image of the stage Irishman had been formulated in London, and would have to be first contested in that city, before an Irish *risorgimento* might blossom. This was a point perceived by the early directors of the Abbey Theatre, who from 1903 onwards insisted on touring their initial successes, like *Riders to the Sea* and *Cathleen Ní Houlihan*, through British cultural centres such as London, Oxford, Cambridge and Edinburgh. Wilde and Shaw were, of course, noted examples of the artist-as-public-entertainer, but they never forgot their Irish origins and they tried, with much success, to liberate the enemy language from its historic freight of meaning for an Irish person.

In spite of this, traditionally they have been excluded from most accounts of the Irish literary revival. Yeats, who asserted that there is no great literature without nationality, found them too international, too transparently translatable, for his taste. They were, he alleged, 'the most complete individualists in the history of literature, abstract, isolated minds without a memory or a landscape.' 'It is this very isolation,' continued Yeats, 'this defect as it seems to me, which has given George Bernard Shaw an equal welcome in all countries, the greatest welcome in his own lifetime any writer has known.'[1]

1. W. B. Yeats, Introduction to *The King of the Great Clock Tower*.

It is, nevertheless, possible to see Wilde and Shaw as cultural godfathers of the Irish renaissance. All roads taken by revivalist authors do not lead back to Yeats, and many of the major playwrights were, like Wilde and Shaw, both radical and socialist. The dramas of Synge, for example, owe much to Wilde, in their celebration of 'the power of a lie' and in their author's pursuit of a linguistic art 'more beautiful than nature'. Similarly, Beckett's cult of elegant desperation, as well as his assertion that it is the shape of a sentence that counts, may be traced to his doomed precursor at Portora and Trinity College. In his autobiography, Yeats generously acknowledged his deep indebtedness to Wilde. His concept of the Mask or anti-self is based on Wilde's theory that one must study to become the opposite of all that one is by nature and inheritance. Yeatsian *sprezzatura* has its roots in that Wildean nonchalance which is actually the outcome of rigorous rehearsal; and the idea of a recurring choice between 'perfection of the life, or of the work' was first mooted by Wilde, who claimed to have put his genius into his life and only his talent into his work.

In much the same fashion, later dramatists owe a great deal to Shaw. Both Seán O'Casey and Brendan Behan record in their autobiographies the shock of recognition on reading *John Bull's Other Island*, of which both *Purple Dust* and *The Hostage* are updated versions, recounting the comical progress of the English in Ireland. A Shavian tradition of playwriting runs through the work of Denis Johnston in the 1930s up to the present day, when it reappears in a play of Eoghan Harris's, *Souper Sullivan* (1984).

Recent reinterpretations of the Irish renaissance as an attempt to increase the autonomy of the individual are more hospitable than Yeats to the notion of Wilde and Shaw as dynamic contributors to the national revival. Wilde was, to the end of his days, a militant Irish republican; and Shaw used his considerable influence to castigate the wrongs of England in Ireland. If the texts of Synge, Joyce and O'Casey are concerned with the rights of sons to usurp fathers, of women to challenge men, and of people to shake off an oppressive past, then both Wilde and Shaw may fairly be described as participants in, as well as promoters of, the national recovery. Even their perceived weaknesses, such as the tendency to allow the artist to be overriden by the entertainer, had an instructive value for men like Yeats and Joyce. If Wilde and Shaw had not toppled the stage Irishman from his plinth and cleared the necessary intellectual space, it is doubtful whether Yeats and Synge could ever have set up a successful theatre in Dublin, and certain that much subsequent Irish writing would have taken a very different course.

'Was there ever an Irish man of genius who did not get himself turned into an Englishman as fast as he could?' asked Henry Craik in an immortal line.[2] No better illustration could be found than the career of Oscar Wilde, which began with his arrival in the Oxford of 1874. There he began to dedicate himself to the noble art of the pose. According to Yeats, Wilde in England 'perpetually performed a play which was in all things the opposite of all that he had known in childhood and youth. He never put off completely his wonder at opening his eyes every morning on his own beautiful house and in remembering that he had dined yesterday with a Duchess.'[3] The home that Wilde had abandoned in Dublin was, on the other hand, 'dirty, untidy and daring', presided over by two eccentric parents who seemed to Yeats to have stepped straight out of a bad stage-Irish melodrama. Sir William Wilde, although a most eminent surgeon and scholar, was reputed to be the dirtiest man in Dublin, 'beyond soap and water,' reported Shaw, 'as his Nietzschean son was beyond good and evil.'[4] Sir William's studies of the antiquities and archaeology of Ireland were matched by Lady Wilde's collections of folklore, her militant feminism and her outpourings of nationalist verse. To her second son she bequeathed a love of the theatrical and a conviction of the rights of women to work and to political activity. 'Why should there be one law for men, and another for women?' asks Jack in *The Importance of Being Earnest*, a play that is a satire on the manic Victorian urge to antithesis. Wilde's is an art of inversion, where each side exemplifies qualities that we would normally expect in its opposite, as every dichotomy dichotomizes. The traditional contrast in the comedy of manners between corrupt city slickers and unfallen rural characters is exposed as a gross simplification. Jack and Algy's cynicism is seen to be a mere front for an unquenchable openness to new experience, while the apparent innocence of the country Canon Chasuble is seen to conceal a more sinister kind of knowingness. This inversion of the audience's expectations may also be found in the play's depiction of sexuality. Thus it is the women who read heavy works of German philosophy and attend university courses, while the men lounge elegantly on sofas. The men are filled with romantic impetuosity and breathless surges of emotion, but it is the women who cynically discuss the finer points of the male physique. When Algy proposes to Cecily, it is *she* who runs her fingers through his hair and asks if it curls naturally. ('Yes, darling, with a little help from others.') Lord Bracknell, for his part, knows that a man's place is in the home, for, in the words of his daughter, 'once a man begins to neglect his domestic duties he becomes painfully effeminate, does he not? And I don't like that. It makes men so very attractive.' In all these scenes Wilde is applying his doctrine of the androgyny of the healthy personality. This would find immortal expression in the wisecrack that 'All women become like their mothers. That is their tragedy. No man does. That's his.' The apparent sexism of the first half of the jibe is fully exploded by the sharp feminist intelligence of the conclusion.

Antithesis was the master-key to the entire Victorian cast of mind, causing people to make absolute divisions not just between English and Irish, but also between men and women, good and evil, and so on. Wilde saw that by this mechanism the English male could attribute to the Irish all those traits of poetry, emotion and soft charm which a stern Victorian code had forced him to deny in himself; but he knew from experience that

2. Letter from Henry Craik to John Forster, John Forster Collection, MS. 48.E.25. British Library, London.
3. W. B. Yeats, *Autobiographies* (London: Macmillan, 1955), p. 138.
4. G. B. Shaw, 'My Memories of Oscar Wilde' in Richard Ellmann (ed.), *Oscar Wilde: A Collection of Critical Essays* (Englewood Cliffs, New Jersey: Prentice Hall, 1969), p. 93.

the two peoples are a lot more alike than they care to admit — that the Irish are as often cold, polite and calculating as the English are sentimental, emotional and violent. In the same fashion, Wilde saw Victorian men demand that their women epitomize those virtues of softness, domesticity and fidelity which a harsh business ethic had led them to suppress in themselves. In *The Importance of Being Earnest* Wilde showed that such an antithesis quite simply does not work. As often as not, it is the women in that play who are businesslike in making cynical economic calculations about a proposed marriage, while the men remain steadfastly impractical. Far from being an exponent of the witty paradox, Wilde is interested in the moment of modernism when the ancient antithesis dissolves to reveal an underlying unity. Like Yeats, he could see that talent perceives differences, but only genius discerns unity.

This same inversion of conventional expectations explains the pose adopted by Wilde in England. All the norms of his childhood were now to be reversed. His father had been laughed at by society, so he would mock society first. His father had been an unkempt, fluent Irishman, so he would be a fastidious, urbane Englishman. From his mother Wilde had inherited a gigantic and ungainly body, which recalled all too painfully the gorilla-like form of the stage Irishman in Tenniel's cartoons.[5] To disarm such racialist critics, the young dandy concealed his bulky frame with costly clothes and studied the art of elegant deportment. The ease with which Wilde effected the transition from stage Irishman to stage Englishman was his ultimate comment on the hollowness of the antithesis, on the emptiness of both notions.

In rejecting this manic urge to antithesis, Wilde satirized the determinism of Victorians as diverse as Marx and Carlyle, who believed that upbringing and social conditioning determined consciousness. The belief that the Irishman was the prisoner of heredity, diet and climate, like the conviction that woman is by nature docile, subservient and deferential, were twin attributes of Victorian determinism. This determinism is taken to its *reductio ad absurdum* in Wilde's account of two girls, each of whom accepts that it is her ineluctable destiny to love a man named Ernest. The very plot of the play is an example of a determinism so extreme as to render the concept idiotic and banal. Its machinery creaks with an over-obviousness that is clearly designed to subvert the convention of the well-made play by carrying it to an outrageous degree. Algy predicts that the girls will call each other sister only after they have called one another other names as well; and, sure enough, within ten minutes, Cecily and Gwendolen are embarked on a vicious quarrel, as life imitates art with grim predictability. The girls, precisely because they seem to have been more exposed to Victorian education than the men, show a touching faith in determinism. Ever since Cecily had heard of her wicked uncle, she could think of nothing else. But it is not a belief in determinism that prompts Algy to play along with her charade of fictional letters and engagements between them. Rather, he expresses deep admiration for the fertile imagination of a girl who had the courage to reject the tedious all-female regime of Miss Prism and reincarnate some of the missing male elements in the Ernest who is a pure concoction of her mind. Like the androgynous Wilde, she rejects the notion of an antithesis between herself and others, because she has already recognized the existence of that antithesis in herself. In doing so, she also rejects that other great fiction of the Victorians, the black-and-white distinction between good and evil. Just before meeting her wicked uncle she says: 'I have never met any really wicked person before. I feel rather frightened. I am so afraid he will look just like everyone else.' Wilde is one of the first modernist writers to take for subject not the knowledge of good and evil, but what Lionel Trilling was later to call the knowledge of good-and-evil. He insists that men and women know themselves in all their aspects and that they cease to suppress those attributes that they may find painful or unflattering.

Yet the Victorian Englishman continued to attribute to the Irish all those emotions and impulses that his strict code had led him to deny in himself. Thus, if John Bull was industrious and reliable, Paddy was held to be indolent and contrary; if the former was mature and rational, the latter must be unstable and emotional; if the Englishman was adult and manly, the Irishman must be childish and feminine. So the Irish joined hands with those other two persecuted minorities, women and children; and at the root of many an Englishman's suspicions of the Irish was an unease

5. H. Montgomery Hyde, *Oscar Wilde* (London: Eyre Methuen, 1977), p. 232. On Sir John Tenniel, see books cited in next note.

at the woman or child who lurked within himself. The implications of this equation have been spelled out by Perry Curtis — either as woman or as child, the Irishman was incapable of self-government.[6] The flaunted effeminacy of Wilde, no less than his espousal of the inner world of the child in his stories, may well be a sly comment on these hidden fears. All his essays on Ireland question the assumption that, just because the British are industrious and rational, the Irish must be lazy and illogical. The man who believed that a truth in art is that whose opposite is also true was quick to point out that every good man has an element of the woman in him, just as every sensitive Irishman must have a secret Englishman within himself — and *vice versa*. With his sharp intelligence, Wilde saw that the image of the stage Irishman tells us far more about English fears than Irish realities, just as the still-vibrant Irish joke tells us far less about the Irishman's foolishness than about the Englishman's persistent and poignant desire to say something funny. In his case, Wilde opted to say that something funny for the English, in a life-long performance of Englishness which constituted a parody of the very notion. By becoming more English than the English, Wilde was able to invert, and ultimately to challenge, all the time-honoured myths about Ireland.

To his mortification and delight, Wilde found that his English mask seldom seemed to fit. The more he suppressed his inherited personality, the more it seemed to erupt into self-assertion. 'The two great turning-points in my life', he wrote in *De Profundis*, 'were when my father sent me to Oxford and society sent me to prison.' It is a revealing equation. In both institutions he learned just what it is to be an outsider, an uninvited guest, an Irishman in England. To his Oxford friends he was not so much an Anglo-Irishman as a flashy and fastidious Paddy, with 'a suspicion of brogue' and 'an unfamiliar turn to his phrasing'. At Oxford he took to signing himself 'Oscar Fingal O'Flahertie Wills Wilde', filling two lines of college notepaper with the indisputable proof of his Celtic identity. His flirtation with catholicism at Magdalen College was rather more serious than that of his peers. For an Englishman, the catholic church evoked incense and mariolatry, but for an Irishman, as Montgomery Hyde has remarked, it was the historic faith of a tenacious people. For his devotion to the Scarlet Lady, Wilde was punished by virtual exclusion from his half-brother's will at a time when he was sorely in need of funds.

Oxford strengthened in Wilde the conviction that an Irishman discovers himself only when he goes abroad, just as it reinforced his belief that 'man is least himself when he talks in his own person', but 'give him a mask and he will tell you the truth.' This Nietzschean idea was implanted in Wilde by the simple experience of being an Irishman in England. Years later, when Charles Stewart Parnell was at the height of his political power in 1889, Wilde wrote in celebration of his intellect, which 'at home ... had but learned the pathetic weakness of nationality, but in a strange land realized what indomitable forces nationality possesses.' Wilde saw his own literary career as running parallel to that of Parnell, another urbane Irishman who surprised the English by his haughty self-control. No English cartoonist ever dared to depict Parnell as a monkey or an ape, a treatment meted out to many Irish leaders in the previous hundred years.

The final proof that Wilde was neither a snob nor an anglophile may be found in the attacks on class-society in his plays and in his extraordinarily bloodthirsty statements on the Irish Question. When the Chief Secretary, Cavendish, and the Under-Secretary, Burke, were assassinated in Dublin's Phoenix Park in 1882, even the more militant leaders of Irish opinion denounced the killings; but not Wilde, who remarked laconically to an American audience that 'England is to blame. She is reaping the fruit of seven centuries of injustice.' Always a separatist, Wilde poured scorn on the latest English debate about 'how best to misgovern Ireland'. In a review of J. A. Froude's *The Two Chiefs of Dunboy* he ridiculed its theory that Celts will only thrive under the rule of Anglo-Saxons. Froude had indicted the Anglo-Irish ascendancy not for its cruelty, but for its inefficiency in enforcing the law. 'Mr. Froude admits the martyrdom of Ireland,' joked Wilde, 'but regrets that [it] was not completely carried out.' Froude had endorse Matthew Arnold's comment on the inability of the Celt to cope with the tyranny of fact, to the great disgust of Wilde, in whose moral lexicon the word 'fact' enjoyed a low estimate. 'The

6. L. Perry Curtis Jnr., *Anglo-Saxons and Celts: A Study of Anti-Irish Prejudice in Victorian England* (Bridgeport, Connecticut: Conference on British Studies, 1968); and *Apes and Angels: The Irishman in Victorian Caricature* (Washington, DC: Smithsonian Institution Press, 1971).

Irish, [Mr. Froude] tells us, had disowned the facts of life and the facts of life had proved the strongest.' Wilde closed his review with a wicked inversion of the author's original purpose: 'As a record, however, of the incapacity of a Teutonic to rule a Celtic people against their own wishes his book is not without value', mischievously adding the afterthought that: 'There are some who will welcome with delight the idea of solving the Irish question by doing away with the Irish people.' Wilde seemed to be one of that number, for he had appeared to endorse the policy with his own attempt to solve a crisis of identity by suppressing all trace of his parental inheritance. But the ploy was purely parodic, an attempt to protest against a situation by mimicking it to an absurd extreme, just as Swift's *A Modest Proposal* — that Irish infants be roasted as meat for English tables — was intended as a metaphorical account of the realities of British policy at the time.

OSCAR WILDE
(1854-1900)

from: THE HAPPY PRINCE AND OTHER TALES (1888)

[The title-story of a collection published in 1888, and one of the most famous examples of children's fiction, 'The Happy Prince' has been endlessly dramatized and filmed. Influenced less by the Gaelic fairy-lore collected by his mother than by his own reading of Hans Christian Anderson, the story is a parable of the costs to society when individuals worship art. Hence Wilde's claim that his stories were 'an attempt to mirror modern life in a form remote from reality'. Beneath the beautiful surfaces of the tale may be found a deeply protestant suspicion of images and image-making.]

THE HAPPY PRINCE

High above the city, on a tall column, stood the statue of the Happy Prince. He was gilded all over with thin leaves of fine gold, for eyes he had two bright sapphires, and a large red ruby glowed on his sword-hilt.

He was very much admired indeed. 'He is as beautiful as a weathercock,' remarked one of the Town Councillors who wished to gain a reputation for having artistic tastes; 'only not quite so useful,' he added, fearing lest people should think him unpractical, which he really was not.

'Why can't you be like the Happy Prince?' asked a sensible mother of her little boy who was crying for the moon. 'The Happy Prince never dreams of crying for anything.'

'I am glad there is some one in the world who is quite happy,' muttered a disappointed man as he gazed at the wonderful statue.

'He looks just like an angel,' said the Charity Children[1] as they came out of the cathedral in their bright scarlet cloaks, and their clean white pinafores.

'How do you know?' said the Mathematical Master, 'you have never seen one.'

'Ah! but we have, in our dreams,' answered the children; and the Mathematical Master frowned and looked very severe, for he did not approve of children dreaming.

One night there flew over the city a little Swallow. His friends had gone away to Egypt six weeks before, but he had stayed behind, for he was in love with the most beautiful Reed. He had met her early in the spring as he was flying down the river after a big yellow moth, and had been so attracted by her slender waist that he had stopped to talk to her.

'Shall I love you?' said the Swallow, who liked to come to the point at once, and the Reed made him a low bow. So he flew round and round her, touching the water with his wings, and making silver ripples.

1. Orphans and other disadvantaged children kept in charitable institutions. cf. William Blake's poem 'Holy Thursday'.

This was his courtship, and it lasted all through the summer.

'It is a ridiculous attachment,' twittered the other Swallows, 'she has no money, and far too many relations'; and indeed the river was quite full of Reeds. Then, when the autumn came, they all flew away.

After they had gone he felt lonely, and began to tire of his lady-love. 'She has no conversation,' he said, 'and I am afraid that she is a coquette, for she is always flirting with the wind.' And certainly, whenever the wind blew, the Reed made the most graceful curtsies. 'I admit that she is domestic,' he continued, 'but I love travelling, and my wife, consequently, should love travelling also.'

'Will you come away with me?' he said finally to her; but the Reed shook her head, she was so attached to her home.

'You have been trifling with me,' he cried, 'I am off to the Pyramids. Good-bye!' and he flew away.

All day long he flew, and at night-time he arrived at the city. 'Where shall I put up?' he said; 'I hope the town has made preparations.'

Then he saw the statue on the tall column. 'I will put up there,' he cried; 'it is a fine position with plenty of fresh air.' So he alighted just between the feet of the Happy Prince.

'I have a golden bedroom,' he said softly to himself as he looked round, and he prepared to go to sleep; but just as he was putting his head under his wing a large drop of water fell on him. 'What a curious thing!' he cried, 'there is not a single cloud in the sky, the stars are quite clear and bright, and yet it is raining. The climate in the north of Europe is really dreadful. The Reed used to like the rain, but that was merely her selfishness.'

Then another drop fell.

'What is the use of a statue if it cannot keep the rain off?' he said; 'I must look for a good chimney-pot,' and he determined to fly away.

But before he had opened his wings, a third drop fell, and he looked up, and saw — Ah! what did he see?

The eyes of the Happy Prince were filled with tears, and tears were running down his golden cheeks. His face was so beautiful in the moonlight that the little Swallow was filled with pity.

'Who are you?' he said.

'I am the Happy Prince.'

'Why are you weeping then?' asked the Swallow; 'you have quite drenched me.'

'When I was alive and had a human heart,' answered the statue, 'I did not know what tears were, for I lived in the Palace of Sans-Souci,[2] where sorrow is not allowed to enter. In the daytime I played with my companions in the garden, and in the evening I led the dance in the Great Hall. Round the garden ran a very lofty wall, but I never cared to ask what lay beyond it, everything about me was so beautiful. My courtiers called me the Happy Prince, and happy indeed I was, if pleasure be happiness. So I lived, and so I died. And now that I am dead they have set me up here so high that I can see all the ugliness and all the misery of my city, and though my heart is made of lead yet I cannot choose but weep.'

'What, is he not solid gold?' said the Swallow to himself. He was too polite to make any personal remarks out loud.

'Far away,' continued the statue in a low musical voice, 'far away in a little street there is a poor house. One of the windows is open, and through it I can see a woman seated at a table. Her face is thin and worn, and she has coarse, red hands, all pricked by the needle, for she is a seamstress. She is embroidering passion-flowers on a satin gown for the loveliest of the Queen's maids-of-honour to wear at the next Court-ball. In a bed in the corner of the room her little boy is lying ill. He has a fever, and is asking for oranges. His mother has nothing to give him but river water, so he is crying. Swallow, Swallow, little Swallow, will you not bring her the ruby out of my sword-hilt? My feet are fastened to this pedestal and I cannot move.'

'I am waited for in Egypt,' said the Swallow. 'My friends are flying up and down the Nile, and talking to the large lotus-flowers. Soon they will go to sleep in the tomb of the great King. The King is there himself in his painted coffin. He is wrapped in yellow linen, and embalmed with spices. Round his neck is a chain of pale green jade, and his hands are like withered leaves.'

'Swallow, Swallow, little Swallow,' said the Prince, 'will you not stay with me for one night, and be my messenger? The boy is so thirsty, and the mother so sad.'

'I don't think I like boys,' answered the Swallow. 'Last summer, when I was staying on the river,

2. French: without care. The famous name of the cottage retreat of Frederick the Great of Prussia (1712-86), it became fashionable as a name for houses and homes in Victorian England.

there were two rude boys, the miller's sons, who were always throwing stones at me. They never hit me, of course; we swallows fly far too well for that, and besides, I come of a family famous for its agility; but still, it was a mark of disrespect.'

But the Happy Prince looked so sad that the little Swallow was sorry. 'It is very cold here,' he said; 'but I will stay with you for one night, and be your messenger.'

'Thank you, little Swallow,' said the Prince.

So the Swallow picked out the great ruby from the Prince's sword, and flew away with it in his beak over the roofs of the town.

He passed by the cathedral tower, where the white marble angels were sculptured. He passed by the palace and heard the sound of dancing. A beautiful girl came out on the balcony with her lover. 'How wonderful the stars are,' he said to her, 'and how wonderful is the power of love!' 'I hope my dress will be ready in time for the State-ball,' she answered; 'I have ordered passion-flowers to be embroidered on it; but the seamstresses are so lazy.'

He passed over the river, and saw the lanterns hanging to the masts of the ships. He passed over the Ghetto, and saw the old Jews bargaining with each other, and weighing out money in copper scales. At last he came to the poor house and looked in. The boy was tossing feverishly on his bed, and the mother had fallen asleep, she was so tired. In he hopped, and laid the great ruby on the table beside the woman's thimble. Then he flew gently round the bed, fanning the boy's forehead with his wings. 'How cool I feel,' said the boy, 'I must be getting better'; and he sank into a delicious slumber.

Then the Swallow flew back to the Happy Prince, and told him what he had done. 'It is curious,' he remarked, 'but I feel quite warm now, although it is so cold.'

'That is because you have done a good action,' said the Prince. And the little Swallow began to think, and then he fell asleep. Thinking always made him sleepy.

When day broke he flew down to the river and had a bath. 'What a remarkable phenomenon,' said the Professor of Ornithology as he was passing over the bridge. 'A swallow in winter!' And he wrote a long letter about it to the local newspaper. Every one quoted it, it was full of so many words that they could not understand.

'Tonight I go to Egypt,' said the Swallow, and he was in high spirits at the prospect. He visited all the public monuments, and sat a long time on top of the church steeple. Wherever he went the Sparrows chirruped, and said to each other, 'What a distinguished stranger!' so he enjoyed himself very much.

When the moon rose he flew back to the Happy Prince. 'Have you any commissions for Egypt?' he cried; 'I am just starting.'

'Swallow, Swallow, little Swallow,' said the Prince, 'will you not stay with me one night longer?'

'I am waited for in Egypt,' answered the Swallow. 'Tomorrow my friends will fly up to the Second Cataract. The river-horse couches there among the bulrushes, and on a great granite throne sits the God Memnon.[3] All night long he watches the stars, and when the morning star shines he utters one cry of joy, and then he is silent. At noon the yellow lions come down to the water's edge to drink. They have eyes like green beryls, and their roar is louder than the roar of the cataract.'

'Swallow, Swallow, little Swallow,' said the Prince, 'far away across the city I see a young man in a garret. He is leaning over a desk covered with papers, and in a tumbler by his side there is a bunch of withered violets. His hair is brown and crisp, and his lips are red as a pomegranate, and he has large and dreamy eyes. He is trying to finish a play for the Director of the Theatre, but he is too cold to write any more. There is no fire in the grate, and hunger has made him faint.'

'I will wait with you one night longer,' said the Swallow, who really had a good heart. 'Shall I take him another ruby?'

'Alas! I have no ruby now,' said the Prince; 'my eyes are all that I have left. They are made of rare sapphires, which were brought out of India a thousand years ago. Pluck out one of them and take it to him. He will sell it to the jeweller, and buy food and firewood, and finish his play.'

'Dear Prince,' said the Swallow, 'I cannot do that'; and he began to weep.

'Swallow, Swallow, little Swallow,' said the Prince, 'do as I command you.'

So the Swallow plucked out the Prince's eye, and flew away to the student's garret. It was easy enough to get in, as there was a hole in the roof. Through this he darted, and came into the room. The young man had his head buried in his hands, so he did not hear the flutter of the bird's wings, and

3. A black statue of Thebes in Egypt, which emitted sweet music when warmed by the sun.

when he looked up he found the beautiful sapphire lying on the withered violets.

'I am beginning to be appreciated,' he cried; 'this is from some great admirer. Now I can finish my play,' and he looked quite happy.

The next day the Swallow flew down to the harbour. He sat on the mast of a large vesel and watched the sailors hauling big chests out of the hold with ropes. 'Heave a-hoy!' they shouted as each chest came up. 'I am going to Egypt!' cried the Swallow, but nobody minded, and when the moon rose he flew back to the Happy Prince.

'I am come to bid you good-bye,' he cried.

'Swallow, Swallow, little Swallow,' said the Prince, 'will you not stay with me one night longer?'

'It is winter,' answered the Swallow, 'and the chill snow will soon be here. In Egypt the sun is warm on the green palm-trees, and the crocodiles lie in the mud and look lazily about them. My companions are building a nest in the Temple of Baalbec,[4] and the pink and white doves are watching them, and cooing to each other. Dear Prince, I must leave you, but I will never forget you, and next spring I will bring you back two beautiful jewels in place of those you have given away. The ruby shall be redder than a red rose, and the sapphire shall be as blue as the great sea.'

'In the square below,' said the Happy Prince, 'there stands a little match-girl. She has let her matches fall in the gutter, and they are all spoiled. Her father will beat her if she does not bring home some money, and she is crying. She has no shoes or stockings, and her little head is bare. Pluck out my other eye, and give it to her, and her father will not beat her.'

'I will stay with you one night longer,' said the Swallow, 'but I cannot pluck out your eye. You would be quite blind then.'

'Swallow, Swallow, little Swallow,' said the Prince, 'do as I command you.'

So he plucked out the Prince's other eye, and darted down with it. He swooped past the match-girl, and slipped the jewel into the palm of her hand. 'What a lovely bit of glass,' cried the little girl; and she ran home, laughing.

Then the Swallow came back to the Prince. 'You are blind now,' he said, 'so I will stay with you always.'

4. Syrian temple to Jupiter and Bacchus (1st to 3rd century A.D.). Originally the cult centre of a local Baal, the god was identified with Jupiter after the Romans had colonized the area.

'No, little Swallow,' said the poor Prince, 'you must go away to Egypt.'

'I will stay with you always,' said the Swallow, and he slept at the Prince's feet.

All the next day he sat on the Prince's shoulder, and told him stories of what he had seen in strange lands. He told him of the red ibises, who stand in long rows on the banks of the Nile, and catch gold fish in their beaks; of the Sphinx, who is as old as the world itself, and lives in the desert, and knows everything; of the merchants, who walk slowly by the side of their camels, and carry amber beads in their hands; of the King of the Mountains of the Moon, who is as black as ebony, and worships a large crystal; of the great green snake that sleeps in a palm-tree, and has twenty priests to feed it with honey-cakes; and of the pygmies who sail over a big lake on large flat leaves, and are always at war with the butterflies.

'Dear little Swallow,' said the Prince, 'you tell me of marvellous things, but more marvellous than anything is the suffering of men and of women. There is no Mystery so great as Misery. Fly over my city, little Swallow, and tell me what you see there.'

So the Swallow flew over the great city, and saw the rich making merry in their beautiful houses, while the beggars were sitting at the gates. He flew into dark lanes, and saw the white faces of starving children looking out listlessly at the black streets. Under the archway of a bridge two little boys were lying in one another's arms to try and keep themselves warm. 'How hungry we are!' they said. 'You must not lie here,' shouted the Watchman, and they wandered out into the rain.

Then he flew back and told the Prince what he had seen.

'I am covered with fine gold,' said the Prince, 'you must take it off, leaf by leaf, and give it to my poor; the living always think that gold can make them happy.'

Leaf after leaf of the fine gold the Swallow picked off, till the Happy Prince looked quite dull and grey. Leaf after leaf of the fine gold he brought to the poor, and the children's faces grew rosier, and they laughed and played games in the street. 'We have bread now!' they cried.

Then the snow came, and after the snow came the frost. The streets looked as if they were made of silver, they were so bright and glistening; long icicles like crystal daggers hung down from the eaves of the houses, everybody went about in furs, and the little boys wore scarlet caps and skated on the ice.

The poor little Swallow grew colder and colder, but he would not leave the Prince, he loved him too well. He picked up crumbs outside the baker's door when the baker was not looking, and tried to keep himself warm by flapping his wings.

But at last he knew that he was going to die. He had just strength to fly up to the Prince's shoulder once more. 'Goodbye, dear Prince!' he murmured, 'will you let me kiss your hand?'

'I am glad that you are going to Egypt at last, little Swallow,' said the Prince, 'you have stayed too long here; but you must kiss me on the lips, for I love you.'

'It is not to Egypt that I am going,' said the Swallow. 'I am going to the House of Death. Death is the brother of Sleep, is he not?'

And he kissed the Happy Prince on the lips, and fell down dead at his feet.

At that moment a curious crack sounded inside the statue, as if something had broken. The fact is that the leaden heart had snapped right in two. It certainly was a dreadfully hard frost.

Early the next morning the Mayor was walking in the square below in company with the Town Councillors. As they passed the column he looked up at the statue: 'Dear me! how shabby the Happy Prince looks!' he said.

'How shabby indeed!' cried the Town Councillors, who always agreed with the Mayor, and they went up to look at it.

'The ruby has fallen out of his sword, his eyes are gone, and he is golden no longer,' said the Mayor; 'in fact, he is little better than a beggar!'

'Little better than a beggar,' said the Town Councillors.

'And here is actually a dead bird at his feet!' continued the Mayor. 'We must really issue a proclamation that birds are not to be allowed to die here.' And the Town Clerk made a note of the suggestion.

So they pulled down the statue of the Happy Prince. 'As he is no longer beautiful he is no longer useful,' said the Art Professor at the University.

Then they melted the statue in a furnace, and the Mayor held at meeting of the Corporation to decide what was to be done with the metal. 'We must have another statue, of course,' he said, 'and it shall be a statue of myself.'

'Of myself,' said each of the Town Councillors, and they quarrelled. When I last heard of them they were quarrelling still.

'What a strange thing!' said the overseer of the workmen at the foundry. 'This broken lead heart will not melt in the furnace. We must throw it away.' So they threw it on a dustheap where the dead Swallow was also lying.

'Bring me the two most precious things in the city,' said God to one of His Angels; and the Angel brought Him the leaden heart and the dead bird.

'You have rightly chosen,' said God, 'for in my garden of Paradise this little bird shall sing for evermore, and in my city of gold the Happy Prince shall praise me.'

MR. FROUDE'S BLUE BOOK (ON IRELAND) (1889)

[This review of J. A. Froude's *The Two Chiefs of Dunboy* was published in *Pall Mall Gazette*, 13 April 1889, p. 3. Its uncompromising critique of British imperialism in Ireland may be due, in part, to the influence of Wilde's mother, 'Speranza', but is inspired mainly by Wilde's admiration for Charles Stewart Parnell, the leader of the Irish Party at Westminster and a man already being called 'the uncrowned king of Ireland'.]

Blue Books are generally dull reading, but Blue Books on Ireland have always been interesting. They form the record of one of the great tragedies of modern Europe. In them England has written down her indictment against herself, and has given to the world the history of her shame. If in the last century she tried to govern Ireland with an insolence that was intensified by race-hatred and religious prejudice, she has sought to rule her in this century with a stupidity that is aggravated by good intentions. The last of these Blue Books, Mr. Froude's[1] heavy novel, has appeared, however, somewhat too late. The society that he describes has long since passed away. An entirely new factor has appeared in the social development of the country, and this factor is the Irish-American, and his influence. To mature its powers, to concentrate its action, to learn the secret of its own strength and of England's weakness, the Celtic intellect has had to

1. J. A. Froude was a noted nineteenth-century historian of the English in Ireland. A 'blue book' was a report on aspects of governmental policy.

cross the Atlantic. At home it had but learned the pathetic weakness of nationality; in a strange land it realized what indomitable forces nationality possesses. What captivity was to the Jews, exile has been to the Irish. America and American influence has educated them. Their first practical leader is an Irish American.[2]

But while Mr. Froude's book has no practical relation to modern Irish politics, and does not offer any solution of the present question, it has a certain historical value. It is a vivid picture of Ireland in the latter half of the eighteenth century, a picture often false in its lights and exaggerated in its shadows, but a picture none the less. Mr. Froude admits the martyrdom of Ireland, but regrets that the martyrdom was not completely carried out. His ground of complaint against the executioner is not his trade, but his bungling. It is the bluntness, not the cruelty, of the sword that he objects to. Resolute government, that shallow shibboleth of those who do not understand how complex a thing the art of government is, is his posthumous panacea for past evils. His hero, Colonel Goring, has the words Law and Order ever on his lips, meaning by the one the enforcement of unjust legislation, and implying by the other the suppression of every fine natural aspiration. That the Government should enforce iniquity, and the governed submit to it, seems to be to Mr. Froude, as it certainly is to many others, the true ideal of political science. Like most pen-men he overrates the power of the sword. Where England has had to struggle she has been wise. Where physical strength has been on her side, as in Ireland, she has been made unwieldy by that strength. Her own strong hands have blinded her. She has had force, but no direction.

There is, of course, a story in Mr. Froude's novel. It is not simply a political disquisition. The interest of the tale, such as it is, centres round [*sic*] two men, Colonel Goring and Morty Sullivan, the Cromwellian and the Celt. These men are enemies by race, and creed, and feeling. The first represents Mr. Froude's cure for Ireland. He is a resolute Englishman, with strong Non-conformist tendencies, who plants an industrial colony on the coast of Kerry, and has deep-rooted objections to that illicit trade with France, which in the last century was the sole method by which the Irish people were enabled to pay their rents to their absentee land lords. Colonel Goring bitterly regrets that the Penal Laws against Catholics are not vigorously carried out. He is a '*Police* at any price' man:

> And this, said Goring scornfully, is what you call governing Ireland, hanging up your law like a scarecrow in the garden till every sparrow has learned to make a jest of it. Your Popery Acts! Well, you borrow them from France. The French Catholics did not choose to keep the Huguenots among them, and recalled the Edict of Nantes. As they treated the Huguenots, so you said to all the world that you would treat the Papists. You borrowed from the French the very language of your statute, but they are not afraid to stand by their law, and you are afraid to stand by yours. You let the people laugh at it, and in teaching them to despise one law you teach them to despise all laws — God's and man's alike. I cannot say how it will end, but I can tell you this, that you are training up a race with the education which you are giving them that will astonish the world by and by.

Mr. Froude's resume of the History of Ireland is not without power, though it is far from being really accurate. The Irish, he tells us, had disowned the facts of life and the facts of life had proved the strongest. England, unable to tolerate anarchy so near their shores, consulted the Pope. The Pope gave them leave to interfere, and the Pope had the best of the bargain. For the English brought him in, and the Irish kept him there. England's first settlers were Norman nobles. They became more Irish than the Irish, and England found herself in this difficulty. To abandon Ireland would be discreditable, to rule it as a province would be contrary to English tradition. She then tried to rule by dividing, and failed. The Pope was too strong for her. At last she made her great political discovery. What Ireland wanted was evidently an entirely new population of the same race and the same religion as her own. The new policy was partly carried out:

> Elizabeth first, and then James, and then Cromwell replanted the island, introducing English, Scots, Huguenots, Flemings, Dutch, tens of thousands of families of vigorous and earnest Protestants who brought their industries along with them. Twice the Irish tried to drive out this new element. They failed. But England had no sooner accomplished her long

2. Parnell, whose mother was American.

task than she set herself to work to spoil it again. She destroyed the industries of her colonists by her trade laws. She set the Bishops to rob them of their religion.... As for the gentry, the purpose for which they had been introduced into Ireland was unfulfilled. They were but alien intruders, who did nothing, who were allowed to do nothing. The time would come when an exasperated population would demand that the land should be given back to them, and England would then, perhaps, throw the gentry to the wolves, in the hope of a momentary peace. But her own turn would follow. She would be face to face with the old problem, either to make a new conquest or to retire with disgrace.

Political disquisitions of this kind, and prophecies after the event, are found all through Mr. Froude's book, and on almost every second page we come across aphorisms[3] on the Irish character, on the teachings of Irish history, and on the nature of England's mode of government. Some of these represent Mr. Froude's own views, others are entirely dramatic, and introduced for the purpose of characterization. We append some specimens. As epigrams, they are not very felicitous, but they are interesting from some points of view.

Irish society grew up in happy recklessness. Insecurity added rest to enjoyment.

We Irish must either laugh or cry, and if we went in for crying, we should all hang ourselves.

Too close a union with the Irish had produced degeneracy both of character and creed in all the settlements of English.

We age quickly in Ireland with the whisky and the broken heads.

The Irish leaders cannot fight. They can make the country ungovernable, and keep an English army occupied in watching them.

No nation can ever achieve a liberty that will not be a curse to it, except by arms in the field.

The Irish are taught from their cradles that English rule is the cause of all their miseries. They were as ill off under their own chiefs; but they would bear from their natural leaders what they will not bear from us, and if we have not made their lot more wretched, we have not made it any better.

Patriotism? Yes! Patriotism of the Hibernian order. That the country has been badly treated, and is poor and miserable. This is the patriot's stock in trade. Does he want it mended? Not he. His own occupation would be gone.

Irish corruption is the twin brother of Irish eloquence.

England will not let us break the heads of our scoundrels: she will not break them herself: we are a free country, and must take the consequences.

The functions of the Anglo-Irish Government were to do what ought not to be done, and to leave undone what ought to be done.

The Irish race have always been noisy, useless, and ineffectual. They have produced nothing, they have done nothing which it is possible to admire. What they are that they have always been, and the only hope for them is that their ridiculous Irish nationality should be buried and forgotten.

The Irish are the best actors in the world.

Order is an exotic in Ireland. It has been imported from England, but it will not grow. It suits neither soil nor climate. If the English wanted order in Ireland, they should have left none of us alive.

When ruling powers are unjust, nature reasserts her rights.

Even anarchy has its advantages.

Nature keeps an accurate account. The longer a bill is left unpaid, the heavier the accumulation of interest.

You cannot live in Ireland without breaking laws on one side or another. *Pecca fortiter*,[4] therefore, as Luther says.

The animal spirits of the Irish remained when all else was gone, and if there was no purpose in their lives they could at least enjoy themselves.

The Irish peasants can make the country hot for the Protestant gentlemen, but that is all they are fit for.

As we said before, if Mr. Froude intended his book to help the Tory Government to solve the

3. Wilde was himself fascinated by epigram and aphorism, but most of his (unlike Froude's) would challenge rather than confirm the conventional wisdom.

4. Sin strongly.

Irish question he has entirely missed his aim. The Ireland of which he writes has disappeared. As a record, however, of the incapacity of a Teutonic to rule a Celtic people against their own wishes his book is not without value. It is dull, but dull books are very popular at present, and as people have grown a little tired of talking about 'Robert Elsmere,'[5] they will probably take to discussing 'The Two Chiefs of Dunboy.' There are some who will welcome with delight the idea of solving the Irish question by doing away with the Irish people. There are others who will remember that Ireland has extended her boundaries, and that we have now to reckon with her not merely in the Old World but also in the New.

5. Best-selling novel about faith and doubt (published in 1888) by Mrs Humphrey Ward (1851-1920), who believed that Christianity could be revitalized by addressing social issues.

from:
THE PICTURE OF DORIAN GRAY (1891)

[The novel, a *succès de scandale*, appeared in 1891 and these introductory epigrams were doubtless included by Wilde to forestall (and perhaps also to foment) the outrage of Victorian moralists. This same strategy would later be adopted by Synge in prefaces to controversial plays, introduced (e.g. *The Tinker's Wedding*) with the assertion that 'the drama does not teach or prove anything'.

At the heart of Dorian Gray is a guilty secret — Dorian remains eternally the beautiful youth, but in an attic recess his portrait rapidly takes on the coarse corruptions of age, registering the effects of the sitter's increasingly dissolute life. The book appeared in the year in which Wilde took up with Lord Alfred Douglas.]

PREFACE

The artist is the creator of beautiful things.

To reveal art and conceal the artist is art's aim.

The critic is he who can translate into another manner or a new material his impression of beautiful things.

The highest as the lowest form of criticism is a mode of autobiography.

Those who find ugly meanings in beautiful things are corrupt without being charming. This is a fault.

Those who find beautiful meanings in beautiful things are the cultivated. For these there is hope.

They are the elect to whom beautiful things mean only Beauty.

There is no such thing as a moral or an immoral book. Books are well written, or badly written. That is all.

The nineteenth century dislike of Realism is the rage of Caliban[1] seeing his own face in a glass.

The nineteenth century dislike of Romanticism is the rage of Caliban not seeing his own face in a glass.

The moral life of man forms part of the subject-matter of the artist, but the morality of art consists in the perfect use of an imperfect medium.

No artist desires to prove anything. Even things that are true can be proved.

No artist has ethical sympathies. An ethical sympathy in an artist is an unpardonable mannerism of style.

No artist is ever morbid. The artist can express everything.

Thought and language are to the artist instruments of an art.

Vice and virtue are to the artist materials for an art.

From the point of view of form, the type of all the arts is the art of the musician. From the point of view of feeling, the actor's craft is the type.

All art is at once surface and symbol.

Those who go beneath the surface do so at their peril.

Those who read the symbol do so at their peril.

It is the spectator, and not life, that art really mirrors.

Diversity of opinion about a work of art shows that the work is new, complex, and vital.

When critics disagree the artist is in accord with himself.

1. A primitive and bestial man, native to the sunny island in Shakespeare's *The Tempest*; a churl. To treat art as a mirror, Wilde says in *The Decay of Lying*, would 'reduce genius to the position of a cracked looking-glass', falsely rendering art as subordinate to life. Joyce, in the opening chapter of *Ulysses*, plays on these conceits, when Stephen Dedalus suggests that 'the cracked looking-glass of a servant' is a proper symbol of Irish folk-revivalism.

We can forgive a man for making a useful thing as long as he does not admire it. The only excuse for making a useless thing is that one admires it intensely.

All art is quite useless.

from: INTENTIONS (1891)

['Intentions: The Decay of Lying' is one of four critical essays published together in 1891 with much revision. Its dialogic form permits Wilde to explore contradictory propositions, and allows him to register the essential criticisms of the artistic code to which he adheres. Such dialogism, modelled on that of those classic Greek authors whom Wilde revered, was extremely influential. Many of Yeats's poems take the form of dialogue, between Self and Soul, or Hic and Ille; and even apparently monologic texts such as 'Easter 1916' are shown, on inspection, to contain rival personal and public voices. The Stephen Dedalus who, in the National Library scene of *Ulysses*, enunciates an interpretation of Shakespeare and concludes by saying that he no longer believes his own theory is working consciously in this Wildean mode. Scott Fitzgerald, another admirer, said that the test of a first-rate intelligence was its ability to hold opposed ideas in the head without losing the capacity to function. Wilde's philosophy of 'both/and', rather than 'either/or', is one of the many features that places him in a tradition of Irish, as opposed to English, writing.]

THE DECAY OF LYING

. . . VIVIAN: No. There is one more passage,[1] but it is purely practical. It simply suggests some methods by which we could revive this lost art of Lying.

CYRIL: Well, before you read it to me, I should like to ask you a question. What do you mean by saying that life, 'poor, probable, uninteresting human life,' will try to reproduce the marvels of art? I can quite understand your objection to art being treated as a mirror. You think it would reduce genius to the position of a cracked looking-glass. But you don't mean to say that you seriously believe that Life imitates Art, that Life in fact is the mirror, and Art the reality?

VIVIAN: Certainly I do. Paradox though it may seem — and paradoxes are always dangerous things — it is none the less true that Life imitates art far more than Art imitates life. We have all seen in our own day in England how a certain curious and fascinating type of beauty, invented and emphasised by two imaginative painters, has so influenced Life that whenever one goes to a private view or to an artistic salon one sees, here the mystic eyes of Rossetti's dream, the long ivory throat, the strange square-cut jaw, the loosened shadowy hair that he so ardently loved, there the sweet maidenhood of 'The Golden Stair,' the blossom-like mouth and weary loveliness of the 'Laus Amoris,' the passion-pale face of Andromeda, the thin hands and lithe beauty of the Vivien in 'Merlin's Dream.'[2] And it has always been so. A great artist invents a type, and Life tries to copy it, to reproduce it in a popular form, like an enterprising publisher. Neither Holbein nor Vandyck[3] found in England what they have given us. They brought their types with them, and Life with her keen imitative faculty set herself to supply the master with models. The Greeks, with their quick artistic instinct, understood this, and set in the bride's chamber the statue of Hermes or of Apollo, that she might bear children as lovely as the works of art that she looked at in her rapture or her pain. They knew that Life gains from Art not merely spirituality, depth of thought and feeling, soul-turmoil or soul-peace, but that she can form herself on the very lines and colours of art, and can reproduce the dignity of Pheidias as well as the grace of Praxiteles.[4] Hence came their objection to realism. They disliked it on purely social grounds. They felt that it inevitably makes people ugly, and they were perfectly right. We try to improve the conditions of the race by means of good air, free sunlight, wholesome water, and hideous bare buildings for the better housing of the lower orders.

1. Vivian has argued that Nature has good intentions, but that only Art can fully carry them out; and that Art is really a form of exaggeration and selective overemphasis, a veil and not a mirror.

2. Dante Gabriel Rossetti (1828-82), Pre-Raphaelite painter and poet. These are the names of some of his paintings. The Pre-Raphaelite Brotherhood, founded in 1848, brought a new moral and literary seriousness to painting, and protested against the ugliness and squalor of contemporary industrial society.

3. Hans Holbein, the Younger (1497-1543), German realistic portrait-painter, engraver and illustrator of Luther's Bible. A friend of Erasmus, he visited England in the 1520s and again in the 1530s. Van Dyck (1599-1641), the Dutch court painter and disciple of Rubens, refined Holbein's techniques.

4. Pheidias, Greek sculptor of Zeus, who also designed the Parthenon for the Athenian ruler Pericles. Praxiteles, Athenian sculptor, whose 'Hermes Burying the Infant Dionysus' was discovered at Olympia.

But these things merely produce health, they do not produce beauty. For this, Art is required, and the true disciples of the great artist are not his studio-imitators, but those who become like his works of art, be they plastic as in the Greek days, or pictorial as in modern times; in a word, Life is Art's best, Art's only pupil.

As it is with the visible arts, so it is with literature. The most obvious and the vulgarest form in which this is shown is in the case of the silly boys who, after reading the adventures of Jack Sheppard or Dick Turpin,[5] pillage the stalls of unfortunate apple-women, break into sweet-shops at night, and alarm old gentlemen who are returning home from the city by leaping out on them in suburban lanes, with black masks and unloaded revolvers. This interesting phenomenon, which always occurs after the appearance of a new edition of either of the books I have alluded to, is usually attributed to the influence of literature on the imagination. But this is a mistake. The imagination is essentially creative and always seeks for a new form. The boy-burglar is simply the inevitable result of life's imitative instinct. He is Fact, occupied as Fact usually is, with trying to reproduce Fiction, and what we see in him is repeated on an extended scale throughout the whole of life. Schopenhauer[6] has analysed the pessimism that characterises modern thought, but Hamlet invented it. The world has become sad because a puppet was once melancholy. The Nihilist, that strange martyr who has no faith, who goes to the stake without enthusiasm, and dies for what he does not believe in, is a purely literary product. He was invented by Tourgénieff, and completed by Dostoieffski.[7] Robespierre came out of the pages of Rousseau as surely as the People's Palace rose out of the *débris* of a novel.[8] Literature always anticipates life. It does not copy it, but moulds it to its purpose. The nineteenth century, as we know it, is largely an invention of Balzac. Our Luciens de Rubempré, our Rastignacs, and De Marsays made their first appearance on the stage of the *Comédie Humaine*.[9] We are merely carrying out, with footnotes and unnecessary additions, the whim or fancy or creative vision of a great novelist. I once asked a lady, who knew Thackeray intimately, whether he had had any model for Becky Sharp. She told me that Becky was an invention, but that the idea of the character had been partly suggested by a governess who lived in the neighbourhood of Kensington Square, and was the companion of a very selfish and rich old woman. I inquired what became of the governess, and she replied that, oddly enough, some years after the appearance of *Vanity Fair*, she ran away with the nephew of the lady with whom she was living, and for a short time made a great splash in society, quite in Mrs. Rawdon Crawley's[10] style, and entirely by Mrs. Rawdon Crawley's methods. Ultimately she came to grief, disappeared to the Continent, and used to be occasionally seen at Monte Carlo and other gambling places. The noble gentleman from whom the same great sentimentalist drew Colonel Newcome died, a few months after *The Newcomes* had reached a fourth edition, with the word 'Adsum' on his lips.[11] Shortly after Mr. Stevenson published his curious psychological story of transformation,[12] a friend of mine, called Mr. Hyde, was in the north of London, and being anxious to get to a railway station, took what he thought would be a short cut, lost his way, and found himself in a network of mean, evil-looking streets. Feeling rather nervous he began to walk extremely fast, when suddenly out of an archway ran a child right between his legs. It fell on the pavement, he tripped over it, and trampled upon it. Being of course very much frightened and a little hurt, it began to scream, and in a few seconds the whole street was full of rough people who came pouring out of the houses like ants. They surrounded him, and asked him his name. He was just about to give it when he suddenly remembered the opening incident in Mr.

5. Noted highwaymen and bandits.
6. Arthur Schopenhauer (1788-1860), German philosopher of pessimism, obstinacy and misogyny, especially in *The World as Will and Idea* (1818).
7. Ivan Turgenev (1818-83). His *Fathers and Sons* (1862) portrays a nihilist hero in Bazarov. Wilde is probably thinking too of Fyodor Dostoevsky's *The Insulted and the Injured* (1861), which he reviewed in 1887.
8. Perhaps the reference here is to the Crystal Palace of 1851, an exhibition and recreational centre as renowned for the bric-à-brac it contained as for its revolutionary design.
9. Honoré de Balzac (1799-1850) wrote the 91 novels and stories of *La Comédie Humaine* between 1827 and 1847. The characters named appear in *Le Père Goriot* and *Les Illusions Perdues*, among others.
10. Actually, Becky Sharp, the heroine of Thackeray's novel *Vanity Fair* (1848), whose secret marriage to Rawdon Crawley infuriates his cynical and aristocratic family.
11. In William Makepeace Thackeray's novel *The Newcomes* (1853-55), Colonel Newcome dies with the word 'Adsum' (I am present) on his lips; he was answering God's calling of his name.
12. Robert Louis Stevenson's *The Strange Case of Dr Jekyll and Mr Hyde* (1886).

Stevenson's story. He was so filled with horror at having realized in his own person that terrible and well written scene, and at having done accident[al]ly, though in fact, what the Mr. Hyde of fiction had done with deliberate intent, that he ran away as hard as he could go. He was, however, very closely followed, and finally he took refuge in a surgery, the door of which happened to be open, where he explained to a young assistant, who happened to be there, exactly what had occurred. The humanitarian crowd were induced to go away on his giving them a small sum of money, and as soon as the coast was clear he left. As he passed out, the name on the brass door-plate of the surgery caught his eye. It was 'Jekyll'. At least it should have been.

Here the imitation, as far as it went, was of course accidental. In the following case the imitation was self-conscious. In the year 1879, just after I had left Oxford, I met at a reception at the house of one of the Foreign Ministers a woman of very curious exotic beauty. We became great friends, and were constantly together. And yet what interested most in her was not her beauty, but her character, her entire vagueness of character. She seemed to have no personality at all, but simply the possibility of many types. Sometimes she would give herself up entirely to art, turn her drawing-room into a studio, and spend two or three days a week at picture-galleries or museums. Then she would take to attending race-meetings, wear the most horsey clothes, and talk about nothing but betting. She abandoned religion for mesmerism, mesmerism for politics, and politics for the melodramatic excitements of philanthropy. In fact, she was a kind of Proteus, and as much a failure in all her transformations as was that wondrous sea-god when Odysseus laid hold of him. One day a serial began in one of the French magazines. At that time I used to read serial stories, and I well remember the shock of surprise I felt when I came to the description of the heroine. She was so like my friend that I brought her the magazine, and she recognized herself in it immediately, and seemed fascinated by the resemblance. I should tell you, by the way, that the story was translated from some dead Russian writer, so that the author had not taken his type from my friend. Well, to put the matter briefly, some months afterwards I was in Venice, and finding the magazine in the reading-room of the hotel, I took it up casually to see what had become of the heroine. It was a most piteous tale, as the girl had ended by running away with a man absolutely inferior to her, not merely in social station, but in character and intellect also. I wrote to my friend that evening about my views on John Bellini, and the admirable ices at Florio's, and the artistic value of gondolas, but added a postscript to the effect that her double in the story had behaved in a very silly manner. I don't know why I added that, but I remember I had a sort of dread over me that she might do the same thing. Before my letter had reached her, she had run away with a man who deserted her in six months. I saw her in 1884 in Paris, where she was living with her mother, and I asked her whether the story had had anything to do with her action. She told me that she had felt an absolutely irresistible impulse to follow the heroine step by step in her strange and fatal progress, and that it was with a feeling of real terror that she had looked forward to the last few chapters of the story. When they appeared, it seemed to her that she was compelled to reproduce them in life, and she did so. It was a most clear example of this imitative instinct of which I was speaking, and an extremely tragic one.

However, I do not wish to dwell any further upon individual instances. Personal experience is a most vicious and limited circle. All that I desire to point out is the general principle that Life imitates Art far more than Art imitates Life, and I feel sure that if you think seriously about it you will find that it is true. Life holds the mirror up to Art, and either reproduces some strange type imagined by painter or sculptor, or realizes in fact what has been dreamed in fiction. Scientifically speaking, the basis of life — the energy of life, as Aristotle would call it — is simply the desire for expression, and Art is always presenting various forms through which this expression can be attained. Life seizes on them and uses them, even if they be to her own hurt. Young men have committed suicide because Rolla did so, have died by their own hand because by his own hand Werther died.[13] Think of what we owe to the imitation of Christ, of what we owe to the imitation of Caesar.

CYRIL: The theory is certainly a very curious one, but to make it complete you must show that Nature, no less than Life, is an imitation of Art. Are you prepared to prove that?

13. Famous cases of suicide in Romantic literature.

VIVIAN: My dear fellow, I am prepared to prove anything.

CYRIL: Nature follows the landscape painter then, and takes her effects from him?

VIVIAN: Certainly. Where, if not from the Impressionists, do we get those wonderful brown fogs that come creeping down our streets, blurring the gas-lamps and changing the houses into monstrous shadows? To whom, if not to them and their master, do we owe the lovely silver mists that brood over our river, and turn to faint forms of fading grace curved bridge and swaying barge? The extraordinary change that has taken place in the climate of London during the last ten years is entirely due to this particular school of Art. You smile. Consider the matter from a scientific or a metaphysical point of view, and you will find that I am right. For what is Nature? Nature is no great mother who has borne us. She is our creation. It is in our brain that she quickens to life. Things are because we see them, and what we see, and how we see it, depends on the Arts that have influenced us. To look at a thing is very different from seeing a thing. One does not see anything until one sees its beauty. Then, and then only, does it come into existence. At present, people see fogs, not because there are fogs, but because poets and painters have taught them the mysterious loveliness of such effects. There may have been fogs for centuries in London. I dare say there were. But no one saw them, and so we do not know anything about them. They did not exist till Art had invented them. Now, it must be admitted, fogs are carried to excess. They have become the mere mannerism of a clique, and the exaggerated realism of their method gives dull people bronchitis. Where the cultured catch an effect, the uncultured catch cold. And so, let us be humane, and invite Art to turn her wonderful eyes elsewhere. She has done so already, indeed. That white quivering sunlight that one sees now in France, with its strange blotches of mauve, and its restless violet shadows, is her latest fancy, and, on the whole, Nature reproduces it quite admirably. Where she used to give us Corots and Daubignys, she gives us now exquisite Monets and entrancing Pissarros.[14] Indeed there are moments, rare, it is true, but still to be observed from time to time, when Nature becomes absolutely modern. Of course she is not always to be relied upon. The fact is that she is in this unfortunate position. Art creates an incomparable and unique effect, and, having done so, passes on to other things. Nature, upon the other hand, forgetting that imitation can be made the sincerest form of insult, keeps on repeating this effect until we all become absolutely wearied of it. Nobody of any real culture, for instance, ever talks now-a-days about the beauty of a sunset. Sunsets are quite old-fashioned. They belong to the time when Turner was the last note in art. To admire them is a distinct sign of provincialism of temperament. Upon the other hand they go on. Yesterday evening Mrs. Arundel insisted on my going to the window, and looking at the glorious sky, as she called it. Of course I had to look at it. She is one of those absurdly pretty Philistines, to whom one can deny nothing. And what was it? It was simply a very second-rate Turner, a Turner of a bad period, with all the painter's worst faults exaggerated and overemphasized.[15] Of course, I am quite ready to admit that Life very often commits the same error. She produces her false Renés and her sham Vautrins, just as Nature gives us, on one day a doubtful Cuyp, and on another a more than questionable Rousseau.[16] Still, Nature irritates one more when she does things of that kind. It seems so stupid, so obvious, so unnecessary. A false Vautrin might be delightful. A doubtful Cuyp is unbearable. However, I don't want to be too hard on Nature. I wish the Channel, especially at Hastings, did not look quite so often like a Henry Moore,[17] grey pearl with yellow lights, but then, when Art is more varied, Nature will, no doubt, be more varied also. That she imitates Art, I don't think even her worst enemy would deny now. It is the one thing that keeps her in touch with civilized man. But have

14. The French painters, Corot and Daubigny, were noted for lucid portraits of persons at work, while Monet and Pissarro were praised for their vague and impressionistic canvasses, striking but seldom lucid.

15. J. M. W. Turner (1775-1851), the greatest of English Romantic painters, was famous for his pre-Impressionistic experiments in luminosity and colour.

16. François René Chateaubriand (1768-1848), author of *René* (1805), the hero of which is devoured by a secret sorrow. Vautrin is the arch criminal of Balzac's *La Comédie Humaine*. Aelbert Cuyp (1620-91), one of the foremost Dutch landscape artists, has had an improbably large number of paintings attributed to him. The reference to Jean Jacques Rousseau (1712-78) is an echo of the earlier indication that the French revolutionary, Robespierre, was a living imitation of Rousseau's fictional man of virtue.

17. A nineteenth-century British landscape artist, not to be confused with the twentieth-century abstract sculptor.

I proved my theory to your satisfaction?

CYRIL: You have proved it to my dissatisfaction, which is better. But even admitting this strange imitative instinct in Life and Nature, surely you would acknowledge that Art expresses the temper of its age, the spirit of its time, the moral and social conditions that surround it, and under whose influence it is produced.

VIVIAN: Certainly not! Art never expresses anything but itself. This is the principle of my new aesthetics; and it is this, more than that vital connection between form and substance, on which Mr. Pater dwells,[18] that makes music the type of all the arts. Of course, nations and individuals, with that healthy natural vanity which is the secret of existence, are always under the impression that it is of them that the Muses are talking, always trying to find in the calm dignity of imaginative art some mirror of their own turbid passions, always forgetting that the singer of life is not Apollo, but Marsyas.[19] Remote from reality, and with her eyes turned away from the shadows of the cave, Art reveals her own perfection, and the wondering crowd that watches the opening of the marvellous, many-petalled rose fancies that it is its own history that is being told to it, its own spirit that is finding expression in a new form. But it is not so. The highest art rejects the burden of the human spirit, and gains more from a new medium or a fresh material than she does from any enthusiasm for art, or from any lofty passion, or from any great awakening of the human consciousness. She develops purely on her own lines. She is not symbolic of any age. It is the ages that are her symbols.

Even those who hold that Art is representative of time and place and people, cannot help admitting that the more imitative an art is, the less it represents to us the spirit of its age. The evil faces of the Roman emperors look out at us from the foul porphyry and spotted jasper in which the realistic artists of the day delighted to work, and we fancy that in those cruel lips and heavy sensual jaws we can find the secret of the ruin of the Empire. But it was not so. The vices of Tiberius could not destroy that supreme civilization, any more than the virtues of the Antonines could save it. It fell for other, for less interesting reasons. The sibyls and prophets of the Sistine may indeed serve to interpret for some that new birth of the emancipated spirit that we call the Renaissance; but what do the drunken boors and brawling peasants of Dutch art tell us about the great soul of Holland? The more abstract, the more ideal an art is, the more it reveals to us the temper of its age. If we wish to understand a nation by means of its art, let us look at its architecture or its music.

CYRIL: I quite agree with you there. The spirit of an age may be best expressed in the abstract ideal arts, for the spirit itself is abstract and ideal. Upon the other hand, for the visible aspect of an age, for its look, as the phrase goes, we must of course go to the arts of imitation.

VIVIAN: I don't think so. After all, what the imitative arts really give us are merely the various styles of particular artists, or of certain schools of artists. Surely you don't imagine that the people of the Middle Ages bore any resemblance at all to the figures on medieval stained glass, or in medieval stone and wood carving, or on medieval metal-work, or tapestries, or illuminated MSS. They were probably very ordinary-looking people, with nothing grotesque, or remarkable, or fantastic in their appearance. The Middle Ages, as we know them in art, are simply a definite form of style, and there is no reason at all why an artist with this style should not be produced in the nineteenth century. No great artist ever sees things as they really are. If he did, he would cease to be an artist. Take an example from our own day. I know that you are fond of Japanese things. Now, do you really imagine that the Japanese people, as they are presented to us in art, have any existence? If you do, you have never understood Japanese art at all. The Japanese people are the deliberate self-conscious creation of certain individual artists. If you set a picture by Hokusai, or Hokkei, or any of the great native painters, beside a real Japanese gentleman or lady, you will see that there is not the slightest resemblance between them. The actual people who live in Japan are not unlike the general run of English people; that is to say, they are extremely commonplace, and have nothing curious or extraordinary about them. In fact the whole of Japan is a pure invention. There is no such country,

18. Walter Pater (1839-94), Oxford classicist and art critic; his cult of intense sensation greatly appealed to Wilde, who described Pater's *Studies in the History of the Renaissance* (1873) as 'the holy writ of beauty'.

19. Apollo, Greek sun-god, patron of poetry, music and archery; Marsyas, Greek satyr, punished for appropriating a flute tossed aside by Athene, and, after being defeated by Apollo in a musical contest, he was flayed by a knife.

there are no such people. One of our most charming painters went recently to the Land of the Chrysanthemum in the foolish hope of seeing the Japanese. All he saw, all he had the chance of painting, were a few lanterns and some fans. He was quite unable to discover the inhabitants, as his delightful exhibition at Messrs. Dowdeswell's Gallery showed only too well. He did not know that the Japanese people are, as I have said, simply a mode of style, an exquisite fancy of art. And so, if you desire to see a Japanese effect, you will not behave like a tourist and go to Tokio. On the contrary, you will stay at home, and steep yourself in the work of certain Japanese artists, and then, when you have absorbed the spirit of their style, and caught their imaginative manner of vision, you will go some afternoon and sit in the Park or stroll down Piccadilly, and if you cannot see an absolutely Japanese effect there, you will not see it anywhere. Or, to return again to the past, take as another instance the ancient Greeks. Do you think that Greek art ever tells us what the Greek people were like? Do you believe that the Athenian women were like the stately dignified figures of the Parthenon frieze, or like those marvellous goddesses who sat in the triangular pediments of the same building? If you judge from the art, they certainly were so. But read an authority, like Aristophanes for instance. You will find that the Athenian ladies laced tightly, wore high-heeled shoes, dyed their hair yellow, painted and rouged their faces, and were exactly like any silly fashionable or fallen creature of our own day. The fact is that we look back on the ages entirely through the medium of Art, and Art, very fortunately, has never once told us the truth.

CYRIL: But modern portraits by English painters, what of them? Surely they are like the people they pretend to represent?

VIVIAN: Quite so. They are so like them that a hundred years from now no one will believe in them. The only portraits in which one believes are portraits where there is very little of the sitter, and a very great deal of the artist. Holbein's drawings of the men and women of his time impress us with a sense of their absolute reality. But this is simply because Holbein compelled life to accept his conditions, to restrain itself within his limitations, to reproduce his type, and to appear as he wished it to appear. It is style that makes us believe in a thing — nothing but style. Most of our modern portrait painters are doomed to absolute oblivion. They never paint what they see. They paint what the public sees, and the public never sees anything.

CYRIL: Well, after that I think I should like to hear the end of your article.

VIVIAN: With pleasure. Whether it will do any good I really cannot say. Ours is certainly the dullest and most prosaic century possible. Why, even Sleep has played us false, and has closed up the gates of ivory, and opened the gates of horn. The dreams of the great middle classes of this country, as recorded in Mr. Myers's two bulky volumes on the subject and in the Transactions of the Psychical Society, are the most depressing things that I have ever read.[20] There is not even a fine nightmare among them. They are commonplace, sordid, and tedious. As for the Church I cannot conceive anything better for the culture of a country than the presence in it of a body of men whose duty it is to believe in the supernatural, to perform daily miracles, and to keep alive that mythopoeic faculty which is so essential for the imagination. But in the English Church a man succeeds, not through his capacity for belief, but through his capacity for disbelief. Ours is the only Church where the sceptic stands at the altar, and where St. Thomas is regarded as the ideal apostle. Many a worthy clergyman, who passes his life in admirable works of kindly charity, lives and dies unnoticed and unknown; but it is sufficient for some shallow uneducated passman out of either University to get up in his pulpit and express his doubts about Noah's ark, or Balaam's ass,[21] or Jonah and the whale, for half of London to flock to hear him, and to sit open-mouthed in rapt admiration at his superb intellect. The growth of common sense in the English Church is a thing very much to be regretted. It is really a degrading concession to a low form of realism. It is silly, too. It springs from an entire ignorance of psychology. Man can believe the impossible, but man can never believe the improbable. However, I must read the end of my article:

'What we have to do, what at any rate it is our duty to do, is to revive this old art of Lying. Much of course may be done, in the way of educating the public, by amateurs in the domestic circle, at

20. F. W. H. Myers (1843-1901) was a founder of the Society for Psychical Research in 1882. His two-volume *Phantasms of the Living* (1886) dealt for the most part with telepathy.

21. Numbers, Chapter 22.

literary lunches, and at afternoon teas. But this is merely the light and graceful side of lying, such as was probably heard at Cretan dinner parties. There are many other forms. Lying for the sake of gaining some immediate personal advantage, for instance — lying with a moral purpose, as it is usually called — though of late it has been rather looked down upon, was extremely popular with the antique world. Athena laughs when Odysseus tells her "his words of sly devising," as Mr. William Morris phrases it,[22] and the glory of mendacity illumines the pale brow of the stainless hero of Euripidean tragedy, and sets among the noble women of the past the young bride of one of Horace's most exquisite odes.[23] Later on, what at first had been merely a natural instinct was elevated into a self-conscious science. Elaborate rules were laid down for the guidance of mankind, and an important school of literature grew up round the subject. Indeed, when one remembers the excellent philosophical treatises of Sanchez[24] on the whole question, one cannot help regretting that no one has ever thought of publishing a cheap and condensed edition of the works of that great casuist. A short primer, "When to Lie and How," if brought out in an attractive and not too expensive a form, would no doubt command a large scale, and would prove of real practical service to many earnest and deep-thinking people. Lying for the sake of the improvement of the young, which is the basis of home education, still lingers amongst us, and its advantages are so admirably set forth in the early books of Plato's *Republic* that it is unnecessary to dwell upon them here. It is a mode of lying for which all good mothers have peculiar capabilities, but it is capable of still further development, and has been sadly overlooked by the School Board. Lying for the sake of a monthly salary is of course well known in Fleet Street, and the profession of a political leader-writer is not without its advantages. But it is said to be a somewhat dull occupation, and it certainly does not lead to much beyond a kind of ostentatious obscurity. The only form of lying that is absolutely beyond reproach is Lying for its own sake, and the highest development of this is, as we have already pointed out, Lying in Art. Just as those who do not love Plato more than Truth cannot pass beyond the threshold of the Academe, so those who do not love Beauty more than Truth never know the inmost shrine of Art. The solid stolid British intellect lies in the desert sands like the Sphinx in Flaubert's marvellous tale, and fantasy, *La Chimère*, dances round it, and calls to it with her false, flute-toned voice. It may not hear her now, but surely some day, when we are all bored to death with the commonplace character of modern fiction, it will hearken to her and try to borrow her wings.

'And when that day dawns, or sunset reddens how joyous we shall all be! Facts will be regarded as discreditable, Truth will be found mourning over her fetters, and Romance, with her temper of wonder, will return to the land. The very aspect of the world will change to our startled eyes. Out of the sea will rise Behemoth and Leviathan, and sail round the high-pooped galleys, as they do on the delightful maps of those ages when books on geography were actually readable. Dragons will wander about the waste places, and the phoenix will soar from her nest of fire into the air. We shall lay our hands upon the basilisk, and see the jewel in the toad's head. Champing his gilded oats, the Hippogriff[25] will stand in our stalls, and over our heads will float the Blue Bird singing of beautiful and impossible things, of things that are lovely and that never happen, of things that are not and that should be. But before this comes to pass we must cultivate the lost art of Lying.'

CYRIL: Then we must certainly cultivate it at once. But in order to avoid making any error I want you to tell me briefly the doctrines of the new aesthetics.

VIVIAN: Briefly, then, they are these. Art never expresses anything but itself. It has an independent life, just as Thought has, and develops purely on its own lines. It is not necessarily realistic in an age of realism, nor spiritual in an age of faith. So far from being the creation of its time, it is usually in direct opposition to it, and the only history that it preserves for us is the history of its own progress. Sometimes it returns upon its footsteps, and revives some antique form, as happened in the archaistic movement of late Greek Art, and in the pre-Raphaelite movement of our own day. At other

22. William Morris (1834-96), painter, poet and political agitator. His writings rejected a drab industrialism and called for a return to more organic medieval values.
23. Euripides, *Orestes* and possibly Horace, *Odes*, III, 7: 'Quid fles, Asteric?' ('Asteric, why are you crying?)
24. Francisco Sanchez (1552-1623), a Portuguese philosopher who was opposed to every form of superstition. His great work is *Why Nothing Can Be Known* (1581).
25. Griffin-headed winged horse of medieval fable.

times it entirely anticipates its age, and produces in one century work that it takes another century to understand, to appreciate, and to enjoy. In no case does it reproduce its age. To pass from the art of a time to the time itself is the great mistake that all historians commit.

The second doctrine is this. All bad art comes from returning to Life and Nature, and elevating them into ideals. Life and Nature may sometimes be used as part of Art's rough material, but before they are of any real service to art they must be translated into artistic conventions. The moment Art surrenders its imaginative medium it surrenders everything. As a method Realism is a complete failure, and the two things that every artist should avoid are modernity of form and modernity of subject-matter. To us, who live in the nineteenth century, any century is a suitable subject for art except our own. The only beautiful things are the things that do not concern us. It is, to have the pleasure of quoting myself, exactly because Hecuba is nothing to us that her sorrows are so suitable a motive for a tragedy. Besides, it is only the modern that ever becomes old-fashioned. M. Zola[26] sits down to give us a picture of the Second Empire. Who cares for the Second Empire now? It is out of date. Life goes faster than Realism, but Romanticism is always in front of Life.

The third doctrine is that Life imitates Art far more than Art imitates Life. This results not merely from Life's imitative instinct, but from the fact that the self-conscious aim of Life is to find expression, and that Art offers it certain beautiful forms through which it may realize that energy. It is a theory that has never been put forward before, but it is extremely fruitful, and throws an entirely new light upon the history of Art.

It follows, as a corollary from this, that external Nature also imitates Art. The only effects that she can show us are effects that we have already seen through poetry, or in paintings. This is the secret of Nature's charm, as well as the explanation of Nature's weakness.

The final revelation is that Lying, the telling of beautiful untrue things, is the proper aim of Art. But of this I think I have spoken at sufficient length. And now let us go out on the terrace, where 'droops the milk-white peacock like a ghost,'[27] while the evening star, 'washes the dusk with silver'. At twilight nature becomes a wonderfully suggestive effect, and is not without loveliness, though perhaps its chief use is to illustrate quotations from the poets. Come! We have talked long enough.

26. Emile Zola (1840-1902), French naturalist novelist, whose descriptions of sex, alcoholism and hard labour in the 1880s shocked and impressed many.

27. Alfred Lord Tennyson, *The Princess*, vii, 165.

THE IMPORTANCE OF BEING EARNEST (1895)

THE PERSONS OF THE PLAY

JOHN WORTHING, *J.P.*
ALGERNON MONCRIEFF
REV. CANON CHASUBLE, *D.D.*
MERRIMAN, *Butler*
LANE, *Manservant*
LADY BRACKNELL
HON. GWENDOLEN FAIRFAX
CECILY CARDEW
MISS PRISM, *Governess*

['I am just finishing a new play which, as it is quite non-sensical and has no serious interest, will I hope bring me in a lot of red gold', wrote Wilde in 1894. *The Importance of Being Earnest* was written at speed during a sojourn in the seaside town of Worthing, Sussex. It is widely regarded as one of the most perfect English comedies, sparkling in dialogue, if rather less brilliant in its plotting and characterization. Although billed as 'a trivial comedy for serious people', the play is, in fact, a clever and sustained essay on the nature of the imagination, the proper function of an education, the ethics of ambiguity, and the formation of the modern woman.

At the opening night, on 14 February 1895, the audience rose and cheered. Despite the dramatist's arrest on 5 April, and the embarrassments that followed, the play continued its run until 8 May, but with Wilde's name removed from programmes and posters. Even after 86 performances, the production did not break even, the losses being attributed to the popular scandal. On its second revival in 1909, it ran for almost a year and earned its promoters a great deal of money. It has been enormously popular all over the world ever since.]

ACT I

SCENE — *Morning room in* ALGERNON's *flat in Half-Moon Street.*[1] *The room is luxuriously and*

1. A chic quarter of London's west end.

artistically furnished. The sound of a piano is heard in the adjoining room.

LANE *is arranging afternoon tea on the table, and after the music has ceased,* ALGERNON *enters.*

ALGERNON: Did you hear what I was playing, Lane?

LANE: I didn't think it polite to listen, sir.

ALGERNON: I'm sorry for that, for your sake. I don't play accurately — anyone can play accurately — but I play with wonderful expression. As far as the piano is concerned, sentiment is my forte. I keep science for Life.

LANE: Yes, sir.

ALGERNON: And, speaking of the science of Life, have you got the cucumber sandwiches cut for Lady Bracknell?

LANE: Yes, sir. (*Hands them on a salver*)

ALGERNON: (*Inspects them, takes two, and sits down on the sofa*) Oh! . . . by the way, Lane, I see from your book that on Thursday night, when Lord Shoreman and Mr. Worthing were dining with me, eight bottles of champagne are entered as having been consumed.

LANE: Yes, sir; eight bottles and a pint.

ALGERNON: Why is it that at a bachelor's establishment the servants invariably drink the champagne? I ask merely for information.

LANE: I attribute it to the superior quality of the wine, sir. I have often observed that in married households the champagne is rarely of a first-rate brand.

ALGERNON: Good Heavens! Is marriage so demoralizing[2] as that?

LANE: I believe it *is* a very pleasant state, sir. I have had very little experience of it myself up to the present. I have only been married once. That was in consequence of a misunderstanding between myself and a young person.

ALGERNON: (*Languidly*) I don't know that I am much interested in your family life, Lane.

LANE: No, sir; it is not a very interesting subject. I never think of it myself.

ALGERNON: Very natural, I am sure. That will do, Lane, thank you.

LANE: Thank you, sir.

LANE *goes out.*

ALGERNON: Lane's views on marriage seem somewhat lax. Really, if the lower orders[3] don't set us a good example, what on earth is the use of them? They seem, as a class, to have absolutely no sense of moral responsibility.

Enter LANE.

LANE: Mr. Ernest Worthing.

Enter JACK. LANE *goes out.*

ALGERNON: How are you, my dear Ernest? What brings you up to town?

JACK: Oh, pleasure, pleasure! What else should bring one anywhere? Eating as usual, I see, Algy!

ALGERNON: (*stiffy*) I believe it is customary in good society to take some slight refreshment at five o'clock. Where have you been since last Thursday?

JACK: (*Sitting down on the sofa*) In the country.

ALGERNON: What on earth do you do there?

JACK: (*Pulling off his gloves*) When one is in town one amuses oneself. When one is in the country one amuses other people. It is excessively boring.

ALGERNON: And who are the people you amuse?

JACK: (*Airily*) Oh, neighbours, neighbours.

ALGERNON: Got nice neighbours in your part of Shropshire?[4]

JACK: Perfectly horrid! Never speak to one of them.

ALGERNON: How immensely you must amuse them! (*Goes over and takes sandwich*) By the way, Shropshire is your county, is it not?

JACK: Eh? Shropshire? Yes, of course. Hallo! Why all these cups? Why cucumber sandwiches? Why such reckless extravagance in one so young? Who is coming to tea?

ALGERNON: Oh! merely Aunt Augusta and Gwendolen.

JACK: How perfectly delightful!

ALGERNON: Yes, that is all very well; but I am afraid Aunt Augusta won't quite approve of your being here.

JACK: May I ask why?

ALGERNON: My dear fellow, the way you flirt with Gwendolen is perfectly disgraceful. It is almost as bad as the way Gwendolen flirts with you.

JACK: I am in love with Gwendolen. I have come up to town expressly to propose to her.

ALGERNON: I thought you had come up for pleasure? . . . I call that business.

JACK: How utterly unromantic you are!

2. Algernon means 'depressing', Lane 'corrupting'.

3. cf. The famous comment: 'As for living, our servants will do that for us' in the drama *Axël* (1890) by Philippe Villiers de L'Isle Adam (1838-89).

4. Later Jack will admit that the estate is in Hertfordshire. This is the first of many acts of deceit, committed by all major characters in the play.

ALGERNON: I really don't see anything romantic in proposing. It is very romantic to be in love. But there is nothing romantic about a definite proposal. Why, one may be accepted. One usually is, I believe. Then the excitement is all over. The very essence of romance is uncertainty. If ever I get married, I'll certainly try to forget the fact.

JACK: I have no doubt about that, dear Algy. The Divorce Court was specially invented for people whose memories are so curiously constituted.

ALGERNON: Oh! there is no use speculating on that subject. Divorces are made in Heaven —— (JACK *puts out his hand to take a sandwich.* ALGERNON *at once interferes*) Please don't touch the cucumber sandwiches. They are ordered specially for Aunt Augusta. (*Takes one and eats it*)

JACK: Well, you have been eating them all the time.

ALGERNON: This is quite a different matter. She is my aunt. (*Takes plate from below*) Have some bread and butter. The bread and butter is for Gwendolen. Gwendolen is devoted to bread and butter.

JACK: (*Advancing to table and helping himself*) And very good bread and butter it is too.

ALGERNON: Well, my dear fellow, you need not eat as if you were going to eat it all. You behave as if you were married to her already. You are not married to her already, and I don't think you ever will be.

JACK: Why on earth do you say that?

ALGERNON: Well, in the first place girls never marry the men they flirt with. Girls don't think it right.

JACK: Oh, that is nonsense!

ALGERNON: It isn't. It is a great truth. It accounts for the extraordinary number of bachelors that one sees all over the place. In the second place, I don't give my consent.

JACK: Your consent!

ALGERNON: My dear fellow, Gwendolen is my first cousin. And before I allow you to marry her, you will have to clear up the whole question of Cecily. (*Rings bell*)

JACK: Cecily! What on earth do you mean? What do you mean, Algy, by Cecily? I don't know anyone of the name of Cecily.

Enter LANE.

ALGERNON: Bring me that cigarette case Mr. Worthing left in the smoking-room the last time he dined here.

LANE: Yes, sir.

LANE *goes out.*

JACK: Do you mean to say you have had my cigarette case all this time? I wish to goodness you had let me know. I have been writing frantic letters to Scotland Yard[5] about it. I was very nearly offering a large reward.

ALGERNON: Well, I wish you would offer one. I happen to be more than usually hard up.

JACK: There is no good offering a large reward now that the thing is found.

Enter LANE *with the cigarette case on a salver.* ALGERNON *takes it at once.* LANE *goes out.*

ALGERNON: I think that is rather mean of you, Ernest, I must say. (*Opens case and examines it*) However, it makes no matter, for, now that I look at the inscription inside, I find that the thing isn't yours after all.

JACK: Of course it's mine. (*Moving to him*) You have seen me with it a hundred times, and you have no right whatsoever to read what is written inside. It is a very ungentlemanly thing to read a private cigarette case.

ALGERNON: Oh! it is absurd to have a hard-and-fast rule about what one should read and what one shouldn't. More than half of modern culture depends on what one shouldn't read.

JACK: I am quite aware of the fact, and I don't propose to discuss modern culture. It isn't the sort of thing one should talk of in private. I simply want my cigarette case back.

ALGERNON: Yes; but this isn't your cigarette case. This cigarette case is a present from someone of the name of Cecily, and you said you didn't know anyone of that name.

JACK: Well, if you want to know, Cecily happens to be my aunt.

ALGERNON: Your aunt!

JACK: Yes. Charming old lady she is, too. Lives at Tunbridge Wells. Just give it back to me, Algy.

ALGERNON: (*Retreating to back of sofa*) But why does she call herself Cecily if she is your aunt and lives at Tunbridge Wells? (*Reading*) 'From little Cecily with her fondest love.'

JACK: (*Moving to sofa and kneeling upon it*) My dear fellow, what on earth is there in that? Some aunts are tall, some aunts are not tall. That is a matter that surely an aunt may be allowed to decide for herself. You seem to think that every aunt

5. London police headquarters.

should be exactly like your aunt! That is absurd! For Heaven's sake give me back my cigarette case. (*Follows Algy round the room*)

ALGERNON: Yes. But why does your aunt call you her uncle? 'From little Cecily, with her fondest love to her dear Uncle Jack.' There is no objection, I admit, to an aunt being a small aunt, but why an aunt, no matter what her size may be, should call her own nephew her uncle, I can't quite make out. Besides, your name isn't Jack at all; it is Ernest.

JACK: It isn't Ernest; it's Jack.

ALGERNON: You have always told me it was Ernest. I have introduced you to everyone as Ernest. You answer to the name of Ernest. You look as if your name was Ernest. You are the most earnest looking person I ever saw in my life. It is perfectly absurd your saying that your name isn't Ernest. It's on your cards. Here is one of them. (*Taking it from case*) 'Mr. Ernest Worthing, B. 4, The Albany.' I'll keep this as a proof that your name is Ernest if ever you attempt to deny it to me, or to Gwendolen, or to anyone else. (*Puts the card in his pocket*)

JACK: Well, my name is Ernest in town and Jack in the country, and the cigarette case was given to me in the country.

ALGERNON: Yes, but that does not account for the fact that your small Aunt Cecily, who lives at Tunbridge Wells, calls you her dear uncle. Come, old boy, you had much better have the thing out at once.

JACK: My dear Algy, you talk exactly as if you were a dentist. It is very vulgar to talk like a dentist when one isn't a dentist. It produces a false impression.

ALGERNON: Well, that is exactly what dentists always do. Now, go on! Tell me the whole thing. I may mention that I have always suspected you of being a confirmed and secret Bunburyist; and I am quite sure of it now.

JACK: Bunburyist? What on earth do you mean by a Bunburyist?

ALGERNON: I'll reveal to you the meaning of that incomparable expression as soon as you are kind enough to inform me why you are Ernest in town and Jack in the country.

JACK: Well, produce my cigarette case first.

ALGERNON: Here it is. (*Hands cigarette case*) Now produce your explanation, and pray make it improbable. (*Sits on sofa*)

JACK: My dear fellow, there is nothing improbable about my explanation at all. In fact it's perfectly ordinary. Old Mr. Thomas Cardew, who adopted me when I was a little boy, made me in his will guardian to his granddaughter, Miss Cecily Cardew. Cecily, who addresses me as her uncle from motives of respect that you could not possibly appreciate, lives at my place in the country under the charge of her admirable governess, Miss Prism.[6]

ALGERNON: Where is that place in the country, by the way?

JACK: That is nothing to you, dear boy. You are not going to be invited.... I may tell you candidly that the place is not in Shropshire.

ALGERNON: I suspected that, my dear fellow! I have Bunburyed all over Shropshire on two separate occasions. Now, go on. Why are you Ernest in town and Jack in the country?

JACK: My dear Algy, I don't know whether you will be able to understand my real motives. You are hardly serious enough. When one is placed in the position of guardian, one has to adopt a very high moral tone on all subjects. It's one's duty to do so. And as a high moral tone can hardly be said to conduce very much to either one's health or one's happiness, in order to get up to town I have always pretended to have a young brother of the name of Ernest, who lives in the Albany, and gets into the most dreadful scrapes. That, my dear Algy, is the whole truth pure and simple.

ALGERNON: The truth is rarely pure and never simple. Modern life would be very tedious if it were either, and modern literature a complete impossibility!

JACK: That wouldn't be at all a bad thing.

ALGERNON: Literary criticism is not your forte, my dear fellow. Don't try it. You should leave that to people who haven't been at a University. They do it so well in the daily papers. What you really are is a Bunburyist.[7] I was quite right in saying you were a Bunburyist. You are one of the most advanced Bunburyists I know.

JACK: What on earth do you mean?

ALGERNON: You have invented a very useful young brother called Ernest, in order that you may be able to come up to town as often as you like. I

6. Perhaps the name puns on 'misprision', oversight or neglect of duty in respect of a crime (cf. the explanation of her background in the final act).

7. cf. Wilde — 'man is least himself when he talks in his own person, but give him a mask and he will tell you the truth.' ('The Critic as Artist: A Dialogue, Part 2', *The Artist as Critic*, p. 389.)

have invented an invaluable permanent invalid called Bunbury, in order that I may be able to go down into the country whenever I choose. Bunbury is perfectly invaluable. If it wasn't for Bunbury's extraordinary bad health, for instance, I wouldn't be able to dine with you at Willis's tonight, for I have been really engaged[8] to Aunt Augusta for more than a week.

JACK: I haven't asked you to dine with me anywhere tonight.

ALGERNON: I know. You are absurdly careless about sending out invitations. It is very foolish of you. Nothing annoys people so much as not receiving invitations.

JACK: You had much better dine with your Aunt Augusta.

ALGERNON: I haven't the smallest intention of doing anything of the kind. To begin with, I dined there on Monday, and once a week is quite enough to dine with one's own relations. In the second place, whenever I do dine there I am always treated as a member of the family, and sent down with either no woman at all, or two. In the third place, I know perfectly well whom she will place me next to, tonight. She will place me next Mary Farquhar, who always flirts with her own husband across the dinner table. That is not very pleasant. Indeed, it is not even decent ... and that sort of thing is enormously on the increase. The amount of women in London who flirt with their own husbands is perfectly scandalous. It looks so bad. It is simply washing one's clean linen in public. Besides, now that I know you to be a confirmed Bunburyist, I naturally want to talk to you about Bunburying. I want to tell you the rules.

JACK: I'm not a Bunburyist at all. If Gwendolen accepts me, I am going to kill my brother, indeed I think I'll kill him in any case. Cecily is a little too much interested in him. It is rather a bore. So I am going to get rid of Ernest. And I strongly advise you to do the same with Mr. ... with your invalid friend who has the absurd name.

ALGERNON: Nothing will induce me to part with Bunbury, and if you ever get married, which seems to me extremely problematic, you will be very glad to know Bunbury. A man who marries without knowing Bunbury has a very tedious time of it.

JACK: That is nonsense. If I marry a charming girl like Gwendolen, and she is the only girl I ever saw in my life that I would marry, I certainly won't want to know Bunbury.

ALGERNON: Then your wife will. You don't seem to realize, that in married life three is company and two is none.

JACK: (*Sententiously*) That, my dear young friend, is the theory that the corrupt French Drama[9] has been propounding for the last fifty years.

ALGERNON: Yes; and that the happy English home has proved in half the time.

JACK: For heaven's sake, don't try to be cynical. It's perfectly easy to be cynical.

ALGERNON: My dear fellow, it isn't easy to be anything nowadays. There's such a lot of beastly competition about. (*The sound of an electric bell is heard*) Ah! that must be Aunt Augusta. Only relatives, or creditors, ever ring in that Wagnerian[10] manner. Now, if I get her out of the way for ten minutes, so that you can have an opportunity for proposing to Gwendolen, may I dine with you tonight at Willis's?

JACK: I suppose so, if you want to.

ALGERNON: Yes, but you must be serious about it. I hate people who are not serious about meals. It is so shallow of them.

Enter LANE.

LANE: Lady Bracknell and Miss Fairfax.

ALGERNON *goes forward to meet them. Enter* LADY BRACKNELL *and* GWENDOLEN.

LADY BRACKNELL: Good afternoon, dear Algernon, I hope you are behaving very well.

ALGERNON: I'm feeling very well, Aunt Augusta.

LADY BRACKNELL: That's not quite the same thing. In fact the two things rarely go together. (*Sees* JACK *and bows to him with icy coldness*)

ALGERNON: (*To* GWENDOLEN) Dear me, you are smart!

GWENDOLEN: I am always smart! Aren't I, Mr. Worthing?

JACK: You're quite perfect, Miss Fairfax.

GWENDOLEN: Oh! I hope I am not that. It would leave no room for developments, and I intend to develop in many directions.

GWENDOLEN *and* JACK *sit down together in the corner.*

8. i.e. committed to be present at her party.

9. The English, who saw themselves as morally superior, liked to speak of French decadence. A London performance of Wilde's *Salomé* was banned by the Lord Chamberlain in 1892, but the play was produced later in Paris.

10. Suggestive of the dramatic and emotionally intense compositions of Richard Wagner (1813-83).

LADY BRACKNELL: I'm sorry if we are a little late, Algernon, but I was obliged to call on dear Lady Harbury. I hadn't been there since her poor husband's death. I never saw a woman so altered: she looks quite twenty years younger. And now I'll have a cup of tea, and one of those nice cucumber sandwiches you promised me.

ALGERNON: Certainly, Aunt Augusta. (*Goes over to teatable*)

LADY BRACKNELL: Won't you come and sit here, Gwendolen?

GWENDOLEN: Thanks, mamma, I'm quite comfortable where I am.

ALGERNON: (*Picking up empty plate in horror*) Good heavens! Lane! Why are there no cucumber sandwiches? I ordered them specially.

LANE: (*Gravely*) There were no cucumbers in the market this morning, sir. I went down twice.

ALGERNON: No cucumbers!

LANE: No, sir. Not even for ready money.[11]

ALGERNON: That will do, Lane, thank you.

LANE: Thank you, sir.

ALGERNON: I am greatly distressed, Aunt Augusta, about there being no cucumbers, not even for ready money.

LADY BRACKNELL: It really makes no matter, Algernon. I had some crumpets[12] with Lady Harbury, who seems to me to be living entirely for pleasure now.

ALGERNON: I hear her hair has turned quite gold from grief.[13]

LADY BRACKNELL: It certainly has changed its colour. From what cause I, of course, cannot say. (ALGERNON *crosses and hands tea*) Thank you. I've quite a treat for you tonight, Algernon. I am going to send you down with Mary Farquhar. She is such a nice woman, and so attentive to her husband. It's delightful to watch them.

ALGERNON: I am afraid, Aunt Augusta, I shall have to give up the pleasure of dining with you tonight after all.

LADY BRACKNELL: (*Frowning*) I hope not, Algernon. It would put my table completely out. Your uncle would have to dine upstairs. Fortunately he is accustomed to that.

ALGERNON: It is a great bore, and, I need hardly say, a terrible disappointment to me, but the fact is I have just had a telegram to say that my poor friend Bunbury is very ill again. (*Exchanges glances with* JACK) They seem to think I should be with him.

LADY BRACKNELL: It is very strange. This Mr. Bunbury seems to suffer from curiously bad health.

ALGERNON: Yes; poor Bunbury is a dreadful invalid.[14]

LADY BRACKNELL: Well, I must say, Algernon, that I think it is high time that Mr. Bunbury made up his mind whether he was going to live or to die. This shilly-shallying with the question is absurd. Nor do I in any way approve of the modern sympathy with invalids. I consider it morbid. Illness of any kind is hardly a thing to be encouraged in others. Health is the primary duty of life. I am always telling that to your poor uncle, but he never seems to take much notice . . . as far as any improvement in his ailments goes. I should be obliged if you would ask Mr. Bunbury, from me, to be kind enough not to have a relapse on Saturday, for I rely on you to arrange my music for me. It is my last reception, and one wants something that will encourage conversation, particularly at the end of the season[15] when everyone has practically said whatever they had to say, which, in most cases, was probably not much.

ALGERNON: I'll speak to Bunbury, Aunt Augusta, if he is still conscious, and I think I can promise you he'll be all right by Saturday. Of course the music is a great difficulty. You see, if one plays good music, people don't listen, and if one plays bad music, people don't talk. But I'll run over the programme I've drawn out, if you will kindly come into the next room for a moment.

LADY BRACKNELL: Thank you, Algernon. It is very thoughtful of you. (*Rising, and following* ALGERNON) I'm sure the programme will be delightful, after a few expurgations. French songs I cannot possibly allow. People always seem to think that they are improper, and either look shocked, which is vulgar, or laugh, which is worse. But

11. Lane betrays his master's financial embarrassment, just as earlier he had been accused of disloyalty for drinking Algernon's champagne.
12. Like muffins, a quintessentially English food.
13. A line in iambic pentameter. Wilde wrote that 'as one knows the poet by his fine music, so one can recognize the liar by his rich, rhythmic utterance' (*The Decay of Lying*). Synge employed similar iambic lines throughout *The Playboy of the Western World* (1907).
14. A fashionable literary complaint in the 1890s, invalidism was often associated with saintliness or piety.
15. The period of summer coming-out parties, at which debutantes were introduced to society. By the end of the season, young women such as Gwendolen were painfully anxious to secure partners.

German sounds a thoroughly respectable language, and indeed, I believe is so. Gwendolen, you will accompany me.

GWENDOLEN: Certainly, mamma.

LADY BRACKNELL *and* ALGERNON *go into the music room,* GWENDOLEN *remains behind.*

JACK: Charming day it has been, Miss Fairfax.

GWENDOLEN: Pray don't talk to me about the weather, Mr. Worthing. Whenever people talk to me about the weather, I always feel quite certain that they mean something else. And that makes me so nervous.

JACK: I do mean something else.

GWENDOLEN: I thought so. In fact, I am never wrong.

JACK: And I would like to be allowed to take advantage of Lady Bracknell's temporary absence . . . .

GWENDOLEN: I would certainly advise you to do so. Mamma has a way of coming back suddenly into a room that I have often had to speak to her about.

JACK: (*Nervously*) Miss Fairfax, ever since I met you I have admired you more than any girl . . . I have ever met since . . . I met you.[16]

GWENDOLEN: Yes, I am quite aware of the fact. And I often wish that in public, at any rate, you had been more demonstrative. For me you have always had an irresistible fascination. Even before I met you I was far from indifferent to you. (JACK *looks at her in amazement*) We live, as I hope you know, Mr. Worthing, in an age of ideals. The fact is constantly mentioned in the more expensive monthly magazines, and has reached the provincial pulpits, I am told: and my ideal has always been to love someone of the name of Ernest. There is something in that name that inspires absolute confidence.[17] The moment Algernon first mentioned to me that he had a friend called Ernest, I knew I was destined to love you.

JACK: You really love me, Gwendolen?

GWENDOLEN: Passionately!

JACK: Darling! You don't know how happy you've made me.

GWENDOLEN: My own Ernest!

JACK: But you don't really mean to say that you couldn't love me if my name wasn't Ernest?

GWENDOLEN: But your name is Ernest.

JACK: Yes, I know it is. But supposing it was something else? Do you mean to say you couldn't love me then?

GWENDOLEN: (*Glibly*) Ah! that is clearly a metaphysical speculation, and like most metaphysical speculations[18] has very little reference at all to the actual facts of real life, as we know them.

JACK: Personally, darling, to speak quite candidly, I don't much care about the name of Ernest . . . I don't think the name suits me at all.

GWENDOLEN: It suits you perfectly. It is a divine name. It has a music of its own. It produces vibrations.

JACK: Well, really, Gwendolen, I must say that I think there are lots of other much nicer names. I think Jack, for instance, a charming name.

GWENDOLEN: Jack? . . . No, there is very little music in the name Jack, if any at all, indeed. It does not thrill. It produces absolutely no vibrations. . . . I have known several Jacks, and they all, without exception, were more than usually plain. Besides, Jack is a notorious domesticity for John! And I pity any woman who is married to a man called John. She would probably never be allowed to know the entrancing pleasure of a single moment's solitude. The only really safe name is Ernest.

JACK: Gwendolen, I must get christened[19] at once — I mean we must get married at once. There is not time to be lost.

GWENDOLEN: Married, Mr. Worthing?

JACK: (*Astounded*) Well . . . surely. You know that I love you, and you led me to believe, Miss Fairfax, that you were not absolutely indifferent to me.

GWENDOLEN: I adore you. But you haven't proposed to me yet. Nothing has been said at all about marriage. The subject has not even been touched on.

JACK: Well . . . may I propose to you now?

GWENDOLEN: I think it would be an admirable opportunity. And to spare you any possible disappointment, Mr. Worthing, I think it only fair to tell you quite frankly beforehand that I am fully determined to accept you.

16. The only occasion on which Jack is lost for words, his inarticulateness here suggesting a depth of genuine emotion.
17. The German critic Schiller said that art helped man to overcome 'the earnestness of duty', yet the English novelist, George Eliot, described duty as 'peremptory and absolute'.
18. Wilde mocks the famous English distrust of abstraction. cf. 'Thinking is the most unhealthy thing in the world . . . . Fortunately, in England at any rate, thought is not catching' (*The Decay of Lying*).
19. Wilde himself, apparently, was christened twice — first in a protestant church and later, at the age of one, he was taken by his mother to a catholic priest.

JACK: Gwendolen!

GWENDOLEN: Yes, Mr. Worthing, what have you got to say to me?

JACK: You know what I have got to say to you.

GWENDOLEN: Yes, but you don't say it.

JACK: Gwendolen, will you marry me? (*Goes on his knees*)

GWENDOLEN: Of course I will, darling. How long you have been about it! I am afraid you have had very little experience in how to propose.

JACK: My own one, I have never loved anyone in the world but you.

GWENDOLEN: Yes, but men often propose for practice. I know my brother Gerald does. All my girlfriends tell me so. What wonderfully blue eyes you have, Ernest! They are quite, quite blue. I hope you will always look at me just like that, especially when there are other people present.

Enter LADY BRACKNELL.

LADY BRACKNELL: Mr. Worthing! Rise, sir, from this semi-recumbent posture. It is most indecorous.

GWENDOLEN: Mamma! (*He tries to rise; she restrains him*) I must beg you to retire. This is no place for you. Besides, Mr. Worthing has not quite finished yet.

LADY BRACKNELL: Finished what, may I ask?

GWENDOLEN: I am engaged to Mr. Worthing, mamma.

They rise together.

LADY BRACKNELL: Pardon me, you are not engaged to anyone. When you do become engaged to someone, I, or your father, should his health permit him, will inform you of the fact. An engagement should come on a young girl as a surprise, pleasant or unpleasant, as the case may be. It is hardly a matter that she could be allowed to arrange for herself. . . . And now I have a few questions to put to you, Mr. Worthing. While I am making these inquiries, you, Gwendolen, will wait for me below in the carriage.

GWENDOLEN: (*Reproachfully*) Mamma!

LADY BRACKNELL: In the carriage, Gwendolen! (GWENDOLEN *goes to the door. She and* JACK *blow kisses to each other behind* LADY BRACKNELL*'s back.* LADY BRACKNELL *looks vaguely about as if she could not understand what the noise was. Finally turns round*) Gwendolen, the carriage!

GWENDOLEN: Yes, mamma. (*Goes out, looking back at* JACK)

LADY BRACKNELL: (*Sitting down*) You can take a seat, Mr. Worthing. (*Looks in her pocket for notebook and pencil*)

JACK: Thank you, Lady Bracknell, I prefer standing.

LADY BRACKNELL: (*Pencil and notebook in hand*) I feel bound to tell you that you are not down on my list of eligible young men, although I have the same list as the dear Duchess of Bolton has. We work together, in fact. However, I am quite ready to enter your name, should your answers be what a really affectionate mother requires. Do you smoke?

JACK: Well, yes, I must admit I smoke.

LADY BRACKNELL: I am glad to hear it. A man should always have an occupation of some kind. There are far too many idle men in London as it is. How old are you?

JACK: Twenty-nine.

LADY BRACKNELL: A very good age to be married at. I have always been of opinion that a man who desires to get married should know either everything or nothing. Which do you know?

JACK: (*After some hesitation*) I know nothing, Lady Bracknell.

LADY BRACKNELL: I am pleased to hear it. I do not approve of anything that tampers with natural ignorance. Ignorance is like a delicate exotic fruit; touch it and the bloom is gone. The whole theory of modern education is radically unsound. Fortunately in England, at any rate, education produces no effect whatsoever. If it did, it would prove a serious danger to the upper classes, and probably lead to acts of violence in Grosvenor Square.[20] What is your income?

JACK: Between seven and eight thousand a year.

LADY BRACKNELL: (*Makes a note in her book*) In land, or in investments?

JACK: In investments, chiefly.

LADY BRACKNELL: That is satisfactory. What between the duties expected of one during one's lifetime, and the duties exacted from one after one's death, land has ceased to be either a profit or a pleasure. It gives one position, and prevents one from keeping it up.[21] That's all that can be said about land.

JACK: I have a country house with some land, of course, attached to it, about fifteen hundred acres, I

20. Fashionable locale for the wealthy and genteel.

21. cf. 'Property not merely has duties, but has so many duties that its possession is to a large extent a bore' (*The Soul of Man Under Socialism*).

believe; but I don't depend on that for my real income. In fact, as far as I can make out, the poachers are the only people who make anything out of it.

LADY BRACKNELL: A country house! How many bedrooms? Well, that point can be cleared up afterwards. You have a town house, I hope? A girl with a simple, unspoiled nature, like Gwendolen, could hardly be expected to reside in the country.

JACK: Well, I own a house in Belgrave Square, but it is let by the year to Lady Bloxham. Of course, I can get it back whenever I like, at six months' notice.

LADY BRACKNELL: Lady Bloxham? I don't know her.

JACK: Oh, she goes about very little. She is a lady considerably advanced in years.

LADY BRACKNELL: Ah, nowadays that is no guarantee of respectability of character. What number in Belgrave Square?

JACK: 149.

LADY BRACKNELL: (*Shaking her head*) The unfashionable side. I thought there was something. However, that could easily be altered.

JACK: Do you mean the fashion, or the side?

LADY BRACKNELL: (*Sternly*) Both, if necessary, I presume. What are your politics?

JACK: Well, I am afraid I really have none. I am a Liberal Unionist.[22]

LADY BRACKNELL: Oh, they count as Tories. They dine with us. Or come in the evening,[23] at any rate. Now to minor matters. Are your parents living?

JACK: I have lost both my parents.

LADY BRACKNELL: Both? ... That seems like carelessness. Who was your father? He was evidently a man of some wealth. Was he born in what the Radical papers call the purple of commerce, or did he rise from the ranks of aristocracy?

JACK: I am afraid I really don't know. The fact is, Lady Bracknell, I said I had lost my parents. It would be nearer the truth to say that my parents seem to have lost me.... I don't actually know who I am by birth. I was ... well, I was found.[24]

LADY BRACKNELL: Found!

JACK: The late Mr. Thomas Cardew, an old gentleman of a very charitable and kindly disposition, found me, and gave me the name of Worthing, because he happened to have a first-class ticket for Worthing in his pocket at the time. Worthing is a place in Sussex. It is a seaside resort.

LADY BRACKNELL: Where did the charitable gentleman who had a first-class ticket for this seaside resort find you?

JACK: (*Gravely*) In a handbag.

LADY BRACKNELL: A handbag?

JACK: (*Very seriously*) Yes, Lady Bracknell. I was in a handbag — a somewhat large, black leather handbag, with handles to it — an ordinary handbag, in fact.

LADY BRACKNELL: In what locality did this Mr. James, or Thomas, Cardew come across this ordinary handbag?

JACK: In the cloak room at Victoria Station. It was given to him in mistake for his own.

LADY BRACKNELL: The cloak room at Victoria Station?

JACK: Yes. The Brighton line.

LADY BRACKNELL: The line is immaterial. Mr. Worthing, I confess I feel somewhat bewildered by what you have just told me. To be born, or at any rate, bred in a handbag, whether it had handles or not, seems to be to display a contempt for the ordinary decencies of family life that remind one of the worst excesses of the French Revolution. And I presume you know what that unfortunate movement led to? As for the particular locality in which the handbag was found, a cloak room at a railway station might serve to conceal a social indiscretion[25] — has probably, indeed, been used for that purpose before now — but it could hardly be regarded as an assured basis for a recognized position in good society.

JACK: May I ask you then what you would advise me to do? I need hardly say I would do anything in the world to ensure Gwendolen's happiness.

LADY BRACKNELL: I would strongly advise you, Mr. Worthing, to try and acquire some relations as

22. A political group that was progressive on social questions, but staunchly conservative in opposing Gladstone's Home Rule Bills for Ireland.
23. The Irish, even the Unionists, were still regarded as semi-outsiders in the London of the 1890s. Wilde has been described by Mary McCarthy as an 'uninvited guest' whose sin was 'making himself too much at home'.
24. The notion of the self-invented man pervades the writings of Shaw, Nietzsche, Yeats and Joyce. Where nineteenth-century authors emphasized the establishment of parental lineage (such scenes are parodied at the end of the play), modernists preferred to disrupt all ideas of chronological progress.
25. That is, as a place to deposit an unwanted child.

soon as possible, and to make a definite effort to produce at any rate one parent, of either sex, before the season is quite over.[26]

JACK: Well, I don't see how I could possibly manage to do that. I can produce the handbag at any moment. It is in my dressing room at home. I really think that should satisfy you, Lady Bracknell.

LADY BRACKNELL: Me, sir! What has it to do with me? You can hardly imagine that I and Lord Bracknell would dream of allowing our only daughter — a girl brought up with the utmost care — to marry into a cloak room, and form an alliance with a parcel? Good morning, Mr. Worthing!

LADY BRACKNELL *sweeps out in majestic indignation.*

JACK: Good morning! (ALGERNON, *from the other room, strikes up the Wedding March.* JACK *looks perfectly furious, and goes to the door*) For goodness' sake don't play that ghastly tune, Algy! How idiotic you are!

The music stops, and ALGERNON *enters cheerily.*

ALGERNON: Didn't it go off all right, old boy? You don't mean to say Gwendolen refused you? I know it is a way she has. She is always refusing people. I think it is most ill-natured of her.

JACK: Oh, Gwendolen is as right as a trivet.[27] As far as she is concerned, we are engaged. Her mother is perfectly unbearable. Never met such a Gorgon[28] ... I don't really know what a Gorgon is like, but I am quite sure that Lady Bracknell is one. In any case, she is a monster, without being a myth, which is rather unfair.... I beg your pardon, Algy, I suppose I shouldn't talk about your own aunt in that way before you.

ALGERNON: My dear boy, I love hearing my relations abused. It is the only thing that makes me put up with them at all. Relations are simply a tedious pack of people who haven't got the remotest knowledge of how to live, nor the smallest instinct about when to die.

JACK: Oh, that is nonsense!

ALGERNON: It isn't!

JACK: Well, I won't argue about the matter. You always want to argue about things.

ALGERNON: That is exactly what things were originally made for.

JACK: Upon my word, if I thought that, I'd shoot myself.... (*A pause*) You don't think there is any chance of Gwendolen becoming like her mother in about a hundred and fifty years, do you, Algy?

ALGERNON: All women become like their mothers. That is their tragedy. No man does. That's his.

JACK: Is that clever?

ALGERNON: It is perfectly phrased! and quite as true as any observation in civilized life should be.

JACK: I am sick to death of cleverness. Everybody is clever nowadays. You can't go anywhere without meeting clever people. The thing has become an absolute public nuisance. I wish to goodness we had a few fools left.

ALGERNON: We have.

JACK: I should extremely like to meet them. What do they talk about?

ALGERNON: The fools? Oh! about the clever people, of course.

JACK: What fools!

ALGERNON: By the way, did you tell Gwendolen the truth about your being Ernest in town, and Jack in the country?

JACK: (*In a very patronizing manner*) My dear fellow, the truth[29] isn't quite the sort of thing one tells to a nice sweet refined girl. What extraordinary ideas you have about the way to behave to a woman!

ALGERNON: The only way to behave to a woman is to make love to her, if she is pretty, and to someone else if she is plain.

JACK: Oh, that is nonsense.

ALGERNON: What about the young lady whose guardian you are? Miss Cardew! What about your brother? What about the profligate Ernest?

JACK: Oh! Cecily is all right. Before the end of the week I shall have got rid of my brother. I'll say he died in Paris of apoplexy. Lots of people die of apoplexy, quite suddenly, don't they?

ALGERNON: Yes, but it's hereditary, my dear fellow. It's a sort of thing that runs in families. You had much better say a severe chill.

JACK: You are sure a severe chill isn't hereditary, or anything of that kind?

ALGERNON: Of course it isn't!

JACK: Very well, then. My poor brother Ernest is

26. cf. Nietzsche: 'If you haven't had a good father, you had better invent one.'
27. i.e. in perfect health. A trivet is a secure tripod, used to hold pots over a fire.
28. A horror, one of three female monsters (Stheno, Euryale and Medusa) in Greek myth, with hissing serpents for hair.
29. The first of many explorations of the meaning of the word.

carried off suddenly in Paris, by a severe chill. That gets rid of him.

ALGERNON: But I thought you said that . . . Miss Cardew was a little too much interested in your poor brother Ernest? Won't she feel his loss a good deal?

JACK: Oh, that is all right. Cecily is not a silly romantic girl, I am glad to say. She has got a capital appetite, goes on long walks, and pays no attention at all to her lessons.

ALGERNON: I would rather like to see Cecily.

JACK: I will take very good care you never do. She is excessively pretty, and she is only just eighteen.

ALGERNON: Have you told Gwendolen yet that you have an excessively pretty ward who is only just eighteen?

JACK: Oh! one doesn't blurt these things out to people. Cecily and Gwendolen are perfectly certain to be extremely great friends. I'll bet you anything you like that half an hour after they have met, they will be calling each other sister.

ALGERNON: Women only do that when they have called each other a lot of other things first. Now, my dear boy, if we want to get a good table at Willis's, we really must go and dress. Do you know it is nearly seven?

JACK: (*Irritably*) Oh! it always is nearly seven.

ALGERNON: Well, I'm hungry.

JACK: I never knew you when you weren't. . . .

ALGERNON: What shall we do after dinner? Go to the theatre?

JACK: Oh no! I loathe listening.

ALGERNON: Well, let us go the club?

JACK: Oh, no! I hate talking.

ALGERNON: Well, we might trot around to the Empire[30] at ten?

JACK: Oh no! I can't bear looking at things. It is so silly.

ALGERNON: Well, what shall we do?

JACK: Nothing!

ALGERNON: It is awfully hard work doing nothing. However, I don't mind hard work where there is no definite object of any kind.

Enter LANE.

LANE: Miss Fairfax.

Enter GWENDOLEN. LANE *goes out*.

ALGERNON: Gwendolen, upon my word!

GWENDOLEN: Algy, kindly turn your back. I have something very particular to say to Mr. Worthing.

ALGERNON: Really, Gwendolen, I don't think I can allow this at all.

GWENDOLEN: Algy, you always adopt a strictly immoral attitude towards life. You are not quite old enough to do that.

ALGERNON *retires to the fireplace*.

JACK: My own darling!

GWENDOLEN: Ernest, we may never be married. From the expression on mamma's face I fear we never shall. Few parents nowadays pay any regard to what their children say to them. The old-fashioned respect for the young is fast dying out. Whatever influence I ever had over mamma, I lost at the age of three. But although she may prevent us from becoming man and wife, and I may marry someone else, and marry often, nothing that she can possibly do can alter my eternal devotion to you.

JACK: Dear Gwendolen!

GWENDOLEN: The story of your romantic origin, as related to me by mamma, with unpleasing comments, has naturally stirred the deeper fibres of my nature. Your Christian name has an irresistible fascination. The simplicity of your character makes you exquisitely incomprehensible to me. Your town address at the Albany I have. What is your address in the country?

JACK: The Manor House, Woolton, Hertfordshire.

ALGERNON, *who has been carefully listening, smiles to himself, and writes the address on his shirt-cuff. Then picks up the Railway Guide.*

GWENDOLEN: There is a good postal service, I suppose? It may be necessary to do something desperate. That of course will require serious consideration. I will communicate with you daily.

JACK: My own one!

GWENDOLEN: How long do you remain in town?

JACK: Till Monday.

GWENDOLEN: Good! Algy, you may turn round now.

ALGERNON: Thanks, I've turned round already.

GWENDOLEN: You may also ring the bell.

JACK: You will let me see you to your carriage, my own darling?

GWENDOLEN: Certainly.

JACK: (*To* LANE, *who now enters*) I will see Miss Fairfax out.

LANE: Yes, sir.

JACK *and* GWENDOLEN *go off*. LANE *presents several*

30. A west end London music hall.

letters on a salver to ALGERNON. *It is to be surmised that they are bills, as* ALGERNON, *after looking at the envelopes, tears them up.*

ALGERNON: A glass of sherry, Lane.

LANE: Yes, sir.

ALGERNON: Tomorrow, Lane, I'm going Bunburying.

LANE: Yes, sir.

ALGERNON: I shall probably not be back till Monday. You can put up my dress clothes, my smoking jacket, and all the Bunbury suits. . . .

LANE: Yes, sir. (*Handing sherry*)

ALGERNON: I hope tomorrow will be a fine day, Lane.

LANE: It never is, sir.

ALGERNON: Lane, you're a perfect pessimist.

LANE: I do my best to give satisfaction, sir.

Enter JACK. LANE *goes off.*

JACK: There's a sensible, intellectual girl! the only girl I ever cared for in my life. (ALGERNON *is laughing immoderately*) What on earth are you so amused at?

ALGERNON: Oh, I'm a little anxious about poor Bunbury, that is all.

JACK: If you don't take care, your friend Bunbury will get you into a serious scrape some day.

ALGERNON: I love scrapes. They are the only things that are never serious.

JACK: Oh, that's nonsense, Algy. You never talk anything but nonsense.

ALGERNON: Nobody ever does.

JACK *looks indignantly at him, and leaves the room.* ALGERNON *lights a cigarette, reads his shirt-cuff, and smiles.*

ACT II

SCENE — *Garden at the Manor House, Woolton. A flight of grey stone steps leads up to the house. The garden, an old-fashioned one, full of roses. Time of year, July. Basket chairs, and a table covered with books, are set under a large yew tree.*

MISS PRISM *discovered seated at the table.* CECILY *is at the back watering flowers.*

MISS PRISM: (*Calling*) Cecily, Cecily! Surely such a utilitarian occupation as the watering of flowers is rather Moulton's duty than yours? Especially at a moment when intellectual pleasures await you. Your German grammar is on the table. Pray open it at page fifteen. We will repeat yesterday's lesson.

CECILY: (*Coming over very slowly*) But I don't like German. It isn't at all a becoming language. I know perfectly well that I look quite plain after my German lesson.[1]

MISS PRISM: Child, you know how anxious your guardian is that you should improve yourself in every way. He laid particular stress on your German, as he was leaving for town yesterday. Indeed, he always lays stress on your German when he is leaving for town.

CECILY: Dear Uncle Jack is so very serious! Sometime he is so serious that I think he cannot be quite well.

MISS PRISM: (*Drawing herself up*) Your guardian enjoys the best of health, and his gravity of demeanour is especially to be commended in one so comparatively young as he is. I know no one who has a higher sense of duty and responsibility.

CECILY: I suppose that is why he often looks a little bored when we three are together.

MISS PRISM: Cecily! I am surprised at you. Mr. Worthing has many troubles in his life. Idle merriment and triviality would be out of place in his conversation. You must remember his constant anxiety about that unfortunate young man his brother.

CECILY: I wish Uncle Jack would allow that unfortunate young man, his brother, to come down here sometimes. We might have a good influence over him, Miss Prism. I am sure you certainly would. You know German, and geology, and things of that kind influence a man very much. (*Begins to write in her diary*)

MISS PRISM: (*Shaking her head*) I do not think that even I could produce any effect on a character that according to his own brother's admission is irretrievably weak and vacillating. Indeed I am not sure that I would desire to reclaim him. I am not in favour of this modern mania for turning bad people into good people at a moment's notice. As a man sows so let him reap. You must put away your diary, Cecily. I really don't see why you should keep a diary at all.

CECILY: I keep a diary in order to enter the wonderful secrets of my life. If I didn't write them down I should probably forget all about them.

MISS PRISM: Memory, my dear Cecily, is the diary that we all carry about with us.

1. German sobriety was considered a trusty counter to French triviality and decadence.

CECILY: Yes, but it usually chronicles the things that have never happened, and couldn't possibly have happened. I believe that Memory is responsible for nearly all the three-volume novels that Mudie[2] sends us.

MISS PRISM: Do not speak slightingly of the three-volume novel, Cecily. I wrote one myself in earlier days.

CECILY: Did you really, Miss Prism? How wonderfully clever you are! I hope it did not end happily? I don't like novels that end happily. They depress me so much.

MISS PRISM: The good ended happily, and the bad unhappily. That is what Fiction means.

CECILY: I suppose so. But it seems very unfair. And was your novel ever published?

MISS PRISM: Alas! no. The manuscript unfortunately was abandoned. I use the word in the sense of lost or mislaid. To your work, child, these speculations are profitless.

CECILY: (*Smiling*) But I see dear Dr. Chasuble coming up through the garden.

MISS PRISM: (*Rising and advancing*) Dr. Chasuble! This is indeed a pleasure.

Enter CANON CHASUBLE.

CHASUBLE: And how are we this morning? Miss Prism, you are, I trust, well?

CECILY: Miss Prism has just been complaining of a slight headache. I think it would do her so much good to have a short stroll with you in the Park, Dr. Chasuble.

MISS PRISM: Cecily, I have not mentioned anything about a headache.

CECILY: No, dear Miss Prism, I know that, but I felt instinctively that you had a headache. Indeed I was thinking about that, and not about my German lesson, when the Rector came in.

CHASUBLE: I hope Cecily, you are not inattentive.

CECILY: Oh, I am afraid I am.

CHASUBLE: That is strange. Were I fortunate enough to be Miss Prism's pupil, I would hang upon her lips. (MISS PRISM *glares*) I spoke metaphorically. — My metaphor was drawn from bees. Ahem! Mr. Worthing, I suppose, has not returned from town yet?

MISS PRISM: We do not expect him till Monday afternoon.

CHASUBLE: Ah yes, he usually likes to spend his Sunday in London. He is not one of those whose sole aim is enjoyment, as, by all accounts, that unfortunate young man his brother seems to be. But I must not disturb Egeria[3] and her pupil any longer.

MISS PRISM: Egeria? My name is Laetitia, Doctor.

CHASUBLE: (*Bowing*) A classical allusion merely, drawn from the Pagan authors. I shall see you both no doubt at Evensong?[4]

MISS PRISM: I think, dear Doctor, I will have a stroll with you. I find I have a headache after all, and a walk might do it good.

CHASUBLE: With pleasure, Miss Prism, with pleasure. We might go as far as the schools and back.

MISS PRISM: That would be delightful. Cecily, you will read your Political Economy in my absence. The chapter on the Fall of the Rupee you may omit. It is somewhat too sensational. Even these metallic problems have their melodramatic side. (*Goes down the garden with* DR. CHASUBLE)

CECILY: (*Picks up books and throws them back on table*) Horrid Political Economy! Horrid Geography! Horrid, horrid German!

Enter MERRIMAN *with a card on a salver.*

MERRIMAN: Mr. Ernest Worthing has just driven over from the station. He has brought his luggage with him.

CECILY: (*Takes the card and reads it*) 'Mr. Ernest Worthing, B. 4, The Albany, W.' Uncle Jack's brother! Did you tell him Mr. Worthing was in town?

MERRIMAN: Yes, Miss. He seemed very much disappointed. I mentioned that you and Miss Prism were in the garden. He said he was anxious to speak to you privately for a moment.

CECILY: Ask Mr. Ernest Worthing to come here. I suppose you had better talk to the housekeeper about a room for him.

MERRIMAN: Yes, Miss.

MERRIMAN *goes off.*

CECILY: I have never met any really wicked person before. I feel rather frightened. I am so afraid he will look just like everyone else. (*Enter* ALGERNON, *very gay and debonair*) He does!

ALGERNON: (*Raising his hat*) You are my little cousin Cecily, I'm sure.

2. A circulating library, specializing in romantic novels.

3. In classical mythology, a goddess. Legend recounts that the nymph Egeria gave advice and counsel to Numa, the second king of Rome.

4. The daily church service of evening prayer and Bible readings.

CECILY: You are under some strange mistake. I am not little. In fact, I believe I am more than usually tall for my age. (ALGERNON *is rather taken aback*) But I am your cousin Cecily. You, I see from your card, are Uncle Jack's brother, my cousin Ernest, my wicked cousin Ernest.

ALGERNON: Oh! I am not really wicked at all, cousin Cecily. You mustn't think that I am wicked.

CECILY: If you are not, then you have certainly been deceiving us all in a very inexcusable manner. I hope you have not been leading a double life, pretending to be wicked and being really good all the time. That would be hypocrisy.

ALGERNON: (*Looks at her in amazement*) Oh! Of course I have been rather reckless.

CECILY: I am glad to hear it.

ALGERNON: In fact, now you mention the subject, I have been very bad in my own small way.

CECILY: I don't think you should be so proud of that, though I am sure it must have been very pleasant.

ALGERNON: It is much pleasanter being here with you.

CECILY: I can't understand how you are here at all. Uncle Jack won't be back till Monday afternoon.

ALGERNON: That is a great disappointment. I am obliged to go up by the first train on Monday morning. I have a business appointment that I am anxious . . . to miss.

CECILY: Couldn't you miss it anywhere but in London?

ALGERNON: No: the appointment is in London.

CECILY: Well, I know, of course, how important it is not to keep a business engagement, if one wants to retain any sense of the beauty of life, but still I think you had better wait till Uncle Jack arrives. I know he wants to speak to you about your emigrating.

ALGERNON: About my what?

CECILY: Your emigrating. He has gone up to buy your outfit.

ALGERNON: I certainly wouldn't let Jack buy my outfit. He has no taste in neckties at all.

CECILY: I don't think you will require neckties. Uncle Jack is sending you to Australia.

ALGERNON: Australia? I'd sooner die.

CECILY: Well, he said at dinner on Wednesday night, that you would have to choose between this world, the next world, and Australia.

ALGERNON: Oh, well! The accounts I have received of Australia and the next world are not particularly encouraging. This world is good enough for me, cousin Cecily.

CECILY: Yes, but are you good enough for it?

ALGERNON: I'm afraid I'm not that. That is why I want you to reform me. You might make that your mission, if you don't mind, cousin Cecily.

CECILY: I'm afraid I've no time, this afternoon.

ALGERNON: Well, would you mind my reforming myself this afternoon?

CECILY: It is rather Quixotic of you. But I think you should try.

ALGERNON: I will. I feel better already.

CECILY: You are looking a little worse.

ALGERNON: That is because I am hungry.

CECILY: How thoughtless of me. I should have remembered that when one is going to lead an entirely new life, one requires regular and wholesome meals. Won't you come in?

ALGERNON: Thank you. Might I have a buttonhole first? I never have any appetite unless I have a buttonhole first.

CECILY: A Maréchal Niel?[5] (*Picks up scissors*)

ALGERNON: No, I'd sooner have a pink rose.

CECILY: Why? (*Cuts a flower*)

ALGERNON: Because you are like a pink rose, cousin Cecily.

CECILY: I don't think it can be right for you to talk to me like that. Miss Prism never says such things to me.

ALGERNON: Then Miss Prism is a shortsighted old lady. (CECILY *puts the rose in his buttonhole*) You are the prettiest girl I ever saw.

CECILY: Miss Prism says that all good looks are a snare.

ALGERNON: They are a snare that every sensible man would like to be caught in.

CECILY: Oh! I don't think I would care to catch a sensible man. I shouldn't know what to talk to him about.

They pass into the house. MISS PRISM *and* DR. CHASUBLE *return.*

MISS PRISM: You are too much alone, dear Dr. Chasuble. You should get married. A misanthrope I can understand — a womanthrope, never!

CHASUBLE: (*With a scholar's shudder*) Believe me, I do not deserve so neologistic a phrase. The precept as well as the practice of the Primitive Church was distinctly against matrimony.

5. A yellow rose, named after one of Napoleon III's generals.

MISS PRISM: (*Sententiously*) That is obviously the reason why the Primitive Church has not lasted up to the present day. And you do not seem to realize, dear Doctor, that by persistently remaining single, a man converts himself into a permanent public temptation. Men should be more careful; this very celibacy leads weaker vessels astray.

CHASUBLE: But is a man not equally attractive when married?

MISS PRISM: No married man is ever attractive except to his wife.

CHASUBLE: And often, I've been told, not even to her.

MISS PRISM: That depends on the intellectual sympathies of the woman. Maturity can always be depended on. Ripeness can be trusted. Young women are green. (DR. CHASUBLE *starts*) I spoke horticulturally. My metaphor was drawn from fruits. But where is Cecily?

CHASUBLE: Perhaps she followed us to the schools.

Enter JACK *slowly from the back of the garden. He is dressed in the deepest mourning, with crape hat-band and black gloves.*

MISS PRISM: Mr. Worthing!

CHASUBLE: Mr. Worthing?

MISS PRISM: This is indeed a surprise. We did not look for you till Monday afternoon.

JACK: (*Shakes* MISS PRISM'*s hand in a tragic manner*) I have returned sooner than I expected. Dr. Chasuble, I hope you are well?

CHASUBLE: Dear Mr. Worthing, I trust this garb of woe does not betoken some terrible calamity?

JACK: My brother.

MISS PRISM: More shameful debts and extravagance?

CHASUBLE: Still leading his life of pleasure?

JACK: (*Shaking his head*) Dead!

CHASUBLE: Your brother Ernest dead?

JACK: Quite dead.

MISS PRISM: What a lesson for him! I trust he will profit by it.

CHASUBLE: Mr. Worthing, I offer you my sincere condolence. You have at least the consolation of knowing that you were always the most generous and forgiving of brothers.

JACK: Poor Ernest! He had many faults, but it is a sad, sad blow.

CHASUBLE: Very sad indeed. Were you with him at the end?

JACK: No. He died abroad; in Paris, in fact. I had a telegram last night from the manager of the Grand Hotel.

CHASUBLE: Was the cause of death mentioned?

JACK: A severe chill, it seems.

MISS PRISM: As a man sows, so shall he reap.

CHASUBLE: (*Raising his hand*) Charity, dear Miss Prism, charity! None of us are perfect. I myself am peculiarly susceptible to draughts. Will the interment take place here?

JACK: No. He seemed to have expressed a desire to be buried in Paris.

CHASUBLE: In Paris! (*Shakes his head*) I fear that hardly points to any very serious state of mind at the last. You would no doubt wish me to make some slight allusion to this tragic domestic affliction next Sunday. (JACK *presses his hand convulsively*) My sermon on the meaning of the manna in the wilderness can be adapted to almost any occasion, joyful, or, as in the present case, distressing. (*All sigh*) I have preached it at harvest celebrations, christenings, confirmations, on days of humiliation and festal days. The last time I delivered it was in the Cathedral, as a charity sermon on behalf of the Society for the Prevention of Discontent among the Upper Orders. The Bishop, who was present, was much struck by some of the analogies I drew.

JACK: Ah! That reminds me, you mentioned christenings, I think, Dr. Chasuble? I suppose you know how to christen all right? (DR. CHASUBLE *looks astounded*) I mean, of course, you are continually christening, aren't you?

MISS PRISM: It is, I regret to say, one of the Rector's most constant duties in this parish. I have often spoken to the poorer classes on the subject. But they don't seem to know what thrift is.

CHASUBLE: But is there any particular infant in whom you are interested, Mr. Worthing? Your brother was, I believe, unmarried, was he not?

JACK: Oh yes.

MISS PRISM: (*Bitterly*) People who live entirely for pleasure usually are.

JACK: But it is not for any child, dear Doctor. I am very fond of children. No! the fact is, I would like to be christened myself, this afternoon, if you have nothing better to do.

CHASUBLE: But surely, Mr. Worthing, you have been christened already?

JACK: I don't remember anything about it.

CHASUBLE: But have you any grave doubts on the subject?

JACK: I certainly intend to have. Of course I don't

know if the thing would bother you in any way, or if you think I am a little too old now.

CHASUBLE: Not at all. The sprinkling, and, indeed, the immersion of adults is a perfectly canonical practice.

JACK: Immersion!

CHASUBLE: You need have no apprehensions. Sprinkling is all that is necessary, or indeed I think advisable. Our weather is so changeable. At what hour would you wish the ceremony performed?

JACK: Oh, I might trot round about five if that would suit you.

CHASUBLE: Perfectly, perfectly! In fact I have two similar ceremonies to perform at that time. A case of twins that occurred recently in one of the outlying cottages on your own estate. Poor Jenkins the carter, a most hard-working man.

JACK: Oh! I don't see much fun in being christened along with other babies. It would be childish. Would half-past five do?

CHASUBLE: Admirably! Admirably! (*Takes out watch*) And now, dear Mr. Worthing, I will not intrude any longer into a house of sorrow. I would merely beg you not to be too much bowed down by grief. What seem to us bitter trials are often blessings in disguise.

MISS PRISM: This seems to me a blessing of an extremely obvious kind.

Enter CECILY *from the house.*

CECILY: Uncle Jack! Oh, I am pleased to see you back. But what horrid clothes you have got on! Do go and change them.

MISS PRISM: Cecily!

CHASUBLE: My child! my child!

CECILY *goes towards* JACK; *he kisses her brow in a melancholy manner.*

CECILY: What is the matter, Uncle Jack? Do look happy! You look as if you had toothache, and I have got such a surprise for you. Who do you think is in the dining room? Your brother!

JACK: Who?

CECILY: Your brother Ernest. He arrived about half an hour ago.

JACK: What nonsense! I haven't got a brother!

CECILY: Oh, don't say that. However badly he may have behaved to you in the past he is still your brother. You couldn't be so heartless as to disown him. I'll tell him to come out. And you will shake hands with him, won't you, Uncle Jack? (*Runs back into the house*)

CHASUBLE: These are very joyful tidings.

MISS PRISM: After we had all been resigned to his loss, his sudden return seems to me peculiarly distressing.

JACK: My brother is in the dining room? I don't know what it all means. I think it is perfectly absurd.

Enter ALGERNON *and* CECILY *hand in hand. They come slowly up to* JACK.

JACK: Good heavens! (*Motions* ALGERNON *away*)

ALGERNON: Brother John, I have come down from town to tell you that I am very sorry for all the trouble I have given you, and that I intend to lead a better life in the future.

JACK *glares at him and does not take his hand.*

CECILY: Uncle Jack, you are not going to refuse your own brother's hand?

JACK: Nothing will induce me to take his hand. I think his coming down here disgraceful. He knows perfectly well why.

CECILY: Uncle Jack, do be nice. There is some good in everyone. Ernest has just been telling me about his poor invalid friend Mr. Bunbury whom he goes to visit so often. And surely there must be much good in one who is kind to an invalid, and leaves the pleasures of London to sit by a bed of pain.

JACK: Oh! he has been talking about Bunbury, has he?

CECILY: Yes, he has told me all about poor Mr. Bunbury, and his terrible state of health.

JACK: Bunbury! Well, I won't have him talk to you about Bunbury or about anything else. It is enough to drive one perfectly frantic.

ALGERNON: Of course I admit that the faults were all on my side. But I must say that I think that Brother John's coldness to me is peculiarly painful. I expected a more enthusiastic welcome, especially considering it is the first time I have come here.

CECILY: Uncle Jack, if you don't shake hands with Ernest, I will never forgive you.

JACK: Never forgive me?

CECILY: Never, never, never!

JACK: Well, this is the last time I shall ever do it. (*Shakes hands with* ALGERNON *and glares*)

CHASUBLE: It's pleasant, is it not, to see so perfect a reconciliation? I think we might leave the two brothers together.

MISS PRISM: Cecily, you will come with us.

CECILY: Certainly, Miss Prism. My little task of reconciliation is over.

CHASUBLE: You have done a beautiful action today, dear child.

MISS PRISM: We must not be premature in our judgments.

CECILY: I feel very happy.

They all go off.

JACK: You young scoundrel, Algy, you must get out of this place as soon as possible. I don't allow any Bunburying here.

Enter MERRIMAN.

MERRIMAN: I have put Mr. Ernest's things in the room next to yours, sir. I suppose that is all right?

JACK: What?

MERRIMAN: Mr. Ernest's luggage, sir. I have unpacked it and put it in the room next to your own.

JACK: His luggage?

MERRIMAN: Yes, sir. Three portmanteaus, a dressing case, two hat-boxes, and a large luncheon basket.

ALGERNON: I am afraid I can't stay more than a week this time.

JACK: Merriman, order the dogcart[6] at once. Mr. Ernest has been suddenly called back to town.

MERRIMAN: Yes, sir.

Goes back into the house.

ALGERNON: What a fearful liar you are, Jack. I have not been called back to town at all.

JACK: Yes, you have.

ALGERNON: I haven't heard anyone call me.

JACK: Your duty as a gentleman calls you back.

ALGERNON: My duty as a gentleman has never interfered with my pleasures in the smallest degree.

JACK: I can quite understand that.

ALGERNON: Well, Cecily is a darling.

JACK: You are not to talk of Miss Cardew like that. I don't like it.

ALGERNON: Well, I don't like your clothes. You look perfectly ridiculous in them. Why on earth don't you go up and change? It is perfectly childish to be in deep mourning for a man who is actually staying for a whole week with you in your house as a guest. I call it grotesque.

JACK: You are certainly not staying with me for a whole week as a guest or anything else. You have got to leave ... by the four-five train.

ALGERNON: I certainly won't leave you so long as you are in mourning. It would be most unfriendly. If I were in mourning you would stay with me, I suppose. I should think it very unkind if you didn't.

JACK: Well, will you go if I change my clothes?

ALGERNON: Yes, if you are not too long. I never saw anybody take so long to dress, and with such little result.

JACK: Well, at any rate, that is better than being always overdressed as you are.

ALGERNON: If I am occasionally a little overdressed, I make up for it by being always immensely overeducated.

JACK: Your vanity is ridiculous, your conduct an outrage, and your presence in my garden utterly absurd. However, you have got to catch the four-five, and I hope you will have a pleasant journey back to town. This Bunburying, as you call it, has not been a great success for you. (*Goes into the house*)

ALGERNON: I think it has been a great success. I'm in love with Cecily, and that is everything. (*Enter* CECILY *at the back of the garden. She picks up the can and begins to water the flowers*) But I must see her before I go, and make arrangements for another Bunbury. Ah, there she is.

CECILY: Oh, I merely came back to water the roses. I thought you were with Uncle Jack.

ALGERNON: He's gone to order the dogcart for me.

CECILY: Oh, is he going to take you for a nice drive?

ALGERNON: He's going to send me away.

CECILY: Then have we got to part?

ALGERNON: I am afraid so. It's very painful parting.

CECILY: It is always painful to part from people whom one has known for a very brief space of time. The absence of old friends one can endure with equanimity. But even a momentary separation from anyone to whom one has has just been introduced is almost unbearable.

ALGERNON: Thank you.

Enter MERRIMAN.

MERRIMAN: The dogcart is at the door, sir.

ALGERNON *looks appealingly at* CECILY.

CECILY: It can wait, Merriman ... for ... five minutes.

MERRIMAN: Yes, Miss.

Exit MERRIMAN.

ALGERNON: I hope, Cecily, I shall not offend you if I state quite frankly and openly that you seem to me to be in every way the visible personification of absolute perfection.

6. A horse-drawn, two-wheeled carriage, often used by hunters and their dogs.

CECILY: I think your frankness does you great credit, Ernest. If you will allow me I will copy your remarks into my diary. (*Goes over to table and begins writing in diary*)

ALGERNON: Do you really keep a diary? I'd give anything to look at it. May I?

CECILY: Oh no. (*Puts her hand over it*) You see, it is simply a very young girl's record of her own thoughts and impressions, and consequently meant for publication. When it appears in volume form I hope you will order a copy. But pray, Ernest, don't stop. I delight in taking down from dictation. I have reached 'absolute perfection.' You can go on. I am quite ready for more.

ALGERNON: (*Somewhat taken aback*) Ahem! Ahem!

CECILY: Oh, don't cough, Ernest. When one is dictating one should speak fluently and not cough. Besides, I don't know how to spell a cough. (*Writes as* ALGERNON *speaks*)

ALGERNON: (*Speaking very rapidly*) Cecily, ever since I first looked upon your wonderful and incomparable beauty, I have dared to love you wildly, passionately, devotedly, hopelessly.

CECILY: I don't think that you should tell me that you love me wildly, passionately, devotedly, hopelessly. Hopelessly doesn't seem to make much sense, does it?

ALGERNON: Cecily!

Enter MERRIMAN.

MERRIMAN: The dogcart is waiting, sir.

ALGERNON: Tell it to come round next week, at the same hour.

MERRIMAN: (*Looks at* CECILY, *who makes no sign*) Yes, sir.

MERRIMAN *retires.*

CECILY: Uncle Jack would be very much annoyed if he knew you were staying on till next week, at the same hour.

ALGERNON: Oh, I don't care about Jack. I don't care for anybody in the whole world but you. I love you, Cecily. You will marry me, won't you?

CECILY: You silly boy! Of course. Why, we have been engaged for the last three months.

ALGERNON: For the last three months?

CECILY: Yes, it will be exactly three months on Thursday.

ALGERNON: But how did we become engaged?

CECILY: Well, ever since dear Uncle Jack first confessed to us that he had a younger brother who was very wicked and bad, you of course have formed the chief topic of conversation between myself and Miss Prism. And of course a man who is much talked about is always very attractive. One feels there must be something in him after all. I daresay it was foolish of me, but I fell in love with you, Ernest.

ALGERNON: Darling! And when was the engagement actually settled?

CECILY: On the 14th of February last. Worn out by your entire ignorance of my existence, I determined to end the matter one way or the other, and after a long struggle with myself I accepted you under this dear old tree here. The next day I bought this little ring in your name, and this is the little bangle with the true lovers' knot I promised you always to wear.

ALGERNON: Did I give you this? It's very pretty, isn't it?

CECILY: Yes, you've wonderfully good taste, Ernest. It's the excuse I've always given for your leading such a bad life. And this is the box in which I keep all your dear letters. (*Kneels at table, opens box, and produces letters tied up with blue ribbon*)

ALGERNON: My letters! But my own sweet Cecily, I have never written you any letters.

CECILY: You need hardly remind me of that, Ernest. I remember only too well that I was forced to write your letters for you. I always wrote three times a week, and sometimes oftener.

ALGERNON: Oh, do let me read them, Cecily?

CECILY: Oh, I couldn't possibly. They would make you far too conceited. (*Replaces box*) The three you wrote me after I had broken off the engagement are so beautiful, and so badly spelled, that even now I can hardly read them without crying a little.

ALGERNON: But was our engagement ever broken off?

CECILY: Of course it was. On the 22nd of last March. You can see the entry if you like. (*Shows diary*)'Today I broke off my engagement with Ernest. I feel it is better to do so. The weather still continues charming.'

ALGERNON: But why on earth did you break it off? What had I done? I had done nothing at all. Cecily, I am very much hurt indeed to hear you broke it off. Particularly when the weather was so charming.

CECILY: It would hardly have been a really serious engagement if it hadn't been broken off at least once. But I forgave you before the week was out.

ALGERNON: (*Crossing to her, and kneeling*) What a perfect angel you are, Cecily.

CECILY: You dear romantic boy. (*He kisses her, she puts her fingers through his hair*) I hope your hair curls naturally, does it?

ALGERNON: Yes, darling, with a little help from others.

CECILY: I am so glad.

ALGERNON: You'll never break off our engagement again, Cecily?

CECILY: I don't think I could break it off now that I have actually met you. Besides, of course, there is the question of your name.

ALGERNON: (*Nervously*) Yes, of course.

CECILY: You must not laugh at me, darling, but it had always been a girlish dream of mine to love someone whose name was Ernest. (ALGERNON *rises,* CECILY *also*) There is something in that name that seems to inspire absolute confidence. I pity any poor married woman whose husband is not called Ernest.

ALGERNON: But, my dear child, do you mean to say you could not love me if I had some other name?

CECILY: But what name?

ALGERNON: Oh, any name you like — Algernon — for instance. . . .

CECILY: But I don't like the name of Algernon.

ALGERNON: Well, my own dear, sweet, loving little darling, I really can't see why you should object to the name of Algernon. It is not at all a bad name. In fact, it is rather an aristocratic name. Half of the chaps who get into the Bankruptcy Court are called Algernon. But seriously, Cecily . . . (*Moving to her*) . . . if my name was Algy, couldn't you love me?

CECILY: (*Rising*) I might respect you, Ernest, I might admire your character, but I fear that I should not be able to give you my undivided attention.

ALGERNON: Ahem! Cecily! (*Picking up hat*) Your Rector here is, I suppose, thoroughly experienced in the practice of all the rites and ceremonials of the Church?

CECILY: Oh, yes. Dr. Chasuble is a most learned man. He has never written a single book, so you can imagine how much he knows.

ALGERNON: I must see him at once on a most important christening — I mean on most important business.

CECILY: Oh!

ALGERNON: I shan't be away more than half an hour.

CECILY: Considering that we have been engaged since February the 14th, and that I only met you today for the first time, I think it is rather hard that you should leave me for so long a period as half an hour. Couldn't you make it twenty minutes?

ALGERNON: I'll be back in no time. (*Kisses her and rushes down the garden*)

CECILY: What an impetuous boy he is! I like his hair so much. I must enter his proposal in my diary.

Enter MERRIMAN.

MERRIMAN: A Miss Fairfax has just called to see Mr. Worthing. On very important business, Miss Fairfax states.

CECILY: Isn't Mr. Worthing in his library?

MERRIMAN: Mr. Worthing went over in the direction of the Rectory some time ago.

CECILY: Pray ask the lady to come out here; Mr. Worthing is sure to be back soon. And you can bring tea.

MERRIMAN: Yes, Miss.

Goes out.

CECILY: Miss Fairfax! I suppose one of the many good elderly women who are associated with Uncle Jack in some of his philanthropic work in London. I don't quite like women who are interested in philanthropic work. I think it is so forward of them.

Enter MERRIMAN.

MERRIMAN: Miss Fairfax.

Enter GWENDOLEN.

Exit MERRIMAN.

CECILY: (*Advancing to meet her*) Pray let me introduce myself to you. My name is Cecily Cardew.

GWENDOLEN: Cecily Cardew? (*Moving to her and shaking hands*) What a very sweet name! Something tells me that we are going to be great friends. I like you already more than I can say. My first impressions of people are never wrong.

CECILY: How nice of you to like me so much after we have known each other such a comparatively short time. Pray sit down.

GWENDOLEN: (*Still standing up*) I may call you Cecily, may I not?

CECILY: With pleasure!

GWENDOLEN: And you will always call me Gwendolen, won't you?

CECILY: If you wish.

GWENDOLEN: Then that is all quite settled, is it not?

CECILY: I hope so.

A pause. They both sit down together.

GWENDOLEN: Perhaps this might be a favourable opportunity for my mentioning who I am. My father is Lord Bracknell. You have never heard of papa, I suppose?

CECILY: I don't think so.

GWENDOLEN: Outside the family circle, papa, I am glad to say, is entirely unknown. I think that is quite as it should be. The home seems to me to be the proper sphere for the man. And certainly once a man begins to neglect his domestic duties he becomes painfully effeminate, does he not? And I don't like that. It makes men so very attractive. Cecily, mamma, whose views on education are remarkably strict, has brought me up to be extremely shortsighted; it is part of her system; so do you mind my looking at you through my glasses?

CECILY: Oh! not at all, Gwendolen. I am very fond of being looked at.

GWENDOLEN: (*After examining* CECILY *carefully through a lorgnette*[7]) You are here on a short visit, I suppose.

CECILY: Oh no! I live here.

GWENDOLEN: (*Severely*) Really? Your mother, no doubt, or some female relative of advanced years, resides here also?

CECILY: Oh no! I have no mother, nor, in fact, any relations.

GWENDOLEN: Indeed?

CECILY: My dear guardian, with the assistance of Miss Prism, has the arduous task of looking after me.

GWENDOLEN: Your guardian?

CECILY: Yes, I am Mr. Worthing's ward.

GWENDOLEN: Oh! It is strange he never mentioned to me that he had a ward. How secretive of him! He grows more interesting hourly. I am not sure, however, that the news inspires me with feelings of unmixed delight. (*Rising and going to her*) I am very fond of you, Cecily; I have liked you ever since I met you! But I am bound to state that now that I know that you are Mr. Worthing's ward, I cannot help expressing a wish you were — well just a little older than you seem to be — and not quite so very alluring in appearance. In fact, if I may speak candidly ——

CECILY: Pray do! I think that whenever one has anything unpleasant to say, one should always be quite candid.

GWENDOLEN: Well, to speak with perfect candour, Cecily, I wish that you were fully forty-two, and more than usually plain for your age. Ernest has a strong upright nature. He is the very soul of truth and honour. Disloyalty would be as impossible to him as deception. But even men of the noblest possible moral character are extremely susceptible to the influence of the physical charms of others. Modern, no less than Ancient History, supplies us with many most painful examples of what I refer to. If it were not so, indeed, History would be quite unreadable.

CECILY: I beg your pardon, Gwendolen, did you say Ernest?

GWENDOLEN: Yes.

CECILY: Oh, but it is not Mr. Ernest Worthing who is my guardian. It is his brother — his elder brother.

GWENDOLEN: (*Sitting down again*) Ernest never mentioned to me that he had a brother.

CECILY: I am sorry to say they have not been on good terms for a long time.

GWENDOLEN: Ah! that accounts for it. And now that I think of it I have never heard any man mention his brother. The subject seems distasteful to most men. Cecily, you have lifted a load from my mind. I was growing almost anxious. It would have been terrible if any cloud had come across a friendship like ours, would it not? Of course you are quite, quite sure that it is not Mr. Ernest Worthing who is your guardian?

CECILY: Quite sure. (*A pause*) In fact, I am going to be his.

GWENDOLEN: (*Inquiringly*) I beg your pardon?

CECILY: (*Rather shy and confidingly*) Dearest Gwendolen, there is no reason why I should make a secret of it to you. Our little county newspaper is sure to chronicle the fact next week. Mr. Ernest Worthing and I are engaged to be married.

GWENDOLEN: (*Quite politely, rising*) My darling Cecily, I think there must be some slight error. Mr. Ernest Worthing is engaged to me. The announcement will appear in the *Morning Post* on Saturday at the latest.

CECILY: (*Very politely, rising*) I am afraid you must be under some misconception. Ernest proposed to me exactly ten minutes ago. (*Shows diary*)

GWENDOLEN: (*Examines diary through her lorgnette carefully*) It is certainly very curious, for he asked me to be his wife yesterday afternoon at 5:30. If you would care to verify the incident, pray do so. (*Produces diary of her own*) I never travel without

7. Eyeglasses with a handle.

my diary. One should always have something sensational to read in the train. I am so sorry, dear Cecily, if it is any disappointment to you, but I am afraid *I* have the prior claim.

CECILY: It would distress me more than I can tell you, dear Gwendolen, if it caused you any mental or physical anguish, but I feel bound to point out that since Ernest proposed to you he clearly has changed his mind.

GWENDOLEN: (*Meditatively*) If the poor fellow has been entrapped into any foolish promise I shall consider it my duty to rescue him at once, and with a firm hand.

CECILY: (*Thoughtfully and sadly*) Whatever unfortunate entanglement my dear boy may have got into, I will never reproach him with it after we are married.

GWENDOLEN: Do you allude to me, Miss Cardew, as an entanglement? You are presumptuous. On an occasion of this kind it becomes more than a moral duty to speak one's mind. It becomes a pleasure.

CECILY: Do you suggest, Miss Fairfax, that I entrapped Ernest into an engagement? How dare you? This is no time for wearing the shallow mask of manners. When I see a spade I call it a spade.

GWENDOLEN: (*Satirically*) I am glad to say that I have never seen a spade. It is obvious that our social spheres have been widely different.

Enter MERRIMAN, *followed by the footman. He carries a salver, tablecloth, and plate stand.* CECILY *is about to retort. The presence of the servants exercises a restraining influence, under which both girls chafe.*

MERRIMAN: Shall I lay tea here as usual, Miss?

CECILY: (*Sternly, in a calm voice*) Yes, as usual.

MERRIMAN *begins to clear table and lay cloth. A long pause.* CECILY *and* GWENDOLEN *glare at each other.*

GWENDOLEN: Are there many interesting walks in the vicinity, Miss Cardew?

CECILY: Oh! yes! a great many. From the top of one of the hills quite close one can see five counties.

GWENDOLEN: Five counties! I don't think I should like that. I hate crowds.

CECILY: (*Sweetly*) I suppose that is why you live in town?

GWENDOLEN *bites her lip, and beats her foot nervously with her parasol.*

GWENDOLEN: (*Looking round*) Quite a well-kept garden this is, Miss Cardew.

CECILY: So glad you like it, Miss Fairfax.

GWENDOLEN: I had no idea there were any flowers in the country.

CECILY: Oh, flowers are as common here, Miss Fairfax, as people are in London.

GWENDOLEN: Personally I cannot understand how anybody manages to exist in the country, if anybody who is anybody does. The country always bores me to death.

CECILY: Ah! This is what the newspapers call agricultural depression, is it not? I believe the aristocracy are suffering very much from it just at present. It is almost an epidemic amongst them, I have been told. May I offer you some tea, Miss Fairfax?

GWENDOLEN: (*With elaborate politeness*) Thank you. (*Aside*) Detestable girl! But I require tea!

CECILY: (*Sweetly*) Sugar?

GWENDOLEN: (*Superciliously*) No, thank you. Sugar is not fashionable any more.

CECILY *looks angrily at her, takes up the tongs and puts four lumps of sugar into the cup.*

CECILY: (*Severely*) Cake or bread and butter?

GWENDOLEN: (*In a bored manner*) Bread and butter, please. Cake is rarely seen at the best houses nowadays.

CECILY: (*Cuts a very large slice of cake, and puts it on the tray*) Hand that to Miss Fairfax.

MERRIMAN *does so, and goes out with footman.* GWENDOLEN *drinks the tea and makes a grimace. Puts down cup at once, reaches out her hand to the bread and butter, looks at it, and finds it is cake. Rises in indignation.*

GWENDOLEN: You have filled my tea with lumps of sugar, and though I asked most distinctly for bread and butter, you have given me cake. I am known for the gentleness of my disposition, and the extraordinary sweetness of my nature, but I warn you, Miss Cardew, you may go too far.

CECILY: (*Rising*) To save my poor, innocent, trusting boy from the machinations of any other girl there are no lengths to which I would not go.

GWENDOLEN: From the moment I saw you I distrusted you. I felt that you were false and deceitful. I am never deceived in such matters. My first impressions of people are invariably right.

CECILY: It seems to me, Miss Fairfax, that I am trespassing on your valuable time. No doubt you have many other calls of a similar character to make in the neighbourhood.

Enter JACK.

GWENDOLEN: (*Catching sight of him*) Ernest! My own Ernest!

JACK: Gwendolen! Darling! (*Offers to kiss her*)

GWENDOLEN: (*Drawing back*) A moment! May I ask if you are engaged to be married to this young lady? (*Points to* CECILY)

JACK: (*Laughing*) To dear little Cecily! Of course not! What could have put such an idea into your pretty little head?

GWENDOLEN: Thank you. You may! (*Offers her cheek*)

CECILY: (*Very sweetly*) I knew there must be some misunderstanding, Miss Fairfax. The gentleman whose arm is at present round your waist is my dear guardian, Mr. John Worthing.

GWENDOLEN: I beg your pardon?

CECILY: This is Uncle Jack.

GWENDOLEN: (*Receding*) Jack! Oh!

Enter ALGERNON.

CECILY: Here is Ernest.

ALGERNON: (*Goes straight over to* CECILY *without noticing anyone else*) My own love! (*Offers to kiss her*)

CECILY: (*Drawing back*) A moment, Ernest! May I ask you — are you engaged to be married to this young lady?

ALGERNON: (*Looking round*) To what young lady? Good heavens! Gwendolen!

CECILY: Yes! to good heavens, Gwendolen, I mean to Gwendolen.

ALGERNON: (*Laughing*) Of course not! What could have put such an idea into your pretty little head?

CECILY: Thank you. (*Presenting her cheek to be kissed*) You may.

ALGERNON *kisses her.*

GWENDOLEN: I felt there was some slight error, Miss Cardew. The gentleman who is now embracing you is my cousin, Mr. Algernon Moncrieff.

CECILY: (*Breaking away from* ALGERNON) Algernon Moncrieff! Oh! (*The two girls move towards each other and put their arms round each other's waists as if for protection*) Are you called Algernon?

ALGERNON: I cannot deny it.

CECILY: Oh!

GWENDOLEN: Is your name really John?

JACK: (*Standing rather proudly*) I could deny it if I liked, I could deny anything if I liked. But my name certainly is John. It has been John for years.

CECILY: (*To* GWENDOLEN) A gross deception has been practised on both of us.

GWENDOLEN: My poor wounded Cecily!

CECILY: My sweet wronged Gwendolen!

GWENDOLEN: (*Slowly and seriously*) You will call me sister, will you not?

They embrace. JACK *and* ALGERNON *groan and walk up and down.*

CECILY: (*Rather brightly*) There is just one question I would like to be allowed to ask my guardian.

GWENDOLEN: An admirable idea! Mr. Worthing, there is just one question I would like to be permitted to put to you. Where is your brother Ernest? We are both engaged to be married to your brother Ernest, so it is a matter of some importance to us to know where your brother Ernest is at present.

JACK: (*Slowly and hesitatingly*) Gwendolen — Cecily — it is very painful for me to be forced to speak the truth. It is the first time in my life that I have ever been reduced to such a painful position, and I am really quite inexperienced in doing anything of the kind. However I will tell you quite frankly that I have no brother Ernest. I have no brother at all. I never had a brother in my life, and I certainly have not the smallest intention of ever having one in the future.

CECILY: (*Surprised*) No brother at all?

JACK: (*Cheerily*) None!

GWENDOLEN: (*Severely*) Had you never a brother of any kind?

JACK: (*Pleasantly*) Never. Not even of any kind.

GWENDOLEN: I am afraid it is quite clear, Cecily, that neither of us is engaged to be married to anyone.

CECILY: It is not a very pleasant position for a young girl suddenly to find herself in. Is it?

GWENDOLEN: Let us go into the house. They will hardly venture to come after us there.

CECILY: No, men are so cowardly, aren't they?

They retire into the house with scornful looks.

JACK: This ghastly state of things is what you call Bunburying, I suppose?

ALGERNON: Yes, and a perfectly wonderful Bunbury it is. The most wonderful Bunbury I have ever had in my life.

JACK: Well, you've no right whatsoever to Bunbury here.

ALGERNON: That is absurd. One has a right to Bunbury anywhere one chooses. Every serious Bunburyist[8] knows that.

8. Wilde, who claimed his was a trivial play for serious people, liked paradox.

JACK: Serious Bunburyist! Good heavens!

ALGERNON: Well, one must be serious about something, if one wants to have any amusement in life. I happen to be serious about Bunburying. What on earth you are serious about I haven't got the remotest idea. About everything, I should fancy. You have such an absolutely trivial nature.

JACK: Well, the only small satisfaction I have in the whole of this wretched business is that your friend Bunbury is quite exploded. You won't be able to run down to the country quite so often as you used to do, dear Algy. And a very good thing too.

ALGERNON: Your brother is a little off-colour, isn't he, dear Jack? You won't be able to disappear to London quite so frequently as your wicked custom was. And not a bad thing either.

JACK: As for your conduct towards Miss Cardew, I must say that your taking in a sweet, simple, innocent girl like that is quite inexcusable. To say nothing of the fact that she is my ward.

ALGERNON: I can see no possible defence at all for your deceiving a brilliant, clever, thoroughly experienced young lady like Miss Fairfax. To say nothing of the fact that she is my cousin.

JACK: I wanted to be engaged to Gwendolen, that is all. I love her.

ALGERNON: Well, I simply wanted to be engaged to Cecily. I adore her.

JACK: There is certainly no chance of your marrying Miss Cardew.

ALGERNON: I don't think there is much likelihood, Jack, of you and Miss Fairfax being united.

JACK: Well, that is no business of yours.

ALGERNON: If it was my business, I wouldn't talk about it. (*Begins to eat muffins*) It is very vulgar to talk about one's business. Only people like stockbrokers do that, and then merely at dinner parties.

JACK: How you can sit there, calmly eating muffins when we are in this horrible trouble, I can't make out. You seem to me to be perfectly heartless.

ALGERNON: Well, I can't eat muffins in an agitated manner. The butter would probably get on my cuffs. One should always eat muffins quite calmly. It is the only way to eat them.

JACK: I say it's perfectly heartless your eating muffins at all, under the circumstances.

ALGERNON: When I am in trouble, eating is the only thing that consoles me.[9] Indeed, when I am in really great trouble, as anyone who knows me intimately will tell you, I refuse everything except food and drink. At the present moment I am eating muffins because I am unhappy. Besides, I am particularly fond of muffins. (*Rising*)

JACK: (*Rising*) Well, that is no reason why you should eat them all in that greedy way. (*Takes muffins from* ALGERNON)

ALGERNON: (*Offering tea cake*) I wish you would have tea cake instead. I don't like tea cake.

JACK: Good heavens! I suppose a man may eat his own muffins in his own garden.

ALGERNON: But you have just said it was perfectly heartless to eat muffins.

JACK: I said it was perfectly heartless of you, under the circumstances. That is a very different thing.

ALGERNON: That may be. But the muffins are the same. (*He seizes the muffin dish from* JACK)

JACK: Algy, I wish to goodness you would go.

ALGERNON: You can't possibly ask me to go without having some dinner. It's absurd. I never go without my dinner. No one ever does, except vegetarians and people like that. Besides I have just made arrangements with Dr. Chasuble to be christened at a quarter to six under the name of Ernest.

JACK: My dear fellow, the sooner you give up that nonsense the better. I made arrangements this morning with Dr. Chasuble to be christened myself at 5:30, and I naturally will take the name of Ernest. Gwendolen would wish it. We can't both be christened Ernest. It's absurd. Besides, I have a perfect right to be christened if I like. There is no evidence at all that I ever have been christened by anybody. I should think it extremely probable I never was, and so does Dr. Chasuble. It is entirely different in your case. You have been christened already.

ALGERNON: Yes, but I have not been christened for years.

JACK: Yes, but you have been christened. That is the important thing.

ALGERNON: Quite so. So I know my constitution can stand it. If you are not quite sure about your ever having been christened, I must say I think it rather dangerous your venturing on it now. It might make you very unwell. You can hardly have forgotten that someone very closely connected with you was very nearly carried off this week in Paris by a severe chill.

9. Cursed with a gargantuan appetite and an ungainly body, Wilde was fascinated by the appeal of food to the insecure.

JACK: Yes, but you said yourself that a severe chill was not hereditary.

ALGERNON: It usen't to be, I know — but I daresay it is now. Science is always making wonderful improvements in things.

JACK: (*Picking up the muffin dish*) Oh, that is nonsense; you are always talking nonsense.

ALGERNON: Jack, you are at the muffins again! I wish you wouldn't. There are only two left. (*Takes them*) I told you I was particularly fond of muffins.

JACK: But I hate tea cake.

ALGERNON: Why on earth then do you allow tea cake to be served up for your guests? What ideas you have of hospitality!

JACK: Algernon! I have already told you to go. I don't want you here. Why don't you go!

ALGERNON: I haven't quite finished my tea yet! and there is still one muffin left.

JACK *groans, and sinks into a chair.* ALGERNON *still continues eating.*

ACT III

SCENE — *Morning room at the Manor House*

GWENDOLEN *and* CECILY *are at the window, looking out into the garden.*

GWENDOLEN: The fact that they did not follow us at once into the house, as anyone else would have done, seems to me to show that they have some sense of shame left.

CECILY: They have been eating muffins. That looks like repentance.

GWENDOLEN: (*After a pause*) They don't seem to notice us at all. Couldn't you cough?

CECILY: But I haven't got a cough.

GWENDOLEN: They're looking at us. What effrontery!

CECILY: They're approaching. That's very forward of them.

GWENDOLEN: Let us preserve a dignified silence.

CECILY: Certainly. It's the only thing to do now.

Enter JACK *followed by* ALGERNON. *They whistle some dreadful popular air from a British Opera.*

GWENDOLEN: This dignified silence seems to produce an unpleasant effect.

CECILY: A most distasteful one.

GWENDOLEN: But we will not be the first to speak.

CECILY: Certainly not.

GWENDOLEN: Mr. Worthing, I have something very particular to ask you. Much depends on your reply.

CECILY: Gwendolen, your common sense is invaluable. Mr. Moncrieff, kindly answer me the following question. Why did you pretend to be my guardian's brother?

ALGERNON: In order that I might have an opportunity of meeting you.

CECILY: (*To* GWENDOLEN) That certainly seems a satisfactory explanation, does it not?

GWENDOLEN: Yes, dear, if you can believe him.

CECILY: I don't. But that does not affect the wonderful beauty of his answer.

GWENDOLEN: True. In matters of grave importance, style, not sincerity is the vital thing.[1] Mr. Worthing, what explanation can you offer to me for pretending to have a brother? Was it in order that you might have an opportunity of coming up to town to see me as often as possible?

JACK: Can you doubt it, Miss Fairfax?

GWENDOLEN: I have the gravest doubts upon the subject. But I intend to crush them. This is not the moment for German scepticism. (*Moving to* CECILY) Their explanations appear to be quite satisfactory, especially Mr. Worthing's. That seems to me to have the stamp of truth upon it.

CECILY: I am more than content with what Mr. Moncrieff said. His voice alone inspires one with absolute credulity.

GWENDOLEN: Then you think we should forgive them?

CECILY: Yes. I mean no.

GWENDOLEN: True! I had forgotten. There are principles at stake that one cannot surrender. Which of us should tell them? The task is not a pleasant one.

CECILY: Could we not both speak at the same time?

GWENDOLEN: An excellent idea! I nearly always speak at the same time as other people. Will you take the time from me?

CECILY: Certainly.

GWENDOLEN *beats time with uplifted finger.*

GWENDOLEN and CECILY: (*Speaking together*) Your Christian names are still an insuperable barrier. That is all!

JACK and ALGERNON: (*Speaking together*) Our Christian names! Is that all? But we are going to be christened this afternoon.

1. cf. 'All bad poetry springs from genuine feeling' (*The Decay of Lying*).

GWENDOLEN: (*To* JACK) For my sake you are prepared to do this terrible thing?

JACK: I am.

CECILY: (*To* ALGERNON) To please me you are ready to face this fearful ordeal?

ALGERNON: I am!

GWENDOLEN: How absurd to talk of the equality of the sexes! Where questions of self-sacrifice are concerned, men are infinitely beyond us.

JACK: We are. (*Clasps hands with* ALGERNON)

CECILY: They have moments of physical courage of which we women know absolutely nothing.

GWENDOLEN: (*To* JACK) Darling!

ALGERNON: (*To* CECILY) Darling. (*They fall into each other's arms*)

Enter MERRIMAN. *When he enters he coughs loudly, seeing the situation.*

MERRIMAN: Ahem! Ahem! Lady Bracknell!

JACK: Good heavens!

Enter LADY BRACKNELL. *The couples separate in alarm.*

Exit MERRIMAN.

LADY BRACKNELL: Gwendolen! What does this mean?

GWENDOLEN: Merely that I am engaged to be married to Mr. Worthing, mamma.

LADY BRACKNELL: Come here. Sit down. Sit down immediately. Hesitation of any kind is a sign of mental decay in the young, of physical weakness in the old. (*Turns to* JACK) Apprised, sir, of my daughter's sudden flight by her trusty maid, whose confidence I purchased by means of a small coin, I followed her at once by a luggage train. Her unhappy father is, I am glad to say, under the impression that she is attending a more than usually lengthy lecture by the University Extension Scheme on the Influence of a permanent income on Thought. I do not propose to undeceive him. Indeed I have never undeceived him on any question. I would consider it wrong. But of course, you will clearly understand that all communication between yourself and my daughter must cease immediately from this moment. On this point, as indeed on all points, I am firm.

JACK: I am engaged to be married to Gwendolen, Lady Bracknell!

LADY BRACKNELL: You are nothing of the kind, sir. And now, as regards Algernon! . . . Algernon!

ALGERNON: Yes, Aunt Augusta.

LADY BRACKNELL: May I ask if it is in this house that your invalid friend Mr. Bunbury resides?

ALGERNON: (*Stammering*) Oh! No! Bunbury doesn't live here. Bunbury is somewhere else at present. In fact, Bunbury is dead.

LADY BRACKNELL: Dead! When did Mr. Bunbury die? His death must have been extremely sudden.

ALGERNON: (*Airily*) Oh! I killed Bunbury this afternoon. I mean poor Bunbury died this afternoon.

LADY BRACKNELL: What did he die of?

ALGERNON: Bunbury? Oh, he was quite exploded.

LADY BRACKNELL: Exploded! Was he the victim of a revolutionary outrage?[2] I was not aware that Mr. Bunbury was interested in social legislation. If so, he is well punished for his morbidity.

ALGERNON: My dear Aunt Augusta, I mean he was found out! The doctors found out that Bunbury could not live, that is what I mean — so Bunbury died.

LADY BRACKNELL: He seems to have had great confidence in the opinion of his physicians. I am glad, however, that he made up his mind at the last to some definite course of action, and acted under proper medical advice. And now that we have finally got rid of this Mr. Bunbury, may I ask, Mr. Worthing, who is that young person whose hand my nephew Algernon is now holding in what seems to me a peculiary unnecessary manner?

JACK: That lady is Miss Cecily Cardew, my ward.

LADY BRACKNELL *bows coldly to* CECILY.

ALGERNON: I am engaged to be married to Cecily, Aunt Augusta.

LADY BRACKNELL: I beg your pardon?

CECILY: Mr. Moncrieff and I are engaged to be married, Lady Bracknell.

LADY BRACKNELL: (*With a shiver, crossing to the sofa and sitting down*) I do not know whether there is anything peculiarly exciting in the air of this particular part of Hertfordshire, but the number of engagements that go on seems to me considerably above the proper average that statistics have laid down for our guidance. I think some preliminary inquiry on my part would not be out of place. Mr. Worthing, is Miss Cardew at all connected with any of the larger railway stations in London? I merely desire information. Until yesterday I had no idea that there were any families or persons whose origin

2. Anarchist bombings were a feature of the 1890s in major European cities.

was a Terminus.[3]

JACK *looks perfectly furious, but restrains himself.*

JACK: (*In a clear, cold voice*) Miss Cardew is the granddaughter of the late Mr. Thomas Cardew of 149, Belgrave Square, S.W.; Gervase Park, Dorking, Surrey; and the Sporran, Fifeshire, N.B.[4]

LADY BRACKNELL: That sounds not unsatisfactory. Three addresses always inspire confidence, even in tradesmen. But what proof have I of their authenticity?

JACK: I have carefully preserved the Court Guides[5] of the period. They are open to your inspection, Lady Bracknell.

LADY BRACKNELL: (*Grimly*) I have known strange errors in that publication.

JACK: Miss Cardew's family solicitors are Messrs. Markby, Markby, and Markby.

LADY BRACKNELL: Markby, Markby, and Markby? A firm of the very highest position in their profession. Indeed I am told that one of the Mr. Markbys is occasionally to be seen at dinner parties. So far I am satisfied.

JACK: (*Very irritably*) How extremely kind of you, Lady Bracknell! I have also in my possession, you will be pleased to hear, certificates of Miss Cardew's birth, baptism, whooping cough, registration, vaccination, confirmation, and the measles; both the German and the English variety.

LADY BRACKNELL: Ah! A life crowded with incident, I see; though perhaps somewhat too exciting for a young girl. I am not myself in favour of premature experiences. (*Rises, looks at her watch*) Gwendolen! the time approaches for our departure. We have not a moment to lose. As a matter of form, Mr. Worthing, I had better ask you if Miss Cardew has any little fortune?

JACK: Oh! about a hundred and thirty thousand pounds in the Funds.[6] That is all. Good-bye, Lady Bracknell. So pleased to have seen you.

LADY BRACKNELL: (*Sitting down again*) A moment, Mr. Worthing. A hundred and thirty thousand pounds! And in the Funds! Miss Cardew seems to me a most attractive young lady, now that I look at her. Few girls of the present day have any really solid qualities, any of the qualities that last, and improve with time. We live, I regret to say, in an age of surfaces. (*To* CECILY) Come over here, dear. (CECILY *goes across*) Pretty child! your dress is sadly simple, and your hair seems almost as Nature might have left it. But we can soon alter all that. A thoroughly experienced French maid produces a really marvellous result in a very brief space of time. I remember recommending one to young Lady Lancing, and after three months her own husband did not know her.

JACK: (*Aside*) And after six months nobody knew her.

LADY BRACKNELL: (*Glares at* JACK *for a few moments. Then bends, with a practised smile, to* CECILY) Kindly turn round, sweet child (CECILY *turns completely round*) No, the side view is what I want. (CECILY *presents her profile*) Yes, quite as I expected. There are distinct social possibilities in your profile. The two weak points in our age are its want of principle and its want of profile. The chin a little higher, dear. Style largely depends on the way the chin is worn. They are worn very high, just at present. Algernon!

ALGERNON: Yes, Aunt Augusta!

LADY BRACKNELL: There are distinct social possibilities in Miss Cardew's profile.

ALGERNON: Cecily is the sweetest, dearest, prettiest girl in the whole world. And I don't care twopence about social possibilities.

LADY BRACKNELL: Never speak disrespectfully of Society, Algernon. Only people who can't get into it do that. (*To* CECILY) Dear child, of course you know that Algernon has nothing but his debts to depend upon. But I do not approve of mercenary marriages. When I married Lord Bracknell I had no fortune of any kind. But I never dreamed for a moment of allowing that to stand in my way. Well, I suppose I must give my consent.

ALGERNON: Thank you, Aunt Augusta.

LADY BRACKNELL: Cecily, you may kiss me!

CECILY: (*Kisses her*) Thank you, Lady Bracknell.

LADY BRACKNELL: You may also address me as Aunt Augusta for the future.

CECILY: Thank you, Aunt Augusta.

LADY BRACKNELL: The marriage, I think, had better take place quite soon.

ALGERNON: Thank you, Aunt Augusta.

CECILY: Thank you, Aunt Augusta.

LADY BRACKNELL: To speak frankly, I am not in favour of long engagements. They give people the opportunity of finding out each other's character

3. The destination-point on a bus or rail route.
4. North Britain, in other words, Scotland.
5. Lists of the foremost families in the realm, indicating their projects and lands, published by the royal stationers.
6. State-sponsored bonds.

before marriage, which I think is never advisable.

JACK: I beg your pardon for interrupting you, Lady Bracknell, but this engagement is quite out of the question. I am Miss Cardew's guardian, and she cannot marry without my consent until she comes of age. That consent I absolutely decline to give.

LADY BRACKNELL: Upon what grounds may I ask? Algernon is an extremely, I may almost say an ostentatiously, eligible young man. He has nothing, but he looks everything. What more can one desire?

JACK: It pains me very much to have to speak frankly to you, Lady Bracknell, about your nephew, but the fact is that I do not approve at all of his moral character. I suspect him of being untruthful.

ALGERNON *and* CECILY *look at him in indignant amazement.*

LADY BRACKNELL: Untruthful! My nephew Algernon? Impossible! He is an Oxonian.[7]

JACK: I fear there can be no possible doubt about the matter. This afternoon, during my temporary absence in London on an important question of romance, he obtained admission to my house by means of the false pretence of being my brother. Under an assumed name he drank, I've just been informed by my butler, an entire pint bottle of my Perrier-Jouet, Brut, '89; a wine I was specially reserving for myself. Continuing his disgraceful deception, he succeeded in the course of the afternoon in alienating the affections of my only ward. He subsequently stayed to tea, and devoured every single muffin. And what makes his conduct all the more heartless is, that he was perfectly well aware from the first that I have no brother, that I never had a brother, and that I don't intend to have a brother, not even of any kind. I distinctly told him so myself yesterday afternoon.

LADY BRACKNELL: Ahem! Mr. Worthing, after careful consideration I have decided entirely to overlook my nephew's conduct to you.

JACK: That is very generous of you, Lady Bracknell. My own decision, however, is unalterable. I decline to give my consent.

LADY BRACKNELL: (*To* CECILY) Come here, sweet child. (CECILY *goes over*) How old are you, dear?

CECILY: Well, I am really only eighteen, but I always admit to twenty when I go to evening parties.

LADY BRACKNELL: You are perfectly right in making some slight alteration. Indeed, no woman should ever be quite accurate about her age. It looks so calculating.... (*In a meditative manner*) Eighteen, but admitting to twenty at evening parties. Well, it will not be very long before you are of age and free from the restraints of tutelage. So I don't think your guardian's consent is, after all, a matter of any importance.

JACK: Pray excuse me, Lady Bracknell, for interrupting you again, but it is only fair to tell you that according to the terms of her grandfather's will Miss Cardew does not come legally of age till she is thirty-five.

LADY BRACKNELL: That does not seem to me to be a grave objection. Thirty-five is a very attractive age. London society is full of women of the very highest birth who have, of their own free choice, remained thirty-five for years. Lady Dumbleton is an instance in point. To my own knowledge she has been thirty-five ever since she arrived at the age of forty, which was many years ago now. I see no reason why our dear Cecily should not be even still more attractive at the age you mention than she is at present. There will be a large accumulation of property.

CECILY: Algy, could you wait for me till I was thirty-five?

ALGERNON: Of course I could, Cecily. You know I could.

CECILY: Yes, I felt it instinctively, but I couldn't wait all that time. I hate waiting even five minutes for anybody. It always makes me rather cross. I am not punctual myself, I know, but I do like punctuality in others, and waiting, even to be married, is quite out of the question.

ALGERNON: Then what is to be done, Cecily?

CECILY: I don't know, Mr. Moncrieff.

LADY BRACKNELL: My dear Mr. Worthing, as Miss Cardew states positively that she cannot wait till she is thirty-five — a remark which I am bound to say seems to me to show a somewhat impatient nature — I would beg of you to reconsider your decision.

JACK: But my dear Lady Bracknell, the matter is entirely in your own hands. The moment you consent to my marriage with Gwendolen, I will most gladly allow your nephew to form an alliance with my ward.

LADY BRACKNELL: (*Rising and drawing herself up*) You must be quite aware that what you propose is out of the question.

7. Former student of Oxford University.

JACK: Then a passionate celibacy is all that any of us can look forward to.

LADY BRACKNELL: This is not the destiny I propose for Gwendolen. Algernon, of course, can choose for himself. (*Pulls out her watch*) Come, dear; (GWENDOLEN *rises*) we have already missed five, if not six, trains. To miss any more might expose us to comment on the platform.

Enter DR. CHASUBLE.

CHASUBLE: Everything is quite ready for the christenings.

LADY BRACKNELL: The christenings, sir! Is not that somewhat premature!

CHASUBLE: (*Looking rather puzzled, and pointing to* JACK *and* ALGERNON) Both these gentlemen have expressed a desire for immediate baptism.

LADY BRACKNELL: At their age? The idea is grotesque and irreligious! Algernon, I forbid you to be baptized. I will not hear of such excesses. Lord Bracknell would be highly displeased if he learned that that was the way in which you wasted your time and money.

CHASUBLE: Am I to understand then that there are to be no christenings at all this afternoon?

JACK: I don't think that, as things are now, it would be of much practical value to either of us, Dr. Chasuble.

CHASUBLE: I am grieved to hear such sentiments from you, Mr. Worthing. They savour of the heretical views of the Anabaptists,[8] views that I have completely refuted in four of my unpublished sermons. However, as your present mood seems to be one peculiarly secular, I will return to the church at once. Indeed, I have just been informed by the pew-opener that for the last hour and a half Miss Prism has been waiting for me in the vestry.

LADY BRACKNELL: (*Starting*) Miss Prism! Did I hear you mention a Miss Prism?

CHASUBLE: Yes, Lady Bracknell. I am on my way to join her.

LADY BRACKNELL: Pray allow me to detain you for a moment. This matter may prove to be one of vital importance to Lord Bracknell and myself. Is this Miss Prism a female of repellent aspect, remotely connected with education?

CHASUBLE: (*Somewhat indignantly*) She is the most cultivated of ladies, and the very picture of respectability.

8. Radical protestant sect of the seventeenth century, denounced by Luther for their heretical views on baptism.

LADY BRACKNELL: It is obviously the same person. May I ask what position she holds in your household?

CHASUBLE: (*Severely*) I am a celibate, madam.

JACK: (*Interposing*) Miss Prism, Lady Bracknell, has been for the last three years Miss Cardew's esteemed governess and valued companion.

LADY BRACKNELL: In spite of what I hear of her, I must see her at once. Let her be sent for.

CHASUBLE: (*Looking off*) She approaches; she is nigh.

Enter MISS PRISM *hurriedly*.

MISS PRISM: I was told you expected me in the vestry, dear Canon. I have been waiting for you there for an hour and three quarters. (*Catches sight of* LADY BRACKNELL *who has fixed her with a stony glare,* MISS PRISM *grows pale and quails. She looks anxiously round as if desirous to escape*)

LADY BRACKNELL: (*In a severe, judicial voice*) Prism! (MISS PRISM *bows her head in shame*) Come here, Prism! (MISS PRISM *approaches in a humble manner*) Prism! Where is that baby? (*General consternation.* THE CANON *starts back in horror.* ALGERNON *and* JACK *pretend to be anxious to shield* CECILY *and* GWENDOLEN *from hearing the details of a terrible public scandal*) Twenty-eight years ago, Prism, you left Lord Bracknell's house, Number 104, Upper Grosvenor Street, in charge of a perambulator[9] that contained a baby, of the male sex. You never returned. A few weeks later, through the elaborate investigations of the Metropolitan police, the perambulator was discovered at midnight, standing by itself in a remote corner of Bayswater. It contained the manuscript of a three-volume novel of more than usually revolting sentimentality. (MISS PRISM *starts in involuntary indignation*) But the baby was not there! (*Everyone looks at* MISS PRISM) Prism! Where is that baby?

A pause.

MISS PRISM: Lady Bracknell, I admit with shame that I do not know. I only wish I did. The plain facts of the case are these. On the morning of the day you mention, a day that is forever branded on my memory, I prepared as usual to take the baby out in its perambulator. I had also with me a somewhat old, but capacious handbag, in which I had intended to place the manuscript of a work of fiction that I had written during my few unoccupied hours. In a moment of mental abstraction, for

9. A small carriage for a child; a pram.

which I never can forgive myself, I deposited the manuscript in the bassinette,[10] and placed the baby in the handbag.

JACK: (*Who has been listening attentively*) But where did you deposit the handbag?

MISS PRISM: Do not ask me, Mr. Worthing.

JACK: Miss Prism, this is a matter of no small importance to me. I insist on knowing where you deposited the handbag that contained that infant.

MISS PRISM: I left it in the cloak room of one of the larger railway stations in London.

JACK: What railway station?

MISS PRISM: (*Quite crushed*) Victoria. The Brighton line. (*Sinks into a chair*)

JACK: I must retire to my room for a moment. Gwendolen, wait here for me.

GWENDOLEN: If you are not too long, I will wait here for you all my life.

Exit JACK *in great excitement.*

CHASUBLE: What do you think this means, Lady Bracknell?

LADY BRACKNELL: I dare not even suspect, Dr. Chasuble. I need hardly tell you that in families of high position strange coincidences are not supposed to occur. They are hardly considered the thing.

Noises heard overhead as if someone was throwing trunks about. Everyone looks up.

CECILY: Uncle Jack seems strangely agitated.

CHASUBLE: Your guardian has a very emotional nature.

LADY BRACKNELL: This noise is extremely unpleasant. It sounds as if he was having an argument. I dislike arguments of any kind. They are always vulgar, and often convincing.

CHASUBLE: (*Looking up*) It has stopped now.

The noise is redoubled.

LADY BRACKNELL: I wish he would arrive at some conclusion.

GWENDOLEN: This suspense is terrible. I hope it will last.

Enter JACK *with a handbag of black leather in his hand.*

JACK: (*Rushing over to* MISS PRISM) Is this the handbag, Miss Prism? Examine it carefully before you speak. The happiness of more than one life depends on your answer.

MISS PRISM: (*Calmly*) It seems to be mine. Yes, here is the injury it received through the upsetting of a Gower Street omnibus[11] in younger and happier days. Here is the stain on the lining caused by the explosion of a temperance beverage, an incident that occurred at Leamington. And here, on the lock, are my initials. I had forgotten that in an extravagant mood I had had them placed there. The bag is undoubtedly mine. I am delighted to have it so unexpectedly restored to me. It has been a great inconvenience being without it all these years.

JACK: (*In a pathetic voice*) Miss Prism, more is restored to you than this handbag. I was the baby you placed in it.

MISS PRISM: (*Amazed*) You!

JACK: (*Embracing her*) Yes . . . mother!

MISS PRISM: (*Recoiling in indignant astonishment*) Mr. Worthing! I am unmarried!

JACK: Unmarried! I do not deny that is a serious blow. But after all, who has the right to cast a stone against one who has suffered? Cannot repentance wipe out an act of folly? Why should there be one law for men, and another for women? Mother, I forgive you. (*Tries to embrace her again*)

MISS PRISM: (*Still more indignant*) Mr. Worthing, there is some error. (*Pointing to* LADY BRACKNELL) There is the lady who can tell you who you really are.

JACK: (*After a pause*) Lady Bracknell, I hate to seem inquisitive, but would you kindly inform me who I am?

LADY BRACKNELL: I am afraid that the news I have to give you will not altogether please you. You are the son of my poor sister, Mrs. Moncrieff, and consequently Algernon's elder brother.

JACK: Algy's elder brother! Then I have a brother after all. I knew I had a brother! I always said I had a brother! Cecily — how could you have ever doubted that I had a brother? (*Seizes hold of* ALGERNON) Dr. Chasuble, my unfortunate brother. Miss Prism, my unfortunate brother. Gwendolen, my unfortunate brother. Algy, you young scoundrel, you will have to treat me with more respect in the future. You have never behaved to me like a brother in all your life.

ALGERNON: Well, not till today, old boy, I admit. I did my best, however, though I was out of practice. (*Shakes hands*)

GWENDOLEN: (*To* JACK) My own! But what own are you? What is your Christian name, now that you have become someone else?

10. A basket or cradle, equipped with a hood.

11. A bus (literally, the Latin means 'for every person').

JACK: Good heavens! . . . I had quite forgotten that point. Your decision on the subject of my name is irrevocable, I suppose?

GWENDOLEN: I never change, except in my affections.

CECILY: What a noble nature you have, Gwendolen!

JACK: Then the question had better be cleared up at once. Aunt Augusta, a moment. At the time when Miss Prism left me in the handbag, had I been christened already?

LADY BRACKNELL: Every luxury that money could buy, including christening, had been lavished on you by your fond and doting parents.

JACK: Then I was christened! That is settled. Now, what name was I given? Let me know the worst.

LADY BRACKNELL: Being the eldest son you were naturally christened after your father.

JACK: (*Irritably*) Yes, but what was my father's christian name?

LADY BRACKNELL: (*Meditatively*) I cannot at the present moment recall what the General's christian name was. But I have no doubt he had one. He was eccentric, I admit. But only in later years. And that was the result of the Indian climate, and marriage, and indigestion, and other things of that kind.

JACK: Algy! Can't you recollect what our father's christian name was?

ALGERNON: My dear boy, we were never even on speaking terms. He died before I was a year old.

JACK: His name would appear in the Army Lists of the period, I suppose, Aunt Augusta?

LADY BRACKNELL: The General was essentially a man of peace, except in his domestic life. But I have no doubt his name would appear in any military directory.

JACK: The Army Lists of the last forty years are here. These delightful records should have been my constant study. (*Rushes to bookcase and tears the books out*) M. Generals ... Mallam, Maxbohm, Magley, what ghastly names they have — Markby, Migsby, Mobbs, Moncrieff! Lieutenant 1840, Captain, Lieutenant Colonel, Colonel, General 1869, christian names, Ernest John. (*Puts book very quietly down and speaks quite calmly*) I always told you, Gwendolen, my name was Ernest, didn't I? Well it is Ernest after all. I mean it naturally is Ernest.

LADY BRACKNELL: Yes, I remember now that the General was called Ernest. I knew I had some particular reason for disliking the name.

GWENDOLEN: Ernest! My own Ernest! I felt from the first that you could have no other name!

JACK: Gwendolen, it is a terrible thing for a man to find out suddenly that all his life he has been speaking nothing but the truth. Can you forgive me?

GWENDOLEN: I can. For I feel that you are sure to change.

JACK: My own one!

CHASUBLE: (*To* MISS PRISM) Laetitia! (*Embraces her*)

MISS PRISM: (*Enthusiastically*) Frederick! At last!

ALGERNON: Cecily! (*Embraces her*) At last!

JACK: Gwendolen! (*Embraces her*) At last!

LADY BRACKNELL: My nephew, you seem to be displaying signs of triviality.

JACK: On the contrary, Aunt Augusta, I've now realized for the first time in my life the vital Importance of Being Earnest.

GEORGE BERNARD SHAW

(1856-1950)

George Bernard Shaw was another writer who treated England, and indeed the world, as a gigantic laboratory in which he could define what it meant to be an Irishman. Raised as a protestant in Dublin, Shaw came to read the life of St Joan as a parable of emergent protestantism in a catholic-dominated society. The peasant girl who follows the dictates of her inner voices, in the conviction that no mere priest may come between her and her God, is represented in Shaw's play (1923) as the first protestant mystic. His story, after all, was in many respects similar to hers — the shy youth from the provinces comes to the capital city and by sheer charisma and will-power subjugates all former masters.

Equally, in a play like *Arms and the Man* (1894), the word 'Bulgaria' might be replaced, without undue strain, by the word 'Ireland'. The satire on an aristocracy slouching aimlessly in the absence of a suitable war is the work of a man who noted the same combination of 'hardy bodies' and 'timid souls' in the Anglo-Irish ascendancy. The final bidding-scene between the bourgeois Bluntschli and the aristocrat Sergius recalls Shaw's own observations on the discrepancies of wealth between the Shaws (who had a baronet in the family, but no money) and their bespoke tailor (who sent his son to public school, and kept a country-house and yacht).

In the face of their growing poverty, the 'downstart' Shaws were dropped by Dublin society. Having lost a class, Shaw entered no other, but became instead a life-long anatomizer of the hidden injuries of rank. He came to associate Dublin with failure and derision, and the London, to which he emigrated at the age of twenty, with socialism, fraternity and the will-to-change manifest in a truly protestant ethic. His father had been a broken alcoholic and a failure in business; his mother, though good-natured, was undisciplined and neglected her son for a career in music. 'All the work of disciplining and educating myself, which should have been done for me as a child, I had to do myself.'[1] The consequence was that Shaw sprang from his own conception of himself, as 'G.B.S.', a pure self-creation. When the Four Courts in Dublin were bombed in 1923, and public records destroyed, Shaw announced: 'I am an Irishman without a birth certificate.'[2] Lacking an adequate lineage in Dublin, he chose instead to be born again in London as the child of his own writings, 'G.B.S.'.

He never forgot the land of his birth, however, and *John Bull's Other Island* (1904) is the proof. 'I could have become a poet like Yeats or Synge,' he boasted, 'but I prided myself on thinking clearly and therefore could not stay. Whenever I took a problem, I always pursued it to its logical conclusion, and inevitably it resolved itself into a comedy. . . . England had conquered Ireland, so there was nothing for it but to come over and conquer England.'[3]

Shaw was a highly successful playwright by the time he offered *John Bull's Other Island* as 'a patriotic contribution to the Irish Literary Theatre'. The offer may well have been tongue-in-cheek, given the harshly anti-Yeatsian approach of a play which, anyway, called for technical resources well beyond those of the infant Abbey Theatre. Yeats politely declined the offer, insisting to Shaw that 'Ireland is still an island' whose people are uninterested, as yet, in the differences between Irish and English character.[4] This was, of course, the very point Shaw had made in his play — that because most Irish persons have never set foot outside of Ireland, they cannot truly be said to know themselves. In the play, the defrocked priest, Peter Keegan, found wonders in Oxford that he had never seen in Ireland, but on his return home he discovered that the wonders had been there all the time. 'I did not know what my own house was like,' he concludes, 'because I had never been outside it.' In similar fashion, the mock-villain Broadbent discovers what it means to be an Englishman only when he pays a visit to Ireland. 'Ireland,' wrote Shaw, 'is the only spot on earth which still produces the ideal Englishman of history.' *John Bull's Other Island* is Shaw's attempt to show how the peoples of the two islands spend most of their time acting an approved part before their neighbour's eyes; these assigned parts are seen as impositions by the other side rather than as opportunities for true self-expression. In the play stereotypes are exploded, for it is the Englishman Tom Broadbent who is a romantic duffer, while the Irishman Larry Doyle is a cynical realist. The underlying reasoning is sound, for the Irish have become fact-facers through harsh poverty, while the English have enjoyed a scale of wealth so great that it allows them to indulge their victims with expansively sentimental gestures.

On the one hand, Broadbent cynically plots the ruin of the village of Roscullen and packs a gun before his visit to the place; on the other hand, he fills his head with sentimental stage-Irish claptrap

1. G.B. Shaw, *An Autobiography: Selected from His Writings*, edited by Stanley Weintraub (London: Reinhardt, 1970), p. 61.
2. The remark was made to playwright Denis Johnston and is quoted by Michael Holroyd, 'GBS and Ireland', *Sewanee Review*, Vol. LXXXIV, No. 1 (Winter 1976), 39.
3. Quoted by Hesketh Pearson, *George Bernard Shaw* (London: Methuen, 1961), p. 247.
4. See M.J. Sidnell, 'Yeats and Shaw', in Robert O'Driscoll and Lorna Reynolds (eds), *Theatre and Nationalism in Twentieth Century Ireland*, (London: Oxford University Press, 1974).

about the charm of rural Irish life. As his cynical Irish partner observes, he keeps these separate ideas in watertight compartments, with 'all the compartments warranted impervious to anything it doesnt suit you to understand'. So Broadbent is charmed by the antics of Tim Haffigan, a stage Irishman who wishes him the top-o-the-mornin', until Doyle exposes him as a fraud and an imposter, born not in Ireland but in the streets of Glasgow. Doyle insists that the Stage Irishman is a creation of the British folk mind: 'All he [Haffigan] has to do is to sit there and drink your whiskey while you humbug yourself', he warns Broadbent, but to no avail, for the English partner attributes this anger to 'the melancholy of the Keltic race'. Doyle remarks that sweeping generalizations about the Celtic race constitute the most insidiously aggressive ploy of all the tactics used by imperialistic Englishmen. Such talk does more harm than ten coercion acts, because it gives rise to the feeling, bitterly and wittily mocked by Seamus Deane, that 'if the Celts stay quaint they will also stay put'.[5]

Yet Doyle himself submits to such Arnoldian thinking in his long speech on the Irishman's inability to face facts and to abandon the world of dreaming: 'An Irishman's imagination never lets him alone, never convinces him, never satisfies him; but it makes him that he cant face reality nor deal with it nor handle it nor conquer it: he can only sneer at them that do....' Arnold, of course, found this charming and quaint, whereas Doyle finds it frustrating and negative. As an empirical fact-facing Irishman, he felt uneasy in his own country — his youthful desire was to learn how to do something and then to get out of Ireland in order to have the chance to do it. The play itself seems to suggest that an Irishman will succeed far better in England than in Ireland, where the only successful men are all English. In Ireland, Broadbent plays the role of amateur of the Celts, the English liberal in search of round towers and fresh-faced colleens. So Broadbent, by his outrageous antics in the role of English duffer, manages to see only the Ireland he has come to see, a land of buffoons, derisive laughter and Celtic whimsy, where a pig can be taken for a ride in his car and an Englishman voted the fittest man to represent Roscullen in parliament. Broadbent adopts the protective coloration of the stage-English buffoon, to the enormous entertainment of the natives, who reciprocate by adopting the protective coloration of the stage-Irish peasant, taking tea at the wrong time of the day and laughing hysterically at every event that ensues. Larry Doyle foresees that, for his antics, Broadbent will not be laughed out of town but will be rewarded with Larry's girl and Larry's seat in Westminster: 'He'll never know theyre laughing at him; and while theyre laughing he'll win the seat.'

The driver who ferried Broadbent into Roscullen told him that the finest hotel in Ireland was there, but there is no hotel — just seventeen pubs. Aunt Jude excuses the driver: 'Sure he'd say hwatever was the least trouble to himself and the pleasantest to you'. This is the psychology that underlies the acting of all parties, both Irish and English. On the Irish side, Patsy Farrell, the callow labourer, exudes an air of helpless silliness which, says Shaw, is 'not his real character, but a cunning developed by his constant dread of a hostile dominance, which he habitually tries to disarm and tempt into unmasking by pretending to be a much greater fool than he really is. Englishmen think him half-witted, which is exactly what he intends them to think.' This, however, is precisely the strategy adopted already by the conquering Englishman, for, according to Larry Doyle, 'the Englishman does what the caterpillar does. He instinctively makes himself look like a fool, and eats up all the real fools at his ease while his enemies let him alone and laugh at him for being a fool like the rest. Oh, nature is cunning! cunning!' In other words, at root the English and Irish are identical peoples, who have nevertheless decided to perform extreme versions of Englishness and Irishness to one another in an attempt to wrest a material advantage from the unsuspecting audience of each performance. Each group projects onto the other all those attributes that they have denied in themselves, but at bottom both peoples are alike. This socialist perception is embodied in Hodson, Broadbent's servant, who does indeed find in Ireland the flexibility of mind to disown his master and to point to the common cause of the dispossessed Irish labourer and the exploited English proletariat.

Shaw's play, like Wilde's career, is a radical socialist critique of the Anglo-Irish antithesis so beloved of the Victorians and, it must be stressed, of that last Victorian, W.B. Yeats. By the simple expedient of presenting a romantic Englishman and

5. Seamus Deane, 'Irish Poetry and Irish Nationalism', in Douglas Dunn (ed.), *Two Decades of Irish Writings* (Cheadle, Cheshire: Carcanet Press, 1975), p. 16.

an empirical Irishman, *John Bull's Other Island* mocks the ancient stereotype. Of course, that is not the end of the story, for, by his performance of absurd sentimentality, Broadbent effectively takes over the entire village on the terms most favourable to himself, while Larry Doyle loses his cynical self-composure in the face of the ruin of his people. Larry's discriminating intellect paralyzes him into inactivity, for he has grown too subtle and too cynical, foolish in his very cleverness, whereas Broadbent's blinkered vision is finally what allows him to be so efficient, so clever in his very foolishness. In the end, the Anglo-Irish antithesis is questioned, but only to be reasserted in a slightly modified form.[6] It is left to the prophetic Peter Keegan to explain Boadbent's efficient victory: 'Let not the right side of your brain know what the left side doeth. I learnt at Oxford that this is the secret of the Englishman's strange power of making the best of both worlds.' By mastering the stereotype, by pretending to be a stage-fool, Broadbent has eaten up all the real fools, just as Larry predicted. Ireland has on this occasion been a useful laboratory for another English experiment.

It is no accident that the British Prime Minister Arthur Balfour should have attended Shaw's play with cabinet colleagues on four separate occasions, or that King Edward VII should have broken his chair while laughing at the production. After all, the play gratified English vanity, by managing at once to criticize the old stereotype and at the same time to suggest that it was true in a deeper and subtler way. English audiences not only found their ancient prejudices confirmed by a witty Irish playwright, but could leave the theatre with unexpected and clever evidence in support of their ancient bias. It was all too fitting that Shaw should have described himself as a faithful servant of the British people. There is a real sense in which his own play is itself an artistic casualty of the vice of compartmentalization which he satirizes. The plot issues in an emphatic victory for the efficient and romantic Englishman, but all the subversive witticisms have been uttered by a cynical but ineffectual Irishman. This was the very same dualism that Shaw detected in the comedies of Wilde, each of which contains some scathing witticisms at the expense of the institutions of British class society, but whose power to disturb is wholly disarmed by the reassuringly conventional nature of Wilde's plots. In such plots, the aristocratic society always wins out, as in *The Importance of Being Earnest,* where Lady Bracknell can marry off her Gwendolen to a young man of her own exalted class. Both Wilde and Shaw are finally English writers in the strict terms of Shaw's own definition of Englishness as a talent for keeping ideas separate in watertight compartments. The right side of the dramatist's brain never knows what the left doeth, and the plots of their plays are entirely at variance with the subversive one-liners and jokes. All of which is a measure of the artistic constraints on any socialist dramatist who sought a career in the London of the time.

Yeats's solution to this dilemma was to gather a native Irish audience and create a native Irish theatre in Dublin — to express Ireland to herself rather than run the risk of exploiting her for the foreigner. He accepted the Anglo-Irish antithesis, but only on condition that he was allowed to reinterpret it in a more flattering light. Whereas the English had called the Irish backward, superstitious and uncivilized, the Gaelic revivalists created an idealized counter-image, which saw her as pastoral, mystical, admirably primitive. Yet such a counter-image was not wholly effective, if only because it elevated a single aspect of Ireland into a type of the whole. 'Connaught for me is Ireland', said Yeats; but Ireland is not Connaught — rather she is a patchwork quilt of cultures, as she was before the Normans invaded. George Watson has devoted a valuable section of *Irish Identity and the Literary Revival* to an elaboration of this point, showing how Yeats's folklorism confirmed the traditional image of the Irish as subservient and menial — only now they were deemed menial in colourful and interesting new ways. 'The cracked looking-glass of a servant' was how Joyce's hero Stephen described such an art. It is an apt image, not just of Yeats's hopeless rehabilitation of the modes of deference but also of Joyce's own escape into modernism, for what a cracked looking-glass really shows is not a single but a multiple self.

JOHN BULL'S OTHER ISLAND (1904)

[Before Shaw had even sent the manuscript of *John Bull's Other Island* to Yeats, he had already planned an opening

6. A. Turco Jnr., *Shaw's Moral Vision* (Ithaca, New York: Cornell University Press, 1976), p. 178.

at the Royal Court Theatre in London for November 1904. It was hugely popular, due 'to the fact that in it the typical Englishman was sentimental and successful, which is how he likes to see himself, while the typical Irishman was clever and was assumed to be unsuccessful on no evidence whatever' (Hesketh Pearson, *George Bernard Shaw* (London: Methuen, 1961), p. 247).

Even Yeats was impressed by this thoroughly anti-Yeatsian play. 'It astonishes me that you have been so long in London', he wrote to Shaw, 'and yet have remembered so much'. (See M. Holroyd, 'GBS and Ireland' *Sewanee Review*, Vol. LXXXIV, No. 1 (Winter 1976), 51.) However, he found Shaw's very intensity about Irish affairs overwhelming rather than illuminating, alleging that sometimes the author's seriousness leaps upon the stage, knocks the characters over, and insists on having all the conversation to itself.

Shaw's diagnosis of Irish ills is certainly comprehensive, but his prescriptions for a cure are much less emphatic. This has led some to opine that, far from being knocked over by the author's seriousness, Shaw's characters finally escape his grasp. The final act is somewhat inconclusive, since the price of Keegan's wisdom and insight is an inability to act in any given situation. And yet, if properly played, this is one of Shaw's most memorable scenes, in which he espouses, for the first time, that visionary mode which would characterize many great, later plays. Moreover, his refusal of an emphatic conclusion is a deliberate strategy to compel the audience to consider the full complexities of the situation for itself.

The play, in fact, works on a number of levels, having one meaning in Dublin, another in London; and that, of course, is one of its central points. Like all problem plays, it raises ethical, religious and political questions in such a manner as to leave us in radical uncertainty about their proper resolution.]

CHARACTERS

TOM BROADBENT	HODSON
LARRY DOYLE	FATHER DEMPSEY
TIM HAFFIGAN	PATSY FARRELL
PETER KEEGAN	CORNELIUS DOYLE
NORA REILLY	MATTHEW HAFFIGAN
AUNT JUDY	BARNEY DORAN

ACT I

Great George Street, Westminster, is the address of Doyle and Broadbent, civil engineers. On the threshold one reads that the firm consists of Mr. Laurence Doyle and Mr. Thomas Broadbent, and that their rooms are on the first floor. Most of these rooms are private; for the partners, being bachelors and bosom friends, live there; and the door marked Private, next the clerks' office, is their domestic sitting room as well as their reception room for clients. Let me describe it briefly from the point of view of a sparrow on the window sill. The outer door is in the opposite wall, close to the right hand corner. Between this door and the left hand corner is a hatstand and a table consisting of large drawing boards on trestles, with plans, rolls of tracing paper, mathematical instruments, and other draughtsman's accessories on it. In the left hand wall is the fireplace, and the door of an inner room between the fireplace and our observant sparrow. Against the right hand wall is a filing cabinet, with a cupboard on it, and nearer, a tall office desk and stool for one person. In the middle of the room a large double writing table is set across, with a chair at each end for the two partners. It is a room which no woman would tolerate, smelling of tobacco, and much in need of repapering, repainting, and recarpeting; but this is the effect of bachelor untidiness and indifference, not want of means; for nothing that Doyle and Broadbent themselves have purchased is cheap; nor is anything they want lacking. On the walls hang a large map of South America, a pictorial advertisement of a steamship company, an impressive portrait of Gladstone,[1] *and several caricatures of Mr. Balfour*[2] *as a rabbit and Mr. Chamberlain as a fox by Francis Carruthers Gould.*[3]

At twenty minutes to five o'clock on a summer afternoon in 1904, the room is empty. Presently the outer door is opened, and a valet comes in laden with a large Gladstone bag[4] *and a strap of rugs. He carries them into the inner room. He is a respectable valet, old enough to have lost all alacrity and acquired an air of putting up patiently with a great deal of trouble and indifferent health. The luggage belongs to* BROADBENT, *who enters after the valet. He pulls off*

1. William Ewart Gladstone (1809-98), British Liberal leader and four times prime minister, who disestablished the Irish protestant church (1869), introduced two Land Bills (1870, 1881) and two Home Rule Bills (1886, 1893), yet died with his mission 'to pacify Ireland' unfulfilled.
2. Arthur Balfour (1848-1930), a Conservative statesman and repressive chief secretary for Ireland in the 1890s. He became British prime minister in 1902 and was staunchly opposed to Home Rule for Ireland. Attended Shaw's play accompanied by cabinet colleagues.
3. Joseph Chamberlain (1836-1914), radical Birmingham supporter of Gladstone, he later opposed the First Home Rule Bill, taunting both Parnell and Gladstone for its inadequacies. Increasingly baffled by Irish nationalism, he opposed the separatist claim, resigning over the Home Rule issue to form the Liberal Unionists. Later, Shaw refers to Broadbent's 'smarting under Mr Chamberlain's economic heresy'. Gould, whose real name was Bernard Partridge, did black-and-white drawings for the satirical magazine *Punch*.
4. A travelling bag or portmanteau, opening out flat, named after the British prime minister.

his overcoat and hangs it with his hat on the stand. Then he comes to the writing table and looks through the letters waiting there for him. He is a robust, full-blooded, energetic man in the prime of life, sometimes eager and credulous, sometimes shrewd and roguish, sometimes portentously solemn, sometimes jolly and impetuous, always buoyant and irresistible, mostly likeable, and enormously absurd in his most earnest moments. He bursts open his letters with his thumb, and glances through them, flinging the envelopes about the floor with reckless untidiness whilst he talks to the valet.

BROADBENT: (*Calling*) Hodson.

HODSON: (*In the bedroom*) Yes sir.

BROADBENT: Don't unpack. Just take out the things Ive worn; and put in clean things.

HODSON: (*Appearing at the bedroom door*) Yes sir. (*He turns to go back into the bedroom*)

BROADBENT: And look here! (HODSON *turns again*) Do you remember where I put my revolver?

HODSON: Revolver, sir! Yes sir. Mr. Doyle uses it as a paper-weight, sir, when he's drawing.

BROADBENT: Well, I want it packed. Theres a packet of cartridges somewhere, I think. Find it and pack it as well.

HODSON: Yes sir.

BROADBENT: By the way, pack your own traps[5] too. I shall take you with me this time.

HODSON: (*Hesitant*) Is it a dangerous part youre going to, sir? Should I be expected to carry a revolver, sir?

BROADBENT: Perhaps it might be as well. I'm going to Ireland.

HODSON: (*Reassured*) Yes sir.

BROADBENT: You dont feel nervous about it, I suppose?

HODSON: Not at all, sir. I'll risk it, sir.

BROADBENT: Ever been in Ireland?

HODSON: No sir. I understand it's a very wet climate, sir. I'd better pack your india-rubber overalls.

BROADBENT: Do. Wheres Mr. Doyle?

HODSON: I'm expecting him at five, sir. He went out after lunch.

BROADBENT: Anybody been looking for me?

HODSON: A person giving the name of Haffigan has called twice today, sir.

BROADBENT: Oh, I'm sorry. Why didnt he wait? I told him to wait if I wasnt in.

5. personal luggage.

HODSON: Well sir, I didn't know you expected him; so I thought it best to — to — not to encourage him, sir.

BROADBENT: Oh, he's all right. He's an Irishman, and not very particular about his appearance.

HODSON: Yes sir: I noticed that he was rather Irish.

BROADBENT: If he calls again let him come up.

HODSON: I think I saw him waiting about, sir, when you drove up. Shall I fetch him, sir?

BROADBENT: Do, Hodson.

HODSON: Yes sir. (*He makes for the outer door*)

BROADBENT: He'll want tea. Let us have some.

HODSON: (*Stopping*) I shouldnt think he drank tea, sir.

BROADBENT: Well, bring whatever you think he'd like.

HODSON: Yes sir. (*An electric bell rings*) Here he is, sir. Saw you arrive, sir.

BROADBENT: Right. Shew him in. (HODSON *goes out.* BROADBENT *gets through the rest of his letters before* HODSON *returns with the visitor*)

HODSON: Mr. Affigan.

HAFFIGAN *is a stunted, shortnecked, smallheaded man of about 30, with a small bullet head, a red nose, and furtive eyes. He is dressed in seedy black, almost clerically, and might be a tenth-rate schoolmaster ruined by drink. He hastens to shake* BROADBENT'S *hand with a show of reckless geniality and high spirits, helped out by a rollicking stage brogue. This is perhaps a comfort to himself, as he is secretly pursued by the horrors of incipient delirium tremens.*

HAFFIGAN: Tim Haffigan, sir, at your service. The top o the mornin to you, Misther Broadbent.

BROADBENT: (*Delighted with his Irish visitor*) Good afternoon, Mr. Haffigan.

TIM: An is it the afthernoon it is already? Begorra,[6] what I call the mornin is all the time a man fasts afther breakfast.

BROADBENT: Havent you lunched?

TIM: Divil a lunch![7]

BROADBENT: I'm sorry I couldnt get back from Brighton in time to offer you some; but —

TIM: Not a word, sir, not a word. Sure itll do

6. A Hiberno-English corruption of 'By God'. The phrase, like 'top o the morning' and others used by Haffigan, was a stock-in-trade of the nineteenth-century stage Irishman in English music halls. Hence also Haffigan's confusion of the sound-values 't' and 'th', which are not discriminated in the Irish language.

7. i.e. no lunch.

tomorrow. Besides, I'm Irish, sir: a poor aither, but a powerful dhrinker.

BROADBENT: I was just about to ring for tea when you came. Sit down, Mr. Haffigan.

TIM: Tay is a good dhrink if your nerves can stand it. Mine can't.

HAFFIGAN *sits down at the writing table, with his back to the filing cabinet.* BROADBENT *sits opposite him.* HODSON *enters empty-handed; takes two glasses, a siphon, and a tantalus*[8] *from the cupboard; places them before* BROADBENT *on the writing table; looks ruthlessly at* HAFFIGAN, *who cannot meet his eye; and retires.*

BROADBENT: Try a whisky and soda.

TIM: (*Sobered*) There you touch the national wakeness, sir. (*Piously*) Not that I share it meself. Ive seen too much of the mischief of it.

BROADBENT: (*Pouring the whisky*) Say when.

TIM: Not too sthrong. (BROADBENT *stops and looks inquiringly at him*) Say half-an-half. (BROADBENT, *somewhat startled by this demand, pours a little more, and again stops and looks*) Just a dhrain more: the lower half o the tumbler doesnt hold a fair half. Thankya.

BROADBENT: (*Laughing*) You Irishmen certainly do know how to drink. (*Pouring some whisky for himself*) Now thats my poor English idea of a whisky and soda.

TIM: An a very good idea it is too. Dhrink is the curse o me unhappy counthry. I take it meself because Ive a wake heart and a poor digestion; but in principle I'm a teetoatler.

BROADBENT: (*Suddenly solemn and strenuous*) So am I, of course. I'm a Local Optionist[9] to the backbone. You have no idea, Mr Haffigan, of the ruin that is wrought in this country by the unholy alliance of the publicans, the bishops, the Tories, and The Times. We must close the public-houses at all costs. (*He drinks*)

TIM: Sure I know. It's awful. (*He drinks*) I see youre a good Liberal like meself, sir.

BROADBENT: I am a lover of liberty, like every true Englishman, Mr Haffigan. My name is Broadbent. If my name were Breitstein,[10] and I had a hooked nose and a house in Park Lane, I should carry a Union Jack handkerchief and a penny trumpet, and tax the food of the people to support the Navy League, and clamor for the destruction of the last remnants of national liberty —

TIM: Not another word. Shake hands.

BROADBENT: But I should like to explain —

TIM: Sure I know every word youre goin to say before yev said it. *I* know the sort o man yar. An so youre thinkin o comin to Ireland for a bit?

BROADBENT: Where else can I go? I am an Englishman and a Liberal; and now that South Africa has been enslaved and destroyed,[11] there is no country left to me to take an interest in but Ireland. Mind: I dont say that an Englishman has not other duties. He has a duty to Finland and a duty to Macedonia. But what sane man can deny that an Englishman's first duty is his duty to Ireland? Unfortunately, we have politicians here more unscrupulous than Bobrikoff, more bloodthirsty than Abdul the Damned;[12] and it is under their heel that Ireland is now writhing.

TIM: Faith, theyve reckoned up with poor oul Bobrikoff anyhow.

BROADBENT: Not that I defend assassination: God forbid! However strongly we may feel that the unfortunate and patriotic young man who avenged the wrongs of Finland on the Russian tyrant was perfectly right from his own point of view, yet every civilized man must regard murder with abhorrence. Not even in defence of Free Trade would I lift my hand against a political opponent, however richly he might deserve it.

TIM: I'm sure you wouldnt; and I honor you for it. Youre goin to Ireland, then, out o sympithy: is it?

BROADBENT: I'm going to develop an estate there for the Land Development Syndicate, in which I am interested. I am convinced that all it needs to make it pay is to handle it properly, as estates are handled in England. You know the English plan, Mr Haffigan, dont you?

TIM: Bedad I do, sir. Take all you can out of Ireland and spend it in England: thats it.

8. A case in which decanters are visible, but locked up.
9. A group that campaigned for the right of individual communities to decide whether to allow licensed premises to open.
10. The first of many hints that much English nationalism is the creation of Jews, anxious to impatriate themselves. See Larry Doyle's later remarks on patriotic songs by German Jews.
11. The Boer War (1899-1902) ended with the Peace of Vereeniging after a brutal campaign of farm-burning and concentration camps had forced the Boers to surrender. The war divided Britain's Liberal Party, but united the Parnellites and anti-Parnellites of the Irish Party at Westminster, in support of the Boers.
12. Sultan Abdul Hamid II of Turkey (1842-1918) was forced to promise reforms after his part in the massacres of Armenians in Turkey 1894-96. General Nikolay Ivanovich Bobrikoff (1839-1904), the ruthless Governor General of Finland, was assassinated on 16 June 1904. He is mentioned in the 'Aeolus' episode of Joyce's *Ulysses* (133.16).

BROADBENT: (*Not quite liking this*) My plan, sir, will be to take a little money out of England and spend it in Ireland.

TIM: More power to your elbow! an may your shadda never be less! for youre the broth of a boy[13] intirely. An how can I help you? Command me to the last dhrop o me blood.

BROADBENT: Have you ever heard of Garden City?

TIM: (*Doubtfully*) D'ye mane Heavn?

BROADBENT: Heaven! No: it's near Hitchin. If you can spare half an hour I'll go into it with you.

TIM: I tell you hwat, Gimme a prospectus. Lemmy take it home and reflect on it.

BROADBENT: Youre quite right: I will. (*He gives him a copy of Ebenezer Howard's book,*[14] *and several pamphlets*) You understand that the map of the city — the circular construction — is only a suggestion.

TIM: I'll make a careful note o that. (*Looking dazedly at the map*)

BROADBENT: What I say is, why not start a Garden City in Ireland?

TIM: (*With enthusiasm*) Thats just what was on the tip o me tongue to ask you. Why not? (*Defiantly*) Tell me why not.

BROADBENT: There are difficulties. I shall overcome them; but there are difficulties. When I first arrive in Ireland I shall be hated as an Englishman. As a Protestant, I shall be denounced from every altar. My life may be in danger. Well, I am prepared to face that.

TIM: Never fear, sir. We know how to respict a brave innimy.

BROADBENT: What I really dread is misunderstanding. I think you could help me to avoid that. When I heard you speak the other evening in Bermondsey at the meeting of the National League, I saw at once that you were — You wont mind my speaking frankly?

TIM: Tell me all me faults as man to man. I can stand anything but flatthery.

BROADBENT: May I put it in this way? that I saw at once that you are a thorough Irishman, with all the faults and all the qualities of your race: rash and improvident but brave and goodnatured; not likely to succeed in business on your own account perhaps, but eloquent, humorous, a lover of freedom, and a true follower of that great Englishman Gladstone.

TIM: Spare me blushes. I mustnt sit here to be praised to me face. But I confess to the goodnature: it's an Irish wakeness. I'd share me last shillin with a friend.

BROADBENT: I feel sure you would, Mr Haffigan.

TIM: (*Impulsively*) Damn it! call me Tim. A man that talks about Ireland as you do may call me anything. Gimy a howlt o that whisky bottle. (*He replenishes*)

BROADBENT: (*Smiling indulgently*) Well, Tim, will you come with me and help to break the ice between me and your warmhearted, impulsive countrymen?

TIM: Will I come to Madagascar or Cochin China wid you? Bedad I'll come to the North Pole wid you if yll pay me fare; for the divil a shillin I have to buy a third class ticket.

BROADBENT: Ive not forgotten that, Tim. We must put that little matter on a solid English footing, though the rest can be as Irish as you please. You must come as my — my — well, I hardly know what to call it. If we call you my agent, theyll shoot you. If we call you a bailiff, theyll duck you in the horsepond. I have a secretary already; and —

TIM: Then we'll call him the Home Secretary and me the Irish Secretary.[15] Eh?

BROADBENT: (*Laughing industriously*) Capital. Your Irish wit has settled the first difficulty. Now about your salary —

TIM: A salary, is it? Sure I'd do it for nothin, only me cloes ud disgrace you; and I'd be dhriven to borra money from your friends: a thing thats agin me nacher.[16] But I wont take a penny more than a hundherd a year. (*He looks with restless cunning at* BROADBENT, *trying to guess how far he may go*)

BROADBENT: If that will satisfy you —

TIM: (*More than reassured*) Why shouldnt it satisfy me? A hundherd a year is twelve pound a month, isnt it?

BROADBENT: No. Eight pound six and eightpence.

TIM: Oh murdher! An I'll have to sind five timmy poor oul mother in Ireland. But no matther: I said a hundherd; and what I said I'll stick to, if I have to starve for it.

13. Characteristic English phrase to describe a robust stage-Irishman.
14. Sir Ebenezer Howard (1850-1928), an English town-planner, was the principal founder of the garden-city movement. His *Garden Cities of Tomorrow* (1902) outlined a model self-sustaining town that combined urban conveniences and industries with the advantages of an agricultural location.
15. Pun on titles of two ministerial officials in government.
16. nature.

BROADBENT: (*With business caution*) Well, let us say twelve pounds for the first month. Afterwards, we shall see how we get on.

TIM: Youre a gentleman, sir. Whin me mother turns up her toes, you shall take the five pounds off; for your expinses must be kep down wid a sthrong hand; an — (*He is interrupted by the arrival of* BROADBENT'S *partner*)

MR LAURENCE DOYLE *is a man of 36, with cold grey eyes, strained nose, fine fastidious lips, critical brows, clever head, rather refined and goodlooking on the whole, but with a suggestion of thinskinnedness and dissatisfaction that contrasts strongly with* BROADBENT'S *eupeptic*[17] *jollity.*

He comes in as a man at home there, but on seeing the stranger shrinks at once, and is about to withdraw when BROADBENT *reassures him. He then comes forward to the table, between the two others.*

DOYLE: (*Retreating*) Youre engaged.

BROADBENT: Not at all, not at all. Come in. (*To* TIM) This gentleman is a friend who lives with me here: my partner, Mr Doyle. (*To* DOYLE) This is a new Irish friend of mine, Mr Tim Haffigan.

TIM: (*Rising with effusion*) Sure it's meself thats proud to meet any friend o Misther Broadbent's. The top o the mornin to you, sir! Me heart goes out teeye both. It's not often I meet two such splendid speciments iv the Anglo-Saxon race.

BROADBENT: (*Chuckling*) Wrong for once, Tim. My friend Mr Doyle is a countryman of yours.
TIM *is noticeably dashed by this announcement. He draws in his horns at once, and scowls suspiciously at* DOYLE *under a vanishing mask of good-fellowship: cringing a little, too, in mere nerveless fear of him.*

DOYLE: (*With cool disgust*) Good evening. (*He retires to the fireplace, and says to* BROADBENT *in a tone which conveys the strongest possible hint to* HAFFIGAN *that he is unwelcome*) Will you soon be disengaged?

TIM: (*His brogue decaying into a common would-be genteel accent with an unexpected strain of Glasgow in it*) I must be going. Avnmpoartnt engeegement in the west end.

BROADBENT: (*Rising*) It's settled, then, that you come with me.

TIM: Ashll be verra pleased to accompany ye, sir.

BROADBENT: But how soon? Can you start tonight? from Paddington.[18] We go by Milford Haven.

TIM: (*Hesitating*) Well — A'm afraid — A (DOYLE *goes abruptly into the bedroom, slamming the door and shattering the last remnant of* TIM'S *nerve. The poor wretch saves himself from bursting into tears by plunging again into his role of daredevil Irishman. He rushes to* BROADBENT; *plucks at his sleeve with trembling fingers; and pours forth his entreaty with all the brogue he can muster, subduing his voice lest* DOYLE *should hear and return*) Misther Broadbent: dont humiliate me before a fella counthryman. Look here: me cloes is up the spout. Gimmy a fypoun-note — I'll pay ya next Choosda[19] whin me ship comes home — or you can stop it out o me month's sallery. I'll be on the platform at Paddnton punctial an ready. Gimmy it quick, before he comes back. You wont mind me axin, will ye?

BROADBENT: Not at all. I was about to offer you an advance for travelling expenses. (*He gives him a bank note*)

TIM: (*Pocketing it*) Thank you. I'll be there half an hour before the thrain starts. (LARRY *is heard at the bedroom door, returning*) Whisht:[20] he's comin back. Goodbye an God bless ye. (*He hurries out almost crying, the £5 note and all the drink it means to him being too much for his empty stomach and overstrained nerves*)

DOYLE: (*Returning*) Where the devil did you pick up that seedy swindler? What was he doing here? (*He goes up to the table where the plans are, and makes a note on one of them, referring to his pocket book as he does so*)

BROADBENT: There you go! Why are you so down on every Irishman you meet, especially if he's a bit shabby? poor devil! Surely a fellow-countryman may pass you the top of the morning without offence, even if his coat is a bit shiny at the seams.

DOYLE: (*Contemptuously*) The top of the morning! Did he call you the broth of a boy? (*He comes to the writing table*)

BROADBENT: (*Triumphantly*) Yes.

DOYLE: And wished you more power to your elbow?

BROADBENT: He did.

DOYLE: And that your shadow might never be less?

BROADBENT: Certainly.

DOYLE: (*Taking up the depleted whisky bottle and*

17. cheerful, pertaining to good digestion.
18. Mainline railway station in London, from where the Irish boat train departed.
19. Tuesday.
20. Be silent.

shaking his head at it) And he got about half a pint of whisky out of you.

BROADBENT: It did him no harm. He never turned a hair.

DOYLE: How much money did he borrow?

BROADBENT: It was not borrowing exactly. He shewed a very honorable spirit about money. I believe he would share his last shilling with a friend.

DOYLE: No doubt he would share his friend's last shilling if his friend was fool enough to let him. How much did he touch you for?

BROADBENT: Oh, nothing. An advance on his salary — for travelling expenses.

DOYLE: Salary! In Heaven's name, what for?

BROADBENT: For being my Home Secretary, as he very wittily called it.[21]

DOYLE: I dont see the joke.

BROADBENT: You can spoil any joke by being cold blooded about it. I saw it all right when he said it. It was something — something really very amusing — about the Home Secretary and the Irish Secretary. At all events, he's evidently the very man to take with me to Ireland to break the ice for me. He can gain the confidence of the people there, and make them friendly to me. Eh? (*He seats himself on the office stool, and tilts it back so that the edge of the standing desk supports his back and prevents his toppling over*)

DOYLE: A nice introduction, by George! Do you suppose the whole population of Ireland consists of drunken begging letter writers, or that even if it did, they would accept one another as references?

BROADBENT: Pooh! nonsense! he's only an Irishman. Besides, you dont seriously suppose that Haffigan can humbug me, do you?

DOYLE: No: he's took lazy to take the trouble. All he has to do is to sit there and drink your whisky while you humbug yourself. However, we neednt argue about Haffigan, for two reasons. First, with your money in his pocket he will never reach Paddington: there are too many public houses on the way. Second, he's not an Irishman at all.

BROADBENT: Not an Irishman! (*He is so amazed by the statement that he straightens himself and brings the stool bolt upright*)

DOYLE: Born in Glasgow. Never was in Ireland in his life. I know all about him.

BROADBENT: But he spoke — he behaved just like an Irishman.

DOYLE: Like an Irishman!! Man alive, dont you know that all this top-o-the-morning and broth-of-a-boy and more-power-to-your-elbow business is got up in England to fool you, like the Albert Hall concerts of Irish music? No Irishman ever talks like that in Ireland, or ever did, or ever will. But when a thoroughly worthless Irishman comes to England, and finds the whole place full of romantic duffers like you, who will let him loaf and drink and sponge and brag as long as he flatters your sense of moral superiority by playing the fool and degrading himself and his country, he soon learns the antics that take you in. He picks them up at the theatre or the music hall. Haffigan learnt the rudiments from his father, who came from my part of Ireland. I knew his uncles, Matt and Andy Haffigan of Rosscullen.

BROADBENT: (*Still incredulous*) But his brogue?

DOYLE: His brogue! A fat lot you know about brogues! Ive heard you call a Dublin accent that you could hang your hat on, a brogue. Heaven help you! you dont know the difference between Connemara and Rathmines.[22] (*With violent irritation*) Oh, damn Tim Haffigan! lets drop the subject: he's not worth wrangling about.

BROADBENT: Whats wrong with you today, Larry? Why are you so bitter?

DOYLE *looks at him perplexedly; comes slowly to the writing table; and sits down at the end next the fireplace before replying.*

DOYLE: Well: your letter completely upset me, for one thing.

BROADBENT: Why?

DOYLE: Your foreclosing this Rosscullen mortgage and turning poor Nick Lestrange out of house and home has rather taken me aback; for I liked the old rascal when I was a boy and had the run of his park to play in. I was brought up on the property.

BROADBENT: But he wouldnt pay the interest. I had to foreclose on behalf of the Syndicate. So now I'm off to Rosscullen to look after the property myself. (*He sits down at the writing table opposite* LARRY, *and adds, casually, but with an anxious glance at his partner*) Youre coming with me, of course?

DOYLE: (*Rising nervously and recommencing his restless movements*) Thats it. Thats what I dread. Thats what has upset me.

21. But Tim Haffigan had suggested that he be Broadbent's Irish, not Home, Secretary.

22. A wild, rugged region of west Connacht, contrasted with a fashionable Dublin suburb.

BROADBENT: But dont you want to see your country again after 18 years absence? to see your people? to be in the old home again? to —

DOYLE: (*Interrupting him very impatiently*) Yes, yes: I know all that as well as you do.

BROADBENT: Oh well, of course (*with a shrug*) if you take it in that way, I'm sorry.

DOYLE: Never you mind my temper: it's not meant for you, as you ought to know by this time. (*He sits down again, a little ashamed of his petulance; reflects a moment bitterly; then bursts out*) I have an instinct against going back to Ireland: an instinct so strong that I'd rather go with you to the South Pole than to Rosscullen.

BROADBENT: What! Here you are, belonging to a nation with the strongest patriotism! the most inveterate homing instinct in the world! and you pretend youd rather go anywhere than back to Ireland. You dont suppose I believe you, do you? In your heart —

DOYLE: Never mind my heart: an Irishman's heart is nothing but his imagination. How many of all those millions that have left Ireland have ever come back or wanted to come back? But whats the use of talking to you? Three verses of twaddle about the Irish emigrant 'sitting on the stile, Mary,' or three hours of Irish patriotism in Bermondsey or the Scotland Division of Liverpool, go further with you than all the facts that stare you in the face. Why, man alive, look at me! You know the way I nag, and worry, and carp, and cavil, and disparage, and am never satisfied and never quiet, and try the patience of my best friends.

BROADBENT: Oh, come, Larry! do yourself justice. Youre very amusing and agreeable to strangers.

DOYLE: Yes, to strangers. Perhaps if I was a bit stiffer to strangers, and a bit easier at home, like an Englishman, I'd be better company for you.

BROADBENT: We got on well enough. Of course you have the melancholy of the Keltic race —

DOYLE: (*Bounding out of his chair*) Good God!!!

BROADBENT: (*Slyly*) — and also its habit of using strong language when theres nothing the matter.

DOYLE: Nothing the matter! When people talk about the Celtic race, I feel as if I could burn down London. That sort of rot does more harm than ten Coercion Acts.[23] Do you suppose a man need be a Celt to feel melancholy in Rosscullen? Why, man, Ireland was peopled just as England was; and its breed was crossed by just the same invaders.

BROADBENT: True. All the capable people in Ireland are of English extraction. It has often struck me as a most remarkable circumstance that the only party in parliament which shews the genuine old English character and spirit is the Irish party. Look at its independence, its determination, its defiance of bad Governments, its sympathy with oppressed nationalities all the world over! How English!

DOYLE: Not to mention the solemnity with which it talks old-fashioned nonsense which it knows perfectly well to be a century behind the times. Thats English, if you like.

BROADBENT: No, Larry, no. You are thinking of the modern hybrids that now monopolize England. Hypocrites, humbugs, Germans, Jews, Yankees, foreigners, Park Laners, cosmopolitan riffraff.[24] Dont call them English. They dont belong to the dear old island, but to their confounded new empire; and by George! theyre worthy of it; and I wish them joy of it.

DOYLE: (*Unmoved by this outburst*) There! You feel better now, dont you?

BROADBENT: (*Defiantly*) I do. Much better.

DOYLE: My dear Tom, you only need a touch of the Irish climate to be as big a fool as I am myself. If all my Irish blood were poured into your veins, you wouldnt turn a hair of your constitution and character. Go and marry the most English Englishwoman you can find, and then bring up your son in Rosscullen; and that son's character will be so like mine and so unlike yours that everybody will accuse me of being his father. (*With sudden anguish*) Rosscullen! oh, good Lord, Rosscullen! The dullness! the hopelessness! the ignorance! the bigotry!

BROADBENT: (*Matter-of-factly*) The usual thing in the country, Larry. Just the same here.

DOYLE: (*Hastily*) No, no: the climate is different. Here, if the life is dull, you can be dull too, and no great harm done. (*Going off into a passionate dream*) But your wits cant thicken in that soft moist air, on those white springy roads, in those misty rushes and brown bogs, on those hillsides of granite rocks and magenta heather. Youve no such colors in the sky, no such lure in the distances, no such sadness in the evenings. Oh, the dreaming! the

23. Repressive government measures enacted throughout the nineteenth century to stamp out resistance in Ireland.

24. bohemian types.

dreaming! the torturing, heart-scalding, never satisfying dreaming, dreaming, dreaming, dreaming! (*Savagely*) No debauchery that ever coarsened and brutalized an Englishman can take the worth and usefulness out of him like that dreaming. An Irishman's imagination never lets him alone, never convinces him, never satisfies him; but it makes him that he cant face reality nor deal with it nor handle it nor conquer it: he can only sneer at them that do, and (*bitterly, to* BROADBENT) be 'agreeable to strangers,' like a good-for-nothing woman on the streets. (*Gabbling at* BROADBENT *across the table*) It's all dreaming, all imagination. He cant be religious. The inspired Churchman that teaches him the sanctity of life and the importance of conduct is sent away empty; while the poor village priest that gives him a miracle or a sentimental story of a saint, has cathedrals built for him out of the pennies of the poor. He cant be intelligently political: he dreams of what the Shan Van Vocht[25] said in ninetyeight.[26] If you want to interest him in Ireland youve got to call the unfortunate island Kathleen ni Hoolihan[27] and pretend she's a little old woman. It saves thinking. It saves working. It saves everything except imagination, imagination, imagination; and imagination's such a torture that you cant bear it without whisky. (*With fierce shivering self-contempt*) At last you get that you can bear nothing real at all: youd rather starve than cook a meal; youd rather go shabby and dirty than set your mind to take care of your clothes and wash yourself; you nag and squabble at home because your wife isnt an angel, and she despises you because youre not a hero; and you hate the whole lot round you because theyre only poor slovenly useless devils like yourself. (*Dropping his voice like a man making some shameful confidence*) And all the while there goes on a horrible, senseless, mischievous laughter. When youre young, you exchange drinks with other young men; and you exchange vile stories with them; and as youre too futile to be able to help or cheer them, you chaff and sneer and taunt them for not doing the things you darent do yourself. And all the time you laugh! laugh! laugh! eternal derision, eternal envy, eternal folly, eternal fouling and staining and degrading, until, when you come at last to a country where men take a question seriously and give a serious answer to it, you deride them for having no sense of humor, and plume yourself on your own worthlessness as if it made you better than them.

BROADBENT: (*Roused to intense earnestness by* DOYLE's *eloquence*) Never despair, Larry. There are great possibilities for Ireland. Home Rule[28] will work wonders under English guidance.

DOYLE: (*Pulled up short, his face twitching with a reluctant smile*) Tom: why do you select my most tragic moments for your most irresistible strokes of humor?

BROADBENT: Humor! I was perfectly serious. What do you mean? Do you doubt my seriousness about Home Rule?

DOYLE: I am sure you are serious, Tom, about the English guidance.

BROADBENT: (*Quite reassured*) Of course I am. Our guidance is the important thing. We English must place our capacity for government without stint at the service of nations who are less fortunately endowed in that respect; so as to allow them to develop in perfect freedom to the English level of self-government, you know. You understand me?

DOYLE: Perfectly. And Rosscullen will understand you too.

BROADBENT: (*Cheerfully*) Of course it will. So thats all right. (*He pulls up his chair and settles himself comfortably to lecture* DOYLE) Now, Larry, Ive listened carefully to all youve said about Ireland; and I can see nothing whatever to prevent your coming with me. What does it all come to? Simply that you were only a young fellow when you were in Ireland. Youll find all that chaffing and drinking and not knowing what to be at in Peckham just the same as in Donnybrook.[29] You looked at Ireland with a boy's eyes and saw only boyish things. Come back with me and look at it with a man's; and get a better opinion of your country.

DOYLE: I daresay youre partly right in that: at all events I know very well that if I had been the son of a laborer instead of the son of a country landagent,

25. *Sean-bhean bhocht* is Gaelic for 'poor old woman', one of many metaphorical designations of Ireland as female.
26. 1798, a year of widespread rebellion when the Shan Van Vocht sang that 'the French are on the sea'.
27. W. B. Yeats wrote a nationalist play (*Cathleen Ni Houlihan*, 1902) suggesting that this old woman would again walk like a radiant young queen, when young men were willing to kill and die for her.
28. A proposal to restore a native parliament to an Ireland that would still remain a possession of Britain, based on a famous nineteenth-century Saxonist theory that Celts could thrive only under English rule.
29. Suburbs of London and Dublin respectively.

I should have struck more grit than I did. Unfortunately I'm not going back to visit the Irish nation, but to visit my father and Aunt Judy and Nora Reilly and Father Dempsey and the rest of them.

BROADBENT: Well, why not? Theyll be delighted to see you, now that England has made a man of you.

DOYLE: (*Struck by this*) Ah! you hit the mark there, Tom, with true British inspiration.

BROADBENT: Common sense, you mean.

DOYLE: (*Quickly*) No I dont: youve no more common sense than a gander. No Englishman has any common sense, or ever had, or ever will have. Youre going on a sentimental expedition for perfectly ridiculous reasons, with your head full of political nonsense that would not take in any ordinarily intelligent donkey; but you can hit me in the eye with the simple truth about myself and my father.

BROADBENT: (*Amazed*) I never mentioned your father.

DOYLE: (*Not heeding the interruption*) There he is in Rosscullen, a landagent who's always been in a small way because he's a Catholic, and the landlords are mostly Protestants. What with land courts reducing rents and Land Purchase Acts[30] turning big estates into little holdings, he'd be a beggar if he hadnt taken to collecting the new purchase instalments instead of the old rents. I doubt if he's been further from home than Athenmullet for twenty years. And here am I, made a man of, as you say, by England.

BROADBENT: (*Apologetically*) I assure you I never meant —

DOYLE: Oh, dont apologize: it's quite true. I daresay Ive learnt something in America and a few other remote and inferior spots; but in the main it is by living with you and working in double harness with you that I have learnt to live in a real world and not in an imaginary one. I owe more to you than to any Irishman.

BROADBENT: (*Shaking his head with a twinkle in his eye*) Very friendly of you, Larry, old man, but all blarney.[31] I like blarney; but it's rot, all the same.

DOYLE: No it's not. I should never have done anything without you; though I never stop wondering at that blessed old head of yours with all its ideas in watertight compartments, and all the compartments warranted impervious to anything it doesnt suit you to understand.

BROADBENT: (*Invincible*) Unmitigated rot, Larry, I assure you.

DOYLE: Well, at any rate you will admit that all my friends are either Englishmen or men of the big world that belongs to the big Powers. All the serious part of my life has been lived in that atmosphere: all the serious part of my work has been done with men of that sort. Just think of me as I am now going back to Rosscullen! to that hell of littleness and monotony! How am I to get on with a little country landagent that ekes out his 5 per cent with a little farming and a scrap of house property in the nearest country town? What am I to say to him? What is he to say to me?

BROADBENT: (*Scandalized*) But youre father and son, man!

DOYLE: What difference does that make? What would you say if I proposed a visit to your father?

BROADBENT: (*With filial rectitude*) I always made a point of going to see my father regularly until his mind gave way.

DOYLE: (*Concerned*) Has he gone mad? You never told me.

BROADBENT: He has joined the Tariff Reform League.[32] He would never have done that if his mind had not been weakened. (*Beginning to declaim*) He has fallen a victim to the arts of a political charlatan who —

DOYLE: (*Interrupting him*) You mean that you keep clear of your father because he differs from you about Free Trade, and you dont want to quarrel with him. Well, think of me and my father! He's a Nationalist and a Separatist. I'm a metallurgical chemist turned civil engineer. Now whatever else metallurgical chemistry may be, it's not national. It's international. And my business and yours as civil engineers is to join countries, not to separate them. The one real political conviction that our business has rubbed into us is that frontiers are hindrances and flags confounded nuisances.

BROADBENT: (*Still smarting under Mr Chamberlain's economic heresy*) Only when there is a protective tariff —

DOYLE: (*Firmly*) Now look here, Tom; you want

30. These allowed tenants to buy portions of the estates once held by Anglo-Irish landlords.

31. Idle talk, colourful spoofing, often in flattery. The Blarney Stone in County Cork is reputed to confer on those who kiss it the gift of eloquence.

32. This League called for the imposition of taxes on imports.

to get in a speech on Free Trade; and youre not going to do it: I wont stand it. My father wants to make St George's Channel[33] a frontier and hoist a green flag on College Green;[34] and I want to bring Galway within 3 hours of Colchester and 24 of New York. I want Ireland to be the brains and imagination of a big Commonwealth, not a Robinson Crusoe island. Then theres the religious difficulty. My Catholicism is the Catholicism of Charlemagne or Dante, qualified by a great deal of modern science and folklore which Father Dempsey would call the ravings of an Atheist. Well, my father's Catholicism is the Catholicism of Father Dempsey.

BROADBENT: (*Shrewdly*) I dont want to interrupt you, Larry; but you know this is all gammon.[35] These differences exist in all families; but the members rub on together all right. (*Suddenly relapsing into portentousness*) Of course there are some questions which touch the very foundations of morals; and on these I grant you even the closest relationships cannot excuse any compromise or laxity. For instance —

DOYLE: (*Impatiently springing up and walking about*) For instance, Home Rule, South Africa, Free Trade, and putting the Church schools on the Education Rate. Well, I should differ from my father on every one of them, probably, just as I differ from you about them.

BROADBENT: Yes; but you are an Irishman; and these things are not serious to you as they are to an Englishman.

DOYLE: What! not even Home Rule!

BROADBENT: (*Steadfastly*) Not even Home Rule. We owe Home Rule not to the Irish, but to our English Gladstone. No, Larry: I cant help thinking that theres something behind all this.

DOYLE: (*Hotly*) What is there behind it? Do you think I'm humbugging you?

BROADBENT: Dont fly out, old chap. I only thought —

DOYLE: What did you think?

BROADBENT: Well, a moment ago I caught a name which is new to me: a Miss Nora Reilly, I think. (DOYLE *stops dead and stares at him with something like awe*) I dont wish to be impertinent, as you know, Larry; but are you sure she has nothing to do with your reluctance to come to Ireland with me?

DOYLE: (*Sitting down again, vanquished*) Thomas Broadbent: I surrender. The poor silly-clever Irishman takes off his hat to God's Englishman. The man who could in all seriousness make that recent remark of yours about Home Rule and Gladstone must be simply the champion idiot of all the world. Yet the man who could in the very next sentence sweep away all my special pleading and go straight to the heart of my motives must be a man of genius. But that the idiot and the genius should be the same man! how is that possible? (*Springing to his feet*) By Jove, I see it all now. I'll write an article about it, and send it to *Nature*.[36]

BROADBENT: (*Staring at him*) What on earth —

DOYLE: It's quite simple. You know that a caterpillar —

BROADBENT: A caterpillar!!!

DOYLE: Yes, a caterpillar. Now give your mind to what I am going to say; for it's a new and important scientific theory of the English national character. A caterpillar —

BROADBENT: Look here, Larry: dont be an ass.

DOYLE: (*Insisting*) I say a caterpillar and I mean a caterpillar. Youll understood presently. A caterpillar (BROADBENT *mutters a slight protest, but does not press it*) when it gets into a tree, instinctively makes itself look exactly like a leaf; so that both its enemies and its prey may mistake it for one and think it not worth bothering about.

BROADBENT: Whats that got to do with our English national character?

DOYLE: I'll tell you. The world is as full of fools as a tree is full of leaves. Well, the Englishman does what the caterpillar does. He instinctively makes himself look like a fool, and eats up all the real fools at his ease while his enemies let him alone and laugh at him for being a fool like the rest. Oh, nature is cunning! cunning! (*He sits down, lost in contemplation of his word-picture*)

BROADBENT: (*With hearty admiration*) Now you know, Larry, that would never have occurred to me. You Irish people are amazingly clever. Of course it's all tommy rot; but it's so brilliant, you know! How the dickens do you think of such things! You really must write an article about it: theyll pay you something for it. If *Nature* wont have it, I can

33. A stretch of sea between south-east Ireland and the coast of Britain.
34. Seat of Grattan's parliament in Dublin, 1782-1800.
35. chatter, especially that designed to distract attention from the central issues. May derive from the game of backgammon.
36. A periodical founded in 1869 to provide the public with information on scientific matters.

get it into *Engineering* for you: I know the editor.

DOYLE: Lets get back to business. I'd better tell you about Nora Reilly.

BROADBENT: No: never mind. I shouldnt have alluded to her.

DOYLE: I'd rather. Nora has a fortune.

BROADBENT: (*Keenly interested*) Eh? How much?

DOYLE: Forty per annum.

BROADBENT: Forty thousand?

DOYLE: No, forty. Forty pounds.

BROADBENT: (*Much dashed*) Thats what you call a fortune in Rosscullen, is it?

DOYLE: A girl with a dowry of five pounds calls it a fortune in Rosscullen. Whats more, £40 a year is a fortune there; and Nora Reilly enjoys a good deal of social consideration as an heiress on the strength of it. It has helped my father's household through many a tight place. My father was her father's agent. She came on a visit to us when he died, and has lived with us ever since.

BROADBENT: (*Attentively, beginning to suspect* LARRY *of misconduct with* NORA, *and resolving to get to the bottom of it*) Since when? I mean how old were you when she came?

DOYLE: I was seventeen. So was she: if she'd been older she'd have had more sense than to stay with us. We were together for 18 months before I went up to Dublin to study. When I went home for Christmas and Easter, she was there. I suppose it used to be something of an event for her; though of course I never thought of that then.

BROADBENT: Were you at all hard hit?

DOYLE: Not really. I had only two ideas at that time: first, to learn to do something; and then to get out of Ireland and have a chance of doing it. She didnt count. I was romantic about her, just as I was romantic about Byron's heroines or the old Round Tower[37] of Rosscullen; but she didnt count any more than they did. Ive never crossed St George's Channel since for her sake — never even landed at Queenstown[38] and come back to London through Ireland.

BROADBENT: But did you ever say anything that would justify her in waiting for you?

DOYLE: No, never. But she is waiting for me.

BROADBENT: How do you know?

37. An ancient symbol of Ireland, a tall, thin, circular edifice in which monks hid themselves and religious treasures from invading Norsemen.

38. The port of Cobh, near Cork city, at which transatlantic liners berthed.

DOYLE: She writes to me — on her birthday. She used to write on mine, and send me little things as presents; but I stopped that by pretending that it was no use when I was travelling, as they got lost in the foreign post-offices. (*He pronounces post-offices with the stress on offices, instead of on post*)

BROADBENT: You answer the letters?

DOYLE: Not very punctually. But they get acknowledged at one time or another.

BROADBENT: How do you feel when you see her handwriting?

DOYLE: Uneasy. I'd give £50 to escape a letter.

BROADBENT: (*Looking grave, and throwing himself back in his chair to intimate that the cross-examination is over, and the result very damaging to the witness*) Hm!

DOYLE: What d'ye mean by Hm!

BROADBENT: Of course I know that the moral code is different in Ireland. But in England it's not considered fair to trifle with a woman's affections.

DOYLE: You mean that an Englishman would get engaged to another woman and return Nora her letters and presents with a letter to say he was unworthy of her and wished her every happiness?

BROADBENT: Well, even that would set the poor girl's mind at rest.

DOYLE: Would it? I wonder! One thing I can tell you; and that is that Nora would wait until she died of old age sooner than ask my intentions or condescend to hint at the possibility of my having any. You dont know what Irish pride is. England may have knocked a good deal of it out of me; but she's never been in England; and if I had to choose between wounding that delicacy in her and hitting her in the face, I'd hit her in the face without a moment's hesitation.

BROADBENT: (*Who has been nursing his knee and reflecting, apparently rather agreeably*) You know, all this sounds rather interesting. Theres the Irish charm about it. Thats the worst of you: the Irish charm doesnt exist for you.

DOYLE: Oh yes it does. But it's the charm of a dream. Live in contact with dreams and you will get something of their charm: live in contact with facts and you will get something of their brutality. I wish I could find a country to live in where the facts were not brutal and the dreams not unreal.

BROADBENT: (*Changing his attitude and responding to* DOYLE's *earnestness with deep conviction: his elbows on the table and his hands clenched*) Dont despair, Larry, old boy: things may look black; but there will be a great change after the next election.

DOYLE: (*Jumping up*) Oh, get out, you idiot!

BROADBENT: (*Rising also, not a bit snubbed*) Ha! ha! you may laugh; but we shall see. However, dont let us argue about that. Come now! you ask my advice about Miss Reilly?

DOYLE: (*Reddening*) No I dont. Damn your advice! (*Softening*) Lets have it, all the same.

BROADBENT: Well, everything you tell me about her impresses me favorably. She seems to have the feelings of a lady; and though we must face the fact that in England her income would hardly maintain her in the lower middle class —

DOYLE: (*Interrupting*) Now look here, Tom. That reminds me. When you go to Ireland, just drop talking about the middle class and bragging of belonging to it. In Ireland youre either a gentleman or youre not. If you want to be particularly offensive to Nora, you can call her a Papist; but if you call her a middle-class woman, Heaven help you!

BROADBENT: (*Irrepressible*) Never fear. Youre all descended from the ancient kings: I know that. (*Complacently*) I'm not so tactless as you think, my boy. (*Earnest again*) I expect to find Miss Reilly a perfect lady; and I strongly advise you to come and have another look at her before you make up your mind about her. By the way, have you a photograph of her?

DOYLE: Her photographs stopped at twenty-five.

BROADBENT: (*Saddened*) Ah yes, I suppose so. (*With feeling, severely*) Larry: youve treated that poor girl disgracefully.

DOYLE: By George, if she only knew that two men were talking about her like this —!

BROADBENT: She wouldnt like it, would she? Of course not. We ought to be ashamed of ourselves, Larry. (*More and more carried away by his new fancy*) You know, I have a sort of presentiment that Miss Reilly is a very superior woman.

DOYLE: (*Staring hard at him*) Oh! you have, have you?

BROADBENT: Yes I have. There is something very touching about the history of this beautiful girl.

DOYLE: Beau—! Oho! Heres a chance for Nora! and for me! (*Calling*) Hodson.

HODSON: (*Appearing at the bedroom door*) Did you call, sir?

DOYLE: Pack for me too. I'm going to Ireland with Mr Broadbent.

HODSON: Right, sir. (*He retires into the bedroom*)

BROADBENT: (*Clapping* DOYLE *on the shoulder*) Thank you, old chap. Thank you.

ACT II

Rosscullen. Westward a hillside of granite rock and heather slopes upward across the prospect from south to north. A huge stone stands on it in a naturally impossible place, as if it had been tossed up there by a giant. Over the brow, in the desolate valley beyond, is a round tower. A lonely white high road trending away westward past the tower loses itself at the foot of the far mountains. It is evening; and there are great breadths of silken green in the Irish sky. The sun is setting.

A man with the face of a young saint, yet with white hair and perhaps 50 years on his back, is standing near the stone in a trance of intense melancholy, looking over the hills as if by mere intensity of gaze he could pierce the glories of the sunset and see into the streets of heaven. He is dressed in black, and is rather more clerical in appearance than most English curates are nowadays; but he does not wear the collar and waistcoat of a parish priest. He is roused from his trance by the chirp of an insect from a tuft of grass in a crevice of the stone. His face relaxes: he turns quietly, and gravely takes off his hat to the tuft, addressing the insect in a brogue which is the jocular assumption of a gentleman and not the natural speech of a peasant.

THE MAN: An is that yourself, Misther Grasshopper? I hope I see you well this fine evenin.

THE GRASSHOPPER: (*Prompt and shrill in answer*) X.X.

THE MAN: (*Encouragingly*) Thats right. I suppose now youve come out to make yourself miserable by admyerin the sunset?

THE GRASSHOPPER: (*Sadly*) X.X.

THE MAN: Aye, youre a thrue Irish grasshopper.

THE GRASSHOPPER: (*Loudly*) X.X.X.

THE MAN: Three cheers for ould Ireland, is it? That helps you to face out the misery and the poverty and the torment, doesnt it?

THE GRASSHOPPER: (*Plaintively*) X.X.

THE MAN: Ah, it's no use, me poor little friend. If you could jump as far as a kangaroo you couldnt jump away from your own heart an its punishment. You can only look at Heaven from here: you cant reach it. There! (*pointing with his stick to the sunset*) thats the gate of glory, isnt it?

THE GRASSHOPPER: (*Assenting*) X.X.

THE MAN: Sure it's the wise grasshopper yar to

know that. But tell me this, Misther Unworldly Wiseman:[1] why does the sight of Heaven wring your heart an mine as the sight of holy wather wrings the heart o the divil? What wickedness have you done to bring that curse on you? Here! where are you jumpin to? Wheres your manners to go skyrocketin like that out o the box in the middle o your confession (*he threatens it with his stick*)?

THE GRASSHOPPER: (*Penitently*) X.

THE MAN: (*Lowering the stick*) I accept your apology; but dont do it again. And now tell me one thing before I let you go home to bed. Which would you say this counthry was: hell or purgatory?

THE GRASSHOPPER: X.

THE MAN: Hell! Faith I'm afraid youre right. I wondher what you and me did when we were alive to get sent here.

THE GRASSHOPPER: (*Shrilly*) X.X.

THE MAN: (*Nodding*) Well, as you say, it's a delicate subject; and I wont press it on you. Now off widja.

THE GRASSHOPPER: X.X. (*It springs away*)

THE MAN: (*Waving his stick*) God speed you! (*He walks away past the stone towards the brow of the hill. Immediately a young laborer, his face distorted with terror, slips round from behind the stone*)

THE LABORER: (*Crossing himself repeatedly*) Oh glory be to God! glory be to God! Oh Holy Mother an all the saints! Oh murdher! murdher! (*Beside himself, calling*) Fadher Keegan! Fadher Keegan!

THE MAN: (*Turning*) Who's there? Whats that? (*He comes back and finds the laborer, who clasps his knees*) Patsy Farrell! What are you doing here?

PATSY: Oh for the love o God dont lave me here wi dhe grasshopper. I hard it spakin to you. Dont let it do me any harm, Father darlint.

KEEGAN: Get up, you foolish man, get up. Are you afraid of a poor insect because I pretended it was talking to me?

PATSY: Oh, it was no pretendin, Fadher dear. Didnt it give three cheers n say it was a divil out o hell? Oh say youll see me safe home, Fadher; n put a blessin on me or somethin (*he moans with terror*).

KEEGAN: What were you doing there, Patsy, listnin? Were you spyin on me?

PATSY: No, Fadher: on me oath an soul I wasnt: I was waitn to meet Masther Larry n carry his luggage from the car; n I fell asleep on the grass; n you woke me talkin to the grasshopper; n I hard its wicked little voice. Oh, d'ye think I'll die before the year's out, Fadher?

KEEGAN: For shame, Patsy! Is that your religion, to be afraid of a little deeshy[2] grasshopper? Suppose it was a divil, what call have you to fear it? If I could ketch it, I'd make you take it home widja in your hat for a penance.

PATSY: Sure, if you wont let it harm me, I'm not afraid, your riverence. (*He gets up, a little reassured. He is a callow, flaxen polled, smoothfaced, downy chinned lad, fully grown but not yet fully filled out, with blue eyes and an instinctively acquired air of helplessness and silliness, indicating, not his real character, but a cunning developed by his constant dread of a hostile dominance, which he habitually tries to disarm and tempt into unmasking by pretending to be a much greater fool than he really is. Englishmen think him half-witted, which is exactly what he intends them to think. He is clad in corduroy trousers, unbuttoned waistcoat, and coarse blue striped shirt*)

KEEGAN: (*Admonitorily*) Patsy: what did I tell you about callin me Father Keegan an your reverence? What did Father Dempsey tell you about it?

PATSY: Yis, Fadher.

KEEGAN: Father!

PATSY: (*Desperately*) Arra, hwat am I to call you? Fadher Dempsey sez youre not a priest; n we all know youre not a man; n how do we know what ud happen to us if we shewed any disrespect to you? N sure they say wanse[3] a priest always a priest.

KEEGAN: (*Sternly*) It's not for the like of you, Patsy, to go behind the instruction of your parish priest and set yourself up to judge whether your Church is right or wrong.

PATSY: Sure I know that, sir.

KEEGAN: The Church let me be its priest as long as it thought me fit for its work. When it took away my papers it meant you to know that I was only a poor madman, unfit and unworthy to take charge of the souls of the people.

PATSY: But wasnt it only because you knew more Latn than Father Dempsey that he was jealous of you?

KEEGAN: (*Scolding him to keep himself from smiling*) How dar you, Patsy Farrell, put your own wicked little spites and foolishnesses into the heart

1. Pun on the name of Worldly Wiseman, a character in John Bunyan's *The Pilgrim's Progress* (1678).

2. tiny.

3. once.

of your priest? For two pins I'd tell him what you just said.

PATSY: (*Coaxing*) Sure you wouldnt—

KEEGAN: Wouldnt I? God forgive you! youre little better than a heathen.

PATSY: Deedn I am, Fadher: it's me bruddher the tinsmith in Dublin youre thinkin of. Sure he had to be a freethinker when he larnt a thrade and went to live in the town.

KEEGAN: Well, he'll get to Heaven before you if youre not careful, Patsy. And now you listen to me, once and for all. Youll talk to me and pray for me by the name of Pether Keegan, so you will. And when youre angry and tempted to lift your hand agen the donkey or stamp your foot on the little grasshopper, remember that the donkey's Pether Keegan's brother, and the grasshopper Pether Keegan's friend. And when youre tempted to throw a stone at a sinner or a curse at a beggar, remember that Pether Keegan is a worse sinner and a worse beggar, and keep the stone and the curse for him the next time you meet him. Now say God bless you, Pether, to me before I go, just to practise you a bit.

PATSY: Sure it wouldnt be right, Fadher. I cant—

KEEGAN: Yes you can. Now out with it; or I'll put this stick into your hand an make you hit me with it.

PATSY: (*Throwing himself on his knees in an ecstasy of adoration*) Sure it's your blessin I want, Fadher Keegan. I'll have no luck widhout it.

KEEGAN: (*Shocked*) Get up out o that, man. Dont kneel to me: I'm not a saint.

PATSY: (*With intense conviction*) Oh in throth yar, sir. (*The grasshopper chirps.* PATSY, *terrified, clutches at* KEEGAN's *hands*) Dont set it on me, Fadher: I'll do anythin you bid me.

KEEGAN: (*Pulling him up*) You bosthoon,[4] you! Dont you see that it only whistled to tell me Miss Reilly's comin? There! Look at her and pull yourself together for shame. Off widja to the road: youll be late for the car if you dont make haste (*bustling him down the hill*). I can see the dust of it in the gap already.

PATSY: The Lord save us! (*He goes down the hill towards the road like a haunted man*)

NORA REILLY *comes down the hill. A slight weak woman in a pretty muslin print gown (her best), she is a figure commonplace enough to Irish eyes; but on the inhabitants of fatter-fed, crowded, hustling and bustling modern countries she makes a very different impression. The absence of any symptoms of coarseness or hardness or appetite in her, her comparative delicacy of manner and sensibility of apprehension, her fine hands and frail figure, her novel accent, with the caressing plaintive Irish melody of her speech, give her a charm which is all the more effective because, being untravelled, she is unconscious of it, and never dreams of deliberately dramatizing and exploiting it, as the Irishwomen in England do. For Tom Broadbent therefore, an attractive woman, whom he would even call ethereal. To Larry Doyle, an everyday woman fit only for the eighteenth century, helpless, useless, almost sexless, an invalid without the excuse of disease,[5] an incarnation of everything in Ireland that drove him out of it. These judgments have little value and no finality; but they are the judgments on which her fate hangs just at present.* KEEGAN *touches his hat to her; he does not take it off.*

NORA: Mr Keegan: I want to speak to you a minute if you dont mind.

KEEGAN: (*dropping the broad Irish vernacular of his speech to* PATSY) An hour if you like, Miss Reilly: youre always welcome. Shall we sit down?

NORA: Thank you. (*They sit on the heather. She is shy and anxious; but she comes to the point promptly because she can think of nothing else*) They say you did a gradle[6] o travelling at one time.

KEEGAN: Well, you see I'm not a Mnooth man (*he means that he was not a student at Maynooth College*).[7] When I was young I admired the older generation of priests that had been educated in Salamanca.[8] So when I felt sure of my vocation I went to Salamanca. Then I walked from Salamanca to Rome, an sted in a monastery there for a year. My pilgrimage to Rome taught me that walking is a better way of travelling than the train; so I walked from Rome to the Sorbonne in Paris; and I wish I could have walked from Paris to Oxford; for I was very sick on the sea. After a year of Oxford I had to walk to Jerusalem to walk the Oxford feeling off me. From Jerusalem I came back to Patmos, and spent six months at the monastery of Mount Athos. From that I came to Ireland and settled down as a parish priest until I went mad.

4. loutish fellow (Ir. *bastún*).

5. Shaw here revises the Yeatsian image of Ireland as woman.

6. a measure, a good deal.

7. St Patrick's College, Maynooth, Co. Kildare, a national seminary for training catholic priests.

8. Roman catholic seminary in Spain, from which many Irish priests graduated in the seventeenth and eighteenth centuries, when the Penal Statutes outlawed Irish seminaries.

NORA: (*Startled*) Oh dont say that.

KEEGAN: Why not? Dont you know the story? how I confessed a black man and gave him absolution? and how he put a spell on me and drove me mad?

NORA: How can you talk such nonsense about yourself? For shame!

KEEGAN: It's not nonsense at all: it's true — in a way. But never mind the black man. Now that you know what a travelled man I am, what can I do for you? (*She hesitates and plucks nervously at the heather. He stays her hand gently*) Dear Miss Nora: dont pluck the little flower. If it was a pretty baby you wouldnt want to pull its head off and stick it in a vawse[9] o water to look at. (*The grasshopper chirps:* KEEGAN *turns his head and addresses it in the vernacular*) Be aisy, me son: she wont spoil the swing-swong in your little three. (*To* NORA, *resuming his urbane style*) You see I'm quite cracked; but never mind: I'm harmless. Now what is it?

NORA: (*Embarrassed*) Oh, only idle curiosity. I wanted to know whether you found Ireland — I mean the country part of Ireland, of course — very small and backwardlike when you came back to it from Rome and Oxford and all the great cities.

KEEGAN: When I went to those great cities I saw wonders I had never seen in Ireland. But when I came back to Ireland I found all the wonders there waiting for me. You see they had been there all the time; but my eyes had never been opened to them. I did not know what my own house was like, because I had never been outside it.

NORA: D'ye think thats the same with everybody?

KEEGAN: With everybody who has eyes in his soul as well as in his head.

NORA: But really and truly now, werent the people rather disappointing? I should think the girls must have seemed rather coarse and dowdy after the foreign princesses and people? But I suppose a priest wouldnt notice that.

KEEGAN: It's a priest's business to notice everything. I wont tell you all I noticed about women; but I'll tell you this. The more a man knows, and the farther he travels, the more likely he is to marry a country girl afterwards.

NORA: (*Blushing with delight*) Youre joking, Mr Keegan: I'm sure yar.

KEEGAN: My way of joking is to tell the truth. It's the funniest joke in the world.

NORA: (*Incredulous*) Galong[10] with you!

KEEGAN: (*Springing up actively*) Shall we go down to the road and meet the car? (*She gives him her hand and he helps her up*) Patsy Farrell told me you were expecting young Doyle.

NORA: (*Tossing her chin up at once*) Oh, I'm not expecting him particularly. It's a wonder he's come back at all. After staying away eighteen years he can hardly expect us to be very anxious to see him: can he now?

KEEGAN: Well, not anxious perhaps; but you will be curious to see how much he's changed in all these years.

NORA: (*With a sudden bitter flush*) I suppose thats all that brings him back to look at us, just to see how much weve changed. Well, he can wait and see me be candlelight: I didnt come out to meet him: I'm going to walk to the Round Tower (*going west across the hill*).

KEEGAN: You couldnt do better this fine evening. (*Gravely*) I'll tell him where youve gone. (*She turns as if to forbid him; but the deep understanding in his eyes makes that impossible; and she only looks at him earnestly and goes. He watches her disappear on the other side of the hill; then says*) Aye, he's come to torment you; and youre driven already to torment him. (*He shakes his head, and goes slowly away across the hill in the opposite direction, lost in thought*).

By this time the car has arrived, and dropped three of its passengers on the high road at the foot of the hill. It is a monster jaunting car,[11] *black and dilapidated, one of the last survivors of the public vehicles known to earliest generations as Beeyankiny cars, the Irish having laid violent tongues on the name of their projector, one Bianconi, an enterprising Italian. The three passengers are the parish priest,* FATHER DEMPSEY; CORNELIUS DOYLE, LARRY'S *father; and* BROADBENT, *all in overcoats and as stiff as only an Irish car could make them.*

The priest, stout and fatherly, falls far short of that finest type of countryside pastor which represents the genius of priesthood; but he is equally far above the base type in which a strong-minded unscrupulous peasant uses the Church to extort money, power, and privilege. He is a priest neither by vocation nor

9. vase.

10. Get along.

11. Horse-drawn carriage, with side-facing seats, used for pleasure outings.

ambition, but because the life suits him. He has boundless authority over his flock, and taxes them stiffly enough to be a rich man. The old Protestant ascendency is now too broken to gall him. On the whole, an easygoing, amiable, even modest man as long as his dues are paid and his authority and dignity fully admitted.

CORNELIUS DOYLE *is an elder of the small wiry type, with a hardskinned, rather worried face, clean shaven except for sandy whiskers blanching into a lustreless pale yellow and quite white at the roots. His dress is that of a country-town man of business: that is, an oldish shooting suit, with elastic sided boots quite unconnected with shooting. Feeling shy with* BROADBENT, *he is hasty, which is his way of trying to appear genial.*

BROADBENT, *for reasons which will appear later, has no luggage except a field glass and a guide book. The other two have left theirs to the unfortunate* PATSY FARRELL, *who struggles up the hill after them, loaded with a sack of potatoes, a hamper, a fat goose, a colossal salmon, and several paper parcels.*

CORNELIUS *leads the way up the hill, with* BROADBENT *at his heels. The priest follows.* PATSY *lags laboriously behind.*

CORNELIUS: This is a bit of a climb, Mr Broadbent; but it's shorter than goin round be the road.

BROADBENT: (*Stopping to examine the great stone*) Just a moment, Mr Doyle: I want to look at this stone. It must be Finian's diecast.

CORNELIUS: (*In black bewilderment*) Hwat?

BROADBENT: Murray describes it. One of your great national heroes — I cant pronounce the name — Finian Somebody, I think.

FATHER DEMPSEY: (*Also perplexed, and rather scandalized*) Is it Fin McCool[12] you mean?

BROADBENT: I daresay it is. (*Referring to the guide book*) Murray says that a huge stone, probably of Druidic origin, is still pointed out as the die cast by Fin in his celebrated match with the devil.

CORNELIUS: (*Dubiously*) Jeuce[13] a word I ever heard of it!

FATHER DEMPSEY: (*Very seriously indeed, and even a little severely*) Dont believe any such nonsense, sir. There never was any such thing. When people talk to you about Fin McCool and the like, take no notice of them. It's all idle stories and superstition.

BROADBENT: (*Somewhat indignantly; for to be rebuked by an Irish priest for superstition is more than he can stand*) You dont suppose I believe it, do you?

FATHER DEMPSEY: Oh, I thought you did. D'ye see the top o the Roun Tower there? thats an antiquity worth lookin at.

BROADBENT: (*Deeply interested*) Have you any theory as to what the Round Towers were for?

FATHER DEMPSEY: (*A little offended*) A theory? Me! (*Theories are connected in his mind with the late Professor Tyndall, and with scientific scepticism generally: also perhaps with the view that the Round Towers are phallic symbols*)[14]

CORNELIUS: (*Remonstrating*) Father Dempsey is the priest of the parish, Mr Broadbent. What would he be doing with a theory?

FATHER DEMPSEY: (*With gentle emphasis*) I have a knowledge of what the Roun Towers were, if thats what you mean. They are the forefingers of the early Church, pointing us all to God.

PATSY, *intolerably overburdened, loses his balance, and sits down involuntarily. His burdens are scattered over the hillside.* CORNELIUS *and* FATHER DEMPSEY *turn furiously on him, leaving* BROADBENT *beaming at the stone and the tower with fatuous interest.*

CORNELIUS: Oh, be the hokey,[15] the sammin's broke in two! You schoolpid[16] ass, what d'ye mean?

FATHER DEMPSEY: Are you drunk, Patsy Farrell? Did I tell you to carry that hamper carefully or did I not?

PATSY: (*Rubbing the back of his head, which has almost dinted a slab of granite*) Sure me fut[17] slipt. Howkn I carry three men's luggage at wanst?

FATHER DEMPSEY: You were told to leave behind what you couldnt carry, an go back for it.

PATSY: An whose things was I to lave behind? Hwat would your reverence think if I left your hamper behind in the wet grass; n hwat would the masther say if I left the sammin and the goose be the

12. Legendary leader of Fianna, a troop of mercenary soldiers who defended the shores of Ireland against invaders. Gaelic: *Fionn Mac Cumhaill.*
13. Deuce.
14. John Tyndall (1820-93), an Irish physicist. He was a prolific lecturer and writer, and a popularizer of science, who aroused controversy over his views on the relationship between science and theology.
    Various improbable theories about the Round Towers of Ireland flourished among antiquarians in the late eighteenth and early nineteenth centuries before the work of George Petrie (1790-1886) put an end to the speculation in an essay of 1833.
15. A petty expletive, of unknown origin.
16. stupid.
17. foot.

side o the road for annywan to pick up?

CORNELIUS: Oh, youve a dale to say for yourself, you butther-fingered omadhaun.[18] Waitll Ant Judy sees the state o that sammin: she'll talk to you. Here! gimmy that birdn that fish there; an take Father Dempsey's hamper to his house for him; n then come back for the rest.

FATHER DEMPSEY: Do, Patsy. And mind you dont fall down again.

PATSY: Sure I —

CORNELIUS: (*Bustling him up the hill*) Whisht! heres Ant Judy.

PATSY *goes grumbling in disgrace, with* FATHER DEMPSEY's *hamper.*

AUNT JUDY *comes down the hill, a woman of 50, in no way remarkable, lively and busy without energy or grip, placid without tranquility, kindly without concern for others: indeed without much concern for herself: a contented product of a narrow, strainless life. She wears her hair parted in the middle and quite smooth, with a flattened bun at the back. Her dress is a plain brown frock, with a woollen pelerine*[19] *of black and aniline mauve over her shoulders, all very trim in honor of the occasion. She looks round for* LARRY; *is puzzled; then stares incredulously at* BROADBENT.

AUNT JUDY: Surely to goodness thats not you, Larry!

CORNELIUS: Arra how could he be Larry, woman alive? Larry's in no hurry home, it seems. I havent set eyes on him. This is his friend, Mr Broadbent. Mr Broadbent: me sister Judy.

AUNT JUDY: (*Hospitably: going to* BROADBENT *and shaking hands heartily*) Mr Broadbent! Fancy me takin you for Larry! Sure we havnt seen a sight of him for eighteen years, n he ony a lad when he left us.

BROADBENT: It's not Larry's fault: he was to have been here before me. He started in our motor an hour before Mr Doyle arrived, to meet us at Athenmullet, intending to get here long before me.

AUNT JUDY: Lord save us! do you think he's had n axidnt?[20]

BROADBENT: No: he's wired to say he's had a breakdown and will come on as soon as he can. He expects to be here at about ten.

AUNT JUDY: There now! Fancy him trustn himself in a motor and we all expectn him! Just like him! he'd never do anything like anybody else. Well, what cant be cured must be injoored. Come on in, all of you. You must be dyin for your tea, Mr Broadbent.

BROADBENT: (*With a slight start*) Oh, I'm afraid it's too late for tea (*he looks at his watch*).

AUNT JUDY: Not a bit: we never have it airlier than this. I hope they gave you a good dinner at Athenmullet.

BROADBENT: (*Trying to conceal his consternation as he realizes that he is not going to get any dinner after his drive*) Oh — er — excellent, excellent. By the way, hadnt I better see about a room at the hotel? (*They stare at him*)

CORNELIUS: The hotel!

FATHER DEMPSEY: Hwat hotel?

AUNT JUDY: Indeedn youre not goin to a hotel. Youll stay with us. I'd have put you into Larry's room, ony the boy's pallyass[21] is too short for you; but we'll make a comfortable bed for you on the sofa in the parlor.

BROADBENT: Youre very kind, Miss Doyle; but really I'm ashamed to give you so much trouble unnecessarily. I shant mind the hotel in the least.

FATHER DEMPSEY: Man alive! theres no hotel in Rosscullen.

BROADBENT: No hotel! Why, the driver told me there was the finest hotel in Ireland here. (*They regard him joylessly*)

AUNT JUDY: Arra would you mind what the like of him would tell you? Sure he'd say hwatever was the least trouble to himself and the pleasantest to you, thinkin you might give him a thruppeny bit for himself or the like.

BROADBENT: Perhaps theres a public house.

FATHER DEMPSEY: (*Grimly*) Theres seventeen.

AUNT JUDY: Ah then, how could you stay at a public house? theyd have no place to put you even if it was a right place for you to go. Come! is it the sofa youre afraid of? If it is, you can have me own bed. I can sleep with Nora.

BROADBENT: Not at all, not at all: I should be only too delighted. But to upset your arrangements in this way —

CORNELIUS: (*Anxious to cut short the discussion, which makes him ashamed of his house; for he guesses* BROADBENT's *standard of comfort a little more accurately than his sister does*) Thats all right: itll be no trouble at all. Hweres Nora?

18. From Irish *amadán* (foolish person, idiot).

19. Woman's cape, with long pointed ends coming down at the front.

20. an accident.

21. paillasse, straw-filled mattress.

AUNT JUDY: Oh, how do I know? She slipped out a little while ago: I thought she was goin to meet the car.

CORNELIUS: (*Dissatisfied*) It's a queer thing of her to run out o the way at such a time.

AUNT JUDY: Sure she's a queer girl altogether. Come. Come in: come in.

FATHER DEMPSEY: I'll say good-night, Mr Broadbent. If theres anything I can do for you in this parish, let me know. (*He shakes hands with* BROADBENT)

BROADBENT: (*Effusively cordial*) Thank you, Father Dempsey. Delighted to have met you, sir.

FATHER DEMPSEY: (*Passing on to* AUNT JUDY) Good-night, Miss Doyle.

AUNT JUDY: Wont you stay to tea?

FATHER DEMPSEY: Not to-night, thank you kindly: I have business to do at hime. (*He turns to go, and meets* PATSY FARRELL *returning unloaded*) Have you left that hamper for me?

PATSY: Yis, your reverence.

FATHER DEMPSEY: Thats a good lad (*going*).

PATSY: (*To* AUNT JUDY) Fadher Keegan sez —

FATHER DEMPSEY: (*Turning sharply on him*) Whats that you say?

PATSY: (*Frightened*) Fadher Keegan —

FATHER DEMPSEY: How often have you heard me bid you call Mister Keegan in his proper name, the same as I do? Father Keegan indeed! Cant you tell the difference between your priest and any ole madman in a black coat?

PATSY: Sure I'm afraid he might put a spell on me.

FATHER DEMPSEY: (*Wrathfully*) You mind what I tell you or I'll put a spell on you thatll make you lep. D'ye mind that now? (*He goes home*)

PATSY *goes down the hill to retrieve the fish, the bird, and the sack.*

AUNT JUDY: Ah, hwy cant you hold your tongue, Patsy, before Father Dempsey?

PATSY: Well, hwat was I to do? Father Keegan bid me tell you Miss Nora was gone to the Roun Tower.

AUNT JUDY: An hwy couldnt you wait to tell us until Father Dempsey was gone?

PATSY: I was afeerd o forgetn it; and then may be he'd a sent the grasshopper or the little dark looker into me at night to remind me of it. (*The dark looker is the common grey lizard, which is supposed to walk down the throats of incautious sleepers and cause them to perish in a slow decline*)

CORNELIUS: Yah, you great gaum,[22] you! Widjer grasshoppers and dark lookers! Here: take up them things and let me hear no more o your foolish lip. (PATSY *obeys*) You can take the sammin under your oxther.[23] (*He wedges the salmon into* PATSY'S *axilla*)

PATSY: I can take the goose too, sir. Put it on me back n gimmy the neck of it in me mouth.

CORNELIUS *is about to comply thoughtlessly*

AUNT JUDY: (*Feeling that* BROADBENT'S *presence demands special punctiliousness*) For shame, Patsy! to offer to take the goose in your mouth that we have to eat after you! The masterll bring it in for you.

PATSY: Arra what would a dead goose care for me mouth? (*He takes his load up the hill*)

CORNELIUS: Hwats Nora doin at the Roun Tower?

AUNT JUDY: Oh, the Lord knows! Romancin, I suppose. Praps she thinks Larry would go there to look for her and see her safe home.

BROADBENT: Miss Reilly must not be left to wait and walk home alone at night. Shall I go for her?

AUNT JUDY: (*Contemptuously*) Arra hwat ud happen to her? Hurry in now, Corny. Come, Mr Broadbent: I left the tea on the hob to draw; and itll be black if we dont go in an drink it.

They go up the hill. It is dusk by this time.

BROADBENT *does not fare so badly after all at* AUNT JUDY'S *board. He gets not only tea and bread-and-butter, but more mutton chops than he has ever conceived it possible to eat at one sitting. There is also a most filling substance called potato cake. Hardly have his fears of being starved been replaced by his first misgiving that he is eating too much and will be sorry for it tomorrow, when his appetite is revived by the production of a bottle of illicitly distilled whisky, called potcheen, which he has read and dreamed of (he calls it pottine) and is now at last to taste. His goodhumor rises almost to excitement before* CORNELIUS *shews signs of sleepiness. The contrast between* AUNT JUDY'S *table service and that of the south and east coast hotels at which he spends his Fridays-to-Tuesdays when he is in London, seems to him delightfully Irish. The almost total atrophy of any sense of enjoyment in* CORNELIUS, *or even any desire for it or toleration of the possibility of life being something better than a round of sordid worries, relieved by tobacco, punch, fine mornings, and petty successes in buying and selling, passes with his guest as the whimsical affection*

22. gormless one, fool.
23. oxter, armpit.

of a shrewd Irish humorist and incorrigible spendthrift. AUNT JUDY *seems to him an incarnate joke. The likelihood that the joke will pall after a month or so, and is probably not apparent at any time to born Rosculleners, or that he himself unconsciously entertains* AUNT JUDY *by his fantastic English personality and English mispronunciations, does not occur to him for a moment. In the end he is so charmed, and so loth to go to bed and perhaps dream of prosaic England, that he insists on going out to smoke a cigar and look for* NORA REILLY *at the Round Tower. Not that any special insistence is needed; for the English inhibitive instinct does not seem to exist in Rosscullen. Just as* NORA's *liking to miss a meal and stay out at the Round Tower is accepted as a sufficient reason for her doing it, and for the family going to bed and leaving the door open for her, so* BROADBENT's *whim to go out for a late stroll provokes neither hospitable remonstrance nor surprise. Indeed* AUNT JUDY *wants to get rid of him whilst she makes a bed for him on the sofa. So off he goes, full fed, happy and enthusiastic, to explore the valley by moonlight.*

The Round Tower stands about half an Irish mile from Rosscullen, some fifty yards south of the road on a knoll with a circle of wide greensward on it. The road once ran over this knoll; but modern engineering has tempered the level to the Beeyankiny car by carrying the road partly round the knoll and partly through a cutting; so that the way from the road to the tower is a footpath up the embankment through furze and brambles.

On the edge of this slope, at the top of the path, NORA *is straining her eyes in the moonlight, watching for* LARRY. *At last she gives it up with a sob of impatience, and retreats to the hoary foot of the tower, where she sits down discouraged and cries a little. Then she settles herself resignedly to wait, and hums a song — not an Irish melody, but a hackneyed English drawing room ballad of the season before last — until some slight noise suggests a footstep, when she springs up eagerly and runs to the edge of the slope again. Some moments of silence and suspense follow, broken by unmistakable footsteps. She gives a little gasp as she sees a man approaching.*

NORA: Is that you, Larry? (*Frightened a little*) Who's that?

BROADBENT's *voice from below on the path*: Dont be alarmed.

NORA: Oh, what an English accent youve got!

BROADBENT: (*Rising into view*) I must introduce myself —

NORA: (*Violently startled, retreating*) It's not you! Who are you? What do you want?

BROADBENT: (*Advancing*) I'm really so sorry to have alarmed you, Miss Reilly. My name is Broadbent. Larry's friend, you know.

NORA: (*Chilled*) And has Mr Doyle not come with you?

BROADBENT: No. Ive come instead. I hope I am not unwelcome.

NORA: (*Deeply mortified*) I'm sorry Mr Doyle should have given you the trouble, I'm sure.

BROADBENT: You see, as a stranger and an Englishman, I thought it would be interesting to see the Round Tower by moonlight.

NORA: Oh, you came to see the tower. I thought — (*confused, trying to recover her manners*) Oh, of course. I was so startled. It's a beautiful night, isnt it?

BROADBENT: Lovely. I must explain why Larry has not come himself.

NORA: Why should be come? He's seen the tower often enough: it's no attraction to him. (*Genteelly*) An what do you think of Ireland, Mr Broadbent? Have you ever been here before?

BROADBENT: Never.

NORA: An how do you like it?

BROADBENT: (*Suddenly betraying a condition of extreme sentimentality*) I can hardly trust myself to say how much I like it. The magic of this Irish scene, and — I really dont want to be personal, Miss Reilly; but the charm of your Irish voice —

NORA: (*Quite accustomed to gallantry, and attaching no seriousness whatever to it*) Oh, get along with you, Mr Broadbent! Youre breaking your heart about me already, I daresay, after seeing me for two minutes in the dark.

BROADBENT: The voice is just as beautiful in the dark, you know. Besides, Ive heard a great deal about you from Larry.

NORA: (*With bitter indifference*) Have you now? Well, thats a great honor, I'm sure.

BROADBENT: I have looked forward to meeting you more than to anything else in Ireland.

NORA: (*Ironically*) Dear me! did you now?

BROADBENT: I did really. I wish you had taken half as much interest in me.

NORA: Oh, I was dying to see you, of course. I daresay you can imagine the sensation an Englishman like you would make among us poor Irish people.

BROADBENT: Ah, now youre chaffing me, Miss

Reilly; you know you are. You mustnt chaff me. I'm very much in earnest about Ireland and everything Irish. I'm very much in earnest about you and about Larry.

NORA: Larry has nothing to do with me, Mr Broadbent.

BROADBENT: If I really thought that, Miss Reilly, I should — well, I should let myself feel that charm of which I spoke just now more deeply than I — than I —

NORA: Is is making love to me you are?

BROADBENT: (*Scared and much upset*) On my word I believe I am, Miss Reilly. If you say that to me again I shant answer for myself; all the harps of Ireland are in your voice. (*She laughs at him. He suddenly loses his head and seizes her arms, to her great indignation*) Stop laughing: do you hear? I am in earnest: in English earnest. When I say a thing like that to a woman, I mean it. (*Releasing her and trying to recover his ordinary manner in spite of his bewildering emotion*) I beg your pardon.

NORA: How dare you touch me?

BROADBENT: There are not many things I would not dare for you. That does not sound right perhaps; but I really — (*he stops and passes his hand over his forehead, rather lost*)

NORA: I think you ought to be ashamed. I think if you were a gentleman, and me alone with you in this place at night, you would die rather than do such a thing.

BROADBENT: You mean that it's an act of treachery to Larry?

NORA: Deed I dont. What has Larry to do with it? It's an act of disrespect and rudeness to me: it shews what you take me for. You can go your way now; and I'll go mine. Good-night, Mr Broadbent.

BROADBENT: No, please, Miss Reilly. One moment. Listen to me. I'm serious: I'm desperately serious. Tell me that I'm interfering with Larry; and I'll go straight from this spot back to London and never see you again. Thats on my honor: I will. Am I interfering with him?

NORA: (*Answering in spite of herself in a sudden spring of bitterness*) I should think you ought to know better than me whether youre interfering with him. Youve seen him oftener than I have. You know him better than I do, by this time. Youve come to me quicker than he has, havnt you?

BROADBENT: I'm bound to tell you, Miss Reilly, that Larry has not arrived in Rosscullen yet. He meant to get here before me; but his car broke down; and he may not arrive until to-morrow.

NORA: (*Her face lighting up*) Is that the truth?

BROADBENT: Yes: thats the truth. (*She gives a sigh of relief*) Youre glad of that?

NORA: (*Up in arms at once*) Glad indeed! Why should I be glad? As weve waited eighteen years for him we can afford to wait a day longer, I should think.

BROADBENT: If you really feel like that about him, there may be a chance for another man yet. Eh?

NORA: (*Deeply offended*) I suppose people are different in England, Mr Broadbent; so perhaps you dont mean any harm. In Ireland nobody'd mind what a man'd say in fun, nor take advantage of what a woman might say in answer to it. If a woman couldnt talk to a man for two minutes at their first meeting without being treated the way youre treating me, no decent woman would ever talk to a man at all.

BROADBENT: I dont understand that. I dont admit that. I am sincere; and my intentions are perfectly honorable. I think you will accept the fact that I'm an Englishman as a guarantee that I am not a man to act hastily or romantically; though I confess that your voice had such an extraordinary effect on me just now when you asked me so quaintly whether I was making love to you —

NORA: (*Flushing*) I never thought —

BROADBENT: (*Quickly*) Of course you didnt: I'm not so stupid as that. But I couldnt bear your laughing at the feeling it gave me. You — (*again struggling with a surge of emotion*) you dont know what I — (*he chokes for a moment and then blurts out with unnatural steadiness*) Will you be my wife?

NORA: (*Promptly*) Deed I wont. The idea! (*Looking at him more carefully*) Arra, come home, Mr Broadbent; and get your sense back again. I think youre not accustomed to potcheen punch in the evening after your tea.

BROADBENT: (*Horrified*) Do you mean to say that I — I — I my God! that I appear drunk to you, Miss Reilly?

NORA: (*Compassionately*) How many tumblers had you?

BROADBENT: (*Helplessly*) Two.

NORA: The flavor of the turf prevented you noticing the strength of it. Youd better come home to bed.

BROADBENT: (*Fearfully agitated*) But this is such a horrible doubt to put into my mind — to — to —

For Heaven's sake, Miss Reilly, am I really drunk?

NORA: (*Soothingly*) Youll be able to judge better in the morning. Come on now back with me, an think no more about it. (*She takes his arm with motherly solicitude and urges him gently towards the path*)

BROADBENT: (*Yielding in despair*) I must be drunk: frightfully drunk; for your voice drove me out of my senses — (*he stumbles over a stone*). No: on my word, on my most sacred word of honor, Miss Reilly, I tripped over that stone. It was an accident: it was indeed.

NORA: Yes, of course it was. Just take my arm, Mr Broadbent, while we're goin down the path to the road. Youll be all right then.

BROADBENT: (*Submissively taking it*) I cant sufficiently apologize, Miss Reilly, or express my sense of your kindness when I am in such a disgusting state. How could I be such a bea — (*he trips again*) damn the heather! my foot caught in it.

NORA: Steady now, steady. Come along: come. *He is led down to the road in the character of a convicted drunkard. To him there is something divine in the sympathetic indulgence she substitutes for the angry disgust with which one of his own countrywomen would resent his supposed condition. And he has no suspicion of the fact, or of her ignorance of it, that when an Englishman is sentimental he behaves very much as an Irishman does when he is drunk.*

ACT III

Next morning BROADBENT *and* LARRY *are sitting at the ends of a breakfast table in the middle of a small grass plot before* CORNELIUS DOYLE'S *house. They have finished their meal, and are buried in newspapers. Most of the crockery is crowded upon a large square black tray of japanned metal. The teapot is of brown delft ware. There is no silver; and the butter, on a dinner plate, is en bloc. The background to this breakfast is the house, a small white slated building, accessible by a half-glazed door. A person coming out into the garden by this door would find the table straight in front of him, and a gate leading to the road half way down the garden on his right; or, if he turned sharp to his left, he could pass round the end of the house through an unkempt shrubbery. The mutilated remnant of a huge plaster statue, nearly dissolved by the rains of a century, and vaguely resembling a majestic female in Roman draperies, with a wreath in her hand, stands neglected amid the laurels. Such statues, though apparently works of art, grow naturally in Irish gardens. Their germination is a mystery to the oldest inhabitants, to whose means and tastes they are totally foreign.*

There is a rustic bench, much soiled by the birds, and decorticated[1] *and split by the weather, near the little gate. At the opposite side, a basket lies unmolested because it might as well be there as anywhere else. An empty chair at the table was lately occupied by* CORNELIUS, *who has finished his breakfast and gone in to the room in which he receives rents and keeps his books and cash, known in the household as 'the office.' This chair, like the two occupied by* LARRY *and* BROADBENT, *has a mahogany frame and is upholstered in black horsehair.*

LARRY rises and goes off through the shrubbery with his newspaper. HODSON *comes in through the garden gate, disconsolate.* BROADBENT, *who sits facing the gate, augurs the worst from his expression.*

BROADBENT: Have you been to the village?

HODSON: No use, sir. We'll have to get everything from London by parcel post.

BROADBENT: I hope they made you comfortable last night.

HODSON: I was no worse than you were on that sofa, sir. One expects to rough it here, sir.

BROADBENT: We shall have to look out for some other arrangement. (*Cheering up irrepressibly*) Still, it's no end of a joke. How do you like the Irish, Hodson?

HODSON: Well, sir, theyre all right anywhere but in their own country. Ive known lots of em in England, and generally liked em. But here, sir, I seem simply to hate em. The feeling come over me the moment we landed at Cork, sir. It's no use my pretendin, sir: I cant bear em. My mind rises up agin their ways, somehow: they rub me the wrong way all over.

BROADBENT: Oh, their faults are on the surface: at heart they are one of the finest races on earth. (HODSON *turns away, without affecting to respond to his enthusiasm*) By the way, Hodson —

HODSON: (*Turning*) Yes, sir.

BROADBENT: Did you notice anything about me last night when I came in with that lady?

HODSON: (*Surprised*) No, sir.

BROADBENT: Not any — er —? You may speak frankly.

HODSON: I didnt notice nothing, sir. What sort of thing did you mean, sir?

1. Deprived of bark or husk.

BROADBENT: Well — er — er — well, to put it plainly, was I drunk?

HODSON: (*Amazed*) No, sir.

BROADBENT: Quite sure?

HODSON: Well, I should a said rather the opposite, sir. Usually when youve been enjoying yourself, youre a bit hearty like. Last night you seemed rather low, if anything.

BROADBENT: I certainly have no headache. Did you try the pottine, Hodson?

HODSON: I just took a mouthful, sir. It tasted of peat: oh! something horrid, sir. The people here call peat turf. Potcheen and strong porter is what they like, sir. I'm sure I dont know how they can stand it. Give me beer, I say.

BROADBENT: By the way, you told me I couldnt have porridge for breakfast; but Mr Doyle had some.

HODSON: Yes, sir. Very sorry, sir. They call it stirabout, sir: thats how it was. They know no better, sir.

BROADBENT: All right: I'll have some tomorrow.

HODSON *goes to the house. When he opens the door he finds* NORA *and* AUNT JUDY *on the threshold. He stands aside to let them pass, with the air of a well trained servant oppressed by heavy trials. Then he goes in.* BROADBENT *rises.* AUNT JUDY *goes to the table and collects the plates and cups on the tray.* NORA *goes to the back of the rustic seat and looks out at the gate with the air of a woman accustomed to have nothing to do.* LARRY *returns from the shrubbery.*

BROADBENT: Good morning, Miss Doyle.

AUNT JUDY: (*Thinking it absurdly late in the day for such a salutation*) Oh, good morning. (*Before moving his plate*) Have you done?

BROADBENT: Quite, thank you. You must excuse us for not waiting for you. The country air tempted us to get up early.

AUNT JUDY: N d'ye call this airly, God help you?

LARRY: Aunt Judy probably breakfasted about half past six.

AUNT JUDY: Whisht, you! draggin the parlor chairs out into the gardn n givin Mr Broadbent his death over his meals out here in the cold air. (*To* BROADBENT) Why d'ye put up with his foolishness, Mr Broadbent?

BROADBENT: I assure you I like the open air.

AUNT JUDY: Ah galong! How can you like whats not natural? I hope you slept well.

NORA: Did anything wake yup with a thump at three o'clock? I thought the house was falling. But then I'm a very light sleeper.

LARRY: I seem to recollect that one of the legs of the sofa in the parlor had a way of coming out unexpectedly eighteen years ago. Was that it, Tom?

BROADBENT: (*Hastily*) Oh, it doesnt matter: I was not hurt — at least — er —

AUNT JUDY: Oh now what a shame! An I told Pasty Farrll to put a nail in it.

BROADBENT: He did, Miss Doyle. There was a nail, certainly.

AUNT JUDY: Dear oh dear!

An oldish peasant farmer, small, leathery, peat-faced, with a deep voice and a surliness that is meant to be aggressive, and is in effect pathetic – the voice of a man of hard life and many sorrows – comes in at the gate. He is old enough to have perhaps worn a long tailed frieze coat and knee breeches in his time; but now he is dressed respectably in a black frock coat, tall hat, and pollard[2] *colored trousers; and his face is as clean as washing can make it, though that is not saying much, as the habit is recently acquired and not yet congenial.*

THE NEW-COMER: (*At the gate*) God save all here! (*He comes a little way into the garden*)

LARRY: (*Patronizingly, speaking across the garden to him*) Is that yourself, Matt Haffigan? Do you remember me?

MATTHEW: (*Intentionally rude and blunt*) No. Who are you?

NORA: Oh, I'm sure you remember him, Mr Haffigan.

MATTHEW: (*Grudgingly admitting it*) I suppose he'll be young Larry Doyle that was.

LARRY: Yes.

MATTHEW: (*To* LARRY) I hear you done well in America.

LARRY: Fairly well.

MATTHEW: I suppose you saw me brother Andy out dhere.

LARRY: No. It's such a big place that looking for a man there is like looking for a needle in a bundle of hay. They tell me he's a great man out there.

MATTHEW: So he is, God be praised. Wheres your father?

AUNT JUDY: He's inside, in the office, Mr Haffigan, with Barney Doarn n Father Dempsey.

MATTHEW, *without wasting further words on the company, goes curtly into the house.*

LARRY: (*Staring after him*) Is anything wrong with old Matt?

2. tree-bark brown.

NORA: No. He's the same as ever. Why?

LARRY: He's not the same to me. He used to be very civil to Masther Larry: a deal too civil, I used to think. Now he's as surly and stand-off as a bear.

AUNT JUDY: Oh sure he's bought his farm in the Land Purchase. He's independent now.

NORA: It's made a great change, Larry. Youd harly know the old tenants now. Youd think it was a liberty to speak t'dhem — some o dhem. (*She goes to the table, and helps to take off the cloth, which she and* AUNT JUDY *fold up between them*)

AUNT JUDY: I wonder what he wants to see Corny for. He hasnt been here since he paid the last of his old rent; and then he as good as threw it in Corny's face, I thought.

LARRY: No wonder! Of course they all hated us like the devil. Ugh! (*Moodily*) Ive seen them in that office, telling my father what a fine boy I was, and plastering him with compliments, with your honor here and your honor there, when all the time their fingers were itching to be at his throat.

AUNT JUDY: Deedn why should they want to hurt poor Corny? It was he that got Matt the lease of his farm, and stood up for him as an industrious decent man.

BROADBENT: Was he industrious? Thats remarkable, you know, in an Irishman.

LARRY: Industrious! That man's industry used to make me sick, even as a boy. I tell you, an Irish peasant's industry is not human: it's worse than the industry of a coral insect. An Englishman has some sense about working: he never does more than he can help — and hard enough to get him to do that without scamping[3] it; but an Irishman will work as if he'd die the moment he stopped. That man Matthew Haffigan and his brother Andy made a farm out of a patch of stones on the hillside: cleared it and dug it with their own naked hands and brought their first spade out of their first crop of potatoes. Talk of making two blades of wheat grow where one grew before![4] those two men made a whole field of wheat grow where not even a furze bush had ever got its head up between the stones.

BROADBENT: That was magnificent, you know. Only a great race is capable of producing such men.

LARRY: Such fools, you mean! What good was it to them? The moment theyd done it, the landlord put a rent of £5 a year on them, and turned them out because they couldnt pay it.

AUNT JUDY: Why couldnt they pay as well as Billy Byrne that took it after them?

LARRY: (*Angrily*) You know very well that Billy Byrne never paid it. He only offered it to get possession. He never paid it.

AUNT JUDY: That was because Andy Haffigan hurt him with a brick so that he was never the same again. Andy had to run away to America for it.

BROADBENT: (*Glowing with indignation*) Who can blame him, Miss Doyle? Who can blame him?

LARRY: (*Impatiently*) Oh, rubbish! whats the good of the man thats starved out of a farm murdering the man thats starved into it? Would you have done such a thing?

BROADBENT: Yes. I—I—I—I— (*stammering with fury*) I should have shot the confounded landlord, and wrung the neck of the damned agent, and blown the farm up with dynamite, and Dublin Castle[5] along with it.

LARRY: Oh yes: youd have done great things; and a fat lot of good youd have got out of it, too! Thats an Englishman all over! make bad laws and give away all the land, and then, when your economic incompetence produces its natural and inevitable results, get virtuously indignant and kill the people that carry out your laws.

AUNT JUDY: Sure never mind him, Mr Broadbent. It doesnt matter, anyhow, because theres harly[6] any landlords left; and therell soon be none at all.

LARRY: On the contrary, therll soon be nothing else; and the Lord help Ireland then!

AUNT JUDY: Ah, youre never satisfied, Larry. (*To* NORA) Come on, alanna,[7] an make the paste for the pie. We can leave them to their talk. They dont want us (*she takes up the tray and goes into the house*).

BROADBENT: (*Rising and gallantly protesting*) Oh, Miss Doyle! Really, really —

NORA, *following* AUNT JUDY *with the rolled-up cloth in her hands, looks at him and strikes him dumb. He watches her until she disappears; then comes to* LARRY *and addresses him with sudden intensity.*

3. A less common word for 'skimping'.
4. Jonathan Swift: 'And, he gave it for his opinion, that whoever could make two ears of corn, or two blades of grass to grow upon a spot of ground where only one grew before; would deserve better of mankind, and do more essential service to his country, than the whole race of politicians put together.' (*Gulliver's Travels*, Book II, Ch. 7).
5. The seat of British administration in Ireland.
6. hardly.
7. A term of endearment in Irish, 'my child'.

BROADBENT: Larry.

LARRY: What is it?

BROADBENT: I got drunk last night, and proposed to Miss Reilly.

LARRY: You hwat??? (*He screams with laughter in the falsetto Irish register unused for that purpose in England*)

BROADBENT: What are you laughing at?

LARRY: (*Stopping dead*) I dont know. Thats the sort of thing an Irishman laughs at. Has she accepted you?

BROADBENT: I shall never forget that with the chivalry of her nation, though I was utterly at her mercy, she refused me.

LARRY: That was extremely improvident of her. (*Beginning to reflect*) But look here: when were you drunk? You were sober enough when you came back from the Round Tower with her.

BROADBENT: No, Larry, I was drunk, I am sorry to say. I had two tumblers of punch. She had to lead me home. You must have noticed it.

LARRY: I did not.

BROADBENT: She did.

LARRY: May I ask how long it took you to come to business? You can hardly have known her for more than a couple of hours.

BROADBENT: I am afraid it was hardly a couple of minutes. She was not here when I arrived; and I saw her for the first time at the tower.

LARRY: Well, you are a nice infant to be let loose in this country! Fancy the potcheen going to your head like that!

BROADBENT: Not to my head, I think. I have no headache; and I could speak distinctly. No: potcheen goes to the heart, not to the head. What ought I to do?

LARRY: Nothing. What need you do?

BROADBENT: There is rather a delicate moral question involved. The point is, was I drunk enough not to be morally responsible for my proposal? Or was I sober enough to be bound to repeat it now that I am undoubtedly sober?

LARRY: I should see a little more of her before deciding.

BROADBENT: No, no. That would not be right. That would not be fair. I am either under a moral obligation or I am not. I wish I knew how drunk I was.

LARRY: Well, you were evidently in a state of blithering sentimentality, anyhow.

BROADBENT: That is true, Larry: I admit it. Her voice has a most extraordinary effect on me. That Irish voice!

LARRY: (*Sympathetically*) Yes, I know. When I first went to London I very nearly proposed to walk out with a waitress in an Aerated Bread shop because her Whitechapel accent was so distinguished, so quaintly touching, so pretty —

BROADBENT: (*Angrily*) Miss Reilly is not a waitress, is she?

LARRY: Oh, come! The waitress was a very nice girl.

BROADBENT: You think every Englishwoman an angel. You really have coarse tastes in that way, Larry. Miss Reilly is one of the finer types: a type rare in England, except perhaps in the best of the aristocracy.

LARRY: Aristocracy be blowed! Do you know what Nora eats?

BROADBENT: Eats! what do you mean?

LARRY: Breakfast: tea and bread-and-butter, with an occasional rasher,[8] and an egg on special ocasions: say on her birthday. Dinner in the middle of the day, one course and nothing else. In the evening, tea and bread-and-butter again. You compare her with your Englishwomen who wolf down from three to five meat meals a day; and naturally you find her a sylph. The difference is not a difference of type: it's the difference between the woman who eats not wisely but too well, and the woman who eats not wisely but too little.

BROADBENT: (*Furious*) Larry: you — you — you disgust me. You are a damned fool. (*He sits down angrily on the rustic seat, which sustains the shock with difficulty*)

LARRY: Steady! stead-eee! (*He laughs and seats himself on the table*)

CORNELIUS DOYLE, FATHER DEMPSEY, BARNEY DORAN, *and* MATTHEW HAFFIGAN *come from the house.* DORAN *is a stout bodied, short armed, roundheaded, red haired man on the verge of middle age, of sanguine temperament, with an enormous capacity for derisive, obscene, blasphemous, or merely cruel and senseless fun, and a violent and impetuous intolerance of other temperaments and other opinions, all this representing energy and capacity wasted and demoralized by want of sufficient training and social pressure to force it into beneficent activity and build a character with it; for* BARNEY *is by no means either stupid or weak. He is recklessly untidy as to his person;*

8. slice of bacon.

but the worst effects of his neglect are mitigated by a powdering of flour and mill dust; and his unbrushed clothes, made of a fashionable tailor's sackcloth, were evidently chosen regardless of expense for the sake of their appearance.

MATTHEW HAFFIGAN, *ill at ease, coasts the garden shyly on the shrubbery side until he anchors near the basket, where he feels least in the way. The priest comes to the table and slaps* LARRY *on the shoulder.* LARRY, *turning quickly, and recognizing* FATHER DEMPSEY, *alights from the table and shakes the priest's hand warmly.* DORAN *comes down the garden between* FATHER DEMPSEY *and* MATT*; and* CORNELIUS, *on the other side of the table, turns to* BROADBENT, *who rises genially.*

CORNELIUS: I think we all met las night.

DORAN: I hadnt that pleasure.

CORNELIUS: To be sure, Barney: I forgot. (*To* BROADBENT, *introducing* BARNEY) Mr Doran. He owns that fine mill you noticed from the car.

BROADBENT: (*Delighted with them all*) Most happy, Mr Doran. Very pleased indeed.

DORAN, *not quite sure whether he is being courted or patronized, nods independently.*

DORAN: Hows yourself, Larry?

LARRY: Finely, thank you. No need to ask you.

DORAN *grins; and they shake hands.*

CORNELIUS: Give Father Dempsey a chair, Larry.

MATTHEW HAFFIGAN *runs to the nearest end of the table and takes the chair from it, placing it near the basket; but* LARRY *has already taken the chair from the other end and placed it in front of the table.* FATHER DEMPSEY *accepts that more central position.*

CORNELIUS: Sit down, Barney, will you; and you, Matt.

DORAN *takes the chair* MATT *is still offering to the priest; and poor* MATTHEW, *outfaced by the miller, humbly turns the basket upside down and sits on it.* CORNELIUS *brings his own breakfast chair from the table and sits down on* FATHER DEMPSEY'S *right.* BROADBENT *resumes his seat on the rustic bench.* LARRY *crosses to the bench and is about to sit down beside him when* BROADBENT *holds him off nervously.*

BROADBENT: Do you think it will bear two, Larry?

LARRY: Perhaps not. Dont move. I'll stand. (*He posts himself behind the bench*)

They are all now seated, except LARRY*; and the session assumes a portentous air, as if something important were coming.*

CORNELIUS: Praps youll explain, Father Dempsey.

FATHER DEMPSEY: No, no: go on, you: the Church has no politics.

CORNELIUS: Were yever thinkin o goin into parliament at all, Larry?

LARRY: Me!

FATHER DEMPSEY: (*Encouragingly*) Yes, you. Hwy not?

LARRY: I'm afraid my ideas would not be popular enough.

CORNELIUS: I dont know that. Do you, Barney?

DORAN: Theres too much blatherumskite[9] in Irish politics: a dale too much.

LARRY: But what about your present member? Is he going to retire?

CORNELIUS: No: I dont know that he is.

LARRY: (*Interrogatively*) Well? then?

MATTHEW: (*Breaking out with surly bitterness*) Weve had enough of his foolish talk agen lanlords. Hwat call has he to talk about the lan, that never was outside of a city office in his life?

CORNELIUS: We're tired of him. He doesnt know hwere to stop. Every man cant own land; and some men must own it to employ them. It was all very well when solid men like Doran an Matt were kep from ownin land. But hwat man in his senses ever wanted to give land to Patsy Farrll an dhe like o him?

BROADBENT: But surely Irish landlordism was accountable for what Mr Haffigan suffered.

MATTHEW: Never mind hwat I suffered. I know what I suffered adhout you tellin me. But did I ever ask for more dhan the farm I made wid me own hans? tell me that, Corny Doyle, and you that knows. Was I fit for the responsibility or was I not? (*Snarling angrily at* CORNELIUS) Am I to be compared to Patsy Farrll, that doesnt harly know his right hand from his left? What did he ever suffer, I'd like to know?

CORNELIUS: Thats just what I say. I wasnt comparin you to your disadvantage.

MATTHEW: (*Implacable*) Then hwat did you mane be talkin about givin him lan?

DORAN: Aisy, Matt, aisy. Youre like a bear with a sore back.

MATTHEW: (*Trembling with rage*) An who are you, to offer to taitch me manners?

9. rubbishy talk, compound of 'blather' (talk) and 'skite' (pointless action).

FATHER DEMPSEY: (*Admonitorily*) Now, now, now, Matt! none o dhat. How often have I told you youre too ready to take offence where none is meant? You dont understand: Corny Doyle is saying just what you want to have said. (*To* CORNELIUS) Go on, Mr Doyle; and never mind him.

MATTHEW: (*Rising*) Well, if me lan is to be given to Patsy and his like, I'm goin oura dhis.[10] I —

DORAN: (*With violent impatience*) Arra who's goin to give your lan to Patsy, yowl fool ye?

FATHER DEMPSEY: Aisy, Barney, aisy. (*Sternly, to* MATT) I told you, Matthew Haffigan, that Corny Doyle was saying nothin against you. I'm sorry your priest's word is not good enough for you. I'll go, sooner than stay to make you commit a sin against the Church. Good morning, gentlemen. (*He rises. They all rise, except* BROADBENT)

DORAN: (*To* MATT) There! Sarve you dam well right, you cantankerous oul noodle.

MATTHEW: (*Appalled*) Dont say dhat, Fadher Dempsey. I never had a thought agen you or the Holy Church. I know I'm a bit hasty when I think about the lan. I ax[11] your pardon for it.

FATHER DEMPSEY: (*Resuming his seat with dignified reserve*) Very well: I'll overlook it this time. (*He sits down. The others sit down, except* MATTHEW. FATHER DEMPSEY, *about to ask* CORNY *to proceed, remembers* MATTHEW *and turns to him, giving him just a crumb of graciousness*) Sit down, Matt. (MATTHEW, *crushed, sits down in disgrace, and is silent, his eyes shifting piteously from one speaker to another in an intensely mistrustful effort to understand them*) Go on, Mr Doyle. We can make allowances. Go on.

CORNELIUS: Well, you see how it is, Larry. Round about here, weve got the land at last; and we want no more Goverment meddlin. We want a new class o man in parliament: one dhat knows dhat the farmer's the real backbone o the country, n doesnt care a snap of his fingers for the shoutn o the riff-raff in the towns, or for the foolishness of the laborers.

DORAN: Aye; an dhat can afford to live in London and pay his own way until Home Rule comes, instead o wantin subscriptions and the like.

FATHER DEMPSEY: Yes: thats a good point, Barney. When too much money goes to politics, it's the Church that has to starve for it. A member of parliament ought to be a help to the Church instead of a burden on it.

LARRY: Heres a chance for you, Tom. What do you say?

BROADBENT: (*Deprecatory, but important and smiling*) Oh, I have no claim whatever to the seat. Besides, I'm a Saxon.

DORAN: A hwat?

BROADBENT: A Saxon. An Englishman.

DORAN: An Englishman. Bedad I never heard it called dhat before.

MATTHEW: (*Cunningly*) If I might make so bould, Fadher, I wouldnt say but an English Prodestn mightnt have a more indepindent mind about the lan, an be less afeerd to spake out about it, dhan an Irish Catholic.

CORNELIUS: But sure Larry's as good as English: arnt you, Larry?

LARRY: You may put me out of your head, father, once for all.

CORNELIUS: Arra why?

LARRY: I have strong opinions which wouldnt suit you.

DORAN: (*Rallying him blatantly*) Is it still Larry the bould Fenian?[12]

LARRY: No: the bold Fenian is now an older and possibly foolisher man.

CORNELIUS: Hwat does it matter to us hwat your opinions are? You know that your father's bought his place here, just the same as Matt's farm n Barney's mill. All we ask now is to be let alone. Youve nothin against that, have you?

LARRY: Certainly I have. I dont believe in letting anybody or anything alone.

CORNELIUS: (*Losing his temper*) Arra what d'ye mean, you young fool? Here Ive got you the offer of a good seat in parliament; n you think yourself mighty smart to stand there and talk foolishness to me. Will you take it or leave it?

LARRY: Very well: I'll take it with pleasure if youll give it to me.

CORNELIUS: (*Subsiding sulkily*) Well, why couldnt you say so at once? It's a good job youve made up your mind at last.

DORAN: (*Suspiciously*) Stop a bit: stop a bit.

MATTHEW: (*Writhing between his dissatisfaction and his fear of the priest*) It's not because he's your

10. out of this.
11. ask.
12. A member of an insurrectionist group, named after the Fianna, which rose in abortive rebellion against the British in 1867.

son that he's to get the sate.[13] Fadher Dempsey: wouldnt you think well to ask him what he manes about the lan?

LARRY: (*Coming down on* MATT *promptly*) I'll tell you, Matt. I always thought it was a stupid, lazy, good-for-nothing sort of thing to leave the land in the hands of the old landlords without calling them to a strict account for the use they made of it, and the condition of the people on it. I could see for myself that they thought of nothing but what they could get out of it to spend in England; and that they mortgaged and mortgaged until hardly one of them owned his own property or could have afforded to keep it up decently if he'd wanted to. But I tell you plump and plain, Matt, that if anybody thinks things will be any better now that the land is handed over to a lot of little men like you, without calling you to account either, theyre mistaken.

MATTHEW: (*Sullenly*) What call have you to look down on me? I suppose you think youre everybody because your father was a land agent.

LARRY: What call have you to look down on Patsy Farrell? I suppose you think youre everybody because you own a few fields.

MATTHEW: Was Patsy Farrll ever ill used as I was ill used? tell me dhat.

LARRY: He will be, if ever he gets into your power as you were in the power of your old landlord. Do you think, because youre poor and ignorant and half-crazy with toiling and moiling[14] morning noon and night, that youll be any less greedy and oppressive to them that have no land at all than old Nick Lestrange, who was an educated travelled gentleman that would not have been tempted as hard by a hundred pounds as youd be by five shillings? Nick was too high above Patsy Farrell to be jealous of him; but you, that are only one little step above him, would die sooner than let him come up that step; and well you know it.

MATTHEW: (*Black with rage, in a low growl*) Lemmy oura dhis. (*He tries to rise; but* DORAN *catches his coat and drags him down again*) I'm goin, I say. (*Raising his voice*) Leggo me coat, Barney Doran.

DORAN: Sit down, yowl omadhaun, you. (*Whispering*) Dont you want to stay an vote agen him?

FATHER DEMPSEY: (*Holding up his finger*) Matt! (MATT *subsides*) Now, now, now! come, come! Hwats all dhis about Patsy Farrll? Hwy need you fall out about him?

LARRY: Because it was by using Patsy's poverty to undersell England in the markets of the world that we drove England to ruin Ireland. And she'll ruin us again the moment we lift our heads from the dust if we trade in cheap labor; and serve us right too! If I get into parliament, I'll try to get an Act to prevent any of you from giving Patsy less than a pound a week (*they all start, hardly able to believe their ears*) or working him harder than youd work a horse that cost you fifty guineas.

DORAN: Hwat!!!

CORNELIUS: (*Aghast*) A pound a — God save us! the boy's mad.

MATTHEW, *feeling that here is something quite beyond his powers, turns openmouthed to the priest, as if looking for nothing less than the summary excommunication of* LARRY.

LARRY: How is the man to marry and live a decent life on less?

FATHER DEMPSEY: Man alive, hwere have you been living all these years? and hwat have you been dreaming of? Why, some o dhese honest men here cant make that much out o the land for dhemselves, much less give it to a laborer.

LARRY (*Now thoroughly roused*) Then let them make room for those who can. Is Ireland never to have a chance? First she was given to the rich; and now that they have gorged on her flesh, her bones are to be flung to the poor, that can do nothing but suck the marrow out of her. If we cant have men of honor own the land, lets have men of ability. If we cant have men with ability, let us at least have men with capital. Anybody's better than Matt, who has neither honor, nor ability, nor capital, nor anything but mere brute labor and greed in him, Heaven help him!

DORAN: Well, we're not all foostherin[15] oul doddherers like Matt. (*Pleasantly, to the subject of this description*) Are we, Matt?

LARRY: For modern industrial purposes you might just as well be, Barney. Youre all children: the big world that I belong to has gone past you and left you. Anyhow, we Irishmen we never made to be farmers; and we'll never do any good at it. We're like the Jews: the Almighty gave us brians, and bid

13. seat.

14. working hard.

15. frenetically clumsy. From Irish *fuadar*, hurry.

us farm them, and leave the clay and the worms alone.

FATHER DEMPSEY: (*With gentle irony*) Oh! is it Jews you want to make of us? I must catechize you a bit meself, I think. The next thing youll be proposing is to repeal the disestablishment[16] of the so-called Irish Church.

LARRY: Yes: why not? (*Sensation*)

MATTHEW: (*Rancorously*) He's a turncoat.

LARRY: St Peter, the rock on which our Church was built, was crucified head downwards for being a turncoat.

FATHER DEMPSEY: (*With a quiet authoritative dignity which checks* DORAN, *who is on the point of breaking out*) Thats true. You hold your tongue as befits your ignorance, Matthew Haffigan; and trust your priest to deal with this young man. Now, Larry Doyle, whatever the blessed St Peter was crucified for, it was not for being a Prodestan. Are you one?

LARRY: No. I am a Catholic intelligent enough to see that the Protestants are never more dangerous to us than when they are free from all alliances with the State. The so-called Irish Church is stronger today than ever it was.

MATTHEW: Fadher Dempsey: will you tell him dhat me mother's ant was shot and kilt dead in the sthreet o Rosscullen be a soljer in the tithe war? (*Frantically*) He wants to put the tithes on us again. He—

LARRY: (*Interrupting him with overbearing contempt*) Put the tithes on you again! Did the tithes ever come off you? Was your land any dearer when you paid the tithe to the parson than it was when you paid the same money to Nick Lestrange as rent, and he handed it over to the Church Sustentation Fund? Will you always be duped by Acts of Parliament that change nothing but the necktie of the man that picks your pocket? I'll tell you what I'd do with you, Matt Haffigan: I'd make you pay tithes to your own Church. I want the Catholic Church established in Ireland: thats what I want. Do you think that I, brought up to regard myself as the son of a great and holy Church, can bear to see her begging her bread from the ignorance and superstition of men like you? I would have her as high above worldly want as I would have her above worldly pride or ambition. Aye; and I would have Ireland compete with Rome itself for the chair of St Peter and the citadel of the Church; for Rome, in spite of all the blood of the martyrs, is pagan at heart to this day, while in Ireland the people is the Church and the Church the people.

FATHER DEMPSEY: (*Startled, but not at all displeased*) Whisht, man! youre worse than mad Pether Keegan himself.

BROADBENT: (*Who has listened in the greatest astonishment*) You amaze me, Larry. Who would have thought of your coming out like this! (*Solemnly*) But much as I appreciate your really brilliant eloquence, I implore you not to desert the great Liberal principle of Disestablishment.

LARRY: I am not a Liberal: Heaven forbid! A disestablished Church is the worst tyranny a nation can groan under.

BROADBENT: (*Making a wry face*) Dont be paradoxical, Larry. It really gives me a pain in my stomach.

LARRY: Youll soon find out the truth of it here. Look at Father Dempsey! he is disestablished: he has nothing to hope or fear from the State; and the result is that he's the most powerful man in Rosscullen. The member for Rosscullen would shake in his shoes if Father Dempsey looked crooked at him. (FATHER DEMPSEY *smiles, by no means averse to this acknowledgment of his authority*) Look at yourself! you would defy the established Archbishop of Canterbury ten times a day; but catch you daring to say a word that would shock a Nonconformist! not you. The Conservative party today is the only one thats not priestridden — excuse the expression, Father (FATHER DEMPSEY *nods tolerantly*) — because it's the only one that has established its Church and can prevent a clergyman becoming a bishop if he's not a Statesman as well as a Churchman.

He stops. They stare at him dumbfounded, and leave it to the priest to answer him.

FATHER DEMPSEY: (*Judicially*) Young man: youll not be the member for Rosscullen; but dheres more in your head than the comb will take out.

LARRY: I'm sorry to disappoint you, father; but I told you it would be no use. And now I think the candidate had better retire and leave you to discuss his successor. (*He takes a newspaper from the table and goes away through the shrubbery amid dead silence, all turning to watch him until he passes out of sight round the corner of the house*)

16. The protestant Church of Ireland was disestablished in 1869, i.e. it was no longer afforded official recognition by the state, entitling its clergy to tithes from the people.

DORAN: (*Dazed*) Hwat sort of a fella is he at all at all?

FATHER DEMPSEY: He's a clever lad: dheres the making of a man in him yet.

MATTHEW: (*In consternation*) D'ye mane to say dhat yll put him into parliament to bring back Nick Lesthrange on me, and to put tithes on me, and to rob me for the like o Patsy Farrll, because he's Corny Doyle's son?

DORAN: (*Brutally*) Arra hould your whisht:[17] who's goin to send him into parliament? Maybe youd like us to send you dhere to thrate dhem to a little o your anxiety about dhat dirty little podato patch o yours.

MATTHEW: (*Plaintively*) Am I to be towld dhis afther all me sufferins?

DORAN: Och, I'm tired o your sufferins. Weve been hearin nothin else ever since we was childher but sufferins. Hwen it wasnt yours it was somebody else's; and hwen it was nobody else's it was ould Irelan's. How the divil are we to live on wan anodher's sufferins?

FATHER DEMPSEY: Thats a thrue word, Barney Doarn; only your tongue's a little too familiar wi dhe divil. (*To* MATT) If youd think a little more o the sufferins of the blessed saints, Matt, an a little less o your own, youd find the way shorter from your farm to heaven. (MATT *is about to reply*) Dhere now! dhats enough! we know you mean well; an I'm not angry with you.

BROADBENT: Surely, Mr Haffigan, you can see the simple explanation of all this. My friend Larry Doyle is a most brilliant speaker; but he's a Tory: an ingrained old-fashioned Tory.

CORNELIUS: N how d'ye make dhat out, if I might ask you, Mr Broadbent?

BROADBENT: (*Collecting himself for a political deliverance*) Well, you know, Mr Doyle, theres a strong dash of Toryism in the Irish character. Larry himself says that the great Duke of Wellington was the most typical Irishman that ever lived. Of course thats an absurd paradox; but still theres a great deal of truth in it. Now I am a Liberal. You know the great principles of the Liberal Party. Peace —

FATHER DEMPSEY: (*Piously*) Hear! hear!

BROADBENT: (*Encouraged*) Thank you. Retrenchment — (*he waits for further applause*).

MATTHEW: (*Timidly*) What might rethrenchment mane now?

17. keep silent.

BROADBENT: It means an immense reduction in the burden of the rates and taxes.

MATTHEW: (*Respectfully approving*) Dhats right. Dhats right, sir.

BROADBENT: (*Perfunctorily*) And, of course, Reform.

CORNELIUS:
FATHER DEMPSEY: } (*Conventionally*) Of course.
DORAN:

MATTHEW: (*Still suspicious*) Hwat does Reform mane, sir? Does it mane altherin annythin dhats as it is now?

BROADBENT: (*Impressively*) It means, Mr Haffigan, maintaining those reforms which have already been conferred on humanity by the Liberal Party, and trusting for future developments to the free activity of a free people on the basis of those reforms.

DORAN: Dhats right. No more meddlin. We're all right now: all we want is to be let alone.

CORNELIUS: Hwat about Home Rule?

BROADBENT: (*Rising so as to address them more imposingly*) I really cannot tell you what I feel about Home Rule without using the language of hyperbole.

DORAN: Savin Fadher Dempsey's presence, eh?

BROADBENT: (*Not understanding him*) Quite so — er — oh yes. All I can say is that as an Englishman I blush for the Union. It is the blackest stain on our national history. I look forward to the time — and it cannot be far distant, gentlemen, because Humanity is looking forward to it too, and insisting on it with no uncertain voice — I look forward to the time when an Irish legislature shall arise once more on the emerald pasture of College Green, and the Union Jack — that detestable symbol of a decadent Imperialism — be replaced by a flag as green as the island over which it waves: a flag on which we shall ask for England only a modest quartering in memory of our great party and of the immortal name of our grand old leader.

DORAN: (*Enthusiastically*) Dhats the style, begob! (*He smites his knee, and winks at* MATT)[18]

MATTHEW: More power to you, sir!

BROADBENT: I shall leave you now, gentlemen, to your deliberations. I should like to have enlarged on the services rendered by the Liberal Party to the religious faith of the great majority of the people of Ireland; but I shall content myself with saying that

18. by gosh, by God.

in my opinion you should choose no representative who — no matter what his personal creed may be — is not an ardent supporter of freedom of conscience, and is not prepared to prove it by contributions, as lavish as his means will allow, to the great and beneficent work which you, Father Dempsey! (*Father Dempsey bows*), are doing for the people of Rosscullen. Nor should the lighter but still most important question of the sports of the people be forgotten. The local cricket club —

CORNELIUS: The hwat!

DORAN: Nobody plays bat n ball here, if dhats what you mane.

BROADBENT: Well, let us say quoits.[19] I saw two men, I think, last night — but after all, these are questions of detail. The main thing is that your candidate, whoever he may be, shall be a man of some means, able to help the locality instead of burdening it. And if he were a countryman of my own, the moral effect on the House of Commons would be immense! tremendous! Pardon my saying these few words: nobody feels their impertinence more than I do. Good morning, gentlemen. (*He turns impressively to the gate, and trots away, congratulating himself, with a little twist of his head and cock of his eye, on having done a good stroke of political business*)

HAFFIGAN: (*Awestruck*) Good morning, sir.

THE REST: Good morning. (*They watch him vacantly until he is out of earshot*)

CORNELIUS: Hwat d'ye think, Father Dempsey?

FATHER DEMPSEY: (*Indulgently*) Well, he hasnt much sense, God help him; but for the matter o that, neether has our present member.

DORAN: Arra musha[20] he's good enough for parliament:[21] what is there to do there but gas a bit, an chivy the Goverment, an vote wi dh Irish party?

CORNELIUS: (*Ruminatively*) He's the queerest Englishman *I* ever met. When he opened the paper dhis mornin the first thing he saw was that an English expedition had been bet in a battle in Inja[22] somewhere; an he was as pleased as Punch! Larry told him that if he'd been alive when the news o Waterloo came, he'd a died o grief over it. Bedad I dont think he's quite right in his head.

DORAN: Divil a matther if he has plenty o money. He'll do for us right enough.

MATTHEW: (*Deeply impressed by* BROADBENT, *and unable to understand their levity concerning him*) Did you mind what he said about rethrenchment? That was very good, I thought.

FATHER DEMPSEY: You might find out from Larry, Corny, what his means are. God forgive us all! it's poor work spoiling the Egyptians, though we have good warrant for it; so I'd like to know how much spoil there is before I commit meself. (*He rises. They all rise respectfully*)

CORNELIUS: (*Ruefully*) I'd set me mind on Larry himself for the seat; but I suppose it cant be helped.

FATHER DEMPSEY: (*Consoling him*) Well, the boy's young yet; an he has a head on him. Goodbye, all. (*He goes out through the gate*)

DORAN: I must be goin, too. (*He directs* CORNELIUS's *attention to what is passing in the road*) Look at me bould Englishman shakin hans wid Fadher Dempsey for all the world like a candidate on election day. And look at Fadher Dempsey givin him a squeeze an a wink as much as to say It's all right, me boy. You watch him shakin hands with me too: he's waitn for me. I'll tell him he's as good as elected. (*He goes, chuckling mischievously*)

CORNELIUS: Come in with me, Matt. I think I'll sell you the pig after all. Come in an wet the bargain.[23]

MATTHEW: (*Instantly dropping into the old whine of the tenant*) I'm afeerd I cant afford the price, sir. (*He follows* CORNELIUS *into the house*)

LARRY, *newspaper still in hand, comes back through the shrubbery.* BROADBENT *returns through the gate.*

LARRY: Well? What has happened?

BROADBENT: (*Hugely self-satisfied*) I think Ive done the trick this time. I just gave them a bit of straight talk; and it went home. They were greatly impressed: everyone of those men believes in me and will vote for me when the question of selecting a candidate comes up. After all, whatever you say, Larry, they like an Englishman. They feel they can trust him, I suppose.

LARRY: Oh! theyve transferred the honor to you, have they?

BROADBENT: (*Complacently*) Well, it was a pretty obvious move, I should think. You know, these fellows have plenty of shrewdness in spite of their

19. A game in which heavy, flat rings are thrown at a stake in the ground.
20. *musha:* from Irish 'más ea', *if that is so* — often in Hiberno-English, meaning 'anyway'.
21. Irish nationalists commitment to parliament was always conditional. Many texts of the Gaelic Revival are satires on the parliamentary process.
22. India.
23. have a drink to seal the bargain.

Irish oddity. (HODSON *comes from the house.* LARRY *sits in* DORAN's *chair and reads*) Oh, by the way, Hodson —

HODSON: (*Coming between* BROADBENT *and* LARRY) Yes, sir?

BROADBENT: I want you to be rather particular as to how you treat the people here.

HODSON: I havnt treated[24] any of em yet, sir. If I was to accept all the treats they offer me I shouldnt be able to stand at this present moment, sir.

BROADBENT: Oh well, dont be too standoffish, you know, Hodson. I should like you to be popular. If it costs anything I'll make it up to you. It doesnt matter if you get a bit upset at first: theyll like you all the better for it.

HODSON: I'm sure youre very kind, sir; but it dont seem to matter to me whether they like me or not. I'm not going to stand for parliament here, sir.

BROADBENT: Well, I am. Now do you understand?

HODSON: (*Making up at once*) Oh, I beg your pardon, sir, I'm sure. I understand, sir.

CORNELIUS: (*Appearing at the house door with* MATT) Patsy'll drive the pig over this evenin, Matt. Goodbye. (*He goes back into the house*)

MATT *makes for the gate.* BROADBENT *stops him.* HODSON, *pained by the derelict basket, picks it up and carries it away behind the house.*

BROADBENT: (*Beaming candidatorially*) I must thank you very particularly, Mr Haffigan, for your support this morning. I value it because I know that the real heart of a nation is the class you represent, the yeomanry.[25]

MATTHEW: (*Aghast*) The yeomanry!!!

LARRY: (*Looking up from his paper*) Take care, Tom! In Rosscullen a yeoman means a sort of Orange Bashi-Bazouk.[26] In England, Matt, they call a freehold farmer a yeoman.

MATTHEW: (*Huffily*) I dont need to be insthructed be you, Larry Doyle. Some people think no one knows anythin but dhemselves. (*To* BROADBENT, *deferentially*) Of course I know a gentleman like you would not compare me to the yeomanry. Me own granfather was flogged in the sthreets of Athenmullet be them when they put a gun in the thatch of his house an then went and found it there, bad cess[27] to them!

BROADBENT: (*With sympathetic interest*) Then you are not the first martyr of your family, Mr Haffigan?

MATTHEW: They turned me out o the farm I made out of the stones o Little Rosscullen hill wid me own hans.

BROADBENT: I have heard about it; and my blood still boils at the thought. (*Calling*) Hodson —

HODSON: (*Behind the corner of the house*) Yes, sir. (*He hurries forward*)

BROADBENT: Hodson: this gentleman's sufferings should make every Englishman think. It is want of thought rather than want of heart that allows such iniquities to disgrace society.

HODSON: (*Prosaically*) Yes, sir.

MATTHEW: Well, I'll be goin. Good mornin to you kindly, sir.

BROADBENT: You have some distance to go, Mr Haffigan: will you allow me to drive you home?

MATTHEW: Oh sure it'd be throublin your honor.

BROADBENT: I insist: it will give me the greatest pleasure, I assure you. My car is in the stable: I can get it round in five minutes.

MATTHEW: Well, sir, if you wouldnt mind, we could bring the pig Ive just bought from Corny —

BROADBENT: (*With enthusiasm*) Certainly, Mr Haffigan: it will be quite delightful to drive with a pig in the car: I shall feel quite like an Irishman. Hodson: stay with Mr Haffigan; and give him a hand with the pig if necessary. Come, Larry; and help me. (*He rushes away through the shrubbery*)

LARRY: (*Throwing the paper ill-humoredly on the chair*) Look here, Tom! here, I say! confound it! — (*he runs after him*)

MATTHEW: (*glowering disdainfully at* HODSON, *and sitting down on* CORNELIUS's *chair as an act of social self-assertion*) N are you the valley?

HODSON: The valley? Oh, I follow you: yes: I'm Mr Broadbent's valet.

MATTHEW: Ye have an aisy time of it: you look purty sleek. (*With suppressed ferocity*) Look at me! Do *I* look sleek?

HODSON: (*Sadly*) I wish I ad your ealth: you look as ard as nails. I suffer from an excess of uric acid.

MATTHEW: Musha what sort o disease is zhouragassid? Didjever suffer from injustice and starvation? Dhats the Irish disease. It's aisy for you to talk o sufferin, an you livin on the fat o the land

24. In this case, stood a drink.
25. A class of small, freehold farmers, below gentlemen but above labourers.
26. One of the class of irregular mounted troops in the Turkish military service.
27. bad luck; 'cess' literally means 'tax'.

wid money wrung from us.

HODSON: (*Suddenly dropping the well-spoken valet, and breaking out in his native cockney*)[28] Wots wrong with you, aold chep? Ez ennybody been doin ennythink to you?

MATTHEW: Anythin timmy! Didnt your English masther say that the blood biled in him to hear the way they put a rint[29] on me for the farm I made wid me own hans, and turned me out of it to give it to Billy Byrne?

HODSON: Ow, Tom Broadbent's blad boils pretty easy over ennything that eppens aht of his aown cantry. Downt you be tiken in by my aowl men, Peddy.

MATTHEW: (*Indignantly*) Paddy yourself! How dar you call me Paddy?

HODSON: (*Unmoved*) You jast keep your air on and listen to me. You Awrish people are too well off: thets wots the metter with you. (*With sudden passion*) You talk of your rotten little fawm cause you mide it by chackin a few stowns dahn a ill! Well, wot prawce maw grenfawther, Oi[30] should lawk to knaow, that fitted ap a fust clawss shop and built ap a fust clawss dripery business in Landon by sixty years work, and then was chacked aht of it on is ed at the end of is lease withaht a penny for his goodwill. You talk of evictions! you that cawnt be moved until youve ran ap ighteen months rent. Oi once ran ap four weeks in Lembeth wen Oi was aht of a job in winter. They took the door off its inges[31] and the winder aht of its seshes[32] on me, an gev maw wawf pnoomownia.[33] Oi'm a widower nah. (*Between his teeth*) Gawd! when Oi think of the things we Englishmen as to pat ap with, and eah you Awrish ahlin[34] abaht your silly little grievances, and see the wy you mike it worse for haz[35] by the rotten wiges[36] youll cam over and tike and the rotten plices youll sleep in, I jast feel that I could tike the aowl bloomin British awland[37] and mike you a present of it, jast to let you fawnd aht wot reel awdship's lawk.[38]

MATTHEW: (*Starting up, more in scandalized incredulity than in anger*) D'ye have the face to set up England agen Ireland for injustices an wrongs an disthress an sufferin?

HODSON: (*With intense disgust and contempt*) Ow, chack it, Peddy. Cheese it.[39] You danno wot awdship is owver eah: all you knaow is ah to ahl abaht it. You tike the biscuit at thet, you do. Oi'm a Owm Ruler, Oi em. Do you know woy?

MATTHEW: (*Equally contemptuous*) D'ye know, yourself?

HODSON: Yus Oi do. It's because Oi want a little attention pide to my aown cantry; and thetll never be as long as your cheps are ollerin at Westminister as if nowbody mettered but your own bloomin selves. Send em beck to ell or C'naught, as good aowld English Cramwell said. I'm jast sick of Awrland. Let it gow. Cat the caible. Mike it a present to Germany to keep the aowl Kyzer[40] busy for a wawl; and give poor aowld England a chawnce; thets wot Oi say.

MATTHEW: (*Full of scorn for a man so ignorant as to be unable to pronounce the word Connaught, which practically rhymes with bonnet in Ireland, though in* HODSON's *dialect it rhymes with untaught*) Take care we dont cut the cable ourselves some day, bad scran[41] to you! An tell me dhis: have yanny Coercion Acs in England? Have yanny Removable magisthruts? Have you Dublin Castle to suppress every newspaper dhat takes the part o your own counthry?

HODSON: We can beyive ahrselves withaht sich things.

MATTHEW: Bedad youre right. It'd ony be waste o time to muzzle a sheep. Here! wheres me pig? God forgimmy for talkin to a poor ignorant craycher like you!

HODSON: (*Grinning with good-humoured malice, too convinced of his own superiority to feel his withers wrung*) Your pig'll ev a rare doin in that car, Peddy. Forty mawl an ahr dahn that rocky line will strawk it pretty pink, you bet.

MATTHEW: (*Scornfully*) Hwy cant you tell a raisonable lie when youre about it? What horse can go forty mile an hour?

HODSON: Orse! Wy, you silly aowl rotter, it's not a orse: it's a mowtor. Do you spowse Tom Broadbent ud gow himself to fetch a orse?

MATTHEW: (*In consternation*) Holy Moses! dont

28. Dialect of inner-city Londoners.
29. rent.
30. I.
31. hinges.
32. window out of its sashes.
33. gave my wife pneumonia.
34. hear you Irish howling.
35. us.
36. wages.
37. island.
38. find out what real hardship's like.
39. Give over, stop it.
40. Kaiser, German King.
41. fare, provisions.

tell me it's the ingine[42] he wants to take me on.

HODSON: Wot else?

MATTHEW: Your sowl to Morris Kelly![43] why didnt you tell me that before? The divil an ingine he'll get me on this day. (*His ear catches an approaching teuf-teuf*) On murdher! it's comin afther me: I hear the puff-puff of it. (*He runs away through the gate, much to* HODSON's *amusement. The noise of the motor ceases; and* HODSON, *anticipating* BROADBENT's *return, throws off the cockney and recomposes himself as a valet.* BROADBENT *and* LARRY *come through the shrubbery.* HODSON *moves aside to the gate*)

BROADBENT: Where is Mr Haffigan? Has he gone for the pig?

HODSON: Bolted, sir! Afraid of the motor, sir.

BROADBENT: (*Much disappointed*) Oh, thats very tiresome. Did he leave any message?

HODSON: He was in too great a hurry, sir. Started to run home, sir, and left his pig[44] behind him.

BROADBENT: (*Eagerly*) Left the pig! Then it's all right. The pig's the thing: the pig will win over every Irish heart to me. We'll take the pig home to Haffigan's farm in the motor: it will have a tremendous effect. Hodson!

HODSON: Yes, sir?

BROADBENT: Do you think you could collect a crowd to see the motor?

HODSON: Well, I'll try, sir.

BROADBENT: Thank you, Hodson: do.

HODSON *goes out through the gate.*

LARRY: (*Desperately*) Once more, Tom, will you listen to me?

BROADBENT: Rubbish! I tell you it will be all right.

LARRY: Only this morning you confessed how surprised you were to find that the people here shewed no sense of humor.

BROADBENT: (*Suddenly very solemn*) Yes: their sense of humor is in abeyance: I noticed it the moment we landed. Think of that in a country where every man is a born humorist! Think of what it means! (*Impressively*) Larry: we are in the presence of a great national grief.

LARRY: Whats to grieve them?

BROADBENT: I divined it, Larry: I saw it in their faces. Ireland has never smiled since her hopes were buried in the grave of Gladstone.

LARRY: Oh, whats the use of talking to such a man? Now look here, Tom. Be serious for a moment if you can.

BROADBENT: (*Stupent*)[45] Serious! I!!!

LARRY: Yes, you. You say the Irish sense of humor is in abeyance. Well, if you drive through Rosscullen in a motor car with Haffigan's pig, it wont stay in abeyance. Now I warn you.

BROADBENT: (*Breezily*) Why, so much the better! I shall enjoy the joke myself more than any of them. (*Shouting*) Hallo, Patsy Farrell, where are you?

PATSY: (*Appearing in the shrubbery*) Here I am, your honor.

BROADBENT: Go and catch the pig and put it into the car: we're going to take it to Mr. Haffigan's. (*He gives* LARRY *a slap on the shoulders that sends him staggering off through the gate, and follows him buoyantly, exclaiming*) Come on, you old croaker! I'll shew you how to win an Irish seat.

PATSY: (*Meditatively*) Bedad, if dhat pig gets a howlt o the handle o the machine — (*He shakes his head ominously and drifts away to the pigsty*)

42. engine — i.e. motor-car.
43. Your soul to the devil.
44. The stage Irish clown appeared with pig in close attendance, in keeping with English views of Irish primitivism. Cartoonists often depicted Irish rebels as markedly porcine.
45. In a state of stupor or amazement.

ACT IV[1]

The parlor in CORNELIUS DOYLE's *house. It communicates with the garden by a half glazed door. The fireplace is at the other side of the room, opposite the door and windows, the architect not having been sensitive to draughts. The table, rescued from the garden, is in the middle; and at it sits* KEEGAN, *the central figure in a rather crowded apartment.* NORA, *sitting with her back to the fire at the end of the table, is playing backgammon across its corner with him, on his left hand.* AUNT JUDY, *a little further back, sits facing the fire knitting, with her feet on the fender. A little to* KEEGAN's *right, in front of the table, and almost sitting on it, is* BARNEY DORAN. *Half a dozen friends of his, all men, are between him and the open door, supported by others outside. In the corner behind them is the sofa, of mahogany and horsehair, made up as a bed for* BROADBENT. *Against the wall behind* KEEGAN *stands a mahogany sideboard. A door*

1. Many of Shaw's scenes are musically patterned, as in the ensuing contrast between Doran's falsetto and Keegan's grave locutions.

leading to the interior of the house is near the fireplace, behind AUNT JUDY. *There are chairs against the wall, one at each end of the sideboard.* KEEGAN'S *hat is on the one nearest the inner door; and his stick is leaning against it. A third chair, also against the wall, is near the garden door.*

There is a strong contrast of emotional atmosphere between the two sides of the room. KEEGAN *is extraordinarily stern: no game of backgammon could possibly make a man's face so grim.* AUNT JUDY *is quietly busy.* NORA *is trying to ignore* DORAN *and attend to her game.*

On the other hand DORAN *is reeling in an ecstasy of mischievous mirth which has infected all his friends. They are screaming with laughter, doubled up, leaning on the furniture and against the walls, shouting, screeching, crying.*

AUNT JUDY: (*As the noise lulls for a moment*) Arra hold your noise, Barney. What is there to laugh at?

DORAN: It got its fut into the little hweel — (*he is overcome afresh; and the rest collapse again*)

AUNT JUDY: Ah, have some sense: youre like a parcel o childher.[2] Nora: hit him a thump on the back: he'll have a fit.

DORAN: (*With squeezed eyes, exsufflicate with cachinnation*)[3] Frens, he sez to dhem outside Doolan's: I'm takin the gintleman that pays the rint for a dhrive.

AUNT JUDY: Who did he mean be that?

DORAN: They call a pig that in England. Thats their notion of a joke.

AUNT JUDY: Musha God help them if they can joke no better than that!

DORAN: (*With renewed symptoms*) Thin —

AUNT JUDY: Ah now dont be tellin it all over and settin yourself off again, Barney.

NORA: Youve told us three times, Mr Doran.

DORAN: Well but whin I think of it —!

AUNT JUDY: Then dont think of it, alanna.

DORAN: Dhere was Patsy Farrll in the back sate wi dhe pig between his knees, n me bould English boyoh in front at the machinery, n Larry Doyle in the road startin the injine wid a bed winch. At the first puff of it the pig lep out of its skin and bled Patsy's nose wi dhe ring in its snout. (*Roars of laughter:* KEEGAN *glares at them*) Before Broadbint knew hwere he was, the pig was up his back and over into his lap; and bedad the poor baste did credit to Corny's thrainin of it; for it put in the fourth speed wid its right crubeen[4] as if it was enthered for the Gordn Bennett.[5]

NORA: (*Reproachfully*) And Larry in front of it and all! It's nothin to laugh at, Mr Doran.

DORAN: Bedad, Miss Reilly, Larry cleared six yards sideways at wan[6] jump if he cleared an inch; and he'd a cleared seven if Doolan's granmother hadnt cotch him in her apern[7] widhout intindin to. (*Immense merriment*)

AUNT JUDY: Ah, for shame, Barney! the poor old woman! An she was hurt before, too, when she slipped on the stairs.

DORAN: Bedad, maam, she's hurt behind now; for Larry bouled her over like a skittle. (*General delight at this typical stroke of Irish Rabelaisianism*)

NORA: It's well Mr Doyle wasnt killed.

DORAN: Faith it wasnt o Larry we were thinkin just dhen, wi dhe pig takin the main sthreet o Rosscullen on market day at a mile a minnit. Dh ony[8] thing Broadbint could get at wi dhe pig in front of him was a fut brake; n the pig's tail was undher dhat; so that whin he thought he was putn non the brake he was ony squeezin the life out o the pig's tail. The more he put the brake on the more the pig squealed n the fasther he dhruv.

AUNT JUDY: Why couldnt he throw the pig out into the road?

DORAN: Sure he couldnt stand up to it, because he was spanchelled-like[9] between his seat and dhat thing like a wheel on top of a stick between his knees.

AUNT JUDY: Lord have mercy on us!

NORA: I dont know how you can laugh. Do you, Mr Keegan?

KEEGAN: (*Grimly*) Why not? There is danger, destruction, torment! What more do we need to make us merry? Go on, Barney: the last drops of joy are not squeezed from the story yet. Tell us again how our brother was torn asunder.

DORAN: (*Puzzled*) Whose bruddher?

KEEGAN: Mine.

NORA: He means the pig, Mr Doran. You know his way.

DORAN: (*Rising gallantly to the occasion*) Bedad

2. children.
3. exploding with loud laughter.
4. pig's trotter.
5. A famous early car-race.
6. one.
7. apron.
8. only.
9. spancelled, stuck.

I'm sorry for your poor bruddher, Misther Keegan; but I recommend you to thry him wid a couple o fried eggs for your breakfast tomorrow. It was a case of Excelsior[10] wi dhat ambitious baste; for not content wid jumpin from the back seat into the front wan, he jumped from the front wan into the road in front of the car. And —

KEEGAN: And everybody laughed!

NORA: Dont go over that again, please, Mr Doran.

DORAN: Faith be the time the car went over the poor pig dhere was little left for me or anywan else to go over except wid a knife an fork.

AUNT JUDY: Why didnt Mr Broadbent stop the car when the pig was gone?

DORAN: Stop the car! He might as well ha thried to stop a mad bull. First it went wan way an made fireworks o Molly Ryan's crockery stall; an dhen it slewed round an ripped ten fut o wall out o the corner o the pound. (*With enormous enjoyment*) Begob, it just tore the town in two and sent the whole dam market to blazes. (NORA *offended, rises*)

KEEGAN: (*Indignantly*) Sir!

DORAN: (*Quickly*) Savin your presence, Miss Reilly, and Misther Keegan's. Dhere! I wont say anuddher word.

NORA: I'm surprised at you, Mr Doran. (*She sits down again*)

DORAN: (*Reflectively*) He has the divil's own luck, that Englishman, annyway; for hwen they picked him up he hadnt a scratch on him, barrn hwat the pig did to his cloes. Patsy had two fingers out o jynt;[11] but the smith pulled them sthraight for him. Oh, you never heard such a hullaballoo as there was. There was Molly cryin Me chaney,[12] me beautyful chaney! n oul Matt shoutin Me pig, me pig! n the polus[13] taking the number o the car, n not a man in the town able to speak for laughin —

KEEGAN: (*With intense emphasis*) It is hell: it IS hell. Nowhere else could such a scene be a burst of happiness for the people.

CORNELIUS *comes in hastily from the garden, pushing his way through the little crowd.*

CORNELIUS: Whisht your laughin, boys! Here he is. (*He puts his hat on the sideboard, and goes to the fireplace, where he posts himself with his back to the chimneypiece*)

10. going one better.
11. joint.
12. china crockery.
13. police.

AUNT JUDY: Remember your behavior, now.

Everybody becomes silent, solemn, concerned, sympathetic. BROADBENT *enters, soiled and disordered as to his motoring coat: immensely important and serious as to himself. He makes his way to the end of the table nearest the garden door, whilst* LARRY, *who accompanies him, throws his motoring coat on the sofa bed, and sits down, watching the proceedings.*

BROADBENT: (*Taking off his leather cap with dignity and placing it on the table*) I hope you have not been anxious about me.

AUNT JUDY: Deedn we have, Mr Broadbent. It's a mercy you werent killed.

DORAN: Kilt! It's a mercy dheres two bones of you left houldin together. How dijjescape at all at all? Well, I never thought I'd be so glad to see you safe and sound again. Not a man in the town would say less (*murmurs of kindly assent*). Wont you come down to Doolan's and have a dhrop o brandy to take the shock off?

BROADBENT: Youre all really too kind; but the shock has quite passed off.

DORAN: (*Jovially*) Never mind. Come along all the same and tell us about it over a frenly[14] glass.

BROADBENT: May I say how deeply I feel the kindness with which I have been overwhelmed since my accident? I can truthfully declare that I am glad it happened, because it has brought out the kindness and sympathy of the Irish character to an extent I had no conception of.

SEVERAL PRESENT: Oh, sure youre welcome!
Sure it's only natural.
Sure you might have been kilt.

A young man, feeling that he must laugh or burst, hurries out. BARNEY *puts an iron constraint on his features.*

BROADBENT: All I can say is that I wish I could drink the health of everyone of you.

DORAN: Dhen come an do it.

BROADBENT: (*Very solemnly*) No: I am a teetotaller.

AUNT JUDY: (*Incredulously*) Arra since when?

BROADBENT: Since this morning, Miss Doyle. I have had a lesson (*he looks at* NORA *significantly*) that I shall not forget. It may be that total abstinence has already saved my life; for I was astonished at the steadiness of my nerves when death stared me in the face today. So I will ask you to excuse me. (*He collects himself for a speech*)

14. friendly.

Gentlemen: I hope the gravity of the peril through which we have all passed — for I know that the danger to the bystanders was as great as to the occupants of the car — will prove an earnest of closer and more serious relations between us in the future. We have had a somewhat agitating day: a valuable and innocent animal has lost its life: a public building has been wrecked: an aged and infirm lady has suffered an impact for which I feel personally responsible, though my old friend Mr Laurence Doyle unfortunately incurred the first effects of her very natural resentment. I greatly regret the damage to Mr Patrick Farrell's fingers; and I have of course taken care that he shall not suffer pecuniarily by his mishap. (*Murmurs of admiration at his magnaminity, and a voice* 'Youre a gentleman, sir'). I am glad to say that Patsy took it like an Irishman, and, far from expressing any vindictive feeling, declared his willingness to break all his fingers and toes for me on the same terms (*subdued applause, and* 'More power to Patsy!'). Gentleman: I felt at home in Ireland from the first (*rising excitement among his hearers*). In every Irish breast I have found that spirit of liberty (*A cheery voice* 'Hear Hear'), that instinctive mistrust of the Government (*A small pious voice, with intense expression,* 'God bless you, sir!'), that love of independence (*A defiant voice,* 'Thats it! Independence!'), that indignant sympathy with the cause of oppressed nationalities abroad (*A threatening growl from all: the ground-swell of patriotic passion*) and with the resolute assertion of personal rights at home, which is all but extinct in my own country. If it were legally possible I should become a naturalized Irishman; and if ever it be my good fortune to represent an Irish constituency in parliament, it shall be my first care to introduce a Bill legalizing such an operation. I believe a large section of the Liberal party would avail themselves of it. (*Momentary scepticism*) I do. (*Convulsive cheering*) Gentlemen: I have said enough. (*Cries of* 'Go on') No: I have as yet no right to address you at all on political subjects; and we must not abuse the warm-hearted Irish hospitality of Miss Doyle by turning her sitting room into a public meeting.

DORAN: (*Energetically*) Three cheers for Tom Broadbent, the future member for Rosscullen!

AUNT JUDY: (*Moving a half knitted sock*) Hip hip hurray!

The cheers are given with great heartiness, as it is by this time, for the more humorous spirits present, a question of vociferation or internal rupture.

BROADBENT: Thank you from the bottom of my heart, friends.

NORA: (*whispering to* DORAN) Take them away, Mr Doran. (DORAN *nods*)

DORAN: Well, good evenin, Mr Broadbent; an may you never regret the day you wint dhrivin wid Haffigan's pig! (*They shake hands*) Good evenin, Miss Doyle.

General handshaking, BROADBENT *shaking hands with everybody effusively. He accompanies them to the garden and can be heard outside saying Good-night in every inflexion known to parliamentary candidates,* NORA, AUNT JUDY, KEEGAN, LARRY, *and* CORNELIUS *are left in the parlor.* LARRY *goes to the threshold and watches the scene in the garden.*

NORA: It's a shame to make game of him like that. He's a gradle more good in him than Barney Doran.

CORNELIUS: It's all up with his candidature. He'll be laughed out o the town.

LARRY: (*Turning quickly from the doorway*) Oh no he wont: he's not an Irishman. He'll never know theyre laughing at him; and while theyre laughing he'll win the seat.

CORNELIUS: But he cant prevent the story getting about.

LARRY: He wont want to. He'll tell it himself as one of the most providential episodes in the history of England and Ireland.

AUNT JUDY: Sure he wouldnt make a fool of himself like that.

LARRY: Are you sure he's such a fool after all, Aunt Judy? Suppose you had a vote! which would you rather give it to? the man that told the story of Haffigan's pig Barney Doran's way or Broadbent's way?

AUNT JUDY: Faith I wouldnt give it to a man at all. It's a few women they want in parliament to stop their foolish blather.

BROADBENT: (*Bustling into the room, and taking off his damaged motoring overcoat, which he puts down on the sofa*) Well, thats over. I must apologize for making a speech, Miss Doyle; but they like it, you know. Everything helps in electioneering.

LARRY *takes the chair near the door; draws it near the table; and sits astride it, with his elbows folded on the back.*

AUNT JUDY: I'd no notion you were such an orator, Mr Broadbent.

BROADBENT: Oh, it's only a knack. One picks it up on the platform. It stokes up their enthusiasm.

AUNT JUDY: Oh, I forgot. Youve not met Mr Keegan. Let me introjoosha.[15]

BROADBENT: (*Shaking hands effusively*) Most happy to meet you, Mr Keegan. I have heard of you, though I have not had the pleasure of shaking your hand before. And now may I ask you — for I value no man's opinion more — what you think of my chances here.

KEEGAN: (*Coldly*) Your chances, sir, are excellent. You will get into parliament.

BROADBENT: (*Delighted*) I hope so. I think so. (*Fluctuating*) You really think so? You are sure you are not allowing your enthusiasm for our principles to get the better of your judgment?

KEEGAN: I have no enthusiasm for your principles, sir. You will get into parliament because you want to get into it enough to be prepared to take the necessary steps to induce the people to vote for you. That is how people usually get into that fantastic assembly.

BROADBENT: (*Puzzled*) Of course. (*Pause*) Quite so. (*Pause*) Er — yes. (*Buoyant again*) I think they will vote for me. Eh? Yes?

AUNT JUDY: Arra why shouldn't they? Look at the people they do vote for!

BROADBENT: (*Encouraged*) Thats true: thats very true. When I see the windbags, the carpet-baggers, the charlatans, the — the — the fools and ignoramuses who corrupt the multitude by their wealth, or seduce them by spouting balderdash to them, I cannot help thinking that an Englishman with no humbug about him, who will talk straight common sense and take his stand on the solid ground of principle and public duty, must win his way with men of all classes.

KEEGAN: (*Quietly*) Sir: there was a time, in my ignorant youth, when I should have called you a hypocrite.

BROADBENT: (*Reddening*) A hypocrite!

NORA: (*Hastily*) Oh I'm sure you dont think anything of the sort, Mr Keegan.

BROADBENT: (*Emphatically*) Thank you, Miss Reilly: thank you.

CORNELIUS: (*Gloomily*) We all have to stretch it a bit in politics: hwats the use o pretendin we dont?

BROADBENT: (*Stiffly*) I hope I have said or done nothing that calls for any such observation, Mr Doyle. If there is a vice I detest — or against which my whole public life has been a protest — it is the vice of hypocrisy. I would almost rather be inconsistent than insincere.

KEEGAN: Do not be offended, sir: I know that you are quite sincere. There is a saying in the Scripture which runs — so far as the memory of an oldish man can carry the words — Let not the right side of your brain know what the left side doeth. I learnt at Oxford that this is the secret of the Englishman's strange power of making the best of both worlds.

BROADBENT: Surely the text refers to our right and left hands. I am somewhat surprised to hear a member of your Church quote so essentially Protestant a document as the Bible; but at least you might quote it accurately.

LARRY: Tom: with the best intentions youre making an ass of yourself. You dont understand Mr Keegan's peculiar vein of humour.

BROADBENT: (*Instantly recovering his confidence*) Ah! it was only your delightful Irish humor, Mr Keegan. Of course, of course. How stupid of me! I'm so sorry. (*He pats* KEEGAN *consolingly on the back*) John Bull's wits are still slow, you see. Besides, calling me a hypocrite was too big a joke to swallow all at once, you know.

KEEGAN: You must also allow for the fact that I am mad.

NORA: Ah, dont talk like that, Mr Keegan.

BROADBENT: (*Encouragingly*) Not at all, not at all. Only a whimsical Irishman, eh?

LARRY: Are you really mad, Mr Keegan?

AUNT JUDY: (*Shocked*) Oh, Larry, how could you ask him such a thing?

LARRY: I dont think Mr Keegan minds. (*To* KEEGAN) Whats the true version of the story of that black man you confessed on his deathbed?

KEEGAN: What story have you heard about that?

LARRY: I am informed that when the devil came for the black heathen, he took off your head and turned it three times round before putting it on again; and that your head's been turned ever since.

NORA: (*Reproachfully*) Larry!

KEEGAN: (*Blandly*) That is not quite what occurred. (*He collects himself for a serious utterance: they attend involuntarily*) I heard that a black man was dying, and that the people were afraid to go near him. When I went to the place I found an elderly Hindoo, who told me one of those tales of unmerited misfortune, of cruel ill luck, of relentless persecution by destiny, which sometimes wither the commonplaces of consolation on the lips of a

15. introduce you.

priest. But this man did not complain of his misfortunes. They were brought upon him, he said, by sins committed in a former existence. Then, without a word of comfort from me, he died with a clear-eyed resignation that my most earnest exhortations have rarely produced in a Christian, and left me sitting there by his bedside with the mystery of this world suddenly revealed to me.

BROADBENT: That is a remarkable tribute to the liberty of conscience enjoyed by the subjects of our Indian Empire.

LARRY: No doubt; but may we venture to ask what is the mystery of this world?

KEEGAN: This world, sir, is very clearly a place of torment and penance, a place where the fool flourishes and the good and wise are hated and persecuted, a place where men and women torture one another in the name of love; where children are scourged and enslaved in the name of parental duty and education; where the weak in body are poisoned and mutilated in the name of healing, and the weak in character are put to the horrible torture of imprisonment, not for hours but for years, in the name of justice. It is a place where the hardest toil is a welcome refuge from the horror and tedium of pleasure, and where charity and good works are done only for hire to ransom the souls of the spoiler and the sybarite. Now, sir, there is only one place of horror and torment known to my religion; and that place is hell. Therefore it is plain to me that this earth of ours must be hell,[16] and that we are all here, as the Indian revealed to me — perhaps he was sent to reveal it to me — to expiate crimes committed by us in a former existence.

AUNT JUDY: (*Awestruck*) Heaven save us, what a thing to say!

CORNELIUS: (*Sighing*) It's a queer world: thats certain.

BROADBENT: Your idea is a very clever one, Mr Keegan: really most brilliant: *I* should never have thought of it. But it seems to me — if I may say so — that you are overlooking the fact that, of the evils you describe, some are absolutely necessary for the preservation of society, and others are encouraged only when the Tories are in office.

LARRY: I expect you were a Tory in a former existence; and that is why you are here.

BROADBENT: (*With conviction*) Never, Larry, never. But leaving politics out of the question, I find the world quite good enough for me: rather a jolly place, in fact.

KEEGAN: (*Looking at him with quiet wonder*) You are satisfied?

BROADBENT: As a reasonable man, yes. I see no evils in the world — except, of course, natural evils — that cannot be remedied by freedom, self-government, and English institutions. I think so, not because I am an Englishman, but as a matter of common sense.

KEEGAN: You feel at home in the world, then?

BROADBENT: Of course. Dont you?

KEEGAN: (*From the very depths of his nature*) No.

BROADBENT: (*Breezily*) Try phosphorus pills. I always take them when my brain is overworked. I'll give you the address in Oxford Street.[17]

KEEGAN: (*Enigmatically: rising*) Miss Doyle: my wandering fit has come on me: will you excuse me?

AUNT JUDY: To be sure: you know you can come in n nout as you like.

KEEGAN: We can finish the game some other time, Miss Reilly. (*He goes for his hat and stick*)

NORA: No: I'm out with you (*she disarranges the pieces and rises*). I was too wicked in a former existence to play backgammon with a good man like you.

AUNT JUDY: (*Whispering to her*) Whisht, whisht, child! Dont set him back on that again.

KEEGAN: (*To* NORA) When I look at you, I think that perhaps Ireland is only purgatory, after all. (*He passes on to the garden door*)

NORA: Galong with you!

BROADBENT: (*Whispering to* CORNELIUS) Has he a vote?

CORNELIUS: (*Nodding*) Yes. An theres lotsle vote the way he tells them.

KEEGAN: (*At the garden door, with gentle gravity*) Good evening, Mr Broadbent. You have set me thinking. Thank you.

BROADBENT: (*Delighted, hurrying across to him to shake hands*) No, really? You find that contact with English ideas is stimulating, eh?

KEEGAN: I am never tired of hearing you talk, Mr Broadbent.

BROADBENT: (*Modestly remonstrating*) Oh come! come!

KEEGAN: Yes, I assure you. You are an extremely interesting man. (*He goes out*)

16. Shaw held, in many essays, that the truly damned were those who were happy in hell.

17. A London thoroughfare then noted for pharmacists.

BROADBENT: (*Enthusiastically*) What a nice chap! What an intelligent, broadminded character, considering his cloth! By the way, I'd better have a wash. (*He takes up his coat and cap, and leaves the room through the inner door*)

NORA *returns to her chair and shuts up the backgammon board.*

AUNT JUDY: Keegan's very queer today. He has his mad fit on him.

CORNELIUS: (*Worried and bitter*) I wouldnt say but he's right after all. It's a contrairy world. (*To* LARRY) Why would you be such a fool as to let Broadbent take the seat in parliament from you?

LARRY: (*Glancing at Nora*) He will take more than that from me before he's done here.

CORNELIUS: I wish he'd never set foot in my house, bad luck to his fat face! D'ye think he'd lend me £300 on the farm, Larry? When I'm so hard up, it seems a waste o money not to mortgage it now it's me own.

LARRY: *I* can lend you £300 on it.

CORNELIUS: No, no; I wasnt putn in for that. When I die and leave you the farm I should like to be able to feel that it was all me own, and not half yours to start with. Now I'll take me oath Barney Doarn's going to ask Broadbent to lend him £500 on the mill to put in a new hweel; for the old one'll harly hol together. An Haffigan cant sleep with covetn that corner o land at the foot of his medda[18] that belongs to Doolan. He'll have to mortgage to buy it. I may as well be first as last. D'ye think Broadbent'd len me a little?

LARRY: I'm quite sure he will.

CORNELIUS: Is he as ready as that? Would he len me five hundred, d'ye think?

LARRY: He'll lend you more than the landll ever be worth to you; so for Heaven's sake be prudent.

CORNELIUS: (*Judicially*) All right, all right, me son: I'll be careful. I'm goin into the office for a bit. (*He withdraws through the inner door, obviously to prepare his application to* BROADBENT)

AUNT JUDY: (*Indignantly*) As if he hadnt seen enough o borryin when he was an agent without beginnin borryin himself! (*She rises*) I'll borry him, so I will. (*She puts her knitting on the table and follows him out, with a resolute air that bodes trouble for* CORNELIUS)

LARRY *and* NORA *are left together for the first time since his arrival. She looks at him with a smile that perishes as she sees him aimlessly rocking his chair, and reflecting, evidently not about her, with his lips pursed as if he were whistling. With a catch in her throat she takes up* AUNT JUDY's *knitting, and makes a pretence of going on with it.*

NORA: I suppose it didnt seem very long to you.

LARRY: (*Starting*) Eh? What didnt?

NORA: The eighteen years youve been away.

LARRY: Oh, that! No: it seems hardly more than a week. I've been so busy — had so little time to think.

NORA: Ive had nothin else to do but think.

LARRY: That was very bad for you. Why didnt you give it up? Why did you stay here?

NORA: Because nobody sent for me to go anywhere else, I suppose. Thats why.

LARRY: Yes: one does stick frightfully in the same place, unless some external force comes and routs one out. (*He yawns slightly; but as she looks up quickly at him, he pulls himself together and rises with an air of waking up and setting to work cheerfully to make himself agreeable*) And how have you been all this time?

NORA: Quite well, thank you.

LARRY: Thats right. (*Suddenly finding that he has nothing else to say, and being ill at ease in consequence, he strolls about the room humming distractedly*)

NORA: (*Struggling with her tears*) Is that all you have to say to me, Larry?

LARRY: Well, what is there to say? You see, we know each other so well.

NORA: (*A little consoled*) Yes: of course we do. (*He does not reply*) I wonder you came back at all.

LARRY: I couldnt help it. (*She looks up affectionately.*) Tom made me. (*She looks down again quickly to conceal the effect of this blow. He whistles another stave; then resumes*) I had a sort of dread of returning to Ireland. I felt somehow that my luck would turn if I came back. And now here I am, none the worse.

NORA: Praps it's a little dull for you.

LARRY: No: I havnt exhausted the interest of strolling about the old places and remembering and romancing about them.

NORA: (*Hopefully*) Oh! You do remember the places, then?

LARRY: Of course. They have associations.

NORA: (*Not doubting that the associations are with her*) I suppose so.

LARRY: M'yes. I can remember particular spots where I had long fits of thinking about the countries

18. meadow.

I meant to get to when I escaped from Ireland. America and London, and sometimes Rome and the east.

NORA: (*Deeply mortified*) Was that all you used to be thinking about?

LARRY: Well, there was precious little else to think about here, my dear Nora, except sometimes at sunset, when one got maudlin and called Ireland Erin, and imagined one was remembering the days of old, and so forth. (*He whistles Let Erin Remember*)[19]

NORA: Did jever get a letter I wrote you last February?

LARRY: Oh yes; and I really intended to answer it. But I havnt had a moment; and I knew you wouldnt mind. You see, I am so afraid of boring you by writing about affairs you dont understand and people you dont know! And yet what else have I to write about? I begin a letter; and then I tear it up again. The fact is, fond as we are of one another, Nora, we have so little in common — I mean of course the things one can put in a letter — that correspondence is apt to become the hardest of hard work.

NORA: Yes: it's hard for me to know anything about you if you never tell me anything.

LARRY: (*Pettishly*) Nora: a man cant sit down and write his life day by day when he's tired enough with having lived it.

NORA: I'm not blaming you.

LARRY: (*Looking at her with some concern*) You seem rather out of spirits. (*Going closer to her, anxiously and tenderly*) You havnt got neuralgia, have you?

NORA: No.

LARRY: (*Reassured*) I get a touch of it sometimes when I am below par. (*Absently, again strolling about*) Yes, yes. (*He gazes through the doorway at the Irish landscape, and sings, almost unconsciously, but very expressively, an air from Offenbach's Whittington*)[20]

NORA, *who has been at first touched by the tenderness*

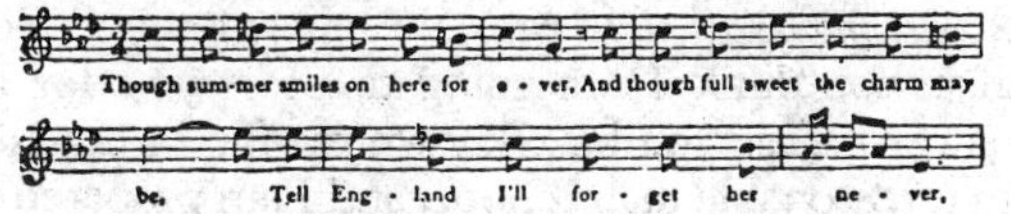

of his singing, puts down her knitting at this very unexpected sentiment, and stares at him. He continues until the melody soars out of his range, when he trails off into whistling Let Erin Remember.

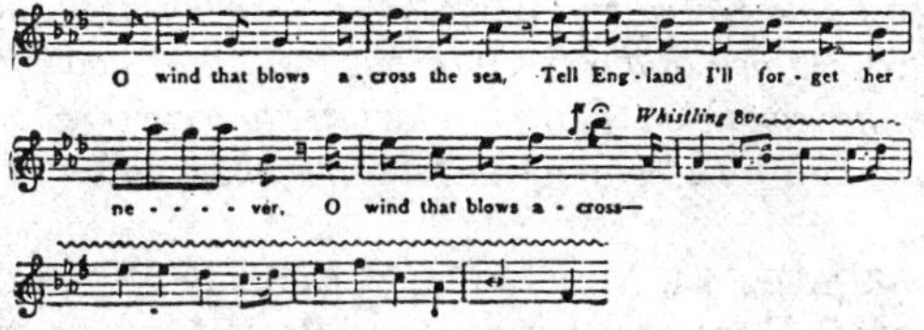

I'm afraid I'm boring you, Nora, though youre too kind to say so.

NORA: Are you wanting to get back to England already?

LARRY: Not at all. Not at all.

NORA: Thats a queer song to sing to me if youre not.

LARRY: The song! Oh, it doesnt mean anything: it's by a German Jew, like most English patriotic sentiment. Never mind me, my dear: go on with your work; and dont let me bore you.

NORA: (*Bitterly*) Rosscullen isnt such a lively place that I am likely to be bored by you at our first talk together after eighteen years, though you dont seem to have much to say to me after all.

LARRY: Eighteen years is a devilish long time, Nora. Now if it had been eighteen minutes, or even eighteen months, we should be able to pick up the interrupted thread, and chatter like two magpies. But as it is, I have simply nothing to say; and you seem to have less.

NORA: I — (*her tears choke her; but she keeps up appearances desperately*)

LARRY: (*Quite unconscious of his cruelty*) In a week or so we shall be quite old friends again. Meanwhile, as I feel that I am not making myself particularly entertaining, I'll take myself off. Tell Tom Ive gone for a stroll over the hill.

NORA: You seem very fond of Tom, as you call him.

LARRY: (*The triviality going suddenly out of his voice*) Yes: I'm fond of Tom.

NORA: Oh, well, dont let me keep you from him.

LARRY: I know quite well that my departure will be a relief. Rather a failure, this first meeting after eighteen years, eh? Well, never mind: these great sentimental events always are failures; and now the worst of it's over anyhow. (*He goes out through the garden door*)

NORA, *left alone, struggles wildly to save herself from*

19. Thomas Moore, *Irish Melodies* (1808-34).
20. Jacques Offenbach (1819-80), French composer of operettas. *Whittington* is one of the lesser known ones. In 1889 Shaw wrote: '... Offenbach's music is wicked. It is abandoned stuff: every accent in it is a snap of the fingers in the face of moral responsibility ....' (*Shaw on Music*, edited by E. Bentley (New York, 1955), p. 201).

breaking down, and then drops her face on the table and gives way to a convulsion of crying. Her sobs shake her so that she can hear nothing; and she has no suspicion that she is no longer alone until her head and breast are raised by BROADBENT, *who, returning newly washed and combed through the inner door, has seen her condition, first with surprise and concern, and then with an emotional disturbance that quite upsets him.*

BROADBENT: Miss Reilly, Miss Reilly. Whats the matter? Dont cry: I cant stand it: you musnt cry. (*She makes a choked effort to speak, so painful that he continues with impulsive sympathy*) No: dont try to speak: it's all right now. Have your cry out: never mind me: trust me. (*Gathering her to him, and babbling consolatorily*) Cry on my chest: the only really comfortable place for a woman to cry is a man's chest: a real man, a real friend. A good broad chest, eh? not less than forty-two inches — no: dont fuss: never mind the conventions: we're two friends, arnt we? Come now, come, come! It's all right and comfortable and happy now, isn't it?

NORA: (*Through her tears*) Let me go. I want me hankerchief.

BROADBENT: (*Holding her with one arm and producing a large silk handkerchief from his breast pocket*) Heres a handkerchief. Let me (*he dabs her tears dry with it*). Never mind your own: it's too small: it's one of those wretched little cambric handkerchiefs —

NORA: (*Sobbing*) Indeed it's a common cotton one.

BROADBENT: Of course it's a common cotton one — silly little cotton one — not good enough for the dear eyes of Nora Cryna —

NORA: (*Spluttering into a hysterical laugh and clutching him convulsively with her fingers while she tries to stifle her laughter against his collar bone*) Oh dont make me laugh: please dont make me laugh.

BROADBENT: (*Terrified*) I didnt mean to, on my soul. What is it? What is it?

NORA: Nora Creena, Nora Creena.

BROADBENT: (*Patting her*) Yes, yes, of course, Nora Creena, Nora acushla[21] (*he makes cush rhyme to plush*) —

NORA: Acushla (*she makes cush rhyme to bush*).

BROADBENT: Oh, confound the language! Nora darling — my Nora — the Nora I love —

21. 'Creena' and 'acushla' are Irish terms of endearment, 'heart' and 'pulse'.

NORA: (*Shocked into propriety*) You mustnt talk like that to me.

BROADBENT: (*Suddenly becoming prodigiously solemn and letting her go*) No, of course not. I dont mean it. At least I do mean it; but I know it's premature. I had no right to take advantage of your being a little upset; but I lost my self-control for a moment.

NORA: (*Wondering at him*) I think youre a very kind-hearted man, Mr Broadbent; but you seem to me to have no self-control at all (*she turns her face away with a keen pang of shame and adds*) no more than myself.

BROADBENT: (*Resolutely*) Oh yes, I have: you should see me when I am really roused: then I have TREMENDOUS self-control. Remember: we have been alone together only once before; and then, I regret to say, I was in a disgusting state.

NORA: Ah no, Mr Broadbent: you wernt disgusting.

BROADBENT: (*Mercilessly*) Yes I was: nothing can excuse it: perfectly beastly. It must have made a most unfavorable impression on you.

NORA: Oh, sure it's all right. Say no more about that.

BROADBENT: I must, Miss Reilly: it is my duty. I shall not detain you long. May I ask you to sit down. (*He indicates her chair with oppressive solemnity. She sits down wondering. He then, with the same portentous gravity, places a chair for himself near her; sits down; and proceeds to explain*) First, Miss Reilly, may I say that I have tasted nothing of an alcoholic nature today.

NORA: It doesnt seem to make as much difference in you as it would in an Irishman, somehow.

BROADBENT: Perhaps not. Perhaps not. I never quite lose myself.

NORA: (*Consolingly*) Well, anyhow, youre all right now.

BROADBENT: (*Fervently*) Thank you, Miss Reilly: I am. Now we shall get along. (*Tenderly, lowering his voice*) Nora: I was in earnest last night. (NORA *moves as if to rise*) No: one moment. You must not think I am going to press you for an answer before you have known me for 24 hours. I am a reasonable man, I hope; and I am prepared to wait as long as you like, provided you will give me some small assurance that the answer will not be unfavorable.

NORA: How could I go back from it if I did? I sometimes think youre not quite right in your head,

Mr Broadbent, you say such funny things.

BROADBENT: Yes: I know I have a strong sense of humor which sometimes makes people doubt whether I am quite serious. That is why I have always thought I should like to marry an Irishwoman. She would always understand my jokes. For instance, you would understand them, eh?

NORA: (*Uneasily*) Mr Broadbent: I couldnt.

BROADBENT: (*Soothingly*) Wait: let me break this to you gently, Miss Reilly: hear me out. I daresay you have noticed that in speaking to you I have been putting a very strong constraint on myself, so as to avoid wounding your delicacy by too abrupt an avowal of my feelings. Well, I feel now that the time has come to be open, to be frank, to be explicit. Miss Reilly: you have inspired in me a very strong attachment. Perhaps, with a woman's intuition, you have already guessed that.

NORA: (*Rising distractedly*) Why do you talk to me in that unfeeling nonsensical way?

BROADBENT: (*Rising also, much astonished*) Unfeeling! Nonsensical!

NORA: Dont you know that you have said things to me that no man ought to say unless — unless — (*she suddenly breaks down again and hides her face on the table as before*) Oh, go away from me: I wont get married at all: what is it but heartbreak and disappointment?

BROADBENT: (*Developing the most formidable symptoms of rage and grief*) Do you mean to say that you are going to refuse me? that you dont care for me?

NORA: (*Looking at him in consternation*) Oh, dont take it to heart, Mr Br —

BROADBENT: (*Flushed and almost choking*) I dont want to be petted and blarneyed. (*With childish rage*) I love you. I want you for my wife. (*In despair*) I cant help your refusing. I'm helpless: I can do nothing. You have no right to ruin my whole life. You — (*a hysterical convulsion stops him*).

NORA: (*Almost awestruck*) Youre not going to cry, are you? I never thought a man could cry. Dont.

BROADBENT: I'm not crying. I—I—I leave that sort of thing to your damned sentimental Irishmen. You think I have no feeling because I am a plain unemotional Englishman, with no powers of expression.

NORA: I dont think you know the sort of man you are at all. Whatever may be the matter with you, it's not want of feeling.

BROADBENT: (*Hurt and petulant*) It's you who have no feeling. Youre as heartless as Larry.

NORA: What do you expect me to do? Is it to throw meself at your head the minute the word is out o your mouth?

BROADBENT: (*Striking his silly head with his fists*) Oh, what a fool! what a brute I am! It's only your Irish delicacy: of course, of course. You mean Yes. Eh? What? Yes? yes? yes?

NORA: I think you might understand that though I might choose to be an old maid, I could never marry anybody but you now.

BROADBENT: (*Clasping her violently to his breast, with a crow of immense relief and triumph*) Ah, thats right, thats right: thats magnificent. I knew you would see what a first-rate thing this will be for both of us.

NORA: (*Incommoded and not at all enraptured by his ardor*) Youre dreadfully strong, an a gradle too free with your strength. An I never thought o whether it'd be a good thing for us or not. But when you found me here that time, I let you be kind to me, and cried in your arms, because I was too wretched to think of anything but the comfort of it. An how could I let any other man touch me after that?

BROADBENT: (*Moved*) Now thats very nice of you, Nora: thats really most delicately womanly (*he kisses her hand chivalrously*).

NORA: (*Looking earnestly and a little doubtfully at him*) Surely if you let one woman cry on you like that youd never let another touch you.

BROADBENT: (*Conscientiously*) One should not. One ought not, my dear girl. But the honest truth is, if a chap is at all a pleasant sort of chap, his chest becomes a fortification that has to stand many assaults: at least it is so in England.

NORA: (*Curtly, much disgusted*) Then youd better marry an Englishwoman.

BROADBENT: (*Making a wry face*) No, no: the Englishwoman is too prosaic for my taste, too material, too much of the animated beefsteak about her. The ideal is what I like. Now Larry's taste is just the opposite: he likes em solid and bouncing and rather keen about him. It's a very convenient difference; for weve never been in love with the same woman.

NORA: An d'ye mean to tell me to me face that youve ever been in love before?

BROADBENT: Lord! yes.

NORA: I'm not your first love!

BROADBENT: First love is only a little foolishness and a lot of curiosity: no really self-respecting woman would take advantage of it. No, my dear Nora: Ive done with all that long ago. Love affairs always end in rows. We're not going to have any rows: we're going to have a solid four-square home: man and wife: comfort and common sense. And plenty of affection, eh (*he puts his arm round her with confident proprietorship*)?

NORA: (*Coldly, trying to get away*) I dont want any other woman's leavings.

BROADBENT: (*Holding her*) Nobody asked you to, maam. I never asked any woman to marry me before.

NORA: (*Severely*) Then why didnt you if youre an honorable man?

BROADBENT: Well, to tell you the truth, they were mostly married already. But never mind! there was nothing wrong. Come! dont take a mean advantage of me. After all, you must have had a fancy or two yourself, eh?

NORA: (*Conscience-stricken*) Yes. I suppose Ive no right to be particular.

BROADBENT: (*Humbly*) I know I'm not good enough for you, Nora. But no man is, you know, when the woman is a really nice woman.

NORA: Oh, I'm no better than yourself. I may as well tell you about it.

BROADBENT: No, no: lets have no telling: much better not. *I* shant tell you anything: dont you tell me anything. Perfect confidence in one another and no tellings: thats the way to avoid rows.

NORA: Dont think it was anything I need be ashamed of.

BROADBENT: I dont.

NORA: It was only that I'd never known anybody else that I could care for; and I was foolish enough once to think that Larry —

BROADBENT: (*Disposing of the idea at once*) Larry! Oh, that wouldnt have done at all, not at all. You dont know Larry as I do, my dear. He has absolutely no capacity for enjoyment: he couldnt make any woman happy. He's as clever as be-blowed;[22] but life's too carthly for him: he doesnt really care for anything or anybody.

NORA: Ive found that out.

BROADBENT: Of course you have. No, my dear: take my word for it, youre jolly well out of that. There! (*swinging her round against his breast*) thats much more comfortable for you.

NORA: (*With Irish peevishness*) Ah, you mustnt go on like that. I dont like it.

BROADBENT: (*Unabashed*) Youll acquire the taste by degrees. You mustnt mind me: it's an absolute necessity of my nature that I should have somebody to hug occasionally. Besides, it's good for you: itll plump out your muscles and make em elastic and set up your figure.

NORA: Well, I'm sure! if this is English manners! Arnt you ashamed to talk about such things?

BROADBENT: (*In the highest feather*)[23] Not a bit. By George, Nora, it's a tremendous thing to be able to enjoy oneself. Lets go off for a walk out of this stuffy little room. I want the open air to expand in, Come along. Co-o-ome along. (*He puts her arm into his and sweeps her out into the garden as an equinoctial gale might sweep a dry leaf*)

Later in the evening, the grasshopper is again enjoying the sunset by the great stone on the hill; but this time he enjoys neither the stimulus of KEEGAN's *conversation nor the pleasure of terrifying* PATSY FARRELL. *He is alone until* NORA *and* BROADBENT *come up the hill arm in arm.* BROADBENT *is still breezy and confident; but she has her head averted from him and is almost in tears.*

BROADBENT: (*Stopping to snuff up the hillside air*) Ah! I like this spot. I like this view. This would be a jolly good place for a hotel and a golf links. Friday to Tuesday, railway ticket and hotel all inclusive. I tell you, Nora, I'm going to develop this place. (*Looking at her*) Hallo! Whats the matter? Tired?

NORA: (*Unable to restrain her tears*) I'm ashamed out o me life.

BROADBENT: (*Astonished*) Ashamed! What of?

NORA: Oh, how could you drag me all round the place like that, telling everybody that we're going to be married, and introjoocing me to the lowest of the low, and letting them shake hans with me, and encouraging them to make free with us? I little thought I should live to be shaken hans with be Doolan in broad daylight in the public street of Rosscullen.

BROADBENT: But, my dear, Doolan's a publican: a most influential man. By the way, I asked him if his wife would be at home tomorrow. He said she would; so you must take the motor car round and call on her.

NORA: (*Aghast*) Is it me call on Doolan's wife!

22. bedamned.

23. In the finest spirits.

BROADBENT: Yes, of course: call on all their wives. We must get a copy of the register and a supply of canvassing cards. No use calling on people who havnt votes. Youll be a great success as a canvasser, Nora: they call you the heiress; and theyll be flattered no end by your calling, especially as youve never cheapened yourself by speaking to them before — have you?

NORA: (*Indignantly*) Not likely, indeed.

BROADBENT: Well, we mustnt be stiff and stand-off, you know. We must be thoroughly democratic, and patronize everybody without distinction of class. I tell you I'm a jolly lucky man, Nora Cryna. I get engaged to the most delightful woman in Ireland; and it turns out that I couldnt have done a smarter stroke of electioneering.

NORA: An would you let me demean meself like that, just to get yourself into parliament?

BROADBENT: (*Buoyantly*) Aha! Wait til you find out what an exciting game electioneering is: youll be mad to get me in. Besides, youd like people to say that Tom Broadbent's wife had been the making of him? that she got him into parliament? into the Cabinet, perhaps, eh?

NORA: God knows I dont grudge you me money! But to lower meself to the level of common people —

BROADBENT: To a member's wife, Nora, nobody is common provided he's on the register. Come, my dear! it's all right: do you think I'd let you do it if it wasnt? The best people do it. Everybody does it.

NORA: (*Who has been biting her lip and looking over the hill, disconsolate and unconvinced*) Well, praps you know best what they do in England. They must have very little respect for themselves. I think I'll go in now. I see Larry and Mr Keegan coming up the hill; and I'm not fit to talk to them.

BROADBENT: Just wait and say something nice to Keegan. They tell me he controls nearly as many votes as Father Dempsey himself.

NORA: You little know Peter Keegan. He'd see through me as if I was a pane o glass.

BROADBENT: Oh, he wont like it any the less for that. What really flatters a man is that you think him worth flattering. Not that I would flatter any man: dont think that. I'll just go and meet him. (*He goes down the hill with the eager forward look of a man about to greet a valued acquaintance. Nora dries her eyes, and turns to go as* LARRY *strolls up the hill to her*)

LARRY: Nora. (*She turns and looks at him hardly, without a word. He continues anxiously, in his most conciliatory tone*) When I left you that time, I was just as wretched as you. I didnt rightly know what I wanted to say; and my tongue kept clacking to cover the loss I was at. Well, Ive been thinking ever since; and now I know what I ought to have said. Ive come back to say it.

NORA: Youve come too late, then. You thought eighteen years was not long enough, and that you might keep me waiting a day longer. Well, you were mistaken. I'm engaged to your friend Mr Broadbent; and I'm done with you.

LARRY: (*Naïve*) But that was the very thing I was going to advise you to do.

NORA: (*Involuntarily*) Oh you brute! to tell me that to me face!

LARRY: (*Nervously relapsing into his most Irish manner*) Nora, dear, dont you understand that I'm an Irishman, and he's an Englishman. He wants you; and he grabs you. *I* want you; and I quarrel with you and have to go on wanting you.

NORA: So you may. Youd better go back to England to the animated beefsteaks youre so fond of.

LARRY: (*Amazed*) Nora! (*Guessing where she got the metaphor*) He's been talking about me, I see. Well, never mind: we must be friends, you and I. I dont want his marriage to you to be his divorce from me.

NORA: You care more for him than you ever did for me.

LARRY: (*With curt sincerity*) Yes of course I do: why should I tell you lies about it? Nora Reilly was a person of very little consequence to me or anyone else outside this miserable little hole. But Mrs Tom Broadbent will be a person of very considerable consequence indeed. Play your new part well, and there will be no more neglect, no more loneliness, no more idle regrettings and vain-hopings in the evenings by the Round Tower, but real life and real work and real cares and real joys among real people: solid English life in London, the very centre of the world. You will find your work cut out for you keeping Tom's house and entertaining Tom's friends and getting Tom into parliament; but it will be worth the effort.

NORA: You talk as if I was under an obligation to him for marrying me.

LARRY: I talk as I think. Youve made a very good match, let me tell you.

NORA: Indeed! Well, some people might say he's not done so badly himself.

LARRY: If you mean that you will be a treasure to him, he thinks so now; and you can keep him thinking so if you like.

NORA: I wasnt thinking o meself at all.

LARRY: Were you thinking of your money, Nora?

NORA: I didnt say so.

LARRY: Your money will not pay your cook's wages in London.

NORA: (*Flaming up*) If thats true — and the more shame for you to throw it in me face if it is true — at all events itll make us independent; for if the worst comes to the worst, we can always come back here an live on it. An if I have to keep his house for him, at all events I can keep you out of it; for Ive done with you; and I wish I'd never seen you. So goodbye to you, Mister Larry Doyle. (*She turns her back on him and goes home*)

LARRY: (*Watching her as she goes*) Goodbye. Goodbye. Oh, thats so Irish! Irish both of us to the backbone: Irish! Irish! Iri—

BROADBENT *arrives, conversing energetically with* KEEGAN.

BROADBENT: Nothing pays like a golfing hotel, if you hold the land instead of the shares, and if the furniture people stand in with you, and if you are a good man of business.

LARRY: Nora's gone home.

BROADBENT: (*With conviction*) You were right this morning, Larry. I must feed up Nora. She's weak; and it makes her fanciful. Oh, by the way, did I tell you that we're engaged?

LARRY: She told me herself.

BROADBENT: (*Complacently*) She's rather full of it, as you may imagine. Poor Nora! Well, Mr Keegan, as I said, I begin to see my way here. I begin to see my way.

KEEGAN: (*With a courteous inclination*) The conquering Englishman, sir. Within 24 hours of your arrival you have carried off our only heiress, and practically secured the parliamentary seat. And you have promised me that when I come here in the evenings to meditate on my madness; to watch the shadow of the Round Tower lengthening in the sunset; to break my heart uselessly in the curtained gloaming[24] over the dead heart and blinded soul of the island of the saints, you will comfort me with the bustle of a great hotel and the sight of the little children carrying the golf clubs of your tourists as a preparation for the life to come.

BROADBENT: (*Quite touched, mutely offering him a cigar to console him, at which he smiles and shakes his head*) Yes, Mr Keegan: youre quite right. Theres poetry in everything, even (*looking absently into the cigar case*) in the most modern prosaic things, if you know how to extract it (*he extracts a cigar for himself and offers one to* LARRY, *who takes it*). If I was to be shot for it I couldnt extract it myself; but thats where you come in, you see. (*Roguishly, making up from his reverie and bustling* KEEGAN *good-humoredly*) And then *I* shall wake you up a bit. Thats where I come in: eh? d'ye see? Eh? eh? (*He pats him very pleasantly on the shoulder, half admiringly, half pityingly*) Just so, just so. (*Coming back to business*) By the way, I believe I can do better than a light railway here. There seems to be no question now that the motor boat has come to stay. Well, look at your magnificent river there, going to waste.

KEEGAN: (*Closing his eyes*)
'Silent, O Moyle, be the roar of thy waters.'[25]

BROADBENT: You know, the roar of a motor boat is quite pretty.

KEEGAN: Provided it does not drown the Angelus.

BROADBENT: (*Reassuringly*) Oh no: it wont do that: not the least danger. You know, a church bell can make a devil of a noise when it likes.

KEEGAN: You have an answer for everything, sir. But your plans leave one question still unanswered: how to get butter out of a dog's throat.

BROADBENT: Eh?

KEEGAN: You cannot build your golf links and hotels in the air. For that you must own our land. And how will you drag our acres from the ferret's grip of Matthew Haffigan? How will you persuade Cornelius Doyle to forgo the pride of being a small landowner? How will Barney Doran's millrace agree with your motor boats? Will Doolan help you to get a license for your hotel?

BROADBENT: My dear sir: to all intents and purposes the syndicate I represent already owns half Rosscullen. Doolan's is a tied house; and the brewers are in the syndicate. As to Haffigan's farm and Doran's mill and Mr Doyle's place and half a dozen others, they will be mortgaged to me before a month is out.

KEEGAN: But pardon me, you will not lend them more on their land than the land is worth; so they

24. twilight, dusk.

25. Thomas Moore, 'The Song of Fionnuala'.

will be able to pay you the interest.

BROADBENT: Ah, you are a poet, Mr Keegan, not a man of business.

LARRY: We will lend everyone of these men half as much again on their land as it is worth, or ever can be worth, to them.

BROADBENT: You forget, sir, that we, with our capital, our knowledge, our organization, and may I say our English business habits, can make or lose ten pounds out of land that Haffigan, with all his industry, could not make or lose ten shillings out of. Doran's mill is a superannuated folly: I shall want it for electric lighting.

LARRY: What is the use of giving land to such men? they are too small, too poor, too ignorant, too simpleminded to hold it against us: you might as well give a dukedom to a crossing sweeper.

BROADBENT: Yes, Mr Keegan: this place may have an industrial future, or it may have a residential future: I cant tell yet; but it's not going to be a future in the hands of your Dorans and Haffigans, poor devils!

KEEGAN: It may have no future at all. Have you thought of that?

BROADBENT: Oh, I'm not afraid of that. I have faith in Ireland. Great faith, Mr Keegan.

KEEGAN: And we have none: only empty enthusiasms and patriotisms, and emptier memories and regrets. Ah yes: you have some excuse for believing that if there be any future, it will be yours; for our faith seems dead, and our hearts cold and cowed. An island of dreamers who wake up in your jails, of critics and cowards whom you buy and tame for your own service, of bold rogues who help you to plunder us that they may plunder you afterwards.

BROADBENT: (*A little impatient of this unbusiness-like view*) Yes, yes; but you know you might say that of any country. The fact is, there are only two qualities in the world: efficiency and inefficiency, and only two sorts of people: the efficient and the inefficient. It dont matter whether theyre English or Irish. I shall collar this place, not because I'm an Englishman and Haffigan and Co are Irishmen, but because theyre duffers, and I know my way about.

KEEGAN: Have you considered what is to become of Haffigan?

LARRY: Oh, we'll employ him in some capacity or other, and probably pay him more than he makes for himself now.

BROADBENT: (*Dubiously*) Do you think so? No no: Haffigan's too old. It really doesnt pay now to take on men over forty even for unskilled labor, which I suppose is all Haffigan would be good for. No: Haffigan had better go to America, or into the Union,[26] poor old chap! He's worked out, you know: you can see it.

KEEGAN: Poor lost soul, so cunningly fenced in with invisible bars!

LARRY: Haffigan doesnt matter much. He'll die presently.

BROADBENT: (*Shocked*) Oh come, Larry! Dont be unfeeling. It's hard on Haffigan. It's always hard on the inefficient.

LARRY: Pah! what does it matter where an old and broken man spends his last days, or whether he has a million at the bank or only the workhouse dole? It's the young men, the able men, that matter. The real tragedy of Haffigan is the tragedy of his wasted youth, his stunted mind, his drudging over his clods and pigs until he has become a clod and a pig himself — until the soul within him has smouldered into nothing but a dull temper that hurts himself and all around him. I say let him die, and let us have no more of his like. And let young Ireland take care that it doesnt share his fate, instead of making another empty grievance of it. Let your syndicate come —

BROADBENT: Your syndicate too, old chap. You have your bit of the stock.

LARRY: Yes: mine if you like. Well, our syndicate has no conscience: it has no more regard for your Haffigans and Doolans and Dorans than it has for a gang of Chinese coolies. It will use your patriotic blatherskite and balderdash to get parliamentary powers over you as cynically as it would bait a mousetrap with toasted cheese. It will plan, and organize, and find capital while you slave like bees for it and revenge yourselves by paying politicians and penny newspapers out of your small wages to write articles and report speeches against its wickedness and tyranny, and to crack up your own Irish heroism, just as Haffigan once paid a witch a penny to put a spell on Billy Byrne's cow. In the end it will grind the nonsense out of you, and grind strength and sense into you.

BROADBENT: (*Out of patience*) Why cant you say a simple thing simply, Larry, without all that Irish exaggeration and talky-talky? The syndicate is a perfectly respectable body of responsible men of

26. The poorhouse, where the destitute retired to die.

good position. We'll take Ireland in hand, and by straightforward business habits teach it efficiency and self-help on sound Liberal principles. You agree with me, Mr Keegan, dont you?

KEEGAN: Sir: I may even vote for you.

BROADBENT: (*Sincerely moved, shaking his hand warmly*) You shall never regret it, Mr Keegan: I give you my word for that. I shall bring money here: I shall raise wages: I shall found public institutions: a library, a Polytechnic (undenominational, of course), a gymnasium, a cricket club, perhaps an art school. I shall make a Garden city of Rosscullen: the round tower shall be thoroughly repaired and restored.

KEEGAN: And our place of torment shall be as clean and orderly as the cleanest and most orderly place I know in Ireland, which is our poetically named Mountjoy prison. Well, perhaps I had better vote for an efficient devil that knows his own mind and his own business than for a foolish patriot who has no mind and no business.

BROADBENT: (*Stiffly*) Devil is rather a strong expression in that connexion, Mr Keegan.

KEEGAN: Not from a man who knows that this world is hell. But since the word offends you, let me soften it, and compare you simply to an ass.

LARRY *whitens with anger*.

BROADBENT: (*Reddening*) An ass!

KEEGAN: (*Gently*) You may take it without offence from a madman who calls the ass his brother — and a very honest, useful and faithful brother too. The ass, sir, is the most efficient of beasts, matter-of-fact, hardy, friendly when you treat him as a fellow-creature, stubborn when you abuse him, ridiculous only in love, which sets him braying, and in politics, which move him to roll about in the public road and raise a dust about nothing. Can you deny these qualities and habits in yourself, sir?

BROADBENT: (*Goodhumoredly*) Well, yes, I'm afraid I do, you know.

KEEGAN: Then perhaps you will confess to the ass's one fault.

BROADBENT: Perhaps so: what is it?

KEEGAN: That he wastes all his virtues — his efficiency, as you call it — in doing the will of his greedy masters instead of doing the will of Heaven that is in himself. He is efficient in the service of Mammon,[27] mighty in mischief, skilful in ruin, heroic in destruction. But he comes to browse here without knowing that the soil his hoof touches is holy ground. Ireland, sir, for good or evil, is like no other place under heaven; and no man can touch its sod or breathe its air without becoming better or worse. It produces two kinds of men in strange perfection: saints and traitors. It is called the island of the saints; but indeed in these later years it might be more fitly called the island of the traitors; for our harvest of these is the fine flower of the world's crop of infamy. But the day may come when these islands shall live by the quality of their men rather than by the abundance of their minerals; and then we shall see.

LARRY: Mr Keegan: if you are going to be sentimental about Ireland, I shall bid you good evening. We have had enough of that, and more than enough of cleverly proving that everybody who is not an Irishman is an ass. It is neither good sense nor good manners. It will not stop the syndicate; and it will not interest young Ireland so much as my friend's gospel of efficiency.

BROADBENT: Ah, yes, yes: efficiency is the thing. I dont in the least mind your chaff, Mr Keegan; but Larry's right on the main point. The world belongs to the efficient.

KEEGAN: (*With polished irony*) I stand rebuked, gentlemen. But believe me, I do every justice to the efficiency of you and your syndicate. You are both, I am told, thoroughly efficient civil engineers; and I have no doubt the golf links will be a triumph of your art. Mr Broadbent will get into parliament most efficiently, which is more than St Patrick could do if he were alive now. You may even build the hotel efficiently if you can find enough efficient masons, carpenters, and plumbers, which I rather doubt. (*Dropping his irony, and beginning to fall into the attitude of the priest rebuking sin*) When the hotel becomes insolvent (BROADBENT *takes his cigar out of his mouth, a little taken aback*) your English business habits will secure the thorough efficiency of the liquidation. You will reorganize the scheme efficiently; you will liquidate its second bankruptcy efficiently (BROADBENT *and* LARRY *look quickly at one another; for this, unless the priest is an old financial hand, must be inspiration*); you will get rid of its original shareholders efficiently after efficiently ruining them; and you will finally profit very efficiently by getting that hotel for a few shillings in the pound. (*More and more sternly*) Besides these efficient operations, you will foreclose

27. The god of riches.

your mortgages most efficiently (*his rebuking forefinger goes up in spite of himself*); you will drive Haffigan to America very efficiently; you will find a use for Barney Doran's foul mouth and bullying temper for employing him to slave-drive your laborers very efficiently; and (*low and bitter*) when at last this poor desolate countryside becomes a busy mint in which we shall all slave to make money for you, with our Polytechnic to teach us how to do it efficiently, and our library to fuddle the few imaginations your distilleries will spare, and our repaired Round Tower with admission sixpence, and refreshments and penny-in-the-slot mutoscopes[28] to make it interesting, then no doubt your English and American shareholders will spend all the money we make for them very efficiently in shooting and hunting, in operations for cancer and appendicitis, in gluttony and gambling; and you will devote what they save to fresh land development schemes. For four wicked centuries the world has dreamed this foolish dream[29] of efficiency; and the end is not yet. But the end will come.

BROADBENT: (*Seriously*) Too true, Mr Keegan, only too true. And most eloquently put. It reminds me of poor Ruskin:[30] a great man, you know. I sympathize. Believe me, I'm on your side. Dont sneer, Larry: I used to read a lot of Shelley years ago. Let us be faithful to the dreams of our youth (*he wafts a wreath of cigar smoke at large across the hill*).

KEEGAN: Come, Mr Doyle! is this English sentiment so much more efficient than our Irish sentiment, after all? Mr Broadbent spends his life inefficiently admiring the thoughts of great men, and efficiently serving the cupidity of base money hunters. We spend our lives efficiently sneering at him and doing nothing. Which of us has any right to reproach the other?

BROADBENT: (*Coming down the hill again to* KEEGAN's *right hand*) But you know, something must be done.

KEEGAN: Yes: when we cease to do, we cease to live. Well, what shall we do?

BROADBENT: Why, what lies to our hand.

KEEGAN: Which is the making of golf links and hotels to bring idlers to a country which workers have left in millions because it is a hungry land, a naked land, an ignorant and oppressed land.

BROADBENT: But, hang it all, the idlers will bring money from England to Ireland!

KEEGAN: Just as our idlers have for so many generations taken money from Ireland to England. Has that saved England from poverty and degradation more horrible than we have ever dreamed of? When I went to England, sir, I hated England. Now I pity it.

BROADBENT *can hardly conceive an Irishman pitying England; but as* LARRY *intervenes angrily, he gives it up and takes to the hill and his cigar again.*

LARRY: Much good your pity will do it!

KEEGAN: In the accounts kept in heaven, Mr Doyle, a heart purified of hatred may be worth more than even a Land Development Syndicate of Anglicized Irishmen and Gladstonized Englishmen.

LARRY: Oh, in heaven, no doubt. I have never been there. Can you tell me where it is?

KEEGAN: Could you have told me this morning where hell is? Yet you know now that it is here.[31] Do not despair of finding heaven: it may be no farther off.

LARRY: (*Ironically*) On this holy ground, as you call it, eh?

KEEGAN: (*With fierce intensity*) Yes, perhaps, even on this holy ground which such Irishmen as you have turned into a Land of Derision.

BROADBENT: (*Coming between them*) Take care! you will be quarrelling presently. Oh, you Irishmen, you Irishmen! Toujours Ballyhooly, eh? (LARRY, *with a shrug, half comic, half impatient, turns away up the hill, but presently strolls back on* KEEGAN's *right.* BROADBENT *adds, confidentially to* KEEGAN) Stick to the Englishman, Mr Keegan: he has a bad name here; but at least he can forgive you for being an Irishman.

KEEGAN: Sir: when you speak to me of English and Irish you forget that I am a Catholic. My country is not Ireland nor England, but the whole mighty realm of my Church.[32] For me there are but two countries: heaven and hell; but two conditions of men: salvation and damnation. Standing here

28. An early form of cinematograph.
29. Keegan here reverses the meaning of Doyle's diatribe on 'dreaming' in Act I.
30. John Ruskin (1819-1900), English writer and architectural critic.
31. Milton's *Paradise Lost*, Book I, lines 254-55:
The mind is its own place, and in itself,
Can make a Heav'n of Hell, a Hell of Heav'n.
32. Shaw wrote 'If we could only forget for one moment that we are Irish, and become really Catholic Europeans, there would be some hope for us.' (*The Matter with Ireland*).

between you the Englishman, so clever in your foolishness, and this Irishman, so foolish in his cleverness, I cannot in my ignorance be sure which of you is the more deeply damned; but I should be unfaithful to my calling if I opened the gates of my heart less widely to one than to the other.

LARRY: In either case it would be an impertinence, Mr Keegan, as your approval is not of the slightest consequence to us. What use do you suppose all this drivel is to men with serious practical business in hand?

BROADBENT: I dont agree with that, Larry. I think these things cannot be said too often: they keep up the moral tone of the community. As you know, I claim the right to think for myself in religious matters: in fact, I am ready to avow myself a bit of a — of a — well, I dont care who knows it — a bit of a Unitarian; but if the Church of England contained a few men like Mr Keegan, I should certainly join it.

KEEGAN: You do me too much honor, sir. (*With priestly humility to* LARRY) Mr Doyle: I am to blame for having unintentionally set your mind somewhat on edge against me. I beg your pardon.

LARRY: (*Unimpressed and hostile*) I didnt stand on ceremony with you: you neednt stand on it with me. Fine manners and fine words are cheap in Ireland: you can keep both for my friend here, who is still imposed on by them. *I* know their value.

KEEGAN: You mean you dont know their value.

LARRY: (*Angrily*) I mean what I say.

KEEGAN: (*Turning quietly to the Englishman*) You see, Mr Broadbent, I only make the hearts of my countrymen harder when I preach to them: the gates of hell still prevail against me. I shall wish you good evening. I am better alone, at the Round Tower, dreaming of heaven. (*He goes up the hill*)

LARRY: Aye, thats it! there you are! dreaming! dreaming! dreaming! dreaming!

KEEGAN: (*Halting and turning to them for the last time*) Every dream is a prophecy: every jest is an earnest in the womb of Time.

BROADBENT: (*Reflectively*) Once, when I was a small kid, I dreamt I was in heaven. (*They both stare at him*) It was a sort of pale blue satin place, with all the pious old ladies in our congregation sitting as if they were at a service; and there was some awful person in the study at the other side of the hall. I didnt enjoy it, you know. What is it like in your dreams?

KEEGAN: In my dreams it is a country where the State is the Church and the Church the people: three in one and one in three.[33] It is a commonwealth in which work is play and play is life: three in one and one in three. It is a temple in which the priest is the worshipper and the worshipper the worshipped: three in one and one in three. It is a godhead in which all life is human and all humanity divine: three in one and one in three. It is, in short, the dream of a madman. (*He goes away across the hill*)

BROADBENT: (*Looking after him affectionately*) What a regular old Church and State Tory he is! He's a character: he'll be an attraction here. Really almost equal to Ruskin and Carlyle.[34]

LARRY: Yes; and much good they did with all their talk!

BROADBENT: Oh tut, tut, Larry! They improved my mind: they raised my tone enormously. I feel sincerely obliged to Keegan: he has made me feel a better man: distinctly better. (*With sincere elevation*) I feel now as I never did before that I am right in devoting my life to the cause of Ireland. Come along and help me to choose the site for the hotel.

33. Keegan is playing on St Patrick's famous explanation of the mystery of the Trinity by use of a shamrock, Ireland's national emblem: 'I bind unto myself the Name/The strong name of the Trinity/By invocation of the same,/The Three-in-One, and One-in-Three.'

34. Thomas Carlyle (1795-1881), celebrated talker and author of *Sartor Resartus* (1833) and *Past and Present* (1843). His philosophy of vitalism, seeing energy as a sign of the godhead, was greatly influential.

JOHN BULL'S OTHER ISLAND

PREFACE FOR POLITICIANS (TO THE FIRST EDITION IN 1906)

[If Shaw was wary of pat prescriptions at the end of *John Bull's Other Island*, then in his many prefaces and postfaces to that work he was not. Anti-Shavians find in this very proliferation of commentaries proof positive that Shaw failed to achieve a full artistic embodiment of his insights in the play itself. Apologists argue that, on the contrary, Shaw was too much the artist to enforce his personal political opinions in a form as objective as the drama. His successive re-readings of his own work admirably demonstrate the way in which the meaning of a text is changed not just by location — the Dublin version of the play may not be the same as the London version — but also by the historical moment into which it is inserted. Far from being a series of 'I-told-you-sos', these essays are a fascinating account of the complexities of textual reception, and a brilliant series of analyses of the fluctuating fortunes of Anglo-Irish relations in the early decades of the 20th century.]

John Bull's Other Island was written in 1904 at the request of Mr William Butler Yeats, as a patriotic contribution to the repertory of the Irish Literary Theatre. Like most people who have asked me to write plays, Mr Yeats got rather more than he bargained for. The play was at that time beyond the resources of the new Abbey Theatre, which the Irish enterprise owed to the public spirit of Miss A. E. F. Horniman (an Englishwoman, of course), who, twelve years ago, played an important part in the history of the modern English stage as well as in my own personal destiny by providing the necessary capital for that memorable season at the Avenue Theatre which forced my Arms and The Man and Mr Yeats's Land of Heart's Desire on the recalcitrant London playgoer, and gave a third Irish playwright, Dr John Todhunter, an opportunity which the commercial theatres could not have afforded him.[1]

There was another reason for changing the destination of John Bull's Other Island. It was uncongenial to the whole spirit of the neo-Gaelic movement, which is bent on creating a new Ireland after its own ideal, whereas my play is a very uncompromising presentment of the real old Ireland. The next thing that happened was the production of the play in London at the Court Theatre by Messrs Vedrenne and Barker, and its immediate and enormous popularity with delighted and flattered English audiences. This constituted it a successful commercial play, and made it unnecessary to resort to the special machinery or tax the special resources of the Irish Literary Theatre for its production.

HOW TOM BROADBENT TOOK IT

Now I have a good deal more to say about the relations between the Irish and the English than will be found in my play. Writing the play for an Irish audience, I thought it would be good for them to be shewn very clearly that the loudest laugh they could raise at the expense of the absurdest Englishman was not really a laugh on their side; that he would succeed where they would fail; that he could inspire strong affection and loyalty in an Irishman who knew the world and was moved only to dislike, mistrust, impatience and even exasperation by his own countrymen; that his power of taking himself seriously, and his insensibility to anything funny in danger and destruction, was the first condition of economy and concentration of force, sustained purpose, and rational conduct. But the need for this lesson in Ireland is the measure of its demoralizing superfluousness in England. English audiences very naturally swallowed it eagerly and smacked their lips over it, laughing all the more heartily because they felt that they were taking a caricature of themselves with the most tolerant and large-minded goodhumor. They were perfectly willing to allow me to represent Tom Broadbent as infatuated in politics, hypnotized by his newspaper leader-writers and parliamentary orators into an utter paralysis of his common sense, without moral delicacy or social tact, provided I made him cheerful, robust, goodnatured, free from envy, and above all, a successful muddler-through in business and love. Not only did no English critic allow that the success in business of Messrs English Broadbent and Irish Doyle might possibly have been due to some extent to Doyle, but one writer actually dwelt with much feeling on the pathos of Doyle's failure as an engineer (a circumstance not mentioned nor suggested in my play) in contrast with Broadbent's solid success. No doubt, when the play is performed in Ireland, the Dublin critics will regard it as self-evident that without Doyle Broadbent would have become bankrupt in six months. I should say, myself, that the combination was probably much more effective than either of the partners would have been alone. I am persuaded further — without pretending to know more about it than anyone else — that Broadbent's special contribution was simply the strength, self-satisfaction, social confidence and cheerful bumptiousness that money, comfort, and good feeding bring to all healthy people; and that Doyle's special contribution was the freedom from illusion, the power of facing facts, the nervous industry, the sharpened wits, the sensitive pride of the imaginative man who has fought his way up through social persecution and poverty. I do not say that the confidence of the Englishman in Broadbent is not for the moment justified. The virtues of the English soil are not less real because they consist of

1. John Todhunter (1839-1916), poet and dramatist, had his play *A Comedy of Sighs* (1894) put on at the Avenue Theatre as a curtain-raiser to Yeats's *The Land of Heart's Desire*. The play failed and was replaced by Shaw's *Arms and the Man*.

coal and iron, not of metaphysical sources of character. The virtues of Broadbent are not less real because they are the virtues of the money that coal and iron have produced. But as the mineral virtues are being discovered and developed in other soils, their derivative virtues are appearing so rapidly in other nations that Broadbent's relative advantage is vanishing. In truth I am afraid (the misgiving is natural to a by-this-time slightly elderly playwright) that Broadbent is out of date.[2] The successful Englishman of today, when he is not a transplanted Scotchman or Irishman, often turns out on investigation to be, if not an American, an Italian, or a Jew, at least to be depending on the brains, the nervous energy, and the freedom from romantic illusions (often called cynicism) of such foreigners for the management of his sources of income. At all events I am persuaded that a modern nation that is satisfied with Broadbent is in a dream. Much as I like him, I object to be governed by him, or entangled in his political destiny. I therefore propose to give him a piece of my mind here, as an Irishman, full of an instinctive pity for those of my fellow-creatures who are only English.

WHAT IS AN IRISHMAN?

When I say that I am an Irishman I mean that I was born in Ireland, and that my native language is the English of Swift and not the unspeakable jargon of the mid-XIX century London newspapers. My extraction is the extraction of most Englishmen: that is, I have no trace in me of the commercially imported North Spanish strain which passes for aboriginal Irish:[3] I am a genuine typical Irishman of the Danish, Norman, Cromwellian, and (of course) Scotch invasions. I am violently and arrogantly Protestant by family tradition; but let no English Government therefore count on my allegiance: I am English enough to be an inveterate Republican and Home Ruler. It is true that one of my grandfathers was an Orangeman; but then his sister was an abbess; and his uncle, I am proud to say, was hanged as a rebel. When I look round me on the hybrid cosmopolitans, slum poisoned or square pampered, who call themselves Englishmen today, and see them bullied by the Irish Protestant garrison as no Bengalee now lets himself be bullied by an Englishman; when I see the Irishman everywhere standing clear-headed, sane, hardily callous to the boyish sentimentalities, susceptibilities, and credulities that make the Englishman the dupe of every charlatan and the idolater of every numskull, I perceive that Ireland is the only spot on earth which still produces the ideal Englishman of history. Blackguard, bully, drunkard, liar, foulmouth, flatterer, beggar, backbiter, venal functionary, corrupt judge, envious friend, vindictive opponent, unparalleled political traitor: all these your Irishman may easily be, just as he may be a gentleman (a species extinct in England, and nobody a penny the worse); but he is never quite the hysterical, nonsense-crammed, fact-proof, truth-terrified, unballasted sport of all the bogey panics and all the silly enthusiasms that now calls itself 'God's Englishman.' England cannot do without its Irish and its Scots today, because it cannot do without at least a little sanity.

THE PROTESTANT GARRISON

The more Protestant an Irishman is — the more English he is, if it flatters you to have it put that way, the more intolerable he finds it to be ruled by English instead of Irish folly. A 'loyal' Irishman is an abhorrent phenomenon, because it is an unnatural one. No doubt English rule is vigorously exploited in the interests of the property, power, and promotion of the Irish classes as against the Irish masses. Our delicacy is part of a keen sense of reality which makes us a very practical, and even, on occasion, a very coarse people. The Irish soldier takes the King's shilling and drinks the King's health; and the Irish squire takes the title deeds of the English settlement and rises uncovered to the strains of the English national anthem. But do not mistake this cupboard loyalty for anything deeper. It gains a broad base from the normal attachment of every reasonable man to the established government as long as it is bearable; for we all, after a certain age, prefer peace to revolution and order to chaos, other things being equal. Such considerations produce loyal Irishmen as they produce loyal Poles and Fins, loyal Hindoos, loyal Filipinos, and faithful slaves. But there is nothing more in it than that. If there is an entire lack of gall in the feeling of the Irish gentry towards the English, it is because the Englishman is always gaping admiringly at the Irishman as at some clever child

2. This portion of the Preface was actually written in 1906, two years after the first performance of the play.
3. Shaw refers here to the theory that the Celts or Milesians first came to Ireland from the Iberian peninsula.

prodigy. He overrates him with a generosity born of a traditional conviction of his own superiority in the deeper aspects of human character.[4] As the Irish gentleman, tracing his pedigree to the conquest or one of the invasions, is equally convinced that if this superiority really exists, he is the genuine true blue heir to it, and as he is easily able to hold his own in all the superficial social accomplishments, he finds English society agreeable, and English houses very comfortable, Irish establishments being generally straitened by an attempt to keep a park and a stable on an income which would not justify an Englishman in venturing upon a wholly detached villa.

OUR TEMPERAMENTS CONTRASTED

But however pleasant the relations between the Protestant garrison and the English gentry may be, they are always essentially essentially of the nature of an *entente cordiale*[5] between foreigners. Personally I like Englishmen much better than Irishmen (no doubt because they make more of me) just as many Englishmen like Frenchmen better than Englishmen, and never go on board a Peninsular and Oriental steamer when one of the ships of the Messageries Maritimes[6] is available. But I never think of an Englishman as my countryman. I should as soon think of applying that term to a German. And the Englishman has the same feeling. When a Frenchman fails to make the distinction, we both feel a certain disparagement involved in the misapprehension. Macaulay,[7] seeing that the Irish had in Swift an author worth stealing, tried to annex him by contending that he must be classed as an Englishman because he was not an aboriginal Celt. He might as well have refused the name of Briton to Addison because he did not stain himself blue and attach scythes to the poles of his sedan chair. In spite of all such trifling with facts, the actual distinction between the idolatrous Englishman and the fact-facing Irishman, of the same extraction though they be, remains to explode those two hollowest of fictions, the Irish and English 'races.' There is no Irish race any more than there is an English race or a Yankee race. There *is* an Irish climate, which will stamp an immigrant more deeply and durably in two years, apparently, than the English climate will in two hundred. It is reinforced by an artificial economic climate which does some of the work attributed to the natural geographic one; but the geographic climate is eternal and irresistible, making a mankind and a womankind that Kent, Middlesex, and East Anglia cannot produce and do not want to imitate.

How can I sketch the broad lines of the contrast as they strike me? Roughly I should say that the Englishman is wholly at the mercy of his imagination, having no sense of reality to check it. The Irishman, with a far subtler and more fastidious imagination, has one eye always on things as they are. If you compare Moore's visionary Minstrel Boy with Mr Rudyard Kipling's quasi-realistic Soldiers Three, you may yawn over Moore or gush over him, but you will not suspect him of having had any illusions about the contemporary British private; whilst as to Mr Kipling, you will see that he has not, and unless he settles in Ireland for a few years will always remain constitutionally and congenitally incapable of having, the faintest inkling of the reality which he idolizes as Tommy Atkins.[8] Perhaps you have never thought of illustrating the contrast between English and Irish by Moore and Mr Kipling, or even by Parnell and Gladstone. Sir Boyle Roche[9] and Shakespear may seem more to your point. Let me find you a more dramatic instance. Think of the famous meeting between the Duke of Wellington, that intensely Irish Irishman, and Nelson, that intensely English Englishman. Wellington's contemptuous disgust at Nelson's theatricality as a professed hero, patriot, and rhapsode, a theatricality which in an Irishman would have been an insufferably vulgar affectation, was quite natural and inevitable. Wellington's formula for that kind of thing was a well-known Irish one: 'Sir: dont be a damned fool.' It is the

4. Joyce's Englishman Haines, in the opening chapter of *Ulysses* (also set in 1904), is another example of this phenomenon. A sentimental Celticist, like Broadbent, he takes the precaution of coming to his beloved Ireland armed with a gun.
5. friendly alliance.
6. The 'P and O' was an English firm; the 'Messageries Maritimes' French.
7. Thomas Babington Macaulay (1800-59), popular apologist for industrialization and progress, especially in his *History of England* (1849-61).
8. 'The Minstrel Boy' is one of Thomas Moore's *Irish Melodies*. Rudyard Kipling (1865-1936) published *Soldiers Three* in 1890. Tommy Atkins became a standard name for the British soldier in 1815.
9. Sir Boyle Roche (1743-1807), Irish parliamentarian, was celebrated for his absurdities and the Irish 'bulls' that he regularly perpetrated. Hence the comparison with Shakespeare is a comparison of the ridiculous with the sublime.

formula of all Irishmen for all Englishmen to this day. It is the formula of Larry Doyle for Tom Broadbent in my play, in spite of Doyle's affection for Tom. Nelson's genius, instead of producing intellectual keenness and scrupulousness, produced mere delirium. He was drunk with glory, exalted by his fervent faith in the sound British patriotism of the Almighty, nerved by the vulgarest anti-foreign prejudice, and apparently unchastened by any reflections on the fact that he had never had to fight a technically capable and properly equipped enemy except on land, where he had never been successful. Compare Wellington, who had to fight Napoleon's armies, Napoleon's marshals, and finally Napoleon himself, without one moment of illusion as to the human material he had to command, without one gush of the 'Kiss me, Hardy' emotion which enabled Nelson to idolize his crews and his staff, without forgetting even in his dreams that the normal British officer of that time was an incapable amateur (as he still is) and the normal British soldier a never-do-well (he is now a depressed and respectable young man). No wonder Wellington became an accomplished comedian in the art of anti-climax, scandalizing the unfortunate Croker,[10] responding to the demand for glorious sentiments by the most disenchanting touches of realism, and, generally, pricking the English windbag at its most explosive crises of distention. Nelson, intensely nervous and theatrical, made an enormous fuss about victories so cheap that he would have deserved shooting if he had lost them, and, not content with lavishing splendid fighting on helpless adversaries like the heroic De Brueys or Villeneuve (who had not even the illusion of heroism when he went like a lamb to the slaughter), got himself killed by his passion for exposing himself to death in that sublime defiance of it which was perhaps the supreme tribute of the exquisite coward to the King of Terrors (for, believe me, you cannot be a hero without being a coward: supersense cuts both ways), the result being a tremendous effect on the gallery. Wellington, most capable of captains, was neither a hero nor a patriot: perhaps not even a coward; and had it not been for the Nelsonic anecdotes invented for him — 'Up guards, and at em' and so forth — and the fact that the antagonist with whom he finally closed was such a master of theatrical effect that Wellington could not fight him without getting into his limelight, nor overthrow him (most unfortunately for us all) without drawing the eyes of the whole world to the catastrophe, the Iron Duke would have been almost forgotten by this time. Now that contrast is English against Irish all over, and is the more delicious because the real Irishman in it is the Englishman of tradition, whilst the real Englishman is the traditional theatrical foreigner.

The value of the illustration lies in the fact that Nelson and Wellington were both in the highest degree efficient, and both in the highest degree incompatible with one another on any other footing than one of independence. The government of Nelson by Wellington or of Wellington by Nelson is felt at once to be a dishonorable outrage to the governed and a finally impossible task for the governor.

I daresay some Englishman will now try to steal Wellington as Macaulay tried to steal Swift. And he may plead with some truth that though it seems impossible that any other country than England could produce a hero so utterly devoid of common sense, intellectual delicacy, and international chivalry as Nelson, it may be contended that Wellington was rather an eighteenth century aristocratic type, than a specifically Irish type. George IV and Byron, contrasted with Gladstone, seem Irish in respect of a certain humorous blackguardism, and a power of appreciating art and sentiment without being duped by them into mistaking romantic figments for realities. But faithlessness and the need for carrying off the worthlessness and impotence that accompany it, produce in all nations a gay, sceptical, amusing, blaspheming, witty fashion which suits the flexibility of the Irish mind very well; and the contrast between this fashion and the energetic infatuations that have enabled intellectually ridiculous men, without wit or humor, to go on crusades and make successful revolutions, must not be confused with the contrast between the English and Irish idiosyncrasies. The Irishman makes a distinction which the Englishman is too lazy intellectually (the intellectual laziness and slovenliness of the English is almost beyond belief) to make. The Englishman, impressed with the dissoluteness of the faithless wits of the Restoration and the Regency, and with the victories of the wilful zealots of the patriotic,

10. John Wilson Croker (1780-1857), Irish historian and Tory MP, notorious for his review of Keats's *Endymion*. The *Croker Papers* (1884) contain letters from the Duke of Wellington.

religious, and revolutionary wars, jumps to the conclusion that wilfulness is the main thing. In this he is right. But he overdoes his jump so far as to conclude also that stupidity and wrongheadedness are better guarantees of efficiency and trustworthiness than intellectual vivacity, which he mistrusts as a common symptom of worthlessness, vice, and instability. Now in this he is most dangerously wrong. Whether the Irishman grasps the truth as firmly as the Englishman may be open to question; but he is certainly comparatively free from the error. That affectionate and admiring love of sentimental stupidity for its own sake, both in men and women, which shines so steadily through the novels of Thackeray would hardly be possible in the works of an Irish novelist. Even Dickens, though too vital a genius and too severely educated in the school of shabby-genteel poverty to have any doubt of the national danger of fatheadedness in high places, evidently assumes rather too hastily the superiority of Mr Meagles to Sir John Chester and Harold Skimpole.[11] On the other hand, it takes an Irishman years of residence in England to learn to respect and like a blockhead. An Englishman will not respect nor like anyone else. Every English statesman has to maintain his popularity by pretending to be ruder, more ignorant, more sentimental, more superstitious, more stupid than any man who has lived behind the scenes of public life for ten minutes can possibly be. Nobody dares to publish really intimate memoirs of him or really private letters of his until his whole generation has passed away, and his party can no longer be compromised by the discovery that the platitudinizing twaddler and hypocritical opportunist was really a man of some perception as well as of strong constitution, peg-away industry, personal ambition, and party keenness.

ENGLISH STUPIDITY EXCUSED

I do not claim it as a natural superiority in the Irish nation that it dislikes and mistrusts fools, and expects its political leaders to be clever and humbug-proof. It may be that if our resources included the armed force and virtually unlimited money which push the political and military figureheads of England through bungled enterprises to a muddled success, and create an illusion of some miraculous and divine innate English quality that enables a general to become a conqueror with abilities that would not suffice to save a cabman from having his licence marked, and a member of parliament to become Prime Minister with the outlook on life of a sporting country solicitor educated by a private governess, we should lapse into gross intellectual sottishness, and prefer leaders who encouraged our vulgarities by sharing them, and flattered us by associating them with purchased successes, to our betters. But as it is, we cannot afford that sort of encouragement and flattery in Ireland. The odds against which our leaders have to fight would be too heavy for the fourth-rate Englishmen whose leadership consists for the most part in marking time ostentatiously until they are violently shoved, and then stumbling blindly forward (or backward) wherever the shove sends them. We cannot crush England as a Pickford's van might crush a perambulator. We are the perambulator and England the Pickford. We must study her and our real weaknesses and real strength; we must practise upon her slow conscience and her quick terrors; we must deal in ideas and political principles since we cannot deal in bayonets; we must outwit, outwork, outstay her; we must embarrass, bully, even conspire and assassinate when nothing else will move her, if we are not all to be driven deeper and deeper into the shame and misery of our servitude. Our leaders must be not only determined enough, but clever enough to do this. We have no illusions as to the existence of any mysterious Irish pluck, Irish honesty, Irish bias on the part of Providence, or sterling Irish solidity of character, that will enable an Irish blockhead to hold his own against England. Blockheads are of no use to us: we were compelled to follow a supercilious, unpopular, tongue-tied, aristocratic Protestant Parnell, although there was no lack among us of fluent imbeciles, with majestic presences and oceans of dignity and sentiment, to promote into his place could they have done his work for us. It is obviously convenient that Mr Redmond should be a better speaker and rhetorician than Parnell; but if he began to use his powers to make himself agreeable instead of making himself reckoned with by the enemy; if he set to work a manufacture and support English shams

11. Mr. Meagher is a lovable character in Charles Dickens's *Little Dorrit* (1857-58); Sir John Chester, a smooth villain in *Barnaby Rudge* (1841); Harold Skimpole, a selfish hypocrite in *Bleak House* (1852-53).

and hypocrisies instead of exposing and denouncing them; if he constituted himself the permanent apologist of doing nothing, and, when the people insisted on his doing something, only roused himself to discover how to pretend to do it without really changing anything, he would lose his leadership as certainly as an English politician would, by the same course, attain a permanent place on the front bench.[12] In short, our circumstances place a premium on political ability whilst the circumstances of England discount it; and the quality of the supply naturally follows the demand. If you miss in my writings that hero-worship of dotards and duffers which is planting England with statues of disastrous statesmen and absurd generals, the explanation is simply that I am an Irishman and you an Englishman.

IRISH PROTESTANTISM REALLY PROTESTANT

When I repeat that I am an Irish Protestant, I come to a part of the relation between England and Ireland that you will never understand unless I insist on explaining it to you with that Irish insistence on intellectual clarity to which my English critics are so intensely recalcitrant.

First, let me tell you that in Ireland Protestantism is really Protestant. It is true that there is an Irish Protestant Church (disestablished some 35 years ago) in spite of the fact that a Protestant Church is, fundamentally, a contradiction in terms. But this means only that the Protestants use the word Church to denote their secular organization, without troubling themselves about the metaphysical sense of Christ's famous pun, 'Upon this rock I will build my church.' The Church of England, which a reformed Anglican Catholic Anti-Protestant Church, is quite another affair. An Anglican is acutely conscious that he is not a Wesleyan; and many Anglican clergymen do not hesitate to teach that all Methodists incur damnation. In Ireland all that the member of the Irish Protestant Church knows is that he is not a Roman Catholic. The decorations of even the 'lowest' English Church seem to him to be extravagantly Ritualistic and Popish. I myself entered the Irish Church by baptism, a ceremony performed by my uncle in 'his own church.' But I was sent, with many boys of my own denomination, to a Wesleyan school where the Wesleyan catechism was taught without the least protest on the part of the parents, although there was so little presumption in favor of any boy there being a Wesleyan that if all the Church boys had been withdrawn at any moment, the school would have become bankrupt. And this was by no means analogous to the case of those working class members of the Church of England in London, who send their daughters to Roman Catholic schools rather than to the public elementary schools. They do so for the definite reason that the nuns teach girls good manners and sweetness of speech, which have no place in the County Council curriculum. But in Ireland the Church parent sends his son to a Wesleyan school (if it is convenient and socially eligible) because he is indifferent to the form of Protestantism, provided it is Protestantism. There is also in Ireland a characteristically Protestant refusal to take ceremonies and even sacraments very seriously except by way of strenuous objection to them when they are conducted with candles or incense. For example, I was never confirmed, although the ceremony was specially needed in my case as the failure of my appointed godfather to appear at my baptism had led to his responsibilities being assumed on the spot, at my uncle's order, by the sexton. And my case was a very common one, even among people quite untouched by modern scepticisms. Apart from the weekly churchgoing, which holds its own as a respectable habit, the initiations are perfunctory, the omissions regarded as negligible. The distinction between churchman and dissenter, which in England is a class distinction, a political distinction, and even occasionally a religious distinction, does not exist. Nobody is surprised in Ireland to find that the squire who is the local pillar of the formerly established Church is also a Plymouth Brother[13] and, except on certain special or fashionable occasions, attends the Methodist meeting-house. The parson has no priestly character and no priestly influence: the High Church curate of course exists and has his vogue among religious epicures of the other sex; but the general attitude of his

12. This supposition turned out to be largely prophetic. By taking the English promise of Home Rule as a basis for Irish enlistment in the war effort, John Redmond (see footnote 19 of *O'Flaherty VC*, p. 506) effectively lost the leadership of Irish nationalist opinion.

13. A fundamentalist protestant sect that originated in Dublin in 1827.

congregation towards him is that of Dr Clifford.[14] The clause in the Apostles' Creed professing belief in a Catholic Church is a standing puzzle to Protestant children; and when they grow up they dismiss it from their minds more often than they solve it, because they really are not Catholics but Protestants to the extremest practicable degree of individualism. It is true that they talk of church and chapel with all the Anglican contempt for chapel; but in Ireland the chapel means the Roman Catholic church, for which the Irish Protestant reserves all the class rancor, the political hostility, the religious bigotry, and the bad blood generally that in England separates the Establishment from the non-conforming Protestant organizations. When a vulgar Irish Protestant speaks of a 'Papist' he feels exactly as a vulgar Anglican vicar does when he speaks of a Dissenter. And when the vicar is Anglican enough to call himself a Catholic priest, wear a cassock, and bless his flock with two fingers, he becomes horrifically incomprehensible to the Irish Protestant Churchman, who, on his part, puzzles the Anglican by regarding a Methodist as tolerantly as an Irishman who likes grog regards an Irishman who prefers punch.[15]

A FUNDAMENTAL ANOMALY

Now nothing can be more anomalous, and at bottom impossible, than a Conservative Protestant party standing for the established order against a revolutionary Catholic party. The Protestant is theoretically an anarchist as far as anarchism is practicable in human society: that is, he is an individualist, a free-thinker, a self-helper, a Whig, a Liberal, a mistruster and vilifier of the State, a rebel. The Catholic is theoretically a Collectivist, a self-abnegator, a Tory, a Conservative, a supporter of Church and State one and undivisible, an obeyer. This would be a statement of fact as well as of theory if men were Protestants and Catholics by temperament and adult choice instead of by family tradition. The peasant who supposed that Wordsworth's son would carry on the business now the old gentleman was gone was not a whit more foolish than we who laugh at his ignorance of the nature of poetry whilst we take it as a matter of course that a son should 'carry on' his father's religion. Hence, owing to our family system, the Catholic Churches are recruited daily at the font by temperamental Protestants, and the Protestant organizations by temperamental Catholics, with consequences most disconcerting to those who expect history to be deducible from the religious professions of the men who make it.

Still, though the Roman Catholic Church may occasionally catch such Tartars as Luther and Voltaire, or the Protestant organizations as Newman and Manning,[16] the general run of mankind takes its impress from the atmosphere in which it is brought up. In Ireland the Roman Catholic peasant cannot escape the religious atmosphere of his Church. Except when he breaks out like a naughty child he is docile; he is reverent; he is content to regard knowledge as something not his business; he is a child before his Church, and accepts it as the highest authority in science and philosophy. He speaks of himself as a son of the Church, calling his priest father instead of brother or Mister. To rebel politically, he must break away from parish tutelage and follow a Protestant leader on national questions. His Church naturally fosters his submissiveness. The British Government and the Vatican may differ very vehemently as to whose subject the Irishman is to be; but they are quite agreed as to the propriety of his being a subject. Of the two, the British Government allows him more liberty, giving him as complete a democratic control of local government as his means will enable him to use, and a voice in the election of a formidable minority in the House of Commons, besides allowing him to read and learn what he likes — except when it makes a tuft-hunting onslaught on a seditious newspaper.[17] But if he dared to claim a voice in the selection of his parish priest, or a representative at the Vatican, he would be denounced from the altar as an almost inconceivable blasphemer; and his educational opportunities are so restricted by his Church that he is heavily handicapped in every walk of life that requires any

14. John Clifford (1836-1923), English baptist divine; 'the uncrowned king of militant nonconformity', he was a radical in politics and a liberal evangelical in theology.
15. Grog is spirits and water, a more fiery drink than punch, which is usually modified by sugar or lemon.
16. John Henry Newman (1801-90) and Henry Edward Manning (1808-92) were converts to the Roman catholic church. Both became cardinals and famous controversialists.
17. Tuft-hunting is a sycophantic attempt to please people in power. The reference is to the suppression of Arthur Griffith's newspaper *The United Irishman* in 1906 by the Dublin Castle authorities.

literacy. It is the aim of his priest to make him and keep him a submissive Conservative; and nothing but gross economic oppression and religious persecution could have produced the strange phenomenon of a revolutionary movement not only tolerated by the Clericals, but, up to a certain point, even encouraged by them. If there is such a thing as political science, with natural laws like any other science, it is certain that only the most violent external force could effect and maintain this unnatural combination of political revolution with Papal reaction, and of hardy individualism and independence with despotism and subjugation.

That violent external force is the clumsy thumb of English rule. If you would be good enough, ladies and gentlemen of England, to take your thumb away and leave us free to do something else than bite it, the unnaturally combined elements in Irish politics would fly asunder and recombine according to their proper nature with results entirely satisfactory to real Protestantism.

THE NATURE OF POLITICAL HATRED

Just reconsider the Home Rule question in the light of that very English characteristic of the Irish people, their political hatred of priests. Do not be distracted by the shriek of indignant denial from the Catholic papers and from those who have witnessed the charming relations between the Irish peasantry and their spiritual fathers. I am perfectly aware that the Irish love their priests as devotedly as the French loved them before the Revolution or as the Italians loved them before they imprisoned the Pope in the Vatican. They love their landlords too: many an Irish gentleman has found in his nurse a foster-mother more interested in him than his actual mother. They love the English, as every Englishman who travels in Ireland can testify. Please do not suppose that I speak satirically: the world is full of authentic examples of the concurrence of human kindliness with political rancor. Slaves and schoolboys often love their masters; Napoleon and his soldiers made desperate efforts to save from drowning the Russian soldiers under whom they had broken the ice with their cannon; even the relations between nonconformist peasants and country parsons in England are not invariably unkindly; in the southern States of America planters are often traditionally fond of negroes and kind to them, with substantial returns in humble affection; soldiers and sailors often admire and cheer their officers sincerely and heartily; nowhere is actual personal intercourse found compatible for long with the intolerable friction of hatred and malice. But people who persist in pleading these amiabilities as political factors must be summarily bundled out of the room when questions of State are to be discussed. Just as an Irishman may have English friends whom he may prefer to any Irishman of his acquaintance, and be kind, hospitable, and serviceable in his intercourse with Englishmen, whilst being perfectly prepared to make the Shannon run red with English blood if Irish freedom could be obtained at that price; so an Irish Catholic may like his priest as a man and revere him as a confessor and spiritual pastor whilst being implacably determined to seize the first opportunity of throwing off his yoke. This is political hatred: the only hatred that civilization allows to be mortal hatred.

THE REVOLT AGAINST THE PRIEST

Realize, then, that the popular party in Ireland is seething with rebellion against the tyranny of the Church. Imagine the feelings of an English farmer if the parson refused to marry him for less than £20, and if he had virtually no other way of getting married! Imagine the Church Rates revived in the form of an unofficial Income Tax scientifically adjusted to your taxable capacity by an intimate knowledge of your affairs verified in the confessional! Imagine being one of a peasantry reputed the poorest in the world, under the thumb of a priesthood reputed the richest in the world! Imagine a Catholic middle class continually defeated in the struggle of professional, official, and fashionable life by the superior education of its Protestant competitors, and yet forbidden by its priests to resort to the only efficient universities in the country! Imagine trying to get a modern education in a seminary of priests, where every modern book worth reading is on the index,[18] and the earth is still regarded, not perhaps as absolutely flat, yet as being far from so spherical as Protestants allege! Imagine being forbidden to read this preface because it proclaims your own grievance! And imagine being bound to submit to all this because the popular side must hold together at all costs in

18. *Index Librorum Prohibitorum* — a list of books proscribed by the Roman catholic church.

the face of the Protestant enemy! That is, roughly, the predicament of Roman Catholic Ireland.

PROTESTANT LOYALTY: A FORECAST

Now let us have a look at Protestant Ireland. I have already said that a 'loyal' Irishman is an abhorrent phenomenon, because he is an unnatural one. In Ireland it is not 'loyalty' to drink the English king's health and stand uncovered to the English national anthem: it is simply exploitation of English rule in the interests of the property, power, and promotion of the Irish classes as against the Irish masses. From any other point of view it is cowardice and dishonor. I have known a Protestant go to Dublin Castle to be sworn in as a special constable, quite resolved to take the baton and break the heads of a patriotic faction just then upsetting the peace of the town, yet back out at the last moment because he could not bring himself to swallow the oath of allegiance tendered with the baton. There is no such thing as genuine loyalty in Ireland. There is a separation of the Irish people into two hostile camps: one Protestant, gentlemanly, and oligarchical; the other Roman Catholic, popular, and democratic. The oligarchy governs Ireland as a bureaucracy deriving authority from the king of England. It cannot cast him off without casting off its own ascendancy. Therefore it naturally exploits him sedulously, drinking his health, waving his flag, playing his anthem, and using the foolish word 'traitor' freely in its cups. But let the English Government make a step towards the democratic party, and the Protestant garrison revolts at once, not with tears and prayers and anguish of soul and years of trembling reluctance, as the parliamentarians of the XVII century revolted against Charles I, but with acrid promptitude and strident threatenings. When England finally abandons the garrison by yielding to the demand for Home Rule, the Protestants will not go under, nor will they waste much time in sulking over their betrayal, and comparing their fate with that of Gordon left by Gladstone to perish on the spears of heathen fanatics.[19] They cannot afford to retire into an Irish Faubourg St Germain. They will take an energetic part in the national government, which will be sorely in need of parliamentary and official forces independent of Rome. They will get not only the Protestant votes, but the votes of Catholics in that spirit of toleration which is everywhere extended to heresies that happen to be politically serviceable to the orthodox. They will not relax their determination to hold every inch of the government of Ireland that they can grasp; but as that government will then be a national Irish government instead of as now an English government, their determination will make them the vanguard of Irish Nationalism and Democracy as against Romanism and Sacerdotalism,[20] leaving English Unionists grieved and shocked at their discovery of the true value of an Irish Protestant's loyalty.

But there will be no open break in the tradition of the party. The Protestants will still be the party of Union, which will then mean, not the Repeal of Home Rule, but the maintenance of the Federal Union of English-speaking commonwealths, now theatrically called the Empire.[21] They will pull down the Union Jack without the smallest scruple; but they know the value of the Channel Fleet, and will cling closer than brothers to that and any other Imperial asset that can be exploited for the protection of Ireland against foreign aggression or the sharing of expenses with the British taxpayer. They know that the Irish coast is for the English invasion-scaremonger the heel of Achilles, and that they can use this to make him pay for the boot.

PROTESTANT PUGNACITY

If any Englishman feels incredulous as to this view of Protestantism as an essentially Nationalist force in Ireland, let him ask himself which leader he, if he were an Irishman, would rather have back from the grave to fight England: the Catholic Daniel O'Connell or the Protestant Parnell. O'Connell organized the Nationalist movement only to draw its teeth, to break its determination, and to declare that Repeal of the Union was not worth the shedding of a drop of blood. He died in the bosom of his Church, not in the bosom of his country. The Protestant leaders, from Lord Edward Fitzgerald[22] to Parnell, have never divided their devotion. If any

19. Charles George Gordon (1833-85) was the English military leader who besieged Khartoum without full authorization. Gladstone punished him for this by delaying the sending of reinforcements. Gordon was killed in the fighting.

20. Ecclesiocracy, or priest-ridden politics.
21. This was also the policy advocated by Sir Horace Plunkett.
22. Lord Edward Fitzgerald (1763-98), Irish patriot and member of the Anglo-Irish aristocracy, who joined the United Irishmen in 1796 but was captured and mortally wounded before the 1798 Rebellion.

Englishman thinks that they would have been more sparing of blood than the English themselves are, if only so cheap a fluid could have purchased the honor of Ireland, he greatly mistakes the Irish Protestant temper. The notion that Ireland is the only country in the world not worth shedding a drop of blood for is not a Protestant one, and certainly not countenanced by English practice. It was hardly reasonable to ask Parnell to shed blood *quant. suff.*[23] in Egypt to put an end to the misgovernment of the Khedive and replace him by Lord Cromer[24] for the sake of the English bondholders, and then to expect him to become a Tolstoyan[25] or an O'Connellite in regard to his own country. With a wholly Protestant Ireland at his back he might have bullied England into conceding Home Rule; for the insensibility of the English governing classes to philosophical, moral, social considerations — in short, to any considerations which require a little intellectual exertion and sympathetic alertness — is tempered, as we Irish well know, by an absurd susceptibility to intimidation.

For let me halt a moment here to impress on you, O English reader, that no fact has been more deeply stamped into us than that we can do nothing with an English Government unless we frighten it, any more than you can yourself. When power and riches are thrown haphazard into children's cradles as they are in England, you get a governing class without industry, character, courage, or real experience; and under such circumstances reforms are produced only by catastrophes followed by panics in which 'something must be done.' Thus it costs a cholera epidemic to achieve a Public Health Act, a Crimean War to reform the Civil Service, and a gunpowder plot[26] to disestablish the Irish Church. It was by the light, not of reason, but of the moon, that the need for paying serious attention to the Irish land question was seen in England. It cost the American War of Independence and the Irish Volunteer movement to obtain the Irish parliament of 1782, the constitution of which far overshot the nationalist mark of today in the matter of independence.

It is vain to plead that this is human nature and not class weakness. The Japanese have proved that it is possible to conduct social and political changes intelligently and providentially instead of drifting along helplessly until public disasters compel a terrified and inconsiderate rearrangement. Innumerable experiments in local government have shewn that when men are neither too poor to be honest nor too rich to understand and share the needs of the people — as in New Zealand, for example — they can govern much more providently than our little circle of aristocrats and plutocrats.

THE JUST ENGLISHMAN

English Unionists, when asked what they have to say in defence of their rule of subject peoples, often reply that the Englishman is just, leaving us divided between our derision of so monstrously inhuman a pretension, and our impatience with so gross a confusion of the mutually exclusive functions of judge and legislator. For there is only one condition on which a man can do justice between two litigants, and that is that he shall have no interest in common with either of them, whereas it is only by having every interest in common with both of them that he can govern them tolerably. The indispensable preliminary to Democracy is the representation of every interest: the indispensable preliminary to justice is the elimination of every interest. When we want an arbitrator or an umpire, we turn to a stranger: when we want a government, a stranger is the one person we will not endure. The Englishman in India, for example, stands, a very statue of justice, between two natives. He says, in effect, 'I am impartial in your religious disputes because I believe in neither of your religions. I am impartial in your conflicts of custom and sentiment because your customs and sentiments are different from, and abysmally inferior to, my own. Finally, I am impartial as to your interests, because they are both equally opposed to mine, which is to keep you both equally powerless against me in order that I may extract money from you to pay salaries and pensions to myself and my fellow Englishmen as judges and rulers over you. In return for which you get the inestimable benefit of a government that does absolute justice as between Indian and Indian, being wholly preoccupied with the maintenance of

23. in sufficient, i.e. necessary, quantity.
24. Lord Cromer (1841-1917), administrator and diplomat, became agent and consul general in Egypt in 1883 and was the *de facto* ruler of the country until 1907. The khedive was the Ottoman viceroy.
25. Count Leo Tolstoy (1828-1910), Russian novelist and pacifist.
26. An abortive conspiracy to blow up the Houses of Parliament and James I on 5 November 1605, led by Robert Catesby and various co-conspirators, including Guy Fawkes — all staunch Roman catholics.

absolute injustice as between India and England.'

It will be observed that no Englishman, without making himself ridiculous, could pretend to be perfectly just or disinterested in English affairs, or would tolerate a proposal to establish the Indian or Irish system in Great Britain. Yet if the justice of the Englishman is sufficient to ensure the welfare of India or Ireland, it ought to suffice equally for England. But the English are wise enough to refuse to trust to English justice themselves, preferring democracy. They can hardly blame the Irish for taking the same view.

In short, dear English reader, the Irish Protestant stands outside that English Mutual Admiration Society which you call the Union or the Empire. You may buy a common and not ineffective variety of Irish Protestant by delegating your powers to him, and in effect making him the oppressor and you his sorely bullied and bothered catspaw and military maintainer; but if you offer him nothing for his loyalty except the natural superiority of the English character, you will — well, try the experiment, and see what will happen! You would have a ten-times better chance with the Roman Catholic; for he has been saturated from his youth up with the Imperial idea of foreign rule by a spiritually superior international power, and is trained to submission and abnegation of his private judgment. A Roman Catholic garrison would take its orders from England and let her rule Ireland if England were Roman Catholic. The Protestant garrison simply seizes on the English power; uses it for its own purposes; and occasionally orders the English Government to remove an Irish secretary who has dared to apply English ideas to the affairs of the garrison. Whereupon the English Government abjectly removes him, and implores him, as a gentleman and a loyal Englishman, not to reproach it in the face of the Nationalist enemy.

Such incidents naturally do not shake the sturdy conviction of the Irish Protestant that he is more than a match for any English Government in determination and intelligence. Here, no doubt, he flatters himself; for his advantage is not really an advantage of character, but of comparative directness of interest, concentration of force on one narrow issue, simplicity of aim, with freedom from the scruples and responsibilities of world-politics. The business is Irish business, not English; and he is Irish. And his object, which is simply to secure the dominance of his own caste and creed behind the power of England, is simpler and clearer than the confused aims of English Cabinets struggling ineptly with the burdens of empire, and biassed by the pressure of capital anywhere rather than in Ireland. He has no responsibility, no interest, no status outside his own country and his own movement, which means that he has no conscience in dealing with England; whereas England, having a very uneasy conscience, and many hindering and hampering responsibilities and interests in dealing with him, gets bullied and driven by him, and finally learns sympathy with Nationalist aims by her experience of the tyranny of the Orange party.

IRISH CATHOLICISM FORECAST

Let us suppose that the establishment of a national government were to annihilate the oligarchic party by absorbing the Protestant garrison and making it a Protestant National Guard. The Roman Catholic laity, now a cipher, would organize itself; and a revolt against Rome and against the priesthood would ensue. The Roman Catholic Church would become the official Irish Church. The Irish parliament would insist on a voice in the promotion of churchmen; fees and contributions would be regulated; blackmail would be resisted; sweating in conventual factories and workshops would be stopped; and the ban would be taken off the universities.[27] In a word, the Roman Catholic Church, against which Dublin Castle is powerless, would meet the one force on earth that can cope with it victoriously. That force is Democracy, a thing far more Catholic than itself. Until that force is let loose against it, the Protestant garrison can do nothing to the priesthood except consolidate it and drive the people to rally round it in defence of their altars against the foreigner and the heretic. When it *is* let loose, the Catholic laity will make as short work of sacerdotal tyranny in Ireland as it has done in France and Italy. And in doing so it will be forced to face the old problem of the relations of Church and State. A Roman Catholic party must submit to Rome: an anti-clerical Catholic party must of necessity become an Irish Catholic party. The Holy Roman Empire, like the other Empires, has no future except as a Federation of national Catholic Churches; for Christianity can no more escape

27. The ecclesiastical ban on Roman catholics attending Trinity College, Dublin was removed only in 1970. Shaw's predictions in this passage proved less than realistic.

Democracy than Democracy can escape Socialism. It is noteworthy in this connection that the Anglican Catholics have played and are playing a notable part in the Socialist movement in England in opposition to the individualist Secularists of the urban proletariat; but they are quit of the preliminary dead lift that awaits the Irish Catholic. Their Church has thrown off the yoke of Rome, and is safely and permanently Anglicized. But the Catholic Church in Ireland is still Roman. Home Rule will herald the day when the Vatican will go the way of Dublin Castle, and the island of the saints assume the headship of her own Church. It may seem incredible that long after the last Orangeman shall lay down his chalk for ever, the familiar scrawl on every blank wall in the north of Ireland 'To hell with the Pope!' may reappear in the south, traced by the hands of Catholics who shall have forgotten the traditional counter legend, 'To hell with King William'[28] (of glorious, pious, and immortal memory); but it may happen so. 'The island of the saints' is no idle phrase. Religious genius is one of our national products; and Ireland is no bad rock to build a Church on. Holy and beautiful is the soul of Catholic Ireland: her prayers are lovelier than the teeth and claws of Protestantism, but not so effective in dealing with the English.

ENGLISH VOLTAIREANISM

Let me familiarize the situation by shewing how closely it reproduces the English situation in its essentials. In England, as in France, the struggle between the priesthood and the laity has produced a vast body of Voltaireans.[29] But the essential identity of the French and English movements has been obscured by the ignorance of the ordinary Englishman, who, instead of knowing the distinctive tenets of his church or sect, vaguely believes them to be the eternal truth as opposed to the damnable error of all the other denominations. He thinks of Voltaire as a French 'infidel,' instead of as the champion of the laity against the official theocracy of the State Church. The Nonconformist leaders of our Free Churches are all Voltaireans. The warcry of the Passive Resisters is Voltaire's war-cry, 'Écrasez l'infâme.'[30] No account need be taken of the technical difference between Voltaire's 'infâme' and Dr Clifford's. One was the unreformed Roman Church of France; the other is the reformed Anglican Church; but in both cases the attack has been on a priestly tyranny and a professional monopoly. Voltaire convinced the Genevan ministers that he was the philosophic champion of their Protestant, Individualistic, Democratic Deism against the State Church of Roman Catholic France; and his heroic energy and beneficence as a philanthropist, which now only makes the list of achievements on his monument at Ferney[31] the most impressive epitaph in Europe, then made the most earnest of the Lutheran ministers glad to claim a common inspiration with him. Unfortunately Voltaire had an irrepressible sense of humor. He joked about Habakkuk;[32] and jokes about Habakkuk smelt too strongly of brimstone to be tolerated by Protestants to whom the Bible was not a literature but a fetish and a talisman. And so Voltaire, in spite of the church he 'erected to God,' became in England the bogey-atheist of three generations of English ignoramuses, instead of the legitimate successor of Martin Luther and John Knox.[33]

Nowadays, however, Voltaire's jokes are either forgotten or else fall flat on a world which no longer venerates Habakkuk; and his true position is becoming apparent. The fact that Voltaire was a Roman Catholic layman, educated at a Jesuit college, is the conclusive reply to the shallow people who imagine that Ireland delivered up to the Irish democracy — that is, to the Catholic laity — would be delivered up to the tyranny of the priesthood.

SUPPOSE!

Suppose, now, that the conquest of France by Henry V of England had endured, and that France in the XVIII century had been governed by an English viceroy through a Huguenot bureaucracy and a judicial bench appointed on the understanding that loyalty for them meant loyalty to

28. King William of Orange, who defeated the catholic army of James II at the battle of the Boyne (1690), thereby establishing protestant ascendancy in Ireland.
29. anti-clericals.
30. Put an end to infamy (French). The catch-phrase was used by Voltaire in his writings and correspondence.
31. In 1758 Voltaire bought an estate, Ferney-Voltaire, on the French-Swiss border near Geneva. It became famous as a centre of his various crusades against intolerance and oppression.
32. Habakkuk was a minor prophet of the Old Testament.
33. John Knox (*c.* 1512-72), a leading radical protestant preacher and the dominant figure in the establishment of the Church of Scotland.

England, and patriotism a willingness to die in defence of the English conquest and of the English Church, would not Voltaire in that case have been the meanest of traitors and self-seekers if he had played the game of England by joining in its campaign against his own and his country's Church? The energy he threw into the defence of Calas and Sirven[34] would have been thrown into the defence of the Frenchmen whom the English would have called 'rebels'; and he would have been forced to identify the cause of freedom and democracy with the cause of 'l'infâme.' The French revolution would have been a revolution against England and English rule instead of against aristocracy and ecclesiasticism; and all the intellectual and spiritual forces in France, from Turgot to De Tocqueville,[35] would have been burnt up in mere anti-Anglicism and nationalist dithyrambs instead of contributing to political science and broadening the thought of the world.

What would have happened in France is what has happened in Ireland; and that is why it is only the small-minded Irish, incapable of conceiving what religious freedom means to a country, who do not loathe English rule. For in Ireland England is nothing but the Pope's policeman. She imagines she is holding the Vatican cardinals at bay when she is really strangling the Voltaires, the Foxes and Penns, the Cliffords, Hortons, Campbells, Walters, and Silvester Hornes, who are to be found among the Roman Catholic laity as plentifully as among the Anglican Catholic laity in England.[36] She gets nothing out of Ireland but infinite trouble, infinite confusion and hindrance in her own legislation, a hatred that circulates through the whole world and poisons it against her, a reproach that makes her professions of sympathy with Finland and Macedonia[37] ridiculous and hypocritical, whilst the priest takes all the spoils, in money, in power, in pride, and in popularity.

IRELAND'S REAL GRIEVANCE

But it is not the spoils that matter. It is the waste, the sterilization, the perversion of fruitful brain power into flatulent protest against unnecessary evil, the use of our very entrails to tie our own hands and seal our own lips in the name of our honor and patriotism. As far as money or comfort is concerned, the average Irishman has a more tolerable life — especially now that the population is so scanty — than the average Englishman. It is true that in Ireland the poor man is robbed and starved and oppressed under judicial forms which confer the imposing title of justice on a crude system of bludgeoning and perjury. But so is the Englishman. The Englishman, more docile, less dangerous, too lazy intellectually to use such political and legal power as lies within his reach, suffers more and makes less fuss about it than the Irishman. But at least he has nobody to blame but himself and his fellow countrymen. He does not doubt that if an effective majority of the English people made up their minds to alter the Constitution, as the majority of the Irish people have made up their minds to obtain Home Rule, they could alter it without having to fight an overwhelmingly powerful and rich neighboring nation, and fight, too, with ropes round their necks. He can attack any institution in his country without betraying it to foreign vengeance and foreign oppression. True, his landlord may turn him out of his cottage if he goes to a Methodist chapel instead of to the parish church. His customers may stop their orders if he votes Liberal instead of Conservative. English ladies and gentlemen who would perish sooner than shoot a fox do these things without the smallest sense of indecency and dishonor. But they cannot muzzle his intellectual leaders. The English philosopher, the English author, the English orator can attack every abuse and expose every superstition without strengthening the hands of any common enemy. In Ireland every such attack, every such exposure, is a service to England and a stab to Ireland. If you expose the tyranny and rapacity of the Church, it is an argument in favor of Protestant ascendancy. If you denounce the nepotism and jobbery of the new local authorities, you are demonstrating the unfitness of

34. Jean Calas and Elisabeth Sirven were two protestant victims of Catholic prejudice in France in the 1760s. Voltaire took up their cause and mobilized public opinion against these judicial crimes.
35. A. R. Jacques Turgot (1727-81), intellectual and financier; his dismissal from the post of controller general of France in 1776 was a prelude to the subsequent national bankruptcy. Alexis de Tocqueville (1805-59), the famous French political theorist and historian, wrote *Democracy in America* (1835-39) and *The Ancien Régime and the Revolution* (1850).
36. All these were opponents of despotic or intolerant church authorities and governments in British history.
37. Until 1898 the Russians respected Finland's autonomy, but the intensive Russification campaign of Tsar Nicholas II provoked determined resistance. Macedonia is a region of the Balkans, claimed by the Bulgarians, the Greeks and the Serbs in the latter part of the nineteenth century.

the Irish to govern themselves, and the superiority of the old oligarchical grand juries.

And there is the same pressure on the other side. The Protestant must stand by the garrison at all costs: the Unionist must wink at every bureaucratic abuse, connive at every tyranny, magnify every official blockhead, because their exposure would be a victory for the Nationalist enemy. Every Irishman is in Lancelot's position: his honor rooted in dishonor stands; and faith unfaithful keeps him falsely true.[38]

THE CURSE OF NATIONALISM

It is hardly possible for an Englishman to understand all that this implies. A conquered nation is like a man with cancer: he can think of nothing else, and is forced to place himself, to the exclusion of all better company, in the hands of quacks who profess to treat or cure cancer. The windbags of the two rival platforms are the most insufferable of all windbags. It requires neither knowledge, character, conscience, diligence in public affairs, nor any virtue, private or communal, to thump the Nationalist or Orange tub: nay, it puts a premium on the rancor or callousness that has given rise to the proverb that if you put an Irishman on a spit you can always get another Irishman to baste him. Jingo oratory in England is sickening enough to serious people: indeed one evening's mafficking[39] in London produced a determined call for the police. Well, in Ireland all political oratory is Jingo oratory; and all political demonstrations are maffickings. English rule is such an intolerable abomination that no other subject can reach the people. Nationalism stands between Ireland and the light of the world. Nobody in Ireland of any intelligence likes Nationalism any more than a man with a broken arm likes having it set. A healthy nation is as unconscious of its nationality as a healthy man of his bones. But if you break a nation's nationality it will think of nothing else but getting it set again. It will listen to no reformer, to no philosopher, to no preacher, until the demand of the Nationalist is granted. It will attend to no business, however vital, except the business of unification and liberation.

That is why everything is in abeyance in Ireland pending the achievement of Home Rule. The great movements of the human spirit which sweep in waves over Europe are stopped on the Irish coast by the English guns of the Pigeon House Fort.[40] Only a quaint little offshoot of English pre-Raphaelitism called the Gaelic movement has got a footing by using Nationalism as a stalking-horse, and popularizing itself as an attack on the native language of the Irish people, which is most fortunately also the native language of half the world, including England. Every election is fought on nationalist grounds; every appointment is made on nationalist grounds; every judge is a partisan in the nationalist conflict; every speech is a dreary recapitulation of nationalist twaddle; every lecture is a corruption of history to flatter nationalism or defame it; every school is a recruiting station; every church is a barrack; and every Irishman is unspeakably tired of the whole miserable business, which nevertheless is and perforce must remain his first business until Home Rule makes an end of it, and sweeps the nationalist and the garrison hack together into the dustbin.

There is indeed no greater curse to a nation than a nationalist movement, which is only the agonizing symptom of a suppressed natural function. Conquered nations lose their place in the world's march because they can do nothing but strive to get rid of their nationalist movements by recovering their national liberty. All demonstrations of the virtues of a foreign government, though often conclusive, are as useless as demonstrations of the superiority of artificial teeth, glass eyes, silver windpipes, and patent wooden legs to the natural products. Like Democracy, national self-government is not for the good of the people: it is for the satisfaction of the people: One Antonine emperor, one St Louis, one Richelieu,[41] may be worth ten democracies in point of what is called good government; but there is no satisfaction for the people in them. To deprive a dyspeptic of his dinner and hand it over to a man who can digest it

38. Alfred, Lord Tennyson, *Lancelot and Elaine* (1859), lines 870-71: 'His honour rooted in dishonour stood,/And faith unfaithful kept him falsely true.'
39. Hysterical rejoicing, such as occurred in the streets of London at the news of the relief of Mafeking (1900), during the Boer War.
40. Armoury for British forces on the south side of Dublin Bay.
41. Antoninus Pius (A.D. 86-161), Roman emperor who devoted himself to promoting the happiness of his people. Louis XI, king of France 1461-83, and Cardinal Richelieu (1585-1642) were among the greatest of French rulers and statesmen.

better is a highly logical proceeding; but it is not a sensible one. To take the government of Ireland away from the Irish and hand it over to the English on the ground that they can govern better would be a precisely parallel case if the English had managed their own affairs so well as to place their superior faculty for governing beyond question. But as the English are avowed muddlers — rather proud of it, in fact — even the logic of that case against Home Rule is not complete. Read Mr Charles Booth's account of London, Mr Rowntree's account of York,[42] and the latest official report on Dundee; and then pretend, if you can, that Englishmen and Scotchmen have not more cause to hand over their affairs to an Irish parliament than to clamor for another nation's cities to devastate and another people's business to mismanage.

A NATURAL RIGHT

The question is not one of logic at all, but of natural right. English universities have for some time past encouraged an extremely foolish academic exercise which consists in disproving the existence of natural rights on the ground that they cannot be deduced from the principles of any known political system. If they could, they would not be natural rights but acquired ones. Acquired rights are deduced from political constitutions; but political constitutions are deduced from natural rights. When a man insists on certain liberties without the slightest regard to demonstrations that they are not for his own good, nor for the public good, nor moral, nor reasonable, nor decent, nor compatible with the existing constitution of society, then he is said to claim a natural right to that liberty. When, for instance, he insists on living, in spite of the irrefutable demonstrations of many able pessimists, from the author of the book of Ecclesiastes to Schopenhauer,[43] that life is an evil, he is asserting a natural right to live. When he insists on a vote in order that his country may be governed according to his ignorance instead of the wisdom of the Privy Council, he is asserting a natural right to self-government. When he insists on guiding himself at 21 by his own inexperience and folly and immaturity instead of by the experience and sagacity of his father, or the well-stored mind of his grandmother, he is asserting a natural right to independence. Even if Home Rule were as unhealthy as an Englishman's eating, as intemperate as his drinking, as filthy as his smoking, as licentious as his domesticity, as corrupt as his elections, as murderously greedy as his commerce, as cruel as his prisons, and as merciless as his streets, Ireland's claim to self-government would still be as good as England's. King James the First proved so cleverly and conclusively that the satisfaction of natural rights was incompatible with good government that his courtiers called him Solomon.[44] We, more enlightened, call him Fool, solely because we have learnt that nations insist on being governed by their own consent — or, as they put it, by themselves and for themselves — and that they will finally upset a good government which denies them this even if the alternative be a bad government which at least creates and maintains an illusion of democracy. America, as far as one can ascertain, is much worse governed, and has a much more disgraceful political history than England under Charles I; but the American Republic is the stabler government because it starts from a formal concession of natural rights, and keeps up an illusion of safeguarding them by an elaborate machinery of democratic election. And the final reason why Ireland must have Home Rule is that she has a natural right to it.

A WARNING

Finally, some words of warning to both nations. Ireland has been deliberately ruined again and again by England. Unable to compete with us industrially, she has destroyed our industries by the brute force of prohibitive taxation. She was perfectly right. That brute force was a more honorable weapon than the poverty which we used to undersell her. We lived with and as our pigs, and let loose our wares in the Englishman's market at prices which he could compete with only by living like a pig himself. Having the alternative of stopping our industry altogether, he very naturally

42. Charles Booth (1840-1916), author of the monumental inquiry *Life and Labour of the People of London* (17 vols, 1891-1903). Seebohm Rowntree (born 1871) wrote a similar work on a smaller scale, *Poverty: A Study of Town Life* (1901), the setting of which was York.

43. Schopenhauer's *The World as Will and Idea* (1818) was an influential work throughout the nineteenth century. The general theme of the Old Testament book of Ecclesiastes is the vanity of human life.

44. James I of England (James VI of Scotland) who lived from 1566 to 1621 is reputedly the author of *True Law of Free Monarchies* (1598), in which he argues against the notion that the king is elected by and responsible to the people.

and properly availed himself of it. We should have done the same in his place. To bear malice against him on that score is to poison our blood and weaken our constitutions with unintelligent rancor. In wrecking all the industries that were based on the poverty of our people England did us an enormous service. In omitting to do the same on her own soil, she did herself a wrong that has rotted her almost to the marrow. I hope that when Home Rule is at last achieved, one of our first legislative acts will be to fortify the subsistence of our people behind the bulwark of a standard wage, and to impose crushing import duties on every English trade that flourishes in the slum and fattens on the starvation of our unfortunate English neighbors.

DOWN WITH THE SOLDIER!

Now for England's share of warning. Let her look to her Empire; for unless she makes it such a Federation for civil strength and defence that all free peoples will cling to it voluntarily, it will inevitably become a military tyranny to prevent them from abandoning it; and such a tyranny will drain the English taxpayer of his money more effectually than its worst cruelties can ever drain its victims of their liberty. A political scheme that cannot be carried out except by soldiers will not be a permanent one. The soldier is an anachronism of which we must get rid. Among people who are proof against the suggestions of romantic fiction there can no longer be any question of the fact that military service produces moral imbecility, ferocity, and cowardice, and that the defence of nations must be undertaken by the civil enterprise of men enjoying all the rights and liberties of citizenship, and trained by the exacting discipline of democratic freedom and responsibility. For permanent work the soldier is worse than useless: such efficiency as he has is the result of dehumanization and disablement. His whole training tends to make him a weakling. He has the easiest of lives: he has no freedom and no responsibility. He is politically and socially a child, with rations instead of rights, treated like a child, punished like a child, dressed prettily and washed and combed like a child, excused for outbreaks of naughtiness like a child, forbidden to marry like a child, and called Tommy like a child. He has no real work to keep him from going mad except housemaid's work: all the rest is forced exercise, in the form of endless rehearsals for a destructive and terrifying performance which may never come off, and which, when it does come off, is not like the rehearsals. His officer has not even housekeeper's work to keep him sane. The work of organizing and commanding bodies of men, which builds up the character and resource of the large class of civilians who live by it, only demoralizes the military officer, because his orders, however disastrous or offensive, must be obeyed without regard to consequences: for instance, if he calls his men dogs, and perverts a musketry drill order to make them kneel to him as an act of personal humiliation, and thereby provokes a mutiny among men not yet thoroughly broken in to the abjectness of the military condition, he is not, as might be expected, shot, but, at worst, reprimanded, whilst the leader of the mutiny, instead of getting the Victoria Cross and a public testimonial, is condemned to five years' penal servitude by Lynch Law (technically called martial law) administered by a trade union of officers. Compare with this the position of, for instance, our railway managers or our heads of explosive factories. They have to handle large bodies of men whose carelessness or insubordination may cause wholesale destruction of life and property; yet any of these men may insult them, defy them, or assault them without special penalties of any sort. The military commander dares not face these conditions: he lives in perpetual terror of his men, and will undertake their command only when they are stripped of all their civil rights, gagged, and bound hand and foot by a barbarous slave code. Thus the officer learns to punish, but never to rule; and when an emergency like the Indian Mutiny[45] comes, he breaks down; and the situation has to be saved by a few untypical officers with character enough to have retained their civilian qualities in spite of the messroom. This, unfortunately, is learnt by the public, not on the spot, but from Lord Roberts[46] fifty years later.

Besides the Mutiny we have had the Crimean and South African wars, the Dreyfus affair[47] in

45. A rebellion against British rule 1857-58, originating in the Bengal army of the East India Company, but eventually supported by some of the civilian population in the subcontinent's northern and central regions.

46. Lord Roberts (1832-1914) won the Victoria Cross in the Indian Mutiny, later became commander of the British forces in Ireland (1895). As commander-in-chief of the imperial forces in South Africa (1899-1900), he directed the campaign that captured Pretoria.

47. Alfred Dreyfus, an Alsatian Jewish army officer on the French general staff, was falsely imprisoned for treason in 1894. The Dreyfus

France, the incidents of the anti-militarist campaign by the Social-Democrats in Germany, and now the Denshawai affair in the Nile delta,[48] all heaping on us sensational demonstrations of the fact that soldiers pay the penalty of their slavery and outlawry by becoming, relatively to free civilians, destructive, cruel, dishonest, tyrannical, hysterical, mendacious, alarmists at home and terrorists abroad, politically reactionary, and professionally incapable. If it were humanly possible to militarize all the humanity out of a man, there would be absolutely no defence to this indictment. But the military system is so idiotically academic and impossible, and renders its victims so incapable of carrying it out with any thoroughness except when, in an occasional hysterical outburst of terror and violence, that hackneyed comedy of civil life, the weak man putting his foot down, becomes the military tragedy of the armed man burning, flogging, and murdering in a panic, that a body of soldiers and officers is in the main, and under normal circumstances, much like any other body of laborers and gentlemen. Many of us count among our personal friends and relatives officers whose amicable and honorable character seems to contradict everything I have just said about the military character. You have only to describe Lynch courts and acts of terrorism to them as the work of Ribbonmen, Dacoits, Moonlighters, Boxers,[49] or — to use the general term most familiar to them — 'natives,' and their honest and generous indignation knows no bounds: they feel about them like men, not like soldiers. But the moment you bring the professional side of them uppermost by describing precisely the same proceedings to them as the work of regular armies, they defend them, applaud them, and are ready to take part in them as if their humanity had been blown out like a candle. You find that there is a blind spot on their moral retina, and that this blind spot is the military spot.

The excuse, when any excuse is made, is that discipline is supremely important in war. Now most soldiers have no experience of war; and to assume that those who have are therefore qualified to legislate for it, is as absurd as to assume that a man who has been run over by an omnibus is thereby qualified to draw up wise regulations for the traffic of London. Neither our military novices nor our veterans are clever enough to see that in the field, discipline either keeps itself or goes to pieces; for humanity under fire is a quite different thing from humanity in barracks: when there is danger the difficulty is never to find men who will obey, but men who can command. It is in time of peace, when an army is either a police force (in which case its work can be better done by a civilian constabulary) or an absurdity, that discipline is difficult, because the wasted life of the soldier is unnatural, except to a lazy man, and his servitude galling and senseless, except to a docile one. Still, the soldier is a man, and the officer sometimes a gentleman in the literal sense of the word; and so, what with humanity, laziness, and docility combined, they manage to rub along with only occasional outbursts of mutiny on the one side and class rancor and class cowardice on the other.

They are not even discontented; for the military and naval codes simplify life for them just as it is simplified for children. No soldier is asked to think for himself, to judge for himself, to consult his own honor and manhood, to dread any consequence except the consequence of punishment to his own person. The rules are plain and simple; the ceremonies of respect and submission are as easy and mechanical as a prayer wheel; the orders are always to be obeyed thoughtlessly, however inept or dishonorable they may be. As the late Laureate[50] said in the two stinging lines in which he branded the British soldier with the dishonor of Esau, 'theirs not to reason why, theirs but to do and die.' To the moral imbecile and political sluggard these conditions are as congenial and attractive as they are abhorrent and intolerable to the William Tell temperament. Just as the most incorrigible criminal is always, we are told, the best behaved convict, so the man with least conscience and initiative makes the best behaved soldier, and that not wholly through mere fear of punishment, but through a genuine fitness for and consequent happiness in the childlike military life. Such men dread freedom and responsibility as a weak man dreads a risk or a heavy

affair split the France of the Third Republic so severely that the repercussions of the case survived long after Dreyfus's innocence had been established.

48. An instance of British military stupidity and violence in Egypt in June 1906 to which Shaw devotes a later section of this Preface.

49. The names, respectively, of Irish, Indian, Irish and Chinese groups, all given to organized violence against the established (British) authorities.

50. Alfred, Lord Tennyson (1809-92) in 'The Charge of the Light Brigade'.

burden; and the objection to the military system is that it tends to produce such men by a weakening disuse of the moral muscles. No doubt this weakness is just what the military system aims at, its ideal soldier being, not a complete man, but a docile unit of cannon-fodder which can be trusted to respond promptly and certainly to the external stimulus of a shouted order, and is intimidated to the pitch of being afraid to run away from a battle. It may be doubted whether even in the Prussian heyday of the system, when floggings of hundreds and even thousands of lashes were matters of ordinary routine, this detestable ideal was ever realized; but your courts-martial are not practical enough to take that into account: it is characteristic of the military mind continually to ignore human nature and cry for the moon instead of facing modern social facts and accepting modern democratic conditions. And when I say the military mind, I repeat that I am not forgetting the patent fact that the military mind and the humane mind can exist in the same person; so that an officer who will take all the civilian risks, from city traffic to fox-hunting, without uneasiness, and who will manage all the civil employees on his estate and in his house and stables without the aid of a Mutiny Act, will also, in his military capacity, frantically declare that he dare not walk about in a foreign country unless every crime of violence against an Englishman in uniform is punished by the bombardment and destruction of a whole village, or the wholesale flogging and execution of every native in the neighborhood, and also that unless he and his fellow officers have power, without the intervention of a jury, to punish the slightest self-assertion or hesitation to obey orders, however grossly insulting or disastrous those orders may be, with sentences which are reserved in civil life for the worst crimes, he cannot secure the obedience and respect of his men, and the country will accordingly lose all its colonies and dependencies, and be helplessly conquered in the German invasion which he confidently expects to occur in the course of a fortnight or so. That is to say, in so far as he is an ordinary gentleman he behaves sensibly and courageously; and in so far as he is a military man he gives way without shame to the grossest folly, cruelty, and poltroonery.[51] If any other profession in the world had been stained by these vices, and by false witness, forgery, swindling, torture, compulsion of men's families to attend their executions, digging up and mutilation of dead enemies, all wantonly added to the devastation proper to its own business, as the military profession has been within recent memory in England, France, and the United States of America (to mention no other countries), it would be very difficult to induce men of capacity and character to enter it. And in England it is, in fact, largely dependent for its recruits on the refuse of industrial life, and for its officers on the aristocratic and plutocratic refuse of political and diplomatic life, who join the army and pay for their positions in the more or less fashionable clubs which the regimental messes provide them with — clubs which, by the way, occasionally figure in ragging scandals as circles of extremely coarse moral character.

Now in countries which are denied Home Rule: that is, in which the government does not rest on the consent of the people, it must rest on military coercion; and the bureaucracy, however civil and legal it may be in form and even in the character of its best officials, must connive at all the atrocities of military rule, and become infected in the end with the chronic panic characteristic of militarism. . . .

TWENTYFOUR YEARS LATER.[52] The sequel to these events confirmed my unheeded warning with a sanguinary completeness of which I had no prevision. At Easter 1916 a handful of Irishmen seized the Dublin Post Office and proclaimed an Irish Republic, with one of their number, a schoolmaster named Pearse, as President. If all Ireland had risen at this gesture it would have been a serious matter for England, then up to her neck in the war against the Central Empires. But there was no response: the gesture was a complete failure. All that was necessary was to blockade the Post Office until its microcosmic republic was starved out and made ridiculous. What actually happened would be incredible if there were not so many living witnesses of it. From a battery planted at Trinity College (the Irish equivalent of Oxford University), and from a warship in the river Liffey, a bombardment was poured on the centre of the ciy which reduced more than a square mile of it to such a condition that when, in the following year, I was taken through Arras and Ypres to shew me what the German

51. dastardy, lack of spirit.

52. 1929.

artillery had done to these cities in two and a half years, I laughed and said, 'You should see what the British artillery did to my native city in a week.' It would not be true to say that not one stone was left upon another; for the marksmanship was so bad that the Post Office itself was left standing amid a waste of rubbish heaps; and enough scraps of wall were left for the British Army, which needed recruits, to cover with appeals to the Irish to remember Belgium lest the fate of Louvain[53] should befall their own hearths and homes.

Having thus worked up a harebrained romantic adventure into a heroic episode in the struggle for Irish freedom, the victorious artillerists proceeded to kill their prisoners of war in a drawn-out string of executions. Those who were executed accordingly became not only national heroes, but the martyrs whose blood was the seed of the present Irish Free State. Among those who escaped was its first President. Nothing more blindly savage, stupid, and terror-mad could have been devised by England's worst enemies. It was a very characteristic example of the mentality produced by the conventional gentleman-militarist education at Marlborough and Sandhurst[54] and the conventional gentleman-diplomatist education at Eton and Oxford, Harrow and Cambridge. Is it surprising that the Russian Soviet Government, though fanatically credulous as to the need for popular education, absolutely refused to employ as teachers anyone who had been touched by the equivalent public school and university routine in Russia, and stuck to its resolution even at the cost of carrying on for some years with teachers who were hardly a day ahead of their pupils?

But the Post Office episode was eclipsed by an event which was much more than an episode, as it shattered the whole case for parliamentary government throughout the world. The Irish Nationalists, after thirty years of constitutional procedure in the British Parliament, had carried an Act to establish Irish Home Rule,[55] as it was then called, which duly received the royal assent and became a statute of the realm.[56] Immediately the British officers on service in Ireland mutinied, refusing to enforce the Act or operate against the northern Orangemen who were openly arming themselves to resist it. They were assured of support by their fellow-officers at home. The Act was suspended after prominent English statesmen had taken part in the military manoeuvres of the Orangemen. The Prime Minister publicly pledged himself that Belfast, the Orange capital, would not in any case be coerced. In short, the Act was shelved under a threat of civil war; and the Clan na Gael,[57] which in America had steadfastly maintained that the constitutional movement was useless, as England would in the last resort repudiate the constitution and hold Ireland against the Irish by physical force, and had been rebuked, lectured, and repudiated by the parliamentary Home Rulers for a whole generation for saying so, was justified. The Catholic Irish accordingly armed themselves and drilled as Volunteers in spite of the hostility of the Government, which meanwhile gave every possible assistance to the parallel preparations of the Orangemen. An Irish parliament (or Dail) sat in Dublin and claimed to be the national government.[58] Irish courts were set up for the administration of Irish justice; Irish order was kept by Irish police; Irish taxes were collected by Irish officials; and British courts were boycotted. Upon this interesting but hopeless attempt to ignore British rule the Government let loose a specially recruited force (known to history as the Black and Tans) with *carte blanche* to kill, burn, and destroy, save only that they must stop short of rapine. They wrecked the Irish courts and produced a state of anarchy. They struck at the Irish through the popular co-operative stores and creameries, which they burnt. The people found a civil leader in Arthur Griffith and a military one in Michael Collins. The Black and Tans had the British Government at their back: Collins had the people at his back. He threatened that for every creamery or co-operative store or cabin or cottage burnt by the Black and Tans he would burn two country houses of the Protestant gentry. The country houses that were not burnt were raided at night and laid under contribution for needed supplies. If the occupants reported the raid, the house was burnt. The Black and Tans and the

53. The university library of this Belgium town was destroyed by German forces in 1914. Propaganda about German atrocities in Belgium was particularly intense in catholic Ireland.

54. Marlborough College is an English public school. Sandhurst is the headquarters of the Royal Military Academy for the training of officer cadets for the British army.

55. In 1912.

56. In 1914.

57. Irish-American organization, literally, in Irish, 'Family of the Gaels'.

58. In 1919.

ordinary constabulary were treated as enemies in uniform: that is, they were shot at sight and their stations burnt; or they were ambushed and killed in petty battles. Those who gave warnings or information of any helpful kind to them were mercilessly executed without privilege of sex or benefit of clergy. Collins, with allies in every street and hamlet, proved able to carry out his threat. He won the crown of the Reign of Terror; and the position of the Protestant gentry became unbearable.

Thus by fire and bullet, murder and torture and devastation, a situation was produced in which the British Government had either to capitulate at the cost of a far more complete concession of self-government to Ireland than that decreed by the repudiated Home Rule Act, or to let loose the military strength of England in a Cromwellian reconquest, massacre, and replantation which it knew that public opinion in England and America would not tolerate; for some of the most conspicuous English champions of Ulster warned the Government that they could stand no more of the Black and Tan terrorism. And so we settled the Irish Question, not as civilized and reasonable men should have settled it, but as dogs settle a dispute over a bone.

Future historians will probably see in these catastrophes a ritual of human sacrifice without which the savages of the twentieth century could not effect any redistribution of political power or wealth. Nothing was learnt from Denshawai or the Black and Tan terror. In India, which is still struggling for self-government, and obviously must finally have it, a military panic led to the cannonading of a forbidden public meeting at Amritsar, the crowd being dealt with precisely as if it were a body of German shocktroops rushing the British trenches in Flanders.[59] In London the police would have broken a score or two of heads and dragged a handful of ringleaders to the police courts. And there was the usual combination of mean spite with hyperbolical violence. Indians were forced to crawl past official buildings on their hands and knees. The effect was to make British imperial rule ridiculous in Europe, and implacably resented in India.

In Egypt the British domination died of Denshawai; but at its deathbed the British Sirdar was assassinated, whereupon the British Government, just then rather drunk after a sweeping election victory secured by an anti-Russian scare, announced to an amazed world that it was going to cut off the Nile at its source and destroy Egypt by stopping its water supply. Of course nothing happened but an ignominious climb down; but the incident illustrates my contention that our authority, when it is too far flung (as our patriotic rhapsodists put it),[60] goes stark mad at the periphery if a pin drops. As to what further panics and atrocities will ensue before India is left to govern itself as much as Ireland and Egypt now are I am in the dark until the event enlightens me. But on the folly of allowing military counsels to prevail in political settlements I may point to the frontiers established by the victors after the war of 1914-18. Almost every one of these frontiers has a new war implicit in it, because the soldier recognizes no ethnographical, linguistic, or moral boundaries: he demands a line that he can defend, or rather that Napoleon or Wellington could have defended; for he has not yet learnt to think of offence and defence in terms of airplanes which ignore his Waterloo ridges. And the inevitable nationalist rebellions against these military frontiers, and the atrocities by which they are countered, are in full swing as I write.

Meanwhile, John Bull's Other Island, though its freedom has destroyed all the romantic interest that used to attach to it, has become at last highly interesting to the student of political science as an experiment in political structure. Protestant Ulster, which armed against the rest of Ireland and defied the British Parliament to the cry of 'We wont have it,' meaning that they would die in the last ditch singing 'O God, our help in ages past'[61] rather than suffer or tolerate Home Rule, is now suffering and indeed hugging Home Rule on a much more homely scale than the Home Rulers ever demanded or dreamt of; for it has a Belfast Home Rule Parliament instead of an Irish one. And it has allowed Catholic Ireland to secure the Irish parliament. Thus, of the two regional parliaments

59. In Amritsar, Punjab on 13 April 1919, British troops under General Reginald Dyer fired on Indians who were demonstrating against the extension of the British government's emergency powers to combat subversive activity. Some 379 unarmed Indians were killed in the massacre and 1,200 injured.

60. Rudyard Kipling, 'Recessional': 'God of our fathers, known of old, Lord of our far-flung battle-line,/ Beneath whose awful Hand we hold/ Dominion over palm and pine —'.

61. Isaac Watts (1674-1748), 'Psalm 90'.

which have been established on a sectarian basis, Protestant Ulster has been left with the smaller. Now it happens that Protestant Ulster is industrial Ireland and Catholic Ireland agricultural Ireland. And throughout the world for a century past the farmer, the peasant, and the Catholic have been the bulwark of the industrial capitalists against the growing political power of the industrial proletariat organized in trade unions, Labor parties, and the ubiquitous sodalities of that new ultra-Catholic Church called Socialism.

From this defensive alliance the Ulster employers, blinded by an obsolete bigotry and snobbery, have deliberately cut themselves off. In my preface of 1906, and again in my 1912 preface to a six-penny edition of this play called the Home Rule edition, I exhorted the Protestants to take their chance, trust their grit, and play their part in a single parliament ruling an undivided Ireland. They did not take my advice. Probably they did not even read it, being too deeply absorbed in the History of Maria Monk,[62] or the latest demonstration that all the evil in the world is the work of an underground conspiracy entitled by them 'the Jesuits.' It is a pity they did not begin their political education, as I began mine, by reading Karl Marx. It is true that I had occasion to point out that Marx was not infallible; but he left me with a very strong disposition to back the economic situation to control all the other situations, religious, nationalist, or romantic, in the long run. And so I do not despair of seeing Protestant Ulster seeking the alliance it repudiated. The Northern Parliament will not merge into the Oireachtas;[63] for until both of them are superseded by a completely modernized central government, made for action and not for obstruction, they will remain more effective as regional parliaments than they would be as national ones; but they will soon have to take counsel together through conferences which will recur until they become a permanent institution and finally develop into what the Americans call Congress, or Federal Government of the whole island. No doubt this will be received in Belfast (if noticed at all) with shouts of 'We wont have it.' But I have heard that cry before, and regard it as a very hopeful sign that they will have it gladly enough when they have the luck to get it.

AYOT ST LAWRENCE,
November 1929.

COMPOSITE AUTOBIOGRAPHY (1969)

[Shaw, who spent most of his life talking about himself, never wrote an autobiography, although he is widely believed to have 'ghosted' parts of three early biographies of himself. 'The best autobiographies are confessions', he remarked in old age, 'but if a man is a deep writer, all his works are confessions'. The following extracts serve to sketch something of the Shavian background. The extracts are from the *Composite Autobiography* (*Vol. I, 1856-98*), edited by Stanley Weintraub, 1969.]

'THE MOTHER'

When my mother grew up, she knew thorough-bass as taught by her musicmaster Johann Bernhard Logier (famous in Dublin as the inventor of the chiroplast, a mechanical finger exerciser which set his piano pupils all wrong); she could repeat two of La Fontaine's fables in French with perfect pronunciation; she could carry herself with complete dignity; and she could have worked as a ragpicker without losing her entire conviction that she was a lady, of a species apart from servants and common persons. But she could not housekeep on a small income; she had no notion of the value of money; she detested her grand aunt and regarded all that had been taught her as religion and discipline as tyranny and slavery. Consequently, as she was naturally very humane, she abandoned her own children to the most complete anarchy. Both my parents, as it happened, were utterly uncoercive.

In due time she was floated in Dublin society to get married. Among other persons with whom she came in contact was George Carr Shaw, an apparently harmless gentleman of forty, with a squint and a vein of humor which delighted in anti-climax, and would have made him an appreciative listener for Charles Lamb. He was a member of a large family which spoke of itself as 'the Shaws,' and got invited, on the strength of a second cousinship, to Bushy Park, the seat of the bachelor Sir Robert Shaw, Bart., as to whom see

62. Maria Monk, *The Awful Disclosures of Maria Monk* (New York, 1836), a popular and lurid account of life in a catholic convent. It is mentioned in the 'Wandering Rocks' episode of *Ulysses*.
63. Irish name for the Irish political system, comprising the President, the Senate (upper house) and Dáil (lower house).

Burke's Landed Gentry. George Carr Shaw seemed very safe company for my carefully guarded mother, because nobody could conceive his having the audacity, the enterprise, nor the means, to marry anybody, even if it could be supposed that his years or his squint could appeal to so well brought-up a female as Miss Lucinda Elizabeth Gurly. He was therefore well spoken of to her by her relatives as a quite eligible person to know in a general social way. They forgot that, having never been taught what marriage really means, nor experienced impecuniosity, she might marry any adventurer without knowing how much she was doing.

Her tragedy came about by external pressure of a sort that nobody could have foreseen....

I can only imagine the hell into which my mother descended when she found out what shabby-genteel poverty with a drunken husband is like. She told me once that when they were honeymooning in Liverpool (of all places) she opened her bridegroom's wardrobe and found it full of empty bottles. In the first shock of the discovery she ran away to the docks to get employed as a stewardess and be taken out of the country. But on the way she was molested by some rough docklanders and had to run back again.

I have elsewhere recorded how, when my father, taking me for a walk, pretended in play to throw me into the canal, he very nearly did it. When we got home I said to my mother as an awful and hardly credible discovery 'Mamma: I think Papa is drunk.' This was too much for her. She replied 'When is he anything else?'

It is a rhetorical exaggeration to say that I have never since believed in anything or anybody; but the wrench from my childish faith in my father as perfect and omniscient to the discovery that he was a hypocrite and a dipsomaniac was so sudden and violent that it must have left its mark on me....

My mother's salvation came through music. She had a mezzo-soprano voice of extraordinary purity of tone; and to cultivate it she took lessons from George John Vandeleur Lee, already well established in Dublin as an orchestral conductor, an organizer of concerts, and a teacher of singing so heterodox and original that he depended for his performances on amateurs trained by himself, and was detested by his professional rivals, whom he disparaged as voice wreckers, as indeed they mostly were. He extended this criticism to doctors, and amazed us by eating brown bread instead of white, and sleeping with the window open, both of which habits I acquired and have practised ever since. His influence in our household, of which he at last became a member, accustomed me to the scepticism as to academic authority which still persists in me.

He not only made my mother sing by a method that preserved her voice perfectly until her death at over eighty but gave her a Cause and a Creed to live for.

Those who know my play Misalliance, in which the lover has three fathers, will note that I also had a natural father and two supplementaries, making three varieties for me to study. This widened my outlook very considerably. Natural parents should bear in mind that the more supplementaries their children find, at school or elsewhere, the better they will know that it takes all sorts to make a world. Also that though there is always the risk of being corrupted by bad parents, the natural ones may be — probably ten per cent of them actually are — the worst of the lot.

'THE FATHER'

My parents took no moral responsibility for me. I was just something that happened to them and had to be put up with and supported. I never suffered the meddlesomeness of those morbidly conscientious parents who are so busy with their children's characters that they have no time to look after their own. I cannot remember having ever heard a single sentence uttered by my mother in the nature of moral or religious instruction. My father made an effort or two. When he caught me imitating him by pretending to smoke a toy pipe he advised me very earnestly never to follow his example in any way; and his sincerity so impressed me that to this day I have never smoked, never shaved, and never used alcoholic stimulants. He taught me to regard him as an unsuccessful man with many undesirable habits, as a warning and not as a model. In fact he did himself some injustice lest I should grow up like him; and I now see that this anxiety on his part was admirable and lovable; and that he was really just what he so carefully strove not to be: that is, a model father....

... Let me tell you a story of my father. When I was a child, he gave me my first dip in the sea in Killiney Bay. He prefaced it by a very serious exhortation on the importance of learning to swim, culminating in these words 'When I was a boy of only fourteen, my knowledge of swimming enabled me to save your Uncle Robert's life.' Then, seeing that I was deeply impressed, he stooped, and added confidentially in my ear 'and, to tell you the truth, I never was so sorry for anything in my life afterwards.' He then plunged into the ocean, enjoyed a thoroughly refreshing swim, and chuckled all the way home.

Now I have never aimed consciously at anti-climax:[1] it occurs naturally in my work. But there is no doubt some connection between my father's chuckling and the enjoyment produced in the theatre by my comedic methods....

'THE SCHOOL'

Why did the Model School[2] afflict me with a shame which was more or less a psychosis? I have told elsewhere that my esthetic hatred of poverty and squalor, and of the species of human animal they produce, was acquired not at the Model School, where the boys were not worse clad and fed than I, but in the slums into which my nursemaid took me on her visits to her friends when she was supposed to be exercising me in the parks. I hated these experiences intensely. My artist nature, to which beauty and refinement were necessities, would not accept poor people as fellowcreatures, nor slum tenements as fit for human habitation. To me they were places where I could not possibly live. The mental process thus set up culminated some fifty years later in my play Major Barbara, in which the millionaire saint, Andrew Undershaft, thunders his doctrine that poverty is not the natural and proper punishment of vice, but a social crime compared to which our sporadic murders and thefts are negligible....

At the Model School I had already asserted myself in another direction. The reading lessons in history ignored Ireland and glorified England. I always substituted Ireland for England in such dithyrambs.[3] The boys wondered what would happen to me. But the teacher smiled and said nothing. I was, in fact, a young Fenian in my political sympathies, such as they were....

'THE EXILE'

I did not set foot in Ireland again until 1905, and not then on my own initiative. I went back to please my wife; and a curious reluctance to retrace my steps made me land in the south and enter Dublin through the backdoor from Meath rather than return as I came, through the front door on the sea. In 1876 I had had enough of Dublin. James Joyce in his Ulysses had described, with a fidelity so ruthless that the book is hardly bearable, the life that Dublin offers to its young men, or, if you prefer to put it the other way, that its young men offer to Dublin. No doubt it is much like the life of young men everywhere in modern urban civilization. A certain flippant futile derision and belittlement that confuses the noble and serious with the base and ludicrous seems to me peculiar to Dublin; but I suppose that is because my only personal experience of that phase of youth was a Dublin experience; for when I left my native city I left that phase behind me, and associated no more with men of my age until, after about eight years of solitude in this respect, I was drawn into the Socialist revival of the early eighties, among Englishmen intensely serious and burning with indignation at very real and very fundamental evils that affected all the world; so that the reaction against them bound the finer spirits of all the nations together instead of making them cherish hatred of one another as a national virtue. Thus, when I left Dublin I left (a few private friendships apart) no society that did not disgust me. To this day my sentimental regard for Ireland does not include the capital. I am not enamored of failure, of poverty, of obscurity, and of the ostracism and contempt which these imply; and these were all that Dublin offered to the enormity of my unconscious ambition. The cities a man likes are the cities he has conquered. Napoleon did not turn from Paris to sentimentalize over Ajaccio, nor Catherine from St Petersburg to Stettin as the centre of her universe.

... I never thought of myself as destined to become what is called a great man: indeed I was diffident to the most distressing degree; and I was

1. The ending to a Shavian play is often ambiguous and oddly unemphatic. The diagnostic early acts invariably seem much stronger than the closing ones, which, as in *John Bull's Other Island*, shun the prescriptive. A noted unmasker, Shaw is less famous for positive proposals.
2. The Central Model School, Marlborough Street, Dublin, attended mainly by the sons of lower middle-class shopkeepers and tradesmen, all catholic, although in theory the school was non-denominational. As a result of his attendance, Shaw was shunned by other protestant boys and 'lost caste'. He dropped out in protest after six months.
3. Ancient greek hymns, or rapturous poems.

ridiculously credulous as to the claims of others to superior knowledge and authority. But one day in the office I had a shock. One of the apprentices, by name C. J. Smyth, older than I and more a man of the world, remarked that every young chap thought he was going to be a great man. On a really modest youth this commonplace would have had no effect. It gave me so perceptible a jar that I suddenly became aware that I had never thought I was to be a great man simply because I had always taken it as a matter of course. The incident passed without leaving any preoccupation with it to hamper me; and I remained as diffident as ever because I was still as incompetent as ever. But I doubt whether I ever recovered my former complete innocence of subconscious intention to devote myself to the class of work that only a few men excel in, and to accept the responsibilities that attach to its dignity.

Now this bore directly on my abandonment of Dublin, for which many young Irishmen of today find it impossible to forgive me. My business in life could not be transacted in Dublin out of an experience confined to Ireland. I had to go to London just as my father had to go to the Corn Exchange. London was the literary centre for the English language, and for such artistic culture as the realm of the English language (in which I proposed to be king) could afford. There was no Gaelic League[4] in those days, nor any sense that Ireland had in herself the seed of culture. Every Irishman who felt that his business in life was on the higher planes of the cultural professions felt that he must have a metropolitan domicile and an international culture: that is, he felt his first business was to get out of Ireland. I had the same feeling. For London as London, or England as England, I cared nothing.... But as the English language was my weapon, there was nothing for it but London....

4. A society founded in 1893 for the preservation of the Irish language and culture. It was so successful that by turn of the century it aimed at the restoration of Irish throughout Ireland.

THE PROTESTANTS OF IRELAND (1912)

[Shaw delivered this address on 6 December 1912 in the Memorial Hall, London, in the same year as the Ulster Volunteer Force was founded to fight Home Rule. The speech later appeared in a pamphlet, *What Irish Protestants Think: Speeches on Home Rule*.]

I am an Irishman; my father was an Irishman, and my mother an Irishwoman; and my father and my mother were Protestants, who would have been described by a large section of their fellow countrymen in the ruder age when I was young sanguinary Protestants. Many of the duties of my mother were shared by an Irish nurse, who was a Catholic, and she never put me to bed without sprinkling me with Holy Water. What is there to laugh at in an Irish Catholic woman sprinkling with Holy Water — and you know what Holy Water meant to her — a little Protestant infant, whose parents grossly underpaid her? The fact that you can laugh at the underpayment of a poor Irishwoman shews how this open wound of the denial of our National rights is keeping us a hundred years behind the rest of the world on social and industrial questions. I shall make a few jokes for you presently, as you seem to expect them from me; but I beg you not to laugh at them until I come to them. To my mind this relation of mine to my old nurse is not a thing to be laughed at. It is a pathetic and sacred relation, and it disposes completely of the notion that between the Catholic and the Irish Protestant there be any natural animosity.

Though I have been before the British public as a political speaker for thirty years, this is the first time I have ever spoken in public on the subject of Home Rule. During that period I have taken part more or less in all the General Elections at which Home Rule was at stake. I have heard English party politicians desperately trying to excite themselves about it, and to excite their audiences about it; and I have never once heard them succeed. You may take it from me that the British electorate does not care a rap about Home Rule or Ireland. It is hard enough to induce them to take an interest in their own affairs, it is impossible to make them take an interest in ours. Why should they? They know too well that they do not govern us any more than they govern themselves. Ireland is not governed by Englishmen, but by a handful of Irishmen who exploit our country in the name of England as far as the Irish democracy will stand it.

My own personal feeling in the matter is curiously unreasonable. I will not defend it; but I will tell you what it is. My career has been in many respects a most deserving one. I have displayed all the virtues set out in Smiles's Self-Help.[1] I have won a position of some distinction [a voice: 'That was the Holy Water'] — well, many less plausible explanations are current. But the confession I have to make is that, while none of these distinctions which I have achieved by the exercise of the copybook virtues has ever given me a moment's self-complacency, the mere geographical accident of my birth, for which I deserve no credit whatever — this fact that I am an Irishman — has always filled me with a wild and inextinguishable pride. I am also proud of being a Protestant, though Protestantism is to me a great historic movement of Reformation, Aspiration, and Self-Assertion against spiritual tyrannies rather than that organization of false gentility which so often takes its name in vain in Ireland. Already at this meeting pride in Protestantism as something essentially Irish has broken out again and again. I cannot describe what I feel when English Unionists are kind enough to say, 'Oh, you are in danger of being persecuted by your Roman Catholic fellow countrymen. England will protect you.' I would rather be burnt at the stake by Irish Catholics than protected by Englishmen. We Protestants know perfectly well that we are quite able to take care of ourselves, thank you. I do not want to banish religion from politics, though I do want to abolish the thing miscalled religion in this controversy from the world altogether. I want to bring religion back into politics. There is nothing that revolts me in the present state of things more than the unnatural religious calm in Ireland. I do not want a peaceful Ireland in that sense. I want a turbulent Ireland. All free and healthy nations are full of the turbulence of controversy, political, religious, social: all sorts of controversy. Without it you can have no progress, no life.

In Ireland we Protestant Nationalists dare not utter a controversial word lest we should be misunderstood on the great question of national rights. I have much to say in criticism of Catholicism in Ireland; but I dare not say it lest I should be supposed to speaking on behalf of Unionism. I have quite as much to say in criticism of Irish Protestantism; but that, too, I must not say lest I should discredit my Protestant colleagues against the day when they will have to claim their share in the self-government of Ireland — and let me say that it will be an important share; for our Catholics are far too amiable and indulgent to take care of public money as Protestants do. The Local Government Act of 1898 made a revolutionary change from the most extreme form of Oligarchy to the most extreme form of Democracy; but we Protestants are kept out of the local council because it is feared that the return of a Protestant would be a triumph for Unionism. The denial of Home Rule corrupts every election and every division in Parliament. Consider the Land Purchase Acts; to some of us they are the salvation of Ireland. To me they are its damnation — the beginning of landlordism all over again on a poorer and therefore a worse and more oppressive scale. Many thought as I did; but we all had to be unanimous in support of the Acts, because to oppose them would have been to go over to the enemy. We Irish Protestants are bound and gagged at every turn by the Union.

As to the persecution scare, I decline to give any guarantees. I am not going to say, 'Please, kind English masters, if you give us Home Rule we will be good boys.' We will persecute and be persecuted if we like, as the English do; we are not children: we do not offer conditions of good behavior as the price of our national rights. No nation should be called upon to make such conditions. Wherever there is a Church, that Church will persecute if it can; but the remedy for that is Democracy. We Protestants will take our chance. If you come to that, think of the chances our Catholic priesthood is taking! Look at what has happened to them in Free France! Look at what has happened to them in Rome itself! Many of them would be glad enough to be safe in the island of the saints. I am far more anxious about the future of the unfortunate English when they lose us. What will they do without us to think for them? The English are a remarkable race; but they have no commonsense. We never lose our commonsense. The English people say that if we got Home Rule we should cut each other's throats. Who has a better right to cut them? They are very glad to get us to cut the throats of their enemies. Why should we not have the same privilege among ourselves? What will prevent it? The natural resistance of the other Irishmen.

Mr Chairman, what I have said must not be taken as a reasoned case for Home Rule as a good bargain for the parties. This is not what we are here

1. Samuel Smiles (1812-1904) won much success with his studies of the protestant ethic, starting with *Self-Help* (1859), and followed by such titles as *Character*, *Thrist*, and *Duty*.

for; and it is not what the question will finally turn on. I leave such special pleading to the lawyers who are ashamed to call themselves Irishmen, though they have no objection to be called Irish officials. What I have uttered is a purposely unguarded expression of the real feelings and instincts of a Protestant Irishman.

A NOTE ON AGGRESSIVE NATIONALISM (1913)

[This article appeared in *The New Statesman* on 12 July 1913, which happens to be the festive day of Ulster Unionists, who, by tradition, mark their political power over their catholic and Irish nationalist neighbours by ostentatious marches to the beat of a Lambeg drum.]

The world seems just now to have made up its mind that self-consciousness is a very undesirable thing and Nationalism a very fine thing. This is not a very intelligent conclusion; for, obviously, Nationalism is nothing but a mode of self-consciousness, and a very aggressive one at that. It is, I think, altogether to Ireland's credit that she is extremely tired of the subject of herself. Even patriotism, which in England is a drunken jollity when it is not a Jewish rhapsody, is in Ireland like the genius of Jeremiah, a burning fire shut up in the bones, a pain, a protest against shame and defeat, a morbid condition which a healthy man must shake off if he is to keep sane. If you want to bore an Irishman, play him an Irish melody, or introduce him to another Irishman. The modern Irish theatre began with the Kathleen ni Houlihan of Mr Yeats and Lady Gregory's Rising of the Moon, in which the old patriotism stirred and wrung its victims; but when the theatre thus established called on Young Ireland to write Irish plays and found a national school of drama, the immediate result was a string of plays of Irish life — and very true to life they were — in which the heroines proclaimed that they were sick of Ireland and rated[1] their Nationalist husbands for sacrificing all the realities of life to senseless Fenian maunderings, and the heroes damned Ireland up hill and down dale in the only moments of enthusiasm their grey lives left possible.

Abroad, however, it is a distinction to be an Irishman; and accordingly the Irish in England flaunt their nationality. An Englishman who had married an Irishwoman once came to me and asked me could I give him the name of any Englishman who had ever done anything. He explained that his wife declared that all England's statesmen, all her warriors, all her musical composers, all her notables of every degree were Irishmen, and that the English could not write their names until the Irish taught them. I suggested Gladstone. 'She says he was an Irishman' was the reply. After this, it was clear that the man's case was desperate; so I left him to his fate.

From this you may gather that the reaction against the Nationalist variety of self-consciousness does not, unfortunately, mean a reaction against conceit, against ignorance, against insular contempt for foreigners, against bad manners and the other common human weaknesses which sometimes masquerade as patriotism. Ireland produces virulent varieties of all of them; for it is, on the whole, a mistake to suppose that we are a nation of angels. You can always find something better than a good Englishman and something worse than a bad one; but this is not so in Ireland: a bad Irishman is the vilest thing on earth, and a good one is a saint. Thackeray's Barry Lyndon[2] is a very accurate sketch of the sort of thoroughpaced scoundrel Ireland can produce, not when she is put to it, but quite wantonly, merely for the fun of being mischievous. In point of conceit, Ireland, especially Northern Ireland, can stagger humanity. The Ulster Unionist is not a shrewd calculator who, on a careful estimate of the pressure of public opinion on any Government which should try to coerce Belfast into submission to a Dublin Parliament, concludes that he can safely bluff Home Rule out of Ulster: he really believes, as so many of the Boer farmers[3] believed, that he can fight and conquer the British Empire, or any other empire that is not Ulster and Protestant. This is not a respectable infatuation; and if there were nothing else to be considered except the salvation of the Ulsterman's soul, it would be a positive duty for the British Empire to blow him sky high to convince him that even a Unionist God (and he believes in no other, and therefore does not really believe in God at all) has

1. i.e. berated.

2. *The Luck of Barry Lyndon*, a novel by W. M. Thackeray, whose eponymous hero is an Irishman.

3. South African militant whites who rose against the British, with the assistance of such Irish nationalists as Major John MacBride (husband of Maud Gonne).

occasionally to look beyond Down and Antrim.

A new siege of Derry[4] under a capable commander would be an invaluable corrective to the old one, as it would last about ten minutes, and end in an ignominious surrender of as much of Derry as might be left. But these military moral lessons, fashionable as they are, cost more than the souls of the regenerated (not to mention the bodies of those they kill) are worth; and it would, I think, be more sensible to make Ulster an autonomous political lunatic asylum, with Sir Edward Carson[5] as head keeper, and an expensive fleet and a heavily fortified frontier to hold against the Pope, than to thwart its inclinations in any way. The alternative, if England would stand it, would be to make Ulster a province of England, and have the Education Acts and the Factory Acts applied in the English manner; but I doubt if Ulster would tamely submit to be identified with a country where men touch their hats to a Roman Catholic duke of Norfolk, and meet him at dinner as if he were their equal. On the whole, the notion of a Kingdom of Orangia (Ibsen invented the name in The Master Builder) is the more amusing. When it came to paying for the frontier fortifications and the new Harland and Wolff[6] fleet, the South would smile sunnily.

What will finally settle the Ulster question, probably, is just the old-fashioned romantic Nationalism of which the South is so deadly tired. That hackneyed fisherman who saw the round towers of other days in the waves beneath him shining,[7] pursued his not very lucrative occupation on the banks of Lough Neagh, and was no doubt an Orangeman. Now it happens that the true Ulsterman is a harsh father; and his son's chief joy when he is old enough to dare to differ from his violent and bigoted parent is to profess every opinion that can defy and exasperate the old man. And, indeed, it is clear, as the world is now constituted, that prudent young men should aim at being as unlike Orangemen and as like human beings as possible, even as in the South the young men are discovering that in point of insufferableness there is not a halfpenny to choose between a Nationalist and an Orangeman. Thus, though the Protestant boys will still carry the drum, they will carry it under the green flag, and realize that the harp, the hound, and the round tower are more satisfactory to the imagination than that stupidest of decorative designs the Union Jack, which, it must be admitted, is, considered merely as a decorative design, the most resourceless of patterns. And the change can be effected without treachery to England; for if my personal recollection does not deceive me, the Gaelic League began in Bedford Park, London, W., after a prolonged incubation in Somerset House.

It is not very long since I stood on the coast of Donegal and asked two boys how many languages they had. They had three. One was English, which they spoke much better than it is ever spoken in England. The second was Irish, which they spoke with their parents. The third was the language invented by the Gaelic League, which I cannot speak (being an Irishman), but which I understand to be in its qualities comparable to a blend of Esperanto with fifth-century Latin. Why should not Ulster adopt this strange tongue? Its very name suggests Scotland, which is what the present vernacular of the North also suggests.

The truth is that all the Nationalist inventions that catch on now are not Irish at all. For instance, the admirable comedies of Synge, who, having escaped from Ireland to France, drew mankind in the manner of Molière, and discreetly assured the public that this was merely the human nature of the Blasket Islands,[8] and that, of course, civilized people never admired boastful criminals nor esteemed them according to the atrocities they pretended to commit. The Playboy's real name was Synge; and the famous libel on Ireland (and who is Ireland that she should not be libeled as other countries are by their great comedians?) was the truth about the world.

4. The protestant Apprentice Boys held the city against the attacking Jacobite army in 1689.
5. A founding-father of twentieth-century Ulster unionism.
6. A noted shipbuilding firm in Belfast, with a mainly protestant workforce.
7. Thomas Moore, 'Let Erin remember the days of old', from *Irish Melodies*: 'as the fisherman strays . . . He sees the round towers of other days/In the wave beneath him shining.'
8. Small, windswept islands off the west Kerry coast, later featured in the writings of Thomas O'Crohan and Peig Sayers.

from:
HOW TO SETTLE THE IRISH QUESTION (1917)

[In November 1917 Shaw was urged by the editor of the *Daily Express* to contribute an essay on the deteriorating situation in Ireland. He was initially reluctant to write for a conservative paper, which represented all that he most scorned; but the editor, R. D. Blumenfeld, prevailed upon him, with the argument that Shaw might regard his article as missionary work among the enemy rather than cosy preaching to the already-converted. The piece appeared not just in the *Daily Express*, but in a number of Irish papers, in November 1917, and in some leading American journals in the following weeks.]

... Surely, of all sorts of dependence, the most abjectly wretched is that in which a minor State is helplessly dependent on a powerful neighbor, who accepts no responsibility for her and shares nothing with her, but makes her soil the no-man's-land between two frontiers hostile when war breaks out. If the English had a pennyworth of political sagacity instead of being, as they are, incorrigible Sinn Feiners almost to the last man, they would long ago have brought the Irish Separatists to their senses by threatening them with independence. It is as plain as the stars in heaven that if England tried to cast Ireland off, it would be necessary for Ireland, if she could, to make war on England, as Lincoln made war on Jefferson Davis, to maintain the Union.[1] Yet here are these two sets of fools: one repudiating an invaluable alliance in the name of freedom, and the other insisting on conferring the boon by force in the guise of conquest. How Irish on the part of the English! How English on the part of the Irish!

Sinn Fein has one other pseudo-practical cry: Fiscal Autonomy. And if Sinn Fein does not think better of it, Sinn Fein will get what it is inconsiderately demanding. For here again it is quite clear that England has everything to gain and Ireland everything to lose by separate banking accounts. It means shilling telegrams for Ireland and ninepenny ones for England, with postage rates to correspond. It means grants-in-aid to all the English counties for housing, education, public health, roads, and railways, out of the colossal fund of British rent nationalized by supertaxation, and nothing for the Irish counties. It means rents and taxes collected in Ireland spent in munition-making in England.

When Blücher[2] saw London he said, 'What a city to loot!' That is how I, as an Irish Socialist, feel about London and her ground rents. Sinn Fein wants to protect London from me, and thinks that in doing so it will be protecting Dublin. *Sancta simplicitas!*[3] The beggar refuses to pool with the millionaire; and the millionaire, terrified, calls for horse, foot, and artillery to force the beggar to rifle his pockets. When people ask me what Sinn Fein means, I reply that it is Irish for John Bull. . . .

1. Shaw is referring to the American Civil War (1861-65), sparked when Abraham Lincoln (1809-65) was elected US president. Jefferson Davis (1808-89) was the president of the Southern confederacy.
2. Gebhard Leberecht von Blücher (1742-1819), the Prussian field marshal who fought with Wellington at the battle of Waterloo in 1815.

3. Sacred simplicity!

O'FLAHERTY V.C.
A RECRUITING PAMPHLET (1915)

[Late in 1915, the officials of the Vice-Regal Lodge in Dublin voiced to Shaw their concern at the failure of the drive to recruit Irish troops for the British army. Shaw criticized their campaign as an ineffective call to romantic British patriotism, and advised them instead to appeal to practical Irish self-interest. He submitted a drafting poster, outling concrete reasons why Irishmen should enlist, but it was never used by the Dublin authorities. Moreover, his short 1915 recruiting play, *O'Flaherty V.C.*, had its proposed production at the Abbey Theatre cancelled, due to pressure from Dublin Castle, which presumably considered its perceptive comedy quite inappropriate to its avowed purpose.

'VC' stands for Victoria Cross, the highest honour for bravery which the British army can bestow. A number of Irishmen won it in both world wars.

O'Flaherty V.C. was, as it transpired, not performed until many years after the war had ended.]

It may surprise some people to learn that in 1915 this little play was a recruiting poster in disguise. The British officer seldom likes Irish soldiers; but he always tries to have a certain proportion of them in his battalion, because, partly from a want of common sense which leads them to value their lives less than Englishmen do (lives are really less worth living in a poor country), and partly because even the most cowardly Irishman feels obliged to outdo an Englishman in bravery if possible, and at least to set a perilous pace for him, Irish soldiers give impetus to those military operations which require for their spirited execution more devilment than prudence.

Unfortunately, Irish recruiting was badly bungled in 1915. The Irish were for the most part

Roman Catholics and loyal Irishmen, which means that from the English point of view they were heretics and rebels. But they were willing enough to go soldiering on the side of France and see the world outside Ireland, which is a dull place to live in. It was quite easy to enlist them by approaching them from their own point of view. But the War Office insisted on approaching them from the point of view of Dublin Castle. They were discouraged and repulsed by refusals to give commissions to Roman Catholic officers, or to allow distinct Irish units to be formed. To attract them, the walls were covered with placards headed REMEMBER BELGIUM. The folly of asking an Irishman to remember anything when you want him to fight for England was apparent to everyone outside the Castle: FORGET AND FORGIVE would have been more to the point. Remembering Belgium and its broken treaty led Irishmen to remember Limerick and its broken treaty;[1] and the recruiting ended in a rebellion, in suppressing which the British artillery quite unnecessarily reduced the centre of Dublin to ruins, and the British commanders killed their leading prisoners of war in cold blood morning after morning with an effect of long drawn out ferocity. Really it was only the usual childish petulance in which John Bull does things in a week that disgrace him for a century, though he soon recovers his good humor, and cannot understand why the survivors of his wrath do not feel as jolly with him as he does with them. On the smouldering ruins of Dublin the appeals to remember Louvain were presently supplemented by a fresh appeal. IRISHMEN: DO YOU WISH TO HAVE THE HORRORS OF WAR BROUGHT TO YOUR OWN HEARTHS AND HOMES? Dublin laughed sourly.

As for me, I addressed myself quite simply to the business of obtaining recruits. I knew by personal experience and observation what anyone might have inferred from the records of Irish emigration, that all an Irishman's hopes and ambitions turn on his opportunities of getting out of Ireland. Stimulate his loyalty, and he will stay in Ireland and die for her; for, incomprehensible as it seems to an Englishman, Irish patriotism does not take the form of devotion to England and England's king. Appeal to his discontent, his deadly boredom, his thwarted curiosity and desire for change and adventure, and, to escape from Ireland, he will go abroad to risk his life for France, for the Papal States, for secession in America, and even, if no better may be, for England. Knowing that the ignorance and insularity of the Irishman is a danger to himself and to his neighbors, I had no scruple in making that appeal when there was something for him to fight which the whole world had to fight unless it meant to come under the jack boot of the German version of Dublin Castle.

There was another consideration, unmentionable by the recruiting sergeants and war orators, which must nevertheless have helped them powerfully in procuring soldiers by voluntary enlistment. The happy home of the idealist may become common under millennial conditions. It is not common at present. No one will ever know how many men joined the army in 1914 and 1915 to escape from tyrants and taskmasters, termagants and shrews, none of whom are any the less irksome when they happen by ill-luck to be also our fathers, our mothers, our wives and our children. Even at their amiablest, a holiday from them may be a tempting change for all parties. That is why I did not endow O'Flaherty V.C. with an ideal Irish colleen for his sweetheart, and gave him for his mother a Volumnia[2] of the potato patch rather than an affectionate parent from whom he could not so easily have torn himself away.

I need hardly say that a play thus carefully adapted to its purpose was voted utterly inadmissible; and in due course the British Government, frightened out of its wits for the moment by the rout of the Fifth Army, ordained Irish Conscription, and then did not dare to go through with it. I still think my own line was the more businesslike. But during the war everyone except the soldiers at the front imagined that nothing but an extreme assertion of our most passionate prejudices, without the smallest regard to their effect on others, could win the war. Finally the British blockade won the war; but the wonder is that the British blockhead did not lose it. I suppose the enemy was no wiser. War is not a sharpener of wits; and I am afraid I gave great offence by keeping my head in this matter of Irish recruiting. What can I do but apologize, and publish the play now that it can no longer do any good?

1. By the Treaty of Limerick (1691), Irish catholics were promised rights that were immediately afterwards abrogated by the Penal Laws.

2. Volumnia, in Shakespeare's *Coriolanus*, is the proud and imperious mother of the hero. She rejoices in her son's exploits, but saves Rome from the enemy at her son's expense.

At the door of an Irish country house in a park. Fine summer weather: the summer of 1915. The porch, painted white, projects into the drive; but the door is at the side and the front has a window. The porch faces east; and the door is in the north side of it. On the south side is a tree in which a thrush is singing. Under the window is a garden seat with an iron chair at each end of it.

The last four bars of God Save the King are heard in the distance, followed by three cheers. Then the band strikes up It's a Long Way to Tipperary[1] *and recedes until it is out of hearing.*

PRIVATE O'FLAHERTY V.C. *comes wearily southward along the drive, and falls exhausted into the garden seat. The thrush utters a note of alarm and flies away. The tramp of a horse is heard.*

A GENTLEMAN'S VOICE: Tim! Hi! Tim! (*He is heard dismounting*)

A LABORER'S VOICE: Yes, your honor.

THE GENTLEMAN'S VOICE: Take this horse to the stables, will you?

A LABORER'S VOICE: Right, your honor. Yup there. Gwan now. Gwan. (*The horse is led away*)

GENERAL SIR PEARCE MADIGAN, *an elderly baronet in khaki, beaming with enthusiasm, arrives.* O'FLAHERTY *rises and stands at attention.*

SIR PEARCE: No, no, O'Flaherty: none of that now. Youre off duty. Remember that though I am a general of forty years service, that little Cross of yours gives you a higher rank in the roll of glory than I can pretend to.

O'FLAHERTY: (*Relaxing*) I'm thankful to you, Sir Pearce; but I wouldnt have anyone think that the baronet of my native place would let a common soldier like me sit down in his presence without leave.

SIR PEARCE: Well, youre not a common soldier, O'Flaherty: youre a very uncommon one; and I'm proud to have you for my guest here today.

O'FLAHERTY: Sure I know, sir. You have to put up with a lot from the like of me for the sake of the recruiting. All the quality[2] shakes hands with me and says theyre proud to know me, just the way the king said when he pinned the Cross on me. And it's as true as I'm standing here, sir, the queen said to me 'I hear you were born on the estate of General Madigan,' she says; 'and the General himself tells me you were always a fine young fellow.' 'Bedad, Mam,' I says to her, 'if the General knew all the rabbits I snared on him, and all the salmon I snatched on him, and all the cows I milked on him, he'd think me the finest ornament for the county jail he ever sent there for poaching.'

SIR PEARCE: (*Laughing*) Youre welcome to them all, my lad. Come! (*he makes him sit down again on the garden seat*) sit down and enjoy your holiday (*he sits down on one of the iron chairs: the one at the doorless side of the porch*).

O'FLAHERTY: Holiday, is it? I'd give five shillings to be back in the trenches for the sake of a little rest and quiet. I never knew what hard work was til I took to recruiting. What with the standing on my legs all day, and the shaking hands, and the making speeches, and — whats worse — the listening to them, and the calling for cheers for king and country, and the saluting the flag til I'm stiff with it, and the listening to them playing God Save the King and Tipperary, and the trying to make my eyes look moist like a man in a picture book, I'm that bet that I hardly get a wink of sleep. I give you my word, Sir Pearce, that I never heard the tune of Tipperary in my life till I came back from Flanders;[3] and already it's drove me to that pitch of tiredness of it that when a poor little innocent slip of a boy in the street the other night drew himself up and saluted and began whistling it at me, I clouted his head for him, God forgive me.

SIR PEARCE: (*Soothingly*) Yes, yes: I know. *I* know. One does get fed up with it: Ive been dog tired myself on parade many a time. But still, you know, theres a gratifying side to it, too. After all, he is our king; and it's our own country, isn't it?

O'FLAHERTY: Well, sir, to you that have an estate in it, it would feel like your country. But the divil a perch of it ever I owned. And as to the king, God help him, my mother would have taken the skin off my back if I'd ever let on to have any other king than Parnell.[4]

SIR PEARCE: (*Rising, painfully shocked*) Your

1. Popular recruiting and marching song among infantry in World War I.
2. gentry, upper-class.
3. Belgian region overlapping parts of Holland and France in which many Irishmen lost their lives during battles with the Germans.
4. Charles Stewart Parnell, leader of the Irish Party at Westminster, was known popularly as 'the uncrowned king of Ireland'. Even in 1915, some people believed that he was not dead, but would return in triumph from a hiding-place in the hills.

mother! What are you dreaming about, O'Flaherty? A most loyal woman. Always most loyal. Whenever there is an illness in the Royal Family, she asks me every time we meet about the health of the patient as anxiously as if it were yourself, her only son.

O'FLAHERTY: Well, she's my mother; and I wont utter a word agen her. But I'm not saying a word of lie when I tell you that that old woman is the biggest kanatt[5] from here to the cross of Monasterboice.[6] Sure she's the wildest Fenian and rebel, and always has been, that ever taught a poor innocent lad like myself to pray night and morning to St Patrick to clear the English out of Ireland the same as he cleared the snakes. Youll be surprised at my telling you that now, maybe, Sir Pearce?

SIR PEARCE: (*unable to keep still, walking away from* O'FLAHERTY) Surprised! I'm more than surprised, O'Flaherty. I'm overwhelmed. (*Turning and facing him*) Are you — are you joking?

O'FLAHERTY: If youd been brought up by my mother, sir, youd know better than to joke about her. What I'm telling you is the truth; and I wouldnt tell it to you if I could see my way to get out of the fix I'll be in when my mother comes here this day to see her boy in his glory, and she after thinking all the time it was against the English I was fighting.

SIR PEARCE: Do you mean to say you told her such a monstrous falsehood as that you were fighting in the German army?

O'FLAHERTY: I never told her one word that wasnt the truth and nothing but the truth. I told her I was going to fight for the French and for the Russians; and sure who ever heard of the French or the Russians doing anything to the English but fighting them? That was how it was, sir. And sure the poor woman kissed me and went about the house singing in her old cracky voice that the French was on the sea, and theyd be here without delay, and the Orange will decay, says the Shan van Vocht.[7]

SIR PEARCE: (*Sitting down again, exhausted by his feelings*) Well, I never could have believed this. Never. What do you suppose will happen when she finds out?

O'FLAHERTY: She mustnt find out. It's not that she'd half kill me, as big as I am and as brave as I am. It's that I'm fond of her, and cant bring myself to break the heart in her. You may think it queer that a man should be fond of his mother, sir, and she having bet him from the time he could feel to the time she was too slow to ketch him; but I'm fond of her; and I'm not ashamed of it. Besides, didnt she win the Cross for me?

SIR PEARCE: Your mother! How?

O'FLAHERTY: By bringing me up to be more afraid of running away than of fighting. I was timid by nature; and when the other boys hurted me, I'd want to run away and cry. But she whaled[8] me for disgracing the blood of the O'Flahertys until I'd have fought the divil himself sooner than face her after funking a fight. That was how I got to know that fighting was easier than it looked, and that the others was as much afeard of me as I was of them, and that if I only held out long enough theyd lose heart and give up. Thats the way I came to be so courageous. I tell you, Sir Pearce, if the German army had been brought up by my mother, the Kaiser would be dining in the banqueting hall at Buckingham Palace this day, and King George[9] polishing his jack boots for him in the scullery.

SIR PEARCE: But I dont like this, O'Flaherty. You cant go on deceiving your mother, you know. It's not right.

O'FLAHERTY: Cant go on deceiving her, cant I? It's little you know what a son's love can do, sir. Did you ever notice what a ready liar I am?

SIR PEARCE: Well, in recruiting a man gets carried away. I stretch it a bit occasionally myself. After all, it's for king and country. But if you wont mind my saying it, O'Flaherty, I think that story about your fighting the Kaiser and the twelve giants of the Prussian guard singlehanded would be the better for a little toning down. I dont ask you to drop it, you know; for it's popular, undoubtedly; but still, the truth is the truth. Dont you think it would fetch in almost as many recruits if you

5. Or kanitt, a stink, a repulsive person.
6. Monasterboice, Co. Louth is noted for the remains of a monastic settlement founded by St Buithe probably towards the end of the fifth century.
7. The Old Woman, i.e. Ireland, who sang of French military help coming by sea, and who would walk again like a young queen when young men were willing to die for her.
8. flogged, thrashed.
9. George V (1865-1936), king of the United Kingdom from 1910 until his death. The British and German royal families were closely connected.

reduced the number of guardsmen to six?

O'FLAHERTY: Youre not used to telling lies like I am, sir. I got great practice at home with my mother. What with saving my skin when I was young and thoughtless, and sparing her feelings when I was old enough to understand them, Ive hardly told my mother the truth twice a year since I was born; and would you have me turn round on her and tell it now, when she's looking to have some peace and quiet in her old age?

SIR PEARCE: (*Troubled in his conscience*) Well, it's not my affair, of course, O'Flaherty. But hadnt you better talk to Father Quinlan about it?

O'FLAHERTY: Talk to Father Quinlan, is it! Do you know what Father Quinlan says to me this very morning?

SIR PEARCE: Oh, youve seen him already, have you? What did he say?

O'FLAHERTY: He says 'You know, dont you' he says 'that it's your duty, as a Christian and a good son of the Holy Church, to love your enemies?' he says. 'I know it's my juty as a soldier to kill them' I says. 'Thats right, Dinny,' he says: 'quite right. But' says he 'you can kill them and do them a good turn afterwards to shew your love for them' he says; 'and it's your duty to have a mass said for the souls of the hundreds of Germans you say you killed' says he; 'for many and many of them were Bavarians and good Catholics' he says. 'Is it me that must pay for masses for the souls of the Boshes?'[10] I says. 'Let the King of England pay for them' I says; 'for it was his quarrel and not mine.'

SIR PEARCE: (*Warmly*) It is the quarrel of every honest man and true patriot, O'Flaherty. Your mother must see that as clearly as I do. After all, she is a reasonable, well disposed woman, quite capable of understanding the right and the wrong of the war. Why cant you explain to her what the war is about?

O'FLAHERTY: Arra, sir, how the divil do I know what the war is about?

SIR PEARCE: (*Rising again and standing over him*) What! O'Flaherty: do you know what you are saying? You sit there wearing the Victoria Cross for having killed God knows how many Germans; and you tell me you dont know why you did it!

O'FLAHERTY: Asking your pardon, Sir Pearce, I tell you no such thing. I know quite well why I kilt them. I kilt them because I was afeard that, if I didnt, theyd kill me.

SIR PEARCE: (*Giving it up, and sitting down again*) Yes, yes, of course; but have you no knowledge of the causes of the war? of the interests at stake? of the importance — I may almost say — in fact I will say — the sacred rights for which we are fighting? Dont you read the papers?

O'FLAHERTY: I do when I can get them. Theres not many newsboys crying the evening paper in the trenches. They do say, Sir Pearce, that we shall never beat the Boshes until we make Horatio Bottomley Lord Leftnant of England.[11] Do you think thats true, sir?

SIR PEARCE: Rubbish, man! theres no Lord Lieutenant in England: the king is Lord Lieutenant. It's a simple question of patriotism. Does patriotism mean nothing to you?

O'FLAHERTY: It means different to me than what it would to you, sir. It means England and England's king to you. To me and the like of me, it means talking about the English just the way the English papers talk about the Boshes. And what good has it ever done here in Ireland? It's kept me ignorant because it filled up my mother's mind, and she thought it ought to fill up mine too. It's kept Ireland poor, because instead of trying to better ourselves we thought we was the fine fellows of patriots when we were speaking evil of Englishmen that was as poor as ourselves and maybe as good as ourselves. The Boshes I kilt was more knowledgable men than me; and what better am I now that Ive kilt them? What better is anybody?

SIR PEARCE: (*Huffed, turning a cold shoulder to him*) I am sorry the terrible experience of this war — the greatest war ever fought — has taught you no better, O'Flaherty.

O'FLAHERTY: (*Preserving his dignity*) I dont know about it's being a great war, sir. It's a big war; but thats not the same thing. Father Quinlan's new church is a big church: you might take the little old chapel out of the middle of it and not miss it. But my mother says there was more true religion in the old chapel. And the war has taught me that may be she was right.

SIR PEARCE: (*Grunts sulkily*)!!

O'FLAHERTY: (*Respectfully but doggedly*) And theres another thing it's taught me too, sir, that

10. The Bosch, or Germans.

11. Horatio Bottomley (1860-1933), newspaper editor and proprietor.

concerns you and me, if I may make bold to tell it to you.

SIR PEARCE: (*Still sulky*) I hope it's nothing you oughtnt to say to me, O'Flaherty.

O'FLAHERTY: It's this, sir: that I'm able to sit here now and talk to you without humbugging you; and thats what not one of your tenants or your tenants' childer[12] ever did to you before in all your long life. It's a true respect I'm shewing you at last, sir. Maybe youd rather have me humbug you and tell you lies as I used, just as the boys here, God help them, would rather have me tell them how I fought the Kaiser, that all the world knows I never saw in my life, than tell them the truth. But I cant take advantage of you the way I used, not even if I seem to be wanting in respect to you and cocked up[13] by winning the Cross.

SIR PEARCE: (*Touched*) Not at all, O'Flaherty. Not at all.

O'FLAHERTY: Sure whats the Cross to me, barring the little pension it carries? Do you think I dont know that theres hundreds of men as brave as me that never had the luck to get anything for their bravery but a curse from the sergeant, and the blame for the faults of them that ought to have been their betters? Ive learnt more than youd think, sir; for how would a gentleman like you know what a poor ignorant conceited creature I was when I went from here into the wide world as a soldier? What use is all the lying, and pretending, and humbugging, and letting on, when the day comes to you that your comrade is killed in the trench beside you, and you dont as much as look round at him until you trip over his poor body, and then all you say is to ask why the hell the stretcher-bearers dont take it out of the way. Why should I read the papers to be humbugged and lied to by them that had the cunning to stay at home and send me to fight for them? Dont talk to me or to any soldier of the war being right. No war is right; and all the holy water that Father Quinlan ever blessed couldnt make one right. There, sir! Now you know what O'Flaherty V.C. thinks; and youre wiser so than the others that only knows what he done.

SIR PEARCE: (*Making the best of it, and turning goodhumoredly to him again*) Well, what you did was brave and manly, anyhow.

O'FLAHERTY: God knows whether it was or not, better than you nor me, General. I hope He wont be too hard on me for it, anyhow.

SIR PEARCE: (*Sympathetically*) Oh yes: we all have to think seriously sometimes, especially when we're a little run down. I'm afraid weve been overworking you a bit over these recruiting meetings. However, we can knock off for the rest of the day; and tomorrow's Sunday. Ive had about as much as I can stand myself. (*He looks at his watch*) It's teatime. I wonder whats keeping your mother.

O'FLAHERTY: It's nicely cocked up the old woman will be, having tea at the same table as you, sir, instead of in the kitchen. She'll be after dressing in the heighth of grandeur; and stop she will at every house on the way to shew herself off and tell them where she's going, and fill the whole parish with spite and envy. But sure, she shouldnt keep you waiting, sir.

SIR PEARCE: Oh, thats all right: she must be indulged on an occasion like this. I'm sorry my wife is in London: she'd have been glad to welcome your mother.

O'FLAHERTY: Sure, I know she would, sir. She was always a kind friend to the poor. Little her ladyship knew, God help her, the depth of divilment that was in us: we were like a play to her. You see, sir, she was English: that was how it was. We was to her what the Pathans and Senegalese[14] was to me when I first seen them: I couldnt think, somehow, that they were liars, and thieves, and backbiters, and drunkards, just like ourselves or any other Christians. Oh, her ladyship never knew all that was going on behind her back: how would she? When I was a weeshy[15] child, she gave me the first penny I ever had in my hand; and I wanted to pray for her conversion that night the same as my mother made me pray for yours; and —

SIR PEARCE: (*Scandalized*) Do you mean to say that your mother made you pray for my conversion?

O'FLAHERTY: Sure and she wouldnt want to see a gentleman like you going to hell after she nursing your own son and bringing up my sister Annie on the bottle. That was how it was, sir. She'd rob you; and she'd lie to you; and she'd call down all the blessings of God on your head when she was selling you your own three geese that you thought had been ate by the fox the day after youd finished

12. children.
13. made proud.

14. Colonized African peoples.
15. tiny.

fattening them, sir; and all the time you were like a bit of her own flesh and blood to her. Often has she said she'd live to see you a good Catholic yet, leading victorious armies against the English and wearing the collar of gold that Malachi won from the proud invader.[16] Oh, she's the romantic woman is my mother, and no mistake.

SIR PEARCE: (*In great perturbation*) I really cant believe this, O'Flaherty. I could have sworn your mother was as honest a woman as ever breathed.

O'FLAHERTY: And so she is, sir. She's as honest as the day.

SIR PEARCE: Do you call it honest to steal my geese?

O'FLAHERTY: She didnt steal them, sir. It was me that stole them.

SIR PEARCE: Oh! And why the devil did you steal them?

O'FLAHERTY: Sure we needed them, sir. Often and often we had to sell our own geese to pay you the rent to satisfy your needs; and why shouldnt we sell your geese to satisfy ours?

SIR PEARCE: Well, damn me!

O'FLAHERTY: (*Sweetly*) Sure you had to get what you could out of us; and we had to get what we could out of you. God forgive us both!

SIR PEARCE: Really, O'Flaherty, the war seems to have upset you a little.

O'FLAHERTY: It's set me thinking, sir; and I'm not used to it. It's like the patriotism of the English. They never thought of being patriotic until the war broke out; and now the patriotism has took them so sudden and come so strange to them that they run about like frightened chickens, uttering all manner of nonsense. But please God theyll forget all about it when the war's over. Theyre getting tired of it already.

SIR PEARCE: No, no: it has uplifted us all in a wonderful way. The world will never be the same again, O'Flaherty. Not after a war like this.

O'FLAHERTY: So they all say, sir. I see no great differ myself. It's all the fright and the excitement; and when that quiets down theyll go back to their natural divilment and be the same as ever. It's like the vermin: itll wash off after a while.

SIR PEARCE: (*Rising and planting himself firmly behind the garden seat*) Well, the long and short of it is, O'Flaherty, I must decline to be a party to any attempt to deceive your mother. I thoroughly disapprove of this feeling against the English, especially at a moment like the present. Even if your mother's political sympathies are really what you represent them to be, I should think that her gratitude to Gladstone[17] ought to cure her of such disloyal prejudices.

O'FLAHERTY: (*Over his shoulder*) She says Gladstone was an Irishman, sir. What call would he have to meddle with Ireland as he did if he was wasnt?

SIR PEARCE: What nonsense! Does she suppose Mr Asquith[18] is an Irishman?

O'FLAHERTY: She wont give him any credit for Home Rule, sir. She says Redmond[19] made him do it. She says you told her so.

SIR PEARCE: (*Convicted out of his own mouth*) Well, I never meant her to take it up in that ridiculous way. (*He moves to the end of the garden seat on* O'FLAHERTY's *left*) I'll give her a good talking to when she comes. I'm not going to stand any of her nonsense.

O'FLAHERTY: It's not a bit of use, sir. She says all the English generals is Irish. She says all the English poets and great men was Irish. She says the English never knew how to read their own books until we taught them. She says we're the lost tribes of the house of Israel and the chosen people of God.[20] She says that the goddess Venus, that was born out of the foam of the sea, came up out of the water in Killiney Bay off Bray Head.[21] She says that Moses built the seven churches, and that Lazarus was buried in Glasnevin.[22]

16. Malachi the Second (948-1022), high king of Ireland who (with Brian Boru) expelled Norse invaders, taking the collar of the Norwegian prince Tomar as booty, having crushed his army at Dublin in 996. The line is a quotation from Thomas Moore's song 'Let Erin remember the days of old'.

17. See Note 1 to *John Bull's Other Island* (p. 424).

18. H. H. Asquith, Liberal leader and prime minister, introduced the Home Rule Bill on 11 April 1912. It was put on the statute book, for implementation after the war, but Asquith was ousted by Lloyd George in November 1916.

19. John Redmond, leader of the Nationalist Party at Westminster, he urged Irishmen to enlist in the British army during World War I, in return for the promise of Home Rule. He threatened to resign after the executions of 1916, but gradually lost ground to Sinn Féin activists, before his humiliation and death in 1918.

20. The equation of Irish and Israelites as a lost, but chosen, people was a commonplace in Gaelic poetry for centuries.

21. A scenic bay, to the south of Dublin, next to Bray Head, and noted as a holiday resort. One of Shaw's few periods of happiness in youth occurred when, at the age of ten, he was taken to live with his mother in a cottage at nearby Dalkey.

22. The seven churches traditionally are associated with the monastic settlements of Glendalough in County Wicklow. Glasnevin is a cemetery on the north side of Dublin.

SIR PEARCE: Bosh! How does she know he was? Did you ever ask her?

O'FLAHERTY: I did, sir, often.

SIR PEARCE: And what did she say?

O'FLAHERTY: She asked me how did I know he wasnt, and fetched me a clout on the side of my head.

SIR PEARCE: But have you never mentioned any famous Englishman to her, and asked her what she had to say about him?

O'FLAHERTY: The only one I could think of was Shakespear, sir; and she says he was born in Cork.

SIR PEARCE: (*Exhausted*) Well, I give it up (*he throws himself into the nearest chair*) The woman is — Oh, well! No matter.

O'FLAHERTY: (*Sympathetically*) Yes, sir: she's pigheaded and obstinate: theres no doubt about it. She's like the English: they think theres no one like themselves. It's the same with the Germans, though theyre educated and ought to know better. Youll never have a quiet world til you knock the patriotism out of the human race.

SIR PEARCE: Still, we —

O'FLAHERTY: Whisht,[23] sir, for God's sake: here she is.

The GENERAL *jumps up.* MRS O'FLAHERTY *arrives, and comes between the two men. She is very clean, and carefully dressed in the old fashioned peasant costume: black silk sunbonnet with a tiara of trimmings, and black cloak.*

O'FLAHERTY: (*Rising shyly*) Good evening, mother.

MRS O'FLAHERTY: (*Severely*) You hold your whisht, and learn behaviour while I pay my juty to his honor. (*To* SIR PEARCE, *heartily*) And how is your honor's good self? And how is her ladyship and all the young ladies? Oh, it's right glad we are to see your honor back again and looking the picture of health.

SIR PEARCE: (*Forcing a note of extreme geniality*) Thank you, Mrs O'Flaherty. Well, you see weve brought you back your son safe and sound. I hope youre proud of him.

MRS O'FLAHERTY: And indeed and I am, your honor. It's the brave boy he is; and why wouldnt he be, brought up on your honor's estate and with you before his eyes for a pattern of the finest soldier in Ireland. Come and kiss your old mother, Dinny darlint. (O'FLAHERTY *does so sheepishly*) Thats my own darling boy. And look at your fine new uniform stained already with the eggs youve been eating and the porter[24] youve been drinking. (*She takes out her handkerchief; spits on it; and scrubs his lapel with it*) Oh, it's the untidy slovenly one you always were. There! It wont be seen on the khaki: it's not like the old red coat[25] that would shew up everything that dribbled down to it. (*To* SIR PEARCE) And they tell me down at the lodge that her ladyship is staying in London, and that Miss Agnes is to be married to a fine young nobleman. Oh, it's your honor that is the lucky and happy father! It will be bad news for many of the young gentlemen of the quality round here, sir. Theres lots thought she was going to marry young Master Lawless —

SIR PEARCE: What! That — that — that bosthoon![26]

MRS O'FLAHERTY: (*Hilariously*) Let your honour alone for finding the right word! A big bosthoon he is indeed, your honor. Oh, to think of the times and times I have said that Miss Agnes would be my lady as her mother was before her! Didnt I, Dinny?

SIR PEARCE: And now, Mrs O'Flaherty, I daresay you have a great deal to say to Dennis that doesnt concern me. I'll just go in and order tea.

MRS O'FLAHERTY: Oh, why would your honor disturb yourself? Sure I can take the boy into the yard.

SIR PEARCE: Not at all. It wont disturb me in the least. And he's too big a boy to be taken into the yard now. He has made a front seat for himself. Eh? (*He goes into the house*)

MRS O'FLAHERTY: Sure he has that, your honor. God bless your honour! (*The* GENERAL *being now out of hearing, she turns threateningly to her son with one of those sudden Irish changes of manner which amaze and scandalize less flexible nations, and exclaims*) And what do you mean, you lying young scald,[27] by telling me you were going to fight agen the English? Did you take me for a fool that couldnt find out, and the papers all full of you shaking hands with the English king at Buckingham Palace?

O'FLAHERTY: I didnt shake hands with him: he shook hands with me. Could I turn on the man in

23. Keep your silence!

24. A dark sweet ale brewed from black malt.

25. The historic uniform of British soldiers, known in Ireland (and elsewhere) as 'redcoats'.

26. churl, clumsy fellow.

27. heart-scald, heart-breaker.

his own house, before his own wife, with his money in my pocket and in yours, and throw his civility back in his face?

MRS O'FLAHERTY: You would take the hand of a tyrant red with the blood of Ireland —

O'FLAHERTY: Arra hold your nonsense, mother: he's not half the tyrant you are, God help him. His hand was cleaner than mine that had the blood of his own relations[28] on it, may be.

MRS O'FLAHERTY: (*Threateningly*) Is that a way to speak to your mother, you young spalpeen?[29]

O'FLAHERTY: (*Stoutly*) It is so, if you wont talk sense to me. It's a nice thing for a poor boy to be made much of by kings and queens, and shook hands with by the heighth of his country's nobility in the capital cities of the world, and then to come home and be scolded and insulted by his own mother. I'll fight for who I like; and I'll shake hands with what kings I like; and if your own son is not good enough for you, you can go and look for another. Do you mind me now?

MRS O'FLAHERTY: And was it the Belgians learned you such brazen impudence?

O'FLAHERTY: The Belgians is good men; and the French ought to be more civil to them, let alone their being half murdered by the Boshes.

MRS O'FLAHERTY: Good men is it! Good men! to come over here when they were wounded because it was a Catholic country, and then to go to the Protestant Church because it didnt cost them anything, and some of them to never go near a church at all. Thats what you call good men!

O'FLAHERTY: Oh, youre the mighty fine politician, arnt you? Much you know about Belgians or foreign parts or the world youre living in, God help you!

MRS O'FLAHERTY: Why wouldnt I know better than you? Amment I your mother?

O'FLAHERTY: And if you are itself, how can you know what you never seen as well as me that was dug into the continent of Europe for six months, and was buried in the earth of it three times with the shells bursting on the top of me? I tell you I know what I'm about. I have my own reasons for taking part in this great conflict. I'd be ashamed to stay at home and not fight when everybody else is fighting.

MRS O'FLAHERTY: If you wanted to fight, why couldnt you fight in the German army?

O'FLAHERTY: Because they only get a penny a day.

MRS O'FLAHERTY: Well, and if they do itself, isnt there the French army?

O'FLAHERTY: They only get a hapenny a day.

MRS O'FLAHERTY: (*Much dashed*) Oh murder! They must be a mean lot, Dinny.

O'FLAHERTY: (*Sarcastic*) Maybe youd have me join the Turkish army, and worship the heathen Mahomet that put a corn in his ear and pretended it was a message from the heavens when the pigeon come to pick it out and eat it. I went where I could get the biggest allowance for you; and little thanks I get for it!

MRS O'FLAHERTY: Allowance, is it! Do you know what the thieving blackguards did on me? They came to me and they says, 'Was your son a big eater?' they says. 'Oh, he was that' says I: 'ten shillings a week wouldnt keep him.' Sure I thought the more I said the more theyd give me. 'Then' says they, 'thats ten shillings a week off your allowance' they says, 'because you save that by the king feeding him.' 'Indeed!' says I: 'I suppose if I'd six sons, youd stop three pound a week from me, and make out that I ought to pay you money instead of you paying me.' 'Theres a fallacy in your argument' they says.

O'FLAHERTY: A what?

MRS O'FLAHERTY: A fallacy: thats the word he said. I says to him, 'It's a Pharisee[30] I'm thinking you mean, sir; but you can keep your dirty money that your king grudges a poor old widow; and please God the English will be bet yet for the deadly sin of oppressing the poor'; and with that I shut the door in his face.

O'FLAHERTY: (*Furious*) Do you tell me they knocked ten shillings off you for my keep?

MRS O'FLAHERTY: (*Soothing him*) No, darlint: they only knocked off half a crown.[31] I put up with it because Ive got the old age pension; and they know very well I'm only sixty two; so Ive the better of them by half a crown a week anyhow.

O'FLAHERTY: It's a queer way of doing business.

28. i.e. members of his own family.
29. A journeyman, travelling poet or tradesman, especially in the eighteenth century. From Irish *spailpín*.
30. Hypocritical ministers of the law — literally, an elite Jewish sect, with rigid rules, who clashed frequently with Jesus Christ, on the grounds that they wanted people to follow regulations while he wanted them simply to please God.
31. A quarter of ten shillings in the old currency.

If theyd tell you straight out what they was going to give you, you wouldnt mind; but if there was twenty ways of telling the truth and only one way of telling a lie, the Government would find it out. It's in the nature of governments to tell lies.

TERESA DRISCOLL, *a parlor maid, comes from the house.*

TERESA: Youre to come up to the drawingroom to have your tea, Mrs. O'Flaherty.

MRS O'FLAHERTY: Mind you have a sup of good black tea for me in the kitchen afterwards, acushla.[32] That washy drawingroom tea will give me the wind if I leave it on my stomach. (*She goes into the house, leaving the two young people alone together*)

O'FLAHERTY: Is that yourself, Tessie? And how are you?

TERESA: Nicely, thank you. And hows yourself?

O'FLAHERTY: Finely, thank God. (*He produces a gold chain*) Look what Ive brought you, Tessie.

TERESA: (*Shrinking*) Sure I dont like to touch it, Denny. Did you take it off a dead man?

O'FLAHERTY: No: I took it off a live one; and thankful he was to me to be alive and kept a prisoner in ease and comfort, and me left fighting in peril of my life.

TERESA: (*Taking it*) Do you think it's real gold, Denny?

O'FLAHERTY: It's real German gold, anyhow.

TERESA: But German silver isnt real, Denny.

O'FLAHERTY: (*His face darkening*) Well, it's the best the Bosh could do for me, anyhow.

TERESA: Do you think I might take it to the jeweller next market day and ask him?

O'FLAHERTY: (*Sulkily*) You may take it to the divil if you like.

TERESA: You neednt lose your temper about it. I only thought I'd like to know. The nice fool I'd look if I went about shewing off a chain that turned out to be only brass!

O'FLAHERTY: I think you might say Thank you.

TERESA: Do you? I think you might have said something more to me than 'Is that yourself?' You couldnt say less to the postman.

O'FLAHERTY: (*His brow clearing*) Oh, is that whats the matter? Here! come and take the taste of the brass out of my mouth. (*He seizes her and kisses her*)

TERESA, *without losing her Irish dignity, takes the kiss as appreciatively as a connoisseur might take a glass of wine, and sits down with him on the garden seat.*

TERESA: (*As he squeezes her waist*) Thank God the priest cant see us here!

O'FLAHERTY: It's little they care for priests in France, alanna.

TERESA: And what had the queen on her, Denny, when she spoke to you in the palace?

O'FLAHERTY: She had a bonnet on without any strings to it. And she had a plakeen[33] of embroidery down her bosom. And she had her waist where it used to be, and not where the other ladies had it.[34] And she had little brooches in her ears, though she hadnt half the jewelry of Mrs Sullivan that keeps the popshop in Drumpogue. And she dresses her hair down over her forehead, in a fringe like. And she has an Irish look about her eyebrows. And she didnt know what to say to me, poor woman! and I didnt know what to say to her, God help me!

TERESA: Youll have a pension now with the Cross, wont you, Denny?

O'FLAHERTY: Sixpence three farthings a day.

TERESA: That isnt much.

O'FLAHERTY: I take out the rest in glory.

TERESA: And if youre wounded, youll have a wound pension, wont you?

O'FLAHERTY: I will, please God.

TERESA: Youre going out again, arnt you, Denny?

O'FLAHERTY: I cant help myself. I'd be shot for a deserter if I didnt go; and may be I'll be shot by the Boshes if I do go; so between the two of them I'm nicely fixed up.

MRS O'FLAHERTY: (*Calling from within the house*) Tessie! Tessie darlint!

TERESA: (*Disengaging herself from his arm and rising*) I'm wanted for the tea table. Youll have a pension anyhow, Denny, wont you, whether youre wounded or not?

MRS O'FLAHERTY: Come, child, come.

TERESA: (*Impatiently*) Oh, sure I'm coming. (*She tries to smile at* DENNY, *not very convincingly, and hurries into the house*)

O'FLAHERTY: (*Alone*) And if I do get a pension itself, the divil a penny of it youll ever have the spending of.

MRS O'FLAHERTY: (*As she comes from the porch*) Oh, it's a shame for you to keep the girl from her

32. my pulse, love. The Irish word *cuisle* means pulse.

33. small platform or square.

34. By use of tight corsetry, then fashionable.

juties, Dinny. You might get her into trouble.

O'FLAHERTY: Much I care whether she gets into trouble or not! I pity the man that gets her into trouble. He'll get himself into worse.

MRS O'FLAHERTY: Whats that you tell me? Have you been falling out with her, and she a girl with a fortune of ten pounds?

O'FLAHERTY: Let her keep her fortune. I wouldnt touch her with the tongs if she had thousands and millions.

MRS O'FLAHERTY: Oh fie for shame, Dinny! why would you say the like of that of a decent honest girl, and one of the Driscolls too?

O'FLAHERTY: Why wouldn't I say it? She's thinking of nothing but to get me out there again to be wounded so that she may spend my pension, bad scran[35] to her!

MRS O'FLAHERTY: Why, whats come over you, child, at all at all?

O'FLAHERTY: Knowledge and wisdom has come over me with pain and fear and trouble. Ive been made a fool of and imposed upon all my life. I thought that covetious sthreal[36] in there was a walking angel; and now if ever I marry at all I'll marry a Frenchwoman.

MRS O'FLAHERTY: (*Fiercely*) Youll not, so; and dont you dar repeat such a thing to me.

O'FLAHERTY: Wont I, faith! Ive been as good as married to a couple of them already.

MRS O'FLAHERTY: The Lord be praised, what wickedness have you been up to, you young blackguard?

O'FLAHERTY: One of them Frenchwomen would cook you a meal twice in the day and all days and every day that Sir Pearce himself might go begging through Ireland for, and never see the like of. I'll have a French wife, I tell you; and when I settle down to be a farmer I'll have a French farm, with a field as big as the continent of Europe that ten of your dirty little fields here wouldnt so much as fill the ditch of.

MRS O'FLAHERTY: (*Furious*) Then it's a French mother you may go look for; for I'm done with you.

O'FLAHERTY: And it's no great loss youd be if it wasnt for my natural feelings for you; for it's only a silly ignorant old countrywoman you are with all your fine talk about Ireland: you that never stepped beyond the few acres of it you were born on!

MRS O'FLAHERTY: (*Tottering to the garden seat and showing signs of breaking down*) Dinny darlint, why are you like this to me? Whats happened to you?

O'FLAHERTY: (*Gloomily*) Whats happened to everybody? thats what I want to know. Whats happened to you that I thought all the world of and was afeard of? Whats happened to Sir Pearce, that I thought was a great general, and that I now see to be no more fit to command an army than an old hen? Whats happened to Tessie, that I was mad to marry a year ago, and that I wouldnt take now with all Ireland for her fortune? I tell you the world's creation is crumbling in ruins about me; and then you come and ask whats happened to me?

MRS O'FLAHERTY: (*Giving way to wild grief*) Ochone! ochone![37] my son's turned agen me. Oh, whatll I do at all at all? Oh! oh! oh! oh!

SIR PEARCE: (*Running out of the house*) Whats this infernal noise? What on earth is the matter?

O'FLAHERTY: Arra hold your whisht, mother. Dont you see his honor?

MRS O'FLAHERTY: Oh, sir, I'm ruined and destroyed. Oh, wont you speak to Dinny, sir: I'm heart scalded with him. He wants to marry a Frenchwoman on me, and to go away and be a foreigner and desert his mother and betray his country. It's mad he is with the roaring of the cannons and he killing the Germans and the Germans killing him, bad cess[38] to them! My boy is taken from me and turned agen me; and who is to take care of me in my old age after all Ive done for him, ochone! ochone!

O'FLAHERTY: Hold your noise, I tell you. Who's going to leave you? I'm going to take you with me. There now: does that satisfy you?

MRS O'FLAHERTY: Is it take me into a strange land among heathens and pagans and savages, and me not knowing a word of their language nor them of mine?

O'FLAHERTY: A good job they dont: may be theyll think youre talking sense.

MRS O'FLAHERTY: Ask me to die out of Ireland, is it? and the angels not to find me when they come for me!

O'FLAHERTY: And would you ask me to live in Ireland where Ive been imposed on and kept in ignorance, and to die where the divil himself wouldnt take me as a gift, let alone the blessed

35. bad fare.
36. A covetous and feckless woman.
37. Gaelic cry of lamentation.
38. bad luck.

angels? You can come or stay. You can take your old way or take my young way. But stick in this place I will not among a lot of good-for-nothing divils thatll not do a hand's turn but watch the grass growing and build up the stone wall where the cow walked through it. And Sir Horace Plunkett[39] breaking his heart all the time telling them how they might put the land into decent tillage like the French and Belgians.

SIR PEARCE: Yes: he's quite right, you know, Mrs O'Flaherty: quite right there.

MRS O'FLAHERTY: Well, sir, please God the war will last a long time yet; and may be I'll die before it's over and the separation allowance stops.

O'FLAHERTY: Thats all you care about. It's nothing but milch cows we men are for the women, with their separation allowances, ever since the war began, bad luck to them that made it!

TERESA: (*Coming from the porch between the* GENERAL *and* MRS O'FLAHERTY) Hannah sent me out for to tell you, sir, that the tea will be black and the cake not fit to eat with the cold if yous all dont come at wanst.[40]

MRS O'FLAHERTY: (*Breaking out again*) Oh, Tessie darlint, what have you been saying to Dinny at all at all? Oh! oh —

SIR PEARCE: (*Out of patience*) You cant discuss that here. We shall have Tessie beginning now.

O'FLAHERTY: Thats right, sir: drive them in.

TERESA: I havnt said a word to him. He —

SIR PEARCE: Hold your tongue; and go in and attend to your business at the tea table.

TERESA: But amment I telling your honor that I never said a word to him? He gave me a beautiful gold chain. Here it is to shew your honor thats it's no lie I'm telling you.

SIR PEARCE: Whats this, O'Flaherty? Youve been looting some unfortunate officer.

O'FLAHERTY: No, sir: I stole it from him of his own accord.

MRS O'FLAHERTY: Wouldnt your honor tell him that his mother has the first call on it? What would a slip of a girl like that be doing with a gold chain round her neck?

TERESA: (*Venomously*) Anyhow, I have a neck to put it round and not a hank of wrinkles.

At this unfortunate remark, MRS O'FLAHERTY *bounds from her seat; and an appalling tempest of wordy wrath breaks out. The remonstrances and commands of the* GENERAL, *and the protests and menaces of* O'FLAHERTY, *only increase the hubbub. They are soon all speaking at once at the top of their voices.*

MRS O'FLAHERTY: (*Solo*) You impudent young heifer, how dar you say such a thing to me? (TERESA *retorts furiously; the men interfere; and the solo becomes a quartet, fortissimo*). Ive a good mind to clout your ears for you to teach you manners. Be ashamed of yourself, do; and learn to know who youre speaking to. That I maytnt sin! but I dont know what the good God was thinking about when he made the like of you. Let me not see you casting sheep's eyes at my son again. There never was an O'Flaherty yet that would demean himself by keeping company with a dirty Driscoll; and if I see you next or nigh my house I'll put you in the ditch with a flea in your ear: mind that now.

TERESA: Is it me you offer such a name to, you foul-mouthed, dirty minded, lying, sloothering[41] old sow, you? I wouldnt soil my tongue by calling you in your right name and telling Sir Pearce whats the common talk of the town about you. You and your O'Flahertys! setting yourself up agen the Driscolls that would never lower themselves to be seen in conversation with you at the fair. You can keep your ugly stingy lump of a son; for what is he but a common soldier? and God help the girl that gets him, say I! So the back of my hand to you, Mrs O'Flaherty; and that the cat may tear your ugly old face!

SIR PEARCE: Silence. Tessie: did you hear me ordering you to go into the house? Mrs O'Flaherty! (*Louder*) Mrs O'Flaherty!! Will you just listen to me one moment? Please. (*Furiously*) Do you hear me speaking to you, woman? Are you human beings or are you wild beasts? Stop that noise immediately: do you hear? (*Yelling*) Are you going to do what I order you, or are you not? Scandalous! Disgraceful! This comes of being too familiar with you. O'Flaherty: shove them into the house. Out with the whole damned pack of you.

O'FLAHERTY: (*To the women*) Here now: none of that, none of that. Go easy, I tell you. Hold your whisht, mother, will you, or youll be sorry for it after. (*To* TERESA) Is that the way for a decent young

39. Organizer of the Irish Co-operative Agricultural Movement and a staunch advocate of a United Ireland within the British Commonwealth. He became a senator of the Free State in 1922, but removed to England after his house was burned by republicans in 1923.

40. at once.

41. slobbering.

girl to speak? (*Despairingly*) Oh, for the Lord's sake, shut up, will yous? Have yous no respect for yourselves or your betters? (*Peremptorily*) Let me have no more of it, I tell you. Och! the divil's in the whole crew of you. In with you into the house this very minute and tear one another's eyes out in the kitchen if you like. In with you.

The two men seize the two women, and push them, still violently abusing one another, into the house. SIR PEARCE *slams the door upon them savagely. Immediately a heavenly silence falls on the summer afternoon. The two sit down out of breath; and for a long time nothing is said.* SIR PEARCE *sits on an iron chair.* O'FLAHERTY *sits on the garden seat. The thrush begins to sing melodiously.* O'FLAHERTY *cocks his ears, and looks up at it. A smile spreads over his troubled features.* SIR PEARCE, *with a long sigh, takes out his pipe, and begins to fill it.*

O'FLAHERTY: (*Idyllically*) What a discontented sort of an animal a man is, sir! Only a month ago, I was in the quiet of the country out at the front, with not a sound except the birds and the bellow of a cow in the distance as it might be, and the shrapnel making little clouds in the heavens, and the shells whistling, and may be a yell or two when one of us was hit; and would you believe it, sir, I complained of the noise and wanted to have a peaceful hour at home. Well: them two has taught me a lesson. This morning, sir, when I was telling the boys here how I was longing to be back taking my part for king and country with the others, I was lying, as you well knew, sir. Now I can go and say it with a clear conscience. Some like war's alarums; and some likes home life. Ive tried both, sir; and I'm all for war's alarums now. I always was a quiet lad by natural disposition.

SIR PEARCE: Strictly between ourselves, O'Flaherty, and as one soldier to another (O'FLAHERTY *salutes, but without stiffening*), do you think we should have got an army without conscription if domestic life had been as happy as people say it is?

O'FLAHERTY: Well, between you and me and the wall, Sir Pearce, I think the less we say about that until the war's over, the better.

He winks at the GENERAL. *The* GENERAL *strikes a match. The thrush sings. A jay laughs. The conversation drops.*

from: WAR ISSUES FOR IRISHMEN (1918)

[As late as 1918, with Sinn Féin on the rise and talk of Irish sovereignty in the air, the recruitment campaign of the British army in Ireland continued to disappoint its sponsors. Another appeal to Shaw for advice came from Captain Stephen Gwynn of the Irish Recruiting Council. By the time he had come up with his 'open letter', events had overtaken much of his material; and even when the rejigged piece was ready for publication by Maunsel and Company as *War Issues for Irishmen*, the Armistice was declared. Very few copies of the pamphlet ever reached the public.]

... If I say that the Irish people are under very strong obligations to the English people, obligations which it would be the grossest ingratitude to deny or forget, I shall no doubt astonish those bookmade Irish patriots who are too busy reading about the Treaty of Limerick[1] and the feats of Brian Boru[2] to see anything that happens under their noses. But at least they must be dimly conscious that there was an attempt made in Dublin in the Easter of 1916 to establish an independent Irish Republic, and that one of its leaders was a noted Socialist trade unionist named James Connolly who, being captured by the British troops, was denied the right of a prisoner of war, and shot. Now, Connolly owed his position and influence as an Irish National leader to the part he had taken in organizing the great strike of the transport workers in Dublin in 1913, and the remains of his organization was the nucleus of the little army of the Irish Republican Brotherhood. That strike was sustained for many months after it would have exhausted the resources of the Irish workers had they not been aided from abroad. Where did the aid come from? From the reckless generosity of the English unions. The English workers fed, out of their own scanty wages, the Irish strikers and their families for months. I

1. The Treaty of Limerick (1691) secured Williamite rule in Ireland, but its promise to secure also the civil rights of catholics was violated 'before the ink was dry'.
2. Brian Boru (*c.* 941-1014), Irish high king who defeated Norsemen in a key battle at Clontarf in 1014, ending their domination in western Europe.

myself, with Connolly and Mr George Russell,[3] was among the speakers at a huge meeting got up in aid of the strike by Mr James Larkin[4] in London. It was a genuine non-party meeting called by English workers and crowded by thousands of English people, who rallied to the Irish strike with unbounded enthusiasm and with as much money as they could afford, and indeed more than they would have thrown away on that doomed struggle if their heads had been as clear as their sympathies were warm. Connolly got the money by the plea that the cause of Labor was the same cause all the world over, and that as against the idler and the profiteer England and Ireland were 'members one of another.' We did not set up the cry of Sinn Fein then. We did not say 'WE OURSELVES are sufficient to ourselves: you can keep your English money and leave us to take care of ourselves.' We took the money and were glad to get it and spend it. We cannot now with any decency forget Connolly and change the subject to Cromwell and General Maxwell.[5] I have the right to remind the Irish people of this, because I was one of those who asked for the money; and I was cheered to the echo by Englishmen and Englishwomen for doing so. I am an Irishman; and I have not forgotten. English working-class mothers have the right to say to me: 'Our sons are in the trenches, fighting for their lives and liberties and for yours; and some of your sons who took our money when they were starving are leaving them to fight alone.' Not a very heroic position, that, for an Irish movement which is always talking heroics.

Naturally, General Maxwell and the Unionists of the War Office, with the British and Irish Junker[6] class generally, take particularly good care not to remind the Irish people of this obligation. They can hardly hold up Connolly as a hero after shooting him, or claim the payment of debts due to him as debts of honor. They dread that sinking of national differences in the common cause of Labor all over the world far more than they dread a German victory. They will tell you to remember Belgium, to remember Poland, to remember Servia,[7] to remember any place that is far enough off to have no obvious bearing on the relations between you and them; but they will not tell you to remember Dublin and Connolly. And yet it is only through Connolly and the international solidarity that Connolly stood for that the Irish worker can be made to feel that his cause and that of the English worker is a common cause, and that he is in debt to English Labor through a very recent and very big transaction. And the worst of it is that the Nationalists and Sinn Feiners are as guilty of this ungrateful suppression as their Unionist opponents, and as blind to the fact that the Irish workers by themselves are negligible, though in combination with European and American Labor they are part of the only force that can finally make an end of all the empires and turn them into commonwealths of free nations.

Let me turn now from the broad unselfish view to the narrow and interested one; for it is useless to pretend that lads brought up as so many of ours have been, drudging for mean wages on small farms in petty parishes, can be expected to reason like statesmen or to feel obliged to repay benefits that came directly only to workers in cities they never set foot in. To them you must say that, horrible as this war is, it has raised millions of men and their families from a condition not far above savagery to comparative civilization. A trench is a safer place than a Dublin slum; and the men in it are well fed, well clothed, and certain that, whatever the Germans may do to them, at least their own commanders are keenly interested in the preservation of their lives and the maintenance of their health and strength, which is more than can be said of their employers at home. Their wives get a separation allowance; and the children are considered and allowed for too. The huge sums of money that this costs are taken largely from the incomes of rich landlords and capitalists who have to give up one pound out of every three they possess to feed, clothe, and equip the soldier, and keep his wife at home. The wonder is that any man chooses to live in a slum or drudge as a laborer on a farm

3. George Russell (1867-1935), poet, mystic and organizer of the Irish Co-operative Movement, published a famous letter to the masters of Dublin during the 1913 Lockout.
4. James Larkin (1876-1947), leading trade unionist and organizer of the 1913 strike.
5. General Maxwell was military commander of the British forces during the 1916 Rising.
6. Narrow-minded reactionary aristocrat. Named after the Prussian landowners who strenuously clung to their social and political privileges in the nineteenth century.
7. Small nations on whose behalf the Irish were urged to fight with the allies in the Great War.

when he can get into the army. But at least, some of them will say, you do not get blown to bits by high-explosive shells in a slum. Unfortunately, you do. Bombs are raining on civilian slums, farmhouses, and cottages every day in this war; and the rain gets heavier from week to week. If the slums of Ireland have escaped so far, it is only because the slums of England are nearer to the German lines; and the day is not far distant when, if the war goes on, the soldier in his bombproof dug-out will be safer from shells than the slum dweller in his wretched room. The aeroplane and the torpedo are making short work of the safety of the civilian in war. . . .

Biographies/Bibliographies

Oscar Wilde

LIFE. Born at 21 Westland Row, Dublin, on 16 October 1854, Oscar Wilde was the second son of Sir William Wilde, a noted surgeon and antiquary, and Jane Francesca Agnes Elgee, better known by her pen-name 'Speranza', under which she wrote Irish nationalist verse. After an education at Portora Royal School, Enniskillen and Trinity College, Dublin (where he was greatly influenced by the classical scholar J. P. Mahaffy), he went to Magdalen College, Oxford. The Newdigate Prize for his poem 'Ravenna' in 1878, and a lecture tour of North America in 1882, set him on the road to literary fame. In 1884 he married Constance Lloyd in London, and the couple had two sons.

By 1891, however, Wilde had met Lord Alfred Douglas, with whom he embarked on a homosexual relationship. The pair visited Florence, Algiers, and Monte Carlo together in 1894 and 1895, the years of Wilde's greatest artistic fame. In February 1895, Douglas's father, the Marquess of Queensberry, left a card at the Albemarle Club, accusing Wilde of 'posing as a somdomite' [*sic*]. Wilde took Queensberry to court, but without success; and was himself arrested and charged with homosexuality on 5 April, the day of his enemy's acquittal. The jury disagreed, and a second trial ensued, leading to a sentence of two years' hard labour, carried out in Pentonville, Wandsworth and Reading jails.

Released in May 1897, Wilde travelled at once to France, where he was reunited with Douglas. Their relationship was fraught with difficulties, further increased by the news of the death of Wilde's wife in 1898. After sojourns on the Italian and French Mediterranean, he returned to Paris and died there in the Hotel d'Alsace on 30 November 1900.

CHIEF WRITINGS. *Poems* (London: David Bogue, 1881); *The Happy Prince and Other Tales* (London: Nutt, 1888); *The Soul of Man Under Socialism* (initially in *Pall Mall Gazette*, 1891, privately published, London, 1904); *The Picture of Dorian Gray* (London: Ward Lock, 1891); *Intentions* (London: Leipzig, Heinemann and Balestier, 1891); *Lord Arthur Savile's Crime and Other Stories* (London: McIlvaine, 1891); French edition of *Salomé* (Paris: Librairie de l'art independant, 1893); *Lady Windermere's Fan* (London: Elkin Mathews and John Lane, 1893); English edition of *Salomé* (London: Elkin Mathews, 1894); *A Woman of No Importance* (London: Lane, 1894); *De Profundis* (written in jail, 1897, published London: Methuen, 1905); *The Ballad of Reading Gaol* (London: Elkin Mathews, 1898); *The Importance of Being Earnest* (London: Smithers, 1899); *An Ideal Husband* (London: Smithers, 1899); *The Poems of Oscar Wilde* (London: Methuen and Co., 1908); R. Ross (ed.), *Oscar Wilde: Complete Works* 10 vols (New York: Doubleday, 1921); G.F. Maine (ed.), *The Works of Oscar Wilde* (London and Glasgow: Collins, 1948); I. Murray (ed.), *The Complete Shorter Fiction of Oscar Wilde* (Oxford: Oxford University Press, 1979).

BIOGRAPHY AND CRITICISM. The definitive life is Richard Ellmann's *Oscar Wilde* (London: Hamish Hamilton, 1987). H. Montgomery Hyde's *Oscar Wilde* (London: Eyre Methuen, 1976) is best read in conjunction with the same author's *The Trials of Oscar Wilde* (London: Methuen, 1962). Frank Harris's *Oscar Wilde: His Life and Confessions* (New York: Garden City, 1930) is lively but contentious. Philippe Jullian's *Oscar Wilde* (English edition, London: Paladin Books, 1969) is excellent on the French background. Vyvyan Holland's *Son of Oscar Wilde* (London: Hart-Davis, 1954) is of more than domestic interest. *Selected Letters of Oscar Wilde*, edited by Rupert Hart-Davis (London: Oxford University Press, 1962) make a fascinating collection. E.H. Mikhail's *Interviews and Recollections* 2 vols (London: Macmillan, 1978) is useful. Wilde's major criticism was impeccably edited by Richard Ellmann in *The Artist as Critic* (London: W.H. Allen, 1970). See also K. Beckson, *Oscar Wilde: The Critical Heritage* (London: Routledge & Kegan Paul, 1970).

Criticism has concentrated more on the man than the texts, but Christopher Naasser's *Into the Demon Universe* (New Haven: Yale University Press, 1974) can be unreservedly recommended, along with Rodney Shewan's *Oscar Wilde: Art and Egotism* (London: Macmillan, 1977). Alan Bird's *The Plays of Oscar Wilde* (London: Duckworth, 1977) is an unpretentious, if rudimentary, guide. Richard Ellmann's *Oscar Wilde: A Collection of Critical Essays* (Englewood Cliffs, New Jersey: Prentice Hall, 1969), in the Twentieth-Century Views series, encapsulates critiques by Wilde's artistic contemporaries (Yeats, Gide, Mann, Shaw) and successors (Auden, Borges, Mary McCarthy). It can be supplemented by a more academic collection, William Tydeman's *Oscar Wilde: Comedies* (London: Macmillan, 1984) in the Modern Judgements series. Katherine Worth's *Oscar Wilde* (London: Macmillan, 1983) is the best short study of the plays in performance. Essays by Ellmann in *Eminent Domain* (London: Oxford University Press, 1974), *Golden Codgers* (London: Oxford University Press, 1974) and *Four Dubliners* (London: Hamish Hamilton, 1987), and by Susan Sontag in *Against Interpretation* (New York: New Directions, 1966), are indispensable. Owen Dudley Edwards's *The Fireworks of Oscar Wilde* (London: Barrie and Jenkins, 1989) is a useful collection and commentary on Wilde's epigrams. See also S. Mason, *Bibliography of Oscar Wilde*, new edition (London: Bertram Rota, 1967); E.H. Mikhail, *Oscar Wilde: An Annotated Bibliography of Criticism* (London: Macmillan, 1978).

George Bernard Shaw

LIFE. Born in Dublin on 26 July 1856, the son of George Carr Shaw, a 'downstart' protestant businessman with pretensions to aristocracy, and of Lucinda Elizabeth Gurly, a keen musician, whose entanglement with her teacher Vandeleur Lee provided the author with the first of many surrogate fathers. After desultory schooling in Dublin, Shaw worked in an estate agent's office, often collecting rents among poorer sections of the city. He left for London in 1876.

Five unsuccessful novels were written between 1879 and 1883, but the reading of Marx's *Das Kapital* in this period 'made a man of me'. Shaw became a member of Fabian Society in 1884, and went on to great success as a music critic. The study of Ibsen led to a career as a playwright, beginning with *Widowers' Houses* in 1892, and to fame as the drama critic of the *Saturday Review*. In 1898 Shaw married the heiress Charlotte Payne-Townshend and in 1906 the couple went to live permanently at Ayot St Lawrence, Hertfordshire. By then Shaw was established as the leading dramatist of his age, with more than 700 performances of his plays by the Court Theatre over a three-year period.

During World War I, he supported dissident pacifists, as well as criticizing British repression in Ireland. In 1925, he was awarded the Nobel Prize for Literature. The death of his wife in 1943 did not stem the flow from his pen, which continued right up until his death in 1950. He was childless, but left some of his money to the National Gallery of Ireland, where many of his happiest youthful hours had been spent.

CHIEF WRITINGS. *The Quintessence of Ibsenism* (London: Walter Scott, 1890); *Widowers' Houses* (London: Constable, 1892); *Mrs Warren's*

Profession (London: Constable, 1893); *Arms and the Man* (London: Constable, 1894); *Candida* (London: Constable, 1894); *You Never Can Tell* (London: Constable, 1896); *Man and Superman* (London: Constable, 1903); *John Bull's Other Island* (London: Constable, 1904); *Major Barbara* (London: Constable, 1905); *The Doctor's Dilemma* (London: Constable, 1906); *Androcles and the Lion* (London: Constable, 1911); *Pygmalion* (London: Constable, 1912); *Heartbreak House* (London: Constable, 1916); *Back to Methusalah* (London: Constable, 1921); *St Joan* (London: Constable, 1923); *The Intelligent Woman's Guide to Socialism and Capitalism* (London: Constable, 1928); *The Apple Cart* (London: Constable, 1929).

Beginning in 1903, Shaw wrote many Prefaces to his plays, and these can be found in *Collected Plays with their Prefaces* (London: Reinhardt, 1970 ff). The Constable Standard Edition (1930-50, 36 volumes) includes Shaw's major drama criticism, *Our Theatre in the Nineties* (3 volumes), as well as his foremost aesthetic pronouncements in *Major Critical Essays*. The author's erratic but brilliant writings on his native country are collected in *The Matter With Ireland*, edited by David H. Greene and Dan H. Laurence (1962).

BIOGRAPHY AND CRITICISM. Pending complete publication of Michael Holroyd's multi-volume *Life* (London: Chatto and Windus — Vol. I, *The Search for Power* (1988); Vol. II, *The Pursuit of Power* (1989)), the most trusted source is Archibald Henderson's *Man of the Century* (New York: Appleton-Century-Crofts, 1956). Also immensely useful is the composite autobiography, compiled in two volumes from Shaw's writings by Stanley Weintraub, *Shaw: An Autobiography 1856-1898* and *1898-1950* (London: Reinhardt, 1969). Hesketh Pearson's *George Bernard Shaw* (London: Methuen, 1961) is predictably lively.

The *Collected Letters of Bernard Shaw* 4 vols, edited by Dan H. Laurence (London: Reinhardt, 1965) is indispensable.

One of the earliest critical assessments, Eric Bentley's *Bernard Shaw* (New York: New Directions, 1947) remains the best single introduction to life, work and thought. A sensitive recent study, with a feel for the Irish background, is Nicholas Grene's *Bernard Shaw: A Critical View* (London: Macmillan, 1984). Michael Holroyd's essay 'GBS and Ireland' in *Sewanee Review* (Winter 1976) is informative, as is B.C. Rosset's *Shaw of Dublin: The Formative Years* (Pennsylvania: Pennsylvania State University Press, 1964).

Maurice Valency's *The Cart and the Trumpet* (New York: Oxford University Press, 1973) and Alfred Turco's *Shaw's Moral Vision* (Ithaca, New York: Cornell University Press, 1976) valuably assess Shavian ideas as embodied in art; but the most penetrating study of this topic is still Richard Ohmann's *Shaw: The Style and the Man* (Middletown, Connecticut: Wesleyan University Press, 1963). On politics, Paul Hummert's *Bernard Shaw's Marxian Romance* (Omaha: University of Nebraska Press, 1973) is useful, if at times heavy-handed; and Alick West's *A Good Man Fallen among Fabians* (London: Lawrence and Wishart, 1950) still challenges. Rodelle Weintraub's collection of essays by divers hands, *Fabian Feminist: Bernard Shaw and Women* (London: Reinhardt, 1977), is both lively and rigorous; while R.J. Kaufmann's Twentieth-Century Views on *G.B. Shaw* (Englewood Cliffs, New Jersey: Prentice Hall, 1965) skilfully unfolds the range of critical debate.

Martin Meisel's *Shaw and the Nineteenth Century Theatre* (New York: Limelight, 1963) is still the last, exhaustive word on its subject, while Margery Morgan's *The Shavian Playground* (London: Methuen, 1972) has provocative insights into *John Bull's Other Island*. For some debunking of Shavian pretensions, read J.W. Krutch's *'Modernism' in Modern Drama* (Ithaca, New York: Cornell University Press, 1953) and Edmund Wilson's essay in *The Triple Thinkers* (Harmondsworth: Penguin, 1952). On the other hand, Michael Holroyd (ed.), *The Genius of Shaw* (London: Hodder and Stoughton, 1979) is an engaging set of essays by staunch devotees. *The Annual of Bernard Shaw Studies*, edited by Stanley Weintraub, is a most vibrant journal. See also J. P. Wearing (ed.), *G.B. Shaw: An Annotated Bibliography of Writings About Him Vol. I 1871-1930*; D.C. Haberman (ed.), *Vol. III 1957-1978* (Dekalb, Illinois: Northern Illinois University Press, 1986).

TERENCE BROWN, *Editor*

Cultural Nationalism 1880-1930

The cultural nationalism that governed much of the most significant literary and intellectual activity in Ireland between 1880 and 1930 was a force distinct from, though intimately involved with, political nationalism. Cultural nationalism may be taken to mean that conviction (which originated in eighteenth-century Germany, and which was fanned into general life by the fervour of Romanticism) whereby the essential, spiritual life of a people is assumed to subsist in its culture, bequeathed to it from antiquity and prehistory. Language in such an understanding of national identity is what bears the gifts of the past into the present and supplies a living link with a racial spirituality. Indeed, the spirit of a people is vital in their language and in the legends, literature, songs and stories which that language makes available.

As such, cultural nationalism is a useful, even energizing, adjunct to a struggle waged primarily in the interests of a political nationalism whose aim is simply that of legislative independence. And in Ireland the relationship between the two forces was largely of that order. Cultural nationalism offered a rationale according to which the political struggle for independence could be prosecuted with a heightened sense of justification (although, it is necessary to add, many of those who were active in the interests of cultural nationalism would not have seen the matter in such stark terms).

In Ireland the materials necessary to generate a sense of the country's distinctive cultural inheritance were fairly ready to hand by the end of the nineteenth century. Over a century of antiquarian and philological researches, in which European scholarship had played a major role, had unearthed the literary and cultural remains of the Celtic past. French scholars, Ernest Renan (1823-92) and Marie Henri d'Arbois de Jubainville (1827-1910), had given intellectual weight to the idea of the Celt, which had been popularized by Matthew Arnold's derivative though influential essay of 1867, *On the Study of Celtic Literature*, German philological enterprise had rescued texts and grammar from obscurity and, in such translations as Kuno Meyer's *The Voyage of Bran* (1895) or *Four Old Irish Songs of Summer & Winter* (1903), had made this work readily available to the literary imagination.

What crucially was lacking, however, was a distinctive Irish language in which the Irish spirit might be discerned and nurtured. The Gaelic tongue, which had remained in widespread use until the end of the eighteenth century, was facing extinction one hundred years later, the tragic Famine of the later 1840s a *coup de grâce* from which it seemed scarcely capable of recovering. Accordingly, one of the most fraught debates of the period 1880 to 1930 was whether a distinctive Irish identity might be forged in the English language (the mother tongue of most of the island's inhabitants) or whether the revival of Irish was a 'necessity' (in Douglas Hyde's formulation) if the idea of Irish nationhood was to be anything more than a political expediency.

The Irish Literary Revival was a movement that sought to supply the Ireland of the late nineteenth and early twentieth centuries with a sense of its own distinctive identity through the medium of the English language. This movement's main writers and thinkers believed that a general awareness of the splendours and riches of Gaelic literary antiquity and of the residual fires of the Celtic way of life (still burning in rural districts, particularly in the West) would generate a sense of national self-worth and of organic unity, which would give to the political struggle a dignity and purpose it would otherwise lack. Indeed, W. B. Yeats, its primary propagandist, believed that the cultural movement was even a substitute for political activity, and he identified its origins in the trough of political disillusionment that followed the collapse of Parnell's parliamentary campaign for Home Rule in 1886 and his death in 1891. Young men, Yeats believed, took to culture when politics failed them.

Yet, in a predominantly catholic country, it was primarily Irish protestants who involved themselves in this crusade or whose work contributed to it. Among them were Standish James O'Grady (a unionist in politics, but a powerful popularizer of ideas about the Celtic past), W. B. Yeats, AE (George Russell), Lady Augusta Gregory and Douglas Hyde. The reasons why these individuals became so enamoured of things Celtic, so obsessed with the 'matter of Ireland', bears some brief examination, for it was uncharacteristic in the period, if not unknown, for members of their caste and class to be so in quite the ways they were.

Protestant Anglo-Ireland, the ruling elite in nineteenth- century Ireland, had throughout most of the century viewed both Irish political and cultural nationalism with nervous distaste. With rare exceptions (Samuel Ferguson and Thomas Davis), protestant Irishmen had resolutely espoused, when culture interested them at all, an imperial and cosmopolitan view, epitomized in the writings of the great unionist historian, W. E. H. Lecky (1838-1903). That a movement should have developed in which members of the protestant elite supported the cause of an Irish cultural nationalism has drawn much study and comment.

There would be grounds for believing that these writers had simply fallen under the spell of a compelling and fortuitous literary opportunity. In all their writings on the matter of Ireland (and this is especially true of Standish O'Grady), there is an enthusiastic ardour, a buoyant rhetoric that suggests an enraptured discovery of something primal, enthralling in its strangeness. Such an explanation was gratifying to nationalist *amour propre*, for it suggested that even the colonial elite could not blind itself to the incomparable riches of the Irish cultural inheritance, thereby giving substance and aid to political separatism; and in such terms, catholic Ireland, largely supportive of political nationalism, occasionally seemed willing to accept the Literary Revival as a contribution to the more important struggle.

However, it is as an aspect of the dynamics of a late colonial society that the Irish protestant elite's interest in things cultural can more convincingly be explained. Since 1829 and the Catholic Emancipation Act, the protestant elite and its unionist politics had endured recurring crises. The Famine of the 1840s, the Disestablishment of the Church of Ireland in 1869, the Land War of the 1880s and the threat of the Home Rule Bill of 1886 all had impelled a formerly secure and arrogant caste to ponder its future with less than equanimity. A nascent Irish political nationalism, predominantly catholic in complexion and Gaelic in aspiration, was increasingly prepared to view the Anglo-Irish protestant world as simply the alien culture of a garrison society. The doctrines of the Irish Ireland movement, propagated with especial force by D. P. Moran (whose idea of a 'Battle of Two Civilizations' caught a widespread mood) insisted that Ireland's authentic cultural nationalist identity was unquestionably as a Gaelic and catholic nation, in which the Anglo-Irish, English-speaking protestant could have no part. So pervasive was this attitude in nationalist Ireland that even Douglas Hyde (son of a Church of Ireland protestant clergyman) fell under its influence. Indeed, his 1892 lecture, 'The Necessity for De-Anglicising Ireland' (which led to the foundation of the Gaelic League in 1893, an organization dedicated to the revival of the Irish language), argues that Gaelic is crucial to Ireland's distinctive survival. But, in the contradictions and confusion of its argument, this lecture suggests how problematic a thing it was for a member of the protestant Anglo-Irish social caste to espouse the cause of Irish Ireland, since a key element in that movement's ideology was the catholicism of the Irish people and the inauthenticity of the protestant Irish.

In contrast to Douglas Hyde, other descendants of Anglo-Irish landowners, of professional men and protestant clergy, conscious to lesser and greater extents of the threat to their social standing from the increasingly self-assured and powerful majority, sought to popularize a view of Irish identity that might soften the stark outlines of politics, class and sectarianism in the benign glow of culture. Writers like O'Grady, Yeats, AE and Lady Gregory wrote therefore of an ancient Ireland, heroic and self-sacrificially magnificent, in which unity of culture was manifest in a pagan, mythic, rural paradise. In their work, prelapsarian Ireland knows nothing of the political and sectarian strife of the modern; its simple grandeur and other-worldliness are a rebuke to the reductive and strident voices of the aggressively political nationalists. The authentic Celtic tradition, in such a view, was organic and coherent, aristocratic and individualistic. As such, it could be exploited in their writings as a powerful symbolic corrective to the sectarian, exclusivist, democratic and collectivist doctrines of Irish Ireland and modern Irish political nationalism (from which Yeats and his fellow-workers had much to lose).

Nevertheless, the fact that the Literary Revival probably had its opportunistic and self-interested aspects should not obscure the movement's idealism. Lady Gregory, Yeats and AE genuinely believed that in their works they were giving Ireland what it needed, that they were indeed saving the political nationalists from themselves and from the sterile materialism of a merely political creed. While the implicit condescension of such a stance can seem unattractive — a cultivated form of the white man's burden — it *was* the source of much enthusiastic, energetic, genuinely patriotic activity, which made the publication of such works as Standish O'Grady's *History of Ireland: The Heroic Period* (1878-80), Douglas Hyde's *Love Songs of Connacht* (1893), and Lady Gregory's *Cuchulain of Muirthemne* (1902) landmarks of Irish cultural history.

The Irish Literary Revival and its English-language-based cultural nationalism therefore can be understood in relation to these debates about identity and language, a developing sense of colonial insecurity and a nascent aggressive political nationalism. The idealism of both, and their anxiety to achieve cultural self-respect, must also be seen as characteristic phenomena — the crises of the late Victorian period.

Late Victorian British society was marked by a social crisis bred of the threat posed to an increasingly insecure middle class by a large, industrial proletariat, and also by a philosophical and religious crisis, the consequence of new scientific modes of thought. A characteristic Victorian figure was therefore the anxious, perplexed, literary man, whose certainties of class and creed had been undermined by the generally calamitarian mood and by reductionist scientific scepticism. Such a figure in late Victorian Britain was often the child of devoutly evangelical parents, whose chiliastic creed and enthusiastic religiosity he had forsaken, under the twin assaults of social unease and scepticism, for generalized calamitarian anxieties and for 'culture', conceived of as a civilized and humanizing force.

Irish protestantism was afflicted in the period by markedly similar experiences, so that developments within it can be seen as local variants of the broader British crises. In the work of O'Grady, for example, we see a mind formed by the fervent evangelicalism of his immediate family background, disturbed by a profoundly anxious social vision (the Irish 'mob' becomes the equivalent of the English proletariat) and by a sceptical, speculative intelligence. Yet from his evangelical childhood he brings a rhapsodic fervour, expressed in an elevated prose style. Indeed, the apocalyptic note struck in O'Grady's prose, so characteristic of late Victorian literature, is one that recurs throughout the writings of the Irish Literary Revival, often with obvious echoes of the evangelicals' millenarian obsessions. Furthermore, that commonplace of nineteenth-century English literary history, whereby in literary and cultural activity imaginative young men found a substitute for the discipline and sustaining warmth of an intellectually indefensible evangelical fundamentalism (Edmund Gosse's *Father and Son* is the classic English account), had its analogue in protestant Ireland.

John Millington Synge, then, was an entirely typical Victorian when he found his childhood faith undermined by Darwinian evolutionism and when he substituted for that faith, literary and cultural interests:

> Soon after I had relinquished the Kingdom of God I began to take a real interest in the Kingdom of Ireland. My patriotism went round from a vigorous and reasoning loyalty to a temperate nationalism and everything Irish became sacred. (*Autobiography*)

What was distinctive in such an Irish pilgrimage, however, was that in Irish cultural nationalism such a young man could find a vital, socially significant mode of thought and feeling that fully compensated for what had been lost. A Matthew Arnold in Victorian Britain might seek spiritual sustenance for an era of doubt and great social unease in ideas of Hellenized aestheticism, a John Ruskin in a moralizing socialism; but neither had the opportunity to participate in a movement that charged literary and cultural activities with that absolute sense of social significance that nationalism gives to its adherents.

There were, too, in the cultural nationalism of the Revivalist (a term with obvious evangelical associations) things that made it readily explicable as an enterprise with roots quite simply in an Irish protestantism, troubled by the spirit of the age. The eager Celticism of its adherents in part can be explained by the fact that the anglican Church of Ireland had long asserted its own Celtic purity, doubting the Irish authenticity of the Roman communion in a claim of an apostolic succession stretching back to Saint Patrick himself. So the idea of the Celt was not merely the possession of European and British ethnology; it had been the received wisdom of the Church of Ireland since the days of Archbishop Ussher in the early seventeenth century. Moreover, the Irish language had been a familiar property in the Church of Ireland world, where it was valued as a useful tool for the proselytizer. For many Irish protestants, therefore, Gaelic was an accepted accomplishment of assumed utility, even as the emergent catholic, nationalist middle class was earnest to forget its antecedents in and its duties to a Gaelic-speaking peasantry, whose own language it had largely abandoned. In such a context, Lady Augusta Gregory, a compelling figure in the Revival, who acquired Irish in adulthood and who made it a daily practice to read from the New Testament in that language, is less of an exotic than she might appear.

For two further reasons, cultural nationalism was attractive to Irish Victorian minds seeking a sustainable and imaginatively satisfying spirituality. It was largely immune to rational penetration and it gave religious sanction to literary endeavour.

The structure of thought encompassed in the term cultural nationalism is one that allows for a mystical, indefinable sense of spirit (*geist* in German) present in a people, even when it is not immediately observable to the eye of unbelief. Late Victorian petit-bourgeois Irish society — the small farmer on his plot, the fisherman at his trade — may seem an unlikely repository of an ancient spirituality, distinctive and essentially Irish, but so, the doctrine states, it must be. Therefore cultural nationalism, in its unlikely yet compelling claims, has its occult aspects, its capacity to satisfy minds hungry for mystery in an increasingly unmysterious and materialist world. It must assume that the spirit that vitalized a Cuchulain is still dynamic in a reality less obviously heroic than the prehistoric, and it must stimulate a quest for his analogues or avatars in such figures as a Charles Stewart Parnell, or in the figure of a modern revolutionary. So in Irish cultural nationalism we see an illogical blend of radical fervour and occult yearnings, mingled with an evangelical certainty and excitement.

Cultural nationalism invests the records of the past with the spiritual charge of the sacred. Archaic texts are not simply archaeological remnants; they are chapters in the sacred book of the people. The modern Irish writer (often from a background where protestantism had been a religion of the book) is in fact a scribe at work upon a sacred manuscript, his own creation capable of being subsumed in the greater text. There is then, not surprisingly, a recurrent suggestion that the Revival itself was composing a sacred book, its writers merely the priests of a sacred order. At such moments in cultural nationalism, the occult and literature combine to produce a heady brew indeed. George Moore satirized this aspect of the Literary Revival in his autobiographical account, *Hail and Farewell*, but the book itself is ambivalently insecure about its claims to be the sacred text of the movement. That even so sardonic a mind as George Moore's was tempted by the religious sanction that cultural nationalism lent to the act of writing suggests how powerful a narcotic it could be.

In aspiring to participate in the composition of a sacred book of the people, of course, the Revival writers were taking a large step away from the realism, naturalism and subjectivism that had characterized much late nineteenth-century English literature. Their own cultural nationalism encouraged that departure in several further ways.

First, the belief that literature could serve the people by revealing in its sacred pages the true soul of the race, hidden by contemporary appearances under the shroud of convention, meant that writers invested the legends and myths of the past with symbolic powers. So the Irish Literary Revival saw Cuchulain not simply as a mythological personage, but as a figure embodying the truly Irish spirit. Accordingly, his portrayal in modern literature lifts the veil of appearance to reveal a higher reality. As such, Cuchulain appears in the Revivalists' writings as a symbol, his presence a revelation of occult, esoteric truths; and, in so doing, he wrests literature away from mere realism or naturalism. As an image of a universal principle in the Irish world, he transcends any mere subjectivism. For he is so much more than simply a passing mood in author or reader. Cuchulain is the manifestation of an objective, communal reality.

Secondly, the Revivalists' literary involvement with the remains of a primitive people gave an obviously textual, non-realistic quality to their writings. To read their redactions, translations, versions of myth and folk-tale is to realize almost continuously the literariness of literature, that a book is always a book in the making. The *Love Songs of Connacht*, for example, achieves its effect in part by printing Irish and English together. Most of its early readers knew little or no Irish, and the old Gaelic script gave to the experience of reading the work, one imagines, a sense of archaic, esoteric things rendered assimilable by an act of translation. The work is as much a celebration of that act, a testament to literary power, as it is a book of love lyrics.

In its moving away from the dominant modes of nineteenth-century literary production (in which the realist novel had pride of place) towards symbolism, objectivity and the self-reflexive text, the Irish Literary Revival has seemed to many to be intimately associated with the early stages of Modernism. The thrust of its social vision made its role in the broader theatre of the international Modernist movement even more secure.

In seeking as cultural nationalists the essence of the Irish people in the past, in mythology, in an ancient rural civilization, the writers of the Irish Literary Revival revealed themselves as profoundly reactionary, their conservatism seeking confirmation in aristocratic, all too literary nostalgias about race and religion. The Irish people were not the contentious, sectarian, democratic, modernizing men and women encountered daily in the streets, but a heroic Celtic race, sublimely unfitted for the squalid compromises of the modern world. So powerful was the mesmeric attraction of this dream of essence, beside which the refractory problems of mere existence paled into insignificance, that even the revolutionary Patrick Pearse fell under its sway. In his writings we see a committed social visionary and political activist, distracted by images of antique chivalry and archaic purity of creed and blood, a mind compelled by apocalyptic imaginings to deeds of desperation. Indeed, it could be argued that the martyr Pearse had the courage of the Literary Revival's radical conservatism, taking its aesthetics seriously as politics.

It is not surprising that this grandiose, magnificently insubstantial sense of Irish identity should have drawn impatient criticism. George Moore's *Hail and Farewell* contains passages of sustained and malicious satire on the absurdities of the Revivalist's enterprise, although Moore had done his bit to portray Ireland as essentially rural and naively quaint in his *The Untilled Field*. D. P. Moran directed the barrage of his aggressive scorn on the fey trivialities of the Celtic Twilight school (for whom Ireland is an occult secret whose mysteries are best glimpsed in the crepuscular lyric). But it was in the writings of James Joyce that the movement as a whole was to endure a withering, searchingly intelligent critique.

What cannot be gainsaid of the Literary Revival's achievement, however, is that, in creating for the first time an indisputably Irish literature in the English language, these writers gave the Irish people to know that the language of their daily social intercourse could be the basis of an internationally recognised body of creative writing. As such it *did* play its part in that raising of Irish consciousness which was a part of the process that led to legislative independence for most of the island. It also demonstrated that the English language in Ireland, influenced by its long association with Irish speech patterns and modes of thought, was a flexible, mature, subtle instrument, capable of great nobility and energy as well as of sardonic witticism and lyric intensity. Perhaps most importantly of all, it demonstrated, albeit in ways not all Irish people always have found congenial, that the English spoken in Ireland could be the means whereby a society reflected on itself.

STANDISH O'GRADY

(1846-1928)

from:
HISTORY OF IRELAND (1878)

[In his *History of Ireland*, Volume One (1878), subtitled *The Heroic Period*, Standish O'Grady retold the story of Deirdre, whom the Irish Revival writers were to imagine as the Irish Helen. This tale, one of the Ulster cycle of Irish sagas, was to inspire works by W. B. Yeats, Lady Gregory, AE, Synge and James Stephens.]

CHAPTER XXV
DEIRDRE

'Yea, for her sake, on them the fire gat hold.'[1]
Swinburne

When Concobar Mac Nessa was called to the Ard-Rieship of Ulla[2] he celebrated his inauguration by a great banquet at Emain Macha, and all the knights of the Crave Rue were there, and the chiefs and kings of the Clanna Rury, and the kings and ambassadors of the tribes and nations of Erin that were favourable to his succession. There were also there noble ladies, and amongst them the bride of Felim, chief bard of the Ultonians.[3] It was a year of prophecies and portents, and Cathvah, the druid — he who had eaten of the nuts of knowledge[4] — the interpreter of dreams and omens — had announced that an age was then in its inception, which would be renowned to the ends of the earth, and the last age of the world.

That night the Ultonians feasted with more magnificence than had ever before that been used in Erin, and the sounds of revelry arose out of the vast and high Dûn[5] into the night, and the lights glared far and wide, and there was the sound of the harp and of singing voices, for Emain Macha was wholly given over to festivity.

Then about the time that the shrill cry of the cock is first heard, a rapid fear swept like a wind through the whole city, and smote an universal silence, and men held their breaths awaiting some prodigy. Anon there arose upon the night a shrill and agonizing scream, as of an animal pierced, that utters a cry in its agony. And three times the cry shrilled through the city. But simultaneously were heard low thunder-like mutterings, whereat the earth trembled; but this came from the Tayta Brac,[6] wherein was the warlike equipment of all the Red Branch; and aged warriors who had fought under Rury recognised that solemn warning, and they knew what shield it was that announced impending disaster. And, after this, there arose sounds of battle, crash of meeting hosts and shattering spears, the shoutings of warriors, and the war-cries of the Clans of Ulla, and between these noises was heard, far away, the roaring of the sea. Then the prodigy died away, and men saw the reflection of their own fear in the white faces of their comrades.

But in the king's palace the feast was broken up, and the king summoned a council of his great men, and there it was determined that Cathvah the seer should be interrogated concerning the import of the prodigy. Then Cathvah arose with his druidical instruments in his hands, and chanted the chant of divination; and under the power of that chant the veil that hides futurity was rent before his mind, and in a sacred phrenzy he walked towards the Grianan[7] of the women, and the king and his knights followed him reverently. Then he approached the bride of the chief bard of Ulla, singling her out from amongst all the women in the Dûn, and he stood above her and prophesied:

'No common child bearest thou in thy womb, O lady. Beneath thy zone, veiled yet in infancy, I see a woman of wondrous beauty, bright gold her hair, eyes piercing and splendid, tongue full of sweet

1. From A. C. Swinburne's 'Laus Veneris' (1866). In quoting this notorious poem in praise of illicit sexuality, O'Grady seems to be associating the Deirdre of legend with besotted erotic obsession.
2. The high-kingship of Ulster.
3. The inhabitants of Ulster. Crave Rue = Craodh Ruadh (The Red Branch).
4. In the next chapter of his *History of Ireland*, O'Grady tells how there is an invisible fountain in the heart of Ireland, seen only by the invisible Tuatha Dé Danaan. Around the fountain grow seven hazel-trees. Those who eat of the nuts of these trees are filled with knowledge.
5. A fortified dwelling.
6. The name of the armaments' store in Emain Macha (Armagh); from the Irish *Teité Brec(c)*. For suggested meanings of this name, see Tomás O Bróin, '"Craebruad": The Spurious Tradition', *Éigse*, 15 (1973), 103-13.
7. A sun-palace, set apart for the women.

sounds, her countenance like the colour of snow blended with crimson; but out of her beauty shall arise a sword. It is the destruction of the wide territories of Ulla that thou bearest in thy womb, O lady — wasting wars and conflagrations and blood. I see the Red Branch[8] divided against itself, and the sons of Usna slain, and the son of Duthrect, and I see the son of the High King, and Fergus, and many kings of the tribes of Una flying across the boundary into exile, and wars yet greater arising out of that expatriation which shall consume away the children of Iar.'

After this, Concobar convened his council, and he himself desired that the child, when born, should be slain; but it was finally determined that a tower should be built in a remote and inaccessible spot, and that she should be immured there until she died, for they reverenced the interpretations of Cathvah.

The child was born a beautiful blue-eyed babe, and she was called Deirdré, and Concobar selected a prudent and wise woman named Lowrcam, to whom he committed the child, and she was immured according to the resolution of the saba[9] of the kings, at Emain Macha.

The child Deirdré grew up so beautiful, gentle, and tender, that she drew to herself the whole heart's-love of the lady who guarded her, so that her loyalty to the council of the kings, and to Concobar Mac Nessa, was dissolved, and the memory of the portents that attended Deirdré's birth, and the vaticinations of Cathvah, faded away. Therefore she relaxed the severity of that imprisonment, and suffered her to wander in the forest that surrounded the tower, to gather flowers, and listen to the songs of the birds.

There were at this time amongst the knights of the Red Branch three young warriors, the glory of all Ulla for their beauty and their accomplishments, Naysi, and Anly, and Ardan, the three sons of Usna, and they were loved by all who knew them, and chiefly by Fergus Mac Roy, who was the great sheltering tree of all the noblest and best of the young knights. And now that I have likened Fergus to a great sheltering tree, I mind me how afterwards, in the wars of the Tân-bo-Cooalney,[10] one seeing him moving in the fore-front of Queen Meave's host said, 'He seems to me, observing him, to resemble a great tree that stands alone upon the lawn of some noble Dûn.' But to him the children of Usna were dearer than all the rest of the Red Branch. Naysi was the most beautiful of the brothers, black as the raven were his eyebrows and curling hair, and white and ruddy his countenance.

It so happened that, in a great chase, Naysi, the son of Usna, got separated from his companions, and as he wandered through the forest, seeking to recover his way, he came to where was the lonely tower in which Deirdré was immured. But he presented himself to her as she walked among the trees, and the end of that meeting was, that they gave each other their love, and plighted a faithful troth.

Then Naysi took counsel with his brothers, and with the chiefs of his clan, and they were troubled and afraid, and besought him to cease from that upon which he had resolved. But, when they could not persuade him, they resolved to perish along with him before the wrath of the High King, if it were necessary, rather than suffer him to be unbefriended.

So there was a sudden hosting of the clan, and they bore away Deirdré from her tower, and marched rapidly northwards to the Moyle.[11] But at Dûn Kermnah, upon the sea, a fleet was prepared. Thus the Clanna Usna deserted Concobar Mac Nessa, and they passed into Alba,[12] and went into the service of the king of that land.

Then there was great lamentation over all Ulla, for the loss of the children of Usna, and in every Dûn, from Assaroe to Dundalgan, the poets chanted mournful strains about the exile of the sons of Usna, and the wondrous beauty of Deirdré, and the noblest of the youth of Ulla, and of the rest of Eiré, passed into Alba, to see Deirdré, and many of them took service under them, and the Clan Usna grew mightier every day. But Concobar Mac Nessa passed sentence of perpetual banishment and exile against the clan, for he feared the words of the

8. The Order of the Knights of the Red Branch, the warriors of Ulster in the Ulster Cycle.
9. Here seems to mean 'council'; possibly derived from the Irish word *samhadh* meaning a community, especially the members of a religious community or council.
10. *Táin Bó Cúailnge* (The Cattle Raid of Cooley), the central tale of the Ulster or Ulidian cycle, which tells how Cú Chulainn (The Hound of Culann), while still a youth, held up an army of invaders from Connacht while awaiting the arrival of his fellow-Ulstermen, who were under a spell.
11. A district in north-east Ulster.
12. Scotland.

prophet prophesying the Red Branch divided against itself.

But, from the time of their departure, Fergus Mac Roy had no rest, for he was disconsolate for the perpetual exile of Naysi, Anly, and Ardan, and he was wroth with Concobar Mac Nessa, and uttered bitter gibes and scoffs against the High King and his star-gazers. But, in the end, he procured a reversal of the sentence of perpetual exile, and forthwith, taking his household troops, and his sons, Illan the Fair, and Bewney the Ruthless Red, he passed over into Alba; and when the sons of Usna heard of the reversal of the sentence, they gave three shouts of joy, and shed tears of pleasure; but Deirdré uttered three cries of lamentation, and shed tears of sorrow, for she said that evil was impending over the children of Usna. Then Fergus Mac Roy said that they were under his protection, and that no harm could happen them, for that there was no king in Erin who could break through his protection. But Deirdré would not be comforted, and all the day and night she shed tears, and related dreams and omens, and predicted the treachery of Bewney the Ruthless Red; yet they did not give heed to her, but hastened forward the sailing. But innumerable were the lamentations of Deirdré concerning the children of Usna, and they are preserved in the books of the poets. And, both in Alba, before they set out, and while they sailed across the intervening sea, were they warned by many portents. But beside many other, it was permitted them to hear the mournful chanting of the unhappy children of Lear.[13] For, as they rowed across the cold expanse of the Moyle, they heard the children singing, and it was night. There the hands of all the mariners were relaxed, and every oar suspended. Then the whole host wept together, and the warriors and strong men sobbed aloud, when they heard the children singing, for the cry of them, as they sang, pierced the starry night, and dissolved every heart.

After this, they rowed on in silence, and came to Dûn Kermnah, and the children of Usna hastened onward to Emain Macha, trusting in the High King, that he would not violate the protection of Mac Roy.

Nay-the-less, Concobar Mac Nessa gave no heed to the protection of Fergus, for he saw that his authority and sovereignty were set aside, and that now the wars predicted by Cathvah were about to burst, and that Fergus and the children of Usna were confederate against him. Therefore, he made a swift and sudden excursion into the north, with his bravest and most agile warriors; but Fergus Mac Roy had delayed at Dûn Kermnah, having been detained there by a stratagem, and Bewney the Ruthless Red, went over to his side, and betrayed the children of Usna. But Concobar Mac Nessa seized Deirdré and Naysi, Anly and Ardan, and he slew the children of Usna, and Illan the Fair, and many of the Clan Usna, and despised the protection of Fergus Mac Roy.

But, when Fergus Mac Roy heard how his protection had been set at naught, and his son slain, and the sons of Usna, he passed into rebellion, and drew away with him two-thirds of the Red Branch; for wide territories passed into rebellion along with him, and amongst them Cormac Conlingas, the High King's son, and the children of Iar were divided against themselves, and the whole realm was shaken with war, and Emain Macha burned to the ground; but, in the end, Fergus Mac Roy was defeated, and driven over the border into the country of the Olnemacta, west of the Shannon, and all these exiles went into the service of Aileel More and Queen Meave, and Fergus Mac Roy was the greatest of her generals at the breaking out of the wars of the Tan-bo-Coolney.

13. 'The Children of Lir' is one of the tales of the Mythological Cycle. It tells how Lir's children are turned into swans by a jealous step-mother and are doomed to remain as swans for nine hundred years, three hundred of which must be spent on the Mull of Kintyre, on the west coast of Scotland. Release from the spell will come only when the bell of Christianity rings in Ireland, with the coming of St Patrick. The Moyle is the stretch of water between the Mull of Kintyre and Dalriada, on the coast of County Antrim.

from:
HISTORY OF IRELAND (1881)

[The following excerpt is taken from O'Grady's *History of Ireland: Critical and Philosophical* (1881). In its elaborately detailed enthusiasm for Ireland's legendary past, it is both characteristic of the author and seminal for the period. Here indeed is the dawn of the Irish Literary Revival.]

DAWN

There is not perhaps in existence a product of the human mind so extraordinary as the Irish annals.

From a time dating for more than three thousand years before the birth of Christ, the stream of Hibernian history flows down uninterrupted, copious and abounding, between accurately defined banks, with here and there picturesque meanderings, here and there flowers lolling on those delusive waters, but never concealed in mists or lost in a marsh. As the centuries wend their way, king succeeds king with a regularity most gratifying, and fights no battle, marries no wife, begets no children, does no doughty deed of which a contemporaneous note was not taken, and which has not been incorporated in the annals of his country. To think that this mighty fabric of recorded events, so stupendous in its dimensions, so clean and accurate in its details, so symmetrical and elegant, should be after all a mirage and delusion, a gorgeous bubble, whose glowing rotundity, whose rich hues, azure, purple, amethyst and gold, vanish at a touch and are gone, leaving a sorry remnant over which the patriot disillusionized may grieve.

Early Irish history is the creation mainly of the bards. Romances and poems supplied the great blocks with which the fabric was reared. These the chroniclers fitted into their places, into the interstices pouring shot-rubbish, and grouting. The bardic intellect, revolving round certain ideas for centuries, and round certain material facts, namely, the mighty barrows of their ancestors, produced gradually a vast body of definite historic lore, life-like kings and heroes, real-seeming queens. The mechanical intellect followed with perspicuous arrangement, with a thirst for accuracy, minuteness, and verisimilitude. With such quarrymen and such builders the work went on apace, and anon a fabric huge rose like an exhalation,[1] and like an exhalation its towers and pinnacles of empurpled mist are blown asunder and dislimn.

Doubtless the legendary blends at some point with the historic narrative. The cloud and mist somewhere condense into the clear stream of indubitable fact. But how to discern under the rich and teeming mythus of the bards, the course of that slender and doubtful rivulet, or beneath the piled rubbish and dust of the chroniclers, discover the tiny track which elsewhere broadens into the highway of a nation's history. In this minute, circumstantial, and most imposing body of history, where the certain legend exhibits the form of plain and probable narrative, and the certain fact displays itself with a mythical flourish, how there to fix upon any one point and say here is the first truth. It is a task perilous and perplexing.

Descartes[2] commenced his investigations into the nature of the soul, by assuming the certainty of his own existence. Standing upon this adamantine foothold, he sought around him for ground equally firm, which should support his first step in the quagmire of metaphysics. But in the early Irish history, what one solid and irrefutable fact appears upon which we can put foot or hand and say, 'This, at all events, is certain; this that I hold is not mist; this that I stand on is neither water nor mire?' Running down the long list of Milesian[3] kings, chiefs, brehons,[4] and bards, where first shall we pause, arrested by some substantial form in this procession of empty ghosts — how distinguish the man from the shadow, when over all is diffused the same concealing mist, and the eyes of the living and the dead look with the same pale glare? Eocha of the heavy sighs, how shall we certify or how deny the existence of that melancholy man, or of Tiernmas, who introduced the worship of fire? Lara of the ships, did he really cross the sea to Gaul, and return thence to give his name to Leinster, and beget Leinster kings? Ugainey More, did he rule to the Torrian sea, holding sea-coast towns in fee, or was he a prehistoric shadow thrown into the past from the stalwart figure of Niall of the Hostages? Was Morann a real brehon, or fabulous as the collar that threatened to strangle him in the utterances of unjust judgments? Was Ferkeirtney a poet, having flesh and bones and blood, and did Bricrind, the satirist, really compose those bitter ranns[5] for the Ultonians?[6] or were both as ghostly as the prime druid, Amergin, who came into the island with the sons of Milesius, and in a manner beyond all praise, collected the histories of the conquered peoples? Or do we wrong that venerable man whose high-

1. Milton, *Paradise Lost*, Book I, line 711.

2. René Descartes (1596-1650), the author of *Discours de la méthode*, to the most famous proposition of which ('Cogito, ergo sum'; 'I think, therefore I am') O'Grady refers.
3. The peoples, assumed to derive from the Spanish peninsula, who in Celtic mythology defeated the legendary Tuatha Dé Danaan.
4. judges.
5. verses.
6. The inhabitants of Ulster. In this passage, O'Grady is pondering the historical reality of the Irish legends of Celtic antiquity. Niall of the Nine Hostages was king of Ireland 379-405 A.D.

sounding name clung for ages around the estuary of the Avoca?

One thing at all events we cannot deny — that the national record is at least lively. Clear noble shapes of kings and queens, chieftains, brehons, and bards gleam in the large rich light shed abroad over the triumphant progress of the legendary tale. We see Duns[7] snow-white with roofs striped crimson and blue, chariots cushioned with noble skins, with bright bronze wheels and silver poles and yokes. The lively-hearted, resolute steeds gallop past, bearing the warrior and his charioteer with the loud clangour of rattling spears and darts. As in some bright young dawn, over the dewy grass, and in the light of the rising sun, superhuman in size and beauty, their long, yellow hair curling on their shoulders, bound around the temples with torcs of gold, clad in white linen tunics, and loose brattas[8] of crimson silk fastened on the breast with huge wheel brooches of gold, their long spears musical with running rings; with naked knees and bare crown, they cluster round their kings, the chieftains and knights of the heroic age of Ireland.

The dawn of history is like the dawn of the day. The night of the pre-historic epoch grows rare, its dense weight is relaxed; flakes of fleeting and uncertain light wander and vanish; vague shapes of floating mist reveal themselves, gradually assuming form and colour; faint hues of crimson, silver, and gold strike here and there, and the legendary dawn grows on. But the glory of morn though splendid is unsubstantial; the glory of changing and empurpled mist — vapours that conceal the solid face of nature, the hills, trees, streams, and the horizon, holding between us and the landscape a concealing veil, through whose close woof the eye cannot penetrate, and over all a weird strange light.

In the dawn of the history of all nations we see this deceptive light, those glorious and unearthly shapes; before Grecian history, the gods and demigods who fought around Illium;[9] before Roman, the strong legends of Virginius[10] and Brutus;[11] in the dawn of Irish history, the Knights of the Red Branch, and all the glory that surrounded the Court of Concobar Mac Nessa, High King of the Ultonians.

But of what use these concealing glories, these cloudy warriors, and air-built palaces? Why not pass on at once to credible history?

A nation's history is made for it by circumstances, and the irresistible progress of events; but their legends, they make for themselves. In that dim twilight region, where day meets night, the intellect of man, tired by contact with the vulgarity of actual things, goes back for rest and recuperation, and there sleeping, projects its dreams against the waning night and before the rising of the sun.

The legends represent the imagination of the country; they are that kind of history which a nation desires to possess. They betray the ambition and ideals of the people and, in this respect, have a value far beyond the tale of actual events and duly recorded deeds, which are no more history than a skeleton is a man. Nay, too, they have their own reality. They fill the mind with an adequate and satisfying pleasure. They present a rhythmic completeness and a beauty not to be found in the fragmentary and ragged succession of events in time. Achilles[12] and Troy appear somehow more real than Histiaeus and Miletus,[13] Cuculain and Emain Macha than Brian Boru and Kincora.[14]

7. fortified dwellings.
8. cloaks.
9. Troy.
10. In Roman tradition, Verginius killed his daughter Verginia to save her from the lust of a tyrant, thus starting a revolution.
11. The traditional founder of the Roman Republic.

12. A hero of the *Iliad*.
13. Histiaeus was the tyrant of Miletus, who rendered service to Darius during his Scythian campaign (*c.* 512 B.C.). Miletus is the southernmost of the great Ionian cities of Asia Minor.
14. Brian Boru (*c.* 941-1014), victor over the Norsemen at the battle of Clontarf (1014), king of Ireland, whose political base was at Kincora, in the West, near Limerick. Cuchulain's political base was Emain Macha (Armagh), but he and Emain Macha belong to legend, not history.

from:
TORYISM AND THE TORY DEMOCRACY (1886)

[In 1886, the year of the first Home Rule Bill, O'Grady published his political tract, *Toryism and the Tory Democracy*. It includes a diatribe against the landed aristocracy of Ireland whom he felt had neglected their duties as the country's natural leaders. The following extract, from the end of the chapter entitled 'Ireland and the Hour', sets O'Grady's cultural nationalism in the context of his firmly protestant unionist convictions.]

IRELAND AND THE HOUR

... I believe there is no example in history of a lethargic, effete aristocracy such as yours getting reformed from within, and yet as against such a reform I can perceive no very serious obstacle, save the extreme shortness of the time still left you and the strength of the evil habits which you must abandon. He who leaves the right road has little difficulty in returning if he soon discovers his error. A few steps to the right hand or the left, and he is once more upon the way. But you now for some two hundred years have been travelling all awry, travelling like that pilgrim who at the end of his journey on smooth and level ground found himself at length right beneath an impending mountain, from which thunder rolled and fire flashed .... And even if you should now, winged with terror and pricked by sharp conscience, hasten back to the right road — narrow and rough, but the right road for all that — what a way you have to travel, skirting the edge, nay, rather through the bowels of that flaming Mountain!

Of you as a class, as a body of men, I can entertain not the least hope; who, indeed, can? If the times with their words of thunder do not alarm you, do not send you flying like one assailed by murderers from that same snug solicitor's office, parchment-strewn, I know that my words will not, that the words of no man will. These words of mine you will not read, or reading, will not understand. Your enemies will read them, and in the main understand; but you will do neither. For even those of you who have had the grace to remain in the land have grown as earthy and dull as the earth itself. A respectable Dublin publisher informed me recently that he seldom or never received an order from a country gentleman for a new book. 'Such new books as I sell are bought,' he added, 'by Dublin professional men.' You have hunted the fox till, like that old red hunter, you have come to despise your birthright, and all that treats of it, and cultivated crops, till the very clay of the earth is more intelligent than yours. Your serious talk is of bullocks, and, in short, 'Quos Deus vult perdere prius dementat.'[1] Your ancestors, who raised the noble classic buildings of Dublin, loved a Latin quotation. The less ignoble Siren of classicism and culture they were not beyond admiring. Of you now I doubt if one in twenty could translate that hackneyed newspaper phrase. For so, by easy stages, aristocracies run or slide downhill. The heroic ardour goes first, culture and intellectual refinement come and depart. Loyalty to even your own class in due time disappears, and personal worth, the simple cardinal virtues of the private citizen, last of all. These, indeed, still remain with you, and while they last Pandora's box is not empty.

Of you, as a collective body of men, even those of you who have still the grace to remain with us and stick to the sinking ship, I entertain not the least hope. It is for individuals here and there I write this book, knowing that even a very few, such as one might count on the fingers of one hand, if of the right mettle and the right calibre, may be able even now to awake you from your slumbers, and breathe, which I and men like me cannot, some breath of life into your nostrils. Here and there, such men, I believe, are in Ireland, men who look with shame and dismay upon your astonishing stupidity, men of finer mould, more subtle intelligence, of more patriotic spirit and class spirit, of a conscience not seared, of a soul not altogether dead in your trespasses and sins. To you, here and there over Ireland, or outside Ireland, and though but one, or two, or three, I would now address myself, and especially to the young, whose hearts are not yet hardened by contact with the rest or worn out by that grinding attrition.

1. Latin: Whom the gods wish to destroy they first drive mad.

DOUGLAS HYDE

(1860-1949)

from: THE NECESSITY FOR DE-ANGLICISING IRELAND (1892)

[This important statement, from which the following is an extract, was addressed to the National Literary Society in Dublin on 25 November 1892. Hyde was president of the newly formed Society. The address, like so much in his career, reveals Hyde's anxiety to limit the proposed revival of the Irish national spirit to the sphere of 'culture'; it also exposes the difficulties attendant upon such an attempt.]

When we speak of 'The Necessity for De-Anglicising the Irish Nation', we mean it, not as a protest against imitating what is *best* in the English people, for that would be absurd, but rather to show the folly of neglecting what is Irish, and hastening to adopt, pell-mell, and indiscriminately, everything that is English, simply because it *is* English.

This is a question which most Irishmen will naturally look at from a National point of view, but it is one which ought also to claim the sympathies of every intelligent Unionist,[1] and which, as I know, does claim the sympathy of many.

If we take a bird's-eye view of our island today, and compare it with what it used to be, we must be struck by the extraordinary fact that the nation which was once, as every one admits, one of the most classically learned and cultured nations in Europe, is now one of the least so; how one of the most reading and literary peoples has become one of the *least* studious and most *un*-literary, and how the present art products of one of the quickest, most sensitive, and most artistic races on earth are now only distinguished for their hideousness.

I shall endeavour to show that this failure of the Irish people in recent times has been largely brought about by the race diverging during this century from the right path, and ceasing to be Irish without becoming English. I shall attempt to show that with the bulk of the people this change took place quite recently, much more recently than most people imagine, and is, in fact, still going on. I should also like to call attention to the illogical position of men who drop their own language to speak English, of men who translate their euphonious Irish names into English monosyllables, of men who read English books, and know nothing about Gaelic literature, nevertheless protesting as a matter of sentiment that they hate the country which at every hand's turn they rush to imitate.

I wish to show you that in Anglicising ourselves wholesale we have thrown away with a light heart the best claim which we have upon the world's recognition of us as a separate nationality. What did Mazzini[2] say? What is Goldwin Smith[3] never tired of declaiming? What do the *Spectator* and *Saturday Review*[4] harp on? That we ought to be content as an integral part of the United Kingdom because we have lost the notes of nationality, our language and customs.

It has always been very curious to me how Irish sentiment sticks in this half-way house — how it continues to apparently hate the English, and at the same time continues to imitate them; how it continues to clamour for recognition as a distinct nationality, and at the same time throws away with both hands what would make it so. If Irishmen only went a little farther they would become good Englishmen in sentiment also. But — illogical as it appears — there seems not the slightest sign or probability of their taking that step. It is the curious certainty that come what may Irishmen will continue to resist English rule, even though it should be for their good, which prevents many of our nation from becoming Unionists upon the spot. It is a fact, and we must face it as a fact, that although they adopt English habits and copy England in every way, the great bulk of Irishmen

1. A supporter of the political union between Britain and Ireland.

2. Giuseppe Mazzini (1805-72), Genoese propagandist, revolutionary and champion of the movement for Italian unity, known as the Risorgimento.

3. Goldwin Smith (1823-1910), English historian and journalist, who advocated the unity of the Anglo-Saxon peoples.

4. Influential English periodicals of the time.

and Irishwomen over the whole world are known to be filled with a dull, ever-abiding animosity against her, and — right or wrong — to grieve when she prospers, and joy when she is hurt. Such movements as Young Irelandism, Fenianism, Land Leagueism, and Parliamentary obstruction[5] seem always to gain their sympathy and support. It is just because there appears no earthly chance of their becoming good members of the Empire that I urge that they should not remain in the anomalous position they are in, but since they absolutely refuse to become the one thing, that they become the other; cultivate what they have rejected, and build up an Irish nation on Irish lines.

But you ask, why should we wish to make Ireland more Celtic than it is — why should we de-Anglicise it at all?

I answer because the Irish race is at present in a most anomalous position, imitating England and yet apparently hating it. How can it produce anything good in literature, art, or institutions as long as it is actuated by motives so contradictory? Besides, I believe it is our Gaelic past which, though the Irish race does not recognise it just at present, is really at the bottom of the Irish heart, and prevents us becoming citizens of the Empire, as, I think, can be easily proved.

To say that Ireland has not prospered under English rule is simply a truism; all the world admits it, England does not deny it. But the English retort is ready. You have not prospered, they say, because you would not settle down contentedly, like the Scotch, and form part of the Empire. 'Twenty years of good, resolute, grandfatherly government,' said a well-known Englishman, will solve the Irish question.[6] He possibly made the period too short, but let us suppose this. Let us suppose for a moment — which is impossible — that there were to arise a series of Cromwells[7] in England for the space of one hundred years, able administrators of the Empire, careful rulers of Ireland, developing to the utmost our national resources, whilst they unremittingly stamped out every spark of national feeling, making Ireland a land of wealth and factories, whilst they extinguished every thought and every idea that was Irish, and left us, at last, after a hundred years of good government, fat, wealthy, and populous, but with all our characteristics gone, with every external that at present differentiates us from the English lost or dropped; all our Irish names of places and people turned into English names; the Irish language completely extinct; the O's and the Macs dropped; our Irish intonation changed, as far as possible, by English schoolmasters into something English; our history no longer remembered or taught; the names of our rebels and martyrs blotted out; our battle-fields and traditions forgotten; the fact that we were not of Saxon origin dropped out of sight and memory, and let me now put the question — How many Irishmen are there who would purchase material prosperity at such a price? It is exactly such a question as this and the answer to it that shows the difference between the English and Irish race. Nine Englishmen out of ten would jump to make the exchange, and I as firmly believe that nine Irishmen out of ten would indignantly refuse it.

And yet this awful idea of complete Anglicisation, which I have here put before you in all its crudity, is, and has been, making silent inroads upon us for nearly a century.

Its inroads have been silent, because, had the Gaelic race perceived what was being done, or had they been once warned of what was taking place in their own midst, they would, I think, never have allowed it. When the picture of complete Anglicisation is drawn for them in all its nakedness Irish sentimentality becomes suddenly a power and refuses to surrender its birthright.

What lies at the back of the sentiments of nationality with which the Irish millions seem so strongly leavened, what can prompt them to applaud such sentiments as:

They say the British Empire owes much to Irish
hands,
That Irish valour fixed her flag o'er many
conquered lands;
And ask if Erin takes no pride in these her
gallant sons,

5. Young Ireland: a separatist political movement of the 1840s.
Fenianism: a revolutionary separatist movement of the 1860s, forerunner of the Irish Republican Brotherhood.
Land League: a movement led by Michael Davitt in the 1880s, which sought land reform.
Parliamentary obstruction: the filibustering techniques of the Irish Party at Westminster.
6. On 17 May 1886, during a public debate on the Home Rule Bill in St James's Hall, London, Lord Salisbury said of the English government's rule in Ireland: 'Apply that recipe honestly, consistently and resolutely for 20 years.'
7. Oliver Cromwell (1599-1658), English general and statesman, Lord Protector of the Commonwealth 1653-58.

Her Wolseleys[7] and her Lawrences,[8] her Wolfes[9]
and Wellingtons. . . .[10]

Of course it is a very composite feeling which prompts them; but I believe that what is largely behind it is the half unconscious feeling that the race which at one time held possession of more than half Europe, which established itself in Greece, and burned infant Rome, is now — almost extirpated and absorbed elsewhere — making its last stand for independence in this island of Ireland; and do what they may the race of today cannot wholly divest itself from the mantle of its own past. Through early Irish literature, for instance, can we best form some conception of what that race really was, which, after overthrowing and trampling on the primitive peoples of half Europe, was itself forced in turn to yield its speech, manners, and independence to the victorious eagles of Rome. We alone of the nations of Western Europe escaped the claws of those birds of prey; we alone developed ourselves naturally upon our own lines outside of and free from all Roman influence; we alone were thus able to produce an early art and literature, *our* antiquities can best throw light upon the pre-Romanised inhabitants of half Europe, and — we are our father's sons.

There is really no exaggeration in all this, although Irishmen are sometimes prone to overstating as well as to forgetting. Westwood[11] himself declares that, were it not for Irishmen, these islands would possess no primitive works of art worth the mentioning; Jubainville[12] asserts that early Irish literature is that which best throws light upon the manners and customs of his own ancestors the Gauls; and Zimmer,[13] who has done so much for Celtic philology, has declared that only a spurious criticism can make an attempt to doubt about the historical character of the chief persons of our two epic cycles, that of Cuchullain and that of Finn. It is useless elaborating this point; and Dr. Sigerson[14] has already shown in his opening lecture the debt of gratitude which in many respects Europe owes to ancient Ireland. The dim consciousness of this is one of those things which are at the back of Irish national sentiment, and our business, whether we be Unionists or Nationalists, should be to make this dim consciousness an active and potent feeling, and thus increase our sense of self-respect and of honour.

What we must endeavour to never forget is this, that the Ireland of today is the descendant of the Ireland of the seventh century, then the school of Europe and the torch of learning. It is true that Northmen made some minor settlements in it in the ninth and tenth centuries, it is true that the Normans made extensive settlements during the succeeding centuries, but none of those broke the continuity of the social life of the island. Dane and Norman drawn to the kindly Irish breast issued forth in a generation or two fully Irishised, and more Hibernian than the Hibernians themselves, and even after the Cromwellian plantation the children of numbers of the English soldiers who settled in the south and midlands, were, after forty years' residence, and after marrying Irish wives, turned into good Irishmen, and unable to speak a word of English, while several Gaelic poets of the last century have, like Father English, the most unmistakably English names. In two points only was the continuity of the Irishism of Ireland damaged. First, in the north-east of Ulster, where the Gaelic race was expelled and the land planted with aliens, whom our dear mother Erin, assimilative as she is, has hitherto found it difficult to absorb, and in the ownership of the land, eight-ninths of which belongs to people many of whom always lived, or live, abroad, and not half of whom Ireland can be said to have assimilated.

During all this time the continuation of Erin's national life centred, according to our way of looking at it, not so much in the Cromwellian or Williamite landholders who sat in College Green,[15]

7. Garnet Joseph Wolseley, 1st viscount (1833-1913), a County Dublin-born British field marshal, who was instrumental in modernizing the British army.
8. A reference to one or all of a remarkable trio of brothers who served in India: John Laird Mair Lawrence, 1st baron (1811-79), British viceroy and governor general of India, known as 'Saviour of the Punjab'; Sir Henry Montgomery Lawrence (1806-57), brigadier general and chief commissioner in Oudh; Sir George S. Patrick Lawrence (1804-84), a general who served in India. The family boasted an Irish grandfather.
9. James Wolfe (1727-59), commander of the British army at the capture of Quebec from the French in 1759, at which he was killed. His grandfather was reputed to be an Irishman and one of the leading defenders of Limerick in 1651.
10. Arthur Wellesley (1769-1852), 1st duke of Wellington, Dublin-born British military commander. Defeated Napoleon at Waterloo (1815). Prime minister of Britain 1828-30.
11. John Obadiah Westwood (1805-93), English entomologist and palaeographer, who excelled in reproducing old manuscripts.
12. Marie Henri d'Arbois de Jubainville (1827-1910), French historian, linguist and Celticist.
13. Heinrich Zimmer (1851-1910), German linguist and philologist.
14. George Sigerson (1836-1925), physician, scientist, translator and author of *Bards of the Gael and Gall* (1897).
15. The Irish parliament met in College Green in Dublin until the Act of Union in 1800.

and governed the country, as in the mass of the people whom Dean Swift[16] considered might be entirely neglected, and looked upon as hewers of wood and drawers of water; the men who, nevertheless, constituted the real working population, and who were living on in the hopes of better days; the men who have since made America, and have within the last ten years proved what an important factor they may be in wrecking or in building the British Empire. These are the men of whom our merchants, artisans, and farmers mostly consist, and in whose hands is today the making or marring of an Irish nation. But, alas, *quantum mutatus ab illo*![17] What the battleaxe of the Dane, the sword of the Norman, the wile of the Saxon were unable to perform, we have accomplished ourselves. We have at last broken the continuity of Irish life, and just at the moment when the Celtic race is presumably about to largely recover possession of its own country, it finds itself deprived and stript of its Celtic characteristics, cut off from the past, yet scarcely in touch with the present. It has lost since the beginning of this century almost all that connected it with the era of Cuchullain and of Ossian, that connected it with the Christianisers of Europe, that connected it with Brian Boru and the heroes of Clontarf,[18] with the O'Neills and O'Donnells,[19] with Rory O'More,[20] with the Wild Geese,[21] and even to some extent with the men of '98.[22] It has lost all that they had — language, traditions, music, genius, and ideas. Just when we should be starting to build up anew the Irish race and the Gaelic nation — as within our own recollection Greece has been built up anew — we find ourselves despoiled of the bricks of nationality. The old bricks that lasted eighteen hundred years are destroyed; we must now set to, to bake new ones, if we can, on other ground and of other clay. Imagine for a moment the restoration of a German-speaking Greece.

The bulk of the Irish race really lived in the closest contact with the traditions of the past and the national life of nearly eighteen hundred years, until the beginning of this century. Not only so, but during the whole of the dark Penal times[23] they produced amongst themselves a most vigorous literary development. Their schoolmasters and wealthy farmers, unwearied scribes, produced innumerable manuscripts in beautiful writing, each letter separated from another as in Greek, transcripts both of the ancient literature of their sires and of the more modern literature produced by themselves. Until the beginning of the present century there was no county, no barony, and, I may almost say, no townland which did not boast of an Irish poet, the people's representative of those ancient bards who died out with the extirpation of the great Milesian families. The literary activity of even the eighteenth century among the Gaels was very great, not in the South alone, but also in Ulster — the number of poets it produced was something astonishing. It did not, however, produce many works in Gaelic prose, but it propagated translations of many pieces from the French, Latin, Spanish, and English. Every well-to-do farmer could read and write Irish, and many of them could understand even archaic Irish. I have myself heard persons reciting the poems of Donogha More O'Daly,[24] Abbot of Boyle, in Roscommon, who died sixty years before Chaucer was born. To this very day the people have a word for archaic Irish, which is much the same as though Chaucer's poems were handed down amongst the English peasantry, but required a special training to understand. This training, however, nearly every one of fair education during the Penal times possessed, nor did they begin to lose their Irish training and knowledge until after the establishment of Maynooth[25] and the rise of O'Connell.[26] These two events made an end of the Gaelicism of the Gaelic race, although a great number of poets and scribes existed even down to the forties and fifties of the present century, and a few may linger on yet in remote localities. But it may be said, roughly speaking, that the ancient Gaelic civilisation died

16. Jonathan Swift (1667-1745), author of *Gulliver's Travels* and Dean of St Patrick's Cathedral, Dublin.
17. How changed we are from what we were! Vergil, *Aeneid*, II, 274.
18. The battle of Clontarf, at which Brian Boru was slain in conflict with the Danes, was fought near Dublin in 1014.
19. Irish septs who opposed the English conquest in the sixteenth and seventeenth centuries.
20. Rory O'More (1620-52) was an Irish rebel and leader of the 1641 rebellion.
21. Irish earls who fled from Ireland after the Williamite victory at Aughrim and the Treaty of Limerick (1691).
22. The United Irishmen, who attempted revolution in 1798.
23. The eighteenth century, when catholics and dissenters suffered varying degrees of religious persecution and legal discrimination.
24. Donogha More O'Daly (died 1244) was an Irish poet and the most famous member of the greatest family of hereditary poets.
25. A catholic seminary in County Kildare, established in 1795.
26. Daniel O'Connell (1775-1847), the leader who achieved catholic emancipation in 1829.

with O'Connell, largely, I am afraid, owing to his example and his neglect of inculcating the necessity of keeping alive racial customs, language, and traditions, in which with the one notable exception of our scholarly idealist, Smith O'Brien,[27] he has been followed until a year ago by almost every leader of the Irish race.

Thomas Davis[28] and his brilliant band of Young Irelanders came just at the dividing of the line, and tried to give to Ireland a new literature in English to replace the literature which was just being discarded. It succeeded and it did not succeed. It was a most brilliant effort, but the old bark had been too recently stripped off the Irish tree, and the trunk could not take as it might have done to a fresh one. It was a new departure, and at first produced a violent effect. Yet in the long run it failed to properly leaven our peasantry who might, perhaps, have been reached upon other lines. I say they *might* have been reached upon other lines because it is quite certain that even well on into the beginning of this century, Irish poor scholars and schoolmasters used to gain the greatest favour and applause by reading out manuscripts in the people's houses at night, some of which manuscripts had an antiquity of a couple of hundred years or more behind them, and which, when they got illegible from age, were always recopied. The Irish peasantry at that time were all to some extent cultured men, and many of the better off ones were scholars and poets. What have we now left of all that? Scarcely a trace. Many of them read newspapers indeed, but who reads, much less recites, an epic poem, or chants an elegiac or even a hymn?

Wherever Irish throughout Ireland continued to be spoken, there the ancient MSS. continued to be read, there the epics of Cuchullain, Conor MacNessa, Déirdre, Finn, Oscar, and Ossian continued to be told, and there poetry and music held sway. Some people may think I am exaggerating in asserting that such a state of things existed down to the present century, but it is no exaggeration. I have myself spoken with men from Cavan and Tyrone who spoke excellent Irish. Carleton's[29] stories bear witness to the prevalence of the Irish language and traditions in Ulster when he began to write. My friend Mr. Lloyd has found numbers in Antrim who spoke good Irish. And, as for Leinster, my friend Mr. Cleaver informed me that when he lived in Wicklow a man came by from the County Carlow in search of work who could not speak a word of English. Old labourers from Connacht, who used to go to reap the harvest in England and take shipping at Drogheda, told me that at that time, fifty years ago, Irish was spoken by every one round that town. I have met an old man in Wicklow, not twenty miles from Dublin, whose parents always repeated the Rosary in Irish. My friend Father O'Growny,[30] who has done and is doing so much for the Irish language and literature at Maynooth, tells me that there, within twenty miles of Dublin, are three old people who still speak Irish. O'Curry[31] found people within seven miles of Dublin city who had never heard English in their youth at all, except from the car-drivers of the great town. I gave an old man in the street who begged from me, a penny, only a few days ago, saying, '*Sin pighin agad*,'[32] and when he answered in Irish I asked him where he was from, and he said from *Newna* (*n'Eamhain*), i.e., Navan. Last year I was in Canada and out hunting with some Red Indians, and we spent a night in the last white man's house in the last settlement on the brink of the primeval forest; and judging from a peculiarly Hibernian physiognomy that the man was Irish, I addressed him in Gaelic, and to the intense astonishment both of whites and Indians we entered into a conversation which none of them understood; and it turned out that he was from within three miles of Kilkenny, and had been forty years in that country without forgetting the language he had spoken as a child, and I, although from the centre of Connacht, understood him perfectly. When my father was a young boy in the County Leitrim, not far from Longford, he seldom heard the farm labourers and tenants speak anything but Irish amongst themselves. So much for Ulster and Leinster, but Connacht and Munster were until quite recently completely Gaelic. In fact, I may venture to say, that, up to the beginning of the present century, neither man, woman, nor child of the Gaelic race,

27. William Smith O'Brien (1803-64), Irish nationalist and Young Irelander.
28. Thomas Davis (1814-45), a leader of the Young Ireland movement in the 1840s. He contributed poems to *The Nation*, the organ of the movement.
29. William Carleton (1794-1869), novelist and short-story writer. He wrote *Traits and Stories of the Irish Peasantry* (1830-33).
30. Rev. Eugene O'Growney (1863-99), Gaelic scholar, Irish language enthusiast and author of *Simple Lessons in Irish* (1894).
31. Eugene O'Curry (1796-1862), Gaelic scholar.
32. 'There's a penny for you.'

either of high blood or low blood, existed in Ireland who did not either speak Irish or understand it. But within the last ninety years we have, with an unparalleled frivolity, deliberately thrown away our birthright and Anglicised ourselves. None of the children of those people of whom I have spoken know Irish, and the race will from henceforth be changed; for as Monsieur Jubainville says of the influence of Rome upon Gaul, England 'has definitely conquered us, she has even imposed upon us her language, that is to say, the form of our thoughts during every instant of our existence.' It is curious that those who most fear West-Britonism have so eagerly consented to imposing upon the Irish race what, according to Jubainville, who in common with all the great scholars of the continent, seems to regret it very much, is 'the form of our thoughts during every instant of our existence.'

So much for the greatest stroke of all in our Anglicisation, the loss of our language. I have often heard people thank God that if the English gave us nothing else they gave us at least their language. In this way they put a bold face upon the matter, and pretend that the Irish language is not worth knowing, and has no literature. But the Irish language *is* worth knowing, or why would the greatest philologists of Germany, France, and Italy be emulously studying it, and it *does* possess a literature, or why would a German savant have made the calculation that the books written in Irish between the eleventh and seventeenth centuries, and still extant, would fill a thousand octavo volumes.

I have no hesitation at all in saying that every Irish-feeling Irishman, who hates the reproach of West-Britonism, should set himself to encourage the efforts which are being made to keep alive our once great national tongue. The losing of it is our greatest blow, and the sorest stroke that the rapid Anglicisation of Ireland has inflicted upon us. In order to de-Anglicise ourselves we must at once arrest the decay of the language. We must bring pressure upon our politicians not to snuff it out by their tacit discouragement merely because they do not happen themselves to understand it. We must arouse some spark of patriotic inspiration among the peasantry who still use the language, and put an end to the shameful state of feeling — a thousand-tongued reproach to our leaders and statesmen — which makes young men and women blush and hang their heads when overheard speaking their own language.* Maynooth has at last come splendidly to the front, and it is now incumbent upon every clerical student to attend lectures in the Irish language and history during the first three years of his course. But in order to keep the Irish language alive where it is still spoken — which is the utmost we can at present aspire to — nothing less than a house-to-house visitation and exhortation of the people themselves will do, something — though with a very different purpose — analogous to the procedure that James Stephens[33] adopted throughout Ireland when he found her like a corpse on the dissecting table. This and some system of giving medals or badges of honour to every family who will guarantee that they have always spoken Irish amongst themselves during the year. But, unfortunately, distracted as we are and torn by contending factions, it is impossible to find either men or money to carry out this simple remedy, although to a dispassionate foreigner — to a Zeuss, Jubainville, Zimmer, Kuno Meyer, Windisch, or Ascoli,[34] and the rest — this is of greater importance than whether Mr. Redmond or Mr. MacCarthy

*As an instance of this, I mention the case of a young man I met on the road coming from the fair of Tuam, some ten miles away. I saluted him in Irish, and he answered me in English. 'Don't you speak Irish,' said I. 'Well, I declare to God, sir,' he said, 'my father and mother hasn't a word of English, but still, I don't speak Irish.' This was absolutely true for him. There are thousands upon thousands of houses all over Ireland today where the old people invariably use Irish in addressing the children, and the children as invariably answer in English, the children understanding Irish but not speaking it, the parents understanding their children's English but unable to use it themselves. In a great many cases, I should almost say most, the children are not conscious of the existence of two languages. I remember asking a gossoon [boy, from the French *garçon*] a couple of miles west of Ballaghaderreen in the Co. Mayo, some questions in Irish and he answered them in English. At last I said to him, '*Nach labhrann tu Gaedheilg?*' (i.e., 'Don't you speak Irish?') and his answer was, 'And isn't it Irish I'm spaking?' 'No *a-chuisle*,' said I, 'it's not Irish you're speaking, but English.' 'Well then,' said he, 'that's how I spoke it ever!' He was quite unconscious that I was addressing him in one language and he answering in another. On a different occasion I spoke Irish to a little girl in a house near Kilfree Junction, Co. Sligo, into which I went while waiting for a train. The girl answered me in Irish until her brother came in. 'Arrah now, Mary,' said he, with what was intended to be a most bitter sneer; 'and isn't that a credit to you!' And poor Mary — whom I had with difficulty persuaded to begin — immediately hung her head and changed to English. This is going on from Malin Head to Galway, and from Galway to Waterford, with the exception possibly of a few spots in Donegal and Kerry, where the people are wiser and more national.

33. James Stephens (1825-1901), Fenian and revolutionary.
34. Johann Kasper Zeuss (1806-56), German Celticist; Arbois de Jubainville (1827-1910), French historian, linguist and Celticist; Heinrich Zimmer (1851-1910), German linguist and philologist; Kuno Meyer (1858-1919), German Celticist; Ernest Windisch (1844-1918), German linguist; Graziadio Ascoli (1829-1907), Italian linguist.

lead the largest wing of the Irish party for the moment, or Mr. So-and-So succeed with his election petition. To a person taking a bird's-eye view of the situation a hundred or five hundred years hence, believe me, it will also appear of greater importance than any mere temporary wrangle, but, unhappily, our countrymen cannot be brought to see this.

We can, however, insist, and we *shall* insist if Home Rule be carried, that the Irish language, which so many foreign scholars of the first calibre find so worthy of study, shall be placed on a par with — or even above — Greek, Latin, and modern languages, in all examinations held under the Irish Government. We can also insist, and we *shall* insist, that in those baronies where the children speak Irish, Irish shall be taught, and that Irish-speaking schoolmasters, petty sessions clerks, and even magistrates be appointed in Irish-speaking districts. If all this were done, it should not be very difficult, with the aid of the foremost foreign scholars, to bring about a tone of thought which would make it disgraceful for an educated Irishman — especially of the old Celtic race, MacDermotts, O'Conors, O'Sullivans, MacCarthys, O'Neills — to be ignorant of his own language — would make it at least as disgraceful as for an educated Jew to be quite ignorant of Hebrew.

from:
LOVE SONGS OF CONNACHT (ABHRÁIN GRÁDH CHÚIGE CONNACHT (1893)

[*Love Songs of Connacht* is one of the most important of the many renderings which, since the late eighteenth century, had negotiated the relationship between the Irish and English languages and cultures. Hyde's versions of the Irish are distinguished in their own right, but they enhance their appeal by being printed alongside the Gaelic original and by sometimes having an accompanying literal translation. They demonstrate visually the coexistence of the two languages and the process of moving from one to the other. In Hyde's renditions, the English is offered as nothing more than an approximation of the strange and intricate beauty of the original Gaelic. In this example he gives no literal translation for the last stanza of the Gaelic.]

Tá píosa binn eile ann a ḃfáġmaoid an ráḋ ceudna, "reult an eólais" agus is aoiḃinn an ráḋ é. Is ag cur i g céill atá sé go mbíonn eólas dúbalta agus géir-intinn meudaiġṫe go mór, ag an té atá i ngráḋ. Tá an gráḋ mar reult, agus tá sé mar reult-eólais mar ġeall ar an g-caoi ann a n-osglann sé ár g-ceudfaṫa, go mbiḋmíd dúbalta níos eudtroime níos beóḋa agus géire 'ná ḃiamar roiṁe sin. Tuigmid ann sin glóir agus áilleaċt an tsaoġail i rioċt nár ṫuigeamar ariaṁ go dtí sin é. Ag só an píosa air ar laḃras, aḃrán naċ féidir a ṡáruġaḋ i dteanga ar biṫ ar a ṁillseaċt agus ar a ḟíor-ċaoime.

A Óganaiġ an Ċúil Ċeangailte

A óganaiġ an ċúil ċeangailte
Le a raiḃ mé seal i n-éinfeaċt
Ċuaiḋ tu 'réir, an bealaċ so
'S ni ṫáinig tu do m'ḟeuċaint.
Ṡaoil mé naċ ndeunfaiḋe doċar duit
Dá dtiucfá, a's mé d'iarraiḋ,
'S gur b'í do ṗóigín ṫabairfeaḋ sólās
Dá mbeiḋinn i lár an ḟiaḃrais.

Dá mbeiḋeaḋ maoin agam-sa
Agus airgead ann mo ṗóca
Ḋeunfainn bóiṫrín aiṫ-giorraċ
Go doras tiġe mo stóirín,
Mar ṡúil le Dia go g-cluinnfinn-se
Torann binn a ḃróige,
'S is fad an lá ann ar ċodail mé
Aċt ag súil le blas do ṗóige.

A's ṡaoil me a stóirín
Go mbuḋ gealaċ agus grian tu,
A's ṡaoil mé 'nna ḋiaiġ sin
Go mbuḋ sneaċta ar an tsliaḃ tu,
A's ṡaoil mé 'nn a ḋiaiġ sin
Go mbuḋ lóċrann o Ḋia tu,
No gur ab tu an reult-eólais
Ag dul róṁam a's mo ḋiaiġ tu.

Ġeall tu síoda 's saitin dam
Callaiḋe's bróga árda,
A's ġeall tu tar éis sin
Go leanfá tríd an tsnáṁ mé.
Ni mar sin atá mé
Aċt mo sgeaċ i mbeul bearna,
Gaċ nóin a's gaċ maidin
Ag feuċaint tiġe m' aṫar.

TRANSLATION

There is another melodious piece in which we find the same expression, 'star of knowledge,' and a lovely expression it is. It is making us understand it is, that there be's double knowledge and greatly increased sharp-sightedness to him who is in love. The love is like a star, and it is like a star of knowledge on account of the way in which it opens our senses, so that we be double more light, more lively and more sharp than we were before. We understand then the glory and the beauty of the world in a way we never understood it until that. Here is the piece of which I spoke, a song which cannot be surpassed in any language for its sweetness and true gentleness.

Ringleted Youth of My Love

Ringleted youth of my love,
   With thy locks bound loosely behind thee,
You passed by the road above,
   But you never came in to find me;
Where were the harm for you
   If you came for a little to see me,
Your kiss is a wakening dew
   Were I ever so ill or so dreamy.

If I had golden store
   I would make a nice little boreen
To lead straight up to his door,
   The door of the house of my storeen;
Hoping to God not to miss
   The sound of his footfall in it,
I have waited so long for his kiss
   That for days I have slept not a minute.

I thought, O my love! you were so —
   As the moon is, or sun on a fountain,
And I thought after that you were snow,
   The cold snow on top of the mountain;
And I thought after that, you were more
   Like God's lamp shining to find me,
Or the bright star of knowledge before,
   And the star of knowledge behind me.

You promised me high-heeled shoes,
   And satin and silk, my storeen,
And to follow me, never to lose,
   Though the ocean were round us roaring;
Like a bush in a gap in a wall
   I am now left lonely without thee,
And this house I grow dead of, is all
   That I see around or about me.†

†Literally. O youth of the bound back hair, With whom I was once together. You went by this way last night, And you did not come to see me. I thought no harm would be done you If you were to come and to ask for me, And sure it is your little kiss would give comfort. If I were in the midst of a fever.

If I had wealth And silver in my pocket, I would make a handy boreen To the door of the house of my storeen; Hoping to God that I might hear The melodious sound of his shoe, And long (since) is the day on which I slept, But (ever), hoping for the taste of his kiss.

And I thought, my storeen, That you were the sun and the moon, And I thought after that, That you were snow on the mountain, And I thought after that That you were a lamp from God, Or that you were the star of knowledge Going before me and after me.

LADY GREGORY

(1852-1932)

from:
CUCHULAIN OF MUIRTHEMNE (1902)

[Standish O'Grady had introduced Cuchulain as the exemplary hero of pagan Ireland. Lady Gregory added to his prominence by enhancing his tragic status. The death of the great hero became an emblem in Yeats's poetry and drama. The quoted excerpt is the last chapter of the work.]

CHAPTER XX

DEATH OF CUCHULAIN

Cuchulain went on then to the house of his mother, Dechtire, to bid her farewell. And she came out on the lawn to meet him, for she knew well he was going out to face the men of Ireland, and she brought out wine in a vessel to him, as her custom was when he passed that way. But when he took the vessel in his hand, it was red blood that was in it. 'My grief!' he said, 'my mother Dechtire, it is no wonder others to forsake me, when you yourself offer me a drink of blood.' Then she filled the vessel a second, and a third time, and each time when she gave it to him, there was nothing in it but blood.

Then anger came on Cuchulain, and he dashed the vessel against a rock, and broke it, and he said: 'The fault is not in yourself, my mother Dechtire, but my luck is turned against me, and my life is near its end, and I will not come back alive this time from facing the men of Ireland.' Then Dechtire tried hard to persuade him to go back and to wait till he would have the help of Conall. 'I will not wait,' he said, 'for anything you can say; for I would not give up my great name and my courage for all the riches of the world. And from the day I first took arms till this day, I have never drawn back from a fight or a battle. And it is not now I will begin to draw back,' he said, 'for a great name outlasts life.'

Then he went on his way, and Cathbad, that had followed him, went with him. And presently they came to a ford, and there they saw a young girl, thin and white-skinned, and having yellow hair, washing and ever washing, and wringing out clothing that was stained crimson red, and she crying and keening all the time. 'Little Hound,' said Cathbad, 'do you see what it is that young girl is doing? It is your red clothes she is washing, and crying as she washes, because she knows you are going to your death against Maeve's great army. And take the warning now and turn back again.' 'Dear master,' said Cuchulain, 'you have followed me far enough; for I will not turn back from my vengeance on the men of Ireland that are come to burn and to destroy my house and my country. And what is it to me, the woman of the Sidhe[1] to be washing red clothing for me? It is not long till there will be clothing enough, and armour and arms, lying soaked in pools of blood, by my own sword and my spear. And if you are sorry and loth to let me go into the fight, I am glad and ready enough myself to go into it, though I know as well as you yourself I must fall in it. Do not be hindering me any more, then,' he said, 'for, if I stay or if I go, death will meet me all the same. But go now to Emain, to Conchubar and to Emer, and bring them life and health from me, for I will never go back to meet them again. It is my grief and my wound, I to part with them! And O Laeg!' he said, 'we are going away under trouble and under darkness from Emer now, as it is often we came back to her with gladness out of strange places and far countries.'

Then Cathbad left him, and he went on his way. And after a while he saw three hags, and they blind of the left eye, before him in the road, and they having a venomous hound they were cooking with charms on rods of the rowan tree. And he was going by them, for he knew it was not for his good they were there.

But one of the hags called to him: 'Stop a while with us, Cuchulain.' 'I will not stop with you,' said Cuchulain. 'That is because we have nothing better than a dog to give you,' said the hag. 'If we had a grand, big cooking-hearth, you would stop and visit us; but because it is only a little we have to offer you, you will not stop. But he that will not show respect for the small, though he is great, he will get no respect himself.'

Then he went over to her, and she gave him the shoulder-blade of the hound out of her left hand, and he ate it out of his left hand. And he put it down on his left thigh, and the hand that took it was struck down, and the thigh he put it on was struck through and through, so that the strength that was in them before left them.

Then he went down the road of Meadhon-Luachair, by Slieve Fuad, and his enemy, Erc, son of Cairbre, saw him in the chariot, and his sword shining red in his hand, and the light of his courage plain upon him, and his hair spread out like threads of gold that change their colour on the edge of the anvil, under the smith's hand, and the Crow of Battle in the air over his head.

'Cuchulain is coming at us,' said Erc to the men of Ireland, 'and let us be ready for him.' So they made a fence of shields linked together, and Erc put a couple of the men that were strongest here and there, to let on to be fighting one another, that they might call Cuchulain to them; and he put a Druid with every couple of them, and he bid the Druid to ask Cuchulain's spears of him, for it would be hard for him to refuse a Druid. For it was in the prophecy of the children of Calatin that a king would be killed by each one of those spears in that battle.

And he bid the men of Ireland to give out shouts, and Cuchulain came against them in his chariot, doing his three thunder feats, and he used his spear and his sword in such a way, that their heads, and

1. The fairy folk.

their hands, and their feet, and their bones, were scattered through the plain of Muirthemne, like the sands on the shore, like the stars in the sky, like the dew in May, like snow-flakes and hailstones, like leaves of the trees, like buttercups in a meadow, like grass under the feet of cattle on a fine summer day. It is red that plain was with the slaughter Cuchulain made when he came crashing over it.

Then he saw one of the men that was put to quarrel with the other, and the Druid called to him to come and hinder them, and Cuchulain leaped towards them. 'Your spear to me,' cried the Druid. 'I swear by the oath of my people,' said Cuchulain, 'you are not so much in want of it as I am in want of it myself. The men of Ireland are upon me,' he said, 'and I am upon them.' 'I will put a bad name on you if you refuse it to me,' said the Druid. 'There was never a bad name put on me yet, on account of any refusal of mine,' said Cuchulain, and with that he threw the spear at him, and it went through his head, and it killed the men that were on the other side of him.

Then Cuchulain drove through the host, and Lugaid, son of Curoi, got the spear. 'Who is it will fall by this spear, children of Calatin?' said Lugaid. 'A king will fall by it,' said they. Then Lugaid threw the spear at Cuchulain's chariot, and it went through and hit the driver, Laeg, son of Riangabra, and he fell back, and his bowels came out on the cushions of the chariot. 'My grief!' said Laeg, 'it is hard I am wounded.' Then Cuchulain drew the spear out, and Laeg said his farewell to him, and Cuchulain said: 'Today I will be a fighter and a chariot-driver as well.'

Then he saw the other two men that were put to quarrel with one another, and one of them called out it would be a great shame for him not to give him his help. Then Cuchulain leaped towards them. 'Your spear to me, Cuchulain,' said the Druid. 'I swear by the oath my people swear by,' said he, 'you are not in such want of the spear as I am myself, for it is by my courage, and by my arms, that I have to drive out the four provinces of Ireland that are sweeping over Muirthemne today.' 'I will put a bad name upon you,' said the Druid. 'I am not bound to give more than one gift in the day, and I have paid what is due to my name already,' said Cuchulain. Then the Druid said: 'I will put a bad name on the province of Ulster, because of your refusal.'

'Ulster was never dispraised yet for any refusal of mine,' said Cuchulain, 'or for anything I did unworthily. Though little of my life should be left to me, Ulster will not be reproached for me today.' With that he threw his spear at him, and it went through his head, and through the heads of the nine men that were behind him, and Cuchulain went through the host as he did before.

Then Erc, son of Cairbre Niafer, took up his spear. 'Who will fall by this?' he asked the children of Calatin. 'A king will fall by it,' they said. 'I heard you say the same thing of the spear that Lugaid threw a while ago,' said Erc. 'That is true,' said they, 'and the king of the chariot-drivers of Ireland fell by it, Cuchulain's driver Laeg, son of Riangabra.'

With that, Erc threw the spear, and it went through the Grey of Macha. Cuchulain drew the spear out, and they said farewell to one another. And then the Grey went away from him, with half his harness hanging from his neck, and he went into Glas-linn, the grey pool in Slieve Fuad.

Then Cuchulain drove through the host, and he saw the third couple disputing together, and he went between them as he did before. And the Druid asked his spear of him, but he refused him. 'I will put a bad name on you,' said the Druid. 'I have paid what is due to my name today,' said he; 'my honour does not bind me to give more than one request in a day.' 'I will put a bad name upon Ulster because of your refusal.' 'I have paid what is due for the honour of Ulster,' said Cuchulain. 'Then I will put a bad name on your kindred,' said the Druid. 'The news that I have been given a bad name shall never go back to that place I am never to go back to myself; for it is little of my life that is left to me,' said Cuchulain. With that he threw the spear at him, and it went through him, and through the heads of the men that were along with him.

'You do your kindness unkindly, Cuchulain,' said the Druid, as he fell. Then Cuchulain drove for the last time through the host, and Lugaid took the spear, and he said: 'Who will fall by this spear, children of Calatin?' 'A king will fall by it,' said they. 'I heard you saying that a king would fall by the spear Erc threw a while ago.' 'That is true,' they said, 'and the Grey of Macha fell by it, that was the king of the horses of Ireland.'

Then Lugaid threw the spear, and it went through and through Cuchulain's body, and he knew he had got his deadly wound; and his bowels came out on the cushions of the chariot, and his only horse went away from him, the Black Sainglain, with half the harness hanging from his neck, and left his master, the king of the heroes of Ireland, to die upon the plain of Muirthemne.

Then Cuchulain said: 'There is great desire on me to go to that lake beyond, and to get a drink from it.'

'We will give you leave to do that,' they said, 'if you will come back to us after.'

'I will bid you come for me if I am not able to come back myself,' said Cuchulain.

Then he gathered up his bowels into his body, and he went down to the lake. He drank a drink, and he washed himself, and he turned back again to his death, and he called to his enemies to come and meet him.

There was a pillar-stone west of the lake, and his eye lit on it, and he went to the pillar-stone, and he tied himself to it with his breast-belt, the way he would not meet his death lying down, but would meet it standing up. Then his enemies came round about him, but they were in dread of going close to him, for they were not sure but he might be still alive.

'It is a great shame for you,' said Erc, son of Cairbre, 'not to strike the head off that man, in revenge for his striking the head off my father.'

Then the Grey of Macha came back to defend Cuchulain as long as there was life in him, and the hero-light was shining above him. And the Grey of Macha made three attacks against them, and he killed fifty men with his teeth, and thirty with each of his hoofs. So there is a saying: 'It is not sharper work than this was done by the Grey of Macha, the time of Cuchulain's death.'

Then a bird came and settled on his shoulder. 'It is not on that pillar birds were used to settle,' said Erc.

Then Lugaid came and lifted up Cuchulain's hair from his shoulders, and struck his head off, and the men of Ireland gave three great heavy shouts, and the sword fell from Cuchulain's hand, and as it fell, it struck off Lugaid's right hand, so that it fell to the ground. Then they cut off Cuchulain's hand, in satisfaction for it, and then the light faded away from about Cuchulain's head, and left it as pale as the snow of a single night. Then all the men of Ireland said that as it was Maeve had gathered the army, it would be right for her to bring away the head to Cruachan. 'I will not bring it with me; it is for Lugaid that struck it off to bring it with him,' said Maeve. And then Lugaid and his men went away, and they brought away Cuchulain's head and his right hand with them, and they went south, towards the Lifé river.

At that time the army of Ulster was gathering to attack its enemies, and Conall was out before them, and he met the Grey of Macha, and his share of blood dripping from him. And then he knew that Cuchulain was dead, and himself and the Grey of Macha went looking for Cuchulain's body. And when they saw his body at the pillar-stone, the Grey of Macha went and laid his head in Cuchulain's breast: 'That body is a heavy care to the Grey of Macha,' said Conall.

Then Conall went after the army, thinking in his own mind what way he could get satisfaction for Cuchulain's death. For it was a promise between himself and Cuchulain that whichever of them would be killed the first, the other would get satisfaction for his death.

'And if I am the first that is killed,' said Cuchulain at that time, 'how long will it be before you get satisfaction for me?'

'Before the evening of the same day,' said Conall, 'I will have got satisfaction for you. And if it is I that will die before you,' he said, 'how long will it be before you get satisfaction for me?'

'Your share of blood will not be cold on the ground,' said Cuchulain, 'when I will have got satisfaction for you.'

So Conall followed after Lugaid to the river Lifé.

Lugaid was going down to bathe in the water, but he said to his chariot-driver: 'Look out there over the plain, for fear would any one come at us unknown.'

The chariot-driver looked around him. 'There is a man coming on us,' he said, 'and it is in a great hurry he is coming; and you would think he has all the ravens in Ireland flying over his head, and there are flakes of snow speckling the ground before him.'

'It is not in friendship the man comes that is coming like that,' said Lugaid. 'It is Conall Cearnach it is, with Dub-dearg, and the birds that you see after him, they are the sods the horse has scattered in the air from his hoofs, and the flakes of snow that are speckling the ground before him, they are the froth that he scatters from his mouth and from the bit of his bridle. Look again,' said Lugaid, 'and see what way is he coming.' 'It is to the ford he is coming, the same way the army passed over,' said the chariot-driver. 'Let him pass by us,' said

Lugaid, 'for I have no mind to fight with him.'

But when Conall came to the middle of the ford, he saw Lugaid and his chariot-driver, and he went over to them. 'Welcome is the sight of a debtor's face,' said Conall. 'The man you owe a debt to is asking payment of you now, and I myself am that man,' he said, 'for the sake of my comrade, Cuchulain, that you killed. And I am standing here now, to get that debt paid.'

They agreed then to fight it out on the plain of Magh Argetnas, and in the fight Conall wounded Lugaid with his spear. From that they went to a place called Ferta Lugdac. 'I would like that you would give me fair play,' said Lugaid. 'What fair play?' said Conall Cearnach.

'That you and I should fight with one hand,' said he, 'for I have the use of but one hand.'

'I will do that,' said Conall. Then Conall's hand was bound to his side with a cord, and then they fought for a long time, and one did not get the better of the other. And when Conall was not gaining on him, his horse, Dub-dearg, that was near by, came up to Lugaid, and took a bite out of his side.

'Misfortune on me,' said Lugaid, 'it is not right or fair that is of you, Conall.'

'It was for myself I promised to do what is right and fair,' said Conall. 'I made no promise for a beast, that is without training and without sense.'

'It is well I know you will not leave me till you take my head, as I took Cuchulain's head from him,' said Lugaid. 'Take it, then, along with your own head. Put my kingdom with your kingdom, and my courage with your courage; for I would like that you would be the best champion in Ireland.'

Then Conall made an end of him, and he went back, bringing Cuchulain's head along with him to the pillar-stone where his body was.

And by that time Emer had got word of all that had happened, and that her husband had got his death by the men of Ireland, and by the powers of the children of Calatin. And it was Levarcham brought her the story, for Conall Cearnach had met her on his way, and had bade her go and bring the news to Emain Macha; and there she found Emer, and she sitting in her upper room, looking over the plain for some word from the battle.

And all the women came out to meet Levarcham, and when they heard her story, they made an outcry of grief and sharp cries, with loud weeping and burning tears; and there were long dismal sounds going through Emain, and the whole country round was filled with crying. And Emer and her women went to the place where Cuchulain's body was, and they gathered round it there, and gave themselves to crying and keening.

And when Conall came back to the place, he laid the head with the body of Cuchulain, and he began to lament along with them, and it is what he said: 'It is Cuchulain had prosperity on him, a root of valour from the time he was but a soft child; there never fell a better hero than the hero that fell by Lugaid of the Lands. And there are many are in want of you,' he said, 'and until all the chief men of Ireland have fallen by me, it is not fitting there should ever be peace.

'It is grief to me, he to have gone into the battle without Conall being at his side; it was a pity for him to go there without my body beside his body. Och! it is he was my foster-son, and now the ravens are drinking his blood; there will not be either laughter or mirth, since the Hound has gone astray from us.'

'Let us bury Cuchulain now,' said Emer. 'It is not right to do that,' said Conall, 'until I have avenged him on the men of Ireland. And it is a great shouting I hear about the plain of Muirthemne, and it is full the country is of crying after Cuchulain; and it is good at keeping the country and watching the boundaries the man was that is here before me, a cross-hacked body in a pool of blood. And it is well pleased Lugaid, son of Curoi, to be at the killing of Cuchulain, for it was Cuchulain killed the chiefs and the children of Deaguid round Famain, son of Foraoi, and round Curoi, son of Daire himself. And this shouting has taken away my wits and my memory from me,' he said, 'and it is hard for me, Cuchulain not to answer these cries, and I to be without him now; for there is not a champion in Ireland that was not in dread of the sword in his hand. And it is broken in halves my heart is for my brother, and I will bring my revenge through Ireland now, and I will not leave a tribe without wounding, or true blood without spilling, and the whole world will be told of my rout to the end of life and time, until the men of Munster and Connaught and Leinster will be crying for the rising they made against him. And without the spells of the children of Calatin, the whole of them would not have been able to do him to death.'

After that complaint, rage and madness came on Conall, and he went forward in his chariot to follow after the rest of the men of Ireland, the same way as he had followed after Lugaid.

And Emer took the head of Cuchulain in her hands, and she washed it clean, and put a silk cloth about it, and she held it to her breast; and she began to cry heavily over it, and it is what she said:

'Ochone!'[2] said she, 'it is good the beauty of this head was, though it is low this day, and it is many of the kings and princes of the world would be keening it if they knew the way it is now, and the poets and the Druids of Ireland and of Alban; and many were the goods and the jewels and the rents and the tributes that you brought home to me from the countries of the world, with the courage and the strength of your hands!'

And she made this complaint:

'Och, head! Ochone, O head! you gave death to great heroes, to many hundreds; my head will lie in the same grave, the one stone will be made for both of us.

'Och, hand! Ochone, hand, that was once gentle. It is often it was put under my head; it is dear that hand was to me!

'Dear mouth! Ochone, kind mouth that was sweet-voiced telling stories; since the time love first came on your face, you never refused either weak or strong!

'Dear the man, dear the man, that would kill the whole of a great host; dear his cold bright hair, and dear his bright cheeks!

'Dear the king, dear the king, that never gave a refusal to any; thirty days it is tonight since my body lay beside your body.

'Och, two spears! Ochone, two spears! Och, shield! Och, deadly sword! Let them be given to Conall of the battles; there was never any wage given like that.

'I am glad, I am glad, Cuchulain of Muirthemne, I never brought red shame on your face, for any unfaithfulness against you.

'Happy are they, happy are they, who will never hear the cuckoo again for ever, now that the Hound has died from us.

'I am carried away like a branch on the stream; I will not bind up my hair today. From this day I have nothing to say that is better than Ochone!'

And then she said: 'It is long that it was showed to me in a vision of the night, that Cuchulain would fall by the men of Ireland, and it appeared to me Dundealgan to be falling to the ground, and his shield to be split from lip to border, and his sword and his spears broken in the middle, and I saw Conall doing deeds of death before me, and myself and yourself in the one death. And oh! my love,' she said, 'we were often in one another's company, and it was happy for us; for if the world had been searched from the rising of the sun to sunset, the like would never have been found in one place, of the Black Sainglain and the Grey of Macha, and Laeg the chariot-driver, and myself and Cuchulain. And it is breaking my heart is in my body, to be listening to the pity and the sorrowing of women and men, and the harsh crying of the young men of Ulster keening Cuchulain, and Ulster to be in its weakness, and without strength to revenge itself upon the men of Ireland.'

And after she had made that complaint, she brought Cuchulain's body to Dundealgan; and they all cried and keened about him until such time as Conall Cearnach came back from making his red rout through the army of the men of Ireland.

For he was not satisfied to make a slaughter of the men of Munster and Connaught, without reddening his hand in the blood of the men of Leinster as well.

And when he had done that, he came to Dundealgan, and his men along with him, but they made no rejoicing when they went back that time. And he brought the heads of the men of Ireland along with him in a gad,[3] and he laid them out on the green lawn, and the people of the house gave three great shouts when they saw the heads.

And Emer came out, and when she saw Conall Cearnach, she said: 'My great esteem and my welcome before you, king of heroes, and may your many wounds not be your death; for you have avenged the treachery done on Ulster, and now what you have to do is to make our grave, and to lay us together in the grave, for I will not live after Cuchulain.

'And tell me, Conall,' she said, 'whose are those heads all around on the lawn, and which of the great men of Ireland did they belong to?'

And she was asking, and Conall was answering, and it is what she said:

'Tell me, Conall, whose are those heads, for surely you have reddened your arms with them? Tell me the names of the men whose heads are there upon the ground.'

2. A lamentation.

3. A wickerwork basket or receptacle.

And Conall said: 'Daughter of Forgall of the Horses, young Emer of the sweet words, it is in revenge for the Hound of Feats I brought these heads here from the south.'

'Whose is the great black head, with the smooth cheek redder than a rose; it is at the far end, on the left side, the head that has not changed its colour?'

'It is the head of the king of Meath, Erc, son of Cairbre of Swift Horses; I brought his head with me from far off, in revenge for my own foster-son.'

'Whose is that head there before me, with soft hair, with smooth eyebrows, its eyes like ice, its teeth like blossoms; that head is more beautiful in shape than the others?'

'A son of Maeve; a destroyer of harbours, yellow-haired Maine, man of horses; I left his body without a head; all his people fell by my hand.'

'O great Conall, who did not fail us, whose head is this you hold in your hand? Since the Hound of Feats is not living, what do you bring in satisfaction for his head?'

'The head of the son of Fergus of the Horses, a destroyer in every battle-field, my sister's son of the narrow tower; I have struck his head from his body.'

'Whose is that head to the west, with fair hair, the head that is spoiled with grief? I used to know his voice; I was for a while his friend.'

'That is he that struck down the Hound, Lugaid, son of Curoi of the Rhymes. His body was laid out straight and fair, I struck his head off afterwards.'

'Whose are those two heads farther out, great Conall of good judgment? For the sake of your friendship, do not hide the names of the men put down by your arms.'

'The heads of Laigaire and Clar Cuilt, two men that fell by my wounds. It was they wounded faithful Cuchulain; I made my weapons red in their blood.'

'Whose are those heads farther to the east, great Conall of bright deeds? The hair of the two is of the one colour; their cheeks are redder than a calf's blood.'

'Brave Cullain and hardy Cunlaid, two that were used to overcome in their anger. There to the east, Emer, are their heads; I left their bodies in a red pool.'

'Whose are those three heads with evil looks I see before me to the north? Their faces blue, their hair black; even hard Conall's eye turns from them.'

'Three of the enemies of the Hound, daughters of Calatin, wise in enchantments; they are the three witches killed by me, their weapons in their hands.'

'O great Conall, father of kings, whose is that head that would overcome in the battle? His bushy hair is gold-yellow; his head-dress is smooth and white like silver.'

'It is the head of the son of Red-Haired Ross, son of Necht Min, that died by my strength. This, Emer, is his head; the high king of Leinster of Speckled Swords.'

'O great Conall, change the story. How many of the men that harmed him fell by your hand that does not fail, in satisfaction for the head of Cuchulain?'

'It is what I say, ten and seven scores of hundreds is the number that fell, back to back, by the anger of my hard sword and of my people.'

'O Conall, what way are they, the women of Ireland, after the Hound? Are they mourning the son of Sualtim? are they showing respect through their grief?'

'O Emer, what shall I do without my Cuchulain, my fine nurseling, going in and out from me, tonight?'

'O Conall, lift me to the grave. Raise my stone over the grave of the Hound; since it is through grief for him I go to death, lay my mouth to the mouth of Cuchulain.

'I am Emer of the Fair Form; there is no more vengeance for me to find; I have no love for any man. It is sorrowful my stay is after the Hound.'

And after that Emer bade Conall to make a wide, very deep grave for Cuchulain; and she laid herself down beside her gentle comrade, and she put her mouth to his mouth, and she said: 'Love of my life, my friend, my sweetheart, my one choice of the men of the earth, many is the woman, wed or unwed, envied me till today: and now I will not stay living after you.'

And her life went out from her, and she herself and Cuchulain were laid in the one grave by Conall. And he raised the one stone over them, and he wrote their names in Ogham,[4] and he himself and all the men of Ulster keened them.

But the three times fifty queens that loved Cuchulain saw him appear in his Druid chariot, going through Emain Macha; and they could hear him singing the music of the Sidhe.

4. A script of twenty characters used by the ancient British and Irish.

AE (GEORGE RUSSELL)

(1867-1935)

from:
A LETTER TO W.B. YEATS (1896)

[This extract from a letter to Yeats announces, in messianic tones, the coming of the new spiritual redemption that Ireland will bring to the world.]

3 Up Ely Place
2.6.96

Dear W.B.Y—

I am not going to bother you about any derned thing this time but simply to tell you some things about the Ireland behind the veil. You remember my writing to you about the awakening of the ancient fires which I knew about. Well, it has been confirmed from other sources and we are likely to publish it. The gods have returned to Erin and have centred themselves in the sacred mountains and blow the fires through the country. They have been seen by several in vision, they will awaken the magical instinct everywhere, and the universal heart of the people will turn to the old druidic beliefs. I note through the country the increased faith in faery things. The bells are heard from the mounds and sounding in the hollows of the mountains. A purple sheen in the inner air, perceptible at times in the light of day, spreads itself over the mountains. All this I can add my own testimony to. Furthermore, we were told that though now few we would soon be many, and that a branch of the school for the revival of the ancient mysteries to teach real things would be formed here soon. Out of Ireland will arise a light to transform many ages and peoples. There is a hurrying of forces and swift things going out and I believe profoundly that a new Avatar is about to appear and in all spheres the forerunners go before him to prepare. It will be one of the kingly Avatars, who is at once ruler of men and magic sage. I had a vision of him some months ago and will know him if he appears. America is on fire with mysticism just now and the new races are breaking the mould of European thought and psychics abound. Their light reflects itself in Ireland, and the path of connection has been seen. Now I wish you could come over to this county Sligo or wherever you like and absorb this new force. To me enchantment and fairyland are real and no longer dreams .... Yours ever, Geo. W. Russell.

from:
COLLECTED POEMS (1913)

[This poem, with its strange mixture of banality in rhythm and language and visionary assurance, is a typical instance of AE's verse.]

Carrowmore

It's a lonely road through bogland to the lake at Carrowmore,
And a sleeper there lies dreaming where the water laps the shore;
Though the moth-wings of the twilight in their purples are unfurled,
Yet his sleep is filled with music by the masters of the world.

There's a hand as white as silver that is fondling with his hair:
There are glimmering feet of sunshine that are dancing by him there:
And half-open lips of faery that were dyed a faery red
In their revels where the Hazel Tree its holy clusters shed.

'Come away,' the red lips whisper, 'all the world is weary now;
'Tis the twilight of the ages and it's time to quit the plough.
Oh, the very sunlight's weary ere it lightens up the dew,
And its gold is changed and faded before it falls to you.

'Though your colleen's[1] heart be tender, a tenderer heart is near.
What's the starlight in her glances when the stars are shining clear?

1. From the Irish for a girl.

Who would kiss the fading shadow when the
flower-face glows above?
'Tis the beauty of all Beauty that is calling for your
love.'

Oh, the great gates of the mountain have opened
once again,
And the sound of song and dancing falls upon the
ears of men,
And the Land of Youth lies gleaming, flushed with
rainbow light and mirth,
And the old enchantment lingers in the honey-heart
of earth.

GEORGE MOORE

(1852-1933)

from: HAIL AND FAREWELL: SALVE (1912)

[This excerpt from *Salve*, the second volume of Moore's famous trilogy, first published in 1912, recounts a memorable journey by the author and his friend, George Russell (AE). The journey and the conversations belong to the world of the present, but they also represent the period's characteristic effort to renew the spirit of the ancient past in the present and thereby to give Ireland a sense of its own distinctive identity.]

IV

You've punctured! AE said, and I could see that he looked upon the incident as ominous. I can mend your puncture for you, but perhaps the quickest way will be to go back; the shop isn't more than a quarter of a mile from here.

And in it we met a young man, who advanced to meet us on long, thin legs, his blue, Celtic eyes full of inquiry; after listening, I thought sympathetically, to my mishap (he was really thinking of something else) he asked me what he could do for me, and, on my telling him again that I had punctured, he seemed to wake up sufficiently to call his partner, a thick-set man, who seized my machine and told me that he was just tightening a gentleman's wheel for him, but it wouldn't take more than a couple of minutes. In a quarter of an hour .... could I wait that long?

He spoke with a Lancashire burr, and I began to wonder how the Celt and the Saxon had come together, so different were they, and why the red-headed Celt lingered about the shop instead of going to the help of his fellow. And it was to escape from unpleasant thoughts of my country's idleness that I asked him if the language movement was making progress in Dundalk;[1] but when he told me that a branch of the Gaelic League had been started about two years ago, and that he was a constant attendant at the classes, I apologised to him, inwardly, for a hasty judgment, and, seeing in him, perhaps, a future apostle, I commenced preaching. A few people had just dropped in for a chat after dinner, and taking for my text the words that I had heard spoken on the road to Chelsea,[2] I said:

A few days after the voice spoke to me again, this time not out of the clouds, but within a few inches of my ear, and the words that it spoke were, Go to Ireland, go to Ireland, and not long after this second revelation, a force completely outside of myself compelled me to fall upon my knees, and I prayed for the first time for many years. But it was not to any Christian God that I prayed.

AE looked up, hoping, no doubt, that I would not shock the young man's Catholic susceptibilities to the point of his asking me to leave his shop; and, thinking that in saying I had not prayed to a Christian God I had said enough, I admitted that the future religion of Ireland was not our business, but one for the next generation to settle. Our business was to revive the Irish language, for the soul of Ireland was implicit in it, and, pulling out of my pocket a copy of the *Claidheamh Soluis*,[3] I described the aims and ambitions of the paper. But a cloud came into the young man's face and into the faces of the three or four people present, whom I invited to subscribe to it, and the thought dashed

1. A market town and seaport in County Louth, about fifty miles north of Dublin.
2. In *Ave* (the first volume of *Hail and Farewell*), Moore describes how on the road to Chelsea, a district of London, he had heard the summons to go to Ireland, to participate in the revival of Irish literature.
3. *The Sword of Light*, the Gaelic League's periodical.

through my mind that I was being mistaken for an advertising agent, and to remove such sordid suspicion I told them that I had no pecuniary interest in the paper whatever, but was working for the language of our forefathers, and to support this paper (the organ of the League) seemed to me part of the work I had been sent to do in Ireland. The best way to do this was by getting advertisements for the paper, and my way of getting advertisements was simple and advantageous to all parties. I had rented a house in Dublin. The roof was leaking, and a builder had to be called in; he had been given the job of repairing the roof on condition that he advertised in the *Claidheamh Soluis*. The upholsterer had furnished my house under the same conditions, and as soon as I came to live in it I had gone to the butcher, the grocer, the chandler, the greengrocer, the apothecary, the baker, the tailor, the draper, the bootmaker: You shall have my custom if you advertise in the *Claidheamh Soluis* .... And you, sir, having bicycles to sell, might like to do business with me on the same terms.

The young Celt agreed that he would like to do business with me, but, being somewhat slow-witted, said he must refer the matter to his partner.

But why refer it to your partner? I answered. Everybody will advertise if he is sure of getting custom. I am the only advertising agent in the world who can insure a speedy return for the money laid out.

As the young man hesitated, AE took me aside and reminded me that my method was not as applicable to bicycles as to furniture and food, for if I were to buy a bicycle every time I punctured I should have more machines on my hands than it would be possible for me to find use for.

If you'll be good enough to wait till my partner comes back, chimed in the young Celt, I'll be able to give you your answer.

And when the Lancashire man came in with the bicycle on his shoulders, the conditions of sale were explained to him (conditions which I could see by the partner's face he was quite willing to accept).

We shan't get to Slievegullion today if you don't hasten, AE said; but the Lancashire man, loath to lose a chance of selling a bicycle, sent the young Celt along with us, the pretext being to put us on the right road; and we all three pedalled away together, myself riding in the middle, explaining to the Celt that language wears out like a coat, and just as a man has to change his coat when it becomes threadbare, a nation has to change its language if it is to produce a new literature. There could be no doubt about this. Italy had produced a new literature because Italy had changed her language; whereas Greece had not changed hers, and there was no literature in Greece, and there could be none until the modern language had separated itself sufficiently from the ancient.

The young man seemed to wish to interpose a remark, but I dashed into a new theory. Ideas were climatic; the climate of Ireland had produced certain modes of thought, and these could only transpire in the language of the country, for of course language is only the echo of the mind. The young man again tried to interpose a remark, and AE tried too, but neither succeeded in getting heard, for it seemed to me of primary importance to convince the young man that literary genius depended upon the language as much as upon the writer, and Ireland was proof of it, for, though Irishmen had been speaking English for centuries, they had never mastered that language.

If Irishmen would only read English literature, AE shouted from the other side of the road, but they read the daily paper.

But, AE, a nation reads the literature that itself produces. Ireland cannot be as much interested in Shakespeare as England is, or in the Bible, Ireland having accepted the Church of Rome, and the two ways of learning English are through the Bible and Shakespeare.

But there is an excellent Irish translation of the Bible, nearly as good as the English Bible, and AE appealed to the young Celt, who admitted that he had heard that Bedell's Bible[4] was in very good Irish.

But it isn't read in the classes.

And why isn't it read in the classes? I asked.

Well, you see, it was done by a Protestant.

I screamed at him that it was ridiculous to reject good Irish because a Protestant wrote it.

You are a native speaker, sir?

No, I answered, I don't know any Irish.

The young man gazed at me, and AE began to laugh.

You should begin to learn, and I hope you won't

4. In the seventeenth century, the protestant bishop, William Bedell, had the Old Testament translated into Irish. This was published with a translation of the New Testament in London in 1685 and became known as 'Bedell's Bible'.

mind taking this little book from me; it is O'Growney's.[5] I am in the fifth. And now, he said, I don't think I can go any farther with you. The cromlech[6] — you can't miss it when you come to the first gate on the left.

He left us so abruptly that I could not return the book to him, and had to put it into my pocket; and the incident amused AE until we came to a gate about half a mile up the road, which we passed through, coming upon the altar of our forefathers in the middle of a large green field — a great rock poised upon three or four upright stones, nine or ten feet high, and one stone worn away at the base, but rebuilt by some pious hand, for the belief abides that Diarmuid and Grania slept under the cromlech in their flight from Finn.[7]

Traditions are often more truthful than scripts, AE said, and, believing in this as in everything he says, I walked round the cromlech three times, praying, and when my devotions were finished, I returned to AE, who was putting the last touches to a beautiful drawing of the altar, a little nervous lest he should question me as to the prayers I had offered up. But instead of groping in any one's religious belief AE talks sympathetically of Gods ascending and descending in many-coloured spirals of flame, and of the ages before men turned from the reading of earth to the reading of scrolls, and of the earth herself, the origin of all things and the miracle of miracles. AE is extraordinarily forthcoming, and while speaking on a subject that interests him, nothing of himself remains behind, the revelation is continuous, and the belief imminent that he comes of Divine stock, and has been sent into the world on an errand.

I watched him packing up his pastels, and we went together to the warrior's grave at the other end of the field, and stood by it, wondering in the beautiful summer weather what his story might be. And then my memory disappears. It emerges again some miles farther on, for we were brought to a standstill by another puncture, and this second puncture so greatly stirred AE's fears lest the Gods did not wish to see me on the top of their mountain, that it was difficult for me to persuade him to go into the cottage for a basin of water. At last he consented, and, while he worked hard, heaving the tyre from off the wheel with many curious instruments, which he extracted from a leather pocket behind the saddle of his machine, I talked to him of Ireland, hoping thereby to distract his attention from the heat of the day. It was not difficult to do this, for AE, like Dujardin,[8] can be interested in ideas at any time of the day or night, though the sweat pours from his forehead; and I could see that he was listening while I told him that we should have room to dream and think in Ireland when America had drawn from us another million and a half of the population.

Two millions is the ideal population for Ireland and about four for England. Do you know, AE, there could not have been more than two million people in England when Robin Hood and his merry men haunted Sherwood Forest. How much more variegated the world was then! At any moment one might come upon an archer who had just split a willow wand distant a hundred yards, or upon charcoal-burners with their fingers and thumbs cut off for shooting deer, or jugglers standing on each other's heads in the middle of sunlit inter-spaces! A little later, on the fringe of the forest, the wayfarer stops to listen to the hymn of pilgrims on their way to Canterbury! Oh, how beautiful is the world of vagrancy lost to us for ever, AE!

There is plenty of vagrancy still in Ireland, he answered, and we spoke seriously of the destiny of the two countries. As England had undertaken to supply Ireland with hardware, he would not hang the pall cloud of Wolverhampton over Dundalk. The economic conditions of the two countries are quite different, he said, and many other interesting things which would have gladdened Plunkett's[9] heart, but my memory curls and rushes into darkness at the word economic, and a considerable time must have elapsed, for we were well on our way when I heard my own voice saying:

Will this hill never cease?

We're going to Slievegullion.

True for you, I said, for at every half-mile the road gets steeper, which I suppose is always the case

5. Rev. Eugene O'Growney (1863-99), a Gaelic scholar who wrote *Simple Lessons in Irish* (1894).
6. A circle of stones.
7. The elopement of Diarmuid and Gráinne and their pursuit by the elderly Finn is a famous Ossianic tale, a variant of the Deirdre story. Cromlechs and dolmens all over Ireland are known as the bed of Diarmuid and Gráinne, reputed resting places of the lovers in their flight from Finn's vengeance.
8. Edouard Dujardin (1861-1949), French symbolist poet.
9. Sir Horace Plunkett (1854-1932), a pioneer of Irish agricultural co-operation.

when one is going towards a mountain. But, despite the steepness which should have left no doubt upon his mind, AE was not satisfied that we were in the right road, and he jumped off his bicycle to call to a man, who left his work willingly to come to our assistance, whether from Irish politeness or because of the heat of the day, I am still in doubt. As he came towards us his pale and perplexed eyes attracted my attention; they recalled to mind the ratlike faces with the long upper lip that used to come from the mountains to Moore Hall,[10] with banknotes in their tall hats, a little decaying race in knee-breeches, worsted stockings, and heavy shoon, whom our wont was to despise because they could not speak English. Now it was the other way round; I was angry with this little fellow because he had no Irish. His father, he said, was a great Irish speaker, and he would have told us the story of the decline of the language in the district if AE had not suddenly interrupted him with questions regarding the distance to Slievegullion.

If it's to the tip-top you're thinking of going, about another four miles, and he told us we would come upon a cabin about half a mile up the road, and the woman in it would mind our bicycles while we were at the top of the hill, and from her house he had always heard that it was three miles to the top of the mountain; that was how he reckoned it was four miles from where we stood to the lake. He had never been to the top of Slievegullion himself, but he had heard of the lake from those that had been up there, and he thought that he had heard of Finn from his father, but he disremembered if Finn had plunged into the lake after some beautiful queen.[11]

Those who have lived too long in the same place become melancholy, AE. Let him emigrate. He has forgotten his Irish and the old stories that carried the soul of the ancient Gael right down to the present generation. I'm afraid, AE, that ancient Ireland died at the beginning of the nineteenth century and beyond hope of resurrection.

AE was thinking at that moment if the peasant had directed us rightly, and impatient for an answer I continued:

Can the dreams, the aspirations and traditions of the ancient Gael be translated into English? And being easily cast down, I asked if the beliefs of the ancient Gael were not a part of his civilisation and have lost all meaning for us?

That would be so, AE answered, if truth were a casual thing of today and tomorrow, but men knew the great truths thousand[s] of years ago, and it seems to me that these truths are returning, and that we shall soon possess them, not perhaps exactly as the ancient Gael —

I hope that you are right, for all my life is engaged in this adventure, and I think you are right, and that the ancient Gael was nearer to nature than we have ever been since we turned for inspiration to Galilee.

The fault I find with Christianity is that it is no more than a code of morals, whereas three things are required for a religion — a cosmogony, a psychology, and a moral code.

I'm sure you're right, AE, but the heat is so great that I feel I cannot push this bicycle up the hill any farther. You must wait for me till I take off my drawers. And behind a hedge I rid myself of them. You were telling me that the dreams and aspirations and visions of the Celtic race have lost none of their ancient power as they descended from generation to generation.

I don't think they have. And I listened to him telling how these have slept through dream after dream of the manifold nature of man, and how each dream, heroism, or beauty, has laid itself nigh the Divine power it represents. Deirdre was like Helen .... It went to my heart to interrupt him, but the heat was so great that to listen to him with all my soul I must rid myself of the rest of my hosiery, and so once more I retired behind a hedge, and, returning with nothing on my moist body but a pair of trousers and a shirt, I leaned over the handle-bars, and by putting forth all my strength, mental as well as physical, contrived to reach the cottage.

We left our bicycles with the woman of the house and started for the top of the mountain. The spare, scant fields were cracked and hot underfoot, but AE seemed unaware of any physical discomfort. Miraculously sustained by the hope of reaching the sacred lake, he hopped over the walls dividing the fields like a goat, though these were built out of loose stones, every one as hot as if it had just come out of a fire; and I heard him say, as I fell back exhausted among some brambles, that man was not

10. George Moore's ancestral home in County Mayo, where he spent his childhood.
11. Finn and his hounds chased a fawn to Slievegullion, where he encountered a girl weeping for the loss of a gold ring, which had fallen into the lake there. Finn recovered the ring, but when he returned it he was immediately turned into an aged and decrepit man. The girl was one of the fairy-folk and Finn had once spurned her love in favour of her sister. Eventually Finn regained his youth by drinking a magic potion.

a momentary seeming but a pilgrim of eternity.

What is the matter, Moore? Can't you get up?

I am unbearably tired, and the heat is so great that I can't get over this wall.

Take a little rest, and then you'll be able to come along with me.

No, no, I'm certain that today it would be impossible, all the way up that mountain, a long struggle over stones and through heather. No, no! If a donkey or a pony were handy!

He conjured me to rise.

It is very unfortunate, for you will see Finn, and I might see him, too, whether in the spirit or in the flesh I know not; and having seen him, we should come down from that mountain different beings, that I know; but it's impossible.

Get up. I tell you to get up. You must get up.

A lithe figure in grey clothes and an old brown hat bade me arise and walk; his shining grey eyes were filled with all the will he had taught himself to concentrate when, after a long day's work at Pim's[12] as accountant, he retired to his little room and communicated with Weekes and Johnson,[13] though they were miles away; but, great as the force of his will undoubtedly is, he could not infuse in me enough energy to proceed; my body remained inert, and he left me, saying that alone he would climb the mountain, and I saw him going away, and the gritty and grimy mountain showing aloft in ugly outline upon a burning sky.

Going to see Finn, I murmured, and had I strength I would sit with him by the holy lake waiting for the vision; but I may not. He'll certainly spend an hour by the lake, and he will take two hours to come back, and all that time I shall sit in a baking field where there is no shade to speak of. I had struggled into a hazel-copse, but my feet were burnt by the sun and my tongue was like a dry stick. The touch of the hazel-leaves put my teeth on edge, and, remembering that AE would be away for hours, I walked across the field towards the cottage where we had left our bicycles.

May I have a drink of water? I asked, looking over the half-door.

Two women came out of the gloom, and, after talking between themselves, one of them asked wouldn't I rather have a drop of milk? — a fine-looking girl with soft grey eyes and a friendly manner; the other was a rougher, an uglier sort.

I drank from the bowl, and could have easily finished the milk, but lifting my eyes suddenly I caught sight of a flat-faced child with flaxen hair all in curl watching me, and it occurring to me at that moment that it might be his milk I was drinking, I put down the bowl and my hand went to my pocket.

How much is the milk?

You're heartily welcome to it, sir, the young woman answered. Sure, it was only a sup.

No, I must pay you.

But all my money had been left in Dundalk, and I stood penniless before these poor people, having drunk their milk.

My friend will come from the mountain to fetch his bicycle, and he will pay you. Again the young woman said I was welcome to the milk; but I didn't know that AE had any money upon him, and it occurred to me to offer her my vest and drawers. She said she couldn't think of taking them, eyeing them all the while. At last she took them and asked me to sit down and take the weight off my limbs. Thank you kindly, and, sitting on the proffered stool, I asked if they were Irish speakers.

Himself's mother can speak it, and I turned towards the old woman who sat by the ashes of a peat fire, her yellow hands hanging over her knees, her thick white hair showing under a black knitted cap. Her eyes never left me, but she made no attempt to answer my questions. She's gone a little bothered lately and wouldn't know what you'd be asking for. I could make nothing of the younger women, the child and the grandmother only stared. It was like being in a den with some shy animals, so I left a message with them for AE, that I would bicycle on to Dundalk very slowly, and hoped he would overtake me. And it was about two hours after he came up with me, not a bit tired after his long walk, and very willing to tell me how he had had to rest under the rocks on his way to the summit, enduring dreadful thirst, for there was no rill; all were dry, and he had been glad to dip his hat into the lake and drink the soft bog water, and then to lie at length among the heather. So intense was the silence that his thoughts were afraid to move, and he had lain, his eyes roving over boundless space, seeing nothing but the phantom tops of distant mountains, the outer rim of the world, so

12. The name of the department store in Dublin where AE worked as a shop assistant before becoming an organizer in Horace Plunkett's co-operative movement.

13. Two of AE's occultist friends. Charles Johnston was one of the founders of the Dublin lodge of the Theosophical Society. Charles Alexander Weekes (1867-1946) published AE's first book of poems.

did they seem to him. At each end of the crescent-shaped lake there is a great cairn built of cyclopean stones; and into one of these cairns he had descended and had followed the passage leading into the heart of the mountain till he came upon a great boulder, which twenty men could not move, and which looked as if it had been hurled by some giant down there.

Perchance to save the Druid mysteries from curious eyes, I said, and a great regret welled up in me that I had not been strong enough to climb that mountain with him. What have I missed, AE? Oh, what have I missed? And as if to console me for my weakness he told me that he had made a drawing of the cairn, which he would show me as soon as we reached Dundalk. All the while I was afraid to ask him if he had seen Finn, for if he had seen the hero plunge into the lake after the queen's white limbs, I should have looked upon myself as among the most unfortunate of men, and it was a relief to hear that he had not seen Finn. Such is the selfishness of men. He spoke of alien influences, and as we rode down the long roads under the deepening sky, we wondered how the powers of the material world could have reached as far as the sacred lake, violating even the mysterious silence that sings about the Gods. That the silence of the lake had been violated was certain, for the trance that was beginning to gather had melted away; his eyes had opened in the knowledge that the Gods were no longer by him, and seeing that the evening was gathering on the mountain he had packed up his drawings.

But the night will be starlit. If I had been able to get there I shouldn't have minded waiting. Were you on the mountain, now, you would be seeing that horned moon reflected in the crescent-shaped lake. It was faint-hearted of you.

At that moment two broad backs bicycling in front of us explained the sudden withdrawal of the Gods. Our two Christian wayfarers had been prowling about Slievegullion, and our wheels had not revolved many times before we had overtaken them.

We meet again, sir, and your day has been a pleasant one, I hope?

It has been very hot, he answered, too hot for Slievegullion. We couldn't get more than half-way. It was my friend that sat down overcome by the heat.

AE began to laugh.

What is your friend laughing at?

And the story of how my strength had failed me at the third wall was told.

I quite sympathise with you, said the one that had been overcome like myself by the heat. Did the poet get to the top?

Yes, he did, I replied sharply.

And did the view compensate you for the walk?

There is no view, AE answered; only a rim of pearl-coloured mountains, the edge of the world they seemed, and an intense silence.

That isn't enough to climb a thousand feet for, said the chubbier of the two.

But it wasn't for the view he went there, I replied indignantly, but for the Gods.

For the Gods!

And why not? Are there no Gods but yours?

My question was not answered, and at the end of an awkward silence we talked about the wonderful weather and the crops, the ministers showing themselves to be such good fellows that when we came to the inn AE proposed we should ask them to dine with us. A supper of ideas indeed it was, for before our dish of chops came to table they had learnt that Slievegullion was the most celebrated mountain in all Celtic theology. The birthplace of many beautiful gospels, AE said, leaning across the table, so deep in his discourse that I could not do else than insist on his finishing his chop before he unpacked his portfolio and showed the drawing he had made of the crescent-shaped lake. He ate for a little while, but it was impossible to restrain him from telling how Finn had seen a fairy face rise above the waters of the lake and had plunged after it. Whether Finn captured the nymph, and for how long he had enjoyed her, he did not tell, only that when Finn rose to the surface again he was an old man, old as the mountains and the rocks of the world. But his youth was given back to him by enchantment, and of the adventure nothing remained except his snow-white hair, which was so beautiful, and became him so well, that it had not been restored to its original colour. It was on this mountain that Cuchulain had found the fabled horse, Leath Macha,[14] and he told us, in language which still rings in my memory, of the great battle of the ford and the giant chivalry of the Ultonians.[15]

14. The legendary Gray of Macha, Cuchulain's horse.
15. AE is recalling incidents from the *Táin Bó Cúailnge*, in which Cuchulain kept the ford single-handedly against Queen Maeve's

He spoke to us of their untamable manhood, and of the exploits of Cuchulain and the children of Rury, more admirable, he said, as types, more noble and inspiring than the hierarchy of little saints who came later and cursed their memories.

This last passage seemed to conciliate the Presbyterians; they looked approvingly; but AE's soul refuses to recognise the miserable disputes of certain Christian sects. He was thinking of Culain, the smith, who lived in the mountain and who forged the Ultonians their armour.[16] And when that story had been related he remembered that he had not told them of Mananaan Mac Lir, the most remote and most spiritual of all Gaelic divinities, the uttermost God, and of the Feast of Age, the Druid counterpart of the mysteries, and how any one who partook of that Feast became himself immortal.[17]

It is a great grief to me that no single note was taken at the time of that extraordinary evening spent with AE in the inn at Dundalk, eating hard chops and drinking stale beer. The fare was poor, but what thoughts and what eloquence! A short-hand writer should have been by me. She is never with us when she should be. I might have gone to my room and taken notes, but no note was taken, alas! .... A change came into the faces of the Presbyterians as they listened to AE; even their attitudes seemed to become noble. AE did not see them; he was too absorbed in his ideas; but I saw them, and thought the while of barren rocks that the sun gilds for a moment. And then, not satisfied with that simile, I thought how at midday a ray finds its way even into the darkest valley. We had remained in the valley of the senses — our weak flesh had kept us there, but AE had ascended the mountain of the spirit and a Divine light was about him. It is the mission of some men to enable their fellows to live beyond themselves. AE possesses this power in an extraordinary degree, and we were lifted above ourselves.

My memory of that evening is one which Time is powerless to efface, and though years have passed by, the moment is remembered when AE said that a religion must always be exotic which makes a far-off land sacred rather than the earth underfoot; and then he denied that the Genius of the Gael had ever owed any of its inspiration to priestly teaching. Its own folk-tales — our talk is always reported incorrectly, and in these memories of AE there must be a great deal of myself, it sounds indeed so like myself, that I hesitate to attribute this sentence to him; yet it seems to me that I can still hear him speaking it — the folk-tales of Connaught have ever lain nearer to the hearts of the people than those of Galilee. Whatever there is of worth in Celtic song and story is woven into them, imagery handed down from the dim Druidic ages. And did I not hear him say that soon the children of Eri, a new race, shall roll out their thoughts on the hillsides before your very doors, O priests! calling your flocks from your dark chapels and twilit sanctuaries to a temple not built with hands, sunlit, starlit, sweet with the odour and incense of earth, from your altars call them to the altars of the hills, soon to be lit up as of old, soon to be blazing torches of God over the land? These heroes I see emerging. Have they not come forth in every land and race when there was need? Here, too, they will arise. My ears retain memories of his voice when he cried, Ah, my darlings, you will have to fight and suffer; you must endure loneliness, the coldness of friends, the alienation of love, warmed only by the bright interior hope of a future you must toil for but may never see, letting the deed be its own reward; laying in dark places the foundations of that high and holy Eri of prophecy, the isle of enchantment, burning with Druidic splendours, bright with immortal presences, with the face of the everlasting Beauty looking in upon all its ways, Divine with terrestrial mingling till God and the world are one.

But how much more eloquent were thy words than any that my memory recalls! Yet sometimes it seems to me that thy words have floated back almost as thou didst speak them, aggravating the calumny of an imperfect record. But for the record to be perfect the accent of thy voice and the light in thine eyes, and the whole scene — the maculated tablecloth, the chops, everything would have to be reproduced. How vain is art! That hour in the inn in Dundalk is lost for ever — the drifting of the ministers to their beds. Faint, indeed, is the memory of their passing, so faint that it will be better not to attempt to record it, but to pass on to

---

warriors, until the men of Ulster had recovered from a mysterious fatigue.

16. Cuchulain, the hound of Ulster, was so named after he slew the hound that guarded Culain's smithy. Cuchulain was willing to stand guard until a new watch-dog had been trained.

17. Manannan Mac Lir established a ritual feast, which endowed immortality upon the old gods of Ireland, the Tuatha Dé Danaan, who inhabited fairy mounds.

another event, to the portrait which AE drew that evening; for, kept awake by the presences of the Gods on the mountain, he said he must do a portrait of me, and the portrait is a better record of the dream that he brought down with him from the mountain than any words of mine. It hangs in a house in Galway, and it is clearly the work of one who has been with the Gods, for in it my hair is hyacinthine and my eyes are full of holy light. The portrait was executed in an hour, and even this work could not quell AE's ardour. He would have sat up till morning had I allowed him, telling me his theory of numbers, but I said:

Suppose we reserve that theory for tomorrow? Sufficient for the day is the blessing thereof.

from:
THE UNTILLED FIELD (1903)

[The English edition of *The Untilled Field* was published in 1903 (a version in Irish had appeared in 1902). In this collection of tales and stories, Moore included 'The Wedding Gown', a simple, haunting tale of that peasant life the Revival writers admired for its unadulterated innocence.]

THE WEDDING GOWN

It was said, but with what truth I cannot say, that the Roche property had been owned by the O'Dwyers many years ago, several generations past, some time in the eighteenth century. Only a faint legend of this ownership remained; only once had young Mr. Roche heard of it, and it was from his mother he had heard it; among the country people it was forgotten. His mother had told him that his great-great-grandfather, who had made large sums of money abroad, had increased his property by purchase from the O'Dwyers, who then owned, as well as farmed, the hillside on which the Big House stood. The O'Dwyers themselves had forgotten that they were once much greater people than they now were, but the master never spoke to them without remembering it, for though they only thought of themselves as small farmers, dependents on the squire, every one of them, boys and girls alike, retained an air of high birth, which at the first glance distinguished them from the other tenants of the estate. Though they were not aware of it, some sense of their remote origin must have survived in them, and I think that in a still more obscure way some sense of it survived in the country side, for the villagers did not think worse of the O'Dwyers because they kept themselves aloof from the pleasures of the village and its squabbles. The O'Dwyers kept themselves apart from their fellows without any show of pride, without wounding anyone's feelings.

The head of the family was a man of forty, and he was the trusted servant, almost the friend, of the young master. He was his bailiff and his steward, and he lived in a pretty cottage by the edge of the lake. O'Dwyer's aunts — they were old women of sixty-eight and seventy — lived in the Big House; the elder had been cook, and the younger housemaid, and both were now past their work, and they lived full of gratitude to the young master, to whom they thought they owed a great deal. He believed the debt to be all on his side, and when he was away he often thought of them, and when he returned home he went to greet them as he might go to the members of his own family. The family of the O'Dwyers was long-lived, and Betty and Mary had a sister far older than themselves, Margaret Kirwin, 'Granny Kirwin', as she was called, and she lived in the cottage by the lake with her nephew, Alec O'Dwyer. She was over eighty — it was said that she was nearly ninety — but her age was not known exactly. Mary O'Dwyer said that Margaret was nearly twenty years older than she, but neither Betty nor Mary remembered the exact date of their sister's birth. They did not know much about her, for though she was their sister, she was almost a stranger to them. She had married when she was sixteen, and had gone away to another part of the country, and they had hardly heard of her for thirty years. It was said that she had been a very pretty girl, and that many men had been in love with her, and it was known for certain that she had gone away with the son of the gamekeeper of the grandfather of the present Mr. Roche, so you can understand what a very long while ago it was, and how little of the story of her life had come to the knowledge of those living now.

It was certainly sixty years since she had gone away with this young man; she had lived with him in Meath[1] for some years, nobody knew exactly how many years, maybe some nine or ten years, and then

1. County Meath, to the north of Dublin and bordering in the east on the Irish Sea.

he had died suddenly, and his death, it appears, had taken away from her some part of her reason. It was known for certain that she left Meath after his death, and had remained away many years. She had returned to Meath about twenty years ago, though not to the place she had lived in before. Some said she had experienced misfortunes so great that they had unsettled her mind. She herself had forgotten her story, and one day news had come to Galway[2] — news, but it was sad news, that she was living in some very poor cottage on the edge of Navan town[3] where her strange behaviour and her strange life had made a scandal of her. The priest had to inquire out her relations, and it took him some time to do this, for the old woman's answers were incoherent, but he at length discovered she came from Galway, and he had written to the O'Dwyers. And immediately on receiving the priest's letter, Alec sent his wife to Navan, and she had come back with the old woman.

'And it was time indeed that I went to fetch her,' she said. 'The boys in the town used to make game of her, and follow her, and throw things at her, and they nearly lost the poor thing the little reason that was left to her. The rain was coming through the thatch, there was hardly a dry place in the cabin, and she had nothing to eat but a few scraps that the neighbours gave her. Latterly she had forgotten how to make a fire, and she ate the potatoes the neighbours gave her raw, and on her back there were only a few dirty rags. She had no care for anything except for her wedding gown. She kept that in a box covered over with paper so that no damp should get to it, and she was always folding it and seeing that the moth didn't touch it, and she was talking of it when I came in at the door. She thought that I had come to steal it from her. The neighbours told me that that was the way she always was, thinking that someone had come to steal her wedding gown.'

And this was all the news of Margaret Kirwin that Alec O'Dwyer's wife brought back with her. The old woman was given a room in the cottage, and though with food and warmth and kind treatment she became a little less bewildered, a little less like a wild, hunted creature, she never got back her memory sufficiently to tell them all that had happened to her after her husband's death. Nor did she seem as if she wanted to try to remember: she was garrulous only of her early days when the parish bells rang for her wedding, and the furze was in bloom. This was before the Big House on the hill had been built. The hill was then a fine pasture for sheep, and Margaret would often describe the tinkling of the sheep-bells in the valley, and the yellow furze, and the bells that were ringing for her wedding. She always spoke of the bells, though no one could understand where the bells came from. It was not customary to ring the parish bell for weddings, and there was no other bell, so that it was impossible to say how Margaret could have got the idea into her head that bells were ringing for her when she crossed the hill on her way to the church, dressed in the beautiful gown, which the grandmother of the present Mr. Roche had dressed her in, for she had always been the favourite, she said, with the old mistress, a much greater favourite than even her two sisters had ever been. Betty and Mary were then little children and hardly remembered the wedding, and could say nothing about the bells.

Margaret Kirwin walked with a short stick, her head lifted hardly higher than the handle, and when the family were talking round the kitchen fire she would come among them for a while and say something to them, and then go away, and they felt they had seen someone from another world. She hobbled now and then as far as the garden-gate, and she frightened the peasantry, so strange did she seem among the flowers — so old and forlorn, almost cut off from this world, with only one memory to link her to it. It was the spectral look in her eyes that frightened them, for Margaret was not ugly. In spite of all her wrinkles the form of the face remained, and it was easy, especially when her little grandniece was by, to see that sixty-five years ago she must have had a long and pleasant face, such as one sees in a fox, and red hair like Molly.

Molly was sixteen, and her grey dress reached only to her ankles. Everyone was fond of the poor old woman; but it was only Molly who had no fear of her at all, and one would often see them standing together beside the pretty paling that separated the steward's garden from the high road. Chestnut trees grew about the house, and China roses over the walls, and in the course of the summer there would be lilies in the garden, and in the autumn hollyhocks and sunflowers. There were a few fruit-trees a little further on, and, lower down, a stream.

2. County Galway, in the west of Ireland, bounded on the west by the Atlantic Ocean. Galway is the county town.
3. A market town in County Meath.

A little bridge led over the stream into the meadow, and Molly and her grandaunt used to go as far as the bridge, and everyone wondered what the child and the old woman had to say to each other. Molly was never able to give any clear account of what the old woman said to her during the time they spent by the stream. She had tried once to give Molly an account of one long winter when the lake was frozen from side to side. Then there was something running in her mind about the transport of pillars in front of the Big House — how they had been drawn across the lake by oxen, and how one of the pillars was now lying at the bottom of the lake. That was how Molly took up the story from her, but she understood little of it. Molly's solicitude for the old woman was a subject of admiration, and Molly did not like to take the credit for a kindness and pity which she did not altogether feel. She had never seen anyone dead, and her secret fear was that the old woman might die before she went away to service. Her parents had promised to allow her to go away when she was eighteen, and she lived in the hope that her aunt would live two years longer, and that she would be saved the terror of seeing a dead body. And it was in this intention that she served her aunt, that she carefully minced the old woman's food and insisted on her eating often, and that she darted from her place to fetch the old woman her stick when she rose to go. When Margaret Kirwin was not in the kitchen Molly was always laughing and talking, and her father and mother often thought it was her voice that brought the old woman out of her room. So the day Molly was grieving because she could not go to the dance the old woman remained in her room, and not seeing her at tea-time they began to be afraid, and Molly was asked to go to fetch her aunt.

'Something may have happened to her, mother. I daren't go.'

And when old Margaret came into the kitchen towards evening she surprised everyone by her question:

'Why is Molly crying?'

No one else had heard Molly sob, if she had sobbed, but everyone knew the reason of her grief; indeed, she had been reproved for it many times that day.

'I will not hear any more about it,' said Mrs. O'Dwyer; 'she has been very tiresome all day. Is it my fault if I cannot give her a gown to go to the dance?' And then, forgetting that old Margaret could not understand her, she told her that the servants were having a dance at the Big House, and had asked Molly to come to it. 'But what can I do? She has got no gown to go in. Even if I had the money there wouldn't be time to send for one now, nor to make one. And there are a number of English servants stopping at the house; there are people from all parts of the country, they have brought their servants with them, and I am not going to see my girl worse dressed than the others, so she cannot go. She has heard all this, she knows it .... I've never seen her so tiresome before.' Mrs. O'Dwyer continued to chide her daughter; but her mother's reasons for not allowing her to go to the ball, though unanswerable, did not seem to console Molly, and she sat looking very miserable. 'She has been sitting like that all day,' said Mrs. O'Dwyer, 'and I wish that it were tomorrow, for she will not be better until it is all over.'

'But, mother, I am saying nothing; I'll go to bed. I don't know why you're blaming me. I'm saying nothing. I can't help feeling miserable.'

'No, she don't look a bit cheerful,' the old woman said, 'and I don't like her to be disappointed.' This was the first time that old Margaret had seemed to understand since she came to live with them what was passing about her, and they all looked at her, Mrs. O'Dwyer and Alec and Molly. They stood waiting for her to speak again, wondering if the old woman's speech was an accident, or if she had recovered her mind. 'It is a hard thing for a child at her age not to be able to go to the dance at the Big House, now that she has been asked. No wonder there is not a smile on her face. I remember the time that I should have been crying too for a dance, and isn't she the very same?'

'But, Granny, she can't go in the clothes she is wearing, and she has only got one other frock, the one she goes to Mass in. I can't let my daughter ——'

But seeing the old woman was about to speak Alec stopped his wife.

'Let's hear what she has to say,' he whispered.

'There's my wedding gown, it's beautiful enough for anyone to wear. It hasn't been worn since the day I wore it, when the bells were ringing, and I went over the hill to be married; and I've taken such care of it that it is the same as it was that day. Molly will look very nice in it, she will look just as I looked on my wedding day.'

And they stood astonished — father, mother, and daughter — for the old woman, ever since she had come to live with them, had kept her wedding gown sacred from their eyes and hands, closing her door before taking it out to give it the air and strew it with camphor. Only once they had seen it. She had brought it out one day and shown it to them as a child might show a toy; but the moment Mrs. O'Dwyer put out her hand to touch it, Granny had gone away with her gown, and they had heard her shutting the box it was in. Now she was going to lend it to Molly, so she said, but they fully expected her to turn away and to go to her room, forgetful of what she had said. Even if she were to let Molly put the dress on, she would not let her go out of the house with it. She would change her mind at the last minute.

'When does this dancing begin?' she asked, and when they told her she said there would be just time for her to dress Molly, and asked the girl to come into her room. Mrs. O'Dwyer feared the girl would be put to a bitter disappointment, but if Molly once had the gown on she would not oblige her to take it off.

'In my gown you will be just like what I was when the bells were ringing.'

She took the gown out of its box herself, the petticoat and the stockings and the shoes.

'The old mistress gave me all these. Molly has gotten the hair I used to have, and will look like myself. Aren't they beautiful shoes? Look at the buckles, and they'll fit her, for her feet are the same size as mine were.'

Molly's feet went into the shoes just as if they had been made for her, and the gown fitted as well as the shoes, and Molly's hair was arranged according to the old woman's fancy, as she used to wear her own hair when it was thick and red like a fox's.

The girl thought Granny would regret her gifts, and she expected the old woman to follow her into the kitchen and ask her to give back the gown as she was going out of the house. As she stood on the threshold her mother offered her the key; the ball would not be over till five, and Granny said she'd stay up for her.

'I'll doze a bit upon a chair. If I am tired I'll lie down upon my bed. I shall hear Molly; I shan't sleep much. She'll not be able to enter the house without my hearing her.'

It was extraordinary to hear her speak like this, and, a little frightened by her sudden sanity, they tried to persuade her to allow them to lock up the house; but she sat looking into the fire, seemingly so contented that they left her, and for an hour she sat dreaming, seeing Molly young and beautifully dressed in the wedding gown of more than sixty years ago.

Dream after dream went by, the fire had burned low, the sods were falling into white ashes, and the moonlight began to stream into the room. It was the chilliness that had come into the air that awoke her, and she threw several sods of turf on to the fire.

An hour passed, and old Margaret awoke. 'The bells are ringing, the bells are ringing,' she said, and went to the kitchen door; she opened it, and under the rays of the moon she stood lost in memories, for the night of her marriage was just such a night as this one, and she had stood in the garden amid the summer flowers, just as she did now.

'The day is beginning,' she said, mistaking the moonlight for the dawn, and, listening, it seemed to her that she heard once more the sound of bells coming across the hill. 'Yes, the bells are ringing,' she said; 'I can hear them quite clearly, and must hurry and get dressed — I must not keep him waiting.'

And, returning to the house, she went to her box, where her gown had lain so many years; and though no gown was there it seemed to her that there was one, and one more beautiful than the gown she had cherished. It was the same gown, only grown more beautiful. It had passed into softer silk, into a more delicate colour; it had become more beautiful, and holding the dream-gown in her hands, she sat with it in the moonlight thinking how fair he would find her in it. Once her hands went to her hair, and then she dropped them again.

'I must begin to dress myself; I mustn't keep him waiting.'

The moonlight lay still upon her knees, but little by little the moon moved up the sky, leaving her in the shadow.

It was at this moment, as the shadows grew denser about old Margaret, that the child who was dancing at the ball came to think of her who had given her her gown, and who was waiting for her. It was in the middle of a reel she was dancing, and she was dancing it with Mr. Roche, that she felt that something had happened to her aunt.

'Mr. Roche,' she said, 'you must let me go away; I cannot dance any more tonight. I am sure that something has happened to my aunt, the old woman, Margaret Kirwin, who lives with us in the Lodge. It was she who lent me this gown. This was her wedding gown, and for sixty-five years it has never been out of her possession. She has hardly allowed anyone to see it; but she said that I was like her, and she heard me crying because I had no gown to go to the ball, and so she lent me her wedding gown.'

'You look very nice, Molly, in the wedding gown, and this is only a fancy.' Seeing the girl was frightened and wanted to go, he said: 'But why do you think that anything has happened to your aunt?'

'She is very old.'

'But she isn't much older than she was when you left her.'

'Let me go, Mr. Roche; I think I must go. I feel sure that something has happened to her. I never had such a feeling before, and I couldn't have that feeling if there was no reason for it.'

'Well, if you must go.'

She glanced to where the moon was shining and ran down the drive, leaving Mr. Roche looking after her, wondering if after all she might have had a warning of the old woman's death. The night was one of those beautiful nights in May, when the moon soars high in the sky, and all the woods and fields are clothed in the green of spring. But the stillness of the night frightened Molly, and when she stopped to pick up her dress she heard the ducks chattering in the reeds. The world seemed divided into darkness and light. The hawthorn-trees threw black shadows that reached into the hollows, and Molly did not dare to go by the path that led through a little wood, lest she should meet Death there. For now it seemed to her that she was running a race with Death, and that she must get to the cottage before him. She did not dare to take the short cut, but she ran till her breath failed her. She ran on again, but when she went through the wicket she knew that Death had been before her. She knocked twice; receiving no answer she tried the latch, and was surprised to find the door unlocked. There was a little fire among the ashes, and after blowing the sod for some time she managed to light the candle, and holding it high she looked about the kitchen.

'Auntie, are you asleep? Have the others gone to bed?'

She approached a few steps, and then a strange curiosity came over her, and though she had always feared death she now looked curiously upon death, and she thought that she saw the likeness which her aunt had often noticed.

'Yes,' she said, 'she is like me. I shall be like that some day if I live long enough.'

And then she knocked at the door of the room where her parents were sleeping.

D. P. MORAN

(1872-1936)

from:
THE PHILOSOPHY OF IRISH IRELAND (1905)

[The sardonic tone and polemical ambition of D. P. Moran's writing remind us of the formidable opposition to the literary ideals of Synge and Yeats, among others. Moran's exclusive nationalism led him to false predictions, as in this instance, but it had a tonic effect on some of the more elusive notions (e.g. Matthew Arnold's 'natural magic') upon which the new Irish literature in English tried to ground its distinctive claims.]

THE BATTLE OF TWO CIVILIZATIONS

. . . I will now attempt to trace, in broad outline, the influence which the state of things that I have referred to[1] has had upon literary taste and literary production in Ireland, on social progress and the development of polite society, on the Irish attitude

1. Earlier, D. P. Moran had argued that Irish nationalism simple-mindedly had identified all things English as ignoble and all things Irish as noble. This, he believed, was a self-defeating consequence of the conquest, which led to the country's economic dependence on Britain.

towards England, and its powerful bearing upon the economic helplessness and stagnation of the country.

I think I have read somewhere that the great Duke of Marlborough[2] knew no English history except that which he learned from Shakespeare's works. I mention this in order to point out that it takes an Englishman to get the most out of English literature, as it takes a Frenchman to get the most out of French literature. A literature steeped in the history, traditions, and genius of one nation, is at the best only an imperfect tutor to the people of another nation; in fact, the common, half-educated people of another nation will have none of it. The Irish nation has, this century, been brought up on English literature. Of course it never really kindled their minds or imaginations; they were driven to look at literature as a thing not understandable and above them — a position, I need scarcely say, not making for the development of self-respect or intellectual self-dependence. In most cases when they left school they ceased to read anything but the newspapers. Of course there are many exceptions to this generalization. If an Irishman received a higher English education and lost touch with Irish aspirations, he practically became an Englishman, and many people with less advantages, by force of exceptional ability, got their heads above the entanglements around them and breathed something like free air. But I am talking of the common run of men who make up a nation, and not of the few exceptions. Tell me of any ordinary man in Dublin, Cork or elsewhere, who professes an appreciation for the best products of English literature, and I will have no hesitation in informing you that he is an intellectual snob, mostly composed of affectation. Literature, to the common Irishman, is an ingenious collection of fine words which no doubt have some meaning, but which he is not going to presume to understand. A good speaker in Ireland is not a man who talks keen sense well, but one with 'the divil's flow of words'; and Irish 'oratory' has developed into the windiest thing on earth. The state of literature and thought and original intellectual activity of any kind had indeed dropped to a low level. The 'Irish National' literary output chiefly consisted of a few penny magazines in which the most commonplace rhymes were passed off as 'Irish' poetry, and which contained an unceasing and spirit-wearying flow of romances about '48, '98, and other periods, in all of which, of course, Ireland was painted spotless white. Romances in which Irish heroes of a couple of hundred years ago, who probably never spoke a word of English in their lives, were made to prate heroics in English of the 'Seest thou yon battlements' type, were so manifestly absurd, that no one but very young boys could put up with them. Thought was necessarily absent from all this literature, for assuredly the first effort of thought would be to let the light through all this make-believe that passed current as part and parcel of 'Irish National' literature. Criticism had died, and this sort of thing, along with 'oratory', was allowed to swell like soap bubbles all over the land. The Irish people dropped off reading, not from any lack of intellectual desire, but because nowhere was to be found that which would interest them. Then the great rise of cheap periodicals came about in England, and the market in Ireland was flooded with them. Ireland being a poor country, the cheapest class of periodicals only is within the popular resources, and it soon became evident that a great evil was threatening us, and that Ireland was largely feeding on a questionable type of British reading matter. And the commandment — 'Thou shalt be Irish' — was all the while troubling Irish hearts.

A number of writers then arose, headed by Mr. W. B. Yeats, who, for the purposes they set themselves to accomplish, lacked every attribute of genius but perseverance. However, by proclaiming from the house-tops that they were great Irish literary men, they succeeded in attracting that notice from the people of Ireland which the crowd walking up Ludgate Hill would give to five or six men who waved their hands and shouted on top of St. Paul's Cathedral. Practically no one in Ireland understands Mr. Yeats or his school; and one could not, I suggest, say anything harder of literary men. For if a literary man is not appreciated and cannot be understood, of what use is he? He has not served his purpose. The Irish mind, however, was wound down to such a low state that it was in a fit mood to be humbugged by such a school. Ireland, it must be understood, was fully convinced at this time that she possessed an Irish literature in the English language. She pointed proudly to Goldsmith, Sheridan and the rest, and cursed the Saxon when

2. Duke of Marlborough (1650-1722), English general and statesman, hero of the battle of Blenheim (1704).

that dull gentleman asked where particularly did Ireland come in, and then went on in his dull way classing all such literature as English. What is Irish literature? was a simple question which generations of Irishmen for good instinctive reasons fought shy of. They were afraid of the truth. There is manifestly no essential difference between first-class literary work executed by an English-speaking man born in Ireland, and that executed by an English-speaking man born in England. But we had to make a difference, for though we had adopted the English language, it was death to the man who called our writings by their proper name. Another make-believe had to be manufactured.

We put in 'throths' and 'begors' and 'alannas' and 'asthores' by way of Irish seasoning. But though certain classes of ballad and lyric poetry can be written in dialect, as Burns[3] has proved, you cannot rise to dignity or poetry on 'begors' and 'bedads'. There is something essentially mean about the corrupt English of the Irish peasant, particularly when put into cold print; it passes the power of man to write literature in it. Here, then, was an *impasse*. We were all on the look out for somebody to think for us, for we had given up that habit with our language. Matthew Arnold happily came along just in the nick of time, and in a much quoted essay suggested, among other things, that one of the characteristics of Celtic poetry was 'natural magic.'[4] I confess I don't exactly know what 'natural magic' means; and even dare to submit that if each of the words mean anything at all that their meanings are contradictory. But let that pass. We seized on that phrase like hawks. Then we called ourselves Celts — a word which is supposed to stand for a people, but who that people are no one seems to know, and indeed very few care. Beardless boys studying for their degrees, and serious girls were haunted by the phrase; and literary articles and literary discussion were studded with these two words, 'natural magic.' At last we had found the missing gulf, the missing something that separated us from the dull Saxon hind [*sic*], and rejoiced accordingly. We now know the difference between English literature and Irish literature, and satisfied ourselves that Shakespeare was demonstrably a Celt. Then yet another Irish make-believe was born, and it was christened 'The Celtic Note,' Mr. W. B. Yeats standing sponsor for it. The 'Celtic Renaissance' was another name invented about this time, and we were asked to pride ourselves on the influence we had exerted, and would continue to exert on English literature. The birth of the 'Celtic Note,' and the discovery of what Irish literature was really made of, caused a little stir amongst minor literary circles in London, but, much less stir in Ireland itself, where the 'Irish National' demand for *The Mirror of Life*, *The Police Gazette*, and publications of a like kind, showed no signs of weakening. The people, when they showed any evidence of interest whatever, asked what these gentlemen were driving at. Their backers thereupon put them up proudly on a pedestal, and said: 'Hats off, gentlemen; these are mystics.' Never, indeed, was a truer sentence uttered. Mystics they were and are, for a mystic is assuredly a man who deals in mysteries, and mysteries are things which the limited human mind cannot understand. The whole situation was really charged with the comic element. A muddled land which mistook politics for nationality, and English literature for Irish, which confused black with white, was offered the services of a few mystics. 'But, man, it's too many mysteries we have already,' no one had the courage to say, 'and what Ireland wants is not men to muddle her with more mysteries, but men who can solve some of the too many already in stock.' However, it must be admitted that the mystics served a useful purpose, though it was by no means the one they intended. By making a serious and earnest effort to create a distinct Irish literature in English they pushed forward the question, 'What is Irish literature?' The Gaelic League took up a logical and uncompromising position, fought a sharp and, as it proved, a decisive campaign, and last summer Mr. W. B. Yeats formally surrendered his sword, and Irish literature henceforward was not to be thought of outside the Irish language. When exactly, or by what process, Mr. George Moore came to the same conclusion I cannot say. His first public pronouncement, as far as I am aware, was made only a few months ago. The Irish language is now the ultimate goal of the Irish Literary Theatre, and a play in Irish is announced for next year. No man will dare now to say that such a contradiction as Irish literature in the English language does or could exist. And thus in a few years the work of the Young Irelanders and the

3. Robert Burns (1759-96), the Scottish poet.
4. Moran is quoting here from Matthew Arnold's influential essay, 'On the Study of Celtic Literature' (1867).

ideals of Sir Charles Gavan Duffy,[5] 'The Celtic Note,' 'The Celtic Renaissance,' and the whole Irish literary make-believes of a century were weighed in the balance and found wanting; and the triumphant Gaelic League is free to march along as if they had never been.

5. Sir Charles Gavan Duffy (1816-1903), one of the founders in 1842 of *The Nation*, the famous nationalist newspaper, which was the mouthpiece of the Young Ireland group, led by Thomas Davis.

PATRICK PEARSE

(1879-1916)

THE COMING REVOLUTION (1913)

[Published in *An Claidheamh Soluis*, the organ of the Gaelic League, in November 1913, this article marks the moment of transition from the cultural nationalism of Douglas Hyde, president and founder of the Gaelic League in 1893, to the political nationalism of which Pearse was the most eloquent and impassioned exponent. In less than three years, Pearse would be the leader of the Easter Rebellion and subsequently the executed martyr of the Irish nationalist cause.]

NOVEMBER 1913

I have come to the conclusion that the Gaelic League, as the Gaelic League, is a spent force; and I am glad of it. I do not mean that no work remains for the Gaelic League, or that the Gaelic League is no longer equal to work; I mean that the vital work to be done in the new Ireland will be done not so much by the Gaelic League itself as by men and movements that have sprung from the Gaelic League or have received from the Gaelic League a new baptism and a new life of grace. The Gaelic League was no reed shaken by the wind, no mere *vox clamantis*: it was a prophet and more than a prophet. But it was not the Messiah. I do not know if the Messiah has yet come, and I am not sure that there will be any visible and personal Messiah in this redemption: the people itself will perhaps be its own Messiah, the people labouring, scourged, crowned with thorns, agonising and dying, to rise again immortal and impassible. For peoples are divine and are the only things that can properly be spoken of under figures drawn from the divine epos.

If we do not believe in the divinity of our people we have had no business, or very little, all these years in the Gaelic League. In fact, if we had not believed in the divinity of our people, we should in all probability not have gone into the Gaelic League at all. We should have made our peace with the devil, and perhaps might have found him a very decent sort; for he liberally rewards with attorney-generalships [*sic*], bank balances, villa residences, and so forth, the great and the little who serve him well. Now, we did not turn our backs upon all these desirable things for the sake of *is* and *tá*.[1] We did it for the sake of Ireland. In other words, we had one and all of us (at least, I had, and I hope that all you had) an ulterior motive in joining the Gaelic League. We never meant to be Gaelic Leaguers and nothing more than Gaelic Leaguers. We meant to do something for Ireland, each in his own way. Our Gaelic League time was to be our tutelage: we had first to learn to know Ireland, to read the lineaments of her face, to understand the accents of her voice; to re-possess ourselves, disinherited as we were, of her spirit and mind, re-enter into our mystical birthright. For this we went to school to the Gaelic League. It was a good school, and we love its name and will champion its fame throughout all the days of our later fighting and striving. But we do not propose to remain schoolboys for ever.

I have often said (quoting, I think, Herbert Spencer)[2] that education should be a preparation for complete living; and I say now that our Gaelic League education ought to have been a preparation for our complete living as Irish Nationalists. In proportion as we have been faithful and diligent Gaelic Leaguers, our work as Irish Nationalists (by which term I mean people who accept the ideal of, and work for, the realisation of an Irish Nation, by

1. Two forms of the Gaelic verb *to be*, often found troublesome by students of the language.
2. Herbert Spencer (1820-1903), English sociologist and philosopher.

whatever means) will be earnest and thorough, a valiant and worthy fighting, not the mere carrying out of a ritual. As to what your work as an Irish Nationalist is to be, I cannot conjecture; I know what mine is to be, and would have you know yours and buckle yourself to it. And it may be (nay, it is) that yours and mine will lead us to a common meeting-place, and that on a certain day we shall stand together, with many more beside us, ready for a greater adventure than any of us has yet had, a trial and a triumph to be endured and achieved in common.

This is what I meant when I said that our work henceforward must be done less and less through the Gaelic League and more and more through the groups and the individuals that have arisen, or are arising, out of the Gaelic League. There will be in the Ireland of the next few years a multitudinous activity of Freedom Clubs, Young Republican Parties, Labour Organisations, Socialist Groups, and what not; bewildering enterprises undertaken by sane persons and insane persons, by good men and bad men, many of them seemingly contradictory, some mutually destructive, yet all tending towards a common objective, and that objective: the Irish Revolution.

For if there is one thing that has become plainer than another it is that when the seven men met in O'Connell Street to found the Gaelic League,[3] they were commencing, had there been a Liancourt[4] there to make the epigram, not a revolt, but a revolution. The work of the Gaelic League, its appointed work, was that; and the work is done. To every generation its deed. The deed of the generation that has now reached middle life was the Gaelic League, the beginning of the Irish Revolution. Let our generation not shirk *its* deed, which is to accomplish the revolution.

I believe that the national movement of which the Gaelic League has been the soul has reached the point which O'Connell's movement had reached at the close of the series of monster meetings. Indeed, I believe that our movement reached that point a few years ago — say, at the conclusion of the fight for Essential Irish; and I said so at the time. The moment was ripe then for a new Young Ireland Party, with a forward policy; and we have lost much by our hesitation. I propose in all seriousness that we hesitate no longer — that we push on. I propose that we leave Conciliation Hall behind us and go into the Irish Confederation.

Whenever Dr. Hyde, at a meeting at which I have had a chance of speaking after him, has produced his dove of peace, I have always been careful to produce my sword; and to tantalise him by saying that the Gaelic League has brought into Ireland 'Not Peace, but a Sword.' But this does not show any fundamental difference of outlook between my leader and me; for while he is thinking of peace between brother-Irishmen, I am thinking of the sword-point between banded Irishmen and the foreign force that occupies Ireland, and his peace is necessary to my war. It is evident that there can be no peace between the body politic and a foreign substance that has intruded itself into its system; between them war only until the foreign substance is expelled or assimilated.

Whether Home Rule means a loosening of a tightening of England's grip upon Ireland remains yet to be seen. But the coming of Home Rule, if come it does, will make no material difference in the nature of the work that lies before us; it will affect only the means we are to employ, our plan of campaign. There remains, under Home Rule as in its absence, the substantial tasks of achieving the Irish Nation. I do not think it is going to be achieved without stress and trial, without suffering and bloodshed; at any rate, it is not going to be achieved without *work*. Our business here and now is to get ourselves into harness for such work as has to be done.

I hold that before we can do any work, any *men's* work, we must first realise ourselves as men. Whatever comes to Ireland she needs men. And we of this generation are not in any real sense men, for we suffer things that men do not suffer, and we seek to redress grievances by means which men do not employ. We have, for instance, allowed ourselves to be disarmed; and, now that we have the chance of re-arming, we are not seizing it. Professor Eoin Mac Neill[5] pointed out last week that we have at this

3. The Gaelic League (Conradh na Gaeilge) was founded on 31 July 1893 at 9 O'Connell Street, Dublin (then Sackville Street). Douglas Hyde records that ten to twelve people were present. Of these, the best-known, apart from Hyde, were Rev. Eusaby Cleaver (vice-president), Eóin MacNeill (secretary), Seosamh Laoide (treasurer), T. O'Neill Russell and Father William Hayden SJ.

4. Roger du Plessis, duc de Liancourt (1598-1674), French Jansenist.

5. Professor Eóin MacNeill, professor of early Irish history at University College, Dublin, in an article published in the preceding issue of *An Claidheamh Soluis*, had welcomed the formation of the

moment an opportunity of rectifying the capital error we made when we allowed ourselves to be disarmed; and such opportunities, he reminds us, do not always come back to nations.

A thing that stands demonstrable is that nationhood is not achieved otherwise than in arms: in one or two instances there may have been no actual bloodshed, but the arms were there and the ability to use them. Ireland unarmed will attain just as much freedom as it is convenient for England to give her; Ireland armed will attain ultimately just as much freedom as she wants. These are matters which may not concern the Gaelic League, as a body; but they concern every member of the Gaelic League, and every man and woman of Ireland. I urged much of this five or six years ago in addresses to the Ard-Chraobh:[6] but the League was too busy with resolutions to think of revolution, and the only resolution that a member of the League could not come to was the resolution to be a man. My fellow-Leaguers had not (and have not) apprehended that the thing which cannot defend itself, even though it may wear trousers, is no man.

I am glad, then, that the North has 'begun'. I am glad that the Orangemen have armed, for it is a goodly thing to see arms in Irish hands. I should like to see the A. O. H.[7] armed. I should like to see the Transport Workers[8] armed. I should like to see any and every body of Irish citizens armed. We must accustom ourselves to the thought of arms, to the sight of arms, to the use of arms. We may make mistakes in the beginning and shoot the wrong people; but bloodshed is a cleansing and a sanctifying thing, and the nation which regards it as the final horror has lost its manhood. There are many things more horrible than bloodshed; and slavery is one of them.

Ulster Volunteers, since it gave the opportunity to the Irish Volunteers to prepare openly to defend the interests of nationalist Ireland by force of arms. The article was entitled 'The North Began'.
6. The Gaelic League's governing body.
7. The Ancient Order of Hibernians, a catholic nationalist association.
8. The Irish Transport and General Workers Union, which was involved in the great Lockout in Dublin in 1913.

from:
POEMS (1958)

[Written in the last year of Pearse's life, before the Easter Rising, these poems are an integral part of the rebel's last will and testament. His identification with legendary, Gaelic Ireland and his repudiation of his country's oppressors are both features of his sacrificial and fervent mentality.]

I am Ireland

I am Ireland:
I am older than the Old Woman of Beare.[1]

Great my glory:
I that bore Cuchulainn the valiant.

Great my shame:
My own children that sold their mother.

I am Ireland:
I am lonelier than the Old Woman of Beare.

1. A legendary old woman. Her house is an ancient monument on Ballygawley Mountain in County Sligo.

The Rebel

I am come of the seed of the people, the people that sorrow,
That have no treasure but hope,
No riches laid up but a memory
Of an Ancient glory.
My mother bore me in bondage, in bondage my mother was born,
I am of the blood of serfs;
The children with whom I have played, the men and women with whom I have eaten,
Have had masters over them, have been under the lash of masters,
And, though gentle, have served churls;
The hands that have touched mine, the dear hands whose touch is familiar to me,
Have worn shameful manacles, have been bitten at the wrist by manacles,
Have grown hard with the manacles and the task-work of strangers,
I am flesh of the flesh of these lowly, I am bone of their bone,
I that have never submitted;
I that have a soul greater than the souls of my people's masters,
I that have vision and prophecy and the gift of fiery speech,
I that have spoken with God on the top of His holy hill.

And because I am of the people, I understand
 the people,
I am sorrowful with their sorrow, I am hungry
 with their desire:
My heart has been heavy with the grief of
 mothers,
My eyes have been wet with the tears of
 children.
I have yearned with old wistful men,
And laughed or cursed with young men;
Their shame is my shame, and I have reddened
 for it,
Reddened for that they have served, they who
 should be free,
Reddened for that they have gone in want, while
 others have been full,
Reddened for that they have walked in fear of
 lawyers and of their jailers
With their writs of summons and their
 handcuffs,
Men mean and cruel!
I could have borne stripes on my body rather
 than this shame of my people.

And now I speak, being full of vision;
I speak to my people, and I speak in my people's
 name to the masters of my people.
I say to my people that they are holy, that they
 are august, despite their chains,
That they are greater than those that hold them,
 and stronger and purer,
That they have but need of courage, and to call
 on the name of their God,
God the unforgetting, the dear God that loves
 the peoples
For whom He died naked, suffering shame.
And I say to my people's masters: Beware,
Beware of the thing that is coming, beware of
 the risen people,
Who shall take what ye would not give. Did ye
 think to conquer the people,
Or that Law is stronger than life and than men's
 desire to be free?
We will try it out with you, ye that have harried
 and held,
Ye that have bullied and bribed, tyrants,
 hypocrites, liars!

Biographies/Bibliographies

Standish James O'Grady

LIFE. Born in 1846 in Castletown Berehaven, Co. Cork, O'Grady graduated from Trinity College, Dublin and practised law until he forsook that calling to take up writing. His discovery, in his twenty-fourth year, of the history and literature of his native land (he had chanced upon Sylvester O'Halloran's *An Introduction to the Study of the History and Antiquities of Ireland*) led to his life-long enthusiasm for the Irish past. This proved to be his most fruitful literary involvement, for it was his retelling of the ancient Irish sagas that made him a seminal figure in the history of the Irish Literary Revival. His work was crucial in introducing the heroic figure of Cuchulain to the modern consciousness. A staunch unionist in politics and an admirer of Thomas Carlyle's vision of strong leadership, O'Grady also laboured to remind the landlords of Ireland of their duties as political leaders. In this enterprise he was less than successful. Between 1900 and 1906 he edited a journal, *The All-Ireland Review*, in which he presented a radical conservative view of Irish political and social life. With its closure, he largely withdrew from comment on Irish affairs. He left Ireland in 1918 and died ten years later on the Isle of Wight, in the south of England.

CHIEF WRITINGS. *History of Ireland: The Heroic Period* (London: Sampson Low, Searle, Marston and Rivington; Dublin: E. Ponsonby, 1878); *Early Bardic Literature, Ireland* (London: Sampson Low, Searle, Marston and Rivington; Dublin: E. Ponsonby, 1879); *History of Ireland: Cuchulain and His Contemporaries* (London: Sampson Low, Searle, Marston and Rivington; Dublin: E. Ponsonby, 1880); *History of Ireland: Critical and Philosophical* (London: Sampson Low; Dublin: E. Ponsonby, 1881); *The Crisis in Ireland* (Dublin: E. Ponsonby; London: Simpkin and Marshall, 1882); *Toryism and the Tory Democracy* (London: Chapman and Hall, 1886).

BIOGRAPHY AND CRITICISM. Hugh Art O'Grady, *Standish James O'Grady: The Man and His Work* (Dublin: The Talbot Press, 1929); Philip Marcus, *Standish O'Grady* (Lewisburg, Pennsylvania: Bucknell University Press, 1970). Marcus's is the best study of this writer.

Douglas Hyde

LIFE. Born in 1860, of a protestant clerical family, Hyde grew up in Frenchpark, Co. Roscommon, where his father was rector. It was there that he acquired the Irish language which was to remain a life-long interest. Before his entry to Trinity College, Dublin in 1880, he had already begun his collections of Irish folk-tale and song, which were to be the basis of his most important work and publications. Ostensibly a student of the law, at university Hyde continued the studies that were to bear fruit first in the poems he published under the pseudonym *An Craoibhín Aoibhinn* (The Pleasant Little Branch) and subsequently in his scholarly translations of folk-tales and poems of the Gaelic tradition, upon which his chief claim to fame must rest. In 1892 Hyde accepted the presidency of the newly formed National Literary Society and in the year of his marriage (1893) became president of the Gaelic League, which he helped to establish. At its inception, the League sought to revive Irish and create a modern literature in the language without involving culture in politics. Hyde kept the League free of the taint of party politics until 1915, in the years of its greatest influence. When its constitution was changed to admit a separatist political aim, Hyde resigned. He had been appointed professor of modern Irish in University College, Dublin in 1905. He remained in this post, a vigorous and influential teacher, until 1932. In 1938 Douglas Hyde was elected the first President of Ireland and held office until 1944. He died in Dublin in 1949.

CHIEF WRITINGS. *Beside the Fire: A Collection of Irish Gaelic Folk Stories* (London: David Nutt, 1890); *Love Songs of Connacht*, Dublin: Gill, 1893; facsimile edition, Shannon: Irish University Press, 1969); *A*

Literary History of Ireland from the Earliest Times to the Present Day (London: Unwin, 1899; revised and edited by Brian Ó Cuív, London: Ernest Benn; New York: Barnes and Noble, 1967); *The Religious Songs of Connacht* (Dublin: Gill, 1906; facsimile edition, Shannon: Irish University Press, 1972).

BIOGRAPHY AND CRITICISM. Dominic Daly, *The Young Douglas Hyde: The Dawn of the Irish Revolution and Renaissance 1874-1893* (Shannon: Irish University Press, 1974); Lester Conner, 'The Importance of Douglas Hyde to the Irish Literary Renaissance', in R. J. Porter and J. D. Brophy (eds), *Modern Irish Literature* (New York: Twayne, 1972), Vol. I, pp. 95-114. This essay is a thoughtful appreciation of Hyde as writer and man.

Lady Augusta Gregory

LIFE. Lady Gregory was born Isabella Augusta Persse at Roxborough, Co. Galway in 1852, where she grew up. In 1880 she married Sir William Gregory of Coole, Co. Galway, a former governor of Ceylon, who gave her entrance to the broad Victorian world of literary and political society. Her own political attitudes gradually became those of a convinced nationalist and in 1901 she edited a collection of essays on the subject of cultural nationalism, *Ideals in Ireland*. Lady Gregory's commitment to cultural nationalism expressed itself in her assiduous labours to collect the folk-tales and legends of her native region, which she published in five collections. Her knowledge of the Irish language, which she learnt in adulthood, allowed her to translate Irish epic literature into a form of Hiberno-English (Kiltartanese) identified with her own Galway district. She met the poet W.B. Yeats in 1896 and a life-long friendship developed; she made Coole available to him and other writers of the Literary Revival as a place of rest and recuperation. It was there that she, Yeats and her neighbour, Edward Martyn, laid the basis of an Irish Literary Theatre, subsequently The Abbey Theatre. Between her fiftieth and seventy-fifth year she wrote forty plays for the theatre. For much of her later life her preoccupation was to try to persuade the British government to recognize a codicil to her nephew Hugh Lane's will, which bequeathed a collection of Impressionist paintings to the Irish nation. She died at Coole in 1932.

CHIEF WRITINGS. *Ideals in Ireland* (London: Unicorn, 1901); *Cuchulain of Muirthemne* (London: John Murray, 1902); *Gods and Fighting Men* (London: John Murray, 1904); *A Book of Saints and Wonders* (Dundrum: Dun Emer, 1906); *The Kiltartan History Book* (Dublin: Maunsel, 1909); *Seven Short Plays* (Dublin: Maunsel, 1909); *The Kiltartan Wonder Book* (Dublin: Maunsel, 1910); *Irish Folk History Plays*, First Series (London: Putnam, 1912); *Irish Folk History Plays*, Second Series (London: Putnam, 1912); *Our Irish Theatre* (London: Putnam, 1913); *The Kiltartan Poetry Book: Translations from the Irish* (London: Putnam, 1919); *Visions and Beliefs of the West of Ireland* (London: Putnam, 1920); *Seventy Years* (Gerrards Cross: Colin Smythe, 1974); *The Coole Edition of Lady Gregory's Writings* Colin Smythe, T.R. Henn general editors (Gerrards Cross: Colin Smythe; New York: Oxford University Press, 1970).

BIOGRAPHY AND CRITICISM. Hazard Adams, *Lady Gregory* (Lewisburg, Pennsylvania: Bucknell University Press, 1973); Elizabeth Coxhead, *Lady Gregory: A Literary Portrait*, revised edition (Gerrards Cross: Colin Smythe, 1966); Mary Lou Kohfeldt, *Lady Gregory: The Woman Behind the Irish Renaissance* (London: André Deutsch, 1985); Ann Saddlemyer, 'Augusta Gregory, Irish Nationalist', in Joseph Ronsley (ed.), *Myth and Reality in Irish Literature* (Waterloo, Ontario: Wilfrid Laurier University Press, 1977), pp. 29-40; Ann Saddlemyer, *In Defense of Lady Gregory, Playwright* (Dublin: Dolmen Press, 1966). Saddlemyer's essays are the best introduction to this writer.

AE (George Russell)

LIFE. Russell (who took the pseudonym AE) was born in Lurgan, Co. Armagh in 1867. His family moved to Dublin while he was a schoolboy and it was there that he met W.B. Yeats, at the Metropolitan School of Art. With Yeats he became involved in various occult groups, including the Theosophical Society. Russell began work in a draper's shop, but found his true avocation as an organizer for Sir Horace Plunkett's Irish Agricultural Organization Society, a body that encouraged rural co-operation. Throughout his life AE published books of vaguely visionary poems (the literary companions of his equally ethereal paintings) and volumes in which he propounded his spiritual beliefs. It was, however, in his dramatic version of the Deirdre legend that he achieved the greatest literary success. Perhaps his most effective contribution to the period was as a journalist. Two journals that he edited — *The Irish Homestead* (1905-23) and *The Irish Statesman* (1923-30) — asserted some influence in the Ireland of their day and in these AE expressed his vigorously argued socialist vision of a possible Irish society. An idealist in politics and art, he was an inspirational figure and gave considerable support to younger writers and poets. He died in Bournemouth in the south of England in 1935, having left Ireland after his wife's death in 1932.

CHIEF WRITINGS. *Deirdre* (Dublin: Maunsel, 1907); *Collected Poems* (London: Macmillan, 1913); *The National Being* (Dublin and London: Maunsel, 1916); *The Candle of Vision* (London: Macmillan, 1918); *The Interpreters* (London: Macmillan, 1922); *Vale and Other Poems* (London: Macmillan, 1931); *Song and Its Fountains* (London: Macmillan, 1932); *The Avatars: A Futuristic Fantasy* (London: Macmillan, 1933).

BIOGRAPHY AND CRITICISM. Henry Summerfield, *That Myriad-Minded Man: A Biography of G.W. Russell, 'AE'* (Gerrards Cross: Colin Smythe; Totowa, N.J.: Rowan and Littlefield, 1975); Robert Bernard Davis, *George William Russell (AE)* (Boston: Twayne, 1977). These two volumes together amount to a sound estimate of man and writer. John Eglinton (W.K. Magee), *A Memoir of AE* (London: Macmillan, 1937); Richard M. Kain and James H. O'Brien, *George Russell (AE)* (Lewisburg, Pennsylvania: Bucknell University Press, 1976); Henry Summerfield, 'AE as a Literary Critic' in Joseph Ronsley (ed.), *Myth and Reality in Irish Literature* (Waterloo, Ontario, Wilfrid Laurier University Press, 1977), pp. 41-61; Alan Denson, *Printed Writings by George W. Russell: A Bibliography* (Evanston, Illinois: Northwestern University Press, 1961).

George Moore

LIFE. George Moore was born of a landed County Mayo family in Ballyglass in 1852. The religion of his immediate family was catholic, but in most other respects his was the childhood and young manhood of a scion of the protestant ascendancy. His father's death in 1870 allowed for a life of subsidized dilettantism in Paris until, in 1880, the Land War placed the rents from his estates in even greater jeopardy than they had been. This crisis made of Moore a professional writer, who for the next twenty years lived the life of a successful novelist and man of letters in England. With *Esther Waters* (1894) he established for himself a place in the history of English literature, introducing in a successful way the techniques of Zola and Flaubert to English fiction. (He had attempted a more purely Zolaesque experiment in his less successful novel of Irish big house life, *A Drama in Muslin*, in 1886.) His distaste for England in the period of the Boer War and a dissatisfaction with his own work brought Moore back to Ireland in 1901, where he had already advised Yeats on his play *The Countess Cathleen* (1899). For the next ten years he was to figure among the writers of the Literary Revival. In 1903 he produced *The Untilled Field*, a collection of stories that broke new artistic ground in its concentration on Irish rural life and that anticipated the Irish short-story form. In 1905 his novel, *The Lake*, was published — a remarkable portrait of a priest enduring a crisis of conscience. But from this period his finest work was *Hail and Farewell*, an autobiographical *tour de force* in three volumes that lays claim to be his masterpiece. In 1911 Moore again settled in London, where as man of letters he spent the next twenty-two years polishing a style that more and more seemed out of tune with the age. He died, unmarried, in 1933.

CHIEF WRITINGS. *A Modern Lover* (London: Tinsley Brothers, 1883); *A Mummer's Wife* (London: Vizetelly and Co., 1885); *A Drama in*

Muslin (London: Vizetelly and Co., 1886); *Confessions of A Young Man* (London: Swan Sonnenschein, Lowry and Co., 1888); *The Strike at Arlingford* (London: Walter Scott Ltd., 1893); *Esther Waters* (London, Walter Scott Ltd., 1894); *The Bending of the Bough* (London: T. Fisher Unwin; Chicago and New York: Herbert S. Stone and Co., 1900); *The Untilled Field* (London: T. Fisher Unwin; Philadelphia: J.B. Lippincott Company, 1903); *The Lake* (London: William Heinemann, 1905; New York: D. Appleton and Co., 1906); *Hail and Farewell: Ave* (London: William Heinemann; New York: D. Appleton and Co., 1911); *Hail and Farewell: Salve* (London: William Heinemann; New York: D. Appleton and Co., 1912); *Hail and Farewell: Vale* (London: William Heinemann; New York: D. Appleton and Co., 1914); *The Brook Kerith* (London: T. Werner Laurie Ltd; New York: Macmillan, 1916); *Celibate Lives* (London: William Heinemann Ltd; New York: Boni and Liveright, 1927). Note also the twenty volumes in the Ebury Edition (London: William Heinemann, 1937).

BIOGRAPHY AND CRITICISM. Joseph Hone, *The Life of George Moore* (New York: Macmillan, 1936). The definitive bibliography is Edwin Gilcher, *A Bibliography of George Moore* (Dekalb, Illinois: Northern Illinois University Press, 1970); Malcolm Brown, *George Moore: A Reconsideration* (Seattle: University of Washington Press, 1955); Graham Owens (ed.), *George Moore's Mind and Art* (Edinburgh: Oliver and Boyd, 1968); Douglas A. Hughes, *The Man of Wax: Critical Essays on George Moore* (New York: New York University Press, 1971); Janet Egleson Dunleavy, *George Moore: The Artist's Vision, The Storyteller's Art* (Lewisburg, Pennsylvania: Bucknell University Press, 1973); Richard Allen Cave, *A Study of the Novels of George Moore* (Gerrards Cross: Colin Smythe, 1978); Robert Welch (ed.), *The Way Back: Essays on George Moore's The Untilled Field* (Dublin: Wolfhound Press, 1982); Janet Egleson Dunleavy (ed.), *George Moore In Perspective* (Massachusetts: Malton Press; Gerrards Cross: Colin Smythe; Totowa: Barnes and Noble, 1983).

D.P. Moran

LIFE. Born in Waterford in 1872, Moran cut his journalistic teeth in London where he made contact with the Irish Literary Society during the 1890s. He returned to Ireland intending to help revive the Irish language, but delighted in attacking sham and cant (the Citizen's word 'raimeis', in the Cyclops episode of *Ulysses*, was his popularization). He published articles in the *New Ireland Review* from 1898 onwards and in 1900 founded *The Leader* newspaper, of which he remained editor until 1926. Moran was a vigorous advocate of Irish Irelandism, economic self-sufficiency and of a full-blooded nationalism, 'racy of the soil'. He died in Sutton, Co. Dublin, in 1936.

CHIEF WRITINGS. *The Philosophy of Irish Ireland*, Dublin: reprinted from *New Ireland Review*, 1905.

BIOGRAPHY AND CRITICISM. D. McCartney, 'Hyde, D.P. Moran and Irish Ireland' in F.X. Martin (ed.), *Leaders and Men of the Easter Rising* (Ithaca, New York: Cornell University Press, 1967), pp. 43-54.

Patrick Pearse

LIFE. Born in Dublin in 1879, of an English father and an Irish mother, Pearse was educated by the Christian Brothers and at the Royal University (subsequently University College, Dublin). He also read for the Bar at Dublin's King's Inns. Between 1903 and 1909 he edited the Gaelic League's journal, *An Claidheamh Soluis* (The Sword of Light). In 1908 he had founded a school, St Enda's, in Rathfarnham, Co. Dublin, where he practised his educational theories on the nature of a fully human Irish education. Besides journalism, he also wrote plays, stories and poems in the Irish language and a small body of verse in English. As a member of the Irish Volunteers and the Irish Republican Brotherhood, Pearse led the Rising in Dublin at Easter 1916. He died at the hands of a British firing squad on 3 May 1916.

CHIEF WRITINGS. *Political Writings and Speeches* (Dublin: The Talbot Press, 1952); *Poems* (Dublin: The Talbot Press, 1958).

BIOGRAPHY AND CRITICISM. Ruth Dudley Edwards, *Patrick Pearse: The Triumph of Failure* (London: Gollancz, 1977). This is the definitive life. Raymond J. P. Porter, *P.H. Pearse* (New York: Twayne, 1973); Seamus Deane, 'Pearse: Writing and Chivalry' in *Celtic Revivals: Essays in Modern Irish Literature 1880-1980* (London and Boston: Faber and Faber, 1985), pp. 63-74. A cogent and sympathetic literary assessment. See additional bibliography in Volume III, p. 932.

D. E. S. MAXWELL, *Editor*

Irish Drama 1899-1929: The Abbey Theatre

In 1897 W.B. Yeats and two landowners in the west of Ireland, Augusta Lady Gregory and Edward Martyn, recommended the establishment of a 'literary theatre' in Dublin: a concept, not a building. Their aim, declared in a prospectus, was 'to build up a Celtic and Irish school of dramatic literature', distanced both from the English commercial theatre of the time and from the whole English theatrical tradition that had accommodated Farquhar, Congreve, Sheridan, and Goldsmith. Shortly before the first of the Irish Literary Theatre's three Dublin seasons (1899-1901), the novelist George Moore, also a landowner, joined the original trio.

United in proposing an indigenous drama, and lacking native precedent, the founders were at aesthetic odds on the means to their end; and indeed on the exact nature of the end. Martyn advocated as a model the new continental drama, Ibsen particularly. Moore agreed, but regarded Martyn and Yeats as apprentices to his (marginally) greater theatrical experience. Privately, Yeats thought Ibsen a modish realist whose fashion would soon pass. He was attracted to Lady Gregory's translations of Irish heroic legends and peasant tales: images of Irish life to supplant the 'stage Irishman' of popular theatre. He looked also, in a selective way, to the symbolist drama of *fin de siècle* France and was ambitious to restore verse and a non-realist drama to their bygone primacy — 'the theatre of Shakespeare or rather perhaps of Sophocles.'

Largely indifferent to these rarified dissensions, the potential audience was alert to a more narrowly political reckoning of the 'national theatre'. As a corrective to English disparagement, nationalist sentiment demanded faithful, indeed flattering, portrayals of Irish piety. Unionist opinion concurred in these Victorianized notions of respectability, perhaps interpreting impiety as a covert form of political subversion. A movement cultivated by an élite was having to contend with populist aspirations which, orchestrated by Arthur Griffith's newspaper, *The United Irishman*, submitted art to political judgment.

The Irish Literary Theatre's three seasons held the rival theories roughly in balance. Yeats's *The Countess Cathleen*, briefly suspected of heresy, and *Diarmuid and Grania*, written in uneasy partnership with Moore, represented heroic verse drama. Martyn's *The Heather Field* and *Maeve* were laboured imitations of Ibsen. So was Moore's *The Bending of the Bough*, originally Martyn's *The Tale of a Town*, until Martyn rejected Moore's dictatorial 'collaboration.' Douglas Hyde's *Casadh an tSúgáin* (*The Twisting of the Rope*) was an entertaining one-act peasant comedy. Altogether there seemed to be a design for the future: verse-poetic/prose-realist, cosmopolitan/native. Events were to reshape it.

Martyn resigned, disaffected by Yeats's neglect of continental drama; Moore lost interest and went back to England. Relieved of opposition, and sustained by Lady Gregory, Yeats turned to the brothers Frank and Willie Fay, enthusiastic amateurs. They had trained a body of non-professional players for their Irish National Dramatic Company. They believed, with Yeats, in 'the sovereignty of words' and had instructed their players in distinct speech and minimal stage 'business.' Although Frank envisaged a commitment to Irish as necessary to a truly national theatre, he recognized that in practice English had superseded it. The long commerce with Gaelic had given English a distinctively hibernicized character, sanctioning it, in J.M. Synge's words, as 'English that is perfectly Irish in essence.'

In 1902, the Fays' Company presented Yeats's *Cathleen ni Houlihan* and the next year it joined Yeats and Lady Gregory to form the Irish National Theatre Society. This became the Irish National Theatre Society Ltd — the Abbey — in 1904 when it moved to permanent quarters in Abbey Street, the gift of Miss Annie Horniman, an eccentric English admirer of Yeats and a demanding patron. In that year, it put on Yeats's *The Hour Glass* and *The King's Threshold*, James Cousin's *The Racing Lug*, Lady Gregory's first play, *Twenty-Five*; and, auguries of the theatre's accomplishment, Padraic Colum's *Broken Soil* and Synge's *In the Shadow of the Glen*.

Lady Gregory, an indispensable mediator in the early days, did not begin to write plays until she was fifty. Between 1907 and 1927 she gave the Abbey some thirty-seven plays, most of them very popular: folk comedy and tragedy, history plays, translations. If it seems now a more modest achievement than it did to Lady Gregory, or to Yeats, who praised it fulsomely, it was nevertheless suggestive of a dramatic potential in the English speech of her region, Kiltartan in County Galway. It was Synge who absorbed vernaculars, those of Wicklow and the Aran Islands, into an elaborately stylized dramatic rhetoric, to be judged by the power of its artifice, not literal authenticity.

Yeats's work was continuing to keep verse drama alive. Synge, however, was a signal of a decisive turn to prose. His was a prose — 'highly coloured musical language' — acceptable to Yeats. That of Padraic Colum is plainer, closer to its counterparts in life — much reduced, in Yeats's view, by migration from the land and the levelling by formal education and the popular press — in the Midlands, the region about which Colum wrote. Yet his characters' speech does have a subdued poetry.

Colum's plays are much more circumstantially of their place and time than Synge's. Their subjects are the emotional penalties of the hunger for land, now available to tenants for purchase (*The Land*, 1905); the lure of a fiddler's itinerant life, constricted in a cottage farm (*The Fiddler's House*, 1907); the bickering malice of small-town life dispossessing a workhouse master of his minor dignity (*Thomas Muskerry*, 1910). Colum has a keen sense of the historical energies which question the assumptions of their period and enforce change. The 'time' of Ellen's conversation with Matt in *The Land* is a moment of personal decision. It is also the time of an epoch, of 'twenty years for the purchase' of a farm, a continuing home, or an encumbrance that will force emigration to the doubtful opportunities of America. The dialogue keeps delicate hold, beneath what is actually spoken, on both individual relationships and broader social dissolutions.

These consolidations of theory into a somewhat divergent body of writing, indisputably Synge's work of genius, were accompanied by strife both within and outside the Abbey. Synge's plays were consistently a cause of outrage. Maud Gonne walked out of the first performance of *In the Shadow of the Glen*. Riots greeted the supposed defamation of the peasantry's moral and linguistic purity in *The Playboy of the Western World* (1907). Yeats was suspected of subordinating the political struggle to artistic whimsies. More discriminating criticism alleged, especially after Synge's death in 1909, the loss of some primal vigour in the theatre.

The Abbey's management was split, disunited about *The Playboy*, nervous of the anti-clericalism in Synge's *The Tinker's Wedding* (1902-07, not presented until 1971). Miss Horniman detested the Fays and by 1908 had engineered their resignations. In 1910 she withdrew her subsidy, finally convinced that the Abbey was a nest of Republicanism. With Synge dead and Lady Gregory an ally, Yeats was in control. Ironically, it was by this time evident that his ideal poetic theatre was not to be. The appointment of Lennox Robinson, an Abbey dramatist since 1908 (*The Clancy Name*), as play-director (1909-14, 1919-35) acknowledged the realistic bent of the Abbey stage.

There were two interesting exceptions to this general run, neither much encouraged by Yeats: the curious fantasy plays of George Fitzmaurice (*The Pie-Dish*, 1908) and the verse plays of Austin Clarke (*The Son of Learning*, rejected in 1927). Set mostly in the sixth to the twelfth centuries, Clarke's plays constitute another fruitless assault on the twentieth-century resistance to dramatic verse; the disregard for the wondrous region of Fitzmaurice's mannered, riddling prose was a real loss to the Abbey.

The main genealogy was that of Colum's contemporaries and successors: William Boyle (*The*

Building Fund, 1905), Lennox Robinson, T.C. Murray (*Birthright*, 1910), St John Ervine (*Mixed Marriage*, 1911), George Shiels (*Paul Twyning*, 1922); and their explosive culmination, Sean O'Casey (*The Shadow of a Gunman*, 1923). Their theatrical space was the nineteenth-century proscenium stage and they were variously enterprising with the realism its conventions enjoin. At their slightest, they work in documentary paraphrases easily referred to their origins in the world of events. Such was the work of William Boyle, which the Abbey seems to have presented and his audiences to have received as farcical comedy. *The Building Fund* and *The Mineral Workers* (1906) are in fact quite bitter portrayals of rural materialism and sharp practice. Boyle's dialogue, however, with none of the subtly metaphorical implications of Colum's, limits his characters to their immediate circumstances.

Though more diversified, Lennox Robinson's plays resemble Boyle's in their rather constricted regionalism and their dependence on plot manoeuvres, not the enigmas of human behaviour. His earliest work indulges a sub-Ibsenite gloom of murder and family corruption: the 'Cork realist' school. His popular comedy, *Drama at Inish* (1933), laughs at these pretensions: the sombre repertoire of a travelling company incites a small seaside resort to thoughts of suicide and fateful promiscuities (see Volume III, p. 181.

Knowledgeable in the international theatre of the 1920s, Robinson founded the Dublin Drama League in 1919 to import European and American plays. His own *Church Street* (1934) borrows effectively from Pirandello: a young Irish dramatist invents stories about his neighbours which turn out to be — perhaps — true. Robinson's versatile talent commanded a wide range of forms, most at home in skilfully turned, not too demanding, comedy.

Another 'Cork realist', T.C. Murray, has a harrowing awareness of the outcast created, then oppressed, by the compulsions of social and religious codes. In *Aftermath* (1922), a mother contrives her son's debasing marriage. Remarkable for its period, *Autumn Fire* (1924) imbues the marriage of an ageing man to a young girl with a repressed and questing sexuality. The settings, from the harsh and contested landscapes of *Birthright* to drably ensnaring interiors, reflect the characters' destinies.

Although given to melodramatic curtain lines, Murray manages a speech that disturbingly suggests motives and responses beyond the characters' conscious perception. The claustrophobic atmosphere defining his plays comes from the strains between intense passions and their prohibition. Not only are there no winners. There can be none. The characters must simply endure within customary ways, and a strict catholicism which Murray — though his plays are not exercises in moral dogma — implicitly endorses.

There had been stirrings in the North also. In 1904 Bulmer Hobson and David Parkhill founded the Ulster Literary Theatre in Belfast. The company, amateur to the end, survived into the 1930s and developed in kitchen comedy and tragedy a regional variant of the Abbey's style, of which it was not invariably respectful: Lewis Purcell wrote two amusing parodies of the manner. Rutherford Mayne's *The Drone* (1908) was among the most successful comedies of its time, but though Mayne did some other interesting work, the Ulster Literary Theatre cultivated no major dramatist.

The first consequential Northern playwright was St John Ervine. His early plays, *Jane Clegg* (1913) and *The Orangeman* (1914) — both produced in England, show the Fabian influence of his acquaintanceship with Shaw. His inbred unionism frustrated this brief alliance. After his politically stormy Abbey play-directorship (1915-16), Ervine achieved celebrity in England for a succession of fashionable comedies (*The First Mrs Fraser*, 1929).

Ervine's early plays added to the Abbey register an authentic Northern inflection: *Mixed Marriage* (1911), *The Magnanimous Lover* (1912), *John Ferguson* (1915). The historically repetitive Belfast tragedy of *Mixed Marriage* enters an urban vernacular. There, as in his rural settings, vulgarized religious and political imperatives contend with personal decencies. Persuasive studies of the Northern protestant temperament, its obduracy and convivialities, Ervine's characters have their conflicts simplified, more arbitrarily than T. C. Murray's, by plots admitting only bluntly opposed moral systems: as in *John Ferguson* between versions of an Old and a New Testament ethic.

George Shiels, also a Northerner, is a more enigmatic dramatist. First produced by the Ulster Literary Theatre, he gave the Abbey a series of box-office successes, beginning with *Paul Twyning* (1922) and continuing to the late 1940s. Contemporary reviews indicate that the Abbey rendered

Shiels as broad farce, a travesty of his grim world. The early plays, such as *Professor Tim* (1925), innocent enough comedies, occupy a disorderly and deceptive universe whose 'happy endings' entail unsuspected consequences left in wait.

Shiels's plays are amoral moralities, increasingly so as his work developed: base actions, Yeats noted disapprovingly of *Cartney and Kevney* (1927), recorded without judgment. *The Passing Day* (1936) is representative. The narrative concerns the dispositions of John Fibb's will. The real tale is in the emotional manipulations practised by all the characters. With no sense of inconsistency, they appeal to whatever principles may serve their turn, the equity of the outcome 'not the playwright's business'. Feelings are declared rather than registered in a prose holding close to common speech, dominated by the vocabulary of mortgages, bank loans, credit and foreclosures.

Between them these dramatists demonstrate the very considerable range in the metaphorical (Colum, Shiels) and documentary (Boyle, Ervine) statements possible on the realist stage. Synge is a special case. His language is the most elaborate and fantastical of all; and it is language that asserts a reality on the stage itself, beyond straight imitation of actuality. O'Casey, with his synthesis of urban realism and a vernacular poetry, is both Synge's successor and the culmination in these years of the tradition which can, with qualification, be called realist. Synge, O'Casey and Fitzmaurice represent the remarkable achievement of the native drama's first quarter century.

W. B. YEATS

A consistent purpose of Yeats's drama was to displace the theatre of social and psychological realism and a language reduced to its merely informative or explanatory functions. Decrying elaborate décor, stage 'business' and overblown acting, his controlling belief insisted on 'the sovereignty of words' elevated by verse to release the poetic imagination. Yeats envisaged a drama of legend and myth, strongly ritual in form, concerned not with the transient manners of period and place but with the divine and diabolic in human action, 'the deeps of the mind'.

It was perhaps the novelty of his subject, the Irish saga-world, rather than any innate impulse to theatrical experiment, that prompted Yeats to these speculations. Nevertheless, he contemplated the mid-nineties *avant-garde* theatre of Europe and, despite major reservations, found in Maeterlinck and especially in de l'Isle Adam's *Axel* a non-representational drama amenable to his purposes: not external action, but crises of the soul on a stage of 'symbolic and decorative scenery'. From 1916 his ideas cohered around aspects of Japanese Noh drama, plays of dead lovers, gods incarnate, visions. With dance and music, masked actors, moving like marionettes, filled the stage space with a fusion of words and non-verbal effects, 'as a decorator of pottery accepts the roundness of a bowl'.

Despite his aesthetic theories, Yeats did not insulate his drama from life. Often political parables, his plays affirm standpoints. *The Countess Cathleen* (1902) attests his ideal of the Anglo-Irish Big House; *Cathleen ni Houlihan* (1902) is a patriotic call to arms; *Purgatory* (1938) creates a bitter fable of modern Ireland. Even in *At the Hawk's Well* (1916), his fullest exercise of the Noh conventions, the shapes imposed by the successive groupings of players, the hawk-dance, the music, are significant of the play's meaning: Cuchulain, exemplar of the hero, confirms his tragic destiny by his own will and choice. *On Baile's Strand* (1904), the earliest of the Cuchulain plays, demonstrates Yeats's early move away from conventional heroics of the nationalist kind towards a more ritualized and stylized representation of the tragic hero.

Yeats's plays, which he conceived of as expressing 'a moment of intense life', are a debated achievement. They have their incisive dramatic passages, but also their wordy deliberations on choice and motive. The verse is the single voice of the lyric poet dispersed among characters contemplating rather than enacting their situation. Yeats praised the mordant irony that guarded Synge against heroics. He sought the same deflationary counterpointing for his own plays. Hence the Blind Man and the Fool in *On Baile's Strand*; they are the antithesis of Cuchulain's heroism, but perhaps too plainly and schematically so.

J. M. SYNGE

Padraic Colum early identified the nature of Synge's dramatic language, calling it 'a splendid convention.' Its inventive turns discard literal transcription of peasant speech but reproduce its 'energy and extravagance.' Synge's language is not so much a medium as the constituent of his characters' being. Christy in *The Playboy of the Western World* (1907) exists as the creation of his own lavish arias, which for a while seduce the entire village, for a while supersede the reality of his botched parricide, and in the end restore him from humiliation. 'Go on,' he tells his father: 'I'm saying'; and saying is believing. The only reality in Christy's fame, his triumph at the races, collapses when his father appears; but the magic of 'telling stories' wins Old Mahon to Christy's side.

Deirdre of the Sorrows (1910), Synge's only play about the saga people, is a story of romantic love dreading its transience. Deirdre enters into the doom foretold for her and Naisi, dignifying their deaths by composing events into legend, 'a story will be told forever'. The lovers thus commemorated are not ethereal tapestry figures. Theirs is an erotic love; the tangibles of their world are part of it; so, even, is Owen's carnality. Grandeur includes earthy familiarities.

'No drama', Synge wrote, 'can grow out of anything other than the fundamental realities of life.' As Synge applied the dictum, it stressed the growth out of realities. Certainly the cottage or shebeen furnishings of his stage sets were rigorously accurate. His 'fundamental realities', however, were more profoundly determined than at that level of verisimilitude. While Synge's comedy, as he said in another connection, is 'rich and genial and humorous', it does not blink at violence, lust, desolation. He consolidates his 'masterful images', in Yeats's phrases, with the 'slut who keeps the till', 'the foul rag and bone shop of the heart'.

Lurking behind the stage action of *The Playboy* are 'the broken harvest and the ended war', 'the loosèd khaki cutthroats'. On stage, murder is mimicked; Pegeen viciously taunts Christy — 'you swaying and wiggling on the butt of a rope;' she has 'a stale stink of poteen on her;' and she is 'the Lady Helen of Troy ... with a nosegay in her golden shawl.' The love of Christy and Pegeen is both the tender communion of Act III and Pegeen's last despairing cry. So in *Deirdre* the protagonists' love is at once doomed and immortal, sacred and profane. The language dissolves incongruities into a multifaceted truth. While Synge works within the physical form of the proscenium stage, the constant interplay of viewpoints, and between language and the facts it purports to describe, enlarges the apparent fixity of its enclosing shape.

Apart from Deirdre and *Riders to the Sea* (1904), all Synge's plays are comedies, with 'happy endings.' In *The Well of the Saints* (1905) the Douls find happiness in their returned blindness; but it is a happiness that their imagination must constantly renew — 'looking up in our own minds into a grand sky' — defying equally the Saint's illusory heaven and the villagers' bullying conventionality. The tramp's eloquence in *In the Shadow of the Glen* (1903) lures Nora from her husband to a vagabond life of which 'a wet ditch' is as much a part as 'the south wind blowing.'

Nora is not a rural Irish version of the Ibsenist New Woman. She is not responding with a pagan sexuality to the compellingly imaginative wording of an outlaw life. Much of the talk in the play is about talk. The tramp's 'fine bit of talk' — 'blather' to Dan — creates for Nora a perception of reality different from the restricted vision of the life on the smallholding. *The Playboy*, the most assured affirmation of the outcast's triumph, has a happy ending for Christy; for Pegeen it is a loss.

Typically in Synge's plays an intruder challenges the values of a small community. He is at best on the fringes of settled society. He represents the artist at odds with established usages, the wayward imagination with its exhilarating, dangerous liberation. Synge's plays in themselves exemplify the kinds of fiction they employ. They might be read, in one way, as a claim by the colonized to the dispossessing language.

GEORGE FITZMAURICE

Fitzmaurice's first play, *The Country Dressmaker* (1907), is a realistic satire, common enough by then, of acquisitive rural matchmaking. Its impish second-act curtain, a dresserful of crockery collapsing on an empty stage, foreshadows the haunted kitchens of his daringly experimental dramatic fantasies. Without preliminary, they assume a world inhabited by humans and demons.

It begins to take shape in *The Pie-Dish* (1908). Though peopled entirely by humans, it insinuates a diabolic control over Leum Donoghue's twenty years of work on his ornamented pie-dish. As he dies, it drops unfinished from his hands and shatters. Human and crafted clay die together, Leum 'dead and damned'. There is a gruesome tension between the family's bickering over the querulous old man and its oracular occasion:

comedy black enough to include eternal judgment.

The Magic Glasses (1913) fully enters its earthly otherworld. The fey Jaymoney lives in the enchanted visions of his coloured glasses. As the Devil invades the house, he is found dead, 'his jugular cut by the Magic Glasses': another murderous artefact. So in *The Dandy Dolls* (rejected 1913), Roger Carmody, who speaks ambiguously of 'the time I was turning into a man,' is the maker of the dolls which, intact or mutilated, become the prize in a feud — or is it a collusion to seize Roger? — between the Grey Men and the Haj of Burma. Again, talk of the mundane, leaking oven and hole in the thatch, accompanies fabulous visitations. Throughout all, the child (presumably also Roger's creation) sits enigmatic and mute, apart from his song and strange private game, maybe a piece in the larger game. 'They are wicked old children', Fitzmaurice said of the Kerry folk.

The talk is never mundane. Fitzmaurice derived his dramatic speech from the English of his native Kerry. It differs from Lady Gregory's Kiltartanese and, though it has a nearer resemblance, from Synge. Certainly with a more profuse scattering of localisms, Fitzgerald's dialogue shares with Synge's its own echoing, strongly rhythmical stylings of its source.

SEAN O'CASEY

In 1923 the Abbey accepted O'Casey's *The Shadow of a Gunman*. Its period is the Anglo-Irish war, which led to the 1921 Treaty. *Juno and the Paycock* (1924), set during the Civil War after the Treaty, and *The Plough and the Stars* (1926), an anti-heroic treatment of the 1916 Rising, completed his 'Dublin trilogy.' This established O'Casey's reputation, despite the riotous abuse that greeted *The Plough*.

These are plays without heroes, but with, in their common interpretation, heroines: the women who cling to personal loyalty and family bonds, indifferent to the political abstractions spuriously asserted by the men. In *Juno*, only Mrs Boyle stands by Mary in her pregnancy; in *The Plough*, Bessie Burgess gives her life to save Nora Clitheroe. Of the men, Johnny Boyle becomes informer and coward, Jack Clitheroe joins the Citizen Army for show. The men who espouse the beliefs O'Casey held — international communism and working-class solidarity — spout platitudes.

It is of no consequence that O'Casey's plays are at odds with his personal beliefs. The most powerful political image he saw in the Dublin of that time was the failure of Marxism, in particular, to translate itself into the idiom of the slums and tenements. Once organized, into trade union, political party, philosophical system, ideology began to detach itself from the ways in which people really talked and thought and acted. The women too — Mary Boyle chattering about her 'principles,' Bessie Burgess, fanatical unionist, Rosie Redmond enamoured of the oratory outside the pub — are susceptible to the lofty words whose enticement is their comfortable remoteness from actuality: like the Foresters' uniforms, which Mrs Gogan sees as nicer than 'a pantomime'.

It may seem a sceptical set of attitudes. Yet the plays are not disheartening. The confidently realized characters prevail upon our imaginative, if not always our moral, sympathies. In the bustling, communal life of the tenements, O'Casey affirms the workings of humane feelings: unpredictable, fickle, but surviving. It is a comic world where the mock-heroic splendour of the language plays around and outsoars its run-of-the-mill subjects. So Fluther cannot just tell Peter to stop his Bodenstown anecdotes; he extends the mention of memorial leaves into a crescendo of abusive images.

Farce and absurdity pervade O'Casey's plays. Knockabout routines and tumbledown rooms establish a metaphor of a disintegrating society. We see it in *The Shadow of a Gunman:* Seamus Shields's fragile braces that would do Cuchulainn, the spoons that don't add up, are comic, indeed farcical, signs of a world whose structures will never live up to the promise they seem to contain. The recurrent verbal traps and malapropisms belong to the same world; among them are Mrs Henderson's 'parrot talks', the ambitious technicalities of Mr Gallagher's letter, Dolphie's ranting, or, indeed the verbiage of Donal Davoren's 'suffering'. Although farcical, it is not frivolous. It is a world that also contains betrayal and death, the shooting of Minnie Powell, the discovery of the paper typed for her by Davoren, with his name obliterated. The Dublin trilogy, in which farce and tragic (often brutal) experience negotiate, can be seen as realistic 'slices of life' only in a damagingly limiting way.

All O'Casey's later plays are experiments in

form, inaugurated by the expressionist battlefield set, with choric and solo chants, of *The Silver Tassie* (1928), which the Abbey rejected. Oddly, the further O'Casey moved, formally, from realism, the more simply he retailed a Marxist creed of social deliverance; and, ominously apparent in the *Tassie*, the less his control of language. It approaches self-parody, and not only in the serious speeches, where O'Casey was always perilously indulgent of 'fine writing.' Here, even the comic vernacular strains after a surfeit of verbal decoration.

Red Roses for Me (1943) is the sole later play to use a Dublin setting, apart from *The Star Turns Red* (1940), where Dublin is only nominally the location. It conflates the 1911 strike and the 1913 Lockout. Perhaps because the workers are beaten, the play is an elegiac, not a strident, expression of faith. Like all O'Casey's post-Abbey work, it is in search of a stage totality of words, music, dance, costumes, lighting, deliberately gainsaying realism. The common judgment is right, that O'Casey's first three plays are his best; the later work has energy enough to fit out a stage for itself.

The first quarter-century of the Irish dramatic movement constitutes an experiment with the boundaries of realist theatre: a drama working with characters, situations, and a speech recognisably taken from real life; and, formally, accepting the three enclosing walls of the proscenium stage. To Yeats's mind, it achieved crude approximations of reality. Undoubtedly, many Abbey plays, like William Boyle's, were content to tell a plain tale, echoing the newspapers outside the theatre.

At its best, however, Irish drama, was, so to speak, extending the invisible fourth wall of its stage beyond the circumscribing set. Fitzmaurice invites us into kitchens which are the hunting-ground of spirits. Synge suggests that the reality represented to us may be subservient to the ways in which the characters talk about it. O'Casey's characters make adventures of commonplace events. The persuasive agent is language; language that does not reflect reality but discomposes and reconstructs it, while remaining aware that it is playing games which may be halted by the pragmatic rules it is defying.

That the language, in its many variants, is English, is a consequence of political necessity turned to artistic advantage: at the simplest level it displants obsequious 'broguery'. Its subjects are often political too, many of them, as in O'Casey, overtly so. Obliquely, the plays commonly reflect upon social usages that paraphrase types of political behaviour. An obvious instance is the codes, as stated and as tacitly interpreted, within which Shiels's merchants usually can make themselves at home.

More profoundly, and often through the intervention of an outsider as a major character, Irish drama characteristically pits individual fulfilment against the protective, limiting pieties of a community. There is an antagonism between private freedom and agreed convention; they also have in common that they are modes of affirming, whether by communal solidarity or anarchic self-assertion, a purely human power of continuance: fictions, constructions, of multiple kinds, contend with the brutalities and frustrations of life. These, in their elemental state, are the matter of politics.

EDWARD MARTYN

(1859-1923)

THE HEATHER FIELD
(1899)

[*The Heather Field*, presented at the Antient Concert Rooms in Dublin on 9 May 1899, was the second play of the Irish Literary Theatre's first season (Yeats's *The Countess Cathleen* was the first.) The conjunction of these two plays anticipated the forthcoming struggle in the new Irish theatre between poetic and realistic drama. Martyn's debt to Ibsen is obvious. The drawing-room setting, with the mountainside and the ocean beyond, is characteristic of the Norwegian's dramatization of the struggle between the wildness and closed life of the middle classes and the boundless life of the idealistic spirit. Although Yeats overcame Martyn in the dispute for leadership of the new theatre, Martyn's play remains as an important example of the kind of play that constantly would emerge in opposition to the experimental and risky enterprise of Yeatsian drama.]

CHARACTERS

BARRY USSHER, *a landowner, student, philosopher, etc.*
LORD SHRULE, *a neighboring landowner*
LADY SHRULE (LILIAN), *his wife*
CARDEN TYRRELL
MRS. GRACE TYRRELL (*born* DESMOND), *his wife*
KIT, *their son, nine years old*
MILES TYRRELL, *scholar of Trinity College, Dublin, and brother of Carden*
DOCTOR DOWLING } *physicians*
DOCTOR ROCHE }

The action takes place about the year 1890, in CARDEN TYRRELL's *house on the West coast of Ireland.*

ACT I

CARDEN TYRRELL's *library. On the right a door leads to the dining-room and rest of house. On the left is a large empty fire-place. At back through open glass folding-doors a small garden is visible, below which the Atlantic Ocean, flanked by a mountain at left, stretches out to the horizon. Between fire-place and folding-doors stands a writing-table with chairs on either side. At the opposite part of the room near folding-doors is a large sofa. Books in shelves line all walls. In front at the right is another table covered with papers, magazines, etc., which are likewise thrown negligently over other chairs in the room. It is a bright afternoon in the Autumn.*

MILES TYRRELL, *a young light-haired man of about nineteen, dressed in a blue serge suit, is seated at the writing-table in deep study with several books around him. After a pause he looks up wearily, then again bends over his books.*

BARRY USSHER, *a lean man of about two and thirty, of medium height, with dark hair, a short pointed beard, and dressed in a riding-costume of sombre grey, enters from garden at back.*

MILES: (*Starting*) Ah, Barry.

USSHER: (*Throwing his hat and hunting-whip on the sofa*) Hallo, Miles, good morning. I see you are determined to win that gold-medal at Trinity — and become one day Lord Chancellor of Ireland, too, I'll be bound.

MILES: (*With a faint smile*) Lord Chancellor indeed! I shall be lucky if I can pass my examination and then find just so many briefs as will afford me a living.

USSHER: Why are you so despondent? You have ability.

MILES: Perhaps — if there was an opportunity for displaying it. Oh, this is no place to work.

USSHER: I know what you mean. But why not study in your room upstairs?

MILES: I might do that. Still, it is not so much the interruptions. It is the knowledge of what goes on, perpetually.

USSHER: Are things as bad as ever?

MILES: Yes. My brother and his wife cannot agree.

USSHER: How sad it is.

MILES: Oh, if only I had a quiet house to study in like yours. You live there like a sage absorbed in your books and ideas.

USSHER: I fear I also find difficulties in cultivating the tastes that are congenial to me.

MILES: Why?

USSHER: You see, Miles, an unfortunate landowner must devote all his attention to keeping a little of his belongings together in these bad times.

MILES: As if you were affected by bad times — you, with that fine place here joining us, and with your unencumbered estate, and no one depending upon you. You're a lucky fellow. No wonder the luck of Barry Ussher is a byword with the country people.

USSHER: They know nothing about it.

MILES: Well, in any case you seem able to live as you please. You have always means to travel, and never want for anything.

USSHER: So that is your idea of luck, Miles?

MILES: Well, somewhat, I fancy. Isn't it yours?

USSHER: I don't think these things make much difference either way.

MILES: Oh, come, Barry, you can't expect me to believe that.

USSHER: Yes, I mean that what we have on one side is taken away from the other; so the world's lots are more fairly divided than you imagine. Our natures remain much the same at their root. There is always the original pain.

MILES: I suppose you cynical philosophers must invent some grievance from lack of real troubles.

USSHER: No, Miles.

MILES: Well, if you only knew how my brother envies your good fortune.

USSHER: There are others Carden Tyrrell might envy, but he need not envy me. By the way, where is he?

MILES: He is out — I suppose in the heather field.

USSHER: Oh — (*after a short pause*) he has finished all his work there, hasn't he?

MILES: Yes, the young grass is coming up beautifully now. Do you want to see him at once? I can send for him. In any case he is sure to be back soon.

USSHER: That will do. I am in no great hurry.

MILES: You have some business with him?

USSHER: Well, yes. It is about this very subject of land reclamation. I hear he is about to raise another large loan from Government, in order to extend these operations of his.

MILES: Really!

USSHER: So they told me yesterday in Dublin at the Board of Works.

MILES: When Grace hears this, there will be more troubles and disputes.

USSHER: Most likely. What a pity your sister-in-law defeats all her objects by her manner towards Carden.

MILES: Oh, indeed she is very impatient with him. Yet she is good enough in her way too.

USSHER: Precisely; and would probably have made an excellent wife for almost any other man; but for your brother — well, it might have been better if he had never thought of marriage at all.

MILES: What? Surely he might have found some one to suit him. Why should you say such a thing?

USSHER: (*With a frightened look*) Why?

MILES: Yes, Barry. But what is the matter with you?

USSHER: (*Quickly recovering himself*) Oh, nothing, Miles, nothing. I merely meant to say that it would be very difficult for anyone to suit Carden. He is a person so much of himself, you know.

MILES: Ah, it is certainly a great misfortune he ever met Grace. And this estrangement is so extraordinary, for he once used to be so fond of her.

USSHER: Yes, they generally begin that way. I remember just before he became engaged he told me that he thought till then he should never marry, but that at last he had found real happiness. They all say that, you know.

MILES: You may very well philosophise over what is past, Barry. But why did you not then try to dissuade him?

USSHER: Of course I tried to dissuade him then. I did my best.

MILES: Oh, you did, did you?

USSHER: Yes, of course. I warned him against the danger of marrying a girl with whom he was only acquainted so short a time. I entreated him to wait a while at all events, as he was then only twenty-one and she something younger. But all to no purpose. Ah, if he had waited, he could not have failed to discover that she was only marrying him for his means and position, and that she did not in the least care for him. Besides, I was certain from the first that he had no real affection or respect for her.

MILES: Indeed? What made you so certain of that, Barry?

USSHER: Well, you see, Carden and I had been intimate so long. We had been brought up together, in fact, so that I fancy I understood him better than anyone. The sudden overturning of all his ideas at that time seemed to me strange and unnatural. He was like one bewitched. A man's whole nature somehow does not change in a moment. You were too young, Miles, to know him in those days; but he was so ideal, so imaginative, as engaging as some beautiful child who saw nothing real in the world outside his own fairy dreams.

MILES: (*With a baffled look*) I have memories of those days!

USSHER: They are vivid with me. Oh, he always did so fascinate and interest me. What poetry he put into those days of my youth — the days that are dead. (*Pause*) Then to see him suddenly changed, grown even prosy under the power of her influence — it made it impossible for me to consider this attachment of his genuine or likely to endure. And has not the result proved that I was right?

MILES: I fear I must admit, Barry, that you were, alas, a reliable prophet.

USSHER: Oh, I foresaw all. I knew this change could not last. The old, wild nature had to break out again when the novelty was over. It was a misfortune since he was married, but it was inevitable. There are some dispositions too eerie, too ethereal, too untamable for good, steady, domestic cultivation, and if so domesticated they avenge themselves in after time. Ah, foolishly his wife and her friends thought they were going to change Carden to their model of a young man, but the latent, untamable nature was not to be subdued. Its first sign of revolt against suppression was when he began this vast work in the heather field.

MILES: (*With a puzzled look*) Barry, I — I do not understand.

USSHER: Miles, you must admit it was rather an extravagant work. He has sunk a fortune of borrowed capital in the reclamation of that mountain. Look at all the men he employed to root up rocks, and the steam ploughs, too, that have been working during these last years.

MILES: But surely he will obtain a large rent for the rich grass he has made to grow there. That ought to more than compensate for his outlay.

USSHER: Meanwhile interest is accruing. The grass has not grown sufficiently for letting as yet. Then payment of rent cannot follow till long after, always supposing that it ever produces much rent.

MILES: (*Surprised*) Why do you say that? Is not the land good now?

USSHER: Ah, Miles, do you not know that the soil in such places is very wild and untamable? If heather lands are brought into cultivation for domestic use, they must be watched, they must have generous and loving treatment, else their old wild nature may avenge itself. (*He averts his look*)

MILES: (*With mingled wonder and uneasiness*) Avenge itself? How, Barry?

USSHER: Why, the wild heather may break out upon them soon again.

MILES: Oh. (*Then eagerly*) But don't you think Carden has given the best of treatment to the heather field?

USSHER: (*Slowly and gently*) I do not know whether his treatment was sufficiently kind, as farmers say here in West Ireland. Somehow he seemed too impatient for the change. He was hardly considerate enough, perhaps, in the accomplishment of his will.

MILES: (*With dejection*) You evidently think there is something unsatisfactory in the business.

USSHER: Let us hope for the best, Miles. In any case we ought to try and prevent him from embarking on further schemes.

MILES: Do, Barry. If there is one person in the world he will listen to it is you. Besides, you will remove a fresh cause of quarrels with Grace; and who knows but you may be able to do more afterwards. Stop — I see him coming now through the garden.

CARDEN TYRRELL, *a rather powerfully built man of one and thirty, with light hair, spare growth of beard, unsteady eyes, very large forehead, and lower part of face small, dressed negligently in a dark suit, enters from the back.*

TYRRELL: (*Smiling*) Oh, how goes it with you, Barry? You have not favoured us with visits much of late. What have you been doing?

USSHER: Well, I have been in Dublin for one thing.

TYRRELL: So I heard. But is it true you are reducing all your rents?

USSHER: Yes, I have been reducing them somewhat.

TYRRELL: My goodness. I suppose you will end by making the tenants a present of your property. You call me a dreamer, but it seems that I am the practical man.

USSHER: (*Laughing*) Oh, that does not follow at all. I consider it wiser to give a little in time, than later on to have perhaps more wrung from me by the Land Commission.[1]

TYRRELL: But one should never depreciate the value of one's property. I am afraid, Barry, you are mismanaging your affairs. Have you begun yet to reclaim that bog outside your demesne, as I advised?

USSHER: No, Carden.

TYRRELL: There, you see. Well, a fortune is to be made by such work. You would be much better employed at it than at reducing your rents. But, my dear old Barry, there is no use in arguing with you, when you are once set upon a thing. I suppose it is because you knew I would not approve of what you are doing that you have not been to see me for so long.

USSHER: Always suspicious, Carden. But, may I ask why you never come to see me?

TYRRELL: You forget all I have undertaken — all my responsibilities. I have little time.

USSHER: And one would think my time was of no value. Perhaps, Carden, the real reason is that I might possibly not appreciate some of your undertakings and responsibilities.

TYRRELL: (*With a swift shy glance*) Why should you think so?

1. Since 1879, when the Land League was founded, tenants had become increasingly organized and less deferential in their attitudes to landlords. A series of Acts, passed between 1870 and 1891, led to the setting up of land courts and a Land Commission, the purpose of which was to regulate rents and allow tenants to buy out their holdings.

USSHER: (*Smiling*) Oh, I don't know. I was only wondering.

TYRRELL: But why should that prevent me from going to you?

USSHER: Precisely, why indeed? I should never have thought of it, if you had not first suggested the thought.

TYRRELL: Well, you have had no reason to think anything of the kind. Just as if I could be occupied in the way you imagine.

USSHER: It seems odd that you should, Carden.

TYRRELL: Yet you have an idea all the same, that I could.

USSHER: Well, to tell you the truth, I heard yesterday that you were contemplating what seems to me certainly most rash.

TYRRELL: Oh, you did, did you? Let us hear what seems to you most rash.

USSHER: It is true, is it not, that you are about to borrow another large sum of money for new land improvements?

TYRRELL: (*Somewhat confused*) Yes, it is true — well?

USSHER: Well — don't you think you had better not?

TYRRELL: Why not?

USSHER: Don't you think you have done enough work — for the present, at all events? Would it not be better to rest for a time and be sure whether what you have already improved is going to be really successful?

MILES: Yes, Carden, don't you think you ought to wait for a while longer?

TYRRELL: Wait? Why wait, when I know the work must be successful — nay, is already successful?

USSHER: You can scarcely be sure of that yet, Carden.

TYRRELL: Why not?

USSHER: (*Rather confused*) Oh, the nature — (*he hesitates*).

MILES: You can scarcely yet be sure of what the land is capable, you know.

TYRRELL: Can I not see what grass it has produced?

USSHER: Yes, but will that continue?

TYRRELL: (*Scornfully*) Will that continue? Who ever heard so absurd a question? As well ask will the air continue to bear up the birds. Will its myriad life continue to pant underneath the sea? Come, my old friend, my brother, I will not have you talk in this discouraging way and make such insinuations, as if you were indeed nothing more than mere country neighbours, who cannot understand my ideas. No, you must believe in me, and inspire me with heart.

MILES: We do believe in you, Carden, but —

USSHER: We only suggest prudence.

MILES: Be prudent, Carden.

TYRRELL: Oh, but when you understand the matter, you will see how prudent I have been. For it was absolutely necessary to obtain this further loan unless the value of the previous one was to be destroyed.

USSHER: I do not follow you. Will you explain?

TYRRELL: Well, you see, the drainage of the heather field has practically swamped the lands below it; so I now must necessarily drain the water off from them right down to the sea. When I have finished all that grand ramification of drains, I shall have created a whole vast tract of fertile pasture which will double the value of my property. What do you think of that? Why, I believe all you people imagine that I am working in the dark, that I do not know what I am about. But I tell you I have excellent reasons for everything I undertake.

USSHER: Yes, Carden, of course — but you have borrowed a vast sum of money. Take care that the interest you will have to pay the Board of Works does not exceed your income.

TYRRELL: There is no danger, Barry. Have I not told you that my income must be greatly increased?

USSHER: You have indeed. I can only hope most sincerely that it will be so.

TYRRELL: But you still seem to doubt it all the same. (USSHER *is silent*) Oh, come, Barry, this is unfriendly of you. Barry, you are a prophet of evil. Heaven grant that your doubts may be vain, else, oh, I should be the most miserable of men. But they are vain — they are, they are — even despite your other memorable prophecy that, alas, has come too true. Ah, do you remember your warning to me ten years ago?

USSHER: You mean just before your marriage? Yes.

TYRRELL: (*Gloomily*) I wonder had that anything to do with its unhappiness. I wonder if these doubts now will bring misfortune on my present undertakings.

USSHER: (*In a frightened voice*) Carden, for pity's sake stop. Don't speak like that. Forget any doubts I may have now expressed. Forget them — forget them. I was wrong ever to have interfered with my advice. Never will I do so again. No, I have not the right. See, Carden, for all I know you may succeed now. I heartily hope you will. You are determined to, and discouragement might only cause you to fail. No, you must not have a second misfortune to cast at me. Good-bye. (*He prepares to go*)

MILES: Oh, Barry, do not leave us in this way. Think —

TYRRELL: Oh, I am sorry you should take anything I said in that light. I did not mean, Barry, really, to —

USSHER: No, Carden, forgive me, but I was for the moment unnerved by the thought that you should attribute to me any of your ill-luck. No, I hope you will always find me a help to you instead, whenever you may require me.

TYRRELL: Ah, now you are like yourself again, the Barry of other days. I knew you would understand me when I explained everything to you.

USSHER: I hope, Carden, at least I may never be to you the cause of ill-luck.

Exit at back

TYRRELL: Dear old Barry, it makes him positively angry to see me improving my property, because he has not the enterprise to improve his own. But I think I have convinced him that he was mistaken in his estimate of my work.

MILES: You certainly frightened him, Carden. I have never seen him as he was just now.

TYRRELL: Oh, I really did not mean what I said. He only annoyed me by his stupid doubting.

MILES: Still — as a matter of fact long ago he tried to dissuade you from marrying Grace — isn't that so?

TYRRELL: Yes, he was full of doubts and objections then as now — only then he was right. But now — ha, ha — well, I know he is altogether wrong.

MILES: Why do you say you know, Carden? Why are you so certain now?

TYRRELL: Because I see so clearly before me.

MILES: That at least is a comfort. But perhaps he might be wrong in the other matter too. Don't you think it would be well also if you would determine to belie his doubts of long ago as well as of today?

TYRRELL: What do you mean?

MILES: Why, Carden, to try and prove that after all he was wrong when he advised you not to marry Grace.

TYRRELL: (*With a sigh*) Ah — impossible.

MILES: Don't say that, Carden.

TYRRELL: Oh, Miles, you do not understand.

MILES: But have you never tried?

TYRRELL: Tried?

MILES: Yes, tried. You know there is nothing really wrong with her.

TYRRELL: Nothing, nothing — and everything. The same thing that is wrong about me. That is how it is between us.

MILES: But might you not try to fall in just a little with her ways? She is good after all.

TYRRELL: My dear Miles, you don't know what you are talking about. Of course she is good enough. I know that perfectly well. But she has no sense of compromise — no consideration for me at all. She always despised me.

MILES: Oh, Carden, no —

TYRRELL: Oh, but yes. That is why she is so indignant I should take an interest in anything but herself. She would shape my life altogether after her own standard and that of Lady Shrule. I have often given in before, but the result was she became more and more exacting, until at last I found matters quite intolerable. Oh, it is useless to deny that here at least Barry's warnings have come true.

MILES: How extraordinary that you should have changed so toward her — you who once were so devoted.

TYRRELL: Ah, Miles, I have simply found her to be absolutely different from what I had imagined her. I was very young then, very inexperienced. I longed for sympathy, and thought it was easy to find. I idealised women in those days. I believed that they were idealists. Ah, that was my fatal error.

MILES: But surely you don't mean to deny that some are?

TYRRELL: I don't believe any are, really. They may be on an average more fanciful than man, but your true idealist can only be a man. Alas! had I known that then, my fate would have been very different. I thought others were easy to find, in whom I could confide as in Barry.

MILES: Do you consider him an idealist?

TYRRELL: I should think so indeed — a true idealist — only he is in a way so drilled and careful, that he will never let himself go. But he is such a friend, and understands everything! No, I never knew isolation when we were together in our youth. Isolation only began with my marriage, which led me out into a lonely world. Oh, it was a great misfortune. And I have no one to blame but myself.

MILES: And yet — and yet were you really so

much to blame? She was so beautiful.

TYRRELL: Ah, you have said it. There you have found the cause of all the trouble. But Barry would never have wavered.

MILES: Oh, he is a hardened philosopher whom no beauty could soften.

TYRRELL: That is because, unlike most people, he can see the truly beautiful, and so is heedless of shams.

MILES: Shams? And you can speak like that of her beauty? How I remember her on your wedding-day, when I held her train! I was only nine years old then, and thought she was some tall white fairy that had come to live with us. Oh, Carden, think of that time. Its memory might banish much bitterness.

TYRRELL: Too late, too late. You are still very young, Miles. I have outgrown the capacity of such sentiment.

MILES: But you have not outgrown the great kindness of your nature. No, that I could never believe. Ought it not in these difficulties to help you? Why, see how good you are always to me.

TYRRELL: Ah, yes, that is different, Miles.

MILES: And Kit, too — are you not most affectionate and kind to him?

TYRRELL: My poor little son, of course — how could I be otherwise to him? He is really so loveable and such a companion to me. For just now he is wonderfully like what you were, Miles, when you acted as that pretty page. His age besides is the same as yours was then; so that the very sight of him calls back to me the days of my youth. Oh, that happy time before my fatal mistake! Miles, do you remember that time?

MILES: Remember? How well I remember!

TYRRELL: I suppose I had troubles then, as now; but memory has idealised those past scenes, till only their beauty remains, wafted back to me like an aroma from some lost paradise. I feel I shall never know the joy of those days again.

MILES: You must not think such things, Carden. Days as good as these will, I am sure, return.

TYRRELL: Ah, no, Miles — their poetry, never — the hope that shines like a spring-day sun upon our youth! It warms us with such life. It inspires us to attempt so many deeds. With what expectations we travel, for instance. What materials we are to make out of it all. Do you remember when we went abroad together?

MILES: (*Joyfully*) Oh, yes, of course I do, Carden.

TYRRELL: Well, it seems funny that I should have taken you with me then on travels you were too young to appreciate; but I could not bear to leave you who had no protector save me after our father died.

MILES: You kind brother.

TYRRELL: Yes, I carried you off, my little Miles, as you were then.

MILES: And how I enjoyed myself.

TYRRELL: What fairie towns we came to — Boppart on the Rhine with its quaint old houses. Then we sailed our boat through the hills to Lorlei [*sic*], and watched where the river nymphs used long ago to glide, laughing, through the gold-lit depths of the stream.

MILES: Yes, and you told me the legend of their gold — how it was robbed and restored and still guarded by them.

TYRRELL: I did; and you, little practical man that you were, you bent down to the water expecting to see the glitter of the Rhine Gold![2]

MILES: (*Laughing*) The marvellous seemed real in those days.

TYRRELL: Ah, those bright happy days! And do you remember that Sunday morning in Cologne Cathedral when all the boys sang Palestrina[3] so divinely?

MILES: I remember we stood by great iron gates. I looked up in your face and wondered why it shone through its tears.

TYRRELL: How pure the silver voice chords soared to the vaults of stone! Pure as our joy in those days. Fit music for those bright young days.

MILES: Yes, everything seemed joyful then.

TYRRELL: Oh, what brave times we used to have together. You know we were always such friends.

MILES: (*With emotion*) Indeed we always were, Carden. There is no one in the whole world I love as well as you. You have ever been the best of brothers to me.

TYRRELL: (*Goes over mysteriously to* MILES) Then you think, Miles, you will always help me?

MILES: (*Surprised*) Why, Carden, of course.

TYRRELL: (*With anxious intensity*) You will not

2. Martyn was an enthusiastic admirer of Richard Wagner (1813-83). The opera *Das Rheingold (The Rhine Gold*, 1869) is a prologue to the trilogy of *Der Ring des Nibelungen (The Ring of the Nibelung)*.

3. An admirer of Giovanni Pierluigi da Palestrina (*c.* 1525-94), Martyn endowed a choir in Dublin's Pro-Cathedral in the Italian composer's honour and in an attempt to improve the quality of Ireland's church music.

leave me if — if ever I should stand helpless and alone, will you, Miles?

MILES: Good gracious, no — but what makes you imagine such a thing?

TYRRELL: Well, somehow I feel that persons and objects are receding from me and becoming more unreal in these later times. (*Crosses over to sofa at right and kneeling on it with one knee, gazes out at the mountain*) Do you know, Miles, I often think that my life of pain and unrest here is only a dream after all.

MILES: And like a dream this suffering will pass away, Carden, let us hope never to return.

TYRRELL: (*Sadly*) No, oh no, it would be too much to expect that. A dream — a bad dream (*as if suddenly illumined*) yet with intervals too of wakefulness now and then.

MILES: (*Approaching him*) Of wakefulness? What do you mean? When are those intervals?

TYRRELL: When I am out in the heather field.

MILES: (*Anxiously*) The heather field?

TYRRELL: (*With enthusiasm*) Yes, the great mountain field out there (*points out at back*) that it was my ideal to bring to fruitfulness. There I awaken to true life indeed, as I stand looking over the Atlantic; and sea winds sweep against my feet the young grass in its matchless Irish green that gleams a golden green in the Autumn sun today. There I am haunted by those departed joys of my youth — again and again.

MILES: (*With a puzzled look*) There? But why there, Carden? Why there more than anywhere else?

TYRRELL: Oh, you matter-of-fact Miles — still the same as the little wise Miles of long ago, who used to ask such quaint questions. How different we are. Yet how delightful I always find you. 'Why there?' you ask. Ha, ha.

MILES: (*A little disconcerted*) Evidently you consider it a superfluous question. But I think I may very reasonably ask it all the same.

TYRRELL: Well, then, because there after years of joyless stagnation I find myself again in an ideal domain — away from fretful surroundings — alone! except for little Kit, who loves the mountain and its wild flowers. You know, Miles, how like I have said he now looks to what you were in the old days. At moments, indeed, I can hardly believe it is he and not you. So his presence there is no hindrance to that evocation of the past. No, he serves rather to quicken the magic of the heather field.

MILES: (*With sudden emotion*) Oh, to think I could ever have been so much to you. How good you always were to me, Carden.

TYRRELL: I could not help it. You belonged to the beauty of that time.

MILES: All this sounds like the marvellous tales you used to tell me when I was a child. I see your imagination is the same as ever.

TYRRELL: And you call what I tell you only imagination?

MILES: Well, Carden — but what else?

TYRRELL: (*Resignedly*) Ah, I suppose I cannot help you. You too are like Barry, who said the same thing when I once told him of the voices —

MILES: (*With vague alarm*) Voices, Carden? Why — what voices are these?

TYRRELL: Out there — over the mountain. Oh, the vivid brightness of those voices, as they float back from the past on each changing breeze!

MILES: (*Anxiously*) You only heard the wind whistle along the coast. Don't heed it any more, Carden.

TYRRELL: Why should I not heed such celestial song?

MILES: A dream phantom of the desolate mountain.

TYRRELL: No, it is only your words I heard as in a troubled dream.

MILES: (*Gently*) Carden, it is deceiving you — this wonderful imagination.

TYRRELL: What? Imagination again?

MILES: Of course.

TYRRELL: (*Patiently*) Ah, well, I cannot convince you, Miles. But what does it matter? You are delightfully sympathetic to me all the same. I feel this opening of my soul to you has even done me good. Yes, it does me good to be listened to occasionally. It leaves a great peace after it; and I have not felt so peaceful as now for many a day. Indeed, if this could last, it would be almost like the old time again.

GRACE TYRRELL, *a rather tall, thin woman of about thirty but looking younger, with a pale face, brown hair, and an indefinable attractiveness in her outward manner and movements, enters by door at right. She is dressed plainly, but with exceeding neatness. Tyrrell takes a large book from the shelves at back of sofa, on which he now sits and turns over the leaves, suppressing a look of annoyance.*

MILES: (*Going towards her politely*) I suppose you have been out on your rounds this morning as usual, Grace?

GRACE: Yes as usual. Have you been here since breakfast?

MILES: Yes.

GRACE: Studying, I suppose.

MILES: Not much.

GRACE: Why?

MILES: Oh, Barry Ussher was here; and then Carden and I have been talking.

GRACE: And so your morning was wasted, Miles?

MILES: Oh, not wasted, Grace.

GRACE: I think it would have been more profitably employed in working for your examination than in talking to your brother.

MILES: I am not at all so certain you are right.

GRACE: You must admit you have plenty of time for talking without allowing it to interfere with your studies.

TYRRELL: (*Looking up from his book*) It is so hard for us, Miles, is it not, when we are together, to refrain.

GRACE: What you two can have to say perpetually to each other puzzles me. You never visit anywhere nor seem to know what is going on in the neighbourhood.

TYRRELL: If we did, I am certain we shouldn't trouble to speak about it.

GRACE: Oh, indeed.

TYRRELL: No. The subjects that mutually interest us are far different. Among other things, we were talking before you came in over our journey long ago on the Continent. (*Then as if carried away by the subject of the moment*) Look, in this architectural book there are plates representing some buildings we saw then. Here is a Romanesque house at Boppart on the Rhine. It is a unique specimen of domestic architecture in that period. And here — this is the bishop's house at Wurzburg. How beautifully the oriel is poised there at the angle, like a hooded falcon on its perch! What a genius these medieval architects had for soothing with picturesque ideality the restless suffering spirit of their time. To gaze on their work makes one forget oneself and everything else.

GRACE: (*Who the while has been looking about her with an impatient and wearied expression*) Goodness me, what a litter the room is in with all these books and papers.

TYRRELL: (*With a momentary look of humiliation*) Oh!

GRACE: What brought me here, by the way, was to tell you that I must have it thoroughly dusted and tidied at once, as the Shrules come to lunch tomorrow.

TYRRELL: Yes, but what have they got to do with my room?

GRACE: We shall want it to sit in. I could not think of letting anyone see it in its present state.

TYRRELL: (*Fretfully*) Can't you leave my room alone?

GRACE: There! As usual you are disagreeable when your wife wants anything.

TYRRELL: No, but I have a quantity of important papers that it would give me endless trouble at present to sort and put away.

MILES: Oh, why cause him all this inconvenience, Grace? Will not the drawing room suit you just as well?

GRACE: Lord Shrule has had an attack of gout and does not like going upstairs.

MILES: Then bring them here. But you need not upset the room. Everyone knows it's a work-room.

GRACE: I could not think of allowing any strangers to see it in this state.

MILES: I wonder how you can attach so much importance—

GRACE: (*Coldly*) That will do, Miles. As usual you don't know what you are talking about.

MILES: Hei-ho. (*He begins to gather his books together on the writing-table*)

TYRRELL: You are not going, Miles, are you?

MILES: I think I shall try if I can read in the summerhouse outside. *Exit at back, carrying with him his books.*

GRACE: (*Quietly*) Well, I suppose you had better put away all these old papers at once, and let the housemaid come in.

TYRRELL: Impossible. I am too busy.

GRACE: That's what you always say. You imagine yourself the busiest man in the world; and as a matter of fact you have nothing to do.

TYRRELL: Nothing to do?

GRACE: (*Calmly*) What have you to do?

TYRRELL: (*Checking his irritation*) Very well, we won't discuss that old subject. Anyhow I require my papers, as a man comes to see me tomorrow on business connected with them.

GRACE: Who is this man?

TYRRELL: The drainage inspector of the Board of Works.

GRACE: Indeed! Why, I thought he had finished everything here long ago.

TYRRELL: Oh, so he has.

GRACE: Well, what is he coming for now?

TYRRELL: (*Vaguely*) Oh — you see — it would take too long to explain just at present. Besides, you might not understand.

GRACE: (*With a penetrating look*) You know I would understand well enough. But you never were a person to be relied upon. You are now trying to hide something from me. Come, it is as good to tell it to me at once.

TYRRELL: (*Bridling up*) I am not trying to hide anything from you. I don't care whether you know it or not.

GRACE: Well, then, why is this man coming?

TYRRELL: He is to lay out some drains in the valley beneath the heather field.

GRACE: (*Astounded*) What? You don't mean to say you are going to drain all that immense tract of land too?

TYRRELL: Yes. It is necessary now after the other work. So I am going to obtain a new loan from Government to carry it out.

GRACE: A new loan! We shall certainly be ruined this time.

TYRRELL: No — no. Why, can you not see the enormous improvement this work must be to the estate?

GRACE: Oh, that is what you are always saying; and the estate for some years past has been steadily growing worse and worse, until now we are almost reduced to difficulties.

TYRRELL: You are quite mistaken. I tell you we are on the eve of seeing our income doubled. Just consider the rent that must soon be produced by the heather field.

GRACE: (*With a gesture of impatience*) The heather field! Up to this, indeed, it has been nothing but a gigantic loss. And who knows but it may never be anything else? My goodness, can you not wait to see if it will be a success before you swamp the estate with this new debt?

TYRRELL: No, no, every delay is a loss of profit. You do not understand.

GRACE: Oh, I am tired of your always telling me that I do not understand. I understand perfectly that you are bringing us to beggary.

TYRRELL: Well, it is certainly amazing that you should think so. But then, you know, you are never open to reason — never in sympathy with my ideas.

GRACE: How on earth can I be, when like everyone else I believe you to be utterly mistaken in what you are doing?

TYRRELL: I do not mean what I am doing at present — but the whole tenor of my life and ideas. You have never understood them.

GRACE: (*Sharply*) Look here, it's beginning to irritate me, this talk about my not understanding. So I see, you think yourself the great incomprehensible, ha, ha. Well, you are quite mistaken. Everyone understands you. So do I, absolutely. For in spite of all your efforts to be singular, you are a very ordinary person, in whom there is nothing particular to understand.

TYRRELL: (*Helplessly*) What on earth do you mean by always harping on my efforts to be singular? Heaven knows I cannot see how I try to be so.

GRACE: (*With a little laugh, as she taps her foot on the floor*) I suppose you are now habituated to the effort.

TYRRELL: (*Looking at her with a sort of wonder*) Oh, how impossible it is for you ever to know how I have suffered — how I have aspired!

GRACE: (*Impatiently*) Really, it becomes too provoking when you begin talking about these imaginary sufferings and aspirations of yours. What on earth have you to suffer? You are in good health, are you not? Were you not more than fortunate to have married as you did? Have you not independent means? What then can a man like you aspire more to? It is true, of course, that you have crippled your resources by mismanagement and extravagance. But, if you will now be led by me, and put this scheme of drainage out of your head, and if we are economical for a while, the property must recover. Then you can have absolutely nothing to trouble you.

TYRRELL: Oh, this matter-of-fact way you have of looking at things! This simple barren prose of your mind. It is that that is driving me mad.

GRACE: Driving you mad —

Pause, during which they look at each other.

TYRRELL: Well, I suppose you think I am so. (*He waits for her answer*) What an absurd idea! This is another means of annoying me.

GRACE: I must defend myself.

TYRRELL: What do you mean?

GRACE: Seeing you are so bent on ruining our child and me, I can only think of one thing.

TYRRELL: That I am mad?

GRACE *without answering him walks to back.*

TYRRELL: Grace.

GRACE: (*Turning*) Well, what is it?

TYRRELL: Do you mean this?

GRACE: (*Still walking to back*) What did I say?

TYRRELL: You said — I mean you insinuated that — I am mad.

GRACE *does not answer.*

TYRRELL: You do not mean this. Take back what you have said.

GRACE: (*Turning suddenly*) I cannot. (*She still walks to back*)

TYRRELL: Before you go, take back your words. You don't know how they frighten me. Again I beseech you to take back those words. You do not believe what you say.

GRACE: I do believe them. I believe you to be mad. *Exit at back.*

TYRRELL: (*Laughing nervously*) Oh — ha — mad — how can she say such a thing? Mad — who is saner than I am? Ha — ha — I suppose people of her type think everyone who differs from them, mad. How curious! Ah, we have not a single sympathy. That is what it is. (*With a look of terror*) Merciful heaven, is it possible, though, she may be right? Can there possibly be a doubt as to which is the reality and which is the dream? Oh, horror — horror! (*He sinks upon the sofa and covers his face with his hands*)

MILES TYRRELL *carrying his books as before, enters at back.*

MILES: It is rather chilly reading out of doors. As I just saw Grace go through the garden, I may perhaps again have this place to myself. (*Perceiving* TYRRELL) Oh, you here still? Why, Carden, what is the matter with you.

TYRRELL: (*Rising, approaches in a dazed manner, and seems involuntarily to feel his way with his hands*) Nothing — only that persons and things now more than ever seem strangely to recede from me and become more unreal. But you — you, Miles, said you would never leave me (*glances around with a shudder*) if ever I should stand helpless and alone. Oh, Miles, my brother — (*he hides his face on Miles' shoulder*).

MILES: Carden — (*the books fall from his arms on the floor*).

ACT II

The same as last, except that the room is tidied, the window doors at back are closed, vases of flowers stand on the tables from which the papers, etc., have been removed and replaced by sundry drawing-room ornaments. It is the afternoon of the following day.

GRACE TYRRELL *opens the door at right for* LADY SHRULE, *a plain, fashionable-looking woman of about five and thirty, in a riding habit and straw hat which fit her to perfection. She enters somewhat jauntily.*

GRACE: (*Following her*) I thought we might as well sit here after lunch instead of in the drawing room. I know Lord Shrule is not very fond of going upstairs.

LADY SHRULE: No, my husband, dear old man, finds it trying after his attack of gout. Well, upon my word, Grace, this is quite a pretty room. What a pity not to turn all these frowsy books out of it!

GRACE: (*Sighing*) Oh, of course, it ought to be a drawing-room.

LADY SHRULE: Then why don't you make it one?

GRACE: My goodness, Lilian, you know I can do nothing in this house.

LADY SHRULE: I know you have a wretched time of it, dear, with that husband of yours. Still, I cannot help thinking that if, at the beginning, you had really tried, you might have made him more amenable.

GRACE: That sounds very easy. You have no idea what he is.

LADY SHRULE: Oh, nonsense, Grace. Most men have notions before they marry; but they are soon brought to their senses, if their wives are clever. And you are clever; so that is why I say you cannot have tried.

GRACE: I have tried everything, Lilian, although you won't believe it.

LADY SHRULE: What — everything?

GRACE: Yes.

LADY SHRULE: There is one thing I am sure you have never tried.

GRACE: (*Eagerly*) What is that?

LADY SHRULE: Flattery.

GRACE: Lilian, don't be silly. As if there was anything I could flatter him about.

LADY SHRULE: Well, you know, in spite of all, people do say he is clever.

GRACE: (*Impatiently*) I must say I have never found him so.

LADY SHRULE: I confess I never have either. But then I don't see very much of him. To tell you the truth he always seemed to me odd and ridiculous; for he never cared for society, never went to races, dances, or tennis parties, you know, like other people. Still, it might be worth your while to do as I advise. You can hardly imagine what effect it has even on the most unpromising man.

GRACE: That may be, that may be, when they are really superior to one; but to flatter him — ugh — never. (*Half to herself as she turns away*) Besides, it is impossible after yesterday.

LADY SHRULE: (*Pricking up her ears*) Yesterday? What happened yesterday, Grace? (*Goes up to her*) What is the matter, dear?

GRACE: (*Petulantly*) Oh, nothing, Lilian. I did not mean for you to hear.

LADY SHRULE: Oh, but there is something, Grace. I see it by your troubled look. He must have done something dreadful yesterday. Perhaps I might be of help to you. What was it?

GRACE: Well, this. Yesterday I discovered that he has embarked on a new folly which must end in our ruin; and when I tried to remonstrate with him he would not listen to a word I said. Just think, he — he — to treat a person like me this way.

LADY SHRULE: He must be a great savage. But what else can you expect from the life he leads?

GRACE: Quite true. You are perfectly right, Lilian.

LADY SHRULE: What is this new folly you say he has embarked on, Grace?

GRACE: Oh, a monstrous plan of draining another immense morass. As if our means were not already sufficiently crippled by his extravagance in this way.

LADY SHRULE: I should think so, indeed. What a misfortune for you that you ever married him!

GRACE: Yes, what a misfortune!

LADY SHRULE: I have always wondered why you did, Grace. You know you never cared for him. How, indeed, could any girl care for such a man — least of all the Grace Desmond I remember in those days, when we used to meet at every party and ball in the county.

GRACE: Yes, yes, Lilian, I know that. But you see he was a good match at the time; and I thought I would be able to make him sensible, and to lead him; for he was so much in love with me.

LADY SHRULE: Was he ever really, do you think?

GRACE: Oh, I think so; he must have been at first; for then it seemed to me that I used to monopolise all his attention.

LADY SHRULE: How came he to change? Some other woman, I suppose —

GRACE: No — no, there is no one else. I am sure of that. I have watched him closely now for some years.

LADY SHRULE: Nonsense, dear — just as if you could watch him. I tell you it is impossible that a man can exist without loving some woman.

GRACE: Yes — I know we women all think so. But this is quite a case in itself. He is such a queer creature. You canot imagine how strange his ideas are. (*With a certain relief and confidence*) Oh, no, there is no one else; and it is very wicked of you, Lilian, to suggest such a thing.

LADY SHRULE: (*A little nettled*) How then do you account for his behaviour?

GRACE: I cannot think, for I have always been most amiable to him and patient with his eccentricities, which are dreadfully irritating. Gracious, I remember when he first began to weary me with his strange ideas that I could not make head or tail of. So you may be sure, dear, they were sheer nonsense. It was then, when I tried to draw him from such folly, and to centre his interest upon myself, that I noticed a curious change in him. It seemed all at once that I became as nothing to him — that what he loved was something mysterious — beyond me.

LADY SHRULE: Ah, he never loved you, Grace. I am certain, now, he never did.

GRACE: Oh, yes, he must have at first. You should have seen how I made him do almost anything for me. Why, he settled down, entertained, shot, even farmed. Imagine that for him.

LADY SHRULE: (*Composedly*) Well, that was the result? What about the farming, for instance?

GRACE: (*Crestfallen*) Indeed — the only result of the farming has been — the heather field.

LADY SHRULE: Ah, Grace, for all you made him do, you were not able to make him give up the heather field — my poor Grace!

GRACE: (*With violent emotion*) Oh, that folly! That abominable work! With the beginning of it I noticed his first change towards me.

LADY SHRULE: He never loved you, Grace. He is a terrible man. These Tyrrells were always a queer lot. You know the father was very eccentric; and the mother — well, Shrule tells me she went quite out of her mind before she died, at the birth of the young brother. What kind is he, by the way? He is very good-looking, don't you think?

GRACE: Oh, Miles is all right. He is a harmless creature — wonderfully clever at college, I hear. He is certainly amiable, but vexes me occasionally with his foolish admiration for my husband.

LADY SHRULE: Yes, I can imagine how annoying that must be.

GRACE: Yes, and to have that fellow Ussher, too, dropping in to complete the mutual admiration society! Oh, I always disliked him.

LADY SHRULE: I don't think much of him either, with his sad, lonely way of living there in that great place of his. I believe he has it filled with such strange things.

GRACE: Yes, books — and hideous pictures — I have not been there for years. I avoid him as much as possible; for he was always my enemy, and does his best to destroy whatever influence I might have with my husband.

LADY SHRULE: My poor Grace, what a strange crew you have fallen among! This dreadful husband! So at last he is going selfishly to sacrifice you for the gratification of his theories and whims.

GRACE: (*With determination*) He shall not sacrifice me, Lilian. I am certain of that now.

LADY SHRULE: Why, dear, what are you thinking of?

GRACE: All those facts you have mentioned about the Tyrrells only confirm a suspicion that has haunted me for some time.

LADY SHRULE: (*With increasing curiosity*) What suspicion, Grace?

GRACE: That my husband is not in his right senses.

LADY SHRULE: Do you mean you think him mad?

GRACE: Yes, mad.

LADY SHRULE: Oh!

GRACE: Yes, Lilian, I feel there can be no doubt about it now. You know his monstrous extravagance, his wild manner of talking — and then what you tell me about his father and mother. Oh, he must certainly be mad.

LADY SHRULE: I suppose you are right.

GRACE: Of course — that is what it is. Poor man! Measures ought therefore to be taken at once to prevent him from ruining his family.

LADY SHRULE: What measure can you take, Grace?

GRACE: I don't see why I should not commence a legal suit to deprive him of control over the property.

LADY SHRULE: But that would mean placing him under restraint, wouldn't it?

GRACE: I suppose so, if necessary. All I know is that I am determined to prevent this new burden from being put on the estate.

LADY SHRULE: Wouldn't it be well, Grace, if you were first to have medical advice as to the state of your husband's mind?

GRACE: I have already thought of that, Lilian. I have been in communication with Doctor Dowling and Doctor Roche.

LADY SHRULE: What — really?

GRACE: Yes. I believe two doctors are required, are they not, in cases of this sort?

LADY SHRULE: I don't know; but we can ask Shrule.

GRACE: Of course, he is sure to know. How lucky I have you both here.

LADY SHRULE: When do you think of sending for the doctors?

GRACE: Well, Lilian, the sooner the better, if this government loan is to be stopped. (*Hesitating*) Well, the fact is — I have sent for them today.

LADY SHRULE: Today?

GRACE: Yes. Was I not right?

LADY SHRULE: But your husband suspects nothing of this?

GRACE: Good heavens, no! Neither do the doctors as yet. No, I have sent for them upon the plea of their holding a consultation about Kit. As Doctor Roche has been attending him lately off and on for little attacks of feverishness and nausea, their visit will not look in any way suspicious. I will then take care they have conversation with my husband. You see?

LADY SHRULE: What energy and resource you have, dear, to be sure.

GRACE: Ah, when a woman is reduced to such desperate straits as I am at present, it sharpens her wits. But the doctors may arrive now at any moment, and as I must see and prepare them beforehand for this task, let us go out to the end of the shrubbery where we can meet them on their way.

LADY SHRULE: Very well — and you can bring Shrule to join in our consultation afterwards, when he comes from the dining-room.

GRACE: What a comfort, Lilian, to have you both to consult. (*Vehemently*) You must help me. I tell you I must succeed in this undertaking. It means the very existence of my child and me.

CARDEN TYRRELL *enters hastily at the back.*

TYRRELL: Oh, have you finished lunch so soon? How do you do, Lady Shrule? (*They shake hands*) I hope you will excuse my absence. I was very busy all the morning with the Board of Works inspector.

LADY SHRULE: Oh, not at all. Have you finished your business?

TYRRELL: No, but I expect to by tonight. The inspector has gone in before me to lunch; so, with your permission, I will leave you to look after him.

LADY SHRULE: Of course, Mr Tyrrell, we will excuse you. Grace and I were just about to take a stroll around the garden. You will find Shrule in the dining-room.

Exeunt LADY SHRULE *and* GRACE TYRRELL *at back.* CARDEN TYRRELL *gazes after them as they disappear in the garden, then goes to writing table where he searches for something which he cannot find, while he grumbles indistinctly. He looks around the room with an expression of annoyance at its altered condition, then exit by door at right.*

Enter at back BARRY USSHER *and* KIT TYRRELL, *a rather wild though pensive-looking boy with short, fair hair, and dressed in a sailor suit. He has a daisy chain swung across his shoulder, and holds a bunch of wild flowers in his hand.*

KIT: (*Dragging* USSHER *by the sleeve*) Come in, Barry, come in. I missed you yesterday. Have you brought me anything this time?

USSHER: I am afraid nothing this time, Kit. You see, when I left home I did not intend to come here; but on the road I met by chance Doctor Roche, who told me he had been sent for by your mother. So I thought I would just turn in, and see if anything was the matter. There is no one ill, is there?

KIT: No, of course not. They are only bringing him to bother me again. I have nothing the matter with me; and still he is always saying I must not eat this and I must not eat that.

USSHER: What a nasty old fellow!

KIT: Yes, isn't he horrid! He says, too, I mustn't lie on the grass. I suppose he'll soon want to prevent me hunting for wild flowers.

USSHER: That would be a privation, Kit. You love them so much, don't you? What nice ones you have brought in today. Where did you get them — so late, too, in the year?

KIT: Oh, you can't think how I had to search for them here and there through the long grass in the heather field. It is the only place now where any wild flowers are left. How I love being there with father.

USSHER: So you, Kit, have also caught the sickness of the heather field.

KIT: What is this sickness you are all saying I have? I tell you I am quite well. (*With impatience*) Oh, how I wish I were a man.

USSHER: Alas, are you not much better as you are? Why do you want to be a man?

KIT: Because then they could not prevent me doing what I like. I should be a sailor and find out what is beyond that great sea father and I are always looking at from the heather field.

USSHER: Be a sailor, Kit, and give up the wild flowers?

KIT: Oh, I forgot. But should I have to, do you think?

USSHER: I fear you could not gather flowers on the sea, except perhaps a few poor crushed ones, torn from its depths by the storms.

KIT: Then there are some, after all?

USSHER: Yes, down under the sea grow numberless fair flowers whose leaves close softly around many a poor sailor.

KIT: (*Dreamily*) What beautiful flowers!

USSHER: I hope you will never be such a sailor, Kit. No, you are far better as you are! Do not wish to be a man.

KIT: Why, Barry?

USSHER: Because you understand so many things now you never could then. How much nicer to be always a little wildflower elf. In the lives of dream children such as you it is beautiful to think of a heather field!

KIT: Oh, but can they prevent me from going there?

USSHER: They cannot. I will see that old Roche attempts no such tyranny.

KIT: Oh, thank you, Barry. How good you always are!

LORD SHRULE, *an elderly, benevolent-looking man dressed in a somewhat old-fashioned riding costume,* MILES TYRRELL, *and* CARDEN TYRRELL *enter by the door at night.*

LORD SHRULE: Now that the inspector has gone out again to his work, I must say, my dear Carden, I am astounded at hearing of this new expenditure you contemplate. I did not like to speak before him — Ah, Ussher, how do you do? (*To* KIT) And how is my little man?

KIT: (*Holding out his hand*) Very well, thanks.

LORD SHRULE: That's right, that's right. I was saying, my dear Carden, your fresh project of expenditure fills me with amazement. Have you heard about it, Ussher?

USSHER: I have indeed.

LORD SHRULE: Well, does it not seem to you

extremely imprudent — nay, reckles?

USSHER: Oh, you must not ask me, Lord Shrule. Carden seems determined. And, after all, he is the best judge of his own affairs.

TYRRELL: Yes, Barry, that is just it.

LORD SHRULE: Come, come, Carden, you will not mind the advice of an old man who has a long experience in the management of land. Your father and I were always fast friends, and I naturally take a great interest in you and your family.

TYRRELL: I know you have always been very kind, Lord Shrule. Forgive me if I have spoken hastily. I did not mean —

LORD SHRULE: Of course not, my dear Carden, I quite understand you. I fear indeed you must think it rather impertinent of your friends to interfere in your business. But then, as I have said, I consider myself privileged.

TYRRELL: You may be quite sure, Lord Shrule, I could not take anything from you except in good part.

LORD SHRULE: I thought so. Well, let me implore of you, if only for the sake of your family, to desist. This is certainly the wildest scheme I ever heard of, and couldn't pay, even if the drainage were to turn out a success.

TYRRELL: But you forget it is necessary now that the drainage of the heather field falls into this land. I must make a cutting for the water to get to the sea. And then, what is easier than to reclaim the land through which this cutting goes?

LORD SHRULE: My dear Carden, don't mind the cutting — don't mind the heather field. What you have only got to think of is to cease altogether from loading your estate with an ever-growing burden of debt. For goodness' sake leave these works alone. If you continue them you will simply beggar yourself.

TYRRELL: (*Uneasily*) I do not see that at all. The work will be very remunerative. It will double the value of the estate.

LORD SHRULE: Oh, Carden, listen to me. I know well the nature of such works as you are carrying on. I have tried them myself — on a far smaller scale, of course. They never repay their expenditure.

TYRRELL: That is a mere assertion unsupported by argument. On the other hand, I have excellent reasons why I should believe that what I am about to undertake must have the best results. Look at the rich pasture now in the heather field. And am I to suppose that I shall not have the same in the valley when it is reclaimed? Until you can prove logically that I am mistaken, I must continue those works, which I clearly see are so profitable. Am I not right, Barry?

USSHER: I have said I shall never again discourage you, Carden.

LORD SHRULE: Ussher, upon my word I thought you knew better. But I suppose it is useless remonstrating with our friend about his experiments, which amount with him to absolute mania.

GRACE TYRRELL *enters at back.*

GRACE: (*After bowing to* USSHER) Oh, Lord Shrule, we have been waiting for you in the garden. Won't you come? I want to show you my little greenhouse. The plants you gave me are doing so well in it.

LORD SHRULE: I am delighted to hear you say so, Mrs Tyrrell. Let us go and see them. But I hope you will not make me walk much, as I have barely recovered from that last attack of gout, and can only get about as yet quietly on my pony. Let me see, I left my hat in the hall.

GRACE: We can go through there, just as well.

Exeunt LORD SHRULE *and* GRACE TYRRELL *by door at right.*

TYRRELL: It is really too bad that I should be molested thus perpetually with unsolicited advice. All my acquaintances seem to consider it incumbent upon them to interfere in and direct my affairs just like their own. One would think I had no right to do anything. That old fellow, you know, means well; but it is very annoying to be taken to task by a person who really has no right to meddle. Ha! It is too absurd indeed that I should have to defend what I have a perfect right to do.

MILES: I know it must be very trying, Carden.

TYRRELL: I should think so, indeed. And I am not going to stand it any longer. I will live my life as I want, and will take dictation from nobody.

USSHER: But you must expect to be criticised, Carden. That is the penalty, you know, for attempting to do anything.

TYRRELL: Oh, I don't mind any amount of outside criticism — not even the strictures of friends like Lord Shrule, as long as their remarks are not to my face. No, it is other criticism — nearer — that leaves a sting.

MILES: Well, Carden, I am sure Barry and I are not in the habit of finding fault with you. At least we never mean to.

USSHER: Of that, at all events, I am certain.

TYRRELL: No — not you two, kindest and best. It is even nearer home — this criticism and opposition — this hearing perpetually amidst the strain of labour, bitter and disheartening words. That is what is so unbearable.

MILES: Be patient with her, Carden. Grace cannot as yet understand. This is a period of trial. One day you will see her loyally helping and inspiring you.

TYRRELL: (*Impatiently*) Inspiring me! I wish, Miles, you would not use a sublime word in a vulgar sense. When you have more experience you will find that instead of inspiring they more often prevent us from doing anything.

MILES: Oh, Carden, how unlike you! That is more the style of the cynic philosopher there — Barry. See how he is smiling. I am sure he regrets he missed saying such a thing himself instead.

USSHER: Well, really, Miles —

TYRRELL: (*Laughing*) Oh, you dear Miles. You were always the most wonderful body in the world for dispelling bitterness and gloom with that beautiful light you seem to carry about you! (*Hopefully*) Well, two friends such as you ought to compensate me for what I have to bear from others. Bah, I will not mind them. I will be merry while I work; and my work will be incessant, leaving no time for brooding over unpleasant things. And both of you will always be present with me, if difficulties should arise. Yes, with you I know I cannot suffer defeat from the rest.

Enter at back GRACE TYRRELL, DOCTOR DOWLING, *a thick-set man of about forty, dressed in a tweed suit, and* DOCTOR ROCHE, *an elderly, lean, and somewhat prim man, wearing spectacles and black clothes. Looking a bit ill at ease, the Doctors exchange salutations with* TYRRELL, MILES, USSHER, *and* KIT.

KIT: Mother!

GRACE: Yes, my dear?

KIT: Who is that with Doctor Roche?

GRACE: Doctor Dowling.

KIT: Is he coming to see me too?

GRACE: Just to look at you, Kit, that's all.

KIT: But I have nothing the matter with me, mother.

GRACE: Never mind — neither will hurt you — only save you from possible peril — oh, my own sweet boy. (*She kisses him*)

TYRRELL: (*To* GRACE) You cannot think there was cause for summoning these two physicians.

GRACE: (*Vaguely*) Cause? Well — I was a little anxious on the child's account, and thought it best they should consult about him. But I expected to find you alone. (*She glances at* USSHER)

USSHER: (*Taking the hint*) Carden, I must go. I hope there is nothing really the matter with Kit. He doesn't look as if there was.

KIT: Oh, Barry, don't go. You know you promised —

USSHER: Hush, Kit.

TYRRELL: Yes, stay where you are, Barry. There is no reason for making such a mystery of this business. Besides, I must soon go out to the inspector, and we can walk together. (*To* USSHER) By the way, what has become of the Shrules?

GRACE: (*Uneasily*) Oh, Lord Shrule had to return home suddenly about some matter of importance. They both desired me to say goodbye to you.

TYRRELL: So much the better. Well, doctors, I certainly cannot understand the necessity of this consultation. The boy seems to me perfectly well.

GRACE: No, I assure you, Doctor Dowling, he is not so. He is often ill from eating all sorts of unwholesome sweets. How do you find him looking today, Doctor Roche?

ROCHE: He appears healthier, on the whole, I think, Mrs Tyrrell. (*To* KIT) Come here, and let me look well at you, my little man. There, put out your tongue.

KIT: Ah, I suppose, Barry, I must now expect the worst.

USSHER: Never fear, Kit. They don't look as if they mean to do much to you.

GRACE: (*Suspiciously*) I am afraid, Mr. Ussher, you spoil him as much as his father; and I shall get no good of him while you are here. You and Miles ought to take a walk. It would be so nice on this fine day, wouldn't it? But won't you return to dinner? Do return to dinner, Mr. Ussher.

USSHER: No, thank you, Mrs. Tyrrell, I regret I cannot. I shall be going now in a minute with Carden. Kit must not expect any countenance from me.

KIT: But I thought you said you would not let Doctor Roche—

USSHER: Now, Kit, you must do as you are told. Have I not said you needn't fear?

The Doctors look at KIT, *feel his pulse, talk together, etc.*

USSHER: (*Aside to* MILES) Your sister-in-law seems particularly anxious to get rid of us.

MILES: (*Aside to* USSHER, *with an enquiring look*)

Do you really think so? I wonder why.

USSHER: (*Aside to* MILES) I am not certain yet.

TYRRELL: How needless this consultation is, to be sure. There is nothing the matter with the boy.

GRACE: You do well to say so — you, who are the chief cause of his illness.

TYRRELL: I, the cause?

GRACE: Of course you are. He is sick at night from those long days when you keep him out fasting on the mountain, and then feed him with sweets at dinner afterwards. This must all cease.

KIT: Oh, mother, do not prevent me from going to the heather field. I don't want those sweets. I was only sick once.

GRACE: Can you not see, Kit, that I am only acting for your good? (*Sadly, as* KIT *turns*) It is I who fight for his interests, and he leaves me for his father.

TYRRELL: Only sick once, and all this fuss for that! Never mind, Kit. You shall not be prevented. I will take care in future that you get plenty to eat and at proper times. So there will be no danger of sickness again.

KIT: Then you will not let anyone prevent me from going with you, father?

TYRRELL: Ah, you see, Kit, I never could get on without you in the heather field. We should feel so lonely — both of us, shouldn't we?

GRACE *looks significantly at the Doctors, who now begin to observe* TYRRELL *closely.*

KIT: Yes, father, dear.

USSHER: (*Aside to* MILES) The doctors seem strangely inattentive now to Kit and his ailments.

MILES: (*Aside to* USSHER, *with a puzzled expression*) So it seems. What do you think they mean?

USSHER: (*Aside to* MILES) Wait. I have an uncomfortable suspicion. It is well we stayed here.

GRACE: Alas, the child's health must be sacrificed like everything else, I suppose.

TYRRELL: How sacrificed?

GRACE: Oh, to add zest to your infatuation for that mountain —

TYRRELL: Nothing of the kind. If I had known he had ever been ill, I would have taken every precaution, in spite of my infatuation, as you choose to call the interest I take in my work.

DOWLING: Is that your land work, Mr. Tyrrell?

TYRRELL: Yes.

DOWLING: You are an extensive reclaimer of waste land?

TYRRELL: Yes, I fancy there are few in Ireland more extensive.

ROCHE: You are certainly most enterprising.

TYRRELL: Ay, it is a grand work.

DOWLING: And you believe in the possibility of its paying?

TYRRELL: Of course. Wait till you see the profits I shall make. With these I shall extend my works, and with the further profits I shall embark on such a scale of business as in time will enable me to start a company for buying up and reclaiming or reafforesting every inch of waste land in Ireland.

USSHER: That is truly a gigantic scheme, Carden. Look here, I must really be going; and your inspector too must be waiting for you. Let us be off. Come along.

TYRRELL: Oh, wait a minute, Barry. I want to explain. I will go with you directly. (*To the Doctors*) With the far-reaching usefulness of my projects I must become a real benefactor to the country, and in a time, too, when so many quack remedies in the way of legislation are being offered to the public.

ROCHE: True, true. How very interesting.

DOWLING: Upon my word, how interesting.

TYRRELL: Oh, the work is a glorious one. There is something creative about it — this changing the face of a whole country! None of the humdrum, barn-door work of ordinary farming, with its sordid accompaniment of the cattle fair! When from the ideal world of my books those people forced me to such a business, I was bound to find the extreme of its idealisation.

DOWLING: (*Aside to* DOCTOR ROCHE) What the dickens does he mean by that?

ROCHE: You mean you have idealised farming, Mr. Tyrrell?

TYRRELL: Of course, what else? Do you think I could go on doing the dull drudgery they forced upon me? No, I considered how I could elevate it. I pondered and pondered and never rested, until at last there came to me the master-thought of the heather field.

ROCHE: (*Slowly nodding assent*) Oh, indeed. Dear me.

TYRRELL: (*With evident pleasure at the surprise he is creating*) Yes — was it not a discovery? And what contentment it brought after the previous life-drudgery. I felt like returning to my youth's ideals in that free mountain air. Oh! there is magic in those mountain breezes!

DOWLING: All I know, sir, is that the Faculty consider sea air blowing over a mountain bog to be the finest remedy in the world for bile or dyspepsia. (*He looks around him facetiously*)

TYRRELL: (*With an expression of disgust*) So that is the only thought suggested to you by the ethereal mountain breeze! There are some people who can never recognize a beautiful meaning in anything.

DOWLING: Maybe so, Mr. Tyrrell. (*As if struck with an idea*) Do you find any meaning yourself, though, in this mountain air?

TYRRELL: (*Disdainfully*) Do I? Why, of course I do. I find in it a medium between the beauty of the past and myself.

DOWLING: Indeed.

TYRRELL: Yes — nature's ethereal phonograph, as it might be, treasuring for my delight past ecstasies of sound. I hear on its waves those voices floating back to me from —

USSHER: (*With alarm, aside to* MILES) You must take your brother away at once.

DOWLING: What is that you are saying, Mr. Tyrrell?

ROCHE: Voices — you don't mean to say you hear voices?

TYRRELL: I do mean to say it.

DOWLING: Whose voices do you hear?

TYRRELL: Choristers singing of youth in an eternal sunrise!

ROCHE: But you must know that this is all imagination.

TYRRELL: (*Irritably*) Imagination — always imagination. How wearisome that word sounds to me. I tell you there is no such thing as imagination.

DOWLING: That is a bold statement, sir.

TYRRELL: No. You either perceive or you don't perceive. Therefore it vexes me, when I perceive anything, to be told it is only imagination.

GRACE: Wouldn't it be more accurate, then, to call it hallucination?

TYRRELL: (*Hastily to her*) That's always how you enter into the spirit of my ideas.

DOWLING: You can hardly expect her to agree with them.

TYRRELL: (*Resignedly*) No, I suppose there must always be distortion of my meaning.

DOWLING: Then would you mind explaining your meaning?

ROCHE: You told us you hear voices.

TYRRELL: Yes, of course.

ROCHE: Do you ever remember anything they say?

TYRRELL: (*Thinking*) Yes.

DOWLING: Well, would you let us know?

TYRRELL: They keep telling me I am not what I am.

ROCHE: How very strange!

DOWLING: Humph! Do they say anything else, sir?

TYRRELL: They often call me back to my real life.

ROCHE: What do you mean by your real life?

TYRRELL: That life before I wandered into this dream.

DOWLING: And so you think you are only dreaming now?

TYRRELL: How can you tell that you also are not now in a dream?

USSHER: Answer that, if you are able, Doctor.

DOWLING: A man ought to know very well whether he is asleep or awake.

TYRRELL: That is just it; and I know I am in a dream.

USSHER: (*Impatiently*) Really, Carden, I don't see what you gain by discussing your ideas with people who can neither understand nor sympathise with them. Come, come away. I cannot wait any longer.

TYRRELL: (*Rather dejected*) Yes, Barry, I suppose you are right. It was stupid of me. Let us go out. Good evening, Doctors.

USSHER: (*To* TYRRELL) You walk on with Miles and Kit. I just remember I have something to consult Doctor Roche about.

MILES: Come, Carden.

Exeunt at back CARDEN, MILES *and* KIT TYRRELL.

USSHER: (*Very gravely*) Doctor Dowling and Doctor Roche, you were sent for by Mrs. Tyrrell today to consult on a matter altogether different from the health of the little boy.

GRACE: (*Defiantly*) Well, then, and if they were?

USSHER: Your husband fortunately suspects nothing; and I have warned Miles against saying anything to enlighten him.

GRACE: If you consider me in your power, you are greatly mistaken.

USSHER: (*Austerely*) I consider nothing of the sort, Mrs. Tyrrell. You have strangely misunderstood me.

GRACE: I don't know. Anyhow, I have nothing to fear from you. The opinions of Doctor Dowling and Doctor Roche will ensure the success of the measures I have decided upon for the security of the child's interests and mine.

USSHER: You seem very sure as to conclusions

these gentlemen are to arrive at.

GRACE: Well, they know all about my poor husband's reckless expenditure, his inability to act like other people, his futile disputes with the tenantry, and today they have seen how he has conducted himself, and have heard him speak. I hardly think they can have any doubt as to the condition of his mind. What do you say, Doctor Dowling and Doctor Roche?

DOWLING: I am of opinion, ma'am, it is a case of dementia — but curable with proper treatment.

USSHER: Indeed. And what are your reasons for considering it dementia?

DOWLING: The general tenor, Mr. Ussher, of the patient's behavour — his reckless expenditure of his means, as Mrs. Tyrrell says — his queer deranged enthusiasm — and, above all, his talk about hearing voices. There is no more common sign of insanity than for persons to believe that they hear voices.

ROCHE: Quite so. That is by far the most serious symptom in the case.

USSHER: But surely you must see that a highly-gifted man like Carden Tyrrell is not to be judged by your everyday rules. These voices you speak of he heard long ago in happier days. They are only memories made vivid by the force of imagination. Why, he told you as much. Did he not?

DOWLING: That was not the impression conveyed to me.

USSHER: Doctor Roche, you cannot agree with this, I am sure.

ROCHE: Well, really, Mr. Ussher, I fear I must — that is to say, with certain reservations. Our responsibility in certifying to madness is no doubt grave; but then, on the other hand, we would incur a graver responsibility if, by our indulgence, the patient afterwards were to harm himself or anybody else.

GRACE: If he is not restrained he will surely bring the child and me to irreparable ruin. You see he has almost done so already. Oh, think of that, Doctor Roche. You know he is not fit to have the control of anything.

ROCHE: I know there might be some doubt as to the question of madness, if we had nothing more to go upon than these extravagant land improvements of his.

USSHER: (*Eagerly*) Yes.

ROCHE: But then I am confronted by this unpleasant symptom of his hearing voices that have no existence — a most common sign, as you say rightly, Dowling, of insanity.

USSHER: Did not Joan of Arc declare she heard voices calling on her to accomplish a work which proved to be one of the most powerful and practical in history? Was not Socrates firmly convinced that he was in the habit of receiving admonitions from his daemon? I might quote you several other instances of celebrated personages whose imaginations led them to believe they heard voices. Yet no one has ever thought of calling them insane. Come now, Doctor Roche, a man of your experience and culture must admit the truth of what I say.

ROCHE: Ah, Mr. Ussher, I fear all forms of madness might be explained away by your arguments.

GRACE: Of course, Doctor Roche. Pray don't listen to him.

ROCHE: But, at the same time, Mrs. Tyrrell, I am bound to admit that madness partakes more of an infirmity whereby the natural sequence of ideas is disconnected.

USSHER: Quite so, quite so. If you talk with a lunatic you find that you can never keep him to any consecutive line of thought. He is perpetually off here, off there, on some new and irrelevant tangent. You can never obtain a direct answer to a question. His mental process resembles a chain, at intervals unlinked. These are the real symptoms of that pitiful and uninteresting malady. Are they not?

ROCHE: Yes, Mr. Ussher, on the whole you are fairly right.

USSHER: Very well then, are any such symptoms discoverable in Carden Tyrrell? Who is more clearly consecutive in his ideas than he? Discuss any question with him — politics or books — what you will — I am bound he acquits himself ably.

GRACE: And land improvement too, Mr. Ussher. You forget that.

DOWLING: There you just have it, ma'am.

USSHER: His reasons for making these improvements are quite consecutive and rational. (DOCTOR DOWLING *and* GRACE *laugh*) Oh, but I assure you they are so. His work may or may not be practical. Who knows? Personally I agree with you in thinking it is not. Still, that is no plea for trying to deprive him of his liberty and rights. If it were, I fear that many, and those too in responsible positions, might have their freedom of action endangered. It is only common-place and unimaginative people who consider the poetic and original temperament to be a mark of madness.

ROCHE: There is a great deal in what you say, Mr. Ussher. I —

GRACE: (*Alarmed*) Doctor Roche, you cannot be serious? You are not giving in to such arguments?

ROCHE: (*Apologetically*) No — no, Mrs. Tyrrell, I merely admit their truth in a general way. That is all.

USSHER: You are far too clever a man, Doctor, not to see their truth. Then again, think of the gravity and danger of what you propose doing. You know, of course, gentlemen, that you will be asked to confirm on oath before a Commission of Lunacy the opinion you now so rashly form of my friend.

DOWLING: I am quite prepared, Sir, to swear before any Commission.

USSHER: That may be, Doctor Dowling. However, Doctor Roche, the matter doubtless appears in another light to you. You may be quite certain that when Carden Tyrrell is forewarned, he will be particularly careful not to compromise himself at his private examination by the Commission, who will then, of course, ridicule the idea of preventing him from managing his estate. The defeated parties afterwards will be open to an action by their victim for damages, of which action the law costs, whether he succeeds or not, are sure to be considerable on all sides. When this conspiracy —

GRACE: Mr. Ussher, you forget yourself. How dare you?

USSHER: Yes, Mrs. Tyrrell, it is an unpleasant word, but excusable in my resentment of this cruel injustice to my old and best friend. You may be sure, too, it is the word the world will use. Why did the Shrules leave here so suddenly today?

GRACE: (*Haughtily*) You have already heard the reason.

USSHER: I am bound to accept it. But I cannot help suspecting that Lord Shrule invented his excuse.

GRACE: I think we have heard quite enough from you, Mr. Ussher. You are not likely to intimidate us by your threats. (*To the Doctors*) Isn't that so?

DOWLING: Oh, I am prepared to stand by my opinions, ma'am.

GRACE: And you, Doctor Roche?

ROCHE: (*Nervously*) Well, you see, Mrs. Tyrrell, I never held so decided an opinion of the case as my friend Doctor Dowling. I think — for the present — that is to say — perhaps —

GRACE: For the present? Surely you must know that if we do not act at once we shall be too late to prevent the raising of this ruinous loan.

ROCHE: Ah, yes, yes; but I am afraid I cannot make up my mind about the patient as yet. I could not undertake to swear on oath that he is insane.

GRACE: It is quite clear, Doctor Roche, that you are intimidated.

ROCHE: (*Indignantly*) I allow no one to intimidate me, Mrs. Tyrrell.

GRACE: And you will leave the child and me to be ruined?

ROCHE: What can I do? Have I not told you my difficulties?

GRACE: Doctor Roche, we are in your hands. Our fate lies upon your decision. I implore of you not to fail us.

ROCHE: (*Very confused*) You must excuse me, Mrs. Tyrrell; but on consideration I would not venture to grant your request. I have an appointment just now. Pray excuse me. Good afternoon, Mrs. Tyrrell — good afternoon — good afternoon.

Exit, bowing to all, at back.

DOWLING: Well, I suppose after this I am not much use here, so I may as well also be on my way. I am sorry, ma'am, the Doctor was persuaded to change his mind; but he is a nervious, timid man. To me the case seems clear. However, perhaps it is better to do nothing just at present.

He bows, and exit by door at back.

GRACE: (*To* USSHER, *with suppressed anger*) I suppose you are prepared to bear the responsibility you have incurred.

USSHER: Yes — I am prepared to bear it. But did you fully consider the responsibility you were so eager to take upon yourself, Mrs. Tyrrell? I can only hope that you had not considered the question.

GRACE: I do not understand you.

USSHER: I am sorry for it. Is it then so light a matter to imprison a man — and above all such a man as your husband? It would practically mean his death. To take him away from all that he loves — his free life on the mountains, his intimate delight in nature, his interests and occupations, without which life would become for him meaningless — can you not understand the cruelty of this?

GRACE: I have no wish to be cruel. I must only protect myself.

USSHER: Yes — but it seems to me in attempting this protection you are very inexorable — very cruel. And the worst of it is, you appear not to realise the cruelty which you are so ready to inflict.

Have you forgotten that he is your husband, that he once loved you very dearly? Have you forgotten everything except yourself?

GRACE: I have not forgotten my child.

USSHER: You are, of course, bound to think of him, but not, I am sure, to the detriment of your husband. Carden has his rights as well as Kit. Is the father to be wholly sacrificed for the child? (*Pause*) But, Mrs. Tyrrell, were you only thinking of your child?

GRACE: What do you mean?

USSHER: Was there not another reason besides the child which caused you to be so resolute? That personal dislike — remember you and Carden have not been living very amicably for some time.

GRACE: Oh, do you consider that ill-feeling has actuated me in this matter?

USSHER: I don't say so. I only suggest the probability. Are you sure that it is not so?

GRACE: (*Indignantly*) What a base insinuation. No — I am sure it is not so. Of course it is not so. I may no longer care for my husband. Perhaps I never cared much for him. But I know that now I am only thinking of my child. It was for little Kit's sake that I wished —

USSHER: Yes — to imprison his father in a mad-house.

GRACE: I was willing to accept the responsibility. Are you still willing to accept yours? It is a heavy one. There was a chance of saving our fortune; and you have wrecked it. (*With rising anger*) What will you now do to save the child and me from this madman who is devouring our substance?

USSHER: Hush, hush. For heaven's sake do not talk in this manner.

GRACE: Oh, why did you do me this cruel wrong today?

USSHER: I only prevented your doing a cruel wrong.

GRACE: You have done us all a cruel wrong.

USSHER: No — I feel I have done you all a good deed today.

GRACE: (*Scornfully*) A good deed truly — a deed giving power to carry out those projects which are our ruin!

USSHER: Who can tell but that his projects may succeed? Be patient. Be gentle with him. I believe you might win him yet by gentleness from very great extravagance. Try.

GRACE: (*Gloomily*) Too late.

USSHER: Why too late?

GRACE: It was too late from the moment his thoughts first turned to the heather field.

USSHER: (*Starts and looks at her for a moment with vague alarm. Then says very gently*) There is no reason why he should ever learn the part you have played against him today. Henceforth you will be different to him, will you not?

GRACE: (*Gazing steadfastly before her*) Too late.

USSHER: (*Sadly*) Ah — well —

Exit quietly at back.

There is a noise as of some one approaching. GRACE *looks out at back, then recedes to door at right.* CARDEN TYRRELL *enters hurriedly, carrying a sheet of the ordnance map, which he lays upon the writing-table at left and studies, unaware of his wife's presence. She watches him with an expression of gathering anger, then exit sobbing by door at right. He starts and turns to see her just disappear, then sighing he shrugs his shoulders, and resumes his eager study of the map.*

ACT III

Scene. *The same as last, only the place, by the absence of all drawing-room ornaments, has assumed once more its aspect of a library. A fire of fresh ashwood in the large fire-place burns cheerfully, while sunlight streams in through the window-doors at back. A sheet of the ordnance map lies on writing table at left. Several months have passed; and it is now Spring.*

KIT TYRRELL *runs in by door at right carrying a child's kite, which he examines as he kneels down in front of the fire. Measuring out the string at arm's length, he appears dissatisfied. Then, as if suddenly remembering, he runs over to the book-case at back, and climbing up on its ledge he takes from behind the books on an upper row a mass of cord. He returns, and disentangling it ties its end to the cord attached to the kite, which he then carries to the window-doors at back. These he opens, and stands in a flood of sunlight. Outside is heard the singing of birds.*

CARDEN TYRRELL, *somewhat aged and careworn, enters by door at right.*

TYRRELL: (*Half to himself as he watches* KIT) Oh, memories —

KIT: (*After a short pause, perceiving* TYRRELL *and running to him*) Father.

TYRRELL: The little birds are singing in the sunlight to my little bird. Where are you going, Kit?

KIT: I am going to fly the kite. Oh, come out, father, with me to the heather field. There is sure to be a splendid breeze there today.

TYRRELL: (*Sadly*) Ah, the heather field. No, Kit, I cannot.

KIT: You have not been there for such a long time. Why can't you come?

TYRRELL: I can't; it is unbearable to be always followed and watched — and in that place above all others.

KIT: But, father, why don't you tell those policemen to go away?

TYRRELL: I have done so over and over again. They will not go.

KIT: Why why must they watch you, father, dear?

TYRRELL: (*Looks at* KIT *for a moment, then in an unsteady voice as he turns away*) Do not ask me, boy. You would not understand.

KIT: (*Catching* TYRRELL *by the arm*) Really? Yet Barry says that I understand so many things better than if I were a man.

TYRRELL: (*Thoughtfully*) He is right. Only those who become as you are can know the rarest joys of life.

KIT: Then why do you think, father, I would not understand the reason they are watching you?

TYRRELL: Because — because it would appear — well, something incredible to you. There, do not ask boy (*He flings himself moodily into the chair on the outside of the writing-table*)

A short pause.

KIT: (*Coming near*) Father, dear, you are not angry with me?

TYRRELL: No, Kit, only a bit worried by things in general.

KIT: I am sorry if I have ever worried you. I will try not to do it again. I love you. Oh, you don't know how I love you, father.

TYRRELL: (*Throwing his arms around* KIT) My darling, you have never worried me. I could not live without you.

KIT: (*Hiding his face on* TYRRELL's *neck*) Oh, father, father!

TYRRELL: Yes, Kit, you are the little elf that calls up for me the magic of the heather field. Henceforth we must never be divided — you and I.

KIT: Never, oh never, father, dear. You don't know how lonely I feel away from you. I have not been to the heather field for ever so long. It seemed such a sad place when you were not there.

TYRRELL: Even in spite of its wild flowers, Kit? It is time for them now to be coming out again.

KIT: Yes, the heather field will be beginning to look lovely now.

TYRRELL: How I wish I were free to walk among its flowers on this soft spring day.

KIT: Poor father! But would you like me to fetch you some of them? Shall I go?

TYRRELL: Yes, do, Kit. I should like some flowers from the heather field.

BARRY USSHER *enters at back.*

KIT: Oh, there's Barry.

TYRRELL: What — Barry! It is an event when I see anyone now.

USSHER: As if it were not your own doing.

TYRRELL: (*Somewhat ruffled*) You may say what you like for all I care.

USSHER: (*Shrugging his shoulders*) Heigh-ho! Well, Kit, are you glad the winter is over?

KIT: Oh, yes, how horrid and dark it was.

USSHER: I wonder how you ever managed to exist through it. And you never got the pony, after all?

KIT: No — you see when father promised me one he thought he could afford it. But now he cannot, until he lets the heather field. I must wait a while longer. Is not that so, father?

TYRRELL: Yes, Kit, we must wait.

KIT: You know, Barry, I could not think of worrying him any more about the pony.

USSHER: You good little son, there is no need to wait any longer. I have just brought you such a nice pony.

TYRRELL: What is this, Barry? What is this?

USSHER: Out in the yard waiting for you — bridle, saddle and all.

KIT: Oh, thank you, Barry. Father, is he not nice and kind?

TYRRELL: (*Looking at* USSHER) Yes, always the kind friend — always the same.

KIT: Father, I shall ride the pony off to the heather field at once, and get you those flowers.

Exit back

USSHER: How happy the little fellow is.

TYRRELL: You have indeed made him so by your kindness, Barry.

USSHER: Bah — a selfish kindness at most. I tell you, I have not felt for a long time such real happiness as just now when I saw myself looked at like some good spirit by that little face.

TYRRELL: And to think that you who are so lucky, to whom most things come so easy, should say this! Why, even I, with all my troubles, could hardly speak more despondingly. What would you do if you were imprisoned as I am here since those evictions?

USSHER: Your health will be ruined by your obstinacy.

TYRRELL: What can I do? The police have orders never to lose sight of me if I go out. They say I should be shot at otherwise.

USSHER: Ha!

TYRRELL: And you know I never could bear to be followed by a guard. It makes me feel like a criminal. I would much rather stay indoors.

USSHER: (*After thinking for a moment*) Look here, Carden, we ought to leave this place for a while. We will go together. We will travel.

TYRRELL: Impossible. The drainage of the valley could never go on in my absence.

USSHER: Why not? You haven't been near it for ever so long.

TYRRELL: Oh, that doesn't matter in the least. I can direct it just as well from this room. There on the writing table is my map with all the drains marked upon it. The superintendent comes to me at stated intervals, reports the progress of each man's work, and takes the fresh orders which I give him from the map. I assure you it gives me greater pleasure to conduct operations in this way, scientifically, than if I were to go on the ground. One can imagine oneself in such a situation, like Moltke[1] fighting battles from his study.

USSHER: (*Gives a quick look at* TYRRELL. *Then after a short pause*) Well, if you don't leave here, at all events try and settle with those peasants, so that you may dispense with police and be able to go about again.

TYRRELL: Settle? How could I settle with them? The only settlement they would hear of I could never grant. Oh, no — a nice ending, indeed, that would be to our battle!

USSHER: Is there no compromise you will come to?

TYRRELL: I will reinstate the evicted, if they pay in full their rents and the costs I have incurred on their account.

USSHER: Oh, that is no compromise at all.

TYRRELL: Well, it is as much as I can agree to. I told these people when they struck, that I could not afford to give abatements on rents which had already been reduced so much by the Land Commission, and I can less afford to give any now with pressing mortgagees who have not been paid for so long.

USSHER: But would it not be better to get some rent for that land instead of leaving it idle? Others, you know, will not dare to take it from you.

TYRRELL: I cannot help that. I must work it myself.

USSHER: Meanwhile how are you going to pay the mortgagees their interest?

TYRRELL: Oh, there is the great difficulty. The chief mortgagee is most pressing, and threatens to foreclose immediately. I have implored of him again and again to wait until I can let the heather field, but in vain. Miles, whom I expect home this evening, was to have made a final appeal to him in Dublin last night. I can only hope for a favourable result.

USSHER: I think you had better come to terms with those tenants, Carden.

TYRRELL: I shall never give in to them. I shall never voluntarily reduce the value of my property. Besides, if the worst should come, I have always the great resource.

USSHER: What is that?

TYRRELL: The heather field!

USSHER: Carden, take care. It is a dangerous thing — trusting to only one resource.

TYRRELL: (*A little irritated*) What do you mean? Are you too going to join the enemy?

USSHER: (*Uneasily*) No, no, Carden, you do not understand me; but —

TYRRELL: But what?

USSHER: Oh, I should so like to see you on good terms with your people again. I am sure the remembrance of all that friendship with them in the past must make this quarrel unbearable to you.

TYRRELL: Yes, indeed that is true.

USSHER: And this continual watch upon your movements too must be dreadful.

TYRRELL: Dreadful. It is gradually wearing me out. I know I cannot stand it much longer. And most of the long dreary winter I had no one about me whom I could confide in or consult; for Miles has been away at College as you know.

USSHER: Yes, carrying everything before him — I see he has won a scholarship. He is sure of his gold medal now.

TYRRELL: Miles is of the stuff to succeed. I am so

1. General Field-Marshal Graf Helmuth von Moltke (1800-91), commander-general of the German armies during the Franco-Prussian war of 1870-71.

fond of Miles. He was always such a good company.

USSHER: Of course, a most charming boy. I am glad he is to be at home today.

TYRRELL: Indeed his companionship will make a great difference to me, now that I can never get about.

USSHER: (*Anxiously*) Oh, but Carden, you cannot continue in this way. You have always been used to so free a life in the open air. I say this imprisonment will kill you. Already I see a very marked change in your appearance.

TYRRELL: (*Doggedly*) I cannot help it. My past demands that I must suffer. (*With a sigh, he passes to right of doors at back, where he looks out in a reverie*)

USSHER: (*Watching him*) For heaven's sake, Carden, do not be so fatally unreasonable.

TYRRELL: (*After a pause, still looking in the same direction*) No — I am not so. You think those remedies you suggest would avail to relieve me; but they would not.

USSHER: Why not?

TYRRELL: You ask — you who are such a philosopher? Can you not understand the only remedy for me must be something that has no relation whatever with those circumstances that may affect me ill or otherwise?

USSHER: You mean the improvement of circumstances has little to do with bringing contentment.

TYRRELL: I mean that the only remedy must be something which would make me forgetful that I am myself. (*Mysteriously*) Barry, would you believe it, often in moments of darkest anxiety I am arrested by the sight of some flower or leaf or some tiny nook in the garden out there. And oh — I become then at once so peaceful that I care not what may happen to me. I think it is only when we turn to them in our misery that we can really see the exquisite beauty of these things.

USSHER: Ah, Carden, nature is a marvellous sedative. How infinite her ingenuousness amidst all our pains and fears!

TYRRELL: Yes — and just this moment when I looked upon the ocean there and the land awakening with such freshness from its winter sleep, I felt something that no improvement of circumstances could bring. (*Then with a strange enthusiasm*) Oh, to feel that despite all suffering one has the firmament, the earth, the sea! What more can one really require from the world?

USSHER: Ay — true enough. 'For all things were made from these,' to quote the great medieval philosopher.[2] Nevertheless I think I might bring you another and very real sort of relief from this present trouble, if you would but allow me.

TYRRELL: And what if you might? It would only be succeeded by some further trouble. That is the only sort of relief you could ever bring. Ah, there is a trouble past all your remedies.

USSHER: Alas, I fear there are many. How could I pretend otherwise? But will you tell me this particular one?

TYRRELL: I wonder will you understand.

USSHER: Why not, Carden?

TYRRELL: Well then, have you ever seen on earth something beautiful beyond earth — that great beauty which appears in divers ways? And then have you known what it is to go back to the world again?

USSHER: (*Sadly*) I know, I know — the pain of loss —

TYRRELL: Is it not misery? But you have seen the great beauty, have you not? Oh, that immortal beauty — so far away — always so far away.

USSHER: Yes — yes, our ideal of beauty that for ever haunts and eludes us through life. (*With a movement of resignation*) But let us not speak of it any more.

TYRRELL: Why, Barry?

USSHER: Because, as you say, it makes one so miserable in the world, and it is such a hopeless phantom after all.[3]

USSHER: (*Cautiously*) Hush, Carden, I do not know.

TYRRELL: (*Laughing bitterly*) There — just like you, Barry, careful never to let yourself go.

USSHER: No — no, Carden, but you brood too much on these thoughts. You are overworked — you ought really to come away from here. Do let us travel somewhere together for a change.

TYRRELL: Ah, not now — at some future time, perhaps — but not now. My difficulties are gathering before me. I must stand and hew them from my path.

GRACE TYRRELL *enters hurriedly and excitedly by door at right.*

GRACE: (*Pauses when she sees* USSHER, *then to* TYRRELL) Oh, but I suppose you have no secrets from him —

2. John Duns Scotus (*c.* 1265-1308), Scottish scholastic theologian and Franciscan priest.

3. In both the 1899 text and the 1966 reprint, Carden Tyrrell's lines are missing.

TYRRELL: (*Starting*) Well, what is the matter?

GRACE: (*Holding out a paper*) A dreadful-looking man has just handed me this.

TYRRELL: Let me see. (*Takes paper*) Ah —

GRACE: I have so often asked you for money to pay this person.

TYRRELL: I am very sorry. I had nothing to give you.

GRACE: Alas, you always had plenty to squander on that mountain.

TYRRELL: That was Government money, and it could not honestly be expended except on the object for which it was advanced.

GRACE: I am afraid I must have some of it now. I cannot be left in this condition.

TYRRELL: Indeed you shall not have one penny of it.

GRACE: What — you mean to leave me under the stigma of such an insult?

TYRRELL: (*Impatiently*) There is no particular urgency. I will see if I can possibly meet this writ by some money of my own. (*With a painfully distracted look*) Oh, this worry, this worry —

Exit by door at right.

GRACE: Well, Mr. Ussher, I hope you are satisfied now. We are ruined; and my husband is becoming stranger in his behaviour every day. But for you, he might have been cured by this, and the estate in a very different condition.

USSHER: I have nothing, Mrs. Tyrrell, to reproach myself with. I did all for the best.

GRACE: Yes, of course. That is the only satisfaction one ever receives for injuries done through gratuitous interference.

USSHER: Nothing has since happened to convict me of having acted wrongly. I have done you no injury.

GRACE: No injury? Well!

USSHER: You cannot lay to my account this quarrel with the tenants which is the cause of your present difficulties. Goodness knows I have done my best to mend it.

GRACE: (*Impatiently*) Oh, that is only a temporary difficulty. But the estate will be ruined for ever by the great debt from which we should have saved it, if you had not interfered. (*Pause*) Yes — I see how it all will be. The child and I will be driven out, ruined, to battle with the world.

USSHER: Oh, don't think of such a thing, Mrs. Tyrrell. It can never come to that.

GRACE: (*Sadly*) Ah, yes, you destroyed my last chance of saving our home. I might have kept it lovingly for Kit until he grew to be a man; but now I see it must go from us. I shall have to bid everything farewell — the familiar rooms — the garden where I found an occupation for my life — even those common useless things about the house I have been accustomed to look at for years. Oh, you don't know what it is — this parting from those everyday things of one's life.

USSHER: Yes, yes — indeed I do — and from my heart I feel for you.

GRACE: And yet you could have acted as you have.

USSHER: I acted only in good faith. Heaven knows that is the truth.

GRACE: The injury remains still the same.

USSHER: (*With strong emotions*) If it is I who have injured you, Mrs. Tyrrell, you must allow me to make amends.

GRACE: Alas, what amends are possible?

USSHER: Who can tell? I promise you, at least, you shall never, never bid farewell to your home.

GRACE: (*In a trembling voice*) If only what you say might come true.

LADY SHRULE, LORD SHRULE: *and* CARDEN TYRRELL *enter by door at right.*

LORD SHRULE: Carden, I believe the butler was actually going to say 'not at home' to us, if I had not caught sight of you in the hall. Ha, ha.

LADY SHRULE: What a shame, Mr. Tyrrell, to try and prevent me from seeing Grace. How do you do, Grace dear? (*Giving her hand apathetically to* USSHER) How do you do?

LORD SHRULE: (*Shakes hands with* GRACE *and* USSHER) We should have been so disappointed.

TYRRELL: I assure you, Lord Shrule, my attempt to escape is purely an imagination on your part.

LORD SHRULE: Oh, you sly fellow, you think I do not know. You are just like your father when people used to call — although he would never run away from me, I can tell you.

TYRRELL: No more did I. I was only surprised to see you; that was all. When I heard the bell I thought it was Miles come from Dublin. I am anxiously expecting him now at any moment.

LORD SHRULE: Ah, it will be a pleasure to see Miles again. We have all heard of his University triumphs. How proud your poor father would have been.

TYRRELL: Yes, and now delighted to share his satisfaction with you.

LORD SHRULE: Poor Marmaduke — we were such friends. At our very last interview he asked me to keep you and your brother always in mind after he was gone. So I have always felt somewhat like a father towards you both, you know, and with a father's privilege occasionally have given advice.

GRACE: Yes, Lord Shrule, and how I wish your good advice occasionally had been followed.

LORD SHRULE: Ah, we cannot help that, Mrs. Tyrrell. Nothing will ever teach the young save bitter experience.

GRACE: I am sure there has been enough bitter experience; but it seems to have taught nothing at all.

LORD SHRULE: Well, well, I hope it won't be so. Eh, Carden?

TYRRELL: I do not see how my experience can teach me to act differently from my present way of acting. (*Aside to* USSHER) Miles ought to have arrived by this. Oh, I am nearly dead with anxiety to know the news he will bring.

USSHER: (*Aside to* TYRRELL) I hope there will be good news.

LORD SHRULE: Never mind, Mrs. Tyrrell. Carden will come by degrees to see his mistakes.

GRACE: I fear we are now in so bad a way that it does not much matter whether he sees them or not.

LADY SHRULE: No — really, Grace, you do not say so?

GRACE: Oh, Lilian, we are ruined.

LORD SHRULE: Come, come, I am sure it cannot be as bad as that.

TYRRELL: Goodness me, of course, Lord Shrule. On the contrary, in the near future we shall make a fortune.

GRACE: I say we are ruined, utterly, irretrievably.

TYRRELL: No — no —

USSHER: What noise is that? (*Listens, then opens doors at right*) Why, Miles has arrived.

TYRRELL: Miles — oh!

USSHER: There, Carden, for goodness sake be calm.

Enter MILES TYRRELL *by door at right.*

MILES: Carden. (*He grasps his brother by the hand, then greets all the rest*)

TYRRELL: What news, Miles? Will he wait?

MILES: (*Turning away dejectedly*) I did my best, Carden. There is no hope, I fear.

GRACE: No hope? What is this new misfortune? Who won't wait?

MILES: The chief mortgagee.

GRACE: Is he going to foreclose?

MILES: He says so.

LORD SHRULE: Ha — this is a most serious matter.

TYRRELL: But Miles, didn't you explain to him all about the heather field?

MILES: Yes.

TYRRELL: Didn't you assure him that it would soon bring in what would more than pay his interest?

MILES: Indeed I did, Carden.

TYRRELL: Well?

MILES: Well, that only seemed to make him impatient with me. But I used every argument I could think of, and pleaded with him for nearly an hour in his office, until at last he had to get rid of me almost brutally.

TYRRELL: (*With a look of humiliation and despair*) Oh, ruin! ruin!

USSHER: No, no, Carden — it is not yet that. We must see how we can help you through this difficulty.

TYRRELL: (*Quietly*) With all your goodwill, Barry, what can you do now?

USSHER: Who knows? Just keep quiet, and do not distress yourself. Leave it all to me.

TYRRELL: (*Almost staggering*) Yes — such a severe blow — this. It has quite upset me. I am sure you will all excuse me. You, Barry, will see what you can do, won't you? Yes — (*he goes to door at right*)

USSHER: Carden, I hope all will come well.

LORD SHRULE: How much of the property does this mortgage cover?

GRACE: Oh, pretty nearly all, I should think.

TYRRELL: (*Suddenly turning*) All, do you say? No — not all. This vulture cannot touch the heather field! My hope — it is my only hope now, and it will save me in the end. Ha, ha! these wise ones! They did not think the barren mountain of those days worth naming in their deed. But now that mountain is a great green field worth more than all they can seize (*with a strange intensity*) and it is mine — all mine!

Exits by door at right.

LORD SHRULE: (*Throwing up his hands*) Oh dear, oh dear, what infatuation!

GRACE: Yes, indeed, it has caused us all to be cast adrift in the world. Oh, what is to become of me — what is to become of me? (*She sobs in her handkerchief*)

LADY SHRULE: Grace, you must not lose heart.

GRACE: Ah, the final misfortune has come.

LADY SHRULE: We shall try and help you, dear. There.

USSHER: Yes, we must lose no time now to see what can be done for Carden.

LADY SHRULE: You should indeed bestir yourself, Mr. Ussher, and save him; for we have you to thank that he was left in a position to ruin himself.

USSHER: And have not you too, Lady Shrule, to thank yourself for the same thing?

LADY SHRULE: I? How so, pray?

USSHER: Why did you and Lord Shrule disappear so suddenly on that day the doctors were here? Your advocacy would doubtless have made them heedless of my objections.

LADY SHRULE: Ah, why indeed? You know, Shrule, I wanted you to —

LORD SHRULE: Well, well, I could not bear to act in such a way to the son of my old friend. But I suppose in my weakness I did wrong.

USSHER: No, Lord Shrule, you did right. You never could be suspected by any one of doing otherwise.

LORD SHRULE: I hope not, Ussher! Still, I am inclined to think it might have been wiser then to have taken some definite step.

LADY SHRULE: I should think so. Just see what has happened since.

GRACE: Nothing less than the ruin of a helpless woman and her child.

LADY SHRULE: You have, indeed, incurred a nice responsibility, Mr. Ussher.

GRACE: (*To* USSHER) What — what right had you to do my child and me this wrong?

USSHER: I only prevented what I thought a grievous wrong from being done to my friend.

GRACE: It was no wrong — it was for his good — for all our good. In your heart you must know I was right.

USSHER: I have often said, Mrs. Tyrrell, I know nothing of the sort.

LADY SHRULE: Still, you must admit that his actions since more than justify Mrs. Tyrrell in the course she adopted.

LORD SHRULE: Alas, I fear that is the case.

USSHER: I admit he is very wilful and extravagant, but no more. I cannot discover any mental infirmity. His mind has a perfect grasp of ideas.

GRACE: Don't talk of ideas. I have heard enough about them since I was married to give me a horror of them for the rest of my life.

LADY SHRULE: They have certainly caused the wreck of this household.

LORD SHRULE: Oh, I hope not. We must not be too pessimistic. Who can tell? Perhaps the heather field may turn out a success after all!

GRACE: (*With contempt*) The heather field.

LORD SHRULE: If it were to, there can be no doubt but that all would be saved. I wonder how it is going on. Have you been there lately, Mrs. Tyrrell?

GRACE: Of course not, Lord Shrule. The very thought of the place fills me with despair.

MILES: That is a pity, Grace — a great pity, when so much depends upon the success of the heather field.

GRACE: No good can ever come of that abominable work.

MILES: You must not speak such words; no luck can come from such words.

GRACE: I cannot help it.

MILES: Oh, I know you have much to endure, but I cannot remain here and listen to such denunciation of what my brother holds nearest to his heart.

GRACE: I have only said the truth.

MILES: You cannot be certain of this truth. It is not right to speak such words.

Exit by door at right.

LADY SHRULE: My poor Grace.

GRACE: Oh, Lilian.

LADY SHRULE: These troubles are driving you to distraction. You had better leave this place for a while. Will you not come and stay with us?

LORD SHRULE: Oh, yes, won't you stay with us, Mrs. Tyrrell? You might be saved much annoyance and worry.

GRACE: You are both so kind. I shall like to for a little while, certainly. This house has become unbearable of late with debts and difficulties on every side.

LADY SHRULE: Oh, dear, how terrible. You had better leave at once, Grace. Perhaps you might have some of your things seized. Anyhow, bring with you those that you most value. We will take care of them.

GRACE: Thanks, Lilian.

LORD SHRULE: Well then, that is agreed, Mrs. Tyrrell. I am so glad we may be of use to you.

LADY SHRULE: We shall expect you this evening, dear.

GRACE: Yes, I shall get ready at once.

LADY SHRULE: And it is time for us to return home. Goodbye, Mr. Ussher.

USSHER: Goodbye, Lady Shrule.

LORD SHRULE: Goodbye.

Exeunt LADY SHRULE, GRACE TYRRELL *and* LORD SHRULE *by door at right.*

USSHER: (*Gloomily*) Heaven help her — help them all. What is to be done? Stay — I might go security. I would do anything to help them. But would it really be of use? Other difficulties must follow these, so that my whole fortune would not suffice. I will think the matter over. I wonder how the heather field is going on. No one seems to have been there lately.

KIT TYRRELL, *carrying a small white bundle, enters through door at back.*

KIT: (*Placing the bundle on sofa*) Barry, the pony is splendid. I had such galloping over the heather field.

USSHER: Well, did you bring back any flowers?

KIT: They have not yet come out. All I could find there were these little buds in my handkerchief. (*Unties the bundle*) Look.

USSHER: (*With a start*) What — buds of heather? Has your father seen these, Kit?

KIT: Yes, I told him I found them growing all over the heather field.

USSHER: You did, boy; and what did he say?

KIT: Nothing for a while. But he looked — he looked — well, I have never seen him look like that before.

USSHER: Ha. And then?

KIT: Oh, then he seemed to forget all about it. He became so kind, and oh, Barry, what do you think, he called me his 'little brother Miles'. So I am really his brother, he says, after all —

MILES TYRRELL, *in haste and violent trepidation, enters through door at back.*

MILES: Barry, for pity's sake. (*Sees* KIT *and suddenly checks himself, then brings* USSHER *over to fireplace*) Barry, something dreadful has come over Carden. He does not know me.

USSHER: (*In a trembling voice, as he gazes fixedly before him*) The vengeance of the heather field!

MILES: Oh! for pity's sake, come to him. Come to him —

USSHER: Where is he?

MILES: Wandering helpless about the garden. Oh, heavens, what shall we do?

USSHER: (*With suppressed terror*) Let us find him. (*He turns to go*)

CARDEN TYRRELL *appears outside doorway at back. He has a strange, collected look.*

USSHER: (*Starting*) Carden!

TYRRELL: (*Coming in*) Well, Barry? Why, what has happened to you since yesterday? My goodness, you look at least ten years older. (*Glancing at* MILES) Who is that? He was annoying me about something just now in the fuchsia walk.

MILES: Oh, I cannot stand this torture. Carden, dear Carden, look at me —

TYRRELL: (*Retreats like a frightened animal towards* USSHER, *keeping always his eyes fixed on* MILES) Barry, what is the matter with him? Don't leave me alone with him, Barry. Get him to go away.

USSHER: You need not fear him, Carden. (*He signs to* MILES, *who retires with an inconsolable expression and stands by fireplace*)

TYRRELL: (*After a moment, mysteriously*) Barry—

USSHER: Yes, Carden.

TYRRELL: (*Looking cautiously around*) You remember our conversation yesterday.

USSHER: (*Puzzled*) Yesterday? I did not see you yesterday.

TYRRELL: (*With impatience*) We did not walk together on the cliff yesterday, when you advised me not to marry Grace Desmond? What do you mean?

USSHER: (*Suddenly recollecting*) Oh, I remember, I remember. (*Then in a trembling voice*) But Carden — Carden, that was ten years ago. Don't you know that you are now married to her?

TYRRELL: (*With a surprised, baffled look*) I am?

USSHER: (*Very gently*) Yes, indeed.

TYRRELL: (*His expression for a moment grows vaguely painful, then gradually passes into one of vacant calm. After a short pause*) Barry, you are quite right.

USSHER: (*Joyfully*) I knew you would understand me, Carden.

TYRRELL: Yes, I will take your advice. I will not ask her to be my wife.

USSHER: (*With cruel disappointment*) Hopeless — I see it is hopeless now.

TYRRELL: (*Unheeding*) I do not care for her any more. I know now I never cared for her.

USSHER: Do you? Why?

TYRRELL: (*Distressfully*) Oh, I have had such a dreadful dream.

USSHER: A dream?

TYRRELL: I must tell it to you. Let me see, what was it? No — I cannot remember — no — it has gone completely from me before the beauty of the morning. (*Looks at back and stretches out his arms*) Oh, is not this Spring morning divine?

USSHER: But, Carden, can you not see that it is evening?

TYRRELL: Ah, I must have been a long time asleep — a long, long time. Yet it looks like the morning. Yes, it seems as if it would always be morning now for me.

USSHER: (*With interest*) Indeed, is that so?

TYRRELL: Yes — its genius somehow is always about me.

USSHER: And what do you call this genius of the morning?

TYRRELL: (*With a strange ecstasy*) Joy! Joy!

USSHER: (*After looking at him for a while in wonder*) Then, are you happy, Carden?

TYRRELL: Oh, yes, so happy. Why not?

USSHER: (*With hesitation*) You have no troubles, have you?

TYRRELL: Troubles? No, except sometimes in dreams. But oh, when I awake to the joy of this great beauty —

USSHER: Yet — great beauty — is it not for ever far away?

TYRRELL: No — it is forever by me. (*Then as if suddenly recollecting*) Ah, now I can tell you my dreadful dream. (*Slowly*) I dreamed that my lot was to wander through common luxurious life, seeing now and then in glimpses that beauty, but so far away! And when the vision left me — ah, you do not know the anguish I felt in looking again at my lot in life.

USSHER: And this was only a dream?

TYRRELL: (*Fervently*) Thank heaven only a dream! (*He goes to the sofa, where* KIT *all this time has been playing with the heather buds*)

USSHER: (*Meditatively sorrowful*) And are beauty and happiness mere illusions after all? (*Goes towards* MILES) I am dazed in the presence of this awful misfortune.

MILES: (*Approaching* USSHER) Oh, the misery of seeing him like this. He thinks he is living in the old days.

USSHER: It has come upon him again — that eerie ethereal youth I remember so well.

MILES: And for which he would yearn with such fond regret. But Grace and the child. Oh, what is to become of them? I fear their ruin is now certain and complete.

USSHER: (*As if suddenly awakened*) Not so. It may be possible to save them now that there is no danger of further expenditure. And I will save them. I will be security for the payment of all their debts. I will save the estate, if it costs me every penny I have in the world.

MILES: (*Grasping* USSHER *by the hand*) Oh, Barry, this is good of you.

They go towards the fireplace in earnest discourse.

TYRRELL: (*Placing a heather wreath on* KIT'S *head*) There — you are like a young field-faun now.

KIT: What sort of thing is that?

TYRRELL: Why, one of the field-fairies fresh and clean as those soft heather-shoots around your hair —

KIT: (*Delighted*) What — the fairies that live in green hillocks, and dance by the river bank, in the valley over there? Oh, tell me of them again.

TYRELL: Yes, beautiful child-fairies that play with the water nymphs — those sirens, you know, who sing in the wistful depths of the stream. (*With a sudden transport*) Oh, we must go to Lorlei as last year, where the river is lit with their gold. (*Pointing out at back*) See, even now the sky is darkening as in that storm scene of the old legend I told you on the Rhine. See, the rain across a saffron sun trembles like gold harp strings, through the purple Irish Spring!

GRACE TYRRELL *enters by door at right, dressed for going out, with her face thinly veiled and looking altogether younger and more handsome.*

GRACE: (*To* TYRRELL) I am just starting to visit the Shrules for some days.

TYRRELL: (*Turns, surprised*) Miss Desmond — Oh — (*with emotion and signs of struggle*) Oh, where is that beauty now — that music of the morning? (*Suddenly arrested*) Such strange solemn harmonies. (*Listens*) The voices — yes, they are filling the house — those white-stoled children of the morning. (*His eyes after a moment wander slowly to the doorway at back*) Oh, the rainbow! (*To* KIT) Come quick, see the lovely rainbow! (*They go to watch it hand in hand*) Oh, mystic highway of man's speechless longings! My heart goes forth upon the rainbow to that horizon of joy! (*With a fearful exaltation*) The voices — I hear them now triumphant in a silver glory of song!

GRACE: (*Looking bewildered from* MILES *to* USSHER) What — what is all this?

USSHER: Ah, your fears have come true, Mrs. Tyrrell. You have not heard —

GRACE: No. What has happened? For heaven's sake speak.

USSHER: The wild heather has broken out again in the heather field.

Curtain

W. B. YEATS

(1865-1939)

CATHLEEN NI HOULIHAN (1902)

[Writing in the *United Irishman* newspaper in 1902, Yeats said of this play: 'My subject is Ireland and its struggle for independence. The scene is laid in the West of Ireland at the time of the French landing. I have described a household preparing for the wedding of the son of the house.... Into this household comes Cathleen ni Houlihan herself, and the bridegroom leaves his bride, and all the hopes come to nothing. It is the perpetual struggle of the cause of Ireland and every other ideal cause against private hopes and dreams, against all that we mean when we say the world.' Yeats was always aware of the political impact and dimension of the play. In *Last Poems* (1936-39) he returns to it to ask the famous question:

Did that play of mine send out
Certain men the English shot?
('The Man and the Echo')

Certainly, at its first performance by the Irish National Dramatic Company, it would have been difficult to ignore the political aspects of the play's appeal. Maud Gonne played the part of Cathleen. She made it as regal and tragic as possible. Further, the play was more appealing because Yeats had managed to 'get down out of that high window of dramatic verse', as he put it. It was popular with the Dublin audiences. Yeats called it 'the first play of our Irish School of folk-drama', although he went on to wonder if the success of that school arose out of opinion or of a naive ignorance. This query is not accidental. It is at the heart of Yeats's questioning of the relationship between art and politics, between opinion and imagination, between the involvement in this world and the dedication of oneself to another world, to a spiritual principle.

The play was first performed by the Irish National Dramatic Company at St Teresa's Hall, Clarendon Street, Dublin on 2 April 1902.]

PERSONS IN THE PLAY

PETER GILLANE
MICHAEL GILLANE, *his son, going to be married*
PATRICK GILLANE, *a lad of twelve, Michael's brother*
BRIDGET GILLANE, *Peter's wife*
DELIA CAHEL, *engaged to Michael*
THE POOR OLD WOMAN
NEIGHBOURS

Interior of a cottage close to Killala, in 1798.[1] BRIDGET *is standing at a table undoing a parcel.* PETER *is sitting at one side of the fire,* PATRICK *at the other.*

PETER: What is that sound I hear?

PATRICK: I don't hear anything. (*He listens*) I hear it now. It's like cheering. (*He goes to the window and looks out*) I wonder what they are cheering about. I don't see anybody.

PETER: It might be a hurling.[2]

PATRICK: There's no hurling today. It must be down in the town the cheering is.

BRIDGET: I suppose the boys must be having some sport of their own. Come over here, Peter, and look at Michael's wedding clothes.

PETER: (*Shifts his chair to table*) Those are grand clothes, indeed.

BRIDGET: You hadn't clothes like that when you married me, and no coat to put on of a Sunday more than any other day.

1. In 1798, a French army landed at Killala in County Mayo and was joined by a large band of unarmed peasants. After an initial victory, the force was defeated.
2. Hurling, an ancient Irish game, faintly resembling hockey, was encouraged in its modern form by the Gaelic Athletic Association, founded in 1884.

PETER: That is true, indeed. We never thought a son of our own would be wearing a suit of that sort for his wedding, or have so good a place to bring a wife to.

PATRICK: (*Who is still at the window*) There's an old woman coming down the road. I don't know is it here she is coming.

BRIDGET: It will be a neighbour coming to hear about Michael's wedding. Can you see who it is?

PATRICK: I think it is a stranger, but she's not coming to the house. She's turned into the gap that goes down where Maurteen and his sons are shearing sheep. (*He turns towards* BRIDGET) Do you remember what Winny of the Cross-Roads was saying the other night about the strange woman that goes through the country whatever time there's war or trouble coming?

BRIDGET: Don't be bothering us about Winny's talk, but go and open the door for your brother. I hear him coming up the path.

PETER: I hope he has brought Delia's fortune with him safe, for fear the people might go back on the bargain and I after making it. Trouble enough I had making it.

PATRICK *opens the door and* MICHAEL *comes in.*

BRIDGET: What kept you, Michael? We were looking out for you this long time.

MICHAEL: I went round by the priest's house to bid him be ready to marry us tomorrow.

BRIDGET: Did he say anything?

MICHAEL: He said it was a very nice match, and that he was never better pleased to marry any two in his parish than myself and Delia Cahel.

PETER: Have you got the fortune, Michael?

MICHAEL: Here it is.

MICHAEL *puts bag on table and goes over and leans against chimney-jamb.* BRIDGET, *who has been all this time examining the clothes, pulling the seams and trying the lining of the pockets, etc., puts the clothes on the dresser.*

PETER: (*Getting up and taking the bag in his hand and turning out the money*) Yes, I made the bargain well for you, Michael. Old John Cahel would sooner have kept a share of this a while longer. 'Let me keep the half of it until the first boy is born,' says he. 'You will not,' says I. 'Whether there is or is not a boy, the whole hundred pounds must be in Michael's hands before he brings your daughter to the house.' The wife spoke to him then, and he gave in at the end.

BRIDGET: You seem well pleased to be handling the money, Peter.

PETER: Indeed, I wish I had had the luck to get a hundred pounds, or twenty pounds itself, with the wife I married.

BRIDGET: Well, if I didn't bring much I didn't get much. What had you the day I married you but a flock of hens and you feeding them, and a few lambs and you driving them to the market at Ballina?[3] (*She is vexed and bangs a jug on the dresser*) If I brought no fortune I worked it out in my bones, laying down the baby, Michael that is standing there now, on a stook[4] of straw, while I dug the potatoes, and never asking big dresses or anything but to be working.

PETER: That is true, indeed. (*He pats her arm*)

BRIDGET: Leave me alone now till I ready the house for the woman that is to come into it.

PETER: You are the best woman in Ireland, but money is good, too. (*He begins handling the money again and sits down*) I never thought to see so much money within my four walls. We can do great things now we have it. We can take the ten acres of land we have the chance of since Jamsie Dempsey died, and stock it. We will go to the fair at Ballina to buy the stock. Did Delia ask any of the money for her own use, Michael?

MICHAEL: She did not, indeed. She did not seem to take much notice of it, or to look at it at all.

BRIDGET: That's no wonder. Why would she look at it when she had yourself to look at, a fine, strong young man? It is proud she must be to get you; a good steady boy that will make use of the money, and not be running through it or spending it on drink like another.

PETER: It's likely Michael himself was not thinking much of the fortune either, but of what sort the girl was to look at.

MICHAEL: (*Coming over towards the table*) Well, you would like a nice comely girl to be beside you, and to go walking with you. The fortune only lasts for a while, but the woman will be there always.

PATRICK: (*Turning round from the window*) They are cheering again down in the town. Maybe they are landing horses from Enniscrone.[5] They do be cheering when the horses take the water well.

MICHAEL: There are no horses in it. Where

3. A town in Mayo.
4. A bundle of sheaves.
5. A town in County Sligo, not far from Killala.

would they be going and no fair at hand? Go down to the town, Patrick, and see what is going on.

PATRICK: (*Opens the door to go out, but stops for a moment on the threshold*) Will Delia remember, do you think, to bring the greyhound pup she promised me when she would be coming to the house?

MICHAEL: She will surely.

PATRICK *goes out, leaving the door open.*

PETER: It will be Patrick's turn next to be looking for a fortune, but he won't find it so easy to get it and he with no place of his own.

BRIDGET: I do be thinking sometimes, now things are going so well with us, and the Cahels such a good back[6] to us in the district, and Delia's own uncle a priest, we might be put in the way of making Patrick a priest some day, and he so good at his books.

PETER: Time enough, time enough. You have always your head full of plans, Bridget.

BRIDGET: We will be well able to give him learning, and not to send him tramping the country like a poor scholar that lives on charity.

MICHAEL: They're not done cheering yet. (*He goes over to the door and stands there for a moment, putting up his hand to shade his eyes*)

BRIDGET: Do you see anything?

MICHAEL: I see an old woman coming up the path.

BRIDGET: Who is it, I wonder? It must be the strange woman Patrick saw a while ago.

MICHAEL: I don't think it's one of the neighbours anyway, but she has her cloak over her face.

BRIDGET: It might be some poor woman heard we were making ready for the wedding and came to look for her share.

PETER: I may as well put the money out of sight. There is no use leaving it out for every stranger to look at. (*He goes over to a large box in the corner, opens it and puts the bag in and fumbles at the lock*)

MICHAEL: There she is, father! (*An* OLD WOMAN *passes the window slowly. She looks at* MICHAEL *as she passes*) I'd sooner a stranger not to come to the house the night before my wedding.

BRIDGET: Open the door, Michael; don't keep the poor woman waiting.

The OLD WOMAN *comes in.* MICHAEL *stands aside to make way for her.*

OLD WOMAN: God save all here!

PETER: God save you kindly!

OLD WOMAN: You have good shelter here.

PETER: You are welcome to whatever shelter we have.

BRIDGET: Sit down there by the fire and welcome.

OLD WOMAN: (*Warming her hands*) There is a hard wind outside.

MICHAEL *watches her curiously from the door.* PETER *comes over to the table.*

PETER: Have you travelled far today?

OLD WOMAN: I have travelled far, very far; there are few have travelled so far as myself, and there's many a one that doesn't make me welcome. There was one that had strong sons I thought were friends of mine, but they were shearing their sheep, and they wouldn't listen to me.

PETER: It's a pity indeed for any person to have no place of their own.

OLD WOMAN: That's true for you indeed, and it's long I'm on the roads since I first went wandering.

BRIDGET: It is a wonder you are not worn out with so much wandering.

OLD WOMAN: Sometimes my feet are tired and my hands are quiet, but there is no quiet in my heart. When the people see me quiet, they think old age has come on me and that all the stir has gone out of me. But when the trouble is on me I must be talking to my friends.

BRIDGET: What was it put you wandering?

OLD WOMAN: Too many strangers in the house.[7]

BRIDGET: Indeed you look as if you'd had your share of trouble.

OLD WOMAN: I have had trouble indeed.

BRIDGET: What was it put the trouble on you?

OLD WOMAN: My land that was taken from me.[8]

PETER: Was it much land they took from you?

OLD WOMAN: My four beautiful green fields.[9]

PETER: (*Aside to* BRIDGET) Do you think could she be the widow Casey that was put out of her holding at Kilglass[10] a while ago?

BRIDGET: She is not. I saw the widow Casey one time at the market in Ballina, a stout fresh woman.

PETER: (*To* OLD WOMAN) Did you hear a noise of cheering, and you coming up the hill?

6. providing good back, support.

7. i.e. Too many English and Scottish invaders in Ireland.

8. A reference to the seventeenth-century plantations of Ireland by English and Scottish settlers.

9. The four provinces of Ireland: Ulster, Leinster, Munster and Connacht.

10. A village near Killala.

OLD WOMAN: I thought I heard the noise I used to hear when my friends came to visit me. (*She begins singing half to herself*)

I will go cry with the woman,
For yellow-haired Donough is dead,
With a hempen rope for a neckcloth,
And a white cloth on his head, —

MICHAEL: (*Coming from the door*) What is it that you are singing, ma'am?

OLD WOMAN: Singing I am about a man I knew one time, yellow-haired Donough that was hanged in Galway. (*She goes on singing, much louder*)

I am come to cry with you, woman,
My hair is unwound and unbound;
I remember him ploughing his field,
Turning up the red side of the ground,
And building his barn on the hill
With the good mortared stone;
O! we'd have pulled down the gallows
Had it happened in Enniscrone![11]

MICHAEL: What was it brought him to his death?

OLD WOMAN: He died for love of me: many a man has died for love of me.

PETER: (*Aside to* BRIDGET) Her trouble has put her wits astray.

MICHAEL: Is it long since that song was made? Is it long since he got his death?

OLD WOMAN: Not long, not long. But there were others that died for love of me a long time ago.

MICHAEL: Were they neighbours of your own, ma'am?

OLD WOMAN: Come here beside me and I'll tell you about them. (MICHAEL *sits down beside her on the hearth*) There was a red man of the O'Donnells from the north, and a man of the O'Sullivans from the south, and there was one Brian that lost his life at Clontarf by the sea,[12] and there were a great many in the west, some that died hundreds of years ago, and there are some that will die tomorrow.

MICHAEL: Is it in the west that men will die tomorrow?

OLD WOMAN: Come nearer, nearer to me.

11. The song is derived from *Donnchadh Bán* (*Fair-Haired Donough*), perhaps composed by Antoine Raftery (*c.* 1784-1835), the blind poet of Mayo, to whom Yeats refers several times in his poetry.

12. Red Hugh O'Donnell (1571-1602), a leader of the Irish against the Elizabethan invasions. Donal O'Sullivan Beare (1560-1618) also fought the English forces, even after the battle of Kinsale (1601) in which O'Donnell was defeated. Brian Boru, high king of Ireland, died at the battle of Clontarf in 1014, in which the Danes were defeated. All three are tragic, as well as heroic, figures.

BRIDGET: Is she right, do you think? Or is she a woman from beyond the world?

PETER: She doesn't know well what she's talking about, with the want and the trouble she has gone through.

BRIDGET: The poor thing, we should treat her well.

PETER: Give her a drink of milk and a bit of the oaten cake.

BRIDGET: Maybe we should give her something along with that, to bring her on her way. A few pence or a shilling itself, and we with so much money in the house.

PETER: Indeed I'd not begrudge it to her if we had it to spare, but if we go running through what we have, we'll soon have to break the hundred pounds, and that would be a pity.

BRIDGET: Shame on you, Peter. Give her the shilling and your blessing with it, or our own luck will go from us.

PETER *goes to the box and takes out a shilling.*

BRIDGET: (*To the* OLD WOMAN) Will you have a drink of milk, ma'am?

OLD WOMAN: It is not food or drink that I want.

PETER: (*Offering the shilling*) Here is something for you.

OLD WOMAN: This is not what I want. It is not silver I want.

PETER: What is it you would be asking for?

OLD WOMAN: If any one would give me help he must give me himself, he must give me all.

PETER *goes over the table staring at the shilling in his hand in a bewildered way, and stands whispering to* BRIDGET.

MICHAEL: Have you no one to care you in your age, ma'am?

OLD WOMAN: I have not. With all the lovers that brought me their love I never set out the bed for any.

MICHAEL: Are you lonely going the roads, ma'am?

OLD WOMAN: I have my thoughts and I have my hopes.

MICHAEL: What hopes have you to hold to?

OLD WOMAN: The hope of getting my beautiful fields back again; the hope of putting the strangers out of my house.

MICHAEL: What way will you do that, ma'am?

OLD WOMAN: I have good friends that will help me. They are gathering to help me now. I am not afraid. If they are put down today they will get the upper hand tomorrow. (*She gets up*) I must be going to meet my friends. They are coming to help me and I must be there to welcome them. I must call the neighbours together to welcome them.

MICHAEL: I will go with you.

BRIDGET: It is not her friends you have to go and welcome, Michael; it is the girl coming into the house you have to welcome. You have plenty to do; it is food and drink you have to bring to the house. The woman that is coming home is not coming with empty hands; you would not have an empty house before her. (*To the* OLD WOMAN) Maybe you don't know, ma'am, that my son is going to be married tomorrow.

OLD WOMAN: It is not a man going to his marriage that I look to for help.

PETER: (*To* BRIDGET) Who is she, do you think, at all?

BRIDGET: You did not tell us your name yet, ma'am.

OLD WOMAN: Some call me the Poor Old Woman, and there are some that call me Cathleen, the daughter of Houlihan.[13]

PETER: I think I knew some one of that name, once. Who was it, I wonder? It must have been some one I knew when I was a boy. No, no; I remember, I heard it in a song.

OLD WOMAN: (*Who is standing in the doorway*) They are wondering that there were songs made for me; there have been many songs made for me. I heard one on the wind this morning.

(*Sings*)

Do not make a great keening[14]
When the graves have been dug tomorrow.
Do not call the white-scarfed riders[15]
To the burying that shall be tomorrow.
Do not spread food to call strangers
To the wakes that shall be tomorrow;
Do not give money for prayers
For the dead that shall die tomorrow....

They will have no need of prayers, they will have no need of prayers.

MICHAEL: I do not know what that song means, but tell me something I can do for you.

PETER: Come over to me, Michael.

MICHAEL: Hush, father, listen to her.

OLD WOMAN: It is a hard service they take that help me. Many that are red-cheeked now will be pale-cheeked; many that have been free to walk the hills and the bogs and the rushes will be sent to walk hard streets in far countries; many a good plan will be broken; many that have gathered money will not stay to spend it; many a child will be born and there will be no father at its christening to give it a name. They that have red cheeks will have pale cheeks for my sake, and for all that, they will think they are well paid. (*She goes out; her voice is heard outside singing*)

They shall be remembered for ever,
They shall be alive for ever,
They shall be speaking for ever,
The people shall hear them for ever.

BRIDGET: (*To* PETER) Look at him, Peter; he has the look of a man that has got the touch.[16] (*Raising her voice*) Look here, Michael, at the wedding clothes. Such grand clothes as these are! You have a right to fit them on now; it would be a pity tomorrow if they did not fit. The boys would be laughing at you. Take them, Michael, and go into the room and fit them on. (*She puts them on his arm*)

MICHAEL: What wedding are you talking of? What clothes will I be wearing tomorrow?

BRIDGET: These are the clothes you are going to wear when you marry Delia Cahel tomorrow.

MICHAEL: I had forgotten that. (*He looks at the clothes and turns towards the inner room, but stops at the sound of cheering outside*)

PETER: There is the shouting come to our own door. What is it has happened?

Neighbours come crowding in, PATRICK *and* DELIA *with them.*

PATRICK: There are ships in the Bay; the French are landing at Killala!

PETER *takes his pipe from his mouth and his hat off, and stands up. The clothes slip from* MICHAEL's *arm.*

DELIA: Michael! (*He takes no notice*) Michael! (*He turns towards her*) Why do you look at me like a stranger? (*She drops his arm*)

BRIDGET *goes over towards her.*

PATRICK: The boys are all hurrying down the hillside to join the French.

13. The Sean Bhean Bocht (The Poor Old Woman) and Cathleen Ní Houlihan (Cathleen, daughter of Houlihan) are traditional names for Ireland.
14. From the Irish *caoineadh* (wailing or keening), a traditional form of mourning at Irish wakes — gatherings in honour of the dead.
15. Possibly white-robed priests.
16. The touch or stroke was commonly believed to be inflicted by the fairies. It usually caused disfigurement, but was also associated with seduction from the human to the fairy world.

DELIA: Michael won't be going to join the French.

BRIDGET: (*To* PETER) Tell him not to go, Peter.

PETER: It's no use. He doesn't hear a word we're saying.

BRIDGET: Try and coax him over to the fire.

DELIA: Michael, Michael! You won't leave me! You won't join the French, and we going to be married! (*She puts her arms about him, he turns towards her as if about to yield*)

OLD WOMAN'S *voice outside:*

They shall be speaking for ever,
The people shall hear them for ever.

MICHAEL *breaks away from* DELIA, *stands for a second at the door, then rushes out, following the* OLD WOMAN'S *voice.* BRIDGET *takes* DELIA, *who is crying silently, into her arms.*

PETER: (*To* PATRICK, *laying a hand on his arm*) Did you see an old woman going down the path?

PATRICK: I did not, but I saw a young girl, and she had the walk of a queen.

ON BAILE'S STRAND (1904)

[The play was first performed by the Irish National Theatre Society on 27 December 1904 and then altered a good deal by Yeats for an April 1906 production at the Abbey Theatre. The later version is now the definitive text.

On Baile's Strand is one of the cycle of Cuchulain plays. The great hero is, as in the other plays dealing with his career, a victim of a fate that will not allow him to be complete. He is the legendary version of what Yeats called 'the unfinished man', a type both for himself and for Ireland, an example of the person or nation who must relive a painful history over and over until finally it becomes wholly significant. At that point, Cuchulain becomes, or will become, free of his fate.]

PERSONS IN THE PLAY

A FOOL
A BLIND MAN
CUCHULAIN, *King of Muirthemne*
CONCHUBAR, *High King of Uladh*
A YOUNG MAN, *son of Cuchulain*
KINGS AND SINGING WOMEN

A great hall at Dundealgan,[1] *not 'Cuchulain's great ancient house'*[2] *but an assembly-house nearer to the sea. A big door at the back, and through the door misty light as of sea-mist. There are many chairs and one long bench. One of these chairs, which is towards the front of the stage, is bigger than the others. Somewhere at the back there is a table with flagons of ale upon it and drinking-horns. There is a small door at one side of the hall.* A FOOL *and* BLIND MAN, *both ragged, and their features made grotesque and extravagant by masks, come in through the door at the back. The* BLIND MAN *leans upon a staff.*

FOOL: What a clever man you are though you are blind! There's nobody with two eyes in his head that is as clever as you are. Who but you could have thought that the henwife sleeps every day a little at noon? I would never be able to steal anything if you didn't tell me where to look for it. And what a good cook you are! You take the fowl out of my hands after I have stolen it and plucked it, and you put it into the big pot at the fire there, and I can go out and run races with the witches at the edge of the waves and get an appetite, and when I've got it, there's the hen waiting inside for me, done to the turn.

BLIND MAN: (*Who is feeling about with his stick*) Done to the turn.

FOOD: (*Putting his arm round* BLIND MAN'S *neck*) Come now, I'll have a leg and you'll have a leg, and we'll draw lots for the wish-bone. I'll be praising you, I'll be praising you while we're eating it, for your good plans and for your good cooking. There's nobody in the world like you, Blind Man. Come, come. Wait a minute. I shouldn't have closed the door. There are some that look for me, and I wouldn't like them not to find me. Don't tell it to anybody, Blind Man. There are some that follow me. Boann herself out of the river and Fand out of the deep sea.[3] Witches they are, and they come by in the wind, and they cry, 'Give a kiss, Fool, give a kiss', that's what they cry. That's wide enough. All the witches can come in now. I wouldn't have them beat at the door and say, 'Where is the Fool? Why has he put a lock on the door?' Maybe they'll hear

1. Modern Dundalk in County Louth.
2. Lady Gregory, *Cuchulain of Muirthemne* (1902), p. 24.
3. Boann, the river-goddess, after whom the river Boyne is named; Fand (or Fann), wife of Mannanan MacLir, God of the Sea. In one of the Cuchulain legends (*Serglige Con Culainn, The Wasting Sickness of Cú Chulainn*), he wins her love for a time before returning to his earthly wife, Emer.

the bubbling of the pot and come in and sit on the ground. But we won't give them any of the fowl. Let them go back to the sea, let them go back to the sea.

BLIND MAN: (*Feeling legs of big chair with his hands*) Ah! (*Then, in a louder voice as he feels the back of it*) Ah — ah —

FOOL: Why do you say 'Ah-ah'?

BLIND MAN: I know the big chair. It is today the High King Conchubar is coming. They have brought out his chair. He is going to be Cuchulain's master in earnest from this day out. It is that he's coming for.

FOOL: He must be a great man to be Cuchulain's master.

BLIND MAN: So he is. He is a great man. He is over all the rest of the kings of Ireland.

FOOL: Cuchulain's master! I thought Cuchulain could do anything he liked.

BLIND MAN: So he did, so he did. But he ran too wild, and Conchubar is coming today to put an oath upon him that will stop his rambling and make him as biddable as a house-dog and keep him always at his hand. He will sit in this chair and put the oath upon him.

FOOL: How will he do that?

BLIND MAN: You have no wits to understand such things. (*The* BLIND MAN *has got into the chair*) He will sit up in this chair and he'll say: 'Take the oath, Cuchulain. I bid you take the oath. Do as I tell you. What are your wits compared with mine, and what are your riches compared with mine? And what sons have you to pay your debts and to put a stone over you when you die? Take the oath, I tell you. Take a strong oath.'

FOOL: (*Crumpling himself up and whining*) I will not. I'll take no oath. I want my dinner.

BLIND MAN: Hush, hush! It is not done yet.

FOOL: You said it was done to a turn.

BLIND MAN: Did I, now? Well, it might be done, and not done. The wings might be white, but the legs might be red. The flesh might stick hard to the bones and not come away in the teeth. But, believe me, Fool, it will be well done before you put your teeth in it.

FOOL: My teeth are growing long with the hunger.

BLIND MAN: I'll tell you a story — the kings have storytellers while they are waiting for their dinner — I will tell you a story with a fight in it, a story with a champion in it, and a ship and a queen's son that has his mind set on killing somebody that you and I know.

FOOL: Who is that? Who is he coming to kill?

BLIND MAN: Wait, now, till you hear. When you were stealing the fowl, I was lying in a hole in the sand, and I heard three men coming with a shuffling sort of noise. They were wounded and groaning.

FOOL: Go on. Tell me about the fight.

BLIND MAN: There had been a fight, a great fight, a tremendous great fight. A young man had landed on the shore, the guardians of the shore had asked his name, and he had refused to tell it, and he had killed one, and the others had run away.

FOOL: That's enough. Come on now to the fowl. I wish it was bigger. I wish it was as big as a goose.

BLIND MAN: Hush! I haven't told you all. I know who that young man is. I heard the men who were running away say he had red hair, that he had come from Aoife's country,[4] that he was coming to kill Cuchulain.

FOOL: Nobody can do that.

(*To a tune*)

Cuchulain has killed kings,
Kings and sons of kings,
Dragons out of the water,
And witches out of the air,
Banachas and Bonachas[5] and people of the woods.

BLIND MAN: Hush! hush!

FOOL: (*Still singing*)

Witches that steal the milk,
Fomor[6] that steal the children,
Hags that have heads like hares,
Hares that have claws like witches,
All riding a-cock-horse

(*Spoken*)

Out of the very bottom of the bitter black North.

BLIND MAN: Hush, I say!

FOOL: Does Cuchulain know that he is coming to kill him?

4. Aoife is the Scottish warrior queen whom Cuchulain defeats in battle and by whom he has a son, Conlaech. Her country is the Hebrides.
5. Ugly goblins, white-faced and puck-faced respectively.
6. The Fomor or Fomhoire (literally 'under-demons'), a race of demonic beings who were engaged in epic struggles for control of the land of Ireland. They often are confused with the Tuatha De Danann (People of the Goddess Danu) who were themselves defeated by the Gaels, but who, because of their magical powers, were assigned underground to the lower half of Ireland, while the Gaels ruled the upper half. Each chief was assigned a *sidh* or fairy mound, the traditional dwellings of the fairy people, who are associated with the stealing of children and of corn and milk from the human or upper world.

BLIND MAN: How would he know that with his head in the clouds? He doesn't care for common fighting. Why would he put himself out, and nobody in it but that young man? Now if it were a white fawn that might turn into a queen before morning —

FOOL: Come to the fowl. I wish it was as big as a pig; a fowl with goose grease and pig's crackling.

BLIND MAN: No hurry, no hurry. I know whose son it is. I wouldn't tell anybody else, but I will tell you, — a secret is better to you than your dinner. You like being told secrets.

FOOL: Tell me the secret.

BLIND MAN: That young man is Aoife's son. I am sure it is Aoife's son, it flows in upon me that it is Aoife's son. You have often heard me talking of Aoife, the great woman-fighter Cuchulain got the mastery over in the North?

FOOL: I know, I know. She is one of those cross queens that live in hungry Scotland.

BLIND MAN: I am sure it is her son. I was in Aoife's country for a long time.

FOOL: That was before you were blinded for putting a curse upon the wind.

BLIND MAN: There was a boy in her house that had her own red colour on him, and everybody said he was to be brought up to kill Cuchulain, that she hated Cuchulain. She used to put a helmet on a pillarstone and call it Cuchulain and set him casting at it. There is a step outside — Cuchulain's step.

CUCHULAIN *passes by in the mist outside the big door.*

FOOL: Where is Cuchulain going?

BLIND MAN: He is going to meet Conchubar that has bidden him to take the oath.

FOOL: Ah, an oath, Blind Man. How can I remember so many things at once? Who is going to take an oath?

BLIND MAN: Cuchulain is going to take an oath to Conchubar who is High King.

FOOL: What a mix-up you make of everything, Blind Man! You were telling me one story, and now you are telling me another story.... How can I get the hang of it at the end if you mix everything at the beginning? Wait till I settle it out. There now, there's Cuchulain (*he points to one foot*) and there is the young man (*he points to the other foot*) that is coming to kill him, and Cuchulain doesn't know. But where's Conchubar? (*Takes bag from side*) That's Conchubar with all his riches — Cuchulain, young man, Conchubar. — And where's Aoife? (*Throws up cap*) There is Aoife, high up on the mountains in high hungry Scotland. Maybe it is not true after all. Maybe it was your own making up. It's many a time you cheated me before with your lies. Come to the cooking-pot, my stomach is pinched and rusty. Would you have it to be creaking like a gate?

BLIND MAN: I tell you it's true. And more than that is true. If you listen to what I say, you'll forget your stomach.

FOOL: I won't.

BLIND MAN: Listen. I know who the young man's father is, but I won't say. I would be afraid to say. Ah, Fool, you would forget everything if you could know who the young man's father is.

FOOL: Who is it? Tell me now quick, or I'll shake you. Come, out with it, or I'll shake you.

A murmur of voices in the distance.

BLIND MAN: Wait, wait. There's somebody coming.... It is Cuchulain is coming. He's coming back with the High King. Go and ask Cuchulain. He'll tell you. It's little you'll care about the cooking-pot when you have asked Cuchulain that ....

BLIND MAN *goes out by side door.*

FOOL: I'll ask him. Cuchulain will know. He was in Aoife's country. (*Goes up stage*) I'll ask him. (*Turns and goes down stage*) But, no, I won't ask him, I would be afraid. (*Going up again*) Yes, I will ask him. What harm in asking? The Blind Man said I was to ask him. (*Going down*) No, no. I'll not ask him. He might kill me. I have but killed hens and geese and pigs. He has killed kings. (*Goes up again almost to big door*) Who says I'm afraid? I'm not afraid. I'm no coward. I'll ask him. No, no, Cuchulain, I'm not going to ask you.

He has killed kings,
Kings and the sons of kings,
Dragons out of the water,
And witches out of the air,
Banachas and Bonachas and people of the woods.

FOOL *goes out by side door, the last words being heard outside.* CUCHULAIN *and* CONCHUBAR *enter through the big door at the back. While they are still outside,* CUCHULAIN'*s voice is heard raised in anger. He is a dark man, something over forty years of age.* CONCHUBAR *is much older and carries a long staff, elaborately carved or with an elaborate gold handle.*

CUCHULAIN:

Because I have killed men without your bidding
And have rewarded others at my own pleasure,

Because of half a score of trifling things,
You'd lay this oath upon me, and now — and now
You add another pebble to the heap,
And I must be your man, well-nigh your bondsman,
Because a youngster out of Aoife's country
Has found the shore ill-guarded.

CONCHUBAR: He came to land
While you were somewhere out of sight and hearing,
Hunting or dancing with your wild companions.

CUCHULAIN:
He can be driven out. I'll not be bound.
I'll dance or hunt, or quarrel or make love,
Wherever and whenever I've a mind to.
If time had not put water in your blood,
You never would have thought it.

CONCHUBAR: I would leave
A strong and settled country to my children.

CUCHULAIN:
And I must be obedient in all things;
Give up my will to yours; go where you please;
Come when you call; sit at the council-board
Among the unshapely bodies of old men;
I whose mere name has kept this country safe,
I that in early days have driven out
Maeve of Cruachan[7] and the northern pirates,
The hundred kings of Sorcha,[8] and the kings
Out of the Garden in the East of the World.
Must I, that held you on the throne when all
Had pulled you from it, swear obedience
As if I were some cattle-raising king?
Are my shins speckled with the heat of the fire,
Or have my hands no skill but to make figures
Upon the ashes with a stick? Am I
So slack and idle that I need a whip
Before I serve you?

CONCHUBAR: No, no whip, Cuchulain,
But every day my children come and say:
'This man is growing harder to endure.
How can we be at safety with this man
That nobody can buy or bid or bind?
We shall be at his mercy when you are gone;
He burns the earth as if he were a fire,
And time can never touch him.'

CUCHULAIN: And so the tale
Grows finer yet; and I am to obey
Whatever child you set upon the throne,
As if it were yourself!

CONCHUBAR: Most certainly.
I am High King, my son shall be High King;
And you for all the wildness of your blood,
And though your father came out of the sun,
Are but a little king and weigh but light
In anything that touches government,
If put into the balance with my children.

CUCHULAIN:
It's well that we should speak our minds out plainly,
For when we die we shall be spoken of
In many countries. We in our young days
Have seen the heavens like a burning cloud
Brooding upon the world, and being more
Than men can be now that cloud's lifted up,
We should be the more truthful. Conchubar,
I do not like your children — they have no pith,
No marrow in their bones, and will lie soft
Where you and I lie hard.

CONCHUBAR: You rail at them
Because you have no children of your own.

CUCHULAIN:
I think myself most lucky that I leave
No pallid ghost or mockery of a man
To drift and mutter in the corridors
Where I have laughed and sung.

CONCHUBAR: That is not true,
For all your boasting of the truth between us;
For there is no man having house and lands,
That have been in the one family, called
By that one family's name for centuries,
But is made miserable if he know
They are to pass into a stranger's keeping,
As yours will pass.

CUCHULAIN: The most of men feel that,
But you and I leave names upon the harp.

CONCHUBAR:
You play with arguments as lawyers do,
And put no heart in them. I know your thoughts,
For we have slept under the one cloak and drunk
From the one wine-cup. I know you to the bone,
I have heard you cry, aye, in your very sleep,
'I have no son', and with such bitterness
That I have gone upon my knees and prayed
That it might be amended.

CUCHULAIN: For you thought
That I should be as biddable as others

7. Maeve or Medbh, queen of Connacht, whose capital was Cruachan, modern Rathcrogan in County Roscommon. She was commander of the armies sent against Ulster, defeated by Cuchulain.
8. The pirates are the Norse invaders. Sorcha is a region of the Celtic otherworld.

Had I their reason for it; but that's not true;
For I would need a weightier argument
Than one that marred me in the copying,
As I have that clean hawk out of the air
That, as men say, begot this body of mine
Upon a mortal woman.

CONCHUBAR: Now as ever
You mock at every reasonable hope,
And would have nothing, or impossible things.
What eye has ever looked upon the child
Would satisfy a mind like that?

CUCHULAIN: I would leave
My house and name to none that would not face
Even myself in battle.

CONCHUBAR: Being swift of foot,
And making light of every common chance,
You should have overtaken on the hills
Some daughter of the air, or on the shore
A daughter of the Country-under-Wave.[9]

CUCHULAIN:I am not blasphemous.

CONCHUBAR: Yet you despise
Our queens, and would not call a child your own,
If one of them had borne him.

CUCHULAIN: I have not said it.

CONCHUBAR:
Ah! I remember I have heard you boast,
When the ale was in your blood, that there was one
In Scotland, where you had learnt the trade of war,
That had a stone-pale cheek and red-brown hair;
And that although you had loved other women,
You'd sooner that fierce woman of the camp
Bore you a son than any queen among them.

CUCHULAIN:
You call her a 'fierce woman of the camp',
For, having lived among the spinning-wheels,
You'd have no woman near that would not say,
'Ah! how wise!' 'What will you have for supper?'
'What shall I wear that I may please you, sir?'
And keep that humming through the day and night
For ever. A fierce woman of the camp!
But I am getting angry about nothing.
You have never seen her. Ah! Conchubar, had you seen her
With that high, laughing, turbulent head of hers
Thrown backward, and the bowstring at her ear,
Or sitting at the fire with those grave eyes
Full of good counsel as it were with wine,
Or when love ran through all the lineaments
Of her wild body — although she had no child,
None other had all beauty, queen or lover,
Or was so fitted to give birth to kings.

CONCHUBAR:
There's nothing I can say but drifts you farther
From the one weighty matter. That very woman —
For I know well that you are praising Aoife —
Now hates you and will leave no subtlety
Unknotted that might run into a noose
About your throat, no army in idleness
That might bring ruin on this land you serve.

CUCHULAIN:
No wonder in that, no wonder at all in that.
I never have known love but as a kiss
In the mid-battle, and a difficult truce
Of oil and water, candles and dark night,
Hillside and hollow, the hot-footed sun
And the cold, sliding, slippery-footed moon —
A brief forgiveness between opposites
That have been hatreds for three times the age
Of this long-'stablished ground.

CONCHUBAR: Listen to me.
Aoife makes war on us, and every day
Our enemies grow greater and beat the walls
More bitterly, and you within the walls
Are every day more turbulent; and yet,
When I would speak about these things, your fancy
Runs as it were a swallow on the wind.

Outside the door in the blue light of the sea-mist are many old and young KINGS; *amongst them are three* WOMEN, *two of whom carry a bowl of fire. The third, in what follows, puts from time to time fragrant herbs into the fire so that it flickers up into brighter flame.*

Look at the door and what men gather there —
Old counsellors that steer the land with me,
And younger kings, the dancers and harp-players
That follow in your tumults, and all these
Are held there by the one anxiety.
Will you be bound into obedience
And so make this land safe for them and theirs?
You are but half a king and I but half;
I need your might of hand and burning heart,
And you my wisdom.

CUCHULAIN (*Going near to door*):
Nestlings of a high nest,
Hawks that have followed me into the air
And looked upon the sun, we'll out of this
And sail upon the wind once more. This king

9. A name for the Celtic underworld.

Would have me take an oath to do his will,
And having listened to his tune from morning,
I will no more of it. Run to the stable
And set the horses to the chariot-pole,
And send a messenger to the harp-players.
We'll find a level place among the woods,
And dance awhile.

A YOUNG KING: Cuchulain, take the oath.
There is none here that would not have you take it.

CUCHULAIN:
You'd have me take it? Are you of one mind?

THE KINGS: All, all, all, all!

A YOUNG KING: Do what the High King bids you.

CONCHUBAR:
There is not one but dreads this turbulence
Now that they're settled men.

CUCHULAIN: Are you so changed,
Or have I grown more dangerous of late?
But that's not it. I understand it all.
It's you that have changed. You've wives and children now,
And for that reason cannot follow one
That lives like a bird's flight from tree to tree. —
It's time the years put water in my blood
And drowned the wildness of it, for all's changed,
But that unchanged. — I'll take what oath you will:
The moon, the sun, the water, light, or air,
I do not care how binding.

CONCHUBAR: On this fire
That has been lighted from your hearth and mine;
The older men shall be my witnesses,
The younger, yours. The holders of the fire
Shall purify the thresholds of the house
With waving fire, and shut the outer door,
According to the custom; and sing rhyme
That has come down from the old law-makers
To blow the witches out. Considering
That the wild will of man could be oath-bound,
But that a woman's could not, they bid us sing
Against the will of woman at its wildest
In the Shape-Changers that run upon the wind.
(CONCHUBAR *has gone on to his throne*)

THE WOMEN: (*They sing in a very low voice after the first few words so that the others all but drown their words*)
May this fire have driven out
The Shape-Changers that can put
Ruin on a great king's house
Until all be ruinous.
Names whereby a man has known
The threshold and the hearthstone,
Gather on the wind and drive
The women none can kiss and thrive,
For they are but whirling wind,
Out of memory and mind.
They would make a prince decay
With light images of clay
Planted in the running wave;
Or, for many shapes they have,
They would change them into hounds
Until he had died of his wounds,
Though the change were but a whim;
Or they'd hurl a spell at him,
That he follow with desire
Bodies that can never tire
Or grow kind, for they anoint
All their bodies, joint by joint,
With a miracle-working juice
That is made out of the grease
Of the ungoverned unicorn.
But the man is thrice forlorn,
Emptied, ruined, wracked, and lost,
That they follow, for at most
They will give him kiss for kiss
While they murmur, 'After this
Hatred may be sweet to the taste'.
Those wild hands that have embraced
All his body can but shove
At the burning wheel of love
Till the side of hate comes up.
Therefore in this ancient cup
May the sword-blades drink their fill
Of the home-brew there, until
They will have for masters none
But the threshold and hearthstone.

CUCHULAIN: (*Speaking, while they are singing*)
I'll take and keep this oath, and from this day
I shall be what you please, my chicks, my nestlings.
Yet I had thought you were of those that praised
Whatever life could make the pulse run quickly,
Even though it were brief, and that you held
That a free gift was better than a forced. —
But that's all over. — I will keep it, too;
I never gave a gift and took it again.
If the wild horse should break the chariot-pole,
It would be punished. Should that be in the oath?

Two of the WOMEN, *still singing, crouch in front of*

him holding the bowl over their heads. He spreads his hands over the flame.

I swear to be obedient in all things
To Conchubar, and to uphold his children.

CONCHUBAR:
We are one being, as these flames are one:
I give my wisdom, and I take your strength.
Now thrust the swords into the flame, and pray
That they may serve the threshold and the hearthstone
With faithful service.

The KINGS *kneel in a semicircle before the two* WOMEN *and* CUCHULAIN, *who thrusts his sword into the flame. They all put the points of their swords into the flame. The third* WOMAN *is at the back near the big door.*

CUCHULAIN: O pure, glittering ones
That should be more than wife or friend or mistress,
Give us the enduring will, the unquenchable hope,
The friendliness of the sword! —

The song grows louder, and the last words ring out clearly. There is a loud knocking at the door, and a cry of 'Open! open!'

CONCHUBAR:
Some king that has been loitering on the way.
Open the door, for I would have all know
That the oath's finished and Cuchulain bound,
And that the swords are drinking up the flame.

The door is opened by the third WOMAN, *and a* YOUNG MAN *with a drawn sword enters.*

YOUNG MAN: I am of Aoife's country.

The KINGS *rush towards him.* CUCHULAIN *throws himself between.*

CUCHULAIN: Put up your swords.
He is but one. Aoife is far away.

YOUNG MAN:
I have come alone into the midst of you
To weigh this sword against Cuchulain's sword.

CONCHUBAR:
And are you noble? for if of common seed,
You cannot weigh your sword against his sword
But in mixed battle.

YOUNG MAN: I am under bonds
To tell my name to no man; but it's noble.

CONCHUBAR:
But I would know your name and not your bonds.
You cannot speak in the Assembly House,
If you are not noble.

FIRST OLD KING: Answer the High King!

YOUNG MAN:
I will give no other proof than the hawk gives
That it's no sparrow! (*He is silent for a moment, then speaks to all*)
Yet look upon me, kings.
I, too, am of that ancient seed, and carry
The signs about this body and in these bones.

CUCHULAIN:
To have shown the hawk's grey feather is enough,
And you speak highly, too. Give me that helmet.
I'd thought they had grown weary sending champions.
That sword and belt will do. This fighting's welcome.
The High King there has promised me his wisdom;
But the hawk's sleepy till its well-beloved
Cries out amid the acorns, or it has seen
Its enemy like a speck upon the sun.
What's wisdom to the hawk, when that clear eye
Is burning nearer up in the high air?
(*Looks hard at* YOUNG MAN; *then comes down steps and grasps* YOUNG MAN *by shoulder*)
Hither into the light.
(*To* CONCHUBAR) The very tint
Of her that I was speaking of but now.
Not a pin's difference.
(*To* YOUNG MAN) You are from the North,
Where there are many that have that tint of hair —
Red-brown, the light red-brown. Come nearer, boy,
For I would have another look at you.
There's more likeness — a pale, a stone-pale cheek.
What brought you, boy? Have you no fear of death?

YOUNG MAN:
Whether I live or die is in the gods' hands.

CUCHULAIN:
That is all words, all words; a young man's talk.
I am their plough, their harrow, their very strength;
For he that's in the sun begot this body
Upon a mortal woman, and I have heard tell
It seemed as if he had outrun the moon
That he must follow always through waste heaven,
He loved so happily. He'll be but slow

To break a tree that was so sweetly planted.
Let's see that arm. I'll see it if I choose.
That arm had a good father and a good mother,
But it is not like this.

YOUNG MAN: You are mocking me;
You think I am not worthy to be fought.
But I'll not wrangle but with this talkative knife.

CUCHULAIN:
Put up your sword; I am not mocking you.
I'd have you for my friend, but if it's not
Because you have a hot heart and a cold eye,
I cannot tell the reason.
(*To* CONCHUBAR) He has got her fierceness,
And nobody is as fierce as those pale women.
But I will keep him with me, Conchubar,
That he may set my memory upon her
When the day's fading. — You will stop with us,
And we will hunt the deer and the wild bulls;
And, when we have grown weary, light our fires
Between the wood and water, or on some
mountain
Where the Shape-Changers of the morning
come.
The High King there would make a mock of me
Because I did not take a wife among them.
Why do you hang your head? It's a good life:
The head grows prouder in the light of the dawn,
And friendship thickens in the murmuring dark
Where the spare hazels meet the wool-white
foam.
But I can see there's no more need for words
And that you'll be my friend from this day out.

CONCHUBAR:
He has come hither not in his own name
But in Queen Aoife's, and has challenged us
In challenging the foremost man of us all.

CUCHULAIN: Well, well, what matter?

CONCHUBAR: You think it does not matter,
And that a fancy lighter than the air,
A whim of the moment, has more matter in it.
For, having none that shall reign after you,
You cannot think as I do, who would leave
A throne too high for insult.

CUCHULAIN: Let your children
Re-mortar their inheritance, as we have,
And put more muscle on. — I'll give you gifts,
But I'd have something too — that arm-ring, boy.
We'll have this quarrel out when you are older.

YOUNG MAN:
There is no man I'd sooner have my friend
Than you, whose name has gone about the world
As if it had been the wind; but Aoife'd say
I had turned coward.

CUCHULAIN: I will give you gifts
That Aoife'll know, and all her people know,
To have come from me. (*Showing cloak*)
My father gave me this.
He came to try me, rising up at dawn
Out of the cold dark of the rich sea.
He challenged me to battle, but before
My sword had touched his sword, told me his
name,
Gave me this cloak, and vanished. It was woven
By women of the Country-under-Wave
Out of the fleeces of the sea. O! tell her
I was afraid, or tell her what you will.
No; tell her that I heard a raven croak
On the north side of the house, and was afraid.

CONCHUBAR:
Some witch of the air has troubled Cuchulain's
mind.

CUCHULAIN:
No witchcraft. His head is like a woman's head
I had a fancy for.

CONCHUBAR: A witch of the air
Can make a leaf confound us with memories.
They run upon the wind and hurl the spells
That make us nothing, out of the invisible wind.
They have gone to school to learn the trick of it.

CUCHULAIN:
No, no — there's nothing out of common here;
The winds are innocent. — That arm-ring, boy.

A KING:
If I've your leave I'll take this challenge up.

ANOTHER KING:
No, give it me, High King, for this wild Aoife
Has carried off my slaves.

ANOTHER KING: No, give it me,
For she has harried me in house and herd.

ANOTHER KING: I claim this fight.

OTHER KINGS: (*Together*) And I! And I! And I!

CUCHULAIN:
Back! back! Put up your swords! Put up your
swords!
There's none alive that shall accept a challenge
I have refused. Laegaire, put up your sword!

YOUNG MAN:
No, let them come. If they've a mind for it,
I'll try it out with any two together.

CUCHULAIN:
That's spoken as I'd have spoken it at your age.
But you are in my house. Whatever man

Would fight with you shall fight it out with me.
They're dumb, they're dumb. How many of you would meet (*Draws sword*)
This mutterer, this old whistler, this sand-piper,
This edge that's greyer than the tide, this mouse
That's gnawing at the timbers of the world,
This, this — Boy, I would meet them all in arms
If I'd a son like you. He would avenge me
When I have withstood for the last time the men
Whose fathers, brothers, sons, and friends I have killed
Upholding Conchubar, when the four provinces
Have gathered with the ravens over them.
But I'd need no avenger. You and I
Would scatter them like water from a dish.

YOUNG MAN:
We'll stand by one another from this out.
Here is the ring.

CUCHULAIN: No, turn and turn about.
But my turn's first because I am the older.
(*Spreading out cloak*)
Nine queens out of the Country-under-Wave
Have woven it with the fleeces of the sea
And they were long embroidering at it. — Boy,
If I had fought my father, he'd have killed me,
As certainly as if I had a son
And fought with him, I should be deadly to him;
For the old fiery fountains are far off
And every day there is less heat o' the blood.

CONCHUBAR: (*In a loud voice*)
No more of this. I will not have this friendship.
Cuchulain is my man, and I forbid it.
He shall not go unfought, for I myself —

CUCHULAIN: I will not have it.

CONCHUBAR: You lay commands on me?

CUCHULAIN: (*Seizing* CONCHUBAR)
You shall not stir, High King. I'll hold you there.

CONCHUBAR: Witchcraft has maddened you.

THE KINGS: (*Shouting*) Yes, witchcraft! witchcraft!

FIRST OLD KING:
Some witch has worked upon your mind, Cuchulain.
The head of that young man seemed like a woman's
You'd had a fancy for. Then of a sudden
You laid your hands on the High King himself!

CUCHULAIN:
And laid my hands on the High King himself?

CONCHUBAR:
Some witch is floating in the air above us.

CUCHULAIN:
Yes, witchcraft! witchcraft! Witches of the air!
(*To* YOUNG MAN) Why did you? Who was it set you to this work?
Out, out! I say, for now it's sword on sword!

YOUNG MAN: But . . . but I did not.

CUCHULAIN: Out, I say, out, out!

YOUNG MAN *goes out followed by* CUCHULAIN. *The* KINGS *follow them out with confused cries, and words one can hardly hear because of the noise. Some cry,* 'Quicker, quicker!' 'Why are you so long at the door?' 'We'll be too late!' 'Have they begun to fight?' 'Can you see if they are fighting?' *and so on. Their voices drown each other. The three* WOMEN *are left alone.*

FIRST WOMAN: I have seen, I have seen!

SECOND WOMAN: What do you cry aloud?

FIRST WOMAN:
The Ever-living have shown me what's to come.

THIRD WOMAN: How? Where?

FIRST WOMAN: In the ashes of the bowl.

SECOND WOMAN:
While you were holding it between your hands?

THIRD WOMAN: Speak quickly!

FIRST WOMAN: I have seen Cuchulain's roof-tree
Leap into fire, and the walls split and blacken.

SECOND WOMAN: Cuchulain has gone out to die.

THIRD WOMAN: O! O!

SECOND WOMAN:
Who could have thought that one so great as he
Should meet his end at this unnoted sword!

FIRST WOMAN:
Life drifts between a fool and a blind man
To the end, and nobody can know his end.

SECOND WOMAN:
Come, look upon the quenching of this greatness.

The other two go to the door, but they stop for a moment upon the threshold and wail.

FIRST WOMAN:
No crying out, for there'll be need of cries
And rending of the hair when it's all finished.

The WOMEN *go out. There is the sound of clashing swords from time to time during what follows.*

Enter the FOOL, *dragging the* BLIND MAN.

FOOL: You have eaten it, you have eaten it! You have left me nothing but the bones. (*He throws* BLIND MAN *down by big chair*)

BLIND MAN: O, that I should have to endure such a plague! O, I ache all over! O, I am pulled to pieces! This is the way you pay me all the good I have done you.

FOOL: You have eaten it! You have told me lies. I might have known you had eaten it when I saw your slow, sleepy walk. Lie there till the kings come. O, I will tell Conchubar and Cuchulain and all the kings about you!

BLIND MAN: What would have happened to you but for me, and you without your wits? If I did not take care of you, what would you do for food and warmth?

FOOL: You take care of me? You stay safe, and send me into every kind of danger. You sent me down the cliff for gulls' eggs while you warmed your blind eyes in the sun; and then you ate all that were good for food. You left me the eggs that were neither egg nor bird. (BLIND MAN *tries to rise;* FOOL *makes him lie down again*) Keep quiet now, till I shut the door. There is some noise outside — a high vexing noise, so that I can't be listening to myself. (*Shuts the big door*) Why can't they be quiet? Why can't they be quiet? (BLIND MAN *tries to get away*) Ah! you would get away, would you? (*Follows* BLIND MAN *and brings him back*) Lie there! lie there! No, you won't get away! Lie there till the kings come. I'll tell them all about you. I will tell it all. How you sit warming yourself, when you have made me light a fire of sticks, while I sit blowing it with my mouth. Do you not always make me take the windy side of the bush when it blows, and the rainy side when it rains?

BLIND MAN: O, good Fool! listen to me. Think of the care I have taken of you. I have brought you to many a warm hearth, where there was a good welcome for you, but you would not stay there; you were always wandering about.

FOOL: The last time you brought me in, it was not I who wandered away, but you that got put out because you took the crubeen[10] out of the pot when nobody was looking. Keep quiet, now!

CUCHULAIN: (*Rushing in*) Witchcraft! There is no witchcraft on the earth, or among the witches of the air, that these hands cannot break.

FOOL: Listen to me, Cuchulain. I left him turning the fowl at the fire. He ate it all, though I had stolen it. He left me nothing but the feathers.

CUCHULAIN: Fill me a horn of ale!

BLIND MAN: I gave him what he likes best. You do not know how vain this Fool is. He likes nothing so well as a feather.

10. pig's trotter.

FOOL: He left me nothing but the bones and feathers. Nothing but the feathers, though I had stolen it.

CUCHULAIN: Give me that horn. Quarrels here, too! (*Drinks*) What is there between you two that is worth a quarrel? Out with it!

BLIND MAN: Where would he be but for me? I must be always thinking — thinking to get food for the two of us, and when we've got it, if the moon is at the full or the tide on the turn, he'll leave the rabbit in the snare till it is full of maggots, or let the trout slip back through his hands into the stream.

The FOOL *has begun singing while the* BLIND MAN *is speaking.*

FOOL: (*Singing*)

When you were an acorn on the tree-top,
  Then was I an eagle-cock;
Now that you are a withered old block,
  Still am I an eagle-cock.

BLIND MAN: Listen to him, now. That's the sort of talk I have to put up with day out, day in.

The FOOL *is putting the feathers into his hair.* CUCHULAIN *takes a handful of feathers out of a heap the* FOOL *has on the bench beside him, and out of the* FOOL'*s hair, and begins to wipe the blood from his sword with them.*

FOOL: He has taken my feathers to wipe his sword. It is blood that he is wiping from his sword.

CUCHULAIN: (*Goes up to door at back and throws away feathers*) They are standing about his body. They will not awaken him, for all his witchcraft.

BLIND MAN: It is that young champion that he has killed. He that came out of Aoife's country.

CUCHULAIN: He thought to have saved himself with witchcraft.

FOOL: That Blind Man there said he would kill you. He came from Aoife's country to kill you. That Blind Man said they had taught him every kind of weapon that he might do it. But I always knew that you would kill him.

CUCHULAIN: (*To the* BLIND MAN) You knew him, then?

BLIND MAN: I saw him, when I had my eyes, in Aoife's country.

CUCHULAIN: You were in Aoife's country?

BLIND MAN: I knew him and his mother there.

CUCHULAIN: He was about to speak of her when he died.

BLIND MAN: He was a queen's son.

CUCHULAIN: What queen? what queen? (*Seizes* BLIND MAN, *who is now sitting upon the bench*) Was it Scathach? There were many queens. All the rulers there were queens.

BLIND MAN: No, not Scathach.

CUCHULAIN: It was Uathach, then? Speak! speak!

BLIND MAN: I cannot speak; you are clutching me too tightly. (CUCHULAIN *lets him go*) I cannot remember who it was. I am not certain. It was some queen.

FOOL: He said a while ago that the young man was Aoife's son.

CUCHULAIN: She? No, no! She had no son when I was there.

FOOL: That Blind Man there said that she owned him for her son.

CUCHULAIN: I had rather he had been some other woman's son. What father had he? A soldier out of Alba?[11] She was an amorous woman — a proud, pale, amorous woman.

BLIND MAN: None knew whose son he was.

CUCHULAIN: None knew! Did you know, old listener at doors?

BLIND MAN: No, no; I knew nothing.

FOOL: He said a while ago that he heard Aoife boast that she'd never but the one lover, and he the only man that had overcome her in battle.

Pause.

BLIND MAN: Somebody is trembling, Fool! The bench is shaking. Why are you trembling? Is Cuchulain going to hurt us? It was not I who told you, Cuchulain.

FOOL: It is Cuchulain who is trembling. It is Cuchulain who is shaking the bench.

BLIND MAN: It is his own son he has slain.

CUCHULAIN: 'Twas they that did it, the pale windy people.
Where? where? where? My sword against the thunder!
But no, for they have always been my friends;
And though they love to blow a smoking coal
Till it's all flame, the wars they blow aflame
Are full of glory, and heart-uplifting pride,
And not like this. The wars they love awaken
Old fingers and the sleepy strings of harps.
Who did it then? Are you afraid? Speak out!
For I have put you under my protection,
And will reward you well. Dubthach the Chafer?[12]
He'd an old grudge. No, for he is with Maeve.
Laegaire did it! Why do you not speak?
What is this house? (*Pause*) Now I remember all.

(*Comes before* CONCHUBAR'S *chair, and strikes out with his sword, as if* CONCHUBAR *was sitting upon it*)

'Twas you who did it — you who sat up there
With your old rod of kingship, like a magpie
Nursing a stolen spoon. No, not a magpie,
A maggot that is eating up the earth!
Yes, but a magpie, for he's flown away.
Where did he fly to?

BLIND MAN: He is outside the door.

CUCHULAIN: Outside the door?

BLIND MAN: Between the door and the sea.

CUCHULAIN: Conchubar, Conchubar! the sword into your heart! (*He rushes out*)

Pause. FOOL *creeps up to the big door and looks after him.*

FOOL: He is going up to King Conchubar. They are all about the young man. No, no, he is standing still. There is a great wave going to break, and he is looking at it. Ah! now he is running down to the sea, but he is holding up his sword as if he were going into a fight. (*Pause*) Well struck! well struck!

BLIND MAN: What is he doing now?

FOOL: O! he is fighting the waves!

BLIND MAN: He sees King Conchubar's crown on every one of them.

FOOL: There, he has struck at a big one! He has struck the crown off it; he has made the foam fly. There again, another big one!

BLIND MAN: Where are the kings? What are the kings doing?

FOOL: They are shouting and running down to the shore, and the people are running out of the houses. They are all running.

BLIND MAN: You say they are running out of the houses? There will be nobody left in the houses. Listen, Fool!

FOOL: There, he is down! He is up again. He is going out in the deep water. There is a big wave. It has gone over him. I cannot see him now. He has killed kings and giants, but the waves have mastered him, the waves have mastered him!

BLIND MAN: Come here, Fool!

FOOL: The waves have mastered him.

BLIND MAN: Come here!

FOOL: The waves have mastered him.

BLIND MAN: Come here, I say.

FOOL: (*Coming towards him, but looking*

11. Scotland.
12. One of the leading figures in the Ulster cycle.

backwards towards the door) What is it?

BLIND MAN: There will be nobody in the houses. Come this way; come quickly! The ovens will be full. We will put our hands into the ovens.

They go out.

PURGATORY (1938)

[The play was first produced on 10 August 1938 at the Abbey Theatre. It aroused great interest and a good deal of dispute, much of it of a theological cast. Many found its meaning obscure. Yeats explained in an interview (*Irish Independent*, 13 August 1938):

> My plot is my meaning. I think the dead suffer remorse and recreate their old lives as I have described. . . . In my play, a spirit suffers because of its share, when alive, in the destruction of an honoured house; that destruction is taking place all over Ireland today. Sometimes it is the result of poverty, but more often because a new individualistic generation has lost interest in the ancient sanctities.
>
> I know of old houses, old pictures, old furniture that have been sold without apparent regret. In some cases a house has been destroyed by a *mésalliance*. I have founded my play on this exceptional case, partly because of my interest in certain problems of eugenics, partly because it enables me to depict more vividly than would otherwise be possible the tragedy of the house.

The play is profoundly political, involving both a lament for Anglo-Ireland, for old civilization and a tragic sense of the inevitable fate of the aristocratic spirit in the democratic world of the 1930s. The links between eugenics and fascism need not be overemphasized in this case. There is a fury and crudity in Yeats's opinions but, as he consistently maintained from his earliest days as a dramatist, there is a war between opinion and imagination. This play is an instance of that war.]

PERSONS IN THE PLAY

A BOY
AN OLD MAN

Scene — A ruined house and a bare tree in the background

BOY: Half-door, hall door,
Hither and thither day and night,
Hill or hollow, shouldering this pack,
Hearing you talk.

OLD MAN: Study that house.
I think about its jokes and stories;
I try to remember what the butler
Said to a drunken gamekeeper
In mid-October, but I cannot.
If I cannot, none living can.
Where are the jokes and stories of a house,
Its threshold gone to patch a pig-sty?

BOY: So you have come this path before?

OLD MAN: The moonlight falls upon the path,
The shadow of a cloud upon the house,
And that's symbolical; study that tree,
What is it like?

BOY: A silly old man.

OLD MAN: It's like — no matter what it's like.
I saw it a year ago stripped bare as now,
So I chose a better trade.
I saw it fifty years ago
Before the thunderbolt had riven it,
Green leaves, ripe leaves, leaves thick as butter,
Fat, greasy life. Stand there and look,
Because there is somebody in that house.

The BOY *puts down pack and stands in the doorway.*

BOY: There's nobody here.

OLD MAN: There's somebody there.

BOY: The floor is gone, the windows gone,
And where there should be roof there's sky,
And here's a bit of an egg-shell thrown
Out of a jackdaw's nest.

OLD MAN: But there are some
That do not care what's gone, what's left:
The souls in Purgatory that come back
To habitations and familiar spots.

BOY: Your wits are out again.

OLD MAN: Re-live
Their transgressions, and that not once
But many times; they know at last
The consequence of those transgressions
Whether upon others or upon themselves;
Upon others, others may bring help,
For when the consequence is at an end
The dream must end; if upon themselves,
There is no help but in themselves
And in the mercy of God.

BOY: I have had enough!
Talk to the jackdaws, if talk you must.

OLD MAN: Stop! Sit there upon that stone.
That is the house where I was born.

BOY: The big old house that was burnt down?

OLD MAN: My mother that was your grand-dam owned it,
This scenery and this countryside,

Kennel and stable, horse and hound —
She had a horse at the Curragh,[1] and there met
My father, a groom in a training stable,
Looked at him and married him.
Her mother never spoke to her again,
And she did right.
BOY: What's right and wrong?
My grand-dad got the girl and the money.
OLD MAN: Looked at him and married him,
And he squandered everything she had.
She never knew the worst, because
She died in giving birth to me,
But now she knows it all, being dead.
Great people lived and died in this house;
Magistrates, colonels, members of Parliament,
Captains and Governors, and long ago
Men that had fought at Aughrim and the
Boyne.[2]
Some that had gone on Government work
To London or to India came home to die,
Or came from London every spring
To look at the may-blossom in the park.
They had loved the trees that he cut down
To pay what he had lost at cards
Or spent on horses, drink and women;
Had loved the house, had loved all
The intricate passages of the house,
But he killed the house; to kill a house
Where great men grew up, married, died,
I here declare a capital offence.
BOY: My God, but you had luck! Grand clothes,
And maybe a grand horse to ride.
OLD MAN: That he might keep me upon his
level
He never sent me to school, but some
Half-loved me for my half of her:
A gamekeeper's wife taught me to read,
A Catholic curate taught me Latin.
There were old books and books made fine
By eighteenth-century French binding, books
Modern and ancient, books by the ton.
BOY: What education have you given me?
OLD MAN: I gave the education that befits
A bastard that a pedlar got
Upon a tinker's daughter in a ditch.
When I had come to sixteen years old
My father burned down the house when drunk.
BOY: But that is my age, sixteen years old,
At the Puck Fair.[3]
OLD MAN: And everything was burnt;
Books, library, all were burnt.
BOY: Is what I have heard upon the road
the truth,
That you killed him in the burning house?
OLD MAN: There's nobody here but our
two selves?
BOY: Nobody, Father.
OLD MAN: I stuck him with a knife,
That knife that cuts my dinner now,
And after that I left him in the fire.
They dragged him out, somebody saw
The knife-wound but could not be certain
Because the body was all black and charred.
Then some that were his drunken friends
Swore they would put me upon trial,
Spoke of quarrels, a threat I had made.
The gamekeeper gave me some old clothes,
I ran away, worked here and there
Till I became a pedlar on the roads,
No good trade, but good enough
Because I am my father's son,
Because of what I did or may do.
Listen to the hoof-beats! Listen, listen!
BOY: I cannot hear a sound.
OLD MAN: Beat! Beat!
This night is the anniversary
Of my mother's wedding night,
Or of the night wherein I was begotten.
My father is riding from the public-house,
A whiskey-bottle under his arm.
A window is lit showing a young girl.
Look at the window; she stands there
Listening, the servants are all in bed,
She is alone, he has stayed late
Bragging and drinking in the public-house.
BOY: There's nothing but an empty gap in
the wall.
You have made it up. No, you are mad!
You are getting madder every day.
OLD MAN: It's louder now because he rides
Upon a gravelled avenue
All grass today. The hoof-beat stops,
He has gone to the other side of the house,

1. A large plain in County Kildare where horse races have been run for centuries.
2. Battles of 1690-91 in which the protestant cause, under William of Orange, triumphed over the catholic forces of James II, inaugurating the rule of the protestant ascendancy in Ireland.
3. A great fair held in Killorglin, Co. Kerry, traditionally associated with the festival of Lunasa on 1 August. The date was changed by eleven days on the adoption of the Gregorian calendar in 1750.

Gone to the stable, put the horse up.
She has gone down to open the door.
This night she is no better than her man
And does not mind that he is half drunk,
She is mad about him. They mount the stairs.
She brings him into her own chamber.
And that is the marriage-chamber now.
The window is dimly lit again.

Do not let him touch you! It is not true
That drunken men cannot beget,
And if he touch he must beget
And you must bear his murderer.
Deaf! Both deaf! If I should throw
A stick or a stone they would not hear;
And that's a proof my wits are out.
But there's a problem: she must live
Through everything in exact detail,
Driven to it by remorse, and yet
Can she renew the sexual act
And find no pleasure in it, and if not,
If pleasure and remorse must both be there,
Which is the greater?
I lack schooling.
Go fetch Tertullian;[4] he and I
Will ravel all that problem out
Whilst those two lie upon the mattress
Begetting me.
Come back! Come back!
And so you thought to slip away,
My bag of money between your fingers,
And that I could not talk and see!
You have been rummaging in the pack.

The light in the window has faded out.

BOY: You never gave me my right share.
OLD MAN: And had I given it, young as you are,
You would have spent it upon drink.
BOY: What if I did? I had a right
To get it and spend it as I chose.
OLD MAN: Give me that bag and no more words.
BOY: I will not.
OLD MAN: I will break your fingers.

They struggle for the bag. In the struggle it drops, scattering the money. The OLD MAN *staggers but does not fall. They stand looking at each other. The window is lit up. A man is seen pouring whiskey into a glass.*

BOY: What if I killed you? You killed my grand-dad,
Because you were young and he was old.
Now I am young and you are old.
OLD MAN: (*Staring at window*)
Better-looking, those sixteen years —
BOY: What are you muttering?
OLD MAN: Younger — and yet
She should have known he was not her kind.
BOY: What are you saying? Out with it?

OLD MAN *points to window.*

My God! The window is lit up
And somebody stands there, although
The floorboards are all burnt away.
OLD MAN: The window is lit up because my father
Has come to find a glass for his whiskey.
He leans there like some tired beast.
BOY: A dead, living, murdered man!
OLD MAN: 'Then the bride-sleep fell upon Adam':[5]
Where did I read those words?
And yet
There's nothing leaning in the window
But the impression upon my mother's mind;
Being dead she is alone in her remorse.
BOY: A body that was a bundle of old bones
Before I was born. Horrible! Horrible! (*He covers his eyes*)
OLD MAN: That beast there would know nothing, being nothing,
If I should kill a man under the window
He would not even turn his head.

(*He stabs the* BOY)

My father and my son on the same jack-knife!
That finishes — there — there — there — (*He stabs again and again. The window grows dark*)
'Hush-a-bye baby, thy father's a knight,
Thy mother a lady, lovely and bright.'[6]
No, that is something that I read in a book,
And if I sing it must be to my mother,
And I lack rhyme.

4. Tertullian (*c.* 160 - *c.* 225), one of the Latin Fathers of the Church. In treatises such as *De Pudicitia* (*On Modesty*) and *De Exhortatione Castitatis* (*On the Encouragement of Chastity*), he characterized marriage as a form of adultery, and claimed that sexual intercourse involved an inextricable mixture of pleasure and guilt and that this mixture persisted in the soul after death.

5. Dante Gabriel Rossetti (1828-82), 'Eden Bower', line 165.

6. Sir Walter Scott (1771-1832), 'Lullaby of an Infant Chief'.

The stage has grown dark except where the tree stands in white light.

Study that tree.
It stands there like a purified soul,
All cold, sweet, glistening light.
Dear mother, the window is dark again,
But you are in the light because
I finished all that consequence.
I killed that lad because had he grown up
He would have struck a woman's fancy,
Begot, and passed pollution on.
I am a wretched foul old man
And therefore harmless. When I have stuck
This old jack-knife into a sod
And pulled it out all bright again,
And picked up all the money that he dropped,
I'll to a distant place, and there
Tell my old jokes among new men.
(*He cleans the knife and begins to pick up money*)
Hoof-beats! Dear God,
How quickly it returns — beat — beat —!

Her mind cannot hold up that dream.
Twice a murderer and all for nothing,
And she must animate that dead night
Not once but many times!

O God,
Release my mother's soul from its dream!
Mankind can do no more. Appease
The misery of the living and the remorse of the dead.

LADY GREGORY

(1852-1932)

SPREADING THE NEWS (1904)

[On the opening night of the Abbey Theatre proper in the Mechanics' Institute in Abbey Street, Dublin, on 27 December 1904, Lady Gregory's *Spreading the News* shared the bill with Yeats's *On Baile's Strand.* It was appropriate that she who had helped Yeats as a dramatist should inaugurate the theatre with him as a dramatist too. Her one-act plays contributed a great deal to the Abbey's development as a theatre. The Kiltartan dialect in which they were written had its influence upon Synge. But, perhaps more simply, Lady Gregory's vision of Irish life was that of a culture in which an essential and enduring sense of community was constantly being vexed and undermined by harsh economic and political conditions, almost all of which she believed were the result of maladministration by the British authorities. She had a belief in the Abbey as an educative force and revelled in its success in becoming a folk-theatre and in what she called its 'return to the people'. Her conception of the Abbey is very different from that of Yeats. It is simpler, more pragmatic, a kind of 'good work' to which she committed herself on behalf of her country.

She supplied the following note to the play:

The idea of this play first came to me as a tragedy. I kept seeing as in a picture people sitting by the roadside, and a girl passing to the market, gay and fearless. And then I saw her passing by the same place at evening, her head hanging, the heads of others turned from her, because of some sudden story that had risen out of a chance word, and had snatched away her good name.

But comedy and not tragedy was wanted at our theatre to put beside the high poetic work, *The King's Threshold, The Shadowy Waters, On Baile's Strand, The Well of the Saints*; and I let laughter have its way with the little play. I was delayed in beginning it for a while, because I could only think of Bartley Fallon as dull-witted or silly or ignorant, and the handcuffs seemed too harsh a punishment. But one day by the sea at Duras a melancholy man, who was telling me of the crosses he had gone through at home, said — 'But I'm thinking if I went to America, it's long ago today I'd be dead. And it's a great expense for a poor man to be buried in America.' Bartley was born at that moment, and, far from harshness, I felt I was providing him with a happy old age in giving him the lasting glory of that great and crowning day of misfortune.

It has been acted very often by other companies as well as our own, and the Boers have done me the honour of translating and pirating it.]

PERSONS

BARTLEY FALLON
MRS FALLON
JACK SMITH
SHAWN EARLY
TIM CASEY
JAMES RYAN
MRS TARPEY
MRS TULLY
A POLICEMAN (JO MULDOON)
A REMOVABLE MAGISTRATE

Scene: The outskirts of a Fair. An Apple Stall. MRS TARPEY *sitting at it.* MAGISTRATE *and* POLICEMAN *enter.*

MAGISTRATE: So that is the Fair Green. Cattle and sheep and mud. No system. What a repulsive sight!

POLICEMAN: That is so, indeed.

MAGISTRATE: I suppose there is a good deal of disorder in this place?

POLICEMAN: There is.

MAGISTRATE: Common assault?

POLICEMAN: It's common enough.

MAGISTRATE: Agrarian crime, no doubt?

POLICEMAN: That is so.

MAGISTRATE: Boycotting?[1] Maiming of cattle? Firing into houses?

POLICEMAN: There was one time, and there might be again.

MAGISTRATE: That is bad. Does it go any farther than that?

POLICEMAN: Far enough, indeed.

MAGISTRATE: Homicide, then! This district has been shamefully neglected! I will change all that. When I was in the Andaman Islands,[2] my system never failed. Yes, yes, I will change all that. What has that woman on her stall?

POLICEMAN: Apples mostly — and sweets.

MAGISTRATE: Just see if there are any unlicensed goods underneath — spirits or the like. We had evasions of the salt tax in the Andaman Islands.

1. Refusing to buy goods, or have any commercial transactions, as a protest or as a means of coercion. Captain C. C. Boycott (1832-97), a land agent for the Earl of Erne, was a victim of such practices in the 1880s, for refusing to reduce rents in his part of County Mayo.
2. These islands, in the Indian Ocean, were part of the British Empire. The British administration established a penal settlement there in 1858.

POLICEMAN: (*Sniffing cautiously and upsetting a heap of apples*) I see no spirits here — or salt.

MAGISTRATE: (*To* MRS TARPEY) Do you know this town well, my good woman?

MRS TARPEY: (*Holding out some apples*) A penny the half-dozen, your honour.

POLICEMAN: (*Shouting*) The gentleman is asking do you know the town! He's the new magistrate!

MRS TARPEY: (*Rising and ducking*) Do I know the town? I do, to be sure.

MAGISTRATE: (*Shouting*) What is its chief business?

MRS TARPEY: Business, is it? What business would the people here have but to be minding one another's business?

MAGISTRATE: I mean what trade have they?

MRS TARPEY: Not a trade. No trade at all but to be talking.

MAGISTRATE: I shall learn nothing here.

JAMES RYAN *comes in, pipe in mouth. Seeing* MAGISTRATE *he retreats quickly, taking pipe from mouth.*

MAGISTRATE: The smoke from that man's pipe had a greenish look; he may be growing unlicensed tobacco at home. I wish I had brought my telescope to this district. Come to the post-office, I will telegraph for it. I found it very useful in the Andaman Islands.

MAGISTRATE *and* POLICEMAN *go out left.*

MRS TARPEY: Bad luck to Jo Muldoon, knocking my apples this way and that way. (*Begins arranging them*) Showing off he was to the new magistrate.

Enter BARTLEY FALLON *and* MRS FALLON.

BARTLEY: Indeed it's a poor country and a scarce country to be living in. But I'm thinking if I went to America it's long ago the day I'd be dead!

MRS FALLON: So you might, indeed. (*She puts her basket on a barrel and begins putting parcels in it, taking them from under her cloak*)

BARTLEY: And it's a great expense for a poor man to be buried in America.

MRS FALLON: Never fear, Bartley Fallon, but I'll give you a good burying the day you'll die.

BARTLEY: Maybe it's yourself will be buried in the graveyard of Cloonmara before me, Mary Fallon, and I myself that will be dying unbeknownst some night, and no one a-near me. And the cat itself may be gone straying through the country, and the mice squealing over the quilt.

MRS FALLON: Leave off talking of dying. It

might be twenty years you'll be living yet.

BARTLEY: (*With a deep sigh*) I'm thinking if I'll be living at the end of twenty years, it's a very old man I'll be then!

MRS TARPEY: (*Turns and sees them*) Good morrow, Bartley Fallon; good morrow, Mrs. Fallon. Well, Bartley, you'll find no cause for complaining today; they are all saying it was a good fair.

BARTLEY: (*Raising his voice*) It was not a good fair, Mrs Tarpey. It was a scattered sort of a fair. If we didn't expect more, we got less. That's the way with me always; whatever I have to sell goes down and whatever I have to buy goes up. If there's ever any misfortune coming to this world, it's on myself it pitches, like a flock of crows on seed potatoes.

MRS FALLON: Leave off talking of misfortunes, and listen to Jack Smith that is coming the way, and he singing.

Voice of JACK SMITH *heard singing* —

I thought, my first love,
There'd be but one house between you and me,
And I thought I would find
Yourself coaxing my child on your knee.
Over the tide
I would leap with the leap of a swan,
Till I came to the side
Of the wife of the Red-haired man![3]

JACK SMITH *comes in; he is a red-haired man, and is carrying a hayfork.*

MRS TARPEY: That should be a good song if I had my hearing.

MRS FALLON: (*Shouting*) It's 'The Red-haired Man's Wife.'

MRS TARPEY: I know it well. That's the song that has a skin on it! (*She turns her back to them and goes on arranging her apples*)

MRS FALLON: Where's herself, Jack Smith?

JACK SMITH: She was delayed with her washing; bleaching the clothes on the hedge she is, and she daren't leave them, with all the tinkers that do be passing to the fair. It isn't to the fair I came myself, but up to the Five Acre Meadow I'm going, where I have a contract for the hay. We'll get a share of it into tramps[4] today. (*He lays down hayfork and lights his pipe*)

BARTLEY: You will not get it into tramps today. The rain will be down on it by evening, and on myself too. It's seldom I ever started on a journey but the rain would come down on me before I'd find any place of shelter.

JACK SMITH: If it didn't itself, Bartley, it is my belief you would carry a leaky pail on your head in place of a hat, the way you'd not be without some cause of complaining.

A voice heard, 'Go on, now, go on out o' that. Go on I say.'

JACK SMITH: Look at that young mare of Pat Ryan's that is backing into Shaughnessy's bullocks with the dint[5] of the crowd! Don't be daunted, Pat, I'll give you a hand with her. (*He goes out, leaving his hayfork*)

MRS FALLON: It's time for ourselves to be going home. I have all I bought put in the basket. Look at there, Jack Smith's hayfork he left after him! He'll be wanting it. (*Calls*) Jack Smith! Jack Smith! — He's gone through the crowd — hurry after him, Bartley, he'll be wanting it.

BARTLEY: I'll do that. This is no safe place to be leaving it. (*He takes up fork awkwardly and upsets the basket*) Look at that now! If there is any basket in the fair upset, it must be our own basket! (*He goes out to right*)

MRS FALLON: Get out of that! It is your own fault, it is. Talk of misfortunes and misfortunes will come. Glory be! Look at my new egg-cups rolling in every part — and my two pound of sugar with the paper broke —

MRS TARPEY: (*Turning from stall*) God help us, Mrs Fallon, what happened your basket?

MRS FALLON: It's himself that knocked it down, bad manners to him. (*Putting things up*) My grand sugar that's destroyed, and he'll not drink his tea without it. I had best go back to the shop for more, much good may it do him!

Enter TIM CASEY.

TIM CASEY: Where is Bartley Fallon, Mrs Fallon? I want a word with him before he'll leave the fair. I was afraid he might have gone home by this, for he's a temperate man.

MRS FALLON: I wish he did go home! It'd be best for me if he went home straight from the fair green, or if he never came with me at all! Where is he, is it?

3. The song, variously titled 'The Red Man's Wife' or 'The Red-Haired Man's Wife', has been popular for over 200 years. Originally in Irish, it has been translated into English by Douglas Hyde, among others.
4. Possibly slide-cars, carts without wheels but with protruding shafts, called trams, at the rear; they were used principally for transporting hay, turf and manure.
5. pressure, force.

He's gone up the road (*jerks elbow*) following Jack Smith with a hayfork. (*She goes out to left*)

TIM CASEY: Following Jack Smith with a hayfork! Did ever anyone hear the like of that. (*Shouts*) Did you hear that news, Mrs Tarpey?

MRS TARPEY: I heard no news at all.

TIM CASEY: Some dispute I suppose it was that rose between Jack Smith and Bartley Fallon, and it seems Jack made off, and Bartley is following him with a hayfork!

MRS TARPEY: Is he now? Well, that was quick work! It's not ten minutes since the two of them were here, Bartley going home and Jack going to the Five Acre Meadow; and I had my apples to settle up, that Jo Muldoon of the police had scattered, and when I looked round again Jack Smith was gone, and Bartley Fallon was gone, and Mrs Fallon's basket upset, and all in it strewed upon the ground — the tea here — the two pound of sugar there — the egg-cups there —. Look, now, what a great hardship the deafness puts upon me, that I didn't hear the commencement of the fight! Wait till I tell James Ryan that I see below; he is a neighbour of Bartley's, it would be a pity if he wouldn't hear the news! (*She goes out*)

Enter SHAWN EARLY *and* MRS TULLY.

TIM CASEY: Listen, Shawn Early! Listen, Mrs Tully, to the news! Jack Smith and Bartley Fallon had a falling out, and Jack knocked Mrs Fallon's basket into the road, and Bartley made an attack on him with a hayfork, and away with Jack, and Bartley after him. Look at the sugar here yet on the road!

SHAWN EARLY: Do you tell me so? Well, that's a queer thing, and Bartley Fallon so quiet a man!

MRS TULLY: I wouldn't wonder at all. I would never think well of a man that would have that sort of a mouldering[6] look. It's likely he has overtaken Jack by this.

Enter JAMES RYAN *and* MRS TARPEY.

JAMES RYAN: That is great news Mrs Tarpey was telling me! I suppose that's what brought the police and the magistrate up this way. I was wondering to see them in it a while ago.

SHAWN EARLY: The police after them? Bartley Fallon must have injured Jack so. They wouldn't meddle in a fight that was only for show!

MRS TULLY: Why wouldn't he injure him? There was many a man killed with no more of a weapon than a hayfork.

JAMES RYAN: Wait till I run north as far as Kelly's bar to spread the news! (*He goes out*)

TIM CASEY: I'll go tell Jack Smith's first cousin that is standing there south of the church after selling his lambs. (*Goes out*)

MRS TULLY: I'll go telling a few of the neighbours I see beyond to the west. (*Goes out*)

SHAWN EARLY: I'll give word of it beyond at the east of the green. (*Is going out when* MRS TARPEY *seizes hold of him*)

MRS TARPEY: Stop a minute, Shawn Early, and tell me did you see red Jack Smith's wife, Kitty Keary, in any place?

SHAWN EARLY: I did. At her own house she was, drying clothes on the hedge as I passed.

MRS TARPEY: What did you say she was doing?

SHAWN EARLY: (*Breaking away*) Laying out a sheet on the hedge. (*He goes*)

MRS TARPEY: Laying out a sheet for the dead! The Lord have mercy on us! Jack Smith dead, and his wife laying out a sheet for his burying! (*Calls out*) Why didn't you tell me that before, Shawn Early? Isn't the deafness the great hardship? Half the world might be dead without me knowing of it or getting word of it at all! (*She sits down and rocks herself*) O my poor Jack Smith! To be going to his work so nice and so hearty, and to be left stretched on the ground in the full light of the day!

Enter TIM CASEY.

TIM CASEY: What is it, Mrs Tarpey? What happened since?

MRS TARPEY: O my poor Jack Smith!

TIM CASEY: Did Bartley overtake him?

MRS TARPEY: O the poor man!

TIM CASEY: Is it killed he is?

MRS TARPEY: Stretched in the Five Acre Meadow!

TIM CASEY: The Lord have mercy on us! Is that a fact?

MRS TARPEY: Without the rites of the Church or a ha'porth!

TIM CASEY: Who was telling you?

MRS TARPEY: And the wife laying out a sheet for his corpse. (*Sits up and wipes her eyes*) I suppose they'll wake him the same as another?

Enter MRS TULLY, SHAWN EARLY, *and* JAMES RYAN.

MRS TULLY: There is great talk about this work in every quarter of the fair.

6. Various expressions in Irish associate mouldiness with physical weakness and reduced energy.

MRS TARPEY: Ochone![7] cold and dead. And myself maybe the last he was speaking to!

JAMES RYAN: The Lord save us! Is it dead he is?

TIM CASEY: Dead surely, and the wife getting provision for the wake.

SHAWN EARLY: Well, now, hadn't Bartley Fallon great venom in him?

MRS TULLY: You may be sure he had some cause. Why would he have made an end of him if he had not? (*To* MRS TARPEY, *raising her voice*) What was it rose the dispute at all, Mrs Tarpey?

MRS TARPEY: Not a one of me knows. The last I saw of them, Jack Smith was standing there, and Bartley Fallon was standing there, quite and easy, and he listening to 'The Red-haired Man's Wife'.

MRS TULLY: Do you hear that, Tim Casey? Do you hear that, Shawn Early and James Ryan? Bartley Fallon was here this morning listening to red Jack Smith's wife, Kitty Keary that was! Listening to her and whispering with her! It was she started the fight so!

SHAWN EARLY: She must have followed him from her own house. It is likely some person roused him.

TIM CASEY: I never knew, before, Bartley Fallon was great with Jack Smith's wife.

MRS TULLY: How would you know it? Sure it's not in the streets they would be calling it. If Mrs Fallon didn't know of it, and if I that have the next house to them didn't know of it, and if Jack Smith himself didn't know of it, it is not likely you would know of it, Tim Casey.

SHAWN EARLY: Let Bartley Fallon take charge of her from this out so, and let him provide for her. It is little pity she will get from any person in this parish.

TIM CASEY: How can he take charge of her? Sure he has a wife of his own. Sure you don't think he'd turn souper[8] and marry her in a Protestant church?

JAMES RYAN: It would be easy for him to marry her if he brought her to America.

SHAWN EARLY: With or without Kitty Keary, believe me it is for America he's making at this minute. I saw the new magistrate and Jo Muldoon of the police going into the post-office as I came up — there was hurry on them — you may be sure it was to telegraph they went, the way he'll be stopped in the docks at Queenstown![9]

MRS TULLY: It's likely Kitty Keary is gone with him, and not minding a sheet or a wake at all. The poor man, to be deserted by his own wife, and the breath hardly gone out yet from his body that is lying bloody in the field!

Enter MRS FALLON.

MRS FALLON: What is it the whole of the town is talking about? And what is it you yourselves are talking about? Is it about my man Bartley Fallon you are talking? Is it lies about him you are telling, saying that he went killing Jack Smith? My grief that ever he came into this place at all!

JAMES RYAN: Be easy now, Mrs Fallon. Sure there is no one at all in the whole fair but is sorry for you!

MRS FALLON: Sorry for me, is it? Why would anyone be sorry for me? Let you be sorry for yourselves, and that there may be shame on you for ever and at the day of judgment, for the words you are saying and the lies you are telling to take away the character of my poor man, and to take the good name off of him, and to drive him to destruction! That is what you are doing!

SHAWN EARLY: Take comfort now, Mrs Fallon. The police are not so smart as they think. Sure he might give them the slip yet, the same as Lynchehaun.*

MRS TULLY: If they do get him, and if they do put a rope around his neck, there is no one can say he does not deserve it!

MRS FALLON: Is that what you are saying, Bridget Tully, and is that you think? I tell you it's too much talk you have, making yourself out to be such a great one, and to be running down every respectable person! A rope, is it? It isn't much of a rope was needed to tie up your own furniture the day you came into Martin Tully's house, and you never bringing as much as a blanket, or a penny, or a suit of clothes with you and I myself bringing seventy pounds and two feather beds. And now you are stiffer than a woman would have a hundred pounds! It is too much talk the whole of you have. A rope is it? I tell you the whole of this town is full of

7. Alas!
8. This expression dates from the time of the Famine (1845-48) when proselytizing protestant groups offered soup to the starving on condition that they changed their faith.

*James Lynchehaun was a criminal who was sheltered by the people of Achill Island and helped to escape to America. The incident contributed elements to Synge's *Playboy of the Western World*.

9. The former name of present-day Cobh, a port near Cork.

liars and schemers that would hang you up for half a glass of whisky. (*Turning to go*) People they are you wouldn't believe as much as daylight from without you'd get up to have a look at it yourself. Killing Jack Smith indeed! Where are you at all, Bartley, till I bring you out of this? My nice quiet little man! My decent comrade! He that is as kind and as harmless as an innocent beast of the field! He'll be doing no harm at all if he'll shed the blood of some of you after this day's work! That much would be no harm at all. (*Calls out*) Bartley! Bartley Fallon! Where are you? (*Going out*) Did anyone see Bartley Fallon?

All turn to look after her.

JAMES RYAN: It is hard for her to believe any such a thing, God help her!

Enter BARTLEY FALLON *from right, carrying hayfork.*

BARTLEY: It is what I often said to myself, if there is ever any misfortune coming to this world it is on myself it is sure to come!

All turn round and face him.

To be going about with this fork and to find no one to take it, and no place to leave it down, and I wanting to be gone out of this — Is that you, Shawn Early? (*Holds out fork*) It's well I met you. You have no call to be leaving the fair for a while the way I have, and how can I go till I'm rid of this fork? Will you take it and keep it until such time as Jack Smith —

SHAWN EARLY: (*Backing*) I will not take it, Bartley Fallon, I'm very thankful to you!

BARTLEY: (*Turning to apple stall*) Look at it now, Mrs Tarpey, it was here I got it; let me thrust it in under the stall. It will lie there safe enough, and no one will take notice of it until such time as Jack Smith —

MRS TARPEY: Take your fork out of that! Is it to put trouble on me and to destroy me you want? Putting it there for the police to be rooting it out maybe. (*Thrusts him back*)

BARTLEY: That is a very unneighbourly thing for you to do, Mrs Tarpey. Hadn't I enough care on me with that fork before this, running up and down with it like the swinging of a clock, and afeard to lay it down in any place! I wish I never touched it or meddled with it at all!

JAMES RYAN: It is a pity, indeed, you ever did.

BARTLEY: Will you yourself take it, James Ryan? You were always a neighbourly man.

JAMES RYAN: (*Backing*) There is many a thing I would do for you, Bartley Fallon, but I won't do that!

SHAWN EARLY: I tell you there is no man will give you any help or any encouragement for this day's work. If it was something agrarian now —

BARTLEY: If no one at all will take it, maybe it's best to give it up to the police.

TIM CASEY: There'd be a welcome for it with them surely! (*Laughter*)

MRS TULLY: And it is to the police Kitty Keary herself will be brought.

MRS TARPEY: (*Rocking to and fro*) I wonder now who will take the expense of the wake for poor Jack Smith?

BARTLEY: The wake for Jack Smith!

TIM CASEY: Why wouldn't he get a wake as well as another? Would you begrudge him that much?

BARTLEY: Red Jack Smith dead! Who was telling you?

SHAWN EARLY: The whole town knows of it by this.

BARTLEY: Do they say what way did he die?

JAMES RYAN: You don't know that yourself, I suppose, Bartley Fallon? You don't know he was followed and that he was laid down with the stab of a hayfork?

BARTLEY: The stab of a hayfork!

SHAWN EARLY: You don't know, I suppose, that the body was found in the Five Acre Meadow?

BARTLEY: The Five Acre Meadow!

TIM CASEY: It is likely you don't know that the police are after the man that did it?

BARTLEY: The man that did it!

MRS TULLY: You don't know, maybe, that he was made away with for the sake of Kitty Keary, his wife?

BARTLEY: Kitty Keary, his wife! (*Sits down bewildered*)

MRS TULLY: And what have you to say now, Bartley Fallon?

BARTLEY: (*Crossing himself*) I to bring that fork here, and to find that news before me! It is much if I can ever stir from this place at all, or reach as far as the road!

TIM CASEY: Look, boys, at the new magistrate, and Jo Muldoon along with him! It's best for us to quit this.

SHAWN EARLY: That is so. It is best not to be mixed in this business at all.

JAMES RYAN: Bad as he is, I wouldn't like to be an informer against any man.

All hurry away except MRS TARPEY, *who remains behind her stall. Enter* MAGISTRATE *and* POLICEMAN.

MAGISTRATE: I knew the district was in a bad state, but I did not expect to be confronted with a murder at the first fair I came to.

POLICEMAN: I am sure you did not, indeed.

MAGISTRATE: It was well I had not gone home. I caught a few words here and there that roused my suspicions.

POLICEMAN: So they would, too.

MAGISTRATE: You heard the same story from everyone you asked?

POLICEMAN: The same story — or if it was not altogether the same, anyway it was no less than the first story.

MAGISTRATE: What is that man doing? He is sitting alone with a hayfork. He has a guilty look. The murder was done with a hayfork!

POLICEMAN: (*In a whisper*) That's the very man they say did the act; Bartley Fallon himself!

MAGISTRATE: He must have found escape difficult — he is trying to brazen it out. A convict in the Andaman Islands tried the same game, but he could not escape my system! Stand aside — Don't go far — have the handcuffs ready. (*He walks up to* BARTLEY, *folds his arms, and stands before him*) Here, my man, do you know anything of John Smith?

BARTLEY: Of John Smith! Who is he, now?

POLICEMAN: Jack Smith, sir — Red Jack Smith!

MAGISTRATE: (*Coming a step nearer and tapping him on the shoulder*) Where is Jack Smith?

BARTLEY: (*With a deep sigh, and shaking his head slowly*) Where is he, indeed?

MAGISTRATE: What have you to tell?

BARTLEY: It is where he was this morning, standing in this spot, singing his share of songs — no, but lighting his pipe — scrapping a match on the sole of his shoe —

MAGISTRATE: I ask you, for the third time, where is he?

BARTLEY: I wouldn't like to say that. It is a great mystery, and it is hard to say of any man, did he earn hatred or love.

MAGISTRATE: Tell me all you know.

BARTLEY: All that I know — Well, there are the three estates; there is Limbo, and there is Purgatory, and there is —

MAGISTRATE: Nonsense! This is trifling! Get to the point.

BARTLEY: Maybe you don't hold with the clergy so? That is the teaching of the clergy. Maybe you hold with the old people. It is what they do be saying, that the shadow goes wandering, and the soul is tired, and the body is taking a rest — The shadow! (*Starts up*) I was nearly sure I saw Jack Smith not ten minutes ago at the corner of the forge, and I lost him again — Was it his ghost I saw, do you think?

MAGISTRATE: (*To* POLICEMAN) Conscience-struck! He will confess all now!

BARTLEY: His ghost to come before me! It is likely it was on account of the fork! I to have it and he to have no way to defend himself the time he met with his death!

MAGISTRATE: (*To* POLICEMAN) I must note down his words. (*Takes out notebook*) (*To* BARTLEY) I warn you that your words are being noted.

BARTLEY: If I had ha' run faster in the beginning, this terror would not be on me at the latter end! Maybe he will cast it up against me at the day of judgment — I wouldn't wonder at all at that.

MAGISTRATE: (*Writing*) At the day of judgment —

BARTLEY: It was soon for his ghost to appear to me — is it coming after me always by day it will be, and stripping the clothes off in the night time? — I wouldn't wonder at all at that, being as I am an unfortunate man!

MAGISTRATE: (*Sternly*) Tell me this truly. What was the motive of this crime?

BARTLEY: The motive, is it?

MAGISTRATE: Yes, the motive; the cause.

BARTLEY: I'd sooner not say that.

MAGISTRATE: You had better tell me truly. Was it money?

BARTLEY: Not at all! What did poor Jack Smith ever have in his pockets unless it might be his hands that would be in them?

MAGISTRATE: Any dispute about land?

BARTLEY: (*Indignantly*) Not at all! He never was a grabber or grabbed from any one!

MAGISTRATE: You will find it better for you if you tell me at once.

BARTLEY: I tell you I wouldn't for the whole world wish to say what it was — it is a thing I would not like to be talking about.

MAGISTRATE: There is no use in hiding it. It will be discovered in the end.

BARTLEY: Well, I suppose it will, seeing that mostly everybody knows it before. Whisper here now. I will tell no lie; where would be the use? (*Puts his hand to his mouth, and* MAGISTRATE *stoops*) Don't be putting the blame on the parish, for such a thing was never done in the parish before — it was done for the sake of Kitty Keary, Jack Smith's wife.

MAGISTRATE: (*To* POLICEMAN) Put on the handcuffs. We have been saved some trouble. I knew he would confess if taken in the right way.

POLICEMAN *puts on handcuffs.*

BARTLEY: Handcuffs now! Glory be! I always said, if there was ever any misfortune coming to this place it was on myself it would fall. I to be in handcuffs! There's no wonder at all in that.

Enter MRS FALLON, *followed by the rest. She is looking back at them as she speaks.*

MRS FALLON: Telling lies the whole of the people of this town are; telling lies, telling lies as fast as a dog will trot! Speaking against my poor respectable man! Saying he made an end of Jack Smith! My decent comrade! There is no better man and no kinder man in the whole of the five parishes! It's little annoyance he ever gave to anyone! (*Turns and sees him*) What in the earthly world do I see before me? Bartley Fallon in charge of the police! Handcuffs on him! O Bartley, what did you do at all at all?

BARTLEY: O Mary, there has a great misfortune come upon me! It is what I always said, that if there is ever any misfortune —

MRS FALLON: What did he do at all, or is it bewitched I am?

MAGISTRATE: This man has been arrested on a charge of murder.

MRS FALLON: Whose charge is that? Don't believe them! They are all liars in this place! Give me back my man!

MAGISTRATE: It is natural you should take his part, but you have no cause of complaint against your neighbours. He has been arrested for the murder of John Smith, on his own confession.

MRS FALLON: The saints of heaven protect us! And what did he want killing Jack Smith?

MAGISTRATE: It is best you should know all. He did it on account of a love affair with the murdered man's wife.

MRS FALLON: (*Sitting down*) With Jack Smith's wife! With Kitty Keary! — Ochone, the traitor!

THE CROWD: A great shame, indeed. He is a traitor, indeed.

MRS TULLY: To America he was bringing her, Mrs Fallon.

BARTLEY: What are you saying, Mary? I tell you —

MRS FALLON: Don't say a word! I won't listen to any word you'll say! (*Stops her ears*) O, isn't he the treacherous villain? Ohone go deo![10]

BARTLEY: Be quiet till I speak! Listen to what I say!

MRS FALLON: Sitting beside me on the ass-car coming to the town, so quiet and so respectable, and treachery like that in his heart!

BARTLEY: Is it your wits you have lost or is it I myself that have lost my wits?

MRS FALLON: And it's hard I earned you, slaving, slaving — and you grumbling, and sighing, and coughing, and discontented, and the priest wore out anointing you, with all the times you threatened to die!

BARTLEY: Let you be quiet till I tell you!

MRS FALLON: You to bring such a disgrace into the parish. A thing that was never heard of before!

BARTLEY: Will you shut your mouth and hear me speaking?

MRS FALLON: And if it was for any sort of a fine handsome woman, but for a little fistful of a woman like Kitty Keary, that's not four feet high hardly, and not three teeth in her head unless she got new ones! May God reward you, Bartley Fallon, for the black treachery in your heart and the wickedness in your mind, and the red blood of poor Jack Smith that is wet upon your hand!

Voice of JACK SMITH *heard singing.*

The sea shall be dry,
The earth under mourning and ban!
Then loud shall he cry
For the wife of the red-haired man!

BARTLEY: It's Jack Smith's voice — I never knew a ghost to sing before — It is after myself and the fork he is coming! (*Goes back*)

Enter JACK SMITH.

Let one of you give him the fork and I will be clear of him now and for eternity!

MRS TARPEY: The Lord have mercy on us! Red Jack Smith! The man that was going to be waked!

JAMES RYAN: Is it back from the grave you are come?

SHAWN EARLY: Is it alive you are, or is it dead you are?

TIM CASEY: Is it yourself at all that's in it?

10. Alas for ever.

MRS TULLY: Is it letting on you were to be dead?

MRS FALLON: Dead or alive, let you stop Kitty Keary, your wife, from bringing my man away with her to America!

JACK SMITH: It is what I think, the wits are gone astray on the whole of you. What would my wife want bringing Bartley Fallon to America?

MRS FALLON: To leave yourself, and to get quit of you she wants, Jack Smith, and to bring him away from myself. That's what the two of them has settled together.

JACK SMITH: I'll break the head of any man that says that! Who is it says it? (*To* TIM CASEY) Was it you said it? (*To* SHAWN EARLY) Was it you?

ALL TOGETHER: (*Backing and shaking their heads*) It wasn't I said it!

JACK SMITH: Tell me the name of any man that said it!

ALL TOGETHER: (*Pointing to* BARTLEY) It was *him* that said it!

JACK SMITH: Let me at him till I break his head!

BARTLEY *backs in terror. Neighbours hold* JACK SMITH *back.*

JACK SMITH: (*Trying to free himself*) Let me at him! Isn't he the pleasant sort of a scarecrow for any woman to be crossing the ocean with! It's back from the docks of New York he'd be turned (*trying to rush at him again*), with a lie in his mouth and treachery in his heart, and another man's wife by his side, and he passing her off as his own! Let me at him can't you. (*Makes another rush, but is held back*)

MAGISTRATE: (*Pointing to* JACK SMITH) Policeman, put the handcuffs on this man. I see it all now. A case of false impersonation, a conspiracy to defeat the ends of justice. There was a case in the Andaman Islands, a murderer of the Mopsa tribe, a religious enthusiast —

POLICEMAN: So he might be, too.

MAGISTRATE: We must take both these men to the scene of the murder. We must confront them with the body of the real Jack Smith.

JACK SMITH; I'll break the head of any man that will find my dead body!

MAGISTRATE: I'll call more help from the barracks. (*Blows* POLICEMAN'S *whistle*)

BARTLEY: It is what I am thinking, if myself and Jack Smith are put together in the one cell for the night, the handcuffs will be taken off him, and his hands will be free, and murder will be done that time surely!

MAGISTRATE: Come on! (*They turn to the right*)

THE WORKHOUSE WARD (1908)

[In this play we can see the struggle in Lady Gregory's drama between affection for and condescension towards the people whom she portrayed. But part of the play's importance is precisely in its adherence to the local and the 'colourful', something that many Abbey dramatists were to duplicate to the point of monotony.

Lady Gregory's own note to the play reads:

I heard of an old man in the workhouse who had been disabled many years before by, I think, a knife thrown at him by his wife in some passionate quarrel.

One day I heard the wife had been brought in there, poor and sick. I wondered how they would meet, and if the old quarrel was still alive, or if they who knew the worst of each other would be better pleased with one another's company than with that of strangers.

I wrote a scenario of the play, Dr Douglas Hyde getting in plot what he gave back in dialogue, for at that time we thought a dramatic movement in Irish would be helpful to our own as well as to the Gaelic League. Later I tried to rearrange it for our own theatre, and for three players only, but in doing this I found it necessary to write entirely new dialogue, the two old men in the original play obviously talking at an audience in the wards, which is no longer there.

I sometimes think the two scolding paupers are a symbol of ourselves in Ireland — 'it is better to be quarrelling than to be lonesome.' The Rajputs, that great fighting race, when they were told they had been brought under the Pax Britannica and must give up war, gave themselves to opium in its place, but Connacht has not yet planted its poppy gardens.]

PERSONS

MIKE McINERNEY	} Paupers
MICHAEL MISKELL	} Paupers
MRS DONOHOE	A Countrywoman

Scene: A ward in Cloon Workhouse. The two old men in their beds.

MICHAEL MISKELL: Isn't it a hard case, Mike McInerney, myself and yourself to be left here in the bed, and it the feast day of Saint Colman,[1] and the rest of the ward attending on the Mass.

1. 14 March.

MIKE McINERNEY: Is it sitting up by the hearth you are wishful to be, Michael Miskell, with cold in the shoulders and with speckled shins? Let you rise up so, and you well able to do it, not like myself that has pains the same as tin-tacks within in my inside.

MICHAEL MISKELL: If you have pains within in your inside there is no one can see it or know of it the way they can see my own knees that are swelled up with the rheumatism, and my hands that are twisted in ridges the same as an old cabbage stalk. It is easy to be talking about soreness and about pains, and they maybe not to be in it at all.

MIKE McINERNEY: To open me and to analyse me you would know what sort of a pain and a soreness I have in my heart and in my chest. But I'm not one like yourself to be cursing and praying and tormenting the time the nuns are at hand, thinking to get a bigger share than myself of the nourishment and of the milk.

MICHAEL MISKELL: That's the way you do be picking at me and faulting me. I had a share and a good share in my early time, and it's well you know that, and the both of us reared in Skehanagh.

MIKE McINERNEY: You may say that, indeed, we are both of us reared in Skehanagh. Little wonder you to have good nourishment the time we were both rising, and you bringing away my rabbits out of the snare.

MICHAEL MISKELL: And you didn't bring away my own eels, I suppose, I was after spearing in the Turlough? Selling them to the nuns in the convent you did, and letting on they to be your own. For you were always a cheater and a schemer, grabbing every earthly thing for your own profit.

MIKE McINERNEY: And you were no grabber yourself, I suppose, till your land and all you had grabbed wore away from you!

MICHAEL MISKELL: If I lost it itself, it was through the crosses I met with and I going through the world. I never was a rambler and a card-player like yourself, Mike McInerney, that ran through all and lavished it unknown to your mother!

MIKE McINERNEY: Lavished it, is it? And if I did was it you yourself led me to lavish it or some other one? It is on my own floor I would be today and in the face of my family, but for the misfortune I had to be put with a bad next door neighbour that was yourself. What way did my means go from me is it? Spending on fencing, spending on walls, making up gates, putting up doors, that would keep your hens and your ducks from coming in through starvation on my floor, and every four-footed beast you had from preying and trespassing on my oats and my mangolds and my little lock of hay!

MICHAEL MISKELL: O to listen to you! And I striving to please you and to be kind to you and to close my ears to the abuse you would be calling and letting out of your mouth. To trespass on your crops is it? It's little temptation there was for my poor beasts to ask to cross the mering.[2] My God Almighty! What had you but a little corner of a field!

MIKE McINERNEY: And what do you say to my garden that your two pigs had destroyed on me the year of the big tree being knocked, and they making gaps in the wall.

MICHAEL MISKELL: Ah, there does be a great deal of gaps knocked in a twelvemonth. Why wouldn't they be knocked by thunder, the same as the tree, or some storm that came up from the west?

MIKE McINERNEY: It was the west wind, I suppose, that devoured my green cabbage? And that rooted up my Champion potatoes? And that ate the gooseberries themselves from off the bush?

MICHAEL MISKELL: What are you saying? The two quietest pigs ever I had, no way wicked and well ringed. They were not ten minutes in it. It would be hard for them eat strawberries in that time, let alone gooseberries that's full of thorns.

MIKE McINERNEY: They were not quiet, but very ravenous pigs you had that time, as active as a fox they were, killing my young ducks. Once they had blood tasted you couldn't stop them.

MICHAEL MISKELL: And what happened myself the fair day of Esserkelly, the time I was passing your door? Two brazened dogs that rushed out and took a piece of me. I never was the better of it or of the start I got, but wasting from then till now!

MIKE McINERNEY: Thinking you were a wild beast they did, that had made his escape out of the travelling show, with the red eyes of you and the ugly face of you, and the two crooked legs of you that wouldn't hardly stop a pig in a gap. Sure any dog that had any life in it at all would be roused and stirred seeing the like of you going the road!

MICHAEL MISKELL: I did well taking out a summons against you that time. It is a great wonder you not to have been bound over through your lifetime, but the laws of England is queer.

MIKE McINERNEY: What ailed me that I did not

2. A green strip or road, serving as a boundary.

summons yourself after you stealing away the clutch of eggs I had in the barrel, and I away in Ardrahan searching out a clocking hen.[3]

MICHAEL MISKELL: To steal your eggs is it? Is that what you are saying now? (*Holds up his hands*) The Lord is in heaven, and Peter and the saints, and yourself that was in Ardrahan that day put a hand on them as soon as myself? Isn't it a bad story for me to be wearing out my days beside you the same as a spancelled[4] goat. Chained I am and tethered I am to a man that is ramsacking [*sic*] his mind for lies!

MIKE McINERNEY: If it is a bad story for you, Michael Miskell, it is a worse story again for myself. A Miskell to be next and near me through the whole of the four quarters of the year. I never heard there to be any great name on the Miskells as there was on my own race and name.

MICHAEL MISKELL: You didn't, is it? Well, you could hear it if you had but ears to hear it. Go across to Lisheen Crannagh and down to the sea and to Newtown Lynch and the mills of Duras and you'll find a Miskell, and as far as Dublin!

MIKE McINERNEY: What signifies Crannagh and the mills of Duras? Look at all my own generations that are buried at the Seven Churches.[5] And how many generations of the Miskells are buried in it? Answer me that!

MICHAEL MISKELL: I tell you but for the wheat that was to be sowed there would be more side cars and more common cars at my father's funeral (God rest his soul!) than at any funeral ever left your own door. And as to my mother, she was a Cuffe from Claregalway, and it's she had the purer blood!

MIKE McINERNEY: And what do you say to the banshee?[6] Isn't she apt to have knowledge of the ancient race? Was ever she heard to screech or to cry for the Miskells? Or for the Cuffes from Claregalway? She was not, but for the six families, the Hyneses, the Foxes, the Faheys, the Dooleys, the McInerneys. It is of the nature of the McInerneys she is I am thinking, crying them the same as a king's children.

MICHAEL MISKELL: It is a pity the banshee not to be crying for yourself at this minute, and giving you a warning to quit your lies and your chat and your arguing and your contrary ways; for there is no one under the rising sun could stand you. I tell you you are not behaving as in the presence of the Lord!

MIKE McINERNEY: Is it wishful for my death you are? Let it come and meet me now and welcome so long as it will part me from yourself! And I say, and I would kiss the book on it, I to have one request only to be granted, and I leaving it in my will, it is what I would request, nine furrows of the field, nine ridges of the hills, nine waves of the ocean to be put between your grave and my own grave the time we will be laid in the ground!

MICHAEL MISKELL: Amen to that! Nine ridges, is it? No, but let the whole ridge of the world separate us till the Day of Judgement! I would not be laid anear you at the Seven Churches, I to get Ireland without a divide!

MIKE McINERNEY: And after that again! I'd sooner than ten pound in my hand, I to know that my shadow and my ghost will not be knocking about with your shadow and your ghost, and the both of us waiting our time. I'd sooner be delayed in Purgatory! Now, have you anything to say?

MICHAEL MISKELL: I have everything to say, if I had but the time to say it!

MIKE McINERNEY: (*Sitting up*) Let me up out of this till I'll choke you!

MICHAEL MISKELL: You scolding pauper you!

MIKE McINERNEY: (*Shaking his fist at him*) Wait a while!

MICHAEL MISKELL: (*Shaking his fist*) Wait a while yourself!

MRS DONOHOE *comes in with a parcel. She is a countrywoman with a frilled cap and a shawl. She stands still a minute. The two old men lie down and compose themselves.*

MRS DONOHOE: They bade me come up here by the stair. I never was in this place at all. I don't know am I right. Which now of the two of ye is Mike McInerney?

MIKE McINERNEY: Who is it is calling me by my name?

MRS DONOHOE: Sure amn't I your sister, Honor McInerney that was, that is now Honor Donohoe.

MIKE McINERNEY: So you are, I believe. I didn't

3. A sitting hen, a hen that would sit on eggs to hatch them.
4. i.e. hobbled with a rope.
5. Traditionally associated with the monastic settlement of Glendalough in County Wicklow and by extension with a number of monastic sites. The local monastic site in this part of Galway is that of Kilmacduagh, founded in the sixth century by St Colman mac Duach. Seven monuments (not all of them churches) still remain. Crannagh is a townland in County Galway; Duras, also in Galway, is noted for Durras House, once the property of Count Florimond de Basterot, a friend of Lady Gregory, Yeats and Edward Martyn.
6. Irish *bean sídhe* (woman of the fairies); in Irish folklore, a female spirit whose wailing warns of impending death.

know you till you pushed anear me. It is time indeed for you to come see me, and I in this place five year or more. Thinking me to be no credit to you, I suppose, among that tribe of the Donohoes. I wonder they to give you leave to come ask am I living yet or dead?

MRS DONOHOE: Ah, sure, I buried the whole string of them. Himself was the last to go. (*Wipes her eyes*) The Lord be praised he got a fine natural death. Sure we must go through our crosses. And he got a lovely funeral; it would delight you to hear the priest reading the Mass. My poor John Donohoe! A nice clean man, you couldn't but be fond of him. Very severe on the tobacco he was, but he wouldn't touch the drink.

MIKE McINERNEY: And is it in Curranroe you are living yet?

MRS DONOHOE: It is so. He left all to myself. But it is a lonesome thing the head of a house to have died!

MIKE McINERNEY: I hope that he has left you a nice way of living?

MRS DONOHOE: Fair enough, fair enough. A wide lovely house I have; a few acres of grass land . . . the grass does be very sweet that grows among the stones. And as to the sea, there is something from it every day of the year, a handful of periwinkles to make kitchen,[7] or cockles maybe. There is many a thing in the sea is not decent, but cockles is fit to put before the Lord!

MIKE McINERNEY: You have all that! And you without ere a man in the house?

MRS DONOHOE: It is what I am thinking, yourself might come and keep me company. It is no credit to me a brother of my own to be in this place at all.

MIKE McINERNEY: I'll go with you! Let me out of this! It is the name of the McInerneys will be rising on every side!

MRS DONOHOE: I don't know. I was ignorant of you being kept to the bed.

MIKE McINERNEY: I am not kept to it, but maybe an odd time when there is a colic rises up within me. My stomach always gets better the time there is a change in the moon. I'd like well to draw anear you. My heavy blessing on you, Honor Donohoe, for the hand you have held out to me this day.

MRS DONOHOE: Sure you could be keeping the fire in, and stirring the pot with the bit of Indian meal for the hens, and milking the goat and taking the tacklings off the donkey at the door; and maybe putting out the cabbage plants in their time. For when the old man died the garden died.

MIKE McINERNEY: I could to be sure, and be cutting the potatoes for seed. What luck could there be in a place and a man not to be in it? Is that now a suit of clothes you have brought with you?

MRS DONOHOE: It is so, the way you will be tasty[8] coming in among the neighbours at Curranroe.

MIKE McINERNEY: My joy you are! It is well you earned me! Let me up out of this! (*He sits up and spreads out the clothes and tries on coat*) Is that not a good frieze coat . . . and a hat in the fashion . . . (*He puts on hat*)

MICHAEL MISKELL: (*Alarmed*) And is it going out of this you are, Mike McInerney?

MIKE McINERNEY: Don't you hear I am going? To Curranroe I am going. Going I am to a place where I will get every good thing!

MICHAEL MISKELL: And is it to leave me here after you you will?

MIKE McINERNEY: (*In a rising chant*) Every good thing! The goat and the kid are there, the sheep and the lamb are there, the cow does be running and she coming to be milked! Ploughing and seed sowing, blossom at Christmas time, the cuckoo speaking through the dark days of the year! Ah, what are you talking about? Wheat high in hedges, no talk about the rent! Salmon in the rivers as plenty as turf! Spending and getting and nothing scarce! Sport and pleasure, and music on the strings! Age will go from me and I will be young again. Geese and turkeys for the hundreds and drink for the whole world!

MICHAEL MISKELL: Ah, Mike, is it truth you are saying, you to go from me and to leave me with rude people and with townspeople, and with people of every parish in the union, and they having no respect for me or no wish for me at all!

MIKE McINERNEY: Whist[9] and I'll leave you . . . my pipe (*hands it over*); and I'll engage it is Honor Donohoe won't refuse to be sending you a few ounces of tobacco an odd time, and neighbours coming to the fair in November or in the month of May.

MICHAEL MISKELL: Ah, what signifies tobacco?

7. To impart flavour or variety to the staple meal of potatoes.

8. i.e. displaying good taste, elegant.

9. Hush! Be quiet!.

All that I am craving is the talk. There to be no one at all to say out to whatever thought might be rising in my innate mind! To be lying here and no conversable person in it would be the abomination of misery!

MIKE McINERNEY: Look now, Honor.... It is what I often heard said, two to be better than one. ... Sure, if you had an old trouser was full of holes ... or a skirt ... wouldn't you put another in under it that might be as tattered as itself, and the two of them together would make some sort of a decent show?

MRS DONOHOE: Ah, what are you saying? There is no holes in that suit I brought you now, but as sound it is as the day I spun it for himself.

MIKE McINERNEY: It is what I am thinking, Honor .... I do be weak an odd time ... any load I would carry, it preys upon my side ... and this man does be weak an odd time with the swelling in his knees ... but the two of us together it's not likely it is at the one time we would fail. Bring the both of us with you, Honor, and the height of the castle of luck on you, and the both of us together will make one good hardy man!

MRS DONOHOE: I'd like my job! Is it queer in the head you are grown asking me to bring in a stranger off the road?

MICHAEL MISKELL: I am not, ma'am, but an old neighbour I am. If I had forecasted this asking I would have asked it myself. Michael Miskell I am, that was in the next house to you in Skehanagh!

MRS DONOHOE: For pity's sake! Michael Miskell is it? That's worse again. Yourself and Mike that never left fighting and scolding and attacking one another! Sparring at one another like two young pups you were, and threatening one another after like two grown dogs!

MIKE McINERNEY: All the quarrelling was ever in the place it was myself did it. Sure his anger rises fast and goes away like the wind. Bring him out with myself now, Honor Donohoe, and God bless you.

MRS DONOHOE: Well, then, I will not bring him out, and I will not bring yourself out, and you not to learn better sense. Are you making yourself ready to come?

MIKE McINERNEY: I am thinking, maybe ... it is a mean thing for a man that is shivering into seventy years to go changing from place to place.

MRS DONOHOE: Well, take your luck or leave it. All I asked was to save you from the hurt and the harm of the year.

MIKE McINERNEY: Bring the both of us with you or I will not stir out of this.

MRS DONOHOE: Give me back my fine suit so (*begins gathering up the clothes*), till I'll go look for a man of my own!

MIKE McINERNEY: Let you go so, as you are so unnatural and so disobliging, and look for some man of your own, God help him! For I will not go with you at all!

MRS DONOHOE: It is too much time I lost with you, and dark night waiting to overtake me on the road. Let the two of you stop together, and the back of my hand to you. It is I will leave you there the same as God left the Jews! (*She goes out*)

The old men lie down and are silent for a moment.

MICHAEL MISKELL: Maybe the house is not so wide as what she says.

MIKE McINERNEY: Why wouldn't it be wide?

MICHAEL MISKELL: Ah, there does be a good deal of middling poor houses down by the sea.

MIKE McINERNEY: What would you know about wide houses? Whatever sort of a house you had yourself it was too wide for the provision you had into it.

MICHAEL MISKELL: Whatever provision I had in my house it was wholesome provision and natural provision. Herself and her periwinkles! Periwinkles is a hungry sort of food.

MIKE McINERNEY: Stop your impudence and your chat or it will be the worse for you. I'd bear with my own father and mother as long as any man would, but if they'd vex me I would give them the length of a rope as soon as another!

MICHAEL MISKELL: I would never ask at all to go eating periwinkles ....

MIKE McINERNEY: (*Sitting up*) Have you anyone to fight me?

MICHAEL MISKELL: (*Whimpering*) I have not, only the Lord!

MIKE McINERNEY: Let you leave putting insults on me so, and death picking at you!

MICHAEL MISKELL: Sure I am saying nothing at all to displease you. It is why I wouldn't go eating periwinkles, I'm in dread I might swallow the pin.

MIKE McINERNEY: Who in the world wide is asking you to eat them? You're as tricky as a fish in the full tide!

MICHAEL MISKELL: Tricky is it! Oh, my curse and the curse of the four and twenty men upon you!

MIKE McINERNEY: That the worm may chew you from skin to marrow bone! (*Seizes his pillow*)

MICHAEL MISKELL: (*Seizing his own pillow*) I'll leave my death on you, you scheming vagabond!

MIKE McINERNEY: By cripes! I'll pull out your pin feathers! (*Throwing pillow*)

MICHAEL MISKELL: (*Throwing pillow*) You tyrant! You big bully you!

MIKE McINERNEY: (*Throwing pillow and seizing mug*) Take this so, you stobbing ruffian you!

They throw all within their reach at one another, mugs, prayer books, pipes, etc.

JOHN MILLINGTON SYNGE

(1871-1909)

IN THE SHADOW OF THE GLEN (1903)

A PLAY IN ONE ACT

[The folk-story on which Synge based this play ends with the husband triumphant. Synge's version makes Nora the dominant character. She is clearly intended to represent values and qualities superior to Dan Burke's. The workings of this central conflict raise questions: for example, about the consistency of Nora's presentation — her sexuality perhaps seems at odds with her forebodings of death, and her entertaining, on purely materialist grounds, of Michael's proposal. Synge appears to be less interested in plausible psychology than in establishing an overriding tension between domineering conventional ways and a kind of liberation both exciting and dangerous.

The play was first produced on 8 October 1903 in the Molesworth Hall, Camden Street, Dublin by the Irish National Theatre Society. It received a hostile reception from the public and provoked an internal crisis in the Theatre Society itself.]

PERSONS

DAN BURKE, *farmer and herd*
NORA BURKE, *his wife*
MICHAEL DARA, *a young herd*
A TRAMP

SCENE

The last cottage at the head of a long glen in County Wicklow.

Cottage kitchen; turf fire on the right; a bed near it against the wall with a body lying on it covered with a sheet. A door is at the other end of the room, with a low table near it, and stools, or wooden chairs. There are a couple of glasses on the table, and a bottle of whiskey, as if for a wake, with two cups, a tea-pot, and a home-made cake. There is another small door near the bed. NORA BURKE *is moving about the room, settling a few things and lighting candles on the table, looking now and then at the bed with an uneasy look. Someone knocks softly at the door on the left. She takes up a stocking with money from the table and puts it in her pocket. Then she opens the door.*

TRAMP: (*Outside*) Good evening to you, lady of the house.[1]

NORA: Good evening kindly, stranger, it's a wild night, God help you, to be out in the rain falling.

TRAMP: It is surely, and I walking to Brittas from the Aughrim fair.[2]

NORA: Is it walking on your feet, stranger?

TRAMP: On my two feet, lady of the house, and when I saw the light below I thought maybe if you'd a sup of new milk and a quiet decent corner where a man could sleep. . . . (*He looks in past her and sees the body on the bed*) The Lord have mercy on us all!

NORA: It doesn't matter any way, stranger, come in out of the rain.

TRAMP: (*Coming in slowly and going towards the bed*) Is it departed he is?

NORA: It is, stranger. He's after dying on me,[3] God forgive him, and there I am now with a

1. From the traditional Irish phrase, *bean an tí* (woman or lady of the house).
2. All the place-names mentioned here — Brittas, Aughrim, Lough Nahanagan, Glen Malure, Rathvanna, Glen Imaal, Rathdrum, the Seven Churches (at Glendalough) — are in south County Wicklow.
3. He has just died.

hundred sheep beyond on the hills, and no turf drawn for the winter.

TRAMP: (*Looking closely at the body*) It's a queer look is on him for a man that's dead.

NORA: (*Half-humorously*) He was always queer, stranger, and I suppose them that's queer and they living men will be queer bodies after.

TRAMP: Isn't it a great wonder you're letting him lie there, and he not tidied, or laid out itself?

NORA: (*Coming to the bed*) I was afeard, stranger, for he put a black curse on me this morning if I'd touch his body the time he'd die sudden, or let anyone touch it except his sister only, and it's ten miles away she lives, in the big glen over the hill.

TRAMP: (*Looking at her and nodding slowly*) It's a queer story he wouldn't let his own wife touch him, and he dying quiet in his bed.

NORA: He was an old man, and an odd man, stranger, and it's always up on the hills he was, thinking thoughts in the dark mist. (*She pulls back a bit more of the sheet*) Lay your hand on him now, and tell me if it's cold he is surely.

TRAMP: Is it getting the curse on me you'd be, woman of the house? I wouldn't lay my hand on him for the Lough Nahanagan and it filled with gold.

NORA: (*Looking uneasily at the body*) Maybe cold would be no sign of death with the like of him, for he was always cold, every day since I knew him, — and every night, stranger — (*she covers up his face and comes away from the bed*); but I'm thinking it's dead he is surely, for he's complaining a while back of a pain in his heart, and this morning, the time he was going off to Brittas for three days or four, he was taken with a sharp turn. Then he went into his bed and he was saying it was destroyed he was, the time the shadow was going up through the glen, and when the sun set on the bog beyond he made a great lep,[4] and let a great cry out of him, and stiffened himself out the like of a dead sheep.

TRAMP: (*Crosses himself*) God rest his soul.

NORA: (*Pouring him out a glass of whiskey*) Maybe that would do you better than the milk of the sweetest cow in County Wicklow.

TRAMP: The Almighty God reward you, and may it be to your good health. (*He drinks*)

NORA: (*Giving him a pipe and tobacco from the table*) I've no pipes saving his own, stranger, but they're sweet pipes to smoke.

TRAMP: Thank you kindly, lady of the house.

NORA: Sit down now, stranger, and be taking your rest.

TRAMP: (*Filling a pipe and looking about the room*) I've walked a great way through the world, lady of the house, and seen great wonders, but I never seen a wake till this day with fine spirits, and good tobacco, and the best of pipes, and no one to taste them but a woman only.

NORA: Didn't you hear me say it was only after dying on me he was when the sun went down, and how would I go out into the glen and tell the neighbours and I a lone woman with no house near me?

TRAMP: (*Drinking*) There's no offence, lady of the house?

NORA: No offence in life, stranger. How would the like of you passing in the dark night know the lonesome way I was with no house near me at all?

TRAMP: (*Sitting down*) I knew rightly. (*He lights his pipe so that there is a sharp light beneath his haggard face*) And I was thinking, and I coming in through the door, that it's many a lone woman would be afeard of the like of me in the dark night, in a place wouldn't be as lonesome as this place, where there aren't two living souls would see the little light you have shining from the glass.

NORA: (*Slowly*) I'm thinking many would be afeard, but I never knew what way I'd be afeard of beggar or bishop or any man of you at all. (*She looks towards the window and lowers her voice*) It's other things than the like of you, stranger, would make a person afeard.

TRAMP: (*Looking round with a half-shudder*) It is surely, God help us all!

NORA: (*Looking at him for a moment with curiosity*) You're saying that, stranger, as if you were easy afeard.

TRAMP: (*Speaking mournfully*) Is it myself, lady of the house, that does be walking round in the long nights, and crossing the hills when the fog is on them, the time a little stick would seem as big as your arm, and a rabbit as big as a bay horse, and a stack of turf as big as a towering church in the city of Dublin? If myself was easily afeard, I'm telling you, it's long ago I'd have been locked into the Richmond Asylum, or maybe have run up into the back hills with nothing on me but an old shirt, and been eaten with crows the like of Patch Darcy — the Lord have mercy on him — in the year that's gone.

NORA: (*With interest*) You knew Darcy?

4. leap.

TRAMP: Wasn't I the last one heard his living voice in the whole world?

NORA: There were great stories of what was heard at that time, but would anyone believe the things they do be saying in the glen?

TRAMP: It was no lie, lady of the house. . . . I was passing below on a dark night the like of this night, and the sheep were lying under the ditch and every one of them coughing, and choking, like an old man, with the great rain and the fog . . . . Then I heard a thing talking — queer talk, you wouldn't believe at all, and you out of your dreams, — and 'Merciful God,' says I, 'if I begin hearing the like of that voice out of the thick mist, I'm destroyed surely.' Then I run, and I run, and I run, till I was below in Rathvanna. I got drunk that night, I got drunk in the morning, and drunk the day after, — I was coming from the races beyond — and the third day they found Darcy . . . . Then I knew it was himself I was after hearing, and I wasn't afeard any more.

NORA: (*Speaking sorrowfully and slowly*) God spare Darcy, he'd always look in here and he passing up or passing down, and it's very lonesome I was after him a long while (*she looks over at the bed and lowers her voice, speaking very clearly*), and then I got happy again — if it's ever happy we are, stranger — for I got used to being lonesome. (*A short pause; then she stands up*) Was there anyone on the last bit of the road, stranger, and you coming from Aughrim?

TRAMP: There was a young man with a drift[5] of mountain ewes, and he running after them this way and that.

NORA: (*With a half-smile*) Far down, stranger?

TRAMP: A piece only.

She fills the kettle and puts it on the fire.

NORA: Maybe, if you're not easy afeard, you'd stay here a short while alone with himself?

TRAMP: I would surely. A man that's dead can do no hurt.

NORA: (*Speaking with a sort of constraint*) I'm going a little back to the west, stranger, for himself would go there one night and another, and whistle at that place, and then the young man you're after seeing — a kind of a farmer has come up from the sea to live in a cottage beyond — would walk round to see if there was a thing we'd have to be done, and I'm wanting him this night, the way he can go down into the glen when the sun goes up and tell the people that himself is dead.

TRAMP: (*Looking at the body in the sheet*) It's myself will go for him, lady of the house, and let you not be destroying yourself with the great rain.

NORA: You wouldn't find your way, stranger, for there's a small path only, and it running up between two sluigs[6] where an ass and cart would be drowned. (*She puts a shawl over her head*) Let you be making yourself easy, and saying a prayer for his soul, and it's not long I'll be coming again.

TRAMP: (*Moving uneasily*) Maybe if you'd a piece of a grey thread and a sharp needle — there's great safety in a needle, lady of the house — I'd be putting a little stitch here and there in my old coat, the time I'll be praying for his soul, and it going up naked to the saints of God.

NORA: (*Takes a needle and thread from the front of her dress and gives it to him*) There's the needle, stranger, and I'm thinking you won't be lonesome, and you used to the back hills, for isn't a dead man itself more company than to be sitting alone, and hearing the winds crying, and you not knowing on what thing your mind would stay?

TRAMP: (*Slowly*) It's true, surely, and the Lord have mercy on us all!

NORA *goes out.* THE TRAMP *begins stitching one of the tags in his coat, saying the 'De Profundis'*[7] *under his breath. In an instant the sheet is drawn slowly down, and* DAN BURKE *looks out.* THE TRAMP *moves uneasily, then looks up, and springs to his feet with a movement of terror.*

DAN: (*With a hoarse voice*) Don't be afeard, stranger; a man that's dead can do not hurt.

TRAMP: (*Trembling*) I meant no harm, your honour; and won't you leave me easy to be saying a little prayer for your soul?

A long whistle is heard outside.

DAN: (*Listening, sitting up in his bed and speaking fiercely*) Ah, the devil mend her. . . .[8] Do you hear that, stranger? Did ever you hear another woman could whistle the like of that with two fingers in her mouth? (*He looks at the table hurriedly*) I'm destroyed with the drouth,[9] and let you bring me a drop quickly before herself will come back.

5. drove, gathering.

6. water courses.

7. 'Out of the depths', the first two words of the Latin version of Psalm 130, traditionally said on the occasion of a death.

8. A curse: 'may the devil fix her'.

9. thirst.

TRAMP: (*Doubtfully*) Is it not dead you are?

DAN: How would I be dead, and I as dry as a baked bone, stranger?

TRAMP: (*Pouring out the whiskey*) What will herself say if she smells the stuff on you, for I'm thinking it's not for nothing you're letting on to be dead?

DAN: It is not, stranger, but she won't be coming near me at all, and it's not long now I'll be letting on, for I've a cramp in my back, and my hip's asleep on me, and there's been the devil's own fly itching my nose.... It's near dead I was wanting to sneeze, and you blathering about the rain, and Darcy (*bitterly*) — the devil choke him — and the towering church. (*Crying out impatiently*) Give me that whiskey. Would you have herself come back before I taste a drop at all? (TRAMP *gives him the glass and he drinks*).... Go over now to that cupboard, and bring me a black stick you'll see in the west corner by the wall.

TRAMP: (*Taking a stick from the cupboard*) Is it that?

DAN: It is, stranger; it's a long time I'm keeping that stick, for I've a bad wife in the house.

TRAMP: (*With a queer look*) Is it herself, master of the house, and she a grand woman to talk?

DAN: It's herself, surely, it's a bad wife she is — a bad wife for an old man, and I'm getting old, God help me, though I've an arm to me still. (*He takes the stick in his hand*) Let you wait now a short while, and it's a great sight you'll see in this room in two hours or three. (*He stops to listen*) Is that somebody above?

TRAMP: (*Listening*) There's a voice speaking on the path.

DAN: Put that stick here in the bed, and smooth the sheet the way it was lying. (*He covers himself up hastily*) Be falling to sleep now and don't let on you know anything, or I'll be having your life. I wouldn't have told you at all but it's destroyed with the drouth I was.

TRAMP: (*Covering his head*) Have no fear, master of the house. What is it I know of the like of you that I'd be saying a word or putting out my hand to stay you at all? (*He goes back to the fire, sits down on a stool with his back to the bed and goes on stitching his coat*)

DAN: (*Under the sheet, querulously*) Stranger.

TRAMP: (*Quickly*) Whisht, whisht. Be quiet I'm telling you, they're coming now at the door.

NORA *comes in with* MICHAEL DARA, *a tall, innocent young man, behind her.*

NORA: I wasn't long at all, stranger, for I met himself on the path.

TRAMP: You were middling long, lady of the house.

NORA: There was no sign from himself?

TRAMP: No sign at all, lady of the house.

NORA: (*To* MICHAEL) Go over now and pull down the sheet, and look on himself, Michael Dara, and you'll see it's the truth I'm telling you.

MICHAEL: I will not, Nora, I do be afeard of the dead.

He sits down on a stool next the table facing the TRAMP. NORA *puts the kettle on a lower hook of the pot-hooks, and piles turf under it.*

NORA: (*Turning to* TRAMP) Will you drink a sup of tea with myself and the young man, stranger, or (*speaking more persuasively*) will you go into the little room and stretch yourself a short while on the bed. I'm thinking it's destroyed you are walking the length of that way in the great rain.

TRAMP: Is it go away and leave you, and you having a wake, lady of the house? I will not surely. (*He takes a drink from his glass which he has beside him*) And it's none of your tea I'm asking either. (*He goes on stitching*)

NORA *makes the tea.*

MICHAEL: (*After looking at the* TRAMP *rather scornfully for a moment*) That's a poor coat you have, God help you, and I'm thinking it's a poor tailor you are with it.

TRAMP: (*Looks up at him for a moment*) If it's a poor tailor I am, I'm thinking it's a poor herd does be running back and forward after a little handful of ewes the way I seen yourself running this day, young fellow, and you coming from the fair.

NORA: (*Comes back to the table. To* MICHAEL *in a low voice*) Let you not mind him at all, Michael Dara. He has a drop taken, and it's soon he'll be falling asleep.

MICHAEL: It's no lie he's telling, I was destroyed surely.... They were that wilful they were running off into one man's bit of oats, and another man's bit of hay, and tumbling into the red bogs till it's more like a pack of old goats than sheep they were.... Mountain ewes is a queer breed, Nora Burke, and I'm not used to them at all.

NORA: (*Settling the tea things*) There's no one can drive a mountain ewe but the men do be reared in the Glen Malure, I've heard them say, and above by Rathvanna, and the Glen Imaal, men the like of Patch Darcy, God spare his soul, who would walk through five hundred sheep and miss one of them, and he not reckoning[10] them at all.

MICHAEL: (*Uneasily*) Is it the man went queer in his head the year that's gone?

NORA: It is surely.

TRAMP: (*Plaintively*) That was a great man, young fellow, a great man I'm telling you. There was never a lamb from his own ewes he wouldn't know before it was marked, and he'd run from this to the city of Dublin, and never catch for his breath.

NORA: (*Turning round quickly*) He was a great man surely, stranger, and isn't it a grand thing when you hear a living man saying a good word of a dead man, and he mad dying?

TRAMP: It's the truth I'm saying, God spare his soul.

He puts the needle under the collar of his coat, and settles himself to sleep in the chimney-corner. NORA *sits down at the table: their backs are turned to the bed.*

MICHAEL: (*Looking at her with a queer look*) I heard tell this day, Nora Burke, that it was on the path below Patch Darcy would be passing up and passing down, and I heard them say he'd never pass it night or morning without speaking with yourself.

NORA: (*In a low voice*) It was no lie you heard, Michael Dara.

MICHAEL: (*As before*) I'm thinking it's a power[11] of men you're after knowing if it's in a lonesome place you live itself.

NORA: (*Slowly, giving him his tea*) It's in a lonesome place you do have to be talking with someone, and looking for someone, in the evening of the day, and if it's a power of men I'm after knowing they were fine men, for I was a hard child to please, and a hard girl to please (*she looks at him a little sternly*), and it's a hard woman I am to please this day, Michael Dara, and it's no lie, I'm telling you.

MICHAEL: (*Looking over to see that the* TRAMP *is asleep and then, pointing to the dead man*) Was it a hard woman to please you were when you took himself for your man?

NORA: What way would I live and I an old woman if I didn't marry a man with a bit of a farm, and cows on it, and sheep on the back hills?

MICHAEL: (*Considering*) That's true, Nora, and maybe it's no fool you were, for there's good grazing on it, if it is a lonesome place, and I'm thinking it's a good sum he's left behind.

NORA: (*Taking the stocking with money from her pocket, and putting it on the table*) I do be thinking in the long nights it was a big fool I was that time, Michael Dara, for what good is a bit of a farm with cows on it, and sheep on the back hills, when you do be sitting, looking out from a door the like of that door, and seeing nothing but the mists rolling down the bog, and the mists again, and they rolling up the bog, and hearing nothing but the wind crying out in the bits of broken trees were left from the great storm, and the streams roaring with the rain?

MICHAEL: (*Looking at her uneasily*) What is it ails you this night, Nora Burke? I've heard tell it's the like of that talk you do hear from men, and they after being a great while on the back hills.

NORA: (*Putting out the money on the table*) It's a bad night, and a wild night, Michael Dara, and isn't it a great while I am at the foot of the back hills, sitting up here boiling food for himself, and food for the brood sow, and baking a cake when the night falls? (*She puts up the money, listlessly, in little piles on the table*) Isn't it a long while I am sitting here in the winter, and the summer, and the fine spring, with the young growing behind me and the old passing, saying to myself one time, to look on Mary Brien who wasn't that height (*holding out her hand*), and I a fine girl growing up, and there she is now with two children, and another coming on her in three months or four. (*She pauses*)

MICHAEL: (*Moving over three of the piles*) That's three pounds we have now, Nora Burke.

NORA: (*Continuing in the same voice*) And saying to myself another time, to look on Peggy Cavanagh, who had the lightest hand at milking a cow that wouldn't be easy, or turning a cake, and there she is now walking round on the roads, or sitting in a dirty old house, with no teeth in her mouth, and no sense, and no more hair than you'd see on a bit of a hill and they after burning the furze from it. (*She pauses again*)

MICHAEL: That's five pounds and ten notes, a good sum, surely! ... It's not that way you'll be talking, when you marry a young man, Nora Burke, and they were saying in the fair my lambs were the best lambs, and I got a grand price, for I'm no fool now at making a bargain when my lambs are good.

NORA: What was it you got?

MICHAEL: Twenty pound for the lot, Nora Burke .... We'd do right to wait now till himself will be

10. counting.
11. i.e. a great many, from the Irish *is neart*, meaning both 'power' and 'large number'.

quiet a while in the Seven Churches, and then you'll marry me in the chapel of Rathvanna, and I'll bring the sheep up on the bit of a hill you have on the back mountain, and we won't have anything we'd be afeard to let our minds on when the mist is down.

NORA: (*Pouring him out some whiskey*). Why would I marry you, Mike Dara? You'll be getting old, and I'll be getting old, and in a little while, I'm telling you, you'll be sitting up in your bed — the way himself was sitting — with a shake in your face, and your teeth falling, and the white hair sticking out round you like an old bush where sheep do be leaping a gap.

DAN BURKE *sits up noiselessly from under the sheet, with his hand to his face. His white hair is sticking out round his head.*

NORA: (*Goes on slowly without hearing him*). It's a pitiful thing to be getting old, but it's a queer thing surely.... It's a queer thing to see an old man sitting up there in his bed, with no teeth in him, and a rough word in his mouth, and his chin the way it would take the bark from the edge of an oak board you'd have building a door .... God forgive me, Michael Dara, we'll all be getting old, but it's a queer thing surely.

MICHAEL: It's too lonesome you are from living a long time with an old man, Nora, and you're talking again like a herd that would be coming down from the thick mist (*he puts his arm round her*), but it's a fine life you'll have now with a young man, a fine life surely....

DAN *sneezes violently.* MICHAEL *tries to get to the door, but before he can do so,* DAN *jumps out of the bed in queer white clothes, with the stick in his hand, and goes over and puts his back against it.*

MICHAEL: The Son of God deliver us .... (*Crosses himself, and goes backward across the room*)

DAN: (*Holding up his hand at him*) Now you'll not marry her the time I'm rotting below in the Seven Churches, and you'll see the thing I'll give you will follow you on the back mountains when the wind is high.

MICHAEL: (*To* NORA) Get out of it, Nora, for the love of God. He always did what you bid him, and I'm thinking he would do it now.

NORA: (*Looking at the* TRAMP) Is it dead he is or living?

DAN: (*Turning towards her*) It's little you care if it's dead or living I am, but there'll be an end now of your fine times, and all the talk you have of young men and old men, and of the mist coming up or going down. (*He opens the door*) You'll walk out now from that door, Nora Burke, and it's not tomorrow, or the next day, or any day of your life, that you'll put in your foot through it again.

TRAMP: (*Standing up*) It's a hard thing you're saying, for an old man, master of the house, and what would the like of her do if you put her out on the roads?

DAN: Let her walk round the like of Peggy Cavanagh below, and be begging money at the cross roads, or selling songs to the men. (*To* NORA) Walk out now, Nora Burke, and it's soon you'll be getting old with that life, I'm telling you; it's soon your teeth'll be falling and your head'll be the like of a bush where sheep do be leaping a gap.

He pauses; she looks round at MICHAEL.

MICHAEL: (*Timidly*) There's a fine Union[12] below in Rathdrum.

DAN: The like of her would never go there.... It's lonesome roads she'll be going, and hiding herself away till the end will come, and they find her stretched like a dead sheep with the frost on her, or the big spiders, maybe, and they putting their webs on her, in the butt of a ditch.

NORA: (*Angrily*) What way will yourself be that day, Daniel Burke? What way will you be that day and you lying down a long while in your grave? For it's bad you are living, and it's bad you'll be when you're dead. (*She looks at him a moment fiercely, then half turns away and speaks plaintively again*) Yet, if it is itself, Daniel Burke, who can help it at all, and let you be getting up into your bed, and not be taking your death with the wind blowing on you, and the rain with it, and you half in your skin.

DAN: It's proud and happy you'd be if I was getting my death the day I was shut of[13] yourself. (*Pointing to the door*) Let you walk out through that door, I'm telling you, and let you not be passing this way if it's hungry you are, or wanting a bed.

TRAMP: (*Pointing to* MICHAEL) Maybe himself would take her.

NORA: What would he do with me now?

TRAMP: Give you the half of a dry bed, and good food in your mouth.

DAN: Is it a fool you think him, stranger, or is it a fool you were born yourself? Let her walk out of

12. A workhouse, maintained, at a very basic level indeed, through parish funds, to accommodate the poor and destitute.

13. rid of.

that door, and let you go along with her stranger — if it's raining itself — for it's too much talk you have surely.

TRAMP: (*Going over to* NORA) We'll be going now, lady of the house — the rain is falling but the air is kind, and maybe it'll be a grand morning by the grace of God.

NORA: What good is a grand morning when I'm destroyed surely, and I going out to get my death walking the roads?

TRAMP: You'll not be getting your death with myself, lady of the house, and I knowing all the ways a man can put food in his mouth. . . . We'll be going now, I'm telling you, and the time you'll be feeling the cold and the frost, and the great rain, and the sun again, and the south wind blowing in the glens, you'll not be sitting up on a wet ditch the way you're after sitting in this place, making yourself old with looking on each day and it passing you by. You'll be saying one time, 'It's a grand evening by the grace of God,' and another time, 'It's a wild night, God help us, but it'll pass surely.' You'll be saying —

DAN: (*Goes over to them crying out impatiently*) Go out of that door, I'm telling you, and do your blathering below in the glen.

NORA *gathers a few things into her shawl.*

TRAMP: (*At the door*) Come along with me now, lady of the house, and it's not my blather you'll be hearing only, but you'll be hearing the herons crying out over the black lakes, and you'll be hearing the grouse, and the owls with them, and the larks and the big thrushes when the days are warm, and it's not from the like of them you'll be hearing a talk of getting old like Peggy Cavanagh, and losing the hair off you, and the light of your eyes, but it's fine songs you'll be hearing when the sun goes up, and there'll be no old fellow wheezing the like of a sick sheep close to your ear.

NORA: I'm thinking it's myself will be wheezing that time with lying down under the Heavens when the night is cold, but you've a fine bit of talk, stranger, and it's with yourself I'll go. (*She goes towards the door, then turns to* DAN) You think it's a grand thing you're after doing with your letting on to be dead, but what is it at all? What way would a woman live in a lonesome place the like of this place, and she not making a talk with the men passing? And what way will yourself live from this day, with none to care you? What is it you'll have now but a black life, Daniel Burke, and it's not long, I'm telling you, till you'll be lying again under that sheet, and you dead surely.

She goes out with the TRAMP. MICHAEL *is slinking after them, but* DAN *stops him.*

DAN: Sit down now and take a little taste of the stuff, Michael Dara, there's a great drouth on me, and the night is young.

MICHAEL: (*Coming back to the table*) And it's very dry I am surely, with the fear of death you put on me, and I after driving mountain ewes since the turn of the day.

DAN: (*Throwing away his stick*) I was thinking to strike you, Michael Dara, but you're a quiet man, God help you, and I don't mind you at all. (*He pours out two glasses of whiskey, and gives one to* MICHAEL) Your good health, Michael Dara.

MICHAEL: God reward you, Daniel Burke, and may you have a long life and a quiet life, and good health with it. (*They drink*)

from:
THE PLAYBOY OF THE WESTERN WORLD (1907)

[Synge's great play produced one of the Abbey's major riots when it was presented on 16 January 1907. He was believed by many to caricature the Irish peasants as licentious, foul-mouthed and yet childish — a version, in fact, of the stage-Irishman of the British commercial theatre. A play as complex as this is inevitably embroiled in these disputes about national or folk identity because it is concerned to show the process through which personal identity can be found and communal identity lost. It is a play that questions the realities it establishes.

The action takes place on the day after Christy Mahon's arrival at the village pub of Michael James Flaherty on the Mayo coast. By this time Christy has captivated the villagers with his heroic tale of killing his father with a blow of his loy, and has disenchanted Pegeen with her prospective husband, Shawn Keogh. However, old Mahon has turned up in the previous Act, wounded and vengeful, seen only by Christy and the Widow Quin, who promises to 'swear he's a maniac and not your da.']

PERSONS IN THE PLAY

CHRISTY MAHON
OLD MAHON, *his father, a squatter*
MICHAEL JAMES FLAHERTY, *a publican*
MARGARET FLAHERTY, *called* PEGEEN MIKE, *his daughter*

WIDOW QUIN, *a woman of about thirty*
SHAWN KEOGH, *her cousin, a young farmer*
PHILLY CULLEN *and* JIMMY FARRELL, *small farmers*
SARA TANSEY, *town crier*
VILLAGERS
TOWN CRIER

ACT III

Scene as before [Country public-house or shebeen]. *Later in the day.* JIMMY *comes in, slightly drunk.*

JIMMY: (*Calls*) Pegeen! (*Crosses to inner door*) Pegeen Mike! (*Comes back again into the room*) Pegeen!

PHILLY *comes in in the same state.*

(*To* PHILLY) Did you see herself?

PHILLY: I did not; but I sent Shawn Keogh with the ass-cart for to bear him[1] home. (*Trying cupboards, which are locked*) Well, isn't he a nasty man to get into such staggers at a morning wake;[2] and isn't herself the divil's daughter for locking, and she so fussy after that young gaffer,[3] you might take your death with drouth[4] and none to heed you?

JIMMY: It's little wonder she'd be fussy, and he after bringing bankrupt ruin on the roulette man, and the trick-o'-the-loop[5] man, and breaking the nose of the cockshot-man,[6] and winning all in the sports below, racing, lepping,[7] dancing, and the Lord knows what! He's right luck, I'm telling you.

PHILLY: If he has, he'll be rightly hobbled yet, and he not able to say ten words without making a brag[8] of the way he killed his father, and the great blow he hit with the loy.[9]

JIMMY: A man can't hang by his own informing,[10] and his father should be rotten by now.

OLD MAHON *passes window slowly.*

PHILLY: Supposing a man's digging spuds in that field with a long spade, and supposing he flings up the two halves of that skull, what'll be said then in the papers and the courts of law?

1. Michael James, father of Pegeen Mike.
2. A social gathering in the house of the dead person, before the funeral.
3. Christy.
4. thirst.
5. A game played at fairs in which the spectators tried to guess the centre loop of a ring of cords.
6. Another fair game, in which a man allowed missiles to be thrown at him — for a charge.
7. leaping.
8. boast.
9. A spade for digging turf.
10. A man can't give evidence against himself in a capital trial.

JIMMY: They'd say it was an old Dane, maybe, was drowned in the flood.

OLD MAHON *comes in and sits down near door listening.*

Did you never hear tell of the skulls they have in the city of Dublin, ranged out like blue jugs in a cabin of Connaught?

PHILLY: And you believe that?

JIMMY: (*Pugnaciously*) Didn't a lad see them and he after coming from harvesting in the Liverpool boat? 'They have them there,' says he, 'making a show of the great people there was one time walking the world. White skulls and black skulls and yellow skulls, and some with full teeth, and some haven't only but one.'

PHILLY: It was no lie, maybe, for when I was a young lad there was a graveyard beyond the house with the remnants of a man who had thighs as long as your arm. He was a horrid man, I'm telling you, and there was many a fine Sunday I'd put him together for fun, and he with shiny bones, you wouldn't meet the like of these days in the cities of the world.

MAHON: (*Getting up*) You wouldn't, is it? Lay your eyes on that skull, and tell me where and when there was another the like of it, is splintered only from the blow of a loy.

PHILLY: Glory be to God! And who hit you at all?

MAHON: (*Triumphantly*) It was my own son hit me. Would you believe that?

JIMMY: Well, there's wonders hidden in the heart of man!

PHILLY: (*Suspiciously*) And what way was it done?

MAHON: (*Wandering about the room*) I'm after walking hundreds and long scores of miles, winning clean beds and the fill of my belly four times in the day, and I doing nothing but telling stories of that naked truth. (*He comes to them a little aggressively*) Give me a supeen[11] and I'll tell you now.

WIDOW QUIN *comes in and stands aghast behind him. He is facing* JIMMY *and* PHILLY, *who are on the left.*

JIMMY: Ask herself beyond. She's the stuff hidden in her shawl.

WIDOW QUIN: (*Coming to* MAHON *quickly*) You here, is it? You didn't go far at all?

MAHON: I seen the coasting steamer passing, and I got a drouth upon me and a cramping leg, so I

11. a small sup; '-een' is the diminutive form, from Irish *ín*.

said: 'The divil go along with him,' and turned again. (*Looking under her shawl*) And let you give me a supeen, for I'm destroyed travelling since Tuesday was a week.[12]

WIDOW QUIN: (*Getting a glass, in a cajoling tone*) Sit down then by the fire and take your ease for a space. You've a right to be destroyed indeed, with your walking, and fighting, and facing the sun. (*Giving him poteen*[13] *from a stone jar she has brought in*) There now is a drink for you, and may it be to your happiness and length of life.

MAHON: (*Taking glass greedily, and sitting down by fire*) God increase you!

WIDOW QUIN: (*Taking men to the right stealthily*) Do you know what? That man's raving from his wound today, for I met him a while since telling a rambling tale of a tinker had him destroyed. Then he heard of Christy's deed, and he up and says it was his son had cracked his skull. Oh, isn't madness a fright, for he'll go killing someone yet, and he thinking it's the man has struck him so?

JIMMY: (*Entirely convinced*) It's a fright surely. I knew a party was kicked in the head by a red mare, and he went killing horses a great while, till he eat the insides of a clock and died after.

PHILLY: (*With suspicion*) Did he see Christy?

WIDOW QUIN: He didn't. (*With a warning gesture*) Let you not be putting him in mind of him, or you'll be likely summoned if there's murder done. (*Looking round at* MAHON) Whisht![14] He's listening. Wait now till you hear me taking him easy and unravelling all. (*She goes to* MAHON) And what way are you feeling, mister? Are you in contentment now?

MAHON: (*Slightly emotional from his drink*) I'm poorly only, for it's a hard story the way I'm left today, when it was I did tend him from his hour of birth, and he a dunce never reached his second book,[15] the way he'd come from school, many's the day, with his legs lamed under him, and he blackened with his beatings like a tinker's ass. It's a hard story, I'm saying, the way some do have their next and nighest raising up a hand of murder on them, and some is lonesome getting their death with lamentation in the dead of night.

WIDOW QUIN: (*Not knowing what to say*) To hear you talking so quiet, who'd know you were the same fellow we seen pass today?

MAHON: I'm the same surely. The wrack and ruin of threescore years; and it's a terror to live that length, I tell you, and to have your sons going to the dogs against you, and you wore out scolding them, and skelping[16] them, and God knows what.

PHILLY: (*To* JIMMY) He's not raving. (*To* WIDOW QUIN) Will you ask him what kind was his son?

WIDOW QUIN: (*To* MAHON, *with a peculiar look*) Was your son that hit you a lad of one year and a score maybe, a great hand at racing and lepping and licking the world?

MAHON: (*Turning on her with a roar of rage*) Didn't you hear me say he was the fool of men, the way from this out[17] he'll know the orphan's lot, with old and young making game of him, and they swearing, raging, kicking at him like a mangy cur.

A great burst of cheering outside, some way off.

(*Putting his hands to his ears*) What in the name of God do they want roaring below?

WIDOW QUIN: (*With the shade of a smile*) They're cheering a young lad, the champion Playboy of the Western World.

More cheering.

MAHON: (*Going to window*) It'd split my heart to hear them, and I with pulses in my brain-pan for a week gone by. Is it racing they are?

JIMMY: (*Looking from door*) It is, then. They are mounting him for the mule race will be run upon the sands. That's the playboy on the winkered[18] mule.

MAHON: (*Puzzled*) That lad, is it? If you said it was a fool he was, I'd have laid a mighty oath he was the likeness of my wandering son. (*Uneasily, putting his hand to his head*) Faith, I'm thinking I'll go walking for to view the race.

WIDOW QUIN: (*Stopping him, sharply*) You will not. You'd best take the road to Belmullet, and not be dilly-dallying in this place where there isn't a spot you could sleep.

PHILLY: (*Coming forward*) Don't mind her. Mount there on the bench and you'll have a view of the whole. They're hurrying before the tide will rise, and it'd be near over if you went down the pathway through the crags below.

12. since Tuesday of last week.
13. Illegally distilled alcohol.
14. Hush!
15. i.e. his second year of primary schooling.
16. smacking, beating.
17. from now on.
18. i.e. wearing blinkers.

MAHON: (*Mounts on bench,* WIDOW QUIN *beside him*) That's a right view again[19] the edge of the sea. They're coming now from the point. He's leading. Who is he at all?

WIDOW QUIN: He's the champion of the world, I tell you, and there isn't a ha'p'orth[20] isn't falling lucky to his hands today.

PHILLY: (*Looking out, interested in the race*) Look at that. They're pressing him now.

JIMMY: He'll win it yet.

PHILLY: Take your time, Jimmy Farrell. It's too soon to say.

WIDOW QUIN: (*Shouting*) Watch him taking the gate. There's riding!

JIMMY: (*Cheering*) More power to the young lad!

MAHON: He's passing the third.

JIMMY: He'll lick them yet.

WIDOW QUIN: He'd lick them if he was running races with a score itself.

MAHON: Look at the mule he has, kicking the stars.

WIDOW QUIN: There was a lep! (*Catching hold of* MAHON *in her excitement*) He's fallen? He's mounted again! Faith, he's passing them all!

JIMMY: Look at him skelping her!

PHILLY: And the mountain girls hooshing[21] him on!

JIMMY: It's the last turn! The post's cleared for them now!

MAHON: Look at the narrow place. He'll be into the bogs! (*With a yell*) Good rider! He's through it again!

JIMMY: He's neck and neck!

MAHON: Good boy to him! Flames, but he's in!

Great cheering, in which all join.

(*With hesitation*) What's that? They're raising him up. They're coming this way. (*With a roar of rage and astonishment*) It's Christy, by the stars of God! I'd know his way of spitting and he astride the moon. (*He jumps down and makes a run for the door, but* WIDOW QUIN *catches him and pulls him back*)

WIDOW QUIN: Stay quiet, will you? That's not your son. (*To* JIMMY) Stop him, or you'll get a month for the abetting of manslaughter and be fined as well.

JIMMY: I'll hold him.

MAHON: (*Struggling*) Let me out! Let me out, the lot of you, till I have my vengeance on his head today.

WIDOW QUIN: (*Shaking him, vehemently*) That's not your son. That's a man is going to make a marriage with the daughter of this house, a place with fine trade, with a licence, and with poteen too.

MAHON: (*Amazed*) That man marrying a decent and a moneyed girl! Is it mad yous are? Is it in a crazy-house for females that I'm landed now?

WIDOW QUIN: It's mad yourself is with the blow upon your head. That lad is the wonder of the western world.

MAHON: I seen it's my son.

WIDOW QUIN: You see that you're mad. (*Cheering outside*) Do you hear them cheering him in the zigzags of the road? Aren't you after saying that your son's a fool, and how would they be cheering a true idiot born?

MAHON: (*Getting distressed*) It's maybe out of reason that that man's himself.[22] (*Cheering again*) There's none surely will go cheering him. Oh, I'm raving with a madness that would fright the world! (*He sits down with his hand to his head*) There was one time I seen ten scarlet divils letting on they'd cork my spirit in a gallon can; and one time I seen rats as big as badgers sucking the lifeblood from the butt of my lug;[23] but I never till this day confused that dribbling idiot with a likely man. I'm destroyed surely.

WIDOW QUIN: And who'd wonder when it's your brain-pan that is gaping now?

MAHON: Then the blight of the sacred drouth upon myself and him, for I never went mad to this day, and I not three weeks with the Limerick girls drinking myself silly and parlatic[24] from the dusk to dawn. (*To* WIDOW QUIN, *suddenly*) Is my visage astray?

WIDOW QUIN: It is, then. You're a sniggering maniac, a child could see.

MAHON: (*Getting up more cheerfully*) Then I'd best be going to the union[25] beyond, and there'll be a welcome before me, I tell you (*with great pride*), and I a terrible and fearful case, the way that there I was one time, screeching in a straightened waistcoat,[26] with seven doctors writing out my

19. against.
20. halfpennyworth.
21. urging, cheering.
22. It's perhaps impossible that that man could be Christy.
23. the lobe of my ear.
24. paralytic, immobilized by drink.
25. The workhouse, maintained by parish contributions, for the poor and destitute.
26. strait-jacket.

sayings in a printed book. Would you believe that?

WIDOW QUIN: If you're a wonder itself, you'd best be hasty, for them lads caught a maniac one time and pelted the poor creature till he ran out, raving and foaming, and was drowned in the sea.[27]

MAHON: (*With philosophy*) It's true mankind is the divil when your head's astray. Let me out now and I'll slip down the boreen,[28] and not see them so.

WIDOW QUIN: (*Showing him out*) That's it. Run to the right, and not a one will see.

He runs off.

PHILLY: (*Wisely*) You're at some gaming, Widow Quin; but I'll walk after him and give him his dinner and a time to rest, and I'll see then if he's raving or as sane as you.

WIDOW QUIN: (*Annoyed*) If you go near that lad, let you be wary of your head, I'm saying. Didn't you hear him telling he was crazed at times?

PHILLY: I heard him telling a power,[29] and I'm thinking we'll have right sport before night will fall. (*He goes out*)

JIMMY: Well, Philly's a conceited and foolish man. How could that madman have his senses and his brain-pan slit? I'll go after them and see him turn on Philly now. (*He goes*)

WIDOW QUIN *hides poteen behind counter. Then hubbub outside.*

VOICES: There you are! Good jumper! Grand lepper! Darlint boy! He's the racer! Bear him on, will you!

CHRISTY *comes in, in jockey's dress, with* PEGEEN MIKE, SARA, *and other girls and men.*

PEGEEN: (*To crowd*) Go on now, and don't destroy him, and he drenching with sweat. Go along, I'm saying, and have your tug-of-warring till he's dried his skin.

CROWD: Here's his prizes! A bagpipes! A fiddle was played by a poet in the years gone by! A flat and three-thorned blackthorn would lick the scholars out of Dublin town!

CHRISTY: (*Taking prizes from the men*) Thank you kindly, the lot of you. But you'd say it was little only I did this day if you'd seen me a while since striking my one single blow.

TOWN CRIER: (*Outside ringing a bell*) Take notice, last event of this day! Tug-of-warring on the green below! Come on, the lot of you! Great achievements for all Mayo men!

PEGEEN: Go on and leave him for to rest and dry. Go on, I tell you, for he'll do no more.

She hustles crowd out; WIDOW QUIN *following them.*

MEN: (*Going*) Come on, then. Good luck for the while!

PEGEEN: (*Radiantly, wiping his face with her shawl*) Well, you're the lad, and you'll have great times from this out when you could win that wealth of prizes, and you sweating in the heat of noon!

CHRISTY: (*Looking at her with delight*) I'll have great times if I win the crowning prize I'm seeking now, and that's your promise that you'll wed me in a fortnight, when our banns is called.[30]

PEGEEN: (*Backing away from him*) You've right daring to go ask me that, when all knows you'll be starting to some girl in your own townland, when your father's rotten in four months, or five.

CHRISTY: (*Indignantly*) Starting from you, is it? (*He follows her*) I will not, then, and when the airs is warming, in four months or five, it's then yourself and me should be pacing Neifin[31] in the dews of night, the times sweet smells do be rising, and you'd see a little, shiny, new moon, maybe sinking on the hills.

PEGEEN: (*Looking at him playfully*) And it's that kind of a poacher's love you'd make, Christy Mahon, on the sides of Neifin, when the night is down?

CHRISTY: It's little you'll think if my love's a poacher's, or an earl's itself, when you'll feel my two hands stretched around you, and I squeezing kisses on your puckered lips, till I'd feel a kind of pity for the Lord God[32] is all ages sitting lonesome in His golden chair.

PEGEEN: That'll be right fun, Christy Mahon, and any girl would walk her heart out before she'd meet a young man was your like for eloquence, or talk at all.

CHRISTY: (*Encouraged*) Let you wait, to hear me talking, till we're astray in Erris, when Good Friday's by,[33] drinking a sup from a well, and making mighty kisses with our wetted mouths, or gaming in a gap of sunshine, with yourself stretched

27. Possibly a jibe by Synge at Cuchulain's fate in Yeats's *On Baile's Strand* (see above, p. 612).
28. lane.
29. a great deal.
30. Public notice given in church of an intended marriage so that those who know of any impediment (bann) may lodge an objection.
31. A mountain in Mayo, famed in Gaelic poetry and song.
32. the Lord God [who].
33. After Lent, when the season of abstinence has passed.

back unto your necklace, in the flowers of the earth.

PEGEEN: (*In a low voice, moved by his tone*) I'd be nice so, is it?[34]

CHRISTY: (*With rapture*) If the mitred bishops seen you that time, they'd be the like of the holy prophets, I'm thinking, do be straining the bars of Paradise to lay eyes on the Lady Helen of Troy, and she abroad, pacing back and forward, with a nosegay in her golden shawl.

PEGEEN: (*With real tenderness*) And what is it I have, Christy Mahon, to make me fitting entertainment for the like of you, that has such poet's talking, and such bravery of heart.[35]

CHRISTY: (*In a low voice*) Isn't there the light of seven heavens in your heart alone, the way you'll be an angel's lamp to me from this out, and I abroad in the darkness, spearing salmons in the Owen or the Carrowmore?

PEGEEN: If I was your wife I'd be along with you those nights, Christy Mahon, the way you'd see I was a great hand at coaxing bailiffs, or coining funny nicknames for the stars of night.

CHRISTY: You, is it? Taking your death in the hailstones, or in the fogs of dawn.

PEGEEN: Yourself and me would shelter easy in a narrow bush (*with a qualm of dread*); but we're only talking, maybe, for this would be a poor, thatched place to hold a fine lad is the like of you.

CHRISTY: (*Putting his arm round her*) If I wasn't a good Christian, it's on my naked knees I'd be saying my prayers and paters[36] to every jackstraw you have roofing your head,[37] and every stony pebble is paving the laneway to your door.

PEGEEN: (*Radiantly*) If that's the truth I'll be burning candles from this out to the miracles of God that have brought you from the south today, and I with my gowns bought ready, the way that I can wed you, and not wait at all.

CHRISTY: It's miracles, and that's the truth. Me there toiling a long while, and walking a long while, not knowing at all I was drawing all times nearer to this holy day.

PEGEEN: And myself, a girl, was tempted often to go sailing the seas till I'd marry a Jew-man, with ten kegs of gold, and I not knowing at all there was the like of you drawing nearer, like the stars of God.

CHRISTY: And to think I'm long years hearing women talking that talk, to all bloody fools, and this the first time I've heard the like of your voice talking sweetly for my own delight.

PEGEEN: And to think it's me is talking sweetly, Christy Mahon, and I the fright of seven townlands for my biting tongue. Well, the heart's a wonder; and, I'm thinking, there won't be our like in Mayo, for gallant lovers, from this hour today. (*Drunken singing is heard outside*) There's my father coming from the wake, and when he's had his sleep we'll tell him, for he's peaceful then.

They separate.

MICHAEL: (*Singing outside*)

The jailer and the turnkey
They quickly ran us down,
And brought us back as prisoners
Once more to Cavan town.

He comes in supported by SHAWN.

There we lay bewailing
All in a prison bound....[38]

(*He sees* CHRISTY. *Goes and shakes him drunkenly by the hand, while* PEGEEN and SHAWN *talk on the left. To* CHRISTY) The blessing of God and the holy angels on your head, young fellow. I hear tell you're after winning all in the sports below; and wasn't it a shame I didn't bear you along with me to Kate Cassidy's wake, a fine, stout lad, the like of you, for you'd never see the match of it for flows of drink, the way when we sunk her bones at noonday in her narrow grave, there were five men, aye, and six men, stretched out retching speechless on the holy stones.

CHRISTY: (*Uneasily, watching* PEGEEN) Is that the truth?

MICHAEL: It is, then; and aren't you a louty schemer to go burying your poor father unbeknownst when you'd a right to throw him on the crupper[39] of a Kerry mule and drive him westwards, like holy Joseph[40] in the days gone by, the way we could have given him a decent burial, and not have him rotting beyond, and not a Christian drinking a smart drop to the glory of his soul?

34. Pegeen begins, in language less elevated than Christy's, to show a tenderness unusual to her, making Christy's exposure and triumphant departure the more painful.
35. This is one of the many associations made between eloquence and heroism.
36. pater nosters, the Lord's Prayer.
37. i.e. very particular straw in the thatched roof of the cottage.
38. A ballad entitled 'The Prisoner's Lament'.
39. rump, hindquarters.
40. St Joseph, going to Bethlehem for the birth of Christ.

CHRISTY: (*Gruffly*) It's well enough he's lying, for the likes of him.

MICHAEL: (*Slapping him on the back*) Well, aren't you a hardened slayer? It'll be a poor thing for the household man where you go sniffing for a female wife; and (*pointing to* SHAWN) look beyond at that shy and decent Christian I have chosen for my daughter's hand, and I after getting the gilded dispensation[41] this day for to wed them now.

CHRISTY: And you'll be wedding them this day, is it?

MICHAEL: (*Drawing himself up*) Aye. Are you thinking, if I'm drunk itself, I'd leave my daughter living single with a little frisky rascal is the like of you?

PEGEEN: (*Breaking away from* SHAWN) Is it the truth the dispensation's come?

MICHAEL: (*Triumphantly*) Father Reilly's after reading it in gallous[42] Latin, and 'It's come in the nick of time,' says he; 'so I'll wed them in a hurry, dreading that young gaffer who'd capsize the stars.'

PEGEEN: (*Fiercely*) He's missed his nick of time, for it's that lad, Christy Mahon, that I'm wedding now.

MICHAEL: (*Loudly, with horror*) You'd be making him a son to me, and he wet and crusted with his father's blood?

PEGEEN: Aye. Wouldn't it be a bitter thing for a girl to go marrying the like of Shaneen,[43] and he a middling kind of a scarecrow, with no savagery or fine words in him at all?

MICHAEL: (*Gasping and sinking on a chair*) Oh, aren't you a heathen daughter to go shaking the fat of my heart, and I swamped and drownded with the weight of drink? Would you have them turning on me the way that I'd be roaring to the dawn of day with the wind upon my heart? Have you not a word to aid me, Shaneen? Are you not jealous at all?

SHAWN: (*In great misery*) I'd be afeard to be jealous of a man did slay his da.

PEGEEN: Well, it'd be a poor thing to go marrying your like. I'm saying there's a world of peril for an orphan girl, and isn't it a great blessing I didn't wed you before himself came walking from the west or south?

SHAWN: It's a queer story you'd go picking a dirty tramp up from the highways of the world.

PEGEEN: (*Playfully*) And you think you're a likely beau to go straying along with, the shiny Sundays of the opening year, when it's sooner on a bullock's liver you'd put a poor girl thinking than on the lily or the rose?

SHAWN: And have you no mind of[44] my weight of passion, and the holy dispensation, and the drift[45] of heifers I'm giving, and the golden ring?

PEGEEN: I'm thinking you're too fine for the like of me, Shawn Keogh of Killakeen, and let you go off till you'd find a radiant lady with droves of bullocks on the plains of Meath, and herself bedizened in the diamond jewelleries of Pharaoh's ma. That'd be your match, Shaneen. So God save you now! (*She retreats behind* CHRISTY)

SHAWN: Won't you hear me telling you . . .?

CHRISTY: (*With ferocity*) Take yourself from this, young fellow, or I'll maybe add a murder to my deeds today.

MICHAEL: (*Springing up with a shriek*) Murder is it? Is it mad yous are? Would you go making murder in this place, and it piled with poteen for our drink tonight? Go on to the foreshore if it's fighting you want, where the rising tide will wash all traces from the memory of man. (*Pushing* SHAWN *towards* CHRISTY)

SHAWN: (*Shaking himself free, and getting behind* MICHAEL) I'll not fight him, Michael James. I'd liefer[46] live a bachelor, simmering in passions to the end of time, than face a lepping savage the like of him has descended from the Lord knows where. Strike him yourself, Michael James, or you'll lose my drift of heifers and my blue bull from Sneem.

MICHAEL: Is it me fight him, when it's father-slaying he's bred to now? (*Pushing* SHAWN) Go on, you fool, and fight him now.

SHAWN: (*Coming forward a little*) Will I strike him with my hand?

MICHAEL: Take the loy is on your western side.

SHAWN: I'd be afeard of the gallows if I struck with that.

CHRISTY: (*Taking up the loy*) Then I'll make you face the gallows or quit off from this.

41. The dispensation is needed either because marriage is not normally permitted during Lent or because Pegeen and Shawn Keogh are related within one of the degrees of consanguinity disallowed by the church. Synge has already intimated the degree of inbreeding in this isolated community.
42. From 'gallows', meaning 'fine, splendid'.
43. A contemptuous diminutive for Shawn.
44. Do you give no consideration to.
45. drove.
46. rather.

SHAWN *flies out of the door.*

Well, fine weather be after him (*going to* MICHAEL, *coaxingly*), and I'm thinking you wouldn't wish to have that quaking blackguard in your house at all. Let you give us your blessing and hear her swear her faith to me, for I'm mounted on the spring-tide of the stars of luck, the way it'll be good for any to have me in the house.

PEGEEN: (*At the other side of* MICHAEL) Bless us now, for I swear to God I'll wed him, and I'll not renege.

MICHAEL: (*Standing up in the centre, holding on to both of them*) It's the will of God, I'm thinking, that all should win an easy or a cruel end, and it's the will of God that all should rear up lengthy families for the nurture of the earth. What's a single man, I ask you, eating a bit in one house and drinking a sup in another, and he with no place of his own, like an old braying jackass strayed upon the rocks? (*To* CHRISTY) It's many would be in dread to bring your like into their house for to end them, maybe, with a sudden end; but I'm a decent man of Ireland, and I liefer face the grave untimely and I seeing a score of grandsons growing up little gallant swearers by the name of God, than go peopling my bedside with puny weeds the like of what you'd breed, I'm thinking, out of Shaneen Keogh. (*He joins their hands*) A daring fellow is the jewel of the world, and a man did split his father's middle with a single clout should have the bravery of ten, so may God and Mary and St Patrick bless you, and increase you from this mortal day.

CHRISTY *and* PEGEEN: Amen, O Lord!

Hubbub outside. OLD MAHON *rushes in, followed by all the crowd, and* WIDOW QUIN. *He makes a rush at* CHRISTY, *knocks him down, and begins to beat him.*

PEGEEN: (*Dragging back his arm*) Stop that, will you? Who are you at all?

MAHON: His father, God forgive me!

PEGEEN: (*Drawing back*) Is it rose from the dead?

MAHON: Do you think I look so easy quenched with the tap of a loy? (*Beats* CHRISTY *again*)

PEGEEN: (*Glaring at* CHRISTY) And it's lies you told, letting on you had him slitted, and you nothing at all.

CHRISTY: (*Catching* MAHON's *stick*) He's not my father. He's a raving maniac would scare the world. (*Pointing to* WIDOW QUIN) Herself knows it is true.

CROWD: You're fooling Pegeen! The Widow Quin seen him this day, and you likely knew! You're a liar!

CHRISTY: (*Dumbfounded*) It's himself was a liar, lying stretched out with an open head on him, letting on he was dead.

MAHON: Weren't you off racing the hills before I got my breath with the start I had seeing you turn on me at all?

PEGEEN: And to think of the coaxing glory we had given him, and he after doing nothing but hitting a soft blow and chasing northward in a sweat of fear. Quit off from this.

CHRISTY: (*Piteously*) You've seen my doings this day, and let you save me from the old man; for why would you be in such a scorch of haste to spur me to destruction now?

PEGEEN: It's there your treachery is spurring me, till I'm hard set to think you're the one I'm after lacing in my heart-strings half an hour gone by. (*To* MAHON) Take him on from this, for I think bad the world should see me raging for a Munster liar, and the fool of men.

MAHON: Rise up now to retribution, and come on with me.

CROWD: (*Jeeringly*) There's the playboy! There's the lad thought he'd rule the roost in Mayo! Slate him now, mister.

CHRISTY: (*Getting up in shy terror*) What is it drives you to torment me here, when I'd asked the thunders of the might of God to blast me if I ever did hurt to any saving only that one single blow.

MAHON: (*Loudly*) If you didn't, you're a poor good-for-nothing, and isn't it by the like of you the sins of the whole world are commited?

CHRISTY: (*Raising his hands*) In the name of the Almighty God . . . .

MAHON: Leave troubling the Lord God. Would you have Him sending down droughts, and fevers, and the old hen and the cholera morbus?[47]

CHRISTY: (*To* WIDOW QUIN) Will you come between us and protect me now?

WIDOW QUIN: I've tried a lot, God help me, and my share is done.

CHRISTY: (*Looking round in desperation*) And I must go back into my torment is it, or run off like a vagabond straying through the unions with the dust of August making mudstains in the gullet of my throat; or the winds of March blowing on me till I'd take an oath I felt them making whistles of my ribs within?

47. influenza and diarrhoea.

SARA: Ask Pegeen to aid you. Her like does often change.

CHRISTY: I will not, then, for there's torment in the splendour of her like, and she a girl any moon of midnight would take pride to meet, facing southwards on the heaths of Keel. But what did I want crawling forward to scorch my understanding at her flaming brow?

PEGEEN: (*To* MAHON, *vehemently, fearing she will break into tears*) Take him on from this or I'll set the young lads to destroy him here.

MAHON: (*Going to him, shaking his stick*) Come on now if you wouldn't have the company to see you skelped.

PEGEEN: (*Half laughing, through her tears*) That's it, now the world will see him pandied,[48] and he an ugly liar was playing off the hero, and the fright of men.

CHRISTY: (*To* MAHON, *very sharply*) Leave me go!

CROWD: That's it. Now, Christy. If them two set fighting, it will lick the world.

MAHON: (*Making a grab at* CHRISTY) Come here to me.

CHRISTY: (*More threateningly*) Leave me go, I'm saying.

MAHON: I will, maybe, when your legs is limping, and your back is blue.

CROWD: Keep it up, the two of you. I'll back the old one. Now the playboy.

CHRISTY: (*In low and intense voice*) Shut your yelling, for if you're after making a mighty man of me this day by the power of a lie, you're setting me now to think if it's a poor thing to be lonesome it's worse, maybe, go mixing with the fools of earth.

MAHON *makes a movement towards him.*

(*Almost shouting*) Keep off ... lest I do show a blow unto the lot of you would set the guardian angels winking in the clouds above. (*He swings round with a sudden rapid movement and picks up a loy*)

CROWD: (*Half frightened, half amused*) He's going mad! Mind yourselves! Run from the idiot!

CHRISTY: If I am an idiot, I'm after hearing my voice this day saying words would raise the top-knot on a poet in a merchant's town. I've won your racing, and your lepping, and ....

MAHON: Shut your gullet and come on with me.

CHRISTY: I'm going, but I'll stretch you first.

He runs at OLD MAHON *with the loy, chases him out of the door, followed by crowd and* WIDOW QUIN. *There is a great noise outside, then a yell, and dead silence for a moment.* CHRISTY *comes in, half dazed, and goes to fire.*

WIDOW QUIN: (*Coming in hurriedly, and going to him*) They're turning again you. Come on, or you'll be hanged, indeed.

CHRISTY: I'm thinking, from this out, Pegeen'll be giving me praises, the same as in the hours gone by.

WIDOW QUIN: (*Impatiently*) Come by the back door. I'd think bad to have you stifled on the gallows tree.

CHRISTY: (*Indignantly*) I will not, then. What good'd be my lifetime if I left Pegeen?

WIDOW QUIN: Come on, and you'll be no worse than you were last night; and you with a double murder this time to be telling to the girls.

CHRISTY: I'll not leave Pegeen Mike.

WIDOW QUIN: (*Impatiently*) Isn't there the match of her in every parish public, from Binghamstown unto the plain of Meath? Come on, I tell you, and I'll find you finer sweethearts at each waning moon.

CHRISTY: It's Pegeen I'm seeking only, and what'd I care if you brought me a drift of chosen females, standing in their shifts[49] itself, maybe, from this place to the eastern world?

SARA: (*Runs in, pulling off one of her petticoats*) They're going to hang him. (*Holding out petticoat and shawl*) Fit these upon him, and let him run off to the east.

WIDOW QUIN: He's raving now; but we'll fit them on him, and I'll take him in the ferry to the Achill boat.[50]

CHRISTY: (*Struggling feebly*) Leave me go, will you? when I'm thinking of my luck today, for she will wed me surely, and I a proven hero in the end of all.

They try to fasten petticoat round him.

WIDOW QUIN: Take his left hand and we'll pull him now. Come on, young fellow.

CHRISTY: (*Suddenly starting up*) You'll be taking me from her? You're jealous, is it, of her wedding me? Go on from this. (*He snatches up a stool, and threatens them with it*)

48. Beaten like a schoolboy. A pandy bat was a leather strap used in boys' schools.

49. slips, chemises. The word outraged the play's first audiences.

50. The Widow Quin and Sara are still trying to find sanctuary for Christy on the islands of the Mayo coast. Achill is one of those islands.

WIDOW QUIN: (*Going*) It's in the madhouse they should put him, not in jail, at all. We'll go by the back door to call the doctor, and we'll save him so.

She goes out, with SARA, *through inner room. Men crowed in the doorway.* CHRISTY *sits down again by the fire.*

MICHAEL: (*In a terrified whisper*) Is the old lad killed surely?

PHILLY: I'm after feeling the last gasps quitting his heart.

They peer in at CHRISTY.

MICHAEL: (*With a rope*) Look at the way he is. Twist a hangman's knot on it, and slip it over his head, while he's not minding at all.

PHILLY: Let you take it, Shaneen. You're the soberest of all that's here.

SHAWN: Is it me to go near him, and he the wickedest and worst with me? Let you take it, Pegeen Mike.

PEGEEN: Come on, so.

She goes forward with the others, and they drop the double hitch over his head.

CHRISTY: What ails you?

SHAWN: (*Triumphantly, as they pull the rope tight on his arms*) Come on to the peelers,[51] till they stretch you now.

CHRISTY: Me!

MICHAEL: If we took pity on you the Lord God would, maybe, bring us ruin from the law today, so you'd best come easy, for hanging is an easy and a speedy end.

CHRISTY: I'll not stir. (*To* PEGEEN) And what is it you'll say to me, and I after doing it this time in the face of all?

PEGEEN: I'll say, a strange man is a marvel, with his mighty talk; but what's a squabble in your back yard, and the blow of a loy, have taught me that there's a great gap between a gallous story and a dirty deed. (*To men*) Take him on from this, or the lot of us will be likely put on trial for his deed today.

CHRISTY: (*With horror in his voice*) And it's yourself will send me off, to have a horny-fingered hangman hitching slip-knots at the butt of my ear.

MEN: (*Pulling rope*) Come on, will you?

He is pulled down on the floor.

CHRISTY: (*Twisting his legs round the table*) Cut the rope, Pegeen, and I'll quit the lot of you, and live from this out, like the madman of Keel,[52] eating muck and green weeds on the faces of the cliffs.

PEGEEN: And leave us to hang, is it, for a saucy liar, the like of you? (*To men*) Take him on, out from this.

SHAWN: Pull a twist on his neck, and squeeze him so.

PHILLY: Twist yourself. Sure he cannot hurt you, if you keep your distance from his teeth alone.

SHAWN: I'm afeard of him. (*To* PEGEEN) Lift a lighted sod, will you, and scorch his leg.

PEGEEN: (*Blowing the fire with a bellows*) Leave go now, young fellow, or I'll scorch your shins.

CHRISTY: You're blowing for to torture me. (*His voice rising and growing stronger*) That's your kind, is it? Then let the lot of you be wary, for, if I've to face the gallows, I'll have a gay march down, I tell you, and shed the blood of some of you before I die.

SHAWN: (*In terror*) Keep a good hold, Philly. Be wary, for the love of God. For I'm thinking he would liefest wreak his pains on me.

CHRISTY: (*Almost gaily*) If I do lay my hands on you, it's the way you'll be at the fall of night, hanging as a scarecrow for the fowls of hell. Ah, you'll have a gallous jaunt, I'm saying, coaching out through limbo with my father's ghost.

SHAWN: (*To* PEGEEN) Make haste, will you? Oh, isn't he a holy terror, and isn't it true for Father Reilly, that all drink's a curse that has the lot of you so shaky and uncertain now?

CHRISTY: If I can wring a neck among you, I'll have a royal judgment looking on the trembling jury in the courts of law. And won't there be crying out in Mayo the day I'm stretched upon the rope, with ladies in their silks and satins snivelling in their lacy kerchiefs, and they rhyming songs and ballads on the terror of my fate? (*He squirms round on the floor and bites* SHAWN'*s leg*)

SHAWN: (*Shrieking*) My leg's bit on me. He's the like of a mad dog, I'm thinking, the way that I will surely die.

CHRISTY: (*Delighted with himself*) You will, then, the way you can shake out hell's flags of welcome for my coming in two weeks or three, for I'm thinking Satan hasn't many have killed their da in Kerry, and in Mayo too.

OLD MAHON *comes in behind on all fours and looks on unnoticed.*

51. The police. The nickname was particularly applied to members of the Irish constabulary, founded between 1812 and 1818 by Sir Robert Peel, then chief secretary for Ireland, later British prime minister.

52. The madman of Keel, a village in County Mayo, was reputed to live on the line between the shore and the sea and to survive on a diet of seagrass and periwinkles.

MEN: (*To* PEGEEN) Bring the sod, will you?

PEGEEN: (*Coming over*) God help him so. (*Burns his leg*)

CHRISTY: (*Kicking and screaming*) Oh, glory be to God! (*He kicks loose from the table, and they all drag him towards the door*)

JIMMY: (*Seeing* OLD MAHON) Will you look what's come in?

They all drop CHRISTY *and run left.*

CHRISTY: (*Scrambling on his knees face to face with* OLD MAHON) Are you coming to be killed a third time, or what ails you now?

MAHON: For what is it they have you tied?

CHRISTY: They're taking me to the peelers to have me hanged for slaying you.

MICHAEL: (*Apologetically*) It is the will of God that all should guard their little cabins from the treachery of law, and what would my daughter be doing if I was ruined or was hanged itself?

MAHON: (*Grimly, loosening* CHRISTY) It's little I care if you put a bag on her back, and went picking cockles till the hour of death; but my son and myself will be going our own way, and we'll have great times from this out telling stories of the villainy of Mayo, and the fools is here. (*To* CHRISTY, *who is freed*) Come on now.

CHRISTY: Go with you, is it? I will then, like a gallant captain with his heathen slave. Go on now and I'll see you from this day stewing my oatmeal and washing my spuds, for I'm master of all fights from now. (*Pushing* MAHON) Go on, I'm saying.

MAHON: Is it me?

CHRISTY: Not a word out of you. Go on from this.

MAHON: (*Walking out and looking back at* CHRISTY *over his shoulder*) Glory be to God! (*With a broad smile*) I am crazy again. (*Goes*)

CHRISTY: Ten thousand blessings upon all that's here, for you've turned me a likely gaffer[53] in the end of all, the way I'll go romancing through a romping lifetime from this hour to the dawning of the Judgment Day. (*He goes out*)

MICHAEL: By the will of God, we'll have peace now for our drinks. Will you draw the porter, Pegeen?

SHAWN: (*Going up to her*) It's a miracle Father Reilly can wed us in the end of all, and we'll have none to trouble us when his vicious bite is healed.

PEGEEN: (*Hitting him a box on the ear*) Quit my sight. (*Putting her shawl over her head and breaking out into wild lamentations*) Oh, my grief, I've lost him surely. I've lost the only Playboy of the Western World.

53. i.e. you have made me a considerable person, or boss.

LENNOX ROBINSON

(1886-1958)

from: THE WHITEHEADED BOY (1916)

A PLAY IN THREE ACTS

[First produced at the Abbey on 13 December 1916, this play became one of the most popular items in the theatre's repertoire. The triumph of Denis Geoghegan, the whiteheaded boy — that is, the family favourite or pet — is a victory of good spirits and decency over chicanery and deceit. Robinson himself saw the play in retrospect as 'political from beginning to end'; Denis and his family do not directly represent the relationship between Ireland and England. Yet, as in much Irish comic drama, the political implication or possibility lends force to the treatment of the theme of personal liberation.

The play is presented by a persona who governs the stage directions and provides a distancing commentary on the events.]

CHARACTERS

MRS GEOGHEGAN
GEORGE
PETER } *her children*
DENIS }
DONOUGH BROSNAN, *engaged to* JANE
JOHN DUFFY, *Postmaster and Chairman Rural District Council*
AUNT ELLEN

ACT II

The same room again later in the evening and GEORGE *and* PETER *sitting, talking.*

PETER: You think I should take it, then?

GEORGE: I do.

PETER: But supposing it fails?

GEORGE: Aunt Ellen will stick to it for a year or two, and by that time it will have failed or succeeded. If it's a success, you're game ball;[1] if it fails you're no worse off than you are now, and there will always be foolish, contrary people starting them co-operative things;[2] that class is as thick as thieves and lavish with the money; once you get well in with them they'll not desert you. Besides, you knowing all about shopkeeping, you'll be able to make things easier for the locals. Do you understand me?

PETER: I do.

GEORGE: Them co-operatives have never succeeded yet, but if they ever do — 'twould be bad days for us. I'd like to see you there for life, and yet 'twouldn't be well to be too successful.

PETER: Ah, there'll be some sort of a middle course. (*With a wink*)

GEORGE: That's what's in my mind.

PETER: And Donough will marry Jane and come here in my place, and Baby will be up in Dublin, and Denis will be off our hands. Faith, it all fits together as neat as a puzzle.

GEORGE: And you could be giving an eye to Aunt Ellen's bit of land, and not letting her play puck with it[3] with her contrary schemes, and in the end she'll leave it to you, why wouldn't she? She'll forget Denis when the salt water's between them.

PETER: He's been a weight on us for years; we're well rid of him. But all the same, I felt sorry for the poor fellow tonight.

GEORGE: Ah, he'll do first-class in Canada. Sure, all sorts does well out there. I'm only afraid of the mother having the life wore out of me fretting after him.

PETER: She'll get over that in time.

GEORGE: Well, she must. I'm not going back on what I said about Denis. Go he must.

(Here's their aunt)

AUNT ELLEN: George, your mother wants you. She's above in her room.

GEORGE: Is she after going to bed?

AUNT ELLEN: She is not; she can't get this business of Denis out of her mind, the creature.

GEORGE: There's no use in her talking of it to me. My mind is made up; we're all determined. Denis must go.

AUNT ELLEN: Even so, a word from you might quiet her. Anyhow, she won't take rest till she sees you.

GEORGE: I'll go to her so.

(*He's gone. 'Tisn't likely there's anything he can say will quiet her*)

AUNT ELLEN: You'd have to pity her. Denis was always her white-headed boy, and this is a blow to her. Well, we must all go through with it . . . . Tell me, are you coming out to Kilmurray?

PETER: I'm after talking it over with George; he advises me to go.

AUNT ELLEN: He's right. You'll never regret it. I suppose you know all about co-operation?

PETER: Divil a bit. But I can keep a shop.

AUNT ELLEN: That's all we want.

PETER: I'll leave you and the Committee to do the co-operating.

AUNT ELLEN: You'd better come back there with me tomorrow. The sooner you see the Committee the better. Not that there's a fear you won't get it, for I mentioned your name to them and they were agreeable; but it's best to make sure of them; you never know when they wouldn't turn round behind your back and put in an ignorant fellow — a fellow who couldn't weigh a pound of sugar — just because he was a relation of one of them. It's one of the curses of the country, giving positions to relations.

PETER: I agree with you, Aunt.

AUNT ELLEN: They're a jobbing, ignorant crowd out at Kilmurray . . . . There's a knock. Who can it be this hour of night?

PETER: Hannah's snoring this half-hour. I'll see who it is.

(*He's gone and here he is back and* JOHN DUFFY *with him.* JOHN *is one of the solidest men in Ballycolman,*

1. i.e. you are a winner, triumphant.
2. The Irish Co-operative Movement, founded in 1889 by Sir Horace Plunkett, had only partial success. In his book *Ireland in the New Century* (1904), Plunkett criticized the influence of the clergy in repressing individual initiative. He was attacked by both nationalists and unionists. The cooperative movement remained an important contribution to the idea of economic independence through the modernization of agriculture.
3. In the game of hurling, to puck the ball is to strike it hard in the air — hence 'to play puck with it' is to play games with it, by shuttling the land to and fro between her various schemes.

Chairman of the District Council, Chairman of the Race Committee, and a member of every Committee and every League in the village. He has three public houses and a grocery business and the Post Office, and a branch of the National Bank once a month,[4] *and a trade in old hens and eggs, and a terrible turnover in turkeys at Christmas . . . . Oh, a weighty man . . . . Yes, he buried the wife long ago; he has no child but* DELIA. *He's not looking in too pleasant a humour)*

AUNT ELLEN: Oh, good evening, Mr Duffy; you're welcome. I was wondering who the knock might be.

DUFFY: 'Tis late for visits, but I slipped up to see George for a minute.

AUNT ELLEN: He's in the mother's room. Will you tell him, Peter?
(PETER*'s gone to tell* GEORGE) Will you sit down, Mr Duffy . . . . 'Twon't be long to Christmas now.

DUFFY: That's true.

AUNT ELLEN: You're looking well. How's Delia these times?

DUFFY: She's well enough. She got a great throw-over[5] tonight.

AUNT ELLEN: Is that a fact?

DUFFY: Is Denis around?

AUNT ELLEN: He's not. He's gone to bed.

DUFFY: He's going from you, I hear?

AUNT ELLEN: He is indeed, poor boy. It's hard parting from him, but since it's for his advantage we wouldn't stand in his way.
(*Wouldn't anyone believe her the way she says it?*)

DUFFY: To be sure, to be sure.

AUNT ELLEN: I always said he was too clever to be a doctor. When you see the ignorant fellows that are turned into doctors, you can't believe, Mr Duffy, that it takes much wit to cut off a man's leg or to give him a bottle of medicine.

DUFFY: There's something in that.

AUNT ELLEN: Now in Canada he'll find an opening suitable to his smartness. A brother of my own went out there forty years ago and 'tis wonderful the way he got on.

DUFFY: Is it to his people Denis is going?

AUNT ELLEN: It is. He left a troop of sons and daughters after him.

DUFFY: And where do they live?

AUNT ELLEN: They? — Oh, they live in Saint Paul.

DUFFY: I thought that was in the States.

AUNT ELLEN: There's a place of that name in Canada, too. Do you suppose I wouldn't know my own brother's place?

DUFFY: I beg your pardon, ma'am; indeed I meant no such thing. He's in business, I suppose?

AUNT ELLEN: You may say he is, then. By all accounts he owns half the town.

DUFFY: Do you tell me? Denis will have a fine position so.

AUNT ELLEN: Oh, the best in the world. Nothing to do but superintending like, strolling about with his hands in his pockets making other people work, and putting money in the Bank all the time.

DUFFY: Bedad, that sounds a good life. Tell me, what class of business has your brother?

(*That's a facer!*)[6]

AUNT ELLEN: A mixed business, Mr Duffy.

(*Good woman!*)

DUFFY: I see.

(*Here's* PETER *back with* GEORGE)

GEORGE: You were wanting me, John?

DUFFY: I was.

GEORGE: If it's the fertilizer you're after, I didn't get it in yet. I have it ordered a fortnight or more.

DUFFY: 'Tisn't that at all . . . . This is great news about Denis.

GEORGE: Ay.

DUFFY: He's off to Canada?

GEORGE: He is.

DUFFY: Hannah was blowing[7] about a fine place he's going to, and your Aunt was saying the same thing just now. It's a fact I suppose?

GEORGE: That's true.

DUFFY: Lashings of money and nothing to do.

GEORGE: I believe so.

DUFFY: His cousins own the town?

GEORGE: They do.

DUFFY: 'Tis very sudden.

GEORGE: That's the way things come, John. Only this evening it was settled.

AUNT ELLEN: Of course, Denis being so clever, we always looked for something big to turn up for him.

DUFFY: Delia's in a state over it.

4. He was deputed manager of the National Bank which opened a branch in rented premises each month.
5. shock.
6. A stiff question to answer.
7. boasting.

GEORGE: Ah, she needn't be. Indeed, we were all sorry about that, but it couldn't be helped. They were only children, John, and with Denis going off now there was no use going on with it. Delia's a nice little girl; she's too good for Denis —

PETER: That's a fact.

AUNT ELLEN: She'll take up with someone who'll be a deal more suitable.

DUFFY: They've been promised to one another for two years; so soon as he'd be a doctor they were to be married, and now in the heel of the hunt he gets a big position in Canada, he spreads his sails and away with him, leaving her behind. Faith, it looks to me as if you thought she wasn't good enough for him.

(*Didn't I know he was near his temper*)

GEORGE: Indeed, John, you're making a mistake. That's not the way with it at all. It's the other way about.

DUFFY: That's the way I look at it, anyway, and that's the way the neighbours will look at it.

GEORGE: Sure, it's not cross about it you are?

DUFFY: Oh no, not at all. There's nothing in the wide world a man likes better than to have his only child trampled on like dirt, to be left fooled, to be made a mock of by the countryside. Cross? What would make me cross? I never felt in a pleasanter temper than I do this minute.

PETER: You're talking strange.

DUFFY: The two of you will hear stranger talk than this before you've finished with the Duffys.

GEORGE: What do you mean?

DUFFY: I mean that Denis marries Delia, or else ....

GEORGE: He can't marry her.

AUNT ELLEN: Put that notion out of your mind, Mr Duffy.

DUFFY: Then if he won't marry her, I put the matter into the lawyer's hands tomorrow. £1,000 damages.

(*Oh, my God!*)

GEORGE: John!

AUNT ELLEN: Mr Duffy!

PETER: You're raving!

DUFFY: Ay, you think yourselves great people, don't you? You've a brother who's a gentleman, who is much too high up to get married to a Duffy. It's good enough for Delia to be thrown aside like an old shoe when the fancy takes you. She's not good enough to be brought to Canada, to the fine place there that ....

GEORGE: John, wait. I ....

DUFFY: But I'll show you you've mistaken your man. As long as Delia has a father by her she'll not be treated that way. I'll show you! The Duffys aren't people to be trampled on so easy. I've power to my back — and money — more money than you have — and, by the same token, I'll see a lump of yours before I'm done with you. I'll have the smartest lawyer in Ireland on my side. I got all Denis's letters off Delia tonight — oh, there's no doubt of my case. I'll beat you to the wall, I'll bleed you, I'll teach you the way to treat a decent, honest, poor girl who never did you a day's harm only demeaned herself mixing with low, sneaking people the like of the Geoghegans. Good night to you.

GEORGE: Stop, for God's sake, Mr Duffy. You don't know what you're talking about.

DUFFY: Faith, I do, only too well.

GEORGE: 'Tisn't true. All that about Canada isn't true.

DUFFY: Isn't he going there?

GEORGE: He is, but not to ....

DUFFY: That's enough about it.

(*He's going out, but* GEORGE *is holding him back*)

GEORGE: Don't go. Look here, I'm telling you the truth now, the same as if you were a magistrate on the bench. He's going to no situation there; he's been kicked out of this because we're tired of paying his bills.

DUFFY: Do you expect me to believe that?

GEORGE: You must believe it. Aunt Ellen, tell him that what I'm saying is true.

AUNT ELLEN: It's true, every word of it. I've no cousins in Canada, my brother died unmarried, Denis will have to work like a labourer in Canada.

PETER: We're turning him out; he's a useless, idle fellow.

AUNT ELLEN: Delia's well rid of him; a burden he'd be to her.

GEORGE: She'll get a man twice as good before the year's out.

PETER: He's a waster.

GEORGE: No sense at all.

PETER: A gambler, betting all day on horses.

AUNT ELLEN: Cards and drink.

GEORGE: He has his mother's heart broken.

PETER: 'Tis a great escape Delia's having.

GEORGE: They'd be in the Union[8] before they'd be a year married.

8. the workhouse.

AUNT ELLEN: He's a disgrace to the family.

DUFFY: Well, what sort of a fool do you take me to be at all? Haven't I two eyes in my head? Don't I know Denis since the day he was born? Isn't he known to be the cleverest, smartest . . . .

GEORGE: Not at all.

DUFFY: . . . lad in the countryside. Didn't you tell me yourself the way he swept all before him in the College in Dublin?

GEORGE: 'Tisn't true. Three times he's after failing.

DUFFY: Wasn't he going to be set up there in a big house?

PETER: Not at all.

DUFFY: Wasn't his aunt going to leave him all her money?

AUNT ELLEN: He'll never get a penny from me.

DUFFY: And now you'd like me to turn around and disbelieve it all. Ah, you're clever, but you're not clever enough for me.

GEORGE: You're making a mistake. Tonight things turned up.

DUFFY: They did; I know well they did. Canada turned up, a big position turned up, plans and schemes you made to throw us over. I see your game. Tell me George, is St Paul the name of the place Denis is going to?

GEORGE: No.

(*Look at* DUFFY *turning on the aunt*)

DUFFY: Didn't I know you were lying, ye old brazen thing, the way I wouldn't be able to trace him to bring him back to marry my daughter. But I don't care a damn where he is going to. You're right, Delia's well quit of him; she's well quit of the whole troop of the Geoghegans — but I want that £1,000 and I'll have it too.

PETER: It's the truth we're telling you, Mr Duffy. The rest was all lies.

DUFFY: I know well it's liars you all are.

(*Here's* DONOUGH*; he's excited-like*)

DONOUGH: I couldn't go home till I'd congratulated you about Denis. All the people at the concert were talking of it. It's over railways he'll be, I'm told; a sort of railway king.

GEORGE: Oh, my God!

DUFFY: Do you hear that?

DONOUGH: George, my mind's made up; I'm going with him. When he has all that power he'll be able to do something for the man that's going to marry his sister. I'm tired of slaving on here and no nearer marrying Jane than I was five years ago. Now I'll have her out to me before the autumn. What day is he sailing?

AUNT ELLEN: Don't mind what the people are saying, Donough. There's not a word of truth in it all.

DONOUGH: Isn't Denis going to Canada?

AUNT ELLEN: He is, but not . . . .

DONOUGH: Well, then, what's to hinder me going along with him? 'Twill be a queer thing if he doesn't contrive to get me into a good job out there.

GEORGE: He'll do nothing of the sort.

PETER: Put the idea out of your head.

DONOUGH: Why so?

DUFFY: Listen here to me, Donough; I'll tell you the way it is. This family's too high up in themselves for the like of you and me. We're not class enough for them, do you see? The Geoghegans are a great people, the Duffys aren't good enough for them at all. We've been thrown over; Delia's not a fit match for my brave Denis. You'll be the next to go; it couldn't be expected that Jane Geoghegan would marry Donough Brosnan. They have plans of marrying Jane to a lord.

DONOUGH: What's that you say?

GEORGE: Don't mind him, Donough.

DONOUGH: I will mind him.

GEORGE: You can marry Jane tomorrow for all I care. Duffy's mad.

DUFFY: Mad? Take care what you're saying, George Geoghegan. There's a law against slander and abuse as well as against breaking a promise of marriage. Here's my final word to you: Denis marries Delia and takes her with him to Canada.

GEORGE: He can't.

DUFFY: Or he finishes his course in Dublin and marries her when he's a doctor, the very minute he's qualified.

GEORGE: He can't.

DUFFY: Then I bring an action. £1,000 damages. You can take your choice. I'll give you ten minutes to yourselves to talk it over. I've got to go and see Magner for a minute. I'll be back for an answer. Mind, I mean every word I say. The marriage or an action. That's my final word to you, you pack of schemers!

(*He's off — what a slam he gave the door!*)

AUNT ELLEN: He's a terrible man.

GEORGE: That's a nice fix we're in.

PETER: What the divil can we do now?

DONOUGH: I don't understand what it's all about.

GEORGE: We're kicking Denis out to Canada because he's a useless, idle, extravagant fellow, and Duffy has an idea that he's going out to some big place there, and is mad he won't marry Delia.

DONOUGH: Is that the way it is? I never had much belief in Denis.

GEORGE: I wish to God you could get Duffy and the rest to be of the same mind. There's no one in the village will believe the truth.

DONOUGH: Sure, there's nothing harder to believe than the truth.

PETER: But what are we going to do?

GEORGE: Let me think. My head's bursting. What was it Duffy said? Either marry her and take her to Canada, or go through with College; or else the breach of promise .... I won't send him back to College; I'd rather have the breach — 'twouldn't cost me more in the end. Maybe Denis might be ten years in Dublin or twenty years missing his examinations and spending money. Oh, where would it all come from? ... But £1,000 to go to Duffy, or £500 itself — we'd be ruined; we'd never get it back from the shop.

DONOUGH: Yerra, let Duffy bring the case against Denis and bankrupt him. What matter?

GEORGE: Bankrupt him! Do you think I'm the one to stand by and see a Geoghegan broken by a Duffy or anyone else? I'd sooner die in the Union. There's but the one thing for it. Denis must marry her; he must take her with him to Canada.

AUNT ELLEN: He'll do that all right; sure he's mad to marry her.

GEORGE: Call him down here, Peter.

AUNT ELLEN: He's gone to bed I think.

GEORGE: Pull him out of bed, then. This must be settled before Duffy comes back. He'll put the case into the lawyer's hands tomorrow if we don't.

PETER: I'll call him.

(He's gone)

AUNT ELLEN: It's a terrible upset we're in.

GEORGE: It was all your fault with your schemes for saving the family's good name. If we'd told the truth from the first, this wouldn't be on us now.

(He's turning on her)

AUNT ELLEN: That's a queer thing to say to me, George. Small respect you're showing me.

GEORGE: I don't know what I'm saying.

AUNT ELLEN: It looks like it indeed. Anyway, the truth's a dangerous thing to be saying in a little place like Ballycolman.

DONOUGH: It will be all right. Denis will marry Delia, and there'll be no more about it.

GEORGE: I won't have an easy minute till the pair of them are married and gone. Oh Donough, it's an awful thing to be the head of a family. Since the father died I've not had a minute's rest, pulled this way and that way, this one wanting to get married, another going into business, Baby flying up to Dublin, Denis doctoring — many a time I wished I was born an orphan.

AUNT ELLEN: God forgive you.

GEORGE: It's true, Aunt Ellen. Look at the life I've led between you all, and no one ever thinking maybe I'd want to get married, or have a bit of fun, or spend a bit of money. For two pins I'd throw the lot of ye over tomorrow and sail away out of this for ever.

AUNT ELLEN: Yerra talk sense, George; that's no way to be behaving.

GEORGE: There's no escape for me. I'm caught like an old cow with her head in a stall.

(Here's PETER *back with* DENIS. *It was no lie saying he was in bed, look at his striped pyjamas and his elegant dressing gown)*

DENIS: What do you want me for? Haven't you bothered me enough this evening without hauling me out of bed?

GEORGE: Denis, old Duffy has been here raging mad. He threatens a breach of promise unless you marry Delia. You'll have to do it. You'll have to marry her at once.

DENIS: What? Marry Delia?

GEORGE: Yes, and take her to Canada along with you.

DENIS: Oh!

AUNT ELLEN: I knew you'd be delighted. 'Twas breaking your heart parting from her.

DENIS: And what are we to live on in Canada?

GEORGE: You'll find plenty to live on.

AUNT ELLEN: A man's lost without a woman out there, they say. You'd read on the papers the great scarcity of women there is in Canada.

PETER: That's so; she'll be a great addition to you.

AUNT ELLEN: Father Murphy would marry you tomorrow when he knows the hurry you're in.

DENIS: I see .... Listen here to me. Haven't I agreed to everything you've planned for me all my life through. Tonight I agreed to go to Canada because it's your wish; I agreed to break with Delia. Now you want me to take Delia off to Canada, without a position, without a place to go to, with a few pounds in my pocket that wouldn't keep us for a month. Put the idea out of your head; I'll not do it. There's things I'll submit to myself, but I won't ask Delia to share them.

GEORGE: Do you mean to tell me you don't want to marry Delia? You don't care about her?

DENIS: I do care about her. That's why I won't marry her.

GEORGE: That's crazy talk. You'll do all right in Canada.

PETER: You won't be there a week before you'll have a big position.

DONOUGH: You're sure to do fine.

GEORGE: A clever lad like you will get on fast.

DENIS: You hadn't much opinion of my cleverness an hour ago. I'll have to rough it and take my chance with all the others, and as soon as I've made a place for myself I'll marry Delia; but I'll not ask her to share the roughness and poverty you're sending me out to.

GEORGE: Denis don't turn on us like this.

DENIS: You turned on me bitterly tonight, George. You've kicked me out, you've wrecked my life, you've made me give up Delia.

GEORGE: But I want you to marry her now.

DENIS: And I won't. You know why.

GEORGE: I'd give you a few pounds going to Canada.

DENIS: I won't take them.

GEORGE: If you went back to College —

DENIS: I won't go back to College.

AUNT ELLEN: In the name of God, what do you want?

DENIS: I want to be let make my own life in my own way. I want to be let alone and not bothered.

(He's going towards the door)

GEORGE: Where are you off to?

DENIS: To bed, of course — and to Canada.

GEORGE: Will you marry Delia?

DENIS: No.

(And he's gone)

DONOUGH: Wait — Denis — *(He's gone after him)*

(Poor GEORGE. *You'd have to pity him)*

AUNT ELLEN: And Duffy will be here in a minute for his answer.

PETER: Well, it's the breach of promise now, and no mistake.

GEORGE: We're ruined, we're ruined!

AUNT ELLEN: Yerra, not at all. Maybe when the fit of anger passes John Duffy will think better of what he said tonight. But we must stand up to him boldly; don't let on we're afraid of him.

PETER: Maybe he'd come to terms.

GEORGE: I wouldn't demean myself making terms with him. Let him bring us into the courts. I'll face him; I'll not have it said I was afraid of him.

AUNT ELLEN: That's right.

GEORGE: A Geoghegan's as good as a Duffy any day.

AUNT ELLEN: And better. *(There's a knock)* Glory be to God! there he is.

PETER: I suppose I'll have to let him in. 'Twouldn't do to pretend we're all gone to bed.

GEORGE: I'm afraid of no man. Open the door. 'Tis terrible, oh, 'tis terrible! Why did I ever open my lips tonight about Denis? ... I'm wondering ... I'm wondering, Aunt, if you spoke to Duffy yourself tonight? You used to be good friends long ago, I've heard it said. I ... I ....

AUNT ELLEN: To be sure I'll speak to him; a woman can often come around a man. Ye only heat him.

GEORGE: I'll have nothing to do with compromises and settlements, and it's no surrender, as they say in Derry,[9] but — but — do your best for me. Whisht! He's coming. I'll be up to speak to the mother.

(And he slips out one door as PETER *and* DUFFY *come in the other)*

DUFFY: Well, ma'am, I'm back. Where has George gone to?

AUNT ELLEN: He slipped up to speak to his mother. Peter, go and look for him.

(Isn't she cute the way she got rid of PETER*?)*

Won't you sit down?

DUFFY: I'd sooner stand. Two minutes will give me my answer, I suppose.

AUNT ELLEN: Take it easy while you have a chance .... John Duffy, you're a clever man; I don't know a cleverer.

DUFFY: I'm obliged for your good opinion, ma'am.

(How stiff he is)

AUNT ELLEN: That story of Denis being good for nothing is true, but it suits you not to believe it, and you're right. I'd do the same in your case.

DUFFY: You would?

AUNT ELLEN: I would so. Oh, I always gave in you were one of the smartest men in the country

9. 'No Surrender' was the cry of the defenders of the city of Derry in the famous siege of 1689.

.... You're looking to getting a deal of money out of this action?

DUFFY: I am.

AUNT ELLEN: I wonder will you. They're queer, chancey, uncertain things, breach of promise cases. Great expense, a troop of lawyers, terrible harrying in the witness-box and maybe twenty pounds at the end of it all, or the case dismissed. And Delia such a nervous little girl, I wonder you'd like to drag her through the courts.

DUFFY: Don't be afraid for Delia, ma'am. A thousand pounds will cover a deal of blushes.

AUNT ELLEN: A thousand pounds! You'll never see the quarter of it, no, nor a hundred pounds. It's the foolish people who go looking for money in a breach of promise case. The wise ones settle it up between themselves — and you were never a foolish man, Mr Duffy.

DUFFY: I'm foolish enough, anyway, not to let my name be trampled in the dirt. It doesn't suit me to have Delia treated as if she wasn't good enough for a Geoghegan.

AUNT ELLEN: 'Tis a pity. She'll hardly get married so. The lads are shy of having anything to say to a girl was in a breach of promise case — afraid they'd be the next to be hauled up .... What good will that do either of you? A little bit of money now slipped into your hand without bother or lawyers would be more value to you. A clever man would settle the whole thing for fifty pounds.

DUFFY: Would he indeed?

AUNT ELLEN: You know well the Geoghegans are a weak family. If you got a couple of hundred pounds damages itself, who knows would you ever be paid? But it doesn't reflect well on me to have my nephews dragged into Court. Come, Mr Duffy, if I gave you fifty pounds would you withdraw the case?

DUFFY: I've got my senses still, thank God. Fifty pounds? Keep it.

AUNT ELLEN: That's not a civil way to be answering me — and yet we were good friends once — John.

DUFFY: We were.

AUNT ELLEN: I often think of those old days — ah, I suppose you've forgotten them long ago. But we were good friends.

DUFFY: 'Twasn't my fault we weren't closer than friends.

(*After all, he's sitting down and near her too*)

AUNT ELLEN: I remember. Those days are gone long ago .... You'd have given me anything I asked then.

DUFFY: I would.

AUNT ELLEN: Do you remember the day you walked twelve miles to get a red ribbon I'd set my mind on having for the races?

DUFFY: I do.

AUNT ELLEN: And now I'm offering you fifty pounds, and you throw it back in my face as if I was an old hen-woman at a fair.

DUFFY: Fifty pounds is no money at all.

AUNT ELLEN: Sixty, then ... seventy .... Ah, John, you couldn't refuse me ... for the sake of old times ....

DUFFY: A lot you're talking of old times. Look here, Ellen, are you in earnest? Do you want the case stopped?

AUNT ELLEN: I do so.

DUFFY: Then there's a way you can do it.

AUNT ELLEN: Tell it to me.

DUFFY: You can do what I asked you to do when we were boy and girl together.

AUNT ELLEN: Mr Duffy!

DUFFY: Why not? Give me a hundred pounds down, and promise me you'll marry me before Shrove, and I'll let Denis and the Geoghegans go to the divil.

AUNT ELLEN: I could never do it.

DUFFY: You were near doing it fifteen years ago, after I buried the wife.

AUNT ELLEN: I've lived my own life always, I'm too old to change. I wanted freedom. I wanted to live like the birds, I wanted to do what I pleased with my own money.

DUFFY: You've had your freedom, and what have you made out of it? Nothing at all. You've run after crazy schemes, goats and the like: your farm is gone to waste; you're getting on in years, soon you'll be an old woman, Ellen, with no one to look after you, only relations craving for your money. You'd better have me, I'll take care of you, I'll look after you, you'll have all the freedom you want. When you were a girl, Ellen, you were too proud to look at me, and I married Honora Reilly to spite you. After she died on me I asked you again, but you wouldn't have me. You're the only woman I ever wanted. You made me mad tonight with your talk of old times. You must marry me, you must! Never will you regret it ....

AUNT ELLEN: I couldn't, John. I'm old. I'd like to be free.

DUFFY: Good night, so.

AUNT ELLEN: Why are you going?

DUFFY: What use is there in me staying?

AUNT ELLEN: But what about the case?

DUFFY: I'll see the lawyer in the morning.

AUNT ELLEN: You're a hard man. You always get what you want.

DUFFY: I didn't get the one thing I wanted in all the world.

AUNT ELLEN: If I gave you a hundred pounds without the promise?

DUFFY: 'Twouldn't do me.

AUNT ELLEN: Why do you want to marry me?

DUFFY: Contrariness, I suppose.

(He's kissed her, glory be to God!)

AUNT ELLEN: Stop, John! You should be ashamed of yourself.

DUFFY: You'll have me. I see you will.

AUNT ELLEN: You're taking a lot for granted.

DUFFY: I'm taking you, anyway.

(He's kissed her again!)

AUNT ELLEN: You're a terrible man.

DUFFY: Why the divil didn't you let me do that thirty years ago, when we were boy and girl together? I made an offer at it one time, and you slapped me across the face.

AUNT ELLEN: It's what I'd like to do to you this minute.

DUFFY: You may then.

(Look at him sticking his face out to her)

AUNT ELLEN: Get along with you!

DUFFY: Cripes! I'd like to get drunk, I'd like to pull the house down, I'd like to go bawling singing through the streets of Ballycolman!

AUNT ELLEN: I hope you'll do nothing of the kind, a respectable man like you, with a grown daughter and a wife interred.

DUFFY: Don't remind me of her. I'm twenty years old — not a minute more.

AUNT ELLEN: If you keep shouting like that you'll have George down.

DUFFY: Faith, that reminds me .... I'll draw up a paper and you can sign it.

(He's always an eye to business)

AUNT ELLEN: What are you asking me to sign?

DUFFY: A promise to pay me a hundred pounds down, and that you'll marry me before Shrove, provided I drop the case against Denis .... Have you your cheque-book handy?

AUNT ELLEN: It's here in my bag.

DUFFY: Make out a cheque so for me for a hundred pounds.

AUNT ELLEN: It's a whip[10] of money.

DUFFY: Sure, it's not going to pass out of the family. I'll spend it on stocking the farm.

AUNT ELLEN: You're a terrible man .... I suppose you must have your way.

(She's writing him a cheque, it must be a fact that she's in love with him)

DUFFY: Sign there, now.

(She's doing that too. He's got the cheque and the paper signed, and into his breast pocket they go)

AUNT ELLEN: For the love of goodness don't breathe a word of this to the Geoghegans. They'd have my life for making terms with you. I'll find my own way later of telling them about the marriage.

DUFFY: I'll not open my lips. And it would suit me better if they thought I withdrew the case of my own free will. Isn't it like a story on the pictures, Ellen, the way you and I have come together at the end of all.

(More love-making. Look at his arm round her waist)

AUNT ELLEN: Leave go of me; there's someone coming.

(It's GEORGE, *and his Aunt's slipped out. She's in a flutter and no wonder)*

GEORGE: I'm sorry for leaving you so long, Mr Duffy. I was speaking to my mother and that young rascal of a brother of mine. It's no use trying to make him see reason; you might as well be talking to a deaf man.

DUFFY: Is that so?

GEORGE: My aunt was speaking to you?

DUFFY: She was.

GEORGE: I hope you're feeling in a more reasonable way?

DUFFY: Oh, I've reason enough on my side.

GEORGE: There's no use expecting Denis to marry Delia; he'll not do it. What we've got to do, Mr Duffy, is to settle our little differences the best way we can.

DUFFY: That's a fact.

GEORGE: I'm glad to see you taking that view. What use is there going into court? Five minutes friendly talk is better than all the lawyers in the Four Courts .... Come, John, we were always good friends — what will you take to drop the case?

DUFFY: To ...? Five hundred pounds.

(Tch! Tch!)

GEORGE: I mean in earnest.

10. a lot.

DUFFY: I'm speaking in earnest.

GEORGE: I'll give you two hundred.

DUFFY: Put your hand there. There's one condition I make: not a word of this to your family, or anyone. I'd rather have it thought that I withdrew the case myself.

GEORGE: It will suit me, too, to be quiet about this. The family would be mad with me for going behind their backs. My aunt was all for fighting you to the bitter end.

DUFFY: Was she indeed?

GEORGE: Don't mind a word she was saying; she's a cranky old schemer.

DUFFY: Would you believe me telling you she came near striking me tonight?

GEORGE: She did? Don't mind her, John; she didn't mean a word she said.

DUFFY: Faith, there's things she said tonight I'll hold her accountable for .... Tell me, when will you let me have the money?

GEORGE: I'll write a letter to you tonight promising to pay it in six month's time, provided you don't bring up the case. I'll have to look about for the money.

DUFFY: That'll do me. But if I haven't the letter in the morning I'll start with the case.

GEORGE: Oh, you'll have it, never fear.

(*Here's poor* MRS GEOGHEGAN)

MRS GEOGHEGAN: Is that Mr Duffy's voice?

DUFFY: Good night to you, ma'am.

MRS GEOGHEGAN: Is it true what I hear that you're making a set against my poor Denis, that you're going to bring him into the Courts?

DUFFY: That's so.

GEORGE: Don't go into it now, mother, I've been talking it over with Mr Duffy. By tomorrow morning he's likely to see matters in a more reasonable way.

DUFFY: I'm a generous man, ma'am.

(*You are!*)

MRS GEOGHEGAN: I know you are, I'll say no more, only leave it to God and yourself .... Would you oblige me by taking a note down to Delia?

DUFFY: Certainly, ma'am.

GEORGE: What's that, mother?

MRS GEOGHEGAN: Only a letter of goodbye from my poor Denis. There's a note for yourself, too, Mr Duffy.

(*She's half whispering, she doesn't want* GEORGE *to hear, but he's writing the note to* DUFFY *in the corner of the room*)

DUFFY: Thank you, ma'am.

(*It's a thick letter; he can't help himself from opening it*)

MRS GEOGHEGAN: Are you going to bed, George?

GEORGE: I have to write one letter first.

(*Look what* DUFFY's *pulling out of the envelope. Notes! Bank notes ...!*)

DUFFY: .... May the divil ....

MRS GEOGHEGAN: What's the matter, Mr Duffy?

(*She's afraid* GEORGE *will notice and her finger's on her lips*)

DUFFY: Oh, nothing at all, ma'am, nothing at all. I'll be going.

MRS GEOGHEGAN: I hope business is good by you these times?

DUFFY: Business? Oh, business ma'am is good; never better, never better. Well, be the .... Good night to you both.

(*He's gone. Well, well, such strategy and manoeuvring — such lying as you might call it*)

PADRAIC COLUM
(1881-1972)

from:
THE LAND (1905)
AN AGRARIAN COMEDY

[This three-act play was first produced by the Abbey in June 1905. It was one of Colum's most successful forays into the theatre. The moment of experience recorded here is both poignant and bitter. After the oppressions of landlordism recalled by Murtagh Cosgar, ownership of the land becomes another form of imprisonment rather than the achievement of freedom. Colum's language is that of 'the peasant as he is transformed by modern life', in Yeats's description. He is one of the most delicately gifted of the Abbey realists, although, as in Synge and others, the preoccupation with freedom — personal and political — remains as overweening as ever and is as darkly pondered.]

CHARACTERS

MURTAGH COSGAR, *a farmer*
MATT, *his son*
SALLY, *his daughter*
MARTIN DOURAS, *a farmer*
CORNELIUS, *his son*
ELLEN, *his daughter*
A group of men
A group of boys and girls

The scene is laid in the Irish Midlands, present time.

ACT II

Interior of Martin Douras'. The entrance is at back left. There is a dresser against wall back; a table down from dresser; room-doors right and left. The fireplace is below the room-door right; there are stools and chairs about it. There is a little bookcase left of the dresser, and a mirror beside it. There are patriotic and religious pictures on the wall. There are cups and saucers on table, and a teapot beside fire. It is afternoon still. ELLEN DOURAS *is near the fire reading.* CORNELIUS *comes in slowly.*

CORNELIUS: I left the men down the road a bit. We ought to take great pride out of this day, Ellen. Father did more than any of them to bring it about.

ELLEN: He suffered more than any of them. And it's little we'll get out of the day.

CORNELIUS: It's a great thing to have prophesied it, even. We'll be here to see a great change.

ELLEN: There will be no change to make things better!

CORNELIUS: Will you be taking that school, Ellen?

ELLEN: I'll wait a while.

SALLY *coming in; she is hurried.*

SALLY: (*Breathlessly*) Oh, God save you, Cornelius. Tell me, is my father gone? I dread going back and he there! It was all over that baste[1] of a sow that has kept me slaving all through the spring till I don't know whether greens or potatoes is the fittest for her!

CORNELIUS: He didn't go, Sally. I went down a bit of the road myself with the men.

SALLY: Oh, God help me! And I'll have to be going back to boil meal for her now. How are you, Ellen. (*She goes to* ELLEN)

ELLEN: Sit down for a while, Sally; it's a long time since I was speaking to you.

SALLY *sits down beside* ELLEN.

CORNELIUS: I'll leave this paper where they won't be looking for pipe-lights.[2] There are things in that paper I'd like to be saying. (*He takes a newspaper out of his pocket and goes to room right*)

ELLEN: (*To* SALLY, *who has been watching* CORNELIUS) Tell me, Sally, are they always that busy in your house? Is your father as harsh as they say?

SALLY: Father 'ud keep us all working. He's a powerful great man.

ELLEN: Matt will be bringing a wife into the house soon from all I hear. How would your father treat her?

SALLY: Oh, he'd have his way, and she'd have her way, I suppose.

ELLEN: And do you think your father will let him marry?

1. beast.
2. I will put the paper away so that it will not be torn up into strips for lighting pipes from the fire.

SALLY: Sure he must if the boy likes.

ELLEN: What would he say if Matt married a girl without a fortune?

SALLY: In my mother's country there are lots of girls with fortunes that Matt could have.

ELLEN: Supposing he wanted a girl that had no fortune?

SALLY: Oh, I suppose, father would give in in the end. It wouldn't be clay against flint when Matt and father would be to it.[3]

ELLEN: You're a good girl, Sally. If I was Matt's wife, do you think you'd be fond of me?

SALLY: I'd like you as well as another, Ellen.

CORNELIUS *comes down from room.*

CORNELIUS: I suppose they'll be here soon.

ELLEN: I have tea ready for them.

SALLY: Who's coming at all?

CORNELIUS: Some of the boys and girls that are for America. They are going to Gilroy's tonight, and are leaving from that in the morning. They are coming in to see Ellen on their way down.

SALLY: There are a good many going this flight.[4] The land never troubles them them in America, and they can wear fine clothes, and be as free as the larks over the bogs. It's a wonder you never thought of going, Ellen.

ELLEN: Father wouldn't like me to be far from him, and so I went in for the school instead.

SALLY: And now you've got a fine boy like Matt. It was lucky for you to be staying here.

ELLEN: Hush, Sally.

SALLY: Oh, I knew all about it before you talked to me at all. Matt always goes to the place where he thinks you'd be.

ELLEN: (*Rising*) I'll be in the room when the girls come, Cornelius. (*She goes into room left*)

SALLY: (*Going to* CORNELIUS) God help us, but she's the silent creature. Isn't it a wonder she's not filled with talk of him after seeing him today? But Ellen's right. We shouldn't be talking about men, nor thinking about them either; and that's the way to keep them on our hands on the long run. I'll be going myself. (*She goes towards door*)

CORNELIUS: (*Going to her*) Don't be minding Ellen at all, Sally.

SALLY: Well, as high as she is, and as mighty as she is, she came into his own house to see Matt. God between us and harm, Cornelius, maybe they'll be saying I came into your house to see you.

CORNELIUS: Who'll know you came at all? And what isn't seen won't be spoken of.

SALLY: Would you like me to stay, Cornelius?

CORNELIUS: Ay, I would.

SALLY: Divil mind the sow.[5]

They sit down together.

SALLY: (*After a pause*) Would you like me to knit you a pair of socks, Cornelius?

CORNELIUS: Oh, I would, Sally; I'd love to wear them.

SALLY: I'll knit them. We'll be getting rid of the sow tonight, maybe, and I'll have time after that.

CORNELIUS: And you come along the road when I'm herding. I don't want to be going near your father's house.

SALLY: O Cornelius, it won't be lucky for us when father hears about Ellen and Matt.

CORNELIUS: That's true. No man sees his house afire but looks to his rick.[6]

SALLY: Come down a bit of the road with me, Cornelius. The sow will be grunting and grunting, reminding father that I'm away. Och, a minute ago I was as contented as if there was no land or pigs, or harsh words to trouble one. (*She goes to the door*) The boys and girls for America are coming here.

CORNELIUS: Give me your hands to hold, Sally. (*She gives him her hands*) We are as young as any of them after all.

They hold each other's hands, then stand apart.

SALLY: It's a fine time for them to be going when the leaves are opening on the trees.

Three boys and three girls enter. They are dressed for going away.

God save you, girls. Good-bye, Cornelius. I'll have to run like a redshank.[7]

SALLY *goes out.*

CORNELIUS: I'll call Ellen down to you. (*He goes to the room door and calls*) I'm going herding myself. Herding is pleasant when you have thoughts with you. (*He takes up the rod and goes out*)

The girls begin whispering, then chattering.

FIRST GIRL: Sure I know. Every night I'm dreaming of the sea and the great towns. Streets and streets of houses, and every street as crowded as the

3. That is, when Matt and her father clashed, sparks would fly — it would be flint against flint.

4. She means journey, a going away, not travelling on an aeroplane.

5. Let the sow look after herself.

6. He looks to save the hayrick, his next most precious possession.

7. Red-legged bird of the snipe family; the word was also applied to inhabitants of the Scottish highlands and Ireland.

road outside the chapel when the people do be coming from Mass.

FIRST BOY: I could watch the crowd in the street; I would think it better than any sight I ever knew.

SECOND GIRL: And the shops and the great houses.

SECOND BOY: There's no stir here. There's no fine clothes, nor fine manners, nor fine things to be seen.

THIRD BOY: There's no money. One could never get a shilling together here. In America there's money to have and to spend and to send home.

THIRD GIRL: Every girl gets married in America.

ELLEN *comes down.*

ELLEN: I'm glad you came. I have tea ready for you. I can't go to Gilroy's tonight.

Some come to the table and some remain near the door.

A GIRL: (*At table, to* ELLEN) They say that a turf fire like that will seem very strange to us after America. Bridget wondered at it when she came back. 'Do civilized people really cook at the like of them?' said she.

A BOY: It's the little houses with only three rooms in them that will seem strange. I'm beginning to wonder myself at their thatch and their mud walls.

ANOTHER GIRL: Houses in bogs and fields. It was a heartbreak trying to keep them as we'd like to keep them.

A GIRL AT DOOR: Ah, but I'll never forget Gortan and the little road to Aughnalee.

ANOTHER GIRL: I think I'll be lonesome for a long time. I'll be thinking on my brothers and sisters. I nursed and minded all the little ones.

FIRST BOY: A girl like you, Ellen, is foolish to be staying here.

SECOND BOY: She'll be coming in the Fall. We'll be glad to see you, Ellen.

ELLEN: I have no friends in America.

FIRST GIRL: I have no friends there, either. But I'll get on. You could get on better than any of us, Ellen.

SECOND GIRL: She's waiting for her school. It will be a little place by the side of a bog.

THIRD GIRL: (*Going to* ELLEN) There would be little change in that. And isn't it a life altogether different from this life that we have been longing for? To be doing other work, and to be meeting strange people. And instead of bare roads and market-towns, to be seeing streets, and crowds, and theatres.

ELLEN: (*Passionately*) O what do you know about streets and theatres? You have only heard of them. They are finer than anything you could say. They are finer than anything you could think of, after a story, when you'd be young.

A GIRL: You'll be going after all, Ellen.

ELLEN: I won't be going.

FIRST GIRL: Well, maybe you'll be down at Gilroy's. We must go now.

The girls go to the door. ELLEN *goes with them.*

ONE OF THE BOYS: Phil said that an egg was all he could touch while he was on the sea.

SECOND BOY: God help us, if that was all Phil could take.

THIRD BOY: Light your pipes now, and we'll go.

ELLEN *has parted with the girls. The boys light their pipes at fire. They go to door, and shake hands with* ELLEN. *The boys go out.*

ELLEN: Theatres! What do they know of theatres? And it's their like will be enjoying them.

SALLY *comes back. She is more hurried than before.*

SALLY: Ellen! Ellen! I have wonders to tell. Where is Cornelius, at all? He's never here when you have wonders to tell.

ELLEN: What have you to tell?

SALLY: Oh, I don't know how I'll get it all out! Matt and father had an odious falling out, and it was about you. And Matt's going to America; and he's to bring you with him. And Cornelius was saying that if father found out about yourself and Matt —

ELLEN: Sally, Sally, take breath and tell it.

SALLY: Matt is going to America, like the others, and he's taking you with him.

ELLEN: Sally, Sally, is it the truth you're telling?

SALLY: It is the truth. Honest as day, it is the truth.

ELLEN: And I thought I'd be content with a new house. Now we can go away together. I can see what I longed to see. I have a chance of knowing what is in me. (*She takes* SALLY'*s hands*) It's great news you've brought me. No one ever brought me such news before. Take this little cross. You won't have a chance of getting fond of me after all. (*She wears a cross at her throat; she breaks the string, and gives it to* SALLY)

SALLY: I don't know why I was so fervent to tell you. There's the stool before me that myself and Cornelius were sitting on, and he saying — (*She goes to the door*) Here's Matt! Now we'll hear all about it.

ELLEN: So soon; so soon. (*She goes to the mirror. After a pause, turning to* SALLY) Go down the road a bit, when he comes in. Sally, you have a simple mind; you might be saying a prayer that it will be for the best.

SALLY: (*Going to the door muttering*) Go down the road a bit! 'Deed[8] and I will not till I know the whole ins and outs of it. Sure I'm as much concerned in it as herself! 'No man sees his house afire but watches his rick,' he was saying. Ah, there's few of them could think of as fine a thing as that.

MATT *comes in.*

MATT: Well, Sally, were you home lately?

SALLY: I was — leastways as far as the door. Father and oul' Martin were discoursing.[9]

MATT: I've given them something to discoorse about. Maybe you'll be treated better from this day, Sally.

SALLY: O Matt, I'm sorry. (*She goes out*)

MATT: (*Going to* ELLEN) It happened at last, Ellen; the height of the quarrel came.

ELLEN: It was bound to come. I knew it would come, Matt.

MATT: He was a foolish man to put shame on me after all I did for the land.

ELLEN: You had too much thought for the land.

MATT: I had in troth. The others went when there was less to be done. They could not stand him. Even the girls stole away.

ELLEN: There was the high spirit in the whole of you.

MATT: I showed it to him. 'Stop,' said I; 'no more, or I fling lands and house and everything aside.'

ELLEN: You said that.

MATT: Ay. 'Your other children went for less,' said I; 'do you think there's no blood in me at all?'

ELLEN: What happened then?

MATT: 'I'm your last son,' I said; 'keep your land and your twenty years' purchase.[10] I'm with the others; and it's poor your land will leave you, and you without a son to bring down your name. A bit of land, a house,' said I; 'do you think these will keep me here?'

ELLEN: I knew they could not keep you here, Matt. You have broken from them at last; and now the world is before us. Think of all that is before us — the sea, and the ships, the strange life, and the great cities.

MATT: Ay — there before us — if we like.

ELLEN: Surely we like.

MATT: I was always shy of crowds. I'm simple, after all, Ellen, and have no thought beyond the land.

ELLEN: You said that house and land could not keep you. You told him you were going as your brothers went.

MATT: And I felt I was going. I frightened him. He'll be glad to see me back. It will be long before he treats me that way again.

ELLEN: (*Suddenly*) Matt!

MATT: What is it, Ellen?

ELLEN: I don't know — I was upset — thinking of the quarrel (*putting her hands on his shoulders*). My poor Matt. It was about me you quarrelled.

MATT: Ay, he spoke against you. I couldn't put up with that.

ELLEN: He does not know your high spirit. He does not know your strength.

MATT: Ellen, it's no shame for a man to have harsh words said to him when it's about a woman like you.

ELLEN: Let nothing come between us now. I saw you in the winter making drains and ditches, and it wet. It's a poor story, the life of a man on the land.

MATT: I had too much thought for the land.

ELLEN: You had. Have thought for me now. There is no one in fair or market but would notice me. I was never a favourite. I lived to myself. I did not give my love about. You have never offered me anything. In the song a man offers towns to his sweetheart.[11] You can offer me the sights of great towns, and the fine manners, and the fine life.

MATT: Ellen! (*He draws a little away*) It's not me that could offer the like of that. I never had anything to my hand but a spade.

ELLEN: Your brothers — think of them.

MATT: They all left someone behind them. I am the last of my name.

ELLEN: Why should that keep you back?

MATT: His name is something to a man. Could you hear of your own name melting away without unease? And you are a woman. A man feels it more.

ELLEN: I do not understand men. Will you go

8. Indeed.
9. discoursing, holding a discussion.
10. Under the Land Acts, tenant farmers could buy the land they worked over a twenty-year period.
11. As in the famous traditional song, 'Donal Óg', in which the lover promises his beloved a dozen towns.

back to your father's house after he shaming you out of it?

MATT: He'll be glad to see me back. He'll never cast it up to me that I went.

ELLEN: Matt, your father said words against me. Will you go to him and take this hand after that?

MATT: It was little he said against you. It was against your father he spoke.

ELLEN: (*Sinking down on a chair, and putting her hands before her face*) My God! After all my waiting, you talk like that.

MATT: (*Going to her*) Ellen, Ellen, tell me what I can do for you? There's land and houses to be had here. Father will let me have my own way after this.

ELLEN: (*Rising, with anger*) What does it matter to me whether he lets you have your own way or not? Do you think I could go into a farmer's house?

MATT: Ellen!

ELLEN: It's a bad hand I'd make of a farmer's house. I'm not the sort to be in one. I'm not like Sally.

MATT: (*Getting angry*) Don't be talking that way, Ellen Douras.

ELLEN: (*With greater vehemence*) I must be talking like this. If you take me, you will have to go from your father's house. I always knew it. You ought to know it now, Matt Cosgar.

MATT: You didn't know it always. And you have let someone come between us when you talk like that.

ELLEN: I'm not one to be listening to what people say about you. Nor do I be talking in the markets about you.

MATT: I suppose not. You wouldn't have people think you gave any thought to me; I'm not good enough for you. The people you know are better.

ELLEN: You are foolish to be talking like that. You are foolish, I say.

MATT: I know I am foolish. Fit only to be working in drains and ditches in the winter. That's what you think.

ELLEN: Maybe it is.

MATT: Ellen Douras! Ellen Douras! A farmer's roof will be high enough for you some day.

ELLEN: May I never see the day. Go back, go back. Make it up with your father. Your father will be glad of a labourer.

MATT: Maybe you won't be glad if I go back; thinking on what you've said.

ELLEN: I said too much. We don't know each other at all. Go back. You have made your choice. (*She goes up to room left*)

MATT: Very well, then. God above, am I to be treated everywhere like a heifer strayed into a patch of oats? Neither man nor woman will make me put up with this any longer. (*Going to door*) When Ellen Douras wants me, she knows the place to send to. (*He stands at door. There is no sound from room. Going back he speaks loudly*) I'll be waiting two days or three days to hear from Ellen Douras.

There is no sound. MATT *goes out. The room door is thrown open, and* ELLEN *comes down.*

ELLEN: (*Furiously*) Two days or three days he'll wait for me. As if I'd go into Murtagh Cosgar's house. As if I'd go into any farmer's house. As if I'd get married at all, and the world before me. Two days or three days you'll wait. Maybe it's lonesome, weary years you'll be waiting, Matt Cosgar.

CURTAIN

T. C. MURRAY

(1873-1959)

BIRTHRIGHT (1910)

[As in Colum's *The Land*, although in a more sombre vein, we are faced with a family dispute over inheritance, in which the land comes to represent latent feelings, most of which remain inarticulately but broodingly embodied in the figure of the father, Bat Morrissey. In order to deprive one son, Hugh, of the land, he finds an excuse to disinherit him and give it to the younger son, Shane, his favourite, who would otherwise emigrate. The relationship between the father and the sons is a version of the relationship between the father and mother and between the father and the land. It is a study in destructive possession.

The text is the revised version of 1928.]

CHARACTERS

BAT MORRISSEY, *a farmer*
MAURA, *his wife*
HUGH, *his son*
SHANE, *a younger son*
DAN HEGARTY, *a neighbour*

ACT I

Scene: Sunday evening. The interior of a farmhouse kitchen in the County Cork. BAT MORRISSEY *is seated at the fire smoking. He is a hard-faced man of about sixty-five.* MAURA *is sorting a pile of new socks and removing them from the table to the deep window-sill. She is younger than her husband. Her face looks somewhat careworn. There are hints of a refined temperament in her quiet dress and apron, and in the appearance of the kitchen.* DAN HEGARTY *appears in the doorway. He leans comfortably on the half-door, and looks in, saluting them.*

DAN: God bless all here!

MAURA: And you too (*turning round*). Wisha, is that you, Dan Hegarty? Walk in. (*Unbolting the half-door*) Sure it isn't coming from the play you are so soon?

DAN: 'Tis indeed, then, Mrs. Morrissey — though to tell you the honest truth I could hardly boast I saw the match at all.

MAURA: Well, now.

DAN: 'Twas only by a kind of chance like I come to see the finish of it. I missed all the rest o' the play.

BAT: An' that was no loss to you! Them matches are the curse o' the country with their drinking, an' their squabbling, an' their rowing — an' the Lord knows what! So they are.

DAN: Oh I don't know altogether about that now. Sure —

BAT: Well, I knows it. They're good for the publicans an' no one else, and signs on, they're the heads o' them always[1] .... But 'tis the good sense you had yourself, Dan Hegarty, to be keeping far away from them till the play was nearly over — not like some belonging to this house who ought to know better.

DAN: Faith, I don't know altogether about the good sense, Bat. Sure 'twasn't that what kept me away at all.

BAT: An' what else then, I'd like to know? What else?

DAN: Well, then, 'twas this way with us.

MAURA: (*Giving him a chair*) Sit down, Dan.

DAN: Thank you, ma'am. (*Sits down*) The mason and the carpenter, they'll be coming over tomorrow to begin the new house, and 'twas only this morning the girl took it into her head to tell us the bag of flour was nearly out, an' that there was hardly the makings o' bread for our own supper tonight, not to mind the men's breakfast tomorrow morning. So, begor, Sunday and all as it was I had to tackle the horse an' go east to Macroom for a bag of flour — and I tell you 'twasn't too thankful to myself at all I was over it.

MAURA: Well, indeed, it was hard enough on you, and all the young people in the parish going to the match.

DAN: 'Tis many the big curse came out o' me, I tell you — God forgive me! — an' I jogging away to the town, an' meeting all the world against me going to the great match. 'Tis half ashamed like I felt passing the crowds.

BAT: *Ashamed*, is it? Well! well! (*Laughing derisively*) An' I'd like to know now what was there to be ashamed of?

DAN: Sure I could hardly tell that — but, somehow, it was on my mind what 'ud the people be thinking —

BAT: (*With contemptuous pity*) Oh, wisha, Dan Hegarty, 'tis the quare world surely, an' 'tis the quare people that are in it!

DAN: Faith, that's the truth, Bat, an' the quarest people often are them that do be thinking they have the most sense.... But didn't ye hear at all the great work the parish done — an' the best team in Ireland again them?

BAT: (*Dryly*) We didn't then — an' 'tis little we care aither. If they were playing in that field outside I wouldn't cross to the other side o' the road to see them.

DAN: You wouldn't indeed, an' your own son the captain of the team — an' he coming home to you this evening with another gold meddle?

BAT: Another gold meddle! I wouldn't give that much (*snapping his fingers*) for all the meddles there is in the City of Cork. Meddles! ... I tell you, Dan Hegarty, 'twould be better for the peace o' this house if yer brave captain would stay at home an'

1. it's evident, they're always the heads (organizers) of them.

mind his own business! So it would.

DAN: Yerra,[2] don't be talking like that, man. Take the world a small bit aisy.[3] Sure it isn't working on a Sunday you'd have him?

BAT: There's plenty work for a farmer, Sunday as well as Monday.

DAN: Maybe so, but 'tis the small farm we'll all be wanting when we're dead.

BAT: That's not talk at all.

DAN: Sure, man, we might as well break up the team altogether without Hugh in it.... Why, didn't Father Daly himself say the other day — 'twas after he winning the meddle for the great verses he made for the *feis*[4] — 'there isn't,' says he, 'the beating of Hugh Morrissey in Ireland for anything.' (*To* MAURA) 'Twas east at the cross,[5] Mrs. Morrissey, he said it. I heard him myself.

BAT: (*Crossly*) Ah, don't annoy us with Father Daly an' his talk. 'Tis little him or his aquals[6] cares about the likes of us. Destroying the parish he is, since he came into it, taking people away from their work an' putting notions into their heads. Father Daly!

DAN: Yeh, man, don't be talking like that a day like this! There isn't a mother's soul in this parish but yourself that wouldn't be out of his mind with delight this minute, and everyone to be praising his own flesh and blood! (*To* MAURA) I'm sorry in my soul you didn't see the match, Mrs. Morrissey. I nearly killed the little mare and killed myself hurrying back from the town to see if I could see even the end of it. An' 'twas a grand sight surely.

MAURA: Wisha, God help us, Dan, I'm a bit too old now to be going to places like that.

DAN: Wisha indeed, and indeed you're not, ma'am. A person would think the way you talk you were drawing the pension. But sure whatever excuse there was for you there was none at all for himself here.

BAT: We'd look well, begor,[7] Maura an' myself, going to yer tournament! (*Laughs derisively*)

DAN: An' why not, Bat? Why not? The sight o' your son today would be giving you a kind of feeling, maybe, that your best cows and your heaviest pigs could never give you.

BAT: (*Shaking his head*) God help you, Dan Hegarty! An' you a young man just beginning to rear a little family!

DAN: If I am then, Bat Morrissey, I only wish to God one o' them would grow up something like your Hugh! So I would. (*To* MAURA) All the people, and the strangers even, were cheering like mad for him. Half a dozen times you'd be seeing the ball and it flying into the goal posts, an' your heart would be in your mouth thinking the other side had the goal, when you'd see him sending it back again with a puck into the middle of the field. 'Twas like a miracle the way he used to save it every time!

MAURA: Well! well!

DAN: I galloped away when it was over as I wanted to clear away before the crowds, but I gave one look back, an' they were shouldering him, an' cheering mad, an' shouting for him as if it was a member of Parliament he was.

BAT: An' for what now?

DAN: (*With a gasp*) For what?

BAT: Yes — for what, Dan Hegarty?

DAN: Didn't I tell you?

BAT: Is it because he hit a bit of a leather balleen[8] with a twisted stick? Tch! tch! tch! (*Standing up and going towards room*) 'Tis thinking I am that half the world is becoming a pack o' fools. (*Goes into room*)

MAURA: (*Confidentially*) I'd know could you tell me was he hurt at all, Dan?

DAN: I don't know then — I don't think so.... I'm almost sure he wasn't, now that I think of it.

MAURA: Thanks be to the Almighty God an' His Blessed Mother for that!

DAN: Bat isn't himself somehow this evening, Mrs. Morrissey?

MAURA: Shane's going away next Thursday morning that's upsetting him.

DAN: Ah, sure of course, I never thought of that. Wasn't it very sudden now, Mrs. Morrissey, that Shane got the notion to be going to America?

MAURA: 'Twas indeed, God help us. I couldn't speak with the fright when he told me first.

DAN: An' everyone thought he liked the farming greatly?

MAURA: And so he did — I don't know a boy in this townland that liked it better. But he was saying that Hugh would be getting married in a few years, an' then that 'twould be the poor lookout for him

2. Corruption of Irish *A Mhuire* (vocative of 'Mary'), an invocation to the Blessed Virgin.
3. easy.
4. A festival of Irish music, dancing, verse-speaking and storytelling.
5. crossroads.
6. equals.
7. by God.

8. A small ball.

here. An' no matter what I said, or what his father said, or what anyone else said, it made no difference with him. 'Rocking the cradle for Hugh, ye'd want me to be,' says he.[9]

DAN: Well, I suppose he's old enough to know his own business. . . . There's one thing anyway, there's no fear of him in the States.[10]

MAURA: He's very steady, thank God.

DAN: Begor, 'tis too steady he is, if anything. To tell you the honest truth, I'd rather now a fellow with a bit o' spirit in him, so long as he'd have the good sense at the same time — just like Hugh.

MAURA: Sure their nature is God's blessed work and not their own, Dan Hegarty. And 'tis blaming Him you'll be if you talk that way.

DAN: (*Half sceptically*) Well, now then, I suppose you're right there. (*Re-enter* BAT) I was saying to herself, Bat, that Shane will be the great loss to ye?

BAT: 'Tis little you know it, or any other man aither.

DAN: But 'twon't be long, never fear, till the fat checks be coming to you to make up for it!

BAT: *Tá go breagh!*[11] 'Tis going out the money will be an' not coming in, I'm thinking. We can't work this place without extra help — an' good help, too — once Shane is gone from us. An' 'tis robbing to pay labourers now. Eggs they must be getting for breakfast, and tea after dinner. They'd break a man!

DAN: Yeh, man. You'll get used to that in time, like all the rest of us. (*To* MAURA) But sure what made me call was about Shane's trunk. Herself tells me at home that 'tis the very dickens[12] to get me out of a neighbour's chimney corner once I get in there an' begin the bit o' talk. An' faith, I'm thinking, 'tis the truth she's telling.

MAURA: Sure, not at all. 'Tis early yet. Why wouldn't you be a bit neighbourly? And what message have you about the trunk, Dan?

DAN: When I was getting the flour at Ahern's they asked me to bring it. 'Twas Mrs. Ahern herself was there. She said you were hardly outside the town the fair day when the trunks came. Outside in the car it is. I've left the horse down a bit in the boreen.[13] Mrs. Ahern herself put the label on it with the right directions for fear of any mistake. She said you told her.

MAURA: And so I did. I'm very thankful to you, Dan. 'Twas too much trouble entirely, but I was in a fright as it wasn't coming. Thursday, as you know, he'll be going, and I'd want to begin the packing soon, God help us.

DAN: Well, 'tis time for me to be turning home. I'm thinking 'tis in the great state they'll be for the flour. I'll be over Wednesday night to see Shane before he starts on the big journey next day. I hope he'll have the good weather for the voyage. Good-by for the present, Mrs. Morrissey.

MAURA: Good-by, and good luck, Dan.

DAN: (*Half jauntily*) Come along, Bat. Come along.

He goes out, followed by BAT. MAURA *makes the preliminary preparations for supper, pouring water into the kettle, setting it on the hangers*[14] *over the fire, drawing the turf-embers round the pot-oven by the fire, etc.* BAT *returns, bearing on his shoulders an oak-coloured tin trunk with brass lock. He lets it down on the floor.*

BAT: 'Tis a fine trunk, isn't it?

MAURA: (*After a pause*) 'Tis a fine trunk, indeed, but 'tis the fineness of the coffin that's on it.

BAT: 'Tis a very dacent trunk, an' good value for six shillings.

MAURA: (*After a pause*) There was a shiver come over me, and a queer lonesome feeling, when I saw it on your shoulders. 'Twas the same as when you brought in the coffin for little Owen.

BAT: (*Lighting his pipe*) 'Twill do all right.

MAURA: 'Twill, I suppose, God help us. (*She kneels down and opens the trunk*) Isn't it the strong smell there is from it? I don't like it at all. 'Twill stick to the socks and the shirts for a long time.

There is a pause, during which is heard the strong puff-puff of a smoker whose pipe is in danger of going out.

MAURA: Maybe if I burned a small grain of the coffee in it 'twould make it wholesome?

BAT: Yerra, nonsense, woman! (*Puff-puff*) Is it Shane to mind the smell o' the paint? Thank God, he's not that kind. (*Puff-puff*) Sure I've seen him turn the strongest heap o' manure in the country, and he to mind it no more than if 'twas the fresh cut hay he was tossing on top o' the hayfork. (*Puff-puff*)

MAURA: That's true, of course, but all the same, somehow —

9. That is, he would be looking after Hugh's children.
10. There is no fear of his behaving foolishly when he emigrates to the United States.
11. 'O yes indeed' (ironic).
12. i.e. it is very difficult; 'dickens' is a euphemism for 'devil'.
13. lane.
14. Hooked iron bars.

BAT: Have sense, woman, have sense! . . . If 'twas the other boy, now, 'twould be different. There would be some reason then for talking. (*Laying down his pipe*) Do you remember when we were carting out the manure to the western field last March, an' how white he got — like any poor creature of a woman — when myself an' Shane opened the heap; an' there was yourself running to get a drop o' whiskey for him. Well, begor (*laughing ironically*), 'tis something to have a real gentleman in the family.

MAURA: Sure he can't help his nature no more than ourselves.

BAT: 'Tis the quare nature he have — with his sporting, an' his fiddling, an' his *ráiméis*[15] about the Irish — an' the Lord knows what! 'Tis the grand lookout[16] for the future of this place, so it is. He'll be the man to mind it. . . . A fine lookout indeed.

MAURA: I'm sure he'll be able to mind it as well as the next. Isn't he as hardworking as anyone in this side of the parish — except Shane, of course; but sure everyone knows that he's an exception entirely.

BAT: (*Broodingly*) A fine lookout, sure enough.

MAURA: Sure, God help us, everyone have their own faults.

BAT: He have enough o' them for twenty — so he have.

MAURA: Is it poor Hugh? Sure his faults are only the small faults. You're very hard on him, Bat — I don't know why — very, very hard on him entirely.

BAT: (*Angrily*) What's that you're after saying? 'Hard on him!' Hard, is it? That's the quare saying from your mouth. I'd like to know who is hard. When I bought this place thirty years ago with the bit o' money I made in the States what kind was it? Tell that an' spake the truth! Tell it now!

MAURA: A cold place it was surely — a cold, poor place, with more o' the rock, an' the brier, an' the sour weed than the sweet grass.

BAT: Well, an' who blasted every rock that was in it?

MAURA: Sure, 'twas no one but yourself, Bat.

BAT: An' who rooted out the briers, and often tore 'em out with his own two living hands?

MAURA: (*Conciliatory*) 'Twas yourself I know. Alone you did it.

BAT: (*With rising anger*) An' maybe you'd tell me now again who drained the western field that was little better than a bog — an' who built the strong fences an' planted the thorn on them — an' who made the land kind where the grass was that dry an' coarse you'd think 'twas the strings o' the lash on that whip beyond? Tell me that, will you? Tell me that now?

MAURA: Sure, I know, Bat, 'twas yourself — and the good God that gave you the great strength.

BAT: *I'm hard*, am I? I've been out in the darkness before the dawn, an' remained stuck in the trench an' the furrow all day, till the black darkness came on me again, and the moon come up, and the faintness on me that I couldn't walk into this house for staggering no better than a cripple or a man that would be drunk. An' for what, I ask you? For what, Maura? For my brave Hugh, for an idler and a scamp and a-a-a worthless blackguard! I'm hard, Maura, am I?

MAURA: Wisht, sure I didn't mean it. I didn't mean it at all. I didn't, indeed, Bat.

BAT: I'm hard, am I? 'Tis your son is hard, and you know it. The sweat o' my body an' my life is in every inch o' the land, and 'tis little he cares, with his hurling an' his fiddling an' his versifying an' his confounded nonsense! . . . I tell you again — an' mind my words for it — 'tis the black lookout for this place when *he* gets it, an' only for your talk, an' your crying, 'tis that blackguard's name an' not his brother's would be on that trunk there this night!

MAURA: Wouldn't it be the queer thing entirely, Bat, to send the eldest son away, and he with your own father's name on him?

BAT: Would it, then? Would it? Tell me, had I ever to go away myself? What was good enough for me ought to be good enough for my brave Hugh — but of course *I'm* only a poor ignorant ploughman, and he's the scholar. The scholar! God bless us!

MAURA: Don't talk foolish, Bat. Sure no one thinks that way of you, and least of all the boy himself. . . . (*Half musingly*) 'Tis the strange thing surely, his own father to be the only one in the parish that's not proud of him; and everyone talking of him, and the priest himself praising him, and his picture in the paper for the great rhymes he made for the *feis*.

BAT: That's more o' your foolish talk, an' 'tis you have helped to make him the kind he is. Your blood is in him. I see it in every twist and turn of his and every wild foolish thing coming from his mouth. . . . Good God, woman, will his grand rhymes an' his

15. Irish for 'nonsense'. As a hurler and a supporter of the *feis*, Hugh evidently approves of the Gaelic revival.

16. prospect.

bits o' meddles an' his picture and the people's talk pay the rent for us? (*Folding his hands and looking at her with half-contemptuous pity*) Well, surely, 'tis the foolish thing for a farmer to marry any but wan[17] with the true farmer's blood in her. I should have guessed long ago what 'ud come of it when I married wan that had other blood in her veins. (*He goes towards the door and turns round*) But Shane isn't gone yet — and maybe he'd never go! ... Meddles!

He goes out. MAURA *sits on the stool at the fireplace and looks vacantly into the fire.* SHANE *appears at the door and enters. He looks about twenty-three. He is rather low-sized, but the general physique indicates rough strength. There is a slight suggestion of hardness about the lines of the mouth.*

SHANE: Will the supper soon be ready, mother? I feel a bit hungry.

MAURA: (*Starting*) Oh, is that you, Shane? I never heard you coming in. 'Twill be on the table in five or ten minutes. (*Bustling towards dresser and putting cups on the table*) I didn't expect you'd be back so soon.

SHANE: Oh, there's lots o' time.

MAURA: You got a lift, I suppose?

SHANE: No, then, I didn't. I came home across the fields.

MAURA: 'Tis wonderful the haste you must have made so! Dan Hegarty was here only a short while ago, and he had his horse, and he was saying he drove away the very minute the play was over.

SHANE: 'Twas how I left the field before the match was half over.

MAURA: (*Disappointed*) Well! Well!

BAT *reappears in the doorway. They are both unconscious of his presence till he speaks.*

SHANE: It come into my head somehow that Hugh might be after forgetting to close up the gap this morning — he isn't over careful when them matches do be on — and I was thinking that the cows might be in the little patch o' winter cabbage, and as I was troubled about it I come away.

MAURA: Wisha, what a pity now! and Dan Hegarty was saying 'twas a grand sight altogether.

BAT: Was it now? Was it? If 'twas as grand again 'tis the hungry dinner 'twould make for us tomorrow, an' the day after, an' the day after that again.

MAURA: 'Twould so, I suppose.

BAT: You needn't be supposing it at all. You're the quare woman, Maura. 'Tisn't satisfied you are with wan of your sons making a fool of himself.... Have you candles in the house, and the lantern ready for the night?

MAURA: I'll see, Bat. I'll see this minute.... But why so?

BAT: We must be staying up, Shane and myself, with the sow tonight.

MAURA: Oh, I forgot. Sure of course. (*She opens the cupboard*) There's plenty of candles. And as ye'll be in and out from the stall during the night 'twould be as well if Shane brought in a good *cireán*[18] of turf to keep the fire up. Ye'll be wanting a sup o' hot milk or a cup o' tea at the latter end of the night.

SHANE: So we would. I'll bring in a good *bacal*[19] of it after supper.

MAURA *lifts cover of pot-oven to see the cake and removes the steaming kettle to the side of the hearth.* SHANE *and* BAT *sit on either side of the hearth opposite each other.*

SHANE: Do you know I was thinking, an' I coming through the fields that 'twould be no harm for us to be turning in the cows o' nights from this out?

BAT: Sure we never housed them so soon after the Michaelmas?[20]

SHANE: I know, but it looks as if there would be a great frost tonight.

MAURA: I was thinking so, too, from the look in the sky (*pointing west*). Them red furrows in the west over the big hill is ever a token of the gray frost.

SHANE: 'Twould be a lot safer to turn them in.

BAT: Wait till I have a look out myself. (*He goes towards the door for a moment*) 'Tis very chilly. There'll be a hard frost sure enough, and Shane is right. (*He returns to the fireplace*)

There is a noise in the distance.

MAURA: What's that?

SHANE: (*Hurrying to door*) 'Tis the people returning from the play. There's great crowds. I never seen such a sight o' people before. I hear them shouting. They're cheering for Hugh. Listen.

Shouting afar off.

MAURA: (*Shading her eyes*) Glory be to God! was the like ever seen? 'Tis the end of the world you'd

17. one.

18. A ridge, a supply stacked in a ridge shape.

19. load.

20. 29 September, the feast of St Michael the Archangel.

think it was. Where on earth did they all come from? For God's sake, come here and look at them, Bat. They're like a black flood covering the world.

BAT: (*Removing his pipe*) That I may be blind if I will!

SHANE: They've a band too. The mare is up east on the little hill. If they give a blast of music 'twill frighten her. I'll run an' see after her. (*Going*)

MAURA: Wisha, wait till you have a bit to eat? You didn't take a mouthful since one o'clock. She'll be all right, you'll find.

SHANE: I can't. Winnie is always a bit shy, an' 'tis a little thing would take a start out of her. (*Goes away hurriedly*)

BAT: (*With conviction*) 'Tis more an' more I'm seeing the terrible loss that boy will be to us.... Isn't it a pity now the Great Man above didn't take it into His head to send him to us before the other?

MAURA: He knows Himself what's best, glory and honour to His Name. 'Tis queer for us — and the great blindness that's on us all — to be talking that way.

BAT: Yeh, have sense, have sense, woman.

MAURA: It can't be right at all. 'Tis many a man and woman in the big world that's hungry in their hearts for a little crying child this night, and you complaining that have two fine sons. I tell you, it can't be right at all, Bat.

BAT: Yeh, what nonsense! — that's no talk at all.... Where's Hugh? Isn't it time for him to be here now? Maybe 'tis missing the Rosary he'll be again tonight, like last Sunday?

MAURA: I'm sure he'll be here shortly. And sure if he wasn't in for the Rosary same he didn't forget to say it by himself. I was taking a pillow into his room, and 'twas on his two knees I saw him with the beads in his hands.

BAT: You're the great wan entirely for excusing him, no matter what divilment he does be at. 'Tis the quare prop he'll be for this house an' I'm greatly afeard 'tis the foolish thing I'm doing.

MAURA: Ah, sure, don't say that at all.

He goes towards the door slowly, and turns round speaking with measured deliberation.

BAT: 'Tis the foolish thing, Maura, when a man have the choice o' two poles to put under the roof of his house, to take that wan that is wake an' crooked an' rotten, just because it is a year or two older.... An' that's what I'm doing, Maura Morrissey. (*He goes out slowly*)

After an interval HUGH *is heard approaching. He enters with eager step.* MAURA *hastens to meet him. He is an open, lithe-limbed youth of twenty-five. He is in knickers, and his unbuttoned coat hangs loosely about him showing the crimson jersey beneath. In his hand is a hurley.*[21]

HUGH: (*enthusiastically*) Mother, glorious news! We've won the final after a splendid tussle. Isn't it great, and some of the best men in Ireland against us?

MAURA: Is there any hurt on you at all? Don't be telling me anything till I know that first.

HUGH: (*Laughing*) Oh, make your mind easy. I escaped without a scratch.

MAURA: But is it the truth you're telling me?

HUGH: Oh, God knows, mother, it is.

MAURA: (*Doubtingly*) Sure I can't trust you at all since the time your wrist was sprained, and all the lies you told to keep it from me.

HUGH: (*Playfully*) Look here, you foolish little woman, will this set your mind at rest? (*He dances a short sprightly step, whistling an accompaniment at the same time*) Could a man do that and anything to be wrong with him?

MAURA: (*Laughing*) Well, indeed, 'tis hardly. Thanks be to God that brought you home safe! But sure you must be weak with the hunger. I'll have the tea in half a minute. (*She bustles towards fireplace*)

HUGH: Oh, look here, mother, 'tis hardly worth while. I'm in a desperate hurry.

MAURA: (*Surprised*) What's that you're saying?

HUGH: (*Conciliatory*) 'Tis how we're giving a little bit of a supper to the other team over at Pat Lacy's. There was a couple o' pounds left after paying the expenses of the tournament. 'Tis to be at six o'clock, and I just hurried over for a few minutes to tell you not to be staying up for me tonight. It may be half-past ten — or a little bit later — before I'll be home.

MAURA: (*Sitting down despondently*) Oh, wisha! wisha! wisha!

HUGH: Yeh, what's the matter at all? What is it, mother?

MAURA: (*Rising with sudden energy*) Hugh, boy, you'll stay at home this night, won't you? — won't you?

HUGH: And good heavens, why? Why, mother?

MAURA: (*Hesitatingly*) Sure, just to please me, a poor old woman, Hugh, who — who haven't

21. A hurling stick, usually made of ash.

altogether too many pleasures in her life maybe. Won't you, Hugh?

HUGH: How can I, mother? How can I? 'Tis hard on me to be refsing, but sure *I* must be there whoever else will be there.

MAURA: And you won't do that small thing for me! O Hugh! Hugh! Hugh! (*She turns away reproachfully*)

HUGH: For God's sake don't talk like that, mother.... I'd do anything in the world for your sake, and you know it.

MAURA: You'll not go then? I knew you wouldn't refuse me.

HUGH: Mother, look here. I'll not leave this roof tonight if you'll be anyway against it when I tell you how it is with me.

MAURA: Thank God, Hugh, thank God! You don't know the relief it is to my mind. You could be writing a message to say to them you can't come. I'll run out to get some messenger to take it east for you. (*She puts on her shawl hastily, and hurries towards the door*) The bottle of ink is over there near the brass candlestick. (*Going*)

HUGH: Wait, mother, wait a minute. Sure I haven't told you at all about it yet.

MAURA: It don't matter at all, when you're not going. Maybe I'll find some one against the time[22] you'll be writing the letter. (*Going*)

HUGH: But look here, mother.

MAURA: (*Anxiously*) Well?

HUGH: How do you know but 'tis changing your mind you'll be when I tell you the way 'tis with me about the business?

MAURA: (*Troubled*) What is it, then?

HUGH: Here's a note I got from Father Daly. He got a sick call before the match was over, and scribbled it on a leaf of his notebook before he left the field. Curly Twomey that brought it to me.

MAURA: Read it for me yourself. 'Tis cruel hard to make out his writing always, God bless him.

HUGH: Very well. This is what he says:

'DEAR HUGH — I've met the Canon and spoken to him. He has no objection whatever to the club entertaining themselves so long as I hold myself responsible. Unfortunately, I've got a sick call at the other end of the parish and cannot be present. In my absence it will remain entirely with you to see that everything is seemly, and that there is no excess.' Listen to this, mother.

'Delighted with our men today. They were simply magnificent, and their captain's playing superb.

Yours very faithfully,
CHARLES DALY'

HUGH: Well, mother?

MAURA: (*After a pause*) You can't refuse the priest.

HUGH: (*In playful triumph*) Didn't I say you would change your mind?

MAURA: (*Sadly*) You did, indeed.

HUGH: But in any case, why on earth should you be uneasy about me? Surely I am able to take decent care of myself. Father Daly thinks so anyway ... (*half bitterly*). Is it because I had the misfortune to get drunk once in my life — and that three years ago — that you have so little trust in me?

MAURA: Oh, no, no, no, Hugh! 'Tis not that, indeed and indeed. 'Tis upset and troubled I was because of himself. It was, indeed.

HUGH: And why so, mother?

MAURA: (*Conciliatory*) 'Twas how he was in a kind of temper all the evening since Dan Hegarty called with Shane's trunk. Dan would be talking about the goal and the great work entirely you done today, and you know that's the last thing that's good for him to hear. And 'tis greatly afraid I am that he'll be wild entirely with yourself and with us all when he finds you're not in the house for the Rosary tonight.

HUGH: (*Annoyed*) That's most unfortunate! But what can I do? He seems to be getting more and more unreasonable every day. When a man does his big best for six days of the week 'tis hardly fair to grudge him Sunday! ... Well, I'm bound to go all the same, no matter how he'll take it — but, indeed, I've no heart for pleasure now.

MAURA: Ah, well, sure, never mind — 'tis only a little thing after all.

HUGH: I wouldn't care much for myself — I'd just as lief[23] stay at home — but to be thinking of you sitting there quiet all night on that stool, and he opposite you, an' the hard word, an' the bitter word, coming in turn from his lips, and myself to be the cause of it all!

MAURA: Yeh, sure he don't mean the half of what he says. I don't mind him at all — sure, 'tis time for me now to be used to his ways. Don't be thinking of that at all or letting it trouble your mind. 'Tis half

22. by the time.

23. rather.

sorry I am for telling you at all.

HUGH: Oh, nonsense; why shouldn't you, mother? Why shouldn't you, indeed? And where is he now?

MAURA: He's out with Shane. They're looking after the mare, and they're thinking, too, of turning in the cows tonight.

HUGH: So soon? — but there's a frosty chill in the air.... (*More cheerfully*) Look, mother. There's Father Daly's letter. If he says anything show it to him.

MAURA: 'Tis afraid I am 'twould only be making him worse. He can't bear to hear the name of Father Daly. 'Destroying the parish,' he says he is.

HUGH: There's not another priest in all this diocese like him! 'Tis the changed place the parish is since he came into it. And that's the thanks he's getting!

MAURA: 'Tis foolish for anyone to be expecting thanks in this world. 'Tis above he'll be getting a return for all the good he's after doing, so it is.

HUGH: That's about the truth of it, I'm thinking. (*Suddenly*) 'Tis running a bit late, so I'll just run upstairs for a dash of cold water. I want to freshen myself up a bit for the night.... 'Tis too bad, but I suppose we can only let things take their course. He may say nothing after all.

MAURA: Maybe so, maybe so, indeed.

He hastily mounts the stairs to his room. MAURA *prepares a cup of tea, which she is pouring out as he returns. He runs to a glass, tidying his hair.*

You weren't long. Here, take this and a cut of the hot cake. 'Tis easy to get a chill after the hot sweat o' the play, and 'twill warm you a bit.

HUGH: Thanks. Don't mind the cake. I won't eat anything. (*He gulps down the tea*) That was a fine strong cup o' tea. It sent a warm wave like rushing all over me. I'll be going now; and I'm thinking, maybe, 'twould be no harm for all if you showed him the letter — the sight of the priest's name written by his own hand might soften him a bit, you know?

MAURA: Maybe so, then, with the help of God.

HUGH: (*Affectionately*) And, mother, let the door on the latch, and I'll get to bed without disturbing anyone. I won't make a sound. I wouldn't have you wait up for all the world. (*Appealingly*) Sure you won't now?

MAURA: No, I won't indeed, Hugh. I won't indeed. Make your mind easy.... (*Playfully*) Be off with yourself now, sir, I wouldn't have you a minute late after what the priest wrote.

HUGH: (*Pleasantly*) You're right, mother. You're *always* right. Good-by. (*Going*)

MAURA: Good-by, and God direct you!

HUGH *goes out.* MAURA *stands a few moments at the door gazing after him. She returns and rearranges the supper table, removing cup and saucer to the dresser. After an interval a hurried step is heard.* SHANE *enters hastily, and with a show of strong excitement.*

MAURA: What's the matter, Shane?

SHANE: Bad news enough then. The mare that's hurt on us.

MAURA: Virgin Mother! is it the truth you're saying?

SHANE: I'm not much given to joking. 'Tis for the gun I've come to put her out of pain. Her hind leg that's broken. (*He stands on the chair and takes down the gun from the wall. He loads it in both barrels*)

MAURA: *A Thighearna!*[24] Isn't it terrible — terrible altogether? ... And there's the plowing and everything else to be done by us, and no horse with us now — and the little foal not yet weaned.

SHANE: (*Bitterly*) 'Twas the misfortunate match for us! Their cursed band that frightened her. Bad luck to the whole pack an' dice of them! That's what we've got by their tournament. (*He rushes out*)

MAURA: 'Tis the terrible misfortune, surely. 'Tis the great loss entirely.... And Bat, sure 'twill kill him, and he always so proud of the brown mare.... The poor thing, and she always so good and willing, and the great worker for seven long years.

A shot is heard. MAURA *starts and covers her eyes. She remains thus till* SHANE *and* BAT *return.* SHANE *replaces the gun.* BAT *sits down in gloomy silence.*

SHANE: All over, mother. One shot put an end to her.

MAURA: I heard it, God help us.

SHANE: She was the fine mare. She'll be the sore loss to ye.

MAURA: The sore loss, indeed.

SHANE: There wasn't another like her in the townland for the work. 'Tis often I done nearly an acre o' plowing in the day with her, an' next morning she was as willing as ever again to take to the furrow; and it didn't matter whether 'twas uphill or downhill, or on the leven *ban*[25] she was. She was a great little woman — so she was.

MAURA: The poor thing!

24. Irish, 'Lord!'
25. Irish, 'a plain, pasture land'.

SHANE: Do you know there was a kind of quare feeling come over me, an' I turning the gun at her? — a kind of shiver it was, an' a mist before my eyes.

MAURA: The poor dumb creature and she so kind.

SHANE: 'Tis strange I'll be feeling going across in the big ship, an' thinking of the lonely look in her big eyes with the death coming down on them like a dark dream. . . . Ah, well, ye'll have good reason to be remembering the great match whatever I'll do! 'Twas the dear match for ye! Thirty pounds she would be fetching as surely as she'd fetch a farthing . . . . And I suppose now you won't be entitled to any compensation, father?

BAT: (*Lifting his head*) Where's Hugh?

MAURA: He's gone out.

BAT: Call him.

MAURA: There's no use. He's gone this half-hour or so. He won't be back for a bit.

BAT: An' why?

MAURA: The priest that sent for him on some business or other.

SHANE: 'Tis how Hugh's team are giving some kind of a spree to the other hurlers over at the village. I'm told there's to be great doings altogether, and there's to be a dance after.

MAURA: (*With feverish eagerness*) He won't be long at all. He said so going away. 'Tis only a supper they're having. 'Twas the priest himself asked him to look after things, and only for that he wouldn't be there at all. That's God's truth, Bat, so it is!

SHANE: They were saying it was to be a regular spree. But sure, whatever it is, 'twould be quare for the captain to be away from the diversions. 'Twould never do.

BAT: The black trouble is on this house this night, and feasting and drinking he is that should be here.

MAURA: Sure, God help us, he doesn't know it. How could he at all? And if he did, 'tis worse than Shane, or you or me, he'd feel, for he ever an' always loved the poor creature like a human thing.

BAT: A fine mare gone from us and he carousing . . . worth thirty pounds, Shane says. Worth every penny of forty pounds, I says. (*He stands up with an air of strong determination*) Well, 'tis the long lane that have no turning, and my brave Hugh have come to the turning at last.

MAURA: (*In alarm*) What is it you're going to do at all, at all? Look, Bat, there's the priest's letter — written by his own blessed hand this day. (*Offering the letter*) Only for it he'd be here in this kitchen this minute. God knows he would.

BAT *takes the letter. He goes towards the fireplace and with slow deliberation puts it into the fire unread. He watches it burn.*

Mother of God! What are you after doing? The letter that was written by the holy priest! There'll be no luck in this house forever again!

BAT *goes calmly to the shelf over the fireplace, takes down pen and ink, and hands the pen to* SHANE.

SHANE: (*Wonderingly*) What's this for at all?

BAT: Wait. (*He goes to the trunk, takes out his penknife and carefully cuts off the label bearing* SHANE's *name. Handing label to* SHANE) Read that for me.

SHANE: (*Reading*) 'John Morrissey, Passenger Queenstown to Boston, *via* Campania.'

BAT: Good. Cross out the name that's on it, and write over it Hugh Morrissey. Make it plain and big. (SHANE *hesitates, looking questioningly*) What are you stopping for? Don't you understand plain talk?

SHANE: But, father —

BAT: Write it, I tell you, at wanst.[26]

MAURA: But surely, surely, Bat —

He pushes her roughly aside.

BAT: Shut your mouth, woman! 'Tis none o' your business! (*To* SHANE) Write it — and write it at wanst, I say, or 'twill be worse for you!

SHANE *writes slowly and carefully, and hands back the label to his father.*

BAT: (*Looking at label in the stupid manner of a half-illiterate and handing it back to* SHANE) Read it for me.

SHANE: (*Reading*) 'Hugh Morrissey, Passenger Queenstown to Boston, *via* Campania.' (*He returns it to his father, who goes towards the trunk, and with a grim smile reattaches it to the handle*)

BAT: Now, my fine captain, you may drink and feast to the devil!

MAURA *sits in silent grief. There is a look of uncertain emotion on* SHANE's *face as the curtain descends.*

26. at once.

ACT II

Scene: The same. Midnight. There is a candle on the dresser throwing a dull light. In the middle of the room is a table laid for one. MAURA, *worn and troubled, is kneeling at a chair, a Rosary bead in her hand. There is heard the sound of approaching footsteps, and the latch is lifted. She goes to unbolt the door in trembling haste.*

MAURA: Who's there? Is that yourself, Hugh?

HUGH: Open, mother.

She draws the bolt. HUGH *comes in. She bolts the door again.*

MAURA: What kept you at all, at all? I was getting very troubled about you.

HUGH: 'Twas how I couldn't manage to get away. I did my very best, honestly. God knows I did, mother.

MAURA: Sure, of course. I know, I know. But I was half uneasy like with the night passing and no sign of you at all.

HUGH: (*Dismally*) Such a night of it as I'm after going through! 'Tis little notion Father Daly had the kind of task he was setting me! Good Heavens, such a night, mother!

MAURA: 'Twasn't too easy to manage them all, I suppose?

HUGH: Easy? Easy is it? (*Solemnly*) I give you my word for it I'll be very, very slow to undertake the same responsibility again!

MAURA: Well, now.

HUGH: Some of the other team, when they had a small share of drink taken, were as cross as two sticks. 'Twas no joke at all to keep them in pleasant humour. 'Tisn't hard for men when they're after losing a great game to be losing their tempers after it.

MAURA: That's true, indeed.... But isn't it very pale entirely you're looking, Hugh? 'Tis whiter than the candle you are.

HUGH: I'm fagged out after the day. To tell you the honest truth, I never felt so tired in all my life. 'Twas awful to get the fellows away! I thought I could never get the last of them home. They'd stick on till daylight if I'd let them. One by one I had to force them into the wagonette — nearly twenty of them in all. (*Cheerfully*) But, then, sure everything came right in the end.

MAURA: Thank God for that!

HUGH: 'Tis very late, I suppose?

MAURA: The clock is after striking twelve, but I'm thinking it must be a bit fast. I was afraid o' my life I'd be late for Mass this morning, but I was in a good while before the priest came on the altar.

HUGH: (*Reproachfully*) And you stayed up for me after all your promises? Ah, mother, mother, mother!

MAURA: (*Extenuatingly*) Well, now, I did and I didn't. 'Twas how I couldn't sleep. There was a kind of whirl and an aching in my head, and I thought 'twould ease it a bit if I came down here and busied myself a little till you came. There was plenty for me to be doing, I tell you.

HUGH: There you are! — always and ever thinking of everyone's comfort but your own. I'm sore afraid, you foolish little woman, you'll never learn sense. But there's no use talking to you.

MAURA: Wisha, don't be foolish. I've a nice little bit of supper for you here. 'Twill do you good, an' you want it.

HUGH: I couldn't touch a morsel, I'm so dead tired. Honestly, mother.

MAURA: I'll make the tea very hot, and I have a fine drop of goat's milk. 'Twill warm you a bit, and then you can run off to bed. 'Twon't take five minutes altogether.

HUGH: But sure I had tea before leaving Lacy's. Mrs. Lacy herself made me take a cup after all the others going away.

MAURA: What matter? There's a small bit o' meat since the dinner — 'tis the ham, and 'tis very sweet. I thought you'd like it, you're always so fond of the ham.

HUGH: (*Yielding pleasantly*) Very well so, let us have it.

MAURA: 'Twill be ready in half a minute. (*Puts tea to draw*) 'Tis terrible pale entirely you are after the day. You'd frighten a person. Look, while the tea'll be drawing I'll be taking off your boots for you. Put them up there on that little stool. (*Kneels down to remove his boots*)

HUGH: (*Protestingly*) Oh, nonsense, mother; nonsense! I'll take them off myself. I'm all right. I'm only a little tired, that's all.

MAURA: Ah, wisha, can't you let me — to please me this night.

HUGH: (*Half reluctantly*) Well, so, if 'twill please you.

She begins to unfasten the lace when a man's heavy footsteps are heard on the stones outside approaching the door.

MAURA: (*In a half-whisper*) My God, Hugh, your father!

HUGH: And what matter, sure?

MAURA: Whisht! whisht! for God's sake, talk easy.

A hand lifts the latch and tries to push in the bolted door. They keep still.

BAT: (*Outside*) Maura.

There is no answer.

BAT: (*More peremptorily*) Maura! Maura!

There is still no answer. The footsteps are heard moving slowly away from the door.

MAURA: He thinks 'tis in the bed I am. He's going round to the back to rap at the bedroom window. Look, for God's sake! keep out of his way tonight. Run upstairs to your room till he's gone. Do, do, Hugh?

HUGH: Yeh, for what, mother? Have a bit of sense. What's the great harm I'm after doing at all?

MAURA: No harm, no harm, indeed. But he's in the black rage tonight. Ah, do, do! Won't you, Hugh?

HUGH: (*Half vexed*) Mother, do you think 'tis a frightened child, I am?

MAURA: No, no, indeed I don't, Hugh; but there's a great fear in my heart —

HUGH: Yeh, nonsense. There's nothing at all to be troubled about. Nothing whatever. He'll say nothing, and if he does — sure let him.

MAURA: Well, so, won't you promise me not to mind at all whatever he'll be saying? 'Tis queer in himself he is, and greatly upset — for the mare that's after dying on us.

HUGH: What's that you say? Is it Winnie?

MAURA: She's dead. She broke her leg, and Shane had to shoot her. (*Beseechingly*) For the blessed Lord's sake, Hugh, don't heed anything at all your father'll say this night? 'Tis nearly out of his mind he is with the loss o' the mare.

A loud tapping is heard on the window of the bedroom off the kitchen. MAURA *stands in the shadow of the doorway between kitchen and bedroom and feigns to answer from her bed.*

BAT: Maura. Maura.

MAURA: (*In half-drowsy tones*) Who's there?

BAT: (*Roughly*) Maura!

MAURA: Oh, is that yourself, Bat?

BAT: Get up and open the door. You put the bolt on it an' you going to bed. I want a candle, and I can't get in. The wan we have is nearly burned out.

MAURA: Just one minute, Bat — one minute. I'll have it opened against the time[1] you'll be round. (*She re-enters kitchen*) (*Half distractedly*) Promise me, Hugh, for God's sake, you won't take him up whatever he says. Won't you? Won't you? If you don't, God Himself only knows what might come of it. Look, on my two knees I'm begging you.

HUGH: For heaven's sake don't do that mother. I'll do anything you want — anything at all in the wide world. I'll not open my lips this night if you wish it. Now.

MAURA: God bless you, Hugh. God bless you for that, boy.

BAT'S *heavy step is heard again.* MAURA *throws a shawl around her and takes the candle off the dresser. As the latch is lifted she draws the bolt, and with feverish haste hands out the candle over the half-door to* BAT, *who is standing on the doorstep outside. The kitchen is very dimly lit by the glow of the fire.*

BAT: Isn't it a great wandher[2] you wouldn't think of laving the door on the latch, an' we wanting to be in and out? You must be always doing the quare thing an' the sthupid thing, Maura.

MAURA: I didn't notice myself bolting it, somehow, and I going to bed.

BAT: Well, notice it the next time, or 'tis out of your bed you'll have to be marching again — an' serve you right!

MAURA: (*Half-closing the door*) Oh, I'll think of it this time, never mind.

BAT: Well, do so. (*He goes away slowly with the lighted candle in his hand*)

MAURA: (*Fervently*) Oh, thanks be to the Almighty God for that, Hugh! (*She lights a candle. Her hands are trembling*)

HUGH: (*With tender concern*) You're trembling all over, mother.

MAURA: 'Twas foolish o' me to be so frightened, but — but I couldn't help it. Something in my heart that stirred when the latch rattled.

HUGH: Ah, sure, if I thought 'twould be like that at all with you I'd have gone up to the room the time you asked me, an' gladly too. I would, indeed.

MAURA: Sure it don't matter at all now that he's gone.

HUGH: It looked a cowardly thing, somehow, to be running away and a man after doing no wrong at all; but 'tis a lot more cowardly it looks now to be after remaining, and you to be the way you are this minute.

MAURA: Don't say that at all.

HUGH: (*Eagerly*) Look here now. I'll go off straight to my room this minute for fear anything else might be bringing him back a second time. What do you say? Isn't it best?

1. by the time.

2. wonder.

MAURA: Well, maybe, 'twould be just as good. And I can take up the tea to you after.

HUGH: All right so.

He takes a candle and is lighting it at the fire when the latch is lifted again. The door is opened in. MAURA *hastens towards it.* BAT *appears in the doorway.* HUGH *is in the shelter of the deep fireplace.*

BAT: (*To* MAURA) Didn't you go back to bed since? Faith, 'tis hot in your blood you are! The night outside is getting very chilly, an' t'would be no harm for me, I'm thinking, to be putting on my big coat against the frost. (*He advances into the room and sees* HUGH) So the spree is over at last?

MAURA: Wisha, say nothing to him tonight, Bat. He's not well at all. Look at the colour he is, the Lord save us!

BAT: (*In derision*) Yes, look at him! — look at the cut of him![3]

MAURA: (*Appealingly*) Wisha, Bat.

BAT: (*With jeering mimicry*) 'Wisha, Bat.' . . . Ah, Maura, Maura, 'tis you have the good right to be speaking for him — him that has the great love for you, keeping you up in the bitter night till near cockcrow. But sure he wouldn't be a rale[4] gentleman an' he to come home earlier.

MAURA: No, no, Bat, you're wronging him. He didn't keep me up at all — he didn't, indeed. 'Twas the way I couldn't sleep with a queer pain in my head, and I thought 'twould do me good to come down to the fire for a little while.

BAT: (*Thunderingly*) Hush your mouth, you! (*To* HUGH) Have you any tongue in your head tonight, man? Maybe 'tis ashamed of yourself you are at last — you — you half-drunken scoundrel!

MAURA: (*To* HUGH) Don't mind him at all.

HUGH: (*With quiet dignity*) Those are hard words, father, but they're not true words.

MAURA: (*To* HUGH) Don't mind him this night at all, Hugh. Sure, thank God, no one could ever say that of you, and your father, he don't mean it at all.

BAT: (*Half savagely*) Didn't I tell you hush your mouth before? Go in there straight to your bed, an' don't be interfering with what's no concern of yours! Do you hear me?

MAURA: (*Appealingly*) Wisha, Bat —

BAT: Go at wanst, I tell you! Go now!

She goes towards her room, but lingers in the doorway.

Now, sir, I'm going to talk to you, an' 'tis the plain talk I'll give you. You're never in your life to spend another week under this roof.

HUGH *starts and looks incredulous.*

You think I don't mane[5] it. Look here. By God, I swear it!

HUGH: (*Distressfully*) You wouldn't, father — you wouldn't, surely?

BAT: I've sworn it, sir. You'll lave this house instead of your brother on Thursday morning.

HUGH: You're not in earnest — you wouldn't be so hard — you wouldn't, surely? What wrong have I done?

BAT: Ah, 'tis well you're finding your tongue now, you idle scoundrel! Go you must, an' go you will! Maybe 'tis perjuring myself you'd like me to be?

HUGH: 'Tis not, for you're not bound by such an oath. 'Tis unjust, and you know it.

BAT: (*Jeeringly*) Is it so?

HUGH: Ever since I was a little child 'twas told to me that this place would be mine — you told me so yourself.

BAT: I don't care what I told you! This farm is my own and no one else's. I have put the whole work o' my life into it, and I'll do whatever I like with it. And out of this you'll march bag and baggage on Thursday morning! There! (*Taking trunk and flinging it towards him*) You're a great scholar. You'll be able to read that label, I suppose.

MAURA: (*Rushing towards* BAT) In the name of the good God, Bat — for the honour of Mary, His Mother —

He pushes her aside roughly, and goes out uttering half-smothered ejaculations. There is a long pause, HUGH *sinks into a seat, his head buried in his hands. After a while* MAURA *goes to him timidly.*

HUGH: Mother, don't come near me.

MAURA: Oh, Hugh!

HUGH: I'm sick of everything.

MAURA: *Dia linn as mhuire Mháthaír!*[6]

HUGH: The weight o' the world is on my heart . . . and that look on your face . . . 'tis the weight that's crushing it all down.

MAURA: Wisha, don't mind me at all, my poor boy. . . . Won't you be going to bed? 'Tis cold and white and shivering you are.

HUGH: 'Tis nothing — nothing at all. Let me by

3. the appearance of him.
4. real.
5. mean.
6. Irish, 'God and his Mother Mary be with us!'

myself for a bit and I'll be better. 'Tis you want the rest, poor woman, and not I — 'tis, indeed, mother.

MAURA: (*With feigned cheerfulness*) Sure not at all! I was always wonderful for staying up a night. (*Insinuatingly*) Maybe you'll take a cup o' the tea after all? And I'll take a sup with you for the company. Do, Hugh.

HUGH: I couldn't, mother, I couldn't. Don't ask me.

MAURA: I won't then. I won't, Hugh.

HUGH: (*Going to her affectionately*) Let me alone here by the fire for a little bit, mother, and I'll be all right very soon. You won't refuse me my last Sunday night here — you that never refused me anything in my life.

MAURA: Very well, Hugh, boy. I'll go if 'twill please you. *A Mhuire Mháthair!*[7] What a black night!

She leaves the room weeping silently. HUGH *sits on the stool at the fire looking desolately into the dying embers.*

HUGH: All over now. . . . A black night surely. . . . Poor Winnie dead, too, after all her years. Shot. The poor thing! The poor thing! . . . Thursday morning he said. Short shrift enough! 'Tis the hard landlord that gives only three days' notice. Well, 'tis many a better man has travelled the same road before. (*He looks at the trunk. He examines the label*) Shane that wrote it! Shane! How could he do it? The miserable cur! — 'tis only like him. A grabber — a mean, low grabber! Oh, such a piece of treachery! I could — yes, by God! I could choke the mean soul out of him this minute . . . yet for her sake, with her face full of sorrow, I'll say nothing. Poor mother! God help her! God help her!

There is a pause. He is halfway up the stairs, the candle in his hand, when the door opens and SHANE *comes in. There is a look of eager questioning on his face.*

SHANE: For God's sake, Hugh, what's up at all? My father went in for a candle, and ever since he come back he hasn't spoken a word or minded anything at all, but walking up and down the stall in a black silence.

HUGH: It doesn't matter — let me alone.

SHANE: Where's the harm in asking?

HUGH: Let me alone, I ask you, this night!

SHANE: And why so?

HUGH: Why so? Well, because — because the less talk between you and me just now the better maybe for both of us.

SHANE: Well, there's no doubt of it, but you're getting mighty civil, Hugh.

HUGH: Maybe 'tis too civil I am to a grabber.

SHANE: To what?

HUGH: I ask you again to get out of my sight!

SHANE: (*Threateningly*) What's that you said first?

HUGH: (*With a great effort of self-repression*) In God's name, will you go or not?

SHANE: Who's a grabber?

HUGH: You are — and the meanest grabber that ever walked the earth.

SHANE: You drunken brute, if you say that again —

HUGH: (*Hotly*) You're a liar, and I will say it again, and I'll say it till I'm hoarse, for there was never a dirtier grabber in all Ireland than yourself — grabbing a brother's land.

SHANE: That's a lie for you! What right had you to this place — you that never did an honest day's work in your life?

HUGH: What right had I?

SHANE: Yes, yes, what right? Is it because you were born a year or two before me? 'Tis the man's work an' not the reckoning of his years that makes the right! So it is!

HUGH: You may talk and argue till the Day of Judgment, but a grabber — a mean treacherous grabber you are and nothing else!

SHANE: Say that word again and by the Lord God — (*Pauses, choked with passion*)

HUGH: (*Confronting him*) Well, what then? What then, Shaneen?[8] — Shaneen the grabber?

SHANE: (*Making to strike him*) Blast you!

They struggle with each other for a moment in a tempest of blind rage. MAURA *rushes in.*

MAURA: My God, what is it? What is up with ye at all? (*She rushes between them*) Oh, shame, shame, shame, this holy night! Shame for you, Hugh — what has come over you at all? And black shame for you, Shane, and you knowing the great wrong done him — and the heavy load that is on his heart this night!

SHANE: He brought it on himself with his drunken lies. Don't be blaming me.

MAURA: For shame, Shane, don't be saying things like that.

7. 'Mary, Mother (of God)!'

8. Hugh uses the diminutive of Shane to sarcastic effect.

SHANE: The whiskey was cheap tonight.

MAURA: If it was, there was none of it wet his lips, and you know it well, Shane. 'Tis the soft word, and the word of pity, and not the bitter thought should be on your lips this night.

SHANE: I'll say what I like. 'Twas he began it.

MAURA: 'Tis little heed you should be putting on his words an' his heart breaking.

SHANE: Oh, of course, of course. 'Tis the old story — taking his side always. There should be no favourites in this house, nor in any other house, neither.

MAURA: And sure, glory be to God, there isn't, boy?

SHANE: That's not true! — there is favourites here, an' for many a long day, too.

MAURA: Oh, Shane, boy, don't be talking like that. 'Tisn't true at all, and you know it well. Hush!

SHANE: I won't hush! You're always again me, whoever is in the wrong. 'Tisn't today nor yesterday I've seen it. I tell you 'tis the bad thing for any woman to be making distinctions between her own flesh and blood.

MAURA: Oh, Shane, sure you don't mean that at all? 'Tis the awful queer crooked fancy that's come into your mind. But 'tisn't true at all — indeed and indeed it isn't.

SHANE: That's a lie — and an infernal lie!

HUGH: (*Starting up*) That's no way for you to speak to your mother! 'Tis only to a woman the like of you would say it.[9]

SHANE: I don't want no words at all from you while the smell o' the drink is on them.

MAURA: (*Forcing* HUGH *into his seat*) Whisht, whisht, for God's sake! Let us have no more words this blessed night. Say your prayers and go to bed, the two of ye, in the name of God. 'Tis very late. Won't you, Shane? Won't you, boy?

SHANE: I'll go when I'm after saying what I want to say, an' what's on my mind for many a day.

MAURA: Wisha, hush, hush, boy! 'Tis after one o'clock, and we're all dead tired.

SHANE: You says there is no favourite here.

MAURA: Wisha, Shane, *a chuíd!*[10]

SHANE: But I can swear it to you there is. I've seen it again and again since I was able to understand anything.

MAURA: Ah, wisha, Shane, boy, don't be thinking such a queer thought at all. There's no mortal reason for it — whatever put the foolish notion into your head.

SHANE: 'Tis no foolish notion, an' you know it too! When we were small boys an' we sitting there at that table, who always used to be given the white loaf, an' who used to get the strong cake? An' who was it always got the fine cloth from the shops in Macroom, an' which of us had to be wearing the gray homespun that was like what the poorhouse boys do be wearing, an' they walking out the country roads with their schoolmaster? An' who —

MAURA: Glory be to God, what's come over you? Sure ye were only the same to me as two lambs that would be on the one hill, only one o' ye being a bit stronger like than the other.

SHANE: 'Twas damn bad luck to be the strong lamb — so it was!

MAURA: Hugh hadn't the big strength that you had and he growing up, because that he grew so quick, and he had to be coaxed like to bring him on.

SHANE: Well, so, was it because he hadn't the strength that you used to be taking him to the town to see the fair an' the circus, an' leaving me at home thinking bitter things in my heart? An' was it because he hadn't the strength you got the priest to put him on the altar serving the Mass an' never thought o' me?

MAURA: Wisha, God help us, Shane, sure that was only because he was so quick at the learning.

SHANE: Oh, of course — of course! That was only one o' the distinctions you made between us when I was a boy, and if God made me rough, He didn't make me rough enough not to feel them and remember them to this hour. An' when we grew up 'tisn't one nor a dozen distinctions that was made between us, but a hundred and more. How could I have the soft feeling for you, or for him, or for anyone else? An' if I have the black hatred in my heart instead this night, is it your fault or my own?

MAURA: Shane, Shane, don't be saying such awful things. If I ever, ever made a difference 'twas unknownst to me. 'Twas indeed. Before God, I never meant them! I didn't, I — I didn't indeed . . . . (*Breaks off sobbingly*)

HUGH: (*Passionately*) You're a big cowardly brute to torture like that the woman that bore you. By God! I'll not listen to any more of it. If you dare to say another thing to her I'll — look — I'll choke the words in your throat, you — you mean hound, you — you — you miserable cur.

9. i.e. 'A person such as he would say it only to a woman — not to a man.'
10. Irish, 'Enough!'

SHANE: Try it! do! I'll say what I like an' give you no thanks, great a hero as you are.

HUGH: Do it at your peril!

SHANE: You think I'm afraid of you?

MAURA: Ah, hush, let ye; hush, hush! (*To* HUGH) Sure, Shane don't mean at all what he's saying.

SHANE: I do mean it — an' every single word of it.

MAURA: What harm? What harm?

HUGH: (*Scornfully*) What could anyone expect from the likes of him after his treacherous work of this night?

MAURA: Ah, look, look now, the two of ye, have the grace of God about ye and go to bed?

HUGH: Is it me to lie on the same pillow with a man like him this night?

SHANE: No, I'm not a fine gentleman, and I drunk on other people's money —

HUGH: No, you're not, but do you know what you are? Do you? Do you? (*Approaching him threateningly*)

MAURA: Stop! Stop!

HUGH: (*Passionately*) You're a coward and you're a grabber! That's what you are, and nothing else.

At the word 'grabber,' Shane rushes wildly at HUGH. *They get into handgrips and begin to struggle in blind and furious passion.*

MAURA: (*Frantically, rushing out*) Bat! Bat! for God's sake, run! They're killing each other!

The two men reel and stagger blindly. SHANE *is seen to stumble and fall. Struggling onto his feet, he leaps at his brother. The impact brings them both to the ground. There is a horrid thud.* HUGH *lies perfectly still. Gathering himself up,* SHANE *looks on the prostrate figure. He is dazed and horrified. Pity and terror in his voice, he calls* 'Hugh! Hugh!' *There is only a dreadful stillness. He staggers out into the night crying* 'O God! O God!'

MAURA *rushes in and, bending distractedly over the boy's body, cries* 'Hugh! Hugh!' BAT *is seen coming through the doorway, his face tense with alarm, as the curtain falls.*

GEORGE FITZMAURICE

(1878-1963)

from:
THE DANDY DOLLS
(1913)

[Fitzmaurice, much influenced by Synge, developed a strange idiom of his own, which nevertheless suits the strange, grotesque, magical world in which some of his best effects are achieved. Yeats rejected *The Dandy Dolls* in 1913; Austin Clarke's Lyric Theatre Company produced it first in 1945, but it was not produced at the Abbey until 1969. In effect, after 1913, Fitzmaurice began to withdraw from Irish theatrical life. The Abbey put on *The Country Dressmaker* in 1907 and three other plays of Fitzmaurice, the last in 1923. No more were produced in his lifetime. His fantasy would have been a useful counteragent to the realism that dominated the theatre in these years.

In the second of the play's two scenes, the legendary characters — the Grey Man, the Hag of Barna and her son — battle for the newly made dandy doll of the doll-maker, Roger Carmody. In reaction to the effort of making a dandy doll, Roger is regularly overcome with a craving for poultry, especially for the geese of Father James. To stop his thieving, the priest puts a blessing on the doll. But the Grey Man has already laid a plot with Cauth, Roger's wife, to defeat both the Hag and her son and to rid Cauth of Roger, of whom she is weary. To that end, he has left Roger a bottle containing a magic potion.]

CHARACTERS

ROGER CARMODY
CAUTH, *his wife*
HIS CHILD
GREY MAN
HAG'S SON
TIMMEEN
FATHER JAMES
KEERBY, *the priest's clerk*
THE HAG OF BARNA

Scene II — As curtain rises CAUTH *and* ROGER *are still sleeping. It is within a minute of ten o'clock.*

CHILD: (*Playing marbles on floor*) Into my first of nothing, into my second of nothing, into my last of thaw[1] — games! (*Chalks a circle on floor and plays another game*) Pinked! That's a button won. No! By J, I'm fat! (*singing*) 'Oh then, buttercups and daisies, etc.' (*Looks at clock;* CAUTH *and* ROGER *wake up*) Tick-tack! Tick-tack![2]

CAUTH: Stop, you ashy creature, hasn't the Hag's Son ears would hear a sound like that full fifty miles and more? So stop your tick-tack, for might be will of God he'd forget the hour and maybe fall asleep.

Clock strikes.

CHILD: Dong! Dong! Dong!

VOICE: (*Outside*) Open! Open! Open, open, quick!

CAUTH: Stop outside now, you spawn of a mountainy hag![3] Stop outside now, be off and take your hook![4]

VOICE: (*Outside*) It's me. It's Timmeen Faley. Open in the name of God! The Hag's Son is coming in one swoop down from the Barna hills.

CAUTH *opens door;* TIMMEEN *comes in;* HAG'S SON *comes down from room.*

CAUTH: (*To* HAG'S SON) The Hag's Son! You villain, is it in a slit in the window you came, or down a hole in the thatch?

HAG'S SON: Find out if you're fit,[5] and give me none of your vulgar speech. Or is it the way you mistake me for your sweet bolster man?[6] You green and withered female, I might give you a handsome pinch (*pinches her arm; she screams; he faces* TIMMEEN). Good little boy, Timmeen, good little boy. I'd put a finger in your eye, Timmeen Faley.

TIMMEEN: Your talk is bold, Jackeen, the brat from Barna, but your pride might get a fall and your tail be under you when the who shall's[7] finished for the dandy doll.

HAG'S SON: Is it himself will diddle[8] me half-dozing in his chair; or is it herself will diddle me and she quavering after that pinch; or is it you, you little dribbler, will diddle me with only the breath left in you after that spell of the black north wind? Oh, Lord! look at the cut[9] of him, with his little snuffle, his two dead blue eyes flat inside in his head, his little mouth half-open and the couple of ugly teeth showing themselves stuck in his lips; and it's you think yourself a match for me, you mangy puny thing (*loudly*) a match for me, my chest a plate, my hands as hard as steel, every joint as supple as whalebone, and (*wheeling and turning about*) I've the fingers and toes of a midwife, as my gay old mother says.

TIMMEEN: 'Tis laughing I am, and you not knowing I have twenty points in my favour, and the priest after baptizing the dandy doll.

HAG'S SON: (*Laughing shrilly*) A spit for his baptizing, for my old mother, the Hag, took the virtue out of it, and she, the minute he shook the holy water, giving me a puff of her breath in between the two eyes that blew me in a balloon right over the highest peak of the Barna hills. Likewise it's coming herself she is to help her darling son. Ha-ha! is it now you have the points in your favour? Ha-ha? it's now you're getting in dread.

TIMEEN: (*Brandishing fist in* HAG'S SON'*s face*) Up to your pus,[10] Jackeen, if I am, up to your pus! I'm as good as yourself, by damned, and I'm ready for the fray.

HAG'S SON: On for the battle, then, for Fontenoy[11] and glory! On for the battle, then, and this is the way to smadher[12] the grace of priest or parson!

TIMMEEN: And this is the way to break the melt[13] in Jackeen, the brat from Barna.

They rush at doll; they drag it off table; they wheel about trying to take it from each other; re-enter PRIEST *and* KEERBY.

FATHER JAMES: The battle is raging (*handing gun to* KEERBY) Here, hold that gun, till I make the sign of the cross, read from the book, and drive that Hag's Son up the chimley[14] in one mortal flame of

1. Recitation spoken with the eyes closed, while making a choice.
2. The marble that is struck (pinked) does not leave the chalked circle, as the child first thought it had. Thus he says, 'By J[esus], I'm fat [stupid].' The tick-tack does not refer to the old form of backgammon, but simply to the ticking of the clock.
3. offspring of a mountain-dwelling hag.
4. broom.
5. able.
6. bedmate; a bolster is a long pillow.
7. who shall [win] is.
8. fool, cheat.
9. appearance.
10. face.
11. The battle of Fontenoy (1745), during the War of the Austrian Succession, was decided in favour of the French against English, Hanoverian, Austrian and Dutch troops because of the charge of the Irish Brigade, which fought on the side of the French.
12. stain or besmirch, possibly from Irish *smearaim*.
13. the mould, the child carrying the impress of its mother.
14. chimney.

fire. (*Reads from book*) You won't go up the chimley, you won't? Let us see what will come of a clout of a fist. (*Makes at* HAG'S SON *and misses him*)

CAUTH: That's the style, your reverence, murder him, ruin him; but keep me from the power of the Hag and I'll spoil him with the broom, I will.

KEERBY: (*Standing near dresser*) And I'll make a shy at him with the stock of the gun when he comes around to where I am.

The fight continues, all going around in a ring; CAUTH *and the priest make efforts to hit the* HAG'S SON, *who dodges them; sound of a lively jig played on a fife outside.*

CAUTH: (*In terror*) The Hag, the Hag herself! The Hag, the Hag of Barna!

Enter HAG *playing a flute. She is a fantastically dressed old woman.*

THE HAG: (*Taking flute from mouth*) Ha-ha! is it flamming[15] my little boy they are? (*Hits* CAUTH *with flute*) Take that, old snotty nose! go wash your rotten rags and grease your creaking bones!

CAUTH: I'm kilt.[16]

THE HAG: (*Hitting priest*) Ha-ha, shiny green coat, I have slaughtered a flay[17] on the nape of your neck! (*Hits him again*) Take that on the small of your back and scratch yourself!

FATHER JAMES: (*Itching himself*) Botheration! In the name of the Father!

THE HAG: (*To her son*) Fight away, my gamey boy; fight away, my hearty, Your mother is up to your ear (*Singing*) and we'll rise a grand song and we'll rise a grand tune, going back to our home in Barna.

FATHER JAMES: (*Snatching broom from* CAUTH) Give me that broom; no haunted hag shall daunt me; fight, slash, and batter — the power of man shall conquer the power — the power of the witch!

They go round in a ring as before, fighting.

ROGER: (*Rising suddenly from seat near fire*) They are treenahayla[18] and striking wild. Priest, Cauth, and Keerby, it's walloping Timmeen ye are, and thinking you're striking the Hag and the Hag's Son. Divilment, divilment, you're blinked by divilment! Be careful in the name of God! will ye be careful in the name of God! (HAG'S SON *captures doll*) He has it! Lord, he has it! Sure he had to have it, and where's the good in talking, and all to no use, for it's foredoomed I was, it's foredoomed I was. (HAG'S SON *pulls out windpipe*[19] *and blows through it*) But isn't it fierce all the same, and wherefore should this wrong thing be? But to hell with everything, I don't care, and by damned I'll have a goose![20] (*Enter* GREY MAN *unperceived; he goes to other side of table opposite* ROGER) Or a duck, a fat duck — I must have a duck! (*Moving jaws as if in eating*) No, by Jabers,[21] it's a turkey I must have, a good plump turkey! Oh, Lord, the turkey and the gravy fine! (*Sees* GREY MAN) Ah, the Grey Man, the Grey Man!

GREY MAN, *with grim smile, points to bottle;*[22] ROGER *takes hold of it slowly; he puts it to his mouth, shaking like an aspen; he drinks. An explosion; semi-darkness on stage; noise as of a struggle; dim figures of* GREY MAN, ROGER, HAG, *and* HAG'S SON *seen going out,* ROGER *being dragged along; total darkness.* HAG *and* HAG'S SON *heard singing 'My Bonnie Irish Boy';*[23] *song dies away in distance; stage clears.*

FATHER JAMES: Is any one kilt?

KEERBY: 'Tis a wonder we aren't and all devils here.

FATHER JAMES: Give me that gun, you awkward man.

KEERBY: Faith, the gun is innocent, whatever that bottle did he had in his mouth, for, after the report, didn't the bottom of it open like it would on a hinge, and what did I see inside but a batch of the finest horses, black as jet, with red eyes on them, pracing and pawing, fit to be off. The next minute what happened but out they galloped to me in a bully[24] army, and captains, generals, soldiers, with their cannons, swords, and carabines,[25] all in full bloom for war. Faith, this is no house for an honest man.

Exit

CAUTH: (*Rising as if in pain, from prostrate condition*) Bad scran[26] to him! it's scratched and ruinated I am on account of him, and there isn't a screed[27] on me but is destroyed and tore. (*Looking*

15. tricking, deceiving.
16. killed.
17. flea.
18. in a state of confusion, from Irish *trí na chéile.*
19. i.e. the windpipe of the doll.
20. He has been stealing the priest's geese.
21. A corruption of 'Jesus'.
22. Given him by the Grey Man in the previous scene.
23. A song popular since the eighteenth century.
24. fine, splendid.
25. A fire-arm used by mounted soldiers.
26. bad luck to you.
27. shred.

about her vacantly) But the meila murdhre[28] is over, and there isn't a trace of himself on the floor. The doll gone too; and mustn't it have been the rotten doll itself, when your reverence couldn't save it by the power of your calling, and the grace drawn down from the holy heavens above?

FATHER JAMES: 'Tis mysterious surely, and fantastic strange. Well, there's no more to be done, and I might as well be following Keerby.

Re-enter KEERBY.

KEERBY: Your geese is safe, your reverence, for it's the wonderful thing entirely I now have seen. And the Bay of Doon that's ten miles distant looked as near to me as the cabbage haggart[29] outside, and the three grey men were standing on the rock holding up an almighty torch that lit up all the black land lying to the east; and following the light didn't I see Roger being carried away by the Hag and the Son of the Hag. Riding on two Spanish asses they were, holding him between them by a whisker each, and his whiskers were the length of six feet you'd think, and his nose was the length of six feet you'd think, and his eyes were the size of turnips bulging outside his head. Galloping like the wind they were, through the pass of the Barna mountains, sweeping him along with them, for ever and ever, to their woful den in the heart of the Barna hills.

CURTAIN

28. Irish *mile murdail*, literally 'a thousand murders', but used to indicate that a terrible crisis has occurred or, as in this case, passed.

29. haggard, enclosed plot.

SEÁN O'CASEY

(1880-1964)

THE SHADOW OF A GUNMAN (1923)

A TRAGEDY IN TWO ACTS

[The crowded tenement life, vivid and animated, is O'Casey's subject, holding on against political ideologies and their violent expression. Their exponents here are shams (some, like Seumas Shields, pardoned for the amusement they give) and thugs; or, like Minnie Powell, deluded romantics. Donal Davoren, who might represent some imaginative energy, is disabled for that role by his affected language, although it is not entirely certain that O'Casey intended it satirically.

The play was first produced on 12 April 1923 at the Abbey Theatre.]

CHARACTERS

DONAL DAVOREN
SEUMAS SHIELDS, *a pedlar*
TOMMY OWENS
ADOLPHUS GRIGSON
MRS GRIGSON
MINNIE POWELL
} *Residents in the tenement*
MR MULLIGAN, *the landlord*
MR MAGUIRE, *soldier of the IRA*
MRS HENDERSON
MR GALLOGHER
} *Residents of an adjoining tenement*
AN AUXILIARY

A room in a tenement in Hilljoy Square, Dublin.

Some hours elapse between the two acts. The period of the play is May 1920.

ACT I

A return room[1] *in a tenement house in Hilljoy Square.*[2] *At the back two large windows looking out into the yard; they occupy practically the whole of the back wall-space. Between the windows is a cupboard, on the top of which is a pile of books. The doors are open, and on these are hanging a number of collars and ties. Running parallel with the windows is a stretcher bed;*

1. An extra room in a house, usually at the top of a flight of stairs; little more than a large closet.
2. Mountjoy Square on Dublin's north side, once an elegant Georgian square, but by this time a run-down tenement area. O'Casey lived there for some months.

another runs at right angles along the wall at right. At the head of this bed is a door leading to the rest of the house. The wall on the left runs diagonally, so that the fireplace — which is in the centre — is plainly visible. On the mantelshelf to the right is a statue of the Virgin, to the left a statue of the Sacred Heart, and in the centre a crucifix. Around the fireplace are a few common cooking utensils. In the centre of the room is a table, on which are a typewriter, a candle and candlestick, a bunch of wild flowers in a vase, writing materials and a number of books. There are two chairs, one near the fireplace and one at the table. The aspect of the place is one of absolute untidiness, engendered on the one hand by the congenital slovenliness of SEUMAS SHIELDS, *and on the other by the temperament of* DONAL DAVOREN, *making it appear impossible to effect an improvement in such a place.*

DAVOREN *is sitting at the table typing. He is about thirty. There is in his face an expression that seems to indicate an eternal war between weakness and strength; there is in the lines of the brow and chin an indication of a desire for activity, while in his eyes there is visible an unquenchable tendency towards rest. His struggle through life has been a hard one, and his efforts have been handicapped by an inherited and self-developed devotion to 'the might of design, the mystery of colour, and the belief in the redemption of all things by beauty everlasting'.*[3] *His life would drive him mad were it not for the fact that he never knew any other. He bears upon his body the marks of the struggle for existence and the efforts towards self-expression.*

SEUMAS SHIELDS, *who is in the bed next the wall to the right, is a heavily built man of thirty-five; he is dark-haired and sallow-complexioned. In him is frequently manifested the superstition, the fear and the malignity of primitive man.*

DAVOREN: (*Lilting an air as he composes*)
Or when sweet Summer's ardent arms outspread,
Entwined with flowers,
Enfold us, like two lovers newly wed,
Thro' ravish'd hours —
Then sorrow, woe and pain lose all their powers,
For each is dead, and life is only ours.[4]

A woman's figure appears at the window and taps loudly on one of the panes; at the same moment there is loud knocking at the door.

VOICE OF WOMAN AT WINDOW: Are you awake, Mr Shields — Mr Shields, are you awake? Are you goin' to get up today at all, at all?

VOICE AT THE DOOR: Mr Shields, is there any use of callin' you at all? This is a nice nine o'clock: do you know what time it is, Mr Shields?

SEUMAS: (*Loudly*) Yus!

VOICE AT THE DOOR: Why don't you get up, then, an' not have the house turned into a bedlam[5] tryin' to waken you?

SEUMAS: (*Shouting*) All right, all right, all right! The way these oul' ones bawl at a body![6] Upon my soul! I'm beginnin' to believe that the Irish People are still in the stone age. If they could they'd throw a bomb at you.

DAVOREN: A land mine exploding under the bed is the only thing that would lift you out of it.

SEUMAS: (*Stretching himself*) Oh-h-h. I was fast in the arms of Morpheus — he was one of the infernal deities, son of Somnus,[7] wasn't he?

DAVOREN: I think so.

SEUMAS: The poppy was his emblem, wasn't it?

DAVOREN: Ah, I don't know.

SEUMAS: It's a bit cold this morning, I think, isn't it?

DAVOREN: It's quite plain I'm not going to get much quietness in this house.

SEUMAS: (*After a pause*) I wonder what time it is?

DAVOREN: The Angelus[8] went some time ago.

SEUMAS: (*Sitting up in bed suddenly*) The Angelus! It couldn't be that late, could it? I asked them to call me at nine so that I could get Mass before I went on my rounds. Why didn't you give us a rap?

DAVOREN: Give you a rap! Why, man, they've been thundering at the door and hammering at the window for the past two hours, till the house shook to its very foundations, but you took less notice of

3. Part of the credo of the dying painter, Louis Dubedat, in George Bernard Shaw's *The Doctor's Dilemma* (1906), Act IV.
4. A stanza from O'Casey's poem 'Sunshadows', published in *Windfalls* (1934).
5. madhouse.
6. The way these old people shout at a person.
7. Morpheus and Somnus are generally regarded as the gods of sleep, one Greek, the other Roman. Morpheus was in fact one of the thousand children of Hypnus (Sleep).
8. Catholic devotion, practised three times daily, 6am, noon and 6pm. As the bells ring, the prayer of the Annunciation is said — 'The Angel of the Lord declared unto Mary . . . .'

the infernal din that I would take of the strumming of a grasshopper.

SEUMAS: There's no fear of you thinking of any one else when you're at your poetry. The land of Saints and Scholars 'ill shortly be a land of bloody poets. (*Anxiously*) I suppose Maguire has come and gone?

DAVOREN: Maguire? No, he hasn't been here — why, did you expect him?

SEUMAS: (*In a burst of indignation*) He said he'd be here at nine. 'Before the last chime has struck,' says he, 'I'll be coming in on the door,' and it must be — what time is it now?

DAVOREN: Oh, it must be half-past twelve.

SEUMAS: Did anybody ever see the like of the Irish People? Is there any use tryin' to do anything in this country? Have everything packed and ready, have everything packed and ready, have ....

DAVOREN: And have you everything packed and ready?

SEUMAS: What's the use of having anything packed and ready when he didn't come. (*He rises and dresses himself*) No wonder this unfortunate country is at it is, for you can't depend upon the word of a single individual in it. I suppose he was too damn lazy to get up; he wanted the streets to be well aired first. — Oh, Kathleen ni Houlihan, your way's a thorny way.[9]

DAVOREN: Ah me! alas, pain, pain ever, for ever![10]

SEUMAS: That's from Shelley's *Prometheus Unbound*. I could never agree with Shelley, not that there's anything to be said against him as a poet — as a poet — but ....

DAVOREN: He flung a few stones through stained-glass windows.

SEUMAS: He wasn't the first nor he won't be the last to do that, but the stained-glass windows — more than ever of them — are here still, and Shelley is doing a jazz dance down below. (*He gives a snarling laugh of pleasure*)

DAVOREN: (*Shocked*) And you actually rejoice and are exceedingly glad that, as you believe, Shelley, the sensitive, high-minded, noble-hearted Shelley, is suffering the tortures of the damned.

SEUMAS: I rejoice in the vindication of the Church and Truth.

DAVOREN: Bah. You know as little about truth as anybody else, and you care as little about the Church as the least of those that profess her faith; your religion is simply the state of being afraid that God will torture your soul in the next world as you are afraid the Black and Tans[11] will torture your body in this.

SEUMAS: Go on, me boy; I'll have a right laugh at you when both of us are dead.

DAVOREN: You're welcome to laugh as much as you like at me when both of us are dead.

SEUMAS: (*As he is about to put on his collar and tie*) I don't think I need to wash meself this morning; do I look all right?

DAVOREN: Oh, you're all right; it's too late now to start washing yourself. Didn't you wash yourself yesterday morning?

SEUMAS: I gave meself a great rub yesterday. (*He proceeds to pack various articles into an attaché case — spoons, forks, laces, thread, etc*) I think I'll bring out a few of the braces too; damn it, they're worth sixpence each; there's great stuff[12] in them — did you see them?

DAVOREN: Yes, you showed them to me before.

SEUMAS: They're great value; I only hope I'll be able to get enough o' them. I'm wearing a pair of them meself — they'd do Cuchullian,[13] they're so strong. (*Counting the spoons*) There's a dozen in each of these parcels — three, six, nine — damn it, there's only eleven in this one. I better try another Three, six, nine — my God, there's only eleven in this one too, and one of them bent! Now I suppose I'll have to go through the whole bloody lot of them, for I'd never be easy in me mind thinkin' there'd be more than a dozen in some o' them. And still we're looking for freedom — ye gods, it's a glorious country! (*He lets one fall, which he stoops to pick up*) Oh, my God, there's the braces after breakin'.

DAVOREN: That doesn't look as if they were strong enough for Cuchullian.

SEUMAS: I put a heavy strain on them too sudden. There's that fellow Maguire never turned

9. From the poem 'The Passing of the Gael' by Ethna Carberry (1866-1902); it appeared in the volume *The Four Winds of Eirinn* (1902).
10. Shelley, *Prometheus Unbound* (1820); the lines are used as a refrain throughout Act I.
11. Notorious corps of the British army, who fought in the War of Independence 1919-21; so called because of the colours of their uniform.
12. material.
13. The legendary Irish warrior.

up, either; he's almost too lazy to wash himself. (*As he is struggling with the braces the door is hastily shoved in and* MAGUIRE *rushes in with a handbag*) This is a nice nine o'clock. What's the use of you coming at this hour o' the day? Do you think we're going to work be moonlight? If you weren't goin' to come at nine couldn't you say you weren't ....

MAGUIRE: Keep your hair on;[14] I just blew in to tell you that I couldn't go today at all. I have to go to Knocksedan.[15]

SEUMAS: Knocksedan! An' what, in the name o' God, is bringin' you to Knocksedan?

MAGUIRE: Business, business. I'm going out to catch butterflies.

SEUMAS: If you want to make a cod[16] of anybody, make a cod of somebody else, an' don't be tryin' to make a cod o' me. Here I've had everything packed an' ready for hours; you were to be here at nine, an' you wait till just one o'clock to come rushin' in like a mad bull to say you've got to go to Knocksedan! Can't you leave Knocksedan till tomorrow?

MAGUIRE: Can't be did, can't be did, Seumas; if I waited till tomorrow all the butterflies might be dead. I'll leave this bag here till this evening. (*He puts the bag in a corner of the room*) Goodbye ... ee. (*He is gone before* SEUMAS *is aware of it*)

SEUMAS: (*With a gesture of despair*) Oh, this is a hopeless country! There's a fellow that thinks that the four cardinal virtues[17] are not to be found outside an Irish Republic. I don't want to boast about myself — I don't want to boast about myself, and I suppose I could call meself as good a Gael as some of those that are knocking about now — but I remember the time when I taught Irish six nights a week, when in the Irish Republican Brotherhood[18] I paid me rifle levy[19] like a man, an' when the Church refused to have anything to do with James Stephens,[20] I tarred a prayer for the repose of his soul on the steps of the Pro-Cathedral.[21] Now, after all me work for Dark Rosaleen,[22] the only answer you can get from a roarin' Republican to a simple question is 'Goodbye ... ee.' What, in the name o' God, can be bringin' him to Knocksedan?

DAVOREN: Hadn't you better run out and ask him?

SEUMAS: That's right, that's right — make a joke about it! That's the Irish People all over — they treat a joke as a serious thing and a serious thing as a joke. Upon me soul, I'm beginning to believe that the Irish People aren't, never were, an' never will be fit for self-government. They made Balor of the Evil Eye[23] King of Ireland, an' so signs on it[24] there's neither conscience nor honesty from one end of the country to the other. Well, I hope he'll have a happy day in Knocksedan. (*A knock at the door*) Who's that? (*Another knock. Irritably*) Who's that; who's there?

DAVOREN: (*More irritably*) Halt and give the countersign — damn it, man, can't you go and see? SEUMAS *goes over and opens the door. A man of about sixty is revealed, dressed in a faded blue serge suit; a half tall hat*[25] *is on his head. It is evident that he has no love for* SEUMAS, *who denies him the deference he believes is due from a tenant to a landlord. He carries some papers in his hand.*

THE LANDLORD: (*Ironically*) Good day, Mr Shields; it's meself that hopes you're feelin' well — you're lookin' well, anyhow — though you can't always go be looks nowadays.

SEUMAS: It doesn't matter whether I'm lookin' well or feelin' well; I'm all right, thanks be to God.

THE LANDLORD: I've very glad to hear it.

SEUMAS: It doesn't matter whether you're glad to hear it or not, Mr Mulligan.

THE LANDLORD: You're not inclined to be very civil, Mr Shields.

SEUMAS: Look here, Mr Mulligan, if you come here to raise an argument, I've something to do — let me tell you that.

THE LANDLORD: I don't come here to raise no argument; a person ud have small gains argufyin' with you — let me tell you that.

SEUMAS: I've no time to be standin' here

14. Stay calm.
15. A village in north County Dublin.
16. a fool.
17. Faith, Love, Hope and Charity.
18. The IRB, a secret revolutionary association, founded in 1858, which organized the 1916 Rising.
19. A contribution towards the cost of the rifle.
20. Stephens (1825-1901) was the founder of the Irish Revolutionary, later Republican, Brotherhood and a leading member of the Fenians, a nationalist organization that was denounced by the catholic church.
21. He painted a prayer for Stephens on the steps of the main catholic church in Dublin, even though Fenianism had been put under papal ban as long ago as 1870.
22. Traditional name for Ireland.
23. Balor or Balar of the Evil (Baleful) Eye was defeated by Lugh at the battle of Magh Tuiredh. This mythical figure was never king of Ireland, although he was an important leader of the Fomorians, who were finally defeated in this struggle.
24. i.e. it is evident that.
25. A mark of respectability and prosperity.

gostherin'[26] with you — let me shut the door, Mr Mulligan.

THE LANDLORD: You'll not shut no door till you've heard what I've got to say.

SEUMAS: Well, say it then, an' go about your business.

THE LANDLORD: You're very high an' mighty, but take care you're not goin' to get a drop. What a baby you are not to know what brings me here! Maybe you thought I was goin' to ask you to come to tea.

DAVOREN: Ah me! alas, pain, pain ever, for ever!

SEUMAS: Are you goin' to let me shut the door, Mr Mulligan?

THE LANDLORD: I'm here for me rent; you don't like the idea of bein' asked to pay your just an' lawful debts.

SEUMAS: You'll get your rent when you learn to keep your rent-book in a proper way.

THE LANDLORD: I'm not goin' to take any lessons from you, anyhow.

SEUMAS: I want to have no more talk with you, Mr Mulligan.

THE LANDLORD: Talk or no talk, you owe me eleven weeks' rent, an' its marked down again' you in black an' white.

SEUMAS: I don't care a damn if it was marked down in green, white, an' yellow.[27]

THE LANDLORD: You're a terribly independent fellow, an' it ud be fitter for you to be less funny an' stop tryin' to be billickin'[28] honest an' respectable people.

SEUMAS: Just you be careful what you're sayin', Mr Mulligan. There's law in the land still.

THE LANDLORD: Be me sowl[29] there is, an' you're goin' to get a little of it now. (*He offers the papers to* SEUMAS) Them's for you.

SEUMAS: (*Hesitating to take them*) I want to have nothing to do with you, Mr Mulligan.

THE LANDLORD: (*Throwing the papers in the centre of the room*) What am I better?[30] It was the sorry day I ever let you come into this house. Maybe them notices to quit will stop your writin' letters to the papers about me an' me house.

DAVOREN: For goodness' sake, bring the man in, and don't be discussing the situation like a pair of primitive troglodytes.

SEUMAS: (*Taking no notice*) Writing letters to the papers is my business, an' I'll write as often as I like, when I like, an' how I like.

THE LANDLORD: You'll not write about this house at all events. You can blow about the state of the yard, but you took care to say nothin' about payin' rent: oh no, that's not in your line. But since you're not satisifed with the house, you can pack up an' go to another.

SEUMAS: I'll go, Mr Mulligan, when I think fit, an' no sooner.

THE LANDLORD: Not content with keeping the rent, you're startin' to bring in lodgers — (*To* DAVOREN) not that I'm sayin' anythin' again' you, sir. Bringin' in lodgers without as much as be your leave — what's the world comin' to at all that a man's house isn't his own? But I'll soon put a stop to your gallop, for on the twenty-eight of the next month out you go, an' there'll be few sorry to see your back.

SEUMAS: I'll go when I like.

THE LANDLORD: I'll let you see whether you own the house or no.

SEUMAS: I'll go when I like!

THE LANDLORD: We'll see about that.

SEUMAS: We'll see.

THE LANDLORD: Ay, we'll see. (THE LANDLORD *goes out and* SEUMAS *shuts the door*) (*Outside*) Mind you, I'm in earnest; you'll not stop in this house a minute longer than the twenty-eight.

SEUMAS: (*With a roar*) Ah, go to hell!

DAVOREN: (*Pacing the room as far as the space will permit*) What in the name of God persuaded me to come to such a house as this?

SEUMAS: It's nothing when you're used to it; you're too thin-skinned altogether. The oul' sod's got the wind up about you, that's all.

DAVOREN: Got the wind up about me!

SEUMAS: He thinks you're on the run. He's afraid of a raid, and that his lovely property'll be destroyed.

DAVOREN: But why, in the name of all that's sensible, should he think that I'm on the run?

SEUMAS: Sure they all think you're on the run. Mrs Henderson thinks it, Tommy Owens thinks it, Mrs an' Mr Grigson thinks it, an' Minnie Powell thinks it too. (*Picking up his attaché case*) I'd better be off if I'm goin' to do anything today.

26. Wasting time in idle speech.
27. Colours of the Irish national flag, variously described as green, white and yellow or, more accurately, orange.
28. bilking, or avoiding payment.
29. soul.
30. In what way am I better off (for invoking the law)?

DAVOREN: What are we going to do with these notices to quit?

SEUMAS: Oh, shove them up on the mantelpiece behind one of the statues.

DAVOREN: Oh, I mean what action shall we take?

SEUMAS: I haven't time to stop now. We'll talk about them when I come back.... I'll get me own back on that oul' Mulligan yet. I wish to God they would come an' smash his rookery[31] to pieces, for it's all he thinks of, and, mind you, oul' Mulligan would call himself a descendant of the true Gaels of Banba[32] — (*as he goes out*)

Oh, proud were the chieftains of famed Inisfail.
Is truagh gan oidher 'na Vfarradh.
The stars of our sky an' the salt of our soil —[33]

Oh, Kathleen ni Houlihan, your way's a thorny way! (*He goes out*)

DAVOREN: (*Returning to the table and sitting down at the typewriter*) Oh, Donal Og O'Davoren,[34] your way's a thorny way. Your last state is worse than your first. Ah me, alas! Pain, pain ever, for ever. Like thee, Prometheus, no change, no pause, no hope. Ah, life, life, life! (*There is a gentle knock at the door*) Another Fury[35] come to plague me now! (*Another knock, a little louder*) You can knock till you're tired.

The door opens and MINNIE POWELL *enters with an easy confidence one would not expect her to possess from her gentle way of knocking. She is a girl of twenty-three, but the fact of being forced to earn her living, and to take care of herself, on account of her parents' early death, has given her a force and an assurance beyond her years. She has lost the sense of fear (she does not know this), and, consequently, she is at ease in all places and before all persons, even those of a superior education, so long as she meets them in the atmosphere that surrounds the members of her own class. Her hair is brown, neither light nor dark, but partaking of both tints according to the light or shade she may happen to be in. Her well-shaped figure — a rare thing in a city girl — is charmingly dressed in a brown tailor-made costume, her stockings and shoes are a darker brown tint than the costume, and all are crowned by a silk tam-o' shanter*[36] *of a rich blue tint.*

MINNIE: Are you in, Mr Shields?

DAVOREN: (*Rapidly*) No, he's not, Minnie; he's just gone out — if you run out quickly you're sure to catch him.

MINNIE: Oh, it's all right, Mr Davoren, you'll do just as well; I just come in for a drop o' milk for a cup o' tea; I shouldn't be troublin' you this way, but I'm sure you don't mind.

DAVOREN: (*Dubiously*) No trouble in the world; delighted, I'm sure. (*Giving her the milk*) There, will you have enough?

MINNIE: Plenty, lashins,[37] thanks. Do you be all alone all the day, Mr Davoren?

DAVOREN: No, indeed; I wish to God I was.

MINNIE: It's not good for you then. I don't know how you like to be by yourself — I couldn't stick it long.

DAVOREN: (*Wearily*) No?

MINNIE: No, indeed; (*with rapture*) there's nothin' I'm more fond of than a Hooley.[38] I was at one last Sunday — I danced rings round me! Tommy Owens was there — you know Tommy Owens, don't you?

DAVOREN: I can't say I do.

MINNIE: D'ye not? The little fellow that lives with his mother in the two-pair back[39] — (*ecstatically*) he's a gorgeous melodeon[40] player!

DAVOREN: A gifted son of Orpheus, eh?[41]

MINNIE: (*Who never heard of Orpheus*) You've said it, Mr Davoren: the son of poor oul' Battie Owens, a weeshy, dawny,[42] bit of a man that was never sober an' was always talkin' politics. Poor man, it killed him in the long run.

DAVOREN: A man should always be drunk, Minnie, when he talks politics — it's the only way in which to make them important.

MINNIE: Tommy takes after the oul' fellow, too; he's talk from morning till night when he has a few

31. A cluster of tenement houses.
32. Another traditional name for Ireland, derived from that of a female Druid.
33. The opening lines of Thomas Davis's poem, 'Lament for the Milesians', published in *The Spirit of the Nation* (1843). The line in Irish is taken from an earlier poem. It means 'And it is a pity there is no heir of their company' and constitutes the refrain of the song. Inisfail ('Island of destiny') is a name for Ireland generally associated with the Milesians.
34. Davoren here gives himself a resoundingly Gaelic name (Og means 'young') as he identifies himself more fully with the lamentations of Kathleen ni Houlihan.
35. One of the winged goddesses sent to punish crime.
36. A brimless woollen cap, usually worn pulled down at one side. Named after the hero of a poem by Robert Burns.
37. loads, a surfeit.
38. An evening of dancing.
39. Rooms at the back of a tenement.
40. A small accordion.
41. The mythical type of singer, musician and poet.
42. small and delicate.

jars in him. (*Suddenly; for like all of her class,* MINNIE *is not able to converse very long on the one subject, and her thoughts spring from one thing to another*) Poetry is a grand thing, Mr Davoren, I'd love to be able to write a poem — a lovely poem on Ireland an' the men o' '98.[43]

DAVOREN: Oh, we've had enough of poems, Minnie, about '98, and of Ireland, too.

MINNIE: Oh, there's a thing for a Republican to say! But I know what you mean: it's time to give up the writing an' take to the gun. (*Her roving eye catches sight of the flowers in the vase*) What's Mr Shields doin' with the oul' weeds?

DAVOREN: Those aren't Shields', they're mine. Wild flowers is a kindlier name for them, Minnie, than weeds. These are wild violets, this is an *Arum maculatum*, or wake robin, and these are celandines, a very beautiful flower related to the buttercups. (*He quotes*)

One day, when Morn's half-open'd eyes
Were bright with Spring sunshine —
My hand was clasp'd in yours, dear love,
And yours was clasp'd in mine —
We bow'd as worshippers before
The Golden Celandine.[44]

MINNIE: Oh, aren't they lovely, an' isn't the poem lovely, too! I wonder, now, who she was.

DAVOREN: (*Puzzled*) She, who?

MINNIE: Why, the . . . (*Roguishly*) Oh, be the way you don't know.

DAVOREN: Know? I'm sure I don't know.

MINNIE: It doesn't matter, anyhow — that's your own business; I suppose I don't know her.

DAVOREN: Know her — know whom?

MINNIE: (*Shyly*) Her whose hand was clasped in yours, an' yours was clasped in hers.

DAVOREN: Oh, that — that was simply a poem I quoted about the celandine, that might apply to any girl — to you, for instance.

MINNIE: (*Greatly relieved, coming over and sitting beside* DAVOREN) But you have a sweetheart, all the same, Mr Davoren, haven't you?

DAVOREN: I? No, not one, Minnie.

MINNIE: Oh, now, you can tell that to some one else; aren't you a poet an' aren't all the girls fond o' poets?

DAVOREN: That may be, but all the poets aren't fond of girls.

MINNIE: They are in the story-books, ay, and fond of more than one, too. (*With a questioning look*) Are you fond of them, Mr Davoren?

DAVOREN: Of course I like girls, Minnie, especially girls who can add to their charms by the way in which they dress, like you, for instance.

MINNIE: Oh, now, you're on for coddin'[45] me, Mr Davoren.

DAVOREN: No, really, Minnie, I'm not; you are a very charming little girl indeed.

MINNIE: Then if I'm a charmin' little girl, you ought to be able to write a poem about me.

DAVOREN: (*Who has become susceptible to the attractiveness of* MINNIE, *catching her hand*) And so I will, so I will, Minnie; I have written them about girls not half so pretty as yourself.

MINNIE: Ah, I knew you had one, I knew you had one now.

DAVOREN: Nonsense. Every girl a poet writes about isn't his sweetheart; Annie Laurie wasn't the sweetheart of Bobbie Burns.[46]

MINNIE: You needn't tell me she wasn't; 'An' for bonnie Annie Laurie I'd lay me down an' die.' No man ud lay down an' die for any but a sweetheart, not even for a wife.

DAVOREN: No man, Minnie, willingly dies for anything.

MINNIE: Except for his country, like Robert Emmet.[47]

DAVOREN: Even he would have lived on if he could; he died not to deliver Ireland. The British Government killed him to save the British nation.

MINNIE: You're only jokin' now; you'd die for your country.

DAVOREN: I don't know so much about that.

MINNIE: You would, you would, you would — I know what you are.

DAVOREN: What am I?

MINNIE: (*In a whisper*) A gunman on the run!

DAVOREN: (*Too pleased to deny it*) Maybe I am, and maybe I'm not.

MINNIE: Oh, I know, I know, I know. Do you never be afraid?

43. The United Irishmen, who planned the 1798 Rebellion.
44. A stanza from an early poem by O'Casey, 'A Walk With Eros', published in *Windfalls* (1934).
45. kidding, teasing.
46. Annie Laurie (1682-1724) is the subject of the famous song written by her rejected lover William Douglas, not by Robert Burns.
47. The Irish revolutionary (1778-1803) who was executed after an abortive rising in Dublin in 1803.

DAVOREN: Afraid! Afraid of what?

MINNIE: Why, the ambushes of course; *I'm* all of a tremble when I hear a shot go off, an' what must it be in the middle of the firin'?

DAVOREN: (*Delighted at* MINNIE'S *obvious admiration; leaning back in his chair, and lighting a cigarette with placid affectation*) I'll admit one does be a little nervous at first, but a fellow gets used to it after a bit, till, at last, a gunman throws a bomb as carelessly as a schoolboy throws a snowball.

MINNIE: (*Fervently*) I wish it was all over, all the same. (*Suddenly, with a tremor in her voice*) You'll take care of yourself, won't you, won't you, Donal — I mean, Mr Davoren?

DAVOREN: (*Earnestly*) Call me Donal, Minnie; we're friends, great friends now — (*putting his arm around her*) go on, Minnie, call me Donal, let me hear you say Donal.

MINNIE: The place badly needs a tidyin' up ... Donal — there now, are you satisfied? (*Rapidly, half afraid of* DAVOREN'S *excited emotion*) But it really does, it's in an awful state. Tomorrow's a half-day, an' I'll run in an' straighten it up a bit.

DAVOREN: (*Frightened at the suggestion*) No, no, Minnie, you're too pretty for that sort of work; besides, the people of the house would be sure to start talking about you.

MINNIE: An' do you think Minnie Powell cares whether they'll talk or no? She's had to push her way through life up to this without help from any one, an' she's not goin' to ask their leave, now, to do what she wants to do.

DAVOREN: (*Forgetting his timidity in the honest joy of appreciating the independent courage of* MINNIE) My soul within art thou,[48] Minnie! A pioneer in action as I am a pioneer in thought. The two powers that shall 'grasp this sorry scheme of things entire, and mould life nearer to the heart's desire'.[49] Lovely little Minnie, and brave as well; brave little Minnie, and lovely as well!

His disengaged hand lifts up her bent head, and he looks earnestly at her; he is stooping to kiss her, when TOMMY OWENS *appears at the door, which* MINNIE *has left partially open.* TOMMY *is about twenty-five years of age. He is small and thin; his words are uttered in a nasal drawl; his voice is husky, due to frequent drinks and perpetual cigarette-smoking. He tries to get rid of the huskiness by an occasional cough.* TOMMY *is a hero-worshipper, and, like many others, he is anxious to be on familiar terms with those who he thinks are braver than he is himself, and whose approbation he tries to win by an assumption equal to their own. He talks in a staccato manner. He has a few drinks taken — it is too early to be drunk — that make him talkative. He is dressed in a suit of dungarees, and gives a gentle cough to draw attention to his presence.*

TOMMY: I seen nothin' — honest — thought you was learnin' to typewrite — Mr Davoren teachin' you. I seen nothin' else — s'help me God!

MINNIE: We'd be hard put to it if we minded[50] what you seen, Tommy Owens.

TOMMY: Right, Minnie, Tommy Owens has a heart — Evenin', Mr Davoren — don't mind me comin' in — I'm Tommy Owens — live up in the two-pair back, workin' in Ross an' Walpole's — Mr Shields knows me well; you needn't be afraid o' me, Mr Davoren.

DAVOREN: Why should I be afraid of you, Mr Owens, or of anybody else?

TOMMY: Why should you, indeed? We're all friends here — Mr Shields knows me well — all you've got to say is, 'Do you know Tommy Owens?' an' he'll tell you the sort of a man Tommy Owens is. There's no flies on Tommy — got me?

MINNIE: For goodness' sake, Tommy, leave Mr Davoren alone — he's got enough burgeons[51] on him already.

TOMMY: Not a word, Minnie, not a word — Mr Davoren understands me well, as man to man. It's 'Up the Republic' all the time — eh, Mr Davoren?

DAVOREN: I know nothing about the Republic; I have no connection with the politics of the day, and I don't want to have any connection.

TOMMY: You needn't say no more — a nod's as good as a wink to a blind horse — you've no meddlin' or makin' with it, good, bad, or indifferent, pro nor con; I know it an' Minnie knows it — give me your hand. (*He catches* DAVOREN'S *hand*) Two firm hands clasped together will all the power outbrave of the heartless English

48. cf. Shelley, *Epipsychidion*, line 454; '... a soul within the soul ....'
49. Edward FitzGerald (1809-83), *The Rubaiyat of Omar Khayyam* (1859), Stanza 99:

'Ah Love! could you and I with Him conspire
To grasp this Sorry Scheme of Things entire,
Would not we shatter it to bits — and then
Remould it nearer to the Heart's Desire!'

50. cared about.
51. burdens.

tyrant, the Saxon coward an' knave.[52] That's Tommy Owens' hand, Mr Davoren, the hand of a man, a man — Mr Shields knows me well. (*He breaks into song*)

High upon the gallows tree stood the
    noble-hearted three,
By the vengeful tyrant stricken in their bloom;
But they met him face to face with the spirit of
    their race,
And they went with souls undaunted to their
    doom!

MINNIE: (*In an effort to quell his fervour*) Tommy Owens, for goodness' sake ....

TOMMY: (*Overwhelming her with a shout*)

God save Ireland ses the hayros, God save
    Ireland ses we all,
Whether on the scaffold high or the
    battle-field we die.
Oh, what matter when for Ayryinn dear we
    fall![53]

(*Tearfully*) Mr Davoren, I'd die for Ireland!

DAVOREN: I know you would. I know you would, Tommy.

TOMMY: I never got a chance — they never gave me a chance — but all the same I'd be there if I was called on — Mr Shields knows that — ask Mr Shields, Mr Davoren.

DAVOREN: There's no necessity, Tommy; I know you're the right stuff if you got the chance, but remember that he also serves who only stands and waits.[54]

TOMMY: (*Fiercely*) I'm bloody well tired o' waitin' — we're all tired o' waitin'. Why isn't every man in Ireland out with the IRA? Up with the barricades, up with the barricades; it's now or never, now an' for ever, as Sarsfield said at the battle o' Vinegar Hill.[55] Up with the barricades — that's Tommy Owens — an' a penny buys a whistle. Let them as thinks different say different — what do you say, Mr Davoren?

DAVOREN: I say, Tommy, you ought to go up and get your dinner, for if you wait much longer it won't be worth eating.

TOMMY: Oh, damn the dinner; who'd think o' dinner an' Ireland fightin' to be free — not Tommy Owens, anyhow. It's only the Englishman who's always thinkin' of his belly.

MINNIE: Tommy Owens!

TOMMY: Excuse me, Miss Powell, in the ardure ov me anger I disremembered there was a lady present.

Voices are heard outside, and presently MRS HENDERSON *comes into the room, followed by* MR GALLOGHER, *who, however, lingers at the door, too timid to come any further.* MRS HENDERSON *is a massive woman in every way; massive head, arms, and body; massive voice, and a massive amount of self-confidence. She is a mountain of good nature, and during the interview she behaves towards* DAVOREN *with deferential self-assurance. She dominates the room, and seems to occupy the whole of it. She is dressed poorly but tidily, wearing a white apron and a large shawl.* MR GALLOGHER, *on the other hand, is a spare little man with a spare little grey beard and a thin, nervous voice. He is dressed as well as a faded suit of blue will allow him to be. He is obviously ill at ease during his interview with* DAVOREN. *He carries a hard hat, much the worse for wear, under his left arm, and a letter in his right hand.*

MRS HENDERSON: (*Entering the room*) Come along in, Mr Gallicker, Mr Davoren won't mind; it's him as can put you in the way o' havin' your wrongs righted; come on in, man, an' don't be so shy — Mr Davoren is wan ov ourselves that stands for governmint ov the people with the people by the people. You'll find you'll be as welcome as the flowers in May. Good evenin',[56] Mr Davoren, an' God an' His holy angels be between you an' all harm.

TOMMY: (*Effusively*) Come on, Mr Gallicker, an' don't be a stranger — we're all friends here — anything special to be done or particular advice asked, here's your man here.

DAVOREN: (*Subconsciously pleased, but a little timid of the belief that he is connected with the gunmen*) I'm very busy just now, Mrs Henderson, and really ....

MRS HENDERSON: (*Mistaking the reason of his embarrassment*) Don't be put out, Mr Davoren, we

52. Lines from an anonymous ballad, first published in 1850.
53. Patriotic song by T. D. Sullivan (1827-1914), celebrating the heroism of the Manchester Martyrs, three Irishmen hanged in England in 1867 for their part in helping Fenian prisoners to escape from a police van. Before sentence, the three men declared 'God Save Ireland'. The song appeared under this title in *The Nation* in December 1867.
54. John Milton, 'On His Blindness': 'They also serve who only stand and wait.'
55. Patrick Sarsfield, the Jacobite general, died in 1693. Vinegar Hill, in Wexford, was the scene of the final battle of the 1798 Rebellion. Tommy's enthusiasm is in proportion to his ignorance.
56. In many parts of Ireland, the evening means the afternoon.

won't keep you more nor[57] a few minutes. It's not in me or in Mr Gallicker to spoil sport. Him an' me was young once, an' knows what it is to be strolling at night in the pale moonlight, with arms round one another. An' I wouldn't take much an' say there's game in Mr Gallicker still, for I seen, sometimes, a dangerous cock[58] in his eye. But we won't keep you an' Minnie long asunder; he's the letter an' all written. You must know, Mr Davoren — excuse me for not introducin' him sooner — this is Mr Gallicker, that lives in the front drawin'-room ov number fifty-five, as decent an' honest an' quiet a man as you'd meet in a day's walk. An' no signs on it, it's them as 'ill be imposed upon — read the letter, Mr Gallicker.

TOMMY: Read away, Mr Gallicker, it will be attended to, never fear; we know our own know,[59] eh, Mr Davoren?

MINNIE: Hurry up, Mr Gallicker, an' don't be keeping Mr Davoren.

MRS HENDERSON: Give him time, Minnie Powell. Give him time. You must know in all fairity,[60] Mr Davoren, that the family livin' in the next room to Mr Gallicker — the back drawin'-room, to be particular — am I right or am I wrong, Mr Gallicker?

MR GALLOGHER: You're right, Mrs Henderson, perfectly right, indeed — that's the very identical room.

MRS HENDERSON: Well, Mr Davoren, the people in the back drawin'-room, or, to be more particular, the residents — that's the word that's writ in the letter — am I right or am I wrong, Mr Gallicker?

MR GALLOGHER: You're right, Mrs Henderson, perfectly accurate — that's the very identical word.

MRS HENDERSON: Well, Mr Davoren, the residents in the back drawin'-room, as I aforesaid, is nothin' but a gang o' tramps that oughtn't to be allowed to associate with honest, decent, quiet, respectable people. Mr Gallicker has tried to reason with them, and make them behave themselves — which in my opinion they never will — however, that's only an opinion, an' not legal — ever since they have made Mr Gallicker's life a HELL! Mr Gallicker, am I right or am I wrong?

MR GALLOGHER: I'm sorry to say you're right, Mrs Henderson, perfectly right — not a word of exaggeration.

MRS HENDERSON: Well, now, Mr Gallicker, seein' as I have given Mr Davoren a fair account ov how you've situated, an' ov these tramps' cleverality, I'll ask you to read the letter, which I'll say, not because you're there, or that you're a friend o' mine, is as good a letter as was decomposed by a scholar. Now, Mr Gallicker, an' don't forget the top sayin'.[61]

MR GALLOGHER *prepares to read;* MINNIE *leans forward to listen;* TOMMY *takes out a well-worn notebook and a pencil stump, and assumes a very important attitude.*

TOMMY: One second. Mr Gallicker, is this the twenty-first or twenty-second?

MR GALLOGHER: The twenty-first, sir.

TOMMY: Thanks; proceed, Mr Gallicker.

MR GALLOGHER: (*With a few preliminary tremors, reads the letter. Reading*)

TO ALL TO WHOM THESE PRESENTS COME, GREETING

Gentlemen of the Irish Republican Army . . . .

MRS HENDERSON: There's a beginnin' for you, Mr Davoren.

MINNIE: That's some swank.[62]

TOMMY: There's a lot in that sayin', mind you; it's a hard wallop at the British Empire.

MRS HENDERSON: (*Proudly*) Go on, Mr Gallicker.

MR GALLOGHER: (*Reading*)

> I wish to call your attention to the persecution me and my family has to put up with in respect of and appertaining to the residents of the back drawing-room of the house known as fifty-five, Saint Teresa Street, situate in the Parish of St Thomas, in the Borough and City of Dublin. This persecution started eighteen months ago — or to be precise — on the tenth day of the sixth month, in the year nineteen hundred and twenty.

MRS HENDERSON: That's the word I was trying to think ov — precise — it cuts the ground from under their feet — so to speak.

MR GALLOGHER: (*Reading*)

> We, the complainants, resident on the ground floor, deeming it disrespectable . . . .

57. than.
58. look, as in 'cock a look'.
59. we know what we know.
60. honesty.
61. The form of address to the recipient.
62. high style.

MRS HENDERSON: (*With an emphatic nod*) Which it was.

MR GALLOGHER: (*Reading*)

Deeming it disrespectable to have an open hall door, and to have the hall turned into a playground, made a solemn protest, and, in consequence, we the complainants aforesaid has had no peace ever since. Owing to the persecution, as aforesaid specified, we had to take out a summons again them some time ago as there was no Republican Courts[63] then; but we did not proceed again them as me and my wife — to wit, James and Winifred Gallogher — has a strong objection to foreign Courts[64] as such. We had peace for some time after that, but now things have gone from bad to worse. The name calling and the language is something abominable ....

MRS HENDERSON: (*Holding out her hand as a constable would extend his to stop a car that another may pass*) Excuse me, Mr Gallicker, but I think the word 'shockin'' should be put in there after abominable; for the language used be these tramps has two ways o' bein' looked at — for it's abominable to the childer[65] an' shockin' to your wife — am I right or am I wrong, Mr Davoren?

TOMMY: (*Judicially*) Shockin' is a right good word, with a great deal o' meanin', an' ....

MRS HENDERSON: (*With a deprecating gesture that extinguishes* TOMMY) Tommy, let Mr Davoren speak; whatever Mr Davoren ses, Julia Henderson'll abide be.

DAVOREN: (*Afraid to say anything else*) I think the word might certainly be introduced with advantage.

MRS HENDERSON: Go over there, Mr Gallicker, an' put in the word shockin', as aforesaid.

GALLOGHER *goes over to the table, and with a great deal of difficulty enters the word.*

TOMMY: (*To* MR GALLOGHER *as he writes*) Ey, there's two k's in shockin'!

MR GALLOGHER: (*Reading*)

The language is something abominable and shocking. My wife has often to lock the door of the room to keep them from assaulting her. If you would be so kind as to send some of your army or police down to see for themselves we would give them full particulars. I have to be always from home all day, as I work with Mr Hennessy, the harness maker of the Coombe,[66] who will furnish all particulars as to my unvarnished respectability, also my neighbours. The name of the resident-tenant who is giving all this trouble and who, pursuant to the facts of the case aforesaid mentioned, will be the defendant, is Dwyer. The husband of the aforesaid Mrs Dwyer, or the aforesaid defendant, as the case may be, is a seaman, who is coming home shortly, and we beg The Irish Republican Army to note that the said Mrs Dwyer says he will settle us when he comes home. While leaving it entirely in the the hands of the gentlemen of The Republican Army, the defendant, that is to say, James Gallogher of fifty-five St Teresa Street, ventures to say that he thinks he has made out a Primmy Fashy[67] Case against Mrs Dwyer and all her heirs, male and female as aforesaid mentioned in the above written schedule.

NB. If you send up any of your men, please tell them to bring their guns. I beg to remain the humble servant and devoted admirer of the Gentlemen of the Irish Republican Army.

Witness my hand this tenth day of the fifth month of the year nineteen hundred and twenty.

JAMES GALLOGHER

MR GALLOGHER: (*With a modest cough*) Ahem.

MRS HENDERSON: There's a letter for you, Mr Davoren!

TOMMY: It's the most powerfullest letter I ever heard read.

MINNIE: It wasn't you, really, that writ it, Mr Gallicker?

MRS HENDERSON: Sinn Fein Amhain:[68] him an' him only, Minnie, I see him with me own two eyes when me an' Winnie — Mrs Gallicker, Mr Davoren, aforesaid as appears in the letter — was havin' a chat be the fire.

MINNIE: You'd never think it was in him to do it.

MRS HENDERSON: An' to think that the likes ov such a man is to have the sowl-case[69] worried out ov him by a gang o' tramps; but it's in good hands now,

63. Courts set up by the IRA in 1919-21. again = against.
64. British courts.
65. children.
66. One of the oldest areas of Dublin.
67. prima facie, at first sight, on the face of it.
68. We Ourselves Alone.
69. body.

an' instead ov them settlin' yous, Mr Gallicker, it's yous 'ill settle them. Give the letter to Mr Davoren, an' we'll be goin'. (GALLOGHER *gives the letter to* DAVOREN)

MRS HENDERSON: (*Moving towards the door*) I hope you an' Mr Shields is gettin' on all right together, Mr Davoren.

DAVOREN: Fairly well, thanks, Mrs Henderson. We don't see much of each other. He's out during the day, and I'm usually out during the evening.

MRS HENDERSON: I'm afraid he'll never make a fortune out ov what he's sellin'. He'll talk above an hour over a pennorth o' pins. Every time he comes to our place I buy a package o' hairpins from him to give him a little encouragement. I' clare to God I have as many pins now as ud make a wire mattress for a double bed. All the young divils about the place are beginnin' to make a jeer ov him,[70] too; I gave one ov them a mallavogin'[71] the other day for callin' him oul' hairpins!

MR GALLOGHER: (*Venturing an opinion*) Mr Shields is a man of exceptional mental capacity, and is worthy of a more dignified position.

MRS HENDERSON: Them words is true, Mr Gallicker, and they aren't. For to be wise is to be a fool, an' to be a fool is to be wise.

MR GALLOGHER: (*With deprecating tolerance*) Oh, Mrs Henderson, that's a parrotox.

MRS HENDERSON: It may be what a parrot talks, or a blackbird, or, for the matter of that, a lark — but it's what Julia Henderson thinks, any ... whisht, is that a *Stop Press*? (*Outside is heard the shriek of a newsboy calling 'Stop Press'*) Run out, Tommy, an' get it till we see what it is.

TOMMY: I haven't got a make.[72]

MRS HENDERSON: I never seen you any other way, an' you'll always be the same if you keep follyin' your Spearmints, an' your Bumble Bees an' your Night Patrols.[73] (*Shouting to someone outside*) Is that a *Stop Press*, Mrs Grigson?

VOICE OUTSIDE: Yis, an ambush out near Knocksedan.

MRS HENDERSON: That's the stuff to give them. (*Loudly*) Was there anybody hurted?

VOICE OUTSIDE: One poor man killed — some chap named Maguire, the paper says.

DAVOREN: (*Agitated*) What name did she say?

MINNIE: Maguire; did you know him, Mr Davoren?

DAVOREN: Yes — no, no; I didn't know him, no, I didn't know him, Minnie.

MINNIE: I wonder is it the Maguire that does be with Mr Shields?

DAVOREN: Oh no, not at all, it couldn't be.

MRS HENDERSON: Knocksedan? That's in the County Sligo, now, or I'm greatly mistaken — am I right, Mr Gallicker, or am I wrong?

MR GALLOGHER: (*Who knows perfectly well that it is in the County Dublin, but dare not correct* MRS HENDERSON) That's where it is — Knocksedan, that's the very identical county.

MRS HENDERSON: Well, I think we better be makin' a move, Mr Gallicker; we've kep' Mr Davoren long enough, an' you'll find the letter'll be in good hands.

MR GALLOGHER *and* MRS HENDERSON *move towards the door, which when he reaches it* MR GALLOGHER *grips, hesitates, buttons his coat, and turns to* DAVOREN.

MR GALLOGHER: Mr Davoren, sir, on behalf ov meself, James Gallicker, an' Winifred, Mrs Gallicker, wife ov the said James, I beg to offer, extend an' furnish our humble an' hearty thanks for your benevolent goodness in interferin' in the matter specified, particularated[74] an' expanded upon in the letter, mandamus[75] or schedule, as the case may be. An' let me interpretate to you on behalf ov meself an' Winifred Gallicker, that whenever you visit us you will be supernally positive ov a hundred thousand welcomes — ahem.

MRS HENDERSON: (*Beaming with pride for the genius of her friend*) There's a man for you, Mr Davoren! You forgot to mention Biddy and Shaun, Mr Gallicker — (*to* DAVOREN) his two children — it's himself has them trained well. It ud make your heart thrill like an alarm clock to hear them singin' 'Faith ov Our Fathers' an' 'Wrap the Green Flag Roun Me'.[76]

MR GALLOGHER: (*Half apologetically and half proudly*) Faith an' Fatherland, Mrs Henderson, Faith and Fatherland.

70. make fun of him.
71. A verbal mauling.
72. a halfpenny.
73. Names of sweets, candies.
74. particularized.
75. A writ issued from the Queen's bench to an inferior court (Latin, we command).
76. 'Faith of Our Fathers' was a popular and very martial catholic hymn, 'Wrap the Green Flag Round Me, Boys' a popular patriotic song.

MRS HENDERSON: Well, good-day, Mr Davoren, an' God keep you an' strengthen all the men that are fightin' for Ireland's freedom. (*She and* GALLOGHER *go out*)

TOMMY: I must be off too; so long, Mr Davoren, an' remember that Tommy Owens only waits the call. (*He goes out too*)

DAVOREN: Well, Minnie, we're by ourselves once more.

MINNIE: Wouldn't that Tommy Owens give you the sick — only waitin' to hear the call! Ah, then it'll take all the brass bands in the country to blow the call before Tommy Owens ud hear it. (*She looks at her wristlet watch*) Sacred Heart, I've only ten minutes to get back to work! I'll have to fly! Quick, Mr Davoren, write me name in typewritin' before I go — just 'Minnie' (DAVOREN *types the name*) (*Shyly but determinedly*) Now yours underneath — just 'Donal'. (DAVOREN *does so*) Minnie, Donal; Donal, Minnie; goodbye now.

DAVOREN: Here, what about your milk?

MINNIE: I haven't time to take it now. (*Slyly*) I'll come for it this evening.

They both go towards the door.

DAVOREN: Minnie, the kiss I didn't get.

MINNIE: What kiss?

DAVOREN: When we were interrupted; you know, you little rogue, come, just one.

MINNIE: Quick, then.

DAVOREN *kisses her and she runs out.* DAVOREN *returns thoughtfully to the table.*

DAVOREN: Minnie, Donal; Donal, Minnie. Very pretty, but very ignorant. A gunman on the run! Be careful, be careful, Donal Davoren. But Minnie is attracted to the idea, and I am attracted to Minnie. And what danger can there be in being the shadow of a gunman?

ACT II

The same as in Act I. But it is now night. SEUMAS *is in the bed that runs along the wall at back.* DAVOREN *is seated near the fire, to which he has drawn the table. He has a fountain pen in his hand, and is attracted towards the moon, which is shining in through the windows. An open writing-pad is on the table at* DAVOREN'S *elbow. The bag left by* MAGUIRE *is still in the same place.*

DAVOREN:

The cold chaste moon, the Queen of Heaven's
bright isles,
Who makes all beautiful on which she smiles;
That wandering shrine of soft yet icy flame,
Which ever is transformed yet still the same.[1]

Ah, Shelley, Shelley, you yourself were a lovely human orb shining through clouds of whirling human dust. 'She makes all beautiful on which she smiles.' Ah, Shelley, she couldn't make this thrice accursed room beautiful. Her beams of beauty only make its horrors more full of horrors still. There is an ugliness that can be made beautiful, and there is an ugliness that can only be destroyed, and this is part of that ugliness. Donal, Donal, I fear your last state is worse than your first. (*He lilts a verse, which he writes on the pad before him*)

When night advances through the sky with slow
And solemn tread
The queenly moon looks down on life below,
As if she read
Man's soul, and in her scornful silence said:
All beautiful and happiest things are dead.[2]

SEUMAS: (*Sleepily*) Donal, Donal, are you awake? (*A pause*) Donal, Donal, are you asleep?

DAVOREN: I'm neither awake nor asleep: I'm thinking.

SEUMAS: I was just thinkin', too — I was just thinkin' too, that Maguire is sorry now that he didn't come with me instead of going to Knocksedan. He caught something besides butterflies — two of them he got, one through each lung.

DAVOREN: The Irish people are very fond of turning a serious thing into a joke; that was a serious affair — for poor Maguire.

SEUMAS: (*Defensively*) Why didn't he do what he arranged to do? Did he think of me when he was goin' to Knocksedan? How can he expect me to have any sympathy with him now?

DAVOREN: He can hardly expect that now that he's dead.

SEUMAS: The Republicans'll do a lot for him, now. How am I goin' to get back the things he has belongin' to me, either? There's some of them in that bag over there, but that's not quarter of what he

1. Shelley, 'Epipsychidion', lines 281-84.
2. A stanza from O'Casey's own poem, 'Sunshadows', published in *Windfalls* (1934).

had; an' I don't know where he was stoppin', for he left his old digs[3] a week or so ago — suppose there's nothing to be said about my loss; I'm to sing dumb.

DAVOREN: I hope there's nothing else in the bag, besides thread and hairpins.

SEUMAS: What else ud be in it? ... I can't sleep properly ever since they put on this damned curfew.[4] A minute ago I thought I heard some of the oul' ones standin' at the door; they won't be satisfied till they bring a raid on the house; an' they never begin to stand at the door till after curfew.... Are you gone to bed, Donal?

DAVOREN: No; I'm trying to finish this poem.

SEUMAS: (*Sitting up in bed*) If I was you I'd give that game up; it doesn't pay a working man to write poetry. I don't profess to know much about poetry — I don't profess to know much about poetry — about poetry — I don't know much about the pearly glint of the morning dew, or the damask sweetness of the rare wild rose, or the subtle greenness of the serpent's eye — but I think a poet's claim to greatness depends upon his power to put passion in the common people.

DAVOREN: Ay, passion to howl for his destruction. The People! Damn the people! They live in the abyss, the poet lives on the mountain-top; to the people there is no mystery of colour: it is simply the scarlet coat of the soldier; the purple vestments of a priest; the green banner of a party; the brown or blue overalls of industry. To them the might of design is a three-roomed house or a capacious bed. To them beauty is for sale in a butcher's shop. To the people the end of life is the life created for them; to the poet the end of life is the life that he creates for himself; life has a stifling grip upon the people's throat — it is the poet's musician. The poet ever strives to save the people; the people ever strive to destroy the poet. The people view life through creeds, through customs, and through necessities; the poet views creeds, customs, and necessities through life. The people ....

SEUMAS: (*Suddenly, and with a note of anxiety in his voice*) Whisht! What's that? Is that the tappin' again?

DAVOREN: Tappin'. What tappin'?

SEUMAS: (*In an awed whisper*) This is the second night I heard that tappin! I believe it bodes no good to me. There, do you hear it again — a quiet, steady, mysterious tappin' on the wall.

DAVOREN: I hear no tappin'.

SEUMAS: It ud be better for me if you did. It's a sure sign of death when nobody hears it but meself.

DAVOREN: Death! What the devil are you talking about, man?

SEUMAS: I don't like it at all; there's always something like that heard when one of our family dies.

DAVOREN: I don't know about that; but I know there's a hell of a lot of things heard when one of your family lives.

SEUMAS: God between us an' all harm! Thank God I'm where I ought to be — in bed.... It's always best to be in your proper place when such things happen — Sacred Heart! There it is again; do you not hear it now?

DAVOREN: Ah, for God's sake go asleep.

SEUMAS: Do you believe in nothing?

DAVOREN: I don't believe in tappin'.

SEUMAS: Whisht, it's stopped again; I'll try to go asleep for fear it ud begin again.

DAVOREN: Ay, do; and if it starts again I'll be sure to waken you up. (*A pause*)

SEUMAS: It's very cold tonight. Do you feel cold?

DAVOREN: I thought you were goin' asleep?

SEUMAS: The bloody cold won't let me.... You'd want a pair of pyjamas on you. (*A pause*) Did you ever wear pyjamas, Donal?

DAVOREN: No, no, no.

SEUMAS: What kind of stuff is in them?

DAVOREN: (*Angrily*) Oh, it depends on the climate; in India, silk; in Italy, satin; and the Eskimo wears them made from the skin of the Polar bear.

SEUMAS: (*Emphatically*) If you take my advice you'll get into bed — that poem is beginnin' to get on your nerves.

DAVOREN: (*Extinguishing the candle with a vicious blow*) Right; I'm going to bed now, so you can shut up.

Visibility is still maintained from the light of the moon.

SEUMAS: I was goin' to say something when you put out the light — what's this it was? — um, um, oh, ay: when I was comin' in this evenin' I saw Minnie Powell goin' out. If I was you I wouldn't have that one comin' in here.

DAVOREN: She comes in; I don't bring her in, do I?

3. Rented lodgings.
4. The curfew imposed by British forces in Dublin from July 1920 to December 1921 forbade citizens to be outdoors after 8pm, unless with special permission.

SEUMAS: The oul' ones'll be talkin', an' once they start you don't know how it'll end. Surely a man that has read Shelley couldn't be interested in an ignorant little bitch that thinks of nothin' but jazz dances, foxtrots, picture-theatres an' dress.

DAVOREN: Right glad I am that she thinks of dress, for she thinks of it in the right way, and makes herself a pleasant picture to the eye. Education has been wasted on many persons, teaching them to talk only, but leaving them with all their primitive instincts. Had poor Minnie received an education she would have been an artist. She is certainly a pretty girl. I'm sure she is a good girl, and I believe she is a brave girl.

SEUMAS: A Helen of Troy come to live in a tenement! You think a lot about her simply because she thinks a lot about you, an' she thinks a lot about you because she looks upon you as a hero — a kind o' Paris[5] ... she'd give the world an' all to be gaddin' about with a gunman. An' what ecstasy it ud give her if after a bit you were shot or hanged; she'd be able to go about then — like a good many more — singin', 'I do not mourn me darlin' lost, for he fell in his Jacket Green.'[6] An' then, for a year an' a day, all round her hat she'd wear the Tricoloured Ribbon O,[7] till she'd pick up an' marry someone else — possibly a British Tommy with a Mons Star.[8] An' as for bein' brave, it's easy to be that when you've no cause for cowardice; I wouldn't care to have me life dependin' on brave little Minnie Powell — she wouldn't sacrifice a jazz dance to save it.

DAVOREN: (*Sitting on the bed and taking off his coat and vest, preparatory to going to bed*) There; that's enough about Minnie Powell. I'm afraid I'll soon have to be on the run out of this house, too; it is becoming painfully obvious that there is no peace to be found here.

SEUMAS: Oh, this house is all right; barrin' the children, it does be quiet enough. Wasn't there children in the last place you were in too?

DAVOREN: Ay, ten; (*viciously*) and they were all over forty. (*A pause as* DAVOREN *is removing his collar and tie*)

SEUMAS: Everything is very quiet now; I wonder what time is it?

DAVOREN: The village cock hath thrice done salutation to the morn.[9]

SEUMAS: Shakespeare, *Richard III*, Act v, Scene iii. It was Ratcliff said that to Richard just before the battle of Bosworth.... How peaceful the heavens look now with the moon in the middle; you'd never think there were men prowlin' about tryin' to shoot each other. I don't know how a man who has shot anyone can sleep in peace at night.

DAVOREN: There's plenty of men can't sleep in peace at night now unless they know that they have shot somebody.

SEUMAS: I wish to God it was all over. The country is gone mad. Instead of counting their beads now they're countin' bullets; their Hail Marys and Paternosters are burstin' bombs — burstin' bombs, an' the rattle of machine-guns; petrol is their holy water; their Mass is a burnin' buildin'; their De Profundis is 'The Soldiers' Song',[10] an' their creed is, I believe in the gun almighty, maker of heaven an' earth — an' it's all for 'the glory o' God an' the honour o' Ireland'.[11]

DAVOREN: I remember the time when you yourself believed in nothing but the gun.

SEUMAS: Ay, when there wasn't a gun in the country; I've a different opinion now when there's nothin' but guns in the country.... An' you daren't open your mouth, for Kathleen ni Houlihan is very different now to the woman who used to play the harp an' sing 'Weep on, weep on, your hour is past',[12] for she's a ragin' divil now, an' if you only look crooked at her you're sure of a punch in th' eye. But this is the way I look at it — I look at it this way: You're not goin' — you're not goin' to beat the British Empire — the British Empire, by shootin' an occasional Tommy[13] at the corner of an occasional street. Besides, when the Tommies have the wind up — when the Tommies have the wind up they let bang at everything they see — they don't give a God's curse who they plug.

DAVOREN: Maybe they ought to get down off the

5. In Greek legend, Paris abducted Helen of Troy.
6. 'The Jacket(s) Green', a patriotic song by Michael Scanlan (1836-85).
7. A reference to a famous song of the 1798 period, 'The Tri-coloured Ribbon'.
8. The Battle of Mons in Belgium, fought on 23 August 1914, was one of the bloodiest of the early days of World War I; the Mons Star was awarded to honour those British soldiers who had fought up to November 1914.
9. The attribution is correct, but for 'thrice' read 'twice'.
10. Psalm 130 'Out of the depths I cry to thee, O Lord'; 'The Soldier's Song', composed in 1907 by Peadar Kearney (1883-1942), became Ireland's national anthem after 1922.
11. Slogan of the new Free State after 1922?
12. The typically moist sentiment of the Irish nationalist ballad. No specific source has been traced.
13. A private in the British army.

lorry and run to the Records Office to find out a man's pedigree before the plug him.

SEUMAS: It's the civilians that suffer; when there's an ambush they don't know where to run. Shot in the back to save the British Empire, an' shot in the breast to save the soul of Ireland. I'm a Nationalist meself, right enough — a Nationalist right enough, but all the same — I'm a Nationalist right enough; I believe in the freedom of Ireland, an' that England has no right to be here, but I draw the line when I hear the gunmen blowin' about dyin' for the people, when it's the people that are dyin' for the gunmen! With all due respect to the gunmen, I don't want them to die for me.

DAVOREN: Not likely; you object to any one of them deliberately dying for you for fear that one of these days you might accidentally die for one of them.

SEUMAS: You're one of the brave fellows that doesn't fear death.

DAVOREN: Why should I be afraid of it? It's all the same to me how it comes, where it comes, or when it comes. I leave fear of death to the people that are always praying for eternal life; 'Death is here and death is there, death is busy everywhere.'[14]

SEUMAS: Ay, in Ireland. Thanks be to God I'm a daily communicant. There's a great comfort in religion; it makes a man strong in time of trouble an' brave in time of danger. No man need be afraid with a crowd of angels round him; thanks to God for His Holy religion!

DAVOREN: You're welcome to your angels; philosophy is mine; philosophy that makes the coward brave; the sufferer defiant; the weak strong; the ....

A volley of shots is heard in a lane that runs parallel with the wall of the back-yard. Religion and philosophy are forgotten in the violent fear of a nervous equality.

SEUMAS: Jesus, Mary, an' Joseph, what's that?

DAVOREN: My God, that's very close.

SEUMAS: Is there no Christianity at all left in the country?

DAVOREN: Are we ever again going to know what peace and security are?

SEUMAS: If this continues much longer I'll be nothing but a galvanic battery o' shocks.

DAVOREN: It's dangerous to be in and it's equally dangerous to be out.

SEUMAS: This is a dangerous spot to be in with them windows; you couldn't tell the minute a bullet ud come in through one of them — through one of them, an' hit the — hit the — an' hit the ....

DAVOREN: (*Irritably*) Hit the what, man?

SEUMAS: The wall.

DAVOREN: Couldn't you say that at first without making a song about it?

SEUMAS: (*Suddenly*) I don't believe there's horses in the stable at all.

DAVOREN: Stable! What stable are you talking about?

SEUMAS: There's a stable at the back of the house with an entrance from the yard; it's used as a carpenter's shop. Didn't you often hear the peculiar noises at night? They give out that it's the horses shakin' their chains.

DAVOREN: And what is it?

SEUMAS: Oh, there I'll leave you!

DAVOREN: Surely you don't mean ....

SEUMAS: But I do mean it.

DAVOREN: You do mean what?

SEUMAS: I wouldn't — I wouldn't be surprised — wouldn't be surprised — surprised ....

DAVOREN: Yes, yes, surprised — go on.

SEUMAS: I wouldn't be surprised if they were manufacturin' bombs there.

DAVOREN: My God, that's a pleasant contemplation! The sooner I'm on the run out of this house the better. How is it you never said anything about this before?

SEUMAS: Well — well, I didn't want — I didn't want to — to ....

DAVOREN: You didn't want to what?

SEUMAS: I didn't want to frighten you.

DAVOREN: (*Sarcastically*) You're bloody kind!

A knock at the door; the voice of MRS GRIGSON *heard.*

MRS GRIGSON: Are you asleep. Mr Shields?

SEUMAS: What the devil can she want at this hour of the night? (*To* MRS GRIGSON) No, Mrs Grigson, what is it?

MRS GRIGSON: (*Opening the door and standing at the threshold. She is a woman about forty, but looks much older. She is one of the cave-dwellers of Dublin, living as she does in a tenement kitchen, to which only an occasional sickly beam of sunlight filters through a grating in the yard; the consequent general dimness of*

14. Shelley, 'Death':
Death is here and death is there,
Death is busy everywhere.

her abode has given her the habit of peering through half-closed eyes. She is slovenly dressed in an old skirt and bodice; her face is grimy, not because her habits are dirty – for, although she is untidy, she is a clean woman – but because of the smoky atmosphere of her room. Her hair is constantly falling over her face, which she is frequently removing by rapid movements of her right hand) He hasn't turned up yet, an' I'm stiff with the cold waitin' for him.

SEUMAS: Mr Grigson, is it?

MRS GRIGSON: Adolphus, Mr Shields, after takin' his tea at six o'clock — no, I'm tellin' a lie — it was before six, for I remember the Angelus was ringin' out an' we sittin' at the table — after takin' his tea he went out for a breath o' fresh air, an' I haven't seen sign or light of him since. 'Clare to God me heart is up in me mouth, thinkin' he might be shot be the Black an' Tans.

SEUMAS: Aw, he'll be all right, Mrs Grigson. You ought to go to bed an' rest yourself; it's always the worst that comes into a body's mind; go to bed, Mrs Grigson, or you'll catch your death of cold.

MRS GRIGSON: I'm afraid to go to bed, Mr Shields, for I'm always in dread that some night or another, when he has a sup taken, he'll fall down the kitchen stairs an' break his neck. Not that I'd be any the worse if anything did happen to him, for you know the sort he is, Mr Shields; sure he has me heart broke.

SEUMAS: Don't be downhearted, Mrs Grigson; he may take a thought one of these days an' turn over a new leaf.

MRS GRIGSON: Sorra leaf[15] Adolphus'll ever turn over, he's too far gone in the horns[16] for that now. Sure no one ud mind him takin' a pint or two, if he'd stop at that, but he won't; nothin' could fill him with beer, an' no matter how much he may have taken, when he's taken more he'll always say, 'Here's the first today.'

DAVOREN: (*To* SEUMAS) Christ! Is she going to stop talking there all the night?

SEUMAS: 'Sh, she'll hear you; right enough, the man has the poor woman's heart broke.

DAVOREN: And because he has her heart broken, she's to have the privilege of breaking everybody else's.

MRS GRIGSON: Mr Shields.

SEUMAS: Yes?

MRS GRIGSON: Do the insurance companies pay if a man is shot after curfew?

SEUMAS: Well, now, that's a thing I couldn't say, Mrs Grigson.

MRS GRIGSON: (*Plaintively*) Isn't he a terrible man to be takin' such risks, an' not knowin' what'll happen to him? He knows them Societies[17] only want an excuse to do people out of their money — is it after one, now, Mr Shields?

SEUMAS: Aw, it must be after one, Mrs Grigson.

MRS GRIGSON: (*Emphatically*) Ah, then, if I was a young girl again I'd think twice before gettin' married. Whisht! There's somebody now — it's him, I know be the way he's fumblin'. (*She goes out a little way. Stumbling steps are heard in the hall. Outside*) Is that you, Dolphie, dear? (*After a few moments* ADOLPHUS GRIGSON *with* MRS GRIGSON *holding his arm, stumbles into the room*) Dolphie, dear, mind yourself.

GRIGSON: (*He is a man of forty-five, but looks, relatively, much younger than* MRS GRIGSON. *His occupation is that of a solicitor's clerk. He has all the appearance of being well fed; and, in fact, he gets most of the nourishment,* MRS GRIGSON *getting just enough to give her strength to do the necessary work of the household. On account of living most of his life out of the kitchen, his complexion is fresh, and his movements, even when sober, are livelier than those of his wife. He is comfortably dressed; heavy topcoat, soft trilby hat, a fancy coloured scarf about his neck, and he carries an umbrella*) I'm all right; do you see anything wrong with me?

MRS GRIGSON: Of course you're all right, dear; there's no one mindin' you.

GRIGSON: Mindin' me, is it, mindin' me? He'd want to be a good thing that ud mind me. There's a man here — a man, mind you, afraid av nothin' — not in this bloody house anyway.

MRS GRIGSON: (*Imploringly*) Come on downstairs, Dolphie, dear; sure there's not one in the house ud say a word to you.

GRIGSON: Say a word to me, is it? He'd want to be a good thing that ud say anything to Dolphus Grigson. (*Loudly*) Is there anyone wants to say anything to Dolphus Grigson? If there is, he's here — a man, too — there's no blottin' it out — a man.

MRS GRIGSON: You'll wake everybody in the house; can't you speak quiet?

15. Not a leaf.
16. he's too old.

17. Insurance companies and Friendly Societies.

GRIGSON: (*More loudly still*) What do I care for anybody in the house? Are they keepin' me; are they givin' me anything? When they're keepin' Grigson it'll be time enough for them to talk. (*With a shout*) I can tell them Adolphus Grigson wasn't born in a bottle!

MRS GRIGSON: (*Tearfully*) Why do you talk like that, dear? We all know you weren't born in a bottle.

GRIGSON: There's some of them in this house think Grigson was born in a bottle.

DAVOREN: (*To* SEUMAS) A most appropriate place for him to be born in.

MRS GRIGSON: Come on down to bed, now, an' you can talk about them in the mornin'.

GRIGSON: I'll talk about them, now; do you think I'm afraid of them? Dolphus Grigson's afraid av nothin', creepin' or walkin' — if there's any one in the house thinks he's fit to take a fall out av Adolphus Grigson, he's here — a man; they'll find that Grigson's no soft thing.

DAVOREN: Ah me, alas! Pain, pain ever, for ever.

MRS GRIGSON: Dolphie, dear, poor Mr Davoren wants to go to bed.

DAVOREN: Oh, she's terribly anxious about poor Mr Davoren, all of a sudden.

GRIGSON: (*Stumbling towards* DAVOREN, *and holding out his hand*) Davoren! He's a man. Leave it there, mate. You needn't be afraid av Dolphus Grigson; there never was a drop av informer's blood in the whole family av Grigson. I don't know what you are or what you think, but you're a man, an' not like some of the goughers[18] in this house, that ud hang you. Not referrin' to you, Mr Shields.

MRS GRIGSON: Oh, you're not deludin'[19] to Mr Shields.

SEUMAS: I know that, Mr Grigson; go on down, now, with Mrs Grigson, an' have a sleep.

GRIGSON: I tie myself to no woman's apron-strings, Mr Shields; I know how to keep Mrs Grigson in her place; I have the authority of the Bible for that. I know the Bible from cover to cover, Mr Davoren, an' that's more than some in this house could say. And what does the Holy Scripture say about woman? It says, 'The woman shall be subject to her husband', an' I'll see that Mrs Grigson keeps the teachin' av the Holy Book in the letter an' in the spirit. If you're ever in trouble, Mr Davoren, an' Grigson can help — I'm your man — have you me?

DAVOREN: I have you, Mr Grigson, I have you.

GRIGSON: Right; I'm an Orangeman, an' I'm not ashamed av it, an' I'm not afraid av it, but I can feel for a true man, all the same — have *you* got me, Mr Shields?

SEUMAS: Oh, we know you well, Mr Grigson; many a true Irishman was a Protestant — Tone, Emmet an' Parnell.[20]

GRIGSON: Mind you, I'm not sayin' as I agree with them you've mentioned, Mr Shields, for the Bible forbids it, an' Adolphus Grigson'll always abide be the Bible. Fear God an' honour the King — that's written in Holy Scripture, an' there's no blottin' it out. (*Pulling a bottle out of his pocket*) But here, Mr Davoren, have a drink, just to show there's no coolness.

DAVOREN: No, no, Mr Grigson, it's late now to take anything. Go on down with Mrs Grigson, and we can have a chat in the morning.

GRIGSON: Sure you won't have a drink?

DAVOREN: Quite sure — thanks all the same.

GRIGSON: (*Drinking*) Here's the first today! To all true men, even if they were born in a bottle. Here's to King William, to the battle av the Boyne; to the Hobah Black Chapter[21] — that's my Lodge, Mr Davoren; an' to the Orange Lily O. (*Singing in a loud shout*)

An' dud ya go to see the show, each rose an'
pinkadilly O,
To feast your eyes an' view the prize won be the
Orange Lily O.
The Vic'roy there, so debonair, just like a
daffadilly O,
With Lady Clarke, blithe as a lark, approached
the Orange Lily O.
Heigh Ho the Lily O,
The Royal, Loyal Lily O,
Beneath the sky what flower can vie with
Erin's Orange Lily O!

DAVOREN: Holy God, isn't this terrible!

GRIGSON: (*Singing*)

The elated Muse, to hear the news,
jumped like a Connaught filly O,

18. swindlers.
19. alluding.
20. Wolfe Tone (1763-98), leader of the United Irishmen; Emmet, already mentioned in Act I (p. 683) as leader of the 1803 rebellion; Charles Stewart Parnell (1846-91), the leader of the Irish Parliamentary Party.
21. The Orange Order is organized into various chapters and lodges.

As gossip Fame did loud proclaim the
  triumph av the Lily O.
The Lowland field may roses yield,
  gay heaths the Highlands hilly O;
But high or low no flower can show
  like Erin's Orange Lily O.
    Heigh Ho the Lily O,
    The Royal, Loyal Lily O,
Beneath the sky what flower can vie with
  Erin's Or . . . .[22]

While GRIGSON *has been singing, the sound of a rapidly moving motor is heard, faintly at first, but growing rapidly louder, till it apparently stops suddenly somewhere very near the house, bringing* GRIGSON's *song to an abrupt conclusion. They are all startled, and listen attentively to the throbbing of the engines, which can be plainly heard.* GRIGSON *is considerably sobered, and anxiously keeps his eyes on the door.* SEUMAS *sits up in bed and listens anxiously.* DAVOREN, *with a shaking hand, lights the candle, and begins to search hurriedly among the books and papers on the table.*

GRIGSON: (*With a tremor in his voice*) There's no need to be afraid, they couldn't be comin' here.

MRS GRIGSON: God forbid! It ud be terrible if they came at this hour ov the night.

SEUMAS: You never know, Mrs Grigson; they'd rush in on you when you'd be least expectin' them. What, in the name o' God, is goin' to come out of it all? Nobody now cares a traneen[23] about the orders of the Ten Commandments; the only order that anybody minds now is, 'Put your hands up.' Oh, it's a hopeless country.

GRIGSON: Whisht; do you hear them talking outside at the door? You're sure of your life nowhere now; it's just as safe to go everywhere as it is to anywhere. An' they don't give a damn whether you're a loyal man or not. If you're a Republican they make you sing 'God Save the King', an' if you're loyal they'll make you sing 'The Soldiers' Song'. The singin' ud be all right if they didn't make you dance afterwards.

MRS GRIGSON: They'd hardly come here unless they heard something about Mr Davoren.

DAVOREN: About me! What could they hear about me?

GRIGSON: You'll never get some people to keep their mouths shut. I was in the Blue Lion this evening, an' who do you think was there, blowin' out av him, but that little blower, Tommy Owens; there he was tellin' everybody that *he* knew where there was bombs; that *he* had a friend that was a General in the IRA; that *he* could tell them what the Staff was thinkin' av doin'; that *he* could lay his hand on tons av revolvers; that they wasn't a mile from where he was livin', but that *he* knew his own know, an' would keep it to himself.

SEUMAS: Well, God blast the little blower, anyway; it's the like ov him that deserves to be plugged! (*To* DAVOREN) What are you lookin' for among the books, Donal?

DAVOREN: A letter that I got today from Mr Gallogher and Mrs Henderson; I'm blessed if I know where I put it.

SEUMAS: (*Peevishly*) Can't you look for it in the mornin'?

DAVOREN: It's addressed to the Irish Republican Army, and, considering the possibility of a raid, it would be safer to get rid of it.

Shots again heard out in the lane, followed by shouts of 'Halt, halt, halt!'

GRIGSON: I think we had better be gettin' to bed, Debby; it's not right to be keepin' Mr Davoren an' Mr Shields awake.

SEUMAS: An' what made them give you such a letter as that; don't they know the state the country is in? An' you were worse to take it. Have you got it?

DAVOREN: I can't find it anywhere; isn't this terrible!

GRIGSON: Goodnight, Mr Davoren; goodnight, Mr Shields.

MRS GRIGSON: Goodnight, Mr Shields; goodnight, Mr Davoren.

They go out. SEUMAS *and* DAVOREN *are too much concerned about the letter to respond to their goodnights.*

SEUMAS: What were you thinkin' of when you took such a letter as that? Ye gods, has nobody any brains at all, at all? Oh, this is a hopeless country. Did you try in your pockets?

DAVOREN: (*Searching in his pockets*) Oh, thanks be to God, here it is.

SEUMAS: Burn it now, an', for God's sake, don't take any letters like that again. . . . There's the motor goin' away; we can sleep in peace now for the rest of the night. Just to make sure of everything now, have

22. 'The Orange Lily O' dates from the late eighteenth or early nineteenth century. The Orange Order was founded in 1795. The song is a standard item in the Orange repertoire.
23. A wisp of straw, nothing.

a look in that bag o' Maguire's: not that there can be anything in it.

DAVOREN: If there's nothing in it, what's the good of looking?

SEUMAS: It won't kill you to look, will it?

DAVOREN *goes over to the bag, puts it on the table, opens it, and jumps back, his face pale and limbs trembling.*

DAVOREN: My God, it's full of bombs, Mills bombs![24]

SEUMAS: Holy Mother of God, you're jokin'!

DAVOREN: If the Tans come you'll find whether I'm jokin' or no.

SEUMAS: Isn't this a nice pickle to be in? St Anthony,[25] look down on us!

DAVOREN: There's no use of blaming St Anthony; why did you let Maguire leave the bag here?

SEUMAS: Why did I let him leave the bag here; why did I let him leave the bag here! How did I know what was in it? Didn't I think there was nothin' in it but spoons an' hairpins? What'll we do now; what'll we do now? Mother o' God, grant there'll be no raid tonight. I knew things ud go wrong when I missed Mass this mornin'.

DAVOREN: Give over your praying and let us try to think of what is best to be done. There's one thing certain: as soon as morning comes I'm on the run out of this house.

SEUMAS: Thinkin' of yourself, like the rest of them. Leavin' me to bear the brunt of it.

DAVOREN: And why shouldn't you bear the brunt of it? Maguire was no friend of mine; besides, it's your fault; you knew the sort of man he was, and you should have been on your guard.

SEUMAS: Did I know he was gunman; did I know he was a gunman, did I know he was a gunman? Did ....

DAVOREN: Do you mean to tell me that ....

SEUMAS: Just a moment ....

DAVOREN: You didn't know ....

SEUMAS: Just a moment ....

DAVOREN: That Maguire was connected with ....

SEUMAS: (*Loudly*) Just a moment; can't ....

DAVOREN: The Republican Movement? What's the use of trying to tell damn lies!

MINNIE POWELL *rushes into the room. She is only partly dressed, and has thrown a shawl over her shoulders. She is in a state of intense excitement.*

MINNIE: Mr Davoren, Donal, they're all round the house; they must be goin' to raid the place; I was lookin' out of the window an' I seen them; I do be on the watch every night; have you anything? If you have ....

There is heard at street door a violent and continuous knocking, followed by the crash of glass and the beating of the door with rifle butts.

MINNIE: There they are, there they are, there they are!

DAVOREN *reclines almost fainting on the bed;* SEUMAS *sits up in an attitude of agonised prayerfulness;* MINNIE *alone retains her presence of mind. When she sees their panic she becomes calm, though her words are rapidly spoken, and her actions are performed with decisive celerity.*

MINNIE: What is it; what have you got; where are they?

DAVOREN: Bombs, bombs, bombs; my God! in the bag on the table there; we're done, we're done!

SEUMAS: Hail, Mary, full of grace — pray for us miserable sinners — Holy St Anthony, do you hear them batterin' at the door — now an' at the hour of our death — say an act of contrition, Donal — there's the glass gone!

MINNIE: I'll take them to my room; maybe they won't search it; if they do aself,[26] they won't harm a girl. Goodbye ... Donal (*She glances lovingly at* DAVOREN *— who is only semi-conscious — as she rushes out with the bag*)

SEUMAS: If we come through this I'll never miss a Mass again! If it's the Tommies it won't be so bad, but if it's the Tans, we're goin' to have a terrible time.

The street door is broken open and heavy steps are heard in the hall, punctuated with shouts of ''Old the light 'ere', 'Put 'em up', etc. An AUXILIARY *opens the door of the room and enters, revolver in one hand and electric torch in the other. His uniform is black, and he wears a black beret.*

AUXILIARY: 'Oo's 'ere?

SEUMAS: (*As if he didn't know*) Who — who's that?

AUXILIARY: (*Peremptorily*) 'Oo's 'ere?

SEUMAS: Only two men, mister; me an' me mate in t'other bed.

AUXILIARY: Why didn't you open the door?

24. hand grenades.
25. The patron saint of gravediggers.
26. if they do itself, i.e. if they do anyway.

SEUMAS: We didn't hear you knockin', sir.

AUXILIARY: You must be a little awd of 'earing,[27] ay?

SEUMAS: I had rheumatic fever a few years ago, an' ever since I do be a — I do be a little deaf sometimes.

AUXILIARY: (*To* DAVOREN) 'Ow is it you're not in bed?

DAVOREN: I was in bed; when I heard the knockin' I got up to open the door.

AUXILIARY: *You're* a koind blowke[28] you are. Deloighted, like, to have a visit from us, ay? Ay? (*Threatening to strike him*) Why down't you answer?

DAVOREN: Yes, sir.

AUXILIARY: What's your name?

DAVOREN: Davoren, Dan Davoren, sir.

AUXILIARY: You're not an Irishman, are you?

DAVOREN: I-I-I was born in Ireland.

AUXILIARY: Ow, you were, were you; Irish han' proud of it, ay? (*To* SEUMAS) What's *your* name?

SEUMAS: Seuma . . . Oh no; Jimmie Shields, sir.

AUXILIARY: Ow, you're a Selt (*he means a Celt*), one of the Seltic race that speaks a lingo of its ahn,[29] and that's going to overthrow the British Empire — I don't think! 'Ere, where's your gun?

SEUMAS: I never had a gun in me hand in me life.

AUXILIARY: Now; you wouldn't know what a gun is if you sawr one, I suppowse. (*Displaying his revolver in a careless way*) 'Ere, what's that?

SEUMAS: Oh, be careful, please, be careful.

AUXILIARY: Why, what 'ave I got to be careful abaht?

SEUMAS: The gun; it-it-it might go off.

AUXILIARY: An' what prawse[30] if it did; it can easily be relowded. Any ammunition 'ere? What's in that press?[31] (*He searches and scatters contents of press*)

SEUMAS: Only a little bit o' grub; you'll get nothin' here, sir; no one in the house has any connection with politics.

AUXILIARY: Now? I've never met a man yet that didn't say that, but we're a little bit too ikey[32] now to be kidded with that sort of talk.

SEUMAS: May I go an' get a drink o' water?

AUXILIARY: You'll want a barrel of watah before you're done with us. (*The* AUXILIARY *goes about the room examining places*) 'Ello, what's 'ere? A statue o' Christ! An' a Crucifix! You'd think you was in a bloomin' monastery.

MRS GRIGSON *enters, dressed disorderly and her hair awry.*

MRS GRIGSON: They're turning the place upside-down. Upstairs an' downstairs they're makin' a litter of everything! I declare to God, it's awful what law-abidin' people have to put up with. An' they found a pint bottle of whisky under Dolphie's pillow, an' they're drinkin' every drop of it — an' Dolphie'll be like a devil in the mornin' when he finds he has no curer.[33]

AUXILIARY: (*All attention when he hears the word 'whiskey'*) A bottle of whisky, ay? 'Ere, where do you live — quick, where do you live?

MRS GRIGSON: Down in the kitchen — an' when you go down will you ask them not to drink — oh, he's gone without listenin' to me. (*While* MRS GRIGSON *is speaking the* AUXILIARY *rushes out*)

SEUMAS: (*Anxiously to* MRS GRIGSON) Are they searchin' the whole house, Mrs Grigson?

MRS GRIGSON: They didn't leave a thing in the kitchen that they didn't flitter[34] about the floor; the things in the cupboard, all the little odds an' ends that I keep in the big box, an . . . .

SEUMAS: Oh, they're a terrible gang of blaguards[35] — did they go upstairs? — they'd hardly search Minnie Powell's room — do you think, would they, Mrs Grigson?

MRS GRIGSON: Just to show them the sort of a man he was, before they come in, Dolphie put the big Bible on the table, open at the First Gospel of St Peter, second chapter, an' marked the thirteenth to the seventeenth verse in red ink — you know the passages, Mr Shields — (*quoting*)

> 'Submit yourselves to every ordinance of man for the Lord's sake: whether it be to the king, as supreme; or unto governors, as unto them that are sent by him for the punishment of evildoers, an' for the praise of them that do well. . . . Love the brotherhood. Fear God. Honour the King.'[36]

An' what do you think they did, Mr Shields? They

27. hard of hearing. The Auxiliary is a cockney.
28. kind bloke.
29. a language of its own.
30. price.
31. cupboard. Although commonly used in Ireland, 'press' would not be a familiar word to an English soldier.
32. alert, wide-awake.
33. cure for his hangover.
34. scatter.
35. blackguards.
36. I Peter 2. 13-17.

caught a hold of the Bible an' flung it on the floor — imagine that, Mr Shields — flingin' the Bible on the floor! Then one of them says to another — 'Jack,' says he, 'have you seen the light; is your soul saved?' An' then they grabbed hold of poor Dolphie, callin' him Mr Moody an' Mr Sankey[37] an' wanted him to offer up a prayer for the Irish Republic! An' when they were puttin' me out, there they had the poor man sittin' up in bed, his hands crossed on his breast, his eyes lookin' up at the ceilin', an' he singin' a hymn — 'We shall meet in the Sweet Bye an' Bye' — an' all the time, Mr Shields, there they were drinkin' his whisky; there's torture for you, an' they all laughin' at poor Dolphie's terrible sufferins.

DAVOREN: In the name of all that's sensible, what did he want to bring whisky home with him for? They're bad enough sober, what'll they be like when they're drunk?

MRS GRIGSON: (*Plaintively*) He always brings a drop home with him — he calls it his medicine.

SEUMAS: (*Still anxious*) They'll hardly search all the house; do you think they will, Mrs Grigson?

MRS GRIGSON: An' we have a picture over the mantelpiece of King William crossing the Boyne, an' do you know what they wanted to make out, Mr Shields, that it was Robert Emmet, an' the picture of a sacret society!

SEUMAS: She's not listenin' to a word I'm sayin'! Oh, the country is hopeless an' the people is hopeless.

DAVOREN: For God's sake tell her to go to hell out of this — she's worse than the Auxsie.[38]

SEUMAS: (*Thoughtfully*) Let her stay where she is; it's safer to have a woman in the room. If they come across the bombs I hope to God Minnie'll say nothin'.

DAVOREN: We're a pair of pitiable cowards to let poor Minnie suffer when we know that we and not she are to blame.

SEUMAS: What else can we do, man? Do you want us to be done in? If you're anxious to be riddled, I'm not. Besides, they won't harm her, she's only a girl, an' so long as she keeps her mouth shut it'll be all right.

DAVOREN: I wish I could be sure of that.

SEUMAS: D'ye think are they goin', Mrs Grigson? What are they doin' now?

MRS GRIGSON: (*Who is standing at the door, looking out into the hall*) There's not a bit of me that's not shakin' like a jelly!

SEUMAS: Are they gone upstairs, Mrs Grigson? Do you think, Mrs Grigson, will they soon be goin'?

MRS GRIGSON: When they were makin' poor Dolphie sit up in the bed, I 'clare to God I thought every minute I'd hear their guns goin' off, an' see poor Dolphie stretched out dead in the bed — whisht, God bless us, I think I hear him moanin'!

SEUMAS: You might as well be talking to a stone! They're all hopeless, hopeless, hopeless! She thinks she hears him moanin'! It's bloody near time somebody made him moan!

DAVOREN: (*With a sickly attempt at humour*) He's moaning for the loss of his whisky.

During the foregoing dialogue the various sounds of a raid — orders, the tramping of heavy feet, the pulling about of furniture, etc. — are heard. Now a more definite and sustained commotion is apparent. Loud and angry commands of 'Go on', 'Get out and get into the lorry', are heard, mingled with a girl's voice — it is MINNIE'S *— shouting bravely but a little hysterically, 'Up the Republic.'*

MRS GRIGSON: (*From the door*) God save us, they're takin' Minnie, they're takin' Minnie Powell! (*Running out*) What in the name of God can have happened?

SEUMAS: Holy Saint Anthony grant that she'll keep her mouth shut.

DAVOREN: (*Sitting down on the bed and covering his face with his hands*) We'll never again be able to lift up our heads if anything happens to Minnie.

SEUMAS: For God's sake keep quiet or somebody'll hear you; nothin'll happen to her, nothin' at all — it'll be all right if she only keeps her mouth shut.

MRS GRIGSON: (*Running in*) They're after gettin' a whole lot of stuff in Minnie's room! Enough to blow up the whole street, a Tan says! God tonight, who'd have ever thought that of Minnie Powell!

SEUMAS: Did she say anything, is she sayin' anything, what's she sayin', Mrs Grigson?

MRS GRIGSON: She's shoutin' 'Up the Republic' at the top of her voice. An' big Mrs Henderson is fightin' with the soldiers — she's after nearly knockin' one of them down, an' they're puttin' her into the lorry too.

37. Ira David Sankey and Dwight Lyman Moody were nineteenth-century American evangelists who brought their revivalist campaign to Britain in 1873 and 1883.

38. Auxiliary.

SEUMAS: God blast her! Can she not mind her own business? What does she want here — didn't she know there was a raid on? Is the whole damn country goin' mad? They'll open fire in a minute an' innocent people'll be shot!

DAVOREN: What way are they using Minnie, Mrs Grigson; are they rough with her?

MRS GRIGSON: They couldn't be half rough enough; the little hussy, to be so deceitful; she might as well have had the house blew up! God tonight, who'd think it was in Minnie Powell!

SEUMAS: Oh, grant she won't say anything!

MRS GRIGSON: There they're goin' away now; ah, then I hope they'll give that Minnie Powell a coolin'.

SEUMAS: God grant she won't say anything! Are they gone, Mrs Grigson?

MRS GRIGSON: With her fancy stockin's, an' her pom-poms,[39] an' her crêpe-de-chine blouses! I knew she'd come to no good!

SEUMAS: God grant she'll keep her mouth shut! Are they gone, Mrs Grigson?

MRS GRIGSON: They're gone, Mr Shields, an' here's poor Dolphie an' not a feather astray on him. Oh, Dolphie, dear, you're all right, thanks to God; I thought you'd never see the mornin'.

GRIGSON: (*Entering without coat or vest*) Of course I'm all right; what ud put a bother on Dolphie Grigson? — not the Tans anyway!

MRS GRIGSON: When I seen you stretched out on the bed, an' you ... singin' a hymn ....

GRIGSON: (*Fearful of possible humiliation*) Who was singin' a hymn? D'ye hear me talkin' to you — where did you hear me singin' a hymn?

MRS GRIGSON: I was only jokin', Dolphie, dear; I ....

GRIGSON: Your place is below, an' not gosterin' here to men; down with you quick! (MRS GRIGSON *hurriedly leaves the room. Nonchalantly taking out his pipe, filling it, lighting it, and beginning to smoke*) Excitin' few moments, Mr Davoren; Mrs G lost her head completely — panic-stricken. But that's only natural, all women is very nervous. The only thing to do is to show them that they can't put the wind up you; show the least sign of fright an' they'd walk on you, simply walk on you. Two of them come down — 'Put them up', revolvers under your nose — you know, the usual way. 'What's all the bother about?' says I, quite calm. 'No bother at all,' says one of them, 'only this gun might go off an' hit somebody — have you me?'[40] says he. 'What if it does,' says I; 'a man can only die once, an' you'll find Grigson won't squeal.' 'God, you're a cool one,' says the other, 'there's no blottin' it out.'

SEUMAS: That's the best way to take them; it only makes thing worse to show that you've got the wind up. 'Any ammunition here?' says the fellow that come in here. 'I don't think so,' says I, 'but you better have a look,' 'No back talk,' says he, 'or you might get plugged.' 'I don't know of any clause', says I, 'in the British Constitution that makes it a crime for a man to speak in his own room', — with that, he just had a look round, an' off he went.

GRIGSON: If a man keeps a stiff upper front — Merciful God, there's an ambush!

Explosions of two bursting bombs are heard on the street outside the house, followed by fierce and rapid revolver fire. People are heard rushing into the hall, and there is general clamour and confusion. SEUMAS *and* DAVOREN *cower down in the room;* GRIGSON, *after a few moments' hesitation, frankly rushes out of the room to what he conceives to be the safer asylum of the kitchen. A lull follows, punctured by an odd rifle-shot; then comes a peculiar and ominous stillness, broken in a few moments by the sounds of voices and movement. Questions are heard being asked: 'Who was it was killed?' 'Where was she shot?' which are answered by: 'Minnie Powell'; 'She went to jump off the lorry an' she was shot'; 'She's not dead, is she?'; 'They say she's dead – shot through the buzzom!'*[41]

DAVOREN: (*In a tone of horror-stricken doubt*) D'ye hear what they're sayin', Shields, d'ye hear what they're sayin' — Minnie Powell is shot.

SEUMAS: For God's sake speak easy, an' don't bring them in here on top of us again.

DAVOREN: Is that all you're thinking of? Do you realise that she has been shot to save us?

SEUMAS: Is it my fault; am I to blame?

DAVOREN: It is your fault and mine, both; oh, we're a pair of dastardly cowards to have let her do what she did.

SEUMAS: She did it off her own bat[42] — we didn't ask her to do it.

MRS GRIGSON *enters. She is excited and semi-hysterical, and sincerely affected by the tragic occurrence.*

39. A ball of tufted silk or wool, worn on a hat for decoration.

40. do you understand me?

41. bosom.

42. on her own initiative.

MRS GRIGSON: (*Falling down in a sitting posture on one of the beds*) What's goin' to happen next! Oh, Mr Davoren, isn't it terrible, isn't it terrible! Minnie Powell, poor little Minnie Powell's been shot dead! They were raidin' a house a few doors down, an' had just got up in their lorries to go away, when they was ambushed. You never heard such shootin'! An' in the thick of it, poor Minnie went to jump off the lorry she was on, an' she was shot through the buzzom. Oh, it was horrible to see the blood pourin' out, an' Minnie moanin'. They found some paper in her breast, with 'Minnie' written on it, an' some other name they couldn't make out with the blood; the officer kep' it. The ambulance is bringin' her to the hospital, but what good's that when she's dead! Poor little Minnie, poor little Minnie Powell, to think of you full of a life a few minutes ago, an' now she's dead!

DAVOREN: Ah me, alas! Pain, pain, pain ever, for ever! It's terrible to think that little Minnie is dead, but it's still more terrible to think that Davoren and Shields are alive! Oh, Donal Davoren, shame is your portion now till the silver cord is loosened and the golden bowl be broken.[43] Oh, Davoren, Donal Davoren, poet and poltroon,[44] poltroon and poet!

SEUMAS: (*Solemnly*) I knew something ud come of the tappin' on the wall!

43. Ecclesiastes 12.6.
44. contemptible coward.

from:
THE PLOUGH AND THE STARS (1926)

A TRAGEDY IN FOUR ACTS

[The play was first produced on 8 February 1926, at the Abbey. Acts I and II take place in November 1915. The setting of Act II is a public-house, outside which a meeting is being held.]

CHARACTERS in Act II

JACK CLITHEROE (*a bricklayer*), *Commandant in the Irish Citizen Army*
PETER FLYNN, *a labourer; Nora's uncle*
THE YOUNG COVEY, *a fitter; Clitheroe's cousin*
BESSIE BURGESS, *a street fruit-vendor* } *Residents in the tenement*
MRS. GOGAN, *a charwoman* }
FLUTHER GOOD, *a carpenter* }
LIEUTENANT LANGON (*a civil servant*), *of the Irish Volunteers*
CAPTAIN BRENNAN (*a chicken-butcher*), *of the Irish Citizen Army*
ROSIE REDMOND, *a daughter of 'the Digs'*
A BAR-TENDER
A WOMAN
THE FIGURE IN THE WINDOW

ACT II

A commodious public-house at the corner of the street in which the meeting is being addressed from Platform No. 1. It is the south corner of the public-house that is visible to the audience. The counter, beginning at Back about one-fourth of the width of the space shown, comes across two-thirds of the length of the stage, and, taking a circular sweep, passes out of sight to Left. On the counter are beer-pulls, glasses, and a carafe. The other three-fourths of the Back is occupied by a tall, wide, two-paned window. Beside this window at the Right is a small, box-like, panelled snug. Next to the snug is a double swing door, the entrance to that particular end of the house. Farther on is a shelf on which customers may rest their drinks. Underneath the windows is a cushioned seat. Behind the counter at Back can be seen the shelves running the whole length of the counter. On these shelves can be seen the end (or the beginning) of rows of bottles. The BARMAN *is seen wiping the part of the counter which is in view.* ROSIE *is standing at the counter toying with what remains of a half of whisky in a wine-glass. She is a sturdy, well-shaped girl of twenty; pretty, and pert in manner. She is wearing a cream blouse, with an obviously suggestive glad neck;*[1] *a grey tweed dress, brown stockings and shoes. The blouse and most of the dress are hidden by a black shawl. She has no hat, and in her hair is jauntily set a cheap, glittering, jewelled ornament. It is an hour later.*

BARMAN: (*Wiping counter*) Nothin' much doin' in your line tonight, Rosie?

ROSIE: Curse o' God on th' haporth, hardly, Tom. There isn't much notice taken of a pretty petticoat of a night like this.... They're all in a holy mood. Th' solemn-lookin' dials on th' whole o'

1. A low-cut neckline.

them an' they marchin' to th' meetin'. You'd think they were th' glorious company of th' saints, an' th' noble army of martyrs thrampin' through th' sthreets of paradise. They're all thinkin' of higher things than a girl's garthers.... It's a tremendous meetin'; four platforms they have — there's one o' them just outside opposite th' window.

BARMAN: Oh, ay; sure when th' speaker comes (*motioning with his hand*) to th' near end, here, you can see him plain, an' hear nearly everythin' he's spoutin' out of him.

ROSIE: It's no joke thryin' to make up fifty-five shillin's a week for your keep an' laundhry, an' then taxin' you a quid for your own room if you bring home a friend for th' night.... If I could only put by a couple of quid for a swankier outfit,[2] everythin' in th' garden ud look lovely —

BARMAN: Whisht, till we hear what he's sayin'.

Through the window is silhouetted the figure of a tall man who is speaking to the crowd. The BARMAN *and* ROSIE *look out of the window and listen.*

THE VOICE OF THE MAN: It is a glorious thing to see arms in the hands of Irishmen. We must accustom ourselves to the thought of arms, we must accustom ourselves to the sight of arms, we must accustom ourselves to the use of arms.... Bloodshed is a cleansing and sanctifying thing, and the nation that regards it as the final horror has lost its manhood.... There are many things more horrible than bloodshed, and slavery is one of them![3]

The figure moves away towards the Right, and is lost to sight and hearing.

ROSIE: It's th' sacred thruth, mind you, what that man's afther sayin'.

BARMAN: If I was only a little younger, I'd be plungin' mad into th' middle of it!

ROSIE: (*Who is still looking out of the window*) Oh, here's the two gems runnin' over again for their oil!

PETER *and* FLUTHER *enter tumultuously. They are hot, and full and hasty with the things they have seen and heard. Emotion is bubbling up in them, so that when they drink, and when they speak, they drink and speak with the fullness of emotional passion.* PETER *leads the way to the counter.*

PETER: (*Splutteringly to* BARMAN) Two halves... (*To* FLUTHER) A meetin' like this always makes me feel as if I could dhrink Loch Erinn dhry!

FLUTHER: You couldn't feel any way else at a time like this when th' spirit of a man is pulsin' to be out fightin' for th' thruth with his feet thremblin' on th' way, maybe to th' gallows, an' his ears tinglin' with th' faint, far-away sound of burstin' rifle-shots that'll maybe whip th' last little shock o' life out of him that's left lingerin' in his body!

PETER: I felt a burnin' lump in me throat when I heard th' band playin' 'The Soldiers' Song', rememberin' last hearin' it marchin' in military formation, with th' people starin' on both sides at us, carryin' with us th' pride an' resolution o' Dublin to th' grave of Wolfe Tone.[4]

FLUTHER: Get th' Dublin men goin' an' they'll go on full force for anything that's thryin' to bar them away from what they're wantin', where th' slim thinkin' counthry boyo ud limp away from th' first faintest touch of compromization!

PETER: (*Hurriedly to the* BARMAN) Two more, Tom! ... (*To* FLUTHER) Th' memory of all th' things that was done, an' all th' things that was suffered be th' people, was boomin' in me brain.... Every nerve in me body was quiverin' to do somethin' desperate!

FLUTHER: Jammed as I was in th' crowd, I listened to th' speeches pattherin' on th' people's head, like rain fallin' on th' corn; every derogatory thought went out o' me mind, an' I said to meself, 'You can die now, Fluther, for you've seen th' shadow-dhreams of th' past leppin' to life in th' bodies of livin' men that show, if we were without a titther[5] o' courage for centuries, we're vice versa now!' Looka here. (*He stretches out his arm under* PETER'S *face and rolls up his sleeve*) The blood was BOILIN' in me veins!

The silhouette of the tall figure again moves into the frame of the window speaking to the people.

PETER: (*unaware, in his enthusiasm, of the speaker's appearance, to* FLUTHER) I was burnin' to dhraw me sword, an' wave an' wave it over me —

FLUTHER: (*Overwhelming* PETER) Will you stop your blatherin' for a minute, man, an' let us hear what he's sayin'!

VOICE OF THE MAN: Comrade soldiers of the Irish Volunteers and of the Citizen Army, we

2. Finer, more stylish clothes.
3. From Patrick Pearse's speech *The Coming Revolution* (1913).

4. The grave of Wolfe Tone, father-figure of Irish republicanism, is at Bodenstown, Co. Kildare. It is regularly the scene of commemorations and speeches. Pearse spoke there in June 1913. 'The Soldier's Song', composed by Peadar Kearney in 1907, became the Irish national anthem after independence.
5. scrap, iota.

rejoice in this terrible war. The old heart of the earth needed to be warmed with the red wine of the battlefields.... Such august homage was never offered to God as this: the homage of millions of lives given gladly for love of country. And we must be ready to pour out the same red wine in the same glorious sacrifice, for without shedding of blood there is no redemption![6] (*The figure moves out of sight and hearing*)

FLUTHER: (*Gulping down the drink that remains in his glass, and rushing out*) Come on, man; this is too good to be missed!

PETER *finishes his drink less rapidly, and as he is going out wiping his mouth with the back of his hand he runs into* THE COVEY *coming in. He immediately erects his body like a young cock, and with his chin thrust forward, and a look of venomous dignity on his face, he marches out.*

THE COVEY: (*At counter*) Give us a glass o' malt,[7] for God's sake, till I stimulate meself from th' shock o' seein' th' sight that's afther goin' out!

ROSIE: (*All business, coming over to the counter, and standing near* THE COVEY) Another one for me, Tommy; (*To the* BARMAN) th' young gentleman's ordherin' it in th' corner of his eye.

The BARMAN *brings the drink for* THE COVEY, *and leaves it on the counter.* ROSIE *whips it up.*

BARMAN: Ay, houl' on there, houl' on there, Rosie!

ROSIE: (*To the* BARMAN) What are you houldin' on out o' you for? Didn't you hear th' young gentleman say that he couldn't refuse anything to a *nice little bird? (To* THE COVEY) Isn't that right, Jiggs? (THE COVEY *says nothing*) Didn't I know, Tommy, it would be all right? It takes Rosie to size a young man up, an' tell th' thoughts that are thremblin' in his mind. Isn't that right, Jiggs?

THE COVEY *stirs uneasily, moves a little farther away, and pulls his cap over his eyes.*

ROSIE: (*Moving after him*) Great meetin' that's gettin' held outside. Well, it's up to us all, anyway, to fight for our freedom.

THE COVEY: (*To* BARMAN) Two more, please. (*To* ROSIE) Freedom! What's th' use o' freedom, if it's not economic freedom?

ROSIE: (*Emphasizing with extended arm and moving finger*) I used them very words just before you come in. 'A lot o' thricksters,' says I, 'that wouldn't know what freedom was if they got it from their mother.' ... (*To* BARMAN) Didn't I, Tommy?

BARMAN: I disremember.

ROSIE: No, you don't disremember. Remember you said, yourself, it was all 'only a flash in th' pan.' Well, 'flash in th' pan, or no flash in th' pan,' says I, 'they're not goin' to get Rosie Redmond,' says I, 'to fight for freedom that wouldn't be worth winnin' in a raffle!'

THE COVEY: There's only one freedom for th' workin' man: conthrol o' th' means o' production, rates of exchange, an' th' means of disthribution. (*Tapping* ROSIE *on the shoulder*) Look here, comrade, I'll leave here tomorrow night for you a copy of Jenersky's *Thesis on the Origin, Development, an' Consolidation of the Evolutionary Idea of the Proletariat.*[8]

ROSIE: (*Throwing off her shawl on to the counter, and showing an exemplified glad neck, which reveals a good deal of a white bosom*) If y'ass Rosie, it's heart-breakin' to see a young fella thinkin' of anything, or admirin' anything, but silk thransparent stockin's showin' off the shape of a little lassie's legs!

THE COVEY, *frightened, moves a little away.*

ROSIE: (*Following on*) Out in th' park in th' shade of a warm summery evenin', with your little darlin' bridie to be, kissin' an' cuddlin' (*she tries to put her arm around his neck*), kissin' an' cuddlin', ay?

THE COVEY: (*Frightened*) Ay, what are you doin'? None o' that, now; none o' that. I've something else to do besides shinannickin' afther Judies![9]

He turns away, but ROSIE *follows, keeping face to face with him.*

ROSIE: Oh, little duckey, oh, shy little duckey! Never held a mot's[10] hand, an' wouldn't know how to tittle a little Judy! (*She clips him under the chin*) Tittle him undher th' chin, tittle him undher th' chin!

THE COVEY: (*Breaking away and running out*) Ay, go on, now; I don't want to have any meddlin' with a lassie like you!

6. Pearse, *Peace and the Gael* (1915), an article published in the magazine *Spark* in 1915. It is his most extravagant glorification of war and aroused the hostility of James Connolly, his socialist revolutionary partner in 1916 and one of O'Casey's mentors.
7. whiskey.

8. This mock-title shows O'Casey's disdain for (and ignorance of) the pedantic Marxist continental tradition represented by such men as Karl Kautsky (*The Proletarian Revolution and Its Programme*, 1924) and György Lukács (*Reification and the Consciousness of the Proletariat*, 1922). Few continental works were available in translation, but they carried their reputation for jargon before them.
9. i.e. running after girls.
10. young woman's.

ROSIE: (*Enraged*) Jasus, it's in a monasthery some of us ought to be, spendin' our holidays kneelin' on our adorers,[11] tellin' our beads, an' knockin' hell out of our buzzums![12]

THE COVEY: (*Outside*) Cuckoo-oo!

PETER *and* FLUTHER *come in again, followed by* MRS. GOGAN, *carrying a baby in her arms. They go over to the counter.*

PETER: (*With plaintive anger*) It's terrible that young Covey let me pass without proddin' at me! Did you hear him murmurin' 'cuckoo' when we were passin'?

FLUTHER: (*Irritably*) I wouldn't be everlastin' cockin' me ear to hear every little whisper that was floatin' about me! It's my rule never to lose me temper till it would be dethrimental to keep it. There's nothin' derogatory in th' use o' th' word 'cuckoo', is there?

PETER: (*Tearfully*) It's not th' word; it's th' way he says it: he never says it straight out, but murmurs it with curious quiverin' ripples, like variations on a flute!

FLUTHER: Ah, what odds if he gave it with variations on a thrombone! (*To* MRS. GOGAN) What's yours goin' to be, ma'am?

MRS GOGAN: Ah, a half o' malt,[13] Fluther.

FLUTHER: (*To* BARMAN) Three halves, Tommy.

The BARMAN *brings the drinks.*

MRS GOGAN: (*Drinking*) The Foresthers'[14] is a gorgeous dhress! I don't think I've seen nicer, mind you, in a pantomime.... Th' loveliest part of th' dhress, I think, is th' osthrichess plume.... When yous are goin' along, an' I see them wavin' an' noddin' an' waggin', I seem to be lookin' at each of yous hangin' at th' end of a rope, your eyes bulgin' an' your legs twistin' an' jerkin', gaspin' an' gaspin' for breath while yous are thryin' to die for Ireland!

FLUTHER: If any o' them is hangin' at the end of a rope, it won't be for Ireland!

PETER: Are you goin' to start th' young Covey's game o' proddin' an' twartin'[15] a man? There's not many that's talkin' can say that for twenty-five years he never missed a pilgrimage to Bodenstown!

FLUTHER: You're always blowin' about goin' to Bodenstown. D'ye think no one but yourself ever went to Bodenstown?

PETER: (*Plaintively*) I'm not blowin' about it; but there's not a year that I go there but I pluck a leaf off Tone's grave, an' this very day me prayer-book is nearly full of them.

FLUTHER: (*Scornfully*) Then Fluther has a vice versa opinion of them that put ivy leaves into their prayer-books,[16] scabbin'[17] it on th' clergy, an' thryin' to out-do th' haloes o' th' saints be lookin' as if he was wearin' around his head a glittherin' aroree boree allis![18] (*Fiercely*) Sure, I don't care a damn if you slep' in Bodenstown! You can take your breakfast, dinner, an' tea on th' grave in Bodenstown, if you like, for Fluther!

MRS GOGAN: Oh, don't start a fight, boys, for God's sake; I was only sayin' what a nice costume it is — nicer than th' kilts, for, God forgive me, I always think th' kilts is hardly decent.

FLUTHER: Ah, sure, when you'd look at him, you'd wondher whether th' man was makin' fun o' th' costume, or th' costume was makin' fun o' th' man!

BARMAN: Now, then, thry to speak asy, will yous? We don't want no shoutin' here.

THE COVEY *followed by* BESSIE BURGESS *comes in. They go over to the opposite end of the counter, and direct their gaze on the other group.*

THE COVEY: (*To* BARMAN) Two glasses o' malt.

PETER: There he is, now; I knew he wouldn't be long till he folleyed me in.

BESSIE: (*Speaking to* THE COVEY, *but really at the other party*) I can't for th' life o' me undherstand how they can call themselves Catholics, when they won't lift a finger to help poor little Catholic Belgium.[19]

MRS GOGAN: (*Raising her voice*) What about poor little Catholic Ireland?

BESSIE: (*Over to* MRS GOGAN) You mind your own business, ma'am, an stupefy your foolishness be gettin' dhrunk.

PETER: (*Anxiously*) Take no notice of her; pay no attention to her. She's just tormentin' herself

11. knees.
12. bosoms — that is, beating their breasts, while saying 'mea culpa' (my fault).
13. a glass of whiskey.
14. The Irish National Foresters was little more than a friendly society with patriotic leanings and a strikingly smart uniform. The Foresters Hall in Dublin's Parnell Square was used by the IRB in planning the rebellion.
15. thwarting.
16. The ivy leaf was a symbol or memento of Parnell, whom the clergy had opposed after his divorce case in 1890.
17. tricking, putting it on, pretending.
18. Aurora Borealis, the Northern Lights.
19. In the course of its recruiting drive in Ireland, British World War I propaganda made a great issue of the violation of catholic Belgium by the Hun.

towards havin' a row with somebody.

BESSIE: There's a storm of anger tossin' in me heart, thinkin' of all th' poor Tommies,[20] an' with them me own son, dhrenched in water an' soaked in blood, gropin' their way to a shattherin' death, in a shower o' shells! Young men with th' sunny lust o' life beamin' in them, layin' down their white bodies, shredded into torn an' bloody pieces, on th' althar that God Himelf has built for th' sacrifice of heroes!

MRS GOGAN: Isn't it a nice thing to have to be listenin' to a lassie an' hangin' our heads in a dead silence, knowin' that some persons think more of a ball of malt than they do of th' blessed saints.

FLUTHER: Whisht; she's always dangerous an' derogatory when she's well oiled. Th' safest way to hindher her from havin' any enjoyment out of her spite, is to dip our thoughts into the fact of her bein' a female person that has moved out of th' sight of ordinary sensible people.

BESSIE: To look at some o' th' women that's knockin' about, now, is a thing to make a body sigh.... A woman on her own, dhrinkin' with a bevy o' men, is hardly an example to her sex.... A woman dhrinkin' with a woman is one thing, an' a woman dhrinkin' with herself is still a woman — flappers[21] may be put in another category altogether — but a middle-aged married woman makin' herself th' centre of a circle of men is as a woman that is loud an' stubborn, whose feet abideth not in her own house.[22]

THE COVEY: (*To* BESSIE) When I think of all th' problems in front o' th' workers, it makes me sick to be lookin' at oul' codgers goin' about dhressed up like green-accountred figures gone asthray out of a toyshop!

PETER: Gracious God, give me patience to be listenin' to that blasted young Covey proddin' at me from over at th' other end of th' shop!

MRS GOGAN: (*Dipping her finger in the whisky, and moistening with it the lips of her baby*) Cissie Gogan's a woman livin' for nigh on twenty-five years in her own room, an' beyond biddin' th' time o' day to her neighbours, never yet as much as nodded her head in th' direction of other people's business, while she knows some as are never content unless they're standin' senthry over other people'd doin's!

BESSIE *is about to reply, when the tall, dark figure is again silhouetted against the window, and the voice of the speaker is heard speaking passionately.*

VOICE OF SPEAKER: The last sixteen months have been the most glorious in the history of Europe. Heroism has come back to the earth. War is a terrible thing, but war is not an evil thing. People in Ireland dread war because they do not know it. Ireland has not known the exhilaration of war for over a hundred years. When war comes to Ireland she must welcome it as she would welcome the Angel of God![23]

The figure passes out of sight and hearing.

THE COVEY: (*Towards all present*) Dope, dope. There's only one war worth havin': th' war for th' economic emancipation of th' proletariat.

BESSIE: They may crow away out o' them; but it ud be fitther for some o' them to mend their ways, an' cease from havin' scouts out watchin' for th' comin' of th' Saint Vincent de Paul man,[24] for fear they'd be nailed lowerin' a pint of beer, mockin' th' man with an angel face, shinin' with th' glamour of deceit an' lies!

MRS GOGAN: An' a certain lassie standin' stiff behind her own door with her ears cocked listenin' to what's being said, stuffed till she's sthrained with envy of a neighbour thryin' for a few little things that may be got be hard sthrivin' to keep up to th' letther an' th' law, an' th' practices of th' Church!

PETER: (*To* MRS GOGAN) If I was you, Mrs Gogan, I'd parry her jabbin' remarks be a powerful silence that'll keep her tantalizin' words from penethratin' into your feelin's. It's always betther to leave these people to th' vengeance o' God!

BESSIE: Bessie Burgess doesn't put up to know much, never havin' a swaggerin' mind, thanks be to God, but goin' on packin' up knowledge accordin' to her conscience: precept upon precept, line upon line; here a little, an' there a little. But (*with a passionate swing of her shawl*), thanks be to Christ, she knows when she was got, where she was got, an' how she was got; while there's some she knows, decoratin' their finger with a well-polished weddin'

20. British soldiers.

21. Contemporary slang for frivolous and unconventional young women.

22. Proverbs 7.11.

23. Pearse, *Peace and the Gael*. This was an article, not a speech.

24. A man from the catholic charitable society of St Vincent de Paul, who checked the conditions of those who were in receipt of the society's money.

ring, would be hard put to it if they were assed to show their weddin' lines!

MRS GOGAN: (*Plunging out into the centre of the floor in a wild tempest of hysterical rage*) Y' oul' rip of a blasted liar, me weddin' ring's been well earned be twenty years be th' side o' me husband, now takin' his rest in heaven, married to me be Father Dempsey, in th' Chapel o' Saint Jude's, in th' Christmas Week of eighteen hundhred an' ninety-five; an' any kid, livin' or dead, that Jinnie Gogan's had since, was got between th' bordhers of th' Ten Commandments! ... An' that's more than some o' you can say that are kep' from th' dhread o' desthruction be a few drowsy virtues, that th' first whisper of temptation lulls into a sleep, that'll know one sin from another only on th' day of their last anointin', an' that use th' innocent light o' th' shinin' stars to dip into th' sins of a night's diversion!

BESSIE: (*Jumping out to face* MRS GOGAN, *and bringing the palms of her hands together in sharp claps to emphasize her remarks*) Liar to you, too, ma'am, y' oul' hardened thresspasser on other people's good nature, wizenin' up your soul in th' arts o' dodgeries, till every dhrop of respectability in a female is dhried up in her, lookin' at your ready-made manoeuverin' with th' menkind!

BARMAN: Here, there; here, there; speak asy there. No rowin' here, no rowin' here, now.

FLUTHER: (*Trying to calm* MRS GOGAN) Now Jinnie, Jinnie, it's a derogatory thing to be smirchin' a night like this with a row; it's rompin' with th' feelin's of hope we ought to be, instead o' bein' vice versa!

PETER: (*Trying to quiet* BESSIE) I'm terrible dawny,[25] Mrs Burgess, an' a fight leaves me weak for a long time afterwards.... Please, Mrs. Burgess, before there's damage done, thry to have a little respect for yourself.

BESSIE: (*With a push of her hand that sends* PETER *tottering to the end of the shop*) G'way, you little sermonizing, little yella-faced, little consequential, little pudgy, little bum, you!

MRS GOGAN: (*Screaming*) Fluther, leggo! I'm not goin' to keep an unresistin' silence, an' her scattherin' her festherin' words in me face, stirrin' up every dhrop of decency in a respectable female, with her restless rally o' lies that would make a saint say his prayer backwards!

25. weak, feeble.

BESSIE: (*Shouting*) Ah, everybody knows well that th' best charity that can be shown to you is to hide th' thruth as much as our thrue worship of God Almighty will allow us!

MRS GOGAN: (*Frantically*) Here, houl' th' kid, one o' yous; houl' th' kid for a minute! There's nothin' for it but to show this lassie a lesson or two.... (*To* PETER) Here, houl' th' kid, you. (*Before* PETER *is aware of it, she places the infant in his arms*) (*To* BESSIE, *standing before her in a fighting attitude*) Come on, now, me loyal lassie, dyin' with grief for little Catholic Belgium! When Jinnie Gogan's done with you, you'll have a little leisure lyin' down to think an' pray for your king an' counthry!

BARMAN: (*Coming from behind the counter, getting between the women, and proceeding to push them towards the door*) Here, now, since yous can't have a little friendly argument quietly, you'll get out o' this place in quick time. Go on, an' settle your differences somewhere else — I don't want to have another endorsement on me licence.[26]

PETER: (*Anxiously, over to* MRS GOGAN) Here, take your kid back, ower this. How nicely I was picked, now, for it to be plumped into me arms!

THE COVEY: She knew who she was givin' it to, maybe.

PETER: (*Hotly to* THE COVEY) Now, I'm givin' you fair warnin', me young Covey, to quit firin' your jibes an' jeers at me.... For one o' these days, I'll run out in front o' God Almighty an' take your sacred life!

BARMAN: (*Pushing* BESSIE *out after* MRS GOGAN) Go on, now; out you go.

BESSIE: (*As she goes out*) If you think, me lassie, that Bessie Burgess has an untidy conscience, she'll soon show you to th' differ!

PETER: (*Leaving the baby down on the floor*) Ay, be Jasus, wait there, till I give her back her youngster! (*He runs to the door*) Ay, there, ay! (*He comes back*) There, she's afther goin' without her kid. What are we goin' to do with it, now?

THE COVEY: What are we goin' to do with it? Bring it outside an' show everybody what you're afther findin'!

PETER: (*In a panic to* FLUTHER) Pick it up, you, Fluther, an' run afther her with it, will you?

26. A legal stamp that indicated an infraction of the licensing laws. Too many endorsements would lead to a withdrawal of the licence to sell liquor.

FLUTHER: What d'ye take Fluther for? You must think Fluther's a right gom.[27] D'ye think Fluther's like yourself, destitute of a titther of undherstandin'?

BARMAN: (*Imperatively to* PETER) Take it up, man, an' run out afther her with it, before she's gone too far. You're not goin' to leave th' bloody thing here, are you?

PETER: (*Plaintively, as he lifts up the baby*) Well, God Almighty, give me patience with all th' scorners, tormentors, an' twarters that are always an' ever thryin' to goad me into prayin' for their blindin' an' blastin' an' burnin' in th' world to come! (*He goes out*)

FLUTHER: God, it's a relief to get rid o' that crowd. Women is terrible when they start to fight. There's no holdin' them back. (*To* THE COVEY) Are you goin' to have anything?

THE COVEY: Ah, I don't mind if I have another half.

FLUTHER: (*To* BARMAN) Two more, Tommy, me son.

The BARMAN *gets the drinks.*

You know, there's no conthrollin' a woman when she loses her head.

ROSIE *enters and goes over to the counter on the side nearest to* FLUTHER.

ROSIE: (*To* BARMAN) Divil a use o' havin' a thrim little leg on a night like this; things was never worse.... Give us a half till tomorrow, Tom, duckey.

BARMAN: (*Coldly*) No more tonight, Rosie; you owe me for three already.

ROSIE: (*Combatively*) You'll be paid, won't you?

BARMAN: I hope so.

ROSIE: You hope so! Is that th' way with you, now?

FLUTHER: (*To* BARMAN) Give her one; it'll be all right.

ROSIE: (*Clapping* FLUTHER *on the back*) Oul' sport!

FLUTHER: Th' meetin' should be soon over, now.

THE COVEY: Th' sooner th' betther. It's all a lot o' blasted nonsense, comrade.

FLUTHER: Oh, I wouldn't say it was all nonsense. Afther all, Fluther can remember th' time, an' him only a dawny chiselur,[28] bein' taught at his mother's knee to be faithful to th' Shan Van Vok![29]

THE COVEY: That's all dope, comrade; th' sort o' thing that workers are fed on be th' Boorzwawze.[30]

FLUTHER: (*A little sharply*) What's all dope? Though I'm sayin' it that shouldn't: (*catching his cheek with his hand, and pulling down the flesh from the eye*) d'ye see that mark there, undher me eye?... A sabre slice from a dragoon in O'Connell Street! (*Thrusting his head forward towards* ROSIE) Feel that dint in th' middle o' me nut!

ROSIE: (*Rubbing* FLUTHER's *head, and winking at* THE COVEY) My God, there's a holla![31]

FLUTHER: (*Putting on his hat with quiet pride*) A skelp from a bobby's baton at a Labour meetin' in th' Phoenix Park!

THE COVEY: He must ha' hitten you in mistake. I don't know what you ever done for th' Labour movement.

FLUTHER: (*Loudly*) D'ye not? Maybe, then, I done as much, an' know as much about th' Labour movement as th' chancers[32] that are blowin' about it!

BARMAN: Speak easy, Fluther, thry to speak easy.

THE COVEY: There's no necessity to get excited about it, comrade.

FLUTHER: (*More loudly*) Excited? Who's gettin' excited? There's no one gettin' excited! It would take something more than a thing like you to flutther a feather o' Fluther. Blatherin', an', when all is said, you know as much as th' rest in th' wind up!

THE COVEY: Well, let us put it to th' test, then, an' see what you know about th' Labour movement: what's the mechanism of exchange?

FLUTHER: (*Roaring, because he feels he is beaten*) How th' hell do I know what it is? There's nothin' about that in th' rules of our Thrades Union!

BARMAN: For God's sake, thry to speak easy, Fluther.

THE COVEY: What does Karl Marx say about th' Relation of Value to th' Cost o' Production?

FLUTHER: (*Angrily*) What th' hell do I care what he says? I'm Irishman enough not to lose me head be follyin' foreigners!

BARMAN: Speak easy, Fluther.

27. fool.
28. young boy.
29. Shean Bhean Bhoct, Poor Old Woman (Ireland).
30. bourgeoisie.
31. hollow.
32. rascals, pretenders.

THE COVEY: It's only waste o' time talkin' to you, comrade.

FLUTHER: Don't be comradin' me, mate. I'd be on me last legs if I wanted you for a comrade.

ROSIE: (*To* THE COVEY) It seems a highly rediculous thing to hear a thing that's only an inch or two away from a kid, swingin' heavy words about he doesn't know th' meanin' of, an' uppishly thryin' to down a man like Misther Fluther here, that's well flavoured in th' knowledge of th' world he's livin' in.

THE COVEY: (*Savagely to* ROSIE) Nobody's askin' you to be buttin' in with your prate.... I have you well taped,[33] me lassie.... Just you keep your opinions for your own place.... It'll be a long time before th' Covey takes any insthructions or reprimandin' from a prostitute!

ROSIE: (*Wild with humiliation*) You louse, you louse, you! ... You're no man.... You're no man ... I'm a woman, anyhow, an' if I'm a prostitute aself, I have me feelin's.... Thryin' to put his arm around me a minute ago, an' givin' me th' glad eye,[34] th' little wrigglin' lump o' desolation turns on me now, because he saw there was nothin' doin'.... You louse, you! If I was a man, or you were a woman, I'd bate th' puss o' you![35]

BARMAN: Ay, Rosie, ay! You'll have to shut your mouth altogether, if you can't learn to speak easy!

FLUTHER: (*To* ROSIE) Houl' on there, Rosie; houl' on there. There's no necessity to flutther yourself when you're with Fluther.... Any lady that's in th' company of Fluther is goin' to get a fair hunt.... This is outside your province.... I'm not goin' to let you demean yourself be talkin' to a tittherin' chancer.... Leave this to Fluther — this is a man's job. (*To* THE COVEY) Now, if you've anything to say, say it to Fluther, an', let me tell you, you're not goin' to be pass-remarkable[36] to any lady in my company.

THE COVEY: Sure I don't care if you were runnin' all night afther your Mary o' th' Curlin' Hair,[37] but, when you start tellin' luscious lies about what you done for th' Labour movement, it's nearly time to show y'up!

FLUTHER: (*Fiercely*) Is it you show Fluther up? G'way, man, I'd beat two o' you before me breakfast!

THE COVEY: (*Contemptuously*) Tell us where you bury your dead, will you?

FLUTHER: (*With his face stuck into the face of* THE COVEY) Sing a little less on th' high note, or, when I'm done with you, you'll put a Christianable consthruction on things, I'm tellin' you!

THE COVEY: You're a big fella, you are.

FLUTHER: (*Tapping* THE COVEY *threateningly on the shoulder*) Now, you're temptin' Providence when you're temptin' Fluther!

THE COVEY: (*Losing his temper, and bawling*) Easy with them hands, there, easy with them hands! You're startin' to take a little risk when you commence to paw the Covey!

FLUTHER *suddenly springs into the middle of the shop, flings his hat into the corner, whips off his coat, and begins to paw the air.*

FLUTHER: (*Roaring at the top of his voice*) Come on, come on, you lowser;[38] put your mits up now, if there's a man's blood in you! Be God, in a few minutes you'll see some snots flyin' around, I'm tellin' you.... When Fluther's done with you, you'll have a vice versa opinion of him! Come on, now, come on!

BARMAN: (*Running from behind the counter and catching hold of* THE COVEY) Here, out you go, me little bowsey.[39] Because you got a couple o' halves you think you can act as you like. (*He pushes* THE COVEY *to the door*) Fluther's a friend o' mine, an' I'll not have him insulted.

THE COVEY: (*Struggling with the* BARMAN) Ay, leggo, leggo there; fair hunt, give a man a fair hunt! One minute with him is all I ask; one minute alone with him, while you're runnin' for th' priest an' th' doctor.

FLUTHER: (*To the* BARMAN) Let him go, let him go, Tom: let him open th' door to sudden death if he wants to!

BARMAN: (*To* THE COVEY) Go on, out you go an' do th' bowsey somewhere else. (*He pushes* THE COVEY *out and comes back*)

ROSIE: (*Getting* FLUTHER's *hat as he is putting on his coat*) Be God, you put th' fear o' God in his heart that time! I thought you'd have to be dug out of him.... Th' way you lepped out without any of

33. I have taken your measure.
34. A lustful, enticing glance.
35. beat the face off you.
36. not going to pass insulting remarks.
37. Reference to a standard figure in a traditional love song.
38. louse, good-for-nothing.
39. A bowsey is a tough, a pugnacious young man.

your fancy side-steppin'! 'Men like Fluther,' say I to meself, 'is gettin' scarce nowadays.'

FLUTHER: (*With proud complacency*) I wasn't goin' to let meself be malignified by a chancer.... He got a little bit too derogatory for Fluther.... Be God, to think of a cur like that comin' to talk to a man like me!

ROSIE: (*Fixing on his hat*) Did j'ever!

FLUTHER: He's lucky he got off safe. I hit a man last week, Rosie, an' he's fallin' yet!

ROSIE: Sure, you'd ha' broken him in two if you'd ha' hitten him one clatther![40]

FLUTHER: (*Amorously, putting his arm around* ROSIE) Come on into th' snug, me little darlin', an' we'll have a few dhrinks before I see you home.

ROSIE: Oh, Fluther, I'm afraid you're a terrible man for th' women.

They go into the snug as CLITHEROE, CAPTAIN BRENNAN *and* LIEUT. LANGON *of the Irish Volunteers enter hurriedly.* CAPTAIN BRENNAN *carries the banner of The Plough and the Stars, and* LIEUT. LANGON *a green, white, and orange Tri-colour.*[41] *They are in a state of emotional excitement. Their faces are flushed and their eyes sparkle; they speak rapidly, as if unaware of the meaning of what they said. They have been mesmerized by the fervency of the speeches.*

CLITHEROE: (*Almost pantingly*) Three glasses o' port!

The BARMAN *brings the drinks.*

CAPT. BRENNAN: We won't have long to wait now.

LIEUT. LANGON: Th' time is rotten ripe for revolution.

CLITHEROE: You have a mother, Langon.

LIEUT. LANGON: Ireland is greater than a mother.

CAPT. BRENNAN: You have a wife, Clitheroe.

CLITHEROE: Ireland is greater than a wife.

LIEUT. LANGON: Th' time for Ireland's battle is now — th' place for Ireland's battle is here.

The tall, dark figure again is silhouetted against the window. The three men pause and listen.

VOICE OF THE MAN: Our foes are strong, but strong as they are, they cannot undo the miracles of God, who ripens in the heart of young men the seeds sown by the young men of a former generation. They think they have pacified Ireland; think they have foreseen everything; think they have provided against everything; but the fools, the fools, the fools! — they have left us our Fenian dead, and, while Ireland holds these graves, Ireland, unfree, shall never be at peace![42]

CAPT. BRENNAN: (*Catching up The Plough and the Stars*) Imprisonment for th' Independence of Ireland!

LIEUT. LANGON: (*Catching up the Tri-colour*) Wounds for th' Independence of Ireland!

CLITHEROE: Death for th' Independence of Ireland!

THE THREE: (*Together*) So help us God!

They drink. A bugle blows the Assembly. They hurry out. A pause. FLUTHER *and* ROSIE *come out of the snug;* ROSIE *is linking* FLUTHER, *who is a little drunk. Both are in a merry mood.*

ROSIE: Come on home, ower o' that, man. Are you afraid or what? Are you goin' to come home, or are you not?

FLUTHER: Of course I'm goin' home. What ud ail me that I wouldn't go?

ROSIE: (*Lovingly*) Come on, then, oul' sport.

OFFICER'S VOICE: (*Giving command outside*) Irish Volunteers, by th' right, quick march!

ROSIE: (*Putting her arm round* FLUTHER *and singing*)

I once had a lover, a tailor, but he could do
  nothin' for me,
An' then I fell in with a sailor as strong an' as
  wild as th' sea.
We cuddled an' kissed with devotion, till th'
  night from th' mornin' had fled;
An' there, to our joy, a bright bouncin' boy
Was dancin' a jig in th' bed!

Dancin' a jig in th' bed, an' bawlin' for butther
  an' bread.
An' there, to our joy, a bright bouncin' boy
Was dancin' a jig in th' bed!

They go out with their arms round each other.

CLITHEROE'S VOICE: (*In command outside*) Dublin Battalion of the Irish Citizen Army, by th' right, quick march!

40. clatter, blow.
41. The flag of the Irish Citizen Army.
42. From Pearse's funeral oration at the graveside of the Fenian leader, Jeremiah O'Donovan Rossa, on 1 August 1915 (see p. 294).

GEORGE SHIELS

(1886-1949)

from:
THE PASSING DAY (1936)

[As John Fibbs lies dying in hospital, the play re-enacts his last day in his general store. A weakening in his avaricious nature and his fantasy of going on 'the longest cruise in the world' forebode the heart attack which will bring on his final illness. In the following scenes, the cruise, a painfully jocose sexuality, a plot to undo Tom Looney that loses direction, a dialogue toying with 'life' and 'mortality' all convey his decline, culminating in his grotesque dying words. In a more flattened dialect than Ervine's, Shiels brings his aloof observation to bear on the ethos of small-town life in Northern Ireland.

The play was first performed at the Abbey on 13 April 1936.]

CHARACTERS from SCENES IV, V and VI

JOHN FIBBS
PETER FIBBS, *his son*
NURSE
TOM LOONEY
MRS. FIBBS
DAW
DOCTOR

from SCENE IV

John Fibb's store

JOHN: (*Pleased*) Do you think so now? (*Rubs his hands*) I was in hospital one time for a week — oh, long ago — and the nurses were all very kind to me.

NURSE:[1] They couldn't help it, you're such a nice man.

JOHN: Are you telling tickets, Nurse?

NURSE: I was trying to, but this nephew of yours is as hard as nails.

JOHN: Och, Peter, buy a ticket! Don't be stubborn. It's for a good cause.

PETER: Too dear ... seven-and-six.[2]

JOHN: Nonsense! I don't know what the young men are coming to. Give me a ticket, Nurse, if you please. (*Pays for it*)

NURSE: Mr. Fibbs, you're a great gentleman! Thank you very much.

JOHN: Not at all. It's for a good cause. Look at the service the Red Cross rendered in France. I remember at a public meeting in war-time, as Chairman I paid a glowing tribute to the work of the Red Cross in France.

NURSE: That speech has lived. I've heard all about it.... Peter, you'll never be as fine a man as your uncle. Do you hear?

PETER: I'm hearing nothing else ... all the time.

NURSE: It's true.

PETER: If you could do something for that pain in his side, 'twould suit him better than flattery.

NURSE: What pain?

JOHN: In my left side, Nurse ... all about the heart.

NURSE: Yes, you do look rather tired. How long has it been troubling you?

PETER: Hold on! If you're going to start vetting him, I'll get.[3] (*He goes*)

JOHN: It's troubled me for years, Nurse, off and on, but it's worse now.

NURSE: It's this heat wave. You ought to see the Doctor. A man like you can't afford to take risks, and we can't afford to lose you. You're the only gentleman of any public spirit in this town.

JOHN: That's true, Nurse, I never spared myself. I think I overstrained myself during the war at public meetings.

NURSE: Quite likely. I know several who did.... Let me take your pulse.

JOHN: Thanks. Will I put off my coat?

NURSE: No, don't trouble.... Let your hand relax. (*Takes his pulse with her wristlet watch*) Yes, your heart's a bit rocky.

JOHN: Is that dangerous, Nurse?

NURSE: Not terribly.... Have you had a stimulant this morning — an aspirin or anything?

JOHN: You won't mention this, Nurse. I took a little spirits with a friend, I was feeling rather weak.

NURSE: You did the right thing. Nothing better.

JOHN: Of course, I never touch it.

1 The nurse is a cautious ally of Peter.
2. seven shillings and sixpence, about 37 pence in present currency.
3. i.e. get going.

NURSE: We all know that. Have you had a holiday this year?

JOHN: Not yet, Nurse. I've been awful busy. I think I'll take a long sea cruise —

NURSE: Excellent! the longer the better.

JOHN: Away to the Amazon, about ten weeks on the water. A gentleman friend is going with me —

NURSE: Bosh![4] what you want — to make a job of it — is a good nurse. I wish I were going with you!

JOHN: My goodness, that would be a holiday! Of course, you couldn't get off duty, Nurse.

NURSE: Oh, you never know. Where there's a will there's a way.

JOHN: I'd pay your salary and all expenses. You could take my pulse every day, and see that all was right.

NURSE: What would Mrs. Fibbs say?

JOHN: What could she say — if the Doctor ordered it?

NURSE: I'm afraid the Doctor wouldn't order me, worse luck.

JOHN: Well, it's a pity! It's a mortal pity. Life'd be worth living.

NURSE: Wouldn't it? A poem. But when 'twas all over we'd have to crawl back to the old grindstone.

JOHN: Why should we ever come back at all, if we liked it over there? A fine climate, and good health, we could live as cheap there as here.

NURSE: And no public opinion.

JOHN: (*Laughs, an unearthly sort of noise*) My goodness, you're a bright creature! If I was thirty years younger, nothing would stop me. I'd walk away and leave the shop-door open. Let all go to pot.

NURSE: I wish Peter'd a bit of your pluck. I've been trying for ages to get friendly with him, but he won't give a spark.

JOHN: Ach, him! he's hopeless. Only an old woman. I'm at him all the time to tighten up and be a man.

NURSE: Well, the crack's[5] good, but I must tear myself away. (*Shaking hands*) Don't forget about the Amazon. If you can fix it up with the Doctor, I'm game.

JOHN: My goodness! talk about a cruise! (*Puts his arm round her shoulders*) We'd sit all day long on the upper deck, and get all sunburnt.

NURSE: Yes, and at night the big silver moon. By the way, can you play the banjo?

JOHN: No, but I could soon learn. I'm awful fond of music.

NURSE: Never mind. The ship's band'll do as well.

JOHN: Ten weeks on the salt water!

NURSE: With the blue sky over us.

JOHN: A thousand miles away from work and worry!

NURSE: (*Freeing herself gently*) Now if you go on like that — we'll both run away to sea, whether the Doctor orders it or not! (*She goes out: a hand clapped over her mouth, to keep from laughing*)

JOHN: Goodness gracious me! (*Walks about*) Divorce should be made easier . . . and cheaper! . . . .

from SCENE V

The Same

. . . JOHN: (*Producing a small packet*) Have a cigarette, Looney.

LOONEY: (*Takes one*) I didn't think ye smoked, John.

JOHN: Neither I do, Tom. I neither smoke nor drink. (*Lights one*)

LOONEY: Neither do I. (*Lights one*)

JOHN: I soon put Black[1] in his corner, Looney. Says I, Tom Looney's my old friend and neighbour, and if you touch him you touch me.

LOONEY: Sure, I seen it all when I come in. Black hadn't a word to say, nor the face to look up. No jumpin' about over here!

JOHN: He knew better — he knew I'd my eye on him. Says I, I've known Tom Looney for a lifetime, and I won't allow you — or any other man — to lay him on the street. Says I, remember that, Mr. Black.

LOONEY: That 'ud bring him to his senses.

JOHN: Says I, if you push Looney too hard you needn't come back to this town. I'll boycott you all over the place. Then he drew in his horns and said, 'I'll do anything for you, Mr. Fibbs. What do you suggest?' And I said, 'Give Looney another month, and I'll see that all's right.'

LOONEY: I say, I'm proud of ye! He badgered me for over an hour. 'A writ,' says he, 'or a cheque!' Mad as a bull.

4. Rubbish!
5. chat, gossip, conversation.

1. A travelling salesman.

JOHN: He didn't badger me, Looney. . . . If you're ever in a tight corner, Tom, come to me. I'm always here.

LOONEY: Man, if I just had fifty pounds ready money, 'twould put me on my feet. Firm as a rock.

JOHN: I'd like to help you, Looney. You know I would. Don't you know that, Tom?

LOONEY: I do, John. May I never forget ye! You're the only friend I have. Them other fellows 'ud rather see me in the gutter.

JOHN: Yah! that miserable crew! I could buy up the whole lot and never miss it. . . . If I give you fifty pounds, Looney, will you pay it back in three months?

LOONEY: I'll give an IOU.

JOHN: Blazes! I want no IOU. Tom Looney's word of honour is good enough for me. Come over tomorrow morning, Tom.

LOONEY: Man, if you could spare it now! Peter'd be around here in the morning. . . .

JOHN: Wait a minute. Peter left some cash in this drawer. (*Opens drawer*) Lots of money here, Tom. . . . Ten, twenty, thirty, forty, fifty. . . . Put that in your pocket, Tom.

LOONEY: (*Overcome, but pockets the money*) Old — friend . . . old . . . neighbour. May — may I never forget ye! (*Sobs a bit*)

JOHN: Ach, for God's sake, Looney, stop that nonsense. What's fifty pounds to me? Not that! (*Cracks fingers*) Dry your eyes and hold out your glass. . . .

LOONEY: (*Sniffing*) No more! I say, no more for me. The wife'd smell it.

JOHN: My goodness, the bottle's empty! No outcome in them round bottles. Could you get me another bottle, Looney?

LOONEY: Me? No, in sowl,[2] I could not! If I was seen going in to buy whiskey — 'twould ruin me.

JOHN: I've to go to the hotel for dinner. I must have another drink, to make me eat.

LOONEY: Sure, you can get a half'un[3] in the hotel bar; no remarks passed there.

JOHN: Too long to wait, Tom. You must get me a bottle.

LOONEY: I tell ye — blunt — I can't do it! It's easy for you — your wife's away, but mine's over there across the street.

JOHN: What's your wife got to do with it? Are you not master in your own house?

LOONEY: In sowl, I am not!

JOHN: That's bad, Looney. You should be master in your own house. The day we were married, I told the wife, plump and plain, I'll be master in my own house! From that to this she never dared to contradict me.

LOONEY: I say, that was the time to lay down the law — at the outset. After that, d'ye see, it's too late.

JOHN: Tom Looney, could you keep a secret?

LOONEY: Me? to be sure. I'm a close one.

JOHN: I'd mention this to no living man but you, Tom. D'ye know that red-haired Nurse?

LOONEY: I do, well . . . a fine girl. I say, a smasher.

JOHN: She and I are going on a long sea cruise. Away to the Amazon . . . ten weeks on the water.

LOONEY: (*His eyes popping*) Didn't I see her in here this morning?

JOHN: You did. We settled all the details this morning.

LOONEY: I say, gimme the hand! (*Shaking*) It's a bold undertaking. I say, a first-class adventure! It's like something you'd see in *Thompson's Weekly*.

JOHN: You'll never mention it, Looney.

LOONEY: No damn fear! I wouldn't name it in this town for a thousand pounds.

JOHN: Well, I must have a drink. Dan Kelly left in a bottle of poteen[4] — to rub the pains with. Will you try a shot of it?

LOONEY: For the love o' God, talk sense! A shot o' Kelly's poteen 'ud lay ye out as stiff as a corpse.

JOHN: Is it that strong?

LOONEY: I tell ye 'twould take the four feet from a horse! But I'll tell ye a plan. Make hot punch, and put a slice o' lemon and two cloves in it. Then rowl into bed, d'ye see? You'll have no pains the next morning. It cured me.

JOHN: Well, I must try it tonight. I think I'll write some letters now. You can go, Tom.

LOONEY: Before I go — did you look at them papers?

JOHN: I did — examined them very carefully. You won't have to pay a penny. I'll dictate a letter tomorrow morning . . . get you off scot-free.

LOONEY: I say, no wonder you got on in the world. You're a gifted man. You're the brains. (*Gathers up papers*) I'll go now and let you get on with your work. (*Shaking hands*) Old friend, old

2. in soul, absolutely.
3. i.e. a half glass of whiskey.
4. An illicit spirit, often distilled from potatoes.

neighbour, may I never forget ye! Good-bye.

JOHN: Good-bye, Tom. I'll see you tomorrow.

LOONEY: (*Turns at door and, unconsciously, has a last look at* JOHN) Good-bye again, John!

JOHN: Good-bye, Tom.

LOONEY *goes.* JOHN *prepares a dose of poteen and soda.*

from SCENE VI

The Hospital

... MRS FIBBS *and* DAW *come in — he with attaché case.*

MRS FIBBS: My husband is in no condition at present to make a will, Mr. Daw!

DAW: Isn't that a matter for the Doctor? Your husband told me to come back.

MRS FIBBS: My husband isn't responsible. I'm satisfied with whatever arrangements he made today. It's Peter that wants the new will.

PETER: It is not, Aunt. I'm quite content with the old one.

DAW: How is he, Nurse?

NURSE: No change, Mr Daw. One moment talking, and the next drowsy.

DAW: Is he sleeping now?

NURSE: I'll just see. (*Goes to the bedside*) Are you sleeping?

JOHN: (*With a jerk*) You, Rachel! ... I knew you'd come, Rachel.... A good sister to me.

MRS FIBBS: You hear that, Mr Daw? His mind's wandering. He thinks the Nurse is his sister Rachel from Scotland. That man's in no condition to make a new will! I'll contest it....

NURSE: Hush!

JOHN: I left you everything, Rachel ... forty thousand pounds....

MRS FIBBS: Judgement of God!

JOHN: Five pounds to the wife ... five to Peter ... the rest to you, Rachel.... Don't sell Imperial Chemicals.... (*He settles down in the bed*)

NURSE: (*Her finger on his pulse*) Where's the Doctor?

DAW: He'll be here in a moment, Nurse.

NURSE: (*Pause*) Please go and fetch him, Mr Daw....

DOCTOR *comes in.*

DOC: Well?

MRS FIBBS: Save him, Doctor! Save him — for God's sake! if only for a few minutes....

DOC: (*After a moment's examination*) I'm afraid it's too late. He's gone.

MR DAW *shuts his little case with a snap and leaves the room.*

ST JOHN G. ERVINE

(1883-1971)

from: MIXED MARRIAGE (1911)

[Ervine's early plays for the Abbey introduced the North into its dramatic repertoire. He chose controversial subjects and treated them in a dramatic speech founded upon popular idiom. In this instance, John Rainey has agreed to muster protestant support for a strike led by the catholic Michael O'Hara, but withdraws on learning that his son, Hugh, is to marry a catholic girl, Nora. Michael too wants the engagement to be broken, for it threatens the strike. Nora stands firm. Rioting breaks out and Nora is killed when the British army opens fire on a mob outside Rainey's house. There is little difference in the conversations in Acts I and II. The same debates rage and the comic moments add a little to the discriminations the play seeks to make.

Ervine's dialogue is an authentic rendering of Belfast vernacular, and *Mixed Marriage* the first play on the political tensions that have continued to occupy Northern dramatists. The play was first produced at the Abbey on 30 March 1911 by Lennox Robinson.]

CHARACTERS

JOHN RAINEY
MRS RAINEY, *his wife*
TOM RAINEY } *his sons*
HUGH RAINEY }

NORA MURRAY
MICHAEL O'HARA

The scene is laid in the kitchen of a workman's home midway between the Falls Road and the Shankill Road, Belfast, in the year 1904.

from ACT 3

. . . RAINEY: A belave that man Hart's[1] right.

MICHAEL: What!

RAINEY: A belave he's right. It is a Papish plot, the strack.[2] How can A belave anythin' else whin A see it goin' on in me own house. Me son taken thrum[3] me be a Papish wumman!

MICHAEL: Aw, man, ye don't mane that?

RAINEY: A do.

MICHAEL: Ye'll not ondo iv'rything fur the sake o' that?

RAINEY: A'll do no more. A've done wi' it all. A'm not goin' till the Or'nge Hall the night.[4]

MICHAEL: Aw, but ye've promised.

MRS RAINEY: Ye can't go back on yer word.

RAINEY: A can, an' A will.

HUGH: It's a mane thing t' do. Ye think ye'll stap Nora an' me thrum marryin' acause o' the strack, but ye wun't.

NORA: Aw, A nivir thought o' that.

MICHAEL: Will ye go if they give wan another up?

RAINEY: A'm not sure. A har'ly[5] know where A am, yit.[6]

MICHAEL: Man, there's no time t' be lost. Will ye go til[7]the Or'nge Hall the night, an' spake agin Hart if they agree not til marry wan another?

RAINEY: How'll A know they'll kape their word?

MICHAEL: Ye'll have til trust them.

RAINEY: An' if they betray me?

MICHAEL: Ye'll have til lave them til God. Sure, treachery be anny wan else is no rayson fur treachery be you.

HUGH: Ye needn' bother yerself, we'll not agree til that.

MICHAEL: It's not you A'm goin' til ask. Nora, ye know what this means, don't ye? Ye know what we're workin' fur?

NORA: Ay.

MICHAEL: It's a bigger thing nor you are, issen it? Ye know it is, for all ye won't answer. It's Irelan' agin you. Irelan' 's a bigger thing nor you an' Hugh an' me an' all o' us rowled thegither.

NORA: A don't belave it. A'm in the wurl' t' be happy, an' A'll be happy wi' him.

MICHAEL: What'll yer happiness be till ye, if it manes the destruction o' a nation?

NORA: A don't care.

RAINEY: Have ye no thought fur others?

NORA: No, A haven't. On'y fur him an' me.

HUGH: Ye've no thought yerself fur anythin' but yer blin' superstitions an' yer bigotry. You're a man til talk about sacrifice, whin ye'd destroy Irelan' fur yer damned bigotry.

MICHAEL: Don't be talkin' like that. Sure, it's his faith. He can't go back on his faith.

HUGH: A can't go back on Nora.

MICHAEL: Will ye give him up, Nora. It's no good talkin' t' him. He's demented wi' love.

NORA: No, A won't give him up. A need him, A need him.

MICHAEL: What's your need til the wurl's need?

MRS RAINEY: Man, Michael, when yer as ould as A am, ye'll know that yer own need is the wurl's need. It's love that Nora an' Hugh needs, an' it's love the wurl' needs. Ye're wrong til be suggestin' partin' til them. Can't ye see, they're doin' the very thing ye want Irelan' t' do. It's Cathlik an' Prodesan joinin' han's thegither. It's quare ye shud be wantin' til separate them.

MICHAEL: It's acause a want a bigger joinin' o' han's. It's not enough fur a man an' a wumman til join han's. A want til see the whole wurl' at peace.

MRS RAINEY: Ye'll on'y git that be men an' weemen bein' at peace. Him an' her, Mickie, are bigger than the wurl', if ye on'y knew it. That man o' mine can't see fardher nor churches an' Or'nge Lodges, an' all the time there's men an' weemen stan'in' about, waitin' fur somethin' til bring them thegither.

MICHAEL: Aw, but selfishness is the curse o' the wurl'. An' it's the curse o' Irelan' more nor anny

1. Hart is an upper class protestant demagogue imported from Dublin, probably modelled on the unionist leader Edward Carson. 'A belave = 'I believe'.
2. strike. Ervine's phonetic spelling, although a nuisance, is an attempt to render the Northern pronunciation.
3. from.
4. The hall where the local branch of the Orange lodge would meet. The sense is 'I'm not going to the Orange Hall tonight.'
5. hardly, scarcely.
6. yet.
7. to.

other country. They wur alwis thinkin' o' their-selves, the men an' weemen that might ha' saved Irelan'. Whinivir a man's come near deliverin' Irelan', a wumman's stepped in an' destroyed him.[8] It's alwis bin the way since the beginnin'. Alwis, alwis, alwis! There'll be no salvation fur Irelan' til a man is born that dussen care a God's curse fur weemen. They're hangin' about the neck o' the lan', draggin' her down.

MRS RAINEY: Ye're blamin' us fur the follies o' men. Is Nora to blame acause my man's a fool?

RAINEY: A'm no fool. A must stick til the right. It's onnacherl[9] fur a man an' a wumman til live in the same house an' worship in a differ'nt church.

MRS RAINEY: Sure, if they can live in the same lan' they can live in the same house. It's on'y igner'nce an' wickedness an' men wi' foul tongues that makes it hard. John, ye'll be a good man, an' go til the Or'nge Hall the night, an' do yer best t' keep the peace.

RAINEY: A can't go.

HUGH: A'll go meself. A won't belave that the men o' Irelan' will let bigotry destroy them fur ivir.

MICHAEL: Ye can't go. Ye're not an Or'ngeman.

HUGH: A'll git in somehow. If A've spoiled the work, A can mend it again.

MICHAEL: If ye had on'y waited awhile. In a week or two, it 'ud ha' bin all over, an' we'd ha' won. Aw, Mr Rainey, can't ye think o' the danger o' losin' iv'rythin' be yer action. Ye run the risk o' perpetuatin' bigotry an' losin' all we've struck fur. Man, ye can't do the like o' that.

RAINEY: A'll do what ye want if he'll give her up. A wun't go anear the Or'nge Hall if he dussen.

HUGH: An' A wun't give her up A tell ye.

MRS RAINEY: Aw, the wurl' is bein' destroyed be headstrong men. (*To* RAINEY) Will ye go til the Lodge the night, an' lave this over fur awhile. (*To* HUGH) Ye'll promise not til marry her til after yer da's had time til think it over?

HUGH: Ay, A'll do that.

RAINEY: There's nathin' til be thought over. He's determined til marry her, an' she's determined not til change her religion. There's nathin' more til be said. Ye'll git me t' go t' the Lodge the night ondher pretence that mebbe they'll change their min's, an' ye know as well as yer livin', they won't. (*Pointing to* NORA) Luk at that wumman's face. She manes til[10] marry him.

MICHAEL: Wud ye sacrifice all the rest o' us fur them? That's what ye're doin' mind ye. There's a whole townfull o' us, an' ye'll let us go t'wreck an' ruin fur wan man an' a wumman.

MRS RAINEY: Ay, indeed, ye're just as bad as they are.

RAINEY: Ay, ye'll all make me out in the wrong. Ye give me no credit a-tall. A'm on'y an obstinit ould man t' ye. Ye nivir think A'm in earnest about me religion.

TOM: A nivir knew bein' in earnest wus anny excuse fur makin' a fool o' yerself.

RAINEY: Hould yer tongue.

TOM: Naw, A wun't.[11] A've bin putt upon long enough. Ye're an ould fool, that's what ye are; a damned ould fool.

RAINEY: Ye young scoundrel . . . .

MRS RAINEY: Tom, dear, don't ye think ye might go out for a wee walk?

TOM: Naw, A don't want a wee walk. A'm alwis sent out fur a walk whin there's a bit o' bother. A'm a man the same as he is.

MICHAEL: Aw, Tom, don't make it anny worse not it is.

MRS RAINEY: Now, just sit down, the whole o' ye. Dear-a-dear, it's the quare hard work fur a wumman, keepin' men at peace. If there wussen the like o' us in the wurl' ye'd be kickin' wan another iv'ry five minits. Now, what are ye goin' t' do about it all? Are ye goin' t' the Lodge, John?

RAINEY: Naw, A'm not.

MRS RAINEY: Is that ye're last answer?

RAINEY: Ay, it is.

MRS RAINEY: It's a quare pity o' ye. Ye'll be sorry fur this, A tell ye.

RAINEY: A can't help that.

MRS RAINEY: Well, Mickie, an' what are you goin' t' do?

MICHAEL: A don't know. A'll have til think o' somethin'. A'm all throughover.[12] What wi' the slap on the head an' this suddent trouble. A don't know what A'm doin'. A'm near broke wi' grief. A'm the one feels it most. A've dreamt o' this since A wus born, an' now it's near done, this comes an' destroys it. My God, Mrs Rainey, what a wurl'.

8. The reference is probably to Parnell and the divorce proceedings over his liaison with Katharine O'Shea.

9. unnatural.

10. means to.

11. I won't.

12. confused, muddled.

MRS RAINEY: (*Patting him on the back*) Aw, keep yer heart up, Mickie. Mebbe, it'll be all right. A wish there wus Or'ngeweemen. A'd go meself in his place.

HUGH: (*Jumping up*) A'm not an Or'ngeman, but A'll go. Hart issen nayther, an' if they'll let him in, they'll let me. A'll spake til them, an' putt a stop til Hart's nonsense. A'm the one'll do it. A'll not let it be said the peace o' Irelan' wus destroyed be the Raineys.

RAINEY: Ay, ye'll do a quare lot. Ye can't spake?

HUGH: A can spake as good as you.

MRS RAINEY: Aw, can't ye control yer tongues. Ye do too much spakin' atween ye. Ye're consated[13] about yer spakin'.

HUGH: A've nivir spoke afore, but A'll spake the night. A will, A declare til God. A'll put a stap til bigotry.

RAINEY: Will ye tell them why A've refused til have annythin' more til do wi' it?

MRS RAINEY: What wud he be doin' that fur?

RAINEY: Naw, iv coorse not. Ye'll desave[14] them as ye desaved me. D'ye think anny good'll come out o' that?

HUGH: It's noan o' their business who A marry.

NORA: A can't ondherstan' why a man an' a wumman can't git married wi'out iv'ry wan goin' out o' their wits?

MRS RAINEY: Och, they alwis do, dear. Sure, it's the way the wurl's made. Ye have t' putt up wi' it.

TOM: It's a funny soart o' wurl' then.

HUGH: A don't belave the Or'ngemen are such fools as ye make out. They're brave sensible men, a lot o' them, if they wur on'y let alone be them that's supposed t' be their betters.

RAINEY: Will ye tell them why.

HUGH: It's not necessary. It's nathin' t' do wi' it.

RAINEY: Then A'll go meself an' tell them. We'll see who can spake the best then?

MRS RAINEY: Aw, ye cudden go out on a night like this. Sure, ye're gettin' ould.

RAINEY: Lave me alone, will ye. Ye're all conspirin' agin me, but A'll bate ye yit. Gimme me coat, an' let me git out o' this.

MICHAEL: Ye'll have blood on yer han's, Mr Rainey, if ye do that.

RAINEY: A don't care, A tell ye. A'll putt a stap t' this.

MRS RAINEY: Aw, give him his coat, an' let him go, the headstrong ould man.

HUGH: A'll be left whin he comes back.

TOM: Ay, an' so will I.

RAINEY: (*To* MRS RAINEY) A suppose you'll be gone too?

MRS RAINEY: Naw, A think A'll be here. God help ye, ye'll need someone t' luk after ye.

RAINEY: Nathin'll stap me. A've made up me min'. Good-night t' ye. (*To* NORA) Mebbe ye're satisfied, now, me fine girl?

MRS RAINEY: Lave her alone. Aren't ye content wi' the bad work ye've done wi'out proddin' her wi' a knife? G'long wi' ye, an' do yer dirty work, an' don't stan' there hurtin' a girl that nivir done you no harm.

RAINEY: She tuk me son thrum me.

MRS RAINEY: G'long wi' ye, an' make yer spache.[15]

RAINEY *stands for a moment irresolute, then goes out of the house quickly.* MICHAEL *covers his face with his hands. There is a silence, except for the sobbing of* NORA.

TOM: A think A'll go out for a walk.

MRS RAINEY: Ay, do dear.

Exit TOM

MICHAEL: A'll go home.

MRS RAINEY: Ye'll not let this upset ye, Mickie? Ye'll just go on tryin', wun't ye?

MICHAEL: It's the sore work, Mrs Rainey.

MRS RAINEY: Ay, but sure, it 'ud be far sorer not til do it.

HUGH: A'm quare an' sorry, Mickie.

MICHAEL: It's a pity, Hughie. It's a quare pity.

HUGH: We'll not let this bate us.

NORA: No, we wun't. It's us now, that'll have til do the work. We'll all do it. A'll go an' talk til the men in the street, an' mebbe they'll listen til me. A'd 'a' given the wurl' if this hadden happened.

MICHAEL: It's the quare hard job til stap bigotry wance it's started. It runs like lightnin' an' them that tries til stap it has weights hangin' on them til keep them back. A'm afeard it's no good.

MRS RAINEY: It'll be no good, if ye're afeard. Ye must keep yer heart up, that's the way o' the wurl'.

NORA: Ay, that's true. Good-night t' ye, Mrs Rainey.

MR RAINEY: (*Pulling the girl close to her and kissing*

13. conceited.
14. deceive.

15. i.e. make your speech; say your piece.

her very tenderly) Ye'll be a good wife til him, dear, wun't ye?

NORA: A will, indeed.

MRS RAINEY: Good-night, dear. Good-night, Hughie. When ye want me, just run in.

HUGH: A'll come back whin A've got lodgin's fur me things.

MRS RAINEY: A'll have them ready fur ye. Aw, dear, A wish ye wurn't goin'. (HUGH *puts his arms about her and hugs her tightly*) God bless ye, dear.

MICHAEL: Whativir happens, Mrs Rainey, A'm not sorry A knew you.

MRS RAINEY: Ah, well now, that's somethin' til be livin' fur. Sure, the best o' us can't do no more nor that.

MICHAEL: Good-night t' ye.

MRS RAINEY: Come in in the mornin' an' A'll dress yer head fur ye.

MICHAEL: Aw, ye're brave an' kind. A cudden[16] trouble ye.

MRS RAINEY: Sure, it's no trouble a-tall. Good-night, Michael. Good-night, t' ye all.

HUGH: Good-night, ma.

Exeunt HUGH, NORA, *and* MICHAEL

MRS RAINEY: Aw, dear, it's a troublesome wurl'. (*She draws her chair up to the fire and resumes her darning*)

16. I couldn't.

Biographies/Bibliographies

GENERAL. The following studies, chronologically listed, contain important material about the Abbey Theatre, Irish drama, and individual playwrights. They supplement the individual bibliographies given below.

E. Boyd, *Ireland's Literary Renaissance* (Dublin: The Talbot Press; New York: John Lane, 1916; 2nd revised edition New York: Alfred A. Knopf, 1922; reprinted Dublin: Allen Figgis, 1968); *The Contemporary Drama of Ireland* (Dublin: The Talbot Press; London: T. Fisher Unwin, 1918; reprinted Boston: Little, Brown, 1928); D. Byrne, *The Story of Ireland's National Theatre: The Abbey Theatre, Dublin* (Dublin: The Talbot Press, 1929; reprinted New York: Haskell House, 1971); A. E. Malone, *The Irish Drama* (London: Constable; New York: Scribner, 1929; reprinted New York: Benjamin Blom, 1965); Una Ellis-Fermor, *The Irish Dramatic Movement* (London: Methuen, 1939; 2nd edition, 1954; reprinted University Paperbacks, 1967); B. MacNamara, *Abbey Plays 1899-1948* (Dublin: At the Sign of the Three Candles, 1949); P. Kavanagh, *The Story of the Abbey Theatre* (New York: Devin-Adair, 1950; reprinted, 1984); L. Robinson, *Ireland's Abbey Theatre: A History 1899-1951* (London: Sidgwick and Jackson, 1951; reprinted Port Washington, New York: Kennikat Press, 1968); M. Nic Shiubhlaigh, *The Splendid Years* (Dublin: James Duffy, 1955); J. Holloway, *Joseph Holloway's Abbey Theatre*, edited by R. Hogan and M. J. O'Neill (Carbondale and Edwardsville: Southern Illinois University Press; London and Amsterdam: Feffer & Simons, 1967); R. Hogan and M. J. O'Neill (eds), *Joseph Holloway's Irish Theatre*, 3 vols (Dixon, California: Proscenium Press, 1968-70); R. Hogan, *After the Irish Renaissance: A Critical History of the Irish Drama since 'The Plough and the Stars'* (Minneapolis: University of Minnesota Press, 1967; London: Macmillan, 1968); J. W. Flannery, *Miss Annie Horniman of the Abbey Theatre* (Dublin: Dolmen Press; London, Oxford University Press, 1970); F. Fay, *Towards A National Theatre*, edited by R. Hogan (Dublin: Dolmen Press; London: Oxford University Press, 1970); P. Rafroidi et al. (eds), *Aspects of the Irish Theatre* (Lille: Université de Lille, 1972); R. Hogan and J. Kilroy, *The Modern Irish Drama: The Irish Literary Theatre 1899-1901* (Dublin: Dolmen Press; Atlantic Highlands, New Jersey: Humanities Press, 1975); R. Hogan and J. Kilroy, *The Modern Irish Drama: Laying the Foundations, 1902-1904* (Dublin: Dolmen Press; Atlantic Highlands, New Jersey: Humanities Press, 1976); R. J. Finneran, *Anglo-Irish Literature: A Review of Research* (New York: Modern Language Association of America, 1976); supplement, *Recent Research on Anglo-Irish Writers* (New York: Modern Language Association of America, 1983); E. H. Mikhail, *A Research Guide to Modern Irish Dramatists* (Troy, New York: Whitson Publishing Company, 1979); G. J. Watson, *Irish Identity and the Irish Literary Revival; Synge, Yeats, Joyce and O'Casey* (London: Croom Helm; New York: Barnes and Noble, 1979); P. Edwards, *Threshold of a Nation: A Study in English and Irish Drama* (Cambridge: Cambridge University Press, 1979); H. Hunt, *The Abbey: Ireland's National Theatre 1904-1979* (Dublin: Gill and Macmillan, 1980); E. H. Mikhail, *An Annotated Bibliography of Modern Irish Drama* (Troy, New York: Whitson Publishing Company, 1981); H. Kosok (ed.), *Studies in Anglo-Irish Literature* (Bonn: Bouvier, 1982); D. E. S. Maxwell, *A Critical History of Modern Irish Drama, 1891-1980* (Cambridge: Cambridge University Press, 1984); M. Sekine (ed.), *Irish Writers and the Theatre* (Gerrards Cross: Colin Smythe, 1986); C. A. Carpenter, *Modern Drama Scholarship and Criticism 1966-1980* (Toronto and London: University of Toronto Press, 1986); E. H. Mikhail, *The Abbey Theatre* (London: Macmillan, 1988).

ANTHOLOGIES. C. Canfield, *Plays of the Irish Renaissance 1880-1930* (London: Macmillan; New York: Ives Washburn, 1929; reprinted 1932, 1938, 1974); *Plays of Changing Ireland* (New York: Macmillan, 1936); E. Martin Browne, *Three Irish Plays* (Harmondsworth: Penguin Books, 1983); S. Barnet et al. (eds), *The Genius of the Irish Theatre* (New York The New American Library, Mentor, 1960); W. A. Armstrong (ed.), *Classic Irish Drama* (Harmondsworth: Penguin Books, 1964); R. Hogan (ed.), *Seven Irish Plays, 1946-67* (Minneapolis: University of Minnesota Press, 1967); R. Hogan and J. Kilroy (eds), *Lost Plays of the Irish Renaissance* (Newark, Delaware: Proscenium Press; Gerrards Cross: Colin Smythe, 1970).

Edward Martyn

LIFE. Born in Tulira Castle, Ardrahan, Co. Galway in 1859, Martyn studied at Christ Church, Oxford. In 1897 he, Yeats and Lady Gregory co-founded the Irish Literary Theatre, to which he contributed two plays and for which he shouldered financial responsibility. Friction between Martyn, Yeats and George Moore led to his departure from the Abbey. In 1906 he helped to found the Theatre of Ireland and, in 1914, along with Thomas MacDonagh and Joseph Plunkett, both executed after the 1916 Rising, he founded the Irish Theatre. The repertoire was largely continental plays. The theatre survived until 1920. Martyn was a catholic landowner whose political sympathies became more pronouncedly nationalist. He was president of Sinn Féin from 1904 to 1908. Edward Martyn was deeply interested in church music and endowed a chair in the Pro-Cathedral in Dublin to foster improvements in liturgical music. He also took an interest in ecclesiastical art and architecture and spent a great deal of energy in his campaign for their improvement. He died, unmarried, at Tulira Castle in 1923.

CHIEF WRITINGS. *The Heather Field: A Play in Three Acts* and *Maeve: A Psychological Drama in Two Acts* (London: Duckworth, 1899); 'A Plea for A National Theatre in Ireland', *Samhain* No. 1 (October 1901), 14-15; *The Place-Hunters: A Political Comedy in One Act*, The Leader, 26 July 1902; *The Tale of a Town: A Comedy of Affairs in Five Acts* and *An Enchanted Sea: A Play in Four Acts* (Kilkenny: Standish O'Grady; London: Fisher Unwin, 1902); *Grangecolman: A Domestic Drama in Three*

Acts (Dublin: Maunsel, 1912); *The Dream Physician: A Play in Five Acts* (Dublin: The Talbot Press, 1914); 'A Plea for the Revival of the Irish Literary Theatre', *The Irish Review*, 4 April 1914, 79-84. Reprints of *The Heather Field* in Irish Drama Series, Vol. 1, 1966; of *Maeve* in Irish Drama Series, Vol. 2, 1967; of *The Dream Physician* in Irish Drama Series, Vol. 7, 1972 (Chicago: De Paul University).

BIOGRAPHY AND CRITICISM. J MacDonagh, 'Edward Martyn', *The Dublin Magazine* 1 (February 1924), 465-67; D. Gwynn, *Edward Martyn and the Irish Revival* (London: Jonathan Cape, 1930); Sister M.-T. Courtney, *Edward Martyn and the Irish Theatre* (New York: Vintage, 1956); J. Setterquist, *Ibsen and the Beginnings of Anglo-Irish Drama. II: Edward Martyn* (Uppsala: Lundquist, 1960); P. McFate, 'The Bending of the Bough and The Heather Field', *Eire-Ireland* 8 (Spring 1973), 532-61; W. J. Feeney, *Drama in Hardwicke Street: A History of the Irish Theatre Company* (Rutherford: Fairleigh Dickinson University Press; London: Associated University Presses, 1983).

William Butler Yeats

For biography and bibliography, see page 830.

CRITICAL WRITINGS. The Plays: P. Ure, *Yeats the Playwright: A Commentary on Character and Design in the Major Plays* (London: Routledge & Kegan Paul; New York: Barnes and Noble, 1963); H. H. Vendler, *Yeats's 'Vision' and the Later Plays* (Cambridge, Massachusetts: Harvard University Press, 1963); D. R. Clark, *W. B. Yeats and the Theatre of Desolate Reality* (Dublin: Dolmen Press, 1965); L. E. Nathan, *The Tragic Drama of William Butler Yeats: Figures in a Dance* (New York and London: Columbia University Pres, 1965); J. W. Flannery, *W. B. Yeats and the Idea of a Theatre: The Early Abbey Theatre in Theory and Practice* (New Haven and London: Yale University Press, 1976); L. Miller, *The Noble Drama of W. B. Yeats* (Dublin: Dolmen Press; New York: Humanities Press, 1977); R. Taylor, *The Drama of W. B. Yeats. Irish Myth and the Japanese Noh* (New Haven: Yale University Press, 1979); *A Reader's Guide to the Plays of W. B. Yeats* (London: Macmillan; Dublin: Gill and Macmillan, 1984).

Augusta Lady Gregory

For biography and bibliography, see page 560.

J. M. Synge

LIFE. Synge was born in Rathfarnham, Co. Dublin in 1871. His father died the following year and he spent his young life in a family dominated by his mother, grandmother, aunts and his sister. He attended school irregularly, received private tuition and began to rebel against the strict evangelicalism of his upbringing. By the time he attended Trinity College, Dublin (1889-92), the reading of Darwin and his interest in nature had combined to provide him with an alternative, almost mystical faith. He also attended the Royal Irish Academy of Music, became a member of the orchestra (he was proficient on the violin, flute and piano) and in 1893 went to Germany to continue his musical education. Synge turned away from music towards literature and in 1895 went to Paris where he attended lectures in medieval literature and Old Irish at the Sorbonne and became involved with the Irish emigré group there, particularly Stephen MacKenna, Maud Gonne and W. B. Yeats. In 1898, he left Paris for the first of his visits to the Aran Islands, met Lady Gregory and Edward Martyn and resolved to participate in the Irish Literary Theatre. Synge visited Aran on several occasions between 1898 and 1902. In 1903 he finally left Paris, came to Dublin and by 1904 was established as one of the leading figures in the newly founded Abbey Theatre. By then two of his plays had been produced by the Irish National Theatre Company; the Abbey produced three others between 1905 and 1910, with the performance of *The Playboy of the Western World* (1907) and the accompanying riots marking an important moment in the history of the literary movement of the time. His love for the Abbey actress Maire (Molly) O'Neill was shadowed by the progress of Hodgkin's disease, to which he finally succumbed on 24 March 1909.

CHIEF WRITINGS. R. Skelton (ed.), *Collected Works Volume I: Poems* (London: Oxford University Press, 1962); A. Price (ed.), *Collected Works Volume II: Prose* (London: Oxford University Press, 1966); A. Saddlemyer (ed.), *Collected Works Volumes III and IV: Plays* (London: Oxford University Press, 1968); *Letters to Molly: John Millington Synge to Maire O'Neill* (Cambridge, Massachusetts: Belknap Press, 1971); *Some Letters of John M. Synge to Lady Gregory and W. B. Yeats* (Dublin: Cuala Press, 1971).

BIOGRAPHY AND CRITICISM. Lady Gregory, *Our Irish Theatre* (London: Putnam, 1913); D. Corkery, *Synge and Anglo-Irish Literature: A Study* (Dublin and Cork: Cork University Press; London: Longmans, Green, 1931; Cork: Mercier Press, 1966); S. Synge, *Letters to My Daughter: Memories of John Millington Synge* (Dublin: The Talbot Press, 1932); D. H. Greene and E. M. Stephens, *J. M. Synge 1871-1909* (New York: Macmillan, 1959); A. Price, *Synge and Anglo-Irish Drama* (London: Methuen, 1961); D. Gerstenberger, *John Millington Synge* (New York: Twayne, 1964); A. Saddlemyer, *J. M. Synge and Modern Comedy* (Dublin: Dolmen Press, 1968); T. R. Whitaker (ed.), *Twentieth-Century Interpretations of 'The Playboy of the Western World'* (Englewood Cliffs, New Jersey: Prentice Hall, 1969); J. Kilroy, *The 'Playboy' Riots* (Dublin: Dolmen Press, 1971); R. Skelton, *J. M. Synge and His World* (New York: Viking; London: Thames and Hudson, 1971); M. Harmon (ed.), *J. M. Synge Centenary Papers 1971* (Dublin: Dolmen Press, 1972); S. B. Bushrui (ed.), *Sunshine and the Moon's Delight: A Centenary Tribute to John Millington Synge* (Gerrards Cross: Colin Smythe, 1972); E. M. Stephens, *My Uncle John*, edited by Andrew Carpenter (London: Oxford University Press, 1974); N. Grene, *Synge: A Critical Interpretation of the Plays* (London: Macmillan, 1975); K. Worth, *The Irish Drama of Europe: From Yeats to Beckett* (London: The Athlone Press, 1978); D. Kiberd, *Synge and the Irish Language* (London: Macmillan; Totowa, New Jersey: Rowman and Littlefield, 1979); T. O'Brien Johnson, *Synge: The Medieval and the Grotesque* (Gerrards Cross: Colin Smythe; New York: Barnes and Noble, 1982); M. C. King, *The Drama of J. M. Synge* (Syracuse, New York: Syracuse University Press, 1986); E. A. Kopper Jr (ed.), A J.M. Synge Literary Companion (New York: Greenwood Press, 1988).

Lennox Robinson

For biography and bibliography, see Volume III, p. 231.

Padraic Colum

For biography and bibliography, see page 781.

T. C. Murray

LIFE. Thomas Cornelius Murray was born in Macroom, Co. Cork in 1873. He became a schoolteacher and taught in Dublin for over twenty years. He co-founded the Cork Little Theatre with Terence MacSwiney, Con O'Leary and Daniel Corkery and his first play, *Wheel of Fortune*, was produced there in 1909. After *Birthright* was produced by the Abbey in 1910, Murray became one of its leading playwrights. He was director of the Author's Guild of Ireland and was a member of the Irish Academy of Letters. Besides his plays, Murray wrote lyric poetry, a novel and contributed essays to *The Bell*. He died in Dublin in 1959.

CHIEF WRITINGS. *Birthright* (Dublin: Maunsel, 1911); *Maurice Harte* (Dublin: Maunsel, 1912): *Spring and Other Plays* (Dublin: The Talbot Press, 1917); *Aftermath: A Play in Three Acts* (Dublin: The Talbot Press, 1922): *Autumn Fire: A Play in Three Acts* (London: Allen & Unwin, 1925); *Birthright* and *A Pipe in The Fields* (London: Allen & Unwin, 1928); *Michaelmas Eve: A Play in Three Acts* (London: Allen & Unwin, 1932): *Spring Horizon* (London: T. Nelson & Sons, 1937).

BIOGRAPHY AND CRITICISM. D. Macardle, 'The Dramatic Art of T. C. Murray', *The Dublin Magazine* 2 (January 1925), 393-98; T. Hogan, 'T. C. Murray', *Envoy* 3 (November 1950), 138-48; M. O hAodha, 'T. C. Murray and Some Critics', *Studies* 47 (Summer 1958), 185-91; T. Connolly, 'T. C. Murray, The Quiet Man', *The Catholic World* 190 (March 1960), 364-69; T. G. Fitzgibbon, 'The Elements of Conflict in the Plays of T. C. Murray', *Studies* 64 (Spring 1975), 59-65.

George Fitzmaurice

LIFE. Fitzmaurice was born near Listowel, Co. Kerry in 1878, the son of a Church of Ireland clergyman. He spent most of his life in Dublin as a civil servant, apart from a period of service in the British army during World War I. Although the Abbey produced three of his plays in 1907 and 1908, others were rejected and Fitzmaurice withdrew his work from the company. Between 1923, when he had his last Abbey production with *Twixt the Giltinans and the Carmodys*, and 1963, he had very few plays staged and led a quiet and reclusive life. He died in Dublin in 1963.

CHIEF WRITINGS. *Five Plays* (London and Dublin: Maunsel, 1914; Boston: Little, Brown, 1917); A. Clarke and H. Slaughter (eds), *The Plays of George Fitzmaurice. Vol. 1. Dramatic Fantasies* (Dublin: Dolmen Press, 1967); *The Plays of George Fitzmaurice. Vol. 2. Folk Plays* (Dublin: Dolmen Press, 1970); *The Plays of George Fitzmaurice. Vol. 3. Realistic Plays* (Dublin: Dolmen Press, 1970); R. Hogan (ed.), *The Crows of Mephistopheles* (Dublin: Dolmen Press, 1970).

BIOGRAPHY AND CRITICISM. H. K. Slaughter, *George Fitzmaurice and His Enchanted Land* (Dublin: Dolmen Press, 1972); A. E. McGuinness, *George Fitzmaurice* (Lewisburg, Pennsylvania: Bucknell University Press, 1975); C. W. Gelderman, *George Fitzmaurice* (Boston: Twayne, 1979); W. R. Sanger, 'Caught Between Tradition and Experiment: George Fitzmaurice's *The Moonlighter*' in H. Kosok (ed.), *Studies in Anglo-Irish Literature* (Bonn: Bouvier, 1982).

Sean O'Casey

LIFE. Born John Casey in 1880 in Dublin, of a poor protestant family, he was the last of thirteen children and his education was sporadic. From an early age, O'Casey suffered from eye trouble. He worked as a labourer and spent most of his evenings at meetings of various societies and groupings, of which the Gaelic Society, the Irish Transport and General Workers' Union and its offshoot, the Irish Citizen Army, were the most important. He was secretary of the Citizen Army, wrote for the newspaper the *Irish* spent most of his evenings at meetings of various societies and groupings, of which the Gaelic Society, the Irish Transport and General Workers' Union and its offshoot, The Irish Citizen Army, were the most important. He was secretary of the Citizen Army, wrote for the newspaper *The Irish Worker*, and produced a short history of the Citizen Army (1919). He broke with his political friends over the 1916 Rising and, in his portrayal of the crisis, the participation of socialists in a nationalist uprising. After several failures, he had his first play accepted by the Abbey; *The Shadow of a Gunman* was produced in 1923. His other Dublin plays followed. In 1926 the riots that greeted *The Plough and the Stars* both established O'Casey's fame and soured his attitude towards Ireland, further embittered by the rejection by Yeats and Lady Gregory of his play *The Silver Tassie* (1928). O'Casey never again lived in Ireland after 1926. He went to London, befriended Bernard Shaw and Augustus John, received wide acclaim, married and then struggled for some time to find a commercial success comparable to his early triumphs. In 1938 he moved to Devon. In 1955 his first play to be produced in Dublin in almost thirty years, *The Bishop's Bonfire*, aroused some controversy; this was repeated on a larger scale in 1958, when O'Casey withdrew his play *The Drums of Father Ned* because of catholic clerical interference in the Dublin Theatre Festival. He wrote prolifically, but without major success, for the rest of his life, remaining faithful to the communist cause even through the Stalinist trials of the 1930s. He died in Torquay, England in 1964.

CHIEF WRITINGS. *Collected Plays* 4 vols (London: Macmillan; New York: St Martin's Press, 1949-51; reprinted 1962-64); *Mirror in my House: The Autobiographies of Sean O'Casey* 2 vols (New York: Macmillan, 1956); reprinted as *Autobiographies* 2 vols (London: Macmillan, 1963; reprinted Pan Books, 1980; reprinted 2 vols, 1981); R. Hogan (ed.), *Feathers from the Green Crow 1905-1925* (Columbia: University of Missouri Press, 1962; London: Macmillan, 1963); R. Ayling (ed.), *Blasts and Benedictions: Articles and Stories* (London: Macmillan; New York: St Martin's Press, 1967); D. Krause (ed.), *The Letters of Sean O'Casey* 2 vols (London: Macmillan, 1975-80); B. Atkinson (ed.), *The Sean O'Casey Reader* (London: Macmillan, 1985).

BIOGRAPHY AND CRITICISM. D. Krause, *Sean O'Casey: The Man and His Work* (London: MacGibbon & Kee; New York: Macmillan, 1960); R. Hogan, *The Experiments of Sean O'Casey* (New York: St Martin's Press, 1960); S. McCann (ed.), *The World of Sean O'Casey* (London: Frewin, 1966); R. Ayling (ed.), *Sean O'Casey* (London: Macmillan, 1968); S. Cowasjee, *Sean O'Casey* (Edinburgh: Oliver and Boyd, 1968); R. Ayling (ed.), *Sean O'Casey: Modern Judgements* (London: Macmillan, 1969); M. B. Margulies, *The Early Life of Sean O'Casey* (Dublin: Dolmen Press, 1970); H. Goldstone, *In Search of Community: The Achievement of Sean O'Casey* (Cork: Mercier Press, 1973); E. O'Casey, *Sean*, edited by J. C. Trewin (London: Macmillan, 1974); T. Kilroy (ed.), *Twentieth-Century Views: Sean O'Casey* (Englewood Cliffs, New Jersey: Prentice Hall, 1975); D. Krause, *Sean O'Casey and His World* (London: Thames and Hudson, 1976); J. P. Frayne, *Sean O'Casey* (New York: Columbia University Press, 1976); H. Hunt, *Sean O'Casey* (Dublin: Gill and Macmillan, 1980); C. D. Greaves, *O'Casey: Politics and Art* (London: Lawrence and Wishart, 1979); D. Krause and R. G. Lowery (eds), *Sean O'Casey Centenary Essays* (Gerrards Cross: Colin Smythe, 1980); R. J. Lowery (ed.), *Essays on Sean O'Casey's Autobiographies* (Totowa, New Jersey: Barnes and Noble, 1981); H. Kosok, *O'Casey the Dramatist* (Gerrards Cross: Colin Smythe; Totowa, New Jersey: Barnes and Noble, 1985); G. O'Connor, *Sean O'Casey: A Life* (London: Hodder and Stoughton, 1988).

George Shiels

LIFE. Born in Ballymoney, Co. Antrim in 1886, Shiels emigrated as a young man to Canada where, in 1913, he was permanently crippled in a railway accident. He returned to Ireland and began to write plays, at first under the name George Morshiel. The Ulster Literary Theatre produced his earliest work. From 1921, when he was first produced at the Abbey, until 1948, at least one of his plays was staged every year. He died at Ballymoney in 1949.

CHIEF WRITINGS. *Bedmates: A Play in One Act* (Dublin: The Gael Cooperative Society, 1922); *Two Irish Plays: Mountain Dew, A Play in Three Acts* and *Cartney and Kevney, A Comedy in Three Acts* (London: Macmillan, 1930); *The Passing Day: A Play in Six Scenes* and *The Jailbird: A Comedy in Three Acts* (London: Macmillan, 1937); *The Rugged Path: A Play in Three Acts* and *The Summit: A Play in Three Acts* (London: Macmillan, 1942); *Three Plays (Professor Tim, Paul Twyning, The New Gossoon)* (London: Macmillan, 1945); *The Fort Field: A Play in Three Acts* (Dublin: Golden Eagle Books, 1947); *Give Him a House: A Comedy in Three Acts* (Dublin: Golden Eagle Books, 1947); *Grogan and the Ferret: A Comedy in Three Acts* (Dublin: Golden Eagle Books, 1947); *Quin's Secret: A Comedy in Three Acts* (Dublin: Golden Eagle Books, 1947); *The Caretakers: A Play in Three Acts* (Dublin: Golden Eagle Books, 1948); *The Old Broom: A Comedy in Three Acts* (Dublin: Golden Eagle Books, 1948).

BIOGRAPHY AND CRITICISM. T. C. Murray, 'George Shiels, Brinsley MacNamara etc.' in L. Robinson (ed.), *The Irish Theatre: Lectures Delivered During the Abbey Theatre Festival Held in Dublin in August 1938* (London: Macmillan, 1939; reprinted New York: Haskell House, 1971); W. J. Feeney, 'The Rugged Path: A Modern View of Informers', *Eire-Ireland* 2 (Spring 1967), 41-47; D. Kennedy, 'George Shiels: A Playwright at Work', *Threshold* 25 (Summer 1974), 50-58.

St John Ervine

LIFE. St John Greer Ervine was born in Ballymacarret, Belfast in 1883. In 1900 he went to London, met Bernard Shaw and became involved with the Fabian Society. He developed an interest in theatre and had four plays produced at the Abbey between 1911 and 1915. Appointed manager of the Abbey in 1915, he tried to convert it into a repertory theatre and his disastrous influence almost led to the collapse of the company. He served in the Dublin Fusiliers in World War I and was so severely wounded that he had to have a leg amputated. Ervine wrote prolifically for the London theatres and, after 1936, for the Abbey; he also produced several novels, biographies, memoirs and was drama critic for the *New York World* for a time in 1929 and later for *The Observer*. He died in 1971 at Seaton, Devon.

CHIEF WRITINGS. *Four Irish Plays (Mixed Marriage, The Magnanimous Lover, The Critics, The Orangeman)* (Dublin: Maunsel, 1914); *Jane Clegg* (London: Sidgwick and Jackson, 1914); *John Ferguson: A Play in Four Acts* (Dublin: Maunsel, 1915); *Sir Edward Carson and the Ulster Movement* (Dublin: Maunsel, 1915); *Parnell* (Boston: Little, Brown, 1927); *Boyd's Shop: A Comedy in Four Acts* (London: Allen & Unwin, 1936); *Friends and Relations: A Comedy in Three Acts* (London: Allen & Unwin, 1947); *Oscar Wilde: A Present Time Appraisal* (London: Allen & Unwin, 1951); *Bernard Shaw, His Life, Work, and Friends* (New York: William Morrow, 1956).

BIOGRAPHY AND CRITICISM. J. W. Cunliffe, *Modern English Playwrights: A Short History of the English Drama from 1925* (New York and London: Harper, 1927; reprinted. Port Washington, New York: Kennikat Press, 1969); D. Ireland, 'Red Brick City and Its Dramatist: A Note on St. John Ervine' *Envoy* 1 (March 1950), 59-67; S. Hanna Bell, *The Theatre in Ulster: A Survey of the Dramatic Movement in Ulster from 1902 until the Present Day* (Dublin: Gill and Macmillan; Totowa, New Jersey: Rowman and Littlefield, 1972); J. Boyd, 'St. John Ervine, a Biographical Note', *Threshold* 25 (Summer 1974), 101-15; N. Vance, *Irish Literature: A Social History* (Oxford: Blackwell, 1990), chapter V.

SEAMUS DEANE, *Editor*

Poetry 1890–1930

All the poets included below were born before 1900. Antoine Raftery, who wrote in Irish, was 'reborn' before that date. He died in 1835, but he was re-established in the 1890s by Douglas Hyde and Lady Gregory as a type of the Gaelic poet and as an example of the intimacy that existed in Ireland between the poet and his audience. Raftery's poems and songs had become part of the oral tradition of Galway and Mayo. His new sponsors wanted him to become part of the printed tradition in English as well as in Irish, without any loosening of the relationship between the audience and the text. It was, of course, an impossible ambition. Raftery the poet was altered by his translation into print, into English and into the Irish Revival.

By 1890, that Revival was beginning to establish itself as the most remarkable regional response to the metropolitan culture of London and as one of the cultural consequences of the Young Ireland movement and its strenuous assertions of nationality. This was a paradoxical heritage, for English literary culture was dominated, at least in poetry, by those who never moved, as Nietzsche said, 'more than five steps from the hospital'. Tennyson died in 1892 (the year of Yeats's *The Countess Cathleen and Other Poems*) and Swinburne assumed the role of senior poet for the next fifteen or sixteen years. Poetry is suffused, throughout most of the 1890s, with a miasmic, melismatic vagueness, as aestheticism tries to take over from religion and substitutes notions of the self for notions of God. It is an urban rather than an urbane poetry, although the London it refers to is the shot-silk impressionistic city of the painters rather than the grim East End slum of the novelists.

In contrast to this, as has often been said, there is a counter-decadence, associated with Kipling, W.E. Henley and others, as virile and assertive as Lionel Johnson, Ernest Dowson and John Gray are renunciatory and withdrawn. Jingoism and aestheticism are indeed closely allied, throughout this decade and beyond, to the outbreak of the Great War. The same is true in Irish poetry, although there the alliance remains in place for much longer, given the very different political and cultural conditions then prevailing after the fall of Parnell, the formal founding of the Revival, of the Gaelic League, Sinn Féin and the paroxysms of revolt in Ulster in 1912 and in Dublin in 1916. The Irish heritage in poetry is, at this stage, still deriving from the culture of England but doing so in a determinedly separatist fashion. The Celtic Twilight is a regional variation on aestheticism and impressionism; but it is also in its way an attempt to give a more urbane surface to the balladeering nationalism of Young Ireland and its later cohorts. Instead of harps and wolfhounds, it gives us roses and moonlight. But the project, although altered in its idiom, remains the same. The Celt has decided to claim his spiritual destiny. He is the beneficiary of the testament of a century of antiquarians and racial historians. The executor of the will is a reluctant England.

It is appropriate, therefore, that Lionel Johnson, one of the best-known of the English decadent poets, should be an honorary Irishman. Whistler's London was not sufficiently twilit; Yeats's Ireland had more of the tremulous glimmer so beloved of the decadent school. Yet Johnson's poems on Irish subjects are very far from his best. Ireland (and Yeats) managed to be an avocation without ever becoming an inspiration. But Johnson remains relatively unread. His contribution to Irish poetry is important only as a reminder of the appeal of Ireland as a minority cause to the intellectuals and writers of the decadent era. It is Wilde, the Irish exile who became more English than Johnson could ever become Irish, who has produced, in his poems, the outstanding synthesis of aesthetic nostalgia and popular ballad form. Most of Wilde's poetry, including *The Ballad of Reading Gaol*, is vulgar in its facility of feeling and rhythmic automatism. But, as in all of his work, the subversive, even radical, critique of society that is implicit in what he has to say, finds no release within the linguistic conventions which he mocked but by which he remained imprisoned. All the Irish writers in the 1890s were similarly enclosed. As a poet, Joyce was never able to go beyond the linguistic limits of the English decadents and Yeats was well into his forties before he wearied of waiting on the modernist threshold. When dissatisfaction with the existing state of things became sufficiently pronounced, it tended, at this time, to convert itself into mysticism, religiosity, occultism. Wilde, Yeats and AE are the outstanding examples of this turn in the Irish situation.

The most redeeming feature of the poetry of Wilde, Synge, Gogarty, Joyce, Johnson and AE (to a lesser degree) is its technical elegance. Their education was such that they knew enough about metres and verse forms, even the most esoteric, to sustain a poem that was otherwise famished for want of more substantial food. The diet was monotonous: a romantic soufflé served with all the trappings of a full meal. When aestheticism, as a style and an attitude, began to fade in Ireland, it was supplanted by a pastoral nationalism that regarded itself, in the terms of the old *Nation* newspaper, as 'racy of the soil' and the better for that. The shift from the city to the country was regarded as one reason for the greater vitality of the verse that became more admired from about 1905. But it was more than the standard turn from urban to rural, a more dramatic change than in English verse, where aestheticism transmuted, quietly enough, into Georgianism. For the rural territory was Ireland and it bespoke a civilization that was different in kind, not only in degree, from the urban world of the 1890s.

At this point, literary Ireland becomes something very different from literary Dublin, although it is still true that literary Dublin is more excited about the discovery than rural Ireland was, then or since. It is a palimpsest territory, where in excited reverie it is easier to discern Clonmacnoise than Athlone, and Emain Macha than Maynooth. But the element of costume drama involved here cannot be easily dismissed or derided, for the ventriloquism of the poets was matched, over-matched perhaps, by that of the political activists. The Fenians were indeed turning themselves into the Fianna; regionalism was ceasing to be a cultural condition and becoming a political programme (Sinn Féin). In literary terms, there was, if not a breakthrough, at least a breakout from the conventions of Victorian solemnity and aesthetic narcissism. Poetry rediscovered speech, although, in doing so, it also managed to discover a common tongue that was moreover, in terms of the English-language tradition, an uncommon tongue — the speech of the Irish peasantry. Synge, even more than Yeats, exploited this discovery, more successfully in his plays than in his poems, although the folksy element never quite disappears from either. Nevertheless, it was one of the inaugurating moments of Irish modernism. Poetry, lagging behind the drama and the novel, manages to confront the central issue of the need for a new language, another vocabulary, for what most besets it.

One of the more curious manifestations of the Irish pursuit of a new style and vocabulary is what we may call Irish Elizabethanism. Elizabethan literature is read in this period as the source of two opposed modes of writing, analagous to the distinction in English poetry between the decadent and the virile verse of the period from 1890 to 1914. Elizabethan songs are at the heart of Joyce's lyric efforts in poetry. Their appeal seems to lie for him in their elegance, restraint and their lingering, stylized sadness. For Synge, by contrast, the Elizabethan literature is characterized by vigour, fullness of speech, energy. Ireland is to him the Elizabethan country of the modern era. The Irish rediscovery of the Elizabethans is comparable to the Anglo-American rediscovery of the metaphysical poets some twenty years later. The writing of new poetry involves a new reading of the tradition, and it is important to remember that this involved a rereading of the English and the Irish traditions. The first epigraph to George Sigerson's *Bards of the Gael and the Gall* (1897, 2nd edition 1907) is a quotation from Spenser's *A View of the Present State of Ireland*, in which the beauties of Irish poetry are lauded by 'Ireneus'. Since Irish poetry was the only aspect of Gaelic civilization praised by Spenser, the imputation seems to be that here, in the sixteenth century, the two civilizations come together in a mutual literary appreciation. This, it seems, is the origin of the Irish tradition of Gael and Gall, a conception very different from the notion of the Anglo-Irish tradition. The Anglo-Irish tradition is, at this time, more generally understood to refer to a body of writing in English which was, in important ways, distinct both from the Gaelic and from the English traditions. It was only in the 1920s that Yeats found a way of redeeming it from this interstitial fate by claiming that it was throughout informed by the elusive Irish spirit — by then, a profoundly anti-modernist agency that ratified authoritarianism in the name of tradition. Irish Elizabethanism is an early attempt to escape from the dubious 'Celticism' of the Yeatsian vision of the Irish and English past. Once the 'Celt' was replaced by the co-operative action of the Gael and the Gall, the efforts of the nineteenth-century translators could finally be registered in the English-language poetry of men like T. W. Rolleston, William Larminie, Sigerson and their successors.

This is not to say that Irish poetry underwent a very profound revolution at this stage. It was still closely allied to the main developments in English verse and, as decadence and imperial virility gave way to Georgianism and little Englandism, Irish poetry followed suit. There was a prevailing and increasingly provincial orthodoxy; for all their virtues, F. R. Higgins, Padraic Colum, Thomas MacDonagh, Patrick Pearse, Seumas O'Sullivan and Francis Ledwidge are conventional practitioners of it. There are important distinctions between them. Pearse and Ledwidge, in particular, cannot avoid being read in the light of their respective deaths in the Easter Rising and World War I. This does not improve (excuse?) their poetry; but it reminds us that the form of its self-regard is determined by forces other than those of the literary tradition, even though their sense of that may have been impoverished. There is in them a naiveté we do not find in the older generation — Wilde, Joyce, Yeats, Gogarty and others. Their work has something adolescent and autodidactic; they are writing out of an idea of poetry that they have created for themselves out of very little. Thomas MacDonagh's MA thesis on the Elizabethan poet Thomas Campion provides a good example of this naive assertiveness, with its ultimately touching faith in upper-case abstractions — Poetry, Faith, Beauty, Love and all the numinous gods and goddesses of the temple dedicated to Ireland in the name of literature. According to MacDonagh, both in his thesis and the posthumously published *Literature in Ireland* (1916), it is possible to divide English verse into two main types, speech-verse and song-verse (this in the thesis), and to identify a specifically 'Irish mode' of verse, that 'of a people to whom the ideal, the spiritual, the mystic are the true' (this in the book). This is the aesthetic movement politicized. As a way of reading the tradition of poetry in English, most especially since the Elizabethans, it is futile. But as a way of rereading the nationalist tradition and claiming for it an inaugurating power in English-language literature, it is less limiting than it might seem to be. For MacDonagh was at least partly aware of the difference between the literary 'Celtic' idea of Ireland and the more political and culturally hospitable idea of Gaelic civilization. The difference between the Gael and the Celt had been pointed out before by Eóin MacNeill, W. P. Ryan and George Sigerson. Sigerson's *Bards of the Gael and the Gall*, a volume of translations from the earliest period of the Milesian invaders down to the nineteenth century, was important not merely because of the quality of some of the translations themselves, but also for its inclusiveness, its refusal to identify an 'Irish note' in poetry that was peculiar to any one group or that was susceptible to any racial claim. Sigerson, Ryan, MacNeill and others emphasized the mixture of races that constituted the Irish people and derided any notion of an exclusively 'Celtic' spirit. MacDonagh dedicated his book of essays to Sigerson. This is appropriate in many ways, although MacDonagh does waver between the 'Celtic' and the 'Gaelic' determinations of the nature of Irish poetry. His thesis and the essays derived from it do indicate the continuity of the attempt to see the interconnexions as well as the contrasts between the developments, since the Elizabethan period, in English and in Irish verse, and to offer, as a conclusion, the hope that Irish poetry in English might bear witness to its dual heritage.

In 1894, George Sigerson gave a lecture at the opening of the Irish National Literary Society in Dublin on 'Irish Literature: its Origin, Environment and Influence', in which he declared that 'Irish literature is of many blends, not the product of one race but of several.' He went on to confess his dismay in finding that 'some of my patriotic young friends' were ready to decide 'what is and what is not the Irish style in prose and the Irish note in poetry. We all know what is meant. But it is scarcely too much to say that you may search through all the Gaelic literature of the nation, and find many styles, but not this. If it ever existed, it existed outside of our classic literature, in a rustic or plebeian dialect. It must be counted, but to make it exclusive would be to impose fetters on literary expression. As in other countries, there were not one but many styles, differing with the subject, the writer, and the age.' This was a more sensible and ecumenical approach than that of the 'Celtic' school. MacDonagh's critical writing is an abortive attempt to absorb Sigerson's wide tolerance within a theory of English and Irish poetry that was too rudimentary to receive it.

Still, it is a fact often ignored or elided that the 'Celtic' idea of Ireland belonged almost exclusively to Yeats and some of his colleagues in the first phase of the Revival. The replacement of the Celt by the Gael had its effects elsewhere — not only in the poetry of MacDonagh and in the writings of Patrick Pearse, but also in the work of Padraic Colum, F. R. Higgins, Joseph Campbell and, later, Austin Clarke. There was, on their part, a serious attempt to incorporate into their verse some of the technical features of Gaelic poetry, so that as a consequence there would be a fusion of Irish and English modes, of Gael and Gall. In Campbell, in Colum, and sometimes in Higgins, there is an intimacy with the popular folk poetry and songs that lends to some of their best efforts the impersonal quality of the broadsheet poem — precisely the kind of thing that Allingham and Davis, in their different ways, had sought in the previous century.

The emergence of a number of considerable poets from these complicated beginnings is dealt with in other sections of this anthology. Yeats is a case apart; but Austin Clarke, Patrick Kavanagh, Denis Devlin, Brian Coffey, Thomas MacGreevy and Louis MacNeice are perhaps best understood as having been formed in reaction to some of the most fervent pieties of the earlier writers. It is easy now to see the connecting resemblances between Rolleston and Larminie and the nineteenth-century poets, nor is it much more difficult to recognize how fluently they blend with the work of the early twentieth-century writers.

ANTOINE RAFTERY

(*c.* 1784-1835)

[Raftery's poems belonged to the oral tradition until the later part of the nineteenth century when Lady Gregory and Douglas Hyde in particular (in his *Songs of Connacht* of 1903) collected, printed and translated many of them. His belated appearance in print made him into a minor cult figure of the Irish Revival — hence his inclusion at this point. Raftery has neither the training nor the refinement of the eighteenth-century Irish poets, but he was a local legend in County Galway and, by the turn of the century, an emblem of the fading Gaelic literary culture. His poems are, for the most part, songs. Hyde first discovered Raftery when he heard an old man singing 'The County Mayo' and learned the words from him. That was in 1875, 'my first meeting', as he puts it, 'with the wave that Raftery left behind him'. It was 1890 before Hyde found some of Raftery's poems in manuscript in the Royal Irish Academy. Lady Gregory traced twenty-two more in another manuscript. Further researches uncovered a series of poems in the hands of a variety of local people. It was 1903 before Hyde produced his first edition of Raftery. He edited another edition in 1933. The poem may not be by Raftery, but is traditionally ascribed to him.

Mise Raifteri

Mise Raifteri an file
  Lán dóchais agus grádh,
Le súilibh gan solus
  Le ciúnas gan crádh.

Dul sias ar m'aistear
  Le solus mo chroidhe,
Fann agus tuirseach
  Go deireadh mo shlighe.

Féach anois mé
Agus m'aghaidh ar bhalla
Ag seinm ceóil
Do phócaibh falamh.

I Am Raftery

I am Raftery the poet,
Full of hope and love,
With eyes that have no light,
With gentleness that has no misery.

Going west upon my pilgrimage
(Guided) by the light of my heart,
Feeble and tired,
To the end of my road.

Behold me now,
And my face to a wall,
A-playing music
Unto empty pockets.

[Killeaden is close to Raftery's birthplace in County Mayo, and the poem is known by the two titles, 'Cill Liadáin' and 'Condae Mhuigheó'. The Irish text is from Ciarán Ó Coigligh's edition, *Raiftearaí: Amhráin agus Dánta* (Dublin: An Clóchomhar Teoranta, 1987). The translation is by Douglas Hyde. In the first stanza Hyde capitalizes certain key words in an attempt to draw the reader's attention to the fact that in the first four verses 'the eight interlined rhymes are all on the letter *í*, and the four final rhymes in the even lines are on the letter *ó*. The whole poem is constructed on the sounds of *í* (ee), *é* (aé), and *ó*.']

Cill Liadáin

Tiocfaidh an t-earrach is beidh an lá ag síneadh
tar éis na Féil' Bríde agus ardód mo sheol,
is ó chuir mé i mo cheann é ní chónóidh mé choíche,
go seasfaidh mé thíos i lár Chontae Mhaigh Eo.
I gClár Chlainne Mhuiris a bheas mé an chéad oíche,
is i mBalla taobh thíos de is ea a thosós mé ag ól;
go Coillte Mach rachad, go ndéanfad cuairt mhíosa ann,
i bhfogas dhá mhíle do Bhéal an Átha Móir.

Fágaim le huachta go n-éiríonn mo chroíse,
mar a ardaíos an ghaoth, nó mar scaipeas an ceo,
tráth a smaoiním ar Cheara nó ar Ghaileang taobh thíos de,
ar Sceathach an Mhíle is ar Phlánaí Mhaigh Eo.
Cill Liadáin an baile a bhfásann gach ní ann,
tá sméara, sú craobh ann is meas ar gach sórt;
is dá mbeinnse i mo sheasamh ann in gceartlár mo dhaoine,
d'imeodh an aois díom is bheinn arís óg.

Tá cruithneacht is coirce, fás eorna agus lín ann,
seagal breá aoibhinn, arán plúir agus feoil;
lucht déanta uisce beatha gan *licence* ag díol ann,
móruaisle na tíre ann ag imirt is ag ól.
Tá cur agus treabhadh ann, is leasú gan aoileach,
is iomdha sin ní ann nár labhair mé air fós:
áitheanna is muilte ag obair gan scíth ann,
ní íoctar pínn chíosa ann ná dadaidh dá shórt.

Tá an t-uisce sa loch, is an abhainn ag triall ann,
na coracha déanta, is na líonta i gcóir;
tá an liús is an breac is an eascann ina luí ann,
an portán, an faochán, an ronnach, is an rón.
Tá an bradán is an ballach ag preabadh gach oíche ann,
is an liubhán ag triall ann ón bhfarraige mhór;
an *tortoise* is an gliomach is an turbard riabhach,
cnúdáin is iasc ann chomh fairsing le móin.

Tá gach uile shórt maide ann dár féidir cur síos air:
bíonn *sycamore* is *beech* ann, coll, giúsach, is fuinseog,
box agus cuileann, iúr, beith, agus caorthann,
is an dair ghlas le ndéantar bád, long, is crann seoil;
an *logwood*, mahagaine, is gach adhmad dá dhaoire,
is an fíormhaide a dhéanfadh gach uile ghléas ceoil;
úlltoir is sceach gheal ann á ngearradh is á snaidhmeadh
is an tslat ann a dhéanfadh cis, cléibh agus lóid.

Tá an chuach is an smólach ag freagairt a chéile ann,
an lon dubh is an chéirseach ar gor os a gcomhair,
tá an *goldfinch*, is an creabhar, is an *linnet* i *gcage* ann,
an naoscach ag léimnigh, is an fhuiseog ón móin.
Tá an t-iolar as Acaill is an fiach dubh ón gCéis ann,
an seabhac as Loch Eirne is an eala ón Róimh,
is dá mbeifeá ann ar maidin le héirí na gréine,
chloisfeá gach éan acu ag seinm sa ngróbh.

Tá an láir an searrach i bhfochair a chéile ann,
an tseisreach is an céachta, an treabhach is an síol,
na huain ann ar maidin go fairsing ag méiligh,
caoirigh ina dtréada ann is linbh ag mnaoi.
Níl tinneas, níl aicíd, níl galar, níl éag ann,

ach sagairt is cléirigh ag guidhe na naomh;
tá mionnáin ag gabhair is bainbh ag an gcéis ann,
is an loilioch ag géimnigh ag triall ar a lao.

Tá an eilit is an fia is gach uile shórt géim ann,
an mada rua ag léimnigh, an broc is an míol buí;
guth binn na ngadhar is na hadharca dá séideadh,
roimh éiri na gréine a thógfadh do chroí.
Tá marcaigh ar eachraí agus daoine uaisle gléasta
ag fiach i *bplantations* go dtiteann an oích',
siléir go maidin arís ann á réabadh,
ól ag na céadta agus leaba le luí.

Faigheann baintreacha is dílleachtaí cabhair is
réiteach,
slí bia agus éadaí agus talamh gan chíos,
scoláirí bochta, scríobh, scoil and léann ann,
is lucht iarraidh na déirce ann, ag tarraingt is ag
triall.
Sháraigh sé an domhan le gach uile dhea-thréithe,
thug Raiftearaí an chraobh dó ar a bhfaca sé
riamh,
is é deireadh na cainte: saol fada ag Frank Taaffe
ann,
sliocht shinsir Ghaidéalas nár choigil an fial.

Killeaden, *or* County Mayo

Towards the Eve of St. Brigit the days will be
GROWING,
The cock will be CROWING and a home-wind
shall blow,
And I never shall stop but shall ever be GOING
Till I find myself ROVING through the county
May-o.
The first night in Claremorris I hope to put OVER,
And in Balla BELOW IT the cruiskeens shall flow;
In Coilltemach then I'll be living in CLOVER,
Near the place where my HOME IS and the House
that I know.

I solemnly aver it, that my heart rises up,
Even as the wind rises or as the mist disperses,
When I think upon Carra and upon Gallen down
from it,
Upon the Mile-Bush or upon the Plains of Mayo.
Killeaden (is) the village in which everything grows;
There are blackberries and raspberries in it, and
fruit of every kind;
And if I were only to be standing in the middle of
my people,
The age would go from me and I should be
young again.

There be's wheat there and oats, growth of barley
and of flax;
Rye in the ear there, bread of flour, and meat;
People who make 'poteen' selling it there without
a licence,
The great nobles of the country there playing and
drinking.
There is planting and plowing there, and
top-dressing without manure;
There is many a thing there of which I have not
spoken yet,
Kilns and mills working and never resting,
'Sorra' talk there is about a penny of rent nor
anything of the kind.

There is every sort of timber that it were fit to put
down there;
There is sycamore and beech in it, hazel, fir, and
ash,
Box and holly, yew, birch, and rowan-berry,
And the green-oak, of which is made boat and
ship and mast;
The log-wood, mahogany, and every timber no
matter how expensive,
And the fior-mhaide[1] (?) which would make every
musical instrument:
Oltoir[2] and white hawthorn a-cutting and
a-hewing.
And the rod there that would make basket, creels,
and lods.[3]

There is the cuckoo and the thrush answering each
other there,
The blackbird and the ceirseach[4] hatching over
against them,
The goldfinch, the wood-cock, and the linnet in a
cage there,
The snipe leaping up, and the swan from Rome,
The eagle out of Achill and the raven out of Kesh
Corran,
The falcon from Loch Erne and the lark from the
bog,
And if you were to be there in the morning before
rise of sun,

1. the finest of wood.
2. wood of the apple tree.
3. panniers or baskets.
4. The hen blackbird.

Sure you would hear every bird of them
a-singing in the grove.

There is the mare there and the foal, beside one another,
The team-of-six and the plow, the plowman and the seed,
The lambs there in the morning numerously bleating,
There be's sheep and herds, and the woman has a child.
There is no sickness, no disease, no plague, no death there,
But priests and clerics praying to the saints;
The goat has kids, the sow has bonhams,
And the milch-cow is lowing as she goes towards the woman.

The water is in the lake, and the rivers filled,
The weirs are constructed, and the nets in working-order,
The pike and the trout and the eel lying there,
The crab and the periwinkle, the mackerel and seal;
The salmon and the ballach[5] resting there at night,
And the liubhan (little eel, or lamprey?) voyaging thither from the great sea;
The tortoise and the lobster and the grey turbot,
The gurnets and fish are there as plenty as turf.

The fawn and the deer and every kind of game is there,
The red-dog (fox) a-leaping, the badger and the yellow miol (i.e., the hare),
The music of the hounds, and the horns a-blowing,
And with the rise of the sun you would lift up your heart.
There are gentlemen on steeds and horsemen being tried,
Hunting all through until comes the night,
(Then) cellar until morning again a-rending,
Drink for the hundreds and beds to lie down.

The orphan and the widow get assistance and redemption,
A way to get food and clothes, and land without rent;
Poor scholars get writing and schooling and learning there,
And the people who ask alms are drawing and journeying thither.
It overcame the world for all its good qualities,
And Raftery has awarded it the branch, over all that he ever saw;
The end of the talk is this: Long life to Frank Taaffe in it,
The descendant of the Lynch of hospitality, who never spared the hunt.

5. A fish called wrasse.

['Mary Hynes' is the best-known of Raftery's love poems. It is addressed to a local beauty and takes a traditional form, making variations on the *pastourelle*, from which it derives. The translation is by Douglas Hyde, and the Irish text is from Ciarán Ó Coigligh's edition of 1987. Hyde's translation does not follow the newly established sequence of the verses in Irish. In effect, his translation begins with what is now the fourth stanza in the Irish version, continues with the fifth, reverts to the second, continues with the third, reverts to the first, and ends with the sixth. The final two stanzas in the Irish version are untranslated. Once more, Hyde capitalizes words in the first stanza in an attempt to draw attention to the intricate sound patterns of the Irish.]

Máire Ní Eidhin

Is í Máire Ní Eidhin an chiúinbhean bhéasach
is deise méin agus is áille gnaoi,
agus míle cléireach a ghabháil in éineacht
trian a tréithe ní fhéadfadh scríobh.
Bhuail sí Deirdre le breáichte is Véineas
is dá n-abrainn Héilin ler scriosadh an Traí,
seo í an chraobh is cé a d'iarrfadh a héileamh
ar an bpabhsae gléigeal 'tá i mBaile Uí Lia.

De mhullach sléibhe nach aoibhinn aerach
an ní a bheith ag féachaint ar Bhaile Uí Lia,
ag siúl choillte ag baint cnó agus sméara
is gur geall glór éan ann le ceolta sí.
Cad é an bhrí an méid sin go bhfaighfeá léargas
ar bhláth na gcraobh atá lena thaobh?
Is níl gar á shéanadh níos faide ar aon neach,
a spéir na gréine, is tú grá mo chroí.

Dá siúlfá Sasana is an Fhrainc le chéile
an Spáinn, an Ghréig is ar ais arís,
ó bhruach Loch Gréine go béal Loch Eirne
is ní fheicfeá féirín ar bith mar í:
A grua trí lasadh agus a malaí caola
a haghaidh dá réir agus a béal deas faoi.
Scoth ban Éireann, is as ucht an scéil sin,
a thug mé an chraobh duit i mBaile Uí Lia.

Is ag triall chun Aifrinn dom le toil na nGrásta
  bhí an lá ag báistigh agus d'ardaigh an ghaoth,
casadh bruinneall dom le hais Chill Tártan
  agus thit me i láthair i ngrá ar an mnaoi.
D'umhlaíos síos di go múinte mánla
  is do réir a cálach d'fhreagair sí.
Is é a dúirt an ainnir liom: 'beidh m'intinn sásta,
  agus gluais go lá liom go Baile Uí Lia.'

Níor lig mé an tairgse níos faide ar cairde,
  b'ait liom trácht air is gheit mo chroí,
ní raibh le ghabháil againn ach trasna páirce
  agus thug an lá sinn go tóin an tí.
Socraíodh solas chugam, gloine is cárta
  agus cúilín fáinneach le m'ais 'na suí.
Is é a dúirt sí: 'a Raiftearaí, bí ag ól is céad fáilte,
  tá siléar láidir i mBaile Uí Lia.'

A réalt an tsolais, 'gus, a ghrian an fhómhair,
  a chúilín ómra is a chuid den tsaol,
siúil in uaigneas liom go ndéanam comhairle
  faoi choinne an Domhnaigh cá mbéam 'nár suí.
Níor mhór liom ceol duit gach aon tráthnóna
  puins ar bord is dá n-ólfá fíon.
Ach, a Rí na Glóire, go dtriomaí an bóthar
  go bhfaighe mé an t-eolas go Baile Uí Lia.

Is í mo mhian í seach mná na Fódla,
  a ghrá, is, a stórach, is tú a bhreoigh mo chroí
is go mb'fhearr liom póig uait ná saibhreas Sheoirse
  is mura bhfaighe mé fóirthint ní mhairfead mí.
Dá mbeinn pósta le bláth na hóige
  trí Loch an Tóraic is go leanfainn í;
cuanta is cóstaí go siúlfainn is bóithre
  i ndiaidh na seoide atá i mBaile Uí Lia.

Tá a folt ag casadh léi ar dhath na sméara
  ina trilsí réidhe ina diaidh sa drúcht
is 'na soilse lasta ar a brollach gléigeal
  a d'fhág na céadta i ngalar dubhach;
a bráid is gile ná an sneachta séidte
  is lúfar éadrom deas a coiscéim shiúil.
I mo rí dá mbeinnse nó i mo cheannfort Gréagach,
  go ndéanfainn réiteach leat, a bhláth na n-úll.

Mary Hynes, or The Posy Bright

Going to Mass of me, God was GRACIOUS,
  The day came RAINY and the wind did blow,
And near Kiltartan I met a MAIDEN
  Whose love enSLAVED me and left me low.

I spoke to her gently, the courteous MAIDEN,
  And gently and GAILY she answered so:
'Come, Raftery, with me, and let me TAKE YOU
  To Ballylee, where I have to go.'

When I got the offer, I did not put off (its
    acceptance),
  I laughed, and my heart bounded;
We had only to go across the field,
  And we only brought the day to the back of the
    house.[1]
There was laid for us a table on which was a glass
    and quart,
  And the ringletted coolun beside me sitting,
'Twas what she said, 'Raftery be drinking, and a
    hundred welcomes,
  The cellar is strong in Ballylee.'

It is lovely and airy on the side of the mountain
  Looking down upon Ballylee,
Walking in the grass, picking nuts and blackberries,
  The warbling of birds there is all as one as fairy
    music.
What is the good of all that, till you would get a sight
  Of the blossom of the branches who is by its side;
There is no use in denying it, and conceal it from no
    one,
  She is the sky of the sun and the love of my heart.

I travelled England and France together,
  Spain and Greece and back again,
From the brink of Loch Greine to the Mouth of the
    Quay,
  And I never saw a faireen at all like her.
If I were wed to the Blossom of Youth,
  Through Loch an Toraic I would follow her,
Harbours and coasts I would walk, and roads,
  After the jewel-woman who is in Ballylee.

It is Mary Hynes is the courteous, stately woman,
  Of nicest mien and most lovely appearance;
Two hundred clerks, and to put them together,
  One-third of her accomplishments they could
    not write.
She beat Deirdre for fineness, and Venus,
  And if I were to mention Helen by whom Troy
    was destroyed,
But she is the flower of Ireland on account of all
    that,
  The Posy Bright who is in Ballylee.

1. They went to the back of the house to make love for the rest of the day.

O Star of Light, O Sun of Harvest,
  O Amber Coolun, (my) share of the world,
Would you proceed with me, against Sunday,
  Until we take counsel where shall our sitting be.
I would not think it much for you, music every
  Sunday night,
  Punch upon the table, and, if you would drink it,
  wine,
And, O King of Glory, may the road dry,
  Until I find the way to Ballylee.

GEORGE SIGERSON

(1836-1925)

from: BARDS OF THE GAEL AND GALL (1907)

[The first edition of this anthology of translations was published in 1897. The second, expanded version, appeared ten years later. The text below is of the second edition.

Sigerson's volume is one of the most significant of the many anthologies published in the 1890s. Elizabeth Sharp's edition of *Lyra Celtica* (1896) and the better-known *A Treasury of Irish Poetry in the English Tongue* (1900) by Stopford Brooke and T. W. Rolleston, as well as Yeats's *A Book of Irish Verse* (1900), were also important; all these literary-Celtic anthologies had still to compete or conjoin with Martin MacDermott's *The New Spirit of the Nation* (1894) and *Songs and Ballads of Young Ireland* (1896). In fact, the role of anthologies in the development of the Irish Revival is consistently underrated or ignored and the impulses they represented are often indications of the prevailing mood of the decade. Sigerson's volume still retains its prominence in the field for two reasons. It is the most comprehensive of all in its coverage of Irish verse from the beginnings up to the contemporary period. It is also the most sustained, if not always the most successful, act of translation in this period. There is an ambitious effort to find a mode of English that would do some justice to the complexity of the Irish originals. This in itself forced Sigerson, as it later forced others, to abandon some of the conventions of contemporary poetry and to replace them with more direct and colloquial speech and rhythms.

Synge, Colum, Campbell, F. R. Higgins and others were the immediate beneficiaries of Sigerson's effort, even though they also owed a more obvious debt to the translations of Douglas Hyde, the most famous of all the anthologists of these years. The volume is dedicated to Douglas Hyde and to the historian and Parnellite, R. Barry O'Brien. Hyde wrote a preface to a later edition.]

Niall's Dirge

By Queen Gormlai, His Spouse, A.D. 919

[Niall Gleann Dubh, king of Ireland, was killed in battle near Rathfarnham, outside Dublin, in 919. The cleric who administered the last rites had refused him a horse to leave the battlefield — hence the bitterness of the widowed Queen Gormlai. The death of her husband marked the beginning of Gormlai's wretchedness. She is one of the tragic figures of Gaelic literature and is said to have composed this poem while dying from a wound.]

Move, O monk, thy foot away,
Lift it now from Niall's side,
Over-much thou'st cast the clay
Where I would, with him, abide.

Over-long thy task, this day,
Strewing clay o'er Niall slain;
Tread no further, friend, delay, —
Raise it not to meet the plain.

Ah, close not for aye the grave,
Cleric sad, with solemn lay;
From o'er Niall bright and brave
Move, O monk, thy foot away.

Golden King, not thus wert bound
Had I power thy strength to stay,
Leave his pillar, leave his mound,
Move thy foot, O monk, away.

I am Gormlai, who, in gloom,
Sing for him the sorrowing lay;
Stand not there upon his tomb,
Move, O monk, thy foot away.

[The author of 'The Ruined Nest' is unknown. According to Sigerson, it was composed 'long before the fourteenth century'. The poem was first edited and translated by Kuno Meyer in the *Gaelic Journal* (1890) from the fourteenth-century manuscript known as the *Lebor Breac*.]

The Ruined Nest

Sad is yonder blackbird's song,
Well I know what wrought it wrong;
Whosoe'er the deed has done,
Now its nestlings all are gone.

Such a sorrow I, too, know
For such loss, not long ago;
Well, O bird! I read thy state
For a home laid desolate.

How thy heart has burned, nigh broke,
At the rude and reckless stroke!
To lay waste thy little nest
Seems to cowboys but a jest.

Thy clear note called together
Flutt'ring young in new feather;
From thy nest comes now not one —
O'er its mouth the nettle's gone.

Sudden came the callous boys,
Their deed all thy young destroys:
Thou and I one fate deplore —
For my children are no more.

By thy side there used to be
Thy sweet mate from o'er the sea;
The herd's net ensnared her head —
She is gone from thee and dead.

O Ruler of high heaven!
Thou'st laid our loads uneven:
For our friends on ev'ry side
'Mid their mates and children bide.

Hither came hosts of Faery
To waste our home unwary;
Though they left no wound to tell
Brunt of battle were less fell.

Woe for wife; for children, woe!
I, in sorrow's shadow, go;
Not a trace of them I had
Hence my heavy heart is sad.

The Visit of Death

(Author Unknown)

O Youth, so loved and faithless!
  You've covered me with grief,
You mind not my heart breaking
  Nor care to give relief.
How great shall be your shaming
If you save me not from blaming,
Who swore upon the Manual
  To leave me not in grief.

Death will come to seek you
  A short half-hour ere day,
And for each guileful action
  He'll make you strictly pay.
In the small room, lying lonely,
The white shroud round you only,
How gladly you'd do penance
  If then found a way?

I was a happy maiden,
  With gladness in my voice;
You brought the sorrow with you —
  No more can I rejoice.
And now, since you're forsaking,
And your path from me are taking,
If I die through your heart-breaking
  How black will seem your choice!

I'd manage all your household
  With skilful hand so well,
Your hose, and shirt, and raiment
  Would be fairest in the dell.
If care or cloud hung o'er you
To youth I would restore you —
O wed me, and the Glory
  Of God shall with us dwell!

I had once no lack of clothing,
  Of food, or dwelling place,
I earned good fame and found it
  Among my kindred race:
Nor could Gall or Gael upbraid me
Till your false voice — it betrayed me.
But the Envoy I send with you
  Is the Most High King of Grace!

My love! my heart's own neighbour!
How deep tonight my woe,
How dark I'll be tomorrow
When you from me will go!
You've broke death's wall before me
The grave's cold breath blows o'er me,
Yet take one kiss, my Darling!
Before you leave me, so.

A Compliment

(Author Unknown)

Had I for ink the Ocean,
And Earth for paper white
Did ev'ry wing in motion
Give me its quills to write,
Were my reward the rarest —
All Europe's sovran might —
Thy virtues, O my Fairest!
I never could indite.

[Sigerson's note to the next poem is as follows: 'Emer, Cuchulainn's mortal spouse, came upon the lovers with fifty maidens armed with knives to slay Fand. Cuchulainn pledged her protection; but on hearing Emer's pathetic plea, he consoled her, declaring she should always be pleasing to him. Fand could not bear a divided love, and asked to be rejected. Emer also asked, but Fand persisted, and, falling into great grief, departed when she had spoken this lay.']

Fand's Farewell to Cuchulainn

I it is who shall depart,
Though I leave with heavy heart;
Though a hero waits me, fain,
Rather would I here remain!

Rather would I linger here,
Happy serving thee, and near;
Than, though strange to thee it seem,
Rule Aed's[1] court of sunny beam.

Emer, thine be this man still,
Thou shalt garner at thy will;
What my hand reach not, no less
Am I bound in wish to bless.

Many men for me have sued,
Sought in court, in secret woo'd,
Never one have I come nigh
For my path lay pure and high.

Woe to one whose love has gone,
And finds naught to rest upon;
Better who rejected roves
Than be loved not as one loves.

1. Aed or Aedh was the mythological ruler of the land of Faery.

WILLIAM LARMINIE

(*c.*1849-1900)

from: FAND AND OTHER POEMS (1892)

[Larminie was a strong advocate of the use of Gaelic assonance in English poetry. Although he was a skilled theoretician of metrics (see 'The Development of English Metres' in *The Contemporary Review* 66, November 1894), he could not incorporate his theories into his own verse. The two poems given here are by far his best-known. Practically nothing from his other volume, *Glanlua and Other Poems* (1899), survives. *Fand and Other Poems* is dominated by the title poem and by another long narrative poem, 'Moytura'.]

The Nameless Doon[1]

Who were the builders? Question not the silence
That settles on the lake for evermore,
Save when the sea-bird screams and to the islands
The echo answers from the steep-cliffed shore.
O half-remaining ruin, in the lore
Of human life a gap shall all deplore

1. *Dún* (Irish), a fort or castle.

Beholding thee; since thou art like the dead
Found slain, no token to reveal the why,
The name, the story. Some one murdered
We know, we guess; and gazing upon thee,
And, filled with thy long silence of reply,
We guess some garnered sheaf of tragedy;—
Of tribe or nation slain so utterly
That even their ghosts are dead, and on their grave
Springeth no bloom of legend in its wildness;
And age by age weak washing round the islands
No faintest sigh of story lisps the wave.

Consolation

Yes, let us speak; with lips confirming
  The inner pledge that eyes reveal; —
Bright eyes that death shall dim for ever,
  And lips that silence soon shall seal.

Yes, let us make our claim recorded
  Against the powers of earth and sky,
And that cold boon their laws award us —
  Just once to live, and once to die.

Thou say'st that fate is frosty nothing,
  But love the flame of souls that are:—
'Two spirits approach and at their touching
  Behold an everlasting star!'

High thoughts, O love; well! — let us speak them!
  Yet bravely face at least this fate, —
To know the dreams of us that dream them
  On blind unknowing things await.

If years from winters' chill recover,
  If fields are green and rivers run;
If thou and I behold each other,
  Hangs it not all on yonder sun?

So, while that mighty lord is gracious
  With prodigal beam to flood the skies,
Let us be glad that he can spare us
  The light to kindle lovers' eyes,

And die assured should life's new wonder,
  In any world our slumbers break,
These the first words that each will utter,
  'Belovèd, art thou too awake?'

OSCAR WILDE

(1854-1900)

from: THE BALLAD OF READING GAOL (1898)

[Wilde was transferred to Reading Gaol from Wandsworth Prison in November 1895. In 1896, a new occupant arrived, one Charles T. Woolridge, a former trooper in the Royal Horse Guards who had murdered his wife.

Wilde wrote the poem in Berneval in France in 1897, after his release from jail. His choice of the ballad form is in keeping with his new-found religious fervour. In his famous letter from prison, *De Profundis*, he claims that Christ is in every romantic movement in art and cites, among a number of examples, the literary ballads 'The Ancient Mariner', Keats's 'La Belle Dame sans Merci' and Thomas Chatterton's 'Ballad of Charity'. This poem is Wilde's addition to that list. Although it is based on the characteristic ballad stanza (first and third lines in iambic tetrameter, second and fourth in iambic trimeter, with alternate rhyme from the second line), the additional two lines, with the extra rhyme, lead him into occasional difficulties. The rhythm is sometimes clumsy, especially in the trimeter lines. Wilde had been reading A.E. Housman's *A Shropshire Lad* and it had stimulated him to produce this ballad as a broadsheet poem. There were six editions in 1898 alone. It was first included in the 1903 American edition of the *Poems*.]

1

He did not wear his scarlet coat,
  For blood and wine are red,
And blood and wine were on his hands
  When they found him with the dead,
The poor dead woman whom he loved,
  And murdered in her bed.

He walked amongst the Trial Men[1]
In a suit of shabby grey;
A cricket cap was on his head,
And his step seemed light and gay;
But I never saw a man who looked
So wistfully at the day.

I never saw a man who looked
With such a wistful eye
Upon that little tent of blue
Which prisoners call the sky,
And at every drifting cloud that went
With sails of silver by.

I walked, with other souls in pain,
Within another ring,
And was wondering if the man had done
A great or little thing,
When a voice behind me whispered low,
'That fellow's got to swing.'

Dear Christ! the very prison walls
Suddenly seemed to reel,
And the sky above my head became
Like a casque of scorching steel;
And, though I was a soul in pain,
My pain I could not feel.

I only knew what hunted thought
Quickened his step, and why
He looked upon the garish day
With such a wistful eye;
The man had killed the thing he loved,[2]
And so he had to die.

★

Yet each man kills the thing he loves,
By each let this be heard,
Some do it with a bitter look,
Some with a flattering word.
The coward does it with a kiss,
The brave man with a sword!

Some kill their love when they are young,
And some when they are old;
Some strangle with the hands of Lust,
Some with the hands of Gold:
The kindest use a knife, because
The dead so soon grow cold.

Some love too little, some too long,
Some sell, and others buy;
Some do the deed with many tears,
And some without a sigh:
For each man kills the thing he loves,
Yet each man does not die.

He does not die a death of shame
On a day of dark disgrace,
Nor have a noose about his neck,
Nor a cloth upon his face,
Nor drop feet foremost through the floor
Into an empty space.

He does not sit with silent men
Who watch him night and day;
Who watch him when he tries to weep,
And when he tries to pray;
Who watch him lest himself should rob
The prison of its prey.

He does not wake at dawn to see
Dread figures throng his room,
The shivering Chaplain robed in white,
The Sheriff stern with gloom,
And the Governor all in shiny black,
With the yellow face of Doom.

He does not rise in piteous haste
To put on convict-clothes,
While some coarse-mouthed Doctor gloats, and notes
Each new and nerve-twitched pose,
Fingering a watch whose little ticks
Are like horrible hammer-blows.

He does not feel that sickening thirst
That sands one's throat, before
The hangman with his gardener's gloves
Comes through the padded door,
And binds one with three leathern thongs,
That the throat may thirst no more.

He does not bend his head to hear
The Burial Office read,

1. Trial men are prisoners who have the chance of appeal after sentence.
2. The line is an inversion of Bassanio's query to Shylock in *The Merchant of Venice*, IV.1.66: 'Do all men kill the things they do not love?'

Nor, while the anguish of his soul
  Tells him he is not dead,
Cross his own coffin, as he moves
  Into the hideous shed.

He does not stare upon the air
  Through a little roof of glass:
He does not pray with lips of clay
  For his agony to pass;
Nor feel upon his shuddering cheek
  The kiss of Caiaphas.[3]

2

Six weeks the guardsman walked the yard,
  In the suit of shabby grey:
His cricket cap was on his head,
  And his step seemed light and gay,
But I never saw a man who looked
  So wistfully at the day.

I never saw a man who looked
  With such a wistful eye
Upon that little tent of blue
  Which prisoners call the sky,
And at every wandering cloud that trailed
  Its ravelled fleeces by.

He did not wring his hands, as do
  Those witless men who dare
To try to rear the changeling Hope
  In the cave of black Despair:
He only looked upon the sun,
  And drank the morning air.

He did not wring his hands nor weep,
  Nor did he peek or pine,
But he drank the air as though it held
  Some healthful anodyne;
With open mouth he drank the sun
  As though it had been wine!

And I and all the souls in pain,
  Who tramped the other ring,
Forgot if we ourselves had done
  A great or little thing,
And watched with gaze of dull amaze
  The man who had to swing.

3. Caiaphas was the high priest of the Jews; he presided at the trial of Jesus. Judas bargained with him for thirty pieces of silver, to be paid when he kissed Christ. See Luke 3.2; Matthew 26.

For strange it was to see him pass
  With a step so light and gay,
And strange it was to see him look
  So wistfully at the day,
And strange it was to think that he
  Had such a debt to pay.

★

For oak and elm have pleasant leaves
  That in the spring-time shoot;
But grim to see is the gallows-tree,
  With its adder-bitten root,
And, green or dry, a man must die
  Before it bears its fruit!

The loftiest place is that seat of grace
  For which all worldlings try:
But who would stand in hempen band
  Upon a scaffold high,
And through a murderer's collar take
  His last look at the sky?

It is sweet to dance to violins
  When Love and Life are fair:
To dance to flutes, to dance to lutes
  Is delicate and rare:
But it is not sweet with nimble feet
  To dance upon the air!

So with curious eyes and sick surmise
  We watched him day by day,
And wondered if each one of us
  Would end the self-same way,
For none can tell to what red Hell
  His sightless soul may stray.

At last the dead man walked no more
  Amongst the Trial Men,
And I knew that he was standing up
  In the black dock's dreadful pen,
And that never would I see his face
  For weal or woe again.

Like two doomed ships that pass in storm
  We had crossed each other's way:
But we made no sign, we said no word,
  We had no word to say;
For we did not meet in the holy night,
  But in the shameful day.

A prison wall was round us both,
Two outcast men we were:
The world had thrust us from its heart,
And God from out His care:
And the iron gin that waits for Sin
Had caught us in its snare.

3

. . . .

At last I saw the shadowed bars,
Like a lattice wrought in lead,
Move right across the whitewashed wall
That faced my three-plank bed,
And I knew that somewhere in the world
God's dreadful dawn was red.

At six o'clock we cleaned our cells,
At seven all was still,
But the sough and swing of a mighty wing
The prison seemed to fill,
For the Lord of Death with icy breath
Had entered in to kill.

He did not pass in purple pomp,
Nor ride a moon-white steed.
Three yards of cord and a sliding board
Are all the gallows' need:
So with rope of shame the Herald came
To do the secret deed.

We were as men who through a fen
Of filthy darkness grope:
We did not dare to breathe a prayer,
Or to give our anguish scope:
Something was dead in each of us,
And what was dead was Hope.

For Man's grim Justice goes its way,
And will not swerve aside:
It slays the weak, it slays the strong,
It has a deadly stride:
With iron heel it slays the strong,
The monstrous parricide!

We waited for the stroke of eight:
Each tongue was thick with thirst:
For the stroke of eight is the stroke of Fate
That makes a man accursed,
And Fate will use a running noose
For the best man and the worst.

We had no other thing to do,
Save to wait for the sign to come:
So, like things of stone in a valley lone,
Quiet we sat and dumb:
But each man's heart beat thick and quick,
Like a madman on a drum!

With sudden shock the prison-clock
Smote on the shivering air,
And from all the gaol rose up a wail
Of impotent despair,
Like the sound that frightened marshes hear
From some leper in his lair.

And as one sees most fearful things
In the crystal of a dream,
We saw the greasy hempen rope
Hooked to the blackened beam,
And heard the prayer the hangman's snare
Strangled into a scream.

And all the woe that moved him so
That he gave that bitter cry,
And the wild regrets, and the bloody sweats,
None knew so well as I:
For he who lives more lives than one
More deaths than one must die.

4

There is no chapel on the day
On which they hang a man:
The Chaplain's heart is far too sick,
Or his face is far too wan,
Or there is that written in his eyes
Which none should look upon.

So they kept us close till nigh on noon,
And then they rang the bell,
And the warders with their jingling keys
Opened each listening cell,
And down the iron stair we tramped,
Each from his separate Hell.

Out into God's sweet air we went,
But not in wonted way,
For this man's face was white with fear,
And that man's face was grey,
And I never saw sad men who looked
So wistfully at the day.

I never saw sad men who looked
  With such a wistful eye
Upon that little tent of blue
  We prisoners called the sky,
And at every happy cloud that passed
  In such strange freedom by.

But there were those amongst us all
  Who walked with downcast head,
And knew that, had each got his due,
  They should have died instead:
He had but killed a thing that lived,
  Whilst they had killed the dead.

For he who sins a second time
  Wakes a dead soul to pain,
And draws it from its spotted shroud,
  And makes it bleed again,
And makes it bleed great gouts of blood,
  And makes it bleed in vain!

★

Like ape or clown, in monstrous garb
  With crooked arrows starred,
Silently we went round and round
  The slippery asphalte yard;
Silently we went round and round,
  And no man spoke a word.

Silently we went round and round,
  And through each hollow mind
The Memory of dreadful things
  Rushed like a dreadful wind,
And Horror stalked before each man,
  And Terror crept behind.

★

The warders strutted up and down,
  And watched their herd of brutes,
Their uniforms were spick and span,
  And they wore their Sunday suits,
But we knew the work they had been at,
  By the quicklime on their boots.

For where a grave had opened wide,
  There was no grave at all:
Only a stretch of mud and sand
  By the hideous prison-wall,
And a little heap of burning lime,
  That the man should have his pall.

For he has a pall, this wretched man,
  Such as few men can claim:
Deep down below a prison-yard,
  Naked for greater shame,
He lies, with letters on each foot,
  Wrapt in a sheet of flame!

And all the while the burning lime
  Eats flesh and bone away,
It eats the brittle bone by night,
  And the soft flesh by day,
It eats the flesh and bone by turns,
  But it eats the heart alway.

★

For three long years they will not sow
  Or root or seedling there:
For three long years the unblessed spot
  Will sterile be and bare,
And look upon the wondering sky
  With unreproachful stare.

They think a murderer's heart would taint
  Each simple seed they sow.
It is not true! God's kindly earth
  Is kindlier than men know,
And the red rose would but blow more red,
  The white rose whiter blow.

Out of his mouth a red, red rose!
  Out of his heart a white!
For who can say by what strange way,
  Christ brings His will to light,
Since the barren staff the pilgrim bore
  Bloomed in the great Pope's sight?[4]

But neither milk-white rose nor red
  May bloom in prison-air;
The shard, the pebble, and the flint,
  Are what they give us there:
For flowers have been known to heal
  A common man's despair.

4. The reference is to the legend of Tannhauser, who fell in love with Venus and spent seven years with her in the cave of Venusberg. He left, smitten by conscience, to seek forgiveness from the Pope in Rome. The Pope said it was as impossible for Tannhauser to be forgiven as it was for his own dry staff to burgeon. Tannhauser departed in despair; three days later the staff blossomed. The Pope sent for Tannhauser, but he had disappeared with Venus.

So never will wine-red rose or white,
Petal by petal, fall
On that stretch of mud and sand that lies
By the hideous prison-wall,
To tell the men who tramp the yard
That God's Son died for all.

Yet though the hideous prison-wall
Still hems him round and round,
And a spirit may not walk by night
That is with fetters bound,
And a spirit may but weep that lies
In such unholy ground,

He is at peace — this wretched man —
At peace, or will be soon:
There is no thing to make him mad,
Nor does Terror walk at noon,
For the lampless Earth in which he lies
Has neither Sun nor Moon.

They hanged him as a beast is hanged!
They did not even toll
A requiem that might have brought
Rest to his startled soul,
But hurriedly they took him out,
And hid him in a hole.

The warders stripped him of his clothes,
And gave him to the flies:
They mocked the swollen purple throat,
And the stark and staring eyes:
And with laughter loud they heaped the shroud
In which the convict lies.

The Chaplain would not kneel to pray
By his dishonoured grave:
Nor mark it with the blessed Cross
That Christ for sinners gave,
Because the man was one of those
Whom Christ came down to save.

Yet all is well; he has but passed
To Life's appointed bourne:[5]
And alien tears will fill for him
Pity's long-broken urn,
For his mourners will be outcast men,
And outcasts always mourn.

5. destination.

5

I know not whether Laws be right,
Or whether Laws be wrong;
All that we know who lie in gaol
Is that the wall is strong;
And that each day is like a year,
A year whose days are long.

But this I know, that every Law
That men hath made for Man,
Since first Man took his brother's life,
And the sad world began,
But straws the wheat and saves the chaff
With a most evil fan.

This too I know — and wise it were
If each could know the same —
That every prison that men build
Is built with bricks of shame,
And bound with bars lest Christ should see
How men their brothers maim.

With bars they blur the gracious moon,
And blind the goodly sun;
And they do well to hide their Hell,
For in it things are done
That Son of God nor son of Man
Ever should look upon!

★

The vilest deeds like poison weeds,
Bloom well in prison-air;
It is only what is good in Man
That wastes and withers there:
Pale Anguish keeps the heavy gate,
And the Warder is Despair.

For they starve the little frightened child
Till it weeps both night and day:
And they scourge the weak, and flog the fool,
And give the old and grey,
And some grow mad, and all grow bad,
And none a word may say.

Each narrow cell in which we dwell
Is a foul and dark latrine,
And the fetid breath of living Death
Chokes up each grated screen,
And all, but Lust, is turned to dust
In Humanity's machine.

The brackish water that we drink
  Creeps with a loathsome slime,
And the bitter bread they weigh in scales
  Is full of chalk and lime,
And Sleep will not lie down, but walks
  Wild-eyed, and cries to Time.

★

But though lean Hunger and green Thirst
  Like asp with adder fight,
We have little care of prison fare,
  For what chills and kills outright
Is that every stone one lifts by day
  Becomes one's heart by night.

With midnight always in one's heart,
  And twilight in one's cell,
We turn the crank, or tear the rope,[6]
  Each in his separate Hell,
And the silence is more awful far
  Than the sound of a brazen hell.

And never a human voice comes near
  To speak a gentle word:
And the eye that watches through the door
  Is pitiless and hard:
And by all forgot, we rot and rot,
  With soul and body marred.

And thus we rust Life's iron chain
  Degraded and alone:
And some men curse, and some men weep,
  And some men make no moan:
But God's eternal Laws are kind
  And break the heart of stone.

And every human heart that breaks,
  In prison-cell or yard,
Is as that broken box that gave
  Its treasure to the Lord,
And filled the unclean leper's house
  With the scent of costliest nard.[7]

Ah! happy they whose hearts can break
  And peace of pardon win!
How else may man make straight his plan
  And cleanse his soul from Sin?

6. They tore rope to make oakum.
7. Spikenard, a plant whose aromatic roots were used in medicine.

How else but through a broken heart
  May Lord Christ enter in?

★

And he of the swollen purple throat,
  And the stark and staring eyes,
Waits for the holy hands that took
  The Thief to Paradise;
And a broken and a contrite heart
  The Lord will not despise.

The man in red who reads the Law
  Gave him three weeks of life,
Three little weeks in which to heal
  His soul of his soul's strife,
And cleanse from every blot of blood
  The hand that held the knife.

And with tears of blood he cleansed the hand,
  The hand that held the steel:
For only blood can wipe out blood,
  And only tears can heal:
And the crimson stain that was of Cain
  Became Christ's snow-white seal.

6

In Reading gaol by Reading town
  There is a pit of shame,
And in it lies a wretched man
  Eaten by teeth of flame,
In a burning winding-sheet he lies,[8]
  And his grave has got no name.

And there, till Christ call forth the dead,
  In silence let him lie:
No need to waste the foolish tear,
  Or heave the windy sigh:
The man had killed the thing he loved,
  And so he had to die.

And all men kill the thing they love,
  By all let this be heard,
Some do it with a bitter look,
  Some with a flattering word,
The coward does it with a kiss,
  The brave man with a sword!

8. He was buried in lime.

from: THE POEMS OF OSCAR WILDE (1903)

['Requiescat' is probably the most frequently anthologized of all Wilde's poems. The original date of publication is not known, but it appeared in the first edition of Wilde's *Poems* in 1881.]

Requiescat

Tread lightly, she is near
  Under the snow,
Speak gently, she can hear
  The daisies grow.

All her bright golden hair
  Tarnished with rust,
She that was young and fair
  Fallen to dust.

Lily-like, white as snow,
  She hardly knew
She was a woman, so
  Sweetly she grew.

Coffin-board, heavy stone,
  Lie on her breast,
I vex my heart alone,
  She is at rest.

Peace, peace, she cannot hear
  Lyre or sonnet,
All my life's buried here,
  Heap earth upon it.

Avignon

Impressions

1

Les Silhouettes

[First published in 1894, this poem became the first in a sequence that was established by about 1900.]

  The sea is flecked with bars of grey,
  The dull dead wind is out of tune,
  And like a withered leaf the moon
Is blown across the stormy bay.

  Etched clear upon the pallid sand
  Lies the black boat: a sailor boy
  Clambers aboard in careless joy
With laughing face and gleaming hand.

  And overhead the curlews cry,
  Where through the dusky upland grass
  The young brown-throated reapers pass,
Like silhouettes against the sky.

2

La Fuite de la Lune (The Flight of the Moon)

[This second poem in the sequence first appeared in *The Irish Monthly* (1887) as the third of a five-part poem called *Lotus Leaves*. It was slightly modified for its reappearance in this series.]

  To outer senses there is peace,
  A dreamy peace on either hand,
  Deep silence in the shadowy land,
Deep silence where the shadows cease.

  Save for a cry that echoes shrill
  From some lone bird disconsolate;
  A corncrake calling to its mate;
The answer from the misty hill.

  And suddenly the moon withdraws
  Her sickle from the lightening skies,
  And to her sombre cavern flies,
Wrapped in a veil of yellow gauze.

[First published in *The Dramatic Review* (1885), 'The Harlot's House' had two separate editions, in 1904 and 1905, before appearing — with a misprint — in Mosher's edition of the *Poems* (1905). The text here is of the 1904 Folio edition.]

The Harlot's House

We caught the tread of dancing feet,
We loitered down the moonlit street,
And stopped beneath the harlot's house.

Inside, above the din and fray,
We heard the loud musicians play
The 'Treues Liebes Herz' of Strauss.

Like strange mechanical grotesques,
Making fantastic arabesques,
The shadows raced across the blind.

We watched the ghostly dancers spin
To sound of horn and violin,
Like black leaves wheeling in the wind.

Like wire-pulled automatons,
Slim silhouetted skeletons
Went sidling through the slow quadrille.

They took each other by the hand,
And danced a stately saraband;
Their laughter echoed thin and shrill.

Sometimes a clockwork puppet pressed
A phantom lover to her breast,
Sometimes they seemed to try to sing.

Sometimes a horrible marionette
Came out, and smoked its cigarette
Upon the steps like a live thing.

Then, turning to my love, I said,
'The dead are dancing with the dead,
The dust is whirling with the dust.'

But she — she heard the violin,
And left my side, and entered in:
Love passed into the house of lust.

THOMAS WILLIAM ROLLESTON

(1857-1920)

from:
SEA SPRAY: VERSES AND TRANSLATIONS (1909)

['The Dead at Clonmacnois' is a translation of an Irish poem by Angus O'Gillan. Clonmacnoise, a monastic city founded by St Kieran on the banks of the Shannon in the sixth century, is one of the favourite ancient sites for poetic reveries and lamentations of this kind. The point here is that the Christian settlement is built over the pagan, Celtic burial place of the old dynasties. Together, they indicate the depth of the Irish historical record.]

The Dead at Clonmacnois

In a quiet-water'd land, a land of roses,
  Stands Saint Kieran's city fair,
And the warriors of Erinn in their famous generations
  Slumber there.

There beneath the dewy hillside sleep the noblest
  Of the Clan of Conn,
Each below his stone; his name in branching Ogham
  And the sacred knot thereon.

There they laid to rest the Seven Kings of Tara,
  There the sons of Cairbrè sleep —
Battle-banners of the Gael, that in Kieran's plain of crosses
  Now their final hosting keep.

And in Clonmacnois they laid the men of Teffia
  And right many a lord of Breagh;
Deep the sod above Clan Creidè and Clan Connall,
  Kind in hall and fierce in fray.

Many and many a son of Conn the Hundred-Fighter
  In the red earth lies at rest;
Many a blue eye of Clan Colman the turf covers,
  Many a swan-white breast.[1]

1. Conn of the Hundred Battles was a famous, legendary king of Tara; Ogham was an old Irish alphabet, based on a system of strokes and dots; Tara, Co. Meath, is the hill that became the focus of early kingship in Ireland; Cairbre Caithchenn was a notorious usurper of the kingship; Teffia (*recte* Tethra) was a goddess of the sea; the kings of Bregha (Breagh) resided on the banks of the river Boyne; Creidhne (Creidè) was a craftsman-god, a worker in metal; Conall Cernach was one of the heroes of the Ulster Cycle.

SUSAN MITCHELL

(1866-1926)

from: AIDS TO THE IMMORTALITY OF CERTAIN PERSONS IN IRELAND: CHARITABLY ADMINISTERED (1908)

[Susan Mitchell was one of the wittiest writers of her generation. Her book *George Moore* (1916) is the most effective of all the varied responses to the old master of malice. Although some of the objects of her satire are now dated, this volume — also dominated by Moore — demonstrates her light but wounding touch. The text is from the enlarged edition, published in 1913.

The Irish Council Bill of 1907, also known as the Devolution Bill, was a half-hearted version of Home Rule, constituting a compromise between the unionist and Home Rule demands. The proposal was rejected outright by Sinn Féin, by William O'Brien's United Irish League, and by John Redmond and the Irish Parliamentary Party. In fact, the most prominent of the nationalists prepared to accept it was Patrick Pearse.

Mitchell adapts to her satiric purpose the eighteenth-century song, 'The Shan Van Vocht' (The Poor Old Woman — i.e. Ireland), revived by the Young Irelanders in the popular volume *The Spirit of the Nation*.]

The Irish Council Bill, 1907

Is it this you call Home Rule?
Says the Shan Van Vocht.
Do you take me for a fool?
Says the Shan Van Vocht.
To be sending round the hat
Five-and-twenty years for that
Isn't good enough for Pat,
Says the Shan Van Vocht.

And the Lord-Lieutenant too,
Says the Shan Van Vocht,
Is he still to be on view?
Says the Shan Van Vocht.
And all them big police,
Monumentally obese,
Must I go on feeding these?
Says the Shan Van Vocht.

Oh then M.P.s could you do,
Says the Shan Van Vocht,
Nothing better for your screw?
Says the Shan Van Vocht.
I didn't mean your pay
To depend on your delay,
But quite the other way,
Says the Shan Van Vocht.

You rounded on Parnell,
Says the Shan Van Vocht,
You bid him go to hell!
Says the Shan Van Vocht.
You served the Sassenach
When Plunkett got the sack,[1]
On me you've turned your back,
Says the Shan Van Vocht.

Faith it's growing clear to me,
Says the Shan Van Vocht,
That ye like being absentee,
Says the Shan Van Vocht,
At Westminster to appear
On two hundred pounds a year;
Ye'd have empty pockets here,
Says the Shan Van Vocht.

All your promises were vain,
Says the Shan Van Vocht.
I'm turning to Sinn Fein
Says the Shan Van Vocht.
If ye ever travel hence
Unto future Parliaments
'Twill be at your own expense,
Says the Shan Van Vocht.

1. In 1907 Sir Horace Plunkett (1854-1932) resigned from the Recess Committee, which had sought government aid in establishing a Department of Agriculture in 1899. Anti-Parnellites boycotted the committee. In 1908, Plunkett became a supporter of Home Rule. *Sasanach* is the Irish word for Saxon or English person.

['Ode to the British Empire' is a satire on the Church of Ireland, many members of which still lamented the consequences of the Disestablishment of 1869 which deprived them of income, lands and prestige. Tithes had been commuted in the 1830s; landlords were being bought off in the various Land Acts and, as a consequence, church income had fallen.]

Ode to the British Empire

Dedicated to the Archbishops
and Bishops of the Church of Ireland

God of the Irish Protestant,
Lord of our proud Ascendancy,
Soon there'll be none of us extant,
We want a few plain words with thee.
Thou know'st our hearts are always set
On what we get, on what we get.

The landlords with the bonus fly,
The gold upon the plate has ceased;
Without our aristocracy
We sink below the parish priest.
Unless their hire thy labourers get
The Pope may rule in Ireland yet.

You sent us to this Popish land;
Cromwell and William well did smite,
Delivering into our hand
The Hittite and the Jebusite.[1]
The Papishes we burned, and yet
We don't regret, we don't regret.

We did your dirty work for you,
And incidentally likewise
To us some profit did accrue
(You'll understand and sympathise).
Now one by one of each asset
You've robbed us, this we can't forget.

The tithes and the Establishment
You took, but still to you we clung:
Off went each fat emolument,
We smiled although our hearts were wrung.
Beneath that smile our teeth were set,
The worrum wouldn't turrn yet.

1. See Exodus 23.28, 33.2, 34.11 and II Samuel 5.8. The Hittites and Jebusites were enemies of the Chosen People.

Though we were growing moribund,
With all your acts we still agreed;
We had the Sustentation Fund,
You had the Athanasian Creed.
The Commination Service yet
Is ours — and do not you forget![2]

We shouted long, 'God save the King!'
And damned the Papacy to hell.
'Twere easy to reverse the thing
And send you English all to —— well
We needn't mention names, but yet
We'd see you there without regret.

God of the Irish Protestant,
You have grown hideous in our sight;
You're not the kind of god we want.
Rise, Sons of William, rise and smite!
New gods we'll serve, and with them yet
We'll get all there is left to get!

2. The Athanasian Creed, the third of the three principal doctrinal statements of Christianity, is used at morning prayer on the greatest festivals in the Church of England. The Sustentation Fund was administered by the government to provide for needy cases under the Disestablishment Act. Mitchell reverses the usual positions here. The Commination Service, the denunciation of God against sinners, is in the anglican prayer book and is read in church on Ash Wednesday.

[George Moore, born a catholic, made a great fuss about his conversion to protestantism, but found that the Church of Ireland was a little embarrassed by its notorious new recruit — who wished to be baptized over again. So Moore moved into Ely Place in Dublin and resumed the 'pagan' lifestyle to which he was best suited. He proclaimed, with great regularity, that his true religion was art.

The opening line echoes the first line of 'The Vicar of Bray': 'In good King Charles's golden days . . . .' Many of the lines of that anonymous song also end in 'Sir'.]

George Moore becomes the Priest of Aphrodite

In good Victoria's humdrum days
I started my career, Sir,
I from Mayo to France did go,
Where I acted very queer, Sir.
But I my sins repenting sore,
To pious Dublin came, Sir,

And though I find most things a bore,
  I stay here all the same, Sir.
But if you ask me to explain,
  I really cannot say, Sir,
Why I in Dublin still remain
  When I might go away, Sir.

Now I was christened in Mayo,
  Where Popery was in fashion,
But for that error long ago
  I have a great compassion.
I would be christened once again,
  And wear a robe with flounces,
Alas, I'm weighed by stones who then
  Was weighed by pounds and ounces.
But though my form no pretty nurse
  May bear to my baptism, Sir,
I have renounced my country's curse,
  And left the Roman schism, Sir.

When I from Popery did recant,
  And left my dark condition,
To be a simple Protestant
  Was long my sole ambition.
But since my views on Saving Grace
  The Puritans found flighty,
Behold me now in Ely Place
  The priest of Aphrodite.[1]
I'll set her image up on high,
  Within my garden shady,
And every day a wreath I'll lay
  Before my marble lady.

But even this does not explain,
  Nor can I really say, Sir,
Why I in Dublin still remain
  When I might go away, Sir.

1. The Greek goddess of love and beauty.

GEORGE RUSSELL (AE)

(1867-1935)

from:
COLLECTED POEMS (1913)

[Russell's poetry is vaporous, but not whimsically personal or fiercely introverted. With unwearying confidence, he expounds his belief in the supervening power of another world, of which this one is merely a shadow or distortion. He turns readily to mythology and abstraction, for he finds in these the only surviving vocabulary for his beliefs. Ireland is for him, as for many of his contemporaries, an especially privileged and important place because it has kept faith with the spiritual universals that elsewhere have been ignored or forgotten.

It is appropriate that, in one of the poems represented here, Russell should salute Terence MacSwiney, who died on hunger strike in Brixton Prison in 1920. MacSwiney, too, was one of those idealists who believed in the spiritual destiny of Ireland and in the inevitability of its ultimate triumph in the struggle against British rule and British civilization. Russell combined this dedicated mysticism with a wholly pragmatic readiness to get things done, to improve the conditions of Irish life and to help create the basis for economic survival and prosperity. He was an inspirational friend to many of the leading literary and political figures of the period. His final disillusion with Ireland was an emblem of the country's failure to live up to the ideals that he and his friends had helped to create.]

Faith

Here where the loves of others close
The vision of my heart begins.
The wisdom that within us grows
Is absolution for our sins.

We took forbidden fruit and ate
Far in the garden of His mind.
The ancient prophecies of hate
We proved untrue, for He was kind.

He does not love the bended knees,
The soul made wormlike in His sight,
Within whose heaven are hierarchies
And solar kings and lords of light.

Who come before Him with the pride
The Children of the King should bear,
They will not be by Him denied,
His light will make their darkness fair.

To be afar from Him is death
Yet all things find their fount in Him:
And nearing to the sunrise breath
Shine jewelled like the seraphim.

Three Counsellors

It was the fairy of the place,
Moving within a little light,
Who touched with dim and shadowy grace
The conflict at its fever height.

It seemed to whisper 'Quietness,'
Then quietly itself was gone:
Yet echoes of its mute caress
Were with me as the years went on.

It was the warrior within
Who called 'Awake, prepare for fight:
Yet lose not memory in the din:
Make of thy gentleness thy might:

'Make of thy silence words to shake
The long-enthroned kings of earth:
Make of thy will the force to break
Their towers of wantonness and mirth.'

It was the wise all-seeing soul
Who counselled neither war nor peace:
'Only be thou thyself that goal
In which the wars of time shall cease.'

Symbolism

Now when the spirit in us wakes and broods,
Filled with home yearnings, drowsily it flings
From its deep heart high dreams and mystic moods,
Mixed with the memory of the loved earth things:
Clothing the vast with a familiar face;
Reaching its right hand forth to greet the starry race.

Wondrously near and clear the great warm fires
Stare from the blue; so shows the cottage light
To the field labourer whose heart desires
The old folk by the nook, the welcome bright
From the house-wife long parted from at dawn —
So the star villages in God's great depths
  withdrawn.

Nearer to Thee, not by delusion led,
Though there no house fires burn nor bright eyes
  gaze:
We rise, but by the symbol charioted,
Through loved things rising up to Love's own ways:
By these the soul unto the vast has wings
And sets the seal celestial on all mortal things.

Immortality

We must pass like smoke or live within the spirit's
  fire;
For we can no more than smoke unto the flame
  return
If our thought has changed to dream, our will unto
  desire,
  As smoke we vanish though the fire may burn.

Lights of infinite pity star the grey dusk of our days:
Surely here is soul: with it we have eternal breath:
In the fire of love we live, or pass by many ways,
  By unnumbered ways of dream to death.

In Connemara

With eyes all untroubled she laughs as she passes,
  Bending beneath the creel with the seaweed
    brown,
Till evening with pearl dew dims the shining grasses
  And night lit with dreamlight enfolds the sleepy
    town.

Then she will wander, her heart all a laughter,
  Tracking the dream star that lights the purple
    gloom.
She follows the proud and golden races after,
  As high as theirs her spirit, as high will be her
    doom.

Truth

The hero first thought it
To him 'twas a deed:
To those who retaught it,
A chain on their speed.

The fire that we kindled,
A beacon by night,
When darkness has dwindled
Grows pale in the light.

For life has no glory
Stays long in one dwelling,

And time has no story
That's true twice in telling.

And only the teaching
That never was spoken
Is worthy thy reaching,
The fountain unbroken.

The Twilight of Earth

The wonder of the world is o'er:
The magic from the sea is gone:
There is no unimagined shore,
No islet yet to venture on.
The Sacred Hazels' blooms are shed,
The Nuts of Knowledge harvested.

Oh, what is worth this lore of age
If time shall never bring us back
Our battle with the gods to wage
Reeling along the starry track.
The battle rapture here goes by
In warring upon things that die.

Let be the tale of him whose love
Was sighed between white Deirdre's breasts,
It will not lift the heart above
The sodden clay on which it rests.
Love once had power the gods to bring
All rapt on its wild wandering.

We shiver in the falling dew,
And seek a shelter from the storm:
When man these elder brothers knew
He found the mother nature warm,
A hearth fire blazing through it all,
A home without a circling wall.

We dwindle down beneath the skies,
And from ourselves we pass away:
The paradise of memories
Grows ever fainter day by day.
The shepherd stars have shrunk within,
The world's great night will soon begin.

Will no one, ere it is too late,
Ere fades the last memorial gleam,
Recall for us our earlier state?
For nothing but so vast a dream
That it would scale the steeps of air
Could rouse us from so vast despair.

The power is ours to make or mar
Our fate as on the earliest morn,
The Darkness and the Radiance are
Creatures within the spirit born.
Yet, bathed in gloom too long, we might
Forget how we imagined light.

Not yet are fixed the prison bars;
The hidden light the spirit owns
If blown to flame would dim the stars
And they who rule them from their thrones:
And the proud sceptred spirits thence
Would bow to pay us reverence.

Oh, while the glory sinks within
Let us not wait on earth behind,
But follow where it flies, and win
The glow again, and we may find
Beyond the Gateways of the Day
Dominion and ancestral sway.

On Behalf of Some Irishmen Not Followers of Tradition

They call us aliens, we are told,
Because our wayward visions stray
From that dim banner they unfold,
The dreams of worn-out yesterday.
The sum of all the past is theirs,
The creeds, the deeds, the fame, the name,
Whose death-created glory flares
And dims the spark of living flame.
They weave the necromancer's spell,
And burst the graves where martyrs slept,
Their ancient story to retell,
Renewing tears the dead have wept.
And they would have us join their dirge,
This worship of an extinct fire
In which they drift beyond the verge
Where races all outworn expire.
The worship of the dead is not
A worship that our hearts allow,
Though every famous shade were wrought
With woven thorns above the brow.
We fling our answer back in scorn:
'We are less children of this clime
Than of some nation yet unborn

Or empire in the womb of time.
We hold the Ireland in the heart
More than the land our eyes have seen,
And love the goal for which we start
More than the tale of what has been.'
The generations as they rise
May live the life men lived before,
Still hold the thought once held as wise,
Go in and out by the same door.
We leave the easy peace it brings:
The few we are shall still unite
In fealty to unseen kings
Or unimaginable light.
We would no Irish sign efface,
But yet our lips would gladlier hail
The firstborn of the Coming Race
Than the last splendour of the Gael.
No blazoned banner we unfold —
One charge alone we give to youth,
Against the sceptred myth to hold
The golden heresy of truth.

from:
VALE AND OTHER POEMS (1931)

[Terence MacSwiney (1879-1920) was arrested under the notorious Defence of the Realm Act, widely used in Ireland by the British authorities to stifle Irish revolutionary organizations in the 1916-21 period. MacSwiney succeeded Thomas MacCurtain as lord mayor of Cork; MacCurtain had been murdered by members of the Royal Irish Constabulary. After his arrest, MacSwiney embarked on a seventy-four-day hunger strike in London's Brixton Prison. He captured worldwide attention and his funeral through the streets of London was an international event.]

A Prisoner

(Brixton, September 1920)

See, though the oil be low, more purely still and
  higher
The flame burns in the body's lamp. The watchers
  still
Gaze with unseeing eyes while the Promethean will,
The Uncreated Light, the Everlasting Fire,
Sustain themselves against the torturer's desire,
Even as the fabled Titan chained upon the hill.
Burn on, shine here, thou immortality, until
We too can light our lamps at the funereal pyre;
Till we too can be noble, unshakeable, undismayed
Till we too can burn with the holy flame, and know
There is that within us can conquer the dragon pain,
And go to death alone, slowly and unafraid.
The candles of God already are burning row on row:
Farewell, light-bringer; fly to thy fountain again.

LIONEL JOHNSON

(1867-1902)

from:
POEMS (1895)

[One of the 'tragic generation', Johnson sought consolation in catholicism, monarchical opinions, Irish nationalism and, ultimately, in drink. The last killed him. The earlier dedications supplied him with the sources for his formal, musical and melancholy poetry, although the poems on Irish subjects are among his weakest.]

Mystic and Cavalier

Go from me: I am one of those, who fall.
What! hath no cold wind swept your heart at all,
In my sad company? Before the end,
  Go from me, dear my friend!

Yours are the victories of light: your feet
Rest from good toil, where rest is brave and sweet.
But after warfare in a mourning gloom,
  I rest in clouds of doom.

Have you not read so, looking in these eyes?
Is it the common light of the pure skies,
Lights up their shadowy depths? The end is set:
  Though the end be not yet.

When gracious music stirs, and all is bright,
And beauty triumphs through a courtly night;

When I too joy, a man like other men:
Yet, am I like them, then?

And in the battle, when the horsemen sweep
Against a thousand deaths, and fall on sleep:
Who ever sought that sudden calm, if I
Sought not? Yet, could not die.

Seek with thine eyes to pierce this crystal sphere:
Canst read a fate there, prosperous and clear?
Only the mists, only the weeping clouds:
Dimness, and airy shrouds.

Beneath, what angels are at work? What powers
Prepare the secret of the fatal hours?
See! the mists tremble, and the clouds are stirred:
When comes the calling word?

The clouds are breaking from the crystal ball,
Breaking and clearing: and I look to fall.
When the cold winds and airs of portent sweep,
My spirit may have sleep.

O rich and sounding voices of the air!
Interpreters and prophets of despair:
Priests of a fearful sacrament! I come,
To make with you mine home.

The Dark Angel

Dark Angel, with thine aching lust
To rid the world of penitence:
Malicious Angel, who still dost
My soul such subtile violence!

Because of thee, no thought, no thing
Abides for me undesecrate:
Dark Angel, ever on the wing,
Who never reachest me too late!

When music sounds, then changest thou
Its silvery to a sultry fire:
Nor will thine envious heart allow
Delight untortured by desire.

Through thee, the gracious Muses turn
To Furies, O mine Enemy![1]
And all the things of beauty burn
With flames of evil ecstasy.

1. The Furies were the avenging female deities that attended upon the Queen of Hades.

Because of thee, the land of dreams
Becomes a gathering place of fears:
Until tormented slumber seems
One vehemence of useless tears.

When sunlight glows upon the flowers,
Or ripples down the dancing sea:
Thou, with thy troop of passionate powers,
Beleaguerest, bewilderest, me.

Within the breath of autumn woods,
Within the winter silences:
Thy venomous spirit stirs and broods,
O Master of impieties!

The ardour of red flame is thine,
And thine the steely soul of ice:
Thou poisonest the fair design
Of nature, with unfair device.

Apples of ashes, golden bright;[2]
Waters of bitterness, how sweet!
O banquet of a foul delight,
Prepared by thee, dark Paraclete![3]

Thou art the whisper in the gloom,
The hinting tone, the haunting laugh:
Thou art the adorner of my tomb,
The minstrel of mine epitaph.

I fight thee, in the Holy Name!
Yet, what thou dost, is what God saith:
Tempter! should I escape thy flame,
Thou wilt have helped my soul from Death:

The second Death, that never dies,
That cannot die, when time is dead:
Live Death, wherein the lost soul cries,
Eternally uncomforted.

Dark Angel, with thine aching lust!
Of two defeats, of two despairs:
Less dread, a change to drifting dust,
Than thine eternity of cares.

2. The apples of Sodom, deceptively attractive, dissolve into smoke and ashes when they are plucked. Legend has it that they grew near the Dead Sea.
3. The Paraclete is the Holy Ghost, the advocate. The dark Paraclete is Satan.

Do what thou wilt, thou shalt not so,
Dark Angel! triumph over me:
Lonely, unto the Lone I go;[4]
Divine, to the Divinity.

4. Plotinus, in the *Enneads* VI. 9, speaks of the life of the Gods and of happy men as 'a flight of the alone to the alone.'

By the Statue of King Charles at Charing Cross[1]

Sombre and rich, the skies;
Great glooms, and starry plains.
Gently the night wind sighs;
Else a vast silence reigns.

The splendid silence clings
Around me: and around
The saddest of all kings
Crowned and again discrowned.

Comely and calm, he rides
Hard by his own Whitehall:[2]
Only the night wind glides:
No crowds, nor rebels, brawl.

Gone, too, his Court: and yet,
The stars his courtiers are:
Stars in their stations set;
And every wandering star.

Alone he rides, alone,
The fair and fatal king:
Dark night is all his own,
That strange and solemn thing.

Which are more full of fate:
The stars; or those sad eyes?
Which are more still and great:
Those brows; or the dark skies?

Although his whole heart yearn
In passionate tragedy:
Never was face so stern
With sweet austerity.

Vanquished in life, his death
By beauty made amends:
The passing of his breath
Won his defeated ends.[3]

Brief life, and hapless? Nay:
Through death, life grew sublime.
Speak after sentence? Yea:[4]
And to the end of time.

Armoured he rides, his head
Bare to the stars of doom:
He triumphs now, the dead,
Beholding London's gloom.

Our wearier spirit faints,
Vexed in the world's employ:
His soul was of the saints;
And art to him was joy.[5]

King, tried in fires of woe!
Men hunger for thy grace:
And through the night I go,
Loving thy mournful face.

1. The statue of Charles I (1600-49) in Trafalgar Square, London, stands on the original site of the last of the Gothic crosses erected by Edward I to mark the places where the coffin of Queen Eleanor was set down on its way from Nottinghamshire to Westminster Abbey. At that time the village of Charing was halfway between London and Westminster.
2. Charles was executed in front of the royal palace of Whitehall.
3. Charles died nobly and thereby won the admiration and sympathy of many who subsequently helped his son to regain the throne.
4. Charles was not permitted to speak in court.
5. Charles assembled one of the greatest collections of works of art in Europe.

from: IRELAND, AND OTHER POEMS (1897)

[This poem, dedicated to R. Barry O'Brien, the historian and Parnellite, is Johnson's variation on the famous ballad by John Kells Ingram, 'Who Fears to Speak of Ninety-Eight?' (see Volume I, p. 1288). Johnson was anxious to contribute to the centenary celebrations of the 1798 Rebellion. The poem was written in 1893.]

Ninety-Eight

Who fears to speak of ninety-eight?
He, who despairs of Ireland still:
Whose paltry soul finds nothing great
In honest failure: he, whose will,

Feeble and faint in days of gloom,
Takes old defeat for final doom.

Who fears to speak of ninety-eight?
The man, who fears to speak of death:
Who clings and clasps the knees of fate,
And whimpers with his latest breath:
Who hugs his comfort to his heart,
And dares not play a Christian's part.

Who fears to speak of ninety-eight?
The renegade, who sells his trust:
Whose love has rottened into hate,
Whose hopes have withered into dust:
He, who denies, and deems it mad,
The faith his nobler boyhood had.

Who fears to speak of ninety-eight?
The enemy of Ireland fears!
For Ireland undegenerate
Keeps yet the spirit of old years:
He sees, in visions of the night,
A nation arming for the right.

Who fears to speak of ninety-eight?
Not he, who hates a poisonous peace:
For, while the days of triumph wait,
And till the days of sorrow cease,
He, with the Lord of Hosts his friend,
Will fight for Ireland to the end.

Let sword cross sword, or thought meet thought:
One fire of battle thrills them both.
Deliverance only can be wrought
By warfare without stay or sloth:
And by your prayers at Heaven's high gate.
True hearts, that beat in Ninety-Eight.

['Parnell' was first published in the *United Ireland* of 7 October 1893, to mark the second anniversary of Parnell's death.]

Parnell

The wail of Irish winds,
The cry of Irish seas:
Eternal sorrow finds
Eternal voice in these.

I cannot praise our dead,
Whom Ireland weeps so well:
Her morning light, that fled;
Her morning star, that fell.

She of the mournful eyes
Waits, and no dark clouds break:
Waits, and her strong son lies
Dead, for her holy sake.

Her heart is sorrow's home,
And hath been from of old:
An host of griefs hath come,
To make that heart their fold.

Ah, the sad autumn day,
When the last sad troop came
Swift down the ancient way,
Keening a chieftain's name!

Gray hope was there, and dread;
Anger, and love in tears:
They mourned the dear and dead,
Dirge of the ruined years.

Home to her heart she drew
The mourning company:
Old sorrows met the new,
In sad fraternity.

A mother, and forget!
Nay! all her children's fate
Ireland remembers yet,
With love insatiate.

She hears the heavy bells:
Hears, and with passionate breath
Eternally she tells
A rosary of death.

Faithful and true is she,
The mother of us all:
Faithful and true! may we
Fail her not, though we fall.

Her son, our brother, lies
Dead, for her holy sake:
But from the dead arise
Voices, that bid us wake.

Not his, to hail the dawn:
His but the herald's part.
Be ours to see withdrawn
Night from our mother's heart.

JOHN MILLINGTON SYNGE

(1871-1909)

from: POEMS AND TRANSLATIONS (1909)

[In his Preface, Synge declared beliefs about poetry that seem to have more bearing on his plays. Yet the violence of feeling and the attempt to root it in the ordinary and the commonplace are features discernible but not always distinct in his verse:

> In these days poetry is usually a flower of evil or of good, but it is the timber of poetry that wears most surely, and there is no timber that has not strong roots among the clay and worms. Even if we grant that exalted poetry can be kept successful by itself, the strong hints of life are needed in poetry also, to show that what is exalted, or tender, is not made by feeble blood. It may almost be said that before verse can be human again it must learn to be brutal.

This call for vitality and health, for a kind of Elizabethan vigour rather than a Baudelairean decadence, is a description of Synge's own imaginative journey from Paris to the West of Ireland. Nevertheless, a strain of morbidity and anger, stimulated no doubt by ill-health and a consciousness of his approaching death, is braided in with the vigorous vocabulary and embodies the achievement of the young decadent poet, who discovered in the more natural and lyrical idiom of Irish speech an exit from the 'poetic', which had become so powerful and disabling a convention in the 1890s.

Synge died before his poems were published by the Cuala Press. His diffidence about his own powers as a poet was so great that he published only one poem in his lifetime. The first is one of several about the landscape of his native County Wicklow.]

Prelude

Still south I went and west and south again,
Through Wicklow from the morning till the night,
And far from cities, and the sites of men,
Lived with the sunshine and the moon's delight.

I knew the stars, the flowers, and the birds,
The grey and wintry sides of many glens,
And did but half remember human words,
In converse with the mountains, moors, and fens.

To the Oaks of Glencree

My arms are round you, and I lean
Against you, while the lark
Sings over us, and golden lights, and green
Shadows are on your bark.

There'll come a season when you'll stretch
Black boards to cover me:
Then in Mount Jerome I will lie, poor wretch,
With worms eternally.

A Question

I asked if I got sick and died, would you
With my black funeral go walking too,
If you'd stand close to hear them talk or pray
While I'm let down in that steep bank of clay.

And, No, you said, for if you saw a crew
Of living idiots pressing round that new
Oak coffin — they alive, I dead beneath
That board — you'd rave and rend them with your
teeth.

Winter

With little money in a great city

There's snow in every street
Where I go up and down,
And there's no woman, man, or dog
That knows me in the town.

I know each shop, and all
These Jews, and Russian Poles,
For I go walking night and noon
To spare my sack of coals.

The Curse

To a sister of an enemy of the author's who disapproved of 'The Playboy'[1]

Lord, confound this surly sister,
Blight her brow with blotch and blister,

1. The person cursed is said to be Molly Allgood's sister, Mrs Callender, who had disliked Synge's *The Playboy of the Western World*.

Cramp her larynx, lung, and liver,
In her guts a galling give her.
Let her live to earn her dinners
In Mountjoy[2] with seedy sinners:
Lord, this judgment quickly bring,
And I'm Your servant, J. M. Synge.

2. The famous Dublin jail.

from:
POEMS (1962)

[Written in 1908, this poem remained unpublished until 1962 when Robin Skelton included it in *Poems*, Volume I of *J.M. Synge: The Collected Works*. The text is taken from this edition.]

Abroad

Some go to game, or pray in Rome
I travel for my turning home

For when I've been six months abroad
Faith your kiss would brighten God!

In Dream

['In Dream' originally was included in *Vita Vecchia*, a sequence of poems connected by prose narrative, in which Synge tried to deal with an unhappy love affair. The poem was written in 1896 and revised in 1907.]

Again, again, I sinful see
  Thy face, as men who weep
Doomed by eternal Hell's decree
  Might meet their Christ in sleep.

In a Dream

[This poem is also from *Vita Vecchia*. It was written in 1896 and revised in 1907.]

I saw thee start and quake,
When we in face did meet,
I saw dead passion wake
One thrill of yearning sweet.

Then came a change, a wave,
Of bitterness, disdain,
That, through my grassy grave
Will rack my haunted brain.

OLIVER ST JOHN GOGARTY

(1878-1957)

from:
AN OFFERING OF SWANS (1923)

[In his Preface to the Cuala Press edition of this volume, Yeats retold the story which became the occasion of this poem. As a senator of the new state, Gogarty was a target for the IRA irregulars. He was taken from his house by armed men one evening and driven to a deserted house on the banks of the Liffey near Chapelizod. He was not blindfolded, so his return seemed unlikely. Gogarty took the opportunity to escape and dived into the river Liffey. Later he phoned Yeats at his club to know where he could buy two swans, which he had promised to the Liffey if he reached safety after escaping from his captors. Yeats goes on: 'Forced for his safety to leave Ireland for a time, he practised his profession in London and I wonder if it was the excitement of escape, or the new surroundings, his occasional visits to old English country houses, that brought a new sense of English lyric tradition and changed a wit into a poet.'

Gogarty's verse is a mixture of elegance and what Yeats called 'confusion', but he does at times sustain his best effects throughout a single poem. According to Yeats, he 'discovered the rhythm of Herrick and of Fletcher, something different from himself yet akin to himself ....' If there is a seventeenth-century inflection in some of Gogarty's verse, it is indelibly marked by the additional influence of the English poetry of the 1890s. He shares with Joyce a love for that faded, lingering spareness that they both associated with the Elizabethans; similarly, he and Joyce are both fond of the mordant satiric mode, although Joyce excels Gogarty in this. His bitterness was more rooted than Gogarty's playful animosity.]

To the Liffey with the Swans

Keep you these calm and lovely things,
And float them on your clearest water;
For one would not disgrace a King's
Transformed beloved and buoyant daughter.

And with her goes this sprightly swan,
A bird of more than royal feather,
With alban[1] beauty clothed upon:
O keep them fair and well together!

As fair as was that doubled Bird,
By love of Leda so besotten,
That she was all with wonder stirred,
And the Twin Sportsmen[2] were begotten!

1. pure white.
2. Love and War.

from:
WILD APPLES (1928)

The Crab Tree

Here is the crab tree,
Firm and erect,
In spite of the thin soil,
In spite of neglect.
The twisted root grapples
For sap with the rock,
And draws the hard juice
To the succulent top:
Here are wild apples,
Here's a tart crop!

No outlandish grafting
That ever grew soft
In a sweet air of Persia,
Or safe Roman croft;
Unsheltered by steading,[1]
Rock-rooted and grown,
A great tree of Erin,
It stands up alone,
A forest tree spreading
Where forests are gone.

1. The outbuildings of a farmhouse.

Of all who pass by it
How few in it see
A westering remant
Of days when Lough Neagh
Flowed up the long dingles
Its blossom had lit,
Old days of glory
Time cannot repeat;
And therefore it mingles
The bitter and sweet.

It takes from the West Wind
The thrust of the main;
It makes from the tension
Of sky and of plain,
Of what clay enacted,
Of living alarm,
A vitalised symbol
Of earth and of storm,
Of Chaos contracted
To intricate form.

Unbreakable wrestler!
What sapling or herb
Has core of such sweetness
And fruit so acerb?
So grim a transmitter
Of life through mishap,
That one wonders whether
If that in the sap,
Is sweet or is bitter
Which makes it stand up.

Per Iter Tenebricosum[1]

Enough! Why should a man bemoan
A Fate that leads the natural way?
Or think himself a worthier one
Than those who braved it in their day?
If only gladiators died,
Or Heroes, Death would be his pride;
But have not little maidens gone,
And Lesbia's sparrow[2] — all alone?

1. Catullus, *Carmina* III, lines 11-12.
'Qui nunc it per iter tenebricosum
Illuc, unde negant redire quenquam.'
(And now he treads the gloomy track
Whence no one, so they say, comes back.)
2. See *The Poems of Catullus* (Harmondsworth: Penguin Books, 1966), Poem No. 2: 'Lesbia's sparrow,/Lesbia's plaything,/In her lap or at her breast.'

from:
OTHERS TO ADORN (1938)

Ringsend

(After Reading Tolstoi)

I will live in Ringsend
With a red-headed whore,
And the fan-light gone in
Where it lights the hall-door;
And listen each night
For her querulous shout,
As at last she streels in
And the pubs empty out.
To soothe that wild breast
With my old-fangled songs,
Till she feels it redressed
From inordinate wrongs,
Imagined, outrageous,
Preposterous wrongs,
Till peace at last comes,
Shall be all I will do,
Where the little lamp blooms
Like a rose in the stew;
And up the back-garden
The sound comes to me
Of the lapsing, unsoilable,
Whispering sea.

Verse

What should we know,
For better or worse,
Of the Long Ago,
Were it not for Verse:
What ships went down;
What walls were razed;
Who won the crown;
What lads were praised?
A fallen stone,
Or a waste of sands;
And all is known
Of Art-less lands.
But you need not delve
By the sea-side hills
Where the Muse herself
All Time fulfils,
Who cuts with his scythe
All things but hers;
All but the blithe
Hexameters.

THOMAS MACDONAGH

(1878-1916)

from:
SONGS OF MYSELF (1910)

[MacDonagh resigned from his position as a teacher at Patrick Pearse's school, St Enda's, in the summer of 1910; at the same time an important love affair, probably with Mary Maguire (later Mary Colum, wife of Padraic Colum), came to an end. MacDonagh planned a sequence of love sonnets of which 'In Absence' is one. 'After a Year' is an account of the after-effects of this intense emotional attachment. The translations of Irish songs are much more controlled and free from the self-pity that flaws the love poems.]

In Absence

Last night I read your letters once again —
Read till the dawn filled all my room with grey;
Then quenched my light and put the leaves away,
And prayed for sleep to ease my heart's great pain.
But ah! that poignant tenderness made vain
My hope of rest — I could not sleep or pray
For thought of you, and the slow, broadening day
Held me there prisoner of my throbbing brain.

Yet I did sleep before the silence broke,
And dream, but not of you — the old dreams rife
With duties which would bind me to the yoke
Of my old futile, lone, reluctant life:
I stretched my hands for help in the vain strife,
And grasped these leaves, and to this pain awoke.

After a Year

After a year of love
Death of love in a day;

And I who ever strove
To hold love in sure life
Now let it pass away
With no grief and no strife.

Pass — but it holds me yet;
Love, it would seem, may die;
But we can not forget
And can not be the same,
As lowly or as high,
As once, before this came.

Never as in old days
Can I again stoop low;
Never, now fallen, raise
Spirit and heart above
To where once life did show
The lone soul of my love.

None would the service ask
That she from love requires,
Making it not a task
But a high sacrament
Of all love's dear desires
And all life's grave intent.

In an Island

'Mid an isle I stand,
Under its only tree:
The ocean around —
Around life eternity:
'Mid my life I stand,
Under the boughs of thee.

Two Songs from the Irish

I

(*Is truagh gan mise i Sasana*)[1]

'Tis a pity I'm not in England,
  Or with one from Erin thither bound,
Out in the midst of the ocean,
  Where the thousands of ships are drowned.

From wave to wave of the ocean
  To be guided on with the wind and the rain
And O King! that Thou might'st guide me
  Back to my love again!

1. The first line of the poem is a translation of this.

II

(*Táid na réalta 'na seasamh ar an aer*)[1]

The stars stand up in the air,
  The sun and the moon are gone,
The strand of its waters is bare,
  And her sway is swept from the swan.

The cuckoo was calling all day,
  Hid in the branches above,
How my stóirín[2] is fled far away —
  'Tis my grief that I give her my love!

Three things through love I see,
  Sorrow and sin and death —
And my mind reminding me
  That this doom I breathe with my breath.

But sweeter than violin or lute
  Is my love, and she left me behind —
I wish that all music were mute,
  And I to my beauty were blind.

She's more shapely than swan by the strand,
  She's more radiant than grass after dew,
She's more fair than the stars where they stand —
  'Tis my grief that her ever I knew!

1. The first line of the poem translates this.
2. sweetheart.

from:
LYRICAL POEMS (1913)

[In this volume, the last he published, MacDonagh begins to release himself from some of the more conventional attitudinizings of his earlier work. This is most evident in his translation from the Irish and in the short narrative poem 'The Night Hunt'. The son whose birth he celebrates here, Donagh MacDonagh (1912-68), became a poet and broadcaster and co-editor of *The Oxford Book of Irish Verse* (1956).]

The Night Hunt

In the morning, in the dark,
When the stars begin to blunt,
By the wall of Barna Park

Dogs I heard and saw them hunt
All the parish dogs were there,
All the dogs for miles around,
Teeming up behind a hare,
In the dark, without a sound.

How I heard I scarce can tell —
'Twas a patter in the grass —
And I did not see them well
Come across the dark and pass;
Yet I saw them and I knew
Spearman's dog and Spellman's dog
And, beside my own dog too,
Leamy's from the Island Bog.

In the morning when the sun
Burnished all the green to gorse,
I went out to take a run
Round the bog upon my horse;
And my dog that had been sleeping
In the heat beside the door
Left his yawning and went leaping
On a hundred yards before.

Through the village street we passed —
Not a dog there raised a snout —
Through the street and out at last
On the white bog road and out
Over Barna Park full pace,
Over to the Silver Stream,
Horse and dog in happy race,
Rider between thought and dream.

By the stream, at Leamy's house,
Lay a dog — my pace I curbed —
But our coming did not rouse
Him from drowsing undisturbed;
And my dog, as unaware
Of the other, dropped beside
And went running by me there
With my horse's slackened stride.

Yet by something, by a twitch
Of the sleeper's eye, a look
From the runner, something which
Little chords of feeling shook,
I was conscious that a thought
Shuddered through the silent deep
Of a secret — I had caught
Something I had known in sleep.

Wishes for My Son

(*Born on Saint Cecilia's Day*[1] *1912*)

Now, my son, is life for you,
And I wish you joy of it, —
Joy of power in all you do,
Deeper passion, better wit
Than I had who had enough,
Quicker life and length thereof,
More of every gift but love.

Love I have beyond all men,
Love that now you share with me —
What have I to wish you then
But that you be good and free,
And that God to you may give
Grace in stronger days to live?

For I wish you more than I
Ever knew of glorious deed,
Though no rapture passed me by
That an eager heart could heed,
Though I followed heights and sought
Things the sequel never brought.

Wild and perilous holy things
Flaming with a martyr's blood,
And the joy that laughs and sings
Where a foe must be withstood,
Joy of headlong happy chance
Leading on the battle dance.

But I found no enemy,
No man in a world of wrong,
That Christ's word of charity
Did not render clean and strong —
Who was I to judge my kind,
Blindest groper of the blind?

God to you may give the sight
And the clear undoubting strength
Wars to knit for single right,
Freedom's war to knit at length,
And to win, through wrath and strife,
To the sequel of my life.

But for you, so small and young,
Born on Saint Cecilia's Day,

1. St Cecilia is the patron saint of music, especially church music. Her day is 22 November.

I in more harmonious song
Now for nearer joys should pray —
Simpler joys: the natural growth
Of your childhood and your youth,
Courage, innocence, and truth:

These for you, so small and young,
In your hand and heart and tongue.

[Francis Ledwidge's 'Lament for Thomas MacDonagh' (see below, p. 774) probably takes its first line ('He shall not hear the bittern cry') from Ledwidge's memory of this translation of the famous Irish poem, 'An Bonnán Buí' by Cathal Buí Mac Giolla Gunna (*c.*1680-1756).]

The Yellow Bittern

The yellow bittern that never broke out
   In a drinking bout, might as well have drunk;
His bones are thrown on a naked stone
   Where he lived alone like a hermit monk.
O yellow bittern! I pity your lot,
   Though they say that a sot like myself is curst —
I was sober a while, but I'll drink and be wise
   For I fear I should die in the end of thirst.

It's not for the common birds that I'd mourn,
   The black-bird, the corn-crake, or the crane,
But for the bittern that's shy and apart
   And drinks in the marsh from the lone bog-drain.
Oh! if I had known you were near your death,
   While my breath held out I'd have run to you,
Till a splash from the Lake of the Son of the Bird
   Your soul would have stirred and waked anew.

My darling told me to drink no more
   Or my life would be o'er in a little short while;
But I told her 'tis drink gives me health and strength
   And will lengthen my road by many a mile.
You see how the bird of the long smooth neck
   Could get his death from the thirst at last —
Come, son of my soul, and drain your cup,
   You'll get no sup when your life is past.

In a wintering island by Constantine's halls
   A bittern calls from a wineless place,
And tells me that hither he cannot come
   Till the summer is here and the sunny days.
When he crosses the stream there and wings o'er
      the sea
   Then a fear comes to me he may fail in his flight —
Well, the milk and the ale are drunk every drop,
   And a dram won't stop our thirst this night.

SEUMAS O'SULLIVAN

(1879-1958)

from:
VERSES SACRED AND PROFANE (1908)

[The poem below is one of the many poems about Parnell. It is included here, along with Lionel Johnson's, to indicate how feelings about the great leader long survived his death and to what extent the celebration of his death every October (6 October is the precise date) was the conventional occasion for verses dedicated to his heroic memory. The standard literary attitude prevails here: Parnell towers above the littleness of the present day and of those who brought him low. O'Sullivan adheres to the mythic legend by envisaging Parnell's return to a less craven land.]

Glasnevin, 9 October, 1904

They peer about his grave with curious eyes,
And for his sin they pity him, their chief,
With miserable mockery of grief;
Beyond their littleness, serene he lies,
Nor heeds the insult of their sympathies,
This man pre-eminent by strong belief

In his own heart — a little while, for brief
The resting-time is when a hero dies.

Near to God's heart by greatness of thy heart,
And nearer by thy sin, o strong of will!
Send out thy spirit like a sword and kill
Their littleness, no longer dwell apart;
Send forth thy spirit like a flame, and burn
Through these a pathway for thy soul's return.

from: THE EARTH-LOVER AND OTHER VERSES (1909)

The Land War (Prelude)

Sorrow is over the fields,
The fields that never can know
The joy that the harvest yields
When the corn stands row on row.

But alien the cattle feed
Where many a furrow lies,
For the furrows remembered the seed,
And the men have a dream in their eyes.

Not so did the strong men dream
E'er the fathers of these were born,
And their sons have remembered their deeds
As the fields have remembered the corn.

In Mercer Street

Gather 'em, gather 'em, gather 'em O,
He shouts monotonous, jolting slow
His little truck of rags and bones
Over the uneven cobble stones.
Ever about him cling and crowd
The waifs, a many-coloured cloud
All shrilly clamouring, mad with joy,
For sticky sweet, or painted toy;
Hardly a breath is in the air,
Yet every little windmill there
Goes whirling wildly, as tho' it knew
With every turn what rapture flew
Through all the heavy street, and stirred
The stagnant air, till the sad bird
High on the wall, takes heart to sing
And hails the simulated Spring.

from: COLLECTED POEMS (1940)

Dublin (1916)

Even as the empty spaces
That front the intruding sky,
Are the absent faces
In the crowds that pass me by.
The brave salute of John MacBride,
The quick transforming smile,
Thomas MacDonagh's laughing mouth
And eyes of a happy child,
The strange prophetic glance of Pearse,
The half-averted eyes.
Even as the empty spaces
That front the intruding sky,
Are the absent faces
In the crowds that pass me by.

PATRICK PEARSE

(1879-1916)

from: COLLECTED WORKS OF PADRAIC H. PEARSE: PLAYS, POEMS AND STORIES (1917)

[The literary writings of Pearse were assembled in the first volume of his *Collected Works* (1917-22), edited by Desmond Ryan. 'The Fool' and 'The Mother' were written in the autumn of 1915. While in Arbour Hill Prison awaiting court martial between 29 April and 2 May 1916, Pearse wrote 'To My Mother', and 'To My Brother'. These were regarded as seditious by the British commander, General Maxwell, and were included in the court martial papers (see Seamus Ó Buachalla (ed.), *The Literary Writings of Patrick Pearse* (1979), p. 13). 'The Wayfarer' is reputed to have been written on the night before his execution.

The poems included here indicate the potent blend of religious and political dedication that made Pearse so unique. His verse is a credo written in the shadow of revolution and death. No one else managed to make narcissism and nationalism fuse to a comparable degree.]

The Fool

Since the wise men have not spoken, I speak that am only a fool;
A fool that hath loved his folly,
Yea, more than the wise men their books or their counting houses, or their quiet homes,
Or their fame in men's mouths;
A fool that in all his days hath done never a prudent thing,
Never hath counted the cost, nor recked if another reaped
The fruit of his mighty sowing, content to scatter the seed;
A fool that is unrepentant, and that soon at the end of all
Shall laugh in his lonely heart as the ripe ears fall to the reaping-hooks
And the poor are filled that were empty,
Tho' he go hungry.

I have squandered the splendid years that the Lord God gave to my youth
In attempting impossible things, deeming them alone worth the toil.
Was it folly or grace? Not men shall judge me, but God.

I have squandered the splendid years:
Lord, if I had the years I would squander them over again,
Aye, fling them from me!
For this I have heard in my heart, that a man shall scatter, not hoard,
Shall do the deed of today, nor take thought of tomorrow's teen,[1]
Shall not bargain or huxter[2] with God; or was it a jest of Christ's
And is this my sin before men, to have taken Him at His word?

The lawyers have sat in council, the men with the keen, long faces,
And said, 'This man is a fool', and others have said, 'He blasphemeth';
And the wise have pitied the fool that hath striven to give a life
In the world of time and space among the bulks of actual things,
To a dream that was dreamed in the heart, and that only the heart could hold.

O wise men, riddle me this: what if the dream come true?
What if the dream come true? and if millions unborn shall dwell
In the house that I shaped in my heart, the noble house of my thought?
Lord, I have staked my soul, I have staked the lives of my kin
On the truth of Thy dreadful word. Do not remember my failures,
But remember this my faith.

And so I speak.
Yea, ere my hot youth pass, I speak to my people and say:

1. affliction, woe.
2. haggle.

Ye shall be foolish as I; ye shall scatter, not save;
Ye shall venture your all, lest ye lose what is more than all;
Ye shall call for a miracle, taking Christ at His word.
And for this I will answer, O people, answer here and hereafter,
O people that I have loved shall we not answer together?

The Mother

I do not grudge them: Lord, I do not grudge
My two strong sons that I have seen go out
To break their strength and die, they and a few,
In bloody protest for a glorious thing,
They shall be spoken of among their people,
The generations shall remember them,
And call them blessed;
But I will speak their names to my own heart
In the long nights;
The little names that were familiar once
Round my dead hearth.
Lord, thou art hard on mothers:
We suffer in their coming and their going;
And tho' I grudge them not, I weary, weary
Of the long sorrow — And yet I have my joy:
My sons were faithful, and they fought.

Christmas 1915

O King that was born
To set bondsmen free,
In the coming battle,
Help the Gael!

The Wayfarer

The beauty of the world hath made me sad,
This beauty that will pass;
Sometimes my heart hath shaken with great joy
To see a leaping squirrel in a tree,
Or a red lady-bird upon a stalk,
Or little rabbits in a field at evening,
Lit by a slanting sun,
Or some green hill where shadows drifted by
Some quiet hill where mountainy man hath sown
And soon would reap; near to the gate of Heaven;
Or children with bare feet upon the sands
Of some ebbed sea, or playing on the streets
Of little towns in Connacht,
Things young and happy.
And then my heart hath told me:
These will pass,
Will pass and change, will die and be no more,
Things bright and green, things young and happy;
And I have gone upon my way
Sorrowful.

To My Brother[1]

O faithful!
Moulded in one womb,
We two have stood together all the years,
All the glad years and all the sorrowful years,
Own brothers: through good repute and ill,
In direst peril true to me,
Leaving all things for me, spending yourself
In the hard service that I taught to you,
Of all the men that I have known on earth,
You only have been my familiar friend,
Nor needed I another.

1. William Pearse (1881-1916) studied at the Dublin School of Art and in Paris. He joined the Irish Volunteers in 1913 and fought in the Easter Rising. He was executed in Kilmainham Jail on 4 May 1916.

Why Do Ye Torture Me?

Why are ye torturing me, O desires of my heart?
Torturing me and paining me by day and by night?
Hunting me as a poor deer would be hunted on a hill,
A poor long-wearied deer with the hound-pack after him?

There's no ease to my paining in the loneliness of the hills,
But the cry of the hunters terrifically to be heard,
The cry of my desires haunting me without respite, —
O ravening hounds, long is your run!

No satisfying can come to my desires while I live,
For the satisfaction I desired yesterday is no satisfaction,
And the hound-pack is the greedier of the satisfaction it has got, —
And forever I shall not sleep till I sleep in the grave.

Long To Me Thy Coming

Long to me thy coming,
Old henchman of God,
O friend of all friends,
To free me from my pain.

O syllable on the wind,
O footfall not heavy,
O hand in the dark,
Your coming is long to me.

A Rann I Made

A rann[1] I made within my heart
To the rider, to the high king,
A rann I made to my love,
To the king of kings, ancient death.

Brighter to me than light of day
The dark of thy house, tho' black clay;
Sweeter to me than the music of trumpets
The quiet of thy house and its eternal silence.

1. A verse.

Christ's Coming

I have made my heart clean tonight
As a woman might clean her house
Ere her lover come to visit her:
O Lover, pass not by!

I have opened the door of my heart
Like a man that would make a feast
For his son's coming home from afar:
Lovely Thy coming, O Son!

JOSEPH CAMPBELL
(1879-1944)

from: THE RUSHLIGHT (1906)

Who Buys Land

Who buys land
Buys many stones,
Who buys flesh
Buys many bones,
Who buys eggs
Buys many shells,
Who buys Love
Buys nothing else.

Love is a burr
Upon the floor,
Love is a thief
Behind the door.
Who loves leman[1]
For her breath
May quench his fire,
And cry for death!

Love is a bridle,
Love is a load,
Love is a thorn
Upon the road.
Love is the fly
That flits its hour,
Love is the shining
Venom-flower.

Love is a net,
Love is a snare,
Love is a bubble
Blown with air,
Love starts hot
And, waning, cold,
Is withered
In the grave's mould!

1. A beloved, sweetheart.

I Will Go with My Father A-Ploughing

I will go with my father a-ploughing
To the green field by the sea,
And the rooks and the crows and the sea-gulls
Will come flocking after me.
I will sing to the patient horses,
With the lark in the white of the air,
And my father will sing the plough-song
That blesses the cleaving share.

I will go with my father a-sowing
To the red field by the sea,
And the rooks and the gulls and the starlings
Will come flocking after me.
I will sing to the striding sowers,
With the finch on the greening sloe,
And my father will sing the seed-song
That only the wise men know.

I will go with my father a-reaping
To the brown field by the sea,
And the geese and the crows and the children
Will come flocking after me.
I will sing to the tan-faced reapers,
With the wren in the heat of the sun,
And my father will sing the scythe-song
That joys for the harvest done.

O Beautiful Dark Woman

O beautiful dark woman, weep no more.

Weep not for thy princes who have gone from thee: they shall come again.

Cease thy crying and thy lamentation.

Thou shalt be raised up as a star-cluster.

Thy hair shall shine as a river in the dusk, and thine eyes as the blue-bough when the summer is full.

Thy neck and thy breasts shall smell as hazel-saplings fresh peeled.

Thy paps shall flow as well-streams.

Thy sons shall be as shields of findruine[1] about thy feet, and thy daughters as lilies strewn on a mountain altar.

Thy heart shall burn as the heart of red wine, and thy mouth shall utter mead and honey.

So, Beautiful Woman of Sorrows, weep no more.

Weep not for thy princes who have gone from thee: they are upon the Deep.

Cease thy crying and thy lamentation.

The hour of thy deliverance is at hand.

The castled ships draw near: they point their peaks for harbour.

Tomorrow thou shalt hold jubilee, with harps and songs and dancing.

The Shrine

I will make a shrine of the seven woods
That saved my father's seed,
And offer it, with cattle and lands,
To Patraic and Colm and Brigid.

The fruitful palm that Adam found,
The battle-signet of God,
And the maple-tree of Noah's Ark,
And the almond of Moses' Rod.

And the four sweet woods of Calvary Cross,
On which the Man-Christ died,
Cypress and cedar and scented pine,
And birch from Kedron side.[1]

And I will kneel as the Latin stone
That covers the Virgin Tree,
And pray that I may look on the dawn
That breaks on Banba[2] free!

1. Kedron is a stream mentioned in the Bible (John 18.1).
2. A poetical name for Ireland.

from: THE GILLY OF CHRIST (1907)

When Rooks Fly Homeward

When rooks fly homeward
And shadows fall,
When roses fold
On the hay-yard wall,
When blind moths flutter
By door and tree,
Then comes the quiet
Of Christ to me.

When stars look out
On the Children's Path,
And grey mists gather
On carn and rath[1],
When night is one
With the brooding sea,
Then comes the quiet
Of Christ to me.

1. Carn is cairn; a rath is an earthen fort or enclosure.

I Am the Gilly of Christ

I am the gilly[1] of Christ,
The mate of Mary's Son;
I run the roads at seeding time,
And when the harvest's done.

I sleep among the hills,
The heather is my bed;
I dip the termon-well[2] for drink,
And pull the sloe for bread.

No eye has ever seen me,
But shepherds hear me pass,
Singing at fall of even
Along the shadowed grass.

The beetle is my bellman,
The meadow-fire my guide,
The bee and bat my ambling nags
When I have need to ride.

All know me only the Stranger,
Who sits on the Saxons' height:
He burned the bacach's[3] little house
On last St. Brigid's Night.[4]

He sups off silver dishes,
And drinks in a golden horn,
But he will wake a wiser man
Upon the Judgment Morn!

I am the gilly of Christ,
The mate of Mary's Son;
I run the roads at seeding time,
And when the harvest's done.

The seed I sow is lucky,
The corn I reap is red,
And whoso sings the Gilly's Rann[5]
Will never cry for bread.

1. From Irish *giolla*, 'servant'.
2. The Irish word *tearmann* means 'sanctuary, refuge, asylum'. A termon-well is one belonging to a religious foundation.
3. *Bacach* is the Irish word for a tramp or a lame man.
4. Little is known of St Brigid, but she founded a great monastery in Kildare and is buried at Downpatrick with St Patrick and St Columba. Her name is associated with charity and justice and her day is 2 February.
5. A verse.

As I Came Over the Grey, Grey Hills

As I came over the grey, grey hills
And over the grey, grey water,
I saw the gilly leading on,
And the white Christ following after.

Where and where does the gilly lead?
And where is the white Christ faring?
They've travelled the four grey sounds of Orc,
And the four grey seas of Eirinn.

The moon is set and the wind's away,
And the song in the grass is dying,
And a silver cloud on the silent sea
Like a shrouding sheet is lying.

But Christ and the gilly will follow on
Till the ring in the east is showing,
And the awny[1] corn is red on the hills,
And the golden light is glowing!

1. bristly.

from:
THE MOUNTAINY SINGER (1909)

[This is the second, less well-known version of the title poem to this volume. It may be thought of as the Christian companion to the more pagan, 'Gaelic' poem of the same title, printed overleaf.]

I Am the Mountainy Singer (a)

I am the mountainy singer
And I would sing of the Christ
Who followed the paths thro' the mountains
To eat at the people's tryst.

He loved the sun-dark people
As the young man loves his bride,
And he moved among their thatches,
And for them he was crucified.

And the people loved him, also,
More than their houses or lands,

For they had known his pity
And felt the touch of his hands.

And they dreamed with him in the mountains,
And they walked with him on the sea,
And they prayed with him in the garden,
And bled with him on the tree.

Not ever by longing and dreaming
May they come to him now,
But by the thorns of sorrow
That bruised his kingly brow.

I Am the Mountainy Singer (b)

I am the mountainy singer —
The voice of the peasant's dream,
The cry of the wind on the wooded hill,
The leap of the fish in the stream.

Quiet and love I sing —
The carn[1] on the mountain crest,
The cailin[2] in her lover's arms,
The child at its mother's breast.

Beauty and peace I sing —
The fire on the open hearth,
The cailleach[3] spinning at her wheel,
The plough in the broken earth.

Travail and pain I sing —
The bride on the childing bed,
The dark man laboring at his rhymes,
The ewe in the lambing shed.

Sorrow and death I sing —
The canker come on the corn,
The fisher lost in the mountain loch,
The cry at the mouth of morn.

No other life I sing,
For I am sprung of the stock
That broke the hilly land for bread,
And built the nest in the rock!

1. A pile of rough stones that serves as a memorial or as a sepulchral monument.
2. girl.
3. old woman, hag.

from: IRISHRY (1913)

The Gombeen[1]

Behind a web of bottles, bales,
Tobacco, sugar, coffin nails
The gombeen like a spider sits,
Surfeited; and, for all his wits,
As meagre as the tally-board
On which his usuries are scored.

The mountain people come and go
For wool to weave or seed to sow,
White flour to bake a wedding cake,
Red spirits for a stranger's wake.
No man can call his soul his own
Who has the Devil's spoon on loan.

And so behind his web of bales,
Horse halters, barrels, pucaun[2] sails
The gombeen like a spider sits,
Surfeited; and, for all his wits,
As poor as one who never knew
The treasure of the early dew.

1. Irish *gaimbín*: a term of contempt for an exploitative, untrustworthy dealer in land or goods.
2. Irish for a fishing smack, a one-masted boat.

The Old Age Pensioner

He sits over the glimmering coal
With ancient face and folded hands:
His eye glasses his quiet soul,
He blinks and nods and understands.
In dew wetted, in tempest blown,
A Lear at last come to his own.

For fifty years he trenched his field
That he might eat a freeman's bread:
The seasons balked him of their yield,
His children's children wished him dead.
But ransom came to him at length
At the ebb-tide of life and strength.

And so he sits with folded hands
Over the flag of amber fire:
He blinks and nods and understands,
He has his very soul's desire.
In dew wetted, in tempest blown,
A Lear at last come to his own.

PADRAIC COLUM

(1881-1972)

from: THE POET'S CIRCUITS (1960)

[The subtitle of this volume, *Collected Poems of Ireland*, indicates what Colum had in mind when he wrote in the foreword to the collection about this rearrangement of his earlier work: 'In so far as they have a succession, continuity, in so far as they are representative of a countryside, these poems of men and women make a sequence, or . . . a saga. It is as a saga and not as separate pieces that they should be presented. They come under traditional influences: many of the personae are engaged in traditional occupations; some of the poems are reconstructions of traditional songs and are fitted to traditional music; others are translations of pieces that have traditional existence in Gaelic.'

The volume is arranged into eight Circuits — 'The House', 'Field and Road', 'Things More Ancient', 'The Glens', 'The Town', 'Women in the House', 'People on the Road', 'Monuments'. Colum's intimacy with the Gaelic traditions of the countryside helps to give to his poems a degree of detachment and impersonality that counteracts — in most cases — their pastoral sentimentality. This is most evident in his adaptations of traditional songs and prayers.]

Across the Door

The fiddles were playing and playing,
The couples were out on the floor;
From converse and dancing he drew me,
And across the door.

Ah! strange were the dim, wide meadows
And strange was the cloud-strewn sky,
And strange in the meadows the corncrakes,
And they making cry!

The hawthorn bloom was by us,
Around us the breath of the south —
White hawthorn, strange in the night-time —
His kiss on my mouth!

Cradle Song

O men from the fields!
Come gently within.
Tread softly, softly,
O men coming in!

Mavourneen[1] is going
From me and from you,
Where Mary will fold him
With mantle of blue!

From reek of the smoke
And cold of the floor,
And the peering of things
Across the half-door.

O men from the fields!
Soft, softly come through —
Mary puts round him
Her mantle of blue.

1. My darling.

Woman by the Hearth

The little moths are creeping
Across the cottage pane;
On the floor the chickens gather,
And they make talk and complain.

And she sits by the fire
Who has reared so many men;
Her voice is low like the chickens'
With the things she says again:

'The sons that come back do be restless,
They search for the thing to say;
Then they take thought like the swallows,
And the morrow brings them away.

In the old, old days upon Innish,
The fields were lucky and bright,
And if you lay down you'd be covered
By the grass of one soft night.

And doves flew with every burial
That went from Innishore —
Two white doves before the coffined —
But the doves fly no more!'

She speaks and the chickens gather,
And they make talk and complain,
While the little moths are creeping
Across the cottage pane.

Old Woman of the Roads

Oh, to have a little house!
To own the hearth and stool and all!
The heaped-up sods upon the fire,
The pile of turf against the wall!

To have a clock with weights and chains
And pendulum swinging up and down,
A dresser filled with shining delph,
Speckled and white and blue and brown!

I could be busy all the day
Clearing and sweeping hearth and floor,
And fixing on their shelf again
My white and blue and speckled store!

I could be quiet there at night
Beside the fire and by myself,
Sure of a bed and loth to leave
The ticking clock and the shining delph!

Och! but I'm weary of mist and dark,
And roads where there's never a house nor bush,
And tired I am of bog and road,
And the crying wind and the lonesome hush!

And I am praying to God on high,
And I am praying him night and day,
For a little house, a house of my own —
Out of the wind's and the rain's way.

['Poor Scholar' was originally published under the title 'A Poor Scholar of the Forties' in *Wild Earth* (1907) and it evidently refers to the hungry forties of the nineteenth century. The poem is spoken by a scholar or hedge schoolmaster, whose antiquated learning seems especially out of place in the crisis of that decade, which opened with the O'Connellite movement for Repeal of the Union and ended, after the cataclysmic Famine, with the Young Ireland rebellion of 1848. Colum's adopted stance here is characteristically anti-political.]

Poor Scholar

My eyelids red and heavy are
With bending o'er the smold'ring peat.
I know the Æneid now by heart,
My Virgil read in cold and heat,
In loneliness and hunger smart.
  And I know Homer, too, I ween,[1]
  As Munster poets know Ossian.[2]

And I must walk this road that winds
'Twixt bog and bog, while east there lies
A city with its men and books;
With treasures open to the wise,
Heart-words from equals, comrade-looks;
  Down here they have but tale and song,
  They talk Repeal the whole night long.

'You teach Greek verbs and Latin nouns,'
The dreamer of Young Ireland said,
'You do not hear the muffled call,
The sword being forged, the far-off tread
Of hosts to meet as Gael and Gall —
  What good to us your wisdom-store,
  Your Latin verse, your Grecian lore?'

And what to me is Gael or Gall?
Less than the Latin or the Greek —
I teach these by the dim rush-light
In smoky cabins night and week.
But what avail my teaching slight?
  Years hence, in rustic speech, a phrase,
  As in wild earth a Grecian vase!

1. think.
2. James Macpherson (1736-96) 'translated' the Gaelic poems of Ossian, an Irish bard of the third century, in 1765. They played an important role in the Celtic Revival of the late eighteenth century.

from: WILD EARTH, AND OTHER POEMS (1917)

[The words of 'She Moved Through the Fair' are sung to a traditional air, possibly from the seventeenth century.]

She Moved Through the Fair

My young love said to me, 'My brothers won't mind,
And my parents won't slight you for your lack of kind.'
Then she stepped away from me, and this she did say,
'It will not be long, love, till our wedding day.'

She stepped away from me and she moved through the fair,
And fondly I watched her go here and go there,
Then she went her way homeward with one star awake,
As the swan in the evening moves over the lake.

The people were saying no two were e'er wed
But one had a sorrow that never was said,
And I smiled as she passed with her goods and her gear,
And that was the last that I saw of my dear.

I dreamt it last night that my young love came in,
So softly she entered, her feet made no din;
She came close beside me, and this she did say,
'It will not be long, love, till our wedding day.'

Drover

To Meath of the pastures,
From wet hills by the sea,
Through Leitrim and Longford,
Go my cattle and me.

I hear in the darkness
Their slipping and breathing —
I name them the by-ways
They're to pass without heeding;

Then the wet, winding roads,
Brown bogs with black water,
And my thoughts on white ships
And the King o' Spain's daughter.

O farmer, strong farmer!
You can spend at the fair,
But your face you must turn
To your crops and your care;

And soldiers, red soldiers!
You've seen many lands,
But you walk two by two,
And by captain's commands!

O the smell of the beasts,
The wet wind in the morn,
And the proud and hard earth
Never broken for corn!

['I Shall not Die for Thee' is Colum's version of an anonymous seventeenth-century poem, *Ní Bhfuighe Mise Bás Duit*. It appeared in the expanded edition of *Wild Earth*, first published in 1907. Douglas Hyde had included the poem in his *Love Songs of Connacht* (1893).]

I Shall not Die for Thee

O woman, shapely as the swan,
On your account I shall not die:
The men you've slain — a trivial clan —
Were less than I.

I ask me shall I die for these —
For blossom-teeth and scarlet lips?
And shall that delicate swan shape
Bring me eclipse?

Well-shaped the breasts and smooth the skin,
The cheeks are fair, the tresses free —
And yet I shall not suffer death —
God over me!

Those even brows, that hair like gold,
Those languorous tones, that virgin way —
The flowing limbs, the rounded heel
Slight men betray!

Thy spirit keen through radiant mien,
Thy shining throat and smiling eye,
Thy little palm, thy side like foam —
I cannot die!

O woman shapely as the swan,
In a cunning house hard-reared was I:
O bosom white, O well-shaped palm,
I shall not die!

JAMES STEPHENS

(1882-1950)

from: THE HILL OF VISION (1912)

Light-O'-Love

And now, at last, I must away,
But if I tend another fire
In some man's house this you will say
— It is not that her love doth tire:
This is the price she has to pay,
For bread she gets no other way,
Still dreaming of her heart's desire.

And so she went out from the door
While I sat quiet in my chair:
She ran back once, again — no more;
I heard a footstep on the stair,
A lifted latch; one moment fleet
I heard the noises of the street,
Then silence booming everywhere.

from: SONGS FROM THE CLAY (1915)

The Ancient Elf

I am the maker,
The builder, the breaker,
The eagle-winged helper,
The speedy forsaker.

I am the lyre,
The water, the fire,
The tooth of oppression,
The lips of desire.

The snare and the wing,
The honey, the sting;
When you seek for me look
For a different thing.

I, careless and gay,
Never mean what I say,
For my thoughts and my eyes
Look the opposite way.

from: COLLECTED POEMS (1954)

The Snare

I hear a sudden cry of pain!
There is a rabbit in a snare:
Now I hear the cry again,
But I cannot tell from where.

But I cannot tell from where
He is calling out for aid!
Crying on the frightened air,
Making everything afraid!

Making everything afraid,
Wrinkling up his little face!
As he cries again for aid;
— And I cannot find the place!

And I cannot find the place
Where his paw is in the snare!
Little One! Oh, Little One!
I am searching everywhere!

A Glass of Beer

The lanky hank of a she in the inn over there
Nearly killed me for asking the loan of a glass of beer;
May the devil grip the whey-faced slut by the hair,
And beat bad manners out of her skin for a year.

That parboiled ape, with the toughest jaw you will see
On virtue's path, and a voice that would rasp the dead,
Came roaring and raging the minute she looked at me,
And threw me out of the house on the back of my head!

If I asked her master he'd give me a cask a day;
But she, with the beer at hand, not a gill[1] would
  arrange!
May she marry a ghost and bear him a kitten, and
  may
The High King of Glory permit her to get the
  mange.

1. Half-a-pint.

I Am Writer

I am writer,
And do know
Nothing that is false,
Or true:
Have only care
To take it so,
And make it sing,
And make it new:

And make it new
And make it sing,
When, if it's pleasing
Unto you,

Say, I've done
A useful thing
— As your servant
Ought to do.

JAMES JOYCE
(1882-1941)

from:
CHAMBER MUSIC (1907)

[This was Joyce's first published book. The lyrics, modelled on the songs of Shakespeare and other Elizabethans, were written during his student years. Despite the seventeenth-century influence, their melancholy sweetness is characteristically romantic, of the late nineteenth century. As a result of this book, Joyce was able to publish in Ezra Pound's *Imagist Anthology*, although it is an exaggeration to claim that these poems are, in any real sense, imagist. Nevertheless, their frail structures are very carefully and skilfully composed around one or two dominant, if conventional, images.]

II

The twilight turns from amethyst
  To deep and deeper blue,
The lamp fills with a pale green glow
  The trees of the avenue.

The old piano plays an air,
  Sedate and slow and gay;
She bends upon the yellow keys,
  Her head inclines this way.

Shy thoughts and grave wide eyes and hands
  That wander as they list —
The twilight turns to darker blue
  With lights of amethyst.

III

At that hour when all things have repose,
  O lonely watcher of the skies,
  Do you hear the night wind and the sighs
Of harps playing unto Love to unclose
  The pale gates of sunrise?

When all things repose do you alone
  Awake to hear the sweet harps play
  To Love before him on his way,
And the night wind answering in antiphon
  Till night is overgone?

Play on, invisible harps, unto Love,
  Whose way in heaven is aglow
  At that hour when soft lights come and go,
Soft sweet music in the air above
  And in the earth below.

XXXIV

Sleep now, O sleep now,
O you unquiet heart!
A voice crying 'Sleep now'
Is heard in my heart.

The voice of the winter
Is heard at the door.
O sleep, for the winter
Is crying 'Sleep no more.'

My kiss will give peace now
And quiet to your heart —
Sleep on in peace now,
O you unquiet heart!

XXXV

All day I hear the noise of waters
Making moan,
Sad as the sea-bird is, when going
Forth alone,
He hears the winds cry to the waters'
Monotone.

The grey winds, the cold winds are blowing
Where I go.
I hear the noise of many waters
Far below.
All day, all night, I hear them flowing
To and fro.

from: POMES PENYEACH (1927)

[In the winter of 1926-27, Joyce decided to present himself to the public as someone other than the author of *Work in Progress*, which had been having a hostile reception as it appeared in different periodicals. The venture was not a success. Wyndham Lewis and Rebecca West published books in 1927 and 1928 attacking both *Ulysses* and the new work, which was to become *Finnegans Wake*. For West, the new poems were evidence of Joyce's mawkishness and lack of taste.

The first poem in the collection (which numbered only thirteen poems) was written in 1904. 'Tilly' is believed to be obliquely related to Joyce's feelings about his dead mother. But equally, it may be seen as an expressionistic poem, in which Joyce contrasts his own artist's vulnerability with the blind contentment of a characteristic compatriot — who could be a literary or an actual peasant.]

Tilly

He travels after a winter sun,
Urging the cattle along a cold red road,
Calling to them, a voice they know,
He drives his beasts above Cabra.

The voice tells them home is warm.
They moo and make brute music with their hoofs.
He drives them with a flowering branch before him,
Smoke pluming their foreheads.

Boor, bond of the herd,
Tonight stretch full by the fire!
I bleed by the black stream
For my torn bough!

Dublin, 1904

A Flower given to my Daughter

Frail the white rose and frail are
Her hands that gave
Whose soul is sere and paler
Than time's wan wave.

Rosefrail and fair — yet frailest
A wonder wild
In gentle eyes thou veilest,
My blueveined child.

Trieste, 1913

She weeps over Rahoon

Rain on Rahoon falls softly, softly falling,
Where my dark lover lies.
Sad is his voice that calls me, sadly calling,
At grey moonrise.

Love, hear thou
How soft, how sad his voice is ever calling,
Ever unanswered, and the dark rain falling,
Then as now.

Dark too our hearts, O love, shall lie and cold
As his sad heart has lain
Under the moongrey nettles, the black mould
And muttering rain.

Trieste, 1913

Flood

Goldbrown upon the sated flood
The rockvine clusters lift and sway;
Vast wings above the lambent waters brood
Of sullen day.

A waste of waters ruthlessly
Sways and uplifts its weedy mane
Where brooding day stares down upon the sea
In dull disdain.

Uplift and sway, O golden vine,
Your clustered fruits to love's full flood,
Lambent and vast and ruthless as is thine
Incertitude!

Trieste, 1915

Nightpiece

Gaunt in gloom,
The pale stars their torches,
Enshrouded, wave.
Ghostfires from heaven's far verges faint illume,
Arches on soaring arches,
Night's sindark nave.

Seraphim,
The lost hosts awaken
To service till
In moonless gloom each lapses muted, dim,
Raised when she has and shaken
Her thurible.[1]

And long and loud,
To night's nave upsoaring,
A starknell tolls
As the bleak incense surges, cloud on cloud,
Voidward from the adoring
Waste of souls.

Trieste, 1915

1. A container for burning incense that is swung in religious services.

['Ecce Puer' was written in 1932, but did not appear in *Collected Poems* (1936).]

Ecce Puer

Of the dark past
A child is born;
With joy and grief
My heart is torn.

Calm in his cradle
The living lies.
May love and mercy
Unclose his eyes!

Young life is breathed
On the glass;
The world that was not
Comes to pass.

A child is sleeping:
An old man gone.
O, father forsaken,
Forgive your son!

THE HOLY OFFICE[1] (1904)

[The introductory note to this poem in E. Mason and R. Ellmann (eds), *The Critical Writings of James Joyce* (1959) reads as follows:

> Joyce composed this satirical broadside about two months before he left Dublin in 1904. He had it printed but could not afford to pay for it, so the following year, in Pola, he had it printed again and sent the sheets to his brother Stanislaus for distribution to the butts of his satire in Dublin.
>
> In the poem he lumps together Yeats and Russell and their followers, accusing them all of hypocrisy and self-deception. One would hardly suspect from their writings that they had bodies at all; their spirituality has its analogue in female prudery. Joyce, who had always prided himself on his candour and honesty, and was now demonstrating these qualities in *Stephen Hero* and the first stories of *Dubliners*, yokes Aristotle to Christian ritual to claim that his own office is Katharsis, the revelation of what the mummers hide. Then, elevating his metaphor, he condemns them from the mountain-top to which Ibsen and Nietzsche had helped to bring him.

The poem caused great offence among Joyce's friends in Dublin, most of whom felt, with reason, that this was a

1. The title of the poem refers to the office of confession and to the Holy Office, one of the sacred congregations of the papacy, established in 1542 to take the place and continue the work of the Inquisition. It was not until 1917 that it was allocated the work of the Congregation of the Index — that is, the listing of books prohibited on account of the danger they represented to faith and morals. According to Mason and Ellmann, 'There are also overtones of 'the holy office an ostler does for the stallion', *Ulysses*, p. 166, line 664.

strange and bitter return for the help many had given him. The text here is that of the first printing.]

Myself unto myself will give
This name Katharsis-Purgative.
I, who dishevelled ways forsook
To hold the poets' grammar-book,[2]
Bringing to tavern and to brothel
The mind of witty Aristotle,
Lest bards in the attempt should err
Must here be my interpreter:
Wherefore receive now from my lip
Peripatetic scholarship.
To enter heaven, travel hell,
Be piteous or terrible,
One positively needs the ease,
Of plenary indulgences.
For every true-born mysticist
A Dante is, unprejudiced,[3]
Who safe at ingle-nook, by proxy,
Hazards extremes of heterodoxy,
Like him who finds a joy at table
Pondering the uncomfortable.
Ruling one's life by commonsense
How can one fail to be intense?
But I must not accounted be
One of that mumming company[4] —
With him[5] who hies him to appease
His giddy dames'[6] frivolities
While they console him when he whinges
With gold-embroidered Celtic fringes[7] —
Or him who sober all the day
Mixes a naggin in his play[8] —
Or him who conduct 'seems to own',
His preference for a man of 'tone' —
Or him who plays the ragged patch
To millionaires in Hazelhatch
But weeping after holy fast
Confesses all his pagan past[9] —
Or him who will his hat unfix
Neither to malt nor crucifix
But show to all that poor-dressed be
His high Castilian courtesy[10] —
Or him who loves his Master dear[11] —
Or him who drinks his pint in fear[12] —
Or him who once when snug abed
Saw Jesus Christ without his head
And tried so hard to win for us
The long-lost works of Eschylus.[13]
But all these men of whom I speak
Make me the sewer of their clique.
That they may dream their dreamy dreams
I carry off their filthy streams
For I can do those things for them
Through which I lost my diadem,
Those things for which Grandmother Church
Left me severely in the lurch.
Thus I relieve their timid arses,
Perform my office of Katharsis.
My scarlet leaves them white as wool[14]
Through me they purge a bellyful.
To sister mummers one and all
I act as vicar-general[15]
And for each maiden, shy and nervous,

2. This could refer to the fact that, as Mason and Ellmann say, 'Joyce collected the solecisms in the works of his eminent contemporaries.' It could also refer to the fact that he gave up his dissolute ways in 1904 to dedicate himself to the vocation of writing.
3. In a 1903 review of a French translation of Ibsen's first play, *Catilina*, Joyce sneered at the 'young generation', which considered every poetaster to be 'a Dante without the unfortunate prejudices of Dante'.
4. cf. Yeats's 'To Ireland in the Coming Times':
   'Know, that I would accounted be
   True brother of a company
   That sang, to sweeten Ireland's wrong . . . .'
   The mumming company is a derogatory term in particular for the Abbey Theatre, recently established as a new enterprise, distinct from, although inheritor of, the Irish National Theatre.
5. W. B. Yeats.
6. Lady Gregory, Annie E. Horniman, the financial backer of the Abbey, and Maud Gonne MacBride.
7. Mason and Ellmann say this is 'an allusion to the gilt decorations on the books that Yeats published in the 1890s.'
8. The reference is to Synge, whose plays *In the Shadow of the Glen* and *Riders to the Sea* had been produced by the Irish National Theatre Society in 1903-04. Perhaps Joyce is referring to the exuberance of Synge's dramatic language, compared to the sobriety of his general demeanour. naggin = noggin.
9. This reference, and indeed the whole poem, angered Oliver St John Gogarty; it marked the beginning of the end of their friendship.
10. A reference to the fact that Padraic Colum had been given a five-year scholarship by a wealthy American to enable him to write. Colum combined traditional catholic piety with an interest in the pagan past of Irish legend. He and Joyce later became good friends.
11. John Eglinton, pseudonym of W.K. Magee (1868-1961), who worked in the National Library and was to appear later in the 'Scylla and Charybdis' episode of *Ulysses*. His early essays, published between 1894 and 1901, are full of the transcendentalism of Thoreau and Emerson. Courteous and gentlemanly, he neither drank nor belonged to any religious sect. His celibacy was also the occasion for much ribald humour.
12. George Roberts (1873-1953), poet and actor. He was a devoted follower of AE and addressed him as 'Master dear' in a poem.
13. James Starkey (1879-1958), who wrote under the pseudonym Seumas O'Sullivan. He and George Roberts helped to re-establish the publishing firm of Whaley and Company.
14. Isaiah 1.18: 'Though your sins be as scarlet, they shall be as white as snow.'
15. A vicar-general acts in the name of a bishop, usually in administrative duties.

I do a similar kind service.
For I detect without surprise
That shadowy beauty in her eyes,
The 'dare not' of sweet maidenhood
That answers my corruptive 'would'.[16]
Whenever publicly we meet
She never seems to think of it;
At night when close in bed she lies
And feels my hand between her thighs
My little love in light attire
Knows the soft flame that is desire.
But Mammon places under ban
The uses of Leviathan[17]
And that high spirit ever wars
On Mammon's countless servitors,
Nor can they ever be exempt
From his taxation of contempt.
So distantly I turn to view
The shamblings of that motley crew,
Those souls that hate the strength that mine has
Steeled in the school of old Aquinas.
Where they have crouched and crawled and prayed
I stand the self-doomed, unafraid,
Unfellowed, friendless and alone,
Indifferent as the herring-bone,
Firm as the mountain-ridges where
I flash my antlers on the air.[18]
Let them continue as is meet
To adequate the balance-sheet.
Though they may labour to the grave
My spirit shall they never have
Nor make my soul with theirs at one
Till the Mahamanvantara[19] be done:
And though they spurn me from their door
My soul shall spurn them evermore.

16. cf. *Macbeth*, I. 7. 44-45:
    'Letting "I dare not" wait upon "I would",
    Like the poor cat i' th' adage.'
17. Leviathan here is identified with Satan, the heroic individual. cf. Isaiah 27.1, in which Leviathan is 'the fleeing serpent' punished by the Lord — an appropriate image in this context.
18. '... he flung them disdain from his flashing antlers.' *Stephen Hero*.
19. The Hindu 'Great Year'.

GAS FROM A BURNER (1912)

[In September 1909, Joyce, then on a visit to Dublin, signed a contract with the Dublin firm of Maunsel and Company to publish *Dubliners*. But George Roberts, the manager of the firm, began to find reasons first for delaying and then for censoring the manuscript. Negotiations dragged along for three years, until finally Joyce returned to Dublin in July 1912, and brought the matter to a head. Both Joyce and Roberts consulted solicitors; Roberts was advised that the use of actual names for public houses and the like was libellous, and began to demand so many changes that there was no possibility of agreement. At length he decided to accept Joyce's offer to purchase the sheets for the book, which John Falconer, a Dublin printer, had finished. But Falconer, hearing of the dispute, decided he wanted nothing to do with so unpleasant a book, and guillotined the sheets. Joyce left Dublin full of bitterness, which he vented by writing this broadside on the back of his contract with Maunsel and Company for the publication of *Dubliners*, while he was on the train between Flushing and Salzburg.

The notes are from E. Mason and R. Ellmann (eds), *The Critical Writings of James Joyce* (1959). A number of small corrections have been made to the text.]

Ladies and gents, you are here assembled
To hear why earth and heaven trembled
Because of the black and sinister arts
Of an Irish writer in foreign parts.
He sent me a book ten years ago[1]
I read it a hundred times or so,
Backwards and forwards, down and up,
Through both ends of a telescope.
I printed it all to the very last word
But by the mercy of the Lord
The darkness of my mind was rent
And I saw the writer's foul intent.
But I owe a duty to Ireland:
I hold her honour in my hand,
This lovely land that always sent
Her writers and artists to banishment
And in a spirit of Irish fun
Betrayed her own leaders, one by one.
'Twas Irish humour, wet and dry,
Flung quicklime into Parnell's eye;[2]
'Tis Irish brains that save from doom
The leaky barge of the Bishop of Rome
For everyone knows the Pope can't belch
Without the consent of Billy Walsh.[3]
O Ireland my first and only love
Where Christ and Caesar are hand and glove!

1. The speaker is a blend of Roberts and Falconer.
2. This incident, which Joyce also mentions in 'The Shade of Parnell'... occurred at Castlecomer in the summer of 1891, according to Parnell's biographer and friend, R. Barry O'Brien.
3. His Grace the Most Reverend William J. Walsh, D.D., Archbishop of Dublin.

O lovely land where the shamrock grows!
(Allow me, ladies, to blow my nose)
To show you for strictures I don't care a button
I printed the poems of Mountainy Mutton[4]
And a play he wrote (you've read it, I'm sure)
Where they talk of 'bastard', 'bugger' and 'whore'[5]
And a play on the Word and Holy Paul
And some woman's legs that I can't recall
Written by Moore, a genuine gent
That lives on his property's ten per cent:[6]
I printed mystical books in dozens:
I printed the table book of Cousins[7]
Though (asking your pardon) as for the verse
'Twould give you a heartburn on your arse:[8]
I printed folklore from North and South
By Gregory of the Golden Mouth:[9]
I printed poets, sad, silly and solemn:
I printed Patrick What-do-you-Colm:[10]
I printed the great John Milicent Synge
Who soars above on an angel's wing
In the playboy shift[11] that he pinched as swag
From Maunsel's manager's travelling-bag.[12]
But I draw the line at that bloody fellow,
That was over here dressed in Austrian yellow,
Spouting Italian by the hour
To O'Leary Curtis[13] and John Wyse Power[14]
And writing of Dublin, dirty and dear,
In a manner no blackamoor printer could bear.
Shite and onions![15] Do you think I'll print
The name of the Wellington Monument,
Sydney Parade and Sandymount tram,
Downes's cakeshop and Williams's jam?
I'm damned if I do — I'm damned to blazes!
Talk about *Irish Names of Places*![16]
It's a wonder to me, upon my soul,
He forgot to mention Curly's Hole.[17]
No, ladies, my press shall have no share in
So gross a libel on Stepmother Erin.[18]
I pity the poor — that's why I took
A red-headed Scotchman[19] to keep my book.
Poor sister Scotland! Her doom is fell;
She cannot find any more Stuarts to sell.
My conscience is fine as Chinese silk:
My heart is as soft as buttermilk.
Colm can tell you I made a rebate
Of one hundred pounds on the estimate
I gave him for his Irish Review.[20]
I love my country — by herrings I do!
I wish you could see what tears I weep
When I think of the emigrant train and ship.
That's why I publish far and wide
My quite illegible railway guide.
In the porch of my printing institute
The poor and deserving prostitute
Plays every night at catch-as-catch-can
With her tight-breeched British artilleryman
And the foreigner learns the gift of the gab
From the drunken draggletail Dublin drab.
Who was it said: Resist not evil?[21]
I'll burn that book, so help me devil.
I'll sing a psalm as I watch it burn
And the ashes I'll keep in a one-handled urn.
I'll penance do with farts and groans
Kneeling upon my marrowbones.
This very next lent I will unbare
My penitent buttocks to the air
And sobbing beside my printing press
My awful sin I will confess.

4. Joseph Campbell, author of *The Mountainy Singer*, published by Maunsel in 1909.
5. Campbell's *Judgment: a Play in Two Acts*, published by Maunsel in 1912, contains on p. 25 the words 'bastard' and 'whore'.
6. *The Apostle*, published by Maunsel in 1911. Moore's play, in which Christ (the Word) and Paul meet after Christ's death, includes a dialogue between Christ and Mary in which Mary laments her lost beauty. In a long preface Moore surveys the Bible for evidence of sensuality and remarks (p. 9) 'In Samuel we read how David was captured by the sweetness of Bathsheba's legs while bathing . . .', and (p. 26) 'It may be doubted whether Paul always succeeded in subduing these infirmities of the flesh, but we would not love him less, even if we knew that he had loved St. Eunice not wisely but too well.'
7. James Cousins, a Dublin Theosophist and poet. The 'table book' is probably his *Etain the Beloved and Other Poems*, published by Maunsel in 1912.
8. An expression of Joyce's father; see *Ulysses*, p. 102, line 241.
9. Maunsel published Lady Gregory's *Kiltartan History Book* in 1909 and *The Kiltartan Wonder Book* in 1910.
10. Padraic Colum.
11. The word 'shift', spoken by a character in Synge's *Playboy of the Western World*, caused a riot at the Abbey Theatre in 1907; Maunsel published the play in the same year.
12. Roberts was a traveller in ladies' underwear.
13. A Dublin journalist.
14. An official in the Royal Irish Constabulary in Dublin Castle, and a man of considerable cultivation. He figures largely in *Ulysses* in the characters of Jack Power and John Wyse Nolan.
15. An expression of Joyce's father; see *Ulysses*, p. 104, line 329.
16. *The Origin and History of Irish Names of Places*, by Patrick Weston Joyce, no relation to James.
17. A bathing pool at Dollymount, Clontarf.
18. As Dr Oliver Gogarty remarks, in *Mourning Becomes Mrs. Spendlove* (N.Y., 1948) p. 61, Roberts was an Ulster Scot, so Erin is only his stepmother.
19. Roberts himself.
20. The *Irish Review* was edited by Colum from March 1912 to July 1913.
21. Christ, in the Sermon on the Mount.

My Irish foreman from Bannockburn[22]
Shall dip his right hand in the urn
And sign crisscross with reverent thumb
Memento homo[23] upon my bum.

Flushing, September 1912

22. In Scotland.

23. 'Memento, homo, quia pulvis es', the words of the priest on Ash Wednesday as he marks the cross of ashes on the penitent's forehead. forehead.

FRANCIS LEDWIDGE

(1887-1917)

from: SONGS OF THE FIELDS (1916)

June

Broom out the floor now, lay the fender by,
And plant this bee-sucked bough of woodbine there,
And let the window down. The butterfly
Floats in upon the sunbeam, and the fair
Tanned face of June, the nomad gipsy, laughs
Above her widespread wares, the while she tells
The farmers' fortunes in the fields, and quaffs
The water from the spider-peopled wells.

The hedges are all drowned in green grass seas,
And bobbing poppies flare like Elmo's light,[1]
While siren-like the pollen-stained bees
Drone in the clover depths. And up the height
The cuckoo's voice is hoarse and broke with joy.
And on the lowland crops the crows make raid,
Nor fear the clappers of the farmer's boy,
Who sleeps, like drunken Noah, in the shade.

And loop this red rose in that hazel ring
That snares your little ear, for June is short
And we must joy in it and dance and sing.
And from her bounty draw her rosy worth.
Ay! soon the swallows will be flying south,
The wind wheel north to gather in the snow,
Even the roses split on youth's red mouth
Will soon blow down the road all roses go.

1. A corona discharge in the air caused by atmospheric electricity. This luminosity sometimes appears around the masts of ships and church spires.

A Song

My heart has flown on wings to you, away
In the lonely places where your footsteps lie
Full up of stars when the short showers of day
Have passed like ancient sorrows. I would fly
To your green solitude of woods to hear
You singing in the sounds of leaves and birds;
But I am sad below the depth of words
That nevermore we two shall draw anear.

Had I but wealth of land and bleating flocks
And barnfuls of the yellow harvest yield,
And a large house with climbing hollyhocks
And servant maidens singing in the field,
You'd love me; but I own no roaming herds,
My only wealth is songs of love for you,
And now that you are lost I may pursue
A sad life deep below the depth of words.

from: SONGS OF PEACE (1917)

A Twilight in Middle March

Within the oak a throb of pigeon wings
Fell silent, and grey twilight hushed the fold,
And spiders' hammocks swung on half-oped things
That shook like foreigners upon our cold.
A gipsy lit a fire and made a sound
Of moving tins, and from an oblong moon
The river seemed to gush across the ground
To the cracked metre of a marching tune.

And then three syllables of melody
Dropped from a blackbird's flute, and died apart

Far in the dewy dark. No more but three,
Yet sweeter music never touched a heart
Neath the blue domes of London. Flute and reed
Suggesting feelings of the solitude
When will was all the Delphi I would heed,
Lost like a wind within a summer wood
From little knowledge where great sorrows brood.

Lament for Thomas MacDonagh[1]

He shall not hear the bittern cry
In the wild sky, where he is lain,
Nor voices of the sweeter birds
Above the wailing of the rain.

Nor shall he know when loud March blows
Thro' slanting snows her fanfare shrill,
Blowing to flame the golden cup
Of many an upset daffodil.

But when the Dark Cow leaves the moor,
And pastures poor with greedy weeds,
Perhaps he'll hear her low at morn
Lifting her horn in pleasant meads.

1. See above p. 755.

The Shadow People

Old lame Bridget doesn't hear
Fairy music in the grass
When the gloaming's on the mere
And the shadow people pass:
Never hears their slow grey feet
Coming from the village street
Just beyond the parson's wall,
Where the clover globes are sweet
And the mushroom's parasol
Opens in the moonlit rain.
Every night I hear them call
From their long and merry train.
Old lame Bridget says to me,
'It is just your fancy, child.'
She cannot believe I see
Laughing faces in the wild,
Hands that twinkle in the sedge
Bowing at the water's edge
Where the finny minnows quiver,
Shaping on a blue wave's ledge
Bubble foam to sail the river.
And the sunny hands to me
Beckon ever, beckon ever.
Oh! I would be wild and free
And with the shadow people be.

The Herons

As I was climbing Ardan Mor
From the shore of Sheelan lake,
I met the herons coming down
Before the waters wake.

And they were talking in their flight
Of dreamy ways the herons go
When all the hills are withered up
Nor any waters flow.

from:
THE COMPLETE POEMS OF FRANCIS LEDWIDGE (1974)

[These poems were not included in Lord Dunsany's edition of the *Complete Poems* (1919). They were added in Alice Curtayne's 1974 revised edition.]

At Lisnaskea

As I went up thro' Lisnaskea
To weep for thee, my love, my Queen,
I saw thy broken banners there,
Whipping the air with gold and green.

And little ships in flocks of white
Came from the night with flutterings pale,
And there was strong Cuchulain's ghost,
And a Fenian host in glittering mail.

Oh, ever anxious hearts, such dreams
But ill beseem Love's bravery,
Yet, waiting the red signal fire
My golden wire goes pleasantly.

Derry

By day a place of wheels and looms
That struggle in a narrow space,
A shout of children in the slums
And girls with labour-stainèd face.

By night a queen with victory crowned,
For all her years of loud turmoil.
She spreads her beauty all around,
Reflects her glory in the Foyle.

The Sad Queen

I dreamt a young Queen sits alone,
In a strange eastern land unknown.
And all the day she maketh moan
For one departed.

She hears her maids laugh in the hall.
The warders on the palace wall,
The soldiers, to the maidens call
So happy hearted.

She hears the birds sing in the fells,
The river in the twisted dells
As flowing thro' a million bells
Fast to the ocean.

And when her eyes turn to the west
And on the burning hill-top rest,
The secret covered in her breast
Makes little motion.

But O, I'll make a song in Spring
About a little unborn thing
Who one day will rise up a King
And round him gather.

Ten thousand men in war well tried,
Ten thousand vengeful youths beside,
To scour the Kingdoms far and wide
And kill his father.

A Dream

I dreamt last night I met a maiden queen
Who lost the memory of her regal days.
The changing foam of water never took
The wonders of her face. She might have been
The Aphrodite[1] of a country brook
Born in a stony sharp so sweet her praise
Of finny creeks, and moonlight in the reeds
And sounds of twisting water when it leads
The moorhen on her nest. But one came down
And whispered in the windings of her ear,
And on her forehead set a golden crown.
Then all the world grew dark and windy drear.

1. The Greek goddess of love and beauty. She is so called (*aphros* means 'foam' in Greek) because she sprang from the foam of the sea.

FREDERICK ROBERT HIGGINS

(1896-1941)

from:
THE DARK BREED (1927)

The Dark Breed

With those bawneen men I'm one,
In the grey dusk-fall,
Watching the Galway land
Sink down in distress —
With dark men, talking of grass,
By a loose stone wall,
In murmurs drifting and drifting
To loneliness.

Over this loneliness,
Wild riders gather their fill
Of talking on beasts and on fields
Too lean for a plough,
Until, more grey than the grey air,
Song drips from a still,
Through poteen,[1] reeling the dancing —
Ebbing the grief now!

Just, bred from the cold lean rock,
Those fellows have grown;
And only in that grey fire
Their lonely days pass

1. An illicit spirit.

To dreams of far clovers
   And cream-gathering heifers, alone
Under the hazels of moon-lighters,
   Clearing the grass.

Again in the darkness,
   Dull knives we may secretly grease,
And talk of blown horns on clovers
   Where graziers have lain;
But there rolls the mist,
   With sails pulling wind from the seas —
No bullion can brighten that mist,
   O brood of lost Spain.

So we, with the last dark men,
   Left on the rock grass,
May brazen grey loneliness
   Over a poteen still
Or crowd on the bare chapel floor
   Hearing late Mass,
To loosen that hunger
   Broken land never can fill.

Heresy

What peace have I in holy bonds,
From chiselled holiness on stone,
Where croziers, flowering in white bronze,
And fiery minds have finely shown
The grace of God in metal?

So when the quiet shoes my feet
And this hill-pool has cupped the moon,
I'll lie with God and slowly beat
My lonely thought into a tune,
That we may chant together.

Unravelling no gilded prayer,
I'll praise the Scribe, whose burning lines,
On that pure vellum of blue air,
Shoot crimson stars through golden signs
Around the flaming spiral;

And safe beneath those fiery snakes,
His breviary of sleep I'll tell,
Until the shining morning shakes
This calm hill to a laughing bell
And leads the day with singing.

The Fair of Maam

Pursuing my love's wild heart
   From rumours through many a fair,
I roved under miles of pinewood
   Through days of blue dusk air;
To meet the fair day at Maam[1]
   To gather sly rumours of her,
I took the pinewoods for my bed
   And slept until dawn made a stir.

The stir of heifers and young bulls
   Had hoofed soil under the pine,
Through fresh woods smelling of cattle,
   Through dawn airs, moistured and fine;
And I, at a heel of soft herds,
   Stepped from the heavy air
To a green square, gabled with pinewoods —
   The fair-green of Maam fair.

All day in the slapping of bargains
   I sought for word of my love;
And what had crowded my hearing,
   But loud strokes herding each drove,
Horns buckling by bullocks unnozzled;
   Strong words of praise or blame
Were heard from sly ass dealers —
   But never my love's name!

And evening crowded the pinewoods
   When all but my love were seen;
For hearing a reel of fife music
   Rise on the loose fair-green,
Girls hurried from under green timbers
   To dancers grown lively in ale,
To matchmakers, by the bone-fire,
   That welded the female to male.

Then leaving the fair-green of Maam
   The ballad-men sang my love
Until the glens whispered her name
   That hill voices whispered above;
The pools of sunrise had not wet her,
   So I crept where the moonlight creeps
To look on the unknown mountains
   And plunder their blue deeps.

I've lost her, O loved one, O strange one,
   O hunger none other can ease;

1. In County Galway.

Crossroads of the Black Bull deceived me,
  Courtyards by the eastern seas;
Grown peevish, I'm beggared in Maam,
  Its woods are all gone and its fair
Is a memory left to the old men
  Who tether a few goats there.

The Little Clan

Over their edge of earth
  They wearily tread,
Leaving the stone-grey dew —
  The hungry grass;
Most proud in their own defeat,
  These last men pass
This labouring grass that bears them
  Little bread.

Too full their spring tide flowed,
  And ebbing then
Has left each hooker deep
  Within salt grass;
All ebbs, yet lives in their song;
  Song shall not pass
With these most desperate,
  Most noble men!

Then, comfort your own sorrow;
  Time has heard
One groping singer hold
  A burning face;
You mourn no living Troy,
  Then mourn no less
The living glory of
  Each Gaelic word!

Rain

Among those bushy spaces
The grey rain drowns the wind,
Flowing from airy places,
Flowing from hills behind
Her threshold, hushed in grasses;
And now her window-pane
Is caged in brambles casing
The half-light of the rain.
But she has left those grasses,
Then why should I look on
An evening gloss of waters
Without the cloud-blown swan,
Knowing in airy places
The grey rain cannot blur
Those shining airs — the graces
Remembered of her.

A Sheiling of the Music

Violins are crying
  Out across the water,
Through hazel and salley[1]
  And through soft rain they cry;
And no other stir,
  But the yellow stir of rush-light
Touching that window
  Cobwebbed by the sky.

With violins wheening
  Inside that island sheiling,[2]
I hear lost secrets breathing
  Beyond the cairned mound;
And heedless of me waiting
  Sean bends to his playing —
While hazel and salley
  Drip grey light to the ground.

Surely now my love
  Is stolen by the music;
O could I only steal him
  With my heart's sigh
We could steep with those shadows
  And leave the sheiling,
That winks through wet salleys
  Its bleary eye.

Wearily veiling
  The air in greys of evening,
Slow hush of darkness,
  O ease my dreamy pain,
While violins wheening
  Dreamily on water
Are waning, waning
  Softly in rain....

1. willow.
2. Means, variously, a cottage, a summer pasture, and a grassy area in front of a house.

from:
THE GAP OF BRIGHTNESS
(1940)

Song for the Clatter-Bones

God rest that Jewy woman,
Queen Jezebel,[1] the bitch
Who peeled the clothes from her shoulder-bones
Down to her spent teats
As she stretched out of the window
Among the geraniums, where
She chaffed and laughed like one half daft
Titivating her painted hair —

King Jehu[2] he drove to her,
She tipped him a fancy beck;[3]
But he from his knacky side-car spoke,
'Who'll break that dewlapped neck?'
And so she was thrown from the window;
Like Lucifer[4] she fell
Beneath the feet of the horses and they beat
The light out of Jezebel.

That corpse wasn't planted in clover;
Ah, nothing of her was found
Save those grey bones that Hare-foot Mike
Gave me for their lovely sound;
And as once her dancing body
Made star-lit princes sweat,
So I'll just clack: though her ghost lacks a back
There's music in the old bones yet.

1. The wife of Ahab, King of Israel. See II Kings 9.30.
2. See II Kings 9.20.
3. A nod.
4. See Isaiah 14.4, 14.12.

Chinese Winter

From these bare trees
The sticks of last year's nests
Print sad characters against the moon;
While wind-blown moonlight,
Stripping fields to silver,
Scrawls December on each frozen pool.

Light washed on every tree
Roots it in black shadow,
As last year's love now roots me in black night;
And where love danced
Footprints of fiery moments
Flash out memorials in silent ice.

Father and Son

Only last week, walking the hushed fields
Of our most lovely Meath, now thinned by November,
I came to where the road from Laracor leads
To the Boyne river — that seemed more lake than river,
Stretched in uneasy light and stript of reeds.

And walking longside an old weir
Of my people's, where nothing stirs — only the shadowed
Leaden flight of a heron up the lean air —
I went unmanly with grief, knowing how my father,
Happy though captive in years, walked last with me there.

Yes, happy in Meath with me for a day
He walked, taking stock of herds hid in their own breathing;
And naming colts, gusty as wind, once steered by his hand,
Lightnings winked in the eyes that were half shy in greeting
Old friends — the wild blades, when he gallivanted the land.

For that proud, wayward man now my heart breaks —
Breaks for that man whose mind was a secret eyrie,
Whose kind hand was sole signet of his race,
Who curbed me, scorned my green ways, yet increasingly loved me
Till Death drew its grey blind down his face.

And yet I am pleased that even my reckless ways
Are living shades of his rich calms and passions —
Witnesses for him and for those faint namesakes
With whom now he is one, under yew branches,
Yes, one in a graven silence no bird breaks.

O You Among Women

When pails empty the last brightness
Of the well, at twilight-time,
And you are there among women —
O mouth of silence,

Will you come with me, when I sign,
To the far green wood, that fences
A lake inlaid with light?

To be there, O, lost in each other,
While day melts in airy water,
And the drake-headed pike — a shade
In the waves' pale stir!
For love is there, under the breath,
As a coy star is there in the quiet
Of the wood's blue eye.

Biographies/Bibliographies

Antoine Raftery

LIFE. Born in Lios Ard, Co. Mayo probably in 1784, Raftery received some education at a local hedge school. He left at the age of nine when he was blinded by smallpox. His landlords, the Taaffes, encouraged him to some extent, but he left the area after a disagreement with them and became a wandering minstrel in the south Galway area. He died on Christmas Eve 1835. Many stories and legends surrounded him, many of them collected by Lady Gregory and Douglas Hyde. Along with Edward Martyn and many others, they honoured Raftery in August 1900 by erecting a stone on his grave at Killeenin, near Craughwell, Co. Galway. Yeats was also attracted by the legend of Raftery.

CHIEF WRITINGS. D. Hyde (ed.), *Abhráin atá Leaghta ar a Reachtúire. Songs Ascribed to Raftery* in *Songs of Connacht* chapter v (Dublin: Gill and Son, 1903; reprinted New York: Barnes and Noble, 1973; Shannon: Irish University Press, 1979); *Abhráin agus Dánta an Reachtabhraigh* (Baile Átha Cliath: Oifig Díolta Foillseacháin Rialtais, 1933); C. Ó Coigligh (ed.), *Raifteararaí: Amhráin agus Dánta* (Baile Átha Cliath: An Clóchomhar Tta, 1987).

BIOGRAPHY AND CRITICISM. Lady Gregory, in *Poets and Dreamers* (Dublin: Gill and Son, 1903; reprinted Gerrards Cross: Colin Smythe, 1974); B. O'Rourke, 'County Mayo in Gaelic Folksong' in B. O'Hara (ed.), *Mayo. Aspects of Its Heritage* (Galway: Corrib, 1982), pp. 153-56, 291-96; A. Ní Cheannain, *Raifteirí an file* (Baile Átha Cliath: Foilseacháin Náisiúnta, 1984).

George Sigerson

LIFE. Born near Strabane, Co. Tyrone in 1836, Sigerson was educated at Letterkenny Academy, at Paris and at Queen's College, Cork. He translated and edited Charcot's *Diseases of the Nervous System*, became a fellow of the Royal University, professor of biology at University College, Dublin, and, in 1893, president of the National Library Society. He was also a member of the Irish Literary Society and in 1884 was appointed a member of the Royal Commission on Prisons. Sigerson's essays and poems, the latter mostly translations from the Irish, made a considerable impact and his influence is evident in the writings of W. P. Ryan and is acknowledged in the dedication of Thomas MacDonagh's *Literature in Ireland* (1916). His daughter, Dora Sigerson Shorter, became a well-known poet. Sigerson was appointed a senator of the Irish Free State in 1922. He died in Dublin in 1925.

CHIEF WRITINGS. *The Poets and Poetry of Munster* 2nd series (Dublin: John O'Daly, 1860); *Modern Ireland: Its Vital Questions, Secret Societies, and Government* (London: Longmans, Green, Reader and Dyer, 1868; 2nd edition 1869); *History of the Land Classes and Land Tenures of Ireland* (London: Longmans, Green, Reader; Dublin: McGlashan and Gill, 1871); *Political Prisoners at Home and Abroad* (London: Kegan Paul, Trench, Trubner & Co., 1890); *Bards of the Gael and Gall* (London: T. Fisher Unwin, 1897; 2nd enlarged edition, 1907); *The Last Independent Parliament of Ireland* (Dublin: Gill, 1919); *The Easter Song of Sedulius* (Dublin: The Talbot Press, 1922); *Songs and Poems* introduction by P. Colum (Dublin: Duffy, 1927).

William Larminie

LIFE. Larminie was born in Castlebar, Co. Mayo in 1849 or 1850 and was educated at Trinity College, Dublin. He espoused the use of Gaelic assonance in English poetry. Larminie worked for several years at the India Office in London, retired in 1887 and returned to Ireland. He was an influential figure in the Irish Revival, contributing essays to *The Contemporary Review* and collecting folklore material. He died in Bray, Co. Wicklow in 1900.

CHIEF WRITINGS. *Fand and Other Poems* (Dublin: Hodges Figgis, 1892); *West Irish Folktales and Romances* (London: Elliot Stock, 1893); facsimile reprint Shannon: Irish University Press, 1972); *Glanlua and Other Poems* (London: Kegan Paul, 1899).

BIOGRAPHY AND CRITICISM. J. Eglinton, 'William Larminie', *Dublin Magazine*, New Series XIX (April-June 1944), 12-16; P. L. Marcus, *Yeats and the Beginning of the Renaissance* (Ithaca and London: Cornell University Press, 1970), pp. 207-21.

Oscar Wilde

For biography and bibliography, see p. 514.

Thomas William Rolleston

LIFE. Rolleston was born in 1857 near Shinrone, Co. Offaly. He was educated at St Columba's College, Rathfarnham and Trinity College, Dublin. From 1879 to 1883 he lived in Germany, developing an interest in German literature which culminated in his *Life of Lessing* (1889) and his German translation of Walt Whitman's *Leaves of Grass*. On his return to Ireland, he founded *The Dublin University Review*, which he edited 1885-86. He went to London and was first honorary secretary of the irish Literary Society. Rolleston was active in the Arts and Crafts Movement and, during the early years of the century, he was an organizer for the Department of Agriculture. In 1904 he organized the Irish Historic Collection at the St Louis Exhibition. His *Treasury of Irish Poetry*, co-edited with his father-in-law, Stopford Brooke, appeared in 1900. In 1908 he settled in London and was one of the founders of the Rhymers Club. Rolleston died in Hampstead, London in 1920.

CHIEF WRITINGS. *Boycotting: A Reply to Mr. S. Laing* (Dublin: Ponsonby, 1888); *Imagination and Art in Gaelic Literature, being notes on some recent translations from the Gaelic* (Kilkenny: Library of the Nore, 1900); *Ireland, the Empire, and the War* (Dublin: Sealy, Bryars and Walker, 1900); *Sea Spray: Verses and Translations* (Dublin: Maunsel, 1909); *The High Deeds of Finn and other Bardic Romances of Ancient Ireland* (London: Harrap, 1910); *Ireland's Vanishing Opportunity* (Dublin: The Talbot Press, 1919). Trans. *The Teaching of Epictetus* (London: The Camelot Classics, W. Scott, 1886; Chicago: Donohue, Henneberry and Co., 1892; *Life of Gotthold Ephraim Lessing* (London: W. Scott, 1889; reprint, Port Washington, New York/London: Kennikat Press, 1972); *Imagination and Art in Gaelic Literature* (Kilkenny: Kilkenny Moderator, 1900); with Stopford A. Brooke, *A Treasury of Irish Poetry in the English Tongue* (London: Smith, Elder & Co.; New York: Macmillan & Co., 1900); *The High Deeds of Finn* (London: Harrap, 1910; New York:

T. Y. Crowell & Co., 1911); *Myths and Legends of the Celtic Race* (London: Harrap; New York: T. Y. Crowell & Co., 1911); *Whitman and Rolleston: A Correspondence*, edited with an introduction by Horst Frenz (Dublin: Browne and Nolan, 1952).

BIOGRAPHY AND CRITICISM. C. H. Rolleston, *Portrait of an Irishman* (London: Methuen, 1939).

Susan Mitchell

LIFE. Susan Mitchell was born in Carrick-on-Shannon, Co. Leitrim in 1866. She was a friend of the Yeats family with whom she stayed in London, when she went there in 1900 for treatment for an illness that had impaired her hearing. In 1901 she became assistant editor to George Russell (AE) on *The Irish Homestead* and, later, *The Irish Statesman*. She was widely known and admired for her wit and charm. Of all the celebrities whom she knew, it was George Moore who most delighted her by his eccentricities and his hunger for publicity. Mitchell's health was frail. She lived a quiet life with her sister in Dublin, where she died in 1926.

CHIEF WRITINGS. *Aids to the Immortality of Certain Persons in Ireland: Charitably Administered* (Dublin: The New Nation, 1908; enlarged edition Dublin: Maunsel, 1913); *The Living Chalice* (Dublin: Maunsel, 1908); *Frankincense and Myrrh* (Dublin: Cuala Press, 1912); *The Living Chalice and Other Poems* (Dublin and London: Maunsel, 1913); *George Moore* (Dublin: Maunsel, 1916); *Secret Springs of Dublin Song* (Dublin: The Talbot Press, 1918); contributed to *The Abbey Row, Not Edited by W. B. Yeats* (Dublin: Maunsel, 1907).

BIOGRAPHY AND CRITICISM. R. M. Kain, *Susan L. Mitchell* (Lewisburg, Pennsylvania: Bucknell University Press, 1972).

George Russell

For biography and bibliography, see p. 560.

Lionel Johnson

LIFE. Johnson was born in Broadstairs, Kent in 1867, the third son of an Irish army officer. His grandfather had been created baronet for services to the crown during the 1798 Rebellion. Johnson had a brilliant academic career at Winchester College and New College, Oxford, where he came under the influence of Walter Pater. In 1890 he began a career in journalism in London; in 1891 he converted to catholicism and became a member of the Rhymer's Club. Under the influence of Yeats, with whom he developed a close friendship, Johnson began to take an interest in his Irish antecedents and visited Dublin in 1893, where he met many of the leading members of the Revival. With Eleanor Hull, he edited the *Irish Home Reading Magazine* in 1894 and was prominent in the Irish Literary Society in London. Heavy drinking eroded his health. He made a final trip to Ireland in 1898, the year of the 1798 centenary. He died in 1902 after a fall, although it seems that a combination of insomnia, heavy drinking and physical frailty was the real cause of his death.

CHIEF WRITINGS. *The Art of Thomas Hardy* (London: Elkin Matthews and John Lane; New York: Dodd Mead, 1894; new and revised edition 1923); *Poems* (London: Elkin Matthews; Boston: Copeland and Day, 1895); *Ireland, and Other Poems* (London: Elkin Matthews, 1897); *Twenty-one Poems by Lionel Johnson, selected by W. B. Yeats* (Dundrum: Dun Emer Press, 1904); *Selections from the Poems of Lionel Johnson, including some now collected for the first time* with a prefatory memoir by C. Shorter (London: Elkin Matthews, 1908); T. Whittemore (ed.), with L. I. Guiney, *Post Liminum. Essays and Critical Papers* (London: Elkin Matthews, 1911); *Poetical Works* (with preface by Ezra Pound) (London: Elkin Matthews, 1915); *The Religious Poems of Lionel Johnson* (with preface by W. Meynell) (London: Elkin Matthews, 1916); Earl Russell (ed.), *Some Winchester Letters* (London: Elkin Matthews, 1919); R. Shafer (ed.), *Reviews and Critical Papers* (London: Elkin Matthews, 1921); I. Fletcher (ed.), *Collected Poems* (New York: Unicorn Press, 1982).

BIOGRAPHY AND CRITICISM. W. B. Yeats in *Autobiographies* (London: Macmillan, 1955); in D. Donoghue (ed.), *Memoirs* (London: Macmillan, 1972); D. Scott in *Men of Letters* (London: Hodder and Stoughton, 1916); A. W. Patrick, *Lionel Johnson, poète et critique (1867-1902)* (Paris: Flammarion, 1939).

John Millington Synge

For biography and bibliography, see p. 717.

Oliver St John Gogarty

LIFE. Gogarty was born in Dublin in 1878. He was educated at Mungret, Stonyhurst, Clongowes Wood College, the Royal University and the medical school of Trinity College, Dublin. He was a close friend of James Joyce, Robert Yelverton Tyrrell, the classical scholar, and John Pentland Mahaffy, provost of Trinity College 1914-19. He won the Vice-Chancellor's Prize for English Verse in 1902, 1903 and 1905. In the autumn of 1904, he and an Oxford friend shared the Martello tower at Sandycove with James Joyce, an episode celebrated in the opening chapter of *Ulysses*, in which the figure of Buck Mulligan is modelled on Gogarty. He established himself as a successful nose and throat surgeon, was known for his wit and his many sporting interests. His three plays, *Blight* (1917), *A Serious Thing* (1919), and *The Enchanted Trousers* (1919), were produced at the Abbey Theatre, under a pseudonym. A member of the Irish Senate (1922-36), he was kidnapped by republicans during the Civil War and escaped by diving into the river Liffey. His country house at Renvyle, Co. Galway was burned down at this time. Disillusioned with Ireland, Gogarty left for the United States in 1939 and stayed there, save for occasional visits home, until his death in New York in 1957.

CHIEF WRITINGS. (Poetry) *The Ship and Other Poems* (Dublin: The Talbot Press, 1918); *An Offering of Swans* (Dublin: Cuala Press, 1923; London: Eyre and Spottiswoode, 1934); *Wild Apples* (Dublin: Cuala Press, 1928, 1930; New York: J. Cape and H. Smith, *c.* 1929); *Elbow Room* (Dublin: Cuala Press, 1929; New York: Duell, Sloan and Pearce, 1940); *Selected Poems* (New York: Macmillan, 1933; published as *Others to Adorn* (London: Rich and Cowan, 1938); *Perennial* (London: Constable, 1946); *The Collected Poems of Oliver St John Gogarty* (London: Constable, 1951; New York: Devin-Adair, 1954); *Unselected Poems* (Baltimore: Contemporary, 1954).

(Plays) J. F. Carens (ed.), *The Plays of Oliver St John Gogarty* (Newark, Delaware: Proscenium Press, 1971).

(Novels) *Going Native* (New York: Duell, Sloan and Pearce, 1940; London, Constable, 1941); *Mad Grandeur* (Philadelphia and New York: J. B. Lippincott, 1941; London: Constable, 1943); *Mr Petunia* (New York: Creative Age, 1945; London: Constable, 1946).

(Autobiography and Reminiscences) *As I Was Going Down Sackville Street* (London: Rich and Cowan; New York: Reynal and Hitchcock, 1937); *I Follow Saint Patrick* (London: Rich and Cowan; New York: Reynal and Hitchcock, 1938; London: Constable, 1950); *Tumbling in the Hay* (London: Constable; New York: Reynal and Hitchcock, 1939); *It Isn't This Time of Year At All!* (London: MacGibbon and Kee; Garden City, New York: Doubleday, 1954).

(Miscellaneous) *Mourning Becomes Mrs Spendlove and Other Portraits Grave and Gay* (New York: Creative Age, 1948); *Rolling Down the Lea* (London: Constable, 1950); *Intimations* (New York: Abelard, 1950); J. F. Carens (ed.), *Many Lines to Thee: Letters of Oliver St John Gogarty to G. K. A. Bell 1904-07* (Dublin: Dolmen Press, 1971).

BIOGRAPHY AND CRITICISM. W. R. Rodgers, *A Portrait of Oliver St John Gogarty* (London: BBC, 1961); U. O'Connor, *The Times I've Seen; Oliver St John Gogarty* (New York: Obolensky, 1963); in Britain as *Oliver St John Gogarty: A Poet and His Times* (London: Cape, 1964); A. N. Jeffares in *The Circus Animals: Essays on W. B. Yeats* (London: Macmillan, 1970); J. B. Lyons, *Oliver St John Gogarty* (Lewisburg, Pennsylvania: Buckness University Press, 1976); J. F. Carens, *Surpassing Wit: Oliver St John Gogarty, His Poetry and His Prose* (Dublin: Gill and Macmillan, 1979); J. B. Lyons, *Oliver St John Gogarty, The Man of Many Talents: A Biography* (Dublin: Blackwater Press, 1980).

Thomas MacDonagh

LIFE. Thomas MacDonagh was born in Cloughjordan, Co. Tipperary in 1878 and educated at Rockwell College, Cashel. In 1901-03 he joined the Gaelic League while teaching at St Kieran's College in Kilkenny. Between 1903 and 1908 he taught in Fermoy, Co. Cork and became a founder member of the Association of Secondary Teachers. In 1908, he came to Dublin and taught at Patrick Pearse's school, St Enda's College, while studying at University College, Dublin, where he became a lecturer in the English Department in 1911. With James Stephens, Padraic Colum and, later, Joseph Plunkett, he edited *The Irish Review*; in 1914 he co-founded the Irish Theatre with Edward Martyn and Plunkett. He became director of training for the Irish Volunteers in 1913, organized the march to Howth in July 1914 to collect guns in the Howth gun-running incident, organized the parade for the funeral of O'Donovan Rossa in 1915, and in the same year joined the Irish Republican Brotherhood. In April 1916, he was made a member of the secret military council which planned the rebellion of 1916, and he acted as intermediary between Pearse and Eóin MacNeill. He fought in the rebellion and was executed thereafter on 3 May 1916.

CHIEF WRITINGS. *Through the Ivory Gate* (Dublin: Sealy, Byrers and Walker, 1902); *April and May, and other Verses* (Dublin: Sealy, Bryers and Walker, 1903); *When the Dawn is Come* (produced at the Abbey Theatre, 1908) (Dublin: Maunsel, 1908; introduced by C. Garrison with commentary by J. Norstedt, Irish Drama Series, IX, Chicago: De Paul University, 1973); *Songs of Myself* (Dublin: Hodges Figgis, 1910); *Lyrical Poems* (Dublin: Irish Review, 1913); *Thomas Campion and the Art of English Poetry* (Dublin: Hodges Figgis, 1913); *Literature in Ireland: Studies Irish and Anglo-Irish* (Dublin: The Talbot Press, 1916); J. Stephens (ed.), *The Poetical Works of Thomas MacDonagh* (Dublin: The Talbot Press; London: Unwin, 1916); *Pagans* (Dublin: The Talbot Press; London: Unwin, 1920); *Poems*, selected by his sister (Dublin: The Talbot Press, 1925).

BIOGRAPHY AND CRITICISM. D. MacDonagh, 'Plunkett and MacDonagh' in F. X. Martin (ed.), *Leaders and Men of the Easter Rising: Dublin 1916* (London: Methuen, 1967); E. W. and A. Parks, *Thomas MacDonagh: The Man, the Patriot, the Writer* (Athens: University of Georgia Press, 1967); J. A. Norstedt, *Thomas MacDonagh; A Critical Biography* (Charlottesville: University of Virginia Press, 1980).

Seumas O'Sullivan

LIFE. Born James Sullivan Starkey in Dublin in 1879, O'Sullivan was educated at University College, Dublin. He appeared as the Blind Man in Yeats's play, *On Baile Strand*, on the opening night at the Abbey Theatre in December 1904. Later he became co-editor of the Tower Press Booklets (1906-08) and founded the New Nation Press (1909) and *The Dublin Magazine*, of which he was editor from 1923 to 1958. In 1932 he was a founder-member, with Yeats and Shaw, of the Irish Academy of Letters. His most important political friendship was with Arthur Griffith, but his life's work was *The Dublin Magazine*, which nurtured a new generation of writers and became one of the most important literary journals of the century in Ireland. In 1957 O'Sullivan won the Lady Gregory Medal. He died in Dublin in 1958.

CHIEF WRITINGS. *The Twilight People* (Dublin: Whaley; London: A. H. Bullen, 1905); *Verses Sacred and Profane* (Dublin: Maunsel, 1908); *The Earth-Lover and Other Verses* (Dublin: New Nation, 1909); *Poems* (Dublin: Maunsel, 1912); *An Epilogue to the Praise of Angus and other Poems* (Dublin: Maunsel, 1914); *Requiem and Other Poems* (Dublin: privately printed, 1917); *Mud and Purple: Pages from the Diary of a Dublin Man* (Dublin: The Talbot Press, 1917); *The Rosses and Other Poems* (Dublin: Maunsel, 1918); *The Poems of Seumas O'Sullivan* (Boston: B. J. Brimmer, 1923); *Common Adventures: A Book of Prose and Verse* (Dublin: Orwell, 1926); *The Lamplighter, and Other Poems* (Dublin: Orwell, 1929); *Twenty-Five Lyrics* (Bognor Regis, Sussex: Pear Tree Press, 1933); *Poems 1930-1938* (Dublin: Orwell, 1938); *Collected Poems* (Dublin: Orwell, 1940); *Essays and Recollections* (Dublin: The Talbot Press, 1944); *The Rose and Bottle* (Dublin: The Talbot Press, 1946); *Dublin Poems* (New York: Creative Age, 1946).

BIOGRAPHY AND CRITICISM. M. J. MacManus, 'Bibliographies of Irish Authors, no. 3: Seumas O'Sullivan', *Dublin Magazine* 5, no. 3 (1930), 47-50; L. Miller (ed.), *Retrospect: The Work of Seumas O'Sullivan and Estella F. Solomons* (Dublin: Dolmen Press, 1973); A. Clarke, *Poetry in Modern Ireland* (Cork: Mercier Press, 1966); *The Celtic Twilight and the Nineties* (Dublin: Dolmen Press, 1969).

Patrick Pearse

For biography and bibliography, see p. 561 and Volume III, p. 932.

Joseph Campbell

LIFE. Campbell was born in Belfast in 1879. He was an early contributor to the Ulster Literary Theatre and to its journal *Uladh*, of which he became editor. He went to Dublin in 1902, where Padraic Colum introduced him to a number of important literary figures. In 1904, in collaboration with Herbert Hughes, he published *Songs of Uladh*, one of the finest collections of folksongs in an era distinguished for such work. In 1906 he went to London and worked as a teacher and as assistant to Eleanor Hull of the Irish Texts Society. Campbell became secretary of the Irish Literary Society, founded by Yeats. He married and returned to Ireland in 1911, taking a cottage in Glencree, Co. Wicklow. The Abbey Theatre produced his play *Judgment* in April 1912. In 1913, he became involved with the Irish Volunteers and helped with rescue work in Easter Week 1916. He opposed the Treaty of 1921 and was interned for two years during the Civil War. On his release, he emigrated in disillusion to the United States. There, from 1925 to 1939, Campbell pursued the dream of establishing a centre for Irish culture in America. He founded the School of Irish Studies in New York in 1925, the Irish Foundation in 1931 and the journal, *The Irish Review*, in 1934. From 1927-38 he lectured on Irish literature at Fordham University in New York city. In 1939, he returned to his Wicklow cottage, where he lived quietly until his death in 1944.

CHIEF WRITINGS. *The Garden of the Bees and Other Poems* (Belfast: W. Erskine Mayne; Dublin: Gill, 1905); *The Rushlight* (Dublin: Maunsel, 1906); *The Gilly of Christ* (Dublin: Maunsel, 1907); *The Mountainy Singer* (Dublin: Maunsel, 1909; Boston: Four Seas Co., 1919); *Mearing Stones* (Dublin: Maunsel, 1911); *Irishry* (Dublin and London: Maunsel, 1913); *Earth of Cualann* (Dublin and London: Maunsel, 1917); A. Clarke (ed. and introd.), *The Poems of Joseph Campbell* (Dublin: Allen Figgis, 1963).

BIOGRAPHY AND CRITICISM. P. S. O'Hegarty, 'A Bibliography of Joseph Campbell — Seosamh Mac Cathmaoil', *Dublin Magazine* New Series, 15, no. 4 (1940), 58-61; N. Saunders and A. A. Kelly, *Joseph Campbell: Poet and Nationalist 1879-1944 — A Critical Biography* (Dublin: Wolfhound Press, 1988).

Padraic Colum

LIFE. Colum was born in Longford in 1881. He worked for five years as a railway clerk in Dublin before being given a five-year scholarship by a wealthy American to enable him to study and write. He wrote plays for the Abbey between 1905 and 1910, founded *The Irish Review* with Thomas MacDonagh and James Stephens, and won popularity as a poet before he and his wife, Mary, emigrated to the United States in 1914. While there he published a number of translations and books for children. After a three-year spell in France 1930-33, the Colums returned to the USA where they both taught part-time at Columbia University, New York. Mary Colum died in 1957. After her death, he divided his time between the USA and Ireland. Padraic Colum died in Enfield, Connecticut in 1972.

CHIEF WRITINGS. (Plays) *The Land* (1905); *The Fiddler's House* (Dublin: Maunsel, 1907); *Thomas Muskerry* (Dublin: Maunsel, 1910); *Three Plays* (containing all three above) (Dublin and London: Maunsel, 1917; revised edition New York: Macmillan, 1925). See *Lost Plays of the Irish Renaissance*.

(Poems) *Wild Earth* (Dublin: Maunsel, 1907); *Wild Earth, and Other Poems* (New York: Holt; Dublin: Maunsel, 1917); *The Collected Poems of Padraic Colum* (New York: Devin-Adair, 1953); *The Poet's Circuits: Collected Poems of Ireland* (London: Oxford University Press, 1960); *Irish Elegies* (Dublin: Dolmen Press, 1958; augmented editions 1961, 1966).

(Novels) *Castle Conquer* (New York: Macmillan, 1923); *The Flying Swans* (New York: Crown, 1957).

(Biographies) *Ourselves Alone* (New York: Crown, 1959; European edition entitled *Arthur Griffith (1872-1922)* (Dublin: Browne and Nolan, 1959); with Mary Colum, *Our Friend James Joyce* (Garden City, New York: Doubleday, 1958).

(Books for Children) *The King of Ireland's Son* (New York: Macmillan, 1916; London: Harrap, 1920); *The Children of Odin* (New York: Macmillan, 1920; London: Harrap, 1922).

BIOGRAPHY AND CRITICISM. R. J. Loftus, *Nationalism in Modern Anglo-Irish Poetry* (Madison, Wisconsin: University of Wisconsin Press, 1964); pp. 176-80; A. Denson, 'Padraic Colum: An Appreciation with a Checklist of His Publications', *The Dublin Magazine* 6 (Spring 1967), 50-67; Z. Bowen, *Padraic Colum* (Carbondale, Illinois: Southern Illinois University Press, 1970); Z. Bowen and G. Henderson (eds), *The Journal of Irish Literature* (A Padraic Colum Number), 2 (January 1973).

James Stephens

For biography and bibliography, see p. 1219.

James Joyce

For biography and bibliography, see Volume III, p. 86.

Francis Ledwidge

LIFE. Ledwidge was born in Slane, Co. Meath in 1887. Self-educated, he was employed in a number of menial jobs before being taken under the patronage of Lord Dunsany, who gave him access to his library and introduced him to a number of literary figures, including Katharine Tynan and Yeats. On the outbreak of the Great War, he enlisted in Dunsany's regiment, the 10th (Irish) Division. A broken love affair, the news of the Easter Week executions of Thomas MacDonagh and Joseph Plunkett, and the horrors of the war itself imbued his later poetry with an intense sadness which distinguished it from the frail sentiments of his earlier work. On 31 July 1917, Ledwidge was killed near Ypres in Belgium.

CHIEF WRITINGS. *Songs of the Fields* (London: Herbert Jenkins, 1916); *Songs of Peace* (London: Herbert Jenkins, 1917); *Last Songs* (London: Herbert Jenkins, 1918); Lord Dunsany (ed.), *The Complete Poems of Francis Ledwidge* (London: Herbert Jenkins, 1919; newly edited with foreword by A. Curtayne (ed.), (London: Martin, Brian & O'Keeffe, 1974)).

BIOGRAPHY AND CRITICISM. A. Curtayne, *Francis Ledwidge: A Life of the Poet (1887-1917)* (London: Martin, Brian & O'Keeffe, 1972); H. Danielson, *Bibliography of Modern Authors* XI (London: Bookman's Journal, 1921).

Frederick Robert Higgins

LIFE. F. R. Higgins was born in Foxford, Co. Mayo in 1896, of protestant-unionist parentage, but grew up in County Meath. He was a pioneer of the labour movement, founded the first women's magazine in Ireland and, by 1927, had established his reputation as a poet. He became a close friend of Austin Clarke, who helped reaffirm his interest in the Gaelic tradition in poetry. In 1935 Higgins became a director of the Abbey Theatre and later the company's business manager. He died in Dublin in 1941.

CHIEF WRITINGS. *Island Blood* (London: J. Lane, 1925); *The Dark Breed* (London: Macmillan, 1927); *Arable Holdings* (Dublin: Cuala Press, 1933): *The Gap of Brightness* (London: Macmillan, 1940).

BIOGRAPHY AND CRITICISM. S. Beckett, 'Recent Irish Poetry', *Bookman* 77 (August 1934), 235-36; M. J. MacManus, 'A Bibliography of F. R. Higgins', *Dublin Magazine* New Series 12 (1937), 61-67; P. Kavanagh, 'The Gallivanting Poet', *Irish Writing* 3 (November 1947), 63-70; R. Farren, *The Course of Irish Verse* (London: Sheed and Ward, 1948), pp. 128-50; R. J. Loftus, *Nationalism in Modern Anglo-Irish Poetry* (Madison, Wisconsin: University of Wisconsin Press, 1964); R. F. Garratt, *Modern Irish Poetry; Tradition and Continuity from Yeats to Heaney* (Berkeley, Los Angeles and London: University of California Press, 1986), pp. 66-70.

SEAMUS HEANEY, *Editor*

William Butler Yeats

(1865-1939)

Within the history of Irish writing in English, the achievement of W. B. Yeats represents a point of both culmination and origin. He has been rightly named a founder, for it was under the aegis of his creative authority that a modern, self-critical and more or less coherent poetic action established itself in Ireland during the last hundred years. But Yeats can also be thought of as an inheritor, because in him the enterprise of several nineteenth-century writers found its purpose redefined and its aspiration fulfilled. These writers included the poets James Clarence Mangan, Thomas Davis and Samuel Ferguson, names invoked by Yeats in his early poem, 'To Ireland in the Coming Times', as 'a company/That sang, to sweeten Ireland's wrong,/ Ballad and story, rann and song'. With these forebears Yeats consciously identified himself, yet the company of his literary ancestors might also include all those writers who shared the common nineteenth-century plight which James Joyce diagnosed in his essay on James Clarence Mangan: Mangan, in Joyce's bare statement of the case, 'wrote with no native literary tradition to guide him.'

This lack was one that W. B. Yeats deliberately sought to redress. Before Yeats, the Irish poet with most canonical presence at home and abroad had been Thomas Moore (1779-1852), cherished as the author of the exquisite and pathetic *Irish Melodies*. These songs maintained a sentiment of national identity during the nineteenth century, but even though they evoked the martial splendours of the Gael, their effect was palliative rather than inflammatory. Moore, however, was treated by Joyce with less indulgence than the disconsolate Mangan. In *A Portrait of the Artist as a Young Man*, as Stephen Dedalus proceeds under the memorial statue of Moore, which still stands in College Green, Joyce has him observe the statue's 'servile head'; and Stephen goes on to conceive of this representation of Ireland's 'national poet' in terms of its 'indignity', 'a Firbolg in the borrowed cloak of a Milesian'. There may have been a personal Joycean mordancy in this presentation, but fifty years after the death of Moore it was inevitable that he should have become an emblem of nineteenth-century Ireland's cultural and political debilitation. Fifty years after the death of Yeats, on the other hand, it would be both stupid and insensitive to think of him or his art or the figure he cuts as being anything less than dignified, heroic and epoch-making. The abstract, uningratiating lines of the Henry Moore memorial sculpture in St Stephen's Green proclaim a very different message from the one picked up by Stephen Dedalus on College Green: Yeats, whether we think of him as a national bard or as a world poet, has been translated into a universal symbolic force, an energy released and a destiny discharged.

If Yeats's greatness as a writer has grown indisputable, the virtue of his example has not. Much opposition has been engendered by his ultimate embrace of the high aesthetic mode as the basis not only of a poetic but of an ethic as well. At its most extreme, this opposition would impugn Yeats's espousal of an essentially feudal vision in the realm of politics and culture, and disqualify him as a writer because of his momentary attraction to Italian fascism in the 1930s: it might regard his idealization of Major Robert Gregory ('Our Sidney and our perfect man') as an admissible foible, but discover in his sympathy for the hard-line political antics of General Eoin O'Duffy and his Blueshirts an evil symptom. At its least accusatory, the opposition would question the good of being influenced by a poetry so unready to engage sympathetically with the circumstances of life in a bourgeois democracy, so resolutely opposed to the scientific spirit and so dangerously susceptible to being interpreted as a licence for actions at once violent, romantic and nationalist.

As a figure who exerted considerable pressure and influence, and identified himself with various anti-populist causes over a long lifetime, Yeats was never without his detractors. Yet, from the beginning, those most intent on debunking the man or demythologizing the poet were conscious of the gratifying fact that his commitments were selfless and disciplined. Thomas Flanagan has noted that neither George Moore (Yeats's senior) nor James Joyce (his junior) ever doubted that the phenomenon known as the Irish Literary Revival represented the execution of high creative purpose, even though they could find fault with Yeats's way of discharging that purpose on a scale ranging from the ridiculous to the reprehensible. Moore, as a fellow middle-class Dubliner, mocked him for getting carried away by fantasies of aristocratic splendour and Renaissance *hauteur*. Joyce, more indigent and less socially advantaged, was oddly enough enraged by what he perceived as the poet's *downward* mobility and castigated him in his pamphlet, *The Day of the Rabblement* (1901), for his association with 'a platform from which even self-respect should have urged him to refrain.'

Joyce was here referring to Yeats's association, from the late 1890s onwards, with the cultural ambitions of the Irish Literary Theatre, soon to become the Abbey Theatre. Yeats was thereby lending his gift to the nationalist political lobby and, in Joyce's view, abdicating from the artist's proper stance as vigilant solitary, neither susceptible nor attentive to 'the emotion of the multitude.' What Joyce could not know, of course, was that a deep convulsive energy was building in the poet as the effort to bind himself to a national purpose — 'Theatre business, management of men' — collided with his antithetical and more powerful drive to assert the claims of individual personality over every conformity. A decade later, in *Responsibilities* (1914) and *The Wild Swans at Coole* (1919), a poetry of singular clarity and detachment would spring from the tension generated in him between his ideal of service to a new, imagined Ireland and his recognition of the demeaned standards actually preferred by the Ireland in which he was living. It all contributed to the emergence of a new poetic voice, intellectually capable, emotionally renovated and rhetorically well-girded.

Moore and Joyce were not, of course, the only objectors to the Yeatsian programme. As the pre-eminent theorist, visionary and exemplar of a literature based on the category of nationality, Yeats has always been exposed to questioning. Different Irish objectors have voiced different resistances. Quite recently, for example, Seamus Deane (in his *Celtic Revivals*, 1985) has insisted that there is a disparity between the social, political and intellectual realities of the eighteenth-century Anglo-Irish world and the mythic version of them that Yeats's poems both derive from and project. And yet Deane would be the first to acknowledge the unique necessity of Yeats's work in the evolution of the consciousness that would criticize it. When he speaks of Ireland in Yeats's conception 'as if it were a vestigial Greece in a sternly Roman world', or when he links Yeats's vision with 'the old Romantic premise that the world can be seen falsely, in a bleak Newtonian light, or, truly, in a pre-Newtonian aura', he does indeed expose the recalcitrance of Yeats's mind. Yet, equally, he displays a relish and a gratitude for the integrity of the recalcitrance itself. His richly suggestive comments flourish in the expanding imaginative universe of Yeats's whole *oeuvre* in poetry, drama and prose.

It was Yeats's ambition that his work should have just such a fortifying effect upon his subsequent readership. The creation of an Irish audience with international standards, the transformation of 'mob' to 'people', was an aim he cherished from the start. He never saw his art functioning solely as an aspect of his own individuation, never limited its scope to the execution of its own formal and technical possibilities. This is not to say that he was not intensely inspired by the purely writerly exactions of composing and revising, line by line, stanza by stanza, or to deny that he partly resolved the complications of his personal life by confronting and quelling them in his poems. That he did so is self-evident and many of his poems require some knowledge of the broad outline of his life in order to yield up their richest significations. Yet this pressure of personal matter was not in itself sufficient to make art; that whole effort also required the energies of the impersonal drive, always necessary for the transformation of autobiographical data into objective image. It is an impersonal command that is obeyed when a poet seeks to make the poem a thing, thrown free of inchoate inwardness. It is an impersonal law that enforces itself when the ear recognizes a rhythm as inevitable. But in the case of Yeats, this impersonal command began very early to insist that the poetry manifest a definite metaphysical disposition and diffuse the atmosphere of certain congenial landscapes.

This may seem a laboured and roundabout way of saying that the young Yeats wanted to attach himself to Irish subject-matter and settings, and to express the lineaments of an occult doctrine which he found corroborated in the supernatural beliefs and superstitions of the country people of the west of Ireland. These statements are, of course, true, yet it is essential to remember that they refer to the ambitions of a poet, not to the operations of a promoter. The young Yeats certainly had a propagandist and political side to him — 'Red Hanrahan's Song about Ireland,' for example, is in the tradition of the *aisling*, a stealthy genre of political poetry in Irish — and he was indeed fired to commit his imagination to Irish themes by meeting the old Fenian, John O'Leary, and by falling in love with the young and beautiful revolutionary, Maud Gonne, who took the title role in Yeats's subversive play, *Cathleen ni Houlihan* (1902). Yet it is easy to be familiar with all these aspects of the case and not recognize that they represented an artistic problem as well as an artistic opportunity.

Poems, after all, are not bulletins or editorials, and it was precisely the editorial nature of work done by his nineteenth-century company who 'sang, to sweeten Ireland's wrong' that Yeats was intent on correcting. He wanted to verify their general sentiment — chthonic, national, Celtic — by compounding it with the workings of his own psyche and the drama of his own spiritual quest. Typically, he attributed the inspiration for *Cathleen ni Houlihan* to a dream, a circumstance he could hold in reserve to outflank (if necessary) the cause that the play happened to serve. True poetry, he would declare, had to be the speech of the whole man. It was not sufficient that it be the artful expression of daylight opinion and conviction; it had to emerge from a deeper consciousness of things and, in the words of his friend Arthur Symons, be the voice of 'the mystery which lies about us, out of which we have come and into which we shall return.'[1]

The cadence and melancholy of these words recall the 'red-rose-bordered hem' of mystical thought in Yeats's early poetry, a kind of thought that he was determined to unite with more expected thoughts of Irish cultural and political regeneration. Yet that national regeneration was also of original and vital importance to him. Even though subsequent efforts to enshrine the dream in a constituted state might outrage him — his famous Senate speech of 1925 when he deplored the imposition of a ban on divorce upon the Irish protestant minority is one instance of this — and even though the violent impact of the War of Independence and the Civil War would help to rob him of trust in any historically ratified order, Yeats's radical devotion to the potential and otherness of a specifically Irish reality should never be underestimated. This reality would be neither prescriptive nor coercive. In his early conjunction of Neo-Platonic tradition with the deposits of Irish folklore, and in the mature symbolism of his dwelling in a Norman tower conjoined with a thatched cabin, Yeats intended to open and complicate the meaning of Irishness. In fact, his imagined Ireland represented not only a regenerative breakaway from the imperium of Britain but also from the hegemony of orthodox Christianity:

Nor may I less be counted one
With Davis, Mangan, Ferguson,
Because, to him who ponders well,
My rhymes more than their rhyming tell
Of things discovered in the deep,
Where only body's laid asleep.
For the elemental creatures go
About my table to and fro,
That hurry from unmeasured mind
To rant and rage in flood and wind;
Yet he who treads in measured ways
May surely barter gaze for gaze.
('To Ireland in the Coming Times')

This poetry admittedly strikes a more cajoling note than Stephen Dedalus's celebrated line about forging in the smithy of his soul the uncreated conscience of his race; but still, by affirming his

1. In *The Symbolist Movement in Literature* (1899).

poetic entitlement — he treads in 'measured ways' — and by claiming the prerogative to 'barter gaze for gaze' with a pristine source of authority, Yeats here inaugurates his own campaign for 'the spiritual liberation of [his] country.' Hence the search for a style that would have universal command, and the ambition to establish a poetic note that would sound every bit as given, self-born and unquestionable as the myths and symbols of traditional systems of belief.

His success in the pursuit of these aims becomes clear when we open the *Collected Poems* and sense how resourcefully, vigorously and coherently each poem dwells within its own imaginative ether-shield, at a certain intact distance from the reader. The reader, indeed, is constantly made to share the eerie viewpoint that Yeats created for himself in 'The Collar-Bone of a Hare'. There he imagines finding a hare's collar-bone in a region far beyond the world of everyday occurrence, and employing it as a kind of bushman's lorgnette through which that world can be distanced and made strange:

I would find by the edge of that water
The collar-bone of a hare
Worn thin by the lapping of water,
And pierce it through with a gimlet, and stare
At the old bitter world where they marry in
churches,
And laugh over the untroubled water
At all who marry in churches,
Through the white thin bone of a hare.

This is the typical angle of the late nineteenth-century artist and reminds one in particular of Matthew Arnold's plaintively forsaken merman. It also links with the enterprise of the French Symbolists, with whom Yeats felt an immediate sympathy when Arthur Symons introduced him to them in the 1890s. But it possesses an open-air freedom, a folk-song wholesomeness, which distinguishes it from the literature of metropolitan coteries. It is the culmination of Yeats's early manner, evidence of how successfully he fulfilled his ambition to combine the inner weather of sensibility with the inheritance of an Irish landscape and mythology.

Reading Yeats, we are under the sway of a voice that offers both the expansiveness of self-absorbed reverie and the containment of wholly self-conscious utterance, and this is as true of the early work as it is of a magnificent late set-piece such as 'A Dialogue of Self and Soul'. Even a poem as apparently candid and technically uncalculating as 'To Ireland in the Coming Times' harks back to the measure of Milton's 'Il Penseroso', and displays an incipient ability — as Yeatsian as it was Miltonic — to string the sentence out with reinforced syntactical effect over a sequence of rhymes and line-endings. In fact, its very stylistic perfection functions as a distancing device. The poem is a written melody as much as it is the formulation of aims and hopes; its formality operates as transparently between itself and its subjects as the eye-piece made of hare-bone operated between the enchanted poet and the quotidian world.

Yeats's singularity as a writer depended upon this uniquely elaborated command of the strategies of English verse; but it derived also from the off-centre viewpoint he deliberately maintained as a member of occult societies, a student of mystical thought and a practitioner of magic. Even an intelligence as strong and antagonistic as James Joyce's functioned within a set of cultural and intellectual forms that generally were shared and assented to. Homer and classical learning, Roman catholic liturgy and dogma, the medieval corpus of knowledge as represented by Dante and Aquinas: when Joyce began to write, such a keyboard of reference looked as solidly established as the contours of nature. The weapons in his lifelong campaign of detachment and affirmation were at least agreed weapons; calling his protagonist Dedalus, for example, meant that he harnessed a whole system to his own ends. But when Yeats called a character Red Hanrahan or Michael Robartes, no matter how deliberately he might furnish a background in his fiction or in notes to the poems, he still could not endow the new-minted name with such immediate canonical authority. There might well be a reservoir of doctrine and belief which sanctioned the imaginative archetype behind the character, but it had sunk underground. So while Joyce could disdain 'the monkish philosophy' that was his birthright and apparatus, it was, *qua* apparatus, far more immediately efficient than the 'fardel of stories, and of personages, and of emotions' that Yeats had gathered from sources variously poetic, folkloric and esoteric.

We must therefore take special cognizance of the fact that the Dublin of the young Yeats included the Hermetic Society, where he met the Brahmin Mohini Chatterjee, as well as the Contemporary

Club, where he met the founder of the Gaelic League, Douglas Hyde; and that his London included the Order of the Golden Dawn and the magician MacGregor Mathers, as well as soirées with Oscar Wilde and others at the home of W. E. Henley. As a consequence, his everyday routine included practices and meditations based upon 'secret disciplines', just as the everyday routine of his pious Victorian contemporaries might include the rites and prayers of Christianity. One has to conceive of an intelligence naturally solitary, readily combative and happily beset, mounting in confidence and strategy as the wayward, 'unchristened' pursuit of nourishment through symbol and arcane dogma yielded more and more riches. In fact, one has to remember to grant to the occult at least as much formative and directive influence in Yeats's project as one might unthinkingly grant to catholicism in Joyce's. Once this recognition is made, the courage of Yeats's creative undertaking and the far-fetched elaboration of his *oeuvre* stand forth in all their self-born splendour. His endeavour was not only to create an Irish literature cognate with other movements of withdrawal from the imperial, empirical sway of Britain; it was also an attempt to launch upon the world a vision of reality that possessed no surer basis than the ground of his own imagining.

Admittedly, that imagining was conducted in terms that had been 'passed on from generation to generation by poets and painters with some help from philosophers and theologians.' The reality of a world of spirit, the immortality of the soul and its fated reincarnations, the cyclical relations pertaining between the land of the living and the land of the dead, the perviousness of these realms to each other's influence, the possibility of gaining knowledge of the destined shape of things through the study of arcane books and symbols — Yeats's mind was hospitable to these ideas. Ultimately his belief in them may have been provisional, but that did not weaken his devotion to conscripting and extending their heuristic virtue within his writing. Images that we associate with particular phases of his poetry derive from older contexts. The rose, for example, which figures so much in his early work, is one of the emblems of Rosicrucianism (rose and cross) and also recalls Dante's mystical rose of paradisal transfiguration; and the moon, so important in the scheme of his mature symbology in *A Vision* (1925), has been immemorially associated with shifting and change, both physical and psychic.

Still, while one must insist upon the centrality of unorthodox spiritual disciplines in Yeats's life, one must beware of thinking of him as a gullible consumer of superstitions. He possessed a robust, sceptical intelligence and his grasp of what was happening in his own times was at least equal to that of the most secular and topically focussed minds of his generation. His career as a poet spanned fifty years, from *The Wanderings of Oisin* in 1889 to *Last Poems*, posthumously published in 1939, the year of his death. Born in 1865, he lived a life that coincided with an era of convulsive change; Britain and Europe moved out of the pomp and confidence of the high imperial epoch into the devastation of World War I and its aftermath, on through the effects of the Russian Revolution, the rise of fascism in Italy, the Nazi takeover in Germany, the Spanish Civil War and, finally, the months of haunted apprehension before the outbreak of World War II. In Ireland also he witnessed drastic changes. The Easter Rising in 1916 and the ensuing violence that issued first in the creation of the Irish Free State and then in the Irish Civil War meant that the country suffered a national upheaval corresponding to the international upheavals beyond. And to all of these crises Yeats responded within his own idiom, at his own pace. He did record direct responses to some events in Ireland, most notably in his poem 'Easter 1916', but generally the poems did not arise from the immediate stimulus of happenings or from a desire to set down the story. They arose, rather, from the resonance that the happenings produced within his consciousness and from the meditated meaning they engendered there.

Obviously, then, although the historical shocks that ran through the world did affect Yeats, his imagination did not function like an obedient seismograph. Indeed the whole force of his thought worked against those philosophies which regarded the mind's activity as something determined by circumstance and which consequently limited its possibilities to empirical discovery. His initial attraction to Blake, and to the Blakean imperative to create a system or be enslaved by another man's, was followed by his espousal of a Nietzschean, Dionysian will to overbear the golden mean and the agreed consensus. He loved Bishop Berkeley's idealist confidence that all things were 'a dream' and was bold to aver:

That this pragmatical, preposterous pig of a
world, its farrow that so solid seem,
Must vanish on the instant if the mind but
change its theme.

This is as extreme as it is exultant, and it is no wonder that such an imagination was capable of burning itself out as well as burning up that which was fed to it. Yeats's capacity to renew the flame of his inspiration at different periods of his life appears therefore as a triumphant fulfilment of his own prophetic belief in the mind's indomitable resource. Constantly he affirmed the necessity of self-renewal, compulsively he pushed the limits of his own artistic and existential possibilities. Style, he declared, was the equivalent of self-conquest in a writer; he conceded 'The fascination of what's difficult' to be the basis of achievement; and he professed early his belief that 'we must labour to be beautiful'.

Conquest, difficulty, labour: these terms indicate the strenuousness of Yeats's creative endeavour. From the start, he was enamoured of Blake's conviction that energy is eternal delight, yet the development of his own thought brought him more and more to the conclusion that conflict was the inescapable condition of being human. So, as his art matured and the articulation of his beliefs became more clarified and forceful, Yeats's poems typically conveyed a sensation of certitude achieved and contradictions quelled. Poems in which the defiant self is pitted against hostile or disabling conditions — 'An Irish Airman Foresees his Death', 'September 1913', 'Meditations in Time of Civil War' — are complemented by poems that read like discharges of pure, self-possessed energy, poems from which the accidental circumstances have been excluded so that all that remains is the melody and stamina of resurgent spirit — 'The Cold Heaven', 'Byzantium', 'Long-legged Fly'.

The greatest consolidation of his powers happened during his fifties, when several occasions conspired to inaugurate a period of abundant creativity. Like Thomas Hardy's 'darkling thrush', which surprised itself and its creator with a song of 'joy illimited', Yeats too made the unpredictable choice 'to fling his soul/Upon the growing gloom'. In poems that were both a reprise and a resonantly amplified promulgation of all that he had already thought and imagined, he performed new feats of vision and rhetoric. This onset of authority derived from a natural command that came with age and eminence, but it was given further impetus by two related developments in his life: his marriage in 1917 to George Hyde-Lees, and his purchase of a Norman tower at Ballylee, which he had restored as a home for himself and his new bride. Yet it was less as a family man setting up house than as an acclaimed poet entering ritually into his imagined kingdom that Yeats took possession of Thoor Ballylee. The three volumes deriving from occupation of that site are the indispensable harvest of his mature years. The speculations of *A Vision* (1925) and the poetry of *The Tower* (1928) and *The Winding Stair and Other Poems* (1933) have a planetary range and ardour, and incorporate haphazard yet powerfully registered incidents of personal and public life within the orbit of a single, curbing intelligence.

This unifying drive had always been central to Yeats's mind, but its operations reached a climax with the composition of *A Vision*. Although this bold formulation of his system of thought was born out of the automatic writings that George began to produce a few days after their marriage, its dominant motifs had been present to Yeats in different manifestations all through his career. It was as much an arrangement of images into a paradigm of reality as it was a sustained philosophic discourse, and old preoccupations — such as the idea of apocalyptic reversals in history, the doctrine of reincarnation, and the discipline of the mask — began to be reimagined in terms of new conceptions, such as the phases of the moon and the diagram of the gyres. Just as the living individual poet had entered into the traditionally symbolic tower, so he also endeavoured to unite his work of original ratiocination with an ancient body of images and beliefs. Yeats now lived not as a 'bundle of accident and incoherence' but as 'something intended, complete'. He merged his biographical self into the representative figure of the poet/seer, and he spoke as one both empowered and responsible beyond the limits of a private self. Thus, sequences like 'Meditations in Time of Civil War' and 'Nineteen Hundred and Nineteen' have about them the high pitch of sacred rite, and poems like 'Among School Children' and 'A Dialogue of Self and Soul' go beyond the lyric's usual function of giving perfected form to a privileged state of mind and achieve an effulgent, oracular impersonality. More and more, Yeats's poetic voice evacuated all traces of the domestic creature, the flesh and blood sexagenarian, and became instead the mouthpiece of greatly representative imagination:

> Labour is blossoming or dancing where
> The body is not bruised to pleasure soul,
> Nor beauty born out of its own despair,
> Nor blear-eyed wisdom out of midnight oil.
> O chestnut-tree, great-rooted blossomer,
> Are you the leaf, the blossom or the bole?
> O body swayed to music, O brightening glance,
> How can we know the dancer from the dance?

The result of such exorbitant identification of himself with imagined possibilities above and beyond people's actual behaviour was an overweening intensity of utterance which occasionally strained into theatricality. Although it is true that Yeats managed to break the lyric barrier in awesome poems like 'The Statues', where his extravagant leaps of association brought him to a realm of extreme intuition and rhetorical daring, it is also true that a certain coarsening of tone occurred in some of his poetry during the 1930s. What he may have intended as nonchalance can now strike a reader as callousness. His own self-absolution — 'Why should not old men be mad?' — does not necessarily extenuate the rant and licence, and the unease generated by his political leanings at this period is complemented by one's resistance to a strain of violence that disfigures some of the verse.

Nevertheless, the last poems do set a crown upon the lifetime's effort. 'Long-legged Fly' triumphantly celebrates the stamina and quarantine of the heroic artist, yet the very absolutism and exclusiveness of that heroic stance is interrogated in 'The Man and the Echo' and 'Cuchulain Comforted'. In the end, the man's fortitude is at worst cancelled, at best condoned by the echo's empty rebound, and the rattle of Cuchulain's arms is subsumed into the life-in-death music of the bird-shades. These poems correct the histrionic streak Yeats was indulging when he planned to conclude his *Last Poems* — and therefore *Collected Poems* as well — with 'Politics'. 'Politics' shows him playing the old Nineties bohemian in order to affront the earnest Marxist spirit of the Thirties. The poem subtly craves our indulgence by pretending to mock it. Its urge is to flaunt instinctive drives — 'But O that I were young again/And held her in my arms!' — above the demands of the examined life, but such abdication from the world of pain and injustice has been tenderly rebuked by the concluding lines of 'The Man and the Echo':

> But hush, for I have lost the theme,
> Its joy or night seem but a dream;
> Up there some hawk or owl has struck,
> Dropping out of sky or rock,
> A stricken rabbit is crying out,
> And its cry distracts my thought.

'Politics', for all its commendable jauntiness, does not possess the force of lines like these. Here the paradoxical privileges of art are exemplified in a poem that is responsive to the cry of suffering but unable to prevent or to assist; a poem that gives pleasure by enlightening, even as it reveals its helplessness to alleviate. As I have written elsewhere:

> It is the triumph of this art to confront a despair at the very notion of art *as* triumph. Yet it also manages to wrest from the confrontation with such despair a margin of trust that makes the renewal of artistic effort contemplatable .... the Yeatsian drama ends with the poet as Macbeth, still pacing the battlements, just acknowledging the tremor on the fringes of Birnam but refusing to allow his chivalric countenance to quail. The tower as emblem of adversity, as the place of writing, has taken on a final aspect as icon of the absurd.[2]

It is because of this unconsoled modernity of his achievement that Yeats abides many of our questions and, while it is right that the questions continue to be pressed, it is imperative to recognize the immense contribution his work makes to our general intellectual and imaginative resource. Nobody doubts his fundamental importance as the creator of a cultural idea in and for Ireland, but that is only the beginning of his greatness. His extreme exploration of the possibilities of reconciling the human impulse to transcendence and subversion with the antithetical project of continuity and consolidation is universally and inexhaustibly relevant. Naturally, some political aspects of his work have been particularly assailed — and justly defended, as when Elizabeth Cullingford concludes her study of

2. In *The Place of Writing* (Atlanta, Georgia: Scholars Press, 1989), pp. 33-34, 35.

Yeats as a political poet with the proposition that his fascist sympathies are best regarded as part of his 'fantasies' rather than as part of his 'convictions'; but perhaps the general implications of his tough-minded insight that all reality comes to us as the reward of labour have been insufficiently pondered. There is surely political meaning, at once realistic and visionary, in his sense of life as an abounding conflict of energies; in his recognition of the necessity as well as the impossibility of the attempt 'to hold in a single thought reality and justice'; and in his conviction — overriding his sense of hierarchy and election — that even among the Paudeens of this earth, 'There cannot be . . . A single soul that lacks a sweet crystalline cry.'

When all the objections have been lodged, Yeats's work survives as a purely motivated, greatly active power for good. What Andrew Marvell presented as a challenging fantasy — 'roll all our strength, and all/Our sweetness, up into one ball' — Yeats actually achieved. To apply oneself to the densely trustworthy fabric of an *oeuvre* that embodies the power of 'thoughts long knitted into a single thought' is to experience once again the force of what he called 'the spiritual intellect's great work'. This force transmits itself, of course, by poetic means: Yeats's essential gift is his ability to raise a temple in the ear, to make a vaulted space in language through the firmness, in-placeness and undislodgeableness of stanzaic form. But the force is also present in his persistent drive to 'teach the free man how to praise'. His nationalism, for example, was essentially another avenue towards an ideal if unattainable 'Unity of Being'. In fact, nationality possessed for Yeats something of the same resource that the unconscious possessed for Jung, and seemed to promise access to the 'abounding glittering jet' of life lived spontaneously and certainly within its own free terms.

Furthermore, Yeats's incitements to generous self-transcendence, his fostering of all that is unconstrained and enjoys full scope, contribute greatly to the value of his work. Its range is ample, from the autumnal chastities of 'The Wild Swans at Coole' through the jubiliation of 'Coole Park and Ballylee, 1931' to the limb-sweetening fullness of the last stanza of 'Among School Children'. We certainly do not encounter in such work any image of life's surfaces in our world of consumer capitalism and clamant Marxism; but it marvellously promotes the savour of states of being where our social intelligence is animated, our emotional nature is replenished and our best-dreamt possibilities are corroborated.

NOTE

In annotating the following poems, I have made extensive use of A. N. Jeffares's indispensable *A New Commentary on The Collected Poems of W. B. Yeats.* (London: Macmillan, 1984). The texts used are those in the second edition of *The Collected Poems of W. B. Yeats* (London: Macmillan, 1950). The order of the work printed here from *New Poems* (1938) and *Last Poems* (1939) is that established by Richard J. Finneran in *W. B. Yeats: The Poems. A New Edition* (New York and London: Macmillan, 1983).

from: CROSSWAYS (1889)

[Before Yeats committed himself to Irish themes and settings, his sense of the supernatural world exercised itself through Indian scenes and subjects. The Brahmin Mohini Chatterjee, who visited Dublin and spoke to the Hermetic Society in 1885, would have reinforced Yeats's interest in Buddhist thought and imagery.]

The Indian upon God

I passed along the water's edge below the humid trees,
My spirit rocked in evening light, the rushes round my knees,
My spirit rocked in sleep and sighs; and saw the moorfowl pace
All dripping on a grassy slope, and saw them cease to chase
Each other round in circles, and heard the eldest speak:
Who holds the world between His bill and made us strong or weak
Is an undying moorfowl, and He lives beyond the sky.
The rains are from His dripping wing, the moonbeams from His eye.
I passed a little further on and heard a lotus talk:
Who made the world and ruleth it, He hangeth on a stalk,
For I am in His image made, and all this tinkling tide
Is but a sliding drop of rain between His petals wide.

A little way within the gloom a roebuck raised his eyes
Brimful of starlight, and he said: *The Stamper of the Skies,*
He is a gentle roebuck; for how else, I pray, could He
Conceive a thing so sad and soft, a gentle thing like me?
I passed a little further on and heard a peacock say:
Who made the grass and made the worms and made my feathers gay,
He is a monstrous peacock, and He waveth all the night
His languid tail above us, lit with myriad spots of light.

[In the next two poems, Yeats is deliberately combining the note of Irish folk-song with that of English lyric poetry.]

Down by the Salley[1] Gardens

Down by the salley gardens my love and I did meet;
She passed the salley gardens with little snow-white feet.
She bid me take love easy, as the leaves grow on the tree;
But I, being young and foolish, with her would not agree.

In a field by the river my love and I did stand,
And on my leaning shoulder she laid her snow-white hand.
She bid me take life easy, as the grass grows on the weirs;
But I was young and foolish, and now am full of tears.

1. willow.

The Meditation of the Old Fisherman

You waves, though you dance by my feet like children at play,
Though you glow and you glance, though you purr and you dart;
In the Junes that were warmer than these are, the waves were more gay,
When I was a boy with never a crack in my heart.

The herring are not in the tides as they were of old;
My sorrow! for many a creak gave the creel in the cart
That carried the take to Sligo town to be sold,
When I was a boy with never a crack in my heart.

And ah, you proud maiden, you are not so fair when his oar
Is heard on the water, as they were, the proud and apart,
Who paced in the eve by the nets on the pebbly shore,
When I was a boy with never a crack in my heart.

from: THE ROSE (1893)

[Yeats wrote several narrative poems based on Irish sagas and story cycles, following the lead of Sir Samuel Ferguson (1810-86), who had done poetic versions of the old legends. Cuchulain, champion of Ulster, is the central figure in the story cycle telling of the Red Branch, a warrior band who followed King Conchubar (Conor). He is also the hero of the Old Irish epic, *Táin Bó Cúailnge* (*The Cattle Raid of Cooley*). In Yeats's imagination, Cuchulain develops from being a powerful example of the imaginative riches of Celtic tradition into a personal symbolic resource. He becomes a figure through whom the mature Yeats explores the penalties of action and consciousness in his *Four Plays for Dancers* (1921), and through whom, in late poems like 'The Statues' and 'Cuchulain Comforted', Yeats finally opens a passage between the historical and the visionary. The following poem is based upon matter in Jeremiah Curtin's *Myths and Folklore of Ireland* (1890).]

Cuchulain's Fight with the Sea

A man came slowly from the setting sun,
To Emer,[1] raddling raiment in her dun,[2]
And said, 'I am that swineherd whom you bid
Go watch the road between the wood and tide,
But now I have no need to watch it more.'

Then Emer cast the web upon the floor,
And raising arms all raddled with the dye,
Parted her lips with a loud sudden cry.

That swineherd stared upon her face and said,
'No man alive, no man among the dead,
Has won the gold his cars of battle bring.'

'But if your master comes home triumphing
Why must you blench and shake from foot to crown?'

1. Emer, Cuchulain's wife, seems here to be confused with Aoife by whom he had a son, Conlaech.
2. i.e. dyeing cloth with red ochre in her fortress (dun).

Thereon he shook the more and cast him down
Upon the web-heaped floor, and cried his word:
'With him is one sweet-throated like a bird.'[3]

'You dare me to my face,' and thereupon
She smote with raddled fist, and where her son
Herded the cattle came with stumbling feet,
And cried with angry voice, 'It is not meet
To idle life away, a common herd.'

'I have long waited, mother, for that word:
But wherefore now?'
'There is a man to die;
You have the heaviest arm under the sky.'

'Whether under its daylight or its stars
My father stands amid his battle-cars.'

'But you have grown to be the taller man.'

'Yet somewhere under starlight or the sun
My father stands.'
'Aged, worn out with wars
On foot, on horseback or in battle-cars.'

'I only ask what way my journey lies,
For He who made you bitter made you wise.'

'The Red Branch camp in a great company
Between wood's rim and the horses of the sea.
Go there, and light a camp-fire at wood's rim;
But tell your name and lineage to him
Whose blade compels, and wait till they have found
Some feasting man that the same oath has bound.'

Among those feasting men Cuchulain dwelt,
And his young sweetheart close beside him knelt,
Stared on the mournful wonder of his eyes,
Even as Spring upon the ancient skies,
And pondered on the glory of his days;
And all around the harp-string told his praise,
And Conchubar, the Red Branch king of kings,
With his own fingers touched the brazen strings.

At last Cuchulain spake, 'Some man has made
His evening fire amid the leafy shade.
I have often heard him singing to and fro,
I have often heard the sweet sound of his bow.
Seek out what man he is.'
One went and came.
'He bade me let all know he gives his name
At the sword-point, and waits till we have found
Some feasting man that the same oath has bound.'

Cuchulain cried, 'I am the only man
Of all this host so bound from childhood on.'

After short fighting in the leafy shade,
He spake to the young man, 'Is there no maid
Who loves you, no white arms to wrap you round,
Or do you long for the dim sleepy ground,
That you have come and dared me to my face?'

'The dooms of men are in God's hidden place.'

'Your head a while seemed like a woman's head
That I loved once.'
Again the fighting sped,
But now the war-rage in Cuchulain woke,
And through that new blade's guard the old blade broke,
And pierced him.
'Speak before your breath is done.'

'Cuchulain I, mighty Cuchulain's son.'

'I put you from your pain. I can no more.'

While day its burden on to evening bore,
With head bowed on his knees Cuchulain stayed;
Then Conchubar sent that sweet-throated maid,
And she, to win him, his grey hair caressed;
In vain her arms, in vain her soft white breast.
Then Conchubar, the subtlest of all men,
Ranking his Druids round him ten by ten,
Spake thus: 'Cuchulain will dwell there and brood
For three days more in dreadful quietude,
And then arise, and raving slay us all.
Chaunt in his ear delusions magical,
That he may fight the horses of the sea.'
The Druids took them to their mystery,
And chaunted for three days.
Cuchulain stirred,
Stared on the horses of the sea, and heard
The cars of battle and his own name cried;
And fought with the invulnerable tide.

3. Eithne Inguba, Cuchulain's mistress.

[When Yeats spoke of his early practice of combining a personal emotion with a general pattern of myth and symbol, he was describing poems like 'The Rose of the World'. The personal element here involves his famous love for Maud Gonne (1866-1953), while the rose, representing simultaneously spiritual beauty, mystical wisdom and — in a more hovering way — Ireland, provides the 'myth and symbol'.]

The Rose of the World

Who dreamed that beauty passes like a dream?
For these red lips, with all their mournful pride,
Mournful that no new wonder may betide,
Troy passed away in one high funeral gleam,
And Usna's children died.[1]

We and the labouring world are passing by:
Amid men's souls, that waver and give place
Like the pale waters in their wintry race,
Under the passing stars, foam of the sky,
Lives on this lonely face.

Bow down, archangels, in your dim abode:
Before you were, or any hearts to beat,
Weary and kind one lingered by His seat;
He made the world to be a grassy road
Before her wandering feet.

1. Naoise and his brothers, who perished at the hands of King Conchubar. Naoise had stolen away with Deirdre, whom the king had secluded as his betrothed.

The Lake Isle of Innisfree

I will arise and go now, and go to Innisfree,
And a small cabin build there, of clay and wattles made:
Nine bean-rows will I have there, a hive for the honey-bee,
And live alone in the bee-loud glade.

And I shall have some peace there, for peace comes dropping slow,
Dropping from the veils of the morning to where the cricket sings;
There midnight's all a glimmer, and noon a purple glow,[1]
And evening full of the linnet's wings.

I will arise and go now, for always night and day
I hear lake water lapping with low sounds by the shore;
While I stand on the roadway, or on the pavements grey,
I hear it in the deep heart's core.

1. Innisfree means 'Heather Island'.

Who Goes with Fergus?[1]

Who will go drive with Fergus now,
And pierce the deep wood's woven shade,
And dance upon the level shore?
Young man, lift up your russet brow,
And lift your tender eyelids, maid,
And brood on hopes and fear no more.

And no more turn aside and brood
Upon love's bitter mystery;
For Fergus rules the brazen cars,
And rules the shadows of the wood,
And the white breast of the dim sea
And all dishevelled wandering stars.

1. Fergus MacRoy, another figure from the Red Branch, was a king of Ulster who, according to a tale in the Book of Leinster, was tricked out of his crown. Yeats imagines him opting freely for the poetic life of the wild woods.

The Lamentation of the Old Pensioner

Although I shelter from the rain
Under a broken tree,
My chair was nearest to the fire
In every company
That talked of love or politics,
Ere Time transfigured me.

Though lads are making pikes[1] again
For some conspiracy,
And crazy rascals rage their fill
At human tyranny,
My contemplations are of Time
That has transfigured me.

There's not a woman turns her face
Upon a broken tree,

1. In Ireland, pikestaffs were associated particularly with rebellion because of their widespread use in the rising of 1798.

And yet the beauties that I loved
Are in my memory;
I spit into the face of Time
That has transfigured me.

[The following poem is discussed in the introduction (p. 785). It is both the manifesto for a committed national literature and the affirmation of a personal mystical faith.]

To Ireland in the Coming Times

Know, that I would accounted be
True brother of a company
That sang, to sweeten Ireland's wrong,
Ballad and story, rann[1] *and song;*
Nor be I any less of them,
Because the red-rose-bordered hem
Of her, whose history began
Before God made the angelic clan,
Trails all about the written page.
When Time began to rant and rage
The measure of her flying feet
Made Ireland's heart begin to beat;
And Time bade all his candles flare
To light a measure here and there;
And may the thoughts of Ireland brood
Upon a measured quietude.

Nor may I less be counted one
With Davis, Mangan, Ferguson,[2]
Because, to him who ponders well,
My rhymes more than their rhyming tell
Of things discovered in the deep,
Where only body's laid asleep.
For the elemental creatures go
About my table to and fro,
That hurry from unmeasured mind
To rant and rage in flood and wind;
Yet he who treads in measured ways
May surely barter gaze for gaze.
Man ever journeys on with them
After the red-rose-bordered hem.
Ah, faeries, dancing under the moon,
A Druid land, a Druid tune!

While still I may, I write for you
The love I lived, the dream I knew.
From our birthday, until we die,
Is but the winking of an eye;
And we, our singing and our love,
What measurer Time has lit above,
And all benighted things that go
About my table to and fro,
Are passing on to where may be,
In truth's consuming ecstasy,
No place for love and dream at all;
For God goes by with white footfall.
I cast my heart into my rhymes,
That you, in the dim coming times,
May know how my heart went with them
After the red-rose-bordered hem.

1. Yeats's use of this Irish word for a stanza unites him with the movement in the early 1890s for the restoration of the Irish language. The Gaelic League was founded in 1893, the year that also saw the publication of *The Rose*.
2. Yeats here allies himself with the cultural nationalism represented by Thomas Davis (1814-45), James Clarence Mangan (1803-49) and Sir Samuel Ferguson (1810-86).

from: THE WIND AMONG THE REEDS (1899)

[Yeats's own note to 'The Host of the Air' reads: 'This poem is founded on an old Gaelic ballad that was sung and translated for me by a woman at Ballisodare in County Sligo; but in the ballad the husband found the keeners keening his wife when he got to his house.']

The Host of the Air

O'Driscoll drove with a song
The wild duck and the drake
From the tall and the tufted reeds
Of the drear Hart Lake.

And he saw how the reeds grew dark
At the coming of night-tide,
And dreamed of the long dim hair
Of Bridget his bride.

He heard while he sang and dreamed
A piper piping away,
And never was piping so sad,
And never was piping so gay.

And he saw young men and young girls
Who danced on a level place,
And Bridget his bride among them,
With a sad and a gay face.

The dancers crowded about him
And many a sweet thing said,
And a young man brought him red wine
And a young girl white bread.

But Bridget drew him by the sleeve
Away from the merry bands,
To old men playing at cards
With a twinkling of ancient hands.

The bread and the wine had a doom,
For these were the host of the air;
He sat and played in a dream
Of her long dim hair.

He played with the merry old men
And thought not of evil chance,
Until one bore Bridget his bride
Away from the merry dance.

He bore her away in his arms,
The handsomest young man there,
And his neck and his breast and his arms
Were drowned in her long dim hair.

O'Driscoll scattered the cards
And out of his dream awoke:
Old men and young men and young girls
Were gone like a drifting smoke;

But he heard high up in the air
A piper piping away,
And never was piping so sad,
And never was piping so gay.

[Aengus was considered by Yeats to be a Celtic god of youth, beauty and poetry. The poem below was entitled, on first publication, 'A Mad Song', and Yeats's notes to it in *The Wind Among the Reeds* cite parallel stories about men entranced by such apparitions.]

The Song of Wandering Aengus

I went out to the hazel wood,
Because a fire was in my head,
And cut and peeled a hazel wand,
And hooked a berry to a thread;
And when white moths were on the wing,
And moth-like stars were flickering out,
I dropped the berry in a stream
And caught a little silver trout.

When I had laid it on the floor
I went to blow the fire aflame,
But something rustled on the floor,
And some one called me by my name:
It had become a glimmering girl
With apple blossom in her hair[1]
Who called me by my name and ran
And faded through the brightening air.

Though I am old with wandering
Through hollow lands and hilly lands,
I will find out where she has gone,
And kiss her lips and take her hands;
And walk among long dappled grass,
And pluck till time and times are done
The silver apples of the moon,
The golden apples of the sun.

1. Yeats wrote about Maud Gonne in *Autobiographies*: 'Her complexion was luminous, like that of apple blossom through which the light falls, and I remember her standing that first day by a great heap of such blossoms in the window' (p. 123).

['The Heart of the Woman' is an early instance of a motif that persists and deepens all through Yeats's work: the encounter, both terrible and fascinated, between mortal and immortal. See also 'Leda and the Swan', 'Byzantium', 'Ribh at the Tomb of Baile and Aillinn'.]

The Heart of the Woman

O what to me the little room
That was brimmed up with prayer and rest;
He bade me out into the gloom,
And my breast lies upon his breast.

O what to me my mother's care,
The house where I was safe and warm;
The shadowy blossom of my hair
Will hide us from the bitter storm.

O hiding hair and dewy eyes,
I am no more with life and death,
My heart upon his warm heart lies,
My breath is mixed into his breath.

He hears the Cry of the Sedge

I wander by the edge
Of this desolate lake
Where wind cries in the sedge:
Until the axle break

That keeps the stars in their round,
And hands hurl in the deep
The banners of East and West,
And the girdle of light is unbound,
Your breast will not lie by the breast
Of your beloved in sleep.

He wishes for the Cloths of Heaven

Had I the heavens' embroidered cloths,
Enwrought with golden and silver light,
The blue and the dim and the dark cloths
Of night and light and the half-light,
I would spread the cloths under your feet:
But I, being poor, have only my dreams;
I have spread my dreams under your feet;
Tread softly because you tread on my dreams.

[When Mohini Chatterjee visited Dublin in 1885, he taught that 'one should say before sleeping: "I have lived many lives, I have been a slave and a prince .... Everything that has been shall be again."' Here the Buddhist doctrine of reincarnation merges with songs of transformation by Amergin, ur-poet of the Gaels, and by the Welsh sixth-century bard Taliesin.]

He thinks of his Past Greatness when a Part of the Constellations of Heaven

I have drunk ale from the Country of the Young
And weep because I know all things now:
I have been a hazel-tree, and they hung
The Pilot Star and the Crooked Plough
Among my leaves in times out of mind:
I became a rush that horses tread:
I became a man, a hater of the wind,
Knowing one, out of all things, alone, that his head
May not lie on the breast nor his lips on the hair
Of the woman that he loves, until he dies.
O beast of the wilderness, bird of the air,
Must I endure your amorous cries?

from:
IN THE SEVEN WOODS (1904)

['The Folly of Being Comforted' is in the barer idiom which Yeats tried for after the culmination of his 'Celtic Twilight' art in *The Wind Among the Reeds*. Henceforth his range of allusion broadens to include Classical and Renaissance as well as Celtic sources, and his exemplary figures are drawn more and more from the spectrum of the noble, the aristocratic and the tragic.]

The Folly of Being Comforted

One that is ever kind said yesterday:
'Your well-belovèd's[1] hair has threads of grey,
And little shadows come about her eyes;
Time can but make it easier to be wise
Though now it seems impossible, and so
All that you need is patience.'
Heart cries, 'No,
I have not a crumb of comfort, not a grain.
Time can but make her beauty over again:
Because of that great nobleness of hers
The fire that stirs about her, when she stirs,
Burns but more clearly. O she had not these ways
When all the wild summer was in her gaze.'

O heart! O heart! if she'd but turn her head,
You'd know the folly of being comforted.

1. Maud Gonne's.

[Adam's curse was that the human race was doomed to work because of his fall from grace. This poem is about the effort expended by Yeats in doing the work of art and in his cultivation of 'the old high way of love'.]

Adam's Curse

We sat together at one summer's end,
That beautiful mild woman, your close friend,
And you[1] and I, and talked of poetry.
I said, 'A line will take us hours maybe;
Yet if it does not seem a moment's thought,
Our stitching and unstitching has been naught.

Better go down upon your marrow-bones
And scrub a kitchen pavement, or break stones
Like an old pauper, in all kinds of weather;

1. Maud Gonne's sister, Kathleen, and Maud Gonne. Maud Gonne's autobiography records how on one occasion her sister told Yeats — who had complimented her on her dress and on her looks in general — that 'it was hard work being beautiful'. A comparison of that commonsense observation with the grave, formal tone of this poem reveals the 'noble' cast of mind that Yeats now deliberately cultivated.

For to articulate sweet sounds together
Is to work harder than all these, and yet
Be thought an idler by the noisy set
Of bankers, schoolmasters, and clergymen
The martyrs call the world.'

And thereupon
That beautiful mild woman for whose sake
There's many a one shall find out all heartache
On finding that her voice is sweet and low
Replied, 'To be born woman is to know —
Although they do not talk of it at school —
That we must labour to be beautiful.'

I said, 'It's certain there is no fine thing
Since Adam's fall but needs much labouring.
There have been lovers who thought love should be
So much compounded of high courtesy
That they would sigh and quote with learned looks
Precedents out of beautiful old books;
Yet now it seems an idle trade enough.'

We sat grown quiet at the name of love;
We saw the last embers of daylight die,
And in the trembling blue-green of the sky
A moon, worn as if it had been a shell
Washed by time's waters as they rose and fell
About the stars and broke in days and years.

I had a thought for no one's but your ears:
That you were beautiful, and that I strove
To love you in the old high way of love;
That it had all seemed happy, and yet we'd grown
As weary-hearted as that hollow moon.

[Red Hanrahan was a character in Yeats's prose, a folk poet and lover based upon the rambling Irish-language poets of the seventeenth and eighteenth centuries. The following 'song' is Yeats's exercise in one of their favourite genres, the *aisling* or dream vision poem, in which Ireland is symbolized as a numinous woman. The poem is written to Maud Gonne.]

Red Hanrahan's Song about Ireland

The old brown thorn-trees break in two high over
Cummen Strand,
Under a bitter black wind that blows from the left
hand;
Our courage breaks like an old tree in a black wind
and dies,
But we have hidden in our hearts the flame out of
the eyes
Of Cathleen, the daughter of Houlihan.

The wind has bundled up the clouds high over
Knocknarea,[1]
And thrown the thunder on the stones for all that
Maeve can say.
Angers that are like noisy clouds have set our hearts
abeat;
But we have all bent low and low and kissed the
quiet feet
Of Cathleen, the daughter of Houlihan.

The yellow pool has overflowed high up on Clooth-
na-Bare,
For the wet winds are blowing out of the clinging
air;
Like heavy flooded waters our bodies and our blood;
But purer than a tall candle before the Holy Rood
Is Cathleen, the daughter of Houlihan.

1. The supposed burial cairn of Queen Maeve is on top of this mountain in County Sligo.

from: THE GREEN HELMET AND OTHER POEMS (1910)

[After Maud Gonne's marriage to John MacBride in 1903, Yeats's poems to her achieve a new burnish and a tauter rhetoric.]

No Second Troy

Why should I blame her that she filled my days
With misery, or that she would of late
Have taught to ignorant men most violent ways,[1]
Or hurled the little streets upon the great,
Had they but courage equal to desire?
What could have made her peaceful with a mind
That nobleness made simple as a fire,
With beauty like a tightened bow, a kind
That is not natural in an age like this,
Being high and solitary and most stern?
Why, what could she have done, being what she is?
Was there another Troy for her to burn?

1. Maud Gonne was thoroughly engaged in revolutionary politics and resolutely pursuing the end of British rule in Ireland.

The Fascination of What's Difficult

The fascination of what's difficult
Has dried the sap out of my veins, and rent
Spontaneous joy and natural content
Out of my heart. There's something ails our colt[1]
That must, as if it had not holy blood
Nor on Olympus leaped from cloud to cloud,
Shiver under the lash, strain, sweat and jolt
As though it dragged road-metal. My curse on plays[2]
That have to be set up in fifty ways,
On the day's war with every knave and dolt,
Theatre business, management of men.
I swear before the dawn comes round again
I'll find the stable and pull out the bolt.

1. Pegasus, the winged horse, favourite of the Muses.
2. Yeats probably is referring not only to his own work as a dramatist but to his responsibilities as a director of the Abbey Theatre.

['Upon a House Shaken by the Land Agitation', and the five poems that follow it here, are typical of the new, self-consciously profiled 'courtier' image that Yeats cultivated in the first decade of the twentieth century. Familiarity with and acceptance within Lady Gregory's household at Coole Park, Co. Galway underlay his new identification with the 'horseman' strain in Irish life, and signified the incorporation into Yeats's mythology of a second Ireland — 'the Irish nation' of protestant gentry descended from the patriotic generations of Anglo-Irish in the eighteenth century. Henceforth 'native' Ireland meant not just the romance of folk-life and the heritage of legend; for Yeats, it was increasingly synonymous with catholicism and commercialism ('Paudeen'), with self-serving caution ('Romantic Ireland's dead and gone'), and with 'rancorous' politics ('an old foul mouth'). The positive aspect of all this was a new demystified acknowledgment of Yeats's solidarity with his own caste. Yet his honesty to this feeling extended into anti-democratic flourishes which have cost him the sympathy of many readers, and of Marxist critics in particular. Yeats's imagination was unrepentantly hierarchical; and even though his sense of justice complicated his aesthetic instinct, that aesthetic preference remained steadfastly for the high style. His myth of 'protestant' Ireland, for example, had no place for the levelling dissenters of the northern enlightenment nor for the later loyalism of northern unionists.]

Upon a House Shaken by the Land Agitation

How should the world be luckier if this house,
Where passion and precision have been one
Time out of mind, became too ruinous
To breed the lidless eye that loves the sun?
And the sweet laughing eagle thoughts that grow
Where wings have memory of wings, and all
That comes of the best knit to the best? Although
Mean roof-trees were the sturdier for its fall,[1]
How should their luck run high enough to reach
The gifts that govern men, and after these
To gradual Time's last gift, a written speech
Wrought of high laughter, loveliness and ease?

1. Yeats ventures the thought that the civilization produced by the 'big house' tradition would not be compensated for by the breakdown of the estate for the economic advantage of the tenants.

At Galway Races

There where the course is,
Delight makes all of the one mind,
The riders upon the galloping horses,
The crowd that closes in behind:
We, too, had good attendance once,
Hearers and hearteners of the work;
Aye, horsemen for companions,
Before the merchant and the clerk
Breathed on the world with timid breath.
Sing on: somewhere at some new moon,
We'll learn that sleeping is not death,
Hearing the whole earth change its tune,
Its flesh being wild, and it again
Crying aloud as the racecourse is,
And we find hearteners among men
That ride upon horses.

from: RESPONSIBILITIES (1914)

['September 1913' was written in reaction to Dublin Corporation's refusal to build a gallery to house Sir Hugh Lane's proffered collection of Impressionist pictures. The gift was contingent upon this one condition being fulfilled. Yeats makes Lane's opulence of spirit a standard by which contemporary mean-spiritedness is judged.]

September 1913

What need you, being come to sense,
But fumble in a greasy till
And add the halfpence to the pence
And prayer to shivering prayer, until

You have dried the marrow from the bone?
For men were born to pray and save:
Romantic Ireland's dead and gone,
It's with O'Leary[1] in the grave.

Yet they were of a different kind,
The names that stilled your childish play,
They have gone about the world like wind,
But little time had they to pray
For whom the hangman's rope was spun,
And what, God help us, could they save?
Romantic Ireland's dead and gone,
It's with O'Leary in the grave.

Was it for this the wild geese[2] spread
The grey wing upon every tide;
For this that all that blood was shed,
For this Edward Fitzgerald died,
And Robert Emmet and Wolfe Tone,
All that delirium of the brave?
Romantic Ireland's dead and gone,
It's with O'Leary in the grave.

Yet could we turn the years again,
And call those exiles as they were
In all their loneliness and pain,
You'd cry, 'Some woman's yellow hair
Has maddened every mother's son':
They weighed so lightly what they gave.
But let them be, they're dead and gone,
They're with O'Leary in the grave.

1. John O'Leary (1830-1907), Fenian, exile and literary mentor to the young Yeats. Because of his visionary revolutionary politics, he is here associated with the patriotic heroes Lord Edward Fitzgerald (1763-98), Robert Emmet (1778-1803) and Theobald Wolfe Tone (1763-98).
2. Under the terms of the Treaty of Limerick (1691), Irish catholic soldiers who had fought under James II were allowed to leave for France, and large numbers of them did so. These 'Wild Geese' and their descendants fought under the banners of the Irish brigade in the French armies on every major European battlefield.

To a Friend whose Work has come to Nothing

Now all the truth is out,
Be secret and take defeat
From any brazen throat,
For how can you compete,
Being honour bred, with one[1]
Who, were it proved he lies,
Were neither shamed in his own
Nor in his neighbours' eyes?
Bred to a harder thing
Than Triumph, turn away
And like a laughing string
Whereon mad fingers play
Amid a place of stone,
Be secret and exult,
Because of all things known
That is most difficult.

1. William Martin Murphy (1844-1919), owner of the *Irish Independent* and the *Evening Herald* and a strong opponent of Sir Hugh Lane's unsuccessful scheme for a picture gallery. Lane was a nephew of Lady Gregory, who supported him and who is therefore likely to be the 'friend whose work has come to nothing'.

Paudeen

Indignant at the fumbling wits, the obscure spite
Of our old Paudeen in his shop, I stumbled blind
Among the stones and thorn-trees, under morning light;
Until a curlew cried and in the luminous wind
A curlew answered; and suddenly thereupon I thought
That on the lonely height where all are in God's eye,
There cannot be, confusion of our sound forgot,
A single soul that lacks a sweet crystalline cry.[1]

1. Yeats conceives of Paudeen as a pure spirit 'in God's eye'. This vision of Paudeen purified reveals the final sweetness and inclusiveness of Yeats's attitudes.

To a Shade

If you have revisited the town, thin Shade,[1]
Whether to look upon your monument
(I wonder if the builder has been paid)
Or happier-thoughted when the day is spent
To drink of that salt breath out of the sea
When grey gulls flit about instead of men,
And the gaunt houses put on majesty:
Let these content you and be gone again;
For they are at their old tricks yet.

1. Charles Stewart Parnell (1846-91), the Irish parliamentary leader who fell from favour because of his affair with Katharine O'Shea. His monument stands at the northern end of O'Connell Street in Dublin.

A man[2]
Of your own passionate serving kind who had brought
In his full hands what, had they only known,
Had given their children's children loftier thought,
Sweeter emotion, working in their veins
Like gentle blood, has been driven from the place,
And insult heaped upon him for his pains,
And for his open-handedness, disgrace;
Your enemy, an old foul mouth,[3] had set
The pack upon him.
Go, unquiet wanderer,
And gather the Glasnevin coverlet[4]
About your head till the dust stops your ear,
The time for you to taste of that salt breath
And listen at the corners has not come:
You had enough of sorrow before death —
Away, away! You are safer in the tomb.

September 29, 1913

2. Sir Hugh Lane, art collector.
3. William Martin Murphy, newspaper magnate.
4. Parnell is buried in Glasnevin cemetery, Dublin.

Running to Paradise

As I came over Windy Gap
They threw a halfpenny into my cap,
For I am running to Paradise;
And all that I need do is to wish
And somebody puts his hand in the dish
To throw me a bit of salted fish:
And there the king is *but as the beggar.*

My brother Mourteen is worn out
With skelping his big brawling lout,
And I am running to Paradise;
A poor life, do what he can,
And though he keep a dog and a gun,
A serving-maid and a serving-man:
And there the king is *but as the beggar.*

Poor men have grown to be rich men,
And rich men grown to be poor again,
And I am running to Paradise;
And many a darling wit's grown dull
That tossed a bare heel when at school,
Now it has filled an old sock full:
And there the king is *but as the beggar.*

The wind is old and still at play
While I must hurry upon my way
For I am running to Paradise;
Yet never have I lit on a friend
To take my fancy like the wind
That nobody can buy or bind:
And there the king is *but as the beggar.*

Fallen Majesty

Although crowds gathered once if she but showed her face,[1]
And even old men's eyes grew dim, this hand alone,
Like some last courtier at a gypsy camping-place
Babbling of fallen majesty, records what's gone.

The lineaments, a heart that laughter has made sweet,
These, these remain, but I record what's gone. A crowd
Will gather, and not know it walks the very street
Whereon a thing once walked that seemed a burning cloud.

1. Maud Gonne. Yeats attributed her sway over crowds at political meetings to her beauty.

['The Cold Heaven', said by Yeats to be his attempt to describe feelings roused in him by the cold detached sky in winter, grows out of a double sensation of enlargement and exposure, and is typical of the visionary strain that complemented the 'civic' poetry of *Responsibilities*.]

The Cold Heaven

Suddenly I saw the cold and rook-delighting heaven
That seemed as though ice burned and was but the more ice,
And thereupon imagination and heart were driven
So wild that every casual thought of that and this
Vanished, and left but memories, that should be out of season
With the hot blood of youth, of love crossed long ago;
And I took all the blame out of all sense and reason,
Until I cried and trembled and rocked to and fro,
Riddled with light. Ah! when the ghost begins to quicken,
Confusion of the death-bed over, is it sent
Out naked on the roads, as the books say, and stricken
By the injustice of the skies for punishment?

The Magi

Now as at all times I can see in the mind's eye,
In their stiff, painted clothes, the pale unsatisfied ones
Appear and disappear in the blue depth of the sky
With all their ancient faces like rain-beaten stones,
And all their helms of silver hovering side by side,
And all their eyes still fixed, hoping to find once more,
Being by Calvary's turbulence unsatisfied,
The uncontrollable mystery on the bestial floor.

from: THE WILD SWANS AT COOLE (1919)

The Wild Swans at Coole

The trees are in their autumn beauty,
The woodland paths are dry,
Under the October twilight the water
Mirrors a still sky;
Upon the brimming water among the stones
Are nine-and-fifty swans.

The nineteenth autumn has come upon me
Since I first made my count;
I saw, before I had well finished,
All suddenly mount
And scatter wheeling in great broken rings
Upon their clamorous wings.

I have looked upon those brilliant creatures,
And now my heart is sore.
All's changed since I, hearing at twilight,
The first time on this shore,
The bell-beat of their wings above my head,
Trod with a lighter tread.

Unwearied still, lover by lover,
They paddle in the cold
Companionable streams or climb the air;
Their hearts have not grown old;
Passion or conquest, wander where they will,
Attend upon them still.

But now they drift on the still water,
Mysterious, beautiful;
Among what rushes will they build,
By what lake's edge or pool
Delight men's eyes when I awake some day
To find they have flown away?

[Robert Gregory, the 'Irish Airman' of the poem that follows this one, was killed in action on 23 January 1918. 'In Memory of Major Robert Gregory' is one of the first of Yeats's poems to be set in Thoor Ballylee, the Norman tower he purchased in 1917 as a summer home for himself and his new wife, George Hyde-Lees. Its note of seniority and authority derives in part from the emotional and intellectual consolidation that Yeats found in the simultaneous experience of his marriage, his tower and his visitation by ghostly 'instructors' who spoke through his wife's automatic writings and gave him the elements of an integrated system of philosophy and symbols.]

In Memory of Major Robert Gregory

I

Now that we're almost settled in our house
I'll name the friends that cannot sup with us
Beside a fire of turf in th' ancient tower,[1]
And having talked to some late hour
Climb up the narrow winding stair to bed:
Discoverers of forgotten truth
Or mere companions of my youth,
All, all are in my thoughts to-night being dead.

II

Always we'd have the new friend meet the old
And we are hurt if either friend seem cold,
And there is salt to lengthen out the smart
In the affections of our heart,
And quarrels are blown up upon that head;
But not a friend that I would bring
This night can set us quarrelling,
For all that come into my mind are dead.

III

Lionel Johnson[2] comes the first to mind,
That loved his learning better than mankind,

1. Yeats purchased the building from the Congested Districts Board and set about its restoration with the deliberate intention of making it a poetic symbol.
2. Lionel Johnson (1867-1902), poet and critic. Johnson was a member of the Rhymers Club, a group Yeats was associated with in London in the 1890s.

Though courteous to the worst; much falling he
Brooded upon sanctity
Till all his Greek and Latin learning seemed
A long blast upon the horn that brought
A little nearer to his thought
A measureless consummation that he dreamed.

IV

And that enquiring man John Synge[3] comes next,
That dying chose the living world for text
And never could have rested in the tomb
But that, long travelling, he had come
Towards nightfall upon certain set apart
In a most desolate stony place,
Towards nightfall upon a race
Passionate and simple like his heart.

V

And then I think of old George Pollexfen,[4]
In muscular youth well known to Mayo men
For horsemanship at meets or at racecourses,
That could have shown how pure-bred horses
And solid men, for all their passion, live
But as the outrageous stars incline
By opposition, square and trine;[5]
Having grown sluggish and contemplative.

VI

They were my close companions many a year,
A portion of my mind and life, as it were,
And now their breathless faces seem to look
Out of some old picture-book;
I am accustomed to their lack of breath,
But not that my dear friend's dear son,
Our Sidney and our perfect man,[6]
Could share in that discourtesy of death.

VII

For all things the delighted eye now sees
Were loved by him: the old storm-broken trees
That cast their shadows upon road and bridge;
The tower set on the stream's edge;
The ford where drinking cattle make a stir
Nightly, and startled by that sound
The water-hen must change her ground;
He might have been your heartiest welcomer.

VIII

When with the Galway foxhounds he would ride
From Castle Taylor to the Roxborough side
Or Esserkelly plain, few kept his pace;
At Mooneen he had leaped a place
So perilous that half the astonished meet
Had shut their eyes; and where was it
He rode a race without a bit?
And yet his mind outran the horses' feet.

IX

We dreamed that a great painter had been born[7]
To cold Clare rock and Galway rock and thorn,
To that stern colour and that delicate line
That are our secret discipline
Wherein the gazing heart doubles her might.
Soldier, scholar, horseman, he,
And yet he had the intensity
To have published all to be a world's delight.

X

What other could so well have counselled us
In all lovely intricacies of a house
As he that practised or that understood
All work in metal or in wood,
In moulded plaster or in carven stone?
Soldier, scholar, horseman, he,
And all he did done perfectly
As though he had but that one trade alone.

XI

Some burn damp faggots, others may consume
The entire combustible world in one small room
As though dried straw, and if we turn about
The bare chimney is gone black out
Because the work had finished in that flare.

3. John Millington Synge (1871-1909), dramatist of genius and friend of Yeats; he discovered himself artistically on the Aran Islands, wrote for the Abbey Theatre and died young.
4. Yeats's maternal uncle, an experimenter in magic and respecter of the other-wordly beliefs of the country people.
5. In astrology, an aspect of 120° between two planets.
6. Sir Philip Sidney (1554-86), English poet, soldier, courtier, who also died young in battle and became a type of the versatile and integrated 'Renaissance man'.
7. Robert Gregory had studied painting in Paris and had exhibited in London in 1914. An example of his work can be seen in the Municipal Gallery in Dublin.

Soldier, scholar, horseman, he,
As 'twere all life's epitome.
What made us dream that he could comb grey hair?

XII

I had thought, seeing how bitter is that wind
That shakes the shutter, to have brought to mind
All those that manhood tried, or childhood loved
Or boyish intellect approved,
With some appropriate commentary on each;
Until imagination brought
A fitter welcome; but a thought
Of that late death took all my heart for speech.

An Irish Airman Foresees his Death

I[1] know that I shall meet my fate
Somewhere among the clouds above;
Those that I fight I do not hate,
Those that I guard I do not love;
My country is Kiltartan Cross,[2]
My countrymen Kiltartan's poor,
No likely end could bring them loss
Or leave them happier than before.
Nor law, nor duty bade me fight,
Nor public men, nor cheering crowds,
A lonely impulse of delight
Drove to this tumult in the clouds;
I balanced all, brought all to mind,
The years to come seemed waste of breath,
A waste of breath the years behind
In balance with this life, this death.

1. The speaker is Robert Gregory.
2. A crossroads in the district of Kiltartan, near Gregory's home at Coole Park, Co. Galway.

The Collar-Bone of a Hare

Would I could cast a sail on the water
Where many a king has gone
And many a king's daughter,
And alight at the comely trees and the lawn,
The playing upon pipes and the dancing,
And learn that the best thing is
To change my loves while dancing
And pay but a kiss for a kiss.

I would find by the edge of that water
The collar-bone of a hare
Worn thin by the lapping of water,
And pierce it through with a gimlet, and stare
At the old bitter world where they marry in
churches,
And laugh over the untroubled water
At all who marry in churches,
Through the white thin bone of a hare.

The Fisherman

Although I can see him still,[1]
The freckled man who goes
To a grey place on a hill
In grey Connemara clothes
At dawn to cast his flies,
It's long since I began
To call up to the eyes
This wise and simple man.
All day I'd looked in the face
What I had hoped 'twould be
To write for my own race
And the reality;
The living men that I hate,
The dead man that I loved,
The craven man in his seat,
The insolent unreproved,
And no knave brought to book
Who has won a drunken cheer,
The witty man and his joke
Aimed at the commonest ear,
The clever man who cries
The catch-cries of the clown,
The beating down of the wise
And great Art beaten down.

Maybe a twelvemonth since
Suddenly I began,
In scorn of this audience,
Imagining a man,
And his sun-freckled face,
And grey Connemara cloth,
Climbing up to a place
Where stone is dark under froth,
And the down-turn of his wrist
When the flies drop in the stream;
A man who does not exist,
A man who is but a dream;

1. Yeats is literally the 'seer' in this poem, envisaging an imaginary character who creates the standard by which 'the reality' is measured and found wanting.

And cried, 'Before I am old
I shall have written him one
Poem maybe as cold
And passionate[2] as the dawn.'

2. Positive terms in Yeats's vocabulary: cf. his epitaph in 'Under Ben Bulben': 'Cast a cold eye/On life, on death....'

Memory

One had a lovely face,
And two or three had charm,
But charm and face were in vain
Because the mountain grass
Cannot but keep the form[1]
Where the mountain hare has lain.

1. The correct name for the lair that the hare makes in the grass.

Her Praise

She[1] is foremost of those that I would hear praised.
I have gone about the house, gone up and down
As a man does who has published a new book,
Or a young girl dressed out in her new gown,
And though I have turned the talk by hook or crook
Until her praise should be the uppermost theme,
A woman spoke of some new tale she had read,
A man confusedly in a half dream
As though some other name ran in his head.
She is foremost of those that I would hear praised.
I will talk no more of books or the long war
But walk by the dry thorn until I have found
Some beggar sheltering from the wind, and there
Manage the talk until her name come round.
If there be rags enough he will know her name
And be well pleased remembering it, for in the old days,
Though she had young men's praise and old men's blame,
Among the poor both old and young gave her praise.

1. Maud Gonne.

Broken Dreams

There is grey in your hair.[1]
Young men no longer suddenly catch their breath
When you are passing;
But maybe some old gaffer mutters a blessing
Because it was your prayer
Recovered him upon the bed of death.
For your sole sake — that all heart's ache have known,
And given to others all heart's ache,
From meagre girlhood's putting on
Burdensome beauty — for your sole sake
Heaven has put away the stroke of her doom,
So great her portion in that peace you make
By merely walking in a room.

Your beauty can but leave among us
Vague memories, nothing but memories.
A young man when the old men are done talking
Will say to an old man, 'Tell me of that lady
The poet stubborn with his passion sang us
When age might well have chilled his blood.'

Vague memories, nothing but memories,
But in the grave all, all, shall be renewed.
The certainty that I shall see that lady
Leaning or standing or walking
In the first loveliness of womanhood,
And with the fervour of my youthful eyes,
Has set me muttering like a fool.

You are more beautiful than any one,
And yet your body had a flaw:
Your small hands were not beautiful,
And I am afraid that you will run
And paddle to the wrist
In that mysterious, always brimming lake
Where those that have obeyed the holy law
Paddle and are perfect. Leave unchanged
The hands that I have kissed,
For old sake's sake.

The last stroke of midnight dies.
All day in the one chair
From dream to dream and rhyme to rhyme I have ranged
In rambling talk with an image of air:
Vague memories, nothing but memories.

1. Maud Gonne is being addressed.

To a Squirrel at Kyle-na-no[1]

Come play with me;
Why should you run

1. Kyle-na-no (*Coill na gcno* in Irish) means the Wood of the Nuts and is one of the seven woods of Coole.

Through the shaking tree
As though I'd a gun
To strike you dead?
When all I would do
Is to scratch your head
And let you go.

['Ego Dominus Tuus' is Latin for 'I am your master'. It is the phrase spoken to Dante Alighieri (1265-1321) by the 'Lord of Terrible Aspect.' This figure appears in the vision described by Dante at the beginning of *Vita Nuova*: Dante hears it say 'many things among which I could understand but few'. The title, therefore, is probably an indirect affirmation that the highest traditional sanction exists for belief in the reality and authority of visionary knowledge. The poem was written in 1915, two years before Yeats purchased his 'old wind-beaten tower' and began his work on the symbology of *A Vision* (1925); so it is prophetic of these events and must be regarded, in the words of Harold Bloom, as 'not one of Yeats's great poems, but . . . surely one of his most central and troubling.' Bloom also comments upon its 'majestic and unanswerable rhetorical authority' and his whole discussion of the poem in his *Yeats* (1970) is helpful and suggestive.]

Ego Dominus Tuus

Hic.[1] On the grey sand beside the shallow stream
Under your old wind-beaten tower, where still
A lamp burns on beside the open book
That Michael Robartes[2] left, you walk in the moon,
And, though you have passed the best of life, still trace,
Enthralled by the unconquerable delusion,
Magical shapes.

Ille. By the help of an image
I call to my own opposite, summon all
That I have handled least, least looked upon.

Hic. And I would find myself and not an image.

Ille. That is our modern hope, and by its light
We have lit upon the gentle, sensitive mind
And lost the old nonchalance of the hand;
Whether we have chosen chisel, pen or brush,
We are but critics, or but half create,
Timid, entangled, empty and abashed,
Lacking the countenance of our friends.

Hic. And yet
The chief imagination of Christendom,
Dante Alighieri,[3] so utterly found himself
That he has made that hollow face of his
More plain to the mind's eye than any face
But that of Christ.

Ille. And did he find himself
Or was the hunger that had made it hollow
A hunger for the apple on the bough
Most out of reach? and is that spectral image
The man that Lapo and that Guido[4] knew?
I think he fashioned from his opposite
An image that might have been a stony face
Staring upon a Bedouin's horse-hair roof
From doored and windowed cliff, or half upturned
Among the coarse grass and the camel-dung.
He set his chisel to the hardest stone.
Being mocked by Guido for his lecherous life,
Derided and deriding, driven out
To climb that stair and eat that bitter bread,
He found the unpersuadable justice, he found
The most exalted lady loved by a man.

Hic. Yet surely there are men who have made their art
Out of no tragic war, lovers of life,
Impulsive men that look for happiness
And sing when they have found it.

Ille. No, not sing,
For those that love the world serve it in action,
Grow rich, popular and full of influence,
And should they paint or write, still it is action:
The struggle of the fly in marmalade.
The rhetorician would deceive his neighbours,
The sentimentalist himself; while art
Is but a vision of reality.

1. *Hic* is Latin for 'this one'; *Ille* for 'that one'. *Hic* represents the impulse towards 'sincerity', a self-realization based upon self-scrutiny and a scrupulous study of the inward mirror. *Ille* represents the opposite, 'theatrical' impulse, the modelling of the self upon a mask, making one's project the imitation of a hero who calls one *out* of oneself. *Hic* is concerned with the life that finds itself (line 19), *Ille* with the life that seeks its anti-self (line 74). Yeats's attitudes are those of *Ille*.
2. A fictional character invented by Yeats; an initiate of magical societies and an experienced guide to the intricacies of occult learning.
3. Dante's *The Divine Comedy* represents both the summation and the effulgence of the medieval Christian 'vision of reality' (line 48).
4. Lapo degli Uberti and the poet Guido Cavalcanti, both friends of Dante's.

What portion in the world can the artist have
Who has awakened from the common dream
But dissipation and despair?

Hic. And yet
No one denies to Keats love of the world;
Remember his deliberate happiness.

Ille. His art is happy, but who knows his mind?
I see a schoolboy when I think of him,
With face and nose pressed to a sweet-shop
window,
For certainly he sank into his grave
His senses and his heart unsatisfied,
And made — being poor, ailing and ignorant,
Shut out from all the luxury of the world,
The coarse-bred son of a livery-stable keeper —
Luxuriant song.

Hic. Why should you leave the lamp
Burning alone beside an open book,
And trace these characters upon the sands?
A style is found by sedentary toil
And by the imitation of great masters.

Ille. Because I seek an image, not a book.
Those men that in their writings are most wise
Own nothing but their blind, stupefied hearts.
I call to the mysterious one who yet
Shall walk the wet stands by the edge of the stream
And look most like me, being indeed my double,
And prove of all imaginable things
The most unlike, being my anti-self,
And, standing by these characters, disclose
All that I seek; and whisper it as though
He were afraid the birds, who cry aloud
Their momentary cries before it is dawn,
Would carry it away to blasphemous men.[5]

5. Inhabitants of the commonsense world, who are not susceptible to visionary revelation and likely therefore to be scornful of its sacred truths. Yeats is actually subverting the usual meaning of 'blasphemous'.

from:
MICHAEL ROBARTES AND THE DANCER (1921)

[The Easter Rising began in Dublin on 24 April 1916 and ended in surrender five days later. Between 3 and 12 May, fifteen of the leaders were executed, including all those referred to in 'Easter 1916'. (Sir Roger Casement, executed later, made up the 'Sixteen Dead Men' of the next poem.) Yeats started work on the poem almost immediately and significantly appended the date of its completion in the published version. The refrain has become one of his most famous lines and established him as the laureate of the rebellion; yet the poem also acknowledges the prevalent contemporary belief that England would have granted Home Rule to Ireland after World War I in return for the support of the Irish soldiers who enlisted and died with the British army. Yeats salutes the apotheosis of disaffected citizens into immortal names; it is less their specifically political fervour than their sacrifice of themselves to a self-transcending ideal — a mask, an anti-self — which elicits his astonished admiration.]

Easter 1916

I have met them at close of day
Coming with vivid faces
From counter or desk among grey
Eighteenth-century houses.
I have passed with a nod of the head
Or polite meaningless words,
Or have lingered awhile and said
Polite meaningless words,
And thought before I had done
Of a mocking tale or a gibe
To please a companion
Around the fire at the club,
Being certain that they and I
But lived where motley is worn:
All changed, changed utterly:
A terrible beauty is born.

That woman's days were spent
In ignorant good-will,
Her nights in argument
Until her voice grew shrill.
What voice more sweet than hers
When, young and beautiful,
She rode to harriers?
This man had kept a school
And rode our wingèd horse;
This other his helper and friend
Was coming into his force;
He might have won fame in the end,
So sensitive his nature seemed,
So daring and sweet his thought.
This other man I had dreamed

A drunken, vainglorious lout.[1]
He had done most bitter wrong
To some who are near my heart,
Yet I number him in the song;
He, too, has resigned his part
In the casual comedy;
He, too, has been changed in his turn,
Transformed utterly:
A terrible beauty is born.

Hearts with one purpose alone
Through summer and winter seem
Enchanted to a stone
To trouble the living stream.
The horse that comes from the road,
The rider, the birds that range
From cloud to tumbling cloud,
Minute by minute they change;
A shadow of cloud on the stream
Changes minute by minute;
A horse-hoof slides on the brim,
And a horse plashes within it;
The long-legged moor-hens dive,
And hens to moor-cocks call;
Minute by minute they live:
The stone's in the midst of all.

Too long a sacrifice
Can make a stone of the heart.
O when may it suffice?
That is Heaven's part, our part
To murmur name upon name,
As a mother names her child
When sleep at last has come
On limbs that had run wild.
What is it but nightfall?
No, no, not night but death;
Was it needless death after all?
For England may keep faith
For all that is done and said.
We know their dream; enough
To know they dreamed and are dead;
And what if excess of love
Bewildered them till they died?

1. These four are, respectively, Constance Gore-Booth (1868-1927), also known as Countess Markievicz through her marriage to a Polish nobleman; Patrick Pearse (1879-1916), poet, teacher and commandant general of the rebels; Thomas MacDonagh (1878-1916), poet, critic and lecturer in English at University College, Dublin; Major John MacBride (1865-1916), Maud Gonne's abusive husband. The death sentence of the Countess Markievicz was commuted.

I write it out in a verse —
MacDonagh and MacBride
And Connolly[2] and Pearse
Now and in time to be,
Wherever green is worn,
Are changed, changed utterly:
A terrible beauty is born.

September 25, 1916

2. James Connolly (1868-1916), trade union leader, political theorist and organizer of the Citizen Army.

Sixteen Dead Men

O but we talked at large before
The sixteen men were shot,
But who can talk of give and take,
What should be and what not
While those dead men are loitering there
To stir the boiling pot?

You say that we should still the land
Till Germany's overcome;
But who is there to argue that
Now Pearse is deaf and dumb?
And is their logic to outweigh
MacDonagh's bony thumb?

How could you dream they'd listen
That have an ear alone
For those new comrades they have found,
Lord Edward[1] and Wolfe Tone,
Or meddle with our give and take
That converse bone to bone?

1. Lord Edward Fitzgerald (1763-98), United Irishman.

[In 'The Second Coming' Yeats is once more the 'seer'. A 'vast image', which troubles his sight, is plainly described and then interpreted as the omen of a new era.]

The Second Coming

Turning and turning in the widening gyre[1]
The falcon cannot hear the falconer;
Things fall apart; the centre cannot hold;

1. A word of great potency in Yeats's vocabulary, suggestive of unstoppable process, of turbulent action that is part of a larger pattern. Yeats used the geometrical figure of two cones or vortices interpenetrating to represent the simultaneous processes of waxing and waning, rise and fall, which are necessarily at work at any moment

Mere anarchy is loosed upon the world,
The blood-dimmed tide is loosed,[2] and everywhere
The ceremony of innocence is drowned;
The best lack all conviction, while the worst
Are full of passionate intensity.

Surely some revelation is at hand;
Surely the Second Coming is at hand.
The Second Coming! Hardly are those words out
When a vast image out of *Spiritus Mundi*[3]
Troubles my sight: somewhere in sands of the desert
A shape with lion body and the head of a man,
A gaze blank and pitiless as the sun,
Is moving its slow thighs, while all about it
Reel shadows of the indignant desert birds.
The darkness drops again; but now I know
That twenty centuries of stony sleep[4]
Were vexed to nightmare by a rocking cradle,
And what rough beast, its hour come round at last,
Slouches towards Bethlehem to be born?

in the life of an individual or a society. The extreme moment of risen, waxing life (the far-flung base of one cone) is also the moment when there arrives the original movement of new counter-swirling growth (the apex of the other cone, sharp-set at the centre of the wide base). So, when the 'widening gyre' reaches its fullest unwinding circumference, we are to expect a 'Second Coming', a new life which initiates an opposite motion. (Following upon this symmetrical pattern of antitheses, the 'rough beast' will replace the gentle Christ child at the same spot, in Bethlehem.)

2. This poem was written two years after the Russian Revolution of 1917 and during the initial stages of the Irish War of Independence.
3. Yeats defined this as 'a general storehouse of images which have ceased to be a property of any personality or spirit.'
4. In Yeats's scheme of history, the Christian era was now coming to its end, each cycle having a span of two millennia.

from:
THE TOWER (1928)

['Sailing to Byzantium' is a quest poem. The speaker sails out in search of the imagined completion of being that will occur when the natural life dies into its supernatural image, and the effort of artistic creation is fulfilled in the perfected otherness of the work itself. Yeats introduced the poem in 1931, in a BBC broadcast from Belfast, as follows: 'When Irishmen were illuminating the Book of Kells and making the jewelled croziers in the National Museum, Byzantium was the centre of European civilization and the source of its spiritual philosophy, so I symbolize the search for the spiritual life by a journey to that city.']

Sailing to Byanztium

I

That is no country for old men. The young
In one another's arms, birds in the trees
— Those dying generations — at their song,
The salmon-falls, the mackerel-crowded seas,
Fish, flesh, or fowl, commend all summer long
Whatever is begotten, born, and dies.
Caught in that sensual music all neglect
Monuments of unageing intellect.

II

An aged man is but a paltry thing,
A tattered coat upon a stick, unless
Soul clap its hands and sing, and louder sing
For every tatter in its mortal dress,
Nor is there singing school but studying
Monuments of its own magnificence;
And therefore I have sailed the seas and come
To the holy city of Byzantium.

III

O sages standing in God's holy fire[1]
As in the gold mosaic of a wall,
Come from the holy fire, perne in a gyre,[2]
And be the singing-masters of my soul.
Consume my heart away; sick with desire
And fastened to a dying animal
It knows not what it is; and gather me
Into the artifice of eternity.

IV

Once out of nature I shall never take
My bodily form from any natural thing,
But such a form as Grecian goldsmiths make
Of hammered gold and gold enamelling
To keep a drowsy Emperor awake;[3]
Or set upon a golden bough to sing
To lords and ladies of Byzantium
Of what is past, or passing, or to come.

1927

1. Among the famous mosaics in the church of S. Appollinaire Nuovo at Ravenna, which Yeats visited in 1907, there is a frieze representing martyrs and virgins in a blaze of gold leaf.
2. i.e. turn or spin in a spiral movement.
3. Yeats had read that in the Emperor's palace there was a tree made of silver and gold, and artificial birds that sang.

['Meditations in Time of Civil War' and the following sequence, 'Nineteen Hundred and Nineteen', represent the high tide of Yeats's achievement as a public poet. They both appeared in *The Tower* (1928), a volume where Yeats presents himself as a figure of the fully empowered, traditionally authoritative poet, the wisdom-speaker, the memory-keeper, the one who confronts menace with ritual song. The menace was worldwide, brought forth by World War I and the Russian Revolution of 1917, but Yeats apprehended it through the particular circumstances of an Ireland fighting to end British rule and then plunging into a cruel and intimate civil war. These events were symptomatic of the end of an old order of 'ancestral houses' and rich estates with 'flowering lawns'. Yeats braves out the world-change by recognizing that every civilization begins with reversal and destruction (cf. 'The Second Coming'), that its 'greatness' — its munificent flowering — depends upon its 'violence', the initial force and conquest that secured its base. The rhetoric of these poems combines stateliness and intensity in an effort to oppose the tragic recognitions that history is enforcing upon the poet's consciousness; Yeats's art here not only affirms the mind's trust in its own salutary creative powers, but manifests those powers in the aural and visionary excitements of the verse itself.]

Meditations in Time of Civil War

I

Ancestral Houses

Surely among a rich man's flowering lawns,
Amid the rustle of his planted hills,
Life overflows without ambitious pains;
And rains down life until the basin spills,
And mounts more dizzy high the more it rains
As though to choose whatever shape it wills
And never stoop to a mechanical
Or servile shape, at others' beck and call.

Mere dreams, mere dreams! Yet Homer had not sung
Had he not found it certain beyond dreams
That out of life's own self-delight had sprung
The abounding glittering jet,[1] though now it seems
As if some marvellous empty sea-shell flung
Out of the obscure dark of the rich streams,
And not a fountain, were the symbol which
Shadows the inherited glory of the rich.

Some violent bitter man, some powerful man
Called architect and artist in, that they,
Bitter and violent men, might rear in stone
The sweetness that all longed for night and day,
The gentleness none there had ever known;
But when the master's buried mice can play,
And maybe the great-grandson of that house,
For all its bronze and marble, 's but a mouse.

O what if gardens where the peacock strays
With delicate feet upon old terraces,
Or else all Juno from an urn displays
Before the indifferent garden deities;
O what if levelled lawns and gravelled ways
Where slippered Contemplation finds his ease
And Childhood a delight for every sense,
But take our greatness with our violence?

What if the glory of escutcheoned doors,
And buildings that a haughtier age designed,
The pacing to and fro on polished floors
Amid great chambers and long galleries, lined
With famous portraits of our ancestors;
What if those things the greatest of mankind
Consider most to magnify, or to bless,
But take our greatness with our bitterness?

II

My House

An ancient bridge, and a more ancient tower,
A farmhouse that is sheltered by its wall,
An acre of stony ground,
Where the symbolic rose can break in flower,
Old ragged elms, old thorns innumerable,
The sound of the rain or sound
Of every wind that blows;
The stilted water-hen
Crossing stream again
Scared by the splashing of a dozen cows;

A winding stair, a chamber arched with stone,
A grey stone fireplace with an open hearth,
A candle and written page.
Il Penseroso's Platonist[2] toiled on

1. The glittering, jetting fountain is an image of life at its spontaneous, instinctive best; but the exhaustion of the older hierarchical civilization is now better symbolized by the 'empty sea-shell'.

2. In John Milton's poem *Il Penserosa*, the poet writes:
Or let my Lamp at midnight hour
Be seen in some high lonely Tower,
Where I may oft outwatch the *Bear*,
With thrice great *Hermes*, or unsphear,
The spirit of Plato. . . .

In some like chamber, shadowing forth
How the daemonic rage
Imagined everything.
Benighted travellers
From markets and from fairs
Have seen his midnight candle glimmering.

Two men have founded here. A man-at-arms
Gathered a score of horse and spent his days
In this tumultuous spot,
Where through long wars and sudden night alarms
His dwindling score and he seemed castaways
Forgetting and forgot;
And I, that after me
My bodily heirs may find,
To exalt a lonely mind,
Befitting emblems of adversity.

III

My Table

Two heavy trestles, and a board
Where Sato's gift[3], a changeless sword,
By pen and paper lies,
That it may moralise
My days out of their aimlessness.
A bit of an embroidered dress
Covers its wooden sheath.
Chaucer had not drawn breath
When it was forged. In Sato's house,
Curved like new moon, moon-luminous,
It lay five hundred years.
Yet if no change appears
No moon; only an aching heart
Conceives a changeless work of art.
Our learned men have urged
That when and where 'twas forged
A marvellous accomplishment,
In painting or in pottery, went
From father unto son
And through the centuries ran
And seemed unchanging like the sword.[4]
Soul's beauty being most adored,
Men and their business took
The soul's unchanging look;
For the most rich inheritor,
Knowing that none could pass Heaven's door
That loved inferior art,
Had such an aching heart
That he, although a country's talk
For silken clothes and stately walk,
Had waking wits; it seemed
Juno's peacock screamed.[5]

IV

My Descendants

Having inherited a vigorous mind
From my old fathers, I must nourish dreams
And leave a woman and a man behind[6]
As vigorous of mind, and yet it seems
Life scarce can cast a fragrance on the wind,
Scarce spread a glory to the morning beams,
But the torn petals strew the garden plot;
And there's but common greenness after that.

And what if my descendants lose the flower
Through natural declension of the soul,
Through too much business with the passing hour,
Through too much play, or marriage with a fool?
May this laborious stair and this stark tower
Become a roofless ruin that the owl
May build in the cracked masonry and cry
Her desolation to the desolate sky.

The Primum Mobile[7] that fashioned us
Has made the very owls in circles move;
And I, that count myself most prosperous,
Seeing that love and friendship are enough,
For an old neighbour's friendship chose the house
And decked and altered it for a girl's love,[8]
And know whatever flourish and decline
These stones remain their monument and mine.

3. Junzo Sato, Japanese consul at Portland, Oregon, had made Yeats a gift of an ancient family sword after the poet had lectured there in 1922.
4. The sword's changelessness is evidence of the traditional nature of Japanese civilization which Yeats goes on to evoke in the following lines.
5. Omen of traumatic change, of the end of an era that seemed 'unchanging'.
6. Yeats's daughter and son, Anne and Michael, born 26 February 1919 and 22 August 1921 respectively.
7. Prime Mover of the nine spheres of the universe in the Ptolemaic system.
8. Lady Gregory and Yeats's new wife, George Hyde-Lees.

V

The Road at My Door

An affable Irregular,[9]
A heavily-built Falstaffian man,
Comes cracking jokes of civil war
As though to die by gunshot were
The finest play under the sun.

A brown Lieutenant[10] and his men,
Half dressed in national uniform,
Stand at my door, and I complain
Of the foul weather, hail and rain,
A pear-tree broken by the storm.

I count those feathered balls of soot
The moor-hen guides upon the stream,
To silence the envy in my thought;
And turn towards my chamber, caught
In the cold snows of a dream.

VI

The Stare's Nest[11] by My Window

The bees build in the crevices
Of loosening masonry, and there
The mother birds bring grubs and flies.
My wall is loosening; honey-bees,
Come build in the empty house of the stare.

We are closed in, and the key is turned
On our uncertainty; somewhere
A man is killed, or a house burned,
Yet no clear fact to be discerned:
Come build in the empty house of the stare.

A barricade of stone or of wood;
Some fourteen days of civil war;
Last night they trundled down the road
That dead young soldier in his blood:
Come build in the empty house of the stare.

We had fed the heart on fantasies,
The heart's grown brutal from the fare;
More substance in our enmities
Than in our love; O honey-bees,
Come build in the empty house of the stare.

VII

I see Phantoms of Hatred and of the Heart's Fullness and of the Coming Emptiness[12]

I climb to the tower-top and lean upon broken stone,
A mist that is like blown snow is sweeping over all,
Valley, river, and elms, under the light of a moon
That seems unlike itself, that seems unchangeable,
A glittering sword out of the east. A puff of wind
And those white glimmering fragments of the mist sweep by.
Frenzies bewilder, reveries perturb the mind;
Monstrous familiar images swim to the mind's eye.

'Vengeance upon the murderers,' the cry goes up,
'Vengeance for Jacques Molay.'[13] In cloud-pale rags, or in lace,
The rage-driven, rage-tormented, and rage-hungry troop,
Trooper belabouring trooper, biting at arm or at face,
Plunges towards nothing, arms and fingers spreading wide
For the embrace of nothing; and I, my wits astray
Because of all that senseless tumult, all but cried
For vengeance on the murderers of Jacques Molay.

Their legs long, delicate and slender, aquamarine their eyes,
Magical unicorns bear ladies on their backs.
The ladies close their musing eyes. No prophecies,
Remembered out of Babylonian almanacs,
Have closed the ladies' eyes, their minds are but a pool
Where even longing drowns under its own excess;
Nothing but stillness can remain when hearts are full
Of their own sweetness, bodies of their loveliness.

9. The Irregulars were members of the Republican forces, the anti-government side in the Irish Civil War.
10. The lieutenant is a member of the regular army of the newly formed Irish Free State.
11. Yeats says in his own notes to the poem: 'In the west of Ireland we call a starling a stare, and during the civil war one built in a hole in the masonry by my bedroom window.'
12. This title instructs us how best to read what follows: as a more or less literal account of visions that the poet has seen. The 'meaning' of these phantoms resides in their immediate emotional impact, a succession of moods created by the tumult of troopers, the sinister beauty of ladies and unicorns, and the cruel, brazen hawks.
13. Jacques de Molay was the last grand master of the Order of the Knights Templar. He was burned at the stake in Paris in 1314, in what may have been a 'purge' of the order by the papal authorities.

The cloud-pale unicorns, the eyes of aquamarine,
The quivering half-closed eyelids, the rags of cloud or of lace,
Or eyes that rage has brightened, arms it has made lean,
Give place to an indifferent multitude, give place
To brazen hawks. Nor self-delighting reverie,
Nor hate of what's to come, nor pity for what's gone,
Nothing but grip of claw, and the eye's complacency,
The innumerable clanging wings that have put out the moon.

I turn away and shut the door, and on the stair
Wonder how many times I could have proved my worth
In something that all others understand or share;
But O! ambitious heart, had such a proof drawn forth
A company of friends, a conscience set at ease,
It had but made us pine the more. The abstract joy,
The half-read wisdom of daemonic images,
Suffice the ageing man as once the growing boy.

1923

['Nineteen Hundred and Nineteen' was written in 1919 and originally was called 'Thoughts on the Present State of the World', a grand project which may account for the prevalent majestic tone. In the first section Yeats 'rhymes' the sacking of ancient Athens by the Persian forces with the destruction of the old order in Europe and Ireland by the violence of the Great War and of the Irish War of Independence. The mood of the poem sometimes conjures up, and at other times defies, the destruction and collapse that surround the meditative protagonist.]

Nineteen Hundred and Nineteen

I

Many ingenious lovely things are gone
That seemed sheer miracle to the multitude,
Protected from the circle of the moon
That pitches common things about. There stood
Amid the ornamental bronze and stone
An ancient image made of olive wood —
And gone are Phidias' famous ivories
And all the golden grasshoppers and bees.[1]

We too had many pretty toys when young:
A law indifferent to blame or praise,
To bribe or threat; habits that made old wrong
Melt down, as it were wax in the sun's rays;
Public opinion ripening for so long
We thought it would outlive all future days.
O what fine thought we had because we thought
That the worst rogues and rascals had died out.

All teeth were drawn, all ancient tricks unlearned,
And a great army but a showy thing;
What matter that no cannon had been turned
Into a ploughshare? Parliament and king
Thought that unless a little powder burned
The trumpeters might burst with trumpeting
And yet it lack all glory; and perchance
The guardsmen's drowsy chargers would not prance.[2]

Now days are dragon-ridden,[3] the nightmare
Rides upon sleep: a drunken soldiery
Can leave the mother, murdered at her door,
To crawl in her own blood, and go scot-free;
The night can sweat with terror as before
We pieced our thoughts into philosophy,
And planned to bring the world under a rule,
Who are but weasels fighting in a hole.

He who can read the signs nor sink unmanned
Into the half-deceit of some intoxicant
From shallow wits; who knows no work can stand,
Whether health, wealth or peace of mind were spent
On master-work of intellect or hand,
No honour leave its mighty monument,
Has but one comfort left: all triumph would
But break upon his ghostly solitude.

But is there any comfort to be found?
Man is in love and loves what vanishes,
What more is there to say? That country round
None dared admit, if such a thought were his,
Incendiary or bigot could be found
To burn that stump on the Acropolis

1. The treasures of ancient Athens which Yeats evokes include an olive-wood statue sacred to Athena Polias, ivory statues made by the great sculptor Phidias (*c.* 490-417 B.C.), and brooches in the form of grasshoppers and bees.

2. In the second and third stanzas, Yeats alludes to the experience of a generation who grew up in a world of military pomp and empire in the late nineteenth century.

3. The background of this stanza is the 'dragon-ridden' mood of an Ireland caught in the struggle between guerilla fighters and the British auxiliaries and Black and Tans. Yeats refers to atrocities committed by the British near Gort, Co. Galway.

Or break in bits the famous ivories
Or traffic in the grasshoppers or bees.[4]

II

When Loie Fuller's Chinese dancers[5] enwound
A shining web, a floating ribbon of cloth,
It seemed that a dragon of air
Had fallen among dancers, had whirled them round
Or hurried them off on its own furious path;
So the Platonic Year[6]
Whirls out new right and wrong,
Whirls in the old instead;
All men are dancers and their tread
Goes to the barbarous clangour of a gong.

III

Some moralist or mythological poet
Compares the solitary soul to a swan;
I am satisfied with that,
Satisfied if a troubled mirror show it,
Before that brief gleam of its life be gone,
An image of its state;
The wings half spread for flight,
The breast thrust out in pride
Whether to play, or to ride
Those winds that clamour of approaching night.

A man in his own secret meditation
Is lost amid the labyrinth that he has made
In art or politics;
Some Platonist affirms that in the station
Where we should cast off body and trade
The ancient habit sticks,
And that if our works could
But vanish with our breath
That were a lucky death,
For triumph can but mar our solitude.

The swan has leaped into the desolate heaven:
That image can bring wildness, bring a rage
To end all things, to end
What my laborious life imagined, even
The half-imagined, the half-written page;
O but we dreamed to mend
Whatever mischief seemed
To afflict mankind, but now
That winds of winter blow
Learn that we were crack-pated when we dreamed.

IV

We, who seven years ago
Talked of honour and of truth,
Shriek with pleasure if we show
The weasel's twist, the weasel's tooth.

V

Come let us mock at the great
That had such burdens on the mind
And toiled so hard and late
To leave some monument behind,
Nor thought of the levelling wind.

Come let us mock at the wise;
With all those calendars whereon
They fixed old aching eyes,
They never saw how seasons run,
And now but gape at the sun.

Come let us mock at the good
That fancied goodness might be gay,
And sick of solitude
Might proclaim a holiday:
Wind shrieked — and where are they?

Mock mockers after that
That would not lift a hand maybe
To help good, wise or great
To bar that foul storm out, for we
Traffic in mockery.

VI

Violence upon the roads: violence of horses;[7]
Some few have handsome riders, are garlanded
On delicate sensitive ear or tossing mane,
But wearied running round and round in their
courses

4. In peacetime, acts of destruction, such as occurred in ancient Greece or during the 'Troubles' in Ireland, would be unthinkable.
5. Loie Fuller (1862-1928) was an American who led a troupe of Japanese dancers in Paris in the 1890s.
6. The overall, regulating span of the historical cycles.
7. Violence on the roads of contemporary Ireland merges into a vision of dangerous phantoms. In 1899, Yeats had noted that the fairy hosts travelled in whirling winds and that their menacing energies were connected in medieval times with the daughters of Herodias.

All break and vanish, and evil gathers head:
Herodias' daughters have returned again,
A sudden blast of dusty wind and after
Thunder of feet, tumult of images,
Their purpose in the labyrinth of the wind;
And should some crazy hand dare touch a daughter
All turn with amorous cries, or angry cries,
According to the wind, for all are blind.
But now wind drops, dust settles; thereupon
There lurches past, his great eyes without thought
Under the shadow of stupid straw-pale locks,
That insolent fiend Robert Artisson
To whom the love-lorn Lady Kyteler[8] brought
Bronzed peacock feathers, red combs of her cocks.

1919

8. The image of the incubus, Robert Artisson, powerfully sinister in itself, suggests a consciousness evacuated of all compassion, and therefore indicative of the new age. He represents the demon to whom the fourteenth-century witch from Kilkenny, Dame Alice Kyteler, is said to have sacrificed cocks and peacock's eyes.

[The following sonnet on the rape of Leda by Zeus in the shape of a swan links with other occasions in Yeats's poetry, such as the scream of Juno's peacock in *My Table* ('Meditations in Time of Civil War') and the rough beast in 'The Second Coming'. Each of these is a metaphorical embodiment of Yeats's notion of one historical cycle on the wane as another is violently announced. The mild Christian annunciation — winged angel saluting intact virgin with the news that she has miraculously conceived by the power of godhead — is savagely prefigured in this version of the story, where Leda is left pregnant with Helen of Troy. Helen's abduction by Paris was the cause of the Trojan War.]

Leda and the Swan

A sudden blow: the great wings beating still
Above the staggering girl, her thighs caressed
By the dark webs, her nape caught in his bill,
He holds her helpless breast upon his breast.

How can those terrified vague fingers push
The feathered glory from her loosening thighs?
And how can body, laid in that white rush,
But feel the strange heart beating where it lies?

A shudder in the loins engenders there
The broken wall, the burning roof and tower
And Agamemnon dead.
Being so caught up,
So mastered by the brute blood of the air,
Did she put on his knowledge with his power
Before the indifferent beak could let her drop?

1923

[Written after Yeats's visit to a Montessori school in Waterford in 1926, 'Among School Children' begins as an autobiographical reverie, develops into a meditation on the penalties of mortality — age, incompleteness, disappointment — and concludes with a visionary evocation of a state of transcendent fulfilment. It is also a great example of Yeats's use of the *ottava rima* stanza: the combination of purposeful, concentrated argument with a 'complete coincidence between period and stanza' gives his utterance the conclusive, founded, typically 'Yeatsian' quality.]

Among School Children

I

I walk through the long schoolroom questioning;
A kind old nun in a white hood replies;
The children learn to cipher and to sing,
To study reading-books and histories,
To cut and sew, be neat in everything
In the best modern way — the children's eyes
In momentary wonder stare upon
A sixty-year-old smiling public man.[1]

II

I dream of a Ledaean body,[2] bent
Above a sinking fire, a tale that she
Told of a harsh reproof, or trivial event
That changed some childish day to tragedy —
Told, and it seemed that our two natures blent
Into a sphere from youthful sympathy,
Or else, to alter Plato's parable,[3]
Into the yolk and white of the one shell.

1. Yeats visited the school in Waterford in his capacity as a member of the Irish Senate.
2. Yeats constantly associates Maud Gonne with Helen of Troy. Helen (cf. 'Leda and the Swan') was Leda's daughter, fathered by Zeus.
3. Plato's parable is in the *Symposium*.

III

And thinking of that fit of grief or rage
I look upon one child or t'other there
And wonder if she stood so at that age —
For even daughters of the swan can share
Something of every paddler's heritage —[4]
And had that colour upon cheek or hair,
And thereupon my heart is driven wild:
She stands before me as a living child.

IV

Her present image floats into the mind —
Did Quattrocento finger fashion it[5]
Hollow of cheek as though it drank the wind
And took a mess of shadows for its meat?
And I though never of Ledaean kind
Had pretty plumage once — enough of that,
Better to smile on all that smile, and show
There is a comfortable kind of old scarecrow.

V

What youthful mother, a shape upon her lap
Honey of generation had betrayed,
And that must sleep, shriek, struggle to escape
As recollection or the drug decide,
Would think her son, did she but see that shape
With sixty or more winters on its head,
A compensation for the pang of his birth,
Or the uncertainty of his setting forth?[6]

VI

Plato thought nature but a spume that plays
Upon a ghostly paradigm of things;
Solider Aristotle played the taws
Upon the bottom of a king of kings;
World-famous golden-thighed Pythagoras
Fingered upon a fiddle-stick or strings
What a star sang and careless Muses heard:
Old clothes upon old sticks to scare a bird.[7]

VII

Both nuns and mothers worship images,
But those the candles light are not as those
That animate a mother's reveries,
But keep a marble or a bronze repose.
And yet they too break hearts — O Presences
That passion, piety or affection knows,
And that all heavenly glory symbolise —
O self-born mockers of man's enterprise;

VIII

Labour is blossoming or dancing where
The body is not bruised to pleasure soul,
Nor beauty born out of its own despair,
Nor blear-eyed wisdom out of midnight oil.
O chestnut-tree, great-rooted blossomer,
Are you the leaf, the blossom or the bole?
O body swayed to music, O brightening glance,
How can we know the dancer from the dance?

4. A child touched with immortal blood can still live the usual life of other youngsters.
5. The hand of a fifteenth-century artist; in another version, Yeats had referred specifically to Leonardo da Vinci (1452-1519).
6. Yeats has much learned commentary on the neo-Platonic sources of this stanza. An 'unofficial' reading of it might be as follows: What young mother, with an infant on her lap whose soul has been 'betrayed' out of eternity by the father's 'honey of generation', and who has had to go through the stupor and pain of labour — depending on whether she is drugged or wide-awake — would think . . . .?
7. In this stanza, Yeats gives three brilliantly suggestive condensations of the thought of Plato, Aristotle and Pythagoras, the first a believer in the primacy of the ideal world, the second more scientific and down-to-earth (as Alexander the Great's tutor, Aristotle, is imagined using a very unideal schoolteacher's leather strap), and the third a proponent of the idea that the soul transmigrated between the realms of the ideal and the natural.

from: THE WINDING STAIR AND OTHER POEMS (1933)

[A memory of the Gore-Booth sisters, young, free, full of grace and impulse, is dwelt upon and preferred, as an image of possible fullness and spontaneity, to the facts of their dutifully committed later lives. The movement of this poem, undulant and propulsive, contributes greatly to the success of its climax, where an imagined intensity of being — identified with these 'last romantics' among the Anglo-Irish — is promoted over the actual humdrum of routine, 'a fight/With a common wrong or right.']

In Memory of Eva Gore-Booth and Con Markiewicz

The light of evening, Lissadell,[1]
Great windows open to the south,
Two girls in silk kimonos, both
Beautiful, one a gazelle.[2]
But a raving autumn shears
Blossom from the summer's wreath;
The older[3] is condemned to death,
Pardoned, drags out lonely years
Conspiring among the ignorant.
I know not what the younger dreams —
Some vague Utopia — and she seems,
When withered old and skeleton-gaunt,
An image of such politics.
Many a time I think to seek
One or the other out and speak
Of that old Georgian mansion, mix
Pictures of the mind, recall
That table and the talk of youth,
Two girls in silk kimonos, both
Beautiful, one a gazelle.

Dear shadows, now you know it all,
All the folly of a fight
With a common wrong or right.
The innocent and the beautiful
Have no enemy but time;
Arise and bid me strike a match
And strike another till time catch;
Should the conflagration climb,
Run till all the sages know.
We the great gazebo[4] built,
They convicted us of guilt;
Bid me strike a match and blow.

October 1927

1. Lissadell is the Gore-Booth house in County Sligo. Yeats visited there often in 1894-95.
2. The gazelle is Eva (1870-1926), a poet and later a trade union organizer for women in Britain.
3. Constance Gore-Booth (1868-1927) married Count Casimir Dunin-Markievicz in 1900 and became famous in the struggle for Irish independence and its aftermath.
4. A summer house in the grounds of Lissadell; but equally important is the gazebo's association with a point of view that is spacious, contemplative and unconstrained.

[The best help in approaching 'A Dialogue of Self and Soul' is given by Yeats in a letter to Olivia Shakespear, where he calls it 'a new tower poem "Sword and Tower", which is a choice of rebirth rather than deliverance from birth. I make my Japanese sword and its silk covering my symbol of life.' Deliverance from birth is the aspiration of 'Soul' in the finished version, while an embrace of mortal life/lives remains the defiant choice of 'Self'. 'Soul' is still connected with the tower and eternity, 'Self' with the sword and time.]

A Dialogue of Self and Soul

I

My Soul. I summon to the winding ancient stair;
Set all your mind upon the steep ascent,
Upon the broken, crumbling battlement,
Upon the breathless starlit air,
Upon the star that marks the hidden pole;
Fix every wandering thought upon
That quarter where all thought is done:
Who can distinguish darkness from the soul?

My Self. The consecrated blade upon my knees
Is Sato's[1] ancient blade, still as it was,
Still razor-keen, still like a looking-glass
Unspotted by the centuries;
That flowering, silken, old embroidery, torn
From some court-lady's dress and round
The wooden scabbard bound and wound,
Can, tattered, still protect, faded adorn.

My Soul. Why should the imagination of a man
Long past his prime remember things that are
Emblematical of love and war?
Think of ancestral night that can,
If but imagination scorn the earth
And intellect its wandering
To this and that and t'other thing,
Deliver from the crime of death and birth.

My Self. Montashigi,[2] third of his family,
fashioned it
Five hundred years ago, about it lie
Flowers from I know not what embroidery —
Heart's purple — and all these I set
For emblems of the day against the tower
Emblematical of the night,
And claim as by a soldier's right
A charter to commit the crime once more.

1. Junzo Sato was the Japanese consul in Portland, Oregon who gave Yeats the ceremonial sword (see p. 810, note 3).
2. The maker of the sword.

My Soul. Such fullness in that quarter overflows
And falls into the basin of the mind
That man is stricken deaf and dumb and blind,
For intellect no longer knows
Is from the *Ought*, or *Knower* from the *Known* —
That is to say, ascends to Heaven;
Only the dead can be forgiven;
But when I think of that my tongue's a stone.

II

My Self. A living man is blind and drinks his drop.
What matter if the ditches are impure?
What matter if I live it all once more?
Endure that toil of growing up;
The ignominy of boyhood; the distress
Of boyhood changing into man;
The unfinished man and his pain
Brought face to face with his own clumsiness;

The finished man among his enemies? —
How in the name of Heaven can he escape
That defiling and disfigured shape
The mirror of malicious eyes
Casts upon his eyes until at last
He thinks that shape must be his shape?
And what's the good of an escape
If honour find him in the wintry blast?

I am content to live it all again
And yet again, if it be life to pitch
Into the frog-spawn of a blind man's ditch,
A blind man battering blind men;
Or into that most fecund ditch of all,
The folly that man does
Or must suffer, if he woos
A proud woman not kindred of his soul.

I am content to follow to its source
Every event in action or in thought;
Measure the lot; forgive myself the lot!
When such as I cast out remorse
So great a sweetness flows into the breast
We must laugh and we must sing,
We are blest by everything,
Everything we look upon is blest.

[Throughout his mature career, Yeats wrote poems like the following one, in which he reviewed his life's purpose and commitments, celebrated his chosen friends and chosen ground, and rededicated himself to all of them.]

Coole Park and Ballylee, 1931

Under my window-ledge[1] the waters race,
Otters below and moor-hens on the top,
Run for a mile undimmed in Heaven's face
Then darkening through 'dark' Raftery's 'cellar' drop,[2]
Run underground, rise in a rocky place
In Coole demesne, and there to finish up
Spread to a lake and drop into a hole.
What's water but the generated soul?[3]

Upon the border of that lake's a wood
Now all dry sticks under a wintry sun,
And in a copse of beeches there I stood,
For Nature's pulled her tragic buskin on
And all the rant's a mirror of my mood:
At sudden thunder of the mounting swan
I turned about and looked where branches break
The glittering reaches of the flooded lake.

Another emblem there! That stormy white
But seems a concentration of the sky;
And, like the soul, it sails into the sight
And in the morning's gone, no man knows why;
And is so lovely that it sets to right
What knowledge or its lack had set awry,
So arrogantly pure, a child might think
It can be murdered with a spot of ink.

Sound of a stick upon the floor, a sound
From somebody that toils from chair to chair;[4]
Beloved books that famous hands have bound,
Old marble heads, old pictures everywhere;
Great rooms where travelled men and children found
Content or joy; a last inheritor[5]
Where none has reigned that lacked a name and fame
Or out of folly into folly came.

A spot whereon the founders lived and died
Seemed once more dear than life; ancestral trees,

1. At the tower in Ballylee, Co. Galway.
2. The river goes underground before resurfacing in the lakes of Coole demesne. Antoine Raftery (*c.*1784-1835) was the blind — hence 'dark' — Irish poet associated with Ballylee.
3. In neo-Platonic lore, water was considered the generating source of souls.
4. Lady Gregory, aged and infirm; she died in 1932.
5. Lady Gregory's heir, Robert, was killed in the Great War. Hence the ancestral house devolves, guardianless, into an era where 'all is changed'.

Or gardens rich in memory glorified
Marriages, alliances and families,
And every bride's ambition satisfied.
Where fashion or mere fantasy decrees
We shift about — all that great glory spent —
Like some poor Arab tribesman and his tent.

We were the last romantics[6] — chose for theme
Traditional sanctity and loveliness;
Whatever's written in what poets name
The book the people; whatever most can bless
The mind of man or elevate a rhyme;
But all is changed, that high horse riderless,[7]
Though mounted in that saddle Homer rode
Where the swan drifts upon a darkening flood.

6. The attempt made by Lady Gregory, J.M. Synge and Yeats to create an art that embraced what they considered the patrician values of the Anglo-Irish and the traditional folkways and beliefs of the native Irish country people.
7. Pegasus, the winged horse of inspiration. Yeats suggests that an uninspired age is about to obliterate the high pitch of mind and achievement which his Irish literary movement had attained.

Mohini Chatterjee[1]

I asked if I should pray,
But the Brahmin said,
'Pray for nothing, say
Every night in bed,
"I have been a king,
I have been a slave,
Nor is there anything,
Fool, rascal, knave,
That I have not been,
And yet upon my breast
A myriad heads have lain."'

That he might set at rest
A boy's turbulent days
Mohini Chatterjee
Spoke these, or words like these.
I add in commentary,
'Old lovers yet may have
All that time denied —
Grave is heaped on grave
That they be satisfied —
Over the blackened earth
The old troops parade,
Birth is heaped on birth
That such cannonade
May thunder time away,
Birth-hour and death-hour meet,
Or, as great sages say,
Men dance on deathless feet.'

1928

1. Mohini Chatterjee visited Dublin in 1885.

[A thought which Yeats stated simply to Ethel Mannin in a letter in 1938 is explored in greater complexity in 'Byzantium': 'To me all things are made of the conflict of two states of consciousness, beings or persons which die each other's life, live each other's death.' The poem works by analogue and association: Byzantium, its dome, its Emperor's pavement, smithies and golden metal — all suggestive of perfected form, of a pure and absolute condition — are analogues for the purged state of the soul once it has been freed from the complexities, the mire and blood, the bitter furies and gong-tormented predicament it suffers in time and in the body. Yeats's first idea for the poem was to describe souls being carried to Paradise on the backs of dolphins.]

Byzantium

The unpurged images of day recede;
The Emperor's drunken soldiery are abed;
Night resonance recedes, night-walkers' song
After great cathedral gong;
A starlit or a moonlit dome disdains
All that man is,
All mere complexities,
The fury and the mire of human veins.

Before me floats an image, man or shade,[1]
Shade more than man, more image than a shade;
For Hades' bobbin[2] bound in mummy-cloth
May unwind the winding path;
A mouth that has no moisture and no breath
Breathless mouths may summon;
I hail the superhuman;
I call it death-in-life and life-in-death.

Miracle, bird or golden handiwork,
More miracle than bird or handiwork,
Planted on the star-lit golden bough,
Can like the cocks of Hades crow,

1. Since Byzantium is both a city in time and an imagined abode of spirits in an afterlife, the population may be conceived as either living or dead; or as the dead dreaming back through their lives or the living encountering their death.
2. Suggestive of time being reeled and unreeled between Hades, the land of the dead, and the land of the living.

Or, by the moon embittered, scorn aloud
In glory of changeless metal
Common bird or petal
And all complexities of mire or blood.

At midnight on the Emperor's pavement flit
Flames that no faggot feeds, nor steel has lit,
Nor storm disturbs, flames begotten of flame,
Where blood-begotten spirits come
And all complexities of fury leave,
Dying into a dance,
An agony of trance,
An agony of flame that cannot singe a sleeve.

Astraddle on the dolphin's mire and blood,[3]
Spirit after spirit! The smithies break the flood,
The golden smithies of the Emperor!
Marbles of the dancing floor
Break bitter furies of complexity,
Those images that yet
Fresh images beget,
That dolphin-torn, that gong-tormented sea.

1930

3. A natural creature bearing the souls of the dead out of nature, the dolphin is associated with both spirit and body.

from: WORDS FOR MUSIC PERHAPS AND OTHER POEMS (1932)

['Crazy Jane talks with the Bishop' and the two poems that follow it are from a sequence entitled 'Words For Music Perhaps', although Yeats realized that was 'only a name, nobody will sing them.' Louis MacNeice has drawn attention to the probable influence of J. M. Synge, and A. N. Jeffares notes in particular Synge's translations of François Villon, in the imagining of Crazy Jane.]

Crazy Jane talks with the Bishop

I met the Bishop on the road
And much said he and I.
'Those breasts are flat and fallen now,
Those veins must soon be dry;
Live in a heavenly mansion,
Not in some foul sty.'

'Fair and foul are near of kin,
And fair needs foul,' I cried.
'My friends are gone, but that's a truth
Nor grave nor bed denied,
Learned in bodily lowliness
And in the heart's pride.

'A woman can be proud and stiff
When on love intent;
But Love has pitched his mansion in
The place of excrement;
For nothing can be sole or whole
That has not been rent.'

After Long Silence

Speech after long silence; it is right,
All other lovers being estranged or dead,
Unfriendly lamplight hid under its shade,
The curtains drawn upon unfriendly night,
That we descant and yet again descant
Upon the supreme theme of Art and Song:
Bodily decrepitude is wisdom; young
We loved each other and were ignorant.

The Delphic Oracle upon Plotinus

Behold that great Plotinus[1] swim,
Buffeted by such seas;
Bland Rhadamanthus beckons him,
But the Golden Race looks dim,
Salt blood blocks his eyes.

Scattered on the level grass
Or winding through the grove
Plato there and Minos pass,
There stately Pythagoras
And all the choir of Love.[2]

August 19, 1931

1. Third-century philosopher, founder of Neo-Platonic philosophy, whose works were translated by Stephen MacKenna. This poem is based on MacKenna's translation of an account (in Porphyry's *Life of Plotinus*) of what the oracle at Delphi said when he was asked where the soul of Plotinus had gone after death.
2. Yeats imagines the souls of the blessed (Plato and Pythagoras), 'the Golden Race' and the classical sons of God (the judging figures of Rhadamanthus and Minos among them) watching as the soul of Plotinus crosses out of the turmoil of physical life.

from: A WOMAN YOUNG AND OLD (1933)

A Last Confession

What lively lad most pleasured me
Of all that with me lay?
I answer that I gave my soul
And loved in misery,
But had great pleasure with a lad
That I loved bodily.

Flinging from his arms I laughed
To think his passion such
He fancied that I gave a soul
Did but our bodies touch,
And laughed upon his breast to think
Beast gave beast as much.

I gave what other women gave
That stepped out of their clothes,
But when this soul, its body off,
Naked to naked goes,
He it has found shall find therein
What none other knows,

And give his own and take his own
And rule in his own right;
And though it loved in misery
Close and cling so tight,
There's not a bird of day[1] that dare
Extinguish that delight.

1. Presumably a harbinger of the dawn chorus, announcing the end of the lovers' night.

from: A FULL MOON IN MARCH (1935)

[*'Ribh at the Tomb of Baile and Aillinn'*, like the two poems that follow it here, belongs to a group entitled 'Supernatural Songs'. It describes what happens when 'this soul, its body off,/Naked to naked goes,' ('A Last Confession'). Ribh is a hermit figure, a repository of Indian and Celtic lore.]

Ribh at the Tomb of Baile and Aillinn

Because you have found me in the pitch-dark night
With open book you ask me what I do.
Mark and digest my tale, carry it afar
To those that never saw this tonsured head
Nor heard this voice that ninety years have cracked.
Of Baile and Aillinn[1] you need not speak,
All know their tale, all know what leaf and twig,
What juncture of the apple and the yew,
Surmount their bones; but speak what none have
heard.

The miracle that gave them such a death
Transfigured to pure substance what had once
Been bone and sinew; when such bodies join
There is no touching here, nor touching there,
Nor straining joy, but whole is joined to whole;
For the intercourse of angels is a light
Where for its moment both seem lost, consumed.

Here in the pitch-dark atmosphere above
The trembling of the apple and the yew,
Here on the anniversary of their death,
The anniversary of their first embrace,
Those lovers, purified by tragedy,
Hurry into each other's arms; these eyes,
By water, herb and solitary prayer
Made aquiline, are open to that light.
Though somewhat broken by the leaves, that light
Lies in a circle on the grass; therein
I turn the pages of my holy book.[2]

1. Baile and Aillinn were legendary Irish lovers, buried beneath a yew tree and an apple tree respectively.
2. The narrative content here constitutes one aspect of what the poem imports, but equally important is the 'purified' feel of the language, the way a state of vision is suggested in the accumulation of words like water, herb, prayer, aquiline, light, leaves, circle, grass, holy.

Whence had they come?

Eternity is passion, girl or boy
Cry at the onset of their sexual joy
'For ever and for ever'; then awake
Ignorant what Dramatis Personae[1] spake;
A passion-driven exultant man sings out
Sentences that he has never thought;

1. The powers that generate passion are conceived by Yeats as pre-existing dramatic roles that individual lovers must act out.

The Flagellant lashes those submissive loins
Ignorant what that dramatist enjoins,
What master made the lash. Whence had they come,
The hand and lash that beat down frigid Rome?
What sacred drama through her body heaved
When world-transforming Charlemagne[2] was
conceived?

2. Charlemagne (*c.* 742-814), king of the Franks, transformed the world by becoming Holy Roman Emperor and establishing his court at Aachen as a centre of learning.

Meru

Civilisation is hooped together, brought
Under a rule, under the semblance of peace
By manifold illusion; but man's life is thought,
And he, despite his terror, cannot cease
Ravening through century after century,
Ravening, raging, and uprooting that he may come
Into the desolation of reality:
Egypt and Greece, good-bye, and good-bye, Rome!
Hermits upon Mount Meru[1] or Everest,
Caverned in night under the drifted snow,
Or where that snow and winter's dreadful blast
Beat down upon their naked bodies, know[2]
That day brings round the night, that before dawn
His glory and his monuments are gone.

1. In Hindu mythology, a mountain at the centre of Paradise.
2. The wisdom of the hermits is of the kind attained by Ribh — and by the two Chinamen in 'Lapis Lazuli'; it is visionary, prophetic and continuous, with the synoptic view of reality that Yeats puts forward in *A Vision.*

from:
NEW POEMS (1938)

[During Yeats's last years, his poetic effort was to discover a way of triumphing over the destructive circumstances of his own bodily ailments and of outfacing the violent events and ever more violent premonitions that assailed Europe in the late 1930s. In poem after poem, he sought by meditation upon images and by the generation of emotional intensity to concentrate consciousness to the point where it might overbear the mortal and historical conditions that it had to suffer. Here a piece of carved lapis lazuli focuses his meditation until the clamour of political debate and dread of the coming war are comprehended as part of a deep recurrent pattern of reality.]

Lapis Lazuli

For Harry Clifton

I have heard that hysterical women[1] say
They are sick of the palette and fiddle-bow,
Of poets that are always gay,
For everybody knows or else should know
That if nothing drastic is done
Aeroplane and Zeppelin will come out,
Pitch like King Billy bomb-balls in
Until the town lie beaten flat.

All perform their tragic play,
There struts Hamlet, there is Lear,
That's Ophelia, that Cordelia;
Yet they, should the last scene be there,
The great stage curtain about to drop,
If worthy their prominent part in the play,
Do not break up their lines to weep.
They know that Hamlet and Lear are gay;
Gaiety transfiguring all that dread.
All men have aimed at, found and lost;
Black out; Heaven blazing into the head:
Tragedy wrought to its uttermost.
Though Hamlet rambles and Lear rages,
And all the drop-scenes drop at once
Upon a hundred thousand stages,
It[2] cannot grow by an inch or an ounce.

On their own feet they came, or on shipboard,
Camel-back, horse-back, ass-back, mule-back,
Old civilisations put to the sword.
Then they and their wisdom went to rack:
No handiwork of Callimachus,[3]
Who handled marble as if it were bronze,
Made draperies that seemed to rise
When sea-wind swept the corner, stands;
His long lamp-chimney shaped like the stem
Of a slender palm, stood but a day;

1. Yeats disdains strident propagandists who would have poets desert the bohemian aestheticism of the Nineties for the political commitment of the Thirties. He subtly demeans the technological majesty of Zeppelin airships by associating them with the 'bomb-balls' that King William fired during the battle of the Boyne in 1690.
2. The 'it' refers back to 'All men have aimed at, found and lost ... Tragedy wrought to its uttermost.' These lines in turn are glosses upon the tragic destinies embodied by Shakespeare's characters Hamlet, Lear, Cordelia and Ophelia. A précis of the meaning here might run: the poetic imagination offers mankind a sense of the volume and limits of reality, and creates examples of the proper conduct in face of that reality which it is a failure not to imitate.
3. A Greek sculptor of the fifth century B.C. who made a golden lamp for the Erechtheum in Athens.

All things fall and are built again,
And those that build them again are gay.

Two Chinamen, behind them a third,
Are carved in lapis lazuli,
Over them flies a long-legged bird,
A symbol of longevity;
The third, doubtless a serving-man,
Carries a musical instrument.

Every discoloration of the stone,
Every accidental crack or dent,
Seems a water-course or an avalanche,
Or lofty slope where it still snows
Though doubtless plum or cherry-branch
Sweetens the little half-way house
Those Chinamen climb towards, and I
Delight to imagine them seated there;
There, on the mountain and the sky,
On all the tragic scene they stare.
One asks for mournful melodies;
Accomplished fingers begin to play.
Their eyes mid many wrinkles, their eyes,
Their ancient, glittering eyes, are gay.

['An Acre of Grass', like the two poems that follow it, arises from the aging Yeats's impulse towards summation and recapitulation. These are works written in an old man's 'fiery shorthand', and they prepare the way for the much more deeply pondered work of self-estimation and self-inquisition that goes on in 'The Municipal Gallery Revisited', 'The Circus Animals' Desertion' and 'The Man and the Echo'.]

An Acre of Grass

Picture and book remain,
An acre of green grass[1]
For air and exercise,
Now strength of body goes;
Midnight, an old house
Where nothing stirs but a mouse.

My temptation is quiet.
Here at life's end
Neither loose imagination,
Nor the mill of the mind
Consuming its rag and bone,
Can make the truth known.

1. In 1932 Yeats leased Riversdale, a house in Rathfarnham, just outside Dublin, with a fruit garden, a flower garden and lawns.

Grant me an old man's frenzy,
Myself must I remake
Till I am Timon and Lear
Or that William Blake
Who beat upon the wall
Till Truth obeyed his call;

A mind Michael Angelo knew
That can pierce the clouds,[2]
Or inspired by frenzy
Shake the dead in their shrouds;
Forgotten else by mankind,
An old man's eagle mind.

2. Here Yeats's poetry as usual recreates the feel of the state of mind to which he aspires. He does this by piling up names of figures who possessed unappeasable intellectual and creative appetites: Shakespeare's Timon of Athens and King Lear, the artist Michelangelo (1475-1564) and the poet William Blake (1757-1827).

What Then?

His chosen comrades thought at school
He must grow a famous man;
He thought the same and lived by rule,
All his twenties crammed with toil;
'What then?' sang Plato's ghost. 'What then?'

Everything he wrote was read,
After certain years he won
Sufficient money for his need,
Friends that have been friends indeed;
'What then?' sang Plato's ghost. 'What then?'

All his happier dreams came true —
A small old house, wife, daughter, son,
Grounds where plum and cabbage grew,
Poets and Wits about him drew;
'What then?' sang Plato's ghost. 'What then?'

'The work is done,' grown old he thought,
'According to my boyish plan;
Let the fools rage, I swerved in naught,
Something to perfection brought';
But louder sang that ghost, 'What then?'

Beautiful Lofty Things

Beautiful lofty things: O'Leary's noble head;
My father upon the Abbey stage, before him a
raging crowd:

'This Land of Saints,' and then as the applause died out,
'Of plaster Saints'; his beautiful mischievous head thrown back.
Standish O'Grady[1] supporting himself between the tables
Speaking to a drunken audience high nonsensical words;
Augusta Gregory seated at her great ormolu table,
Her eightieth winter approaching: 'Yesterday he threatened my life.
I told him that nightly from six to seven I sat at this table,
The blinds drawn up'; Maud Gonne at Howth station waiting a train,
Pallas Athene[2] in that straight back and arrogant head:
All the Olympians; a thing never known again.

1. With the exception of Standish O'Grady (1846-1928), the historian and novelist, all the characters mentioned in this poem are referred to in the introduction to this section.
2. All through his life Yeats persisted in linking Maud Gonne with heroines of classical antiquity, in this case the famous grey-eyed goddess of the Greeks.

The O'Rahilly

Sing of the O'Rahilly,[1]
Do not deny his right;
Sing a 'the' before his name;
Allow that he, despite
All those learned historians,
Established it for good;
He wrote out that word himself,
He christened himself with blood.
How goes the weather?

Sing of the O'Rahilly
That had such little sense
He told Pearse and Connolly
He'd gone to great expense
Keeping all the Kerry men
Out of that crazy fight;
That he might be there himself
Had travelled half the night.
How goes the weather?

'Am I such a craven that
I should not get the word
But for what some travelling man
Had heard I had not heard?
Then on Pearse and Connolly
He fixed a bitter look:
'Because I helped to wind the clock
I come to hear it strike.'
How goes the weather?

What remains to sing about
But of the death he met
Stretched under a doorway
Somewhere off Henry Street;
They that found him found upon
The door above his head
'Here died the O'Rahilly.
R.I.P.' writ in blood.
How goes the weather?

1. In Irish usage, the definite article added to a surname denotes the leader of the clan/family of that name. The O'Rahilly (1875-1916) was shot during the Easter Rising, in circumstances which Yeats's ballad narrates.

Come Gather round me, Parnellites

Come gather round me, Parnellites,[1]
And praise our chosen man;
Stand upright on your legs awhile,
Stand upright while you can,
For soon we lie where he is laid,
And he is underground;
Come fill up all those glasses
And pass the bottle round.

And here's a cogent reason,
And I have many more,
He fought the might of England
And saved the Irish poor,
Whatever good a farmer's got
He brought it all to pass;
And here's another reason,
That Parnell loved a lass.[2]

And here's a final reason,
He was of such a kind
Every man that sings a song
Keeps Parnell in his mind.

1. Supporters of the great parliamentary leader and agitator for Irish Home Rule, Charles Stewart Parnell (1846-91).
2. Mrs Katharine O'Shea (1845-1921), Parnell's mistress. In 1889, her husband, Captain William Henry O'Shea, cited Parnell as co-respondent in his divorce case.

For Parnell was a proud man,
No prouder trod the ground,
And a proud man's a lovely man,
So pass the bottle round.

The Bishops and the Party[3]
That tragic story made,
A husband that had sold his wife
And after that betrayed;
But stories that live longest
Are sung above the glass,
And Parnell loved his country,
And Parnell loved his lass.

3. The scandal of the divorce case lost Parnell the support of persons of conventional political and religious views.

The Great Day

Hurrah for revolution and more cannon-shot!
A beggar upon horseback lashes a beggar on foot.
Hurrah for revolution and cannon come again!
The beggars have changed places, but the lash goes
on.

[In 'The Municipal Gallery Revisited' Yeats makes a formal claim that he and the members of the literary movement he founded are to be considered along with the famous revolutionaries, politicians and men of action as makers of modern Ireland. The poem can be read as an old man's boast to the young self who wrote 'To Ireland in the Coming Times'.]

The Municipal Gallery Revisited

I

Around me the images of thirty years:[1]
An ambush; pilgrims at the water-side;
Casement[2] upon trial, half hidden by the bars,
Guarded; Griffith[3] staring in hysterical pride;
Kevin O'Higgins'[4] countenance that wears
A gentle questioning look that cannot hide
A soul incapable of remorse or rest;
A revolutionary soldier kneeling to be blessed;

II

An Abbot or Archbishop with an upraised hand
Blessing the Tricolour. 'This is not,' I say,
'The dead Ireland of my youth, but an Ireland
The poets have imagined, terrible and gay.'
Before a woman's portrait suddenly I stand,
Beautiful and gentle in her Venetian way.
I met her all but fifty years ago
For twenty minutes in some studio.

III

Heart-smitten with emotion I sink down,
My heart recovering with covered eyes;
Wherever I had looked I had looked upon
My permanent or impermanent images:
Augusta Gregory's son; her sister's son,
Hugh Lane, 'onlie begetter'[5] of all these;
Hazel Lavery[6] living and dying, that tale
As though some ballad-singer had sung it all;

IV

Mancini's[7] portrait of Augusta Gregory,
'Greatest since Rembrandt,' according to John
Synge;
A great ebullient portrait certainly;
But where is the brush that could show anything
Of all that pride and that humility?
And I am in despair that time may bring
Approved patterns of women or of men
But not that selfsame excellence again.

V

My mediaeval[8] knees lack health until they bend,
But in that woman, in that household where
Honour had lived so long, all lacking found.

1. The poem was written in 1937; the preceding decades had seen Yeats involved with J. M. Synge and Lady Gregory in the Abbey Theatre, and covered the years of political agitation and violent events surrounding the establishment of the Irish Free State.
2. Sir Roger Casement (1864-1916) joined the Irish National Volunteers in 1913. He was found guilty of high treason for arms-dealing in Germany, and was hanged in Pentonville prison, England.
3. Arthur Griffith (1872-1922), Sinn Féin activist, political theorist, editor of the *United Irishman* 1898-1906.
4. Kevin O'Higgins (1892-1927), hard-line minister for justice in the Irish Free State, assassinated on his way to Mass.
5. The quotation is from the opening of the dedication to Shakespeare's Sonnets:
'TO THE ONLIE BEGETTER OF THESE . . .'
6. The second wife of the painter, Sir John Lavery (1856-1941).
7. Antonio Mancini (1852-1930), Italian artist.
8. Medieval perhaps in the sense that his knees have a medieval impulse to bend in respect, as in a court or church.

Childless I thought, 'My children may find here
Deep-rooted things,' but never foresaw its end,
And now that end has come I have not wept;
No fox can foul the lair the badger swept —[9]

VI

(An image out of Spenser and the common tongue).
John Synge, I and Augusta Gregory, thought
All that we did, all that we said or sang
Must come from contact with the soil, from that
Contact everything Antaeus-like[10] grew strong.
We three alone in modern times had brought
Everything down to that sole test again,
Dream of the noble and the beggar-man.

VII

And here's John Synge himself, that rooted man,
'Forgetting human words,' a grave deep face.
You that would judge me, do not judge alone
This book or that, come to this hallowed place
Where my friends' portraits hang and look thereon;
Ireland's history in their lineaments trace;
Think where man's glory most begins and ends,
And say my glory was I had such friends.

9. Edmund Spenser, 'The Ruines of Time': 'He now is gone, the whiles the Foxe is crept/Into the hole, the which the badger swept.'
10. In Greek mythology, Antaeus was a son of the earth, whose strength was renewed by contact with it.

from: LAST POEMS (1939)

[As in the first section of 'Nineteen Hundred and Nineteen', in 'The Statues' Yeats juxtaposes modern Ireland with ancient Greece in order to illuminate and extend his understanding of both. To commemorate the death of Patrick Pearse and the other leaders of the Easter Rising, a statue of Cuchulain, Celtic warrior and type of heroic national virtue, stands in the General Post Office in Dublin. The image of Cuchulain moulded these leaders' sense of destiny, so the logic of the poem might be condensed thus: we know that the mathematical and philosophical system of Pythagoras lay behind the perfection of Greek sculpture; we also know that, for the Greeks, sculpture gave to beauty an ideal form and to passion an ultimate focus. So when Pearse focussed a national destiny by invoking the ideal form of Cuchulain, he was positing — and imaginatively verifying — the existence of an ancient archetypal reality similar to that which Pythagoras brought under intellectual sway. Both Pearse and Pythagoras thereby create conditions for the generation of images which would influence national life, and saved their respective nations from 'vague immensities' and 'formless . . . fury'.]

The Statues

Pythagoras planned it. Why did the people stare?
His numbers, though they moved or seemed to move
In marble or in bronze, lacked character.
But boys and girls, pale from the imagined love
Of solitary beds, knew what they were,
That passion could bring character enough,
And pressed at midnight in some public place
Live lips upon a plummet-measured face.

No! Greater than Pythagoras, for the men
That with a mallet or a chisel modelled these
Calculations that look but casual flesh, put down
All Asiatic vague immensities,
And not the banks of oars that swam upon
The many-headed foam at Salamis.[1]
Europe put off that foam when Phidias
Gave women dreams and dreams their looking-glass.

One image crossed the many-headed, sat
Under the tropic shade, grew round and slow,
No Hamlet thin from eating flies, a fat
Dreamer of the Middle Ages. Empty eyeballs knew
That knowledge increases unreality, that
Mirror on mirror mirrored is all the show.
When gong and conch declare the hour to bless
Grimalkin crawls to Buddha's emptiness.[2]

When Pearse summoned Cuchulain to his side,
What stalked through the Post Office? What intellect,

1. Yeats imagines that the supremacy displayed by the Greeks when they defeated the Persians at the battle of Salamis (480 B.C.) had its origin in the same faculty that allowed Greek sculptors like Phidias (*c.*500–*c.*432 B.C.) to create definitive and imposing forms.
2. This stanza is a variation upon Yeats's constant theme that all things are made from the conflict of states of consciousness which die each other's life and live each other's death. When west defeated east at Salamis, calculation defeated vagueness, form imposed upon emptiness; and yet, since the Buddha image was developed (in Yeats's opinion) from a Greek sculptural influence, east lives by that instance of western death — the death of one form into another. A similar transition involving the intercourse of exhaustion and fulfilment occurs when Grimalkin, image of witchcraft-haunted medieval Europe, crawls to Buddha, symbol of the fullest illumination.

What calculation, number, measurement, replied?
We Irish, born into that ancient sect
But thrown upon this filthy modern tide
And by its formless spawning fury wrecked,
Climb to our proper dark, that we may trace
The lineaments of a plummet-measured face.

April 9, 1938

[Yeats's title, 'News for the Delphic Oracle', might be thought to play with the irreverent import of the phrase, 'I've got news for you.' The Delphic Oracle's version of the afterlife is revised and rendered less ethereal and far more sexually rambunctious.]

News for the Delphic Oracle

I

There all the golden codgers[1] lay,
There the silver dew,
And the great water sighed for love,
And the wind sighed too.
Man-picker Niamh[2] leant and sighed
By Oisin on the grass;
There sighed amid his choir of love
Tall Pythagoras.[3]
Plotinus came and looked about,
The salt-flakes on his breast,
And having stretched and yawned awhile
Lay sighing like the rest.

II

Straddling each a dolphin's back
And steadied by a fin,
Those Innocents re-live their death,
Their wounds open again.
The ecstatic waters laugh because
Their cries are sweet and strange,
Through their ancestral patterns dance,
And the brute dolphins plunge
Until, in some cliff-sheltered bay
Where wades the choir of love
Proffering its sacred laurel crowns,
They pitch their burdens off.[4]

III

Slim adolescence that a nymph has stripped,
Peleus on Thetis stares.[5]
Her limbs are delicate as an eyelid,
Love has blinded him with tears;
But Thetis' belly listens.
Down the mountain walls
From where Pan's[6] cavern is
Intolerable music falls.
Foul goat-head, brutal arm appear,
Belly, shoulder, bum,
Flash fishlike; nymphs and satyrs
Copulate in the foam.

1. The familiar term, denoting indolence and a certain amiability, demystifies the life of the immortals.
2. Niamh 'picked' Oisin for her 'man' when she rode off with him to Tir-na-n-Og.
3. See note 2 to 'The Delphic Oracle upon Plotinus' (p. 819).
4. This stanza imagines the arrival into the classical paradise of the souls of the Holy Innocents slain by King Herod at the birth of Christ. That Judaic spirits are now being admitted to the Hellenic paradise is 'news' indeed for the Delphic oracle.
5. In Greek mythology, Peleus captured and married the nereid, Thetis. Yeats was familiar with a picture of their marriage, by Nicolas Poussin, which hung in the National Gallery of Ireland.
6. A fertility god, horned and goat-footed, flute-player and dweller in caverns.

[Yeats said that the refrain of 'Long-legged Fly' was about the importance of silence in the lives of creative people. The poem concerns the mysterious efficacy that a deed or an act of mind can achieve for the whole of history that follows it.]

Long-legged Fly

That civilisation may not sink,
Its great battle lost,
Quiet the dog, tether the pony
To a distant post;
Our master Caesar is in the tent
Where the maps are spread,
His eyes fixed upon nothing,
A hand under his head.
Like a long-legged fly upon the stream
His mind moves upon silence.

That the topless towers be burnt
And men recall that face,
Move most gently if move you must
In this lonely place.

She thinks, part woman, three parts a child,[1]
That nobody looks; her feet
Practise a tinker shuffle
Picked up on a street.
Like a long-legged fly upon the stream
Her mind moves upon silence.

That girls at puberty may find
The first Adam in their thought,
Shut the door of the Pope's chapel,
Keep those children out.
There on that scaffolding reclines
Michael Angelo.[2]
With no more sound than the mice make
His hand moves to and fro.
Like a long-legged fly upon the stream
His mind moves upon silence.

1. Helen of Troy, whom the dramatist Christopher Marlowe imagined as the agent of destruction of Troy's 'topless towers'.
2. He is imagined at work on his painting of the creation of Adam in the Sistine Chapel of the Vatican Palace.

[The title 'High Talk' seems a mixture of self-mockery and self-approbation. Malachi Stilt-Jack, a reckless, rickety name, all of a piece with the improvisational nature of the poem's movement, is employed to flaunt Yeats's high style — of which the stilts are a sort of caricature. Yeats dramatizes himself once again in a traditional 'role' which allows the personal voice great latitude and ecstasy.]

High Talk

Processions that lack high stilts[1] have nothing that catches the eye.
What if my great-granddad had a pair that were twenty foot high,
And mine were but fifteen foot, no modern[2] stalks upon higher,
Some rogue of the world stole them to patch up a fence or a fire.
Because piebald ponies, led bears, caged lions, make but poor shows,
Because children demand Daddy-long-legs upon his timber toes,
Because women in the upper storeys demand a face at the pane,
That patching old heels they may shriek, I take to chisel and plane.

Malachi Stilt-Jack am I, whatever I learned has run wild,
From collar to collar, from stilt to stilt, from father to child.
All metaphor, Malachi, stilts and all. A barnacle goose
Far up in the stretches of night; night splits and the dawn breaks loose;
I, through the terrible novelty of light, stalk on, stalk on;
Those great sea-horses bare their teeth and laugh at the dawn.

1. As a boy, Yeats owned a pair of stilts and learned to walk on them.
2. Mention of the 'modern' makes explicit the poem's status as a parable of Yeats's romantic reckless old age among the earnest young political poets of the 1930s.

[In 'The Circus Animals' Desertion', the notion of poetic activity as a circus is probably linked to the carnival imagery of the preceding poem, as is the association of different poetic themes with different acts and animals in the show.]

The Circus Animals' Desertion

I

I sought a theme and sought for it in vain,
I sought it daily for six weeks or so.
Maybe at last, being but a broken man,
I must be satisfied with my heart,[1] although
Winter and summer till old age began
My circus animals were all on show,
Those stilted boys, that burnished chariot,
Lion and woman and the Lord knows what.

II

What can I but enumerate old themes?[2]
First that sea-rider Oisin led by the nose

1. Yeats believed two 'counter-truths' which this poem explores: that personal feeling — 'heart' — is the source of his art, but that its expression should be supra-personal. The 'I' of the poet has to be reborn as a 'masterful' image.
2. The 'old themes' that Yeats goes on to enumerate in the second section of the poem were treated first in his narrative poem, *The Wanderings of Oisin* (1889); secondly, in his early play, *The Countess Cathleen* (1899) — both acts of homage and courtship to his 'faery bride', Maud Gonne, whose soul he believed to be 'enslaved' to politics; and thirdly, in his late play, *The Death of Cuchulain*, where a Fool and a Blind Man provide an anti-heroic commentary on the protagonist's tragic end.

Through three enchanted islands, allegorical
 dreams,
Vain gaiety, vain battle, vain repose,
Themes of the embittered heart, or so it seems,
That might adorn old songs or courtly shows;
But what cared I that set him on to ride,
I, starved for the bosom of his faery bride?

And then a counter-truth filled out its play,
The Countess Cathleen was the name I gave it;
She, pity-crazed, had given her soul away,
But masterful Heaven had intervened to save it.
I thought my dear must her own soul destroy,
So did fanaticism and hate enslave it,
And this brought forth a dream and soon enough
This dream itself had all my thought and love.

And when the Fool and Blind Man stole the bread
Cuchulain fought the ungovernable sea;
Heart-mysteries there, and yet when all is said
It was the dream itself enchanted me:
Character isolated by a deed
To engross the present and dominate memory.
Players and painted stage took all my love,
And not those things that they were emblems of.

III

Those masterful images because complete
Grew in pure mind, but out of what began?
A mound of refuse or the sweepings of a street,
Old kettles, old bottles, and a broken can,
Old iron, old bones, old rags, that raving slut
Who keeps the till. Now that my ladder's[3] gone,
I must lie down where all the ladders start,
In the foul rag-and-bone shop of the heart.

3. An echo of the image of the stilt in 'High Talk'.

Politics

'In our time the destiny of man presents its meaning in political terms.' — THOMAS MANN

How can I, that girl standing there,
My attention fix
On Roman or on Russian
Or on Spanish politics?
Yet here's a travelled man that knows
What he talks about,
And there's a politician
That has read and thought,
And maybe what they say is true
Of war and war's alarms,
But O that I were young again
And held her in my arms!

[In 'The Man and the Echo' Yeats uses the convention of the echo poem to dramatize the way that human consciousness (The Man) feels compelled by a reality intuited at an uncrossable distance beyond itself (The Echo). In the dialogue that ensues between them, self-accusation and self-justification are maintained in strenuous equilibrium.]

The Man and the Echo

Man

In a cleft that's christened Alt[1]
Under broken stone I halt
At the bottom of a pit
That broad noon has never lit,
And shout a secret to the stone.
All that I have said and done,
Now that I am old and ill,
Turns into a question till
I lie awake night after night
And never get the answers right.
Did that play of mine[2] send out
Certain men the English shot?
Did words of mine put too great strain
On that woman's reeling brain?[3]
Could my spoken words have checked
That whereby a house lay wrecked?[4]
And all seems evil until I
Sleepless would lie down and die.

Echo

Lie down and die.

1. A glen on Knocknarea mountain, a rocky fastness such as an oracle or sibyl might inhabit.
2. *Cathleen ni Houlihan*, performed in 1902, with Maud Gonne in the title role, had a notably intoxicating effect upon nationalist audiences in Dublin (see p. 597).
3. Margot Ruddock, a young poet whom Yeats encouraged and flirted with, had had a breakdown in the course of a visit to him in 1936.
4. Coole Park, home of Lady Gregory, had been sold by the Department of Forestry to a contractor, who had demolished it.

Man

That were to shirk
The spiritual intellect's great work,
And shirk it in vain. There is no release
In a bodkin[5] or disease,
Nor can there be work so great
As that which cleans man's dirty slate.
While man can still his body keep
Wine or love drug him to sleep,
Waking he thanks the Lord that he
Has body and its stupidity,
But body gone he sleeps no more,
And till his intellect grows sure
That all's arranged in one clear view,
Pursues the thoughts that I pursue,
Then stands in judgment on his soul,
And, all work done, dismisses all
Out of intellect and sight
And sinks at last into the night.

Echo

Into the night.

Man

O Rocky Voice,
Shall we in that great night rejoice?
What do we know but that we face
One another in this place?
But hush, for I have lost the theme,
Its joy or night seem but a dream;
Up there some hawk or owl has struck,
Dropping out of sky or rock,
A stricken rabbit is crying out,
And its cry distracts my thought.

5. Hamlet, in his 'To be or not to be' soliloquy (*Hamlet*, III. 1. 56) considers suicide with 'a bare bodkin' as one way of escaping life's burdens.
6. The echo, bouncing back off rocks, is associated with the voice of sibyls, prophets and hermits, who gain divine authority by their sojourn in fastnesses.

['Cuchulain Comforted' is based on a prose note that Yeats made in early January 1939. It is written in *terza rima*, the three-line stanza form rhyming *ababcbcdc etc.* which Dante employed in *The Divine Comedy*. It is obviously no coincidence that Yeats, two weeks before his death, writes about Cuchulain's arrival in the land of the shades in a stanza that recalls the most famous underworld poem in Western literature. This is a deliberate ritual of farewell where the poet divests himself finally of heroic pride. Cuchulain, his alter ego who strides among the dead, is made to do things in common with cowards and outcasts and, as a result, attains a state where all purpose and function are realized in the song of the bird/soul.]

Cuchulain Comforted

A man that had six mortal wounds, a man
Violent and famous, strode among the dead;
Eyes stared out of the branches and were gone.

Then certain Shrouds that muttered head to head
Came and were gone. He leant upon a tree
As though to meditate on wounds and blood.

A Shroud that seemed to have authority
Among those bird-like things came, and let fall
A bundle of linen. Shrouds by two and three

Came creeping up because the man was still.
And thereupon that linen-carrier said:
'Your life can grow much sweeter if you will

'Obey your ancient rule and make a shroud;
Mainly because of what we only know
The rattle of those arms makes us afraid.

'We thread the needles' eyes, and all we do
All must together do.' That done, the man
Took up the nearest and began to sew.

'Now must we sing and sing the best we can,
But first you must be told our character:
Convicted cowards all, by kindred slain

'Or driven from home and left to die in fear.'
They sang, but had nor human tunes nor words,
Though all was done in common as before;

They had changed their throats and had the throats
of birds.[1]

January 13, 1939

1. In *The Death of Cuchulain*, the dying hero envisages his soul fluttering in front of him like a bird, and cries out with his last breath that 'it is about to sing'.

Biography/Bibliography

LIFE. William Butler Yeats born on 13 June 1865, at Sandymount Avenue, Dublin, eldest child of John Butler Yeats and Susan Mary (*née* Pollexfen). Until the age of sixteen, lives mainly in London, with many visits of varying duration to Sligo, his mother's home county. From 1881 until 1887, lives in Dublin as art student, student of mysticism and apprentice poet; becomes president of Dublin Hermetic Society and a friend of the old Fenian, John O'Leary; associates with various Dublin writers of his own generation such as the mystic AE, the Gaelic revivalist Douglas Hyde, and the poet Katharine Tynan. From 1887, establishes his characteristic pattern of life between Dublin and London, and works actively and resourcefully to establish an Irish literary movement that will release national potential and confirm the image of cultural identity at home and abroad. In 1889, publishes *The Wanderings of Oisin and Other Poems*; lectures on 'Sligo Fairies', edits a collection of Irish folktales and spends Christmas Day with Oscar Wilde. Meets Maud Gonne in 1889 and retains intense involvement with her for the next thirty years; works on his play *The Countess Cathleen* and on an edition of William Blake. In 1890 is initiated into the Order of the Golden Dawn; busy then for years with literary journeywork. Publishes *Countess Kathleen and Various Legends and Lyrics* in 1892; becomes active in founding The National Literary Society, which Douglas Hyde inaugurates in November with his famous lecture on 'The Necessity for De-Anglicizing Ireland'. Publishes his epoch-making *The Celtic Twilight* in 1893 and the next year meets Verlaine in Paris. These years see Yeats's consolidation as the voice of the new 'Celtic' movement in literature and his increasing commitment to the drama. Meets J. M. Synge in Paris in 1896. In 1897, stays with Lady Gregory at Coole Park, collects folklore with her and discusses the possibility of 'Celtic theatre'. Publishes *The Wind Among the Reeds* in 1899. *Cathleen ni Houlihan* produced in 1902; meets James Joyce. In 1903, Maud Gonne marries Major John MacBride, Yeats publishes *In the Seven Woods* and embarks upon a long lecture tour in the United States. The Abbey Theatre is founded in 1904 and for the next decade Yeats is thoroughly involved with its management, its controversies and its triumphs. A 'new' Yeats, less Celtic and more patrician, begins to emerge in the bitter aftermath of the *Playboy* riots (1907) and the rejection of Sir Hugh Lane's picture gallery scheme by Dublin Corporation (1913). Works intermittently with Ezra Pound as secretary, publishes *Responsibilities* in 1914, refuses a knighthood in 1915. In 1916, after the execution of Major MacBride for his part in the Easter Rising, Yeats again proposes to Maud Gonne and is refused, also proposes to and is refused by her daughter, Iseult. In 1917, purchases a Norman tower in County Galway and marries George Hyde-Lees. The tower begins to be restored in 1918 and to be used as summer home during the years of the Anglo-Irish War and the Irish Civil War. Anne Yeats born 1919, Michael Yeats, 1921. Yeats's increasing role as national poet now evident in his condemnation of British policy in Ireland at the Oxford Union in 1921, his appointment as Senator of the Free State in 1922 and the award of the Nobel Prize for Literature in 1923. During these years he is also active composing his esoteric thesaurus, *A Vision* (1925); at the height of his creative powers, he publishes *The Tower* (1928) and *The Winding Stair and Other Poems* (1933). Spends time with the Pound circle at Rapallo in Italy, lectures in the United States, broadcasts occasionally with the BBC. Briefly connected in 1933 with General Eoin O'Duffy's Blueshirt Movement. Remains active for the final years of his life, despite declining health, as dramatist, poet and man of letters, publishing the controversial *Oxford Book of Modern Verse* in 1936, his version of *The Ten Principal Upanishads* in 1937, and *New Poems* in 1938, when *Purgatory* was also produced. He died on 28 January 1939 at Roquebrune in the south of France and was reburied at Drumcliff, Co. Sligo, in accordance with his wishes, in September 1948.

CHIEF WRITINGS. The standard editions are: P. Allt and R. K. Alspach (eds), *The Variorum Edition of the Poems of W. B. Yeats* (London: Macmillan, 1957; corrected 3rd edition, 1966); R. K. Alspach and C.C. Alspach (eds), *The Variorum Edition of the Plays of W. B. Yeats* (New York: Macmillan, 1965; corrected 2nd printing, 1966); *The Collected Poems of W. B. Yeats* (London: Macmillan, 1933; 1949; 1950; eighth impression, 1956 et seq.); R. J. Finneran (ed.), *W. B. Yeats: The Poems. A New Edition* (London: Macmillan, 1983); G. Bornstein (ed.), *W. B. Yeats: The Early Poetry. Manuscript Materials by W. B. Yeats* (Ithaca and London: Cornell University Press, 1987).

For a listing of critical writings about Yeats's plays, see p. 717 of the present volume.

BIOGRAPHY AND CRITICISM.
(a) Biographical
J. M. Hone, *W. B. Yeats, 1865-1939* (London: Macmillan, 1942; 2nd edition 1962); R. Ellmann, *Yeats: The Man and the Masks* (London: Macmillan, 1949); A. N. Jeffares, *Yeats: A New Biography* (London: Century Hutchinson, 1988); J. Kelly and E. Domville (eds), *The Collected Letters of W. B. Yeats, Volume I: 1865-1895* (Oxford: Clarendon Press, 1986).
(b) Critical Writings. Poetry.
L. MacNeice, *The Poetry of W. B. Yeats* (London: Oxford University Press, 1941; reprinted 1967); P. Ure, *Towards a Mythology: Studies in the Poetry of W. B. Yeats* (Liverpool: Liverpool University Press; London: Hodder & Stoughton, 1946); T. R. Henn, *The Lonely Tower: Studies in the Poetry of Yeats* (London: Methuen, 1950; 2nd revised edition London: Methuen; New York: Barnes and Noble, 1965); J. Hall and M. Steinmann (eds), *The Permanence of Yeats: Selected Criticism* (New York: Macmillan, 1950); R. Ellmann, *The Identity of Yeats* (London: Macmillan; New York: Oxford University Press, 1954; reprinted London: Faber and Faber, 1983); F. Kermode, *Romantic Image* (London: Routledge & Kegan Paul, 1957); F. A. C. Wilson, *Yeats's Iconography* (London: Gollancz, 1958); F. A. C. Wilson, *W. B. Yeats and Tradition* (London: Gollancz, 1960); T. R. Whitaker, *Swan and Shadow: Yeats's Dialogue With History* (Chapel Hill: North Carolina University Press, 1959; reprinted 1964); J. Stallworthy, *Between the Lines: W. B. Yeats's Poetry in the Making* (Oxford: Clarendon Press, 1963); G. Melchiori, *The Whole Mystery of Art: Pattern into Poetry in the Work of W. B. Yeats* (London: Routledge & Kegan Paul, 1960); T. Parkinson, *W. B. Yeats: The Later Poetry* (Berkeley and Los Angeles: University of California Press; London: Cambridge University Press, 1965); A. N. Jeffares and K. W. Cross (eds), *In Excited Reverie: A Centenary Tribute to William Butler Yeats 1865-1939* (London: Macmillan, 1965); D. Torchiana, *W. B. Yeats and Georgian Ireland* (Evanston: Northwestern University Press; London: Oxford University Press, 1966); H. Kenner (ed.), *Yeats: Twentieth-Century Views* (Englewood Cliffs, New Jersey: Prentice Hall, 1969); P. L. Marcus, *Yeats and the Beginning of the Irish Renaissance* (Ithaca: Cornell University Press, 1970); H. Bloom, *Yeats* (New York: Oxford University Press, 1970); D. Donoghue, *Yeats* (London: Fontana, 1971); W. H. Pritchard, *W. B. Yeats: A Critical Anthology* (Harmondsworth: Penguin, 1972); D. A. Harris, *Yeats, Coole Park & Ballylee* (Baltimore: Johns Hopkins University Press, 1974); G. M. Harper, *Yeats's Golden Dawn* (London: Macmillan, 1974); E. Cullingford, *Yeats, Ireland and Fascism* (London: Macmillan, 1981); D. Archibald, *Yeats* (Syracuse: Syracuse University Press, 1983); A. N. Jeffares, *A New Commentary on The Collected Poems of W. B. Yeats* (London: Macmillan, 1983); S. Deane, *Celtic Revivals* (London: Faber and Faber, 1985); R. J. Finneran (ed.), *Critical Essays on W. B. Yeats* (Boston: G. K. Hall & Co., 1986).

W. J. Mc CORMACK, *Editor*

Irish Gothic and After
(1820-1945)

Gothic fiction, as initiated by Horace Walpole (1717-97) with his short novel *The Castle of Otranto* (1764), is not easily defined. But the sublime and asymmetrical character of gothic architecture, transformed into verbal intricacy, convoluted plot, emotional intensity — and all this overlaid with implications of supernatural agency — lies behind the literary experiment. In eighteenth-century gothic novels, the supernatural sometimes threatened, only to be ultimately exposed as effects manipulated by clever villains and (for a time) accepted by innocent victims. Emotional intensity usually involved feelings of terror or horror, in which sexual and violent aspects of human experience were not infrequently linked. As for verbal intricacy, this was more often represented by complicated oaths of loyalty, arcane or antique documents, and compromising last wills and testaments. In this last-named connection, one discovers an underlying concern for linkage and continuity, especially for the transmission of property at a time of repeated assaults on the traditional basis of English society. Gothic fiction was rarely the beneficiary of literary grace, and those gothic novels that are remembered still today constitute only a fraction of the vast bulk of such material published in the sixty or so years following *The Castle of Otranto*. Gothicism is a remarkable phenomenon in that it combines a cult of the exotic and the exclusive with uncritical popularity.

This paradox of the gothic novel's readership may be connected with another, more general contradiction. The gothic novel endlessly exposed the violence and corruption that lay behind authority, ancient authority for the most part; in this sense it was a subversive force in the eighteenth century and the period following the French Revolution. At the same time, it tended to glorify antique and elite values in such extended narratives as seemed to exercise a conservative force upon the past. Perhaps we should read gothicism as in part a literary subgenre effectively engaged in a *reformation* of the past, rather than as any revolutionary assault on a contemporary establishment. This reformatory task was quickly taken up in a more refined style by the historical novel proper. Certainly, the *floruit* of the gothic novel in English is seriously curtailed by the emergence of Walter Scott and the end of the Napoleonic Wars.

In Ireland, novelists following in Scott's footsteps were unable to impose the master's distinction between past history and present politics, and as a consequence the gothic mode endured there in a fugitive and discontinuous manner throughout the nineteenth century. By the end of the century, however, the Scott-like historical novel was intellectually bankrupt, and Irish gothicism was redirected into new and unexpected channels. A commercial novelist like Bram Stoker and a sublime poet like W. B. Yeats both found a place for the expiring gothic note, and in their different ways of doing so illuminated a political dimension. The 1930s witnessed a crisis at least as grave as that of the French revolutionary era.

In the 1780s and 1790s, one of the principal publishers of this kind of fiction was the Minerva Press in London.[1] In the lists of its publications, one finds

1. See Dorothy Blakey, *The Minerva Press 1790-1820* (London: Bibliographical Society, 1939).

a large proportion of novels written by women and (even by 1783) novels employing Irish settings or Irish themes. Not all Minerva books were gothic; some were romances of a more insipid quality. But Regina Maria Roche, née Dalton (1765-1845) combined Irish birth and a gothic propensity in several novels on the Minerva lists. *The Children of the Abbey*, Roche's least forgotten novel, was first issued by Minerva in 1796; several Irish editions followed — Cork in 1798, and Belfast as late as 1835/36. Indeed, the book remained available throughout much of the nineteenth century. Its tone, at once gothic and sentimental, can be gauged from a passage in which an aged penitent chooses a ruined chapel in Dunreath Abbey as the place in which to make a late restitution to the heroine:

> Lady Dunreath then took a key from her bosom, with which she opened [an iron box], and took from thence a sealed paper: 'receive,' she said, presenting it to Amanda, 'receive the will of your grandfather: a sacred deposit, intrusted to your care for your brother, the rightful heir to the Earl of Dunreath.[2]

'Sacred deposit' may seem an excessive term for a testamentary document, but *The Children of the Abbey* several times emphasizes the crucial role of written texts as all-too-frail vessels bearing some ineffable value. Immediately before the scene just quoted, the distraught lady has peremptorily ordered Amanda to explain her timely arrival; her terms are crisply exact: 'In the meantime, do you throw upon paper a brief account of your life, that I may know the incidents which so providentially brought you to the abbey.'[3] Some disproportion between incident and providence is to be mediated for her by the throwing of words upon paper.

Other contributors to the pre-history of the Irish gothic include Mrs Kelly (author of *The Ruins of Avondale Priory*, 1796), Mrs F. C. Patrick (*The Irish Heiress*, 1797), 'the Wife of an Officer' who wrote *Most Ghosts!* (1798) and Mrs Colpoys with *The Irish Excursion, or I Fear to Tell You* (1801). The last-mentioned presents the dishonest Irish amid London society, and recommends the Union as a panacea for all political and social ills.

But it is Charles Robert Maturin (1782-1824), Joseph Sheridan Le Fanu (1814-73) and Bram Stoker (1847-1912) who are invoked in the name of a more substantial Irish gothic tradition. Of the three, Le Fanu has the best claim to be regarded as a writer of talent, and the description 'gothic' can be applied to his work only in a general and unsatisfactory way. In his day, Le Fanu was first thought of as an Irish historical novelist (cf. *The Cock and Anchor*, 1845), and later as one of the English 'sensationalist' school of writers of whom Wilkie Collins (1824-89) and Charles Reade (1814-84) were the most successful. Sensationalism was popular, and (unlike the gothic) it thrived on immediate and contemporary themes and anxieties: the maladministration of lunatic asylums, marital cruelty in the suburbs, the 'terrorism' (as Reade saw it) of trade unions. Although Le Fanu managed to avoid these lurid topicalities, his novels of the 1860s cannot be reclassified under the gothic heading: his use of significant architectural setting (in *Uncle Silas* (1864) for example) derives not from the abbeys and castles of Walpole or the Minervans but from that Irish concern with the 'Big House' as a political microcosm, which was inaugurated by Maria Edgeworth's *Castle Rackrent* (1800). As for Charles Robert Maturin, his acknowledged gothic masterpiece, *Melmoth the Wanderer* (1820), remains an eccentric even among his extravagant romances and (un)historical extravaganzas. Bram Stoker is known solely for *Dracula* (1897), the plot of which borrows from a story by Le Fanu and the details of which depend much on information provided by a Hungarian scholar, Armin Vambery. His other stories and novels are remarkable for the way in which sado-masochism is bound up with colonial exploitation: it is a symptomatic feature, not a literary achievement.

One further feature of this oft-remarked Irish gothic tradition which distinguishes it from the school of Walpole is its pronounced lack of interest in the medieval period: nothing earlier than the seventeenth-century wars of religion ever really gripped the imaginations of Maturin, Le Fanu or Stoker, and frequently their excursions to the past are quickly sidetracked into distinctly contemporary concerns. It might be as useful to relate these writers to the French notion of Le Grand Guignol, in which grotesque and macabre incident dominates all else. Named after the principal figure of an eighteenth-century puppet-show, Grand Guignol

2. Despite its many reprintings, the novel is rare. Consequently I am obliged to cite a late edition: see Regina Maria Roche, *The Children of the Abbey* (Manchester: Gleave, 1823), p. 551.
3. ibid., p. 549.

finds a high degree of woodenness perfectly adequate in characterization, for character is to be shown as endlessly manipulatable by powers (fate, inquisitors, aristocratic in-laws and other ghouls) that have been, are, and ever more shall be. Grand Guignol has a direct affinity with the English showground figure, Punch; and it is no coincidence that the Victorian magazine of that name portrayed Irish character as incorrigible. Violent, ungrateful, scheming, rebellious — these characteristics of the Irish, in *Punch*'s eye, were merely superficially altering manifestations of a lack of human character as such, a lack that was to be seen as eternally damning. This Victorian focus is a cynosure for all readers of the Irish gothic, and (to a degree) diminishes the aptness of the term 'gothic'. Yet even when we trace certain preoccupations forward in the writings of William Butler Yeats (1865-1939) and Elizabeth Bowen (1899-1973), the Victorian period remains central. But this is to run ahead too quickly.

Even if the Irish tradition of gothic fiction turns out, on examination, to be a slender one, there are other ways in which such material is of literary significance. Whereas the origins of English gothicism are diverse and obscure — involving the sensibility of a remarkable individual like Walpole, the larger development of literary romanticism, and the growth of aesthetics through the study of concepts such as 'the sublime' — Irish gothic fiction is remarkably explicit in the way it demonstrates its attachment to history and to politics. A shrewd pamphleteer, writing in 1787, prefigured this connection when he described the discountenancing religious instruction of other than that of the established church in state schools as 'a gothic edict against the improvement of our rational faculties'.[4] Certainly, the link is evident in some of the fiction published by London firms like the Minerva Press, especially in the years after 1798. Mrs Kelly's *The Matron of Erin* (1816) did not originate with the Minerva Press, and while it is also relatively late in its attention to the 1798 Rebellion as an exciting topic for fiction, it neatly illustrates the interaction of certain gothic excesses, recent Irish history, and female heroics. The author of *Melmoth the Wanderer* had dealt with similar material in *The Milesian Chief* (1812), and *The Wild Irish Boy* (1808) was written expressly by Maturin as a riposte to *The Wild Irish Girl* (1806) by Sydney, Lady Morgan (*c.* 1783-1859). The Irish gothic, in other words, engages quite promiscuously with other literary subgenres — historical romance, military narrative, and the sentimental novel. Its authors are far from exclusive in their loyalties, and a series of comparisons may reveal the wide-ranging implications of their indiscriminate commerce.

C. R. MATURIN AND W. H. MAXWELL

Melmoth the Wanderer is a highly complex network of interlocking tales that take the reader from seventeenth-century London madhouses to islands in the Indian Ocean. These locations are forms of exotic distance, of course, but the twelfth chapter of the third volume illustrates a number of points about crowd psychology (officially we are concerned with the Spanish Inquisition) by means of two footnotes. The first of these reports the circumstances of the death of the Rev. Dr William Hamilton (1755-97) who was killed in County Donegal by agrarian assassins, and the second (which is even closer to the date of writing) deserves quotation in full:

> In the year 1803, when Emmett's [*sic*] insurrection broke out in Dublin — (*the fact* from which this account is drawn was related to me by an eye witness) — Lord Kilwarden, in passing through Thomas Street, was dragged from his carriage, and murdered in the most horrid manner. Pike after pike was thrust through his body, till at last he was *nailed to a door*, and called out to his murderers to 'put him out of his pain'. At this moment, a shoemaker, who lodged in the garret of an opposite house, was drawn to the window by the horrible cries he heard. He stood at the window, gasping with horror, his wife attempting vainly to drag him away. He saw the last blow struck — he heard the last groan uttered, as the sufferer cried, 'put me out of pain', while sixty pikes were thrusting at him. The man stood at his window as if nailed to it; and when dragged from it, became — an *idiot for life*.[5]

4. [Edward Sheridan] *A Critical Review of the B*[*ishop*] *of Cloyne's Publication*.... By an unbiassed Irishman. 2nd ed. (Dublin: John Chambers, 1787), pp. xx-xxi. Quoted by James Kelly, 'The Context and Course of Thomas Orde's Plan of Education of 1787', *The Irish Journal of Education*, Vol. 20, No. 1 (1986), pp. 3-26; see p. 20.

5. Charles Robert Maturin, *Melmoth the Wanderer; A Tale* edited by Douglas Grant (London: Oxford University Press, 1968), p. 257n.

Here, immediacy of both time and place has replaced the exotic and antique. Moreover, the psychological trait that Maturin is seeking to examine is itself founded on a kind of permanent immediacy: the shoemaker remains transfixed or (as the Freudians might say) fixated by the brief scene he once witnessed. Maturin renders this trait in the very stuff of his writing — Lord Kilwarden is dragged from a carriage and nailed (as it were) to a door; the wife tries to drag the watching shoemaker from the window, but he 'stood at his window as if nailed to it'. These precise verbal repetitions enact a kind of identification between victim and witness which is at the heart of Maturin's novel. Ideally, it aims at an effective abolition of the reader.

The kind of military adventure that Maturin introduced into *The Milesian Chief* is given a different treatment in the novels of William Hamilton Maxwell (1792-1850). Following active service in the British army, Maxwell became a Church of Ireland clergyman posted to remote Ballagh in County Mayo. He began to write a kind of fiction in which rollicking narrative incorporated incidents of military life and harmless picaresque scenes. Though far from gothic in its emotional range — even the thought of battle is purged of any terror for hero and reader alike — Maxwell's fiction shares certain affiliations with the gothic. It is, so to speak, the comic side of Irish gothic, responding to death with frivolous irresponsibility instead of endlessly reiterated excess. *O'Hara* (1825) deals with the 1798 Rebellion in Ulster; one of the stories in *Erin go Bragh* (1859) gives a vivid account of the Emmet rebellion; in other *Adventures*, Maxwell covers the French invasion of County Mayo and the activities of secret societies. All these books are notable for the combination of incidental humour presented against an implicitly violent background which can shift rapidly and evasively from rural Ireland to the wars against Napoleon. Even if Maxwell remains a third-rate novelist, his work identifies several anxieties that underpin Irish gothic fiction. One of these is simply the pressure that contemporary, local and actual events exercise upon an imagination seeking to represent things that are remote in time or space. Maturin's footnote about Emmet is one example; Maxwell's sudden switch of setting to a largely non-fatal military escapade in Spain is another. The Irish gothic officiously fails to exclude the immediate, while the military novel (and Maxwell is the inventor of that sub-genre) manages to disarm death itself.

The Fortunes of Hector O'Halloran and his Man Mark Antony O'Toole (1842) takes the reader from the rural south of Ireland, through Dublin and London, to the Iberian peninsula. The novel opens with an attack on a small castle, although this is prefaced by an apparently unimportant act of naming which should not go unnoticed. Both the attack on property and the bestowing of the names Mark Antony on an orphan/servant indicate, in contrasting proportions and emotional registers, a concern for continuity, or anxiety for the operation of inheritance. In the gothic novel, wrongful disinheritance is an explicit formula in plots that can employ the lost or concealed will, the wicked uncle, scheming baron and so forth, to the same end. But in Maxwell's novel, acts of naming (both explicit and implicit) perform a more discreet function. The orphan in question is the son of a soldier whose Christian name had been Mark:

> 'What's in a name?' said Dr. Hamilton.
>
> 'More than one would suppose, Doctor,' replied my father. 'Our red-headed adjutant married a Bath heiress almost at sight, for after but a two hours' siege she surrendered at discretion, declaring that it was utterly impossible to hold out against a lover whose apellatives were Julius Caesar.'
>
> 'Then add Antony to his patronymic, and your *protégé* will prove irresistible.'
>
> 'Marc Antony be it then,' replied the priest; and in five minutes the ceremony was complete.[6]

With these light-hearted invocations of ancient Roman conquest, the novel proceeds to the besieging of the house by local banditti. In the repulse of insurgent threat, one can read the success of these invocations. By a kind of pathetic overdetermination, Colonel O'Halloran's guard-dog is also named Caesar and so participates in the defence of Irish civilization against the barbarian hordes, a touching detail were it not for the implication that a dog and a catholic servant-boy may derive their names in the same way. Thereafter, the hero of the title and his renamed Sancho Panza set off to recolonize Spain for Maxwell's particular brand of harmless, distinctly unsatirical picaresque, immune to the mortality

6. William Hamilton Maxwell, *The Fortunes of Hector O'Halloran and his Man Mark Anthony O'Toole* (London: Tegg, (n.d.)), p. 12.

normally associated with violence and warfare. The same author's *History of the Irish Rebellion in 1798* (1845) recounts an actual siege (of the Rev. McGhee's house near Hacketstown, Co. Wicklow) in much the same terms, with a line drawing by George Cruikshank to emphasize the grim reality of life and death in Ireland. For good measure it also provides a history of Emmet's rebellion, and thus fleshes out the scanty matter in Maturin's footnote.

But the location of the inaugurating action in *Hector O'Halloran* has a further significance. The year, we are told, is 1795, when British forces have been driven out of the Low Countries and the revolutionaries have established the Batavian republic there. 'In a word, everything was gloomy and discouraging abroad, and at home life and property had no security.' Immediately after this frank analysis, the novel presents the home of the O'Halloran family:

> Yet there were few persons excepting its owner, who, even in peaceful times, would choose Knockloftie for an abiding place. It was an old and dreary-looking fabric — one portion consisting of a dark square tower, the keep of a former stronghold of the O'Hallorans — and the others, additions built at different periods, according to the wants or fancies of succeeding proprietors. The house was perched upon a cliff, which rose in sheer ascent two hundred feet above the beach beneath it. Although sheltered by some high grounds behind, still, as the building looked upon the ocean, it was necessarily exposed and cold; while dwarfed and sickly copse-wood — all that repeated efforts to grow timber could produce — instead of improving the general appearance of the place, gave a silent but striking evidence of its hopeless sterility.[7]

Insecurity . . . sterility . . . these paragraphs rapidly chart an accelerating crisis. But the narrator continues by means of a reversed chronology:

> To my father, however, Knockloftie had hereditary endearments. For five centuries his ancestors had been born and died there; and he clung with a family attachment to that ancient roof-tree, where the O'Hallorans, in better days, had exercised a boundless hospitality, which even yet was chronicled in the traditions of the neighbourhood.[8]

The house is thus perfectly equipped to inaugurate a gothic novel, but the novel follows a different pattern. Moreover, the house itself ceases to play a part in young O'Halloran's destiny, which is to achieve effortlessly in the peninsular war the victory denied to his father in the campaigns of the early 1790s. Two attributes of the house deserve emphasis, the first and lesser being that it is staffed (however informally) by chaplains of both the catholic and the protestant persuasions, and so accommodates the principal allegiances of the surrounding population. By a kind of parallelism, the hero's mother is an English catholic, while his father is a protestant bearing a Gaelic family name. In these strategies, we see how a symbol of a dominant economic order is bedecked in the superficial trappings of *all* the ideological combatants of the epoch, so that it appears to be not just the embodiment of a political class but of all classes and creeds — indeed the embodiment of civilization itself. Initially overloaded with these various representative roles, the house is quickly eclipsed inside the narrative lest the very notion of representation should be too closely considered.

In this process, nomenclature is at least as important as narrative. The house is as often named Knockloftie as its antiquity is emphasized. The Irish reader in 1842 recognized this as the name of an actual house, the home of the Hely Hutchinson family, earls of Donoughmore. Knocklofty is situated on the gentle slopes of the river Suir, near Clonmel in County Tipperary; it is a mid-eighteenth-century house, and *c.* 1795 it was as distinctly lacking in 'hereditary endearments' as its parvenu proprietor, John Hely Hutchinson (1724-94). The Hely Hutchinsons were stars rising rapidly in Irish political and military life (associated in the late eighteenth century with liberal reform and later with undifferentiated careerism), but the novel's association of their house with a five-hundred-year line of O'Hallorans is an exceedingly broad rewriting of history. Maxwell's account of a Whiteboy attack on this architectural synthesis marks an awareness of an insurgent class equally hostile towards venerable O'Hallorans and meteoric Hely Hutchinsons. In due course we find that William Carleton will adapt

7. ibid., p. 2.

8. idem.

certain gothic techniques to recount the attack of another secret society on a far less elevated house.

SYDNEY, LADY MORGAN AND OLIVIA, LADY CLARKE

In gothic novels, with their concentration on ancient families, depraved barons and contested inheritances, aristocratic titles proliferate. Nor is it a coincidence that this literary snobbery should be voraciously consumed by the public during a period when many relatively humble men were concocting pedigrees for themselves. The English gothic novel should probably be regarded as extinct well before Victoria came to the throne in 1837, but its successor in the business of propagating a fictitious aristocracy was the 'silver fork' school of fiction that flourished in the years after 1830.

Sydney and Olivia (died 1845) Owenson were the daughters of Robert Owenson (1744-1812), an impoverished Irish actor of more charm than ability. Their father claimed an uncertain relationship with a number of Irish county families, while their mother was English and methodist. The daughters' education reflected these mixed inheritances of the rakish and the righteous, and both married gentlemen who provided them with impeccable (if minor) noble titles. In a sense, their promotion in society mirrors an aspect of the fashion for gothic. Lady Morgan was renowned for the effusiveness of her characters' sentiments, but her politics (which her sister shared) combined a degree of Whiggish radicalism unknown among the silver fork novelists.

Like the gothic novelists, Lady Morgan has not fared well in the construction of an officially approved canon of fiction in English. She has always retained the interest of some admirers among Irish critics, notably because of her emotional depiction of what is taken to be aboriginal Gaelic culture. In *The Wild Irish Girl* (1806), the Prince of Inismore is presented as being both a contemporary figure, hidden away in the recesses of the Irish landscape, and a Milesian of old: he is, in other words, a disinherited victim of a kind familiar in the gothic portrait gallery, but with the advantage of having a daughter who bears a striking resemblance to the future Lady Morgan. In *O'Donnel; a National Tale* (1814), there is a hero of sorts named Glentworth, who derives from a Lord Glenthorn in Maria Edgeworth's story 'Ennui' (1809), but in the restitution of lost estates that constitutes the novel's principal achievement, more is done by Miss Charlotte O'Halloran than by Glentworth. This Charlotte O'Halloran is a conflation of names, based on two antiquarian writers, Charlotte Brooke (*c.*1740-93) and Sylvester O'Halloran (1728-1807). For good measure, there is also a character called Dexter, who is based on John Wilson Croker (1780-1857). The Charlotte O'Halloran figure, however, is of more interest than the satiric portrait of the young Croker, because she indicates the profound influence that the Celtic antiquarianism of the 1790s had upon nineteenth-century Irish fiction. The name O'Halloran remains a touchstone of dignity even as late as 1842 when Maxwell published *The Fortunes of Hector O'Halloran.* Maria Edgeworth's Count O'Halloran in *The Absentee* (1812) is the most subtle treatment of a social type and a cultural influence.[9]

Morgan's politics remained essentially confused, and her romantic love of freedom linked arms with a fear of popular upheavals. Here too one finds some resemblance to the gothic novel, where an intense investment in the trappings of ancient nobility goes hand in hand with an intermittent recognition of the tendency towards corruption inherent in all exclusive or absolute systems of power. (It is striking how few monarchs figure in these novels, presumably because readers — while they might engineer their own latter-day nobility — could scarcely aspire to the throne itself). Morgan's treatment of this political aspect of her plots relies on two asymmetrical features — the unchanging residual dignity of those who were once powerful but who have been unseated by insurgent or intrusive forces, and the highly mobile advance of others who acquire and possess lands and titles often by means of apostasy. In *The O'Briens and the O'Flahertys* (1827), several kinds of skewed identity are narrated at length. The novel, however, compels not for its plot or even for its extensive genealogies and chronicles but for the rich and at times raucous diversity of its many linguistic discourses. The opening chapter is a series of letters, with addresses given in French: later there is earthy Dublin dialogue, followed by pedantic historiography. The

9. For an exhaustive account of O'Halloran in Maria Edgeworth's fiction, see the introduction to the World's Classics edition of *The Absentee*, edited by W. J. Mc Cormack and Kim Walker (Oxford: Oxford University Press, 1988).

fourth chapter of the first volume — it is a four-volume work — is a lengthy account of two ladies' experience at a mock battle in the Phoenix Park. Proceeding beneath the social whirl and the laughable juxtaposition of idiolects is a searing analysis, at once satirical and sympathetic, of the sexual lives of these two women. The chapter can be sampled admirably in edited form (see below), but one has to judge once again the compulsive nominalism of such fiction and the apparent inability of the author to exclude the scandal of real (as opposed to fictional) history. Here is a preliminary account of the greater of the two ladies as she arrives; although the name she bears is highly significant for the reader of Irish fiction, the initial (mis)identification is even more risqué in that it momentarily brings together her ladyship and the most notorious courtesan of Dublin high society in the late eighteenth century:

> Many among the multitude announced her as the famous Kitty Cutdash; and nodded knowingly as she passed them; but the greater number detected in the beautiful charioteer, the equally famous Albina Countess Knocklofty, the female chief of that great oligarchical family, the Proudforts — a family on which the church rained mitres, the state coronets, and the people — curses.[10]

Lady Clarke was less committed to her career as a writer than her renowned sister. Yet her play, *The Irishwoman* (1819), returns to the question of metropolitan values and provincial origins so pervasive in Irish writing in the first quarter of the nineteenth century. In London Sir Toby is plotting to marry off his niece to the elderly Lord Ancestor, assisted by the forgery of an Irish family tree — 'a pretty piece of work I have had to trump up a pedigree at the mother's side, to compensate for a little defalcation on the father's'.[11] Added to this falsification of class, there is the subplot concerning Chatterton, a quack doctor specialising in 'craniology', the pseudo-science of telling character by reading the bumps on the skull. Chatterton is in fact Irish, but his masquerade as a medical man is augmented by suppression of his Irish origins. In the denouement, it takes an Irishwoman's arrival in London to sort out reality from illusion, in the course of which she rescues a young woman from marriage. When Chatterton gets his hands on Lord Ancestor's head, the result is a dramatic coincidence of several kinds of pretence:

> *Chatterton:* Aye, there they are, my lord, there they are, Sir Toby, there are indeed those very noble organs of patronage and protection, as strongly as I ever felt them developed, except on the cranium of his Grace the Duke of Loftycourt.
>
> *Lord Ancester:* Loftycourt! aye, the Loftycourts came in with the Saxon heptarchy, and are uterine cousins to the Ancestors.[12]

Clarke's essentially feminist play mockingly enacts in the naming of characters that *pretension* to aristocratic pedigree that one finds simultaneously in gothic novels and 'protestant ascendancy' families. Her anxiously titled character, Lord Ancestor, specifies a variation on the Hely Hutchinson residence (Knocklofty) as the epitome of that antique nobility with which he wishes to be associated. If Olivia Clarke cannot be said to be a gothic writer, her theme nonetheless is the very immediate and contemporary invention of a pre-history, upon which the 'gothic proper' can proceed to erect its fantastical castles. Her choice of drama, as distinct from the novel, as a literary medium underlines the inherent tendency of the latter towards a setting in the past. All fiction requires the perfect tense, whereas drama revels in the contemporary. Herein lies further evidence of Maria Edgeworth's originality in *Tales of Fashionable Life* (1809/12).

WILLIAM CARLETON'S 'WILDGOOSE LODGE': FACT AND FICTION

At the risk of paradox, it has to be said that while Irish gothic writing does not amount to a tradition, it is a distinctly protestant tradition. Maturin, Maxwell, the Owenson sisters, Sheridan Le Fanu and Charles Lever, Bram Stoker and Oscar Wilde, Yeats, Synge and Elizabeth Bowen were all attached to some degree to the (once) Established Church of Ireland. Maturin and Maxwell were ordained ministers of the church; Le Fanu was the son of a dean, and even Yeats was the grandson of a

10. Sydney, Lady Morgan, *The O'Briens and the O'Flahertys: A National Tale* (London: Colburn, 1827) Vol. 1, p. 157.
11. Olivia Clarke, *The Irishwoman: A Comedy in Five Acts* (London: Colburn, 1819), p. 4.
12. ibid., p. 39.

clerical home. However, only the earliest of these writers (Maturin) could be described as in any sense a conscientious believer in the orthodoxies of the reformed church, and progressive distance from belief is a more important feature of their background than credal allegiance. Irish gothic in this sense is a distinctive version of a wider Victorian crisis of Christian belief.

Denomination is never wholly separable from class, just as no simple equational formula can be established between a denomination and class. The list of authors given above is noteworthy for its reliance all but exclusively upon the Irish middle classes. A clerical background implicated Huguenot merchant stock (Maturin and Le Fanu) more than it drew on landed estate or high ecclesiastical office. Lever (like Stoker's brother and Wilde's father) was incorporated into Dublin society through the medical profession. Yeats and Bowen had more complex social origins in the countryside, but only Synge and Bowen could cite anything like a long pedigree of land-possessing gentry status. In this essentially bourgeois and conventionally protestant company, William Carleton appears initially as an anomaly.

His background was rural, humble and — in a sense that was becoming decisive at precisely the time of his birth — catholic. For Carleton was born near Clogher in County Tyrone in 1794, the youngest of a family with a direct if diminishing link with Gaelic-speaking Ulster. The Orange Order was founded in the year following his birth, and the sectarian violence that both prompted its foundation and characterized its growth looms large in many of Carleton's novels and tales. 'Confessions of a Reformed Ribbonman' was first published in January 1830 in *The Dublin Literary Gazette, Or Weekly Chronicle of Criticism, Belles Lettres, and Fine Arts*, although it is better known by the title 'Wildgoose Lodge' under which it appeared in Carleton's *Traits and Stories of the Irish Peasantry*.[13] By 1830, its author had converted to the Established Church and set up residence in Dublin as a professional writer; he had, in other words, drastically shifted from his origins to conform (it might appear) to the pattern discerned in Maturin, Lever, Stoker and the others. The tale reproduced below is ostensibly autobiographical, and the manner of its first publication underlined the non-fictional base of the narrative while also pointing out details of authorial intervention. *The Dublin Literary Gazette* prefaced Carleton's anonymous narrative with these words:

> In exhibiting the 'lights and shadows' of Irish life, though we have no desire to conceal or to extenuate, unfairly, the faults and vices of our country-men, we certainly feel no delight in dwelling, over-much, upon the darker side of the picture. Had the following story been a pure fiction, it would not have gained a place in our pages, but like the tale which we had the pleasure of presenting lately to our readers, and to which this forms so deep and melancholy a contrast, it is unfortunately 'a true record'. The source from which it is derived satisfies us of its authenticity.
>
> As affording an insight into the habits and secret actions of a very extraordinary set of wretches, some of whom are said even yet to disgrace the wilder parts of the country, it may well be regarded as a curious and interesting relation, and not the less so, that the spirit which animated these miscreants, is, we trust, fast dying away, and will soon be known only by remembrance.
>
> It will probably be remarked by the observant reader, that the language of the narrator is not uniform, as the style is raised in some places above what is consistent with the condition of the character described. We are not prepared to say that the descriptions have not sometimes been embellished, and the phraseology occasionally raised, but our ribbonman went to school after his reformation.[14]

The question of literary technique, especially technique characteristic of the gothic mode, will be discussed in the headnote to Carleton's tale. We can note here that the alteration of the title to 'Wildgoose Lodge' constitutes a further recognition of the primacy of the Big House in the setting of Irish fiction, while the action of the tale harks back to some of the fiction published by the

13. Carleton's stories went through many versions, and an impressionistic account of the altering text of 'Confessions of a Reformed Ribbonman' may be found in Barbara Hayley, *Carleton's 'Traits and Stories' and the 19th Century Anglo-Irish Tradition* (Gerrards Cross: Colin Smythe, 1983), pp. 123-36.

14. *The Dublin Literary Gazette* No. 4 (23/1/1830), p. [49].

Minerva Press in the years following the Irish Rebellion of 1798. The social conditions that contained even so apparently extreme an incident as the burning of Wildgoose Lodge have been the subject of comment by a local historian, who explicitly refers to Carleton's fiction. The after-effects of the Napoleonic wars feature prominently in his account:

> At length, peace being proclaimed, an unexpected reaction ensued, causing a fearfully sudden change in the social condition of this fine and lately flourishing county . . . Agriculturalists were ruined . . . Corn merchants were involved in bankruptcy, and landlords could not get their rents. The middlemen became insolvent and could no longer exist, but no sympathy or regret was felt for the destruction of that class . . . The harvest of the year 1816 turned out sadly unpropitious . . . Unfortunately a most deplorable calamity was added to the general desolation . . . The unlawful confederacy of Ribbonism, which was considered antagonistic to Orangeism, produced its horribly demoralising and anti-social effects in midnight outrages, incendiarism, and robbery of arms. Two men were tried, condemned, and sentenced to death, for the first attack on Wildgoose Lodge. . . .
>
> It is dreadfully appalling to contemplate human nature in such a hideous aspect as that exhibited by the unfortunate wretch who concocted the infernal plot for the burning of Wildgoose Lodge. His heart must have been steeled by the archfiend, when he, being clerk of the Chapel of Stonetown, could so defile the sanctuary entrusted to his care as to turn it into a Pandemonium for devising and maturing such a dark and barbarous atrocity![15]

The factual basis to the incident at the heart of the tale is readily established. Like other exemplary executions, the hanging of the culprits was noted in the newspapers of the day, especially in the *Belfast News-letter*, a fact that serves to indicate the extent to which north Louth was regarded as being essentially part of the province of Ulster. Local historians continued to report the enduring impact of the attack (29 October 1816) on Wildgoose Lodge, even into the twentieth century.[16] These accounts are helpful to students of William Carleton's fiction, though care should be taken lest the writer's influence on the historians should be confused with what purports to be their objective account of the facts. Two sources predating 'Confessions of a Reformed Ribbonman' are of course immune to this influence: a pamphlet published in Drogheda in 1824, and a private letter written by a catholic priest in April 1818, but published only in 1972. To these may be added an account of the state of public feeling in Louth immediately after the executions which, though written in the 1840s, is independent of local tradition: this account is included in the lengthy reminiscences of a Scotsman, James Anton, who arrived in Ireland with the 42nd Foot Regiment (the Royal Highlanders) in May 1817, and reached Dundalk, Co. Louth in June.[17] The soldier's memoir serves to remind us also that the military life, exploited for largely comic (or comic-heroic) effect in Hamilton Maxwell and for decorative (or satirico-decorative) effect in Lady Morgan, had a grimmer and more local reality in Ireland. What all this material establishes is the essentially factual basis of Carleton's *general* account of the burning of Wildgoose Lodge. Thus (indirectly) the particular narrative perspective can be gauged in the spectrum of gothic techniques of effectively identifying reader and narrator, techniques we have already

15. William Brett, *Reminiscences of Louth . . . from the Period of the Legislative Union of Ireland with Great Britain to the Year 1836* (Enniskillen: Fermanagh Reporter, 1857), pp. 6-7. Various motives for the crime have been proposed: that Lynch (head of the family who were massacred) had refused to become a sworn member of the Ribbonmen and/or had given evidence to the authorities about a previous attack; that the attackers included a man who had tried to marry Lynch's daughter, and so on. It seems clear that Lynch leased or rented the property from the Filgate family and this, together with the genteel term 'lodge', suggests that he belonged to that 'middleman' stratum of Irish rural society that was so hard-pressed in the years after the Napoleonic wars. See the commentary and annotations on Gerald Griffin's *The Collegians* in Volume I of this anthology, pp. 1150-69.

16. Three articles on the *Journal of the County Louth Archaeological and Historical Society* conveniently sift this material: see T. F. G. Paterson, 'The Burning of Wildgoose Lodge', Vol. 12, No. 2 (1950), pp. 159-80; Daniel J. Casey, 'Carleton in Louth', Vol. 17, No. 2 (1970), pp. 97-106; Daniel J. Casey, 'Wildgoose Lodge: The Evidence and the Lore', Vol. 18, No. 2 (1974), pp. 140-64.

17. James Anton, *Retrospect of a Military Life during the Most Eventful Periods of the Last War* (Edinburgh: Lizars, 1841). Anton rose to become quartermaster-sergeant of his regiment, and in the *Retrospect* he admits that he had literary ambitions. His account of the Wildgoose lodge incident (pp. 268-75) indicates original research, but does not wholly rule out the possibility that he had read Carleton's story, although he does not mention it. The account (pp. 261-330) of his stay in Ireland, 1817-25, is generally of high value.

observed in Maturin's deployment of footnotes in *Melmoth the Wanderer*. Yet one important shift between Maturin and Carleton should be noted promptly: the identification that in effect is indicated in Maturin is a masochistic one, in which the reader is all but assimilated to the victim of violence; but in Carleton's first-person narrative the identification is of a passive narrator with the agent (and not the object) of suffering. This 'thirst for accusation' is more fully developed in Sheridan Le Fanu, and much later becomes itself the material for a memorable passage in a poem by W. B. Yeats.

LE FANU AND LEVER

We are now in a position to compare the full-blooded exoticism of Maturin, the exceptional local intensities of Carleton, and the more fragmentary evidences of political allusion in Lady Morgan. The *nominal* presence of the actual and historical within her palpably fictitious narrative also characterizes both the Irish military novels of Maxwell and Charles Lever (1806-72) and the less unified, more discontinuous writings of Maturin and Le Fanu. None of Le Fanu's novels could be accurately described as gothic, though his shorter tales stand in some contrast with their explicit use of the supernatural. Here, the most recurrent theme is retribution, the delayed but inevitable visitation of judgment from the past upon the present. In the short tales, a variety of stock figures (cf. the demon lover in 'Strange Event in the Life of Schalken the Painter', in Volume I, p. 1231) are put to new uses, while the novels struggle to elaborate some (usually) hackneyed situation or plot and to integrate this retributive pattern into the representation of ordinary Victorian social life. But before he was obliged by his publisher to adopt contemporary English settings and the other trappings of sensational fiction, Le Fanu wrote one novel in which many of the problems we have been discussing converge. This is *The House by the Church-yard* (1863), a book as rambling and as tense as anything written by Maturin. Where Maturin ranged across the globe and through the centuries, Le Fanu's ramblings and tensions are strictly focussed in the village of Chapelizod in County Dublin and in the hidden life of his ultimately exposed villain.

We have seen in Volume I (p. 1243) of this anthology how Charles Lever incorporated certain effectively self-contained tales in his novels. The argument is made there that these interpolated tales — fictions within fictions — constitute an attempt at a higher veracity or truthfulness to social reality than that permitted by the agreed conventions of Lever's early novels with their romantic yet decorous pranks, their dashing military capers, and the endless plagiarisms so skilfully exposed by Charles Gavan Duffy. Le Fanu also had recourse to the interpolated tale in order to swell out a novel to the length required by his London publisher; indeed *Uncle Silas* (1864) is an expanded version of a short story written more than twenty years earlier. *The House by the Church-yard* draws on two earlier magazine publications by Le Fanu, and also 'incorporates' a tale so self-contained and so apparently originless as to require further comment.

The tale — it constitutes a single chapter in the novel — is called 'An Authentic Narrative of the Ghost of a Hand', and in it Le Fanu describes how a 'white and plump' hand taps at windows and doors as if to gain admission, and subsequently leaves its print in the dust of a parlour table. The hand is then seen on several occasions inside the house; it is literally disembodied, appearing to resemble a toad in its horrid completeness and integrity. At the climax of this persecution, the tenant of the house, Mr. Prosser

> drew the curtain at the side of the bed, and saw Mrs Prosser lying, as for a few seconds, he mortally feared, dead, her face being motionless, white, and covered with a cold dew; and on the pillow, close beside her head, and just within the curtains [of the bed], was, as he first thought, a toad — but really the same white, fattish hand, the wrist resting on the pillow, and the fingers extended towards her temple.[18]

If this has the shiver-inducing frisson which enthusiasts of the gothic appreciate, we should be all the more careful to adopt a strictly analytical approach, even one which may seem plodding in its philological procedures. The hand is complete in itself but it is, by another reading which cannot be utterly discarded, a fragment, a portion of an unapparent, absent or non-existent body. There is a once-familiar classical allusion by which one refers to fragments as *disjecta membra*, scattered remains as

18. Joseph Sheridan Le Fanu, *The House by the Church-yard* (London: Tinsley, 1863) Vol. I, p. 128.

they might be found on a battlefield. Behind that Latin cliché lies a specific line by the poet Horace — 'disjecti membra poetae' — which translates as 'the remains of a dismembered poet' but which can be interpreted either at a literal level (his arms, legs etc.) or at a literary level (his texts in fragmentary form).

If we look at the chapter about the hand, the *membrum disjectum* that terrifies Mrs Prosser, we find that the chapter itself is curiously cut off from the larger body (the novel) to which we expect to find it attached. Within *The House by the Church-yard*, the incident is pointless; the Prossers are not characters referred to in any other connection; the period of their tenancy has long passed before the action proper begins, and the hand never manifests itself to anyone else. Le Fanu here is writing a psychic narrative that is the exact obverse to that provided by Maturin in his footnote about the Emmet rising. For the shoemaker witnessing Kilwarden's murder, there is an excessive relation between observer and observed; the two merge in Maturin's repeated epithets. For the Prossers, there is an inadequate perception of the observed, all of whose body has been obliterated, excised or repressed to leave only a hand. Maturin's footnote telegraphs urgently from the Spanish Inquisition to Thomas Street, Dublin, levelling boundaries between separate narrative sequences. Le Fanu's chapter holds itself remote from the novel that officially enfolds it.

That larger narrative is labyrinthine in plot and sub-plot, rich in local incident and local colour, voluble in its asides and digressions. If a summary were possible, it would centre on the discovery that the character Paul Dangerfield is really the same person as Charles Archer, who twenty years earlier had committed a fearful crime. Only as a datum of uncertain value can one offer the information that the Dublin of Le Fanu's youth knew a prominent publisher-journalist by the name of Charles Archer: nothing is asserted as to the link between the actual figure and the fictitious character who later bears his name but to say that these *nominal* echoes run through the fiction not only of Le Fanu (where they are legion) but also (as we have seen) in Hamilton Maxwell, in Sydney Morgan, in Charles Lever, and even (vestigially) in Bram Stoker. Nothing is known of any link between the historical Charles Archer and Sheridan Le Fanu (another publisher/journalist), and the macabre scenes of the novel converge on the name with an inscrutable logic. In the private, as opposed to public, life of the novelist, however, there is evidence that goes some way to rendering logical the disjointed chapter already quoted.

Le Fanu's wife was the daughter of George Bennett, a leading Dublin barrister of vigorously conservative views. She and her husband moved into Bennett's house when he retired, and there she died in April 1858. A few days later, in a letter to his mother, Le Fanu wrote a lengthy account of some of Susanna Bennett's highly disturbed dreams:

> . . . she one night thought she saw the curtain of her bed at the side next the door drawn, & the darling old man [i.e. her father] dressed in his usual morning suit, holding it aside, stood close to her looking ten or (I think) twelve years younger than when he died, & with his delightful smile of fondness & affection beaming upon her, I think she also said that his hand rested on the bed clothes as he used to place it. The words were as you say 'There is room in the vault for you, my little Sue'. . . .[19]

Freudians legitimately may have a field day with such material, and we shall harvest a grain or two of psychoanalytical wisdom in due course. For the moment, however, note the resemblances between this letter and the passage from the authentic narrative of the ghost of a hand in *The House by the Church-yard*. There is a bed curtain, and a hand isolated in the prose, and the writing in each case is rhythmically punctuated with nervous intellection — 'as he first thought' . . . '(I think)' — and so forth. Moreover, the connection is reinforced by a further isolated and inexplicable detail in the fiction. Prosser, at the moment when the ghostly hand is discovered by his wife's head, is described thus: 'a heavy ledger, connected with his father-in-law's business being under his arm.' The father-in-law is meaningless in the fiction but explicit in the memoir; and the ledger is itself all but inexplicable in the chapter, yet attaches itself in the most tenuous yet suggestive way to *The House by the Church-yard*. A prologue to the novel evokes a bygone scene only to admit (accidentally at it were) the present reality of a grim factory, commerce, and housing built of 'pale new brick'. Whatever the larger significance of this

19. Le Fanu to Mrs Emma Le Fanu 3 May [1858]; quoted in W. J. McCormack, *Sheridan Le Fanu and Victorian Ireland*, 2nd edition (Dublin: The Lilliput Press, 1990), p. 133.

vestigially evoked present within the novel, once again fiction and documentation engage in a kind of *dance macabre* or annihilating unison. Le Fanu's letter about his father-in-law's visionary activity by the bedside ends with a postscript: 'Will you keep this statement of the dream as I shall want to refer to it, intending to write down all the particulars. . . . [?]' Such a confirmation of the uncanny one might term a *pas du Dieu*, for the manifest basis of Susanna Le Fanu's anxiety had been religious.

Its latent basis (as the Freudians would say) is undoubtedly sexual. In the letter, the visionary Bennett's hand is laid 'as he used to place it' simply on his daughter's bed-clothes. Textually, the fiction is far more suggestive, for the hand of an otherwise excised body 'extended towards her temple'. 'Extended' carries with it not simply the idea of rest but the energy of desire, and in the philological method of Freudian dream-interpretation the temple is not so much metonymic of the head as it is symbolic of the vagina, the sacred grove. Rival males, father and husband, gather in this least integrated chapter of Le Fanu's most disturbing novel. His work, with all its flaws, somehow insists on being described in terms of sexual trauma; it is emasculated, and may be rightly called the *disjecta membra* of — in this case — the novelist. If Le Fanu must be regarded as part of some Irish gothic tradition, it is helpful to recall the several different codes of interpretation — political, psychological and so on — that can be applied to his highly varied literary texts. Charles Lever's interpolations tend to offer, at a level of enhanced story-telling, access to a political or even military reality *less* fictive than the larger narrative. Le Fanu's incorporation of gothic horror may also give access to a sexual history no less violent and considerably more repressed than that openly articulated by his sensationalist plots.

BRAM STOKER AND OSCAR WILDE

The smallness of Dublin's middle-class society, or at least that portion of it which adhered to the reformed churches, is well indicated by a number of interlocking if trivial facts: that Oscar Wilde as a child played with Sheridan Le Fanu's children; that Bram Stoker's wife (Florence Balcombe) had been courted by Wilde; that Stoker borrowed from a story of Le Fanu's ('Carmilla') when he came to write *Dracula* (1897). Florence Balcombe's two youthful beaux subsequently flowered as writers, each with a particularly extreme relation to the gothic inheritance we have been considering. Her husband, Stoker, is now known solely for *Dracula* which, if it is not gothic in any strict sense (is there a strict sense?), is notorious for its unrelenting narration of supernatural and horrific agencies. His unsuccessful rival, Oscar Wilde, is of course renowned as a writer of drama, fiction and criticism in which the gothic mode is discernible only in parodic form and only in one early story, 'The Canterville Ghost'. A deadly earnestness pervades *Dracula* even in its most ludicrous moments, while Wilde's story incorporates the gothic legacy in a comic inventory of fiendish tricks. These two extremes — overkill in the case of Dracula the Undead, and deflationary pragmatism in dealing with Canterville the Incompetent — can be read as rival attempts to renegotiate the formula whereby the peculiarly Irish sub-form of the gothic novel attended to political reality.

Abraham Stoker's background was conventionally middle-class, his brother being a pillar of the medical establishment. He himself entered the civil service, wrote a textbook, and gave little sign of any original talent for the position of manager to Sir Henry Irving, the great actor, a post he took up at the Lyceum Theatre in London in 1878 and held until 1905. His biographical account of Irving is dutiful, and (with all the reservations appropriate to a Victorian man of business) Stoker seems an upright and unremarkable citizen. *Dracula*, then, must be read as a luridly obvious product of what Yeats was soon to call the *anti-self*, its heaping of cannibalistic horror upon sacrilegious horror an inverse statement of Victorian normality.

The book's debts are evident enough. The vampire theme reaches back to John William Polidori (1795-1821), who published a story of this kind in 1819 and tried to foist it on Byron. Setting to some extent, and incident to a specific and measurable extent, owe much to Le Fanu's 'Carmilla', in which vampirism (tinged with lesbianism) is active, though the Transylvanian background of Count Dracula himself may be partly the contribution of Armin Vambery (*c.* 1832-1913), an eccentric but learned Hungarian linguist and traveller who met Stoker during a visit to England. The character who specializes in disposing of the 'undead', Van Helsing, may owe something to the real-life Vambery, but his name also echoes the fictitious Dr Hesselius, whose papers on paranormal experience

Le Fanu's collection of stories (including 'Carmilla') *In a Glass Darkly* (1872) purports to be. However, Stoker's prose eschews the stylistic resourcefulness of his predecessor.

Critical to the enormous success of *Dracula* is its narrative structure: the novel is composed of twenty-seven chapters, which in turn draw on diaries, journals, phonograph recordings, a telegram, a newspaper report, together with shorthand notes and letters written by the various participants in the action. A preliminary authorial note reads:

> How these papers have been placed in sequence will be made clear in the reading of them. All needless matters have been eliminated, so that a history almost at variance with the possibilities of latter-day belief may stand forth as simple fact. There is throughout no statement of past events wherein memory may err, for all the records chosen are exactly contemporary, given from the standpoints and within the range of knowledge of those who made them.[20]

A remote ancestor to this procedure is the epistolary novel of the eighteenth century; a closer antecedent is Wilkie Collins's crime-novel *The Moonstone* (1868). But whereas Collins is concerned with a terrestrial crime — the theft of a diamond — Stoker is intent on evading all such limitations through his focus on a human who cannot ultimately die. The multiple narration of *The Moonstone* is apt to the relative knowledge and ignorance that characterizes crime, concealment and detection; the apparently similar device in *Dracula* camouflages the essentially non-narratable nature of the central theme. This epistemological catch-as-catch-can is then 'balanced' by the sensationalist immediacy of the multiple narrators and their up-to-the-minute records of the action. Stoker is partly right to speak of there being 'no statement of past events wherein memory may err' because the notion of an 'undead' person effectively abolishes the distinction between past and present.

Given that he is the embodiment of this abolition, the presence of the Count wreaks havoc on the characterization of the merely living, mortal figures — Lucy Westenra, Jonathan Harker, Mina Harker, Dr Seward and so forth. The individuality, even uniqueness, which western civilization assumed to be essential to the human personality, undergoes a degree of amalgamation that indicates more than mere incompetence on Stoker's part, more than the conventional woodenness of gothic characterization. The nominal aspect of *Dracula*'s characters takes on an additional force in the absence of any profound characterization. Harker somehow harks or listens, and in this way his name becomes a transparent cipher. Lucy bears the equally unusual surname, Westenra, and if this associates her with western civilization as against the murky powers of the Transylvanian past, it also relates her to the Westenra family (barons of Rossmore) of County Monaghan. Such nominal disruptions, together with this breakdown of the underlying assumption of Victorian psychology, are evident in the linguistic textures of *Dracula*, where middle-class banality masquerading as incomprehension of the Count's real nature is augmented by the device of opening the novel with a journal originally written up in shorthand, by occasional hymns of praise to the portable typewriter, and — crucially — by Van Helsing's incomplete grasp of English grammar. While advances in communications such as shorthand and typing are attached to those who are at the vampire's mercy, the sole figure who can master Dracula is unable to master the English language.

In this novel, the impossible or non-credible element upon which the title-character is founded essentially depends upon the control of language. In Jonathan Harker's (originally) shorthand account of his first morning in Castle Dracula, the Count promptly points to his collection of books, which, however, he refers to by the more intimate term 'these friends'. Harker congratulates the Count on his thorough knowledge of English, to which the latter replies:

> 'I thank you, my friend, for your all too flattering estimate, but yet I fear that I am but a little way on the road I would travel. True, I know the grammar and the words, but yet I know not how to speak them.'[21]

Superficially, the Count is presented here in all the fluency of a costume-drama villain: he has the seducer's gilded tongue, the false modesty of a confident monomaniac. Yet the incorporation of the

20. Bram Stoker, *Dracula* (Harmondsworth: Penguin, 1979), p. [8].

21. ibid., p. 31.

newly arrived Englishman Harker ('my friend') into the Count's linguistic stockpile ('these friends') accomplishes within a single paragraph an underlying feature of Stoker's book — the notion, not yet articulate in anglophone proto-modernism, that language is an arbitrary set of signs, uncertainly linked to some more 'real' reality. What the Count protests to his guest might be conventionally restated to reveal that he does not know 'the soul of the English language'; gesturally and systematically, what the novel delves into is the fear that no such spiritual metaphor is appropriate to language.

Intimacy is the mediating narrative between the ineffable domain of the old-fashioned 'spirit' and the newly discovered unattached randomness of 'language'. The Count is quick to begin the process; it is a *hors d'oeuvre* to his more notorious oral intentions upon the English visitors. By way of contrast, Van Helsing's entrance is delayed, and his ultimate triumph over spiritual evil is marked throughout by linguistic incompetence:

> Now to the historical, for as Madam Mina write not in her stenography, I must, in my cumbrous old fashion, that so each day of us may not go unrecorded.[22]

It is noteworthy that here Van Helsing does not contrast his writing to Mina Harker's native fluency but to her commercial dexterity, and he alludes not to his broken English but to his out-of-date technique — 'cumbrous' encases all this in sentimental obscurity. It goes without saying that *Dracula* is riddled with sexuality, explicit and otherwise; and readers need little reminding that the tragedy of the Count lies in the fact that he is compelled to bite off more than he can screw. What needs to be said is that Van Helsing's verbal formulations in relation to Mina Harker are also marked with sexual innuendo:

> At the first, I tell Madam Mina to sleep; she try, and she succeed. She sleep all the time; till at the last, I feel myself to suspicious grow, and attempt to wake her. But she sleep on, and I may not wake her though I try. I do not wish to try too hard lest I harm her; for I know that she have suffer much, and sleep at times be all-in-all to her. I think I drowse myself, for all of sudden I feel guilt, as though I have done something; I find myself bolt up, with the reins in my hand, and the good horses go along jog, jog, just as ever. I look down and find Madam Mina still sleep.[23]

22. ibid., p. 431.

In a memorandum written by a man speeding across central Europe to extinguish the last of the undead, 'the good horses go along jog, jog' is surely superfluous, one of those needless matters the author had allegedly eliminated. If we keep to the possibilities of latter-day belief, and discount vampirism, then the coincidence of Abraham Stoker's Christian name with his character Van Helsing's takes on an added significance. *Dracula* commenced with a Harker, which is not so far from a Stoker; now it closes with an all-powerful Abraham in suggestive control of Mrs Harker's sleeping and waking. The violence of this, or the element of violation implicit in sexual control, is deflected into the multiple knifing of Dracula by Jonathan Harker and Quincey Morris; and to emphasize the potency of these actions, a child of the Harkers is born on the calendar-day upon which Dracula's assailant (Morris) died, a child whose 'bundles of names links all our little band of men together; but we call him Quincey'.[24] If this is nothing more than sunshine through the nursery window, a commonplace of Victorian fiction, Harker's concluding note reverts to the issue of linguistic accountability:

> I took the papers from the safe where they have been ever since our return so long ago. We were struck with the fact that, in all the mass of material of which the record is composed, there is hardly one authentic document! nothing but a mass of typewriting, except the later notebooks....[25]

Van Helsing's final act of exorcism, then, is to banish any ontological fears this lack of full authenticity might give rise to. He does this by pointing complacently to the living child. After the violent fiction, domestic intimacy can be resumed through a little speech of Van Helsing's which, as it happens, wholly lacks grammatical solecism and broken idiom.

Of course, *Dracula* cannot be summarized solely in terms of its linguistic crises and resolutions. It has a prevailing geographical setting — Transylvania — and a great rigmarole of folk

23. ibid., p. 432.
24. ibid., p. 449.
25. idem.

beliefs, plausible and otherwise. Thus, while it remains an exotic product of 1890's fiction, it is not without lines of connection to more complex novels, even if an important line in this pattern of connection is the cult of the primitive. Two years after the publication of *Dracula*, the Irish folklorist William Larminie (1849-1900) wrote:

> It is clear that just as the meaning and seriousness of life shrink to nothing in the absence of transcendentalism, so does the value of the art shrink which deals with a life from which transcendental belief has disappeared. The life becomes aimless, corrupt, or both, the only point of interest being the pathos of the spectacle of souls robbed of their heritage.[26]

Students of the Irish literary revival are well acquainted with the role of folk material in providing the modern artist with a sense of this endangered transcendental dimension; Yeats strove to harness both the folklorist's methodology and his material to the poetic quest and, as the work of John Millington Synge (1871-1909) and Augusta Lady Gregory (1859-1932) manifestly demonstrates, he was not alone in looking to folk tradition. This recourse to the primitive is no simple matter of a return to native or national roots; it forms part of wider patterns of modernist writing traceable in the writings of Joseph Conrad and D. H. Lawrence, to name but two non-Irish anglophone novelists.

For Larminie, Transylvanian peasant belief in 'the evil eye', as described by Stoker, would not in itself have diminished his interest in *Dracula*. Larminie worked with Yeats and Lady Gregory, and his diagnosis of 'souls robbed of their heritage' fits uncannily Van Helsing's account of the voluptuous women whose living corpses he must assault in order to rescue their souls from the grip of that perverted immortality, the vampire. Yet, despite his background, Stoker rarely refers in his fiction to Ireland or its surviving folk traditions. True, his first novel (*The Snake's Pass*, London, 1891) is set in County Mayo, abounds in sentimental violent incident, and even summons up legends of the French revolutionary invasion. True also that *Dracula* was eventually translated into Irish in 1933, perhaps to mark the accession to power of Eamon de Valera. Essentially, Stoker aligns himself with the London exiles (and not only Shaw and Wilde, but Arthur Conan Doyle and Arthur Sullivan) as against the home-based revivalists, and the gross primitivism of his best-known fiction indicates the compensatory mechanisms at work in this dichotomy of the metropolitan and the provincial. Similarly, his most renowned novel highlights two contrasting but mutually dependent features: the proliferating technologies of commercial office management, and a madly exotic setting. The latter is perched vertiginously between the west and the east, between rival forms of Christianity, between Christianity and rival religions. These regional tensions are then given a kind of horrible stability by the jeopardizing of that biological time which distinguishes between death and life. If one were to look for a complementary image closer to home, then W. B. Yeats's denunciations of industrialized and commercialized England spring to mind — his novella *John Sherman* (1891) and the more trenchant journalism he wrote during the last decade of the nineteenth century.

Transylvania may not have been the military cockpit of Europe that Belgium was to become fifteen years after *Dracula*, but it was historically a frontier region between the Hapsburg and Ottoman empires or, in the late nineteenth century, between British and Russian spheres of interest. Stoker's principal informant on matters Hungarian and Transylvanian, Armin Vambery, had stressed the rivalry — military and commercial — of these great powers in several of his publications.[27] Oscar Wilde's Russian play, *Vera; or, the Nihilists*, was produced in 1883; its published version includes a prologue employing a crude anticipation of Lady Gregory's 'Kiltartanese', a dramatic idiom resembling Irish peasant speech. Joseph Conrad's great novel of Russian terrorism in exile, *Under Western Eyes* (1911), is dedicated to an Irishwoman, Agnes Tobin, who had befriended Synge on her return from the United States. However loosely, *Dracula* attaches itself to aspects of high modernism, to fragmentary aspects of its political and religious preoccupations. *Dracula* gives evidence of some anxieties about language, anxieties we now recognize as the starting point from which the revolutionary linguistics of Ferdinand de Saussure

26. Quoted by John Wilson Foster, *Fictions of the Irish Literary Revival: A Changeling Art* (Syracuse: Syracuse University Press, 1987), p. 155.

27. Among those of Vambery's books translated into English before 1897, see in particular *Central Asia and the Anglo-Russian Frontier Question* (London: Smith, Elder, 1874).

set out. But the whole *irrationale* of the novel is directed towards a return to the securities of a language domesticated and serviceable in the bourgeois world where even Van Helsing is fluently accommodated at last. Borrowing a phrase from American historiography, we can call Stoker's relation to modernism 'a pre-emptive counter-revolution'. Just as it is wrongheaded to read the passage by Larminie just quoted as a startling anticipation of James Joyce's *Dubliners*, so it would be wrong to recruit Stoker to any Anglo-Irish modernist canon.[28]

Oscar Wilde's fiction stands in serene contrast to all this. *The Picture of Dorian Gray* (1891) and the various shorter tales display an ease of narrative advance that instantly shows up the awkward construction and lurid texture of Stoker's writing. Yet there are paradoxes here. Wilde's novel centrally employs the reverse morality of the visual image in a manner not inconsistent with the vampiric avoidance of mirrors, and his shorter fiction repeatedly originated in conversation, in a drawing room transformation of an Irish storytelling tradition which he knew through the researches of both his mother and father. In addition to the family's devotion to things natively Irish, Lady Wilde (née Jane Francesca Elgee, 1826-96) had contributed to the store of Irish gothic writing with translations from the German.[29] Yet while *Vera* and *Dorian Gray* — not to mention *Salomé* (1893) — are not deficient in violent or macabre scenes, it is with a short and more isolated composition that Wilde opens his brief negotiations with gothic writing. 'The Canterville Ghost' first appeared in *Court and Society Review* in 1891, and was collected in *Lord Arthur Savile's Crime and Other Stories* (1891). Unlike Stoker, Wilde's reputation is secured by work other than that included in this section of the anthology, and there is little need to introduce him or his achievement to the reader. What one particularly notes in 'The Canterville Ghost', of course, is its playful acceptance of the fictional nature of gothic convention — hauntings, medieval armour, ineradicable bloodstains, and so forth. On the basis of his easy narration, Wilde builds these familiar devices into an ostentatiously contemporary setting and transforms the ancient clash of dynasties or feuding families into an account of American domestic ingenuity at work in an English country house. The lightness of all this disguises Wilde's insinuation that an invasion of manners is no less an invasion than the Norman conquest: Wilde is as much a political writer as Maria Edgeworth and, like her, he understands that style is a miniature politics. In this light, the fact that the Americans concerned are the family of a diplomat is more than a sop to the glory-hunting readers of *Court and Society Review*, more even than a vehicle for the author's mischievous allusions to republican virtue. Wilde's politics were consistently, if not always evidently, radical.

In contrast again to the heavy-handed Stoker, the child in Wilde's ghost story is a delightfully complex figure. As her name suggests, Virginia is the embodiment of innocence in its most actively sympathetic form, yet she is also the chosen one of the young Duke of Cheshire. Here Wilde's gothic tale has finally turned into a fairy story. In life, things went differently. Wilde's charmed existence was transformed into vilification and imprisonment for criminal homosexual practices. At least one commentator has suggested that the triumphantly voluptuous women at Castle Dracula owed something to the street-carnival of London's whores at the downfall of Wilde. On his release from prison, he acknowledged something of the gothic aspect in his own life by adopting the pseudonym Sebastian Melmoth, after the hero of Charles Robert Maturin's novel. But since Lady Wilde's maternal aunt had married Maturin, Wilde's gesture of disguise merely served to underline a family kinship. The closeness of an Irish Victorian gothic tradition could be confirmed even in its extinction.

J. M. SYNGE'S *WHEN THE MOON HAS SET*

With Yeats, Synge and Bowen, we enter a qualitatively different phase of literary history. Both Stoker and Wilde had sought to terminate the Irish gothic tradition, the first by attempting a total transvaluation in which the drawing room once more would triumph, the second by laughing the gothic out of court. Wilde's radical deliberation, rather than Stoker's conservative trepidation, set the tone for their twentieth-century successors. Yet before the more subtle exploitation or elaboration of the

28. The 'wrongheaded' argument rejected here is advanced by Foster (op. cit.) with specific reference to Joyce's 'The Dead', though with diminishing confidence.
29. See Terence de Vere White, *The Parents of Oscar Wilde: Sir William and Lady Wilde* (London: Hodder and Stoughton, 1967).

supernatural and the terrible got under way, the anxieties of Irish class relations still had something to offer.

Even today, J. M. Synge is too often regarded as the peasant dramatist whom Yeats elegized in the years after 1909. And even among theatre-goers well acquainted with Synge's emphatically non-peasant background, *The Playboy of the Western World* (1907) is thought of as depicting an Irish social reality upon which aesthetic reflection has neither smiled nor frowned. We may insist that the much-repeated (that is, Yeats-repeated) account of the elder poet's urging Synge 'to go to the Aran Islands and find a life that had never been expressed in literature' misleads with its simple-minded notion of literature's expressivity.[30] Yet the more complex relation between dramatic setting, aesthetic mediation and social reality that informs Synge's great plays is comparatively unexplored. In part, responsibility for this must lie with Yeats who, for his own immediate strategic purposes, required of the dead Synge that he haunt Ireland, berating it as a culture which, in him, had rejected its own artistic begetter. In part also we can now see that another mistaken notion — of Synge's dramatic settings being all of a piece, undifferentiatedly Irish and peasantly classless — derives from the ideology of an homogeneous, unified nation in the process of giving birth to itself in the years surrounding 1921.[31]

Synge's early literary experiments were introspective and melancholic. They were located far from the land where Pegeen Mike Flaherty lay awaiting her playboy. By birth he had a better claim to gentry status than any other participant in the Irish literary movement of his day, Edward Martyn excepted. The Synges had come to Ireland in the seventeenth century, acquired landed estates, provided the Church of Ireland with numerous clergy and bishops, and in the early nineteenth century even linked themselves by marriage to the titled classes. But the Victorian era was one of reversal and paradox for the Synges; some of the family became involved with the Plymouth Brethren, an extreme evangelical sect that had originated within the Church of Ireland; some had lost land in the aftermath of the Famine, had turned to the professions as a way of life and had moved into suburban Dublin. John Hatch Synge (1824–72) had become a barrister; after his death, his widow moved her family to a house on Orwell Road, Rathgar. The future author of *In the Shadow of the Glen* grew up with but a distant prospect of the hills in which his first play was to be ostensibly set. His upbringing was restrictively pious, anti-intellectual and philistine.[32]

There were two links with the family's lost prestige, neither of them wholly reassuring. J. M. Synge's second eldest brother became a land agent, and in this subordinate role represented the family throughout the land war of the 1880s. Glanmore, a neo-gothic castle near Ashford in County Wicklow, had once belonged to the playwright's grandfather. But through vagaries of religious affiliation, financial difficulty and a second marriage, this refuge from middle-class Rathgar was no longer in the hands of Synges. As a child J. M. Synge visited the castle, but his more regular point of contact in Wicklow was a smaller farmhouse on higher, poorer land north-west of Ashford which his mother rented for summer holidays. Not only did this distance from the neo-gothic battlements of Glanmore measure the decline in the Synges' financial well-being, it also brought to the young man's attention the means whereby his family had earlier acquired the wealth now so evidently dispersed. This inquiry into the nature of inheritance formed the basis of Synge's first completed play.

It is not clear how Synge came in possession of the material upon which *When the Moon Has Set* is based. During the tumultuous 1880s, his elder brother Edward was involved in enforcing numerous evictions, including some in County Wicklow. Their mother relied on a small annual income from properties in County Galway, and the family were frequently made aware of the threatened stability of real estate in Ireland. Moreover, Synge's late father had borne Christian names that came to him from his great-grandfather, John Hatch of Lissenhall, near Swords, Co. Dublin. This shadowy ancestor of the playwright

30. W. B. Yeats, 'The Tragic Generation' in *Autobiographies* (London: Macmillan, 1955), p. 343.
31. The classic use of Synge's work as an example of 'a national literature' is Daniel Corkery, *Synge and Anglo-Irish Literature* (Cork: Cork University Press, 1931).
32. See the biography edited by Andrew Carpenter from the vast typescript assembled by Synge's nephew and literary executor: *My Uncle John: Edward Stephens's Life of J. M. Synge* (London: Oxford University Press, 1974).

died near the close of the eighteenth century, leaving lands that formed the basis of the Synge's Wicklow estates. The question was — how had Hatch acquired these lands in the first place? — a question doubly disturbing to a youth brought up in a household equally sensitive to ethical niceties and assaults on property.

The play possesses features which are now familiar from our survey of nineteenth-century Irish literature as affected by influences from the gothic novel. Legacy, and the discovery of a will, is central. As in 'Wildgoose Lodge' and the opening pages of *The Fortunes of Hector O'Halloran*, there is an attack on an isolated house. The continental alternative to Irish reality, represented by Napoleon's wars in the last-named novel, is inscribed by Synge in the form of a highly self-consciousness epistle on aesthetics written from Paris to the hero of the play. And as in Wilde's *Vera* and W. B. Yeats's (later) *Cathleen ni Houlihan*, divergences of class and dramatic dialect are explored. Although *When the Moon Has Set* remained unpublished for more than half-a-century after Synge's death, the nervous immediacy of its relation to his own painful maturing as a playwright can still be traced. From an eighteenth-century document preserved in the National Library of Ireland, we can reconstruct by means of summary quotations the events leading up to the death of a Mr Samuel McCracken:

> 1762 May 15 Mr Samuel Macraken of Roundwood in the Co. Wicklow duly made and published his last will . . . and thereof appointed John Hatch . . . his sole Ex[ecuto]r and . . . leaves all his leases . . . to said John Hatch. . . .
> This Will was left by Mr Macraken in the hands of Mr Duffe . . . together with a letter directed to said John Hatch and dated february 25th 1766. . . .
> 1769 Augt 2d He came to town and dined with said John Hatch & on the 4th came to him and complained most grievously of his unfortunate situation, beged [*sic*] that he (said Hatch) wou'd let him go to Lissenhall & that he wou'd there give him a Garret and let him remain there as he cou'd never think of returning to his own House, told him of an affair he had with a maid Servant in his house, that the maid Servant married a man in his Neighbourhood who threatened to prosecute him at the assizes. . . .
> [Hatch and a friend then advised McCracken] that he shoud [*sic*] return home the next morning, go to the assizes of Wicklow the tuesday following. . . .
> Saturday Augst 5th Mr Macraken went to his lodging in the even: and next morning he called on Mr Hatch between seven and 8 o'clock and about 8 set out for his own house, got home about 11 that night, went to Church next morning, dined at home, read prayers to his family in the Evening went to bed about 9 o'clock and was found Dead on the floor of his bed Chamber next morning with his brains blown about and a Discharged Pistol by his side. . . .[33]

But the suicide of McCracken (a cousin of John Hatch's) did not result in a simple execution of the 1765 will in favour of Hatch. A second unwitnessed will was discovered on the old man's death, and the proposed beneficiary of this second will, a nephew named William Stewart, eventually forged a third document in the hope of giving effect to the second. All these delays were resolutely resisted by Hatch, who also took advice as to how he might retain the property to his descendants in the absence of male issue. For Hatch had married Barbara Synge *c.*1765 and their two daughters duly 'married their cousins, the brothers Francis and Samuel Synge, sons of their mother's brother', the Rev. Edward Synge, D.D. (died 1792).[34] From Francis Synge and his wife Elizabeth (née Hatch), the Wicklow properties of Samuel McCracken descended through John Hatch's will to the diversified family of J. M. Synge's day. In particular, the lands of McCracken himself lay precisely where Mrs Synge took her children on their holidays.

A comparison is worthwhile between aspects of this morbid chronicle on the one hand, and the plot of Synge's first completed play on the other. The locations, historical and dramatic, can be reconciled. The episode of an affair between the master of the house and a maid servant is repeated from history into the play. In the latter, however, old Columb Sweeny's letter to his heir repeatedly stresses the honour of his conduct: 'I was

33. National Library of Ireland Ms. 11,333. [Orthography is non-standard.]
34. See *My Uncle John*, p. 5.

scrupulous when I should have been strong', 'No man of our blood has ever been unlawful.' The uncompleted threat to the elder Sweeny is transferred onto the hero, his nephew/namesake, while the sexual offence against marriage is deflected onto the servant, Bride — note her exonerating name — who is pregnant. The dead man's letter, together with the attack on young Columb Sweeny, provides the necessary delay in Synge's play for hero and heroine to overcome their differences and fall acceptably in love. This may be seen as taken over from the historical source in some act of fidelity, but it is held aside from any dramatic implication until well into the last half of the second act. Although the will itself is entirely passed over in silence, the ultimate union of young Sweeny and his cousin, Sister Eileen, is achieved through the reading of successive documents. Their 'marriage' according to the impromptu rites of a solar religion eliminates the implied difference of denominational loyalty between the hero as (protestant) heir to the Big House and the heroine as (catholic) nun. If we read McCracken's affair and suicide, and Hatch's bullying insistence on the original will, as a kind of guilty inheritance, then *When the Moon Has Set* seeks to transform such legacies from the past by means of a unifying myth.

We cannot say with any certainty how J. M. Synge came upon the material quoted above, but certain matters serve to remind us of how close the documentary and the literary have often been in the course of nineteenth-century Irish literature. First, the document quoted at length is part of a brief prepared by John Hatch in connection with his own involvement in McCracken's estate. It is preserved in the Joly Papers in the National Library; John Joly (1857-1933) had been a friend of the Synge family, and was an unsuccessful suitor of Synge's sister Annie in the early 1880s. The decade of the Land War undoubtedly generated discussions of the family's place in the system of inherited real estate upon which Irish society was based, and the quietly dissident J. M. Synge may have noticed the skeletons in the cupboard. Nor is *When the Moon Has Set* irrelevant to a reading of Synge's more mature work. The beautifully ironic essay 'A Landlord's Garden in County Wicklow' (*c.*1903) coolly describes the decline of the nineteenth-century Big House. *Deirdre of the Sorrows*, for all its elaborate use of Gaelic myth, also focuses on a ruling elite divided against itself and shaken by guilt. What a renewed appreciation of the present play can prompt is a fuller awareness of the complexities of setting and allusion in Synge's classic plays.[35]

W. B. YEATS AND *THE WORDS UPON THE WINDOW-PANE*

If Synge was born into a family which had once owned a neo-gothic castle, W. B. Yeats first saw the light of day in a suburban house a few hundred yards from a gothicized eighteenth-century house owned by his uncle, Robert Corbet. But Sandymount Castle was disposed of by its bankrupt owner, though the poet's father continued to regale the boy with stories of its turrets and gardens even after the financial collapse of the Corbets. In John Butler Yeats's mind, the castle was associated with William Morris's poetry, and his son's early interest in Morris's medievalism was part of a larger hostility to the modern, the mechanical and the rational. Yeats requires no summary here, but in connection with the gothic mode it is fair to emphasize his life-long commitment to magic and the occult as well as his youthful love of guild exclusivity. During the years of his London exile, Yeats sought through spiritualism and theosophy to overcome the agnosticism imposed on him (as he thought) by his father's defection from orthodox Christian belief. These various systems and pseudo-sciences were, as Denis Donoghue has persuasively argued, aspects of Yeats's search for power.[36] The supernatural (but not, for the most part, the divine) preoccupied him throughout his life, with Japanese drama providing at least as much illumination as the folklore of the Irish countryside or the trance-transmitted 'automatic' writing of his wife. These many commitments to the supernatural, evident both in the poet's emotional needs and in his intellectual initiatives, frequently manifested themselves in a further preoccupation with history. *A Vision*, the quasi-philosophical system first published in 1925, advances a reading of past and future.

It might seem that Maturin and Le Fanu had much to offer the young Yeats. But he read the century of his birth differently, preferring its poets

35. Such an analysis is advanced in Mary King, *The Drama of J. M. Synge* (London: Fourth Estate, 1985).

36. Denis Donoghue, *Yeats* (London: Fontana/Collins, 1971).

to its novelists, and (with reservations) preferring the local or national to the dislocated settings of *Melmoth* and *The House by the Church-yard*. Nevertheless, as a diligent collector of useful material from popular legend, Yeats sometimes found himself linking folk belief, politics, and Victorian fiction. Thus, in *Fairy and Folk Tales of the Irish Peasantry* (1888), he comments in a note on 'Omens':

> Some families are attended by phantoms of ravens or other birds. When [Terence Bellew] McManus of '48 celebrity, was sitting by his dying brother, a bird of vulture-like appearance came through the window and lighted on the breast of the dying man. The two watched in terror, not daring to drive it off. It crouched there, bright-eyed, till the soul left the body. It was considered a most evil omen. [Joseph Sheridan] Lefanu worked this into a tale.[37]

What Yeats particularly shared with Le Fanu was an interest in the doctrines of Emanuel Swedenborg (1688-1772), especially Swedenborg's system of correspondences, a comprehensive symbology in which every detail of the material/visible world is related to a spiritual value. Le Fanu had employed Swedenborgianism most thoroughly in his novel *Uncle Silas*, but the doctrines had long before attracted the attention of Blake, Goethe, Balzac and Baudelaire, all of whom provide an antecedent to Yeats's evident use of Swedenborgianism in *The Words upon the Window-pane* (first performed in 1930).

The Grand Guignol aspect of the gothic mode, its terror-inducing and blood-bespattered scenes, retained little power to impress a poet immersed in the subtleties of French symbolism. However, the ghost was another matter, for he formed part of a chain linking the past and present, through lines of attachment to place or guilty consequence. Irish Big Houses had ghosts, and Yeats occasionally told Irish ghost stories of a less radically frivolous kind than Wilde's 'The Canterville Ghost'. That the ghost was to be found also in Homer and in the Japanese Noh plays gave him a degree of acceptability that neither Horace Walpole nor Sheridan Le Fanu could wholly compromise. In *Reveries Over Childhood and Youth* (1915), Yeats recorded the rake-hellish pranks of a relative by marriage at Castle Dargan in County Sligo, concluding with a sly insinuation of the man's real or simulated support for the Land League.[38] At some point during this same wartime period, he told a ghost story at a soirée in Charles Ricketts's London home, a story that looks back to Castle Dargan and forward to his exquisitely constructed late play *Purgatory* (1938). Moreover, it unwittingly explicates the breathless conclusion to Maturin's *Women* (1818) and so contributes to an understanding of the interactions between violent incident and gothic convention, between contemporaneity and historical setting, even (ultimately) between social class and modernist literary form. As recorded in Joseph Hone's biography of Yeats, the story told at Ricketts's house was as follows:

> Centuries ago there lived in a castle in Ireland a man and wife. To their abounding sorrow they remained childless despite prayers and pilgrimage. At last, when they had long given up all hope, the woman, to her joy, found herself pregnant. Her husband, who till then had been tender and trusting, became sullen and suspicious, often giving himself up to lonely bouts of drinking. Barely had the child been born when the man, roaring drunk, rushed into the upper chamber where his wife lay. With cries of 'Bastard, bastard' he wrested the baby from her breast, and with the screaming infant in his arms, strode raging from the room. Down the winding wooden stairs he ran into the hall where, all reason fled, he beat and beat the tiny thing against anything he could. From her bed the mother rose and followed ... to arrive too late. Her son was dead. Picking him up from where he had been flung, she turned and slowly climbed the spiral stairs that led to the threshold of her room. She moved as in a trance till, through the open door, the sight of the bed brought her to earth with a spasm of despair. Vehemently clasping the child, in a flash she bent beneath the bar which fenced

37. John Kelly and Eric Domville (eds), *The Collected Letters of W. B. Yeats; Volume One 1865-1895* (Oxford: Clarendon Press, 1986), p. 82n. The tale in question is 'The Watcher' in Le Fanu's anonymous *Ghost Stories and Tales of Mystery* (1851).

38. Yeats, *Autobiographies*, pp. 53-55. The relationship between this passage, the story told at Charles Ricketts's (see below), and the play *Purgatory* is examined at length in W. J. McCormack, *Ascendancy and Tradition in Anglo-Irish Literary History from 1798 to 1939* (Oxford: Clarendon Press, 1985), pp. 373-78.

the stairs, and dropped, like a singed moth, to the stone flood below. The man, his frenzy spent, was overwhelmed with grief. He sought consolation in taking another wife by whom he had other sons. Thus a family was founded and generation followed generation, each living much the same uneventful bucolic lives as those whom they succeeded. Although they cared for their castle and husbanded its lands, each in turn from time to time abandoned himself to the same solitary bouts. The house as a rule was a happy place but, during those spells, when its master was saturated with drink, an ashen woman would drift past him, ascending the curved stairs. Transfixed, he would wait the tragedy that he knew he was doomed only to see when he was drunk. Always with the same simple gesture she would reach the topmost step; always in the same way, pause, then bend, to drop a fluttering mass. Yet when he peered down he could see nothing. With the years the family vice grew like a cancer until it ate away their entire fortune and they were reduced to poverty. To crown their misery fire gutted the castle. The descendant to whom it then belonged was without the money or the desire to re-build. Indolent and inane, he left with few regrets to live in far-distant Dublin. Thenceforth the family and its fount seemed after countless years to have severed every bond. But destinies and traditions are hard to break and one day the grandson of this deserter was drawn to the very spot. His boon companion, killed by the kick of a horse, was to be buried within sight of the crumbling towers. Moved partly by affection for his friend, partly by curiosity to see the place whence his stock had sprung, the survivor of this long line had journeyed to attend the funeral. He met many friends and tippled with them all and, drunk, he found himself at dusk before the sombre shell of a stronghold. There being no door, he walked straight into the empty well up the wall of which had twined the oaken stairs. As he gazed he saw a fragile dishevelled form glide past him up and round the walls as though the steps were still there. Almost at the top she stopped, then with a burst of emotion dived, to disappear. The man knew no surprise. He felt that he had watched this melancholy scene innumerable times before — and for an instant he dimly understood that neither his children nor yet his children's children could ever purge themselves of a crime that they had inherited with their blood.[39]

No similar recitation informs *The Words upon the Window-pane*. But just as *Purgatory* draws on this story, which in turn recalls some pranks of a Yeats relative, reported in *Reveries Over Childhood and Youth*, so *The Words upon the Window-pane* attaches itself to a family history. In the last-named play, the young man who initiates the debate on history and civilization is named John Corbet. He is, at one level, a mocking self-portrait of the playwright: Yeats turned Cambridge postgraduate. But at another he bears a surname that linked the Yeatses to the gothic evidences of what proved to be only a temporary Hypostatic Union. 'Corbet', in the Yeats family annals, spells mortality, brevity. John Butler Yeats had a brother, Robert Corbet Yeats (*c.*1842-57), who died in Sandymount Castle. He had a son, Robert Corbet Yeats, (named after this brother, and younger than the poet) who died in 1873. Finally, there was Robert Corbet of Sandymount Castle whose gothic improvements were lost in bankruptcy.[40]

The play largely revolves round Corbet's questions about Jonathan Swift. The setting is a room in a decaying Dublin house, immediately before, during and after an apparently unsuccessful seance. Yeats deliberately sought to write a popular play, using conversational prose, in which his high themes of cultural decline and imminent collapse might be brought to a wider audience. The intention was something of a paradox, for Yeats held that wider audiences were inimical to culture, its survival or growth. One might deduce from this a certain antagonism on the writer's part towards culture, a longing for some cataclysmic end to the 'manifold illusion' which (in the poem 'Meru') is the cohesive bond in civilization. But paradox works more radically in the material of the play. The seance is a degenerate means of access to spiritual truth, and in this case there is added reason to believe that the medium (Mrs Henderson) is less

39. J.M. Hone, *W.B. Yeats 1865-1939* (London: Macmillan, 1942), pp. 283-84.

40. For a convenient discussion, see William M. Murphy, *The Yeats Family and the Pollexfens* (Dublin: Dolmen Press, 1971).

than reliable. Yet after her shabby performance, Swift's voice rings through the room, cursing his very birth. In this indirect way, the postgraduate Corbet is retrospectively rebuked, not so much for being wrong, but for being inadequate to the depth of inquiry required of him. Corbet initially had declared himself a sceptic on the topic of seances, and had summarized his excursion into this kind of lore with a very short reading-list including 'a wild book by Conan Doyle'. Arthur Conan Doyle (1859-1930), creator of Sherlock Holmes, author of imperialistic adventure stories and supporter of the British cause in South Africa, had devoted his last years to spiritualistic research, prompted to some degree by the death of friends in World War I. Yeats, in part mocking these wistful pursuits of dead friends 'in the beyond', added a trenchant note to the published text of *The Words upon the Window-pane*, emphasizing a wholly non-optimistic outlook in which war and destruction are accepted for some higher reality they may usher in. Speaking to 'the Cellars and Garrets', Yeats suggests to the masses, whom he thus encloses and dominates, that Progress, 'the sole religious myth of modern man, is only two hundred years old.' His own political preferences are clear enough, for such thoughts

> have already deepened our sense of tragedy and somewhat checked the naïver among those creeds and parties who push their way to power by flattering our moral hopes.[41]

The Words upon the Window-pane is a highly complex series of texts-within-texts, with citations of book titles, readings of poems, hymn-singing, the summary of a Cambridge thesis, and the elaborate unconscious ventriloquism of the medium. There is, centrally, a play-within-a play, mediated from the past by the words of Mrs Henderson, reading from an unseen, unwritten, yet determinate script. With infinitely greater delicacy and structural intelligence than Stoker in *Dracula*, Yeats builds up a montage of textual sources, all lacking in ultimate authority yet reassuringly accessible. The climax of the play, and the full emergence of the inner play, comes with the breaking of Mrs Henderson's saucer and the unmediated sound of Swift's voice: 'Perish the day on which I was born!' Instead of Stoker's cosy reconstitution of the domestic circle through the birth of a child and the perfection of Van Helsing's English, Yeats insists on a tragic denouement, stripped of moral hopes and promising nothing but 'the ruin to come'. In the early 1930s, it was difficult to decipher such a play without reference to European politics. If, as we have suggested, Stoker launched a pre-emptive counter-revolution against modernism, we see in the Yeats after 1930 evidence of an urge towards moral cynicism, or formal nihilism. No work of his wholly endorses such an urge. Most acknowledge it by resisting it, as in the lines mock-scornfully advising the reader to

> Leave nothing but the nothings that belong
> To this bare soul . . . .[42]

The privileging of the unmediated spoken word at the end *The Words upon the Window-pane* is a railing against culture, just as the words spoken are a vain attempt to cancel being.

Mention of Van Helsing, however, brings us back to an earlier stage in the evolution of the play. Liam Miller informs us that 'the earliest draft contains a passage which relates the theme to the stories of J. Sheridan Le Fanu, particularly to the collection entitled *In a Glass Darkly*, but this theme was abandoned as the plot developed.'[43] Here we have a measure of the extent to which Yeats could look back to his Victorian predecessors, and derive some artistic advantage from reading the sensational and the gothic. The elimination of the reference to Le Fanu in the play's text has the effect of evacuating all the buzz of historical actuality and social process that intervened between Jonathan Swift and W. B. Yeats. Le Fanu, as Yeats well knew, had strong links with Swift through the Sheridan family and through papers which had descended to him. In its finished form *The Words upon the Window-pane* deviates from the use of sequential and documentary narratives that earlier had characterized the Irish gothic mode. In a wholly un-gothic fashion, the play ends on a note of prophecy masked as nihilism.

41. See Russell K. Alspach and C. C. Alspach (eds), *The Variorum Edition of the Plays of W. B. Yeats* (London: Macmillan, 1966), pp. 962-63.
42. W. B. Yeats, 'Parnell's Funeral' in *Collected Poems* (London: Macmillan, 1963), p. 320.
43. Liam Miller, *The Noble Drama of W. B. Yeats* (Dublin: Dolmen Press, 1977), p. 287.

ELIZABETH BOWEN

The daughter of Henry Cole Bowen, a County Cork landowner of Cromwellian descent, Elizabeth Bowen (1899-1973) had already published several novels by the time *The Words upon the Window-pane* was performed in the Abbey Theatre. For most of her life her milieu was that of the upper-middle-class English literary set, and the most important influence on her work was the fiction of Henry James. Her recurring theme is the isolation and casual betrayal of the young and innocent, especially young women, a theme elaborated in a series of novels and collections of short stories beginning with *Encounters* (1923). London, Paris, the English country house, respectable but deadly-dull seaside resorts provide her with a reliable background for her finely delineated studies in farouche desperation. In *The Last September* (1929) Elizabeth Bowen made rare use of her own Irish origins in a novel that employed the final stages of British occupation as the backdrop to a young girl's encounter with new realities. Her style, deriving not only from James but from Le Fanu, whom she admired, is at once articulate, nervous and controlled. These qualities aided her when, in the years of World War II, she took to writing modern ghost stories, *The Demon Lover and Other Stories* (1945). 'The Happy Autumn Fields' is one of the best of these. It has the added interest of (mutely) juxtaposing Irish and English locations, while also suggesting that this contrast in space or place may be seen as a difference in time.

Leaving aside the vexed question of a gothic survival in twentieth-century literature, we can see that the ghost story is always concerned with time. It may also emphasize guilt or horror, but its essential material is time. War alters perceptions and conceptions of time, and both of the world wars have witnessed a renewed interest in ghost stories. One of the more unlikely consequences of the August 1914 hostilities was that they prevented the Hon. Everard Feilding from bringing Yeats on a trip to Transylvania! Another was the rash of publications linking spiritualism, survival and psychic communication to the slaughter of an entire generation. The very different war experienced by civilians in London during the German bombing raids sharpened the sense of time's elasticity; this is attested in works as qualitatively different as T. S. Eliot's *Four Quartets* and J. W. Dunne's *Experiment with Time*, as well as a score of plays on the theme of 'the second chance' to live through a particular moment. Elizabeth Bowen's Irish Big House inheritance, her reading of Le Fanu and James, and her residence in London for much of the war provided her with ample experience for the writing of ghost stories.

The question of guilt nevertheless requires some further consideration, even in connection with a story such as 'The Happy Autumn Fields', where a character's personal responsibility is scarcely an issue, and where the ghostly element effectively is transposed into wholly structural terms. As the last heir to a Cromwellian legacy, Elizabeth Bowen might have been prey to a sense of guilt in a period of ultimately successful Irish escape from English occupation. There were additional and more urgent prompts to guilty reflection. A relative, Captain Bowen-Colthurst, having impulsively killed the pacifist Francis Skeffington in the aftermath of the 1916 Rising, had been packed off as insane to Broadmoor prison and then as sane to Canada. Yet Elizabeth Bowen's attitude towards the achievement of Irish independence in the years between cousin John's murder of Skeffington and her own first publication as a novelist had been remarkable for its moral balance and humane adjustment to wholly altered circumstances.

The war years, however, brought new difficulties. Independent Ireland remained neutral in the great European conflict between Britain and Germany. Bowen, never wholly at home in either Britain or Ireland, found herself inwardly divided between a sense of commitment to parliamentary/democratic freedom and an opportunity to claim Irish independence. She was not an ardent admirer of British society between the wars, but even the inchoate notion of *decency* proved its superiority to fascism. She made visits to Ireland during which she gathered material for a report to the English authorities on Irish attitudes to the war. Her novel *The Heat of the Day* (1949) probes painfully into such divided loyalties; it concerns a woman who loves a man she is gradually forced to recognize as a traitor to Britain, a woman whose son inherits in mid-war an estate in southern Ireland. Like Samuel Beckett, Louis MacNeice and Francis Stuart, Bowen encountered the war as a challenge to a host of untested assumptions about identity national and personal, about responsibility in its moral and aesthetic forms.

There is a poem by Yeats, published first in part in 1932 and wholly in 1934, which casts a light on the question of an inherent guilt in the writer. It is 'Parnell's Funeral', and these allusions back to the previous century underline the historical importance of the 1930s as the crucible in which a long-crystallizing issue is ultimately tested. Two central stanzas run:

An age is the reversal of an age:
When strangers murdered Emmet,
  Fitzgerald, Tone,
We lived like men that watch a painted stage.
What matter for the scene, the scene once
  gone:
It had not touched our lives. But popular rage,
Hysterica passio dragged this quarry down.
None shared our guilt; nor did we play a part
Upon a painted stage when we devoured his
  heart.

Come, fix upon me that accusing eye.
I thirst for accusation. All that was sung,
All that was said in Ireland is a lie
Bred out of the contagion of the throng,
Saving the rhyme rats hear before they die.
Leave nothing but the nothings that belong
To this bare soul, let all men judge that can
Whether it be an animal or a man.[44]

Like all of Yeats's greatest poems, this one functions on many levels, draws on diverse sources of imagery, mythological as well as political. To those for whom 'the Cretan barb' of the poem's opening stanza is a mystery, Robert Emmet's supposed Speech from the Dock is accessible. And, too often, vice versa, one might say, for all that Yeats demonstrates his ability to draw artistic vigour from vulgar knowledge. One critic has said of the public and plural 'we' in this and other poems that 'the speaker makes himself the scapegoat of an entire coterie', makes himself in effect a 'trapped Daedalus' indicted on charges of 'inaccurate vision, political naivete, precious refusals to act'.[45] In this masterly control of his speaker's dilemma as spokesman for an art all but redundant in the twentieth century, Yeats employs rhetorical elements and dramatic techniques familiar to us from the gothic sub-literature. If he transcends its aesthetic grossness, he does not necessarily avoid wholly the moral terrorism implicit in that legacy.

44. Yeats, *Collected Poems*, pp. 319-20.
45. Daniel A. Harris, *Yeats, Coole Park & Ballylee* (Baltimore and London: Johns Hopkins University Press, 1974), p. 156 and note.

CHARLES ROBERT MATURIN

(1782-1824)

from: MELMOTH THE WANDERER (1820)

[The first two chapters of Maturin's highly complicated gothic novel present an image of Irish rural accommodation that is less conventional than might appear on casual reading. The house in question is not notably large, and its location is comparatively close to Dublin. While the elaborate tale-within-a-tale takes the reader to Restoration London, the Indian Ocean and Spain during the Inquisition, these opening pages very effectively exploit a known Irish scene. Details of young Melmoth's financial dependence echo the author's own difficulties, while the business of a father placing his son under the guardianship of an uncle (commonplace enough of course) is modified effectively in Sheridan Le Fanu's *Uncle Silas* (1864). That the later novel employs an English setting encourages one to interpret the diverted father/son relationship (with a hostile uncle intervening) as analogous to a certain resentment among Irish loyalists at the remoteness of their British sponsors. However this may be, gothic atmosphere has rarely been evoked so powerfully in an Irish setting, and the later footnote allusions to Robert Emmet's rebellion (see Introduction above) benefit from the strength of these opening pages.]

CHAPTER I

Alive again? Then show me where he is;
I'll give a thousand pounds to look upon him.
SHAKESPEARE[1]

In the autumn of 1816, John Melmoth, a student in Trinity College, Dublin, quitted it to attend a dying uncle on whom his hopes for independence chiefly rested. John was the orphan son of a younger brother, whose small property scarce could pay John's college expences; but the uncle was rich, unmarried, and old; and John, from his infancy, had been brought up to look on him with that mingled sensation of awe, and of the wish, without the means to conciliate, (that sensation at once attractive and repulsive), with which we regard a being who (as nurse, domestic, and parent have tutored us to believe) holds the very threads of our existence in his hands, and may prolong or snap them when he pleases.

On receiving this summons, John set immediately out to attend his uncle.

The beauty of the country through which he travelled (it was the county Wicklow)[2] could not prevent his mind from dwelling on many painful thoughts, some borrowed from the past, and more from the future. His uncle's caprice and moroseness, — the strange reports concerning the cause of the secluded life he had led for many years, — his own dependent state, — fell like blows fast and heavy on his mind. He roused himself to repel them, — sat up in the mail,[3] in which he was a solitary passenger, — looked out on the prospect, — consulted his watch; — then he thought they receded for a moment, — but there was nothing to fill their place, and he was forced to invite them back for company. When the mind is thus active in calling over invaders, no wonder the conquest is soon completed. As the carriage drew near the Lodge, (the name of old Melmoth's seat), John's heart grew heavier every moment.

The recollection of this awful uncle from infancy, — when he was never permitted to approach him without innumerable lectures, — *not to be troublesome*, — not to go too near his uncle, — not to ask him any questions, — on no account to disturb the inviolable arrangement of his snuff-box, hand-bell, and spectacles, nor to suffer the glittering of the gold-headed cane to tempt him to the mortal sin of handling it, — and, finally, to pilot himself aright through his perilous course in and out of the apartment without striking against the piles of books, globes, old newspapers, wig-blocks,[4] tobacco-pipes, and snuff-cannisters, not to mention certain hidden rocks of rat-traps and mouldy books beneath the chairs, — together with the final reverential bow at the door, which was to be closed with cautious gentleness, and the stairs to be descended as if he were 'shod with felt'.[5] — This recollection was carried on to his school-boy years, when at Christmas and Easter, the ragged poney, the jest of the school, was dispatched to bring the reluctant visitor to the Lodge, — where his pastime was to sit vis-a-vis to his uncle, without speaking or moving, till the pair resembled Don Raymond and the ghost of Beatrice in the Monk,[6] — then watching him as he picked the bones of lean mutton out of his mess of weak broth, the latter of which he handed to his nephew with a needless caution not to 'take more than he liked,' — then hurried to bed by daylight, even in winter, to save the expence of an inch of candle, where he lay awake and restless from hunger, till his uncle's retiring at eight o'clock gave signal to the governante[7] of the meagre household to steal up to him with some fragments of her own scanty meal, administering between every mouthful a whispered caution not to tell his uncle. Then his college life, passed in an attic in the second square,[8] uncheered by an invitation to the country; the gloomy summer wasted in walking up and down the deserted streets, as his uncle would not defray the expences of his journey; — the only intimation of his existence, received in quarterly epistles, containing, with the scanty but punctual remittance, complaints of the expences of his education, cautions against extravagance, and lamentations for the failure of tenants and the fall of the value of lands. All these recollections came over

1. II *Henry VI*, III. 3. 12-13.
2. The mountainous county immediately south of County Dublin, scene of rebellion in 1798.
3. The coach carrying mail and passengers.
4. Wooden stands on which wigs were hung (to keep them shapely) when they were not being worn.
5. cf. *King Lear*, IV. 6. 189-90: 'to shoe / A troop of horse with felt'.
6. *The Monk* (1796) by M. G. Lewis (1775-1818) is one of the most renowned of gothic novels.
7. housekeeper.
8. Trinity College, Dublin is built on a pattern of rectangles. The term used here is not idiomatic.

him, and along with them the remembrance of that last scene, where his dependence on his uncle was impressed on him by the dying lips of his father.

'John, I must leave you, my poor boy; it has pleased God to take your father from you before he could do for you what would have made this hour less painful to him. You must look up, John, to your uncle for every thing. He has oddities and infirmities, but you must learn to bear with them, and with many other things too, as you will learn too soon. And now, my poor boy, may He who is the father of the fatherless look on your desolate state, and give you favour in the eyes of your uncle.' As this scene rose to John's memory, his eyes filled fast with tears, which he hastened to wipe away as the carriage stopt to let him out at his uncle's gate.

He alighted, and with a change of linen in a handkerchief, (his only travelling equipment), he approached his uncle's gate. The lodge was in ruins, and a barefooted boy from an adjacent cabin ran to lift on its single hinge what had once been a gate, but was now a few planks so villainously put together, that they clattered like a sign in a high wind. The stubborn post of the gate, yielding at last to the united strength of John and his barefooted assistant, grated heavily through the mud and gravel stones, in which it left a deep and sloughy furrow, and the entrance lay open. John, after searching his pocket in vain for a trifle to reward his assistant, pursued his way, while the lad, on his return, cleared the road at a hop step and jump, plunging through the mud with all the dabbling and amphibious delight of a duck, and scare less proud of his agility than of his 'sarving a gentleman.' As John slowly trod the miry road which had once been the approach, he could discover, by the dim light of an autumnal evening, signs of increasing desolation since he had last visited the spot, — signs that penury had been aggravated and sharpened into downright misery. There was not a fence or a hedge round the domain: an uncemented wall of loose stones, whose numerous gaps were filled with furze or thorns, supplied their place. There was not a tree or shrub on the lawn; the lawn itself was turned into pasture-ground, and a few sheep were picking their scanty food amid the pebblestones, thistles, and hard mould, through which a few blades of grass made their rare and squalid appearance.

The house itself stood strongly defined even amid the darkness of the evening sky; for there were neither wings, or offices, or shrubbery, or tree, to shade or support it, and soften its strong harsh outline. John, after a melancholy gaze at the grass-grown steps and boarded windows, 'addressed himself' to knock at the door; but knocker there was none: loose stones, however, there were in plenty; and John was making vigorous application to the door with one of them, till the furious barking of a mastiff, who threatened at every bound to break his chain, and whose yell and growl, accompanied by 'eyes that glow and fangs that grin,'[9] savoured as much of hunger as of rage, made the assailant raise the siege on the door, and betake himself to a well-known passage that led to the kitchen. A light glimmered in the window as he approached: he raised the latch with a doubtful hand; but, when he saw the party within, he advanced with the step of a man no longer doubtful of his welcome.

Round a turf-fire, whose well-replenished fuel gave testimony to the 'master's' indisposition, who would probably as soon have been placed on the fire himself as seen the whole *kish*[10] emptied on it once, were seated the old housekeeper, two or three *followers*, (*i.e.* people who ate, drank, and lounged about in any kitchen that was open in the neighbourhood, on an occasion of grief or joy, all for his honor's sake, and for the great rispict[11] they bore the family), and an old woman, whom John immediately recognized as the doctress of the neighbourhood, — a withered Sybil,[12] who prolonged her squalid existence by practising on the fears, the ignorance, and the sufferings of beings as miserable as herself. Among the better sort, to whom she sometimes had access by the influence of servants, she tried the effects of some simples,[13] her skill in which was sometimes productive of success. Among the lower orders she talked much of the effects of the 'evil eye',[14] against which she boasted a counter-spell, of unfailing efficacy; and while she spoke, she shook her grizzled locks with such witch-like eagerness, that she never failed to communicate to her half-terrified, half-believing audience, some

9. Unidentified.
10. From Irish *cis*: a wickerwork basket for carrying turf.
11. i.e. respect; occasionally Maturin thus indicates dialect pronunciation.
12. A prophetess, an old hag.
13. Traditional herbal remedies.
14. The superstitious belief that certain people have 'the evil eye' which blights those it gazes on is now more popularly associated with remote regions like Transylvania. Its currency in Ireland can be attested throughout the nineteenth century.

portion of that enthusiasm which, amid all her consciousness of imposture, she herself probably felt a large share of; still, when the case at last became desperate, when credulity itself lost all patience, and hope and life were departing together, she urged the miserable patient to confess *'there was something about his heart'*; and when this confession was extorted from the weariness of pain and the ignorance of poverty, she nodded and muttered so mysteriously, as to convey to the bystanders, that she had had difficulties to contend with which were invincible by human power. When there was no pretext, from indisposition, for her visiting either 'his honor's' kitchen, or the cottar's[15] hut, — when the stubborn and persevering convalescence of the whole country threatened her with starvation, — she still had a resource:— if there were no lives to be shortened, there were fortunes to be told; — she worked 'by spells, and by such daubry as is beyond our element'.[16] No one twined so well as she the mystic yarn to be dropt into the lime-kiln pit, on the edge of which stood the shivering inquirer into futurity, doubtful whether the answer to her question of 'who holds?' was to be uttered by the voice of demon or lover.[17]

No one knew so well as she to find where the four streams met, in which, on the same portentous season, the chemise was to be immersed, and then displayed before the fire, (in the name of one whom we dare not mention to 'ears polite'),[18] to be turned by the figure of the destined husband before morning. No one but herself (she said) knew the hand in which the comb was to be held, while the other was employed in conveying the apple to the mouth, — while, during the joint operation, the shadow of the phantom-spouse was to pass across the mirror before which it was performed. No one was more skilful or active in removing every iron implement from the kitchen where these ceremonies were usually performed by the credulous and terrified dupes of her wizardry, lest, instead of the form of a comely youth exhibiting a ring on his white finger, an headless figure should stalk to the rack, (*Anglicè*,[19] dresser), take down a long spit, or, in default of that, snatch a poker from the fireside, and mercilessly take measure with its iron length of the sleeper for a coffin. No one, in short, knew better how to torment or terrify her victims into a belief of that power which may and has reduced the strongest minds to the level of the weakest; and under the influence of which the cultivated sceptic, Lord Lyttleton,[20] yelled and gnashed and writhed in his last hours, like the poor girl who, in the belief of the horrible visitation of the vampire, shrieked aloud, that her grandfather was sucking her vital blood while she slept, and expired under the influence of imaginary horror. Such was the being to whom old Melmoth had committed his life, half from credulity, and (*Hibernicè* speaking) *more than half* from avarice. Among this groupe John advanced, — recognizing some, — disliking more, — distrusting all. The old housekeeper received him with cordiality; — he was always her 'white-headed boy,' she said, — (*imprimis*,[21] his hair was as black as jet), and she tried to lift her withered hand to his head with an action between a benediction and a caress, till the difficulty of the attempt forced on her the conviction that that head was fourteen inches higher than her reach since she had last patted it. The men, with the national deference of the Irish to a person of superior rank, all rose at his approach, (their stools chattering on the broken flags), and wished his honor 'a thousand years, and long life to the back of that; and would not his honor take something to keep the grief out of his heart;' and so saying, five or six red and bony hands tendered him glasses of whiskey all at once. All this time the Sybil sat silent in the ample chimney-corner, sending redoubled whiffs out of her pipe. John gently declined the offer of spirits, received the attention of the old housekeeper cordially, looked askance at the withered crone who occupied the chimney corner, and then glanced at the table, which displayed other cheer than he had been accustomed to see in his 'honor's time.' There was a wooden dish of potatoes, which old Melmoth

15. One who lives in a cottage supplied in return for his labour.
16. cf. 'She works by charms, by spells, by the figure, and such daubery as this is, beyond our element. ...' Shakespeare, *The Merry Wives of Windsor*, IV. 2. 188-90.
17. Traditional formulae for identifying a future husband; see Robert Burns's poem 'Halloween' and his notes.
18. Alexander Pope, 'Epistle to Burlington', line 150: 'Who never mentions Hell to ears polite.'
19. Medieval Latin *Anglice* = in English. Hiberno-English terms for domestic items and for parts of a house differ from standard English in a number of instances.
20. Thomas Lyttleton (1744-79), 2nd baron Lyttleton, was a notorious profligate who was supposedly warned of his imminent death in a dream.
21. imprimis = in the first place. 'White-headed boy' is a term of affection, indicating one who is a favourite. It is not a literal description.

would have considered enough for a week's subsistence. There was the salted salmon, (a luxury unknown even in London. *Vide* Miss Edgeworth's Tales, 'The Absentee').[22]

There was the *slink-veal*,[23] flanked with tripe; and, finally, there were lobsters and *fried* turbot enough to justify what the author of the tale asserts, 'suo periculo,'[24] that when his great grandfather, the Dean of Killala,[25] hired servants at the deanery, they stipulated that they should not be required to eat turbot or lobster more than twice-a-week. There were also bottles of Wicklow ale, long and surreptitiously borrowed from his 'honor's' cellar, and which now made their first appearance on the kitchen hearth, and manifested their impatience of further constraint, by hissing, spitting, and bouncing in the face of the fire that provoked its animosity. But the whiskey (genuine illegitimate potsheen,[26] smelling strongly of weed and smoke, and breathing defiance to excisemen) appeared, the 'veritable Amphitryon'[27] of the feast; every one praised, and drank as deeply as he praised.

John, as he looked round the circle, and thought of his dying uncle, was forcibly reminded of the scene at Don Quixote's departure, where, in spite of the grief caused by the dissolution of the worthy knight, we are informed that 'nevertheless the niece eat her victuals, the housekeeper drank to the repose of his soul, and even Sancho cherished his little carcase.'[28] After returning, 'as he might,' the courtesies of the party, John asked how his uncle was. 'As bad as he can be'; — 'Much better, and many thanks to your honor,' was uttered in such rapid and discordant unison by the party, that John turned from one to the other, not knowing which or what to believe. 'They say his honor has had a fright,' said a fellow, upwards of six feet high, approaching by way of whispering, and then bellowing the sound six inches above John's head. 'But then his honor has had *a cool* since,' said a man who was quietly swallowing the spirits that John had refused. At these words the Sybil who sat in the chimney corner slowly drew her pipe from her mouth, and turned towards the party: The oracular movements of a Pythoness on her tripod[29] never excited more awe, or impressed for the moment a deeper silence. 'It's not *here*,' said she, pressing her withered finger on her wrinkled forehead, 'nor *here*, — nor *here*;' and she extended her hand to the foreheads of those who were near her, who all bowed as if they were receiving a benediction, but had immediate recourse to the spirits afterwards, as if to ensure its effects. — 'It's all *here* — it's all *about the heart*'; and as she spoke she spread and pressed her fingers on her hollow bosom with a force of action that thrilled her hearers. — It's all *here*,' she added, repeating the action (probably excited by the effect she had produced), and then sunk on her seat, resumed her pipe, and spoke no more. At this moment of involuntary awe on the part of John, and of terrified silence on that of the rest, an unusual sound was heard in the house, and the whole company started as if a musket had been discharged among them: — it was the unwonted sound of old Melmoth's bell. His domestics were so few, and so constantly near him, that the sound of his bell startled them as much as if he had been ringing the knell for his own interment. 'He used always to *rap down* for me,' said the old housekeeper, hurrying out of the kitchen; 'he said pulling the bells wore out the ropes.'

The sound of the bell produced its full effect. The housekeeper rushed into the room, followed by a number of women, (the Irish præficae);[30] all ready to prescribe for the dying or weep for the dead, — all clapping their hard hands, or wiping their dry eyes. These hags all surrounded the bed; and to witness their loud, wild, and desperate grief, their cries of 'Oh! he's going, his honor's going, his honor's going,' one would have imagined their lives were bound up in his, like those of the wives in the story of Sinbad the Sailor, who were to be interred alive with their deceased husbands.[31]

22. Maturin refers, not with total accuracy, to the Wicklow dinner-scene in Maria Edgeworth's *The Absentee* (1812). See Volume I of this anthology, p. 1039.
23. The flesh of a prematurely born calf.
24. (Latin) at his own risk.
25. Peter Maturin was dean of Killala in County Mayo from 1724 to 1741.
26. Normally spelled in English 'poteen', from Irish *poitín*, a little pot.
27. Amphitryon was king of Thebes in Greek mythology, impersonated by Zeus, who begot a child on the king's wife; Maturin alludes to Molière's dramatic adaptation of the legend.
28. See the final chapter of Cervantes's great comic novel, *Don Quixote* (1605/1615).
29. A pythoness was a priestess at Delphi who prophesied while sitting on a three-legged stool; pipe-smoking was thought to be a peculiar habit of Irish peasant women.
30. (Latin) professional mourners. Parallels between classical accounts of the *praeficiae* and contemporary Irish 'keeners' occur in Lady Morgan's fiction and other romantic novels.
31. *The Thousand and One Nights* (including the tale of Sinbad) was introduced into Western Europe in a French version by Antoine Galland (12 vols, 1704-17).

Four of them wrung their hands and howled round the bed, while one, with all the adroitness of a Mrs Quickly, felt his honor's feet, and 'upward and upward,' and 'all was cold as any stone.'[32]

Old Melmoth withdrew his feet from the grasp of the hag, — counted with his keen eye (keen amid the approaching dimness of death) the number assembled round his bed, — raised himself on his sharp elbow, and pushing away the housekeeper, (who attempted to settle his nightcap, that had been shoved on one side in the struggle, and gave his haggard, dying face, a kind of grotesque fierceness), bellowed out in tones that made the company start, — 'What the devil brought ye all here?' The question scattered the whole party for a moment; but rallying instantly, they communed among themselves in whispers, and frequently using the sign of the cross, muttered 'The devil, — Christ save us, the devil in his mouth the first word he spoke.' 'Aye,' roared the invalid, 'and the devil in my eye the first sight I see.' 'Where, — where?' cried the terrified housekeeper, clinging close to the invalid in her terror, and half-hiding herself in the blanket, which she snatched without mercy from his struggling and exposed limbs. 'There, there,' he repeated, (during the battle of the blanket), pointing to the huddled and terrified women, who stood aghast at hearing themselves arointed[33] as the very demons they came to banish. 'Oh! Lord keep your honor's head,' said the housekeeper in a more soothing tone, when her fright was over; 'and sure your honor knows them all, is'n't *her* name, — and *her* name, — and *her* name,' — and she pointed respectively to each of them, adding their names, which we shall spare the English reader the torture of reciting, (as a proof of our lenity, adding the last only, Cotchleen O'Mulligan), 'Ye lie, ye b——h,' growled old Melmoth; 'their name is Legion, for they are many,[34] — turn them all out of the room, — turn them all out of doors, — if they howl at my death, they shall howl in earnest, — not for my death, for they would see me dead and damned too with dry eyes, but for want of the whiskey that they would have stolen if they could have got at it,' (and here old Melmoth grasped a key which lay under his pillow, and shook it in vain triumph at the old housekeeper, who had long possessed the means of getting at the spirits unknown to his 'honor'), 'and for want of the victuals you have pampered them with.' '*Pampered*, oh Ch—st!' ejaculated the housekeeper. 'Aye, and what are there so many candles for, all *fours*, and the same below I warrant. Ah! you — you — worthless, wasteful old devil.' 'Indeed, your honor, they are all *sixes*.'[35] 'Sixes, — and what the devil are you burning sixes for, d'ye think it's *the wake* already? Ha?' 'Oh! not yet, your honor, not yet,' chorussed the beldams;[36] 'but in God's good time, your honor knows,' in a tone that spoke ill suppressed impatience for the event. 'Oh! that your honor would think of making your soul.' 'That's the first sensible word you have said,' said the dying man, 'fetch me the prayer-book, — you'll find it there under that old boot-jack, — blow off the cobwebs; — it has not been opened this many a year.' It was handed to him by the old governante, on whom he turned a reproaching eye. 'What made you burn sixes in the kitchen, you extravagant jade? How many years have you lived in this house?' 'I don't know, your honor.' 'Did you ever see any extravagance or waste in it?' 'Oh never, never, your honor.' 'Was any thing but a farthing candle ever burned in the kitchen?' 'Never, never, your honor.' 'Were not you kept as tight as hand and head and heart could keep you, were you not? answer me that.' 'Oh yes, sure, your honor; every *sowl* about us knows that, — every one does your honor justice, that you kept the closest house and closest hand in the country, — your honor was always a good warrant for it,' 'And how dare you unlock my hold before death has unlocked it,' said the dying miser, shaking his meagre hand at her. 'I smelt meat in the house, — I heard voices in the house, — I heard the key turn in the door over and over. Oh that I was up,' he added, rolling in impatient agony in his bed, 'Oh that I was up, to see the waste and ruin that is going on. But it would kill me,' he continued, sinking back on the bolster,[37] for he never allowed himself a pillow; 'it would kill me, — the very thought of it is killing me now.' The women, discomfited and defeated, after sundry winks and whispers, were huddling out of the room, till recalled by the sharp eager tones of old Melmoth. —

32. The paragraph derives from Mistress Quickly's account of Sir John Falstaff's death in *Henry V*, II. 3. 27-28.
33. exorcised, banished.
34. cf. Luke 9. 30 for the story of the man (called Legion because he was possessed by many devils) whom Jesus cured.
35. Candles weighing six to the pound.
36. From the French *belle dame*: hags, old serving women.
37. A long, narrow pillow.

'Where are ye trooping to now? back to the kitchen to gormandize and guzzle? Won't one of ye stay and listen while there's a prayer read for me? Ye may want it one day for yourselves, ye hags.' Awed by this expostulation and menace, the train silently returned, and placed themselves round the bed, while the housekeeper, though a Catholic, asked if his honor would not have a clergyman to give him *the rights*, (rites) of his church.[38] The eyes of the dying man sparkled with vexation at the proposal. 'What for, — just to have him expect a scarf and hatband at the funeral.[39] Read the prayers yourself, you old —; that will save something.' The housekeeper made the attempt, but soon declined it, alleging, as her reason, that her eyes had been watery ever since his honor took ill. 'That's because you had always a drop in them,' said the invalid, with a spiteful sneer, which the contraction of approaching death stiffened into a hideous grin. — 'Here, — is not there one of you that's gnashing and howling there, that can get up a prayer to keep me from it?' So adjured, one of the women offered her services; and of her it might truly be said, as of the 'most desartless man of the watch' in Dogberry's time, that 'her reading and writing came by nature';[40] for she never had been at school, and had never before seen or opened a Protestant prayer book in her life; nevertheless, on she went, and with more emphasis than good discretion, read nearly through the service for the 'churching of women;'[41] which in our prayer-books following that of the burial of the dead, she perhaps imagined was someway connected with the state of the invalid.

She read with great solemnity, — it was a pity that two interruptions occurred during the performance, one from old Melmoth, who, shortly after the commencement of the prayers, turned towards the old housekeeper, and said in a tone scandalously audible, 'Go down and draw the niggers[42] of the kitchen fire closer, and lock the door, and let me *hear it locked*. I can't mind any thing till that's done.' The other was from John Melmoth gliding into the room, hearing the inappropriate words uttered by the ignorant woman, taking quietly as he knelt beside her the prayer-book from her hands, and reading in a suppressed voice part of that solemn service which, by the forms of the Church of England, is intended for the consolation of the departing.[43]

'That is John's voice,' said the dying man; and the little kindness he had ever shewed this unfortunate lad rushed on his hard heart at this moment, and touched it. He saw himself, too, surrounded by heartless and rapacious menials; and slight as must have been his dependence on a relative whom he had always treated as a stranger, he felt at this hour he was no stranger, and grasped at his support like a straw amid his wreck. 'John, my good boy, you are there. — I kept you far from me when living, and now you are nearest me when dying. — John, *read on*.' John, affected deeply by the situation in which he beheld this *poor man*, amid all his wealth, as well as by the solemn request to impart consolation to his dying moments, read on; — but in a short time his voice became indistinct, from the horror with which he listened to the increasing hiccup of the patient, which, however, he struggled with from time to time, to ask the housekeeper if *the niggers were closed*. John, who was a lad of feeling, rose from his knees in some degree of agitation. 'What, are you leaving me like the rest?' said old Melmoth, trying to raise himself in the bed. 'No, Sir,' said John: 'but,' observing the altered looks of the dying man, 'I think you want some refreshment, some support, Sir.' 'Aye, I do, I do, but whom can I trust to get it for me. *They*, (and his haggard eye wandered round the groupe), *they* would poison me.' 'Trust me, Sir,' said John; 'I will go to the apothecary's,[44] or whoever you may employ.' The old man grasped his hand, drew him close to his bed, cast a threatening yet fearful eye round the party, and then whispered in a voice of agonized constraint, 'I want a glass of wine, it would keep me alive for some hours, but there is not one I can trust to get it for me, — *they'd steal a bottle, and ruin me*.' John was greatly shocked. 'Sir, for God's sake, let *me* get a glass of wine for you.' 'Do you

38. The pun would be inaudible, of course, but Maturin evidently wants to make some gestures towards the rightness of old Maturin's denominational loyalties.
39. These emblems of mourning were sometimes provided to the chief mourners at a funeral.
40. cf. Shakespeare, *Much Ado About Nothing*, III. 3. 17 et seq. for Dogberry's original speech, which is further garbled here.
41. The Church of Ireland provides a service for 'the thanksgiving of women after child-birth, commonly called the churching of women'. It now precedes 'the order for the visitation of the sick'.
42. Niggards are devices for reducing the amount of fuel burnt in a grate.
43. Following the Act of Union (1800) there was a single Established Church for England, Wales and Ireland.
44. A shop dispensing medicines. This suggests that a neighbouring town is not too distant.

know where?' said the old man, with an expression in his face John could not understand. 'No, Sir; you know I have been rather a stranger here, Sir.' 'Take this key,' said old Melmoth, after a violent spasm; 'take this key, there is wine in that closet, — *Madeira*. I always told them there was nothing there, but they did not believe me, or I should not have been robbed as I have been. At one time I said it was whiskey, and then I fared worse than ever, for they drank twice as much of it.'

John took the key from his uncle's hand; the dying man pressed it as he did so, and John, interpreting this as a mark of kindness, returned the pressure. He was undeceived by the whisper that followed, — 'John, my lad, don't drink any of that wine while you are there.' 'Good God!' said John, indignantly throwing the key on the bed; then, recollecting that the miserable being before him was no object of resentment, he gave the promise required, and entered the closet, which no foot but that of old Melmoth had entered for nearly sixty years. He had some difficulty in finding out the wine, and indeed staid long enough to justify his uncle's suspicions, — but his mind was agitated, and his hand unsteady. He could not but remark his uncle's extraordinary look, that had the ghastliness of fear superadded to that of death, as he gave him permission to enter his closet. He could not but see the looks of horror which the women exchanged as he approached it. And, finally, when he was in it, his memory was malicious enough to suggest some faint traces of a story, too horrible for imagination, connected with it. He remembered in one moment most distinctly, that no one but his uncle had ever been known to enter it for many years.

Before he quitted it, he held up the dim light, and looked around him with a mixture of terror and curiosity. There was a great deal of decayed and useless lumber, such as might be supposed to be heaped up to rot in a miser's closet; but John's eyes were in a moment, and as if by magic, rivetted on a portrait that hung on the wall, and appeared, even to his untaught eye, far superior to the tribe of family pictures that are left to moulder on the walls of a family mansion. It represented a man of middle age. There was nothing remarkable in the costume, or in the countenance, but *the eyes*, John felt, were such as one feels they wish they had never seen, and feels they can never forget. Had he been acquainted with the poetry of Southey, he might have often exclaimed in his after-life.

Only the eyes had life,
They gleamed with demon light. —
THALABA[45]

From an impulse equally resistless and painful, he approached the portrait, held the candle towards it, and could distinguish the words on the border of the painting, — Jno. Melmoth, anno 1646. John was neither timid by nature, or nervous by constitution, or superstitious from habit, yet he continued to gaze in stupid horror on this singular picture till, aroused by his uncle's cough, he hurried into his room. The old man swallowed the wine. He appeared a little revived; it was long since he had tasted such a cordial, — his heart appeared to expand to a momentary confidence. 'John, what did you see in that room?' 'Nothing, Sir.' 'That's a lie; every one wants to cheat or rob me.' 'Sir, I don't want to do either.' 'Well, what did you see that you — you took notice of?' 'Only a picture, Sir.' 'A picture, Sir! — the original is still alive.' John, though under the impression of his recent feelings, could not but look incredulous. 'John,' whispered his uncle; — 'John, they say I am dying of this and that; and one says it is for want of nourishment, and one says it is for want of medicine, — but, John,' and his face looked hideously ghastly, 'I am dying of a fright. That man,' and he extended his meagre arm towards the closet, as if he was pointing to a living being; 'that man, I have good reason to know, is alive still.' 'How is that possible, Sir?' said John involuntarily, 'the date on the picture is 1646.' 'You have seen it, — you have noticed it,' said his uncle. 'Well,' — he rocked and nodded on his bolster for a moment, then, grasping John's hand with an unutterable look, he exclaimed, 'You will see him again, he is alive.' Then, sinking back on his bolster, he fell into a kind of sleep or stupor, his eyes still open, and fixed on John.

The house was now perfectly silent, and John had time and space for reflection. More thoughts came crowding on him than he wished to welcome, but they would not be repulsed. He thought of his uncle's habit and character, turned the matter over and over again in his mind, and he said to himself, 'The last man on earth to be superstitious. He never thought of any thing but the price of stocks, and the rate of exchange, and my college expences, that

45. Robert Southey (1774-1843) published a poem, 'Thalaba the Destroyer' in 1801; see Book II, verse 5. 10-11.

hung heavier at his heart than all; and such a man to die of a fright, — a ridiculous fright, that a man living 150 years ago is alive still, and yet — he is dying.' John paused, for facts will confute the most stubborn logician. 'With all his hardness of mind, and of heart, he is dying of a fright. I heard it in the kitchen, I have heard it from himself, — he could not be deceived. If I had ever heard he was nervous, or fanciful, or superstitious, but a character so contrary to all these impressions; — a man that, as poor Butler says, in his Remains, of the Antiquarian, would have 'sold Christ over again for the numerical piece of silver which Judas got for him,'[46] such a man to die of fear! Yet he *is* dying,' said John, glancing his fearful eye on the contracted nostril, the glazed eye, the dropping jaw, the whole horrible apparatus of the *facies Hippocratica*[47] displayed, and soon to cease its display.

Old Melmoth at this moment seemed to be in a deep stupor; his eyes lost that little expression they had before, and his hands, that had convulsively been catching at the blankets, let go their short and quivering grasp, and lay extended on the bed like the claws of some bird that had died of hunger, — so meagre, so yellow, so spread. John, unaccustomed to the sight of death, believed this to be only a sign that he was going to sleep; and urged by an impulse for which he did not attempt to account to himself, caught up the miserable light, and once more ventured into the forbidden room, — the *blue chamber* of the dwelling.[48] The motion roused the dying man; — he sat bolt upright in his bed. This John could not see, for he was now in the closet; but he heard the groan, or rather the choaked and guggling rattle of the throat, that announces the horrible conflict between muscular and mental convulsion. He started, turned away; but, as he turned away, he thought he saw the eyes of the portrait, on which his own was fixed, *move*, and hurried back to his uncle's bedside.

Old Melmoth died in the course of that night, and died as he had lived, in a kind of avaricious delirium. John could not have imagined a scene so horrible as his last hours presented. He cursed and blasphemed about three half-pence, missing, as he said, some weeks before, in an account of change with his groom, about hay to a starving horse that he kept. Then he grasped John's hand, and asked him to give him the sacrament. 'If I send to the clergyman, he will charge me something for it, which I cannot pay, — I cannot. They say I am rich, — look at this blanket; — but I would not mind that, if I could save my soul.' And, raving, he added, 'Indeed, Doctor, I am a very poor man. I never troubled a clergyman before, and all I want is, that you will grant me two trifling requests, very little matters in your way, — save my soul, and (whispering) make interest to get me a parish coffin, — I have not enough left to bury me. I always told every one I was poor, but the more I told them so, the less they believed me.'

John, greatly shocked, retired from the bed-side, and sat down in a distant corner of the room. The women were again in the room, which was very dark. Melmoth was silent from exhaustion, and there was a death-like pause for some time. At this moment John saw the door open, and a figure appear at it, who looked round the room, and then quietly and deliberately retired, but not before John had discovered in his face the living original of the portrait. His first impulse was to utter an exclamation of terror, but his breath felt stopped. He was then rising to pursue the figure, but a moment's reflection checked him. What could be more absurd, than to be alarmed or amazed at a resemblance between a living man and the portrait of a dead one! The likeness was doubtless strong enough to strike him even in that darkened room, but it was doubtless only a likeness; and though it might be imposing enough to terrify an old man of gloomy and retired habits, and with a broken constitution, John resolved it should not produce the same effect on him.

But while he was applauding himself for this resolution, the door opened, and the figure appeared at it, beckoning and nodding to him, with a familiarity somewhat terrifying. John now started up, determined to pursue it; but the pursuit was stopped by the weak but shrill cries of his uncle, who was struggling at once with the agonies of death and his housekeeper. The poor woman, anxious for her master's reputation and her own, was trying to put on him a clean shirt and nightcap, and Melmoth, who had just sensation enough to perceive they were taking something from him,

46. Samuel Butler (1612-80); his *Genuine Remains in Verse and Prose* was published posthumously in 1759.

47. The features on the face of a dying person, so called from the description provided by Hippocrates (*c.* 469-399 B.C.).

48. In the story of Bluebeard, a murderous tyrant in Charles Perrault's *Contes du Temps* (1697), entry to one chamber is forbidden on pain of death.

continued exclaiming feebly, 'They are robbing me, — robbing me in my last moments, — robbing a dying man. John, won't you assist me, — I shall die a beggar; they are taking my last shirt, — I shall die a beggar.' — And the miser died.

CHAPTER II

You that wander, scream, and groan,
Round the mansions once your own.
ROWE[1]

A few days after the funeral, the will was opened before proper witnesses, and John was found to be left sole heir to his uncle's property, which, though originally moderate, had, by his grasping habits, and parsimonious life, become very considerable.

As the attorney who read the will concluded, he added, 'There are some words here, at the corner of the parchment, which do not appear to be part of the will, as they are neither in the form of a codicil, nor is the signature of the testator affixed to them; but, to the best of my belief, they are in the handwriting of the deceased.' As he spoke he shewed the lines to Melmoth, who immediately recognized his uncle's hand, (that perpendicular and penurious hand, that seems determined to make the most of the very paper, thriftily abridging every word, and leaving scarce an atom of margin), and read, not without some emotion, the following words: 'I enjoin my nephew and heir, John Melmoth, to remove, destroy, or cause to be destroyed, the portrait inscribed J. Melmoth, 1646, hanging in my closet. I also enjoin him to search for a manuscript, which I think he will find in the third and lower left-hand drawer of the mahogany chest standing under that portrait, — it is among some papers of no value, such as manuscript sermons, and pamphlets on the improvement of Ireland, and such stuff; he will distinguish it by its being tied round with a black tape, and the paper being very mouldy and discoloured. He may read it if he will; — I think he had better not. At all events, I adjure him, if there be any power in the adjuration of a dying man, to burn it.'

After reading this singular memorandum, the business of the meeting was again resumed; and as old Melmoth's will was very clear and legally worded, all was soon settled, the party dispersed, and John Melmoth was left alone.

We should have mentioned, that his guardians appointed by the will (for he was not yet of age) advised him to return to College, and complete his education as soon as proper; but John urged the expediency of paying the respect due to his uncle's memory, by remaining a decent time in the house after his decease. This was not his real motive. Curiosity, or something that perhaps deserves a better name, the wild and awful pursuit of an indefinite object, had taken strong hold of his mind. His guardians (who were men of respectability and property in the neighbourhood, and in whose eyes John's consequence had risen rapidly since the reading of the will), pressed him to accept of a temporary residence in their respective houses, till his return to Dublin. This was declined gratefully, but steadily. They called for their horses, shook hands with the heir, and rode off — Melmoth was left alone.

The remainder of the day was passed in gloomy and anxious deliberation, — in traversing his late uncle's room, — approaching the door of the closet, and then retreating from it, — in watching the clouds, and listening to the wind, as if the gloom of the one, or the murmurs of the other, relieved instead of increasing the weight that pressed on his mind. Finally, towards evening, he summoned the old woman, from whom he expected something like an explanation of the extraordinary circumstances he had witnessed since his arrival at his uncle's. The old woman, proud of the summons, readily attended, but she had very little to tell, — her communication was nearly in the following words: (We spare the reader her endless circumlocutions, her Irishcisms [*sic*], and the frequent interruptions arising from her applications to her snuff-box, and to the glass of whiskey punch with which Melmoth took care to have her supplied). The old woman deposed, 'That his honor (as she always called the deceased) was always intent upon the little room inside his bed-chamber, and reading there, within the last two years; — that people, knowing his honor had money, and thinking it must be there, had broke into that room, (in other words, there was a robbery attempted there), but finding nothing but some papers, they had retired; — that he was so frightened, he had bricked up the window; but *she thought there was more in it than that*, for when his honor missed but a half-penny, he would make the

1. See Nicholas Rowe, *The Fair Penitent* (1703) V, i.

house ring about it, but that, when the closet was bricked up, he never said a word; — that afterwards his honor used to lock himself up in his own room, and though he was never fond of reading, was always found, when his dinner was brought him, hanging over a paper, which he hid the moment any one came into the room, and once there was a great bustle about a picture that he tried to conceal; — that knowing there was an *odd story in the family*, she did her best to come at it, and even went to Biddy Brannigan's, (the medical Sybil before mentioned), to find out the rights of it; but Biddy only shook her head, filled her pipe, uttered some words she did not understand, and smoked on; — that it was but two evenings before his honor *was struck*, (*i.e.* took ill), she was standing at the door of the court, (which had once been surrounded by stables, pigeon-house, and all the usual etceteras of a gentleman's residence, but now presented only a ruinous range of dismantled out-offices, thatched with thistles, and tenanted by pigs), when his honor called to her to lock the door, (his honor was always *keen* about locking the doors early); she was hastening to do so, when he snatched the key from her, swearing at her, (for he was always very keen about locking the doors, though the locks were so bad, and the keys so rusty, that it was always like *the cry of the dead* in the house when the keys were turned); — that she stood aside for a minute, seeing he was angry, and gave him a key, when she heard him utter a scream, and saw him fall across the door-way; — that she hurried to raise him, *hoping* it was a fit; — that she found him stiff and stretched out, and called for help to lift him up; — that then people came from the kitchen to assist; — that she was so bewildered and terrified, she hardly knew what was done or said; but with all her terror remembered, that as they raised him up, the first sign of life he gave was lifting up his arm, and pointing it towards the court, and at that moment she saw the figure of a tall man cross the court, and go out of the court, she knew not where or how, for the outer gate was locked, and had not been opened for years, and they were all gathered round his honor at the other door; — she saw the figure, — she saw the shadow on the wall, — she saw him walk slowly through the court, and in her terror cried, 'Stop him,' but nobody minded her, all being busy about her master; and when he was brought to his room, nobody thought but of getting him to himself again. And further she could not tell. His honor (young Melmoth) knew as much as she, — he had witnessed his last illness, had heard his last words, he saw him die, — how could she know more than his honor.'

'True,' said Melmoth, 'I certainly saw him die; but — you say *there was an odd story in the family*, do you know any thing about it?' 'Not a word, it was long before my time, as old as I am.' 'Certainly it must have been so; but, was my uncle ever superstitious, fanciful?' — and Melmoth was compelled to use many synonymous expressions, before he could make himself understood. When he did, the answer was plain and decisive, 'No, never, never. When his honor sat in the kitchen in winter, to save a fire in his own room, he could never bear the talk of the old women that came in to light their pipes *betimes*, (from time to time). He used to shew such impatience of their superstitious nonsense, that they were fain[2] to smoke them in silence, without the consolatory accompaniment of one whisper about a child that the evil eye had looked on, or another, that though apparently a mewling, peevish, crippled brat all day, went regularly out at night to dance with the *good people* on the top of a neighbouring mountain, summoned thereto by the sound of a bag-pipe, which was unfailingly heard at the cabin door every night.' Melmoth's thoughts began to take somewhat of a darker hue at this account. If his uncle was not superstitious, might he not have been guilty, and might not his strange and sudden death, and even the terrible visitation that preceded it, have been owing to some wrong that his rapacity had done the widow and the fatherless. He questioned the old woman indirectly and cautiously on the subject, — her answer completely justified the deceased. 'He was a man,' she said, 'of a hard hand, and a hard heart, but he was as jealous of another's right as of his own. He would have starved all the world, but he would not have wronged it of a farthing.'

Melmoth's last resource was to send for Biddy Brannigan, who was still in the house, and from whom he at least hoped to hear the odd story that the old women confessed was in the family. She came, and, on her introduction to Melmoth, it was curious to observe the mingled look of servility and command, the result of the habits of her life, which was alternately one of abject mendicity [*sic*], and of

2. willing, glad.

arrogant but clever imposture. When she first appeared, she stood at the door, awed and curtseying in the presence, and muttering sounds which, possibly intended for blessings, had, from the harsh tone and witch-like look of the speaker, every appearance of malediction; but when interrogated on the subject of the story, she rose at once into consequence — her figure seemed frightfully dilated, like that of Virgil's Alecto,[3] who exchanges in a moment the appearance of a feeble old woman for that of a menacing fury. She walked deliberately across the room, seated, or rather squatted herself on the hearth-stone like a hare in her form, spread her bony and withered hands towards the blaze, and rocked for a considerable time in silence before she commenced her tale. When she had finished it, Melmoth remained in astonishment at the state of mind to which the late singular circumstances had reduced him, — at finding himself listening with varying and increasing emotions of interest, curiosity, and terror, to a tale so wild, so improbable, nay, so actually incredible, that he at least blushed for the folly he could not conquer. The result of these impressions was, a resolution to visit the closet, and examine the manuscript that very night.

This resolution he found it impossible to execute immediately, for, on inquiring for lights, the gouvernante confessed the very last had been burnt at *his honor's* wake; and a bare-footed boy was charged to run for life and death to the neighbouring village for candles; and if you could *borry*[4] a couple of candlesticks, added the housekeeper. 'Are there no candlesticks in the house?' said Melmoth. 'There are, honey, plinty, but it's no time to be opening the old chest, for the plated ones, in regard of their being at the bottom of it, and the brass ones that's *in it* (in the house), one of them has no socket, and the other has no bottom.' 'And how did you make shift yourself,'[5] said Melmoth. 'I stuck it in a potatoe,' quoth the housekeeper. So the *gossoon*[6] ran for life and death, and Melmoth, towards the close of the evening, was left alone to meditate.

It was an evening apt for meditation, and Melmoth had his fill of it before the messenger returned. The weather was cold and gloomy; heavy clouds betokened a long and dreary continuance of autumnal rains; cloud after cloud came sweeping on like the dark banners of an approaching host, whose march is for desolation. As Melmoth leaned against the window, whose dismantled frame, and pierced and shattered panes, shook with every gust of wind, his eye encountered nothing but that most cheerless of all prospects, a miser's garden, — walls broken down, grass-grown walks whose grass was not even green, dwarfish, doddered,[7] leafless trees, and a luxuriant crop of nettles and weeds rearing their unlovely heads where there had once been flowers, all waving and bending in capricious and unsightly forms, as the wind sighed over them. It was the verdure of the churchyard, the garden of death. He turned for relief to the room, but no relief was there, — the wainscotting dark with dirt, and in many places cracked and starting from the walls, — the rusty grate, so long unconscious of a fire, that nothing but a sullen smoke could be coaxed to issue from between its dingy bars — the crazy chairs, their torn bottoms of rush drooping inwards, and the great leathern seat displaying the stuffing round the worn edges, while the nails, though they kept their places, had failed to keep the covering they once fastened, — the chimney-piece, which, tarnished more by time than by smoke, displayed for its garniture half a pair of snuffers,[8] a tattered almanack of 1750, a time-keeper dumb for want of repair, and a rusty fowling-piece without a lock. — No wonder the spectacle of desolation drove Melmoth back to his own thoughts, restless and uncomfortable as they were. He recapitulated the Sybil's story word by word, with the air of a man who is cross-examining an evidence, and trying to make him contradict himself.

'The first of the Melmoths, she says, who settled in Ireland, was an officer in Cromwell's army, who obtained a grant of lands, the confiscated property of an Irish family attached to the royal cause. The elder brother of this man was one who had travelled abroad, and resided so long on the Continent, that his family had lost all recollection of him. Their memory was not stimulated by their affection, for there were strange reports concerning the traveller. He was said to be (like the 'damned magician, great

3. One of the Furies in classical mythology; see *Aeneid* VII, 324.
4. i.e. borrow.
5. provide for your needs.
6. boy, from Irish *garsún*.
7. Having lost the top branches, through age or decay.
8. 'garniture' is decoration or embellishment. Snuffers were scissors-like instruments for pinching (and so quenching) a candle; half a set would be quite useless.

Glendower,') 'a gentleman profited in strange concealments.'[9]

It must be remembered, that at this period, and even to a later, the belief in astrology and witchcraft was very general. Even so late as the reign of Charles II Dryden calculated the nativity of his son Charles, the ridiculous books of Glanville were in general circulation, and Delrio and Wierus were so popular, that even a dramatic writer (Shadwell) quoted copiously from them, in the notes subjoined to his curious comedy of the Lancashire witches.[10] It was said, that during the life-time of Melmoth, the traveller paid him a visit; and though he must have then been considerably advanced in life, to the astonishment of his family, he did not betray the slightest trace of being a year older than when they last beheld him. His visit was short, he said nothing of the past or the future, nor did his family question him. It was said that they did not feel themselves perfectly at ease in his presence. On his departure he left them his picture, (the same which Melmoth saw in the closet, bearing date 1646), and they saw him no more. Some years after, a person arrived from England, directed to Melmoth's house, in pursuit of the traveller, and exhibiting the most marvellous and unappeasable solicitude to obtain some intelligence of him. The family could give him none, and after some days of restless inquiry and agitation, he departed, leaving behind him, either through negligence or intention, a manuscript, containing an extraordinary account of the circumstances under which he had met John Melmoth the Traveller (as he was called).

The manuscript and portrait were both preserved, and of the original a report spread that he was still alive, and had been frequently seen in Ireland even to the present century, — but that he was never known to appear but on the approaching death of one of the family, nor even then, unless when the evil passions or habits of the individual had cast a shade of gloomy and fearful interest over their dying hour.

It was therefore judged no favourable augury for the spiritual destination of the last Melmoth, that this extraordinary person had visited, or been imagined to visit, the house previous to his decease.

Such was the account given by Biddy Brannigan, to which she added her own solemnly-attested belief, that John Melmoth the Traveller was still without a hair on his head changed, or a muscle in his frame contracted; — that she had seen those that had seen him, and would confirm their evidence by oath if necessary; — that he was never heard to speak, seen to partake of food, or known to enter any dwelling but that of his family; — and, finally, that she herself believed that his late appearance boded no good either to the living or the dead.

John was still musing on these things when the lights were procured, and, disregarding the pallid countenances and monitory whispers of the attendants, he resolutely entered the closet, shut the door, and proceeded to search for the manuscript. It was soon found, for the directions of old Melmoth were forcibly written, and strongly remembered. The manuscript, old, tattered, and discoloured, was taken from the very drawer in which it was mentioned to be laid. Melmoth's hands felt as cold as those of his dead uncle, when he drew the blotted pages from their nook. He sat down to read, — there was a dead silence through the house. Melmoth looked wistfully at the candles, snuffed them, and still thought they looked dim, (perchance he thought they burned blue, but such thought he kept to himself). Certain it is, he often changed his posture, and would have changed his chair, had there been more than one in the apartment.

He sunk for a few moments into a fit of gloomy abstraction, till the sound of the clock striking twelve made him start, — it was the only sound he had heard for some hours, and the sounds produced by inanimate things, while all living beings around are as dead, have at such an hour an effect indescribably awful. John looked at his manuscript with some reluctance, opened it, paused over the first lines, and as the wind sighed round the desolate apartment, and the rain pattered with a mournful sound against the dismantled window, wished — what did he wish for? — he wished the sound of the wind less dismal, and the dash of the rain less monotonous. — He may be forgiven, it was past midnight, and there was not a human being awake but himself within ten miles when he began to read.

9. For the account of Owen Glendower's magical interests, see I *Henry IV*, III. 1.

10. John Dryden (1631-1700); Joseph Glanvill (1636-80); Anton Delrio (1551-1608); Johann Weyer (or Wierus) (1516-88); Thomas Shadwell (1642-92).

SYDNEY OWENSON, LADY MORGAN

(*c.*1783-1859)

from:
THE O'BRIENS AND THE O'FLAHERTYS (1829)

[It would be wrong to pretend that this novel has any direct link to the gothic tradition, though it would be equally wrong to omit reference to the duel of novels that took place between Lady Morgan (*The Wild Irish Girl*, 1806) and Charles Robert Maturin (*The Wild Irish Boy*, 1808). Lady Morgan (as she became) contributed substantially to the sense of a growing collective body of Irish fiction, and the novel from which the excerpts below are taken is her finest individual contribution to it. The responsiveness of Irish readers (and indeed Irish fictional characters) to gothic detail is lightly indicated by the rapidity with which a figure from the Spanish Inquisition is recognized at a Phoenix Park military review. Morgan's sustained use of French provides a further exotic tincture, of course, but also helps to set off the idiolects of minor figures. Women are central here, and not only as victims in the gothic style.].

CHAPTER IV

THE REVIEW

Sir, you have wrestled well, and overthrown more than your enemies.

As You Like It.[1]

Heated and animated, with the strong excitement of the combat still fluttering in every heart, and throbbing in every pulse, the Irish brigade and their leader stood at rest along the highest ridge of the acclivity — the gaze and admiration of the multitude, who were crowded along its base in vehicles of all sorts, public and private. It was to this spot, where the mock combat had terminated, that Lady Knocklofty urged her restless steeds, though the ascent was steep and the way encumbered. She had followed the progress of the sham fight with the eye, if not with the science, of a practised tactician. The conspicuous form of the young assailant had seldom eluded her observation, through all the evolutions of the corps: and she had perceived that while, with downcast looks and crimsoned cheek, he stood modestly receiving the eulogies of Lord Charlemont, his furtive glances had more than once been directed towards the spot she occupied. The sight of the lynx, and the scent of the hound, are dull instincts when compared with the rapid perception with which a vain woman detects the admiration she has awakened, and the interest she excites.

She now halted, and drew in half way up the hill, flanked to her right by the line of the Irish brigade, and to the left by a confused mass of gigs, noddies,[2] cars, and private carriages, so as to have all approach cut off on that side where Lady Honoria Stratton was placed. Evidently out of spirits and out of temper, silent and sullen, that lady sat enveloped in a white satin cardinal,[3] which she had drawn round her fine figure; her pouting pretty face just peeping above it, like that charming picture of Miss Farren, in a similar costume, which was once the ornament of every dressing room.[4] The fact was, Lady Honoria had not during the day been fortunate — the Lady Lieutenant had kept many of her own particular men, and one in particular, in constant attendance on her vice regal progress; and while several young military and some of the household contrived to squeeze their horses between the wheel of the phaeton,[5] and the acclivity fringed by the Irish brigade, for the purpose of paying their homage to Lady Knocklofty, all Lady Honoria's prospects were bounded by an old shattered carriage, whose hind wheel had got fast locked in that of Lady Knocklofty's phaeton — a most ludicrous *mésalliance!*. . . .

'I wish I could escape from this atmosphere of bad smells,' said Lady Honoria, looking round with disgust; 'pah! we have got into a pretty mess here!'

'What the devil, Albina, could have driven you to take up this position?' demanded an authoritative voice from behind the carriage. Both ladies started,

1. *As You Like It*, I. 2. 270-71.

2. Light, two-wheeled hackney carriages.
3. A woman's cloak, originally of scarlet and with a hood.
4. Elizabeth Farren (*c.* 1759-1829), countess of Derby, actress.
5. A light, four-wheeled, horse-drawn carriage.

and turned round. A gentleman, for whom the two outriders had backed to make way, had got his horse between the hind wheels of the phaeton. He was a tall, fair, slight, cold-looking person, with a phlegmatic countenance and haughty demeanour; but more distinguished by his splendid volunteer uniform, and his blue ribbon and star of St. Patrick, than by any other mark of exterior supremacy. It was Lord Knocklofty. Lady Honoria stood up, and leaned over the back of the phaeton, with a face, from which every trace of ill humour was banished, and was succeeded by radiant smiles. Lady Knocklofty carelessly turned round her head, and without noticing the conjugal inquiry, addressed her steeds with 'Steady now, dears, steady,' continuing to tip their ears with the whip, in a manner to produce a very contrary effect from that her words directed. Lord Knocklofty pressed significantly the fair hand presented to him by Lady Honoria, with the murmured observation of 'How beautiful you are looking today!' Then addressing his wife, he added, 'I say, Albina, do get out of this as soon as you can — what could induce you to drive up this hill?'

'To show my learning, as your Lordship's coachman calls it,' said Lady Knocklofty, playing with her whip, and smiling archly at 'a case of coxcombs,'[6] who were in waiting by the side of the phaeton.

'Your pedantry you mean' said Lady Honoria pointedly.

'Exactly,' said Lord Knocklofty, 'you are a witty creature.'

'More witty than wise,' said Lady Honoria, laughing, 'or I should not trust myself with such a neck-or-nothing driver as her Ladyship here.'

'Why did you let her scramble up this hill?' added Lord Knocklofty, while his lady was talking to one of her *cavalieri serventi*.[7]

'Needs must,' (said Lady Honoria, shrugging her shoulders), 'when the — ' she paused and laughed.

'*Devil drives*, of course,' added Lady Knocklofty, sharply, and suddenly turning round.

'But observe, my dear, your coming with me today was your own proposition.'

Lady Honoria looked mortified, as if her proposition had been her alternative, between coming in Lady Knocklofty's phaeton, or not coming at all.

'Well, at all events get out of this as soon as you can,' said Lord Knocklofty; 'and pray don't tease your horses so, Albina.'

'Why, I'm only tipping them the silk,' said Lord Knocklofty, 'just to keep them alive.'

'I'll be d——d but they'll throw you.'

'I'll be d—— if they do,' said Lady Knocklofty, not with Lady Townly's 'gulp,' but with such a look, and such a smile, and such an accent, that the coarseness of the imprecation was almost neutralized in its utterance, and its very profaneness almost turned into a grace by the dramatic simplicity and archness with which it was given. Such were the manners of the day in Ireland; not so bad, indeed, as in the days of Queen Elizabeth, when fine ladies were wont to '*jurer leur Grand Dieu*,'[8] at every word; nor yet so coarse as when the prettiest lips uttered the broadest *double-entendres* in the time of the Mary Wortleys.[9] Still they were bad enough; *en arrière*[10] with the age, and even in Ireland peculiar to the domineering and ministerial oligarchy, whose lawless power was thus well illustrated by manners as licentious. All the men laughed vociferously at the playful *nonchalance* of Lady Knocklofty's imprecation, who added, in a coaxing tone, to her cold and sullen Lord (himself occupied in listening to some muttered witticisms of Lady Honoria),

'Well, don't be angry, Lord K——, and 'pon honour, and, as O'Mealy says in Macheath, "may me meer slip her shoulder,"[11] if I don't escape out of this, as soon as I can extricate myself from this file of carriages.'

'Why, then, long life to your honour, Marram,[12] I hopes you soon will, plaze Jesus, with the help of God; and that your ladyship's honour will just let go my bit of a hand whill, Marram, which you have kotched here behind to the rare.'[13] . . .

'Famous, by Jove! capital,' exclaimed a pretty boy officer of the Prince's Own,[14] on the watch for Irish fun, expecting a wit in every peasant, and a *bon mot* in every word uttered by the common people.

6. i.e. a set of showy, foolish fellows.
7. The hangers-on of a married woman; in Italy a conventional enough role, but here decidedly more than conventional. The term *cicisbeo* is used similarly to mean the man tolerated by a husband as his wife's lover.

8. to swear by God Almighty.
9. Lady Mary Wortley-Montagu (1689-1762), English wit.
10. backward, in arrears.
11. The reference is to John Gay's *The Beggar's Opera* (1728), of which Captain Macheath is the hero.
12. Marram is evidently intended as a pronunciation of Madam.
13. 'whill' =wheel; 'kotched' = caught; 'rare' = rere.
14. i.e. a regiment of this name.

'Capital! come, we shall have some vastly good fun now. Do draw him out, Lady Knocklofty — now pray!'

'So, friend,' said Lady Knocklofty, 'I see I have got you into a predicament.'

The driver looked at the bright coin thus carelessly thrown at him, and then in the bright eyes of his generous donor, as if he doubted his good luck. 'Sure I a'n't to keep it all, my lady,' he said, dropping his pipe from his mouth, and throwing an expression of gratitude and delight into his mobile countenance.

'Yes, yes,' said the lady, laughing, 'I don't expect any change.'

'Why then, may I never live to have a happy death, if ever I drive the Castle Knockgarrons[15] again, oncet I get rid of my load.'

'Your load!' exclaimed the ladies and the beaux, fixing their eyes on the close blinded carriage. 'Why, have you any one shut up in that old chaise?'

'Is it in the chay?' (said the man, rubbing his head with a slight contraction in the muscles of his face), 'sorrow, christian,[16] how would I? Sure thims returns,' (pointing to the horses), 'fresh as they look and nat a hair turned, the animals—' and he stroked down the necks of the blind and broken-winded beasts, which had scarcely an hair left to turn.

'What do you mean then by getting rid of your load?' said the Prince's Own.

'What do I mane is it, plaze your honour? Why then, what would I mane (scratching his head in evident perplexity), but my own self, Sir? There is many a man would be glad to get rid of himself; and what *better* way could I do it than in drinking long life to her ladyship's honour there.'

'You mean then,' (said Lady Honoria), 'you will get beside yourself as soon as you can.' . . .

'Och, I didn't get in at the scrape at all, but in at the Castle Knock gate shure; to cut across the Phanix, and to shirk that divil's own Knock-maroon hill on the low road; and just made down to the Fifteens,[17] to see if I could not catch a taste of the Castle Knock infantry doing their revolutions, when one sentry driv me here, and another driv me there; and throth, if they'd been army soggers[18] instead of our own volunteers, I wouldn't have been driven out of my own road by any of them: and so they kip driving me here, and driving me there, till I was fairly driven in amongst the quality; and it's how I came by the great honor of being kotched fast by her ladyship; many a bether man's luck afore me, and will again, plaze God.'

A general laugh followed this allusion, which levelling familiarity, which shewed no respect for titles and dignities, hereditary or professional. 'Edward Fitzgerald' was sent to his brother Leinster, to beg he would put off the private play at Carton;[19] as she had got the Dean of ——— to play Filch, who had to preach at St. Patrick's[20] on Sunday, so that his private vocation might not interfere with his public duties. Kilcolman, a young Tipperary Earl, (and descendant of one of Charles the Second's playfellows and ministers), was sent on an embassy, such as his ancestor had occasionally undertaken, at Whitehall — with a single violet to the Lord Lieutenant.[21] He hesitated. 'Go, go,' said Lady Knocklofty, significantly; 'he will understand it.' The Tipperary Earl rode off, with the nobility of six hundred years on his back. An handsome young page was dispatched to the Earl, his papa, to procure tickets for a concert at the Rotunda,[22] at which the noble amateur was to take the lead. Colonel St. Leger, the 'rose of fashion,' with 'Freddys,' 'Franks,' and 'Phils,' 'all honourable men,' were expedited on various missions; while Manser St. George, (one of the last and best of the Irish fine gentlemen in Ireland's most brilliant day,) was sent to the Duchess, begging permission to bring Lord Charles Fitzcharles, of the Prince's Own, to her grace's *petit souper* and blindman's buff that evening.

All flew to execute her 'infinite deal of nothings,'[23] with a zeal and readiness which proved that the 'age of chivalry was not yet passed,'[24] in Ireland. Neither was it. The Irish gallantry of that day had indeed the true smack of the chivalry of

15. Castle Knock is a distinct bordering the Phoenix Park in Dublin and lending its name to one corner of the park; 'garrons' are small, inferior kinds of horse; 'oncet' = once.
16. 'chay' = chaise; 'sorrow' is a form of imprecation in Hiberno-English; 'christian': the usage here is unlikely and may be a misprint.
17. The Fifteen Acres, a parade ground in Dublin's Phoenix Park.
18. soldiers.
19. Carton was principal home of the Dukes of Leinster, near the town of Maynooth, Co. Kildare.
20. St Patrick's Cathedral, Dublin.
21. The chief representative of the crown in Ireland.
22. The Rotunda Rooms at the northern end of Dublin's Sackville Street (now O'Connell Street) were a fashionable venue for concerts.
23. cf. Shakespeare, *The Merchant of Venice*, I. 1. 114.
24. An indirect quotation from Edmund Burke's *Reflections on the Revolution in France* (1790), in the passage praising Marie Antoinette.

the old times. A mixed system of devotion and brutality; in which women, alternately treated as sultanas and as slaves, extorted all homage but that of respect; and excited all feelings, save those of tenderness. Adored today, *délaissées*[25] tomorrow, fashion or passion ruled their momentary ascendant; and the old parts of the *roués*[26] of the French court were played to the life by the *roués* of the Irish, who were all little Richelieus and De Grammonts[27] in their way.

A long-drawn inspiration, as the last of her noble estafettes[28] galloped off, indicated that their liege lady was not sorry to get rid of them. The two great ladies and dear friends, in evident *guignon*[29] with each other, sat *dos à dos*,[30] Lady Honoria, again enveloped in her cardinal, was sulky, and self-concentrated. Lady Knocklofty with looks and spirits all abroad, hummed an air from the Beggar's Opera;[31] and playing her very pretty foot against the side of her phaeton, slipped it in and out of a little zebra shoe, which was the fashion of the day, and an exact type of a slipper, from the seraglio of the Grand Signor.[32]

This movement, conscious or unconscious on the part of the exhibitor, had attracted the eyes, and caused some confusion along the line of the Irish brigade. It more particularly attracted the young leader, who stood in advance of the corps, and who watched the twinkling of the little foot with such a glance as the hawk gives to the fluttering of a young bird nestled near his eiry. The slipper (as might be expected) at last fell to the ground! and the young volunteer, springing from his post, pounced on his pretty prey with a rapidity that distanced all other competitors for the honour of picking it up, and restoring it. With the slipper in one hand, and his cap in the other, he stood beside the phaeton, presenting it gracefully; his colour deepening, and his eyes raised with a look, not confident but intense, to the face of its distinguished owner. Finer eyes might be forgotten; but such eyes, — eyes that awaken emotion, by emitting it, once met, are remembered for ever!

Lady Knocklofty, instead of taking the shoe so respectfully and gracefully offered, looked round for a moment, then putting out her foot, seemed to say by the motion, and the smile more cordial than coquettish, which accompanied it, 'there! you may put it on for your pains!' The look was understood, as it was meant, and the slipper was put on; but with an air of such religious respect, as pilgrims give to the consecrated slipper of St. Peter, when first permitted to kiss with 'holy palmer's kiss'[33] the toe of infallibility.

The enviable office performed, the young volunteer bowed, was thanked with smiles, backed, and resumed his post; from that moment, orders ran along the line, and fuglemen[34] figured in vain.

'*Ma belle*,' said Lady Honoria, who had witnessed this silent intercourse of eyes, (a drama, whose unities were included in an instant of time), '*Ma belle, avec un tel langage on se passe de paroles!*'[35] Lady Knocklofty (still pre-occupied,) started, coloured through her rouge, and asked coldly, 'what do you mean, child?'

'Mean, child! why I mean that you seem to think those "eyes right" there, which you have been endeavouring to set wrong all day, are "*d'assez beaux yeux, pour des yeux de province*".'[36]

'Yes,' said Lady Knocklofty, flirting her whip and smiling, 'they are terrible eyes, that's the truth of it, Honoria. He is altogether a very fine lad; much superior to the creatures he is hustled among. I wonder who he is?'

'Poh! what does it signify who he is? Of course, as O'Mealy said, he is some young tradesman. If he were *any body*, we could not fail to know him. But, be he who he may, gentle or simple, your permitting him to put on your shoe in this public place, was very foolish. We shall have it all in the 'Freeman's Journal' tomorrow, with an epigram from Curran, or Lysaght;[37] or it will be sung as a ballad about the streets, with 'the Duchess's gig';[38]

25. abandoned, cast aside.
26. rakes.
27. Armand Jean du Plessis (1585-1642), cardinal, and duc de Richelieu; Philibert, comte de Gramont (1621-1707). The first was a great statesman, the second a notable courtier. The tone of the passage is, of course, ironic.
28. dispatch riders.
29. bad luck (here, bad temper).
30. back to back.
31. See note 11 above.
32. From the official brothel of the Turkish sultan.
33. The greeting, or blessing of a pilgrim who has returned from Palestine (with a palm branch).
34. Soldiers used as examples for those learning drill; military models.
35. 'My beauty, with such a language one can dispense with words.'
36. 'quite good eyes for a country girl'.
37. The *Freeman's Journal* was a newspaper of the day. John Philpot Curran (1750-1817) and Edward 'Sweet Ned' Lysaght (1763-1811) were both notable wits and song-writers.
38. A 'gig' was a flighty or foolish girl, and there appears to be a reference to a contemporary scandal here.

and I am sure we are unpopular enough already with "the swinish multitude".'[39] . . .

'Why, yes,' said Lady Knocklofty, pointedly, 'you are tolerably aristocratic in *your fancies*, and none under nobility approaches Mrs. Kitty.'

'To be sure,' said Lady Honoria, 'love has no better child's guide than the red book;[40] and the Exchequer is your true Paphos,[41] after all: see, who has governed France for the last fifty years.'

'Do you call that love? I call it calculation,' said Lady Knocklofty, significantly.

'Call it what you please,' said Lady Honoria, colouring slightly, 'but 'tis good taste, *pour le moins*;[42] and that is precisely what you mere home-bred Irishwomen of fashion are perpetually sinning against.'

'We home-bred Irishwomen! And pray, what are you, my dear, pretty, Honoria O'Callaghan, with all your county Cork kindred —

'Pat O'Daisey,
And Mistress Casey,
All blood relations to Lord Donoughmore.'[43]

'Why, my dear, to answer you (with a little variation in the text) from Paddy O'Carrol in the "Register Office,"[44] — It is true, that as ill luck would leave it, "I comed over to Ireland to be born,"[45] but I was never dipped in the Shannon for all that; and, thanks to my father, have lived too much abroad, not to be fully aware of the absurdities of my native home, since, by divine indignation, I have returned to it. It is a sure sign of barbarism when women make a parade of the vices they have not, and even exhibit more of the virtues they have, than is consistent with decency and *bienséance*.[46] You Irishwomen are all, by temperament, cold and vain; you love display, and there is frequently in your flirting manners and unmeaning *allures*, an absence of taste and a want of keeping, which would in other countries put many a woman in keeping, out of countenance. You look, and you sigh, and permit innocent liberties, — all meaning nothing at all, — and then, are rather startled some fine day, when a disappointed admirer turns, heigh presto, into an inveterate enemy; and you find you have lost your reputation, without gaining any thing by the sacrifice. For instance, you have been playing off this foolish boy, merely for the pleasure of turning his head; as Mrs. Colonel O'Gallagher got her husband broke for throwing his regiment into confusion, at a review in Kilkenny, through her coquetting with the fugleman.' . . .

While Lady Honoria was still speaking, a sudden jerk was given to the chaise, which occasioned one of the old blinds to drop down; and the chaise itself was immediately thrown into rapid motion by the wild gallop of the bare-boned, ill-trained steeds, excited by the smacking whip of Barny Houloghan, who dashing on through thick and thin, overturned a noddy, upset a tim[47] whiskey, threw down an old barrow woman, and extricating himself from all obstacles, as he continued his rolling, rattling, jolting, and serpentine course across the park, cleared his way to the gate, and then disappeared; but whether, according to the phrase of romance, 'in the haze of distance,' or in the first ditch that presented itself outside the Park wall, *reste à savoir!*[48]

During the few minutes that the two ladies had been so closely and intimately engaged in their 'colloquy sublime,'[49] Barny, crawling between the two carriages, had contrived to extricate his wheel; and taking advantage of an opening in the file of vehicles, made by the drawing off of the Lady Lieutenant's phaeton, 'which had stopped the way,'[50] he seized the first moment of possible escape, and drove, as the driver of Irish chaises still drive, in utter contempt of consequences, and a total forgetfulness of the frailty of all sublunary things — wheels, springs, traces and bridles included.

39. Another allusion to Edmund Burke (1729-97) who, however, did not refer to 'the swinish multitude' (i.e. all the common people) but to a particular group as 'a swinish multitude'.
40. The *Royal Kalendar*, published from 1767 to 1893, was known as 'the red book'; it listed the nobility and so constituted a useful guide for those in search of a spouse.
41. i.e. exchequer return (indicating wealth) constitutes a useful Book of Revelations. (Saint John the Divine wrote the original Book on the island of Paphos.)
42. at least.
43. This is a variant on the verse ridiculing the Hely Hutchinson family added to Richard Alfred Milliken's 'The Groves of Blarney' (see Volume I of this anthology, p. 1101).
44. Evidently a reference to the Registry of Deeds, where ancestry can be traced.
45. A jibe at those whose Irishness is an accident of birth.
46. propriety.
47. Possibly a 'thimble-full' of whiskey; or a 'Tim Finnegan'.
48. i.e. it remains to be seen.
49. Milton, *Paradise Lost*, Book VIII, line 455.
50. The phrase in quotation marks is thus emphasized because of the Irish substitution of 'stopped' for 'blocked'.

He was almost out of sight before Lady Knocklofty, drawing breath, observed, in allusion to the discovery made by the dropping of the blind, 'How very extraordinary! Did you ever see such figures?'

'I suspected there was some one shut up in that old chaise from the beginning,' said Lady Honoria.

'There is something very mysterious in this,' said Lady Knocklofty, whose imagination was easily mounted. 'I wish Lord K. had seen them. You know there is 500*l.* offered for the taking of Captain Right;[51] and I should not wonder if he was one of those strangely disguised figures — for disguised they certainly were.'

'No, no,' said Lady Honoria, 'there was no Captain Right there; I saw distinctly the far off figure, who sat more prominent than the muffled one next to us. If not the ghost of St. Dominick come down in his character of Grand Inquisitor, to reform his own order in Ireland, it is some intriguing monk from France or Spain, some Abbé Hussey,[52] whom my father and I left digging his own grave in La Trappe, and who, the year after, was figuring away as an intriguing diplomatist, between half the courts in Europe. You perceived the old man was tonsured.'

'Yes; and what a countenance!' said Lady Knocklofty. 'It just met my idea of the monk in the Castle of Otranto;[53] but the other creature looked like a female; though it was so veiled and muffled, it was difficult to make it out. Who, and what could they be?' ....

'By the by, Lord Charles,' said Lady Knocklofty, 'I have engaged you to the Duchess for this evening; and pray get off your regimentals, and put on a romping frock;§ we are going to play blindman's buff at the Castle, in opposition to the Provost's kutch-a-kutch-choo[54] parties, who is obliged to have innocent pastimes for the fellows and their left-handed wives.[55] You must come.'

'I can't indeed; first we cannot go in plain clothes when in garrison, you know, and the chief there; besides, I am particularly engaged this evening.'

'Nonsense! I know there is nothing going on in town this evening. The Duchess expects you, and I command you.'

'Don't signify, I can't tonight, indeed, Lady Knocklofty. I'm in for a frolic, that's the truth of it, a regular set to; the whole party made this week back, expressly——'

'Where, what party? I hope not another drunken bout at Lord Kilcolman's, with those odious Cherokees,[56] who broke all poor Lady Dunshaughlin's new furniture, the other night in Merrion-street.'

'No, I assure you; none of us English belong to that set.'

'Then where can you be engaged this evening? Are you going to play at Daly's? Has the old Marquis got in his rents?'

'Don't know at all; but the fact is, we are going to ....' Here his lordship lowered his voice, and advanced his head; 'but you won't 'peach,[57] either of you, now will you?'

'Honour bright and shining,' said Lady Honoria, laying her hand on her heart; 'but you must not tell us any thing naughty, mind; you must not do like the man in the gallery, the other night, at the theatre, who put the public into a particular confidence about our viceroy, which it was not good manners to allude to.'

'No, no,' said Lord Seymour, 'it is only a frolic, which the lads of ours have entered into, *en esprit de garnison*.[58] You know that one of us was knocked down by a tavern keeper, the other night; so we are going to take a dinner with him today, at the Strugglers, to see fair play, and pay off old scores.'

'The Struggles! what Struggles! where is that?'

'Why, the Strugglers in Wine Tavern-street; a sort of Hole-in-the-Wall, where the Duke and the

§A simple coat of pepper and salt mixture, worn to conceal the impression of powder, by the members of the *haut ton* in Ireland about this period, when romping was the order of the day.

51. Captain Right was the name under which a campaign of agrarian violence was conducted in the early nineteenth century.
52. Thomas Hussey (1741-1803), confidant of Edmund Burke and catholic bishop of Waterford and Lismore; in his youth he had entered the Trappist monastery. The paranoia of the speaker is to be noted.
53. Horace Walpole (1717-97) wrote what is taken to be the first gothic novel, *The Castle of Otranto*. It was published in 1764.
54. 'kutcha' is a Hindi word meaning crude, temporary. In Anglo-Indian usage it is the opposite of 'pukka' (mature, ripe, properly done).
55. John Hely Hutchinson (1724-94) was provost of Trinity College, Dublin from 1774; he was frequently attacked for abusing his powers, and the larger assault on his family (see note 43 above) is sustained here.
56. Kilcolman was the seat of Edmund Spenser (*c.* 1552-99) during his Irish residence; it was burned by the natives as he fled. The name is used here as a generic. 'Cherokees' has the sense of 'hillbillies'.
57. i.e. tell tales (cf. impeach).
58. i.e. in the spirit of the garrison (i.e. in the spirit of their calling).

Chancellor, and some of us, used to go last winter to eat beef-steaks, and drink whiskey punch.'[59]

'Oh, yes! I remember,' said Lady Knocklofty, 'and where *some of you* got into a sad scrape; what was it all about, I forget now?' ....

'Oh, my dear,' interrupted her friend, 'there is no interfering with public duties; and, truth to tell, a little summary justice after the manner of the "tarrers and featherers"[60] themselves, is no bad thing. It is just as well to meet them sometimes on their own ground.'

'Exactly,' said Lord Charles; 'Lady Honoria is quite right. Lady Knocklofty, do your horses stand fire? We shall have the thirty-six rounds before these heroes have done. — Aye, there they go; now for it, *tenex ferme*.'[61]

Her ladyship's answer was lost in the first volley which was fired; the horses stood it well, but with a little pricking of ears, and curvetting[62] of hoofs. The firing now continued by companies, by grand divisions, by subdivisions, obliquely, advancing, and retreating, then by files and in squares, and finally concluded in one tremendous volley, which burst with a crash that resembled the explosion of a volcano. The too spirited steeds of the reckless Lady Knocklofty, overfed and underworked, were startled by the shock, and plunged forward, breaking the traces. Loosely reined, wild, and unmanageable, they dashed down headlong among the troops, with a fearful velocity that scattered all before them, till they were lost in the dense smoke of the artillery, which left the fate of the two ladies in doubt. None of their *cavalieri serventi* had the presence of mind to go to their rescue, till their interference was too late; and when the smoke cleared off, the anxious spectators of this fearful accident were relieved by seeing the horses at rest in the plain below, panting and foaming, but quiet; their heads held by the leader of the Irish brigade, who was coolly directing the groom to adjust the traces. He had sprung down the acclivity, at the first plunge made by the unruly animals, had thrown himself before them in their wild career, and had all the success in his efforts to save the ladies, which such skill, courage, and presence of mind rarely fail to obtain.

The two ladies, though frightened into a misprision of hysterics,[63] had not fainted. They had firmly and wisely held their seats; and as nerves were not the order of the day, and dashing was, they exhibited a fearless contempt of the danger they had escaped, which was ill borne out by their pale faces and quivering lips. The peril over, the phaeton, (whose gaudy panels were either broken or disfigured), was surrounded by gentlemen. Among others, the Lord Lieutenant, and Lord Knocklofty were in anxious attendance, the latter on his wife's friend, and the former on his friend's wife....

59. Wine Tavern Street was notorious in Dublin for illicit drinking dens, brothels, and other 'hells'.
60. Those who punished by smearing people with tar and feathers.
61. hold firm.
62. Leaping with all four feet off the ground.
63. misprision = an act similar to, but of a lesser kind than, another act (cf. misprision of treason); hence a similacrum, imitation, silly approximation.

WILLIAM CARLETON

(1794-1869)

WILDGOOSE LODGE (1830)

[In *The Dublin Literary Gazette* Carleton's story is presented as part of an otherwise unavailable longer autobiographical text, and this contributes to the pressure upon the reader — a characteristic of gothic fiction. Other ritual details are carefully observed — the three times viewing of the weather, the foul weather itself, the passivity of the narrator in relation to the events in which he participates, the centrality of sacrilege, the encounter of difficulty in committing evil, and the fatal overcoming of this difficulty. The fictive specification of protestantism in the victims, together with the concluding biblical allusions, reflect Carleton's conversion to the Church of Ireland and his literary apprenticeship on *The Christian Examiner*. The serial division of the story into two parts exactly reproduces the movement from the place in which the deed is commissioned to the place in which it is executed, and for this reason it is retained here as evidence of the way in which the form of publication affected the reading of Carleton's text.]

CONFESSIONS OF A REFORMED RIBBONMAN
(An owre true tale)

I had read the anonymous summons, but from its general import, I believed it to be one of those special meetings convened for some purpose affecting the general objects and proceedings of the body.[1] At least the terms in which it was conveyed to me, had nothing extraordinary or mysterious in them, beyond the simple fact that it was not to be a general, but a select meeting; this mark of confidence flattered me, and I determined to attend punctually. I was, it is true, desired to keep the circumstance entirely to myself, but there was nothing startling in this, for I had often received summonses of a similar import. I therefore resolved to attend, according to the letter of my instructions, 'on the next night, at the solemn hour of midnight, to deliberate and act upon such matters as should, then and there, be submitted to my consideration.' The morning after I received this message, I arose and resumed my usual occupations; but from whatever cause it may have proceeded, I felt a sense of approaching evil hang heavily upon me; the beats of my pulse were languid, and an undefinable feeling of anxiety pervaded my whole spirit; even my face was pale, and my eye so heavy, that my father and brothers concluded me to be ill; an opinion which I thought at the time to be correct; for I felt exactly that kind of depression which precedes a severe fever. I could not understand what I experienced, nor can I yet, except by supposing that there is in human nature some mysterious faculty, by which, in coming calamities, the approach throws forward the shadow of some fearful evil, and that it is possible to catch a dark anticipation of the sensations which they subsequently produce. For my part I can neither analyze nor define it; but on that day I knew it by painful experience, and so have a thousand others in similar circumstances.

It was about the middle of winter. The day was gloomy and tempestuous almost beyond any other I remember; dark clouds rolled over the hills about me, and a close sleet-like rain fell in slanting drifts that chased each other rapidly to the earth on the course of the blast. The out-lying cattle[2] sought the closest and calmest corners of the fields for shelter; the trees and young groves were tossed about, for the wind was so unusually high that it swept its hollow gusts through them, with that hoarse murmur which deepens so powerfully on the mind the sense of dreariness and desolation.

As the shades of night fell, the storm if possible increased. The moon was half gone, and only a few stars were visible by glimpses, as a rush of wind left a temporary opening in the sky. I had determined, if the storm should not abate, to incur any penalty rather than attend the meeting; but the appointed hour was distant, and I resolved to be decided by the future state of the night.

Ten o'Clock came, but still there was no change; eleven passed, and on opening the door to observe if there were any likelihood of it clearing up, a blast of wind mingled with rain, nearly blew me off my feet; at length it was approaching to the hour of midnight, and on examining a third time, I found it had calmed a little, and no longer rained.

I instantly got my oak stick, muffled myself in my great coat, strapped my hat about my ears, and as the place of meeting was only a quarter of a mile distant, I presently set out.

The appearance of the heavens was louring[3] and angry, particularly in that point where the light of the moon fell against the clouds from a seeming chasm in them, through which alone she was visible. The edges of this were faintly bronzed, but the dense body of the masses that hung piled on each side of her, was black and impenetrable to sight. In no other point of the heavens was there any part of the sky visible; for a deep veil of clouds overhung the horizon, yet was the light sufficient to give occasional glimpses of the rapid shifting which took place in this dark canopy, and of the tempestuous agitation with which the midnight storm swept to and fro beneath.

At length I arrived at a long slated house, situated in a solitary part of the neighbourhood; a little below it ran a small stream, which was now swollen above its banks, and rushing with mimic roar over

1. The Ribbonmen were a secret organization generally associated with the 1820s, several years later than the incident on which Carleton's story was based. However, secret societies had been endemic in the Irish countryside since the 1760s when the Whiteboys came to prominence in Munster.

2. Cattle lying out in the fields during the night.
3. i.e. looking dark and sullen.

the flat meadows beside it. The appearance of the bare slated building in such a night was particularly sombre, and to those like me who knew the purpose to which it was then usually devoted, it was, or ought to have been, peculiarly so. There it stood, silent and gloomy, without any appearance of human life or enjoyment about, or within it: as I approached, the moon once more had broken out of the clouds, and shone dimly upon the glittering of the wet slates and window, with a death-like lustre, that gradually faded away as I left the point of observation, and entered the folding door. It was the parish chapel.

The scene which presented itself here, was in keeping not only with the external appearance of the house, but with the darkness, the storm, and the hour, — which was now a little after midnight. About eighty persons were sitting in dead silence upon the circular[4] steps of the altar; they did not seem to move, and as I entered and advanced, the echo of my footsteps rang through the building with a lonely distinctness, which added to the solemnity and mystery of the circumstances about me. The windows were secured with shutters on the inside, and on the altar a candle was lighting, which burned dimly amid the surrounding darkness, and lengthened the shadow of the altar itself, and of six or seven persons who stood on its upper steps, until they mingled in the obscurity which shrouded the lower end of the chapel. The faces of those who sat on the altar steps were not distinctly visible, yet the prominent and more characteristic features were in sufficient relief, and I observed, that some of the most malignant and reckless spirits in the parish, were assembled. In the eyes of those who stood at the altar, and whom I knew to be invested with authority over the others, I could perceive gleams of some latent and ferocious purpose, kindled, as I soon observed, into a fiercer expression of vengeance, by the additional excitement of ardent spirits, with which they had stimulated themselves to the point of determination that mocked at the apprehension of all future responsibility, either in this world or the next.

The welcome which I received on joining them, was far different from the boisterous good humour which used to mark our greetings on other occasions; just a nod of the head from this or that person, on the part of those *who sat*, with a *ghud dhemur tha thu*,§ in a suppressed voice, even below a common whisper; but, from the standing group, who were evidently the projectors of the enterprise, I received a convulsive grasp of the hand, accompanied by a fierce and desperate look, that seemed to search my eye and countenance, to try if I was a person not likely to shrink from whatever they had resolved to execute. It is surprising to think of the powerful expression which a moment of intense interest or great danger is capable of giving to the eye, the features, and slightest actions, especially in those whose station in society does not require them to constrain nature, by the force of social courtesies, into habits of concealment of their natural emotions. None of the standing group spoke, but as each of them wrung my hand in silence, his eye was fixed on mine, with an expression of drunken confidence and secrecy, and an insolent determination not to be gainsayed without peril. If looks could be translated with certainty, they seemed to say, 'we are bound upon a project of vengeance, and if you do not join us, remember that we *can* revenge.' Along with this grasp, they did not forget to remind me of the common bond by which we were united, for each man gave me the secret grip of Ribbonism in a manner that made the joints of my fingers ache for some minutes after.

There was one present, however — the highest in authority — whose actions and demeanour were calm and unexcited; he seemed to labour under no unusual influence whatever, but evinced a serenity so placid and philosophical, that I attributed the silence of the sitting group, and the restraint which curbed in the out-breaking passions of those who *stood*, entirely to his presence. He was a schoolmaster, who taught his daily school in that chapel, and acted also, on Sunday, in the capacity of clerk to the priest — an excellent and amiable old man, who knew little of his illegal connection, and atrocious conduct.[5]

When the ceremonies of brotherly recognition and friendship were past, the Captain, by which title I will designate the last-mentioned person, stooped, and raising a jar of whiskey on the corner of the altar, held a wine glass to its neck, which he filled, and with a calm nod handed it to me to drink. I shrunk back, with an instinctive horror, at the

§ How are you?

4. Presumably circular = curved, semi-circular.

5. The phrase after the dash refers, of course, to the priest and not to the schoolmaster.

profaneness of such an act, in the house, and on the altar of God, and peremptorily refused to taste the proffered draught. He smiled, mildly, at what he considered my superstition, and added quietly, and in a low voice, 'You'll be wantin' it, I'm thinkin', afther the wettin' you got.' — 'Wet or dry,' said I — 'Stop, man' he replied in the same tone — 'spake lower; but why would'nt you take the whiskey? Sure there's as holy people to the fore as you — did'nt they all take it? — an' I wish we may never do worse than dhrink a harmless glass of whiskey, to keep the could[6] out, any way.' 'Well,' said I, 'I'll just trust to God, and the consequinces, for the could, Paddy, ma bouchal; but a blessed dhrop ov it wo'nt be crossin' my lips, avick; so no more gosther about it — dhrink it yerself, if you like; may-be you want it as much as I do — wherein I've the patthern of a good big-coat upon me, so thick, yer sowl, that if it was rainin' bullocks, a dhrop would'nt get undher the nap ov it.'[7] He gave me a calm, but keen glance, as I spoke. 'Well, Jim,' said he, 'it's a good comrâde you've got for the weather that's in it — but in the mane time, to set you a dacent patthern, I'll just take this myself,' — saying which, with the jar still upon its side, and the fore-finger of his left hand in its neck, he swallowed the spirits. 'It's the first I dhrank tonight,' he added, 'nor would I dhrink it now, only to shew you that I've heart and sperrit[8] to do a thing that we're all bound and sworn to, when the proper time comes' — saying which, he laid down the glass, and turned up the jar, with much coolness, upon the altar.

During this conversation, those who had been summoned to this mysterious meeting were pouring in fast; and as each person approached the altar, he received from one to two or three large glasses of whiskey, according as he chose to limit himself — and, to do them justice, there were not a few of those present, who, in despite of their own desire, and the Captain's express invitation, refused to taste it in the house of God's worship. Such, however, as were scrupulous, he afterwards recommended to take it on the outside of the chapel door, which they did — as by that means, the sacrilege of the act was supposed to be evaded.

About one o'clock they were all assembled except six — at least so the Captain, on looking at a written paper, asserted. 'Now, boys,' said he, in the same low voice, 'we are all present except the thraitors, whose names I am goin' to read to you; not that we are to count thim as thraitors, till we know whether or not it was in their power to come; any how, the night is terrible — but, boys, you're to know, that neither fire nor wather is to prevint yees, when duly summonsed to attind a meeting — particularly whin the summons is widout a name, as you have been tould that there is always something of consequence to be done *thin*.' He then read out the names of those who were absent, in order that the real cause of their absence might be ascertained — declaring, that they would be dealt with accordingly. After this he went, and with his usual caution shut and bolted the door, and having put the key in his pocket, he ascended the steps of the altar, and for some time traversed the little platform from which the priest usually addresses the congregation.

Until this night I never contemplated the man's countenance with any particular interest, but as he walked the platform, I had an opportunity of observing him more closely. He was a little man, apparently not thirty; and on a first view seemed to have nothing remarkable either in his dress or features. I, however, was not the only person whose eye was rivetted upon him at that moment; in fact every one present observed him with equal interest, for hitherto he had kept the object of the meeting perfectly secret, and of course we all felt anxious to know it. It was while he traversed this platform that I scrutinized his features with a hope, if possible, to glean from them some indication of what was passing within; I could, however, mark but little, and that little was at first rather from the intelligence which seemed to subsist between him and those whom I have already mentioned as *standing* against the altar,[9] than from any indications of his own; their gleaming eyes were fixed upon him with an intensity of savage and demon-like hope, which blazed out in flashes of

6. cold.
7. Carleton's rendering of dialect is inconsistent, and reflects the lack of an agreed conventional orthography for Irish speech. Scots dialect, on the other hand, had elaborated a recognized 'written speech' even before Walter Scott commenced his series of Waverley novels in 1814.
'avick' = my son; 'ma bouchal' = *mo bhuachall* (my boy); 'gosther' = talk, chat; 'bullocks' (English) are castrated young cattle, used here to create a colourful equivalent to the standard idiom 'raining cats and dogs'; 'nap' (English) = the raised pile on a coat or rug.
8. spirit.
9. '*standing* against' = leaning against, standing with their backs against (hence showing disrespect to).

malignant triumph, as upon turning, he threw a cool but rapid glance at them, to intimate the progress he was making in the subject to which he devoted the undivided energies of his mind. But in the course of this meditation, I could observe on one or two occasions a dark shade come over his countenance that contracted his brow into a deep furrow, and it was then, for the first time, that I saw the satanic expression of which his face, by a very slight motion of its muscles, was capable; his hands, during this silence, closed and opened convulsively; his eyes shot out two or three baleful glances, first to his confederates, and afterwards vacantly into the deep gloom of the lower part of the chapel; his teeth ground against each other, like those of a man whose revenge burns to reach a distant enemy, and finally, after having wound himself up to a certain determination, his features relaxed into their original calm and undisturbed expression.

At this moment a loud laugh, having something supernatural in it, rang out wildly from the darkness of the chapel; he stopped, and putting his open hand over his brows, peered down into the gloom, and said calmly in Irish, *bee dhu hust ne wulh anam inh* — 'hold your tongue, it is not yet the time.'[10] — Every eye was now directed to the same spot, but, in consequence of its distance from the dim light on the altar, none could perceive the object from which the laugh proceeded. It was by this time, near two o'clock in the morning.

He now stood for a few moments on the platform, and his chest heaved with a depth of anxiety equal to the difficulty of the design he wished to accomplish; 'brothers,' said he, 'for we are all brothers — sworn upon all that's sacred an' holy, to obey whatever them that's over us, maning among ourselves, wishes us to do — are you now ready, in the name of God, upon whose altar I stand, to fulfil yer oath?'

The words were scarcely uttered, when those who had *stood* beside the altar during the night, sprung from their places, and descending its steps rapidly, turned round, and raising their arms exclaimed, 'By all that's sacred an' holy we're willin'.'

In the mean time, those who *sat* upon the steps of the altar, instantly rose, and following the example of those who had just spoken, exclaimed after them, "to be sure — by all that's sacred an' holy we're willin'."

'Now boys,' said the Captain, 'ar'nt yees big fools for your pains? an' *one* of yee's does'nt know what I mane.'

'You're our Captain,' said one of those who had stood at the altar — 'an' has yer ordhers from higher quarthers, of coorse whatever ye command upon us we're bound to obey you in.'

'Well,' said he, smiling, 'I only wanted to thry yees an' by the oath yees tuck, there's not a Captain in the county has as good a right to be proud of his min as I have — well yees won't rue it, may be, when the right time comes; and for that same rason every one of yees must have a glass from the jar; thim that won't dhrink it *in* the chapel can dhrink it *widout*;[11] an' here goes to open the door for them' — he then distributed another large glass to every man who would accept it, and brought the jar afterwards to the chapel door, to satisfy the scruples of those who would not drink within. When this was performed, and all duly excited, he proceeded:

'Now, brothers, you are solemnly sworn to obey me, an' I'm sure there's no thraithur[12] here that 'id parjure himself for a trifle, any how, but *I'm* sworn to obey them that's above me — manin' still among ourselves — an' to shew you that I don't scruple to do it, there goes' — he then turned round, and taking the Missal between his hands, placed it upon the holy altar. Hitherto, every word was uttered in a low precautionary tone; but on grasping the book, he again turned round, and looking upon his confederates with the same satanic expression which marked his countenance before, exclaimed in a voice of deep determination;

'By this sacred an' holy book of God, I will perform the action which we have met this night to accomplish, be that what it may — an' this I swear upon God's book, an' God's altar!' At this moment the candle which burned before him went suddenly out, and the chapel was wrapped in pitchy darkness; the sound as if of rushing wings fell upon our ears, and fifty voices dwelt upon the last words of his oath, with wild and supernatural tones that seemed to echo and to mock what he had sworn. There was a pause, and an exclamation of horror from all present, but the Captain was too cool and steady to be disconcerted; he immediately groped about until he got the candle, and proceeding calmly to a remote corner of the chapel, took up a half-burned turf which lay there,

10. The phonetic rendering of Irish is poor, and here positively ambiguous. The noun and definite article for 'the time' is *an t-am*, whereas the noun *anam* means 'soul'.

11. i.e. without, outside.

12. traitor.

and after some trouble, succeeded in lighting it again. He then explained what had taken place; which indeed was easily done, as the candle happened to be extinguished by a pigeon which sat exactly above it. The chapel, I should have observed, was at this time, like many country chapels, unfinished inside, and the pigeons of a neighbouring dove-cote, had built nests among the rafters of the unceiled roof, which circumstance also explained the rushing of the wings, for the birds had been affrighted by the sudden loudness of the noise. The mocking voices were nothing but the echoes, rendered naturally more awful by the scene, the mysterious object of the meeting, and the solemn hour of the night.

When the candle was again lighted, and these startling circumstances accounted for, the persons whose vengeance had been deepening more and more during the night, rushed to the altar in a body, where each in a voice trembling with passionate eagerness, repeated the oath, and as every word was pronounced, the same echoes heightened the wildness of the horrible ceremony, by their long and unearthly tones. The countenances of these human tigers were livid with suppressed rage — their knit brows, compressed lips, and kindled eyes, fell under the dim light of the taper, with an expression calculated to sicken any heart not absolutely diabolical.

As soon as this dreadful rite was completed, we were again startled by several loud bursts of laughter, which proceeded from the lower darkness of the chapel, and the captain on hearing them, turned to the place, and reflecting for a moment, said in Irish, '*gutsho nish, avohdhes*' — come hither now, boys. A rush immediately took place from the corner in which they had secreted themselves all the night — and seven men appeared, whom we instantly recognized as brothers and cousins of certain persons who had been convicted some time before, for breaking into the house of an honest poor man in the neighbourhood, from whom, after having treated him with a barbarous violence, they took away such fire arms as he kept for his own protection.

It was evidently not the captain's intention to have produced these persons until the oath should have been generally taken, but the exulting mirth with which they enjoyed the success of his scheme betrayed them, and put him to the necessity of bringing them forward somewhat before the concerted moment.

The scene which now took place was beyond all power of description; peals of wild fiend-like yells rang through the chapel, as the party which *stood* on the altar, and that which had crouched in the darkness met; wringing of hands, leaping in triumph, striking of sticks and fire arms against the ground and the altar itself, dancing and cracking of fingers, marked the triumph of some hellish propensity. Even the captain for a time was unable to restrain their fury; but at length he mounted the platform before the altar once more, and with a stamp of his foot, recalled their attention to himself and the matter in hand.

'Boys,' said he, 'enough of this, and too much; an' well for us it is that the chapel is in a lonely place, or our foolish noise might do us no good — let thim that swore so manfully jist now, stand a one side, till the rest kiss the book one by one.'

The proceedings, however, had by this time taken too alarming a shape, for even the captain to compel them to a blindfold oath; the first man he called flatly refused to swear, until he should first hear the nature of the service that was required. This was echoed by the remainder, who taking courage from the firmness of this person, declared generally, that until they first knew the business they were to execute, none of them should take the oath. The captain's lip quivered slightly, and his brow once more knit with the same hellish expression, which I have remarked gave him so much the appearance of an embodied fiend; but this speedily passed away, and was succeeded by a malignant sneer, in which lurked, if there ever did in a sneer, 'a laughing devil,'[13] calmly, determinedly, atrocious.

'It wasn't worth yer whiles to refuse the oath,' said he, mildly, 'for the thruth is, I had next to nothing for ye's to do — not a hand, maybe, would have to *rise*, only jist to look on, an', if any resistance would be made, to shew yerselves; yer numbers would soon make them see that resistance would be no use whatever in the present case. At all evints the oath of *secrecy must* be taken, or woe be to him that will refuse *that*, he wont know the day, the hour, nor the minute, when he'll be made a spatch cock[14] ov.' He then turned round, and placing his right hand on the Missal, swore 'in the presence of God, and before his holy altar, that whatever might take place that night he would keep secret, from man or mortal, except it was the holy priest on his dying day, and that neither

13. Demonic laughter signals the contempt of Satan for his victims.
14. A bird killed, plucked, split open and cooked.

bribery, nor imprisonment, nor death, would wring it from his heart'; having done this, he struck the book violently, as if to confirm the energy with which he swore, and then calmly descending the steps, stood with a serene countenance, like a man conscious of having performed a good action. As this oath did not pledge those who refused to take the other to the perpetration of any specific crime, it was readily taken by all present; preparations were then made to execute what was intended; the half burned turf was placed in a little pot — another glass of whiskey was distributed, and the door being locked by the captain, who kept the key as parish master and clerk, the crowd departed silently from the chapel. The moment that those who lay in the darkness during the night, made their appearance at the altar, we knew at once the persons we were to visit; for, as I said before, these were related to the miscreants whom one of these persons had convicted, in consequence of their midnight attack upon himself and his family. The Captain's object in keeping them unseen was, that those present, not being aware of the duty about to be imposed on them, might have less hesitation against swearing to its fulfilment. Our conjectures were correct, for on leaving the chapel we directed our steps to the house in which this man (the only Protestant in the parish) resided.[15]

The night was still stormy, but without rain; it was rather dark too, though not so as to prevent us from seeing the clouds careering swiftly through the air. The dense curtain which had overhung and obscured the horizon, was now broken, and large sections of the sky were clear, and thinly studded with stars that looked dim and watery, as did indeed the whole firmament, for in some place large clouds were still visible threatening a continuance of severe tempestuous weather. The road appeared washed and gravelly, every dike was full of yellow water, and each little rivulet and larger stream dashed its hoarse music in our ears; the blast, too, was cold, fierce, and wintry, sometimes driving us back to a stand still, and again, when a turn in the road would bring it in our backs, whirling us along for a few steps, with involuntary rapidity. At length the fated dwelling became visible, and a short consultation was held in a sheltered place, between the Captain and the two parties who seemed so eager for its destruction. Their fire arms were now charged, and their bayonets and short pikes, the latter shod and pointed with iron, were also got ready: the live coal which was brought in the small pot, had become extinguished, but to remedy this, two or three persons from the remote parts of the parish, entered a cabin on the wayside, and under pretence of lighting their own and their comrade's pipes, procured a coal of fire, for so they called a lighted turf. From the time we left the chapel until this moment, a most profound silence had been maintained, a circumstance, which, when I considered the number of persons present, and the mysterious and dreaded object of their journey, had a most appalling effect upon my spirits.

At length we arrived within fifty perches[16] of the house, walking in a compact body, and with as little noise as possible; but it seemed as if the very elements had conspired to frustrate our design, for on advancing within the shade of the farm-hedge, two or three persons found themselves up to the middle in water, and on stooping to ascertain more accurately the state of the place, we could see nothing but one immense sheet of it spread like a lake over the meadows which surrounded the spot we wished to reach.

Fatal night! the very recollection of it, when associated with the fearful tempest of the elements, grows, if that were possible, yet more wild and revolting. Had we been engaged in any innocent or benevolent enterprize, there was something in our situation, just now, that had a touch of interest in it to a mind imbued with a relish for the savage beauties of nature. There we stood, about a hundred and thirty in number, our dark forms bent forwards peering into the dusky expanse of water, with its dim gleams of reflected light, broken by the weltering[17] of the mimic waves into ten thousand fragments, whilst the few stars that overhung it in the firmament, appeared to shoot through it in broken lines, and to be multiplied fifty-fold in the many-faced mirror on which we gazed.

Over this was a stormy sky, and around us a darkness through which we could only distinguish, in outline, the nearest objects, whilst the wild wind swept strongly and dismally upon us. When it was discovered that the common pathway to the house

15. Since nothing in reports of the original incident suggests that the victims were protestants, it must be concluded that Carleton (or his editor) has added a sectarian detail.

16. A perch was about 5½ yards.

17. rolling, heaving.

was inundated,[18] we were about to abandon our object, and return home; the Captain, however, stooped down low for a moment, and almost closing his eyes, looked along the surface of the waters, and then raising himself very calmly, said, in his usual quiet tone, 'yees needn't go back, boys, I've found a path, jist follow me.' He immediately took a more circuitous direction, by which we reached a causeway that had been raised for the purpose of giving a free passage to and from the house, during such inundations as the present. Along this we had advanced more than half way, when we discovered a break in it, which as afterwards appeared, had that night been made by the strength of the flood. This, by means of our sticks and pikes, we found to be about three feet deep, and eight yards broad. Again we were at a loss how to proceed, when the fertile brain of the Captain devised a method of crossing it; 'boys,' said he, 'of course you've all played at leap-frog — very well, strip and go in a dozen of you, — lean one upon the shoulders of another from this to the opposite bank, where one must stand facing the outside man, both their shoulders agin one another, that the outside man may be supported — then *we* can creep over you, an' a decent bridge you'll be, any way.' This was the work of only a few minutes, and in less than ten we were all safely over.

Merciful heaven! how I sicken at the recollection of what is to follow — on reaching the dry bank, we proceeded instantly, and in profound silence, to the house; the Captain divided us into companies, and then assigned to each division its proper station. The two parties who had been so vindictive all the night, he kept about himself, for of those who were present they only were in his confidence, and knew his nefarious purpose; their number was about fifteen. Having made these dispositions, he, at the head of about five of them, approached the house on the windy side, for the fiend possessed a coolness which enabled him to seize upon every possible advantage; that he had combustibles about him was evident, for in less than fifteen minutes nearly one half of the house was enveloped in flames. On seeing this, the others rushed over to the spot where he and his gang were standing, and remonstrated earnestly, but in vain; the flames now burst forth with renewed violence, and as they flung their strong light upon the faces of the foremost group, I do think hell itself could hardly present any thing more satanic than their countenances, now worked up into a paroxysm of infernal triumph, at their own revenge. The Captain's look had lost all its calmness, every feature started out into distinct malignity, the curve in his brow was deep, and ran up to the root of the hair, dividing his face into two sections, that did not seem to have been designed for each other. His lips were half open, and the corners of his mouth a little brought back on each side, like those of a man expressing intense hatred and triumph over an enemy, who is in the death-struggle under his grasp. His eyes blazed from beneath his knit eye-brows, with a fire that seemed to have been lighted up in the infernal pit itself. It is unnecessary and only painful to describe the rest of his gang; demons might have been proud of such horrible visages as they exhibited; for they worked under all the power of hatred, revenge, and joy; and these passions blended into one terrific scowl, enough almost to blast any human eye that would venture to look upon it.

When the others attempted to intercede for the lives of the inmates, there were at least fifteen loaded guns and pistols levelled at them; 'another word,' said the Captain, 'an' you're a corpse where you stand, or the first man who will dare to speak for them: no, no, it wasn't to spare them we came here — "No Mercy" is the pass word for the night, an' by the sacred oath I swore beyant in the chapel, any one among yees that will attimpt to shew it, will find none at my hand. Surround the house, boys, I tell ye, I hear them stirring — *No Mercy* — no quarther — is the ordher of the night.'

Such was his command over these misguided creatures, that in an instant there was a ring round the house to prevent the escape of the unhappy inmates, should the raging element give them time to attempt it; for none present dare withdraw themselves from the scene, not only from an apprehension of the Captain's present vengeance, or that of his gang, but because they knew that even had they then escaped, an early and certain death awaited them from a quarter against which they had no means of defence.[19] The hour now was about half past two o'clock. Scarcely had the last words escaped from the Captain's lips, when one of the windows of the house was broken, and a human

18. flooded.

19. It was a central tenet of Ribbonism and other agrarian secret societies that disobedience was ruthlessly punished; notices to this effect usually accompanied the society's threats.

head having the hair in a blaze, was descried, apparently a woman's, if one might judge by the profusion of burning tresses, and the softness of the tones, notwithstanding that it called, or rather shrieked aloud, for help and mercy. The only reply to this was the whoop from the Captain and his gang, of no mercy — 'No Mercy,' and that instant the former, and one of the latter rushed to the spot, and ere the action could be perceived, the head was transfixed with a bayonet and a pike, both having entered it together. The word mercy was divided in her mouth; a short silence ensued, the head hung down on the window, but was instantly tossed back into the flames.

This action occasioned a cry of horror from all present, except the *gang* and their leader, which startled and enraged the latter so much, that he ran towards one of them, and had his bayonet, now reeking with the blood of its innocent victim, raised to plunge it in his body, when dropping the point, he said in a piercing whisper that hissed in the ears of all: 'Its no use *now*, you know, if one's to hang, all will hang; so our safest way, you persave,[20] is to lave none of them to tell the story: ye *may* go now if you wish; but it wont save a hair of your heads. You cowardly set! I knew if I had tould yees the sport, that none of ye except my *own* boys would come, so I jist played a thrick upon you; but remember what you are sworn to, and stand to the oath ye tuck.'

Unhappily, notwithstanding the wetness of the preceding weather, the materials of the house were extremely combustible; the whole dwelling was now one body of glowing flame, yet the shouts and shrieks within, rose awfully above its crackling and the voice of the storm, for the wind once more blew in gusts, and with great violence. The doors and windows were all torn open, and such of those within, as had escaped the flames rushed towards them, for the purpose of further escape, and of claiming mercy at the hands of their destroyers — but whenever they appeared, the unearthly cry of no mercy rung upon their ears for a moment, and for a moment only, for they were flung back at the points of the weapons which the demons had brought with them to make the work of vengeance more certain.

As yet there were many persons in the house, whose cry for life was strong as despair, and who clung to it with all the awakened powers of reason and instinct; the ear of man could hear nothing so strongly calculated to stifle the demon of cruelty and revenge within him, as the long and wailing shrieks which rose beyond the element, in tones that were carried off rapidly upon the blast, until they died away in the darkness that lay behind the surrounding hills. Had not the house been in a solitary situation, and the hour the dead of night, any person sleeping within a moderate distance must have heard them, for such a cry of sorrow deepening into a yell of despair, was almost sufficient to have awakened the dead. It was lost however upon the hearts and ears that heard it: to them, though in justice be it said, to only comparatively a few of them, it was as delightful as the tones of soft and entrancing music.

The claims of the poor sufferers were now modified; they supplicated merely to suffer death *at the hands of their enemies*; they were willing to bear that, provided they should be allowed to escape from the flames; but no, the horrors of the conflagration were calmly and malignantly gloried in by their merciless assassins, who deliberately flung them back into all their tortures. In the course of a few minutes a man appeared upon the side-wall of the house,[21] nearly naked; his figure, as he stood against the sky in horrible relief, was so finished a picture of woe-begone agony and supplication, that it is yet as distinct in my memory as if I were again present at the scene. Every muscle, now in motion by the powerful agitation of his sufferings, stood out upon his limbs and neck, giving him an appearance of desperate strength, to which by this time he must have been wrought; the perspiration poured from his frame, and the veins and arteries of his neck were inflated to a surprising thickness. Every moment he looked down into the thick flames which were rising to where he stood; and as he looked, the indescribable horror which flitted over his features might have worked upon the devil himself to relent. His words were few; 'my child,' said he, 'is still safe, she is an infant, a young creature that never harmed you nor any one — she is still safe. Your mothers, your wives have young innocent children like it — Oh, spare her, think for a moment that it's one of your own, spare it, as you hope to meet a just God, or if you dont, in mercy

20. perceive.

21. It is not clear what the architectural plausibility of this might be; perhaps the figure has climbed onto the gable wall after the roof has fallen in.

shoot me first, put an end to me, before I see her burned.'

The Captain approached him coolly and deliberately. 'You will prosecute no one now, you bloody informer,' said he; 'you will convict no more boys for taking an ould rusty gun an' pistol from you, or for givin' you a neighbourly knock or two into the bargain.' Just then from a window opposite him, proceeded the shrieks of a woman who appeared at it with the infant in her arms. She herself was almost scorched to death; but with the presence of mind and humanity of her sex, she was about to thrust the little babe out of the window. The Captain noticed this, and with characteristic atrocity, thrust, with a sharp bayonet, the little innocent, along with the person who endeavoured to rescue it, into the red flames, where they both perished. This was the work of an instant. Again he approached the man; 'your child is a coal now,' said he, with deliberate mockery, 'I pitched it in myself on the point of this,' showing the weapon, 'and now is your turn,' saying which he clambered up by the assistance of his gang, who stood with a front of pikes and bayonets bristling to receive the wretched man, should he attempt in his despair to throw himself from the wall. The Captain got up, and placing the point of his bayonet against his shoulder, flung him into the fiery element that raged behind him. He uttered one wild and piercing cry, as he fell back, and no more; after this nothing was heard but the crackling of the fire, and the rushing of the blast; all that had possessed life within were consumed, amounting either to eleven or fifteen persons.

When this was accomplished, those who took an active part in the murder, stood for some time about the conflagration, and as it threw its red light upon their fierce faces and rough persons, soiled as they now were with smoke and black streaks of ashes, the scene seemed to be changed to hell, and the murderers to spirits of the damned, rejoicing over the arrival and the torture of a guilty soul. The faces of those who kept aloof from the slaughter, were blanched to the whiteness of death; some of them fainted — and others were in such agitation that they were compelled to leave their comrades. They became actually stiff and powerless with horror; yet to such a scene were they brought by the pernicious influence of Ribbonism.

It was only when the last victim went down, that the conflagration shot up into the air with most unbounded fury. The house was large, deeply thatched, and well furnished; and the broad red pyramid rose up with fearful magnificence towards the sky. Abstractedly it had sublimity, but now it was associated with nothing in my mind but blood and terror. It was not, however, without a purpose that the Captain and his guard stood to contemplate its effect. 'Boys,' said he, 'we had better be sartin' that all's safe; who knows but there might be some of the sarpents crouchin' under a hape of rubbish, to come out and gibbet us tomorrow or next day; we had betther wait a while, any how, if it was only to see the blaze.'

Just then the flames rose majestically to a surprising height; our eyes followed their direction, and we perceived for the first time, that the dark clouds above, together with the intermediate air, appeared to reflect back, or rather to have caught the red hue of the fire; the hills and country about us appeared with an alarming distinctness; but the most picturesque part of it, was the effect or reflection of the blaze on the floods that spread over the surrounding plains. These, in fact, appeared to be one broad mass of liquid copper, for the motion of the breaking waters, caught from the blaze of the high waving column, as reflected in them, a glaring light, which eddied and rose, and fluctuated, as if the flood itself had been a lake of molten fire.

Fire, however, destroys rapidly; in a short time the flames sank — became weak and flickering — bye and bye, they only shot out in fits — the crackling of the timbers died away — the surrounding darkness deepened; and ere long, the faint light was overpowered by the thick volumes of smoke, that rose from the ruins of the house, and its murdered inhabitants.

'Now, boys,' said the Captain 'all is safe, we may go. Remember, every man of you, what you've sworn this night on the book and altar of God — not on a heretic bible. If you perjure yourselves, you may hang us; but let me tell you for your comfort, that if you do, there is them livin' that will take care the lase of your own lives will be but short.'[22] After this we dispersed, every man to his own home.

Reader, not many months elapsed ere I saw the bodies of this Captain, whose name was Paddy Devan, and all those who were actively concerned in the perpetration of this deed of horror, withering

22. This phrase contains muted biblical echoes: cf. I Kings 12. 24; Nehemiah 5. 13.

in the wind, where they hung gibbetted, near the scene of their nefarious villainy; and while I inwardly thanked heaven for my own narrow and almost undeserved escape, I thought in my heart how seldom, even in this world, justice fails to overtake the murderer, and to enforce the righteous judgment of God, 'that whoso sheddeth man's blood, by man shall his blood be shed.'[23]

23. See Genesis 9. 6.

JOSEPH SHERIDAN LE FANU

(1814-73)

from: THE HOUSE BY THE CHURCH-YARD (1861-63)

[After 1848, Joseph Sheridan Le Fanu effectively had abandoned the writing of fiction. His novel of 1863 broke a silence of sixteen years. Like *The Cock and Anchor* (1845) and to a lesser extent *The Fortunes of Colonel Torlogh O'Brien* (1847), *The House by the Church-yard* exploits the colourful history of Ireland in the period after the displacement of King James by William of Orange. In place of the binary opposition of Jacobite and Williamite (adopted from the fiction of Sir Walter Scott, to the extent that it did not simply reproduce politics), Le Fanu now extensively employed heavily brocaded features of the costume-novel of Harrison Ainsworth and others. That is, minute detail as to clothing, diet, popular song, and so on was woven into the plot to build up a sense of period. In Le Fanu, the technique serves a real function and serves it well. His plot concerning concealed evil-doing in an unchallengeably secure regime, and the distractions of highly localized description, reproduce the impossibility of challenging that hegemony while at the same time decorate (and so draw attention to) unease, dissent, subversion, potential revolt, actual criminality.

The House by the Church-yard is thus part of a Victorian Irish reassessment of the eighteenth century, with the anonymous *Leaders of Public Opinion in Ireland* (1861) by W.E.H. Lecky (1838-1903), a highly suggestive contemporary publication. For both Le Fanu and Lecky, Swift is a touchstone; indeed, the title of Le Fanu's novel derives from a playful poem of Swift's, 'On the Little House by the Churchyard of Castleknock', which first appeared in print in 1746. More problematically, catholic clerical influence concerned novelist and historian in the 1860s; Lecky's nervous essay on the topic (see pp. 214-23) was dropped from subsequent editions of *Leaders of Public Opinion in Ireland*, while Le Fanu's fictional Father Roach is a genial, if somewhat patronizing, portrait of a priest surviving (very nicely, thank you) under the Penal Laws.

Le Fanu's resumption of novel-writing followed promptly on the death of his mother in 1861, less promptly but no less significantly on the death of his wife in 1858. Chapelizod, the setting of the new novel, took him close to the scene of his own childhood in the Phoenix Park where his father held a chaplaincy, and likewise to the setting of crucial events in *The Cock and Anchor*. The three novels that he wrote in a burst of energy after his mother's death — *The House by the Church-yard*, *Wylder's Hand* (1864), and *Uncle Silas* (1864) — are concerned with the general theme of resurrection if, by resurrection, we mean for the moment some questionable form of survival after death. The first of the trio opens with the reinterring of a corpse, and only closes when the seeming death of a villain is exposed in the disguised shape of Paul Dangerfield. Perhaps taking a hint from Swift's poem, *The House by the Church-yard* employs a storm for the purpose of scene-setting. The first three chapters proper are printed below, although in the novel a prologue allows the narrator to rhapsodize on the changed appearance of Chapelizod between the time of the action and the time of narration. It was this prologue that attracted James Joyce's attention, though the resurrection motif is also grist to Finnegan's mill.]

CHAPTER I

THE RECTOR'S NIGHT-WALK TO HIS CHURCH

A.D. 1767 — in the beginning of the month of May — I mention it because, as I said, I write from memoranda, an awfully dark night came down on Chapelizod and all the country round.[1]

1. Chapelizod is an old village on the river Liffey, west of Dublin, associated with Iseult (Chapel of Iseult) of the Tristan legend.

I believe there was no moon, and the stars had been quite put out under the 'wet blanket of the night,'[2] which impenetrable muffler overspread the sky with a funereal darkness.

There was a little of that sheet-lightning early in the evening, which betokens sultry weather. The clouds, column after column, came up sullenly over the Dublin mountains, rolling themselves from one horizon to the other into one black dome of vapour, their slow but steady motion contrasting with the awful stillness of the air. There was a weight in the atmosphere, and a sort of undefined menace brooding over the little town, as if unseen crime or danger — some mystery of iniquity — was stealing into the heart of it, and the disapproving heavens scowled a melancholy warning.

That morning old Sally, the rector's housekeeper, was disquieted. She had dreamed of making the great four-post, spare bed, with the dark-green damask curtains — a dream that betokened some coming trouble — it might, to be sure, be ever so small — (it had once come with no worse result than Dr. Walsingham's[3] dropping his purse, containing something under a guinea in silver, over the side of the ferry boat) — but again it might be tremendous. The omen hung over them doubtful.

A large square letter, with a great round seal, as big as a crown piece, addressed to the Rev. Hugh Walsingham, Doctor of Divinity, at his house, by the bridge, in Chapelizod, had reached him in the morning, and plainly troubled him. He kept the messenger a good hour awaiting his answer; and, just at two o'clock, the same messenger returned with a second letter — but this time a note sufficed for reply. ''Twill seem ungracious,' said the doctor, knitting his brows over his closed folio in the study; 'but I cannot choose but walk clear in my calling before the Lord. How can I honestly pronounce hope, when in my mind there is nothing but *fear* — let another do it if he see his way — I do enough in being present, as 'tis right I should.'

It was, indeed, a remarkably dark night — a rush and down-pour of rain! The doctor stood just under the porch of the stout brick house — of King William's date,[4] which was then the residence of the worthy rector of Chapelizod — with his great surtout[5] and cape on — his leggings buttoned up — and his capacious leather 'overalls'[6] pulled up and strapped over these — and his broad-leafed hat tied down over his wig and ears with a mighty silk kerchief. I dare say he looked absurd enough — but it was the women's doing — who always, upon emergencies, took the doctor's wardrobe in hands. Old Sally, with her kind, mild, grave face, and gray locks, stood modestly behind in the hall; and pretty Lilias, his only child, gave him her parting kiss, and her last grand charge about his shoes and other exterior toggery, in the porch; and he patted her cheek with a little fond laugh, taking old John Tracy's, the butler's, arm. John carried a handsome horn-lantern, which flashed now on a roadside bush — now on the discoloured battlements of the bridge — and now on a streaming window. They stept out — there were no umbrellas in those days — splashing among the wide and widening pools; while Sally and Lilias stood in the porch, holding candles for full five minutes after the doctor and his 'Jack-o'-the-lantern,' as he called honest John, whose arm and candle always befriended him in his night excursions, had got round the corner.

Through the back bow-window of the Phœnix, there pealed forth — faint in the distance and rain — a solemn loyal ditty, piped by the tuneful Aldermen of Skinner's Alley,[7] and neither unmusical nor somehow uncongenial with the darkness, and the melancholy object of the doctor's walk, the chant being rather monastic, wild, and dirge-like. It was a quarter past ten, and no other sound of life or human neighbourhood was stirring. If secrecy were an object, it was well secured by the sable sky, and the steady torrent which rolled down with electric weight and perpendicularity, making all nature resound with one long hush — sh—sh—sh—sh— deluging the broad street, and turning the channels and gutters into mimic mill-streams, which snorted and hurtled headlong through their uneven beds, and round the corners towards the turbid Liffey, which, battered all over with the rain, swollen, muddy, and sullen, reeled its

2. cf. *Macbeth*, I. 5. 54.
3. Le Fanu's novels proliferate in surnames with historical overtones. Sir Francis Walsingham (1532-90) was secretary of state to Elizabeth I. He built up an intelligence service and secured the conviction and execution of Mary Queen of Scots.
4. i.e. built in the late seventeenth century.
5. A man's overcoat, resembling a frock coat.
6. Protective trousers worn over one's regular clothes; the term is dated by the OED to 1782 (i.e. later than 1767). Hence perhaps the inverted commas.
7. The Aldermen of Skinner's Alley was the name of a convivial society in eighteenth-century Dublin, less devoted to the memory of William III than to the drinking of many toasts in his honour.

wild way towards the sea, rolling up to the heavens an aspect black as their own.

As they passed by the Phœnix, (a little rivulet, by-the-bye, was spouting down from the corner of the sign; and indeed the night was such as might well have caused that suicidal fowl to abandon all thoughts of self-incremation, and submit to an unprecedented death by drowning), there was no idle officer, or lounging waiter upon the threshold. Military and civilians were all snug in their quarters that night; and the inn, except for the 'Aldermen' in the back parlour, was doing no business. The door was nearly closed, and only let out a tall, narrow slice of candle-light upon the lake of mud, over every inch of which the rain was incessantly drumming.

The doctor's lantern glided by — and then across the street — and so leisurely along the foot-way, by the range of lightless hall-doors toward the Salmon House, also dark; and so, sharp round the corner, and up to the church-yard gate, which stood a little open, as also the church door beyond as was evidenced by the feeble glow of a lantern from within.

I dare say old Bob Martin, the sexton, and grave Mr. Irons, the clerk, were reassured when they heard the cheery voice of the rector hailing them by name. There were now three candles in church; but the edifice looked unpleasantly dim, and went off at the far end into total darkness. Zekiel Irons was a lean, reserved fellow, with a black wig and blue chin, and something shy and sinister in his phiz.[8] I don't think he had entertained honest Bob with much conversation from those thin lips of his during their grizzly *tête-à-tête* among the black windows and the mural tablets that overhung the aisle.

But the rector had lots to say — though deliberately and gravely, still the voice was genial and inspiring — and exorcised the shadows that had been gathering stealthily around the lesser church functionaries. Mrs. Irons' tooth, he learned, was still bad; but she was no longer troubled with 'that sour humour in her stomach.' There were sour humours, alas! still remaining — enough, and to spare, as the clerk knew to his cost. Bob Martin thanked his reverence; 'the cold rheumatism in his hip was better.' Irons, the clerk, replied, 'he had brought two prayer-books.' Bob averred 'he could not be mistaken; the old lady was buried in the near vault; though it was forty years before, he remembered it like last night. They changed her into her lead coffin in the vault — he and the undertaker together — her own servants would not put a hand to her. She was buried in white satin, and with her rings on her fingers. It was her fancy, and so ordered in her will. They said she was mad. He'd know her face again if he saw her. She had a long hooked nose; and her eyes were open. For, as he was told, she died in her sleep, and was quite cold and stiff when they found her in the morning. He went down and saw the coffin today, half an hour after meeting his Reverence.'

The rector consulted his great warming-pan of a watch. It was drawing near eleven. He fell into a reverie, and rambled slowly up and down the aisle, with his hands behind his back, and his dripping hat in them, swinging nearly to the flags — now lost in the darkness — now emerging again, dim, nebulous, in the foggy light of the lanterns. When this clerical portrait came near, he was looking down, with gathered brows, upon the flags, moving his lips and nodding, as if counting them, as was his way. The doctor was thinking all the time upon the one text: — Why should this livid memorial of two great crimes be now disturbed, after an obscurity of twenty-one years, as if to jog the memory of scandal, and set the great throat of the monster baying once more at the old midnight horror?

And as for that old house at Ballyfermot, why any one could have looked after it as well as he. 'Still he must live somewhere, and certainly this little town is quieter than the city, and the people, on the whole, very kindly, and by no means curious.' This latter was a mistake of the doctor's, who, like other simple persons, was fond of regarding others as harmless repetitions of himself. 'And his soujourn will be,' he says, 'but a matter of weeks'; and the doctor's mind wandered back again to the dead, and forward to the remoter consequences of his guilt, so he heaved a heavy, honest sigh, and lifted up his head and slacked his pace for a little prayer, and with that there came the rumble of wheels to the church door.

CHAPTER II

THE NAMELESS COFFIN

Three vehicles with flambeaux, and the clang and snorting of horses came close to the church porch,

8. face — a colloquial abbreviation of physiognomy.

and there appeared suddenly, standing within the disk of candle-light at the church-door, before one would have thought there was time, a tall, very pale, and peculiar looking young man, with very large, melancholy eyes, and a certain cast of evil pride in his handsome face.

John Tracy lighted the wax candles which he had brought, and Bob Martin stuck them in the sockets at either side of the cushion, on the ledge of the pew, beside the aisle, where the prayer-book lay open at 'the burial of the dead,'[1] and the rest of the party drew about the door, while the doctor was shaking hands very ceremoniously with that tall young man, who had now stepped into the circle of light, with a short, black mantle on, and his black curls uncovered, and a certain air of high breeding in his movements. 'He reminded me painfully of him who is gone, whom we name not,' said the doctor to pretty Lilias, when he got home; 'he has his pale, delicately-formed features, with a shadow of his evil passions, too, and his mother's large, sad eyes.'

And an elderly clergyman, in surplice, band, and white wig, with a hard, yellow, furrowed face, hovered in, like a white bird of night, from the darkness behind, and was introduced to Dr. Walsingham, and whispered for a while to Mr. Irons, and then to Bob Martin, who had two short forms placed transversely in the aisle to receive what was coming, and a shovel full of earth — all ready. So, while the angular clergyman ruffled into the front of the pew, with Irons on one side, a little in the rear, both books open; the plump little undertaker, diffusing a steam from his moist garments, making a prismatic halo, round the candles and lanterns as he moved successively by them, whispered a word or two to the young gentleman (Mr. Mervyn, the doctor called him), and Mr. Mervyn disappeared. Dr. Walsingham and John Tracy got into contiguous seats, and Bob Martin went out to lend a hand. Then came the shuffling of feet, and the sound of hard-tugging respiration, and the suppressed, energetic, mutual directions of the undertaker's men, who supported the ponderous coffin. How much heavier, it always seems to me, that sort of load than any other of the same size!

A great oak shell: the lid was outside in the porch, Mr. Tressels was unwilling to screw it down, having heard that the entrance to the vault was so narrow, and apprehending it might be necessary to take the coffin out. So it lies its length with a dull weight on the two forms. The lead coffin inside, with its dusty black velvet, was plainly much older. There was a plate on it with two bold capitals, and a full stop after each, thus:

R. D.
obiit[2] May 11th,
A.D. 1746.
ætat[3] 38.

And above this plain, oval plate was a little bit of an ornament no bigger than a sixpence. John Tracy took it for a star, Bob Martin said he knew it to be a Freemason's order,[4] and Mr. Tressels, who almost overlooked it, thought it was nothing better than a fourpenny cherub. But Mr. Irons, the clerk, knew that it was a coronet; and when he heard the other theories thrown out, being a man of few words, he let them have it their own way, and with his thin lips closed, with their changeless and unpleasant character of an imperfect smile, he coldly kept this little bit of knowledge to himself.

Earth to earth (rumble), dust to dust (tumble), ashes to ashes (rattle).

And now the coffin must go out again and down to its final abode.

The flag that closed the entrance of the vault had been removed. But the descent of Avernus[5] was not facile, the steps being steep and broken, and the roof so low. Young Mervyn had gone down the steps to see it duly placed; a murky, fiery light came up, against which the descending figures looked black and cyclopean.

Dr. Walsingham offered his brother-clergyman his hospitalities; but somehow that cleric preferred returning to town for his supper and his bed. Mervyn also excused himself. It was late; and he meant to stay that night at the Phœnix, and tomorrow designed to make his compliments in person to Dr. Walsingham. So the bilious clergyman from town climbed into the vehicle in which he had come, and the undertaker and his troop got into the hearse and the mourning coach and drove off

1. That is, at the service for the burial of the dead in the Book of Common Prayer (Church of Ireland).
2. died.
3. aged.
4. Freemasonry was organized in Ireland through the Grand Lodge of 1725.
5. A deep lake of sulphur referred to in Virgil's *Aeneid*, synonymous with a dangerous passage through profound darkness.

demurely through the town; but once a hundred yards or so beyond the turnpike, at such a pace that they overtook the rolicking *cortege* of the Aldermen of Skinner's Alley upon the Dublin road, all singing and hallooing, and crowing and shouting scraps of banter at one another, in which recreations these professional mourners forthwith joined them; and they cracked screaming jokes, and drove wild chariot races the whole way into town, to the terror of the divine whose presence they forgot, and whom, though he bawled like a maniac from the window, they never heard, until getting out, when the coach came to standstill, he gave Mr. Tressels a piece of his mind, and that in so alarming a sort, that the jolly undertaker, expressing a funereal concern at the accident, was obliged to explain that all the noise came from the scandalous party they had so unfortunately overtaken, and that 'the drunken blackguards had lashed and frightened his horses to a runaway pace, singing and hallooing in the filthy way he heard, it being a standing joke among such roisters to put quiet tradesmen of his melancholy profession into a false and ridiculous position.' He did not convince, but only half-puzzled the ecclesiastic, who, muttering, 'credat judæus,'[6] turned his back upon Mr. Tressels with an angry whisk, without bidding him good night.

Dr. Walsingham, with the aid of his guide, in the meantime, had reached the little garden in front of the old house, and the gay tinkle of a harpsichord and the notes of a sweet contralto suddenly ceased as he did so; and he said — smiling in the dark, in a pleasant soliloquy, for he did not mind John Tracy — old John was not in the way — 'She always hears my step — always — little Lily, no matter how she's employed,' and the hall-door opened, and a voice that was gentle, and yet somehow very spirited and sweet, cried a loving and playful welcome to the old man.

6. An abbreviated form of Horace's phrase 'Credat Judaeus Apella', meaning, sarcastically, 'Let Apella the Jew believe it!".

CHAPTER III

MR. MERVYN IN HIS INN

The morning was fine — the sun shone out with a yellow splendour — all nature was refreshed — a pleasant smell rose up from tree, and flower, and earth. The now dry pavement and all the row of village windows were glittering merrily — the sparrows twittered their lively morning gossip among the thick ivy of the old church tower — here and there the village cock challenged his neighbour with high and vaunting crow, and the bugle notes soared sweetly into the air from the artillery ground beside the river.

Moore, the barber, was already busy making his morning circuit, serving-men and maids were dropping in and out at the baker's, and old Poll Delany, in her weather-stained red hood, and neat little Kitty Lane, with her bright, young, careful face and white basket, were calling at the doors of their customers with new-laid eggs. Through half-opened hall-doors you might see the powdered servant, or the sprightly maid in her mob-cap in hot haste steaming away with the red-japanned 'tea kitchen'[1] into the parlour. The town of Chapelizod, in short, was just sitting down to its breakfast.

Mervyn, in the meantime, had had his solitary meal in the famous back parlour of the Phœnix, where the newspapers lay, and all comers were welcome. He was by no means a bad hero to look at, if such a thing were needed. His face was pale, melancholy, statuesque — and his large enthusiastic eyes, suggested a story, and a secret — perhaps a horror. Most men, had they known all would have wondered with good Doctor Walsingham, why, of all places in the world, he should have chosen the little town where he now stood for even a temporary residence. It was not a perversity — but rather a fascination. His whole life had been a flight and a pursuit — a vain endeavour to escape from the evil spirit that pursued him — and a chase of a wild chimera.

He was standing at the window, not indeed enjoying, as another man might, the quiet verdure of the scene, and the fragrant air, and all the mellowed sounds of village life, but lost in a sad and dreadful reverie, when in bounces little red-faced, bustling Dr. Toole — the joke and the chuckle with which he had just requited the fat old barmaid still ringing in the passage — 'Stay there, sweetheart,' addressed to a dog squeezing by him, and which screeched as he kicked it neatly round the door-post.

1. The tea-kitchen here is a utensil, perhaps a bowl, decorated with a hard varnish.

'Hey, your most obedient, sir,' cried the doctor, with a short but grand bow, affecting surprise, though his chief object in visiting the back parlour at that moment was precisely to make a personal inspection of the stranger. 'Pray, don't mind me, sir — your — ho! Breakfast ended, eh? Coffee not so bad, sir; rather good coffee, I hold it, at the Phœnix. Cream very choice, sir? — I don't tell 'em so, though (a wink); it might not improve it, you know. I hope they gave you — eh? (he peeped into the cream-ewer, which he turned towards the light, with a whisk). And no disputing the eggs — forty-eight hens in the poultry yard, and ninety ducks in Tresham's little garden, next door to Sturk's. They make a precious noise, I can tell you, when it showers. Sturk threatens to shoot 'em. He's the artillery surgeon here; and Tom Larkin said, last night, it's because they only dabble and quack — and two of a trade, you know — ha! ha! ha! And what a night we had — dark as Erebus[2] — pouring like pumps, by Jove. I'll remember it, I warrant you. Out on business — a medical man, you know, can't always choose — and near meeting a bad accident, too. Anything in the paper, eh? ho! I see, sir — haven't read it. Well, and what do you think — a queer night for the purpose, eh? you'll say — we had a funeral in the town last night, sir — some one from Dublin. It was Tressel's men came out. The turnpike rogue, just round the corner there — one of the worst gossips in the town — and a confounded prying, tattling place it is, I can tell you — knows the driver; and Bob Martin — the sexton, you know — tells me there were two parsons, no less — hey! Cauliflowers in season, by Jove! Old Dr. Walsingham, our rector — a pious man, sir, and does a world of good — that's to say, relieves half the blackguards in the parish — ha! ha! when we're on the point of getting rid of them — but means well, only he's a little bit lazy, and queer, you know; and that rancid, raw-boned parson, Gillespie — how the plague did they pick him up? — one of the mutes told Bob it was he. He's from Donegal; I know all about him; the sourest dog I ever broke bread with — and a mason, if you please, by Jove — a prince pelican! He supped at the Grand Lodge, after labour, one night — *you're* not a mason, I see; tipt you the sign — and his face was so small and so yellow, by Jupiter, I was near squeezing it into the punch-bowl for a lemon — ha! ha! hey?'[3]

Mervyn's large eyes expressed a well-bred but stern surprise. Dr. Toole paused for nearly a minute, as if expecting something in return; but it did not come.

So the doctor started afresh, never perceiving Mervyn's somewhat dangerous aspect —

'Mighty pretty prospects about here, sir. The painters come out by dozens in the summer, with their books and pencils, and scratch away like so many Scotchmen. Ha! ha! ha! If you draw, sir, there's one prospect up the river, by the mills — upon my conscience — but you don't draw?'

No answer.

'A little, sir, maybe? Just for a maggot,[4] I'll wager — like *my* good lady, Mrs. Toole.' A nearer glance at his dress had satisfied Toole that he was too much of a maccaroni[5] for an artist, and he was thinking of placing him upon the Lord Lieutenant's staff. 'We've capital horses here, if you want to go on to Leixlip,' (where — this between ourselves and the reader — during the summer months His Excellency and Lady Townshend[6] resided, and where, the old newspapers tell us, they 'kept a public day every Monday,' and he 'had a levée, as usual, every Thursday.') But this had no better success.

'If you design to stay over the day, and care for shooting, we'll have some ball practice on Palmerstown fair-green today. Seven baronies to shoot for ten and five guineas. One o'clock — hey?'

At this moment entered Major O'Neill, of the Royal Irish Artillery, a small man, very neatly got up, and with a decidedly Milesian[7] cast of countenance, who said little, but smiled agreeably —

'Gentlemen, your most obedient. Ha, doctor; how goes it? — any thing new — any thing *on* the *Freeman*?'[8]

2. In Greek mythology, Erebus was a place of darkness between earth and Hades.

3. Dr Toole tells Mervyn that the gloomy cleric of the night before is a fellow freemason (prince pelican being a masonic rank), and also indicates that Mervyn has failed to recognize a masonic signal or call for identification.

4. i.e. as the fancy takes one. A 'maggot' was a whim.

5. An eighteenth-century dandy who aped continental fashions.

6. George Townshend (1724-1807), 4th viscount and 1st marquis Townshend, was appointed lord lieutenant of Ireland on 19 August 1767, and was sworn in on 14 October 1767. Thus Le Fanu's narrator is running just a little ahead of the facts, for the first line of Chapter I gives the date as 'the beginning of the month of May'.

7. According to one school of proto-historians, the Milesians were early human settlers on the island and so gave their name to what was thought of as aboriginal Irish characteristics.

8. The Dublin newspaper, *The Freeman's Journal*, was founded in 1763.

Toole had scanned that paper, and hummed out, as he rumpled it over, 'nothing — very — particular. Here's Lady Moira's[9] ball: fancy dresses — all Irish; no masks; a numerous appearance of the nobility and gentry — upwards of five hundred persons. A good many of your corps there, Major?'

'Ay, Lord Blackwater, of course, and the General, and Devereux, and little Puddock, and' —

'*Sturk* wasn't,' with a grin, interrupted Toole, who bore that practitioner no good-will. 'A gentleman robbed, by two foot-pads, on Chapelizod-road, on Wednesday night, of his watch and money, together with his hat, wig, and cane, and lies now in a dangerous state, having been much abused; one of them dressed in an old light-coloured coat, wore a wig. By Jupiter, Major, if I was in General Chattesworth's place, with two hundred strapping fellows at my orders, I'd get a commission from Government to clear that road. It's too bad, sir, we can't go in and out of town, unless in a body, after nightfall, but at the risk of our lives. (The convivial doctor felt this public scandal acutely.) The bloody-minded miscreants, I'd catch every living soul of them, and burn them alive in tar-barrels. By Jove! here's old Joe Napper, of Dirty-lane's dead. Plenty of dry eyes after *him*. And stay, here's another row.' And so he read on.

In the meantime, stout, tightly-braced Captain Cluffe, of the same corps, and little dark, hard-faced, and solemn Mr. Nutter, of the Mills, Lord Castlemallard's agent, came in, and half a dozen more, chiefly members of the club, which met by night in the front parlour on the left, opposite the bar, where they entertained themselves with agreeable conversation, cards, backgammon, draughts, and an occasional song by Dr. Toole, who was a florid tenor, and used to give them, 'While gentlefolks strut in silver and satins,' or 'A maiden of late had a merry design,' or some other such ditty, with a recitation by plump little stage-stricken Ensign Puddock, who, in 'thpite of hith lithp,' gave rather spirited imitations of some of the players — Mossop, Sheridan, Macklin, Barry,[10] and the rest. So Mervyn, the stranger, by no means affecting this agreeable society, took his cane and cocked-hat, and went out — the dark and handsome apparition — followed by curious glances from two or three pairs of eyes, and a whispered commentary and criticism from Toole.

He took a meditative ramble in 'His Majesty's Park, the Phœnix'; and passing out at the Castleknock-gate, walked up the river, between the wooded embankments, which make the valley of the Liffey so pleasant and picturesque, until he reached the ferry, which crossing, at the other side he found himself not very far from Palmerstown, through which village his return route to Chapelizod lay.

9. Elizabeth, the wife of the 2nd Earl of Moira, was famous in the latter years of the eighteenth century for her social accomplishments and entertainments; the date here would require reference to her mother-in-law. The military and official figures referred to just below — Blackwater, Devereux — are imaginary.

10. The theatrical names are authentic. The actor Henry Mossop (*c.*1729-*c.*1774) was working in Dublin in 1767. Thomas Sheridan (1719-88) was an actor, lecturer and lexicographer to whose family Le Fanu was related. Charles Macklin (1699-1797) acted in Dublin 1762-70 under Sheridan's auspices. Dublin-born Spranger Barry (1719-77) returned to the London stage in 1767.

BRAM STOKER

(1847-1912)

from: DRACULA (1897)

[What follows is the second last chapter of the novel, in which the various narrators tell of their advance towards Castle Dracula in pursuit of the Count, who is endeavouring to get back from England on board ship. Their assault is divided, with some travelling by river, others by the bank of the river, and Mina and Van Helsing making a third party. The use of extracts from journals and so forth provides for a non-chronological order, and further complicates Stoker's fundamental assault on the notion of time in his abolition of the divisions between death and life. The geographical setting, close to the Carpathian Mountains, is perhaps the most linguistically diverse in Europe. In the fiction, languages and accents also proliferate, and even in this late chapter a new element (Scots dialect) is introduced, increasing pressure on the notion of a shared, non-arbitrary language.

Meanwhile Mina Harker records her offer of cups of tea, and her admiration for Lord Godalming's 'lovely steam launch'; she reaches a crescendo of Victorian complacency in her hymn of praise to money. Money intervenes in the account of the Jewish Hildesheim, where it is compared to the linguistic codes of punctuation. 'Ready money' is on hand, and bills can be settled in English currency even on the Danube. The universal expansion of the English language and English money (the *currency* of each) is a palpable sub-theme. Mina praises her typewriter again, and Morris puts in a good word of advertisement for the Winchester repeating-rifle.

Business as usual among the vampire-hunters.]

CHAPTER XXVI

DR. SEWARD'S DIARY[1]

29 October. — This is written in the train from Varna to Galatz.[2] Last night we all assembled a little before the time of sunset. Each of us had done his work as well as he could; so far as thought, and endeavour, and opportunity go, we are prepared for the whole of our journey, and for our work when we get to Galatz. When the usual time came round Mrs. Harker prepared herself for her hypnotic effort; and after a longer and more strenuous effort on the part of Van Helsing than has been usually necessary, she sank into the trance. Usually she speaks on a hint; but this time the Professor had to ask her questions, and to ask them pretty resolutely, before we could learn anything; at last her answer came:

'I can see nothing; we are still; there are no waves lapping, but only a steady swirl of water softly running against the hawser. I can hear men's voices calling, near and far, and the roll and creak of oars in the rowlocks. A gun is fired somewhere; the echo of it seems far away. There is tramping of feet overhead, and ropes and chains are dragged along. What is this? There is a gleam of light; I can feel the air blowing upon me.'

Here she stopped. She had risen, as if impulsively, from where she lay on the sofa, and raised both her hands, palms upwards, as if lifting a weight. Van Helsing and I looked at each other with understanding. Quincey raised his eyebrows slightly and looked at her intently, whilst Harker's hand instinctively closed round the hilt of his kukri.[3] There was a long pause. We all knew that the time when she could speak was passing; but we felt that it was useless to say anything. Suddenly she sat up, and, as she opened her eyes, said sweetly:

'Would none of you like a cup of tea? You must all be so tired!' We could only make her happy, and so acquiesced. She bustled off to get tea; when she had gone Van Helsing said:

'You see, my friends. *He* is close to land: he has left his earth-chest. But he has yet to get on shore. In the night he may lie hidden somewhere; but if he be not carried on shore, or if the ship do not touch it, he cannot achieve the land. In such case he can, if it be in the night, change his form and can jump or fly on shore, as he did at Whitby.[4] But if the day come before he get on shore, then, unless he be carried he cannot escape. And if he be carried, then the customs men may discover what the box contains. Thus, in fine, if he escape not on shore tonight, or before dawn, there will be the whole day lost to him. We may then arrive in time; for if he escape not at night we shall come on him in daytime, boxed up and at our mercy; for he dare not be his true self, awake and visible, lest he be discovered.'

There was no more to be said, so we waited in patience until the dawn; at which time we might learn more from Mrs. Harker.

Early this morning we listened, with breathless anxiety, for her reponse in her trance. The hypnotic stage was even longer in coming than before; and when it came the time remaining until full sunrise was so short that we began to despair. Van Helsing seemed to throw his whole soul into the effort; at last, in obedience to his will she made reply:

'All is dark. I hear lapping water, level with me, and some creaking as of wood on wood.' She paused, and the red sun shot up. We must wait till tonight.

And so it is that we are travelling towards Galatz in an agony of expectation. We are due to arrive

1. The travellers referred to here are Dr John Seward, Mrs Mina Harker (née Murray), Dr (or Professor) Abraham Van Helsing, Quincey Morris (an American), Jonathan Harker (husband of Mina), Lord Godalming (formerly the Honourable Arthur Holmwood).
2. Varna, a fortified seaport in Bulgaria 300 miles north-east of Sofia. Galatz, a river port in Romania, on the left bank of the Danube.
3. A curved knife used by the Gurkhas of Nepal.
4. Earlier in the novel, Dracula had landed in England, at Whitby on the Yorkshire coast.

between two and three in the morning; but already, at Bucharest, we are three hours late, so we cannot possibly get in till well after sun-up. Thus we shall have two more hypnotic messages from Mrs. Harker; either or both may possibly throw more light on what is happening.[5]

Later. — Sunset has come and gone. Fortunately it came at a time when there was no distraction; for had it occurred whilst we were at a station, we might have not secured the necessary calm and isolation. Mrs. Harker yielded to the hypnotic influence even less readily than this morning. I am in fear that her power of reading the Count's sensations may die away, just when we want it most. It seems to me that her imagination is beginning to work. Whilst she has been in the trance hitherto she has confined herself to the simplest of facts. If this goes on it may ultimately mislead us. If I thought that the Count's power over her would die away equally with her power of knowledge it would be a happy thought; but I am afraid that it may not be so. When she did speak, her words were enigmatical:

'Something is going out; I can feel it pass me like a cold wind. I can hear, far off, confused sounds — as of men talking in strange tongues, fierce-falling water, and the howling of wolves.' She stopped and a shudder ran through her, increasing in intensity for a few seconds, till, at the end, she shook as though in a palsy. She said no more, even in answer to the professor's imperative questioning. When she woke from the trance, she was cold, and exhausted, and languid; but her mind was all alert. She could not remember anything, but asked what she had said; when she was told, she pondered over it deeply, for a long time and in silence.

30 *October, 7 a.m.* — We are near Galatz now, and I may not have time to write later. Sunrise this morning was anxiously looked for by us all. Knowing of the increasing difficulty of procuring the hypnotic trance Van Helsing began his passes earlier than usual. They produced no effect, however, until the regular time when she yielded with a still greater difficulty, only a minute before the sun rose. The Professor lost no time in his questioning; her answer came with equal quickness:

'All is dark. I hear water swirling by, level with my ears, and the creaking of wood on wood. Cattle low far off. There is another sound, a queer one like —' she stopped and grew white, and whiter still.

'Go on; Go on! Speak, I command you!' said Van Helsing in an agonized voice. At the same time there was despair in his eyes, for the risen sun was reddening even Mrs. Harker's pale face. She opened her eyes, and we all started as she said, sweetly and seemingly with the utmost unconcern:

'Oh Professor why ask me to do what you know I can't? I don't remember anything.' Then, seeing the look of amazement on our faces, she said, turning from one to the other with a troubled look:

'What have I said? What have I done? I know nothing, only that I was lying here, half asleep, and I heard you say "go on! speak, I command you!" It seemed so funny to hear you order me about, as if I were a bad child!'

'Oh, Madam Mina' he said, sadly, 'it is proof, if proof be needed, of how I love and honour you, when a word for your good, spoken more earnest than ever, can seem so strange because it is to order her whom I am proud to obey!'

The whistles are sounding; we are nearing Galatz. We are on fire with anxiety and eagerness.

Mina Harker's Journal

30 *October*. — Mr. Morris took me to the hotel where our rooms had been ordered by telegraph, he being the one who could best be spared, since he does not speak any foreign language. The forces were distributed much as they had been at Varna, except that Lord Godalming went to the Vice-Consul as his rank might serve as an immediate guarantee of some sort to the official, we being in extreme hurry. Jonathan and the two doctors went to the shipping agent to learn particulars of the arrival of the *Czarina Catherine*.[6]

5. Note Van Helsing's use of fashionable hypnosis (starting with 'passes' of the hands to induce trance), which simultaneously Sigmund Freud was abandoning and, in so doing, was developing psychoanalysis. Mina's hypnosis-generated account of Dracula's movements is made possible by her earlier contagion; her narrative bears some resemblance to Mrs Henderson's description of Swift in Yeats's *The Words upon the Window-pane* (see below pp. 938-39).

6. Quincey Morris is an American and unacquainted with European languages. The list of tongues in this most oral of novels (yet all of it narrated through manifest forms of written record) is impressive; in addition to Dracula's English, Romanian and/or Hungarian, there is Van Helsing's Dutch, the French and German of the travellers generally, the implied Slovak and Bulgarian of passers-by, Morris's American idiom, various working-men's London accents, and the Yorkshire dialect of Whitby. English is under enormous pressure, and it shows!

Later. — Lord Godalming has returned. The Consul is away, and the Vice-Consul sick; so the routine work has been attended to by a clerk. He was very obliging, and offered to do anything in his power.

Jonathan Harker's Journal

30 *October*. — At nine o'clock Dr. Van Helsing, Dr. Seward, and I called on Messrs. Mackenzie & Steinkoff, the agents of the London firm of Hapgood. They had received a wire from London, in answer to Lord Godalming's telegraphed request, asking them to show us any civility in their power. They were more than kind and courteous, and took us at once on board the *Czarina Catherine* which lay at anchor out in the river harbour. There we saw the Captain, Donelson by name, who told us of his voyage. He said that in all his life he had never had so favourable a run.

'Man!' he said, 'but it made us afeard, for we expeckit that we should have to pay for it wi' some rare piece o' ill luck, so as to keep up the average. It's no canny to run frae London to the Black Sea wi' a wind ahint ye, as though the Deil himself were blawin' on yer sail for his ain purpose. An' a' the time we could no speer a thing. Gin we were nigh a ship, or a port, or a headland, a fog fell on us and travelled wi' us, till when after it had lifted and we looked out, the deil a thing could we see. We ran by Gibraltar wi'oot bein' able to signal; an' till we came to the Dardanelles and had to wait to get our permit to pass, we never were within hail o' aught. At first I inclined to slack off sail and beat about till the fog was lifted; but whiles, I thocht that if the Deil was minded to get us into the Black Sea quick, he was like to do it whether we would or no. If we had a quick voyage it would be no to our miscredit wi' the owners, or no hurt to our traffic; an' the Old Mon who had served his ain purpose wad be decently grateful to us for no hinderin' him.'[7] This mixture of simplicity and cunning, of superstition and commercial reasoning, aroused Van Helsing, who said:

'Mine friend, that Devil is more clever than he is thought by some; and he know when he meet his match!' The skipper was not displeased with the compliment, and went on:

'When we got past the Bosphorus the men began to grumble; some o' them, the Roumanians, came and asked me to heave overboard a big box which had been put on board by a queer lookin' old man just before we had started frae London. I had seen them speer at the fellow, and put out their twa fingers when they saw him, to guard against the evil eye. Man! but the supersteetion of foreigners is pairfectly rideeculous! I sent them aboot their business pretty quick; but as just after a fog closed in on us, I felt a wee bit as they did anent something, though I wouldn't say it was agin the bit box. Well, on we went, and as the fog didn't let up for five days I joost let the wind carry us; for if the Deil wanted to get somewheres — well, he would fetch it up a'reet. An' if he didn't, well we'd keep a sharp look out anyhow. Sure enuch, we had a fair way and deep water all the time; and two days ago, when the mornin' sun came through the fog, we found ourselves just in the river opposite Galatz. The Roumanians were wild, and wanted me right or wrong to take out the box and fling it in the river. I had to argy wi' them aboot it wi' a handspike; an' when the last o' them rose off the deck, wi' his head in his hand, I had convinced them that, evil eye or no evil eye, the property and the trust of my owners were better in my hands than in the river Danube. They had, mind ye, taken the box on the deck ready to fling in, and as it was marked Galatz *viâ* Varna, I thocht I'd let it lie till we discharged in the port an' get rid o't athegither. We didn't do much clearin' that day, an' had to remain the nicht at anchor; but in the mornin', braw an' airly, an hour before sun-up, a man came aboard wi' an order, written to him from England, to receive a box marked for one Count Dracula. Sure enuch the matter was one ready to his hand. He had his papers a' reet, an' glad I was to be rid o' the dam thing, for I was beginnin' masel' to feel uneasy at it. If the Deil did have any luggage aboord the ship, I'm thinkin' it was nane ither than that same![8]

'What was the name of the man who took it?' asked Dr. Van Helsing with restrained eagerness.

'I'll be tellin' ye quick!' he answered, and, stepping down to his cabin, produced a receipt signed 'Immanuel Hildesheim.' Burgen-strasse 16

7. Note the addition of Donelson's Scottish speech, duly rendered at length. Note also that the Scotsman's name appears to be a degenerate form of Donaldson, further evidence of linguistic decay and transmogrification.

8. canny = lucky; ahint = behind; ain = own; speer = peer; twa = two; anent = about; a'reet = alright; enuch = enough; thocht = thought; athegither = altogether; nicht = night; braw = bright; masel = myself; nane ither = none other. A handspike is a sailor's tool.

was the address. We found out that this was all the Captain knew; so with thanks we came away.

We found Hildesheim in his office, a Hebrew of rather the Adelphi Theatre type, with a nose like a sheep, and a fez. His arguments were pointed with specie — we doing the punctuation — and with a little bargaining he told us what he knew.[9] This turned out to be simple but important. He had received a letter from Mr. de Ville of London, telling him to receive, if possible before sunrise so as to avoid customs, a box which would arrive at Galatz in the *Czarina Catherine*. This he was to give in charge to a certain Petrof Skinsky, who dealt with the Slovaks who traded down the river to the port. He had been paid for his work by an English bank note, which had been duly cashed for gold at the Danube International Bank. When Skinsky had come to him, he had taken him to the ship and handed over the box, so as to save porterage. That was all he knew.

We then sought for Skinsky, but were unable to find him. One of his neighbours, who did not seem to bear him any affection, said that he had gone away two days before, no one knew whither. This was corroborated by his landlord who had received by messenger the key of the house together with the rent due, in English money. This had been between ten and eleven o'clock last night. We were at a standstill again.

Whilst we were talking one came running and breathlessly gasped out that the body of Skinsky had been found inside the wall of the churchyard of St. Peter, and that the throat had been torn open as if by some wild animal. Those we had been speaking with ran off to see the horror, the women crying out 'this is the work of a Slovak!' We hurried away lest we should have been in some way drawn into the affair, and so detained.

As we came home we could arrive at no definite conclusion. We were all convinced that the box was on its way, by water, to somewhere; but where that might be we would have to discover. With heavy hearts we came home to the hotel to Mina.

When we met together, the first thing was to consult as to taking Mina again into our confidence. Things are getting desperate, and it is at least a chance, though a hazardous one. As a preliminary step, I was released from my promise to her.

9. Harker's anti-semitism is obvious enough: 'specie' is a hard, negotiable coin.

Mina Harker's Journal

30 *October, evening.* — They were so tired and worn out and dispirited that there was nothing to be done till they had some rest; so I asked them all to lie down for half an hour whilst I should enter everything up to the moment. I feel so grateful to the man who invented the 'Traveller's' typewriter, and to Mr. Morris for getting this one for me. I should have felt quite astray doing the work if I had to write with a pen. . . .

It is all done; poor dear, dear Jonathan, what he must have suffered, what must he be suffering now. He lies on the sofa hardly seeming to breathe, and his whole body appears in collapse. His brows are knit; his face is drawn with pain. Poor fellow, maybe he is thinking, and I can see his face all wrinkled up with the concentration of his thoughts. Oh! if I could only help at all. . . . I shall do what I can. . . .

I have asked Dr. Van Helsing, and he has got me all the papers that I have not yet seen. . . . Whilst they are resting, I shall go over all carefully, and perhaps I may arrive at some conclusion. I shall try to follow the Professor's example, and think without prejudice on the facts before me. . . .

I do believe that under God's providence I have made a discovery. I shall get the maps and look over them. . . .

I am more than ever sure that I am right. My new conclusion is ready, so I shall get our party together and read it. They can judge it; it is well to be accurate, and every minute is precious.

Mina Harker's Memorandum

(Entered in her Journal)

Ground of inquiry. — Count Dracula's problem is to get back to his own place.

(a) He must be *brought back* by some one. This is evident; for had he power to move himself as he wished he could go either as man, or wolf, or bat, or in some other way. He evidently fears discovery or interference, in the state of helplessness in which he must be — confined as he is between dawn and sunset in his wooden box.

(b) *How is he to be taken?* — Here a process of exclusions may help us. By road, by rail, by water?

1. *By Road.* — There are endless difficulties, especially in leaving a city.

(*x*) There are people; and people are curious, and

investigate. A hint, a surmise, a doubt as to what might be in the box, would destroy him.

(*y*) There are, or there might be, customs and octroi[10] officers to pass.

(*z*) His pursuers might follow. This is his greatest fear; and in order to prevent his being betrayed he has repelled, so far as he can, even his victim — me!

2. *By Rail.* — There is no one in charge of the box. It would have to take its chance of being delayed; and delay would be fatal, with enemies on the track. True, he might escape at night; but what would he be, if left in a strange place with no refuge that he could fly to. This is not what he intends; and he does not mean to risk it.

3. *By Water.* — Here is the safest way, in one respect, but with most danger in another. On the water he is powerless except at night; even then he can only summon fog and storm and snow and his wolves. But were he wrecked, the living water would engulf him, helpless; and he would indeed be lost. He could have the vessel drive to land; but if it were unfriendly land, wherein he was not free to move, his position would still be desperate.

We know from the record that he was on the water; so what we have to do is to ascertain *what* water.

The first thing is to realise exactly what he has done as yet; we may, then, get a light on what his later task is to be.

Firstly. — We must differentiate between what he did in London as part of his general plan of action, when he was pressed for moments and had to arrange as best he could.

Secondly we must see, as well as we can surmise it from the facts we know of, what he has done here.

As to the first, he evidently intended to arrive at Galatz, and sent invoice to Varna to deceive us lest we should ascertain his means of exit from England; his immediate and sole purpose then was to escape. The proof of this, is the letter of instructions sent to Immanuel Hildesheim to clear and take away the box *before sunrise*. There is also the instruction to Petrof Skinsky. These we must only guess at; but there must have been some letter or message, since Skinsky came to Hildesheim.

That, so far, his plans were successful we know. The *Czarina Catherine* made a phenomenally quick journey — so much so that Captain Donelson's suspicions were aroused; but his superstition united with his canniness played the Count's game for him, and he ran with his favouring wind through fogs and all till he brought up blindfold at Galatz.[11] That the Count's arrangements were well made, has been proved. Hildesheim cleared the box, took it off, and gave it to Skinsky. Skinsky took it — and here we lose the trail. We only know that the box is somewhere on the water, moving along. The customs and the octroi, if there be any, have been avoided.

Now we come to what the Count must have done after his arrival — *on land*, at Galatz.

The box was given to Skinsky before sunrise. At sunrise the Count could appear in his own form. Here, we ask why Skinsky was chosen at all to aid in the work? In my husband's diary, Skinsky is mentioned as dealing with the Slovaks who trade down the river to the port; and the man's remark, that the murder was the work of a Slovak, showed the general feeling against his class. The Count wanted isolation.

My surmise is, this: that in London the Count decided to get back to his Castle by water, as the most safe and secret way. He was brought from the Castle by Szgany, and probably they delivered their cargo to Slovaks who took the boxes to Varna, for there they were shipped for London. Thus the Count had knowledge of the persons who could arrange this service. When the box was on land, before sunrise or after sunset, he came out from his box, met Skinsky and instructed him what to do as to arranging the carriage of the box up some river. When this was done, and he knew that all was in train, he blotted out his traces, as he thought, by murdering his agent.

I have examined the map and find that the river most suitable for the Slovaks to have ascended is either the Pruth or the Sereth.[12] I read in the typescript that in my trance I heard cows low and water swirling level with my ears and the creaking of wood. The Count in his box, then, was on a river in an open boat — propelled probably either by oars or poles, for the banks are near and it is working against stream. There would be no such sound if floating down stream.

Of course it may not be either the Sereth or the

10. A duty on goods brought into a town.

11. Mina Harker's command of nautical terms is sudden — further indication of the proliferation of slang and idiom in the novel.

12. The Pruth flows into the Danube below Garatz; the Sereth flows into the Danube five miles above Galatz. The Bistritza joins the Sereth near Baku. Stoker's geographical references are generally accurate.

Pruth, but we may possibly investigate further. Now of these two, the Pruth is the more easily navigated, but the Sereth is, at Fundu, joined by the Bistritza which runs up round the Borgo pass. The loop it makes is manifestly as close to Dracula's Castle as can be got by water.'

When I had done reading, Jonathan took me in his arms and kissed me. The others kept shaking me by both hands, and Dr. Van Helsing said:

'Our dear Madam Mina is once more our teacher. Her eyes have seen where we were blinded. Now we are on the track once again, and this time we may succeed. Our enemy is at his most helpless; and if we can come on him by day, on the water, our task will be over. He has a start, but he is powerless to hasten, as he may not leave his box lest those who carry him may suspect; for them to suspect would be to prompt them to throw him in the stream where he perish. This he knows, and will not. Now men, to our Council of War; for, here and now, we must plan what each and all shall do.'

'I shall get a steam launch and follow him,' said Lord Godalming.

'And I, horses to follow on the bank lest by chance he land,' said Mr. Morris.

'Good!' said the Professor, 'both good. But neither must go alone. There must be force to overcome force if need be; the Slovak is strong and rough, and he carries rude arms.' All the men smiled, for amongst them they carried a small arsenal. Said Mr. Morris:

'I have brought some Winchesters;[13] they are pretty handy in a crowd, and there may be wolves. The Count, if you remember, took some other precautions; he made some requisitions on others that Mrs. Harker could not quite hear or understand. We must be ready at all points.' Dr. Seward said:

'I think I had better go with Quincey. We have been accustomed to hunt together, and we two, well armed, will be a match for whatever may come along. You must not be alone Art. It may be necessary to fight the Slovaks, and a chance thrust — for I don't suppose these fellows carry guns — would undo all our plans. There must be no chances, this time; we shall not rest until the Count's head and body have been separated, and we are sure that he cannot re-incarnate.' He looked at Jonathan as he spoke, and Jonathan looked at me. I could see that the poor dear was torn about in his mind. Of course he wanted to be with me; but then the boat service would, most likely, be the one which would destroy the . . . the . . . the . . . Vampire. (Why did I hesitate to write the word?) He was silent awhile, and during his silence Dr. Van Helsing spoke:

'Friend Jonathan, this is to you for twice reasons. First, because you are young and brave and can fight, and all energies may be needed at the last; and again that it is your right to destroy him — that — which has wrought such woe to you and yours. Be not afraid for Madam Mina; she will be my care, if I may. I am old. My legs are not so quick to run as once; and I am not used to ride so long or to pursue as need be, or to fight with lethal weapons. But I can be of other service; I can fight in other way. And I can die, if need be, as well as younger men. Now let me say that what I would is this: while you, my Lord Godalming, and friend Jonathan go in your so swift little steamboat up the river, and whilst John and Quincey guard the bank where perchance he might be landed, I will take Madam Mina right into the heart of the enemy's country. Whilst the old fox is tied in his box, floating on the running stream whence he cannot escape to land — where he dares not raise the lid of his coffin-box lest his Slovak carriers should in fear leave him to perish — we shall go in the track where Jonathan went, — from Bistritz over the Borgo, and find our way to the Castle of Dracula. Here, Madam Mina's hypnotic power will surely help, and we shall find our way — all dark and unknown otherwise — after the first sunrise when we are near that fateful place. There is much to be done, and other places to be made sanctify, so that that nest of vipers be obliterated.' Here Jonathan interrupted him hotly:

'Do you mean to say, Professor Van Helsing, that you would bring Mina, in her sad case and tainted as she is with that devil's illness, right into the jaws of his death-trap? Not for the world! Not for Heaven or Hell!' He became almost speechless for a minute, and then went on:

'Do you know what the place is? Have you seen that awful den of hellish infamy — with the very moonlight alive with grisly shapes, and every speck of dust that whirls in the wind a devouring monster in embryo? Have you felt the Vampire's lips upon your throat?' Here he turned to me, and as his eyes

13. The Winchester repeating-rifle achieved fame in facilitating the near-genocide of Amerindian tribes. Morris appears here much as the firearms trader does in the classic western.

lit on my forehead, he threw up his arms with a cry: 'Oh, my God, what have we done to have this terror upon us!' and he sank down on the sofa in a collapse of misery. The Professor's voice, as he spoke in clear, sweet tones, which seemed to vibrate in the air, calmed us all:

'Oh my friend, it is because I would save Madam Mina from that awful place that I would go. God forbid that I should take her into that place. There is work — wild work — to be done there, that her eyes may not see. We men here, all save Jonathan, have seen with their own eyes what is to be done before that place can be purify. Remember that we are in terrible straits. If the Count escape us this time — and he is strong and subtle and cunning — he may choose to sleep him for a century; and then in time our dear one' — he took my hand — 'would come to him to keep him company, and would be as those others that you, Jonathan, saw. You have told us of their gloating lips; you heard their ribald laugh as they clutched the moving bag that the Count threw to them. You shudder; and well may it be. Forgive me that I make you so much pain, but it is necessary. My friend, is it not a dire need for the which I am giving, if need be, my life? If it were that anyone went into that place to stay, it is I who would have to go, to keep them company.'

'Do as you will'; said Jonathan, with a sob that shook him all over, 'We are in the hands of God!'

Later. — 'Oh, it did me good to see the way that these brave men worked. How can women help loving men when they are so earnest, and so true, and so brave! And, too, it made me think of the wonderful power of money! What can it not do when it is properly applied; and what might it do when basely used. I felt so thankful that Lord Godalming is rich, and that both he and Mr. Morris, who also has plenty of money, are willing to spend it so freely. For if they did not, our little expedition could not start, either so promptly or so well equipped, as it will within another hour. It is not three hours since it was arranged what part each of us was to do; and now Lord Godalming and Jonathan have a lovely steam launch, with steam up ready to start at a moment's notice. Dr. Seward and Mr. Morris have half a dozen beautiful horses, well appointed. We have all the maps and appliances of various kinds that can be had. Professor Van Helsing and I are to leave by the 11.40 train tonight for Veresti, where we are to get a carriage to drive to the Borgo Pass. We are bringing a good deal of ready money, as we are to buy a carriage and horses. We shall drive ourselves, for we have no one whom we can trust in the matter. The Professor knows something of a great many languages, so we shall get on all right. We have all got arms, even for me a large-bore revolver; Jonathan would not be happy unless I was armed like the rest. Alas! I cannot carry one arm that the rest do; the scar on my forehead forbids that. Dear Dr. Van Helsing comforts me by telling me that I am fully armed as there may be wolves; the weather is getting colder every hour, and there are snow-flurries which come and go as warnings.

Later. — It took all my courage to say good-bye to my darling. We may never meet again. Courage, Mina! the Professor is looking at you keenly; his look is a warning. There must be no tears now — unless it may be that God will let them fall in gladness.

Jonathan Harker's Journal

October 30. *Night.* — I am writing this in the light from the furnace door of the steam launch; Lord Godalming is firing up. He is an experienced hand at the work, as he has had for years a launch of his own on the Thames, and another on the Norfolk Broads.[14] Regarding our plans, we finally decided that Mina's guess was correct, and that if any waterway was chosen for the Count's escape back to his Castle, the Sereth and then the Bistritza at its junction, would be the one. We took it, that somewhere about the 47th degree, north latitude, would be the place chosen for the crossing the country between the river and the Carpathians. We have no fear in running at good speed up the river at night; there is plenty of water, and the banks are wide enough apart to make steaming, even in the dark, easy enough. Lord Godalming tells me to sleep for a while, as it is enough for the present for one to be on watch. But I cannot sleep — how can I with the terrible danger hanging over my darling, and her going out into that awful place.... My only comfort is that we are in the hands of God. Only for that faith it would be easier to die than to live, and so be quit of all the trouble. Mr. Morris and Dr. Seward were off on their long ride before we started; they

14. Godalming is lighting the boiler-fires on the launch. The Norfolk Broads constitute an extensive inland waterway system in East Anglia.

are to keep up the right bank, far enough off to get on higher lands where they can see a good stretch of river and avoid the following of its curves. They have, for the first stages, two men to ride and lead their spare horses — four in all, so as not to excite curiosity. When they dismiss the men, which shall be shortly, they shall themselves look after the horses. It may be necessary for us to join forces; if so they can mount our whole party. One of the saddles has a movable horn, and can be easily adapted for Mina, if required.[15]

It is a wild adventure we are on. Here, as we are rushing along through the darkness, with the cold from the river seeming to rise up and strike us; with all the mysterious voices of the night around us, it all comes home. We seem to be drifting into unknown places and unknown ways; into a whole world of dark and dreadful things. Godalming is shutting the furnace door....

31 *October*. — Still hurrying along. The day has come, and Godalming is sleeping. I am on watch. The morning is bitterly cold; the furnace heat is grateful, though we have heavy fur coats. As yet we have passed only a few open boats, but none of them had on board any box or package of anything like the size of the one we seek. The men were scared every time we turned our electric lamp on them, and fell on their knees and prayed.

1 *November*, *evening*. — No news all day; we have found nothing of the kind we seek. We have now passed into the Bistritza; and if we are wrong in our surmise our chance is gone. We have overhauled every boat, big and little. Early this morning, one crew took us for a Government boat, and treated us accordingly. We saw in this a way of smoothing matters, so at Fundu, where the Bistritza runs into the Sereth, we got a Roumanian flag which we now fly conspicuously. With every boat which we have overhauled since then this trick has succeeded; we have had every deference shown to us, and not once any objection to whatever we chose to ask or do. Some of the Slovaks tell us that a big boat passed them, going at more than usual speed as she had a double crew on board. This was before they came to Fundu, so they could not tell us whether the boat turned into the Bistritza or continued on up the Sereth. At Fundu we could not hear of any such boat, so she must have passed there in the night. I am feeling very sleepy; the cold is perhaps beginning to tell upon me, and nature must have rest some time. Godalming insists that he shall keep the first watch. God bless him for all his goodness to poor dear Mina and me.

2 *November*, *morning*. — It is broad daylight. That good fellow would not wake me. He says it would have been a sin to, for I slept so peacefully and was forgetting my trouble. It seems brutally selfish of me to have slept so long, and let him watch all night; but he was quite right. I am a new man this morning; and, as I sit here and watch him sleeping, I can do all that is necessary both as to minding the engine, steering, and keeping watch. I can feel that my strength and energy are coming back to me. I wonder where Mina is now, and Van Helsing. They should have got to Veresti about noon on Wednesday. It would take them some time to get the carriage and horses; so if they had started and travelled hard, they would be about now at the Borgo Pass. God guide and help them! I am afraid to think what may happen. If we could only go faster! but we cannot; the engines are throbbing and doing their utmost. I wonder how Dr. Seward and Mr. Morris are getting on. There seem to be endless streams running down from the mountains into this river, but as none of them are very large — at present, at all events, though they are terrible doubtless in winter and when the snow melts — the horsemen may not have met much obstruction. I hope that before we get to Strasba we may see them; for if by that time we have not overtaken the Count, it may be necessary to take counsel together what to do next.

Dr. Seward's Diary

2 *November*. — Three days on the road. No news, and no time to write it if there had been, for every moment is precious. We have had only the rest needful for the horses; but we are both bearing it wonderfully. Those adventurous days of ours are turning up useful. We must push on; we shall never feel happy till we get the launch in sight again.

3 *November*. — We heard at Fundu that the launch had gone up the Bistritza. I wish it wasn't so cold. There are signs of snow coming; and if it falls heavy it will stop us. In such case we must get a sledge and go on, Russian fashion.

4 *November*. — Today we heard of the launch having been detained by an accident when trying to

15. Ladies sometimes ride side-saddle. The conventional saddle-horn, fixed in the middle for male security, would thus be awkward.

force a way up the rapid. The slovak boats get up all right, by aid of a rope, and steering with knowledge. Some went up only a few hours before. Godalming is an amateur fitter himself, and evidently it was he who put the launch in trim again. Finally, they got up the Rapids all right, with local help, and are off on the chase afresh. I fear that the boat is not any better for the accident; the peasantry tell us that after she got upon the smooth water again, she kept stopping every now and again so long as she was in sight. We must push on harder than ever; our help may be wanted soon.

Mina Harker's Journal

31 *October*. — Arrived at Veresti at noon. The Professor tells me that this morning at dawn he could hardly hypnotize me at all, and that all I could say was: 'dark and quiet.' He is off now buying a carriage and horses. He says that he will later on try to buy additional horses, so that we may be able to change them on the way. We have something more than 70 miles before us. The country is lovely, and most interesting; if only we were under different conditions, how delightful it would be to see it all. If Jonathan and I were driving through it alone what a pleasure it would be. To stop and see people, and learn something of their life, and to fill our minds and memories with all the colour and picturesqueness of the whole wild, beautiful country and the quaint people! But, alas! —

Later. — Dr. Van Helsing has returned. He has got the carriage and horses; we are to have some dinner, and to start in an hour. The landlady is putting us up a huge basket of provisions; it seems enough for a company of soldiers. The Professor encourages her, and whispers to me that it may be a week before we can get any good food again. He has been shopping too, and has sent home such a wonderful lot of fur coats and wraps, and all sorts of warm things. There will not be any chance of our being cold.

We shall soon be off. I am afraid to think what may happen to us. We are truly in the hands of God. He alone knows what may be, and I pray Him, with all the strength of my sad and humble soul, that He will watch over my beloved husband; that whatever may happen, Jonathan may know that I loved him and honoured him more than I can say, and that my latest and truest thought will be always for him.

JOHN MILLINGTON SYNGE

(1871-1909)

WHEN THE MOON HAS SET

[J. M. Synge brought a two-act version of his first play to Coole Park in September 1901, only to have it rejected by Lady Gregory and W. B. Yeats as unacceptable for the Abbey Theatre. He subsequently reworked the play into a one-act version, and there are indications that a three-act version was also commenced. In other words, *When the Moon Has Set* preoccupied Synge for much of his creative life, and its origins clearly reach back into the years of his preparation for literature. His study of music, his reading in continental literature, and of course his sojourn in Paris, are obviously reflected in the dialogue between Sister Eileen and Columb Sweeny. In addition to the parallel between the Sweeny inheritance in the play and the historical material summarized in the introduction to this section of the anthology, a further parallel indicates the significance of this text for its author. Quite simply, some drafts of the play have the word 'me' written in beside the protagonist's name.

The most surprising of the many textual intrusions into the dialogue (letters, quotations) is surely the lengthy passage from the great catholic mystic, Saint Teresa of Avila (1515-82), almost at the end of the play. Columb's quotation is in French, seventeenth- or eighteenth-century French, to judge by the spelling meticulously transcribed by Synge. Teresa wrote in Spanish, so we can conclude that the playwright is drawing here on somewhat unexpected spiritual resources, explored perhaps during his months in Paris. However, there is more to the reference than can be appreciated through a translation. Before entering the religious life, Teresa considered marrying one of her cousins — Columb and Eileen are cousins, and beyond that there are autobiographical parallels in Synge's emotional life. Teresa, like Eileen in the play, was a nun, but the imagery of her writing was emotional (even erotic) in a way that Columb seems keen to emulate. The ecstasy of Saint Teresa became a theme for artists (cf. Bernini's great sculpture) in which explicit sexual rapture is evident. This is what Columb coyly intends when he remarks that Eileen could hardly find the book moral. As saints go, Teresa was a prolific writer, and Synge may be have noted among her works one called *El Castillo Interior* (The Interior Castle). The teresan recommendation of a spiritual abode, in place of earthly ones, is analogous (at a higher level) to the broad movement of the play in which a decaying inheritance, and an isolated house, are to be abandoned for a natural-religious quest.

What the characters refer to as 'the avenging lunatic' cannot be regarded as a successful dramatic device in the play. But the role of Stephen Costello, together with the isolated house, the postponed will, and of course the shooting, emphasize once again a congruence of early nineteenth-century literary tropes and late nineteenth-century social anxieties. Synge's play tends to wallow in this and simultaneously seeks to escape from it by means of lofty aesthetic reasoning, evasive French phrasing, and an unconvincing invocation of the sun-god. Nevertheless, the play does show Synge at work in search of a dramatic idiom that will be refined only when he discards the (so-called) 'big house' setting into which he was nearly born. Certain uses of props — for example Bride's blowing on the fire with her mouth — show an awareness of the symbolic power of simple and domestic actions. We should hesitate therefore to distinguish too drastically between this play and the mature work. Thematically, if not stylistically, *When the Moon Has Set* anticipates Synge's last play, *Deirdre of the Sorrows*, in its attention to a senescent ruling elite, a divided society, and the impact of sexuality upon these hitherto untroubled male preserves.

The text reproduced below is essentially that of the two-act version as edited by Mary C. King for *Long Room* (the bulletin of the Friends of the Library, Trinity College, Dublin). The present editor has standardized Synge's eccentric typing (use of capitals etc.) in a few particulars.]

SISTER EILEEN, a young nun
COLUMB SWEENY, her distant cousin
MRS BYRNE, a family servant
BRIDE, a young country girl
PAT KAVANAGH, an old man
SISTER DORA, a nun

ACT I

Old family library. Many books are in shelves round the walls and in the corner, a gun, dog-whips etc. are lying as if thrown carelessly together. A turf fire has burnt low on the hearth, and a lamp is lighting on the table where there are several old books and a pile of manuscript. The fireplace with a large portrait above it is on the right opposite a large window. The principal door is near the middle of the scene, but there is another near the window. A harp stands in the corner.

SISTER EILEEN, *a young nun, is standing near the table making a large bow of crape, such as is placed on a house door after a death. She holds it up for a moment, and then, laying it carefully on the table, she goes over, rubs the frost from the window, and looks out, shading her eyes with her hand. In a moment she turns back slowly to the table, handles the MS. carelessly, and then picks up a leaf and reads in a low, clear voice.*

SISTER EILEEN: 'Every life is a symphony and the translation of this sequence into music and from music again, for those who are not musicians, into literature, or painting or sculpture, is the real effort of the artist. The emotions which pass through us have neither end nor beginning, are a part of eternal sensations, and it is this almost cosmic element in the person which gives all personal art a share in the dignity of the world.

'Biography, even autobiography, cannot give this revelation, for the deeds of a man's lifetime are impersonal and concrete, might have been done by anyone, while art is the expression of the abstract beauty of the person.

'Every writer. . . .'

A clock strikes the four quarters and one o'clock. She puts down the MS. and goes back to the window. In a moment she appears to see something, looks at the fire, and goes quickly to the door after touching the bell-pull. Calls in a clear voice but not loudly.

SISTER EILEEN: Bride — Bride — Bring up some turf, the fire is nearly out, and I see lights on the avenue.

She goes back again to the window. BRIDE *— young country girl — comes in with her apron full of turf, and kneels down to arrange the fire.* MRS BYRNE, *an old servant, hurries in after her with her apron up to her eyes.*

MRS BYRNE: Did you say they were coming, Sister Eileen?

SISTER EILEEN: I see a light through the trees.

MRS BYRNE: (*Looking out*) That's the doctor's carriage, they're coming along by the bog. (*Half sobbing to herself*) Ah, the Lord have mercy on us, and isn't it a sad story altogether, the poor young man going out in the night and the great cold, and then his honour to die all in a minute.

SISTER EILEEN: (*Looking out*) Will they soon come to the door?

MRS BYRNE: At once now, Sister Eileen, they're in the last turn through the wood.

SISTER EILEEN: Perhaps you had better go down and tell the doctor what has happened, there's no use bringing him in so late in the night.

MRS BYRNE: I will, Sister Eileen. (*She goes out*)

SISTER EILEEN: (*Going over to the fireplace, where* BRIDE *is blowing the turf with her mouth*) You cannot light it?

BRIDE: (*Talking with plaintive western intonation*) The turf's wet, Sister Eileen, for the roof has fallen in on the turf house with the weight of snow on it, and I haven't a bit of sticks in the whole house. I told Murphy to bring some bog-wood with him out of the town — you can't find a stick here anyplace with the snow lying on the earth — but he hasn't come back, the Lord knows what's keeping him.

SISTER EILEEN: (*Half to herself*) He should not have been sent at all and then he could have gone for the doctor instead of Mr Columb. (*She kneels down by the fire*) I think I could arrange that better.

BRIDE: (*Watching her*) You cannot, Sister Eileen. You're not used to the turf.

SISTER EILEEN: Long ago I could have done it.

BRIDE: I do have to laugh when I see Mr Columb and he making the fire, he throws it all about as if it was coal he had.

SISTER EILEEN: When he was a boy .... (*She stops to listen.* COLUMB *comes in behind them in a heavy coat buttoned up to his chin*)

COLUMB: How suddenly the end came at last.

SISTER EILEEN: (*Standing up and rubbing the turf from her hands*) We expected it. — I wish I had not let you go out in the snow. It was no use.

COLUMB: You were quite right.

SISTER EILEEN: Your uncle died without any pain. The attack he had when you went out did not last, and we thought he was better. He passed away merely from weakness. I was in the room, and I did not know he was dead.

COLUMB: I suppose it is the best way to die. I would have been here sooner, but I missed my way at the second crossing of the roads. I have got stupid about the dark.

SISTER EILEEN: It is well you were not lost.

COLUMB: I met a queer man talking to himself under some trees and I asked him the way to the doctor's. He came back with me to the cross roads and told me how I was to go, I don't know who he can have been he asked several times for my uncle and his voice seemed to remind me of someone, yet I think he was almost mad.

BRIDE *starts slightly and looks round with interest.*

SISTER EILEEN: I am afraid there are many people about here who are not sane. (*She moves towards the door*)

COLUMB: (*Throwing off his coat*) Won't you sit down?

SISTER EILEEN: I have to see Sister Dora, and tell her you have come in. She is going to sit up I am so tired.

COLUMB: Then come down again before you go to bed .... I want to talk to somebody the house is so dismal.

SISTER EILEEN: Is it so late in the night...?

COLUMB: Come for a little while. You will not sleep just yet.

SISTER EILEEN: (*With hesitation*) If you like I will come down for a few minutes. (*She goes out*)

COLUMB: (*Going over to the fire: speaking to* BRIDE) The snow and wind are getting worse.

BRIDE: (*Turning towards him*) Your honour seen no sign of the car?[1]

COLUMB: We passed it at the ford — where the bridge has fallen down. It had been kept back by the snow drifts, and the branches that have been blown out of the trees.

BRIDE: Was the old man from the back gate-lodge upon it, your honour?

COLUMB: There was an old man sitting on the seat next Murphy; it may have been him.

BRIDE: That was him, your honour, that was my father. He went into the town this morning to see my mother, and I suppose he waited the way he could come home with the car. I was afeard he might have drink taken and be fallen in the snow.

COLUMB: I was talking to that old man yesterday, but I did not know you were his daughter .... You are not like him.

BRIDE: He's a very innocent poor man, God help him, but my mother is like a lady. (*Putting on more*

1. The car in question is of course horse-drawn.

turf) I'm told they do call her 'your ladyship,' below in the Asylum.[2]

COLUMB: (*With a movement of surprise*) Is that where she is?

BRIDE: It is your honour. She's there a good bit now, but they say she doesn't be lonesome in it at all, there do be so many coming in from all the houses in the country. (*Blows the turf for a moment with her mouth, and sits up rubbing the smoke from her eyes*) My uncle is a bit queer too, one time and another. I'm thinking it was him your honour seen this night upon the roads, for he does be always walking round like yourself, God bless you, a fine handsome man, and it's two years now since we seen him, though we've heard tell this last while, it wasn't far off from us he was at all.

COLUMB: (*Lighting a cigarette from the fire*) Then it was your voice I was thinking of. Is he a tall man with a stoop, and a sort of beard, I could not see of what colour?

BRIDE: That's himself, your honour, He's a Costello from an old Castillian family,[3] and it's fine people they were, and it's no lie I'm telling you. For my mother was a big tall woman herself, and I had an aunt that's dead, who was the finest girl, I've heard them say, you'ld find in the whole world. She was reared with the nuns (*looking round at him with a curious expression*) and maybe you've heard his honour speak of her, God rest his soul. (*Crosses herself*)

COLUMB: I do not remember it. I have not often talked with my uncle.

There is a noise of wheels under the window. BRIDE *goes over and looks out.*

BRIDE: There's the car going round, and it's a long time they've been. (*Coming back and looking at the fire*) The fire'll burn now and you'll have warmth for the night.

COLUMB: (*Holding out his hands with a movement of relief*) We want it in a storm like this.

BRIDE: It's true for you, your honour. We were thinking it's destroyed you'ld be, walking alone through the night and the great cold, and you not used to anything but the big towns of the world.

A low uncertain tap is heard at the door.

COLUMB: (*to* BRIDE) Who is that?

BRIDE *goes over to the door and whispers to some one outside, then she comes over again towards the fire.*

BRIDE: It is the old man has brought a letter for you out of the town, and he has a little drink taken has made him say he'll give it to no one but into your own hand.

COLUMB: Bring him in.

BRIDE *goes over to the door and brings in old* PAT KAVANAGH. *He is poorly dressed and a little unsteady on his feet.*

PAT: (*To* COLUMB *who stands up to meet him*) Your honour will be sick and sorry after your uncle dying on you, and you out in the snow, but it's a rich man you'll be from this day, and may the Lord preserve you.

COLUMB: You have a letter?

PAT: I have, your honour, and I was thinking I would do right to give it into your own hand, for there are queer people in this house, and round about it.

COLUMB *takes the letter, and* PAT *hesitates as if he wished to speak.*

COLUMB: (*Looking up at him again*) You saw your wife?

PAT: I seen her, your honour, and she as comfortable as any lady in England, France, or Germany, walking round in the Asylum with fine shoes on her feet. (*Looking towards the door and coming closer to* COLUMB) There's another thing. Did ever you hear tell of the sister of the mother of that girl Biddy?

COLUMB: Of your wife's sister? I heard of her tonight.

PAT: It will be queer things you heard?

COLUMB: That she was a fine girl. — That is all.

PAT: There's a power to tell. My head's tired with the perishing cold of the air (*putting up his hand to his head*) and maybe it will be better that I tell you the whole story in the morning, if the Almighty God keep us alive, but there's one thing, my wife and that girl had a brother . . . (*leaning out and whispering*) the maddest man is left walking in the world, and he has sworn his Bible oath he'll shoot the next heir, cousin or descendent [*sic*] of his honour, God rest his soul, who comes down into the place. (*Holding up his hand to mark his words*) I seen that man tonight, and he walking along, and talking to himself, below by the crossing of the roads.

COLUMB: I think I saw him also . . . . He is a tall man with a stoop?

2. The play's topographical references beyond the house — to 'the Asylum', 'Tonagee' — are consistent with an implied setting near Rathdrum in County Wicklow. The Synges used to holiday just north-east of the town, which had an asylum.
3. This pedigree for the fairly common Irish surname invokes a very remote and hypothetical past, but underlines the theme of social decline elsewhere evident in the play.

PAT: (*With astonishment*) That's him, your honour, and you seen him yourself?

COLUMB: He showed me the way to the doctor's.

PAT: And you talked together?

COLUMB: He walked besides me for half a mile, and told me how I should go.

PAT: The Lord have mercy on us all —

SISTER EILEEN *taps lightly and comes in. When she sees* PAT *and* BRIDE *she stops.*

COLUMB: (*To* SISTER EILEEN) Please come in, I was expecting you. (*To* PAT) We can talk about the whole matter in the morning. You want rest tonight. (*Motioning them to the door*) Goodnight, Goodnight Bride.

PAT: Goodnight your honour, and may the Almighty God preserve and prosper you. (*They go out*)

COLUMB: (*To* SISTER EILEEN) You have arranged everything?

SISTER EILEEN: For the time being. Sister Dora is staying in the room.

COLUMB: I will write the letters, that have to be written, in the morning, there will be time enough before the hour for the post.

SISTER EILEEN: What did Pat want so late in the night?

COLUMB: He brought me a letter out of the town and he would give it to no one but myself. He has been drinking a little.

COLUMB *pushes an armchair to the fire for* SISTER EILEEN. *She sits down. Looking at the letter in his hand.*

SISTER EILEEN: Read it if you wish.

COLUMB: (*Opening it*) It is from one of my friends in Paris. I had not time to bid him goodbye, but I left a line for him the morning I travelled. (*Looking through the letter*) I might read some of it out to you if you like.

SISTER EILEEN: Do, if it is interesting.

COLUMB: Wait till I see. He talks first about my leaving, and his money troubles, then ... yes, this is interesting. 'I have been at an exhibition looking at Rodin's Eve.[4] One would almost think the old malin had wished to show how le bon Dieu[5] had made a mess of his first attempt to model the strange shape of woman, but apart from the form the thing is full of curious passion. I have been drawing and playing very little, and yesterday Jeanette came and sat in studio so that I could do nothing but talk. Have you noticed all the wit one lavishes on women? It would be possible to write an article on the "Lost Gems of the Jester", to show the misery of a man who is only articulate with girls, and spreads out humour, and fancies before them which he knows are never understood. You remember Rousseau's — "C'était la seule fois de ma vie, mais je fus sublime."[6] — We are all Rousseaus now, I have never said anything to a man that was worth saying to a woman, and rarely said anything to a woman that was not fit for a man .... Et ton heritage? Mes têtes de mort te saluent.[7] My compliments to the little Irish pigs that eat filth all their lives that you may prosper. Ever etc. ....' (*He puts the letter back in the envelope and turns to* SISTER EILEEN) What do you think of it?

SISTER EILEEN: It is clever I suppose, but there is bravado in it .... Is he a good man?

COLUMB: He is interesting. He lives in a low room draped in black from the floor to the ceiling. He has a black quilt on his bed and two skulls on his chimney-piece with girls' hats on them. His matches are in a coffin, and his clock is a gallows. He sits there whenever he is not at work and drinks absinthe and vermouth.

SISTER EILEEN: You should make him live more wisely or he will go out of his mind.

COLUMB: He seems to think that the dreams and the excitement are worth the danger. For the matter of that in the life of the cloisters, and in this life of Ireland, men go mad every hour and you do not ask them to change.

SISTER EILEEN: There is nothing here or in the

4. Auguste Rodin (1840-1917), French sculptor. There is a letter from Synge to his fiancée, Molly Algood, in which Rodin's work also features:

> I had a very pleasant afternoon at the Mackennas — they have a charming old house full of excellent things that they have picked up, among other [things] a little bronze statuette by Rodin — you have seen his work at Harcourt [Gallery, Dublin] — which he gave to Mrs. MacK(enna).

See Ann Saddlemyer (ed.), *Letters to Molly: John Millington Synge to Marie O'Neill 1906-1909* (Cambridge, Massachusetts: Belknap Press, 1971), p. 272. This letter is dated 31 August (1908), and so is much later than Synge's early work on the play.

5. *malin* = rogue; *le bon Dieu* = the good Lord.
6. Jean-Jacques Rousseau (1712-78), French-Swiss philosopher whose *Confessions* (1781) include several youthful passions. The quotation can be rendered, 'It was the one act of folly in my life, but I was splendid!'
7. 'And what about your inheritance? My death's-heads salute you.' Note that the use of French, proper in quoting Rousseau, is now extended to a more informal domain, and this continues throughout the play until Bride's pregnancy and the embrace of Columb and Eileen are both inscribed through this non-colloquial medium.

religious life to make men mad .... It is different in Paris.

A gust of wind howls through the house. SISTER EILEEN *shudders and looks round at the window.*

COLUMB: Madness is caused by the killing out or exaggeration of some part of the personality, and life here has been withered away by men that are held up in contrast to the French till we are more degenerate than they are.

MRS BYRNE *comes in with a notebook in her hand.*

MRS BYRNE: There is a note-book was under the head of his bed. (*She gives it to* COLUMB, *and then goes over and closes the shutters*) Don't open them shutters for the length of this night, your honour.

COLUMB: Why?

MRS BYRNE: The dogs is howling in the lane and there's more than common death around this house tonight. You'll be needing nothing more?

COLUMB: Nothing more, Goodnight Mrs Byrne.

MRS BYRNE: Goodnight your honour. (*She goes out*)

SISTER EILEEN: (*Looking at the notebook*) They must have gone on settling the room after I had come down.

COLUMB: I suppose we should see what is in it. (*Opening the notebook*) There is a little drawing of a girl and a slip of paper. (*Reads*) 'In the box between the library windows I have left my will and a letter to be read by my heir' — Some keys are with it. It must be that box behind you.

SISTER EILEEN: (*Who has taken up the drawing*) Are you going to read it?

COLUMB: I do not know that I am his heir.

SISTER EILEEN: This girl's face is like some face I have seen.

COLUMB: (*Looking over her shoulder*) It is like Bride, I think.

SISTER EILEEN: Like Bride? ... I believe you are right.

COLUMB: There is curious story about an aunt of hers that old Pat was going to tell me tonight, but his head was not clear enough.

He puts the paper back in the note-book, and lays it on the table. SISTER EILEEN *has still the drawing in her hand. Another gust of wind howls at the window.*

SISTER EILEEN: (*Starting*) I never minded wind before but these nights I have been sitting with your uncle it has begun to terrify me ... I ought to go to bed, if it rises any more I will not be able to sleep.

COLUMB: Wait a little longer I am going to warm some Burgundy, it will do both of us good. (*He opens an old press*[8] *and takes out two curiously formed wine glasses with a saucepan and decanter. Then he arranges the turf, pours some wine into the saucepan and puts it on the fire*)

SISTER EILEEN: (*Still looking at the drawing*) I wonder if your uncle drew this picture himself. There is a whimsical sadness in the girl's face that is wonderfully caught.

COLUMB: (*Getting up from the fire*) Let me see it again. It reminds me a little of my friend in the black room. Not by any physical resemblance, but by something much vaguer — something in the quality of her sadness.

SISTER EILEEN: I don't think the sadness that is in that face would make anyone live in a black room. It is not so material.

COLUMB: (*Getting a bellows out of the corner and going back to the fire*) You are not just to my friend. He is an extraordinary man, and plays very wonderfully on the cello. (*He stirs the fire and spills a little of the wine*) I have spilt some of it, I must put in some more.

SISTER EILEEN: Shall I hand you the decanter? (*She gives it to him*)

COLUMB: Thank you. (*He pours out a little more wine, and gives the decanter back to her. She puts it down on top of the MSS. on the table and then picks it up hastily*)

SISTER EILEEN: Look what I have done, I have stained your MSS. I am so sorry.

COLUMB: What page is it?

SISTER EILEEN: One that begins — 'Every life is a symphony'.

COLUMB: Then it does not matter. That is only in the rough.

SISTER EILEEN: (*Drying the page with her handkerchief*) I read that page when you were out but I did not quite understand it.

COLUMB: If you saw it with the context you would find it simple enough, but it is not easy to explain to you in fragments. (*Blows the fire slowly*) Music is such a direct expression of the human personality that if we know music it is not easy to take up any point of psychology without finding some strange likeness to the things music has expressed. In these notes on the symphony I am trying to point out that this supreme 'form' of art is a reflection of the sequence that each person, and, in

8. In Irish speech a 'press' is a cupboard with doors, a locker; the usage was standard English until the late nineteenth century.

a sense, all humanity, tends to pass through in life. The two subjects on which all our glory is constructed are the facts of love and death. (*Laying down the bellows and picking up the MSS, he selects a page*) That might jar on you tonight. (*He looks for another*) After dealing with the first movement that is filled with passion and excitement I go on to the next. (*Reading*) 'The position of the slow movement after the climax of the opening is also wonderfully suggestive. This sigh of beautiful relief, which comes as an explanation rather than a mere cessation of an excitement that is always pain, is the last utterance of man. A cycle of experience is the only definite unity, and when all has been passed through, and every joy and pain has been resolved in one passion of relief, the only rest that can follow is in the dissolution of the person.' (*He pauses for a moment and the wine boils over*) My wine is ready. (*He pours out two glasses*) Trinquez.[9] You do not often have patients who mix you warm liquers [*sic*] in the small hours of the night.

SISTER EILEEN: I do not: but you are not my patient.

COLUMB: Are you sure? (*Drinking*) C'est bien bon.[10] What a beautiful glow I have made in the turf. May I smoke?

SISTER EILEEN: If you like.

COLUMB: (*Lighting a long pipe*) That is better. (*A pause while he smokes eagerly*)

SISTER EILEEN: (*Looking up at the picture over the chimney-piece*) How much he changed since that picture was done. Yet he cannot have been old.

COLUMB: I remember him first when he came to my grand Aunt's funeral, he was not more than thirty five.

SISTER EILEEN: I was eleven when she died .... He must have been about fifty.

COLUMB: This night reminds me of the days we spent in the woods between her death and the funeral. Do you remember them?

SISTER EILEEN: Not clearly.

COLUMB: You ought to. When we once catch the 'style' of our lives we find refrains of excitement in all we think and do.

SISTER EILEEN: I remember the flowers we picked for the grave ... I do not remember the excitement.

9. 'Clink' (glasses together).
10. 'It's pretty good.'

COLUMB: (*slowly*) It was wonderful weather in June, and our sense of death seemed only strong enough to throw out the whirl of life among the trees. Then the intimate feeling I had of the splendour of the world changed my friendship for you and gave me my first mood of romance. Till that time I had been divided between a vague affection for my people and a dream world where I lived with my imagination, but in that week the death shadow behind the glory of the woods transfigured your reality, and lifted you up to the level of my dreams .... It was my first wakening chord of love and death.

A pause. In a lull in the storm a stifled noise is heard under the windows.

COLUMB: What is that?

SISTER EILEEN: It sounded like some one coughing in the trees.

COLUMB: (*Goes over to the window, opens the shutters and looks from behind the blind*) The snowing is over, and the stars have come out.

SISTER EILEEN: (*Going after him*) Can you see anything?

COLUMB: It is too dark but the moon will rise in a few minutes. Look at the light on that little cloud above Tonagee.

SISTER EILEEN: When the moon rises it will be as bright as day the snow is so white.

COLUMB: Did you hear? That was certainly a cough.

SISTER EILEEN: It may have been some of the animals.

COLUMB: I hope it is not the avenging lunatic.

SISTER EILEEN: What do you mean?

COLUMB: When Pat brought me the letter while you were up stairs, he told me that there is a lunatic about the place who has sworn to kill every new propriator [*sic*] who comes here. It is because of the girl my uncle had the drawing of in his note-book.

SISTER EILEEN: But is there really a lunatic?

COLUMB: It seems that it was the man who showed me the way when I was out.

SISTER EILEEN: (*Shivering*) Come back to the fire. You are safe in any case tonight. (*She sits down in her chair and* COLUMB *stands at the other side of the fireplace*)

COLUMB: Are you superstitious?

SISTER EILEEN: Hardly.

COLUMB: A strange thing happened the night I got your telegram. I spent the evening with my friend who wrote me this letter in his black room.

After midnight we pulled back the black curtains and looked out across the Pantheon[11] .... What is that?

SISTER EILEEN: It is only the ivy flapping on the window.

COLUMB: I am getting nervous .... We looked out across the Pantheon and somebody was wandering about in the shadow calling out with the curious intonation of French beggars 'Mes frères prenez garde à vous,'[12] ... When I got home I found your telegram. It makes me feel uncomfortable. (*He walks up and down the room*)

SISTER EILEEN: Sit down and don't be foolish. (*She finishes her glass of wine*)

COLUMB: Let me give you some more wine. (*He fills the glasses again and drinks*)

A clock strikes the four quarters and two o'clock.

SISTER EILEEN: I must soon go to bed.

COLUMB: Don't leave me just yet. My nerves have been at a tension ever since I came here, and tonight I feel as if a movement might snap them.

SISTER EILEEN: You are easily overcome.

COLUMB: If you had been brought from Paris to find yourself at the foot of a desolate mountain between a dead man and a nun with vague madness and risk about you, you would feel what I mean. We are at an ultimate climax of desolation yet, (*he throws more turf on the fire*) yet through it all it is possible to find a strange impulse of joy.

SISTER EILEEN: (*Picking up the bow of crepe and arranging the ribbons*) Death is always solemn, I do not feel your climax of desolation ... and I do not feel your joy.

COLUMB: Then you were different when you were a child. You felt the supreme moment of satisfaction we had on the threshold of a house shrouded with death as thoroughly as I did.

SISTER EILEEN: That is only some fancy you have conjured up.

COLUMB: The thing is universal wherever people are not ashamed to be human. All funeral games and Irish wakes are due to this feeling. (*Drinking*) Everywhere there is an imperious reaction from the weight of death .... Even now my gaiety is rising.

SISTER EILEEN: (*Standing up*) You must not talk like that .... You have no reverence for your uncle.

COLUMB: That is the point, my child. It is the reaction ... the scherzo has its place in the symphony even after a dead march.

A pause while she stands looking at him with the crepe in her hand. He finishes his glass and stands up.

COLUMB: Ah, ma fille, n'est-il pas malheureux de voir des gens comme toi.[13]

SISTER EILEEN: What do you mean?

COLUMB: I mean that there is a time to weep and a time to laugh.

Wind howls through the house.

SISTER EILEEN: (*Shivering*) If there is a time to laugh you have not chosen yours very judiciously ... unless it is your inheritance that excites you.

COLUMB: (*Coming over to her*) That is cruel and absurd. Do you think a few pounds would make any man play with death? You seem unable to penetrate even the vestibule of an old crâne[14] like mine.

SISTER EILEEN: I did not mean to be cruel, it is hard to understand you.

COLUMB: Hard for you, I salute all my sensations even those that are beggarly or half insane, you will not recognize any that do not come to you in the livery of the saints. You have ceased to be human and now your soul is as unnatural as the toe of a Chinese princess.[15]

SISTER EILEEN: (*Half turning away*) I do not even know what you call a natural person.

COLUMB: I mean a person who has contrived a hierarchy of all his moods and passions .... If you were natural you would feel the glory of this moment. Death has passed near us. We are lost in a wilderness of branches. Yet this room with the old oak chairs and books is exquisitely beautiful. Our Burgundy in these tapered glasses is like a draught of perfurmed jewels. The turf and tobacco have filled the air with incense and draped that beautiful haze about the corners of the ceiling .... You will not answer completely. You are asking yourself if it is right to sit up with me. Parasitic ideas are holding you back from the ecstasy of freedom.

SISTER EILEEN: (*Moving from the fire*) It is time for me to go. I do not like the way you are talking.

11. A familiar name (deriving from the temple in Rome, later a Christian church) for the church of Ste Genevieve in Paris, and for the district in which it stands.
12. 'Brothers, take care of yourselves.'
13. 'Ah, my girl, isn't it unlucky to set eyes on the likes of you?'
14. Literally 'skull', thus 'an old head like mine'.
15. It was customary for the Chinese to bind the feet of a female child of noble birth in order to preserve their delicate size. Synge's interest in oriental matters partly derives from his knowledge of French culture (and thus, French colonialism in Africa and elsewhere) and also from his reading of Lafcadio Hearn (1850-1904) to whom he sometimes claimed a distant family relationship. Hearn was partly educated in Ireland. Later he became a Japanese citizen.

The cry for freedom in this world is only the pretext we use to get license for the lower portion of our nature.

COLUMB: You mistake me utterly. No sane man thinks that the draught of bodily freedom can sate the divine intricacy of the soul. It is too simple. But in the ultimate symphony of the emotions the animal note is heard far away sounding a beautiful and passionate rhythm with unappeasible [*sic*] lamentation. It has the puissance[16] of the drum yet it is only a note .... Your ideals are as rudimentary as Gregorian chants,[17] mine have known freedom, they have the rage of the orchestra.

SISTER EILEEN: There is nothing to keep these theories from leading people to all kinds of wickedness. (*She lights her candle that is on a side table*)

COLUMB: Why?

SISTER EILEEN: Vague excitement without law or rule cannot make people good.

COLUMB: The most beautiful melody may excite a man to love his own wife or his neighbour's. It is important that there are beautiful melodies and that men love. We may neglect accidents. Yet if men are born clean the excitement of life forms round them in a clear atmosphere where no parasite with thick leaves can flourish.

SISTER EILEEN: (*Going to the window*) The wind has fallen and the moon is shining on the snow.

COLUMB: Life is made for luxuriance. You elide the tumult of passion and stifle what is puissant into one mode of the exquisite. It is a capital error.

SISTER EILEEN: Come and look at these trees and the line of the hills. This white moonlight seems to be the type of all I wish for.

COLUMB: (*Following her to the window*) The divine chastity of the earth is only a mood. It will pass in its turn. In three months at this hour these trees will be filled with a tumult of love, another mood that is divine....

SISTER EILEEN: The moonlight is better ... Unless people have the perfect calm that comes with purity and faith their lives are never beautiful.

COLUMB: The only calm of importance is the calm of the man who feels the vortex of passion and death straining beneath him and is able to deride it. Have you noticed the triumphant wail that breaks out from the poised ecstasy of Beethoven, or the muscles of Michael Angelo[18] that have grown monstrous and weary with struggling in chaos for the knees of God, and have slackened at length for the passionate rest of desperation?

SISTER EILEEN: I think there is somebody in the yew trees ... It is only a shadow ... Beethoven's and Michael Angelo's work are filled with faith — like all beautiful works — you must not cite them against me.

COLUMB: Their faith is cosmic faith. Perhaps you deny it. Take Rabelais.[19] You don't know him. Then take the magnificient Kermesse of Rubens[20] in the Louvre with its superb symphony of red and its one dancing wave of men and women, where every limb rages with its particular passion of desire. That is an ultimate utterance which knows nothing of your faith.

SISTER EILEEN: If you go on thinking like that I don't know where you will end. Surely it is right to live by what is divine in us not by what is gross.

COLUMB: Birth and love if they are gross are less so than the putrifying corpse which is the real heaven of the Christians. I say it again, the two poles of existence from which all our emotions are derived lead at last to the joy where we begin or to the horrible corpse where we end.

SISTER EILEEN: You are blotting out the beauty of life.

COLUMB: I am defending its glory. We may be right to drape love in the beauty of death till it becomes chaste, and to love death till it becomes vital, but we are not right to distort the dual puissance of the mind. The world is a mode of the Divine exaltation and every sane fragment of force ends in a fertile passion that is filled with joy. It is the infertile excitements that are filled with death. That is the whole moral and aesthetic of the world.

SISTER EILEEN: You would say that prayer is not fertile yet it is not filled with death.

COLUMB: Prayer is the veiled cry of power before the shadow of its own annihilation. No emotion is simple, and we can find the whole range of exaltation at any moment of rapture. The death cry of the peasants and the dances of Algiers both

16. power.
17. Plainsong, the basis of church music from the 6th century, named after Pope Gregory the Great.
18. Michelangelo Buonarotti (1475-1564), Italian sculptor, painter and poet.
19. François Rabelais (*c.*1494-1553), French comic and satirical writer.
20. Peter Paul Rubens (1577-1640), Flemish painter of both religious and vigorous secular works. A 'kermesse' is a village fair, a popular subject for painters in Rubens's day.

contain the 'crescendo', which is all we know.[21] We have two sources of passion two results of passion, but passion itself is alone.

SISTER EILEEN: Look at that man in the trees ..... A tall man ... He is pointing to us.

COLUMB: It is the avenging lunatic.

A shot is fired and COLUMB *falls on the floor.* SISTER EILEEN *pulls the bell-pull, and then bends over* COLUMB *who is nearly insensible.* SISTER DORA *runs in followed by* BRIDE *and* MRS BYRNE *both half dressed.*

SISTER EILEEN: Some one fired at him through the window. I do not think he is very badly hurt. (*To* MRS BYRNE) Send Murphy for the doctor, and bring something to carry him on.

BRIDE: The master's chair?

SISTER EILEEN: That would do.

BRIDE *and* MRS BYRNE *runs out.*

MRS BYRNE: (*As she is going out*) It was Stephen Costello did that, Ah, the bloody villain.

SISTER DORA: (*To* SISTER EILEEN) You are dressed still. I thought you were tired.

SISTER EILEEN: I have been talking to my cousin, it is so long since I have seen him.

BRIDE *brings in an invalid chair. They put* COLUMB *into it and the two nurses wheel him out.* MRS BYRNE *comes in as they are at the door.*

MRS BYRNE: Murphy is gone for the doctor and he won't be long at all with the clearness of the moon.

The nurses go out.

MRS BYRNE: The Lord have mercy on us all, Biddy, was there ever a night the like of this night? Two weeks ago we were all quiet and easy in our minds, and now where are we going at all, with sickness, and murder, and death .... Bring that lamp with you they'll be wanting all sorts below. (*She goes out*).

BRIDE *is following her with the lamp in her hand.*

MRS BYRNE: (*Calling from outside*) Is the fire safe, Biddy, don't be burning the house.

BRIDE: (*Standing in the doorway*) It is going out, Mrs Byrne, the turf's wet and it'll all be black in a minute. (*She goes out*)

CURTAIN

21. Note again the orientalist element, Algiers being a popular subject for French painters of a certain school.

ACT II

Same scene: clear evening in June. MRS BYRNE *is laying a little table near the window with tea-things for two people.* COLUMB *comes in with his hat on and his arm in a sling.*

COLUMB: (*Talking a little listlessly, as if pre-occupied*) It has been a beautiful evening.

MRS BYRNE: It is true for you, and isn't it a grand thing to see the like of it in the month of June, and isn't it a grand thing your honour's getting his health for the fine time of the year.

COLUMB: (*Pointing from the window*) I have just been up to that white stone you can see above the Inchavor.

MRS BYRNE: The Lord bless us to walk all that way and no one along with you. It's lonesome you must have been after Sister Eileen being beside you every hour in the day for three months or beyond it.

COLUMB: How is Pat?

MRS BYRNE: He's going down[1] this time and no mistake. The priest's been with him and they say he'll be like to go in the night, God help him.

COLUMB: You have been down this evening?

MRS BYRNE: I have not, your honour, but there was a second cousin of his in here a while ago on his way home into the hills, and it was he was telling me. He'd been down at the town this morning — down at the assizes.

COLUMB: (*Turning quickly*) Then he saw Stephen Costello's trial?

MRS BYRNE: Well, he did your honour.

COLUMB: What was done?

MRS BYRNE: Dr. Burke below did all the swearing they wanted, and then they put the poor fellow into a kind of a Criminal Asylum for the rest of his life, the Lord have mercy on him. (*Sighing to herself*) He was a fine bit of a chap at one time, and they were fine people altogether, but it's a long way they're after coming down through the world.

COLUMB: (*Turning to the window again, and speaking as if to change the subject*) Sister Eileen has not yet come in yet?

MRS BYRNE: She has not, your honour (*Looking out beside him*) She had a right to come home to her tea. What good can she do there with the old man dying before her?

COLUMB: I suppose she will come presently. Bride can look after him.

1. dying.

MRS BYRNE: She can indeed your honour, and isn't there Mrs Brady as well does be in there sitting beside him. (*Listening*) There's somebody now. maybe she's after coming up thro' the wood.

SISTER EILEEN *comes in.*

SISTER EILEEN: I am very late. Old Pat is dying, and I did not like to leave him they are so ignorant.

COLUMB: I have just come in.

SISTER EILEEN: Where did you go?

MRS BYRNE: He went up (*pointing from the window*) to where you see the big white stone of the selvage[2] of the hill.

SISTER EILEEN: That is much too far.

MRS BYRNE: (*Taking up her tray*) Sure, he's well now and I think it's soon he'll be walking away from us altogether. (*Goes out of the room muttering to herself*) The likes of him would be too lonesome in it when herself is gone away.

SISTER EILEEN *moves about the room putting ferns and foxgloves she has brought with her into bowls of water.* COLUMB *is leaning on the windowsill.*

SISTER EILEEN: She is right. I shall soon have to go.

COLUMB: Don't let us talk of it, I am too doleful tonight.

SISTER EILEEN: (*Looking around with surprise*) Everything is so beautiful I thought you would be perfectly happy.

COLUMB: There is an anguish in this splendour of June. One feels one's mortality .... the furzebushes are withering already, and the hawthorn is decayed.

SISTER EILEEN: What would you do if you had been sitting all the evening by a death bed as I have.

The light begins to get low.

COLUMB: (*Talking slowly*) It is natural for old men to die. This pageant of blossom that fades in a few hours is far more terrible. Don't you realise the irony of beautiful life? Diamonds and rubies that do not feel are beautiful for ever, but women and flowers fulfil their task of propagation and wither in a day. It is sadder than death.

SISTER EILEEN: With some women an inward beauty comes instead of the other. (*Still moving about the room*) When a man's strength and intelligence begin to fail, it must be worse than for us.

2. Usually, a 'selvage' is a border or hem turned in so that the cloth cannot unravel; hence (rarely) any kind of border or edge, especially (in minerealogy, *c.* 1757) 'a thin layer of clayey or earthy matter surrounding a metalliferous vein'. Is Synge recording a distinctive Wicklow idiom of *c.*1900 here?

COLUMB: It is worse beyond comparison. A man who is very young cannot express, a man who is not very young cannot experience. After thirty we go out among the woods and kiss the lips of girls in wild efforts to remember. A man is sterile when he is beautiful, and withered when he produces. He cannot be satisfied. I am speaking of artists: women and artists are akin....

MRS BYRNE: (*Bringing in the teapot, and a little lamp*) I'm destroyed running, and the Lord knows when we'll get another girl. Biddy'll be too grand now with her bit of an old farm all to herself.

COLUMB: Have the letters come?

MRS BYRNE: They have not, your honour. Murphy was minding the cow that calved last night and he couldn't go for them till a while ago.

She goes out. SISTER EILEEN *sits down at the table and pours out the tea:* COLUMB *is still at the window.*

COLUMB: It has been a wonderful sunset. I wish I could work again. We have nothing to express but the cycle of the seasons, and I am saturated — soaked — with it tonight....

SISTER EILEEN: Your tea is ready.

COLUMB: This illness has brought me a relapse into puberty, I have the envy I used to have of the wild plants that crush and strangle each other in a cold rage of growth.

SISTER EILEEN *covers his cup with a saucer.*

COLUMB: (*Speaking very slowly*) I used to sit all day and look out into the green clefts of a chestnut, behind my window, or at a bit of hedge under it where hemlock, and docks, and woodbine grew with a strange rankness of green.

SISTER EILEEN: Do come and have your tea.

COLUMB: (*Coming to the table*) I am a fool tonight. This illness has made me weak. (*He sits down and goes on talking without uncovering his cup*) Music is the only art that can express the first animal frenzy. In the orchestra it is a divine hymn, in literature, or painting, it is horrible. I suppose music catches the passions at a mood that is more abstract than the mood of words.

SISTER EILEEN: (*Uncovering his cup and putting it before him*) Are you going to turn musician again, they say tastes sometimes change after a wound.

COLUMB: If a wound has to be nursed it is not wonderful that tastes should change. (*Drinking*) I am sorry to hear that old Pat is so bad.

SISTER EILEEN: He is past seventy. At that age death is not very terrible to an old man like him.

COLUMB: (*Moodily*) Death is always terrible....

The last few nights — I suppose because I am not strong — I have been haunted by that appalling sensation in which we realize the gulf of annihilation we are being whirled into .... I suppose you have felt it also.

SISTER EILEEN: Sometimes when I am too tired. It is a kind of nightmare.

COLUMB: A very terrible kind .... At one time it worked all over my consciousness and I used to walk about by the Seine wondering how the men and women could go on with their working and love-making in face of this stupendous doom. Then a beautiful 'bonne'[3] came to work in the window opposite mine and I forgot it.

SISTER EILEEN: It was well to shake it off. (*Taking his cup*) Let me give you some more tea, that must be cold. I don't know what you will do when you have to attend to yourself again.

COLUMB: I don't intend to.

SISTER EILEEN: What do you intend?

COLUMB: To keep you.

SISTER EILEEN: You must not talk like that.

COLUMB: It would be a supreme crime for you to leave me. The worst vice is slight compared with the guiltiness of a man or woman who defies the central order of the world.

SISTER EILEEN: And my religion?

COLUMB: You are changing every day. You have learned in Kilgreine[4] that the world is wider than a nut-shell.

SISTER EILEEN: I have changed a little.

COLUMB: You will change a great deal more. Our faculty for change is not bounded .... What remains in me now of the person you knew when I was a child?

SISTER EILEEN: Very little.

COLUMB: Yet you think we may live for ever and be still the same.

SISTER EILEEN: Something has remained.

COLUMB: Scars, ma fille.[5]

SISTER EILEEN: What makes you so wretched this evening?

COLUMB: Many things. Did you hear about Stephen Costello's trial?

SISTER EILEEN: Dr Burke came in to see Pat on his way home and told me about it.

COLUMB: Fully?

SISTER EILEEN: He had not time, but he took me out to the door when he was going away, and showed me a photograph that was taken in the prison. It is so like the drawing your uncle had in his note-book.

COLUMB: Some one told me they were twins. That would account for the resemblance .... What has become of the drawing. I have not seen it since the night I was shot?

SISTER EILEEN: I locked it up where I keep the money. I did not want the servants to see it. (*She goes over and unlocks a drawer in a writing table and takes out the note-book. Then gives it to* COLUMB)

COLUMB: We have never read the letter my uncle left for me to read.

SISTER EILEEN: We might read it bye-and-bye.

COLUMB: (*Opening the note-book*) There is the drawing.

SISTER EILEEN: (*Looking at it*) Yes, it is exactly like him, except that the sorrow in his face is much more terrible. (*Giving it back to him*)

COLUMB: It is a horrible story .... It makes me unutterably wretched.

SISTER EILEEN: (*Looking at him*) If you had more real knowledge of the misery that is in the world, you would not think as you do .... I could not live if I thought that this life was the end of everything.

COLUMB: That is a girl's fancy. Many people who think as I do, live like you, yet are happier than I am.

SISTER EILEEN: I do not understand them.

COLUMB: Why should we be more unhappy than the birds that are singing outside? .... They are shot and maimed and tortured yet they go on singing, and what does the earth care, or what do we care, for the units? The world is an orchestra where every living thing plays one entry and then gives his place to another. We must be careful to play all the notes. It is for that we are created. If we play them well we are not exorbitantly wretched.

SISTER EILEEN: The only notes many of us can play are very few and painful.

COLUMB: No one pretends to ignore the bitterness of disease and death. It is an immense infinite horror, and the more we learn to set the real value on the vitality of life the more we will dread death. Yet any horror is better than the stagnation of belief.

3. serving maid.
4. The place-name, or house-name, now revealed so late in the play is the anglicized version of the Irish *Cill Gréine* (church of the sun) or *Coill Gréine* (wood of the sun). The confusion of the two separate elements in the common Hiberno-English prefix 'Kil' is apt here, where Synge fuses religious and natural imagery.
5. my girl.

SISTER EILEEN: I do not know what you mean. (*She begins tuning the harp in the corner*)

COLUMB: There is stagnation in everything that has been once mature. (*He gets up and walks about the room*) The world orchestra has been playing in oratorio for two thousand years and the thing has become effete. Now the players have gone out to gain new powers in lonely exaltation. The people who rebel from the law of God are not those who are essaying strange notes in the dark alleys of the world but the fools who linger in the aisles droning their withered chants with senile intonation....

SISTER EILEEN: You are talking riddles. (*She begins playing softly*)

COLUMB: I mean that in the Christian synthesis each separate faculty has been dying of atrophy. The synthesis has fallen. The imagination has wandered away to grow puissant and terrible again, in lonely vigils where she sits and broods among things that have been touched by madmen and things that have the smell of death on them and books written with the blood of horrible crimes. The intellect has peered down into the tumult of atoms and up into the stars till she has forgotten her complements in the personality, and the instinct for practical joy has taught anarchists to hate in the passion of their yearning for love .... In the end men will grow human again with a more wonderful manhood. Every passion will unite in new discords resolving in what are to us inconceivable harmonies.[6]

SISTER EILEEN: How do you know all that?

COLUMB: I don't know it.

SISTER EILEEN: I mean why do you believe it?

COLUMB: I don't believe it ... It is young and fertile, what you believe in is barren and decayed.

SISTER EILEEN: Then you don't care for what is true.

COLUMB: (*With a gesture of impatience*) The only truth a wave knows is that it is going to break. The only truth a bud knows is that it is going to expand and flower. The only truth we know is that we are a flood of magnificent life the fruit of some frenzy of the earth. If what I have said to you is false it does not matter. The European races may be swept away, humanity itself may die out, but a turmoil of life is within us. It has come from eternity, and I suppose will go on for eternity.

SISTER EILEEN: It is simpler to believe in God.

COLUMB: I will believe in millions of them if you like, but I have no doubt they care as little for us as we care for the sorrows of an ant-hill. (*He moves his hand over his face*)

SISTER EILEEN: What shall I sing to you? You must not get excited.

COLUMB: Sing anything you choose. (*She sings 'the Culfion'*[7] *and then leaves the harp*). I wonder if the post has come.

SISTER EILEEN: (*Looking out*) I think I hear Murphy coming up the road.

COLUMB: Then it will be here in a few minutes.

SISTER EILEEN: Are you expecting anything? The news of the trial will not be in the papers till tomorrow.

COLUMB: I expect nothing in particular, but I always hope for news from Paris. My friend may write to me again though I have never answered the letter that came the night of my mishap.... Perhaps he thinks I have forgotten him.

SISTER EILEEN: (*Turning round from the window*) Would you like me to write for you.... You could dictate to me.

COLUMB: I would be delighted. It is very kind of you.

SISTER EILEEN: (*Sitting down at a writing table with paper before her*) Not too fast.

COLUMB: (*Walking about the room, smoking a cigarette*):

> Dear O'Neill,
>
> I have been laid up, and though I am better again I can only write by dictation.
>
> When I got over here the place interested me in a way I did not expect. The old-fashioned Irish conservatism and morality seemed to have evolved a melancholy degeneration worse than anything in Paris. Everyone seemed to be taking his friends to the asylum or bringing them back from it.
>
> After two or three days my uncle died and a couple of hours later an individual with an

6. This paragraph, bringing together scientific (atoms), artistic (imagination), religious (vigils) and political (anarchists) terms and a violent and morbid imagery, picks up all too many topics from fin de siècle debates. An observation, practically buried here, surfaced far more clearly in a preface that Synge wrote for his *Poems* in December 1908: 'It may almost be said that before verse can become human again it must learn to be brutal.' This in turn may owe something to the *Journal* of the Goncourt brothers (see entry for 3 September 1855) which we know Synge was reading.

7. A traditional Irish praise-song and air; the title means 'Fair-headed one'.

avenging obsession put a charge of buckshot into my shoulder.

A distant cousin of mine — a nun — who had been nursing my uncle stayed on here and took care of me. It has been a curious moment. I could look out from my bed into the woods and watch the spring beginning. I had forgotten the marvellousness of the world. Soft grey days came first with quiet clouds and the woods grew purple with sap, while a few birches that stood out before them like candlesticks with wrought silver stems, covered themselves with a dull mist of red. Then the hazels came out and hung the woods with straight earrings of gold that gave relief in their simplicity among the tangled boughs. One morning after rain spectres of pale green and yellow and pink seemed to be looking out between the trees. Then everything stood quiet for a moment till a warm week came at the beginning of May and the whole country broke out into wonderful glory — infinitely timid greens and yellows and whites, and birds singing everywhere, and strange odours creeping up into my room.

I used to lie in the evening while my cousin sat in her white veil by the window with the twilight on the hills behind her and read out old leather books from my uncle's library. We do wrong to seek a foundation for ecstasy in philosophy or in the hidden things of the spirit. When life is at its simplest without anything beyond or before it the mystery is greater than we can endure. Every leaf and flower and insect is full of deeper wonder than any signs the cabbalists[8] have invented. I am wearying my writer — the nun I spoke of. The interest of the present moment is to know whether she will give up her religion and remain with me —

SISTER EILEEN: I won't write that.

COLUMB: Please don't interrupt me — 'or add another to the unhealthy women of Ireland who scorn the rules of life and the beauty that is possible and only possible within them'....

SISTER EILEEN: (*Getting up*) I won't write it.

COLUMB: Well put in that I will write when I am able, and let me sign. (*He leans over her and signs with his left hand*). Look what I am doing. Steady me.

She helps him.

MRS BYRNE: (*Coming in behind them*) There is a letter has come for Sister Eileen (*Giving it to her*) Will you be wanting the big lamp. I don't know if I put oil in it these two days?

COLUMB: (*Looking at it*) There is oil enough I think, but would you kindly pull over that box from between the windows, it is not heavy and I want to look at some things that are in it.

MRS BYRNE: (*Pulling it over*) That is a box the master would look at now and again, but I never rightly knew what was in it. (*Gathers up the tea-things*) You'll be needing nothing more?

SISTER EILEEN: Please tell Murphy that I must go to town[9] by the first train in the morning. I suppose he can drive me down.

MRS BYRNE: To be sure he can. (*With a queer look at* COLUMB) So you're going off from us at last?

SISTER EILEEN: I am going tomorrow.

MRS BYRNE: You'll be needing nothing more?

COLUMB: Nothing more, goodnight Mrs Byrne.

MRS BYRNE: Good-night your honour. (*She goes out*)

COLUMB: (*With a change in his voice*) What is this talk of your going away from me tomorrow?

SISTER EILEEN: I have heard from the Superior.[10] She is short of nurses, so she wrote to Dr Burke to know when I would be free. He answered that you were nearly well, so I am to go tomorrow. It would have been better if you had let me go last week.

COLUMB: (*Walking over to the window*) Cannot you wait a few days longer?

SISTER EILEEN: I am afraid not possibly. (*Looking at her watch*) I must soon go and pack.

COLUMB: But I am so helpless still.

SISTER EILEEN: You can get an attendant. You do not need a nurse.

COLUMB: Tonight I wanted you to open this box, we were going to read the paper of my uncle's.

SISTER EILEEN: I can do that for you, of course. My packing does not take long. Where is the key?

COLUMB: It is one of these. (*He gives her a bunch of keys*)

SISTER EILEEN: (*Tries a couple and opens the box*) There is a portfolio with papers.

COLUMB: (*Taking the portfolio*) That should be it. Yes, here is the paper. There are two rings fastened

8. The vogue for the occult was in full flower in Europe at this time.

9. Presumably to Dublin.

10. The nun in charge of a convent or order.

to the top, a wedding ring and another. What beautiful stones!

SISTER EILEEN: (*Still kneeling by the box*) There is a silk dress in the box also.

COLUMB: Let us see it.

SISTER EILEEN: (*Holding it up*) It is a beautiful brocade. That peculiar green tint is exceptionally rare. My mother had a piece but not nearly so fine as this is.

COLUMB: It looks as if it would fit you. You would be superb.

SISTER EILEEN: (*Throwing it down on a chair*) If you talk like that I will go away.

COLUMB: We have to read this first; it will not take long. What time is it?

SISTER EILEEN: Past twelve. We have been dawdling over everything.

COLUMB: (*Moving towards the reading lamp, passes the window and stops for a moment to look out*) This is the first night of summer. Do you hear the night-jars?[11] It would be a fine night to hunt moths in. They will be thronging in here when the moon sets, yet we must keep the window open, the honey-suckle is so delicious.

SISTER EILEEN: (*Going over to the window near him and taking a long breath of the air*) How sweet the air is. I shall miss this fragrance when I am nursing in town.

COLUMB: All the world seems to be crying out to you not to condemn yourself to an endless vigil with disease .... In a few years you will be ugly and callous, then you will die and rot .... There will be divine nights like this night, divine odours and colours, and birds crying on the heather but nothing will reach you. Don't you realise that if we spent every instant of our vigour writhing with beautiful ecstasies yet when death came we would not have known all the earth meant us to know?

SISTER EILEEN: (*With a stifled voice*) Are you going to read the paper of your uncle's?

COLUMB: (*Going over to the little lamp and unfolding the paper*) We must light the big lamp, I cannot see with this one.

SISTER EILEEN: (*Lighting it*) There is not much oil.

COLUMB: It will last for a while. (*Sits down with the paper and begins to read*)

'I have never known you or wished to know you, but as you will live in my house, I want to leave you a word that you may not live in it as I did.

'My life has gone to ruin because I misunderstood love and because I was scrupulous when I should have been strong. I treated women as if they were gods and they treated me as if I might be damned for their amusement.

'When I was a young man I read Goethe and Heine,[12] the men who were most prominent in literature at that time, and I learned things from them that made the women of my country avoid me because they were pious, and the men because they were stupid.

'If you love a woman subdue her. You will not love a woman it is not lawful to love. No man of our blood has ever been unlawful. If you live in the country live with the country, and find a woman who will understand with you the mysteries of growth and life. Let her know as you will know the two twilights and the quietness of the night. Neglect nothing, for God is in the earth and not above it. In the wet elm leaves trailing in the lanes in autumn, in the deserted currents of the streams, and in the breaking out of the sap, there are joys that collect all the joy that is in religion and art.... Be careful of my books. The dress and the rings were made for a woman I once hoped to marry. She was poor. She died afterwards, and her brother became crazy. He would have shot me but some vow restrained him. He thought I had wronged her....'

When he has finished SISTER EILEEN *still sits looking before her.*

COLUMB: (*After a pause*) Even the dead cry out to you .... Their scruples have brought the death of one woman — that is implied — the madness of her brother, the misery of my uncle, and now nearly my own death and your perversion.... It is almost amusing.

SISTER EILEEN: (*Masters herself with an effort and stands up*) I don't think you will find it very easy to subdue women against their will.

COLUMB: It is their will that is to be subdued. It is not thought difficult. God is with us. It is the

11. The night-jar is a bird that gains its name from the whirring noise the male makes during incubation of the eggs; its other name, the goat-sucker, is also derisively applied to natives of County Wicklow. Synge was highly informed both in naturalist matters and in the lore of County Wicklow.

12. Johann Wolfgang von Goethe (1749-1832), the greatest writer of German literature; Heinrich Heine (1797-1856), German lyric poet of radical disposition. Both men were regarded as 'immoral' by the standards of bourgeois society.

beauty of strength, and not the weakness of beauty that men need in love.

SISTER EILEEN: I must go.

COLUMB: (*Standing before her*) You must stay.

SISTER EILEEN: I cannot. Do not make me angry. After that letter from the Superior I cannot wait any longer. I will be gone before you awake in the morning. You had better go away for a while, you would be lonely here till you are quite strong. Good-bye.

COLUMB: (*Turning towards the window*) Wait, there is somebody on the path. (*Looking out*) It is Bride I think, she may want something for her father.

SISTER EILEEN: I will bring her in through the greenhouse, the servants would not hear her if she called them.

SISTER EILEEN *goes through a side door and is heard calling 'Bride, Bride' . . . . They come in together.*

SISTER EILEEN: What has happened?

BRIDE: He is dead Sister Eileen. Mrs Brady's husband was drunk, and he came up and took herself away before the moon was set. Then I was there a while with the old man, and a little after twelve he gave a sort of turn, and I went over, and he was dead in the bed. Then I was afeard to be there and no-one along with me, so I came up to see would Mrs Byrne go down to keep me from being lonesome. I can't leave him altogether, and I can't stay there by myself. (*She puts her apron up to her eyes*)

COLUMB: I am sure Mrs Byrne will go with you, and you can take Murphy if you think there is anything he can do for you.

BRIDE: Thank your honour, and may the Lord reward you.

COLUMB: You will be very lonely now without the old man.

BRIDE: I'm destroyed crying: but what good is in it. We must be satisfied, and what man at all can be living forever.[13]

SISTER EILEEN: What will you do? I suppose you will stay in service.

BRIDE: I will not Sister Eileen I will be married in two months or three.

COLUMB: Who are you going to marry?

BRIDE: Pat Murphy, your honour. It's a long time we are keeping company and it's time we were married, and now I have the farm and the cow he'll marry me as soon as I take him.

COLUMB: (*Takes a bit of candle off a candle-stick on the chimney piece, lights it and gives it to* BRIDE) That will light you, you know your way.

BRIDE: Thank your honour. (*She goes out*)

COLUMB: Did you notice anything?

SISTER EILEEN: What do you mean?

COLUMB: The girl is enceinte.[14]

SISTER EILEEN: Oh, Columb.

COLUMB: (*Going to the window*) She is nobler than you are. (*Speaking very slowly*) I am not a woman. I cannot judge of your feelings. Yet I know, you have a passionate instinct for children. Far down in below the level of your creed you know that motherhood, the privilege that lifts women up to share in the pain and passion of the earth, is more holy than the vows you have made. (*Looking out*) Look at the light of the dawn working round from the north, the sun will soon go up again.

SISTER EILEEN *goes over and looks out beside him.*

COLUMB: Let us come to the point ... Some destiny — I half believe in destiny — has brought us together, and no delusion is going to put us asunder.

SISTER EILEEN: I have been very wrong to let you talk to me as I have done .... But I am going back to my true life tomorrow, and I will ask for forgiveness.

COLUMB: You will not forget Kilgreine. A day will come when you will mourn over your barrenness .... I do not blame you. I only blame the creed that has distorted the nature God made for you in the beginning.

SISTER EILEEN: (*Goes back to the table: stands for a moment, then picks up an old book*) May I take Sainte Theresa with me as a remembrance? You are not likely to read her.[15]

COLUMB: Take it if you wish, yet for you the book is not moral.

The book slips through her fingers, and falls on the floor.

SISTER EILEEN: (*Picking it up*) Look where it has opened — 'Faites que je désire vrayment que toutes personnes m'abhorrent puisque je vous ay tant de fois laissé, m'aymant moy-même avec tant de

13. This speech is echoed at the end of Maurya's famous lament which closes *Riders to the Sea*: 'No man at all can be living for ever, and we must be satisfied.'

14. French: carrying a child.

15. Saint Teresa of Avila (1515-82), the Spanish nun and mystic. Her writings include a spiritual autobiography and *The Way to Perfection*.

fidélité. Qu'est-ce ceci, mon Dieu? Que pensons-nous tirer de aymer les creatures?'[16] ... I cannot see any more, the lamp is going out, and the printing is so old and curious.

COLUMB: The dawn is coming. I can see the green of the beeches. Look at the wonderful light in the east.

SISTER EILEEN: (*Hesitates for a moment then goes back to the window, speaking almost piteously*) The dawn reminds me of sick people.

COLUMB: (*Looks at her for a moment, then straightens himself, and speaks with decision*) You will not see many more.

SISTER EILEEN: Why?

COLUMB: You could have lived like a lily on a dunghill. I am going to gather you.

SISTER EILEEN: I would wither.

COLUMB: Before this splendour of the morning you cannot be a hypocrite. You know that you love me. Your being is throbbing with the wild impulse of life. The tempest of beauty that has put strange patterns on moths and touched the clouds and eggs of birds with purple, is filling you with radiance. Why will you worship the mania of Sainte Theresa? Your own beauty, your own expression of the divinity of woman, is holier than she is. People worship the folly of others when they have not courage to do a thing that is fit to be worshipped. They renounce when they have not courage to retain. You have power and courage. I adjure you to use them.

SISTER EILEEN: (*Leaning her elbows on the sill, and speaking very slowly*) I can see the purple of the heather ... the smell of the elders is making me dream ....[17] I don't know what to do you are giving me such pain and yet ....

COLUMB: (*Nearly with triumph*) Listen, there is the first note of the birds. I used to know their order of entry as they come out singly as the stars at night.

SISTER EILEEN: I see the first touch of red on Tonagee.

COLUMB: When the sun comes up over the ridge I will ask you to be my wife. You cannot refuse. The trees might as well refuse to grow fragrant and green when it is May, or the birds to sing before the dawn .... There are the larks, and the wrens; you have half an hour. I don't try to persuade you. I don't touch you. It is quite unnecessary. The world will persuade you. The breath that touched the waters and trees, and drew out this forest of leaves, and sent quivering voices to chant in them is making you a vocal existence.... There is the willow warbler, you have a quarter of an hour. Will you go and put this dress about you? I am not in a humour for blasphemy.

SISTER EILEEN *takes the green dress and goes out without looking at him.*

COLUMB: (*As she is in the doorway*) Do not be long. We must not disappoint the priest of day.

She goes out.

COLUMB: (*Alone at the window, speaking slowly with wonder in his voice*) Every life is a symphony .... It is this cosmic element in the person which gives all personal art, and all sincere life, and all passionate love a share in the dignity of the world .... If art is the expression of the abstract beauty of the person there are times when the person is the expression of the beauty that is beyond the world....

SISTER EILEEN *comes in dressed in the old green silk dress, which is cut low at the neck. She reaches the window just as the red morning light sweeps into the room.* COLUMB *is still looking out.*

SISTER EILEEN: (*In a low voice*) Columb I have come back to you.

COLUMB: (*Turning towards her*) You are infinitely beautiful, and you have done a great action. It is far more painful and noble to break through the creeds into life than to go down with them into the pit of abnegation .... You have had a double development, your soul has been growing like a germinating seed, and your mind like a moth within the mask of the chrysalis. Now the seedstalk has split the mask and you are born again ....[18] It is the beauty of your spirit that has set you free, and your emancipation is more exquisite than any that is possible for men who are redeemed by logic. You cannot tell me why you have changed, that is your glory. As the moth comes out of its mask to a new sphere of odour and colour and flight, so you have come out to live in a new sphere of beautiful love .... Listen to the tumult the birds are making in

16. Let it be as I truly desire, that all despise me since I have too often abandoned you, loving myself too faithfully. What is this, my God? What are we thinking of to refrain from giving love to creatures? . . .
17. Elder trees grow prolifically in Ireland, and especially in Wicklow.
18. 'Mask' is a technical term in entomology where it is 'the enlarged labium of the larval and pupal dragon-fly'. Columb's transference of it to seeds and seed-stalks links a more common sexual metaphor with the idea of truth-telling, unmasking.

the trees. That is our marriage hymn. Without love this world would be a loathsome sandhill, and a soul without love is not a great deal better .... Speak to me, I want to hear you, your voice will have a new cadence from today.

SISTER EILEEN: I seem to be in a dream that is wider than I am ... I hope God will forgive me. I cannot help it.

COLUMB: How many people ask to be forgiven for the most divine instant of their lives? The world of habit is diseased .... We will go out among the trees. The red glow is faded and day is come. Here is the ring that was the sorrowful heirloom of my uncle. Give me your hand .... I, the male power, have overcome with worship you, the credulous beauty, the reader of Sainte Theresa. From our harmonized discord new notes will rise. In the end we will assimilate with each other and grow senseless and old. We have incarnated God, and been a part of the world. That is enough. In the Name of the Summer, and The Sun, and the whole World, I wed you as my wife.[19]

They go out enlacés.[20]

19. This nature-religion echoes the benediction of orthodox Christianity, 'In the name of the Father, and the Son, and the Holy Ghost', even to the point where sun echoes son and whole echoes holy.
20. '[with arms] entwined'. Note the conclusive union through an exclusive (or at least excluding) language.

OSCAR WILDE

(1854-1900)

THE CANTERVILLE GHOST (1891)

[Many of Wilde's stories are concerned, however whimsically, with crime, its concealment or expiation, and this is no exception. Indeed, the presence of a political figure (albeit an ambassador) allows Wilde to air a certain radical disenchantment with established society. The story draws lightly on the author's experiences when travelling in America in 1882, and weaves in a host of literary allusions and half-allusions. Both these factors serve to illustrate the question of a tension, or even conflict, between different periods of time, a conflict resolved in the story by Virgina's laying the ghost to rest by carrying out the injunction inscribed in the words upon the window-pane. The theme of love conquering death runs through many of Wilde's fairy stories, where the peculiar sexlessness of love is less evident than here, in the person of fifteen-year-old engaged to be married yet also referred to as 'a little girl'.

The text used here is that edited by Isobel Murray (Oscar Wilde, *The Complete Shorter Fiction*, Oxford: Oxford University Press, 1979) whose annotations I have also drawn on in a few of my own.]

A Hylo-idealistic[1] Romance

I

When Mr. Hiram B. Otis, the American Minister, bought Canterville Chase,[2] every one told him he was doing a very foolish thing, as there was no doubt at all that the place was haunted. Indeed, Lord Canterville himself, who was a man of the most punctilious honour, had felt it his duty to mention the fact to Mr. Otis when they came to discuss terms.

'We have not cared to live in the place ourselves,' said Lord Canterville, 'since my grand-aunt, the Dowager Duchess of Bolton, was frightened into a fit, from which she never really recovered, by two skeleton hands being placed on her shoulders as she

1. Hylo-idealism is the philosophical theory that holds that 'reality belongs to the immediate object of belief as such.'
2. A chase is an area of unenclosed parkland that might be used in a steeplechase or some other kind of horserace. It is found occasionally in the names of large houses or estates; cf. Curragh Chase (home of the de Vere family) in County Limerick.

was dressing for dinner, and I feel bound to tell you, Mr. Otis, that the ghost has been seen by several living members of my family, as well as by the rector of the parish, the Rev. Augustus Dampier, who is a Fellow of King's College, Cambridge. After the unfortunate accident to the Duchess, none of our younger servants would stay with us, and Lady Canterville often got very little sleep at night, in consequence of the mysterious noises that came from the corridor and the library.'

'My Lord,' answered the Minister, 'I will take the furniture and the ghost at a valuation. I come from a modern country, where we have everything that money can buy; and with all our spry young fellows painting the Old World red, and carrying off your best actors and prima-donnas, I reckon that if there were such a thing as a ghost in Europe, we'd have it at home in a very short time in one of our public museums, or on the road as a show.'

'I fear that the ghost exists,' said Lord Canterville, smiling, 'though it may have resisted the overtures of your enterprising impresarios. It has been well known for three centuries, since 1584 in fact, and always makes its appearance before the death of any member of our family.'

'Well, so does the family doctor for that matter, Lord Canterville. But there is no such thing, sir, as a ghost, and I guess the laws of Nature are not going to be suspended for the British aristocracy.'

'You are certainly very natural in America,' answered Lord Canterville, who did not quite understand Mr. Otis's last observation, 'and if you don't mind a ghost in the house, it is all right. Only you must remember I warned you.'

A few weeks after this, the purchase was concluded, and at the close of the season the Minister and his family went down to Canterville Chase. Mrs. Otis, who, as Miss Lucretia R. Tappen, of West 53rd Street, had been a celebrated New York belle, was now a very handsome, middle-aged woman, with fine eyes, and a superb profile. Many American ladies on leaving their native land adopt an appearance of chronic ill-health, under the impression that it is a form of European refinement, but Mrs. Otis had never fallen into this error. She had a magnificent constitution, and a really wonderful amount of animal spirits. Indeed, in many respects, she was quite English, and was an excellent example of the fact that we have really everything in common with America nowadays, except, of course, language. Her eldest son, christened Washington by his parents in a moment of patriotism, which he never ceased to regret, was a fair-haired, rather good-looking young man, who had qualified himself for American diplomacy by leading the German[3] at the Newport Casino for three successive seasons, and even in London was well known as an excellent dancer. Gardenias and the peerage were his only weaknesses. Otherwise he was extremely sensible. Miss Virginia E. Otis was a little girl of fifteen, lithe and lovely as a fawn, and with a fine freedom in her large blue eyes. She was a wonderful amazon, and had once raced old Lord Bilton on her pony twice round the park, winning by a length and a half, just in front of the Achilles statue, to the huge delight of the young Duke of Cheshire, who proposed for her on the spot, and was sent back to Eton that very night by his guardians, in floods of tears. After Virginia came the twins, who were usually called 'The Stars and Stripes,' as they were always getting swished.[4] They were delightful boys, and with the exception of the worthy Minister the only true republicans of the family.

As Canterville Chase is seven miles from Ascot, the nearest railway station, Mr. Otis had telegraphed for a waggonette to meet them, and they started on their drive in high spirits. It was a lovely July evening, and the air was delicate with the scent of the pinewoods. Now and then they heard a wood pigeon brooding over its own sweet voice, or saw, deep in the rustling fern, the burnished breast of the pheasant. Little squirrels peered at them from the beech-trees as they went by, and the rabbits scudded away through the brushwood and over the mossy knolls, with their white tails in the air. As they entered the avenue of Canterville Chase, however, the sky became suddenly overcast with clouds, a curious stillness seemed to hold the atmosphere, a great flight of rooks passed silently over their heads, and, before they reached the house, some big drops of rain had fallen.

Standing on the steps to receive them was an old woman, neatly dressed in black silk, with a white cap and apron. This was Mrs. Umney, the housekeeper, whom Mrs. Otis, at Lady Canterville's earnest request, had consented to keep on in her

3. An intricate dance similar to the cotillion or quadrille. The Newport referred to is the fashionable seaside resort on Rhode Island.

4. flogged, whipped.

former position. She made them each a low curtsey as they alighted, and said in a quaint, old-fashioned manner, 'I bid you welcome to Canterville Chase.' Following her, they passed through the fine Tudor hall into the library, a long, low room, panelled in black oak, at the end of which was a large stained-glass window. Here they found tea laid out for them, and, after taking off their wraps, they sat down and began to look round, while Mrs. Umney waited on them.

Suddenly Mrs. Otis caught sight of a dull red stain on the floor just by the fireplace and, quite unconscious of what it really signified, said to Mrs. Umney, 'I am afraid something has been spilt there.'

'Yes, madam,' replied the old housekeeper in a low voice, 'blood has been spilt on that spot.'

'How horrid,' cried Mrs. Otis; 'I don't at all care for blood-stains in a sitting-room. It must be removed at once.'

The old woman smiled, and answered in the same low, mysterious voice, 'It is the blood of Lady Eleanore de Canterville, who was murdered on that very spot by her own husband, Sir Simon de Canterville, in 1575. Sir Simon survived her nine years, and disappeared suddenly under very mysterious circumstances. His body has never been discovered, but his guilty spirit still haunts the Chase. The blood-stain has been much admired by tourists and others, and cannot be removed.'

'That is all nonsense,' cried Washington Otis; 'Pinkerton's Champion Stain Remover and Paragon Detergent[5] will clean it up in no time,' and before the terrified housekeeper could interfere he had fallen upon his knees, and was rapidly scouring the floor with a small stick of what looked like a black cosmetic. In a few moments no trace of the blood-stain could be seen.

'I knew Pinkerton would do it,' he exclaimed triumphantly, as he looked round at his admiring family; but no sooner had he said these words than a terrible flash of lightning lit up the sombre room, a fearful peal of thunder made them all start to their feet, and Mrs. Umney fainted.

'What a monstrous climate!' said the American Minister calmly, as he lit a long cheroot. 'I guess the old country is so over-populated that they have not enough decent weather for everybody. I have always been of opinion that emigration is the only thing for England.'

'My dear Hiram,' cried Mrs. Otis, 'what can we do with a woman who faints?'

'Charge it to her like breakages,' answered the Minister; 'she won't faint after that;' and in a few moments Mrs. Umney certainly came to. There was no doubt, however, that she was extremely upset, and she sternly warned Mr. Otis to beware of some trouble coming to the house.

'I have seen things with my own eyes, sir,' she said, 'that would make any Christian's hair stand on end, and many and many a night I have not closed my eyes in sleep for the awful things that are done here.' Mr. Otis, however, and his wife warmly assured the honest soul that they were not afraid of ghosts, and, after invoking the blessings of Providence on her new master and mistress, and making arrangements for an increase of salary, the old housekeeper tottered off to her own room.

II

The storm raged fiercely all that night, but nothing of particular note ocurred. The next morning, however, when they came down to breakfast, they found the terrible stain of blood once again on the floor. 'I don't think it can be the fault of the Paragon Detergent,' said Washington, 'for I have tried it with everything. It must be the ghost.' He accordingly rubbed out the stain a second time, but the second morning it appeared again. The third morning also it was there, though the library had been locked up at night by Mr. Otis himself, and the key carried upstairs. The whole family were now quite interested; Mr. Otis began to suspect that he had been too dogmatic in his denial of the existence of ghosts, Mrs. Otis expressed her intention of joining the Psychical Society, and Washington prepared a long letter to Messrs. Myers and Podmore on the subject of the Permanence of Sanguineous Stains when connected with Crime. That night all doubts about the objective existence of phantasmata were removed for ever.

The day had been warm and sunny; and, in the cool of the evening, the whole family went out to drive. They did not return home till nine o'clock,

5. Wilde here echoes the name of Pinkerton's National Detective Agency, founded in Chicago in 1850; in fact Allan Pinkerton (1819-84) was Scottish by birth, a radical Chartist in his early days, a campaigner against slavery in the United States and an organizer of the Union's secret service in the early days of the American Civil War.

when they had a light supper. The conversation in no way turned upon ghosts, so there were not even those primary conditions of receptive expectation which so often precede the presentation of psychical phenomena. The subjects discussed, as I have since learned from Mr. Otis, were merely such as form the ordinary conversation of cultured Americans of the better class, such as the immense superiority of Miss Fanny Davenport over Sara Bernhardt[6] as an actress; the difficulty of obtaining green corn, buckwheat cakes, and hominy,[7] even in the best English houses; the importance of Boston in the development of the world-soul;[8] the advantages of the baggage check system in railway travelling; and the sweetness of the New York accent as compared to the London drawl. No mention at all was made of the supernatural, nor was Sir Simon de Canterville alluded to in any way. At eleven o'clock the family retired, and by half-past all the lights were out. Some time after, Mr. Otis was awakened by a curious noise in the corridor, outside his room. It sounded like the clank of metal, and seemed to be coming nearer every moment. He got up at once, struck a match, and looked at the time. It was exactly one o'clock. He was quite calm, and felt his pulse, which was not at all feverish. The strange noise still continued, and with it he heard distinctly the sound of footsteps. He put on his slippers, took a small oblong phial out of his dressing-case, and opened the door. Right in front of him he saw, in the wan moonlight, an old man of terrible aspect. His eyes were as red burning coals; long grey hair fell over his shoulders in matted coils; his garments, which were of antique cut, were soiled and ragged, and from his wrists and ankles hung heavy manacles and rusty gyves.[9]

'My dear sir,' said Mr. Otis, 'I really must insist on your oiling those chains, and have brought you for that purpose a small bottle of the Tammany Rising Sun Lubricator.[10] It is said to be completely efficacious upon one application, and there are several testimonials to that effect on the wrapper from some of our most eminent native divines. I shall leave it here for you by the bedroom candles, and will be happy to supply you with more should you require it.' With these words the United States Minister laid the bottle down on a marble table, and, closing his door, retired to rest.

For a moment the Canterville ghost stood quite motionless in natural indignation; then, dashing the bottle violently upon the polished floor, he fled down the corridor, uttering hollow groans, and emitting a ghastly green light. Just, however, as he reached the top of the great oak staircase, a door was flung open, two little white-robed figures appeared, and a large pillow whizzed past his head! There was evidently no time to be lost, so, hastily adopting the Fourth Dimension of Space as a means of escape, he vanished through the wainscoting, and the house became quite quiet.

On reaching a small secret chamber in the left wing, he leaned up against a moonbeam to recover his breath, and began to try and realise his position. Never, in a brilliant and uninterrupted career of three hundred years, had he been so grossly insulted. He thought of the Dowager Duchess, whom he had frightened into a fit as she stood before the glass in her lace and diamonds; of the four housemaids, who had gone off into hysterics when he merely grinned at them through the curtains of one of the spare bedrooms; of the rector of the parish, whose candle he had blown out as he was coming late one night from the library, and who had been under the care of Sir William Gull ever since, a perfect martyr to nervous disorders; and of old Madame de Tremouillac, who, having wakened up one morning early and seen a skeleton seated in an armchair by the fire reading her diary, had been confined to her bed for six weeks with an attack of brain fever, and, on her recovery, had become reconciled to the Church, and broken off her connection with that notorious sceptic Monsieur de Voltaire.[11] He remembered the terrible night when the wicked Lord Canterville was found choking in his dressing-room, with the knave of diamonds half-way down his throat, and confessed, just before he died, that he had cheated Charles James Fox out of £50,000 at Crockford's[12] by means of that very card, and swore that the ghost had made

6. Fanny Davenport (1850-98) was an American actress, but she never rivalled the French actress Sarah Bernhardt (1844-1923), regarded as one of the finest tragedians of all time.
7. Originally a red Indian dish, made of coarsely ground maize kernels.
8. Boston was the intellectual centre of the Transcendentalist Movement in the mid-nineteenth century.
9. fetters, shackles.
10. Tammany echoes Tammany Hall, the New York headquarters of the Democratic party and synonymous with political corruption.
11. The name assumed by François-Marie Arouet (1694-1778), French philosopher.
12. Charles James Fox (1749-1806), a liberal Whig statesman. William Crockford (1775-1844) established his famous London gambling club twenty-one years after Fox's death.

him swallow it. All his great achievements came back to him again, from the butler who had shot himself in the pantry because he had seen a green hand tapping at the window pane, to the beautiful Lady Stutfield, who was always obliged to wear a black velvet band round her throat to hide the mark of five fingers burnt upon her white skin, and who drowned herself at last in the carp-pond at the end of the King's Walk. With the enthusiastic egotism of the true artist he went over his most celebrated performances, and smiled bitterly to himself as he recalled to mind his last appearance as 'Red Reuben, or the Strangled Babe,' his *début* as 'Gaunt Gibeon, the Blood-sucker of Bexley Moor,' and the *furore* he had excited one lovely June evening by merely playing ninepins with his own bones upon the lawn-tennis ground. And after all this, some wretched modern Americans were to come and offer him the Rising Sun Lubricator, and throw pillows at his head! It was quite unbearable. Besides, no ghost in history had ever been treated in this manner. Accordingly, he determined to have vengeance, and remained till daylight in an attitude of deep thought.

III

The next morning, when the Otis family met at breakfast, they discussed the ghost at some length. The United States Minister was naturally a little annoyed to find that his present had not been accepted. 'I have no wish,' he said, 'to do the ghost any personal injury, and I must say that, considering the length of time he has been in the house, I don't think it is at all polite to throw pillows at him' — a very just remark, at which, I am sorry to say, the twins burst into shouts of laughter. 'Upon the other hand,' he continued, 'if he really declines to use the Rising Sun Lubricator, we shall have to take his chains from him. It would be quite impossible to sleep, with such a noise going on outside the bedrooms.'

For the rest of the week, however, they were undisturbed, the only thing that excited any attention being the continual renewal of the blood-stain on the library floor. This certainly was very strange, as the door was always locked at night by Mr. Otis, and the windows kept closely barred. The chameleon-like colour, also, of the stain excited a good deal of comment. Some mornings it was a dull (almost Indian) red, then it would be vermilion, then a rich purple, and once when they came down for family prayers, according to the simple rites of the Free American Reformed Episcopalian Church, they found it a bright emerald-green. These kaleidoscopic changes naturally amused the party very much, and bets on the subject were freely made every evening. The only person who did not enter into the joke was little Virginia, who, for some unexplained reason, was always a good deal distressed at the sight of the blood-stain, and very nearly cried the morning it was emerald-green.

The second appearance of the ghost was on Sunday night. Shortly after they had gone to bed they were suddenly alarmed by a fearful crash in the hall. Rushing downstairs, they found that a large suit of old armour had become detached from its stand, and had fallen on the stone floor, while, seated in a high-backed chair, was the Canterville ghost, rubbing his knees with an expression of acute agony on his face. The twins, having brought their pea-shooters with them, at once discharged two pellets on him, with that accuracy of aim which can only be attained by long and careful practice on a writing-master, while the United States Minister covered him with his revolver, and called upon him, in accordance with Californian etiquette, to hold up his hands! The ghost started up with a wild shriek of rage, and swept through them like a mist, extinguishing Washington Otis's candle as he passed, and so leaving them all in total darkness. On reaching the top of the staircase he recovered himself, and determined to give his celebrated peal of demoniac laughter. This he had on more than one occasion found extremely useful. It was said to have turned Lord Raker's wig grey in a single night, and had certainly made three of Lady Canterville's French governesses give warning before their month was up. He accordingly laughed his most horrible laugh, till the old vaulted roof rang and rang again, but hardly had the fearful echo died away when a door opened, and Mrs. Otis came out in a light blue dressing-gown. 'I am afraid you are far from well,' she said, 'and have brought you a bottle of Dr. Dobell's tincture. If it is indigestion, you will find it a most excellent remedy.' The ghost glared at her in fury, and began at once to make preparations for turning himself into a large black dog, an accomplishment for which he was justly renowned, and to which the family doctor always attributed the permanent idiocy of Lord

Canterville's uncle, the Hon. Thomas Horton.[13] The sound of approaching footsteps, however, made him hesitate in his fell purpose, so he contented himself with becoming faintly phosphorescent, and vanished with a deep churchyard groan, just as the twins had come up to him.

On reaching his room he entirely broke down, and became a prey to the most violent agitation. The vulgarity of the twins, and the gross materialism of Mrs. Otis, were naturally extremely annoying, but what really distressed him most was, that he had been unable to wear the suit of mail. He had hoped that even modern Americans would be thrilled by the sight of a Spectre In Armour, if for no more sensible reason, at least out of respect for their national poet Longfellow,[14] over whose graceful and attractive poetry he himself had whiled away many a weary hour when the Cantervilles were up in town. Besides, it was his own suit. He had worn it with great success at the Kenilworth tournament, and had been highly complimented on it by no less a person than the Virgin Queen herself.[15] Yet when he had put it on, he had been completely overpowered by the weight of the huge breastplate and steel casque, and had fallen heavily on the stone pavement, barking[16] both his knees severely, and bruising the knuckles of his right hand.

For some days after this he was extremely ill, and hardly stirred out of his room at all, except to keep the blood-stain in proper repair. However, by taking great care of himself, he recovered, and resolved to make a third attempt to frighten the United States Minister and his family. He selected Friday, the 17th of August, for his appearance, and spent most of that day in looking over his wardrobe, ultimately deciding in favour of a large slouched hat with a red feather, a winding-sheet frilled at the wrists and neck, and a rusty dagger. Towards evening a violent storm of rain came on, and the wind was so high that all the windows and doors in the old house shook and rattled. In fact, it was just such weather as he loved. His plan of action was this. He was to make his way quietly to Washington Otis's room, gibber at him from the foot of the bed, and stab himself three times in the throat to the sound of low music. He bore Washington a special grudge, being quite aware that it was he who was in the habit of removing the famous Canterville blood-stain, by means of Pinkerton's Paragon Detergent. Having reduced the reckless and foolhardy youth to a condition of abject terror, he was then to proceed to the room occupied by the United States Minister and his wife, and there to place a clammy hand on Mrs. Otis's forehead, while he hissed into her trembling husband's ear the awful secrets of the charnel-house. With regard to little Virginia, he had not quite made up his mind. She had never insulted him in any way, and was pretty and gentle. A few hollow groans from the wardrobe, he thought, would be more than sufficient, or, if that failed to wake her, he might grabble at the counterpane with palsy-twitching fingers. As for the twins, he was quite determined to teach them a lesson. The first thing to be done was, of course, to sit upon their chests, so as to produce the stifling sensation of nightmare. Then, as their beds were quite close to each other, to stand between them in the form of a green, icy-cold corpse, till they became paralysed with fear, and finally, to throw off the winding-sheet, and crawl round the room, with white, bleached bones and one rolling eyeball, in the character of 'Dumb Daniel, or the Suicide's Skeleton,' a *rôle* in which he had on more than one occasion produced a great effect, and which he considered quite equal to his famous part of 'Martin the Maniac, or the Masked Mystery.'

At half-past ten he heard the family going to bed. For some time he was disturbed by wild shrieks of laughter from the twins, who, with the light-hearted gaiety of schoolboys, were evidently amusing themselves before they retired to rest, but at a quarter past eleven all was still, and, as midnight sounded, he sallied forth. The owl beat against the window panes, the raven croaked from the old yew-tree, and the wind wandered moaning round the house like a lost soul; but the Otis family slept unconscious of their doom, and high above the rain and storm he could hear the steady snoring of the Minister for the United States. He stepped stealthily out of the wainscoting, with an evil smile

13. Wilde may be poking fun at William Thomas Horton (1864-1919), an English devotee of mystical and psychical wisdom, and a friend of Yeats's. There was also Thomas Horton (died 1649), one of the regicides who signed Charles I's death-warrant: he died in Ireland remarkably soon after the king's execution.

14. Henry Wadsworth Longfellow (1807-82), the American poet whose 'The Skeleton in Armour' (1841) is one of Wilde's sources (or targets).

15. A satiric reference to the extravagant and absurd 'medieval' tournament at Kenilworth Castle, Warwickshire in 1886. It was a spectacular example of the Victorian blend of the pseudo-traditional and patriotic elements.

16. Scraping skin off.

on his cruel, wrinkled mouth, and the moon hid her face in a cloud as he stole past the great oriel window,[17] where his own arms and those of his murdered wife were blazoned in azure and gold. On and on he glided, like an evil shadow, the very darkness seeming to loathe him as he passed. Once he thought he heard something call, and stopped; but it was only the baying of a dog from the Red Farm, and he went on, muttering strange sixteenth-century curses, and ever and anon brandishing the rusty dagger in the midnight air. Finally he reached the corner of the passage that led to luckless Washington's room. For a moment he paused there, the wind blowing his long grey locks about his head, and twisting into grotesque and fantastic folds the nameless horror of the dead man's shroud. Then the clock struck the quarter, and he felt the time was come. He chuckled to himself, and turned the corner; but no sooner had he done so, than, with a piteous wail of terror, he fell back, and hid his blanched face in his long, bony hands. Right in front of him was standing a horrible spectre, motionless as a carven image, and monstrous as a madman's dream! Its head was bald and burnished; its face round, and fat, and white; and hideous laughter seemed to have writhed its features into an eternal grin. From the eyes streamed rays of scarlet light, the mouth was a wide well of fire, and a hideous garment, like to his own, swathed with its silent snows the Titan form. On its breast was a placard with strange writing in antique characters, some scroll of shame it seemed, some record of wild sins, some awful calendar of crime, and, with its right hand, it bore aloft a falchion[18] of gleaming steel.

Never having seen a ghost before, he naturally was terribly frightened, and, after a second hasty glance at the awful phantom, he fled back to his room, tripping up in his long winding sheet as he sped down the corridor, and finally dropping the rusty dagger into the Minister's jack-boots, where it was found in the morning by the butler. Once in the privacy of his own apartment, he flung himself down on a small pallet-bed, and hid his face under the clothes. After a time, however, the brave old Canterville spirit asserted itself, and he determined to go and speak to the other ghost as soon as it was daylight. Accordingly, just as the dawn was touching the hills with silver, he returned towards the spot where he had first laid eyes on the grisly phantom, feeling that, after all, two ghosts were better than one, and that, by the aid of his new friend, he might safely grapple with the twins. On reaching the spot, however, a terrible sight met his gaze. Something had evidently happened to the spectre, for the light had entirely faded from its hollow eyes, the gleaming falchion had fallen from its hand, and it was leaning up against the wall in a strained and uncomfortable attitude. He rushed forward and seized it in his arms, when, to his horror, the head slipped off and rolled on the floor, the body assumed a recumbent posture, and he found himself clasping a white dimity[19] bedcurtain, with a sweeping-brush, a kitchen cleaver, and a hollow turnip lying at his feet! Unable to understand this curious transformation, he clutched the placard with feverish haste, and there, in the grey morning light, he read these fearful words:

YE OTIS GHOSTE.

Ye Onlie True and Originale Spook.

Beward of Ye Imitationes.

All others are Counterfeite.

The whole thing flashed across him. He had been tricked, foiled, and outwitted! The old Canterville look came to his eyes; he ground his toothless gums together; and, raising his withered hands high above his head, swore, according to the picturesque phraseology of the antique school, that when Chanticleer[20] had sounded twice his merry horn, deeds of blood would be wrought, and Murder walk abroad with silent feet.

Hardly had he finished this awful oath when, from the red-tiled roof of a distant homestead, a cock crew. He laughed a long, low, bitter laugh, and waited. Hour after hour he waited, but the cock, for some strange reason, did not crow again. Finally, at half-past seven, the arrival of the housemaids made

17. A bay window.
18. A short and slightly curved medieval sword.
19. A cotton fabric with woven stripes or squares.
20. The traditional name for the crowing cock in Chaucer's 'The Nun's Priest's Tale'.

him give up his fearful vigil, and he stalked back to his room, thinking of his vain oath and baffled purpose. There he consulted several books of ancient chivalry, of which he was exceedingly fond, and found that, on every occasion on which this oath had been used, Chanticleer had always crowed a second time. 'Perdition seize the naughty fowl,'[21] he muttered, 'I have seen the day when, with my stout spear, I would have run him through the gorge, and made him crow for me an 'twere in death!' He then retired to a comfortable lead coffin, and stayed there till evening.

IV

The next day the ghost was very weak and tired. The terrible excitement of the last four weeks was beginning to have its effect. His nerves were completely shattered, and he started at the slightest noise. For five days he kept his room, and at last made up his mind to give up the point of the blood-stain on the library floor. If the Otis family did not want it, they clearly did not deserve it. They were evidently people on a low, material plane of existence, and quite incapable of appreciating the symbolic value of sensuous phenomena. The question of phantasmic apparitions, and the development of astral bodies, was of course quite a different matter, and really not under his control. It was his solemn duty to appear in the corridor once a week, and to gibber from the large oriel window on the first and third Wednesdays in every month, and he did not see how he could honourably escape from his obligations. It is quite true that his life had been very evil, but, upon the other hand, he was most conscientious in all things connected with the supernatural. For the next three Saturdays, accordingly, he traversed the corridor as usual between midnight and three o'clock, taking every possible precaution against being either heard or seen. He removed his boots, trod as lightly as possible on the old worm-eaten boards, wore a large black velvet cloak, and was careful to use the Rising Sun Lubricator for oiling his chains. I am bound to acknowledge that it was with a good deal of difficulty that he brought himself to adopt this last mode of protection. However, one night, while the family were at dinner, he slipped into Mr. Otis's bedroom and carried off the bottle. He felt a little humiliated at first, but afterwards was sensible enough to see that there was a great deal to be said for the invention, and, to a certain degree, it served his purpose. Still, in spite of everything, he was not left unmolested. Strings were continually being stretched across the corridor, over which he tripped in the dark, and on one occasion, while dressed for the part of 'Black Isaac, or the Huntsman of Hogley Woods,' he met with a severe fall, through treading on a butter-slide, which the twins had constructed from the entrance of the Tapestry Chamber to the top of the oak staircase. This last insult so enraged him, that he resolved to make one final effort to assert his dignity and social position, and determined to visit the insolent young Etonians the next night in his celebrated character of 'Reckless Rupert, or the Headless Earl.'

He had not appeared in this disguise for more than seventy years: in fact, not since he had so frightened pretty Lady Barbara Modish by means of it, that she suddenly broke off her engagement with the present Lord Canterville's grandfather, and ran away to Gretna Green[22] with handsome Jack Castletown, declaring that nothing in the world would induce her to marry into a family that allowed such a horrible phantom to walk up and down the terrace at twilight. Poor Jack was afterwards shot in a duel by Lord Canterville on Wandsworth Common, and Lady Barbara died of a broken heart at Tunbridge Wells before the year was out, so, in every way, it had been a great success. It was, however, an extremely difficult 'make-up,' if I may use such a theatrical expression in connection with one of the greatest mysteries of the supernatural, or, to employ a more scientific term, the higher-natural world, and it took him fully three hours to make his preparations. At last everything was ready, and he was very pleased with his appearance. The big leather riding-boots that went with the dress were just a little too large for him, and he could only find one of the two horse-pistols, but, on the whole, he was quite satisfied, and at a quarter past one he glided out of the wainscoting and crept down the corridor. On

21. 'Ruin seize thee' opens Thomas Gray's 'The Bard', and 'perdition catch my soul' is from Shakespeare (*Othello*, III. 3. 90). Much of the landscape description of the story is of course similarly constructed from gothic and sensationalist clichés.

22. A village in Scotland, on the border with England, where eloping couples were married by the blacksmith from 1754 until 1940, when such marriages became illegal.

reaching the room occupied by the twins, which I should mention was called the Blue Bed Chamber, on account of the colour of its hangings, he found the door just ajar. Wishing to make an effective entrance, he flung it wide open, when a heavy jug of water fell right down on him, wetting him to the skin, and just missing his left shoulder by a couple of inches. At the same moment he heard stifled shrieks of laughter proceeding from the four-post bed. The shock to his nervous system was so great that he fled back to his room as hard as he could go, and the next day he was laid up with a severe cold. The only thing that at all consoled him in the whole affair was the fact that he had not brought his head with him, for, had he done so, the consequences might have been very serious.

He now gave up all hope of ever frightening this rude American family, and contented himself, as a rule, with creeping about the passages in list[23] slippers, with a thick red muffler round his throat for fear of draughts, and a small arquebuse,[24] in case he should be attacked by the twins. The final blow he received occurred on the 19th of September. He had gone downstairs to the great entrance-hall, feeling sure that there, at any rate, he would be quite unmolested, and was amusing himself by making satirical remarks on the large Saroni[25] photographs of the United States Minister and his wife, which had now taken the place of the Canterville family pictures. He was simply but neatly clad in a long shroud, spotted with churchyard mould, had tied up his jaw with a strip of yellow linen, and carried a small lantern and a sexton's spade. In fact, he was dressed for the character of 'Jonas the Graveless, or the Corpse-Snatcher of Chertsey Barn,' one of his most remarkable impersonations, and one which the Cantervilles had every reason to remember, as it was the real origin of their quarrel with their neighbour, Lord Rufford. It was about a quarter past two o'clock in the morning, and, as far as he could ascertain, no one was stirring. As he was strolling towards the library, however, to see if there were any traces left of the blood-stain, suddenly there leaped out on him from a dark corner two figures, who waved their arms wildly above their heads, and shrieked out 'BOO!' in his ear.

Seized with a panic, which, under the circumstances, was only natural, he rushed for the staircase, but found Washington Otis waiting for him there with the big garden-syringe; and being thus hemmed in by his enemies on every side, and driven almost to bay, he vanished into the great iron stove, which, fortunately for him, was not lit, and had to make his way home through the flues and chimneys, arriving at his own room in a terrible state of dirt, disorder, and despair.

After this he was not seen again on any nocturnal expedition. The twins lay in wait for him on several occasions, and strewed the passages with nutshells every night to the great annoyance of their parents and the servants, but it was of no avail. It was quite evident that his feelings were so wounded that he would not appear. Mr. Otis consequently resumed his great work on the history of the Democratic Party, on which he had been engaged for some years; Mrs. Otis organised a wonderful clam-bake,[26] which amazed the whole country; the boys took to lacrosse, euchre,[27] poker, and other American national games; and Virginia rode about the lanes on her pony, accompanied by the young Duke of Cheshire, who had come to spend the last week of his holidays at Canterville Chase. It was generally assumed that the ghost had gone away, and, in fact, Mr. Otis wrote a letter to that effect to Lord Canterville, who, in reply, expressed his great pleasure at the news, and sent his best congratulations to the Minister's worthy wife.

The Otises, however, were deceived, for the ghost was still in the house, and though now almost an invalid, was by no means ready to let matters rest, particularly as he heard that among the guests was the young Duke of Cheshire, whose grand-uncle, Lord Francis Stilton, had once bet a hundred guineas with Colonel Carbury that he would play dice with the Canterville ghost, and was found the next morning lying on the floor of the card-room in such a helpless paralytic state, that though he lived on to a great age, he was never able to say anything again but 'Double Sixes.' The story was well known at the time, though, of course, out of respect to the feelings of the two noble families, every attempt was made to hush it up; and a full

23. woollen.
24. A long-barrelled gun.
25. When Wilde was in New York, he posed (twenty times) for the photographer, Napoleon Sarony.
26. An American outdoor social gathering at which clams and fish are eaten.
27. An American card game.

account of all the circumstances connected with it will be found in the third volume of Lord Tattle's *Recollections of the Prince Regent and his Friends*. The ghost, then, was naturally very anxious to show that he had not lost his influence over the Stiltons, with whom, indeed, he was distantly connected, his own first cousin having been married *en secondes noces*[28] to the Sieur de Bulkeley, from whom, as every one knows, the Dukes of Cheshire are lineally descended. Accordingly, he made arrangements for appearing to Virginia's little lover in his celebrated impersonation of 'The Vampire Monk, or, the Bloodless Benedictine,' a performance so horrible that when old Lady Startup saw it, which she did on one fatal New Year's Eve, in the year 1764, she went off into the most piercing shrieks, which culminated in violent apoplexy, and died in three days, after disinheriting the Cantervilles, who were her nearest relations, and leaving all her money to her London apothecary. At the last moment, however, his terror of the twins prevented his leaving his room, and the little Duke slept in peace under the great feathered canopy in the Royal Bedchamber, and dreamed of Virginia.

V

A few days after this, Virginia and her curly-haired cavalier went out riding on Brockley meadows, where she tore her habit so badly in getting through a hedge, that, on their return home, she made up her mind to go up by the back staircase so as not to be seen. As she was running past the Tapestry Chamber, the door of which happened to be open, she fancied she saw some one inside, and thinking it was her mother's maid, who sometimes used to bring her work there, looked in to ask her to mend her habit. To her immense surprise, however, it was the Canterville Ghost himself! He was sitting by the window, watching the ruined gold of the yellowing trees fly through the air, and the red leaves dancing madly down the long avenue.[29] His head was leaning on his hand, and his whole attitude was one of extreme depression. Indeed, so forlorn, and so much out of repair did he look, that little Virginia, whose first idea had been to run away and lock herself in her room, was filled with pity, and determined to try and comfort him. So light was her footfall, and so deep his melancholy, that he was not aware of her presence till she spoke to him.

'I am so sorry for you,' she said, 'but my brothers are going back to Eton tomorrow, and then, if you behave yourself, no one will annoy you.'

'It is absurd asking me to behave myself,' he answered, looking round in astonishment at the pretty little girl who had ventured to address him, 'quite absurd. I must rattle my chains, and groan through keyholes, and walk about at night, if that is what you mean. It is my only reason for existing.'

'It is no reason at all for existing, and you know you have been very wicked. Mrs. Umney told us, the first day we arrived here, that you had killed your wife.'

'Well, I quite admit it,' said the Ghost petulantly, 'but it was a purely family matter, and concerned no one else.'

'It is very wrong to kill any one,' said Virginia, who at times had a sweet Puritan gravity, caught from some old New England ancestor.

'Oh, I hate the cheap severity of abstract ethics! My wife was very plain, never had my ruffs properly starched, and knew nothing about cookery. Why, there was a buck I had shot in Hogley Woods, a magnificent pricket,[30] and do you know how she had it sent up to table? However, it is no matter now, for it is all over, and I don't think it was very nice of her brothers to starve me to death, though I did kill her.'

'Starve you to death? Oh, Mr. Ghost, I mean Sir Simon, are you hungry? I have a sandwich in my case. Would you like it?'

'No, thank you, I never eat anything now; but it is very kind of you, all the same, and you are much nicer than the rest of your horrid, rude, vulgar, dishonest family.'

'Stop!' cried Virginia stamping her foot, 'it is you who are rude, and horrid, and vulgar, and as for dishonesty, you know you stole the paints out of my box to try and furbish up that ridiculous blood-stain in the library. First you took all my reds, including the vermilion, and I couldn't do any more sunsets, then you took the emerald-green and the chrome-yellow, and finally I had nothing left but indigo and Chinese white, and could only do moonlight scenes, which are always depressing to look at, and not at all easy to paint. I never told on

28. in a second marriage.

29. Echoes of Tennyson's 'Maud' and Coleridge's 'Christabel' occur in this sentence.

30. A two-year-old male fallow deer.

you, though I was very much annoyed, and it was most ridiculous, the whole thing; for who ever heard of emerald-green blood?'

'Well, really,' said the Ghost, rather meekly, 'what was I to do? It is a very difficult thing to get real blood nowadays, and, as your brother began it all with his Paragon Detergent, I certainly saw no reason why I should not have your paints. As for colour, that is always a matter of taste: the Cantervilles have blue blood, for instance, the very bluest in England; but I know you Americans don't care for things of this kind.'

'You know nothing about it, and the best thing you can do is to emigrate and improve your mind. My father will be only too happy to give you a free passage, and though there is a heavy duty on spirits of every kind, there will be no difficulty about the Custom House, as the officers are all Democrats. Once in New York, you are sure to be a great success. I know lots of people there who would give a hundred thousand dollars to have a grandfather, and much more than that to have a family ghost.'

'I don't think I should like America.'

'I suppose because we have no ruins and no curiosities,' said Virginia satirically.

'No ruins! no curiosities!' answered the Ghost; 'you have your navy and your manners.'

'Good evening; I will go and ask papa to get the twins an extra week's holiday.'

'Please don't go, Miss Virginia,' he cried; 'I am so lonely and so unhappy, and I really don't know what to do. I want to go to sleep and I cannot.'

'That's quite absurd! You have merely to go to bed and blow out the candle. It is very difficult sometimes to keep awake, especially at church, but there is no difficulty at all about sleeping. Why, even babies know how to do that, and they are not very clever.'

'I have not slept for three hundred years,' he said sadly, and Virginia's beautiful blue eyes opened in wonder; 'for three hundred years I have not slept, and I am so tired.'

Virginia grew quite grave, and her little lips trembled like rose-leaves. She came towards him, and kneeling down at his side, looked up into his old withered face.

'Poor, poor Ghost,' she murmured; 'have you no place where you can sleep?'

'Far away beyond the pinewoods,' he answered, in a low dreamy voice, 'there is a little garden. There the grass grows long and deep, there are the great white stars of the hemlock flower, there the nightingale sings all night long. All night long he sings, and the cold, crystal moon looks down, and the yew-tree spreads out its giant arms over the sleepers.'

Virginia's eyes grew dim with tears, and she hid her face in her hands.

'You mean the Garden of Death,' she whispered.

'Yes, Death. Death must be so beautiful. To lie in the soft brown earth, with the grasses waving above one's head, and listen to silence. To have no yesterday, and no tomorrow. To forget time, to forgive life, to be at peace. You can help me. You can open for me the portals of Death's house, for Love is always with you, and Love is stronger than Death[31] is.'

Virginia trembled, a cold shudder ran through her, and for a few moments there was silence. She felt as if she was in a terrible dream.

Then the Ghost spoke again, and his voice sounded like the sighing of the wind.

'Have you ever read the old prophecy on the library window?'

'Oh, often,' cried the little girl, looking up; 'I know it quite well. It is painted in curious black letters, and it is difficult to read. There are only six lines:

When a golden girl can win
Prayer from out the lips of sin,
When the barren almond bears,
And a little child gives away its tears,
Then shall all the house be still
And peace come to Canterville.

But I don't know what they mean.'

'They mean,' he said sadly, 'that you must weep with me for my sins, because I have no tears, and pray with me for my soul, because I have no faith, and then, if you have always been sweet, and good, and gentle, the Angel of Death will have mercy on me. You will see fearful shapes in darkness, and wicked voices will whisper in your ear, but they will not harm you, for against the purity of a little child the powers of Hell cannot prevail.'

Virginia made no answer, and the Ghost wrung his hands in wild despair as he looked down at her bowed golden head. Suddenly she stood up, very

31. Biblical echoes: cf. Song of Solomon 8. 6-7.

pale, and with a strange light in her eyes. 'I am not afraid,' she said firmly, 'and I will ask the Angel to have mercy on you.'

He rose from his seat with a faint cry of joy, and taking her hand bent over it with old-fashioned grace and kissed it. His fingers were as cold as ice, and his lips burned like fire, but Virginia did not falter, as he led her across the dusky room. On the faded green tapestry were broidered little huntsmen. They blew their tasselled horns and with their tiny hands waved to her to go back. 'Go back! little Virginia,' they cried, 'go back!' but the Ghost clutched her hand more tightly, and she shut her eyes against them. Horrible animals with lizard tails, and goggle eyes, blinked at her from the carven chimney-piece, and murmured 'Beware! little Virginia, beware! we may never see you again,' but the Ghost glided on more swiftly, and Virginia did not listen. When they reached the end of the room he stopped, and muttered some words she could not understand. She opened her eyes, and saw the wall slowly fading away like a mist, and a great black cavern in front of her. A bitter cold wind swept round them, and she felt something pulling at her dress. 'Quick, quick,' cried the Ghost, 'or it will be too late,' and, in a moment, the wainscoting had closed behind them, and the Tapestry Chamber was empty.

VI

About ten minutes later, the bell rang for tea, and, as Virginia did not come down, Mrs. Otis sent up one of the footmen to tell her. After a little time he returned and said that he could not find Miss Virginia anywhere. As she was in the habit of going out to the garden every evening to get flowers for the dinner-table, Mrs. Otis was not at all alarmed at first, but when six o'clock struck, and Virginia did not appear, she became really agitated, and sent the boys out to look for her, while she herself and Mr. Otis searched every room in the house. At half-past six the boys came back and said that they could find no trace of their sister anywhere. They were all now in the greatest state of excitement, and did not know what to do, when Mr. Otis suddenly remembered that, some few days before, he had given a band of gipsies permission to camp in the park. He accordingly at once set off for Blackfell Hollow, where he knew they were, accompanied by his eldest son and two of the farm-servants. The little Duke of Cheshire, who was perfectly frantic with anxiety, begged hard to be allowed to go too, but Mr. Otis would not allow him, as he was afraid there might be a scuffle. On arriving at the spot, however, he found that the gipsies had gone, and it was evident that their departure had been rather sudden, as the fire was still burning, and some plates were lying on the grass. Having sent off Washington and the two men to scour the district, he ran home, and despatched telegrams to all the police inspectors in the country, telling them to look out for a little girl who had been kidnapped by tramps or gipsies. He then ordered his horse to be brought round, and, after insisting on his wife and the three boys sitting down to dinner, rode off down the Ascot road with a groom. He had hardly, however, gone a couple of miles, when he heard somebody galloping after him, and, looking round, saw the little Duke coming up on his pony, with his face very flushed and no hat. 'I'm awfully sorry, Mr. Otis,' gasped out the boy, 'but I can't eat any dinner as long as Virginia is lost. Please, don't be angry with me; if you had let us be engaged last year, there would never have been all this trouble. You won't send me back, will you? I can't go! I won't go!'

The Minister could not help smiling at the handsome young scapegrace,[32] and was a good deal touched at his devotion to Virginia, so leaning down from his horse, he patted him kindly on the shoulders, and said, 'Well, Cecil, if won't go back I suppose you must come with me, but I must get you a hat at Ascot.'

'Oh, bother my hat! I want Virginia!' cried the little Duke, laughing, and they galloped on to the railway station. There Mr. Otis inquired of the station-master if any one answering to the description of Virginia had been seen on the platform, but could get no news of her. The station-master, however, wired up and down the line, and assured him that a strict watch would be kept for her, and, after having bought a hat for the little Duke from a linen-draper, who was just putting up his shutters, Mr. Otis rode off to Bexley, a village about four miles away, which he was told was a well-known haunt of the gipsies, as there was a large common next to it. Here they roused up the rural policeman, but could get no information from him, and, after riding all over the common, they turned their horses' heads

32. An incorrigible scamp.

homewards, and reached the Chase about eleven o'clock, dead-tired and almost heart-broken. They found Washington and twins waiting for them at the gate-house with lanterns, as the avenue was very dark. Not the slightest trace of Virginia had been discovered. The gipsies had been caught on Brockley meadows, but she was not with them, and they had explained their sudden departure by saying that they had mistaken the date of Chorton Fair, and had gone off in a hurry for fear they might be late. Indeed, they had been quite distressed at hearing of Virginia's disappearance, as they were very grateful to Mr. Otis for having allowed them to camp in his park, and four of their number had stayed behind to help in the search. The carp-pond had been dragged, and the whole Chase thoroughly gone over, but without any result. It was evident that, for that night at any rate, Virginia was lost to them; and it was in a state of the deepest depression that Mr. Otis and the boys walked up to the house, the groom following behind with the two horses and the pony. In the hall they found a group of frightened servants, and lying on a sofa in the library was poor Mrs. Otis, almost out of her mind with terror and anxiety, and having her forehead bathed with eau-de-cologne by the old housekeeper. Mr. Otis at once insisted on her having something to eat, and ordered up supper for the whole party. It was a melancholy meal, as hardly any one spoke, and even the twins were awestruck and subdued, as they were very fond of their sister. When they had finished, Mr. Otis, in spite of the entreaties of the little Duke, ordered them all to bed, saying that nothing more could be done that night, and that he would telegraph in the morning to Scotland Yard[33] for some detectives to be sent down immediately. Just as they were passing out of the dining-room, midnight began to boom from the clock tower, and when the last stroke sounded they heard a crash and a sudden shrill cry; a dreadful peal of thunder shook the house, a strain of unearthly music floated through the air, a panel at the top of the staircase flew back with a loud voice, and out on the landing, looking very pale and white, with a little casket in her hand, stepped Virginia. In a moment they had all rushed up to her. Mrs. Otis clasped her passionately in her arms, the Duke smothered her with violent kisses, and the twins executed a wild war-dance round the group.

33. The headquarters of the police force of Metropolitan London.

'Good heavens! child, where have you been?' said Mr. Otis, rather angrily, thinking that she had been playing some foolish trick on them. 'Cecil and I have been riding all over the country looking for you, and your mother has been frightened to death. You must never play these practical jokes any more.'

'Except on the Ghost! except on the Ghost!' shrieked the twins, as they capered about.

'My own darling, thank God you are found; you must never leave my side again,' murmured Mrs. Otis, as she kissed the trembling child, and smoothed the tangled gold of her hair.

'Papa,' said Virginia quietly, 'I have been with the Ghost. He is dead, and you must come and see him. He had been very wicked, but he was really sorry for all that he had done, and he gave me this box of beautiful jewels before he died.'

The whole family gazed at her in mute amazement, but she was quite grave and serious; and, turning round, she led them through the opening in the wainscoting down a narrow secret corridor, Washington following with a lighted candle, which he had caught up from the table. Finally, they came to a great oak door, studded with rusty nails. When Virginia touched it, it swung back on its heavy hinges, and they found themselves in a little low room, with a vaulted ceiling, and one tiny grated window. Imbedded in the wall was a huge iron ring, and chained to it was a gaunt skeleton, that was stretched out at full length on the stone floor, and seemed to be trying to grasp with its long fleshless fingers an old-fashioned trencher and ewer,[34] that were placed just out of its reach. The jug had evidently been once filled with water, as it was covered inside with green mould. There was nothing on the trencher but a pile of dust. Virginia knelt down beside the skeleton, and, folding her little hands together, began to pray silently, while the rest of the party looked on in wonder at the terrible tragedy whose secret was now disclosed to them.

'Hallo!' suddenly exclaimed one of the twins, who had been looking out of the window to try and discover in what wing of the house the room was situated. 'Hallo! the old withered almond-tree has blossomed. I can see the flowers quite plainly in the moonlight.'

34. trencher: a wooden board on which food was cut or served; ewer: a large jug or pitcher.

'God has forgiven him,' said Virginia gravely, as she rose to her feet, and a beautiful light seemed to illumine her face.

'What an angel you are!' cried the young Duke, and he put his arm round her neck, and kissed her.

VII

Four days after these curious incidents a funeral started from Canterville Chase at about eleven o'clock at night. The hearse was drawn by eight black horses, each of which carried on its head a great tuft of nodding ostrich-plumes, and the leaden coffin was covered by a rich purple pall, on which was embroidered in gold the Canterville coat-of-arms. By the side of the hearse and the coaches walked the servants with lighted torches, and the whole procession was wonderfully impressive. Lord Canterville was the chief mourner, having come up specially from Wales to attend the funeral, and sat in the first carriage along with little Virginia. Then came the United States Minister and his wife, then Washington and the three boys, and in the last carriage was Mrs. Umney. It was generally felt that, as she had been frightened by the ghost for more than fifty years of her life, she had a right to see the last of him. A deep grave had been dug in the corner of the churchyard, just under the old yew-tree, and the service was read in the most impressive manner by the Rev. Augustus Dampier. When the ceremony was over, the servants, according to an old custom observed in the Canterville family, extinguished their torches, and, as the coffin was being lowered into the grave, Virginia stepped forward, and laid on it a large cross made of white and pink almond-blossoms. As she did so, the moon came out from behind a cloud, and flooded with its silent silver the little churchyard, and from a distant copse a nightingale began to sing. She thought of the ghost's description of the Garden of Death, her eyes became dim with tears, and she hardly spoke a word during the drive home.

The next morning, before Lord Canterville went up to town, Mr. Otis had an interview with him on the subject of the jewels the ghost had given to Virginia. They were perfectly magnificent, especially a certain ruby necklace with old Venetian setting, which was really a superb specimen of sixteenth-century work, and their value was so great that Mr. Otis felt considerable scruples about allowing his daughter to accept them.

'My Lord,' he said, 'I know that in this country mortmain[35] is held to apply to trinkets as well as to land, and it is quite clear to me that these jewels are, or should be, heirlooms in your family. I must beg you, accordingly, to take them to London with you, and to regard them simply as a portion of your property which has been restored to you under certain strange conditions. As for my daughter, she is merely a child, and has as yet, I am glad to say, but little interest in such appurtenances of idle luxury. I am also informed by Mrs. Otis, who, I may say, is no mean authority upon Art — having had the privilege of spending several winters in Boston when she was a girl — that these gems are of great monetary worth, and if offered for sale would fetch a tall price. Under these circumstances, Lord Canterville, I feel sure that you will recognise how impossible it would be for me to allow them to remain in the possession of any member of my family; and, indeed, all such vain gauds and toys, however suitable or necessary to the dignity of the British aristocracy, would be completely out of place among those who have been brought up on the severe, and I believe immortal, principles of Republican simplicity. Perhaps I should mention that Virginia is very anxious that you should allow her to retain the box, as a memento of your unfortunate but misguided ancestor. As it is extremely old, and consequently a good deal out of repair, you may perhaps think fit to comply with her request. For my own part, I confess I am a good deal surprised to find a child of mine expressing sympathy with mediævalism in any form, and can only account for it by the fact that Virginia was born in one of your London suburbs shortly after Mrs. Otis had returned from a trip to Athens.'

Lord Canterville listened very gravely to the worthy Minister's speech, pulling his grey moustache now and then to hide an involuntary smile, and when Mr. Otis had ended, he shook him cordially by the hand, and said, 'My dear sir, your charming little daughter rendered my unlucky ancestor, Sir Simon, a very important service, and I and my family are much indebted to her for her marvellous courage and pluck. The jewels are clearly hers, and, egad, I believe that if I were heartless enough to take them from her, the wicked old fellow would be out of his grave in a fortnight,

35. A provision of law whereby land is held to be inalienable (by sale or however) from the owning family.

leading me the devil of a life. As for their being heirlooms, nothing is an heirloom that is not so mentioned in a will or legal document, and the existence of these jewels has been quite unknown. I assure you I have no more claim on them than your butler, and when Miss Virginia grows up I daresay she will be pleased to have pretty things to wear. Besides, you forget, Mr. Otis, that you took the furniture and the ghost at a valuation, and anything that belonged to the ghost passed at once into your possession, as, whatever activity Sir Simon may have shown in the corridor at night, in point of law he was really dead, and you acquired his property by purchase.'

Mr. Otis was a good deal distressed at Lord Canterville's refusal, and begged him to reconsider his decision, but the good-natured peer was quite firm, and finally induced the Minister to allow his daughter to retain the present the ghost had given her, and when, in the spring of 1890, the young Duchess of Cheshire was presented at the Queen's first drawing-room on the occasion of her marriage, her jewels were the universal theme of admiration. For Virginia received the coronet, which is the reward of all good little American girls, and was married to her boy-lover as soon as he came of age. They were both so charming, and they loved each other so much, that every one was delighted at the match, except the old Marchioness of Dumbleton, who had tried to catch the Duke for one of her seven unmarried daughters, and had given no less than three expensive dinner-parties for that purpose, and, strange to say, Mr. Otis himself. Mr. Otis was extremely fond of the young Duke personally, but, theoretically, he objected to titles, and, to use his own words, 'was not without apprehension lest, amid the enervating influences of a pleasure-loving aristocracy, the true principles of Republican simplicity should be forgotten.' His objections, however, were completely overruled, and I believe that when he walked up the aisle of St. George's, Hanover Square, with his daughter leaning on his arm, there was not a prouder man in the whole length and breadth of England.

The Duke and Duchess, after the honeymoon was over, went down to Canterville Chase, and on the day after their arrival they walked over in the afternoon to the lonely churchyard by the pine-woods. There had been a great deal of difficulty at first about the inscription on Sir Simon's tomb-stone, but finally it had been decided to engrave on it simply the initials of the old gentleman's name, and the verse from the library window. The Duchess had brought with her some lovely roses, which she strewed upon the grave, and after they had stood by it for some time they strolled into the ruined chancel of the old abbey. There the Duchess sat down on a fallen pillar, while her husband lay at her feet smoking a cigarette and looking up at her beautiful eyes. Suddenly he threw his cigarette away, took hold of her hand, and said to her, 'Virginia, a wife should have no secrets from her husband.'

'Dear Cecil! I have no secrets from you.'

'Yes, you have,' he answered, smiling, 'you have never told me what happened to you when you were locked up with the ghost.'

'I have never told any one, Cecil,' said Virginia gravely.

'I know that, but you might tell me.'

'Please don't ask me, Cecil, I cannot tell you. Poor Sir Simon! I owe him a great deal. Yes, don't laugh, Cecil, I really do. He made me see what Life is, and what Death signifies, and why Love is stronger than both.'

The Duke rose and kissed his wife lovingly.

'You can have your secret as long as I have your heart,' he murmured.

'You have always had that, Cecil.'

'And you will tell our children some day, won't you?'

Virginia blushed.

W.B. YEATS

(1865-1939)

THE WORDS UPON THE WINDOW-PANE (1934)

[There are two immediate contexts within Yeats's work in which this play should be read. He had begun *The Resurrection* in 1925/26 but did not complete it until *The Words upon the Window-pane* had been produced in November 1930. Both are prose plays, though *The Resurrection* incorporates some excellent, practically independent, poems. Both deal with the re-emergence of a figure thought to be dead — Christ and Swift — and of course neither figure is seen by the audience. Both plays surround this absent, potent character with a cast of carefully graded commentators, ranging from the comprehending to the sceptical. But the relation between the two plays is anticipated in a much earlier note in Yeats's Journal (*c.*December 1908): 'The immortals are mortal, the mortals immortal, each living in the others' death and dying in the others' life.' A version of these words, a fragment of Heraclitus, is repeated at the end of *The Resurrection.*

The religious and mystical theme thus identified in both plays can be contrasted to a sexual theme linking the present play with the Crazy Jane poems on which Yeats was working during the same period. The physicality of the poetry complements the bodily absence of Jonathan Swift, Esther Johnson and Hester Van Homrigh in the play. The two women exercise a sexual power over Swift, even in the world of shades on which the play reports. For all that severe rebuke characterizes what we hear of his exchange with Vanessa, and the dialogue with Stella deals with a kind of Platonism, there is no mistaking the libidinous nature of the energies at work. Vanessa alluringly refers to the flesh as 'white ivory dice', and though Stella is strictly chaste, the poem of hers that is quoted teaches 'How wit and virtue from within/Can spread a smoothness o'er the skin'. An application of Platonic idealism to cosmetics, perhaps. Certainly, among the attendance at the seance a skittish sexuality is given some room for manoeuvre. Miss Mackenna insists on sitting beside the only young man present on the first occasion she has met him.

The title of the poem, and seemingly the original idea for the play, came to Yeats when he learned of two lines of doggerel scratched on a window at Fairfield, the Dublin home of Oliver St John Gogarty:

Mary Kilpatrick – very young
Ugly face and pleasant tongue.

The action is based on the doctrine of what Yeats elsewhere calls 'the dreaming back'. According to Emanuel Swedenborg, the soul after death undergoes a reversal of the events of life, rather like the unwinding of cotton from a spool. Traumatic events may be 'relived' several times before they are sloughed off, and it is in this process that 'the murderer repeats his murder'. By combining this notion, together with the more banal activity of communicating with a dead person through a seance, Yeats sets up the drama of Swift's brief, un-final, and tormented 'resurrection'.

A number of considerations, now external to the play as we have it, may be learned from Yeats's preparatory drafts. At one moment in its evolution, *The Words upon the Window-pane* contained a passage in which the seance is compared to the magicians' island in *Gulliver's Travels* (Book III, Chapter 7), where the illustrious dead (including Brutus and the Younger Cato) were called up. However, this was dropped. The names of characters changed several times during these early versions. In one draft, the character we now call Dr Trench was called John Mackenna, and the final Miss Mackenna was then Mary Duncan. Moreover, this Mackenna/Trench opened the play in dialogue with some literary references later abandoned:

MACKENNA: Through a glass darkly seems old fashioned now as Uncle Silas reads as well as ever.

CORBET: Her making the one good influence on Uncle Silas a Swedenborgian shows where her interests lay.

MACKENNA: Yes, that kind of thing runs in my mother's family. Sheridan Lefanu was her uncle. If you had heard the talk I have heard from my mother and from my old aunt, you would understand how in after life such things become an obsession....

The allusion to Joseph Sheridan Le Fanu's *Uncle Silas: A Tale of Bartram-Haugh* (1864) and *In a Glass Darkly* (1872) is clear enough. But the feminine possessive adjective 'her' for their author is wholly inexplicable. Before naming the older man John Mackenna, Yeats had toyed with the idea of calling him John Lefanu. These excised references to the Victorian family linking Swift to Yeats's own generation lend weight to the theory — it can be no more — that T.C. Irwin's poem 'Swift' is a further nineteenth-century source for the play. The more personal significance of the family-name, Corbet, for the playwright has been discussed earlier (p. 851); to those Victorian associations we can add a coincidence linking the playwright almost to a Swiftian succession; the Rev. Francis Corbet was dean of St Patrick's Cathedral from 1747 (two years after Swift's death) until 1775.

Yeats himself wrote an Introduction to the play, in which he made it clear that John Corbet is frequently guilty of 'overstatement'. Nevertheless, he used Corbet's exposition of Swift as a vehicle for political ideas of his own, notably his opposition to democracy and progress. It can be observed through material provided in the notes that Yeats reworked sometimes flippant, or at least casually caustic, material from Swift's correspondence to create a far more orotund and tragic voice. The idea of Swift 'foreseeing' democracy is anachronistic in several respects: as a churchman he was hostile to visionaries, and as a politician he rarely indulged in anything approaching prophecy. Democracy in the sense revitalized by the French Revolution, of course, lay forty years ahead even at the time of the dean's death in 1745. It was an established and endangered concept in the years when Yeats was working on the play.]

In memory of Lady Gregory
in whose house it was written[1]

PERSONS IN THE PLAY

DR. TRENCH
MISS MACKENNA
JOHN CORBET
CORNELIUS PATTERSON
ABRAHAM JOHNSON
MRS. MALLET
MRS. HENDERSON

A lodging-house room, an armchair, a little table in front of it, chairs on either side. A fireplace and window. A kettle on the hob and some tea-things on a dresser. A door to back and towards the right. Through the door one can see an entrance hall. The sound of a knocker. MISS MACKENNA *passes through and then she re-enters hall together with* JOHN CORBET, *a man of twenty-two or twenty-three, and* DR. TRENCH, *a man of between sixty and seventy.*

DR. TRENCH (*In hall*): May I introduce John Corbet, one of the Corbets of Ballymoney,[2] but at present a Cambridge student? This is Miss Mackenna, our energetic secretary.

They come into room, take off their coats.

MISS MACKENNA: I thought it better to let you in myself. This country is still sufficiently medieval to make spiritualism an undesirable theme for gossip. Give me your coats and hats, I will put them in my own room. It is just across the hall. Better sit down; your watches must be fast. Mrs. Henderson is lying down, as she always does before a séance. We won't begin for ten minutes yet. (*She goes out with hats and coats*)

DR. TRENCH: Miss Mackenna does all the real work of the Dublin Spiritualists' Association.[3] She did all the correspondence with Mrs. Henderson, and persuaded the landlady to let her this big room and a small room upstairs. We are a poor society and could not guarantee anything in advance. Mrs. Henderson has come from London at her own risk. She was born in Dublin and wants to spread the movement here. She lives very economically and does not expect a great deal. We all give what we can. A poor woman with the soul of an apostle.

JOHN CORBET: Have there been many séances?

DR. TRENCH: Only three so far.

JOHN CORBET: I hope she will not mind my scepticism. I have looked into Myers' *Human Personality* and a wild book by Conan Doyle,[4] but am unconvinced.

DR. TRENCH: We all have to find the truth for ourselves. Lord Dunraven, then Lord Adare, introduced my father to the famous David Home.[5] My

1. Yeats completed the play in October 1930, while he was staying with Lady Gregory at Coole Park, Co. Galway. However, he had been working on it for some time previously, having broken off from the task of completing 'The Resurrection'.
2. The phrase 'the Corbets of Ballymoney' suggests that Corbet belongs to a family of some social position. Ballymoney is a common enough Irish place-name, there being places of the name in Counties Wexford and Antrim. Later in the play Corbet is said to be, simply, from Cambridge. For the significance of the family name for Yeats, and for his changes of characters' names in the composition of the play, see the Introduction to this section (p. 851), and the headnote.
3. The Dublin Hermetical Society was founded in 1885, and later became the Dublin Theosophical Society. Although these bodies were involved in more arcane matters than seances, it seems clear that Yeats has the societies of his early loyalty in mind. A draft names the street in which the house of the play is located as Nottingham Street, whereas in fact the Hermetical Society met in York Street, Dublin. The parallel of English town-names confirms the parallel between the societies.
4. Frederic William Henry Myers (1843-1901), one of the founders of the Society for Psychical Research, published *Human Personality and its Survival of Bodily Death* in 1903. Yeats appears to have been familiar with the book by 1908 when he made an approving, if inaccurate, reference to it in a speech to the British Association (see John P. Frayne and Colton Johnson (eds), *Uncollected Prose by W.B. Yeats* Vol. II (London: Macmillan, 1975, pp. 367-68)). Arthur Conan Doyle (1859-1930), the creator of Sherlock Holmes, published a *History of Spiritualism* in 1926, and had been absorbed in such studies since the period of World War I.
5. Edwin Richard Windham Wyndham-Quin (1812-71), became 3rd earl of Dunraven in 1850; as Viscount Adare he had sat in the House

father often told me that he saw David Home floating in the air in broad daylight, but I did not believe a word of it. I had to investigate for myself, and I was very hard to convince. Mrs. Piper, an American trance medium, not unlike Mrs. Henderson, convinced me.

JOHN CORBET: A state of somnambulism and voices coming through her lips that purport to be those of dead persons?

DR. TRENCH: Exactly: quite the best kind of mediumship if you want to establish the identity of a spirit. But do not expect too much. There has been a hostile influence.

JOHN CORBET: You mean an evil spirit?

DR. TRENCH: The poet Blake said that he never knew a bad man that had not something very good about him.[6] I say a hostile influence, an influence that disturbed the last séance very seriously. I cannot tell you what happened, for I have not been at any of Mrs. Henderson's séances. Trance mediumship has nothing new to show me — I told the young people when they made me their President that I would probably stay at home, that I could get more out of Emanuel Swedenborg[7] than out of any séance. (*A knock*) That is probably old Cornelius Patterson; he thinks they race horses and whippets in the other world, and is, so they tell me, so anxious to find out if he is right that he is always punctual. Miss Mackenna will keep him to herself for some minutes. He gives her tips for Harold's Cross.[8]

MISS MACKENNA *crosses to hall door and admits* CORNELIUS PATTERSON. *She brings him to her room across the hall.*

JOHN CORBET: (*Who has been wandering about*) This is a wonderful room for a lodging-house.

DR. TRENCH: It was a private house until about fifty years ago. It was not so near the town in those days, and there are large stables at the back. Quite a number of notable people lived here. Grattan was born upstairs; no, not Grattan, Curran[9] perhaps — I forget — but I do know that this house in the early part of the eighteenth century belonged to friends of Jonathan Swift, or rather of Stella.[10] Swift chaffed her in the *Journal to Stella* because of certain small sums of money she lost at cards probably in this very room. That was before Vanessa appeared upon the scene.[11] It was a country-house in those days, surrounded by trees and gardens. Somebody cut some lines from a poem of hers upon the window-pane — tradition says Stella herself. (*A knock*) Here they are, but you will hardly make them out in this light.

They stand in the window. CORBET *stoops down to see better.* MISS MACKENNA *and* ABRAHAM JOHNSON *enter and stand near door.*

---

of Commons as Conservative MP for Glamorgan 1837-51. He was a scholar in the fields of architecture and archaeology. Daniel Douglas Home (1833-86) was a Scottish spiritualist, specializing in seance communications, whose acts of levitation were attested by various well-known individuals, including Dunraven. Yeats has given an incorrect Christian name, for whatever reason.

6. William Blake (1757-1827), English poet and visionary whose works Yeats helped to edit in his youth.
7. Emanuel Swedenborg (1688-1772), Swedish engineer, philosopher and visionary; the fullest statement of his mystical system is the *Arcana Coelestia* in 20 volumes.
8. Harold's Cross is a Dublin suburb. Its suggestive power here is considerable. The place had been used for public executions and was associated (almost as fatally) with a number of important political figures: John Keogh (1740-1817), the wealthy and radical leader of Irish catholic opinion in the 1790s, owned a fine house (Mount Jerome) there; Robert Emmet (1778-1803) was arrested in the district and subsequently was executed in Dublin. In the course of the nineteenth century, a limited liability company had transformed the grounds of Keogh's house into a large cemetery, with a consequent depressing effect on the value of property in the area. The Yeats family lived on Harold's Cross Road *c.*1884-87, following a decline in their financial position. Without naming the district, Yeats described its dreariness in *Reveries Over Childhood and Youth* (1915), and repeated the complaint as late as 1922 in a letter to Lady Gregory. (See John Kelly and Eric Domville (eds), *The Collected Letters of W.B. Yeats* Vol. 1 (Oxford: Clarendon Press, 1986), p. 9.) A course for greyhound-racing was more recently established at Harold's Cross, and it is to this that Dr Trench directly alludes. More generally, all these aspects of Harold's Cross history are touched on in the play: death, the association of patriots like Grattan and Curran, and the decay of once dignified houses.
9. John Philpot Curran (1750-1817), political orator, lawyer and poet, was born in Newmarket, Co. Cork, and so may be ruled out of any fact-grubbing inquiry. Henry Grattan (1746-1820), political orator and MP for Dublin, was born in Fishamble Street, Dublin. Trench's uncertainty as to which of the two great eighteenth-century orators was born in the house is part of Yeats's gradual breakdown of the objective framework in which such a play (with its title) inevitably finds its point of commencement. It is also part of the erosion of Trench's authority, preparatory for the emergence of Swift's dead authority.
10. Those of Jonathan Swift's private letters, of 1710-13, known by their later collective title as the *Journal to Stella*, include numerous allusions to card-play, but the households most frequently named do not appear to have any relation to families or individuals mentioned in the play. Curran may be dismissed from the argument (see note 9 above), but the Grattan family was close to Swift, so close indeed that two Grattans were named by him as his executors. The orator Grattan's father, James Grattan, had been recorder of Dublin. Thus, the Grattans had close links with Swift and with the public life of Dublin. Nevertheless, Yeats leaves the eighteenth-century occupiers of the house unspecified.
11. The woman whom Swift called Vanessa was Hester (or Esther) Van Homrigh (1688-1723). Her father, Bartholemew Van Homrigh (died 1703), a naturalized Dutchman, was the lord mayor of Dublin who in 1697 obtained from King William III the mayoral collar that is still used to this day.

ABRAHAM JOHNSON: Where is Mrs. Henderson?

MISS MACKENNA: She is upstairs; she always rests before a séance.

ABRAHAM JOHNSON: I must see her before the séance. I know exactly what to do to get rid of this evil influence.

MISS MACKENNA: If you go up to see her there will be no séance at all. She says it is dangerous even to think, much less to speak, of an evil influence.

ABRAHAM JOHNSON: Then I shall speak to the President.

MISS MACKENNA: Better talk the whole thing over first in my room. Mrs. Henderson says that there must be perfect harmony.

ABRAHAM JOHNSON: Something must be done. The last séance was completely spoiled.

A knock.

MISS MACKENNA: That may be Mrs. Mallet; she is a very experienced spiritualist. Come to my room, old Patterson and some others are there already. (*She brings him to the other room and later crosses to hall door to admit* MRS. MALLET)

JOHN CORBET: I know those lines well — they are part of a poem Stella wrote for Swift's fifty-fourth birthday.[12] Only three poems of hers — and some lines she added to a poem of Swift's — have come down to us, but they are enough to prove her a better poet than Swift. Even those few words on the window make me think of a seventeenth-century poet, Donne or Crashaw.[13] (*He quotes*)

You taught how I might youth prolong
By knowing what is right and wrong,
How from my heart to bring supplies
Of lustre to my fading eyes.

How strange that a celibate scholar, well on in life, should keep the love of two such women! He met Vanessa in London at the height of his political power. She followed him to Dublin. She loved him for nine years, perhaps died of love, but Stella loved him all her life.

DR. TRENCH: I have shown that writing to several persons, and you are the first who has recognised the lines.

JOHN CORBET: I am writing an essay on Swift and Stella for my doctorate at Cambridge. I hope to prove that in Swift's day men of intellect reached the height of their power — the greatest position they ever attained in society and the State, that everything great in Ireland and in our character, in what remains of our architecture, comes from that day; that we have kept its seal longer than England.

DR. TRENCH: A tragic life: Bolingbroke, Harley, Ormonde, all those great Ministers that were his friends, banished and broken.[14]

JOHN CORBET: I do not think you can explain him in that way — his tragedy had deeper foundations. His ideal order was the Roman Senate, his ideal men Brutus and Cato. Such an order and such men had seemed possible once more, but the movement passed and he foresaw the ruin to come, Democracy, Rousseau, the French Revolution; that is why he hated the common run of men, — 'I hate lawyers, I hate doctors,' he said, 'though I love Dr. So-and-so and Judge So-and-so' — that is why he wrote *Gulliver*, that is why he wore out his brain, that is why he felt *saeva indignatio*, that is why he sleeps under the greatest epitaph in history. You remember how it goes? It is almost finer in English than in Latin: 'He has gone where fierce indignation can lacerate his heart no more.'[15]

12. The woman whom Swift called Stella was Esther Johnson (1687-1728). He met her in 1689 in Sir William Temple's household at Moor Park in Surrey. The poem is 'Stella to Dr Swift on his Birthday November 30, 1721' (see Volume I of the anthology, pp. 457-58).
13. John Donne (1573-1631), Richard Crashaw (*c.*1613-49), English religious poets, the first a cradle catholic but later conforming, the second becoming a catholic as a young man. The second of the quoted lines should read: 'By knowing what was right and wrong.'
14. These prominent politicians were charged with high crimes and misdemeanours in 1715: Henry Saint-John (1678-1751), 1st viscount Bolingbroke; Robert Harley (1661-1724), 1st earl of Oxford, who had been named lord treasurer in 1711; and James Butler (1665-1745), 2nd duke of Ormonde, who had been lord lieutenant of Ireland in 1713. Swift's *An Enquiry into the Behaviour of the Queen's Last Ministry* deals with the background. See also note 29 below.
15. The paragraph is studded with names. By Brutus and Cato is probably indicated Marcius Junius Brutus (85-42 B.C.) and Marcius Porcius Cato (234-149 B.C.), though the younger Marcius Porcius Cato (95-46 B.C.) shared the same Roman virtues of stoic austerity. In *Du Contrat social* (1762) and other writings, the Swiss-French philosopher, Jean-Jacques Rousseau (1712-78), presented a proto-democratic theory of society which was generally thought to have anticipated French revolutionary practice in the 1790s. The letter of Swift to Alexander Pope (29 September 1725) echoed here actually reads:

> I have ever hated all Nations professions and Communityes and all my love is towards individualls for instance I hate the tribe of Lawyers, but I love Councellor such a one, Judge such a one for so with Physicians (I will not Speak of my own Trade) Soldiers, English, Scotch, French; and the rest but principally I hate and detest that animal called man, although I hartily love John, Peter, Thomas and so forth....

Swift's Latin epitaph was composed by himself, and includes the phrase: 'ubi saeve indignatio ulterius cor lacerare nequit'. Yeats 'translated' the epitaph in September 1930:

Swift has sailed into his rest;
Savage indignation there
Cannot lacerate his breast.
Imitate him if you dare,
World-besotted traveller; he
Served human liberty.

ABRAHAM JOHNSON *comes in, followed by* MRS. MALLET *and* CORNELIUS PATTERSON.

ABRAHAM JOHNSON: Something must be done, Dr. Trench, to drive away the influence that has destroyed our séances. I have come here week after week at considerable expense. I am from Belfast. I am by profession a minister of the Gospel, I do a great deal of work among the poor and ignorant. I produce considerable effect by singing and preaching, but I know that my effect should be much greater than it is. My hope is that I shall be able to communicate with the great Evangelist Moody. I want to ask him to stand invisible beside me when I speak or sing, and lay his hands upon my head and give me such a portion of his power that my work may be blessed as the work of Moody and Sankey[16] was blessed.

MRS. MALLET: What Mr. Johnson says about the hostile influence is quite true. The last two séances were completely spoilt. I am thinking of starting a tea-shop in Folkestone.[17] I followed Mrs. Henderson to Dublin to get my husband's advice, but two spirits kept talking and would not let any other spirit say a word.

DR. TRENCH: Did the spirits say the same thing and go through the same drama at both séances?

MRS. MALLET: Yes — just as if they were characters in some kind of horrible play.

DR. TRENCH: That is what I was afraid of.

MRS. MALLET: My husband was drowned at sea ten years ago, but constantly speaks to me through Mrs. Henderson as if he were still alive. He advises me about everything I do, and I am utterly lost if I cannot question him.

CORNELIUS PATTERSON: I never did like the Heaven they talk about in churches: but when somebody told me that Mrs. Mallet's husband ate and drank and went about with his favourite dog, I said to myself, 'That is the place for Corney Patterson'. I came here to find out if it was true, and I declare to God I have not heard one word about it.

ABRAHAM JOHNSON: I ask you, Dr. Trench, as President of the Dublin Spiritualists' Association, to permit me to read the ritual of exorcism appointed for such occasions. After the last séance I copied it out of an old book in the library of Belfast University. I have it here. (*He takes paper out of his pocket*)

DR. TRENCH: The spirits are people like ourselves, we treat them as our guests and protect them from discourtesy and violence, and every exorcism is a curse or a threatened curse. We do not admit that there are evil spirits. Some spirits are earth-bound — they think they are still living and go over and over some action of their past lives, just as we go over and over some painful thought, except that where they are thought is reality. For instance, when a spirit which has died a violent death comes to a medium for the first time, it re-lives all the pains of death.

MRS. MALLET: When my husband came for the first time the medium gasped and struggled as if she was drowning. It was terrible to watch.

DR. TRENCH: Sometimes a spirit re-lives not the pain of death but some passionate or tragic moment of life. Swedenborg describes this and gives the reason for it. There is an incident of the kind in the *Odyssey*,[18] and many in Eastern literature; the murderer repeats his murder, the robber his robbery, the lover his serenade, the soldier hears the trumpet once again. If I were a Catholic I would say that such spirits were in Purgatory. In vain do we write *requiescat in pace*[19] upon the tomb, for they must suffer, and we in our turn must suffer until God gives peace. Such spirits do not often come to séances unless those séances are held in houses where those spirits lived, or where the event took place. This spirit which speaks those incomprehensible words and does not answer when spoken to is of such a nature. The more patient we are, the more quickly will it pass out of its passion and its remorse.

ABRAHAM JOHNSON: I am still convinced that the spirit which disturbed the last séance is evil. If I may not exorcise it I will certainly pray for protection.

16. Ira David Sankey (1840-1908) and Dwight Lyman Moody (1837-99), American revivalist preachers and hymn-writers.

17. A port and seaside resort on the south-east coast of England. It is worth noting how most of the people assembled for the seance are associated with dispersal: Johnson comes from Belfast and will return there, Corbet studies at Cambridge, Mrs Mallet wishes to go to Folkestone, and Mrs Henderson (though born in Dublin) has come from Glasgow.

18. In *A Vision* Yeats provides an instance from Homer's *Odyssey* contrasting 'Heracles passing through the night, bow in hand, and Heracles the freed spirit, a happy god among the gods'. In the latter case, Heracles has gained release from the repetitive pattern of the afterlife described here. (See *A Vision* (London: Macmillan, 1962), p. 226.)

19. May He/She Rest in Peace, traditionally used by catholics in alluding reverently to the dead; summarized in the initials RIP.

DR. TRENCH: Mrs. Henderson's control, Lulu, is able and experienced and can protect both medium and sitters, but it may help Lulu if you pray that the spirit find rest.

ABRAHAM JOHNSON *sits down and prays silently, moving his lips.* MRS. HENDERSON *comes in with* MISS MACKENNA *and others.* MISS MACKENNA *shuts the door.*

DR. TRENCH: Mrs. Henderson, may I introduce to you Mr. Corbet, a young man from Cambridge and a sceptic, who hopes that you will be able to convince him?

MRS. HENDERSON: We were all sceptics once. He must not expect too much from a first séance. He must persevere. (*She sits in the armchair, and the others begin to seat themselves*).

MISS MACKENNA *goes to* JOHN CORBET *and they remain standing.*

MISS MACKENNA: I am glad that you are a sceptic.

JOHN CORBET: I thought you were a spiritualist.

MISS MACKENNA: I have seen a good many séances, and sometimes think it is all coincidence and thought-transference. (*She says this is a low voice*) Then at other times I think as Dr. Trench does, and then I feel like Job — you know the quotation — the hair of my head stands up. A spirit passes before my face.[20]

MRS. MALLET: Turn the key, Dr. Trench, we don't want anybody blundering in here. (DR. TRENCH *locks door*) Come and sit here, Miss Mackenna.

MISS MACKENNA: No, I am going to sit beside Mr. Corbet.

CORBET *and* MISS MACKENNA *sit down.*

JOHN CORBET: You feel like Job tonight?

MISS MACKENNA: I feel that something is going to happen, that is why I am glad that you are a sceptic.

JOHN CORBET: You feel safer?

MISS MACKENNA: Yes, safer.

MRS. HENDERSON: I am glad to meet all my dear friends again and to welcome Mr. Corbet amongst us. As he is a stranger I must explain that we do not call up spirits, we make the right conditions and they come. I do not know who is going to come; sometimes there are a great many and the guides choose between them. The guides try to send somebody for everybody but do not always succeed. If you want to speak to some dear friend who has passed over, do not be discouraged. If your friend cannot come this time, maybe he can next time. My control is a dear little girl called Lulu who died when she was five or six years old. She describes the spirits present and tells us what spirit wants to speak. Miss Mackenna, a verse of a hymn, please, the same we had last time, and will everyone join in the singing.

They sing the following lines from Hymn 564, Irish Church Hymnal

'Sun of my soul, Thou Saviour dear,
It is not night if Thou be near:
O may no earth-born cloud arise
To hide Thee from Thy servant's eyes.'[21]

(MRS. HENDERSON *is leaning back in her chair asleep*)

MISS MACKENNA: (*To* JOHN CORBET) She always snores like that when she is going off.

MRS. HENDERSON: (*In a child's voice*) Lulu so glad to see all her friends.

MRS. MALLET: And we are glad you have come, Lulu.

MRS. HENDERSON: (*In a child's voice*) Lulu glad to see new friend.

MISS MACKENNA: (*To* JOHN CORBET) She is speaking to you.

JOHN CORBET: Thank you, Lulu.

MRS. HENDERSON: (*In a child's voice*) You mustn't laugh at the way I talk.

JOHN CORBET: I am not laughing, Lulu.

MRS. HENDERSON: (*In a child's voice*) Nobody must laugh. Lulu does her best but can't say big long words. Lulu sees a tall man here, lots of hair on face (MRS. HENDERSON *passes her hands over her cheeks and chin*), not much on the top of his head (MRS. HENDERSON *passes her hand over the top of her head*), red necktie, and such a funny sort of pin.

MRS. MALLET: Yes. . . . Yes. . . .

MRS. HENDERSON: (*In a child's voice*) Pin like a horseshoe.

MRS. MALLET: It's my husband.

MRS. HENDERSON: (*In a child's voice*) He has a message.

MRS. MALLET: Yes.

20. Job 4.15: 'Then a spirit passed before my face; the hair of my flesh stood up. . . .'

21. The first stanza from a popular hymn by John Keble (1792-1866). (The fourth stanza is sung later in the play.) The *Irish Church Hymnal* is the collection of hymns prescribed for use in the Church of Ireland (once the Established Church, of which Swift was a dignitary), the reference confirming the non-catholic ambience of the group at the seance.

MRS. HENDERSON: (*In a child's voice*) Lulu cannot hear. He is too far off. He has come near. Lulu can hear now. He says . . . he says, 'Drive that man away!' He is pointing to somebody in the corner, that corner over there. He says it is the bad man who spoilt everything last time. If they won't drive him away, Lulu will scream.

MISS MACKENNA: That horrible spirit again.

ABRAHAM JOHNSON: Last time he monopolised the séance.

MRS. MALLET: He would not let anybody speak but himself.

MRS. HENDERSON: (*In a child's voice*) They have driven that bad man away. Lulu sees a young lady.

MRS. MALLET: Is not my husband here?

MRS. HENDERSON: (*In a child's voice*) Man with funny pin gone away. Young lady here — Lulu thinks she must be at a fancy dress party, such funny clothes, hair all in curls — all bent down on floor near that old man with glasses.

DR. TRENCH: No, I do not recognize her.

MRS. HENDERSON: (*In a child's voice*) That bad man, that bad old man in the corner, they have let him come back. Lulu is going to scream. O. . . . O. . . . (*In a man's voice*) How dare you write to her? How dare you ask if we were married? How dare you question her?

DR. TRENCH: A soul in its agony — it cannot see us or hear us.

MRS. HENDERSON: (*Upright and rigid, only her lips moving, and still in a man's voice*) You sit crouching there. Did you not hear what I said? How dared you question her? I found you an ignorant little girl without intellect, without moral ambition. How many times did I not stay away from great men's houses, how many times forsake the Lord Treasurer, how many times neglect the business of the State that we might read Plutarch together![22]

ABRAHAM JOHNSON *half rises*. DR. TRENCH *motions him to remain seated.*

DR. TRENCH: Silence!

ABRAHAM JOHNSON: But, Dr. Trench. . . .

DR. TRENCH: Hush — we can do nothing.

MRS. HENDERSON: (*Speaking as before*) I taught you to think in every situation of life not as Hester Vanhomrigh would think in that situation, but as Cato or Brutus would, and now you behave like some common slut with her ear against the keyhole.

JOHN CORBET: (*To* MISS MACKENNA) It is Swift, Jonathan Swift, talking to the woman he called Vanessa. She was christened Hester Vanhomrigh.

MRS. HENDERSON: (*In Vanessa's voice*) I questioned her, Jonathan, because I love. Why have you let me spend hours in your company if you did not want me to love you? (*In Swift's voice*) When I rebuilt Rome in your mind it was as though I walked its streets. (*In Vanessa's voice*) Was that all, Jonathan? Was I nothing but a painter's canvas? (*In Swift's voice*) My God, do you think it was easy? I was a man of strong passions and I had sworn never to marry. (*In Vanessa's voice*) If you and she are not married, why should we not marry like other men and women? I loved you from the first moment when you came to my mother's house and began to teach me. I thought it would be enough to look at you, to speak to you, to hear you speak. I followed you to Ireland five years ago and I can bear it no longer. It is not enough to look, to speak, to hear. Jonathan, Jonathan, I am a woman, the women Brutus and Cato loved were not different. (*In Swift's voice*) I have something in my blood that no child must inherit. I have constant attacks of dizziness; I pretend they come from a surfeit of fruit when I was a child.[23] I had them in London. . . . There was a great doctor there, Dr. Arbuthnot;[24] I told him of those attacks of dizziness, I told him of worse things. It was he who explained. There is a line of Dryden's. . . . (*In Vanessa's voice*) O, I know — 'Great wits are sure to madness near allied'.[25] If you had children, Jonathan, my blood would make them healthy. I will take your hand, I will lay it upon my heart — upon the Vanhomrigh blood that has been healthy for generations. (MRS.

22. The passage 'reports' a conversation between Swift and Vanessa, in which Swift rebukes her for questioning Stella about their relationship. Romantic speculations about Swift and his two female intimates proliferated in the nineteenth century (and after!). The Irish poet, Thomas Caulfield Irwin (1823-92), composed a narrative describing Swift's alleged ride to Vanessa's home at Celbridge. Co. Kildare, silently to fling down a letter strongly rebuking her for approaching Stella. The lord treasurer referred to may be taken to be Harley — see note 14 above. Plutarch (*c*.46-*c*.126) was a Greek essayist and biographer from whom much of our knowledge of the ancients' lives derives.

23. cf. Swift to Henrietta Howard (1681-1767), sometime countess of Suffolk, on 19 August 1727: 'About two hours before you were born, I got my Giddyness by eating a hundred golden pippins at a time, at Richmond, and when you were four years and a quarter old bating two days, having made a fine seat about twenty miles farther in Surrey where I used to read and sleep, there I got my deafness, and these two friends have visited me, one or the other, every year since, and being old acquaintance have now thought fit to come together.'

24. John Arbuthnot (1667-1735), a close friend of Swift and Pope.

25. cf. John Dryden, 'Absalom and Achitophel', I, 163.

HENDERSON *slowly raises her left hand*) That is the first time you have touched my body, Jonathan. (MRS. HENDERSON *stands up and remains rigid. In Swift's voice*) What do I care if it be healthy? What do I care if it could make mine healthy? Am I to add another to the healthy rascaldom and knavery of the world? (*In Vanessa's voice*) Look at me, Jonathan. Your arrogant intellect separates us. Give me both your hands. I will put them upon my breast. (MRS. HENDERSON *raises her right hand to the level of her left and then raises both to her breast*) O, it is white — white as the gambler's dice — white ivory dice. Think of the uncertainty. Perhaps a mad child — perhaps a rascal — perhaps a knave — perhaps not, Jonathan. The dice of the intellect are loaded, but I am the common ivory dice. (*Her hands are stretched out as though drawing somebody towards her*) It is not my hands that draw you back. My hands are weak, they could not draw you back if you did not love as I love. You said that you have strong passions; that is true, Jonathan — no man in Ireland is so passionate. That is why you need me, that is why you need children, nobody has greater need. You are growing old. An old man without children is very solitary. Even his friends, men as old as he, turn away, they turn towards the young, their children or their children's children. They cannot endure an old man like themselves. (MRS. HENDERSON *moves away from the chair, her movements gradually growing convulsive*) You are not too old for the dice, Jonathan, but a few years if you turn away will make you an old miserable childless man. (*In Swift's voice*) O God, hear the prayer of Jonathan Swift, that afflicted man, and grant that he may leave to posterity nothing but his intellect that came to him from Heaven. (*In Vanessa's voice*) Can you face solitude with that mind, Jonathan? (MRS. HENDERSON *goes to the door, finds that it is closed*) Dice, white ivory dice. (*In Swift's voice*) My God, I am left alone with my enemy? Who locked the door, who locked me in with my enemy? (MRS. HENDERSON *beats upon the door, sinks to the floor and then speaks as Lulu*) Bad old man! Do not let him come back. Bad old man does not know he is dead. Lulu cannot find fathers, mothers, sons that have passed over. Power almost gone. (MRS. MALLET *leads* MRS. HENDERSON, *who seems very exhausted, back to her chair. She is still asleep. She speaks again as Lulu*) Another verse of hymn. Everybody sing. Hymn will bring good influence.

(*They sing*)

'If some poor wandering child of Thine
Have spurned today the voice divine,
Now, Lord, the gracious work begin;
Let him no more lie down in sin.'

During the hymn MRS. HENDERSON *has been murmuring* 'Stella', *but the singing has almost drowned her voice. The singers draw one another's attention to the fact that she is speaking. The singing stops.*

DR. TRENCH: I thought she was speaking.

MRS. MALLET: I saw her lips move.

DR. TRENCH: She would be more comfortable with a cushion, but we might wake her.

MRS. MALLET: Nothing can wake her out of a trance like that until she wakes up herself. (*She brings a cushion and she and* DR. TRENCH *put* MRS. HENDERSON *into a more comfortable position*)

MRS. HENDERSON: (*In Swift's voice*) Stella.

MISS MACKENNA: (*To* JOHN CORBET) Did you hear that? She said 'Stella'.

JOHN CORBET: Vanessa has gone, Stella has taken her place.

MISS MACKENNA: Did you notice the change while we were singing? The new influence in the room?

JOHN CORBET: I thought I did, but it must have been fancy.

MRS. MALLET: Hush!

MRS. HENDERSON: (*In Swift's voice*) Have I wronged you, beloved Stella? Are you unhappy? You have no children, you have no lover, you have no husband. A cross and ageing man for friend — nothing but that. But no, do not answer — you have answered already in that poem you wrote for my last birthday. With what scorn you speak of the common lot of women 'with no endowments but a face —'

Before the thirtieth year of life
A maid forlorn or hated wife.

It is the thought of the great Chrysostom[26] who wrote in a famous passage that women loved according to the soul, loved as saints can love, keep their beauty longer, have greater happiness than women loved according to the flesh. That thought has comforted me, but it is a terrible thing to be responsible for another's happiness. There are moments when I doubt, when I think Chrysostom

26. St John (345-407), a Greek commentator on New Testament writings; known as Chrysostom (golden-mouthed) because of his eloquence.

may have been wrong. But now I have your poem to drive doubt away. You have addressed me in these noble words:

You taught how I might youth prolong
By knowing what is right and wrong;
How from my heart to bring supplies
Of lustre to my fading eyes;
How soon a beauteous mind repairs
The loss of chang'd or falling hairs;
How wit and virtue from within
Can spread[27] *a smoothness o'er the skin.*

JOHN CORBET: The words upon the window-pane!

MRS. HENDERSON: (*In Swift's voice*) Then, because you understand that I am afraid of solitude, afraid of outliving my friends — and myself — you comfort me in that last verse — you overpraise my moral nature when you attribute to it a rich mantle, but O how touching those words which describe your love:

Late dying may you cast a shred
Of that rich mantle o'er my head;
To bear with dignity my sorrow,
One day alone, then die tomorrow.

Yes, you will close my eyes, Stella. O, you will live long after me, dear Stella, for you are still a young woman, but you will close my eyes. (MRS. HENDERSON *sinks back in chair and speaks as Lulu*) Bad old man gone. Power all used up. Lulu can do no more. Good-bye, friends. (MRS. HENDERSON, *speaking in her own voice*) Go away, go away! (*She wakes*) I saw him a moment ago, has he spoilt the séance again?

MRS. MALLET: Yes, Mrs. Henderson, my husband came, but he was driven away.

DR. TRENCH: Mrs. Henderson is very tired. We must leave her to rest. (*To* MRS. HENDERSON) You did your best and nobody can do more than that. (*He takes out money*)

MRS. HENDERSON: No.... No. ... I cannot take any money, not after a séance like that.

DR. TRENCH: Of course you must take it, Mrs. Henderson. (*He puts money on table, and* MRS. HENDERSON *gives a furtive glance to see how much it is. She does the same as each sitter lays down his or her money*)

MRS. MALLET: A bad séance is just as exhausting as a good séance, and you must be paid.

MRS. HENDERSON: No.... No.... Please don't. It is very wrong to take money for such a failure.

MRS. MALLET *lays down money.*

CORNELIUS PATTERSON: A jockey is paid whether he wins or not. (*He lays down money*)

MISS MACKENNA: That spirit rather thrilled me. (*She lays down money*)

MRS. HENDERSON: If you insist, I must take it.

ABRAHAM JOHNSON: I shall pray for you tonight. I shall ask God to bless and protect your séances. (*He lays down money*)

All go out except JOHN CORBET *and* MRS. HENDERSON

JOHN CORBET: I know you are tired, Mrs. Henderson, but I must speak to you. I have been deeply moved by what I have heard. This is my contribution to prove that I am satisfied, completely satisfied. (*He puts a note on the table*)

MRS. HENDERSON: A pound note — nobody ever gives me more than ten shillings, and yet the séance was a failure.

JOHN CORBET: (*Sitting down near* MRS. HENDERSON) When I say I am satisfied I do not mean that I am convinced it was the work of spirits. I prefer to think that you created it all, that you are an accomplished actress and scholar. In my essay for my Cambridge doctorate I examine all the explanations of Swift's celibacy offered by his biographers and prove that the explanation you selected was the only plausible one. But there is something I must ask you. Swift was the chief representative of the intellect of his epoch, that arrogant intellect free at last from superstition. He foresaw its collapse. He foresaw Democracy, he must have dreaded the future. Did he refuse to beget children because of that dread? Was Swift mad? Or was it the intellect itself that was mad?

MRS. HENDERSON: Who are you talking of, sir?

JOHN CORBET: Swift, of course.

MRS. HENDERSON: Swift? I do not know anybody called Swift.

JOHN CORBET: Jonathan Swift, whose spirit seemed to be present tonight.

MRS. HENDERSON: What? That dirty old man?

JOHN CORBET: He was neither old nor dirty when Stella and Vanessa loved him.

MRS. HENDERSON: I saw him very clearly just as I woke up. His clothes were dirty, his face covered with boils. Some disease had made one of his eyes swell up, it stood out from his face like a hen's egg.[28]

27. The original has 'Send out'.

28. cf. Swift's cousin, Mrs Martha Whiteway, to the earl of Orrery,

JOHN CORBET: He looked like that in his old age. Stella had been dead a long time. His brain had gone, his friends had deserted him. The man appointed to take care of him beat him to keep him quiet.

MRS. HENDERSON: Now they are old, now they are young. They change all in a moment as their thought changes. It is sometimes a terrible thing to be out of the body, God help us all.

DR. TRENCH: (*At doorway*) Come along, Corbet, Mrs. Henderson is tired out.

JOHN CORBET: Good-bye, Mrs. Henderson. (*He goes out with* DR. TRENCH).

All the sitters except MISS MACKENNA, *who has returned to her room, pass along the passage on their way to the front door.* MRS. HENDERSON *counts the money, finds her purse, which is in a vase on the mantelpiece, and puts the money in it.*

MRS. HENDERSON: How tired I am! I'd be the better of a cup of tea. (*She finds the teapot and puts kettle on fire, and then as she crouches down by the hearth suddenly lifts up her hands and counts her fingers, speaking in Swift's voice.*) Five great Ministers that were my friends are gone, ten great Ministers that were my friends are gone. I have not fingers enough to count the great Ministers that were my friends and that are gone.[29] (*She wakes with a start and speaks in her own voice*) Where did I put that tea-caddy? Ah! there it is. And there should be a cup and saucer. (*She finds the saucer*) But where's the cup? (*She moves aimlessly about the stage and then, letting the saucer fall and break, speaks in Swift's voice*) Perish the day on which I was born![30]

22 November 1742: 'About six weeks ago, in one night's time, his left eye swelled as large as an egg, and the lid Mr. Nichols [his surgeon] thought would mortify, and very large boils appeared under his arms and body.'

29. Towards the end of his life Swift compiled lists of his friends, dead and living, and marked them with judgments like 'ungrateful', 'indifferent'. In a letter to Pope, 2 February 1736, he wrote: 'I was t'other day recollecting twenty Seven great Ministers or men of Wit and Learning, who are all dead, and all of my Acquaintance within twenty years past.' Note how the voice of Swift here repeats, but enhances, Trench's remark (see note 14 above) about Swift's friends.
30. cf. Job 3. 3: 'Let the day perish wherein I was born, and the night in which it was said, There is a man child conceived.'

ELIZABETH BOWEN

(1899-1973)

from:
THE DEMON LOVER AND OTHER STORIES (1945)

[In its very structure 'The Happy Autumn Fields' encapsulates Elizabeth Bowen's position during the war, her time divided between London under the blitz and her County Cork home, Bowen's Court. Her periodical returns to Ireland during these years were linked to her work for the British Ministry of Information 'ascertaining Irish attitudes to the war, specifically ... the question of the Treaty Ports in the south and west of Ireland, to which Churchill tried to persuade de Valera to allow British access.' While in Ireland she also began compiling a history of her family home, and wrote the book (published in 1942 as *Bowen's Court*) back in London under the bombs. Hermione Lee notes that 'there are Victorian diary entries in *Bowen's Court* which provide the source of "The Happy Autumn Fields".'

Essentially the story is a 'double helix' narrative, with two strands interwoven but never explicitly connecting. A woman in her bombed-out London house finds an album of Victorian photographs: a young woman walking in a nineteenth-century landscape mentally anticipates some future threat or jeopardy. Each thinks the other, somehow, as a thought. This structure may owe something to Sheridan Le Fanu's far more lurid double narrative involving women, the vampiric tale 'Carmilla' from *In a Glass Darkly* (1872).

The quotation in the title from Alfred Tennyson provides an indirect, and generalized, fixed point in one timetable. The term 'jacquerie' links the disorder and violence of the other timetable back to the Victorian period: the *Oxford English Dictionary* cites a usage of 1882 that is curiously apt: 'in many districts of Ireland the anti-landlord agitation ... has changed an agrarian movement into a true jacquerie.'

THE HAPPY AUTUMN FIELDS[1]

The family walking party, though it comprised so many, did not deploy or straggle over the stubble but kept in a procession of threes and twos. Papa, who carried his Alpine stick, led, flanked by Constance and little Arthur. Robert and Cousin Theodore, locked in studious talk, had Emily attached but not quite abreast. Next came Digby and Lucius, taking, to left and right, imaginary aim at rooks. Henrietta and Sarah brought up the rear.

It was Sarah who saw the others ahead on the blond stubble, who knew them, knew what they were to each other, knew their names and knew her own. It was she who felt the stubble under her feet, and who heard it give beneath the tread of the others a continuous different more distant soft stiff scrunch. The field and all these outlying fields in view knew as Sarah knew that they were Papa's. The harvest had been good and was now in: he was satisfied — for this afternoon, he had made the instinctive choice of his most womanly daughter, most nearly infant son. Arthur, whose hand Papa was holding, took an anxious hop, a skip and a jump to every stride of the great man's. As for Constance — Sarah could often see the flash of her hat-feather as she turned her head, the curve of her close bodice as she turned her torso. Constance gave Papa her attention but not her thoughts, for she had already been sought in marriage.

The landowner's daughters, from Constance down, walked with their beetle-green, mole or maroon skirts gathered up and carried clear of the ground, but for Henrietta, who was still ankle-free. They walked inside a continuous stuffy sound, but left silence behind them. Behind them, rooks that had risen and circled, sun striking blue from their blue-black wings, planed one by one to the earth and settled to peck again. Papa and the boys were dark-clad as the rooks but with no sheen, but for their white collars.

It was Sarah who located the thoughts of Constance, knew what a twisting prisoner was Arthur's hand, felt to the depths of Emily's pique at cousin Theodore's inattention, rejoiced with Digby and Lucius at the imaginary fall of so many rooks. She fell back, however, as from a rocky range, from the converse of Robert and Cousin Theodore. Most she knew that she swam with love at the nearness of Henrietta's young and alert face and eyes which shone with the sky and queried the afternoon.

She recognized the colour of valediction, tasted sweet sadness, while from the cottage inside the screen of trees wood-smoke rose melting pungent and blue. This was the eve of the brothers' return to school. It was like a Sunday; Papa had kept the late afternoon free; all (all but one) encircling Robert, Digby and Lucius, they walked the estate the brothers would not see again for so long. Robert, it could be felt, was not unwilling to return to his books; next year he would go to college like Theodore; besides, to all this they saw he was not the heir. But in Digby and Lucius aiming and popping hid a bodily grief, the repugnance of victims, though these two were further from being heirs than Robert.

Sarah said to Henrietta: 'To think they will not be here tomorrow!'

'*Is* that what you are thinking about?' Henrietta asked, with her subtle taste for the truth.

'More, I was thinking that you and I will be back again by one another at table....'

'You know we are always sad when the boys are going, but we are never sad when the boys have gone.' The sweet reciprocal guilty smile that started on Henrietta's lips finished on those of Sarah. 'Also,' the young sister said, 'we know this is only something happening again. It happened last year, and it will happen next. But oh how should I feel, and how should you feel, if it were something that had not happened before?'

'For instance, when Constance goes to be married?'

'Oh, I don't mean *Constance*!' said Henrietta.

'So long,' said Sarah, considering, 'as, whatever it is, it happens to both of us?' She must never have to wake in the early morning except to the birdlike stirrings of Henrietta, or have her cheek brushed in the dark by the frill of another pillow in whose hollow did not repose Henrietta's cheek. Rather than they should cease to lie in the same bed she prayed they might lie in the same grave. 'You and I will stay as we are,' she said, 'then nothing can touch one without touching the other.'

'So you say; so I hear you say!' exclaimed Henrietta, who then, lips apart, sent Sarah her most tormenting look. 'But I cannot forget that you chose

1. 'In looking on the happy Autumn-fields
And thinking of the days that are no more.'
Tennyson, 'The Princess' (1847) II, 20-21.

to be born without me; that you would not wait —' But here she broke off, laughed outright and said: 'Oh, *see*!'

Ahead of them there had been a dislocation. Emily took advantage of having gained the ridge to kneel down to tie her bootlace so abruptly that Digby all but fell over her, with an exclamation. Cousin Theodore had been civil enough to pause beside Emily, but Robert, lost to all but what he was saying, strode on, head down, only just not colliding into Papa and Constance, who had turned to look back. Papa, astounded, let go of Arthur's hand, whereupon Arthur fell flat on the stubble.

'Dear me,' said the affronted Constance to Robert.

Papa said. 'What is the matter there? May I ask, Robert, where you are going, sir? Digby, remember that is your sister Emily.'

'Cousin Emily is in trouble,' said Cousin Theodore.

Poor Emily, telescoped in her skirts and by now scarlet under her hatbrim, said in a muffled voice: 'It is just my bootlace, Papa.'

'Your bootlace, Emily?'

'I was just tying it.'

'Then you had better tie it. — Am I to think, ' said Papa, looking round them all, 'that you must all go down like a pack of ninepins because Emily has occasion to stoop?'

At this Henrietta uttered a little whoop, flung her arms round Sarah, buried her face in her sister and fairly suffered with laughter. She could contain this no longer; she shook all over. Papa, who found Henrietta so hopelessly out of order that he took no notice of her except at table, took no notice, simply giving the signal for the others to collect themselves and move on. Cousin Theodore, helping Emily to her feet, could be seen to see how her heightened colour became her, but she dispensed with his hand chillily, looked elsewhere, touched the brooch at her throat and said: 'Thank you, I have not sustained an accident.' Digby apologized to Emily, Robert to Papa and Constance. Constance righted Arthur, flicking his breeches over with her handkerchief. All fell into their different steps and resumed their way.

Sarah, with no idea how to console laughter, coaxed, 'Come, come, come,' into Henrietta's ear. Between the girls and the others the distance widened; it began to seem that they would be left alone.

'And why not?' said Henrietta, lifting her head in answer to Sarah's thought.

They looked around them with the same eyes. The shorn uplands seemed to float on the distance, which extended dazzling to tiny blue glassy hills. There was no end to the afternoon, whose light went on ripening now they had scythed the corn. Light filled the silence which, now Papa and the others were out of hearing, was complete. Only screens of trees intersected and knolls made islands in the vast fields. The mansion and the home farm[2] had sunk for ever below them in the expanse of woods, so that hardly a ripple showed where the girls dwelled.

The shadow of the same rook circling passed over Sarah then over Henrietta, who in their turn cast one shadow across the stubble. 'But, Henrietta, we cannot stay here for ever.'

Henrietta immediately turned her eyes to the only lonely plume of smoke, from the cottage. 'Then let us go and visit the poor old man. He is dying and the others are happy. One day we shall pass and see no more smoke; then soon his roof will fall in, and we shall always be sorry we did not go today.'

'But he no longer remembers us any longer.'

'All the same, he will feel us there in the door.'

'But can we forget this is Robert's and Digby's and Lucius's goodbye walk? It would be heartless of both of us to neglect them.'

'Then how heartless Fitzgeorge is!' smiled Henrietta.

'Fitzgeorge is himself, the eldest and in the Army. Fitzgeorge I'm afraid is not an excuse for us.'

A resigned sigh, or perhaps the pretence of one, heaved up Henrietta's still narrow bosom. To delay matters for just a moment more she shaded her eyes with one hand, to search the distance like a sailor looking for a sail. She gazed with hope and zeal in every direction but that in which she and Sarah were bound to go. Then — 'Oh, but Sarah, here *they* are, coming — they are!' she cried. She brought out her handkerchief and began to fly it, drawing it to and fro through the windless air.

In the glass of the distance, two horsemen came into view, cantering on a grass track between the fields. When the track dropped into a hollow they dropped with it, but by now the drumming of hoofs was heard. The reverberation filled the land, the

2. A farmyard attached to the residence of a landowner.

silence and Sarah's being; not watching for the riders to reappear she instead fixed her eyes on her sister's handkerchief which, let hang limp while its owner intently waited, showed a bitten corner as well as a damson stain. Again it became a flag, in furious motion. — 'Wave too, Sarah, wave too! Make your bracelet flash!'

'They must have seen us if they will ever see us,' said Sarah, standing still as a stone.

Henrietta's waving at once ceased. Facing her sister she crunched up her handkerchief, as though to stop it acting a lie. 'I can see you are shy,' she said in a dead voice. 'So shy you won't even wave to *Fitzgeorge*?'

Her way of not speaking the *other* name had a hundred meanings; she drove them all in by the way she did not look at Sarah's face. The impulsive breath she had caught stole silently out again, while her eyes — till now at their brightest, their most speaking — dulled with uncomprehending solitary alarm. The ordeal of awaiting Eugene's approach thus became for Sarah, from moment to moment, torture.

Fitzgeorge, Papa's heir, and his friend Eugene, the young neighbouring squire, struck off the track and rode up at a trot with their hats doffed. Sun striking low turned Fitzgeorge's flesh to coral and made Eugene blink his dark eyes. The young men reined in; the girls looked up at the horses. 'And my father, Constance, the others?' Fitzgeorge demanded, as though the stubble had swallowed them.

'Ahead, on the way to the quarry, the other side of the hill.'

'We heard you were all walking together,' Fitzgeorge said, seeming dissatisfied.

'We are following.'

'What, alone?' said Eugene, speaking for the first time.

'Forlorn!' glittered Henrietta, raising two mocking hands.

Fitzgeorge considered, said 'Good' severely, and signified to Eugene that they would ride on. But too late: Eugene had dismounted. Fitzgeorge saw, shrugged and flicked his horse to a trot; but Eugene led his slowly between the sisters. Or rather, Sarah walked on his left hand, the horse on his right and Henrietta the other side of the horse. Henrietta, acting like somebody quite alone, looked up at the sky, idly holding one of the empty stirrups. Sarah, however, looked at the ground, with Eugene inclined as though to speak but not speaking. Enfolded, dizzied, blinded as though inside a wave, she could feel his features carved in brightness above her. Alongside the slender stepping of his horse, Eugene matched his naturally long free step to hers. His elbow was through the reins; with his fingers he brushed back the lock that his bending to her had sent falling over his forehead. She recorded the sublime act and knew what smile shaped his lips. So each without looking trembled before an image, while slow colour burned up the curves of her cheeks. The consummation would be when their eyes met.

At the other side of the horse, Henrietta began to sing. At once her pain, like a scientific ray, passed through the horse and Eugene to penetrate Sarah's heart.

We surmount the skyline: the family come into our view, we into theirs. They are halted, waiting, on the decline to the quarry. The handsome statufied group in strong yellow sunshine, aligned by Papa and crowned by Fitzgeorge, turn their judging eyes on the laggards, waiting to close their ranks round Henrietta and Sarah and Eugene. One more moment and it will be too late; no further communication will be possible. Stop oh stop Henrietta's heartbreaking singing! Embrace her close again! Speak the only possible word! Say — oh, say what? Oh, the word is lost!

'Henrietta . . .'

A shock of striking pain in the knuckles of the outflung hand — Sarah's? The eyes, opening, saw that the hand had struck, not been struck: there was a corner of a table. Dust, whitish and gritty, lay on the top of the table and on the telephone. Dull but piercing white light filled the room and what was left of the ceiling; her first thought was that it must have snowed. If so, it was winter now.

Through the calico stretched and tacked over the window came the sound of a piano: someone was playing Tchaikowsky badly in a room without windows or doors. From somewhere else in the hollowness came a cascade of hammering. Close up, a voice: 'Oh, *awake*, Mary?' It came from the other side of the open door, which jutted out between herself and the speaker — he on the threshold, she lying on the uncovered mattress of a bed. The speaker added: 'I had been going away.'

Summoning words from somewhere she said: 'Why? I didn't know you were here.'

'Evidently — Say, who is "Henrietta"?'

Despairing tears filled her eyes. She drew back her hurt hand, began to suck at the knuckle and whimpered, 'I've hurt myself.'

A man she knew to be 'Travis', but failed to focus, came round the door saying: 'Really I don't wonder.' Sitting down on the edge of the mattress he drew her hand away from her lips and held it: the act, in itself gentle, was accompanied by an almost hostile stare of concern. 'Do listen, Mary,' he said. 'While you've slept I've been all over the house again, and I'm less than ever satisfied that it's safe. In your normal senses you'd never attempt to stay here. There've been alerts, and more than alerts,[3] all day; one more bang anywhere near, which may happen at any moment, could bring the rest of this down. You keep telling me that you have things to see to — but do you know what chaos the rooms are in? Till they've gone ahead with more clearing, where can you hope to start? And if there *were* anything you could do, you couldn't do it. Your own nerves know that, if you don't: it was almost frightening, when I looked in just now, to see the way you were sleeping — you've shut up shop.'

She lay staring over his shoulder at the calico window. He went on: 'You don't like it here. Your self doesn't like it. Your will keeps driving your self, but it can't be driven the whole way — it makes its own get-out: sleep. Well, I want you to sleep as much as you (really) do. But *not* here. So I've taken a room for you in a hotel; I'm going now for a taxi; you can practically make the move without waking up.'

'No, I can't get into a taxi without waking.'

'Do you realize you're the last soul left in the terrace?'

'Then who is that playing the piano?'

'Oh, one of the furniture-movers in Number Six. I didn't count the jaquerie;[4] of course *they're* in possession — unsupervised, teeming, having a high old time. While I looked in on you in here ten minutes ago they were smashing out that conservatory at the other end. Glass being done in in cold blood — it was brutalizing. You never batted an eyelid; in fact, I thought you smiled.' He listened. 'Yes, the piano — they are highbrow all right. You know there's a workman downstairs lying on your blue sofa looking for pictures in one of your French books?'

'No,' she said, 'I've no idea who is there.'

'Obviously. With the lock blown off your front door anyone who likes can get in and out.'

'Including you.'

'Yes. I've had a word with a chap about getting that lock back before tonight. As for you, you don't know what is happening.'

'I did,' she said, locking her fingers before her eyes.

The unreality of this room and of Travis's presence preyed on her as figments of dreams that one knows to be dreams can do. This environment's being in semi-ruin struck her less than its being some sort of device or trap; and she rejoiced, if anything, in its decrepitude. As for Travis, he had his own part in the conspiracy to keep her from the beloved two. She felt he began to feel he was now unmeaning. She was struggling not to contemn[5] him, scorn him for his ignorance of Henrietta, Eugene, her loss. His possessive angry fondness was part, of course, of the story of him and Mary, which like a book once read she remembered clearly but with indifference. Frantic at being delayed here, while the moment awaited her in the cornfield, she all but afforded a smile at the grotesquerie of being saddled with Mary's body and lover. Rearing up her head from the bare pillow, she looked, as far as the crossed feet, along the form inside which she found herself trapped: the irrelevant body of Mary, weighted down to the bed, wore a short black modern dress, flaked with plaster. The toes of the black suède shoes by their sickly whiteness showed Mary must have climbed over fallen ceilings; dirt engraved the fate-lines in Mary's palms.

This inspired her to say: 'But I've made a start; I've been pulling out things of value or things I want.'

For answer Travis turned to look down, expressively, at some object out of her sight, on the floor close by the bed. '*I* see,' he said, 'a musty old leather box gaping open with God knows what — junk, illegible letters, diaries, yellow photographs, chiefly plaster and dust. Of all things, Mary! — after a missing will?'

'Everything one unburies seems the same age.'

'Then what are these, where do they come from — family stuff?'

3. i.e. bomb alerts, air-raid warnings.
4. A jacquerie is a peasant uprising. (Bowen's individual spelling of the word has been retained since it occurs in all editions.)

5. despise.

'No idea,' she yawned into Mary's hand. 'They may not even be mine. Having a house like this that had empty rooms must have made me store more than I knew, for years. I came on these, so I wondered. Look if you like.'

He bent and began to go through the box — it seemed to her, not unsuspiciously. While he blew grit off packets and fumbled with tapes she lay staring at the exposed laths of the ceiling, calculating. She then said: 'Sorry if I've been cranky, about the hotel and all. Go away just for two hours, then come back with a taxi, and I'll go quiet. Will that do?'

'Fine — except why not now?'

'*Travis . . .*'

'Sorry. It shall be as you say . . . You've got some good morbid stuff in this box, Mary — so far as I can see at a glance. The photographs seem more your sort of thing. Comic but lyrical. All of one set of people — a beard, a gun and pot hat, a schoolboy with a moustache, a phaeton drawn up in front of mansion, a group on steps, a *carte de visite*[6] of two young ladies hand-in-hand in front of a painted field —'

'*Give that to me!*'

She instinctively tried and failed, to unbutton the bosom of Mary's dress: it offered no hospitality to the photograph. So she could only fling herself over on the mattress, away from Travis, covering the two faces with her body. Racked by that oblique look of Henrietta's she recorded, too, a sort of personal shock at having seen Sarah for the first time.

Travis's hand came over her, and she shuddered. Wounded, he said: 'Mary . . .'

'Can't you leave *me* alone?'

She did not move or look till he had gone out saying: 'Then, in two hours.' She did not therefore see him pick up the dangerous box, which he took away under his arm, out of her reach.

They were back. Now the sun was setting behind the trees, but its rays passed dazzling between the branches into the beautiful warm red room. The tips of the ferns in the jardinière[7] curled gold, and Sarah, standing by the jardinière, pinched at a leaf of scented geranium. The carpet had a great centre wreath of pomegranates, on which no tables or chairs stood, and its whole circle was between herself and the others.

No fire was lit yet, but where they were grouped was a hearth. Henrietta sat on a low stool, resting her elbow above her head on the arm of Mamma's chair, looking away intently as though into a fire, idle. Mamma embroidered, her needle slowed down by her thoughts; the length of tatting with roses she had already done overflowed stiffly over her supple skirts. Stretched on the rug at Mamma's feet, Arthur looked through an album of Swiss views, not liking them but vowed to be very quiet. Sarah, from where she stood, saw fuming cataracts and null eternal snows as poor Arthur kept turning over the pages, which had tissue paper between.

Against the white marble mantelpiece stood Eugene. The dark red shadows gathering in the drawing-room as the trees drowned more and more of the sun would reach him last, perhaps never: it seemed to Sarah that a lamp was lighted behind his face. He was the only gentleman with the ladies: Fitzgeorge had gone to the stables, Papa to give an order; Cousin Theodore was consulting a dictionary; in the gunroom Robert, Lucius and Digby went through the sad rites, putting away their guns. All this was known to go on but none of it could be heard.

This particular hour of subtle light — not to be fixed by the clock, for it was early in winter and late in summer and in spring and autumn now, about Arthur's bed-time — had always, for Sarah, been Henrietta's. To be with her indoors or out, upstairs or down, was to share the same crepitation.[8] Her spirit ran on past yours with a laughing shiver into an element of its own. Leaves and branches and mirrors in empty rooms became animate. The sisters rustled and scampered and concealed themselves where nobody else was in play that was full of fear, fear that was full of play. Till, by dint of making each other's hearts beat violently, Henrietta so wholly and Sarah so nearly lost all human reason that Mamma had been known to look at them searchingly as she sat instated for evening among the calm amber lamps.

But now Henrietta had locked the hour inside her breast. By spending it seated beside Mamma, in young imitation of Constance the Society daughter, she disclaimed for ever anything else. It had always been she who with one fierce act destroyed any toy

6. A small photographic portrait mounted on a card.
7. An ornamental stand or receptacle for plants or flowers.
8. A rattling or crackling sound.

that might be outgrown. She sat with straight back, poising her cheek remotely against her finger. Only by never looking at Sarah did she admit their eternal loss.

Eugene, not long returned from a foreign tour, spoke of travel, addressing himself to Mamma, who thought but did not speak of her wedding journey. But every now and then she had to ask Henrietta to pass the scissors or tray of carded wools, and Eugene seized every such moment to look at Sarah. Into eyes always brilliant with melancholy he dared begin to allow no other expression. But this in itself declared the conspiracy of still undeclared love. For her part she looked at him as though he, transfigured by the strange light, were indeed a picture, a picture who could not see her. The wallpaper now flamed scarlet behind his shoulder. Mamma, Henrietta, even unknowing Arthur were in no hurry to raise their heads.

Henrietta said: 'If I were a man I should take my bride to Italy.'

'There are mules in Switzerland,' said Arthur.

'Sarah,' said Mamma, who turned in her chair midly, 'where are you, my love; do you never mean to sit down?'

'To Naples,' said Henrietta.

'Are you not thinking of Venice?' said Eugene.

'No,' returned Henrietta, 'why should I be? I should like to climb the volcano. But then I am not a man, and am still less likely ever to be a bride.'

'Arthur . . .' Mamma said.

'Mamma?'

'Look at the clock.'

Arthur sighed politely, got up and replaced the album on the circular table, balanced upon the rest. He offered his hand to Eugene, his cheek to Henrietta and to Mamma; then he started towards Sarah, who came to meet him. 'Tell me, Arthur,' she said, embracing him, 'what did you do today?'

Arthur only stared with his button blue eyes. 'You were there too; we went for a walk in the cornfield, with Fitzgeorge on his horse, and I fell down.' He pulled out of her arms and said: 'I must go back to my beetle.' He had difficulty, as always, in turning the handle of the mahogany door. Mamma waited till he had left the room, then said: 'Arthur is quite a man now; he no longer comes running to me when he has hurt himself. Why, I did not even know he had fallen down. Before we know, he will be going away to school too.' She sighed and lifted her eyes to Eugene. 'Tomorrow is to be a sad day.'

Eugene with a gesture signified his own sorrow. The sentiments of Mamma could have been uttered only here in the drawing-room, which for all its size and formality was lyrical and almost exotic. There was a look like velvet in darker parts of the air; sombre window draperies let out gushes of lace; the music on the piano-forte bore tender titles, and the harp though unplayed gleamed in a corner, beyond sofas, whatnots,[9] armchairs, occasional tables that all stood on tottering little feet. At any moment a tinkle might have been struck from the lustres' drops of the brighter day, a vibration from the musical instruments, or a quiver from the fringes and ferns. But the towering vases upon the consoles,[10] the albums piled on the tables, the shells and figurines on the flights of brackets, all had, like the alabaster Leaning Tower of Pisa, an equilibrium of their own. Nothing would fall or change. And everything in the drawing-room was muted, weighted, pivoted by Mamma. When she added: 'We shall not feel quite the same,' it was to be understood that she would not have spoken thus from her place at the opposite end of Papa's table.

'Sarah,' said Henrietta curiously, 'what made you ask Arthur what he had been doing? Surely you have not forgotten today?'

The sisters were seldom known to address or question one another in public; it was taken that they knew each other's minds. Mamma, though untroubled, looked from one to the other. Henrietta continued: 'No day, least of all today, is like any other — Surely that must be true?' she said to Eugene. 'You will never forget my waving my handkerchief?'

Before Eugene had composed an answer, she turned to Sarah: 'Or *you*, them riding across the fields?'

Eugene also slowly turned his eyes on Sarah, as though awaiting with something like dread her answer to the question he had not asked. She drew a light little gold chair into the middle of the wreath of the carpet, where no one ever sat, and sat down. She said: 'But since then I think I have been asleep.'

'Charles the First walked and talked half an hour after his head was cut off,'[11] said Henrietta mockingly. Sarah in anguish pressed the palms of her

9. Portable stands with shelves, for displaying ornaments.

10. i.e. console-tables, tables supported by a bracket affixed to a wall.

11. Charles I was beheaded on 30 January 1649 outside the palace of Whitehall in London.

hands together upon a shred of geranium leaf.

'How else,' she said, 'could I have had such a bad dream?'

'That must be the explanation!' said Henrietta.

'A trifle fanciful,' said Mamma.

However rash it might be to speak at all, Sarah wished she knew how to speak more clearly. The obscurity and loneliness of her trouble was not to be borne. How could she put into words the feeling of dislocation, the formless dread that had been with her since she found herself in the drawing-room? The source of both had been what she must call her dream. How could she tell the others with what vehemence she tried to attach her being to each second, not because each was singular in itself, each a drop condensed from the mist of love in the room, but because she apprehended that the seconds were numbered? Her hope was that the others at least half knew. Were Henrietta and Eugene able to understand how completely, how nearly for ever, she had been swept from them, would they not without fail each grasp one of her hands? — She went so far as to throw her hands out, as though alarmed by a wasp. The shred of geranium fell to the carpet.

Mamma, tracing this behaviour of Sarah's to only one cause, could not but think reproachfully of Eugene. Delightful as his conversation had been, he would have done better had he paid this call with the object of interviewing Papa. Turning to Henrietta she asked her to ring for the lamps, as the sun had set.

Eugene, no longer where he had stood, was able to make no gesture towards the bell-rope. His dark head was under the tide of dusk; for, down on one knee on the edge of the wreath, he was feeling over the carpet for what had fallen from Sarah's hand. In the inevitable silence rooks on the return from the fields could be heard streaming over the house; their sound filled the sky and even the room, and it appeared so useless to ring the bell that Henrietta stayed quivering by Mamma's chair. Eugene rose, brought out his fine white handkerchief and, while they watched, enfolded carefully in it what he had just found, then returning the handkerchief to his breast pocket. This was done so deep in the reverie that accompanies any final act that Mamma instinctively murmured to Henrietta: 'But you will be my child when Arthur has gone.'

The door opened for Constance to appear on the threshold. Behind her queenly figure globes approached, swimming in their own light: these were the lamps for which Henrietta had not rung, but these first were put on the hall tables. 'Why, Mamma,' exclaimed Constance, 'I cannot see who is with you!'

'Eugene is with us,' said Henrietta, 'but on the point of asking if he may send for his horse.'

'Indeed?' said Constance to Eugene. 'Fitzgeorge has been asking for you, but I cannot tell where he is now.'

The figures of Emily, Lucius and Cousin Theodore criss-crossed the lamplight there in the hall, to mass behind Constance's in the drawing-room door. Emily, over her sister's shoulder, said: 'Mamma, Lucius wishes to ask you whether for once he may take his guitar to school' — 'One objection, however,' said Cousin Theodore, 'is that Lucius's trunk is already locked and strapped.' 'Since Robert is taking his box of inks,' said Lucius, 'I do not see why I should not take my guitar.' — 'But Robert,' said Constance, 'will soon be going to college.'

Lucius squeezed past the others into the drawing-room in order to look anxiously at Mamma, who said: 'You have thought of this late; we must go and see.' The others parted to let Mamma, followed by Lucius, out. Then Constance, Emily and Cousin Theodore deployed and sat down in different parts of the drawing-room, to await the lamps.

'I am glad the rooks have done passing over,' said Emily, 'they make me nervous.' — 'Why?' yawned Constance haughtily, 'what do you think could happen?' Robert and Digby silently came in.

Eugene said to Sarah: 'I shall be back tomorrow.'

'But, oh —' she began. She turned to cry: 'Henrietta!'

'Why, what is the matter?' said Henrietta, unseen at the back of the gold chair. 'What could be sooner than tomorrow?'

'But something terrible may be going to happen.'

'There cannot fail to be tomorrow,' said Eugene gravely.

'*I* will see that there is tomorrow,' said Henrietta.

'You will never let me out of your sight?'

Eugene, addressing himself to Henrietta, said: 'Yes, promise her what she asks.'

Henrietta cried: 'She *is* never out of my sight. Who are you to ask me that, you Eugene? Whatever tries to come between me and Sarah becomes nothing. Yes, come tomorrow, come sooner, come

— when you like, but no one will ever be quite alone with Sarah. You do not even know what you are trying to do. It is *you* who are making something terrible happen. — Sarah, tell him that this is true! Sarah —'

The others, in the dark on the chairs and sofas, could be felt to turn their judging eyes upon Sarah, who, as once before, could not speak—

— The house rocked: simultaneously the calico window split and more ceiling fell, though not on the bed. The enormous dull sound of the explosion died, leaving a minor trickle of dissolution still to be heard in parts of the house. Until the choking stinging plaster dust had had time to settle, she lay with lips pressed close, nostrils not breathing and eyes shut. Remembering the box, Mary wondered if it had been again buried. No, she found, looking over the edge of the bed: that had been unable to happen because the box was missing. Travis, who must have taken it, would when he came back no doubt explain why. She looked at her watch, which had stopped, which was not surprising; she did not remember winding it for the last two days, but then she could not remember much. Through the torn window appeared the timelessness of an impermeably clouded late summer afternoon.

There being nothing left, she wished he would come to take her to the hotel. The one way back to the fields was barred by Mary's surviving the fall of ceiling. Sarah was right in doubting that there would be tomorrow: Eugene, Henrietta were lost in time to the woman weeping there on the bed, no longer reckoning who she was.

At last she heard the taxi, then Travis hurrying up the littered stairs. 'Mary, you're all right, Mary — *another*?' Such a helpless white face came round the door that she could only hold out her arms and say: 'Yes, but where have *you* been?'

'You said two hours. But I wish —'

'I have missed you.'

'Have you? Do you know you are crying?'

'Yes. How are we to live without natures? We only know inconvenience now, not sorrow. Everything pulverizes so easily because it is rot-dry; one can only wonder that it makes so much noise. The source, the sap must have dried up, or the pulse must have stopped, before you and I were conceived. So much flowed through people; so little flows through us. All we can do is imitate love or sorrow. — Why did you take away my box?'

He only said: 'It is in my office.'

She continued: 'What has happened is cruel: I am left with a fragment torn out of a day, a day I don't even know where or when; and now how am I to help laying that like a pattern against the poor stuff of everything else? — Alternatively, I am a person drained by a dream. I cannot forget the climate of those hours. Or life at that pitch, eventful — not happy, no, but strung like a harp. I have had a sister called Henrietta.'

'And I have been looking inside your box. What else can you expect? — I have had to write off this day, from the work point of view, thanks to you. So could I sit and do nothing for the last two hours? I just glanced through this and that — still, I know the family.'

'You said it was morbid stuff.'

'Did I? I still say it gives off something.'

She said: 'And then there was Eugene.'

'Probably. I don't think I came on much of his except some notes he must have made for Fitzgeorge from some book on scientific farming. Well, there it is: I have sorted everything out and put it back again, all but a lock of hair that tumbled out of a letter I could not trace. So I've got the hair in my pocket.'

'What colour is it?'

'Ash-brown. Of course, it is a bit — desiccated. Do you want it?'

'No,' she said with a shudder. 'Really, Travis, what revenges you take!'

'I didn't look at it that way,' he said puzzled.

'Is the taxi waiting?' Mary got off the bed and, picking her way across the room, began to look about for things she ought to take with her, now and then stopping to brush her dress. She took the mirror out of her bag to see how dirty her face was. 'Travis —' she said suddenly.

'Mary?'

'Only, I —'

'That's all right. Don't let us imitate anything just at present.'

In the taxi, looking out of the window, she said: 'I suppose, then, that I am descended from Sarah?'

'No,' he said, 'that would be impossible. There must be some reason why you should have those papers, but that is not the one. From all negative evidence Sarah, like Henrietta, remained unmarried. I found no mention of either, after a certain date, in the letters of Constance, Robert or Emily, which makes it seem likely both died young.

Fitzgeorge refers, in a letter to Robert written in his old age, to some friend of their youth who was thrown from his horse and killed, riding back after a visit to their home. The young man, whose name doesn't appear, was alone; and the evening, which was in autumn, was fine though late. Fitzgeorge wonders, and says he will always wonder, what made the horse shy in those empty fields.'

Biographies/Bibliographies

Charles Robert Maturin

For biography and bibliography, see Volume I, p. 1171.

Sydney Owenson, Lady Morgan

LIFE. Sydney Owenson was born (too romantically to be reliable) on Christmas Day 1783 on board a ship in the middle of the Irish Sea. Her father was an actor-manager, who retained some contact with his Gaelic antecedents. Sydney published versions of Irish melodies, with the help of Alicia Le Fanu, but is best known as a romantic novelist and travel-writer. Following the great success of *The Wild Irish Girl* in 1806, she was taken up by polite society in Dublin, and in 1809 the Duke and Duchess of Abercorn (in whose retinue she had found a home) arranged for her to marry their physician, Sir Charles Morgan. The Morgans made a witty and attractive couple, and the novelist pursued her own career in literature, earning as she went the undying hatred of Tory critics like John Wilson Croker. Following the defeat of Napoleon in 1815, she travelled to France but the resulting book was received very hostilely. Her views of Italy won the admiration of Lord Byron, but not of the pope nor of the King of Sardinia, both of whom banned the book. Her best fiction (*The O'Briens and the O'Flahertys*, 1829) was written on the eve of catholic emancipation, and her career was at its zenith. In 1837, she was granted a government pension by the Whigs, with which she retired to London. Her husband died in 1843. A prolific and financially successful author, she died in London in 1859, long after her reputation had begun to wane.

CHIEF WRITINGS. *Poems* (Dublin: Stewart, 1801); *St. Clair; or the Heiress of Desmond* (London: Harding, 1803); *A Few Reflections Occasioned by the Perusal of a Work Entitled 'Familiar Epistles . . . On the Present State of the Irish Stage'* (Dublin: Parry, 1804); *The Novice of Saint Dominick* 4 vols (London: Phillips, 1805); *Twelve Original Hibernian Melodies, with English Words* (London: Preston, [1805]); *The Wild Irish Girl: A National Tale* 3 vols (London: Phillips, 1806); *The Lay of an Irish Harp; or Metrical Fragments* (London: Phillips, 1807); *Patriotic Sketches of Ireland* 2 vols (London: Phillips, 1807); *Woman; or, Ida of Athens* (London: Longman, 1809); *The Missionary: An Indian Tale* (London: Stockdale, 1811); *O'Donnel: A National Tale* 3 vols (London: Colburn, 1814); *France* 2 vols (London: Colburn, 1817); *Florence Macarthy: An Irish Tale* 4 vols (London: Colburn, 1818); *Italy* 2 vols (London: Colburn, 1821); *Letter to the Reviewers of 'Italy'* (London: Colburn, 1824); *Absenteeism* (London: Colburn, 1825); *The O'Briens and the O'Flahertys: A National Tale* 4 vols (London: Colburn, 1829); *The Book of the Boudoir* 2 vols (London: Colburn, 1829); *France in 1829-1830* 2 vols (London: Saunders & Otley, 1830); *Dramatic Scenes from Real Life* 2 vols (London: Saunders & Otley, 1833); *The Princess; or, The Beguine* 3 vols (London: Bentley, 1834); *Woman and her Master* 2 vols (London: Colburn, 1840); *The Book without a Name* 2 vols, jointly with Sir T.C. Morgan (London: Colburn, 1841); *Letter to Cardinal Wiseman* (London: Westerton, 1851); *Passages from my Autobiography* (London: Bentley, 1859).

BIOGRAPHY AND CRITICISM. Many works were promptly written in answer to Lady Morgan, especially in relation to her French experiences. Of nineteenth-century publications, see W.J. Fitzpatrick, *Lady Morgan: Her Career, Literary and Personal* (London, 1860); also H. Hepworth Dixon (ed.), *Lady Morgan's Memoirs: Autobiography, Diary and Correspondence* 2 vols (London, 1863).

The best twentieth-century study is Lionel Stevenson, *The Wild Irish Girl: The Life of Sydney Owenson, Lady Morgan 1776-1859* (London: Chapman & Hall, 1936). See also Thomas Flanagan, *The Irish Novelists 1800-1850* (New York: Columbia University Press, 1959), pp. 109-64; Tom Dunne, 'Fiction as "the best history of nations": Lady Morgan's Irish Novels' in Tom Dunne (ed.), *The Writer as Witness; Literature as Historical Evidence* (Cork: Cork University Press, 1987), pp. 133-59.

William Carleton

For biography and bibliography, see p. 205.

Joseph Sheridan Le Fanu

For biography and bibliography, see Volume I, p. 1298.

Abraham (Bram) Stoker

LIFE. Abraham Stoker was born in Dublin in 1847. After a brief career in the Dublin civil service, Stoker (like Shaw and Wilde) moved to London where Arthur Conan Doyle (the son of an Irish artist) was already engaged in writing popular fiction. Apart from writing, Stoker's career was devoted to the management of the Lyceum Theatre from 1878 to 1905. He married fellow-Dubliner Florence Balcombe, whom Wilde had earlier courted. He died in London in 1912. His work, while it rarely possesses literary merit in the accepted sense, has been widely disseminated in American editions, piracies, translations, stage- and film-adaptations; the figure of Dracula has given rise to a sub-genre of horror writing. In relation to his Irish origins, one should note that *The Snake's Pass* (1891) is ostensibly set in rural Ireland, and that *Dracula* was translated into Irish by Seán O Cuirrín (Baile Atha Cliath: Oifig Diolta Foillseacháin Rialtais, 1933). Stoker's brother, Sir Thornley Stoker, was sometime president of the Royal College of Surgeons in Ireland.

CHIEF WRITINGS. Fiction: *Under the Sunset* (London: Sampson, Low, 1882); *The Snake's Pass* (London: Sampson, Low, 1891); *The Watter's Mou'* (Westminster: Constable, 1895); *The Shoulder of Shasta* (Westminster: Constable, 1895); *Dracula* (Westminster: Constable, 1897); *Miss Betty* (London: Pearson, 1898); *The Mystery of the Sea* (New York: Doubleday, 1902); *The Jewel of the Seven Stars* (London: Heinemann, 1903); *The Man* (London: Heinemann, 1905); *Lady Athlyne* (London: Heinemann, 1908); *Snowbound* (London: Collier, 1908); *The Lady of the Shroud* (London: Heinemann, 1909); *The Lair of the White Worm* (London: Rider, [1911]); *Dracula's Guest and Other Weird Stories* (London: Routledge, 1914).

Non-Fiction: *University of Dublin; College Historical Society; Address delivered . . . November 13, 1872* (Dublin: Charles, 1872); *The Duties of Clerks of Petty Sessions in Ireland* (Dublin: Falconer, 1879); *A Glimpse of America* (London: Sampson, Low, 1886); *Sir Henry Irving and Miss Ellen Terry* (New York: Doubleday, [1899]); *Personal Reminiscences of Henry Irving* 2 vols (London: Heinemann, 1906); *Famous Impostors* (London: Sidgwick and Jackson, 1910).

BIOGRAPHY AND CRITICISM. Harry Ludlam, *A Biography of Dracula; The Life Story of Bram Stoker* (London: Foulsham, 1962). Republished as *A Biography of Bram Stoker* (London: New English Library, 1977); Phyllis A. Roth, *Bram Stoker* (Boston: Twayne, 1982); Richard Dalby, *Bram Stoker; A Bibliography of First Editions* (London: Dracula Press, 1983).

John Millington Synge

For biography and bibliography, see p. 717.

Oscar Wilde

For biography and bibliography, see p. 514.

William Butler Yeats

For biography and bibliography, see p. 830.

Elizabeth Bowen

LIFE. Born in Dublin in 1899, Elizabeth Bowen went to England in 1907. She spent most of the following thirty-three years there. In 1923 she married Alan Cameron, moved to Oxford two years later and became well-known in London and Oxford literary circles. In 1930, on the death of her father, she inherited Bowen's Court, the family home in County Cork. She stayed there regularly thereafter, although she still spent most of her time in England. In 1937 she became a member of the Irish Academy of Letters. On the outbreak of war in 1939, Elizabeth Bowen became an air-raid warden in London and in 1940 returned to Ireland to work for the British Ministry of Information, sending back regular reports on the state of feeling and opinion in Ireland. During the war years she travelled between London, Dublin and Bowen's Court. She received an honorary doctorate from Trinity College, Dublin in 1949. In 1951 she moved to Bowen's Court. Her husband died in 1952. In the same year she received an honorary doctorate from Oxford University. During the 1950s she spent a good deal of time teaching in the United States. In 1959 she sold Bowen's Court; the next year it was demolished by the new owner. She died in London in 1973 and was buried at Farahay churchyard, on the former estate of Bowen's Court.

CHIEF WRITINGS. *Encounters* (London: Sidgwick and Jackson, 1923; New York: Boni and Liveright, 1925); *Anne Lee's and Other Stories* (London: Sidgwick and Jackson; New York: Boni and Liveright, 1926); *The Hotel* (London: Constable, 1927; New York: Dial Press, 1928; London: Cape, reprinted 1969, 1981); *Joining Charles and Other Stories* (London: Constable; New York: Dial Press, 1929); *The Last September* (London: Constable; New York: Dial Press, 1929; London: Cape, 1948; Penguin Books, 1988); *Friends and Relations* (London: Constable; New York: Dial Press, 1931); *To the North* (London: Gollancz, 1932; New York: Knopf, 1933); *The Cat Jumps and Other Stories* (London: Gollancz, 1934); *The House in Paris* (London: Gollancz, 1935; New York: Knopf, 1936; London: Cape, 1982); *The Death of the Heart* (London: Gollancz, 1935; New York: Knopf, 1936; London: Readers' Union and Cape, 1949); *Look at All Those Roses* (London: Gollancz; New York: Knopf, 1941); *Bowen's Court* (London: Longmans, Green; New York: Knopf, 1942; 2nd edition with Afterword, London: Longmans, Green; New York: Knopf, 1964; introduction by H. Lee, London: Virago, 1984); *Seven Winters: Memories of a Dublin Childhood* (Dublin: Cuala Press, 1942; London: Longmans, Green, 1943; republished as *Seven Winters: Memories of a Dublin Childhood and Afterthoughts: Pieces on Writing* New York: Knopf, 1962); *The Demon Lover and Other Stories* (London: Cape, 1945; published as *Ivy Gripped the Steps* New York: Knopf, 1946); *The Heat of the Day* (London: Cape, 1949; reprinted 1982; New York: Knopf, 1949); *Collected Impressions* (London: Longmans, Green; New York: Knopf, 1950); *The Shelbourne: A Centre in Dublin Life for More Than a Century* (London: George G. Harrap, 1951; published in the United States as *The Shelbourne Hotel* New York: Knopf, 1951); *Early Stories* (New York: Knopf, 1951); *A World of Love* (London: Cape; New York: Knopf, 1955); *Stories by Elizabeth Bowen* (New York: Knopf, 1959); *The Little Girls* (London: Cape; New York: Knopf, 1964); *A Day in the Dark and Other Stories* (London: Cape, 1965); *Eva Trout or Changing Scenes* (New York: Knopf, 1968; London: Cape, 1969); *Pictures and Conversations:* with a foreword by S.C. Brown (London: Allen Lane, 1975); *Irish Stories* (Swords, Co. Dublin: Poolbeg Press, 1978); *The Collected Stories of Elizabeth Bowen* with an introduction by Angus Wilson (London: Cape, 1980); *The Mulberry Tree: Writings of Elizabeth Bowen* selected and introduced by H. Lee (London: Virago, 1986).

BIOGRAPHY AND CRITICISM. W. Heath, *Elizabeth Bowen: An Introduction* (Madison: University of Wisconsin Press, 1961); A. Allen, *Elizabeth Bowen* (New York: Twayne, 1971); H. Blodgett, *Patterns of Reality: Elizabeth Bowen's Novels* (The Hague: Mouton, 1975); E. J. Kenny, *Elizabeth Bowen* (Lewisburg, Pennsylvania; Bucknell University Press, 1975); V. Glendinning, *Elizabeth Bowen: Portrait of a Writer* (London: Weidenfeld and Nicolson, 1977); H. Lee, *Elizabeth Bowen: An Estimation* (London: Vision; Totowa, New Jersey: Barnes and Noble, 1981); P. Craig, *Elizabeth Bowen* (Harmondsworth: Penguin Books, 1986).

LUKE GIBBONS, *Editor*

Constructing the Canon: Versions of National Identity

Nationalism stands between Ireland and the light of the world. Nobody in Ireland of any intelligence likes Nationalism any more than a man with a broken arm likes having it set. A healthy nation is as unconscious of its nationality as a healthy man of his bones. But if you break a nation's nationality it will think of nothing else but getting it set again. It will listen to no reformer, to no philosopher, to no preacher, until the demand of the Nationalist is granted. It will attend to no business, however vital, except the business of unification and liberation.

from: George Bernard Shaw's 'Preface for Politicians' in *John Bull's Other Island* (1904).

REVIVALISM: CONSTRUCTING THE CANON

In his *Irish Literary Portraits* (1935), John Eglinton confessed that, although he was a renegade from the Literary Revival, Ireland still held a lasting fascination for him as a country 'whose poets all made the mistake of going into politics'.[1] He might have extended this to Irish cultural life in general, where intellectual movements invariably are brought back to their point of origin, to their national provenance, as if they were returning to the scene of a crime.

It is often said that Irish culture is characterized by a resistance to theory, by the lack of a vigorous intellectual tradition. Irish creative writers are more than adequately represented in the pantheon of world literature, but in the case of critical or intellectual enquiry, the Irish contribution, with a few notable exceptions, seems conspicuous by its absence. It is not as if abstract thought is beyond the reach of 'the Irish mind', for in Matthew Arnold's *The Study of Celtic Literature* (1867), the locus classicus for the myth of the imaginative Celt, it was the tendency to get lost in abstraction, 'the abstract, severe character of the Druidical religion', which prevented a more practical, down-to-earth approach to worldly affairs. It was not intellect, but the steam intellect which was missing in Irish society. The Celt revolted against 'the despotism of fact', but was only too willing to fasten on to an *ideal*, no matter how impractical its material realization turned out to be. The ideal in question, the unspoken source of Arnold's anxiety about the 'manifold striving' of the Celt, was, of course, Irish nationalism.

In a curious book entitled *A Short History of Celtic Philosophy*, published in 1920, Herbert Moore Pim sought to establish an unbroken tradition of idealist thought in Ireland, from the ancient Druids, through to Johannes Scottus (Ériugena) and down to George Berkeley and Francis Hutcheson in the

1. John Eglinton, *Irish Literary Portraits* (London: Macmillan, 1935; reprinted Freeport, New York: Books for Libraries, 1967), p. 11.

eighteenth century.[2] What is of interest here is not the wishful thinking of Moore Pim's own philosophy, but his insistence that all intellectual activity, even at the most rarified level, was an expression of an underlying Celtic *mentalité*, a manifestation of 'the Irish mind'. It is perhaps this, more than any alleged deficiency in the Celtic temperament, that is responsible for the arrested development of an intellectual tradition in Ireland. From the late eighteenth century, but more particularly from the nineteenth century, important initiatives in Irish intellectual life were judged, not by Enlightenment standards of reason and progress, but by where they stood on the unfinished business of the national question. No field of enquiry seemed exempt from this imperative. Even the natural sciences, the theoretical vanguard of the Enlightenment, were enlisted in the service of the nationalist ideal. The first volume of *The Transactions of the Royal Irish Academy* (1787), for example, made it clear that whatever fostered 'the cultivation of useful arts and sciences . . . cannot but prove of the greatest national advantage. . . . Animated by such encouragements the Irish nation are called to exert themselves'.[3] Intellectual currents tended to be channelled into those aspects of scientific research that lent themselves to the growth of self-reliance and national esteem. Geology is a case in point. The ease with which the universal gave way to the local is evident in the founding principles of the Geological Society of Dublin (1832), which aimed to investigate 'the mineral structure of Earth, and more particularly Ireland', in the firm belief that its findings would be 'acceptable to the patriot and the man of science alike'[4] — as if the interests of the nation and universal reason could only converge. If we are to believe Gordon Herries Davies, the remit of national renewal extended not only to geology, but even to the outer reaches of mathematics:

> It needs to be emphasized that Griffith's geological map of Ireland is just as much a manifestation of the Irish creative genius as is Orpen's *The Holy Well* — that in Salmon's *Conic Sections* we see an Irish mind at work just as surely as we see de Valera's mind at work in Ireland's 1937 constitution.[5]

One field where pressing local exigencies cut across the universal pretensions of an aspiring 'science' was political economy. In 1912, in an astringent polemic against the economic orthodoxies of the day, Tom Kettle, the newly appointed professor of national economics at the National University in Dublin, addressed himself to 'the gibe' that a chair of national economics made no more sense than a chair of 'National Trigonometry'. Kettle had no difficulty conceding that ' in the sphere of the highly abstract sciences any limiting particularity is certainly incongruous', but he was not prepared to admit economics to this privileged domain. Economics, in his view, did not follow iron laws of necessity but is 'soaked and steeped' in the 'history and temperament' of a specific country. This applied even to what, following nineteenth-century Irish commentators, he insisted on calling *English* classical economy: universality came easily to an imperial power that took the entire world as its playground. Ireland was not simply an exception to the rule of *laissez-faire*, but was the reef on which the whole system of universal free trade foundered. In arguing thus, Kettle cited the precedent of a nineteenth-century Irish school of political economy that included Charles Bastable and John Kells Ingram, although, strangely, he omits John Elliot Cairnes, the Irish economist whose work led both John

2. Johannes Scottus (Ériugena), born in Ireland in the ninth century, is generally credited with being the founder of scholastic philosophy. George Berkeley (1685–1753), the famous idealist philosopher, was born in County Kilkenny and was educated at Trinity College, Dublin. Francis Hutcheson (1694–1746), the foremost exponent of the 'moral sense' school of philosophy, was born in County Down and taught in Dublin. The opening sentence in the introduction to a recent book, *The Irish Mind*, viz. 'Surprisingly, there has never been a study specifically devoted to Ireland's contribution to the world of thought', overlooks Moore Pim's speculative venture into the field. (See R. Kearney (ed.), *The Irish Mind: Exploring Intellectual Traditions* (Dublin: Wolfhound Press; Atlantic Highlands, New Jersey: Humanities Press Inc., 1985), p. 7.)
3. *Transactions of the Royal Irish Academy* Vol. 1 (Dublin: George Bonham, 1787), pp. xi, xvi.
4. See Jean Archer, 'Science Loners: the *Journal of the Geological Society of Dublin* and its successors', in Barbara Hayley and Enda MacKay (eds), *300 Years of Irish Periodicals* (Dublin: Association of Irish Learned Journals, 1987), pp. 50–51.
5. Gordon L. Herries Davies, 'Irish Thought in Science' in R. Kearney (ed.), *The Irish Mind*, p. 310. Sir Richard Griffith (1784–1878), geologist and civil engineer, devised the valuation scheme for the Irish system (1852). His *Geological Map of Ireland* (1855) became the standard reference for the Ordnance Board. George Salmon (1818–1904) was a mathematician and theologian and was appointed provost of Trinity College, Dublin in 1888. His *Conic Sections* (1847) became a standard work on the subject. Sir William Orpen (1878–1931) was one of the leading Irish painters at the turn of the century. *The Holy Well* (c. 1913–14) is one of his few paintings that deal with themes related to the Irish Revival.

Stuart Mill and J. M. Keynes to question the basic premisses of the *laissez-faire* system.[6] For Bastable, the nation always came between the individual, *homo economicus*, and the world at large. In the case of Kells Ingram, the subordination of 'the dismal science' to the rhetoric of nationalism was more complete, for he became known to Irish readers not as a political economist but, much to his chagrin, as the author of a rousing ballad that came to be one of the anthems of popular nationalism: 'Who fears to speak of '98?'

Given this tendency to subsume all intellectual energies, even the 'cold philosophy' of science, into a nationalist project, it is not surprising that literature was also expected to serve this end. If economic laws were circumscribed by the history and temperament of a nation, then literature played a key role in forming this national temperament. For Patrick Pearse, nationalism was not just a political ideology but revealed itself 'in all the arts, all the institutions, all the inner life, all the actions and goings forth of the nation'.[7] There was little room in this for a universal, humanist vision, for a body of creative work that addressed itself to the eternal verities of humanity and nature, the individual and the cosmos. To the urbane sensibility of the critic John Eglinton, this indicated a basic lack of authenticity in Irish culture as if, like T. S. Eliot's Prufrock, it was preoccupied with mundane cultural problems but was mute in the face of the 'overwhelming questions' of life and death. Eglinton, who approached nature with the reverence of Wordsworth and human nature with the suspicion of Nietzsche, was determined that Irish culture should expand its horizons to take in not just the national but the human condition. 'It is by a "thought movement" rather than by a "language movement" ', he wrote, 'that Ireland will have to show that it holds the germs of true nationality'.[8] In the introduction to *Dana*, 'a magazine of independent thought', co-founded with the socialist Frederick Ryan, Eglinton asked rhetorically:

> Man and nature — what more do we want? The difficulty is to begin: and to make a beginning is especially difficult in a country like Ireland, where our bards and prophets have never learned to deal directly and as men with the elements of human nature, and to dispense with traditional methods and traditional themes.

Dana's radical humanism led it to adopt a combative stance towards many of the religious and nationalist pieties that, in its view, were strangling the birth of a truly independent, assertive Irish culture. This hardly endeared it to the leading lights of the Gaelic revival, and the magazine folded after twelve issues. Although Eglinton and Ryan frequently were charged with betraying the cause of Ireland, the most significant aspect of their critical enterprise was that it emanated from *within* the shifting boundaries of the nationalist revival, and not from some alleged neutral vantage-point outside the political ferment of the time. Neither Eglinton nor Ryan was interested in the kind of liberal ecumenism that looked for common ground as a means of burying internal differences and conflicts. Whatever disagreements Eglinton had with 'official' nationalism, it did not prevent him from recommending the volatile figure of John Mitchel as the ideal of a nationalist whose writings possessed universal as well as local resonance. By the same token, Frederick Ryan was capable of puncturing some of the more inflated sentiments of the Gaelic League, but not on the conventional grounds that it mixed culture (a supposedly disinterested pursuit) with politics. On the contrary, Ryan feared that it might divert attention *away* from politics, from the social and economic problems of a dependent country seeking independence. Ryan's outlook was thoroughly internationalist but, like Tom Kettle, he was careful to distinguish this from a shallow cosmopolitanism which, in an Irish context, was simply imperialism masquerading under the guise of universal or civilizing values.

The question of cosmopolitanism was to become one of the most contentious issues in the formative years of the Revival. With the wisdom of hindsight, it is customary to read back into the early decades of the century a 'battle of two civilizations' (to use D. P. Moran's phrase), in which advanced nationalists were at one in promoting a form of

6. For a discussion of the importance of Cairnes in nineteenth-century economic thought, see pp. 184–92 and p. 207 above. See also Tom Boylan and Timothy P. Foley, 'John Elliot Cairnes, John Stuart Mill and Ireland: Some Problems for Political Economy' in Antoin E. Murphy (ed.), *Economists and the Irish Economy* (Dublin: Irish Academic Press, 1984).
7. Patrick H. Pearse, 'The Spiritual Nation', in *Political Writings and Speeches* (Dublin: The Phoenix Publishing Co., 1924), p. 302.
8. John Eglinton, 'Preface' to *Bards and Saints*, The Tower Press Booklets (first series), No. V (Dublin: Maunsel & Co., 1906), p. 11.

cultural isolationism, a narrow provincialism, while the Anglo-Irish and other enlightened forces sought a more outgoing *rapprochement* with the rest of the world. That this is too neat an opposition is clear from the fact that some of the most spirited attacks on cosmopolitanism came from leading Anglo-Irish figures such as W. B. Yeats, and A. E. (George Russell), while 'Irish Irelanders', such as Arthur Clery, a leading contributor to D. P. Moran's *The Leader*, argued that nationalism and cosmopolitanism were not contradictory ideals. The most concerted attempt to link international with nationalist ideals came not from 'Irish Irelanders' or Anglo-Irish writers, but from within the ranks of socialism. No sooner had James Connolly begun the arduous task of establishing a socialist movement in Ireland than the central Marxist tenets of progress and universal freedom, inherited from the Enlightenment, came under pressure from nationalist ideology. Connolly could write of the non-sectarian basis of socialism that it 'is neither freethinker nor Christian, Turk nor Jew . . . it is only HUMAN',[9] but this broad, humanist vision could not easily dispense with the rival claims of nationalism. Hence he was forced to bring about a marriage of convenience between what appeared to be unlikely partners — international socialism and cultural nationalism: 'I consider the free expression of Nationality', Connolly wrote, 'to be as desirable in the interest of humanity in general, as the free expression of individuality is to the nation'.[10]

On closer examination, however, it seems that Connolly's version of Marxism was in fact well-disposed towards the advances of nationalism from the outset. For one thing, his impatience with the philosophical end of socialism — the penchant for speculation 'about materialism and philosophy and ethics and sex and embryology and monogamy and physiology and monism and platonism and determinism'[11] — led him to reject theory as a framework for socialist strategy: instead, the revolutionary 'must first of all learn to look inward upon Ireland for his justification, rest his arguments upon the facts of Irish history'. This emphasis on concrete historical practice, rather than on the refinement of theory, complemented another aspect of Connolly's Marxism, namely his tendency to look towards the (historical) *nation* rather than the (abstract) *state* as the focus for political mobilization. Although the aversion to political institutions and organizations can partly be attributed to Connolly's syndicalism, the idea that modes of production are circumscribed by the cultural and historical exigencies of the nation is hardly compatible with the syndicalist view that revolutionary struggle is exclusively economic in character. Seán O'Faoláin has gone so far as to claim that it was Connolly who introduced the Gaelic mystique, the myth of a continuous nation, into cultural nationalism, but this, as we shall see, is mistaken. The scholarly rationale for this shift in emphasis from the state to the nation was provided by the historical researches of Eóin MacNeill, one of the founders of the Gaelic League and the first president of the Irish Volunteers, from whose ranks the Easter Rising of 1916 was planned.

MacNeill argued that Irish nationality was not a political construct, an affair of government or state, but was instead the legacy of an enduring nation that had existed in Ireland before the Norman conquest. The notion of *continuity* was central here since an unbroken tradition, stretching back to the earliest times, was deemed necessary to secure the legitimacy of Ireland's claim to be a separate nation. For this reason, MacNeill felt compelled to take issue with the sentiments expressed in Thomas Davis's ballad 'A Nation Once Again', on the grounds that it implied that Ireland was not already a nation. One of the difficulties with maintaining a belief in an uninterrupted tradition, however, was that it seemed to run counter to another basic article of faith in nationalism, namely that the English conquest had uprooted and fractured a thriving native culture, an island of saints and scholars. The problem of explaining permanence in the midst of change might have been overcome by positing the existence of a pure, indestructible Irish *race*, surviving all kinds of adversity and oppression, but MacNeill rejected this biologism out of hand, as did one of the most important popularizers of his ideas, Aodh de Blacam:

> It is clear that any attempt to base the Irish Nation on racialism is absurd from the outset [wrote de Blacam]. Such an attempt has never been made

9. *Workers' Republic*, 17 June 1899.
10. *Workers' Republic*, 2 December 1899. In a witty rhetorical stratagem, Connolly argued that being Irish and part of an international socialist movement is no more anomalous than being Irish and a member of the universal or 'Catholic' church (*The Harp*, November 1909).
11. *The Harp*, May 1909.

by any Nationalist of authority. Gaelicism, then, is in no sense racial, and the Gaelic nation offers a welcome to its citizenship to the child of any race if he, living in Ireland, accepts the sovereignty of the Irish nation.

This is an important corrective to the misconception that Irish nationalism, in its most zealous forms at any rate, is bound up with racialism, but it still left writers like de Blacam with the problem of accounting for an enduring Irish identity. 'Gaelicism', de Blacam insisted, 'is not so artificial a thing that it can be killed by a break in its continuity.' It was at this point that the spiritual nation, the Gaelic mystique, made its presence felt. Ironically, this mystical notion of an essential Irish identity persisting throughout all social upheavals was to prove most attractive to writers like de Blacam, AE and the socialist W. P. Ryan, who were intent on *material* reforms, and thus had a particular interest in maintaining a sense of continuity in the midst of substantial social change. These agrarian reformers were captivated by the cooperative potential of Irish agriculture, and looked to the existence of a pre-conquest Gaelic commonwealth, a form of Celtic communism, to establish a native pedigree for their cooperative ideals. W. P. Ryan's spiritual socialism was such that he published a visionary tract entitled *The Celt and the Cosmos* (1913), an inspired attempt to fuse metaphysical and economic speculation. James Connolly, however, was more interested in the plough than in the stars. Although fascinated by the communal structure of ancient Gaelic society, he argued that there was no direct line of descent between this and present-day struggles. At most, it was a valuable aid in countering arguments that socialism was an 'alien' ideology, a modern import into Irish society. Connolly's profound grasp of history as a transformative rather than as a preservative agent made him all too aware of the breaks and discontinuities in the 'Irish tradition'.

The lack of importance accorded in cultural debates to race, in the strict biological sense, meant that, even in the writings of advanced nationalists such as de Blacam, it was possible to allow an element of discontinuity in the 'native heritage', and to construe 'Gaeldom' as a composite of many races, peoples and creeds. With the cultural retrenchment following the founding of the state in 1922, this porous version of the nation became more difficult to sustain. Nationalist propagandists, or at least those with close affiliations to catholicism, felt it was their turn to strike back against the Empire, and particularly against the dominant position of the Anglo-Irish in higher education, the arts and intellectual culture in Ireland. One of the main sites of contention became cultural history itself, which was still labouring under Ascendancy interpretations of the past as exemplified in the work of historians such as W. E. H. Lecky. Considered from this Anglo-Irish position, the resurgence of the Irish nation was primarily a protestant affair, owing its origins to the writings of William Molyneux, Swift, Bishop Berkeley and, of course, to Grattan's parliament. This narrow perspective on the past, the view from the 'Big House', was challenged by Daniel Corkery's *The Hidden Ireland* (1924), a polemical essay in retrieval which sought to restore the native tradition, as represented in Munster poetry, to its central place in Irish history. Corkery was prepared to concede that Anglo-Irish figures such as Swift were concerned with the plight of the native Irish, but only on humanitarian grounds — and humanism of this kind, in his eyes, was a poor substitute for an active identification with nationalism.

Corkery reserved his most thoroughgoing assault on the colonial character of Anglo-Irish literature for the opening chapter of his *Synge and Anglo-Irish Literature* (1931). The exclusivist thrust of his redefinition of the Irish cultural canon can be seen as part of a protectionist mentality which found expression in the censorship legislation of the 1920s, the religious triumphalism of the Eucharistic Congress in 1932, and the economic policies of de Valera's government, which came to power in 1932. The loss of the Aran Islands as a nationalist shrine to J. M. Synge's exuberant vision of the west of Ireland was redeemed by the discovery of a new 'school' of native writing, centring on the Blasket Islands in County Kerry, whose bleak primitivism was more in keeping with the ascetic outlook of the 1930s. In retrospect, these decades have come to be seen as the Irish version of the Dark Ages, a period in which the enclosure of Irish culture, so avidly sought by advanced nationalists since the beginning of the Revival, was finally achieved. The dogmatic stance of an editorial in *The Catholic Bulletin* in 1924 seems to be symptomatic of the cultural introversion of nationalist ideology. Taking issue with the suggestion that the Irish nation is an amalgam of several cultural traditions, the writer states:

> All other elements have no place in Irish national life, literature and tradition . . . We are not a national conglomerate, not a national patchwork specimen; the poetry of life of what Aodh de Blacam calls Belfast can only be Irish by being assimilated by Gaelic literature.[12]

Yet the mention of de Blacam in this context shows that statements of this kind cannot be taken as fully representative of nationalist opinion. It is often assumed that one has to step *outside* the confines of the separatist tradition — to, for example, the pages of the liberal *Irish Statesman* edited by AE — to find acceptance of cultural diversity in Irish society. Yet the most trenchant critique of Corkery's 'monocular vision' (to use Seamus Heaney's term) came from *within* the ranks of advanced nationalism, in the form of an article written by de Blacam entitled 'The Other Hidden Ireland'. Corkery, according to de Blacam, 'shewed as little sympathy for the Anglo-Irish as Lecky shewed for the Gael', and he proceeded to develop this point by arguing that nationalism did not entail a one-dimensional view of Irish culture:

> One of the errors in modern criticism is to assume that everything found in Irish [i.e. the Irish language] is *ipso facto* a Catholic production, an expression of the true Irish spirit, as if everything in good English from Milton to Mitchel should be regarded as the voice of England. In truth, Gaelic literature, although overwhelmingly Catholic, does contain some works of a diverse mind.

The point here is not that de Blacam was a liberal at heart, for in many ways he was an even more ardent nationalist than Daniel Corkery. It is, rather, that a belief in cultural diversity is not the sole prerogative of those who stood outside the ranks of the Gaelic tradition, and who proceeded subsequently to construe all nationalists as speaking with one intolerant voice. While the 'Irishness' of writers such as Swift was a continuing source of controversy throughout this period, other Anglo-Irish writers were disenfranchised to such an extent that the question of their Irishness did not even arise. Writing in 1938 about the threat posed by Anglo-American popular culture to Irish identity, Michael Tierney could state that: 'the difficulty in which we find ourselves is only made more apparent by the belief that the Gaelic cause is advanced when H. G. Wells, *Bram Stoker* and the latest American song-numbers are translated into the Irish language.'[13] It is a measure of the expansive nature of de Blacam's view of Irishness that he included the Dublin-born author of *Dracula* and indeed the Irish Gothic tradition (which gave rise to Bram Stoker) in his pioneering survey, *A First Book of Irish Literature* (1934). Nor was de Blacam alone in his insistence on the multi-faceted character of Irish identity. Writing thirty years earlier, at the beginning of the Revival, the Irish Irelander Arthur Clery rejected any monolithic approach that would seek to exclude alternative or dissident strands in Irish culture:

> This strange method of criticism, a method we ourselves, unhappily, are only too ready to submit to and adopt, arises from the . . . fallacy . . . of supposing all things Irish to be uniform and conformable to one pattern. . . . We must be prepared to meet with many and various Irish natures, and must not attribute every deviation from the conventional type to English ancestry.

12. Quoted in Terence Brown, *Ireland: A Social and Cultural History, 1921–1979* (London: Fontana, 1981), p. 63.

13. Michael Tierney, 'Politics and Culture: Daniel O'Connell and the Gaelic Past', *Studies*, Vol. 27 (1938), 358–59. My italics.

I. NATIONAL LITERATURE: THE PREOCCUPATION WITH THE PAST

JOHN EGLINTON

(1868–1961)

from: LITERARY IDEALS IN IRELAND (1899)

[One of the first critical controversies of the Literary Revival took place in the columns of the Dublin *Daily Express* in 1898 between John Eglinton and W. B. Yeats, with AE and William Larminie later joining in. It created such public interest that it was published in book form. The exchange of views on the role of the past in Irish literature, and the extent to which national literature could be great literature with a universal appeal, presaged many of the themes that were to dominate critical debates in Ireland in the twentieth century. Yeats later wrote of the controversy that it 'was a stirring row while it lasted and we were all very angry'.]

WHAT SHOULD BE THE SUBJECTS OF NATIONAL DRAMA?

Supposing a writer of dramatic genius were to appear in Ireland, where would he look for the subject of a national drama? This question might serve as a test of what nationality really amounts to in Ireland — a somewhat trying one, perhaps, yet it is scarcely unfair to put the question to those who speak of our national literature with hardly less satisfaction in the present than confidence in the future. Would he look for it in the Irish legends, or in the life of the peasantry and folk-lore, or in Irish history and patriotism, or in life at large as reflected in his own consciousness? There are several reasons for thinking that the growing hopes of something in store for national life in this country are likely to come to something. In the great countries of Europe, although literature is apparently as prosperous as ever and is maintained with a circumstance which would seem to ensure it eternal honour, yet the springs from which the modern literary movements have been fed are probably dried up — the springs of simplicity, hope, belief, and an absolute originality like that of Wordsworth. If also, as seems likely, the approaching ages on the Continent are to be filled with great social and political questions and events which can hardly have immediate expression in literature, it is quite conceivable that literature, as it did once before, would migrate to a quiet country like Ireland, where there is no great tradition to be upset or much social sediment to be stirred up, and where the spectacle of such changes might afford a purely intellectual impulse. More important, of course, and certain than any such chances from without is the positive feeling of encouragement which is now taking the place of the hatreds and despondencies of the past. We may think that the peasantry are outside the reach of culture, that the gentry exhaust their function in contributing able officers to the British army, and that, frankly, there is nothing going on in the political or ecclesiastical or social life of Ireland on which to rest any but the most sober hopes for the future, still no one can say that political feebleness or stagnation might not be actually favourable to some original manifestation in the world of ideas. What Renan[1] says, in speaking of the Jews, that 'a nation whose mission it is to revolve in its bosom spiritual truths is often weak politically,' may be used with regard to Ireland as an argument that at least nothing stands in its way in this direction.

1. Ernest Renan (1823–92), the French scholar whose *The Poetry of the Celtic Races* (1859) exerted a considerable influence on the Celticism of Matthew Arnold, and by extension on the Celtic Revival. His five-volume *History of the People of Israel* (1887–93) was based on the premise that 'national distress raises up prophets, by compelling ardent minds to fall back on the pleasures of imagination, which are the real ones.' (*History of the People of Israel*, Third Division, London: Chapman and Hall, 1891, p. xii).

The ancient legends of Ireland undoubtedly contain situations and characters as well suited for drama as most of those used in the Greek tragedies which have come down to us. It is, nevertheless, a question whether the mere fact of Ireland having been the scene of these stories is enough to give an Irish writer much advantage over anyone else who is attracted by them, or whether anything but belles lettres, as distinguished from a national literature, is likely to spring from a determined preoccupation with them. Belles lettres seek a subject outside experience, while a national literature, or any literature of a genuine kind, is simply the outcome and expression of a strong interest in life itself. The truth is, these subjects, much as we may admire them and regret that we have nothing equivalent to them in the modern world, obstinately refuse to be taken up out of their old environment and be transplanted into the world of modern sympathies. The proper mode of treating them is a secret lost with the subjects themselves. It is clear that if Celtic traditions are to be an active influence in future Irish literature they must seem to us worthy of the same compliment as that paid by Europe to the Greeks; we must go to them rather than expect them to come to us, studying them as closely as possible, and allowing them to influence us as they may. The significance of that interest in folk-lore and antiquities, which is so strong in this country, can hardly be different from that of the writings of Herder[2] and others in German literature, and may lie in this, that some hint is caught in such studies of the forgotten mythopœic secret.

As to Irish history and the subjects which it offers — a well-known Scotch Professor once said that Ireland was not a nation because it had never had a Burns nor a Bannockburn.[3] It is, however, as reasonable to think that these glorious memories of Scottish nationality will form a drag on its further evolution as that the want of a peasant poet, or of a recollection of having at least once given the Saxons a drubbing, will be fatal to an attempt to raise people above themselves in this country by giving expression to latent ideals. Ireland must exchange the patriotism which looks back for the patriotism which looks forward. The Jews had this kind of patriotism, and it came to something, and the Celtic peoples have been remarkable for it. The Saxon believes in the present, and, indeed, it belongs to him. The Romance nations, from whose hold the world has been slipping, can hardly be expected just yet to give up the consolations of history.

In short, we need to realise in Ireland that a national drama or literature must spring from a native interest in life and its problems and a strong capacity for life among the people. If these do not, or cannot exist, there cannot exist a national drama or literature. In London and Paris they seem to believe in theories and 'movements,' and to regard individuality as a noble but 'impossible' savage;[4] and we are in some danger of being absorbed into their error. Some of our disadvantages are our safeguards. In all ages poets and thinkers have owed far less to their countries than their countries have owed to them.

2. Johann Gottfried Herder (1744–1803), one of the architects of German Romanticism, pioneered the study of folklore. His enthusiasm for Macpherson's *Ossian* added considerably to the vogue for the Celtic periphery in Romanticism.

3. The battle of Bannockburn (1314) in which Scottish forces led by Robert the Bruce inflicted a historic defeat on the English army under Edward II, which was trying to relieve Stirling Castle.

4. The expression 'noble savage' is associated with Jean Jacques Rousseau's (1712–78) idealization of primitive simplicity in his *Discourse on the Origin of Inequality* (1775). However, Rousseau never used the term: it was coined by John Dryden in his *Almanzar* (1670) and was popularized by Denis Diderot.

W. B. YEATS

(1865–1939)

from: LITERARY IDEALS IN IRELAND (1899)

A NOTE ON NATIONAL DRAMA

Mr. Yeats added these words, as a postscript, to an article on 'The Poetry and Stories of Miss Nora Hopper':[1]

I had some thought of replying to an article headed, 'What should be the Subjects of a National Drama?' in your issue of last Saturday, but found, when I considered the matter, that this article, which I had already finished, answered the most important of your contributor's arguments. He said that 'these subjects' (ancient legends) 'obstinately refuse to be taken out of their old environment and be transplanted into the world of modern sympathies. The proper mode of treating them is a secret lost with the subjects themselves.' And I have given the example of Ibsen, whose 'Peer Gynt' founded on 'these subjects' is not only 'national literature,' the very thing your contributor said it could not be, but the chief glory of 'the national literature' of its country, and the example of Wagner, whose dramas, also founded upon 'these subjects,' are becoming to Germany what the Greek Tragedies were to Greece. . . .

All great poets — Dante not less than Homer and Shakespeare — speak to us of the hopes and destinies of mankind in their fullness; because they have wrought their poetry out of the dreams that were dreamed before men became so crowded upon one another, and so buried in their individual destinies and trades, that every man grew limited and fragmentary. If you were to take out of poetry the personages and stories and metaphors, that first, it may be, visited the shepherds and hunters, who lived before men tilled the ground, not merely its substance, but its language would crumble to nearly nothing. Modern poetry grows weary of using over and over again the personages and stories and metaphors that have come to us through Greece and Rome, or from Wales and Brittany through the middle ages, and has found new life in the Norse and German legends. William Morris's 'Sigurd,'[2] if it is as fine as it seemed to me some years ago, may yet influence the imagination of Europe, and Henrik Ibsen's 'Peer Gynt' and 'The Heroes of Heligoland' are already great influences, while Richard Wagner's dramas of 'The Ring,' are, together with his mainly Celtic 'Parsival' [*sic*] and 'Lohengrin,' and 'Tristan and Iseult,' the most passionate influence in the arts of Europe. The Irish legends, in popular tradition and in old Gaelic literature, are more numerous, and as beautiful as the Norse and German legends, and alone among great European legends have the beauty and wonder of altogether new things. May one not say, then, without saying anything improbable, that they will have a predominant influence in the coming century, and that their influence will pass through many countries?

Miss Hopper merely describes the Temple of the Heroes as being on an island of the Shannon,[3] and is sometimes even less certain about the places of her legends, though she has much feeling for landscape; and this uncertainty is, I believe, a defect in her method. Our legends are always associated with places, and not merely every mountain and valley, but every strange stone and little coppice has its legend, preserved in written or unwritten tradition. Our Irish romantic movement has arisen out of this tradition, and should always, even when it makes new legends about traditional people and things, be haunted by places. It should make Ireland, as Ireland and all other lands were in ancient times, a holy land to her own people. Had Aodh[4] brought

1. W. B. Yeats took an active role in promoting the poetry of Norah Hopper (1871–1906) and was particularly impressed by her first collection, *Ballads in Prose* (1894).

2. William Morris's epic poem, 'Sigurd the Volsung', was completed in 1876. It recast Icelandic sagas from a modern standpoint, contrasting the heroism of a former age with the squalor of modern life.

3. Yeats proposed a specific site for his Castle of the Heroes on Mac Dermot's island, Lough Key, near Boyle, Co. Roscommon.

4. A character in Norah Hopper's poetry who may have influenced the poet Aodh in Yeats's story 'The Binding of the Hair' (1896).

his gifts to any of the traditional sacred places, and had the emotion of the place and its history been in the story, the dreamy beauty of his sacrifice would have grown more beautiful from mixing with ancient beauty and with the beauty of sun and moon burning over an island or hill or hollow that is a part of the scenery of our lives.

JOHN EGLINTON

NATIONAL DRAMA AND CONTEMPORARY LIFE

I am sorry that Mr. Yeats, in his recent article on Miss Norah Hopper's poems, should have taken for granted that my intention in raising the question I did was combative, as, in truth, I simply wished to put it as clearly as possible, without suggesting any definite answer. It should hardly have occurred to me to put it at all, but that Mr. Yeats' own dramatic poems seemed to open up the possibility of a drama with a distinctive note in this country.

Mr. Yeats mentions Ibsen's 'Peer Gynt' and Wagner's musical dramas as examples of national literature founded on the ancient legends of the authors' countries. I should say at once that I did not deny the possibility of a poet being inspired by the legends of his country; it would be strange indeed if he did not sometimes look towards them. The extent to which a great poetic intelligence, supremely interested in life, would use these legends for his images and themes would depend a good deal on the kind and degree of interest prevalent concerning them. If they yielded him typical situations and characters, such as Shakespeare looked for in legend and history, I fancy his joy would be great to discover these in stories which were the peculiar heritage of his country, and known to every one in it. But in the hands of such a poet these characters and situations become entirely new creations by virtue of the new spirit and import which he puts into them; the mode of treating them as they exist in tradition is a lost secret, but the power to make them live again in a new way is a secret of which the artist must be possessed. Prospero, in the 'Tempest,' lying in Shakespeare's mind, drew the vitality by which he still lives from that source. Brutus and Cassius in 'Julius Cæsar' are rather reincarnations of Romans in the Elizabethan age than archæologically Romans. Finn and Cuculain, if they are to appear once more in literature — and I, for one, shall welcome them — must be expected to take up on their broad shoulders something of the weariness and fret of our age, if only to show how lightly they may be carried, and to affright with shadowing masses of truth, such as mortals hurl not now, the uneasy seats of error. . . .

There are two conceptions of poetry, mutually antagonistic so far, and not to be reconciled except in the life-work of another great poet, of which one may be called Wordsworthian, which regards the poetic consciousness as acting from within outward and able to confer on even common things the radiance of the imagination; the other, to which those who are rather in sympathy with art than with philosophy are inclined, regards the poet as passive to elect influences and endowing old material with new form. The first regards the poet as a seer and a spiritual force; the second as an aristocratic craftsman. The first looks to man himself as the source of inspiration; the second to tradition, to the forms and images in which old conceptions have been embodied — old faiths, myths, dreams. The weakness of the first is an inclination to indifference toward the form and comeliness of art, as in Whitman; while the second, if it hold aloof from the first, cuts itself asunder from the source of all regeneration in art. The bias of the first is toward naked statement, hard fact, dogmatism; the bias of the second toward theory, diffuseness, insincerity. The latter appears to me to be the bias of belles lettres at present. The poet looks too much away from himself and from his age, does not feel the facts of life enough, but seeks in art an escape from them. Consequently, the art he achieves cannot be the expression of the age and of himself — cannot be representative or national.

The whole subject of the drama derives an interest from a consideration of the weakness of the present century in this respect. English literature, as a recent writer in the American 'Dial'[1] says, has nothing to show but Shelley's 'Cenci';[2] and the same writer urges that the drama is the 'top achievement of the human intellect.'

1. *The Dial*, a literary periodical founded in Chicago in 1880, became one of the most influential periodicals of the modernist movement, attracting contributors such as W. B. Yeats, T. S. Eliot, Ezra Pound, and e.e. cummings.
2. A Jacobean-style verse tragedy, set in sixteenth-century Italy, written by Shelley in 1819 but not staged during his lifetime.

W. B. YEATS

JOHN EGLINTON AND SPIRITUAL ART

Mr. John Eglinton wrote recently that though 'the ancient legends of Ireland undoubtedly contain situations and characters as well suited for drama as most of those used in Greek tragedies,' yet 'these subjects,' meaning old legends in general, 'refuse to be taken up out of their old environments, and be transplanted into the world of modern sympathies. The proper mode of treating them is a secret lost with the subjects themselves.' I might have replied by naming a good part of modern literature; but as he spoke particularly of drama I named Ibsen's 'Peer Gynt,' which is admittedly the chief among the national poems of modern Norway; and Wagner's musical dramas, which I compared with the Greek tragedies, not merely because of the mythological substance of 'The Ring' and of 'Parsifal,' but because of the influence both words and music are beginning to have upon the intellect of Germany and of Europe, which begins to see the German soul in them. . . .

His second article abandons the opinion — an opinion that I thought from the beginning a petulance of rapid writing — that ancient legends 'cannot be transplanted into the world of modern sympathies,' and thinks that a poet 'may be inspired by the legends of his country,' but goes on to distinguish between 'two conceptions of poetry mutually antagonistic, two ways of treating legends and other things.' I am glad to discuss these distinctions with him, for I think it a misfortune that Mr John Eglinton, whose influence on Irish opinion may yet be great, should believe, as I understand him to believe, in popular music, popular painting, and popular literature. He describes the 'conception' of poetry, he believes me to prefer, as preferred 'by those who are rather in sympathy with art than with philosophy,' as regarding the poet as 'an aristocratic craftsman' as looking for 'the source of inspiration' to 'the forms and images, in which old conceptions have been embodied — old faiths, myths, dreams,' and as seeking 'in poetry an escape from the facts of life'; and he describes the 'conception' he himself prefers and calls Wordsworthian as looking 'to man himself as the source of inspiration,' and as desiring a poetry that expresses 'its age' and 'the facts of life,' and is yet, strange to say, 'a spiritual force' and the work of 'a seer.'

I will restate these distinctions in the words of the younger Hallam, in his essay on Tennyson; one of the most profound criticisms in the English language.[1] Arthur Hallam described Tennyson, who had then written his earlier and greater, but less popular poems, as belonging to 'the æsthetic school' founded by Keats and Shelley — 'A poetry of sensation rather than of reflection,' 'a sort of magic producing a number of impressions too multiplied, too minute, and too diversified to allow of our tracing them to the causes, because just such was the effect, even so boundless and so bewildering, produced' on the imagination of the poet 'by the real appearance of nature.' This poetry, the work of men whose 'fine organs' 'have trembled with emotion at colours and sounds and movements unperceived by duller

1. Arthur Hallam (1811–33), whose brilliant essay on Tennyson was published in the *Englishman's Magazine* in 1831 when Hallam was only twenty years of age.

temperaments,' must always, he thinks, be unpopular because dull temperaments shrink from, or are incapable of the patient sympathy and exaltation of feeling needful for its understanding. He contrasts it with the popular school, the school he thinks Wordsworth belonged to, in all but his highest moments, which 'mixes up' anecdotes and opinions and moral maxims for their own sake — the things dull temperaments can understand — with what is sometimes the poetry of a fine temperament, but is more often an imitation.

This poetry of the popular school is the poetry of those 'who are rather in sympathy' with philosophy than with art, and resembles those paintings one finds in every Royal Academy surrounded by crowds, which 'are rather in sympathy' with anecdotes or pretty faces of babies than with good painting. It is the poetry of the utilitarian and the rhetorician and the sentimentalist and the popular journalist and the popular preacher, but it is not the poetry of 'the seer,' the most 'aristocratic' of men, who tells what he alone has tasted and touched and seen amid the exaltation of his senses; and it is not a 'spiritual force,' though it may talk of nothing but spiritual forces, for a spiritual force is as immaterial and as imperceptible as the falling of dew or as the first greyness of dawn. Why, too, should Mr. John Eglinton, who is a profound transcendentalist, prefer a poetry which is, like all the lusts of the market place, 'an expression of its age' and of 'the facts of life,' the very phrases of the utilitarian criticism of the middle century — to a poetry which seeks to express great passions that are not in nature, though 'the real appearance of nature' awakens them; 'ideas' that 'lie burningly on the divine hand,' as Browning calls them, 'the beauty that is beyond the grave,' as Poe calls them?[2]

The Belgian poet, M. Verhaeren, has also discussed these 'two conceptions of poetry,'[3] and has described the one as founded on physical science and the other as founded upon transcendental science, and has shown that 'the bias of belles lettres at present,' of which Mr. John Eglinton complains, has accompanied a renewed interest in transcendental science. And it may well be that men are only able to fashion into beautiful shapes the most delicate emotions of the soul, spending their days with a patience like the patience of the middle ages in the perfect rounding of a verse, or in the perfect carving of a flower, when they are certain that the soul will not die with the body and that the gates of peace are wide, and that the watchers are at their places upon the wall.

I believe that the renewal of belief, which is the great movement of our time, will more and more liberate the arts from 'their age' and from life, and leave them more and more free to lose themselves in beauty, and to busy themselves, like all the great poetry of the past and like religions of all times, with 'old faiths, myths, dreams,' the accumulated beauty of the age. I believe that all men will more and more reject the opinion that poetry is a 'criticism of life,'[4] and be more and more convinced that it is a revelation of a hidden life, and that they may even come to think 'painting, poetry, and music' 'the only means of conversing with eternity left to man on earth.' I believe, too, that, though a Homer or a Dante or a Shakespeare may have used all knowledge, whether of life or of philosophy, or of mythology or of history, he did so, not for the sake of the knowledge, but to shape to a familiar and intelligible body something he had seen or experienced in the exaltation of his senses. I believe, too, that the difference between good and bad poetry is not in its preference for legendary, or for unlegendary subjects, or for a modern or for an archaic treatment, but in the volume and intensity of its passion for beauty, and in the perfection of its workmanship; and that all criticism that forgets these things is mischievous, and doubly mischievous in a country of unsettled opinion.

2. Yeats is adapting here Poe's statement, in *The Poetic Principle* (1850), that 'loveliness' is 'inspired by an ecstatic prescience of the glories beyond the grave'.
3. Emile Verhaeren (1855–1916), Belgian poet and dramatist. His ideas on modern poetry were brought together in a lecture on 'French Poetry of Today', delivered at Oxford in 1901.
4. See Matthew Arnold, 'The Study of Poetry', in *Essays in Criticism*, Second Series (1888): poetry is 'a criticism of life under the conditions fixed for such a criticism by the laws of poetic truth and poetic beauty'.

JOHN EGLINTON

MR. YEATS AND POPULAR POETRY

The remark criticised by Mr. Yeats, that 'these subjects [ancient legends] refuse to be taken up out of their old environment and be transplanted into the world of modern sympathies,' and that 'the proper mode of treating them, as they exist in tradition, is a secret lost with the subjects themselves,' was not exactly a 'petulance of rapid writing,' but, on the whole, I am ready to accept responsibility for it. At any rate, its falsity is not apparent in the light of the examples he mentions — Ibsen's 'Peer Gynt' and Wagner's musical dramas. When a great legend or narrative comes down to us from antiquity — as, for instance, the Biblical story of David — it does so in a certain form, the form in which it has spontaneously clothed itself, and which fits it as the body fits the soul. No one could improve upon the story of David, unless, by a miracle, he could introduce some new and transforming element into his conception of it. In like manner, the Irish legends have come down to us in a certain form and language, proper to the original conception of them, and they can only be made to live again by something new added to them out of the author's age and personality. As an instance of an old legend or narrative so transformed in the mind of a great and serious artist we might mention Milton's 'Samson,' which is thus the utterance of Milton's age as much as if the whole conception were original. On the other hand, Morris's 'Sigurd' or Ferguson's 'Congal,'[1] to whatever praise either of them is entitled, is not in the same way an original poem or the utterance of the author's age, as the highest poetry always is. To emphasize this truth is not 'mischievous,' but serviceable in this or in any country where a serious desire for a truly original literature exists.

The facts of life with which poetry is concerned are not the complex and conventional facts, but the simple and universal. This age cannot have a realistic poet, as it fondly dreams, because poetry is ideal and not realistic. The kinematograph,[2] the bicycle, electric tramcars, labour-saving contrivances, etc, are not susceptible of poetic treatment, but are, in fact, themselves the poetry, not without a kind of suggestiveness, of a scientific age, with which the poetry of Greek and Hebrew tradition vainly endeavours to vie. It is no wonder that an age which has achieved this concrete type of poetry should be content with an attitude of simple politeness toward those dreamers who walk with their heads in a cloud of vision; we can understand its being so better than we can its genial invitation to our poetic dreamers to apply their visionary faculty and quaint rhythmic trick to a treatment of the mechanical triumphs of modern life, as Homer treated the manners and customs of an heroic age. The epics of the present are the steam-engine and the dynamo, its lyrics the kinematograph, phonograph, etc., and these bear with them the hearts of men as the Iliad and Odyssey of former days uplifted the youth of antiquity, or as the old English ballads expressed the mind of a nation in its childhood. When the poetic and mythopœic faculty deserted the disillusioned Greeks they began to speculate on the nature of poetry, and when the moderns, perceiving a certain void in their lives, have begun to ask for an ideal poetic art springing directly out of modern life, it has been found necessary to investigate the origin and nature of poetry. The further these investigations are carried, the greater confirmation will that theory of poetry receive which is so honourably associated with the name of Wordsworth, and which has been adopted and carried forward by Carlyle, Ruskin, Emerson, Whitman, and others; a theory for the statement of which we may refer to the fragment prefixed by Wordsworth to the 'Excursion.'[3] It is to give the cause of idealism into the hands of the Philistines to allow for a moment that poetry is less a 'fact of life' than business or engine-screeching. Far better fall into a ridiculous attitude of hostility toward modern tendencies, like Ruskin or the grim Carlyle, who refused to consider as poetry what was not rooted in the facts of life, or to regard such facts of life as could not be illustrated by poetry as other than 'phantasms.'

1. Sir Samuel Ferguson's epic poem 'Congal' (1872), regarded as one of the major achievements of nineteenth-century Irish poetry.
2. Eglinton's prescient remark, that cinema is the poetry of the scientific age, was made only two years after the introduction of cinema in Ireland in 1896.
3. Wordsworth's 'Preface to *The Excursion*' (1814) exhorts the poet to combine lofty sentiments with 'low matter', the minutiae of contemporary life.

It is curious that the poetry which has been most a fact of the life of the nineteenth century in England, and has been most universal in its appeal, should be called with some propriety 'Wordsworthian' — after a man who was certainly without great poetic talent or artistic faculty, but who, simply because he was right, and by virtue of his simplicity and seriousness, reached, as Emerson rightly said, the high-water mark of poetry in this century. With Wordsworth, except at his best, we need not concern ourselves. If, at his best, he is a popular poet, which is doubtful, it is surely in the sense in which Shakespeare and the Bible are popular rather than as Hall Caine and Marie Corelli,[4] or even Byron and Swinburne, are so; and it is not clear that such a popularity need be considered as greatly to his discredit. It is rather a sign that poetry is much more of a fact of life than is commonly supposed, and that a man has only to be original to be universal. The poetry of thought in this century — the poetry of Wordsworth, Tennyson, Browning — is more important than the poetry of art and artifice — the poetry of Coleridge, Rossetti, Swinburne — because of its higher seriousness and more universal appeal; because it is more concerned with the facts of life and is more inspired by faith and hope; because it expresses its age better and what is best in the age.

'I fear,' said Blake to Crabb Robinson,[5] 'that Wordsworth loves nature,' and Mr. Yeats, as a philosopher, though not, we are glad to believe, as a poet, would no doubt sympathise with that solicitude. The writer whom he so greatly admires, Villiers de l'Isle Adam,[6] cherished a particular objection to the sun and daylight; and Paul Verlaine,[7] whose influence Mr. Yeats would perhaps consider less baneful in this country than that of Wordsworth, acknowledged that he 'hated to hear the laugh of a healthy man.' But really, what do the symbolists, who talk so much of the 'exaltation of the senses,' mean exactly by saying that the 'poetic passion is not in nature,' and that art is to be 'liberated from life.' Life is nothing but what we make it, and we do not alter its substance by twisting it into an abnormality. If the transcendent realities do not exist in the normal human consciousness, they do not exist in 'poetry, music, and painting,' or at all. Mr. Yeats thinks that Shakespeare interested himself in life and humanity consciously for the sake of his art. This is a matter of opinion; but we think it more likely that Shakespeare's interest in life was a broadly human and representative interest, and that this was the source and power of his art. Art which only interests itself in life and humanity for the sake of art may achieve the occult triumphs of the symbolist school, but humanity will return its indifference in kind, and leave it to the dignity and consolation of 'unpopularity.'

4. Hall Caine (1853–1931) and Marie Corelli (1855–1924), bestselling authors of pot-boiler novels at the turn of the century. Marie Corelli could count Oscar Wilde and James Joyce among her avid readers.
5. Henry Crabb Robinson (1775–1867), confidant of Blake, Wordsworth, Coleridge and Hazlitt. His diaries and letters, first published in 1869, offer valuable insights into the lives of the leading figures in the Romantic movement.
6. Villiers de l'Isle Adam (1838–89), whose symbolist drama *Axel* (1890) exerted a profound influence on Yeats, and inspired Edmund Wilson's famous critical study, *Axel's Castle* (1931).
7. Paul Verlaine (1844–96), leading French poet associated with the Symbolist movement.

II. UNIVERSAL VERSUS NATIONAL IDEALS

THOMAS KETTLE

(1880–1916)

from: THE DAY'S BURDEN (1910)

[In this lecture, delivered at St Patrick's College, Maynooth on 5 December 1912, Tom Kettle argues that the 'universal' laws of economics are subject to national constraints, in both the political and historical sense. The subordination of economics to politics means that the rule of *laissez-faire* is always subject to state intervention, and the nation stands between the individual and abstract, universal laws.]

THE ECONOMICS OF NATIONALISM

The science of economics is commonly held to be lamentably arid and dismal. If that is your experience of it, blame the economists. For the slice of life, with which economics has to deal, vibrates and, so to say, bleeds with human actuality. All science, all exploration, all history in its material factors, the whole epic of man's effort to subdue the earth and establish himself on it, fall within the domain of the economist. His material consists of the ordinary man in the ordinary business of mundane life, that, namely, of getting a living. This means more than food, clothes, and shelter. The highest activities of art and religion can function only under material forms. Churches have to be paid for as well as factories; you can no more get a bar of Caruso[1] for nothing than you can get a bar of soap for nothing.

Economics, moreover, is committed to an analysis not only of the production, but also of the distribution of wealth. In other words, it has to face formally the vast and dismaying problem of poverty. In the accomplishment of these tasks, moreover, the economist, preoccupied with one mode of organization among mankind, must necessarily consider the influence on it of other modes devised or evolved for other ends. Politics imposes itself on him. He can evade the political aspect of his material only by evading reality.

I

It is to a special hinterland of this last tract of territory that I wish to direct your minds tonight. Our inquiry is simple enough, and begins, as far as concerns myself, with a personal examination of conscience. Does the title National Economics amount to a contradiction in terms? If it does not, and if the nation holds a legitimate place in economic life and thought, is it that of a blessing or that of a nuisance? And if it is beneficent can we formulate an economic ideal fitted to express the self-realization of a nation which is resolute to realize itself?

A good many critics, endowed with that verbal deftness so characteristic of Irish critics, have said to me: 'You have a Chair of National Economics in your college. Have you also by any chance a Chair of National Trigonometry or National Biology?' The gibe does not go home. So long as you keep to the sphere of the highly abstract sciences any limiting particularity is certainly incongruous. But as you pass from the greyness of theory to the golden-green foliage of the tree of life, to the rich and endless differentiation of concrete fact, the incongruity diminishes. A National Mathematics is absurd; a National Biology is not quite so absurd, seeing that every country has its own peculiar flora and fauna. When you come to a National Economics the incongruity has wholly disappeared. Plainly you can constitute for each nation under that title a branch of Descriptive Economics. Plainly since one nation is at one stage of growth, and another at another, and since the economy of each is, so to say, steeped and soaked in its temperament and history, your corpus of fact will in each case be strongly individual. Plainly

1. Enrico Caruso (1873–1921), born in Naples, became the greatest operatic tenor of the early twentieth century.

you will have in each case a separate therapeutic. But I suggest to you that the doctrine of nationalism in economics goes far deeper than that.

Nationality is a principle of organization. You may regard it as ultimate and good, or as transitory and bad, and there is no narrowly scientific test by which either view can be dismissed. But in accordance with your first standpoint your whole outlook is determined. Now, there is no doubt that the classical or English school of Political Economy did appear in its early years to be an almost irresistible solvent of nationalism. You will find in Toynbee's *Industrial Revolution*[2] two curiously similar judgements to that effect left on record by two such conflicting contemporaries as Coleridge and Napoleon. The reasons are in no way mysterious. The classicists were all for freedom – free trade, free contract, free competition — and nationalism appeared to them under the form of restrictions on freedom. Internal tolls were disappearing: why should not the custom-house disappear? Self-contained manor and self-contained town had been fused by a long historical process into the nation: why should not the nations be fused into a world-economy? The tides seemed to be setting in that direction. Capital was becoming at once more powerful and more fluid, and there is in capital an inherent cosmopolitanism. Labour moved towards internationalism as an essential part of its 'gospel of deliverance'. What were armies and navies but the watch-dogs of the rich? What were national flags and songs but parts of a ritual which they employed to intoxicate and exploit the poor? 'The proletariat,' cried out Marx in his thunderous manifesto, 'has no father-land.' The whole thought of that period is, indeed, dyed in the grain with cosmopolitanism. And then there comes that sudden upheaving renaissance, and nationalism is there as a colossal fact.

The simplest account of the change is that it was a spontaneous outgush from the deep wells of human nature, and from the overlaid but unexhausted springs of history. From that time on to our own, every nation sets deliberately about the task of self-realization, material and intellectual.

The English bias towards the 'classical' economy was readily intelligible. Dominating the world she took her dominance for granted: she was unconscious of her nationality in the sense in which an entirely healthy man is unconscious of his digestion: and she devised a regime under which every other nation should be, in reference to her, a pupil and a tributary. But as the forces of growth matured and expanded in other nations, they declined to Peter-Pan it to England.[3] And so effective was their refusal that if you turn to a contemporary German textbook you will find the three periods of modern economic thought formally classified as (1) Mercantilism, (2) Liberalism, and (3) Nationalism. . . .

'Cosmopolitanism,' says Turgénev in *Rudin*,'is all twaddle . . . Even the ideal face must have an individual expression.'[4] This humanity, to the worship of which you are to butcher nationalism, is too vast, too vague, too bloodless an abstraction. Our arms are not long enough to fold it in an embrace. Ireland I feel equal to, and Dublin, and that windy Atlantic cliff, straining out against the ocean and the sunset, and that farmer to whom I spoke at Tralee fair, and that publican in Tyrone, and the labourers, spoiled by unemployment, who come to me at my house nearly every day, and for whom I can get no work. But as for the world as a whole, even its geography is too large for my head, to say nothing of its problems, and its emotions are too large for my heart. What is humanity? You and I and the man around the corner, or over the sea, are humanity. And if it is the nature of us all to come to amplest self-expression by living our lives here and now, for a community which is small enough to know and to love, then by 'transcending' national categories you do not enrich, you impoverish, humanity.

Nationalism, indeed, like every other fine faith, has the misfortune to be judged less by its core of dogma than by its shell of superstition. Tariffism and militarism are its apes, not the authentic sons of its house. The parallel to which appeal has been made avails here also. If I knock you down in the street, or, when you call on me, slam the door in

2. Arnold Toynbee (1852–83). His one book, *The Industrial Revolution*, which was published posthumously in 1885, popularized the idea that the industrial revolution (a term he coined) was one of the world's great historical events.

3. That is, they refused to remain in an underdeveloped state. The reference is to the eponymous hero of J. M. Barrie's *Peter Pan* (1904), which relates the story of a boy who refused to grow up.

4. Ivan Turgenev, *Rudin* (1856), Chapter 12. *Rudin* deals with the vicissitudes of a cosmopolitan intellectual in Russian society in the mid-nineteenth century.

your face, they are beyond all doubt impressive proofs of the fact that I enjoy an existence separate from yours. But there are other and better proofs, as, for instance, to buy from you, to learn from you, to feed, foster, or help you. There are better ways of putting heads together than banging them together. In precisely the same way a nation degrades and cancels nationalism by choosing to identify it with isolation or aggressiveness.[5] The first blunder is at war with the conscience of all ages: a character as Goethe says, can fashion itself only in the stream of the world.[6] The second is certainly at war with the conscience of this age. To receive hospitably, and assimilate deeply; to toil, to think, and to communicate without penury or reserve — these remain the marks of a strong nation as of a strong man. Free trade in ideas as in commodities is the desired regime of those who have attained maturity. But it is a strange altruism which bids me not only give myself, but slay myself, so that at the end of the process there is no basis left either for self-regarding or for altruistic action. I must own myself in order to give myself.

Curiously enough, it is in the writings of contemporary theorists of continental socialism that we find the most eloquent repudiation of Professor Cannan's philosophy.[7] Practice had preceded theory. Labour once thought – in the days of the *Communist Manifesto* — that its destiny centred in cosmopolitanism.[8] On that basis it sought to construct an International, but it failed, and the failure led to a notable transformation of Marxism. Today you have an International that possesses reality because its roots are in nationalism.[9]

We Nationalists may appeal to the authoritative words of Professor Sombart in his *Socialism and the Social Movement*:[10] 'Marx's opinion, "The working-classes have no fatherland," is being replaced by another, "If that is so, let us give them one." . . . The view is gaining ground among Socialists — indeed especially among them — that all civilization has its roots in nationality, and that civilization can reach its highest development only on the basis of nationality.' He goes on to quote glowing and splendid passages from David and Pernerstorfer,[11] to one of which we may appeal: 'Socialism and national idea are thus not opposed to each other; they rather supplement each other. Every attempt to weaken the national idea is an attempt to lessen the precious possessions of mankind. . . . Socialism wants to organize, and not disintegrate, humanity. But in the organisms of mankind, not individuals but nations, are the tissues, and if the whole organism is to remain wholly healthy, it is necessary for the tissues to be healthy.'

As for your capitalist who, in those days, was a cosmopolitan, he is now in every country a jingo. Herr Goldenberg is no sooner settled in Park Lane than you find his name heading the list of subscriptions to Lord Roberts's Conscription League.[12]

The general significance of the new politics is twofold. It substitutes an organic for the old atomistic conception of economic life. And in establishing the nation as a principle of organization it establishes it also as a principle of sacrifice, and therein provides the only basis of Protection that is not intellectually disreputable.

II

Such 'sentimentalities' will strike strangely and even harshly on the ears of those who have been bred up to believe that political economy began with Adam

5. Kettle here is distancing himself from the economic protectionism advocated by Arthur Griffith's Sinn Féin movement.
6. See Goethe's *Torquato Tasso* (1790), Act I, Scene 2: 'A talent is formed in stillness, a character in the world's torrent.'
7. Edwin Cannan (1861–1935), English economist. In *The Economic Outlook* (1912) he argued that international socialism was incompatible with nationalism.
8. This refers to Karl Marx and Friedrich Engels's famous statement in *The Communist Manifesto* (1848): 'The working men have no country. . . . National differences and antagonism between peoples are daily more and more vanishing, owing to the development of the bourgeoisie, to freedom of commerce, to the world market, to uniformity in the mode of production and in the conditions of life corresponding thereto. The supremecy of the proletariat will cause them to vanish still faster.'
9. Kettle attended the 7th Congress of the Second International at Stuttgart in 1907 which conducted an intense debate on the role of nationalism and the socialist movement. See his essay 'International Socialists' in *The Day's Burden* (1910, revised edition 1937).
10. Werner Sombart (1863–1941). His *Socialism and the Social Movement* (1896) was first published in pamphlet form as a sympathetic treatment of Marxism, but by 1914 the 10th edition had grown to a violent anti-Marxist tract of almost a thousand pages.
11. Eduard Heinrich (Rudolph) David (1863–1930), a revisionist leader of the German Social Democratic Party. Englebert Pernerstorfer (1850–1918), a prominent propagandist in the German Social Democratic Party with strong German nationalist views.
12. Frederick Roberts (1832–1914), the last commander in chief of the British army, become president of the National Service League in 1905.

Smith and ended with John Stuart Mill,[13] and that between 1780 and 1850 the laws underlying the business life of mankind were defined, once and for all, in immutable formulae. The line of thought suggested by them is very ill represented in English text-books. There is a reason for the lacuna, as for most things, and it lies on the surface. If you want a full appreciation of the significance of health you must go not to the athlete's gymnasium, but to the hospital ward. If you want an appreciation of the value of national freedom and unity, you must go, not to the one nation which entered the Steam Age with these foundations of greatness deeply established, but to one of those which, during the nineteenth century, had to work out their salvation, political and economic, through blood and tears.

During the period of crystallization of the classical economy the industrial hegemony of Great Britain was absolute. Her supremacy in coal, in iron, in shipping, in machinery, in the technique of manufacture was unchallenged. On this basis the great theorists, like Ricardo,[14] implicitly, if not deliberately, proceeded. The system which they evolved was at once too English in matter, too abstract in method, and too dogmatic in tone. Protests against its exclusiveness, its insularity, could be multiplied from the pages of continental economics. Thus Adolph Wagner, the great Austrian master, summarizing Roscher,[15] a precursor, in his *Foundations*, writes:

> They [the English school] have a tendency to rely solely on abstract deduction, and to exaggerate its importance . . . ; in theory, but especially in practice, they isolate economic phenomena too radically from the other social phenomena with which they are intimately associated; they assign to economic phenomena and institutions, and to their solutions of economic questions, a character too absolute, instead of assigning only that relative and historical character which is proper to all the facts of history; their verdict on Free Trade, and its results, is in many respects erroneous, and a great deal too optimistic; they efface the State too completely, and misunderstand its role as regulator of the national economy.

This judgement, which is not precisely a condemnation of scientific principles, but rather a methodological admonition, may now be said to be universally accepted. It is interesting to note that one of the first, and most influential, writers to propagate it in English was John Kells Ingram. Still more interesting is it to note the essential identity of the human reality behind it with that behind 'Who Fears to Speak of '98?' The red fire of passion has been transmuted into the illumination of science, but here, as always, Ingram voices the revolt of the small nations against the czarism, scientific and political, of the great.[16]

The reaction in economics is most adequately represented by the German historical school. Of its leaders, from List and Roscher to Schmoller[17] and Wagner, it is not too much to say that every nerve and fibre of their science quivers with nationalism. . . .

That the historical school should also be, under another aspect, the national school, can occasion no surprise. On the one hand, if you turn to history at all the first fact that impresses itself is the colossal fact of nationality: on the other, every concrete nationality is in origin, form and tendency an historical product.

So much for what we may style the rehabilitation of the national idea. I may seem to you to have laboured it too much with something of a Falstaffian parade of erudition: if so, the explanation is obvious. When you come to mix in the actual life of our contemporary Ireland, you will find everybody on

13. Adam Smith (1723–90), the founder of modern economic theory. His *Wealth of Nations* was published in 1776. John Stuart Mill (1806–73), one of the leading intellectual figures in nineteenth-century Britain, whose *Principles of Political Economy* was published in 1848.
14. David Ricardo (1772–1823), English economist, published his major work, *Principles of Political Economy and Taxation*, in 1817. He entered parliament as a member for Portarlington in Ireland, a borough with only twelve constituents and which he never visited.
15. Adolf Wagner (1835–1917), Austrian economist who laid particular emphasis on the role of the state and 'historical-legal' categories in the application of economic laws to particular countries. His views were greatly influenced by the German economist Wilhelm Roscher (1817–94), who was one of the earliest to challenge the ahistorical and universal basis of economic laws as elaborated by Adam Smith.
16. John Kells Ingram (1823–1907), who wrote the youthful ballad 'Who Fears to Speak of '98?' in 1843, was actually a unionist in politics. His extensive work in economics was preoccupied with applying Comtean positivist principles to the historical method in political economy. His best-known work was *A History of Political Economy* (1888).
17. Friedrich List (1789–1846), the German economist whose economic nationalism and advocacy of protectionism exerted a considerable influence on the writings of Arthur Griffith. His main work, *The National System of Political Economy*, was published in 1841. Gustav von Schmoller (1838–1917) was one of the leading economists associated with the historical school.

the one side concerned about national self-realization, political and economic. You will find everybody on the other parrotting [*sic*] forth the perennial nonsense that the Irish question is not political but purely economic. You will turn to some standard text-book for enlightenment — in the nature of things it will be an English text-book — and you will be confused and discouraged to find principles, which you greatly value, either cheapened or ignored. I have tried to suggest to you that there is an historical explanation for all this. Continental experience comes much closer to ours than does English experience, and continental thought, is, as a result, a much truer source of guidance. To offer a purely economic solution for a politico-economic problem, such as ours, is futile, and even absurd. It is as if a doctor were to tell his patient, that once his lungs are brought back to health, it does not matter whether there is an aneurism in his heart or not.

It should be added that the line of criticism suggested is fully valid only as against the popularizers, not as against the masters of the English school.

III

The acceptance of the national as against the individual, of the organic as against the atomistic, point of view, transforms nearly every economic problem. . . .

We have already quoted one great Irishman, Dr Ingram; we now fall back on another, Professor Bastable,[18] both of Trinity College, Dublin: 'To understand the position taken up by the modern opponents of Free Trade [writes Professor Bastable in his *Commerce of Nations*], it is, above all, essential to recognize that the key-note of their system is nationality. . . . The claims of the nation as a whole are accentuated, and regarded as far more important than those of the individual, or the world at large.'

The nation has a continuity of existence to which none of its children can pretend. It has been from of old; it will still be long after the dust of this generation has been blown about the barren plains, or sealed within the iron hills. Given such an organism, so extended in space and time, it is reasonable to sacrifice the welfare of a part of it to that of the whole, and to sacrifice its own present to its future. The nation is held to be entitled to require from each of its citizens, even in time of peace, tax-contributions which will be spent on great public objects in which assuredly he has no bread-and-butter interest; in time of war, it will exact from him his property, his service in arms, and finally his blood.

The nation does not live by bread alone, but, if its bread fails, the special type of culture of which it is the representative must perish. Is it not clear, then, that if the industrial and cultural strength of a people is compromised by the trend of its trade, the government of that people has the right to interfere, to impose minor economic sacrifices on this or that class, for the behoof of the community, and even to lay burdens on the whole community for the benefit of its future citizens in the same spirit in which a father will work hard, and live sparely, in order to secure for his children a place in the sun? . . .

18. Charles Bastable (1855–1945), born in County Cork, professor of political economy, Trinity College, Dublin 1882–1932, was the author of several works on economics, most notably *The Theory of International Trade* (1887) and *The Commerce of Nations* (1892). He emphasized the relevance of sociological and historical factors to economic analysis.

STOPFORD A. BROOKE

(1832–1916)

from: A TREASURY OF IRISH POETRY IN THE ENGLISH TONGUE (1900)

[In this early confrontation between advanced nationalist and Anglo-Irish critics, D. P. Moran, editor of *The Leader*, throws down the nationalist gauntlet to Stopford Brooke and T. W. Rolleston, who had attempted to broaden the definition of 'Irishness' to include non-nationalist writers associated with Trinity College, Dublin. The fact that these anglophile poets gave their allegiance to nature rather than to the nation comes in for characteristically scathing criticism from Moran.

Moran's review was published in *The Leader* on 22 December 1900. Rolleston's reply and Moran's response appeared on 5 January 1901.]

. . . When the book was first projected, I wished to include nothing in it which did not reach a relatively high standard of excellence. But I soon discovered — and this was strongly urged by my brother Editor[1] — that the book on those lines would not at all represent the growth or the history of Irish poetry in the English language. Moreover, our original purpose had already been carried out by Mr. Yeats in his too brief Anthology,[2] and it was advisable that we should adopt a different aim. It must also be said, with some sorrow, that the Irish poetry of the first sixty years of this century would not reach, except in a very few examples, the requirements of a high standard of excellence. Art is pleased with the ballads, war songs, political and humorous poetry, and with the songs of love and of peasant life, but she does not admit them into her inner shrine. It is only quite lately that modern Irish poetry can claim to be fine art. . . .

The modern movement, justly occupied more with poetry for its own sake than with poetry in aggression against England, has passed into a quieter land, with wider horizons. Its indwellers have larger aims and aspirations than the poets who preceded them. What is universal in poetry is greater to them than any particular; what belongs to human nature all over the world is more to them than what belongs to any special nation. Nevertheless, they remain, as they ought to remain, distinctively Irish. But they pass beyond Ireland also. They desire to do work which may be united with the great and beautiful Song of the whole world. While they love Ireland dearly and fill their work with the spirit of Ireland, they also wish to be inhabitants of that high Land of Art, where there is neither English nor Irish, French nor German, but the spirit of loveliness alone.

This new movement took two lines, which ran parallel to one another, like two lines of railway. But now and again, as lines of railway meet and intersect at stations, these two mingled their motives, their subjects, and their manner. But, on the whole, they ran without touching; and one followed the English and the other the Irish tradition. The poets who kept the first line, and who are placed in Book VI.,[3] have been so deeply influenced by Wordsworth, Keats, and in part by Shelley, that even when they write on Irish subjects the airs of England breathe and the waters of England ripple in their poetry. It is impossible not to admire the subtlety, tenderness, and love of nature of these poets, but their place is apart in an Anthology of Irish poetry. They have not kept, along with their devotion to their art, the spirit of their native land. They are descended from the English poets; and if they were to read out their poems on Knocknarea,[4] Queen Maeve, and with her the Fairy Race of Ireland, would drive them from her presence, gently, for they are bards, but inevitably, and transport them on the viewless winds to England.

The other line on which Irish verse ran was backward to the recovery of the old Celtic stories

1. This refers to Brooke's co-editor, T. W. Rolleston (1857–1920).
2. W. B. Yeats, *A Book of Irish Verse*, selected from modern writers with an introduction and notes (London: Methuen, 1895).
3. Book VI, the controversial section of the anthology, included as 'Irish' certain poets associated with Trinity College, Dublin, who were either indifferent to Irish themes or, as in the case of the eminent critic Edward Dowden, hostile towards Irish nationalism.
4. Knocknarea, a mountain overlooking Sligo town, was the legendary burial place of Queen Maeve of Connacht, and featured prominently in the poetry of W. B. Yeats.

and their modernising in poetry, and forward to the creation of a new form of the Celtic spirit. The poets who did and are doing this work, while they have studied and honoured the great masters of song, and, as they write in English, the English masters, have yet endeavoured to secure and retain in their poetry not only the national and spiritual elements of the character of the Irish people, but also that appealing emotion which lives like a soul in the natural scenery of Ireland, and makes it, at least for Irishmen, transcend all other scenery by depth and range of sentiment. . . .

Amid the varied aims of these poets there is one element common to them all. It is their Nationalism. That nationalism has on the whole ceased to be aggressive against England, and that is all the better. Poetry has no national feuds. But the nationalism which, in love of Ireland, sets itself in poetry towards the steady evolution of the Celtic nature, and the full representation of its varied elements — that is vital in these poets, and is vital to the life, growth, and flowering of Irish poetry. Irish poetry, if it is to be a power in literature, must be as Irish as English poetry is English. It has now gained what of old it wanted. It has gained art. Its work is no longer the work of amateurs. Its manner and melody are its own. Its matter is not yet as great as it ought to be for the creation of poetry of the higher ranges. The Subject-matter of mankind has been only lightly or lyrically treated in Ireland, or only in such side issues as mysticism or religion or reanimation of the past. A graver, larger, and more impassioned treatment of those weighty human issues which live in the present, but are universal in the nature of man, is necessary before Irish poetry can reach maturity.

As to the other great Subject-matter — outward Nature as seen and felt by man — that, I am surprised to find, considering the feeling of the Celt for natural scenery, has received no adequate treatment from the Irish poets. What they have as yet done in this way is not to be compared with the work of English or French poets; moreover, the aspects of nature in Ireland, the special sentiment and soul of natural scenery in Ireland, so varied from sky to sea and from sea to land, so distinguished and so individual, have not, save in a few scattered lines, been expressed — I had almost said, have not been perceived — by the poets who live in that scenery. A vast subject-matter, then, almost untouched, lies before the future Irish poets.

I have said that Art has only shown itself of late in the Irish poetry of this century; nor is there any attempt on my part to claim for the poems in this book a lofty place in literature. The river of Irish poetry in the English language is yet in its youth. It rose a hundred years ago in the far-off hills, and wrought its turbulent way down the channelled gorge it carved for its stream out of its own mountains. Other streams have joined it, bearing with them various waters; and it has only just now issued from the hills, and begun to flow in quieter and lovelier lands, glancing from ripple to pool and from pool to ripple, among woods and meadows, happy, and making its lovers happy. It is the youngest child of the Goddess Poesy. Let it be judged as a youth. In time, if it remain true to its country's spirit, the stream that has just emerged from the mountain torrent will become a noble river.

D. P. MORAN

(1871–1936)

from: THE LEADER (1900)

MORE MUDDLE

The anthology that uttered its bitter cry into our confiding ears a few weeks ago is now fully and completely a citizen of the world. We are not in love with it; but neither do we wish to pick it to the bone. It certainly has a Trinity College liver, and we do not pretend that we maintain a philosophic calm when we contemplate any of the works or pomps of Trinity College.

The introduction of the Rev. Stopford Brooke — a well-known and eminent authority on English literature — for some reason or other, gives us a fit of the nerves. We are belonging to a school of thought that has left all that preface behind us. Yet we are aware that for a large number, perhaps the majority of Anglo-Ireland, that preface is a star that would beckon to them from the West. But once you have crossed the bar between Anglo-Ireland and Ireland, an anthology of this kind will have little or no interest for you. What is not real Irish you would as lief, in fact you would prefer, to have real English. The preface discloses the fact that the Rev. Stopford Brooke is not aware of the advance that has been made in recent years. We don't blame him. He is president of the Irish Literary Society of London, and anyone in that position is not likely to learn much of Ireland. There are people in Dublin with better facilities for understanding present-day Ireland who know less. For our taste, and looking at the matter for the moment from the Anglo-Irish point of view, there is too much cosmopolitan philosophy about the preface, and about the selections of poetry or rhyme in the volume. The preface deals much with what appears to be art in the abstract, or at least art above and independent of nationality. We will not discuss the possibility of divorcing art from nationality, or suggest that the fact that Ireland at present is of no particular nationality has a direct connection with the fact that she has no art or appreciation of art. It is enough for us to know that art, in the sense in which we understand Mr. Stopford Brooke to treat of it, has no human interest for Ireland as at present developed. We have many a weary road to travel before we get into that rarified atmosphere.

The symbolic school is largely represented.[1] In fact, this is where the anthology differs from those that have gone before. We have nothing to say against symbolism — provided we understand it. Our 'Celtic' symbolists appear to us to have coined their own symbols independently, so that before you could understand one of their poems you should go through a course of lectures in the particular technique of their symbolism. We have no Anglo-Irish poet that we know who can talk straight to the heart as Burns talked to the heart of Scotland.

One must judge a book from the point of view of the audience it makes a bid for. If this book makes a bid for an English audience, well and good — we are not interested in England; and there is so much to be done, and done immediately, in Ireland, we do not care what English people think of Ireland or her Anglo-Irish efforts at poetry. We do not know that there is any extensive audience in Ireland to which this volume could be addressed. The plain people — in whom we are interested — are already familiar with the older ballads and pieces in this anthology; they have come across them in a score of different books; and, as for the new additions, they may be all very well in their way, but they do not interest us, and it is very improbable that they will interest them. We are convinced of this — Men developed in Trinity College, even when they try to be national, can never — with, perhaps, one exception to prove the rule[2] — reach the heart of Ireland. They have had an excellent education, no doubt, and are full of the courtesies that come with culture; but the Irish Papist, sitting by his turf fire, or carrying on his trade or profession, is full of hopes and fears, and longings and thoughts, that they will never wot of.[3] The haze of Trinity is around them, and the glamour of the Gael surrounds us. They may write about that glamour, may even annex the phrase, but they will never get into it. The price of Trinity is exile from the Gael — even the Anglo-Gael. Their very interest in us, let our judgment convince us as strongly as it will that it is genuine and whole-hearted, grates on us like patronage. Cannot we be allowed our turf and our glamour, cannot we be allowed to nurse the sweets that come even to those who have been beaten but not conquered, cannot we be allowed to wait for singers of our own who, too, have tasted the gall of patronage, the grim sullenness that comes with unadmitted defeat, the surging hopes of final victory? Even Mr. Yeats does not understand us, and he has yet to write even one line that will strike a chord of the Irish heart. He dreams dreams. They may be very beautiful and 'Celtic,' but they are not ours. The 'stately verse of the Protestant Primate of Ireland'[4] – what interest has it for us? What have we done, what great sin

1. 'The symbolic school' refers to inclusion of poets such as W. B. Yeats, AE, Lionel Johnson and Althea Gyles in Section V of the anthology.

2. 'The exception to prove the rule' is Douglas Hyde (1860–1949), co-founder of the Gaelic League. Hyde entered Trinity College in 1880 to study divinity and law, and was awarded an LL.D in 1888. Of course, the exception can only confirm, never 'prove', the rule.

3. i.e. know of.

4. William Alexander (1824–1911), appointed protestant primate of Ireland in 1897, was the author of several books of verse.

have we committed, that Professor Dowden[5] should be put into an anthology, as if he could possess the cunning to strike a note to which the heart of Ireland would respond? Was it a solemn, grave sense of humour that placed '*From* Actæon,' by Mr. William Wilkins, in an Irish anthology, or suggested that Mr. G. A. Greene's lines to the Italian Lakes, the lakes of the land where he was born, should be classed as *Irish* poetry?[6]

If there is anything that is wanting in Ireland at the present day it is preciseness of thought and a meaning for words. This anthology is as muddling as our politicians. The Trinity College department of it indicates to us that even our men of university education are in a hopeless bog as to what is what. We will welcome anything in English about Ireland, or coming out of Ireland, that strikes our hearts or fires our imaginations; but we draw the line at Professor Dowden and William Wilkins.

5. Edward Dowden (1843–1913), one of the most eminent literary critics of his time, was the first professor of English literature at Trinity College, Dublin, a post he held from 1867 to 1913. His patrician disdain for the national aspects of the Literary Revival led to a protracted controversy with Yeats. In the eyes of advanced nationalists, he represented Trinity College's 'alien influence' in Ireland.

6. William Wilkins (born 1852) was a Trinity graduate and headmaster of the High School, Dublin. He published *Songs of Study* in 1891. George Greene (born 1853) spent his early life in Italy, and later taught English at Alexandra College, Dublin. His *Italian Lyricists of Today* was published in 1893. In the late 1890s, Greene became an ardent supporter of the Gaelic revival, a fact that seems to have escaped Moran's notice.

T. W. ROLLESTON

(1857–1920)

THE BROOKE-ROLLESTON ANTHOLOGY (1901)

Sir — I am not going to discuss your judgment upon the 'Treasury of Irish Poetry,' recently edited by Mr. Stopford Brooke and myself. Your article of last week can scarcely be considered a criticism on that work, and in any case I am content to let it speak for itself. But apropos of this book you lay down the law about certain general principles of Irish literature on which I should like to have a word with you, if, as I gather, the LEADER believes free discussion to be the nursing-mother of truth.

You begin by telling us that Mr. Brooke's preface 'discloses the fact that he is not aware of the advance that has been made [in Ireland] in recent years.' How does it disclose that? Because, you tell us, 'there is too much cosmopolitan philosophy about the preface,' it 'deals much with art in the abstract,' and 'art, in the sense in which we understand Mr. Stopford Brooke to treat of it, has no human interest for Ireland as at present developed. We have many a weary road to travel before we get into that rarified atmosphere.'

So it appears first, that Mr. Brooke is writing as if Ireland were much more backward than she actually is, and, secondly, that he imagines her to have reached a stage which in reality she has yet a long and weary journey to attain. I shall venture to criticize this pronouncement in a sentence of your own: 'If there is anything that is wanting in Ireland at the present day it is preciseness of thought and a meaning for words.'

But is it true that educated Irishmen are incapable of understanding a discussion of 'art in the abstract' or of enjoying anything in literature but some form of 'sunburstery'?[1] I do not for a moment believe it, but if it were so, then so much the worse for them, and the sooner they begin to open their minds and develop their tastes the better. I should not have thought that a paper calling itself the LEADER would endeavour to hold them back.

We all admire the vigour and intelligence with which the LEADER tackles political and economic

1. The 'sunburst' gained popularity as a symbol of a cultural awakening in the 1840s.

questions. But I think in dealing with literary questions it will appear to most men of letters to be 'moving about in worlds not realized.'[2] The secret of the LEADER's power is its crusade against *ráimeis*,[3] but if *ráimeis* means a passion for sweeping generalizations and rhetorical sentiments that have no relation to solid facts, then your excursions into literary criticism are *ráimeis* as pure as any of the gems of the platform and the press that you have held up to our derision. Looked at in the light of facts, is it not a little ridiculous to see a worthy gentleman sitting at a desk in Dublin and pronouncing gravely from that watch-tower that he and he alone knows what reaches or does not reach the 'Irish heart,' and what ought, or ought not, to be written for it? Mr. Yeats, it appears, 'has yet to write even one line that will strike a chord of the Irish heart.' Well, I know many Irish hearts that have been deeply moved by Mr. Yeats's poetry, and some as Irish in the strictest Gaelic sense as that which beats under the LEADER's waistcoat. What title have you to rule all these out with a stroke of the pen simply because they understand and like what you do not? By a still more sweeping generalization you tell us that 'men developed in Trinity College, even where they try to be national, can never — with, perhaps, one exception to prove the rule — reach the heart of Ireland.' Is it *ráimeis*, or what is it, that puts forward this dictum as a criticism on a collection of poetry, that out of more than 120 authors includes just thirty-two who have had anything to do with Trinity? But upon this dictum, too, let us turn the light of facts. Let us glance down the avenue of Irish history for the last hundred years. Among the names of men that in one way or another have deeply influenced the history and touched the heart of Ireland I think you will hardly omit those of Grattan, Wolfe Tone, Emmet, Curran, Moore, Thomas Davis (fancy Thomas Davis trying to be national!), Ingram, Ferguson, Aubrey de Vere, Standish O'Grady, Douglas Hyde. Which of these Trinity men forms your one dubious exception? Not all of them, probably, are known or understood by the peasant 'sitting by his turf fire,' though indeed most are. But show us who, among those outside the influences of Trinity, have more conspicuously influenced Irish life than these? The poets of the so-called 'Celtic-revival' of today are mostly non-university men, but, apparently, they do not please you any the more for that. Show us then the men who have succeeded where all these have failed?

You say in one sentence, 'The Irish Papist, sitting by his turf fire, or carrying on his trade or profession, is full of hopes and fears, and longings, and thoughts that they (men of Trinity College) will never wot of.' If you have any serious meaning in this remark it appears to mean that you are going back I know not how many generations to the dismal conception of an Ireland divided into water-tight compartments, with a separate religion in each, and no common thought, no national sentiment, among them all. In that case the LEADER has certainly very much to learn from a journal which has sometimes been called its prototype — *The Nation* of fifty years ago.[4] You cannot build a nation that way, nor a literature either. Literature is, and ought to be, coloured by local circumstances, local traditions, instincts, beliefs and what not, but it has a vast fund of material common to all humanity by dealing with which it can touch all humanity. Are Davis and Ferguson and Yeats and A.E. to be nothing to the Irish Catholic because he is a Catholic, and are De Vere and Griffin and Mangan to be nothing to me because I am a Protestant? The question may be left to answer itself; or, rather, it may be said that the Irish people have sufficiently answered it already. I think you owe it to your readers to tell us plainly whether you wish to reverse that decision.

Yours truly,

T. W. Rolleston

2. The line is from Wordsworth's 'Ode. Intimations of Immortality from Recollections of Early Childhood'.
3. Irish for 'nonsense', one of the many colourful terms of abuse in Moran's critical vocabulary.
4. The *Nation* newspaper, founded in 1842, made a decisive contribution to the politicization of Irish cultural nationalism. Two of its founders, the protestant Thomas Davis (1814–45) and the catholic John Blake Dillon (1816–66) attended Trinity College, Dublin. The third, the catholic Charles Gavan Duffy (1816–1903), was educated at an all-protestant school.

D. P. MORAN

OUR REPLY (1901)

We regret that Mr. Rolleston should juggle words in his attempt to make a point against us. By reference to our article it will be apparent that when we expressed the view that Mr. Brooke was not aware of the advance that Ireland had recently made, we referred to the advance towards the Gaelic, or Irish, point of view. Most men interested in their country and its literature have, we believe, advanced towards the Gaelic League position. Mr. Brooke, and indeed we may add Mr. Rolleston, do [*sic*] not appear to appreciate the extent of that advance. It also appears plain to us that, before we become cosmopolitan in art, or in anything else, we must first resume our nationality; we believe it is impossible to appreciate what we styled 'art in the abstract' unless we first become really English or really Irish; and before we reach Mr. Brooke's rarified atmosphere, where, according to him 'there is neither English nor Irish, French nor German, but the spirit of loveliness alone,' we must go through the intermediate stage of being one thing or another, Irish or English. We will never get there *via* mongrel-land. These two views may be altogether wrong, or they may not; but we see no contradiction between them. However, they give Mr. Rolleston a chance to attempt a thrust at us. We set it out again: 'So it appears, first, that Mr. Brooke is writing as if Ireland were much more backward than she actually is, and secondly, that he imagines her to have reached a stage which in reality she has yet a long and weary journey to attain.' We certainly believe, to quote Mr. Rolleston's own words, that 'free discussion is the nursing mother of truth,' but we would suggest to him that juggling with phrases only traps the unwary, and is at the best a very poor substitute for wit.

Mr. Rolleston is in reality an educated Englishman who thinks that he is an Irishman, whilst we belong to the legion who have awakened to the fact that they ought to have been brought up Irish, but were educated West Britons.[1] There is, therefore, a gulf between us and men like Mr. Rolleston, and in our several outlooks on many matters affecting Ireland, we must agree to differ.

Mr. Rolleston charges us that in literary matters we 'are moving about in worlds not realised' when it surely ought to be clear to him that our aim and only claim is to keep before our readers' attention the world in which their minds ought to move; a world certainly not yet realised, but which Ireland must proceed to realise if it is to become an intellectual entity. We merely warn them that anthologies of *Irish* poetry in *English* belong to a mongrel school of thought that we have left behind us.

Mr. Rolleston is welcome to accuse us of *ráimeis*, but such accusations are scarcely argument. He is entitled to state that we say we alone know this, that, or the other, as we are to point out that an expression of opinion is not necessarily a claim to the monopoly of wisdom. Like many of our critics, Mr. Rolleston appears not to have read our first article in our first number. From that article we, therefore, quote the following: 'We profess to be no oracle, and we ask no man, not even the humblest, to swallow our views, but rather to consider them and agree with or reject them as he may think fit.'

Now we come to Trinity. There are, it appears, only 32 out of 120 of his authors who have been raised in that atmosphere. But, how many of the verses of the remainder have been published in previous anthologies? Surely Mr. Rolleston does not want us to refer to 'The Night Before Larry was Stretched,' and other lyrics, that have done faithful service in the many anthologies and collections that have gone before? We referred to the Trinity College instalment of verses and rhymes because that struck us as being the feature of the book that was new. Mr. Rolleston turns back upon the roll of Trinity during the past century, though our expression of opinion only concerned Trinity of the present, and not Trinity of the days of Moore and Emmet. The solitary exception we had in our mind was Douglas Hyde.

We very much regret that Mr. Rolleston allowed himself to do anything calculated to stir up the dangerous spirit of bigotry at the end of his letter. There is a little too much of that on the Ascendancy side already. But Mr. Rolleston is mistaken if he

1. 'West Briton', a derogatory term for Irish anglophiles, was popularized by D. P. Moran.

thinks that we are going to turn white at the tune of 'Croppies Lie Down.'[2] We stated some views, and if Mr. Rolleston did not feel that he was belonging to the 'superior' section, he would not insult us — we are sure nothing was further from his mind than to intend to do so — he would not insult us by asking us if we had any meaning in what we said. We repeat that we do not, in the main, believe that any man brought up in Trinity can reach the heart of the common Irishman. We do want to go back many generations. We want to go back to the Gael, the matrix of the Irish nation. We beg to remind Mr. Rolleston that Ireland produced philosophers, poets, and men of action, before Trinity produced an 'atmosphere'; and he ought to know by this time that we look upon the ascendancy[3] of the Pale, dating chiefly from Grattan's time, as the leading cause of the stagnation and vulgarity of modern Ireland. We want to raise the Gael again, to induce men to speak to him rather than to cosmopolitan lovers, or affected lovers, of nebulous symbolism. We want to induce him to speak out from his own heart. If we thought that these things were impossible of attainment we would give up our propaganda, and advise the people to become British as quickly as they could. We know that there are many of our friends — sincere in a narrow and bigoted way — who think that we poor Croppies should not open our mouths until our sympathetic masters of the Pale give us their permission. If the Gael is to be raised, the proper place for the sympathetic Palesman is behind the Gael until he becomes absorbed. But it would appear the price of the tolerance, and of the alliance, of the Pale is that the Gael speaks under his breath, and says 'Thank you,' when one per cent of the former graciously smiles upon him. We have no dismal conception of Ireland; we are conscious of no religious bigotry — at the same time we do not intend to allow ourselves to be walked upon by anyone. Ireland has two religions, and the chief dismal thing about it appears to us to be that the majority cannot talk of their religion above their breath, for fear of appearing bigoted, intolerant, and offending our patronisers. You can't say 'Papist' but the Ascendancy gets a conscientious scruple. They have had the power so long that they shudder and imagine abominations when a Croppy dares to lift his head. And between the supineness and cringe of some of the modern Croppies, and the intolerance and bigotry of the Ascendancy, we are indeed, in many respects, a dismal people.

2. 'Croppies' is a pejorative term applied to republican insurgents in 1798 on account of their short-cropped hairstyle, modelled on the French revolutionaries.
3. The term 'ascendancy', signifying the ruling Anglo-Irish caste, came into popular currency in the 1780s and early 1790s.

JOHN EGLINTON and FREDERICK RYAN

(1874–1913)

from: DANA (1904)

[In their manifesto for *Dana*, a 'magazine of independent thought', the editors, John Eglinton and Frederick Ryan, attempted to place humanism and wider philosophical questions on the agenda in Irish cultural debates. Their innovative and provocative magazine lasted for twelve issues, from May 1904 to April 1905. The extract below introduced the first issue].

Of the various forms which patriotic ambition takes in the minds of Irishmen at the present time, perhaps the most generally favoured, and the least impracticable, is a zeal for the promotion of a national literature. To whom does it not seem a worthy dream, and to whom can it appear entirely chimerical, that humanity in this island should have a voice, should commune with itself and with nature, and this by simply using the human elements which may be presumed to be not less abundant and potential here than elsewhere? Man and nature — what more do we want? The difficulty is to begin: and to make a beginning is especially difficult in a country like Ireland, where our bards and prophets have never learned to deal directly and as men with the elements of human nature, and to dispense with traditional methods and traditional themes. We are in the position of a marooned civilian who has struck his last lucifer match in a desolate isle, and who, with the intention of broiling the fish which he has snared, or the beast which he has slain, is making his first pathetic efforts with flints or with dry sticks.

Since the days of the worthy Thomas Davis, who made a great, a noble, and an epoch-making effort to turn the national spirit in the direction of literature, Irish literary enterprise has concerned itself mainly with the aim of securing the nationality of Irish literature by the choice of Irish subjects, the revival of the Irish language, and so forth. The indefeasible right of humanity in this island to think and feel for itself on all matters has not so far been the inspiring dream of our writers. The endeavour to achieve through the sincere confessions of poets and the strenuous operation of thought the elemental freedom of the human mind, which is really the essential of all independent and therefore national literature, has hardly made its appearance in the Irish literary movement. The neglect of this essential was the fatal defect in the campaign of Davis and his colleagues against the provincial spirit in this country. They carefully skirted and stepped aside from the fundamental questions of life and thought which lay in their way, and they set the fashion — which has lasted to this day and is the cause of a certain hollowness in the pretensions of Irish literature — of trying of promote an artificial and sentimental unity in Irish life by carefully ignoring all those matters as to which Irishmen as thinking and unthinking beings hold diverse opinions. 'Oh,' it is still said, if anyone shows a disposition to broach such questions, 'the time has not yet come for that!' Now, we differ from the general opinion in thinking that fundamental questions are those which first of all require to be seen to, and it is mainly to provide some outlet for honest opinion on all such matters that this little magazine comes into being.

Davis and his colleagues, when they wrote, found themselves instinctively addressing, not the Catholic peasantry who formed the staple of the Irish nation, but the fringe of thinking men and women in Ireland, whose interests were those of thinking men and women elsewhere, and whom Davis and his band sought to draw into sympathy with the cause of Irish nationality. This is apparent in the argumentative style of all that they wrote. And in truth it is not worth while seeking to address any other audience. Yet it must be owned that with regard to this public which they really addressed, and chiefly because they waived essential questions, their arguments were wasted. Davis and his band became the heroes, not of that public which they sought to convince, but of a public which never needed to be convinced by their arguments — that warm-hearted, loyal-minded and ever expectant Irish public, whose literary needs are ministered unto by the nationalist press, but who at any hint of the broaching of fundamental questions of life and thought are strangely scared and silent.

Let us not be suspected of any disposition to be truculent or nasty in the cause of what is called Free Thought. In truth, the more distinctively religious press in this country does not present a standard impossible to emulate in the furtherance of the gospel of peace and good-will to men. We would simply assume that people are sincere when they advocate tolerance, understanding by tolerance not a conspiracy of silence in regard to fundamental and essential matters, but a willingness to allow the freest expression of thought in regard to these. We would have our magazine, however, not merely a doctrinaire but a literary, or rather a humanist, magazine; and we would receive and print contributions in prose and in verse which are the expression of the writer's individuality with greater satisfaction than those which are merely the belligerent expression of opinion. Each writer is of course responsible for the opinions contained in his own contribution, and the editors, beyond the responsibility of selection, are by no means bound by the views of any contributor. We invite the thinkers, dreamers and observers dispersed throughout Ireland and elsewhere, who do not despair of humanity in Ireland, to communicate through our pages their thoughts, reveries and observations; and we venture to hope that a magazine, starting with such general designs, should profit by whatever is genuine in the new life and movement which of late years have manifested themselves in the country.

ARTHUR CLERY

(1879–1932)

from: DUBLIN ESSAYS (1919)

[In this frank, retrospective appraisal of the Irish Ireland movement, Arthur Clery concedes that its high-minded idealism led to a form of rigidity and puritanism. This killjoy culture may have been appealing to purists but did not prove attractive to the vast majority of the population, who found reality demanding enough, without having to attend to ideals as well.]

IRELAND, IRISH AND OTHERWISE (A LECTURE TO AN IRISH IRELAND AUDIENCE)

. . . To the new generation the Gaelic movement is an ultimate fact; a thing that seems to have lasted forever. They never remember a time when there was not a Gaelic League. . . .

To the older generation it is different. We saw the sunrise. We watched the first struggle with the clouds. Learning Irish was in our day a very different process from studying French or Latin or Greek. We were 'alive in that dawn,'[1] and drank of the first enthusiasm, deep or shallow as our nature was, but it was wine all the time. What a wild hope was that of twenty years agone: to revive a dying nation through its language. The schoolboy of today who gets slapped with the same melancholy resignation for missing his Irish, as for neglecting his algebra, must look on matters in a very different light. The dawn with its magic colours is long past, and the noonday sun, as it scorches you, is a very commonplace object. Only when it is veiled by dark clouds do we think of it at all.

The star of Irish Ireland, when it first shone forth in our sky, was, and still is, a five-pointed one: language, industries, music, dancing and games. Literature falls under language, music includes song. Of the five points, only two were in any sense novel — language and dancing. The worst enemies of Ireland, just as they admired our scenery, had usually appreciated our music, as far as they were able, which was not as a rule very far. For to appreciate Irish song, without a knowledge of Gaelic, is a hopeless task. I have occasionally met people whose dislike of Irish manufacture extended even to our music; but these are the people who would prefer foreign grapes to home grapes. The advocacy of Irish industries is, of course, as old as Dean Swift and as new as the latest Chief Secretary.[2] The great movement, which has captured most of what is best in Irish manhood for native games and sports, goes back to 1884, the days of Croke and Cusack, the period of the land war.[3] Only the lowest classes in Dublin, and also the upper-middle and a small part of the lower-middle class of Dublin, and some other towns stand aside from Irish games. The rest of the country is solid in their favour. It is often thought nowadays that the Gaelic Athletic movement is in some way the fruit of the Gaelic League or Irish Ireland movement. It belongs to the previous generation.

The characteristic of the Irish Ireland movement, as it came to be known, was that it combined all these diverse and yet related elements into a single rule of life, giving to language study a place in the national programme, which it had never held before. For it made Gaelic its key-note, insisting on the importance and practicability of the study and use of Irish by every Irish Nationalist. It thus substituted for, or at least added to, the purely political concept of national endeavour then in vogue, a complexus of duties, activities and enthusiasms covering a very wide area and penetrating into the deepest recesses of our social life. Under the impulse of a single aim, it made war on many different fronts, carrying on a number of campaigns with varying fortunes, all

1. See William Wordsworth, *The Prelude*, Book XI, II, 108–09: 'Bliss was it in that dawn to be alive / But to be young was very heaven!'

2. Jonathan Swift's pamphlet *A Proposal for the Universal Use of Irish Manufacture* (1720) was the first influential expression of the case for economic nationalism in Ireland.

3. Michael Cusack (1847–1907) was the founder of the Gaelic Athletic Association, established at Thurles, Co. Tipperary in 1884. Thomas Croke (1824–1902), archbishop of Cashel, was the first patron of the GAA and is commemorated in the name of its headquarters, Croke Park, Dublin.

directed to a common purpose, to save the national soul of Ireland. It was in this way that an importance seemingly disproportionate came to be attached by the new movement to quite trifling things, a dance, a song, a game, much as men cherish the feasts and fasts or pious observances of a faith, not for themselves, but as sentinels of that for which they stand. Among Irish Irelanders it became no venial matter to eat apples from an un-Irish tree. For the battle for any one point was looked upon as the battle for all. This was the strength of the new movement. It would tolerate no harpists clothed in English shoddy,[4] or cricketers studying Irish, or hurlers singing music-hall songs. No one has ever yet ventured to waltz at an Irish college. My friend and frequent editor, Mr. D. P. Moran, in his brilliant philosophy of Irish Ireland and in the weekly paper in which he hammered home its doctrines, did much to win acceptance for this point of view. The name IRISH IRELAND itself very justly expresses it.

The new movement drew its strength from discipline and self-restraint. Discipline can rouse as deep a fervour as liberty. It has made more converts in every age. Once its forces were fairly mobilized, about the turn of the century, they advanced with the irresistible onset of a conquering army. The movement spread like wildfire through the country. But after a time the onset slackened; resistance gathered from various quarters. When the first fervour had passed, say about the middle of the first decade of the century, the advance of Irish Ireland may be said to have been held up. The opposition sprang from various causes. Each point in the Irish Ireland programme hurt somebody. One man wanted his socks and another his songs. One man wanted Rugby football[5] and another two steps. They all wanted ease, without study. The Irish Ireland movement called on them to abandon all these things. It was not so much that they became actively hostile to Irish Ireland — though some did — but rather they admired it as we admire heroic virtue from a safe distance. Men came to have the same sort of patronizing admiration for Irish Ireland as, say, for the monks of Mount Melleray.[6]

When the advance of Irish Ireland, to continue the martial metaphor, was held up, its forces did what any other forces would do in the circumstances. They dug themselves in, and a sort of trench warfare may be said to have ensued ever since. Certain territory the Irish Ireland forces occupied very firmly; within that territory their will prevailed, but the Ireland that was Irish came to be separated from the Ireland that was otherwise by a very clear line of demarcation, a line of severance not less well marked because it divided men's souls and not the solid earth.

Within the territory of Irish Ireland, the Gaelic language was fairly widely spread. Men read Irish papers, or at least papers that wrote about Irish. As for class distinction, the only class they troubled themselves about were language classes. It was not true, as native speakers believed, that all Irish Irelanders rode bicycles and said lá breaᵹ,[7] but they had other peculiarities. They could all dance and dance well. They said they never waltzed, but one sometimes had doubts about the truth of the statement. They could all sing. If some sang strangely, well, perhaps it was a very special kind of sean-nós.[8] 'Irish Irelanders' were not all poets or hurlers (or poetesses and experts at camóᵹuiḋeaċt)[9] but the proportion of poets and even of hurlers among them was larger than that in the outer world. In reality, cycling was the pastime of the Irish Irelander rather than any more traditional sport. Irish Irelanders were usually temperate, often total abstainers, always earnest, self-sacrificing, of high character. This is the army that, for near a quarter of a century, has held the trenches of Irish Ireland.

But, what of the other Ireland, that paradox, un-Irish Ireland? We may for the moment leave out of account the Unionists huddled in the far distance. They have a dim Ireland of their own, a thing so faint and tenuous that it is little more than a shadow cast across the face of Britain, and yet they cling, sometimes even cling passionately, to this shadow. The other Ireland, lying beyond the lines of the Gael, is far from being Unionist, whatever else it

4. Cheap clothing made of woollen or cotton rags.
5. Rugby football originated in Rugby School, England in 1823, and was established at an institutional level in the 1870s. In Ireland, it was generally associated with the Anglo-Irish, and this led to the prohibition on the playing on rugby in the controversial Rule 27 of the articles of the Gaelic Athletic Association.
6. A Trappist monastery in County Waterford, renowned for its devotion to silence and seclusion from the world.
7. Irish: 'fine day'.
8. Irish: refers to a distinctive style of traditional singing.
9. The game of hurling as played by females.

may be. A Unionist at an election cannot poll ten votes, male or female, out of its population. It is sincerely anti-Unionist; but it comprises every variety of political opinion from the out and out rebel to the most stodgy Whig. When I speak of the rebel perhaps some of you will think of that cunning play, *Sable and Gold*,[10] produced at the Abbey Theatre a few weeks ago, in which one character, Gregory, an Irish Irelander of over-tense nerves, who in the end proves a coward, is contrasted with Paul, a representative of that other uncaring Ireland of which I now speak, who meets death with courage. If this contrast is intended as typical, it certainly is not supported by the facts. No one can say that Irish Irelanders have shown themselves wanting in courage. The profession of anti-national and anti-militarist sentiments is not usually associated with military qualities. But for good or for evil, Paul in the play does stand for a great class, perhaps the largest class of our fellow-countrymen, sound at heart, but only at heart. Or would it be more true to say that every Irishman has in him a Paul and a Gregory, a striver after ideals and a complacent cynic. It depends upon which half of him gets the upper hand. In *Irish* Ireland one type prevails, in 'otherwise' Ireland the cynics and the complacents have it all their own way . . . .

I come now to a point where I speak with some hesitation. The commonplace man has rather a peculiar feeling towards Irish Ireland and all its works, something I conceive like the feeling that a great many people in religious agreement with Y. M. C. ideals have towards the Young Men's Christian Association. As I said earlier in the lecture, Irish Irelanders are, for the most part, men of high character. That's the difficulty. High character and elevated ideals inevitably carry a suggestion of puritanism and intellectualism. And of all things on earth, these are the two that frighten the commonplace man most. It is bad enough to ask him to attend a class, but to ask him to amuse himself with idealists, male and female, of high character. Nothing will make him do that. You point to the amusements of Irish Ireland, its brightening influences, the fact that the tea is always good at céiliḋs,[11] never at dances. None of those things will take the bad taste out of his mouth, the taste of high character. Its alleged relaxations are much too tight for him; he can't amuse himself that way. In fact it's one of the difficulties of a country situate as Ireland is, that for the middle class at least, it is only the high life, the ideal life, that is left to the native population and the national side. The commonplace unideal life of card-tables, bars, billiard saloons, music halls, race meetings and betting shops is for the most part conquered by the forces working against the country. That is a tremendous extent of territory to leave in the enemies' hands. The strength of the G.A.A., as distinguished from the other and newer elements of Irish Ireland, is in great part derived from the fact that, while it has an ideal, it has also a large side that is not in the least ideal, but rather makes an appeal to the average human. Ordinary men brought within the ambit of the G.A.A. by circumstances must often be under the same sort of silent compulsion to be Irish, that ordinary men outside its influence are commonly subjected to to make them anti-Irish.

Much of what has gone before is, perhaps, more true of the situation existing a few years ago than of the situation today. Events have been working in favour of Irish Ireland, and it has now a tremendous opportunity if it can seize it. It has for the moment the eager sympathy of numberless people outside its own boundaries, in fact of the vast majority of the native population. The man in the 'pub' and even the man on the racecourse are in its favour. The national party of the day incorporates its doctrines in its programme. How is it to turn this new situation to account, and make converts of its sympathizers? The old methods and the old programme will hardly do. Even Christianity itself underwent developments in formal unessentials when it came out of the catacombs. I am the first to recognize the great importance of moral qualities and high ideals to any movement, above all to a forward movement. They have been an immense strength to Irish Ireland. But if, to continue our metaphor, the campaign is to pass from a trench warfare to a war of movement, if Irish Ireland is to conquer the population as a whole — as Sinn Fein has already done in politics[12] — it must be with a rule of life, which, not only enthusiasts

10. Maurice Dalton's play, *Sable and Gold*, was performed at the Abbey Theatre in September 1918, and published by Maunsel and Roberts in 1922 in the Abbey Theatre Series, second series, Vol. 9.

11. Irish: refers to a dance where the entertainment is provided by Irish music and dancing.

12. Sinn Féin, which finally espoused republicanism in 1917, had won an overwhelming triumph in the general election of 1918.

and intellectuals, but the population as a whole can live up to. Of course it will have its counsels of perfection, but you must have a place for the inconsistent weakling, who perpetually falls away from national grace. You must put up with the man who is quite willing to have his son taught Irish, but won't learn it himself, who plays the wrong sort of games, sings the wrong sort of songs. Excommunication must become a rare process, only to be invoked for the gravest crimes. In fact you will have to be content with a sound heart, without asking too closely whether it is accompanied by a sound head. Above all you must make it clear that high character, whether high living or high thinking, is *not* a condition of belonging to your communion.

And you must do this freely and not grudgingly. Some may think these very dangerous suggestions, involving as they do, if not a lowering of the flag, at least the relaxation of a discipline that has been the glory of our forces, that has given them so much of their efficiency. So far the suggestions are tentative. They can be worked out by others. But we all feel that a new situation and a new generation has [*sic*] arisen, a generation remarkably tolerant of those who have gone before them, yet having enlarged ideals of its own. With such men and in such a situation, with a sympathy so widespread in favour of the Irish point of view, some change in the rule and the programme that has done service these twenty years is necessary. The golden moment has come at last; the youth of Ireland are eager to be its saviours; but they will save it in their own way.

III. NATION, STATE AND CULTURAL IDENTITY

EÓIN MAC NEILL

(1867–1945)

OUR WHIG INHERITANCE (1936)

[This short article, which appeared in the November 1936 issue of *Ireland Today*, is the most concise expression of Eóin Mac Neill's argument, developed over the course of thirty years' research, that Gaelic Ireland possessed no concept of the *state* but looked instead to the *nation* for a common identity. The primacy accorded to the nation over the state exerted a profound influence on the subsequent development of Irish politics, and was partly responsible for placing cultural matters, rather than questions of material power, at the forefront of the struggle for national independence.]

Our sad decay in Kirk and State
surpasses my descriving,
the Whigs came oer us for a curse
and we hae done wi thriving.
Awa, Whigs, awa![1]

The fundamental difference between the Nation and the State' — Nicholas Murray Butler.[2]

On more than one public occasion I have invited people to think about this. Perhaps they do not like to think about it. We really do not like to think about anything. We would rather repeat watchwords and catchwords and other big words and phrases, or ruminate over our feelings and emotions.

There was a man who used to take a hand in various public discussions some years ago in Dublin. He had never been required to learn Latin, but he was a great reader of various periodicals and he had picked up the phrase *ad hoc* with some notion of what it meant. He couldn't talk to you for ten minutes — he could easily talk for ten times ten minutes, but he could not talk for ten minutes without working in *ad hoc*. In truth, this man's *ad hoc* was usually a great deal more *ad hoc* than a lot of

1. 'Awa, Whigs, Awa', a Jacobite song, collected in James Hogg's *The Jacobite Relics of Scotland* (Edinburgh, 1819), Song XLVI.

2. Nicholas Murray Butler (1862–1947), president of Columbia University, New York 1902–47, and world statesman. In 1931 he shared the Nobel Peace Prize with Jane Addams.

the big words that are enunciated in our daily discussions. For example, Imperialism. It is given out in speeches and heard by audiences, evidently on the assumption that the speaker and the hearers know what it means and are agreed about the meaning of it. If a five-minute silence could be provided on one of these occasions, and if the speaker and each of the hearers got a slip of paper and a pencil and wrote down what he or she understood Imperialism to mean, the collected result would perhaps throw some light on the nature of what is called Public Opinion. Just at present, Fascism might be a better test. If a guess may be ventured, it would not be surprising to find that a meeting of Communists, that is of persons who like to imagine that they are Communists, would describe or define Fascism for the most part in such terms as to make it appear that the grand Superfascist of our time is not Mussolini or Hitler, but Stalin.

I repeat the invitation to think whether Nicholas Murray Butler is right in saying that there is a difference, and a fundamental difference, between a Nation and a State, and what that difference is. If we claim to be patriotic, we surely ought to be reasonably clear in our minds about the objects of our patriotism. Some years ago, there was a debate or a discussion in the Seanad[3] about the Government policy in the matter of the Irish language. The official report showed that, in the minds of speakers of different sections, but most markedly in the minds of those Senators who, even though they were of the party supporting the Government, were not in complete accord with its language policy, Nation and State meant the same thing — at least they had not thought enough about it to recognise any fundamental difference. To that extent, the Seanad may have been thoroughly representative of what is called Public Opinion.

Nevertheless, it is part of our national position, and it is either implied or expressed in the politics of our Nationalist parties, past and present, that the fundamental difference exists in Ireland and for Ireland. Our claims to political autonomy, to having a State of our own, have never been based and could not have been based on Ireland's having existed in former times as a State. They were based, and rightly based, on the existence of an Irish Nation throughout the ages of Irish history. For seven centuries and a half, the only form of State that existed in Ireland was the Dublin Bureaucracy, which was consistently anti-Irish and anti-national. Before that, there was only the Highkingship, rather a symbol of the sense of national unity than an operative political institution.

The confusion in the minds of Senators goes back some time. I have seen somewhere the saying ascribed to Henry Grattan — I do not find it in the recent life of Grattan by Roger McHugh — that he assisted at the birth of an Irish nation and also at its funeral.[4] If Grattan said that, or anything like it, Irish people of our time would repudiate the saying or laugh at it. Grattan did not even take part in the establishment of an Irish State, in spite of the statutory declarations here and in England of Irish parliamentary independence. The Dublin Bureaucracy continued to rule the land, and the failure to bring it under the authority of the Irish Parliament shows Grattan's incompetence as a statesman. The confusion is present in the words of Thomas Davis's ballad, 'A Nation Once Again,' for certainly what Davis meant was an independent State, and a ballad was perhaps the most effective thing to plant the confusion in the popular mind. If his essays had been as well known as his ballads, there would be no doubt what he thought about the fundamental difference. For example, he begins his essay on the Irish language with the words 'A Nation should guard its language'[5] — declaring this to be the duty of the Irish Nation at a time when there was no Irish State.

Future historians may recognise that the dominant characteristic of this time of ours is not the great advance made in physical science and invention, but in the popular acceptance of the political theory of State absolutism. The spread of this doctrine, like *ad hoc*, is one of the fruits of the Renaissance. It is rooted in admiration of the grandeur of pagan and imperial Rome. From the small circles of Renais-

3. Seanad Éireann (the Irish Senate) is the upper house of the Oireachtas or Irish parliament.

4. The reference is to Roger McHugh, *Henry Grattan* (Dublin: The Talbot Press; London: Duckworth, 1936). Phrases proximate to this were used by Grattan in his anti-Union speeches of 14 February and 26 May 1800.

5. Thomas Davis's essay 'The Irish Language' appeared in two parts in *The Nation* on 1 April and 30 December 1843. The Gaelic League published it as a pamphlet in 1916. The essay contains this phrase, but does not begin with it.

sance intelligentsia it has spread and spread until now it is carried by journalism and political propaganda into almost every highway and byway of the world. It is gradually becoming, if it has not already become, the real religion of a large part of the human race. By the real religion, I mean what the words mean and no rhetorical figure of speech. 'The Pagan worship of the State' is a phrase quoted in translation of the words of His Holiness Pius XI.[6] Its attitude towards other religions is varied. Sometimes it favours them so long as they appear to serve its own purposes. Sometimes it gives them a sort of contemptuous toleration. Its favours and its toleration may be calculated to deceive even the elect. In our own day, in more than one country, the great god State has begun to speak in the words of the First Commandment.

Here in Ireland, nobody has yet expressly proclaimed the doctrine of State Absolutism under that name, but the jurists have a name of their own that means the same thing, sovereign independence, and with this name we have all been made familiar. Sovereign means absolute internally, and independent means absolute externally.

State absolutism was the main cause of the Great War of 1914. If another Great War comes, State absolutism will be the cause of it. If ruin threatens civilisation in our time, the cause of ruin will be the growth of State absolutism into a popular creed.

The prophet of Statism — to shorten the phrase into one word, based on the French word *étatisme* — was Nicholas Machiavelli. His disciple, the statesman of the policy of Henry VIII., was Thomas Cromwell. In the course of time, statism became the creed of the English Whigs. From them it passed over to the Protestant patriots of Ireland and their Deistic offshoots,[7] and from these to the other Nationalist political parties who succeeded them. This Whig inheritance is potent, we might say it is sacred, among us at present.

If some think I am writing paradoxes, it is because they don't really think and don't want to think. They accept the Whig idea as if it came down to them from Mount Sinai. The Whigs came over us for a curse, and there is more yet to be said about that curse. It is the real curse of Cromwell — Thomas,[8] not Oliver.

6. The antagonism to the state in catholic ideology found expression in the 1930s in the corporatist or vocational movement. It gathered substantial support from leading catholic intellectuals, who saw in Eamon de Valera's nationalization programme evidence of 'creeping' state socialism. The encyclical referred to is *Quadregesimo Anno* (1931). The actual words are 'the twentieth-century idolatry, more irrational than any under paganism, is that of the omnipotent state.'

7. Mac Neill is referring here to the 'real' Whigs or proto-republicans who enjoyed considerable influence in the Dublin of the 1720s under the patronage of Lord Molesworth. They are construed by Mac Neill as forerunners of Grattan's parliament, whereas they could just as easily be seen as the precursors of modern republicanism.

8. Thomas Cromwell (*c.* 1485–1540), Henry VIII's closest adviser, was responsible for drafting most of the Reformation legislation and for securing its passage though parliament.

AODH DE BLACAM

(1890–1951)

from: TOWARDS THE REPUBLIC (1918)

[In this extract from the second edition of Aodh de Blacam's *Towards the Republic*, 'Gaeldom' is dissociated from its grounding in nineteenth-century Celticism and racial theory and is replaced with a more open-ended *cultural* definition of the nation. Consequently, de Blacam is able to elaborate a more inclusive, and multifaceted, but nonetheless distinctively Gaelic, Ireland.

CHAPTER II

THE MAKINGS OF THE NATION

. . . The sole bond of Irish Nationality is — and always was — the native Gaelic culture, and whatever the changing details may be, the underlying motive of every strong national movement can be traced to *the restoration of Gaelicism*. Movements and causes in Ireland may always be observed to succeed or fail in proportion as they approximate to Gaelic tradition. The existence of the Gaelic norm as the public ideal is the most unmistakable phenomenon of Irish life. In proportion as artists work back to Gaelic origins, so does their work gain in conviction, colour and success. In proportion as they have read deeply of Gaelic literature, the work of our poets and story-tellers possesses for the general Irish public 'grip' and reality. In proportion as our publicists are absorbed in Gaelic ideals are they trusted and loved like the Sinn Fein leaders, in distinction to the distrusted and contemned children of Anglicisation.

It is not be be supposed that Gaelicism is a narrow racial cause. When we say that all things non-Gaelic in Ireland are foreign we do not mean that nobody has any part in Irish-Ireland save people who, like many folk in Donegal today, can trace their personal descent back to Niall of the Nine Hostages,[1] and thence, theoretically, to the ancestor of the Milesian race. We merely mean that *the Gael is the normal national type*, and that divergence of that type is a mark of foreign influence, interests or allegiance. Indeed, nobody with an elementary knowledge of modern racial science would so far err as to suppose that anything like homogeneity of race exists in Ireland any more than in any other European nation. Even an unscientific glance at any Irish assembly will detect a score of different types. The old mythological story of the Milesian nation has now long gone by the board. We know that primitive Ireland was populated by immigrations from many sources — the earliest large immigration, that of the Tuatha de Dannan, being, according to Dr. Sigerson,[2] of a Teutonic origin; for did they not come from the North, as Scandinavians would, and were they not, Teuton-like, famed for their musical and magical arts? As for the Celts, no one knows who they were, and we know from the Latin authors that when they populated Gaul they were already a race of mixed types. We know that an Ireland of mixed tribes was compounded into a nation sometime early in the Christian Era (query: by the universal change from pasturage to agriculture?) and that the united nation received numerous immigrations of Norsemen and Normans, and later of Anglo-Saxon Englishry.

So long as Gaelic culture remained dominant in Ireland, all these races were in turn absorbed and moulded to the national type. In a patriarchal country, names count for nothing as evidence of origin, for in such countries nothing is commoner as a social custom than the legal fiction by which foreigners are admitted to the body corporate on the adoption of the clan name. Hence, nobody knows less about his origin in Ireland that an *O* or a *Mac*. He may be descended from any race which ever entered Ireland before modern times when names were fixed. It is impossible to estimate, therefore, what proportion of bearers of Celtic names are of Celtic origin — until such time as ethnologists shall measure all our skulls, when surprising conclusions may be looked for. The possession of a non-Celtic name, again, is no evidence of non-Celtic ancestry, for Celtic names were for long illegal, and those who, in the Pale, adopted English names and entered the towns, thus cutting themselves from the clan influence, transmitted those foreign names to later generations. On the other hand, we find bearers of names like Keating, Nugent, Walsh, Hackett and Fitzgerald, of known non-native origin, among the leading classics of Irish literature and the leading champions of Gaelic nationality.

Hence it is clear that any attempt to base the Irish Nation on racialism is absurd from the outset. Such an attempt has never been made by any Nationalist of authority. Gaelicism, then, is in no sense racial, and the Gaelic nation offers a welcome to its citizenship to the child of any race if he, living in Ireland, accepts the sovereignty of the Irish Nation. But for all this, Gaelicism is none the less real: it is no whit artificial. . . .

[In the second extract from *Towards the Republic*, de Blacam looks back to the communal structure of ancient Irish society in support of his argument that the state in pre-Conquest Ireland was decentralized, and was a cultural rather than a political entity. The modern bureaucratic state, in effect, is dissolved into a more diffuse anterior nation.]

1. An ancient high king who, reputedly, captured St Patrick as a boy and brought him to Ireland.
2. Dr George Sigerson (1836–1925), author of *Bards of the Gael and Gall* (1897), was among the first to attempt to sever Gaelic culture from the racial underpinnings of Celticism. He sought to establish Teutonic as well as the conventional Mediterranean origins for the ancient Irish, a project not unrelated to his own northern European background.

CHAPTER III

THE GAELIC STATE

. . . As we look back to the communal Gaelic State, we see in its constitution the explanation of the Gaelic nation's survival through ages of unparalleled bloody persecution. The communal ownership of the land accounts for that sturdy personal independence which preserved the physical virility of the race, and which, by giving every man his personal stake in the state, made settled, patriotic citizens. Under systems where the farmers are the creatures of large landlords, independence, security, expansive virility are less to be looked for. But it was not alone the fact that every man had his stake in the Gaelic State that made the nation so hard to destroy. It was the many-headedness, as of the hydra, of the Irish constitution that perplexed the enemy, who knew not where to strike. It is true that the Irish State of pre-Invasion days was weak in central authority. Long peace — the Norsemen round the coast had long softened into useful commercial Irish citizens — had left Ireland careless of the need for a strong military monarchy, and when the most unscrupulous and most militaristic nation of Europe sent ravaging armies into Ireland, there was a tragic want of ruthlessness in the opposition that was offered. A strong mediaeval monarchy would not have been content to pen the invaders into Dublin; it would have swept the last intruder into the sea, and with a strong naval effort carried the war into the enemy's camp to teach a wholesome lesson.

And yet this want of centralisation proved, in a sense, the nation's salvation. Had the Irish State hung upon central institutions, the destruction thereof would have meant the nation's destruction. Thus one great battle might have ended Irish independence. As it was, the real bond of Irish Nationality was enthusiastic loyalty to the national culture. It was a spiritual bulwark that no material force could break. Economically, the state was based on self-supporting stateships, and before foreign power could establish itself, each of these stateships had separately to be reduced. Each stateship had its pasturage, tillage, lea, wood, and fresh or salt-water fisheries; in all of which each of its citizens had his stake. Each stateship, again, had its own craftsmen, jurists, physicians and bards: a complete apparatus for independent and varied life. Each stateship produced its own food, clothing, weapons, and cultural ministrations. The arts and crafts were, so to speak, by-industries of agriculture; and hence, so long as the land was held, the complete life of the Gael could thrive in local perfection. A nation thus vitally strong in every part was, as a whole, an organism that could not be quelled save by the extirpation of the race. So long as the people could cling to the soil — and often a clan swept completely from its holdings won its way back — the national life continued in almost full intensity, while the self-sufficiency of every clan made strangers seek absorption so as to enjoy the civic privileges that were otherwise denied.

We thus may learn one of the most important lessons of Irish history, viz., that *the national war was also a social war*. The Irish Nation, when truly Gaelic, *fought its battle upon the social plane*. By preserving a Gaelic society, the nation survived. Gaelicism of life was the hardest thing for the enemy to destroy, and it was only in the last century, when he partially succeeded, with his National Schools[1] (wickedest weapon ever forged) that the nation lost for a while resiliency and the power of absorption and recovery. There is a lesson in this for today. England can deport our politicians, defeat our armed men, strangle with her censorship our diplomatic efforts; but while no means of resistance on our part is to be discarded because it can in the extreme be overborne, yet we do well to remember that England's only argument, Force, cannot prevail against social endeavour. England cannot prevent us from forming and preserving a Gaelic society, and in proportion as Irish social endeavour is united and resolved, the might of England in Ireland will be rendered nugatory.

Along the western counties, where the Irish language still predominates, traces of the life of the stateships linger to this day. There are little groups of parishes almost completely self-supporting, although imported food and manufactured goods are now beginning to penetrate through the accursed gombeen-shops.[2] Here neighbours co-operate to build the houses and make furniture. The superb

1. The National School system of primary schooling, the first of its kind in the world, was introduced into Ireland in 1831.
2. 'Gombeenman' is the term used to describe a usurer or moneylender in rural Ireland. It often refers to a large shop owner who wields considerable influence in a locality by extending credit to his customers at exorbitant rates.

bedding, of touch-delighting woollen texture, and the clothing of the people are from local looms. The food is mainly the good local produce — oatbread and heather-honey are there. In co-operative labours and in a thousand pleasing social traits, the observer may see relics of a very different life from that of Anglicised Ireland, and may cast himself back in vision to the full-blooded life of pre-Famine days, and so to the Ireland of days before the Dispossession. Here there are literature and song and social wealth of life flourishing in the Gaelic tongue, and a happy existence is enjoyed in complete independence of all the tawdry works and pomps of the English-speaking world. You may meet strong farmers who have never heard of John Redmond,[3] so virile, so self-sufficient, are the surviving fragments of the Gaelic polity.

Gaelicism is not so artificial a thing that it can be killed by a break in its continuity. Its principles are instinctive to the Irish people, and though the traditional Gaelic State has been beaten back to the Atlantic verge, its familiar lineaments have strangely begun to re-appear in the fields that it seemed forever to have left. The nation having recovered the land and so acquired security for self-expression, has mysteriously begun, as we may say, to crystallise out in its old form. As by some strange *avatar* the old economic methods have begun to assert themselves in modern conditions. . . .

3. John Redmond (1856–1918), leader of the Irish Parliamentary Party 1900–18. His desire to consolidate Irish claims to Home Rule by calling on nationalists to enlist in the British army during World War I led to the final break between constitutional nationalists and the republican movement.

JAMES CONNOLLY

(1868–1916)

from: ERIN'S HOPE (1896)

[This extract from an early pamphlet of James Connolly's is the most influential exposition of the argument that a form of 'primitive communism' existed in pre-colonial Ireland. Unlike Aodh de Blacam, however, Connolly sees no hope of restoring or recovering this ancient social order, though he does call into question the assumption, common to advocates of both capitalism and socialism, that capitalism always be equated with social progress.]

IRELAND BEFORE THE CONQUEST

Before the time of the conquest, the Irish people knew nothing of absolute property in land. The land belonged to the entire sept; the chief was little more than managing member of the association. The feudal idea which came in with the conquest was associated with foreign dominion, and has never to this day been recognized by the moral sentiment of the people.

In these few words of Mr. John Stuart Mill[1] the impartial student may find the key for unravelling the whole tangled skein of Irish politics. Latter-day politicians, both on the English and Irish side, have done their utmost to familiarize the public mind with the belief that the Irish question arises solely out of the aspirations of the Irish people to have more complete control over the internal administration of the affairs of their country than it is possible for them to exercise while the seat of government is located at Westminster, and that, therefore, some form of local self-government, as, for instance, Mr. Gladstone's Home Rule Bill[2] is all that is needed to

1. John Stuart Mill, *England and Ireland* (London: Longmans, Green, Reader and Dyer, 1865), p. 12. This pamphlet criticized the application of English principles of property and *laissez-faire* to Irish economic conditions, and played a part in bringing about a major change in liberal attitudes towards Ireland. This, in turn, paved the way for Gladstone's first Land Act (1870) and subsequent reforms.
2. W. E. Gladstone introduced two Home Rule Bills, in 1886 and 1892, both of which were defeated.

settle this question, and lay forever the troubled spirit of Irish discontent. According to this luminous(?) exposition of Irish history, we are to believe that the two nations have for seven hundred years been engaged in unceasing warfare, that the one country (Ireland) has during all that time been compelled to witness the merciless slaughter of her children by famine, pestilence and the sword; that each succeeding generation has witnessed a renewal of the conflict and a renewal of the martyrdom, until the sensitive mind recoils from a perusal of Irish history as from the records of a shambles, and all, forsooth, because Irishmen and Englishmen could not agree upon the form of political administration best suited for Ireland.

If this new reading of Irish history were true the intelligent foreigner might be forgiven for rating at a very low standard the intelligence of two nations which during seven hundred years had not evolved a satisfactory solution of such a simple question. At precisely the same low standard may safely be rated the political acumen of the English and Irish party leaders who are today complacently trotting out the discredited abortion of Home Rule as a sovereign remedy for Ireland's misery.

The Irish question has, in fact, a much deeper source than a mere difference of opinion on forms of government. Its real origin and inner meaning lay in the circumstances that the two opposing nations held fundamentally different ideas upon the vital question of property in land. Recent scientific research by such eminent sociologists as Letourneau,[3] Lewis Morgan,[4] Sir Henry Maine,[5] and others has amply demonstrated the fact that common ownership of land formed the basis of primitive society in almost every country. But whereas in the majority of countries now called civilized such primitive communion had almost entirely disappeared before the dawn of history, and had at no time acquired a higher status than that conferred by the social sanction of unlettered and uneducated tribes, in Ireland the system formed part of the well-defined social organization of a nation of scholars and students, recognized by Chief and Tanist, Brehon[6] and Bard, as the inspiring principle of their collective life, and the basis of their national system of jurisprudence. Such a striking fact will, of course, be interpreted in many ways, according to the temperament and political or racial sympathies of the reader. The adherent of the present order of society will regard it as proof of the Irish incapacity for assimilating progressive ideas, and will, no doubt, confidently assert that this incapacity is the real source of Ireland's misery, since it has unfitted her sons for the competitive scramble for existence, and so fore-doomed them to the lot of hewers of wood and drawers of water.

The ardent student of sociology, who believes that the progress of the human race through the various economic stages of communism, chattel slavery, feudalism, and wage-slavery, has been but a preparation for the higher ordered society of the future; that the most industrially advanced countries are but, albeit often unconsciously, developing the social conditions which, since the breakup of universal tribal communism, have been rendered historically necessary for the inauguration of a new and juster economic order, in which social, political and national antagonism will be unknown, will perhaps regard the Irish adherence to clan ownership at such a comparatively recent date as the Seventeenth Century as an evidence of retarded economical development, and therefore a real hindrance to progress. But the sympathetic student of history, who believes in the possibility of a people by political intuition anticipating the lessons afterwards revealed to them in the sad school of experience, will not be indisposed to join with the ardent Irish patriot in his lavish expressions of admiration for the sagacity of his Celtic forefathers, who foreshadowed in the democratic organization of the Irish clan the more perfect organization of the free society of the future.

Whichever be the true interpretation of Irish history, one fact at least stands out clear and undeniable, viz., that the conflict between the rival systems of land ownership was the pivot around which

3. Charles Letourneau (1831–1902), an eminent French anthropologist influenced by evolutionary theory.
4. Lewis Morgan's classic anthropological study, *Ancient Society* (1877), laid the basis for the concept of 'primitive communism' in the writings of Marx and Engels.
5. Sir Henry Maine (1822–88), a Scottish legal historian who pioneered the study of legal anthropology.
6. 'Tanist' refers to the heir apparent to a chieftain in the old Gaelic order. A variant of the term, 'Tánaiste', is the present title for the deputy prime minister in the Irish government. 'Brehon' (a judge) is generally associated with the ancient legal system in Ireland.

centered all the struggles and rebellions of which that history has been so prolific. The Irish regarded with inveterate hostility their English rulers, at all times set little store upon promises of incorporation within the pale of the constitution, and rose with enthusiasm under their respective rebel chiefs, because they regarded this as the all-important question, because in their eyes English rule and Dublin parliaments were alike identified as the introducers and upholders of the system of feudalism and private ownership of land, as opposed to the Celtic system of clan or common ownership, which they regarded, and, I think, rightly, as the pledge at once of their political and social liberty.

The English Government were also astute enough to perceive that the political or national subjection of Ireland was entirely valueless to the conquerors while the politically subjected nation remained in possession of economic freedom. Consequently, we find that the first stipulation made to the Irish tribe upon its submission always provided that the lands of the tribe should be regarded as the private property of the chief; that he should therefore accept them as a grant from the crown, from which he should in future hold them; that he should drop his Irish title, which proclaimed him the freely elected chief of a free community, and should instead accept an English title, such as duke or earl, and in all things conform to English ideas of civilization and social order. All these stipulations were in the last degree repugnant to Irish ideas. The chief, as Mill has justly observed, was but the managing member of the tribal association, although in the stress of constant warfare they usually limited their choice to the members of one or two families; yet the right of election was never abdicated by the tribesmen. Whenever the seductions of English gold overmastered the patriotism of an Irish chief, and succeeded in inducing his acceptance of the alien property system and the alien title (as in the case of Art O'Neil and Nial Garbh O'Donnell, the Queen's O'Reilly and the Queen's Maguire),[7] they immediately elected another chief in his stead; and from that moment the unfortunate renegade became an outlaw from his own people, and could only appear in his native territory under an escort of English spears.

The Irish system was thus on a par with those conceptions of social rights and duties which we find the ruling classes today denouncing so fiercely as 'Socialistic.' It was apparently inspired by the democratic principle that property was intended to serve the people, and not by the principle so universally acted upon at present, viz., that the people have no other function in existing than to be the bondslaves of those who by force or by fraud have managed to possess themselves of property. They did not, indeed, regard all forms of productive property as rightfully belonging to the community; but when we remember that the land alone was at that time of importance, all other forms of property being insignificant by comparison, we see that they were as Socialistic as the industrial development of their time required. The English civilization against which they fought was, on the other hand, thoroughly individualistic; and, as it triumphed, we are reaping the fruits today in the industrial disputes, the agricultural depressions, the poorhouses, and other such glorious institutions in Church and State as we are permitted the luxury of enjoying in common with our fellow-subjects in this 'integral portion of the British Empire.' The results of the change on the national life of Erin are well illustrated in the scornful words in which Aubrey De Vere apostrophises the 'new race' of exploiters which then arose:

The chiefs of the Gael were the people embodied;
The chiefs were the blossoms, the people the root.
Their conquerors, the Normans, high-souled and high-blooded,
Grew Irish at last from the scalp to the foot.
And ye, ye are hirelings and satraps, not nobles —
Your slaves they detest you, your masters, they scorn.
The river lies on, but the sun-painted bubbles
Pass quickly, to the rapids incessantly borne.[8]

7. In 1600, Art O'Neill and Niall Garbh O'Donnell were bought over to the English cause by Sir John Dowcra, a defection that proved a major blow to Hugh O'Neill and Red Hugh O'Donnell's campaign against Elizabeth. Following the flight of Hugh O'Neill and Red Hugh O'Donnell to the Continent in 1607, the lands of the Maguires of Fermanagh and the O'Reilly's of Cavan were confiscated and 'regranted' under English titles.

8. Aubrey de Vere, 'The New Race', in *The Poetic Works of Aubrey de Vere*, Vol. V (London: Macmillan, 1897), p. 137.

SOCIALISM AND REVOLUTIONARY TRADITIONS (1900)

[In this article, an editorial from *The Workers' Republic* of 26 June 1900, Connolly criticizes the hold of tradition on nationalist thinking, arguing that a constant harkening back to the past impedes the attainment of genuine progress. However, he adds the important rider that, of all political activists, socialists in Ireland can ill afford to dispense with history.]

Perhaps among no people in Europe is the love of tradition so strong as amongst the Irish. In this country every popular movement, or, what is perhaps not quite the same, every movement aiming at popularity, harks back to the misty past for its justification, and reckons itself thrice happy indeed if amid the imperfect records of another generation it can trace a resemblance between its own organisation and the institutions, methods, and practices of our forefathers. This reverence for traditional practices, this idealising of past institutions has both its good and its bad sides. Its good side may be briefly stated to consist in the fact that it provides the multitude, who are not too prone to weigh well the consequences of their public acts, with a standard of national and public morality and achievement which all but the most depraved instinctively desire to live up to. As a man of high moral character and strong personality often succeeds in lifting all associated with him up towards his own moral level, so in Ireland the high-water mark of the past marks the zero below which the present will not willingly fall.

Thus this reverence for traditional effort and aspiration supplies to the most uneducated in Ireland that strong sense of public duty and public spirit which we find to be totally lacking in the same class in countries such as England, where ninety nine out of every hundred are totally ignorant even of the names of the men, or of the character of the movements, which won for Englishmen that political freedom of which they boast so much — and utilise so little.

But the Cult of Tradition may be, and in Ireland undoubtedly is, cultivated to an extent which often makes it not only ridiculous but positively harmful. Heedless of the fact that the world moves, and that the political conditions which dictated a specific course of action to the patriots of the past have been profoundly modified ere our days, the present generation is led to believe that it will attain to the greatest height of patriotic wisdom by striving in all things to mould its political organisations upon the exact lines and methods of previous efforts after the same ideal. Thus the enthusiastic nationalist revering the memory of Wolfe Tone strives sedulously to imitate him, forgetting alike that Tone's greatness lay in the fact that he imitated nobody, and that the line of action required at a time when the democracy were [*sic*] unenfranchised, can hardly be accepted as a rule of conduct when the suffrage is widespread, and public bodies generally under popular control.

The Home Rule trickster also knows how to play upon our Irish love of the past. We all know of one political organisation in Ireland which is named after the revolutionists of 1798, which has a weekly organ sailing under the same title as that of the revolutionists of 1867, and which in spite of all this play upon revolutionary tradition is the most bitter and treacherous foe of the revolutionary nationalists of today.[1]

We know also that all during the centennial year of 1798 the Home Rule gentry traded without scruple upon the memory of the heroes of that revolutionary year, and lost no opportunity of declaring that they themselves would have been rebels under similar conditions, ignoring the great truth — the recognition of which forms the point of difference between their attitude and that of the Socialist Republicans — that, while changed conditions do necessitate changed methods of realising an ideal, they do not necessarily involve the abandonment of that ideal, if in itself good.[2]

The revolutionary nationalist worships the ideal and adheres to the methods of the past; Home Rulers profess to worship at the same shrine, but adopt neither the ideals nor the methods of past revolutionists; and the Socialist Republicans adhere to the high ideal of national freedom sought for in the past, go beyond it to a fuller ideal which we conceive to flow

1. This refers to William O'Brien's United Irish League, a rural-based breakaway from the Home Rule party, founded in 1898, and its newspaper, the *Irish People* (1899–1908), edited by O'Brien.
2. The facility with which pillars of the nationalist community, such as the Home Rule Party, could participate in the centenary celebrations of the 1798 Rebellion was the subject of an earlier scathing editorial by Connolly, 'Wolfe Tone and his "Admirers" ', *The Workers' Republic*, 5 August 1899.

from national freedom as a natural and necessary consequence, but reject as utterly unsuited to present conditions the methods of bygone generations.

We AGITATE for the Revolution; let those who will, CONSPIRE for it; when the hour for action arrives our only rivalry need be as to which shall strike the most effective blows against the common enemy.

IV. CRITICAL NATIONALISM

THOMAS MACDONAGH

(1878–1916)

from: LITERATURE IN IRELAND, STUDIES IRISH AND ANGLO-IRISH (1916)

[Although quickly elevated into the pantheon of nationalist martyrs after his execution in 1916, Thomas MacDonagh had a very complex relationship to cultural, and militant, nationalism. Critics have interpreted MacDonagh's participation in the Rising as an attempt to satisfy a deep, messianic impulse, yet it seems to have been a last-minute affair rather than the fulfilment of a historic life mission. His one major critical work, *Literature in Ireland*, attempted to set a new agenda for Anglo-Irish literature, and was also a casualty of the Rising. The book is an amalgam of both new material and previously published articles and was assembled in great haste (there are even reports that he worked on the proofs during the Rising). As a result, it is disjointed in structure and is difficult to anthologize. Therefore, various key statements in his book are presented here, rather than a continuous argument. The passages have been chosen to illustrate MacDonagh's views on 'the Irish mode' and cultural exclusiveness; the process of translation; and the question of tradition and discontinuity. On all these questions, MacDonagh breaks with what are commonly seen as nationalist orthodoxies.]

IV

IRISH AND ENGLISH

. . . Matthew Arnold in his essay *On the Study of Celtic Literature*, largely a work of fiction, has written interestingly of the Celtic Note, using the name in a sense of his own. He has been rather apprehended than understood; and with later writers the meaning has become vaguer. This is due, at least in part, to the vagueness of the two terms, 'Celtic' and 'Note.' I propose, in my study of the metrical effect of poems like *Cashel of Munster*,[1] to use instead my term, the Irish Mode. With the rhythm goes a certain emotion, as distinctly Celtic or Irish, no doubt; but emotions alone are unsafe guides. . . .

1. Sir Samuel Ferguson's 'Cashel of Munster' was published in his *Lays of the Western Gael* (1865).

V

ANGLO-IRISH AUTHORS

. . . I have little sympathy with the criticism that marks off subtle qualities in literature as altogether racial, that refuses to admit natural exceptions in such a naturally exceptional thing as high literature, attributing only the central body to the national genius, the marginal portions to this alien strain or that. It may be quite true that John Keats owed the quality of his work to his half Cornish, half Welsh origin. I can say only that I find it difficult to prove — as difficult as to prove, for instance, that a man of quite other extraction might also have produced work of similar quality. French poetry on the whole has lacked the lyric note. One need not for that agree with a recent writer that the French poets who have the more intense lyric gift must have been of foreign extraction. Less still need one agree that a great lyric poetry may not come to France any day and from the lips of French poets.

My definite conclusions are three:

First, that an Anglo-Irish literature, worthy of a special designation, could come only when English had become the language of the Irish people, mainly of Gaelic stock;[2] and when the literature was from, by, of, to and for the Irish people.

Second, that the ways of life and the ways of thought of the Irish people — the manners, customs, traditions and outlook, religious, social, moral, — have important differences from the ways of life and of thought which have found expression in other English literature.

Third, that the English language in Ireland has an individuality of its own, and the rhythm of Irish speech a distinct character.

If, with some of the best modern critics, we divide literature into poetry and science, the one to be attributed to the intuitive faculties and the other to the intellectual, it may seem that my conclusions have reference only to the science, the logical and the intellectual. That is not quite so: but this work is itself a work of science in that sense; it is a study, an analysis, aiming at the logical, at a clear intellectual grasp of its subject; dealing with literature and language, literature and nationality, and the like, rather than with the wind that bloweth where it listeth or with the utterances, in terms of sense and wit, of mystic things.

It will be seen also that these conclusions bar out from my study the works of some Irish-born writers of the first importance, of Swift, of Goldsmith, of Sheridan — in short, of all but the more characteristically Irish authors of the nineteenth and twentieth centuries.

What then will the historian of Anglo-Irish literature have to deal with? Who are the characteristically Irish writers that come within the scope of his study? — What poets, what novelists, what dramatists, what essayists, what historians, what orators?

The poets of the Irish Mode are evidently his quarry. Moore in the beginning is of them, Mangan, Ferguson. Callanan has a few good poems; Edward Walsh a few.[3] The best of the later poets must be reckoned under this head, down to George Sigerson, Douglas Hyde, and W. B. Yeats, the elder poets of the present day.

Equally within his scope are the explicitly patriotic poets, many of whom have no other subjects than national ones, and yet who have not in our ears, for all their Gaelic words, the Irish accent of Ferguson. Such are Davis and the poets of the *Nation*. Such on the whole are, in our days, Gerald Griffin and William Allingham. Such in much of their work are Emily Lawless and Alice Milligan.[4] There are a few poets, like Aubrey de Vere, whose main work cannot be referred either to the Irish Mode or to living Irish patriotism, yet who are definitely Anglo-Irish. There are a few, like Lionel Johnson and Nora Chesson[5] who were born and who lived their whole lives out of Ireland, and yet are truly Irish. Others, whose relations with Ireland and Irish life were slight, have been included in Anglo-Irish anthologies and the like — Edgar Allen Poe, Emily Brontë, Arthur O'Shaughnessy, Edward Fitzgerald.[6] The connection of some of these with the subject is, however, too slender a link to depend on. . . .

The Anglo-Irish prose authors offer little difficulty; although their prose, except when it is a record of peasant speech, has nowhere the distinct characteristics of Anglo-Irish verse. The novelists are Maria Edgeworth, Charles Mathurin [*sic*], William Carleton, Charles Lever, Samuel Lover, Gerald Griffin, J. Sheridan Lefanu, the Banims and some more recent writers; the orators, Grattan, Flood, Curran, Robert Emmet (by virtue of his one speech), Daniel O'Connell, Richard Lalor Sheil, Butt and a few others; the historians of literary stature, Mitchel and Lecky. The few Irish dramatists of the nineteenth century, from Macklin to the foundation of the Irish Literary Theatre, have little importance in

2. That MacDonagh's use of 'Gaelic stock' was devoid of any racial connotations is clear from his early statement 'some of us who live in Ireland, of Gaelic stock, even of Gaelic speech, are for all that more Greek than Gael. It is difficult to fix the zone.' (*Literature in Ireland*, p. 29).
3. J. J. Callanan (1795–1829), Cork romantic poet, influenced by Byron. Edward Walsh (1805–50), poet, translator and folklorist with strong nationalist sympathies.
4. Gerald Griffin (1803–40), the first important native catholic novelist, wrote *The Collegians* (1829). William Allingham (1824–89), an Irish poet who spent much of his life in England, wrote little of direct nationalist interest. The Hon. Emily Lawless (1845–1913) was a novelist and historical writer who addressed national themes in her work, but did not subscribe to nationalist politics. Alice Milligan (1866–1953) edited the influential periodical *Shan Van Vocht* (i.e. Poor Old Woman, an allegorical name for Ireland) and was a prolific poet.
5. Lionel Johnson (1867–1902), born and educated in England, was a convert to catholicism, and became an influential figure in the Revival in the 1890s. Nora Hopper Chesson (1871–1906), born in Exeter, was a poet championed by Yeats in the 1890s for her 'Celtic' qualities.
6. Arthur O'Shaughnessy (1844–81), a mid-Victorian poet of dreamy verse. Edward Fitzgerald (1809–83), the celebrated translator of *The Rubaiyat of Omar Khayyam* (1859).

literature. The political essayists are Davis, Fintan Lalor and their fellows.

The names of these authors answer my question of six terms above. There is one other group of authors whose work is, in one sense of the world, more Anglo-Irish than that of any of the writers I have mentioned here, with the exception perhaps of such men as Mangan and Ferguson. I refer to the great translators, those pioneers of Irish studies who rendered the Old Irish poems and sagas into an English which gained from the originals a distinct power and beauty. The importance of the work of Eugene O'Curry, John O'Donovan, Whitley Stokes, Standish Hayes O'Grady,[7] can scarcely be overestimated. With these scholars stands George Petrie. Apart from them, not a scholar like them, yet looking in the same direction, stands the strange imaginative Standish James O'Grady. The latest of the great scholar translators, Kuno Meyer,[8] is a German, who, by his own work and that of his disciples, has added wealth of matter and grace of manner to the new literature.

7. John O'Donovan (1809–61), the great nineteenth-century antiquary and scholar. His major work was a critical translation of the *Annals of the Four Masters* (1848–57). He worked on the Ordnance Survey Expedition (1834) with Eugene O'Curry (1796–1862), a self-educated scholar and antiquarian who became professor of Irish history and archaeology at the new Catholic University in Dublin in 1855. Standish Hayes O'Grady (1832–1915), a scholar and antiquary, came under the tutelage of O'Donovan and O'Curry. His principal work was *Silva Gadelica* (1892), a critical edition and translation of ancient Irish manuscripts.

8. Kuno Meyer (1858–1919), German scholar and translator, who made a major contribution to modern Gaelic scholarship.

VII

ON TRANSLATION

. . . One word more remains to say — of the importance, even the necessity, of translation in this literature of ours. Some of our poems from the Irish are re-creations. This is due immediately to the difference of metaphor in the two languages, and fundamentally to that greater difference of tradition, which is at once the cause and the sum and the effect of all our differences here.A phrase like 'the star of knowledge' in Douglas Hyde's translation *Ringleted Youth of My Love* has a value that can rarely be given to such metaphors in English poetry.

I thought, O my love! you were so
  As the moon is, or sun on a fountain,
And I thought after that you were snow,
  The cold snow on the top of the mountain:
And I thought after that you were more
  Like God's lamp shining to find me,
Or the bright star of knowledge before
  And the star of knowledge behind me.

The phrase thus literally rendered is unexpected and exciting in a strange language of different metaphors and different logic. The translations are in a way finer than the originals. The 'star of knowledge' has been used too often in Gaelic poems to have that new magic now. And other lines in the poem,

'Like a bush in a gap in the wall
  I am now left lonely without thee,'

which are commonplace in Irish, have here a winning grace.

The literature of a race goes at first to the pails of those who have previously drawn from the well of life of its parent race. Chaucer is full of translations from the work of his own people, the Normans, and from writers among other peoples from whom his people derived culture. Elizabethan literature is full of translations and adaptations from older literatures in consonance with the new national life of England, not from the too Eastern or the too Western literatures. Shakespeare 'stole' all his plots and translated many of his sonnets and songs. Later poets derive from Chaucer, from Shakespeare and his contemporaries, from Milton. With the exception of the returned refugees to the court of Louis Quatorze, they no longer to any great extent find their originals abroad. Our characteristic ways of thought and ways of life in Ireland have been expressed in Irish: other ways, which we have in common with other peoples, have been expressed in other languages. Mangan and Padraic Colum go to Arabic as well as to Irish for their originals . . . .

At present a large amount of translation is natural. Later, when we have expressed again in English all the emotions and experiences expressed already in Irish, this literature will go forward, free from translation. Through the English language has come a freshening breath from without: with the Gaelic Renaissance has come a new stirring of national consciousness: these two have been the great influences in all new literatures. At that I can leave it, at that freshening and that stirring of it. It is well for us that our workers are poets and our poets workers.

'The more a man gives his life to poetry,' said Francis Thompson,[9] 'the less poetry he writes.' And it is well too that here still that cause which is identified, without underthought of commerce, with the cause of God and Right and Freedom, the cause which has been the great theme of our poetry, may any day call the poets to give their lives in the old service.

9. Francis Thompson (1859–1907), poet and mystic. His spiritual poetry enjoyed considerable vogue in literary circles in Dublin at the turn of the century.

VIII

IRISH LITERATURE

. . . The Gaelic Renaissance is only beginning. It can never be of just the same importance and influence as the Classic. It goes back to a literature of a different kind from the Greek and Latin, a literature almost entirely anonymous, a literature without epic or dramatic verse, a literature, as far as poetry is concerned, of fragments — little personal poems, nature poems, religious poems, short dramatic monologues and dramatic lyrics interspersed in prose tales. And yet it has been claimed for this remnant of literature, and claimed by the best authority in the matter, Doctor Kuno Meyer, that as 'the earliest voice from the dawn of West European civilization, it is the most primitive and original among the literatures of Western Europe.' Most original, and of not least intrinsic worth. It is a fragment. It must not be judged as if it were a fragment of a literature of the Hellenic kind. . . .

The Gaelic Renaissance means to us not only the revival of interest in this old Irish literature, the revival of interest in the civilization, the culture and the history of ancient Ireland, the enthusiasm, the adventure, the pride, the satisfaction, the emotion that are quickened by the discovery of the old monuments, but, added to these, the study of modern Irish as a language capable of literature, the interest in the fragments and traditions that have survived, the reconstruction of our new state on some of the old foundations, and so, patriotism. A recent writer has lamented that instead of the Classic there did not take place in the fourteenth century a Gaelic Renaissance. Of course, the lament and all discussion of it is futile. I listen dreamily to it. To the speakers of the Romance languages, to the readers of Romance literatures, the Classic Renaissance was such as to a strange people, who had seen only the statues of men of our race, would be the sight of the living models. The remarkable thing about the coming of the Classic Renaissance is not its coming in the fourteenth century, but its not coming earlier. The coming was inevitable. It was long prepared for. And when we use the same word, Renaissance, for the Gaelic revival, springing from the rediscovery of the ancient language and literature, and branching now into a double literature in two languages, we do not claim that it is quite the counterpart of the Classic. The old literature that was to be discovered, the ancient Irish art, were not in such consonance even with what of literature and art we still held, as were Classic literature and art with those of mediæval Europe, with the culture that still held allegiance to Rome and had memories of ancient Greece. Still at the heart of that lament for a Gaelic Renaissance five hundred years ago is this truth, that if history had been different the ancient culture and the ancient literature of our people might have had a more powerful influence on the culture and literature of Europe. The Celtic peoples had kindred memories with ours though they had changed their speech. Of Gaelic influence in literature, in art, in music, there have always been the sure marks and the sure effects, as has been pointed out by Dr. Sigerson[10] and others, but only during the last century has it come home and thriven.

This is not the place to attempt a history of the Revival. I propose here rapidly to survey portions of the literature of ancient Ireland and to come thence to the literature and prospects of today. The poems of Old Irish are from eight to fourteen centuries old. There has been in the intervening period a steady enough stream of literature in Middle and Modern Irish; but my ignorance of all but a small amount of this and my sympathy with the way of the old time send me back to the beginning and then draw me home to the new age opening now.

The themes of Early Irish Literature are many of them the themes of modern romantic literature — in lyric poetry, nature and humanity: — nature: the joy of natural things; the joy of the earth's beauty, the woods and the birds in the woods; the delight of

10. See George Sigerson, *Bards of the Gael and Gall* (1897). MacDonagh dedicated his book to Sigerson.

summer, season surpassing, grateful to dwellers in a northern land; the terror of the white winter when not a bell is heard and no crane talks, when shapes are all gone; the joy of the sea, the plain of Ler, with its witching song, the delightful home of ships, the image of Hell with its dread tempest: — humanity: men and women, love and destiny: humanity at odds with life: a king and a hermit; a girl who died for love; a warrior who kept his tryst after death; Deirdre, the predestined of sorrow, winning some joy from life before her fate falls; an old woman who has seen the passing away of her famous beauty, who sees the ebb tide carrying away her years, who sees the flood-wave foaming in for others. Later, after the English are settled in the land, not humanity but the nation, Kathleen ni Houlihan, is our heroic theme. The manifestations of nationality are symbolised by man and nature. . . . And so all Irish Literature is set down as vague, mysterious, obscure. Nothing could be more clear, more direct, more gem-like, hard and delicate and bright, than the earlier lyric poetry, nothing more surely true to nature, full of natural piety, nothing of another kind greater in suggestion, however brief in form. Not till the advent of Wordsworth comes there anything like this intimacy with nature into other modern literature. Not till we listen to the voice of Shelley do we hear in other lyric poetry such prophecy of song as has come down through folk poetry in Irish, a lyric poetry which, as Mr. John Eglinton said some years ago, 'has far more in common with the later developments of English poetry — with poems, for example, like Shelley's *When the Lamp is Shattered* or George Meredith's *Love in a Valley* — than anything produced by the wits of the London coffee houses.'[11]

The themes of the old sagas have been used by many in our day as the story of the Trojan war has been used by many nations that read Greek. Deirdre is to us

> the morning star of loveliness,
> Unhappy Helen of a western land.*

They have not been used as successfully as the Greek models. They are not the inheritance of this alien civilization. They require different standards. To quote Mr. John Eglinton again: 'These subjects, much as we may admire them and regret that we have nothing equivalent to them in the modern world, obstinately refuse to be taken up out of their old environment, and be transplanted into the world of modern sympathies. The proper mode of treating them is a secret lost with the subjects themselves.' It is possible, of course that, while I write, these *dicta* are being disproved. It would be vain, even if unluckily we wished it or could do it, to set bounds to literary genius, which is always breaking new soil, or rather always coming in a new manifestation. It is at its best and highest a new epiphany. Some in our day or after our day may make a great new literature in the tradition of this old world of Early Irish Literature. But I rather expect that the literature of tomorrow will be in terms of the life of tomorrow, and that the old world is too different, too far apart, too much wronged now, I fear, by misrepresentation, by false praise that would make it good of another kind than of its way of goodness, by false blame that would call its culture barbarism, its strength brutality or impropriety, its mysticism magic, its austere sincerity in literature a defect of power and richness, its power and richness, when it has such, exaggeration. We may admit that we cannot now feel those old emotions at first heart, so to put it. We have not reverence for the same things. We cannot pray to the old gods. We could not blaspheme the old gods. We are of a different day; a different light shines upon us. History is between us and our heroes. We cannot rid our memories of the glories and the calamities of our story, of the mighty things, of the futile things. Our thought is woven of the stuff of memory and elder thought and of a knowledge that has gained on this side and lost on that like an island in the sea. Our dreams are children dreams and parent dreams. A part of the old world lives in us; to a large part we are alien not in speech only but in feeling, in sense, in instinct, in vision. We are true to the best of the old literature when we are true to that part of it which we inherit now in the twentieth century, when we discover in ourselves something of its good tradition, something that has remained true by the changing standards and measures.

I have quoted the phrase 'the earliest voice from the dawn of West European civilization'; but I should not like to be taken as meaning that this old

* *The Three Sorrows of Story-Telling: Deirdre*, by Douglas Hyde.

11. John Eglinton, 'The Best Irish Poem' in *Bards and Saints* (Dublin: Maunsel & Co., 1906), p. 48.

literature is a beginning in itself, a first stammering, a simple babbling of simple things on the lips of a people just articulate. It is probably nothing of the kind. These pieces are but stray survivors of stray written records of poems that strayed down for a long time by oral tradition. . . .

Do I take from its honour in holding that we have not in Old, Middle and Modern Irish a complete, continued literature; that, excuse it as you may by the many good reasons of history, it is a literature thwarted and frustrated in many forms, and in the last two centuries or more a literature in decadence? Rather I think that I hold a higher hope in looking for a new literature from now. If the works of some of our contemporaries be not the first stammerings of a new literature that will have to go to school again, then they are the final senile babblings of one moribund.

To the eyes of criticism, Irish literature, after having suffered unparalleled persecution under the long terror of English rule, still suffers wrong even from its Irish admirers. It has in the first place been used as quarry by modern authors in English. The result, as I have pointed out, has not been fortunate. Deirdre,[12] the subject of many plays, is an 'unhappy Helen' indeed. . . .

The poets have used the frame of Irish story as a frame whereon to weave the palpable stuff of their vision and their interpretation of the heroic in life. Their vision is a mistranslation; not for the first time has the world owed a beautiful thing to a mistranslation of genius. The original is a work of genius in another way of beauty. And yet for all that I have said here, for all their error of half-heard words, the poets may be nearer to the rhythm of the ancient song than those of us who spell the words in full. Some of the ancient tales, some passages in the epics, are altogether incredible and impossible to our modern ways of thought and life here. May they not have other than their apparent meanings? They have the impossibility of the fairy tale. Perhaps they have the enduring truth of the fairy tale, of the parable, of the fable, which is truer than a history that owes so much to accident and whim and personality. . . .

12. Deirdre, one of the celebrated heroines of Irish mythology, was the subject of plays by W. B. Yeats and J. M. Synge.

We are the children of a race that, through need or choice, turned from Irish to English. We have now so well mastered this language of our adoption that we use it with a freshness and power that the English of these days rarely have. But now also we have begun to turn back to the old language, not old to us. The future poets of the country will probably be the sons and daughters of a generation that learned Irish as a strange tongue; the words and phrases of Irish will have a new wonder for them; the figures of speech will have all their first poetry. Carlyle says of Imagination: 'Metaphors are her stuff; examine language — what, if you except some primitive elements, what is it but metaphors, recognised as such or no longer recognised, still fluid and florid, or now solid-grown and colourless?'[13] The metaphors of Irish will not be colourless to the fresh eyes of the next generation, though the language be their native idiom. Perhaps the temporary abandonment of Irish has not been an unmitigated disaster, now that its revival is assured. A language that transmits its literature mainly by oral tradition cannot, if spoken only by thousands, bequeath as much to posterity as if spoken by millions. The loss of idiom and of literature is a disaster. But, on the other hand, the abandonment has broken a tradition of pedantry and barren conventions; and sincerity gains thereby. The *aisling*[14] is now at last dead; the simple beautiful folk-songs in which recent Irish literature is richer perhaps than any other, are more likely to serve as models than the vain word-weaving of the bards. The writers of the *dán díreach*[15] became at last, to use a mistranslated phrase, mere 'schoolmen of condensed speech,' but their verse at worst had the high virtue of restraint. Their successors became fluent, eloquent craftsmen of skilful word-music. The poets of the next age will learn from the faults of both schools; they will make restraint a canon of their art, not a pedantry; they will know that the too facile use of the adjective is a vice, and verse-music a snare. Let us postulate continuity, but continuity in the true way.

13. Thomas Carlyle, *Sartor Resartus* (1836), Book I, Chapter IX.
14. A visionary poem about Ireland, based usually on a dream.
15. i.e. 'straight verse', a highly artificial form of bardic poetry measured by syllables, not accents.

JOHN EGLINTON

from: BARDS AND SAINTS (1906)

[In this essay, 'The De-Davisisation of Irish Literature', Eglinton argues that national literature can become great only when it addresses itself to universal rather than local themes. It was precisely this approach that Daniel Corkery attacked in his *Synge and Anglo-Irish Literature*. Eglinton ends on a discordant note, arguing that literature should seek to prise open the internal divisions and conflicts in a country, rather than attempt to resolve them. More than anything, this flew in the face of the nationalist emphasis on social and ideological cohesion.]

THE DE-DAVISISATION OF IRISH LITERATURE

It has been said that during the Middle Ages great men as a rule distinguished themselves in another country than that of their birth. If this may be still said of eminent men born in Ireland, it is easy enough to understand why it should be so, in respect to men of action and administrative faculty; but that literary men and men of thought are still impelled to leave this country in order to 'find themselves' may be taken in association with a statement which is sometimes made, that Ireland has not as yet emerged properly out of the Middle Ages. To speak candidly, if cosmopolitanism be a fault, it has not always been the fault of these gifted sons of Ireland, from the time of Scotus Erigena,[1] that they have become cosmopolitan, since they, as a rule, have remembered that they were Irishmen, while the mother-country has never had the heart to take much pride in pure intellectual achievement. The only distinctive national literary tradition, within its own coasts, acknowledged by Ireland, is mainly the creation of Thomas Davis, and had its point of departure in the anger felt by that excellent patriot when, as a young lawyer, he was brought into contact with the crass worldliness and provincialism of the official and professional classes of Dublin, to which he himself belonged. The nationalism which he was driven to adopt was not exactly, perhaps, the ideal nationalism of his 'Address to the Historical Society,' with which he began his career, but suffered a little from compromise, as perhaps all ideal principles must do when practically applied. There are worldly people in every nation: a successful New York Irishman, for instance, is possibly as worldly a type as could be found; but in the nature of the case, the worldly people in Ireland were those descendants of the 'English Colony,' who still monopolised the prosperity of the country. To the inert weight of provincialism and indifference to the ideal of these people, Davis gave the somewhat fallacious name of Anglicism, or Anglicisation, and turned with passion to the great peasant population of Celtic Ireland, with its ancient language and history, its affiliation to the soil and geography of the country, its long-suffering under centuries of persecution, its freedom, at all events, from what he describes as 'that damned thing . . . call it Yankeeism or Englishism, which measures prosperity by exchangeable value, measures duty by gain, and limits desire to clothes, food and respectability.'[2] It was, no doubt, a worldly time in England especially, the time of Bentham's influence and of the successes of Macaulay:[3] and already at that time in England there had arisen in the person of a Scottish peasant, Thomas Carlyle,[4] a prophet against worldliness, whose influence was already rousing the talent of the strongest writer whom the national cause of Ireland has yet had on its side, John Mitchel. It was Davis, however, who gave a sort of religious or idealistic status to modern Irish patriotism which it has retained; for since Davis the true religion of the Irish Nationalist has been patriotism; and it remains to be decided whether this confusion of two essentially different things,

1. Johannes Scottus (Ériugena) (*c.*810–77), an Irish philosopher who taught at the court of Charles the Bald, was one of the key exponents of mystical thought in the Middle Ages.

2. From Davis's letter to Daniel Owen Madden, quoted in Charles Gavan Duffy, *Young Ireland: A Fragment of Irish History*, Vol. 1 (London: T. Fisher Unwin, 1896), p. 138.

3. Jeremy Bentham (1748–1832), philosopher and legal theorist, was a founder of the Utilitarian movement. Thomas Babington Macaulay (1800–59), politician and historian, was one of the most prominent Whig intellectuals of his day. Davis's letter to Madden (see note 2 above) was a concerted attack on Whig and Utilitarian principles.

4. Thomas Carlyle (1795–1881), Scottish critic and historian, was one of the most prominent critics of Utilitarianism, and exerted a considerable influence on the Young Ireland movement.

idealism and patriotism, has bestowed upon Irish national literature the germs of new developments or is not rather that which must be got rid of before even the meaning of the term 'national literature' is understood.

The genius of Davis himself (who, it must be remembered, died at the age of thirty-one, after a few years of activity, and so was prevented from becoming, what perhaps he might have become to a full extent, a kind of Irish Lessing)[5] succeeded in giving Ireland a brilliant journal, but not exactly literature. The one book of the '48 Movement — written by a kind of accident, and still (though in an exceptional way) *out* of Ireland — was the work of a man, in some respects, of a less admirable character than Davis, yet his superior in that abnormal power of spiritualised egoism which makes the writing-man. It was the lion-hearted, if somewhat wrong-headed Mitchel, who began to use a hearty directness of statement in regard to all matters which affected or interested him, which had hardly been heard in Ireland since the days of Dean Swift. In his Journal and Correspondence (or those fragments of it which are given in his Life by Dillon) as compared with the writings of Davis, we can see the difference between literature and rhetoric, which is mainly that, while rhetoric has in mind some particular audience, literature is the faithful and unbiassed rendering of the individual impression. The two elements of rhetoric and literature meet in that kind of writing, designed to catch the attention of the average man in his average hours, to which, not very happily, we give the name 'journalism'; and in journalism Davis (who indeed was rather an ideal editor than what Mr. T. W. Rolleston has called him, 'the ideal Irishman') succeeded so well that he and his colleagues imposed the tradition of their newspaper on Irish national literature. What the Irish nationalist, as instructed by Davis, means by 'national literature,' is not the interpretation of the soul of a people, still less the emancipation of the national mind by means of individual utterance, but — no doubt a very good thing — the expression of such sentiments as help to exalt an Irishman's notion of the excellence and importance of the race to which he belongs. Our friends, the Gaelic Leaguers, who hold that the English language at the best is an unsuitable vehicle of thought for Irishmen, and who have lately shown signs of ingratitude to the memory of Davis, are ready, no doubt, to accept this implied qualification of his praise, and to use it as an argument on their side; but in the *Jail Journal*[6] of Mitchel, written far away from an audience, and in order to satisfy an overmastering need of self-expression, we do at last get literature, a book so successful in giving expression to the instincts and antipathies of Irish nationality, that, in face of it, any further talk of the inefficiency of the English language in Ireland is somewhat audacious. The literary interest of this book was at once recognised in Paris by M. Emile Montégut, who devoted to it a lengthy article in the *Revue des Deux Mondes* (Tome 10, 1855); an article which every Irishman, who wishes to 'see himself as others see him,' should read. Mitchel afterwards wrote of himself as a man who 'but once in his life [1847–8] was possessed by a great cause, whose whole life and energy converged themselves once to one focus, and were then dissipated into the general atmosphere'; but it is quite certain that so far as concerns his literary activity — for we are not here concerned with the political principles which brought him into unpleasant relations with two Governments, and very nearly with a third, and which allowed him to become the fierce champion of slavery — no other book of his has half the literary value of the *Jail Journal*, which, for many young Irish patriots, has made him the Defoe of the hulks.[7]

There is a class of enthusiasts who pin their faith to an order of things which might have been, if something else had not happened. Thus, a goodly number hold that Christianity was an unpardonable infraction of the pagan ideal. To others, the Renaissance appears to have been the great mistake. A larger number, of course, regret the movements represented by Luther and Rousseau. English music, it is claimed, was certain of a fine career of national development, if the burly Handel had not thrown it out of its bearings. And so on. There is more to be said for the language movement, no doubt, than that it is merely the championship of

5. Gottfried Ephraim Lessing (1729–81), the great German critic and dramatist, who helped to free German letters from an overpowering French influence.

6. Mitchel's classic contribution to prison literature was published in 1854.

7. The lethal irony of Daniel Defoe's pamphlet *The Shortest Way with the Dissenters* (1702) led to his imprisonment in 1703. He immortalized his experience of imprisonment and the pillory in *Hymn to the Pillory* (1703).

one of these lost causes; one must indeed be blind not to see the poetry of this proposal to raise up around our coasts, not Bishop Berkeley's impracticable wall of brass,[8] but a still more irrefragable[9] if impalpable safeguard of nationality in a language bristling with difficulties to a foreigner, but within full of the kindly converse of hearts unsealed at last. It must be confessed, however, that when Anglo-Irish literature has brought us at least so far as the literary integrity and hearty directness of John Mitchel, it seems a pity if the 'Language Movement' is to transport literature in this country back again to that point where the good Davis left it, to that region, which has become now somewhat insipid, in which all private differences are sunk, and in which the Irishman has to speak in his national rather than in his human capacity. For the questions which divide household and nation against themselves, religious, political, fundamental questions, these are the questions in respect to which the literary man must have the license of a prophet; it is these which he looks on as his peculiar region; it is these upon which literature, more than any other agency, can hope to shed some light. Literature must be free as the elements; if that is to be cosmopolitan it must be cosmopolitan. Literature, even when it is really national, is not a matter about which any nation, fortunately for its peace of mind, gives itself great concern. It proceeds quietly in the pursuit of truth and wisdom, and occasionally attracts attention to itself as an elemental force by an electric discharge of thought: whereupon follows, as a rule, one of those regrettable movements already mentioned, and the relegation of the reigning system of thought to the status of a lost cause. If the Irish nation is a literary nation it is a very wonderful nation. But no! the 'cold chain of silence'[10] will never be lifted from the soul of Ireland save by men using the homely directness of utterance, and, without much doubt, the speech of John Mitchel; and one would like to live to see the day of what might be termed, without any disrespect to Davis, the de-Davisisation of Irish national literature, that is to say, the getting rid of the notion that in Ireland, a writer is to think, first and foremost, of interpreting the nationality of his country, and not simply of the burden which he has to deliver. The expression of nationality, literature cannot fail to be; and the richer, more varied and unexpected that expression the better.

8. This refers to Bishop Berkeley's famous hypothetical question in *The Querist*, no.134 (1735–37), as to whether Ireland could surround itself with a wall of brass and do without foreign commerce.
9. i.e. inviolable.
10. From Thomas Moore's poem 'Dear Harp of my Country': 'Dear Harp of my Country! in darkness I found thee,/The cold chain of silence had hung oe'r thee long. . . .' In a footnote to his poem, Moore explains that among the ancient Irish a 'chain of silence' was shook by the bards to bring about a cessation of hostilities by warriors. Moore acknowledges that he borrowed the figure from 'a rebellious, but beautiful song' by the United Irishman, William Drennan: 'When Erin first rose'. See Volume I, p. 1,064 for Moore's poem and p. 327 of Volume III for the Drennan poem.

FREDERICK RYAN

(1874–1913)

from: DANA (1904)

[In this and the succeeding article, both published in *Dana* in late 1904, Frederick Ryan attacks the Gaelic League idea that the restoration of the Irish language is sufficient to guarantee national freedom. He stresses the centrality of *material* factors in any genuine independence movement, but is careful not to dismiss the desirability of cultural freedom. Cultural struggle helps to promote the feeling of indifference to imperial culture, which is a true expression of national self-confidence, rather than the antagonism to all things foreign, which is really an admission of cultural inferiority.]

IS THE GAELIC LEAGUE A PROGRESSIVE FORCE?

The Gaelic League has assuredly now reached a point when the task of examining and estimating its total effect on the national life ought to be undertaken in a fair and unprejudiced spirit. It is not, however, suggested for a moment that the following pages contain more than hints for such an undertaking; but these hints are put forward for what they may be worth.

That the Gaelic League is popular goes without saying. It may or may not be popular with the governing classes — though from them it has met with a benevolent neutrality, if not an encouragement, which no previous national movement ever received — but it is certainly popular with the people, the Church, and the press. In fact, the Gaelic League has got to the stage when its 'popularity' might well be embarrassing to its best friends. There is an old proverb which warns us to beware when all men praise us, and at times the unanimous chorus of approval of the Gaelic League from all quarters might well rouse suspicion. Its work is applauded by Cardinal Logue,[1] Mr. W B. Yeats, Sir Horace Plunkett[2] and *The United Irishman* newspaper, Lord Monteagle[3] and the *Freeman's Journal*, Mr John Redmond[4] and the *Leader*.[5] And assuredly if the League is tending to realise the ultimate objects of some of these men and newspapers, it cannot be tending to realise the objects of others of them.

Now, obviously, the League propaganda centres in the language, the revival of the ancient tongue of Ireland. Other allied movements, and of these I shall speak presently, are collateral and subsidiary. But the revival of the language is the pivot on which the Gaelic League turns. On what scientific grounds, then, is the revival of Irish urged? It is pressed on the ground that it was once the national language of Ireland, and that in adopting it again Ireland will be differentiating herself from all other nations and proving her own individuality. Moreover it is contended that English literature and habits of thought are debased and debasing, whilst the Irish language and literature is superior and elevating.

These arguments have always appeared to me rather faulty. In the first place individuality in man or nation is not a thing to be directly sought; it is a by-product of the whole nature. When a man has to deliberately emphasise his individuality by artificially doing something out of the common, real individuality is at a minimum. What really gives a noble distinction to a man or nation is not the language they speak or the kind of dress they wear; it is their culture, their science, their art. When we meet a man whose conversation and bearing exhibit independence of character and freshness of outlook we say we have met a man of 'individuality.' But 'individuality' is probably the last thing of which such a one is consciously thinking. And I confess when I see the young men and women rushing to acquire the rudiments of Irish (and it seldom gets beyond that) in order to show they are not as other nations, the phenomenon seems to me to have something of pathos in it. Let me, however, not be misunderstood. The desire for political independence is admirable; that counts for real manhood. Only a nation of slaves would contentedly resign themselves to be governed by another nation. But the mere desire to speak another language does not of necessity at all correlate with the active desire for political freedom. On the contrary the Gaelic League leaders do not seem to be at all such keen lovers of liberty as plenty of the mere English-speaking Irishmen before them. To make Irish, or even the desire to acquire it, the test of Nationalism would shut out some of the best men who have served the cause of Irish liberty in the past. Parnell, for instance, assuredly wrought for Ireland at least as well, according to his lights, as any man who ever lived; but Parnell did not know Irish or endeavour to learn it. In fact it has often seemed to me that the language-movement has acted as a soothing rather than a stimulating influence on the political movement. If the Irish people could be lulled to rest with a new toy in the shape of a new tongue, their English governors need not grieve. And it is to a realisation of this fact that I attribute, in some degree, the participation in Gaelic League work of men who would not connect themselves with any other national work whatever. One of the historic methods

1. Michael Logue (1839–1924), archbishop of Armagh and primate of All-Ireland 1887–1924. A conservative in social policies, he was an ardent supporter of the Gaelic League, but a strong critic of Sinn Féin during the War of Independence.
2. Sir Horace Plunkett (1854–1932), unionist MP and founder of the co-operative movement in Irish agriculture.
3. Lord Monteagle of Brandon (1849–1926), a 'progressive' Anglo-Irish landlord who supported Horace Plunkett's co-operative movement.
4. John Redmond, leader of the Home Rule party from 1900 until his death in 1918.
5. *The United Irishman* was founded by Arthur Griffith in 1899, and was the forerunner of the *Sinn Féin* weekly, which Griffith launched in 1906; *The Freeman's Journal* was founded in 1763, and identified with the constitutional Nationalist Party; *The Leader* was established by D. P. Moran in 1900 as the organ of the 'Irish Ireland' movement.

of political reactionaries is to turn any really progressive movement into harmless channels; a foreign war is a favourite device for accomplishing such an end; it provides a distraction and produces a crop of military problems in place of the political ones which previously occupied the stage. May not a language movement, then, unconsciously serve a similar end? And if the people are content to let the substance of liberty go for the gew-gaw of a new grammar, so much the better — for the reactionaries. In short, I want to know how men are necessarily to be made better Nationalists, by which term I mean active lovers of Irish liberty, by knowing Irish, or how the fact of being English-speaking in any way hinders them in that respect. Swift, Wolfe Tone, Moore, Davis, Duffy, Mangan, Fintan Lalor, Mitchel, D'Arcy McGee,[6] John O'Leary, Speranza,[7] Carleton, Kickham, Banim[8] the Sullivans,[9] John Boyle O'Reilly,[10] Standish O'Grady, and Yeats — all these, and I have named, at random, poets, politicians, economists, historians, and men of letters, all these wrote in English. And surely to argue that the language which was good enough for them to sing their love of Ireland in, and preach to Ireland in, is not good enough for us, savours somewhat of priggishness. In fact one might challenge any Gaelic Leaguer to produce from *Irish* literature a list of inspirers at all comparable to that I have given of writers in English. It is not surely the language a man writes in that matters, it is the mind that moves him. And when I see the young scholars of the League substituting the 'Love Songs of Connacht' for 'The Last Conquest of Ireland (Perhaps),'[11] and that is what is tending to take place, I ask myself, is this a step forward or backward? Because there is undoubtedly a good deal of extravagance, to use a mild word, in the claim that mediæval Irish literature can supply the place for a modern mind of modern literature. And in saying this I do not in the least disparage the beauty of the old literature in its place and as a light on the age that produced it. But as each age has to live in itself and face its own problems, so we have to live by present lights and not by those of, say, Brian,[12] who himself had to do the same.

The truth is, however, that most of the leaders of the Gaelic League appear to desire a return to mediævalism, in thought, in literature, in pastimes, in music, and even in dress. And the fact that this desire is impossible of realisation does not affect those who proclaim it, and does not lessen its practical injuriousness. . . .

Let me, however, not be thought to be making a partisan case. All public movements and especially such subtle movements as that under discussion have mixed and diverse results, and their total effect cannot be expressed in any single formula. Thus there is to be set on the other side of the account the fact that the League has brought a spirit of study into the country, has evoked a great amount of self-sacrificing work that in itself compels admiration, whatever its ultimate result, and in addition has stimulated a feeling of indifference for England that is a needed variation on the traditional Irish attitude towards England of appeal, apology and abuse. When the prowess and glory of England are sung to us in every key, it is well occasionally to frankly admit that we have nothing in our own history to exactly compare with the England of Clive, of the Chinese Opium War, of the African Concentration Camps and the Peaceful Mission to Tibet.[13] But such moments of reminiscence should be judiciously restricted. A nation is not morally raised by dwelling on its own past glories or its neighbours' present sins; it is raised by increasing its ability to deal with its present problems, political, economic, and social,

6. Thomas D'Arcy McGee (1825–68), journalist and historian. Active in the Young Ireland movement, his subsequent denunciation of the physical force policies of the Fenians led to his assassination in Canada.
7. Speranza was the pen name of Lady Wilde (1826–96), Oscar Wilde's mother. She contributed poetry to *The Nation* and published several works on folklore.
8. John Banim (1798–1842) and Michael Banim (1796–1874), Kilkenny-born novelists who flourished in the 1820s. Their major work, *The Boyne Water* (1826), earned them the epithet 'the Irish Walter Scott'.
9. A. M. Sullivan (1830–84), journalist and historian, joined *The Nation* in 1855 but was opposed to Fenianism. His *Story of Ireland* (1870) was the bible of popular nationalism. T. D. Sullivan (1827–1914), brother to A. M., was a journalist and poet. His most famous poem, 'God Save Ireland', written to commemorate the Manchester Martyrs in 1867, became one of the anthems of catholic nationalism.
10. John Boyle O'Reilly (1844–90), journalist and poet, became one of the most prominent Fenian organizers in the United States after he escaped from transportation to Australia in 1868.
11. Douglas Hyde's collection of translations, *Love Songs of Connacht*, was published in 1893. John Mitchel's *The Last Conquest of Ireland (Perhaps)* was published in 1861. Ryan is referring to the possibility that charming love poetry might supplant the revolutionary fervour of Mitchel's writings.
12. Brian Boru (*c.*941–1014), high king of Ireland and victor at the battle of Clontarf in 1014.
13. Ryan is referring here to some of the more rapacious examples of English imperialism.

in a spirit of equity and a spirit of knowledge. But these beneficent spirits can be evoked and nourished quite efficiently, it seems to me, without putting on Ireland the enormous burden of adopting what is now virtually a new language, for no better reason than the sentimental one that she once spoke it. The truth is that, given the solution of our political problem, the solution of the others will merely depend on all the modern light we can get; whilst the stress laid on the teaching of Gaelic tends to obscure even some of these. Thus, for instance, the degradation of taste deplored by Father Dinneen[14] and others is not the result of speaking English; it is a result of the industrial system, of long hours and fatiguing work in towns, with scanty leisure, and is more or less characteristic of all modern industrial communities. So far, however, from evading that industrialism most Gaelic Leaguers stand for its extension, without, at the same time, bothering themselves much or sympathising much with the attempts to control and mitigate its evils by socialist reformers in other countries. No mediæval literature can possibly supply any guidance on these complicated but inevitable issues, and though the mythical prowess of Cuchullain and the beauty of Maeve may be fine imaginative themes, they may be overdone. Assuredly in the realms of modern science there are stories as wonderful and at least more profitable than the careers of fabled gods and demi-gods in the Ireland of a thousand years ago.

14. Father Patrick Dinneen (1860–1934), compiler of a famous Irish/English dictionary, and author of *Lectures on the Irish Language Movement* (1904), which deplored the influence of English literature on Irish culture.

ON LANGUAGE AND POLITICAL IDEALS

II

. . . the best way of beginning in a somewhat complex discussion is to define our terms and our starting-points. Until we realise our ends we cannot measure how far a certain policy will bring such ends nearer. Now, one standard of judgment is brought out vividly in an able article in *An Claidheamh Soluis*,[1] which I venture to put first. Dealing with my article the *United Irishman*[2] had said: 'We do not believe there is any but an insignificant minority of Gaelic Leaguers who would hesitate to sacrifice the language if the impossible could take place, and the choice were between the language and freedom.' By way of answer as much to the *United Irishman* as to me, the *Claidheamh Soluis* lays down the following doctrine:

> There is here an opposition of two things which are on totally different planes — nationality and political autonomy. The Irish language is an essential of Irish nationality. It is more, it is its chief depository and safeguard. When the Irish language disappears, Irish nationality will *ipso facto* disappear, and for ever. Political autonomy, on the other hand, can be lost and recovered, and lost again and recovered again. It is an accidental and external thing necessary, indeed, to the complete working out of a national destiny, necessary, in many cases, to the continued existence of a people, but not in itself an essential of nationality. There is such a thing as a nation in bondage. Ireland is such, the Boers are such, Poland is such. Now, if Ireland were to lose her language — which is, remember, an essential of her nationality — there might conceivably be a free state in Ireland at some future date; but that state would not be the Irish nation, for it would have parted from the body of traditions which constitute Irish nationality. The people which would give up its language in exchange for political autonomy would be like the prisoner who would sell his soul to the Evil One that he might be freed from his bodily chains.

That is to say, a nation, miserably poor, without political status, without education, oppressed by another nation, taxed to extinction-point, is to be preferred to a free nation, politically mistress of her own destinies, educated and prosperous, speaking a language not 'her own' only in the sense that it is spoken by the great majority of her people at a later

1. *An Claidheamh Soluis* (The Sword of Light), the newspaper of the Gaelic League, was edited by Patrick Pearse, who wrote the article to which Ryan is referring.
2. *The United Irishman*, edited by Arthur Griffith, looked towards parliamentary abstentionism and economic protectionism, rather than cultural nationalism per se, as the basis of independence.

date than the previous one. The theorem crystallises that metaphysical habit of regarding politics which I am afraid is one of our constitutional vices in this country. If the loss of language be the crucial loss which nothing can ever repair, then Ireland *is* hopelessly gone, sold to the Evil One, whatever that phrase, capital letters and all, may exactly mean. For the great majority of Irishmen *have* given up the language which Ireland at one time spoke; unless, indeed, the theorem before mentioned be modified to the extent of positing that the Irish people who are now re-learning Gaelic would be engaged in a useless task if there were not in the country a remnant of native Gaelic speakers. If that remnant disappeared, then Irish 'nationality' would *ipso facto* have disappeared, and the efforts of the rest would be futile.

It is possibly my limitation, but these speculations transport me to a region where the foothold is so slippery that one is not sure of a step, and the propositions are often so vague and indefinite as to be negligible. As to the kind of nation that is desirable I have a very clear notion; but as to the 'spirit of nationality,' and whether a distinctive language is an essential or accidental part of that spirit, whether political autonomy is or is not an essential of nationality, all this is a species of speculation in which you arrive at any desired conclusion by first giving your terms and phrases the required meaning. One could easily so define nationality as to make it *include* political autonomy as an essential and *exclude* language as accidental.

A nation which has its laws, its finance, its educational system, its administrative habits, and its civil service shaped by the ideas of another nation, would certainly appear to have lost some of the most effective means of moulding character. And as an example, the United States is developing a local patriotism, evidenced in the war with Spain, as strong as exists anywhere, and has as definitely marked habits of industry (whether admirable or otherwise) and as distinctive manners as any nation in Europe, though it has not a separate language.

III

Much more profitable, however, it seems to me, than such theorising is the problem of how to create in Ireland a people, healthy, educated, cultured in the best sense, with sufficient material comfort, developing their minds and their bodies to the end of maximising life, sensitive to intellectual and moral values, and conducting their national life on lines of justice, and freedom, and good faith. That is, in outline, the standard by which, I submit, we should judge proposals and policies. Had we the political power in Ireland, there are a hundred things we should strive for so as to attain that standard. For instance (and I merely take these as examples), we should set up the best system of primary and secondary instruction that the total experience of other countries suggests, with a system of popular university education, free of access to every boy and girl who could reasonably profit by it. We should endeavour to throw the burden of taxation on the wealthy and landlord classes, with a heavy income tax on unearned wealth; and out of such revenues we should provide sufficient old-age pensions for those who need them, and in that way extinguish the abominable workhouse system. We should set our faces against anything like protective duties on food or manufactured articles by which the cost of living is raised on the many for the benefit of the landlord or the capitalist, as the case may be. But we should have an efficient system of factory laws by which the health of the workers would be safeguarded, and we should further raise the position of the farm labourers, perhaps the most neglected class in all Ireland today.[3] We should immediately nationalise the railways and canals as monopolies that pressingly need control, and out of the profits of such administration we might well build harbours round the coast for the proper development of the fisheries; indeed the fishing industry itself might well be nationalised and put on a stable basis.

Now in all this, which is but outline and beginning, I do not exactly know whether we should be stimulating the spirit of nationality or not, and I do not really see that it matters. We should be doing something finer and better — we should be making a strong, and cultivated, and self-reliant people. And the reason, I confess, why I stand for Irish independence is because by it alone can we obtain the machinery to produce this. No alien administration can possibly produce it. When we have the

3. Ryan is here criticizing the type of protectionist policies that later came to be associated with Sinn Féin.

control of our own affairs we may perhaps leave undone many of the things mentioned, and do many foolish things into the bargain. But then at least the responsibility will be ours alone, and responsibility is the beginning of wisdom. Then, those of us who desire democratic progress must fight for our view as best we can, and, if defeated, accept defeat for the time as best we may, recognising that in a civilised nation the decision of the majority is the final court of appeal. . . .

V

Let me, however, in taking leave of this discussion endeavour to sum up. In the Gaelic League are some of the best and most enthusiastic workers in Ireland, and it would be strange if their magnetism had not affected many other good movements. All that goes without saying, and nothing that I have written, I hope, suggests the contrary. And these workers love Ireland, and strive to the best of their belief for her welfare. I claim also to be a lover of Ireland. Though by 'Ireland' I do not mean any 'literary' or mystic entity or any 'nationality' divorced from the real life of the people. By Ireland I mean the peasants in the fields, the workers in the factories, the teachers in the schools, the professors in the colleges, and all others who labour in Ireland and desire to make this people a great people, an intellectual people, a noble people. But in building up that people we must, I submit, keep our eyes fixed on the permanent standards of right and wrong, of good politics and bad, and less and less on the mere ebb and flow of national impulse. Our desire should be not to copy England or any other nation, still less to aimlessly differentiate ourselves from other nations, but to choose the best from all nations. It is an ignoble thing to be a sycophant; it is a foolish thing to be a factious antagonist. If we possess a good method or a useful custom it is unwise to abandon it merely because another nation which we dislike has it too. When the hurricanes of national and racial antagonism die away we must always come back to equity, to utility, and to righteousness. And having at present in our possession, through the operation of many causes, for some of which we are ourselves responsible, a language which unlocks the temples of vast knowledge, and provides a means of world-wide intercourse, we should scrupulously survey our course before parting with it, and critically ask ourselves whether any permanent good we wish to achieve could not as easily be achieved without such sacrifice.

ARTHUR GRIFFITH

(1871–1922)

from: SINN FÉIN (1913)

[In this backhanded tribute to Frederick Ryan after his death, Arthur Griffith attempts to disenfranchise him of his nationalist credentials, arguing that a materialist approach to culture is unacceptable to those like himself who look to nationality as the 'soul' of Ireland. Griffith's attack on Ryan's cultural materialism and internationalist approach to anti-imperialism took place on the eve of the Great Lock-out in Dublin, which brought about a decisive break between Griffith's bourgeois nationalism, and socialist republicanism. Griffith's obituary appeared in *Sinn Fein* on 12 April 1913.]

THE DEATH OF FREDERICK RYAN

All who knew Mr. Frederick Ryan personally will regret to learn that he is dead. Mr. Ryan was one of the members of the Celtic Literary Society,[1] and

1. The Celtic Literary Society was founded by William Rooney in 1893, and included Arthur Griffith, John O'Leary and F. Hugh O'Donnell among its members. It was transformed into Cumann na nGaedheal in 1900, the forerunner of the Sinn Féin party (1906).

the only one who was not or did not become a Nationalist, although he was once perilously near being saved. His mind was essentially that of the English mid-Victorian philosophical Radicals, but much more sincere than any of them save only Wilfrid Blunt,[2] to whom in honesty and courage of conviction he bore a strong affinity. Progress — the Brotherhood of Man, and all the other cants which English Radicalism exudes with a gurgle in its throat seemed real things to Frederick Ryan. He believed in them with a fervency that astonished those to whom they were merely strings to pull the stupid population with. The nation seemed to him a small thing — even an obstructive thing — to the apotheosis of man, and the suffering Egyptian had not less claim on him than his own countrymen. All this false and partial view of life — this creed that man has any other obligation than to do his duty and to do it where it lies to his hand — this curious belief that a man can realise himself otherwise than through the nation and that human brotherhood can be brought about by the supersession of the nation, was a sincere view with Frederick Ryan. He wrote for us — and he wrote against us — he came to us, he went from us, he came back again and he went away again, but he was always sincere, always preaching the truth as he conceived it — which is all any preacher or teacher can do. At one time he almost fell under the fascination of the Irish-Ireland Revival, and if he had succumbed to the Gael in him we know few men whose intellectual powers, thawed by the national sun from a frozen cosmopolitanism, could have served Ireland as well. Detestation of oppression and sympathy with suffering filled his heart, and a belief in the inherent nobility of man possessed his mind. And these things he sought to use as his driving-power in place of Nationalism. Years ago, under the signature of 'Irial', Frederick Ryan contributed occasionally to our columns, and in *Dana* and the Egyptian Nationalist papers which he edited has left work which, granted his premises, have been rarely equalled in the English language for lucidity of statement and strength of argument. A play, *The Laying of the Foundations*, too good although topical not to be revised and revived, and a small volume of essays, *Criticism and Courage*, comprise all he has written outside journalism. As a man he was honourable, generous and fearless. His death, indeed, removes another *man* from the world — a species somewhat rare. It also removes the only man in Ireland who ever drifted into the cosmopolitan heresy in our time who was a real loss to Nationalism . . . . The Frederick Ryan who is dead was an idealist who would have immolated himself at any moment to serve his ideals. Whether the ideals be right or wrong, such men are the saviours of the world — they blow through its stagnant atmosphere, sometimes blowing off the hats of the just as well as the unjust, but nevertheless sweetening the air.

Beannacht De lena anam![3]

2. Wilfrid Scawen Blunt (1840–1922), English radical and implacable anti-imperialist activist in Ireland, India and Egypt. Frederick Ryan edited his paper, *Egypt*.

3. Literally: 'The Blessings of God on his soul'.

from:
SINN FEIN (1913)

[In an outraged response to Griffith's notice of Ryan's death, Francis Sheehy-Skeffington stated that Griffith's attempt to define 'a Nationalist' so as to exclude Fred Ryan is a characteristic example of what Ryan used to reprobate as a 'metaphysical' way of looking at concrete questions. Sheehy-Skeffington rejected Griffith's narrow view that 'A Nationalist is one who sets the interest of his nation above democracy and aristocracy'. He concluded with a question addressed directly to Griffith:
'Fred Ryan was an advocate of the complete political independence of the Irish people; he desired to see them absolutely free to work out their own destinies without foreign intervention. Why should you seek to deny him the title of Nationalist because his vision of what might and should be done in and by a free Ireland was different from yours?' Griffith's reply to Sheehy-Skeffington follows.]

RESPONSE TO SHEEHY-SKEFFINGTON

We did not deny Mr. Ryan the title of Nationalist because his vision of what a free Ireland ought to do was different from ours, but because he himself implied, like Mr. Skeffington in his present letter, that a nation was nothing more than a collection of human beings, and that the interests of the nation were nothing more than the interests of the said human beings — a body without a soul. The castaways on a coral island would have been as much a nation to Mr. Ryan as the Ireland that stretches back to Emain Macha.[1] No doubt Mr. Ryan loved Ireland as a geometrician might love an equilateral triangle, but he loved half-a-dozen other countries in equal fashion. Egypt, Persia, China were as much to him as his own country, and those who held that the business of a man is with his own nation and that no man has a right to give his services to another nation howsoever in need of them while his own is in straits were Obscurantists. When we say we love Ireland we do not mean by Ireland the peasants in the fields, the workers in the factories, the teachers in the schools, the professors in the colleges — we mean the soul into which we were born and which was born into us.[2] If this be a metaphysical way of looking at concrete questions we shall remain in the metaphysical pit along with the unenlightened world that existed before Rousseau and the Manchester school[3] whom poor Ryan so implicitly accepted as the repository of the wisdom of all the ages. As to Mr. Skeffington's questions, 'his nation' is a man's ancestral title on the earth, which it is his first duty and point of honour to maintain, and as to the 'solution' of problems in democracy and aristocracy, the business of the nation is not to let any 'problem' or its 'solution' interfere with its continued existence as a distinctive and conserving force. The man who declared he wanted National freedom in order to promote social reform did not understand the meaning of the nation.

1. The Irish name for Armagh. It was the capital of Ulster in ancient Ireland, and the home of the Red Branch Knights, who feature so prominently in the mythic cycle of Cuchulain. With the introduction of Christianity by St Patrick in the fifth century, it was established as the primatial see of Ireland.
2. It is interesting to compare this mystical version of cultural nationalism with Griffith's position, as cited by Ryan himself, nine years earlier, in which he stated that nationalists would be willing to sacrifice the Irish language for political freedom. See 'On Language and Political Ideals', p. 1000, note 2 above.
3. Jean Jacques Rousseau (1712–78), the great Genevan political philosopher. The Manchester School was the name coined by Disraeli to describe the intellectual leadership of the movement which led to the abolition of the Corn Laws in 1846. It is generally associated with the advocacy of classic *laissez-faire* and liberal trade principles, particularly as enunciated by David Ricardo and John Bright.

V. NATIONALISM: EXCLUSIVISM OR CULTURAL DIVERSITY?

ARTHUR CLERY

from: IRISH ESSAYS (1919)

[In this essay, written before he became a fully fledged member of the 'Irish Ireland' movement, Clery seeks to reclaim some of the great Anglo-Irish writers for an Irish rather than an English literary tradition. In this reprinted version, he appends a dissenting footnote qualifying his earlier views, but the fact of reprinting the essay in the strained cultural climate of 1919 seems to speak for itself.]

. . . [The] great masters of prose I would put forward as the true representatives of our genius in so far as it has taken form in English.* To Gaelic our best

*Twenty years after, I see this essay full of the cock-sureness of a young fellow in his twentieth year, insensible to the poetic revival around him, clinging to received opinions with the strange loyalty of youth, failing to

verse belongs; to English our prose. It is a well-observed phenomenon of all literatures that a period of great poetry is succeeded by a cycle of prose-writers. Our era of poetry occurred while we still spoke our native language. That era is now unhappily almost past. The eighteenth century saw the coming of our age of prose, and, owing to the circumstances of the time, the expression of our thoughts and feelings under this form clothed itself in the English tongue. To search in our English literature of the last two centuries for any analogue to the poetic harvest of earlier ages is to act upon a mistaken principle. The dainty English versifiers of recent times are no true counterpart to the mighty Gaelic creators of the past. We should rather look for a development, and that development we should seek to find embodied in a period of excellence in the more sober art; and we do find it represented in the works of our great eighteenth-century writers. As Plato and the orators were a natural development of Aristophanes and the tragedians; as Shakespeare and his compeers found their successors in Addison, Richardson, and the prose-verse of Pope, so Swift and Goldsmith, Steele and Berkeley, Sheridan and Bourke [*sic*] are the lineal descendants of our lyrists and our epicists.

To offer any proof of the greatness of such writers would be a useless task. All mankind has already admitted it. The attacks we have to parry, in asserting our claim to them, are of a different kind. The energies of successive generations of English *litérateurs* [*sic*] have been devoted to proving they were not our countrymen. As the success of a descendant ennobles Chinese ancestors, so the performance of any great achievement by an Irishman results in the transplanting of his family-tree to the richer soil. Famous Irishmen become English after death. The finding of a grandfather in Lincoln follows close on the discovery of a great-aunt in Sussex, and we are forthwith informed that our mighty humorist was mistaken as to his nationality, and his humour really an alien product. The evidence of character is then brought forward to back that of genealogy. It is pointed out that Swift and Berkeley were not Irishmen, because they were not formed on the model of Goldsmith, and sometimes, with nicer refinement, that Goldsmith was not one either because he was not the counterpart of Bourke. The method by which a standard of Irish character has been arrived at in our neighbour country is indeed not a little peculiar. No one ever thinks of criticising John Bright or Sir Robert Peel[1] upon the basis of their powers of beef-consumption, or their resemblance to a Punch caricature of John Bull.[2] But a corresponding method is commonly applied to determine the nationality of distinguished Irishmen. Irish characters are subjected, not to analysis, but to a strange sort of synthesis. A composite nature is made up out of the most *outré* characteristics of Bourke, Swift, Goldsmith, and Sheridan; an imaginary being as witty as Swift, as rhetorical as Bourke, as improvident as Goldsmith, as intemperate as Steele or Sheridan is conceived and dubbed the typical Irishman. It is then discovered that each of these writers lacked something of this strange ideal; that the writings of the Drapier and the Citizen of the World[3] are simple in style, that Bourke was not witty, that Swift used to walk to bed unassisted, and actually had, when he died, a balance at his bankers. They are all straightway set down as un-Irish, and sentenced to eternal transportation across the Channel.

This strange method of criticism, a method we ourselves, unhappily, are only too ready to submit to and adopt, arises from the same fallacy which we have had to consider before, that of supposing all things Irish to be uniform and conformable to some one pattern. Characters, however, are quite as various in our island as in the rest of the world. There are economical Irishmen as there are lavish ones. Bourke, the only eighteenth-century writer with a pure Irish pedigree, spent his leisure hours in vain but desperate attempts to make a joke. This, however, would not justify us joining a distinguished

notice that few or none of the writers mentioned were of the native population. The writer was probably not then aware that the best Gaelic poetry belongs to the eighteenth century. — A. E. C.

1. John Bright (1811–89), Liberal politician, was a leading crusader against the Corn Laws, and a representative of the 'Manchester School' of economic thought. Sir Robert Peel (1788–1850), British Conservative prime minister 1834–35 and 1841–46, resigned from office following the repeal of the Corn Laws in 1846.
2. *Punch* magazine, founded in 1841, became the leading English illustrated comic periodical of the nineteenth century. Its beefy, convivial cartoon of John Bull, the personification of England, contrasted starkly with the magazine's savage, simian depictions of the Irish.
3. Jonathan Swift's *The Drapier's Letters* (1724) contained an early exposition of the case for economic nationalism. They were allegedly written by a Dublin draper as a protest against a new coinage system ('Wood's Half-pence') in Ireland. Oliver Goldsmith's *The Citizen of the World* (1760–61) was a series of satirical letters by a fictional Chinaman, dealing mainly with English social manners (see Volume I, pp. 671–74).

lady writer in her flight to the conclusion that the native Irish are not a witty people, and what is known as Irish humour is really a Saxon quality. We must be prepared to meet with many and various Irish natures, and must not attribute every deviation from the conventional type to English ancestry. This plea of English pedigree is indeed the customary excuse for robbing us of our best authors. Walt Whitman is never claimed as an English writer. Mark Twain preserves his nationality after death. But hereditary ownership is alleged in all Irishmen whose families may have been originally derived from England. However sharp the line which divides their characters, different though they be amongst themselves, from those formed in the other island, no explanation is ever sought in the all-important factors of national absorption, and, above all, education. The theory that man is wholly the product of his time and circumstance may not be altogether true. Yet certainly the conditions of bringing up and early surroundings must have no small share in the formation of character and mental development. To call Laurence Sterne an Irishman is the mere pedantry of birth registration. But if it was found that in Norman times such families as the Fitzgeralds became more Irish than the Irish themselves, why should not a similar phenomenon explain the characters of our Goldsmiths and our Sheridans? Nay, if a foreign pedigree cannot rob Athens of her Pericles, or France of her Napoleon, why should our great men alone be the creatures of genealogy?. . . .

In the works of the eighteenth-century writers five great strains appear. Whether in the writings of Berkeley, the Plato of the English language, the deepest thought is to be found, is a subject for the unparliamentary discussions of philosophers. But that of all thinkers he enshrined his thought product in the purest prose, that his instrument of expression is attuned to the most delicate harmony, is conceded even by his most bitter opponents. To the music of Berkeley's style, the ease of Steele's tea-table essays, and the beautiful simplicity of Goldsmith, a simplicity that yet found, perhaps, its sweetest expression in the *Vicar of Wakefield*, form a fitting counterpart. In his embodiment of comedy, the third great strain, Goldsmith is also pre-eminent. *She Stoops to Conquer* needs no exposition. The theatre or the library has made it familiar to all of us. Criticism could only repeat those expressions of admiration that all mankind has already bestowed on it. Poor Oliver's comedy seems destined to outlast all other plays, except, indeed, the masterpieces of his countryman, Sheridan. For the latter's wit appears fated to outlive even the fame of his oratory. The woes of the dowagers of Oude drew tears from a crowded House of Commons,[4] the humours of Charles Surface and Mrs. Malaprop[5] seem likely to divert humanity for ever. Yet of the mighty strain of oratory, Sheridan was one of the most splendid exponents. With Bourke and Grattan he made up that triad of inspired speakers who have made eloquence peculiarly our own. To his fame, Byron, twenty years later, bore witness. As to his companions, it is no exaggeration to say that in the Revolution drama, Bourke, towering above Mirabeau,[6] held amongst the orators a position no less exalted than that of Bonaparte among the men of action; whilst as to Grattan, though true oratory is now but little in vogue, it is safe to forecast that with a juster standard of taste and a more generous appreciation of the power and harmony of voice, he will once again be regarded as a mighty master by all who seek to be enthralled or to enthrall the minds of men.

Whether Swift, for it is with this master of satire the fifth great strain I would conclude, was justified in abandoning his party and some of his principles in order to maintain others which he considered of paramount importance, is a problem of political ethics of which I cannot hope to offer any solution in this paper.

The specific gravity of Wood's halfpence is now a matter of little concern.[7] But the question of the nationality of the greatest satirist the world has ever seen cannot but be of supreme interest. We must of necessity feel a certain pride and affection, mingled though they be with awe, when we look on that vast nature-fighting spirit that once pulsated in our midst.

4. This refers to Sheridan's greatest speech in the House of Commons, an impassioned plea on behalf of the dowager princesses of Oudh in India, whose fortunes were brutally expropriated by Warren Hastings and the East India Company. Members of Parliament are supposed to have wept at the pathos of Sheridan's peroration, which lasted for almost six hours.
5. Charles Surface, a rakish character in Sheridan's *The School for Scandal* (1777). Mrs Malaprop, a character in Sheridan's *The Rivals* (1775), was famous for her solecisms.
6. Comte de Mirabeau (1749–91) was the most influential leader in the early phases of the French Revolution. The revolution was the subject of a powerful denunciation by Edmund Burke in his *Reflections on the Revolution in France* (1790).
7. See note 3 above.

Yet, from all claim to the Dean of St. Patrick's Thackeray would debar us.[8] Always an enemy to an Irishman, he was only too glad to sever Swift from his compatriots, that he might vivisect him at greater leisure before his spinster-audiences in England. In his superficial essay he pressed home a certain harshness that we find mingled with the Dean's character, to prove it was un-Irish. It is this view, unhappily, that has gained currency in our country in later times. Cheap editions of Thackeray and of Macaulay[9] — the latter of whom having no space for Swift in his corridor of heroes was obliged, according to the canons of his art, to place him in his gallery of villains — have begotten ideas directly at variance with tradition. People whose grandfathers still tell pleasant tales of Swift, and who, had they been his contemporaries, would have thought it an honour to join his bodyguard, and probably have doubted whether Mr. Wood or Chief Justice Whitshed[10] more nearly resembled anti-Christ, now see in the great Dean only a churlish and un-Irish boor.

Yet this was not the man that Vanessa longed for, that Stella loved. Though he was harsh as the bard of old, none the less Swift's nature was Irish. But its nationality was obscured by the demoniac influences that beset his existence; it was an Irish nature, but an Irish nature permeated with vitriol. In his soul the beautiful and the repulsive were strangely mingled. Charitable beyond measure, loving his friends and loved by them, using his genius ever for the good of his fellows, the flowers that he culled withered beneath his touch. The awful malady of hating for its imperfections that which he loved, tainted all. His benevolence for his fellow-man was unparalleled, yet his fellow-men form without distinction the subject of his direst satire. The betterment of his native country appears to have been the great object of his existence, but towards that country he seems to have professed throughout his life only feelings of horror and indignation. Nor can we doubt that it was hatred of himself and hatred of common humanity that prevented that union with Stella, which might have done so much to bring back his desolate spirit from the dry places into which it had wandered.

Swift's was a life of good deeds and ghoul-faced sorrows. He craved not our pity, yet he deserved it. Still, though we pity, we cannot but exult; for we may not forget that, dreadful as were the conditions under which his genius worked, that reasoning that could scatter armies, that plain-spoken rhetoric that could stir nations to their depths, that wit that could lash humanity, are one and all but portions of the heritage of our national mind. It is to the product of that mind that I have tried to afford definition, and, in some way, criticism, in this paper. Our national soul has had two great embodiments. First, the literature of the Gaelic language, in which poetry flourished, with which it expired, and with whose revival I, for one, hope it may again take life; secondly, the splendid works of the eighteenth century, a true embodiment of our national genius, that, taking fresh life under new forms, as it had once been pre-eminent in poetry, so now established an empire over prose. Overshadowing the reflected efforts of contemporary poets, Irish writers, though of English race, the famous authors inspired by it, wits, orators, essayists, philosophers, took captive the conquering English tongue, and moulded in it that vast and imperishable monument that will preserve the memory of our race, when, to the dead century, be added yet another, and yet to that another and another.

8. See Thackeray's statement in his essay on Swift in *The English Humourists of the Eighteenth Century* (1853): 'That Swift was born at No. 7, Hoey's Court, Dublin, on the 30th November, 1667, is a certain fact, of which nobody will deny the sister island the honour and glory; but, it seems to me, he was no more an Irishman than a man born of English parents at Calcutta is a Hindoo.' Ironically, proponents of an exclusivist Irish nationalism, such as Daniel Corkery, would agree with these sentiments.
9. Thomas Babington Macaulay (1800–59), English historian and statesman whose *History of England from the Accession of James the Second* expounded the Whig version of history.
10. William Whitshed (1656–1727), chief justice of King's Bench in Ireland 1714, was a target of Swift's ridicule in *The Drapier's Letters* because of his prominent role in the 'Wood's Half-pence' affair.

DANIEL CORKERY

(1878–1964)

from: SYNGE AND ANGLO-IRISH LITERATURE (1931)

['On Anglo-Irish Literature', the opening chapter of Daniel Corkery's *Synge and Anglo-Irish Literature* (1931), is a manifesto for an exclusivist approach to Irish identity based solely on 'native' culture. Corkery rightly considered Synge to be the main obstacle in expunging the Anglo-Irish from the cultural canon, and his book takes up many of the arguments that surfaced in the aftermath of the *Playboy* riots in 1907. Although Corkery's views are often taken to be characteristic of cultural nationalism, they did not meet with anything like unanimity in nationalist circles. Corkery realized this, and in subsequent writings tried to counteract the influence of nationalists as diverse as Thomas MacDonagh and Aodh de Blacam, who attempted a more complex engagement with different cultural traditions on the island.]

I

. . . Anglo-Irish literature . . . as the phrase is understood, is mostly the product of Irishmen who neither live at home nor write primarily for their own people. Furthermore the criticism by which it is assessed is not Irish, nor even Anglo-Irish. These facts admitted, the foreign critic would recall how powerful are the moulds of a literature, how tyrannously, when once established, they shape out the subsequent individual books although these may come to be written under altered conditions and even in newly-discovered lands. That foreigner would reason thus: Anglo-Irish literature is a homogeneous thing, first fashioned in Ireland for Ireland, pregnant of Irish mind, of the genius of the isle. Those expatriate writers are Irishmen, he would continue, steeped in the traditions of this literature: its idiom is their idiom; its thoughts their thoughts; expatriation, it is true, may be having some distorting effect on the moulds, but native moulds are not easily changed, hardly ever shattered: the literature then that those expatriate writers, helped by these moulds, produce, is Anglo-Irish literature.

That foreign critic in reasoning thus would be certain he was right; we know he would be wrong. He would be taking for granted that this expatriation is a new thing; that the moulds of the literature were laid before it began; that there was a time when Anglo-Irish was a normal literature, written at home for the homeland. Of course there never was such a time. The moulds are not native to us for they were never fashioned at the bidding of the people of this land: in their making the intention, whether willing or unwilling makes no difference, was not to canalize some share of Irish consciousness so that that consciousness would the better know itself. The intention was rather to discover some easy way in which the strange workings of that consciousness might entertainingly be exhibited to alien eyes. Expatriation is not of today, nor of yesterday. It has been a chronic disease from Goldsmith's time, Steele's time, Sheridan's time, Burke's time, Moore's time, Prout's time,[1] Wilde's time, to our own time of Shaw, Joyce and Moore. Expatriation is, therefore, an older feature in this literature than the very moulds of it. The moulds can have been fashioned only by expatriate hands, and such expatriates as we have described: writers who did not labour for their own people. From the beginning then though we may think of this literature as a homogeneous thing, we cannot think of it as an indigenous thing. Its moulds therefore cannot have been fashioned to express the genius of Ireland in the English language. If in later years certain writers tried to do this, as some have tried, the unnatural homogeneity of these moulds proved their greatest enemy, so inflexible they have ever been.

II

We know the outlines of the history of this literature. Its earliest moulds cannot be distinguished from those of contemporary English literature. Later, it certainly did develop somewhat different moulds, which can be distinguished. These second-period

1. Father Prout was the pen name of Francis Sylvester Mahony (1804–66), a defrocked priest whose remarkable satirical essays on Irish literature and other themes were collected in *The Reliques of Father Prout* (1836).

moulds we may speak of as Colonial moulds. The earliest writers never thought of themselves as cut off from English life or letters; the Colonial writers felt they were; they frequently protest that they are as truly English as the English born in India, as those who have gone thither: their writing at all is often an effort to keep in communion with their kind. Their books may be all regarded as an account of this strange country they are condemned to, written not for their brothers and co-mates in exile — not even for them! — but for their kinsfolk in England. Maria Edgeworth's *Castle Rackrent* is the best specimen of this style of literature.[2] No other book did as much in the creation of what was to prove the most favoured of the moulds which subsequent writers were to use. This Colonial literature was written to explain the quaintness of the humankind of this land, especially the native humankind, to another humankind that was not quaint, that was standard, normal. All over the world is not that the note of Colonial literature? The same note is found everywhere in Kipling's Indian books. From Edgeworth's *Absentee* to *John Bull's Other Island* is a far cry, yet in Shaw's play we have the same theme, with some variations of course.[3] In between, what scores of books have been written in which an Englishman is brought to Ireland and is taken around while a current of comment is poured in his ear, not that he may really understand what he sees, but that he may know that what he sees is only the scum of the milk: he may be a bit of a fool, this Englishman, but still he is normal; he is not one of a lesser breed; and it is really his unsuspecting normality that makes it necessary for the guide to hint that things even more strange lurk unknown to him in the background. In this way the writer can also prove his own intimate acquaintanceship with the life of a strange land and a stranger people. Instructed through history, through the poetry written in Irish by the quaint ones in the background, what an exhibition of crass obtuseness that assumption of intimacy now appears to us!

It was natural for the Ascendancy folk of this second period to write in this Colonial manner, for what are all their books but travellers' tales? It is true that often the traveller was born in the strange land he must write of, but then his father was a traveller if he himself was not, or his grandfather or great-grandfather — and why not take after one's kind? But it is also true that similar books were written by native-born Catholic Irishmen whose forbears had not come out of England. *The Collegians*, by Gerald Griffin, is an example.[4] In this we have an Englishman to whom the quaintness of the folk is exhibited with the accompanying stream of comment, exactly in the Colonial manner. This normal Englishman is really the symbol of the public for whom the book was written; and the writer of it, Gerald Griffin, may be taken as the type of the non-Ascendancy writer who under the stress of the literary moulds of his time wrote Colonial literature.

In Ascendancy literature the leading theme from the start has been: the decline and fall of an Ascendancy 'Big House.' Maria Edgeworth started this hare also, and the hunt still goes on. Within the last few years we have had *The Big House of Inver* by Somerville and Ross, and *The Big House* by Lennox Robinson;[5] and in perhaps every decade of years, from Miss Edgeworth's time to our own, one can discover a book with the self-same theme. Synge, in his simple way, unaware that this was the leading theme in Anglo-Irish literature, thought that he had discovered the theme for himself; he writes: '. . . and if a play-wright chose to go through the Irish country houses he would find material, it is likely, for many gloomy plays that would turn on the dying away of these old families.'[6] It is as well he himself never wrote such a play, for he had no feeling for history, and the theme is historical, the recognition of which fact makes the moderns, like Mr. Lennox Robinson, treat it very differently from the older writers, like Maria Edgeworth. Sweet are the uses of adversity![7] *Castle Rackrent* falls from generation to generation because the family had lost their virtue, but Mr. Robinson's *Big House* falls because the whole Ascendancy had lost their virtue.

2. *Castle Rackrent* (1800) is often described as the first regional novel in the English language.
3. Maria Edgeworth, *The Absentee* (1812). George Bernard Shaw's *John Bull's Other Island* (1904) contains, in fact, a parodic treatment of the stage-Irishman, though Corkery is correct in emphasizing that it was addressed primarily to an English audience.
4. The novelist Gerald Griffin (1803–40) even moved to London in 1823 to establish a reputation as a writer, but gave up, as he put it, because of 'the fickleness of public literary taste'. He subsequently joined the Christian Brothers and entered a monastery.
5. Somerville and Ross, *The Big House of Inver* (1925); Lennox Robinson, *The Big House* (1926).
6. The quotation is from J. M. Synge's *In Wicklow, West Kerry and Connemara* (1910).
7. *As You Like It*, II.1.12.

This difference between *Castle Rackrent* and Robinson's *Big House* or Somerville and Ross's *Big House of Inver* — the sense that in telling of the fall of one 'big house' they are describing the fate of the whole Ascendancy, teaches us that this Ascendancy literature is not impervious to the teaching that comes with the passing years. For all that, *The Big House of Inver* is quite as much written for the English people as *Castle Rackrent* was, more than a hundred years before.

The strain of literature just described forms the mass of Anglo-Irish literature — if it be correct so to describe it. It is all written for their motherland, England, by spiritual exiles. Personally many of those writers would deny this description of themselves, but it is their works and not themselves we are to go by. It is not however to be thought that all the books which make up this mass of Colonial literature are all equally colonial. Many of the writers did it more naturally, like Sir Andrew Aguecheek,[8] and we can readily segregate the more Colonial from the less Colonial books by asking does the book live by English or Irish suffrage? *Castle Rackrent* for instance lives by English suffrage, but Gerald Griffin's *The Collegians* lives by Irish suffrage. Again, the work of Somerville and Ross lives mostly by English suffrage; while Carleton's[9] work — written quite obviously under Ascendancy influence — lives by Irish suffrage; and so one may go through the list. . . .

III

I recall being in Thurles at a hurling match for the championship of Ireland. There were 30,000 onlookers. They were as typical of this nation as any of the great crowds that assemble of Saturday afternoons in England to witness Association football matches are typical of the English nation. It was while I looked around on that great crowd I first became acutely conscious that as a nation we were without self-expression in literary form. The life of this people I looked upon — there were all sorts of individuals present, from bishops to tramps off the road — was not being explored in a natural way by any except one or two writers of any standing. And even of the one or two, I was not certain, their efforts being from the start so handicapped. It was impossible to feel that one could pose such Anglo-Irish writers as the world knows of against that multitude. To use the American phrase, the writers would not belong. One could not see Yeats, A. E., Stephens, Dunsany,[10] Moore, Robinson, standing out from that gathering as natural and indigenous interpreters of it. On the other hand there seems to be no difficulty in posing Galsworthy, Masefield, Bennett, Wells, against corresponding assemblies in England. Those writers do belong. They give the crowd a new significance: through them we may look with better eyes at the massed people of England. The crowd equally deepens the significance of the written word: what stranger, learned in English literature, recollecting it, would not be glad to find himself in their midst, viewing them, listening to them? He might surely well forget the footballing.

Some one here may say that literature is not a mirror of the mob mind. But one does not think of such English writers as we have named as mirroring the mob mind, nor of its being mirrored by the writers of an earlier day — Meredith, George Eliot, Dickens, Thackeray. We are not thinking of the crowd as such, but as an assembly of a number of the nation's individual souls. Those English crowds are 100 per cent English; and the writers who best express the individual souls that make them up are 100 per cent English.* It was never otherwise, it never will be otherwise. The writers in a normal country are one with what they write of. The life of every other people they gaze upon from without, but the life of their own people they cannot get outside of. That is why they belong. The position they thus occupy in the life they deal with has no resemblance to the position occupied by the world-famous Anglo-Irish writers in the life they are supposed to deal with. . . .

8. A foolish character in Shakespeare's *Twelfth Night*, who played roles to win the admiration of others. *Twelfth Night*, II.3.83–84.
9. William Carleton (1794–1869), the most considerable nineteenth-century Irish novelist, was of a catholic background, but in some of his writings he identified with protestant attacks on the influence of the catholic church in Ireland.

*At this point it may be well to recall Rupert Brooke's: *If I should die*. —

10. Lord Dunsany (1878–1957), man of letters and novelist, wrote in a distinctively 'Celtic twilight' vein, and his reputation now rests largely on his fantasy novels, particularly *The Sword of Welleran* (1908) and *The King of Elfland's Daughter* (1924).

V

If this reasoning is right we now know why that crowd of 30,000 human souls I saw in Thurles — a crowd with a national tradition behind them — are still left unuttered in literature. And we may in the light of such reasoning begin to understand curious traits in the literature as it exists, traits that show it to be exotic, not national, not normal, not natural.

A national literature foretells the nation's future. Eighty years ago, sixty years ago, Prout, Lever, Maginn, Lover, others,[11] were accepted by the English-speaking world as the genuine voice of the Irish nation. One wonders if any foreign critic thought it worth his while to forecast the future of this nation in the light of their pages. How interesting now to come on such a forecast! The Irish peasant, with no national assets in his possession outside his own knowledge that he was the native of the isle, during that period fought for the soil of Ireland, and by his own grit and courage, became possessed of it. Not only does he now possess the soil; he also fills the highest offices in the country, in Church, in State, in Learning — everywhere. This the literature of Lover and his compeers hardly promised. Extinction rather than distinction was what it threatened, laughing, 'with foreign jaws,' as it did so. The future conquest of the soil was part of Irish consciousness: if it were not, the thing could not have come to pass; and anyway those of us who have read Irish poetry know that it has for many centuries been one of the deepest things in Irish consciousness; our 'national' writers however either were not aware of it, or, aware of it, could not or would not give it utterance. Yet this literature, so little at one with the national consciousness, is called variously Irish literature and Anglo-Irish literature! And no school of criticism has arisen in Ireland to warn us that if this literature in the future is to be more trustworthy, its creators must not go the way Prout and the others travelled; indeed by laughing 'with foreign jaws' at the 100 per cent type of Irishman, such critics as we have urge the young writers on to the selfsame disastrous road. If Maginn and his fellows were absorbed in the Irish scene, had to write of it for native eyes and not for London drawing-rooms, they could not but have felt that already the disintegration of the Ascendancy in Ireland was setting in. The literature they produced is typical of Anglo-Irish literature in the mass. We do not say that now and then that literature does not send forward-struggling beams; what we assert is that of all living literatures its message has been most often and most utterly belied by what the years have brought to pass. It has always failed to speak the secret things in the nation's soul. Only at rarest moments does it penetrate the superficialities of Irish life; so that one does not wonder if the foreigner who browses on its 'glamorous' pages picture [*sic*] us as given over either to a wild whirl of fox-hunting and rioting, or as spell-bound by fairies that troop nightly from our prehistoric ruins, moping out an existence not wholly in this world nor quite beyond it.

VII

The three great forces which, working for long in the Irish national being, have made it so different from the English national being, are: (1) The Religious Consciousness of the People; (2) Irish Nationalism; and (3) The Land.

Now the mentality of that crowd of 30,000 I looked upon in Thurles was chiefly the result of the interplay of these three forces. To let one's mind, filled with this thought, rest on that crowd, scanning the faces for confirmation of it, and then suddenly to shift one's thought on to the mass of Anglo-Irish literature, is to turn from solid reality to a pale ghost. For, for instance, who can name a novel dealing adequately with their religious consciousness? Yet this religious consciousness is so vast, so deep, so dramatic, even so terrible a thing, occasionally creating wreckage in its path, tumbling the weak things over, that when one begins to know it, one wonders if it is possible for a writer to deal with any phase whatever of Irish life without trenching[12] upon it. To adopt the convention of Anglo-Irish literature, that is, either to leave it out, or to substitute for it the wraith-like wisps of vanished beliefs that still float in the minds of a tiny percentage of the people, is to cut out the heart of the mystery. So firm is the texture of that consciousness that one may

11. In nationalist circles, 'Father Prout', Charles Lever (1806–72), William Maginn (1794–1842), and Samuel Lover (1797–1868), were synonymous with popularizing 'the stage Irishman' for the amusement of English audiences.

12. i.e. without encroaching.

sometimes think that only about Irish life can a really great sex novel be written in these days; for the subject can have no great attraction for the serious artist except where the moral standards are rigid, and the reactions transcend the lusts and the shiverings of the mortal flesh. (Mr. James Joyce has gone astray — although that very texture we have spoken of nearly succeeded in holding him fast.) We may perhaps know that genuine Anglo-Irish literature has come into being when at every hand's turn that religious consciousness breaks in upon it, no matter what the subject, as it does in the Greek plays — comedies as well as tragedies — or as it does in mediæval art, grotesques and all.

As for Irish nationalism, how can normal countries understand it? If one cannot live in Ireland long enough to have it penetrate one's being, driving one although quite a foreigner to take sides, as has so often happened, the only other way to get to know it is to learn the Irish language and read the poetry in it: for such is the nature of Irish nationalism that it demands sincerity, intensity, style for its utterance, in other words, poetry. We who have lived in Ireland in recent years, who have seen what we have seen, need no further instruction to believe that prose is no medium to express it in, nor more than it was for the Jews in their ancient captivity. Like all forces, it wrecks as well as saves. We here are not concerned with the wisest way of dealing with it; we would only point out that it it one of the deepest things in Irish life, searching into the souls of men, drawing sanction, as it does, from hundreds of battlefields, slaughterings, famines, exoduses, as well as from hundreds of heroic lives and the piety of verse. Yet in the eyes of the world, taught of what the world calls 'Irish' literature, that force is a thing for derision, fitted rather for comic than for serious treatment in literature. What a curious message for 'Irish' literature to deliver to the world — as if a fishmonger should cry out rotten fish! Topsy-turvy cannot sing, it seems, except in a cracked voice. A stranger, one fancies, could from the pages of Conrad gather a truer idea of the nature of Irish nationalism than from the heaped-up books of this literature the world knows of.[13] One may be sure we are come upon genuine Anglo-Irish literature when, as with the force just spoken of, that spirit of Irish nationalism expresses itself almost in every page, no matter what the nature of the expression may be, direct or indirect, heroic or grotesque, or perverse, but not alien-minded.

Of the Land as a force in Irish life, we may, the better to contrast it with the same force in English life, recall that according to the late Sir William Butler,[14] there have been no peasants in England since Queen Elizabeth's reign. Overstatement or not, today in England only 6 per cent of the people work on the land, whereas Ireland, in a sense, is a peasant-ridden country, 53 per cent of the people actually working in the fields. It will then be understood that when under the domination of a national movement, certain writers in Ireland began to deal with this force in their novels and plays, they undertook pioneer service to their country. It also will be understood that while from certain Continental schools of literature they learned a little, from England they learned nothing. It was a doubly new experience for writers such as these, first to have to fend for themselves without help from England, secondly to find they had hitched their wagon to a living force. What wonder that those of them who most deeply sank themselves in their subject wrote far above their accustomed pitch? Darrell Figgis with his *Children of Earth*; T. C. Murray's *Birthright* and *Autumn Fire*; Seamus O'Kelly's *Wet Clay*; Padraic Colum's *Castle Conquer*; Lysaght's *The Gael* may be taken as evidence of this.[15] The Land then is a huge force in Irish life. It is not however as universal in it as the other two; one cannot therefore predicate its breaking in upon every page, yet one can understand how when true Anglo-Irish literature comes to be written, if ever, for a long time the Land must lie behind the literature in some such way as the freeing of the serfs lies behind Russian literature — with political rather than social affinities. Only after long years will those political memories drift from the consciousness of the Irish people.

13. Joseph Conrad's lack of sympathy for Irish nationalism was well known, particularly after his refusal to sign a petition for clemency in the case of Roger Casement, who was hanged for 'treason' in August 1916.

14. Sir William Butler (1838–1911), author and soldier. Although he was of Irish origin, he distinguished himself in the British army. He wrote numerous travel books and biographies.

15. The characteristic feature of the authors whom Corkery mentions is their realistic treatment of rural life: Darrell Figgis's novel, *Children of Earth* (1918); T. C. Murray's plays *Birthright* (1910) and *Autumn Fire* (1924); Seamus O'Kelly's novel *Wet Clay* (1922); Padraic Colum's novel *Castle Conquer* (1923); and Edward Lysaght's novel *The Gael* (1919).

These forces exist in all countries; in Ireland they have however been so hardened and sharpened, given, by centuries of onslaught, such momentum, that only such other countries as have also been or are still enslaved can feel with any fitting comprehension the intensity they have now acquired. For one who has come earnestly to know them, to recognise them in the build, the attitude, the eyes of our men and women — how visibly portrayed they were in those faces in Thurles! — it is impossible for such a one to take seriously such Anglo-Irish literature as exists. So measured against life itself, as it were, it has not begun to be.

AODH DE BLACAM

from: STUDIES (1934)

[In this critical rejoinder to Daniel Corkery, Aodh de Blacam elaborates on his earlier view that 'Gaeldom' is a composite of many races and creeds. Although his argument rests on a slender foundation, his desire to stress the 'Irish' rather than the 'Anglo' component of the Anglo-Irish, and his emphasis on the internal diversity of Irish culture, was in marked contrast to Corkery's cultural exclusivism. The review was published in *Studies*, Vol. XXIII, No. 91 (September 1934).]

THE OTHER HIDDEN IRELAND

Professor Daniel Corkery's book, *The Hidden Ireland*, has kept Irish literary and historical criticism in a ferment ever since its appearance nine years ago. It challenged that version of late Irish history which was set forth by Lecky[1] and followed by almost all later writers, at home and abroad. In effect, it said: Lecky described only the shell of Ireland; he ignored the real national life and culture; from him the real Ireland was hidden; he saw only the Ascendancy. Prof. Corkery drew a majestic picture of the secret Ireland of the Gael. His art convinced readers for whom the actual historical *data* long had been available in duller books. However, he did not tell the whole story of the Gaelic side of Irish history, neglected by Lecky and others who wrote before the revival of Gaelic studies. He dealt only with Munster, and Northern Gaels have resented his slighting treatment of Gaelic themes outside Munster.* He shewed as little sympathy for the Anglo-Irish as Lecky shewed for the Gael. If Lecky was partial, so was he. To dismiss Anglo-Ireland as unworthy of a Gael's study, however, is hurtful to Gaelic interests, seeing that a large part of Gaelic and Catholic thought was expressed, during two centuries, in English. The task of the just historian is to depict Irish history with the Gaeltacht[2] as the core, but also to dissect the anglicised sphere, recovering whatsoever belongs to the nation and discarding only what is alien through and through.

Justly to understand Anglo-Irish history, we must make a bold departure from accepted opinion. We may find that there is a 'hidden' Anglo-Ireland as well as a 'hidden' Gaeldom. . . .

We need not marvel, then, if we should find in being an accepted Anglo-Irish version of Anglo-Irish history which is open to challenge. Nay, but it has appeared this very year in that *History of the Church of Ireland*, which is put forward, apparently, as an official account of itself by the Irish Protestant Church. The historical errors in this work have been

1. William Edward Hartpole Lecky (1838–1903), historian and unionist politician (representing Trinity College, Dublin). His classic five-volume *A History of Ireland in the Eighteenth Century* was published in 1892, and looked at Irish history mainly from an Anglo-Irish viewpoint.

*'The book has one very serious fault — the treatment of the Ulster poets. Corkery's criticism of Lecky might well be applied to his own work on the subject' — Rev. L. Murray in Introduction to *Amhráin Sheumais Mhic Chuarta* (1925).

2. Native Irish-speaking areas.

discussed by the Rev. John Ryan, S.J., in STUDIES, and (from a Protestant standpoint) by a writer in the *Times Literary Supplement*; but we hardly need to dwell on errors of fact to presume a mistaken bias when we find that the editor of this history of a body claiming descent from St. Patrick is ignorant of the Irish language, and that his authors, who deal with the 'Celtic' period, are equally ignorant of what surely is a main part of their subject. Conceive a book on French history written by a man who knew no French, and so was ignorant of all French literature in the original and the accent of French life; nay, but conceive such an author controverting French tradition and yet posing, despite his bad qualifications, as the true inner interpreter of French history!

Grant, then, that Anglo-Irish history is written by those who stress the 'Anglo'; mark that this school of opinion has been in charge of Anglo-Irish records for an age and that almost all independent opinion has died out through obvious causes. Is there another plausible reading of Anglo-Irish history? Are there facts which emphatically anglicised writers would be likely to obscure as Protestant writers have obscured certain facts in the English past and as Whig writers have obscured facts in the Scottish past? We think so. The anglicising party in Irish Protestantism has prevailed, because the Protestant Church was a State church and because the State was set on the extinction of all things Gaelic. However, official policy and historical conditions often are at variance, and so it was (as this essay contends) in Anglo-Ireland. Let the case be summarised in propositions.

(1.) Both Gaelic writers, like Dr. Corkery, and Anglo-Irish writers often err by surveying only a section of the true historical field. The identification of Gael with Catholic is plausible in a study of Jacobite Munster, but it collapses at once if we survey the whole Gaelic field from Kerry to the Hebrides. The schism of the sixteenth century cut geographically across the Gaelic world. Scotland and that part of Ulster which was infiltrated, not planted, became Protestant even before the plantation of Ulster. On the other hand, a big non-Gaelic population in Leinster remained Catholic. Hence, we find Gaelic Protestants and non-Gaelic Catholics at the very outset of the period.

(2.) Three big Plantations followed, which affected the racial map of Ireland in all the provinces. It is a fact that English planters were assimilated in three provinces. Those planters who were not assimilated were the Ulster planters, who were mainly Scottish (*i.e.* Gaelic) by blood. The last Plantation, that after the Williamite war, was that which produced the phenomenon of Ascendancy.

(3.) There was much more intermarriage between the races and creeds formerly than in recent times. This we may see by the absorption of Cromwellian settlers, the anxiety of Protestant writers, the tales of abductions, also by Anglo-Irish pedigrees, few of which, save in the landlord class, fail to shew repeated crossing with the old race during the century before Emancipation, and even after. The recovery of Catholic discipline after Emancipation was the main check on mixed marriage, now almost extinct, to the great benefit of religion and domestic peace.

(4.) Not merely was the black and white cleavage between Gall and Gael less distinct in former days as to blood, but community of occupation brought the two together more than now. Old-fashioned rural life made parishes self-contained. In field and fair, the Protestant minority (even if pure English as to blood) could not but pick up the language of the majority.†

(5.) The general knowledge of Irish by Protestants throughout rural districts, which resulted from these factors, can be demonstrated. We might take the poets Comyn in Clare and Fitzgerald in Waterford county, so well described by Dr. Corkery, as examples of Protestants who were indistinguishable from their Catholic neighbours in Gaelic culture in the Penal days. Farther back, the dispute among Protestant prelates in the seventeenth century as to whether services should be conducted in Irish‡ shews how considerable was the use of Irish among the Protestants of the seventeenth century. Bishop Bedell[3] wanted Irish-speaking clergy and Irish prayers for existing congregations, whereas the anglicising party (which prevailed) wished to spread the English language. The tone of the difference shews that Bedell's desire was not simply for Irish as a proselytising agency. Already, moreover, a Protestant version in Irish of the New Testament had

†The small-holding districts of the Ulster border and the Donegal Gaeltacht shew to this day a community of occupation and of speech.

‡Dr. Douglas Hyde's *Literary History of Ireland* gives typical *dicta*.

3. William Bedell (1571–1642), appointed Bishop of Kilmore and Ardagh in 1629, under whose supervision the Bible was translated into Irish.

been made by Bishop Daniel (Uilleam O Domhnaill), and we have the testimony of Stanihurst[4] that, in Elizabeth's day, Irish was 'gaggled' throughout the Pale. Down to the proselytising movement of the nineteenth century there was a certain slender thread of Protestant Gaelic activity, as when sermons by Tillotson[5] and other Protestant divines were translated, in despite of the official policy of anglicisation. When John Wesley[6] brought Methodism to Ireland, his followers soon found the need for preachers in Irish if they were to reach the Protestant common people, neglected by their prelates in Ireland as in England; Gaelic preachers were appointed and it is recorded how one of these addressed troops in Bandon in 1798 in Gaelic after failing to make himself understood in English — they were Scots. As for the Presbyterians, they were largely Gaelic-speaking when they came from Scotland, and they remained so till a late date. Everyone knows the tale of how their Dr. Neilson (author of an Irish grammar published in 1806) was arrested in 1798, after preaching in Irish in County Down, on suspicion of treason. A predecessor of John Mitchel's father in Newry was a Gaelic speaker from Scotland; he used to go down into County Louth to preach to a Gaelic-speaking congregation near Dundalk. Until seventy years ago a course of Irish was part of the training of Presbyterian clergy. When Cardinal Logue was a young curate in Ballybofey, he was the cordial friend of the Rev. Mr. Steele, a Presbyterian clergyman who preached on alternate Sundays in Irish.

These notes shew that there certainly is a *stratum* in Anglo-Irish history when the Protestant people were largely Gaelic-speaking, and in some places predominantly so; that they were interpenetrated with Gaelic influences and largely by Gaelic blood. Some might claim that Irish Protestants, by rights, are as un-English as the Scots. Suffice it here to make the modest claim that their history never can be written justly until the Gaelic *stratum* has been explored, instead of ignored. Obviously, it must have left a great mark on the Anglo-Irish mind. To some of us an intangible kind of evidence is strong: I mean the rhythm of natural speech. No Englishman can write a ballad in the 'Irish mode,'* but it is a matter of common experience that Irish Protestants have the very accent in their popular verse.† Gaelic ancestry is manifest here to such a critic as McDonagh [*sic*]. A scrutiny of popular Anglo-Irish writings, as distinct from works that bear the classical discipline of the University of Dublin, would be fruitful. What would we not give to recover those ballads which Goldsmith wrote in student days, indulging a racy genius that he restrained in his formal literary work! Traces of the Gaelic *stratum* in Irish Protestantism are found, not merely in the Anglo-Irish accent, however, but in Gaelic letters. One of the errors in modern criticism is to assume that everything found in Irish is *ipso facto* a Catholic production, an expression of the true Irish spirit, as if everything in good English from Milton to Mitchel should be regarded as the voice of England. In truth, Gaelic literature, although overwhelmingly Catholic, does contain some works of a diverse mind. . . .

We may make bold, perhaps, to claim that Anglo-Ireland could have become completely Gaelic as it became completely English if, from 1700 to 1750, the balance had not been turned by certain factors.

One factor was emigration. It might be objected to the theory of a big Protestant Gaelic *stratum* that it left disproportionately small traces; but this takes a different aspect when we read of the enormous emigration of Protestants throughout the eighteenth century. 'For nearly three-quarters of a century,' writes Lecky,‡ 'the drain of the energetic Protestant population continued, and their places, when occupied at all, were occupied by a Catholic cottier population. . . . The famine of 1740 and 1741 gave an immense impulse to the movement, and it is said that for several years the Protestant emigrants from Ulster annually amounted to about 12,000. . . . They went with hearts burning with indignation, and in the War of Independence they were almost to a man on the side of the insurgents.' In a word, the typical Protestant common folk emigrated in

4. Richard Stanihurst (1547–1618), politician and historian. A convert to catholicism, he wrote one of the earliest histories of Ireland in 1577.
5. John Tillotson (1630–94), English preacher, was chaplain to Charles II, and a noted opponent of catholicism. He became Archbishop of Canterbury in 1691.
6. John Wesley (1703–91), the founder of methodism, visited Ireland twenty-one times, beginning in 1747.

*Thomas McDonagh [*sic*], *Literature in Ireland*.
†Witness such extravagances as 'The Night before Larry was Stretched,' and some Orange ballads even.
‡*History of Ireland in the Eighteenth Century*, Vol. I, Chap. II.

such vast numbers as to change the complexion of Anglo-Irish life.

The second factor was the official policy of the Protestant Church and the University of Dublin, its adjunct. As we have seen, the very men who most wished to create a national Church used that institution to discourage the use of the national language. As for the University, it was founded expressly for the propagation of the English culture in Ireland; and if we do find one of its earliest professors an O Huiginn,* a scion of a bardic house, he was engaged because he would be useful in the work of anglicisation. In the seventeenth century, the University, like Ussher[7] himself, was not unfriendly to Irish historical studies. In the eighteenth, however, its distinctive bent was settled unmistakably for anglicisation and classicism. Swift and Berkeley were both the greatest and the most typical of the *alumni* of Trinity College, Dublin. Nay, but their genius became its very *genius loci*. From them Trinity learnt to pride itself on a 'hard intellectual light.' Their philosophy may be traced in all the most characteristic sons of Trinity since their day — Swift's scepticism, Berkeley's subjectivism, the classical detachment from the living nation which we see in both. Trained in Trinity, the leaders of the Irish Protestant Church almost all have borne the mark that Swift left on the Anglo-Irish spirit. An Ussher might be a 'fundamentalist' Protestant, with a bias towards rigorism; but, since Swift, Irish Protestant leadership has been virtually Modernist. A religion thus detached from traditionalism could not but tell against the racy old Gaelic culture. The creator of Gulliver, who saw the world as a cruel phantasmagoria, could not love the things to which the Gael was loyal; the author of a subjectivist philosophy could not encourage the blunt Gaelic realism. Their disciples were alien to the Gaelic spirit. Hence educated Protestantism tended steadily to the detachment of its people from the old life.

It was among the common folk, so largely swept away by emigration, that the strain of Gaelic tradition lingered faintly, and racy Irish sympathies persisted. When a patriotic movement appeared in Protestant Ulster, in revolt against the Ascendancy, it was natural that Gaelic ideas should reappear. So we find the United Irishmen of Belfast publishing a Gaelic magazine in 1795; and the Corkman, Thomas Russell, on becoming librarian there, takes up Irish studies together with other Protestant patriots.[8] In the house of the Protestant Dr. James MacDonnell, in what now is Belfast's main thoroughfare, Gaelic poets, harpers and scribes meet with the comrades of Wolfe Tone, among them Whitley Stokes, who financed an Irish dictionary and was forbear of a grand family of Gaelic scholars; and the doctor himself is lamented in a Gaelic elegy in 1845. The Gaelic tradition, in fact, pouring in from the Glens, nearly captured Protestant Belfast, with a Scottish tinge; it was the political *débâcle* that prevented the uprise of a Protestant Ulster Gaelicism, corresponding to the Gaelicism of the Highlands. We observe, among the United Irishmen of the North, a strong sense that the Irish language is as much theirs as any other part of the Irish heritage, and their remarkable devotion to it, and to traditional music, refutes the now popular theory that they were merely subversive revolutionaries under French influence. Indeed, the notion that it belongs only to the Catholics never appears save under the anti-Gaelic aegis of Trinity.† To the persistence of a quiet affection for the old language we may trace the place in Anglo-Irish speech of what Dr. Corkery calls '"green" things that never had any existence at all in the imagination of the Gael' — the Shamrock, the Harp, the Round Tower, the Shillelagh and sundry other emblems that he enumerates. The truth is that these 'green' emblems moved Catholics at least as much as Protestants. The Shillelagh ('whatever that may be,' as Dr. Corkery says) may have been made a bugbear by the stage-Irish curiosity shops, but it certainly is not a bastard creation of the Protestant mind; for we find it in a grand old Penal ballad, 'Bold Phelim Brady':

*Cf. *The Poems of Tadhg Dall O Huiginn*, Introduction by Miss E. Knott.

†As recently as the youth of the present writer's father, Protestants in Newry (an industrial Ulster town where complete anglicisation might be expected) talked Irish to the incoming country folk on market days, and many were proud of whatever Gaelic they knew — few seem to have regarded it as 'not theirs.'

7. James Ussher (1581–1656), archbishop of Armagh 1625–56. Though he attempted to prevent the use of Irish in the Church of Ireland by, among other things, obstructing Bedell's Irish translation of the Bible, he was an avid student of early Irish history.

8. In 1795, the first issue of *Bolg an Tsolair* (*Gaelic Magazine*) was issued from the offices of the United Irishman newspaper, *The Northern Star*. Thomas Russell (1767–1803), one of the leading United Irishmen, was appointed as the first librarian of the Linen Hall library, Belfast, in 1894. He was hanged following the uprising led by Robert Emmet in 1803.

At pattern[9] or fair I could twist my shillela
And trip through a jig with my brogues bound
with straw.‡

The other 'green' things, if taken *seriatim*, could be shewn to have had an authentic place in that phase of our culture when the people were English-speaking with recent Gaelic memories. They have been cheapened, made ugly by separation from context and by hackneyed use; but they had their place once as faithful emanations from the Gaelic into English. When the United Irishmen made *Erin go bragh*[10] their password, their spelling might be bad, but they were using the correct Irish of the North, with the dative *Eirinn* as nominative: foolish would we be to dismiss the phrase for which men died as 'green.'

The obscured *stratum* of Protestant Gaelicism deserves to be explored for another reason. It is a known truth that off-shoots of nations often preserve old traits more exactly than the living stem.* Old customs often are fossilised in the foreign body. So we find the Protestant Church, in its 'rural deaneries,' preserving the memory of small episcopal sees which were absorbed by bigger sees long before the Reformation. Many traits of the Anglo-Irish tradition, therefore, may give us glimpses of old times. An unhistorical attitude towards 'green' things leads Dr. Corkery to the astonishing statement that St. Patrick 'was never a national piety among the Irish.' What! — did Dr. Corkery never read the story of St. Patrick's fight-to-be for the men of Ireland on the Judgment Day, when he will insist on being their judge? The fable, though droll, expresses a national idea of the Saint which can be traced back to the eleventh or twelfth century before ever the Anglo-Irish were imagined.† What other nation has two great pilgrimages to sites connected with its patron,[11] ascribes peculiar rights to him on the Last Day, and puts him in the very centre of its creative literature as when the whole Fenian saga is supposed to be narrated to St. Patrick? If the Anglo-Irish give a tremendous prominence to St. Patrick, it is because they found it already existent; they accepted it, like the climate. If they have made much of the wearing of the shamrock, they do but confirm the existence of that observance in the old nation. The stress which they have laid upon the harp is perfectly historical; the harp held pride of place in our culture down to the mid-Penal days,[12] but economic causes obliged the poorer classes, then Catholic, to transfer favour to the formerly despised pipes; thus, the harp became the preserve of the more prosperous, the Anglo-Irish, who preserved its tradition for us, if we do not despise our own past. We find in the Anglo-Irish, and in the Scots Gaels, parts of the old fabric of life throughout Gaeldom, disguised sometimes or perverted, but necessary to be studied when we try to reconstruct times before the convulsion.

The upshot of all this is that to identify *Catholic* with *Gael*, as it is bad religion, so it is bad history. It is a sort of Irish Nazi-ism. The Catholic body in Ireland always, since the first invasion, has included non-Gaels in high places; St. Patrick himself was no Gael; Catholicism and racialism are mutually destructive. On the other hand, whereas the Gaelic world once was a unit of blood, speech, tradition, faith, from the South of Ireland to the North of Scotland, a big part fell away from the Faith, and the character of its members was transformed. Religion, as we know, transforms the type where the blood is identical; in contiguous Scottish parishes you may see Calvinistic dourness contrasting abruptly with the Catholic way of life, as if different nations met there. The anglicisation of leaders was the agent by which the division was brought about, as when clans followed their chiefs in Scotland into Presbyterianism, and the anglicisation of the Irish Protestant Church buttressed it against pervasive Catholicism. . . .

To ask Protestants, or Anglo-Irish folk, to take up Gaelic studies is not to demand more of them than a due pious interest in their own antecedents. The complete boycott of Irish things, even on the

‡The word Shillelagh, so spelt from the influence of the place-name, may be the pure Gaelic *síleála*, 'trouble' (*cf.* Dineen's *Dictionary*), used in droll manner, as when we call a boxer's fist *Bás gan sagart*.

*Cf. A. J. Toynbee, *A Study of History* (1934), in which such examples are given as the purity of the French culture in Canada under alien sovereignty and of the Castilian preserved by Jews in the Near-East. Cf. Elizabethan English in Modern Ireland.

†Rev. Paul Grosjean, S.J. in *Scottish Gaelic Studies*, III, 1.

9. i.e. a patron saint's day.
10. Irish: 'Ireland for ever'.
11. Croagh Patrick, Co. Mayo, and St Patrick's Purgatory, Lough Derg, Co. Donegal.
12. de Blacam is presumably referring to the harper Turlough O'Carolan (1670–1738), the 'last of the Irish Bards', who learned his craft under the patronage of the old Gaelic Mac Dermott Roe family in north County Roscommon.

census paper, which Lord Craigavon's[13] Northern Government practises, is unhistorical as well as illiberal; perhaps, for this very reason, it will fail, since the call of the blood must assert itself in the Ulster Protestants some day. All penal action against Irish culture is a mark of the inner fear that it will conquer — one does not penalise Esperanto!

In all countries, truth in history is the greatest of healers. We who desire spiritual reunion must wish that the Anglo-Irish will cease to rest on the political *Anglo* and will give its due place to the historic *Irish*, or Gaelic, in their past. To do this will be for the community to follow the path of so many individuals, back to the position where the roads divided and beyond which there lies the happier unity, spiritual peace.

13. Lord Craigavon (1871–1940), unionist politician and first prime minister of Northern Ireland 1921–40.

Biographies/Bibliographies

John Eglinton

LIFE. John Eglinton, the pseudonym of William Kirkpatrick Magee, was born in Dublin in 1868. He became one of the foremost critics to emerge during the Literary Revival. He worked as assistant librarian in the National Library of Ireland until 1922. Influenced by German philosophy, American Transcendentalism and above all by William Wordsworth, he sought to broaden the horizons of the Revival beyond national boundaries. A school friend and later critical adversary of Yeats, he nevertheless enjoyed the distinction of having a selection of his writings made by the poet in 1905. His relationship with Joyce was more strained, which is hardly surprising in view of the fact that he turned down for publication an early version of *A Portrait of the Artist*. Still, Joyce admired his critical intelligence and, in the National Library episode in *Ulysses*, Eglinton is the one critic deemed worthy to challenge Stephen's interpretation of Shakespeare. In his critical writings, Eglinton questioned almost every premise of the Revival – the mythologizing of the past, the emphasis on the local rather than the universal, the subordination of the individual to national ideals. In *Dana*, a magazine of 'independent thought' which he edited with Frederick Ryan, he extended this critique to both the intellectual dogmatism of the catholic church, and the kind of insipid liberalism that is content to 'agree to differ'. Both foreclosed genuine intellectual debate. For Eglinton, criticism came from *within*, and played a vital role in regenerating intellectual movements. He did not consider his critical stance towards the Revival to be incompatible with his 'Irishness', but his opponents thought otherwise.

As national debates grew increasingly doctrinaire, he became a marginal figure, an intellectual exile even before he left Ireland in 1923. He died in Bournemouth in 1961.

CHIEF WRITINGS. *Two Essays on the Remnant* (Dublin: Whaley, 1894); *Literary Ideals in Ireland*, with W. B. Yeats, A. E. and W. Larminie (London: T. Fisher Unwin; Dublin: Daily Express Office, 1899. reprint, New York: Lemma Publishing Corporation, 1973); *Pebbles from a Brook* (Kilkenny and Dublin: Standish O'Grady, 1901); *Some Essays and Passages by John Eglinton*, selected by W. B. Yeats (Dublin: Dun Emer, 1905); *Bards and Saints* (Dublin: Tower Press Booklets, Maunsel, 1906); *Anglo-Irish Essays* (Dublin: The Talbot Press; London: T. Fisher Unwin, 1917); edited and translated G. Moore, *Letters to Edouard Dujardin* (New York: Crosby Gaige, 1929); *Irish Literary Portraits* (London: Macmillan, 1935. reprint, Freeport, New York: Books for Libraries, 1967); *A Memoir of A. E.* (London: Macmillan, 1937); ed. *Letters of George Moore, with an Introduction by John Eglinton, to Whom they were Written* (Bournemouth: Sydenham, [1942]); *Confidential; or, Take it or Leave It* (London: Fortune, 1951).

BIOGRAPHY AND CRITICISM. Ernest Boyd, 'An Irish Essayist: John Eglinton' in *Appreciations and Depreciations: Irish Literary Studies* (Dublin: The Talbot Press; London: T. Fisher Unwin, 1917); Ernest Boyd, *Ireland's Literary Renaissance* (Dublin: Maunsel & Co.; New York: John Lane Co., 1916); Daniel S. Lenoski, 'Yeats, Eglinton, and Aestheticism', *Éire-Ireland* Vol. XIV, No. 4 (Winter 1979), 91–108.

William Butler Yeats

For biography and bibliography, see p. 830.

Thomas Kettle

LIFE. Thomas Kettle was born in north County Dublin in 1880. He attended University College, Dublin, where he shared the reputation of being the leading intellectual figure in student circles with his close friend, James Joyce. President of the radical Young Ireland branch of the Home Rule affiliated United Irish League, he was MP for East Tyrone 1906–10. In 1909, he was appointed professor of national economics in the new National University in Dublin. Described as an 'international nationalist', Kettle was secretly buying arms in Belgium for the Irish Volunteers when war broke out in 1914. His experience of German atrocities led him to devote all his energies to a war effort that he considered necessary to defend Belgium. 'My only counsel to Ireland,' he wrote, 'is that in order to become deeply Irish, she must become European.' He gave evidence on behalf of Eóin Mac Neill at the latter's court martial following the Easter Rising of 1916. Kettle was killed at the battle of the Somme later that year.

CHIEF WRITINGS. Translated with introduction, L. Paul Dubois, *Contemporary Ireland* (Dublin: Maunsel & Co.; New York: The Baker and Taylor Co., 1908); *The Day's Burden: Studies, Literary and Political* (Dublin: Maunsel & Co.; New York: Charles Scribner's Sons, 1910. [reissued with additional essays, Dublin: Browne and Nolan, 1937]); Introduction to Daniel Halevy, *The Life of Friedrich Nietzsche* (London: T. Fisher Unwin; New York: The Macmillan Co., 1911); *Home Rule Finance. An Experiment in Justice* (Dublin: Maunsel & Co., 1911); *The Open Secret of Ireland* (London: W. J. Ham-Smith, 1912); *Poems and Parodies* (London: Duckworth & Son, 1913; New York: F. A. Stokes Co., 1914); Edited with introduction, *Irish Orators and Oratory* (London: T. F. Unwin; New York: Frederick A. Stokes Company [1916]); *The Ways of War*, with a memoir by Mary S. Kettle (Dublin: The Talbot Press; New York: Charles Scribner's Sons, 1917); *An Irishman's Calendar*, compiled by Mary S. Kettle (Dublin: Browne & Nolan, 1938).

BIOGRAPHY AND CRITICISM. Arthur Clery, 'Thomas Kettle', in *Dublin Essays* (Dublin: Maunsel & Co., 1919); Roger McHugh, 'Thomas Kettle and Francis Sheehy-Skeffington' in Conor Cruise O'Brien (ed.), *The Shaping of Modern Ireland* (London: Routledge & Kegan Paul, 1960); J. B. Lyons, *The Enigma of Tom Kettle* (Dublin: The Glendale Press, 1983).

Stopford A. Brooke

LIFE. Stopford Augustus Brooke was born near Letterkenny, Co. Donegal in 1832. Ordained in 1857, he was appointed a chaplain-in-ordinary to Queen Victoria in 1867. He seceded from Church of England in 1880, becoming a unitarian. A prolific writer, he published critical studies of Milton, Shakespeare, Tennyson and Browning, and his *Primer of English Literature* sold over half-a-million copies. He was active as a lecturer, organizer and writer in the early years of the Literary Revival. He died in 1916.

CHIEF WRITINGS. *English Literature* (London: Macmillan & Co., New York: D. Appleton & Co., 1876); *The Need and Use of Getting Irish Literature into the English Tongue: An Address* (London: T. Fisher Unwin, 1895); *Coercion, Concession and Home Rule* (London: National Press Agency, n.d.); ed. with T. W. Rolleston, *A Treasury of Irish Poetry in the English Tongue* (London: Smith Elder & Co.; New York: Macmillan & Co., 1900).

D. P. Moran

For biography and bibliography, see p. 561.

Frederick Ryan

LIFE. Frederick Ryan was one of the few truly independent voices of the Literary Revival. He was born in 1874. A socialist, and a strong believer in secularism and internationalism, he joined James Connolly's Irish Socialist Republican Party and later became national secretary of the Socialist Party of Ireland, founded in 1909. He was, with Tom Kettle and Thomas MacDonagh, a member of the dissident Young Ireland branch of the United Irish League, and was a prolific contributor to nationalist publications. He co-edited two magazines, *Dana* (with John Eglinton) in 1904, and *The National Democrat* (with Francis Sheehy-Skeffington) in 1907. His internationalism led him to take an active interest in Egyptian nationalism, and at the end of 1907 he took up a post in Cairo as editor of the *Egyptian Standard*. Ryan returned to Ireland in 1909, but spent the last two years of his life in London as editor of Wilfrid Scawen Blunt's paper, *Egypt*. He was a member of the Celtic Literary Society and acted as secretary of the Irish National Theatre Society before it became the Abbey Theatre in 1904. A play of his, a pioneering realist satire entitled *The Laying of the Foundations*, was produced in 1902. His only book, *Criticism and Courage*, was published in 1906 as part of the Tower Press series under the editorship of James Connolly and Seamus O'Sullivan. He died in London in 1913.

CHIEF WRITINGS. *Criticism and Courage* (Dublin: Tower Press Booklets, Maunsel, 1906); *The Laying of the Foundations* (Act II only) in Robert Hogan and James Kilroy (eds), *Lost Plays of the Irish Renaissance* (Newark, Delaware: Proscenium Press, 1970); Manus O'Riordan (ed.), *Socialism, Democracy and the Church* by Frederick Ryan (Dublin: Labour History Workshop, 1984); Manus O'Riordan (ed.), *Sinn Fein and Reaction* by Frederick Ryan (Dublin: Labour History Workshop, 1984).

BIOGRAPHY AND CRITICISM. Francis Sheehy-Skeffington, 'Frederick Ryan — the Saint of Irish Rationalism', *The Irish Review*, May 1913.

T. W. Rolleston

For biography and bibliography, see p. 782.

Arthur Clery

LIFE. Arthur Clery was one of the most original contributors to national debates in the early part of the century. He was born in 1879. He attended University College, Dublin, where he was a prominent figure in the Literary and Historical Society, which also included James Joyce and Tom Kettle among its membership. Clery was, along with Kettle, one of the few Irish reviewers of Joyce's first publication *Chamber Music* (1909). He wrote for D. P. Moran's *The Leader* under the pseudonym 'Chanel', and a collection of his articles was published in *The Idea of a Nation* (1907). He was appointed professor of law in the new National University, Dublin, in 1910, and in 1916 defended Eóin Mac Neill after the Easter Rising. His republican views seem to have militated against his being raised to the bench after the founding of the state, and in 1927 he refused to take the oath of allegiance on being elected to the Dáil. A novel, *The Coming of the King*, appeared in 1909 and, in 1919, he published his *Dublin Essays*, a collection of articles on subjects as diverse as the suffrage movement, Irish dialect, rugby football, and Irish culture and society. He died in 1932.

CHIEF WRITINGS. 'Chanel', *The Idea of a Nation* (Dublin: James Duffy & Co., 1907); 'Arthur Synon', *The Coming of the King* (Dublin: The Iona Series, Catholic Truth Society of Ireland, 1909); *Dublin Essays* (Dublin: Maunsel & Co., 1919).

BIOGRAPHY AND CRITICISM. William Dawson, 'Arthur Clery, 1979–1932', *Studies*, Vol. XXII, No. 85 (March 1933).

Eóin Mac Neill

For biography and bibliography, see p. 368.

Aodh de Blacam

LIFE. Aodh de Blacam was born in London in 1890, of Ulster parentage, and was a convert to catholicism. He attended the Gaelic League in London, and moved to Ireland in 1915 to work as a journalist with *The Enniscorthy Echo*. His activities as a publicist for Sinn Féin led to his imprisonment during the War of Independence. A prolific writer, he published political propaganda, scholarly and critical studies, historical biographies, travel books, devotional works, novels, drama, poetry, children's stories and translations from Irish, Latin and Spanish. Under the pseudonym 'Roddy the Rover' he contributed a daily column to *The Irish Press* for nearly twenty years, as well as a provocative monthly column to the catholic periodical *The Irish Monthly*. A socialist during the War of Independence, albeit with a strong spiritual leavening, his religious fervour gradually moved him in the opposite direction so that by the late 1930s he was one of the most vocal propagandists for Franco's Spain. His republican sympathies surfaced again towards the end of his life when he pursued a short unsuccessful career in politics as a Clann na Poblachta candidate and subsequently worked for the Department of Health under Dr Noel Browne. He died in 1951.

CHIEF WRITINGS. *Towards the Republic: A Study of New Ireland's Social and Political Aims* (Dublin: T. Kiersey, 1918); *The Ship that Sailed Too Soon, and other stories* (Dublin: Maunsel & Co., 1919); *The Druid's Cave: A tale of mystery and adventure for young people of seven to seventy* (Dublin: Whelan & Sons, 1920); *What Sinn Fein Stands For* (Dublin: Mellifont Press; London: Chapman & Todd, 1921); *From a Gaelic Outpost* (Dublin: Catholic Truth Society of Ireland, 1921); *Gaelic Literature Surveyed* (Dublin and Cork: The Talbot Press, 1929). [Reissued, with additional chapter by Eoghan Ó hAnluain, Dublin:

The Talbot Press, 1973]; *A First Book of Irish Literature* (Dublin: The Talbot Press, 1934). Port Washington, New York: reprint, London: Kennikat Press, 1970; *A Life Story of Wolfe Tone* (Dublin: The Talbot Press; London: Rich & Cowan, 1935); *The Black North*, with foreword by Eamon de Valera (Dublin: M. H. Gill & Son Ltd., 1938); *St. Patrick, Apostle of Ireland* (Milwaukee: The Bruce Publishing Co., 1941).

James Connolly

For biography and bibliography, see p. 810.

Thomas MacDonagh

For biography and bibliography, see p. 780.

Arthur Griffith

For biography and bibliography, see p. 370.

Daniel Corkery

For biography and bibliography, see Volume III, p. 127.

AUGUSTINE MARTIN, *Editor*

Prose Fiction 1880–1945

William Butler Yeats was fifteen when our period begins but his spirit and influence haunt the age. The two tales that represent him here are not short stories in the modern sense, but one of them, 'The Adoration of the Magi,' reminded the young James Joyce of the great Russian masters and impressed him so much that he had his artist-protagonist in *Stephen Hero* learn it and 'The Tables of the Law' by heart. Yeats's collection of tales, *The Secret Rose* (1897), has as its basic theme 'the war of spiritual with natural order'. Beginning in pagan Ireland, the volume spans 'twenty centuries of stony sleep', leading to a modern apocalypse. His publisher, Bullen, disliked the two last stories, 'The Tables of the Law' and 'The Adoration of the Magi', and excluded them from the volume, but later had them published together in pamphlet form. The stories are permeated with the aestheticism of the decade, the ornate Paterian style, the Wildean extravagance, the sense of the artist as priest and victim. They also usher in the Irish Literary Revival: with three traditional Kerry story-tellers as latter-day Magi, the new dispensation is foreseen as an emphatically Irish affair. In the historical scheme that Yeats excogitated throughout his life, the 'didactic middle ages' were inimical to the artistic impulse — hence the fate of the outcast gleeman. In the same system, the modern era, with Michael Robartes as its prophet and mage, would see the return of the savage god, the unicorn of the second story's climax.

Emily Lawless's *Hurrish* (1886), on the other hand, belongs more to the previous age, being one of the last 'regional' novels of the nineteenth century. The chief characteristic of regionalist fiction is its desire to explain local conditions — whether exotic, quaint or wretched — to a distant audience. Though often weakened by extra-literary anxieties — most commonly a plea for understanding — it has an honourable tradition, stretching back through Carleton and Griffin to Maria Edgeworth. It tends to peter out in the R. M. stories of Somerville and Ross and such works as Jane Barlow's *Irish Idylls* (1892) towards the century's end. The fiction of George Moore, Gerald O'Donovan, and Seumas O'Kelly shares with the regional mode an equal, perhaps even a greater, determination to get the facts of landscape and character right; but with them there is no special pleading and little sense of a foreign audience. The sense of an indigenous readership and criticism adumbrated by the policies of *The Nation* (1842) had become a reality with the centripetal energies of the Literary Revival in the last years of the century.

Hurrish differs from its author's first novel, *Grania* (1892) — a highly charged romantic drama set on the Aran Islands — in that it enters seriously upon the anarchic politics of Ireland during a crucial period of contemporary history, the Land War. Gladstone, who declared the book essential reading for anyone who wanted to understand Ireland, came to power for the second time in 1880 and initiated the series of enlightened Land Acts that brought final peace to the Irish agrarian scene in the Wyndham Act of 1903. Every conceivable shade of political opinion is represented in the novel, from the fanatical republicanism of Old Brigid, through the sly 'enlightened patriotism' of Maurice Brady, to the misunderstood idealism of the 'improving landlord', Mr Pierce

O'Brien of Donore. These representative concerns show the novel's continuity with the peasant fictions of John Banim and William Carleton, while the rough-hewn characterization, the violence and the simple contrast between good and evil — all present in the extract below — partake of a Victorian melodrama found equally in Boucicault and Dickens.

The Real Charlotte (1894) with its 'Big House' setting is also a novel with an ancestry, reaching back in its case through George Moore's *Muslin* and Lever's *Charles O'Malley* to Maria Edgeworth's *Ormond*. But the universal quality of its touch, especially in handling the classic theme of class and character, the sense of unredeemed wickedness in its eponymous heroine, and the subliminal aura of decay that is exuded from these county manor-houses, transcend region and history alike. It is strange that the novel's modernity and strong moral realism should admit such a contemptuous tone towards the 'natives', who in the R. M. narratives are merely picturesque; here they are represented in a few corrosive vignettes as beneath moral consideration. *The Real Charlotte* is perhaps most significant in being the last unselfconscious novel of this 'Big House' tradition. As the new century progressed, these houses increasingly came under threat from within and without. Their fate furnishes Yeats with one of his most plangent poetic themes. The vengeful flames that light up the closing pages of Seán O'Faoláin's 'Midsummer Night Madness' and Elizabeth Bowen's *The Last September* are violent witness to their glory and their doom.

It is often stated that Irish political and intellectual life went into recession after the death of Parnell and stayed there until the century's end, if not indeed until 1916. Joyce's *Dubliners* and much of Yeats's *Responsibilities* — those companions of the greasy till — seem to support that view. Yet the Gaelic League, Sinn Féin, Horace Plunkett's Co-operative Movement and Yeats's own national theatre characterize it as a time of energetic transition. Even that most reactionary of bodies, the Roman catholic church in Ireland, was not immune, as can be seen in George Moore's short stories, and more dramatically in the contrast between the fiction of Canon Sheehan and Gerald O'Donovan. In *My New Curate* Sheehan presents his diocesan priests as secure in the certitude of a dogmatic world established by the first Vatican Council (1870) where papal infallibility had been proclaimed, though against the wish and vote of Archbishop MacHale of Tuam. The genial arguments that enliven their conversation are conducted within the secure boundaries laid down by a church constituted as a citadel against the modern age. The 'radicalism' of the new curate, Father Letheby, goes no further than the co-operative programmes of Horace Plunkett. Father Ralph in Gerald O'Donovan's novel is engaged in the same co-operative activities among his flock, but under the eye of less sympathetic superiors. It is 1907 and the pope had produced his encyclical on modernism, giving the forces of reaction a convenient weapon with which to move against suspected liberals within the clergy. O'Donovan's novel dramatizes the conflict that arises when a priest is ordered to submit formally to the decree (Lamentabili) that preceded the encyclical. The author, in real life Jeremiah O'Donovan, left the priesthood rather than submit. The lives of other liberal priests, such as the two Maynooth professors, Walter McDonald and Michael O'Hickey, immortalized in O'Casey's *Drums Under the Windows* (1945), were made miserable by this conflict, which in the long run gave the Irish church one of the most conservative theologies in Christendom.

It is another aspect of this theology that the saintly Father MacTurnan confronts in Moore's 'A Letter to Rome'. This earnest little priest occupies the epicentre of Moore's despairing rural cosmos in his short story collection *The Untilled Field* (1903). In its two companion stories, 'The Playhouse in the Waste' and the much anthologized 'Julie Cahill's Curse', Moore's narrator, a pragmatical agent of the co-operative movement engaged in promoting cottage industries throughout the 'congested districts' of the west, encounters poverty, apathy and clerical obscurantism of the kind that defeated Father Ralph. The hopelessness of rural Ireland has seldom been so vividly portrayed as in the priest's arguments with the engineer or the description of the peasant's hovel in the middle of the bog. The pastor's quixotic plan to save the people from protestantism, and the optimism of his faith, throw the wretchedness of his situation into even sharper relief, while demonstrating the short story's potential for social commentary and spiritual insight.

Frank O'Connor has assured us that with Moore's *The Untilled Field* 'the Irish short story became a fact'. How it came about is a curiosity of cultural history. When Moore returned to Ireland in 1899, he was asked by his friends to write some stories that might be translated into Irish so as to provide models for young writers in the language revival movement. The stories, undertaken playfully in the first instance, appeared in *The Irish Monthly* with parallel texts in Irish. Moore had as his model *The Sportsman's Sketch-Book*, whose author, Ivan Turgenev, also an expatriate landlord, he had known in his Paris years. As he proceeded, Moore saw the possibility of making the stories into 'a portrait of my people'. In its first form the book had framing stories at the beginning and the end with the sculptor, John Rodney — prototype for Joyce's Stephen Dedalus — deploring the condition of Ireland in the aesthetic idiom of the time. But Moore removed these from the second edition probably because they obscured the serious sense of engagement with his material that marks the greater stories in the volume. These stories, of which 'A Letter to Rome' is a good example, embody the qualities that are to dominate the subsequent tradition: the colloquial language, deriving in part from the art of the oral story-teller; the intimate concern with social realities; the organic form, indifferent to surprise and suspense, the more routine exigencies of plot.

Consciousness of the short story as a modern art form came gradually. The sketch, the idyll, the tale and the anecdote are to be found in abundance through the nineteenth century and survive here and there even today. When George Birmingham set about assembling a volume of Irish short stories in 1932 he agonized a little over definitions. Having ruled out Jane Barlow's 'idylls', he came to Joyce's *Dubliners*: 'Are they stories or not? I decided, perhaps wrongly, that some of them are and some of them are not. I have picked out one that is.' His choice is 'A Painful Case' which, with its tragic action and ironic denouement, satisfies the most atavistic need for narrative suspense. His own story, 'The Deputation', an amiable cliffhanger of small-town intrigue, local colour and country humours, looks backward towards the idyll and the anecdote. Shan Bullock's 'A State Official', on the other hand, though it was written before 1893, has much of the psychological concentration and social analysis — not to say prophecy — that we admire in the short fiction of Moore and Seán O'Faoláin. The fate of Dan the postmaster is a stark foreshadowing of the plight of civilized tolerance in present-day Ulster.

Perhaps even more than the novel, the short story reflected the dialogue between the writer and his evolving society. Its narrow focus permitted intensities of concentration unsustainable in the longer form. With Joyce it quietly dramatized the half-apprehended unhappiness of Dublin citizens trying to keep the best side out towards companions equally lonely, venal and unfulfiled. James Stephens, whose imagination tended to seek the extremes — either of realism or fantasy — dramatizes in 'Hunger' the quiet desperation of an innocent Dublin family facing the sort of social conditions that brought on the Great Lockout of 1913. Stephens was in Paris when that event convulsed Dublin and he wrote a fierce anti-clerical letter to James Connolly's *Irish Worker* in support of the strikers. In 'Hunger', the artistic distillation of that anger, his sympathies find expression in a work of universal resonance.

Seumas O'Kelly, whose first collection of idyllic sketches, *By the Stream of Kilmeen* (1906), had provoked the scorn of Joyce in his Roman exile — 'beautiful, pure faithful Connacht girls and lithe, broad-shouldered, young Connacht men' — matured to write the stories in *Waysiders* (1917) and his greatest story, 'The Weaver's Grave' (1919), which is too long to include here. 'The Building', however, dramatizes the condition of the peasant in terms as archetypal and disturbing as James Stephens's depiction of the urban worker. In a bleak epiphany that foreshadows 'the clayey hours' of Patrick Kavanagh's *The Great Hunger*, one can see the pull of the soil dragging down the artistic impulse with an almost sinister predetermination. Although O'Kelly was a nationalist — he died at the desk of his newspaper, *Nationality*, as a result of a raid on its offices in 1918 — there is no evidence of it in his fiction, which concentrates on rural themes, especially the Irish obsession with land, its pieties and importunities.

Daniel Corkery, whose name was to epitomize cultural nationalism, began in his short-story collection of 1916, *A Munster Twilight*, with similar explorations of rural experience. He was, however, the first to respond to the armed struggle in fictional terms, and his collection, *The Hounds of Banba* (1920), set the tone for his Cork disciples, Frank O'Connor and Seán O'Faoláin, as well as the Aran-born Liam O'Flaherty. 'On the Heights' is the epitome of Corkery's theme, style, and technique. An underlying topos of *A Munster Twilight* had been 'the Holy Land of Ireland', sanctified by the immemorial tread of saints and scholars. The young Irish-speaking guerillas with trench-coat and bicycle are seen romantically reaching across the generations to old men who had carried the torch in previous generations. For Corkery, who had never seen action, the Easter Rising had a sacramental efficacy: it had redeemed the land on which St Finbarr had walked. These stories are written out of the heat of that conviction and they carry all its naive ardour. They undoubtedly reflect a widely felt emotion of the time. The compunction of O'Connor, the disillusion of O'Faoláin and the bitter witness of O'Flaherty are yet to come.

The elation of Corkery's young guerilla on the heights finds a dismal antiphon in the climb of O'Flaherty's battle-weary gunmen to their tavern in the mountains. In the horror and disappointment of the Civil War there is no comfort for these unlovely pilgrims in the possibility that saints may have trodden there before them. The savage malediction of the tavern-keeper's wife constitutes an ironic threnody on the 'terrible beauty' that had so infatuated Corkery. O'Flaherty has dealt finely with the violence out of which modern Ireland was born in novels like *The Informer*, *The Assassin* and *Insurrection*, but never more memorably than in those short stories like 'The Sniper' and 'Civil War', where a moment of vivid action is made to symbolize in personal terms the implications of the larger conflict.

Like O'Flaherty, the 'Cork realists', O'Connor and O'Faoláin, took part in the armed struggle and like him they lived to look back on it all with mixed emotions. Their first collections, *Guests of the Nation* (1931) and *Midsummer Night Madness* (1932) may well have been tainted a little by the complexion of the new state after a decade of native rule. In political terms O'Connor's great title story is the more prophetic while O'Faoláin's bears the more vivid witness to the social scene. In 'Guests of the Nation' the psychological interplay between the reluctant rebels, Noble and Bonaparte, the professional soldiers, Hawkins and Belcher, and the dogged vengefulness of Jeremiah Donovan adds up to a grievous indictment of war. Its political background is a still unsettled country where remnants of the IRA are trying to destabilize the new state. When the anti-Treaty party, Fianna Fáil under Eamon de Valera, comes to power in 1932, the diehard 'republican' prisoners are released, but the issue of partition is gaining cumulative force. The retributive politics of O'Connor's fable are eventually to become the legacy of modern Ireland.

In O'Faoláin's Stevey, the patriot gone to seed, we have a sinister proleptic image of a new breed of Irish politician; his idealism is shrunken into class hatred and vengefulness; his sexual puritanism finds its ground in drunken hypocrisy; and the portrait is chillingly authentic. The nationalists have, of course, a decent representative in the narrator, who tries to hold the ring between old Henn and Stevey, unlovely versions of the old order and the new. In this tableau one might without too much straining of the parallels see the author himself as editor of *The Bell*, fighting the race of philistines, censors, bigots and obscurantists a decade on into the century. Such forces in fact were getting a stranglehold on the nation's consciousness as the story was being written, most notably in the Censorship of Publications Act of 1926, to which O'Faoláin himself was soon to fall victim.

In the hands of Mary Lavin and Francis MacManus the short story relinquished satire and prophecy — as it did for the majority of O'Connor's, O'Faoláin's and O'Flaherty's work — for the quiet depiction of personal experience amid the rhythms of middle-class life in a settled Ireland. Both writers were too young to suffer the traumata of armed uprising or guerilla war. MacManus is better known for his novels of Kilkenny life, most notably *Watergate*, *This House Was Mine* and *The Greatest of These*, the last being a version of the 'catholic novel' whose contemporary exponents were Greene, Waugh, Mauriac and Bernanos abroad, Kate O'Brien and O'Faoláin in Ireland. 'Old Clothes, Old Glory', from his one short-story collection, *Pedlar's Pack*, yields an exquisite cameo of an Ireland not often represented in literature.

Mary Lavin's two novels, *The House in Clewe Street* (1945) and *Mary O'Grady* (1950), one about provincial, the other about urban, experience, share with MacManus a steady contemplation of Irish mores; but her work in the short story over four decades is of a higher order. Sitting apart from the public debates that flickered across the screen of the nation's life — de Valera's new Constitution, the Economic War, the Blueshirts, neutrality, censorship — she has fashioned perhaps the most complete fictional tapestry of middle Ireland about its daily business. Her mastery of the organic form — her exemplars are Chekhov, Joyce, Katherine Mansfield — enables her to record with unhurried vividness the tensions of family life on the big farm and in the small town, the drama of love and money, the attrition of time in human relationships, the heart as a lonely hunter. 'In the Middle of the Fields', the title story of her 1967 collection, is a superb example of her art and craft.

Although the novel in English is traditionally a secular art form, religious experience is seldom long absent from its Irish manifestation. The religious scruples of adolescence and the final crisis of belief explored by Joyce in *A Portrait* are echoed in low-key protestant resonances by Forrest Reid in *Peter Waring*. His best novel, it combines the social realism of his first, *The Kingdom of Twilight* (1904), and the childhood fantasy of *Young Tom* (1944), the last volume of his Tom Barber trilogy begun in the early 1930s. The more adult implications of religious faith raised in *Father Ralph* are developed by Kate O'Brien in a succession of novels of Irish upper middle-class experience, of which *The Land of Spices*, *Mary Lavelle*, *As Music and Splendour* and *The Ante-Room* are the most memorable. Always working with characters who are both intelligent and educated, Kate O'Brien is at her best in the drama of moral choice. Though death is busy in the fiction of these sixty years, it is Kate O'Brien alone, in *The Ante-Room*, who gives us an Irish hero who dies for love.

Religion takes on different connotations with the savage realism of Patrick MacGill in his northern wastes and Brinsley MacNamara in his claustrophic midlands. MacGill, a literary freebooter owing little to any school or movement, turned his experiences as migrant potato-picker, navvy and soldier into angry and committed narratives of social protest. His unromantic account of a boating disaster in *The Rat-Pit* contrasts sharply with Peadar O'Donnell's dashing description of a hazardous sea-crossing in the extract from *Islanders*. Whether MacGill was influenced by Zola's naturalism — as has been claimed — or whether his fierce sense of social injustice responded to the intolerable social conditions that he experienced at first hand, he is the one writer who has depicted in Ireland and Scotland a human milieu bearing every mark of what we have come to call the 'third world'. But the primitive faith that sustains his starving pilgrims allows few luxuries of moral choice.

It is sometimes innocently assumed that the power of the clergy and the catholic middle classes had to wait on the establishment of the Free State to come into its own. MacNamara's first and most notorious novel, *The Valley of the Squinting Windows* (1918), published between the Easter Rising and the Civil War, anatomizes a self-righteous rural community dominated by the most malignant alliance of faith and fatherland, Christ and Caesar. Very much a young man's book, its moral anger issues often in rude caricature and intrusive polemic. The absence in the novel of a decent human being, apart from the victimized heroine and the local schoolmaster, based on the author's father, diminishes its impact. Slung on the boundary between social realism and satiric fantasy, it misses that element of aesthetic distance that might have converted its heat to light. The subsequent persecution of the writer and his father, who was driven from his school on foot of its publication, soured his creative life while impelling him towards some interesting experiments in prose fiction. In *The Clanking of Chains* (1920) he pursues his unrepentant satire on Irish village life — so often idealized by writers like Lady Gregory and Seumas O'Kelly — this time courageously taking the cult of nationalism as his prime target. Arguably his finest work is *The Various Lives of Marcus Igoe* (1929), a reflexive fiction dealing with the multiple personae of the hero's character, and the relation between personality in life and fiction. In exploring the frontiers of realism and fantasy, the book belongs in that tradition of experimental fiction that includes James Stephens, Eimar O'Duffy, Austin Clarke and Flann O'Brien in the first four decades of the century.

The affinities between James Stephens and Eimar O'Duffy are remarkable. Each wrote a book on the Easter Rising: Stephens's vivid factual description of the street fighting in *The Insurrection in Dublin* (1916) compares vividly with O'Duffy's fictional account of the same event in his great sprawling novel of the period, *The Wasted Island*. Both were socialists, and both embodied a subversive social vision in those curious novels where fact and fantasy are so boldly intermingled. O'Duffy, the younger of the two, followed Stephens in debunking the Celtic heroes: Stephens had reincarnated Cú Chulainn for comic effect in his fantasy, *The Demi-Gods* (1914). Austin Clarke chose, instead of the heroic age, the monastic world of medieval Ireland as the site of his three historical novels, *The Bright Temptation*, *The Singing Men at Cashel* and *The Sun Dances at Easter*. By the introduction of invented and mythic personages — the Prumpolaun, Sile na gCich — and nightmare landscapes — Glen Bolcan — and enacting a shrewd parallel between medieval and modern Ireland, Clarke achieves a social satire similar to that of Stephens and O'Duffy.

So many novels of the Anglo-Irish protestant tradition end with country mansions being put to the torch that one might easily conclude that it was a universal historical fact rather than a respected literary convention. Since it had an obvious symbolism and a basis in contemporary fact, it was, for a writer with a sense of form, an excellent way to end a novel. In fact the two most celebrated Big Houses in Ireland, Lady Gregory's Coole Park and Elizabeth Bowen's family home, Bowen's Court — she has written a brilliant history of it under that title — were peacefully demolished because of economic necessity. And the novel of the Big House was to revive dramatically in the decades that followed in the work of William Trevor, Jennifer Johnston, Andrew Ganley, Molly Keane, Aidan Higgins and John Banville. Yet that tradition, looking out in arrogant decline through the windows of Somerville and Ross, alive with energy and innocence in Joyce Cary's *A House of Children* and in tragi-comic collapse with O'Faoláin's 'Midsummer Night Madness' has hardly produced a work equal to Elizabeth Bowen's *The Last September*. The unreal conversations of the old people on the terrace while army lorries patrol the roads; the doomed romance of the young heroine with an officer of the garrison and her sense of obsolescence in such moments as when the gunman walks past her in the darkness; the book's autumnal blend of nostalgia and imminence, the ease of its style and the symmetry of its structure recommend it as perhaps the most perfect novel in this stubborn and brilliant tradition.

The prose fiction of the period from 1880 to 1945 begins in the agrarian conflicts of the Land War and ends with the last phase of that struggle, the Economic War (1932–38) when de Valera refused to pay the land annuities to the British government and was punished by serious trade tariffs on Irish goods entering Britain. In the nature of things, the literature reflecting these economic stringencies did not surface until the following decades – as for instance in such a novel as Mervyn Wall's *Leaves for the Burning* or Flann O'Brien's *An Béal Bocht* (*The Poor Mouth*). The period saw the most decisive rise of nationalism in Irish history; the founding of the Volunteers, its infiltration by the militant IRB, the 1916 Rising, the War of Independence and the founding of the Free State. It saw the organizing of Labour under James Connolly and Jim Larkin, the great Strike/Lockout of 1913 and the emergence of a Labour Party that became the chief opposition in the Dáil up to 1927, when Fianna Fáil under de Valera gave up its policy of abstention and took its place in parliament. From that point on, the parliamentary division was between the policies of Cosgrave's Cumann na nGaedheal which tended to adapt to Irish purposes the institutions of the colonial power, and those of de Valera's Fianna Fáil which sought to emphasize everything indigenous and distinctive in culture and polity: Irish as the first official language, the rhetoric and mythology of republicanism, the promotion of Irish games, dances, rituals, the ideal of a simple pastoral lifestyle. In short, the country was divided between two middle-class ideologies. The extreme republicans, the gentry and the socialists became variously marginalized. A powerful constant in all of this activity and apparent change was the catholic church, which had effective control of education from the British regime and whose conservative social doctrines tended to dominate legislation.

As is evident from the literature presented in this section, the writers responded consistently to these drifts and developments, having established their own organs of response, most notably the Abbey Theatre, founded in 1904, and a succession of journals such as Griffith's *United Irishman* (1899), Russell's *The Irish Homestead* (1895) and *Irish Statesman* (1923), D. P. Moran's *The Leader* (1900), Colum's *Irish Review* (1912), Seumus O'Sullivan's *The Dublin Magazine* (1923) and down to Seán O'Faoláin's *The Bell* (1940). The most consistent focus of attention and of satire was, predictably, the catholic clergy. With the triumphalist developments exemplified in *Father Ralph*, it became almost inevitable that the writer's insistence on intellectual freedom would find the Irish religious atmosphere inimical to the artistic enterprise. The running battle between writer and priest is in fact one of the distressing and enlivening patterns of the entire period.

A good deal of the criticism levelled at the clergy

was justified, for, despite outstanding individuals like Finlay, McDonald, Russell and O'Hickey, the church tended to be as authoritarian, obscurantist and socially conservative as the people and politicians allowed it to be. Many of the great radical individuals died in the Troubles and the reactionary aspirations of the majority were well served by a church that seemed content not only to secure their hegemony but to take the criticism for it as well. In a society inchoate and unsettled, the church provided one constant and recognizable focus for the artist's discontent and was the only institution solid enough to take the full charge of his satire. The resultant anti-clericalism is quite unlike its continental counterparts in seldom being associated with atheism, often with sincere religious practice. It tended to evaporate when the second Vatican Council of 1962–63 reversed so many oppressive tendencies of the first. As our period ends, the Irish Literary Revival expires with the death of Yeats in 1939, but the revolution in prose fiction begun by Moore and Joyce at the turn of the century finds new exponents with Beckett and Flann O'Brien two years before Joyce's death in 1941. For the Irish prose writer — as much as for the dramatist — it had been a period of strenuous experiment, of varied and consistent achievement.

EMILY LAWLESS

(1845–1913)

from: HURRISH (1886)

[Set in the violent period of the Land War (1879–91), the novel centres upon the tragedy of Hurrish O'Brien, an honest tenant farmer working out a frugal existence in the Burren country of County Clare. A widower, he lives with his mother, Bridget, a fierce old woman of fanatical Fenian sympathies, his three small children and a sensitive young niece by marriage called Alley. In the rough-hewn, melodramatic plot, Hurrish is afflicted with the murderous enmity of his distant cousin, Mat Brady, a creature of simian repulsiveness. Hurrish is friendly with Mat's ambitious brother, Maurice, whom he hopes may marry Alley some day. He even promises Maurice that he will not injure Mat whatever the provocation. The land is so unsettled that every violent action is likely to be read in a dozen different ways. The chapter below narrates the circumstances in which the innocent hero commits an action that is to set him on a path of disaster, ultimately leading to his death.]

CHAPTER X

HURRISH'S CRIME

It was the day of the half-yearly fair at Ballyvaughan,[1] the metropolis, in some sort, of the Burren. Like a good many other metropolises, it is not particularly conveniently situated as regards that area of which it is the nucleus. Lying upon the sea-shore to the extreme north of the region, it suggests, and is, a fishing much more than an agricultural centre. The straggling single street sloping directly down to the harbour consists of some three or perhaps four dozen whitewashed structures, the more important ones slated, the rest thatched and overtopped in summer with a gorgeous nodding crown of wild flowers —

1. Ballyvaughan and other place-names refer to actual locations in County Clare, and the topography, flora and fauna of the Burren are rendered with vivid fidelity to the facts.

sedums,[2] poppies, snap-dragons — town-gardens of a distinctively Irish pattern!

Hurrish had some calves to dispose of, and had brought them overnight to Ballyvaughan, their chance of a good sale being naturally better if not previously overtired. Feeling uneasy towards evening as to what might be taking place at home, with Mat Brady so close at hand and himself away, he left the calves in charge of Lep[3] and a herdsman, and walked all the way back to his cabin, arriving there about midnight, and starting again by cock-crow next morning.

Early as it was, every one was astir to give him his stirabout,[4] and see him off. Little Katty came toddling across the floor from the other room, half-naked, and rosy with sleep, and seized him by the flap of his coat, as he sat upon a low stool hastily devouring that satisfying form of nourishment.

'Dada, bring Katty sugey-shtick,' she whispered, rubbing her little rough head like some small tame animal against his sleeve, and looking up in his face with an insinuating grin.

It was an appeal which Hurrish, even at his busiest, could never resist. He picked Miss Katty up on his knee, and gave her a mouthful of the stirabout, by way perhaps of an instalment.

'Sugey-shtick indade! git out wid ye, yer imperint Kitteen,' he said, admiringly. 'D'ye think yer dada has nought to do but be goin' round the town gettin' you sugar-shticks! Be aff this instant minute.' He set her down and got up himself, taking his blackthorn from where it was lounging at ease against a corner of the wall as he passed.

Katty, however, was not to be daunted. With a crow of delight, she trotted after him to the door, where she again repeated her demand, laying hold of the formidable blackthorn as she did so to enforce it.

'Alley, Alley Sheehan! Och, Alley, cum quick! I'm held! I'm cotched![5] sure I won't be able to get away to Ballyvaughan this day! Kitteen's houldin' ov me! Och, wirrastrue[6] wirrastrue, what will I do at all, at all?' he exclaimed, pretending to shake the stick violently, while the child capered and shrieked with delight at the other end of it.

Alley ran to the rescue, and picked up Katty, still capering and shouting, in her arms. Hurrish, however, delayed yet a minute longer to kiss the little red and brown face thus brought nearer to a level with his own.

'Maybe I'll be seein' Morry[7] over beyant,' he whispered, with a glance towards his mother, who was still by the fire. 'Have ye ere a bit ov message for him, Alley 'cushla!'[8]

Alley did not immediately answer. She twisted the stocking she had been knitting around the needles, so as to keep their points from Miss Katty's wriggling pink legs, and looked down.

'I dun know as I have, Hurrish, an' I dun know as he'd care 'bout wan aither,' she said, not coquettishly, but seriously.

Hurrish looked disturbed.

'Blur an' agers,[9] Alley, don't be sayin' sich things!' he said, in a tone of eager remonstrance. 'Sure the pore bhoy luvs ye as he luvs his own sowl! he luvs yer very shadow on the rocks, as any wan wid half an oye can see. Yer thinkin' he's a bit heady these toimes — that's what's in yer moind. But after all what wonder? — so much, as he's thought ov — ivery wan in the whole counthry rinning afther him, an' consultin' wid him! — Sure if he wasn't a troifle 'bove hisself 't wud be *onnatural*. But he has the good heart Morry has, an' that's at the bottom ov all. He's not loike one ov thim bodaghs,[10] so set up whin they're a bit 'bove themselves that there is no holdin' thim — loike an ass-cart that takes itself for a coach-and-four — so proud, the spalpeens,[11] they wudn't shtop and spake to the mother that bore thim! Morry's not that sort, divil a bit. He has the good heart, an' that's iverything in this mortial world!'

Alley sighed. Hurrish must know best, she thought, but still —

'The fact is, yer too young an' ignarant, Alley, to ondershtand the granjeur there is in Morry, an' that's the truth,' Hurrish went on, in a tone of superiority. 'There is not the aqual of him in Clare —

2. rock plants.
3. Short for Leprecaun, Hurrish's dog.
4. porridge.
5. caught.
6. An exclamation of distress, from the Irish 'a Mhuire is trua' (O Mary 'tis pity).
7. Short for 'Maurice' (Brady). beyant = beyond.
8. 'a cushla' (my love) from the Irish *a cuisle*, literally 'my pulse'.
9. Probably a Hiberno-English corruption of *plúr an gharra* - 'flower of the garden', a conventional endearment for a pretty girl.
10. Plural of Irish *bodach* (churl).
11. hired labourers, from the Irish *spailpín*.

not in twinty counties round, so there isn't. He'll be a gran' man yet, as I've telled ye offen, you wait an' see if he isn't — top an' king of thim all! An' 'tis yourself'll be gran' thin too! Trath, 't 'ill be a wonder if ye spake to any ov us 't all!'

Alley smiled a little, but rather sadly. 'I don't want to be gran', she said, almost tearfully.

'Och, Alley asthore,[12] what's cum t'ye 't all? Most of the colleens does be allays changin' and choppin' their moinds, I know, loike the sky, that's blue wan minute an' rid the nixt, but I thought you were better than to go on wid sich wark. Don't ye know 'tis wicked to be choppin' an changin' yer moind wid a man? Is it breakin' his heart ye want wid sich talk?'

Alley made no reply. She looked up at Hurrish earnestly for a minute, as if about to speak. Then, with a sudden blush, she turned away, and appeared to be absorbed in arranging Miss Katty's disarranged garment — a somewhat complicated task, one of that young lady's fat legs having just succeeded in getting through a considerable aperture in her little red flannel petticoat.

Satisfied that his exhortation had had its due effect, Hurrish pursued his way, turning up Gortnacoppin, alongside of its milky torrent, fed by the violent rain of the day before. It was a lovely morning. The sun was still low, and the rocks which overhung the path flung heavy violet shadows before his feet. Everything seemed to be either violet or blue, — a sort of spiritualised blue, such as these desolate limestone regions sometimes show in clear weather. The wet places, where a slow ooze crept over the rocks, showed a faintly bluish iridescence, the blue-grey sheets of rock, the grey-blue sweeps of sky, the blue-grey sweeps of Atlantic — it was all steeped in light, penetrated with light, pathetic, solitary, ethereal — a spiritualised world, fitted, one would say, for anchorites and pious souls 'enskyed and sainted,'[13] whose traffic is less with this warm substantial earth of ours than with the unfamiliar heavens.

Hurrish, his thoughts filled chiefly now with his calves, tramped on, his shadow flinging itself in exaggerated bigness upon the weather-worn surfaces, his iron-studded shoes awaking sharp echoes upon the level rocks. Trailing branches of pale pink spiny rose dangled out of the crevices overhead; masses of blood-red crane's-bill dotted the pale grey sheets of limestone, and the dwarfed bushes of hawthorn which rise out of the stony dykes were white with blossom.

He had reached the amphitheatre where the oratories[14] stood, and where the stream disappears with a great rushing, bubbling noise into the bowels of the earth, when his eye was caught by a large object, conspicuously white amongst the surrounding greyness, lying close to a reddish granite boulder, raised, as many of these iceberg-dropped 'foreign' boulders[15] are, upon a foot or stalk of limestone, which, protected by its cover, has remained intact, while the rock surrounding it has been gradually worn away.

Striding up to the spot, he discovered that the white object was no other than a sheep, — one of his *own* sheep, stark, stiff, and dead, a hideous gash across its innocent white throat telling but too plainly how it had come by its end.

Hurrish loved his beasts, not merely for their money value, but with that natural liking of a warm-hearted man for anything living that he calls his own. Next to his children, to Maurice Brady, and Alley, they were, perhaps, the things he cared for most in the world. A hot tide of anger rushed through his veins, and his cheerful, open face grew suddenly red and corrugated with passion, as he looked fiercely round in search of the perpetrator of the deed. As usual, however, none was to be seen.

He was still standing there looking down at the dead beast, when he was startled by a slight but significant sound. The thin clear whistle of a bullet whizzed past close to his head, and the next second the bullet itself fell flattened off the granite boulder beside him, while, at the same moment, the solitary valley rang with the report of a gun.

Hurrish started upright, and, with an instinct of self-preservation, ran to the other side of the boulder, thus putting it between himself and the direction from which the shot had come. He was only just in time! Another bullet whizzed by, grazing his shoulder as it did so, striking against the rock, and again falling deadened at his feet, while again the

12. Irish: vocative *a stór* (dear, darling).
13. *Measure for Measure*, I.4.34.
14. Beehive-shaped stone huts where medieval Irish anchorites dwelt.
15. Geologically, 'erratic boulders' deposited by the ice-mass as it melted in its slide towards the Atlantic.

report resounded through the silence, dying away only when it had crossed the watershed, a faint prolonged echo returning with a hollow boom from the valley beyond.

Although a minute before the valley had seemed bare as a man's hand, no idea of supernatural agency on this occasion occurred to his brain. Leprechauns and ghosts are known to throw stones, and even to upset curaghs,[16] but no one, even in Connaught, has ever heard of their firing a gun! The question which now arose was, how was he to look round the corner of the boulder without thereby offering a mark to the enemy who had twice missed him so narrowly? A sudden idea struck him. Stooping down to where the boulder was raised, as already explained, upon a limestone foot or pedestal, in the same way that a mushroom is raised by its stalk, he peeped through the worn-away space below, and was thus able to command the whole of the valley before him. Straight in front lay the little group of oratories, the oblique rays of the rising sun gleaming upon their low grey roofs, and upon the white cross set as a pious symbol above the tiny doorway, and, underneath this white cross, in the very doorway itself of the one nearest to him, he saw a face — the red, repulsive, baboon-like face of Mat Brady peering out as an animal's face peers from its lair, the light catching upon the barrel of a gun which he held in his hands.

Hurrish's indolent, good-tempered soul was roused to fury in a moment at this sight. Mat Brady it was, then, that had fired at him! Mat equally of course that had killed his sheep! *Mat*, whom he had spared a dozen times after the most outrageous provocations! *Mat*, who, by the unwritten laws of the neighbourhood, stood condemned to death! It was the quarry attacking the hunter — the criminal assaulting his judge; the last drop in the long gathering cup of wrath! All the man's previous provocations rushed through his brain in a single fiery moment, as a flame rushes through a pile of inflammable materials. Every other consideration, — his own desire to avoid quarrels — his recent promise to Maurice, — everything went for nothing before that suddenly uprisen fire of vengeance. Clutching the blackthorn in his hand, and utterly heedless of the danger to himself, he rushed from behind his defence, up the hill, over the steep rocks, springing across the fissures, straight upon the little pious hermitage, with its innocent small white cross, and that hideous brutalised face in the middle of its ruined doorway.

The suddenness of the impulse proved his salvation. If Mat Brady had kept calm, now was his opportunity. He had not provided, however, against the emergency. His gun was unloaded, and, being a muzzle-loader, required time to recharge. Unarmed, he was, as he well knew, no match for Hurrish. Panic seized his soul, and he sprang from his lair and turned to flee. To scramble through that narrow doorway, however, took time. Hardly had he got himself free from it, and begun to ascend the stony incline, before Hurrish's step was close at his heels, Hurrish's voice sounded in his ears. Then, like a beast, he turned at bay, and like a beast's was the face which presented itself, — the lowering brown, the huge jaw, the mouth distorted and gnashing with rage and terror! A hideous sight — to dream of not to tell[17] — a man in the likeness of a beast, worse than the very ugliest variety with hoofs or claws.

His gun being useless in any other way, he tried to club it; before he had time to do so, however, Hurrish had struck it out of his hands, and the next instant 'crash,' with one sweeping, annihilating blow, the blackthorn had descended like a sledge-hammer full upon his head, — not on the top, where the thickness of skull would have defied any blow, but a little to one side, full on the temple — that part, owing to the position of his head, having come uppermost; and with an oath, strangled in its very utterance, Mat Brady fell backwards, and lay at full length upon the ground, his head striking against a rock with a dull hideous thud as he descended.

Hurrish remained where he was — the blackthorn ready for action — waiting to see him rise. He would not strike even Mat Brady when he was *down*. Minute followed minute, however, and still no sign of life. The echoes awakened by the struggle died slowly away, as a roughened circle dies upon a still pool. The uncouth body lay there quietly at his feet like a log that had been felled for burning. Could he be shamming death? Why did he not get up? What was the meaning of it? That the man could be dead,

16. More commonly 'curraghs': canoe-shaped boats made from tarred canvas stretched over a timber frame.

17. cf. Samuel T. Coleridge, 'Christabel', Part I, line 252.

or even badly hurt, did not at first occur to him. Death from a single blow of a stick is almost unknown, particularly in Ireland, where the weapon is in much repute and constant practice. He was stunned simply — 'knocked silly,'— and would get up again in another minute. He waited accordingly, expecting to see the chest begin to heave, the eyes to open, the hands to clench themselves — waited and waited. Minute slowly followed minute, but still Mat Brady neither stirred nor showed any signs of returning animation.

Puzzled, and rather startled, Hurrish at length stooped down over the fallen man, took hold of him by an arm, and lifted him into a sitting position. His head fell back, however, limply upon one shoulder, the other hand and arm hung down helplessly at his side, his eyes, partially opened, looked up at the sky with a hideous distorted expression, but without any sign of life. A cold sense of discomfort began to creep over the other. He had seen dead men before — men, too, who had come to their deaths by violent means — and he began to have an uneasy suspicion that this one before him closely resembled them; an uneasy recollection, too, that his own arm had come down with very unmistakable velocity.

Laying Mat Brady down upon the rock, he sped back to the stream, and returned with his felt hat full of water, which he dashed into his late adversary's face, then waited anxiously to see the effect. There was no effect at all! The water poured off the man's face as it would off a stone: not the twinkle of an eyelid, not the slightest quivering motion, followed the experiment. The sudden collapse of that mass of animal strength, a few minutes ago so brimful of life and of vindictive passion, had something terrifying about it. It was so utterly unexpected, that there seemed to Hurrish to be something uncanny, almost supernatural, about it, — like the trick of an evil goblin. The unbroken silence of the stony amphitheatre, too, was appalling. Had there been any one to share the situation, it would not have been nearly so bad. It was not the mere fact of Brady being killed, so much as the whole circumstances, — the suddenness, the unaccountableness of the phenomenon, — that quelled him. He felt daunted, as if a cold hand had been unexpectedly laid upon him in the height of his passion.

What was to be done? that was the next question. If Mat Brady was really dead — and it must be owned that it looked uncomfortably like it, — then his own safety must be provided for. What was he to do? Where was he to go? As to giving himself voluntarily up to the authorities, and explaining the unintentionalness of the homicide, — *that* idea, needless to say, did not occur to him for a moment. It would have been repugnant to every sentiment of his class, in whose eyes the law is the Arch enemy, — the one thing which it behoves every man, in honour no less than in self-defence, to avoid having any dealings with. There was a rule, however, for such cases — a very well established and habitually followed one. This rule was, quietly to walk away, and betake yourself to your customary occupations as rapidly as possible, leaving to the next passer-by the duty of finding the body, raising the hue and cry, and sending, if he thought fit, for the police.

Hurrish smiled grimly to himself as he thought of the police. Much good they would do! The strong arm of the law, the first thing that a man so circumstanced in almost any other country in the world would have thought of, was the last that troubled him. He thought of his own people, — what *they* would say and think. His mind glanced to his mother, and a sudden intense disgust filled him, as he thought of her satisfaction; of Alley, and he caught his breath in a prayer that she, at least, might never know his share in the deed. Then he thought of Maurice, and with that thought followed a rush of grief — of grief so violent that it seemed to tear its way through the man's whole body. What *would* Morry say? What *would* he do? It was not fear for himself which prompted the thought. It was the bitterness of feeling that he had been betrayed into doing the very thing that he had sworn to Morry that for his sake he would never do, or allow, if possible, any one else to do. When he remembered the promise given only one short week before, he felt like dashing his own brains out then and there against the rocks. Not that he believed for an instant in any of those threats which the other had uttered. That Maurice, despite his own solemn declarations to that effect, would dream of denouncing him to the Government, was an idea which did not so much as cross his brain. To one of his bringing up it would, in fact, have seemed the one *impossible* thing; the thing which — no matter with what excuse, or under what provocation — no man could do without being branded as a traitor throughout the remainder of his life. It was entirely the personal point of view, the personal relations between their two selves, that made him miserable. The thought that he and Morry could never be friends again — never, never, in all their lives, — nearly drove him mad. He had no hope either that he would fail to recognise his handiwork, — nay, he would almost have preferred that he should know it. That remorse and bitter accusing self-reproach which, as regards the dead man, hardly troubled him at all, he felt acutely, — as acutely as any man so circumstanced could feel it, — as regards the dead man's brother. He would have given all that he possessed, or ever hoped to possess in the world, to bring Mat Brady back to life again, — not for his own sake, not the least from any sense of the innate sinfulness of the deed, not even from any dread of the possible consequences to himself, but solely and wholly for the sake of his promise to Morry.

Odd thoughts, you will say, for a homicide! — for one whom the law, could it lay its hands upon him, would unhesitatingly proclaim a murderer; but they were none the less the first that did occur to him. An anomalous state of affairs begets, no doubt, anomalous ideas, and, as far as remorse went, Hurrish's ideas were pretty much those which would have passed through the brain of any other Irishman in his position, even where provocation had not made his act to some extent excusable — nay, even where there had been no provocation at all.

Meanwhile there was the recognised rule, and to have a prescribed rule to follow is always an immense comfort and repose to the mind. With a calmness which, to those unacquainted with so abnormal a state of affairs, would have seemed incredible, he left the body and walked leisurely down the hill, crossing the dead man's own ground as he did so. He did not even think of breaking into pieces or otherwise destroying the stick with which the deed had been committed. He simply thrust it into the heart of a large furze bush, the first he passed, pulled his coat down, buttoned it over his shirt, which was slightly stained by his own wound, brushed off the mud and dirt which had adhered to him, felt along his neck to make sure that the wound was not of a sufficiently serious character to signify; then — without another glance at the dead man — walked away across the slope, and up the sheep-track leading towards the high-road. Next — remembering that it might be as well not to be seen there at that precise moment, particularly as he would shortly have to pass a police-barrack — he turned to the left, threading his way between a number of boulders standing on end one behind the other; crossed the base of a hill, — its name, to be topographically accurate, was Cashlaundrumlahanah — keeping its ridged mass between him and the road. Then — still keeping away from the main route — he struck off toward the sea, under a tall nearly vertical sweep of cliff, and along a track which would bring him in time, he knew, to Ballyvaughan.

When within about four miles of his destination, what with the head of the sun and his rapid walking, perhaps, too, a little with the emotions of the morning, he began to grow thirsty, so turned aside at Gleninagh to have a drink out of the famous well there. It was approached by a couple of stone steps, and covered over with an arch surmounted by a cross. Hurrish hastily climbed the steps, and taking up a vessel, left benevolently for the service of passers-by, drank long and thirstily. He was in the act, having done so, of putting the drinking-cup down again, when he suddenly perceived, with some dismay, that it was a skull; another and much older one, of which this was evidently the successor, lay a little way off on the ledge, half covered with green mould. It was not exactly a pleasant incident, especially to one whose morning's work had been what Hurrish's had been! It was a comfort, however, to reflect there was nothing actually unlucky about it. On the contrary, skulls were formerly, and in some places are still, considered absolutely indispensable to the proper efficaciousness of a holy well. By the time he reached Ballyvaughan, Hurrish, at any rate, had nearly forgotten the incident. The fair was drawing to an end, so there was no time to lose, and in the course of ten minutes he found himself engaged in a brisk chaffer[18] with a gentleman from Mayo, a large grazier, who wanted to get the whole of his stock of calves at at least four shilling a-head under what their owner considered their value, — Burren calves fetching, as every one knows, better prices than those of any other district in Ireland.

Not merely was he not alarmed, but — save when he thought of his promise to Morry — Hurrish was not even particularly disturbed by his morning's work. He had not, of course, intended to kill Mat Brady, and in cold blood would never, under any

18. bargaining session.

circumstances, have done so. But this had been far from cold blood. The man had shot at him deliberately and treacherously from behind shelter, and, armed only with his trusty blackthorn, he had rushed upon him, struck down his defences, had brought the stick down — once — once only — upon his head. He had not even struck him again. That first sledge-hammer blow had done the work, and the man had fallen. To a great degree it was an accident, for who would ever have believed that a single blow, however delivered, would have struck the life out of that great powerful man-mountain? Hurrish knew nothing, it need hardly be said, about the mechanism of the human anatomy, but in blind rage, without calculation or thought at all, he had, as chance directed, brought his stick down upon the one spot in that huge mass of strength where life could have been extinguished by such a blow — as a hunter by good fortune may chance with his first bullet to reach the one vulnerable spot in the carcass of some brute, which would otherwise have gored him to death. It had been the work of chance, — perhaps even of Providence, — and as such he accepted it modestly, without any self-glorification, beyond the habitual satisfaction he found in his own strength, but certainly without an iota of that horror, dismay, and personal remorse which would have filled the breast of a man less inured to hearing of deeds of violence. He even forgot it by moments, when the bargaining grew brisk and exciting; and although, when the calves were all sold, and his hands for the moment unoccupied, it rushed back upon him with vivid realisation, it was less with a sense of horror than with a feeling that a new epoch of his life had been reached, an important turning-point which it behoved him to guard carefully, so that he might not be led away by this one act into sharing others where the justification might be less clear.

Before the reader resolves to be utterly disgusted with this callousness, and to dismiss Hurrish O'Brien once and for ever as a monster of brutality, he must first kindly consent to take the circumstances of his life a little into consideration. We are all children of our environment — the good no less than the bad, — products of that particular group of habits, customs, traditions, ways of looking at things, standards of right and wrong, which chance has presented to our still growing and expanding consciousness. Hurrish's history must so far have been very imperfectly told if it has not been realised that he was well disposed and kindly above the average; pitiful, and disposed to use his strength for good rather than evil. Yet the fact that he had just been guilty, no matter with what justification, of another's death did not — nay, *could* not — present itself to his mind with any of that sharply-defined horror, that passion of self-dismay and self-reproach, that it would have awakened in the mind of many a far less kindly and, in his way, conscientious man, who had been unused to hearing violence and bloodshed spoken of as the natural panacea for all the disagreements which may happen to arise between man and man. He would rather it had not happened, — when he thought of Morry and his promise to him, — very *much* rather. But as unfortunately it had happened, he resolved in his own mind that, as soon as ever he could with safety to himself, he would pay for masses to be said for the repose of Mat Brady's soul — feeling that he was certainly acting generously; for had not Brady been the aggressor? had he not come out that morning with the express purpose of killing himself? — an intention which only the merest accident had hindered him from carrying out. Moreover, if the matter had ended the other way, and he, Hurrish, been the one to have been killed, he felt perfectly convinced that Mat Brady would never for a moment have thought of having masses offered up for the repose of *his* soul!

GEORGE MOORE
(1852–1933)

from:
THE UNTILLED FIELD
(1903)

[This short story is one of a suite that appear in Moore's *The Untilled Field* (1903) about the most desolate parishes in his imaginary landscape; the other two are the much anthologized 'Julia Cahill's Curse' and 'The Playhouse in the Waste' in which the saintly Father MacTurnan also features.]

A LETTER TO ROME

One morning the priest's housekeeper mentioned as she gathered up the breakfast things, that Mike Mulhare had refused to let his daughter Catherine marry James Murdoch until he had earned the price of a pig.

'This is bad news,' said the priest, and he laid down the newspaper.

'And he waiting for her all the summer! Wasn't it in February last that he came out of the poor-house? And the fine cabin he had built for her! He'll be that lonesome, he'll be going to America.'

'To America!' said the priest.

'Maybe it will be going back to the poor-house he'll be, for he'll never earn the price of his passage at the relief works.'[1]

The priest looked at her for a moment as if he did not catch her meaning, and then a knock came at the door, and he said:

'The inspector is here, and there are people waiting for me.'

And while he was distributing the clothes he had received from Manchester, he argued with the inspector as to the direction the new road should take; and when he came back from the relief works, there was his dinner. He was busy writing letters all the afternoon; it was not until he had handed them to the post-mistress that his mind was free to think of poor James Murdoch, who had built a cabin at the end of one of the famine roads in a hollow out of the way of the wind. From a long way off the priest could see him digging his patch of bog.

And when he caught sight of the priest he stuck his spade in the ground and came to meet him. He wore a pair of torn corduroy trousers out of which two long naked feet appeared; and there was a shirt, but it was torn, the wind thrilled in a naked breast, and the priest thought his housekeeper was right, that James must go back to the poor-house. There was a wild look in his eyes, and he seemed to the priest like some lonely animal just come out of its burrow. His mud cabin was full of peat smoke, there were pools of green water about it, but it had been dry, he said, all the summer; and he had intended to make a drain.

'It's hard luck, your reverence, and after building this house for her. There's a bit of smoke in the house now, but if I got Catherine I wouldn't be long making a chimney. I told Mike he should give Catherine a pig for her fortune, but he said he would give her a calf when I bought the pig, and I said, "Haven't I built a fine house and wouldn't it be a fine one to rear him in." '

And they walked through the bog, James talking to the priest all the way, for it was seldom he had anyone to talk to.

'Now I must not take you any further from your digging.'

'Sure there's time enough,' said James, 'amn't I there all day.'

'I'll go and see Mike Mulhare myself,' said the priest.

'Long life to your reverence.'

'And I will try to get you the price of the pig.'

'Ah, 'tis your reverence that's good to us.'

The priest stood looking after him, wondering if he would give up life as a bad job and go back to the poor-house. But while thinking of James Murdoch,

1. Relief works, such as the building of roads and piers to provide employment for Ireland's rural poor, were set up during the Great Famine of 1846–47. Though discontinued in more prosperous areas of the country, they persisted in such 'congested districts' as west Mayo of the 1890s where the story is set. Poor-houses or 'Unions' had existed in Ireland since the English Poor Law of 1834 had been extended to the country in 1838. Dreaded by the tenant farmers, the poor-houses sometimes provided the only alternative to starvation if the money for a 'passage' to America could not be found.

he was conscious of an idea; it was still dim and distant, but every moment it emerged, it was taking shape.

Ireland was passing away. In five and twenty years, if some great change did not take place, Ireland would be a Protestant country. 'There is no one in this parish except myself who has a decent house to live in,' he murmured; and then an idea broke suddenly in his mind. The Greek priests were married. They had been allowed to retain their wives in order to avert a schism. Rome had always known how to adapt herself to circumstances, and there was no doubt that if Rome knew Ireland's need of children Rome would consider the revocation of the decree — the clergy must marry.

He walked very slowly, and looking through the peat stacks he saw St Peter's rising above a rim of pearl-coloured mountains, and before he was aware of it he had begun to consider how he might write a letter to Rome. Was it not a fact that celibacy had only been made obligatory in Ireland in the twelfth century?

When he returned home, his housekeeper was anxious to hear about James Murdoch, but the priest sat possessed by the thought of Ireland becoming a Protestant country; and he had not moved out of his chair when the servant came in with his tea. He drank his tea mechanically, and walked up and down the room, and it was a long time before he took up his knitting. But that evening he could not knit, and he laid the stocking aside so that he might think. Of what good would his letter be? A letter from a poor parish priest asking that one of the most ancient decrees should be revoked! The Pope's secretary would pitch his letter into the waste paper basket. The Pope would be only told of its contents! The cardinals are men whose thoughts move up and down certain narrow ways, clever men no doubt, but clever men are often the dupe of conventions. All men who live in the world accept the conventions as truths. And the idea of this change in ecclesiastical law had come to him because he lived in a waste bog.

But was he going to write the letter? He could not answer the question! Yes, he knew that sooner or later he must write this letter. 'Instinct,' he said, 'is a surer guide than logic. My letter to Rome was a sudden revelation.' The idea had fallen as it were out of the air, and now as he sat knitting by his own fire-side it seemed to come out of the corners of the room.

'When you were at Rathowen,'[2] his idea said, 'you heard the clergy lament that the people were leaving the country. You heard the bishop and many eloquent men speak on the subject, but their words meant little, but on the bog road the remedy was revealed to you.

'The remedy lies with the priesthood. If each priest were to take a wife about four thousand children would be born within the year, forty thousand children would be added to the birth-rate in ten years. Ireland would be saved by her priesthood!'

The truth of this estimate seemed beyond question, nevertheless, Father MacTurnan found it difficult to reconcile himself to the idea of a married clergy. One is always the dupe of prejudice. He knew that and went on thinking. The priests live in the best houses, eat the best food, wear the best clothes; they are indeed the flower of the nation, and would produce magnificent sons and daughters. And who could bring up their children according to the teaching of our holy church as well as priests?

So did his idea speak to him, unfolding itself in rich variety every evening. Very soon he realised that other advantages would accrue, beyond the addition of forty thousand children to the birth-rate, and one advantage that seemed to him to exceed the original advantage would be the nationalisation of religion, the formation of an Irish Catholicism suited to the ideas and needs of the Irish people.

In the beginning of the century the Irish lost their language, in the middle of the century the characteristic aspects of their religion. He remembered that it was Cardinal Cullen who had denationalised religion in Ireland.[3] But everyone recognised his mistake, and how could a church be nationalised better than by the rescission of the decree? Wives and the begetting of children would attach the priests to the soil of Ireland. It could not be said that anyone loved his country who did not contribute to its maintenance. He remembered that the priests leave Ireland on foreign missions, and he said: 'Every Catholic who leaves Ireland helps to bring about the very thing that Ireland has been struggling against for centuries — Protestantism.'

This idea talked to him, and, one evening, it said,

2. There is no township named Rathowen in County Mayo; Moore's stories tend to be unspecific with place-names.

3. Paul Cullen (1803–78), archbishop of Dublin 1852–78, was the great champion of ultramontanism in the Ireland of his time. (See note 5 to Sheehan's *My New Curate*, p. 1041).

'Religion, like everything else, must be national,' and it led him to contrast cosmopolitanism with parochialism. 'Religion, like art, came out of parishes,' he said. Some great force was behind him. He must write! He must write. . . .

He dropped the ink over the table and over the paper, he jotted down his ideas in the first words that came to him until midnight; he could see his letter in all its different parts, and when he slept it floated through his sleep.

'I must have a clear copy of it before I begin the Latin translation.'

He had written the English text thinking of the Latin that would come after, and very conscious of the fact that he had written no Latin since he had left Maynooth, and that a bad translation would discredit his ideas in the eyes of the Pope's secretary, who was doubtless a great Latin scholar.

'The Irish priests have always been good Latinists,' he murmured as he hunted through the dictionary.

The table was littered with books, for he had found it necessary to create a Latin atmosphere before beginning his translation. He worked principally at night, and one morning about three he finished his translation, and getting up from his chair he walked to the whitening window. His eyes pained him, and he decided he would postpone reading over what he had written till morning.

His illusions regarding his Latin were broken. He had laid his manuscript on a table by his bedside, and on awakening he had reached out his hand for it, but he had not a page when he dropped it; and the manuscript lay on the floor while he dressed. He went into his breakfast, and when he had eaten his breakfast his nerve failed him. He could not bring himself to fetch the manuscript, and it was his housekeeper who brought it to him.

'Ah,' he said, 'it is tasteless as the gruel that poor James Murdoch is eating.' And taking a volume from the table —, 'St. Augustine's Confessions' — he said, 'what diet there is here!'

He stood reading. There was no idiom, he had used Latin words instead of English. At last he was interrupted by the wheels of a car stopping at his door. Father Meehan! Meehan could revise his Latin! None had written such good Latin at Maynooth as Meehan.

'My dear Meehan, this is indeed a pleasant surprise.'

'I thought I'd like to see you. I drove over. But — I am not disturbing you . . . You've taken to reading again. St. Augustine! And you're writing in Latin!'

Father James's face grew red, and he took the manuscript out of his friend's hand.

'No, you mustn't look at that.'

And then the temptation to ask him to overlook certain passages made him change his mind.

'I was never much of a Latin scholar.'

'And you want me to overlook your Latin for you. But why are you writing Latin?'

'Because I am writing to the Pope. I was at first a little doubtful, but the more I thought of this letter the more necessary it seemed to me.'

'And what are you writing to the Pope about?'

'You see Ireland is going to become a Protestant country.'

'Is it?' said Father Meehan, and he listened a little while. Then, interrupting his friend, he said:

'I've heard enough. Now, I strongly advise you not to send this letter. We have known each other all our lives. Now my dear MacTurnan —'

Father Michael talked eagerly, and Father MacTurnan sat listening. At last Father Meehan saw that his arguments were producing no effect, and he said:

'You don't agree with me.'

'It isn't that I don't agree with you. You have spoken admirably from your point of view, but our points of view are different.'

'Take your papers away, burn them!'

Then, thinking his words were harsh, he laid his hand on his friend's shoulder and said:

'My dear MacTurnan, I beg of you not to send this letter.'

Father James did not answer; the silence grew painful, and Father Michael asked Father James to show him the relief works that the Government had ordered.

They walked to where the poor people were working, but important as these works were the letter to Rome seemed more important to Father Michael, and he said:

'My good friend, there isn't a girl that would marry us; now is there? There isn't a girl in Ireland who would touch us with a forty foot pole. Would you have the Pope release the nuns from their vows?'

'I think exceptions should be made in favour of those in orders. But I think it would be for the good of Ireland if the secular clergy were married.'

'That's not my point. My point is that even if the decree was rescinded we should not be able to get wives. You've been living too long in the waste, my dear friend. You've lost yourself in a dream. We shouldn't get a penny. Our parishioners would say, "Why should we support that fellow and his family?" That's what they'd say.'

'We should be poor, no doubt,' said Father James. 'But not so poor as our parishioners. My parishioners eat yellow meal, and I eat eggs and live in a good house.'

'We are educated men, and should live in better houses.'

'The greatest saints live in deserts.'

And so the argument went on until the time came to say good-bye, and then Father James said:

'I shall be glad if you will give me a lift on your car. I want to go to the post-office.'

'To post your letter?'

'The idea came to me — it came swiftly like a lightning flash, and I can't believe that it was an accident. If it had fallen into your mind with the suddenness that it fell into mine, you would believe that it was an inspiration.'

'It would take a good deal to make me believe I was inspired,' said Father Michael, and he watched Father James go into the post-office to register his letter.

As he went home Father James met a long string of peasants returning from their work. The last was Norah Flynn, and the priest blushed deeply. It was the first time he had looked on one of his parishioners in the light of a possible spouse; he entered his house frightened, and when he looked round his parlour he asked himself if the day would come when he should see Norah Flynn sitting opposite to him in his arm-chair. And his face flushed deeper when he looked towards the bedroom door, and he fell on his knees and prayed that God's will might be made known to him.

During the night he awoke many times, and the dream that had awakened him continued when he had left his bed, and he wandered round and round the room in the darkness, seeking a way. At last he reached the window and drew the curtain, and saw the dim dawn opening out over the bog.

'Thank God,' he said, 'it was only a dream — only a dream.'

And lying down he fell asleep, but immediately another dream as horrible as the first appeared, and his housekeeper heard him beating on the walls.

'Only a dream, only a dream,' he said.

He lay awake, not daring to sleep lest he might dream. And it was about seven o'clock when he heard his housekeeper telling him that the inspector had come to tell him they must decide what direction the new road should take. In the inspector's opinion it should run parallel with the old road. To continue the old road two miles further would involve extra labour; the people would have to go further to their work, and the stones would have to be drawn further. The priest held that the extra labour was of secondary importance. He said that to make two roads running parallel with each other would be a wanton humiliation to the people.

But the inspector could not appreciate the priest's arguments. He held that the people were thinking only how they might earn enough money to fill their bellies.

'I don't agree with you, I don't agree with you,' said the priest. 'Better go in the opposite direction and make a road to the sea.'

'Well, your reverence, the Government do not wish to engage upon any work that will benefit any special class. These are my instructions.'

'A road to the sea will benefit no one. . . . I see you are thinking of the landlord. But there is no harbour; no boat ever comes into that flat, waste sea.'

'Well, your reverence, one of these days a harbour may be made, whereas an arch would look well in the middle of the bog, and the people would not have to go far to their work.'

'No, no. A road to the sea will be quite useless; but its futility will not be apparent — at least, not so apparent — and the people's hearts will not be broken.'

The inspector seemed a little doubtful, but the priest assured him that the futility of the road would satisfy English ministers.

'And yet these English ministers,' the priest reflected, 'are not stupid men; they are merely men blinded by theory and prejudice, as all men are who live in the world. Their folly will be apparent to the next generation, and so on and so on for ever and ever, world without end.'

'And the worst of it is,' the priest said, 'while the people are earning their living on these roads their fields will be lying idle, and there will be no crops next year.'

Father MacTurnan began to think of the cardinals and the transaction of business in the Vatican; cardinals and ministers alike are the dupes of convention. Only those who are estranged from habits and customs can think straightforward.

'If, instead of insisting on these absurd roads, the Government would give me the money, I should be able to feed the people at a cost of about a penny a day, and they would be able to sow their potatoes. And if only the cardinals would consider the rescission of the decree on its merits Ireland would be saved from Protestantism.'

Some cardinal was preparing an answer — an answer might be even in the post. Rome might not think his letter worthy of an answer.

A few days afterwards the inspector called to show him a letter he had just received from the Board of Works, and Father James had to write many letters and had to go to Dublin, and in the excitement of these philanthropic activities the emigration question was forgotten. He was talking to the inspector about the possibility of obtaining a harbour when the postman handed him a letter.

'This is a letter from Father Moran. The Bishop wishes to see me. We will continue the conversation tomorrow. It is eight miles to Rathowen, and how much further is the Palace?'

'A good seven,' said the inspector. 'You're not going to walk it, your reverence?'

'Why not? In four hours I shall be there.' He looked at his boots first, and hoped they would hold together; and then he looked at the sky, and hoped it would not rain.

The sky was dim; all the light seemed to be upon the earth; a soft, vague sunlight floated over the bog. Now and again a yellow-hammer rose above the tufts of coarse grass and flew a little way. A line of pearl-coloured mountains showed above the low horizon, and he had walked eight miles before he saw a pine-wood. Some hundred yards further on there was a green field, but under the green sod there was peat, and a man and a boy were cutting it. The heather appeared again, and he had walked ten miles before he was clear of whins[4] and heather.

He walked on, thinking of his interview with the Bishop, and was nearly at the end of his journey when he noticed that one of his shoes had come unsewn, and he stopped at a cabin; and while the woman was looking for a needle and thread he mopped his face with a great red handkerchief that he kept in the pocket of his threadbare coat — a coat that had once been black, but had grown green with age and weather. He had outwalked himself, and feeling he would be tired, and not well able to answer the points that the Bishop would raise, he decided to rest awhile. The woman had found some beeswax, and he stopped half an hour stitching his shoe under the hawthorn that grew beside the cabin.

He was still two miles from the Palace, and this last two miles proved very long. He arrived footsore and covered with dust, and he was so tired that he could hardly get up from his chair to receive Father Moran when he came into the parlour.

'You seem to have walked a long way, Father MacTurnan.'

'About fifteen miles. I shall be all right presently. I suppose his Grace does not want to see me at once.'

'Well, that's just it. His Grace sent me to say he would see you at once. He expected you earlier.'

'I started the moment I received his Grace's letter. I suppose his Grace wishes to see me regarding my letter to Rome.'

The secretary hesitated, coughed, and Father MacTurnan wondered why Father Moran looked at him so intently. He returned in a few minutes, saying that his Grace was sorry that Father MacTurnan had had so long a walk. He hoped that he would rest awhile and partake of some refreshment. . . . The servant brought in some wine and sandwiches, and the secretary returned in half an hour. His Grace was now ready to receive him. Father Moran opened the library door, and Father MacTurnan saw the Bishop — a short, alert man, about fifty-five, with a sharp nose and grey eyes and bushy eyebrows. He popped about the room and gave his secretary many orders. Father MacTurnan wondered if the Bishop would ever finish talking to his secretary. He seemed to have finished, but a thought suddenly struck him, and he followed his secretary to the door, and Father MacTurnan began to fear that the Pope had not decided to place the Irish clergy on the same footing as the Greek clergy. If he had, the Bishop's interest in these many various matters would have subsided: his mind would be engrossed by the larger issue. On returning from the door his Grace passed Father MacTurnan without speaking to him, and going to his writing table he began to search amid his papers. At last Father MacTurnan said:

4. gorse.

'Maybe your Grace is looking for my letter to Rome?'

'Yes,' said his Grace, 'do you see it?'

'It's under your Grace's hand, those blue papers.'

'Ah yes,' and his Grace leaned back in his armchair, leaving Father MacTurnan standing.

'Won't you sit down, Father MacTurnan?' he said casually. 'You've been writing to Rome, I see, advocating the revocation of the decree of celibacy. There's no doubt the emigration of Catholics is a very serious question. So far you have got the sympathy of Rome, and, I may say of myself; but am I to understand that it was your fear for the religious safety of Ireland that prompted you to write this letter?'

'What other reason could there be?'

Nothing was said for a long while, and then the Bishop's meaning began to break in his mind; his face flushed, and he grew confused.

'I hope your Grace doesn't think for a moment that —'

'I only want to know if there is anyone — if your eyes ever went in a certain direction, if your thoughts ever said, "Well, if the decree is revoked —" '

'No, your Grace, no. Celibacy has been no burden to me — far from it. Sometimes I feared that it was celibacy that attracted me to the priesthood. Celibacy was a gratification rather than a sacrifice.'

'I am glad,' said the Bishop, and he spoke slowly and emphatically, 'that this letter was prompted by such impersonal motives.'

'Surely, your Grace, His Holiness did not suspect —'

The Bishop murmured an euphonious Italian name, and Father MacTurnan understood that he was speaking of one of the Pope's secretaries.

'More than once,' said Father MacTurnan, 'I feared that if the decree were revoked, I should not have had sufficient courage to comply with it.'

And then he told the Bishop how he had met Norah Flynn on the road. An amused expression stole into the Bishop's face, and his voice changed.

'I presume you do not contemplate making marriage obligatory; you do not contemplate the suspension of the faculties of those who do not take wives?'

'It seems to me that exception should be made in favour of those in orders, and, of course in favour of those who have reached a certain age like your Grace.'

The Bishop coughed, and pretended to look for some paper which he had mislaid.

'This was one of the many points that I discussed with Father Michael Meehan.'

'Oh, so you consulted Father Meehan,' the Bishop said, looking up.

'He came in one day I was reading over my Latin translation before posting it. I'm afraid the ideas that I submitted to the consideration of His Holiness have been degraded by my very poor Latin. I should have wished Father Meehan to overlook my Latin, but he refused. He begged of me not to send the letter.'

'Father Meehan,' said his Grace, 'is a great friend of yours. Yet nothing he could say could shake your resolution to write to Rome?'

'Nothing,' said Father MacTurnan. 'The call I received was too distinct and too clear for me to hesitate.'

'Tell me about this call.'

Father MacTurnan told the Bishop that the poor man had come out of the workhouse because he wanted to be married, and that Mike Mulhare would not give him his daughter until he had earned the price of a pig. 'And as I was talking to him I heard my conscience say, "No one can afford to marry in Ireland but the clergy." We all live better than our parishioners.'

And then, forgetting the Bishop, and talking as if he were alone with his God, he described how the conviction had taken possession of him — that Ireland would become a Protestant country if the Catholic emigration did not cease. And he told how this conviction had left him little peace until he had written his letter.

The priest talked on until he was interrupted by Father Moran.

'I have some business to transact with Father Moran now,' the Bishop said, 'but you must stay to dinner. You have walked a long way, and you are tired and hungry.'

'But, your Grace, if I don't start now, I shall not get home until nightfall.'

'A car will take you back, Father MacTurnan. I will see to that. I must have some exact information about your poor people. We must do something for them.'

Father MacTurnan and the Bishop were talking together when the car came to take Father MacTurnan home, and the Bishop said:

'Father MacTurnan, you have borne the loneliness of your parish a long while.'

'Loneliness is only a matter of habit. I think, your Grace, I'm better suited to the place than I am for any other. I don't wish any change, if your Grace is satisfied with me.'

'No one will look after the poor people better than yourself, Father MacTurnan. But,' he said, 'it seems to me there is one thing we have forgotten. You haven't told me if you succeeded in getting the money to buy the pig.'

Father MacTurnan grew very red. . . . 'I had forgotten it. The relief works —'

'It's not too late. Here's five pounds, and this will buy him a pig.'

'It will indeed,' said the priest, 'it will buy him two!'

He had left the palace without having asked the Bishop how his letter had been received at Rome, and he stopped the car, and was about to tell the driver to go back. But no matter, he would hear about his letter some other time. He was bringing happiness to two poor people, and he could not persuade himself to delay their happiness by one minute. He was not bringing one pig, but two pigs, and now Mike Mulhare would have to give him Norah and a calf; and the priest remembered that James Murdoch had said — 'What a fine house this will be to rear them in.' There were many who thought that human beings and animals should not live together; but after all, what did it matter if they were happy? And the priest forgot his letter to Rome in the thought of the happiness he was bringing to two poor people. He could not see Norah Mulhare that night; but he drove down to the famine road, and he and the driver called till they awoke James Murdoch. The poor man came stumbling across the bog, and the priest told him the news.

PATRICK AUGUSTINE (CANON) SHEEHAN

(1852–1913)

from: MY NEW CURATE (1900)

[*My New Curate*, Canon Sheehan's third and most popular novel, presents, in elaborate and leisurely detail, the life of a parish in County Cork towards the end of the last century. The book's greatest strength is its narrator, Father Dan Hanrahan, the humane, learned and humorous parish priest who observes and records the efforts of his new curate, Father Letheby, during his one year's ministry in the parish of Kilronan. Father Letheby is earnest, energetic and talented, determined upon social reforms among the poor. He sets up a factory and a fishing industry, refusing to be discouraged by apathy, indifference or bad luck. The play of feeling between the two main characters animates a narrative that is effectively without plot. But the proceedings of an Irish parish of the time are vividly preserved in its daily work and play, its rituals and beliefs and especially in the concerns of the catholic clergy whose role was so crucial in every detail of its existence.]

CHAPTER XVII

A CLERICAL SYMPOSIUM

There is no law, supernatural or natural, forbidding us (who, if we have not many of the crosses, neither have we many of the pleasures of this life) from meeting sometimes, and carrying out St. Paul's prescriptions in the matter of hospitality. I believe, indeed, his words — and he was a wise, kind saint — apply principally to bishops; but why should not we imitate our superiors afar off, and practise the kindly virtue? It is good to meet sometimes and exchange opinions; it softens the asperities of daily life, makes the young think reverently of the old, and the old charitably of the young. At least, these are my views, and acting upon them there is always an open door and a *Céad Milé Fáilte*[1] for a brother; and a few times in the year I try to gather around me my dear friends, and thus to cement those bonds of friendship that make life a little more pleasant, and, perhaps, may keep our memories green. Sometimes, indeed, my dear old friends object to face a drive of eight or ten miles on a cold night in winter; but the young fellows always come. Nothing but extreme urgency would keep them away from an evening with Daddy Dan.[2] Now, we have no nonsense — no soups, nor entrées, which some of my more fashionable confrères are at present affecting, if you please; but a plain turkey and ham, and a roast leg of mutton, and a few little trimmings to fill up vacant spaces. There is an old tradition, too, in Ireland, which I keep to pretty closely — never to invite more than the Muses, nor less than the Graces;[3] but on this occasion — it was during the Octave of the Epiphany[4] — I departed from the custom, and, owing to a few disappointments, the ominous number of thirteen sat down to dinner. I must say, however, it had not a paralyzing effect on the appetites of my guests, nor did they appear to have any apprehensions of a sudden call to the places where turkeys and good mutton are not appreciated. There were a few jokes about the intolerable longevity of certain parish priests; and when my curate, who occupied the vice-chair with infinite grace and dignity, remarked in his own grand style that 'really Da Vinci's "Last Supper" was responsible for that unhallowed superstition, and there really was nothing in it,' some few wags professed themselves greatly relieved, and showed it by new-born zeal in the avocations of the evening. My duties as host engrossed all my attention, until the table was cleared for action; and the call for coffee from eight out of thirteen guests recalled me to my favourite meditation on the mighty yet silent revolution that is progressing in the Irish Church.

I have been now in touch with three generations of Irish priests, each as distinct from the other, and marked by as distinctive characteristics, as those which differentiate an Anglican parson from a mediæval monk. My early education was coloured by contact with the polished, studious, timid priests, who, educated in Continental seminaries, introduced into Ireland all the grace and dignity and holiness, and all the dread of secular authority with the slight tendency to compromise, that seemed to have marked the French clergy, at least in the years immediately succeeding the revolutions and the Napoleonic wars. These were the good men who fraternized with landlords, and lent their congregations to a neighbouring parson on the occasion of some governmental visitation; who were slightly tinged with Gallican ideas, and hated progress and the troubles that always accompany it. They were holy, good, kindly men, but they could hardly be called officers of the Church Militant.[5] Then came Maynooth, which, founded on governmental subsidies,[6] poured from its gates the strongest, fiercest, most fearless army of priests that ever fought for the spiritual and temporal interests of the people — men of large physique and iron constitutions, who spent ten hours a day on horseback, despised French claret, loved their people and chastised them like fathers, but were prepared to defend them with their lives and the outpouring of their blood against their hereditary enemies. Intense in their faith, of stainless lives and spotless reputations, their words cut like razors, and their hands smote like lightning; but they had the hearts of mothers for the little ones of their flocks. They had the classics at their fingers' ends, could roll out lines from Virgil or Horace at an after-dinner speech, and had a profound contempt for English literature. In theology they were rigorists, too much disposed to defer absolution and to give long penances. They had a cordial dislike for new devotions, believing that Christmas and Easter Communion was quite enough for ordinary sanctity. Later on they became more generous, but they clung

1. A traditional Irish greeting, literally 'A Hundred Thousand Welcomes'.
2. An affectionate title used by his parishioners for the narrator, Father Dan.
3. In Greek mythology the three Graces, sister goddesses, were givers of charm and beauty. The Muses, nine sister goddesses, were each regarded as the protectress of a different art or science.
4. i.e. within eight days of the Christian feast of the Epiphany, or Little Christmas, which celebrates the 'showing forth' of the infant Jesus to the Gentiles in the persons of the Magi. The occasion probably encouraged especial hospitality.
5. 'Gallican' ideas tended to express themselves in Ireland in terms of a nationalist rather than an ultramontane catholicism (see note 3 to Moore's 'A Letter to Rome', p. 1035). The Church was seen as comprising three orders: the church suffering in purgatory, the church triumphant in heaven, the church militant on earth. Sheehan is permitting himself a mild pun on the last of these three.
6. The national catholic seminary of St Patrick's College, Maynooth was founded in 1795 for the education of priests. It received from the start a yearly subsidy from the British government which was generously increased in 1844 under Peel's ministry.

with tenacity to the Brown Scapular[7] and the First Sunday[8] of the month. I am quite sure they have turned somersaults in their graves since the introduction of the myriad devotions that are now distracting and edifying the faithful. But they could make, and, alas! too often perhaps for Christian modesty, they did make, the proud boast that they kept alive the people's faith, imbued them with a sense of the loftiest morality, and instilled a sense of intense horror for such violations of Church precepts as a *communicatio cum hereticis in divinis*,[9] or the touching of flesh meat on a day of abstinence. I believe I belong to that school, though my sympathies are wide enough for all. And as in theology, I am quite prepared to embrace Thomists, and Scotists, and Molinists, Nominalists and Realists[10] in fraternal charity, so, too, am I prepared to recognize and appreciate the traits and characteristics of the different generations of clerics in the Irish Church. Sometimes, perhaps, through the vanity that clings to us all to the end, I play the part of 'laudator temporis acti,'[11] and then the young fellows shout:

'Ah, but Father Dan, they were giants in those days.'

And the tags and shreds of poor human nature wave in the wind of flattery; and I feel grateful for the modest appreciation of a generation that has no sympathy with our own.

Then, down there, below the water-line of gray heads is the coming generation of Irish priests, who, like the *lampadephoroi*[12] of old in the Athenian games, will take the torch of faith from our hands and carry it to the Acropolis of Heaven — clean-cut, small of stature, keen-faced, bicycle-riding, coffee-drinking, encyclopædic young fellows, who will give a good account of themselves, I think, in the battles of the near future. It is highly amusing to a distinterested spectator, like myself, to watch the tolerant contempt with which the older generation regards the younger. They have as much contempt for coffee as for ceremonies, and I think their mistakes in the latter would form a handsome volume of *errata*, or add another appendix to our valuable compendiums. To ask one of these old men to pass a cup of coffee is equivalent to asking a Hebrew of the strict observance to carve a ham, or a Hindoo to eat from the same dish with a Christian. And many other objects that the passing generation held in high esteem are 'gods of the Gentiles'[13] to the younger. They laugh profanely at that aureole of distinction that used hang around the heads of successful students, declaring that a man's education only commences when he leaves college, and that his academical training was but the sword exercise of the gymnasium; and they speak dreadful things about evolution and modern interpretation, and the new methods of hermeneutics, and polychrome Bibles; and they laugh at the idea of the world's creation in six days; and altogether, they disturb and disquiet the dreams of the staid and stately veterans of the Famine years, and make them forecast a dismal future for Ireland when German metaphysics and coffee will first impair, and then destroy, the sacred traditions of Irish faith. And yet, these young priests inherit the best elements of the grand inheritance that has come down to them. Their passionate devotion to their faith is only rivalled by their passionate devotion to the Motherland. Every one of them belongs to that great world-wide organization of Priests Adorers, which, cradled in the dying years of our century, will grow to a gigantic stature in the next; for at last it has dawned upon the world that around this sacred doctrine and devotion, as around an oriflamme,[14] the great battles of the twentieth century will rage. And they have as tender and passionate a love for the solitary isle in the wintry western seas as ever brought a film to the eyes of

7. A sacramental consisting of two squares of material held together by two strings and worn around the neck as a sign of lay affiliation to the Carmelite Order.
8. Benediction, a short devotional service, was initially celebrated on the first Sunday of the month on its introduction to the church liturgy *c.* 1820.
9. Literally 'joining with heretics in divine services'. It was strictly forbidden for catholics to attend the services of other religions.
10. Thomists, adherents of St Thomas Aquinas (1225–74) whose thought, largely based on Aristotle, superseded the Scotist, largely Neo-Platonic, theories of the Irish philosopher Johannes Duns Scottus (Ériugena) (*c.* 810–77). Molinists tended to Quietism, a belief adumbrated by the Spanish Jesuit, Louis Molina (1627–96), that grace entered the soul in moments of passive, suspended will. Realists followed Aristotle/Aquinas in asserting the objective existence of things, as opposed to the Nominalist/Idealist view that things exist only in as far as we name them.
11. Literally 'praiser of times past'.
12. Literally 'torch-carriers', athletes who passed a torch from one to the other in Athenian relay-races held at night. It became a metaphor for the passing on of scholarly truth from one generation to the next.
13. II Chronicles, 32.17.
14. A bandarole or small banner hanging from a lance, first worn by kings of France in honour of St Denis: hence a rallying symbol in a battle for sacred values.

exile, or lighted the battle fires in the hearts of her heroes and kings. And with all my ancient prejudices in favour of my own caste, I see clearly that the equipments of the new generation are best suited to modern needs. The bugle-call of the future will sound the retreat for the ancient cavalry and the Old Guard, and sing out, Forward the Light Brigade!

This evening, as usual, the conversation was discursive. It ranged over the whole area of human knowledge and experience, from the price of a horse to Lehmkuhl's Latinity,[15] and from the last political speech to the ever-lasting question, ever discussed and never decided, What is meant by the month's residence as a condition for the acquisition of a domicile?[16] That horrible drug was irritating the nerves of the younger men, until I heard, as in a dream, a Babel of voices: 'The two Ballerini' — 'They'll never arrest him' — 'He'll certainly fire on the people' — 'Daniel never wrote that book, I tell you' — ''Tis only a ringbone' — 'Fifty times worse than a sprain' — 'He got it in the Gregorian University'[17] — 'Paddy Murray, George Crolly' — 'I admire Balfour[18] for his profound knowledge of metaphysics' — 'Did you see the article in the *Record*[19] about the Spanish dispensation?' — 'He's got a first-class mission in Ballarat'[20] — 'No, the lessons were from the Scripture occurring' — 'I don't think we're bound to these Masses' — ''Twas a fine sermon, but too flowery for my tastes' — 'Yes, we expect a good Shrove[21] this year' — 'His *Data of Ethics* won't stand examination' — 'Our fellows will lick yours well next time' — 'Picking the grapes and lemons at Tivoli' — 'Poor old Kirby, what an age he is' — '"Twilight and evening bell, and after that the dark, And may there be no sadness of farewell, when I embark,"[22] that's the way it runs' — 'He cut in his physic year, and is running a paper in Boston' — 'It is up now to thirty-five shillings a ton, and will go higher,' etc., etc. The older men, under the more kindly influence, were calm as sophomores. Amidst the whirlpool of words, they clung to two sheet-anchors — O'Connell in politics, and St. Alphonsus in theology.[23]

At last, the conversation simmered down into an academic debate, whether the centripetal system, which concentrates all Irish students in Maynooth, or the centrifugal, which sends them scampering over the Continent to the ancient universities, was the better. This was a calm, judicious tournament, except now and again, when I had to touch the gong, and say:

'Gentlemen, only three at a time, if you please.'

It was a curious thing to notice that those who had studied in Maynooth were very much in favour of a Continental education; and those who had been in foreign universities were rather inclined to give the verdict for Maynooth.

'You see,' said one, 'it is an education in itself to go abroad. It means expansion, and expansion is education. Then you have the immense advantage of being able to learn and master the foreign languages and literature, and nowadays a man that can't speak French at least is a very helpless creature.'

'You take it for granted,' replied another, 'that residence abroad ensures a knowledge of French. I spent six years in the seminary at N____, and except *cela va sans dire, tant pis*, and a few other colloquialisms, which you will find on the last page of an English dictionary, I might as well have been in Timbuctoo.'

'Well,' said my curate — and though he is not very popular, somehow or other his words appear to carry great weight — 'I must confess that the regret of my life is that I had not an opportunity of studying in Rome, just as the hope of my life is that I shall see Rome before I die. I consider that the greatest Irish college in the world, in numbers and in the influence that arises from intellectual superiority, should be somewhere within the shadows of the Seven Hills.'

'Why not transfer the Dunboyne,[24] with all its

15. Augustine Lehmkuhl S.J. (1834–1918) wrote *Theologia Moralis* (1883–84). Like all such catholic works, it was written in Latin.
16. Technical terms concerning marriage: weddings normally took place where the bride had her domicile.
17. A catholic college in Rome, famous for theology.
18. Arthur James Balfour (1848–1930), chief secretary in Ireland 1887–91.
19. *Irish Ecclesiastical Record*, founded by Cardinal Cullen in 1864, to promote his ultramontane policies for the Irish church. The *Record* promulgated and explained papal doctrine in terms of universal catholicism; hence the topicality of an issue like the 'Spanish dispensation'.
20. A town in Australia, some seventy miles from Melbourne. It became a boom settlement as a result of the 1851 gold rush.
21. Shrove, days before Lent when the faithful come for confession; also for marriage, which is not solemnised between Shrove and Easter.
22. Alfred Lord Tennyson, 'Crossing the Bar' (1889), stanza 3.
23. Daniel O'Connell (1775–1847), Irish constitutional nationalist; St Alphonsus Liguori (1696–1787), an Italian churchman and equally a moderate advocate of the via media in moral theology.
24. Dunboyne Institute at Maynooth, Co. Kildare.

endowments and emoluments, to Rome?' asked a young, eager fellow, who says he can read the Office, going ten miles an hour on the bicycle.

''Twouldn't ever do,' said a Roman student; 'you must be brought up in Rome to understand its spirit. Transplanted shoots never thrive there.'

'Psha!' said an old Maynooth man, who had been listening impatiently to these suggestions; 'we forgot more theology in Maynooth than you ever learned.'

'I don't want to disparage your knowledge of theology, Father,' said my curate, sweetly, 'but you know there are other elements in priestly education besides the mere propositions, and the *solvuntur objecta*[25] of theology. And it is in Rome these subtle and almost intangible accomplishments are acquired.'

Now, this was getting a little warm; so I winked at a young fellow down along the table, and he took the hint promptly, and cried out: 'Look here, Father Dan, this is tiresome. Tell us how you managed the Irish Brigade in France in the fifties.[26] Weren't they going to throw Marseilles into the sea?'

'Now, now,' said I, 'that won't do. I'm not going to be trotting out that old chestnut at every dinner party. Let us have a song!'

And we had, and a good many of them — dear old Irish melodies that would melt an icicle and put blood into a marble statue. No nonsense at my table, I assure you. No operatic rubbish, but genuine Irish music, with the right lilt and the right sentiment. I did let a young fellow once sing, 'I Dreamt that I Dwelt in Marble Halls';[27] but I told him never to repeat it. But it was worth while going miles to hear my curate singing, in his own fine voice, that superb ballad of that true and gentle patriot, Thomas Davis, 'The mess-tent is full, and the glasses are set.'[28]

Dear me! what a mercurial race we are; and how the mercury runs up and down in the barometer of our human hearts! I could see the young priests' faces whitening at the words:

> 'God prosper old Ireland! You'd think them afraid,
> So pale grew the chiefs of the Irish Brigade!'

and softening out in lines of tenderness when the end came:

> 'For, on far foreign fields, from Dunkirk to Belgrade,
> Lie the soldiers and chiefs of the Irish Brigade.'

Then we had 'The West's Awake,' and 'Dear Land,' and then we all arose and sang together, 'God bless the Pope, the great, the good.'[29] I was going to say 'sang in unison,' but I am afraid I should be trespassing on the sacred precincts of truth; yet if that grand old man in Rome, that electric spark in the vase of alabaster, sitting in that lonely chamber, behind the long, empty, gas-lit state apartments, could hear those voices there above the western seas, he would surely realize more keenly what he understands already, that he can always call upon his Irish reserves to ring, as with a fence of steel, the chair and the prerogatives of Peter.

Then came the 'Good-nights.' I pulled aside an old friend, a great theologian, who has all kinds of musty, dusty, leather-bound, water-stained volumes on his shelves.

'Did you ever hear,' I whispered, 'of a mysterious thing, called the *Kampaner Thal*?'[30]

'Never,' he said, emphatically.

'You couldn't conjecture what it is?'

'No,' he said, with deliberation; 'but I can aver it is neither Greek, Latin, nor Irish.'

'Would you mind looking up your cyclopædias,' I pleaded, 'and letting me know immediately that you find it?'

'Of course,' he replied. Then, jerking his thumb over his shoulder: 'I suppose it is this chap?'

'It is,' I said. 'He reads a good deal —'

'Look here, Father Dan, I don't know what we're coming to. Did you ever see such a sight as that table tonight?'

'Never,' I replied, resignedly.

25. A theological procedure, 'the solving of objections'.
26. An extra-parliamentary grouping of Liberal MPs formed in 1851 to oppose the Ecclesiastical Titles Bill; it had Cardinal Cullen's support and in time became known derisively as the 'Pope's Brass Band'. Hence Father Dan's evasiveness.
27. A romantic aria from *The Bohemian Girl* by Michael William Balfe (1807–70).
28. 'The Battle of the Irish Brigade' by Thomas Osborne Davis (1818–45), celebrating a triumph of one of the original Irish brigades on the battlefields of Europe after the Treaty of Limerick (1691). The indented quotations are from the same ballad. 'The West's Awake' and 'Dear Land' are also by Davis.
29. A popular catholic hymn.
30. The title of a philosophic dialogue which a Captain Ormsby reads to Father Dan in the next chapter of the novel; no author is mentioned.

'Would any one believe, when we came on the mission, that we'd live to see such things? Why, these fellows talk up to us as if we were their equals. Don't you remember when a curate daren't open his mouth at table?'

'Of course,' I replied, demurely.

'And it is only now I am beginning to discover the vagaries of this chap of mine. Do you know what he wants? A shrine, if you please — some kind of picture, with candles lighting before it all day. "Can't you say your Rosary," I said, "like your betters?" No, he should have the shrine. And now he wants to force on Benediction every Sunday — not every first Sunday of the month, but every Sunday, if you please. And he has a big red lamp, burning in what he calls his oratory. You can see it miles away. I say to the boys, "Don't be afraid to put to sea at night now, boys. Begor, ye've got a lighthouse at last." Well, good-bye! What's this thing you want?'

And he jotted down the name, I presume phonetically, in his note-book. Now, mind, that man has not had a scandal in his parish for fourteen years; and he is up to his neck in securities for half the farmers of the district.

All this time, shrinking into an obscure corner of the hall, was my Curé d'Ars,[31] as I call him. He now came forward to say good night, his thin face wreathed in smiles, and his two hands stretched out in thankfulness.

'Good night, Father Dan, and a thousand thanks. I never spent a pleasanter evening. What fine young fellows! So clever, so jolly, and so edifying! Won't it be a satisfaction for us when we are going to leave behind us such splendid safeguards of the faith?'

His curate was waiting respectfully. He now got the little man into his great-coat, and buttoned it from collar to boot; the latter murmuring his thanks all the time:

31. St Jean-Baptiste Vianney (1786–1859), a saintly French parish priest, was popularly known as the Curé d'Ars.

'Dear me! dear me! what a trouble I am! Many thanks! Many thanks! There, now I am all right!'

Then his muffler was wrapped carefully around his neck by this big grenadier, and his gloves were drawn over his hands.

'Dear me! dear me! how good! how kind! I'm a regular mummy! a real Egyptian mummy, Father Dan! Good night! good night! Dear me, what a pleasant gathering!'

And the stalwart curate lifted him on his car, as if he were an infant.

A few days later we had a long chat over many things, I and my curate.

When he was going he said:

'That was a real jolly evening, Father Dan! I never enjoyed anything so much!'

'Yes,' I said, 'and you had a splendid audience for that noble song!'

'Yes, indeed; they were very kind.'

'Oh, I don't mean *in foro interno*,' I said, 'but *in foro externo*.[32] There was a crowd outside the window!'

'My God!' he cried, quite shocked. 'What a scandal!'

'Not a bit of it,' I said; 'you've gone up a hundred per cent. in the estimation of the villagers. There was a real fight for the window-sill. But your friend, Jem Deady, captured it.'

He looked dreadfully annoyed.

'Jem says that he kept awake all night trying to remember the notes; and if you'd give him the words of the song and whistle it —'

'What!' said Father Letheby, like a pistol-shot.

'And if you'd give him two or three audiences — I suppose he means rehearsals on the piano — he is quite sure —'

! !! !!!

Dear me; how some people despise popularity!

32. The 'inner forum', as distinct from the 'outer forum'.

EDITH OENONE SOMERVILLE

(1858–1949) and

VIOLET FLORENCE MARTIN

(1862–1915)

from: THE REAL CHARLOTTE (1894)

[*The Real Charlotte* is the most accomplished work of Edith Somerville and Violet Martin, who wrote under the pen-name 'Martin Ross'.The novel's complex action culminates in these four chapters. In the forefront of the action is the spirited, naive, rather common, heroine, Francie, a 'Dublin Jackeen' who has strayed among the treacheries of Anglo-Irish society in County Cork. In the background is the evil genius of the novel, Charlotte Mullen, who, having contrived Francie's downfall, is preparing to leave Rosemount — where she has been staying in the absence of Francie's husband — to clear the way for catastrophe. Charlotte had brought Francie together with the worthless English officer, Gerald Hawkins, whom Francie had rejected when she discovered that he was already engaged. She has married Roddy Lambert, agent of Sir Christopher Dysart, a rich local landowner. Lambert has always been Charlotte's secret passion. As this extract opens, Francie is torn between her obligations to Lambert and her revived infatuation for Hawkins.]

CHAPTER XLVIII

The question, ten days afterwards, to anyone who had known all the features of the case, would have been whether Francie was worth Christopher's act of championing.

At the back of the Rosemount kitchen-garden the ground rose steeply into a knoll of respectable height, where grew a tangle of lilac bushes, rhododendrons, seringas, and yellow broom. A gravel path wound ingratiatingly up through these, in curves artfully devised by Mr. Lambert to make the most of the extent and the least of the hill, and near the top a garden-seat was sunk in the bank, with laurels shutting it in on each side, and a laburnum 'showering golden tears' above it. Through the perfumed screen of the lilac bushes in front unromantic glimpses of the roof of the house were obtainable — eyesores to Mr. Lambert, who had concentrated all his energies on hiding everything nearer than the semi-circle of lake and distant mountain held in an opening cut through the rhododendrons at the corner of the little plateau on which the seat stood. Without the disturbance of middle distance the eye lay at ease on the far-off struggle of the Connemara mountains, and on a serene vista of Lough Moyle; a view that enticed forth, as to a playground, the wildest and most foolish imaginations, and gave them elbow-room; a world so large and remote that it needed the sound of wheels on the road to recall the existence of the petty humanities of Lismoyle.

Francie and Hawkins were sitting there on the afternoon of the day on which Lambert was expected to come home, and as the sun, that had stared in at them through the opening in the rhododendrons when they first went there, slid farther round, their voices sank in unconscious accord with the fading splendours of the afternoon, and their silences seemed momently more difficult to break. They were nearing the end of the phase that had begun in the wood at Bruff, impelled to its verge by the unspoken knowledge that the last of the unthinking, dangerous days was dying with the sun, and that a final parting was looming up beyond. Neither knew for certain the mind of the other, or how they had dropped into this so-called friendship that in half a dozen afternoons had robbed all other things of reality, and made the intervals between their meetings like a feverish dream. Francie did not dare to think much about it; she lived in a lime-light glow that surrounded her wherever she went, and all the world outside was dark. He was going in a fortnight, in ten days, in a week; that was the only fact that the future had held for her since Captain Cursiter had met them with the telegram in his hand on the lake shore at Bruff. She forgot her resolutions; she forgot her pride; and before she reached home that afternoon the spell of the new phase, that was the old, only intensified by forgiveness, was on her. She shut her eyes, and blindly gave house-room in her heart to the subtle passion that came in the garb of an old friend, with a cant about compassion on its lips, and perfidious promises that its life was only for a fortnight.

To connect this supreme crisis of a life with such a person as Mr. Gerald Hawkins may seem incongruous; but Francie was not aware of either crisis or incongruity. All she knew of was the enthralment that lay in each prosaic afternoon visit, all she felt, the tired effort of conscience against fascination. Her emotional Irish nature, with all its frivolity and recklessness, had also, far down in it, an Irish girl's moral principle and purity; but each day she found it more difficult to hide the truth from him; each day the under-currents of feeling drew them helplessly nearer to each other. Everything was against her. Lambert's business had, as he expected, taken him to Dublin, and kept him there; Cursiter, like most men, was chary of active interference in another man's affairs, whatever his private opinion might be; and Charlotte, that guardian of youth, that trusty and vigilant spy, sat in her own room writing interminable letters, or went on long and complicated shopping expeditions whenever Hawkins came to the house.

On this golden, still afternoon, Francie strayed out soon after lunch, half dazed with unhappiness and excitement. Tonight her husband would come home. In four days Hawkins would have gone, as eternally, so far as she was concerned, as if he were dead; he would soon forget her, she thought, as she walked to and fro among the blossoming apple trees in the kitchen-garden. Men forgot very easily, and, thanks to the way she had tried her best to make him think she didn't care, there was not a word of hers to bring him back to her. She hated herself for her discretion; her soul thirsted for even one word of understanding, that would be something to live upon in future days of abnegation, when it would be nothing to her that she had gained his respect, and one tender memory would be worth a dozen self-congratulations.

She turned at the end of the walk and came back again under the apple trees; the ground under her feet was white with fallen blossoms; her fair hair gleamed among the thick embroidery of the branches, and her face was not shamed by their translucent pink and white. At a little distance Eliza Hackett, in a starched lilac calico, was gathering spinach, and meditating no doubt with comfortable assurance on the legitimacy of Father Heffernan's apostolic succession, but outwardly the embodiment of solid household routine and respectability. As Francie passed her she raised her decorous face from the spinach-bed with a question as to whether the trout would be for dinner or for breakfast; the master always fancied fish for his breakfast, she reminded Francie. Eliza Hackett's tone was distant, but admonitory, and it dispelled in a moment the visions of another now impossible future that were holding high carnival before Francie's vexed eyes. The fetter made itself coldly felt, and following came the quick pang of remorse at the thought of the man who was wasting on her the best love he had to give. Her change of mood was headlong, but its only possible expression was trivial to absurdity, if indeed any incident in a soul's struggle can be called trivial. Some day, further on in eternity, human beings will know what their standards of proportion and comparison are worth, and may perhaps find the glory of some trifling actions almost insufferable.

She gave the necessary order, and hurrying into the house brought out from it the piece of corduroy that she was stitching in lines of red silk as a waistcoat for her husband, and with a childish excitement at the thought of this expiation, took the path that led to the shrubbery on the hill. As she reached its first turn she hesitated and stopped, an idea of further and fuller renunciation occurring to her. Turning, she called to the figure stooping among the glossy rows of spinach to desire that the parlour-maid should say that this afternoon she was not at home. Had Eliza Hackett then and there obeyed the order, it is possible that many things would have happened differently. But fate is seldom without a second string to her bow, and even if Francie's message had not been delayed by Eliza Hackett's determination to gather a pint of green gooseberries before she went in, it is possible that Hawkins would none the less have found his way to the top of the shrubbery, where Francie was sewing with the assiduity of Penelope.[1] It was about four o'clock when she heard his step coming up the devious slants of the path, and she knew as she heard it that, in spite of all her precautions, she had expected him. His manner and even his look had nothing now in them of the confident lover of last year; his flippancy was gone, and when he began by reproaching her for having hidden from him, his face was angry and wretched, and he spoke like a person who had been seriously and unjustly hurt. He was more in love than he had ever been before, and he was taking it badly, like a fever that the chills of opposition were driving back into his system.

She made excuses as best she might, with her eyes bent upon her work.

'I might have been sitting in the drawing-room now,' he said petulantly; 'only that Miss Mullen had seen you going off here by yourself, and told me I'd better go and find you.'

An unreasoning fear came over Francie, a fear as of something uncanny.

'Let us go back to the house,' she said; 'Charlotte will be expecting us.' She said it to contradict the thought that had become definite for the first time. 'Come; I'm going in.'

Hawkins did not move. 'I suppose you forget that this is Wednesday, and that I'm going on Saturday,' he replied dully. 'In any case you'll not be much good to Charlotte. She's gone up to pack her things. She told me herself she was going to be very busy, as she had to start at six o'clock.'

Francie leaned back, and realised that now she had no one to look to but herself, and happiness and misery fought within her till her hands trembled as she worked.

Each knew that this was, to all intents and purposes, their last meeting, and their consciousness was charged to brimming with unexpressed farewell. She talked of indifferent subjects; of what Aldershot[2] would be like, of what Lismoyle would think of the new regiment, of the trouble that he would have in packing his pictures, parrying, with a weakening hand, his efforts to make every subject personal; and all the time the laburnum drooped in beautiful despair above her, as if listening and grieving, and the cool-leaved lilac sent its fragrance to mingle with her pain, and to stir her to rebellion with the ecstasy of spring-time. The minutes passed barrenly by, and, as has been said, the silences became longer and more clinging, and the thoughts that filled them made each successive subject more bare and artificial. At last Hawkins got up, and walking to the opening cut in the shrubs, stood, with his hands in his pockets, looking out at the lake and the mountains. Francie stitched on; it seemed to her that if she stopped she would lose her last hold upon herself; she felt as if her work were a talisman to remind her of all the things that she was in peril of forgetting. When, that night, she took up the waistcoat again to work at it, she thought that her heart's blood had gone into the red stitches.

It was several minutes before Hawkins spoke. 'Francie,' he said, turning round and speaking thickly, 'are you going to let me leave you in this — in this kind of way? Have you realised that when I go on Saturday it's most likely — it's pretty certain, in fact — that we shall never see each other again?'

'Yes, I have,' she said, after a pause of a second or two. She did not say that for a fortnight her soul had beaten itself against the thought, and that to hear it in words was as much as her self-command could bear.

'You seem to care a great deal!' he said violently; 'you're thinking of nothing but that infernal piece of work, that I loathe the very sight of. Don't you think you could do without it for five minutes, at all events?'

She let her hands drop into her lap, but made no other reply.

'You're not a bit like what you used to be. You seem to take a delight in snubbing me and shutting me up. I must say, I never thought you'd have turned into a prig!' He felt this reproach to be so biting that he paused upon it to give it its full effect. 'Here I am going to England in four days, and to India in four months, and it's ten to one if I ever come home again. I mean to volunteer for the very first row that turns up. But it's just the same to you, you won't even take the trouble to say you're sorry.'

'If you had taken the trouble to answer my letters last autumn, you wouldn't be saying these things to me now,' she said, speaking low and hurriedly.

1. Penelope, the faithful wife of Odysseus, kept her suitors at bay by promising to choose between them when she had finished an embroidery which she stitched by day and unstitched by night.
2. A famous military barracks in England to which Hawkins must report before his departure to India.

'I don't believe it! I believe if you had cared about me then you wouldn't treat me like this now.'

'I *did* care for you,' she said, while the hard-held tears forced their way to her eyes; 'you made me do it, and then you threw me over, and now you're trying to put the blame on me!'

He saw the glisten on her eyelashes, and it almost took from him the understanding of what she said.

'Francie,' he said, his voice shaking, and his usually confident eyes owning the infection of her tears, 'you might forget that. I'm miserable. I can't bear to leave you!' He sat down again beside her, and, catching her hand, kissed it with a passion of repentance. He felt it shrink from his lips, but the touch of it had intoxicated him, and suddenly she was in his arms.

For a speechless instant they clung to each other; her head dropped to his shoulder, as if the sharp release from the tension of the last fortnight had killed her, and the familiar voice murmured in her ear:

'Say it to me — say you love me.'

'Yes I do — my dearest —' she said, with a moan that was tragically at variance with the confession. 'Ah, why do you make me so wicked!' She snatched herself away from him, and stood up, trembling all over. 'I wish I had never seen you — I wish I was dead.'

'I don't care what you say now,' said Hawkins, springing to his feet, 'you've said you loved me, and I know you mean it. Will you stand by it?' he went on wildly. 'If you'll only say the word I'll chuck everything overboard — I can't go away from you like this. Once I'm in England I can't get back here, and if I did, what good would it be to me? He'd never give us a chance of seeing each other, and we'd both be more miserable than we are, unless — unless there was a chance of meeting you in Dublin or somewhere —?' He stopped for an instant. Francie mutely shook her head. 'Well, then, I shall never see you.'

There was silence, and the words settled down into both their hearts. He cursed himself for being afraid of her, she, whom he had always felt to be his inferior, yet when he spoke it was with an effort.

'Come away with me out of this — come away with me for good and all! What's the odds? We can't be more than happy!'

Francie made an instinctive gesture with her hand while he spoke, as if to stop him, but she said nothing, and almost immediately the distant rush and rattle of a train came quietly into the stillness.

'That's his train!' she exclaimed, looking as startled as if the sound had been a sign from heaven. 'Oh, go away! He mustn't meet you coming away from here.'

'I'll go if you give me a kiss,' he answered drunkenly. His arms were round her again, when they dropped to his side as if he had been shot.

There was a footstep on the path immediately below the lilac bushes, and Charlotte's voice called to Francie that she was just starting for home and had come to make her adieux.

CHAPTER XLIX

Christopher Dysart drove to Rosemount next morning to see Mr. Lambert on business. He noticed Mrs. Lambert standing at the drawing-room window as he drove up, but she left the window before he reached the hall door, and he went straight to Mr. Lambert's study without seeing her again.

Francie returned listlessly to the seat that she had sprung from with a terrified throb of the heart at the thought that the wheels might be those of Hawkins' trap, and, putting her elbow on the arm of the chair, rested her forehead on her hand; her other hand drooped over the side of the chair, holding still in it the sprig of pink hawthorn that her husband had given her in the garden an hour before. Her attitude was full of languor, but her brain was working at its highest pressure, and at this moment she was asking herself what Sir Christopher would say when he heard that she had gone away with Gerald. She had seen him vaguely as one of the crowd of contemptuous or horror-stricken faces that had thronged about her pillow in the early morning, but his opinion had carried no more restraining power than that of Aunt Tish, or Uncle Robert, or Charlotte. Nothing had weighed with her then; the two principal figures in her life contrasted as simply and convincingly as night and day, and like night and day, too, were the alternative futures that were in her hand to choose from. Her eyes were open to her wrong-doing, but scarcely to her cruelty; it could not be as bad for Roddy, she thought, to live without her as for her to stay with him and think of Gerald in India, gone away from her for ever. Her reasoning power was easily mastered, her conscience was a thing of habit, and not fitted to grapple with this turbulent passion.

She swept towards her ruin like a little boat staggering under more sail than she can carry. But the sight of Christopher, momentary as it was, had startled for an instant the wildness of her thoughts; the saner breath of the outside world had come with him, and a touch of the self-respect that she had always gained from him made her press her hot forehead against her hand, and realise that the way of transgressors would be hard.

She remained sitting there, almost motionless, for a long time. She had no wish to occupy herself with anything; all the things about her had already the air of belonging to a past existence; her short sovereignty was over, and even the furniture that she had, a few weeks ago, pulled about and rearranged in the first ardour of possession seemed to look at her in a decorous, clannish way, as if she were already an alien. At last she heard the study door open, and immediately afterwards, Christopher's dog-cart went down the drive. It occurred to her that now, if ever, was the time to go to her husband and see whether, by diplomacy, she could evade the ride that he had asked her to take with him that afternoon. Hawkins had sent her a note saying that he would come to pay a farewell visit, a cautiously formal note that anyone might have seen, but that she was just as glad had not been seen by her husband, and at all hazards she must stay in to meet him. She got up and went to the study with a nervous colour in her cheeks, glancing out of the hall window as she passed it, with the idea that the threatening grey of the sky would be a good argument for staying at home. But if it rained, Roddy might stay at home too, she thought, and that would be worse than anything. That was her last thought as she went into the study.

Lambert was standing with his hands in his pockets, looking down at the pile of papers and books on the table, and Francie was instantly struck by something unwonted in his attitude, something rigid and yet spent, that was very different from his usual bearing. He looked at her with heavy eyes, and going to his chair let himself drop into it; then, still silently, he held out his hand to her. She thought he looked older, and that his face was puffy and unattractive, and in the highly-strung state of her nerves she felt a repugnance to him that almost horrified her. It is an unfortunate trait of human nature that a call for sympathy from a person with whom sympathy has been lost has a repellent instead of an attractive power, and if a strong emotion does not appear pathetic, it is terribly near the ludicrous. In justice to Francie it must be said that her dominant feeling as she gave Lambert her hand and was drawn down on to his knee was less repulsion than a sense of her own hypocrisy.

'What's the matter, Roddy?' she asked, after a second or two of silence, during which she felt the labouring of his breath.

'I'm done for,' he said, 'that's what's the matter.'

'Why! what do you mean?' she exclaimed, turning her startled face half towards him, and trying not to shrink as his hot breath struck on her cheek.

'I've lost the agency.'

'Lost the agency!' repeated Francie, feeling as though the world with all the things she believed to be most solid were rocking under her feet. 'Do you mean he's after dismissing you?'

Lambert moved involuntarily, from the twitch of pain that the word gave him. It was this very term that Lismoyle would soon apply to him, as if he were a thieving butler or a drunken coachman.

'That's about what it will come to,' he said bitterly. 'He was too damned considerate to tell me so today, but he's going to do it. He's always hated me just as I have hated him, and this is his chance, though God knows what's given it to him.'

'You're raving!' cried Francie incredulously; 'what on earth would make him turn you away?' She felt that her voice was sharp and unnatural, but she could not make it otherwise. The position was becoming momently more horrible from the weight of unknown catastrophe, the sight of her husband's suffering and the struggle to sympathise with it, and the hollow disconnection between herself and everything about her.

'I can't tell you — all in a minute,' he said with difficulty. 'Wouldn't you put your arm round my neck, Francie, as if you were sorry for me? You might be sorry for me, and for yourself too. We're ruined. Oh my God!' he groaned, 'we're ruined!'

She put her arm round his neck, and pity, and a sense that it was expected of her, made her kiss his forehead. At the touch of her lips his sobs came suddenly and dreadfully, and his arms drew her convulsively to him. She lay there helpless and dry-eyed, enduring a wretchedness that in some ways was comparable to his own, but never becoming merged in the situation, never quite losing her sense of repulsion at his abasement.

'I never meant to touch a farthing of his — in the long run —' he went on, recovering himself a little; 'I'd have paid him back every half-penny in the end — but, of course, he doesn't believe that. What does he care what I say!'

'Did you borrow money from him, or what was it?' asked Francie gently.

'Yes, I did,' replied Lambert, setting his teeth; 'but I didn't tell him. I was eaten up with debts, and I had to — to borrow some of the estate money.' It was anguish to lower himself from the pedestal of riches and omnipotence on which he had always posed to her, and he spoke stumblingly. 'It's very hard to explain these things to you — it's — it's not so unusual as you'd think — and then, before I'd time to get things square again, some infernal mischief-maker has set him on to ask to see the books, and put him up to matters that he'd never have found out for himself.'

'Was he angry?' she asked, with the quietness that was so unlike her.

'Oh, I don't know — I don't care —' moving again restlessly in his chair; 'he's such a rotten, cold-blooded devil, you can't tell what he's at.' Even at this juncture it gave him pleasure to make little of Christopher to Francie. 'He asked me the most beastly questions he could think of, in that d —— d stammering way of his. He's to write to me in two or three days, and I know well what he'll say,' he went on with a stabbing sigh; 'I suppose he'll have it all over the country in a week's time. He's been to the bank and seen the estate account, and that's what's done me. I asked him plump and plain if he hadn't been put up to it, and he didn't deny it, but there's no one could have known what was paid into that account but Baker or one of the clerks, and they knew nothing about the fines — I mean — they couldn't understand enough to tell him anything. But what does it matter who told him. The thing's done now, and I may as well give up.'

'What will you do?' said Francie faintly.

'If it wasn't for you I think I'd put a bullet through my head,' he answered, his innately vulgar soul prompting him to express the best thought that was in him in conventional heroics, 'but I couldn't leave you, Francie — I couldn't leave you —' he broke down again — 'it was for our honeymoon I took the most of the money —' He could not go on, and her whole frame was shaken by his sobs.

'Don't, Roddy, don't cry,' she murmured, feeling cold and sick.

'He knows I took the money,' Lambert went on incoherently; 'I'll have to leave the country — I'll sell everything —' he got up and began to walk about the room — 'I'll pay him — damn him — I'll pay him every farthing. He sha'n't have it to say he was kept waiting for his money! He shall have it this week!'

'But how will you pay him if you haven't the money?' said Francie, with the same lifelessness of voice that had characterised her throughout.

'I'll borrow the money — I'll raise it on the furniture; I'll send the horses up to Sewell's, though God knows what price I'll get for them this time of year, but I'll manage it somehow. I'll go out to Gurthnamuckla this very afternoon about it. Charlotte's got a head on her shoulders —' He stood still, and the idea of borrowing from Charlotte herself took hold of him. He felt that such trouble as this must command her instant sympathy, and awaken all the warmth of their old friendship, and his mind turned towards her stronger intelligence with a reliance that was creditable to his ideas of the duties of a friend. 'I could give her a bill of sale on the horses and furniture,' he said to himself.

His eyes rested for the first time on Francie, who had sunk into the chair from which he had risen, and was looking at him as if she did not see him. Her hair was ruffled from lying on his shoulder, and her eyes were wild and fixed, like those of a person who is looking at a far-off spectacle of disaster and grief.

CHAPTER L

The expected rain had not come, though the air was heavy and damp with the promise of it. It hung unshed, above the thirsty country, looking down gloomily upon the dusty roads, and the soft and straight young grass in the meadows; waiting for the night, when the wind would moan and cry for it, and the newborn leaves would shudder in the dark at its coming.

At three o'clock Francie was sure that the afternoon would be fine, and soon afterwards she came downstairs in her habit, and went into the drawing-room to wait for the black mare to be brought to the door. She was going to ride towards Gurthnamuckla to meet Lambert, who had gone there some time before; he had made Francie promise to meet him on his way home, and she was going to keep her word. He had become quite a different person to her since the morning, a person who no longer appealed to her admiration or her confidence, but solely and distressingly to her pity. She had always thought of him as invincible, self-sufficing, and possessed of innumerable interests besides herself; she knew him now as dishonest and disgraced, and miserable, stripped of all his pretensions and vanities, but she cared for him today more than yesterday. It was against her will that his weakness appealed to her; she would have given worlds for a heart that did not smite her at its claim, but her pride helped out her compassion. She told herself that she could not let people have it to say that she ran away from Roddy because he was in trouble.

She felt chilly, and she shivered as she stood by the fire, whose unseasonable extravagance daily vexed the righteous soul of Eliza Hackett. Hawkins' note was in her hand, and she read it through twice while she waited; then, as she heard the sound of wheels on the gravel, she tore it in two and threw it into the fire, and, for the second time that morning, ran to the window.

It was Christopher Dysart again. He saw her at the window and took off his cap, and before he had time to ring the bell, she had opened the hall door. She had, he saw at once, been crying, and her paleness, and the tell-tale heaviness of her eyes, contrasted pathetically with the smartness of her figure in her riding habit, and the boyish jauntiness of her hard felt hat.

'Mr. Lambert isn't in, Sir Christopher,' she began at once, as if she had made up her mind whom he had come to see; 'but won't you come in?'

'Oh — thank you — I — I haven't much time — I merely wanted to speak to your husband,' stammered Christopher.

'Oh, please come in,' she repeated, 'I want to speak to you.' Her eyes suddenly filled with tears, and she turned quickly from him and walked towards the drawing-room.

Christopher followed her with the mien of a criminal. He felt that he would rather have been robbed twenty times over than see the eyes that, in his memory, had always been brilliant and undefeated, avoiding his as if they were afraid of him, and know that he was the autocrat before whom she trembled. She remained standing near the middle of the room, with one hand on the corner of the piano, whose gaudy draperies had, even at this juncture, a painful sub-effect upon Christopher; her other hand fidgeted restlessly with a fold of the habit that she was holding up, and it was evident that whatever her motive had been in bringing him in, her courage was not equal to it. Christopher waited for her to speak, until the silence became unendurable.

'I intended to have been here earlier,' he said, saying anything rather than nothing, 'but there was a great deal to be got through at the Bench today, and I've only just got away. You know I'm a magistrate now, and indifferently minister justice —'

'I'm glad I hadn't gone out when you came,' she interrupted, as though, having found a beginning, she could not lose a moment in using it. 'I wanted to say that if you — if you'll only give Roddy a week's time he'll pay you. He only meant to borrow the money, like, and he thought he could pay you before; but, indeed, he says he'll pay you in a week.' Her voice was low and full of bitterest humiliation, and Christopher wished that before he had arraigned his victim, and offered him up as an oblation to his half-hearted sense of duty, he had known that his infirmity of purpose would have brought him back three hours afterwards to offer the culprit a way out of his difficulties. It would have saved him from his present hateful position, and what it would have saved her was so evident, that he turned his head away as he spoke, rather than look at her.

'I came back to tell your husband that — that he could arrange things in — in some such way,' he said, as guiltily and awkwardly as a boy. 'I'm sorry — more sorry than I can say — that he should have spoken to you about it. Of course, that was my fault. I should have told him then what I came to tell him now.'

'He's gone out now to see about selling his horses and the furniture,' went on Francie, scarcely realising all of Christopher's leniency in her desire to prove Lambert's severe purity of action. Her mind was not capable of more than one idea — one, that is, in addition to the question that had monopolised it since yesterday afternoon, and Christopher's method of expressing himself had never been easily understood by her.

'Oh, he mustn't think of doing that!' exclaimed Christopher, horrified that she should think him a Shylock, demanding so extreme a measure of restitution; 'it wasn't the actual money question that — that we disagreed about; he can take as long as he likes about repaying me. In fact — in fact you can tell him from me that — he said something this morning about giving up the agency. Well, I — I should be glad if he would keep it.'

He had stultified himself now effectually; he knew that he had acted like a fool, and he felt quite sure that Mr. Lambert's sense of gratitude would not prevent his holding the same opinion. He even foresaw Lambert's complacent assumption that Francie had talked him over, but he could not help himself. The abstract justice of allowing the innocent to suffer with the guilty was beyond him; he forgot to theorise, and acted on instinct as simply as a savage. She also had acted on instinct. When she called him in she had nerved herself to ask for reprieve, but she never hoped for forgiveness, and as his intention penetrated the egotism of suffering, the thought leaped with it that, if Roddy were to be let off, everything would be on the same footing that it had been yesterday evening. A blush that was incomprehensible to Christopher swept over her face; the grasp of circumstances relaxed somewhat, and a jangle of unexplainable feelings confused what self-control she had left.

'You're awfully good,' she began half hysterically. 'I always knew you were good; I wish Roddy was like you! Oh, I wish I was like you! I can't help it — I can't help crying; you were always too good to me, and I never was worth it!' She sat down on one of the high stiff chairs, for which her predecessor had worked beaded seats, and hid her eyes in her handkerchief. 'Please don't talk to me; please don't say anything to me —' She stopped suddenly. 'What's that? Is that anyone riding up?'

'No. It's your horse coming round from the yard,' said Christopher, taking a step towards the window, and trying to keep up the farce of talking as if nothing had happened.

'My horse!' she exclaimed, starting up. 'Oh yes, I must go and meet Roddy. I mustn't wait any longer.' She began, as if unconscious of Christopher's presence, to look for the whip and gloves that she had laid down. He saw them before she did, and handed them to her.

'Good-bye,' he said, taking her cold, trembling hand, 'I must go too. You will tell your husband that it's — it's all right.'

'Yes. I'll tell him. I'm going to meet him. I must start now,' she answered, scarcely seeming to notice what he said, and withdrawing her hand from his, she began hurriedly to button on her gloves.

Christopher did not wait for further dismissal, but when his hand was on the door, her old self suddenly woke.

'Look at me letting you go away without telling you a bit how grateful I am to you!' she said, with a lift of her tear-disfigured eyes that was like a changeling of the look he used to know; 'but don't you remember what Mrs. Baker said about me, that "you couldn't expect any manners from a Dublin Jackeen"?'

She laughed weakly, and Christopher, stammering more than ever in an attempt to say that there was nothing to be grateful for, got himself out of the room.

After he had gone, Francie gave herself no time to think. Everything was reeling round her as she went out on to the steps, and even Michael the groom thought to himself that if he hadn't the trap to wash, he'd put the saddle on the chestnut and folly the misthress, she had that thrimulous[1] way with her when he put the reins into her hands, and only for it was the mare she was riding he wouldn't see her go out by herself.

It was the first of June, and the gaiety of the spring was nearly gone. The flowers had fallen from the hawthorn, the bluebells and primroses were vanishing as quietly as they came, the meadows were already swarthy, and the breaths of air that sent pale shimmers across them, were full of the unspeakable fragrance of the ripening grass. Under the trees, near Rosemount, the shadowing greenness had saturated the daylight with its gloom, but out among the open pastures and meadows the large grey sky seemed almost bright, and, in the rich sobriety of tone, the red cattle were brilliant spots of colour.

The black mare and her rider were now on thoroughly confidential terms, and, so humiliatingly interwoven are soul and body, as the exercise quickened the blood in her veins, Francie's incorrigible youth rose up, and while it brightened her eyes and drove colour to her cheeks, it whispered that somehow or other happiness might come to her. She rode fast till she reached the turn to Gurthnamuckla, and there, mindful of her husband's injunctions that she was not to ride up to the house, but to wait for him on the road, she relapsed into a walk.

As she slackened her pace, all the thoughts that

1. folley = follow; thrimulous is a dialect word probably combining 'tremulous' and 'trembling'.

she had been riding away from came up with her again. What claim had Roddy on her now? She had got him out of his trouble, and that was the most he could expect her to do for him. He hadn't thought much about the trouble he was bringing on her; he never as much as said he was sorry for the disgrace it would be to her. Why should she break her heart for him and Gerald's heart too? — as she said Hawkins' name to herself, her hands fell into her lap, and she moaned aloud. Every step the mare was taking was carrying her farther from him, but yet she could not turn back. She was changed since yesterday; she had seen her husband's soul laid bare, and it had shown her how tremendous were sin and duty; it had touched her slumbering moral sense as well as her kindness, and though she rebelled she did not dare to turn back.

It was not till she heard a pony's quick gallop behind her, and looking back, saw Hawkins riding after her at full speed, that she knew how soon she was to be tested. She had scarcely time to collect herself before he was pulling up the pony beside her, and had turned a flushed and angry face towards her.

'Didn't you get my note? Didn't you know I was coming?' he began in hot remonstrance. Then, seeing in a moment how ill and strange she looked, 'What's the matter? Has anything happened?'

'Roddy came home yesterday evening,' she said, with her eyes fixed on the mare's mane.

'Well, I know that,' interrupted Hawkins. 'Do you mean that he was angry? Did he find out anything about me? If he did see the note I wrote you, there was nothing in that.' Francie shook her head. 'Then it's nothing? It's only that you've been frightened by that brute,' he said, kicking his pony up beside the mare, and trying to look into Francie's downcast eyes. 'Don't mind him. It won't be for long.'

'You mustn't say that,' she said hurriedly. 'I was very wrong yesterday, and I'm sorry for it now.'

'I know you're not!' he burst out, with all the conviction that he felt. 'You can't unsay what you said to me yesterday. I sat up the whole night thinking the thing over and thinking of you, and at last I thought of a fellow I know out in New Zealand, who told me last year I ought to chuck the army and go out there.' He dropped his reins on the pony's neck, and took Francie's hand. 'Why shouldn't we go there together, Francie? I'll give up everything for you, my darling!'

She feebly tried to take her hand away, but did not reply.

'I've got three hundred a year of my own, and we can do ourselves awfully well on that out there. We'll always have lots of horses, and it's a ripping climate — and — and I love you, and I'll always love you!'

He was carried away by his own words, and, stooping his head, he kissed her hand again and again.

Every pulse in her body answered to his touch, and when she drew her hand away, it was with an effort that was more than physical.

'Ah! stop, stop,' she cried. 'I've changed — I didn't mean it.'

'Didn't mean what?' demanded Hawkins, with his light eyes on fire.

'Oh, leave me alone,' she said, turning her distracted face towards him. 'I'm nearly out of my mind as it is. What made you follow me out here? I came out so as I wouldn't see you, and I'm going to meet Roddy now.'

Hawkins' colour died slowly down to a patchy white. 'What do you think it was that made me follow you? Do you want to make me tell you over again what you know already?' She did not answer, and he went on, trying to fight against his own fears by speaking very quietly and rationally. 'I don't know what you're at, Francie. I don't believe you know what you're saying. Something must have happened, and it would be fairer to tell me what it is, than to drive me distracted in this sort of way.'

There was a pause of several seconds, and he was framing a fresh remonstrance when she spoke.

'Roddy's in great trouble. I wouldn't leave him,' she said, taking refuge in a prevarication of the exact truth.

Something about her told Hawkins that things were likely to go hard with him, and there was something, too, that melted his anger as it rose; but her pale face drew him to a height of passion that he had not known before.

'And don't you think anything about *me*?' he said with a breaking voice. 'Are you ready to throw me overboard just because he's in trouble, when you know he doesn't care for you a tenth part as much as I do? Do you mean to tell me that you want me to go away, and say good-bye to you for ever? If you do, I'll go, and if you hear I've gone to the devil, you'll know who sent me.'

The naïve selfishness of this argument was not perceived by either. Hawkins felt his position to be almost noble, and did not in the least realise what he was asking Francie to sacrifice for him. He had even forgotten the idea that had occurred to him last night, that to go to New Zealand would be a pleasanter way of escaping from his creditors than marrying Miss Coppard. Certainly Francie had no thought of his selfishness or of her own sacrifice. She was giddy with struggle; right and wrong had lost their meaning and changed places elusively; the only things that she saw clearly were the beautiful future that had been offered to her, and the look in Roddy's face when she had told him that wherever he had to go she would go with him.

The horses had moved staidly on, while these two lives stood still and wrestled with their fate, and the summit was slowly reached of the long hill on which Lambert had once pointed out to her the hoof-prints of Hawkins' pony. The white road and the grey rock country stretched out before them, colourless and discouraging under the colourless sky, and Hawkins still waited for his answer. Coming towards them up the tedious slope was a string of half-a-dozen carts, with a few people walking on either side; an unremarkable procession, that might have meant a wedding, or merely a neighbourly return from market, but for a long, yellow coffin that lay, hemmed in between old women, in the midmost cart. Francie felt a superstitious thrill as she saw it; a country funeral, with its barbarous and yet fitting crudity, always seemed to bring death nearer to her than the plumed conventionalities of the hearses and mourning coaches that she was accustomed to. She had once been to the funeral of a fellow Sunday-school child in Dublin, and the first verse of the hymn that they had sung then, came back, and began to weave itself in with the beat of the mare's hoofs.

'Brief life is here our portion,
  Brief sorrow, short-lived care,
The life that knows no ending,
  The tearless life is there.'[2]

'Francie, are you going to answer me? Come away with me this very day. We could catch the six o'clock train before any one knew — dearest, if you love me —' His roughened, unsteady voice seemed to come to her from a distance, and yet was like a whisper in her own heart.

'Wait till we are past the funeral,' she said, catching, in her agony, at the chance of a minute's respite.

At the same moment an old man, who had been standing by the side of the road, leaning on his stick, turned towards the riders, and Francie recognised in him Charlotte's retainer, Billy Grainy. His always bloodshot eyes were redder than ever, his mouth dribbled like a baby's, and the smell of whisky poisoned the air all around him.

'I'm waitin' on thim here this half-hour,' he began, in a loud drunken mumble, hobbling to Francie's side, and moving along beside the mare, 'as long as they were taking her back the road to cry her at her own gate. Owld bones is wake, asthore,[3] owld bones is wake!' He caught at the hem of Francie's habit to steady himself; 'be cripes! Miss Duffy was a fine woman, Lord ha' maircy on her. And a great woman! And divil blasht thim that threw her out of her farm to die in the Union[4] — the dom ruffins.'[5]

As on the day, now very long ago, when she had first ridden to Gurthnamuckla, Francie tried to shake his hand off her habit; he released it stupidly, and staggering to the side of the road, went on grumbling and cursing. The first cart, creaking and rattling under its load of mourners, was beside them by this time, and Billy, for the benefit of its occupants, broke into a howl of lamentation.

'Thanks be to God Almighty, and thanks be to His Mother, the crayture had thim belonging to her that would bury her like a Christian.' He shook his fist at Francie. 'Ah-ha! go home to himself and owld Charlotte, though it's little thim regards you —' He burst into drunken laughter, bending and tottering over his stick.

Francie, heedless of the etiquette that required that she and Hawkins should stop their horses till the funeral passed, struck the mare, and passed by him at a quickened pace. The faces in the carts were all turned upon her, and she felt as if she were enduring, in a dream, the eyes of an implacable tribunal; even the mare seemed to share in her

2. The words are by James Mason Neale (1818–66), translated from the Latin 'Hic breve vivitur'.

3. 'Old bones are weak, my dear.'
4. Poor Law Union. Charlotte had been responsible for the eviction that drove the deceased to the poor-house.
5. damned ruffians.

agitation, and sidled and fidgeted on the narrow strip of road, that was all the space left to her by the carts. The coffin was almost abreast of Francie now, and her eyes rested with a kind of fascination on its bare, yellow surface. She became dimly aware that Norry the Boat[6] was squatted beside it on the straw, when one of the other women began suddenly to groan and thump on the coffin-lid with her fists, in preparation for a burst of the Irish Cry,[7] and at the signal Norry fell upon her knees, and flung out her arms inside her cloak, with a gesture that made her look like a great vulture opening its wings for flight. The cloak flapped right across the mare's face, and she swerved from the cart with a buck that loosened her rider in the saddle, and shook her hat off. There was a screech of alarm from all the women, the frightened mare gave a second and a third buck, and at the third Francie was shot into the air, and fell, head first, on the road.

6. One of Charlotte's servants.
7. The ritual keening at funerals.

CHAPTER LI

The floor of the potato loft at Gurthnamuckla had for a long time needed repairs, a circumstance not in itself distressing to Miss Mullen, who held that effort after mere theoretical symmetry was unjustifiable waste of time in either housekeeping or farming. On this first of June, however, an intimation from Norry that 'there's ne'er a pratie[1] ye have that isn't ate with the rats,' given with the thinly-veiled triumph of servants in such announcements, caused a truculent visit of inspection to the potato loft; and in her first spare moment of the afternoon, Miss Mullen set forth with her tool-basket, and some boards from a packing-case, to make good the breaches with her own hands. Doing it herself saved the necessity of taking the men from their work, and moreover ensured its being properly done.

So she thought, as, having climbed the ladder that led from the cowhouse to the loft, she put her tools on the ground, and surveyed with a workman's eye the job she had set herself. The loft was hot and airless, redolent of the cowhouse below, as well as of the clayey mustiness of the potatoes that were sprouting in the dirt on the floor, and even sending pallid, worm-like roots down into space through the cracks in the boards. Miss Mullen propped the window-shutter open with the largest potato, and, pinning up her skirt, fell to work.

1. potato.

She had been hammering and sawing for a quarter of an hour when she heard the clatter of a horse's hoofs on the cobble-stones of the yard, and, getting up from her knees, advanced to the window with caution and looked out. It was Mr. Lambert, in the act of pulling up his awkward young horse, and she stood looking down at him in silence while he dismounted, with a remarkable expression on her face, one in which some acute mental process was mixed with the half-unconscious and yet all-observant recognition of an intensely familiar object.

'Hullo, Roddy!' she called out at last, 'is that you? What brings you over so early?'

Mr. Lambert started with more violence than the occasion seemed to demand.

'Hullo!' he replied, in a voice not like his own, 'is that where you are?'

'Yes, and it's where I'm going to stay. This is the kind of fancy work I'm at,' brandishing her saw; 'so if you want to talk to me you must come up here.'

'All right,' said Lambert, gloomily, 'I'll come up as soon as I put the colt in the stable.'

It is a fact so improbable as to be worth noting, that before Lambert found his way up the ladder, Miss Mullen had unpinned her skirt and fastened up the end of a plait that had escaped from the massive coils at the back of her head.

'Well, and where's the woman that owns you?' she asked, beginning to work again, while her visitor stood in obvious discomfort, with his head touching the rafters, and the light from the low window striking sharply up against his red and heavy eyes.

'At home,' he replied, almost vacantly. 'I'd have been here half an hour ago or more,' he went on after a moment or two, 'but the colt cast a shoe, and I had to go on to the forge beyond the cross to get it put on.'

Charlotte, with a flat pencil in her mouth, grunted responsively, while she measured off a piece of board, and, holding it with her knee on the body of a legless wheelbarrow, began to saw it across. Lambert looked on, provoked and disconcerted by this engrossing industry. With his brimming sense of collapse and crisis, he felt that even this temporary delay of sympathy was an unkindness.

'That colt must be sold this week, so I couldn't afford to knock his hoof to bits on the hard road.' His manner was so portentous that Charlotte looked up again, and permitted herself to remark on what had been apparent to her the moment she saw him.

'Why, what's the matter with you, Roddy? Now I come to see you, you look as if you'd been at your own funeral.'

'I wish to God I had! It would be the best thing could happen me.'

He found pleasure in saying something to startle her, and in seeing that her face became a shade hotter than the stifling air and the stooping over her work had made it.

'What makes you talk like that?' she said, a little strangely, as it seemed to him.

He thought she was moved, and he immediately felt his position to be more pathetic than he had believed. It would be much easier to explain the matter to Charlotte than to Francie, he felt at once; Charlotte understood business matters, a formula which conveyed to his mind much comfortable flexibility in money affairs.

'Charlotte,' he said, looking down at her with eyes that self-pity and shaken self-control were moistening again, 'I'm in most terrible trouble. Will you help me?'

'Wait till I hear what it is and I'll tell you that,' replied Charlotte, with the same peculiar, flushed look on her face, and suggestion in her voice of strong and latent feeling. He could not tell how it was, but he felt as if she knew what he was going to say.

'I'm four hundred pounds in debt to the estate, and Dysart has found it out,' he said, lowering his voice as if afraid that the spiders and wood-lice might repeat his secret.

'Four hundred,' thought Charlotte; 'that's more than I reckoned'; but she said aloud, 'My God! Roddy, how did that happen?'

'I declare to you I don't know how it happened. One thing and another came against me, and I had to borrow this money, and before I could pay it he found out.'

Lambert was a pitiable figure as he made his confession, his head, his shoulders, and even his moustache drooping limply, and his hands nervously twisting his ash plant.

'That's a bad business,' said Charlotte reflectively, and was silent for a moment, while Lambert realised the satisfaction of dealing with an intelligence that could take in such a situation instantaneously, without alarm or even surprise.

'Is he going to give you the sack?' she asked.

'I don't know yet. He didn't say anything definite.'

Lambert found the question hard to bear, but he endured it for the sake of the chance it gave him to lead up to the main point of the interview. 'If I could have that four hundred placed to his credit before I see him next, I believe there'd be an end of it. Not that I'd stay with him,' he went on, trying to bluster, 'or with any man that treated me this kind of way, going behind my back to look at the accounts.'

'Is that the way he found you out?' asked Charlotte, taking up the lid of the packing-case and twisting a nail out of it with her hammer. 'He must be smarter than you took him for.'

'Someone must have put him up to it,' said Lambert, 'someone who'd got at the books. It beats me to make it out. But what's the good of thinking of that? The thing that's setting me mad is to know how to pay him.' He waited to see if Charlotte would speak, but she was occupied in straightening the nail against the wall with her hammer, and he went on with a dry throat. 'I'm going to sell all my horses, Charlotte, and I daresay I can raise some money on the furniture; but it's no easy job to raise money in such a hurry as this, and if I'm to be saved from being disgraced, I ought to have it at once to stop his mouth. I believe if I could pay him at once he wouldn't have spunk enough to go any further with the thing.' He waited again, but the friend of his youth continued silent. 'Charlotte, no man ever had a better friend, through thick and thin, than I've had in you. There's no other person living that I'd put myself under an obligation to but yourself. Charlotte, for the sake of all that's ever been between us, would you lend me the money?'

Her face was hidden from him as she knelt, and he stooped and placed a clinging, affectionate hand upon her shoulder. Miss Mullen got up abruptly, and Lambert's hand fell.

'All that's ever been between us is certainly a very weighty argument, Roddy,' she said with a smile that deepened the ugly lines about her mouth, and gave Lambert a chilly qualm. 'There's a matter of three hundred pounds between us, if that's what you mean.'

'I know, Charlotte,' he said hastily. 'No one

remembers that better than I do. But this is a different kind of thing altogether. I'd give you a bill of sale on everything at Rosemount — and there are the horses out here too. Of course, I suppose I might be able to raise the money at the bank or somewhere, but it's a very different thing to deal with a friend, and a friend who can hold her tongue too. You never failed me yet, Charlotte, old girl, and I don't believe you'll do it now!'

His handsome, dark eyes were bent upon her face with all the pathos he was master of, and he was glad to feel tears rising in them.

'Well, I'm afraid that's just what I'll have to do,' she said, flinging away the nail that she had tried to straighten, and fumbling in her pocket for another; 'I may be able to hold my tongue, but I don't hold with throwing good money after bad.'

Lambert stood quite still, staring at her, trying to believe that this was the Charlotte who had trembled when he kissed her, whose love for him had made her his useful and faithful thrall.

'Do you mean to say that you'll see me ruined and disgraced sooner than put out your hand to help me?' he said passionately.

'I thought you said you could get the money somewhere else,' she replied, with undisturbed coolness, 'and you might know that coming to me for money is like going to the goat's house for wool. I've got nothing more to lend, and no one ought to know that better than yourself!'

Charlotte was standing, yellow-faced and insolent, opposite to Lambert, with her hands in the pockets of her apron; in every way a contrast to him, with his flushed forehead and suffused eyes. The dull, white light that struck up into the roof from the whitewashed kitchen wall, showed Lambert the furrowed paths of implacability in his adversary's face, as plainly as it showed her his defeat and desperation.

'*You've* got no more money to lend, d'ye say!' he repeated, with a laugh that showed he had courage enough left to lose his temper; 'I suppose you've got all the money you got eighteen months ago from the old lady lent out?[2] 'Pon my word, considering you got Francie's share of it for yourself, I think it would have been civiller to have given her husband the first refusal of a loan! I daresay I'd have given you as good interest as your friends in Ferry Lane!'

Charlotte's eyes suddenly lost their exaggerated indifference.

'And if she ever had the smallest claim to what ye call a share!' she vociferated, 'haven't you had it twenty times over? Was there ever a time that ye came cringing and crawling to me for money that I refused it to ye? And how do you thank me? By embezzling the money I paid for the land, and then coming to try and get it out of me over again, because Sir Christopher Dysart is taught sense to look into his own affairs, and see how his agent is cheating him!'

Some quality of triumph in her tone, some light of previous knowledge in her eye, struck Lambert.

'Was it you told him?' he said hoarsely, 'was it you spoke to Dysart?'

Every now and then in the conduct of her affairs, Miss Mullen permitted the gratification of her temper to take the place of the slower pleasure of secrecy.

'Yes, I told him,' she answered, without hesitation.

'You went to Dysart, and set him on to ruin me!' said Lambert, in a voice that had nearly as much horror as rage in it.

'And may I ask you what you've ever done for me,' she said, gripping her hammer with a strong, trembling hand, 'that I was to keep your tricks from being found out for you? What reason was there in God's earth that I wasn't to do my plain duty by those that are older friends than you?'

'What reason!' Lambert almost choked from the intolerable audacity and heartlessness of the question. 'Are you in your right mind to ask me that? You, that's been like a — a near relation to me all these years, or pretending to be! There was a time you wouldn't have done this to me, you know it damned well, and so do I. You were glad enough to do anything for me then, so long as I'd be as much as civil to you, and now, I suppose, this is your dirty devilish spite, because you were cut out by someone else!'

She did not flinch as the words went through and through her.

'Take care of yourself!' she said, grinning at him, 'perhaps you're not the one to talk about being cut out! Oh, I don't think ye need look as if ye didn't understand me. At all events, all ye have to do is to

2. The 'old lady' is Mrs Mullen, Charlotte's aunt, who died early in the novel.

go home and ask your servants — or, for the matter of that, anyone in the streets of Lismoyle — who it is that's cut ye out, and made ye the laughing-stock of the country?'

She put her hand on the dusty beam beside her, giddy with her gratified impulse, as she saw him take the blow and wither under it.

She scarcely heard at first the strange and sudden sound of commotion that had sprung up like a wind in the house opposite. The windows were all open, and through them came the sound of banging doors and running footsteps, and then Norry's voice screaming something as she rushed from room to room. She was in the kitchen now, and the words came gasping and sobbing through the open door.

'Where's Miss Charlotte? Where is she? O God! O God! Where is she? Miss Francie's killed, her neck's broke below on the road! O God of Heaven, help us!'

Neither Charlotte nor Lambert heard clearly what she said, but the shapeless terror of calamity came about them like a vapour and blanched the hatred in their faces. In a moment they were together at the window, and at the same instant Norry burst out into the yard, with outflung arms and grey hair streaming. As she saw Lambert, her strength seemed to go from her. She staggered back, and, catching at the door for support, turned from him and hid her face in her cloak.

WILLIAM BUTLER YEATS

(1865–1939)

from: THE SECRET ROSE (1897)

['The Crucifixion of the Outcast' is the fourth story in Yeats's collection of mystical stories, *The Secret Rose* (1897), in which he wished, as he announces in the 'Dedication', to dramatize 'the war of spiritual with natural order'. The collection spans Irish history from pagan times to the modern age. Yeats had intended to include 'The Adoration of the Magi' (and another story, 'The Tables of the Law') but omitted them for political reasons. The present story is adapted from a medieval Irish story, 'The Vision of Mac Conglinne', in which the minstrel triumphed over the Abbot.]

THE CRUCIFIXION OF THE OUTCAST

A man, with thin brown hair and a pale face, half ran, half walked, along the road that wound from the south to the town of Sligo. Many called him Cumhal, the son of Cormac, and many called him the Swift Wild Horse; and he was a gleeman,[1] and he wore a short parti-coloured doublet, and had pointed shoes, and a bulging wallet. Also he was of the blood of the Ernaans,[2] and his birthplace was the Field of Gold; but his eating and sleeping places were in the five kingdoms of Eri,[3] and his abiding-place was not upon the ridge of the earth. His eyes strayed from the tower of what was later the Abbey of the White Friars to a row of crosses which stood out against the sky upon a hill a little to the eastward of the town, and he clenched his fist, and shook it at the crosses. He knew they were not empty, for the birds were fluttering about them; and he thought how, as like as not, just such another vagabond as himself had been mounted on one of them; and he muttered: 'If it were hanging or bow-stringing, or stoning or beheading, it would be bad enough. But to have the birds pecking your eyes and the wolves eating your feet! I would that the red wind of the Druids had withered in his cradle the soldier of

1. A travelling minstrel or poet.

2. Probably descendants of Erannan, one of the forty chiefs of the Milesians, the last of the legendary conquerors of Ireland recorded in *The Book of Invasions*.

3. Eire (Ireland), which was divided in ancient times into five provinces (*cuig cúigí*): Ulster, Leinster, Connacht and two Munsters.

Dathi[4] who brought the tree of death out of barbarous lands, or that the lightning, when it smote Dathi at the foot of the mountain, had smitten him also, or that his grave had been dug by the green-haired and green-toothed merrows[5] deep at the roots of the deep sea.'

While he spoke, he shivered from head to foot, and the sweat came out upon his face, and he knew not why, for he had looked upon many crosses. He passed over two hills and under the battlemented gate, and then round by a left-hand way to the door of the Abbey. It was studded with great nails, and when he knocked at it he roused the lay brother who was the porter, and of him he asked a place in the guest-house. Then the lay brother took a glowing turf on a shovel, and led the way to a big and naked outhouse strewn with very dirty rushes; and lighted a rush-candle fixed between two of the stones of the wall, and set the glowing turf upon the hearth and gave him two unlighted sods and a wisp of straw, and showed him a blanket hanging from a nail, and a shelf with a loaf of bread and a jug of water, and a tub in a far corner. Then the lay brother left him and went back to his place by the door. And Cumhal the son of Cormac began to blow upon the glowing turf that he might light the two sods and the wisp of straw; but the sods and the straw would not light, for they were damp. So he took off his pointed shoes, and drew the tub out of the corner with the thought of washing the dust of the highway from his feet; but the water was so dirty that he could not see the bottom. He was very hungry, for he had not eaten all that day, so he did not waste much anger upon the tub, but took up the black loaf, and bit into it, and then spat out the bite, for the bread was hard and mouldy. Still he did not give way to his anger, for he had not drunken these many hours; having a hope of heath beer or wine at his day's end, he had left the brooks untasted, to make his supper the more delightful. Now he put the jug to his lips, but he flung it from him straightway, for the water was bitter and ill-smelling. Then he gave the jug a kick, so that it broke against the opposite wall, and he took down the blanket to wrap it about him for the night. But no sooner did he touch it than it was alive with skipping fleas. At this, beside himself with anger, he rushed to the door of the guest-house, but the lay brother, being well accustomed to such outcries, had locked it on the outside; so he emptied the tub and began to beat the door with it, till the lay brother came to the door and asked what ailed him, and why he woke him out of sleep. 'What ails me!' shouted Cumhal; 'are not the sods as wet as the sands of the Three Rosses? and are not the fleas in the blanket as many as the waves of the sea and as lively? and is not the bread as hard as the heart of a lay brother who has forgotten God? and is not the water in the jug as bitter and as ill-smelling as his soul? and is not the foot-water the colour that shall be upon him when he has been charred in the Undying Fires?' The lay brother saw that the lock was fast, and went back to his niche, for he was too sleepy to talk with comfort. And Cumhal went on beating at the door, and presently he heard the lay brother's foot once more, and cried out at him, 'O cowardly and tyrannous race of monks, persecutors of the bard and the gleeman, haters of life and joy! O race that does not draw the sword and tell the truth! O race that melts the bones of the people with cowardice and with deceit!'

'Gleeman,' said the lay brother, 'I also make rhymes; I make many while I sit in my niche by the door, and I sorrow to hear the bards railing upon the monks. Brother, I would sleep, and therefore I make known to you that it is the head of the monastery, our gracious abbot, who orders all things concerning the lodging of travellers.'

'You may sleep,' said Cumhal. 'I will sing a bard's curse on the abbot.' And he set the tub upside-down under the window, and stood upon it, and began to sing in a very loud voice. The singing awoke the abbot, so that he sat up in bed and blew a silver whistle until the lay brother came to him. 'I cannot get a wink of sleep with that noise,' said the abbot. 'What is happening?'

'It is a gleeman,' said the lay brother, 'who complains of the sods, of the bread, of the water in the jug, of the foot-water, and of the blanket. And now he is singing a bard's curse upon you, O brother

4. The reference is to Nathi (Nath I), later changed to Dathi, a Connacht king who was famous as a raider of Britain and Gall. He was a contemporary of Niall of the Nine Hostages, the first historical high king of Ireland, who brought St Patrick back to Ireland from a British raid. Dathi died at the foot of the Alps and his soldiers brought him home for burial at the royal site of Cruachain in Connacht. Yeats is crediting him with bringing the cross, symbol of Christianity, to Ireland from Christian Europe. See T. F. O'Rahilly, *Early Irish History and Mythology* (Dublin: Dublin Institute for Advanced Studies, 1946), p. 211.
5. mermaids. From the Irish *Muirrúghach*.

abbot, and upon your father and your mother, and your grandfather and your grandmother, and upon all your relations.'

'Is he cursing in rhyme?'

'He is cursing in rhyme, and with two assonances in every line of his curse.'

The abbot pulled his night-cap off and crumpled it in his hands, and the circular grey patch of hair in the middle of his bald head looked like the cairn upon Knocknarea,[6] for in Connacht they had not yet abandoned the ancient tonsure. 'Unless we do somewhat,' he said, 'he will teach his curses to the children in the street, and the girls spinning at the doors, and to the robbers upon Ben Bulben.'[7]

'Shall I go, then,' said the other, 'and give him dry sods, a fresh loaf, clean water in a jug, clean foot-water, and a new blanket, and make him swear by the blessed Saint Benignus, and by the sun and moon, that no bond be lacking, not to tell his rhymes to the children in the street, and the girls spinning at the doors, and the robbers upon Ben Bulben?'

'Neither our Blessed Patron nor the sun and moon would avail at all,' said the abbot; 'for tomorrow or the next day the mood to curse would come upon him, or a pride in those rhymes would move him, and he would teach his lines to the children, and the girls, and the robbers. Or else he would tell another of his craft how he fared in the guest-house, and he in his turn would begin to curse, and my name would wither. For learn, there is no steadfastness of purpose upon the roads, but only under roofs and between four walls. Therefore I bid you go and awaken Brother Kevin, Brother Dove, Brother Little Wolf, Brother Bald Patrick, Brother Bald Brandon, Brother James, and Brother Peter. And they shall take the man, and bind him with ropes, and dip him in the river that he shall cease to sing. And in the morning, lest this but make him curse the louder, we will crucify him.'

'The crosses are all full,' said the lay brother.

'Then we must make another cross. If we do not make an end of him another will, for who can eat and sleep in peace while men like him are going about the world? We would stand shamed indeed before blessed Saint Benignus, and sour would be his face when he comes to judge us at the Last Day, were we to spare an enemy of his when we had him under our thumb! Brother, there is not one of these bards and gleemen who has not scattered his bastards through the five kingdoms, and if they slit a purse or a throat, and it is always one or the other, it never comes into their heads to confess and do penance. Can you name one that is not heathen in his heart, always longing after the Son of Lir, and Aengus, and Bridget, and the Dagda, and Dana the Mother, and all the false gods of the old days; always making poems in praise of those kings and queens of the demons, Finvaragh, whose home is under Cruachmaa, and Red Aodh of Cnoc-na-Sidha, and Cliona of the Wave, and Aoibheal of the Grey Rock, and him they call Donn of the Vats of the Sea;[8] and railing against God and Christ and the blessed Saints?' While he was speaking he crossed himself, and when he had finished he drew the night-cap over his ears to shut out the noise, and closed his eyes and composed himself to sleep.

The lay brother found Brother Kevin, Brother Dove, Brother Little Wolf, Brother Bald Patrick, Brother Bald Brandon, Brother James, and Brother Peter sitting up in bed, and he made them get up. Then they bound Cumhal, and they dragged him to the river, and they dipped him in it at the place which was afterwards called Buckley's Ford.

'Gleeman,' said the lay brother, as they led him back to the guest-house, 'why do you ever use the wit which God has given you to make blasphemous and immoral tales and verses? For such is the way of your craft. I have, indeed, many such tales and verses wellnigh by rote, and so I know that I speak true! And why do you praise with rhyme those demons, Finvaragh, Red Aodh, Cliona, Aoibheal and Donn? I, too, am a man of great wit and learning, but I ever glorify our gracious abbot, and Benignus our Patron, and the princes of the province. My soul

6. A small mountain outside Sligo town with a cairn or burial mound on its summit to mark the grave of the legendary Queen Maeve.
7. A mountain in County Sligo that is mentioned frequently in Yeats's writings.

8. Son of Lir: Manannan Mac Lir, the Irish sea-god; Aengus: the Irish god of love; Bridget: a goddess associated with the Boyne Valley; Dagda: a powerful god, father of Aengus, wife of Boann, patroness of the river Boyne; Dana the Mother: the Tuatha De Danann — fairy host of Irish mythology – are literally 'the People of the Goddess Dana'; Finvaragh: probably Findabair, daughter of Queen Maeve, who lived at Cruachan in Connacht: hence 'her home is under Cruachmaa'; Red Aodh of Cnoc-na-Sidha: literally 'Red-haired Hugh of the Fairy Mountain' i.e. no-one specific; Cliona of the Wave: the 'Wave of Cliona', named after the goddess, is in the bay of Glandore, Co. Cork; Aoibheal of the Grey Rock: a goddess associated with the Clare coast; Donn of the Vats of the Sea: probably the deity associated with life after death, centred on the island, Teach Doinn – Donn's House – off south County Cork.

is decent and orderly, but yours is like the wind among the salley gardens.[9] I said what I could for you, being also a man of many thoughts, but who could help such a one as you?'

'Friend,' answered the gleeman, 'my soul is indeed like the wind, and it blows me to and fro, and up and down, and puts many things into my mind and out of my mind, and therefore am I called the Swift Wild Horse.' And he spoke no more that night, for his teeth were chattering with the cold.

The abbot and the monks came to him in the morning, and bade him get ready to be crucified, and led him out of the guest-house. And while he still stood upon the step a flock of great grass-barnacles passed high above him with clanking cries. He lifted his arms to them and said, 'O great grass-barnacles, tarry a little, and mayhap my soul will travel with you to the waste places of the shore and to the ungovernable sea!' At the gate a crowd of beggars gathered about them, being come there to beg from any traveller or pilgrim who might have spent the night in the guest-house. The abbot and the monks led the gleeman to a place in the woods at some distance, where many straight young trees were growing, and they made him cut one down and fashion it to the right length, while the beggars stood round them in a ring, talking and gesticulating. The abbot then bade him cut off another and shorter piece of wood, and nail it upon the first. So there was his cross for him; and they put it upon his shoulder, for his crucifixion was to be on the top of the hill where the others were. A half-mile on the way he asked them to stop and see him juggle for them; for he knew, he said, all the tricks of Aengus the Subtle-hearted. The old monks were for pressing on, but the young monks would see him: so he did many wonders for them, even to the drawing of live frogs out of his ears. But after a while they turned on him, and said his tricks were dull and a little unholy, and set the cross on his shoulders again. Another half-mile on the way and he asked them to stop and hear him jest for them, for he knew, he said, all the jests of Conan the Bald,[10] upon whose back a sheep's wool grew. And the young monks, when they had heard his merry tales, again bade him take up his cross, for it ill became them to listen to such follies. Another half-mile on the way, he asked them to stop and hear him sing the story of White-breasted Deirdre, and how she endured many sorrows, and how the sons of Usna died to serve her.[11] And the young monks were mad to hear him, but when he had ended they grew angry, and beat him for waking forgotten longings in their hearts. So they set the cross upon his back and hurried him to the hill.

When he was come to the top, they took the cross from him, and began to dig a hole for it to stand in, while the beggars gathered round, and talked among themselves. 'I ask a favour before I die,' says Cumhal.

'We will grant you no more delays,' says the abbot.

'I ask no more delays, for I have drawn the sword, and told the truth, and lived my dream, and am content.'

'Would you, then, confess?'

'By sun and moon, not I; I ask but to be let eat the food I carry in my wallet. I carry food in my wallet whenever I go upon a journey, but I do not taste of it unless I am wellnigh starved. I have not eaten now these two days.'

'You may eat, then,' says the abbot, and he turned to help the monks dig the hole.

The gleeman took a loaf and some strips of cold fried bacon out of his wallet and laid them upon the ground. 'I will give a tithe to the poor,' says he, and he cut a tenth part from the loaf and the bacon. 'Who among you is the poorest?' And thereupon was a great clamour, for the beggars began the history of their sorrows and their poverty, and their yellow faces swayed like Gabhra Lough when the floods have filled it with water from the bogs.

He listened for a little, and, says he, 'I am myself the poorest, for I have travelled the bare road, and by the edges of the sea; and the tattered doublet of parti-coloured cloth upon my back and the torn pointed shoes upon my feet have ever irked me, because of the towered city full of noble raiment which was in my heart. And I have been the more alone upon the roads and by the sea because I heard

9. The 'salley gardens' are mentioned again in Yeats's adaptaton of the folk-song 'Down by the Salley Gardens'.

10. Warrior and satirist of the Fenian narratives. When his head was stuck to the floor by an enemy's magic, his companions pulled him free, leaving hair and skin behind. To cure his baldness, a sheep's skin was grafted to his skull.

11. One of the most famous of Irish legends, much favoured by Yeats. Deirdre and the Sons of Usna were killed because of the sexual jealousy and treachery of King Conchubhar.

in my heart the rustling of the rose-bordered dress of her who is more subtle than Aengus the Subtle-hearted, and more full of the beauty of laughter than Conan the Bald, and more full of the wisdom of tears than White-breasted Deirdre, and more lovely than a bursting dawn to them that are lost in the darkness. Therefore, I award the tithe to myself; but yet, because I am done with all things, I give it unto you.'

So he flung the bread and the strips of bacon among the beggars, and they fought with many cries until the last scrap was eaten. But meanwhile the monks nailed the gleeman to his cross, and set it upright in the hole, and shovelled the earth into the hole, and trampled it level and hard. So then they went away, but the beggars stayed on, sitting round the cross. But when the sun was sinking, they also got up to go, for the air was getting chilly. And as soon as they had gone a little way, the wolves, who had been showing themselves on the edge of a neighbouring coppice, came nearer, and the birds wheeled closer and closer. 'Stay, outcasts, yet a little while,' the crucified one called in a weak voice to the beggars, 'and keep the beasts and the birds from me.' But the beggars were angry because he had called them outcasts, so they threw stones and mud at him, and one that had a child held it up before his eyes and said that he was its father, and cursed him, and thereupon they left him. Then the wolves gathered at the foot of the cross, and the birds flew lower and lower. And presently the birds lighted all at once upon his head and arms and shoulders, and began to peck at him, and the wolves began to eat his feet. 'Outcasts,' he moaned, 'have you all turned against the outcast?'

THE ADORATION OF THE MAGI

I was sitting reading late into the night a little after my last meeting with Aherne,[1] when I heard a light knocking on my front door; and found upon the doorstep three very old men with stout sticks in their hands, who said they had been told I would be up and about, and that they were to tell me important things. I brought them into my study, and when the peacock curtains had closed behind us, I set their chairs from them close to the fire, for I saw that the frost was on their great-coats of frieze and upon the long beards that flowed almost to their waists. They took off their great-coats, and leaned over the fire warming their hands, and I saw that their clothes had much of the country of our time, but a little also, as it seemed to me, of the town life of a more courtly time. When they had warmed themselves — and they warmed themselves, I thought, less because of the cold of the night than because of a pleasure in warmth for the sake of warmth — they turned towards me, so that the light of the lamp fell full upon their weather-beaten faces, and told the story I am about to tell. Now one talked and now another, and they often interrupted one another, with a desire, like that of countrymen, when they tell a story, to leave no detail untold. When they had finished they made me take notes of whatever conversation they had quoted, so that I might have the exact words, and got up to go, and when I asked them where they were going, and what they were doing, and by what names I should call them, they would tell me nothing, except that they had been commanded to travel over Ireland continually, and upon foot and at night, that they might live close to the stones and the trees and at the hours when the Immortals are awake.

I have let some years go by before writing out this story, for I am always in dread of the illusions which came of that inquietude of the veil of the Temple, which M. Mallarmé considers a characteristic of our times;[2] and only write it now because I have grown to believe that there is no dangerous idea which does not become less dangerous when written out in sincere and careful English.

The three old men were three brothers, who had lived in one of the western islands from their early manhood, and had cared all their lives for nothing except for those classical writers and old Gaelic writers who expounded an heroic and simple life. Night after night in winter, Gaelic story-tellers would chant old poems to them over the poteen;[3] and night after night in summer, when the Gaelic story-tellers were at work in the fields or away at the fishing, they would read to one another Virgil and

1. Owen Aherne, hero of Yeats's related apocalyptic story, 'The Tables of the Law', is a recurrent persona in his poetry and prose fiction. He is probably based on the character of the poet Lionel Johnson.

2. Stéphane Mallarmé (1842–98), the French Symbolist poet who had characterized the *fin de siècle* as the 'inquiétude du voile dans le temple'. Yeats adapted the phrase for the title of a chapter of his *Autobiographies*, 'The Trembling of the Veil'.

3. An illicit spirit.

Homer, for they would not enjoy in solitude, but as the ancients enjoyed. At last a man, who told them he was Michael Robartes,[4] came to them in a fishing-boat, like Saint Brendan drawn by some vision and called by some voice; and told them of the coming again of the gods and the ancient things; and their hearts, which had never endured the body and pressure of our time, but only of distant times, found nothing unlikely in anything he told them, but accepted all simply and were happy. Years passed, and one day, when the oldest of the old men, who had travelled in his youth and thought sometimes of other lands, looked out on the grey waters, on which the people see the dim outline of the Islands of the Young — the Happy Islands where the Gaelic heroes live the lives of Homer's Phaeacians[5] — a voice came out of the air over the waters and told him of the death of Michael Robartes. While they were still mourning, the next oldest of the old men fell asleep whilst he was reading out the Fifth Eclogue of Virgil,[6] and a strange voice spoke through him, and bid them set out for Paris, where a dying woman would give them secret names and thereby so transform the world that another Leda would open her knees to the swan, another Achilles beleaguer Troy.[7]

They left their island, and were at first troubled at all they saw in the world, and came to Paris, and there the youngest met a person in a dream, who told him they were to wander about at hazard until those who had been guiding their footsteps had brought them to a street and a house, whose likeness was shown him in the dream. They wandered hither and thither for many days, until one morning they came into some narrow and shabby streets, on the south of the Seine, where women with pale faces and untidy hair looked at them out of the windows; and just as they were about to turn back because Wisdom could not have alighted in so foolish a neighbourhood, they came to the street and the house of the dream. The oldest of the old men, who still remembered some of the modern languages he had known in his youth, went up to the door and knocked, and when he had knocked, the next in age to him said it was not a good house, and could not be the house they were looking for, and urged him to ask for somebody who could not be there and go away. The door was opened by an old over-dressed woman, who said, 'O, you are her three kinsmen from Ireland. She has been expecting you all day.' The old men looked at one another and followed her upstairs, passing doors from which pale and untidy women thrust out their heads, and into a room where a beautiful woman lay asleep, another woman sitting by her.

The old woman said, 'Yes, they have come at last; now she will be able to die in peace,' and went out.

'We have been deceived by devils,' said one of the old men, 'for the Immortals would not speak through a woman like this.'

'Yes,' said another, 'we have been deceived by devils, and we must go away quickly.'

'Yes,' said the third, 'we have been deceived by devils, but let us kneel down for a little, for we are by the death-bed of one that has been beautiful.' They knelt down, and the woman sitting by the bed whispered, and as though overcome with fear, and with lowered head, 'At the moment when you knocked she was suddenly convulsed and cried out as I have heard a woman in childbirth and fell backward as though in a swoon.' Then they watched for a little the face upon the pillow and wondered at its look, as of unquenchable desire, and at the porcelain-like refinement of the vessel in which so malevolent a flame had burned.

Suddenly the second oldest of them crowed like a cock, till the room seemed to shake with the crowing. The woman in the bed still slept on in her death-like sleep, but the woman who sat by her head crossed herself and grew pale, and the youngest of the old men cried out, 'A devil has gone into him, and we must begone or it will go into us also.' Before they could rise from their knees, a resonant chanting voice came from the lips that had crowed and said:

'I am not a devil, but I am Hermes[8] the Shepherd

4. Michael Robartes, the hero of Yeats's other apocalyptic tale, 'Rosa Alchemica', a key persona in his prose and poetry. He is probably based on his Rosicrucian friend, MacGregor Mathers.
5. A happy island community which welcomed Homer's Odysseus ashore on his voyage home after the Trojan War.
6. Yeats must mean the Fourth Eclogue, sometimes called Virgil's 'messianic' eclogue because of its mention of a marvellous child who will bring in a new golden age.
7. Later, in his play *The Resurrection*, Yeats echoes this sentiment in an introductory song:

   Another Troy must rise and set,
   Another lineage feed the crow,
   Another Argo's painted prow
   Drive to a flashier bauble yet.

8. Hermes Trismegistus, known in Latin as Mercurius, in Egyptian as Thoth, is also the patron of authors, having invented writing.

of the Dead, I run upon the errands of the gods, and you have heard my sign. The woman who lies there has given birth, and that which she bore has the likeness of a unicorn and is most unlike man of all living things, being cold, hard and virginal. It seemed to be born dancing; and was gone from the room wellnigh upon the instant, for it is of the nature of the unicorn to understand the shortness of life. She does not know it has gone, for she fell into a stupor while it danced, but bend down your ears that you may learn the names that it must obey.' Neither of the other two old men spoke, but doubtless looked at the speaker with perplexity, for the voice began again: 'When the Immortals would overthrow the things that are today and bring the things that were yesterday, they have no one to help them, but one whom the things that are today have cast out. Bow down and very low, for they have chosen this woman in whose heart all follies have gathered, and in whose body all desires have awakened; this woman who has been driven out of Time and has lain upon the bosom of Eternity.'

The voice ended with a sigh, and immediately the old man awoke out of sleep, and said, 'Has a voice spoken through me, as it did when I fell asleep over my Virgil, or have I only been asleep?'

The oldest of them said, 'A voice has spoken through you. Where has your soul been while the voice was speaking through you?'

'I do not know where my soul has been, but I dreamed I was under the roof of a manger, and I looked down and I saw an ox and an ass; and I saw a red cock perching on the hay-rack; and a woman hugging a child; and three old men in chain armour kneeling with their heads bowed very low in front of the woman and the child. While I was looking the cock crowed and a man with wings on his heels swept up through the air, and as he passed me, cried out, "Foolish old men, you had once all the wisdom of the stars." I do not understand my dream or what it would have us do, but you who have heard the voice out of the wisdom of my sleep know what we have to do.'

Then the oldest of the old men told him they were to take the parchments they had brought with them out of their pockets and spread them on the ground. When they had spread them on the ground, they took out of their pockets their pens, made of three feathers which had fallen from the wing of the old eagle that is believed to have talked of wisdom with Saint Patrick.

'He meant, I think,' said the youngest, as he put their ink-bottles by the side of the rolls of parchment, 'that when people are good the world likes them and takes possession of them, and so eternity comes through people who are not good or who have been forgotten. Perhaps Christianity was good and the world liked it, so now it is going away and the Immortals are beginning to awake.'

'What you say has no wisdom,' said the oldest, 'because if there are many Immortals, there cannot be only one Immortal.'

'Yet it seems,' said the youngest, 'that the names we are to take down are the names of one, so it must be that he can take many forms.'

Then the woman on the bed moved as in a dream, and held out her arms as though to clasp the being that had left her, and murmured names of endearment, and yet strange names, 'Harsh sweetness,' 'Dear bitterness,' 'O solitude,' O terror,' and after lay still for a while. Then her voice changed, and she, no longer afraid and happy but seeming like any dying woman, murmured a name so faintly that the woman who sat by the bed bent down and put her ear close to her mouth.

The oldest of the old men said in French, 'There must have been yet one name which she had not given us, for she murmured a name while the spirit was going out of the body,' and the woman said, 'She was merely murmuring over the name of a symbolist painter she was fond of. He used to go to something he called the Black Mass, and it was he who taught her to see visions and to hear voices.'

This is all the old men told me, and when I think of their speech and of their silence, of their coming and of their going, I am almost persuaded that had I followed them out of the house, I would have found no footsteps on the snow. They may, for all I or any man can say, have been themselves Immortals: immortal demons, come to put an untrue story into my mind for some purpose I do not understand. Whatever they were, I have turned into a pathway which will lead me from them and from the Order of the Alchemical Rose.[9] I no longer live an elaborate and haughty life, but seek to lose myself among the prayers and the sorrows of the multitude. I pray best

9. A fictional name for the Order of the Golden Dawn which Yeats and Mathers belonged to in the 1890s. It figures prominently in 'Rosa Alchemica'.

in poor chapels, where frieze coats brush against me as I kneel, and when I pray against the demons I repeat a prayer which was made I know not how many centuries ago to help some poor Gaelic man or woman who had suffered with a suffering like mine:

Seacht b-páidreacha fó seacht
Chuir Muire faoi n-a Mac,
Chuir Brighid faoi n-a brat,
Chuir Dia faoi n-a neart,
Eidir sinn 'san Sluagh Sidhe,
Eidir sinn 'san Sluagh Gaoith.

Seven paters seven times,
Send Mary by her Son,
Send Bridget by her mantle,
Send God by His strength,
Between us and the faery host,[10]
Between us and the demons of the air.

10. The Irish 'fairy host' was believed to be a troop of phantom horsemen who were borne on the wind.

SHAN F. BULLOCK

(1865–1935)

from: THE AWKWARD SQUADS (1893)

[This portrait of a humane and courageous Ulsterman attempting to retain his charity and independence in the face of tribal retribution is not just uncannily true to so much human experience, but unhappily prophetic of the tragedy that has overtaken his providence a hundred years after his story is recorded.]

A STATE OFFICIAL

Right in the heart of Cavan, sheltered on all sides by hills, and scattered aimlessly along two roads which there meet, cross, and wander on, stands the village of Raheen. In a generous moment you might say it numbered twenty houses, all thickly whitewashed, heavily thatched, and preserving a stillness that might be taken as peaceful or dull as the humour required.

Coming down the hill on which, amid its mouldering graves, stands the parish church, and over which lies the road to the railway, you see right in front, under an arch of spreading beech branches, the village shop cleverly placed on an angle made by the crossing roads; and to the left a low grey wall over which peep the white chimneys of a row of thatched cottages. These last really make the village; without them (and the shop maybe) two roads would meet at a hamlet after their wanderings across the hills.

But, besides this mere numerical and purely local importance, the cottages still preserve a certain air of distinction, first assumed when a tyrannical, to be sure, yet, on the whole, intelligent, government decided that they should shelter a branch of the Imperial post office. It is gone now; but some time, oh long years ago, if, one evening in June, you had leant over the low grey wall and looked down, you would have seen, across a trim, gay little garden and behind a wealth of hanging creepers, an open window framing the bent head of old Dan the cobbler and village postmaster. The *tip tap* of his hammer would have come with a soothing regularity and seemed to be the only sign of life — at that hour it would certainly be the only sound — in the place. After the dust of the road you would have found it pleasant to lean there on the cool stones, and, with that dull beating in your ears, let your eyes wander idly over the homely garden, the old brown thatch, then across the roof towards the fading green of the hills.

But presently the sound would cease; then, looking, you would have seen Dan lean forward, turn a leaf in a book that lay on the window-ledge before him, read fixedly for a moment, and, with a smile on his old face, look up at yourself. For your elbows would rest on stones that were shiny from long rubbing by the coats of gossips who had stood there, sometimes by the hour, cracking a sly joke with the garrulous old man.

Had you remained longer that evening, however, you would have seen a thin, ugly man turn down by the end of the wall, cross the garden, and, regardless of tender flowers, tramp clumsily to Dan's window.

'Hello!' said Dan, looking up and pushing his spectacles up his brow. 'That's sudden. Ah, it's you, Micky! Well, God be with ye, me son, anyway; but you're a powerful bad friend to the light.'

'Yis,' said the man, 'I suppose I am — but no matter. I want to say a word to ye.'

'Say on, me son,' said Dan, reaching to close his book, and putting down his hammer. 'As the wise man said: "There's a time for all things".'

'I want to know, Dan,' said the other, stooping and resting his hands on the window-sill, 'if you've thought better o' what ye said th' other night? Ha' ye changed yir mind?'

'Eh, avick?[1] What's that?' said Dan sharply. 'Changed me mind? — that's what I seldom do. What about?'

'Ye know.'

'I forgot then.'

'About the man that's occupyin' Widow Reilly's farm — are ye goin' to do like another?'

'Ah!' said Dan, 'that's it, is it? An' why should I do like another? Eh?'

'It's no use bleatherin'!'[2] answered the man irritably. 'Ye know what I mane — in plain words will ye quit spakin' or havin' anythin' to do wi' the man?'

'Why should I, Micky? Answer me that. Why *should* I look your way for advice?'

'It's not me. I do as I'm bid — so must you. The man's betrayed the cause by takin' an evicted woman's farm — ye know that. So long as he's there he's a traitor to the cause, an' them that has dealin's with him are worse.'[3]

'The *cause!*' broke in Dan with a scornful laugh. 'Ye call it a cause to leave a man without a bite to eat or a dud[4] to wear, or a soul to cross words with! D'ye call it a cause to let wee childer[5] starve an' a woman to fret?'

'Ye may quit!' said the man abruptly. 'Say no more; ivery word takes ye deeper. Is that your answer?'

'Micky Flynn,' said Dan, rising and, the better to look severe, dragging his spectacles down to his nose, 'from you or any other man I take no counsel when I try to do right. Ye call it a *cause*. I say it's hellish persecution! The man has harmed no-one, neither have his childer; he's only done what *you* think wrong. An' who are you, Micky Flynn, to judge another? *I* think he's done no harm, Micky; an' cause or no cause I'm goin' to think lek that.' He stooped and laid his hand on the closed book. 'Here's where I get me counsel, Micky — here I read' — he shook a warning finger at the man — ' "*This above all — to thine own self be true, and it must —*" '[6]

The man turned away with a foul exclamation of disgust and spat on the flowers, walked to the gate, and there wheeled round.

'Ye may talk yir fool's clack[7] to yirself, now,' he shouted back. 'Be God, yi'll have time enough, ye bleatherin' ould rogue!'

Dan leaned across the sill and looked at his flowers. 'Ah!' said he, 'it's well there's rain comin'; it'll help to wipe out the divil's hoof-tracks.' Then he laughed, and closing the window lit a candle and sat down on his stool.

The unsteady light fell softly on all the mad disorder of the room — the litter on the floor, the rolls of leather in the corner, the lasts on the wall hanging over pictured newspaper cuttings, the little official desk strewn with old pens, cheap stationery, dirty copies of rules and regulations — fell softly on all that and on the sturdy old figure of the postmaster. He laughed softly to himself, and wagged his head gravely.

'Well, well,' said he, 'after all these years o' peace an' quiet to come to this! Spoke to lek that! What next? What's goin' to come to me? Well, well; time'll tell "*This above all*",' he muttered slowly, ' "*To thine own self be true — to thine own self be true*".'

He reached for his book, and, holding the candle close to his face, began turning the leaves and reading a line here and there on a chance page.

1. Literally 'my son' (Irish, *a mhic*), but generally used as an affectionate form of address.
2. blathering.
3. Throughout Ireland in the nineteenth century boycotts were placed on the homes of evicted tenant farmers, and enforced by secret societies. Since this is Ulster, there may be a hint of sectarianism in the cause as mentioned. The reference to Gladstone later in the story suggests that its milieu is protestant.
4. clothes.
5. children.
6. Polonius's advice to Laertes continues: 'and it must follow, as the night the day, / Thou canst not then be false to any man', *Hamlet*, I. 3. 56–57.
7. chatter.

' "*My way of life is fallen into the sere, the yellow leaf*" — ah, ah!'[8]

' "*Rude am I in my speech.*"[9] Just so, just so!'

' "*I am a very foolish, fond old man . . . climbing sorrow . . . serpent's tooth.*"[10] Poor old Lear, Lord help all like him!'

Presently he looked up and, pushing back his glasses, declaimed in a measured sing-song:

' "*There's a divinity that shapes our ends, rough-hew them how we will.*"[11] That's good, that's what I wanted — that's somethin' to sleep on — that an' th' other. What's this it is? Oh, ay! "*This above all. . . . There's a divinity.*".'

Repeating the phrases over and over to himself, he rose and busied himself about the room, arranging his tools, tidying his desk, looking out his work for the morrow.

' "*There's a divinity*",' he kept on repeating; then suddenly stopped, and holding up a piece of wax-end: ' "Shapes our *ends!*" ' he said with a soft chuckle. 'I wonder if it takes a divinity to shape this?'

And laughing at his little joke he bolted the door and went to bed.

The next morning, his flowers watered and wed,[12] his frugal breakfast over, and his little kitchen swept and tidied, Dan with his book open before him, and breathing the sweet morning freshness of his garden, was again at his work, hammering and sewing, reading and muttering, laughing softly betimes to himself and looking up through his spectacles at the wall. But though he looked up often no-one that morning leant on the stones to exchange greetings or jokes; sometimes footsteps sounded from the road; sometimes a neighbour passed close to the wall; once or twice someone looked furtively towards the open window; but no-one spoke; and for the first time for many years the stool at Dan's elbow where usually his neighbours waited for the post, was vacant.

'Eh?' he would say, looking round at the empty stool and up at the wall. 'Eh? well, well!'

Then the post came, carried by a lad who that morning seemed peculiarly gruff and silent, and Dan, for a while sinking his trade and putting on the air of importance becoming a state official, carefully sorted the letters and placed them in order on his desk.

'Now,' said he, turning to his work again, '*now* they'll come — they *must* come now; they *must*.'

Only children came that morning — children who seemed suddenly to be smitten with an unusual awkwardness and shyness, as they stopped before the window or came to the door of Dan's room and asked if there were any letters for Mammy, please.

'Come in, Mary, agra!'[13] Dan called cheerily to the first who came; 'come in, me girl, an' I'll give ye a flower. Ye can't come? Well, well! Where's your Daddy the day? Eh? Where's your tongue, Mary?'

The child suddenly raised her hand from her lips to her eyes, and began to cry.

'Oh!' she sobbed, 'please Dan, Mammy says I mustn't spake to ye.'

Dan's eyes swiftly became grave behind his spectacles.

'Ah!' he said. 'Well, well!' — then, without a word, handed the child the letter.

With the next it was the same, and the next — after that he questioned no more. And all that day he sat silent, his book for the most part neglected, and his heart heavy; not one came to his little room, not one paused to speak to him, not one looked over the wall, except towards evening, when Dan, more by habit than will, raising his eyes, saw a dark, ugly face, that scowled on him for a moment and was gone.

So three days passed; and the fourth morning saw Dan cobbler no longer, but postmaster only. The last job of mending had been taken away (by a child, as usual); for the first time in his working life he had not a stitch to sew. For three days he had been left to his thoughts and his book — in that time only once had he heard a friendly voice, and that belonged to the man for whom he was suffering. His heart was heavy; his flowers had not their old sweet power over him; even Shakespeare could not wholly catch his thoughts; his eyes were grown very sorrowful, and his brow was troubled.

'Well, well,' he would say, 'well, well! Am I asleep

8. *Macbeth*, V. 3. 16–17.
9. *Othello*, I. 3. 80–81: 'Rude am I in my speech,/ And little bless'd with the soft phrase of peace.' Othello is confronting the Venetian Senate, pleading a soldier's privilege.
10. *King Lear*, IV. 7. 60 and I. 4. 311–12.
11. *Hamlet*, V. 2. 9–10.
12. Dialect usage for 'weeded'.

13. From the Irish *a gradh* (my love).

or awake? Is it me at all? What have I done? What am I to do?'

For the hundredth time he reviewed his position. He was cut off from the world — a social outlaw. He had no work, would have none. He could get food only by walking far to a town where he was not known. He had the few shillings a week that made his official salary, and a few pounds in the savings bank — could he keep life with that? He had that one friend — a dull fellow, as it happened, without a laugh in his body, whom, besides, it was dangerous just then to visit. His own thoughts, himself, bare life, his little cottage and garden — could he do with just that?

Such was his position, and such it would be for long and long — till he yielded. Was it worth while? he asked. Should he yield? He did no-one any good by holding out — not one, not even that dull friend. He was pleasing himself, injuring himself. Should he yield? he asked himself that fourth morning, sitting on his stool beside his open window waiting for the children to come for the letters. Mechanically his hand reached for his book of wisdom and opened its old, tattered pages.

' "*This above all*",' he said in a little while, raising his beaming face to the wall. ' "*This above all, to thine own self be true.*" An' what's th' other? "*There's a divinity that shapes our ends.*" Just so, Dan; that's your reason. By the Lord, Dan, you're a sinner at heart; only for the old book you'd be a limb of Satan!'

So he accepted his position; and for a time bore his lot cheerfully, passing the long days as best he might — working in his garden, whitewashing his cottage inside and out and repairing its thatch, reading his one book by the open window; sometimes, at night, dressing in his Sunday clothes, and with his hat jauntily cocked and a flower in his coat, whistling and singing defiantly as he slowly paraded up and down the street or past his neighbours' open doors.

For a time — say, a few weeks longer — he bore himself bravely; then, with a sudden rush, was borne in upon him a full sense of his cruel, unutterable loneliness. A living man shut in a tomb; a tongue quickly smitten dumb; a world suddenly changed from life and laughter to grim, gloomy silence; as such, in such, he found himself. Could he endure that — he by nature so sociable and kindly, who, lately, had been the life of the village — its half-understood philosopher, wit, sage, politician; he who had delighted in the talk and society of his neighbours as much as in his own musings? Could he endure silence, loneliness, not for a day or a week, but for long, perhaps very long? He was doing right; but that did not bring comfort enough — indeed was but cold comfort, seeing that doing right brought only trouble. He could bear hunger, privation, neglect; but silence, loneliness, this death in life, these he could not bear. He felt he must talk or go mad. And all round him for miles and miles there was not one with whom he could chat pleasantly for an hour in the day — only an hour. . . .

Yes, there was another; he, at least, would listen patiently.

So Dan took his book, and, climbing the hill behind the shop, came at last to a hovel by the wayside, where, bending over a small peat fire, he found a miserable old man, clad in rags, crippled with age, dirty beyond belief, and with only bare life lighting his eyes. Here was someone who would listen, even if he could not answer; a relic almost of life, mumbling childishly about himself and his pains, sometimes knitting his brows as his tongue fashioned an old-time phrase, or his mind was troubled with a sudden, half-realized memory.

'Ah!' he would mutter, 'it's shivery cowld the day. Tell me, did — did — was it true that they disestablished the Church, Gladshtone? — ach, no! — ach, a bad man!' [14]

And so he muttered now and then, whilst Dan read by the hour, or stopped to expound a passage, or, coming at last to his favourite lines, made them the text of a long harangue in which his tongue freed his mind of the irritating, ugly burden gathering through those days of silence.

'Ach, a bad man!' was the response, or one equally vague. 'Ach, a bad man!'

But for all his squalor and witlessness, the old cripple was a human being who listened to Dan and did not keep his face from him; who turned his head and said 'Good morning' when Dan entered, and followed him with lifeless old eyes as he went — a human being to whom Dan could talk, and who answered as best he could.

This was very well, so far; but, returning one day

14. In 1869 the Liberal prime minister, W. E. Gladstone, put through his act to disestablish the (anglican) Church of Ireland, which from 1871 became a voluntary body like any other religion in Ireland.

from one of these morning visits; feeling, for all his recent effort, a great desire to talk (really, it may be, a craving for fellowship and sympathy), an almost irresistible impulse to shout aloud, or to go to the nearest house and there compel conversation; and wondering betimes how best he should put behind him the long remaining hours of the day, suddenly, right in view of the village, the thought came to him: why not go and talk? Who might hinder him? People might not answer; but they could not refuse to hear.

The notion made him laugh and slap his leg as he stood pondering on the road. It would be a good way to pay back men's cruelty; it would give himself pleasure and then annoyance; perhaps — yes, perhaps — he might be able to mingle wisdom with his talk, and so gradually bring them round to his charitable point of view.

'Yes,' he said aloud, slapping his leg once more, and beaming at the thought of the funny, clever old codger he still was; 'yes, begob, it's a good idea — a good idea, me son! Dan, you're not done with yet! I'll try it this very night. Mebbe, mebbe —' And turning over the may-be's in his mind, he went slowly, but not sadly, home.

That evening, with his book under his arm, and a big rose in his black chapel coat, Dan went out; and taking his stand about the crossing of the roads, before the shop and within hearing of the cottages, there, with a humorous glint in his eye which sometimes belied the seriousness of his face, read, expounded, and discoursed.

Had you been in Raheen that fine summer's evening, enjoying the rich warmth of the sunset, perhaps, as you leaned at the old spot across the wall; you must certainly have watched the scene with interest — the laughing, bare-armed women at the doors; the men lounging against the wall, wondering whether Dan were knave or fool; the children in the dusty, yellow street, clustering, open-eyed, round the old man just then raising his voice in a part serious, part humorous discourse on Truth even in politics to one's self, and the Divinity that even in politics shapes man's ends. You would have found the scene interesting; perhaps, had you known what lay behind it all, you might have found it pathetic.

Only, the villagers clearly found in it nothing but amusement and a little welcome excitement; for, a night or two after saw Dan talking to bare white walls, the doors all closed, the children's voices coming merrily over the roofs from the back. But Dan was not discomfited. He moved closer to the cottages, and raised his voice louder in a more personal and less humorous harangue — yes, waxed bold; and one night, entering a house, stood with his back to the door and spoke his soul concerning the cause and its adherents.

This, in the opinion of his neighbours, was more than amusing and not to be tolerated. He might talk nonsense outside as much as he chose; but a man's hearthstone was private, and the cause was sacred. He might be cracked — no doubt he was; but he had sense enough left to do harm and talk black heresy.

He had one more chance; and, recklessly, almost foolishly abused it. Then a party of men, with blackened faces and carrying guns visited him as he sat in his kitchen reading by candle light. They entered silently; and, having surrounded him with a ring of threatening muzzles, one of their number, in forcible language, made clear to the trembling, haggard old man the character and blackness of his offence and the swift punishment that would follow its repetition.

Did he hear? shouted the man, and fired at the roof.

Then, silently they went out, and left the old man to stagger to bed with a pain at his heart.

The next morning another opened the postbag; and now, people say that sometimes at night, if you lean over the wall, across the rotting flower-beds you will see a laughing, muttering old man behind a closed window, hammering and reading away.

GEORGE A. BIRMINGHAM

(1865–1950)

from:
THE ADVENTURES OF DR WHITTY (1913)

['The Deputation' is a characteristic short story by a writer fascinated by the humours and vagaries of Irish life in its social, religious and political manifestations. Birmingham's desire for tolerance and understanding is evident in this genial fable of innocent intrigue and affectionate contretemps in a Connacht township.]

THE DEPUTATION

Ballintra is a small town on the coast of Connacht. It was a matter of surprise to everyone who took an interest in such matters when Mr. Willoughby, shortly after his coming to Ireland as Chief Secretary,[1] announced his intention of visiting Ballintra. No high Government official had been there within living memory, for these gentlemen are always so feverishly anxious to get on to somewhere else, that they cannot afford time to go to places which are not on the way to anywhere; and Ballintra, standing on the shore of a deep bay, is the end of a *cul-de-sac*. Its visitors, when they want to go away from it, must travel again the road by which they came.

'It's likely,' said Michael Geraghty, discussing the advent of the Chief Secretary at the bar of the Imperial Hotel, 'that he'll be taking his dinner up at the big house along with Colonel Beresford.'

Thady Glynn, the proprietor of the hotel, sniffed. He did not like Colonel Beresford, who was the principal landlord of the neighbourhood.

'And I wouldn't wonder,' said Michael Geraghty, 'if he'd sleep the night there.'

'He will not, then,' said Thady. 'He'll neither eat nor sleep in the town, but he'll be off out of it again as quick as he can.'

Thady's opinion, given from behind his own bar, naturally carried great weight. He was an important man in Ballintra. His position as Chairman of the Urban Council and President of the local branch of the League[2] placed him above the reach of contradiction.

'I was only making the suggestion,' said Michael meekly. 'It's yourself would know if anyone does.'

'I do know,' said Thady.

His information turned out to be perfectly accurate.

The Chief Secretary's motor car was timed to arrive in Ballintra at twelve o'clock and to leave again as soon as possible afterwards. The Reverend Mother who presided over the convent and the industrial school was the first to make up her mind to receive the Chief Secretary. It was settled that he should stop at the convent, inspect the school, and make the acquaintance of Father Henaghan, the parish priest. The arrangement was quite satisfactory to the ecclesiastical authorities; but it did not appear how the rest of the people would benefit by the inspection. Men looked to Thady Glynn to suggest some way of getting tangible advantage from the visit of Mr. Willoughby. Thady hesitated. He did not see what the Chief Secretary could do for him. He was already a J.P.,[3] in virtue of his position as Chairman of the Urban District Council. He did not know of any other honour or any emolument which the Chief Secretary could bestow. While he hesitated Dr. Whitty came before the public with a plan. It was not very original, but it seemed practical. He suggested that Mr. Willoughby should be asked to build a pier for the benefit of the town.

Michael Geraghty warmly supported the doctor. He was by profession a builder and contractor, and was the only man in Ballintra to whom the contract for building a pier could possibly be given. He was of opinion that a handsome profit might be realized out of the work. He spent an evening working out sums on a sheet of paper, and came to the conclusion that he ought to clear £200 at least out of quite a

1. There was no chief secretary of this name.

2. Probably the Irish National Land League, a broadly based organization for agrarian reform founded by Parnell and others in 1879.

3. Justice of the Peace.

small pier, and might make much more if the inspector who passed his work turned out to be a fool. He called on the doctor the next morning and expressed his intention of doing all in his power to secure the pier.

'It'll be a great benefit to the people of this district,' he said, 'if so be we get the pier. Many's the time there might be a fine catch of mackerel took, or herring or the like, if only there was some way of landing them. But what's the good of going out and taking the trouble to catch the fish when a man'd only be losing his life trying to land them at the slip[4] there is in it, and him maybe with a wife and family depending on him?'

'That's all right, Michael,' said the doctor.

'It's the most thing that would be a real benefit to the people,' went on Geraghty, 'would be to have a good pier. There's more lives would be saved and more money brought into the place —'

'That's all right. You keep that sort of talk for the Chief Secretary. Lay out the bodies of the drowned fishermen in the street if you like when he's coming into the town. Range out the widows and orphans in rows. Show him piles of empty packing cases that might be full of fish if only we had a pier. That sort of thing will impress him, I've no doubt. But you needn't shoot it off at me.'

Michael Geraghty looked at the doctor dubiously. Then he smiled slowly.

'What you want, Doctor,' he said, 'is to provide employment for the starving inhabitants of this town, the decent poor fellows that would be willing to work and earn what would keep themselves and their families in comfort if so be there was work in it to be got. And with the help of God there will be work when they've given us the money to build the pier. It's the poor you're thinking of, Doctor, and I respect you for it.'

'I am not thinking of the poor. Don't you be getting it into your head that I'm either a politician or a philanthropist. I'm going to run this pier scheme through because, when there's money going, we may as well get our whack of it here in Ballintra as let it be grabbed by some other place. That's what I'm thinking of. What's in your mind is the profit you'll make out of the job yourself. Devil the other idea there is in your head this minute.'

4. A slipway, a sloping ramp.

Michael Geraghty smiled again. Then he winked slowly.

'You're a smart man, Doctor,' he said. 'You're a mighty smart man. I've always said it of you, and I'll say it again.'

'It's not just as easy as you might be inclined to think,' said the doctor, 'to get the promise of a pier. There was a time when any man that wanted a pier could get it for the asking, and have it stuck down on any spot on the whole coast of Connacht that he chose to mention. But those days are past. They're getting very particular now about piers. The last two Chief Secretaries have looked a long time at £1,000 before they spent it on a pier.'

'It's a damned shame then,' said Geraghty. 'What's the good of our keeping up a Chief Secretary at all if he won't — it's enough to set a man against the Government altogether, so it is.'

'What we've got to do,' said the doctor, 'is to face this Chief Secretary with a deputation of the most respectable and influential possible kind, the sort of deputation that he can't possibly refuse to listen to.'

'That'll be all right,' said Geraghty. 'There'll be yourself and me and Father Henaghan and —'

'Certainly not. Neither you nor I will be on the deputation at all. We're no use. No Chief Secretary in his senses would listen to what we had to say. Father Henaghan we'll have, of course. He'll introduce the deputation as soon as ever he's finished conducting the Chief Secretary round the industrial school at the convent.'

'He'll do it,' said Geraghty.

'Of course he will. He loves going on deputations. Then I'll go on to the Rev. Mr. Jackson and —'

'The Protestant minister!' said Geraghty. 'What does he know about piers, or about Chief Secretaries for that matter?'

'Nothing,' said the doctor. 'But he'll be mighty useful to us. What impresses a Chief Secretary more than anything else is a union of all creeds for a common good object. When he see Father Henaghan and Mr. Jackson standing hand in hand in front of his motor car he'll be prepared to give us a lighthouse if we want it, let alone a paltry pier.'

'Maybe the Rev. Jackson won't go with you. I'm told he's a queer sort of man.'

'He's an excellent man. I was attending his children when they had the measles last month, and I happen to know that he's a most charitable man. When I tell him all you've been saying about the poor fellows that are out of work, and the benefit the building operations will be to them in the way of wages, he'll join the deputation at once. There's no difficulty whatever so far. The next two people we must secure are Colonel Beresford and Thady Glynn.'

'Be dam,' said Geraghty, 'but you'll not be able to get them — not the both of them; though I don't say but you might get either the one or the other.'

'We must have both, Michael, however we manage it. If we don't get the Colonel, the Chief Secretary will be inclined to think that the whole thing is a got-up job, and that there's no real need of a pier.'

'He might think that surely.'

'He might and would. What's more, speaking between ourselves, he'd be perfectly right if he did. That's why we must have the Colonel.'

'He'll not join,' said Geraghty, 'not if he knows that Thady Glynn is to be one of the party. He hates Thady worse than the devil. And if Thady's left out —'

'We can't leave Thady out possibly. As Chairman of all the different Boards and Leagues about the place he's a most important man. He'll impress the Chief Secretary tremendously.'

'If you left him out he'd go round and rise the minds of the people against the pier, so as they'd get up a petition to have it carted away, if so be that it was stuck down in the middle of the street.'

'Exactly. That's another reason why we must have Thady. We won't get the pier without him.'

'You'll not get both him and the Colonel,' said Geraghty despondingly. 'The thing couldn't be done. No man living could do it. If the Colonel goes, then Thady'll refuse, for he doesn't like the Colonel any more than the Colonel likes him; and if you have Thady engaged, the Colonel will swear by this and by that he'll not go near the Chief Secretary — not if he was never to see a Chief Secretary again as long as he lived.'

'When I say I must have them both I mean to get them both. Listen to me now, Michael. I'm going round now to Father Henaghan and the Rev. Mr. Jackson. They'll agree all right. Just you drop into the hotel and see Thady Glynn. Tell him I sent you to ask him to go on the deputation. Tell him that I'm asking Colonel Beresford, and that I'm pretty sure the Colonel will agree. In fact, you might go as far as to say that the Colonel has agreed. Then come back here and tell me what Thady says.'

'I can tell you that this minute. He'll say that he'll see you and the Colonel and the Chief Secretary and the pier and town of Ballintra a mighty long way off before he goes on any such expedition.'

'Go you off and do as I bid you,' said the doctor, 'and let me run this show my own way.'

Michael Geraghty was back in the doctor's house in less than an hour. He had drunk two bottles of porter and a glass of whisky, but he was not at all cheered. He feared that the doctor's plan was doomed to failure. Thady Glynn had violently refused to have anything to do with the deputation. He had cursed Dr. Whitty for a meddlesome young fool. He had expressed a passionate detestation of Colonel Beresford. He had threatened to have letters written to the paper exposing the whole pier scheme as a dodge — a dastardly and cowardly plot — to seduce the League from the true principles of democracy. It was, he declared, a scandal that a well-known enemy of the popular will, like Colonel Beresford, should be associated with a movement of the kind. Michael, who knew the power and influence of Thady Glynn, felt that there was no hope at all of getting anything out of the Chief Secretary. He made his report to the doctor.

'Didn't I tell you,' he said at the end of it, 'that it's the way things would be? Anybody might have known it.'

Dr. Whitty received the news with the greatest cheerfulness.

'That's all right,' he said. 'That's exactly what I hoped he'd say.'

'You're easy satisfied, then, if you're pleased with that.'

'I'm going up to the Colonel now,' said the doctor. 'Do you come in here tomorrow at two o'clock, when I'll be at home for my dinner, and I'll tell you what's the next thing you have to say to Thady Glynn.'

Dr. Whitty mounted his bicycle and rode to the entrance of the demesne. He greeted the gate-keeper's child cheerfully, and then sped up the long, shady avenue. He found Colonel Beresford cutting exhausted blossoms off his rose trees in front of the house. He introduced his business without delay.

'You've heard,' he said, 'that the new Chief Secretary, Mr. Willoughby, is to pass through the town the day after tomorrow. We were thinking of getting up a deputation to wait upon him in the hope that he might build us a pier at Ballintra.'

'Why the devil should he build a pier in Ballintra?' asked the Colonel.

'Oh, we're not particular as to its being a pier. A railway or anything else would do quite as well. We only suggest a pier because it's the usual thing.'

'But why should he build anything?'

'I don't know why; but, as a matter of fact — you must have observed it yourself, Colonel — all Chief Secretaries build a lot of things when they first come over. I suppose they think it'll make them popular with the people. It doesn't, of course, but they don't find that out for a long time. What we feel is that if there are piers and things going we may as well get our share as not.'

'Very well. If a man's fool enough to build a pier in a place like this, get it if you can, by all means. I suppose you'll put it somewhere out of the way, so that it won't interfere with the fishing boats.'

'Of course we will. I'm glad you take the view you do of it, Colonel, because we want you to form one of our deputation.'

'Who else is going on it? I'm not going to mix myself up with a pack of blackguards simply to swindle a Chief Secretary out of a pier.'

'Mr. Jackson, the rector, has just promised to be one.'

The Colonel grunted. He had no very high opinion of Mr. Jackson's ability, but he was not prepared to describe him as a blackguard.

'And Father Henaghan.'

'And who else?'

'You, Colonel.'

'Look here, Doctor, there's no use dribbling out the names one by one in this way. Sooner or later you've got to own up to it that Thady Glynn is to be one of the party. I may as well tell you straight that I'm not going to mix myself up with that fellow. I wouldn't do it if it was to establish a naval dockyard in the bay. I wouldn't do it if you promised me £1,000. That blackguard hasn't missed an opportunity of abusing me in the most scurrilous way for the last ten years. I'd do a good deal to oblige you, Doctor, but I won't walk about with my arm round Glynn's neck to please any Chief Secretary in Christendom; so it's no use your asking me.'

'Michael Geraghty —' said the doctor.

'I don't care a hang about Michael Geraghty. I suppose he thinks that if there's a pier he'll get the building of it.'

'He does, of course. But what I wanted to tell you was that Michael Geraghty says that Thady Glynn won't go on the deputation. It appears he cursed and swore like mad when he heard of it, and flatly refused to act.'

'Did he? I'm surprised at that. I'd have thought he'd simply have loved it.'

'It appears that he doesn't, though. Now, if I were you, Colonel, I'd put a spoke in Thady Glynn's wheel. He thinks we can't get the pier without him. You come forward and get it for us, and Thady will be the sickest man in Ballintra for the next eighteen months.'

The Colonel chuckled. He was not at all averse to getting the better of Thady if he could. After a little more persuasion he agreed to form part of the deputation.

'Good,' said the doctor. 'We'll count on you. The day after tomorrow, at half-past twelve o'clock outside the convent. Don't forget.'

The following evening Michael Geraghty, carefully instructed by Dr. Whitty, and fully alive to the delicate nature of the negotiation before him, strolled into the hotel and approached the bar. He ordered a bottle of porter from Thady Glynn, and then approached his business obliquely.

'It's wonderful,' he said, 'the spite that some men has — men that ought to know better — against the people of this country and all that might be for their good.'

'That's true,' said Thady Glynn.

'You'd hardly believe it now,' said Geraghty, 'but no sooner did the old colonel above, at the big house, hear your name mentioned in connection with the forthcoming deputation to the Chief Secretary —'

'I'm not going on it. I told you that before.'

'— than he turned on the doctor, and "damned scoundrel" was the mildest words he used. I wouldn't care to be repeating to you the rest of what he said.'

'Did he, then?'

'He did, and more. He said there'd be no pier got without he went and asked for it.'

'Did he say that?'

'He did. And, of course, it was the truth. Who'd give a pier to the likes of us when the gentry says a pier's not wanted in the locality?'

'Was it me he called a damned scoundrel?'

'It was. Maybe I oughtn't to have repeated the like; but it's out now, and if you hadn't heard it from me you would from another; so it's as well as it is.'

'I'll teach him,' said Thady. 'I'll give him a lesson he'll remember.'

'What's the use of talking? You couldn't. What does he care for the likes of you? There's only one thing that would vex him, and that's what you couldn't do.'

'What's that?'

'Get the pier for us. He'd be mad if he heard that we'd got it in spite of him. But you couldn't do it, so where the use?'

'I could do it if I laid myself down to the job.'

'You could not. You're angry this minute, Mr. Glynn, if you'll excuse my saying so. You're angry, and small blame to you. You think you could do anything, the way he has you rose by the language he used; but you couldn't get the pier. The Chief Secretary wouldn't listen to what you'd say.'

'He would listen, and it would be the worse for him if he did not. I'd have a question asked in Parliament if he didn't listen to me, and that's what he wouldn't like.'

'Anyway, you won't do it,' said Geraghty. 'Aren't you after saying this minute that nothing would make you go on the deputation?'

'I may have said that, but if I did, it was because I thought it was a got-up job with them behind it that hasn't the good of the people in their hearts. But I see now I was wrong about that. You can tell the doctor I'll go, and what's more, I'll do my best. What time is it to be?'

'It's twelve o'clock,' said Geraghty. 'That's the hour fixed for the visit to the industrial school above at the convent, and the deputation is to meet him when he comes out.'

'You may tell the doctor, I'll be there.'

'I'll take another bottle of porter,' said Geraghty, 'the way I'll wish you luck.'

The Chief Secretary and his wife, a charming lady in a mauve dress of Irish tweed, reached Ballintra in good time. Accompanied by Father Henaghan and conducted by the Reverend Mother, they entered the convent just as the town clock struck twelve. At ten minutes past twelve Dr. Whitty arrived and was cheered by the crowd which had watched the arrival of the motor car. Five minutes later the Rev. J. Jackson, rector of the parish, came up. He had put on a silk hat, of somewhat antiquated shape, for the occasion. He looked hot and nervous. The crowd, which was in an exceptionally good humour, cheered him too. At twenty minutes past twelve Thady Glynn and Michael Geraghty strolled up together from the hotel and took up a position just outside the convent gate. Someone in the crowd began to sing, 'God save Ireland'.[5] The prayer, considering that Thady Glynn was a prominent leader of public opinion in the country, was appropriate, but it was sung without any malicious intent. There was no thought in anyone's mind that Mr. Glynn might be a difficulty in the way of the Almighty. Then Colonel Beresford drove up in a smart dog-cart drawn by a well-groomed horse. The singing ceased at once. An Irish crowd is always courteous, and it was felt quite rightly that a prayer for the welfare of Ireland would be regarded as an insult to Colonel Beresford. Dr. Whitty watched the scene anxiously, casting hurried glances from the dog-cart to the convent gate, and back from the convent gate to the dog-cart. He saw Mr. Thady Glynn start, saw him make a remark which he supposed, from the gesticulation which accompanied it, to be a violent oath. The Colonel drove on. Dr. Whitty saw Michael Geraghty seize Thady by the arm and whisper eagerly to him. Then the Colonel pulled up his horse with a jerk and sat glaring furiously in the direction of the convent gate. Dr. Whitty felt that there was not a moment to be lost. He darted forward and took his place beside the Colonel's trap.

'Good morning, Colonel. You're just in time. The Chief Secretary is in the convent. He'll be out in two minutes. Mr. Jackson is here, and Father Henaghan is inside. We're all ready. Jump down.'

The Colonel, by way of reply, jammed his whip into its socket, raised his arm, and pointed a finger at Thady Glynn. Dr. Whitty leaned towards him and spoke in a clear whisper.

'I know. It's that beast Thady Glynn. He's come here to make himself objectionable, with all the corner boys about the place after him. He'll start them hooting or booing, or something, directly the Chief Secretary comes out. I was afraid he'd do something of the sort. But never mind. Father Henaghan will introduce the deputation. It'll be all right.'

The Colonel squared himself, as military men do, and assumed an appearance of great determination. Dr. Whitty glanced over his shoulder and observed

5. Far from being an innocent prayer for Ireland, the song's title and chorus claim to be the dying words of Allen, Larkin and O'Brien, the 'Manchester Martyrs', Fenian activists controversially executed in 1867.

with pleasure that Thady Glynn was standing his ground. Michael Geraghty had acted on his instructions and told Thady that Colonel Beresford had come to persuade the Chief Secretary not to give the pier. The Colonel got out of his trap and stalked majestically across the road. Mr. Jackson joined him. Dr. Whitty watched the convent door anxiously. The situation was critical. He sincerely hoped that the Chief Secretary would not be delayed by any unhallowed desire to see more than the Reverend Mother wanted to show him. He need not have been anxious. Mr. Willoughby was a man of tact. He asked only the proper questions and patted the heads of no girls except those brought immediately under his notice. At half-past twelve precisely he shook hands with the Reverend Mother and stepped out of the convent door. The Colonel, Mr. Jackson, and Thady Glynn approached him. Father Henaghan left Mrs. Willoughby, to whom he had been chatting, hurried to the front, and took off his hat.

'It's my pleasing duty, sir,' he said, 'to introduce to you a deputation which, for its representative character, has never been equalled in this neighbourhood.'

The crowd, led by Michael Geraghty, cheered loudly. Mr. Willoughby took off his hat. His wife bowed from the background.

'The Rev. Mr. Jackson,' said Father Henaghan, 'is the Protestant rector of the parish, a gentleman respected by all classes and creeds for his charity and Christian conduct. And I may say, sir, that in this parish all creeds live together in harmony and good-fellowship.'

Mr. Jackson, hat in hand, took a step forward and bowed to Mr. Willoughby. Mr. Willoughby shook him warmly by the hand. The crowd cheered again.

'This,' said Father Henaghan, 'is Colonel Beresford. I make no doubt but you've heard of him before now, and I may say —'

Dr. Whitty watched Thady Glynn. Fortunately the crowd cheered again. Thady hesitated, scowling heavily.

'I may say,' continued Father Henaghan, 'that the fact of Colonel Beresford's presence with us today is a proof that the request we are about to make is reasonable and just.'

The Chief Secretary shook Colonel Beresford's hand, and introduced him to Mrs. Willoughby, who smiled pleasantly. The crowd cheered vociferously.

'This,' said Father Henaghan, taking the unwilling Thady Glynn by the arm and leading him forward, 'is my particular friend, Mr. Glynn, of the Imperial Hotel. A leading man, sir, in this neighbourhood, a J.P., and the Chairman of the Board of Guardians.'

Colonel Beresford grew extremely red in the face. Dr. Whitty suspected that he was only restrained from swearing by the presence of Mrs. Willoughby. The Colonel was before all a gentleman, and respected the feelings of the lady beside him. Dr. Whitty edged a little away from him.

'What this deputation wishes to lay before you,' said Father Henaghan, 'is the drawback that this town suffers from the want of a pier. It's well known that the development of the fisheries of this coast is one of the greatest boons which a sympathetic Government could confer on our poor people.'

He ambled on, encouraged by the cheers of the crowd, totally unconscious of the passions which his introductions had excited. Even Dr. Whitty, who had no reason to look forward with pleasure to the immediate future, began to wish that he would stop. In the end, of course, he did stop. All men must, even when they speak on a topic so entrancing as the development of Irish fisheries. The Chief Secretary's reply was brief but satisfactory. He said that nothing gratified him more than to observe the union of classes and creeds in Ireland. The country, he thought, had been too long divided into hostile factions. In the deputation which had met him that day he saw a plain proof that the days of division were past and a happier epoch at hand. He added that the inhabitants of Ballintra might count upon having the pier they wanted. He himself would see to it that the necessary money was forthcoming. Then he shook hands with each member of the deputation, placed his wife in the motor car, gave an order to the driver, and departed.

'Dr Whitty,' said the Colonel, 'you have grossly abused my confidence, sir. I trusted your word as I might have trusted the word of a gentleman. I find —'

'The man you have to blame, Colonel,' said the doctor, 'is Michael Geraghty. Michael told me distinctly that Thady Glynn absolutely refused to go on the deputation. I had every reason to believe what he said. I did believe it. I believe still that it was true at the time he told it to me. Come now, Colonel, be reasonable. You can't hold me responsible because Glynn changed his mind at the last moment.'

'I do hold you responsible,' said the Colonel; 'I —'

'If Geraghty wasn't fighting for his life this minute,' said Dr. Whitty, 'and getting the worst of it from Thady Glynn, I'd call him to corroborate what I say. Look at that.'

He pointed to the spot where Michael Geraghty was trying to ward off the blows aimed at his head by Thady Glynn. Father Henaghan, with uplifted hands, was dancing about on the outskirts of the fray trying to restore peace.

'Look at that,' said Dr. Whitty. 'Thady's pretty near as angry as you are.'

Colonel Beresford had a sense of humour. He glanced at Thady and his victim, glared at the doctor, glanced at Father Henaghan, smiled at the doctor, and finally got into his trap and drove off.

In the evening Michael Geraghty came round to the doctor's house and complained of the awkward position in which he had been placed.

'Thady Glyn,' he said, 'was terrible angry. Only for Father Henaghan he'd have had me killed.'

'You're all right,' said the doctor. 'I can't see what you have to complain of. You've no bones broken and you've got the pier.'

'Thady'll never speak to me again in this world.'

'He will. So soon as ever he finds out that you're going to make £200 out of that pier he'll be as friendly as ever he was. Why, man, it would be a terrible thing for him if you spent all that money anywhere but in his shop.'

GERALD O'DONOVAN

(1871–1942)

from: FATHER RALPH (1913)

[*Father Ralph*, of which these are the two last chapters, is the first and most powerful of Gerald O'Donovan's novels. Its first sentence is 'It was his mother's idea that Ralph O'Brien should be a priest.' The novel traces the progress of his early, sheltered education in Dublin, the removal of his family to Inniscar in the Irish midlands where he attends a diocesan catholic seminary, his graduation to Maynooth and ordination to the priesthood. Ralph O'Brien's progressive activities among the people bring him into disfavour with his selfish, conservative superior, Father Molloy, and the bishop. The conflict comes to a head when the bishop returns from Rome bearing the pope's condemnation of Modernism in 1907. The decree marks the consolidation of central papal authority proclaimed at the Vatican Council of 1869–70 when Pius IX had proclaimed papal infallability.]

CHAPTER XXVII

For some weeks Ralph was busily occupied. An epidemic of typhus broke out in an outlying district of the parish. There were two nurses for seven houses, and it was impossible to get any attendance, as the people in the neighbourhood were panic-stricken, and would not go near the infected houses. Father Hardy was on vacation, and Father Molloy said he was too busy over the Seminary collection to do any sick calls. Ralph and Father Dempsey took turns in helping the nurses, often staying up all night.

The bishop arrived home, and was received at the railway station by the brass band. Darcy read an address written by Father Molloy. The bishop in reply made a glowing speech on the wisdom of the Pope, whose unceasing care of his people would be manifest when the great encyclical,[1] a copy of which he had the happiness to have in his pocket, was read in the churches. It would gladden the Pope's heart to hear that the bearer of his encyclical had received such a magnificent welcome, worthy alike of the great occasion and of the holiness of the people.

Ralph, who had spent the night in one of the fever houses, heard all this next day from Father Dempsey.

1. The encyclical letter, entitled *Pascendi Dominici Gregis* (1907), in which Pope Pius X refuted Modernism — 'the synthesis of all heresies' — which sought to interpret the Scriptures in the light of contemporary liberalism.

'Your absence was remarked on by his lordship. I said you were on a sick call, but he was none too pleased. He said it showed a lack of zeal, not to be present to welcome one's bishop after a long absence.'

'Have you heard what's in the encyclical?'

'Not a word, only Molloy said this morning that it was a great document for keeping young cubs on the leash.'

At night, when he opened a newspaper, Ralph found the encyclical in full, sharing the front page with 'Princely Reception of the Bishop of Bunnahone[2] in his historic diocese.' He read the encyclical through. It was on the lines outlined by Boyle. He sighed hopelessly when he came to the end. He was tired from want of sleep, and he had some difficulty in keeping awake. The paper fell to the floor, and he awoke with a start. He was not asleep then! There would be some days yet. He could not leave these people who were ill. If there were no fresh cases, all danger would be passed in less than a week.

He slept badly all night. He sat up once, thinking he heard a knock: it was only a window rattling. Half asleep, he seemed to be working desperately against time to get something done. He tried to think what the work was, or what was the danger that threatened to prevent it; turned restlessly from side to side in a vain effort to remember, until at last he fell into a dreamless sleep.

He awoke refreshed, and lay quite still, without thought, listening to the swish of the blind, moved to and fro by the wind through the open window. He drew the bed-clothes tightly round him, feeling vaguely restless. The fever patients of course! He jumped out of bed. The crisis was expected today in the last bad case, John Feeney. While dressing, he thought of his mother with a pang. He felt a dull, physical aching all over him.

Did she care for him? Something in her eluded him. She had loved him so much. What had come between them? Religion? That would have drawn them closer.

He sat with a boot in his hand for fully five minutes, his eyes fixed on the sunlight, making curious patterns on the wall-paper. His mind went back over all their relations in the past. . . .

He felt hard and resentful for a moment, then a wave of pity swept over him. Her heart had become as flint. Fear had driven out love, had crushed even her mother's love for her son. He recalled incident after incident that marked crises in her life — the growth of her idea of a tyrannical God. . . .

He stood up and clenched his fists. He wanted to pull down something. The shadow of the waving branches of the tree outside the window danced gaily on the wall, and seemed to mock him. The room was stuffy, stifling. He threw up the sash from the bottom, and drew in deep breaths of air.

The Church to which he had offered his life had done this. It had separated his mother from him. It had so influenced her gentle timid nature as to dehumanize her. Fear of the God it had given her to worship had narrowed her interests, first to her family, and then to herself. . . . She would sacrifice her husband and her son, to propitiate the anger of a monster. . . .

He saw her grovelling before a colossal stone idol with a malignant grin on its cynical deformed face. . . .

He felt that he must have more air. He hurriedly finished dressing and went out. Unconsciously he took the road to Feeney's house. His feeling of resentment against the Church gave way to an intense longing to be with his mother. . . .

A fresh warm wind from the sea was like the touch of a soft hand on his face. He was back again in the nursery cuddling on his mother's knee, his cheek on her hand, her fragrant breath deliciously fanning his hair. . . .

No decree should keep her from him. She could never cease to love him. . . .

The nurse met him on Feeney's doorstep. The crisis had come in the night, quite normally. He was now sleeping quietly.

Ralph looked at his watch and suddenly remembered that he was to have said mass at the convent at seven o'clock. It was now after eight. He muttered some excuse to the nurse and ran rapidly along the deserted road. He met the old Reverend Mother on the bridge in the convent grounds. She looked keenly at him over her spectacles.

'You are too late. We waited an hour; the nuns have had breakfast.'

'I am very sorry, Reverend Mother.'

'Sister Elizabeth now,' she said with a faint smile. She continued to look at him. 'We shall walk here for a few minutes,' she said with a sigh, turning

2. A fictional name for Clonfert, where O'Donovan served as a priest.

down a side-path along the river. She fingered her beads, as she walked slowly and with difficulty. She stopped at a seat and sat down.

'There is a lot of gossip in the convent,' she said, her eyes on her beads.

'That is nothing unusual,' Ralph said, uneasily, with a smile.

'Don't,' she said gently, 'I feel it too much.' She drew her spectacles up over her clouded eyes.

'The bishop told Reverend Mother. He was here yesterday and was very angry. You are to be punished. Poor boy, poor boy,' she added, under her breath. 'There is to be a special conference next Thursday, Reverend Mother says. He will then make known his decision, not too severe because of your good mother, he said.'

'You seem to know all about it,' Ralph said harshly.

'He tells Reverend Mother everything,' she said simply.

His face had grown rigid. She looked at him anxiously. 'You will bear up . . . and not be proud.'

He laughed, but seeing her pained look he said gently —

'You have been very kind to me. Wherever I go I shall always remember it. I am probably leaving. . . .'

'This parish?' she asked eagerly.

'The priesthood — the Church, as far as the Church is concerned.' The words, in his harsh staccato voice, sounded to him as if some one else had spoken. He had taken the decision for granted since last night, but had not put it into words. He felt numbed.

'My God! my God!' the nun said, swaying on the seat.

He was acutely conscious of the sounds which burned his brain, the murmur of the stream, the sobbing of the nun, voices from the school in the distance, twittering of birds on the lawn.

'Oh, dear God, save him!' He felt the touch of the old nun's hand on his. He returned the pressure.

'You haven't lost your religion?' she said timidly.

A lark rose across the stream and seemed to flood the air with melody.

'I am only trying to find it.'

The nun sat absorbed in thought, or prayer, for she fingered her beads rapidly. Ralph's eyes wandered over the grounds in front. Sound and sight were no longer painful. He drank in the beauty of the wonderful autumn colouring, brown and gold against the light green of the well-mown grass and the harsher green of evergreens gleaming in the sun. The autumn day had all the freshness of spring and the genial warmth of early summer. A weight seemed to have fallen from his spirit. . . .

'Where will you go?'

'I don't know. Anywhere,' he restrained himself because of the sad tone in the nun's voice. 'Where I can breathe and live.' He felt inclined to sing. It was joyful to be alive. 'I was dead and now I live,' he said under his breath.

His eyes fell on the old nun's face, drawn and aged, and the joyful mood passed away.

She shook her head sadly.

'I am too old to understand. There is so much to do in Bunnahone. . . .' Her voice trailed off in a murmur.

'Mother, if I could stay I would. All I see clearly is that I must go — all the rest is dark enough, God knows,' he said drearily.

'Poor boy!' she said. 'I suppose we must all seek God in our own way.'

His eyes roamed round the grounds. It was all so peaceful — late purple and scarlet flowers against the green, the faint drone of the voices of two nuns saying the rosary along a path near by, a hoarse murmur from the schools, a deeper chord in harmony with the voice of the stream. It was the peace of the old, of death. . . .

A clock chimed the hour. 'I must go,' she said. She held his hand, and said gravely —

'There were so many things I intended to say, but somehow I cannot say them. The soul of another is like a trackless wood at night — impenetrable. I won't meddle, but I will pray. May God be ever with you.'

He crossed the road, and opened the door of his house in a dream. Some letters were on the study table. He opened one, with the episcopal seal, in Father Magan's handwriting — a formal announcement of a special conference to consider 'the recent important pronouncements of the Pope, and to take steps for their enforcement.' He dropped it idly. Ann came in and asked if he had breakfasted. He stared at her awhile, seemed to consider the question with great gravity, and said 'no' solemnly.

'What's coming over you?' she said, looking at him suspiciously. He didn't reply, and she left the room grumbling.

He took up his letters again, and read them with little interest. He ate a good breakfast, wandered about his rooms, opened a newspaper, glanced at the headings, and put it by. He went to the bookshelves. There was nothing to read. He lit a pipe, strolled into the garden, and lopped off some dead flowers. He had a restless feeling that he had a lot to do, but he did not know where to begin. Thursday was the conference day. Why put off his preparation for leaving till then, since he had already come to a decision? Ought he to see his mother now, or wait till after Thursday? There was Ann to consider. What was to become of her? He shrank from considering anything.

Father Dempsey called, and was full of the coming conference. The bishop was writing a loyal address to the Pope, which Father Molloy was to propose, and Magan to second. There was some plan to have some of the young priests sign some document. 'Sure no one ought to mind,' he said anxiously, 'about signing a thing like that. What is it but a little bit of paper? There isn't much meaning in theology anyway. I read over that decree myself, and it is only a lot of bother about trifles. It might be the soundest theology in the world that's condemned in it for all I can remember of my reading in Maynooth. You'll sign anything you're asked?' he said eagerly. 'If for nothing else, but to spite Molloy and Magan, who think you're in for a fall.'

Ralph smiled at the naïveté of the priest, whose simple face glowed with sympathy. He would have told him of his resolve, but he wished to avoid endless talk with no common basis of argument; and no possibility of agreement, or even of understanding. He turned the conversation to the Irish language, in his zeal for which Father Dempsey soon forgot Ralph's troubles.

During the days preceding the conference he hated being alone. He was glad of any routine work that gave him no time for thought. He haunted the workhouse, the asylum, the schools, and visited most of the old people in the village. He begged Father Dempsey to spend the evenings with him, and to accompany him on long walks across country. Except Father Dempsey, who soon saw that Ralph did not wish to discuss his position, he avoided everyone he knew with any intimacy. Father Dempsey told him, 'It has gone the rounds of the town that you are in some trouble,' and he was conscious of curious looks cast on him in the street. One old woman, who begged him to help her pay a fine she had incurred at the petty sessions court for drunkenness, offered him her sympathy, saying, 'We're all liable to trouble from the drop of drink, sure I'm sorry to hear you have got into the same trouble yourself.'

The conference met in the bishop's dining-room. When Ralph arrived, within a few minutes of the appointed hour, most of the priests had already come, and stood around the large room in groups. Father Duff was sitting by the fire surrounded by several priests.

'Molloy tried a march on me,' he said, loudly, so as to be heard by Father Molloy, who sat at the head of the table, next an armchair evidently reserved for the bishop, 'but he overreached himself. These two priests think they're very clever, but sorra bit they know of the country, no more than a child in arms. Unless they change their tune, and give up being bill servers for gombeen men,[3] the people'll give them the go-by.'

'Right, Father Duff, right,' a little apple-cheeked priest shouted joyfully, slapping his leg. 'What do you say to that now, Molloy?'

Father Molloy flushed and pretended not to hear.

'Hush,' said a tall sardonic-looking man, 'don't you see that he's busy studying the decree?'

'He'd make as much out of it as a pig would out of the alphabet,' said Father Duff, contemptuously.

'The Miss Hinnisseys gave him a lesson on it last night. Hardy, who is dead jealous of him, told me,' the sardonic man said solemnly.

'I never said a word of the kind,' Hardy said heatedly.

'I have it on the best authority,' the apple-faced man said, 'that Hardy is getting inside Molloy there. He turns the music for Miss Katie. Molloy was never able to do that as he couldn't tell one note from another. Miss Katie used to have to tread on his toe, when she wanted a page turned over.'

There was a general laugh. Father Duff caught Ralph's eye.

'Come here, Ralph,' he said loudly. 'There has been some whispering going on agin you, behind backs. I want to let the people know who are doing it,' he glared at Molloy, and then at Magan, who was shuffling uneasily by the fireplace, his face a deep

3. Grasping shopkeepers achieving power by credit and moneylending.

purple, 'even if they are precious relations of mine itself, that if I hear any more of it, I'll read their characters for them.'

'Do you hear that now, Molloy?' the apple-cheeked man said, 'I know I wouldn't have Father Duff's tongue agin me for a good deal.'

Father Molloy turned the papers in front of him nervously. 'I only do my duty,' he said aggressively.

'Molloy and duty!' said the sardonic man, mockingly.

Several priests laughed.

'What's this decree about, anyway?' the apple-cheeked man said.

'I don't know what it's about,' Father Duff said angrily, 'and I care less, but I won't have it made a handle for Molloy's spite.'

The bishop entered, and all the priests stood up. Having said the 'Veni sancte Spiritus,'[4] he took his seat at the head of the table. Ralph sat between Father Duff and Father Devine, half-way down the long table.

'Reverend Fathers. . . .' the bishop began.

'My lord, I beg leave to interrupt your lordship,' a chinless florid priest said, standing up. 'Gentlemen, this is the first opportunity we have of welcoming, all of us together, his lordship the bishop on his return from the Holy City of Rome. Our hearts were filled with woe and sorrow during his long absence, and are bursting with joy now that he's come back among us again. Our consolation is that he was giving the same good advice to the Holy Father that he's always ready to give to us. In the name of all your devoted priests, my lord, I bid your lordship a hearty welcome.'

Several priests rapped the bare mahogany table loudly with their knuckles.

'And I might be at home getting in my potatoes on a fine day like this. And the frost coming on too,' Father Duff said, across the table to Father Sheldon, who sat with his eyes closed, his clasped hands resting on the table in front of him.

'Muldoon is making a bid for a parish,' the sardonic man said in a stage whisper. There was a jeering laugh at the end of the table.

'Gentlemen,' the bishop said. 'This eloquent expression of your devotion touches me deeply. It is a fitting prelude to the business we have in hand. You have all read the decree Lamentabili?[5] . . .'

'I never saw it,' Father Duff said gruffly. 'Nor I'; 'Nor I'; several voices repeated down the table.

'You have all read the decree Lamentabili?' the bishop repeated firmly.

'Of course we have, my Lord,' Father Muldoon said eagerly.

'Whist,[6] man,' the apple-cheeked man said under his breath, 'sure it's a book about card playing — I wouldn't let on I read it if I were you.'

'And you join with the Holy Father, and every good priest and bishop throughout the world,' the bishop continued, 'in detestation of the errors condemned by it.'

'What are they, my lord?' Father Duff asked.

'This facetiousness should be reserved for a less solemn occasion,' the bishop said testily.

'It's like buying a pig in a poke,' Father Duff said, fretfully, to Ralph. 'Do you know what he's talking about?'

'May I read the address now, my lord?' Father Molloy asked.

'Yes, yes,' the bishop said hastily, having apparently lost the thread of his remarks, searching among his papers for his notes.

Father Molloy stood up, cleared his throat, and read —

'We, the priests of the diocese of Bunnahone in conference assembled, having carefully considered the propositions condemned in the Bull Lamentabili, and the remarks of our Holy Father, the Pope, thereon in the Encyclical Pascendi Gregis, wish unanimously to place on record our horror that such blasphemous views as those condemned by the Holy Father should be held by any who call themselves Catholics. We wish at the same time to assure his Holiness that those errors are unknown and unheard of in this historic diocese, where all the priests and people, under the direction of their devoted bishop, think and act only in accordance with the mind and will of the Holy See.'

'I second it,' Father Magan said, popping up when Father Molloy sat down.

'That is satisfactorily done,' the bishop said,

4. Literally 'Come Holy Spirit', a prayer/hymn appropriate to the opening of religious conferences.

5. *Lamentabili sane exitu* (With truly lamentable results) was the title of the decree of July 1907 that preceded the encyclical letter.

6. Be quiet.

rubbing his hands together. 'Ours will be one of the first in. The Holy Father will be delighted.'

'It's easy pleasing him then,' Father Duff said, yawning. 'Would you tell me now, Ralph, what it's all about?'

'Nero fiddling while Rome burns,' Ralph said shortly.

'It's joking you are.'

'Not at all. Some one will be thrown to the lions presently.'

'Well, I'm glad to see you in good spirits anyway, even if I can't understand you.'

A pained look crossed Father Sheldon's drawn face. He understood, Ralph thought. His eyes wandered round the table. The bishop was speaking in a low tone to Father Molloy. Two priests next Father Sheldon were discussing the price of cattle. The apple-cheeked priest, grown serious, asserted loudly that tenants who had purchased their land ought to pay double dues to the priest. Father Hardy whispered behind his hand to Father Muldoon — 'Drop in at the parochial house before you leave; there's sure to be a game on with all the lads in town.'

The bishop rapped the table, and said, 'Silence. There are just a few more formalities, and I think we shall have done a memorable day's work. First I wish to appoint a board to act as censors of books, and to carry out generally the wishes of our Holy Father embodied in his encyclical; they are the vicar-general, Father Doyle, the president of the Seminary, Father Magan, and the esteemed administrator of this parish, Father Molloy. The best interests of the Church may be safely entrusted to their wisdom and learning.'

'Can Molloy read?' the sardonic-looking priest said gravely to the apple-cheeked priest.

'He makes a boast of reading the newspaper, and he was once seen reading a penny dreadful.'[7]

'Gentlemen, this business is most serious,' the bishop said, again rapping the table. 'There is only one other matter. I have drawn up a declaration, repudiating all the so-called modernist errors, which I shall ask all the young priests, under five years ordained, to repeat after me. Priests of longer service are too wise, I am sure,' he looked meaningly at Father Sheldon, who still sat with eyes closed, 'to hold any views condemned by our Holy Father. Young priests sometimes lack discretion. Would you stand up please, gentlemen, priests of under five years on the mission.'

A dozen or more priests stood up. Ralph remained seated. Devine, who was standing beside him, pulled his sleeve.

'For the love of God, stand up,' he said anxiously.

'There'll be some fun now,' Hardy whispered joyfully to Muldoon.

Father Molloy whispered to the bishop.

'You are not five years ordained, Father O'Brien,' the bishop said suavely.

'No.'

'Do you refuse to make the declaration?'

'Yes.'

'For God's sake, think of what you're doing,' Devine said, in an agonized whisper that was heard all over the room.

'Crikey!' said the apple-cheeked man, 'think of anyone taking that gibberish seriously.'

'You leave me no option, but to suspend you from the exercise of Orders until you come to your senses,' the bishop said with a frown.

'For shame, my lord! the poor lad,' said Father Duff.

'If you don't respect your own years, respect your bishop, sir,' said the bishop, angrily.

'He's very young. He's sure to do what's right. Maybe like myself, he couldn't make head or tail of the whole thing. To suspend him now! Think of the disgrace of it, and he partly of my own rearing too,' the old man said feebly.

'Silence!' the bishop said loudly. He glared at Father Duff, was about to speak, but checked himself. He bundled his papers together, and stood up.

'You didn't read the declaration, my lord,' Father Molloy said.

'In view of our address to the Holy Father, I don't wish to mar the harmony of our meeting. This matter is adjourned.' He knelt on his chair, said a prayer hurriedly, and left the room.

'You'll give in. It's going against God Himself, for He speaks through the mouth of the Pope,' Devine said eagerly to Ralph.

'I don't understand it at all,' said Father Duff, weakly. He passed his hand over his eyes. 'Sheldon'll be able to tell me. He knows a power of things.'

Father Sheldon seemed to wake up from a dream. He crossed the room and put his hand on Ralph's shoulder.

7. A cheap, lurid book or magazine.

'I never found it harder to keep silent. You believe me, and forgive me?' he said wistfully. 'If I spoke I should have said too much.'

'Yours is the harder part,' Ralph said, holding out his hand.

'Is it the end?' Father Sheldon's voice trembled as he put the question.

'Yes . . .'

Father Sheldon pressed his hand.

CHAPTER XXVIII

As Ralph left the room he was conscious of the curious eyes of a group of priests by the door. Two, whom he knew rather well, turned their backs on him. Whe he passed there was a jeering laugh, followed by 'that will be a cooler for him, anyway.' Another voice said, 'Young pup, setting himself up as better than his neighbours. I hope the lord'll give it to him hot.'

There was some delay in the hall while Father Duff was putting on his overcoat. 'I'm well rid of him' came through the open dining-room door, in Father Molloy's voice. 'You see what happens any man that stands up agin me. I flatten him out sooner or later.' 'The widow will shut her purse now,' another voice said. Father Molloy laughed. 'No fear; the lord has her in his fist.'

'I'll tell that skunk what I think of him,' Father Duff said, furiously angry, advancing to the door with his overcoat half on.

Ralph pulled him back. 'It's not worth while; much worse will be said later.'

'I'm afraid so,' Father Sheldon said sadly.

They restrained Father Duff with difficulty.

'I'll not come back for any dinner here,' he said, 'it would poison me. Did any one ever hear the like?' he added, standing on the sidewalk; 'to suspend a man for nothing. If it was drink now, or women, there'd be some meaning in it! But theology! I often heard it said that theology never did a man any good, but I never thought that it could do any harm. You give us a bit to eat, Ralph, and I'll see if I can't set all this to rights.'

Ralph glanced helplessly at Father Sheldon, who finally prevailed on Father Duff to go home with him.

'Let is be as you say,' he said reluctantly. 'I hope ye aren't keeping anything back from me. You ought to know by this, Ralph, that I'd give my heart to serve you.'

When the two priests had gone, Ralph walked home slowly. He hesitated at Mrs. Fahy's door, but decided not to go in; even her broad charity would shrink from him when she found out that he had given up the priesthood.

In his study he felt lonely and bitter; not even Father Duff would understand. He laughed cynically at the recollection of the conference. His dream had ended in a farce. His protest would furnish an idle laugh for one of Father Molloy's card parties.

What was he to do? Give up this house. The furniture belonged to Inniscar;[1] his books he would try to keep. There was Ann; he shrank from an explanation with Ann. Would she be as hard as his mother? He was wrong in thinking that his mother could be hard; when she knew that he was in real trouble her heart would soften towards him again. . . . But she was going into a convent; would she give up the idea and live with him? The memory of her look — hard, implacable — as he left the drawing-room on his last visit came back to him; a feeling of fear overcame him. He struggled against it. She could not hold out against his love. He would break down that iron wall that stood between them. He said aloud, 'I will see her. She will understand; she is my mother.' He sank back exhausted in his chair. He looked at his hands, which felt nerveless, half expecting to see them bruised, so vivid was his sense of having battered at a wall.

He went out and walked to and fro rapidly in his small garden. He tried to shake off the depressed feelings that prevented any effort to think out his position clearly. His mind was such a poor thing, he thought, almost powerless against the dumb, overwhelming forces of its own background, a fitful light shedding a stray gleam here and there through the wrack that seemed to envelop it.

He plucked idly at the dead leaves of a rose-tree. The blooms had long since gone, the leaves had withered, yet in the spring the tree would again renew its youth. This procession of life was universal, in religion as well as in the rose-tree. His whole life had been a slow awakening to this truth. Use and habit and memory made him cling to the dead leaves while as yet the new buds had not forced them to fall.

1. Ralph's mother's house.

There was no conflict between the new life and the old. He would take with him all the religious values that meant so much to him. He was simply choosing life instead of death. . . .

For that was what the Church was doing — cutting itself off from the sources of life: in a few years it must wither and die. . . .

A feeling of peace stole over him, and he worked for awhile selecting the books he would take with him. He piled them in a corner of his study, sat at his desk, and began a letter to the bishop resigning his mission. As he wrote the opening sentence the lines became blurred, and he sat helplessly staring at what seemed to his clouded eyes a blank sheet. An intense longing to stay came back to him. His justification of himself was a string of meaningless words. Others, better than he, were staying. It would regain for him his mother's affection. He saw a vision of an ideal Church with which he was at one. . . .

It faded away almost at once, and his mind dwelt on the actual Church as he knew it. His one hope of its regeneration had been crushed. . . .

He took up his pen and finished the letter, formally resigning, and added that henceforward he considered himself a layman. He took it himself and handed it in at the bishop's door. He heard the sound of loud laughter from the dining-room, and the clatter of plates. As the door closed on him he had a feeling of having done some necessary work, and a desire for food. He hurried home and got Ann to cook him a hasty meal.

'Why aren't you at the big dinner at the bishop's?' she asked, as she served him.

He hesitated a moment. 'I am leaving,' he said.

'To see your mother belike.'[2]

He explained incoherently. When she grasped what he meant, the plate she held in her hands fell to the ground, and she stood transfixed, with her hands extended as if she still held it. Something comic in her attitude provoked a smile, which froze on his lips when he saw the horror on her face and her glazed eyes staring at him.

'The disgrace of it,' she said feebly. 'I once knew a silenced priest in Dublin, who used to hang round the public-houses begging for drinks.'

His head sunk between his shoulders. He wished that he had gone away silently. He should have to pay a bitter price for his freedom in the pain he inflicted on all who loved him. He suffered, but they suffered too, and the thought of their suffering was his heaviest blow. He could feel resentment against the ecclesiastical machine, against its time-servers and self-seekers, but not against those who, unquestioning, regarded it as the voice of God. Acts of authority might seem cruel to them, or unscrupulous, but they were God's actions and must be right.

She put her apron to her eyes and began to cry. She fell on her knees, stretched out her arms, and said passionately —

'I reared you as if you were my own son. Don't go agin me and God now.'

He shook his head sadly, deeply moved. 'Have pity on me, Ann. I must go,' he said, holding out his hand appealingly.

'Ask God to pity you,' she said sternly. 'Though I doubt but He's hardened His heart agin you.'

She left the room, and he sat staring at the table, forgetting the food. After a while she came back and removed the things with a set face, without speaking. He sat on, staring vacantly in front of him. A few vague, unconnected memories passed through his mind. He heard a coal fall from the fire, and waited for another to fall as if his fate depended on it. Ann came in and said —

'Father Devine is in the study. He wants to see you.'

He stood up, hesitated, and sat down again. 'I can't go through this again,' he thought. 'I should only say things that would pain him.'

'Tell him I can't see him,' he said to Ann. 'I'm not at home to any one.'

'And you sitting there,' she said, bridling. 'He's a good young priest, and might put the fear of God into you,' she added more gently.

He smiled wearily, saying, 'I'm not at home to any one.'

He heard Father Devine protesting in the hall, and Ann's voice: 'Leave him to God for the present at any rate. They're a queer, obstinate lot, the O'Briens, when the fit is on them.'

After dark he went for a walk. He tried to make plans for his future, but his thoughts wandered. He must leave Bunnahone at once: but he must see his mother first — came back again and again like a refrain. There was Ann to arrange for, and he must get some secular clothes and some money. What he should do after leaving Bunnahone he shirked

2. perhaps, maybe.

thinking of. It would depend on his mother. He thought of her now in a detached, disinterested way, without fear or hope. . . .

Exhausted from want of food he looked round him curiously, and in the dim light of stars recognized the Inniscar gateway. He stood at the gate for a few minutes. It was too late to call now. He sighed and turned back. Hunger made his thoughts clearer. Should he fit in anywhere in the world of which he knew so little? Almost as unknown to him as the twinkling stars that crowded the dark blue vault above his head. Would he ever again get in touch with people?

It was late when he got home. Ann had not gone to bed, and he found a tray in his study with some supper. He ate heartily, and was sitting down to smoke when Ann came in.

'Will you be wanting hot water for an early mass tomorrow?'

He winced. He had said his last mass.

'The usual time. I am not saying mass,' he said brusquely.

'The whole town is full of your going,' she said angrily. 'It's soon they scattered it. 'Twas an unlucky day you came among the likes of them. If you'd only been a Carmelite, it'd be a different story today. If you'd only go to Father Eusebius[3] and let him lift a hand over you, you'd be made right yet, maybe,' she said eagerly, her voice softening.

He made no reply. 'You're going, then?' she said dully.

He nodded.

'I'll never hold my head high again,' she said sadly, lingering by the door.

He told her that he was about to arrange for a small annuity for her.

'You'll do nothing of the kind,' she said angrily. 'I've enough laid by to see me to my grave without trenching[4] on the little you have. Besides, it wouldn't be lucky money. All the same, I'm glad you made the offer,' she added with a break in her voice. 'I'll pray that God'll give you grace to repent.'

At breakfast next morning Ann handed him a letter.

'Larry Gallagher has just rode in with it. It's from the mistress. Larry wanted to see you right or wrong. He knows there's something up, but I wouldn't gratify him that far. I sent him skadaddling.'[5]

Ralph opened the envelope, which bore no name, and unfolded the letter nervously. It ran —

'You have broken my heart. The bishop drove out yesterday evening immediately on getting your letter and broke the dreadful news to me. My son is a priest. When you have again made submission to our Holy Church, which you have outraged and scandalized, a mother's heart will be open to you, but, until then, I have no son. If you have forgotten your duty to our holy religion, thank God mine has become clearer to me. As some reparation to God for your wicked action, I have made a vow neither to see you, nor to write to, nor receive letters from you, while you persevere in your impenitence and hardness of heart. It rests with you to make that time long or short, as your kind bishop is ready at any time to receive you back on your making full submission, and expressing regret for the scandal you gave at the conference. His kindness of heart, and gentle, tolerant spirit in the whole matter should move even you.

'In a few days I hope to begin my life of reparation in the convent. I shall pray for you constantly. It is a consolation to me that Inniscar will be turned into a house of prayer, as the saintly bishop has consented to accept it as his residence, so that holy mass will be regularly celebrated in the chapel. May God in His mercy bring you back to the true fold.

'In Christ,

'HILDA O'BRIEN'

He read the letter twice before its import came home to him, and even then he grasped it only vaguely. He finished his breakfast, looking at the letter, which lay open beside his plate, curiously from time to time. His emotions were all dried up, and his mind reacted feebly to external impressions. He stared at the signature, 'In Christ, Hilda O'Brien' — his mother? he thought wonderingly. Suddenly he began to cry. His whole frame was shaken by sobs. He experienced a feeling of utter loneliness, a miserable aching feeling of absolute desertion. His mind became clearer. The thinking

3. A Carmelite friar who had recommended Ann to the O'Brien family. He is mentioned in the first chapter of the novel.
4. encroaching.
5. Usually skedaddling: rushing off hurriedly.

half of him seemed to consider the feeling half with curiosity. He had not cried since his childhood. He had no recollection of ever having cried at all. Why did he cry? Did tears always bring this feeling of desolation? He exerted all his will-power fruitlessly to stay the sobs that hurt him physically. He ceased to think and to will, and the sobs slowly died away.

He got up from the table, and again took up the letter and read it. He laughed bitterly. It reminded him — he wondered vaguely why — of the glossy stuff of which the bishop's coats were made: it was so smug. It was Hilda O'Brien in Christ, with the bishop at her elbow, who wrote the letter, not his mother. Was it possible to save her from the meaningless jumble of words with which she had fettered her heart?

He got his bicycle and rode rapidly to Inniscar, determined to make an effort to see her. He would pierce the artificial barrier that divided them. He turned over in his mind the arguments he would use, even the appeals he would make to her feelings. . . .

The maid who opened the door looked confused.

'My mother? Kate. Where is she?'

The maid began to cry. 'She told me to say if you came that she wouldn't see you, Master Ralph — Father Ralph, I mean. I don't know what's up with her at all at all.'

'Where is she?'

'She's in the chapel, but you can't get in. She has the door bolted on the inside.'

He walked rapidly down the corridor that led to the chapel, and turned the handle of the door. It did not yield; he shook the door impatiently. He could hear the swish of a skirt on the carpet, and he knocked loudly.

'Who's there?' His heart stopped at the cold sound of his mother's voice.

'It is I, mother — Ralph. I must see you.'

There was a few moments' silence.

'Have you submitted to the bishop?'

'Let me see you, mother. I shall explain everything. You must understand, you will understand.'

'Have you submitted to the bishop?'

'No, but I can explain. When you understand, everything will be all right.'

'I cannot break my vow. I shall pray for you.'

'It may be the last time we shall see one another. You won't refuse me?' he said despairingly.

He listened intently, and heard the swish of the skirt receding. After a few moments there was no sound except the beating of his own heart, and the ticking of a clock in the corridor.

He called again, shook the door, beat on it with his hands, but there was no response. He lingered at the door for a few minutes, turned away, came back again, and turned the handle gently, and finding it still unyielding, sighed and walked towards the entrance hall. The maid stood red-eyed where he had left her.

'I could have told you, Master Ralph. She won't stir out until I tell her you're not in the house.'

He nodded to her absent-mindedly, and, mounting his bicycle, rode rapidly home. His one thought was to get away from every one, from everything. There was the mid-day train. He could catch that. . . .

Ann opened the door. She had been crying, and looked angry.

'I'm leaving by the next train,' he said.

'I'm not sorry. If it was only to the Carmelities I'd die happy,' she said, raising her apron to her eyes. 'I had to go down the town, and I could hear the track of Father Molloy's tongue. It's a queer world, and he's a good priest, and you're a bad one. My head is moidered[6] with a power of thinking,' she added weakly.

He packed quickly; wrote, rapidly but clearly, minute directions for Ann as to the disposal of his things, and had, after sending his bags to the station, some minutes to spare. He walked round the garden, touching unconsciously, as he had once seen an infant touch flowers, with the tip of his fingers, rose-trees which he had himself planted. He was troubled for a moment about some chrysanthemums now in bloom which an early frost would kill. He looked towards the sea, and suffered a keen disappointment that the mountains in the distance were hidden by clouds.

He rang for Ann, and handed her the paper of directions, his address in Dublin, and Boyle's address in London.

'It must be good-bye now,' he said holding out his hand. 'I'll write.'

'I'd like to kiss you once,' she said brokenly. 'I was a hard woman by religion, when I used to carry you in my arms. And I don't believe I ever kissed you, but I'd like to do it now.'

6. confused, stupefied.

She threw her arms around him, and pressed him to her heart, weeping bitterly.

'It's queer that I never felt for you before as I do now, and you going wrong too. But I'll never believe that you're bad through and through. If you'd see Father Eusebius, he'd make you as good as new.'

He pressed her hand warmly, and rushed off. He had barely time to get his ticket. Through the ticket-office window he saw Father Molloy sitting, dangling his short legs, on a high stool. He asked for a single ticket to Dublin.

'Isn't it a return you want, Father?' the clerk said, looking at him curiously.

'A single ticket, please,' he said shortly.

Father Molloy laughed.

Ralph had a momentary feeling of resentment which passed away before he reached the platform. He met Darcy at the door, and said 'Good morning,' cheerfully. Darcy half raised his hand to his hat, dropped it, and turned away deliberately, without speaking. Ralph gazed after him in astonishment. Boyle's warning recurred to him, and he smiled faintly. A small group of men standing between him and the door of his carriage, a few of whom he knew intimately, turned their backs and sidled away as he approached. 'Didn't you hear that he's turned a Protestant?' he heard some one say behind his back. This, then, was the beginning of the boycott, the innuendo, and calumny, of which Boyle had warned him, he thought, as he took his seat. As the train was about to start old Byrne put his head, breathlessly, into Ralph's compartment.

'Oh. Here you are. I was afeard I'd miss you. I only heard a few minutes ago.' The whistle sounded and the train began to move. He grasped Ralph's hand. There was a hiss from the group standing near. Byrne turned round and faced Father Molloy, who had appeared at the booking-office door. 'It's a blasted shame,' he said angrily, 'and I don't care who hears me. And you're only a lot of damned cowards,' he added, turning to the group that had hissed.

Ralph was alone in the compartment. He sat still for awhile, his eyes fixed on the bay, along which the train skirted, and the mountains rising sheer on the far side. The throbbing of the engine seemed to prolong the hiss. He stood up and stretched his limbs. If that scene on the platform represented his country, and with a pang he felt that it did, he was without a country. The speed of the train increased, and the mountains, clear in the autumn sunlight, seemed to fly past. Cut off by his family, by his Church, by his country — the voice of the train dinned in his ears in a rapid ceaseless refrain. The sounds mocked him. The mountain, in the pale watery sunlight, seemed to wear a sneer. He sat down again, hunched in a corner, oppressed by a sense of overwhelming defeat and failure. Gone, gone, gone, family, Church, country, gone, gone, gone . . . seemed to pierce his brain and sear it. . . .

He got through his business in Dublin in a sort of dream. In the eyes of tailors and outfitters he read a mute accusation. . . .

One morning, as he was buttoning his Roman collar, his eyes fell on unopened cardboard boxes piled on a chair at the end of his room. He unpacked the boxes, and laid a lounge suit with a tie and collar on the bed.

He took off his clerical collar and proceeded to dress in the secular clothes. He made several efforts to knot his tie. It was years since he had worn one, and he had forgotten how to knot it. Every new effort resulted in a more hopeless failure. He shut his eyes at length, and trusted to the memory of his fingers with complete success.

In some obscure way the incident helped him. His languor passed away. He finished dressing with a new sense of power. For the first time he noticed the view from his bedroom window, the pond in Stephen's Green, the Dublin mountains looming blue and mysterious beyond the intervening houses and smoke. He looked again at the pond, a small boy was throwing bread to the ducks, and the memory of his own childhood came back to him. He felt young again, and had a momentary impulse to join the little boy and feed the ducks, too. He laughed joyously.

He took up his clerical collar and looked at it curiously. He smiled as he thought of how he had dreaded laying it aside. And now, there was only a sense of escape from bondage, of freedom. . . .

He stood on the deck of the Holyhead mail boat, his eyes fixed on the receding Irish coast. The sands at Merrion, Howth Head, Bray Head, the Wicklow mountains, recalled youthful dreams. In the blind groping way which is the way of life, he felt that he had been true to them. Life was larger than his vision of it, and where he had read failure life marked advance.

He walked the deck with a springy step, breathing

an east wind, that made his face smart, with a sense of victory.

'I have found myself at last,' he said under his breath. His blood surged through his veins, and he went back to the stern. The sun, falling slant-wise on the foam in the wake of the boat, made a track of molten silver. On the horizon land had faded to a blue outline. He gazed at it longingly until the last faint grey disappeared, and the sea everywhere met the sky.

He turned round and braced himself again to the east wind. Only one dream had faded into the sea, he thought. . . .

And then?

FORREST REID

(1875–1947)

from: PETER WARING (1937)

[In *Peter Waring*, a radical revision of *Following Darkness* (1912), Forrest Reid produces a *bildungsroman* of protestant experience centred on Belfast, similar in many respects to Joyce's account of catholic adolescence in Dublin. Peter is unhappy with his cold schoolmaster father in rural Newcastle, Co. Down, happy only when by himself with his dog, Remus, in the countryside or visiting with the motherly Mrs Carroll in her big house, Derryaghy, a privilege rarely granted him by his lonely parent. Peter is even less comfortable during school term in Belfast where he stays with his relations, the McAllisters. He is especially repelled by his coarse-grained cousin George, with whom he must share a bedroom, and who insists on showing him his hoard of pornographic photographs. The extracts that follow trace the hero's feelings of sexual guilt, religious confusion and spiritual alienation over a crucial Christmas vacation as he contemplates the prospect of going back to the city.]

CHAPTER 31

The thought of that return lay like a perpetual shadow at the back of my mind, yet it was several days before I could screw up my courage to the point of mentioning it to my father. Then one morning after breakfast I did so.

'There is something I want to say to you,' I began nervously, and, though he had been about to rise from the table, he instantly adopted an attitude of attention so excessively attentive that it had the effect of striking me dumb. I forgot the careful phrases I had prepared while dressing, and could only stammer out awkwardly that I wished to leave the McAllisters and choose a lodging for myself.

The revival of the question, I saw, was not pleasing to him, and I hadn't expected it to be. 'You're very self-willed,' he said slowly and drily, and I knew that I hadn't moved him in the least.

Nevertheless I made a second attempt. 'It's not because I'm self-willed,' I said. 'It's because I don't like sleeping with George.'

It was as much as I *could* say, but he dismissed it quietly. 'Why? You have your own bed, haven't you?'

'Yes.'

'And George is your cousin.'

'I know he is my cousin. What difference does that make?' But I saw that it was hopeless.

'It's just this sort of nonsense,' my father exclaimed impatiently, 'that makes me doubt the wisdom of allowing you to go to Derryaghy. It gives you a taste for luxuries, so that you turn up your nose at people who have to live in a simpler way.'

'It isn't a question of luxuries,' I muttered under my breath, and the words had a kind of dreary irony.

But he was determined to see in my persistence only a caprice, or an obstinate struggle to get my own way. True, he offered a sort of conventional excuse. 'I didn't know when I arranged for you to live with Aunt Margaret that they wouldn't be able to give you a room for yourself. On the other hand, I don't consider that a sufficient reason for taking you away now you *are* there. It would amount almost to an insult. But I told you this when I wrote to you, and I can see no purpose in going over it again.'

None indeed, so I said no more.

It was Christmas Eve. During the night there had been a heavy fall of snow, and on the hard frozen ground it lay unmelted to the edge of the sea. All morning I sat beside the fire reading, but after dinner, about three o'clock, I took Remus for a walk over the golf-links. The snow was several inches deep, but crisp and dry on the surface. I had not slept well — what sleep I got being broken by bad dreams — and I determined now to go for a really long walk, so as to be sure to sleep tonight. In spite of the prospect of staying at Derryaghy, in spite of this frosty exhilarating weather, in spite of the fact that I would be getting a Christmas-box from Mrs. Carroll tomorrow, and probably letters from Katherine and Owen,[1] my thoughts were gloomy and depressed. Never before had I looked so closely into myself, and never had I found so little there to comfort me. I felt too dejected even to be angry with my father. I knew that for months past my mind had been submitted to an influence which had acted on my imagination and senses like an unwholesome stimulant. Yet certain seeds, I supposed, could only have taken root within me, could only have sprung up so quickly, because they had found a soil apt to receive them; and I remembered my father's habitual attitude of mistrust. Had he then, all along, been justified? I thought of the book I had been reading that morning — a book written for boys and all about boys — and I compared the characters in it with myself — compared the darkness that weighed upon me now with the troubles they had experienced. It seemed to me that I must be different from every boy in that book — from the bad just as much as from the good. I had feelings which apparently none of them felt. I wondered if I were really different, or if the book were untrue? — but how could I ever find out unless I confided in someone, and unless I were truthfully answered? At present I was hopelessly shut in to the little circle of my own desires and feelings. Owen, whom I knew better than any other boy — what, after all, did I know about him except what he cared to tell me? I knew no one but myself, and of myself I knew much that filled me with shame.

My self-examination had brought me to a standstill. A deep silence overhung the earth. Behind me were the white frozen mountains; on either side was an endless stretch of snow; and before me was the dark and sullen sea. The day was closing in, and already more light rose from the ground than fell from the sky overhead. Snow had begun again to fall — a few flakes, drifting and fluttering down out of the grey clouds. But I knew this was only the beginning, and that there would be more soon. I walked to the edge of the sea, and watched the cold desolate waves rolling in to break at my feet. At that moment I felt infinitely alone.

Alone spiritually, and alone as one might be in a dead or dying world. The whirling flakes of snow fell ever faster out of the winter sky; the barren, frost-bound land was wrapped in stillness; the only sound I heard came from the breaking waves. And it seemed to me that the darkness gradually approaching was like the final extinction of life, and I could imagine that there would be no further awakening — that the end had at last been reached.

It was Remus who aroused me from this dreaming. I had forgotten him, and he begun now to urge me to come on, with a peculiar note in his voice, as if he were less impatient than distressed and anxious. He jumped up against me, and I knelt down in the snow, hugging him, while his warm red tongue passed rapidly over my face. I held him closely, and his black muzzle was pressed into my cheek.

CHAPTER 33

If I had been reluctant in the beginning to go to the McAllisters, my return was more reluctant still, nevertheless the day arrived when I bid good-bye to my father and went back. I found no change in them, though they may have noticed a change in me, for I kept as much to myself as I could, and when with them took less trouble to try to be sociable. I was in a strangely unsettled condition — restless and inclined to take the darkest view of things. The short damp winter days — mild enough, but with never a gleam of sunshine in them — did not help me. The continual greyness, the wet muddy roads, the murky atmosphere and frequent rain — these seemed to have a far more depressing effect in town than in the country; or it may have been that I was more

1. Katherine is Peter's sweetheart, whose offhand response to his Christmas gift takes up most of Chapter 32. Owen is a serious and sensitive schoolfriend in Belfast.

susceptible just now to their influence.

For I was in a brooding discontented state of mind, and except for an occasional walk with Owen there was nothing to rouse me out of it. I wanted to get rid of a burden that was oppressing me; I longed for sympathy and understanding; I longed for guidance, even if I could not follow it. I was bewildered, divided in my mind; my mind itself was a ferment of doubts, desires, resolutions, struggles and despairs. I cannot have been either to Owen or to anybody else a very cheerful companion.

There was the worldly problem; for notwithstanding a high opinion of my own intelligence, there were periods when I saw my life as doomed to failure and myself to disaster. There was the more urgent moral problem — the problem of sin and damnation — over which I pondered, seeing in damnation a condition of mind that attracts evil, and from which no evil can be hidden. When I was with Owen all this grew fainter and even disappeared. He may have had, in fact I knew he had, his own problems, but they were not the same as mine, and to me he seemed completely free from everything that made my life just now so difficult. That is why I could not talk to him about it, and why he must have found me unusually silent and dull: yet I had an increasing and at last intense desire to confide in somebody.

Only it must be someone who would understand. In spite of my revolt against Christianity my thoughts at times turned in that direction. Not because I felt any stirrings of religious emotion: it was not the lack of faith which troubled me: it was simply that an idea of confession hovered before me as a necessary preliminary to any counsel that could be of much use. And after all, was not the Church there for that purpose? But the Church, in this sense, meant an individual — somebody I could trust. And having got thus far, my next step seemed plain.

CHAPTER 34

Yet the matter was not so simple as I at first imagined. One excellent result it did have, and that was to make Sunday, hitherto the flattest day of the week, now the most absorbing, while I went from church to church seeking a possible confessor. In nearly every case I could tell at once that I had not found him, and I was on the point of giving up the idea as impracticable, when one Sunday evening chance took me to Saint Mary Magdalene's. The clergyman who conducted the service was a man well past middle-age. He looked frail and ascetic, with an expression on his worn face as if he had come through a good deal before he had emerged from the struggle victorious. At least, that was how he impressed me, though the struggle may have been merely against ill health. He preached a sermon which, while slightly vague, appealed to my imagination. Even the weakness of his voice, and the unusual quietness of his manner, had upon me the strange effect of making what he said more real. His very dispassionateness suggested a quality of spiritual vision. He struck me as a man who had been unhappy, and therefore, if he had found peace, I thought he must, too, have found the secret of living. I returned to hear him several times, and although my first impression was not strengthened, neither was it effaced. Finally I persuaded Owen to come with me, but Owen could see nothing in him at all.

Far from shaking me in my view, this unfavourable opinion helped to confirm it. Not through perversity, but merely because I felt that the person I was in search of would not be likely to appeal to Owen. I did not want a primarily intellectual person; I wanted one who out of his own, perhaps unorthodox experience, would understand. That night I wrote a letter to the Rev. Henry Applin, asking if I might come to see him, and, if I might, would he tell me when.

[In Chapter 35 Peter rehearses his doubts and hesitations with Owen, who is unsympathetic to any form of 'confession'.]

CHAPTER 36

Since the new year I had been working harder than I had ever done in my life before. The Intermediate examinations would be taking place in June, but this was not my reason: it was merely that I had discovered that on the plea of work I could shut myself up alone in the evenings, and that the work itself kept me from brooding over other things.

I was brooding over them, nevertheless, on the following Wednesday, when I got home from school; and after I had had my dinner, I went out to brood over them again. In four and a half hours, I reflected, I should be knocking at Mr. Applin's door. What would be the result? How did one begin a conversation of that sort? Perhaps it happened oftener than I imagined.

At this juncture, by what I took to be an almost miraculous coincidence, I found myself approaching the open door of a Roman Catholic Church. There, I told myself, if all else failed me, was my way out. Or so it appeared for perhaps five seconds. Then I saw that it would not do. I was completely ignorant, of course, yet it *seemed* highly improbable that a person of an alien sect would be allowed to walk in, make his confession, and walk out again. Things were never so simple as all that, and even for the orthodox there probably would be preliminaries — some kind of preparation.

In spite of this, I could not resist the impulse to go inside and sit down near one of the confessionals. The name of the priest, Father Dempsey, was printed in large letters above it; but I supposed he would only come there by appointment; it was hardly likely that he lurked *perpetually* within that shrouded cabinet. On the other hand, he might have certain fixed hours when he was at home to his penitents, as a doctor is at home to his patients — say from four till six every afternoon. With this the question arose — Was I a penitent? — and there could be little doubt as to the answer — that I much more closely resembled a patient. In fact I didn't quite know what I was. But I continued to sit on, in the faint hope of seeing somebody coming out or going in. I thought that merely by looking at such a person I might learn something — get some kind of assurance or encouragement.

This hope was not fulfilled. Three little girls, busy with their beads, temporarily suspended their devotions in order to glance at me and whisper. The only other person in the church was a middle-aged woman, who was kneeling before an altar, above which hung a large bright oleograph of the Madonna and Child. This woman's lips never ceased to move, and her eyes were fixed on the picture, which was modern and ugly — though surely, I thought, the subject had been painted often and beautifully enough by the old masters. Then I saw a fat sallow little priest — his chin, upper lip and cheeks blue from much shaving — come waddling down the aisle, and I wondered if he were Father Dempsey.

The curiosity that had drawn me into the church was rapidly ebbing. Everything — the smell of stale incense, the lighted candles, the cheap gaudy decorations — now struck me as vulgar and repellent. It all somehow seemed wrong — gross rather than spiritual — and my idea of confessing to a priest seemed wrong too. I rose and went out, the last thing I noticed being a thick sediment of dirt at the bottom of the stoup of holy water.

After tea I went up to my bedroom — George's and mine — and got out my books. On my way home I had felt half inclined not to go to Mr. Applin, but as the time passed I grew more and more restless. Work, at all events, was out of the question. I wished I had not gone into that church. It was this, I knew, that had discouraged me; and yet what valid connection had it with the step I proposed to take? True, I had not liked it, but what I had disliked was essentially superficial — the tawdriness and bad taste — and to allow oneself to be influenced by such things would be as stupid as to refuse to read a book because its binding happened to be unattractive.

I looked at my watch. It was already after eight, and I decided that I would take a stroll in the park, and then, if I felt more in the mood, go on to Mr. Applin's.

I remained in the park till closing time: then I went for a walk. It was now getting late, but I was not very far from the house, and turned in that direction.

I rang the bell and asked if Mr. Applin was home. Yes, the servant told me: who should she say wished to see him?

I gave her my name, and remained standing in the porch for a longish time before she returned. Would I step this way. Just straight on up. And I obeyed her, feeling, now that the decisive moment was reached, less nervous than I had felt all evening.

At the top of a flight of stairs she opened a door, and I entered a large, untidy, lamp-lit study. There were bookshelves against the walls, yet the floor and most of the chairs were littered with books and papers. At the same moment a tall, thin, stooping figure rose from a table near the window, removing, as he did so, a green shade from his forehead. I was conscious of tired eyes that looked at me out of a pale emaciated face, and I was conscious, too, that either my imagination had deceived me, or that Mr. Applin became another person when he was preaching.

My impression of him now, at all events, was quite different from my earlier impression. His manner of greeting me was not exactly distant, not exactly chilly, yet it produced a discouraging effect — the effect, simply, that he was tired, and that he had no idea either who I was or what I wanted. I sat down in the chair towards which he motioned me, and wished that I had stayed at home.

'You are Peter Waring?' he said. My letter, in fact, was lying on the table he had just quitted.

'Yes,' I answered, and the conversation lapsed.

He had taken a chair opposite mine, and he leaned a little forward, the tips of his fingers joined, and swollen blue veins showing under the loose, wrinkled skin of his hands. He was much older than I had supposed — ten years at least — for I had taken him to be about sixty. He was wearing a shabby grey jacket, and I noticed that one of the buttons near the top was of a different colour from the others. My desire to confide in him had completely vanished. I glanced round the unfamiliar room and maintained an awkward silence. It struck me that most likely he thought I had come either for a subscription to a cricket club or for a testimonial — something of that kind anyhow.

'I got your letter,' he murmured. 'You wish to speak to me? You are not a member of my congregation, I think?'

'No. I come sometimes in the evenings.'

I was thankful now that in my letter I had said nothing of my real purpose, and he evidently hadn't the least suspicion of it. On the other hand, I was left with apparently no purpose at all, and this renewed my embarrassment.

'Yes, yes — I understand,' he went on, though what he understood was not precisely clear. 'Well, don't be afraid. If I can do anything for you I shall be very glad.'

I thanked him, and again became tongue-tied. It would have been absolutely impossible for me to have said what I had come to say, and nothing else occurred to me. He was too old, too far away; it would have been like stretching out your hands to try to warm them at the grey ashes in an early morning grate. I could see that he was making an effort to be kind — or at least to be attentive and courteous — only I felt that if I stated my business and said good-bye, it would be what he would like best.

'I think I had better write,' I brought out at last.

It was idiotic, and indeed appeared to surprise him. 'Write?' he echoed, raising his eyebrows. 'But why? You *have* written! What is it all about?' The last words were spoken somewhat querulously — even with a hint of senile impatience.

And at that moment there came a tap at the door, and a faded, elderly lady, possibly his daughter, entered, carrying a small tray, on which were two biscuits and a tumbler of hot milk. She bowed to me and wished me good evening.

I wished *her* good evening: I wanted nothing now but to get away as quickly as possible. Suppose I had been in the middle of my confession when the tray had been brought in! The whole thing was becoming dismally comic.

'Are you in business or at school?' Mr. Applin asked me, between two sips of milk. 'You will excuse my drinking this while it is hot; but I had a funeral this afternoon and I'm afraid I may have caught a chill.'

'Certainly,' I answered hurriedly. 'I hope you haven't. I mean, I hope you haven't caught a chill. I'm sorry for disturbing you. I've really nothing to say. It's only that I liked your sermons very much and wanted to tell you so. Please forgive me.' I got up.

'Sit down — sit down,' he exclaimed, suddenly smiling. 'It was a kind thought. . . . Most kind.' And he really did look pleased, and much more animated.

So I sat down again and he continued to drink his milk — with small, soundless, delicate sips. But the ice was now broken, his doubts — if he had had any — were removed, and he asked me to what church I belonged, where I went to school, and other similar questions. In the end we became almost chatty. A black and white cat, who had come in hopefully with the milk and biscuits, was now purring around my legs, and I stroked the cat and told Mr. Applin about Remus. Before I left he made me promise to come again.

Yet just as I was going out a sort of vague suspicion of other things did appear to float into his consciousness. He detained me, with his hand on my shoulder, looking as if he dimly felt that he had perhaps failed somewhere. 'When you first came in,' he said, 'I got an impression that something might be worrying you, that you had something on your mind.' He paused, and for an instant I saw in him just a glimmer of what I had seen when I had first thought of this visit — for an instant I was on the point of resuming my seat and telling him what I had come to tell him. But I felt that he did not really want me to, that he would be happier if I didn't; and next moment indeed, with a little sigh of relief, he made it impossible by wishing me good night. 'And when you come again you won't be so shy?' he added, smiling wanly.

He did not accompany me downstairs but stood on the landing till I had opened the hall-door. And as I pulled it after me, and walked on down the garden path, I knew I should never go back, and that I would appeal to nobody else.

SEUMAS O'KELLY

(*c.*1875–1918)

from: WAYSIDERS (1917)

[The land is perhaps the predominant theme in the novels and short stories of Seumas O'Kelly. 'The Building', from his 1917 volume *Waysiders*, dramatises the struggle between the artistic impulse and the pull of the soil in the life of an ambitious young peasant.]

THE BUILDING

Martin Cosgrave walked up steadily to his holding after Ellen Miscal had read to him the American letter. He had spoken no word to the woman. It was not every day that he had to battle with a whirl of thoughts. A quiet man of the fields, he only felt conscious of a strong impulse to get back to his holding up on the hill. He had no clear idea of what he would do or what he would think when he got back to his holding. But the fields seemed to cry out to him, to call him back to their companionship, while all the wonders of the resurrection were breaking in fresh upon his life.

Martin Cosgrave walked his fields and put his flock of sheep scurrying out of a gap with a whistle. His holding and the things of his holding were never so precious to his sight. He walked his fields with his hands in his pockets and an easy, solid step upon the sod. He felt a bracing sense of security.

Then he sat up on the mearing.[1]

The day was waning. It seemed to close in about his holding with a new protection. The mood grew upon him as the shadows deepened. A great peace came over him. The breeze stirring the grass spread out at his feet seemed to whisper of the strange unexpected thing that had broken in upon his life. He felt the splendid companionship of the fields for the master.

Suddenly Martin Cosgrave looked down at his cabin. Something snapped as his eyes remained riveted upon it. He leapt from the mearing and walked out into the field, his hands this time gripping the lapels of his coat, a cloud settling upon his brow. In the centre of the field he stood, his eyes still upon the cabin. What a mean, pokey, ugly little dirty hovel it was! The thatch was getting scraggy over the gables and sagging at the back. In the front it was sodden. A rainy brown streak reached down to the little window looking like the claw of a great bird upon the walls. He had been letting everything go to the bad. That might not signify in the past. But now. . . .

'Rose Dempsey would never stand the like,' he said to himself. 'She will be used to grand big houses.'

He turned his back upon the cabin near the boreen[2] and looked up to the belt of beech trees swaying in the wind on the crest of the hill. How did he live there most of his life and never see that it was a place fashioned by the hand of nature for a house? Was it not the height of nonsense to have trees there making music all the long hours of the night without a house beside them and people sleeping within it? In a few minutes the thought had taken hold of his mind. Limestone — beautiful limestone — ready at hand in the quarry not a quarter of a mile down the

1. Hiberno-English for 'boundary fence.'

2. Irish *boithrín* (little road).

road. Sand from the pit at the back of his own cabin. Lime from the kiln beyond the road. And his own two hands! He ran his fingers along the muscles of his arms. Then he walked up the hill.

Martin Cosgrave, as he walked up the hill, felt himself wondering for the first time in his life if he had really been foolish to have run away from his father's cabin when he had been young. Up to this he had always accepted the verdict of the people about him that he had been a foolish boy 'to go wandering in strange places.' He had walked along the roads to many far towns. Then he had struck his friend, the building contractor. He had been a useful worker about a building house. At first he had carried hods of mortar and cement up ladders to the masons. The business of the masons he had mastered quickly. But he had always had a longing to hold a chisel in one hand and a mallet in the other at work upon stone. He had drifted into a quarry, thence to a stone-cutting yard. After a little while he could not conceal his impatience with the mere dressing of coping stones or the chiselling out of tombstones to a pattern. Then he saw the man killed in the quarry. He was standing quite near to him. The chain of the windlass went and the poor man had no escape. Martin Cosgrave had heard the crunch of the skull on the boulder, and some of the blood was spattered upon his boots. He was a man of tense nerves. The sight of blood sickened him. He put on his coat, left the quarry, and went walking along the road.

It was while he walked along the road that the longing for his home came upon him. He tramped back to his home above Kilbeg. His father had been long dead, but by his return he had glorified the closing days of his mother's life. He took up the little farm and cut himself off from his wandering life when he had fetched the tools from his lodgings in the town beside the quarries.

By the time Martin Cosgrave had reached the top of the hill he had concluded that he had not, after all, been a foolish boy to work in far places. 'The hand of God was in it,' he said reverently with his eyes on the beech trees that made music on the crest of the hill.

He made a rapid survey of the place with his keen eyes. Then he mapped out the foundation of the building by driving the heel of his boot into the green sod. He stepped back among the beech trees and looked out at the outlined site of the building. He saw it all growing up in his mind's eye, at first a rough block, a mere shell, a little uncertain and unsatisfactory. Then the uncertainties were lopped off, the building took shape, touch after touch was added. Long shadows spread out from the trees and wrapped the fields. Stars came out in the sky. But Martin Cosgrave never noticed these things. The building was growing all the time. There was a firm grasp of the general scheme, a realization of what the building would evolve that no other building ever evolved, what it would proclaim for all time. The passing of the day and the stealth of the night could not claim attention from a man who was living over a dream that was fashioning itself in his mind, abandoning himself to the joy of his creation, dwelling longingly upon the details of the building, going over and, as it were, feeling it in every fibre, jealous of the effect of every stone, tracing the trend and subtlety of every curve, seeing how one touch fitted in and enhanced the other and how all carried on the meaning of the whole.

When he came down from the hill there was a spring in Martin Cosgrave's step. He swung his arms. The blood was coursing fast through his veins. His eyes were glowing. He would need to make a map of the building. It was all burned clearly into his brain.

From under the bed of his cabin he pulled out the wooden box. It had not been opened since he had fetched it from the far town. He held his breath as he threw open the lid. There they lay, the half-forgotten symbols of his old life. Worn mallets, chisels, the head of a broken hod with the plaster still caked into it, a short broad shovel for mixing mortar, a trowel, a spirit level, a plumb, all wrapped loosely in a worn leather apron. He took the mallets in his hand and turned them about with the quick little jerks that came so naturally to him. Strength for the work had come into his arms. All the old ambitions which he thought had been stifled with his early manhood sprang to life again.

As he lay in his bed that night Martin Cosgrave felt himself turning over and over again the words in the letter which Rose Dempsey had sent to her aunt, Ellen Miscal, from America. 'Tell Martin Cosgrave,' the letter read, 'that I will be back home in Kilbeg by the end of the spring. If he has no wish for any other girl I am willing to settle down.' Beyond the announcement that her sister Sheela would be with her for a holiday, the letter 'brought no other account.' But what an account it had brought to

Martin Cosgrave! The fields understood — the building would proclaim.

Early in the morning Martin Cosgrave went down to Ellen Miscal to tell her what to put in the letter that was going back to Rose Dempsey in America. Martin Cosgrave walked heavily into the house and stood with his back against the dresser. He turned the soft black hat about in his hands nervously and talked like one who was speaking sacred words.

'Tell her,' he said, 'that Martin Cosgrave had no thought for any other person beyond herself. Tell her to be coming back to Kilbeg. Tell her not to come until the late harvest.'

Ellen Miscal, who sat over the sheet of writing paper on the table, looked up quickly as he spoke the words. As she did so she was conscious of the new animation that vivified the idealistic face of Martin Cosgrave. But he did not give her time to question him.

'I have my own reasons for asking her to wait until the harvest,' he said, with some irritation.

He stayed at the dresser until Ellen Miscal had written the letter. He carried it down to the village and posted it with his own hand, and he went and came as gravely as if he had been taking part in some solemn ritual.

II

That day the building was begun. Martin Cosgrave tackled the donkey and drew a few loads of limestone from the nearby quarry. Some of the neighbours who came his way found him a changed man, a silent man with his eager face set, a man in whose eyes a new light shone, a quiet man of the fields into whose mind a set purpose had come. He struggled up the road with his donkey-cart, his hand gripping the shaft to hasten the steps of the slow brute, his limbs bent to the hill, his head down at the work. By the end of the week a pile of grey-blue stones was heaped up on the crest of the hill. The walls of the fields had been broken down to make a carway. Late into the night when the donkey had been fed and tethered the neighbours would see Martin Cosgrave moving about the pile of grey-blue stones, sorting and picking, arranging in little groups to have ready to his hands. 'A house he is going to put up on the hill,' they would say, lost in wonder.

The spring came, and with it all the strenuous work on the land. But Martin Cosgrave went on with the building. The neighbours shook their heads at the sight of neglect that was gathering about his holding; they said it was flying in the face of Providence when Martin Cosgrave weaned all the lambs from the ewes one day, long before their time, and sold them at the fair to the first bidder that came his way. Martin Cosgrave did so because he wanted money and was in a hurry to get back to his building.

'What call has a man to be destroying himself like that?' the neighbours asked each other.

Martin Cosgrave knew what the neighbours were saying about him. But what did he care? What thought had any of them for the heart of a builder? What did any of them know beyond putting a spade in the clay and waiting for the seasons to send up growing things from the seed they scattered by their hands? What did they know about the feel of the rough stone in the hand and the shaping of it to fit into the building, the building that day after day you saw rising up from the ground by the skill of your hand and the art of your mind? What could they in Kilbeg know of the ship that would plough the ocean in the harvest bearing Rose Dempsey home to him? For all their ploughing and their sowing, what sort of a place had any of them led a woman into? They might talk away. The joy of the builder was his. The beech trees that made music all day beside the building he was putting up to the sight of all the world had more understanding of him than all the people of the parish.

Martin Cosgrave had no help. He kept his work from such an early hour in the morning until such a late hour of the night that the people marvelled at his endurance. But as the work went on the people would talk about Martin Cosgrave's building in the fields and tell strangers of it at the markets. They said that the like of it had never been seen in the countryside. It was to be 'full of little turrets and the finest of fancy porches and a regular sight of bulging windows.' One day that Martin Cosgrave heard a neighbour speaking about the 'bulging windows' he laughed a half-bitter, half-mocking laugh.

'Tell them,' he said, 'that they are cut-stone tracery windows to fit in with the carved doors.' These cut-stone windows and carved doors cost Martin Cosgrave such a length of time that they provoked the patience of the people. Out of big slabs of stone he had worked them, and sometimes he would ask the neighbours to give him a hand in the shifting of these slabs. But he was quick to resent any interference. One day a stone-cutter from the quarry went up on the scaffold, and when Martin Cosgrave saw him he went white to the lips and cursed so bitterly that those standing about walked away.

When the shell of the building had been finished Martin Cosgrave hired a carpenter to do all the woodwork. The woodwork cost money. Martin Cosgrave did not hesitate. He sold some of his sheep, sold them hurriedly, and as all men who sell their sheep hurriedly, he sold them badly. When the carpentry had been finished, the roofing cost more money. One day the neighbours discovered that all the sheep had been sold. 'He's beggared now,' they said.

The farmer who turned the sod a few fields away laboured in the damp atmosphere of growing things, his mind filled with thoughts of bursting seeds and teeming barns. He shook his head at sight of Martin Cosgrave above on the hill bent all day over hard stones; whenever he looked up he only caught the glint of a trowel, or heard the harsh grind of a chisel. But Martin Cosgrave took no stock of the men reddening the soil beneath him. Whenever his eyes travelled down the hill-side he only saw the flock of crows that hung over the head of the digger. The study of the veins of limestone that he turned in his hands, the slow moulding of the crude shapes to their place in the building, the rhythm and swing of the mallet in his arm, the zest with which he felt the impact of the chisel on the stone, the ring of forging steel, the consciousness of mastery over the work that lay to his hands — these were the things that seemed to him to give life a purpose and man a destiny. He would whistle a tune as he mixed the mortar with the broad shovel, for it gave him a feeling of the knitting of the building with the ages. He pitied the farmer who looked helplessly upon his corn as it was beaten to the ground by the first storm that blew from the sea; he was upon a work that would withstand the storms of centuries. The scent of lime and mortar greeted his nostrils. When he moved about the splinters crunched under his feet. Everything around him was hard and stubborn, but he was the master of it all. In his dreams in the night he would reach out his hands for the feel of the hard stone, a burning desire in his breast to put it into shape, to give it nobility in the scheme of a building.

It was while Martin Cosgrave walked through the building that Ellen Miscal came to him with the second letter from America. The carpenter was hammering at something below. The letter said that Rose Dempsey and her sister, Sheela, would be home in the late harvest. 'With all I saw since I left Kilbeg,' Rose Dempsey wrote, 'I never saw one that I thought as much of as Martin Cosgrave.'

When Ellen Miscal left him, Martin Cosgrave stood very quietly looking through the cut-stone tracery window. The beech trees were swaying slowly outside. Their music was in his ears.

Then he remembered that he was standing in the room where he would take Rose Dempsey in his arms. It was here he would tell her of all the bitter things he had locked up in his heart when she had gone away from him. It was here he would tell her of the day of resurrection, when all the bitter thoughts had burst into flower at the few words that told of her return. It was that day of great tumult within him that thought of the building had come into his mind.

When Martin Cosgrave walked out of the room the carpenter and a neighbour boy were arguing about something at the foot of the stairs.

'It's too steep, I'm telling you,' the boy was saying.

'What do you know about it?'

'I know this much about it, that if a little child came running down the stairs he'd be apt to fall and break his neck.'

Then the two men went out, still arguing.

Martin Cosgrave sat down on one of the steps of the stairs. A child running down the steps! His child! A child bearing his name! He would be prattling about the building. He would run across that landing, swaying and tottering. His little voice would fill the building. Arms would be reaching out to him. They would be the soft white arms of Rose Dempsey, or maybe, they would be the arms that raised up the building — his own strong arms. Or it might be that he would be carrying down the child and handing him over the rails there into the outspread arms of Rose Dempsey. She would be reaching out for the child with the newly-kindled light of motherhood in her eyes, the passion of a young mother in her welcoming voice. A child with his very name — a child that would grow up to be a man and hand down the name to another, and so on during the generations. And with the name would go down the building, the building that would endure, that would live, that was immortal. Did it all come to him as a sudden revelation, springing from the idle talk of a neighbour boy brought up to work from one season to another? Or was it the same thing that was behind the forces that had fired him while he had worked at the building? Had it not all come into his life the evening he stood among his fields with his eyes on the crest of the hill?

Ah, there had been a great building surely, a building standing up on the hill, a great, a splendid building raised up to the sight of all the world, and with a greater building, a building raised up from the sight of all men, the building of a name, the moulding of hearts that would beat while time was, a building of immortal souls, a building into which God would breath His breath, a building which would be heard of in heaven, among the angels, through all the eternities, a building living on when all the light was gone out of the sun, when oceans were as if they had never been, a name, a building, living when the story of all the worlds and all the generations would be held written upon a scroll in the lap of God. . . . The face of the dreamer as he abandoned himself to this thoughts was pallid with a half-fanatical emotion.

The neighbours were more awed than shocked at the change they saw increasing in Martin Cosgrave. He had grown paler and thinner, but his eyes were more tense, had in them, some of the neighbours said, the colour of the limestone. He was more and more removed from the old life. He walked his fields without seeing the things that made up the old companionship. His whole attitude was one of detachment from everything that did not savour of the crunch of stone, the ring of steel on the walls of a building. He only talked rationally when the neighbours spoke to him of the building. They had heard that he had gone to the money-lender, and mortgaged every perch of his land. 'It was easy to know how work of the like would end,' they said.

One day a stranger was driving by on his car, and when he saw the building he got down, walked up the hill, and made a long study of it. On his way down he met Martin Cosgrave.

'Who built the house on the hill?' he asked.

'A simple man in the neighbourhood,' Martin Cosgrave made answer, after a little pause.

'A simple man!' the stranger exclaimed, looking at Martin Cosgrave with some disapproval. 'Well, he has attempted something anyway. He may not have succeeded, but the artist is in him somewhere. He has created a sort of — well, lyric — in stone on that hill. Extraordinary!'

The stranger hesitated before he hit on the word lyric. He got up on his car and drove away muttering something under his breath.

Martin Cosgrave could have run up the hill and shouted. He could have called all the neighbours together and told them of the strange man who had praised the building.

But he did none of these things. He had work waiting to his hand. A hunger was upon him to feel his pulse beating to the throb of steel on stone. From the road he made a sweep of a drive up to the building. The neighbours looked open-mouthed at the work for the days it went on. 'Well, that finishes Martin Cosgrave anyway,' they said.

Martin Cosgrave rushed the making of the drive; he took all the help he could get. The boys would come up after their day's work and give him a hand. While they worked he was busy with his chisel upon the boulders of limestone which he had set up on either side of the entrance gate. Once more he felt the glamour of life — the impact of forging steel on stone was thrilling through his arms, the stone was being moulded to the direction of his exulting mind.

When he had finished with the boulders at the entrance gate the people marvelled. The gate had a glory of its own, and yet it was connected with the scheme of the building on the hill palpably enough for even their minds to grasp it. When the people looked upon it they forgot to make complaint of the good land that was given to ruin. One of them had expressed the general vague sentiment when he said, 'Well, the kite[3] has got its tail.'

In the late harvest Martin Cosgrave carried up all the little sticks of furniture from his cabin and put it in the building. Then he sent for Ellen Miscal. When the woman came she looked about the place in amazement.

'Well, of all the sights in the world!' she exclaimed.

Martin Cosgrave was irritated at the woman's attitude.

'We'll have to make the best of it,' he said, looking at the furniture. 'I will be marrying Rose Dempsey in the town some days after she lands.'

'Rose would never like the suddenness of that,' her aunt protested. 'She can be staying with me and marrying from my house.'

3. A bird of prey with a long forked tail.

'I saw the priest about it,' Martin Cosgrave said impatiently. 'I will have my way, Ellen Miscal. Rose Dempsey will come up to Kilbeg my wife. We will come in the gate together, we will walk in to the building together. I will have my way.'

Martin Cosgrave spoke of having his way in the impassioned voice of the fanatic, of his home-coming with his bride in the half-dreamy voice of the visionary.

'Have your way, Martin, have your way,' the woman said. 'And,' she added, rising, 'I will be bringing up a few things to put into your house.'

III

Martin Cosgrave spent three days in the town awaiting the arrival of Rose Dempsey. The boat was late. He haunted the railway station, with hungry eyes scanned the passengers as each train steamed in. His blood was on fire in his veins for those three days. What peace could a man have who was waiting to get back to his building and to have Rose Dempsey going back with him, his wife?

Sometimes he would sit down on the railway bench on the platform, staring down at the ground, smiling to himself. What a surprise he had in store for Rose! What would he say to her first? Would he say anything of the building? No, he would say nothing at all of the building until they drove across the bridge and right up to the gate! 'Rose,' he would then say, 'do you remember the hill — the place under the beech trees?' She was sure to remember that place. It was there they had spent so much time, there he had first found her lips, there they had quarrelled! And Rose would look up to that old place and see the building! What would she think? Would she feel about it as he felt himself? She would, she would! What sort of look would come into her face? And what would he be able to tell her about it at all? . . . He would say nothing at all about it; that would be the best way! They would say nothing to each other, but walk in the gate and up the drive across the hill, the hill they often ran across in the old days! They would be quite silent, and walk into the house silently. The building, too, would be silent, and he would take her from one room to another in silence, and when she had seen everything he would look into her eyes and say, 'Well?' It would be all so like a wonderful story, a day of magic! . . . Martin Cosgrave sprang from the bench and went to the edge of the platform, staring down the long level road, with its two rails tapering almost together in the distance. Not a sign of a train. Would it never come in? Had anything happened the boat? He walked up and down with energy, holding the lapel of his coat, saying to himself, 'I must not be thinking of things like this. It is foolishness. Whatever is to happen will happen, and that's all about it. I am quite at ease, quite cool!'

At last it came, steaming and blowing. Windows were lowered, carriage doors flew open, people ran up and down. Martin Cosgrave stood a little away, tense, drawn, his eyes sweeping down the people. Suddenly something shot through him; an old sensation, an old thrill, made his whole being tingle, his mind exult, and then there was the most exquisite relaxation. How long it was since he felt like this before! His eyes were burning upon a familiar figure that had come from a carriage, the figure of a girl in a navy blue coat and skirt, her back turned, struggling with parcels, helped by the hands of invisible people from within the carriage. Martin Cosgrave strode down the platform, eagerness, joy, sense of proprietorship, already in his stride.

'Rose!' he exclaimed while the girl's back was still turned to him.

His voice shook in spite of him. The woman turned about sharply.

Martin Cosgrave gave a little start back. It was not Rose Dempsey, but her sister, Sheela. How like Rose she had grown!

'Martin!' she exclaimed, putting out her hand. He gave it a hurried shake and then searched the railway carriage with burning eyes. The people he saw there were all strangers, tired-looking travellers. When he turned from the railway carriage Sheela Dempsey was rushing with her parcels into a waiting-room. He strode after her. He looked at the girl. How unlike Rose she was after all! Nobody — nobody — could ever be like Rose Dempsey!

'Where is Rose?' he asked.

Sheela Dempsey looked up into the face of Martin Cosgrave and saw there what she had half-dreaded to see.

'Martin,' she said, 'Rose is not coming home.'

Martin Cosgrave gripped the door of the waiting-room. The train whistled outside and glided from the station. He heard a woman's cheerful voice cry out a conventional 'good-bye, good-bye,' and through the window he saw the flutter of a dainty handkerchief. A truck was wheeled past the waiting-room. There was the crack of a whip and some cars rattled away over the road. Then there was silence.

Sheela Dempsey walked over to him and laid a hand upon his shoulder. When she spoke her voice was full of an understanding womanly sympathy.

'Don't be troubling over it, Martin,' she said, 'Rose is not worth it.' She spoke her sister's name with some bitterness.

Vaguely Martin Cosgrave looked into the girl's eyes. He read there in a dim way what the girl could not say of his sister.

It was all so strange! The waiting-room was so bare, so cold, so grey, so like a sepulchre. What could Sheela Dempsey with all her womanly understanding, with all her quick intuition, know of the things that happened beside her? How could she have ears for the crashing down of the pillars of the building that Martin Cosgrave had raised up in his soul? How could she have eyes for the wreck of the structure that was to go on through all the generations? What thought had she of the wiping out of a name that would have lived in the nation and continued for all time in the eternities, a tangible thing in heaven among the immortals when the stars had all been burned out in the sky?

Martin Cosgrave drove home from the railway station with Sheela Dempsey. He sat without a word, not really conscious of his surroundings as they covered the miles. The girl reached across the side-car, touching him lightly on the shoulder.

'Look!' she exclaimed.

Martin Cosgrave looked up. The building stood in the moonlight on the crest of the hill. He bade the driver pull up, and then got down from the car.

'Who owns the house?' Sheela Dempsey asked.

'I do. I put it up on the hill for Rose.'

There was silence for some time.

'How did you get it built, Martin?' Sheela Dempsey asked, awe in her tone.

'I built it myself,' he answered. 'I wonder has Rose as good a place? What sort of building is she in tonight?'

Martin Cosgrave did not notice the sudden quiver in the girl's body as he put the question. But she made no reply, and the car drove on, leaving Martin Cosgrave standing alone at the gate of the building.

The faint sweep of the drive lay before him. It led his eyes up to the crest of the hill. There it was standing shadowy against the sky, every delicate outline clear to his vision. The beech trees were swaying beside it, reaching out like great shapeless arms in the night, blurred and beckoning and ghostly. A little vein of their music sounded in his ears. How often had he listened to that music and the things it had sung to him! It made him conscious of all the emotion he had felt while he had put up the building on the hill.

The joy of the builder swept over him like a wave. He was within the rising walls again, his hands among the grey-blue shapes, the measured stroke of the mallet swinging for the shifting chisel, the throb of steel going through his arms, the grind of stone was under his hands, the stone dust dry upon his lips, his eyes quick and keen, his arms bared, the shirt at his breast open, his whole body tense, tuned, to the desire of the conscious builder. . . . Once more he moved about the carpet of splinters, the grateful crunch beneath his feet, his world a world of stubborn things, rejoicing in the power of direction and mastery over it all. And always at the back of his mind and blending itself with the work was the thought of a ship forging through the water at the harvest, a ship with white sails spread to the winds. Had not thought for the building come into his mind when dead things sprang to life in the resurrection of his hopes?

Martin Cosgrave turned away from the gate. He walked down where the shadow of the mearing was faint upon the road. He turned up the boreen closed in by the still hedges. He stumbled over the ruts. He stood at the cabin door and looked up at the sky with soulless eyes. The animation, the inspiration, that had vivified his face since the building had been begun had died. The face no longer expressed the idealist, the visionary. His eyes swept the sky for a purpose. It was the look of the man of the fields, the man who had thought for his crops, who was near to the soil.

He had not looked a final and anxious, a peasant look, at the sky from his cabin-door in the night since he had embarked upon the building. He was conscious of that fact after a little. He wondered if it was a vague stirring in his heart that made him do it, a vague craving for the old companionship of the fields this night of bitterness. They were the fields, the sod, the territory of his forefathers, the inheritance of his blood. Who was he that he should put up a great building on the hill? What if he had risen for a little on his wings above the common flock?

The night air was heavy with the scent of the late dry harvest and all that the late dry harvest meant to the man nurtured on the side of a wet hill. The sheaves of corn were stooked in his neighbour's fields. Yesterday he had sacrificed the land to the building; tomorrow he would sacrifice the building to the land. Martin Cosgrave knew, the stars seemed to know, what a message, a voice, a command, would come like a wave through the generations of his blood sweeping him back to a common tradition. The cry for service on the land was beginning to stir somewhere. It would come to him in a word, a word sanctified upon the land by the memory of a thousand sacrifices and a thousand struggles, the only word that held magic for his race, the one word — redemption![4] He looked up at the building, made a vague motion of his hand that was like an act of renunciation, and laughed a laugh of terrible bitterness.

'Look,' he cried, 'at the building Martin Cosgrave put up on the hill?'

He moved to the cabin-door, his feet heavy upon the uneven ground as the feet of any of the generations of men who had ever gone that way before. He pressed the cabin-door with his fist. With a groan it went back shakily over the worn stone threshold, sticking when it was only a little way open. All was quiet, black, damp, terrible as chaos, inside. Martin Cosgrave hitched forward his left shoulder, went in sideways, and closed the crazy door against the pale world of moonlight outside.

4. Primarily meaning that he will redeem the debts on his land, but probably carrying — like 'sacrifices' and 'renunciation' — its religious connotations.

DANIEL CORKERY

(1878–1964)

from: THE HOUNDS OF BANBA (1920)

[*The Hounds of Banba* is devoted to the Irish War of Independence and in most of its stories we share the thoughts of the same young revolutionary on the run. 'On the Heights', with its breathless sense of pursuit, its operatic decor of storm and mountain-top, its romantic confrontation between old Fenian and the young IRA man, not only typifies the tone and theme of the volume, but catches what seems to have been the mood of the time.]

ON THE HEIGHTS

I

A stranger handed in a little slip of paper at the door of the farmhouse in Acharas where I had been hiding for several weeks: within ten minutes of receiving it I was on my bicycle, was flying at break-neck speed down mountainy bohereens,[1] one after another, crossing through watercourses without dismounting, and skimming the sharp corners of boulders by half inches or less. And yet I was all but caught! Only for their hooting, as their motor swerved from the main road, I had ridden into their arms. I caught that hoot! hoot! and flung from my path by very instinct; slap-dash in among the rocks and furze I went, went as far as I could, then threw myself off on the heather, and breathing like a swimmer after a long swim against time, could do nothing but wait, helpless. Puffing and panting on my knees, I could see them between the rocks: with frowning determination they were putting their heavy military motor at the hill, and I recognised the sergeant in charge. 'Mullery!' I gasped, and grabbed my handlebar again by instinct. If I fell into Mullery's hands, it meant five years: he was a man that would swear

1. lanes.

anything. When they had gone by, I mounted again, and swept into Gougane Barra[2] by the back road, and was just making on for Keimaneigh when something spoke in my ear — perhaps it was the old Gaelic saints who lie there at rest — 'They will have set a watch in Keimaneigh: take the mountains.' And so, instead of taking the comfortable if heavy road through the Pass of Keimaneigh, I made straight for Coomroe, facing the great walls of rock that enclose that most impressive of mountain glens. I have never heard that any other mortal ever pushed a bicycle up the one thousand eight hundred feet of jagged rock that hangs above the inches[3] there; but I did it, how I do not know, unless it was the vision of that dogged face in the motor car that kept me ever pushing on and on and up and up.

As I shoved, dragged, slided [*sic*], lifted my wheels up the rocks, the sweat ran freely and warmly down my back and limbs. I gave it no thought, I felt no weariness. But when I reached the summit and expected to see the sun again, a cold sea wind struck me, refreshed me, and then, suddenly, chilled me; and up before me rose a wall of white mist. I looked for the mountain-peaks that used to guide me there, but none were visible in the cloud. Feeling it all around me, licking and stroking me, and remembering how warm it had been in the coom,[4] I knew I was making into a night of rain; and there are no wetter hills in the whole of Munster. As I went forward I tried to recollect the whereabouts of the nearest house in those forlorn uplands, but all my landmarks were blotted out. I came suddenly on a close-huddled flock of black-faced mountainy sheep; they looked at me and scampered off into the mists with timid cries; they, too, seemed to be waiting for the rain. I felt lonelier than before. The pursuit was over and done with — years ago, it appeared. I thought of it no more. Could I make the Coomahola river before nightfall, was the only question that would rise up in my mind, as I pushed my bicycle now over the shale and then through growths of fragrant bog-myrtle. And it would come into my mind, too, that though I was making forward with fair speed I was doing no good, for I did not know where I was going. Yet somehow I feared to stop. I stumbled on and on, till suddenly I saw beside me a flat table of rock, about two feet high, as perfectly shaped as if stonecutters had worked at it. Before I had willed it, it seemed, I was sitting on it with a sense of delicious ease. 'I will think out exactly where I am and where I will go,' I said, comforting myself with a pretence of will power that I knew well was but a pretence. Then down came the rain, slanting from the south-west.

II

I bowed my head to it in sheer hopelessness — and that action it was that saved me. Beneath my eyes I saw certain light marks on the ground, not wheel marks — they were not more than two feet six apart, and besides they were not cut into the ground. I was instantly following them. I knew what they were. They were the marks of a 'tray,' as the peasants of that place call it both in Irish and English — a sort of light sleigh on which they bring down the cut turf from places in the uplands that are too steep for horse and cart. These marks meant a house, sooner or later. With the greatest care I kept to them. And soon I began to come on other signs of human ways and strivings — a cairn of stones, a first effort at a clearance, then a crazy sort of boundary fence, long abandoned to its own will, then at last two forked stakes in the ground, a young ash sapling laid across them, closing a gap. I blessed the human touch: the pious hands of husbandry had made it! Then I struck the path.

The night thickened, and the rain thickened; but now with the path beneath my feet, all broken shale it was, I did not mind. I thought I might leave my bicycle there until I had found the house, which I knew to be somewhere in the darkness. I laid it in the dripping heather and made more swiftly on. (I recovered it next day, clean as a new pin.) A waft of turf smoke struck me. I breathed it in with wide nostrils. My spirits rose, I could shout out. Then in a pit of darkness beneath me to the right I saw the tiny little eye of a lamplit window, warm-coloured, and looking as if its kindly gleam had been peering out that way on the hills for thousands and thousands of years, so steady it was. I used no caution. I made for it through the blackness, and lost the path. I

2. Gougane Barra, the region in which Corkery's story is set, amid the mountains of west Cork, is associated with many early Irish saints, most particularly Finnbarr, patron of Cork, whose name — in Irish, Fionn Barra — is probably contained in the place-name.
3. i.e. islands, from the Irish *inse*.
4. narrow valley.

found myself stumbling down the side of a little ravine — I splashed through a leaping stream, I almost fell upon the door. I banged it with my fist. I heard movement within, a collie whined, voices whispered. I could not wait. I banged again, and the rain pelted my warm wrist. I caught the latch and shook the door. 'Open! Open!' I cried. Within, I heard the bolts being withdrawn.

A low-toned, uncertain voice spoke in my face: 'Who are you? What is it you want? Come in. You're all wet.'

A dull-looking, middle-aged man and his wife, a soft-featured, kindly creature, drew back from me, and continued to stare at me; I felt annoyed at their doubtful reception; there was no heartiness in it.

'I'm wet all right,' I said, trying to speak calmly; but then I added with a bitterness I could not help, 'there are more than me on the hills these times, and better than me.'

By these words I would give them to understand why I was on the hills.

The man's jaw fell; he looked at his wife; they stared at me helplessly, even more stupidly than before, I thought, and more frigidly. He came one step towards me and whispered:

'Maybe you'd speak low? Maybe you would?'

What did he mean?

'Draw up to the fire; take your coat off,' the woman said, handing me a towel to wipe my face.

'Why should I speak low? Is there anyone sick?' I said, looking at the poor staring creature that was man of the house.

'No, no; there's no one sick, thanks be to God; glory be to His Holy Name!'

He was smiling at me in an indeterminate sort of way, his jaw hanging. He was a weak-mouthed man, I could see. He went doddering away. His wife pointed to the door in the partition at the end of the room.

'The old man, his father — he's asleep within, and he's noisy if anyone wakes him.'

That then was why I should speak low. I understood. I had met such old men before — Lears, but Lears who get the best of the bargain, maintaining their rights of property to the very day that they have to step into the grave. We found ourselves speaking in whispers, all three of us, I trying to explain how I found the track to their lonely door and they wondering how I had missed the wider track across the hills. After all, they were a good-hearted couple, and could enjoy a chat — if one carried it on in whispers.

The man raised his head suddenly: we all listened. The winds were coming up from Bantry Bay, they were roaring upon the roof. As we listened, in flew the door with a crash, the fire was scattered on the hearth, the sheep dog sprang from his sleep, planted his legs and howled at the storm. We all flung ourselves on the door. In the sudden tumult I forgot myself. As we got the door to I shouted with vast enjoyment:

'There! there! stay outside now — with Sergeant Mullery,' I added under my breath.

'Hush! hush! sir; lave ye.'[5]

Both man and wife were terrified, it seemed. They were looking towards the end of the room.

I put my hand to my mouth, hunching my shoulders, and turning like them towards the unseen sleeper — how we leap at moments back into our childhood! But too late, too late. Three dreadful blows were struck on that partition towards which we were all looking, and an aged but vigorous and indignant voice cried out above the storm in ringing Irish:

'Am I to be kept always in the dark? Ever and always! Look at me, and I for the last hour killed with listening to your foolery — and dogs — and giggling — and the stranger's voice stunning me; and 'tisn't worth your while, Shawn, to come in with a little word.'

Man and wife were trying to smile at me; but I could see that they were used to getting the worse of it. They did not know what was best to do.

'I'll answer him,' I said. They clutched me.

'No, no,' they were whispering warmly in my face; 'no, sir; no sir.'

I cried out in Irish as ringing as his own:

'You'd drive a stranger from your door, this night?' Half in jest, half in earnest, I spoke the words. The winds were roaring with a great voice; I could hear the cataracts pouring.

''Tis no decent person would be travelling the hills this night,' I was answered, and there was suspicion and challenge in the tones.

'There's a more decent person on your floor this night,' I answered back, and in spite of myself my voice was hard and rough, 'a more decent person

5. i.e. leave off talking, be quiet.

than ever walked this hungry land since St. Finnbarr left it, travelling to the east.'

'Left it and blessed it,' the voice answered me in triumph.

'I doubt it,' I answered, and my anger was gone; and there came swiftly over me a joyousness to think of the two of us shouting at each other there in that lonely land with the roaring storm outside, grandest of orchestras.

'I doubt it,' I cried, in a great voice.

'He did,' he answered.

'I doubt it.'

''Tis well known; the authors say so!'

My heart opened to him! How often I had heard that or similar phrases from his like! 'Se adeir na h-ughdair. . . .'[6]

'If he did, ye ought to remember it, and not drive a stranger from. . . .'

'There's no one doing the like; but haven't I the right to complain if my son will not tell me who 'tis comes in or goes out? Come in to me, Shawn, and let you make the stranger his meal, Nora.'

Shawn went into him, having first looked despairingly at his wife, who smiled back encouragingly. I felt I had not fathomed any one of the three of them.

'He'll be in his sleep in a moment,' she said to me in a whisper. 'You gave him his answer.' She was more courageous than the man.

III

I made free with the big teapot of black tea she made me, and with the lovely bread, laughing to myself and yet wondering. After a while Shawn returned to us on tiptoe from the old man's room, and, silenced, we could hear the deep and vigorous breathing of his father.

I began telling them of the detestable war bread the people in the cities and towns had to eat, and of the great scarcity of everything among them; they sighed over them, the poor creatures! And so the night passed. I began to wonder why they did not suggest retiring, for it was now near midnight. I began to yawn involuntarily, and to measure the settle[7] with my eyes. I had often slept on one. They were again confused. At last the man, who was certainly an extraordinarily gentle creature, touched my sleeve shyly and said: 'The only place we have for you to sleep in is with himself,' he nodded towards the partition. I was just about to say, 'What about the settle?' when I thought suddenly that there were but the two rooms in the house; I glanced about and saw that the press on which the candle was lighting was of course a folded-up bedstead. Yet I didn't answer: I did not relish the thought of sleeping with a person I had just quarrelled with.

'You could slip in — quietly. He sleeps sound.'

I smiled at him.

'Go in,' I said, throwing myself erect, 'and tell him the police and the soldiers are on my track, and see what he'll say?'

I felt sure that anyone who kept the 'authors' in his thoughts would not refuse a corner of his bed to a rapparee.[8] I was surprised how they took my words! Had they not known it?

'No, no,' they both cried warmly at me; 'not that way at all,' the man moved about the flags in trouble.[9]

''Tis better say no word about the soldiers or police at all,' the wife urged; 'only that 'tis how a tourist is after losing his way in the fogs, a tourist was fishing in Loch Fada. Go on, Shawn, and tell him that; 'tis a story will do no one any harm.'

I consented, and Shawn went very timidly into his father's presence. We listened; yet there was no noise between them, no squabbling at all. He came out gesturing that the way was clear. About midnight I stepped very carefully over the old man's rather bulky figure, to take my share of the huge old bed.

'Out the candle,' he growled at me. Timidly enough I mumbled an apology, and did so. Outside, the winds shrieked among the upland gullies and the waters fell in them.

IV

I awoke with some dim feeling of annoyance. It was pitch dark and the storm was still roaring, but near by was an unceasing whisper, a sharp hissing of breath between teeth and lips: the old man, hunched up in the bed, was praying. I dozed off again, and again I woke, and the hissing was still going on beside me. He was, I suspected, carrying out a

6. Irish: the authors say so.
7. A wooden seat, for two or more persons, with a high back and arms.
8. Irish, *ropaire*: an old-fashioned word for an outlaw.
9. i.e. shuffled uneasily on the flagstones (of the floor).

practice of fifty or sixty years' standing. To the roaring winds outside he was deaf: he knew their voices better than I. I was listening to them, to him, thankful for the nest of warmth and peace I found myself in. I would occasionally hear the rattle of his beads, and from the sound could guess at their huge size. Dozing again, I heard him gather them up; and then I am quite clear I heard the words, '. . . and for the souls of all the men they put to death in Dublin!'[10] His voice fell to a whisper, and a vigorous 'Amen!' finished his prayers, as with a clasp. He shrugged the clothes up about his shoulders, groped under the pillow, and settled himself to sleep. A sudden rush of thought and feeling swept over me. 'The souls of all the men they put to death in Dublin,' I repeated, and I thought of this lonely old man praying for them in this unknown cabin on the uplands. In the phrase of the people, I was glorified to think of it.

V

Yet presently I fell to wondering why his son and his son's wife had implored me not to tell him that I was a hunted man on the hills. I could not understand it.

VI

I awoke in the bright morning to find the old man's fingers touching and feeling my brow with great gentleness. He started when my eyes glared up at him. It was then I saw him for the first time with any distinctness. He had a fringe of white, wool-white whiskers in under his shaven chin; he looked like a shepherd in an old play or in a picture; but there was a keenness and a sharpness about the brow — an alertness that made one forget this first thought of him. Seeing how he had started, I greeted him in good Irish. He smiled at me:

'You're no tourist was fishing Loch Fada,' he said, knowingly. I listened a moment; there was no stir in the room outside. I felt sure they had not yet risen, had not yet been speaking to him. The sun was bathing the hills, a robin was singing. Even in the little darksome cabin there was an air of freshness and gladness.

'What am I, then?' I said.

'You're no tourist,' he said again, with the same wise and, I thought, encouraging smile.

'But what am I?'

'I'll tell you: you're one of them!' He gave me a slow, antique wink; it was like a gesture. 'I was one of them myself and I young,' he added. He flung up his head.

'It wasn't I told you I was a tourist.'

'No, 'twas himself. But you, 'twas yourself, and no one else, told me — told me what I know. Brother,' he said, using the familiar word among the Gaels, 'you were dreaming . . . powerful dreams!' What wild foolery had I been crying out in my sleep! His eyes were full of vision — my dreams!

''Twill come to pass,' he said, 'the authors foretold it.' I had no reply, except to stare at him, his face aglow, bending upon mine.

'But isn't this a pitiful thing,' he grew mournful above me, 'that man outside, that son of mine — he's a thing without courage, he's like a sheep after being worried by the dogs, he is that! He'd be afraid to hang a bit of green on the door, or to keep a gun in the house. I'm sick and tired of him. But look, forgive me the welcome I gave you: these times there do be men in plain clothes going from house to house, innocent-looking slobs of men, gathering up information, and that pair outside, I must be watching them. 'Tisn't too much I'd tell them.' He repeated that solemn wink of his.

VII

I left him still in his bed, and I sat at breakfast with the two others.

'You got on all right with himself?'

'I did, I did, then.'

'He's a bit cross sometimes; he was a Fenian in the old days.'[11]

'He told me so.'

They looked sharply at me. They were wondering how much he had told me. And in that state of mind I left them.

10. Sixteen leaders of the Easter Rising of 1916 were executed.

11. There had been an armed Fenian (Republican) uprising in 1867.

JAMES STEPHENS

(1882–1950)

from:
THE CROCK OF GOLD (1912)

[A central concern in the intricate plot of James Stephens's prose fantasy, *The Crock of Gold*, is the gentle abduction of the shepherd, Caitilin Ni Murrachu, by the god Pan, who is paying his first visit to Ireland. Her droll father, Meehawl Mac Murrachu, missing her but not knowing the implications of her plight, repairs to the book's intellectual hero, the Philosopher, to whom people resort when they have exhausted 'those extremes of elucidation, the parish priest and the tavern.' In the first extract here, from Book One, Chapter VII, the Philosopher, by means of shrewd questioning, has identified the enemy.]

. . . 'Who was this traveller?'

'I never saw him,' said Meehawl, 'but one day I went a few perches up the hill and I heard him playing — thin, squeaky music it was, like you'd be blowing out of a tin whistle. I looked about for him everywhere, but not a bit of him could I see.'

'Eh?' said the Philosopher.

'I looked about —' said Meehawl.

'I know,' said the Philosopher. 'Did you happen to look at your goats?'

'I couldn't well help doing that,' said Meehawl.

'What were they doing?' said the Philosopher eagerly.

'They were pucking each other across the field, and standing on their hind legs and cutting such capers that I laughed till I had a pain in my stomach at the gait of them.'

'This is very interesting,' said the Philosopher.

'Do you tell me so?' said Meehawl.

'I do,' said the Philosopher, 'and for this reason — most of the races of the world have at one time or another —'

'It's my little daughter, Caitilin, sir,' said Meehawl.

'I'm attending to her,' the Philosopher replied.

'I thank you kindly,' returned Meehawl.

The Philosopher continued —

'Most of the races of the world have at one time or another been visited by this deity, whose title is the "Great God Pan", but there is no record of his ever having journeyed to Ireland, and, certainly within historic times, he has not set foot on these shores. He lived for a great number of years in Egypt, Persia, and Greece, and although his empire is supposed to be world-wide, this universal sway has always been, and always will be, contested; but nevertheless, however sharply his empire may be curtailed, he will never be without a kingdom wherein his exercise of sovereign rights will be gladly and passionately acclaimed.'

'Is he one of the old gods, sir?' said Meehawl.

'He is,' replied the Philosopher, 'and his coming intends no good to this country. Have you any idea why he should have captured your daughter?'

'Not an idea in the world.'

'Is your daughter beautiful?'

'I couldn't tell you, because I never thought of looking at her that way. But she is a good milker, and as strong as a man. She can lift a bag of meal under her arm easier than I can; but she's a timid creature for all that.'

'Whatever the reason is I am certain that he has the girl, and I am inclined to think that he was directed to her by the Leprecauns of the Gort. You know they are at feud with you ever since their bird was killed?'

'I am not likely to forget it, and they racking me day and night with torments.'

'You may be sure,' said the Philosopher, 'that if he's anywhere at all it's at Gort na Cloca Mora he is, for, being a stranger, he wouldn't know where to go unless he was directed, and they know every hole and corner of this countryside since ancient times. I'd go up myself and have a talk with him, but it wouldn't be a bit of good, and it wouldn't be any use your going either. He has power over all grown people so that they either go and get drunk or else they fall in love with every person they meet, and commit assaults and things I wouldn't like to be telling you about. The only folk who can go near him at all are little children, because he has no power over them until they grow to the sensual age, and then he exercises lordship over them as over everyone else. I'll send my two children with a message to him to say that he isn't doing the decent thing, and that if he doesn't let the girl alone and go back to his own country we'll send for Angus Óg.'

'He'd make short work of him, I'm thinking.'

'He might surely; but he may take the girl for himself all the same.'

'Well, I'd sooner he had her than the other one, for he's one of ourselves anyhow, and the devil you know is better than the devil you don't know.'

'Angus Óg is a god,' said the Philosopher severely.

'I know that, sir,' replied Meehawl; 'it's only a way of talking I have. But how will your honour get at Angus? for I heard say that he hadn't been seen for a hundred years, except one night only when he talked to a man for half an hour on Kilmasheogue.'

'I'll find him, sure enough,' replied the Philosopher.

'I'll warrant you will,' replied Meehawl heartily as he stood up. 'Long life and good health to your honour,' said he as he turned away.

The Philosopher lit his pipe.

'We live as long as we are let,' he said, 'and we get the health we deserve. Your salutation embodies a reflection on death which is not philosophic. We must acquiesce in all logical progressions. The merging of opposites is completion. Life runs to death as to its goal, and we should go towards that next stage of experience either carelessly as to what must be, or with a good, honest curiosity as to what may be.'

'There's not much fun in being dead, sir,' said Meehawl.

'How do you know?' said the Philosopher.

'I know well enough,' replied Meehawl. . . .

[The children fail in their embassy, so the Philosopher sets out to confront Pan and, having found Caitilin naked in the sunshine outside the god's cave on the hillside, he engages Pan in mental fight on the subject of virtue. The next extract is from Book Two, Chapter X.]

. . . Now, what is virtue?' —

Pan, who had listened with great courtesy to these remarks, here broke in on the Philosopher.

'Virtue,' said he, 'is the performance of pleasant actions.'

The Philosopher held the statement for a moment on his forefinger.

'And what, then, is vice!' said he.

'It is vicious,' said Pan, 'to neglect the performance of pleasant actions.'

'If this be so,' the other commented, 'philosophy has up to the present been on the wrong track.'

'That is so,' said Pan. 'Philosophy is an immoral practice because it suggests a standard of practice impossible of being followed, and which, if it could be followed, would lead to the great sin of sterility.'

'The idea of virtue,' said the Philosopher, with some indignation, 'has animated the noblest intellects of the world.'

'It has not animated them,' replied Pan; 'it has hypnotized them so that they have conceived virtue as repression and self-sacrifice as an honourable thing instead of the suicide which it is.'

'Indeed,' said the Philosopher; 'this is very interesting, and if it is true the whole conduct of life will have to be very much simplified.'

'Life is already very simple,' said Pan; 'it is to be born and to die, and in the interval to eat and drink, to dance and sing, to marry and beget children.'

'But it is simply materialism,' cried the Philosopher.

'Why do you say "but"?' replied Pan.

'It is sheer, unredeemed animalism,' continued his visitor.

'It is any name you please to call it,' replied Pan.

'You have proved nothing,' the Philosopher shouted.

'What can be sensed requires no proof.'

'You leave out the new thing,' said the Philosopher. 'You leave out brains. I believe in mind above matter. Thought above emotion. Spirit above flesh.'

'Of course you do,' said Pan, and he reached for his oaten pipe.

The Philosopher ran to the opening of the passage and thrust Caitilin aside. 'Hussy,' said he fiercely to her, and he darted out.

As he went up the rugged path he could hear the pipes of Pan, calling and sobbing and making high merriment on the air.

HUNGER
(1918)

[Stephens first published this long short story as a booklet in 1918, under the pseudonym James Esse. From internal evidence, it is set in Dublin after the Lockout of 1913 and before the outbreak of the Great War.]

I

On some people misery comes unrelentingly. It comes with such a continuous rage that one might say destruction had been sworn against them and that they were doomed beyond appeal, or hope.

That seemed to her to be the case as she sat, when her visitor had departed, looking on life as it had moved about her; and she saw that life had closed on her, had crushed her, and that there was nothing to be said about it, and no one to be blamed.

She was ten years married, and she had three children. One of them had fallen when he was a baby, and had hurt his back so badly that the dispensary doctor instructed her not to let him walk for a few years.

She loved all her children, but this child she loved greatly; for she had to do more for him than for the others. Indeed she had to do everything for him, and she did not grudge doing it. He was the eldest and he was always with her. The other youngsters were with her as screamings, as demands, to be attended to and forgotten, but he was with her as a companion eye, a consciousness to whom she could talk and who would reply to her, and who would not, could not, by any means get into mischief.

Her husband was a house-painter, and when work was brisk he got good wages: he could earn thirty-five shillings a week when he was working.

But his work was constant only in the summer months: through the bad weather there was no call for him, for no one wanted house-painting done in the winter; and so the money which he earned in the fine months had to be stretched and made to cover the dead months.

Nor were these five months to be entirely depended upon: here and there in a week days would be missed, and with that his Society dues had to be paid, for he would pay these though he starved for it.

II

Wages which have to be stretched so lengthily give but the slenderest sum towards a weekly budget. It was she who had to stretch them, and the doing of it occupied all the time she could spare for thinking.

She made ends meet where nothing was but ends, and they met just over the starvation line.

She had not known for years what it was like not to be hungry for one day; but life is largely custom; and neither she nor her husband nor the children made much complaint about a condition which was normal for them all, and into which the children had been born.

They could scarcely die of hunger for they were native to it. They were hunger. There was no other hunger but them: and they only made a noise about food when they saw food.

If she could have got work how gladly she would have taken it! How gladly she would have done it! Sweated work! Any work! so it brought in if it was no more than a few coppers in the day. But the children were there, three of them, and all were young and one was a cripple.

Her own people, and those of her husband, lived, existed, far away in the country. They could not take the children off her hands. She could not give a neighbour anything to look after them while she went out working. She was held to them as fast as if she were chained to them; and, for to think in such cases is only to be worried, there was no use in thinking about it. She had already all the worry she could deal with, and she wanted no more.

She remembered a tale that she had laughed at, when she was young, about a woman who had been circumstanced as she was now. This woman used to put her two children into a box, for she had to go out every day to work in order that she might feed them; and she kept them in the box so that they might not injure themselves during her absence.

It was a good idea, but the children came out of the box hunchbacks, and so stunted in their growth that it might be said they never grew thereafter. It might have been better for the children, and easier for them, if they had died; anyhow, their mother died, and the poor little oddities went to the work-house; and must all their lives have got all the jeers which their appearance sanctioned.

There was nothing to be done; even her husband had long ago given up thinking of how this could be arranged; and although she still, and continually, thought about it, she knew that nothing could be done.

III

Her husband was a jolly man; he used to make up lists of gigantic feeds they would have when the ship came home (what ship he did not say, nor was it understood that he expected one), and he or she or the children would remind each other of foods which had been left out of his catalogue; for no food of which they knew the name could justly be omitted from their future.

He was a robust man, and could have eaten a lot had he got it. Indeed he had often tempted his wife to commit an act of madness and have one wild blow-out; for which, as she pointed out to him, they would have to pay by whole days of whole starvation, instead of the whole days of semi-hunger to which they were accustomed.

This was the only subject on which they came nigh to quarrelling, and he brought it forward with fortnightly regularity.

Sometimes she went cold at the thought that on some pay-day he might go in for a wild orgy of eating, and perhaps spend half a crown. Less than that sum could not nearly fill him; and the double of it would hardly fill him the way he needed to be filled; for he wanted to be filled as tightly as a drum, and with such a weight and abundance of victual that he could scarcely be lifted by a crane.

But he was an honourable man, and she knew that he would not do this unless she and the children were with him and could share and go mad with him. He was very fond of them, and if she could have fed him on her own flesh she would have sacrificed a slice or two, for she was very fond of him.

IV

The mild weather had come, and he got a cut in his hand, which festered and seemed stubbornly incurable. The reason was that the gaunt man was not fed well enough to send clean blood down to doctor his cut hand. In the end he did get over it; but for three weeks he had been unable to work, for who will give employment to a man whose hand looks like a poultice or a small football?

The loss of these three weeks almost finished her.

The distinguishing mark of her family had been thinness, it was now bonyness.

To what a food-getting fervour was she compelled! She put the world of rubbish that was about her through a sieve; and winnowed nourishment for her family where a rat would have unearthed disappointment.

She could not beg; but she did send her two children into the street, and sometimes one of these got a copper from a passing stranger. Then, like the call of a famished crow who warns his brothers that he has discovered booty, that youngster gave out a loyal squeal for his companion; and they trotted home with their penny. The sun shone on the day they got a penny; on the days when they got nothing the sun might bubble the tar and split the bricks, but it did not shine.

Her man returned to his work, and if she could hold on they would be able to regain the poverty of a few months previously, but which now beamed to her as distant, unattainable affluence.

She could hold on, and she did; so that they tided feebly across those evil days; and came nigh at last to the longed-for scarcity which yet was not absolute starvation; and whereby they could live in the condition of health to which they were accustomed, and which they recognised and spoke of as good health.

They could not absolutely come to this for at least a year. Provision had still to be made for the lean months to come; the winter months; and more than three weeks' wages which should have been skimmed in this precaution had been unprofitable, had not existed. The difference had to be made up by a double skimming of the present wage; which must also pay the present necessities, and recoup the baker and grocer for the few weeks' credit these shop people had given her.

In all, their lot for a long time was not to be envied, except by a beast in captivity: and envied only by him because he lusts for freedom and the chance of it as we lust for security and the destruction of chance.

V

The winter came — the winter will come tho' the lark protest and the worm cries out its woe — and she entered on that period with misgiving, with resolution, and with a facing of everything that might come.

What bravery she had! What a noble, unwearying courage; when in so little a time, and at so small a pain, she might have died!

But such an idea did not come to her head. She looked on the world, and she saw that it was composed of a man and three children; while they lasted she could last, and when they were done it would be time enough to think of personal matters and her relation to things.

Before the summer had quite ended, e'er autumn had tinted a leaf, the war broke out; and with its coming there came insecurity. Not to her, not to them. They had no standard to measure security by. It came to the people who desire things done, and who pay to have doors varnished or window-frames painted. These people drew silently but resolutely from expense; while he and she and the children sunk deeper into their spending as one wallows into a bog.

The prices of things began to increase with a cumulative rapidity, and the quality of things began to deteriorate with equal speed. Bread and the eater of it came to a grey complexion. Meat was no more. The vegetables emigrated with the birds. The potato got a rise in the world and recognised no more its oldest friends. Nothing was left but the rain; and the rain came loyally.

They, those others, could retrench and draw in a little their horns; but from what could she retreat? What could she avoid? What could she eliminate, who had come to the bare bone and shank of life? The necessity for the loaf comes daily, recurs pitilessly from digestion to digestion, and with the inexorable promptitude of the moon the rent collector wanes and waxes.

They managed.

She and he managed.

Work still was, although it was spaced and intervalled like a storm-blown hedge. Here was a week and there another one, and from it they gleaned their constricted existence.

They did not complain; for those who are down do not complain. Nor did they know they were down. Or, knowing it, they did not admit their downness. For to front so final a fact is to face with naked hands a lion; and to admit is to give in. Is to be washed away. To be lost and drowned. To be anonymous; unhelpable; alive no more; but debris, or a straw which the wind takes and sails, or tears, or drifts, or rots, to powder and forgetfulness.

A bone in a world of bones! And they gnawed these bones until it seemed that nothing moved in the world except their teeth.

VI

The winter came, and his work stopped as it always did in that season.

He got jobs cleaning windows. He got jobs at the docks hoisting things which not Hercules nor the devil himself could lift. But which he could lift, or which his teeth and the teeth of his children detached from the ground as from foundations and rivettings.

He got a job as a coalman; and as a night-watchman sitting in the angle of a black street before a bucket of stinking coal, which had been a fire until the rain put it out. Today he had a job; but tomorrow and for a week he had none.

With what had been saved, skimmed, strained from the summer wages; with what came from the jobs; with the pennies that the children unearthed from strangers as though they dug in those loath souls for coin, they lived through the winter, and did not feel that they had passed through an experience worthy of record, or that their endurance might have been rewarded with medals and a pension.

They were living, as we all manage, amazingly, to live: and if others had an easier time that was their chance. But this was their life, and there were those who were even worse off than they were.

For they paid the rent! And, when that was done, what a deed had been accomplished! How notable an enemy circumvented!

VII

The spring came; but it brought no leaves to their tree. The summer came; but it did not come to them; nor warn them of harvest and a sickle in the yield.

There was no building done that summer; the price of material had gone up and the price of wages. The contractors did not care for that prospect, and the client, remembering taxes and the war, decided to wait.

And her husband had no work!

Almost he had even given up looking for work. He would go out of the house and come into the house and go out of the house again; and he and she would look at each other in a dumb questioning.

It was strange how he had arranged with himself not to look at the children. How he had even arranged that their whimperings should seem to be inaudible, and their very presences invisible! And they, having raked his coming as with search-lights, and discovering that he brought nothing, looked at him no more.

They looked at her. They projected themselves to her, about her, upon her, into her. . . .

A wolf-mother, thus badgered and possessed,

would have escaped from her young by mercifully or unmercifully slaughtering them. But she still could preserve her soul, her tenderness. Yet, if a whole infinity of tenderness seemed to be preserved for the children, a major, a yet more marvellous, tenderness was reserved for her man — it was without words, without action. It was without anything whatever. It was itself alone. Unproven, unquestioned, unending. To be perceived, received, only by the soul, and from the soul, or not to be received or perceived at all.

Sometimes she would say — not that she had anything to say, but to ease her husband's heart with a comradely word —

'Any chance today, do you think?'

And he would reply:

'Chance!'

And he would sit down to brood upon the lapsing word.

They were not angry; they had not the blood to be angry with; for to be wrathful you must be well fed or you must be drunk.

The youngest child died of an ill which, whatever it was at the top, was hunger at the bottom; and she grew terrified. She heard that there was work to be had in the Munition Factories in Scotland, and by some means she gathered together the fare and sent her husband across the sea.

'Write, if you can,' said she, 'the minute you get a place.'

'Yes,' he replied.

'And send us what you can spare,' she said. 'Send something this week if you can.'

'Yes,' he said.

And he went away.

And she went into the streets to beg.

VIII

She left the boy behind in his chair, and brought the other little one with her.

She was frightened, for one can be arrested for begging. And she was afraid not to beg, for one can die of hunger.

How well she knew those streets! and yet she did not know them in this aspect! These were atrocious streets!

She got a penny here and a penny there, and she bought bread. Sometimes even she bought a twist of tea. She could manage until the end of the week; until her man sent the money.

She had thoughts of singing at the corners of streets, as she had so often seen done by the toneless, ashen-faced women, who creak rusty music at the passer, and fix him with their eyes. But she was ashamed; and no song that she could remember seemed suitable; and she only could remember bits of songs; and she knew that her voice would not work for her, but that it would creak and mourn like a rusty hinge.

Her earnings were small, for she could not get in touch with people. That too is a trade and must be learned. They recognised her at a distance as a beggar, and she could only whisper to the back of a head or a cold shoulder.

Sometimes when she went towards a person that person instantly crossed the road and walked for a while hastily.

Sometimes people fixed upon her a prohibitive eye and she drew back from them humbled; her heart panting and her eyes hot at the idea that they took her for a beggar.

At times a man, without glancing at her, stuck a hand in a pocket and gave her a penny without halting in his stride.

One day she got twopence; one day she got sixpence; one day she got nothing.

But she could hold out to the end of the week.

IX

The end of the week came, but it brought no letter.

'It will come tomorrow,' she said.

'He is in a strange country,' she thought in panic. 'He must have missed the post, God help him!'

But on the next day there was no letter; nor any letter on the day after; and on the day that succeeded to it there was no letter.

'He . . . !' she said.

But she could not speculate on him. She knew him too well, and she knew that this was not he; he could no more leave them in the lurch than he could jump across Ireland in one jump.

'He has not got work,' she said.

And she saw him strayed and stranded; without a hand; without a voice; bewildered and lost among strangers; going up streets and down streets; and twisting himself into a maze, a dizziness of loneliness and hunger and despair.

Or, she said:

'The submarines had blown up the ship that was coming with the money.'

The week went by; another came, and still she did not hear from him. She was not able to pay the rent.

She looked at the children; and then she looked away from them distantly to her strayed husband; and then she looked inwardly on herself, and there was nothing to see.

She was down.

No littlest hope could find a chink to peer through. And while she sat, staring at nothing, in an immobile maze of attention, her mind — she had no longer a heart, it had died of starvation — her mind would give a leap and be still; and would leap again, as though an unknown, wordless action were seeking to be free; seeking to do something; seeking to disprove stagnation, and powerlessness, and death; and a little burning centre of violence hung in her head like a star.

She followed people with her eyes, sometimes a little way with her feet, saying to herself:

'The pockets of that man are full of money; he would rattle if he fell.'

Or:

'That man had his breakfast this morning; he is full of food to the chin; he is round and tight and solid, and he weighs a ton.'

She said:

'If I had all the money of all the people in this street I should have a lot of money.'

She said:

'If I owned all the houses in this street I should have a lot of money.'

The rent collector told her imperatively that she must leave at the end of the week, and the children called to her for bread, clamorously, unceasingly, like little dogs that yap and whine and cannot be made to stop.

X

Relief kitchens had been started in various parts of the city, but she only heard of them by chance; and she went to one. She told a lady in attendance her miserable tale, and was given the address of a gentleman who might assist her. He could give her a ticket which would enable her to get food; and he might be able to set her in the way of earning what would pay the rent.

This lady thought her husband had deserted her; and she said so, without condemnation, as one states a thing which has been known to happen; and the poor woman agreed without agreeing, for she did not believe it.

But she did not argue about the matter, for now that she accepted food, she accepted anything that came with it, whether it was opinions or advice. She was an acceptor, and if she claimed to possess even an opinion it might jeopardise her chance of getting anything.

She set out for the house of the gentleman who could give her the ticket which would get her food to bring home to the children.

He lived at some distance, and when she got to his house the servant told her he had gone to his office; at his office she was informed that he had gone out. She called three times at the office, and on the third time she was told that he had come in, but had gone home.

She trudged to his house again; and would have been weary, but that her mind had lapsed far, far, from her trudging feet; and when the mind is away the body matters nothing.

Where was her mind? At times it was nowhere. It was gone from her body and from material things. It might be said to have utterly quitted that tenement, and to be somehow, somewhere, refuged from every fear, havened from every torment and eased of every memory that could deject it. She was life and a will; or, if these are but one, she was the will to be, obscure, diligent, indefatigable.

And then, again, as at the opening of a door, her mind, laden with recollections of time and space, of deeds and things and thwartings, was back in the known and incredible room, looking at the children, listening to them, consoling them; telling them that in a little while she should be home again, and that she would bring them food.

They had not eaten anything for — how long was it? Was it a year? Had they ever eaten? And one of them was sick!

She must get back. She had been away too long. But she must go forward before she could go back.

She must get the ticket which was food and hope

and a new beginning, or a respite. Then she should be able to look about her. The children would go to sleep; and she could plan and contrive and pull together those separated and dwindling ends.

She came to the gentleman's house. He was in, and she told him her story, and how her case was desperate.

He also believed that her husband had deserted her; and he promised to write by that night's post to find out the truth about the man, and to see that he was punished for his desertion.

He had no tickets with him; he had used them all, for the hungry people in Dublin were numerous; work was slack everywhere, and those who had never before applied for assistance were now obliged to do so by dreadful necessity. He gave her some money, and promised to call at her room on the following day to investigate her case.

She went homewards urgently, and near home she bought bread and tea.

When she got in the crippled boy turned dull, dumb eyes upon her; and she laughed at him excitedly, exultantly; for she had food; lots of it, two loaves of it.

But the other child did not turn to her, and would not turn to her again, for he was dead; and he was dead of hunger.

XI

She could not afford to go mad, for she still had a boy, and he depended on her with an utter helpless dependence.

She fed him and fed herself; running from him in the chair to that other in its cot, with the dumb agony of an animal who must do two things at once, and cannot resolve which thing to do.

She could not think; she could hardly feel. She was dulled and distressed and wild. She was weakened by misery and tormented by duties; and life and the world seemed a place of busynesses, and futilities, and unending, unregulated, demands upon her.

A neighbour, hearing that persistent trotting over her head, came up to the room to remonstrate, and remained to shed for her the tears which she could not weep herself. She, too, was in straits, and had nothing more to give than those tears; and the banal iterations which are comfort because they are kindness.

Into this place the gentleman called on the following day to investigate, and was introduced to a room swept almost as clean of furniture as a dog kennel is; to the staring, wise-eyed child who lived in a chair; and to the quiet morsel of death that lay in a cot by the wall.

He was horrified, but he was used to sights of misery; and he knew that when things have ceased to move they must be set moving again; and that all he could do was to remove some of the impediments which he found in the path of life, so that it might flow on before it had time to become stagnant and rotten.

He took from the dry-eyed, tongue-tied woman all the immediate worry of death. He paid the rent, and left something to go on with as well; and he promised to get her work either in his house or at his office, but he would get her work to do somehow.

XII

He came daily; and each day, in reply to her timid question as to her husband, he had nothing to say except that enquiries were being made.

On the fifth day he had news, and he would have preferred any duty, however painful, to the duty of telling her his news.

But he told it, sitting on the one chair; with his hand over his eyes, and nothing of his face visible except the mouth which shaped and spoke sentences.

The munition people in Scotland reported that a man of the name he was enquiring for had applied for work, and had been taken on a fortnight after his application. The morning after he began work he was found dead in a laneway. He had no lodgings in the city; and at the post-mortem examination it was found that he had died of hunger and exposure.

She listened to that tale; looking from the gentleman who told it to her little son who listened to it. She moistened her lips with her tongue; but she could not speak, she could only stammer and smile.

The gentleman also sat looking at the boy.

'We must set this young man up,' said he heavily. 'I shall send a doctor to look him over today.'

And he went away all hot and cold; beating his hands together as he walked; and feeling upon his shoulders all the weariness and misery of the world.

JOYCE CARY

(1888–1957)

from: A HOUSE OF CHILDREN (1941)

[The Maylins' party, in itself a remarkable vignette of an Anglo-Irish childhood on the Inishowen Peninsula in Donegal, marks one decisive stage in the growing consciousness of the novel's young hero, Evelyn. He is on summer holidays at his Aunt's house, Dunamara, where Pinto, mentioned in the first paragraph, is their eccentric summer tutor. Frances and Delia are his older Dunamara cousins, and Frances's opening observation is somewhat prophetic since the novel ends with the elopement of Pinto and her sister. But the novel's chief interest is what happens in Evelyn's mind. He is six years old, younger than his brother, Harry, and senior to his fearful little cousin, Anketel. It is all observed with what A. N. Jeffares has called Cary's 'shrewd knowledge of and unsentimental sympathy for children'.]

CHAPTER 14

Though Frances had told us that Pinto would go to ruin and that his destruction would lie at our door, he got almost at once a much better job. He became tutor to the only son of some people called Maylin at their place ten miles south of Dunvil.[1] The Maylins were rich and good-natured. They were both fat and red-faced and rheumatic. They gave very fine parties, especially at Christmas, when the little husband would push his wife, in a wheel-chair, through the lower rooms, and guests would go up to talk to her. She, however, would do all the talking, uttering cries of laughter like a parrakeet, and waving her crutch to warn you that she had still something to say, when she had finished laughing.

The Maylin Christmas party was four parties in one. It started at four with babies, went on with children till seven or eight; then the young people danced till eleven, and, finally, there was a ball till morning. But some of the young girls stayed for the first half of the ball. I've heard that the Maylins followed this plan to get all their winter hospitality into one day. They themselves did not appear except once at each party. They even dined by themselves and went to bed during the ball.

The Jubilee Christmas was the first Harry and I had spent in Ireland for some years. We went to half a dozen parties, but no vestige of any of them remains to me except a drive in the snow, when the car took the ditch because the skid would not hold the road; and the Maylin party. That, I believe, has been preserved by pure anticipation. Both Harry and I looked forward to it with such intense expectation that we could not sleep. Yet we both knew what parties were like, and though we enjoyed them, we preferred, on the whole, some expedition or hunt. We knew also what happened at parties; games and dances and that nothing else could happen at the Maylins'; but we discussed for three days what would happen there.

'I wonder what we'll do at the Maylins'?'

'I suppose there'll be games.'

Then both of us, taken aback by the small reach of our own imagination, would ponder a moment and Harry would say: 'And dances, of course.'

'Oh, yes, Roger de Coverley.'[2]

Again we were dashed. Yet we both agreed that the Maylins' would be a wonderful party. All our expectation, that life held new delights for us round every corner, was fixed on the Maylin party.

Part of our excitement, no doubt, arose from the fact that we were going without Robert, the four of us alone in the first carriage. Robert refused to go. He said he hated parties. Robert, as we knew afterwards, had started badly at school by making a public fool of himself. He had tried to follow Cousin Philip's advice. But he told no one, not even his mother or Delia, about this catastrophe. He showed the effects only by his quietness, his sudden love of being alone, and sometimes a perplexed, absent-minded look when anyone spoke to him, as if he could not understand ordinary meanings.

1. A fictional name for Derry.

2. A popular country dance.

Robert was out of our lives, and Harry was our senior. But this promotion could not explain Kathy's or my or Anketel's excitement.

We were asked to the first, the youngest children's party, for though Harry was already a boarder at school, as senior in charge, he was sent with me, and I was sent with Anketel. I don't know why Kathy was not put in charge of Anketel, but there was a legend even among grown-ups that Anketel preferred any other to take care of him.

We were silent in the carriage, too excited to speak. Only once Harry gave a deep sigh and said: 'They've got two hundred people coming — with grown-ups.'

Silent and oppressed we were led through a large hall into the cloak-room, and then I found myself in a small parlour full of books, with twenty or thirty other children, who stood round the walls with faces so grave and anxious that one would have thought they had all committed some crime. I have seen the same expression in criminals about to be charged, and in a very warm-hearted girl just about to be married. Nervous tension, the feeling of an important crisis, produced the same oppressed gravity in both. While we stood gazing at each other, Harry, who had waited while Kathy found a hook to button her shoes, walked slowly in, and with the same serious face, stopped for a moment, stared round at us, and then went directly to a corner of the bookshelf, from which he pulled out a dictionary. There was a copy, at Dunamara, of the same dictionary which Harry had been reading that afternoon. Harry's first term at a private school seemed to have had no special effect on him, except to give him a passion for encyclopædias and dictionaries.

He sat down on a chair in a corner and began reading the dictionary, as if he had come for no other purpose.

Harry spent almost the whole time of the party reading his dictionary. Afterwards going home in the carriage he asked me to notice the frosforescence of the lough. I asked him what frosforescence was, and he said: 'It's cold and bright. It's due to little jelly-fish.'

He spoke this with the voice of a mystic contemplating wonders. Harry had enjoyed himself. But when he sat down with the dictionary I was left standing against the wall, holding Anketel's hand in such painful shyness that I did not know where to look. Yet I was still overwhelmed by the thought: 'This is the Maylins' party.'

Some grown-up girls now came in and set the children to play oranges and lemons and hunt the slipper. They were experienced girls, elder sisters, and they simply pushed or carried the guests to the allotted places, dumped them on the floor and joined their senseless hands, and then propelled them through the movements of the game. In hunt the slipper four of these grown-ups, sitting like giants in the circle, had the game to themselves, three laughing and throwing the slipper to each other while a fourth chased it; and the small children, the smallest present, sat and gazed at them with awe.

One girl called to another: 'None of them are actually crying,' and another answered in the same tone of hilarious congratulation, which struck upon our ears as assumed and special to the occasion: 'Yes, we're doing rather well.'

Anketel completed my embarrassment by refusing to join any game. As soon as he was invited to hunt the slipper he flew to a chair, climbed upon it, turned himself round and sat down with the air of taking a place for the evening.

I was in terror that some grown-up would attempt to drag him into the game, in case he might fight or scream and I should be disgraced. I begged him to play, but he shook his head firmly.

'Didn't you want to come to the party?'

He nodded.

'But playing is what you do at a party.'

Two grown-up girls joined us and pleaded with him. 'You won't have to do anything — just sit on the floor and pretend you're playing.'

'They won't give *you* the slipper, will they?' I appealed to the girls, who at once promised Anketel complete freedom from responsibility.

Anketel had turned very pale, but he still shook his head. Then suddenly he got off the chair and rushed out of the room. I dutifully followed, but, finding a dance in the next room, was seized and set dancing with a girl who wanted a partner. We did not speak, and as I did not know even what the dance was, we trod on each other's toes. Suddenly Kathy rescued me and made me dance with her, teaching me how to polka. I would have resented having to dance with my cousin Kathy if it had not been at the Maylins' party. It was the fashion to resent everything Kathy did or said to us, to say that she was bossy and selfish. In fact, she was a sensible child, who was always getting us out of trouble, inventing lies for us, smuggling away wet, torn or dirty clothes when we fell out of trees or into the muddy river; or interceding for us with Uncle Herbert, who had a weakness for little girls.

Also she was affectionate and longed for affection. Her father was dead, her mother had married again and had other children. I think Kathy was unhappy at home and looked forward all the year to holidays with us. On the first day of meeting us, she would flush deeply and run up to us as if to kiss us, then check herself and take our hands. We could see that she was almost crying with delight, with relief; her mouth would shake and tears come into her lashes. She would say: '*Isn't* it lovely? Isn't it *lovely*?'

Then Harry would answer, calmly: '*What's* lovely, do you mean the weather?' or I would say carelessly: 'Hullo, Kathy.' I don't know when this fashion to snub Kathy began. She was not ugly. She had very pretty dark brown eyes and bronze hair, even thicker than Frances'. Her voice was hard, but nearly all girls of that age have hard voices. She could play all games with us and even throw a ball, quite as well as I. But because she needed our affection and sought it, we treated her always like an intruder. Perhaps like small animals, our instinct was to pursue only the female who ran away from us, and Kathy, in showing us her affection, was breaking some rule of nature, as cruel and stupid as most of her sexual arrangements.

When Kathy was pursued she could be loved. At Crowcliff the year before Cousin Tom Foley, who was nearly fourteen, had fallen in love with Kathy, and at once Harry had been furiously jealous. He had claimed Kathy, and there had been several fights in which Harry would have been defeated if Kathy herself had not taken his part. I, too, had been in love with Kathy for an hour or two, during a wet picnic, when Harry was away with measles. But since then we had both treated her with consistent brutality. It had been the idea to crush Kathy in every possible way. We even boasted of a successful snub.

At nine Kathy had already a horizontal wrinkle of perplexity between her eyebrows. She looked at us often with blank wonder, asking herself no doubt what crime she had committed, and how she could discover it and make up for it without offending us further. We, feeling her perplexity on such occasions, always looked still more calm and indifferent.

CHAPTER 15

But on this evening, at the Maylins, because I had forgotten the ideas which governed our schoolroom at Dunamara, I was delighted to see Kathy and showed it. My real feeling for Kathy, which was like a brother's, something deeper than affection, instinctive and primitive, was allowed to show itself in the frank relief and satisfaction with which I grasped her hand and cried: 'What are they doing, Kathy? It isn't anything I know, is it?'

Kathy, as usual, blushed to her eyes in pleasure of this warmth of greeting and began at once, with anxious and responsible care, to teach me the steps while I was as polite and deferential with her as if she had been another of the strange girls who, in puffed silk sleeves and frilled and tucked frocks, soberly danced or conversed round me, frowning over their partner's shoulders with looks of preoccupation and anxiety. They, too, were using every moment of the party.

I danced with Kathy for a long time and thanked her effusively for teaching me the steps. Afterwards we went through a lancers together where all the girls, with shrill angry voices, cried out instructions to their partners, and thrusting them furiously away at the end of each figure, shouted: 'Grand chain — do think what you're doing.'

All of us were instructors or pupils; one saw nothing but humble-looking boys carefully performing awkward motions and little girls beckoning at them or blushing for them. At the end of the dance loud angry discussions broke out about who had spoilt what figure and who had torn somebody's frock. The loud voices and frowning faces and angry gestures were those of a fight. Yet when someone proposed another set we clapped and cried out in chorus: 'Please, please.' All faces were full of eagerness, as if for a treat. We wanted it all again, anxieties, reproaches, instruction. I suppose we felt that this was life, that we were finding out how to do it; and that the finding out was itself engrossing. We had not come to the party for pleasure, but to be engrossed.

Some time during these dances I fell in love with Kathy — I kept on looking at her and laughing with pleasure. She seemed to me charming, kind; the nicest girl I have ever met. I began to prance round her as I used to jump aimlessly round my father's legs, running into him. Kathy was gravely delighted.

At nine she was far more mature than I, and I dare say her feelings were deeper and stronger. She kept on restraining my wild leaps, smiling in an embarrassed way, and saying: 'You must dance the steps.' But her voice was full of apology, and when the dance was over we walked into the passage with our arms round each other's waists and agreed we would never love anyone else. Kathy kept saying: 'But do you really want to marry me?' and every time I assured her she sighed deeply and murmured: 'Oh, dear, isn't it lovely here — isn't it a lovely party? It's the loveliest day of my life.' We even kissed each other, and I could see that this meant a great deal to Kathy; it was a pledge.

CHAPTER 16

After tea, of course, all our decorum, our sense of an important occasion, vanished. I had sat next Kathy at tea and we had even held hands, feeding ourselves with the other; but suddenly I jumped down and darted away from her, with a tribe of boys. Drunk with sugar cake and sweets, wearing paper caps, we flew through the rooms yelling, often revolving on our axes, pirouetting because we knew we would soon reach the end of the rooms, and be obliged to turn back.

Now again, in this riot, I came upon Anketel, being implored by two ladies to come to tea. I saw that he was nearly in tears, so I said to them hastily: 'It's no good — he never does anything you ask him — he's my brother, so I know he won't.'

I called Anketel my brother instead of my cousin to make them believe me. They did believe me and went away. I also flew away, leaving Anketel in the ante-room. At some time later when I rushed through the hall to find a partner for Roger de Coverley, I saw him sitting there, on a hard wood hall chair, in the big cold marble-paved room, completely alone. But I pretended not to see him. I had indeed already invented a lie for Frances, that Anketel had run away from me. I knew that Anketel would not contradict me, since, in his silent way, he was extremely loyal to us all. I was already at ease in my mind.

The sequel next day was unexpected. Anketel told Frances that I had been very kind to him and that he had loved the party. What's more, it seemed that he had enjoyed himself. For weeks afterwards he played at parties, by himself; a game which consisted in moving round in circles, and uttering a murmuring noise, broken now and then by sharp, loud cries.

CHAPTER 17

I myself, now free from responsibility, and, as I say, partly drunk, danced a Roger de Coverley, in which several children were battered into tears. We leaped together, stamped our feet, and when the time came to pass under the hands of the top couple, ran our heads against the behinds of the couple in front, and tried to push them down.

I was especially excited to recognise Kathy in the line of girls opposite me, two or three down. She was not drunk. She had been too busy at tea, giving me the best cakes, to eat much herself. She kept looking at me with a perplexed, mournful expression, and these looks caused me explosions of laughter, not malicious, but purely drunken. Indeed, I felt guilty towards Kathy, but my guilt, like all my other reactions, passed at once into wild leaps and shouts of laughter; into a desire for violence. Our dance grew into a war dance. Some of the girls, except the older ones like Kathy, were rougher than the boys. My partner, a fat creature with a red doll-like face, shrieked like an engine whistle, and then, uttering an insane laugh, with protruded stomach and arms held back, rushed against me and bumped into me so violently that I nearly fell. But I got the idea and I also began to bump my stomach against my neighbour's. All of us danced the whole time with our own steps. Even when I stood in the line, watching the end boy and the end girl preparing their *pas de deux* between the lines, I jumped up and down, yelled, and hopped in complete circles, turning my back on the rest. All of us were trying to make as much noise and turmoil as possible, because the noise, as we had discovered, and the wildness of our own kicks and prances, were themselves exciting.

It was during one of these stimulating performances, if not of Roger de Coverley then of some other tribal dance, that a red-cheeked boy, I think he was the brother of my former partner, the Dutch doll, suddenly said to me: 'I say, this is rather dull, isn't it? — jumping about with a lot of kids, it's silly.'

I was in the act of jumping myself round, on both feet, in fits of laughter; and the red-cheeked boy had been one of the noisiest of the party; but the moment he spoke to me in this critical and superior tone, a rapid change began to take place in my mood. It was not instantaneous, because I was never very quick to catch a new suggestion; a change of social atmosphere. I stared at him in open-mouthed surprise for some seconds. But during all this time the change, which may be described as a kind of crystallisation in the chaotic whirl of my brain, was in rapid progress. Fortunately, as it struck me afterwards, I did not say anything at once, I did not blurt out that I was enjoying myself. It was not till the crystallisation was finished, and I had a clear, sharp-edged knowledge, both feeling and idea, of the new situation, that I answered. I stopped jumping about, screwed my face in an expression similar to the red-cheeked boy's, and said: 'Yes, but it always is at the Maylins', isn't it?'

As I said, I had never been to the Maylins' party before. But the red-cheeked boy accepted my statement with respect. He put his hands in his pockets and said: 'Why do they always expect us to hop about with kids in frocks?'

'It's silly, isn't it?'

'I can't stand parties.'

'Neither can I.'

'Let's clear off and do something sensible.'

'I've been wanting to do that for a long time.'

We had already withdrawn from the laughing, jumping crowd, and now when my partner rushed up to me and began shrieking at me and trying to tell me what to do, I shook myself free and walked off with a scornful air. I felt all at once contemptuous of the games going on round me; the music; the paper caps, the yelling and romping children; I began even to feel that I had been a victim, and that I had been obliged to dance and play against my will.

'What shall we do?' the red-cheeked boy asked me. Obviously, he did not know what to do. For some time, in fact, we simply wandered about with our hands in our pockets. At last even I noticed that we were rather bored. Yet we still felt superior to the other children for amusing themselves with childish games, and kept on criticising their idea of amusement and the party. I remember standing watching some uproarious game of puss-in-the-corner, from a doorway, and feeling the most intense longing to shout advice to the corners, and even to rush in and join the game; yet I am sure my face was still fixed in a calm and aloof scorn and my voice still drawled: 'Silly, aren't they?'

'They don't even play it properly,' the other said, moved, I suppose, by my own temptation to give instructions and catch puss on his own account. We lounged there for a long time, envying and despising the happy players. It was as though some command had forbidden us to enjoy childish games, and this, I suppose, is the actual fact. For even though it operated upon me by means of an idea presented by the red-cheeked boy, that idea found in me an instant response. Something in me, unnoticed till that moment, was waiting for just such an idea to give it form and action.

CHAPTER 18

I don't mean that nature or some mysterious power ended my childhood at eight years old. I don't know when my childhood ended or if it is all ended now. The only certain distinction I can find between childhood and maturity is that children grow in experience and look forward to novelty; that old people tend to be set. This does not mean even that children enjoy life more keenly than grown-ups, they are only more eager for experience. Grown-ups live and love, they suffer and enjoy far more intensely than children; but for the most part, on a narrower front. For the average man or woman of forty, however successful, has been so battered and crippled by various accidents that he has gradually been restricted to a small compass of enterprise. Above all, he is perplexed. He has found out numerous holes and inconsistencies in his plan of life and yet he has no time to begin the vast work of making a new one. He is like a traveller who, when he has reached the most dangerous part of his journey among deep swamps and unknown savages, discovers all at once that his map is wrong, his compass broken, his ammunition damp, his rifle crooked, and his supplies running short. He must push on at high speed, blindly, or fail altogether and fail his companions. I think that is the reason for the special sadness of nearly all grown-up faces, certainly of all those which you respect; you read in their lines of repose, the sense that there is no time to begin again, to get things right. The greater a grown man's power of enjoyment, the stronger his faith, the deeper and more continuous his feeling of the waste of life, of happiness, of youth and love, of himself.

But for children life seems endless, and they do not know a grief that has no cure.

PATRICK MACGILL

(1891–1963)

from: THE RAT-PIT (1915)

[MacGill's novel tells the desolate story of the Ryans, a poor family living around the turn of the century on the poverty-stricken seaboard of County Donegal where the author grew up. Like its forerunner, *Children of the Dead End* (1914), it tells an archetypal story of a people torn between starvation at home and the ignominy of migrant labour as 'tatie-hokers' — potato-diggers — in rural Scotland. In Chapter IV of the present novel Fergus Ryan walks out on his family but sends them money for a while from his employment in Liverpool. In the second extract here, the young heroine, Norah Ryan, becomes the uncomprehending register of a traditional way of life with its oral culture — as seen in her mother's repertory of folk-tales — dying on its feet. Norah is portrayed amid the squalor of her Scottish exile, on her pitiable journey through poverty to prostitution — where she meets her brother again — and death.]

CHAPTER VIII

THE TRAGEDY

I

Often a youth leaves Donegal and goes out into the world, does well for a time, writes frequently home to his own people, sends them a sum of money in every letter (which shows that he is not a spendthrift), asking them for a little gift in return, a scapular blessed by the priest, or a bottle of water from the holy well (which shows that he has not forgotten the faith in which he was born); but in the end he ceases to write, drops out of the ken of his people and disappears. The father mourns the son for a while, regrets that the usual money-order is not forthcoming, weeps little, for too much sentiment is foreign to the hardened sensibilities of the poor; the mother tells her beads and does not fail to say one extra decade for the boy or to give a hard-earned guinea to the priest for masses for the gasair's[1] soul. Time rapidly dries their tears of regret, their sorrow disappears and the more pressing problems of their lives take up their whole interests again. In later years they may learn that their boy died of fever in a hospital, or was killed by a broken derrick-jib, or done to death by a railway train. 'Them foreign parts were always bad,' they may say. 'Black luck be with the big boat, for it's few it takes back of the many it takes away!'

A year had passed since James Ryan last heard from Fergus his son. No word came of the youth, and none of the Frosses people, great travellers though the young of Frosses were, had ever come across him in any corner of the world.

'We are missing the blue pieces of paper,'[2] Mary Ryan said to her husband one evening in the late autumn, fully three years after Fergus's departure. She now spent her days sitting at the fire, and though her health was not the best it had greatly improved within recent years. 'They were the papers!' she exclaimed. 'They could buy meal in the town of Greenanore and pay the landlord his rent. Maybe the gasair is dead!'

'Maybe he is,' the husband answered. He was a man of few words and fewer ideas. Life to him, as to the animals of the field, was naturally simple. He married, became the father of many children, all unnecessary to an overcrowded district, and most of them were flicked out by death before they were a year old. Once every eighteen months James Ryan's wife became suddenly irritable and querulous and asked her husband to leave the house for a while. The cattle were allowed to remain inside, the husband went out and walked about in the vicinity of his home for two or three hours. From time to time he would go up to the door and call out: 'Are you all right, Mary?' through the keyhole. 'I am all right, Shemus,' she would answer, and the man would resume his walk. When the wife allowed him to come in he always found that his family had increased in number.

One day a child was born to him, and its third breath killed it. It was the seventh, and the year was a bad one. Potatoes lay rotting in the fields, and the

1. i.e. boy's. From Irish *gasúr*.

2. Money orders from abroad.

peat being wet refused to burn. Somehow James Ryan felt a great relief when the child was buried. Twelve children in all were born to him, and ten of these died before they reached the age of three. 'The hunger took them, I suppose,' he said, and never wept over any of his offspring, and even in time forgot the names of most of those who were dead. The third who came to him was the boy Fergus; Norah was the youngest of all.

'Maybe, indeed, he is dead,' he repeated to his wife. 'I suppose there is nothing for it but to put out the curragh[3] to the fishing again.'

'And never catch anything,' said his wife, as if blaming him for the ill-luck. 'It is always the way. . . . If Fergus would send a few gold guineas now it would be a great help.'

'It would be a great help.'

'We could keep Norah at school for another year.'

'We could.'

'And then send her to the convent like a lady.'

'Just.'

'When are you going to put the curragh out again?'

'Maybe this very night,' answered the husband. 'It is now Michaelmas a week past. There were blue lights seen out beyond the bar last night, and a sea-gull dropped from the sky and fell dead on the rocks of Dooey. The same happened ten years ago, and at that time there was a big catch out by Arranmore.'

'Then you had better go out tonight, for there is not much money in the tea-pot this minute.'

'The byre[4] cost a big penny,' said James Ryan, and he spoke as if regretting something.

'It did that, and the house does not look half as well with the cattle gone from it.' So saying the woman turned over some live turf on the pile of potatoes that was toasting beside the fire, and rising emptied part of the contents of a jug of milk into a bowl. 'It is a wonder that Norah is not in,' she remarked. 'She should be back from school over an hour ago.'

3. A canoe-like boat, tarred canvas stretched over a timber frame.
4. cowshed.

II

At that moment Norah entered, placed her cotton satchel and books on the window sill, and sat down to her meal. She was a winsome girl, neat, delicate and good-looking. She had grown taller; her tresses were glossier, her clear grey eyes, out of which the radiance of her pure soul seemed to shine, were dreamy and thoughtful. She was remarkable for a pure and exquisite beauty, not alone of body, but of mind. She was dressed in peasant garb, but her clothes, though patched and shabby, showed the lines of her well-formed figure to advantage. Her feet were small, an unusual thing amongst country children who run about bare-footed, and her dainty little hands matched her feet to perfection. Her accomplishments were the knowledge of a few Irish songs and country dances, and her intellectual gifts could be summed up in the words, simple innocence.

'Are you getting on well with your lessons, Norah?' asked the father.

Every day for the last two years, on her return from school, he asked a similar question and took no heed of the answer, which was always the same.

'I am getting on very well, father.'

'He's going out to the fishing tonight,' said the mother, handing a bowl of milk to Norah and pointing her finger at her husband.

'Any letter from Fergus?' asked the girl.

'Never a word,' said the mother. 'Maybe one will be here tomorrow.'

'Tomorrow never comes,' said James Ryan. He had heard somebody use this phrase years ago and he repeated it almost hourly ever since. 'It is off on the curragh that I am going now.'

He rose and went out. The dusk had fallen and a heaven of brilliant stars glittered overhead. A light gust of wind surged up angrily for a moment and swept along the ground, crooning amidst rock and boulder. Outside James Ryan stood for a moment and looked up at the sky, his thoughts running on the conversation which had just taken place inside. 'Tomorrow never comes,' he repeated and hurried towards the sea.

Mary Ryan lit the paraffin lamp which hung from the great beam that stretched across the middle of the house. The rushlight was now used no longer; the oil lamp had taken its place in most of the houses in Frosses. Norah finished her meal and turned to her books. For a long while there was silence in the cabin, but outside the wind was rising, whirling round the corners and sweeping in under the door.

'Tell me a story, mother,' Norah said, putting her books aside and curling up like a pretty ball on the earthen floor in front of the fire.

'All right, I will tell you a story, silly baby that you are!' said the old woman, sitting down on the hassock by the hearth. 'Will it be about the wee red-headed man with the flock of goats before him, and the flock of goats behind him, and the salmon tied to the laces of his brogues[1] for supper?'

'Not that one, a maghair,[2] I know it myself.'

'Will it be about Kitty the Ashy pet who said "Let you be combing there, mother, and I'll be combing here," and who went up the Bay of Baltic, carrying the Rock of Cattegat on her shoulders?'

'I know that one, mother.'

'And the Bonnie Bull of Norway you know as well. Then it will be about the cat that would not dress its whiskers if it wasn't in front of the biggest looking-glass in all the world. The biggest looking-glass in all the wide world is the broad ocean in a calm.'

'Not that one, mother.'

'You are hard to please this very night. I will tell you the story of the little green-coated boy who wandered on the rainy roads. . . . There's the wind rising. Mercy of God be on your father if the sea is out of order!'

Mary Ryan began the story which she knew by heart, having heard it so often from the lips of her own mother. Here, it may be remarked, most of the folk stories of Donegal are of Norwegian or Danish origin and have in many cases been so well preserved that the Scandinavian names of people and places are retained in the stories until the present day.

'Once upon a time when cows were kine and when eagles of the air built their nests in the beards of giants, a little green-coated boy with a stick in his hand and a bundle of bannocks[3] over his shoulder went out on the rainy roads to push his fortune —'

1. shoes.
2. Irish: *a mhathair* (mother).
3. Hard oaten cakes.

III

'I'm going to marry a prince when I get very old, mother,' said Norah, interrupting the story-teller. 'Prince Charming, for that's what the girl did in the fairy stories when she grew up and got old at twenty or twenty-one. She was very poor at first and did nothing grand, but stopped at home, sweeping the floor and washing dishes. Then one night an old woman came down the chimney and told the girl to go to a dance, and the girl didn't leave the dance in time and she lost one of her slippers and — Oh! it was a great story, mother. I read it in a book that Fergus had.'

'You were reading those books, too!'

'Just only that one, mother, and Fergus didn't like it at all. He said it was very silly!'

'So it was, alannah, when it put thoughts like that into your head. Marry Prince Charming, and you going to be a holy nun! Nuns never marry like that.'

'Don't they? Well, I'll not marry a Prince Charming. I'll marry one of the White Horsemen who are under the mountain of Aileach.'

'But nuns never marry anybody.'

'They don't?' exclaimed Norah in a puzzled voice. Then with childish irrelevance: 'But tell me the story about the White Horsemen of Aileach, mother. That's the best story of all.'

'Long, long ago, when the red-haired strangers came to Ireland, they put nearly everybody to the sword; the old and young, the fit and feeble, and mind you, Ireland was in worse than a bad way,' the mother began, drifting easily into her narrative. 'Ireland was a great place in those days with castles and kings. Kings, Norah! There were five of them; now there isn't even one in the four corners of the country. But the red-haired strangers came like a storm from the sea and there was no standing before them. Red were their swords, red as their hair, but not with rust but with the blood of men, women, and children. And the chieftains of Ireland and the men of Ireland could make no stand against the enemy at all. "What am I to do?" cried the Ardrigh, the top king of the whole country, speaking from the door of his own castle. "There will soon be no Ireland belonging to me, it will all go to the red-haired strangers." Then up spoke an old withered stick of a man, that nobody knew, and who had been listening to the words of the King.

' "Have you asked the Chieftain of the White Horsemen for help?"

' "I never met him, decent stranger," answered the King. "I know him not."

' "Go to the sea when it strikes in storm on the coast of Tir Conail," said the old man to the king, "and call out to Maanan MacLir for aid and he'll send to your help his ten score and ten white horsemen. You'll see the white horses far out, rearing on the top of the waves, every steed pawing the ocean and all mad for the fight before them."

'Well, to cut a long story short, the King did as he was told and called to the White Horsemen to come and help him, and they came, ten score of them and ten, with their shields shining like polished silver and lances bright as frosty stars. Down from the North they rode, driving the foe on in front of them, and never was seen such a rout, neither in the days that went before nor the days that came after. The White Horsemen cut their way right through mountains in their haste to get to the other side; for nothing could stand against their lances. Nobody could go as quickly as them, not even the red-haired strangers who were in such a hurry to get out of their way.

'And when victory was theirs, the White Horsemen came back here to Tir Conail and stood on the verge of the ocean while Maanan MacLir headed his horse out on the waves. But lo, and behold! the steed could no longer gallop across the water. The poor animal sank into the sea and the chieftain was nearly drowned. At that moment a voice, nobody knew where it came from, called to Maanan MacLir:

' "Long enough has the sea called for the rest and quiet that was not given to it by the white horses of MacLir. Never more will the sea bend under them; now it will break apart and let them through!"

'When they heard these words the White Horsemen turned away from the sea and went galloping to the foot of the Mountain of Aileach. When they arrived there the mountain raised itself upon one side just like the lid of a kettle and Maanan MacLir and his White Horsemen disappeared under it. Since that day they have never been seen again.'

'But the mountain didn't close on top of them, did it?' asked Norah.

'Of course it did. Isn't it closed to this very day?'

'And will it be a true story?'

'True, child!' exclaimed the mother. 'Sure the mountain is there to this very hour. And besides, Saint Columbkille talks about it in his prophecies.'

'Then the White Horsemen will come out again?'

'They'll come out when the great war comes,' said the mother. 'And that will be when there are roads round every mountain like the frills round the cap of an old woman. It will start, the great war, when the nights lengthen and the year grows brown, between the seasons of scythe and sickle; murder and slaughter, madder than cattle in the heat of summer, will run through the land, and the young men will be killed and the middle-aged men and the old. The very crutches of the cripples will be taken out to arm the fighters, and the bed-ridden will be turned three times three in their beds to see if they are fit to go into the field of battle. Death will take them all, for that is how it is to be; that way and no other. And when they're all gone it will be the turn of the White Horsemen, who have been waiting for the great war ever since they chased the red-haired strangers from the country. They'll come out from under Aileach when the day arrives, ten score and ten of them with silver shields and spears, bright as stars on a frosty night. They'll fight the foe and win and victory will come to Ireland. These are the words of the great saint, Columbkille.'![1]

'Are the White Horsemen very tall, mother?' asked Norah, her eyes alight with enthusiastic interest.

'Tall is not the word!'

'High as a hill?'

'Higher!'

'As Sliab a Tuagh?'[2]

'It's as nothing compared to one of the men of Maanan MacLir.'

'Then I'll marry one of the White Horsemen,' said Norah, decision in her clear voice. 'I'll live in a castle, polish his lance and shield, and — Who will that be at the door?'

1. Maanan MacLir is the legendary god of the sea in Celtic mythology. Aileach is a hill-fort outside Derry. Prophecies, attributed to Colmcille, foretell the expulsion of the invader from Ireland by the sleeping warriors who lie below the hill.
2. *Sliabh* is Irish for 'mountain'. This is the name of a mountain in County Donegal.

IV

Norah paused. Someone was moving outside as if fumbling for the latch; then a tall, heavily-bearded man pushed the door of the cabin inwards and entered, bringing with him a terrific gust of wind that almost shook the house to its foundations. On his face was a scared look, and his clothes were dripping wet, although it was not raining.

'Was it himself?' cried the old woman, alluding to her husband and speaking to the man who entered.

It was evident from the tone in which she spoke that she anticipated something terrible.

'It was himself,' said the man in a low, hoarse voice. 'He's coming on the flat of two oars. God bless us! But it is a black heart that the sea has.'

With these words the visitor went out again, and the excited voices of men could be heard floating on the wind.

'It's your father, Norah,' said the old woman. 'He went down with the curragh, I'm thinking; down through the black water. Mother of God! but it's the sea that has the black heart! There they are coming with him. Open the door wider, Norah!'

The girl, who had risen from her seat, pulled the door inwards and placed a stone against the sill to keep it open. She felt as if a thousand pins were pricking her legs; her head was heavy, her fingers felt enormous and when they pressed against the door it seemed to Norah as if they did not belong to her at all. Outside it was very dark, the heavens held no stars and it looked as if the howling gale had whirled them away. In the darkness a torch swayed in the wind, and behind the torch black forms of men and white, pallid faces could be discerned. Norah's mind turned to the stories which her mother had been telling her. She knew it was wrong to think of them at that moment but she felt an inordinate desire to laugh at something; what she wanted to laugh at she did not know; why she wanted to laugh she could not fathom.

'Are they coming, Norah?' asked the old woman, rising from her seat and hobbling with difficulty towards the door. 'Mother of Christ! but the hand of God is heavy on me this night of nights! Children of my own and man of my own, all, all going away from me! I'll see the last of them go down into the grave before me, for with my hard cough and the long sickness I'll outlive them all: that is the will of God. Ten sons and daughters of my body; every one of them gone, and one away in black foreign parts. . . . Are they coming, Norah?'

The woman reached the door and leant against the jamb for support. The torch was flaring outside and very near.

'Watch that you don't set the thatch on fire!' a voice cried.

Two men entered the house, the water streaming from their clothes and each holding a burdened oar in his hands. Across the oars a sail was bound tightly, and cold in death on the sail lay James Ryan, his grey beard sticking out stiffly, his eyes open, his head shaking from side to side, his bare feet blue with the cold. The oars, which brushed sharply against the old woman in passing, were laid on the floor and the dead man was placed on the bed.

'I'm sweatin' like a pig!' said one of the bearers, and he rubbed his wrinkled brow violently with the back of his hand.

'Watch the thatch!' someone outside shouted. The torch was extinguished and a crowd of men entered the cabin. An old red-haired fisherman lifted the oars; the sail was rolled into a bundle and carried out again. Pools of water formed on the floor and tracks of wet feet showed all over it. The old woman hobbled back to her bed and gazed long and earnestly at her husband; some of the men took off their hats; one was smoking, another dressed a bleeding foot and told how he hit it against a sharp rock when carrying the dead man up from the sea; several of the neighbouring women were already in the house. Maire a Crick was on her knees by the bedside.

'I am used to it now,' said the old woman, as she sorted the blankets on the bed with her withered hands. 'Ten sons and daughters, and another away and maybe never hearing from him again. . . . Himself said when he was going out that the morrow never comes.'

She sat down on the edge of the bed, ran her fingers over the wet clothes of her husband, opened his vest, put her hand on his heart, shook her head sadly and buttoned the coat again.

'Just when he was putting out the wind caught him, and he dropped like a stone over the side of the curragh,' the red-haired fisherman was saying. 'But the boat was no good anyway. It is one of the Congested Districts Board's[1] boats that he should have.'

'Where would he get the money to buy one?' asked Maire a Crick, turning round from the prayer which she was saying for the dead man.

'The money can be paid in instalments,' answered the red fisherman. He spoke the Gaelic, as nearly everybody in Frosses did, but the words 'instalments' and 'Congested Districts Board' were said in English. 'Ten pounds the new boats cost, and there is five years allowed for paying the money.'

1. The Congested Districts Board was set up in 1891 to ease conditions in the poorer areas of the west of Ireland.

'The Congested Districts Board is going to be a great help,' someone remarked.

'Is the curragh safe?' asked Mary Ryan, turning round. She was still sitting beside the bed, turning over the clothes with lean, shaky fingers.

'It is at the bottom,' said a neighbour, Eamon Doherty by name. 'It was rotten anyhow, and it hadn't been in wet water for close on two years. . . . Now, I wonder what made Shemus go out on it?'

'Nothing atall, atall left,' said the old woman in a feeble voice. 'If I only had the curragh even. . . . And himself dead after all the times that the sea has bent under him! Never to see him again, never! Isn't it hard to think that a thing like that could be?'

Whereupon, saying this she began to cry, at first quietly, but afterwards, as if getting warmed to the task, more loudly, until her sobs could be heard a hundred yards away from the house.

'If I only had the curragh left!' she repeated time and again.

Norah approached the bed timidly. She had been weeping silently by the door ever since the corpse had been carried in. Death was here in the house; it had already taken possession of her father. And it was with her also. Not tonight nor tomorrow, but at the end of forty years or of fifty, and was it not all the same? And what was this death? She did not know; she only thought it cruel and strange. Her own helplessness in face of such a crisis almost overpowered her. For death there was no help, from it there was no escape. It was all powerful and terrible. Tomorrow and tomorrow might come and go, but her father would lie still and unheeding. He would not return, he could not return. This fact hammered at her mind, and the cruelty of her own thoughts tortured her. She tried to think of something apart from the tragedy, but ever her mind reverted to the one and same dreadful subject. Of a great fact she was certain; one that would never be contradicted. Her father was dead; thousands of years might pass and one truth would still remain unquestioned. Her father was dead. 'To think of it!' she said in a low voice. 'Dead for ever!'

She went down on her knees by the bedside but could not pray. God was cruel; He had no mercy. She sobbed no longer, but with wide, tearless eyes she gazed at the face of her father. It had now become yellow, the lips blue, the nose was pinched and the eyes sunken. The water from his clothes was dripping underneath the bed, and she could hear the drip-drip of it falling on the floor.

Everything in the house had suddenly taken on a different aspect. The bed appeared strange to her; so did the fire, the low droning voices of the neighbours, and the play of light and shadow on the walls. The old cat sitting on top of the dresser, gazing down at her, had a curious look in its wide-open eyes; the animal seemed to have changed in some queer way. Outside the wind was beating against the house and wailing over the chimney. Never in her life before had she heard such a melancholy sob in the wind.

CHAPTER XV

DRUDGERY

I

New potatoes were urgently needed and the potato merchant told Jim to get as many as possible dug on the first afternoon. No sooner had the squad come to the farmhouse than they were shown out to the fields where the green shaws,[1] heavy with rain, lay in matted clusters across the drills. Every step taken relieved the green vegetable matter of an enormous amount of water, which splashed all over the workers as they stumbled along to their toil.

Work started. The men threw out the potatoes with short three-pronged graips;[2] the women girt bags round their waists, went down on their knees and followed the diggers, picking up the potatoes which they threw out. Two basin-shaped wicker baskets without handles were supplied to each woman; one basket for the good potatoes and the other for 'brock,' pig-food.

'It's the devil's job, as the man said,' old Maire a Glan remarked as she furrowed her way through the slushy earth. 'What d'ye think of it, Judy Farrel?' But Judy, struggling with a potato stem, did not deign to answer.

Maire was a hard worker; and it was her boast that she never had had a day's illness in her life. The story had got abroad that she never missed a stitch in a stocking while giving birth to twins, and the woman never contradicted the story. She gathered after Eamon Doherty's 'graip'; old Eamon with a

1. The stalks and leaves of potatoes and turnips.
2. Pronged forks with which potatoes were dug loose.

head rising to a point almost and a very short temper.

Biddy Wor, the mother of seven children, 'all gone now to all the seven ends of the world,' as she often pathetically remarked, gathered the potatoes that Murtagh Gallagher threw out. Biddy's hair was as white as snow, except on her chin, where a dozen or more black hairs stood out as stiffly as if they were starched.

Owen Kelly, another of the diggers, was very miserly and was eternally complaining of a pain in the back. Micky's Jim assured him that a wife was the best cure in the world for a sore back. But Owen, skinflint that he was, considered a wife very costly property and preferred to live without one. He dug for Judy Farrel, the stunted little creature with the cough. She was a very quiet little woman, Judy, had very little to say and, when speaking, spoke as if her mouth was full of something. When pulling the heavy baskets, weighted with the wet clay, she moaned constantly like a child in pain.

Two sisters worked in the squad, Dora and Bridget Doherty, cheery girls, who spoke a lot, laughed easily, and who were similar in appearance and very ugly. Dora worked with Connel Dinchy, son of Oiney Dinchy, an eel-stomached youth over six foot in height and barely measuring thirty-four inches round the chest. He was a quiet, inoffensive fellow, who laughed down in his throat, and every fortnight he sent all his wages home to his parents. Bridget Doherty gathered potatoes for one of the strange men. Both girls were blood relations of Murtagh Gallagher. The other strange man worked in conjunction with Gourock Ellen; Norah Ryan gathered for Willie the Duck; and Ellen's companion, who was known as Annie — simply Annie — crawled in the clay after Thady Scanlon, a first cousin of Micky's Jim. When the baskets were full, Dermod Flynn emptied the potatoes into large barrels supplied for the purpose.

The women worked hard, trying to keep themselves warm. Norah Ryan became weary very soon. The rain formed into a little pond in the hollow of her dress where it covered the calves of her legs. Seeing that the rest of the women were rising from time to time and shaking the water off their clothes, she followed their example, and when standing, a slight dizziness caused her to reel unsteadily and she almost overbalanced and fell. She went down on her knees hurriedly, as she did not want Micky's Jim to see her tottering. If this was noticed he might think her unfit for the job. For the rest of the afternoon she crawled steadily, fearing to rise, and wondered how Gourock Ellen, who was giving voice to a loose and humorous song, could sing on such a day. What troubled Norah most were the sharp pebbles that came in contact with her knees as she dragged herself along. They seemed to pierce through rags and flesh at each movement, and at times she could hardly refrain from crying aloud on account of the pain. Before night, and when she knew that her knees were bleeding, she had become almost indifferent to bodily discomforts.

All the time she was filled with an insatiable longing for home. The farm looked out on the Clyde — the river was a grey blur seen through the driving rain, and a boat passing by attracted her attention.

'Is it an Irish boat?' she asked Willie the Duck, who was whistling softly to himself.

'Aye, sure,' answered Willie without raising his head.

'I wish that I was goin' home in it,' she said plaintively.

'Ireland's much better than this dirty country,' said Maire a Glan, speaking loud enough for the Scotchwoman Annie to hear her.

II

When six o'clock came round Jim pulled out his watch, looked at it severely for a moment and shouted: 'Down graips and run home to yer warm supper!'

'Home!' repeated Maire a Glan, rising awkwardly to her knees. 'Mother of Jesus! it is a home! An old byre and no less, as the man said. Shame be on ye, Micky's Jim!'

'We have no grub and no siller,'[1] said Gourock Ellen, rising briskly and loosing the clay-coated sack from around her waist. 'I'm up to my thighs in clabber,'[2] she added.

'We'll not let ye starve as long as there's a bit at all goin',' said Micky's Jim.

'We'd be pigs if we ate all ourselves when other people have nothin',' remarked Maire a Glan.

1. drink. From Irish *síl* (a drop or trickle).
2. mud.

When the squad went back to the farm a ploughman, a flat-footed, surly fellow with a hare-lip, showed them their quarters in the steading.[3] 'First I'll show ye where ye're to roost,' said the man, and led the way into an evil-smelling byre, the roof of which was covered with cobwebs, the floor with dung. A young fellow, with a cigarette in his mouth, was throwing the manure through a trap-door into a vault underneath. On both sides of the sink, which ran up the middle, was a row of stalls, each stall containing two iron stanchions to which chains used for tying cattle were fastened.

'No need to tie any of ye to the chains, is there?' asked the man with the hare-lip, laughing loudly. 'When ye go to bed at night, close the trap-door,' he continued. 'It will keep the smell of the midden[4] away from you!'

'Aye, sure,' said Willie the Duck.

'Oh! ye're here again, are ye?' asked the ploughman. 'Have ye got the music murderer with ye? This way to see where yer eatin' room is,' said the man, without waiting to hear Willie the Duck's answer to his question.

The byre was built on the shoulder of a hillock; the midden was situated in a grotto hollowed underneath. Behind the dung-hill, in the grotto, the three-legged stove was standing, and already a fire which old Eamon Doherty had kindled was sparkling merrily.

'Watch yerself'!' shouted the ploughman to Dermod Flynn, who was crossing the dung-hill on the way towards the fire. 'That young rascal above will throw down a graipful of dung of yer head if ye're not careful.'

Maire a Glan filled the pot with clean white potatoes and placed them over the blaze. The ploughman sat down on an upended box and lit his pipe; Micky's Jim took the squad back to the byre, which was not fairly clean, and proceeded to make bunks for the night. Four or five level boxes were placed on the floor of each stall, a pile of hay was scattered about on top, and over this was spread two or three bags sewn together in the form of a sheet; sacks filled with straw served as pillows, a single blanket was given to each person, and two of the party had to sleep in each stall.

'Who's goin' to sleep with me?' asked Micky's Jim.

'I will,' said Murtagh Gallagher.

'Ye snore like a pig!'

'What about me?' asked Owen Kelly.

'Ye kick like a colt.'

'Will I do?' asked Willie the Duck.

'Ye do!' cried Micky's Jim, 'ye that was chased out of the graveyard with a squad of worms. None of ye will sleep with me; Dermod Flynn is the man I want. Help me to make the bed, Dermod Flynn,' he said to the youth who was standing beside him.

'It's a fine place this,' said Gourock Ellen as she spread a pile of hay over the boxes in the stalls. 'A gey guid[5] place!'

'D'ye know who slept in that stall last night?' asked Jim.

'A heifer like mysel' maybe,' said Ellen. 'And indeed it had a muckle[6] better place than I had under the bridge.'

'The potatoes are nearly ready,' shouted Maire a Glan, sticking her wrinkled head round the corner of the door.

There was a hurried rush down to the midden. Boxes were upended to serve as seats, the maid-servant at the farm came out in brattie,* shorgun,† and brogues, and sold milk at a penny a pint to the diggers. All, with the exception of Annie, Ellen, and Owen Kelly, bought a pennyworth; Micky's Jim bought a pennyworth for Ellen, Marie a Glan shared her milk with Annie, and Owen Kelly bought only a halfpennyworth, half of which he kept for his breakfast on the following morning.

The potatoes were not ready yet; the water bubbled and spluttered in the pot and shot out in little short spurts on every side. Ellen complained of her legs; they had been horribly gashed during the day and were now terribly sore. She lifted up her clothes as far as her thighs and rubbed a wet cloth over the wounds. Micky's Jim tittered; Dermod Flynn blushed, turned away his head and looked at Norah Ryan. Ellen noticed this and, smiling sarcastically, began to hum:

*An apron made of coarse cloth.

†Short gown. The uniform of the female farm servant: the sleeves of the blouse reach the elbows, the hem of the skirt covers the knees.

3. The outbuildings of a farm.
4. dung-hill.

5. Scottish dialect: a fine good place.
6. much.

When I was a wee thing and lived wi' my granny,
Oh! it's many a caution my granny gied me;
She said: 'Now, be wise and beware of the boys,
And don't let your petticoats over yer knee!'

As she finished the song, Ellen winked at Micky's Jim and Jim winked back. Then she hit her thigh with her hand and shouted: 'Not a bad leg that for an old one, is it?'

The potatoes were now emptied into a wicker basket, the water running through the bottom into the midden. The men and women sat round the basket, their little tins of milk in their hands, and proceeded to eat their supper. The potato was held in the left hand, and stripped of its jacket with the nail of the right thumb. Gourock Ellen used a knife when peeling, Willie the Duck ate potato, pelt and all.

While they were sitting an old, wrinkled, and crooked man came across the top of the dung-hill, sinking into it almost up to his knees and approached the fire. His clothes were held on by strings, he wore a pair of boots differing one from the other in size, shape, and colour. Indeed they were almost without shape, and the old man's toes, pink, with black nails, showed through the uppers.

Gourock Ellen handed him three large potatoes from the basket.

'God bless ye, for it's yerself that has the kindly heart, decent woman,' said the old fellow in a feeble voice, and he began to eat his potatoes hurriedly like a dog. Dermod handed him part of a tin of milk and blushed at the profuse thanks of the stranger.

'It's a fine warm place that ye are inside of this night,' said the old fellow when he had finished his meal.

'It's a rotten place,' said Dermod Flynn.

'It's better nor[7] lyin' under a hedge,' answered the old man.

'Or under a bridge,' Gourock Ellen remarked, lifting her dress again; then, as if some modest thought had struck her, dropping it suddenly.

'Why do ye lie under a hedge?' Dermod asked, and the old man thereupon gave a rambling account of his misfortunes, which included a sore back and inability to labour along with sound men. He had come from Mayo years ago and had worked at many a hard job since then, both in England and Scotland. Now that he was a homeless old man nobody at all wanted him.

When the party went up to the byre he stretched out his old thin limbs by the fire and fell into the easy slumber of old age. Suddenly he awoke with a start to find the fire still burning brightly and a beautiful girl with long hair flung over her shoulders looking at him. It was Norah Ryan; the old man thought for a moment that he was looking at an angel.

'God be good to me!' he cried, crossing himself; 'but who is yerself?' Then as recollection brought him a face seen at the fire, he exclaimed: 'Arrah, sure it's yerself that is the colleen I was after seein' sittin' here a minute ago. Now, isn't it a good cheery fire?'

'Have ye any home to go to?' asked Norah.

'Never a home,' said the old man, resting one elbow in the ashes. 'There is nothin' but the rainy roads and the hardships for a man like me.'

'But could ye not get inside of some house for the night?'

'God look on yer wit!' said the old fellow, laughing feebly. 'Ye're just new over, I'll warrant, and ye haven't come to learn that they have forgotten all about kindness in this country. They do not want the man with no roof-tree over his head here. They're all black and bitter Protestants.'

'So I heard say.'

'Ye'll be one of the right sort, I'll go bail.'

'I'm a Catholic.'

'Ah! that's it! The Catholics are the best, and I'm one meself just as ye are, girsha.[8] Have ye a penny to spare for one of yer own kind?'

'Are ye goin' back to Ireland again?' asked Norah, drawing the weasel-skin purse from the pocket of her steaming dress.

'If only I had the price of the boat, I'd go in a minute,' said the man, fixing greedy eyes on the purse which Norah held in her hand. 'But I'm very poor, and mind ye I'm one of yer own sort. Maybe ye have a sixpence to spare,' he said.

Norah possessed a two-shilling piece, all the money she had in the world, and she needed it badly herself. But the desire to help the old man overmastered her, and she handed him the florin. Followed by the garrulous thanks of her penniless countryman she hurried back to the byre, feeling in some curious way ashamed of her kindness.

7. than.

8. girl.

III

A candle fixed on top of a stanchion threw a dim light over the byre, and long black shadows danced on roof and wall. A strong, unhealthy odour pervaded the whole building; the tap at one end was running, and as the screw had been broken the water could not be turned off. Micky's Jim sat in a cattle-trough sewing bags together with a packing needle; these were to be used as a quilt. Dermod Flynn, who was undressing, slipped beneath the blankets with his trousers still on as Norah Ryan came in, but Willie the Duck, stripped to the pelt, stood for a moment laughing stupidly, the guttering candle lighting up his narrow, hairy face and sunken chest.

Old Owen Kelly was already in bed.

'This place is a lot better than where we slept last year,' he called to Micky's Jim.

'Where did ye sleep last year?' asked Dermod Flynn.

'In the pig-sty,' said Jim. 'We were almost eaten alive by the blue lice.'

The women undressed in the shadow at the far end of the stalls, and from time to time Micky's Jim peeped round the corner. When the women looked up he would shout out: 'I see something,' and whistle lightly between the thumb and middle finger of his right hand. The Irishwomen undressed under the blankets, the two strange women, careless and indifferent to the jibes of Micky's Jim, stripped off to their chemises in full view of the occupants of the byre. Annie and Gourock Ellen had quarrelled about something; they were not going to sleep together that night.

'Ye have to sleep with me, lass,' said Gourock Ellen to Norah.

'All right,' said the young girl quietly, seeing no reason why she should not sleep with a strange woman. As she spoke she went down on her knees to say her prayers.

'Say one prayer for me, just a short one,' said Ellen in a low tone.

'All right, decent woman,' answered the girl.

'I'll put the light out now,' shouted Micky's Jim after a short interval. 'The women will not be ashamed to go on takin' off their clothes now.'

The light went out, but Jim suddenly relit the candle, and the guttering blaze again flared weakly through the gloom. There was a hurried movement of naked flesh in the women's quarters and a precipitate scampering under the blankets.

'That was a mortal sin, Micky's Jim,' Norah Ryan said in a low voice, and in her tones there was a suspicion of tears.

BRINSLEY MacNAMARA

(1890–1963)

from: THE VALLEY OF THE SQUINTING WINDOWS (1918)

[As its title suggests, *The Valley of the Squinting Windows* is a work of satire in which the village community of Garradrimna — the author's title for his native Delvin, Co. Westmeath — is made to stand for Irish rural life in its less acceptable features of puritan hypocrisy, calumny and intolerance. Rebecca Kerr, an attractive and sensitive young Donegal woman, comes as an assistant teacher to this midland community, where she falls in love with Ulick Shannon, a pleasant but feckless son of a local rich landowner. When she becomes aware that she is pregnant, her letter informing Ulick is opened and read by the postmistress, who divulges its message to Mrs Wyse, head of the girls' school; it is subsequently read by Ulick's uncle, who conceals its contents from his nephew. As Chapter 29 opens, Rebecca is about to receive the weight of the town's malice.]

CHAPTER 29

More than ever on this morning was Rebecca aware that the keen eye of Mrs. Wyse was upon her as she moved about the schoolroom. One of the bigger girls was despatched to the other school for Monica McKeon and Master Donnellan's assistant came in to Mrs. Wyse. She nodded the customary greeting to Rebecca as she passed in. This interview was unusual at such an early hour of the day. But it was never the custom of either of them to tell her of what they were talking. As she busied herself teaching the very smallest of the children she felt that the eyes of both women were upon her.

After what appeared to be a very long time Monica passed out.[1] On this second occasion she looked loftily across her glasses and gave no nod of acknowledgment to Rebecca. Rebecca blushed at this open affront. She felt that Mrs. Wyse must have something against her, something she had told Monica just now. . . . And now the principal was exceedingly busy with her pen as if writing a hurried note. . . . Rebecca heard the high, coarse voice raised in command:

'Euphemia McGoldrick,[2] I want you!'

Then came the timid 'Yes, ma'am!' of Euphemia.

'Here are two letters, child. Take this one to Father O'Keeffe, your parish priest, and this to your mother, like a good child.'

'Yes'm!'

Some fear of unknown things began to stir in the breast of Rebecca. This connection of Mrs. McGoldrick with Mrs. Wyse's occupation of the morning seemed to announce some dragging of her into the matter. But as yet, although her mind moved tremulously in its excitement, she had, curiously enough, no suspicion of what was about to happen. It could not be that Mrs. Wyse had suspected. Oh, not at all. There was still no danger. But it might be a near thing. . . . Already she had begun to wonder would Ulick come tonight. But of course he would come. He was not such a bad fellow. And he might be taken up with his own condition just now. He had missed his examination in Dublin: missed it, maybe, through his foolishness in coming to see her. . . . But already she had thoroughly blamed herself for this. . . . To ease the pain of her mind she went busily about her work. She knew that the eye of Mrs. Wyse was upon her and that the very best way of defeating it was by putting on this air of industry. The day, in its half-hour divisions, was passing rapidly towards noon.

1. i.e. went out.
2. The daughter of Rebecca Kerr's landlady.

A little girl came quickly in to say that Father O'Keeffe was coming up the road. Rebecca glanced out of the window and, sure enough, there he was upon his big, fat, white horse coming into the yard. She heard his loud cries calling into the Boys' School 'for a chap to come out and hold his horse.' When the boy came to do his bidding he held forth at great length upon the best way of leading 'King Billy' around the yard.

Then the reverend manager of Tullahanogue Schools moved into the female portion of the establishment. At the door he twisted his round face into an aspect of severity which was still humorous in its alien incongruity. Here also he removed his hat from his head, which was white and bald like the apex of an egg above the red curve of his countenance. It was his custom to visit the schools of which he was manager, thus precociously to make up in some way for what he lacked in educational knowledge and enthusiasm. As his short, squat figure moved up the passage by the desks, the massive head bowed low upon the broad chest and the fat finger of both hands coiled behind his back, he was not at all unlike an actor made up as Napoleon Bonaparte. His voice was disciplined in the accents of militarism and dictatorship.

Rebecca noticed on the instant that today he was as one intensified. He began to slap his legs continuously with his silver-mounted riding whip. He did not speak to her as he passed in. But, although it caused her heart to flutter for a moment, this appeared to her as no unusual occurrence. He never took notice of her unless when she called at the vestry after Mass upon occasion to deliver up a slice of her salary in Dues and Offerings. Then the Napoleonic powerfulness disappeared and he fell to talking, with laughter in his words, about the richness of Royal Meath[3] in comparison with the wild barrenness of Donegal.

He moved up to where Mrs. Wyse was at work. Rebecca could distinctly hear the loud 'Well, what's your best news?' with which he always prefaced his conversations. In low whispers they began to communicate. . . . It was not till now that she began to have immense doubts as to the purpose of his

3. The novel is set in the rich pasturelands of Royal Meath, the Celtic kingdom that predated the Elizabethan division of Ireland into counties. Rebecca is from north-western County Donegal.

visit, and already she was trembling in presence of the little children.

'An example of her, Father!'

'Oh, yes, an example of her. Nothing less, Mrs. Wyse!'

The words came down to Rebecca clearly through the deep silence that had fallen upon the school since the entrance of Father O'Keeffe. The bigger girls were listening, listening in a great hush of patience, for all that had to be reported when they went home. Each one was preparing for her respective examination —

'Was there any one in the school today?'

'Yes, mother.'

'Who, the inspector?'

'No, the Priest!'

'Father O'Keeffe?'

'Well, anything else?'

'He was talking to Mrs. Wyse.'

'And what was he saying?'

'I couldn't hear, mother, so I couldn't.'

'And why didn't you listen? What am I slaving myself to send you to school for?'

And so they were listening with such eagerness now. They were looking down at Rebecca as if she were the object of the whole discussion. Her thoughts were beginning to well into a swirling unconsciousness. . . . Great sounds, like those of roaring cataracts and the drumming of mighty armies were rolling up to her ears.

Father O'Keeffe and Mrs. Wyse now came down the schoolroom together. As they passed Rebecca, Father O'Keeffe beckoned to her with his riding-whip in the way one might call to a very inferior hireling. Shaken by unique and powerful impulses, she went out into the hall-way to meet her superiors. . . . Instantaneously she knew what had happened — they knew.

'Well, isn't this a nice thing?' began Father O'Keeffe.

'Ye might say it's a nice thing, Father!' echoed Mrs. Wyse.

'An enormous thing!'

'A terrible thing! Father!'

'You're a nice lady!' he said, addressing Rebecca angrily. 'To come into a parish where there is none save decent people to leave a black disgrace upon it and you going away!'

'Was ever the like known, Father? And just imagine her keeping it so secret. Why, we thought there was nothing in this affair with Ulick Shannon. There was such an amount of cuteness in the way they used to meet at times and in places we never knew of. In the woods, I suppose!'

Father O'Keeffe was addressing her directly again.

'Why, when I think of the disgrace of this school and all that, it drives me near mad.'

'And, mind you, the shocking insult it is to me and to the little children.'

'The shocking insult to you and to the little children. True for you, Mrs. Wyse.'

'And when I think of how you have contrived to besmirch the fair name of one of the fine, respectable families of the parish, gentlemen, as you might say, without one blot upon their escutcheon.'

'People as high up as the Houlihans of Clonabroney.'[4]

'People as high up as the Houlihans of Clonabroney, Mrs. Wyse.'

His eye was upon Rebecca with a sudden gleam.

'When I think of that, I consider it an enormous offence. . . .' She did not flinch before them. She was thinking only of the way in which they had come to hear it. . . . She was concerned now that Ulick should not suffer, that his grand family name should not be dragged down with hers. . . . If he had not come to her she would have slipped away without a word. . . . And now to think that it had become public. The previous burning of her mind had been nothing to this. . . . But Father O'Keeffe was still speaking:

'Listen to me, girl! You are to go from hence, but not, as you may imagine, to the place from whence you came. For this very evening I intend to warn your pastor of your lapse from virtue while in our midst, so that you may not return to your father's house and have no more hope of teaching in any National school within the four seas of Ireland.'

'That is only right and proper, Father!' put in Mrs. Wyse.

Rebecca was not listening or else she might have shuddered within the shadow of the torture his words held for her. In these moments she had soared far beyond them. . . . Through the high mood in which she was accepting her tragedy she was

4. Rebecca had been a private tutor to two children whose mother was a 'Houlihan of Clonabroney'.

becoming exalted. . . . What glorious moments there would be, what divine compensation in whispering of the torture surrounding its beginning to the little child when it came?

'So now, Rebecca Kerr, I command you to go forth from this school and from the little children that you corrupt towards your own abomination by further presence among them.'

As he moved angrily out of the school she moved quietly, and without speaking a word, to take her coat and hat down from the rack.

'Oh, wait!' commanded Mrs. Wyse, 'you must not leave until three, until you have made an example of yourself here in a way that all the children may bring home the story. God knows it will be the hard thing for them to be telling their mothers when they go home. The poor little things!'

Rebecca stood there desolately alone in the hallway through the remainder of the afternoon. In one aspect she appeared as a bold child being thus corrected by a harsh superior. On many more occasions than appeared absolutely necessary Monica McKeon passed and re-passed her there as she stood so lonely. The assistant of the Boys' School was a model of disdain as, with her lip curled, she looked away out over her glasses. And ever and anon Mrs. Wyse passed in and out, muttering mournfully to her:

'The cheek of that now, before the children and all!'

And the elder girls moved about her in a procession of sneering. They knew, and they were examining her for the purpose of giving full accounts when they went home.

But, occasionally, some of the little ones would come and gaze up into her eyes with wild looks. Although they did not know why, they seemed to possess for her an immense mute pity.

'Poor Miss Kerr!' they would say, stroking her dress, but their big sisters would come and whisk them away.

'Don't touch her. She's dirty —' Then Monica would pass again. At last she heard the merciful stroke of three.

[Rebecca, having packed her bags in McGoldrick's house, and waited in vain for her lover, Ulick, prepares to depart for the nearby railway town of Kilaconnaghan (Longford).]

CHAPTER 30

. . . Outside the garden gate of Sergeant McGoldrick Charlie Clarke was waiting for her with his motor-car. Her trunk had been put in at the back. This was an unholy job for a saintly chauffeur, but it was Father O'Keeffe's command and his will must be done. When the news of it had been communicated to him he had said a memorable thing:

'Well, now, the quare jobs a religious man has sometimes to do; but maybe these little punishments are by way of satisfaction for some forgotten and far-distant sin!'

Rebecca understood his anxiety to have her off his hands as she saw him jump in behind the wheel at her approach. She got in beside her poor trunk, and presently the car would be ready to start. There was not a trace of any of the McGoldrick family to be seen. . . . But there was a sudden breaking through the green hedge upon the other side of the road, and Janet Comaskey stood beside the car. Rebecca was surprised by the sudden appearance of the little, mad girl at this moment.

'Miss Kerr, Miss Kerr!' she called. 'I got this from God. God told me to give you this!'

The car started away, and Rebecca saw that the superscription on the letter she had been handed was in the pronounced Vere Foster[1] style of Master Donnellan.[2] Doubtless it was some long-winded message of farewell from the kind-hearted master, and she would not open it now. It would be something to read as she moved away towards Dublin.

Just now her eyes were being filled by the receding pageant of the valley, that place of all earth's places which had so powerfully arrayed its villainy against her. . . . And to think that he had not come. . . . It was the Valley of Hinnom[3]. . . . Yes, to think that he had not come after all she had been to him, after all the love of her heart she had given him. No word could ever, ever pass between them again. They were

1. Vere Foster (1819–1900), an Anglo-Irish philanthropist who, among many other activities, devised copy-books to teach children proper handwriting.
2. Based on the author's father, Master Donnellan is the only portrayal of a mature decent person, apart from the heroine, in the novel. It is a matter of history that MacNamara senior lost his post in Delvin school as a result of the publication, which was burnt publicly in the village.
3. The valley of Gehenna, infamous in the Bible for human sacrifice and other abominations.

upon the very brink of the eternity of separation. She knew now that for all the glory in which she had once beheld him, he must shrivel down to the bitter compass of a little, painful memory. Oh, God! to think he had not replied to her letter, and the writing of it had given her such pain.

They were at the station of Kilaconnaghan. Charlie Clarke had not spoken all through the journey, but now he came up to her indignantly, as if very vexed for being compelled to speak to her at all, and said: 'The fare is one pound!'

The words smote her with a little sense of shock. She had been expecting something by way of climax. She was very certain in her consciousness that the valley would not let her slip thus quietly away — A pound for the journey, although it was Father O'Keeffe who had engaged the car — She must pay this religious robber a huge price for the drive. There rushed through her mind momentarily a mad flash of rebellion. The valley was carrying its tyranny a little too far. . . . She would not pay. . . . But almost immediately she was searching for a note in her purse. . . . There were so very few of them now. Yet she could not leave the valley with any further little stain upon her. They would talk of a thing like this for years and years.

With a deadly silence hanging over him and fearful thoughts coming into his mind, Myles Shannon had kept himself and his nephew Ulick at work all through the day. After tea in the lonely dining-room he fetched in his inky account books, which had been neglected for many a month. His nephew would here have work to occupy him for the remainder of the evening and probably far into the night. Ulick was glad of the task, for his mind was very far from being at ease.

Then Mr. Shannon took £100 from the old-fashioned bureau in the parlour, which held, with the other things, all his papers and accounts, and while the evening was yet high went down towards the house of Sergeant McGoldrick to see Rebecca Kerr. Around a bend of the road he encountered Charlie Clarke on his way back from Kilaconnaghan, where he had been delayed upon a bazaar business.

The saintly chauffeur at once put on the brakes. This was Mr. Myles Shannon and some one worth speaking to. He bowed a grovelling salute.

'You're out pretty late?' said Mr. Shannon.

'Oh, yes!' And then he went on to describe his work of the evening. He felt inclined to offer his condolence to Mr. Shannon in a most respectful whisper, but thought better of it at the last moment.

'And no one knows where she has gone?'

'No one. She has disappeared from the valley.'

'She went away very suddenly.'

'Yes, Father O'Keeffe saw that, in the public interest, she should disappear after this fashion. The motor car was a help, you know.'

Charlie Clarke offered to drive Mr. Shannon to his home. No word passed between them as they drew up the avenue to the lonely house among the trees.

In the train, moving on towards Dublin, Rebecca Kerr had just opened the letter from Master Donnellan. It contained a £5 note. . . . This was like a cry of mercy and pardon for the valley. . . . The rich fields of Meath were racing by.

EIMAR O'DUFFY

(1893–1935)

from:
THE WASTED ISLAND (1919)

[O'Duffy's long and sometimes rather shapeless novel on Ireland in the years leading up to the Easter Rising of 1916 combines the *bildungsroman* with political and social satire. It traces the growth to manhood of Bernard Lascelles, son of a titled Huguenot doctor and a catholic mother whose 'veins flowed with the attenuated blood of a very ancient Ulster clan'. The divided loyalties of the young hero's soul are made the ground of conflict in O'Duffy's fictional world. The potent early influence of his travelled uncle, Christopher O'Reilly, fortifies him against the anglicizing forces of an English boarding school.

The novel embodies most of the issues that agitated pre-revolutionary Dublin: Sinn Féin, the Literary Revival, the Boer War, the Labour struggle, recruitment for the British army, the founding of the Volunteers (with whom Bernard enlists), playing an active part in the Howth gun-running. He is imprisoned twice in the course of the novel's action and loses his fiancée, Mabel Harvey, whose mother deplores his politics. The novel is further significant in letting us see the action from the viewpoint of the catholic middle classes, and refracting it through the incessant discussions of Bernard and his friends, Brian Mallow, Hector O'Flaherty, Hugo McGurk, Stephen O'Dwyer, Cyril Umpleby — those who go to the Front or to the barricades, or those who, like Stephen, obey the order of Eóin MacNeill, chief of staff of the Volunteers, who countermanded the Rising.]

CHAPTER XVI

CATASTROPHE

1

All Dublin — that is to say, all Dublin that felt that it really counted and a good proportion that had no idea that it didn't — was at Fairyhouse Races on Monday. The society papers said all Dublin was there, and as definitions are valuable to students and statisticians let it here be stated that in this context 'all Dublin' means and includes five peers, six baronets, eleven knights, two generals, an indeterminate number of colonels, captains, and subalterns, some hundreds of untitled gentry, and some thousands of the commonalty: with women and children over and above. The Earl and Countess of Ringsend were there, with their son Lord Sandymount. Sir Swithin and Lady Mallaby Morchoe were there; and Sir Marmaduke and Lady Perry; and Sir John and Lady Bonegraft (newly titled and striving to appear unconscious of it); Mr. and Mrs. Gunby Rourke were there; and Sir Eugene Lascelles; and Mrs. Harvey (whose newly acquired son-in-law had evidently been a sound investment). It was a most brilliant assembly.

The refreshment-room behind the Grand Stand hummed with conversation during the luncheon hour.

'How dowdy Lady Inchicore is!' said Mrs. Moffat to Mrs. Metcalfe. 'Really, my dear, if I were a Countess I think I'd treat myself to a new hat now and then.'

'It's a long time since Mrs. Harvey appeared in society,' said Mrs. Metcalfe. 'Has she come in for money?'

'My dear, haven't you heard?' said Mrs. Moffat, and proceeded to explain. . . .

'How well Sir Eugene bears his sorrow!' said Lady Bonegraft to Mrs. Gunby Rourke. 'So brave and patriotic of him, isn't it?'

Sir Eugene at the moment was enjoying a paternal flirtation with a pert little miss of seventeen. Sir John Bonegraft, who hated him, interrupted heavily, saying:

'Hello, Lascelles! Is that boy of yours out of jail yet?'

Sir Eugene flushed angrily and said:

'I know nothing whatever about him.' Whereat Sir John emitted his thumping laugh and went off to mimic him to Sir Marmaduke Perry. . . .

A young man came into the refreshment-room breathless with excitement and blurted out to the first person he saw:

'Heard the news? . . . Ructions in town . . . Sinn Feiners out . . . Shooting everybody . . . The Castle taken . . .'

People pressed round him eager for news, which however was received with incredulity.

'A mere street riot, I'm sure,' said Sir Eugene Lascelles.

'No. They've got the Castle.'

'Disloyal beggars!'

'What's all the excitement?' someone asks, pressing into the circle. The story is told again. There is a babel of questions and comments.

'Sin Fainars: what are they?'

'But they've got the Castle. . . .'

'It's all nonsense.'

'They ought to be shot.'

'I *knew* this would happen.'

'This weak-kneed Government!'

'What can you expect with a man like Birrell?'[1]

'German gold, you may be sure . . . .'

'And in the middle of the Great War too!'

'I hope they'll all be shot.'

'I'll bet it's all over by this time.'

These are samples of the more intelligent of the

1. Augustine Birrell (1850–1933), chief secretary for Ireland 1907–16. His failure to avert the Rising led to his retirement from politics.

remarks which filled the air. The excitement lasted for some ten or fifteen minutes, but for lack of definite information it quickly subsided, and incredulity took its place. Interest returned to the races. . . .

The road was packed with pedestrians and vehicles when it was all over. The humble commonalty footed it to the station, or cycled, or crowded in half-dozens on to outside cars, while motors of every description, humming, hooting and screaming, threaded their courses Dublinwards through this chattering, jangling confusion. Mr. and Mrs. Gunby Rourke in their magnificent Rolls Royce were the first to extricate themselves from the multitude and hasten down a clear road towards the city, to their ultimate undoing; for at the end of a long suburban road they came upon the outermost of the barricades.

It was a ramshackle structure. An overturned tramcar made up nearly half of it; the remainder consisting of a couple of motor-cars, half a dozen bicycles, a few paving-stones, some sandbags, and the pillage of a second-hand furniture shop. There was a gap at one end. The fortification was manned by five men in the grey-green uniform of the Volunteers, and rifles could be seen projecting from the windows of the houses that flanked it. The inhabitants of the district, respectable and ragged, stood about staring, grumbling, or cursing.

'Halt!' rang out the voice of one of the garrison; and, as if to guarantee the seriousness of the command, there burst forth the sound of rifle-fire from a distant quarter of the city.

'Don't mind him,' said Mrs. Gunby Rourke to her chauffeur, who had slackened speed. 'Drive for the gap.'

'I'll blow your brains out if you do,' said the Volunteer, whereat the great Rolls Royce stopped dead.

'What impertinence!' cried Mrs. Gunby Rourke. 'Drive on, Jennings.'

'We'd best go back, madam,' said Jennings.

'Ye'll do nothing of the sort, then,' said the sentry. 'If ye move wan inch I'll shoot ye dead.'

'This is outrageous!' said Mrs. Gunby Rourke. 'What can we do, Arthur?'

'I'm afraid we must bow to the inevitable, dear,' said Mr. Gunby Rourke.

Another Volunteer, evidently a section-commander, now came out of one of the houses and crossed the barricade.

'We'll have to commandeer this car,' he said, fingering the handle of a revolver at his belt. 'May I ax ye to step out?'

Mrs. Gunby Rourke was perfectly furious at this. 'Do you know who I am, sir?' she demanded.

'Ye may be the Empress o' Chiney, ma'am, but we've got to finish this barricade, and that car o' yours'll just do it.'

Mrs. Gunby Rourke was almost speechless with indignation. She gasped incoherently and then turned on her husband, who was lying back in his seat passively smoking a cigar.

'Are you going to sit there quietly and hear me insulted?' she asked.

Mr. Gunby Rourke waved his cigar helplessly and said:

'What can one do, my dear?'

'Do!' exclaimed his wife, and became incoherent again.

'Arrah, be aisy, ma'am,' said the Volunteer. 'We won't do y'anny harm, an' when the Republic's established sure we'll give ye compensation for the car. Will ye dismount if ye please?'

Mrs. Gunby Rourke turned her outraged eyes to heaven and sat still, but her husband and the chauffeur alighted.

'Come along, my dear,' said the former. 'We must yield to superior force for the moment, but they'll all be shot in a few days.'

Mrs. Gunby Rourke made no answer, but, seeing the Volunteer lovingly fondle the handle of his revolver, she descended from the car and walked off on her husband's arm. The Rolls Royce was stuffed into the gap in the barricade.

2

A shot and its echo sounded in the far distance. Bernard dropped the book he was reading and listened. Another shot rang out close at hand. Then silence.

He heard someone come down the stairs at a run, and in a moment John Malone burst into the room.

'Did you hear it?' he cried. 'They're suppressing the Volunteers!'

Another distant shot was heard, followed by two others in rapid succession. A chill sense of realisation came to Bernard.

'It isn't that,' he said. 'It's a rebellion.'

'Hurroosh!' cried Malone. 'I guess I'm going for my gun.' And he rushed out.

At the same moment Bernard heard the tramp of feet in the street outside, and going to the window he saw a squad of men in green uniforms marching up the street.

'Foiled again,' he muttered; and added: 'Poor devils!'

Malone returned, carrying his rifle.

'Aren't you coming?' he said.

Bernard knew it would be useless to enter into a discussion with him, so he merely said:

'Not yet. Don't wait for me.'

Malone disappeared. Bernard went out a few minutes later. Hurrying down Harcourt Street, he was struck by the unnatural quietness everywhere. Traffic seemed to have been suspended, and people stood at their doors or in little groups on the sidewalks, talking in subdued tones, with every now and again an anxious glance down the street in the direction of Stephen's Green. Arriving at the corner Bernard saw a little bunch of people being hustled out of the Park by some of the Citizen Army,[2] who, as soon as the last of the civilians had been thrust outside closed the gate and secured it with a lock and chain. In a shrubbery inside the railings half a dozen of the men in green were digging entrenchments. The people who had been expelled from the Green stood staring at them, and from the open doors and windows of all the houses in the neighbourhood the inhabitants were staring hard. Passers-by in the street stopped and stared in their turn. There seemed to be nothing else for people to do but to stare: they were too much puzzled and stupefied to talk. An ominous silence reigned over all, broken only by the clink and scrape of the tools of the trench-diggers and the occasional pop of a distant rifle.

Bernard had no time to stop and stare. He walked on along the east side of the square until he reached Grafton Street, where he stopped abruptly on seeing a section of his own company marching towards him. Bernard succeeded in catching the commander's eye and raised his hand, whereupon the latter halted his men, came over to Bernard, saluted, and stood to attention.

'How's this, Muldoon?' asked Bernard. 'How did you come to be mobilised without me.'

'Captain Skehan mobilised us, sir,' replied Muldoon.

'*Captain* Skehan?' queried Bernard.

'Yes, sir. He showed us his promotion order signed by Commandant-General Pearse. . . . I thought you'd been promoted to the Staff maybe, Captain.'

'Not exactly, Muldoon,' said Bernard. 'In fact, I rather fancy I've been cashiered.'

'I'm sorry to hear that, Captain.'

'This rebellion isn't an Executive affair at all, you know. It's a mutiny against the President as a matter of fact. The whole thing's a frightful mix-up and there's no time to explain it. I'm going down to Headquarters now to see what can be done. Meanwhile, what'll you do?'

'I suppose I'll have to carry out me orders, Captain. But between ourselves I don't know what we're out for. We'll be bet for certain.'

'Something may be done yet. Where are Headquarters, by the way?'

'At the G.P.O., Captain.'

'Very well. I suppose you'd better carry on for the present.'

Muldoon saluted and returned to his men. Bernard resumed his way, passed down Grafton Street and Westmoreland Street, and, arriving at O'Connell Bridge, ran into Stephen and Hector.

'Well,' said Stephen, 'what do you think of this piece of lunacy?'

'Can nothing be done?' asked Bernard.

'Look,' said Stephen, and pointed down Sackville Street. The Republican Tricolour of Orange, White and Green was flying from the roof of the General Post Office.

'There's been a scrap already,' said Hector. 'A party of Lancers[3] went down the street about ten minutes ago and were fired on. Three were killed.'

'Nothing can stop it now,' said Stephen.

There was a burst of firing far away on the south side of the city.

'Attack on Portobello Barracks, I suppose,' suggested Hector.

Excited groups of people were standing about on and near the bridge discussing the situation. Stray words from some of them reached Bernard's ears: 'Bloody fools!' 'What the hell do they think they're

2. A militia founded by James Connolly in the interest of the trade union movement; committed to the nationalist cause in the Rising.

3. A regiment of horse-soldiers, the first to charge the GPO.

up to?' 'I hope they'll all be shot.'

'The Republic doesn't seem to be exactly popular,' observed Hector. 'Physical force won't have much stock in the country when the dust-up is over.'

'I hope to Heaven the country'll keep quiet,' said Stephen. 'How did things look where you were?'

'They didn't seem at all anxious to come out,' replied Bernard.

'I bet they won't like abandoning Dublin,' said Hector.

'Well, let's hope they'll have the sense to do it all the same,' said Stephen.

'I don't know that sense is everything,' said Bernard. He was looking at the flag of Ireland flying in the breeze, and a longing seized him to fight and die in its defence. He was in the grip of hot emotions. The spirit of the rebels of all the ages was calling to him; the music of Ireland was playing to him; the anger of Ireland was thrilling him; reason was being swamped in floods of passion. Stephen, reading all this in his face, said quietly:

'This rebellion will be the ruin of Ireland. It'll be crushed in a few days; the country will be conscripted; and when the people see the damage done they'll react to constitutionalism for another generation and the Union will have a fresh lease of life.'

'I suppose so,' said Bernard.

'Hello, you chaps!' said a voice suddenly, and turning round they were faced by Fergus Moore. They had not seen him for over a year, so they were startled by the change in his appearance, constitutionally wrecked as he was by long-continued dissipation.

'Where are you off to?' asked Hector.

'I'm going down to the G.P.O. to see if they can spare me a rifle.'

'I gave you credit for more sense,' said Stephen. 'Don't you know that this piece of lunacy is going to be the ruin of the country?'

'Who can be sure of anything? And what matter, anyway? I've lived a rotten life, so I may as well die decently.'

'At your country's expense?' said Stephen.

'If you saw D.T.'s in front of you, you wouldn't split hairs over the morality of a fight that gives you a chance to die game, would you? I'd like to kill an Englishman or two, anyway.'

'There's no canteen in the G.P.O.,' said Stephen drily.

'That's unworthy of you, Ward,' replied Moore. 'But I'm going to my death, so I salute you. Good-bye, all.'

He shook hands sentimentally with the three and marched off towards the Post Office.

'I thought that kind of character didn't exist outside novels,' said Hector. 'Who says Sidney Carton's[4] improbable now.'

'Those who go seeking death never find it,' said Stephen. 'I bet you Moore will come out of this scatheless: which is more than will happen to more useful poor fellows.'

Suddenly Bernard cried:

'Hello! Here's Umpleby!' and the others looking round saw the little man approaching from the direction of D'Olier Street. He was loaded up with equipment, carried a Howth rifle[5] on his shoulder, and was quite breathless.

'Oh, I'm so glad to have met you,' he puffed. 'What's the meaning of it all? I was mobilised for a route march, but it looks more like a rebellion. I thought we'd cancelled that. . . .'

Stephen explained the position.

'But,' said Umpleby, tentatively scanning Stephen's face, 'er . . . doesn't honour require that we should throw in our lot with our comrades?' He was hoping with all his heart that it didn't, and his brow was knit with anxiety.

'I can't answer for your honour,' said Stephen bluntly, 'but personally I'm going home.'

Umpleby heaved a sigh of relief. Here was good company to err with.

'I'll do the same,' he said. 'Meanwhile I think I'll rid myself of these superfluous and incriminating impedimenta.' Without more ado he divested himself of his accoutrements and dumped them, rifle and all, over the parapet of the bridge into the Liffey.

'Now I think I'll run off home,' he said. 'My wife will be very anxious about me.' (Distant firing.) 'Hear that? She'll think they're all hitting me. . . . Good-bye, boys.' He shook hands hurriedly and scuttled back down D'Olier Street.

'I suppose I may as well be off home too,' said Bernard.

'No. Come along to the Neptune with us,' said Stephen. 'We can get you a room. We may as well

4. The drink-sodden, romantic hero of Dickens's *A Tale of Two Cities* (1859).
5. One of the shipload of rifles landed illegally at Howth Harbour on 26 July 1914.

stick together in case of trouble.'

Bernard was glad of the invitation. Since Mabel's defection and the loss of Eugene and Willoughby solitude had become intolerable to him. He craved for human society, and now above all he needed the support of Stephen's strong will and character. Hector supplemented the invitation in his bluff way, and Bernard accepted it.

'Let's stroll on then,' said Stephen.

They crossed the bridge and walked down Sackville Street, which was a chaos of strange sights. In the upper stories of many shops the windows had been smashed and then barricaded with furniture, behind which could be seen the green-clad forms of Volunteer sentinels silently waiting. The street was still thronged with wondering people, who walked about, stood and stared, or flung jibes at the imperturbable garrisons of the shops. Excited children ran hither and thither, and a ring of them, with not a few of their elders commingled, was gathered round the body of the horse that had been slain in the affray with the Lancers. At the end of Abbey Street some Volunteers were erecting a barricade of bicycles and rolls of paper under the curious and not very friendly gaze of a crowd of spectators. The toilers seemed to be embarrassed by this publicity, and a pink-and-white youth who acted as sentry was shyly endeavouring to make the crowd stand back. Someone chaffed him rudely, whereat he blushed and desisted from his efforts. He was a bashful revolutionary.

Bernard and his friends walked on and arrived opposite the Post Office, whose windows had been smashed and barricaded like those of the shops.

'I'd just like to go in and tell our friends what I think of them,' said Hector.

'You'd only get shot for your pains,' said Stephen.

Bernard drew their attention to a small crowd collected at the base of Nelson's Pillar, evidently reading a poster of some kind. He went over, followed by the others, and from the outskirts of the crowd read:

POBLACHT NA HEIREANN[6]
THE PROVISIONAL GOVERNMENT
of the
IRISH REPUBLIC
TO THE PEOPLE OF IRELAND

Irishmen and Irishwomen: In the name of God and of the dead generations from which she receives her old tradition of nationhood, Ireland, through us, summons her children to her flag and strikes for her freedom. . . .

There were too many heads in the way to read any farther, and the others called to him to come on. The three continued their walk. When they reached the Parnell Monument, Bernard turned back, and saw once more the flag waving in the wind, the sunlight enriching its gold and green.

'It seems a shame to desert them,' he said.

'You're right,' said Hector. 'I hate leaving them in the lurch like that.'

'Look here, you two,' said Stephen. 'Do you, or do you not, believe that this rebellion is going to be ruinous to Ireland?' There was no answer. 'Well then,' he resumed, 'have sense and come on. If these people are bent on wrecking the country we're not going to help them, anyhow.'

'But the rank-and-file?' said Bernard.

'Indeed I'm sorry for them,' said Stephen, 'but I don't see how we can help them. We did what we could these last few days.'

There was nothing more to be said. They turned their backs on the Post Office, walked on in silence, and in five minutes were at the Neptune Hotel. In the hall they met McGurk, fully equipped and armed.

'What are you up to, Hugo?' asked Hector in surprise.

'I'm going into this bloody rebellion,' replied McGurk.

'Don't be an ass, Hugo,' said Stephen.

'Ah, sure, I know it's absurd,' said McGurk. 'But I can't be deserting the poor boys.'

'You'd rather desert your country instead?' said Stephen.

'Sure this finishes Ireland for our time,' said McGurk, 'so we might as well go down with it. We'll all be shot, anyway, whether we fight or not.'

'That doesn't make it right to fight, Hugo.'

'What matter? I want to kill a few of them bloody English before I die, anyhow.'

Plainly he was not to be argued with.

'Well,' said Hector, 'good luck.'

'Good luck, boys.'

And Hugo McGurk made his sally.

'What splendid material these fellows are going to waste,' said Stephen.

6. Republic of Ireland.

'The best stuff in Ireland,' added Hector . . .

After lunch Bernard crossed town to pay a visit of warning and reassurance to his mother. The poor lady could not understand the situation at all: it was enough for her to know that her son would not be in the fighting, and she made him promise faithfully to take care of himself and not to stir out of doors.

In the evening he returned to the Neptune Hotel. The aspect of the streets was unchanged; no troops had as yet appeared on the scene; but the distant sound of sustained firing from three different directions indicated that fighting had already begun on the outskirts of the city. In Sackville Street the crowds had increased, but they were of a different complexion from those of the morning. Dusk had sent respectable people to their homes and lured forth the under-world in search of loot. All the ragged, starving, and deformed population of the slums was abroad and looting had already begun. Two sweet-shops and a boot-shop had been broken into and plundered to the very walls, and a draper's was being rapidly stripped when Bernard appeared on the scene. The dead horse still lay in the centre of the street, but attracted no more attention. Ragged children ran about clad in all kinds of finery. Old women staggered along with sacks bulging with loot. Drunken harlots danced and sang. The crash of another window brought every one racing in its direction for more plunder. The shouts of quarrelling thieves rang through the air. In the distance was the muffled roar of the fighting.

Bernard passed on. A dirty dishevelled young woman wearing a gorgeous hat and with a sealskin coat over her tattered blouse and skirt was dancing in the middle of the street yelling:

'The Volunteers is up! Ireland's free! Hurroo!'

Another equally repulsive creature was shouting obscenities at the garrison of the Post Office.

'Up th' Alleys an' to hell wid the Kayzer!' she shrieked.

Grim and silent stood the Post Office in the gloom. The tricolour hung limp from its staff. Bernard walked on. The uproar in Sackville Street sank to a murmur and finally died away.

6

'Things are quieter this morning,' observed Hugo McGurk on Friday.

He and his section held a house commanding one of the canal bridges. Every window-pane in the building had been smashed and the embrasures were fortified with sand-bags, mattresses, and articles of furniture. These ramparts had been riddled and splintered by bullets, and the front of the house was chipped and spotted and scarred all over, for the position had been under fire most of the previous day. The garrison had originally numbered eight, but two had been slain, and three of the survivors wore bandages. Smoke-grimed, hungry, and exhausted, they had scarcely left their posts at the windows for close on eighteen hours, but their spirits were still undaunted. No heart could fail under McGurk's cheery command.

Grimmest and most fearless of all the garrison was the grizzled recruit John Malone.[1] Firing with deadly speed and accuracy he had done more to repel yesterday's assaults than all the rest of his companions put together. Towards the end of the day a bullet had pierced his right forearm, but he had barely given time to allow it to be bandaged before he was back at his post dealing out death once more. It was to him that McGurk's remark had been addressed.

'I guess things will be all the hotter when they come,' he replied. 'I tell you, sergeant, this has been some fight. Well worth living for, my son.'

The sentry from the roof entered the room just then and saluted McGurk.

'Troops massing at the end of the road,' he reported.

McGurk made the round of his defences.

'Hold your fire till you're sure to hit, boys,' he said. 'Mulligan keep your head down. We can't afford any more casualties . . . . Kelly, don't waste your ammunition . . . . Now, boys, they're coming . . . .'

A tornado of firing burst forth as he spoke. Bullets came through the windows and pattered on the opposite walls. The rooms were filled with smoke and dust. A motor lorry came down the street and on to the bridge. Then there was an explosion and it came to a standstill. Malone had emptied his magazine into the bonnet. Soldiers poured out from

1. Malone was an actual participant in this famous defence of Mount Street Bridge where the Volunteers inflicted huge casualties on a regiment of Sherwood Forresters.

it and made a rush for the house. Down went three of them: a few ran back: half a dozen came storming at the garden gate. The man at the window over the hall-door dropped his empty rifle and fired both barrels of a shot-gun loaded with buckshot into the midst of them. Four fell, and the remainder ran away screaming with pain. More soldiers came pouring over the bridge. Malone, hurrying not at all, but still firing with the same monotonous regularity, picked off man after man and drove the survivors behind the waggon for shelter. Some of them began shooting from this piece of cover, and Mulligan fell dead with a bullet in his brain.

'Steady, boys!' cried McGurk. 'Heads down! Shoot slow.'

There was a lull in the combat. A bandaged warrior stepped up to McGurk.

'Ammunition nearly gone,' he said.

'Well, well,' said McGurk. 'We'll have to retreat, I suppose.' He thought a moment. 'Have you any ammunition left, Malone?' he shouted.

'Plenty,' called back Malone.

'Well, the rest of you fall back over the roofs,' said McGurk. 'You take command of them, Mick. Me and Malone will hold the rear for a bit. Carry on now.'

The man saluted and marched off with his three comrades.

'Here they are again,' cried Malone, and reopened fire. McGurk dropped behind a sand-bag and did the same. His shooting was wilder than Malone's and not so effective, but he did some damage all the same. It was, however, hopeless for these two to stop the enemy's rush. Over the bridge it came and into the garden. A teribile explosion told of bombs flung at the door, and at that moment Malone gave a cry of pain and rolled over. McGurk rushed to his side.

'I'm done,' said Malone. 'You'd better git.' And he died.

It was too late to retreat. Down went the door with a crash and the enemy surged into the hall and up the stairs. McGurk rushed out on to the landing. *Bang!* went his last cartridge and the foremost soldier dropped. On came the others, a tall man and a little man at their head. McGurk at the stair-head crossed bayonets with the tall man, and the little man tried to run in under his guard. McGurk knocked up the tall man's rifle and dealt the little man a kick in the stomach that sent him reeling. Back and forward went McGurk's bayonet like the tongue of a snake, jabbing the tall man in the chest. Before he could withdraw it another man leapt over the body of the little man and stabbed McGurk in the side. McGurk uttered a curse and went back a step. Another man thrust at him, wounding his thigh. With a roar of anger McGurk clubbed his rifle and smashed in his assailant's head, but at the same moment he was wounded again by another foe. Then at last he fell and the whole band swarmed up and over him, trampling the life out of him. . . .

Once more the tumult of war crashed over the city. With redoubled intensity the big guns boomed and the machine-guns rattled, and gallantly the diminishing rifles of the Volunteers answered back. The Post Office, heart and brain of the insurrection, was being shelled. After twenty minutes of intense bombardment those who watched saw the Republican Flag become obscured by a cloud of smoke. Up from the roof rushed a swirling black column, and soon afterwards a long flame curled up out of one of the windows and licked at the foot of the flag-staff. Little figures could be discerned running about on the roof desperately fighting the flames amid a hail of bullets. Their efforts were useless. Out of the windows and through the roof leaped the red blaze. Soon the whole interior was irretrievably involved and the building had become a vast raging furnace. With a crash the whole internal structure fell in and a gigantic pillar of smoke and flame and sparks and incandescent fragments shot up into the sky. Down came the sparks again in a glittering cascade; up rushed another fury of flames; down rolled the smoke in coiling, fuming billows, spreading themselves abroad or dissipating themselves in filmy clouds. Soon nothing was left of the building but the four bare walls, from one corner of which the flag still flew. It was still flying over the red glowing embers when night fell. For an hour after dark it still fluttered feebly in the breeze. Then suddenly the staff lurched forward and went down.

from: KING GOSHAWK AND THE BIRDS (1926)

[Because the notorious capitalist, King Goshawk, has determined to cage all the song-birds of the world, the Philosopher has gone to the Celtic heaven, Tir-na-nÓg, and brought back Cuchulain, the Irish hero, to do battle against the evils of the modern world. He purchases a body from a decrepit grocer's assistant and persuades the hero's soul to inhabit it for his sojourn in Dublin. The Ireland to which Cuchulain returns is O'Duffy's satiric version of the new Irish Free State, a nation sadly at odds with the country dreamed of by the cast of revolutionaries who had borne their various parts in *The Wasted Island*. Because a hero is, by the narrator's definition, 'a person of superabundant vitality and predominant will, with no sense of responsibility or humour', the collision between Cuchulain and the venal world of modern Ireland provides endless opportunity for satiric humour of a kind similar to that developed in Stephens's *The Crock of Gold*, and further refined in Flann O'Brien's *At Swim-Two-Birds*!]

CHAPTER VIII

HOW CUCHULAIN COURTED A GIRL OF DRUMCONDRA

The new geasa[1] that were laid upon Cuchulain were that he should not again go forth alone until, by the Philosopher's instruction, he should have become thoroughly acquainted with the manners and customs of the people. So for the next two days the hero applied himself diligently to this course of study. But when the third day dawned, because of a prick and urge of the flesh, together with a dancing of the blood and a singing of the spirit, that could no longer brook such inaction, with the temerity that had once brought dark disaster and woe upon Conaire Mor,[2] he broke his geasa and sallied forth by himself till he came to the district of Drumcondra.

There he beheld a young girl leaning over the garden gate of her father's house, watching the people go by in the sunshine. When she saw the young man looking at her, she blushed and smiled; for the spirit of Cuchulain had imparted to the smug features of Robert Emmett Aloysius O'Kennedy a moiety of the beauty and the fire that in the olden times had won the love of Aoife, and Emer, and Fand, and Blanadh, and Niamh, and of three times fifty queens that came to Emain Macha[3] from the four quarters of the earth to look upon the Hound of Ulster.[4] Cuchulain, turning to the maiden, saw that she was fair: for though she was pasty-faced and lanky of figure, yet she was pleasing to the eyes of Robert Emmett Aloysius O'Kennedy, through which he looked upon the world. O'Kennedy's body was thus smitten with a yearning for the damsel which infected even the soul of Cuchulain, so that he stopped and spoke to her, saying:

'Fair maiden, you are beautiful as a morn of spring when the cherries are in bloom.'

'Galong out o that,'[5] answered the girl, smirking.

'Nay,' said Cuchulain, 'send me not away from your gracious presence, for truly your voice is like the love-song of birds on a musky evening, and the Twin Stars shed not sweeter light than your wondrous eyes.'

The girl blushed fiery red, and kicked the gate nervously with her shabby toe; but she made no answer. Then Cuchulain said:

'Bid me again to go, and like the lightning I will be gone: for no woman yet asked me a boon that I refused her. Nevertheless, bid me not; for bitter is the air that is not sweetened by your breath. Speak, therefore: shall I go or stay?'

'Sure, why would you go?' said the girl. 'I was only joking.'

Then Cuchulain kissed with his ambrosial lip the grubby finger-tips of the maiden; and he said:

'In the gardens of Paradise the winds play a melody as of silver flutes over the golden heads of the swaying asphodels. But now my desire is for a cool spot by a woodland stream, amid odours of fern and damp earth, with wild hyacinths, maybe, in the long grass, or wood anemones, and yourself stretched beside me, plashing your white feet in the water.'

The girl, playing with a faded ribbon on her blouse, thrust it between her teeth and giggled. Cuchulain, watching her, said:

'My thirst is for the honey that is gathered from a bed of scarlet flowers.'

'I don't care for the kind you get in them combs,' said the girl. 'I prefer the bottled stuff. But I like jam best.'

Silence fell between them at that; but presently the girl, thinking he would have invited her for a

1. Irish: literally 'taboos', often laid on warriors in heroic literature.
2. The hero of an Irish 'King Tale' entitled 'The Destruction of Da Dearga's Hostel'.
3. Present-day Armagh, ancient headquarters of Ulster's warriors.
4. The hero's name means the Hound of Cullen.
5. 'Go along out of that.' In other words, 'I don't believe you!'

walk or to the pictures but had been prevented by shyness, said: 'What was it you wanted to ask me about?'

Cuchulain answered: 'My desire is for two snowy mountains, rose-crowned, that are fenced about with thorns and barriers of ice. What shall I do to melt the ice and turn aside the menace of the thorns?'

'What do you mean?' asked the maiden.

Then said Cuchulain: 'It is your fair bosom that is the fruit of my desiring, and your red lips ripe for kissing, and your warm white body to be pressed to mine in the clasp of love.'

'O you dirty fellow!' cried the girl, and turning, she fled into her house.

Cuchulain would have pursued her, but a tap on the shoulder made him turn round, and he found himself confronted by two men of singular aspect. Their clothing was all white, though somewhat soiled, with buttons of ivory and facings of swansdown. On their heads they wore helmets in the likeness of a sitting dove; and they carried batons of some white metal wrought in the shape of a lily. On their collars were these words in letters of ivory: CENSOR MORUM.[6]

The official who had tapped him addressed Cuchulain saying: 'What were you wanting with that girl?'

Cuchulain, mindful of his geasa, restraining his desire to smite him, answered: 'That, sir, is a matter between her and me.'

'Now, then,' said the Censor, 'none of your lip. I've reason to suspect that you were asking her more than the time of day; and I've power to put you under arrest unless you can give me a satisfactory explanation.'

'I can tell you nothing of what passed between us,' said Cuchulain, 'without the consent of the lady.'

'Tush, sir,' said the Censor. 'You must be one of those foreigners if you think we would so outrage the modesty of our Womanhood by questioning them on such a subject. Come, now. What is your explanation?'

More difficult was Cuchulain's task to bridle his wrath at that moment than once had been the feat of bridling the Grey of Macha[7] by the dark lake near Sliabh Fuaith. The veins of his forehead stood out like black and knotted cords; his collar at his neck was scorched deep brown; his heart missed seven beats; but calling to mind the calm visage of the Philosopher, he put constraint on his voice and said: 'I was making love.'

'With matrimonial intent?' asked the Censor, entering the reply in his lambskin-covered notebook.

'I do not understand you,' said Cuchulain.

'Do you want to marry the girl?' explained the other Censor.

'Indeed, no,' said Cuchulain. 'There are no marriages in heaven.'

'Then you must come with us,' said the Censors, laying hands on him.

'Whither?' asked Cuchulain.

'To the Lothario Asylum,' said the Censors, and began to haul him away between them.

'Dogs!' cried Cuchulain. 'Let me be'; and he put forth his strength so that his feet dug deep holes in the stone pathway, and the Censors could not move him. Thereupon these raised their lily-shaped truncheons to beat purity into the son of Lugh:[8] but he, taking them up one in each hand, entwined the right leg of the one with the left leg of the other in a truelove knot, and left them there on the pavement for the gathering throngs to admire.

6. Latin: Censor of Morals.

7. One of Cuchulain's two legendary horses.

8. Lugh of the Long Arm, Cuchulain's divine father.

PEADAR O'DONNELL

(1893–1986)

from: ISLANDERS (1928)

[In this extract from *Islanders*, Peadar O'Donnell dramatizes a heroic incident in the life of the people of Inniscara, his fictional island off the coast of Donegal. Charlie Doogan's sister — married to Miley Ferry — is in danger of dying in childbirth. But the island is storm-bound; the fishermen have broken two boats in an attempt to get to the mainland for a doctor.]

CHAPTER XXIII

Charlie Doogan's concern for Peggy was deep and strong. Indeed, all his fondest ties had centred in her until she had left to marry Miley Ferry. After that he was almost a stranger at his own hearth. It is true his relationship with her of late years had not been as in the days before she married Miley. She was his champion in those far-off days, when he was struggling for the freedom of his middle teens. It was she used to watch for him while he shaved; she bought him his first white collar — it was for a Patrick's Night dance in Arranmore. She often wheedled an odd sixpence for him on a day of a regatta. And she alone took pride in his great strength — he remembered how she encouraged him in his weight-throwing and rowing. He was remembering Peggy across the casual years that had passed since he had drifted. And now, she wanted a doctor, how badly he didn't know. Sickness was beyond the range of his experience, and its place in his understanding was vague. He was troubled about Peggy, not really roused on her behalf. He had laboured to launch the boat, as he would have laboured in any attempt on such a day, putting the whole weight of his body into the struggle, troubled, but not roused.

He wished to see his mother. He set off across the beach to Peggy's. She was in the kitchen when he went in. Tears were trickling down her face when she looked at him, and just then Peggy was crying, her great, unrestrained crying, that was so like a child's. Charlie had heard grown-up people cry on occasions at wakes, or a convoy,[1] but it had been the crying of grown-up people. This was different. Not since the day Peggy cut her foot on a black bottle had he heard sobbing that came straight from the heart like that.

He laid hard fingers on his mother's arm. 'Is that our Peggy?' he asked, almost hissed. The mother buried her face in her hands, and her body shook.

'It's her, and she won't be long in it, either,' Mary Neil Rodgers[2] said.

'I never knew, God, I never knew,' Charlie said, running out of the house.

1. A translation of the Irish word *tionnlacan*, a word for the escorting of bereaved relations to a funeral, or of emigrants to a railway station or harbour.
2. The midwife.

CHAPTER XXIV

The men saw Charlie come out of Miley's, and come towards them. He seemed scarcely to bend to the blast, but to sweep through it without staggering. A sense of a new force let loose among the storm came to them.

'Heavens above, but that boy minds me of his grandfather!' Manus O'Donnell said, and then they were all silent until he came to them. He sought out Manus O'Donnell.

'Manus,' he said, 'you were a great man in a curragh;[1] how'd ye get off the island?'

Manus was silent for a moment. ''Twas a day like this yer grandfather, God rest his soul, went from the Point,' Manus said.

'Ye were there, Manus?' Charlie said.

'I was,' Manus agreed quietly.

'Ye planted the curragh on a swell that was sweepin' in an' he was off with the back-wash. I heard him tell it. I mind fine.' He looked at the beach. 'It's a question of bein' through the first breaker 'fore it bursts.'

'It's that,' Manus said; 'an' of not lettin' the next or the next catch ye with its broken top.'

1. A canoe-shaped boat; a timber frame covered with tarred canvas.

'I'm goin' in a curragh,' Charlie said.

The men moved on their feet; nobody spoke.

'Ye'll help me get the curragh planted. Take it out in yer arms to where the wave spendin' itself will about reach yer waists. Ye can have ropes on ye to keep ye from the wash pullin' ye out. I'll scoot out an' try an' get across the neck of the first wave before it bursts deep. Then I'll let it drive me. I must do that.'

Nobody stirred. Charlie turned to Phil.

'Help me, Phil.'

'It's madness, Charlie,' Phil said, taking a chew of tobacco.

Charlie turned from them and made towards a curragh.

'I was waitin' for this; he's his grandfather over again; God bless him, an' his stock were men,' Manus said.

They watched him untie the ropes. Phil sighed. 'Ah, well, in God's Name,' he said, crossing himself.

The others followed Phil's lead. They carried the curragh to the Point. Charlie kicked off his boots.

'Take off the gansey,'[2] Manus advised.

Four men with ropes round their waists held the curragh. The group on the shore held the other ends of the ropes. A wave boiled over and swept forward.

'Now,' Charlie said.

The four men raced into the surf. The curragh floated in their hands; Charlie flopped into it. He shot out with the first ebb of the wave. The staggering men were helped ashore, going reluctantly backward, their eyes on the curragh.

2. sweater.

CHAPTER XXV

He got across the first wave just as foam began to rise from its crest. He was going down its neck when it broke. Into the trough in front of him a wave was tumbling white. He floundered for a moment in the trough, rose hurriedly to the next swell, and again just managed to get across, not, however, until he had shipped some water. It was a mighty tussle, full of skill, and strength, and blessed with luck.

Once clear of the surf, he drove before the storm, delaying, hurrying, once or twice trusting blindly, but racing, racing across the waters. His black, hatless head, his set, granite-hued face dripping wet; strong, supple arms, fingers of steel. And as he drove, the storm seemed suddenly to sing of triumph, to back him up against the waters, and the latter to roll after him and shoot up challengingly before him, not because they could win, but because they had the persistence of the stupid. He shouted; he knew not why, but he shouted . . . just opened his mouth and roared, plying his paddle with grand stroke, and god-like confidence. He growled when a swell slipped water into the curragh; laughed when he broke the face of a crumbling wave. And then he thought of Peggy. 'And she won't be long in it either.' Mary Neil's words were in the blast. He drove his bending paddle deeper into the tossing water, and forged forward, using strength mostly, almost scorning to use caution.

He landed under the shelter of the Point near Burtonport barefooted, soaked in salt water, and now the thought of Peggy so strong on him, that for the first time since he left the island he was frightened.

'Was I long? Was I long?' he muttered. And then he raced up the fields to the doctor's house.

CHAPTER XXVI

Doctor Wilson was in his third year as dispensary doctor in the Rosses.[1] His sister, Ruth, spent a great deal of her time with him. She had long wished to live in the Rosses and to know its people. It was a desire born of the Abbey Theatre, and fostered by short trips to Kerry and Connemara.[2] She had made friends with the local people, especially with the fishermen, who let her accompany them when they went out, testifying to her popularity by declaring that she brought them luck. The women folk, however, held her a little apart; their thoughts and their lives were largely matters for speculation; she had little access to their minds, and she knew it. An elderly aunt lived with the brother and sister. She interested herself in their creature comforts, and considered she was exercising guardianship over them while they grew up and got sense.

During the long storm the doctor had been out

1. The seaboard region of north Donegal, not to be confused with Yeats's Rosses in County Sligo.
2. The early playwrights of the Abbey Theatre, most particularly John Millington Synge, favoured settings on the west coast of Ireland.

but little, except to go daily to the post-office; Ruth went with him in the car to visit a few patients. They were now collected round a bright fire, and immersed in the post. Ruth was absorbed in the story of a swimming match in Dublin; the doctor was idly perusing an advertising leaflet.

'I see the Prince of Wales[3] had a wonderful reception in Canada,' the aunt said, speaking out of the folds of the *Daily Mail*. 'Dear me, how he works! I think he is just splendid.'

'I can't get over Stasia Byrne winning that half-mile. I could always swim rings round her,' Ruth said.

Puff, puff, from the doctor's pipe.

'How the natives love the prince. One old fellow walked two hundred miles to be present at the reception. That's a lesson to some of those at home,' thus the aunt.

'Stasia will be up in her hat. But what a freak photo of her! Give me a cigarette, Dick.'

'Ruth, dear, you're smoking too many cigarettes,' the aunt objected, without laying down her paper.

The brother and sister smiled, and the latter stretched out her crossed legs to rest them on a chair, and reached for a book. 'Let me get back to my *Conqueror*,' she said. 'What a lovable type that man Hamilton[4] was. 'Pon my word, one would be justified in anything to beget a son like that.'

'Ruth!'

'Auntie!'

'You hurt me,' the aunt complained.

Ruth sat up and threw impulsive arms around her aunt, gave her a hug, and then lay back again. 'I'll be good, Auntie. It's that storm; don't you feel it? It has the sea raging, the earth trembling, it can't leave us serene. Moses —'

The exclamation wrung from her by the sudden hammering at the door. And then the room door was flung open.

'My God! The Danes have landed — a Viking,' she added with vigour, commenting on the man who had entered. He was tall; he was drenched; he was excited; his face was pale, rugged, granite-like. His hair was black and short, scattered irregularly, as heavy rain flattens hair. He was bare-footed; he wore a sleeveless vest. It was Charlie Doogan.

The doctor and the aunt got to their feet. Charlie spoke first.

'My sister's very bad,' he said. 'Ye're wanted, quick.'

'Where to?'

'Inniscara.'

'Good heavens!' the doctor commented.

'She's very bad,' Charlie urged.

'Confinement?' the doctor asked.

Charlie nodded.

Then the aunt spoke. 'The doctor couldn't go now. He'll go the very first minute it settles,' she assured him.

Charlie's eyes were on the speaker, then they shifted to Ruth.

He said: 'They say she'll die if the doctor doesn't come now.'

The doctor walked to the window. 'How did you come?' he asked.

'A curragh,' Charlie said.

'What?' Ruth protested. 'A curragh? You never came in a curragh in that?'

'We broke two boats,' Charlie said simply. 'It was the only chance.'

Tears started suddenly in Ruth's eyes, just a sudden passing wave of emotion.

'How am I to get there?' the doctor asked thoughtfully.

'There's drifters[5] down here; wan of them'll go,' Charlie said.

Ruth nodded. 'I was thinking of that,' she said. 'The *Gola Star* boys will go first shot.'

'But the doctor couldn't go out in that,' the aunt persisted.

The doctor put his hand on her shoulder. 'That lunatic came in a curragh.'

'She's very bad, doctor,' Charlie pleaded; 'if we could hurry.'

'I'll be ready in a minute,' the doctor decided.

'I'm coming,' Ruth said.

The doctor halted, with his hand on the knob of the door, and frowned.

'Fiddlesticks, Dick. Now, be a sport.'

'Well, well, if the drifter goes —' the doctor yielded.

'It will,' she said. '*Gola Star* will go.'

The doctor hurried off to get ready.

3. Edward, later to become Edward VIII, visited Canada in 1919.
4. Alex Hamilton is the hero of *Conqueror* (1902), a novel by Franklin Atherton (1857–1948).
5. Medium-sized boats equipped with oar and sail.

'This poor man will get his death,' the aunt said.

Ruth looked at Charlie. No half-drowned man ever was so imposing, she thought. 'You'll have to get a change of things,' she said.

But he only smiled at her, and shook his head. 'I'll have the drifter ready, an' we'll be waitin',' and before they could say anything more to him he was gone.

LIAM O'FLAHERTY

(1896–1984)

from: THE MOUNTAIN TAVERN AND OTHER STORIES (1929)

[This great short story stands side by side with Frank O'Connor's 'Guests of the Nation' and Seán O'Faoláin's 'Midsummer Night Madness' as a dramatization of war and its havoc upon the human family. That the action concerns civil war makes its message all the more terrible and prophetic.]

THE MOUNTAIN TAVERN

Snow was falling. The bare, flat, fenceless road had long since disappeared. Now the white snow fell continuously on virgin land, all level, all white, all silent, between the surrounding dim peaks of the mountains. Through the falling snow, on every side, squat humps were visible. They were the mountain peaks. And between them, the moorland was as smooth as a ploughed field. And as silent, oh, as silent as an empty church. Here, the very particles of the air entered the lungs seemingly as big as pebbles and with the sweetness of ripe fruit. An outstretched hand could almost feel the air and the silence. There was absolutely nothing, nothing at all, but falling flakes of white snow, undeflected, falling silently on fallen snow.

Up above was the sky and God perhaps, though it was hard to believe it; hard to believe that there was anything in the whole universe but a flat white stretch of virgin land between squat mountain peaks and a ceaseless shower of falling snow-flakes.

There came the smell of human breathing from the east. Then three figures appeared suddenly, dark, although they were covered with snow. They appeared silently, one by one, stooping forward. The leading man carried his overcoat like a shawl about his head, with a rifle, butt upwards, slung on his right shoulder and two cloth ammunition belts slung across his body. He wore black top boots. His grim young eyes gazed wearily into the falling snow and his boots, scarcely lifted, raked the smooth earth, scattering the fallen snow-flakes.

The second man wore a belted leather coat, of which one arm hung loose. With the other hand he gripped his chest and staggered forward, with sagging, doddering head. A pistol, pouched in a loose belt, swung back and forth with his gait. There was blood on his coat, on his hand and congealed on his black leggings, along which the melting snow ran in a muddy stream. There was a forlorn look in his eyes, but his teeth were set. Sometimes he bared them and drew in a deep breath with a hissing sound.

The third man walked erect. He wore no overcoat and his head was bare. His hair curled and among the curls the snow lay in little rows like some statue in winter. He had a proud, fearless face, bronzed, showing no emotion nor weariness. Now and again, he shook his great body and the snow fell with a rustling sound off his clothes and off the heavy pack he carried. He also had two rifles wrapped in a cape under his arm; and in his right hand he carried a small wooden box that hung from a leather strap.

They walked in each other's tracks slowly. Rapidly the falling snow filled up the imprints of their feet. And when they passed there was silence again.

The man in front halted and raised his eyes to look ahead. The second man staggered against him, groaned with pain and gripped the other about the body with his loose hand to steady himself. The third man put the wooden box on the ground and shifted his pack.

'Where are we now?' he said.

His voice rang out, hollow, in the stillness and several puffs of hot air, the words, jerked out, like steam from a starting engine.

'Can't say,' muttered the man in front. 'Steady, Commandant. We can't be far now. We're on the road anyway. It should be there in front. Can't see, though. It's in a hollow. That's why.'

'What's in a hollow, Jack?' muttered the wounded man. 'Let me lie down here. It's bleeding again.'

'Hold on, Commandant,' said the man in front. 'We'll be at the Mountain Tavern in half a minute. Christ!'

'Put him on my back,' said the big man. 'You carry the stuff.'

'Never mind. I'll walk,' said the wounded man. 'I'll get there all right. Any sign of them?'

They peered into the falling snow behind them. There was utter silence. The ghostly white shower made no sound. A falling curtain.

'Lead on then,' said the big man. 'Lean on me, Commandant.'

They moved on. The wounded man was groaning now and his feet began to drag. Shortly he began to rave in a low voice. Then they halted again. Without speaking, the big man hoisted his comrade, crosswise, on his shoulders. The other man carried the kit. They moved on again.

The peak in front became larger. It was no longer a formless mass. Gradually, through the curtain of snow, it seemed to move towards them and upwards. The air became still more thin. As from the summit of a towering cliff, the atmosphere in front became hollow; and soon, through the haze of snow, they caught a glimpse of the distant plains, between two mountain peaks. There below it lay, like the bottom of a sea, in silence. The mountain sides sank down into it, becoming darker; for it did not snow down there. There was something, after all, other than the snow. But the snowless, downland earth looked dour and unapproachable.

'It must be here,' the leading man said again. 'Why can't we see it? It's just under the shelter of that mountain. There is a little clump of pine trees and a barn with a red roof. Sure I often had a drink in it. Where the name of God is it, anyway?'

'Go on. Stop talking,' said the curly-headed man.

'Can't you be easy?' muttered the leading man, moving ahead and peering into the snow that made his eyelids blink and blink. 'Supposing this is the wrong road, after all. They say people go round and round in the snow. Sure ye could see it from the other end, four miles away in clear weather, two storey high and a slate roof with the sun shining on it. It's facing this way too, right on the top of the hill, with a black board, "Licensed to Sell."[1] Man called Galligan owns it. I'd swear by the Cross of Christ we must be up on it.'

'Hurry on,' snapped the curly man. 'There's a gurgle in his throat. Jesus! His blood is going down my neck. Why can't you hurry on, blast it?'

'Hey, what place is that?' cried the leading man, in a frightened voice. 'D'ye see a ruin?'

They halted. A moment ago there had been nothing in front but a curtain of falling snow, beyond which, as in a child's sick dream, the darkening emptiness of the snowless lowland approached, tumbling like a scudding black cloud. Now a crazy blue heap appeared quite close. Suddenly it heaved up out of the snow. It was a ruined house. There was a smell from it too. From its base irregular tufts of smoke curled up spasmodically; dying almost as soon as they appeared and then appearing again.

The two men watched it. There was no emotion in their faces. They just looked, as if without interest. It was too strange. The *Mountain Tavern* was a smoking ruin.

'It's gone west,' murmured the leading man.

'Eh?' shouted the curly man. 'Gone did ye say?'

'Aye. Burned to the ground. See?'

'Well?'

'God knows. We're up the pole.'[2]

Suddenly the curly man uttered a cry of rage and staggered forward under his load. The other man opened his mouth wide, drew in an enormous breath and dropped his head wearily on his chest. Trailing his rifle in the snow behind him, he reeled forward, shaking his head from side to side, with his under lip trembling. Then he began to sing foolishly under his breath. There were people around the ruined house. And as the two men, with their dying comrade, came into view, quite close, these people stopped and gaped at them. There was a woman in front of the house, on the road, sitting on an upturned barrel. She was a thin woman with a long pointed nose and thin black hair that hung in disorder on

1. 'Licensed to Sell Wine and Spirits', a sign outside most Irish public houses.
2. 'We're in trouble.'

her thin neck, with hairpins sticking in it. She had a long overcoat buttoned over her dress and a man's overcoat about her shoulders. She held a hat with red feathers on it in her right hand, by the rim. Two children, wrapped in queer clothes, stood beside her, clinging to her, a boy and a girl. They also were thin and they had pointed noses like their mother. One man was pulling something out of a window of the ruined house. Another man, within the window, had his head stuck out. He had been handing out something. Another man was in the act of putting a tin trunk on a cart, to which a horse was harnessed, to the right of the house. All looked, gaping, at the newcomers.

'God save all here,' said the curly man, halting near the woman.

Nobody replied. The other man came up and staggered towards the woman, who was sitting on the upturned barrel. The two children, silent with fear, darted around their mother, away from the man. They clutched at her, muttering something inaudibly.

'Is that you, Mrs. Galligan?'

'It is then,' said the woman in a stupid, cold voice. 'And who might you be?'

'We're Republican soldiers,'[3] said the curly man. 'I have a dying man here.'

He lowered the wounded man gently to the ground. Nobody spoke or moved. The snow fell steadily.

'Mummy, mummy,' cried one of the children, 'there's blood on him. Oh! mummy.'

The two children began to howl. The dying man began to throw his hands about and mutter something. A great rush of blood flowed from him.

'In the name of the Lord God of Heaven,' yelled the curly man, 'are ye savages not to move a foot? Eh? Can't ye go for a doctor? Is there nothing in the house?'

He stooped over the dying man and clutching him in his arms, he cried hoarsely:

'Easy now, Commandant. I'm beside ye. Give us a hand with him, Jack. We'll fix the bandage.'

The two of them, almost in a state of delirium, began to fumble with the dying man. The children wept. The dying man suddenly cried out:

'Stand fast. Stand fast boys. Stand. . . .'

Then he made a violent effort to sit up. He opened his mouth and did not close it again.

The woman looked on dazed, with her forehead wrinkled and her lips set tight. The three men who had been doing something among the ruin began to come up slowly. They also appeared dazed, terrified.

'He's gone,' murmured the curly man, sitting erect on his knees. 'God have mercy on him.'

He laid the corpse flat on the ground. The blood still flowed out. The other soldier took off his hat and then, just as he was going to cross himself, he burst into tears. The three men came close and looked on. Then they sheepishly took off their hats.

'Is he dead?' said one of them.

The curly man sat back on his heels.

'He's dead,' he said. 'The curse o' God on this country.'

'And what did ye say happened?'

'Ambush back there. Our column got wiped out. Haven't ye got anything in the house?'

The woman laughed shrilly. The children stopped crying.

'Is there nothing in the house, ye daylight robber?' she cried. 'Look at it, curse ye. It's a black ruin. Go in. Take what ye can find, ye robber.'

'Robbers!' cried the soldier who had been weeping. 'Come on, Curly. Stand by me. I'm no robber. God! Give me a drink. Something to eat. Christ! I'm dyin'.'

He got to his feet and took a pace forward like a drunken man. The curly-headed soldier caught him.

'Keep yer hair on, Jack,' he said.

'Look at what ye've done,' cried the woman. 'Ye've blown up the house over me head. Ye've left me homeless and penniless with yer war. Oh! God, why don't ye drop down the dome of Heaven on me?'

'Sure we didn't blow up your house,' cried the curly soldier. 'An' we lookin' for shelter after trampin' the mountains since morning. Woman, ye might respect the dead that died for ye.'

The woman spat and hissed at him.

'Let them die. They didn't die for me,' she said. 'Amn't I ruined and wrecked for three long years with yer fightin', goin' back and forth, lootin' and turnin' the honest traveller from my door? For three long years have I kept open house for all of ye and now yer turnin' on one another like dogs after a bitch.'

3. Republican soldiers, called 'Irregulars' later in the story, were the anti-government forces in the Irish Civil War and were opposed to the Free State soldiers, who appear eventually in the narrative.

'None o' that now,' cried the hysterical soldier, trying to raise his rifle.

'Hold on, man,' cried one of the other men. 'She has cause. She has cause.'

He grew excited and waved his hands and addressed his own comrades instead of addressing the soldiers.

'The Republicans came to the house this morning,' he cried. 'So Mr. Galligan told me an' he goin' down the road for McGilligan's motor. The Republicans came, he said. And then . . . then the Free Staters came on top of them and the firing began. Women and children out, they said, under a white flag. So Galligan told me. "They damn near shot me," says he to me, "harbourin' Irregulars under the new act." Shot at sight, or what's worse, they take ye away on the cars, God knows where. Found in a ditch. None of us, God blast my soul if there is a word of a lie in what I am sayin', none of us here have a hand or part in anything. Three miles I came up in the snow when Mr. Galligan told me. Says he to me, "I'll take herself and the kids to aunt Julia's in McGilligan's motor." '

'Where did they go?' said the curly soldier.

'I was comin' to that,' said the man, spitting in the snow and turning towards the woman. 'It's with a bomb they did it, Galligan said to me. Something must have fallen in the fire. They stuck it out, he said. There were six men inside. Not a man came out without a wound. So he said. There were two dead. On the door they took'em away. They took 'em all off in the cars. And they were goin' to take Mr. Galligan too. There you are now. May the Blessed Virgin look down on here. An' many's a man 'll go thirsty from this day over the mountain road.'

'Aye,' said the woman. 'For twenty years in that house, since my father moved from the village, after buyin' it from Johnny Reilly.'

'Twenty years,' she said again.

'Can't ye give us something to eat?' cried the hysterical man, trying to break loose from the curly soldier, who still held him.

'There's nothing here,' muttered a man, 'until Mr. Galligan comes in the motor. He should be well on the way now.'

'They were all taken,' said the curly soldier.

'All taken,' said the three men, all together.

'Sit down, Jack,' said the curly soldier.

He pulled his comrade down with him on to the snow. He dropped his head on his chest. The others looked at the soldiers sitting in the snow. The others had a curious, malign look in their eyes. They looked at the dazed, exhausted soldiers and at the corpse with a curious apathy. They looked with hatred. There was no pity in their eyes. They looked steadily without speech or movement, with the serene cruelty of children watching an insect being tortured. They looked patiently, as if calmly watching a monster in its death agony.

The curly-headed soldier suddenly seemed to realize that they were watching him. For he raised his head and peered at them shrewdly through the falling snow. There was utter silence everywhere, except the munching sound made by the horse's jaws as he chewed hay. The snow fell, fell now, in the fading light, mournfully, blotting out the sins of the world.

The soldier's face, that had until then shown neither fear nor weariness, suddenly filled with despair. His lips bulged out. His eyes almost closed. His forehead gathered together and he opened his nostrils wide.

'I'm done,' he said. 'It's no use. Say, men. Send word that we're here. Let them take us. I'm tired fightin'. It's no use.'

No one spoke or stirred. A sound approached. Strange to say, no one paid attention to the sound. And even when a military motor lorry appeared at the brow of the road, nobody moved or spoke. There were Free State soldiers on the lorry. They had their rifles pointed. They drew near slowly. Then, with a rush, they dismounted and came running up.

The two Republican soldiers put up their hands, but they did not rise to their feet.

'Robbers,' screamed the woman. 'I hate ye all. Robbers.'

Her husband was there with them.

'Mary, we're to go in the lorry,' he said to her. 'They're goin' to look after us they said. Fr. Considine went to the barracks.'

'The bloody robbers,' she muttered, getting off the barrel.

'Who's this?' the officer said, roughly handling the corpse.

He raised the head of the corpse.

'Ha!' he said. 'So we got him at last. Eh? Heave him into the lorry, boys. Hurry up. Chuck 'em all in.'

They took away the corpse and the prisoners.

There was a big dark spot where the corpse had lain. Snow began to fall on the dark spot.

They took away everybody, including the horse and cart. Everybody went away, down the steep mountain road, into the dark lowland country, where no snow was falling. All was silent again on the flat top of the mountain.

There was nothing in the whole universe again but the black ruin and the black spot where the corpse had lain. Night fell and snow fell, fell like soft soothing white flower petals on the black ruin and on the black spot where the corpse had lain.

AUSTIN CLARKE

(1896–1974)

from: THE BRIGHT TEMPTATION (1932)

[*The Bright Temptation* is one of three prose romances written by Austin Clarke about medieval Ireland, the others being *The Singing Men at Cashel* (1936) and *The Sun Dances at Easter* (1952). It rehearses an obsessive theme in the poet's work, the struggle between the spirit and the flesh, authority and freedom in the Irish psyche. Aidan, a clerical student in the monastery of Cluanmore, is separated from his brethren in the novel's first chapter and is launched on an adventurous journey round Ireland. His celibacy is frequently threatened, most especially by a beautiful and innocent girl, Ethna, whose love he reluctantly declines in the interests of chastity, believing it to be a snare of the Evil One. In this, the novel's penultimate chapter, the young novice has returned to his walled monastery.]

CHAPTER TWENTY-FOUR

'IT IS THE FEAST-DAY OF SAINT NESSAN!'[1]

Aidan left the ridge with that eager cry. He had been overcome at first by fears when he saw the festive fires at Cluanmore.[2] But his fears had only been a delusion — a last attempt by the Evil One to keep him from returning to his duty. The saint had warned him of the cunning temptations which would assail his mind. In his ignorance he had listened to the whisperings of the Tempter: he had almost yielded to an impulse of distrust. He quickened his steps, anxious to forget that moment of unworthy hesitation.

'I should have remembered at once. It shows that my mind is still disturbed.'

Saint Nessan was the founder of Cluanmore, and every year his feast-day was an occasion of rejoicing. Aidan remembered the great procession which had been held last year. Three scholars of European fame had arrived in a ship from Tarentum[3] with gifts of altar wine and frankincense, being on their way to the birthplace of Saint Cathaldus in Munster. The celebrations at Cluanmore, in their honour, had lasted all day. Boats were coming, were going, across the Shannon from daybreak. Multitudes gathered along the river-banks.

The King-Bishop of Cashel[4] had ridden there at noon with nine companies of the Eoghanacht.[5] Aidan gazed in awe at the great ecclesiastic, for he wore foreign mail under his rich gold-stitched cope. Great knee'd and sworded, he remained all the time on horseback among his armed clergy and nobles. The young student had been ill at ease, wondering what

1. No saint of that name is recorded as living in the region of the Shannon basin where the novel is set, although there was a St Nessan in County Wicklow.
2. Cluanmore, Irish for 'Big meadow', is a common Irish place-name, but there was no monastery of that name on the Shannon.
3. The Irish saint, Cathaldus, was Bishop of Tarentum in southern Italy in the 7th century.
4. Probably Cormac MacCuilleanáin, hero of Clarke's subsequent novel, *The Singing Men at Cashel*. The four archdioceses of Ireland — Armagh, Tuam, Dublin and Cashel – were established at the Synod of Kells in 1152.
5. Young acolytes.

strange politics or disputes divided Ireland. Better — he had thought — the quiet studies, the discipline, the daily peace of Cluanmore.

The King-Bishop and his nobles had left in an hour, but the celebrations lasted until nightfall. Beacons were kindled along the river-bank, large as the paschal fires, for at Cluanmore the old Irish date of Easter was still kept, despite the controversies which had shaken the schools of Europe.[6] Aidan, as he went to his cell that night, paused with a few scholars, listening in pride to the pious voices that came across the waters, watching the ranked oars leave a fiery wake.

He was glad to think that he would come back to his school on the feast-day of Saint Nessan, for he could mingle among the departing crowds without questions or difficulty. He could go quietly to the students' quarters and delay his explanations until the morrow. He was strangely excited as he went along the dark road, and his heart began to beat so violently that he had to stop at times in order to quieten his mind. He could hear the murmuring of the crowds, but it was still faint though he had almost reached the outer enclosure of Cluanmore. The entire congregation must be down at the far end of the shore. The companies were leaving, and he fancied that he heard the creak of rowlocks, the last cries of benediction.

The night had become tense, silent, around him. He must be passing under the high mounded wall of the outer enclosure. There were trees on his right, for he could catch the rustle of the leaves. His imagination was fevered so that he listened with anxiety to every stir around him. He must not delay; the night might be full of dangers. He would not be safe until he was behind the enclosure. He stopped for a moment in the darkness, and, with a pang, the thought of Ethna lit his mind. He seemed to see her face, pale and sad, reproaching him. She was calling him back, she was warning him. Why was she warning him not to return to Cluanmore? He fought desperately against the temptation; he tried to conceal from his mind her loveliness. He knew that the last moment of temptation had come, that he must escape from himself.

Distracted by his thoughts, he left the road, he scrambled down into the dried fosse.[7] He ran along the fosse as quickly as he could. He stopped again to listen under the wall. He could hear the rustle of leaves on the other side of the road. The earthen wall was faced with large stones, and as he ran his hand along it he could feel the gaps between them. A desperate impulse seized him, and without stopping to think he climbed the mound, slid across the top and dropped into the enclosure of Cluanmore.

He was safe at last. No violence or danger could reach him now. His trials were over and he had conquered himself.

Tears of gratitude were in his eyes as he stood there in the darkness. He felt beneath his feet that blessed earth. He was at peace. Never again would he venture so rashly from that place of meditation and knowledge. He would attend carefully at all his classes, he would study hard, striving to forget his own desires, to please the teachers who believed in him. He wondered at what part of the enclosure he had entered. He must be at the extreme corner, for the murmur of the crowds by the river sounded faint. The low murmur made the silence around him more intense.

He had gone a few steps when he was stopped by some obstruction in the darkness. He groped carefully by the rounded wall and knew that he had come to a cell. There were other cells on every side of him, for he could make out vague circular shapes in the darkness. The cells were empty and silent. None of the monks had come back yet from the shore. A feeling of awe filled him. He must be in the Trian of the Elders,[8] and the students were strictly forbidden to go there.

He had made a mistake in crossing the mounded wall. It had been an impatient and foolish act. He should have followed the causeway until he came to the main entrance. He would not have been noticed, even the erenachs[9] were mingling with the crowd at the river-side. He was a student once more, and the sense of discipline filled him with uneasiness. If he were discovered in the forbidden Trian, he would be brought before the Abbot and punished. He must make his way as quickly as possible to his own

6. In the 7th century there was a vigorous debate — the paschal controversy — between Ireland and Rome regarding the date of Easter. Some Irish monasteries adhered to the old date established by St Patrick, resisting the reformed calendar of Pope Gregory the Great.

7. trench, ditch (Latin fossa).

8. Trian is Irish for third part. One-third of the monastic enclosure was reserved for the Elders, or senior monks.

9. Monastic clergy who shaved or tonsured their heads.

quarters before the monks came back. For several minutes he groped his way among the cells, alarm filling him as he realised that he had lost himself in the darkness. The cells were strangely silent as he stumbled past them. There were so many of them. He must be going round in a circle. At last, with a cry of relief, he came on the open street between the rows of cells. But he had only gone a little way when he stopped. Steps were coming towards him in the night.

The steps were strange and terrible. Their hollow echoes among the deserted cells sent a cold shiver through him.

'It is the Abbot himself.'

He crouched behind one of the cells, appalled by that thought. The Abbot was coming nearer. He could hear that slow tread down the empty street. But the Abbot was not alone. There were other steps, and he could hear harsh guttural voices. It could not be the Abbot and the monks. But what were foreigners doing in the forbidden Trian? The rumbling voices filled him with fear. There was something strange about them, something horrible. He almost imagined that demons were talking in the darkness. Stories of evil apparitions, which he had heard about in class, came to his feverish mind. The awful steps, the voices, were coming towards the very cell behind which he was hidden.

Aidan glided away, but as soon as he had got behind the next cell he took to his heels. He had run for several yards before he ventured to stop again. He could hear nothing except the far murmuring of the crowd by the shore. Had he been needlessly alarmed by those steps in the lonely Trian of the Elders? He had felt like a truant. His imagination was over-excited; he was suffering from the strain of his journey. He must control himself, banish his imaginary fears. There were low walls of a smithy on his left. He was astray in the quarter of the metal-workers. He groped along a wall and, turning a corner, saw in the distance the round-tower, half shadowed, half crimsoned by the hidden bonfires. Beneath the tower were clustered, like dark pent-houses, the roofs of the seven churches.

He had only gone back a few paces when he lost sight of the tower again. He stood bewildered in the darkness before he realised that a high building loomed in front of him. He felt his way along the wall, and became uneasy again. He could not make out what building it was in the darkness. He imagined, for a wild moment, that the Evil One was frustrating him, trying to prevent him from reaching his own cell. He was still hesitating there when he heard the voices of clerics in the distances. They were passing with torches between the churches, and, by the brief flicker, he saw above him the carven wolf-heads on the coigns. He was standing under the Teampull Diarmuid.[10] He knew it at once by those cornices, even though he had never been close to the building before. But he must get away as quickly as he could. He must not be found loitering there, for the temple was in the forbidden quarter.

He made his way past the ancient doorway, and as he did so catechumens[11] hurried past in the distance. The glow of their torches raced along the wall of the Teampull so that the cornices started up with mitred heads and animal shapes. The fantastic carvings vanished again in the night, but not before Aidan had seen a figure crouching beneath them which made him recoil in horror.

Hidden in the remote shadows of the temple wall was a naked woman.

Only for a second had Aidan seen that woman, and he could scarcely believe his own senses. The Devil was mocking him with an evil vision, for no female was even permitted to enter the holy precincts of Cluanmore. But he knew instinctively that his eye could not have deceived him. Too clearly had he seen her repulsive face, seen the lewd smile she gave him as the torchlight swept over her shameless breasts and showed that their black tops were erect. The shadows in which she was dwarfed had hidden her abdomen, but he knew she was bow-legged and that her arms were akimbo. Never could he have imagined, even in Glen Bolcan,[12] so horrible a sight. The woman vanished into the darkness again, but he still remembered her mocking smile.

The scholar's mind was alive with the wildest fancies as he dashed away from the Teampull. He had not been mistaken in the fishing bailey:[13] the woman had been hiding in that house opposite the weaver's door where he had eaten the bread. She

10. Temple of Dermot. The wanderings of Aidan and Ethna are paralled with the journeys of the pagan lovers Diarmuid (Dermot) and Grainne (Grania) of Irish legend.

11. Those preparing to become Christians.

12. Earlier in the novel (Chapter Twenty-One) Aidan visits this mythical valley filled with mad unhappy people, especially those tormented by sins of sex.

13. A space enclosed by a fortified outer wall.

must have followed him stealthily along the road. The leaves had rustled as he crossed the rampart, she had made her way after him into Cluanmore. Even in that holy enclosure he was no longer safe from sin. Its peace and protection were gone; he was once more in the power of the Devil. If he could only reach the crowd by the shore he could mingle among the students. She could not come there among the crowds. The darkness was alive with dangers. He felt as he ran that at any moment naked woman would seize him by the arm, drag him back to the shadows of the Teampull.

Little wonder that Aidan was scared, for he had seen Cile-na-gCich.[14]

He had never heard, in fact, of the obscene female image which was carven on the outside wall of certain chapels at that time. Gazing in spiritual disgust on this image, which revealed the true repulsiveness of womankind, the clergy shrank from the impurity of sin, they snatched their souls from the danger of eternal damnation. True comment of the Celtic-Romanesque age upon the nature of woman, the crumbling image of Cile-na-gCich still lingers on ancient ruins, half hidden by nettles, by thistles, so that the simple are affrighted by its evil eye. On Lustymore Island, in Kilnaboy, on that forsaken oratory by the waters of Lough Erne, on the very pillar of Adamnan[15] at Tara, she dwells in loneliness. But at dark, poets say that Sheila of the Paps still goes by misty short-cut, by dark wood, hastening, like the spirit of offended Irish womanhood, to the pillows of the tonsured. In that midnight hour of temptation the good clergy hear around them the horrid whispers of the confession-box.

'King of Sunday, save me!'

Believing that the woman was gaining on him, Aidan raced in the darkness across the wide quadrangle of Cluanmore. The seven churches were blacker against the glow of the bonfires. The murmuring of the multitudes by the river had increased. If he could only get to the shadow of the main buildings he would be safe. Something was glittering on the ground in front of him. As he darted past, he saw to his horror that it was one of the great chalices of Cluanmore. He knew at once by the burnished gold and silver, by the livid swarm of its jewels. But why was the sacred vessel lying there in the middle of the quadrangle? A chill premonition of evil passed through him. But he dared not stop, for that woman was pressing towards him in the darkness.

Why was the noise of the crowd so loud? Hundreds must be shouting as they hurried behind the churches. A mighty shadow loomed against the ruddy light, it took and enclosed him in darkness.

He started back, then with a cry of relief he stumbled forward again. He was safe at last. He had found sanctuary, for he was under the high-cross of Cluanmore.

But his joyful relief lasted only for a second. Tumult was on every side of him. In the air above evil spirits were in combat around the sculptured cross. Suddenly the plinth was torchlit, and the interlaced snakes were unknotting themselves as rapidly as they could, the small figures of scriptural kings or centaurs were in flight.[16] Melchisedech[17] was unsceptred, Cain pursued Abel once more, and the little Garden of Eden was astir with idle leaves.

'The pillar is alive!'

Aidan shrank back again, but the clamour was wilder. Shrill above that clamour rose the voice of the woman. He broke from the wheel-shadow[18] of the cross. The open doorway of the Daimhliag[19] was only a few yards away. He heard the prayers of the congregation within the nave. Evil spirits were combating in the night; the clergy had fled for protection to the cathedral.

He had no sooner got to the recessed arches of the doorway than his eyes were smarting with the smoke of pitch-pine. Fantastic in that smoke were the eel's-head and cat's-head moulding, the chamfered ledges, the carven heads above them. He thought at first that the cathedral was on fire, but from its gloom came the prayers of the congregation and above them the voice of the woman.

Peering through the changes of smoke, Aidan saw

14. A misprint for Sile-na-gGich, more often anglicized Sile-na-Gig from the Irish Síle na gCioch (Sheila of the Paps). This mysterious image is to be found, as Clarke relates, in medieval church enclosures all over Ireland.
15. Adamnán (*c.* 624–704) was abbot of Iona from 679 until his death.
16. Aidan imagines that the serpentine, biblical designs on the pillars are dissolving and giving way to such pagan images as centaurs — half-human, half-horse.
17. Type for Judeo-Christian priesthood: Psalms 110.4: 'a priest forever according to the order of Melchisedech'.
18. Celtic crosses have stone circles at the intersection.
19. Literally 'Stone-Church', central church of the enclosure.

a sight which held him in fascinated horror.

Triumphant, enthroned upon the high-altar, amid torchlight and shadowy smoke, was a strange woman. But she was not the horrible creature who had pursued him from the Teampull, for she was massive of limb and richly clad. Her red tresses were interwound, were coiled from her brows; her white arms were raised in exultation. Her breasts were of hammered metal, but each nipple was of gold. Her mailed body was half hidden by a broidered vestment of sea-purple, but her large thighs were naked, torched, as she leaned back upon that throne.

She triumphed where the holy offices of Man had alone been performed, where the sacrifical mysteries had been celebrated, the chanting of Latin heard daily. Her voice was lifted in a barbaric chant; she rose, she flung back her arms, and at their bidding the smoke of that rite was stayed.

More horrible still — in the gloom of that nave the clerics were congregated, worshipping with bowed heads before her.

'The monks have gone mad! They have gone mad!'

Aidan's sense was reeling as he clutched the pillar beside him for support. He felt, as on the night in Glen Bolcan, the insane reality of what he saw. But even as he stared at the praying monks they raised their peaked cowls. A hoarse roar came from their hidden throats. They stirred slowly, and the gloom was smithied with the clank of iron. They raised their heads higher in the gloom, and the horrified student saw their cowls become helmets, their habits change into mail. They were armed men, and above their shadowed shoulders was the flash of battle-axes.

'The Danes! The Danes!'[20]

Too late Aidan knew the awful death which awaited him. Fool that he had been to have lost himself in vain thought, to have believed himself the victim of especial temptations during the last hours of his journey. He had been warned by the haymakers and girls as they fled along the hills, but in his folly he had ignored them. He had been warned by the turf-man carrying the crone on his back, but he had not stayed to listen. He might have known only too well why every field was deserted, the road so lonely. He might have known why the fishermen had fled in boats with their families. Fool that he had been, he had closed his eyes against every warning. He had walked into the very encampment of death.

'The Danes! The Danes!'

Long since, the clergy of Cluanmore had fled to remote hiding-places or to the lake-schools. At the first warning the students had been ordered to abandon their cells. All had known the omens, seen fiery spectacles in the clouds; for the very air was alive with phantom companies or outcry when the northmen's ships were on their way to Ireland. The followers of Odin and Thor,[21] hating the Christian creed which had been promulgated in the icy north by force of arms, spared not the pious in their desire for revenge. Aidan knew his awful fate at last. He had walked straight into Cluanmore. He was alone, helpless, in the armed camp of the Danes. He had come back to his own death.

Even in that moment thronged with thoughts he had been seen. Through the smoke and torchlight the eye of the priestess had discovered him. Her white arm, outstretched, pointed towards him in denunciation. He heard the sudden roar of the jarls[22] and vikings, but he only saw that woman pointing to him. Terrible in her strength was the priestess, even as Ota, the wife of Turgesius,[23] when she delivered her oracles from the desecrated altar of Clonmacnoise.

Aidan had staggered back from the smoke; leaping down the step, he was half-way around the corner of the Daimhliag. There was a roar behind him, beyond him. Voices were gathering as he swerved; the darkness had become a shuttle of fire and steel. He was running for his life. Already he felt in imagination the agonising pain of battle-axes as they cleft through the bone into his very brain. Already he felt in his sinking bowels the tortures of blades finding his blood. The Danars would trample him down with their iron feet, they would fling his mangled body into the river. He would sink once

20. Although the bulk of Viking invaders were Norse, the Irish tended to refer to them as *Danair* or Danes, a term quickly synonymous with barbarian.

21. Viking deities.

22. Scandinavian nobles.

23. From 832 A.D. up to his defeat and death by King Malachi in 845, Turgesius ravaged Ireland, placing fleets on many of its major rivers. His wife Ota performed pagan rites on the high altar of Clonmacnoise.

more through that cold darkness. He seemed to feel the gasping, choking moment of his death. He would sink through the darkness, he would be plunged in mortal sin into the tortures of eternity. But he did not want to die, he did not want to be tortured for all eternity. He was young and he had scarcely lived. He wanted madly to live. Existence was a menace, a roar around him in the darkness; it was a mystery of cruelty, of pain. But he had only one life, and he wanted madly to live and to be happy. In memory, the pale face of Ethna was lit before him; she seemed to be looking at him, trying to save him. But he would never see her again; he would never hear her voice. She would search for him; she would never know that he had been killed, that he was lost in eternal darkness.

There was a tumult among the dark churches behind him. Death was rushing towards him from those broken altars. He had turned, he was running in the opposite direction. He was lost among the cells where, only a night ago, scholars had prayed and slept in peace. He knew well that deserted street of beaten clay as he ran down it. He stopped halfway, his eyes dazed.

Hundreds of armed men were massed against the glow of the watch-fires, shouting as they stirred beneath the weft of standards that divided them. He was coming to the central camp of the Danars, and it was crowded, astir with sharp edges, with terrible shadows. For a second he saw that encampment of iron men, noisy with change, brilliant with death.

He dashed to the left, but in a swirl of smoke or flame the monstrous crests of dragons rose between him and the waters. Those gigantic heads might have been reared by the creatures that Torbach[24] and his scribes encircled within the illuminated gospel-page. The Piasts,[25] which had been banished by Saint Patric, were returning broodily along the Shannon. Terrible were the carven prows of the warships, furled, roped inside the currents, as they showed their dragonish jaws against the snaffles of flame.

But Aidan saw those decks no more, for he was halfway back among the cells. The mounded wall of the outer enclosure rose before him, and he scrambled to the top. The tumult was less as his feet touched the soft earth below. He was running along the fosse outside Cluanmore. He was hurrying, like a possessed creature, in the darkness of the dyke. . . .

He could not remember how he had got to the ridge a few miles beyond Cluanmore. He had crossed the causeway into the rustle of leaves. He had plunged through brakes,[26] stumbled across furrows until he found a track beyond the last field. It must have taken him a long time to reach the ridge, for the path was steep and overgrown. Once, indeed, he had lost his way in a waste of briars, but he had found the track again as he stumbled, scratched his arms in the darkness. Only when he got to the ridge and stopped to take a breath did he venture to look back for the first time.

Far below the tower and seven churches of Cluanmore were dark against the ruddy glow of the beacons. Even while he looked a great flame rose behind the eaves, and the tower was illuminated. The Danars were sacking the holy city; they were setting fire to the refectory, to the libraries. Faintly in the night came the roar of the distant multitude by the Shannon, as the conflagration spread, and he could see clearly the streets of cells, the black deserted churches.

Such was the destruction of Cluanmore.

Aidan left the ridge. In the darkness there was no sound save that of the pasture through which he sped. It seemed to him that the mockery of the night had been an evil dream, a mad impossibility of the past. He did not think of the population which had fled from the holy school. The shock had left a sense of emptiness in his mind. His school had vanished. He was without shelter or hope. Cluanmore had become a place of lust and cruelty, an armed camp of death.

Half an hour later Aidan flung himself exhausted in the bracken beneath a little wood of quickentrees. The quietness of the night around him was strange. He felt the dewy fronds of the brackens; they were cool, soft to his touch. He had escaped from death, he was safe and all his life was before him. The thought came to him with a strange exhilaration as he fingered the dewy fronds. The shock had left him numb, and he could not even

24. Torbach was a famous scribe, Abbot of Armagh 807–08. He commissioned the Book of Armagh.

25. Serpents; there is a pious tradition that Patrick drove them out of Ireland.

26. Dense undergrowth, thickets.

pray; but something was happening to him that he did not understand. Faintly his own youth, from which he had fled, was returning, and his imagination had won its own victory. Softly, faintly his youth returned, and he felt in the stillness that sense of gentleness which he had known for the first time when he lay captive in the little wood of Monarua.

Once more he felt that sense of trust, and as he yielded to his own imagination the memory of his love grew bright, triumphed. He saw Ethna again with all his mind, and knew truly that though he had forsaken her, she would forgive him. She moved to him, gently, happily, through the light of his own mind. He heard her voice like the music of drowsiness; it became clear, urgent, as he listened from the bracken. He was back in the firelight by their cave, and she was speaking.

'I would have gone back every night, Aidan, to the little wood at Monarua, hoping I would find you again.'

And he replied:

'I would have come back there, Ethna. I know that I would have found my way there, despite every danger.'

Tears were in his eyes as he repeated those words — words which he had tried to forget. In his mind he could still see her, hear her urgent voice. The terror of Cluanmore was gone. He was filled with hope and courage.

The crescent moon was in the south as Aidan left the wood. His curls were tangled on his brow, his eyes were wide open, tremulous, as he turned to the sky. He was younger, gentler than Diarmuid that night he sought for Grania when she was lost. His cheeks were thin and pale, yet on them, fiery as the shadowed flush of the foxglove, was the love-spot of youth. Deer-like and swift from the lair of his visions was the scholar as he left the quicken-trees that night.

KATE O'BRIEN

(1897–1974)

from: THE ANTE-ROOM (1934)

[*The Ante-Room* is one of Kate O'Brien's most concentrated fictions, focusing as it does on the dilemma of conscience posed to her sensitive and intellectual heroine in the course of a single weekend. The novel is divided into three books corresponding to the three days of Hallowe'en, *The Eve of All Saints, The Feast of All Saints* and *The Feast of All Souls*. With the opening of the third book the novel's action is approaching its climax. The scene is the large town house in Mellick (Kate O'Brien's native Limerick) where the unmarried Agnes is managing a household comprising her mother, Teresa, who is dying, her father and her brother, Reggie, who is invalided through syphilis. Agnes is in love with Vincent, husband of her beloved sister, Marie-Rose; both have come on a visit for the long weekend. Dr Curran, her mother's physician, has proposed marriage to Agnes, not realizing the intensity of her passion for Vincent and his love for her.]

BOOK III

THE FIRST CHAPTER

Vincent waited for her near the tunnel of fir-trees, and as he saw the moonlight assault their darkness to reveal her, he thought that if ever the stage was set for the barn-stormer's play, it was now; if ever two characters were correctly placed to exemplify to an excited gallery that love is the lord of all, it was he and she.

She was before him, halted — her eyes more incandescent than the stars, her breath a frosty garland.

He trembled.

'It's cold,' he said.

'I'm burning.'

She laid a hand on his to prove it, and her fire was not to be endured. He took her in his arms.

'Warm me,' he cried.

Line for line, bone for bone, they seemed to fit together as if by heaven grooved to take each other, as if the platonic split was mended here, and a completed creature stood united to itself at last. 'He that loveth the danger —' [1]a desperate angel cried again to Agnes, but a voice from heaven was not the one most likely at this minute to attain to her. And she might have answered that indeed this danger merited love.

'It's cold, Agnes; I'm cold.'

She was not astonished or shocked at herself. One plane of her mind was certainly thinking: He and I are Catholics, and he is married and his wife is my sister — but against the fantastic proclamation of his mouth on her hair, on her neck, such prose was still as thin as the angel's voice. And yet she knew that she was cheating heaven and him. For what was happening was impossible, and yet it was impossible to deny it.

She turned her face that he might look in it — and his, by some new light which was too brilliant to be happiness, was changed so that it startled her.

But he spoke in a happy tone.

'You're too little,' he said, 'too slim and little to warm a man.'

She put her hand against his face, and marvelled at how natural it was to touch him.

'My darling,' she said. But then a stupid violence of trembling shook her. She closed her eyes and wondered at the space that lay between one second and the next.

She felt herself being lifted, being carried. She opened her eyes as he set her down on the floor of the garden-house. She opened her eyes, and looking round her at the shadowy, familiar little room, full of memories, full of croquet hoops and guns and rusty garden treasures, full of impedimenta of scattered brothers, vanished childhood, she remembered with integrity, as with a violent blow, who she was and what she had come to do. She moved away from Vincent, far, far away across the little room. He sprang to catch her, but she flung up a hand of absolute denial, and he paused, becoming statue-quiet in a strip of light that fell about him. She sought the shadows.

'I came to ask a favour of you,' she said. Then, looking at him, reconsidered the word 'favour.' 'Oh no, not a favour.'

'Don't ask it!'

'Can *you* endure things, then?'

He hesitated.

'I must.'

'I can't! But even if I could — must *she*?'

'What has *she* to bear?'

'Ah, Vincent!'

'She was disillusioned before my mind was filled with you.'

'Now she's unhappy.'

'If that were true, her way back couldn't be through me.'

'You're hard.'

'When two people lose the knack of being at peace, it's gone. And she and I never really had it.'

'But what's to happen?'

'There's a fantasy-life —'

'No use to Marie-Rose.'

'Oh, it's no *use* to anyone! But it *is* one's servant, and it decorates some hours.'

'It's waste!'

'It's nothing of the kind. It's sheer starvation.'

'But is *she* to wither at your pleasure?'

'She won't wither. I told her tonight — you heard me — that she'd be happy. She thought I was making a magic prophecy, but I was only talking common sense. She said to you that she wanted to weep for the coldness of her heart. She often says that. You see, she knows she's not vulnerable. I've done things to her that I hope she's never told you. I've sneered at her and humiliated her. I've thwarted her feelings when my own were stone-dead, and the next day I've despised her for coldness. I've treated her vanity as if it were a loathsome thing — oh, there isn't a mental humiliation or torture that some devil in me hasn't tried on her at one time or another — but, heaven be praised, she hasn't understood! She hasn't imagination, you see, and so I've really never done anything more serious than enrage her —'

Agnes pressed her hand against her breast as though she were wounded.

'But if you had?' she whispered in horror. 'If one of your shots had hit the little thing?'

'Then there might have been a hope,' he said.

'Vincent! She loves you! Why, even today she told me —'

'Believe me, she'll be happy. "Her heart is in the right place," as the saying goes.'

'And is that a crime?'

1. Book of Wisdom 3.26: 'He that loveth the danger shall perish therein.'

'No. Only an advantage.'

'You gave her no peace till she accepted you. I remember that. I was about.'

'Yes. You were about.' He laughed. 'Oh heavens, heavens, don't say that!'

'You're very unscrupulous.'

'Well, if I can't speak of things as they are, to *you* —!'

She moved towards him and then drew back.

'I have no love for my wife. Right or wrong — that is true.'

Agnes sank to the low bench that ran against the wall, and covered her face with her hands. In a stride he came and was on his knees before her. His arms went round her, he laid his forehead against her breast.

She held him to her and let him be. Staring beyond him to the garden, she thought about the ease of love. To her cool mind it had sometimes seemed that the initial expressions of tenderness to someone who was — however adored — a stranger, would be difficult to the point of impossibility. It had never occurred to her that the danger of passion might lie not in its novelty but in its naturalness. And now it was the latter which paralysed her. She reflected that it had not been so earlier in the night when Dr. Curran kissed her, and she smiled above Vincent's head. This was her day, apparently. But in William Curran's arms she had not felt natural; she was sure of that because of the sensation of anxiety she experienced as to how the embrace should end. Her hand moved over the quiet head on her breast, as she thought triumphantly that with this lover she could end or begin a million caresses without taking half a thought. William Curran's kiss had had the vast, dark comfort of a mystery, a strangeness hiding weary life a second, an anæsthetic — that was it.

Here was no anæsthetic, but only a wound unalleviated. There was no hope for this septic wound.

'I came out here,' she said, 'to ask your help in arranging something.'

He moved and looked up at her. Keeping his arm about her he turned sideways to see her better, squatting on his heels. She took courage.

'We mustn't see each other again,' she said.

He threw back his head.

'That at least can't happen to us, love!'

'Ah, but I beg of you!'

'I told you *not* to ask your favour!'

'You talk as if you were a god!'

He sprang to his feet and strode about the little room.

'Even if I'm not, where could you hide from me?'

'Here, for a while, if you'd do as I ask — because my duty is here just now — some of it.'

'All of it!'

'Oh no! My real duty is to God, and Marie-Rose, and should take me miles from here.'

'Your duty to God?'

She sighed wearily.

'Don't pretend this isn't a sin.'

His tradition, as Catholic as hers, allowed him no protest. She went on, speaking very softly:

'If you say it isn't, you have to say a great many other things. In fact you have to say you don't believe in the Church. But I do believe in it.'

'So do I,' he said, 'though I wonder why!'

'I don't believe there's a "why", a reasonable one, anyway.' She paused and looked away to the stars. 'At school I always suspected that there are no real reasons for belief.'

'But they gave you some.'

'I never needed them.'

'Still — all the childishness, and all the cruelties and lapses —'

'They matter humanly — but, if the story was fifty times worse, they wouldn't really matter anything to my belief. Because that's a natural thing, that it's just silly to bludgeon with facts. I feel that in the end the Church is right, only we can't see it except in our own terms — we can't see it, well, transfigured. And I think we will, when we're dead. So all the wrong things —'

'Don't matter? Sins don't matter?'

'Oh — they do!'

'But they are committed.'

'Yes, that's different. You can be honest, and choose to commit a sin.'

'Oh, love, you're so judicial!'

She laughed. If this was how a judge had to flog himself to justice!

'Yesterday, before you came — how long ago it seems! — I went to confession,' she said. 'I hadn't been for ten weeks —'

'You didn't know I was coming?'

'Oh, I knew. I was sick with thinking of you; I was ashamed and exhausted. It was a shock to know I would have to see you again while I was so — out of hand. And then Uncle Tom came and suggested special prayers for mother — and I couldn't go to communion for her unless I cleaned my heart of you — and so I did, just before you came. And I was full of self-confidence then — oh, I was happy, Vincent!'

'I saw you.'

'Ever since, I swear I've tried to hold on to the courage confession gave me! But your being here, and your audacity this time — and the unhappiness of everyone — oh, it's all too much! I'm going to end it.'

'How?'

'I want your promise that you won't come to Mellick for a year. I promise not to go to Dublin.'

'Even if I promised — what's a year?'

'At the end of it, if — if mother is no longer here — I — I'll marry Dr. Curran, if he'll have me.'

He wheeled about. His hand struck violently against the table, rattling the guns that lay there.

'You'll marry Dr. Curran. And then ask me and my wife on a congratulatory visit?'

'No.'

'You called me unscrupulous just now!'

'He would know about this — and he needn't have me.'

'Oh no, he needn't! Most men, as you know, would look you over and pass you by.'

'One did.'

'Oh, love — don't *you* get angry, too.'

'I *am* angry! Vincent, Vincent — can't you see? Because of one silly mistake the feelings of four people must be lacerated! — and if they're not, or even if, letting them take their chance, any shot is made at least to save the decencies, to save understanding, and peace and pride and responsibility and usefulness, to save the innocent — you look at me as if I were obscene!'

He came and took her up into his arms.

'Ah, my heart! my darling!' he cried, his whole frame shaking —

'Oh, stop it! Stop, I say!' She pressed her hands on to his breast to escape, but he would not let her go.

'You used the word "obscene",' he said. 'Then let me tell you there is only one obscenity for me — and that is, to imagine he might have you!'

'Ah, but you're mad!'

'What does that alter? I have no hopes, but if you take away the fantasies that keep me quiet —'

'Who could do that?'

'He could. The man who — had you. I'd never see you as you are again. He kissed you tonight — I saw him. For a second it was as if — as if someone had said you were dead.'

She grew limp in his arms. She seemed to lose the argument.

Dead? she pondered. I wonder what I'd feel if I had to die now?

There was a deathly weariness upon her face. He drew her down on to the bench and sat in silence by her.

'I was thinking about death today,' he said. 'No, not so much about death really as about mother.'

'What was your mother like?'

He hesitated.

'A bit like me — I think — in her face. She was small, of course.' He laughed. 'As little as you.'

'I'm tall.'

'She used to say that too.' He bent forward and clasped his hands together between his knees. 'The only way I can explain mother to you,' he said, 'is this. She used to make me feel something that you do too — a kind of finality of appreciation — a stillness, as if her mere being alive justified everything. It's a lovely, cool sensation, and although it's love, I suppose, it has nothing to do with the other feeling, of wanting to touch you. Perhaps it's the sort of thing some absolutely perfect work of art should cause — but, still, it's warmer than that, and it's surer. It's that you *see* perfection, in your own image, alive and walking — and it's a comfort somehow. . . .'

Agnes said nothing. His voice had a vibration in it that she dared not answer.

'One day I said to mother — "I hope I'll think of you when I'm dying." She asked me why I said that, and I couldn't explain. But *you* see what I mean, don't you? The best thing that there was, the most superb — the most complete apology for life — that'd be a good idea to hold on to then. Now, I suppose it's you I'd see —'

'No, no — you'd think of her —'

'I don't know. When I'm tired the two of you get mixed in my head. But she wasn't ever, I should think, as beautiful as you. Only she had the trick you have — of somehow being perfection!'

She took his hands and kissed them.

'It seems to me,' she said, 'that she passed on that trick to you! Oh, I love you so much, so much!'

He knelt again to gather her against him. She felt him trembling violently, and that his face was wet against her throat.

'If you're ever the mother of a son,' he sobbed, 'oh, don't die until he's hardened to the idea!'

'I'd be afraid to have a child! There's too much in this business of attachment!'

'Oh Agnes, Agnes!'

'I shall love you all my life, I imagine,' she said, 'I cannot think that any number of years or centuries could change the thing I feel when I remember you or look at you. Of course, they say that years change everything, but I don't believe it. I shall love you always — and there are only two things possible to me. Either I keep you out of sight and mind, and marry someone else — oh Vincent, let me speak! — or, if you refuse me that, I'll give you my vow of chastity, and go away at once, right, right away, a thousand miles from Ireland, and live an old maid devoted to good works, and never come home again!'

'You can't do that.'

'If I have to, I can. I can invent an illness. I can make some arrangement for mother and the household.'

'You'd die of grief.'

'Not die.'

'I'd find you.'

'I'd think of a way to make that impossible.'

'You're talking madly.'

'I expect I am.'

'And if you stay — and marry, what is the advantage then?'

'Oh, there are many. I would spare myself and Marie-Rose a separation which might never end. I would gratify and even make happy a man who's worth that trouble, the only man, except you, whom I have felt I could be a good wife to. I would have occupations and responsibilities, and things to fill the days and make me tired at night. Companionship, too, instead of exile. Oh, sturdy facts to keep me sane, and build a barrier between us! Am I asking too much? Am I being shrewd and vulgar?'

'Perhaps. I don't know.'

He got up, and walked to the door. He leant against its frame, his hands in his pockets, his head in the air.

'There is another alternative, my darling.'

'What is it? Tell me.'

'You said just now that people can be honest, and choose to commit a sin.'

'Ah —!'

'You did say that?'

'But I only meant you could be honest, or insolent if you like — with *God*.'

'Of course. But I hadn't thought of cheating the world. I meant that you need not be alone in exile. We could go together.'

He shut his eyes, and dropped and slowed his voice on the last sentence. He was speaking a fantasy out loud at last, he was suggesting that it might take shape. He saw the ancient, sunlit world of the further Mediterranean, white-shored islands and blue waters, broken temples, red-sailed ships. He saw his love amid these things that she thought strange to her, while muleteers and fishermen and beggars marked her rare grace with smiles of atavistic reminiscence. He heard the music of a flute. He saw a sickle moon beyond an open window. The voice of the sea, like an old god counselling, would guide them through their passion into sleep.

'We would go together, dear love.'

They would stay far away for ever, so that no mud flung by the righteous should disfigure them. They would stay among the simple, ancient peoples who, whether thinking Christianly or paganly, take their courtesy from the sweet morning of their world and are disinclined to make astonishment about forbidden love. Her beauty would be their fatal explanation everywhere on those shores where men have eyes, and in any case he would love her so much that it would be obvious he had no right to her. He smiled, and turned to look upon her face. For all her fears of too much caring, she must give him children. Children playing their first games on the Ægean hills and Adriatic rocks, children with her for mother, would be so lucky already that namelessness would be a joke. And she would grow old with a divine, noncombatant reluctance, a rueful grace like that which was his mother's. She would grow old and he with her, and then there would be death and for their sin whatever theologians meant by hell. And it would have to be hell indeed to make its cause regrettable. For if it left a man his human memories —

Agnes wondered why this alternative had never once occurred to her. She had, she saw now, allowed for every issue of their situation except this — that she should take and keep him. She had sought escape from love by many means, by plans of absolute evasion or of compromise on the one hand, and on the other by surrender to such dreams and hungers as she had the day before confessed. And the latter device by its very revelation of herself to her was perhaps, she thought, as true a barrier between her and him as flight from his living presence might be. For fantasy had taught her that once to surrender to the reality it shadowed would be for ever to surrender — and that was simply never to be done. So even tonight, however close he held her, however exquisite the game of 'just this once', and 'this last minute', she knew all the time that she was cheating him and having it both ways — because she burnt to be his lover, and that was rapture, but she knew, some inexorable censor in her knew that it would never happen, and that the wildest danger was not danger.

Was she ignoble then? Was all her struggle falsity, and she content to lose her spirit's virginity while saving her ridiculous, mortal body? Did she love this man at all?

She leant forward on the bench. Her elbows were on her knees, her chin in her hands. She stared at him and tenderness overflowed in all her nerves and senses, flooding the problem of her hardness. Indeed, indeed she loved him — and her spirit by its own roads fled to meet him in that far country of their mutual peace where she knew he wandered dreaming now. She could not have named the places that he saw them in, or told whether there would be snow or sand or cobblestones beneath their feet; she only knew that she was with him in his paradise and that it was hers because he was there. Ah, yes — she could at least assure herself she loved him, for would she not grow old delightedly like this, just sitting here to satisfy her eyes on his relaxed and gentle beauty, content, though blindfold from the images of his thought, to follow its mood which his dreamer's face evoked?

If she loved him then, and if only sin and her immortal soul prevented — ah, but how vast a barricade! Yes, yes, but still her own affair? Her own and God's. But God could surely take some fraction of responsibility for the needs He planted in His helpless creatures? He gave you grace and the moral law and the True Church. And put *Him* in my path, she retorted softly and gladly, thrust Him down into my life and gave me eyes to see Him! Who had said that before today? Ah, William Curran! And he had thought it was a sign of heaven's mercy? Vincent — I can't help it. I do love you. Come back from far away, my darling — come back and take me with you —

He turned to her again and moved his hands in lazy gesture, as if to say how simple everything was.

'We'll never be parted then,' he said.

Never be parted. What was the good of denying so natural a plan?

She lifted her head from the indolent cupping of her hands. Sighing a little she felt, without moving at all, that she had crossed the small space between them and was in his heart, in safety.

He was turned full round towards her, not dreaming now, but speculative. He was thinking of the chances and crudities, the necessities and indignities which were this girl's unalterable human part as surely as another's; he thought of the savagery and lasciviousness of passion, and the surprising isolation from each other of participants in its zenith; he thought of the fatuous egotism of love; of the wounds that malice gives, and the stupidity of good intentions; of the final impenetrability of one mind by another, however in need, however caring; he thought of the world's burden and tale of disillusionment, of how all things tarnish into a regret; into disease and age. He thought of the encroaching worm, and at last of her white bones, clean, dissociated, nameless in the dark. Against it all he had only the unwise mania of his worship; for treading the terrible pattern he had no more than his illicit, unreliable hand to give her.

But there was *her* hand for him; there was her magnitude. And passion, which held together as many as it destroyed. They might come through. Against the story of the world.

He smiled at her beauty and the tender fall of moonlight on her.

She said: 'We'll never be together.'

She spoke softly, yet to both the words were a hard ripple of pistol-shots. But Agnes, as she heard them issue from her astonished lips, understood their truth. For a ghost passed before her eyes then, and had no doubt selected them.

Marie-Rose was the ghost, and she had chosen well. They were the only possible words.

Vincent did not move, but it seemed to Agnes that his eyes drew back into black, alien caverns, gathering a wild blaze, so that they were not blue eyes, but burning coals.

She looked up into them and felt lost, stupid, impotent, indifferent. She could never explain this withering blast of fact, this discovery of the residuum of herself.

Silence swelled hideously, but she had to let it be. She marvelled that it held so vast a shock, so much sense of bitterness and grievance. Two minutes ago — was it? — there had been no question that they could ever be together. What, then, did this plain denial murder? An unreality? Had they dreamt so deeply in that little space of time? Had they so nimbly taken for granted the romantic fate of lovers for ever banished to the sun? So that the pricking of a second's myth seemed the taking of a life?

For him, the dreamer, it was so. He had travelled so far into illusion since presenting her with *his* alternative that her words had somewhat the same effect on his body and mind as if, after years of love, she had betrayed him. The pain was breath-taking.

'What did you say?' he asked, using his voice delicately lest it should whimper.

But she still had no energy.

'You heard,' she said.

'Yes.' He put a hand to his forehead, then let it fall. What was the matter? There was a confusion somewhere, a hiatus. He had misunderstood something. But as a bull will unawares gather his own rage while feeling stunned, he became himself before he knew it.

'What game is this?' he snarled. 'See-saw?'

'It was, I suppose. But the see-saw's down now — finished.'

'Why?'

'Marie-Rose.'

He drew himself up, and when he spoke she could feel his lips sneering.

'And she is *my* responsibility,' he said, 'the burden on *my* conscience.'

Agnes felt inclined to laugh.

'Conventionally, yes.'

'The whole trouble is in that convention — that I have a wife.'

'No. I see now, after tonight, that however I might boast and pray and fight, I would never be *safe* from sin just because you're married —'

'Oh, sweet —'

'And whatever the law is, is doesn't matter a scrap to me that I'm your wife's sister —'

'Well then?'

'But your wife is Marie-Rose.'

'I'm not so ruthless as I sound, my darling. I whirled her into marriage, and adored her for a while. I'll reckon with the remorse and misery of that. But leave it to me, since it *is* mine! Don't pry!'

'I'm not prying. I'm not thinking about you at all.'

'What *do* you mean, then?'

'You talked just now about her not being vulnerable and how your worst unkindness never did more than enrage her. That frightened me, but for a few minutes it seemed that you must be right, that she isn't vulnerable. You see, I'm so much in love with you that it was easy to think that anyone whom you couldn't really hurt must be — rather hard. And perhaps she is. But she isn't completely — I could hurt her. Perhaps I'm the only person who could —'

'Oh, as children you adored each other —'

'If your mother were alive you'd never ask me to run away with you.'

He winced. 'She *isn't* alive.'

'Marie-Rose and I adored each other, as you say. And I didn't marry, and she didn't marry happily. So the devotion was not brushed aside. I think that now I'm the only living soul she feels safe with — and look at me!'

She flung out her hands in comment on them both.

'Supposing what you say is true,' he cried, 'why should she be spared? Why should the lucky person with only one tender spot be saved at the expense of those who're raw all over?'

'Or supposing that you're so little exacting that you only ask one fellow-creature for a real relationship —'

'You'd let her drag on in misery with a man who drives her mad?'

'Since she still wants you, and you can't set her free. Let her at least have the kind of life she decorates so well, and the certainty of me. It isn't much.'

'She'd be happier if I went — in the end.'

'Perhaps. But not if I did.'

'You're very sure of her blind faith in you.'

'I'd have the same in her. Vincent, my darling — understand. It's so long ago since I began to relate everything in life to Marie-Rose. I was a baby when I first discovered how pretty and gay she was. And she was kind to me always! Once someone told me I was the plainest girl in the school, and Marie-Rose gave me no peace until I told her what had upset me. The revenge she took! The way she lampooned that plain little girl before the Junior School! I think I'd have died for her that night!'

'And she has long ago forgotten it.'

'The only point is that *I* haven't. Or a million other things. She made a kind of revelation of growing up! She was such fun!'

'And now, for that — I am to do without you.'

'Her eyes — they'd be bewildered! Oh, they'd haunt me, Vincent!'

'Why didn't you say this an hour ago?'

'I didn't understand it then — I came out here quite honestly to try and find a solution. Oh, I was tempted, too, by the thought of being alone with you. But all the time something I couldn't quite get at kept insisting that I was a cheat to talk to you of love. Still, when you said we could go away together —'

'Yes?'

'Then for a minute — oh, my darling!'

'God!'

'But this other thing would have been there all the same.'

'You love her more than me.'

'I've never thought about how I love her.'

He made no answer, no movement. He continued to lean wearily against the frame of the door. She crossed the little room suddenly, as if to touch or comfort him, but then swerved and leant against the opposite doorpost. Moonlight made a dividing stream between them.

He considered her desperately. She was the one thing he asked of life. He was in the habit of having what he wanted. She loved him with passion, each contact proclaimed their aching physical sympathy. But she was virgin and could not foresee the real claims of her senses. If they were once revealed to her —

'If I were to take you now,' he said, 'if I were to make you my mistress tonight —'

She closed her eyes.

'Are you afraid?'

'Not of you,' she said.

'Listen. I could take you now; I could rape you, ruin you — there are heaps of words. You'd be hurt and bruised and miserable and a great deal disillusioned — but still, if you loved me, you would begin perhaps to see what I mean, what I'm asking for. You might begin to understand that there's one thing in the world which may be worth regrets and dishonours —'

'Yes, of course — *we'd* have our *quid pro quo*. There's only one person who'd get nothing out of the bargain.'

'And you would *never* forget that? There's *nothing* I could do?'

'Nothing. If there were, I'd hate you for doing it.'

'Hate me?'

'It would be as if you'd killed her. I can't explain. I suppose the things we've always known are the last we understand. Probably the whole affair was settled that night in Junior Recreation.'

He understood. Violence and passion could have their tortured minute if he insisted, but they could not retrace, unplait, unravel the long slow weaving of childhood. It was the sort of fact he grasped with fatalism, which told him also that it was the child of that inexorable making whom he loved in the woman now before him. Had she been differently woven, by happy accident, he might have won and would not have wanted her.

All the cards were on the table then — and the game was over. There seemed to be nothing to say.

'I don't seem to have done much good by coming out here to talk,' said Agnes.

'But surely, yes. Isn't everything settled now?'

'Not for me.'

He looked at her resentfully. See-saw again?

'We've settled that there's no use in loving each other. But we haven't decided how to stop it.'

'I'm not going to.'

'I am. I can't face turning into a crazy old maid.'

'So you want me to face the spectacle of your marriage to Curran?'

'Or let me go away as soon as I can, and promise not to follow me.'

'How about Marie-Rose?'

'She could come to where I was sometimes. We could write. Some day I'd come back.'

'With your love for me well scotched?'

'I suppose so.'

'I am to take my choice?'

'Vincent — don't talk in that hateful voice —'

'I'm sorry you find it "hateful!" '

'Well, I do.'

Two o'clock struck. The bells of Mellick had their usual tussle in announcing the small hour. When silence came back Vincent and Agnes were still motionless against their doorposts.

'I believe we're quarrelling,' she said.

'Oh, let's not bother! We're too tired.'

'Yes. We must go in. Won't you help me at all about the future?'

He looked across the stream of moonlight and

studied her with attention. Her face was turned to him in direct appeal. It was — he informed himself coldly, for he was very tired — a divine triumph of a face, to be learnt and re-learnt in many lives; a boy's face and a woman's, the face of an archangel and of a lost little girl.

'If I never see you again, I shall be, when I have got used to it, quite dead and bored. If I am occasionally permitted to see you under his smug patronage I shall live in hell. Either way will be hard on Marie-Rose. Which would *you* choose?'

'The first.'

'And exact your vow to be a crazy old maid?'

'Not crazy, perhaps.'

'Give me time. Give me until tomorrow!'

'I wanted to have no excuse for discussing it again.'

'Why this mania for tidiness?'

'I'm sick of the mess of things. Father, Mother, Reggie, Dr. Curran, you, Marie-Rose — myself — it seems as if someone ought to try to tidy something!'

'Oh, I agree. Life has no shape.'

'How tired your voice is!'

'Not hateful?'

'Oh!'

With a young, wild sob she came to him.

'Not hateful ever! The dearest, dearest, dearest voice! Ah, you! My heart, my darling!'

They clung together.

'And it is love that has beaten us,' he whispered.

'I wonder — I don't know.'

'She's very lucky — Marie-Rose.'

'I thought that three years ago,' said Agnes, with bitter tenderness.

He looked down hungrily into her lifted face.

'Ah, you're so sweet to me,' he said, 'so sweet and generous, and I am a selfish, sulky fool who's made a mess of life for you!'

She ran her hand along his face.

'Yes, you're selfish and sulky,' she said, with a tenderness that set his heart pounding.

'My love! My foolish love! How can I make sure that you'll be happy sometime?'

She put a hand on his mouth. Her eyes filled with tears.

''Ssh. There's no way. But I'll grow middlingly content and so will you, and we'll be middle-aged eventually.'

'That's no good; you'll be glorious then.'

'And so will you.'

She turned her face against his shoulder a minute, then lifted it again.

'I'm going in now,' she said, 'but before I go I'll kiss you — your darling mouth.' She trailed her fingers over it.

She thought that they might part in tenderness; her idea was to reach him in a gentle expression of love, a caress of resignation. That would explain and pacify, and somehow set them free. It seemed that his eyes resisted her, and were afraid, but she drew his head down unrelentingly till their mouths met.

Then she understood her sentimental mistake. There was no pacification here, or freedom. There was no such thing — she ought to have known — as kissing him good-bye and saying 'God bless you.' Love had been painful in fantasy, but here in its clumsy truth it was anguish, with the worst of it that its moment must pass, that there must be an end of the pang of insatiability.

Open-eyed they kissed, she hardly recognising his brilliant eyes, yet very sure that they were his. As more and more he forced her body to the hard slant of his embrace, as the storms of their breasts became one and their mouths gave only thirst for thirst, she understood her own innocence.

He also saw that this kiss was a trap. Long ago he had grown sick of the kisses of flippancy, and afterwards in married life had come to hate those of anger and remorse. He had imagined every aspect of love with Agnes, but because he had to keep a show of decorum had never in the centre of his heart allowed that the intermittent high moments of any earthly passion could be to the last edge of imaginability worth while. He had managed, that is to say, to keep a film of incredulity between himself and the final absurdities of his romanticism. An inner, consoling doctrine of his was that he could visualise what life could not supply.

Now that was gone. From her mouth he was drawing in a poisonous vitality, an irrational knowledge of happiness which made it as clear as light to him that life, contrary to his comforting idea, could justify a dreamer. Could, but would not. From her mouth he was drinking credulity, conviction. In her kiss he was able to measure the finality of his desire for her and its cruel rightness. It was as he had alternately dreamt and denied it — heaven, and the gateway to a further heaven. Useless now and henceforward to drag up the old argument, that in embrace the beloved being too near for focusing, and the sensations of the body too violent for sensitive analysis, she might be anyone, her uniqueness having done its work and been lost in the darkness of desire. That was not so. The world was sick of perpetual kissing and yearning, of which far too much fuss was made — but once in a while a man might know his fate. And here was his, denied him.

He folded her against him.

'I cannot live without you,' he said.

Her arms were round his neck.

'Or I without you.'

'This is love — it hardly ever happens.'

She drooped, drew back from him.

'You mean — it never happens.'

Her face had a look of death. Looking into his, drained and weary. 'I'm sorry,' she said, 'I — I thought it would be no harm to kiss you — once.'

He put his hand under her chin and smiled at her. 'You little love,' he whispered, 'it was no harm.'

'Will you forgive me?' she asked him. 'Will you forgive me for everything?'

'What is everything?'

She paused and looked about her perplexedly.

'Marie-Rose.'

'You were my fate,' he said. 'It is something to have seen that, even now.'

'She is our fate. Ah, little Rose!' She withdrew from his arms. 'I must go in,' she said wearily. 'I must go in.'

They looked at each other, and understood that there was not another word to say.

Agnes passed under the fir-trees and through the cold garden slowly, not as she had come. She shivered a little. That coming had been a fool's errand; it had done no more than prove to her, in one silly kiss, that she could not do without what she must never have. There was no hope or courage anywhere now. Only starvation. Only disgust with everything that was not he, and that for that reason might be hers.

Vincent, still leaning against the doorpost, also thought of her kiss and its lesson — that he could not do without what he could never have.

[Through the second and third chapters Teresa's illness deepens; her brother, Father Tom, is in close attendance as death appears imminent. The possibility of an alliance of convenience between the hopeless Reggie and the acquisitive Nurse Cunningham begins to emerge. Dr Curran feels certain that Agnes will accept his proposal of marriage while the frustrated love between Agnes and Vincent grows more desperate.]

THE FOURTH CHAPTER

Agnes was not in the dining-room when the doctor entered it, but came there immediately after him. She had been with the other members of the family in the drawing-room, she said.

'They're wondering if they may see Mother, and they're afraid to see her.'

'They needn't be afraid. I've told Nurse Cunningham they may pay her a quick, quiet visit now. They'll find her very happy.'

'Happy?'

'Yes. Sit down — that's right. You look extremely tired.'

'Happy? Is it that she doesn't know yet?'

'It's that she doesn't care now about her own fate — and no state of mind can be so happy, I should think. Listen. She had a curious piece of news for me just now — curious, but good. It seems that Nurse Cunningham is going to marry your brother.'

Agnes's face became in a wave of lightning speed suffused in red, and then drained white again before a breath could be taken.

'Marry — Reggie?'

'Yes.'

'But —'

'She knows about him. A formal marriage — which will give him companionship and a very competent protection and care. It's an excellent idea.'

Agnes stood up.

'I think it's horrible —' she whispered.

'Nothing of the kind. It's a miraculous answer to all your prayers. She's a nurse and a woman of the world, and yet kind and livable with and human, and she wants to do it. She's made your mother absolutely happy.'

'How queer!' Agnes said.

'You're being a bit sentimental,' he suggested gently.

'But what motive can she possibly have?'

He smiled at the rich young woman who had never been poor and unprotected.

'Dear girl! Look round you! That hard-working

creature upstairs has not known security since she was born, I imagine!'

'And she's prepared to marry — Reggie for money?'

'More admirable than to marry a better man for that reason.'

Agnes fidgeted about the room. She was immensely confused, by her own horror and acknowledgment of its folly, by pity and bitter gladness for her mother, pity and distaste for her new sister-in-law — and a general, smudgy feeling of discomfort. She was not helped by the certainty that this man knew of those mixed sensations, and was resolute to tidy them up for her.

'In any case,' his voice went on. 'there is nothing dishonest in marrying for money.'

'Oh, I'm not bothering about dishonesty!'

'Why bother about anything? There's nothing in this to bother about. It's a clear contract — as a marriage should be. In this the services which the wife will offer are not the usual ones, but they will be the more exacting for that. In return, perhaps her reward is more secure. Your brother is a rich man, and —'

'Please!'

'But you must listen to me —'

'I won't. I know you're talking sense — only I feel — dirty, somehow.'

'You're cruel.'

'I expect so. But be satisfied now. You've been very skilful in breaking the news and getting me to toe the line' — she smiled at him. 'I promise not to be foolish and unhappy over it.'

'You're beginning to know me,' he said. 'In any case, I was rather neatly blackmailed, as I see it now' — he smiled reminiscently — 'into getting you to take the matter calmly.'

She raised her delicate brows.

'Nurse Cunningham, fearful for your health, tells me that you spent most of last night in the garden. A clever move. She knows very well that I am far more human than gentlemanly. A gentleman would know that where you spend your nights is your business and not his, but an ordinary man who's in love with you won't be able to refrain from mentioning the curious news, in the hope — or fear — of an explanation. And so — because of this deplorable humanity — you know that you are in Nurse Cunningham's power up to a point, and she knows that you know, and that you won't be excessively haughty — as on occasion you can be — about her perfectly legitimate arrangement of her future.'

'You sound as if you read Miss Braddon.'[1]

'Well, I do. And her heroines are always voluble in explanation of themselves.'

'Oh, I'll explain. But not today. I can't be voluble today.'

She dropped on to the window-seat and looked at him appealingly.

'Love, I was only joking,' he cried, 'or — half joking.'

'It wouldn't make you happy — my explanation,' she said.

'Well — if I could even think that it made you a little —'

She leant against the window-glass and kept looking out at the bare garden.

'No. It has nothing to do with happiness. I don't quite know what I mean — what I'm talking about.'

'Don't try to. You're very tired.'

There was silence now between them, broken only by the whispering of the fire, and occasional soft footfalls in the room above, her mother's room. Someone was potting at rooks again; someone was pacing a horse on the road.

'Have you ever noticed that some days are always themselves, year after year?' Agnes asked him idly. 'Good Friday is like that. It's always the most exquisite, heart-breaking day, with a thrill in it that one is ashamed of. And All Souls' Day is like this — leaden and silent, and full of fear —'[2]

'But the worst of today is over now, and for your mother it has turned out to be an intensely happy day.'

'Yes. I wish I could feel that more.'

'How do you feel?'

'Oh — All Souls' Day feeling! Cold and frightened —'

'I can't bear that.'

'It'll pass. This news about — about Reggie is, funnily enough, a bit of a personal solution for me, I suppose.'

'It will loosen your ties here, after your mother is gone.'

1. Mary Elizabeth Braddon (1837–1915), popular author of sensational romantic novels, notably *Lady Audley's Secret* (1862).
2. In catholic practice All Souls' Day is devoted to the souls in Purgatory; the faithful make church visits and offer prayers of intercession that these suffering souls 'may be released from their sins'.

'Yes. I could go away then — right out of his sight — without rousing suspicions or making a scene. Father and Reggie would be off my mind.' She spoke idly, to herself, not to him.

'Out of his sight?'

'Yes.' She turned and faced him, the truth and its desolation in her face. 'Vincent. Out of his sight.'

'And what about mine?'

'Please!' The voice was small and pitiful. 'I have no room in me for more trouble today.'

He lost the sense of his own hunger for her, as so often by a mere trick of voice or attitude she could make him do. Lost it in apprehension of her hunger. Ah! the clumsiness of life to wound its best like this!

'Today will pass, like any other day,' he promised her.

'I'll be glad of that.'

'Poor day!'

She laughed unsteadily. 'Don't try to coax me,' she said, with kindness. 'That's what you're trying to do — and it's waste of time. I feel as if I had some kind of poison in me — as if I were dying here this minute — half dead.'

'Ah, my dear heart!'

'Please, please! Oh, how I pity you!' She got up and gently brushed aside his begging hands. 'I must go and see Mother. She'll wonder at my being so long.'

She left him and went upstairs. On the corridor she met her father, who looked uneasy, worried. He paused before her and tried to read her face.

'Have you heard, my dear? Have you heard?'

'Yes, Father,' she said, too weary to give him any clue to her feelings.

'It's for the best, my dear,' he ventured. 'It's for the best, I think. Good news, child, good news.'

She patted his hand.

'Yes,' she said, 'it's making her happy.'

She passed on into the sick-room.

There are too many people here, she thought, with a shock. Nurse Cunningham was crocheting beside the fire, and Reggie stood and fidgeted in her vicinity. His world, in wasteful fashion, had been rebuilt beneath his feet; Agnes, with a twinge of savage jealousy, turned her eyes from him. Uncle Tom sat by her mother's bed, and Marie-Rose, deft and quiet, stood arranging flowers before the statue of Our Lady.

Too many people, Agnes thought again. They'll exhaust her.

But the figure in the bed was very quiet, and the face of her mother startled Agnes when she bent above it. This is happiness, she thought, and wondered if even here she did not grudge it.

'Mother darling,' she said tenderly.

Teresa smiled at her.

'You know?' she croaked, and Agnes nodded.

'God is good,' the broken voice went on. 'Always He is good. He never fails us.'

Agnes looked at her uncle, and wondered what he made of this answer to his intercessions. But his face gave her no clue. His eyes were on Teresa, and his lips moved in a prayer which he allowed to become audible. 'Tu rex gloriæ, Christe. Tu Patris sempiternus. . . .'[3]

'Du bist die Ruh,'[4] Marie-Rose sang under her breath.

Agnes thought: They are all alive, even Mother. But I'm dying. Vincent, if I could only die — oh, Vincent, darling —

3. 'You, Christ, king of glory. You eternal Father . . .' — phrases from catholic prayer.

4. 'You are Sorrow.' The words, from the second strophe of a poem by Friedrich Rückert (1788–1866), were set to music by Franz Schubert (*Werke*, Leipzig, 1884–97, 7.64.iii).

THE FIFTH CHAPTER

Vincent, walking towards the rose-garden, smiled at Dr. Curran's irritability, and had the impression of already considering it from the other side of death. But I can count on him, all the same, he thought. He has wits — that's quite true. He'll know exactly what I mean.

He entered the little dark garden-house and sat down on the bench. He looked about it with a sense of affection and familiarity, for he seemed now to have lived a long time in association with it. He felt very tired, and was glad that there was no more thinking to do. All that was over, that long soliloquy that had begun when her kiss ended — how many hours or days ago? He believed that he had slept a little, dreamt a little, during it. But that had not seemed to break the thread of thought.

The potentialities of simple things were vast, he thought. A gun — his eyes rested on several — could accomplish a number of simple and complicated things, and a rose — he looked out at the frozen bushes — could be any fool's delight or the symbol which in love and poetry and mysticism it was. People were always kissing each other — and no bones broken — and then she kissed you.

He went to the table, where three guns lay that he had been cleaning. Like a careful stage manager he appraised the table's effect, the opened oil-bottle, the scattered rags. The Snyder, with its breach open and empty. The little old Westbury Richards, which had a defective piston spring, loaded. He, a gun expert, had discovered how to control this defect, but it could be made to seem a source of accident. He touched the Spencer repeater, but then picked up the Westbury Richards again. A short, awkward weapon — its eccentricities and age attracted him. He carried it to the door of the hut, raised it and killed a hurrying rook. Reluctantly he put it back upon the table.

He took off his coat and threw it on the floor. He smeared the oil-rags on his hands and ruffled up his hair.

Everything was in order. His affairs and his will. But they always were. It would be a grief for everyone — and then it would be over, and they could live. No one but she — and her quick-witted lover – would dream that it was not an accident. For even if it crossed Marie-Rose's mind, Agnes, the cherisher, would know how to scotch the thought. But it wouldn't. Marie-Rose *knew* him, she would say, and did not know how deep was the misery of their marriage. All the better time for going. No suspicion anywhere. But in a house already so troubled — was it a very fine cruelty to add this shock of sadness? Perhaps, but Teresa was near death, and much protected by morphia; it would not really reach her heart or make much difference now. And for the others, the sooner they can flower again, with all their sorrows buried — why, the better. Now is the time, he insisted to himself, when they have given me coroner's evidence of accident with general talk of shooting and cleaning old guns. Now is the time — while I still know how to love her and the only honest way to give her up. It must be *now*. I cannot take her terms. I cannot live to torture her. If she takes another and is happy in my sight, oh, God, you see, you know! And if I drive her out of sight, and waste and spoil her! But that's impossible. She'll find this cruel, what I do. She won't know what to think at first, or where to turn. She'll cry —

He sat on the bench and shut his eyes. To his own amazement he was trembling and sobbing now. Oh, it was madness to think about her tears — it was the straight way back to sanity, the road he could not take.

He stood again — in frozen calm. His eyes were glazed as if sightless. He had done with life — for every good reason, not all of them cruel or selfish. It was his own affair if he put his own valuation on one girl. There was no explanation except in him, and he must be allowed it. His mother would listen to him and call him no hard names. And he would find her soon — in spite of the sin he was going to commit. Yes, it was a sin — but would God show him an alternative? To end things in one crime, or to live in an unending vulgar guilt? Agnes would see what he meant. Oh, surely Agnes would? He was going to hurt her almost to death, and still, in the end, she would see and understand. Hurt, or dead, or what you will, he was safe with her. And life and death didn't really matter, in a way, once you knew that.

He closed his glazed, tired eyes. Last night, last night. He would think of it for only one minute more. He laid his hands on the Richards, and remembered the stars of last night's sky, which would take their happy places again tonight. Perseus he had noticed, but not Andromeda. And Orion's sword was clear.[1] Then she had come, her eyes defeating all the planets, and her breath had been like a white wreath. 'I've come to ask a favour,' she had said. Oh, Agnes, Agnes, I ask a favour now. I ask for evermore your dear forgiveness. I ask you the impossible, you gentle heart — that you won't cry or grieve for me. But understand! Oh, Agnes — understand! Don't cry! Don't cry! Be merciful, and promise not to cry! My love, forgive me!

He leant upon the gun, reflecting that the essential was to hit the brain, making it seem as if the weapon had gone off while he bent over it to adjust the inessential screw he had this morning loosened. So long as Curran took his cues up firmly — ah, he was tired. The metal was getting warm against his face. No need to press upon the muzzle. That would seem unnatural. He could stand straighter and trust his aim. Last night. Dear love, last night — *Du bist die*

1. Vincent may be contrasting his position with that of Perseus, who saved his beloved, Andromeda, from a monster in the Greek legend. Orion is the hunter.

Ruh. Die Ruh. He remembered leaning on a gun in the garden at home on a sunny day, leaning like this, and talking to his mother. It was summer and she was sewing. She had said: 'Don't lean on it, Vin. It will mark your face.' Darling mother. He smiled. He could see every detail of her smile. Darling mother. He pulled the trigger, his thoughts far off in boyhood.

Limerick. January 18th, 1931

ELIZABETH BOWEN

(1899–1973)

from: THE LAST SEPTEMBER (1929)

[The heroine of the novel is Lois, niece of Sir Richard Naylor at whose country house, Danielstown, in County Cork, the novel is set. The time is autumn 1920, when the Auxiliaries — a military force recruited largely from demobbed British officers after the Great War — were added to the Royal Irish Constabulary and the Black and Tans, in the fight against the IRA. Lois is in love with Gerald Lesworth, a young English officer of the local garrison, who is probably part of the patrol circling the estate in the opening extract. The Montmorencys, Hugo and Francie, old friends and cousins of the Naylors are their house guests as the novel opens. Hugo had briefly loved Lois's mother, Laura, who has been dead for several years. Lois's cousin, Laurence, is nephew to Lady Naylor, also referred to as Aunt Myra; he is spending his long vocation with his aunt and uncle at Danielstown. As they sit on the terrace in this opening extract, Lois, conscious of Gerald's role out in the unfriendly darkness, becomes an uneasy register for the strange sense of elegy and crisis that informs the novel's action.]

BOOK ONE

CHAPTER 4

Lois was sent upstairs for the shawls; it appeared that a touch of dew on the bare skin might be fatal to Lady Naylor or Mrs Montmorency. On the stairs, her feet found their evening echoes; she dawdled, listening. When she came down everybody was on the steps — at the top, on the wide stone plateau — the parlourmaid looking for somewhere to put the coffee tray. Mrs Montmorency sat in the long chair; her husband was tucking a carriage rug round her knees. 'If you do that,' Lois could not help saying, 'she won't be able to walk about, which is the best part of sitting out.'

No one took any notice: Mr Montmorency went on tucking.

'Haven't you got a wrap for yourself?' said Lady Naylor. Lois took a cushion and sat on the top step with her arms crossed, stroking her elbows. 'I shouldn't sit there,' her aunt continued; 'at this time of night stone will strike up through anything.'

'If you don't get rheumatism now,' added Francie, 'you will be storing up rheumatism.'

'It will be my rheumatism,' said Lois as gently as possible, but added inwardly: 'After you're both dead.' A thought that fifty years hence she might well, if she wished, be sitting here on the steps — with or without rheumatism — having penetrated thirty years deeper ahead into Time than they could, gave her a feeling of mysteriousness and destination. And she was fitted for this by being twice as complex as their generation — for she must be: double as many people having gone to the making of her.

Laurence, looking resentfully round for somewhere to sit — she had taken the only cushion — said: 'I suppose you think ants cannot run up your legs if you cannot see them?'

Mr Montmorency surprised her by offering a cigarette. He had a theory, he said, that ants did not like cigarette smoke. The air was quiet now, the flame ran up his match without a tremble. 'The ants are asleep,' she said, 'they disappear into the cracks of the steps. They don't bite, either; but the idea is horrid.'

'Don't you want a chair?' When she said she didn't, he settled back in his own. Creaks ran through the wicker, discussing him, then all was quiet. He was not due to leave the ship in which they were all rushing out into Time till ten years after the others, though it was to the others that he belonged. Turning half round, she watched light breathe at the tips of the cigarettes; it seemed as though everybody were waiting. Night now held the trees with a toneless finality. The sky shone, whiter than glass, fainting down to the fretted leaf-line, but was being steadily drained by the dark below, to which the grey of the lawns, like smoke, as steadily mounted. The house was highest of all with toppling immanence, like a cliff.

'I don't think,' said Francie, 'I remember anything so — so quiet as evenings here.'

'Trees,' said Laurence, shifting his pipe. His shirt-front was high above them, he stood by the door with his foot on the scraper.

'This time tomorrow,' said Lady Naylor, 'we shall want to be quiet — after the tennis party.' She let out a sigh that hung in the silence, like breath in cold air.

'Oh yes, the party! The tennis party. . . .'

'Francie, did I tell you who were coming?'

'You told her,' said Laurence. 'I heard you.'

'It is the people who don't play tennis who make it so tiring.'

Something about the way, the resigned way, Francie's hands lay out on the rug gave her the look of an invalid. 'It is a good thing,' said Sir Richard, 'you two never went out to Canada. I never liked the idea myself; I was very much against it at the time, if you remember.'

'I was divided about it myself,' said Hugo. 'It seemed worth trying, and yet there was so much against it. I don't know that I should have done very much good — I wonder.'

They wondered with him, with degrees of indifference. Lois stroked her dress — the feel of the stuff was like cobwebs, sticky and damp. There must be a dew falling.

'Oh!' cried Francie. '*Listen!*'

She had so given herself to the silence that the birth of sound, after which the others were still straining, had shocked her nerves like a blow. They looked, from the steps, over a bay of fields, between the plantations, that gave on a sea of space. Far east, beyond the demesne: a motor, straining cautiously out of the silence. A grind, an anguish of sound as it took the hill.

'Patrols,' said Laurence.

Hugo reached out and pressed a hand on to Francie's rug. 'Patrols,' he told her, translating the information.

Sir Richard explained severely: 'Out every night — not always in this direction.'

'They're early; it's half-past nine. Now I wonder. . . .'

The sound paused, for a moment a pale light showed up the sky in the darkness. Then behind the screen of trees at the skyline, demesne boundary, the sound moved shakily, stoopingly, like someone running and crouching behind a hedge. The jarring echoed down the spines of the listeners. They heard with a sense of complicity.

'A furtive lorry is a sinister thing.'

'Laurence, it isn't furtive!' said Lady Naylor. 'Can't you be ordinary? If it wouldn't be taken in some absurd kind of way as a demonstration, I should ask the poor fellows in to have coffee.'

'They're careful enough,' said Hugo impatiently. It seemed that the lorry took pleasure in crawling with such a menace along the boundary, marking the scope of peace of this silly island, undermining solitude. In the still night sound had a breathlessness, as of intention.

'The roads are so rough,' said Lois: she could see the wary load lurching into the hedges. 'I wonder now,' she added, 'who is with the patrol tonight?'

'Someone you know?' cried Francie. But Sir Richard, who did not like his friends to be distracted from him by lorries any more than by introspection or headaches or the observation of nature, bore this down with one of his major chords:

'The lower tennis court, Hugo' — waving sideways into the darkness — 'is not what it used to be. Some cattle got on to it after the rain and destroyed it. It's had rolling enough to level a mountain, but it won't be the same for a long time. D'you remember the fours we had on that court that summer — wasn't it nineteen-six — you and I and O'Donnell and poor John Trent?'

'I do. Now was it James O'Donnell or Peter that went to Ceylon?'

'That was a great summer; I never remember a summer like it. We had the hay in by the end of June.'

The lorry ground off east towards Ballyhinch;

silence sifting down on its tracks like sand. Their world was clear of it and a pressure lightened. Once more they could have heard a leaf turn in the trees or a bird shifting along a branch. But they found it was now very dark. Francie shivered, and Lady Naylor, rising formally, said she thought they should go in. 'Poor John Trent,' she added, gathering up her cushions, 'never got over that trouble he had with the Sheehans over the Madder[1] fishing. It went into court, you know, and of course he lost. We always told him to keep it out of court. He was very obstinate.'

'He was indeed,' said Sir Richard. 'He made an enemy of Sheehan and it's not a good thing to have made an enemy. Though of course he's dead nowadays, so it may not matter.'

'It may to the Archie Trents. . . . Laurence, help Uncle Richard in with the long chair, and remember to bring in your own chair afterwards.'

'I never had a chair.'

'Oh, they haven't lighted the lamp in the hall. That is too bad! I am lost without Sarah — do you remember Sarah, Francie? She died, you know.'

Lois, sitting still among rising, passing and vaguely searching figures, cried: 'But it's only just beginning! You're missing the whole point. I shall walk up the avenue.'

Francie went in, groping; trailing her rug. The three men, carrying wicker chairs, converged at the door: the chairs jostled. They all put them down and apologized. Lois repeated: '*I* shall walk up the avenue.' But having arranged an order of procedure they all passed on into the house, creaking and bumping. She walked down the steps alone: she wanted to be alone, but to be regretted.

'Mind you don't get locked out!' her uncle shouted after her. The glass doors shut with a rattle.

Lois walked alone up the avenue, where she had danced with Gerald. She thought what a happy night that had been, and how foolish Mr Montmorency now thought them. He had seemed annoyed at her being young when he wasn't. She could not hope to explain that her youth seemed to her also rather theatrical and that she was only young in that way because people expected it. She had never refused a role. She could not forgo that intensification, that kindling of her personality at being considered very happy and reckless, even if she were not. She could not hope to assure him she was not enjoying anything he had missed, that she was now unconvinced and anxious but intended to be quite certain, by the time she was his age, that she had once been happy. For to explain this — were explanation possible to so courteous, ironical and unfriendly a listener — would, she felt, be disloyal to herself, to Gerald, to an illusion both were called upon to maintain.

Just by the lime, in that dancing night, she had missed a step and sagged on his arm, which tightened. His hand slid up between her shoulders; then, as she steadied back to the rhythm, down again. They had set out laughing, noisy and conscious, but soon had to save their breath. Gerald's cheek, within an inch of her own, was too near to see. All the way up, he had not missed a step; he was most dependable. And remembering how the family had just now gone into the house — so flatly, so unregrettingly, slamming the glass doors — she felt *that* was what she now wanted most — his eagerness and constancy. She felt, like a steady look from him, the perfectness of their being together.

'Oh, I do want you!'

But he was very musical, he conducted a jazz band they had at the barracks: while reaching out in her thoughts she remembered, the band would be practising now. She was disappointed. To a line of tune the thought flung her, she danced on the avenue.

A shrubbery path was solid with darkness, she pressed down it. Laurels breathed coldly and close: on her bare arms the tips of leaves were timid and dank, like tongues of dead animals. Her fear of the shrubberies tugged at its chain, fear behind reason, fear before her birth; fear like the earliest germ of her life that had stirred in Laura. She went forward eagerly, daring a snap of the chain, singing; a hand to the thump of her heart, dramatic with terror. She thought of herself as forcing a pass. In her life — deprived as she saw it — there was no occasion for courage, which like an unused muscle slackened and slept.

High up a bird shrieked and stumbled down through dark, tearing the leaves. Silence healed, but kept a scar of horror. The shuttered-in drawing-room, the family sealed in lamplight, secure and bright like flowers in a paperweight — were desirable, worth much of this to regain. Fear curled back from the carpet-border. . . . Now, on the path: grey

1. A trout river in the neighbourhood.

patches worse than the dark: they slipped up her dress knee-high. The laurels deserted her groping arm. She had come to the holly, where two paths crossed.

First, she did not hear footsteps coming, and as she began to notice the displaced darkness thought what she dreaded was coming, was there within her — she was indeed clairvoyant, exposed to horror and going to see a ghost. Then steps, hard on the smooth earth; branches slipping against a trench-coat. The trench-coat rustled across the path ahead, to the swing of a steady walker. She stood by the holly immovable, blotted out in her black, and there passed within reach of her hand, with the rise and fall of a stride, a resolute profile, powerful as a thought. In gratitude for its fleshliness, she felt prompted to make some contact: not to be known seemed like a doom: extinction.

'It's a fine night,' she would have liked to observe; or, to engage his sympathies: 'Up Dublin!' or even — since it was in her uncle's demesne she was straining under a holly — boldly — 'What do you want?'

It must be because of Ireland he was in such a hurry; down from the mountains, making a short cut through their demesne. Here was something else that she could not share. She could not conceive of her country emotionally: it was a way of living, an abstract of several landscapes, or an oblique frayed island, moored at the north but with an air of being detached and washed out west from the British coast.

Quite still, she let him go past in contemptuous unawareness. His intentions burnt on the dark an almost visible trail; he might well have been a murderer he seemed so inspired. The crowd of trees, straining up from passive disputed earth, each sucking up and exhaling the country's essence — swallowed him finally. She thought: 'Has he come for the guns?'[2] A man in a trench-coat had passed without seeing her: that was what it amounted to.

She ran back to tell, in excitement. Below, the house waited; vast on its west side, with thin yellow lines round the downstairs shutters. It had that excluded, sad, irrelevant look outsides of houses take in the dark. Inside, they would all be drawing up closer to one another, tricked by the half-revelation of lamplight. 'Compassed about,' thought Lois, 'by so great a cloud of witnesses. . . .'[3] Chairs standing round dejectedly; upstairs, the confidently waiting beds; mirrors vacant and startling; books read and forgotten, contributing no more to life; dinner-table certain of its regular compulsion; the procession of elephants that throughout uncertain years had not broken file.

But as Lois went up the steps breathlessly, her adventure began to diminish. It held ground for a moment as she saw the rug dropped in the hall by Mrs Montmorency sprawl like a body across the polish. Then confidence disappeared, in a waver of shadow, among the furniture. Conceivably, she had just surprised life at a significant angle in the shrubbery. But it was impossible to speak of this. At a touch from Aunt Myra adventure became literary, to Uncle Richard it suggested an inconvenience; a glance from Mr Montmorency or Laurence would make her encounter sterile.

But what seemed most probable was that they would not listen. . . . She lighted her candle and went up to bed — uncivilly, without saying good night to anyone. Her Uncle Richard, she afterwards heard, was obliged to sit up till twelve o'clock. He had not been told she was in, so did not think it right to lock up the house.

[As the novel nears its end, the political situation has grown more unstable, while the love between Lois and Gerald has become at once deeper and more complicated. Lady Naylor's disapproval and the lovers' failure to understand each other have made their most recent meeting at once a declaration of undying love and a parting of the ways. In the last paragraphs of Book Three, Chapter 23, the novel's penultimate chapter, the tragedy that has haunted the action from the start begins to materialize when Gerald fails to return from a trip to Cork. The scene is the military barracks at Clonmore.]

BOOK THREE

CHAPTER 23

. . . The world did not stand still, though the household at Danielstown and the Thompsons' lunch party took no account of it. The shocking news reached Clonmore that night, about eight

2. There has been reference in Chapter 2 to guns buried in the woods.
3. Epistle of St Paul to the Hebrews, 12.1.

o'clock. It crashed upon the unknowingness of the town like a wave that for two hours, since the event, had been rising and toppling, imminent. The news crept down streets from door to door like a dull wind, fingering the nerves, pausing. In the hotel bars, heads went this way and that way, quick with suspicion. The Fogartys'[1] Eileen, called by a friend while she was clearing away the supper, cried 'God help him!' and stumbled up to Mr Fogarty's door, blubbered. Mr Fogarty dropped his glass and stood bent some time like an animal, chin on the mantelpiece. Philosophy did not help; in this thickening brain actuality turned like a mill-wheel. His wife, magnificent in her disbelief, ran out, wisps blowing, round the square and through the vindictively silent town.

Barracks were closed, she could not get past the guards; for once she was at a loss, among strangers. She thought mechanically 'His mother,' and pressed her hands up under her vast and useless bosom. Trees in the square, uneasy, shifted dulled leaves that should already have fallen under the darkness. The shocking news, brought in at the barrack gates officially, produced an abashed silence, hard repercussions, darkness of thought and a loud glare of electricity. In Gerald's room some new music for the jazz band, caught in a draught, flopped over and over. An orderly put it away, shocked. All night some windows let out, over the sandbags, a squeamish, defiant yellow.

Mrs Vermont[2] heard when Timmy had just gone out; he was to be out all night with a patrol. She was to sleep alone, she could not bear it. Past fear, she ran to the Rolfes' hut. She spent the night there, sobbing, tearing off with her teeth the lace right round her handkerchief. Captain Rolfe kept bringing her hot whisky. 'I can't, I can't, not whisky; it's so awful.' They all felt naked and were ashamed of each other, as though they had been wrecked. From the hut floor — where they had danced — the wicker furniture seemed to rise and waver.

'Percy, where did he — how was he —?'

'Through the head.'

'Then it didn't —?'

'Oh no. Probably instantaneous.'

'Oh, *don't*! Oh, Percy, how can you!'

Denise repeated: 'I can't believe it.' And while the others sickly, furtively stared, she tried to press from her hair the waves she had had put in that morning. 'You know. I *can't* believe it. Can you, Betty? It's so . . . extraordinary.'

'Why can't we all go home? Why did we stay here? Why don't we all go home? That's what I can't understand.'

'Percy, can *you* believe it? I mean, I remember him coming in and standing against this table —'

'Oh, don't! — Percy, what became of *them*? Where did they go? Those devils!'

'Oh, got right away.'

'Didn't anyone hear anything, any firing? I mean, didn't it make a noise? . . . Couldn't they be tortured — why should they just be hanged or shot? Oh, I do think, I mean, I do think when you think —'

'Well, we've got to get 'em, haven't we? Look, just try —'

'Oh, I *can't*, I tell you — Why can't we all go home!'

'Percy, leave her *alone*! Oh God, my head; I shall cut my hair off. I mean, he came in and stood there against that table. Why did they get just Gerald? — Oh, yes, I know there was the sergeant — but *he* won't die; I know he won't die . . . I can't believe it! Percy, *can* you believe it? Percy, say something.'

Betty sobbed: 'I should like to — oh, I should like to — Those beasts, those beasts!'

'Look, you two girls go to bed.'

'Oh, how can we!'

'Oh, why isn't Timmy here? I mean, when I think of Timmy, and out all night — *I* can't understand the King, I can't understand the Government: *I* think it's awful!'

But they went to bed — Percy spent the night on two chairs — and lay in what seemed to both an unnatural contiguity, reclasping each other's fingers, talking of 'Him', of 'you know who' and 'that boy' in the eager voices, low-pitched and breaking, kept as a rule to discuss the intimacies of their marriages. In the same moment they fell, dimly shocked at each other, asleep. Then Denise saw Lois clearly, standing affectedly on the Danielstown steps with a tin of biscuits, a room full of mirrors behind her. And Betty woke with surprise to hear herself say: 'What I mean is, it seems so odd that he shouldn't

1. The Fogartys are local friends of the military. Lois had spent the night at their house after a recent dance.
2. Mrs Betty Vermont, whose husband, Timmy, is still out on patrol, is a close friend of Mrs Denise Rolfe, wife of Captain Percy Rolfe. Recently arrived from England, they are known as 'the girl wives'.

really have meant anything.'[3]

They heard an early bugle shivering in the rain.

3. When the 'girl wives' had attempted to drop in on Danielstown, they had been skilfully repulsed by Lois, who had fed them biscuits from a tin on the steps of the great house.

CHAPTER 24

Mr Daventry[1] arrived before the postman. He had not paid an unofficial visit since he had been in Ireland; it seemed to him odd there should be nothing to search for, nobody to interrogate. It was early, wet tarnished branches came cheerfully through the mist. He had come to the gate with a convoy on its way over to Ballyhinch; two lorries had ground into silence and waited for him at the gate, alarming the cottagers. He walked up the avenue lightly and rapidly: nothing, at the stage things had reached for him, mattered. And superciliously he returned the stare of the house.

He rang and made his demand. Lois came out slowly, dumb with all she must begin to say — for who could an anxious waiting officer be but Gerald? 'Really. . . .' Lady Naylor had said, with a glance at the clock, advising her to put down her table napkin. And Francie, smiling, had covered up her egg for her.

'You?' she now said while everything, the importance of everything, faintly altered. 'Come and have breakfast.'

He told her that there had been a catastrophe yesterday, west of Clonmore: a patrol with an officer and an N.C.O. had been ambushed, fired on at a cross-roads. The officer — Lesworth — was instantly killed, the N.C.O. shot in the stomach. The enemy made off across country, they did not care for sustained fire, in spite of the hedges. The men did what they could for the sergeant.

'Will he die?'

'Probably.'

'And Gerald was killed?'

'Yes. Would you —?'

'I'm all right, thank you.'

'Right you are.' He turned round and stood with his back to her. She asked what time it had happened; he said about six o'clock. She thought how accurate Gerald was and how anxious, last time, he had been to establish just *when* she had been happy because of him, on what day, for how long. 'They'd been out all the afternoon?' They both saw the amazed white road and dust, displaced by the fall, slowly settling. 'As a matter of fact,' said Daventry, 'we were mostly ready for things. I don't suppose — if he knew at all — it mattered.' 'No, I don't suppose, to oneself, it ever would matter much.' But she thought of Gerald in the surprise of death. He gave himself up to surprise with peculiar candour.

'Thank you for coming.'

'I was passing this way anyhow.'

'But still, there was no reason why you should take the trouble.'

Daventry glanced at her, then at the gravel under his feet, without speculation. Cold and ironical, he was a stay;[2] he was not expecting anything of her. He finally said: 'It seemed practical. Would you like me to — shall I just let the others know?' She nodded, wondering where to go, how long to stay there, how to come back. Her mind flooded with trivialities. She wondered who would go up to the tennis this afternoon, if there would be anyone left who did not know, who would expect him; she wondered what would become of the jazz band.[3] She saw for days ahead she must not deny humanity, she would have no privacy. 'As a matter of fact, they are expecting me back to breakfast.'

But at the thought of Francie's tender and proud smile, covering up her egg, she was enlightened and steadied by grief, as at the touch of finger-tips. She went into the house and up to the top to meet what was waiting. Life, seen whole for a moment, was one act of apprehension, the apprehension of death. Daventry, staring at her in memory — she was, after all, a woman — went into the hall. Here, it pleased him to think of Gerald socially circumspect under the portraits.

He waited. The dining-room door swung open on a continued argument; they came out one by one, each on the threshold, balanced momentarily like a ball on a fountain by the shock of seeing him. 'Lady

1. Mr Daventry is an enigmatic figure. A mere subaltern at Clonmore, he had been a major in the war, and is still suffering from shell-shock. He seems to have desired Lois and felt jealous of Gerald.

2. prop, support.

3. Gerald had been its conductor.

Naylor?' he said to Francie. 'Oh *no*!' She seemed appalled at the supposition. 'Isn't . . . Mr Lesworth here?' 'Not today.' Lady Naylor came last and stared hardest: really, the Army seemed to be inexhaustible. He told her. 'Oh, no!' she said quickly, as though to prevent something. He told her the circumstances. 'Oh — *no*,' she repeated, and turned in appeal to her husband. 'That is . . . that is too bad,' said Sir Richard and in despairing confusion touched her shoulder. He looked back into the dining-room at the chairs and plates and table, incredible in their survival.

The fact was, they did not at all care for the look of Mr Daventry. They felt instinctively that he had come here to search the house. Lady Naylor, still statuesque from the shock, made, even, a little disdainful gesture, a kind of: 'Here's everything.' He, unconscious of her impression of being brought to book, remained staring darkly and piercingly past her. Behind her, across the dark dining-room, he saw through a window the lawn striped with mist and sunshine. In Clonmore it had rained that morning: they seemed to have escaped that too. She said sharply: 'Where's Lois?'

'I'm afraid I don't know,' he replied, indifferent.

'She — you have —?'

'Oh, yes.'

Her defensive dropped; she said with heartbroken eyes on his face: 'You know, we knew him so well. He came out here so often to tennis. It seems queer that one can't — that one never — He was so —'

'Yes, he was, wasn't he?'

'His mother, he used to tell me about his mother. Who will write? I should like to write to her. Yes, I want very much to write to her. I think she might like — we did know him so well, you see — Richard, don't you think I — ?'

But Sir Richard had slipped away quietly; he was an old man, really, outside all this, and did not know what to do. He was wondering, also, about the Connors. Peter Connor's friends — they knew everything, they were persistent: it did not do to imagine. . . .

Mr Daventry said that was all, he thought; he must go now. He took leave with unfriendly courtesy and went off abruptly, with an air that obliterated them, as though he had never been into their house at all. Then she exclaimed, recollecting herself: '*He* must be unhappy; I ought to have said something.' There was so much to do now, more than would fit into a morning; she had some idea of postponing lunch. And hearing the postman, she half thought, terrified by a sense of exposure: 'Suppose there should be a — suppose he should have —'

But there was no letter for Lois from Gerald.

No one was on the steps to hear the news from the postman; he went away disappointed. Lady Naylor thought firmly: 'Now I must go and find Lois.' But she did not go; things seemed to delay her. She looked into the drawing-room to see whether something — she wasn't certain what — was there. Francie, red-eyed, looked guiltily over the back of the sofa. They did not say anything. The room became so sharply painful that Lady Naylor almost exclaimed: 'Lois has not done the flowers!'

It was Laurence who, walking about the grounds unguardedly, was exposed to what they all dreaded. He came on Lois, standing beside a holly tree. She could have moved away, but seemed not so much rooted as indifferent.

'It's all right,' she explained, and added: 'I'm just thinking.'

His look became almost personal, as though he had recognized her. He said: 'I think I should. I expect — I don't know — one probably gets past things.'

'But look here, there are things that one can't —' (She meant: 'He loved me, he believed in the British Empire.') 'At least, I don't want to.'

'Perhaps you are right,' he said, studying, with an effort of sight and comprehension, some unfamiliar landscape.

'Well, don't stop, Laurence. You're going somewhere, aren't you?'

'Nowhere particular. Not if you —'

'No, I don't specially. Though if it has to be anyone, you.'

Taking this for what it was worth, he went on, brushing awkwardly past her against the laurels.

A fortnight later, Mrs Trent[4] drove over, the very evening of her return from the North. She had been inexpressibly bored up there and wished to complain. Lady Naylor, delighted, came out to meet her; it was like old times again.

'The house feels empty. They've gone, you know.'

4. The Trents are Anglo-Irish neighbours, living at nearby Castle Trent.

'Yes, dear me. I was sorry not to have seen the last of Hugo and poor little Francie. What about their bungalow?'

'Oh, that was just an idea; they are quite off it. Bungalows inland seem so pointless, cliffs are so windy and one cannot live on a flat coast. No, they think now of going to Madeira.'

'Then they won't un-store the furniture?'

'I don't think so; they never cared for it much.'

'It's a pity he never did go to Canada.' Mrs Trent looked round at the pleasant fields and lawns, the trees massive and tarnished, the windows that from their now settled emptiness seemed to have gained composure. Her sense of home-coming extended even to Danielstown. She went on: 'How's Richard? And listen: are you getting in your apples? — we haven't begun. They never get anything done when I'm away. And tell me: how's Lois?'

'Oh, gone, you know.'

'*Gone*? Oh, the school of art!'

'Oh no,' said Lady Naylor, surprised. 'Tours. For her French, you know. And to such an interesting, cultivated family; she is really fortunate. I never have been happy about her French. As I said to her, there will be plenty of time for Italian.'

'Oh, that's splendid,' Mrs Trent said vaguely but warmly. 'Then of course you must feel quiet. Did she and Laurence travel over together?'

'She seemed so offended at being thought incompetent and he was worried at the idea of looking after her luggage, so we sent them over separately; he crossed Wednesday, she Friday. Both nights, I hear, it was rough. . . . Yes, it's been sad here, lately, we've been so much shocked and distressed about that unfortunate young Lesworth. I think I felt it particularly; he had been out here so much and seemed so glad to talk, and had come, in a way, to depend on one. Though it was a shock, too, for Lois. You see they had played tennis so often and were beginning to be quite friends. She did not take it as hard as I feared, girls of her generation seem less sensitive, really . . . I don't know; perhaps that is all for the best. And of course she has so many interests. But it was terrible, wasn't it? I still think: how terrible. But he did have a happy life. I wrote that to his mother; I said, it must always be some consolation to think how happy his life had been. He quite beamed, really; he was the life and soul of everything. And she wrote back — I did not think tactfully, but of course she would be distracted — that it was *her* first consolation to think he died in so noble a cause.'

Mrs Trent had for a moment an uneasy, exposed look. She said: 'It was heroic,' and glanced down awkwardly at her gloves. She missed a dog, she felt unstayed, there was no dog.

'Heroic,' said Lady Naylor, and scanned the skies with eager big-pupilled eyes that reflected the calm light. 'Although,' she added, half in surprise, 'he could not help it. . . . But come in now and tell Richard about the North, he will be amused, though sorry that you were dull. To tell you the truth, we both rather feared you might be. Ah, don't mind the time, I'm sure it's early; come in, come in!'

But Mrs Trent could not, she was a punctilious person and wore a wrist-watch. She had not even sent round her dog-cart to the back; a man was walking the cob up and down the avenue. 'A flying visit,' said Lady Naylor mournfully, having prolonged the conversation by half an hour. Then Mrs Trent climbed briskly into the dog-cart and gathered the reins up; they sighed at each other their resignation to parting.

'Then we see you on Tuesday. Be sure and come early, before the Hartigans.' To the domestic landscape, Mrs Trent nodded an approving farewell. 'Every autumn, it strikes me this place looks really its best.'

'To tell you the truth, I really believe it does. There is something in autumn,' said Lady Naylor. She remained on the steps looking after the trap, her hands restlessly, lightly folded. Some leaves spun down from the gate with a home-coming air.

The two did not, however, again see Danielstown at such a moment, such a particular happy point of decline in the short curve of the day, the long curve of the season. Here, there were no more autumns, except for the trees. By next year light had possessed itself of the vacancy, still with surprise. Next year, the chestnuts and acorns pattered unheard on the avenues, that, filmed over with green already, should have been dull to the footsteps — but there were no footsteps. Leaves, tottering down the slope on the wind's hesitation, banked formless, frightened, against the too clear form of the ruin.

For in February, before those leaves had visibly budded, the death — execution, rather — of the three houses, Danielstown, Castle Trent, Mount Isabel, occurred in the same night. A fearful scarlet ate up the hard spring darkness; indeed, it seemed that an extra day, unreckoned, had come to abortive birth that these things might happen. It seemed, looking from east to west at the sky tall with scarlet, that the country itself was burning; while to the north the neck of mountains before Mount Isabel was frightfully outlined. The roads in unnatural dusk ran dark with movement, secretive or terrified; not a tree, brushed pale by wind from the flames, not a cabin pressed in despair to the bosom of night, not a gate too starkly visible but had its place in the design of order and panic. At Danielstown, half-way up the avenue under the beeches, the thin iron gate twanged (missed its latch, remained swinging aghast) as the last unlit car slid out with the executioners bland from accomplished duty. The sound of the last car widened, gave itself to the open and empty country and was demolished. Then the first wave of silence that was to be ultimate flowed back, confident, to the steps. Above the steps, the door stood open hospitably upon a furnace.

Sir Richard and Lady Naylor, not saying anything, did not look at each other, for in the light from the sky they saw too distinctly.

SEÁN O'FAOLÁIN

(1900–)

from: MIDSUMMER NIGHT MADNESS AND OTHER STORIES (1932)

[If Frank O'Connor's fiction 'Guests of the Nation' epitomizes the pity and terror of armed conflict in the shaping of modern Ireland, O'Faoláin's 'Midsummer Night Madness' is prophetic of the social and moral tensions of the new nation. The narrator, in the mould of Corkery's heroic cyclist in 'On the Heights', finds himself caught between the eccentric swagger of the old Anglo-Irish as reproduced by Major Henn, and the coarse, retributive morality of Stevey, type for all that may turn sour and hypocritical in the fledgling state.]

MIDSUMMER NIGHT MADNESS

For a second I looked back into the city, down through the smoke at the clustered chimney pots and roofs on whose purples and greens and blues the summer night was falling as gently as dust, falling too on the thousand tiny beacons winking and blinking beneath me to their starry counterparts above. It was just on the curfew hour and the last few laggard couples went hurrying past me, their love-making ended abruptly for the night, lest the Tans[1] in their roaring Lancia patrol cars should find them conspicuous on the empty white streets of the city. Then, mounting my bicycle, I turned to the open fields and drew in a long draught of their sweetness, their May-month sweetness, as only a man could who had been cooped up for months past under one of those tiny roofs, seeing the life of men and women only through a peephole in a window blind, seeing these green fields only in the far distance from an attic skylight. I left the last gas lamp behind, and the pavement end, and rode on happily into the country.

Yet, though the countryside was very sweet to me after all those months among the back yards, I was worried and watchful lest I should run into a chance patrol or raiding party. I kept listening, not to the chorus of the birds, not to the little wind in the bushes by the way, but nervously to every distant, tiny sound — the chuckle of a wakeful goose or hen in a near-by farmyard, or the fall of water coming suddenly within earshot, or some animal starting away from the hedge where I surprised its drowsing heavy head. Once I halted dead, my grip tight on

1. Black and Tans, a name applied to a body of men recruited in 1919, from British soldiers who had fought in the Great War, to assist the Royal Irish Constabulary in the Irish War of Independence which provides the background to the story.

the brakes, when a donkey brayed suddenly and loudly as if he were laughing at the intense quietness of the night. Fallen hawthorn blossoms splashed with their lime the dust of the road, and so narrow were the boreens[2] in places that the lilac and the dog rose, hung with wisps of hay, reached down as if to be plucked. Under the overhanging trees I could smell the pungent smell of the laurel sweating in the damp night air. And all about me the dead silence of the coming night, the heavy silence, drowsy with the odors of the night flowers and the cut meadows, unless a little stream trickled over the road and my wheels made a great double splash as they crossed it.

I was on my way to the townlands of Farrane and Kilcrea,[3] to see why to all appearances the local battalion had been completely inactive for the last three or four months. That portion of my task I did not relish, for I had known and been friendly with Stevey Long, the commandant, ever since the chances of revolution threw us together. Still, I should be free of the open fields for a few days, and there was enough romance left in the revolution for me to be excited at the thought that I was to stay at a house I had known and wondered at since childhood; I might even see and meet, if he were still alive, its strange mad owner whom as children we thought more terrifying than any of the ogres in the fairy books — old Henn of Henn Hall.

I could hardly credit that he was still alive, for even when we were very young my mother always spoke of him as 'that old divil of a Henn.' And an old devil he was, living up there all alone, in what she used to call his 'rooky-rawky' of a house, never married but always in a state of marriage with some woman or other. He began, I could well believe, with women of his own class, officers' wives from the barracks at B——, or Cork, or perhaps with what we used to call 'horsy women' from some neighbouring or English hunt. But, judging by his later life, he cannot have been overparticular at any time in his choice of women, and many a tinted London trollop must have walked his fields, looking in utter boredom at the gulls flying after the plough or the rain hanging in the bare trees, until finally, like all her predecessors and successors of many years, she in her turn cursed Henn and his hall, and Ireland and all belonging to it, and went back gladly to the flickering city lights and the back streets, and the familiar loved smells of gaslit theatres and stuffy hansom cabs. A man who lived by the things of the body — women, wine, hunting, fishing, shooting.

My mother often told us how as she and a crowd of schoolgirl friends were returning from their first Communion one cold autumn afternoon they entered his fields to take a short way by the river to their homes, removing their new shoes and stockings as they always did when they left the high road. They came on Henn — and he was a grown man then — standing in his pelt by the river, ready for a swim. She used to shudder as she told how he chased them, and they ran from him, screaming with fear, throwing away the new shoes and stockings as they ran, their legs all torn on the withered rushes of the bog and the furzed hedgetops, not daring to look back to see if the naked 'madman' were catching up with them, until, as she said, they had left his fields 'forty miles behind,' and panting and exhausted they ran into their homes. Henn must have been delighted with his frolic, and I can see him, running back for his swim, his long legs and his long neck, that gave him the nickname of Henn's Neck, cutting through the air as he ran. He must have been especially delighted when in the late evening the fathers and brothers of the children came looking here and there timidly for the little blue or red socks and the black shoes. It was only one of many such escapades that spread the name and legend of madness that clung to him through his life. We needed few such warnings to avoid him and his estate. We used to say to each other, somebody's warning half understood, that if Henn caught a little girl 'he'd salt her,'[4] and we went in mortal terror of him and his salting for years. We used to say that he had wires hidden under his fields and if you crossed even one of his ditches bells would ring up in the hall and he would come galloping on a white horse with his hungry hounds to salt you.

2. lanes.
3. Typical Irish place-names but not identifiable on the landscape of the story, where the region is rural Cork, the rivers Lee and Bride real, the townlands deliberately unspecific.
4. In parts of Ireland the *droit de seigneur* – landlord's right to the first night with the brides of his tenants – survived among the Anglo-Irish gentry into the nineteenth century, and its memory much longer in the minds of the people.

It was a wonderful old house to look at, sitting up on its own high hill, its two gable chimneys like two cocked ears and all its empty windows gazing wide-eyed down the river valley — very tall, with a wide door whose steps curled down and around like moustaches. The façade was a pale rain-faded pink at the end, but if was often called The Red House, and if it was ever really *red* it must have been visible for miles to anyone driving westward to Crookstown along the valley, following the little river and its dark line of woods. Yet, as I tried to recall it now, only one impression remained, for we came into the city when I was quite young and there I soon forgot the hall. But at least two or three times afterwards my father took me on an unusually long walk in that direction and each time when he returned he said to my mother, 'We could just see The Red House up the valley beyond Kilnaglory'; and each time she said, 'Glory be to God, I wonder is that old divil alive yet?' and told us all over again how he chased them in his pelt when they were little children.

One of these walks was on a soft wintry day with packed clouds threatening to drop rain every minute, and the Lee and the Bride in flood, and the tall bare beeches with the rooks' nests in their tiptops swayed and swung in the hard wind. The roads were muddy in places and there were many potholes full of rain or liquid dung and they were all wrinkled in the breeze and the flooded river ran frothing and brown by the very edge of the road. Off up the sodden valley, high on its rounded hill, sat Henn's house, and it was really more red than pink that day because of the rain, and as we looked at it one solitary window showed a light. At the same time the cold yellow sky behind it was turning to a most marvellous red as of blood, and the scarlet light blackened every leafless twig and tree trunk that stood against it and every ditch and scooped riverbank, and lastly the road and the very sky itself became swarthy, and there was light only in the waves curling the river and the potholes of the road. When the solitary window shone, my father said, 'That's old Henn.' I pictured him as an old man with a beard and long claw-hands half into the glowing ashes, so that I said, 'I think, Father, it's going to be thunder and lightning,' and he looked and said, 'It might,' and to my joy we turned our backs on Henn and his house and faced for the lights and the crowds and the shop windows of the city.

Really, I am sure, that was not Henn; he would have been down at the bridge head with his rods and his basket and his gillie.[5] But whenever those same winter rains streamed down the curtainless windows now, would he not have to stand watching, back bent — if indeed he still lived — shivering in the bay, and return to crouch sadly — not so far removed from my childish picture of him — over his perpetual summer-to-summer fire?

You may pity him as I tell you of him, but I, riding along the darkling lanes that night, had nothing in my heart for him but hate. He was one of the class that had battened for too long on our people. I was pleased to think that if he lived he lived only in name; that if he had any physique left now he would need it all to attract even the coarsest women. No London light-o'-love would be attracted to his ruin of a house now for other reasons; the farmers' daughters for miles around would shun him like the plague; and even maids who came from a distance would not be in the place a day without hearing all about him from the neighbours. Perhaps the travelling tinker-women would have to suffice? But, thinking of the big Red House, with its terraced lawns, and its cypresses and its yews, and its great five-mile estate wall, all built by the first Henn, the founder not only of his line but of an industry — glassmaking, and long since disappeared from Ireland — I could not believe even such a house would fall so low.

As I came to a crossways where my road dropped swiftly downhill the tenting chestnuts filled the lanes with darkness, and under my wheels the laid dust was soft as velvet. Before I took this last turn on my way I looked back the road I had come and saw upthrown behind the hill the distant glow of the city's lights, a furnace glow that made me realize how near and how far were the roofs and chimneys I had left. But as I looked I saw, too, how the clouds were gathering like pale flowers over the inky sky and even as I dropped silently downhill the first drops beat the fronded layers above. On my left, high as two men, rose the estate walls that had once kept the whole countryside at bay, but could not now (gapped and crumbling) keep a fox out or a chicken in. I passed two great entrance gates sunk in the weeds. Then the pale ghostlike pillars of the

5. Irish *giolla*: servant attending on a fisherman.

third gate came into view across a gap in the tunnel where the rain was beating down the dust, gradually changing its pattering blows for the hissing sound of a real downpour. Head bowed I raced across the unsheltered patch and edged my bicycle through the creaking gate and was just abreast of the little Gothic door of the lodge when it swung open and a woman stepped suddenly through the laurels and caught my arm, saying roughly and passionately as she did so:

'Stevey, why did you go away? Henn was down again tonight. Stevey, I. . . .'

The rain beat down on us, blotting out stars and moon alike.

Then she saw her mistake, and dropped my hand.

'I'm sorry,' she said. 'I thought. . . .'

I laughed to put her at her ease.

'You thought I was Stevey Long.'

She turned and went back to the door and seeing me, from there, look after her she cried out roughly:

'Go on!'

And because I was slow in moving for all the falling rain, she cried again:

'Go on about your business! Go on!'

'What a rough creature!' I was saying to myself as I began to wheel my bicycle up the avenue, when I heard her steps behind me. She beckoned and drew me back into the shadow of one of the sheltering trees beside the little house, leaned insinuatingly close to me, fingering my lapel, and said in a hollow mannish voice:

'You know Stevey Long?'

'Yes, of course I do.'

'Are you the boy he was bringing to the hall to stay?'

'Yes.'

'He told me about you. You know him well, don't you?'

'I know Stevey for a long time.'

'He told me you were in jail with him once.'

'Did he tell you that? I was. Oh, yes! Stevey and I had many a bout together.'

She paused. Then in a low, trembling voice she said, 'Do you know his girl?'

'His girl?'

'Yes. He told me all about her. He said you know her too. Tell me . . . where is she?'

Her voice was strained against the leash. I did not want to be caught by her country trickery, and I looked into her face by the light of the little window, from eye to eye searching for the truth. Seeing me hesitate she caught my arm fiercely.

'Tell me!'

'Why, I suppose you are Stevey's girl,' I bantered.

'Tell me, boy! She sent him letters to jail, didn't she? Oh, for Christ's sake, go on and tell me!'

She had me by the two arms now, her full bosom almost touching mine, so close to me that I could see the pouches under her eyes, her mouth dragged down wet and sensual, the little angry furrow between her eyebrows. The wind shook the heavy leaves of the chestnuts and as they scattered benediction on us the light from the little Gothic window shone on these wet leaves, and on her bosom and chest and knees. For a second I thought her blue apron drooped over her too rich, too wide hips. Since I did not speak she shook me like a dog and growled at me as fiercely as a dog.

'I don't know,' I said. 'She just sent letters to us, to Stevey, of course, and cigarettes and fruit and things — that's all. I don't know!'

She threw me away so that I all but stumbled over my bike.

'I knew it was true,' she moaned. 'I knew it was true when they said it.'

'But anyone might write him a letter. . . .'

'He denied it. He denied he ever got a letter from her.' In open country it is surprising how the voice sometimes echoes. Under those trees her voice resounded so that I feared she would be heard up at the hall or down in the village. 'The liar! He's going to marry that wan. That's the wan he wants. The shcut![6] And look what he's going to do now!'

Her great bosom rose and fell in rage.

'Do?' I asked. 'What is he going to do?'

'Who'd mind Henn? I ought to know. But Stevey! With his grand talk. He said *he'd* never harm me. But I won't marry him! I won't marry him! I won't! I won't!'

And she turned and ran into the lodge, leaving me with the feeling that this hall and estate and countryside had an unpleasant, real life of its own, a life that would spoil for me the few days of quietness that I had been dreaming of this last hour as I cycled between the hedgerows. I scarcely noticed that the sudden summer shower had ceased as I made slowly up the mossed drive, dark with unpruned trees and black laurel. Everything here too seemed to send up

6. i.e. scut: pup, blackguard.

its sweetness into the soft wet air, even the weeds bursting through the gravel, and when I came to the front of the house the great dark cypresses in the wet failing light were plumes of billowy smoke against the sky. I was now on the terrace before the hall, and as I looked down into the valley to where the sound of the waters of the Bride rose murmuring through the air purified by the shower, I almost expected to see the old libertine come floating up like a spectre or a long-legged ogre through the hills.

I found my way, as I had been instructed to do, to the rear of the house and in by the servants' quarters to the great kitchen. The pale still light of a candle on the table filled the room, and at the foot of the table beneath it was a basin of dusty milk. Before the embers an old sheep dog yawned and stretched his legs. I sat down by the fire and, glad of the rest, began to try to understand what it was that so troubled the girl at the lodge, with her passionate raging outburst against Stevey, and her cry, 'I won't marry him! I won't marry him!' But almost on my heels I heard the sound of feet mashing the gravel outside and she came into the kitchen.

'Put on some turf, boy,' she said at once. 'And blow up the fire.'

As I laid on the brown peat and sat by the side of the machine turning its handle she began to lay the table for my supper. Then we heard somebody else approach outside, and with a sudden shake of her fist to me by way of warning, she opened the door to Stevey. To her he gave a mere 'Hullo, Gypsy.' To me he gave a cordial 'Here we are again,' and he shook my hand several times and told me how glad he was to see me safe and sound.

Sullenly the girl broke in on us with, 'Put the kettle on, Stevey, for the boy's supper,' and sent me out to the rain barrel for water. I rose and went, and as I passed the window, there she was struggling out of his arms like a wild animal. When I returned she was again by the table, and he was bending down over the fire, swinging the great iron kettle forward on its crane to be filled. I lay back in the old basket chair and watched him move silently about the kitchen, finding everything where he expected to find it, his fair flock of curls all about his neck and brow like a mountainy sheep, his knees flinging apart at every step as they always did, and his hangdog head and his rounded shoulders more slouched than ever.

Since they would not speak to one another I began to ask random questions: the name of this or that townland; whether this or that family were still alive; and they answered civilly enough but would never talk a word to one another.

A nice companionable house I have come to! I was grumbling to myself; and a nice pair of quarrelsome suspicious lovers! And I was wondering if I should really have come to this house at all, or if I was to have any pleasure in my few days of freedom, when suddenly Gypsy broke silence to say that a lorryload of Tans had gone past two hours ago on the valley road, 'roaring,' she said, 'with the great venom and the drink,' shooting over the thatch of the houses in the village; they had killed a child and gone on without a thought, laughing at the terror of the villagers. At that Stevey burst into a terrible profane rage, but he caught my eye and fell silent. He knew my thought — if he had not been so inactive for the past four months the Tans would not be roaring their way so daringly through his territory now.

'Did anyone come to warn me?' he asked.

'Aye. The girl of the Mullinses.' And she added, 'The boys are wild tonight.'

I wished Stevey would turn to see me looking at him. I had something to go on already and I was looking forward to my talk with him when the girl would leave us to ourselves. But his mind began to wander from the Tans and he began to hum moodily to himself like a man with something gnawing at his brain, until, at last, unable to keep silent any longer he came out with a very casual, 'Was, eh, was Henn down tonight, Gyp?'

'He knows what he'd get if he came.'

At once everything changed. Stevey burst suddenly into a wild roar of song, his old favourite, the barcarole from *Hoffman*.[7] He echoed it through the empty house. Even Gypsy gave me a wry smile as she bade me sit up to supper.

'By God, John,' he cried at me, 'we'll give those bastards of Tans something to think about. Won't we, girl?'

And he caught her up, whirling her into a corner of the room so that she screamed with sudden delight and in mock fear of his rough hands. Stevey drew a long comical face at his stupidity, and she smoothed herself down and said she was all right, and so they

7. The barcarolle is from the grand opera *The Tales of Hoffman* by Jacques Offenbach (1819–80).

sat in a corner of the huge fireplace while I, with my back to them, ate my salted rashers and my country bread and butter.

'Eat up there, John,' he said; and then I felt they were kissing secretly.

'I am ready for it,' I said.

'That's the man,' said Stevey, and they kissed again and she giggled to herself, and turning I found her tousling his already wild mop because he was making too free of her where she sat on his knee.

'She has great titties, John,' said Stevey coarsely, and she slapped his face for that, and as I went on with my supper I heard him kiss her in return. So they made their love in the dark corner, shamelessly, until I was almost finished and ready for Stevey, and then they rose suddenly and left me, to walk, as they said, down to the village now that it was so fine in the heel of the day. Stevey waved me aside when I wanted to detain him, saying the night was long and tomorrow was good too. I was alone in the hall, listening to the corncrake at his last dim rattle in the meadows and the doves fluting long and slow in the deep woods.

As I lit my pipe and smoked under the shadow of the fireplace I began to feel that I should not have come to this house at all. True, it was safe enough because it was the home of one of the 'garrison'[8] people, one of those thousand unofficial blockhouses of the English on Irish soil, the last place to be suspected of harboring a rebel. But with Stevey's girl in the same house, this was not a suitable place for the investigator of Stevey's shortcomings. I chewed crossly over this for a while, until, as when I came along the road, the quietness and the peace gradually drove it all out of my head. The city, I thought, would by now be empty as if it had been deserted, the Lancias booming along the naked streets, their searchlights shooting down the dark lanes and the side alleys, and the funereal *tramp-tramp* of the patrols taking with them from every door they passed its heavy sigh of suspended fear. All this Stevey had escaped. Not for him as for us, for months on end, the sight of a rusted roof in a city back yard, the stale odor of airless bedrooms. Strange to think that one could work better in that sort of a room than where the walls were deep in grass, and the springtime rain green-dripping from the trees into water butts and cupped flowers.

The great front door banged, its echoes thundering, and steps clanked in the front hall. Another door opened and was closed again. The night had settled down about the hall, seeped into the woods, calming the doves. Only the old tireless corncrake kept up his ceaseless cry. A door opened again. Steps shuffled along the passage and halted; then an old man's voice coughed and called wheedlingly:

'Gypsy?'

Again the old voice wheedled, now almost at the kitchen door:

'Is he gone, Gypsy? Are you there, my pretty?'

The shuffling came nearer and the stick-tapping and coughing, and Mad Henn stood peering at me around the candle flame. I knew him at once by his long collarless neck and his stork's legs and his madman's face beaked and narrow like a hen. He wore a little faded bowler hat cocked airily on one side of his head, and over his shoulders and draping his body a rug. He had the face of a bird, mottled and bead-eyed, and his hair, tawny in streaks with the glister of oil, had one lock at the back that stood out like a cock's comb.

As he looked at me for a moment he pulled the loose flesh of his throat and scraped with one finger the tawny scum about his lips as if he were trying to remember whether he might not have asked me to come there or had some business with me that he had forgotten. I stood up awkwardly.

'Gyspy is gone for a walk with Stevey, Mr. Henn,' I said.

'And who might you be, young man, if I might ask a polite question?' — his eyebrows working up and down with irritation and the strain of having to speak.

'I . . . I'm a friend of Mr. Long's.'

He sniffed so that a drop fell from his beaked nose.

'Mr. Long,' he muttered in scorn. 'So you're another one of 'em, are you?'

'I don't quite understand,' I said, and mentally cursed Stevey for not having arranged things better. For the old fellow began to pound with his heel on the floor and his legs and hands twitched for rage so that I expected him every second to turn me out of his house at the point of his stick.

'I suppose, I say,' he piped sardonically again, 'I

8. The Anglo-Irish protestant Ascendancy were frequently known as the 'garrison', holding the country for Britain; hence their residences are 'blockhouses' or military forts commanding strategic points throughout the country.

suppose you're another one of our new patriots? Eh? Eh? I suppose you think you can walk into any man's house and sit on his armchair and drink his liquor? Eh? And threaten him if he protests against you for a cad and a bully? Eh? You're another of 'em, are you?'

He held a decanter in his right hand; it was filled with dancing liquor. I thought it best to humour him.

'I beg your pardon, Mr. Henn,' I said as humbly as I knew how, for I did not want a quarrel with the old devil. 'I'm sorry if I have intruded. But I didn't mean to. I think I have made a mistake — and I'll try if I can find the servant, or find Stevey, that is . . . wherever they are . . . just now.'

It was a very undignified speech, but it seemed to strike the old man with astonishment.

'Ho?' he said. 'This is a new one! Quite polite in fact. You're not very long on the road, young man,' he added with an air of bitter experience.

'That's all right,' I said, as I turned sullenly to go.

He halted me as I laid my hand on the door latch. Where I was going to I did not know.

'Here! It is all right. Your apology is perfectly all right. Don't go, boy. Don't you go.'

'At the word *here* I noticed how tenderly he said his *r's* — *here*, and *your*, and *perfectly*. It was the last bit of blazonry he preserved, marking him off for all his degradation as one of the conquering race.

We looked at one another silently; then, in quite another tone, as coolly and politely as if he were speaking across his decanter in a club:

'Will you have a drink?'

I looked at him in surprise.

'Come along. I should like to talk to you. You are the first of your kind that I have met who seems to have any bit of education. We'll have a whiskey and soda. Will you join me?'

I returned, largely because I did not know what else to do; and our feet went clanking on the hall flags as if the whole house were a vault, and indeed there was everywhere a musty smell of rooms long abandoned or never tended. His drawing room was just as I expected, a good room but like a ragged tramp. At the farther end was a great superfluous fire and standing by it he poured me out a jorum of whiskey in a glass whose crevices were brown with the encrustations of years, all the time peering at me around the side of a pink-bowled oil lamp whose unshaded light made everything look even more drab and dirty — the bare uncarpeted floor, the fine marble fireplace mottled and cracked, the china cabinets with broken glass and no china in them; and I remembered the look of the yards with their rusted churns and staveless barrels, and everywhere the fur of mildew and green damp.

'Here! Drink that,' he said, pouring himself another glass and throwing it off at a gulp, raw. 'That's the way to take your liquor. I suppose you'll empty the siphon in yours, eh? Hum! If you didn't have a revolver stuck in your back pockets what would you young fellows have over us? Oh, you're stronger — but have you more grit? Let me look at you.'

As I stood up for the drink, he peered at me.

'Ah!' he wailed. 'There's only one thing I regret, one thing I've lost, and that's clear eyes. The whole year is all like foggy autumn to me. I see the trees and the woods as if they were clouded in mist. It's a great blessing. I go out on a fine evening like this evening and it's like an evening in winter to me when the light fails at four o'clock in the afternoon and every hill is a valley and every tree is twice as far away.'

His streaming eyes strayed to the caverns of the fire, but the flames shone dully in the milky cataracts of the old fading pink-shot pupils.

'Why are you in this business, tell me?' he asked of a sudden.

'I believe in it,' I said.

He threw up his hand in disgust.

'I believed in things once,' he said. 'I had ideas about the people, the people on my land. I thought I'd get them to do things with their land — I was ready to help them with loans and advice. I'd tell them how to drain it, how to grow more variety of vegetables, how to make money out of their gardens selling the produce in the city, and how to make better butter and keep their eggs clean. . . .'

He sniffed a long sneer at himself and pulled his throat and looked absently into the fire.

'Look at them today. As dirty as ever, as poor as ever, as backward as ever, and I suppose they blame people like us for it all. If they had my land they'd know how to farm it, they think. But why haven't they done anything with their own? Why? Why?'

He was a hot-tempered old fellow, flying into a temper at a second's warning.

'But you're a city boy, you know nothing of the people. It's people like us who know Ireland. We belong to it — we who've grown up on the land and know it and the people on it.'

'Your people were merchants,' I said coldly.

'They made their money on bottles,' he said, reaching for the whiskey. 'And I've spent their money on bottles,' he added with the air of a man who has often made the same joke and grown serious over it. Then as he began to pour the liquor out tremblingly he turned savagely on me. 'And who makes glass in Ireland now?' he wheezed. 'When we stopped, why didn't somebody else take it up? They could make lovely glass in Ireland at one time. It might have became a great, a distinctive national industry, and everywhere you'd see the men blowing the glass into lovely shapes. People would be coming from abroad to see them. I've seen them as a lad. *Pouf!* And there you had a globe of glass. Shining, coloured, glowing. Oh, no! Oh, no! What do we see in the shop windows now?' he cried, leaning forward and baring his rotting, easily moved teeth. 'Cobblers! Yah! A race of cobblers. That's what we are — a race of cobblers! They hadn't it in them. They hadn't it in them!'

I saw for the first time how deep the hate on his side could be, as deep as the hate on ours, as deep and as terrible.

'Oh, that all began two centuries ago,' I cried back at him. 'It was the union with England that ruined us and our industries.[9] Can't you see that? It ruined you. It ruined your glass business. Aren't you part of Ireland as much as us?'

'Ach! It's always the same. This ruined us, and that ruined us, and the other ruined us. I tell you I'm ashamed to be called an Irishman, and in fact I'm not an Irishman. I'm a colonist — a planter — whatever you like – one of those that tried to come and do something with you people. Why didn't the people fight for their rights when they had a parliament?'

I tried to answer, but he wouldn't let me, spilling his liquor all over the hearth in his rage.

'I know what you'll say. But look at the Welsh, and look at the Scotch. They haven't a parliament and they have prospered. What's to stop us from making our linens and our woven silks, from weaving patterns into them like the Italians and the Slavs? Where are our crafts? What can we show? What have we ever done? Except dig ditches and plough fields? Why haven't we stuffs, yes, stuffs, stuffs, stuffs, of our own — stuffs', — how he spat it out! — 'that any woman would love to fold around her body, stuffs she'd love to feel against her flesh? Coloured, brilliant, delicate stuffs?'

And he began to rub his little hands down his thighs.

'Oh, fantastic!' I said, and leaned back from him smiling.

'Ah, there's your revolver man talking! But it could be done. Or why don't we export bulbs or cut flowers like the Dutch and the French and the Channel Islanders?'

'It's impossible. The climate.'

'Pah! It's on our side. The Gulf Stream would do it.'

'The Gulf Stream?'

Mad Henn!

'Yes! It warms our southern shores. You can grow acacias in Kerry in the open air in midwinter.' (A rush of delicate *r*'s here.) 'I've picked London pride on the mountains in early March. Jasmine, lilacs, fuchsias. . . .'

'Fuchsia isn't a cut flower,' I taunted. 'Nor a bulb!'

He twitched in every limb, dashed his glass into the fire, banged the hearth with his stick, and stuttered all the rest he had to say to me:

'It grows, it grows, I tell you it grows wild in midwinter. In the open air. You're a damned obstinate young fellow. And wallflower, lily of the valley, freesia, gardenia, arbutus, mignonette. All sorts of delicate ferns. A marvellous, but a lost, opportunity. These things will bring them in more money than potatoes. But they tread on them. It's so silly, really, because it's just like treading on gold.'

'But the people are farmers.'

'What are the Germans, the Dutch, the Belgians? Ah!' (It was a long-drawn-out 'Ah!' of sweet memories.) 'I know the people. You city fellows don't know them.' Then his voice fell. 'I know their women.'

He rubbed his little hands again and tapped me on the knee.

'I know every sort of woman: English women, French women, Italians; I've even known a Russian woman. The Russians are like the Irish, you know. But too stubborn and too obstinate and too proud. Prouder even than the Irish. And not one of them

9. The Act of Union (1800) transferred the Irish parliament to Westminster with unhappy consequences for Irish industry.

all can equal the Irish woman — of the right sort. But they're airy. You have to bind them down with a brutal religion or they'd fly over the fields from you. Don't you feel that too, eh?'

And he cocked his hat even still further over on one ear and laughed a little elfish laugh of delight and his loose lock behind almost curled like a drake's tail. He poked the embers with his stick. He filled my glass in spite of me — delighted like all old bachelors whose club days and dancing days are done to have anyone at all who will talk with them.

'Ah! Yes,' he sighed as he poured my whiskey, 'the women are all right. So lovely and plump. Muscular from the fields. Arms . . . right!' (He moulded them with the bottle in his hand.) 'Breasts like tulips. Lovely! Lovely! But you don't know. You only know the city. The city! Puh! I wouldn't give that much for a city woman.'

I threw off his whiskey neat.

'Why shouldn't I know the country?' I said. 'By damn, but I do! As well as you, better than you. I know their women. Many a mouse I moused with their women. What's more than that, I was born in the country and born right here in this townland. My mother was born and is buried and my grandmother and all her people before her down there in Kilcrea churchyard. I lived in the townland of Farrane myself as a child and my father lived there before me.'

I thought he shrank into himself at that, pulling down his long neck like a snail or a tortoise at the approach of danger.

'What's your name?' he asked quietly.

I told him.

'I remember your mother well,' he said. 'She held land from me. And I remember your father. He was stationed at Kilcrea.[10] I met him first at an eviction on my land. They shoved a red-hot poker through the door at him and he caught it; and, by God, he pulled it from them, so he did. A fine man.'

'I remember that,' I said, quiet myself, too, now.

'No, boy, no,' he said sadly. 'That was a long time ago.'

'Oh, but, I do well,' I cried. 'I remember the bandage on his hand.'

'Not at all,' and he smacked the stick on the side of the marble fireplace. 'This was a long time ago. Forty years or more. Forty years or more' — and as he said it his eyes strayed, rheum wet, from me to the fire and back to me again as if he were trying to see my father in me and those dead years that were gone from him for ever.

'Where is he now?' he asked.

'He's dead,' I said.

'Ah, and is he dead?'

'Yes.'

'And your mother?'

'She is dead,' I answered quietly.

'Ah!'

He looked into the embers. They glowed faintly in his all but sightless balls — a quietness more than the night fallen on him secretly and unexpectedly. Just then a step resounded on the hall flags and the door opened and in came the dark, muscular Gypsy, behind her Stevey, slouching as ever. He did not see me. He gave the old man a low 'Good night.' Henn did not reply, but he raised a feeble hand and took the girl's fingers in his palm. His was as tiny as hers. The fire shone pink between his bony fingers, ridged with the veins and threaded with the thousand wrinkles of age. As their eyes met, his lean neck curved up to her lovingly.

'Have you had a nice walk, pretty?'

'Yes, down to the bridge at the pub.'

Before him how delicately her lips said *down*, with a voluptuous upward curve at the corners of her mouth so that they swept into her cheeks as the curved initials on his ring swept into the gold. Her sullen eyes went soft. In this light she almost looked beautiful. His hand wandered over her arm as he asked the next question: a question as familiar as Sunday. She smiled as she replied.

'Was there anything rising?' he asked.

'Down by the bridge they're leppin',' she said.

'It's the breeze. There's always a breeze fluting down that side of the valley.'

Stevey laughed loudly at them both, and his voice was rough and coarse beside the rich voice of the girl and the cultured voice of the old man.

'Leppin'? Rise? Rise, how are you! That was me spittin' when she wasn't looking.'

'Oh, then, there was a rise,' she cried. 'I saw their silver bellies shining as they leaped.'

'Ooh!' mocked Stevey. 'Bellies! Naughty word! Ooh!'

Henn gripped his stick until it trembled and his

10. An autobiographical touch: O'Faoláin's father was a sergeant in the Royal Irish Constabulary. In his memoir, *Vive Moi!*, the writer describes an incident similar to the eviction narrative here.

knuckles strained the skin white. He snapped at Stevey.

'If the girl says there was a rise, there was. Aren't you enough of a gentleman not to contradict her?'

But his voice trembled as if he were half afraid of his own daring. In a second Stevey was in one of his violent passions.

'I don't want any English pimp to tell me what to do or not to do with the girl, or any girl. Mind that!'

Henn's hand shook, and all his legs as he pulled himself up on his stick, taller when he stood than any of us, his bent back straightened, made gigantic by the great shadow that climbed the wall behind him. I could see what a man he was in his heyday, what a figure on a horse, wielding the rod from the top of a rock, a wiry, bony giant. There was almost majesty in him as he pointed his trembling stick to the door and faced down to Stevey with:

'Leave my house, sir. I'll not be bullied any longer by you — not an hour.'

'And I'll leave it,' cried Stevey, 'when and only when I choose. I'll not be ordered by *you*. Who the hell do you think you are ordering? Do you think you can order *me*? Ho, and but let me tell you, Mr. Alexander Henn, I'm *staying* here.'

I could see he had taken drink while down at the pub, and the devil was in his eyes; he skipped across the hearth by the side of Henn and flopped mockingly into the chair the old man had just left. Then he stretched out his hand for Henn's glass on the mantelpiece, and wiping the side of it on his coat sleeve raised it in mockery of the old man. There was silence for a second and then Gypsy laughed, and the laugh cut through Henn. He raised his stick and lashed at the hand that held the empty glass in the air, and as the splinters fell I leaped, Henn thrusting his face across my arm into Stevey's face, Gypsy barely holding back Stevey's fist before it crashed into the old rheumy, half-blind eyes. Henn was all but weeping for vanity, for that laughter of the girl at his age and infirmity. All he could say between his sobs was, 'You young ruffian. You ruffian. You ruffian . . . .'

I thrust Stevey back. Henn turned to me.

'This young woman. If anything should happen to her, which God forbid. . . .'

'Oh, you hypocrite,' cried Stevey, turning to the empty air for somebody to appeal to. 'Oh, listen to that! God! God forbid! Oh, the hypocrisy of it!'

'Yes, yes, yes,' I appealed and implored Gypsy to take him away and pushed him from us, and the girl dragged him, and pushed him, and persuaded him out of the room. She was entirely cool as if abuse and quarrelling and coarse talk were nothing to her. I put the old man in his chair and filled a glass for him and left him and found Stevey sullenly akimbo on the top of the steps. He was ashamed, I felt, to have played his heroics opposite me and I thought he might not have quarrelled with old Henn if he had known I was there. I stood beside him without speaking until he said he was sorry he had broken out like that since it would ruin my chances of staying at the hall. I could not tell of what else he was thinking, but I was thinking to myself, Where shall I go now? For I could neither remain in the hall nor go with Stevey. My hopes of a quiet, serene night were vanished. We stood in silence and looked down into the night. A frightened bird fluttered in the woods; a star fell in a graceful, fatal swoop, vanishing in mid-air as if a mighty hand had scratched the sky with light.

Biting his nails, Stevey said, 'Tell Gypsy I want her.'

I went back to the drawing room, where the girl and the old man stood by the window.

'Stevey wants to talk to you,' I said; and when she went tramping wearily, heavily, from the room I looked at Henn and he looked back at me and neither of us spoke. As I looked away again through the shining window I could see the old man's eyes fixed on me. At last I buttoned my coat about me and turned to him.

'I suppose I'd better be going,' I said.

'Going? Where are you going?'

'I don't know really, but. . . .'

'Hum! You were to stay here, I take it, eh? Another uninvited guest?'

After a long hesitation I answered, 'Yes — I was. I was. I may even stay in your hay barn yet, for all you know. Good night,' I concluded. 'I'm glad to have met you.'

'No, boy. I won't say good night. And you won't stay in my hay barn, because I have none. Stay where you intended to stay. Even though you didn't choose to ask me, stay. If not for your own sake, for your father's and mother's sake.'

He rose and went slowly and feebly to the door, his half-emptied bottle in his hand.

'Could I stop you,' he said, 'if you wanted to stay here a month? Stay! And be damned to ye!'

'I won't,' I said.

He turned to me at the door.

'Please do stay,' he pleaded, nodding his head many times to encourage me. 'Stay, stay, stay.'

He was maudlin with the excitement and the liquor.

'Will you stay?' he asked again.

I looked out into the dark. I thought to myself, It must be near to eleven or midnight.

'Thanks very much,' I said; and being satisfied he waved his bony hand, slipping his bottle into the great pocket of his swallow-tailed coat. Then he turned and went, his little hat perched on one side of his head and his rug trailing after him on the uncarpeted floor.

I sat by the table and looked about me again: at the tablecloth like a gypsy's shawl, at the dusty lace curtains dragged to the ends of their poles; and everything my eyes fell on mocked him and his desires. Lovely woven silks, he had said. And woven linens? And stuffs such as women might love to feel? And such strange flowers and bulbs as the Dutch and the Channel Islanders grew, freesia, gardenia, mignonette? What a liar, I thought; and bitterly I was pleased to end the triad, calling him (as the farming folk had called him for fifty years) a lunatic and a libertine.

Gypsy returned. I told her I was staying in the house, and once more she went and returned. We heard Stevey's steps vanish down the drive, and then silently she took a candle and lit me upstairs to bed. As we went I asked her what her name was, and she said:

'My name's Gammle.'

'Indeed,' I said, thoughtlessly.

'Why *indeed*?' she asked, halting in her step and looking at me.

'Nothing,' I said. 'It's just a strange name.'

I did not tell her I was thinking that the name was well known in North Cork for a tinker tribe, in Charleville and Doneraile and the borders of Limerick and up into Clare.

'Good night,' she said, and left me in a great, empty, musty room, the bed all tousled and the bedclothes soiled, and yellow. I lay down as I stood. To the sound of the branches of the trees tapping on the bare window I dozed and slept.

I awoke, wide-eyed of a sudden insomnia, to the rusted, wailing drone of an old phonograph in the room below me. By the light of the moon I looked at my watch; it was past twelve o'clock, an hour when cities begin to live and the fields are fast asleep. It reminded me of the years when I had lain awake for hours listening to late parties singing their way homeward before the war and curfew sent us all to our beds. I would be awake again now until the dawn broke. Rising peevishly I went to the door, opening it in time to hear a new record begin its nasal introductory speech: *This is an Edison Bell recawrd; number one seven nine nine, songs from the awpera of Dawn Giovanni by Mozart*. And then through the hollow-sounding house the stifled music of one of the loveliest of all operas; and humming with the singer, or rather behind the singer, came old bleareyed, maudlin Henn's cracked and drunken voice:

'Batti; batti. . . .',[11]

I bade sleep good night, and dragging on my pants sat on the edge of the bed, my coat about my shoulders, smoking a cigarette. I watched the branches beating on the panes, the laurels shivering and shining in the tangled garden beneath my window, the Bride rain-laden far below glinting between its gall-black alders under the starry sky.

'Questo é il fin di chi fa mal. . . .'[12]

The pair and their song died slowly. Then silence fell. Henn kicked his enamel chamber pot until it rang. Croaking and humming the love song he shuffled out on his landing. I leaned over the banister and watched him stumble down the stairs, out of the house, onto the gravelled drive and out of sight into the dark.

One by one I began to hear them — those innumerable, inexplicable sounds that are to be heard at night in a house when all the casual day sounds are still; timbers that stretch and contract, little insects that make a great creaking noise. I pulled on my boots and went down to the open door and out on the avenue and down towards the cottage in the track of Henn. Here a chill wind was blowing last year's leaves high in the air, but near the lodge where the drive fell sharply down to the gates under the trees clawing their high ditches dust lay in soft whispering drifts — soft and white as snow under the moon, so soft that as I stood by the little deserted lodge peering curiously in through one of the windows I might have been a rabbit or a fox for all the warning I gave

11. 'Beat; beat. . . .'
12. Literally, 'This is the end of him who does evil.'

anyone who might be inside. A shaft of wavering light lay thrown across the tiny hallway from another room. There they were, Gypsy and Henn: she with her skirt drawn above her knees, an old coat over the warm skin of her bare shoulders, toasting her shins to a little flickering fire — Henn, as he did the first time I saw them together, holding her fingers in his palm and leaning forward over her round knee to see into her eyes.

I watched the unequal pair looking at one another long, silently, seeming not to say one word to each other, her dark head bowed sidelong to his lips, her fallen lashes on her cheeks; he, with a smile foolish yet tender sagging his quivering mouth apart, his old hat cocked forward on eyes that streamed their water to his cheeks. And yet, though he was old and decaying, and she warm-fleshed, white to her teeth, full of the pride of youth, and — Henn was right — her breasts like tulips fully blown, if anything too magnificently full, he could, for all that, raise his hand now with so much languid grace to feel their roundness, hold the precious globe for one moment, so lightly, so fondly on his fingers before his withered hand fell as if in despair into her lap, that finer women than Gypsy might well have smiled, as she smiled now, with head turning slow from that flattering gesture of the epicure, with long slow-drawn sighs at the uselessnes of such praise from him.

To which of these men, I wondered, had she given herself?

With her hair dragged on the ridge of her chair and her head falling lower on her bosom until her eyes were caught in the embers of the fire, she permitted him to move aside her skirt, ever so little, from her bare knee, and caress it with his withered hand as softly as if it were swan's-down, caress it even after the glow of the fire shone on her eyes drowned in tears, caress it while she sat rigid with misery, her moans breaking out in trembling waves to the whispering night outside. And yet not one word from Henn; only as if hoping that his old hand could quiet her childlike sobs, he caressed and caressed and looked and looked doglike into her face.

I could not bear those doglike eyes of the old libertine, nor those sighs and sobs of the young girl. Stumbling away from the light of the little window and out of the creaking gate I found myself walking on and on under the tenting chestnuts in the windy dust-blown lane, up and along the highway I had come that evening, too moved to return and sit alone in my unkempt bedroom in the hall. Suddenly country and freedom seemed a small thing under this austere darkness, with that pair, heavy with one another's sorrow, down in the weather-streaked decaying cottage.

With the memory of those drooping mother's breasts and that large mother's belly on the young girl, and the look of pity on the old libertine's face, I find myself walking aimlessly on and on; until across the black valley there rises a leaping yellow flame, and through the night air on the night wind the crackle of burning timber.

The flames through the trees were now flickering like a huge bonfire. Running down the lanes toward Henn Hall I could see from time to time as I ran the distant outline of windows, a gable end, a chimney silhouetted against the glowing air. At the lodge the little light was still shining in the window. Without looking through I knocked and knocked until padding feet came along the floor and the girl's voice said:

'Who is it? Who's there?'

'A fire!' I cried. 'What can we do? Across the valley, a big house.' And in my excitement I cried out, 'Where's Mad Henn?'

She answered through the door.

'He's not here. Isn't he at the hall?'

She opened an inch or two of the door and looked out at me with frightened eyes.

'Whose house is it?' she asked.

'I don't know. It's straight over the river — straight across there.'

Holding her clothes about her body she stepped to the corner of the lodge and looked across at the blazing house.

'It's Blake's,' she said. 'We can't do anything. They may come over here. Where's Henn?' she asked then, suddenly terrified.

'I thought he was here.'

She stared at me, astonished, yet full of cunning that was mingled with fright for Henn.

'Isn't he at the hall?' she insisted nervously.

'Maybe,' I stuttered. 'Yes, I suppose he *is* at the hall.'

'Did you try?'

'I was out walking,' I said.

'Walking!'

There was a pause.

'What time is it?' she asked.

As I peered at my watch, saying, 'It's well after one o'clock,' I could see her eyes looking at me with fear and suspicion, and having spied on her I was ashamed to look up. Then, slowly, I understood why she was watching me in that way. She thought that my coming there that night, a man 'on the run,' had something to do with this burning house, that I had caused it, as a reprisal, an act of revenge, and that in some way Henn too would suffer by it, and that Stevey, probably, had been the man who carried it out. Such reprisals were as yet rare in the country and it had never occurred to me that this was one until I saw the fear and distrust and hate in her eyes.

'A nice time for walking,' she said shortly, and raced down the slope of the ditch and up to the hall and there she knocked on the heavy hen's-head knocker until the countryside resounded and even a dog, somewhere across the fields, began to *bark-bark* at our *knock-knock-knock* on the echoing door. I tried to explain myself.

''Tis why I came to the country — to sleep. I get insomnia. So I got up and came out.'

'How did you get out? Henn keeps the key in his room.'

'The door was open.'

There was no sound from the house.

'My God,' she moaned. 'what's happened to him?'

Then in her fear and rage and suspicion she turned on me, a tigress robbed of her mate — and even in that instant I remember saying to myself, Oho! So it's Henn, is it?

'Where is he?' she cried. 'What did ye do with him? Christ blast ye all, what did ye do to him?'

Her voice was echoed by the stony face of the house, thrown back into the fields and echoed again and again by the barking dog.

'I know nothing about him,' I said angrily. 'He's probably dead drunk. Knock him up.'

And I clouted the hen's head until my hand ached. Not a sound but the dog over the fields, now thoroughly aroused, and the crackling of the flames across the valley, and, within, the old sheep dog howled mournfully.

The girl caught my arm in fear.

'It's the dog crying before somebody dies.'

'Is that a window?'

'Is it the I.R.A. that burnt it?' she asked, looking up and then over her shoulder.

'I know nothing about it. How can we get in?'

'It's for the child the Tans killed. Ye've done something to Alec? Ye've surely done something to Alec!'

We found a little scullery window open. I clambered in and let her in at the front door. We climbed the dark stairs, the dog flopping along behind, and up to his room. We found him in his bed, snoring on his stomach with the weight of drink, his nightshirt crumpled above his bare knees, and on his head a fluff-laden nightcap of scarlet wool. Ashamed of the sight of him with his dirty toes and the engrimed creases across the base of his neck and halfway up his skull Gypsy shook him madly into a gasping wakefulness, straightened his cap on his head as if he were a child, and covered his shoulders as he sat up in bed looking about him at the angry waving light like a picture of Juan in hell.

'Are you all right?' she asked.

'I — yes — I'm all right. But. . . .'

'Look.' She pointed and he looked.

'My God!' he cried. 'Totty Blake's.'

His eyes bulged as he looked, and trying to master himself he shambled across the floor to stoop in the open window in his shirt.

'Oh! My God! My God!' was all he could say, and then, 'Do you hear them? Do you hear the noise?'

'The flames?' I said.

'No! The rooks. They'll never nest there again. They're ruined with the heat.'

And he began to tousle his cap and sank on his knees crying like a child. Gypsy stood over him where he knelt.

'The Blakes will be likely coming here for the night.'

He stood up at once like a hardened toper, and turned to us.

'Go down,' he said, 'and lay the table for them, and set the fire going. And you, boy, go, like a good fellow, and give her a hand.'

Gypsy went. I thought he was unable to look after himself and tried to coax him from the window.

'I'll stay here,' I whispered. 'It's cold, you know. You must dress now. I'll help you. Come on.'

He flung my arm aside, peevishly.

'Am I a child?' he roared.

I left him in a palsy of trembling, dragging his nightshirt over his head, rump naked, fumbling for his clothes by the pale light of the candle and the fluttering light of the burning house.

In silence we set about blowing the seed of fire on

the hearth into flame, and I dipped the kettle in the dark water of the butt and the crane swung it slowly over the fire. The false dawn of the fire and the distant rooks cawing with fright had awakened the doves and all the birds on this side of the valley and the night was sweet with their music. From time to time as we passed from kitchen to parlour with ware or food we halted to look at the fire that sometimes seemed to have died away and sometimes flared up more madly than ever before. There Henn joined me and we waited there, wondering if the Blakes would come or if we should go back to bed and try to sleep out the end of the night. At last he drew me into the room and filled out a drink for himself, while I yawned, dry-eyed for lack of sleep.

'I don't know where else the Blakes can go,' he said. 'Though if there was another house within three miles of them they'd rather die than come under my roof. I'm sorry for his two tits of sisters, though.'

'Only two women?' I asked wearily.

'Philamena and Agatha. Two sour tits. And the captain, their father. That's all that's there. Oh, but Philamena *is* a sour bitch. I chalked that very word on the door of the church about her when I was six — got whipped for it too. And she never spoke a word to me after. And I gave Agatha a penny at the age of eight if she'd let me swing her so high that I could see her drawers. They never let her see me after that. I once went,' he said, throwing back his liquor, 'I once went to church to a Handel service, and I had to run out of it when I saw the two virgins singing away *"To us a child is born; to us a son is given."*[13] Ah!' he snarled. 'They're sour titties. Vinegar for milk they have. Sour and old and virginal.'

He was getting angry with them, I could see.

'They'd just raise their hands in horror at a girl like . . . at a girl that would, that would. . . .'

I stood in the corner of the window watching the sparks rising and falling endlessly like fireflies, silenced as one is always silenced by a raging fire, to think of calamity on one's doorstep.

'Gypsy,' says Henn, suddenly rising and going to another window, 'Gypsy was sick tonight.'

'Bad?' I asked sleepily.

'Bad? Not yet.'

'Not yet?'

'That's what I said. Didn't you hear me?'

'Yes.'

He came shuffling over to me on his stick.

'The girl is ruined,' he said, peering into my eyes, that filled with shame as he looked at them.

'What do you mean by that?'

'Gypsy is going to be a mother.'

I answered his stare.

For answer I looked angrily over the valley at the house. What did it matter to him what I thought? What would all the country think when they heard it? Another servant of Henn's — it was an old story — about to bear a child.

'I'll not be blamed,' he cried and his tubes were hoarse with passion. 'I am not to be blamed.'

'What does the girl say?'

'How does she know?'

And he went back to his glass and his fire.

Up the avenue in a shadowy mass, singing and shouting, came the incendiaries, Stevey at their head, ready for anything, drunk with whiskey and triumph. Had it been six months later, he could safely have burned half the houses in the district and we should not have dared, nor cared, nor had the time, nor even wished in the heat of passion — for things grew very hot by then — to question what he did. But tonight I ran to the door determined to thwart him. He faced up the steps and shouted for Henn, Henn the whore, Henn the cock, the Henn's neck, and all about him shouted with him out of the dark.

'Henn! Henn! Come out, you whore![14] Come out, Henn!'

There was a glint of a revolver in one man's hand as I ran down the steps and faced up to Stevey.

'What rotten sort of soldier are you?' I shouted at him.

'What do you mean?' he cried.

'Is that what you call soldiering?' I shouted into his face, pointing across the valley at the burning ruin. For an instant he looked at it, and then to his men and at me.

'Aha!' he shouted. 'We burnt the bastards out, didn't we, boys? And damn right well they deserved it.'

They shouted it back to him, their memories full of the days when their people died of starvation by

13. A chorus from 'Messiah'.

14. 'Whore', more commonly pronounced 'hoor', is applied as a term of abuse, and even affection, to the male in everyday Irish speech.

the roadsides and the big houses looked on in portly indifference.

'And we'll burn Henn out,' cried Stevey, and made a drive for the steps. I caught him and swung him about while Henn hung over the iron railings and croaked down at us:

'If I had a gun! Oh, if I only had a gun!'

'Shut up,' I shouted at him. The crowd was nasty enough without this.

'Oh, for a gun!' he persisted. 'Just for one minute. . . .'

'Go in, blast you,' I shouted at him while Gypsy tried to drag him from the steps.

'You're fine fellows! Oh, you're great fellows,' I taunted them. 'You haven't, between the lot of you, fired a single shot in all this district for four months. Unless you shot a sitting hare or a tame fox. It's what you'd do by the look of you. And now you go and burn a couple of women out in the middle of the night. Oh, you're grand soldiers entirely. You cowardly mob!'

'You keep your tongue quiet,' from Stevey. He was a head higher than me.

'I'm here to talk to you,' I said, 'and I'll give you and your men my talk now, if you want it. Let me tell you you have the reputation of being the tamest commandant. . . .'

He flew into a passion at once and drew his revolver at me. At once the country fellows skipped between us. They didn't at all like this business of drawing a gun on one of their own. They began to mutter and pluck at Stevey, and to signal me to hold my peace. But I knew my man.

'Now, now, Long!' they muttered. 'Be aisy now, Long.'

'You won't bully me,' I said. 'Why don't you use your gun on the Tans?'

He turned to them.

'Are you going to be stopped by a city caffler?'[15]

And to me:

'We know what Henn is.'

'What am I?' croaked Henn, who was still grasping the railings, with Gypsy trying to persuade him to come in.

'What did Henn ever do to *you*?' I asked.

'Aye, what did I ever do to you?' gasped Henn, hoarse with excitement, sweeping his little hat off his head and leaning down over the railings like a man giving a speech. 'What did I do to you? What did I ever do to you or yours?'

'Aha!' Stevey shouted up to him. 'You whore master' — and I thought he'd blow the old man's brains out. 'What do *you* know what's mine or yours?'

Utterly beyond himself he pointed with his gun at Gypsy, and shook his fist in the old man's eyes.

'Look at that girl. What did you do to her? Answer that or you'll not have a house by morning.'

Then quite without warning the rest of them turned and raced over the lawn into the surrounding night. Only one waited to pluck Stevey by the arm and whisper:

'It's the Blakes. They're coming. Come away out of this. They'll know us.'

'I don't care about the Blakes,' said Stevey, too intent on having his way with Henn that night to care about anything else. 'Ask him!' he said to me. 'Ask him what did he do to that girl? Ask him that!'

'Stevey, Stevey,' implored the girl as she tried still to induce Henn to move.

I dragged Stevey to one side as Henn, who had also seen the Blakes come up the drive swaying with the weight of the bundles they bore, stood down on the steps to meet them, his hat in his hand like an ambassador or a prince receiving his guests, his head like a gander's head, jigging up and down as he bowed them in; and as the two old maids came timidly up to him, peering here and there in their fear, and the portly captain, their father, brought up the rear, peeping over their shoulders because he was almost as blind as Henn, they all looked more like frightened ganders and geese than human beings able to look to themselves. They clustered together on their way up the steps, Henn wheezing about not being 'quite up to the tiptop of readiness,' and saying, 'You have me at a disadvantage, Miss Blake. But come in. A cup of hot tea, now. A shot of Martell's, Captain? Most regrettable! Terrible! This way, now. Allow me. This way. That's right — there we are. . . .' And so into the hall with his visitors.

When they were gone the dark figures gathered about us again.

'I'll make that man marry the girl,' said Stevey under his breath to me, 'or I'll burn this house to the very ground.'

'We'll burn him out,' they growled, the lust for destruction in their blood.

'He'll marry the girl, or he'll have no house over

15. prevaricator.

his head by morning.'

'But the man is eighty if he's a day,' I implored, 'and the girl is a mere slip of a girl. Is she twenty itself?'

'Well, he ruined her,' said Stevey up to my mouth, as if he would force the words into it.

'I do not believe it,' I said.

Another shower had begun to fall by now, growing heavier drop by drop, dimming the starlight and shimmering dark about the distant fire. Stevey waved his hand to his fellows.

'The city fellows are a lot of help to us,' he said. 'But I'll show you. I'm not going to stand here all night in the rain talking with you.'

He rushed past me up the steps and into the house with his mob after him. I managed to stop him at the door of the drawing room and we parleyed there for a while, whispering angrily as we peeped through the cracked door. There, where fifty years ago he had leaned across the shining walnut to his lights-o'-love, smiling quizzically down on them from his swan's neck, approving the painted lips, the tilted eyebrows, always gracious to them, however cynical, perpetually on the smile, only leaning back from his scandalous whispering when the butler laid a new course or refilled his glass — there, now, he offered his smoke-tainted tea to the two silent, miserable old maids.

'Oh, yes, do drink a cup of tea, Miss Blake,' and he puffs out his cheeks to encourage her. 'Just one?'

'Thank you. I don't believe I really want one, Mr. Henn.'

'Oh, just one cup. Just one.'

They sat straight-backed and unbending, trying hard not to keep looking over the valley at their ruined home. They looked at the soiled tablecloth, the unequal ware, the tarnished silver, or at one another, or at the old captain, their father, who sat sucking his brandy, heavy jowled and heavy bodied, by Henn's fire. They looked at Gypsy, who, careless of her ungainly, ungirlish shape, danced superfluous attendance on them, full of pity for their misfortune, glad to be in the presence of real ladies even for an hour.

So they were sitting when Stevey burst out of my grip into the middle of them, calling on Henn so loudly that they almost screamed.

'Henn,' he said, 'we want you.'

'Don't go, Henn,' said the captain at once, as if he felt as much for his own sake as for Henn's that it was better they should all cling together now.

'What do you want now?' stuttered Henn.

'I want you to come too, Gypsy,' said Stevey.

'Oh, Stevey, Stevey,' said the girl, utterly ashamed before the company.

'Come on, Henn,' bullied Stevey. 'Or will I tell my business here?'

'Out with it,' says the captain.

'One minute now,' pleaded Henn.

I thought it best to get the matter over, and went up to the old man and whispered that it would be best to come. I could not keep those fellows in hand for him any longer.

'Don't go, Henn,' said the captain again.

'No, no,' said the old maids, with the same thought as their father in their minds that even Henn was better than nothing in their extremity, homeless as they were at this hour of the morning.

He rose and went into the kitchen and Stevey and Gypsy and I after him. There he turned and faced us, looking down over us all, even over Stevey himself. Stevey returned his glare. The girl sat with her head in her hands by the fire. I looked at the rain spitting on the dark window. When Stevey had finished, all Henn could say was, 'You liar, you liar!' And all the girl could do was weep and say, 'My misfortune. My misfortune. My misfortune.' Even when I went to her and put my hand on her shoulder she only burst away from me and cried to let her alone, let her alone in her misfortune; for God's sake to let her alone in her misfortune; and sat at the table hiding her face in her hands, shaken with tears.

'You liar!' muttered Henn.

'I'm no liar,' cried Stevey.

The girl wept with renewed shame that no man would own her. Henn looked at her and said very gently to me:

'Supposing I won't marry her?'

'No harm will come to your person,' I said, and faced Stevey on that.

'Your house will go the way of Blake's,' said Stevey, and faced me on that. 'If not tonight, tomorrow night, and if not then, the night after. But if I have to wait a year to do it, up it will go.'

I shook the wretched girl by the shoulder.

'Do you want to marry this old man?' I cried into her ear.

She gave no reply.

'Speak up, Gypsy,' said Stevey. 'You will marry him, won't you? You said you would.'

She said not a word now.

'I'll not marry her,' said Henn.

Stevey had cunning enough to play his last card.

'Then tell your Blake friends to get out of this house, if they have sense. Or, I'll do it.'

Henn stopped him at the door.

'Don't! Don't do that!'

And thereupon he sank into a chair with a sudden dizziness, and I had to hold him up from falling sidelong to the floor.

'Gypsy,' I said, 'get a sup of whiskey.'

'Alec!' she said, going to him, and he took her hand, her little hand, in his when she stood by his side and said his name. 'Alec! Will I get a sup of brandy?'

There was silence for a few minutes, with only the noise of the rain cat-pattering against the window and the three of us over Henn. At last he began to whisper through his fingers, and I leaned down to hear him.

'Will she marry me?' he was whispering while the spittle dropped like a cow's spittle between his fingers to the flagged floor.

'Now!' cried Stevey triumphantly. 'Gypsy! Will you have him?'

In her deep man's voice she replied:

'And who else would have me now? Since others won't — others that have their own life and their own plans and plots?'

And seeing that the old man was not in need of help she went out of the kitchen, holding her stomach in her little palms, murmuring as she went.

'I will, if he will.'

I pushed Stevey before me from the kitchen and leaving Henn to himself we drove the rest of the chaps before us from the hall, into the darkness, now rain-arrowy and old. From the great front door I watched them go tramping down the avenue and as I, too, turned to go upstairs to my bed I heard Henn, back in the drawing room, trying once more to play the host with his smoky tea and his patched ware. I wondered as I tramped upstairs if he was thinking that, with this young wife, he might begin life again.

From my bed I heard the summer downpour drip about the house and occasionally spit down the chimney on the damp papers stuffed in the grate, tainting all the room with their sooty reek. Not until late noon did I hear another sound, and then it was the birds singing and the croaking corncake and the doves in the high woods, and when I rose the whole house was radiant with sunshine reflected from the fields and the trees. There was nobody about the house but Gypsy. The Blakes had gone since early morning. Henn did not leave his bed for several days. Stevey I could find nowhere and the local men said he was gone into Kerry, swearing he would only return to make Henn keep to his promise. Two days I waited for him and searched about for news of him, and then I called a meeting of his battalion and replaced him by a new commandant.

One evening I left Henn Hall as I had come, but before I went I visited Henn in his room to say good-bye and I found him sitting over his fire, drinking punch and reading an *Anglers' Annual* of thirty years ago.

'Be careful of yourself, boy,' he warned as I turned to leave him.

'Oh, yes,' I said. 'I'll be careful.'

'Do you believe Long's story?' he said then, leaning forward to me.

'I have no cause,' I parried, 'to believe or disbelieve anybody.'

He leaned back and stared at the fire.

'Anyway,' he said after a while, 'I'm going to marry her. She's as good as the next, and better than some, even though she *is* only a tinker's daughter. Besides,' he added proudly, 'if it's a boy 'twill keep the name alive.'

As if he were a Hapsburg or a Bourbon.

One night two months or so later we heard in our back-yard bedroom that a strange pair left Cork for Dublin that afternoon on the mail express, all their dozen or so of trunks and bags labelled forward to an address in Paris. The woman, in a massive hat with a scarlet feather, had flaunted her way to her carriage; the old man, her husband, hobbling and shuffling along behind her. His travelling coat almost completely hid him, its tail touching the ground, its coat collar up about his ears, and so weak did his eyes appear to be that even in the dim filtered light of the station he had cocked his hat forward over his eyebrows and shaded his eyes with his withered hand as he walked. But I found it too painful to think of him with his scraps of governess French, guiding his tinker wife through the boulevards, the cafés, the theatres, seeing once more the lovely women gay in their hour. Anyway, we had more serious things to think of then.

FRANK O'CONNOR

(1903–66)

from: GUESTS OF THE NATION (1931)

['Guests of the Nation', the title story of O'Connor's first collection, is perhaps our most vivid account of hostage-taking and its effect on the human family. His sense of character and setting – observant, witty and compassionate – intensifies our sense of disquiet as the impersonal tyranny of war slowly penetrates to the heart of that human company in the remote farmhouse. The horror of the events is never allowed to rob the victims and executioners – even Donovan, awkward emissary of death – of their humanity. The tragedy of Ireland's modern history has seldom been presented in fiction with such economy and power.]

GUESTS OF THE NATION

I

At dusk the big Englishman, Belcher, would shift his long legs out of the ashes and say 'Well, chums, what about it?' and Noble and myself would say 'All right, chum' (for we had picked up some of their curious expressions), and the little Englishman, Hawkins, would light the lamp and bring out the cards. Sometimes Jeremiah Donovan would come up and supervise the game, and get excited over Hawkins' cards, which he always played badly, and shout at him, as if he was one of our own. 'Ah, you divil, why didn't you play the tray?'[1]

But ordinarily Jeremiah was a sober and contented poor devil like the big Englishman, Belcher, and was looked up to only because he was a fair hand at documents, though he was slow even with them. He wore a small cloth hat and big gaiters over his long pants, and you seldom saw him with his hands out of his pockets. He reddened when you talked to him, tilting from toe to heel and back, and looking down all the time at his big farmer's feet. Noble and myself used to make fun of his broad accent, because we were both from the town.

I could not at the time see the point of myself and Noble guarding Belcher and Hawkins at all, for it was my belief that you could have planted that pair down anywhere from this to Claregalway[2] and they'd have taken root there like a native weed. I never in my short experience saw two men take to the country as they did.

They were passed on to us by the Second Battalion[3] when the search for them became too hot, and Noble and myself, being young, took them over with a natural feeling of responsibility, but Hawkins made us look like fools when he showed that he knew the country better than we did.

'You're the bloke they call Bonaparte,' he says to me. 'Mary Brigid O'Connell told me to ask what you'd done with the pair of her brother's socks you borrowed.'

For it seemed, as they explained it, that the Second had little evenings, and some of the girls of the neighbourhood turned up, and, seeing they were such decent chaps, our fellows could not leave the two Englishmen out. Hawkins learned to dance 'The Walls of Limerick', 'The Siege of Ennis' and 'The Waves of Tory' as well as any of them, though he could not return the compliment, because our lads at that time did not dance foreign dances on principle.[4]

So whatever privileges Belcher and Hawkins had with the Second they just took naturally with us, and after the first couple of days we gave up all pretence of keeping an eye on them. Not that they could have got far, because they had accents you could cut with a knife, and wore khaki tunics and overcoats with civilian pants and boots, but I believe myself they never had any idea of escaping and were quite content to be where they were.

It was a treat to see how Belcher got off with the old woman in the house where we were staying. She

1. i.e. the three.

2. A townland north of Galway city on the river Clare.
3. Through the War of Independence (1919–21), in which the action takes place, the chief military unit of the IRA was the battalion.
4. Cultural nationalist organizations of the time, the Gaelic League and the Gaelic Athletic Association, discouraged foreign games and dances.

was a great warrant to scold,[5] and cranky even with us, but before ever she had a chance of giving our guests, as I may call them, a lick of her tongue, Belcher had made her his friend for life. She was breaking sticks, and Belcher, who had not been more than ten minutes in the house, jumped up and went over to her.

'Allow me, madam,' he said, smiling his queer little smile. 'Please allow me,' and he took the hatchet from her. She was too surprised to speak, and after that, Belcher would be at her heels, carrying a bucket, a basket or a load of turf. As Noble said, he got into looking before she leapt, and hot water, or any little thing she wanted, Belcher would have ready for her. For such a huge man (and though I am five foot ten myself I had to look up at him) he had an uncommon lack of speech. It took us a little while to get used to him, walking in and out like a ghost, without speaking. Especially because Hawkins talked enough for a platoon, it was strange to hear Belcher with his toes in the ashes come out with a solitary 'Excuse me, chum,' or 'That's right, chum.' His one and only passion was cards, and he was a remarkably good card player. He could have skinned myself and Noble, but whatever we lost to him, Hawkins lost to us, and Hawkins only played with the money Belcher gave him.

Hawkins lost to us because he had too much old gab, and we probably lost to Belcher for the same reason. Hawkins and Noble argued about religion into the early hours of the morning, and Hawkins worried the life out of Noble, who had a brother a priest, with a string of questions that would puzzle a cardinal. Even in treating of holy subjects, Hawkins had a deplorable tongue. I never met a man who could mix such a variety of cursing and bad language into any argument. He was a terrible man, and a fright to argue.[6] He never did a stroke of work, and when he had no one else to argue with, he got stuck in the old woman.

He met his match in her, for when he tried to get her to complain profanely of the drought she gave him a great comedown[7] by blaming it entirely on Jupiter Pluvius[8] (a deity neither Hawkins nor I had ever heard of, though Noble said that among the pagans it was believed that he had something to do with the rain). Another day he was swearing at the capitalists for starting the German war[9] when the old lady laid down her iron, puckered up her little crab's mouth and said: 'Mr Hawkins, you can say what you like about the war, and think you'll deceive me because I'm only a simple poor countrywoman, but I know what started the war. It was the Italian Count that stole the heathen divinity out of the temple of Japan. Believe me, Mr. Hawkins, nothing but sorrow and want can follow people who disturb the hidden powers.'

A queer old girl, all right.

II

One evening we had our tea and Hawkins lit the lamp and we all sat into cards. Jeremiah Donovan came in too, and sat and watched us for a while, and it suddenly struck me that he had no great love for the two Englishmen. It came as a surprise to me because I had noticed nothing of it before.

Late in the evening a really terrible argument blew up between Hawkins and Noble about capitalists and priests and love of country.

'The capitalists pay the priests to tell you about the next world so that you won't notice what the bastards are up to in this,' said Hawkins.

'Nonsense, man!' said Noble, losing his temper. 'Before ever a capitalist was thought of people believed in the next world.'

Hawkins stood up as though he was preaching. 'Oh, they did, did they?' he said with a sneer. 'They believed all the things you believe — isn't that what you mean? And you believe God created Adam, and Adam created Shem, and Shem created Jehoshophat.[10] You believe all that silly old fairytale about Eve and Eden and the apple. Well listen to me, chum! If you're entitled to a silly belief like that, I'm entitled to my own silly belief — which is that the first thing your God created was a bleeding capitalist, with morality and Rolls-Royce complete. Am I right, chum?' he says to Belcher.

'You're right, chum,' says Belcher with a smile,

5. i.e. a great expert at scolding. A warrant confers authority and, by association, expertise.
6. i.e. very argumentative.
7. i.e. put him in his place.
8. Jupiter: chief of the Olympian gods. Although the old woman's deity is not recorded anywhere, *pluvia* is the Latin for rain.
9. The Great War, 1914–18.
10. Unrelated Bible personages and places are jumbled together to produce deliberate nonsense; creation is confused with begetting.

and he got up from the table to stretch his long legs into the fire and stroke his moustache. So, seeing that Jeremiah Donovan was going, and that there was no knowing when the argument about religion would be over, I went out with him. We strolled down to the village together, and then he stopped, blushing and mumbling, and said I should be behind, keeping guard. I didn't like the tone he took with me, and anyway I was bored with life in the cottage, so I replied by asking what the hell we wanted to guard them for at all.

He looked at me in surprise and said: 'I thought you knew we were keeping them as hostages.'

'Hostages?' I said.

'The enemy have prisoners belonging to us, and now they're talking of shooting them,' he said. 'If they shoot our prisoners, we'll shoot theirs.'

'Shoot Belcher and Hawkins?' I said.

'What else did you think we were keeping them for?' he said.

'Wasn't it very unforeseen of you not to warn Noble and myself of that in the beginning?' I said.

'How was it?' he said. 'You might have known that much.'

'We could not know it, Jeremiah Donovan,' I said. 'How could we when they were on our hands so long?'

'The enemy have our prisoners as long and longer,' he said.

'That's not the same thing at all,' said I.

'What difference is there?' said he.

I couldn't tell him, because I knew he wouldn't understand. If it was only an old dog that you had to take to the vet's, you'd try and not get too fond of him, but Jeremiah Donovan was not a man who would ever be in danger of that.

'And when is this to be decided?' I said.

'We might hear tonight,' he said. 'Or tomorrow or the next day at latest. So if it's only hanging round that's a trouble to you, you'll be free soon enough.'

It was not the hanging round that was a trouble to me at all by this time. I had worse things to worry about. When I got back to the cottage the argument was still on. Hawkins was holding forth in his best style, maintaining that there was no next world, and Noble saying that there was; but I could see that Hawkins had had the best of it.

'Do you know what, chum?' he was saying with a saucy smile. 'I think you're just as big a bleeding unbeliever as I am. You say you believe in the next world, and you know just as much about the next world as I do, which is sweet damn-all. What's heaven? You don't know. Where's heaven? You don't know. You know sweet damn-all! I ask you again, do they wear wings?'

'Very well, then,' said Noble. 'They do. Is that enough for you? They do wear wings.'

'Where do they get them then? Who makes them? Have they a factory for wings? Have they a sort of store where you hand in your chit and take your bleeding wings?'

'You're an impossible man to argue with,' said Noble. 'Now, listen to me —' And they were off again.

It was long after midnight when we locked up and went to bed. As I blew out the candle I told Noble. He took it very quietly. When we'd been in bed about an hour he asked if I thought we should tell the Englishmen. I didn't, because I doubted if the English would shoot our men. Even if they did, the Brigade officers, who were always up and down to the Second Battalion and knew the Englishmen well, would hardly want to see them plugged. 'I think so too,' said Noble. 'It would be great cruelty to put the wind up them now.'

'It was very unforeseen of Jeremiah Donovan, anyhow,' said I.

It was next morning that we found it so hard to face Belcher and Hawkins. We went about the house all day, scarcely saying a word. Belcher didn't seem to notice; he was stretched into the ashes as usual, with his usual look of waiting in quietness for something unforeseen to happen, but Hawkins noticed it and put it down to Noble being beaten in the argument of the night before.

'Why can't you take the discussion in the proper spirit?' he said severely. 'You and your Adam and Eve! I'm a Communist, that's what I am. Communist or Anarchist, it all comes to much the same thing.' And he went round the house, muttering when the fit took him: 'Adam and Eve! Adam and Eve! Nothing better to do with their time than pick bleeding apples!'

III

I don't know how we got through that day, but I was very glad when it was over, the tea things were cleared away, and Belcher said in his peaceable way: 'Well, chums, what about it?' We sat round the table and Hawkins took out the cards, and just then I heard Jeremiah Donovan's footsteps on the path and a dark presentiment crossed my mind. I rose from the table and caught him before he reached the door.

'What do you want?' I asked.

'I want those two soldier friends of yours,' he said, getting red.

'Is that the way, Jeremiah Donovan?' I asked.

'That's the way. There were four of our lads shot this morning, one of them a boy of sixteen.'

'That's bad,' I said.

At that moment Noble followed me out, and the three of us walked down the path together, talking in whispers. Feeney, the local intelligence officer, was standing by the gate.

'What are you going to do about it?' I asked Jeremiah Donovan.

'I want you and Noble to get them out; tell them they're being shifted again; that'll be the quietest way.'

'Leave me out of that,' said Noble, under his breath.

Jeremiah Donovan looked at him hard.

'All right,' he says. 'You and Feeney get a few tools from the shed and dig a hole by the far end of the bog. Bonaparte and myself will be after you. Don't let anyone see you with the tools. I wouldn't like it to go beyond ourselves.'

We saw Feeney and Noble go round to the shed and went in ourselves. I left Jeremiah Donovan to do the explanations. He told them that he had orders to send them back to the Second Battalion. Hawkins let out a mouthful of curses, and you could see that though Belcher didn't say anything, he was a bit upset too. The old woman was for having them stay in spite of us, and she didn't stop advising them until Jeremiah Donovan lost his temper and turned on her. He had a nasty temper, I noticed. It was pitch dark in the cottage by this time, but no one thought of lighting the lamp, and in the darkness the two Englishmen fetched their topcoats and said goodbye to the old woman.

'Just as a man makes a home of a bleeding place, some bastard at headquarters thinks you're too cushy and shunts you off,' said Hawkins, shaking her hand.

'A thousand thanks, madam,' said Belcher. 'A thousand thanks for everything' — as though he'd made it up.

We went round to the back of the house and down towards the bog. It was only then that Jeremiah Donovan told them. He was shaking with excitement.

'There were four of our fellows shot in Cork this morning and now you are to be shot as a reprisal.'

'What are you talking about?' snaps Hawkins. 'It's bad enough being mucked about as we are without having to put up with your funny jokes.'

'It isn't a joke,' said Donovan. 'I'm sorry, Hawkins, but it's true,' and begins on the usual rigmarole about duty and how unpleasant it is. I never noticed that people who talk a lot about duty find it much of a trouble to them.

'Oh, cut it out!' said Hawkins.

'Ask Bonaparte,' said Donovan, seeing that Hawkins wasn't taking him seriously. 'Isn't it true, Bonaparte?'

'It is,' I said, and Hawkins stopped.

'Ah, for Christ's sake, chum!'

'I mean it, chum,' I said.

'You don't sound as if you mean it.'

'If he doesn't mean it, I do,' said Donovan, working himself up.

'What have you against me, Jeremiah Donovan?'

'I never said I had anything against you. But why did your people take out four of our prisoners and shoot them in cold blood?'

He took Hawkins by the arm and dragged him on, but it was impossible to make him understand that we were in earnest. I had the Smith and Wesson in my pocket and I kept fingering it and wondering what I'd do if they put up a fight for it or ran, and wishing to God they'd do one or the other. I knew if they did run for it, that I'd never fire on them. Hawkins wanted to know was Noble in it, and when we said yes, he asked us why Noble wanted to plug him. Why did any of us want to plug him? What had he done to us? Weren't we all chums? Didn't we understand him and didn't he understand us? Did we imagine for an instant that he'd shoot us for all the so-and-so officers in the so-and-so British Army?

By this time we'd reached the bog, and I was so sick I couldn't even answer him. We walked along the edge of it in the darkness, and every now and then Hawkins would call a halt and begin all over again, as if he was wound up, about our being chums, and I knew that nothing but the sight of the grave would convince him that we had to do it. And all the time I was hoping that something would happen; that they'd run for it or that Noble would take over the responsibility from me. I had the feeling that it was worse on Noble than on me.

IV

At last we saw the lantern in the distance and made towards it. Noble was carrying it, and Feeney was standing somewhere in the darkness behind him, and the picture of them so still and silent in the bogland brought it home to me that we were in earnest, and banished the last bit of hope I had.

Belcher, on recognising Noble, said: 'Hallo, chum,' in his quiet way, but Hawkins flew at him at once, and the argument began all over again, only this time Noble had nothing to say for himself and stood with his head down, holding the lantern between his legs.

It was Jeremiah Donovan who did the answering. For the twentieth time, as though it was haunting his mind, Hawkins asked if anybody thought he'd shoot Noble.

'Yes, you would,' said Jeremiah Donovan.

'No, I wouldn't, damn you!'

'You would, because you'd know you'd be shot for not doing it.'

'I wouldn't, not if I was to be shot twenty times over. I wouldn't shoot a pal. And Belcher wouldn't — isn't that right, Belcher?'

'That's right, chum,' Belcher said, but more by way of answering the question than of joining in the argument. Belcher sounded as though whatever unforeseen thing he'd always been waiting for had come at last.

'Anyway, who says Noble would be shot if I wasn't? What do you think I'd do if I was in his place, out in the middle of a blasted bog?'

'What would you do?' asked Donovan.

'I'd go with him wherever he was going, of course. Share my last bob[11] with him and stick by him through thick and thin. No one can ever say of me that I let down a pal.'

'We've had enough of this,' said Jeremiah Donovan, cocking his revolver. 'Is there any message you want to send?'

'No, there isn't.'

'Do you want to say your prayers?'

Hawkins came out with a cold-blooded remark that even shocked me and turned on Noble again.

'Listen to me Noble,' he said. 'You and me are chums. You can't come over to my side, so I'll come over to your side. That show you I mean what I say? Give me a rifle and I'll go along with you and the other lads.'

Noble answered him. We knew that was no way out.

'Hear what I'm saying?' he said. 'I'm through with it. I'm a deserter or anything else you like. I don't believe in your stuff, but it's no worse than mine. That satisfy you?'

Noble raised his head, but Donovan began to speak and he lowered it again without replying.

'For the last time, have you any messages to send?' said Donovan in a cold, excited sort of voice.

'Shut up, Donovan! You don't understand me, but these lads do. They're not the sort to make a pal and kill a pal. They're not the tools of any capitalist.'

I alone of the crowd saw Donovan raise his Webley to the back of Hawkins's neck, and as he did so I shut my eyes and tried to pray. Hawkins had begun to say something else when Donovan fired, and as I opened my eyes at the bang, I saw Hawkins stagger at the knees and lie out flat at Noble's feet, slowly and as quiet as a kid falling asleep, with the lantern-light on his lean legs and bright farmer's boots. We all stood very still, watching him settle out in the last agony.

Then Belcher took out a handkerchief and began to tie it about his own eyes (in our excitement we'd forgotten to do the same for Hawkins), and, seeing it wasn't big enough, turned and asked for the loan of mine. I gave it to him, and he knotted the two together and pointed with his foot at Hawkins.

'He's not quite dead,' he said. 'Better give him another.'

Sure enough, Hawkins's left knee was beginning to rise. I bent down and put my gun to his head; then recollecting myself, I got up again. Belcher understood what was in my mind.

'Give him his first,' he said. 'I don't mind. Poor bastard, we don't know what's happening to him now.'

I knelt and fired. By this time I didn't seem to know what I was doing. Belcher, who was fumbling a bit awkwardly with the handkerchiefs, came out with a laugh as he heard the shot. It was the first time I had heard him laugh and it sent a shudder

11. shilling.

down my back; it sounded so unnatural.

'Poor bugger!' he said quietly. 'And last night he was so curious about it all. It's very queer, chums, I always think. Now he knows as much about it as they'll ever let him know, and last night he was all in the dark.'

Donovan helped him to tie the handkerchiefs about his eyes. 'Thanks, chum,' he said. Donovan asked if there were any messages he wanted sent.

'No, chum,' he said. 'Not for me. If any of you would like to write to Hawkins's mother, you'll find a letter from her in his pocket. He and his mother were great chums. But my missus left me eight years ago. Went away with another fellow and took the kid with her. I like the feeling of a home, as you may have noticed, but I couldn't start another again after that.'

It was an extraordinary thing, but in those few minutes Belcher said more than in all the weeks before. It was just as if the sound of the shot had started a flood of talk in him and he could go on the whole night like that, quite happily, talking about himself. We stood around like fools now that he couldn't see us any longer. Donovan looked at Noble, and Noble shook his head. Then Donovan raised his Webley, and at that moment Belcher gave his queer laugh again. He may have thought we were talking about him, or perhaps he noticed the same thing I'd noticed and couldn't understand it.

'Excuse me, chums,' he said. 'I feel I'm talking the hell of a lot, and so silly, about my being so handy about a house and things like that. But this thing came on me suddenly. You'll forgive me, I'm sure.'

'You don't want to say a prayer?' asked Donovan.

'No, chum,' he said. 'I don't think it would help. I'm ready, and you boys want to get it over.'

'You understand that we're only doing our duty?' said Donovan.

Belcher's head was raised like a blind man's, so that you could only see his chin and the top of his nose in the lantern-light.

'I never could make out what duty was myself,' he said. 'I think you're all good lads, if that's what you mean. I'm not complaining.'

Noble, just as if he couldn't bear any more of it, raised his fist at Donovan, and in a flash Donovan raised his gun and fired. The big man went over like a sack of meal, and this time there was no need for a second shot.

I don't remember much about the burying, but that it was worse than all the rest because we had to carry them to the grave. It was all mad lonely with nothing but a patch of lantern-light between ourselves and the dark, and birds hooting and screeching all round, disturbed by the guns. Noble went through Hawkins's belongings to find the letter from his mother, and then joined his hands together. He did the same with Belcher. Then, when we'd filled in the grave, we separated from Jeremiah Donovan and Feeney and took our tools back to the shed. All the way we didn't speak a word. The kitchen was dark and cold as we'd left it, and the old woman was sitting over the hearth, saying her beads. We walked past her into the room, and Noble struck a match to light the lamp. She rose quietly and came to the doorway with all her cantankerousness gone.

'What did ye do with them?' she asked in a whisper, and Noble started so that the match went out in his hand.

'What's that?' he asked without turning round.

'I heard ye,' she said.

'What did you hear?' asked Noble.

'I heard ye. Do you think I didn't hear ye, putting the spade back in the houseen?'[12]

Noble struck another match and this time the lamp lit for him.

'Was that what ye did to them?' she asked.

Then, by God, in the very doorway, she fell on her knees and began praying, and after looking at her for a minute or two Noble did the same by the fireplace. I pushed my way out past her and left them at it. I stood at the door, watching the stars and listening to the shrieking of the birds dying out over the bogs. It is so strange what you feel at times like that that you can't describe it. Noble says he saw everything ten times the size, as though there was nothing in the whole world but that little patch of bog with the two Englishmen stiffening into it, but with me it was as if the patch of bog where the Englishmen were was a million miles away, and even Noble and the old woman, mumbling behind me, and the birds and the bloody stars were all far away, and I was somehow very small and very lost and lonely like a child astray in the snow. And anything that happened to me afterwards, I never felt the same about again.

12. little house, shed.

MARY LAVIN

(1912–)

from:
A SINGLE LADY (1951)

['A Visit to the Cemetery' is one of a suite of stories concerning the humdrum destiny of a small-town family, the Grimeses, which includes Alice and Liddy, the heroines of the present story. Other tales in the series are 'The Little Prince', 'Frail Vessel' and 'An Old Boot'.]

A VISIT TO THE CEMETERY

What a pity she had to be buried here!' said Alice, for about the hundredth time since their mother died, as she took the key from her younger sister Liddy and struggled with the corroded iron gate of the old cemetery as it was called since the new plot had been opened outside the town.

The New Plot was about a mile outside the town, on a nice dry hill that commanded a fine view of the countryside. And it was just a nice walk out to it, not too far; but above all not too near.

'I can't think why on earth they ever put a cemetery here in the middle of the town,' cried Alice, as the lock turned at last but the heavy old gate refused to budge.

'Oh Alice!' Liddy had to laugh at her older sister's ignorance, because of course the cemetery was far older than the town. It was the site of an old friary of which only one stump now remained, sticking up like an old tooth rotted down to its obstinate root, but which, upon the open fields, must once have floated free as an island.

Alice, however, was not concerned with antiquity.

'Come on,' she cried. She had got the gate to open. The next minute they were inside, finding their way through the neglected grass and high rank nettles by following the faint track of the funeral, still visible after four months. There was no real path anywhere now, and funerals had to make their way on foot, in and out, worm-like, between the tottering tombstones. No hearse had entered the place in living memory; coffins had to be shouldered into their last resting-place.

'Mind your clothes!' cried Alice sharply, because she still had memories of the humiliation she suffered at the funeral, when the mourners, themselves included, came out into the street with burs stuck all over their good black clothes.

'I'm all right,' said Liddy. She was holding up her skirt but all the same they both had to stop more than once where their dresses caught in the briars.

But at last they got to their mother's grave and knelt down quickly, crossing themselves before their knees touched the clay and, as they brought their hands together again in front of them, closing their eyes tightly.

For the next minute or two their lips moved with the quick pecking movements of a bird, as they got through what might almost at some previous date have been decided upon as their mother's ration, so neatly did they come to an end together. Yet they did not immediately make the sign of the cross, neither wanting to be the first to make a move. But after all someone had to do it, and so at last Liddy glanced across at Alice and raised her eyebrows questioningly.

At once, just as if she had been audibly addressed, Alice answered.

'I am. Are you?' she said, and she began to bless herself and got to her feet. Liddy also scrambled to her feet.

'That grass was damp,' she said a little crossly, and she began to rub her knees.

'It's always damp in this old place,' said Alice very crossly. 'I always say I'll bring something with me to kneel on — even an old newspaper — but I forget it every time.' She, too, rubbed her knees, but it was her black dress that concerned her most and lifting up the hem she submitted her skirt to a close scrutiny. 'I'll never forget those burs,' she said.

'Nor I,' said Liddy, but she didn't bother to look at her dress because after all they had to make their way back to the gate again.

Wasn't it a wonder no one took any care of the place? Even to scythe the weeds would be such a help. But then of course hardly anyone ever came here; except themselves.

What a lonely place it was, she thought, and

although where she stood she could hear the voices of people talking in the street outside, and only a little further away shouts and the thudding of a ball in the ball-alley,[1] it seemed to her for a minute that she was cut off from them in some way so that though she heard them they would not hear her, not even if she were to scream at the top of her voice.

But that was absurd: why should she scream? It was broad daylight and she wasn't a child any longer. And there was Alice a few feet away calling out to her impatiently.

'Are you coming?' cried Alice.

But Liddy still loitered, and as if she had never been in it before, she looked around the old cemetery. As far as they could be seen in the rank growth in which they were submerged, there wasn't a tombstone or a headstone that wasn't slanted or tottering. It was almost as if the earth had quaked and the quiet dead had been momentarily dislodged and settled down again in postures, unquiet and disorderly.

And ah — just behind their mother's headstone there was an unsightly grave where a rabbit — no it must have been a badger — had burrowed, and from it, yes, though Liddy averted her eyes abruptly — yes, from it a large bleached bone had been dislodged.

Almost falling forward into the high grass she ran after Alice, but when she caught up with her, she stopped again and brought Alice to a standstill with her.

'Poor mother!' she cried. 'I can't help thinking how much nicer and cleaner it would have been for her in the new cemetery!'

'Isn't that what I'm always saying!' Alice looked at her. Liddy was so slow sometimes. 'Are you coming or are you not?' she cried, pulling her sleeve free and going on a few steps.

'Alice?'

Alice didn't want to turn around, but there was something in Liddy's voice that made her turn back. Liddy was standing just where she left her, looking backward at their mother's grave.

'What?'

Alice knew her voice was grumpy, but she really wanted to get to the gate. She hated this place.

And Liddy looked as if she was prepared to stay there for ever.

'Do you ever think about it at all, Alice?'

What she meant Alice both knew and did not know, so she took her choice.

'I don't know what you're talking about,' she said.

Liddy turned around slowly and in her eyes there was an expression that could not be misread or misunderstood.

'It's so awful,' she said, 'isn't it?' and she shuddered.

Almost as quickly as Liddy herself had averted her eyes from the bone on the grave, Alice averted hers from her sister.

'Oh, Liddy!' she exclaimed impatiently. 'If I thought you were going to take on like this I'd never have come with you.' She paused, casting around in her mind for some way to smooth out the awkwardness of the moment. 'After all we must all die — we know that,' she said lamely.

But Liddy was incorrigible.

'That's what I mean,' she said quietly.

Alice was at a loss.

'Well, after all we can console ourselves that it's only the body that is buried, the soul . . . .'

Not exactly rudely, however, and not exactly impatiently, Liddy shrugged her shoulders.

'I sometimes think that's the worst of it,' she said, in a voice so low Alice had to bend forward to hear it. 'I can never believe that I won't go on feeling: feeling the cold and the damp — you know, even after —'

'Liddy! Liddy!' Alice stumbled across the tufted grass to her. If she said a single other word of the sentence she would have clapped her hands over her mouth.

But Liddy didn't finish it. She had begun to sob softly.

'And to think,' she said after a minute, 'that in a few years, perhaps sooner, poor Father —' she sobbed, 'just think of it — poor Father will be put down here too.'

This was dreadful. Alice felt helpless. She always knew Liddy felt things differently from her, but she never knew her to carry on like this. She couldn't think what to do, and when at that moment near her foot she saw a white bone she gave it a kick. Hateful place: it was all bones. That one might have been brought in by some mongrel, but it could just as easily be a human bone: the place was disgusting. It was enough to give anyone the creeps. Oh, if only Mother had been buried in the new cemetery where

1. Handball was a popular sport in Irish provincial towns.

everything was so neat and orderly Liddy would not have got into this state! Jem Flagg, the grave-digger up at the new cemetery, always boasted that he'd give five pounds to anyone that found a bone after him!

'Well, thanks be to goodness we won't be buried here, anyway!' she said impulsively.

'We won't?' Liddy looked up in such surprise that the tears that were slowly rolling down her cheeks were jerked abruptly into the air.

'Of course not,' Alice cried. 'Not unless we are old maids!' But that seemed so untoward a thing that she made a playful grimace. Then, seeing that Liddy had smiled, if wanly, she put on an arch expression. 'We'll be buried with our husbands,' she said.

'Oh, Alice!' Liddy knew that Alice used to talk about boys with her friends, but she had never said anything like that to her before. She felt herself blushing, and was furious about it until she saw that Alice was blushing a little too.

'It's true!' said Alice defensively. 'The first death in the family means that you have to buy a plot — surely you know that! That's why mother was buried here, because of that baby she had before any of us, the one that died. Father bought a plot here then, and now even though it's years and years ago since then, and there is a new cemetery now, mother had to be buried here, and so will Father. But there aren't any more plots to be got here now, thanks be to God, so our husbands will have to provide them — in the new cemetery — thanks be to God again!'

Our husbands: it was an intoxicating thought. Liddy looked across the graveyard to the gate; it was turning out to be a beautiful evening, although you wouldn't notice that in the graveyard, everything was so dark with the ivy, and the old stones with their shadows overlapping everywhere, made a sort of double gloom.

Although there was hardly room for two to walk together, she recklessly linked her arm in her sister's and began to move towards the gate. A great feeling of sisterly affection had come over her, and it seemed to her that it wasn't just a matter of chance that they had picked this evening to come out together. It was as if something for a long time suppressed in her at last had begun to force upwards towards the light.

'Just think, Alice — about that baby, I mean. Mother was younger than us — than you, anyway — when that baby was born, and we —' she hesitated.

'I know,' said Alice glumly. 'I was just thinking that myself a few minutes ago. But times were different then; girls were encouraged to have boys then: not like now when it's the very opposite.'

'You mean Father would —'

'He'd be just wild, and you know that as well as I do. And he will probably be ten times more strict now because he used to rely on mother to look after us.'

'Poor Mother! She wasn't very strict at all.'

'I expect that was because she was so ill for the past few years. You remember everyone said it was a happy release for her.'

'I suppose it was, in a way,' said Liddy.

But they had reached the gate at last, and she sighed. Their adventure for the day was over. It was a pity they started out so early in a way; if they started half an hour later they would be coming in the gate now instead of going out. And she was right about the evening; there was a remarkable change in the air, it was like an evening in spring, and just as they stepped out into the street a breeze that came up out of nowhere, oh, so fresh and sweet, blew their skirts around them like an umbrella around its stem. It would be such a nice evening to go for a walk, outside the town; to hold up their faces, to look, to smell, and above all to talk; to talk.

'Oh, isn't it too bad, Alice,' she cried, as if it was the first time anyone had expressed the idea —

'— that she wasn't buried in the New Cemetery?' Liddy nodded eagerly. 'It must be lovely up there on an evening like this: we could walk around and read the names on the stones — they're all names we know: not like in this old place. I don't suppose —' she hesitated — 'I wonder if —'

'You mean — walk out that way?' said Alice, taking up her meaning immediately, but she looked frightened. 'We didn't tell them at home that we were going to a walk.'

'We said we were going to the cemetery, didn't we?' cried Libby. 'We didn't say which one!' She gave Alice's arm a pull. 'Oh, come on,' she cried. 'I've something to tell you, anyway. I've kept it a secret, but I think I could tell you now.'

For a minute Alice was almost livid with jealousy. Could it be possible that Liddy had a boy: Liddy who was two years younger than her. And she hadn't had a single flutter.[2] Unless you counted what

2. A flirtation.

happened after the choir the other evening. She wondered what Liddy would think about it? She might tell her as they went along.

'Come on so,' she cried. 'We'll chance it.'

They almost forgot to lock the gate.

'What about this,' cried Liddy when she managed to get the key out of the lock.

They were supposed to hand it back where they got it, at the parochial house.

'Oh, we'll leave it back on the way home,' said Alice. She was impatient to start.

But before they set out, one after the other, the sisters went over to the iron gate and gave it a push to see that it was locked, and to make doubly sure Liddy put her shoulder to it.

'It's locked all right,' she said. 'Come on.'

from:
IN THE MIDDLE OF THE FIELDS (1967)

['In the Middle of the Fields', the title story of Mary Lavin's 1967 collection, is one of those studies of longing and loneliness that she pursued with such intensity in her middle years.]

IN THE MIDDLE OF THE FIELDS

Like a rock in the sea, she was islanded by fields, the heavy grass washing about the house, and the cattle wading in it as in water. Even their gentle stirrings were a loss when they moved away at evening to the shelter of the woods. A rainy day might strike a wet flash from a hay barn on the far side of the river. Not even a habitation! And yet she was less lonely for him here in Meath than elsewhere. Anxieties by day, and cares, and at night vague, nameless fears, these were the stones across the mouth of the tomb. But who understood that? They thought she hugged tight every memory she had of him. What did they know about memory? What was it but another name for dry love and barren longing? They even tried to unload upon her their own small purposeless memories. 'I imagine I see him every time I look out there,' they would say as they glanced nervously over the darkening fields when they were leaving. 'I think I ought to see him coming through the trees.'

Oh, for God's sake! she'd think. She'd forgotten him for a minute.

It wasn't him she saw when she looked out at the fields. It was ugly tufts of tow and scutch[1] that whitened the tops of the grass and gave it the look of a sea in storm, spattered with broken foam. That grass would have to be topped. And how much would it cost?

At least Ned, the old herd, knew the man to do it for her. 'Bartley Crossen is your man, Ma'am. Your husband knew him well.'

Vera couldn't place him at first. Then she remembered. 'Oh, yes, that's his hay barn we see, isn't it? Why, of course. I know him well, by sight.' And so she did, splashing past on the road in his big muddy car, the wheels always caked with clay, and the wife in the front seat beside him.

'I'll get him to call around and have a word with you, Ma'am,' said the herd.

'Before dark,' she cautioned.

But there was no need to tell Ned. The old man knew how she always tried to be upstairs before it got dark, locking herself into her bedroom, which opened off the room where the children slept, praying devoutly that she wouldn't have to come down again for anything, above all, not to answer the door. That was what in particular she dreaded: a knock after dark.

'Ah, sure, who'd come near you, Ma'am, knowing you're a woman alone with small children that might be wakened and set crying? And, for that matter, where could you be safer than in the middle of the fields, with the innocent beasts asleep around you?' If he himself had come to the house late at night for any reason, to get hot water to stoup[2] the foot of a beast, or to call the vet, he took care to shout out long before he got to the gable. 'It's me, Ma'am!' he'd shout.

'Coming! Coming!' she'd cry, gratefully, as quick on his words as their echo. Unlocking her door, she'd run down and throw open the hall door. No matter what the hour! No matter how black the night!

'Go back to your bed now, you Ma'am,' he'd say

1. Terms borrowed from the flax industry to denote rough grass; 'tow' means 'uncleansed flax'; to 'scutch' means to beat flax in the process of curing it.
2. Wash by immersion.

from the darkness, where she could see the swinging yard lamp coming nearer and nearer like the light of a little boat drawing near to a jetty. 'I'll put out the lights and let myself out.' Relaxed by the thought that there was someone in the house, she would indeed scuttle back into bed, and, what was more, she'd be nearly asleep when she'd hear the door slam. It used to sound like the slam of a door a million miles away. There was no need to worry. He'd see that Crossen came early.

It was well before dark when Crossen did drive up to the door. The wife was with him, as usual, sitting up in the front seat the way people sat up in the well of little tub traps long ago, their knees pressed together, allowing no slump. Ned had come with them, but only he and Crossen got out.

'Won't your wife come inside and wait, Mr. Crossen?' she asked.

'Oh, not at all, Ma'am. She lies sitting in the car. Now, where's the grass that's to be cut? Are there any stones lying about that would blunt the blade?' Going around the gable of the house, he looked out over the land.

'There's not a stone or a stump in it,' Ned said. 'You'd run your blade over the whole of it while you'd be whetting it twenty times in another place.'

'I can see that,' said Bartley Crossen, but absently, Vera thought. He had walked across the lawn to the rickety wooden gate that led into the pasture, and leaned on it. He didn't seem to be looking at the fields at all though, but at the small string of stunted thorns that grew along the riverbank, their branches leaning so heavily out over the water that their roots were almost dragged clear of the clay. When he turned around he gave a sigh. 'Ah, sure, I didn't need to look. I know it well,' he said. As she showed surprise, he gave a little laugh, like a young man. 'I courted a girl down there when I was a lad,' he said. 'That's a queer length of time ago now, I can tell you.' He turned to the old man. 'You might remember.' Then he looked back at her. 'I don't suppose you were born then Ma'am,' he said, and there was something kindly in his look and in his words. 'You'd like the mowing done soon, I suppose? How about first thing in the morning?'

Her face lit up. But there was the price to settle. 'It won't be as dear as cutting meadow, will it?'

'Ah, I won't be too hard on you, Ma'am,' he said. 'I can promise you that.'

'That's very kind of you,' she said, but a little doubtfully.

Behind Crossen's back, Ned nodded his head in approval. 'Let it go at that, Ma'am,' he whispered as they walked back towards the car. 'He's a man you can trust.'

When Crossen and the wife had driven away, Ned reassured her again. 'A decent man,' he said. Then he gave a laugh, and it was a young kind of laugh for a man of his age. 'Did you hear what he said about the girl he courted down there? Do you know who that was? It was his first wife. You know he was twice married? Ah, well, it's so long ago I wouldn't wonder if you never heard it. Look at the way he spoke about her himself, as if she was some girl he'd all but forgotten. The thorn trees brought her to his mind. That's where they used to meet, being only youngsters, when they first took up with each other.

'Poor Bridie Logan! She was as wild as a hare. And she was mad with love, young as she was. They were company-keeping while they were still going to school. Only nobody took it seriously, him least of all, maybe, till the winter he went away to the agricultural college in Clonakilty. They started writing to each other then. I used to see her running up to the postbox at the crossroads every other evening, and sure, the whole village knew where the letter was going. His people were fit to be tied when he came home in the summer and said he wasn't going back, but was going to marry Bridie. All the same, his father set them up in a cottage on his own land. It's the cottage he uses now for stall-feeds, it's back of his new house. Oh, but you can't judge it now for what it was then. Giddy and all as she was, as lightheaded as a thistle, you should have seen the way Bridie kept that cottage. She'd have had it scrubbed away if she didn't start having a baby. He wouldn't let her take the scrubbing brush into her hands after that.'

'But she wasn't delicate, was she?'

'Bridie? She was as strong as a kid goat, that one. But I told you she was mad about him, didn't I? Well, after she was married to him she was no better. Worse, I'd say: She couldn't do enough for him. It was like as if she was driven on by some kind of a fever. You'd only to look in her eyes to see it. Do you know! From that day to this, I don't believe I ever saw a woman so full of going as that one. Did you ever happen to see little birds flying about in the air like they were flying for the divilment of it and nothing else? And did you ever see the way they give a sort of little leap in the air, like they were forcing themselves to go a bit higher still, higher than they ought? Well, it struck me that was the way Bridie was acting, as she rushed about that cottage doing this and doing that to make him prouder and prouder of her. As if he could be any prouder than he was already with her condition getting noticeable.'

'She didn't die in childbed?'

'No. Not in a manner of speaking, anyway. She had the child, nice and easy, and in their own cottage too, only costing him a few shillings for one of those women that went in for that kind of job long ago. And all went well. It was no time till she was let up on her feet again. I was there the first morning she had the place to herself. She was up and dressed when I got there, just as he was going out to milk.

' "Oh, it's great to be able to go out again," she said, taking a great breath of the morning air as she stood at the door looking after him. "Wait, why don't I come with you to milk?" she called out after him. Then she threw a glance back at the baby to make sure it was asleep in its crib by the window.

' "It's too far for you, Bridie," he said. The cows were down in a little field alongside the road, at the foot of the hill below the village. And knowing she'd start coaxing him, Bartley made off as quick as he could out of the gate with the cans. "Good man!" I said to myself. But the next thing I knew, Bridie had darted across the yard.

' "I can go on the bike if it's too far to walk," she said. And up she got on her old bike, and out she pedalled through the gate.

' "Bridie, are you out of your mind?" Bartley shouted as she whizzed past him.

' "Arrah, what harm can it do me?" she shouted back.

'I went stiff with fright looking after her. And I thought it was the same with him, when he threw down the cans and started down the hill after her. But looking back on it, I think it was the same fever as always was raging in her that was raging in him, too. Mad with love, that's what they were, both of them, she only wanting to draw him on, and he only too willing.

' "Wait for me!" he shouted, but before she'd even got to the bottom she started to brake the bike, putting down her foot like you'd see a youngster do, and raising up such a cloud of dust we could hardly see her.'

'She braked too hard?'

'Not her! In the twinkle of an eye she'd stopped the bike, jumped off, turned it round, and was pedalling madly up the hill again to meet him, with her head down on the handle-bars like a racing cyclist. But that was the finish of her.'

'Oh, no! What *happened*?'

'She stopped pedalling all of a sudden, and the bike half stopped, and then it started to slide back down the hill, as if it had skidded on the loose gravel at the side of the road. That's what we both thought happened, because we both began to run down the hill too. She didn't get time to fall before we got to her. But what use was that? It was some kind of internal bleeding that took her. We got her into the bed, and the neighbours came running, but she was gone before night.'

'Oh, what a dreadful thing to happen! And the baby?'

'Well, it was a strong child. And it grew into a fine lad. That's the fellow that drives the tractor for him now, the oldest son, Barty they called him not to confuse him with Bartley.'

'Well, I suppose his second marriage had more to it, when all was said and done.'

'That's it. And she's a good woman, the second one. Look at the way she brought up that child of Bridie's, and filled the cradle, year after year, with sons of her own. Ah sure, things always work out for the best in the end, no matter what!' the old man said, and he started to walk away.

'Wait a minute, Ned,' Vera called after him urgently. 'Do you really think he forgot about her, until today?'

'I'd swear it,' said the old man. Then he looked hard at her. 'It will be the same with you, too,' he added kindly. 'Take my word for it. Everything passes in time and is forgotten.'

As she shook her head doubtfully, he shook his emphatically. 'When the tree falls, how can the shadow stand?' he said. And he walked away.

I wonder! she thought as she walked back to the house, and she envied the practical country people who made good the defaults of nature as readily as the broken sod knits back into the sward.

Again that night, when she went up to her room, Vera looked down towards the river and she thought of Crossen. Had he really forgotten? It was hard for her to believe, and with a sigh she picked up her hairbrush and pulled it through her hair. Like everything else about her lately, her hair was sluggish and hung heavily down, but after a few minutes under the quickening strokes of the brush, it lightened and lifted, and soon it flew about her face like the spray over a weir. It had always been the same, even when she was a child. She had only to suffer the first painful drag of the bristles when her mother would cry out, 'Look! Look! That's electricity!' And a blue spark would shine for an instant like a star in the grey depths of the mirror. That was all they knew of electricity in those dim-lit days when valleys of shadow lay deep between one piece of furniture and another. Was it because rooms were so badly lit then that they saw it so often, that little blue star? Suddenly she was overcome by longing to see it again, and, standing up impetuously, she switched off the light. It was just then that, down below, the iron fist of the knocker was lifted and, with a strong, confident hand, brought down on the door. It was not a furtive knock. She recognised that even as she sat stark with fright in the darkness. And then a voice that was vaguely familiar called out from below.

'It's me, Ma'am. I hope I'm not disturbing you?'

'Oh, Mr. Crossen!' she cried out with relief, and unlocking her door, she ran across the landing and threw up a window on that side of the house. 'I'll be right down!' she called.

'There's no need to come down, Ma'am,' he shouted. 'I only want one word with you.'

'Of course I'll come down.' She went back and got her dressing-gown and was about to pin up her hair, but as she did she heard him stomping his feet on the gravel. It had been a mild day, but with night a chill had come in the air, and for all that it was late spring, there was a cutting east wind coming across the river. 'I'll run down and let you in from the cold,' she called, and, twisting up her hair, she held it against her head with her hand without waiting to pin it, and she ran down the stairs in her bare feet and opened the hall door.

'Oh? You were going to bed, Ma'am?' he said apologetically when she opened the door. And where he had been so impatient a minute beforehand, he stood stock-still in the open doorway. 'I saw the lights were out downstairs when I was coming up the drive,' he said contritely. 'But I didn't think you'd gone up for the night.'

'Not at all,' she lied, to put him at his ease. 'I was just upstairs brushing my hair. You must excuse me,' she added, because a breeze from the door was blowing her dressing-gown from her knees, and to pull it across she had to take her hand from her hair, so the hair fell down about her shoulders. 'Would you mind closing the door for me?' she said, with some embarrassment, and she began to back up the stairs. 'Please go inside to the sitting-room off the hall. Put on the light. I'll be down in a minute.'

Although he had obediently stepped inside the door, and closed it, he stood stoutly in the middle of the hall. 'I shouldn't have come in,' he said. 'You were going to bed,' he cried, this time in an accusing voice as if he dared her to deny it. He was looking at her hair. 'Excuse my saying so, Ma'am, but I never saw such a fine head of hair. God bless it!' he added quickly, as if afraid he had been too familiar. 'Doesn't a small thing make a big differ,' he said impulsively. 'You look like a young girl.'

In spite of herself, she smiled with pleasure. She wanted no more of this kind of talk, all the same. 'Well, I don't feel like one,' she said sharply.

What was meant for a quite opposite effect, however, seemed to delight him and put him wonderfully at ease. 'Ah sure, you're a sensible woman, I can see that,' he said, and, coming to the foot of the stairs, he leaned comfortably across the newel post. 'Let you stay the way you are, Ma'am,' he said. 'I've only one word to say to you. Let me say here and now and be off about my business. The wife will be waiting up for me, and I don't want that.'

She hesitated. Was the reference to his wife meant to put *her* at ease? 'I think I ought to get my slippers,' she said cautiously. Her feet were cold.

'Oh, yes, you should put on your slippers,' he said, only then seeing that she was in her bare feet. 'But as to the rest, I'm long gone beyond taking any account of what a woman has on her. I'm gone beyond taking notice of women at all.'

But she had seen something to put on her feet. Under the table in the hall there was a pair of old boots belonging to Richard, with fleece lining in them. She hadn't been able to make up her mind to give them away with the rest of his clothes, and although they were big and clumsy on her, she often stuck her feet into them when she came in from the fields with mud on her shoes. 'Well, come in where it's warm, so,' she said. She came back down the few steps and stuck her feet into the boots, and then she opened the door of the sittingroom. She was glad she'd come down. He'd never have been able to put on the light. 'There's something wrong with the centre light,' she said as she groped along the skirting board to find the plug of the reading lamp. It was in an awkward place, behind the desk. She had to go down on her knees.

'What's wrong with it?' he asked, as, with a countryman's interest in practicalities, he clicked the switch up and down to no effect.

'Oh, nothing much, I'm sure,' she said absently. 'There!' She had found the plug, and the room was lit up with a bright white glow.

'Why don't you leave the plug in the socket?' he asked critically.

'I don't know,' she said. 'I think someone told me it's safer, with reading lamps, to pull the plugs out at night. There might be a short circuit, or mice might nibble at the cord, or something. I forget what I was told. I got into the habit of doing it, and now I keep on.' She felt a bit silly.

But he was concerned about it. 'I don't think any harm could be done,' he said gravely. Then he turned away from the problem. 'About tomorrow, Ma'am,' he said, somewhat offhandedly, she thought. 'I was determined I'd see you tonight, because I'm not a man to break my word, above all, to a woman.'

What was he getting at?

'Let me put it this way,' he said quickly. 'You'll understand, Ma'am, that as far as I am concerned, topping land is the same as cutting hay. The same time. The same labour. The same cost. And the same wear and tear on the blade. You understand that?'

On her guard, she nodded.

'Well now, Ma'am, I'd be the first to admit that it's not quite the same for you. For you, topping doesn't give the immediate return you'd get from hay.'

'There's *no* return from topping,' she exclaimed crossly.

'Oh, come now, Ma'am! Good grassland pays as well as anything. You know you won't get nice sweet pickings for your beasts from neglected land, but only dirty old tow grass knotting under their feet. It's just that it's not a quick return, and so, as you know, I told you I'd be making a special price for you.'

'I do know,' she said impatiently. 'But I thought that part of it was settled and done.'

'Oh, I'm not going back on it, if that's what you think,' he said affably. 'I'm glad to do what I can for you, Ma'am, the more so seeing you have no man to attend to these things for you, but only yourself alone.'

'Oh, I'm well able to look after myself,' she said, raising her voice.

Once again her words had an opposite effect to what she intended. He laughed good-humouredly. 'That's what all women like to think,' he said. 'Well, now,' he went on in a different tone of voice, and it annoyed her to see he seemed to think something had been settled between them, 'it would suit me, and I'm sure it's all the same to you, if we could leave your little job till later in the week, say till nearer to the time of haymaking generally. Because by then I'd have the cutting bar in good order, sharpened and ready for use. Whereas now, while there's still a bit of ploughing to be done here and there, I'll have to be chopping and changing, between the plough and the mower, putting one on one minute and the other the next.'

'As if anyone is still ploughing this time of the year! Who are you putting before me?' she demanded.

'Now, take it easy, Ma'am. I'm not putting anyone before you, leastways, not without getting leave first from you.'

'Without telling me you're not coming, you mean.'

'Oh, now, Ma'am, don't get cross. I'm only trying to make matters easy for everyone.'

She was very angry now. 'It's always the same story. I thought you'd treat me differently. I'm to wait till after this one, and after that one, and in the end my fields will go wild.'

He looked a bit shamefaced. 'Ah now, Ma'am, that's not going to be the case at all. Although, mind you, some people don't hold with topping, you know.'

'I hold with it.'

'Oh, I suppose there's something in it,' he said reluctantly. 'But the way I look at it, cutting the weeds in July is a kind of topping.'

'Grass cut before it goes to seed gets so thick at the roots no weeds can come up,' she cried, so angry she didn't realise how authoritative she sounded.

'Faith, I never knew you were so well up, Ma'am,' he said, looking at her admiringly, but she saw he wasn't going to be put down by her. 'All the same now, Ma'am, you can't say a few days here or there could make any difference?'

'A few days could make all the difference. This farm has a gravelly bottom to it, for all it's so lush. A few days of drought could burn it to the butt. And how could I mow it then? And what cover would there be for the "nice sweet pickings" you were talking about a minute ago?' Angrily, she mimicked his own accent without thinking.

He threw up his hands. 'Ah well, I suppose a man may as well admit when he's bested,' he said. 'Even by a woman. And you can't say I broke my promise.'

'I can't say but you tried hard enough,' she said grudgingly, although she was mollified that she was getting her way. 'Can I offer you anything?' she said then, anxious to convey an air of finality to their discussion.

'Not at all, Ma'am. Nothing, thank you. I'll have to be getting home.'

'I hope you won't think I was trying to take advantage of you,' he said as they went towards the door. 'It's just that we must all make out as best we can for ourselves, isn't that so? Not but you are well able to look after yourself, I must say. No one ever thought you'd stay on here after your husband died. I suppose it's for the children you did it?' He looked up the well of the stairs. 'Are they asleep?'

'Oh, long ago,' she said indifferently. She opened the hall door.

The night air swept in. But this time, from far away, it brought with it the fragrance of new-mown hay. 'There's hay cut somewhere already,' she exclaimed in surprise. And she lifted her face to the sweetness of it.

For a minute, Crossen looked past her out into the darkness, then he looked back at her. 'Aren't you never lonely here at night?' he asked suddenly.

'You mean frightened?' she corrected quickly and coldly.

'Yes! Yes, that's what I meant,' he said, taken aback. 'Ah, but why would you be frightened? What safer place could you be under the sky than right here with your own fields all about you.'

What he said was so true, and he himself as he stood there, with his hat in his hand, so normal and natural it was indeed absurd to think that he would no sooner have gone out the door than she would be scurrying up the stairs like a child. 'You may not believe it,' she said, 'but I am scared to death sometimes. I nearly died when I heard your knock on the door tonight. It's because I was scared that I was upstairs,' she said, in a further burst of confidence. 'I always go up the minute it gets dark. I don't feel so frightened upstairs.'

'Isn't that strange now?' he said, and she could see he found it an incomprehensibly womanly thing to do. He was sympathetic all the same. 'You shouldn't be alone. That's the truth of the matter,' he said. 'It's a shame.'

'Oh, it can't be helped,' she said. There was something she wanted to shrug off in his sympathy, while at the same time she appreciated the kindliness. 'Would you like to do something for me?' she asked impulsively. 'Would you wait and put out the lights down here and let me get back upstairs before you go? Ned often does that for me if he's working here late.' After she had spoken she felt foolish, but she saw at once that, if anything, he thought it only too little to do for her. He was genuinely troubled about her. And it wasn't only the present moment that concerned him; he seemed to be considering the whole problem of her isolation and loneliness.

'Is there nobody could stay here with you, at night even? It would have to be another woman, of course,' he added quickly, and her heart was warmed by the way, without a word from her, he rejected that solution out of hand. 'You don't want another woman about the place,' he said flatly.

'Oh, I'm all right, really. I'll get used to it,' she said.

'It's a shame, all the same,' he said. He said it helplessly, though, and he motioned her towards the stairs. 'You'll be all right for tonight, anyway. Go on up the stairs now, and I'll put out the lights.' He had already turned around to go back into the sitting-room.

Yet it wasn't quite as she intended for some reason, and it was somewhat reluctantly that she started up the stairs.

'Wait a minute! How do I put out this one?' he called out from the room before she was halfway up.

'Oh, I'd better put out that one myself,' she said, thinking of the awkward position of the plug. She ran down again, and, going past him into the little room, she knelt and pulled at the cord. Instantly the room was deluged in darkness. And instantly she felt that she had done something stupid. It was not like turning out a light by a switch at the door and being able to step back into the lighted hall. She got to her feet as quickly as she could, but as she did, she saw that Crossen was standing in the doorway. His bulk was blocked out against the hall light behind him. 'I'll leave the rest to you,' she said to break the peculiar silence that had come down on the house. But he didn't move. He stood there, the full of the doorway, and she was reluctant to brush past him.

Why didn't he move? Instead he caught her by the arm, and, putting out his other hand, he pressed his palm against the door-jamb, barring her way.

'Tell me,' he whispered, his words falling over each other, 'are you never lonely at all?'

'What did you say?' she said in a clear voice, because the thickness of his voice sickened her. She had barely heard what he said. Her one thought was to get past him.

He leaned forward. 'What about a little kiss?' he whispered, and to get a better hold on her he let go the hand he had pressed against the wall, but before he caught at her with both hands she had wrenched her all free of him, and, ignominiously ducking under his armpit, she was out next minute into the lighted hall.

Out there, because light was all the protection she needed from him, the old fool, she began to laugh. She had only to wait for him to come sheepishly out. But there was something she hadn't counted on; she hadn't counted on there being anything pathetic in his sheepishness, something really pitiful in the way he shambled into the light, not raising his eyes. And she was so surprisingly touched that before he had time to utter a word she put out her hand. 'Don't feel too bad,' she said. 'I didn't take offence.'

Still he didn't look at her. He just took her hand and pressed it gratefully, his face turned away. And to her dismay she saw that his nose was running water. Like a small boy, he wiped it with the back of his fist, streaking his face. 'I don't know what came over me,' he said slowly. 'I'm getting on to be an old man. I thought I was beyond all that.' He wiped his face again. 'Beyond letting myself go, anyway,' he amended miserably.

'Oh, it was nothing,' she said.

He shook his head. 'It wasn't as if I had cause for what I did.'

'But you did nothing,' she protested.

'It wasn't nothing to me,' he said dejectedly.

For a minute, they stood there silent. The hall door was still ajar, but she didn't dare to close it. What am I going to do with him now, she thought, I'll have him here all night if I'm not careful. What time was it, anyway? All scale and proportion seemed to have gone from the night. 'Well, I'll see you in the morning, Mr Crossen,' she said, as matter-of-factly as possible.

He nodded, but made no move to go. 'You know I meant no disrespect to you, Ma'am, don't you?' he said, looking imploringly at her. 'I always had a great regard for you. And for your husband, too. I was thinking of him this very night when I was coming up to the house. And I thought of him again when you came to the door looking like a young girl. I thought what a pity it was him to be taken from you, and you both so young. Oh, what came over me at all? And what would Mona say if she knew?'

'But surely you wouldn't tell her? I should certainly hope not,' Vera cried, appalled. What sort of a figure would she cut if he told the wife about her coming down in her bare feet with her hair down her back. 'Take care would you tell her!'[3] she warned.

'I don't suppose I ought,' he said, but he said it uncertainly and morosely, and he leaned back against the wall. 'She's been a good woman, Mona. I wouldn't want anyone to think different. My sons could tell you. She's been a good mother to them all these years. She never made a bit of difference between them. Some say she was better to Barty than to any of them. She reared him from a week old. She was living next door to us, you see, at the time I was left with him,' he said. 'She came in that first night and took him home to her own bed, and, mind you, that wasn't a small thing for a woman who knew nothing about children, not being what you'd call a young girl, in spite of the big family she gave me afterwards. She took him home and looked after him, although it isn't every woman would care to be responsible for a newborn baby. That's a thing a man doesn't forget easy. There's many I know would say that if she hadn't taken him someone else would, but no one only her would have done it the way she did. She used to keep him all day in her own cottage, feeding him and the rest of it. But at night, when I'd be back from the fields, she'd bring him home and leave him down in his little crib by the fire alongside of me. She used to let on she had things to

3. Hiberno-English idiom: 'Think what would happen if you did tell her' (i.e. 'Don't tell her').

do in her own place, and she'd slip away and leave us alone, but that wasn't her real reason for leaving him. She knew the way I'd be sitting looking into the fire, wondering how I'd face the long years ahead, and she left the child there with me to distract me from my sorrow. And she was right. I never got long to brood. The child would give a cry, or whinge, and I'd have to run out and fetch her to him. Or else she'd hear him herself maybe, and run in without me having to call her at all. I used often think she must have kept every window and door in her place open, for fear she'd lose a sound from either of us. And so, bit by bit, I was knit back into a living man. I often wondered what would have become of me if it wasn't for her. There are men and when the bright way closes to them there's no knowing but they'll take a dark way. And I was that class of man. I told you she used to take the little fellow away in the day and bring him back at night? Well, of course, she used to take him away again coming on to the real dark of night. She used to keep him in her own bed. But as the months went on and he got bigger, I could see she hated taking him away from me at all. He was beginning to smile and play with his fists and be real company. "I wonder ought I leave him with you tonight," she'd say then, night after night. And sometimes she'd run in and dump him down in the middle of the big double bed in the room off the kitchen, but the next minute she'd snatch him up again. "I'd be afraid you'd overlie him. You might only smother him, God between us and all harm!" '

' "You'd better take him," I'd say, I used to hate to see him go myself by this time. All the same, I was afraid he'd start crying in the night, and what would I do then? If I had to go out for her in the middle of the night, it could cause a lot of talk, there was talk enough as things were, I can tell you, although there was no grounds for it. I had no more notion of her than if she wasn't a woman at all. Would you believe that? But one night when she took him up and put him down, and put him down and took him up, and went on and went on about leaving him or taking him, I had to laugh. "It's a pity you can't stay along with him, and that would settle all," I said. I was only joking her, but she got as red as fire, and next thing she burst out crying. But not before she'd caught up the child and wrapped her coat around him. Then, after giving me a terrible look, she ran out the door with him. Well, that was the beginning of it. I'd no idea she had any feelings for me. I thought it was only for the child. But men are fools, as women well know, and she knew before me what was right and proper for us both. And for the child too. Some women have great insight into these things. That night God opened my eyes to the woman I had in her, and I saw it was better I took her than wasted away after the one that was gone. And wasn't I right?'

'Of course you were right,' she said quickly.

But he had slumped back against the wall, and the abject look came back into his eyes. 'And to think I shamed her as well as myself.'

I'll never get rid of him, Vera thought desperately. 'Ah, what ails you?' she cried impatiently. 'Forget it, can't you?'

'I can't,' he said simply.

'Ah, for heaven's sake. It's got nothing to do with her at all.'

Surprised, he looked up at her. 'You're not blaming yourself, surely? he asked.

She'd have laughed at that if she hadn't seen she was making headway. Another stroke and she'd be rid of him. 'Why are you blaming any of us?' she cried. 'It's got nothing to do with any of us, with you, or me, or the woman at home waiting for you. It was the other one you should blame, that girl, your first wife, Bridie! Blame her!' The words had broken uncontrollably from her. For a moment, she thought she was hysterical and that she could not stop. 'You thought you could forget her,' she cried, 'but see what she did to you when she got the chance.'

He stood for a moment at the open door. 'God rest her soul,' he said, without looking back, and he stepped into the night.

FRANCIS MacMANUS

(1909–65)

from: THE PEDLAR'S PACK (1944)

['Old Clothes — Old Glory' is from Francis MacManus's only collection of short pieces, *The Pedlar's Pack*. Dealing with the fanaticism of a young man for hurling, Ireland's ancient field game, he dramatizes an aspect of Irish life rarely treated of in literature, yet strangely relevant to the modern cosmopolitan scene.]

OLD CLOTHES — OLD GLORY

He came upon me before I had time, really, to recognize him and to make plans for escape, the mean plans that one makes in such circumstances. I was loitering on the quays above O'Connell Bridge in front of a second-hand bookshop, and so I couldn't decently plead that I was in a hurry. I know I was ashamed afterwards of the thought, especially when I looked on his sunken cheeks, stubbled black, and the cold eyes that had a queer light in them, all like the emaciated face of a holy man in a dark, smouldering Spanish painting. Also as we spoke, I remembered the few scraps of his story.

He shook my hand vaguely, and while I tried to place him, he said, pointing to his hat and smiling gravely: 'Look. That's Micky Cregan of Cork's hat. And this is Petey Power's overcoat, Petey Power of Limerick. He played a horse of a game last year, didn't he? And this is Marty Lanigan's suit. He's a terribly good-natured chap. Look it, I had only to walk into his house and he ga' me it, and his mother ga' me me dinner. And look at the shoes. They're like feathers on me feet. Jim Brett's. He trains the lads. And me tie, that's a dandy. Jimmy Crosse of Tipp.[1] ga' me that. I'm dressed for the match, amn't I?'

The odd light was in his eye as he belted up the bulky overcoat. Then I recognized him.

It wasn't the list of names that defined him in my memory, names of hurlers who had made throats go hoarse for cheering at finals in Croke Park, All-Ireland hurlers who were marked off for glory. It was the swaggering hitch of his shoulders that fixed him for me. I remembered Matty O'Meara.

'How are you, Matty?'

He ignored the courtesy. 'Will the lads carry it off on Sunday?' he asked.

'Sunday?'

'The All-Ireland. I'm up for it.'

'So soon, Matty?'

That was on Friday. It would be like him to be there, days before.

'I walked', he added.

When I was a growing lad, Matty O'Meara seemed to be a full-grown man. Of course he wasn't anything of the sort, but a young, lean, wiry fellow who, like his father and his brothers, a good family all, did a bit of gardening in our town. Matty's gardening was harmless, as my mother knew.

No sooner would he be out of sight of the house and the grown-ups, than he'd draw out a hurley from a ridge of potatoes or a heap of stones, slide his hands along it to finger the grain, and then begin to drive at the air. The odd light used to settle into his eyes then. The whole mind of the man, the power and control of his limbs, were focused on the balancing and swinging of that hurley.

'How's that, lads?' he'd shout to an unseen audience.

He'd pick up a pebble or a frostbitten potato and play at lobbing and pucking as if he had a real ball. Long graceful drives he had, and after every swing he'd stand still in a pose, his bare muscular arms crooked towards his left shoulder and the hurley curved around behind his head.

'How's that, lads? Matty O'Meara of Toomeveara[2] won't be in it with me.'

From morning till night he'd practise like that, as long as nobody urged him to take the spade to the

1. The All-Ireland Hurling Championship is contested between certain Irish counties among which 'Tipp', County Tipperary, is one of the foremost.

2. A village in Tipperary noted for hurling.

garden. There were a few other men like Matty in the town, men from whom he took his pattern. There was one in particular who for years and years as a paper-boy practised both hands with tiny pebbles for handball, pebbles that demanded exquisite precision to be struck at all by the palm of the hand or to be slung by crooked fingers. He became champion of Ireland. Matty, too, was shaping to be a champion, successor to the man of whom he was a namesake, for Matty O'Meara of Toomeveara was one of the most renowned goalkeepers of a long generation.

Our Matty would be a second and greater champion.

In those days, the town spawned little local hurling clubs. These were the breeding ground of a number of fine hurlers who earned their place in Croke Park at many a final. Matty wasn't a member of any particular club, but he hung around them all, playing with this team and that, now out in the field where he was a failure, now in the goal where he wasn't too bad. Then, one Sunday he played a miraculous game in goal, and some selectors were impressed, for Matty was told that he would get his chance of being tried out for the County team.

He walked the town in the evenings with a more rakish slant on his cap, a new swagger on his shoulders and a brighter glow in his cold eyes. He walked the streets with his hurley in his hand, the symbol and instrument of his craft and profession.

'Matty O'Meara of Toomeveara!' someone would call out.

'How's that, lads?' he'd respond, and shifting his hurley deftly, he'd hold it up as if he were stopping and deadening a high ball. 'Wait till Sunday, lads. Wait till Sunday.'

It was the first, and I think the last time I heard him laughing.

He trained for that Sunday as no man ever trained before. He didn't do any gardening, although there was plenty to be done. It wasn't that he could afford to miss a day's work. No. But a champion was in the making, a champion was about to be tested, and the name of the O'Meara of Toomeveara would fade like an old moon. What was earning a living compared to that? Or eating and drinking and going to bed of nights?

Matty stood against the gable-end of a house on which a goal had been marked with chalk, while other lads and myself pelted him with hurling balls from every angle. He was to stop them as they poured in.

I've seen good goalkeepers, men whose calculated movement, whose swift action following close on swift but careful thought, was a delight, something to remember like music or fine dancing, or a piece of good verse. Rhythm, speed, coolness, all blended perfectly.

With his back to the gable-end, Matty was the incarnation of greatness. Remember, we could pelt balls, usually old and sodden, with force and accuracy, and we could direct them as we pleased; and sometimes we'd feint, making a deceptive swing of our arms, and then suddenly let go. I don't care. I don't care, but Matty leaped, sprang, slid and cast himself down, and somehow the blade of the hurley would snake out, meet the ball and stop it dead with a most satisfactory smack. Every angle, almost every ball! He would continue at that while our shoulders ached, and his eyes would burn and he would cheer himself.

He turned out to play before the selectors on that Sunday, and his togs were immaculate, his new cap was jaunty, and as he trailed his hurley, yellow with linseed oil, at his heels, a crowd of children followed him. He swaggered down to his goal, waved his hand to the crowd at the posts, who cried: 'Come on, Matty. The hard Matty O'Meara of Toomeveara', and not a man of them could have guessed that every word they uttered would be fuel for the vision's frenzy.

'Not a blade of grass will I let through,' he cried, 'not a breath.'

But then he did. He saved the first ball that sailed in hard, saved it in a free goal mouth and drove it comfortably up the field. Then, a ball dropped down out of the sky and he caught it among a ruck of struggling men, twisted and wriggled for space, swung and cleared again. It was grand. He stood in a pose. The crowd howled and whooped. His eyes were like a cat's in the dark.

'How's that, lads?'

'You'll be in Croke Park, Matty.'

'Come on, Stonewall O'Meara.'

And so he was ruined by whatever vision shook before his eyes and blinded him, for, after that, balls that a schoolboy could have stopped dribbled past him while he fumbled and staggered.

When the match was over, he sat down alone in the ditch, far apart from the rest. He was pale as dried clay. Nobody spoke to him, nobody offered a word to ease that pain which wrinkled his forehead and beaded his skin with perspiration, nobody except the young lads.

'Come on and dress yourself, Matty.'

'Don't take it so hard. It's nothing.'

He looked up dully, swaying his head.

'You'll do it yet, Matty.'

'O'Meara of Toomeveara.'

'Them was two great saves.'

Vision came back into his eyes as he said: 'Warn't they, though, warn't they? I'll do it yet. It's nothing. Them was great saves. I'll do it yet.'

Then, weeks later, we heard that they had taken him away and locked him up in the asylum. We were told that his father and brothers could get no good of him and that he had begun to rise early in the mornings, almost with the first spark of the day, to go out into the fields behind the house with a hurley. That wasn't the worst of it. He could not be spoken to or checked. He would threaten with the hurley.

One night when it was just dark, he arose from his stool in his father's kitchen where he had been sitting silent, went down to a lower room and presently reappeared dressed in his hurling togs and with his stick in his hand.

'Where are you going at this hour of the night, son, in the name of God?'

'Keep back. The match. The match. I'll do it this time.'

They followed him out and discerned him in the dark, I suppose, by the white gleaming of the shorts that he had always kept spotless. He walked into the field behind the house and began to shout, to fill the night with cries, so that neighbours came to their doors and windows while men gathered out with bicycle lamps and lanterns.

'O'Meara of Toomeveara', he shouted. 'Come on, lads. Not a breath I'll let in. Here's the stonewall. Hoo! Hoo! Hurroo!'

They crept up to him. He didn't notice them nor the lamps that lit up the grass. He was crouching out in the dark like a man tensed in a goal who faces a whirl of hurlers from which a ball may light out like a bullet. He was shouting, turning his head to answer, as though all behind him were people whose roars tore through his soul like supreme joy. Suddenly, he straightened up as a lamp glowed on his face, fingered his cap and sighed. Tears glistened on his cheeks.

They led him away easily.

Those were the things I recalled as we stood on the Dublin quay, beside the bookshop.

'I walked', said he, 'all the way.'

'That's a long walk', I said.

'I've been all over Ireland. All the hurlers know me. Matty O'Meara of Toomeveara. But it's cold in the nights when you're caught out, and I'll have to take care of myself. The lads might be needing me. Your poor mother was good to me, God rest her. Look what I have on me.' Once more he pointed to the hat, the overcoat, the suit, the tie and the light shoes, and reeled off the names of men who could shake thousands. 'I'm dressed, amn't I? In the clothes of the best of 'em.'

'Who has a better right, Matty?'

The grave smile transfigured his cadaverous jaws and his sad mouth. He held his hands together, the left below the right, and moved his arms as though he swung a hurley. Then, with the light warming his cold eyes, sharpening his face, he wheeled from me, saying: 'I'll see you in Croke Park on Sunday', and set off down the quays, his mind astray on some field. And I knew that of all the thousands who would be packed in the Park for the All-Ireland Final, even of all the men on the field itself, he would be the one in whom the fire of the game would mount to a consuming frenzy as he stood in the clothes of the champions and became all of them at once, every one.

MICHAEL McLAVERTY

(1907–)

from: THE GAME COCK AND OTHER STORIES (1947)

[This is a typical McLaverty story. The illegality of cock-fighting, the ruined big house near the grand-parents' farm, the sense of a vivid but marginalized life, all surround and give deeper implication to the small saga of the trip to Toome and the cock-fights. The story was subsequently published in McLaverty's *Collected Short Stories* (Swords, Co. Dublin: Poolbeg Press, 1978).]

THE GAME COCK

When I was young we came to Belfast and my father kept a game cock and a few hens. At the back of the street was waste ground where the fowl could scrape, and my father built a shed for them in the yard and sawed a hole in the back door so that they could hop in and out as they took the notion. In the mornings our cock was always first out on the waste ground.

We called him Dick, but he was none of your ordinary cocks, for he had a pedigree as long as your arm, and his grandfather and grandmother were of Indian breed. He was lovely to look at, with his long yellow legs, black glossy feathers in the chest and tail, and reddish streaky neck. In the long summer evenings my father would watch him for hours, smiling at the way he tore the clayey ground with his claws, coming on a large earwig, and calling the hens to share it. But one day when somebody lamed him with a stone, my father grew so sad that he couldn't take his supper.

We had bought him from Jimmy Reilly, the blind man, and many an evening he came to handle him. I would be doing my school exercise at the kitchen table, my father, in his shirt sleeves, reading the paper. A knock would come to the door, and with great expectancy in his voice my father'd say, 'That's the men now. Let them in, son.'

And when I opened the door I'd say, 'Mind the step!' and in would shuffle wee Johnny Moore leading the blind man. They'd sit on the sofa; Jimmy Reilly, hat on head, and two fists clasped round the shank of the walking stick between his legs; and Johnny Moore with a stinking clay pipe in his mouth.

As soon as they started the talk I'd put down my pen and listen to them.

'Sit up to the fire, men, and get a bit of the heat.'

'That's a snorer[1] of a fire you've on, Mick,' would come from the blind man.

'What kind of coals is them?' says Johnny Moore, for he had my father pestered with questions.

'The best English; them's none of your Scotch slates!'

'And what's the price of them a ton?'

'They cost a good penny,' my father would answer crossly.

'And where do you get them?'

The blind man's stick would rattle on the kitchen tiles and he'd push out his lower lip, stroke his beard and shout, 'They're good coals, anyway, no matter where they're got.' And then add in his slow natural voice, 'How's the cock, Mick?'

'He's in great fettle, Jimmy. He's jumping out of his pelt.'[2] And he'd tell how the comb was reddening and how he had chased Maguire's dunghill of a rooster from about the place. And the blind man would smile and say, 'That's the stuff! He'll soon have the walk to himself; other cocks would annoy him.'

With a lighted candle I would be sent out to the yard to lift Dick off the roost. The roosts were low so that the cock wouldn't bruise his feet when flying to the ground. He'd blink his eyes and cluck-cluck in his throat when I'd bring him into the gas-light and hand him to the blind man.

Jimmy fondled him like a woman fondling a cat. He gently stroked the neck and tail, and then stretched out one wing and then the other. 'He's in great condition. We could cut his comb and wattles any time and have him ready for Easter.' And he'd put him down on the tiles and listen to the scrape of his claws. Then he'd feel the muscles on the thighs,

1. Northern Irish dialect form of English; 'snorer' = a great fire, perhaps even a fire that is so hot it would put you to sleep.
2. 'Pelt' is skin. The cock is vibrant with energy.

and stick out his beard with joy, 'There's no coldness about that fella, Mick. He has shoulders on him as broad as a bulldog. Aw, my lovely fella,' feeling the limber[3] of him as his claws pranced on the tiles. 'He'll do us credit. A hould you he'll win a main.'[4]

My father would stuff his hands in his pockets and rise off his heels, 'And you think he's doing well, Jimmy?'

'Hould yer tongue, man, I wish I was half as fit,' Jimmy would answer, his sightless eyes raised to the ceiling.

And one evening as they talked like this about the cock and forthcoming fights, Johnny Moore sneaked across to the table and gave me sums out of his head: *A ropemaker made a rope for his marrying daughter, and in the rope he made twenty knots and in each knot he put a purse, and in each purse he put seven threepenny bits and nine half-pennies. How much of a dowry did the daughter get?*

I couldn't get the answer and he took the pipe from his mouth and laughed loudly, 'The scholars, nowadays, have soft brains. You can't do it with your pencil and paper and an old man like me can do it in my head.'

My face burned as I said, 'But we don't learn them kind of sums.' He laughed so much that I was glad when it was time for him to lead the blind man home.

A few evenings afterwards they were back again; the blind man with special scissors to cut Dick's comb and wattles. Jimmy handed the scissors to my father, then he held the cock, his forefinger in its mouth and his thumb at the back of its head.

'Now, Mick,' said he, 'try and cut it with one stroke.'

When my sisters saw the chips of comb snipped off with the scissors and the blood falling on the tiles they began to cry, 'That's a sin, father! That's a sin!'

'Tush, tush,' said my father, and the blood on his sleeves. 'He doesn't feel it. It's just like getting your hair cut. Isn't that right, Jimmy?'

'That's right; just like getting your toenails cut.'

But when Dick clucked and shook his head with pain, my sisters cried louder and were sent out to play, and I went into the scullery to gather cobwebs to stop the bleeding.

In a few days the blood had hardened and Dick was his old self again. The men came nearly every night and talked about the cock fights to be held near Toome[5] at Easter. They made plans for Dick's training and arranged how he was to be fed.

About a fortnight before the fights my father got a long box and nailed loose sacking over the front to keep it in darkness. Dick was put into this and his feathers and tail were clipped. For the first two days he got no feed so as to keep his weight down. Then we gave him hard-boiled eggs, but they didn't agree with him and made him scour. The blind man recommended a strict diet of barley and barley water. 'That's the stuff to keep his nerves strong and his blood up. A hould you it'll not scour him.'[6]

Every morning we took him from his dark box and gave him a few runs up and down the yard. Johnny Moore had made a red flannel bag stuffed with straw, and Dick sparred at this daily, and when he had finished my father would lift him in his arms, stroke him gently, and sponge the feet and head. Day by day the cock grew peevish, and once when he nebbed[7] at me I gave him a clout that brought my father running to the yard.

The night before the fights the steel spurs were tied on him to see how he would look in the pit. 'Ah, Jimmy, if you could see him,' said my father to the blind man. 'He's the picture of health.'

The blind man fingered his beard and putting a hand in his pocket, took out a few pound notes and spat on them for luck. 'Put that on him tomorrow. There's not another cock this side of the Bann[8] nor in all County Derry that could touch him.' Even Johnny Moore risked a few shillings, and the next morning before five o'clock my father wakened me to go to Toome.

It was Easter Monday and there were no trams running early so we set off to walk to the Northern Counties Railway to catch the half-six train. The cock was in a potato bag under my arm, and I got orders not to squeeze him, while my father carried the overcoats and a gladstone[9] filled with things for

3. litheness.
4. 'I'll bet you he'll win a lot'.

5. A predominantly catholic town in County Antrim, about thirty miles from Belfast.
6. 'I guarantee it won't damage him.' 'Scour' means to clean out, so the diet won't act as a severe laxative.
7. pecked. The neb is the beak.
8. The river Bann divides east from west Ulster.
9. A large leather bag, named after the British prime minister William Ewart Gladstone (1809–98).

my Granny, who lived near the place where the cocks were to fight.

The streets were deserted, and our feet echoed in the chill air. Down the Falls Road we hurried. The shopblinds were pulled down, the tram lines shining, and no smoke coming from the chimneys. At the Public Baths my father looked at his watch and then stood out in the road to see the exact time by the Baths' clock.

'Boys-a-boys, my watch is slow. We'll need to hurry.' In the excitement the cock got his neb out and pecked at me. I dropped the bag, and out jumped the cock and raced across the tram lines, the two of us after him.

'Don't excite him, son. Take him gently.' We tried to corner him in a doorway, my father with his hand outstretched calling in his sweetest way, 'Dick, Dick, Dicky.' But as soon as he stooped to lift him, the cock dived between his legs, and raced up North Howard Street, and stood contemplating a dark-green public lavatory.

'Whisht,'[10] said my father, holding my arm as I went to go forward. 'Whisht! If he goes in there we'll nab him.'

The cock stood, head erect, and looked up and down the bare street. Then he scraped each side of his bill on the step of the lavatory and crowed into the morning.

'Man, but that's the brazen tinker of a cock for you,' said my father, looking at his watch. And then, as if Dick were entering the hen-shed, in he walked and in after him tiptoed my father, and out by the roofless top flew the cock with a few feathers falling from him.

I swished him off the top and he flew for all he was worth over the tram lines, down Alma Street and up on a yard wall.

'We'll be late for the train if we don't catch him quick, and maybe have the peelers[11] down on us before we know where we are.'

Up on the wall I was heaved and sat with legs astride. The cock walked away from me, and a dog in the yard yelped and jumped up the back door.

'I'm afraid, Da, I'm afraid.'

'Come down out of that and don't whinge there.'

A baby started to cry and a man looked out of a window and shouted, 'What the hell's wrong?'

'We're after a cock,' replied my father apologetically.

The man continued to lean out of the window in his shirt, and a woman yelled from the same room, 'Throw a bucket of water round them, Andy. A nice time of the morning to be chasing a bloody rooster.'

Here and there a back door opened and barefooted men in their shirts and trousers came into the entry. They all chased after Dick.

'Ah, easy, easy,' said my father to a man who was swiping at Dick savagely with a yard-brush. 'Don't hit him with that.'

By this time the cock had walked half way down the entry, still keeping to the top of the yard walls. Women shouted and dogs barked, and all the time I could hear my father saying, 'If we don't catch him quick we'll miss the train.'

'Aw,' said one man, looking at the scaldy[12] appearance of the cock. 'Sure he's not worth botherin' about. There's not as much on him as'd set a rat-trap.'

My father kept silent about Dick's pedigree for he didn't want anyone to know about the cockfights, and maybe have the police after us.

We had now reached the end of the entry and Dick flew off the wall and under a little handcart that stood in a corner. Five men bunched in after him, and screeching and scolding the cock was handed to my father.

'I can feel his heart going like a traction engine,' he said, when we were on the road again. 'He'll be bate.[13] The blind man's money and everybody's money will be lost. Lost!'

We broke into a trot, I carrying the gladstone, and my father the cock and the overcoats. Along York Street we raced, gazing up at the big clocks and watching the hands approach half-six. Sweat broke out on us and a stitch came in my side, but I said nothing as I lagged behind trying to keep pace.

We ran into the station and were just into the carriage when out went the train.

'Aw-aw-aw,' said my father, sighing out all his breath in one puff. 'I'm done. Punctured! That's a nice start for an Easter Monday!'

He took off his hard hat and pulled out a handkerchief. His bald head was speckled with sweat and

10. 'Quiet.'
11. police.
12. 'Scaldy' is a dialect word for 'balded'; young birds that are still without feathers are called 'scaldies'.
13. beaten.

the hat had made a red groove on his brow. He puffed and ah-ee-d so many times I thought he'd faint, and I sat with my heart thumping, my shirt clammy with sweat, waiting with fear for what he'd say. But he didn't scold me.

'It was my own fault,' he said. 'I should have tied a bit of string round the neck of the bag. He'll be bate! He'll be bate!'

He took the spurs from his pocket and pulled the corks off the steel points. 'I might as well strap them on a jackdaw as put them on Dick this day, for he'll be tore asunder after that performance.'

As the train raced into the country we saw the land covered with a thin mist, and ploughed fields with shining furrows. The cold morning air came into the carriage; it was lovely and fresh. My father's breathing became quieter, and he even pointed out farms that would make great 'walks' for cocks. It was going to be a grand day: a foggy sun was bursting through, and crows flew around trees that were laden with their nests.

Dick was taken from the bag and petted; and then my father stretched himself out on the seat and fell asleep. I watched the telegraph wires rising and falling, and kept a lookout for the strange birds that were cut out in the hedge near Doagh.

When we came to Toome my father tied the neck of the bag with a handkerchief and sent me on in front for fear the police might suspect something. The one-streeted village was shady and cool, the sun skimming the housetops. Pieces of straw littered the road, and a few hens stood at the closed barrack door, their droppings on the doorstep.

We passed quickly through the silent village and turned on to the long country road that led to my Granny's. Behind us the train rumbled and whistled over the bridge; and then across the still country came the dull cheer of the Bann waterfall and the wind astir in the leafing branches. Once my father told me to sit and rest myself while he crossed a few fields to a white cottage. It wasn't long until he was back again. 'I've got the stuff in my pocket that'll make him gallop. The boys in Lough Beg made a run of poteen[14] for Easter.'

When we reached my Granny's she was standing at the door, a string garter fallen round her ankle, and a basin in her hand; near her my Uncle's bicycle was turned upside down and he was mending a puncture. They had great welcome for us and smiled when my father put the poteen on the table. He took tumblers from the dresser, filled one for my Granny, and in another he softened a few pieces of bread for the cock.

My Granny sat at the fire and at every sip she sighed and held the glass up to the light. 'Poor fellas, but they run great risks to make that. None of your ould treacle about the Lough Beg stuff . . . made from the best of barley.'

As she sipped it she talked to me about my school, and the little sense my father had in his head to be bothering himself about game cocks and maybe land himself in jail; and when the car came up for him she went to the door and waved him off. 'Mind the peelers,' she shouted. 'Ye'd never know where they'd be sniffing around.'

During the day I played about the house and tormented the tethered goat, making her rise on her hind legs. I went to the well at the foot of the field and carried a bucket of water to my Granny, and she said I was a big, strong man. Later my Uncle brought me through the tumbled demesne wall and showed me where he had slaughtered a few trees for the fire. I talked to him about Dick and I asked him why he didn't keep game cocks. He laughed at me and said, 'I wouldn't have them about the place. They destroy the hens and make them as wild as the rooks.' I didn't talk any more about game cocks, but all the time as we walked to the Big House I thought about Dick and wondered would he win his fights. The Big House was in ruins, crows were nesting in the chimneys, and the lake was covered with rushes and green scum. When I asked my uncle where were all the ladies and gentlemen and the gamekeeper, he spat through the naked windows and replied, 'They took the land from the people and God cursed them.'

When we came back my Granny was standing at the door looking up and down the road wondering what was keeping my father. A few fellows coming from the cockfights passed on bicycles, and soon my father arrived. He was in great form, his face red, and his navy blue trousers covered with clay.

The cock's comb was scratched with blood, his feathers streaky, and his eyes half shut. He was left in the byre[15] until the tea was over. While my father

14. Lough Beg is a townland near Toome. Poteen is an illegally distilled spirit, made from barley and various other ingredients. When ready, the poteen was 'run off' into containers.

15. cowshed.

was taking the tea he got up from the table and stood in the middle of the floor telling how Dick had won his fights. 'Five battles he won and gave away weight twice.'

'Take your tea, Mick, and you can tell us after,' my Granny said, her hands in her sleeves, and her feet tapping the hearth.

He would eat for a few minutes and he'd be up again. 'Be the holy frost if ye'd seen him tumbling the big Pyle cock from Derry it'd have done yer heart good. I never seen the like of it. Aw, he's a great battler. And look at the morning he put in on them yard walls . . . up and down a dozen streets he went, running and flying and crowing. And then to win his fights. Wait till Jimmy Reilly hears about this and the nice nest egg I have for him. The poteen was great stuff. A great warrior!' And he smiled in recollection.

I was glad when he was ready for home and gladder still when we were in the train where I made the wheels rumble and chant: . . . *They took the land from the people . . . God cursed them*.

It was dark when we reached Belfast and I carried Dick in the potato bag. We got into a tram at the station; the lights were lit and we sat downstairs. The people were staring at my father, at the clabber[16] on his boots and the wrinkles on his trousers. But he paid no heed to them. In the plate glass opposite I could see our reflections; my father was smiling with his lips together, and I knew he was thinking of the cock.

'He's very quiet, Da,' I whispered. 'The fightin' has fairly knocked the capers out of him.'

'Aw, son, he's a great warrior,' and he put his hand in his pocket and slipped me a half crown. 'I'll get his photo took as soon as he's his old self again.'

I held the money tightly in my hand, and all the way home I rejoiced that Johnny Moore wasn't with us, for he would have set me a problem about a half-crown.

In the kitchen I left the bag on the floor and sat on the sofa, dead tired. My father got down the olive oil to rub on Dick's legs, but when he opened the bag the cock never stirred. He took him out gently and raised his head, but it fell forward limply, and from the open mouth blood dripped to the floor.

'God-a-God, he's dead!' said my father, stretching out one of the wings. He held up the cock's head in the gaslight and looked at him. Then he put him on the table without a word and sat on a chair. For awhile I said nothing, and then I asked quietly, 'What'll you do with him, Da?'

He turned and looked at the cock, stretched on the table. 'Poor Dick!' he said. And I felt a lump rise in my throat.

Then he got up from the chair. 'What'll I do with him! What'll I do with him! I'll get him stuffed! That's what I'll do!'

16. mud.

Biographies/Bibliographies

Emily Lawless

LIFE. Emily Lawless was born in Kildare in 1845. Her father was Valentine Browne Lawless, 3rd baron Cloncurry. The family had come to prominence in the previous generation because of the involvement of the 2nd Baron Cloncurry in the United Irishmen, the Catholic Emancipation and the anti-Tithe campaigns. Emily was educated privately and travelled a great deal in Europe. Her novel *Hurrish* (1886) brought her to the attention of Gladstone, with whom she corresponded. She also befriended Sir Horace Plunkett and Shan Bullock and retained close ties with the British political establishment in Ireland. In politics, she remained a loyalist, although she was sympathetic to the need for serious land reform in Ireland. Her father and two of her sisters committed suicide. Emily, disillusioned with developments in Ireland, particularly in relation to the Home Rule controversy, retired to a life of seclusion in Surrey, England. She became increasingly eccentric as her health weakened. She died in Surrey in 1913.

CHIEF WRITINGS. *A Chelsea Householder* 3 vols (London: Sampson and Low, 1882); *Ireland: with additional chapters by Mrs. A. Bronson* (London: Fisher Unwin, 1885; 5th edition 1892; revised edition 1912); *A Millionaire's Cousin* (London: Macmillan; New York: Holt, 1885); *Hurrish. A Study* 2 vols (Edinburgh: W. Blackwood and Sons; New York: Harper, 1886; 6th edition London: Methuen, 1895); *Major Lawrence, F.L.S.* 3 vols (London: John Murray; New York: Holt, 1887); *Plain Frances Mowbray and other tales* (London: John Murray, 1889); *With Essex in Ireland* (London: Smith, Elder & Co., 1890; new edition London: Methuen, 1902); *Grania: The Story of an Island* 2 vols (London: Smith, Elder & Co., 1892); *Maelcho: A Sixteenth Century Narrative* 2 vols (London: Smith, Elder & Co.; New York: D. Appleton & Co., 1894); *Traits and Confidences* (London: Methuen & Co., 1897); *A Garden Diary. September 1899–September 1900* (London: Methuen & Co., 1901); *With the Wild Geese,* introduction by Stopford A. Brooke (London: Isbister, 1902); *Maria Edgeworth* (London: Macmillan, 1904); *The Book of Gilly: Four Months out of a Life* (London: Smith, Elder & Co., 1906); with Shan F. Bullock, *The Race of Castlebar* (London: John Murray, 1913); *The Inalienable Heritage and other poems* (London: privately printed, 1914).

BIOGRAPHY AND CRITICISM. P. Fallon (ed. and introduction), *The Poems of Emily Lawless* (Dublin: Dolmen Press, 1965); B. W. Brewer, '"She Was a Part of It": Emily Lawless (1845-1913)', *Eire — Ireland* 18, No. 4 (Winter 1983), 119–31; J. M. Cahalan, *The Irish Novel: A Critical History* (Dublin: Gill and Macmillan, 1988), pp. 80–83.

George Moore

For biography and bibliography, see p. 560.

Patrick Augustine (Canon) Sheehan

LIFE. Patrick Sheehan was born in Mallow, Co. Cork in 1852, educated at St Colman's College, Fermoy, and afterwards at St Patrick's College, Maynooth. Ordained a priest at Cork in 1875, he was sent on the English mission as a curate to Plymouth and Exeter. He returned to a curacy in Mallow in the Cork diocese, where he continued to work until his appointment as parish priest of Doneraile in 1885. He was still at Doneraile when raised to the position of canon in 1903, and its communal life furnished him with a model for much of his Irish fiction. His first two novels, *Geoffrey Austin, Student* (1897) and *The Triumph of Failure* (1898), both dealing with the growing pains of a sensitive catholic adolescent, achieved immediate success. *My New Curate* — an Irish response to George Eliot's *Scenes from Clerical Life* — first appeared in *The American Ecclesiastical Review* (1898–89) and was published as a book in Boston (1900) and in Britain as late as 1928. Sheehan's work was translated into several languages, achieving perhaps its greatest critical celebrity in Germany. His most popular novel with Irish readers — apart from *My New Curate* — is the historical romance, *Glenanaar* (1905), with its memorable characterization of Daniel O'Connell. His discursive writings, as in his *Early Essays and Lectures* (1906) — with its three-part essay on 'The German Universities', reveal him as a man of learned curiosity and wide cultural sympathies, though deeply imbued with that Jansenist distrust of sexuality so common in the clergy of his generation. He was a brilliant linguist, well read in the Classics, in English and American literature and in the cultures of France and Germany. He seems to have been happy in his pastoral ministry, an ardent constitutional nationalist whose persistent desire was that Ireland would achieve in time something of the cultural amenity of contemporary Europe. Canon Sheehan died in Doneraile, Co. Cork in 1913.

CHIEF WRITINGS. *Geoffrey Austin, Student* (Dublin: M. H. Gill, 1897); *The Triumph of Failure* (London: Burns & Oates, 1898); *Cithara Mea* (poems) (Boston: Marlier, Callanan, 1900); *My New Curate* (Boston: Marlier, 1900); *Luke Delmege* (London: Longmans, 1901); *Under the Cedars and the Stars* (essays) (Dublin: Browne and Nolan, 1903); *Lost Angel of a Ruined Paradise* (London: Longmans, 1904); *Glenanaar* (London: Longmans, 1905); *A Spoiled Priest, and Other Stories* (London: Unwin, 1905); *Early Essays and Lectures* (London: Longmans, 1906); *Lisheen* (London: Longmans, 1907); *Canon Sheehan's Short Stories* (London: Burns & Oates, 1908); *Parerga* (essays) (London: Longmans, 1908); *The Blindness of Dr Gray* (London: Longmans, 1909); *The Intellectuals* (London: Longmans, 1911); *The Queen's Fillet* (London: Longmans, 1911); *Miriam Lucas* (London: Longmans, 1912); *The Graves at Kilmorna* (London: Longmans, 1915); *Sermons*, ed. M. J. Phelan (Dublin and London: Maunsel, 1920); *The Literary Life, and Other Essays* (Dublin and London: Maunsel and Roberts, 1921); *Poems* (Dublin and London: Maunsel and Roberts, 1921); *Tristram Lloyd*, completed by Rev. Henry Gaffney (Dublin and Cork: The Talbot Press, 1929).

BIOGRAPHY AND CRITICISM. H. J. Heuser, *Canon Sheehan of Doneraile* (London: Longmans, 1917); Arthur P. A. Coussens, *Sheehan, zijn liven en zijn werken* (Brugge, 1923); Francis Boyle, *Canon Sheehan, A Sketch of His Life and Works* (Dublin: Gill, 1927); Benedict Kiely, 'Canon Sheehan: The Reluctant Novelist', *Irish Writing* No. 37 (Autumn 1957); Francis MacManus, 'The Fate of Canon Sheehan', *The Bell* No. 15 (November 1947); Terence Brown, 'Canon Sheehan and the Catholic Intellectual' in Robert Welch and Suheil Badi Bushrui (eds), *Literature and the Art of Creation* (Gerrards Cross: Colin Smythe; Totowa, New Jersey: Barnes and Noble, 1955); Terence Brown, 'Canon Sheehan and the Catholic Intellectual' in *Ireland's Literature: Selected Essays* (Mullingar, Co. Westmeath: The Lilliput Press; Totowa, New Jersey: Barnes and Noble, 1988), pp. 65–76.

Edith Somerville and Martin Ross

LIFE. Edith Oenone Somerville and 'Martin Ross' achieved their greatest fame for their two brilliant sketch-books, *Experiences of an Irish R.M.* and *Further Experiences of an Irish R.M.*, and their great novel of the Anglo-Irish Ascendancy, *The Real Charlotte*. Edith Somerville, the senior partner of the team, was born in 1858 in Corfu where her father was an officer in the British armed forces. She returned with him to the family home, Drishane, in Castletownsend, Co. Cork, the following year, where she spent most of her life and where she found a setting for her fictions. She was educated at Alexandra College, Dublin, and went on to study painting at London, Paris and Düsseldorf. She remained a keen and accomplished artist with brush and pencil for the rest of her life. She died unmarried, at Drishane in 1949.

In 1886 Edith Somerville met her Galway cousin, Violet Martin, and their strange literary partnership began. Violet Florence Martin, who took the pen-name 'Martin Ross', was born at Ross House, Co. Galway in 1862 and was educated at Alexandra College, Dublin. Like her cousin, she had a passion for horse-riding which led to a disastrous hunting accident in 1898 from which she never quite recovered. There was a mystical relationship between the two authors which enabled them to communicate after Violet's death at Cork in 1915.

CHIEF WRITINGS. *An Irish Cousin* 2 vols (London: Richard Bentley, 1889); *Naboth's Vineyard* (London: Spencer Blackett, 1891); *Through Connemara in a Governess Cart* (London: W. H. Allen, 1893); *The Real Charlotte* 3 vols (London: Ward and Downey, 1894); *Beggars on Horseback* (Edinburgh and London: William Blackwood, 1895); *The Silver Fox* (London: Lawrence and Bullen, 1898); *Some Experiences of an Irish R.M* (London: Longmans, Green, 1899); *Some Irish Yesterdays* (London: Longmans, Green, 1906); *Further Experiences of an Irish R.M.* (London: Longmans, Green, 1908); *Irish Memories* (London: Longmans, Green, 1917); *Mount Music* (London: Longmans, Green, 1919); *The Big House of Inver* (London: William Heinemann, 1925); *French Leave* (London: William Heinemann, 1928).

BIOGRAPHY AND CRITICISM. Geraldine Dorothy Cummins, *Dr. E. OE. Somerville* (London: Andrew Dakers, 1952); Maurice Collis, *Somerville and Ross* (London: Faber and Faber, 1968); Violet Powell, *The Irish Cousins* (London: Heinemann, 1970); John Cronin, *Somerville and Ross* (Lewisburg, Pennsylvania: Bucknell University Press, 1972); Hilary Robinson, *Somerville and Ross: A Critical Appreciation* (Dublin: Gill and Macmillan; New York: St Martin's Press, 1980); Gifford Lewis, *Somerville and Ross: The World of the Irish R.M.* (London: (Penguin, 1985); Gifford Lewis (ed.), *The Selected Letters of Somerville and Ross* (London: Faber and Faber, 1989).

William Butler Yeats

For biography and bibliography, see p. 830.

Shan Bullock

LIFE. Shan F. Bullock was born to a protestant family in Crom, Co. Fermanagh in 1865. His father was a bailiff, so he was familiar from the start with the sort of agrarian-sectarian conflict enacted in the story by which he is represented here. Having spent some time on his father's farm, Bullock went to London and worked in the British civil service for most of his life. His first publication, a collection of tales entitled *The Awkward Squads* (1893), whose title story deals drolly with the rival religious factions and their clumsy attempts to organize into militias. His experiences as a civil servant issued in the novel *Robert Thorne: The Story of a London Clerk* (1907). His most impressive work was probably *Thomas Andrews, Shipbuilder* (1912), which deals with the construction of *The Titanic*, though *By Thrasna River*, in which he recalls both the exultation and bitterness of farm life in his native Fermanagh, is equally vivid. His outwardly uneventful life ended in Cheam, Surrey, in February 1935.

CHIEF WRITINGS. *The Awkward Squads and Other Stories* (London: Cassell, 1893); *By Thrasna River* (London: Ward Lock and Bowden, 1895); *Ring o' Rushes* (London: Ward Lock and Bowden, 1896); *The Charmer* (London: Bowden, 1897); *The Barrys* (London: Harper, 1899); *Irish Pastorals* (London: Grant Richards; New York: McClure, Phillips, 1901); *The Squireen* (London: Methuen, 1903); *The Red Leaguers* (London: Methuen, 1903); *Dan the Dollar* (Dublin: Maunsel, 1905); *The Cubs* (London: Laurie, 1906); *Robert Thorne* (London: Laurie, 1907); *A Laughing Matter* (London: Laurie, 1907); *Master John* (London: Laurie, 1909); *Hetty* (London: Laurie, 1911); *Thomas Andrews, Shipbuilder* (Dublin and London: Maunsel, 1912, published in the United States as *A 'Titanic' Hero* (Baltimore: Norman, Remington, 1913)); with Emily Lawless, *The Race of Castlebar* (London: John Murray, 1913); *Mr Ruby Jumps the Traces* (London: Chapman and Hall, 1917); *Mors et Vita* (poems) (London: Laurie, 1923); *The Loughsiders* (London: Harrap, 1924); *Gleanings* (poems) (Sutton, Surrey: William Pile, 1926); *After Sixty Years* (London: Sampson Low, 1931).

BIOGRAPHY AND CRITICISM. John Wilson Foster, *Forces and Themes in Ulster Fiction* (Dublin: Gill and Macmillan; Totowa, New Jersey: Rowan and Littlefield, 1974); Benedict Kiely, *Modern Irish Fiction — A Critique* (Dublin: Golden Eagle Books, 1950); Augustine Martin (ed.), *The Genius of Irish Prose* (Cork: Mercier Press, 1985); John Wilson Foster, *Fictions of the Irish Literary Revival* (Dublin: Gill and Macmillan; Syracuse: Syracuse University Press, 1987).

George A. Birmingham (J. O. Hannay)

For biography and bibliography, see Volume III, p. 557.

Gerald O'Donovan (Jeremiah O'Donovan)

LIFE. Born in County Down in 1871, Jeremiah O'Donovan was of a Cork family; his father moved around Ireland building piers. His education in Cork, Galway and Sligo led in 1889 to his acceptance by St Patrick's College, Maynooth, where he studied for the priesthood. He was ordained to the diocese of Clonfert in 1895 and appointed to a curacy at Kilmalinogue and Lickmassy, moving to Loughrea, Co. Galway in 1896. A man of progressive ideas, O'Donovan espoused the co-operative policies of Horace Plunkett, swiftly becoming, along with Edward Martyn, Connacht's representative on the Irish Agricultural Organisation Society. His cultural enthusiasms attracted artists like Jack B. Yeats and Sarah Purser to work on the new cathedral at Loughrea, and the Abbey Theatre to perform there.

With a change of bishop in 1903, O'Donovan found his social and cultural ambitions for the diocese increasingly frustrated. In 1904 he left the priesthood and subsequently the catholic church. It is believed that George Moore's portrait of Father Gogarty in *The Lake* is based on O'Donovan, who was a friend of the author. He carried on a freelance career in London, and was for a year (1910–11) subwarden of Toynbee Hall in London's east end. His first and best novel, *Father Ralph*, was published to critical acclaim in 1913; the sixth and last, *The Holy Tree*, was published in 1922.

During the Great War O'Donovan worked in the British Department of Propaganda, and later as a reader in the publishing house of Collins. His marriage in 1910 brought him three children, one of whom died tragically in youth. In his last years he lived in Albury, Surrey, where he died of cancer in July 1942.

CHIEF WRITINGS. *Father Ralph* (London: Macmillan, 1913); *Waiting* (London: Macmillan, 1914); *Conquest* (London: Constable, 1920); *How They Did It* (London: Methuen, 1920); *Vocations* (London: Martin Secker, 1921); *The Holy Tree* (London: Heinemann, 1922).

BIOGRAPHY AND CRITICISM. Peter Costello, *The Heart Grown Brutal* (Dublin: Gill and Macmillan; Totowa, New Jersey: Rowman and Littlefield, 1978); Norrys O'Connor, 'The Irish Uncle Tom's Cabin' in *Changing Ireland* (Cambridge, Mass.: Harvard University Press, 1924); John Wilson Foster, *Fictions of the Irish Literary Revival* (Dublin: Gill and Macmillan; Syracuse: Syracuse University Press, 1987).

Forrest Reid

LIFE. Forrest Reid was born in Belfast in 1875, of a protestant, mercantile family that had experienced mixed fortunes in the world of shipping. He was educated locally, then apprenticed to the tea trade, which eventually he abandoned in favour of Cambridge. There he became a close friend of E. M. Forster, who admired his talent and encouraged him in his work. On graduating, Reid returned to Belfast, where he pursued a career as a novelist, autobiographer and critic for the rest of his inconspicuous life. His first novel, *The Kingdom of Twilight* (1904) had a modest success, but it was with *Following Darkness* (1912), later rewritten as *Peter Waring*, that he found his full strength. The three most prominent themes in Reid's fiction are his hatred of urban squalor — dramatized especially in his Belfast sequences — an almost mystical sense of nature, and the intensity of male friendship, particularly between adolescent boys. His two autobiographies, *Apostate* (1926) — which deals with his loss of faith — and *Private Road* (1940), provide useful information on his artistic development as well as being vivid works of literature. His book on W.B. Yeats (1915) seems to have been the first full-length study of the great poet. He died in Warrenpoint, Co. Down in 1947.

CHIEF WRITINGS. *The Kingdom of Twilight* (London: Unwin, 1904); *The Garden God* (London: David Nutt, 1905); *The Bracknels* (London: Edward Arnold, 1911), rewritten as *Denis Bracknel* (London: Faber, 1947); *Following Darkness* (London: Edward Arnold, 1912) rewritten as *Peter Waring* (London: Faber, 1937; Belfast: Blackstaff Press, 1976); *The Gentle Lover* (London: Edward Arnold, 1913); *At the Door of the Gate* (London: Edward Arnold, 1915); *W. B. Yeats, A Critical Study* (London: Martin Secker, 1915); *The Spring Song* (London: Edward Arnold, 1916); *A Garden by the Sea* (Dublin: The Talbot Press; London: Unwin, 1918); *Pirates of the Spring* (Dublin: The Talbot Press; London: Unwin, 1919); *Pender among the Residents* (London: Collins, 1922); *Apostate* (London: Constable, 1926; London: Faber, 1947); *Demaphon* (London: Collins, 1927); *Walter de la Mare: A Critical Study* (London: Faber, 1929); *Uncle Stephen* (London: Faber, 1931); *Brian Westby* (London: Faber, 1934); *The Retreat; or the Machinations of Henry* (London: Faber, 1936); *Private Road* (London: Faber, 1940); *Young Tom; or Very Mixed Company* (London: Faber, 1944).

BIOGRAPHY AND CRITICISM. E. M. Forster, *Abinger Harvest* (London: Arnold, 1936); E. M. Forster, *Two Cheers for Democracy* (London: Arnold, 1951); Russell Burlington, *Forrest Reid: A Portrait and a Study* (London: Faber, 1953); John Wilson Foster, *Forces and*

Themes in Ulster Fiction (Dublin: Gill and Macmillan; Totowa, New Jersey: Rowman and Littlefield, 1974); Mary Bryan, *Forrest Reid* (Boston: Twayne, 1976);.

Seumas O'Kelly

LIFE. Seumas O'Kelly was born, probably in 1875, at Mobhill, Loughrea, Co. Galway. After a rudimentary education locally, he entered journalism, working first on the *Connaught Leader*, moving on in 1903 to Skibbereen's *Southern Star*, and in 1906 to *The Leinster Leader* in Naas, Co. Kildare. While in Naas he produced his first, remarkably uncertain, collection of short stories, *By the Stream of Kilmeen* (1906), and made the acquaintance of Arthur Griffith, Padraic Colum and other figures of the Irish Literary Revival. His writing became more assured and varied. His play, *The Shuiler's Child*, was produced at the Abbey Theatre in 1909 and, amidst strenuous journalistic activity, he was writing the fiction that was to culminate in such novels as *The Lady of Deerpark* (1917), *Wet Clay* (1922) and his masterpiece in the short story from, 'The Weaver's Grave' (1919). He moved to a staff job on *The Saturday Evening Post* in 1912, but because of ill health was forced to return to *The Leinster Leader* in 1915, resuming its editorship when his brother, Michael, was arrested by the British in 1916. He took over Arthur Griffith's paper, *Nationality*, when Griffith was deported in 1918. When the Crown forces raided its office in Harcourt Street later that year, O'Kelly died of a resultant heart attack. A radio adaptation of 'The Weaver's Grave' by Michael O'hAodha won the Italia Prize for Radio Éireann in 1961.

CHIEF WRITINGS. *The Shuiler's Child* (Dublin: Maunsel, 1909; Chicago: De Paul University, 1971); *The Bribe* (play) (London: Maunsel, 1914; Dublin: James Duffy, 1952); *The Lady of Deerpark* (London: Methuen, 1917); *Waysiders* (Dublin: The Talbot Press; London: Unwin, 1917; New York: Stokes, 1919); *Ranns and Ballads* (Dublin: Candle, 1918); *The Golden Barque and the Weaver's Grave* (Dublin: The Talbot Press; London: Unwin, 1919); *The Leprecaun of Kilmeen* (Dublin: Martin Lester, 1920); *Hillsiders* (Dublin: The Talbot Press; London: Unwin, 1921); *Wet Clay* (Dublin: The Talbot Press; London: Unwin, 1922); *The Land of Loneliness and Other Stories*, selected with Introduction by Eamon Grennan (Dublin: Gill and Macmillan, 1969).

BIOGRAPHY AND CRITICISM. George Brandon Saul, *Seumas O'Kelly* (Lewisburg, Pennsylvania: Bucknell University Press, 1971); Anne Clune, 'Seumas O'Kelly' in Patrick Rafroidi and Terence Brown (eds), *The Irish Short Story* (Gerrards Cross, Bucks: Colin Smythe; Atlantic Highlands, New Jersey: Humanities Press, 1979); Augustine Martin (ed.), *The Genius of Irish Prose* (Cork: Mercier Press, 1985); John Wilson Foster, *Fictions of the Irish Literary Revival* (Dublin: Gill and Macmillan; Syracuse: Syracuse University Press, 1987).

Daniel Corkery

For biography and bibliography, see Volume III, p. 127.

James Stephens

LIFE. James Stephens was born in the north-side Dublin slums in 1882 and spent much of his childhood in the Meath Industrial School, Dublin. He was working as a clerk in a solicitor's office on Merrion Square when George Russell (AE) read one of his poems in Arthur Griffith's paper, *Sinn Fein*. Encouraged by Russell and his circle, Stephens rapidly became a central and prolific figure of the Literary Revival, his *annus mirabilis* being 1912 when his novel, *The Charwoman's Daughter*, his prose fantasy, *The Crock of Gold*, and his second book of lyrics, *The Hill of Vision*, appeared on both sides of the Atlantic. Stephens and his future wife, 'Cynthia', went to live in Paris in 1912, from which was published his short-story collection, *Here Are Ladies*, and his second fantasy in prose, *The Demi-Gods*. He returned to Dublin in 1915 to take up his duties as registrar of the National Gallery. The 1916 Rising prompted him to write a vivid and circumstantial day-by-day account of the street-fighting, *The Insurrection in Dublin*. The following years were devoted to translations of Gaelic poetry, in *Reincarnations* and, the retelling of old Irish saga and epic literature, in *Deirdre, In the Land of Youth,* and in *Irish Fairy Tales*. In 1922 Stephens went to live in London where, in the 1930s, he became a popular literary broadcaster for the BBC. His creative energies seem to have declined in the English years, which yielded a few short stories and two slim volumes of verse. He died in London in 1950.

CHIEF WRITINGS. *Insurrections* (poems) (Dublin: Maunsel; New York: Macmillan, 1909); *The Hill of Vision* (Dublin: Maunsel; New York: Macmillan, 1912); *The Charwoman's Daughter* (London: Macmillan, 1912). American title: *Mary, Mary* (Boston: Small, Maynard, 1912); *The Crock of Gold* (London: Macmillan, 1912; New York: Macmillan, 1913); *Here Are Ladies* (London and New York: Macmillan, 1913); *The Demi-Gods* (London and New York: Macmillan, 1914); *Songs from the Clay* (poems) (London and New York: Macmillan, 1915); *The Adventures of Seamus Beg and The Rocky Road to Dublin* (London and New York: Macmillan, 1915); *The Insurrection in Dublin* (Dublin: Maunsel; New York: Macmillan, 1916); *Hunger: A Dublin Story* (Dublin: Candle Press, 1918); *Reincarnations* (London and New York: Macmillan, 1918); *Irish Fairy Tales* (London and New York: Macmillan, 1920); *Deirdre* (London and New York: Macmillan, 1923); *In the Land of Youth* (London and New York: Macmillan, 1924); *Collected Poems* (London and New York: Macmillan, 1926); *Etched in Moonlight* (stories) (London and New York: Macmillan, 1928); *Strict Joy* (London and New York: Macmillan, 1931); *Kings and the Moon* (London and New York: Macmillan, 1938); Lloyd Frankenberg (ed.), *James Stephens, a Selection* (London: Macmillan, 1962); Lloyd Frankenberg (ed.), *James, Seamus and Jacques* (London and New York: Macmillan 1974); Richard Finneran (ed.), *Letters of James Stephens* (London and New York: Macmillan, 1974); Patricia McFate (ed.), *The Uncollected Prose of James Stephens* (London: Macmillan, 1983).

BIOGRAPHY AND CRITICISM. Hilary Pyle, *James Stephens, His Work and an Account of his Life* (London: Routledge & Kegan Paul, 1965); Augustine Martin, *James Stephens, A Critical Study* (Dublin: Gill and Macmillan; Totowa, New Jersey, 1977).

Joyce Cary

LIFE. Born in 1888 in Derry, Arthur Joyce Lunel Cary lived to inherit Castle Cary — the setting for his Irish fictions — in the Inishowen Peninsula, after his father's death in 1937. In the tradition of so many Irish planter families, he was educated in England, going up to Oxford in 1910 and taking his law degree in 1913. In his active and adventurous career he worked with Horace Plunkett in the Irish Co-operative Movement, fought with a Montenegrin battalion in the 1912–13 war, served in the colonial service in Nigeria, worked on films in Ethiopia and India, lectured in the United States. He worked in London as an air-raid warden in 1945. His prolific output included essays, journalism, broadcasts, lectures, short stories and the novels that made him one of the major writers of the twentieth century — most notably his first great trilogy, *Herself Surprised*, *To be a Pilgrim*, and *The Horse's Mouth*. Joyce Cary died in Oxford in 1957.

CHIEF WRITINGS. *Castle Corner* (London: Gollancz, 1938); *Mister Johnson* (London: Gollancz, 1939; New York: Harper, 1951); *Charley is my Darling* (London: Michael Joseph, 1940; New York: Harper, 1960); *A House of Children* (London: Michael Joseph, 1941; New York: Harper, 1956); *The Case for African Freedom* (London: Secker and Warburg, 1941); *Herself Surprised* (London: Michael Joseph, 1941); *To be a Pilgrim* (London: Michael Joseph, 1942); *The Horse's Mouth* (London: Michael Joseph, 1944); *The Moonlight* (London: Michael Joseph, 1946; New York: Harper, 1947); *A Fearful Joy* (London: Michael Joseph, 1949; New York: Harper, 1950); *Prisoner of Grace* (London: Michael Joseph; New York: Harper, 1952); *Except the Lord* (London: Michael Joseph; New York: Harper, 1953); *Not Honour More* (London: Michael Joseph; New York: Harper, 1955); *Spring Song and Other Stories* (London: Michael Joseph, 1960).

The definitive Carfax edition of Cary's fiction began publication by Michael Joseph in 1950.

BIOGRAPHY AND CRITICISM. Andrew Wright, *Joyce Cary: A Preface to his Novels* (London: Chatto & Windus, 1959); Walter Ernest Allen, *Joyce Cary*, revised edition (London: Longmans, 1963, Writers and Their Work Series, No. 41); Charles G. Hoffman, *The Comedy of Freedom* (Pittsburgh; University of Pittsburgh Press, 1964); Malcolm Foster, *Joyce Cary, A Biography* (Boston: Houghton Mifflin, 1968); Barbara Fisher, *Joyce Cary: The Writer and his Theme* (Gerrards Cross: Colin Smythe, 1980); *Joyce Cary Remembered: In Letters and Interviews by his Family and Others* (Gerrards Cross: Colin Smythe; New York: Barnes and Noble, 1988).

Patrick MacGill

LIFE. Patrick MacGill was born in 1891 on a small farm in the Glenties, Co. Donegal, the eldest of eleven children. He left school at the age of twelve to work as a farm labourer, before migrating to Scotland to earn his living as a potato-picker and later as an itinerant labourer on the roads and railways. These experiences prompted such early publications as *Gleanings from a Navvy's Scrapbook* (1911), *Songs of a Navvy* and *Songs of the Dead End*. One of his most enduring achievements, his novel, *Children of the Dead End* (1914), appeared just before he enlisted as a private with the London Irish Rifles at the outbreak of World War I. Its sequel, *The Rat-Pit* — also set in Ireland and Scotland, came out in the following year. He served throughout the war and embodied some of his bitter accounts of the experience in *The Amateur Army* (1915) and *The Great Push: An Episode in the Great War* (1916). Returning to civilian life, MacGill continued to write up to 1937, living inconspicuously until he died in 1963. He went to the United States in 1930 and lived there until his death in 1963. Though popular and significant, his work attracted almost no attention from the literary critics. His reputation seemed altogether eclipsed until the publication of his best novels by Caliban Books in 1983. Both his literary and humanitarian achievements are now celebrated by an important annual summer school in his native Glenties.

CHIEF WRITINGS. *Gleanings from a Navvy's Scrapbook* (Derry: The Derry Journal, 1911); *Songs of a Navvy* (Windsor: P. MacGill, 1911); *Songs of the Dead End* (London: Year Book Press, 1912) *Children of the Dead End* (London: Herbert Jenkins, 1914); *The Amateur Army* (London: Herbert Jenkins, 1915); *The Rat-Pit* (London: Herbert Jenkins, 1915); *Red Horizon* (London: Herbert Jenkins, 1916); *The Great Push: An Episode in the Great War* (London: Herbert Jenkins, 1916); *Glenmornan* (London: Herbert Jenkins, 1919); *Lanty Hanlon: A Comedy of Irish Life* (London: Herbert Jenkins, 1922); *Moleskin Joe* (London: Herbert Jenkins, 1923); *Tulliver's Mill* (London: Herbert Jenkins, 1934); *The House at the World's End* (London: Herbert Jenkins, 1935).

The following titles were republished in hardback and paperback, by Caliban Books: *Children of the Dead End, The Rat-Pit, Lanty Hanlon, Moleskin Joe, Glenmornan* (all in 1983); *Red Horizon, The Great Push: An Episode in the Great War, Patrick MacGill: The Navvy Poet*, incorporating the bulk of his verse (these in 1984).

Brinsley MacNamara (John Weldon)

LIFE. Brinsley MacNamara — pen-name for John Weldon — was born in 1890 in Delvin, Co. Westmeath, one of seven children. His father was the local schoolmaster, James Weldon, whose destiny was to be severely altered by his son's literary activities. In 1910 MacNamara joined the Abbey Players and went with them on their first tour of the United States in 1911. Having spent two years in America working freelance, he returned to Ireland in 1913. For the next five years he lived in Delvin writing occasional pieces for the journals and newspapers and working on his first novel, *The Valley of the Squinting Windows*. When the book appeared in 1918, the impact of its satire on village life was such as to bring almost unprecedented odium on the author and his family. The book was burned publicly in Delvin and was condemned throughout the country; his school having been boycotted, MacNamara's father had to leave the region. The author spent the rest of his life in Quin, Co. Clare and Dublin where he continued to write novels, short stories and plays for the Abbey, *The Clanking of Chains* (1920) and *The Various Lives of Marcus Igoe* (1929) being the best of the fiction. Of his nine plays for the Abbey, *Margaret Gillan* (1933) is notable for its uncompromising realism and *Look at the Heffernans* (1926) was one of the theatre's most popular comedies during those rather lean theatrical years. MacNamara succeeded James Stephens as registrar of the National Gallery in 1924, became a member of the Irish Academy of Letters, and was briefly a director of the Abbey Theatre in 1935, resigning, paradoxically, in protest at the production of O'Casey's *The Silver Tassie* in that year. He died in Dublin in 1963.

CHIEF WRITINGS. *The Valley of the Squinting Windows* (London: Sampson, Low, Marston, 1918); *The Clanking of Chains* (Dublin: Maunsel, 1920); *The Mirror in the Dusk* (Dublin and London: Maunsel and Roberts, 1921); *Look at the Heffernans* (Dublin: The Talbot Press, 1926); *The Various Lives of Marcus Igoe* (London: Sampson, Low, Marston, 1929); *Margaret Gillan* (London: George Allen and Unwin, 1934); *Some Curious People* (short stories) (Dublin: The Talbot Press, 1945); *Michael Caravan* (Dublin: The Talbot Press, 1946); *The Whole Story of X.Y.Z.* (Belfast: H. R. Carter, 1951); *The Glorious Uncertainty* (Dublin: P. J. Bourke, n.d.).

BIOGRAPHY AND CRITICISM. Robert Hogan, *After the Irish Renaissance* (Minneapolis: University of Minnesota Press, 1967); Benedict Kiely, *Modern Irish Fiction — A Critique* (Dublin: Golden Eagle Books, 1950); Michael McDonnell, 'Brinsley MacNamara: A Checklist', *Journal of Irish Literature* 4 (May 1975); Andrew E. Malone, 'Brinsley MacNamara: An Appreciation', *The Dublin Magazine*, July 1929; Donnchadh A. Meehan, 'Of Four Fantasies', *The Bookman*, December 1948; Augustine Martin (ed.), *The Genius of Irish Prose* (Cork: Mercier Press, 1985); John Wilson Foster, *Fictions of the Irish Literary Revival* (Dublin: Gill and Macmillan; Syracuse: Syracuse University Press, 1987); Padraic O'Farrell, *The Burning of Brinsley MacNamara* (Dublin: The Lilliput Press, 1990).

Eimar O'Duffy

LIFE. Eimar Ultan O'Duffy was born in Dublin in 1893, the son of a fashionable dentist, and was educated at the English Jesuit boarding school, Stonyhurst, and afterwards at University College, Dublin. Having graduated in dentistry, he experimented unsuccessfully for a time with playwriting, while joining the Irish Republican Brotherhood and becoming a captain in the Irish Volunteers, which the militant IRB sought to infiltrate. He was with the faction that alerted Eóin MacNeill to the plans for the Easter Rising, which MacNeill then countermanded. These events and the rebellion itself are dramatized in his long novel *The Wasted Island* (1919). O'Duffy's literary experiments during this period included a lively historical romance, *The Lion and the Fox* (1922), a satire of Irish culture and mores, *Printer's Errors* (1922), and a comic romance set in the time of the War of Independence, entitled *Miss Rudd and Some Lovers* (1923). Up to 1925 O'Duffy worked as a teacher and then in the Department of External Affairs of the new state. He left the country in 1925, moving his family to England and working for a time as a journalist in Paris. In 1926 he published *King Goshawk and the Birds*, the first of a satiric trilogy that included *The Spacious Adventures of the Man in the Street* and *Asses in Clover*. O'Duffy's critique of the capitalist attitude to finance within the social structure — a crucial theme in the trilogy — found formal expression in his discursive *Life and Money* (1933). His attempts to make a living by writing detective stories failed as his health continued to deteriorate. He died at New Malden, Surrey in 1935.

CHIEF WRITINGS. *The Wasted Island* (Dublin: Martin Lester, 1919); revised London: Macmillan 1929); *The Lion and the Fox* (Dublin: Martin Lester, 1922); *Printer's Errors* (Dublin: Martin Lester, 1922; London: Leonard Parsons, 1922); *Miss Rudd and Some Lovers*, (Dublin: The Talbot Press, 1923); *King Goshawk and the Birds* (London: Macmillan, 1926); *The Spacious Adventures of the Man in the Street* (London: Macmillan, 1928); *Asses in Clover* (London: Putnam, 1933). *The Journal of Irish Literature* No. 7 (1978) reprinted *Printer's Errors* and an early play, *Bricriu's Feast*.

BIOGRAPHY AND CRITICISM. Robert Hogan, *Eimar O'Duffy* (Lewisburg, Pennsylvania: Bucknell University Press, 1972); Augustine Martin (ed.), *The Genius of Irish Prose* (Cork: Mercier Press, 1985); John Wilson Foster, *Fictions of the Irish Literary Revival* (Dublin: Gill and Macmillan; Syracuse: Syracuse University Press, 1987), Chapter 13, 'The Kingdom of Fantasy'.

Peadar O'Donnell

LIFE. Peadar O'Donnell was born in Meenmore, Co. Donegal in 1893; he was educated locally and at St Patrick's Teacher Training College, Dublin. He worked as a primary teacher for some years before joining the Irish Transport and General Workers' Union in 1918, his first step in a career dedicated to left-wing causes. In the following year he joined the IRA and took part in the Black-and-Tan War. He opposed the Treaty and went on active service with the republican irregulars. He was arrested in July 1922 and was jailed for two years. His literary career began dramatically with two novels in quick succession, *Storm* (1925) and *Islanders* (1927). Among the journals he edited were *An tOglach* and *An Phoblacht* — both republican organs — and more significantly, *The Bell*, which he took over from Seán O'Faoláin in 1946. In his fiction the struggle for social justice, often symbolized in a communal life of the poor in Gaelic Ireland, is a constant theme. His three autobiographical works, *The Gates Flew Open* (1932), *Salud! An Irishman in Spain* (1937) and *There Will be Another Day* (1963), are testimony to a life of energetic commitment to national regeneration and social justice. He died in Dublin in 1986.

CHIEF WRITINGS. *Storm* (Dublin: The Talbot Press, 1925); *Islanders* (London: Jonathan Cape, 1928; New York: retitled *The Way it Was with Them*, Putnam, 1928); *Adrigoole* (London: Jonathan Cape; New York: Putnam, 1929); *The Knife* (London: Jonathan Cape, 1930; retitled *There Will be Fighting*, New York: Putnam, 1931); *The Gates Flew Open* (London: Jonathan Cape, 1932); *Wrack* (play) (London: Jonathan Cape, 1933); *On the Edge of the Stream* (London: Jonathan Cape, 1934); *Salud! An Irishman in Spain* (London: Methuen, 1937); *The Big Windows* (London: Jonathan Cape, 1955; reprinted London: Allison and Busby; Dublin: O'Brien Press, 1983); *There Will be Another Day* (Dublin: Dolmen Press, 1963); *Proud Island* (Dublin: O'Brien Press, 1975).

BIOGRAPHY AND CRITICISM. Frank O'Connor, *The Lonely Voice* (Cleveland: World, 1962; London: Macmillan, 1963); Paul Doyle, 'Peadar O'Donnell: Checklist, *Bulletin of Bibliography* 28 (January-March 1971); Grattan Freyer, *Peadar O'Donnell* (Lewisburg, Pennsylvania: Bucknell University Press, 1973); Michael McInerney, *Peadar O'Donnell: Irish Social Rebel* (Dublin: O'Brien Press, 1976).

Liam O'Flaherty

For biography and bibliography, see Volume III, p. 128.

Austin Clarke

For biography and bibliography, see Volume III, p. 168.

Kate O'Brien

LIFE. Kate O'Brien, born in 1897 in Limerick to a middle-class, catholic family, was educated at Laurel Hill Convent and later at University College, Dublin. In the years that followed, she worked as a governess in Spain and as a journalist on the *Manchester Guardian*. Her first literary success was a play, *Distinguished Villa* (1926), but she turned quickly to the novel, *Without My Cloak* (1931) winning both the Hawthornden and James Tait Black Memorial prizes. Her novels, by and large, explore the complexities of the Irish catholic conscience, bringing to the theme an intellectual European sensibility. Perhaps her greatest novel is *That Lady* (1946), a historical fiction set in sixteenth-century Spain. Her travel books, *Farewell, Spain* and *My Ireland*, achieved a richly deserved popularity and her biography, *Teresa of Avila*, is a proto-feminist portrait of a great woman. Kate O'Brien spent her rather secluded life between Spain, England and Ireland. She died in Faversham, Kent in 1974.

CHIEF WRITINGS. *Distinguished Villa* (London: E. Benn, 1926); *Without My Cloak* (London: Heinemann; New York, Doubleday, Doran, 1931); *The Ante-Room* (London: Heinemann; New York: Doubleday, 1934; reprinted Dublin: Arlen House, 1980; London: Virago, 1989); *Mary Lavelle* (London: Heinemann; New York: Doubleday, 1936); *Farewell, Spain* (London: Heinemann; New York: Doubleday, 1937); *Pray for the Wanderer* (London: Heinemann; New York: Doubleday, Doran, 1938); *The Land of Spices* (London: Heinemann, 1941); *English Diaries and Journals* (London: Collins, 1943); *The Last of Summer* (London: Heinemann; New York: Doubleday, Doran, 1943; reprinted London: Virago, 1990); *That Lady* (London: Heinemann; published as *For One Sweet Grape* New York: Doubleday, 1946); *That Lady* (play) (New York: Harper, 1949); *Teresa of Avila* (London: Max Parrish; New York; Sheed and Ward, 1951); *The Flower of May* (London: Heinemann; New York: Harper, 1953); *As Music and Splendour* (New York: Harper, 1958); *My Ireland* (New York: Hastings House, 1962).

BIOGRAPHY AND CRITICISM. Augustine Martin (ed.), *The Genius of Irish Prose* (Cork: Mercier Press, 1985); Lorna Reynolds, *Kate O'Brien, A Literary Portrait* (Gerrards Cross: Colin Smythe, 1987); Adele M. Dalsimer, *Kate O'Brien: A Critical Study* (Dublin: Gill and Macmillan, 1990).

Elizabeth Bowen

For biography and bibliography, see p. 949.

Seán O'Faoláin

For biography and bibliography, see Volume III, p. 127.

Frank O'Connor

For biography and bibliography, see Volume III, p. 127.

Mary Lavin

LIFE. Born in 1912 in Walpole, Massachusetts, of Irish parents, Mary Lavin spent the first eleven years of her life in America. Then her father returned to Ireland, where he settled for a time with his family in the town of Athenry, Co. Galway, the model for such provincial town settings as in 'A Visit to the Cemetery'. At the end of 1922 the family moved to Dublin, where the future novelist was educated at Loreto College and University College, Dublin (she took her M.A. in 1937). She began to publish short stories in the late 1930s and, in 1942, the year of her marriage to William Walsh, a Dublin lawyer, established her reputation with *Tales from Bective Bridge*. While the short story is her chosen form, she has written two highly successful novels, *The House in Clewe Street* and *Mary O'Grady*, both republished by Virago Press. With her husband she bought the Abbey Farm at Bective, Co. Meath, the setting for many of her stories of rural Irish life. It is the setting for 'In the Middle of the Fields', one of those many studies of widowhood written after the death of her husband in 1954. Her steady output of short stories brought her a world reputation; she won two Guggenheim awards, the James Tait Black Memorial Prize, the Katherine Mansfield Prize, the Ella Lynam Cabot Award, The Eire Society Gold Medal, the Literary Award of the American Irish Foundation, the Gregory Gold Medal and an honorary doctorate from the National University of Ireland. In 1969 she married Michael MacDonald Scott, dean of the School of Irish Studies, then in Dublin. An exponent of the organic form, Mary Lavin has described her approach to the short story in these terms: 'Short story writing — for me — is only looking closer than normal into the human heart. The vagaries and contrarieties there to be found have their own integral design.' (Preface to *Selected Stories*, New York, 1959).

CHIEF WRITINGS. *Tales from Bective Bridge* (Boston: Little, Brown, 1942; London: Michael Joseph, 1943); *The Long Ago and Other Stories* (London: Michael Joseph, 1944); *The House in Clewe Street* (London: Michael Joseph, 1945; Boston: Little, Brown, 1946); *The Becker Wives and Other Stories* (London: Michael Joseph, 1946); *At Sally Gap and Other Stories* (Boston: Little, Brown, 1947); *Mary O'Grady* (Boston: Little, Brown; London: Michael Joseph, 1950); *A Single Lady and Other Stories* (London: Michael Joseph, 1951); *The Patriot Son and Other Stories* (London: Michael Joseph, 1956); *Selected Stories* (New York: Macmillan, 1959); *The Great Wave and Other Stories* (London and New York: Macmillan, 1961); *The Stories of Mary Lavin* (London: Longman, 1972; London: Constable, 1964); *In the Middle of the Fields and Other Stories* (London: Constable, 1967); *Happiness and Other Stories* (London: Constable, 1969); *Collected Stories* (Boston: Houghton Mifflin, 1971); *The Second Best Children in the World* (Volume I Boston: Houghton Mifflin, 1972); *A Memory and Other Stories* (London: Constable, 1972; Boston: Houghton Mifflin, 1973); *The Stories of Mary Lavin*, Volume II (London: Constable, 1974); *The Shrine and Other Stories* (London: Constable, 1977); *A Family Likeness and Other Stories* (London: Constable, 1985); *Collected Stories* 3 vols (London: Constable, 1985); *Mary O'Grady*, with Afterword by Augustine Martin (London: Virago Press, 1987); *The House in Clewe Street*, with Afterword by Augustine Martin (London: Virago Press, 1988).

BIOGRAPHY AND CRITICISM. A. Martin, 'A Skeleton Key to the Stories of Mary Lavin' *Studies* No. 52 (Winter 1963); F. O'Connor, *The Lonely Voice, A Study of the Modern Short Story* (London: Macmillan; Cleveland and New York; World, 1963); P. A. Doyle, 'Mary Lavin: A Checklist', *The Papers of the Bibliographical Society of America* 63 (1969), 317–21; Z. Bowen, *Mary Lavin* (Lewisburg, Pennsylvania: Bucknell University Press; London: Associated University Presses, 1975); A. A. Kelly, *Mary Lavin. A Quiet Rebel* (Dublin: Wolfhound Press, 1978); P. Rafroidi and T. Brown (eds), *The Irish Short Story* (Gerrards Cross: Colin Smythe; Atlantic Highlands, New Jersey: Humanities Press, 1979); R. F. Peterson, *Mary Lavin* (Boston: Twayne, 1979); *Irish University Review*, Mary Lavin Special Issue, Vol. 9, No. 2 (Autumn 1979).

Francis MacManus

LIFE. Francis MacManus, born in Kilkenny in 1909, was educated locally, at St Patrick's Training College, Drumcondra and at University College, Dublin. He taught secondary school for some twenty years before joining Radio Éireann in 1948, where he became head of features, a position that gave him the opportunity to encourage a generation of young Irish writers. Apart from his steady output in fiction, MacManus published biographies of Boccaccio and St Columban. His first novel was *Stand and Give Challenge* (1934), the first volume of a trilogy on eighteenth-century Ireland with the Waterford poet, Donnacha Ruadh MacConmara, as its central figure. In 1937 he began that series of novels based on the farming life of County Kilkenny for which he was celebrated and of which *Watergate* and *This House Was Mine* are the finest. He was elected to the Irish Academy of Letters and founded the perennial radio series, the Thomas Davis Lectures. He died in Dublin in 1965.

CHIEF WRITINGS. *Stand and Give Challenge* (Dublin: The Talbot Press, 1934); *Candle for the Proud* (Dublin: The Talbot Press, 1936; London: Sheed and Ward, 1937); *Pedlar's Pack: Stories, Sketches, Essays, Verse* (Dublin: The Talbot Press, 1944); *This House Was Mine* (Dublin: The Talbot Press, 1937); *Men Withering* (Dublin: The Talbot Press, 1939); *The Wild Garden* (Dublin: The Talbot Press, 1940); *Flow On, Lovely River* (Dublin: The Talbot Press, 1941); *Watergate* (Dublin: The Talbot Press, 1942); *The Greatest of These* (Dublin: The Talbot Press, 1943); *Statue For a Square* (Dublin: The Talbot Press, 1945); *Boccaccio* (London: Sheed & Ward, 1947); *The Fire in the Dust* (London: Jonathan Cape, 1950); *The American Son* (London: Jonathan Cape, 1959); *St Columban* (Dublin: Clonmore & Reynolds, 1963); ed. *The Years of the Great Test 1922–39* (Cork: Mercier Press, 1967).

BIOGRAPHY AND CRITICISM. Benedict Kiely, *Modern Irish Fiction — A Critique* (Dublin: Golden Eagle Books, 1950); Augustine Martin (ed.), *The Genius of Irish Prose* (Cork: Mercier Press, 1985).

Michael McLaverty

LIFE. Born in Carrickmacross, Co. Monaghan in 1907, McLaverty spent part of his childhood on Rathlin Island, off the north Antrim coast. He was educated in Belfast, at St Malachy's College and at Queen's University. After graduation with an M.Sc., he became a teacher of mathematics. He remained in the profession for the rest of his working life, becoming a headmaster at St Thomas's Secondary School on the Falls Road in Belfast. He befriended a number of younger writers, John McGahern and Seamus Heaney among them, and was a notable figure on the Northern literary scene until his retirement in 1972.

CHIEF WRITINGS. *Call My Brother Back* (London and New York: Longmans, Green, 1939; reissued Dublin: Allen Figgis, 1970); *Lost Fields* (New York and Toronto: Longmans, Green, 1941); *The White Mare and Other Stories* (Newcastle, Co. Down: Mourne Press, 1943); *In This Thy Day* (London: Jonathan Cape, 1945); *The Game Cock and Other Stories* (New York: Devin-Adair, 1947); *The Three Brothers* (London: Jonathan Cape, 1948); *Truth in The Night* (New York: Macmillan, 1951); *School for Hope* (London: Jonathan Cape, 1954); *The Choice* (London: Jonathan Cape, 1958); *The Brightening Day* (New York: Macmillan, 1965); *The Road to the Shore and Other Stories* (Swords, Co. Dublin: Poolbeg Press, 1976); *Collected Short Stories* (Swords, Co. Dublin: Poolbeg Press, 1978); S. Hillan King (ed.), *In Quiet Places: The Uncollected Stories, Letters and Critical Prose of Michael McLaverty* (Swords, Co. Dublin: Poolbeg Press, 1989).

BIOGRAPHY AND CRITICISM. J. W. Foster, *Forces and Themes in Ulster Fiction* (Dublin: Gill and Macmillan; Totowa, New Jersey: Rowman and Littlefield, 1974), pp. 36–47, 59–63; J. M. Cahalan, *The Irish Novel: A Critical History* (Dublin: Gill and Macmillan, 1988), pp. 194–96.

INDEX OF FIRST LINES OF POEMS

VOLUME II

The first lines of excerpts are indicated by an ellipsis.

GENERAL INDEX

VOLUME II

This index includes only those names that have particular importance for the texts in this volume. Names that occur only in annotations and in fleeting references have been excluded.

Bold numerals indicate text selections; italic numerals indicate biographical and bibliographical listings; roman numerals indicate other references.

THE FIELD DAY ANTHOLOGY OF IRISH WRITING

THE FIELD DAY ANTHOLOGY OF IRISH WRITING

VOLUME III

General Editor: Seamus Deane
Associate Editors: Andrew Carpenter, Jonathan Williams

Derry
Field Day Publications
Distributed by Faber & Faber Limited

First published in 1991
by Field Day Publications, Foyle Arts Centre,
Old Foyle College, Lawrence Hill, Derry,
Northern Ireland BT48 7NJ

Distributed by Faber & Faber Limited
3 Queen Square
London WC1N 3AU

For the Set of Three Volumes ISBN 0 946755 20 5

Typeset in Ireland by Phototype-Set Ltd, Drumcondra, Dublin.
Printed in the United States by Kingsport Press

1 2 3 4 5 6 7 8 9 0

Contents

NORTHERN PROTESTANT ORATORY AND WRITING 1791-1985

TOM PAULIN, *Reader in English, University of Nottingham, England*

AUTOBIOGRAPHY AND MEMOIRS 1890-1988

SEAMUS DEANE

CHALLENGING THE CANON: REVISIONISM AND CULTURAL CRITICISM

LUKE GIBBONS, *Faculty of Communications, Dublin City University, Dublin*

IRISH FICTION 1965-1990

JOHN WILSON FOSTER, *Department of English, University of British Columbia, Vancouver, Canada*

CONTEMPORARY DRAMA 1953-1986

D.E.S. MAXWELL, *formerly Department of English, York University, Ontario, Canada*

CONTEMPORARY IRISH POETRY

DECLAN KIBERD, *Department of English, University College, Galway*

SEAMUS DEANE, *Editor*

James Joyce

(1882-1941)

Before Joyce, Irish writers had been compelled to define themselves within the conventions of an English-speaking world. Their Irish backgrounds and experiences made this difficult, because in Ireland many of those conventions and protocols of law, manners, custom, economic thought, literary form, class and political deference simply did not obtain. The recording of Irish difference in these matters encouraged the production of writings that had a greater sociological than literary value. The registering of Irish protest brought into existence a considerable prison literature and much polemical historical writing and reminiscence. Most of the attempts to create a literature that was rooted in the actualities of Irish experience were hampered by the fact that the audience for them was largely English; therefore, the fact of Irish difference was transmuted into an acceptance of Irish quaintness and, on that premise, the idea of Irish national character could be formulated and adapted to benign or malign purposes. It seemed to many commentators on Irish affairs that there was an ineradicable distinction between the Irish and the English as such and that the Irish problem, no matter how charitably or brutally confronted, always would remain, in one form or another, as an enduring expression of that distinction. The imperial power established a norm and the Irish deviation from that was considered to be a matter of amusement or distaste.

In one sense, the choice facing Irish writers was simple. They could repudiate Ireland as provincial, if interesting, and go to the metropolitan centre of London, where their writing could address more general issues and be liberated from the endless cycle of Ireland's subjugation and rebellion and from its marginalized and maimed culture. On the other hand, they could enter upon the act of repossession through translation, the double translation of the largely Gaelic past into modern English and the modification of English that would be the consequence of success. This led to a series of disputes centring on the need felt by some to deanglicize Ireland and by others to hibernicize England or, at least, the English language. Allied to this was the conviction that there were important respects in which Irish experience was an alternative to English experience, not simply an ancillary curiosity. The almost fetishistic concern with Ireland as the last of the Celtic nations, or as the former harbinger of Christianity to the Middle Ages, or as the national culture which queried the assumptions of the world-imperial power more challengingly than any other, feeds off and is fed by this conviction. Ireland is not, in this light, a peripheral culture, but a central one masked in peripherality. The aim, then, politically and aesthetically, is to unmask that culture and demonstrate its otherness in relation to England and its unique importance to the world.

Both Yeats and Joyce embarked on this project and, astonishingly, both brought it to a successful conclusion, although by entirely different means. Like any revolutionary, Yeats believed in the need for secret societies, propaganda and an ultimate renovation of a decayed world. His revolutionary methods demanded great powers of organization and a degree of political acumen in the handling of different factions. These he had in abundance. Joyce, on the other hand, was a lonely anarchist, a man who repudiated all that he had inherited and spent his life in perfecting the ultimate weapon of destruction that would restore everything to its primal, unstructured essence. His revolution was a carefully phased, cumulative business. One of its subtlest and most unexpected turns was its dismantling of the stereotype of the revolutionist himself — in this case, Stephen Dedalus and his replacement by a version of Everyman, first as Leopold Bloom and then as HCE in *Finnegans Wake*. Most of all, Joyce portrayed his heroic rebel as a foreigner within his native culture and as a native in his peregrine sojourns in the other, foreign world. He discovered that the form of Ireland's desire for centrality was merely a symptom of its anxiety about peripherality. Joyce sought to redirect that desire and, in so doing, had to reconsider the issues of language and form which Irish nationalism, in its political and literary manifestations, had raised.

All the important Irish writers from 1880 to 1950, from Wilde to Beckett, are self-conscious about the virtuosity of their language. Wilde, Shaw, Moore, Yeats, Synge, Joyce, O'Casey and Beckett are linguistic performers, showing how completely they are in possession of a language that is, in varying ways, not natively their own. It is something they have created, as well as something by which they have been made creative. Sometimes even their names participate in this process. Wilde becomes Oscar, Shaw becomes GBS, Yeats becomes WBY and John Casey becomes John Cassidy and then Seán O'Casey. Like Moore, O'Casey, when he writes autobiography, writes in the third person about himself as, in his peculiar way, does Joyce when he writes about Stephen in *A Portrait of the Artist as a Young Man*. There is intimacy and distance, strangely combined, here. Imported vocabularies predominate. Moore finds several — in Paris, in London, in the West of Ireland and in Dublin; Shaw finds vocabularies in Darwinism and socialism; Yeats in occultism; Beckett in verticalism and in Descartes; Synge in Irish country speech; O'Casey in Dublin street speech and in the Bible. These imports are consumed with great aplomb, but they retain that flavour of glamour and foreignness which somehow earns these writers the reward of being *echt Irische*, true natives. Joyce dominates them all in this respect, because he was not only an absorber of foreign vocabularies, but finally made English itself foreign and, in doing so, fulfilled his credentials as an Irish writer of this period. Yet, to finish as such an omnivorous consumer, he had an odd beginning as a penurious stylist. This is a crucial aspect of his complicated development.

Dubliners is a series of economical accounts of betrayed desire. The paralysis that pervades the city and its inhabitants is like a plague generated from within. The city is closed; there are no exits, just struggles to escape. The style is not only a mimicry of this condition. It is also self-consciously a style, a formal equivalent to and description of a preordained state. Everything is limited — the range of vocabulary, the syntactical manoeuvres, the allegorical possibilities. The extremity of the general and individual situations is defined by the restraint with which they are presented. Yet the comparative monotony of the language, its constant treading on the threshold of larger meanings that prove elusive, enforces the sense of an alienation that is within the words themselves. This is a language that is foreign to the native situation it describes. It is naturalistic but with a longing for symbol. It cannot attain the symbolic level because to do so would betray the actuality. But that is the point. Language involves a betrayal of experience. It is not, even under the most fastidiously severe control, coincident with it. This is Joyce's obsession. Ireland, the land of betrayers and betrayals, duplicates in its literature the betrayal at the heart of its own condition. Where language is felt to be treacherous, and treachery is native, then language is a betrayal of a betrayal. This makes foreignness important. The only path to foreignness is that of exile, and in exile one is forced to take account of a foreign language and of the foreignness of language. Joyce, in other words, resumes the debates of the nineteenth century in Ireland about the relationship between native and foreign culture and the co-operative effort that would recast one in terms of the other. But in his case the debate was carried further: to the consideration of the status of language itself and the dialectic between that which was immediate, given and native — experience — and that which was secondary, stylized and foreign — language.

For all that, Joyce remained, at one level, an anti-clerical Irish nationalist with socialist leanings, close to Fenianism and even closer to the position of Michael Davitt. It is ironically appropriate that he should have expounded this position in the Italian language, in his lectures and newspaper articles for a Triestine audience. Joyce's struggle with his heritage is both linguistic and political. Ireland's two masters — the British and the Roman catholic empires — provided two languages which Ireland needed to dismantle and repossess for the sake of intellectual freedom. Joyce is insistent on the interconnection between these two; like the Fenians, he saw the church as one of the instruments of British power in Ireland, as well as a power in its own right for which Ireland was merely an instrument in its struggle to regain its lost influence in England. Irish nationalists, who saw Britain only as the enemy, were, like the Citizen in *Ulysses*, monocular, Cyclopean revolutionaries, who were willing to suffer the enslavement of catholicism while protesting against the enslavement of imperialism. In the story of Parnell's downfall, the British and catholic forces had combined to destroy an Irish leader, enabled to do so in the end by the Irish themselves, who had betrayed their leader and had also thereby betrayed the degree to which they were still enslaved. The sexual scandal at the heart of the Parnell crisis only emphasized the alliance between British Victorianism and catholic Jansenism. It is not surprising that Joyce should have tried to counter the dual British-Roman catholic spiritual monarchy by attributing to sexual freedom a central role in his rebellion against the established powers. As is often the case in early modernist literature, the sexual relationship is seen as the ultimately private area that has been invaded and conquered by the forces of political and social convention. Mind, body and feeling are shackled by religious and political chains, and not even an intellectual Houdini like Stephen can escape from them. The wonderful freedom of Molly Bloom rests on her refusal even to acknowledge these chains. For her, they are phantom bonds upon which men confer reality and by which they therefore bind themselves.

The language of catholicism is inverted by Stephen into the language of his aesthetic theory both in *A Portrait* and in *Ulysses*. However, in the later novel its deficiencies are glaringly obvious and are in proportion to its ingenuity. In trying to annihilate the female principle — the figure of the mother — Stephen does little more than display the homology between Irish catholicism and Irish nationalism as maternally based and provincial myths. He does not and cannot bring his proposed heresy any further because it is dependent for its intellectual coherence upon a denial of feeling and, most especially, upon a denial of the feelings that govern the sexual life. It is a theory without vitality or, if you like, without the vitalism that is Molly's (and Joyce's) response to the dismembered experience of Irish history. Catholicism supplies the idea of wholeness; it provides the connection with European and world history, or at least a connection with these which is independent of and prior to the connection furnished by the British imperial system. But it disallows love, it disavows freedom and it is a friend to imperial oppression and an enemy to the desire for liberation that even a maimed nationalism retains.

The language of the Empire, on the other hand, while it has its specialized aspects, particularly in literature, is the language of everyday use. To invert it is to invert everything that is within the range of conventional speech and writing. The techniques necessary for this are multiple and dislocating — interior monologue, parody, pastiche, typographical variation, systems of interconnection borrowed from encyclopaedias, dictionaries, catechisms, advertising posters, puns, slips of the tongue, dreams, propaganda, gossip, chance meetings. All these are used in *Ulysses*. In *Finnegans Wake* language is disordered to the point of deliquescence, at which words, syllables and sounds melt into one another so confusedly that the English that predominates is seen as an emergent rather than as a developed language. It is both foreign and familiar, beginning to be familiar and yet remaining indisputably foreign. It is a literary way of reimagining English in Irish terms, to bring it back towards its original matrix and so let it develop within the confines of a human narrative to which Irish experience is central. This is Joyce's brilliant, complicated way of solving the centrality-peripherality issue, although the Herculean labour involved in such a reconstitution of language may be thought by his readers to be excessive in its demands. Nevertheless, it is a demonstration of the Babel that the monoglot empire produces in its conquered territories, a reverse translation of the single imperial language into all its contributory parts, as well as a rewriting of that language in terms of the history of the country that had consistently found cultural ways and means to disclaim the reality of political and economic subjugation. The cultural triumph of this version of Irish nationalism is to make the English language a peculiarly Irish possession. The arrogance of Joyce's attempt makes the effort to revive the Irish language seem a comparatively modest ambition.

It is therefore instructive to see Joyce's fiction in conjunction with his political writings. There is nothing extraordinary in the political writings themselves, although his view of James Clarence Mangan and his consistent view of Ireland as a culture that needs reclamation both have an important bearing on the literary work, for all the fiction has a formal characteristic that is a Joycean response to the fact of suppression. Each of the four great books — *Dubliners*, *A Portrait*, *Ulysses* and *Finnegans Wake* — ends with the liberation of a voice that had been initially suppressed. In 'The Dead', the last story in *Dubliners*, it is the voice of the dead that finally speaks through the song that recalls Michael Furey and also recalls to Gabriel and Gretta the feelings that have been deadened in their own marriage. 'Ivy Day in the Committee Room' is the prelude to 'The Dead'. In it, the same gesture is repeated. After a sequence of shadowy references, the name of Parnell emerges from the chiaroscuro of the committee room and, almost as in a seance, the voice of Parnell is heard through the medium of the poem that ends the story. Extinguished, then revived, then revitalized, Parnell returns to dominate the text that had been dominated by his absence. So too in *A Portrait*, Stephen, at first overwhelmed by the political, literary and religious views and vocabularies of his elders, rebels and resists to the point at which his voice finally takes over the narration of the story, and his declaration of faith in the entirely other discipline of art and soul that will redeem his race supervenes over all else. In *Ulysses*, it is the voice of Molly, first heard in Episode 4, then silenced, which closes and retrospectively alters the story that Ulysses-Bloom and Telemachus-Stephen until then had possessed. In *Finnegans Wake*, the suppressed letter, finally delivered, releases the forgiving and lyrical voice of Anna Livia Plurabelle as she leaves her daughter to time and the river and herself rejoins the ocean of eternity. Formally, all the novels enact the liberation of a voice from paralysis, silence, suppression. In his 1907 essay, 'Ireland at the Bar', Joyce goes back twenty-five years to the Maamtrasna murders in County Galway for which an innocent man, Myles Joyce, was hanged. This Joyce knew no English and was tried in an English-speaking court without the benefit of translation:

> The figure of this dumbfounded old man, a remnant of a civilisation not ours, deaf and dumb before his judge, is a symbol of the Irish nation at the bar of public opinion.

That is, in its way, a Joycean epiphany. This Joyce is silent in the face of a victimizing injustice, and his silence is reproduced in a world that therefore cannot hear him or plead his cause. It is out of such a silence that Joyce's language rises, out of a culture 'not ours', beyond representation in a world that is equally 'not ours'. It is in Myles Joyce's incompetence that James Joyce's mastery has its source.

It is of course true that Joyce wrote about Dublin rather than Ireland, even though his Dublin includes all Irish history and all world history in his gigantesque version of its geography and history. He ransacked his own and other people's memories and libraries for details, quite sure, it seems, that in any part one could discover the lineaments of the whole. He lived, as a man, out of the city he lived in as a writer. Perhaps this was the only way in which the actual place could sustain itself in his imagination as a mythical site. His legendary place owes some of its magical quality to the fidelity he bestowed upon its detail. Yet in reproducing even its most sordid and unappealing aspects, he betrayed it, in the benign sense, to the world as the archetypal city, a monument to a terrible history in a dream landscape. In her autobiography, *Life and the Dream* (1947), Mary Colum remembers Joyce's answer when he was asked where he would like best to live:

> 'In a city of about half a million population, an old city built on a river with a woman's name.'
> 'And with a castle inside a courtyard,' I suggested, 'a villainous castle with a villainous history.' He nodded.

from:
JAMES CLARENCE MANGAN (1907)

[This is Joyce's second Italian lecture, translated from the manuscript entitled 'Giacomo Clarenzio Mangan'. It incorporates passages from the address on Mangan that

Joyce delivered in 1902 to the Literary and Historical Society of University College, Dublin and which was published in the university magazine *St Stephen's*. Both essays, but this one in particular, contribute to the myth of Mangan as the doomed romantic poet who embodied in his life and writings the essence of the Irish nation's condition. There are similarities between Joyce's view of Mangan's relationship to Ireland and his own. The posture of heroic integrity, the claim to radical intimacy with Ireland's soul, and the obscurity that is borne for the sake of art are all Joycean features. The difference is that Ireland's incompletion, which Mangan represented in his career, will be overcome in Joyce's completeness. What nationalism had failed to do, Joyce's art would bring to fruition — the articulation of Ireland as a totality rather than the duplicating of its fragmentation.]

There are certain poets who, in addition to the virtue of revealing to us some phase of the human conscience unknown until their time, also have the more doubtful virtue of summing up in themselves the thousand contrasting tendencies of their era, of being, so to speak, the storage batteries of new forces. For the most part, it is in the latter role rather than the former that they come to be appreciated by the masses, who are by nature unable to evaluate any work of true self-revelation, and so hasten to recognize by some act of grace the incalculable aid that the individual affirmation of a poet gives to a popular movement. The most popular act of grace in such cases is a monument, because it honours the dead while it flatters the living. It has also the supreme advantage of finality, since, to tell the truth, it is the most polite and effective way to assure a lasting oblivion of the deceased. In logical and serious countries, it is customary to finish the monument in a decent manner, and have the sculptor, the city officials, orators, and a great crowd of people attend the unveiling. But in Ireland, a country destined by God to be the eternal caricature of the serious world,[1] even when the monuments are for the most popular men, whose character is most amenable to the will of the people, they rarely get beyond the laying of the foundation stone. In the light of the foregoing, perhaps I can give you an idea of the Cimmerian[2] night that enfolds the name of Clarence Mangan when I say that, to the detriment of the noted generosity of the Emerald Isle, up to now no ardent spirit has thought of laying the restless ghost of the national poet with the foundation stone and the usual wreaths. Perhaps the unbroken peace in which he lies will have become so pleasant for him that he will be offended (if mortal accents ever come to that world beyond the grave) at hearing his spectral quiet disturbed by a countryman in exile,[3] at hearing an amateur talk about him in a strange tongue before well-wishing foreigners. . . .

. . . after a childhood passed in the midst of domestic cruelties, misfortunes, and misery, he became a clerk in a third-rate notary's office. He had always been a child of quiet and unresponsive nature, secretly given to the study of various languages, retiring, silent, preoccupied with religious matters, without friends or acquaintances. When he began to write, he immediately attracted the attention of the cultured, who recognized in him an exalted lyrical music and a burning idealism that revealed themselves in rhythms of extraordinary and unpremeditated beauty, to be found, perhaps, nowhere else in the range of English literature except in the inspired songs of Shelley. Thanks to the influence of some literary men, he obtained a position as assistant in the great library of Trinity College, Dublin, a rich treasure of books three times as large as the Victor Emmanuel Library in Rome[4] . . . . There it was that his biographer and friend Mitchel[5] saw him for the first time, and in the preface to the poet's works, he describes the impression made on him by this thin little man with the waxen countenance and the pale hair, who was sitting on the top of a ladder with his legs crossed, deciphering a huge, dusty volume in the dim light.

In this library Mangan passed his days in study and became a competent linguist. He knew well the Italian, Spanish, French and German languages and literatures, as well as those of England and Ireland, and it appears that he had some knowledge of oriental languages, probably some Sanskrit and Arabic. From time to time he emerged from that

1. Joyce used this phrase again in 'Ireland, Island of Saints and Sages' (see p. 7 below).
2. The darkness of the underworld in Greek mythology.

3. The one occasion on which Joyce refers to himself as an exile.
4. The National Library of Italy.
5. John Mitchel (1815-75), a leading member of Young Ireland, edited Mangan's poems: *Poems by James Clarence Mangan* with a biographical introduction by John Mitchel (New York: Haverty, 1859). Mitchel was the first important figure to recruit Mangan as a nationalist poet.

studious quiet to contribute some poems to the revolutionary newspapers,[6] but he took little interest in the nightly meetings of the party. He passed his nights far away. His dwelling was a dark and dingy room in the old city, a quarter of Dublin that even today has the significant name 'The Liberties'.[7] His nights were so many Stations of the Cross among the disreputable dives of 'The Liberties', where he must have made a very strange figure in the midst of the choice flower of the city's low-life — petty thieves, bandits, fugitives, pimps and inexpensive harlots. It is strange to say (but it is the consensus of opinion among his countrymen, who are always ready to testify in such matters) that Mangan had nothing but purely formal intercourse with this underworld. He drank little, but his health was so weakened that drinking produced an extraordinary effect on him. The death mask that is left to us shows a refined, almost aristocratic face, in whose delicate lines it is impossible to discover anything but melancholy and great weariness.

I understand that pathologists deny the possibility of combining the pleasures of alcohol with those of opium, and it seems that Mangan soon became convinced of this fact, because he began to take narcotic drugs immoderately. Mitchel tells us that toward the end of his life Mangan looked like a living skeleton. His face was fleshless, barely covered with a skin as transparent as fine China. His body was gaunt, his eyes, behind whose infrequent glimmerings seemed to be hidden the horrible and voluptuous memories of his visions, were large, fixed, and vacant, his voice slow, weak, and sepulchral. He descended the last steps toward the grave with frightening rapidity. He became mute and ragged. He ate hardly enough to keep body and soul together, until one day he collapsed suddenly while he was walking in the street. When he was carried to the hospital, a few coins and a worn book of German poetry were found in his pockets. When he died, his miserable body made the attendants shudder, and some charitable friends paid the cost of his sordid burial.

So lived and died the man that I consider the most significant poet of the modern Celtic world, and one of the most inspired singers that ever used the lyric form in any country. It is too early, I think, to assert that he must live forever in the drab fields of oblivion, but I am firmly convinced that if he finally emerges into the posthumous glory to which he has a right, it will not be by the help of any of his countrymen. Mangan will be accepted by the Irish as their national poet on the day when the conflict will be decided between my native land and the foreign powers — Anglo-Saxon and Roman Catholic, and a new civilization will arise, either indigenous or completely foreign....

Although he wrote such a wonderful English style, he refused to collaborate with the English newspapers or reviews; although he was the spiritual focus of his time, he refused to prostitute himself to the rabble or to make himself the loud-speaker of politicians. He was one of those strange abnormal spirits who believe that their artistic life should be nothing more than a true and continual revelation of their spiritual life, who believe that their inner life is so valuable that they have no need of popular support, and thus abstain from proffering confessions of faith, who believe, in sum, that the poet is sufficient in himself, the heir and preserver of a secular patrimony, who therefore has no urgent need to become a shouter, or a preacher, or a perfumer.

Now what is this central idea that Mangan wants to hand down to posterity? All his poetry records injustice and tribulation, and the aspiration of one who is moved to great deeds and rending cries when he sees again in his mind the hour of his grief. This is the theme of a large part of Irish poetry, but no other Irish poems are full, as are those of Mangan, of misfortune nobly suffered, of vastation of soul so irreparable. ... Poetry considers many of the idols of the market place unimportant — the succession of the ages, the spirit of the age, the mission of the race. The poet's central effort is to free himself from the unfortunate influence of these idols that corrupt him from without and within, and certainly it would be false to assert that Mangan has always made this effort. The history of his country encloses him so straitly that even in his hours of extreme individual passion he can barely reduce its walls to ruins. He cries out in his life and in his mournful verses against the injustice of despoilers, but almost never laments a loss greater than that of buckles and banners. He inherits the latest and worst part of a tradition upon which no divine hand has ever traced a boundary, a tradition which is loosened and

6. The reference is to *The Nation* newspaper, founded in 1842 as the organ of the Young Ireland movement.

7. The area around St Patrick's Cathedral, just to the west of the city centre. The name was originally a legal term denoting the area over which a person's or corporation's rights or immunities extended.

divided against itself as it moves down the cycles. And precisely because this tradition has become an obsession with him, he has accepted it with all its regrets and failures and would pass it on just as it is. The poet who hurls his lightning against tyrants would establish upon the future an intimate and crueller tyranny. The figure that he adores has the appearance of an abject queen to whom, because of the bloody crimes that she has committed and the no less bloody crimes committed against her by the hands of others, madness has come and death is about to come, but who does not wish to believe that she is about to die, and remembers only the rumour of voices that besiege her sacred garden and her lovely flowers that have become *pabulum aprorum*, food for wild boars. Love of grief, despair, high-sounding threats — these are the great traditions of the race of James Clarence Mangan, and in that impoverished figure, thin and weakened, an hysterical nationalism receives its final justification.

In what niche of the temple of glory should we place his image? If he has never won the sympathy of his own countrymen, how can he win that of foreigners? Doesn't it seem probable that the oblivion that he would almost have desired awaits him? Certainly he did not find in himself the force to reveal to us triumphant beauty, the splendour of truth that the ancients deify. He is a romantic, a herald manqué, the prototype of a nation manqué, but with all that, one who has expressed in a worthy form the sacred indignation of his soul cannot have written his name in water.[8] In those vast courses of multiplex life that surround us, and in that vast memory which is greater and more generous than ours, probably no life, no moment of exaltation is ever lost; and all those who have written in noble disdain have not written in vain, although, weary and [desperate, they have never heard the silver laughter of wisdom.][9]

8. John Keats's epitaph: 'Here lies one whose name was writ in water'.
9. The words in parenthesis are supplied from the 1902 essay on Mangan.

from:
IRELAND, ISLAND OF SAINTS AND SAGES (1907)

[This excerpt is from the first of three lectures that Joyce delivered at the Università Popolare in Trieste in March 1907. His audience would have been able to sympathize with his attitudes, given Trieste's own struggle to escape from Austrian rule.

The first part of the lecture is a sketch of early Christian Ireland. Thereafter, Joyce launches on a description of the modern history of Ireland and her subjugation by British imperialism and Roman catholicism. The question, which he raises in different forms but answers in no satisfactory way, concerns the legitimacy of nationalism. It seems that he would have welcomed a republican secular nationalism; what he saw was a nationalism that was justified in its opposition to British imperialism, but shackled by its fidelity to a catholicism that was no more than an instrument of that same imperialism in Ireland. Neither protestant nor catholic nationalism would be liberating. Ireland still awaited, with increasing impatience, the movement that would lead to a genuine revival.

The text for this and the following excerpts from lectures and newspaper articles is that given in E. Mason and R. Ellmann (eds), *The Critical Writings of James Joyce* (New York: The Viking Press, Compass Books Edition, 1964).]

. . . But while these last stars[1] still reminded the European nations of Ireland's past glory, a new Celtic race was arising, compounded of the old Celtic stock and the Scandinavian, Anglo-Saxon, and Norman races. Another national temperament rose on the foundation of the old one, with the various elements mingling and renewing the ancient body. The ancient enemies made common cause against the English aggression, with the Protestant inhabitants (who had become *Hibernis Hiberniores*, more Irish than the Irish themselves) urging on the Irish Catholics in their opposition to the Calvinist and Lutheran fanatics from across the sea, and the descendants of the Danish and Norman and Anglo-Saxon settlers championing the cause of the new Irish nation against the British tyranny.

Recently, when an Irish member of parliament was making a speech to the voters on the night before an election, he boasted that he was one of the ancient race and rebuked his opponent for being the descendant of a Cromwellian settler. His rebuke provoked a general laugh in the press, for, to tell the truth, to exclude from the present nation all who are descended from foreign families would be impossible, and to deny the name of patriot to all those

1. The reference is to Johannes Scottus (Ériugena) (*c.*.810-*c.*877) and others, the last great medieval thinkers and scholars of the Irish Christian church.

who are not of Irish stock would be to deny it to almost all the heroes of the modern movement — Lord Edward Fitzgerald, Robert Emmet, Theobald Wolfe Tone and Napper Tandy, leaders of the uprising of 1798, Thomas Davis and John Mitchel, leaders of the Young Ireland movement, Isaac Butt, Joseph Biggar, the inventor of parliamentary obstructionism, many of the anticlerical Fenians, and, finally, Charles Stewart Parnell, who was perhaps the most formidable man that ever led the Irish, but in whose veins there was not even a drop of Celtic blood.[2]

In the national calendar, two days, according to the patriots, must be marked as ill-omened — that of the Anglo-Saxon and Norman invasion, and that, a century ago, of the union of the two parliaments. Now, at this point, it is important to recall two piquant and significant facts. Ireland prides itself on being faithful body and soul to its national tradition as well as to the Holy See. The majority of the Irish consider fidelity to these two traditions their cardinal article of faith. But the fact is that the English came to Ireland at the repeated requests of a native king, without, needless to say, any great desire on their part, and without the consent of their own king, but armed with the papal bull of Adrian IV and a papal letter of Alexander. They landed on the east coast with seven hundred men, a band of adventurers against a nation; they were received by some native tribes, and in less than a year, the English King Henry II celebrated Christmas with gusto in the city of Dublin. In addition, there is the fact that parliamentary union was not legislated at Westminster but at Dublin, by a parliament elected by the vote of the people of Ireland, a parliament corrupted and undermined with the greatest ingenuity by the agents of the English prime minister, but an Irish parliament nevertheless. From my point of view, these two facts must be thoroughly explained before the country in which they occurred has the most rudimentary right to persuade one of her sons to change his position from that of an unprejudiced observer to that of a convinced nationalist.

On the other hand, impartiality can easily be confused with a convenient disregard of facts, and if an observer, fully convinced that at the time of Henry II Ireland was a body torn by fierce strife and at the time of William Pitt was a venal and wicked mess of corruption, draws from these facts the conclusion that England does not have many crimes to expiate in Ireland, now and in the future, he is very much mistaken. When a victorious country tyrannizes over another, it cannot logically be considered wrong for that other to rebel. Men are made this way, and no one who is not deceived by self-interest or ingenuousness will believe, in this day and age, that a colonial country is motivated by purely Christian motives. These are forgotten when foreign shores are invaded, even if the missionary and the pocket Bible precede, by a few months, as a routine matter, the arrival of the soldiers and the uplifters. If the Irishmen at home have not been able to do what their brothers have done in America, it does not mean that they never will, nor is it logical on the part of English historians to salute the memory of George Washington and profess themselves well content with the progress of an independent, almost socialist, republic in Australia while they treat the Irish separatists as madmen.

A moral separation already exists between the two countries....

The reasons for this difference in temperament, which has now become a commonplace of the phrase-makers of Fleet Street,[3] are in part racial and in part historical. Our civilization is a vast fabric, in which the most diverse elements are mingled, in which nordic aggressiveness and Roman law, the new bourgeois conventions and the remnant of a Syriac religion[4] are reconciled. In such a fabric, it is useless to look for a thread that may have remained pure and virgin without having undergone the influence of a neighbouring thread. What race, or what language (if we except the few whom a playful will seems to have preserved in ice, like the people of Iceland) can boast of being pure today? And no race has less right to utter such a boast than the race now living in Ireland. Nationality (if it really is not a convenient fiction like so many others to which the scalpels of present-day scientists have given the coup de grâce) must find its reason for being rooted in something that surpasses and transcends and informs changing things like blood and the human word....

I find it rather naïve to heap insults on England

2. All these well-known figures were protestant and of English or Norman stock.

3. The street in London in which most newspaper offices were situated.

4. That is, Christianity.

for her misdeeds in Ireland. A conqueror cannot be casual, and for so many centuries the Englishman has done in Ireland only what the Belgian is doing today in the Congo Free State,[5] and what the Nipponese dwarf will do tomorrow in other lands. She enkindled its factions and took over its treasury. By the introduction of a new system of agriculture, she reduced the power of the native leaders and gave great estates to her soldiers. She persecuted the Roman church when it was rebellious and stopped when it became an effective instrument of subjugation. Her principal preoccupation was to keep the country divided, and if a Liberal English government that enjoyed the full confidence of the English voters were to grant a measure of autonomy to Ireland tomorrow, the conservative press of England would immediately begin to incite the province of Ulster against the authority of Dublin.[6]

She was as cruel as she was cunning. Her weapons were, and still are, the battering-ram, the club, and the rope; and if Parnell was a thorn in the English side, it was primarily because when he was a boy in Wicklow he heard stories of the English ferocity from his nurse. A story that he himself told was about a peasant who had broken the penal laws and was seized at the order of a colonel, stripped, bound to a cart, and whipped by the troops. By the colonel's orders, the whipping was administered on his abdomen in such a way that the miserable man died in atrocious pain, his intestines falling out onto the roadway.

The English now disparage the Irish because they are Catholic, poor, and ignorant; however, it will not be so easy to justify such disparagement to some people. Ireland is poor because English laws ruined the country's industries, especially the wool industry, because the neglect of the English government in the years of the potato famine allowed the best of the population to die from hunger, and because under the present administration, while Ireland is losing its population and crimes are almost non-existent, the judges receive the salary of a king, and governing officials and those in public service receive huge sums for doing little or nothing. . . .

Nor is it any harder to understand why the Irish citizen is a reactionary and a Catholic, and why he mingles the names of Cromwell and Satan when he curses. For him, the great Protector of civil rights is a savage beast who came to Ireland to propagate his faith by fire and sword. He does not forget the sack of Drogheda and Waterford, nor the bands of men and women hunted down in the furthermost islands by the Puritan, who said that they would go 'into the ocean or into hell', nor the false oath that the English swore on the broken stone of Limerick.[7] How could he forget? Can the back of a slave forget the rod? The truth is that the English government increased the moral value of Catholicism when they banished it.

Now, thanks partly to the endless speeches and partly to Fenian violence, the reign of terror is over. The penal laws have been revoked. Today, a Catholic in Ireland can vote, can become a government employee, can practise a trade or profession, can teach in a public school, can sit in parliament, can own his own land for longer than thirty years, can keep in his stalls a horse worth more than 5 pounds sterling, and can attend a Catholic mass, without running the risk of being hanged, drawn, and quartered by the common hangman. But these laws have been revoked such a short time ago that a Nationalist member of parliament who is still living was actually sentenced by an English jury to be hanged, drawn, and quartered for the crime of high treason by the common hangman (who is a mercenary in England, chosen by the sheriff from among his mercenary colleagues for conspicuous merit in diligence or industry).

The Irish populace, which is ninety per cent Catholic, no longer contributes to the maintenance of the Protestant church, which exists only for the well-being of a few thousand settlers. It is enough to say that the English treasury has suffered some loss, and that the Roman church has one more daughter. With regard to the educational system, it allows a few streams of modern thought to filter slowly into

5. Leopold II of Belgium organized the Congo Free State in 1885 with himself as absolute monarch and chief stockholder of the company formed to exploit its resources. By 1904 reports in the international press of abuses against the native people who worked in the mines and on the rubber plantations provoked an outcry of protest. The atrocities were documented by Roger Casement (1864-1916).

6. This did in fact happen five years later with the Home Rule crisis. The Conservative Party and the press supported Ulster unionism against the British government and the idea of a Home Rule government in Dublin.

7. The Treaty of Limerick (1691), which ended the Williamite wars in Ireland, guaranteed Irish catholics religious toleration. The protestant Irish parliament broke this clause in the treaty and passed the system of penal laws which extinguished the catholics as a political force in the country in the eighteenth century.

the arid soil. In time, perhaps there will be a gradual reawakening of the Irish conscience, and perhaps four or five centuries after the Diet of Worms,[8] we will see an Irish monk throw away his frock, run off with some nun, and proclaim in a loud voice the end of the coherent absurdity that was Catholicism and the beginning of the incoherent absurdity that is Protestantism.

But a Protestant Ireland is almost unthinkable. Without any doubt, Ireland has been up to now the most faithful daughter of the Catholic church. . . .

Is this country destined to resume its ancient position as the Hellas of the north some day? Is the Celtic mind, like the Slavic mind which it resembles in many ways, destined to enrich the civil conscience with new discoveries and new insights in the future? Or must the Celtic world, the five Celtic nations, driven by stronger nations to the edge of the continent, to the outermost islands of Europe, finally be cast into the ocean after a struggle of centuries? Alas, we dilettante sociologists are only second-class augurers. We look and peer into the innards of the human animal, and, after all, confess that we see nothing there. Only our supermen know how to write the history of the future.

It would be interesting, but beyond the scope I have set myself tonight, to see what might be the effects on our civilization of a revival of this race. The economic effects of the appearance of a rival island near England, a bilingual, republican, self-centred, and enterprising island with its own commercial fleet, and its own consuls in every port of the world. And the moral effects of the appearance in old Europe of the Irish artist and thinker — those strange spirits, frigid enthusiasts, sexually and artistically untaught, full of idealism and unable to yield to it, childish spirits, ingenuous and satirical, 'the loveless Irishmen', as they are called. But in anticipation of such a revival, I confess that I do not see what good it does to fulminate against the English tyranny while the Roman tyranny occupies the palace of the soul.[9]

I do not see the purpose of the bitter invectives against the English despoiler, the disdain for the vast Anglo-Saxon civilization, even though it is almost entirely a materialistic civilization, nor the empty boasts that the art of miniature in the ancient Irish books, such as the *Book of Kells*, the *Yellow Book of Lecan*, the *Book of the Dun Cow*, which date back to a time when England was an uncivilized country, is almost as old as the Chinese, and that Ireland made and exported to Europe its own fabrics for several generations before the first Fleming arrived in London to teach the English how to make bread. If an appeal to the past in this manner were valid, the fellahin of Cairo would have all the right in the world to disdain to act as porters for English tourists. Ancient Ireland is dead just as ancient Egypt is dead. Its death chant has been sung, and on its gravestone has been placed the seal. The old national soul that spoke during the centuries through the mouths of fabulous seers, wandering minstrels, and Jacobite poets disappeared from the world with the death of James Clarence Mangan. With him, the long tradition of the triple order of the old Celtic bards ended; and today other bards, animated by other ideals, have the cry.

One thing alone seems clear to me. It is well past time for Ireland to have done once and for all with failure. If she is truly capable of reviving, let her awake, or let her cover up her head and lie down decently in her grave forever. 'We Irishmen,' said Oscar Wilde one day to a friend of mine,[10] 'have done nothing, but we are the greatest talkers since the time of the Greeks.' But though the Irish are eloquent, a revolution is not made of human breath and compromises. Ireland has already had enough equivocations and misunderstandings. If she wants to put on the play that we have waited for so long, this time let it be whole, and complete, and definitive. But our advice to the Irish producers is the same as that our fathers gave them not so long ago — hurry up! I am sure that I, at least, will never see that curtain go up, because I will have already gone home on the last train.

8. In 1521 at Worms, a city on the Rhine, Martin Luther was summoned before Emperor Charles V to defend his protestant teachings. He refused to renounce them and was formally declared to be an outlaw.
9. Lord Byron, 'Childe Harolde's Pilgrimage', Canto II, stanza 6, has the phrase, 'palace of the soul', first used by Edmund Waller (1606-87) in 'Of Tea' in *Poems* (1645).

10. The 'friend' was Yeats.

from: THE HOME RULE COMET (1910)

[This excerpt is from the sixth of the nine articles Joyce wrote about Ireland and Irish affairs for the Triestine newspaper *Il Piccolo della Sera* between 1907 and 1912. Looking at the new situation created by the general election of December 1910 in Britain, he forecasts a double betrayal — of Ireland by England and of Ireland by herself. The incompatability between the Irish and the 'Anglo-Saxon' system is a theme often broached by Joyce. He is, in that respect, an inheritor of the arguments of previous generations of Irish nationalists and English liberals (Matthew Arnold, for example) in his belief that the English system is too materialistic for the more 'spiritual' and imaginative Irish.]

The idea of Irish autonomy has gradually become surrounded with a pallid and tenuous substantiality, and just a few weeks ago, when a royal decree dissolved the English parliament,[1] something pale and wavering was seen dawning in the East. It was the Home Rule comet, vague, distant, but as punctual as ever. The sovereign Word which in an instant made twilight fall on the demi-gods at Westminster had called from the darkness and the void the obedient and unknowing star.

This time, however, it could be made out very poorly because the skies were cloudy. The fog which usually covers the British shores grew so thick that it cloaked them in a fixed and impenetrable cloud bank, behind which could be heard the orchestral music of the electoral elements in discord — the fiddles of the nobles agitated and hysterical, the raucous horns of the people, and, from time to time, a passing phrase on the Irish flutes. . . .

In the midst of such confusions it is easy to understand how the dispatches contradict themselves, and announce that Home Rule is at the door, and write its obituary six hours later. The uninitiated cannot be too sure in the case of comets, but at any rate the passage of the celestial body so long awaited has been communicated to us by the official observatory.

Last week, the Irish leader Redmond[2] proclaimed the happy news to a crowd of fishermen. English democracy, he said, has broken the power of the Lords once and for all,[3] and within a few weeks, perhaps, Ireland will have her independence. Now, it is necessary to be a voracious nationalist to be able to swallow such a mouthful. As soon as it is seated on the ministerial benches, the Liberal cabinet will be confronted by a conglomeration of troubles, among which the foremost is the double balance.[4] When this matter is settled for good or for bad, peers and commoners will declare a treaty of peace in honour of the coronation of George V.[5] So far the way is clear, but only prophets can tell us where a government as heterogeneous as the present one will end. To remain in power, will it try to appease the Welsh and the Scots with ecclesiastical and agrarian measures? If the Irish exact autonomy as the price for the support of their votes, will the cabinet hasten to blow the dust off one of their many Home Rule bills and present it to the House again?

The history of Anglo-Saxon liberalism teaches us the answer to these and similarly ingenuous questions very clearly. The Liberal ministers are scrupulous men, and once again the Irish problem will cause symptomatic rifts in the body of the cabinet, in the face of which it will plainly appear that the English electorate really did not authorize the government to legislate in its favour. And, following the Liberal strategy (which aims to wear down the separatist sentiment slowly and secretly, while creating a new, eager social class, dependent, and free from dangerous enthusiasms, by means of partial concessions), if the government introduces a reform bill, or the semblance of one, which Ireland will haughtily refuse, will not that be the propitious moment for the intervention of the Conservative party? Faithful to its cynical tradition of bad faith, will it not take this occasion to declare the Irish dictatorship intolerable, and start a campaign to reduce the number of Irish members from 80 to 40 on the basis of the depopulation, more unique than rare in a civilized country, which was and still is the bitter fruit of misgovernment?

1. The dissolution of parliament had been brought on by the refusal of the House of Lords to accept the 'people's budget' of David Lloyd George in 1909. In the budget, ambitious, social reforms were to be paid for by a land tax, higher death duties, and a supertax on incomes over £3,000.
2. John Redmond (1856-1918), since 1900 leader of the reunited Irish Parliamentary Party.
3. Herbert Asquith, the British prime minister, needed Redmond's support in his struggle with the House of Lords. Before the 1910 election, Asquith made a public commitment to Home Rule for Ireland. The Parliament Act of 1911 restricted the power of the House of Lords and asserted the legislative supremacy of the Commons. In return, Redmond got the Home Rule Bill of 1912.
4. The double balance between the Liberals and the Unionists, each of whom won 272 seats in the election, rested on the Labour Party, with 47 votes, and the Irish Party, with 84 votes.
5. George V became king in 1910 at the height of the struggle between Asquith and the House of Lords.

The connection, then, between the abolition of the Lords' veto and the granting of autonomy to the Irish is not as immediate as some would have us believe. In the final count, that is the business of the English themselves, and admitting that the English people no longer have the worship for their spiritual and temporal fathers that they once had, it is still probable that they will proceed with the reform of the upper house as slowly and cautiously as they are proceeding with the reform of their medieval laws, with the reform of their pompous and hypocritical literature, with the reform of their monstrous judicial system. And in anticipation of these reforms, it will matter very little to the credulous ploughman in Ireland whether Lord Lansdowne or Sir Edward Grey[6] rules the lot of the Ministry of Foreign Affairs.

The fact that Ireland now wishes to make common cause with British democracy should neither surprise nor persuade anyone. For seven centuries she has never been a faithful subject of England. Neither, on the other hand, has she been faithful to herself. She has entered the British domain without forming an integral part of it. She has abandoned her own language almost entirely and accepted the language of the conqueror without being able to assimilate the culture or adapt herself to the mentality of which this language is the vehicle. She has betrayed her heroes, always in the hour of need and always without gaining recompense. She has hounded her spiritual creators into exile only to boast about them. She has served only one master well, the Roman Catholic Church, which, however, is accustomed to pay its faithful in long term drafts.

What long term alliance can exist between this strange people and the new Anglo-Saxon democracy? The phrase-makers who speak so warmly about it today will soon see (if they do not see it already) that between the English nobles and the English workers there is a mysterious communion of blood; and that the highly praised Marquis of Salisbury[7], a refined gentleman, spoke not only for his caste but for his race when he said: 'Let the Irish stew in their own juice.'

6. Henry Petty-Fitzmaurice (1845-1927), 5th marquis of Lansdowne, was British foreign secretary 1900-05, but his appointment was widely criticized. Viscount Edward Grey (1862-1933), Grey of Falloden, succeeded him and served as foreign secretary until 1916, the longest continuous tenure of that office.
7. Lord Salisbury (1830-1903), British prime minister 1885-86, 1886-92, 1895-1902. He was a confirmed unionist.

from: THE SHADE OF PARNELL (1912)

[This essay, the seventh in the sequence for *Il Piccolo della Sera*, shows Joyce's hatred for the English liberalism exemplified by Gladstone and for the treachery of the Irish in aiding the hypocritical English to destroy their own great leader. The mythical status that Joyce gives to Parnell is part and not cause of the legend that grew around the leader both within and without literary circles. Ultimately, Joyce admires Parnell's disdain and the nobility that was enhanced in him by the recognition of the inevitable treachery of others. These aspects of Parnell, like some of those he found in Mangan, are incorporated into Joyce's own myth of himself.]

By passing the bill for parliamentary autonomy on its second reading,[1] the House of Commons has resolved the Irish question, which, like the hen of Mugello, looks newborn, though it is a hundred years old. The century which began with the transaction of buying and selling the Dublin parliament is now closing with a triangular pact between England, Ireland, and the United States.[2] It was graced with six Irish revolutionary movements which, by the use of dynamite, rhetoric, the boycott, obstructionism, armed revolt, and political asssassination,[3] have succeeded in keeping awake the slow and senile conscience of English Liberalism.

The present law was conceived, in the full maturity of time, under the double pressure of the Nationalist party at Westminster which has been jumbling up the workings of the British legislative body for half a century, and the Irish party across the Atlantic, which is blocking the greatly desired

1. The Third Home Rule Bill was introduced to the House of Commons in April 1912. It was January 1913 before it passed its third reading. The House of Lords delayed it for two years and it was signed into law in September 1914, was suspended for the duration of the Great War and was finally superseded by the Government of Ireland Act 1920.
2. Joyce seems to be claiming that the Home Rule Bill of 1912 was linked to the Arbitration Treaty between England and the United States, signed in August 1911. There is no foundation for this view, although it is true that the Arbitration Treaty issue had aroused Irish-American opposition to any hint of an alliance between England and the USA at least since 1904.
3. There were more than six. They include: O'Connell's campaign for catholic emancipation; his later campaign for the repeal of the Union; the Tithe War of 1834; the Young Ireland movement and the rising of 1848; the Fenian organization and the rising of 1867, followed by dynamiting campaigns in Britain and the Phoenix Park murders of 1882; the Land War of the 1880s; and the obstructionist tactics of the Home Rule campaign carried on in the House of Commons by the Irish Parliamentary Party.

Anglo-American alliance. Conceived and moulded with masterful cunning and art, the law forms a worthy capstone to the tradition handed down to posterity by that pluterperfect[4] Liberal statesman, William Gladstone. It suffices to say that, while it reduces the strong phalanx of 103 Irish members actually represented at Westminster to a band of 40 representatives, it pushes these into the arms of the little Labour party; and from this incestuous embrace there will probably be born a coalition which will operate from the left, that is to say from the Liberal party's point of operations in its campaign against Conservatism to the extreme left.

Into its tangle of financial qualifications, there is no chance of penetrating. At any rate, the Irish government about to be born will have to cover a deficit ably created by the British treasury, either by manipulation of local and imperial taxes, or by a reduction of its administrative expenses, or by an increase in direct taxes, in any case provoking the disillusioned hostility of the middle and lower classes. The Irish separatist party would like to reject this Greek gift, which makes the Chancellor of the Exchequer in Dublin a titular minister fully responsible to the taxpayers and at the same time dependent on the British cabinet, one who has the power to tax without being able to control the collections of his department — a transmitter which cannot work unless the dynamo at London sends a current of the necessary voltage.

It doesn't matter — there is an appearance of autonomy. At the recent national assembly held at Dublin, the recriminations and protests of the Nationalists who belong to the bitterly sceptical school of John Mitchel[5] did not disturb the popular rejoicing very much. The representatives, grown old in the constitutional struggle and weakened by so many years of deluded hopes, hailed in their speeches the end of a long era of misunderstanding. A young orator, Gladstone's nephew,[6] invoked the name of his uncle amid the frenzied acclamation of the crowd, and hailed the prosperity of the new nation. Within two years at the most, with or without the consent of the House of Lords, the doors of the old Irish parliament will be reopened; and Ireland, released from its century-old prison, will walk forth toward the palace like a new bride, escorted by musicians and ritual bridal torches. A grand-nephew of Gladstone, if there is one, will scatter flowers beneath the feet of the sovereign; but there will be a ghost at the banquet — the shade of Charles Parnell.

His most recent critic has tried to minimize the greatness of this strange spirit by pointing out the different sources of his agile parliamentary tactics. But even if we grant the historical critic that obstructionism was invented by Biggar and Ronayne,[7] that the doctrine of the independence of the Irish party was launched by Gavan Duffy,[8] that the Agrarian League was the creation of Michael Davitt,[9] these concessions only make more conspicuous the extraordinary personality of a leader who, without forensic gifts or any original political talent, forced the greatest English politicians to carry out his orders; and, like another Moses, led a turbulent and unstable people from the house of shame to the verge of the Promised Land.

The influence exerted on the Irish people by Parnell defies critical analysis. He had a speech defect and a delicate physique; he was ignorant of the history of his native land; his short and fragmentary speeches lacked eloquence, poetry, and humour; his cold and formal bearing separated him from his own colleagues; he was a Protestant, a descendant of an aristocratic family, and, as a crowning disgrace, he spoke with a distinct English accent. He would often come to meetings an hour or an hour and a half late without apologizing. He would neglect his correspondence for weeks on end. The applause and anger of the crowd, the abuse and praise of the press, the denunciations and defence of the British ministers never disturbed the melancholy serenity of his character. It is even said that he did not know by sight many of those who sat with him on the Irish benches. When the Irish people presented him with a national gratuity of 40,000 pounds sterling in 1887,[10] he put the cheque into his billfold, and in the speech which he delivered to the

4. Translation of Joyce's Italian epithet *sopraperfetto*.
5. John Mitchel (1815-75), the fiercest and most bitter of the Young Irelanders.
6. This is not Gladstone's nephew, but his son, Herbert John (Viscount) Gladstone (1854-1930), who was sympathetic to Home Rule or, failing that, to some form of self-government for Ireland.
7. Two Irish Parliamentary Party MPs. Joseph Biggar (1828-90) is generally credited with initiating the policy of obstruction. Joseph P. Ronayne (1822-76) was MP for Cork.
8. Sir Charles Gavan Duffy (1816-1903) was a founder of the Independent Irish Party in 1852.
9. Michael Davitt (1846-1906) played a vital role in the founding of the Land League in 1879.
10. The Parnell Tribute of 1883 raised over £37,000.

immense gathering made not the slightest reference to the gift which he had received.

When he was shown the copy of *The Times* containing the famous autograph letter which would have proved his implication in the barbarous assassination in the Phoenix Park, he put his finger on one letter in the handwriting and said simply, 'I have not made an 's' that way since '78.' Later, when the inquiries of the Royal Commission revealed the conspiracy which had been formed against him and the perjurer and forger Pigott blew out his brains in a Madrid hotel, the House of Commons, without regard to party, greeted Parnell's entrance with an ovation that remains without precedent in the annals of the British Parliament. Is it necessary to say that Parnell made no response to the ovation with a smile or a bow or a gesture, but merely passed to his place beyond the aisle and sat down? Gladstone was probably thinking of this incident when he called the Irish leader an intellectual phenomenon.

Nothing more unusual can be imagined than the appearance of this intellectual phenomenon in the midst of the moral suffocation of Westminster. Now, looking back at the scene of the drama and hearing again the speeches that shook the minds of his listeners, it is useless to deny that all the eloquence and all those triumphs of strategy begin to smell stale. But time is kinder to the 'uncrowned king' than to the jester and the phrase-maker. The light of his sovereign bearing, mild and proud, silent and disconsolate, makes Disraeli look like a diplomatic opportunist who dines when he can at rich men's houses, and Gladstone like an imposing major domo who has gone to night school. How lightly Disraeli's wit and Gladstone's culture weigh in the balance today. Today how flimsy seem the studied gibes, the greasy locks, and the stupid novels of Disraeli; and the high-sounding periods, the Homeric studies, the speeches on Artemis and on marmalade of Gladstone.[11]

Although Parnell's strategy was to make use of any English party, Liberal or Conservative, at his pleasure, a nexus of circumstances involved him in the Liberal movement. Gladstonian liberalism was an inconstant algebraic symbol whose coefficient was the movement's political pressure and whose index was his personal profit. While he temporized in internal politics, contradicting and justifying himself in turn, he always maintained (as much as he was capable of it) a sincere admiration for liberty in the house of others. It is necessary to keep in mind this elastic quality of Gladstone's liberalism in order to understand the nature and magnitude of Parnell's task.

To put it in few words, Gladstone was a self-seeking politician. He raged at the restless iniquity of O'Connell in 1835,[12] but he was the English legislator who proclaimed the moral and economic necessity for Irish autonomy. He thundered against the admission of Jews to public office, but he was the minister who, for the first time in English history, raised a Jew to the peerage.[13] He spoke fiercely against the Boers who rebelled in 1881, but after the defeat of Majuba he concluded a treaty with Transvaal which the English themselves called a cowardly surrender.[14] In his first parliamentary speech he warmly defended against Earl Grey's accusation of cruelty his own father, a rich slave owner in Demerara who had made two million francs from the sale of human flesh, while in his last letter to another 'childhood friend', the Duke of Westminster, he invoked all the lightning available on the head of the great assassin of Constantinople.[15]

Parnell, convinced that such liberalism would yield only to force, united behind him every element of Irish life and began to march, treading on the verge of insurrection. Just six years after his entrance into Westminster he held in his hands the fate of the government. He was imprisoned, but in his cell at Kilmainham he concluded a pact with the ministers who had imprisoned him.[16] When the

11. Benjamin Disraeli (1804-81), British prime minister 1868, 1874-80, was renowned as a novelist and, to a lesser extent, as a wit. Gladstone wrote copiously and ponderously on all kinds of subjects, from his *Studies on Homer and the Homeric Age* (1858) to his miscellaneous essays, collected in 7 volumes as *Gleanings of Past Years* (1879).

12. Gladstone objected to O'Connell's pact with Lord Melbourne during the Tithe War of 1834.

13. Nathan, Baron Rothschild (1840-1915) was the first member of the Jewish faith to become a peer, in 1885. His father had been the first Jew to become an MP.

14. At the battle of Majuba Hill in February 1881, during the first Boer War, a British force was annihilated. In August 1881 the Pretoria Convention ended the war. By this agreement, Britain recognized the independence of the Transvaal.

15. Gladstone denounced Abdul Hamid II, sultan of Turkey, as inhuman in a letter to the Duke of Westminster in 1897. It was published as a pamphlet, *Letter to the Duke of Westminster*. The issue was the behaviour of the Turks during the Graeco-Turkish war of 1897.

16. The Kilmainham Treaty of 1882 was an agreement between Parnell and Gladstone, designed to defuse the deteriorating situation in Ireland.

attempt at blackmail failed with Pigott's confession and suicide,[17] the Liberal government offered him a portfolio. Parnell not only refused it, he ordered all his followers as well to refuse ministerial duties, and forbade the municipalities and public corporations in Ireland to receive officially any member of the British royal house until the English government should restore autonomy to Ireland. The Liberals had to accept these humiliating conditions, and in 1886 Gladstone read the first Home Rule Bill at Westminster.

Parnell's fall came in the midst of these events like lightning from a clear sky. He fell hopelessly in love with a married woman, and when her husband, Captain O'Shea, asked for a divorce, the ministers Gladstone and Morley[18] openly refused to legislate in favour of Ireland if the sinner remained as head of the Nationalist Party. Parnell did not appear at the hearings to defend himself. He denied the right of a minister to exercise a veto over the political affairs of Ireland, and refused to resign.

He was deposed in obedience to Gladstone's orders. Of his 83 representatives only 8[19] remained faithful to him. The high and low clergy entered the lists to finish him off. The Irish press emptied on him and the woman he loved the vials of their envy. The citizens of Castlecomer threw quicklime in his eyes.[20] He went from county to county, from city to city, 'like a hunted deer',[21] a spectral figure with the signs of death on his forehead. Within a year he died of a broken heart at the age of 45.

The ghost of the 'uncrowned king' will weigh on the hearts of those who remember him when the new Ireland in the near future enters into the palace 'fimbriis aureis circumamicta varietatibus';[22] but it will not be a vindictive ghost. The melancholy which invaded his mind was perhaps the profound conviction that, in his hour of need, one of the disciples who dipped his hand in the same bowl with him would betray him. That he fought to the very end with this desolate certainty in mind is his greatest claim to nobility.

In his final desperate appeal to his countrymen, he begged them not to throw him as a sop to the English wolves howling around them. It redounds to their honour that they did not fail this appeal. They did not throw him to the English wolves; they tore him to pieces themselves.

17. Richard Pigott (1828-89) forged letters which he sold to *The Times* newspaper in an attempt to implicate Parnell and his party in agrarian crime. The forgery was exposed in a special commission. Pigott shot himself in an hotel in Madrid in February 1889.
18. John Morley (1838-1923), twice chief secretary for Ireland and a confidante and eventual biographer of Gladstone. Gladstone wrote Morley a letter, to be shown to the vice-chairman of the Irish Party, saying that, after the uncontested divorce case, Parnell's continued leadership would render his own 'a nullity'.
19. Possibly a misprint for '18'; in the vote in Committee Room 15, 44 voted against and 26 for retention of Parnell as leader.
20. This incident took place in the course of Parnell's last campaign in County Kilkenny in December 1890. He so incensed his audience by his personal attacks on Michael Davitt that he was showered with slaked lime.
21. R. Barry O'Brien, in *The Life of Charles Stewart Parnell* (London, 1898), described Parnell in 1890 as looking like 'a hunted hind' (II, p. 297). In 'The Tragic Generation' in *Autobiographies*, Yeats noted how 'a quotation from Goethe ran through the papers, describing Irish jealousy. "The Irish seem to me like a pack of hounds, always dragging down some noble stag."' The quotation is from Eckermann's *Conversations with Goethe*, entry for 7 April 1829.
22. Psalms 44. 14-15: 'girded with golden fringes, in varied colours'.

from:
STEPHEN HERO (1904-07)

[Written between 1904 and 1907, *Stephen Hero* is Joyce's most ponderously uncompromising statement of repudiation. His position is essentially anarchist. He refuses all forms of authority — church, state and family — and promotes in their place a radical individualism, of which Stephen as artist is the exemplar. The individualism is so pronounced that Stephen does not pursue the revolutionary political implications, because that would involve adherence to a group and a set of doctrines. Instead, he follows the arguments laid down by Michael Davitt in *The Fall of Feudalism in Ireland* (1904), a book he brought with him to Trieste, and rejects the British-Roman catholic panaceas offered Ireland for her ills. The negativity of his response is pure; it is an aristocratic anarchism, rooted in anger and blossoming as disdain. His father is one of the natural and crucial victims of the young man's chill rejection. Stephen's family is a monument to feudalism, which he exposes by practising what he calls the 'vivisective' modern spirit.

The extract, from Chapter XX, is taken from T. Spencer (ed.), *Stephen Hero. Part of the first draft of 'A Portrait of the Artist as a Young Man'*, revised edition by J. J. Slocum and H. Cahoon (London: Jonathan Cape, 1956). The numbering of the chapters follows this edition, not the corrected sequence that will be followed in a forthcoming edition.]

. . . Stephen's father was quite capable of talking himself into believing what he knew to be untrue. He knew that his own ruin had been his own handiwork but he had talked himself into believing that it was the handiwork of others. He had his son's distaste for responsibility without his son's courage. He was one of those illogical wiseacres with whom no evidence can outreason the first impression. His wife had fulfilled her duties to him with startling literalness and yet she had never been able to expiate the offence of her blood. Misunderstanding such as this, which is accepted as natural in higher social grades, is wrongly refused recognition in the burgher class where it is often found to issue in feuds of insatiable, narrow hatred. Mr Daedalus hated his wife's maiden name with a medieval intensity: it stunk in his nostrils. His alliance therewith was the only sin of which, in the entire honesty of his cowardice, he could accuse himself. Now that he was making for the final decades of life with the painful consciousness of having diminished comfortable goods and of having accumulated uncomfortable habits he consoled and revenged himself by tirades so prolonged and so often repeated that he was in danger of becoming a monomaniac. The hearth at night was the sacred witness of these revenges, pondered, muttered, growled and execrated. The exception which his clemency had originally made in favour of his wife was soon out of mind and she began to irritate him by her dutiful symbolism. The great disappointment of his life was accentuated by a lesser and keener loss — the loss of a coveted fame. On account of a certain income and of certain sociable gifts Mr Daedalus had been accustomed to regard himself as the centre of a little world, the darling of a little society. This position he still strove to maintain but at the cost of a reckless liberality from which his household had to suffer both in deed and in spirit. He imagined that while he strove to retain this infatuating position his home affairs would, through the agency of a son whom he made no effort to understand, in some divine manner right themselves. This hope when indulged in would sometimes embitter his affection for a son whom he thereby acknowledged as superior but, now that he was led to suspect that his hope was fatuous, an embitterment of that affection seemed likely to fix itself permanently among his emotional landmarks. His son's notion of aristocracy was not the one which he could sympathise with and his son's silence during the domestic battles no longer seemed to him a conveyed compliment. He was, in fact, sufficiently acute to observe here a covert menace against castellar rights and he would not have been wrong if he had imagined that his son regarded [these] assistance at these tortuous and obscene monologues as the tribute exacted by a father for affording a wayward child a base of supplies....

Stephen did not consider his parents very seriously. In his opinion they had opened up misleading and unnatural relations between themselves and him and he considered their affection for him requited by a studious demeanour towards them and by a genuine goodwill to perform for them a great number of such material services as, in his present state of fierce idealism, he could look upon as trifles. The only material services he would refuse them were those which he judged to be spiritually dangerous and it is as well to admit that this exception all but nullified his charity for he had cultivated an independence of the soul which could brook very few subjections. Divine exemplars abetted him in this. The phrase which preachers elaborate into a commandment of obedience seemed to him meagre, ironical and inconclusive and the narrative of the life of Jesus did not in any way impress him [with] as the narrative of the life of one who was subject to others. When he had been a Roman Catholic in the proper sense of the term the figure of Jesus had always seemed to him too remote and too passionless and he had never uttered from his heart a single fervent prayer to the Redeemer: it was to Mary, as to a weaker and more engaging vessel of salvation, that he had entrusted his spiritual affairs. Now his enfranchisement from the discipline of the Church seemed to be coincident with an [natural] instinctive return to the Founder thereof and this impulse would have led him perhaps to a consideration of the merits of Protestantism had not another natural impulse inclined him to bring even the self-contradictory and the absurd into order. He did not know, besides, whether the haughtiness of the Papacy was not as derivable from Jesus himself as the reluctance to be pressed beyond 'Amen: I say to you' for an account of anything but he was quite sure that behind the enigmatic utterances of Jesus there was a very much more definite conception than any which could be supposed [to] discoverable behind Protestant theology:

— Put this in your diary, he said to transcriptive Maurice.[1] Protestant Orthodoxy is like Lanty McHale's dog: it goes a bit of the road with everyone.

1. Stephen's brother, who records everything.

— It seems to me that S. Paul trained that dog, said Maurice. . . .

[In Chaper XXII, Stephen, at a loose end in Dublin during the summer vacation, goes into the broken-down area of the Liberties, in the neighbourhood of St Patrick's Cathedral, to observe the people and analyze their condition.]

. . . The summer was dull and warm. Nearly every day Stephen wandered through the slums watching the sordid lives of the inhabitants. He read all the street-ballads which were stuck in the dusty windows of the Liberties. He read the racing names and prices scrawled in blue pencil outside the dingy tobacco-shops, the windows of which were adorned with scarlet police journals. He examined all the book-stalls which offered old directories and volumes of sermons and unheard-of treatises [for] at the rate of a penny each or three for twopence. He often posted himself opposite one of the factories in old Dublin at two o'clock to watch the hands coming out to dinner — principally young boys and girls with colourless, expressionless faces, who seized the opportunity to be gallant in their way. He drifted in and out of interminable chapels in which an old man dozed on a bench or a clerk dusted the woodwork or an old woman prayed before the candle she had lighted. As he walked slowly through the maze of poor streets he stared proudly in return for the glances of stupid wonder that he received and watched from under his eyes the great cow-like trunks of police constables swing slowly round after him as he passed them. These wanderings filled him with deep-seated anger and whenever he encountered a burly black-vested priest taking a stroll of pleasant inspection through these warrens full of swarming and cringing believers he cursed the farce of Irish Catholicism: an island [whereof] the inhabitants of which entrust their wills and minds to others that they may ensure for themselves a life of spiritual paralysis,[1] an island in which all the power and riches are in the keeping of those whose kingdom is not of this world, an island in which Caesar [professes] confesses Christ and Christ confesses Caesar that together they may wax fat upon a starveling rabblement which is bidden ironically to take to itself this consolation in hardship 'The Kingdom of God is within you'.

This mood of indignation which was not guiltless of a certain superficiality was undoubtedly due to the excitement of release and it was hardly countenanced by him before he realised the dangers of being a demagogue. The attitude which was constitutional with him was a silent self-occupied, contemptuous manner and his intelligence, moreover, persuaded him that the tomahawk, as an effective instrument of warfare, had become obsolete. He acknowledged to himself in honest egoism that he could not take to heart the distress of a nation, the soul of which was antipathetic to his own, so bitterly as the indignity of a bad line of verse: but at the same time he was nothing in the world so little as an amateur artist. He wished to express his nature freely and fully for the benefit of a society which he would enrich and also for his own benefit, seeing that it was part of his life to do so. It was not part of his life to undertake an extensive alteration of society but he felt the need to express himself such an urgent need, such a real need, that he was determined no conventions of a society, however plausibly mingling pity with its tyranny, should be allowed to stand in his way, and though a taste for elegance and detail unfitted him for the part of demagogue, [in] from his general attitude he might have been supposed not unjustly an ally of the collectivist politicians, who are often very seriously upbraided by [believers] opponents who believe in Jehovahs, and decalogues[2] and judgments [for] with sacrificing the reality to an abstraction.

That kind of Christianity which is called Catholicism seemed to him to stand in his way and forthwith he removed it. He had been brought up in the belief of the Roman supremacy and to cease to be a Catholic for him meant to cease to be a Christian. The idea that the power of an empire is weakest at its borders requires some modification for everyone knows that the Pope cannot govern Italy as he governs Ireland nor is the Tsar as terrible an engine to the tradesmen of S. Petersburg as he is to the little Russian of the Steppes. In fact in many cases the government of an empire is strongest at its borders and it is invariably strongest there in the case when its power at the centre is on the wane. The waves of the rise and fall of empires do not travel with the rapidity of waves of light and it will be perhaps a considerable time before Ireland will be able to understand that the Papacy is no longer

1. The phrase is from Thomas Carlyle's *On Heroes, Hero-Worship and the Heroic in History* (1841).

2. The ten commandments.

going through a period of anabolism.[3] The bands of pilgrims who are shepherded safely across the continent by their Irish pastors must shame the jaded reactionaries of the eternal city by their stupefied intensity of worship in much the same way as the staring provincial newly arrived from Spain or Africa may have piqued the loyalty of some smiling Roman for whom [the his past had but] the future of his race was becoming uncertain as its past had already become obvious. Though it is evident on the one hand that this persistence of Catholic power in Ireland must intensify very greatly the loneliness of the Irish Catholic who voluntarily outlaws himself yet on the other hand the force which he must generate to propel himself out of so strong and intricate a tyranny may often be sufficient to place him beyond the region of reattraction. It was, in fact, the very fervour of Stephen's former religious life which sharpened for him now the pains of his solitary position and at the same time hardened into a less pliable, a less appeasable enmity molten rages and glowing transports on which the emotions of helplessness and loneliness and despair had first acted as chilling influences . . . .

3. constructive metabolism.

[Stephen has proposed to Emma, a fellow student to whom he is deeply attracted, that she should spend one night with him. She has angrily refused and asked him not to speak to her again. He feels disinclined to tell his brother Maurice or his friend Cranly about the incident. Only Lynch receives this confidence. Here, in Chapter XXV, the event sets off a train of reflections on sexual conventions, the influence of the church and the nature of its appeal to Stephen to forsake his unorthodox opinions.]

. . . The next time Stephen met Emma in the street she did not salute him. He did not tell the incident to anyone but Lynch. From Cranly he expected scant sympathy and he was deterred from speaking of it to Maurice because he had still the elder brother's wish to appear successful. The conversation with Lynch had revealed to him with distressing effect the commonplace side of the adventure. He asked himself seriously and often had he expected that she would have answered 'Yes' to his proposal. His mind, he thought, must have been somewhat unbalanced that morning. And yet when he reconsidered his own defence of his conduct he found it just. The economic aspect of the affair did not present itself to him very vividly and, indeed, was only vivid enough to make him deplore the fact that the solution of moral problems should be so hopelessly entangled with merely material considerations. He was not sufficiently doctrinaire to wish to have his theory put to the test by a general [revulsion] revolution of society but he could not believe that his theory was utterly impracticable. The Roman Catholic notion that a man should be unswervingly continent from his boyhood and then be permitted to achieve his male nature, having first satisfied the Church as to his orthodoxy, financial condition, [and] prospects and general intentions, and having sworn before witnesses to love his wife for ever whether he loved her or not and to beget children for the kingdom of heaven in such manner as the Church approved of — this notion seemed to him by no means satisfactory.

During the train of these reflections the Church sent an embassy of nimble pleaders into his ears. These ambassadors were of all grades and of all types of culture. They addressed every side of his nature in turn. He was a young man with a doubtful future and an unusual character: this was the first salient fact. The ambassadors met it without undue pretence or haste. They stated that it was in their power to make smooth many of the ways which promised to be rough and, by diminishing the hardships of the material nature, to allow the unusual character scope and ease to develop and approve itself. He had deplored the entanglement of merely material considerations in a problem of morals and here, at least, was a warrant that if he chose to give ear to the pleadings of the embassy the moral problem in his case would be set on the road of solving itself free from minor and unworthier cares. He had what he called a 'modern' reluctance to give pledges: no pledges were required. If at the end of five years he still persevered in his obduracy of heart he could still seize upon his individual liberty without fear of being called oath-breaker therefor. The practice of due consideration was an old one and a wise one. He himself was the greatest sceptic concerning the perfervid enthusiasms of the patriots. As an artist he had nothing but contempt for a work which had arisen out of any but the most stable mood of the mind. Was it possible that he would exercise less rigour on his life than he desired to exercise on his art? How could he be guilty of such foolishness, of such cynical subordination of the actual to the abstract, if he honestly believed that an institution is to be accounted valuable in proportion to its nearness to some actual human need or energy and that the epithet 'vivisective' should be applied to the modern spirit as distinguished from the ancient or category-burdened spirit. He desired for himself the life of an artist. Well! And he feared that the Church would obstruct his desire. But, during the formulation of his artistic creed, had he not found item after item upheld for him in advance by the greatest and most orthodox doctor of the Church[1] and was it anything but vanity which urged him to seek out the thorny crown of the heretic while the entire theory, in accordance with which his entire artistic life was shaped, arose most conveniently for his purpose out of the mass of Catholic theology? He could not accept wholeheartedly the offers of Protestant belief: he knew that the liberty it boasted of was often only the liberty to be slovenly in thought and amorphous in ritual. No-one, not the most rabid enemy of the Church, could accuse it of being slovenly in thought: the subtlety of its disquisitions had become a byword with demagogues. No-one again could accuse the Church of being amorphous in ritual. The Puritan, the Calvinist, the Lutheran were inimical to art and to exuberant beauty: the Catholic was the friend of him who professed to interpret or divulge the beautiful. Could he assert that his own aristocratic intelligence and passion for a supremely satisfying order in all the fervours of artistic creation were not purely Catholic qualities? The ambassadors did not labour this point.

Besides, they said, it is a mark of the modern spirit to be shy in the presence of all absolute statements. However sure you may be now of the reasonableness of your convictions you cannot be sure that you will always think them reasonable. If you sincerely regard a pledge as an infringement of human liberty you cannot pledge yourself against following a reactionary impulse which is certain to overtake you some day. You cannot leave out of sight the possibility that your views of the world will change to such an extent that you will regard all interference with the course of affairs as the part of such [who] as can still be deluded by hope. In that case what will have become of your life? You will have wasted it in efforts to save people who have neither inclination nor aptitude for freedom. You believe in an aristocracy: believe also in eminence of the aristocratic class and in the order of society which secures that eminence. Do you imagine that manners will become less ignoble, intellectual and artistic endeavour less conditioned, if the ignorant, enthusiastic, spiritual slovens whom we have subjected subject us? Not one of those slovens understands your aims as an artist or wants your sympathy: we, on the contrary, understand your aims and often are in sympathy with them and we solicit your support and consider your comradeship an honour. You are fond of saying that the Absolute is dead. If that be so it is possible that we are all wrong and if once you accept that as a possibility what remains for you but an intellectual disdain. With us you can exercise your contemptuous faculties when you are recognised as one of the patrician order and you will not even be obliged to grant a truce to the very doctrines, the success of which in the world has secured you your patricianship. Make one with us. Your life will be insured from grosser troubles, your art will be safeguarded against the intrusions of revolutionary notions which no artist of whom history tells us has ever made himself champion. Make one with us, on equal terms. In temper and in mind you are still a Catholic. Catholicism is in your blood. Living in an age which professes to have discovered evolution, can you be fatuous enough to think that simply by being wrong-headed you can recreate entirely your mind and temper or can clear your blood of what you may call the Catholic infection? A revolution such as you desire is not brought about by violence but gradually: and, within the Church you have an opportunity of beginning your revolution in a rational manner. You can sow the seeds in the careful furrows entrusted to you and if your seed is good it will propser. But by going into the unnecessary wilderness and scattering your seed broadcast on all soils what harvest will you have? Everything seems to urge you to a course of moderation, of forbearance, and the purified will can surely display itself quite as well in acceptance as in rejection. The trees do not resent autumn nor does any exemplary thing in nature resent its limitations. Neither then do you resent the limitations of compromise....

1. St Thomas Aquinas (1225-74).

from: DUBLINERS (1914)

['Araby' was added to the sequence of stories in October 1905. It was the eleventh in order of composition. As is always the case with the stories in *Dubliners*, precise factual detail can be accumulated as background, but the range of significance is not increased in proportion. The central action is clear. The world of the charity bazaar which the boy finally reaches is a representation of his muted passion for Mangan's sister. Behind both the passion and the bazaar looms desolation and this takes many detailed forms. There is the bleakness of the daily Dublin surroundings, their claustrophobic meanness; there is the vulgarity of the bazaar itself; there is the cheapness of the boy's ostensibly dedicated passion; there is the tawdriness of the 'Eastern' glamour, productive of so much pallid romanticism; there is the wounding recognition of the boy's own vanity and, with that, the complete sense of estrangement from others.

The informed reader can add to this by noting that there was indeed an Araby bazaar opened in Dublin on 15 May 1894 in aid of Jervis Street Hospital, and that reports of the event stressed the contrast between its bright gaiety and the gloom of the hospital it was designed to fund. It is also possible to see the story in relation to those preceding it as an initiation rite into disappointment, and the consequent bearing it has on the book's preoccupation with what Joyce famously described as Dublin's 'paralysis'. It may be that the young protagonist is entering into something more like a cult than a bazaar. The East was already a tired literary cult, refreshed by its association with the more recent and widespread interest in ritual and magic — an avocation of Yeats and many others associated with the Irish literary revival. The story could be an ironic glance at occultism of this sort and the thin diet it offered to an impoverished imagination. The point is that the reverberations of the story are multiple and yet their extent remains uncertain. To demand an ultimate account of these is to ignore or reduce the elusiveness of the language, which is both strict in its economy and liberal in its allusiveness. The careful equilibrium between these coexistent characteristics gives to this story its peculiarly Joycean flavour. It is neither 'realistic' nor 'symbolic'. It treads the previously invisible path between these apparently opposed modes of writing, thereby becoming a mode unique to itself.]

ARABY[1]

North Richmond Street,[2] being blind, was a quiet street except at the hour when the Christian Brothers' School set the boys free. An uninhabited house of two storeys stood at the blind end, detached from its neighbours in a square ground. The other houses of the street, conscious of decent lives within them, gazed at one another with brown imperturbable faces.

The former tenant of our house, a priest, had died in the back drawing-room. Air, musty from having been long enclosed, hung in all the rooms, and the waste room behind the kitchen was littered with old useless papers. Among these I found a few paper-covered books, the pages of which were curled and damp: *The Abbot*, by Walter Scott, *The Devout Communicant* and *The Memoirs of Vidocq*.[3] I liked the last best because its leaves were yellow. The wild garden behind the house contained a central apple-tree and a few straggling bushes under one of which I found the late tenant's rusty bicycle-pump. He had been a very charitable priest; in his will he had left all his money to institutions and the furniture of his house to his sister.

When the short days of winter came dusk fell before we had well eaten our dinners. When we met in the street the houses had grown sombre. The space of sky above us was the colour of ever-changing violet and towards it the lamps of the street lifted their feeble lanterns. The cold air stung us and we played till our bodies glowed. Our shouts echoed in the silent street. The career of our play brought us through the dark muddy lanes behind the houses where we ran the gauntlet of the rough tribes from the cottages, to the back doors of the dark dripping gardens where odours arose from the ashpits, to the dark odorous stables where a coachman smoothed and combed the horse or shook music from the buckled harness. When we returned to the street light from the kitchen windows had filled the areas. If my uncle was seen turning the corner we hid in the shadow until we had seen him safely housed. Or if Mangan's sister came out on the doorstep to call her brother in to his tea we watched her from our shadow peer up and down the street. We waited to see whether she would remain or go in and, if she remained, we left our shadow and walked up to Mangan's steps

1. The Araby charity bazaar was held in the Central Hall of the Royal Dublin Society in Ballsbridge, Dublin from 15-22 May 1894. The story is set on Saturday, 19 May. The bazaar's official closing time was 10.30 pm.
2. Joyce's family lived at 17 North Richmond Street in the north-east part of Dublin from late 1894 to 1896.
3. Walter Scott's *The Abbot* (1820) is a story about a young boy in service to Mary, Queen of Scots. *The Devout Communicant; or, Pious Meditations and Aspirations for the Three Days Before and the Three Days After Receiving the Holy Eucharist* (1813) was a tract by the English Franciscan, Pacificus (or Robert) Baker (1695-1774). *The Memoirs of Vidocq* (1828-29) by Eugene François Vidocq (1775-1857) is an account of the adventures of a criminal turned detective. They are thought to be spurious.

resignedly. She was waiting for us, her figure defined by the light from the half-opened door. Her brother always teased her before he obeyed and I stood by the railings looking at her. Her dress swung as she moved her body and the soft rope of her hair tossed from side to side.

Every morning I lay on the floor in the front parlour watching her door. The blind was pulled down to within an inch of the sash so that I could not be seen. When she came out on the doorstep my heart leaped. I ran to the hall, seized my books and followed her. I kept her brown figure always in my eye and, when we came near the point at which our ways diverged, I quickened my pace and passed her. This happened morning after morning. I had never spoken to her, except for a few casual words, and yet her name was like a summons to all my foolish blood.

Her image accompanied me even in places the most hostile to romance. On Saturday evenings when my aunt went marketing I had to go to carry some of the parcels. We walked through the flaring streets, jostled by drunken men and bargaining women, amid the curses of labourers, the shrill litanies of shop-boys who stood on guard by the barrels of pigs' cheeks, the nasal chanting of street-singers, who sang a *come-all-you* about O'Donovan Rossa,[4] or a ballad about the troubles in our native land. These noises converged in a single sensation of life for me: I imagined that I bore my chalice safely through a throng of foes. Her name sprang to my lips at moments in strange prayers and praises which I myself did not understand. My eyes were often full of tears (I could not tell why) and at times a flood from my heart seemed to pour itself out into my bosom. I thought little of the future. I did not know whether I would ever speak to her or not or, if I spoke to her, how I could tell her of my confused adoration. But my body was like a harp and her words and gestures were like fingers running upon the wires.

One evening I went into the back drawing-room in which the priest had died. It was a dark rainy evening and there was no sound in the house. Through one of the broken panes I heard the rain impinge upon the earth, the fine incessant needles of water playing in the sodden beds. Some distant lamp or lighted window gleamed below me. I was thankful that I could see so little. All my senses seemed to desire to veil themselves and, feeling that I was about to slip from them, I pressed the palms of my hands together until they trembled, murmuring: *'O love! O love!'* many times.

At last she spoke to me. When she addressed the first words to me I was so confused that I did not know what to answer. She asked me was I going to *Araby*. I forgot whether I answered yes or no. It would be a splendid bazaar, she said; she would love to go.

'And why can't you?' I asked.

While she spoke she turned a silver bracelet round and round her wrist. She could not go, she said, because there would be a retreat that week in her convent. Her brother and two other boys were fighting for their caps and I was alone at the railings. She held one of the spikes, bowing her head towards me. The light from the lamp opposite our door caught the white curve of her neck, lit up her hair that rested there and, falling, lit up the hand upon the railing. It fell over one side of her dress and caught the white border of a petticoat, just visible as she stood at ease.

'It's well for you,' she said.

'If I go,' I said, 'I will bring you something.'

What innumerable follies laid waste my waking and sleeping thoughts after that evening! I wished to annihilate the tedious intervening days. I chafed against the work of school. At night in my bedroom and by day in the classroom her image came between me and the page I strove to read. The syllables of the word *Araby* were called to me through the silence in which my soul luxuriated and cast an Eastern enchantment over me. I asked for leave to go to the bazaar on Saturday night. My aunt was surprised and hoped it was not some Freemason affair.[5] I answered few questions in class. I watched my master's face pass from amiability to sternness; he hoped I was not beginning to idle. I could not call my wandering thoughts together. I had hardly any patience with the serious work of life which, now that it stood between me and my desire, seemed to me child's play, ugly monotonous child's play.

On Saturday morning I reminded my uncle that

4. A 'come-all-you' is a popular song, usually political in nature, which opens with those words. Jeremiah O'Donovan Rossa (1831-1915) was one of the fiercest and most popular of the Fenian leaders.

5. Freemasonry was associated with mysterious rites and rituals of a perverse, anti-catholic nature. It had gained notoriety for its elaborate ritualistic irreligion in the decade of the French Revolution.

I wished to go to the bazaar in the evening. He was fussing at the hallstand, looking for the hat-brush, and answered me curtly:

'Yes, boy, I know.'

As he was in the hall I could not go into the front parlour and lie at the window. I left the house in bad humour and walked slowly towards the school. The air was pitilessly raw and already my heart misgave me.

When I came home to dinner my uncle had not yet been home. Still it was early. I sat staring at the clock for some time and, when its ticking began to irritate me, I left the room. I mounted the staircase and gained the upper part of the house. The high cold empty gloomy rooms liberated me and I went from room to room singing. From the front window I saw my companions playing below in the street. Their cries reached me weakened and indistinct and, leaning my forehead against the cool glass, I looked over at the dark house where she lived. I may have stood there for an hour, seeing nothing but the brown-clad figure cast by my imagination, touched discreetly by the lamplight at the curved neck, at the hand upon the railings and at the border below the dress.

When I came downstairs again I found Mrs. Mercer sitting at the fire. She was an old garrulous woman, a pawnbroker's widow, who collected used stamps for some pious purpose.[6] I had to endure the gossip of the tea-table. The meal was prolonged beyond an hour and still my uncle did not come. Mrs. Mercer stood up to go: she was sorry she couldn't wait any longer, but it was after eight o'clock and she did not like to be out late, as the night air was bad for her. When she had gone I began to walk up and down the room, clenching my fists. My aunt said:

'I'm afraid you may put off your bazaar for this night of Our Lord.'

At nine o'clock I heard my uncle's latchkey in the halldoor. I heard him talking to himself and heard the hallstand rocking when it had received the weight of his overcoat. I could interpret these signs. When he was midway through his dinner I asked him to give me the money to go to the bazaar. He had forgotten.

'The people are in bed and after their first sleep now,' he said.

6. Catholic missions collected stamps and sold them to help finance their various endeavours.

I did not smile. My aunt said to him energetically:

'Can't you give him the money and let him go? You've kept him late enough as it is.'

My uncle said he was very sorry he had forgotten. He said he believed in the old saying: 'All work and no play makes Jack a dull boy.' He asked me where I was going and, when I had told him a second time he asked me did I know *The Arab's Farewell to his Steed*.[7] When I left the kitchen he was about to recite the opening lines of the piece to my aunt.

I held a florin tightly in my hand as I strode down Buckingham Street towards the station. The sight of the streets thronged with buyers and glaring with gas recalled to me the purpose of my journey. I took my seat in a third-class carriage of a deserted train. After an intolerable delay the train moved out of the station slowly. It crept onward among ruinous houses and over the twinkling river. At Westland Row Station a crowd of people pressed to the carriage doors; but the porters moved them back, saying that it was a special train for the bazaar. I remained alone in the bare carriage. In a few minutes the train drew up beside an improvised wooden platform. I passed out on to the road and saw by the lighted dial of a clock that it was ten minutes to ten. In front of me was a large building which displayed the magical name.

I could not find any sixpenny entrance and, fearing that the bazaar would be closed, I passed in quickly through a turnstile, handing a shilling to a weary-looking man. I found myself in a big hall girdled at half its height by a gallery. Nearly all the stalls were closed and the greater part of the hall was in darkness. I recognised a silence like that which pervades a church after a service. I walked into the centre of the bazaar timidly. A few people were gathered about the stalls which were still open. Before a curtain, over which the words *Café Chantant* were written in coloured lamps, two men were counting money on a salver. I listened to the fall of the coins.

Remembering with difficulty why I had come I went over to one of the stalls and examined porcelain vases and flowered tea-sets. At the door of the stall a young lady was talking and laughing with two young gentlemen. I remarked their English accents and listened vaguely to their conversation.

'O, I never said such a thing!'

7. A well-known poem by Caroline Sheridan Norton (1808-77).

'O, but you did!'

'O, but I didn't!'

'Didn't she say that?'

'Yes. I heard her.'

'O, there's a . . . fib!'

Observing me the young lady came over and asked me did I wish to buy anything. The tone of her voice was not encouraging; she seemed to have spoken to me out of a sense of duty. I looked humbly at the great jars that stood like eastern guards at either side of the dark entrance to the stall and murmured:

'No, thank you.'

The young lady changed the position of one of the vases and went back to the two young men. They began to talk of the same subject. Once or twice the young lady glanced at me over her shoulder.

I lingered before her stall, though I knew my stay was useless, to make my interest in her wares seem the more real. Then I turned away slowly and walked down the middle of the bazaar. I allowed the two pennies to fall against the sixpence in my pocket. I heard a voice call from one end of the gallery that the light was out. The upper part of the hall was now completely dark.

Gazing up into the darkness I saw myself as a creature driven and derided by vanity; and my eyes burned with anguish and anger.

IVY DAY[1] IN THE COMMITTEE ROOM

['Ivy Day in the Committee Room' takes place on 6 October 1902, the eleventh anniversary of Charles Stewart Parnell's death. Queen Victoria died in 1901; her successor, Edward VII, visited Ireland in July 1903. The municipal election of the story takes place midway between these events.

The emphasis on kingship, monarchy and election is sustained and deliberate. Ireland is leaderless and is ready to choose, as surrogate for Parnell, an English king whose sexual behaviour is more scandalous than Parnell's. As usual, the story is full of specific details that have possible, but not certain, resonances. The committee room of the election headquarters does indeed refer to Committee Room 15 in the House of Commons, in which Parnell was abandoned by all but a minority of his supporters in 1890-91. The fire that old Jack stirs into reluctant life is perhaps representative of a funeral pyre and of the phoenix flame of Fenianism; the shadows it throws on the wall remind us of the heroic past which darkens the present. The canvassing for votes, the inter-party divisions, the drinking, the cheap, sentimental poem, the inertia, the references to the royal son Edward and other sons who have repudiated their fathers, all intensify the effect of semi-darkness and disillusion that were the bitter fruits of the split by which Irish political life was riven after Parnell's defeat and death.

The central issue of the Dublin municipal elections of 1902 was the response of the incoming candidates to the presentation of a loyal address to Edward VII. The leader of the Sinn Féin party, Arthur Griffith, supported those who refused the address, chiefly the candidates of the Irish Socialist Party, founded by James Connolly in 1896. Connolly was a candidate in another ward in this election, but was defeated because of a violent campaign, orchestrated by the catholic clergy, against him and his socialist ideas. Sinn Féin put up no candidates, in line with its abstentionist policies. The church supported the nationalist Irish Parliamentary Party, which of course was opposed by Parnellites, some of whom backed the socialist candidate. Joyce seems to be repudiating the participation in a parliamentary process that merely reinforces Ireland's dependence on the British state and the catholic church. The election was won by the nationalist candidate.

The story is the eighth in order of composition. It was completed by 1905.]

Old Jack raked the cinders together with a piece of cardboard and spread them judiciously over the whitening dome of coals. When the dome was thinly covered his face lapsed into darkness but, as he set himself to fan the fire again, his crouching shadow ascended the opposite wall and his face slowly re-emerged into light. It was an old man's face, very bony and hairy. The moist blue eyes blinked at the fire and the moist mouth fell open at times, munching once or twice mechanically when it closed. When the cinders had caught he laid the piece of cardboard against the wall, sighed and said:

'That's better now, Mr. O'Connor.'

Mr. O'Connor, a grey-haired young man, whose face was disfigured by many blotches and pimples, had just brought the tobacco for a cigarette into a shapely cylinder but when spoken to he undid his handiwork meditatively. Then he began to roll the tobacco again meditatively and after a moment's thought decided to lick the paper.

1. The ivy leaf was worn as a symbol of mourning for Parnell because of its association with his estate, Avondale, near Rathdrum, Co. Wicklow. Since it was evergreen, it was also an emblem of regeneration and loyalty.

'Did Mr. Tierney say when he'd be back?' he asked in a husky falsetto.

'He didn't say.'

Mr. O'Connor put his cigarette into his mouth and began to search his pockets. He took out a pack of thin pasteboard cards.

'I'll get you a match,' said the old man.

'Never mind, this'll do," said Mr. O'Connor.

He selected one of the cards and read what was printed on it:

MUNICIPAL ELECTIONS

ROYAL EXCHANGE WARD

Mr. Richard J. Tierney, P.L.G., respectfully solicits the favour of your vote and influence at the coming election in the Royal Exchange Ward.[2]

Mr. O'Connor had been engaged by Mr. Tierney's agent to canvass one part of the ward but, as the weather was inclement and his boots let in the wet, he spent a great part of the day sitting by the fire in the Committee Room in Wicklow Street with Jack, the old caretaker. They had been sitting thus since the short day had grown dark. It was the sixth of October, dismal and cold out of doors.

Mr. O'Connor tore a strip off the card and, lighting it, lit his cigarette. As he did so the flame lit up a leaf of dark glossy ivy in the lapel of his coat. The old man watched him attentively and then, taking up the piece of cardboard again, began to fan the fire slowly while his companion smoked.

'Ah, yes,' he said, continuing, 'it's hard to know what way to bring up children. Now who'd think he'd turn out like that! I sent him to the Christian Brothers and I done what I could for him, and there he goes boosing about. I tried to make him someway decent.'

He replaced the cardboard wearily.

'Only I'm an old man now I'd change his tune for him. I'd take the stick to his back and beat him while I could stand over him — as I done many a time before. The mother, you know, she cocks him up with this and that . . . .'

'That's what ruins children,' said Mr. O'Connor.

'To be sure it is,' said the old man. 'And little thanks you get for it, only impudence. He takes th'upper hand of me whenever he sees I've a sup taken. What's the world coming to when sons speaks that way to their father?'

'What age is he?' said Mr. O'Connor.

'Nineteen,' said the old man.

'Why don't you put him to something?'

'Sure, amn't I never done at the drunken bowsy ever since he left school? "I won't keep you," I says. "You must get a job for yourself." But, sure, it's worse whenever he gets a job; he drinks it all.'

Mr. O'Connor shook his head in sympathy, and the old man fell silent, gazing into the fire. Someone opened the door of the room and called out:

'Hello! Is this a Freemason's meeting?'[3]

'Who's that?' said the old man.

'Where are you doing in the dark?' asked a voice.

'Is that you, Hynes?' asked Mr. O'Connor.

'Yes. What are you doing in the dark?' said Mr. Hynes, advancing into the light of the fire.

He was a tall slender young man with a light brown moustache. Imminent little drops of rain hung at the brim of his hat and the collar of his jacket-coat was turned up.

'Well, Mat,' he said to Mr. O'Connor, 'how goes it?'

Mr. O'Connor shook his head. The old man left the hearth, and after stumbling about the room returned with two candlesticks which he thrust one after the other into the fire and carried to the table. A denuded room came into view and the fire lost all its cheerful colour. The walls of the room were bare except for a copy of an election address. In the middle of the room was a small table on which papers were heaped.

Mr. Hynes leaned against the mantelpiece and asked:

'Has he paid you yet?'[4]

'Not yet,' said Mr. O'Connor. 'I hope to God he'll not leave us in the lurch tonight.'

Mr. Hynes laughed.

'O, he'll pay you.Never fear', he said.

2. The Royal Exchange Ward is in central Dublin. Tierney is a Poor Law Guardian (P.L.G.), an elected administrator of the Poor Law Unions, or administrative units, set up initially in 1834 and subsequently revised.

3. Hynes asks this because of the atmosphere of darkness and secrecy associated with freemasonry. The word 'bowsy', some lines earlier, is Dublin slang for a person of no worth.

4. He is asking O'Connor if Tierney has paid him yet for canvassing on his behalf. This is an early instance of the multiple references to payment for political favours, including payment for betrayal.

'I hope he'll look smart about it if he means business,' said Mr. O'Connor.

'What do you think, Jack?' said Mr. Hynes satirically to the old man.

The old man returned to his seat by the fire, saying:

'It isn't but he has it, anyway. Not like the other tinker.'

'What other tinker?' said Mr. Hynes.

'Colgan,' said the old man scornfully.

'Is it because Colgan's a working-man you say that? What's the difference between a good honest bricklayer and a publican — eh? Hasn't the working-man as good a right to be in the Corporation as anyone else — ay, and a better right than those shoneens[5] that are always hat in hand before any fellow with a handle to his name? Isn't that so, Mat?' said Mr. Hynes, addressing Mr. O'Connor.

'I think you're right,' said Mr.O'Connor.

'One man is a plain honest man with no hunker-sliding[6] about him. He goes in to represent the labour classes. This fellow you're working for only wants to get some job or other.'

'Of course, the working-classes should be represented,' said the old man.

'The working-man,' said Mr. Hynes, 'gets all kicks and no halfpence.[7] But it's labour produces everything. The working-man is not looking for fat jobs for his sons and nephews and cousins. The working-man is not going to drag the honour of Dublin in the mud to please a German monarch.'[8]

'How's that?' said the old man.

'Don't you know they want to present an address of welcome to Edward Rex if he comes here next year?[9] What do we want kowtowing to a foreign king?'

'Our man won't vote for the address,' said Mr. O'Connor. 'He goes in on the Nationalist ticket.'[10]

'Won't he?' said Mr. Hynes. 'Wait till you see whether he will or not. I know him. Is it Tricky Dicky Tierney?'

'By God! perhaps you're right, Joe,' said Mr. O'Connor. 'Anyway, I wish he'd turn up with the spondulics.'[11]

The three men fell silent. The old man began to rake more cinders together. Mr. Hynes took off his hat, shook it and then turned down the collar of his coat, displaying, as he did so, an ivy leaf in the lapel.

'If this man was alive,' he said, pointing to the leaf, 'we'd have no talk of an address of welcome.'

'That's true,' said Mr. O'Connor.

'Musha, God be with them times!' said the old man. 'There was some life in it then.'

The room was silent again. Then a bustling little man with a snuffling nose and very cold ears pushed in the door. He walked over quickly to the fire, rubbing his hands as if he intended to produce a spark from them.

'No money, boys,' he said.

'Sit down here, Mr. Henchy,' said the old man, offering him his chair.

'O, don't stir, Jack, don't stir,' said Mr. Henchy.

He nodded curtly to Mr. Hynes and sat down on the chair which the old man vacated.

'Did you serve Aungier Street?'[12] he asked Mr. O'Connor.

'Yes,' said Mr. O'Connor, beginning to search his pockets for memoranda.

'Did you call on Grimes?'

'I did.'

'Well? How does he stand?'

'He wouldn't promise. He said: "I won't tell anyone what way I'm going to vote." But I think he'll be all right.'

'Why so?'

'He asked me who the nominators were; and I told him. I mentioned Father Burke's name. I think it'll be all right.'

Mr. Henchy began to snuffle and to rub his hands over the fire at a terrific speed. Then he said:

'For the love of God, Jack, bring us a bit of coal. There must be some left.'

The old man went out of the room.

'It's no go,' said Mr. Henchy, shaking his head. 'I asked the little shoeboy, but he said: "Oh, now, Mr. Henchy, when I see the work going on properly I

5. A contemptuous word for those who establish their respectability through sycophancy towards the powerful. It refers especially to Irish people who display this trait towards the English. The diminutive suffix of the Irish Seán refers to John (Bull), a collective nickname for the English.
6. duplicity.
7. Monkeys were led about to collect halfpennies by performing tricks. They were kicked if their performance was unsatisfactory.
8. The English monarchy was of German (Hanoverian) extraction.
9. The Dublin Corporation finally refused an address of welcome when Edward VII did arrive, but other district councils provided one.
10. He was representative of the Irish Parliamentary Party, led by John Redmond.
11. the money.
12. He is asking if O'Connor canvassed Aungier Street, a nearby thoroughfare.

won't forget you, you may be sure." Mean little tinker! 'Usha, how could he be anything else?'[13]

'What did I tell you, Mat?' said Mr. Hynes. 'Tricky Dicky Tierney.'

'O, he's as tricky as they make 'em,' said Mr. Henchy. 'He hasn't got those little pigs' eyes for nothing. Blast his soul! Couldn't he pay up like a man instead of: "O, now, Mr. Henchy, I must speak to Mr. Fanning.... I've spent a lot of money"? Mean little shoeboy of hell! I suppose he forgets the time his little old father kept the hand-me-down shop in Mary's Lane.'

'But is that a fact?' asked Mr. O'Connor.

'God, yes,' said Mr. Henchy. 'Did you never hear that? And the men used to go in on Sunday morning before the houses were open to buy a waistcoat or a trousers — moya![14] But Tricky Dicky's little old father always had a tricky little black bottle up in a corner. Do you mind now?[15] That's that. That's where he first saw the light.'

The old man returned with a few lumps of coal which he placed here and there on the fire.

'That's a nice how-do-you-do,' said Mr. O'Connor. 'How does he expect us to work for him if he won't stump up?'[16]

'I can't help it,' said Mr. Henchy. 'I expect to find the bailiffs in the hall when I go home.'

Mr. Hynes laughed and, shoving himself away from the mantelpiece with the aid of his shoulders, made ready to leave.

'It'll be all right when King Eddie comes,' he said. 'Well, boys, I'm off for the present. See you later. 'Bye, 'bye.'

He went out of the room slowly. Neither Mr. Henchy nor the old man said anything, but, just as the door was closing, Mr. O'Connor, who had been staring moodily into the fire, called out suddenly: ''Bye, Joe.'

Mr. Henchy waited a few moments and then nodded in the direction of the door.

'Tell me,' he said across the fire, 'what brings our friend in here? What does he want?'

''Usha, poor Joe!' said Mr. O'Connor, throwing the end of his cigarette into the fire, 'he's hard up like the rest of us.'

Mr. Henchy snuffled vigorously and spat so copiously that he nearly put out the fire, which uttered a hissing protest.

'To tell you my private and candid opinion,' he said, 'I think he's a man from the other camp. He's a spy of Colgan's, if you ask me. "Just go round and try and find out how they're getting on. They won't suspect you." Do you twig?'[17]

'Ah, poor Joe is a decent skin,' said Mr. O'Connor.

'His father was a decent respectable man,' Mr. Henchy admitted. 'Poor old Larry Hynes! Many a good turn he did in his day! But I'm greatly afraid our friend is not nineteen carat. Damn it, I can understand a fellow being hard up, but what I can't understand is a fellow sponging. Couldn't he have some spark of manhood about him?'

'He doesn't get a warm welcome from me when he comes,' said the old man. 'Let him work for his own side and not come spying around here.'

'I don't know,' said Mr. O'Connor dubiously, as he took out cigarette-papers and tobacco. 'I think Joe Hynes is a straight man. He's a clever chap, too, with the pen. Do you remember that thing he wrote...?'

'Some of these hillsiders and fenians[18] are a bit too clever if you ask me,' said Mr. Henchy. 'Do you know what my private and candid opinion is about some of those little jokers? I believe half of them are in the pay of the Castle.'[19]

'There's no knowing,' said the old man.

'O, but I know it for a fact,' said Mr. Henchy. 'They're Castle hacks.... I don't say Hynes.... No, damn it, I think he's a stroke above that.... But there's a certain little nobleman with a cock-eye — you know the patriot I'm alluding to?'

Mr. O'Connor nodded.

'There's a lineal descendant of Major Sirr[20] for you if you like! O, the heart's blood of a patriot! That's a fellow now that'd sell his country for fourpence — ay — and go down on his bended knees

13. The sneering references ('shoeboy', 'tinker') are to Tierney, the man for whom he is working.
14. Ironic, because in fact the men were going in for a drink, before the public houses opened.
15. 'Do you remember now?'
16. i.e. gives the required money.
17. 'Do you understand, catch on?'
18. Fenians were often on the run and were caricatured as living in hiding in the hills. The Fenians supported the Parnellite faction after the split.
19. By this he means that they were hired by the British administration, which worked from Dublin Castle.
20. Major Henry Charles Sirr (1764-1861) was an Irish officer of the British army during the 1798 Rebellion. He arrested Lord Edward Fitzgerald and was notorious for his brutality and his use of informers.

and thank the Almighty Christ he had a country to sell.'

There was a knock at the door.

'Come in!' said Mr. Henchy.

A person resembling a poor clergyman or a poor actor appeared in the doorway. His black clothes were tightly buttoned on his short body and it was impossible to say whether he wore a clergyman's collar or a layman's, because the collar of his shabby frock-coat, the uncovered buttons of which reflected the candlelight, was turned up about his neck. He wore a round hat of hard black felt. His face, shining with raindrops, had the appearance of damp yellow cheese save where two rosy spots indicated the cheekbones. He opened his very long mouth suddenly to express disappointment and at the same time opened wide his very bright blue eyes to express pleasure and surprise.

'O Father Keon!' said Mr. Henchy, jumping up from his chair. 'Is that you? Come in!'

'O, no, no, no!' said Father Keon quickly, pursing his lips as if he were addressing a child.

'Won't you come in and sit down?'

'No, no, no!' said Father Keon, speaking in a discreet indulgent velvety voice. 'Don't let me disturb you now! I'm just looking for Mr. Fanning....'

'He's round at the *Black Eagle*,' said Mr. Henchy. 'But won't you come in and sit down a minute?'

'No, no, thank you. It was just a little business matter,' said Father Keon. 'Thank you, indeed.'

He retreated from the doorway and Mr. Henchy, seizing one of the candlesticks, went to the door to light him downstairs.

'O, don't trouble, I beg!'

'No, but the stairs is so dark.'

'No, no, I can see.... Thank you, indeed.'

'Are you right now?'

'All right, thanks.... Thanks.'

Mr. Henchy returned with the candlestick and put it on the table. He sat down again at the fire. There was silence for a few moments.

'Tell me, John,' said Mr. O'Connor, lighting his cigarette with another pasteboard card.

'Hm?'

'What is he exactly?'

'Ask me an easier one,' said Mr. Henchy.

'Fanning and himself seem to me very thick. They're often in Kavanagh's together. Is he a priest at all?'

'Mmmyes, I believe so.... I think he's what you call a black sheep. We haven't many of them, thank God! but we have a few.... He's an unfortunate man of some kind....'[21]

'And how does he knock it out?'[22] asked Mr. O'Connor.

'That's another mystery.'

'Is he attached to any chapel or church or institution or ——.'

'No,' said Mr. Henchy, 'I think he's travelling on his own account.... God forgive me,' he added, 'I thought he was the dozen of stout.'[23]

'Is there any chance of a drink itself?' asked Mr. O'Connor.

'I'm dry too,' said the old man.

'I asked that little shoeboy three times,' said Mr. Henchy, 'would he send up a dozen of stout. I asked him again now, but he was leaning on the counter in his shirt-sleeves having a deep goster[24] with Alderman Cowley.'

'Why didn't you remind him?' said Mr. O'Connor.

'Well, I couldn't go over while he was talking to Alderman Cowley. I just waited till I caught his eye, and said: "About that little matter I was speaking to you about...." "That'll be all right, Mr. H.," he said. Yerra, sure the little hop-o'-my-thumb has forgotten all about it.'

'There's some deal on in that quarter,' said Mr. O'Connor thoughtfully. 'I saw the three of them hard at it yesterday at Suffolk Street corner.'

'I think I know the little game they're at,' said Mr. Henchy. 'You must owe the City Fathers money nowadays if you want to be made Lord Mayor. Then they'll make you Lord Mayor. By God! I'm thinking seriously of becoming a City Father myself. What do you think? Would I do for the job?'

Mr. O'Connor laughed.

'So far as owing money goes ....'

'Driving out of the Mansion House,' said Mr. Henchy, 'in all my vermin,[25] with Jack here

21. The implication is that Father Keon has been silenced by his bishop because of some serious misdemeanour. He hints that the priest is an alcoholic.
22. 'How does he make a living?'
23. The boy bringing the twelve bottles of stout.
24. conversation, gossip.
25. The Mansion House is the residence of the lord mayor of Dublin. On formal occasions the mayor would ride in a ceremonial coach wearing the ermine-trimmed (vermin) robes of office.

standing up behind me in a powdered wig — eh?'

'And make me your private secretary, John.'

'Yes. And I'll make Father Keon my private chaplain. We'll have a family party.'

'Faith, Mr. Henchy,' said the old man, 'you'd keep up better style than some of them. I was talking one day to old Keegan, the porter. "And how do you like your new master, Pat?" says I to him. "You haven't much entertaining now," says I. "Entertaining!" says he. "He'd live on the smell of an oil-rag." And do you know what he told me? Now, I declare to God, I didn't believe him.'

'What?' said Mr. Henchy and Mr. O'Connor.

'He told me: "What do you think of a Lord Mayor of Dublin sending out for a pound of chops for his dinner?[26] How's that for high living?" says he. "Wisha! wisha," says I. "A pound of chops," say he, "coming into the Mansion House." "Wisha!" says I, "what kind of people is going at all now?"'

At this point there was a knock at the door, and a boy put in his head.

'What is it?' said the old man.

'From the *Black Eagle*,' said the boy, walking in sideways and depositing a basket on the floor with a noise of shaken bottles.

The old man helped the boy to transfer the bottles from the basket to the table and counted the full tally. After the transfer the boy put his basket on his arm and asked:

'Any bottles?'

'What bottles?' said the old man.

'Won't you let us drink them first?' said Mr. Henchy.

'I was told to ask for bottles.'

'Come back tomorrow,' said the old man.

'Here, boy!' said Mr. Henchy, 'will you run over to O'Farrell's and ask him to lend us a corkscrew — for Mr. Henchy, say. Tell him we won't keep it a minute. Leave the basket there.'

The boy went out and Mr. Henchy began to rub his hands cheerfully, saying:

'Ah, well, he's not so bad after all. He's as good as his word, anyhow.'

'There's no tumblers,' said the old man.

'O, don't let that trouble you, Jack,' said Mr. Henchy. 'Many's the good man before now drank out of the bottle.'

'Anyway, it's better than nothing,' said Mr. O'Connor.

'He's not a bad sort,' said Mr. Henchy, 'only Fanning has such a loan of him. He means well, you know, in his own tinpot way.'

The boy came back with the corkscrew. The old man opened three bottles and was handing back the corkscrew when Mr. Henchy said to the boy:

'Would you like a drink, boy?'

'If you please, sir,' said the boy.

The old man opened another bottle grudgingly, and handed it to the boy.

'What age are you?' he asked.

'Seventeen,' said the boy.

As the old man said nothing further the boy took the bottle, said: 'Here's my best respects, sir,' to Mr. Henchy, drank the contents, put the bottle back on the table and wiped his mouth with his sleeve. Then he took up the corkscrew and went out of the door sideways, muttering some form of salutation.

'That's the way it begins,' said the old man.

'The thin edge of the wedge,' said Mr. Henchy.

The old man distributed the three bottles which he had opened and the men drank from them simultaneously. After having drunk each placed his bottle on the mantelpiece within hand's reach and drew in a long breath of satisfaction.

'Well, I did a good day's work today,' said Mr. Henchy, after a pause.

'That so, John?'

'Yes. I got him one or two sure things in Dawson Street, Crofton and myself. Between ourselves, you know, Crofton (he's a decent chap, of course), but he's not worth a damn as a canvasser. He hasn't a word to throw to a dog. He stands and looks at the people while I do the talking.'

Here two men entered the room. One of them was a very fat man, whose blue serge clothes seemed to be in danger of falling from his sloping figure. He had a big face which resembled a young ox's face in expression, staring blue eyes and a grizzled moustache. The other man, who was much younger and frailer, had a thin, clean-shaven face. He wore a very high double collar and a wide-brimmed bowler hat.

'Hello, Crofton!' said Mr. Henchy to the fat man. 'Talk of the devil . . . .'

'Where did the boose come from?' asked the young man. 'Did the cow calve?'

26. T. C. Harrington was lord mayor of Dublin 1901-04. He was known for his working-class background and tastes. Since he was also a staunch Parnellite, he was open to jibes of this sort from the anti-Parnellite supporters of the Parliamentary Party.

'O, of course, Lyons spots the drink first thing!' said Mr. O'Connor, laughing.

'Is that the way you chaps canvass,' said Mr. Lyons, 'and Crofton and I out in the cold and rain looking for votes?'

'Why, blast your soul,' said Mr. Henchy, 'I'd get more votes in five minutes than you two'd get in a week.'

'Open two bottles of stout, Jack,' said Mr. O'Connor.

'How can I?, said the old man, 'when there's no corkscrew?'

'Wait now, wait now!' said Mr. Henchy, getting up quickly. 'Did you ever see this little trick?'

He took two bottles from the table and, carrying them to the fire, put them on the hob. Then he sat down again by the fire and took another drink from his bottle. Mr. Lyons sat on the edge of the table, pushed his hat towards the nape of his neck and began to swing his legs.

'Which is my bottle?' he asked.

'This lad,' said Mr. Henchy.

Mr. Crofton sat down on a box and looked fixedly at the other bottle on the hob. He was silent for two reasons. The first reason, sufficient in itself, was that he had nothing to say; the second reason was that he considered his companions beneath him. He had been a canvasser for Wilkins, the Conservative, but when the Conservatives had withdrawn their man and, choosing the lesser of two evils, given their support to the Nationalist candidate, he had been engaged to work for Mr. Tierney.[27]

In a few minutes an apologetic *Pok!* was heard as the cork flew out of Mr. Lyons' bottle. Mr. Lyons jumped off the table, went to the fire, took his bottle and carried it back to the table.

'I was just telling them, Crofton,' said Mr. Henchy, 'that we got a good few votes today.'

'Who did you get?' asked Mr. Lyons.

'Well, I got Parkes for one, and I got Atkinson for two, and I got Ward of Dawson Street. Fine old chap he is, too — regular old toff,[28] old Conservative! "But isn't your candidate a Nationalist?" said he. "He's a respectable man," said I. "He's in favour of whatever will benefit this country. He's a big ratepayer," I said. "He has extensive house property in the city and three places of business and isn't it to his own advantage to keep down the rates? He's a prominent and respected citizen," said I, "and a Poor Law Guardian, and he doesn't belong to any party, good, bad, or indifferent." That's the way to talk to 'em.'

'And what about the address to the King?' said Mr. Lyons, after drinking and smacking his lips.

'Listen to me,' said Mr. Henchy. 'What we want in this country, as I said to old Ward, is capital. The King's coming here will mean an influx of money into this country. The citizens of Dublin will benefit by it. Look at all the factories down by the quays there, idle! Look at all the money there is in the country if we only worked the old industries, the mills, the shipbuilding yards and factories. It's capital we want.'

'But look here, John,' said Mr. O'Connor. 'Why should we welcome the King of England? Didn't Parnell himself . . . .'

'Parnell,' said Mr. Henchy, 'is dead. Now, here's the way I look at it. Here's this chap come to the throne after his old mother keeping him out of it till the man was grey. He's a man of the world, and he means well by us. He's a jolly fine decent fellow, if you ask me, and no damn nonsense about him. He just says to himself: "The old one never went to see these wild Irish.[29] By Christ, I'll go myself and see what they're like." And are we going to insult the man when he comes over here on a friendly visit? Eh? Isn't that right, Crofton?'

Mr. Crofton nodded his head.

'But after all now,' said Mr. Lyons argumentatively, 'King Edward's life, you know, is not the very . . . .'[30]

'Let bygones be bygones,' said Mr. Henchy. 'I admire the man personally. He's just an ordinary knockabout like you and me. He's fond of his glass of grog and he's a bit of a rake, perhaps, and he's a good sportsman. Damn it, can't we Irish play fair?'

'That's all very fine,' said Mr. Lyons. 'But look at the case of Parnell now.'

'In the name of God,' said Mr. Henchy, 'where's

27. The Irish Conservative Party, unionist in outlook and therefore opposed to Home Rule, preferred even the Home Rule party to the socialists.
28. Slang for somebody rich, well-dressed and upper-class.
29. In fact the 'old one' (Queen Victoria) did visit Ireland in 1849, 1853, 1861 and 1900. On the last occasion she had received an address of welcome from Dublin Corporation.
30. While Prince of Wales, Edward's relations with married women had been exposed in a divorce trial. The contrast with the reaction to Parnell's case is obvious.

the analogy between the two cases?'

'What I mean,' said Mr. Lyons, 'is we have our ideals. Why, now, would we welcome a man like that? Do you think now after what he did Parnell was a fit man to lead us? And why, then, would we do it for Edward the Seventh?'

'This is Parnell's anniversary,' said Mr. O'Connor, 'and don't let us stir up any bad blood. We all respect him now that he's dead and gone — even the Conservatives,' he added, turning to Mr. Crofton.

Pok! The tardy cork flew out of Mr. Crofton's bottle. Mr. Crofton got up from his box and went to the fire. As he returned with his capture he said in a deep voice:

'Our side of the house respects him because he was a gentleman.'

'Right you are, Crofton!' said Mr. Henchy fiercely. 'He was the only man that could keep that bag of cats in order. "Down, ye dogs! Lie down, ye curs!" That's the way he treated them. Come in, Joe! Come in!' he called out, catching sight of Mr. Hynes in the doorway.

Mr. Hynes came in slowly.

'Open another bottle of stout, Jack,' said Mr. Henchy. 'O, I forgot there's no corkscrew! Here, show me one here and I'll put it at the fire.'

The old man handed him another bottle and he placed it on the hob.

'Sit down, Joe,' said Mr. O'Connor, 'we're just talking about the Chief.'

'Ay, ay!' said Mr. Henchy.

Mr. Hynes sat on the side of the table near Mr. Lyons but said nothing.

'There's one of them, anyhow,' said Mr. Henchy, 'that didn't renege him. By God, I'll say for you, Joe! No, by God, you stuck to him like a man!'

'O, Joe,' said Mr. O'Connor suddenly. 'Give us that thing you wrote — do you remember? Have you got it on you?'

'O, ay!' said Mr. Henchy. 'Give us that. Did you ever hear that. Crofton? Listen to this now: splendid thing.'

'Go on,' said Mr. O'Connor. 'Fire away, Joe.'

Mr. Hynes did not seem to remember at once the piece to which they were alluding, but, after reflecting a while, he said:

'O, that thing is it.... Sure, that's old now.'

'Out with it, man!' said Mr. O'Connor.

''Sh, 'sh,' said Mr. Henchy. 'Now, Joe!'

Mr. Hynes hesitated a little longer. Then amid the silence he took off his hat, laid it on the table and stood up. He seemed to be rehearsing the piece in his mind. After a rather long pause he announced:

THE DEATH OF PARNELL

6th October, 1891

He cleared his throat once or twice and then began to recite:

He is dead. Our Uncrowned King is dead.
    O, Erin, mourn with grief and woe
For he lies dead whom the fell gang
    Of modern hypocrites laid low.

He lies slain by the coward hounds
    He raised to glory from the mire;
And Erin's hopes and Erin's dreams
    Perish upon her monarch's pyre.

In palace, cabin or in cot
    The Irish heart where'er it be
Is bowed with woe — for he is gone
    Who would have wrought her destiny.

He would have had his Erin famed,
    The green flag gloriously unfurled,
Her statesmen, bards and warriors raised
    Before the nations of the World.

He dreamed (alas, 'twas but a dream!)
    Of Liberty: but as he strove
To clutch that idol, treachery
    Sundered him from the thing he loved.

Shame on the coward, caitiff[31] hands
    That smote their Lord or with a kiss
Betrayed him to the rabble-rout
    Of fawning priests — no friends of his.

My everlasting shame consume
    The memory of those who tried
To befoul and smear th' exalted name
    Of one who spurned them in his pride.

31. base, cowardly.

He fell as fall the mighty ones,
Nobly undaunted to the last,
And death has now united him
With Erin's heroes of the past.

No sound of strife disturb his sleep!
Calmly he rests: no human pain
Or high ambition spurs him now
The peaks of glory to attain.

They had their way: they laid him low.
But Erin, list, his spirit may
Rise, like the Phoenix from the flames,
When breaks the dawning of the day,

The day that brings us Freedom's reign.
And on that day may Erin well
Pledge in the cup she lifts to Joy
One grief — the memory of Parnell.

Mr. Hynes sat down again on the table. When he had finished his recitation there was a silence and then a burst of clapping: even Mr. Lyons clapped. The applause continued for a little time. When it has ceased all the auditors drank from their bottles in silence.

Pok! The cork flew out of Mr. Hynes' bottle, but Mr. Hynes remained sitting, flushed and bareheaded on the table. He did not seem to have heard the invitation.

'Good man, Joe!' said Mr. O'Connor, taking out his cigarette papers and pouch the better to hide his emotion.

'What do you think of that, Crofton?' cried Mr. Henchy. 'Isn't that fine? What?'

Mr. Crofton said that it was a very fine piece of writing.

from: A PORTRAIT OF THE ARTIST AS A YOUNG MAN (1916)

Et ignotas animum dimittit in artes
Ovid, *Metamorphoses*, VIII, 18

[The epigraph — 'And he sets his mind to work upon unknown arts' — indicates a central figure in Joyce's *A Portrait*. The passage in Ovid is describing Daedalus's creation of wings so that he and his son Icarus may fly free from the Cretan labyrinth. Icarus flies too close to the sun; his wings, made of wax and feathers, melt and he falls into the sea. The relationship between the father and the son is pictured as analogous to that between classical (Daedalus) and romantic (Icarus) art. But it is seen in a more complex fashion too. Stephen-Icarus is flying from the Irish labyrinth by a rejection of the parental culture in which he has become ensnared. In doing so, he undergoes the risk of liberating himself from incarceration at the expense of his capacity to feel love. His will to be himself — comparable in some respects to the titanic pride of Ibsen's hero Brand in the play of that name — may conclude in a disdainful and traumatized narcissism. He is both Daedalus and Icarus, an artificer and a doomed, romantic youth. In the excerpts chosen (from the opening and closing of the novel), we see how Stephen begins by receiving the world and its words, including the story of another doomed father-hero — Parnell — and ends by replacing that world with the words of his own diary. The narrator who quotes others has a curious triumph in learning ultimately to quote himself. Although there is an element of triumph, it is not without an ironical subversion. The political and religious weight of Irish culture and history is almost lifted away by the end of the novel. But Stephen's relationship with his mother, and the complex transference of his theory of artistic independence from the language of catholic theology, remind us of the simple fact that his idea of freedom is dependent upon the power with which he can re-evoke the sense of imprisonment. His freedom is dependent on that which denied it; it consists in denying the power of his culture's denial.

The text is that of the Viking Critical Library edition, edited by Chester G. Anderson (New York: The Viking Press, 1968).]

I

Once upon a time and a very good time it was there was a moocow coming down along the road and this moocow that was coming down along the road met a nicens little boy named baby tuckoo....

His father told him that story: his father looked at him through a glass: he had a hairy face.

He was baby tuckoo. The moocow came down the road where Betty Byrne lived: she sold lemon platt.[1]

O, the wild rose blossoms
On the little green place.[2]

1. Sticks of barley-sugar.
2. The lines are from a popular song, 'Lily Dale' by F. H. Thompson, which has as chorus:
   'Oh! Lily, sweet Lily, dear Lily Dale,
   Now the wild rose blossoms
   O'er her little green grave,
   'Neath the trees in the flow'ry vale.'

He sang that song. That was his song.

O, the green wothe botheth.

When you wet the bed first it is warm then it gets cold. His mother put on the oilsheet. That had the queer smell.

His mother had a nicer smell than his father. She played on the piano the sailor's hornpipe for him to dance. He danced:

Tralala lala
Tralala tralaladdy
Tralala lala
Tralala lala.

Uncle Charles and Dante clapped. They were older than his father and mother but uncle Charles was older than Dante.

Dante had two brushes in her press.[3] The brush with the maroon velvet back was for Michael Davitt and the brush with the green velvet back was for Parnell.[4] Dante gave him a cachou every time he brought her a piece of tissue paper.

The Vances lived in number seven. They had a different father and mother. They were Eileen's father and mother. When they were grown up he was going to marry Eileen. He hid under the table. His mother said:

— O, Stephen will apologise.

Dante said:

— O, if not, the eagles will come and pull out his eyes.

Pull out his eyes,
Apologise,
Apologise,
Pull out his eyes.

Apologise,
Pull out his eyes,
Pull out his eyes,
Apologise.[5]

The wide playgrounds were swarming with boys. All were shouting and the prefects urged them on with strong cries. The evening air was pale and chilly and after every charge and thud of the footballers the greasy leather orb flew like a heavy bird through the grey light. He kept on the fringe of his line, out of sight of his prefect, out of the reach of the rude feet, feigning to run now and then. He felt his body small and weak amid the throng of players and his eyes were weak and watery. Rody Kickham was not like that: he would be captain of the third line[6] all the fellows said.

Rody Kickham was a decent fellow but Nasty Roche was a stink. Rody Kickham had greaves in his number and a hamper in the refectory.[7] Nasty Roche had big hands. He called the Friday pudding dog-in-the-blanket. And one day he had asked:

— What is your name?

Stephen had answered:

— Stephen Dedalus.

Then Nasty Roche had said:

— What kind of a name is that?

And when Stephen had not been able to answer Nasty Roche had asked:

— What is your father?

Stephen had answered:

— A gentleman.

Then Nasty Roche had asked:

— Is he a magistrate?

He crept about from point to point on the fringe of his line, making little runs now and then. But his hands were bluish with cold. He kept his hands in the sidepockets of his belted grey suit. That was a belt round his pocket. And belt was also to give a fellow a belt. One day a fellow had said to Cantwell:

— I'd give you such a belt in a second.

Cantwell had answered:

— Go and fight your match. Give Cecil Thunder a belt. I'd like to see you. He'd give you a toe in the rump for yourself.

That was not a nice expression. His mother had told him not to speak with the rough boys in the

3. cupboard.

4. Charles Stewart Parnell (1846-91), the leader of the Irish Parliamentary Party until his fall in 1890 after a divorce case. Michael Davitt (1846-1906), founder-member of the Land League, had co-operated with Parnell in the years 1879-82. After that time, their political views diverged once again. Davitt was early and prominent in demanding that Parnell be removed from the party leadership in 1890.

5. Adapted from Song XXIII in *Divine Songs Attempted in Easy Language for the Use of Children* (London, 1715) by Isaac Watts. The song itself derives from Proverbs 30. 17: 'The eye that mocketh at his father, and despiseth to obey his mother, the ravens of the valley shall pick it out, and the young eagles shall eat it.'

6. The students at Clongowes Wood, a Jesuit college that Joyce attended in County Kildare, were divided by age into three groups or lines. Those under thirteen were in the third line; those under fifteen were in the lower line; those from fifteen to eighteen were in the higher line.

7. He had shin-guards in his locker and a basket of food, sent from home, in the dining-hall.

college. Nice mother! The first day in the hall of the castle when she had said goodbye she had put up her veil double to her nose to kiss him: and her nose and eyes were red. But he had pretended not to see that she was going to cry. She was a nice mother but she was not so nice when she cried. And his father had given him two fiveshilling pieces for pocket money. And his father had told him if he wanted anything to write home to him and, whatever he did, never to peach on[8] a fellow. Then at the door of the castle the rector had shaken hands with his father and mother, his soutane fluttering in the breeze, and the car had driven off with his father and mother on it. They had cried to him from the car, waving their hands:

— Goodbye, Stephen, goodbye!

— Goodbye, Stephen, goodbye!

He was caught in the whirl of a scrimmage and, fearful of the flashing eyes and muddy boots, bent down to look through the legs. The fellows were struggling and groaning and their legs were rubbing and kicking and stamping. Then Jack Lawton's yellow boots dodged out the ball and all the other boots and legs ran after.[9] He ran after them a little way and then stopped. It was useless to run on. Soon they would be going home for the holidays. After supper in the studyhall he would change the number pasted up inside his desk from seventy-seven to seventysix.

It would be better to be in the studyhall than out there in the cold. The sky was pale and cold but there were lights in the castle. He wondered from which window Hamilton Rowan had thrown his hat on the haha and had there been flowerbeds at that time under the windows.[10] One day when he had been called to the castle the butler had shown him the marks of the soldiers' slugs in the wood of the door and had given him a piece of shortbread that the community ate. It was nice and warm to see the lights in the castle. It was like something in a book. Perhaps Leicester Abbey was like that. And there were nice sentences in Doctor Cornwell's Spelling Book.[11] They were like poetry but they were only sentences to learn the spelling from.

Wolsey died in Leicester Abbey
Where the abbots buried him.
Canker is a disease of plants,
Cancer one of animals.[12]

It would be nice to lie on the hearthrug before the fire, leaning his head upon his hands, and think on those sentences. He shivered as if he had cold slimy water next his skin. That was mean of Wells to shoulder him into the square ditch because he would not swop his little snuffbox for Wells's seasoned hacking chestnut, the conqueror of forty.[13] How cold and slimy the water had been! A fellow had once seen a big rat jump into the scum. Mother was sitting at the fire with Dante waiting for Brigid to bring in the tea. She had her feet on the fender and her jewelly slippers were so hot and they had such a lovely warm smell! Dante knew a lot of things. She had taught him where the Mozambique Channel was and what was the longest river in America and what was the name of the highest mountain in the moon.[14] Father Arnall knew more than Dante because he was a priest but both his father and uncle Charles said that Dante was a clever woman and a wellread woman. And when Dante made that noise after dinner and then put up her hand to her mouth: that was heartburn.

A voice cried far out on the playground:

— All in!

Then other voices cried from the lower and third lines:

— All in! All in!

The players closed around, flushed and muddy,

8. inform, tell tales on someone.
9. The football game is rugby, in which the ball is hooked back from the scrum.
10. Archibald Hamilton Rowan (1751-1834), a member of the United Irishmen, escaped from an armed escort of British troops while being conducted to prison. He took refuge in Clongowes Wood Castle, the building that later became the Jesuit school. It is said that the troops opened fire on him just as he closed the library door. He threw his hat on to the ha-ha, a sunken fence or moat surrounding the house, to give the impression that he had escaped by the window. In fact, he hid in a secret room in the castle.
11. James Cornwell (1812-1902) and Alexander Allen (1814-42) were the co-authors of *A Grammar for Beginners* (London, 1838).
12. Thomas, Cardinal Wolsey (*c.* 1475-1530), the most famous counsellor of Henry VIII and lord chancellor of England 1515-29. He died at Leicester Abbey on the way to London to stand trial for high treason. The sentences cited here are meant to show different clausal constructions common in English.
13. Chestnut championships are popular in schools in the autumn when the chestnuts have fallen. In the game, chestnuts hung on a string are struck alternately by the contestants until one breaks. A seasoned chestnut can become a 'conqueror of forty'.
14. Dante Riordan's knowledge is random and shallow; to the boy it appears exotic and authoritative. This is more important than the specifics of her information or than any indication, as strained after by commentators, that these items have a 'catholic' reference.

and he went among them, glad to go in. Rody Kickham held the ball by its greasy lace. A fellow asked him to give it one last: but he walked on without even answering the fellow. Simon Moonan told him not to because the prefect was looking. The fellow turned to Simon Moonan and said:

— We all know why you speak. You are McGlade's suck.[15]

Suck was a queer word. The fellow called Simon Moonan that name because Simon Moonan used to tie the prefect's false sleeves behind his back and the prefect used to let on to be angry. But the sound was ugly. Once he had washed his hands in the lavatory of the Wicklow Hotel and his father pulled the stopper up by the chain after and the dirty water went down through the hole in the basin. And when it had all gone down slowly the hole in the basin had made a sound like that: suck. Only louder.

To remember that and the white look of the lavatory made him feel cold and then hot. There were two cocks that you turned and water came out: cold and hot. He felt cold and then a little hot: and he could see the names printed on the cocks. That was a very queer thing.

And the air in the corridor chilled him too. It was queer and wettish. But soon the gas would be lit and in burning it made a light noise like a little song. Always the same: and when the fellows stopped talking in the playroom you could hear it.

It was the hour for sums. Father Arnall wrote a hard sum on the board and then said:

— Now then, who will win? Go ahead, York! Go ahead, Lancaster![16]

Stephen tried his best but the sum was too hard and he felt confused. The little silk badge with the white rose on it that was pinned on the breast of his jacket began to flutter. He was no good at sums but he tried his best so that York might not lose. Father Arnall's face looked very black but he was not in a wax:[17] he was laughing. Then Jack Lawton cracked his fingers and Father Arnall looked at his copy-book and said:

— Right. Bravo Lancaster! The red rose wins. Come on now, York! Forge ahead!

Jack Lawton looked over from his side. The little silk badge with the red rose on it looked very rich because he had a blue sailor top on. Stephen felt his own face red too, thinking of all the bets about who would get first place in elements,[18] Jack Lawton or he. Some weeks Jack Lawton got the card for first and some weeks he got the card for first. His white silk badge fluttered and fluttered as he worked at the next sum and heard Father Arnall's voice. Then all his eagerness passed away and he felt his face quite cool. He thought his face must be white because it felt so cool. He could not get out the answer for the sum but it did not matter. White roses and red roses: those were beautiful colours to think of. And the cards for first place and second place and third place were beautiful colours too: pink and cream and lavender. Lavender and cream and pink roses were beautiful to think of. Perhaps a wild rose might be like those colours and he remembered the song about the wild rose blossoms on the little green place. But you could not have a green rose. But perhaps somewhere in the world you could.

The bell rang and then the classes began to file out of the rooms and along the corridors towards the refectory. He sat looking at the two prints of butter on his plate but could not eat the damp bread. The tablecloth was damp and limp. But he drank off the hot weak tea which the clumsy scullion, girt with a white apron, poured into his cup. He wondered whether the scullion's apron was damp too or whether all white things were cold and damp. Nasty Roche and Saurin drank cocoa that their people sent them in tins. They said they could not drink the tea; that it was hogwash. Their fathers were magistrates, the fellows said.

All the boys seemed to him very strange. They had all fathers and mothers and different clothes and voices. He longed to be at home and lay his head on his mother's lap. But he could not: and so he longed for the play and study and prayers to be over and to be in bed.

He drank another cup of hot tea and Fleming said:

— What's up? Have you a pain or what's up with you?

— I don't know, Stephen said.

15. A sycophant, one who plays up to the prefect to win favour.
16. In the English Wars of the Roses (1455-85), Lancaster had as symbol the red rose and York the white rose. Ireland supported York, the losing side.
17. bad temper, rage.
18. The elements consisted of spelling, grammar, writing, arithmetic, geography, history and Latin. Members of the first line would learn the basic principles — the elements — of these disciplines.

— Sick in your breadbasket,[19] Fleming said, because your face looks white. It will go away.

— O yes, Stephen said.

But he was not sick there. He thought that he was sick in his heart if you could be sick in that place. Fleming was very decent to ask him. He wanted to cry. He leaned his elbows on the table and shut and opened the flaps of his ears. Then he heard the noise of the refectory every time he opened the flaps of his ears. It made a roar like a train at night. And when he closed the flaps the roar was shut off like a train going into a tunnel. That night at Dalkey the train had roared like that and then, when it went into the tunnel, the roar stopped. He closed his eyes and the train went on, roaring and then stopping; roaring again, stopping. It was nice to hear it roar and stop and then roar out of the tunnel again and then stop.

Then the higher line fellows began to come down along the matting in the middle of the refectory, Paddy Rath and Jimmy Magee and the Spaniard who was allowed to smoke cigars and the little Portuguese who wore the woolly cap. And then the lower line tables and the tables of the third line. And every single fellow had a different way of walking.

He sat in a corner of the playroom pretending to watch a game of dominos and once or twice he was able to hear for an instant the little song of the gas. The prefect was at the door with some boys and Simon Moonan was knotting his false sleeves. He was telling them something about Tullabeg.[20]

Then he went away from the door and Wells came over to Stephen and said:

— Tell us, Dedalus, do you kiss your mother before you go to bed?

Stephen answered:

— I do.

Wells turned to the other fellows and said:

— O, I say, here's a fellow says he kisses his mother every night before he goes to bed.

The other fellows stopped their game and turned round, laughing. Stephen blushed under their eyes and said:

— I do not.

Wells said:

— O, I say, here's a fellow says he doesn't kiss his mother before he goes to bed.

They all laughed again. Stephen tried to laugh with them. He felt his whole body hot and confused in a moment. What was the right answer to the question? He had given two and still Wells laughed. But Wells must know the right answer for he was in third of grammar. He tried to think of Wells's mother but he did not dare to raise his eyes to Wells's face. He did not like Wells's face. It was Wells who had shouldered him into the square ditch the day before because he would not swop his little snuffbox for Wells's seasoned hacking chestnut, the conqueror of forty. It was a mean thing to do; all the fellows said it was. And how cold and slimy the water had been! And a fellow had once seen a big rat jump plop into the scum.

The cold slime of the ditch covered his whole body; and, when the bell rang for study and the lines filed out of the playrooms, he felt the cold air of the corridor and staircase inside his clothes. He still tried to think what was the right answer. Was it right to kiss his mother or wrong to kiss his mother? What did that mean, to kiss? You put your face up like that to say goodnight and then his mother put her face down. That was to kiss. His mother put her lips on his cheek; her lips were soft and they wetted his cheek; and they made a tiny little noise: kiss. Why did people do that with their two faces?

Sitting in the studyhall he opened the lid of his desk and changed the number pasted up inside from seventyseven to seventysix. But the Christmas vacation was very far away: but one time it would come because the earth moved round always.

There was a picture of the earth on the first page of his geography: a big ball in the middle of clouds. Fleming had a box of crayons and one night during free study he had coloured the earth green and the clouds maroon. That was like the two brushes in Dante's press, the brush with the green velvet back for Parnell and the brush with the maroon velvet back for Michael Davitt. But he had not told Fleming to colour them those colours. Fleming had done it himself.

He opened the geography to study the lesson; but he could not learn the names of places in America. Still they were all different places that had those different names. They were all in different countries and the countries were in continents and the continents were in the world and the world was in the universe.

He turned to the flyleaf of the geography and read what he had written there: himself, his name and where he was.

19. stomach.

20. Tullabeg was the site of another Jesuit foundation which had merged with Clongowes Wood in 1886.

Stephen Dedalus
Class of Elements
Clongowes Wood College
Sallins
County Kildare
Ireland
Europe
The World
The Universe

That was in his writing: and Fleming one night for a cod[21] had written on the opposite page:

Stephen Dedalus is my name,
Ireland is my nation.
Clongowes is my dwellingplace
And heaven my expectation.

He read the verses backwards but then they were not poetry. Then he read the flyleaf from the bottom to the top till he came to his own name. That was he: and he read down the page again. What was after the universe? Nothing. But was there anything round the universe to show where it stopped before the nothing place began? It could not be a wall but there could be a thin thin line there all round everything. It was very big to think about everything and everywhere. Only God could do that. He tried to think what a big thought that must be but he could think only of God. God was God's name just as his name was Stephen. *Dieu* was the French for God and that was God's name too; and when anyone prayed to God and said *Dieu* then God knew at once that it was a French person that was praying. But though there were different names for God in all the different languages in the world and God understood what all the people who prayed said in their different languages still God remained always the same God and God's real name was God.

It made him very tired to think that way. It made him feel his head very big. He turned over the flyleaf and looked wearily at the green round earth in the middle of the maroon clouds. He wondered which was right, to be for the green or for the maroon, because Dante had ripped the green velvet back off the brush that was for Parnell one day with her scissors and had told him that Parnell was a bad man. He wondered if they were arguing at home about that. That was called politics. There were two sides in it: Dante was on one side and his father and Mr Casey were on the other side but his mother and uncle Charles were on no side. Every day there was something in the paper about it.

It pained him that he did not know well what politics meant and that he did not know where the universe ended. He felt small and weak. When would he be like the fellows in poetry and rhetoric? They had big voices and big boots and they studied trigonometry. That was very far away. First came the vacation and then the next term and then vacation again and then again another term and then again the vacation. It was like a train going in and out of tunnels and that was like the noise of the boys eating in the refectory when you opened and closed the flaps of the ears. Term, vacation; tunnel, out; noise, stop. How far away it was! It was better to go to bed to sleep. Only prayers in the chapel and then bed. He shivered and yawned. It would be lovely in bed after the sheets got a bit hot. First they were so cold to get into. He shivered to think how cold they were first. But then they got hot and then he could sleep. It was lovely to be tired. He yawned again. Night prayers and then bed: he shivered and wanted to yawn. It would be lovely in a few minutes. He felt a warm glow creeping up from the cold shivering sheets, warmer and warmer till he felt warm all over, ever so warm; ever so warm and yet he shivered a little and still wanted to yawn.

The bell rang for night prayers and he filed out of the studyhall after the others and down the staircase and along the corridors to the chapel. The corridors were darkly lit and the chapel was darkly lit. Soon all would be dark and sleeping. There was cold night air in the chapel and the marbles were the colour the sea was at night. The sea was cold day and night: but it was colder at night. It was cold and dark under the seawall beside his father's house. But the kettle would be on the hob to make punch.

The prefect of the chapel prayed above his head and his memory knew the responses:

O Lord, open our lips
And our mouth shall announce Thy praise.
Incline unto our aid, O God!
O Lord, make haste to help us![22]

There was a cold night smell in the chapel. But it was a holy smell. It was not like the smell of the old

21. i.e. as a joke.

22. The opening lines of Matins in the Divine Office.

peasants who knelt at the back of the chapel at Sunday mass. That was a smell of air and rain and turf and corduroy. But they were very holy peasants. They breathed behind him on his neck and sighed as they prayed. They lived in Clane, a fellow said: there were little cottages there and he had seen a woman standing at the halfdoor of a cottage with a child in her arms, as the cars had come past from Sallins. It would be lovely to sleep for one night in that cottage before the fire of smoking turf, in the dark lit by the fire, in the warm dark, breathing the smell of the peasants, air and rain and turf and corduroy. But, O, the road there between the trees was dark! You would be lost in the dark. It made him afraid to think of how it was.

He heard the voice of the prefect of the chapel saying the last prayer. He prayed it too against the dark outside under the trees.

> *Visit, we beseech Thee, O Lord, this habitation and drive away from it all the snares of the enemy. May Thy holy angels dwell herein to preserve us in peace and may Thy blessing be always upon us through Christ, Our Lord. Amen.*[23]

His fingers trembled as he undressed himself in the dormitory. He told his fingers to hurry up. He had to undress and then kneel and say his own prayers and be in bed before the gas was lowered so that he might not go to hell when he died. He rolled his stockings off and put on his nightshirt quickly and knelt trembling at his bedside and repeated his prayers quickly quickly, fearing that the gas would go down. He felt his shoulders shaking as he murmured:

> *God bless my father and my mother and spare them to me!*
> *God bless my little brothers and sisters and spare them to me!*
> *God bless Dante and uncle Charles and spare them to me!*

He blessed himself and climbed quickly into bed and, tucking the end of the nightshirt under his feet, curled himself together under the cold white sheets, shaking and trembling. But he would not go to hell when he died; and the shaking would stop. A voice bade the boys in the dormitory goodnight. He peered out for an instant over the coverlet and saw the yellow curtains round and before his bed that shut him off on all sides. The light was lowered quietly.

The prefect's shoes went away. Where? Down the staircase and along the corridors or to his room at the end? He saw the dark. Was it true about the black dog that walked there at night with eyes as big as carriagelamps? They said it was the ghost of a murderer. A long shiver of fear flowed over his body. He saw the dark entrance hall of the castle. Old servants in old dress were in the ironingroom above the staircase. It was long ago. The old servants were quiet. There was a fire there but the hall was still dark. A figure came up the staircase from the hall. He wore the white cloak of a marshal; his face was pale and strange; he held his hand pressed to his side. He looked out of strange eyes at the old servants. They looked at him and saw their master's face and cloak and knew that he had received his deathwound. But only the dark was where they looked: only dark silent air. Their master had received his deathwound on the battlefield of Prague far away over the sea. He was standing on the field; his hand was pressed to his side; his face was pale and strange and he wore the white cloak of a marshal.[24]

O how cold and strange it was to think of that! All the dark was cold and strange. There were pale strange faces there, great eyes like carriagelamps. They were the ghosts of murderers, the figures of marshals who had received their deathwound on battlefields far away over the sea. What did they wish to say that their faces were so strange?

> *Visit, we beseech Thee, O Lord, this habitation and drive away from it all . . .*

Going home for the holidays! That would be lovely: the fellows had told him. Getting up on the cars in the early wintry morning outside the door of the castle. The cars were rolling on the gravel. Cheers for the rector!

Hurray! Hurray! Hurray!

23. The prayer preceding the concluding lines of Compline, the last of the seven canonical hours in the Divine Office.

24. A member of the Browne family, which had owned Clongowes Wood in the eighteenth century, Maximilian Ulysses (1705-57), count von Browne, became a field-marshal in the Austrian army. He was the son of an Irish Jacobite expatriate. Legend has it that on the day he was killed by the Prussians in the battle of Prague in 1757, his bloodied ghost appeared to the servants in Clongowes Castle.

The cars drove past the chapel and all caps were raised. They drove merrily along the country roads. The drivers pointed with their whips to Bodenstown.[25] The fellows cheered. They passed the holly farmhouse of the Jolly Farmer. Cheer after cheer after cheer. Through Clane they drove, cheering and cheered. The peasant women stood at the half-doors, the men stood here and there. The lovely smell there was in the wintry air: the smell of Clane: rain and wintry air and turf smouldering and corduroy.

The train was full of fellows: a long long chocolate train with cream facings. The guards went to and fro opening, closing, locking, unlocking the doors. They were men in dark blue and silver; they had silvery whistles and their keys made a quick music: click, click: click, click.

And the train raced on over the flat lands and past the Hill of Allen. The telegraphpoles were passing, passing. The train went on and on. It knew. There were coloured lanterns in the hall of his father's house and ropes of green branches. There were holly and ivy round the pierglass and holly and ivy, green and red, twined round the chandeliers. There were red holly and green ivy round the old portraits on the walls. Holly and ivy for him and for Christmas.

Lovely...

All the people. Welcome home, Stephen! Noises of welcome. His mother kissed him. Was that right? His father was a marshal now: higher than a magistrate. Welcome home, Stephen!

Noises...

There was a noise of curtainrings running back along the rods, of water being splashed in the basins. There was a noise of rising and dressing and washing in the dormitory: a noise of clapping of hands as the prefect went up and down telling the fellows to look sharp. A pale sunlight showed the yellow curtains drawn back, the tossed beds. His bed was very hot and his face and body were very hot.

He got up and sat on the side of his bed. He was weak. He tried to pull on his stocking. It had a horrid rough feel. The sunlight was queer and cold.

Fleming said:

— Are you not well?

He did not know; and Fleming said:

25. The burial place of Wolfe Tone (1763-98), the father of Irish republicanism.

— Get back into bed. I'll tell McGlade you're not well.

— He's sick.

— Who is?

— Tell McGlade.

— Get back into bed.

— Is he sick?

A fellow held his arms while he loosened the stocking clinging to his foot and climbed back into the hot bed.

He crouched down between the sheets, glad of their tepid glow. He heard the fellows talk among themselves about him as they dressed for mass. It was a mean thing to do, to shoulder him into the square ditch, they were saying.

Then their voices ceased; they had gone. A voice at his bed said:

— Dedalus, don't spy on us, sure you won't?

Wells's face was there. He looked at it and saw that Wells was afraid.

— I didn't mean to. Sure you won't?

His father had told him, whatever he did, never to peach on a fellow. He shook his head and answered no and felt glad. Wells said:

— I didn't mean to, honour bright. It was only for cod. I'm sorry.

The face and the voice went away. Sorry because he was afraid. Afraid that it was some disease. Canker was a disease of plants and cancer one of animals: or another different. That was a long time ago then out on the playgrounds in the evening light, creeping from point to point on the fringe of his line, a heavy bird flying low through the grey light. Leicester Abbey lit up. Wolsey died there. The abbots buried him themselves.

It was not Wells's face, it was the prefect's. He was not foxing. No, no: he was sick really. He was not foxing. And he felt the prefect's hand on his forehead; and he felt his forehead warm and damp against the prefect's cold damp hand. That was the way a rat felt, slimy and damp and cold. Every rat had two eyes to look out of. Sleek slimy coats, little little feet tucked up to jump, black shiny eyes to look out of. They could understand how to jump. But the minds of rats could not understand trigonometry. When they were dead they lay on their sides. Their coats dried then. They were only dead things.

The prefect was there again and it was his voice that was saying that he was to get up, that Father Minister had said he was to get up and dress and go to the infirmary. And while he was dressing himself as quickly as he could the prefect said:

— We must pack off to Brother Michael because we have the collywobbles![26] Terrible thing to have the collywobbles! How we wobble when we have the collywobbles!

He was very decent to say that. That was all to make him laugh. But he could not laugh because his cheeks and lips were all shivery: and then the prefect had to laugh by himself.

The prefect cried:

— Quick match! Hayfoot! Strawfoot![27]

They went together down the staircase and along the corridor and past the bath. As he passed the door he remembered with a vague fear the warm turfcoloured bogwater, the warm moist air, the noise of plunges, the smell of the towels, like medicine.

Brother Michael was standing at the door of the infirmary and from the door of the dark cabinet on his right came a smell like medicine. That came from the bottles on the shelves. The prefect spoke to Brother Michael and Brother Michael answered and called the prefect sir. He had reddish hair mixed with grey and a queer look. It was queer that he would always be a brother. It was queer too that you could not call him sir because he was a brother and had a different kind of look. Was he not holy enough or why could he not catch up on the others?

There were two beds in the room and in one bed there was a fellow: and when they went in he called out:

— Hello! It's young Dedalus! What's up?

— The sky is up, Brother Michael said.

He was a fellow out of the third of grammar and, while Stephen was undressing, he asked Brother Michael to bring him a round of buttered toast.

— Ah, do! he said.

— Butter you up! said Brother Michael. You'll get your walking papers in the morning when the doctor comes.

— Will I? the fellow said. I'm not well yet.

Brother Michael repeated:

— You'll get your walking papers, I tell you.

He bent down to rake the fire. He had a long back like the long back of a tramhorse. He shook the poker gravely and nodded his head at the fellow out of third of grammar.

Then Brother Michael went away and after a while the fellow out of third of grammar turned in towards the wall and fell asleep.

That was the infirmary. He was sick then. Had they written home to tell his mother and father? But it would be quicker for one of the priests to go himself to tell them. Or he would write a letter for the priest to bring.

Dear Mother

I am sick. I want to go home. Please come and take me home. I am in the infirmary.

Your fond son,

Stephen

How far away they were! There was cold sunlight outside the window. He wondered if he would die. You could die just the same on a sunny day. He might die before his mother came. Then he would have a dead mass in the chapel like the way the fellows had told him it was when Little had died.[28] All the fellows would be at the mass, dressed in black, all with sad faces. Wells too would be there but no fellow would look at him. The rector would be there in a cope of black and gold and there would be tall yellow candles on the altar and round the catafalque. And they would carry the coffin out of the chapel slowly and he would be buried in the little graveyard of the community off the main avenue of limes. And Wells would be sorry then for what he had done. And the bell would toll slowly.

He could hear the tolling. He said over to himself the song that Brigid had taught him.

Dingdong! The castle bell!
Farewell, my mother!
Bury me in the old churchyard
Beside my eldest brother.
My coffin shall be black,
Six angels at my back,
Two to sing and two to pray
And two to carry my soul away.

How beautiful and sad that was! How beautiful the words were where they said *Bury me in the old churchyard!* A tremor passed over his body. How

26. An upset stomach, diarrhoea.
27. Rural recruits to the army often had a wisp of hay tied to the left foot and a wisp of straw to the right foot to make it easier for them to learn to march to the order 'Right, Left!'.
28. A student named Little died of pneumonia at Clongowes in 1890. He would have had a requiem mass in the school chapel.

sad and how beautiful! He wanted to cry quietly but not for himself: for the words, so beautiful and sad, like music. The bell! The bell! Farewell! O farewell!

The cold sunlight was weaker and Brother Michael was standing at his bedside with a bowl of beeftea. He was glad for his mouth was hot and dry. He could hear them playing on the playgrounds. And the day was going on in the college just as if he were there.

Then Brother Michael was going away and the fellow out of third of grammar told him to be sure and come back and tell him all the news in the paper. He told Stephen that his name was Athy and that his father kept a lot of racehorses that were spiffing[29] jumpers and that his father would give a good tip to Brother Michael any time he wanted it because Brother Michael was very decent and always told him the news out of the paper they got every day up in the castle. There was every kind of news in the paper: accidents, shipwrecks, sports and politics.

— Now it is all about politics in the paper, he said. Do your people talk about that too?

— Yes, Stephen said.

— Mine too, he said.

Then he thought for a moment and said:

— You have a queer name, Dedalus, and I have a queer name too, Athy. My name is the name of a town. Your name is like Latin.

Then he asked:

— Are you good at riddles?

Stephen answered:

— Not very good.

Then he said:

— Can you answer me this one? Why is the county Kildare like the leg of a fellow's breeches?

Stephen thought what could be the answer and then said:

— I give it up.

— Because there is a thigh in it, he said. Do you see the joke? Athy is the town in the county Kildare and a thigh is the other thigh.

— O, I see, Stephen said.

— That's an old riddle, he said.

After a moment he said:

— I say!

— What? asked Stephen.

— You know, he said, you can ask that riddle another way?

— Can you? said Stephen.

— The same riddle, he said. Do you know the other way to ask it?

— No, said Stephen.

— Can you not think of the other way? he said.

He looked at Stephen over the bedclothes as he spoke. Then he lay back on the pillow and said:

— There is another way but I won't tell you what it is.

Why did he not tell it? His father, who kept the racehorses, must be a magistrate too like Saurin's father and Nasty Roche's father. He thought of his own father, of how he sang songs while his mother played and of how he always gave him a shilling when he asked for sixpence and he felt sorry for him that he was not a magistrate like the other boys' fathers. Then why was he sent to that place with them? But his father had told him that he would be no stranger there because his grand-uncle had presented an address to the liberator[30] there fifty years before. You could know the people of that time by their old dress. It seemed to him a solemn time: and he wondered if that was the time when the fellows in Clongowes wore blue coats with brass buttons and yellow waistcoats and caps of rabbitskin and drank beer like grownup people and kept greyhounds of their own to course the hares with.

He looked at the window and saw that the daylight had grown weaker. There would be cloudy grey light over the playgrounds. There was no noise on the playgrounds. The class must be doing the themes or perhaps Father Arnall was reading a legend out of the book.

It was queer that they had not given him any medicine. Perhaps Brother Michael would bring it back when he came. They said you got stinking stuff to drink when you were in the infirmary. But he felt better now than before. It would be nice getting better slowly. You could get a book then. There was a book in the library about Holland. There were lovely foreign names in it and pictures of strangelooking cities and ships. It made you feel so happy.

How pale the light was at the window! But that was nice. The fire rose and fell on the wall. It was like waves. Someone had put coal on and he heard voices. They were talking. It was the noise of

29. Rather old-fashioned British slang for 'splendid'.

30. Daniel O'Connell, the leader who won catholic emancipation in 1829.

the waves. Or the waves were talking among themselves as they rose and fell.

He saw the sea of waves, long dark waves rising and falling, dark under the moonless night. A tiny light twinkled at the pierhead where they ship was entering: and he saw a multitude of people gathered by the waters' edge to see the ship that was entering their harbour.[31] A tall man stood on the deck, looking out towards the flat dark land: and by the light at the pierhead he saw his face, the sorrowful face of Brother Michael.

He saw him lift his hand towards the people and heard him say in a loud voice of sorrow over the waters:

— He is dead. We saw him lying upon the catafalque.

A wail of sorrow went up from the people.

— Parnell! Parnell! He is dead!

They fell upon their knees, moaning in sorrow.

And he saw Dante in a maroon velvet dress and with a green velvet mantle hanging from her shoulders walking proudly and silently past the people who knelt by the waters' edge.

A great fire, banked high and red, flamed in the grate and under the ivytwined branches of the chandelier the Christmas table was spread. They had come home a little late and still dinner was not ready: but it would be ready in a jiffy, his mother had said. They were waiting for the door to open and for the servants to come in, holding the big dishes covered with their heavy metal covers.

All were waiting: uncle Charles, who sat far away in the shadow of the window, Dante and Mr Casey, who sat in the easychairs at either side of the hearth, Stephen, seated on a chair between them, his feet resting on the toasted boss.[32] Mr Dedalus looked at himself in the pierglass above the mantelpiece, waxed out his moustache-ends and then, parting his coattails, stood with his back to the glowing fire: and still, from time to time, he withdrew a hand from his coattail to wax out one of his moustache-ends. Mr Casey leaned his head to one side and, smiling, tapped the gland of his neck with his fingers. And Stephen smiled too for he knew now that it was not true that Mr Casey had a purse of silver in his throat. He smiled to think how the silvery noise which Mr Casey used to make had deceived him. And when he had tried to open Mr Casey's hand to see if the purse of silver was hidden there he had seen that the fingers could not be straightened out: and Mr Casey had told him that he had got those three cramped fingers making a birthday present for Queen Victoria.[33]

Mr Casey tapped the gland of his neck and smiled at Stephen with sleepy eyes: and Mr Dedalus said to him:

— Yes. Well now, that's all right. O, we had a good walk, hadn't we, John? Yes... I wonder if there's any likelihood of dinner this evening. Yes... O, well now, we got a good breath of ozone round the Head[34] today. Ay, bedad.

He turned to Dante and said:

— You didn't stir out at all, Mrs Riordan?

Dante frowned and said shortly:

— No.

Mr Dedalus dropped his coattails and went over to the sideboard. He brought forth a great stone jar of whisky from the locker and filled the decanter slowly, bending now and then to see how much he had poured in. Then replacing the jar in the locker he poured a little of the whisky into two glasses, added a little water and came back with them to the fireplace.

— A thimbleful, John, he said, just to whet your appetite.

Mr Casey took the glass, drank, and placed it near him on the mantelpiece. Then he said:

— Well, I can't help thinking of our friend Christopher manufacturing...

He broke into a fit of laughter and coughing and added:

—... manufacturing that champagne[35] for those fellows.

Mr Dedalus laughed loudly.

— Is it Christy? he said. There's more cunning in one of those warts on his bald head than in a pack of jack foxes.

He inclined his head, closed his eyes, and, licking his lips profusely, began to speak with the voice of the hotelkeeper.

31. Parnell's body was brought by ship to Kingstown (now Dun Laoghaire) on 11 October 1891, where it was met by a huge crowd — which, incidentally, included Yeats, who had gone there to meet one of the passengers, Maud Gonne.

32. A hassock or, possibly, a knob on the brass fender.

33. Mr Casey had been jailed and had had to pick oakum, a common chore for criminals.

34. Bray Head, a promontory above the coastal resort of Bray, Co. Wicklow.

35. Presumably 'champagne' here means explosives.

— And he has such a soft mouth when he's speaking to you, don't you know. He's very moist and watery about the dewlaps, God bless him.

Mr Casey was still struggling through his fit of coughing and laughter. Stephen, seeing and hearing the hotelkeeper through his father's face and voice, laughed.

Mr Dedalus put up his eyeglass and, staring down at him, said quietly and kindly:

— What are you laughing at, you little puppy, you?

The servants entered and placed the dishes on the table. Mrs Dedalus followed and the places were arranged.

— Sit over, she said.

Mr Dedalus went to the end of the table and said:

— Now, Mrs Riordan, sit over. John, sit you down, my hearty.

He looked round to where uncle Charles sat and said:

— Now then, sir, there's a bird here waiting for you.

When all had taken their seats he laid his hand on the cover and then said quickly, withdrawing it:

— Now, Stephen.

Stephen stood up in his place to say the grace before meals:

Bless us, O Lord, and these Thy gifts which through Thy bounty we are about to receive through Christ Our Lord. Amen.

All blessed themselves and Mr Dedalus with a sigh of pleasure lifted from the dish the heavy cover pearled around the edge with glistening drops.

Stephen looked at the plump turkey which had lain, trussed and skewered, on the kitchen table. He knew that his father had paid a guinea for it in Dunn's of D'Olier Street and that the man had prodded it often at the breastbone to show how good it was: and he remembered the man's voice when he had said:

— Take that one, sir. That's the real Ally Daly.[36]

Why did Mr Barrett in Clongowes call his pandybat a turkey?[37] But Clongowes was far away: and the warm heavy smell of turkey and ham and celery rose from the plates and dishes and the great fire was banked high and red in the grate and the green ivy and red holly made you feel so happy and when dinner was ended the big plumpudding would be carried in, studded with peeled almonds and sprigs of holly, with bluish fire running around it and a little green flag flying from the top.

It was his first Christmas dinner and he thought of his little brothers and sisters who were waiting in the nursery, as he had often waited, till the pudding came. The deep low collar and the Eton jacket[38] made him feel queer and oldish: and that morning when his mother had brought him down to the parlour, dressed for mass, his father had cried. That was because he was thinking of his own father. And uncle Charles had said so too.

Mr Dedalus covered the dish and began to eat hungrily. Then he said:

— Poor old Christy, he's nearly lopsided now with roguery.

— Simon, said Mrs Dedalus, you haven't given Mrs Riordan any sauce.

Mr Dedalus seized the sauceboat.

— Haven't I? he cried. Mrs Riordan, pity the poor blind.

Dante covered her plate with her hands and said:

— No, thanks.

Mr Dedalus turned to uncle Charles.

— How are you off, sir?

— Right as the mail, Simon.

— You, John?

— I'm all right. Go on yourself.

— Mary? Here, Stephen, here's something to make your hair curl.

He poured sauce freely over Stephen's plate and set the boat again on the table. Then he asked uncle Charles was it tender. Uncle Charles could not speak because his mouth was full but he nodded that it was.

— That was a good answer our friend made to the canon. What? said Mr Dedalus.

— I didn't think he had that much in him, said Mr Casey.

— *I'll pay you your dues, father, when you cease turning the house of God into a pollingbooth.*

— A nice answer, said Dante, for any man calling himself a catholic to give to his priest.

36. The best; the real thing.

37. The pandybat, a leather strap used for punishment, turned the hands turkey-red.

38. A waist-length jacket with a v-shaped back, open in front, that was worn by pupils of Eton College, the English public school.

— They have only themselves to blame, said Mr Dedalus suavely. If they took a fool's advice they would confine their attention to religion.

— It is religion, Dante said. They are doing their duty in warning the people.

— We go to the house of God, Mr Casey said, in all humility to pray to our Maker and not to hear election addresses.

— It is religion, Dante said again. They are right. They must direct their flocks.

— And preach politics from the altar, is it? asked Mr Dedalus.

— Certainly, said Dante. It is a question of public morality. A priest would not be a priest if he did not tell his flock what is right and what is wrong.

Mrs Dedalus laid down her knife and fork, saying:

— For pity's sake and for pity sake let us have no political discussion on this day of all days in the year.

— Quite right, ma'am, said uncle Charles. Now, Simon, that's quite enough now. Not another word now.

— Yes, yes, said Mr Dedalus quickly.

He uncovered the dish boldly and said:

— Now then, who's for more turkey?

Nobody answered. Dante said:

— Nice language for any catholic to use!

— Mrs Riordan, I appeal to you, said Mrs Dedalus, to let the matter drop now.

Dante turned on her and said:

— And am I to sit here and listen to the pastors of my church being flouted?

— Nobody is saying a word against them, said Mr Dedalus, so long as they don't meddle in politics.

— The bishops and priests of Ireland have spoken, said Dante, and they must be obeyed.

— Let them leave politics alone, said Mr Casey, or the people may leave their church alone.

— You hear? said Dante turning to Mrs Dedalus.

— Mr Casey! Simon! said Mrs Dedalus. Let it end now.

— Too bad! Too bad! said uncle Charles.

— What? cried Mr Dedalus. Were we to desert him[39] at the bidding of the English people?

— He was no longer worthy to lead, said Dante. He was a public sinner.

— We are all sinners and black sinners, said Mr Casey coldly.

— *Woe be to the man by whom the scandal cometh!* said Mrs Riordan. *It would be better for him that a millstone were tied about his neck and that he were cast into the depth of the sea rather than that he should scandalise one of these, my least little ones.*[40] That is the language of the Holy Ghost.

— And very bad language if you ask me, said Mr Dedalus coolly.

— Simon! Simon! said uncle Charles. The boy.

— Yes, yes, said Mr Dedalus. I meant about the . . . I was thinking about the bad language of that railway porter. Well now, that's all right. Here, Stephen, show me your plate, old chap. Eat away now. Here.

He heaped up the food on Stephen's plate and served uncle Charles and Mr Casey to large pieces of turkey and splashes of sauce. Mrs Dedalus was eating little and Dante sat with her hands in her lap. She was red in the face. Mr Dedalus rooted with the carvers at the end of the dish and said:

— There's a tasty bit here we call the pope's nose. If any lady or gentleman . . .

He held a piece of fowl up on the prong of the carvingfork. Nobody spoke. He put it on his own plate, saying:

— Well, you can't say but you were asked. I think I had better eat it myself because I'm not well in my health lately.

He winked at Stephen and, replacing the dish-cover, began to eat again.

There was a silence while he ate. Then he said:

— Well now, the day kept up fine after all. There were plenty of strangers down too.

Nobody spoke. He said again:

— I think there were more strangers down than last Christmas.

He looked round at the others whose faces were bent towards their plates and, receiving no reply, waited for a moment and said bitterly:

— Well, my Christmas dinner has been spoiled anyhow.

— There could be neither luck nor grace, Dante said, in a house where there is no respect for the pastors of the church.

Mr Dedalus threw his knife and fork noisily on his plate.

— Respect! he said. Is it for Billy with the lip or

39. Parnell.

40. Luke 17. 1-2.

for the tub of guts up in Armagh?[41] Respect!

— Princes of the church, said Mr Casey with slow scorn.

— Lord Leitrim's coachman,[42] yes, said Mr Dedalus.

— They are the Lord's anointed, Dante said. They are an honour to their country.

— Tub of guts, said Mr Dedalus coarsely. He has a handsome face, mind you, in repose. You should see that fellow lapping up his bacon and cabbage of a cold winter's day. O Johnny!

He twisted his features into a grimace of heavy bestiality and made a lapping noise with his lips.

— Really, Simon, said Mrs Dedalus, you should not speak that way before Stephen. It's not right.

— O, he'll remember all this when he grows up, said Dante hotly — the language he heard against God and religion and priests in his own home.

— Let him remember too, cried Mr Casey to her from across the table, the language with which the priests and the priests' pawns broke Parnell's heart and hounded him into his grave. Let him remember that too when he grows up.

— Sons of bitches! cried Mr Dedalus. When he was down they turned on him to betray him and rend him like rats in a sewer. Lowlived dogs! And they look it! By Christ, they look it!

— They behaved rightly, cried Dante. They obeyed their bishops and their priests. Honour to them!

— Well, it is perfectly dreadful to say that not even for one day in the year, said Mrs Dedalus, can we be free from these dreadful disputes!

Uncles Charles raised his hands mildly and said:

— Come now, come now, come now! Can we not have our opinions whatever they are without this bad temper and this bad language? It is too bad surely.

Mrs Dedalus spoke to Dante in a low voice but Dante said loudly:

— I will not say nothing. I will defend my church and my religion when it is insulted and spit on by renegade catholics.

Mr Casey pushed his plate rudely into the middle of the table and, resting his elbows before him, said in a hoarse voice to his host:

— Tell me, did I tell you that story about a very famous spit?

— You did not, John, said Mr Dedalus.

— Why then, said Mr Casey, it is a most instructive story. It happened not long ago in the county Wicklow where we are now.

He broke off and, turning towards Dante, said with quiet indignation:

— And I may tell you, ma'am, that I, if you mean me, am no renegade catholic. I am a catholic as my father was and his father before him and his father before him again when we gave up our lives rather than sell our faith.

— The more shame to you now, Dante said, to speak as you do.

— The story, John, said Mr Dedalus smiling. Let us have the story anyhow.

— Catholic indeed! repeated Dante ironically. The blackest protestant in the land would not speak the language I have heard this evening.

Mr Dedalus began to sway his head to and fro, crooning like a country singer.

— I am no protestant, I tell you again, said Mr Casey flushing.

Mr Dedalus, still crooning and swaying his head, began to sing in a grunting nasal tone:

O, come all you Roman catholics
That never went to mass.

He took up his knife and fork again in good humour and set to eating, saying to Mr Casey:

— Let us have the story, John. It will help us to digest.

Stephen looked with affection at Mr Casey's face which stared across the table over his joined hands. He liked to sit near him at the fire, looking up at his dark fierce face. But his dark eyes were never fierce and his slow voice was good to listen to. But why was he then against the priests? Because Dante must be right then. But he had heard his father say that she was a spoiled nun and that she had come out of the convent in the Alleghanies when her brother had got the money from the savages for the trinkets and the chainies. Perhaps that made her severe against Parnell. And she did not like him to play with Eileen because Eileen was a protestant and when she was young she knew children that used to play with protestants and the protestants used to make fun of the litany of the Blessed Virgin.

41. Respectively, if not respectfully, the Rev. William Walsh (1841-1921), archbishop of Dublin 1885-1921, and the Rev. Michael Logue (1840-1924), archbishop of Armagh 1887-1924. Both were deeply involved in the fortunes of the Irish Parliamentary Party.

42. Lord Leitrim, one of the most notorious of Irish landlords, was assassinated in 1877. His coachman tried to prevent the attack, thereby imitating the role of the church in protecting British injustice.

Tower of Ivory, they used to say, *House of Gold!*[43] How could a woman be a tower of ivory or a house of gold? Who was right then? And he remembered the evening in the infirmary in Clongowes, the dark waters, the light at the pierhead and the moan of sorrow from the people when they had heard.

Eileen had long white hands. One evening when playing tig[44] she had put her hands over his eyes: long and white and thin and cold and soft. That was ivory: a cold white thing. That was the meaning of *Tower of Ivory*.

— The story is very short and sweet, Mr Casey said. It was one day down in Arklow, a cold bitter day, not long before the chief died. May God have mercy on him!

He closed his eyes wearily and paused. Mr Dedalus took a bone from his plate and tore some meat from it with his teeth, saying:

— Before he was killed, you mean.

Mr Casey opened his eyes, sighed and went on:

— It was down in Arklow one day. We were down there at a meeting and after the meeting was over we had to make our way to the railway station through the crowd. Such booing and baaing, man, you never heard. They called us all the names in the world. Well there was one old lady, and a drunken old harridan she was surely, that paid all her attention to me. She kept dancing along beside me in the mud bawling and screaming into my face: *Priesthunter! The Paris Funds! Mr Fox! Kitty O'Shea!*[45]

— And what did you do, John? asked Mr Dedalus.

— I let her bawl away, said Mr Casey. It was a cold day and to keep up my heart I had (saving your presence, ma'am) a quid of Tullamore in my mouth and sure I couldn't say a word in any case because my mouth was full of tobacco juice.

— Well, John?

— Well. I let her bawl away, to her heart's content, *Kitty O'Shea* and the rest of it till at last she called that lady a name that I won't sully this Christmas board nor your ears, ma'am, nor my own lips by repeating.

He paused. Mr Dedalus, lifting his head from the bone, asked:

— And what did you do, John?

— Do! said Mr Casey. She stuck her ugly old face up at me when she said it and I had my mouth full of tobacco juice. I bent down to her and *Phth!* says I to her like that.

He turned aside and made the act of spitting.

— *Phth!* says I to her like that, right into her eye.

He clapped a hand to his eye and gave a hoarse scream of pain.

— *O Jesus, Mary and Joseph!* says she. *I'm blinded! I'm blinded and drownded!*

He stopped in a fit of coughing and laughter, repeating:

— *I'm blinded entirely.*

Mr Dedalus laughed loudly and lay back in his chair while uncle Charles swayed his head to and fro.

Dante looked terribly angry and repeated while they laughed:

— Very nice! Ha! Very nice!

It was not nice about the spit in the woman's eye. But what was the name the woman had called Kitty O'Shea that Mr Casey would not repeat? He thought of Mr Casey walking through the crowds of people and making speeches from a wagonette. That was what he had been in prison for and he remembered that one night Sergeant O'Neill had come to the house and had stood in the hall, talking in a low voice with his father and chewing nervously at the chinstrap of his cap. And that night Mr Casey had not gone to Dublin by train but a car had come to the door and he had heard his father say something about the Cabinteely road.

He was for Ireland and Parnell and so was his father: and so was Dante too for one night at the band on the esplanade she had hit a gentleman on the head with her umbrella because he had taken off his hat when the band played *God save the Queen* at the end.

Mr Dedalus gave a snort of contempt.

— Ah, John, he said. It is true for them. We are an unfortunate priestridden race and always were and always will be till the end of the chapter.

Uncle Charles shook his head, saying:

— A bad business! A bad business!

Mr Dedalus repeated:

— A priestridden Godforsaken race!

43. Traditional phrases, many of them deriving from the Old Testament, in the Roman catholic Litany of Our Lady.

44. A children's game, more commonly called 'tag'.

45. Parnell is called a priesthunter because he had opposed the clergy in his campaign of 1891. The Paris Funds were so called because the Irish Parliamentary Party kept its funds on deposit in Paris to prevent any possible sequestration of them by the British authorities. Parnell used these funds in his campaign and was accused of misappropriating them to finance his liaison with his mistress, Katharine O'Shea. 'Mr Fox' was one of the assumed names Parnell used in his communications with her.

He pointed to the portrait of his grandfather on the wall to his right.

— Do you see that old chap up there, John? he said. He was a good Irishman when there was no money in the job. He was condemned to death as a whiteboy.[46] But he had a saying about our clerical friends, that he would never let one of them put his two feet under his mahogany.

Dante broke in angrily:

— If we are a priestridden race we ought to be proud of it! They are the apple of God's eye. *Touch them not,* says Christ, *for they are the apple of My eye.*[47]

— And can we not love our country then? asked Mr Casey. Are we not to follow the man that was born to lead us?

— A traitor to his country! replied Dante. A traitor, an adulterer! The priests were right to abandon him. The priests were always the true friends of Ireland.

— Were they, faith? said Mr Casey.

He threw his fist on the table and, frowning angrily, protruded one finger after another.

— Didn't the bishops of Ireland betray us in the time of the union when bishop Lanigan presented an address of loyalty to the Marquess Cornwallis? Didn't the bishops and priests sell the aspirations of their country in 1829 in return for catholic emancipation? Didn't they denounce the fenian movement from the pulpit and in the confession-box? And didn't they dishonour the ashes of Terence Bellew MacManus?[48]

His face was glowing with anger and Stephen felt the glow rise to his own cheek as the spoken words thrilled him. Mr Dedalus uttered a guffaw of coarse scorn.

— O, by God, he cried, I forgot little old Paul Cullen![49] Another apple of God's eye!

Dante bent across the table and cried to Mr Casey:

— Right! Right! They were always right! God and morality and religion come first.

46. A member of an agrarian secret society which first emerged in Tipperary-Kilkenny in the 1780s.

47. cf. Zacharias 2. 8-9.

48. The funeral of Terence Bellew MacManus (1823-60) was organized into a mass demonstration of nationalist feeling in 1861, despite the hostility of the catholic church.

49. Cardinal Paul Cullen (1803-78), archbishop of Dublin 1852-78 and the first Irish cardinal (1866), forbade the use of the Pro-Cathedral in Dublin for the lying-in-state of MacManus in 1861 and was a bitter opponent of the Fenians.

Mrs Dedalus, seeing her excitement, said to her:

— Mrs Riordan, don't excite yourself answering them.

— God and religion before everything! Dante cried. God and religion before the world!

Mr Casey raised his clenched fist and brought it down on the table with a crash.

— Very well, then, he shouted hoarsely, if it comes to that, no God for Ireland!

— John! John! cried Mr Dedalus, seizing his guest by the coatsleeve.

Dante stared across the table, her cheeks shaking. Mr Casey struggled up from his chair and bent across the table towards her, scraping the air from before his eyes with one hand as though he were tearing aside a cobweb.

— No God for Ireland! he cried. We have had too much God in Ireland. Away with God!

— Blasphemer! Devil! screamed Dante, starting to her feet and almost spitting in his face.

Uncle Charles and Mr Dedalus pulled Mr Casey back into his chair again, talking to him from both sides reasonably. He stared before him out of his dark flaming eyes, repeating:

— Away with God, I say!

Dante shoved her chair violently aside and left the table, upsetting her napkinring which rolled slowly along the carpet and came to rest against the foot of an easychair. Mrs Dedalus rose quickly and followed her towards the door. At the door Dante turned round violently and shouted down the room, her cheeks flushed and quivering with rage:

— Devil out of hell! We won! We crushed him to death! Fiend!

The door slammed behind her.

Mr Casey, freeing his arms from his holders, suddenly bowed his head on his hands with a sob of pain.

— Poor Parnell! he cried loudly. My dead king!

He sobbed loudly and bitterly.

Stephen, raising his terrorstricken face, saw that his father's eyes were full of tears . . . .

[In the closing pages of the final chapter, Stephen's own writing takes over. His friends, his parents, his love and his country are all finally rejected for his art.]

V

20 *March:* Long talk with Cranly on the subject of my revolt. He had his grand manner on. I supple

and suave. Attacked me on the score of love for one's mother. Tried to imagine his mother: cannot. Told me once, in a moment of thoughtlessness, his father was sixtyone when he was born. Can see him. Strong farmer type. Pepper and salt suit. Square feet. Unkempt grizzled beard. Probably attends coursing matches. Pays his dues regularly but not plentifully to Father Dwyer of Larras. Sometimes talks to girls after nightfall. But his mother? Very young or very old? Hardly the first. If so, Cranly would not have spoken as he did. Old then. Probably, and neglected. Hence Cranly's despair of soul: the child of exhausted loins.

21 *March, morning:* Thought this in bed last night but was too lazy and free to add it. Free, yes. The exhausted loins are those of Elisabeth and Zachary.[1] Then he is the precursor. Item: he eats chiefly belly bacon and dried figs. Read locusts and wild honey.[2] Also, when thinking of him, saw always a stern severed head or deathmask as if outlined on a grey curtain or veronica. Decollation they call it in the fold. Puzzled for the moment by saint John at the Latin gate.[3] What do I see? A decollated precursor trying to pick the lock.

21 *March, night:* Free. Soulfree and fancyfree. Let the dead bury the dead. Ay. And let the dead marry the dead.[4]

22 *March:* In company with Lynch followed a sizable hospital nurse. Lynch's idea. Dislike it. Two lean hungry greyhounds walking after a heifer.

23 *March:* Have not seen her since that night. Unwell? Sits at the fire perhaps with mamma's shawl on her shoulders. But not peevish. A nice bowl of gruel? Won't you now?

24 *March:* Began with a discussion with my mother. Subject: B.V.M.[5] Handicapped by my sex and youth. To escape held up relations between Jesus and Papa against those between Mary and her son. Said religion was not a lying-in hospital.[6] Mother indulgent. Said I have a queer mind and have read too much. Not true. Have read little and understood less. Then she said I would come back to faith because I had a restless mind. This means to leave church by backdoor of sin and reenter through the skylight of repentance. Cannot repent. Told her so and asked for sixpence. Got threepence.

Then went to college. Other wrangle with little roundhead rogue'seye Ghezzi. This time about Bruno the Nolan.[7] Began in Italian and ended in pidgin English. He said Bruno was a terrible heretic. I said he was terribly burned. He agreed to this with some sorrow. Then gave me recipe for what he calls *risotto alla bergamasca.*[8] When he pronounces a soft *o* he protrudes his full carnal lips as if he kissed the vowel. Has he? And could he repent? Yes, he could: and cry two round rogue's tears, one from each eye.

Crossing Stephen's, that is, my green,[9] remembered that his countrymen and not mine had invented what Cranly the other night called our religion. A quartet of them, soldiers of the ninety-seventh infantry regiment, sat at the foot of the cross and tossed up dice for the overcoat of the crucified.[10]

Went to library. Tried to read three reviews. Useless. She is not out yet. Am I alarmed? About what? That she will never be out again.

Blake wrote:

I wonder if William Bond will die
For assuredly he is very ill.[11]

Alas, poor William!

I was once at a diorama in Rotunda.[12] At the end were pictures of big nobs.[13] Among them William Ewart Gladstone, just then dead. Orchestra played

1. Elisabeth and Zachary were the parents of John the Baptist, the precursor of Christ.
2. John lived on locusts and wild honey during his years in the desert. See Matthew 3.4.
3. John the Baptist was beheaded ('decollated') at the request of Salome after she had danced for Herod. The Church celebrates the decollation of John on 29 August. Christ's face was miraculously imprinted on the cloth with which Veronica, one of the mourners who followed him to Calvary, wiped it. St John the Evangelist was miraculously released from his persecutors near the Latin Gate in Rome. The Feast of St John Before the Latin Gate is celebrated on 6 May. The day also celebrates the dedication of the Basilica of St John Lateran in Rome, dedicated to both John the Baptist and John the Evangelist, precursor and follower.
4. Luke 9.60: 'Jesus said unto him, Let the dead bury their dead: but go thou and preach the kingdom of God.'
5. The Blessed Virgin Mary.
6. This is a theme later developed by Stephen in *Ulysses.* He argues that the relationship between God the Father and God the Son is more central than that between Jesus and his mother Mary.
7. Giordano Bruno of Nola (1548-1600), burned at the stake for heresy by the Inquisition.
8. A rice dish after the manner of Bergamo, a town in northern Italy.
9. St Stephen's Green in the centre of Dublin.
10. Roman soldiers cast dice at the foot of the Cross for Christ's coat.
11. Lines 3 and 4 of William Blake's poem 'William Bond'. The third line begins 'And'.
12. The Rotunda, at the end of O'Connell Street, was used as a place of public entertainment and for public meetings. A diorama was an early mode of image projection.
13. Chiefly British slang for people of social distinction.

O, Willie, we have missed you.[14]

A race of clodhoppers!

25 *March, morning:* A troubled night of dreams. Want to get them off my chest.

A long curving gallery. From the floor ascend pillars of dark vapours. It is peopled by the images of fabulous kings, set in stone. Their hands are folded upon their knees in token of weariness and their eyes are darkened for the errors of men go up before them for ever as dark vapours.

Strange figures advance from a cave. They are not as tall as men. One does not seem to stand quite apart from another. Their faces are phosphorescent, with darker streaks. They peer at me and their eyes seem to ask me something. They do not speak.

30 *March:* This evening Cranly was in the porch of the library, proposing a problem to Dixon and her brother. A mother let her child fall into the Nile. Still harping on the mother.[15] A crocodile seized the child. Mother asked it back. Crocodile said all right if she told him what he was going to do with the child, eat it or not eat it.[16]

This mentality, Lepidus would say, is indeed bred out of your mud by the operation of your sun.[17]

And mine? Is it not too? Then into Nilemud with it!

1 *April:* Disapprove of this last phrase.

2 *April:* Saw her drinking tea and eating cakes in Johnston, Mooney and O'Brien's. Rather, lynxeyed Lynch saw her as we passed. He tells me Cranly was invited there by brother. Did he bring his crocodile? Is he the shining light now? Well, I discovered him. I protest I did. Shining quietly behind a bushel of Wicklow bran.[18]

3 *April:* Met Davin at the cigar shop opposite Findlater's church. He was in a black sweater and had a hurleystick. Asked me was it true I was going away and why. Told him the shortest way to Tara was *via* Holyhead.[19] Just then my father came up. Introduction. Father, polite and observant. Asked Davin if he might offer him some refreshment. Davin could not, was going to a meeting. When we came away father told me he had a good honest eye. Asked me why I did not join a rowingclub. I pretended to think it over. Told me then how he broke Pennyfeather's heart. Wants me to read law. Says I was cut out for that. More mud, more crocodiles.

5 *April:* Wild spring. Scudding clouds. O life! Dark stream of swirling bogwater on which appletrees have cast down their delicate flowers. Eyes of girls among the leaves. Girls demure and romping. All fair or auburn: no dark ones. They blush better. Houp-la!

6 *April:* Certainly she remembers the past. Lynch says all women do. Then she remembers the time of her childhood — and mine if I was ever a child. The past is consumed in the present and the present is living only because it brings forth the future. Statues of women, if Lynch be right, should always be fully draped, one hand of the woman feeling regretfully her own hinder parts.

6 *April, later:* Michael Robartes remembers forgotten beauty and, when his arms wrap her round, he presses in his arms the loveliness which has long faded from the world. Not this. Not at all. I desire to press in my arms the loveliness which has not yet come into the world.[20]

10 *April:* Faintly, under the heavy night, through the silence of the city which has turned from dreams to dreamless sleep as a weary lover whom no caresses move, the sound of hoofs upon the road. Not so faintly now as they come near the bridge: and in a moment as they pass the darkened windows the silence is cloven by alarm as by an

14. Title of a song by the American songwriter Stephen Foster. Gladstone, four times British prime minister, was popular because of his support for Home Rule for Ireland.
15. cf. Polonius on Hamlet in *Hamlet*, II.2.188: 'Still harping on my daughter'.
16. In this old conundrum, the mother replies: 'You are going to eat it.' This confounds the crocodile, who cannot both return the child and eat it.
17. Lepidus in *Antony and Cleopatra*, II. 7. 29-31, says: 'Your serpent of Egypt is bred now of your mud by the operation of your sun. So is your crocodile.'
18. cf. Matthew 5.15.
19. Tara, Co. Meath is the site of the ancient kingship of Ireland. Holyhead is a port in Anglesey, north Wales, and the traditional place for Irish emigrants who take the boat from Dublin to Britain. Joyce is saying that Ireland can be discovered only by leaving it. He is also satirically implying that his method of doing so is superior to that of the writers of the Revival, for whom Tara would have more reality than Holyhead.
20. Yeats's poem 'Michael Robartes remembers Forgotten Beauty', later retitled 'He remembers Forgotten Beauty', in *The Wind Among the Reeds* (1899), lines 1-3:

    'When my arms wrap you round I press
    My heart upon the loveliness
    That has long faded from the world;'

    This is Joyce's renunciation of the Irish Revival and an annunciation of his own project, which he sees as the converse of what Yeats tried to do.

arrow. They are heard now far away, hoofs that shine amid the heavy night as gems, hurrying beyond the sleeping fields to what journey's end — what heart? — bearing what tidings?

11 *April:* Read what I wrote last night. Vague words for a vague emotion. Would she like it? I think so. Then I should have to like it also.

13 *April:* That tundish has been on my mind for a long time. I looked it up and find it English and good old blunt English too. Damn the dean of studies and his funnel! What did he come here for to teach us his own language or to learn it from us? Damn him one way or the other![21]

14 *April:* John Alphonsus Mulrennan has just returned from the west of Ireland. (European and Asiatic papers please copy.)[22] He told us he met an old man there in a mountain cabin. Old man had red eyes and short pipe. Old man spoke Irish. Mulrennan spoke Irish. Then old man and Mulrennan spoke English. Mulrennan spoke to him about universe and stars. Old man sat, listened, smoked, spat. Then said:

— Ah, there must be terrible queer creatures at the latter end of the world.

I fear him. I fear his redrimmed horny eyes. It is with him I must struggle all through this night till day come, till he or I lie dead, gripping him by the sinewy throat till... Till what? Till he yield to me? No. I mean him no harm.

15 *April:* Met her today pointblank in Grafton Street. The crowd brought us together. We both stopped. She asked me why I never came, said she had heard all sorts of stories about me. This was only to gain time. Asked me, was I writing poems? About whom? I asked her. This confused her more and I felt sorry and mean. Turned off that valve at once and opened the spiritual-heroic refrigerating apparatus, invented and patented in all countries by Dante Alighieri.[23] Talked rapidly of myself and my plans. In the midst of it unluckily I made a sudden gesture of a revolutionary nature. I must have looked like a fellow throwing a handful of peas into the air. People began to look at us. She shook hands a moment after and, in going away, said she hoped I would do what I said.

Now I call that friendly, don't you?

Yes, I liked her today. A little or much? Don't know. I liked her and it seems a new feeling to me. Then, in that case, all the rest, all that I thought I thought and all that I felt I felt, all the rest before now, in fact... O, give it up, old chap! Sleep it off!

16 *April:* Away! Away!

The spell of arms and voices: the white arms of roads, their promise of close embraces and the black arms of tall ships that stand against the moon, their tale of distant nations. They are held out to say: We are alone. Come. And the voices say with them: We are your kinsmen. And the air is thick with their company as they call to me, their kinsman, making ready to go, shaking the wings of their exultant and terrible youth.

26 *April:* Mother is putting my new secondhand clothes in order. She prays now, she says, that I may learn in my own life and away from home and friends what the heart is and what it feels. Amen. So be it. Welcome, O life! I go to encounter for the millionth time the reality of experience and to forge in the smithy of my soul the uncreated conscience of my race.

27 *April:* Old father, old artificer, stand me now and ever in good stead.

Dublin 1904
Trieste 1914

from: ULYSSES (1922)

Episode 1: Telemachus. 16 June 1904, 8.00 am. Martello Tower, Sandycove.

[In this first section, Joyce portrays Stephen Dedalus, returned from Paris, entrapped within the confines of a culture that can only represent itself to him in phantasmal or parodied forms. His friend, Buck Mulligan, performs a mock-version of the mass, using his shaving-bowl as chalice, whistling for the fire from heaven (answered by the mailboat leaving Ireland) that will perform the miraculous transformation which, nevertheless, he sees in medical terms as an alteration of the 'white corpuscles'. His 'chalice' is covered by a mirror and razor, and these items gain significance as the chapter develops. The shaving bowl in the parodied mass is held aloft over the

21. In an earlier part of Chapter V, the Dean of Studies, an Englishman, had been bemused by Stephen's use of the word 'tundish' for 'funnel'. Stephen now discovers that the word is English, not Irish.
22. A parody of the style used by newspapers that reported court and social news. This could be copied, since it was not copyrighted. Here an old Gaelic peasant type takes the place of social notabilities; he is the current fad in the literary world of Ireland, one from which Joyce must escape.
23. Dante's ideal of platonic love, embodied in *La Vita Nuova*.

parapet of the martello tower, itself a circular fort, which is in turn ringed by the circle of Dublin Bay. The bowl also reminds Stephen of the vessel into which his mother vomited in her death agony. These three circles — bowl, fort, bay — are directly linked with three environing forces — the church, the British imperial power, the embrace of the great mothering sea and Mother Ireland, from which the mailboat is escaping. Mulligan offers fake escapes — he parodies the church in the mass, he makes fun of the Englishman Haines, who is downstairs in the tower, he converts the sea into a fake Aegean, speaks of Hellenising Ireland, cites the English poet Algernon Swinburne, and, ultimately, dismisses the death of Stephen's mother in brutal physical terms, appropriate to his medical training. He carries in his hands the three emblems of the episode's significance. One is the bowl-chalice, with its fake transubstantiation; the second is the mirror, the emblem of representation, which he also parodies in his discussion of Stephen's theory of Irish art and his citation of Oscar Wilde's distinction between romanticism and naturalism. The third item, the razor, is repeated in his name for Stephen, Kinch, the knifeblade, and in Stephen's own characterization of his art as a lancet, and as a 'cold steel pen', which Mulligan fears; for the blade cuts below the level of appearance and representation and beyond the mockery and parody which is Mulligan's only answer to this traditional emblem of the function of art in relation to experience.

Stephen wants to escape from the rings in which he is entrapped, as in a labyrinth. The maternal sea, mother church, mother England, mother Ireland, are the distorted cultural projections of his own relationship with his mother, who appears to him in ghostly form, a haunting of his conscience, a woman who will not let him be. In order to make his escape, he must rethink the idea of art, he must forsake the emblems of representation and transubstantiation, and, in so doing, must liberate himself from the embrace of his biological and cultural mothers. He is justified in doing so because, if he fails, he will become merely a mocker and usurper like Mulligan, someone who rejects, as does Stephen, the abiding conventions, but whose stance is nothing more than one of dandified negativity. Stephen has to go beyond this.

From the outset, *Ulysses* queries the assumptions underlying Irish, English and European culture by showing to us the grounds for Stephen's repudiation of them and his search for an alternative that will provide a ground for his art and a way of understanding his experience. In Ireland, religion, imperialism and nationalism all, in their different but interconnected ways, have so misrepresented the traditional idea of culture that that idea, as well as Ireland itself, must be abandoned for something new and liberating. The danger is that this abandonment might also involve a refusal of natural feeling. Stephen, in trying to reconceive himself, is ruthless in his drive towards a radical freedom. He is in danger of becoming, literally, in Mulligan's phrase, 'an impossible person'. Within the rings, at the centre of the universe, in the new 'omphalos'. Stephen wants to become father to himself, without any umbilical relation to his maternal culture.]

Stately, plump Buck Mulligan came from the stairhead, bearing a bowl of lather on which a mirror and a razor lay crossed. A yellow dressing-gown, ungirdled, was sustained gently behind him on the mild morning air. He held the bowl aloft and intoned:

— *Introibo ad altare Dei.*[1]

Halted, he peered down the dark winding stairs and called out coarsely:

— Come up, Kinch! Come up, you fearful jesuit![2]

Solemnly he came forward and mounted the round gunrest. He faced about and blessed gravely thrice the tower, the surrounding land and the awaking mountains. Then, catching sight of Stephen Dedalus, he bent towards him and made rapid crosses in the air, gurgling in his throat and shaking his head. Stephen Dedalus, displeased and sleepy, leaned his arms on the top of the staircase and looked coldly at the shaking gurgling face that blessed him, equine in its length, and at the light untonsured hair, grained and hued like pale oak.

Buck Mulligan peeped an instant under the mirror and then covered the bowl smartly.

— Back to barracks! he said sternly.[3]

He added in a preacher's tone:

— For this, O dearly beloved, is the genuine christine:[4] body and soul and blood and ouns.[5] Slow music, please. Shut your eyes, gents. One moment. A little trouble about those white corpuscles. Silence, all.

He peered sideways up and gave a long slow whistle of call, then paused awhile in rapt attention, his even white teeth glistening here and there with

1. 'I will go the altar of God', the opening phrase of the Introit in the Latin mass.
2. cf. Friar Laurence to Romeo in *Romeo and Juliet,* III.3.1: 'Romeo, come forth, come forth, thou fearful man.'
3. Mulligan, after pronouncing his gibberish, is ordering the mock elements of the eucharist to remain in the chalice-bowl under their natural appearances. They are not to issue forth yet transubstantiated. There is also, of course, a reference to Stephen, who has come back to this military barracks of the tower and of Ireland before he could be converted into an artist.
4. In this mock-consecration prayer, Mulligan parodies the name 'Christ' by turning it into a woman's name, a diminutive form (*-in* is a diminutive form in Irish) and an approximation to 'Christian'.
5. 'ouns' is 'wounds' (Christ's).

gold points. Chrysostomos.[6] Two strong shrill whistles answered through the calm.[7]

— Thanks, old chap, he cried briskly. That will do nicely. Switch off the current, will you?[8]

He skipped off the gunrest and looked gravely at his watcher, gathering about his legs the loose folds of his gown. The plump shadowed face and sullen oval jowl recalled a prelate, patron of arts in the middle ages. A pleasant smile broke quietly over his lips.

— The mockery of it! he said gaily. Your absurd name, an ancient Greek![9]

He pointed his finger in friendly jest and went over to the parapet, laughing to himself. Stephen Dedalus stepped up, followed him wearily halfway and sat down on the edge of the gunrest, watching him still as he propped his mirror on the parapet, dipped the brush in the bowl and lathered cheeks and neck.

Buck Mulligan's gay voice went on.

— My name is absurd too: Malachi Mulligan, two dactyls. But it has a Hellenic ring, hasn't it? Tripping and sunny like the buck himself. We must go to Athens. Will you come if I can get the aunt to fork out twenty quid?

He laid the brush aside and, laughing with delight, cried:

— Will he come? The jejune jesuit!

Ceasing, he began to shave with care.

— Tell me, Mulligan, Stephen said quietly.

— Yes, my love?

— How long is Haines going to stay in this tower?

Buck Mulligan showed a shaven cheek over his right shoulder.

— God, isn't he dreadful? he said frankly. A ponderous Saxon. He thinks you're not a gentleman. God, these bloody English! Bursting with money and indigestion. Because he comes from Oxford. You know, Dedalus, you have the real Oxford manner. He can't make you out. O, my name for you is the best: Kinch, the knifeblade.

He shaved warily over his chin.

— He was raving all night about a black panther, Stephen said. Where is his guncase?

— A woful lunatic! Mulligan said. Were you in a funk?

— I was, Stephen said with energy and growing fear. Out here in the dark with a man I don't know raving and moaning to himself about shooting a black panther. You saved men from drowning. I'm not a hero, however. If he stays on here I am off.

Buck Mulligan frowned at the lather on his razorblade. He hopped down from his perch and began to search his trouser pockets hastily.

— Scutter! he cried thickly.

He came over to the gunrest and, thrusting a hand into Stephen's upper pocket, said:

— Lend us a loan of your noserag to wipe my razor.

Stephen suffered him to pull out and hold up on show by its corner a dirty crumpled handkerchief. Buck Mulligan wiped the razorblade neatly. Then, gazing over the handkerchief, he said:

— The bard's noserag! A new art colour for our Irish poets: snotgreen. You can almost taste it, can't you?

He mounted to the parapet again and gazed out over Dublin bay, his fair oakpale hair stirring slightly.

— God! he said quietly. Isn't the sea what Algy calls it: a great sweet mother?[10] The snotgreen sea. The scrotumtightening sea. *Epi oinopa ponton.*[11] Ah, Dedalus, the Greeks! I must teach you. You must read them in the original. *Thalatta! Thalatta!*[12] She is our great sweet mother. Come and look.

Stephen stood up and went over to the parapet. Leaning on it he looked down on the water and on the mailboat clearing the harbourmouth of Kingstown.

— Our mighty mother![13] Buck Mulligan said.

He turned abruptly his grey searching eyes from the sea to Stephen's face.

— The aunt thinks you killed your mother, he said.

6. 'Golden-mouthed', a standard epithet in Greek for an orator. This is the first intermission of Stephen's consciousness as he observes Mulligan.
7. The mailboat is whistling as it leaves Kingstown harbour. Only in exile will the call for transformation be achieved.
8. The divine intervention, the fire from heaven, envisaged as an electric current.
9. Stephen, named after the great artificer of Greek legend, Dedalus, whose son was Icarus, embraces in his name the classical-romantic opposition. He also provides Mulligan with an opportunity for his 'Hellenising' commentary.
10. Algernon Charles Swinburne (1837-1909), in stanza 33 of 'The Triumph of Time' in *Poems and Ballads* (1866):
    'I will go back to the great sweet mother,
    Mother and lover of men, the sea.'
11. 'Over the wine-dark sea' — a recurrent phrase in Homer's *Odyssey*.
12. Greek for 'The sea! The sea!', the cry of the Ten Thousand led by Xenophon when they catch sight of the Black Sea in Xenophon's *Anabasis* IV, vii, 24.
13. A phrase used by the Irish mystic poet George Russell (AE) in various poems.

That's why she won't let me have anything to do with you.
— Someone killed her, Stephen said gloomily.
— You could have knelt down, damn it, Kinch, when your dying mother asked you, Buck Mulligan said. I'm hyperborean[14] as much as you. But to think of your mother begging you with her last breath to kneel down and pray for her. And you refused. There is something sinister in you....

He broke off and lathered again lightly his farther cheek. A tolerant smile curled his lips.
— But a lovely mummer! he murmured to himself. Kinch, the loveliest mummer of them all!

He shaved evenly and with care, in silence, seriously.

Stephen, an elbow rested on the jagged granite, leaned his palm against his brow and gazed at the fraying edge of his shiny black coatsleeve. Pain, that was not yet the pain of love, fretted his heart. Silently, in a dream she had come to him after her death, her wasted body within its loose brown graveclothes giving off an odour of wax and rosewood, her breath, that had bent upon him, mute, reproachful, a faint odour of wetted ashes. Across the threadbare cuffedge he saw the sea hailed as a great sweet mother by the wellfed voice beside him. The ring of bay and skyline held a dull green mass of liquid. A bowl of white china had stood beside her deathbed holding the green sluggish bile which she had torn up from her rotting liver by fits of loud groaning vomiting.

Buck Mulligan wiped again his razorblade.
— Ah, poor dogsbody! he said in a kind voice. I must give you a shirt and a few noserags. How are the secondhand breeks?[15]
— They fit well enough, Stephen answered.

Buck Mulligan attacked the hollow beneath his underlip.
— The mockery of it, he said contentedly. Secondleg they should be. God knows what poxy bowsy[16] left them off. I have a lovely pair with a hair stripe, grey. You'll look spiffing in them. I'm not joking, Kinch. You look damn well when you're dressed.
— Thanks, Stephen said. I can't wear them if they are grey.
— He can't wear them, Buck Mulligan told his face in the mirror. Etiquette is etiquette. He kills his mother but he can't wear grey trousers.

He folded his razor neatly and with stroking palps of fingers felt the smooth skin.

Stephen turned his gaze from the sea and to the plump face with its smokeblue mobile eyes.
— That fellow I was with in the Ship last night, said Buck Mulligan, says you have g.p.i. He's up in Dottyville[17] with Connolly Norman. General paralysis of the insane!

He swept the mirror a half circle in the air to flash the tidings abroad in sunlight now radiant on the sea. His curling shaven lips laughed and the edges of his white glittering teeth. Laughter seized all his strong wellknit trunk.
— Look at yourself, he said, you dreadful bard!

Stephen bent forward and peered at the mirror held out to him, cleft by a crooked crack. Hair on end. As he and others see me. Who chose this face for me? This dogsbody to rid of vermin. It asks me too.
— I pinched it out of the skivvy's room, Buck Mulligan said. It does her all right. The aunt always keeps plainlooking servants for Malachi. Lead him not into temptation. And her name is Ursula.[18]

Laughing again, he brought the mirror away from Stephen's peering eyes.
— The rage of Caliban at not seeing his face in a mirror, he said. If Wilde were only alive to see you![19]

Drawing back and pointing, Stephen said with bitterness:
— It is a symbol of Irish art. The cracked lookingglass of a servant.[20]

Buck Mulligan suddenly linked his arm in Stephen's and walked with him round the tower, his razor and mirror clacking in the pocket where he had thrust them.

14. Nietzsche uses the term to describe the *Übermensch*, the superman, in the first part of his *Antichrist* (1895).
15. breeches, trousers.
16. urchin.
17. Richmond Lunatic Asylum.
18. St Ursula, protectress of the education of the young and a martyr for the estate of virginity.
19. Oscar Wilde, in the Preface to *The Picture of Dorian Gray* (1891): 'The nineteenth century dislike of Realism is the rage of Caliban seeing his own face in the glass. The nineteenth-century dislike of Romanticism is the rage of Caliban not seeing his own face in the glass.'
20. Wilde, *The Decay of Lying* (1889), in *Intentions* (1891). One of the speakers in the dialogue says: 'I can quite understand your objection to art being treated as a mirror. You think it would reduce genius to the position of a cracked looking-glass. But you don't mean to say that you seriously believe that Life imitates Art, that Life in fact is the mirror, and Art the reality?' Stephen, sorely conscious of Ireland's subjugation, adds the phrase 'of a servant'. (See Volume II, p. 384).

— It's not fair to tease you like that, Kinch, is it? he said kindly. God knows you have more spirit than any of them.

Parried again. He fears the lancet of my art as I fear that of his. The cold steel pen.

— Cracked lookingglass of a servant! Tell that to the oxy[21] chap downstairs and touch him for a guinea. He's stinking with money and thinks you're not a gentleman. His old fellow made his tin by selling jalap to Zulus or some bloody swindle or other. God, Kinch, if you and I could only work together we might do something for the island. Hellenise[22] it.

Cranly's arm. His arm.

— And to think of your having to beg from these swine. I'm the only one that knows what you are. Why don't you trust me more? What have you up your nose against me? Is it Haines? If he makes any noise here I'll bring down Seymour and we'll give him a ragging worse than they gave Clive Kempthorpe.

Young shouts of moneyed voices in Clive Kempthorpe's rooms. Palefaces: they hold their ribs with laughter, one clasping another. O, I shall expire! Break the news to her gently, Aubrey! I shall die! With slit ribbons of his shirt whipping the air he hops and hobbles round the table, with trousers down at heels, chased by Ades of Magdalen with the tailor's shears. A scared calf's face gilded with marmalade. I don't want to be debagged! Don't you play the giddy ox with me!

Shouts from the open window startling evening in the quadrangle. A deaf gardener, aproned, masked with Matthew Arnold's face, pushes his mower on the sombre lawn watching narrowly the dancing motes of grasshalms.[23]

To ourselves .... new paganism .... *omphalos.*[24]

Let him stay, Stephen said. There's nothing wrong with him except at night.

Then what is it? Buck Mulligan asked impatiently. Cough it up. I'm quite frank with you. What have you against me now?

They halted, looking towards the blunt cape of Bray Head[25] that lay on the water like the snout of a sleeping whale. Stephen freed his arm quietly.

— Do you wish me to tell you? he asked.

— Yes, what is it? Buck Mulligan answered. I don't remember anything.

He looked in Stephen's face as he spoke. A light wind passed his brow, fanning softly his fair uncombed hair and stirring silver points of anxiety in his eyes.

Stephen, depressed by his own voice, said:

— Do you remember the first day I went to your house after my mother's death?

Buck Mulligan frowned quickly and said:

— What? Where? I can't remember anything. I remember only ideas and sensations. Why? What happened in the name of God?

— You were making tea, Stephen said, and went across the landing to get more hot water. Your mother and some visitor came out of the drawing-room. She asked you who was in your room.

— Yes? Buck Mulligan said. What did I say? I forget.

— You said, Stephen answered, *O, it's only Dedalus whose mother is beastly dead.*

A flush which made him seem younger and more engaging rose to Buck Mulligan's cheek.

— Did I say that? he asked. Well? What harm is that?

He shook his constraint from him nervously.

— And what is death, he asked, your mother's or yours or my own? You saw only your mother die. I see them pop off every day in the Mater and Richmond and cut up into tripes in the dissecting-room. It's a beastly thing and nothing else. It simply doesn't matter. You wouldn't kneel down to pray for your mother on her deathbed when she asked you. Why? Because you have the cursed jesuit strain in you, only it's injected the wrong way. To me it's all a mockery and beastly. Her cerebral lobes are not functioning. She calls the doctor sir Peter Teazle[26] and picks buttercups off the quilt. Humour her till it's over. You crossed her last wish in death and yet you sulk with me because I don't whinge like some hired mute from Lalouette's.[27]

21. clownish.
22. The verb used by Matthew Arnold in *Culture and Anarchy* (1869), in which he opposes the Hellenic and the Hebraic principles, valorizing the Hellenic as liberating, sensual and aesthetic.
23. Two versions of Oxford, one that of the undergraduate romp, the other that of the solemn (but servile) Matthew Arnold figure. Joyce's obsession with servility and the Arnoldian notion of the 'Celtic' is indicated here.
24. Greek for 'navel'; in Greek legend, Delphi is the navel of the universe.
25. Artistic licence. Bray Head cannot be seen from the Martello Tower in Sandycove.
26. A character in Sheridan's *The School for Scandal* (1777).
27. Lalouette's was an undertaker's in Dublin. The reference is to the hiring of mutes as mourners.

Absurd! I suppose I did say it. I didn't mean to offend the memory of your mother.

He had spoken himself into boldness. Stephen, shielding the gaping wounds which the words had left in his heart, said very coldly:

— I am not thinking of the offence to my mother.

— Of what then? Buck Mulligan asked.

— Of the offence to me, Stephen answered.

Buck Mulligan swung round on his heel.

— O, an impossible person! he exclaimed.

He walked off quickly round the parapet. Stephen stood at his post, gazing over the calm sea towards the headland. Sea and headland now grew dim. Pulses were beating in his eyes, veiling their sight, and he felt the fever of his cheeks.

A voice within the tower called loudly:

— Are you up there, Mulligan?

— I'm coming, Buck Mulligan answered.

He turned towards Stephen and said:

— Look at the sea. What does it care about offences? Chuck Loyola,[28] Kinch, and come on down. The Sassenach wants his morning rashers.

His head halted again for a moment at the top of the staircase, level with the roof:

— Don't mope over it all day, he said. I'm inconsequent. Give up the moody brooding.

His head vanished but the drone of his descending voice boomed out of the stairhead:

— And no more turn aside and brood
Upon love's bitter mystery
For Fergus rules the brazen cars.[29]

Woodshadows floated silently by through the morning peace from the stairhead seaward where he gazed. Inshore and farther out the mirror of water whitened, spurned by lightshod hurrying feet. White breast of the dim sea. The twining stresses, two by two. A hand plucking the harpstrings, merging their twining chords. Wavewhite wedded words shimmering on the dim tide.

A cloud began to cover the sun slowly, wholly, shadowing the bay in deeper green. It lay beneath him, a bowl of bitter waters. Fergus' song: I sang it alone in the house, hoilding down the long dark chords. Her door was open: she wanted to hear my music. Silent with awe and pity I went to her bedside. She was crying in her wretched bed. For those words, Stephen: love's bitter mystery.

Where now?

Her secrets: old featherfans, tasselled dancecards, powdered with musk, a gaud of amber beads in her locked drawer. A birdcage hung in the sunny window of her house when he was a girl. She heard old Royce sing in the pantomime of *Turko the Terrible*[30] and laughed with others when he sang:

I am the boy
That can enjoy
Invisibility.

Phantasmal mirth, folded away: muskperfumed.

And no more turn aside and brood.

Folded away in the memory of nature with her toys. Memories beset his brooding brain. Her glass of water from the kitchen tap when she had approached the sacrament. A cored apple, filled with brown sugar, roasting for her at the hob on a dark autumn evening. Her shapely fingernails reddened by the blood of squashed lice from the children's shirts.

In a dream, silently, she had come to him, her wasted body within its loose graveclothes giving off an odour of wax and rosewood, her breath, bent over him with mute secret words, a faint odour of wetted ashes.

Her glazing eyes, staring out of death, to shake and bend my soul. On me alone. The ghostcandle to light her agony. Ghostly light on the tortured face. Her hoarse loud breath rattling in horror, while all prayed on their knees. Her eyes on me to strike me down. *Liliata rutilantium te confessorum turma circumdet: iubilantium te virginum chorus excipiat.*[31]

Ghoul! Chewer of corpses!

No, mother! Let me be and let me live....

28. St Ignatius Loyola (1491-1556), founder of the Society of Jesus (Jesuits) in 1534.
29. From Yeats's poem 'Who Goes with Fergus?', included in *The Rose* (1893) but first a lyric in the play *The Countess Cathleen* (1892), which Joyce saw in 1899.
30. Edward Royce was a member of the company of the Gaiety Theatre, London. The Company performed pantomimes, of which *Turko the Terrible* was one, in the Gaiety Theatre, Dublin. This pantomime was first staged in 1873 and Joyce saw it as a child.
31. From the prayers for the dying in catholic ritual: 'May the lilied throng of radiant confessors encompass thee; may the choir of rejoicing angels welcome thee.'

Episode 3: Proteus. Time: 11.00 am. Sandymount Strand.

[This is the first section in which the interior monologue dominates and, consequently, it can present the reader with initially formidable problems. Although the processes of Stephen's thought are not obscure, the transitions they involve can seem random. Stephen is making his way towards the city centre after teaching his class and talking with his headmaster, Mr Deasy. As in the first excerpt, he is still trying to find some dimension in which he will be free of the pressure of history — Irish or world events — and culture. In his sojourn on the strand, he attempts to go to the very root of the questions about representation and transformation that had been raised in the first section. He sees himself as bounded by time and space or, more precisely, by theories of time and space, which he wishes to test against his own experience. But the philosophical questions raised here do not long survive Stephen's obsessive interest in origin, particularly his own origin and the matter of supplanting that parental doom with a choice of his own, a means of creating himself from a new beginning. Inevitably, this train of thought brings him back to all that he wishes to repudiate: the lost causes of Irish history, here represented by an exiled Fenian in Paris, his mother's derelict family, and emblematic figures like Swift and the early church heretics who were destroyed because they broke with the conventions and beliefs of the majority. An immersion in the actual, which is stifling, or a withdrawal that leads to abstraction, are the alternatives between which he tries to steer. This is the protean chapter of mutation. Opposites blend into one another, time into space and space into time, life into death, beginning into end. Stephen tries to hold his mind at the point where the merging takes place, at that intersection where art happens. It is in words that the relationship between the audible and the visible is incarnated as rhythm. However, this is an improvised conclusion. Stephen is still far from any resolution.]

Ineluctable modality of the visible:[1] at least that if no more, thought through my eyes. Signatures of all things[2] I am here to read, seaspawn and seawrack, the nearing tide, that rusty boot. Snotgreen, bluesilver, rust: coloured signs. Limits of the diaphane.[3] But he adds: in bodies.[4] Then he was aware of them bodies before of them coloured. How? By knocking his sconce against them, sure.[5] Go easy. Bald he was and a millionaire,[6] *maestro di color che sanno.*[7] Limit of the diaphane in. Why in? Diaphane, adiaphane. If you can put your five fingers through it it is a gate, if not a door.[8] Shut your eyes and see.

Stephen closed his eyes to hear his boots crush crackling wrack and shells. You are walking through it howsomever. I am, a stride at a time. A very short space of time through very short times of space. Five, six: the *Nacheinander.*[9] Exactly: and that is the ineluctable modality of the audible. Open your eyes. No. Jesus! If I fell over a cliff that beetles o'er his base,[10] fell through the *Nebeneinander* ineluctably! I am getting on nicely in the dark. My ash sword hangs at my side. Tap with it: they[11] do. My two feet in his boots are at the ends of his legs,[12] *nebeneinander.* Sounds solid: made by the mallet of Los *demiurgos.*[13] Am I walking into eternity along Sandymount strand? Crush, crack, crick, crick. Wild sea money. Dominie Deasy[14] kens them a'.

Won't you come to Sandymount,
Madeline the mare?

1. These words are not in Aristotle, but may be taken as the sort of phrase used in scholastic treatises to exemplify an aspect of Aristotle's thought.
2. 'Signatures of all things' is derived from Jacob Boehme's treatise *De signatura rerum* (1622). Boehme (1575-1624) elaborated a theosophical system in which the world is understood in terms of oppositions, which will finally be overcome on the Last Day, when Christ will triumph over Satan. All things have a visible signature, but they also have a substance not visible to the eye.
3. Limit of that which is perceptible to sight.
4. The reference is to Aristotle and his treatise *De Sensu et Sensibili,* in which he distinguishes between the transparency of air and water and the limited transparency of other things.
5. Stephen likens Aristotle beating his head against the material world to prove its existence to Dr Johnson's refutation of Berkeley by kicking his foot against a stone. Of course, beating one's head against something is also a futile exercise. The world may be independent of our perception of it, yet it may be futile to try to prove this, even though Stephen proceeds with a similar experiment.
6. Medieval versions of Aristotle pictured him as bald (wise) and rich.
7. The phrase, meaning 'master of those who know', with which Dante describes Aristotle, who sits highest in the Castle of Fame in Limbo in *Inferno* IV.131.
8. A parody of Dr Johnson's elaborate definitions in his *A Dictionary of the English Language* (1755).
9. 'One after the other' in the dimension of time. This contrasts with '*Nebeneinander*' (see below), meaning 'one next to the other' in the dimension of space. The reference is to Gotthold Ephraim Lessing's *Laokoon* (1766), in which he distinguishes between poetry on the one hand and painting and sculpture on the other.
10. *Hamlet,* I.4.70-71. The ghost of Hamlet's father beckons him and Horatio pleads with Hamlet not to go:
    'What if it tempt you toward the flood, my lord,
    Or to the dreadful summit of the cliff
    That beetles o'er his base into the sea,
    And there assume some other horrible form,
    Which might deprive your sovereignty of reason,
    And draw you into madness?'
11. Stephen is wearing Mulligan's shoes and trousers.
12. i.e. the blind.
13. Possibly a reference to William Blake's *Milton* I, section 29. The demiurges are intermediate energies, deriving power from God, that create the physical world.
14. Deasy, the headmaster in Stephen's school in Dalkey, knows all the varieties of sea plant and wrack as kinds of money (punning on sea anemone). Joyce trades on the reputation of the Ulster-Scots' fondness for money by giving Deasy the Scots title 'dominie' (master). His knowledge is quite different to that of the earlier 'master', Aristotle.

Rhythm begins, you see. I hear. Acatalectic tetrameter of iambs[15] marching. No, agallop: *deline the mare.*

Open your eyes now. I will. One moment. Has all vanished since? If I open and am for ever in the black adiaphane.[16] *Basta!*[17] I will see if I can see.

See now. There all the time without you: and ever shall be, world without end.[18]

They came down the steps from Leahy's terrace prudently, *Frauenzimmer*:[9] and down the shelving shore flabbily, their splayed feet sinking in the silted sand. Like me, like Algy,[20] coming down to our mighty mother. Number one swung lourdily her midwife's bag, the other's gamp poked in the beach. From the liberties,[21] out for the day. Mrs Florence MacCabe, relict of the late Patk MacCabe, deeply lamented, of Bride Street. One of her sisterhood lugged me squealing into life. Creation from nothing. What has she in the bag? A misbirth with a trailing navelcord, hushed in ruddy wool. The cords of all link back, strandentwining cable of all flesh. That is why mystic monks. Will you be as gods? Gaze in your *omphalos*[22]. Hello! Kinch here. Put me on to Edenville.[23] Aleph, alpha: nought, nought, one.[24]

Spouse and helpmate of Adam Kadmon: Heva, naked Eve.[25] She had no navel. Gaze. Belly without blemish, bulging big, a buckler of taut vellum, no, whiteheaped corn, orient and immortal, standing from everlasting to everlasting.[26] Womb of sin.

Wombed in sin darkness I was too, made not begotten. By them, the man with my voice and my eyes and a ghostwoman with ashes on her breath. They clasped and sundered, did the coupler's will. From before the ages He willed me and now may not will me away or ever. A *lex eterna*[27] stays about Him. Is that then the divine substance wherein Father and Son are consubstantial? Where is poor dear Arius[28] to try conclusions? Warring his life long upon the contransmagnificandjewbangtantiality.[29] Illstarred heresiarch![30] In a Greek watercloset he breathed his last: *euthanasia.*[31] With beaded mitre and with crozier, stalled upon his throne, widower of a widowed see,[32] with upstiffed *omophorion,*[33] with clotted hinderparts.

Airs romped round him, nipping and eager airs. They are coming, waves. The whitemaned seahorses, champing, brightwindbridled, the steeds of Mananaan.[34]

I mustn't forget his letter for the press. And after? The Ship, half twelve. By the way go easy with that money like a good young imbecile. Yes, I must.

His pace slackened. Here. Am I going to aunt Sara's or not? My consubstantial father's voice. Did you see anything of your artist brother Stephen lately? No? Sure he's not down in Strasburg terrace with his aunt Sally? Couldn't he fly a bit higher

15. However this is scanned, the lines are neither catalectic (missing a final stress) nor acatalectic (not missing a final stress). As iambic tetrameters, the missing stress comes at the beginning, not the end (— ' ⌐ ' ⌐ ' ⌐ ' / // ' ⌐ ' ⌐ ').
16. the dark void.
17. *Enough!*
18. Translation of the phrase 'nunc et semper in saecula saeculorum' from the *Gloria Patri,* a traditional profession of faith in the Trinity.
19. (German) 'The room of the women'.
20. Algernon Swinburne (1837-1909), English poet.
21. A poor part of the old city, near St Patrick's Cathedral.
22. Genesis 3.5: The serpent says to Eve, 'ye shall be as gods, knowing good and evil.' To gaze in the navel (*omphalos*) is the traditional contemplative posture.
23. Eden imagined as a telephone area, with the umbilical cords of mankind acting as the telephone cable connecting us to our origins.
24. Eden's telephone number; the first letters of the Hebrew and Greek alphabets with the numbers 001.
25. Adam Kadmon, according to Cabalistic tradition, is the Primordial Man; 'Heva' is a more ancient version of the name 'Eve', deriving from Hebrew *Haj* meaning 'mother of the living'.
26. Cabalistic tradition had it that Eve had no navel since she was not born of woman. The Song of Solomon 7.2 says 'thy belly is like an heap of wheat set about with lilies'. Thomas Traherne (*c.*1632-74), an English metaphysical poet, in the third meditation of the third century in *Centuries of Meditations* (1908), has the words: 'The Corn was Orient and Immortal Wheat, which never should be reaped, nor was ever sown. I thought it had stood from everlasting to everlasting.'
27. eternal law.
28. Arius (*c.*256-336), bishop of Alexandria, denied that the Son was coeternal and consubstantial with the Father. His views were condemned at the Council of Nicaea in 325. Arianism was the first great heresy of the early church.
29. This portmanteau word is a heretical variation on consubstantiality: Arius was against the notion of transcendence and magnificence allowed to Christ, the product of intercourse between his Jewish parents (jewbang). There is probably a reference to the Magnificat, the hymn of the Virgin Mary. This looks forward to Stephen's attack on the supplanting of the mystery of the Trinity by the image of the Holy family in the Scylla and Charybdis episode (below, p. 61).
30. Arius was the ill-starred founder of a heresy, whereas Christ, about whose nature he was heretical, had his coming announced by a favourable star.
31. Athanasius and Sozomen both give this version of the death of Arius. 'Euthanasia' literally means 'good death', and so is ironic here. It also contains the dreadful pun indicating that Arius spent his 'youth in Asia'.
32. Arius was first a member of a consecrated order, called widowers, in the Early Church. His episcopal see is 'widowed' because of his condemnation and death.
33. A vestment worn during the saying of the mass.
34. cf. *Hamlet,* I.4.2: 'It is a nipping and an eager air.'

Mananaan MacLir is the legendary God of the sea in Celtic mythology. Like Proteus, he assumes many forms, and the white horses of the sea are his steeds.

than that, eh? And and and and tell us, Stephen, how is uncle Si? O, weeping God, the things I married into! De boys up in de hayloft. The drunken little costdrawer and his brother, the cornet player. Highly respectable gondoliers![35] And skeweyed Walter sirring his father, no less! Sir. Yes, sir. No, sir. Jesus wept: and no wonder, by Christ!

I pull the wheezy bell of their shuttered cottage: and wait. They take me for a dun,[36] peer out from a coign of vantage.[37]

— It's Stephen, sir.

— Let him in. Let Stephen in.

A bolt drawn back and Walter welcomes me.

— We thought you were someone else.

In his broad bed nuncle Richie, pillowed and blanketed, extends over the hillock of his knees a sturdy forearm. Cleanchested. He has washed the upper moiety.[38]

— Morrow, nephew. Sit down and take a walk.

He lays aside the lapboard whereon he drafts his bills of costs for the eyes of master Goff and master Shapland Tandy, filing consents and common searches and a writ of *Duces Tecum.*[39] A bogoak frame over his bald head: Wilde's *Requiescat.*[40] The drone of his misleading whistle brings Walter back.

— Yes, sir?

— Malt for Richie and Stephen, tell mother. Where is she?

— Bathing Crissie, sir.

Papa's little bedpal. Lump of love.

— No, uncle Richie....

— Call me Richie. Damn your lithia water.[41] It lowers. Whusky!

— Uncle Richie, really....

— Sit down or by the law Harry I'll knock you down.

Walter squints vainly for a chair.

— He has nothing to sit down on, sir.

— He has nowhere to put it, you mug. Bring in our chippendale chair. Would you like a bite of something? None of your damned lawdeedaw airs here. The rich of a rasher fried with a herring? Sure? So much the better. We have nothing in the house but backache pills.

All'erta!

He drones bars of Ferrando's *aria di sortita.* The grandest number, Stephen, in the whole opera.[42] Listen.

His tuneful whistle sounds again, finely shaded, with rushes of the air, his fists bigdrumming on his padded knees.

This wind is sweeter.

Houses of decay, mine, his and all. You told the Clongowes gentry you had an uncle a judge and an uncle a general in the army. Come out of them, Stephen. Beauty is not there. Nor in the stagnant bay of Marsh's library where you read the fading prophecies of Joachim Abbas.[43] For whom? The hundredheaded rabble of the cathedral close. A hater of his kind ran from them to the wood of madness, his mane foaming in the moon, his eyeballs stars. Houyhnhnm, horsenostrilled.[44] The oval equine faces, Temple, Buck Mulligan, Foxy Campbell, Lanternjaws. Abbas[45] father, furious dean, what offence laid fire to their brains? Paff! *Descende, calve, ut ne amplius decalveris.*[46] A garland of grey hair on his comminated head see him me clambering down to the footpace (*descende!*), clutching a monstrance, basiliskeyed.[47] Get down, baldpoll! A choir gives back menace and echo, assisting about the altar's horns,[48] the snorted Latin of jackpriests[49] moving burly in their albs, tonsured

35. Simon Dedalus's acrid opinion of his in-laws and his dislike of Stephen (the Icarus who should fly higher than that) having anything to do with them. 'Highly respectable gondoliers' is a recurrent phrase in the song of Don Alhambra in Gilbert and Sullivan's opera *The Gondoliers* (1889).
36. debt-collector.
37. *Macbeth,* I.6.7.
38. upper half.
39. 'You shall take with you' — the opening words of a search warrant. Stephen's uncle was a law clerk with Messrs Goff and Tandy.
40. Wilde's most cited poem, written after the death of his sister.
41. Lithia water was often prescribed for people suffering from gout.
42. *'All 'erta'* (Look out!) is the first word of the *aria di sortita* (aria of a singer's entrance) in Verdi's opera *Il Trovatore* (1853).
43. Joachim of Floris (the monastery of San Giovanni in Fiore, Italy) (*c.* 1132-1202), in his prophetic work *Expositio in Apocalypsim,* divides history into three ages — those of the Father, the Son and the Holy Ghost. Joyce read this work in Marsh's library, behind St Patrick's Cathedral in Dublin.
44. The reference is to Jonathan Swift, dean of St Patrick's 1713-45, whose misanthropy, madness and creation of the rational horses, the Houyhnhnms, in Book IV of *Gulliver's Travels* are taken to be interconnected.
45. The Latin original of 'abbot', spiritual father.
46. 'Go down, bald-head, lest you become even balder'. This is taken from Joachim's *Concordia* of the Old and New Testaments and is based on the jeering cry of the children of Elisha in II Kings 2.23: 'Ascende calve' (Go up, thou bald head).
47. Stephen sees Joachim as a version of himself, a priest driven mad (like Swift) by a threatening crowd, performing their rite of benediction by descending from the altar clutching a monstrance, a circular spiked receptacle, in the centre of which the host was contained like a single eye, as fatal as the eye of the fabulous basilisk.
48. The wings or sides of the altar.
49. Conventional priests, comfortable in their vocation.

and oiled and gelded, fat with the fat of kidneys of wheat.[50]

And at the same instant perhaps a priest round the corner is elevating it. Dringdring! And two streets off another locking it into a pyx. Dringadring! And in a ladychapel another taking housel all to his own cheek. Dringdring! Down, up, forward, back. Dan Occam thought of that, invincible doctor. A misty English morning the imp hypostasis tickled his brain.[51] Bringing his host down and kneeling he heard twine with his second bell the first bell in the transept (he is lifting his) and, rising, heard (now I am lifting) their two bells (he is kneeling) twang in diphthong.

Cousin Stephen, you will never be a saint. Isle of saints.[52] You were awfully holy, weren't you? You prayed to the Blessed Virgin that you might not have a red nose. You prayed to the devil in Serpentine avenue that the fubsy widow in front might lift her clothes still more from the wet street. *O si, certo!*[53] Sell your soul for that, do, dyed rags pinned round a squaw. More tell me, more still! On the top of the Howth tram alone crying to the rain: *Naked women! Naked women!* What about that, eh?

What about what? What else were they invented for?

Reading two pages apiece of seven books every night, eh? I was young. You bowed to yourself in the mirror, stepping forward to applause earnestly, striking face. Hurray for the Goddamned idiot! Hray! No-one saw: tell no-one. Books you were going to write with letters for titles. Have you read his F? O yes, but I prefer Q. Yes, but W is wonderful. O yes, W. Remember your epiphanies written on green oval leaves, deeply deep, copies to be sent if you died to all the great libraries of the world, including Alexandria? Someone was to read them there after a few thousand years, a mahamanvantara.[54] Pico della Mirandola like.[55] Ay, very like a whale.[56] When one reads these strange pages of one long gone one feels that one is at one with one who once....

The grainy sand had gone from under his feet. His boots trod again a damp crackling mast, razorshells, squeaking pebbles, that on the unnumbered pebbles beats, wood sieved by the shipworm, lost Armada. Unwholesome sandflats waited to suck his treading soles, breathing upward sewage breath, a pocket of seaweed smouldered in seafire under a midden of man's ashes. He coasted them, walking warily. A porterbottle stood up, stogged to its waist, in the cakey sand dough. A sentinel: isle of dreadful thirst. Broken hoops on the shore; at the land a maze of dark cunning nets; farther away chalkscrawled backdoors and on the higher beach a dryingline with two crucified shirts. Ringsend: wigwams of brown steersmen and master mariners. Human shells.[57]

He halted. I have passed the way to aunt Sara's. Am I not going there? Seems not. No-one about. He turned northeast and crossed the firmer sand towards the Pigeonhouse.

— *Qui vous a mis dans cette fichue position?*
— *C'est le pigeon, Joseph.*[58]

Patrice, home on furlough, lapped warm milk with me in the bar MacMahon. Son of the wild goose, Kevin Egan of Paris.[59] My father's a bird,[60] he lapped the sweet *laid chaud* with pink young tongue, plump bunny's face. Lap, *lapin.*[61] He hopes to win in the *gros lots.*[62] About the nature of women

50. Deuteronomy 32. 14.
51. Dan ('Master') William of Occam (*c.* 1285-1349), a scholastic philosopher, known as the invincible doctor, elaborated a theory in which he distinguished between the essence (hypostasis) of a thing and its attributes. This does not seem to be pertinent to what Joyce describes here, since Occam ponders the appearance of Christ at different times and in different places as the bell of consecration rings in different chapels.
52. Variation on the remark attributed to Dryden in relation to Swift in 'Swift' in Johnson's *Lives of the English Poets* (1779-81).
From the seventh century into the Middle Ages, Ireland was known as the Isle of Saints (Insula Sanctorum).
53. 'Yes, indeed'.
54. An ironic glance at Joyce's own youthful collection of 'epiphanies', revelatory and radiant moments. The Hindu term 'mahamanvantara' (great year) indicates an immense span of time, characterized by change and recurrence.
55. Pico della Mirandola (1463-94), the great Italian humanist, who tried to blend Christianity and Cabalistic tradition in his work *Heptaplus.*
56. Polonius to Hamlet in *Hamlet*, III.2.390. Hamlet is describing a cloud that constantly changes form.
57. The dwellings and the stiff shirts drying on the line are both human shells.
58. 'Who has put you in this miserable condition?'
'It is the pigeon, Joseph.'
The lines are from Leo Taxil's *Vie de Jésus* (Paris, 1884), in a scene in which Joseph questions Mary about her pregnancy, which she attributes to the 'pigeon' (dove, Holy Ghost).
59. The reference here is to the son of the exiled Fenian Joseph Casey, here 'Kevin Egan', one of the 'wild geese', the Irish officers who left Ireland after the Treaty of Limerick (1691) and the defeat of the catholic cause. The Wild Geese joined the continental armies and 'Patrice' is following in this tradition, since he is home on military leave ('furlough').
60. A reference to Buck Mulligan's 'The ballad of joking Jesus' from episode 1. 'Goose', 'pigeon' and 'dove' are all interlinked in a catholic-nationalist bond.
61. He laps the warm milk, like a rabbit ('lapin').
62. The great (national) lottery.

he read in Michelet.[63] But he must send me *La Vie de Jésus* by M. Léo Taxil. Lent it to his friend.
— *C'est tordant, vous savez. Moi, je suis socialiste. Je ne crois pas en l'existence de Dieu. Faut pas le dire à mon père.*
— *Il croit?*
— *Mon père, oui.*[64]

Schluss.[65] He laps.

My Latin quarter hat. God, we simply must dress the character. I want puce gloves. You were a student, weren't you? Of what in the other devil's name? Paysayenn. P.C.N., you know: *physiques, chimiques et naturelles.*[66] Aha. Eating your groatsworth of *mou en civet,*[67] fleshpots of Egypt,[68] elbowed by belching cabmen. Just say in the most natural tone: when I was in Paris, *boul'Mich'*,[69] I used to. Yes, used to carry punched tickets to prove an alibi if they arrested you for murder somewhere. Justice. On the night of the seventeenth of February 1904 the prisoner was seen by two witnesses. Other fellow did it: other me. Hat, tie, overcoat, nose. *Lui, c'est moi.*[70] You seem to have enjoyed yourself.

Proudly walking. Whom were you trying to walk like? Forget: a dispossessed. With mother's money order, eight shillings, the banging door of the post office slammed in your face by the usher. Hunger toothache. *Encore deux minutes.* Look clock. Must get. *Fermé.* Hired dog! Shoot him to bloody bits with a bang shotgun, bits man spattered walls all brass buttons.[71] Bits all khrrrrklak in place clack back. Not hurt? O, that's all right. Shake hands. See what I meant, see? O, that's all right. Shake a shake. O, that's all only all right.

You were going to do wonders, what? Missionary to Europe after fiery Columbanus. Fiacre and Scotus on their creeypstools in heaven spilt from their pintpots, loudlatinlaughing: *Euge! Euge!*[72] Pretending to speak broken English as you dragged your valise, porter threepence, across the slimy pier at Newhaven. *Comment?* Rich booty you brought back; *Le Tutu,* five tattered numbers of *Pantalon Blanc et Culotte Rouge*; a blue French telegram, curiosity to show:
— Nother dying come home father.[73]

The aunt thinks you killed your mother. That's why she won't.

Then here's a health to Mulligan's aunt
And I'll tell you the reason why.
She always kept things decent in
The Hannigan famileye.

His feet marched in sudden proud rhythm over the sand furrows, along by the boulders of the south wall. He stared at them proudly, piled stone mammoth skulls. Gold light on sea, on sand, on boulders. The sun is there, the slender trees, the lemon houses.

Paris rawly waking, crude sunlight on her lemon streets. Moist pith of farls of bread, the froggreen wormwood, her matin incense, court the air. Belluomo rises from the bed of his wife's lover's wife, the kerchiefed housewife is astir, a saucer of acetic acid in her hand. In Rodot's Yvonne and Madeleine newmake their tumbled beauties, shattering with gold teeth *chaussons* of pastry, their mouths yellowed with the *pus* of *flan breton.*[74] Faces of Paris men go by, their wellpleased pleasers, curled *conquistadores.*

Noon slumbers. Kevin Egan rolls gunpowder cigarettes through fingers smeared with printer's ink, sipping his green fairy as Patrice his white. About us gobblers fork spiced beans down their gullets. *Un demi setier!*[75] A jet of coffee steam from the burnished caldron. She serves me at his beck. *Il est irlandais. Hollandais? Non fromage. Deux irlandais, nous, Irlande, vous savez? Ah, oui!* She

63. Jules Michelet (1794-1874), French historian, who wrote a book entitled *La Femme* (1861).
64. 'It's painfuly funny, you know. Me, I'm a socialist. I don't believe in the existence of God. Must not say so to my father.'
'He believes?'
'My, father, yes.'
65. (German) End.
66. The faculty of physics, chemistry and biology at the École de Médecine in Paris, where Stephen took a premedical course for a short time. The faculty was popularly known as P.C.N. ('paysayenn').
67. stew.
68. Exodus 16.3.
69. Abbreviated pronunciation of the Boulevard Saint Michel in the Latin Quarter of Paris.
70. 'I am he'. Perhaps a play on Louis XIV's remark, 'L'état, c'est moi'.
71. Joyce's recollection of his failure to cash a money order at a post office which was shut in his face as he arrived, hungry and plagued by toothache.
72. Columbanus (543-615) was one of the greatest of the Irish missionaries to the Continent in the Dark Ages. St Fiacre built a monastery in France and died there. Scotus is probably Johannes Scottus (Ériugena) (*c.*810-*c.*877), the most important philosopher of Christian Ireland. *'Euge!'* means *'Well done!'*
73. This is the telegram Joyce actually received in Paris on Good Friday 1903.
74. *chaussons* are pastry turnovers; *flan breton* is pastry filled with creamy custard.
75. A colloquial term for a measure of wine or beer.

thought you wanted a cheese *hollandais.*[76] Your postprandial, do you know that word? Postprandial. There was a fellow I knew once in Barcelona, queer fellow, used to call it his postprandial. Well: *slainte!*[77] Around the slabbed tables the tangle of wined breaths and grumbling gorges. His breath hangs over our saucestained plates, the green fairy's fang thrusting between his lips.[78] Of Ireland, the Dalcassians, of hopes, conspiracies, of Arthur Griffith now, AE, pimander, good shepherd of men.[79] To yoke me as his yokefellow, our crimes our common cause. You're your father's son. I know the voice. His fustian shirt, sanguineflowered, trembles its Spanish tassels at his secrets. M. Drumont, famous journalist, Drumont, know what he called queen Victoria? Old hag with the yellow teeth. *Vieille ogresse* with the *dents jaunes.*[80] Maud Gonne, beautiful woman, *la Patrie,* M. Millevoye,[81] Félix Faure, know how he died?[82] Licentious men. The *froeken, bonne à tout faire,*[83] who rubs male nakedness in the bath at Upsala. *Moi faire*, she said, *tous les messieurs.*[84] Not this *monsieur*, I said. Most licentious custom. Bath a most private thing. I wouldn't let my brother, not even my own brother, most lascivious thing. Green eyes, I see you. Fang, I feel. Lascivious people.

The blue fuse burns deadly between hands and burns clear. Loose tobaccoshreds catch fire: a flame and acrid smoke light our corner. Raw facebones under his peep of day boy's hat. How the head centre got away, authentic version. Got up as a young bride, man, veil, orangeblossoms, drove out the road to Malahide.[85] Did, faith. Of lost leaders, the betrayed, wild escapes. Disguises, clutched at, gone, not here.

Spurned lover. I was a strapping young gossoon[86] at that time, I tell you. I'll show you my likeness one day. I was, faith. Lover, for her love he prowled with colonel Richard Burke, tanist of his sept, under the walls of Clerkenwell and, crouching, saw a flame of vengeance hurl them upward in the fog.[87] Shattered glass and toppling masonry. In gay Paree he hides, Egan of Paris, unsought by any save by me. Making his day's stations, the dingy printingcase, his three taverns, the Montmartre lair he sleeps short night in, *rue de la Goutte-d'Or,* damascened with flyblown faces of the gone. Loveless, landless, wifeless. She is quite nicey comfy without her outcast man, madame in *rue Gît-le-Cœur,* canary and two buck lodgers. Peachy cheeks, a zebra skirt, frisky as a young thing's. Spurned and undespairing. Tell Pat you saw me, won't you? I wanted to get poor Pat a job one time. *Mon fils,* soldier of France. I taught him to sing *The boys of Kilkenny are stout roaring blades.*[88] Know that old lay? I taught Patrice that. Old Kilkenny: saint Canice, Strongbow's castle on the Nore. Goes like this, *O, O.* He takes me, Napper Tandy,[89] by the hand.

O, O the boysof
Kilkenny . . . .[90]

Weak wasting hand on mine. They have forgotten Kevin Egan, not he them. Remembering thee, O Sion . . . .[91]

---

76. 'He is Irish. Dutch? Not cheese. We are two Irishmen, you understand? Ah, yes!'
77. (Irish) Health!
78. His tongue stained by the drink (absinthe).
79. The span of Irish history from the Munster kings of the Dalcassian line, dating from 300, to Arthur Griffith's Sinn Féin movement of 1904 and AE (George Russell).
80. Édouard Drumont (1844-1917), a virulently anti-semitic journalist.
81. Lucien Millevoye (1850-1918), editor-in-chief of the right-wing periodical *La Patrie,* was a lover of Maud Gonne (1866-1953), Yeats's beloved.
82. Félix Faure (1841-99), president of France 1895-99, reputedly died in the arms of his mistress.
83. 'froeken' (Swedish) and the French phrase both mean 'maid-of-all-work'.
84. Broken French for 'I do all the gentlemen'.
85. James Stephens, the 'head centre' of the Fenians, escaped from Richmond Jail in Dublin in November 1865. He left Ireland by boat from Malahide, in north Dublin, some weeks later. He was not dressed as a bride; this is one of the many ornate versions of the escape.
'Peep of Day Boys', a protestant secret agrarian society, was the original of the Orange Order. Joyce deliberately 'disguises' the Fenian chief as an Orangeman in this series of mutations and disguises.
86. boy, youth (from French garçon).
87. Richard O'Sullivan Burke (1838-1922) was imprisoned in Clerkenwell for his part in organizing the rescue of Fenian prisoners in Manchester in 1867. He was successor-apparent ('tanist') to the clan (sept), meaning the Irish-American Fenian organization, Clan-na-Gael. A Fenian rescue party tried to spring him from jail, causing the Clerkenwell explosion, in which several people died.
88. A popular nineteenth-century song. Egan is not only in exile; he is betrayed by his wife who is comfortable in the Street of the Dead Heart ('*Gît-le-Cœur*') with her two 'buck' lodgers, 'buck' and 'blade' signifying sexual power and promiscuity.
89. James Napper Tandy (1740-1803), United Irishman. The reference is to a line at the opening of the ballad 'The Wearing of the Green': 'I met with Napper Tandy and he shook me by the hand.'
90. Kilkenny takes its name from St Canis (Cill Ceanais). Strongbow, the leader of the Norman invasion of Ireland in 1170, built his castle at Kilkenny. He married the daughter of Dermot MacMurrough, who had invited him to Ireland. There is a link between invasion, exile and sexual betrayal throughout this passage.
91. Psalms 137.1: 'By the rivers of Babylon, there we sat down, yea, we wept, when we remembered Zion.' The catholic Douay version has 'Sion'.

Episode 9: Scylla and Charybdis. Time: 2.00 pm. The National Library.

[This excerpt gives the beginnings of Stephen's theory about Shakespeare's *Hamlet*. As the Homeric allusion in the title indicates, Stephen, like Ulysses, has to find a way between two dangers: the rock on which the monster Scylla dwells and the whirlpool of Charybdis. Joyce embodies these in two characters. One (the Rock) is represented by Buck Mulligan (modelled on Oliver St John Gogarty), who sees everything in gross physical terms; the other is represented by George Russell (AE), who sees everything in an ethereally spiritual mode. Stephen refuses both and seeks some reconciliation between the extremes. His *Hamlet* theory is a parable of that reconciliation, although it is also a revelation of Stephen's own obsessive search for a principle of origin which will not owe a debt to anything or anyone else. The work of art is a coordination of the physical and the spiritual; the relationship between experience and art is created by the artist in such a manner that the artist becomes the father of significance. He creates meaning through beauty; beauty depends upon the reconciliation of opposites. The artist's privilege is, therefore, like Shakespeare's, that of converting the actual into the meaningful. As always with Joyce, actual experience is characterized by betrayal — sexual, political, aesthetic. Fidelity to oneself as an artist is the means by which the betrayal of others is overcome. Even so, the betrayals spoken of here are betrayals of man by woman. Hence the emphasis on the Trinity, the theological concept which, transferred to the plane of aesthetics, allows for a theory of artistic production in which the possibility of sexual betrayal is annihilated. This extraordinary annihilation is, in the whole scheme of the book, seen in an unfavourable contrast with Leopold Bloom's charity in overcoming his betrayal by Molly. Bloom achieves in his life the reconciliation Stephen seeks in his art. Stephen attributes to Shakespeare what he desires for himself.]

... — The sense of beauty leads us astray, said beautifulinsadness Best to ugling Eglinton.[1]

Steadfast John replied severe:

—The doctor[2] can tell us what those words mean. You cannot eat your cake and have it.

Sayest thou so? Will they wrest from us, from me, the palm of beauty?[3]

— And the sense of property, Stephen said. He drew Shylock out of his own long pocket. The son of a maltjobber and moneylender he was himself a cornjobber and moneylender, with ten tods of corn hoarded in the famine riots.[4] His borrowers are no doubt those divers of worship mentioned by Chettle Falstaff who reported his uprightness of dealing.[5] He sued a fellowplayer for the price of a few bags of malt and exacted his pound of flesh in interest for every money lent. How else could Aubrey's ostler and callboy get rich quick?[6] All events brought grist to his mill. Shylock chimes with the jewbaiting that followed the hanging and quartering of the queen's leech Lopez, his jew's heart being plucked forth while the sheeny was yet alive:[7] *Hamlet* and *Macbeth* with the coming to the throne of a Scotch philosophaster with a turn for witchroasting.[8] The lost armada is his jeer in *Love's Labour Lost*.[9] His pageants, the histories, sail fullbellied on a tide of Mafeking enthusiasm.[10] Warwickshire jesuits are tried and we have a porter's theory of equivocation.[11] The *Sea Venture* comes home from Bermudas and the play Renan admired is written with Patsy Caliban, our American cousin.[12] The sugared sonnets follow

1. Richard Best (1872-1959), assistant director of the National Library 1904-23 and director 1924-40. He was at this time an admirer of the aesthetic theories of Oscar Wilde and Walter Pater. John Eglinton was the pseudonym of William Kirkpatrick Magee (1868-1961), essayist and critic, assistant librarian in the National Library 1904-32.
2. Sigmund Freud (1856-1939).
3. Stephen's question refers to an earlier conversation in the Aeolus episode, in which the Greek philosopher Antisthenes had been cited as arguing that Penelope's virtue made her more beautiful than Helen of Troy. Will the moralist rather than the artist be rewarded?
4. Stephen is drawing on contemporary accounts of Shakespeare's life to say that Shakespeare was a tradesman who created Shylock in *The Merchant of Venice* out of his own experience in dealing with money.
5. Henry Chettle (*c.* 1560-*c.* 1607), a London printer and playwright, who is reputed to have been a possible model for Shakespeare's Falstaff. He attributed 'uprightness of dealing' to Shakespeare.
6. In his *Brief Lives* (1698), John Aubrey (1626-97) claims that Shakespeare's father was a butcher; other sources claim that he was an ostler and a prompter in the theatre ('callboy'). He got rich because he sued an apothecary; that is, he exacted his 'pound of flesh', as Shylock did in his business dealings.
7. In 1594, Queen Elizabeth's Jewish physician, Roderigo Lopez, was hanged, drawn and quartered for having accepted a bribe from Spanish agents to poison her. An outbreak of anti-semitism followed. A 'sheeny' is a slang word for Jew.
8. James I (James VI of Scotland), king of England 1603-25, who wrote a book on witchcraft, *Daemonologie* (1597).
9. Don Adriano de Armado is a caricature Spaniard in Shakespeare's *Love's Labour's Lost*. The Spanish Armada was defeated in 1588.
10. In the Boer War, the town of Mafeking was relieved from siege on 17 May 1900; a burst of jingoistic celebration followed in England, as it did in the aftermath of the Armada.
11. The Warwickshire Jesuit Henry Garnet was tried for his involvement in the plot to blow up the king and the Houses of Parliament in November 1605. He defended the doctrine of equivocation at his trial, ironically referred to by the porter in *Macbeth*, II.3.8-12.
12. Joyce draws on contemporary accounts of Shakespeare's life, which claimed that *The Tempest* was in part inspired by the voyage of a ship called the *Sea Venture*, lost in 1609. Ernest Renan (1823-92) admired Shakespeare's last plays and wrote a sequel to *The Tempest*. Caliban, the monster in the play, is called Patsy after the stage-Irishman of

Sidney's.[13] As for fay Elizabeth, otherwise carrotty Bess, the gross virgin who inspired the *Merry Wives of Windsor*, let some meinherr from Almany grope his life long for deephid meanings in the depths of the buckbasket.[14]

I think you're getting on very nicely. Just mix up a mixture of theolologicophilolological. *Mingo, minxi, mictum, mingere.*[15]

— Prove that he was a jew, John Eglinton dared, expectantly. Your dean of studies holds he was a holy Roman.

Sufflaminandus sum.[16]

— He was made in Germany, Stephen replied, as the champion French polisher of Italian scandals.

— A myriadminded man, Mr Best reminded. Coleridge called him myriadminded.[17]

Amplius. In societate humana hoc est maxime necessarium ut sit amicitia inter multos.[18]

— Saint Thomas, Stephen began ...

— *Ora pro nobis*,[19] Monk Mulligan groaned, sinking to a chair.

There he keened a wailing rune:

— *Pogue mahone! Acushla machree!* It's destroyed we are from this day! It's destroyed we are surely![20]

All smiled their smiles.

— Saint Thomas, Stephen smiling said, whose gorbellied works I enjoy reading in the original, writing of incest from a standpoint different from that of the new Viennese school Mr Magee spoke of,[21] likens it in his wise and curious way to an avarice of the emotions.[22] He means that the love so given to one near in blood is covetously withheld from some stranger who, it may be, hungers for it. Jews, whom christians tax with avarice, are of all races the most given to intermarriage. Accusations are made in anger. The christian laws which built up the hoards of the jews (for whom, as for the lollards,[23] storm was shelter) bound their affections too with hoops of steel. Whether these be sins or virtues old Nobodaddy[24] will tell us at doomsday leet. But a man who holds so tightly to what he calls his rights over what he calls his debts will hold tightly also to what he calls his rights over her whom he calls his wife. No sir smile neighbour shall covet his ox or his wife or his manservant or his maidservant or his jackass.[25]

— Or his jennyass, Buck Mulligan antiphoned.

— Gentle Will is being roughly handled, gentle Mr Best said gently.

— Which will? gagged sweetly Buck Mulligan. We are getting mixed.

— The will to live, John Eglinton philosophised, for poor Ann, Will's widow, is the will to die.

— *Requiescat!* Stephen prayed.

What of all the will to do?
It has vanished long ago ...[26]

— She lies laid out in stark stiffness in that second-best bed, the mobled queen, even though you prove that a bed in those days was as rare as a motorcar is now and that its carvings were the wonder of seven parishes. In old age she takes up with gospellers (one stayed with her at New Place and drank a quart of sack the town council paid for but in which bed he slept it skills not to ask) and heard she had a soul. She read or had read to her his chapbooks

nineteenth-century theatre. *Our American Cousin* (1858) is a play by the English dramatist Tom Taylor (1817-80), at a performance of which, in Washington, President Abraham Lincoln was assassinated.

13. Sir Philip Sidney's sonnet sequence *Astrophel and Stella*, composed in the early 1580s, preceded Shakespeare's sonnets, called 'sugared sonnets' by a contemporary, Francis Meres, in his *Palladio Tamia, Wit's Treasury* (1598).
14. Queen Elizabeth, Spenser's Faerie ('fay') Queene, was red-haired ('carrotty') and known as Good Queen Bess. She was reputed to have a gross sense of humour, but her virginity was probably a myth. Tradition has it that she ordered Shakespeare to write *The Merry Wives of Windsor*, a play in which the word 'Buckbasket' occurs several times, often with sexual connotations. The German referred to ('meinherr from Almany') could be Freud or any one of the famous German scholars of Shakespeare.
15. Conjugation of the Latin verb 'to make water' ('miscere' is 'to mix').
16. 'I ought to be extinguished, stopped from speaking'. The reference is to the phrase 'sufflaminandus erat' used by Ben Jonson in his posthumous work *Timber* (1641) where he refers to Shakespeare's almost culpable fluency.
17. Coleridge called Shakespeare 'myriadminded' in *Biographia Literaria* (1817), chapter XV.
18. 'As a generalization [it may be said] in human society that there should be friendly relationships between as many as possible.' Possibly an adaptation from Cicero.
19. 'Pray for us.'
20. The phonetic rendering of the Irish means 'Kiss my arse! Pulse of my heart' and the subsequent phrase is adapted from Synge's *Riders to the Sea* (1904).
21. The school of Freud.
22. St Thomas Aquinas discusses incest in Article 9 of the *Summa Theologica, Secunda Secundae*, Question 154.
23. The Jews and the Lollards, a fourteenth-century group of religious reformers, were both persecuted. They found shelter from the storm at different times in England.
    Polonius to Laertes in *Hamlet*, I.3.62-63:
    'Those friends thou hast, and their adoption tried,
    Grapple them unto thy soul with hoops of steel,'
24. William Blake's name for the God of wrath.
25. *The Winter's Tale*, I.2.196: 'Sir Smile, his neighbour'. In Deuteronomy 6.21, it is forbidden to covet any of these things.
26. The opening lines of 'Sung on a By-Way', a poem by George Russell (AE).

preferring them to the *Merry Wives* and, loosing her nightly waters on the jordan, she thought over *Hooks and Eyes for Believers' Breeches* and *The Most Spiritual Snuffbox to Make the Most Devout Souls Sneeze*. Venus has twisted her lips in prayer.[27] Agenbite of inwit: remorse of conscience.[28] It is an age of exhausted whoredom groping for its god.

— History shows that to be true, *inquit Eglintonus Chronolologos*.[29] The ages succeed one another. But we have it on high authority that a man's worst enemies shall be those of his own house and family. I feel that Russell is right. What do we care for his wife or father? I should say that only family poets have family lives. Falstaff was not a family man. I feel that the fat knight is his supreme creation.

Lean, he lay back. Shy, deny thy kindred, the unco guid.[30] Shy, supping with the godless, he sneaks the cup. A sire in Ultonian Antrim bade it him.[31] Visits him here on quarter days. Mr Magee, sir, there's a gentleman to see you. Me? Says he's your father, sir. Give me my Wordsworth. Enter Magee Mor Matthew, a rugged rough rugheaded kern,[32] in strossers with a buttoned codpiece, his nether stocks bemired with clauber of ten forests, a wand of wilding in his hand.[33]

Your own? He knows your old fellow. The widower.

Hurrying to her squalid deathlair from gay Paris on the quayside I touched his hand. The voice, new warmth, speaking. Dr Bob Kenny is attending her. The eyes that wish me well. But do not know me.

— A father, Stephen said, battling against hopelessness, is a necessary evil. He wrote the play in the months that followed his father's death. If you hold that he, a greying man with two marriageable daughters, with thirtyfive years of life, *nel mezzo del cammin di nostra vita*,[34] with fifty of experience, is the beardless undergraduate from Wittenberg then you must hold that his seventyyear old mother is the lustful queen. No. The corpse of John Shakespeare does not walk the night.[35] From hour to hour it rots and rots.[36] He rests, disarmed of fatherhood, having devised that mystical estate upon his son. Boccaccio's Calandrino[37] was the first and last man who felt himself with child. Fatherhood, in the sense of conscious begetting, is unknown to man. It is a mystical estate, an apostolic succession, from only begetter to only begotten.[38] On that mystery and not on the madonna which the cunning Italian intellect flung to the mob of Europe the church is founded and founded irremovably because founded, like the world, macro and microcosm, upon the void. Upon incertitude, upon unlikelihood. *Amor matris*, subjective and objective genitive,[39] may be the only true thing in life. Paternity may be a legal fiction. Who is the father of any son that any son should love him or he any son?

What the hell are you driving at?

I know. Shut up. Blast you. I have reasons.

Amplius. Adhuc. Iterum. Postea.[40]

Are you condemned to do this?

— They are sundered by a bodily shame so steadfast that the criminal annals of the world, stained with all other incests and bestialities, hardly record its breach. Sons with mothers, sires with daughters, lesbic sisters, loves that dare not speak their name,[41] nephews with grandmothers, jailbirds with keyholes, queens with prize bulls. The son unborn

27. Shakespeare's wife, Anne Hathaway, was allegedly a puritan and would have read tracts like these, both of which were published between 1650 and 1653.
28. *Agenbite of Inwit* is a medieval volume describing the virtues and vices. The title means 'remorse of conscience'. The phrase first appears in episode 1.
29. 'said Eglinton, the Chronologist'.
30. Robert Burns, 'Address to the Unco Guid, or the Rigidly Righteous' (1786-87).
31. Antrim, one of the counties of Ulster, taken by Stephen to be John Eglinton's birthplace.
32. Stephen envisages Magee's puritan father visiting him in the Library. Shakespeare in *The Tragedy of King Richard II*, II.1.155-56 has the lines:
    'Now for our Irish wars:
    We must supplant those rough rug-headed kerns'.
    A kern was a foot-soldier.
33. *Henry V*, III.7.55-57: '. . . and you rode, like a kern of Ireland . . . in your strait strossers' (underpants). 'Clauber' is 'mud'. A 'wilding' is a wild-apple tree.
    See Wordsworth, 'Two April Mornings' (1799):
    'Methinks I see him stand
    As at this moment, with a bough
    Of wilding in his hand.'
34. Dante, 'in the middle of our life's way' — the opening line of the *Inferno*.
35. The Ghost in *Hamlet*, I.5.10 is 'Doom'd for a certain term to walk the night. . . .'
36. *As You Like It*, II. 7.27: 'And then, from hour to hour, we rot and rot'.
37. In Boccaccio's *The Decameron*, Calandrino is persuaded by his friends that he is with child. They pretend to cure him, for a price.
38. In accord with the Nicene Creed, which repudiated the Arian heresy.
39. Either 'love of a mother' for her child or 'love of a mother' by her child.
40. 'In addition. Until now (heretofore). Once again. Hereafter.' These are terms used in scholastic philosophy to indicate phases of the argument.
41. The phrase cited by Oscar Wilde at his trial, from a poem, 'Two Loves', by his friend Lord Alfred Douglas. It refers to homosexual love.

mars beauty: born, he brings pain, divides affection, increases care. He is a new male: his growth is his father's decline, his youth his father's envy, his friend his father's enemy.

In rue Monsieur le Prince I thought it.

— What links them in nature? An instant of blind rut.

Am I a father? If I were?

Shrunken uncertain hand.

— Sabellius, the African, subtlest heresiarch of all the beasts of the field,[42] held that the Father was Himself His Own Son. The bulldog of Aquin,[43] with whom no word shall be impossible, refutes him. Well: if the father who has not a son be not a father can the son who has not a father be a son? When Rutlandbaconsouthamptonshakespeare[44] or another poet of the same name in the comedy of errors[45] wrote *Hamlet* he was not the father of his own son merely but, being no more a son, he was and felt himself the father of all his race, the father of his own grandfather, the father of his unborn grandson who, by the same token, never was born, for nature, as Mr Magee understands her, abhors perfection.[46]

Eglintoneyes, quick with pleasure, looked up shybrightly. Gladly glancing, a merry puritan, through the twisted eglantine.[47]

Flatter. Rarely. But flatter.

— Himself his own father, Sonmulligan told himself. Wait. I am big with child. I have an unborn child in my brain. Pallas Athena![48] A play! The play's the thing![49] Let me parturiate!

He clasped his paunchbrow with both birthaiding hands.

— As for his family, Stephen said, his mother's name lives in the forest of Arden.[50] Her death brought from him the scene with Volumnia in *Coriolanus*.[51] His boyson's death is the deathscene of young Arthur in *King John*.[52] Hamlet, the black prince, is Hamnet Shakespeare.[53] Who the girls in *The Tempest*, in *Pericles*, in *Winter's Tale* are we know.[54] Who Cleopatra, fleshpot of Egypt, and Cressid and Venus are we may guess.[55] But there is another member of his family who is recorded.

— The plot thickens, John Eglinton said.

The quaker librarian, quaking, tiptoed in, quake, his mask, quake, with haste, quake, quack.

Door closed. Cell. Day.

They list. Three. They.

I you he they.

Come, mess . . . .

42. Sabellius, a third-century heretic against the doctrine of the Trinity, mentioned in episode 1 with Arius, Photius and Valentine, other famous heretics of the early church against this doctrine. In Genesis 3.1, 'the serpent was more subtil than any beast of the field.'
43. Aquinas, a Dominican, from 'domini canis' (dog of God), was of the Italian family of Aquino.
44. The three men who were alleged to have written some or all of Shakespeare's works were the 5th Earl of Rutland (1576-1612), Sir Francis Bacon (1561-1626), and the 3rd Earl of Southampton (1573-1624).
45. In *The Comedy of Errors,* two of the main characters are identical twins attended by another pair of identical twins.
46. Eglinton wrote in his *Pebbles from a Brook* (1902): 'Nature abhors perfection'.
47. The phrase 'the twisted eglantine' occurs in Milton's 'L'Allegro'.
48. In Greek legend, Pallas Athena, goddess of wisdom, was born from the head of Zeus.
49. *Hamlet,* II.2.633.
50. Shakespeare's mother was Mary Arden and Arden is the pastoral forest in *As You Like It*.
51. *Coriolanus,* V.3. The play was produced in 1608, the year of Shakespeare's mother's death.
52. Hamnet, Shakespeare's son, died in 1596; the authorities on which Stephen depends here give 1596-97 as the year of Shakespeare's *King John*.
53. Hamlet first appears dressed in black, in mourning for his father. Edward, the Black Prince (1330-76), never succeeded to the English throne because his father, Edward III, outlived him.
54. They are, respectively, Miranda, Marina and Perdita.
55. Cleopatra and Cressida are the sexually seductive heroines, based on Anne Hathaway and contrasting with the heroines of the late plays.

Episode 11: Sirens. Time: 4.00 pm. Ormond Hotel, Ormond Quay.

[In this episode, in which 'the ineluctable modality of the audible' predominates, Leopold Bloom is transfixed by music, which cheats the senses in that it renders him immobile and reminds him of the sexual cheating which has now, at four o'clock, reached its most painful moment. Blazes Boylan, on his way to Molly, comes into the bar of the Ormond Hotel where the siren-barmaids, the 'bronze' Miss Lydia Douce and the 'gold' Miss Mina Kennedy, are playing an elaborate teasing game with their customers. Bloom and his dining-companion, Richie Goulding, eat a meal as the various musical forms are orchestrated around them. Bloom hears more acutely and comprehensively than anyone, for he alone can feel the pain of the jingling sound of Boylan's jaunting car carrying him to Molly's jingling bed, interwoven with the steely ring of the viceregal parade through the Dublin streets and the fulsome lovelorn operatic airs of which Stephen's father, Simon Dedalus, is the expert, yet ruined, exponent. Bloom has to escape this paralyzing music. In observing his intense internal writhings and reactions, we become more aware of the presence of the narrator of the novel, a voice distinct from that of the interior monologue of the protagonist, a voice that controls and orders all that happens, a ventriloquist through whom all speak, while giving the illusion that they speak of their own volition.

This episode is a complex image of the Dublin culture that Joyce loved and had to flee from for the sake of his own integrity. Seductive, glamorous, cheap, treacherous, ultimately paralyzing, it is the culture the son leaves and to which the father succumbs. The alternative father, Bloom, enacts this struggle; his triumph is in his leaving and his leaving is made possible by his keeping a level head in the swirl of enchanting sound. He is a man of words, not music, and he chooses words, having seen how music works and how its tricks are part of the whole system of emotional and intellectual deception to which his fellow-citizens are such willing victims.]

. . . He touched to fair miss Kennedy a rim of his slanted straw. She smiled on him. But sister bronze outsmiled her, preening for him her richer hair, a bosom and a rose.

Smart Boylan bespoke potions.

— What's your cry? Glass of bitter? Glass of bitter, please, and a sloegin for me. Wire in yet?

Not yet. At four she. Who said four?

Cowley's red lugs and bulging apple in the door of the sheriff's office. Avoid. Goulding a chance. What is he doing in the Ormond? Car waiting. Wait.

Hello. Where off to? Something to eat? I too was just. In here. What, Ormond? Best value in Dublin. Is that so? Diningroom. Sit tight there. See, not be seen. I think I'll join you. Come on. Richie led on. Bloom followed bag. Dinner fit for a prince.

Miss Douce reached high to take a flagon, stretching her satin arm, her bust, that all but burst, so high.

— O! O! jerked Lenehan, gasping at each stretch. O!

But easily she seized her prey and led it low in triumph.

— Why don't you grow? asked Blazes Boylan.

Shebronze, dealing from her oblique jar thick syrupy liquor for his lips, looked as it flowed (flower in his coat: who gave him?), and syrupped with her voice:

— Fine goods in small parcels.

That is to say she. Neatly she poured slowsyrupy sloe.

— Here's fortune, Blazes said.

He pitched a broad coin down. Coin rang.

— Hold on, said Lenehan, till I . . . .

— Fortune, he wished, lifting his bubbled ale.

— Sceptre[1] will win in a canter, he said.

— I plunged a bit, said Boylan winking and drinking. Not on my own, you know. Fancy of a friend of mine.

Lenehan still drank and grinned at his tilted ale and at miss Douce's lips that all but hummed, not shut, the oceansong her lips had trilled. Idolores. The eastern seas.[2]

Clock whirred. Miss Kennedy passed their way (flower, wonder who gave), bearing away teatray. Clock clacked.

Miss Douce took Boylan's coin, struck boldly the cashregister. It clanged. Clock clacked. Fair one of Egypt[3] teased and sorted in the till and hummed and handed coins in change. Look to the west. A clack. For me.

— What time is that? asked Blazes Boylan. Four?

O'clock.

Lenehan, small eyes ahunger on her humming, bust ahumming, tugged Blazes Boylan's elbowsleeve.

— Let's hear the time, he said.

The bag of Goulding, Collis, Ward led Bloom by ryebloom flowered tables. Aimless he chose with agitated aim, bald Pat attending, a table near the door. Be near. At four. Has he forgotten? Perhaps a trick. Not come: whet appetite. I couldn't do. Wait, wait. Pat, waiter, waited.

Sparkling bronze azure eyed Blazure's skyblue bow and eyes.

— Go on, pressed Lenehan. There's no-one. He never heard.

— *. . . to Flora's lips did hie.*[4]

High, a high note pealed in the treble clear.

Bronzedouce communing with her rose that sank and rose sought Blazes Boylan's flower and eyes.

— Please, please.

He pleaded over returning phrases of avowal.

— *I could not leave thee . . .*

— Afterwits, miss Douce promised coyly.

1. The name of the horse in the Ascot Gold Cup race on which Lenehan has placed a bet. The actual winner, unwittingly tipped by Bloom, is Throwaway.
2. A line from the song 'The Shade of the Palm' from the light opera *Floradora* (1899): 'Oh my Dolores queen of the eastern sea'.
3. 'Fair one of Eden' is a phrase from the same song; the link between Eve and Cleopatra is a recurrent one in *Ulysses,* since both are regarded as seductive and treacherous.
4. Words adapted from the popular song 'Goodbye, Sweetheart, Goodbye'. The actual phrase is '. . . to floral lips doth hie'.

— No, now, urged Lenehan. *Sonnez la cloche!*[5] O do! There's no-one.

She looked. Quick. Miss Kenn out of earshot. Sudden bent. Two kindling faces watched her bend.

Quavering the chords strayed from the air, found it again, lost chord, and lost and found it, faltering.

— Go on! Do! *Sonnez!*

Bending, she nipped a peak of skirt above her knee. Delayed. Taunted them still, bending, suspending, with wilful eyes.

— *Sonnez!*

Smack. She set free sudden in rebound her nipped elastic garter smackwarm against her smackable a woman's warmhosed thigh.

— *La cloche*! cried gleeful Lenehan. Trained by owner. No sawdust there.

She smilesmirked supercilious (wept! aren't men?), but, lightward gliding, mild she smiled on Boylan.

— You're the essence of vulgarity, she in gliding said.

Boylan, eyed, eyed. Tossed to fat lips his chalice, drank off his chalice tiny, sucking the last fat violet syrupy drops. His spellbound eyes went after, after her gliding head as it went down the bar by mirrors, gilded arch for ginger ale, hock and claret glasses shimmering, a spiky shell, where it concerted, mirrored, bronze with sunnier bronze.

Yes, bronze from anearby.

— *. . . sweetheart, goodbye!*

— I'm off, said Boylan with impatience.

He slid his chalice brisk away, grasped his change.

— Wait a shake, begged Lenehan, drinking quickly. I wanted to tell you. Tom Rochford . . . .

— Come on to blazes, said Blazes Boylan, going.

Lenehan gulped to go.

— Got the horn or what?[6] he said. Wait. I'm coming.

He followed the hasty creaking shoes but stood by nimbly by the threshold, saluting forms, a bulky with a slender.

— How do you do, Mr Dollard?

— Eh? How do? How do? Ben Dollard's vague bass answered, turning an instant from Father Cowley's woe. He won't give you any trouble, Bob. Alf Bergan will speak to the long fellow. We'll put a barleystraw in that Judas Iscariot's[7] ear this time.

Sighing Mr Dedalus came through the saloon, a finger soothing an eyelid.

— Hoho, we will, Ben Dollard yodled jollily. Come on, Simon. Give us a ditty. We heard the piano.

Bald Pat, bothered waiter, waited for drink orders. Power for Richie. And Bloom? Let me see. Not make him walk twice. His corns. Four now. How warm this black is. Course nerves a bit. Refracts (is it?) heat.[8] Let me see. Cider. Yes, bottle of cider.

— What's that? Mr Dedalus said. I was only vamping,[9] man.

— Come on, come on, Ben Dollard called. Begone dull care.[10] Come, Bob.

He ambled Dollard, bulky slops, before them (hold that fellow with the: hold him now) into the saloon. He plumped him Dollard on the stool. His gouty paws plumped chords. Plumped, stopped abrupt.

Bald Pat in the doorway met tealess gold returning. Bothered, he wanted Power and cider. Bronze by the window, watched, bronze from afar.

Jingle a tinkle jaunted.

Bloom heard a jing, a little sound. He's off.[11] Light sob of breath Bloom sighed on the silent bluehued flowers. Jingling. He's gone. Jingle. Hear.

— *Love and War*,[12] Ben, Mr Dedalus said. God be with old times.

Miss Douce's brave eyes, unregarded, turned from the crossblind, smitten by sunlight. Gone. Pensive (who knows?), smitten (the smiting light), she lowered the dropblind with a sliding cord. She drew down pensive (why did he go so quick when I?) about her bronze, over the bar where bald stood

5. 'Sound the bell!' Miss Douce obeys by snapping her garter; Bloom is hearing, below all the sounds, the whirring of the clock as it brings on the moment of his cuckoldry.
6. 'Are you sexually aroused?' Again, by the snapping of the garter or by the approach of the time of his assignation with Molly.
7. The reference is to Reuben J. Dodd, a landlord who is demanding payment of his rent. The attack on a Jewish figure is appropriate here: Bloom is increasingly isolated among his fellow-Irishmen, who band together in their bigotry against the figure of 'the Jew'.
8. Richie Goulding orders a Power's whiskey; Bloom orders a cider and, characteristically, cannot remember whether black clothes reflect or refract heat (they do neither). The same question had occurred to him earlier, in episode 4 (Calypso).
9. improvising.
10. The title of a seventeenth-century drinking song.
11. That is, Boylan has left to meet Molly.
12. Title of a duet for tenor and bass to be sung by Dollard and Dedalus, accompanied by Cowley in the bar.

by sister gold, inexquisite contrast, contrast inexquisite nonexquisite, slow cool dim seagreen sliding depth of shadow, *eau de Nil.*[13]

— Poor old Goodwin was the pianist that night, Father Cowley reminded them. There was a slight difference of opinion between himself and the Collard grand.[14]

There was.

— A symposium all his own, Mr Dedalus said. The devil wouldn't stop him. He was a crotchety old fellow in the primary stage of drink.

— God, do you remember? Ben bulky Dollard said, turning from the punished keyboard. And by Japers I had no wedding garment.

They laughed all three. He had no wed. All trio laughed. No wedding garment.

— Our friend Bloom turned in handy that night, Mr Dedalus said. Where's my pipe, by the way?

He wandered back to the bar to the lost chord pipe.[15] Bald Pat carried two diners' drinks, Richie and Poldy. And Father Crowley laughed again.

— I saved the situation, Ben, I think.

— You did, averred Ben Dollard. I remember those tight trousers too. That was a brilliant idea, Bob.

Father Cowley blushed to his brilliant purply lobes. He saved the situa. Tight trou. Brilliant ide.

— I knew he was on the rocks, he said. The wife was playing the piano in the coffee palace on Saturdays for a very trifling consideration and who was it gave me the wheeze she was doing the other business?[16] Do you remember? We had to search all Holles street to find them till the chap in Keogh's gave us the number. Remember?

Ben remembered, his broad visage wondering.

— By God, she had some luxurious operacloaks and things there.

Mr Dedalus wandered back, pipe in hand.

— Merrion square style. Balldresses, by God, and court dresses. He wouldn't take any money either. What? Any God's quantity of cocked hats and boleros and trunkhose. What?

— Ay, ay, Mr Dedalus nodded. Mrs Marion Bloom has left off clothes of all descriptions.

Jingle jaunted down the quays. Blazes sprawled on bounding tyres.

Liver and bacon. Steak and kidney pie. Right, sir. Right, Pat.

Mrs Marion. Met him pike hoses. Smell of burn. Of Paul de Kock.[17] Nice name he.

— What's this her name was? A buxom lassy. Marion . . . ?

— Tweedy.

— Yes. Is she alive?

— And kicking.

— She was a daughter of. . . .

— Daughter of the regiment.[18]

— Yes, begad. I remember the old drummajor.

Mr. Dedalus struck, whizzed, lit, puffed savoury puff after

— Irish? I don't know, faith. Is she, Simon?

Puff after stiff, a puff, strong, savoury, crackling.

— Buccinator muscle is . . . What? . . . Bit rusty . . . O, she is . . . My Irish Molly, O.[19]

He puffed a pungent plumy blast.

— From the rock of Gibraltar . . . all the way.

They pined in depth of ocean shadow, gold by the beerpull, bronze by maraschino, thoughtful all two. Mina Kennedy, 4 Lismore terrace, Drumcondra with Idolores, a queen, Dolores, silent.

Pat served, uncovered dishes. Leopold cut liverslices. As said before he ate with relish the inner organs, nutty gizzards, fried cods' roes while Richie Goulding, Collis, Ward ate steak and kidney, steak then kidney, bite by bite of pie he ate Bloom ate they ate.

Bloom with Goulding, married in silence, ate. Dinners fit for princes.

By Bachelor's walk jogjaunty jingled Blazes Boylan, bachelor, in sun in heat, mare's glossy rump atrot, with flick of whip, on bounding tyres: sprawled, warmseated, Boylan impatience, ardentbold. Horn. Have you the? Horn. Have you the? Haw haw horn.

Over their voices Dollard bassooned attack,

13. Pale-green cloth, like the colour of 'the water of the Nile' and referring sidelong once more to Cleopatra.
14. A brand-name for a piano.
15. 'The lost chord' is a title of a popular song by Arthur Sullivan, in which the chord of the title brings, for a moment, perfect peace before it is lost. 'Poldy' is a familiar shortening of Bloom's first name, Leopold.
16. 'told me that she was in the second-hand clothes business'.
17. Bloom is recalling his morning conversation with Molly concerning the word 'metempsychosis' (reincarnation of the soul in another body) and the novels of Paul de Kock (1794-1871), a French novelist whose name makes Molly think (mistakenly) that he might be interesting — i.e. pornographic. During this conversation, Molly smelled the burning of the kidneys Bloom had put on to fry.
18. Refers both to Molly and to the opera by Gaetano Donizetti, *La Fille du Régiment* (1840), advertised that day for performance on 17 June 1904.
19. Anonymous ballad, 'My Irish Molly, O'.

booming over bombarding chords:
— *When love absorbs my ardent soul* . . . .[20]

Roll of Bensoulbenjamin rolled to the quivery loveshivery roofpanes.

— War! War! cried Father Cowley. You're the warrior.

— So I am, Ben Warrior laughed. I was thinking of your landlord. Love or money.[21]

He stopped. He wagged huge beard, huge face over his blunder huge.

— Sure, you'd burst the tympanum of her ear, man, Mr Dedalus said through smoke aroma, with an organ like yours.[22]

In bearded abundant laughter Dollard shook upon the keyboard. He would.

— Not to mention another membrane, Father Cowley added. Half time, Ben. *Amoroso ma non troppo.*[23] Let me there.

Miss Kennedy served two gentlemen with tankards of cool stout. She passed a remark. It was indeed, first gentleman said, beautiful weather. They drank cool stout. Did she know where the lord lieutenant was going? And heard steelhoofs ringhoof ring. No, she couldn't say. But it would be in the paper. O, she need not trouble. No trouble. She waved about her outspread *Independent*, searching, the lord lieutenant, her pinnacles of hair slowmoving, lord lieuten. Too much trouble, first gentleman said. O, not in the least. Way he looked that. Lord lieutenant. Gold by bronze heard iron steel.

— . . . . *my ardent soul*
I care not foror the morrow.

In liver grey Bloom mashed mashed potatoes. *Love and War* someone is. Ben Dollard's famous. Night he ran round to us to borrow a dress suit for that concert. Trousers tight as a drum on him. Musical porkers. Molly did laugh when he went out. Threw herself back across the bed, screaming, kicking. With all his belongings on show. O saints above, I'm drenched! O, the women in the front row! O, I never laughed so many. Well, of course that's what gives him the base barreltone. For instance eunuchs. Wonder who's playing. Nice touch. Must be Cowley. Musical. Knows whatever note you play. Bad breath he has, poor chap. Stopped.

Miss Douce, engaging, Lydia Douce, bowed to suave solicitor, George Lidwell, gentleman, entering. Good afternoon. She gave her moist (a lady's) hand to his firm clasp. Afternoon. Yes, she was back. To the old dingdong again.

— Your friends are inside, Mr Lidwell.

George Lidwell, suave, solicited, held a lydiahand.

Jingle.

Bloom ate liv as said before. Clean here at least. That chap in the Burton, gummy with gristle. No-one here: Goulding and I. Clean tables, flowers, mitres of napkins. Pat to and fro. Bald Pat. Nothing to do. Best value in Dub.

Piano again. Cowley it is. Way he sits in to it, like one together, mutual understanding. Tiresome shapers scraping fiddles, eye on the bowend, sawing the cello, remind you of toothache. Her high long snore. Night we were in the box. Trombone under blowing like a grampus, between the acts, other brass chap unscrewing, emptying spittle. Conductor's legs too, bagstrousers, jiggedy jiggedy. Do right to hide them.

Jiggedy jingle jaunty jaunty.

Only the harp. Lovely. Gold glowering light. Girl touched it. Poop of a lovely. Gravy's rather good fit for a. Golden ship.[24] Erin. The harp that once or twice.[25] Cool hands. Ben Howth, the rhododendrons. We are their harps. I. He. Old. Young.[26]

— Ah, I couldn't, man, Mr Dedalus said, shy, listless.

Strongly.

— Go on, blast you! Ben Dollard growled. Get it out in bits.

— *M'appari*,[27] Simon, Father Cowley said.

Down stage he strode some paces, grave, tall in affliction, his long arms outheld. Hoarsely the apple of his throat hoarsed softly. Softly he sang to a dusty

20. A line from the song 'Love and War'.
21. Cowley's landlord was called Love.
22. The reference to the sound of Dollard's voice is also sexual, as Cowley immediately and unnecessarily makes plain. The Virgin, according to medieval traditions, conceived Jesus through her ear — i.e. took in the word of God.
23. 'In a soft and loving style, but not too much so.'
24. Cleopatra's barge in *Antony and Cleopatra* (II.2.197) had a poop that was 'beaten gold'.
25. Tom Moore's famous song from *Irish Melodies*, 'The harp that once through Tara's halls'.
26. That is, men are the harps on which women play. Ben Howth is the promontory at the northern end of Dublin Bay. The rhododendrons in Howth Castle are a famous attraction.
27. A tenor air from Flotow's opera *Martha* (1847). It is sung by Lionel in Act III and is a lament for the lost love of his beloved Martha.

seascape there: *A Last Farewell.*[28] A headland, a ship, a sail upon the billows. Farewell. A lovely girl, her veil awave upon the wind upon the headland, wind around her.

Cowley sang:

— *M'appari tutt'amor:*
Il mio sguardo l'incontr . . .[29]

She waved, unhearing Cowley, her veil, to one departing, dear one, to wind, love, speeding sail, return.

— Go on, Simon.

— Ah, sure, my dancing days are done, Ben . . . . Well . . . .

Mr Dedalus laid his pipe to rest beside the tuningfork and, sitting, touched the obedient keys.

— No, Simon, Father Cowley turned. Play it in the original. One flat.

The keys, obedient, rose higher, told, faltered, confessed, confused.

Up stage strode Father Cowley.

— Here, Simon, I'll accompany you, he said. Get up.

By Graham Lemon's pineapple rock, by Elvery's elephant jingly jogged.[30]

Steak, kidney, liver, mashed, at meat fit for princes sat princes Bloom and Goulding. Princes at meat they raised and drank, Power and cider.

Most beautiful tenor air ever written, Richie said: *Sonnambula.*[31] He heard Joe Maas sing that one night. Ah, what M'Guckin! Yes. In his way. Choirboy style. Maas was the boy. Massboy. A lyrical tenor if you like. Never forget it. Never.[32]

Tenderly Bloom over liverless bacon saw the tightened features strain. Backache he. Bright's bright eye. Next item on the programme. Paying the piper. Pills, pounded bread, worth a guinea a box. Stave it off awhile. Sings too: *Down among the dead men.*[33] Appropriate. Kidney pie. Sweets to the.[34] Not making much hand of it. Best value in. Characteristic of him. Power. Particular about his drink. Flaw in the glass, fresh Vartry water.[35] Fecking[36] matches from counters to save. Then squander a sovereign in dribs and drabs. And when he's wanted not a farthing. Screwed refusing to pay his fare. Curious types.

Never would Richie forget that night. As long as he lived: never. In the gods of the old Royal with little Peake.[37] And when the first note.

Speech paused on Richie's lips.

Coming out with a whopper now. Rhapsodies about damn all. Believes his own lies. Does really. Wonderful liar. But want a good memory.

— Which air is that? asked Leopold Bloom.

— *All is lost now.*[38]

Richie cocked his lips apout. A low incipient note sweet banshee murmured: all. A thrust. A throstle. His breath, birdsweet, good teeth he's proud of, fluted with plaintive woe. Is lost. Rich sound. Two notes in one there. Blackbird I heard in the hawthorn valley. Taking my motives he twined and turned them. All most too new call is lost in all. Echo. How sweet the answer.[39] How is that done? All lost now. Mournful he whistled. Fall, surrender, lost.

Bloom bent leopold ear, turning a fringe of doyley down under the vase. Order. Yes, I remember. Lovely air. In sleep she went to him. Innocence in the moon.[40] Brave. Don't know their danger. Still hold her back. Call name. Touch water.[41] Jingle jaunty. Too late. She longed to go. That's why. Woman. As easy stop the sea. Yes: all is lost.

— A beautiful air, said Bloom lost Leopold. I know it well.

28. A print on the wall illustrates a sunset-and-sea scene for the song 'The Last Farewell', another sentimental tune on the theme of lost love.
29. The opening lines of Lionel's song in *Martha:* 'All love appeared to me, that encounter filled my eyes . . . .' Simon Dedalus sings one of the many English versions of the song.
30. Shops on O'Connell Street (then Sackville Street), indicating Boylan's progress towards Bloom's house in Eccles Street.
31. Earlier Richie Goulding had whistled an air from Vincenzo Bellini's opera *La Sonnambula* (1831). Beginning 'Tutto e sciulto' ('All is lost'), it too is a lament on the part of the hero for the apparent faithlessness of his beloved.
32. Joseph Maas (1847-1886), a famous English lyric tenor. Barton McGuckin (1852-1913) was a well-known Irish tenor, who had admired Joyce's father's tenor voice.
33. The title of an old English song. Bloom is prompted to think of it as he looks at Richie Goulding, who seems to him to have the symptoms of Bright's disease, often caused by too much alcohol. There was at that time no effective treatment.
34. In *Hamlet,* Queen Gertrude scatters flowers on the dead Ophelia, saying 'Sweets to the sweet' (V.1.265); Richie is eating kidneys and suffers from a kidney disease.
35. Water from the river Vartry in Dublin.
36. Stealing in a small way.
37. The Old Royal Theatre in Dublin.
38. Translation of first line of aria 'Tutto e sciulto' from Bellini's *La Sonnambula.*
39. Thomas Moore, 'Echo' from *Irish Melodies:* 'How sweet the answer Echo makes . . . .'
40. The reference is to the sleepwalking of Amina in *La Sonnambula*; she is innocent even though she appears guilty.
41. Bloom is thinking of how sleepwalkers can be wakened — by calling them by name or by letting them touch water.

Never in all his life had Richie Goulding.

He knows it well too. Or he feels. Still harping on his daughter.[42] Wise child that knows her father, Dedalus said.[43] Me?

Bloom askance over liverless saw. Face of the all is lost. Rollicking Richie once. Jokes old stale now. Wagging his ear. Napkinring in his eye. Now begging letters he sends his son with. Crosseyed Walter sir I did sir.[44] Wouldn't trouble only I was expecting some money. Apologise.

Piano again. Sounds better than last time I heard. Tuned probably. Stopped again.

Dollard and Cowley still urged the lingering singer out with it.

— With it, Simon.

— It, Simon.

— Ladies and gentlemen, I am not deeply obliged by your kind solicitations.

— It, Simon.

— I have no money but if you will lend me your attention I shall endeavour to sing to you of a heart bowed down.[45]

By the sandwichbell in screening shadow Lydia, her bronze and rose, a lady's grace, gave and withheld: as in cool glaucous *eau de Nil* Mina to tankards two her pinnacles of gold.

The harping chords of prelude closed. A chord, longdrawn, expectant, drew a voice away.

— *When first I saw that form endearing*...[46]

Richie turned.

— Si Dedalus' voce, he said.

Braintipped, cheek touched with flame, they listened feeling that flow endearing flow over skin limbs human heart soul spine. Bloom signed to Pat, bald Pat is a waiter hard of hearing, to set ajar the door of the bar. The door of the bar. So. That will do. Pat, waiter, waited, waiting to hear, for he was hard of hear by the door.

— ...*Sorrow from me seemed to depart.*

Through the hush of air a voice sang to them, low, not rain, not leaves in murmur, like no voice of strings or reeds or whatdoyoucallthem dulcimers touching their still ears with words, still hearts of their each his remembered lives. Good, good to hear: sorrow from them each seemed to from both depart when first they heard. When first they saw, lost Richie Poldy, mercy of beauty, heard from a person wouldn't expect it in the least, her first merciful lovesoft oftloved word.

Love that is singing: love's old sweet song.[47] Bloom unwound slowly the elastic band of his packet. Love's old sweet *sonnez la* gold. Bloom wound a skein round four forkfingers, stretched it, relaxed, and wound it round his troubled double, fourfold, in octave, gyved them fast.

— *Full of hope and all delighted*....

Tenors get women by the score. Increase their flow.[48] Throw flower at his feet. When will we meet? My head it simply. Jingle all delighted. He can't sing for tall hats. Your head it simply swurls.[49] Perfumed for him. What perfume does your wife? I want to know.[50] Jing. Stop. Knock. Last look at mirror always before she answers the door. The hall. There? How do you? I do well. There? What? Or? Phial of cachous,[51] kissing comfits, in her satchel. Yes? Hands felt for the opulent.[52]

Alas the voice rose, sighing, changed: loud, full, shining, proud.

— *But alas, 'twas idle dreaming*....

Glorious tone he has still. Cork air softer also their brogue.[53] Silly man! Could have made oceans of money. Singing wrong words. Wore out his wife: now sings. But hard to tell. Only the two themselves. If he doesn't break down. Keep a trot for the avenue.[54] His hands and feet sing too. Drink. Nerves overstrung. Must be abstemious to sing. Jenny Lind soup:[55] stock, sage, raw eggs, half pint of cream. For creamy dreamy.

Tenderness it welled: slow, swelling, full it throbbed. That's the chat. Ha, give! Take! Throb, a throb, a pulsing proud erect.

42. Polonius in *Hamlet*, II.2.188-89: 'How say you by that? Still harping on my daughter.'
43. Dedalus says this in episode 6 (Hades).
44. Walter, son of Richie Goulding, is referred to in episode 3, just before Stephen's reflections on 'Houses of decay', now duplicated by Bloom.
45. 'The Heart Bowed Down' is a song from M.W. Balfe's opera *The Bohemian Girl* (1843).
46. Translation of Lionel's song 'M'Appari' in *Martha*.
47. 'Love's Old Sweet Song' (1884), a popular and sentimental air.
48. Sexual activity was said to increase a singer's vocal capacity.
49. This jingle, associated with Boylan as well as with Molly and Bloom's daughter Milly, is cited in episode 4.
50. In episode 5, Martha Clifford asks Bloom, in the PS to her letter, 'Do tell me what kind of perfume does your wife use.'
51. 'Lover of a lozenge eaten to sweeten the breath.'
52. Cited from the pornographic novel *Sweets of Sin*, which Bloom reads in episode 10: '... while his hands felt for the opulent curves inside her deshabille.'
53. A broad, gentle dialectal accent.
54. He means that Simon Dedalus can still perform on occasion, as an aging horse can still trot briskly in the avenue, not on the racecourse.
55. Jenny Lind (1820-87), a Swedish soprano known for her healthy and abstemious diets.

Words? Music? No: it's what's behind.

Bloom looped, unlooped, noded, disnoded.

Blood. Flood of warm jamjam lickitup secretness flowed to flow in music out, in desire, dark to lick flow invading. Tipping her tepping her tapping her topping her. Tup. Pores to dilate dilating. Tup. The joy the feel the warm the. Tup. To pour o'er sluices pouring gushes. Flood, gush, flow, joygush, tupthrob. Now! Language of love.[56]

— ... *ray of hope is* ....

56. The language used here refers to the copulation of animals. The subsequent phrase from 'M'appari' is, in full, 'Not a ray of hope remains'. Bloom is envisaging Molly and Blazes together and feeling the pain of lost love.

Episode 12: Cyclops. Time: 5.00 pm. Barney Kiernan's pub.

[Here Bloom confronts the citizen, the epitome of an exclusive and boastfully provincial Irish nationalism. In the previous episode he had suffered the pain of the cuckold, excluded from his wife's affections and yet unseduced by the charms of the soft siren music that had ensnared Simon Dedalus. Here his Jewishness is made the excuse for excluding him from his country; yet again, Bloom refuses to accept the separation and asserts love of country and his claim to Irishness in a spirit of charity and hospitality, which humiliates the enraged citizen's xenophobic rantings. By now, the narrative is controlled by different voices, those of characteristic Dubliners, flawed by their penchant for vicious gossip, exaggeration, overweening respect for authority and pseudo-rebelliousness. Bloom appears more and more, through these voices, as an extraordinary figure, not susceptible to the embrace of the stereotype in which all the others are easily enfolded.]

... So he starts telling us about corporal punishment and about the crew of tars and officers and rearadmirals drawn up in cocked hats and the parson with his protestant bible to witness punishment and a young lad brought out, howling for his ma, and they tie him down on the buttend of a gun.

— A rump and dozen, says the citizen, was what that old ruffian sir John Beresford[1] called it but the modern God's Englishman calls it caning on the breech.

1. Probably John Beresford (1738-1805), commissioner of revenue in Ireland in the late eighteenth century. He owned a riding school in Dublin which was used in 1797-98 as a torture centre for rebels.

And says John Wyse:

— 'Tis a custom more honoured in the breach than in the observance.[2]

Then he was telling us the master at arms comes along with a long cane and he draws out and he flogs the bloody backside off of the poor lad till he yells meila[3] murder.

— That's your glorious British navy, says the citizen, that bosses the earth. The fellows that never will be slaves,[4] with the only hereditary chamber on the face of God's earth and their land in the hands of a dozen gamehogs and cottonball barons. That's the great empire they boast about of drudges and whipped serfs.

— On which the sun never rises, says Joe.

— And the tragedy of it is, says the citizen, they believe it. The unfortunate yahoos believe it.

They believe in rod, the scourger almighty, creator of hell upon earth, and in Jacky Tar, the son of a gun, who was conceived of unholy boast, born of the fighting navy, suffered under rump and dozen, was scarified, flayed and curried, yelled like bloody hell, the third day he arose again from the bed, steered into haven, sitteth on his beamend till further orders whence he shall come to drudge for a living and be paid.[5]

— But, says Bloom, isn't discipline the same everywhere. I mean wouldn't it be the same here if you put force against force?

Didn't I tell you? As true as I'm drinking this porter if he was at his last gasp he'd try to downface you that dying was living.

— We'll put force against force, says the citizen. We have our greater Ireland beyond the sea. They were driven out of house and home in the black '47. Their mudcabins and their shielings by the roadside were laid low by the batteringram and the *Times* rubbed its hands and told the whitelivered Saxons there would soon be as few Irish in Ireland as redskins in America. Even the Grand Turk sent us his piastres. But the Sassenach tried to starve the nation at home while the land was full of crops that the British hyenas bought and sold in Rio de Janeiro. Ay, they drove out the peasants in hordes. Twenty thousand of them died in the coffinships.

2. Hamlet, speaking of the carousing in Elsinore which has become habitual under Claudius, says it is a custom 'More honour'd in the breach than the observance' (I.4.16).
3. Irish *míle*, a thousand.
4. A line from 'Rule Britannia': 'Britons never will be slaves.'
5. A parody on the Apostles' Creed.

But those that came to the land of the free remember the land of bondage. And they will come again and with a vengeance, no cravens, the sons of Granuaile, the champions of Kathleen ni Houlihan.[6]

— Perfectly true, says Bloom. But my point was....

— We are a long time waiting for that day, citizen, says Ned. Since the poor old woman told us that the French were on the sea and landed at Killala.[7]

— Ay, says John Wyse. We fought for the royal Stuarts that reneged us against the Williamites and they betrayed us. Remember Limerick and the broken treatystone. We gave our best blood to France and Spain, the wild geese. Fontenoy, eh? And Sarsfield and O'Donnell, duke of Tetuan in Spain, and Ulysses Browne of Camus that was fieldmarshal to Maria Teresa. But what did we ever get for it?[8]

— The French! says the citizen. Set of dancing masters! Do you know what it is? They were never worth a roasted fart to Ireland. Aren't they trying to make an entente cordial now at Tay Pay's dinner-party with perfidious Albion! Firebrands of Europe and they always were.[9]

— *Conspuez les français*,[10] says Lenehan, nobbling his beer.

— And as for the Prooshians and the Hanoverians, says Joe, haven't we had enough of those sausage-eating bastards on the throne from George the elector down to the German lad and the flatulent old bitch that's dead?[11]

Jesus, I had to laugh at the way he came out with that about the old one with the winkers on her, blind drunk in her royal palace every night of God, old Vic, with her jorum of mountain dew and her coachman carting her up body and bones to roll into bed and she pulling him by the whiskers and singing him old bits of songs about *Ehren on the Rhine* and come where the boose is cheaper.[12]

— Well, says J. J. We have Edward the peacemaker now.

— Tell that to a fool, says the citizen. There's a bloody sight more pox than pax about that boyo. Edward Guelph-Wettin![13]

— And what do you think, says Joe, of the holy boys, the priests and bishops of Ireland doing up his room in Maynooth in His Satanic Majesty's racing colours and sticking up pictures of all the horses his jockeys rode. The earl of Dublin, no less.[14]

— They ought to have stuck up all the women he rode himself, says little Alf.

And says J. J.:

— Considerations of space influenced their lordships' decision.

— Will you try another, citizen? says Joe.

— Yes, sir, says he. I will.

— You? says Joe.

— Beholden to you, Joe, says I. May your shadow never grow less.

6. The reference to the Famine of 1847 and the words attributed to *The Times* newspaper by John Mitchel and by many others since are part of the nationalist folklore about the cruelty of the English government, the selling of grain from a starving country, the many deaths on the emigrant ships and the subsequent national resurgence in 'Celtic' dress, when Ireland became 'Granuaile' and 'Kathleen ni Houlihan', traditional feminine emblems of the island.
7. The popular ballad 'The Shan Van Vocht' (The Poor Old Woman) celebrates the fact that 'the French are on the sea'. A French force landed at Killala, Co. Mayo in 1798, but after initial success was forced to surrender.
8. In the Williamite wars of the late seventeenth century, Ireland supported the Stuart dynasty under James II, who deserted to the Continent after defeat at the battle of the Boyne in 1690. The Treaty of Limerick of 1691 promised concessions to the Irish catholics, but these were reneged upon by the Irish parliament. Patrick Sarsfield, the Irish general at Limerick, went into exile with his officer corps; this exodus was known as the 'Flight of the Wild Geese'. These soldiers fought in the continental armies and, at the battle of Fontenoy (1745), enabled the French to defeat a British-led alliance. Leopold O'Donnell (1809-67), a descendant of the Wild Geese, became duke of Tetuan and then prime minister of Spain on three occasions between 1854 and 1866. Ulysses Browne was another such descendant, a field-marshal in the Austrian army who was killed at the battle of Prague in 1757. His ghost was supposed to appear at Clongowes Wood castle and he is referred to in Joyce's *A Portrait of the Artist,* chapter I. George, Count de Browne (1698-1792) was born at Camus, Co. Limerick and became a field-marshal in the Russian army.
9. The friendly accord (Entente Cordiale) between England and France was signed in 1904. T.P. ('Tay Pay') O'Connor (1848-1929), an Irish parliamentarian and journalist, founded his most popular newspaper, *T.P.'s Weekly,* in 1902. (He turned down an application for a job from Joyce.) 'perfidious Albion' is a traditional, originally French, phrase for England.
10. 'Scorn the French'.
11. The Hanoverian succession to the English throne began in 1714 with George I; Queen Victoria married Prince Albert, also a German. She died in 1901.
12. Queen Victoria had a strange and dependent relationship with her servant John Brown. It was the subject of much inventive gossip. 'Ehren on the Rhine' is a nineteenth-century song about a soldier's leavetaking of his love.
13. Edward VII was called the 'peacemaker' in the aftermath of the Entente Cordiale; his promiscuity with women earns him this insult about venereal disease. 'Guelph-Wettin' refers to the family names of Victoria and Albert's households.
14. During Edward VII's state visit to Ireland in 1903, he was received in a sycophantic manner by the clergy at Maynooth and his fondness for horseracing was acknowledged in the decoration of the refectory with his racing colours and engravings of two of his favourite horses. Edward had been named earl of Dublin by Queen Victoria in 1849.

— Repeat that dose, says Joe.

Bloom was talking and talking with John Wyse and he quite excited with his dunducketymud-coloured mug on him and his old plumeyes rolling about.

— Persecution, says he, all the history of the world is full of it. Perpetuating national hatred among nations.

— But do you know what a nation means? says John Wyse.

— Yes, says Bloom.

— What is it? says John Wyse.

— A nation? says Bloom. A nation is the same people living in the same place.

— By God, then, says Ned, laughing, if that's so I'm a nation for I'm living in the same place for the past five years.

So of course everyone had the laugh at Bloom and says he, trying to muck out of it:

— Or also living in different places.

— That covers my case, says Joe.

— What is your nation if I may ask? says the citizen.

— Ireland, says Bloom. I was born here. Ireland.

The citizen said nothing only cleared the spit out of his gullet and, gob, he spat a Red bank oyster out of him right in the corner.

— After you with the push, Joe, says he, taking out his handkerchief to swab himself dry.

— Here you are, citizen, says Joe. Take that in your right hand and repeat after me the following words.

The muchtreasured and intricately embroidered ancient Irish facecloth attributed to Solomon of Droma and Manus Tomaltach og MacDonogh, authors of the Book of Ballymote, was then carefully produced and called forth prolonged admiration.[15] No need to dwell on the legendary beauty of the cornerpieces, the acme of art, wherein one can distinctly discern each of the four evangelists in turn presenting to each of the four masters his evangelical symbol, a bogoak sceptre, a North American puma (a far nobler king of beasts than the British article, be it said in passing), a Kerry calf and a golden eagle from Carrantuohill.[16] The scenes depicted on the emunctory[17] field, showing our ancient duns and raths and cromlechs and grianauns and seats of learning and maledictive stones, are as wonderfully beautiful and the pigments as delicate as when the Sligo illuminators gave free rein to their artistic fantasy long long ago in the time of the Barmecides.[18] Glendalough, the lovely lakes of Killarney, the ruins of Clonmacnois, Cong Abbey, Glen Inagh and the Twelve Pins, Ireland's Eye, the Green Hills of Tallaght, Croagh Patrick, the brewery of Messrs Arthur Guinness, Son and Company (Limited), Lough Neagh's banks, the vale of Ovoca, Isolde's tower, the Mapas obelisk, Sir Patrick Dun's hospital, Cape Clear, the glen of Aherlow, Lynch's castle, the Scotch house, Rathdown Union Workhouse at Loughlinstown, Tullamore jail, Castleconnel rapids, Kilballymacshonakill, the cross at Monasterboice, Jury's Hotel, S. Patrick's Purgatory, the Salmon Leap, Maynooth college refectory, Curley's hole, the three birthplaces of the first duke of Wellington, the rock of Cashel, the bog of Allen, the Henry Street Warehouse, Fingal's Cave — all these moving scenes are still there for us today rendered more beautiful still by the waters of sorrow which have passed over them and by the rich incrustations of time.[19]

— Show us over the drink, says I. Which is which?

— That's mine, says Joe, as the devil said to the dead policeman.[20]

— And I belong to a race too, says Bloom, that is

15. One of the great manuscript anthologies, *The Book of Ballymote* (*c.* 1391) was compiled by several scribes, including Solomon O'Droma and Manus O'Duigenan, at the house of Tolmatoch mac Tadgh or MacDonogh.

16. *The Annals of the Four Masters* (*c.*1636) was compiled by four Franciscans. The four evangelists are represented in the Book of Revelation by a winged man with a lance (Matthew, 'bogoak sceptre'), a lion (Mark, 'North American puma', not the British lion), an ox (Luke, 'a Kerry calf'), and an eagle (John, 'the golden eagle from Carrantuohill', the highest mountain in Ireland).

17. Relating to a bodily organ having an excretory function.

18. The reference is to James Clarence Mangan's poem 'The Time of the Barmecides', these being a powerful Persian dynasty of the eighth century. It was standard practice to cite ancient dynasties which were surpassed in antiquity and achievement by the ancient Irish with their forts (duns), ring-forts (raths), dolmens (cromlechs), sun-rooms (grianauns) and commemorative stone monuments (maledictive stones).

19. These are ancient monastic sites (Glendalough, Clonmacnois, Cong Abbey, Monasterboice); places of religious pilgrims (Croagh Patrick, S. Patrick's Purgatory); scenic spots (lakes of Killarney, Glen Inagh and the Twelve Pins, Ireland's Eye, the Green Hills of Tallaght, Lough Neagh's banks, the vale of Ovoca, the glen of Aherlow, Castleconnel rapids, the Salmon Leap, the bog of Allen); famous monuments, landmarks and buildings (Guinness's brewery, Isolde's Tower, the Mapas obelisk, Sir Patrick Dun's hospital, Lynch's castle, the Scotch house, Rathdown Union Workhouse, Tullamore jail, Maynooth college refectory, the rock of Cashel, the Henry Street warehouse, and Fingal's Cave, which is in Scotland, not Ireland). The list is deliberately miscellaneous and comic.

20. Indicating where dead policemen were supposed to go.

hated and persecuted. Also now. This very moment. This very instant.

Gob, he near burnt his fingers with the butt of his old cigar.

— Robbed, says he. Plundered. Insulted. Persecuted. Taking what belongs to us by right. At this very moment, says he, putting up his fist, sold by auction in Morocco like slaves or cattle.[21]

— Are you talking about the new Jerusalem? says the citizen.

— I'm talking about injustice, says Bloom.

— Right, says John Wyse. Stand up to it then with force like men.

That's an almanac picture[22] for you. Mark for a softnosed bullet. Old lardyface standing up to the business end of a gun. Gob, he'd adorn a sweeping-brush, so he would, if he only had a nurse's apron on him. And then he collapses all of a sudden, twisting around all the opposite, as limp as a wet rag.

— But it's no use, says he. Force, hatred, history, all that. That's not life for men and women, insult and hatred. And everybody knows that it's the very opposite of that that is really life.

— What? says Alf.

— Love, says Bloom. I mean the opposite of hatred. I must go now, says he to John Wyse. Just round to the court a moment to see if Martin is there.[23] If he comes just say I'll be back in a second. Just a moment.

Who's hindering you? And off he pops like greased lightning.

— A new apostle to the gentiles, says the citizen. Universal love.[24]

— Well, says John Wyse. Isn't that what we're told. Love your neighbour.

— That chap? says the citizen. Beggar my neighbour is his motto. Love, moya! He's a nice pattern of a Romeo and Juliet.

Love loves to love love. Nurse loves the new chemist. Constable 14A loves Mary Kelly. Gerty MacDowell loves the boy that has the bicycle. M. B. loves a fair gentleman. Li Chi Han lovey up kissy Cha Pu Chow. Jumbo, the elephant, loves Alice, the elephant. Old Mr Verschoyle with the ear trumpet loves old Mrs Verschoyle with the turnedin eye. The man in the brown macintosh loves a lady who is dead. His Majesty the King loves Her Majesty the Queen. Mrs Norman W. Tupper loves officer Taylor. You love a certain person. And this person loves that other person because everybody loves somebody but God loves everybody.

— Well, Joe, says I, your very good health and song. More power, citizen.

— Hurrah, there, says Joe.

— The blessing of God and Mary and Patrick on you, says the citizen.

And he ups with his pint to wet his whistle.

— We know those canters, says he, preaching and picking your pocket. What about sanctimonious Cromwell and his ironsides that put the women and children of Drogheda to the sword with the bible text *God is love* pasted round the mouth of his cannon?[25] The bible! Did you read that skit in the *United Irishman* today about that Zulu chief that's visiting England?[26]

— What's that? says Joe.

So the citizen takes up one of his paraphernalia papers and he starts reading out:

— A delegation of the chief cotton magnates of Manchester was presented yesterday to His Majesty the Alaki of Abeakuta by Gold Stick in Waiting, Lord Walkup of Walkup on Eggs, to tender to His Majesty the heartfelt thanks of British traders for the facilities afforded them in his dominions. The delegation partook of luncheon at the conclusion of which the dusky potentate, in the course of a happy speech, freely translated by the British chaplain, the reverend Ananias Praisegod Barebones,[27] tendered his best thanks to Massa Walkup and emphasised the cordial relations existing between Abeakuta and the British empire, stating that he treasured as one of his dearest possessions an illuminated bible, the volume of the word of God and the secret of England's greatness, graciously presented to him by the white chief woman, the great squaw Victoria, with a personal

21. Jews were obliged to perform compulsory service in Morocco up to 1907.
22. A picture to be chosen for an almanac or calendar.
23. i.e. Martin Cunningham, who returns towards the end of this quoted passage.
24. Like St Paul, who preached Christian love to all, Jews and Gentiles.
25. Cromwell and his army massacred the citizens of Drogheda after a siege in 1649. He justified the slaughter as 'righteous' in the eyes of God (see Volume I, p. 859).
26. Arthur Griffith's newspaper, the *United Irishman*, mocked the British imperial system in passages similar to this.
27. The Alaki of Abeakuta in Nigeria visited England in the summer of 1904. Praisegod Barebones (*c.* 1596-1679), a sectarian preacher, was a member of the 'Barebones Parliament' of 1653 and was notorious for his puritan fanaticism.

dedication from the august hand of the Royal Donor. The Alaki then drank a lovingcup of first-shot usquebaugh[28] to the toast *Black and White* from the skull of his immediate predecessor in the dynasty Kakachakachak, surnamed Forty Warts, after which he visited the chief factory of Cottonopolis and signed his mark in the visitors' book, subsequently executing a charming old Abeakutic wardance, in the course of which he swallowed several knives and forks, amid hilarious applause from the girl hands.

— Widow woman, says Ned. I wouldn't doubt her. Wonder did he put that bible to the same use as I would.

— Same only more so, says Lenehan. And thereafter in that fruitful land the broadleaved mango flourished exceedingly.[29]

— Is that by Griffith? says John Wyse.

— No, says the citizen. It's not signed Shanganagh. It's only initialled: P.[30]

— And a very good initial too, says Joe.

— That's how it's worked, says the citizen. Trade follows the flag.

— Well, says J. J., if they're any worse than those Belgians in the Congo Free State they must be bad. Did you read that report by a man what's this his name is?

— Casement, says the citizen. He's an Irishman.

— Yes, that's the man, says J. J. Raping the women and girls and flogging the natives on the belly to squeeze all the red rubber they can out of them.[31]

— I know where he's gone, says Lenehan, cracking his fingers.

— Who? says I.

— Bloom, says he. The courthouse is a blind. He had a few bob on *Throwaway* and he's gone to gather in the shekels.[32]

28. Whiskey. 'Black and White' is a brand of Scotch whiskey.
29. Lenehan's coarse reference, both sexual and lavatorial, parodies the insemination of religion in colonial countries, which thereafter produce crops that are useless.
30. These were pen-names used by Griffith. 'Shanganagh' is an area south of Dublin, perhaps adopted by Griffith because John Mitchel in his *Jail Journal* mentioned 'the vale of Shanganagh' as one of the last sights he had of Ireland as he was taken away to be transported to Australia.
31. In 1904 Roger Casement (1864-1916), as a member of the British colonial service, published a report on the inhumane treatment of native workers in the Belgian Congo; it produced an outraged public reaction. He later joined Sinn Féin and was hanged for treason in August 1916 after he had tried to smuggle German arms into Ireland.
32. Bloom unwittingly gave Bantam Lyons the tip for the winner, Throwaway, but it is assumed by all that he backed the horse himself. Throwaway came in at twenty to one.

— Is it that whiteeyed kaffir? says the citizen, that never backed a horse in anger in his life?

— That's where he's gone, says Lenehan. I met Bantam Lyons going to back that horse only I put him off it and he told me Bloom gave him the tip. Bet what you like he has a hundred shillings to five on. He's the only man in Dublin has it. A dark horse.

— He's a bloody dark horse himself, says Joe.

— Mind, Joe, says I. Show us the entrance out.

— There you are, says Terry.

Goodbye Ireland I'm going to Gort. So I just went round the back of the yard to pumpship and begob (hundred shillings to five) while I was letting off my (*Throwaway* twenty to) letting off my load gob says I to myself I knew he was uneasy in his (two pints off of Joe and one in Slattery's off) in his mind to get off the mark to (hundred shillings is five quid) and when they were in the (dark horse) pisser Burke was telling me card party and letting on the child was sick (gob, must have done about a gallon) flabbyarse of a wife speaking down the tube *she's better* or *she's* (ow!) all a plan so he could vamoose with the pool if he won or (Jesus, full up I was) trading without a licence (ow!) Ireland my nation says he (hoik! phthook) never be up to those bloody (there's the last of it) Jerusalem (ah!) cuckoos.

So anyhow when I got back they were at it dingdong, John Wyse saying it was Bloom gave the ideas for Sinn Fein to Griffith to put in his paper all kinds of jerrymandering, packed juries and swindling the taxes off of the government and appointing consuls all over the world to walk about selling Irish industries. Robbing Peter to pay Paul. Gob, that puts the bloody kybosh[33] on it if old sloppy eyes is mucking up the show. Give us a bloody chance. God save Ireland from the likes of that bloody mouseabout. Mr Bloom with his argol bargol.[34] And his old fellow before him perpetrating frauds, old Methusalem Bloom, the robbing bagman, that poisoned himself with the prussic acid after he swamping the country with his baubles and his penny diamonds. Loans by post on easy terms. Any amount of money advanced on note of hand. Distance no object. No security. Gob, he's like Lanty MacHale's goat that'd go a piece of the road with every one.[35]

33. puts an end to. Probably from the Irish *cie bais* (cap of death).
34. i.e. gibberish. A combination of 'argy bargy' and the French *argot* (slang).
35. A common expression, used by Joyce in *Stephen Hero*. See p. 16.

— Well, it's a fact, says John Wyse. And there's the man now that'll tell you all about it, Martin Cunningham....

Episode 17: Ithaca. 17 June, 2.00 a.m. Bloom's House, 7 Eccles Street.

[Bloom finally reaches home with Stephen in tow. The meeting and conversation, so long anticipated, degenerates into a comic 'mathematical cathechism', as Joyce called it. 'All events', he explained to his friend Frank Budgen, 'are resolved into their cosmic physical, psychical etc. equivalents....' The result is that, after the hallucinations and extreme subjective distortions of previous episodes, we now enter a universe of frozen, encyclopaedic fact, a world that is entirely other than that of the interior monologue, with its personal associative patterns and emotional variations. In one sense, we understand that the proposed meeting between the father and the son, vicariously pursued in the preceding sixteen sections, is proving abortive. In another sense, Joyce is indicating to the reader that one of the traditional features of the novel — its penchant towards documentary realism — can be pushed to such absurd lengths that the convention of the way in which novels end is under comic and subversive inspection here. More than that, we begin to see also that the two men, for all their imaginative speculations, are in a world that is physically complex but in other respects limiting. The infinite possibilities of theory and desire can be rebuked by the determining influence of physico-chemical laws. Joyce is at this point — not in the next episode — refusing the temptation to close in a resonant appeal to universal resonance. His epic is both a wonderful imaginative enterprise and a physical-chemical event, cast now in a form that has the logical coherence of an encyclopaedia, but which does not, simultaneously, have the kind of significance we conventionally ascribe to a novel. Both encyclopaedia and novel are essentially masses of words arranged in conventional patterns. In reminding us of this, Joyce is forcing the reader to acknowledge the primacy of language and the coercive power of convention in making it comprehensible to us. He is writing a novel that tries to disburden itself of the conventions of the novel to make its penultimate point. Stephen and Bloom are ultimately seen as participators in a cosmic drama so huge in scale that the close-range view we have had of them up to now is shattered, and the careful hour-by-hour timing of the day is rendered almost absurd against the backdrop of ocean, air and sky.

The cosmic scale retains its comic elements, however. There is a coming-together, as well as a separation, in this chapter. It is a cold prelude to Bloom's return to the warmth of his bed and to Molly. The vitalism of that final chapter is not really the true ending of the world; it is an alternative ending. This episode is the other, the first ending. Its most distressing effect is to demystify the nexus of relationships that have been explored hitherto and to demonstrate that the almost ritual meanings — reinforced by the Homeric parallels that have been generated earlier — can be cancelled by a deployment of language which is simply free from the consolations of a fictional tradition that assumes man's at-homeness in the world. With the two protagonists finally at home, we are faced with the spectacle of their alienation from the huge system of world and society which, nevertheless, operates to enable them to do something as simple as making a cup of tea. The comedy of the sequence does not work to reduce its bleakness.]

...What did Bloom see on the range?

On the right (smaller) hob a blue enamelled saucepan: on the left (larger) hob a black iron kettle.

What did Bloom do at the range?

He removed the saucepan to the left hob, rose and carried the iron kettle to the sink in order to tap the current by turning the faucet to let it flow.

Did it flow?

Yes. From Roundwood reservoir in county Wicklow of a cubic capacity of 2400 million gallons, percolating through a subterranean aqueduct of filter mains of single and double pipeage constructed at an initial plant cost of £5 per linear yard by way of the Dargle, Rathdown, Glen of the Downs and Callowhill to the 26 acre reservoir at Stillorgan, a distance of 22 statute miles, and thence, through a system of relieving tanks, by a gradient of 250 feet to the city boundary at Eustace bridge, upper Leeson street, though from prolonged summer drouth and daily supply of 12½ million gallons the water had fallen below the sill of the overflow weir for which reason the borough surveyor and waterworks engineer, Mr Spencer Harty, C. E., on the instructions of the waterworks committee had prohibited the use of municipal water for purposes other than those of consumption (envisaging the possibility of recourse being had to the impotable water of the Grand and Royal canals as in 1893) particularly as the South Dublin Guardians, notwithstanding their ration of 15 gallons per day per pauper supplied through a 6 inch meter, had been convicted of a wastage of 20,000 gallons per night by a reading of their meter on the affirmation of the law agent of the corporation, Mr Ignatius Rice, solicitor, thereby acting to the detriment of another section of the public, selfsupporting taxpayers, solvent, sound.[1]

What in water did Bloom, waterlover, drawer of water, watercarrier, returning to the range, admire?

Its universality: its democratic equality and constancy to its nature in seeking its own level: its vastness in the ocean of Mercator's projection:[2] its unplumbed profundity in the Sundam trench of the Pacific exceeding 8000 fathoms:[3] the restlessness of its waves and surface particles visiting in turn all points of its seaboard: the independence of its units: the variability of states of sea: its hydrostatic quiescence in calm: its hydrokinetic turgidity in neap and spring tides: its subsidence after devastation: its sterility in the circumpolar icecaps, arctic and antarctic: its climatic and commercial significance: its preponderance of 3 to 1 over the dry land of the globe: its indisputable hegemony extending in square leagues over all the region below the subequatorial tropic of Capricorn: the multisecular stability of its primeval basin: its luteofulvous[4] bed: its capacity to dissolve and hold in solution all soluble substances including millions of tons of the most precious metals: its slow erosions of peninsulas and islands, its persistent formation of homothetic islands, peninsulas and downwardtending promontories: its alluvial deposits: its weight and volume and density: its imperturbability in lagoons and highland tarns: its gradation of colours in the torrid and temperate and frigid zones: its vehicular ramifications in continental lakecontained streams and confluent oceanflowing rivers with their tributaries and transoceanic currents, gulfstream, north and south equatorial courses: its violence in seaquakes, waterspouts, Artesian wells, eruptions, torrents, eddies, freshets, spates, groundswells, watersheds, waterpartings, geysers, cataracts, whirlpools, maelstroms, inundations, deluges, cloudbursts: its vast circumterrestrial ahorizontal curve: its secrecy in springs and latent humidity, revealed by rhabdomantic[5] or hygrometric instruments and exemplified by the well by the hole in the wall at Ashtown gate, saturation of air, distillation of dew: the simplicity of its composition, two constituent parts of hydrogen with one constituent part of oxygen: its healing virtues: its buoyancy in the waters of the Dead Sea: its persevering penetrativeness in runnels, gullies, inadequate dams, leaks on shipboard: its properties for cleansing, quenching thirst and fire, nourishing vegetation: its infallibility as paradigm and paragon: its metamorphoses as vapour, mist, cloud, rain, sleet, snow, hail: its strength in rigid hydrants: its variety of forms in loughs and bays and gulfs and bights and guts and lagoons and atolls and archipelagos and sounds and fjords and minches and tidal estuaries and arms of sea: its solidity in glaciers, icebergs, icefloes: its docility in working hydraulic millwheels, turbines, dynamos, electric power stations, bleachworks, tanneries, scutchmills: its utility in canals, rivers, if navigable, floating and graving docks: its potentiality derivable from harnessed tides or watercourses falling from level to level: its submarine fauna and flora (anacoustic, photophobe),[6] numerically, if not literally, the inhabitants of the globe: its ubiquity as constituting 90% of the human body: the noxiousness of its effluvia in lacustrine marshes, pestilential fens, faded flowerwater, stagnant pools in the waning moon.

Having set the halffilled kettle on the now burning coals, why did he return to the stillflowing tap?

To wash his soiled hands with a partially consumed tablet of Barrington's lemonflavoured soap, to which paper still adhered, (bought thirteen hours previously for fourpence and still unpaid for), in fresh cold neverchanging everchanging water and dry them, face and hands, in a long redbordered holland cloth passed over a wooden revolving roller.

What reason did Stephen give for declining Bloom's offer?

That he was hydrophobe, hating partial contact by immersion or total by submersion in cold water,

1. All the facts here are drawn from *Thom's Directory* (1904) and from newspaper reports.
2. On Mercator's two-dimensional projection of the globe, the oceans appear vaster than they actually are.
3. The Sundam Trench off the island of Sumatra in the Pacific.
4. reddish-yellow.
5. Having to do with divination by means of a rod or wand.
6. 'Anacoustic' means without a sense of hearing; 'photophobe' means having an aversion to or fear of light.

(his last bath having taken place in the month of October of the preceding year), disliking the aqueous substances of glass and crystal, distrusting aquacities of thought and language.

What impeded Bloom from giving Stephen counsels of hygiene and prophylactic to which should be added suggestions concerning a preliminary wetting of the head the contraction of the muscles with rapid splashing of the face and neck and thoracic and epigastric region in case of sea or river bathing, the parts of the human anatomy most sensitive to cold being the nape, stomach and thenar[7] or sole of foot?

The incompatibility of aquacity with the erratic originality of genius.

What additional didactic counsels did he similarly repress?

Dietary: concerning the respective percentage of protein and caloric energy in bacon, salt ling and butter, the absence of the former in the lastnamed and the abundance of the latter in the firstnamed.

Which seemed to the host to be the predominant qualities of his guest?

Confidence in himself, an equal and opposite power of abandonment and recuperation.

What concomitant phenomenon took place in the vessel of liquid by the agency of fire?

The phenomenon of ebullition. Fanned by a constant updraught of ventilation between the kitchen and the chimneyflue, ignition was communicated from the faggots of precombustible fuel to polyhedral masses of bituminous coal, containing in compressed mineral form the foliated fossilised decidua of primeval forests which had in turn derived their vegetative existence from the sun, primal source of heat (radiant), transmitted through omnipresent luminiferous diathermanous ether.[8] Heat (convected), a mode of motion developed by such combustion, was constantly and increasingly conveyed from the source of calorification to the liquid contained in the vessel, being radiated through the uneven unpolished dark surface of the metal iron, in part reflected, in part absorbed, in part transmitted, gradually raising the temperature of the water from normal to boiling point, a rise in temperature expressible as the result of an expenditure of 72 thermal units needed to raise 1 pound of water from 50° to 212° Fahrenheit.

What announced the accomplishment of this rise in temperature?

A double falciform ejection of water vapour from under the kettlelid at both sides simulataneously.

For what personal purpose could Bloom have applied the water so boiled?

To shave himself.

What advantages attended shaving by night?

A softer beard: a softer brush if intentionally allowed to remain from shave to shave in its agglutinated lather: a softer skin if unexpectedly encountering female acquaintances in remote places at incustomary hours: quiet reflections upon the course of the day: a cleaner sensation when awaking after a fresher sleep since matutinal noises, premonitions and perturbations, a clattered milkcan, a postman's double knock, a paper read, reread while lathering, relathering the same spot, a shock, a shoot, with thought of aught he sought though fraught with nought might cause a faster rate of shaving and a nick on which incision plaster with precision cut and humected[9] and applied adhered: which was to be done.

Why did absence of light disturb him less than presence of noise?

Because of the surety of the sense of touch in his firm full masculine feminine passive active hand.

What quality did it (his hand) possess but with what counteracting influence?

The operative surgical quality but that he was reluctant to shed human blood even when the end

7. Thenar can refer to the sole of the foot, to the base of the thumb, or to the palm of the hand.

8. An ether that allows for the passage of light and heat. The existence of such a medium was disproved by Einsteinian theory.

9. moistened.

justified the means, preferring, in their natural order, heliotherapy, psychophysicotherapeutics, osteopathic surgery....

Episode 18: Penelope. The bed.

[After so much agonizing on the part of Stephen and Bloom about the relations between parents and children, husband and wife, lover and beloved, betrayal and fidelity, Molly Bloom's soliloquy comes as a relief. Molly is natural and spontaneous in a way neither man can be. Stephen places art above nature, thinking of it as the act of reconciliation, in which nature's breach is healed. His longing for a way of becoming his own father, like the first person of the Trinity, stimulates him both to brilliance and absurdity. Bloom, wounded more palpably than Stephen, is weary of belonging in a vicarious sense; he is substitute Irishman in the view of others — substitute father to Stephen, substitute husband to Molly. He wants actuality and cannot find it through Stephen. Whether he does or not through Molly is a hypothetical question. We can see now that all the narrative inventions have been abandoned for a simple, traditional (if unpunctuated) soliloquy; that it is possible to be in direct contact with experience, whether of the present or of the past. Molly is not plagued by guilt or remorse. All her irritations are minor, all her celebrations are major. Sexual love is for her the abiding joy and pleasure of her existence, although it would be wrong to emphasise the sexuality at the expense of the love. She and Bloom have not had sexual relations in a long time, yet she loves Bloom as she does not love Boylan. There is an implication, no more, that sexual relations will resume after her recognition of Bloom's superiority. More important, Molly does not wince or turn away from what is to come; her memory of the past love, of what happened sixteen years before between her and Leopold among the rhodedendrons on Howth Head is also an anticipation of a future to which she responds positively. For the first time in the novel, the language has no element of parody. It is, instead, almost naive in its haste to catch something of the flow of Molly's ruminations and reactions. The happiness in *Ulysses* is that language can parody anything except the love of life that Molly embodies.]

... no thats no way for him has he no manners nor no refinement nor no nothing in his nature slapping us behind like that on my bottom because I didnt call him Hugh[1] the ignoramus that doesnt know poetry from a cabbage thats what you get for not keeping them in their proper place pulling off his shoes and trousers there on the chair before me so barefaced without even asking permission and standing out that vulgar way in the half of a shirt they wear to be admired like a priest or a butcher or those old hypocrites in the time of Julius Caesar[2] of course hes right enough in his way to pass the time as a joke sure you might as well be in bed with what with a lion God Im sure hed have something better to say for himself an old Lion would O well I suppose its because they were so plump and tempting in my short petticoat he couldnt resist they excite myself sometimes its well for men all the amount of pleasure they get off a womans body were so round and white for them always I wished I was one myself for a change just to try with that thing they have swelling up on you so hard and at the same time so soft when you touch it my uncle John has a thing long I heard those cornerboys saying passing the corner of Marrowbone lane my aunt Mary has a thing hairy because it was dark and they knew a girl was passing it didnt make me blush why should it either its only nature and he puts his thing long into my aunt Marys hairy etcetera and turns out to be you put the handle in a sweepingbrush men again all over they can pick and choose what they please a married woman or a fast widow or a girl for their different tastes like those houses round behind Irish street[3] no but were to be always chained up theyre not going to be chaining me up no damn fear once I start I tell you for their stupid husbands jealousy why cant we all remain friends over it instead of quarrelling her husband found it out what they did together well naturally and if he did can he undo it hes coronado[4] anyway whatever he does and then he going to the other mad extreme about the wife in Fair Tyrants[5] of course the man never even casts a 2nd thought on the husband or wife either its the woman he wants and he gets her what else were we given all those desires for Id like to know I cant help it if Im young still can I its a wonder Im not an old shrivelled hag before my time living with him so cold never embracing me except sometimes when hes asleep the wrong end of me not knowing I suppose who he has any man thatd kiss a womans bottom Id throw my hat at him after that hed kiss anything unnatural where we havent 1 atom of any kind of expression in

1. Boylan's first name is Hugh.

2. Perhaps Molly is thinking of the dress she imagines the Romans wore.
3. In Gibraltar.
4. She means 'cuckolded'.
5. The pulp novel Molly read earlier, mentioned in episode 10.

us all of us the same 2 lumps of lard before ever Id do that to man pfooh the dirty brutes the mere thought is enough I kiss the feet of you senorita theres some sense in that didnt he kiss our halldoor yes he did what a madman nobody understands his cracked ideas but me still of course a woman wants to be embraced 20 times a day almost to make her look young no matter by who so long as to be in love or loved by somebody if the fellow you want isnt there sometimes by the Lord God I was thinking would I go around by the quays there some dark evening where nobodyd know me and pick up a sailor off the sea thatd be hot on for it and not care a pin whose I was only do it off up in a gate somewhere or one of those wildlooking gipsies in Rathfarnham had their camp pitched near the Bloomfield laundry to try and steal our things if they could I only sent mine there a few times for the name model laundry sending me back over and over some old ones odd stockings that blackguard-looking fellow with the fine eyes peeling a switch attack me in the dark and ride me up against the wall without a word or a murderer anybody what they do themselves the fine gentlemen in their silk hats that K C[6] lives up somewhere this way coming out of Hardwicke lane the night he gave us the fish supper on account of winning over the boxing match of course it was for me he gave it I knew him by his gaiters and the walk and when I turned round a minute after just to see there was a woman after coming out of it too some filthy prostitute then he goes home to his wife after that only I suppose the half of those sailors are rotten again with disease O move over your big carcass out of that for the love of Mike listen to him the winds that waft my sighs to thee[7] so well he may sleep and sigh the great Suggester[8] Don Poldo de la Flora[9] if he knew how he came out on the cards this morning hed have something to sigh for a dark man in some perplexity between 2 7s[10] too in prison for Lord knows what he does that I dont know and Im to be slooching around down in the kitchen to get his lordship his breakfast while hes rolled up like a mummy will I indeed did you ever see me running Id just like to see myself at it show them attention and they treat you like dirt I dont care what anybody says itd be much better for the world to be governed by the women in it you wouldnt see women going and killing one another and slaughtering when do you ever see women rolling around drunk like they do or gambling every penny they have and losing it on horses yes because a woman whatever she does she knows where to stop sure they wouldnt be in the world at all only for us they dont know what it is to be a woman and a mother how could they where would they all of them be if they hadnt all a mother to look after them what I never had thats why I suppose hes running wild now out at night away from his books and studies and not living at home on account of the usual rowy house I suppose well its a poor case that those that have a fine son like that theyre not satisfied and I none was he not able to make one it wasnt my fault we came together when I was watching the two dogs up in her behind in the middle of the naked street that disheartened me altogether I suppose I oughtnt to have buried him in that little woolly jacket I knitted crying as I was but give it to some poor child but I knew well Id never have another our 1st death too it was[11] we were never the same since O Im not going to think myself into the glooms about that any more I wonder why he wouldnt stay the night I felt all the time it was somebody strange he brought in instead of roving around the city meeting God knows who nightwalkers and pickpockets his poor mother wouldnt like that if she was alive ruining himself for life perhaps still its a lovely hour so silent I used to love coming home after dances the air of the night they have friends they can talk to weve none either he wants what he wont get or its some woman ready to stick her knife in you I hate that in women no wonder they treat us the way they do we are a dreadful lot of bitches I suppose its all the troubles we have makes us so snappy Im not like that he could easy have slept in there on the sofa in the other room I suppose he was as shy as a boy he being so young hardly 20 of me in the next room hed have heard me on the chamber arrah what harm Dedalus I wonder its like those names in Gibraltar Delapaz Delagracia they had the devils queer names there father

6. King's Counsel.
7. 'The winds that waft my sighs to thee' is the title of a song by H.W. Challis and William V. Wallace.
8. An epithet applied to Odysseus in Book XXIII of the *Odyssey*.
9. A mock name for Bloom, or Poldy as she affectionately knows him. There are many puns and jokes about his name and flowers.
10. Molly's reading of the cards shows Bloom as the King of Clubs, signifying a lonely and secretive man who, for his happiness, needs the understanding of a woman.
11. She is remembering the death of their first child but, unlike Bloom, is not going to dwell on the sad event.

Vilaplana of Santa Maria that gave me the rosary Rosales y OReilly in the Calle las Siete Revueltas and Pisimbo and Mrs Opisso in Governor street O what a name Id go and drown myself in the first river if I had a name like her O my and all the bits of streets Paradise ramp and Bedlam ramp and Rodgers ramp and Crutchetts ramp and the devils gap[12] steps well small blame to me if I am a harum-scarum I know I am a bit I declare to God I dont feel a day older than then I wonder could I get my tongue round any of the Spanish como esta usted muy bien gracias y usted[13] see I havent forgotten it all I thought I had only for the grammar a noun is the name of any person place or thing pity I never tried to read that novel cantankerous Mrs Rubio lent me by Valera[14] with the questions in it all upside down the two ways I always knew wed go away in the end I can tell him the Spanish and he tell me the Italian then hell see Im not so ignorant what a pity he didnt stay Im sure the poor fellow was dead tired and wanted a good sleep badly I could have brought him in his breakfast in bed with a bit of toast so long as I didnt do it on the knife for bad luck or if the woman was going her rounds with the watercress and something nice and tasty there are a few olives in the kitchen he might like I never could bear the look of them in Abrines[15] I could do the criada[16] the room looks all right since I changed it the other way you see something was telling me all the time Id have to introduce myself not knowing me from Adam very funny wouldnt it Im his wife or pretend we were in Spain with him half awake without a Gods notion where he is dos huevos estrellados senor[17] Lord the cracked things come into my head sometimes itd be great fun supposing he stayed with us why not theres the room upstairs empty and Millys[18] bed in the back room he could do his writing and studies at the table in there for all the scribbling he does at it and if he wants to read in bed in the morning like me as hes making the breakfast for 1 he can make it for 2 Im sure Im not going to take in lodgers off the street for him if he takes a gesabo[19] of a house like this Id love to have a long talk with an intelligent welleducated person Id have to get a nice pair of red slippers like those Turks with the fez used to sell or yellow and a nice semi-transparent morning gown that I badly want or a peachblossom dressing jacket like the one long ago in Walpoles only 8/6 or 18/6 Ill just give him one more chance Ill get up early in the morning Im sick of Cohens[20] old bed in any case I might go over to the markets to see all the vegetables and cabbages and tomatoes and carrots and all kinds of splendid fruits all coming in lovely and fresh who knows whod be the 1st man Id meet theyre out looking for it in the morning Mamy Dillon used to say they are and the night too that was her massgoing Id love a big juicy pear now to melt in your mouth like when I used to be in the longing way then Ill throw him up his eggs and tea in the moustachecup she gave him to make his mouth bigger I suppose hed like my nice cream too I know what Ill do Ill go about rather gay not too much singing a bit now and then mi fa pieta Masetto then Ill start dressing myself to go out presto non son piu forte[21] Ill put on my best shift and drawers let him have a good eyeful out of that to make his micky stand for him Ill let him know if thats what he wanted that his wife is fucked yes and damn well fucked too up to my neck nearly not by him 5 or 6 times handrunning theres the mark of his spunk on the clean sheet I wouldnt bother to even iron it out that ought to satisfy him if you dont believe me feel my belly unless I made him stand there and put him into me Ive a mind to tell him every scrap and make him do it out in front of me serve him right its all his own fault if I am an adulteress as the thing in the gallery said[22] O much about it if thats all the harm ever we did in this vale of tears God knows its not much doesnt everybody only they hide it I suppose thats what a woman is supposed to be there for or He wouldnt have made us the way He did so attractive to men then if he wants to kiss my bottom Ill drag open my drawers and bulge it right out in his face as large as life he can stick his tongue 7 miles up my hole as hes there

12. These are all names of streets or steps in Gibraltar.
13. 'How are you? Very well, thank you. And you?'
14. Juan Valera Y Alacala Galiano (1824-1905), Spanish author.
15. A bakery in Gibraltar.
16. 'maid'.
17. 'two fried eggs, sir'.
18. Milly is the Blooms' daughter, at present in boarding school.
19. A summerhouse in a garden.
20. A glancing allusion to the moment in the *Odyssey* in which Odysseus convinces Penelope of his identity because he knows the secret of the construction of their bed. Perhaps Molly is weary of the secret of her bed, which Bloom does not share.
21. Mozart, *Don Giovanni* I. 3. 'I'm sorry for Masetto .... Quick, my strength is failing.' At this point, Zerlina is yielding to Giovanni's urgings and is forsaking Masetto.
22. The reference is to the English version of G. Giacosa's play *The Wife of Scarli* (1897), in which there is an adulterous affair.

my brown part then Ill tell him I want £1 or perhaps 30/- Ill tell him I want to buy underclothes then if he gives me that well he wont be too bad I dont want to soak it all out of him like other women do I could often have written out a fine cheque for myself and write his name on it for a couple of pounds a few times he forgot to lock it up besides he wont spend it Ill let him do it off on me behind provided he doesnt smear all my good drawers O I suppose that cant be helped Ill do the indifferent 1 or 2 questions Ill know by the answers when hes like that he cant keep a thing back I know every turn in him Ill tighten my bottom well and let out a few smutty words smellrump or lick my shit or the first mad thing comes into my head then Ill suggest about yes O wait now sonny my turn is coming Ill be quite gay and friendly over it O but I was forgetting this bloody pest of a thing pfooh you wouldnt know which to laugh or cry were such a mixture of plum and apple no Ill have to wear the old things so much the better itll be more pointed hell never know whether he did it or not there thats good enough for you any old thing at all then Ill wipe him off me just like a business his omission then Ill go out Ill have him eying up at the ceiling where is she gone now make him want me thats the only way a quarter after what an unearthly hour I suppose theyre just getting up in China now combing out their pigtails for the day well soon have the nuns ringing the angelus theyve nobody coming in to spoil their sleep except an odd priest or two for his night office or the alarmclock next door 1 2 3 4 5 what kind of flowers are those they invented like the stars the wallpaper in Lombard street was much nicer the apron he gave me was like that something only I only wore it twice better lower this lamp and try again so as I can get up early Ill go to Lambes there beside Findlaters and get them to send us some flowers to put about the place in case he brings him home tomorrow today I mean no no Fridays an unlucky day first I want to do the place up someway the dust grows in it I think while Im asleep then we can have music and cigarettes I can accompany him first I must clean the keys of the piano with milk whatll I wear shall I wear a white rose[23] or those fairy cakes in Liptons I love the smell of a rich big shop at 7½d a lb or the other ones with the cherries in them and the pinky sugar 11d a couple of lbs of those a nice plant for the middle of the table Id get that cheaper in wait wheres this I saw them not long ago I love flowers Id love to have the whole place swimming in roses God of heaven theres nothing like nature the wild mountains then the sea and the waves rushing then the beautiful country with the fields of oats and wheat and all kinds of things and all the fine cattle going about that would do your heart good to see rivers and lakes and flowers all sorts of shapes and smells and colours springing up even out of the ditches primroses and violets nature it is as for them saying theres no God I wouldnt give a snap of my two fingers for all their learning why dont they go and create something I often asked him atheists or whatever they call themselves go and wash the cobbles off themselves first then they go howling for the priest and they dying and why why because theyre afraid of hell on account of their bad conscience ah yes I know them well who was the first person in the universe before there was anybody that made it all who ah that they dont know neither do I so there you are they might as well try to stop the sun from rising tomorrow the sun shines for you he said the day we were lying among the rhododendrons on Howth head in the grey tweed suit and his straw hat the day I got him to propose to me yes first I gave him the bit of seedcake out of my mouth and it was leapyear like now yes 16 years ago my God after that long kiss I near lost my breath yes he said I was a flower of the mountain yes so we are flowers all a womans body yes that was one true thing he said in his life and the sun shines for you today yes that was why I liked him because I saw he understood or felt what a woman is and I knew I could always get round him and I gave him all the pleasure I could leading him on till he asked me to say yes and I wouldnt answer first only looked out over the sea and the sky I was thinking of so many things he didnt know of Mulvey and Mr Stanhope and Hester and father and old captain Groves and the sailors playing all birds fly and I say stoop and washing up dishes they called it on the pier and the sentry in front of the governors house with the thing round his white helmet poor devil half roasted and the Spanish girls laughing in their shawls and their tall combs and the auctions in the morning the Greeks and the jews and the Arabs and the devil knows who else from all the ends of Europe and Duke street and the fowl market all clucking outside Larby Sharons and the poor donkeys slipping half asleep and the vague fellows in the cloaks asleep in

23. Title of a song, 'Shall I Wear a White Rose or Shall I Wear a Red?'

the shade on the steps and the big wheels of the carts of the bulls and the old castle thousands of years old yes and those handsome Moors all in white and turbans like kings asking you to sit down in their little bit of a shop and Ronda with the old windows of the posadas[24] 2 glancing eyes a lattice hid for her lover to kiss the iron and the wineshops half open at night and the castanets and the night we missed the boat at Algeciras[25] the watchman going about serene with his lamp and O that awful deepdown torrent O and the sea the sea crimson sometimes like fire and the glorious sunsets and the figtrees in the Alameda gardens[26] yes and all the queer little streets and the pink and blue and yellow houses and the rosegardens and the jessamine and geraniums and cactuses and Gibraltar as a girl where I was a Flower of the mountain yes when I put the rose in my hair like the Andalusian girls used or shall I wear a red yes and how he kissed me under the Moorish wall[27] and I thought well as well him as another and then I asked him with my eyes to ask again yes and then he asked me would I yes to say yes my mountain flower and first I put my arms around him yes and drew him down to me so he could feel my breasts all perfume yes and his heart was going like mad and yes I said yes I will Yes.

Trieste-Zurich-Paris
1914-1921

24. Ronda is a picturesque town in Spain; a 'posada' is an inn or townhouse.
25. A town in Spain facing across towards Gibraltar.
26. A well-known promenade and garden on Gibraltar.
27. This wall crosses the upper plateau in Gibraltar.

from: FINNEGANS WAKE (1939)

[The following excerpt from the opening pages of the *Wake* provides no more than the preliminary account of the pattern that will be repeated in ever-thickening grids and meshes throughout. It is a story of the Fall of Man written in 'night-language' which has, as one of its premises, that the history of the individual recapitulates the history of the race. In a similar way, the history of a single nation (Ireland) recapitulates the history of the world. The articulation of this micro-macrocosm relationship is achievable only below the threshold of the conscious mind, at that level where everything that is repressed finds a means by which it can be expressed. The expression, however, is not simply the admission of fault, crime or error; these things are themselves the source of expression. The ten one-hundred letter words that thunder at different points in the text frighten man into speech, and his speech is, in the most radical way, the speech of origin, the questioning about parents, the delivery of the self into the world, the 'crime of birth'. In the *Wake*, the Chapelizod Earwicker family, which includes the parents HCE and ALP, the sons Shem and Shaun and the daughter Issy, are involved in a crisis that has to do with a secret crime and with its revelation. The crime was committed, we can safely say, in Phoenix Park by HCE and is either that of indecent exposure or voyeurism. It was witnessed by others. Shem, as writer, inherits the crime, which he reproduces in writing; Shaun, as sanitary saint, is the brother who will deliver the letter and deliver us from the letter that is supposed to be a plea in defence of HCE, ostensibly written by Shem but actually written 'through' him or his pen by his mother, ALP. As always, the sexual trauma is central in the Joycean narrative, in part because Joyce had absorbed a good deal of Freud and in part because it was the area of experience which then was most heavily censored. It is the act of suppression that creates the taboo; but the taboo is itself a way of masking something that is perfectly natural. Yet from the censoring system grows civilization; from the dismantling of the censoring system grows writing, which is itself integral to civilization. The two are dialectically related, like all the twins that proliferate throughout the work. The *Wake* itself has the temerity to attempt to include within itself almost all previous literature, being in itself a recapitulation of everything already written, a world book that tries to blur the distinction between world and book so that it might, in achieving that unique status, simultaneously be both the culmination of the literary tradition and its origin.

A text such as this cannot be annotated in any comprehensive way. All the voices we listen to here are ancestral, soliloquizers who are repeating, over and over again, the 'tellafun book' of world history and human consciousness. It is a highly programmed work that uses anarchic techniques to achieve its aim, a funeral and a 'funferall'. The 'footnotes' are, therefore, to be taken as sketchy gestures written under the Joycean warning: 'You is feeling like you was lost in the bush, boy? You says: It is a puling sample jungle of words. You most shouts out: Bethicket me for a stump of beech if I have the poultriest notions what the farest he all means.']

riverrun, past Eve and Adam's, from swerve of shore to bend of bay, brings us by a commodius vicus of recirculation back to Howth Castle and Environs.[1]

1. Adam and Eve's church is beside the river Liffey in Dublin. 'Commodius' refers to (a) commodious; (b) the Roman Emperor

Sir Tristram, violer d'amores, fr'over the short sea, had passencore rearrived from North Armorica on this side the scraggy isthmus of Europe Minor to wielderfight his penisolate war:[2] nor had topsawyer's rocks by the stream Oconee exaggerated themselse to Laurens County's gorgios[3] while they went doublin their mumper all the time:[4] nor avoice from afire bellowsed mishe mishe to tauftauf thuartpeatrick;[5] not yet, though venissoon after, had a kidscad buttended a bland old isaac:[6] not yet, though all's fair in vanessy, were sosie sesthers wroth with twone nathandjoe.[7] Rot a peck of pa's malt had Jhem or Shen brewed by arclight and rory end to the regginbrow was to be seen ringsome on the aquaface.[8]

The fall (bababadalgharaghtakamminarronnkonnbronntonnerronntuonnthunntrovarrhounawnskawntoohoohoordenenthurnuk!)[9] of a once wallstrait oldparr is retaled early in bed and later on life down through all christian minstrelsy.[10] The great fall of the offwall entailed at such short notice the pftjschute[11] of Finnegan, erse solid man, that the humptyhillhead of humself prumptly sends an unquiring one well to the west in quest of his tumptytumtoes:[12] and their upturnpikepointandplace is at the knock out in the park where oranges have been laid to rust upon the green since devlinsfirst loved livvy.[13]

What clashes here of wills gen wonts, oystrygods gaggin fishygods![14] Brékkek Kékkek Kékkek Kékkek! Kóax Kóax Kóax! Ualu Ualu Ualu! Quaouauh![15] Where the Baddelaries partisans are still out to mathmaster Malachus Micgranes and the Verdons catapelting the camibalistics out of the Whoyteboyce of Hoodie Head. Assiegates and boomeringstroms.[16] Sod's brood, be me fear!

Commodus, who believed himself to be the reincarnation of Hercules and who eventually was strangled by an athlete called Narcissus (self); (c) a commode, a chamber pot enclosed in a wooden box or frame.

'vicus' is (a) Latin for 'village'; (b) it refers also to the Vico Road, in the village of Dalkey, on the coast of Dublin bay opposite Howth; (c) moreover, it refers to the Italian philosopher Giambattista Vico (1668-1744), who expounded a cyclical theory of history in his work *Scienza nuova* (1725); (d) the emphasis on cycle and circle also brings in the phrase 'vicious circle'.

'Howth Castle and Environs' contains (a) the letters HCE, which will be repeated endlessly throughout the book in various combinations; (b) The castle on Howth Head was built by Sir Amory Tristram, 1st earl of Howth, born in Brittany (North Armorica), who changed his name to St Lawrence. The fusion of 'amo' (Latin 'I love') and 'armo(u)r', with its military reference, is frequent.

2. The Tristan of legend (Tristram in the English version) had spent his youth in Brittany (Armorica), returned to Cornwall and then to Ireland to fetch Isolde for his uncle Mark. He fell in love with her himself and thus violated love. 'Violer d'amores' suggests the instrument 'viola d'amore'. He had not yet (pas encore) arrived; but he had rearrived because this is a recurrent pattern of events which repeats forever ('fr'over'); Armorica is America, from which he comes to fight again (Germain *wiederfechten*) or to yield or fight his 'penisolate war' — the Peninsular War of 1808-13 against Napoleon's armies; Howth and Brittany are peninsulas; a war of love (penis); a lonely war with the pen, or a war with the pen against insularity.
3. 'topsawyer's' refers to (a) Tom Sawyer and his 'twin' Huckleberry Finn, heroes of Mark Twain (King Mark again); the rock of Peter and Christ's 'saw' about his being the foundation rock of the church. There is a Dublin in Laurens (Lawrence) County, Georgia, by the river Oconee, founded by a Dubliner Peter Sawyer, which has as its motto 'Doubling all the time'. 'Giorgio' is a Romany gypsy word for 'young' and also the name of Joyce's son.
4. 'mumper' is number; Dublin is the 'mum', mother, that is doubled here; besides the 'per' recalls French *père* (father).
5. 'avoice from afire' (afar) is the voice of God saying to Moses from the burning bush, 'I am what I am'; 'mishe mishe' is the Irish rendering of this phrase; 'tauf' in German means 'baptize'; St Patrick christianized Ireland, the peat-rick, the land rich in turf, the kingdom of peat and of Pat.
6. 'venissoon' (very soon; 'I came' soon after) refers to Swift's renamed loves, Stella and Vanessa, both of whom were called Esther; Jacob (James), a purveyor of venison, tricked his father Isaac into giving him his blessing by disguising himself in a calfskin so that he would be taken for his brother Esau. Parnell ended the leadership of Isaac Butt.
7. 'all's fair in love and war'; 'vanessy' refers to (a) Vanessa; (b) Irish *bean* for 'woman' (bhean in dative, pronounced 'van') and 'esse' (to be, existence), love being woman's essence; 'sosie' is French for 'twin' and also refers to Susie (Susannah), and 'sesthers' contains 'sisters' and 'Esther'; 'wroth' has 'Ruth' and 'wrath' and 'wreathed with'. 'twone' is 'twin' and 'two in one'; 'nathandjoe' is Nathan and Joseph and is also Jonathan (Swift). All these biblical women were loved by older men and all these men resisted sexual advances of various kinds.
8. Jhem (Shem) and Shen (Shaun), the Earwicker sons, had not yet brewed either Jameson's whiskey or Guinness and Sons stout under the covenant or arc (Ark) or rainbow (German *regenbogen*) of God; but the cycle of God's promise is to be seen 'ringsome' and dewy ('rory' from the Latin *roridus*) on the face of the waters.
9. The hundred-letter word, representing the Fall, the thundercrash, itself contains the word for thunder from ten languages.
10. 'wallstrait' echoes the 'Wall Street' crash of 1929; once this old parent was 'all-straight'. The story of his fall is told over and over, retailed also, and told again and again with a different ending, a new tail on the same tale.
11. From the French *chute* (fall) with onomatopoeic prefix.
12. 'erse' refers to (a) Irish; (b) erstwhile; the Humpty Dumpty fall sends an inquirer to the west to Phoenix Park, for his head is at his Howth and his feet stick up in the Park.
13. His feet 'up turn' at the Turnpike in Chapelizod and at the (Castle)knock gate in Phoenix Park where orange and green, Ireland's colours, have been laid to rest (rust) since the foundation of Dublin (Devlin) on the Liffey (livvy) — also since the foundation of the new state, created by the Treaty of 1921, 'dev's' (de Valera's) 'first' (Document no. 1, as he called it in the quarrels afterwards). The orange and the green states thus created rested and rusted together. Chapelizod (Chapelle d'Iseult, Iseult's chapel) recalls Tristram, Howth Castle and Armorica.
14. 'wills against wonts', desires against prohibitions; Ostrogoths against (German *gegen*) Visigoths, oystermen against fishermen.
15. Brékkek . . . is the chorus of frogs in Hades in *The Frogs* by Aristophanes, thought to be part of his quarrel with Euripides.
16. Badelaire and malchus are types of sword; partisan and verdun are types of lance, and migraine is a fire grenade. 'Baddelaries partisans' may refer to those who support Ares, the god of war and battles, or the Lares, the ghosts of the dead, who always outnumber

Sanglorians, save! Arms apeal with larms, appalling. Killykillkilly: a toll, a toll.[17] What chance cuddleys, what cashels aired and ventilated! What bidimetoloves sinduced by what tegotetabsolvers![18] What true feeling for their's hayair with what strawng voice of false jiccup![19] O here here how hoth sprowled met the duskt the father of fornicationists but, (O my shining stars and body!) how hath fanespanned most high heaven the skysign of soft advertisement![20] But waz iz? Iseut? Ere were sewers?[21] The oaks of ald now they lie in peat yet elms leap where askes lay. Phall if you but will, rise you must: and none so soon either shall the pharce for the nunce come to a setdown secular phoenish.[22]

Bygmester Finnegan, of the Stuttering Hand, freemen's maurer, lived in the broadest way immarginable in his rushlit toofarback for messuages before joshuan judges had given us numbers or Helviticus committed deuteronomy[23] (one yeastyday he sternely struxk his tete in a tub for to watsch the future of his fates but ere he swiftly stook it out again, by the might of moses, the very water was eviparated and all the guenneses had met their exodus so that ought to show you what a pentschanjeuchy chap he was!)[24] and during mighty odd years this man of hod, cement and edifices in Toper's Thorp piled buildung supra buildung pon the banks for the livers by the Soangso.[25] He addle liddle phifie Annie ugged the little craythur. Wither hayre in honds tuck up your part inher.[26] Oftwhile balbulous, mithre ahead, with goodly trowel in grasp and ivoroiled overalls which he habitacularly fondseed,[27] like Haroun Childeric Eggeberth he would caligulate by multiplicables the alltitude and malltitude until he seesaw by neatlight of the liquor wheretwin 'twas born,[28] his roundhead staple of other days to rise in undress maisonry upstanded (joygrantit!), a waalworth of a skyerscape of most eyeful hoyth entowerly,[29] erigenating from next to nothing and celescalating the himals and all,[30] hierarchitectitiptitoploftical, with a burning bush abob

(mathmaster) the living, even when the growth of population is computed by 'mathmaster' Thomas Malthus (Malachus), whose *Essay on Population* foretold that the growth of population would outstrip the means of subsistence. Verdun was one of the bloodiest battles of World War I. Whiteboys were eigtheenth-century agrarian rebels in Ireland, 'hooded' in white. Assegais are African spears, and boomerangs are weapons which, like everything in this episode, return.

17. 'God's blood' or 'Earth's brood' by my 'father' (*fear* is the Irish for 'man'). *Sang* is French for 'blood', 'larme' is tear and in German *larm* is 'noise'; 'Kill', from Irish *chill* (church) is frequent in Irish place-names and the 'toll' may refer to the church tithes, the payment of which in Ireland led to the Tithe War of the 1830s.
18. 'cashels' are castles; the Rock of Cashel in County Tipperary is a collection of ruined buildings; the English poet Robert Herrick wrote the lines, 'Bid me to live, and I will live/Thy protestant to be,/Or bid me love, and I will give/A loving heart to thee.' The words of absolution in Penance, 'ego te absolvo' (I absolve thee) are conflated with the letter 't' to give 'tego', homonym for 'tadgh' (teague) a common name for a catholic in Ireland.
19. 'their's hayair' includes 'their heir', 'their saviour' and 'their hero'; 'hay' is paired with 'straw(ng)'; 'jiccup' includes Jacob, who deceived Isaac. Isaac, associated with Isaac Butt, Parnell's predecessor, brings us back to Parnell himself, the betrayed hero.
20. 'hoth' echoes 'Howth'; 'fane' is both pennant or temple; cf. Isaiah 48.13: 'my right hand hath spanned the heavens'.
21. Wagner's Tristan's first words: 'Was ist? Isolde?'
22. 'the farce for the nonce come to an ultimate secular finish'. 'pharce' also includes the earlier 'arc' of the rainbow that ends in the 'aquaface', and 'phoenix', besides reminding us of rebirth from the 'askes', derives from Irish *fionn uisce* (clear water). 'nunce' includes 'nuns' and contrasts with 'secular' as a moment contrasts with a century (Latin *saecula*); it also includes 'not once'.
23. Ibsen's *The Master Builder* is, in the original, *Bygmester Solness*; *freimaurer* in German is 'freemason'; 'rushlit' (rushlight) is slang for 'liquor'; 'toofarback' refers to a house with two back rooms; a messuage is a dwelling and adjacent lands; Joshua, Judges, Numbers, Leviticus and Deuteronomy are books of the Old Testament; Deuteronomy contains a repetition of the Decalogue; 'Helviticus' may contain a reference to the French philosophe Helvétius, but also emphasizes that the Book Leviticus defined the degrees of consanguinity within which marriage was forbidden.
24. 'yeastyday' (yesterday and Easter Day); Sterne and Swift, author of *A Tale of a Tub* who 'swiftly' withdraws his head from the 'tub', a work full of images of evaporation and evacuation; 'pentschanjeuchy' — 'punch and judy', ('juicy'), 'pentateuch', the five books of Moses; 'guenneses' has 'guinnesses' and also the goinses who meet their 'exodus'.
25. 'Toper's Thorp' could be glossed as the village of the heavy drinker, conceivably Dublin; 'buildung' contains German *bildung* (education). 'hod, cement and edifices' provides us with HCE again. 'Soangso' is 'so-and-so' or the river Hwang-ho.
26. A reference to Alice P. Liddell, Lewis Carroll's model for *Alice's Adventures in Wonderland.* 'hayre in honds' — 'her in hand', 'hare and hounds'; then, 'take up your partner'.
27. Balbus, a Roman wallbuilder, whose name means 'stutter', is here also bibulous, like Finnegan; 'mithre' has a bishop's headgear, mitre; a headband, considered a mark of effeminacy by the Romans; a joint in carpentry, or perhaps echoing 'Mithra', the Persian sun-god; habitaculum (Latin) is 'dwelling-place' which he 'fancied', but also in which he 'founded his seed'.
28. Haroun-al-Raschid, caliph of Baghdad in the *Arabian Nights*; the Frankish kings were called 'Childeric'; 'Eggeberth' is obviously egg-birth and 'caligulate' means both to calculate and to behave (monstrously) like Caligula, the Roman emperor; he sees by night-light, but also in drunkenness (malt, neat, liquor) and sees ('seesaw') double ('wheretwin').
29. The references here include those to the Arthurian round table, free masonry ('undress maisonry'), Woolworth's skyscraper (and fire-escape) in New York, the Eiffel (or awful) Tower ('eyeful'), Howth and height ('hoyth') and resurrection ('to rise', 'upstanded', 'joygrantit').
30. 'erigenating' combines the Irish philosopher Johannes Scottus (Ériugena) with the Latin 'erigo' (I erect) and with originating. In 'celescalating' (climbing a ladder to heaven) the himals (Himalayas, and, in German, *himmel*, the heavens), he emerges from next (German, *nichts*, nothing) to nothing (chaos, emptiness).

off its baubletop and with larrons o'toolers clittering up and tombles a'buckets clottering down.[31]

Of the first was he to bare arms and a name: Wassaily Booslaeugh of Riesengeborg.[32] His crest of huroldry, in vert with ancillars, troublant, argent, a hegoak, poursuivant, horrid, horned.[33] His scutschum fessed, with archers strung, helio, of the second. Hootch is for husbandman handling his hoe.[34] Hohohoho, Mister Finn, you're going to be Mister Finnagain! Comeday morm and, O, you're vine! Sendday's eve and, ah, you're vinegar![35] Hahahaha, Mister Funn, you're going to be fined again!

What then agentlike brought about that tragoady thundersday this municipal sin business?[36] Our cubehouse still rocks as earwitness to the thunder of his arafatas[37] but we hear also through successive ages that shebby choruysh of unkalified muzzlenimiissilehims that would blackguardise the whitestone ever hurtleturtled out of heaven.[38] Stay us wherefore in our search for tighteousness, O Sustainer, what time we rise and when we take up to toothmick and before we lump down upown our leatherbed and in the night and at the fading of the stars! For a nod to the nabir is better than wink to the wabsanti.[39] Otherways wesways like that provost scoffing bedoueen the jebel and the jpysian sea.[40] Cropherb the crunchbracken shall decide.[41] Then we'll know if the feast is a flyday. She has a gift of seek on site and she allcasually ansars helpers, the dreamydeary. Heed! Heed! It may half been a missfired brick, as some say, or it mought have been due to a collupsus of his back promises, as others looked at it. (There extand by now one thousand and one stories, all told, of the same)....[42]

31. The haughty tower of Babel with workmen climbing up and down, some of them rising like Laurence O'Toole, patron saint of Dublin, and some of them falling like the martyred Thomas à Becket, his contemporary.
32. *Hamlet*, V. 1. 31: ''A was the first that ever bore arms' (Adam); 'Wassaily Booslaeugh' contains Vasily Buslaev, hero of a Russian ballad cycle, 'wassail', drunken carousing, prominent early in *Hamlet*, linking with 'boose' and 'laugh'. 'Riesengeborg' means 'mountains of the giants'.
33. The heraldic terms refer to crude strength, fertility and cuckoldry ('hegoak', hegoat and also bogoak); 'horned', *horridus* ('savage' in Latin), pursuit (but 'poursuivant' is also an officer of the College of Arms) and 'in vert' ('in green', also 'invert' with 'ancillars', *ancilla* is Latin for 'handmaiden', sexual in- or per-version echoed in 'hure(e), 'whore'-oldry). This is also a description of the Dublin coat of arms.
34. 'scutschum' is escutcheon; also 'scut' of a 'chum', which may refer to 'helio' (Tim Healy, the leading enemy of Parnell, also Greek *helios*, 'the sun' (son)). The Parnellite escutcheon was divided (fesse is a third of a heraldic field enclosed between two lines) by his second-in-command. 'Hootch' ('hooch' liquor, also 'hoots') for the 'husbandman' (Captain O'Shea or Parnell) 'handling his hoe' (sexual connotation, also 'foe' and 'hero' echoed here).
35. Finn is going to Finn again, as vine or wine is going to vinegar in the 'week' between a Monday morn (norm) and a Sunday eve (Sin Day's Eve). The Fall of Adam and the fall of Parnell are beginnings that lead to ends (fin) and back again.
36. 'agentlike' contains agency, again-like and *eigentlich* (German for really); *tragodia* is Greek for tragedy; 'municipal sin' is a sin pertaining to a region or province, Eden, the world, Ireland.
37. 'cubehouse' is translation of Ka'aba, centre of Islam, also 'cubhouse' or 'clubhouse'; 'earwitness' like 'eyewitness' refers to 'Earwicker', the protagonist, whose name also involves 'earwig'; 'arafatas' includes 'Our Fathers' and *araf*, the Islamic name for purgatory.
38. 'shabby chorus of unqualified Moslems', also 'missal' or 'missile' hymns, 'that would blacken, or make a blackguard of the whitest one (or the stone of Ka'aba at Mecca that came down white but was blackened by sin) that was hurled, thrown over (turned turtle) out of heaven.'
39. 'nabir' includes Arab *nabi* (a prophet) and neighbour; 'wabsanti' has the saints (*santi*) and the 'absent'.
40. Otherwise we sway like the prophet's coffin (Mohammed's coffin is forever suspended), or the provost (John Pentland Mahaffy of Trinity College, Dublin) scoffing 'between the devil ('jebel' — 'bedown the rebel') and the deep blue (Egyptian, gypsy) sea'. Mahaffy scoffed at the Irish language and refused the rebels the use of Trinity for a meeting. He wrote about Egyptian papyri and Irish history.
41. 'Cropherb the crunchbracken', perhaps 'Robert the hunchback', an obscure reference, involving the notion that the Jews, as nomadic herdsmen (cropherbs) forsook the Egyptians and made their obscure language proverbial. Robert Atkinson, professor of languages at Trinity College, Dublin, was cited by Mahaffy as dismissing the Irish language. Joyce refers to this in the speech of Professor McHugh in the Aeolus episode of *Ulysses*.
42. 'flyday' is Friday, a f(e)astday in the church; 'seek on site' includes 'second sight'; 'dreamydeary' includes 'dromedary', which perhaps refers back to 'crunchbracken' and 'hunchback'. There are now, as in the *Arabian Nights*, 1001 stories of the 'collupsus' (collapse, the Fall), all the same story.

Biography/Bibliography

LIFE. Born in Rathgar, Dublin in 1882. In 1887, the family moved to Bray, Co. Wicklow. From 1888 to 1891, Joyce attended Clongowes Wood College, a Jesuit school, in County Kildare. In June 1891 he was withdrawn from the college because his father had lost his job. In this year he wrote *Et Tu, Healy!* on the betrayal and death of Parnell; the work has not survived. In 1892, the family moved to Blackrock, south of Dublin. The next year, the family moved to Dublin and Joyce attended the Christian Brothers School in North Richmond Street. In April 1893, he enrolled at the Jesuit school, Belvedere College, where he remained until 1898. In 1899, as a student at University College, Dublin, he refused to sign the students' protest against Yeats's play *The Countess Cathleen*. In 1900 Joyce read the essay 'Drama and Life' before the college's Literary and Historical Society, published an article 'Ibsen's New Drama' in the *Fortnightly Review*, and wrote a play, no longer extant, titled *A Brilliant Career*. In 1901, he published his attack on the Irish Literary Theatre, *The Day of the Rabblement*; his article on James Clarence Mangan was published in the college magazine, *St. Stephen's*, in 1902. He graduated that year in modern languages and went to Paris; with the help of Yeats and Lady Gregory, he wrote a number of reviews for the Dublin *Daily Express*. In 1903, he was called home from Paris because his mother was dying. She died in August. His essay-story 'A Portrait of the Artist' was rejected by the magazine *Dana* in 1904 and he began to rewrite it as *Stephen Hero.* He began publishing stories (which later would appear in *Dubliners*), in AE's journal *The Irish Homestead*; poems of his appeared in various magazines. He lived in the Martello Tower, Sandycove with Oliver St John Gogarty and taught for a time in a school in Dalkey. In June 1904 he met Nora Barnacle; they left Dublin together and travelled to Paris, Zurich, Trieste and Pola, where he began to teach English at the Berlitz language school. In 1905 they moved to Trieste. Joyce submitted the first version of *Dubliners* to Grant Richards. Their son Giorgio was born. In 1906 they moved to Rome where Joyce worked in a bank. In 1907, the family returned to Trieste. *Chamber Music* was published; Joyce wrote articles for the newspaper *Il Piccolo della Sera*, the story 'The Dead' and began to rewrite *Stephen Hero* as *A Portrait of the Artist as a Young Man.* In 1909, Joyce visited Dublin twice, once to sign a contract with Maunsel for the publication of *Dubliners* and once to organize the Cinematograph Volta. In 1910, he returned to Trieste. The cinema venture failed and Maunsel postponed the publication of *Dubliners.* In 1911, in deep discouragement, Joyce threw the manuscript of *A Portrait* into the fire. It was rescued by his sister Eileen. In 1912, Joyce and his family made a last trip to Ireland, visiting Dublin and Galway. The printer destroyed the edition of *Dubliners.* Joyce wrote the satiric poem, 'Gas from a Burner'. In 1914, *A Portrait* was published serially in the London magazine *The Egoist* and Grant Richards published *Dubliners.* The writing of *Ulysses* and the play *Exiles* was begun. After the outbreak of war, the Joyce family moved to Zurich. Ezra Pound, Yeats and Edmund Gosse helped him to the receipt of a grant from the British Treasury Fund in 1916 and *A Portrait* was published in New York. In 1917, he received the first of many gifts of money from Harriet Weaver and underwent his first eye operation, in London. In 1918, the New York magazine, *The Little Review*, serialized parts of *Ulysses*, and *Exiles* was published. *The Egoist* serialized five installments of *Ulysses.* Joyce returned to Trieste. In 1920, the year he first met Ezra Pound, he moved to Paris. Serialization of *Ulysses* was stopped by a complaint from the Society for the Prevention of Vice. Sylvia Beach, Adrienne Monnier, Valéry Larbaud and Pound were now sponsoring Joyce's career. In 1922, on Joyce's birthday, 2 February, Sylvia Beach's Shakespeare and Company published *Ulysses.* In 1923, he began the writing of *Finnegans Wake*, the first fragment of which was published in the *Transatlantic Review* (Paris) under the title 'Work in Progress'. Between 1927 and 1938, seventeen installments of 'Work in Progress' were published in the Parisian journal *transition* by Eugene Jolas. In 1931, Joyce and Nora were married in London. Lucia Joyce (b. 1907) had a breakdown in 1932 which led to her hospitalization in Switzerland the next year. After a court ruling that it was not pornographic, *Ulysses* was published in New York in 1934; Joyce's *Collected Poems* were published in 1936. *Finnegans Wake* was published in 1939 in London and New York. After the outbreak of war, the Joyces returned to France. Forced to leave in 1940, they went to Zurich, where Joyce died on 13 January 1941.

CHIEF WRITINGS. First editions only are given here, except in the case of *Stephen Hero.*
Chamber Music (London: Elkin Matthews, 1907); *Dubliners* (London: Grant Richards, 1914); *A Portrait of the Artist as a Young Man* (London: Egoist Press; New York: B. W. Huebsch, 1916); *Exiles* (London: Grant Richards; New York: B. W. Huebsch, 1918); *Ulysses* (Paris: Shakespeare & Co., 1922); *Pomes Penyeach* (Paris: Shakespeare & Co., 1927); *Collected Poems* (New York: Black Sun Press, 1936); *Finnegans Wake* (London: Faber and Faber; New York: B. W. Huebsch, 1939); T. Spencer (ed.), *Stephen Hero* (Norfolk, Connecticut: New Directions; London: Jonathan Cape, 1944); 2nd edition New Directions, 1955; revised edition with introduction and notes by J. J. Slocum and H. Cahoon (London: Jonathan Cape, 1956; New Directions, 1963; London: Four Square, 1966); O. A. Silverman (ed.), *Epiphanies* (Buffalo: University of Buffalo, 1956); S. Gilbert (ed.), *Letters of James Joyce* Vol. I (London: Faber and Faber; New York, The Viking Press, 1957); E. Mason and R. Ellmann (eds), *The Critical Writings of James Joyce* (London: Faber and Faber; New York: The Viking Press, 1959); T. E. Connolly (ed.), *Scribbledehobble* (London: Oxford University Press; Evanston, Illinois: Northwestern University Press, 1961); R. Ellmann (ed.), *The Letters of James Joyce* Vols II and III (London: Faber and Faber; New York: The Viking Press, 1966); R. Ellmann (ed.), *Giacomo Joyce* (London: Faber and Faber, 1968); R. Ellmann (ed.), *Selected Letters* (New York: The Viking Press; London: Faber and Faber, 1975).

CRITICAL EDITIONS OF TEXTS. R. Scholes (ed.), *Dubliners* (London: Cape, 1967; New York: The Viking Press, 1968); further corrected edition, R. Scholes and A. Walton Litz (New York: The Viking Press, 1969); C. G. Anderson (ed.), *A Portrait of the Artist as a Young Man* (New York: The Viking Press; London: Cape, 1964; reprinted New York: The Viking Press, 1968); H. W. Gabler et al (eds), *Ulysses: The Critical and Synoptic Edition* 3 vols (New York: Garland, 1984); corrected text New York: Random House; London: The Bodley Head; Harmondsworth: Penguin Books, 1986); see also M. Groden et al (eds), *The James Joyce Archive* 63 vols (New York: Garland, 1977-79); R. Ellmann and A. Walton Litz (eds), with the assistance of J. Whittier-Ferguson, *James Joyce. Poems and Shorter Writings, including Epiphanies, Giacomo Joyce and A Portrait of the Artist as a Young Man* (London: Faber and Faber, 1990).

BIOGRAPHY AND CRITICISM. (a) Biography: R. Ellmann, *James Joyce* (New York, London: Oxford University Press, 1959; new edition New York: Oxford University Press, 1982).
(b) General Criticism: D. Attridge and D. Ferrer (eds), *Post-structuralist Joyce. Essays from the French* (Cambridge: Cambridge University Press, 1984); A. Burgess, *Here Comes Everybody: An Introduction to James Joyce for the Ordinary Reader* (London: Faber and Faber, 1965); published in the USA as *Re Joyce* (New York: Norton, 1965); *Joysprick* (London: André Deutsch, 1973); R. H. Deming (ed.), *James Joyce: The Critical Heritage* 2 vols (London and Boston: Routledge & Kegan Paul, 1970); S. Givens (ed.), *James Joyce: Two Decades of Criticism* (New York: Vanguard Press, 1948; 2nd ed. 1963); H. Kenner, *Dublin's Joyce* (London: Chatto and Windus, 1955; Boston: Beacon Press, 1962; Bloomington, Indiana: Indiana University Press, 1966); H. Kenner, *Joyce's Voices* (London: Faber and Faber, 1978); H. Levin, *James Joyce: A Critical Introduction* (Norfolk, Connecticut: New Directions, 1941; revised edition 1960); A. W. Litz, *The Art of James Joyce* (London: Oxford University Press, 1961); C. McCabe, *James Joyce and the Revolution of the Word* (London: Macmillan, 1978); (ed.), *James Joyce: New Perspectives* (Brighton: Harvester Press; Bloomington: Indiana University Press, 1982); M. Magalaner and R. M. Kain, *Joyce: The Man, The Work and the Reputation* (New York: New York University Press, 1956); D. Manganiello, *Joyce's Politics* (London and Boston: Routledge & Kegan Paul, 1980); J. Mitchel Morse, *The Sympathetic Alien: James Joyce and Catholicism* (New York: New York University Press, 1959); P. Parrinder, *James Joyce* (Cambridge: Cambridge University Press, 1984); J.-M. Rabaté, *Joyce: Portrait de l'Auteur en Autre Lecteur* (Brussels: Cistre, 1984); F. Senn, *Nichts Gegen Joyce: Joyce Versus Nothing* (Zurich: Haffmans Verlag, 1985); D. Attridge (ed.), *The Cambridge Companion to James Joyce* (Cambridge: Cambridge University Press, 1990).

Dubliners
E. Brandabur, *A Scrupulous Meanness: A Study of Joyce's Early Work* (Urbana, Chicago, London: University of Illinois Press, 1971); J. R. Baker and T. F. Staley (eds), *James Joyce's Dubliners: A Critical Handbook* (New York: Wadsworth, 1969); M. Beja (ed.), *Dubliners and A Portrait of the Artist as a Young Man* Casebook Series (London: Macmillan, 1973); C. Hart (ed.), *James Joyce's Dubliners: Critical Essays* (New York: The Viking Press, 1969); M. Magalaner, *Time of Apprenticeship: The Fiction of the Young James Joyce* (London, New York, Toronto: Abelard Schuman, 1959); D. T. Torchiana, *Backgrounds for Joyce's Dubliners* (Boston, London, Sydney: Allen & Unwin, 1986).

A Portrait of the Artist as a Young Man
T. E. Connolly (ed.), *Joyce's Portrait: Criticism and Critiques* (New York: Appleton-Century-Crofts, 1962); W. E. Morris and C. A. Nault Jr. (eds), *Portraits of An Artist: A Casebook on James Joyce's A Portrait of the Artist as a Young Man* (New York: Odyssey Press, 1962); R. S. Ryf, *A New Approach to Joyce: The Portrait of the Artist as a Guidebook* (Berkeley and

Los Angeles: University of California Press, 1962); R. Scholes and R. M. Kain, *The Workshop of Daedalus: James Joyce and the Raw Material for A Portrait of the Artist as a Young Man* (Evanston, Illinois: Northwestern University Press, 1965); K. Sullivan, *Joyce Among the Jesuits* (New York: Columbia University Press, 1958).

Ulysses
R. M. Adams, *Surface and Symbol: The Consistency of James Joyce's Ulysses* (New York: Oxford University Press, 1962); H. Blamires, *The New Bloomsday Book: A Guide Through Joyce's Ulysses: The Corrected Text* (London: Routledge & Kegan Paul, 1989); F. Budgen, *James Joyce and the Making of Ulysses* (London: Grayson and Grayson, 1934; with additional material, Bloomington: Indiana University Press, 1960; London: Oxford University Press, 1972); R. Ellmann, *Ulysses on the Liffey* (London: Faber and Faber, 1972); M. French, *The Book As World: James Joyce's Ulysses* (Cambridge, Massachusetts and London: Harvard University Press, 1976); S. Gilbert, *James Joyce's Ulysses: A Study* (London: Faber, 1930; new edition, Faber; New York: Vintage, 1952; The Viking Press, 1966), S. L. Goldberg, *The Classical Temper* (London: Faber and Faber, 1961); M. Groden, *Ulysses in Progress* (Princeton: Princeton University Press, 1977); D. Hayman, *Ulysses: The Mechanics of Meaning* (Englewood Cliffs, New Jersey: Prentice Hall, 1970); R. Kain, *Fabulous Voyager: James Joyce's Ulysses* (New York: The Viking Press, 1959); H. Kenner, *Ulysses* (London: Allen & Unwin, 1980); K. Lawrence, *The Odyssey of Style in Ulysses* (Princeton: Princeton University Press, 1981); W. M. Schutte, *Joyce and Shakespeare: A Study in the Meaning of Ulysses* (New Haven: Yale University Press, 1957); S. Stanley, *The Argument of Ulysses* (Columbus: Ohio State University Press, 1965).

Finnegans Wake
J. S. Atherton, *The Books at the Wake* (London: Faber and Faber, 1959; New York: The Viking Press, 1960); B. Benstock, *Joyce-again's Wake: An Analysis of Finnegans Wake* (Seattle: University of Washington Press, 1965); J. Campbell and H. M. Robinson, *A Skeleton Key to Finnegans Wake* (New York: Harcourt Brace, 1944; London: Faber and Faber, 1947); A. Glasheen, *A Third Census of Finnegans Wake: An Index of Characters and their Roles* (Berkeley: University of California Press, 1977); C. Hart, *Structure and Motif in 'Finnegans Wake'* (London: Faber and Faber, 1962; Evanston, Illinois: Northwestern University Press, 1962); C. Hart, *A Concordance to Finnegans Wake* (Minneapolis: University of Minnesota Press, 1963); D. Hayman, *A First-Draft Version of Finnegans Wake* (Austin: University of Texas Press, 1962); R. McHugh, *The Sigla of Finnegans Wake* (London: Edward Arnold, 1976); M. Norris, *The Decentered Universe of Finnegans Wake: A Structuralist Analysis* (Baltimore and London: Johns Hopkins University Press, 1976); W. Y. Tindall, *A Reader's Guide to Finnegans Wake* (London: Thames and Hudson, 1969).

Guides
D. Gifford and R. J. Seidman, *Notes for Joyce: Dubliners and A Portrait of the Artist as a Young Man* (London: Faber and Faber, 1959; New York: E. P. Dutton, 1967, 2nd edition Berkeley: University of California Press, 1982); *Notes for Joyce: An Annotation of James Joyce's Ulysses* (New York: E. P. Dutton, 1974, revised edition Berkeley: University of California Press, 1989); R. McHugh, *Annotations to Finnegans Wake* (Baltimore and London: Johns Hopkins University Press, 1980); W. Thornton, *Allusions in Ulysses* (Chapel Hill, N.C.: University of North Carolina Press, 1961).

Bibliographies
J. J. Slocum and H. Cahoon, *A Bibliography of James Joyce 1882-1941* (New Haven: Yale University Press, 1953; reprinted Westport, Connecticut: Greenwood, 1971); R. H. Deming, *A Bibliography of James Joyce Studies* 2nd edition (Boston: G. K. Hall, 1977); T. J. Jackson, *James Joyce: A Guide to Research* (New York: Garland, 1982). See also the listings published quarterly in the *James Joyce Quarterly* (Tulsa, Oklahoma).

TERENCE BROWN, *Editor*

The Counter Revival:

Provincialism and Censorship 1930-65

Literary activity in the Irish Free State and in the Republic of Ireland (established in 1949) was affected by the deep social conservatism that marked the newly independent state and by the narrowly defined nationalism that was its ideological support. A largely rural society, in which the farmers and the grocers of the small towns throughout the country determined the moral and intellectual climate, the twenty-six counties of southern Ireland (following the partition of 1920, the six northern counties remained under British rule) in the 1920s and 1930s began a period of self-imposed cultural confinement and provincialism that was to be intensified by the enforced isolation of the war years (1939-45).

The innate conservatism of a majority of the people within the new state's jurisdiction was given ideological respectability by the official nationalism propagated by government party and opposition alike, and emotional sustenance by the moral approval of a vigorously puritanical church. In a dominant Irish Ireland consensus, ideas about Irish identity — compacted of a restrictive catholicism, which emphasized the perils of uninhibited sexuality, and a limited vision of Gaelic tradition, which emphasized its rural roots — were the substance of the nationalism that lent legitimacy to the new political order. Severe restrictions on economic and vocational opportunity, in a society where high levels of emigration were accepted almost as a law of nature (only one son could inherit a farm), accentuated the newly independent state's tendency to settle within the cautiously conservative moulds that nineteenth-century Ireland had bequeathed to it. There were sharp distinctions between the classes in relation to the ownership of land and capital, a less than adventurous tradition of native investment, a low level of industrialization and a prudent cost accounting management of the national exchequer.

In this context, a Draconian literary censorship was established by the Censorship of Publications Act of 1929. This Act, originally conceived of and drafted to respond (not unreasonably) to the problem of genuinely pornographic works in a threatening age of mass communication, became a weapon of cultural and social control. As such, it was accepted by most Irish people as a necessary bulwark against external threats to the Gaelic and catholic identity, which was felt to constitute the *raison d'être* of that Irish independence for which the martyrs of 1916 had given their lives. Accordingly, in the thirty-eight years in which its provisions were vigorously applied (a revision of the law in 1967 significantly liberalized its operations), the great majority of the modern literary classics fell under the Irish Censor's interdict and therefore were unavailable to more than a very small minority of Irish people. Although the threat to Irish national purity was generally perceived to be an external one (and Ireland has not been unique as a post-revolutionary, twentieth-century society in seeing the world in this starkly Manichean manner), Irish writers too fell foul of this notorious legislative instrument. Almost no Irish author of note remained unscathed and, although the curious recognition afforded to Irish writers by interdiction in their own country may have enhanced some international reputations, the local effects of this legislation necessarily must have been deforming for society and artist alike.

Among the various deformations that may be attributed to the Censorship Act and its primitive application was that of literary isolation for the Irish writer and a disabling provincialism for the society in which he or she worked. That invigorating interchange between a society and its writers, where ideas both indigenous and imported circulate freely, did not exist in an Ireland which seemed to choose a narrow self-absorption and a rejection of current existence in a celebration of a rigidly defined national essence. Consequently, the major developments in European intellectual and artistic life (to which Irishmen in the persons of Joyce, Yeats and Beckett contributed notably in the period) were almost completely ignored in Ireland, and much writing was produced which reflected on a provincial society apparently undisturbed by the tremors that were shaking the foundations in the rest of Europe. It would be possible, indeed, to read through a good deal of the Irish literature of the period without being aware either of the rise of fascism or of the costly experiment of Soviet communism. The threats posed to individual human dignity by totalitarianism of one kind or another and to man's understanding of himself by scientific, philosophical and psychological revolution, are subjects that scarcely engaged the Irish writer in those years and most certainly did not engage the society in which he worked. That society concerned itself with provincial issues of personal morality and national identity. Rare efforts to relate these to the wider twentieth-century context of post-colonial experience did little to disturb the general acquiescence in provincial modes of social life, thought and artistic production. Eamon de Valera, the longest-serving chief executive in the period (1932-48 was his longest occupancy) may have attempted to align Ireland with other small countries in the League of Nations before World War II, but his efforts did little to make the majority conscious of anything beyond their shores. Even the Irish missionary movement, which took numerous young men and women to the five continents and which might have allowed Ireland a perspective on the general phenomenon of colonialism, aligning its experience with that of other colonized societies, was conducted in terms barely distinguishable from the imperial values that had energized the European missionary movement of the nineteenth century.

It was perhaps inevitable that the Ireland of the 1930s and 1940s should have been a less exhilarating, more provincial place for the writer and artist than the years before the 1916 Rising and the War of Independence. Then, a broadly inclusive cultural nationalism had given a sense of authenticity to literary and artistic endeavour, and the ideals of romantic nationalism had demanded a passionate and heroic symbolism. In a more constricted period in the first decades of independence, when nationalism became precisely and exclusively identified with the Irish Ireland movement, the idea of the Celt, of a mysterious yet ennobling Irishness, became altogether more difficult to celebrate. For the Irish Ireland movement insisted that the only authentic Irish identity was the rural Gaelic/catholic one (its political muscle showed in the government-directed attempt to Gaelicize the education system). This view, of course, could be sustained only when the complicated social composition of the island as a whole was ignored and when the manifest existence of an indigenous English-language literature was denied.

In propagating this myopic view, the Irish Ireland movement was assisted by the writings of an able polemicist, Daniel Corkery, whose powerful if narrowly intense studies of Irish literary and cultural history were considerably influential. His works *The Hidden Ireland* (1925) and *Synge and Anglo-Irish Literature* (1931) gave intellectual sanction to an attitude that in its less refined form often expressed itself as a strident xenophobia or a bigoted social triumphalism.

In such a context, realism seemed the appropriate artistic mode. Ideals had apparently diminished to a day-to-day pragmatism. The fervour of revolutionary hope had dissipated in the disillusionment that followed the Civil War of 1922-23 (when the new state suppressed those elements in the independence movement who believed that the 1921 Treaty with Britain was a betrayal of the republican cause). The actual facts of Irish sectarian division could no longer be relegated to insignificance in a unifying vision of national culture. So AE (George Russell), in *The Irish Statesman* in 1928, identified the prevailing social climate as one of reaction to the heady years of romantic aspiration that preceded the Treaty. The emergence in newly independent Ireland of a significant body of realistic prose in the 1920s and the two succeeding decades suggests that AE was measuring the social temperature correctly.

AE's *Irish Statesman* (founded in 1923) had made strenuous efforts to maintain the idealism of the pre-revolutionary period. Throughout the 1920s he preached with repetitive fervour that the Irish tradition was composed of many elements and that the nation would ignore this fact at its peril. Instead of Irish Ireland's view of the Gaelic catholic tradition as an assimilative power, which would in time absorb all other cultural formations in the country, AE envisaged a broad cultural synthesis, which would give birth to a more richly composed Irish identity. In the homiletic columns of his journal, AE was making a special plea for the cultural distinctiveness of Anglo-Ireland in general and for the literature of the Literary Revival in particular. The new Ireland, however, was inclined to view both as the irrelevant properties of the *ancien régime*. So it is a note of argumentation and advocacy that makes AE's own writings in *The Irish Statesman* part of the new realism. For, instead of visionary enthusiasm, his journal is notable for its debates, controversies, vigorous polemics, and its attentive analyses of everyday events in the new state. In his columns we see the emergence in modern Ireland of the writer as social critic, as attentive to economic theory and practice as he is to aesthetic doctrine. In this conception, the writer must serve almost as an opposition political party, constantly challenging the monolithic assumptions of the prevailing social consensus.

The Irish Statesman ceased publication in 1930 (following a libel action). In the 1930s, only *Ireland Today* for a brief period (1936-38) attempted to emulate its blend of literary and social concern until it was forced to close after agitation from right-wing catholic associations — of the kind AE had feared — against its support of the republican cause in the Spanish Civil War. But in 1940 the Irish short-story writer and novelist, Seán O'Faoláin, founded *The Bell*, which for sixteen years was to offer sustained, systematic criticism of the Irish social order and an outlet for a great deal of new writing by Irish writers. O'Faoláin edited the magazine for six years, when it was at its most contentious and stimulating.

The Bell informed its readers in a subtitle that it was 'A Survey of Irish Life', and in his first editorial, 'This Is Your Magazine', O'Faoláin insisted that it would be governed by no ideological imperative, but would be open to the full reality of whatever life might exist in Ireland. Its recurrent note throughout O'Faoláin's editorship is a plea for 'honesty' and 'realism', and a cold-eyed assessment of the country's resources and state of development. There is, too, an open-minded concern to seek that real Ireland wherever it may be found — in the North, among the Anglo-Irish, as well as in the Gaelic/catholic Ireland of official approval. Instead of a sterile, antiquated nationalism, O'Faoláin advocates a practical, experimental patriotism:

> This Ireland is young and earnest. She knows that somewhere, among the briars and brambles, there stands the reality which the generations died to reach — not you notice the Ideal; our generation is too sober to talk much about Ideals, though we may think of it by any fine name there is, the Holy Grail, the Sacred Altar, the dream we have called by those hundred names now gone out of date.[1]

What distinguished O'Faoláin's critique of newly independent Ireland in *The Bell* from that of AE in *The Irish Statesman* was that it was rooted in a more realistically historical analysis of the social order. When AE rather plaintively pleaded for cultural synthesis, it had been in a vain effort to deny the social reality of a sectarian Ireland in which a catholic majority, long denied political power, wished to maintain and extend its recently established hegemony. O'Faoláin quite simply accepted that this was the fact of the matter and identified the new state's Irish Ireland consensus as the ideological underpinning of a middle-class *putsch*. Against this ideology he waged persistent polemical war, characterizing the nationalist myth of the antiquity and heroic splendour of the Gael as an idealistic fantasy, which distracted government and people alike from the urgent task of nation-building in an economically and socially deprived country.

In six years of editorials in *The Bell*, O'Faoláin produced a body of biting, pungent, common-sensical, clearly argued realistic analyses of current Irish society. *The Bell*, indeed, was almost the only counterweight to the ideological monolith of independent Ireland. The censorship of books particularly drew O'Faoláin's wrath, the Gaelic revival was excoriated as mere jobbery, the romantic image of the Irish peasant (celebrated in poems, sermons and bishops' pastorals) was denounced as a denial of the dismal social reality of rural Ireland and of the country's inadequate industrialization. O'Faoláin's primary theme was that Ireland was not a great,

1. Seán O'Faoláin, 'This Is Your Magazine', *The Bell*, Vol. 1, No. 1 (October 1940).

restored nation but 'a country at the beginning of its creative history, and at the end of its revolutionary history'. In attending in so systematic and committed a way to the creative possibilities of Irish society, O'Faoláin amply deserved the praise that an American commentator on Irish affairs lavished on him when he wrote that O'Faoláin's writings in *The Bell* amounted to

> the fullest analytic description of contemporary Ireland, and of its strengths, faults and derivations ever given. More than anything else these writings, close in manner and approach to the best eighteenth century pamphleteering, justify his title as first Irish man of letters.[2]

In assuming the burden of social criticism in the new Ireland, O'Faoláin performed a vital function in maintaining the sense of ideological alternatives. In strictly literary terms his work was also significant, despite his own sense that his years at the editorial desk had been ill-spent — a distraction from the more serious and agreeable business of his art. For O'Faoláin's editorials and articles allowed of the possibility that the notion of literature in Ireland might encompass the discursive essay, the work of the cultural analyst, the social historian, the pamphleteer. His writings were and remain a challenge to the Irish tendency to see only in lyric poetry, fiction and drama the expression of a creative imagination.

O'Faoláin was of course a novelist and short-story writer of distinction. The period 1930-60 was notable in Irish literary history for the emergence of the short-story as a characteristically Irish form. The period's dominant realism, which AE had anticipated and identified, found expression in a body of short prose fictions which took as their thematic material the everyday life of ordinary Irish men and women. These tales were touched by the sociological impulses that had governed such periodicals as *The Irish Statesman* and *The Bell*. Taken together, they present a portrait of a post-revolutionary, petit bourgeois society in a state of transition. An archaic, isolated rural society, with its own customs, laws and values, is presented at moments when the new modernizing forces of church, state and law interfere with immemorial practice. In this body of work, individual liberty, creativity and emotional fulfilment are constantly seen as victims of an oppressively provincial mode of life. Notions of respectability, morality and convention smother the revolutionary energies that had erupted in the years before Independence. The characteristic movement of the Irish short story is therefore towards a moment when buried emotion is recognized but rarely acted upon.

Various explanations suggest themselves to account for the emergence of the short story as a form consonant with Irish social and cultural experience in this period. The anecdotal, expository, intimate voice adopted by the narrators in so many of these works may owe something to the Irish tradition of the *seanachai* (the oral story-teller, whose tales recounted local incidents of note). In such a view, the Irish short story is simply the modern expression in the legible world of Irish oral tradition. A speaking voice is imitated which, as Thomas Kilroy has noted of Irish fiction in general, 'is a voice heard over and over again, whatever its accents, a voice with a supreme confidence in its own histrionics, one that assumes with its audience a shared ownership of the told tale and all that it implies: a taste for anecdote, an unshakable belief in the value of human actions, a belief that life may be adequately encapsulated into stories that require no reference, no qualifications, beyond their own selves'.[3]

More complicatedly, the Irish short-story form may be understood as a symptom of a society undergoing change. Frank O'Connor, one of the form's most distinguished practitioners, in his book on the short story, *The Lonely Voice* (1963), associates the short story in general with such a social condition. He argues that the short story gives voice to the feeling of submerged populations and peoples. But it is of course only when a society, a people, or an individual senses some form of social, cultural or national superimposition that the metaphor of submergence becomes apposite. In Ireland in the twentieth century, the old Gaelic, rural civilization, with its distinctive folk idioms, lore and music, was being submerged by the new modernizing, essentially urban social order of the towns and cities. But the Ireland of the small towns — nationalist, catholic, petit bourgeois — also sensed itself to be a submerged population in the wider context of the British Isles. At the frontiers

2. John V. Kelleher, 'Seán O'Faoláin', *Atlantic Monthly*, CXCIX (May 1957), 68.

3. Thomas Kilroy, 'Teller of Tales', *The Times Literary Supplement* (17 March 1972), p. 301.

between these various superimpositions, the short story emerges as a form appropriate to a sense of submergence and transition; for the form itself seems transitional, poised, as Declan Kiberd has noted, 'like its authors, between the profane world of contemporary literature and the pious world of the folk'.[4] The short story in purely formal terms also seems transitional, functioning at literary boundaries, in part work to be performed with the communal speaking voice determining its histrionics, in part work to be savoured on the page in privacy and silence.

O'Connor's account of the sociology of the short story suggests furthermore why its dominant mood has been lyrical. In a submerged population, where the provincial mind senses its own social impotence, definitions of selfhood must perforce involve private feeling, romantic imagination and defeat. A lyric form is an aesthetic acquiescence in the general sense of powerlessness, an artistic making-do. This is how Sean O'Faoláin himself accounted for the dominance of the short story in the Irish fiction of the period. A depressed provincial world had little to offer the realist prose writer (as he argued in 1949):

> The life now known, or knowable to any modern Irish writer is either the traditional, entirely simple life of the farm (simple intellectually speaking); or the groping, ambiguous, rather artless urban life of these same farmers' sons and daughters who have, this last twenty-five years, been taking over the cities and towns from the Anglo-Irish. . . .
>
> In such an unshaped society there are many subjects for little pieces, that is for the short-story writer; the novelist or the dramatist loses himself in the general amorphism, unthinkingness, brainlessness, egalitarianism and general unsophistication.[5]

So the characteristic Irish short story deals in an oppressive, authoritarian environment, where law, politics and the iron regimen of economic life determine existence. The tale itself achieves a moment of lyric definition, an epiphany, in which protagonist, narrator, author and reader all share, as if momentarily transcending the bleak condition of life to which the story itself is attentive. 'What one searches for and what one enjoys in a short story,' wrote O'Faoláin, 'is a special distillation of personality, a unique sensibility which has recognized and selected at once a subject that, above all other subjects, is of value to the writer's temperament and to his alone — his counterpart, his perfect opportunity to project himself.'[6]

There were prose writers in the period who refused to be limited by the short story's realistic mode with its defining lyricism. In their works, the dismal provincial absurdities of post-independence Ireland could be represented only in the dimension of fantasy. Of these, Flann O'Brien's *At Swim-Two-Birds* (1939) is a minor masterpiece, a nihilistic extravaganza, which absorbs Irish experience into the endlessly fictive world of mere textuality. The story-shaped world subverts a realist's grasp on a conventional and depressed social scene. Here anecdote runs riot, the epic mode encounters the sordid, the parodic meets the poetic. An endless literary inventiveness is the febrile artistic response to a social and cultural enervation that O'Brien in another of his manifestations (as Myles na gCopaleen) treated to an angry, witty, and satiric castigation. *At Swim-Two-Birds* makes language itself its subject, in a society where a language and culture had died and were proving incapable of resurrection. A weary sense that the only possible life in present-day Ireland is the linguistic makes *At Swim-Two-Birds* perhaps the most damning indictment of post-independence Ireland in the period. For in that strange, comic, frightening book, one senses language facing death for want of anything truly worthwhile to say. It should not surprise that in his next novel, *The Third Policeman*, Flann O'Brien attempted to write a language of the dead.

4. Declan Kiberd, 'Story-Telling: The Gaelic Tradition' in P. Rafroidi and T. Brown (eds), *The Irish Short Story* (Lille: Publications de l'université de Lille III, 1979), p. 15.
5. 'The Dilemma of Irish Letters', *The Month*, Vol. 2, No. 6 (1949), 373, 375-76.
6. Seán O'Faoláin, *The Short Story* (London: Collins, 1948), pp. 37-38.

AE (GEORGE RUSSELL)

(1867-1935)

from: THE IRISH STATESMAN (1928)

[In this editorial in *The Irish Statesman*, AE attempts to rationalize his disappointment at developments in the Irish Free State since Independence. The essay was published on 29 December 1928, at the end of a year that had seen the assassination of the Minister for Justice, Kevin O'Higgins, and the entry of Fianna Fáil into the arena of parliamentary politics, Dáil Éireann. AE accurately identifies realism as the dominant social mood, which was to intensify in the 1930s.]

SEVEN YEARS' CHANGE

It is now seven years since we ceased to be ruled from Westminster, and we assumed control over our own affairs. There is a myth, which may have some scientific foundation for all we know, to the effect that there is a complete change in the atomic structure of the human body every seven years. We doubt if this applies to a nation even if it applies to the individuals who compose it. The country and the people have very much the same kind of character as they had before the European war. There are differences of course. Every nation has oscillations within its own being. Every action leads to a reaction. Every passion develops its antitoxin. There is a kind of logic in all developments and reactions in the national being, whether in politics, literature, art or economic theory. We see these inevitable reactions in the history of all cultures and civilisations. In literature the classical is superseded by the romantic, the romantic by the realistic, the realistic by the symbolist. The history of philosophy shows every great thinker reacting in some fashion from the dominant figure preceding him. We see the logic so clearly in past history that we think we should be able to prophecy the next stage in our own development. But, in truth, the future eludes us. We may be quite certain that the logic of reaction will be maintained, but we cannot say whether the reaction will zigzag to right or left or up or down. We can see that the passionate moods preceding the truce,[1] with their high idealism and their devilry, have subsided. The nation at present is frankly realistic in its politics. It is concerned about economics, about the organisation of its farmers, the development of industry, the Shannon scheme,[2] electricity, sugar beet, inland fisheries, butter, eggs, cattle, horses, quite admirable interests, but the inevitable reaction from the mood of seven years ago, when the world was well lost for freedom. The disregard of human life which was rampant before the truce has been replaced by a national hatred of violence. No party desiring the confidence of the voters talks at all about physical force in our politics. Men who half a dozen years ago believed their militant mood was immortal find somehow the spring of that heroic mentality has mysteriously dried up, not because they are afraid, not because they have reasoned themselves into another course of action. It is like the action of the sun, which sucks up moisture and leaves everything dry in the fields. That dryness comes not because of any action by plant or soil, but because of something else. There is simply no moisture left and the subsiding of violence has come about by some mysterious power in the national being, and the militant find simply that the desire to use physical force is no longer in them.

The people who were quiescent during the Anglo-Irish war, who lay low because of the danger, are having their period of activity. They now are militant about books, newspapers, cinemas, short skirts, dances, which they would like to suppress. There were others who lay low during the Anglo-Irish war, the jobbers and grafters with whom the fighters who were honest would have no truck. The jobbers and grafters would not join secret societies which there was an element of danger to life in membership [*sic*]. Now these folk

1. The truce between the British government and Dáil Éireann, which came into operation on 11 July 1921, ended the War of Independence and allowed for the negotiations that bore fruit in the Treaty with Britain, which came into effect at the end of that year.
2. Between 1925 and 1929 a major electrical power station was constructed at Ardnacrusha, near Limerick. It exploited the river Shannon as a source of energy.

are joining some secret and sectarian associations to get jobs or business, and Ministers who are honest will have a tough fight to prevent these upsetting the work of the Civil Service Commission and the Public Appointments Commission, which were established so that merit alone would be the test. These sectarian associations wish membership of themselves to be the qualification. They cry out because they can no longer make membership of themselves or relationships the lever to secure positions, and they would like to dominate the panels or the commissions. From quiescence when there was danger these groups have jumped into activity, when there is no danger to their skins. We believe the heart of Ireland is sound and that once it realises what danger there is in these associations it will act, so that they will become contemptible to national sentiment. But there is a real danger to the integrity of our institutions when thousands of people who are members of secret associations are in politics, in local government, in law, so that one can never be certain why votes are given for this cause or that, or why nominations for positions are made. It becomes most important to have national integrity preserved because the process of creating an organic unity of people and institutions in the Free State has been going on very rapidly during the past seven years, and it is vital to us when the organisation is complete that its institution will maintain integrity and impartiality in public affairs.

Ireland before the Treaty had no other organic unity than that provided by national sentiment. Such unity as there was was subjective. Our railways were run by several companies. Now there is but one railway system. There used to be several hundred dairy societies, each marketing its butter for itself. Now eighty per cent market their produce through one organisation. Our political parties have accepted the organic unity created by the Oireachtas,[3] and whatever their differences may be they work inside it and use it as the instrument for national action. The forty odd boards have been merged in a few departments with a logic for their existence. In another year the genius for organisation will have brought it about that electricity for lighting or power purposes will be generated in one centre and distributed through the entire country. The organisation of farmers is going on steadily. The rationalisation of industry here is delayed, but it is inevitable and there are signs here and there of a tendency to form combines. All this has been fostered by Ministers who are inspired by the Time spirit which in every country is sweeping the unorganised into great national organisations, so that the State may have the swift free movement of the athletic individual, and have a mechanism Ministers can control, and national problems be made manageable which they can never be while agriculture and industry are unorganised. All this is realistic and contrasts with the spirit of seven years ago, when people were judged by their moods, their beliefs, their idealisms, rather than by any other criterion. Now we are inclined to judge by technical competence, whether a man can do a job, whether the mechanism will work. But though there is this change or reaction it would be wrong to assume that there is not a very sincere patriotic spirit behind these new activities. We are sure there is. We find in a decade that the militarist has become pacifist. The cowards are becoming brave when there is no danger. The unorganised are becoming organised. The idealists in politics and literature are becoming realists. Should we not be able to foresee any new reactions or zigzagging from current moods? We ought to be, but we cannot. Our intuition is that our revolutions are going to be intellectual, and that the next generation will be interested in science, our writers in psychology, that is, they will be intellectual rather than idealistic as they were a generation ago, or realistic as the most prominent are at present. We may be quite mistaken. But it is worth while noting the changes in national psychology, and the logic which underlies them. We have faith that if the Irish will really use their intellect they can make their country one of the most brilliant in Europe. If they yield to the obscurantists who want people to read nothing or think nothing, there can be only national decay. We believe the Irish intellect will awaken just because there are so many who want to dose it with moral bromides, and we are certain it will resist.

3. The Irish legislature, composed (under the provisions of the Constitution established by the Treaty) of the King or Queen and two chambers, Dáil Eireann and Seanad Eireann. The Constitution of 1937 replaced the King with the President.

GEORGE BERNARD SHAW

(1856-1950)

from: THE IRISH STATESMAN (1928)

[The proposal to enact a Censorship of Publications Act provoked a lively controversy, in which many well-known writers participated vigorously. In *The Irish Statesman* (17 November 1928) George Bernard Shaw added his acerbic voice to the literary opposition to the proposed Act.]

THE CENSORSHIP

It is a convention to assume that there is nothing people like more than political liberty. As a matter of fact there is nothing they dread more. Under the feeble and apologetic tyranny of Dublin Castle[1] we Irish were forced to endure a considerable degree of compulsory freedom. The moment we got rid of that tyranny we rushed to enslave ourselves. We gave our police power to seize any man's property and to put upon him the onus of proving that it belonged to him. We declared that as prison would not deter Irishmen from evildoing they must be savagely flogged; and when evildoers were flogged they were imprisoned for long periods lest the flogging should provoke them to commit fresh crimes. When gunmen were all over the place we made it a crime for anyone to possess a weapon to protect himself against gunmen. We are too much afraid of our peaceful citizens to arm them, and too much afraid of brawlers not to suspect a brawler in every peaceful citizen. We are afraid to let a fellow citizen practise fine art because he (or she) might take advantage of our ignorance of art to cheat or corrupt us. Miss Mia Cranwill,[2] the Irish Benvenuto Cellini[3] (I am not referring to her private life) is to be driven out of the country by the sellers of the dullest and commonest English silver goods under a regulation which a medieval guild in the last stage of decay would have refused to believe possible in a sane community.

We shall never be easy until every Irish person is permanently manacled and fettered, gagged and curfewed, lest he should punch our heads or let out the truth about something. It is useless to remonstrate. As Mark Twain said, the average man is a coward. The latest demonstration of Irish abjectness is the supplanting of constitutional law by the establishment of a Censorship extending in general terms to all human actions, but specifically aimed at any attempt to cultivate the vital passion of the Irish people or to instruct it in any function which is concerned with that passion. It is, in short, aimed at the extermination of the Irish people as such to save them from their terror of life and of one another. The Jews aspired to a state in which 'none should make them afraid'; but they proposed to live to enjoy it, each Jew sitting up, alive and hearty, under his own vine and fig tree. We hope for no peace until we lie dead, each under his own headstone, forgetting that when it comes to the point we shall be afraid to die lest the devil should use us worse than even our dreaded fellow-creatures.

Since it would be vain to appeal to the Irish people, I turn to the Church, which is not Irish, but Catholic. Is it going to submit to this amateur Inquisition which is eliciting triumphant chuckles of 'We told you so' from Ulster? Does it realize the ghastly change that threatens its temples in the Unfree State at the suggestion of Sir William Joynson Hicks,[4] the most resolute No Popery man in England, and of a raving Orangeman who supplies Ireland with English papers and declares that he would rather murder his children than trust them uncensored.[5] I am on cordial personal terms with both of these sturdy Protestants; but I hardly expected to see the Catholic Church coming to heel at their whistle.

1. The administrative centre of English colonial rule in Ireland.
2. Mia Cranwill (1880-1972) was an Irish miniaturist whose work in designing jewellery and enamelled metals on symbolic and Celtic themes was much admired during the Irish Literary Revival.
3. Benvenuto Cellini (1500-71), a Florentine goldsmith and metal-worker who turned to large-scale sculpture. His *Autobiography*, written between 1558 and 1562, gives a racy account of the complications of his private life.
4. Sir William Joynson Hicks (1865-1932) was the first Viscount Brentford and a Conservative politician.
5. Possibly a reference to John Charles Malcolm Eason (1880-1976) who became managing director of Eason and Son, the Irish bookseller and newspaper distributor, in 1926. A liberal, Eason did support, however, some censorship of literature and especially of films. He made a submission to the Committee on Evil Literature, which body prepared the way for the Censorship of Publications Act of 1929.

All those figures of the dead Christ, with their strong appeal to the pity and love of Irish girls (who has not seen them weeping and praying before such figures?) must be melted or smashed, and the girls referred to St. Thomas Aquinas[6] for instruction in purely intellectual religious emotion. All the handsome brave St. Joans must be chopped up for firewood. The boys who feel that they can pray to St. Joan when they cannot pray with any heart to the distantly august Trinity will cease to pray, and interest themselves in getting rich quickly. The Catherines and Margarets with their long tresses, teaching the young to associate loveliness with blessedness, will be torn down, leaving their adorers to associate loveliness with debauchery, like all Censors. The Mother of God herself will be spared only on condition that she be made repulsively ugly lest she should 'excite sexual passion', a course which must end in her complete banishment lest the ugliness should excite abhorrence. The Faith will wither at the root and perish. The Iconoclast will rejoice and exult.

Then what of the priest? Clearly his splendid vestments at the altar cannot be tolerated by the Censors: his carnal good looks must be masked in Genevan black. The gilded shrine must be replaced by a cricket pavilion locker and the incense replaced by assafoetida;[7] for did not Mahomet say 'There are three supremely delightful things: perfume, woman, and prayer; and the greatest of these delights is prayer.' And what is incense but perfume? Clearly if Mahomet had been an Irishman he would not have wasted his time praying when he could get all his soul's troubles settled for him by a Censorship.

As to singing in churches, its sensuous appeal must be severely censored under the Act. In London the contrast between the virility and charm of the singing in Westminster Cathedral and the wretched bawling of the opera choruses has struck everyone who has compared them; and I cannot believe that the Irish cathedrals do not equally eclipse the Gaiety Theatre. But under the Censorship the Mass will be sung in Ireland by the choristers of the musical comedy stage, because their efforts could not possibly warm the most susceptible female heart.

These fleshly and artistic snares of the devil are, however, mere trifles. What of the priest as confessor, counsellor, spiritual adviser, teacher of youth? If innocent youths or maidens going from a sheltered home into the world are warned by their pastor of the perils of venereal disease, away with him to prison for corrupting the young. If the wives and husbands of his congregation come to him for help in the domestic troubles brought on them by their ignorance, and he brings the ancient wisdom of his Church to their relief (his supply of modern scientific treatises on the subject being cut off) away with him at once: the priest who would mention such things in conversation with a lady is no better than Dr. Marie Stopes.[8] If, in his counsels to schoolboys, he makes any reference to homosexuality, unfrock him and cast him forth to share an eternity of burning brimstone with Miss Radclyffe Hall.[9]

And when all these monstrous follies are being perpetrated by way of purifying Ireland the Church will be blamed for it. Already it is said on all hands that the Censorship Bill is the Church's doing. It will certainly be the Church's undoing unless the Church stands openly by its anti-Puritan tradition. The notion that Raphael[10] was less inspired, or otherwise inspired, when he painted the history of Cupid and Psyche than when he painted the Transfiguration, has no warrant in Church doctrine.

(By the way, what is to be done with the National Gallery under the Act?)

What we have to consider in judging the special aim of the Bill is that life, especially married life, is unnecessarily troubled and occasionally wrecked because we have no technique of marriage; and this ignorance is produced by the deliberate suppression of all responsible information on the subject. England has an expert instructress in the person of Dr. Marie Stopes; and the result is that —

6. St Thomas Aquinas (1224/5-74), the most renowned catholic theologian and philosopher, and the embodiment of the intellectual, scholastic approach to religion.
7. The gum resin of a family of oriental plants, used in medicine as an anti-spasmodic.
8. Dr Marie Stopes (1880-1958), an early advocate of family planning.
9. Marguerite Radclyffe Hall (1883-1943) is chiefly remembered for her novel *The Well of Loneliness* (1928), which openly treated of a lesbian theme. It occasioned a trial for obscenity and was banned, although it was republished in 1949.
10. Raphael, more properly Raffaello Sanzio (1483-1520), was one of the most famous painters of the Italian Renaissance. The ceiling of the Villa Farnesina in Rome shows the story of Psyche. The *Transfiguration* in the Vatican, an altarpiece displaying the moment when Christ's divinity shone through his human form, was unfinished at his death.

quite apart from the special technique of Birth Control, which she has at all events rescued from the uncontradicted, and in Ireland presently to become the legally uncontradictable, advertisements of the underground trade in 'specialities' — numbers of unhappy marriages have been set right by her instruction. The Irish people will not be allowed to consult either Dr. Stopes or their spiritual directors. Of clandestine instruction there will be plenty; but as nobody will be allowed to criticise it, or even to mention it, everything that is evil in it will be protected and nourished, and everything that is honest and enlightening in it will be discredited and suppressed.

But we must not let our vision be narrowed by the specific and avowed objects of the Act, which are, to prevent our learning the truth about the various methods of Birth Control (some of them in urgent need of criticism) now in irresistible use, and to hide from us the natural penalties of prostitution until we have irrevocably incurred them, often quite innocently at second hand. The matter of Censorship as opposed to constitutional law is bigger than these, its meanest instances. Ireland is now in a position of special and extreme peril. Until the other day we enjoyed a factitious prestige as a thorn in the side of England, or shall I say, from the military point of view, the Achilles heel of England? We were idealized by Pity, which always idealizes the victim and the underdog. The island was hymned as one of saints, heroes, bards, and the like more or less imaginary persons. Every Don Quixote in Europe and America, and even actually in China, made a Dulcinea[11] of Kathleen ni Houlihan and the Dark Rosaleen. We thought ourselves far too clever to take ourselves at the Quixotic valuation; but in truth even the most cynically derisive Dubliners (detestable animals!) overrated us very dangerously; and when we were given a free hand to make good we found ourselves out with a shock that has taken all the moral pluck out of us as completely as physical shell shock. We can recover our nerve only by forcing ourselves to face new ideas, proving all things, and standing by that which is good. We are in a world in which mechanical control over nature and its organization has advanced more in a single century than it had done before in a whole epoch. But the devil of it is that we have made no corresponding advance in morals and religion. We are abject cowards when confronted with new moral ideas, and insanely brave when we go out to kill one another with a physical equipment of artificial volcanoes and atmospheres of poison, and a mental equipment appropriate to stone axes and flint arrow heads. We incite our young men to take physical risks which would have appalled the most foolhardy adventurers of the past; but when it is proposed to allow a young woman to read a book which treats sexual abnormalities as misfortunes to be pitied instead of horrors to be screamed at and stoned, an Irishman arises in the face of England and madly declares that he is prepared in the interests of family life to slay his children rather than see them free to read such a work. What sort of family life his daughter has led him since he made this amazing exhibition of Irish moral panic is a matter for shuddering conjecture; but however dearly he has paid at his own fireside for his terrors, he can hardly have got worse than he deserves.

The moral is obvious. In the nineteenth century all the world was concerned about Ireland. In the twentieth, nobody outside Ireland cares twopence what happens to her. If she holds her own in the front of European culture, so much the better for her and for Europe. But if, having broken England's grip of her, she slops back into the Atlantic as a little grass patch in which a few million moral cowards are not allowed to call their souls their own by a handful of morbid Catholics, mad with heresyphobia, unnaturally combining with a handful of Calvinists mad with sexphobia (both being in a small and intensely disliked minority of their own co-religionists) then the world will let 'these Irish' go their own way into insignificance without the smallest concern. It will no longer even tell funny stories about them. That was what happened to so mighty a power as the Spanish Empire; and in magnitude we are to the Spanish Empire what a crumb is to a loaf.

By the way, the reality behind that poetic fiction, 'the Irish race', has a good deal of Spanish blood in it. The seed of Torquemada is in the Irish soil as well as the seed of Calvin.[12]

Let us beware!

11. A mistress or sweetheart — the name of Don Quixote's lover in Cervantes's novel.

12. Tomás de Torquemada (1420-98), a Spanish Dominican monk who was made Grand Inquisitor of the Spanish Inquisition in 1483. John Calvin (1509-64), a French protestant theologian, author of *Institutes of the Christian Religion* (1536) and the founder of a theocratic, despotic government in Geneva in 1541. Both men are notorious for their intolerance.

DANIEL CORKERY
(1878-1964)

from: THE HIDDEN IRELAND (1925)

[In his introduction to *The Hidden Ireland*, the short-story writer and critic, Daniel Corkery, employed the world of eighteenth-century Gaelic poets in Munster to offer a version of an Irish Ireland ideology. This expressed the nativist ethos of the new state in terms of a narrow cultural nationalism, a return to the native hearth. The book was highly influential in the 1930s and 1940s.]

IV

Reading those re-discovered poets day after day, I was more and more struck with the extent to which the modes of Mediæval literature survived in them. At first I felt merely curious; but somehow becoming aware that the whole trend of modern literature was towards those self-same long discarded modes, I grew to think that here was such a justification for reviving the language as overshadowed all others.

In this place it is not feasible, even if one were able, to take such a wide or penetrating view of modern literature as would show whether or not Renaissance moulds are being flung aside as no longer of use. One must be satisfied to sketch out roughly certain lines of thought which give us to feel a great struggle going on in modern literature between the dying spirit of the Renaissance and the re-discovered spirit of Nationality. It is not today nor yesterday that this fight began. What is every Romantic movement, every *Sturm und Drang* movement, but a skirmish in it? Does not every such movement begin by an increased consciousness that the breadth, movement, colour of life, the romance of it, cannot be poured into classical moulds? (Of course, the moulds are not really Classical at all; they are only Classical at second-hand; they are Renaissance.) It is the surface-movement, the surface-flush of life that at first seems to protest against the inflexibility, the too-regulated shapeliness, the too-restricted colouring that those Renaissance modes insist upon, for all their size and grandeur. Then the pageantry of the past, where surface-movement, surface-colour, are less mixed with other elements, joins in the protest and clamours for expression. But it does not matter to the argument which of the two comes first; the thing to insist upon is that every Romantic movement is a national effort to discover for present needs forms other than the Classical forms.

It has to be insisted upon that Renaissance standards are not Greek standards. Greek standards in their own time and place were standards arrived at by the Greek nation; they were national standards. Caught up at second-hand into the art-mind of Europe — thus becoming international, their effect was naturally to whiten the youthfully tender national cultures of Europe. That is, the standards of a dead nation killed in other nations those aptitudes through which they themselves had become memorable. Since the Renaissance there have been, strictly speaking, no self-contained national cultures in Europe. The antithesis of Renaissance art in this regard is national art. To some it must seem as if the Renaissance has justified itself in thus introducing a common strain into the art-consciousness of all European countries. That common strain was certainly brilliant, shapely, worldly-wise, strong, if not indeed gigantic, overabounding in energy, in life! Yet all the time there was a latent weakness in it, a strain, a sham strength, an uneasy energy, a death in life. It always protested too much. Dissembling always, it was never simple-hearted enough to speak plainly, and so, intensely. It therefore dazzles us rather than moves us. If it has justified itself, then should we swap Rheims cathedral for St Peter's and Rouen for St Paul's! 'One would, however, swap Dante for Shakespeare?'[1] — Yes, but what did Shakespeare's native wood-notes wild know of the Unities?[2] Happy England! — so naïvely ignorant of the Renaissance at the close of the sixteenth century. Unhappy France! — where even before Shakespeare was born they had ceased to develop their native Christian literary modes, had indeed begun to fling them aside for those of Euripides and Seneca.[3] The

1. An imagined response to T. S. Eliot on Dante and Shakespeare in *The Sacred Wood* (1920).
2. The unities of action, place and time in classical drama.
3. Euripides (*c.* 485-*c.* 406 B.C.), a Greek tragedian. Seneca (*c.* 4 B.C.-65 A.D.), a Roman philosopher, dramatist and statesman. French classical drama of the seventeenth century, especially the plays of Racine, was strictly modelled on classical forms.

edifice they built up in after years upon these borrowed alien modes is both noble and vast, perhaps even great, but it is not either a Rheims or a Rouen: its appeal to the spirit has less in it both of magic and depth. The Renaissance may have justified itself, but not, we feel, either on the plane of genuine Christian art or genuine pagan art. It is not as intense or as tender as the one, nor so calm, majestic and wise as the other.*

A Romantic movement is not usually thought of as a violent effort to re-discover the secret power that lay behind Greek art; yet in essence that is what every Romantic movement has been. The personal note, the overweening subjectivity, that marks such movements is a protest against the externality of Renaissance moulds. The local colour, the religious *motif*, the patriotic *motif*, these are an adventure in rough life rather than in the pale meadows of death. That is, every Romantic movement is right in its intention: it seeks to grow out of living feeling, out of the here and now, even when it finds its themes in the past, just as Greek art, which also looked for themes in its people's past, grew up out of the living feeling of its own time and place. The Renaissance would hold by a dead age and a dead land.

There is perhaps no tongue in Europe that has not had its Romantic movement, or movements. If we are destined to see no more, it is simply that the Old Man of the Sea has been flung from our backs, that the Renaissance is dead.

The Renaissance, artificial from the start, rootless, had sometime to die. Dead, what could succeed it except a return to national standards? Whether or not we feel that every literature in Europe is doing this may be a question of knowledge. But it is not necessary to take them in turn and observe their courses. Let us rather ask ourselves: What language in Europe since the French Revolution — which outburst, for all its Classicism, really meant the overthrow of the Renaissance — has done the greatest work in literature? The answer is the Russian. That literature, born too late to share deeply in the wares of the Renaissance, is at once the most national and the most significant of all modern literatures. A memorable and comforting fact — pointing out the way of light and freedom.

Note again, the influence that other late comers in the field of world-literatures, such as Danish, Norwegian, Swedish, are having on the world of letters. It is the literatures of these countries that are really the pathfinders of today. Note again, how impossible it would have been for America to make any progress in literature if Whitman[4] had not arisen to slay the New Englanders. Still further observe the huge extent to which dialect is entering into the stuff of modern literature in almost all countries. Imagine what Racine[5] would say to Eugene O'Neill![6] Dialect is the language of the common people; in literature it denotes an almost overweening attempt to express the here and now, that, in its principle, is anti-Renaissance.

If one confined his attention to English, it would be interesting to show how truly modern is A. E. Housman's[7] *Shropshire Lad*, how old-fashioned Francis Thompson:[8] Housman, the Saxon, the Nationalist; Thompson, the Latinist, the child of the Renaissance. Again, an interesting contrast could be made between Hardy,[9] the delineator of a rural parish, and Shaw, whose country is the world, though, of course, Shaw is anything but pure Renaissance. He is not old-fashioned through and through.

But indeed in a hundred different ways it could be shown that in every live country, literature is creeping back to the national hearth, as if it would there find a mother tongue in which to express its

*When writing this I had forgotten that Wilde had more brilliantly said the same thing: 'To me one of the things in history the most to be regretted is that the Christ's own Renaissance, which has produced the Cathedral at Chartres, the Arthurian cycle of legends, the life of St Francis of Assisi, the art of Giotto, and Dante's *Divine Comedy*, was not allowed to develop on its own lines, but was interrupted and spoiled by the dreary Classical Renaissance that gave us Petrarch, and Raphael's frescoes, and Palladian architecture, and formal French tragedy, and St Paul's Cathedral, and Pope's poetry, and everything that is made from without and by dead rules, and does not spring from within through some spirit informing it.' — *De Profundis.*

4. Walt Whitman (1819-92), whose *Leaves of Grass*, from its first edition in 1855 to its final edition in 1891-92, replaced the conventionalities of the prim New England tradition in poetry with a simple, natural and colloquial style.
5. Jean Baptiste Racine (1639-99), the greatest of the French classical dramatists, was an artist who achieved his effects within formal and rigorous restrictions.
6. Eugene O'Neill (1888-1953), an American dramatist, noted for his experimentations in many theatrical forms.
7. A. E. Housman (1859-1936), an English poet, whose *A Shropshire Lad* (1896) treats Shropshire, a county on the England-Wales border, as an ideal regional domain.
8. Francis Thompson (1859-1907), an English catholic poet, best-known for his poems 'The Hound of Heaven' and 'The Kingdom of God'.
9. Thomas Hardy (1840-1928), who recreated his native region of south-east England as the Wessex of his novels and poems.

judgment on such human souls as most deeply move its affections.

If another line of argument be necessary, one could institute an interesting comparison between the art which Renaissance standards have most tongue-tied and that which fortunately has never known them — Sculpture and Music. What a difference! It is almost the difference between Life and Death. The value of this argument is that it sufficiently answers those to whom Europe without the Renaissance is unthinkable. One certainly does not hold that Music has not been influenced, and deeply influenced, by the Renaissance spirit, but the question all through is not one so much of 'spirit' as 'mode': in music we have, happily, clear evidence that modern Europe could invent art-forms when put to it — all out of its own head! If only it could have done so in Sculpture! Music is really the one triumph of modern Europe in art.

This aspect of the value of Irish poetry — how it brings the mind right into the stream of modern literature, as far at least as expression is concerned — struck me more and more while reading these forgotten poets, although, of course, the tradition in which they lived failing more and more, they are the least Gaelic of Gaelic poets. Indeed it seems to me that nearly all modern poets in English are trying, never, however, with the same triumphant success, to write lyrics in the manner of Keating's[10] 'A Bhean Lán de Stuaim'. When they succeed in doing so the Old Man of the Renaissance will have been flung from the shoulders of our civilisation.

10. Geoffrey Keating (*c.* 1580-*c.* 1650), Gaelic poet and historian. The title of this classic Irish poem means 'Lady Full of Guile'. In it a man renounces sexual pleasure in language that is itself deeply sensual and sexual in its appeal. It is not certain that Keating is the author.

SEÁN O'FAOLÁIN

(1900-)

from: THE BELL (1943)

[In an editorial in *The Bell* (June 1943) Seán O'Faoláin took the opportunity afforded by some particularly fatuous examples of Irish Ireland myopia, to launch an assault on the new Irish social order, tracing its origins and identifying its conservative ideological assumptions.]

THE STUFFED-SHIRTS

A few weeks ago in Dublin, at a Convention of the Gaelic Athletic Association — a body which has done a great deal of fine work in reviving through sport the spirit of manhood among our people — it was proposed that the Minister for Defence be at once removed from office. If any Irishman outside Ireland (for within Ireland we have become pretty alert to the meaning of these motions) should read that sentence he will probably conclude that the Minister for Defence has been grossly remiss in his work: possibly that he has not built up our Air Force, or that our Tank Corps are under strength. The actual complaint was that some members of the Army play golf, or hockey, or soccer — which are not 'national games'. With a world-war raging at our shores, boiling up from the Papuans to the Aleutians, from Iceland down to Madagascar, I think that this is, of all recent Celtic lunacies, the most lunatic that I have ever met.

But, about the same week, a whole batch of zanies seemed to have performed a mass-escape from Grangegorman Asylum! A second idealist proposed at the Dublin Corporation that the Press be henceforth prevented (note how constructive they all are) from reporting the details of unpleasant crimes: this, in Holy Ireland where such things do not happen; in a country where the Press is almost sepulchral in its reticence; where courts are commonly cleared at the slightest provocation; where Press reports are frequently killed by editors out of sheer human sympathy; and where it is a firm Press tradition that newspapers just will not exploit any human embarrassment, or any purely personal misfortune outside crime. The next straws-in-the-hair were the Censors: they banned the last two volumes of Marcel Proust's *A la Recherche du Temps Perdu*:[1]

1. Marcel Proust (1871-1922), whose famous novel of 1913-27 was translated into English as *Remembrance of Things Past* (1922-31).

this, in a country where, I suppose, about .02 of the population ever heard of Proust, and where the rest (in the old joke) think Sodom has something to do with Begorrah. A fourth gentleman, down in Limerick — he might be called the anti-Marx brother — of the name of O'Mahony was meanwhile raising Cain crucified because the Readers' Union of London[2] had refused to send him any more books — for the very good reason, that he had, on his own admission, refused to send out to R.U. members in Limerick their last choice, a book by H. G. Wells.[3] Mr. O'Mahony was maintaining, in fact, that it was his duty, and right, to censor the Readers' Union choice for these members. There were other blokes dodging about in the shrubbery, quacking at us through their fingers, but it is enough; and a good bag at that. It is enough to make one sit down and seriously try to find out what on earth has happened to our native Irish mixture of realism and humour.

The only thing to do is to look back and see just where the crack began. Goodness knows if I am right — and when fissures appear they probably break all over the place — but I have come to the conclusion that where the crack began was about 1913; and that it was wide open in 1922: and that what came crawling out of it was an appalling and quite alien, stuffed-shirt, middle-class mentality.

The year 1913, it may be remembered, was the year of the great Dublin Tramway Strike, when Mr. William Martin Murphy,[4] a 'strong man' of the old régime, locked-out his workers, organised his fellow-employers, set to starve the poor of the city, and unwittingly created a fermentation of ideas that long outlasted the strike. It was the year, too, of the founding of the Irish Citizen Army.[5] It was, in addition, the year of Carson's[6] defiance of the British Government and his enrolment of the Ulster Volunteers; which gave birth in turn to the Irish Volunteers in the South; who were, in turn, to raise the Rebellion of 1916. In 1913 Revolution was on its way.

2. An English book club.
3. H. G. Wells (1866-1946), a prolific English novelist and journalist, whom Irish conservatives regarded suspiciously as an atheist and propagandist for modern freethinking.
4. William Martin Murphy (1844-1919), businessman and newspaper owner. He led the Dublin employers against the trade unions in the dispute that led to the 1913 Lockout in Dublin.
5. Founded in 1913 by James Connolly (1868-1916), labour leader, socialist and one of the executed leaders of the 1916 Rebellion.
6. Edward Carson (1854-1935), lawyer and political leader of Ulster opposition to Home Rule from 1912.

So far, good. But what lay behind those dramatic incidents is more important — the old, multiple, traditional life to be sought and found in every cabin in the country. This is the social history of our times which has been almost wholly subserved to their political history. That human background may be summed up in three commonplace observations.

The first observation of all social historians is that the more powerful elements in every country use the weaker elements to exploit Nature for them. Here the more powerful men were not ourselves, whom a too devoted love of ancient custom had debilitated and made unadaptable; they were the various Tudor and pre-Tudor conquistadors who broke us on the wheel of our own conservatism, and whose descendants exploited us for centuries afterwards in a manner as ruthless as it was natural. We shared the fate, that is, of all races who had grown old in the joints, and, in a too-remote Gaelic isolation, ignored the threats of approaching World Change.

The second commonplace of social history is that there can be only one satisfactory outcome to Conquest — the assimilation of races into a new, hybrid society. And native Ireland was, to a great extent, thus assimilated. We adopted the English language (perforce); English law (perforce — we still rule ourselves by means of it); and most modern European customs and ideas were passed on to us by Britain. Indeed, the sum of our local story is that long before 1900 we had become part and parcel of the general world-process — with a distinct English pigmentation.

On the other hand the original and subsequent colonists had taken on an Irish colouring — Butlers, Fitzgeralds, Lacys, MacMurroughs, de Burgos, de Angulos (who became Burkes and Costellos respectively), Boyles, Floods, Grattans, Magennises, Wilmots, Hydes, Cunninghams, Redmonds, Parnells, Skeffingtons, and so on — all men of Norman, Tudor, or Cromwellian Conquistador descent. This mutual absorption, however, must be fairly swift, generous, and mutually advantageous if it is to succeed; and it was too slow in Ireland and never generous enough to be a complete success.

Now we come to the third and most important commonplace of social history. As the powerful parasite begins to enjoy the fruits of victory he inevitably shares them with those whom he exploits. Fumbling and foolish Handy Andy[7] making ludicrous mistakes with his squire's letters, and his soda-water, and his silver forks is all the time learning far more than merely waiting at table: so is Tom, Dick, and 'Arry, Sans Culotte,[8] Simon Bolivar,[9] Hyder Ali,[10] Lajos Kossuth,[11] or Dan O'Connell.[12] Besides it is the grace of civilisation that men become ashamed of crude exploitation and sincerely wish to help and share with the weaker — at first, no doubt, out of pity and human charity, but, gradually, on terms of human responsibility, duty and liberal emotion. The whole history of Grattan's Parliament[13] here is this history of this growth of fellowship between colonists and natives. The history of the whole colonial empire of Britain shows just the same process, and sometimes reveals (as in India) the same fatal evils of adjournment and procrastination.[14] So your weaker element steadily gains in strength, and your stronger as steadily grows less powerful. The last stage of the process is generally a sharp economic struggle. All liberal emotion begins to vanish. Old ties snap. Ancient memories revive. The basic fight remains the same but is now expressed in national or political terms. That is what happened here from O'Connell to Davitt[15] — 1800 to 1900 and after.

The social history of modern Ireland, when we thus clear it of the murky smoke and flame of patriotic emotion, had been, up to 1913, the history of a gradual undoing of the economic exploitation of the peasant which followed the original military conquest. All through the nineteenth century, in Land Act after Land Act, and in various other reforms, the people were slowly lifting their backs and lifting their heads. By 1898 the farmer had already won real political power on the establishment of the County Councils, under the new Local Government Act. By 1905 he was getting solid possession of his land. All the time, his sons were going steadily into business, clerical posts, crafts, trades, and the professions, so that a native town-class had become consolidated by the first decade of this century. By 1914, except for Home Rule, and the economic hang-over of Time, the country-folk had retrieved an astonishing amount of ground. In fact, many of the remaining larger evils such as Emigration, then attributed to misgovernment, have proved insoluble even under native rule.

When one thus considers the whole record up to 1913 it is only natural that our people should have wanted, mainly, this material basis of Freedom, and that the title of Freedom should wait on the solid meaning of it. The people had wanted, first and foremost, fair play, solid leases, education — the elements of existence. In their circumstances no politicians who tried to lead them without a social policy could have succeeded: and none who tried, like Butt,[16] did succeed. Even O'Connell failed after Emancipation, and it was not until Davitt founded the Land League that the people rose again. Once the Land Acts had been won, John Redmond[17] was the weaker for it: as every politician is always the weaker for a lack of material grievances — so much so that his success in perceiving them is threatened by his success in removing them; and he as often goes down in defeat less because he has been a failure than because he has been a success.

The final social picture around our time is given objectively and dispassionately in Elizabeth Bowen's *Bowen's Court*,[18] which covers the whole story of a typical Big House, as in the south we call the home of the big landowners, from the Cromwellian Plantations on. Anybody who has read that book must have seen that towards the end the Big House had ceased to be a fortress: it had become something between a besieged city — besieged by

7. A stage-Irish servant, hero of Samuel Lover's novel, *Handy Andy* (1842).
8. Literally, 'without knee-breeches': a republican of the poorer classes in Paris during the French Revolution. By extension, an extreme republican, a fierce revolutionary.
9. Simon Bolivar (1783-1830), soldier-statesman and revolutionary, who overthrew Spanish rule in Venezuela, Colombia, Ecuador and Peru.
10. Hyder Ali (1722-82), Muslim ruler of Mysore, who fought the British in the Anglo-French Wars.
11. Lajos Kossuth (1802-94), leader of the Hungarian struggle for independence from Austria in 1848-49.
12. Daniel O'Connell (1775-1847), known in Ireland as 'The Liberator', led the movement for catholic emancipation, conceded in 1829, and for the repeal of the Union of Ireland and Britain. In 1938 O'Faoláin published his well-known study of O'Connell, *King of the Beggars*.
13. A popular name for the Irish parliament that won a measure of legislative independence from England in 1782. Henry Grattan (1746-1820) was its leading orator and political figure.
14. This editorial was written four years before India and Pakistan won independence.
15. Michael Davitt (1846-1906), founder of the Irish National Land League in 1879, an organization of tenants against landlords, which played a decisive role in the struggle for land reform and Home Rule.
16. Isaac Butt (1813-79), barrister and politician, who founded the Home Rule movement in 1870.
17. John Redmond (1856-1918) became leader of the Irish Parliamentary Party in 1900.
18. Bowen's Court in County Cork was the novelist Elizabeth Bowen's family home. Although the book was published in 1942, she did not return to live there until 1952, remaining until 1960. She died in 1973.

growing economic pressure — and an anachronistic remnant of such dearly-bought grace and incomplete comfort that it had already become 'quaint' to English visitors (or even funny: e.g., Somerville and Ross)[19] while all about it there was growing up a sturdy peasant society, whose grace and comfort was a hundred times, a thousand times, more incomplete, but whose outlook for the future was rosily promising. All this is, of course, part of the now neglected story of the magnificent labours of the Irish Parliamentary Party, and of the generations who supported it by all those methods of political agitation, not short of violence, initiated by Dan O'Connell — who was indubitably the greatest political agitator who ever lived.

That is the material ground of 1913 and after. And since it is often remarked that the meaning and value of ideas depend not only on themselves but on the nature of the soil on which they fall, this retrospect is essential in order to remember what kind of soil took in the ideas of Sinn Fein.[20]

But here we meet the most important thing of all. The last great political movement before Sinn Fein was the Land League — i.e., a rural movement. Sinn Fein was a town movement, started by a townsman (Arthur Griffith),[21] and plugged by townsmen almost without exception. There was, probably for that reason, far more sheer idealism about the original Sinn Fein movement than any other previous political movement; except only that other townsman's movement, The Young Irelanders.[22] That very fact gave it its strength. It rose above all material appeals. It was, like the Young Irelanders, inventing a sentiment, an ethic, almost a philosophy of life out of the material struggle.

But let us not deceive ourselves. If the country people were roused by that appeal, as to this day they can still be roused by some old magician of that remaining little clan, such as Mr. de Valera,[23] it was not because they were not interested in the material advantages of freedom but because, thanks to the Irish Party and the Land Leaguers, they had — as I have shown — a firm grip on most of the possible material advantages already. They had turned the corner of the bare struggle for existence, and could at last take risks out of crystal-pure and unselfish patriotism. As we know, they took them nobly.

For the townspeople, however, there was far more yet to be gained and as the movement increased in power the idealism took on a more material shape. Those generations in the towns and cities had developed an incipient social sense. In some, such as the socialist James Connolly,[24] that sense was strong and clear. He was always trying to interpret abstract terms like 'Freedom' in human forms. In most this was little more than an instinct. I think Griffith had little of it. Instinctively Sinn Fein hated the sight of Dublin Castle society; of snob-Catholics, whom they called Cawstle Cawtholics; a good deal of the attraction of the Gaelic language and Gaelic games was that they belonged to the life of the common people and brought us closer to the rude cradle of our history: we all had an instinctive mistrust of what one may call clubby people.

That is why I go back to 1913 and all that. Politics became, after 1913, as urbanised as they ever can become in a country where 51 per cent. of the people are engaged in agriculture and where 63 per cent. live outside towns and cities. The people who ultimately profited by the success of Sinn Fein, as the farmers had profited by the Land League, were mainly townspeople. Then the farmers' sons took a sudden step up. They became, from 1922 on, our new industrialists, business-men, Civil Servants, professionals. (In recent years many of the urban and village poor have also profited by our improved social services.) That was where the break came.

Had these new men had any real sense of history they would have wanted to weld the new Ireland

19. Edith Somerville (1858-1949) and 'Martin Ross' (pseud. Violet Martin, 1862-1915) were Irish novelists and short-story writers, best known for the comic sketches in *Some Experiences of an Irish R.M.* (1899), although their novel *The Real Charlotte* (1894) revealed a darker and grimmer aspect of Irish life.
20. Sinn Féin, meaning 'We Ourselves', was the movement founded by Arthur Griffith (see below) in Dublin in 1905, to encourage Irish political and economic self-sufficiency and independence. Although many republicans disagreed with Griffith's economic doctrines, the term Sinn Féin was associated throughout the 1917-22 period with all the militant and political activists who fought for the Irish separatist cause.
21. Arthur Griffith (1871-1922) was also editor of the influential periodicals the *United Irishman* and *Sinn Féin*, in which he promoted his ideas about Irish self-reliance and economic independence.
22. The Young Ireland movement was led by Thomas Davis (1814-45), a journalist and pamphleteer. It was a literary-political movement dedicated to the revival of the Irish national spirit.
23. Eamon de Valera (1882-1975), Irish freedom fighter, politician, long-serving Taoiseach (Prime Minister) and finally President of the Republic of Ireland (1959-73). He founded the powerful Fianna Fáil (Soldiers of Destiny) political party in 1926 and was its leader until 1959. de Valera was the dominant influence in the formulation of the Constitution of Ireland in 1937 and was the chief architect of the independent Irish state.
24. See note 5 above.

into a coherent society. They did not. They cut their roots, as so often happens with their like. The final stage of the Revolution around 1922 became — and is to this day — a middle-class *putsch*. It was not a society that came out of the maelstrom. It was a class. You had only to look about you in the streets — at the the crowds of motor-cars, at the over-dressed women, or in their homes at the cheap mass-produced furniture, to see that they had lost their own world and were lost in the new.

Now, with all that in mind, if we look at the face of Ireland, at this date, many things become clear. The foremost is illustrated by the fact that about two-thirds of our representatives in the Dáil are townsmen. In the Senate likewise, name after name is that of a cityman or a townsman — with only a very dubious one-fourth from the country. There is, obviously, no question as to who is running this country, or in whose major interest it is being run: so that Mr. de Valera may think that he is representing his twenty-five acre farmer of North Cork, but in practice nothing he wishes to do can be done unless his solid urban backing agrees. In any case the economic policy of the present government has been an industrialist's policy.

But behind politicians are those organisations which pretend to represent, and often affect public opinion. It was in this critical period after 1922 that bodies like the Gaelic League, and the Gaelic Athletic Association, even semi-religious bodies like the Catholic Truth Society, or purely cultural bodies like the Irish Academy of Letters, could have done a great deal to direct us. Alas, most of them were just as lost as the politicians. I have shown in other articles how the Gaelic League, for example, sold itself to politics, became vulgarised, forgot its true cultural function, with the result, obvious now to all, that the Gaelic language became synonymous in the popular mind with racketeering and inefficiency. Worst of all, the Labour movement hastened to cash-in on self-government, and threw ideas and idealism overboard: so thoroughly that when I, myself, interviewed the present leader of that Party in January, 1934, he refused to admit that his Party was 'Socialist.'[25] (And, incidentally, because I recorded the fact the *Daily Herald* refused to print it.) In the Election of 1923 Farmers were 10 per cent. of the Dáil; in 1932 they were under 3 per cent.; and in 1938 there were none at all. Semi-masonic (Catholic) bodies rose overnight; and pietistic bodies flourished as never before. Everything was so swallowed up by the middle-class *putsch* that by the time Mr. de Valera — who had so far resisted it — came into power it swallowed him and his 'republicans' up, too.

Look at the most idealistic, if wrong-headed, young organisation we have today, Ailtiri na hAiseirghe (The Masons of the Resurrection):[26] one has only to glance at its unmistakable policy to see its origin, and to guess — which is the fact — that the main interest in it comes from the Civil Service, industrialists, and, surprisingly, but it is so, one or two of the landed gentry.

One need probe no further. It is plain that our generation has lost all sense of its origins. The healthy, generous, humane sweep of feeling that we associate with the traditions of our countryside no longer runs through society or political life. The very history being pumped into our children in the schools and the image of life being offered to them is all alien alike to our nature and to fact. It is a complete fairy-tale — I have examined scores of these books and speak by the book — based on a fanciful Celtophilism of which you will find no living example if you get on your bicycle and wander through the countryside in search of its exponents. The main notion of it is that we have since the dawn of our history been united here in our efforts to eject all foreign ways, peoples, manners, and customs — which is, of course, arrant nonsense: on this fancy there has been piled up a gospel of the sanctity of the West and the evil of the East, the generative power and utter purity of all native custom and tradition, as handed down by an army of, mainly legendary, saints and heroes; a thirst for not only what little remains of this custom and tradition but for the revival of what of it is actually dead or obsolescent; a drive towards authoritarianism to enforce these ideas and a censorship of cold-blooded economic pressure (which we all feel, and which business-men carefully watch) to down everybody who opposes them. This farrago is called Nationalism.

There is here a very interesting continental analogy which deserves an article to itself. In the first half of the nineteenth century there grew up in

25. This was William Norton (1900-63), who led the Irish Labour Party from 1932 to 1963.

26. More properly, 'Architects of the Renaissance', a right-wing republican nationalist organization.

Russia a group of Nationalists called Slavophils. They adored the native soil, declared that Russia was killing her native strength by imitation of Germany, as Germany had done with France before Frederick the Great,[27] and before Lessing, Schelling, and Herder[28] raised the cry of national culture. These Slavophils were opposed by the Westerners who wanted Russia to learn from Europe, to progress, to be modern. There was a very similar clash in modern China. Now, both these ideas were generative, if only by virtue of their conflict, but the point is that those Slavophils evoked sympathy mainly from just the same class of people as our rabid Nationalists — the middle-class stuffed-shirts, Civil Servants, landed gentry, professionals. For like our Nationalists they wanted not Change but the momentary *status quo*. They liked to think of the peasant safe in his cabin, the worker safe at his bench, the lord safe in his manor, and the Czar safe in his palace. And some, I agree, may well say, Why not? They had just the same colossal evangelism, the same Messianic delusion as our Celtophils — one of whom declared recently and rather vulgarly: 'Ireland must be the shop-window of Christianity for the world.' The Russian historian Kluchevsky[29] said it better when he called Russia 'this dirty village cradle in which restlessly tosses and helplessly cries the future of the world.' And like ours they had the same alluring watchwords of Tradition, Piety, Custom, Obedience, Authority.

Our Celtophils — many of them misguided idealists, for whom one can have a great respect and a great regard, mind you — think themselves revolutionaries and democrats. They think, in everything they do, to apply the words of Father Gannon, S.J.,[30] on the Censorship, that they are working 'in the interests of the common people.' I see in them only reaction, conservatism, sentimentality, and intellectual cowardice. I feel that if you took every element of them, from the Gaelic League to the Catholic Truth Society, the Censorship Board to the Aiseirghe, The Knights of Columbanus to the Legion of Mary, and rubbed them all into a ball they would stick into an indecipherable lump like plasticine — and you could pull the bits apart, and make little homunculi of them again, and not one of them would notice any difference. They are all different names for the same thing — a lump of mush softened out by the manipulations of that uprooted middle-class which has cashed-in on 1913-1922, all of whom, instinctively no doubt rather than in callous deliberation, see in this kind of thing a bulwark against those final changes that they naturally fear and would do anything to prevent.

So, the Gaelic Athletic Association has its own good work to do in fostering sport: the Gaelic League has its own good work to do in the revival of the Gaelic language: the bookseller of Limerick has his own good work to do in selling intelligent books: the Dublin councillor need not look for unpleasant stories in the Press, he will find them in the slums of his own Ward. They have all (unknown to themselves) in one way or another been lured to play politics — the politics of buttressing the fake-society which is being thrust on us by the successors of Mr. William Martin Murphy and his colleagues — rather than help to form the kind of society that liberal men would shape for the people who rose in 1913 and were thwarted in 1922. And if, here, the G.A.A. should ask, 'What have Gaelic games, or golf, or even soccer to do with any sort of social policy?' — we answer: 'Nothing. That is the point. It is just a smoke-screen of Bunk.' For these things are all one vast smoke-screen sent up to hide the corruption of this bastard thing that we have unforeseeingly created out of martyrdom and blood.

How differently we had once dreamed it all! We had not merely seen the English flag and the English army go, and the Royal Irish Constabulary, and the sepoys of Dublin Castle. That was but the clearance. We had not merely seen even those first steps of the new thing — land for the landless, homes for the poor, factories rising, rivers harnessed, a fair share of our own people in business, an end to emigration and unemployment. That was but the framework. We had looked forward to seeing all classes united, all religions equal, all races welded, all ideas welcome, that hammering and clanging of a young nation at work which Milton so

27. Frederick the Great (1712-86), king of Prussia from 1740, was a remarkable general and challenged French hegemony in eighteenth-century Europe.
28. G. E. Lessing (1729-81), a German critic and playwright; J. G. von Herder (1744-1803), a German philosopher and critic and a leading figure in the *Sturm und Drang* movement; and F. von Schelling (1775-1854), a philosopher, were influential figures in the formation of the new national spirit in Germany in the late eighteenth and early nineteenth centuries.
29. V. O. Kliuchevski (1841-1911), Russian historian.
30. Father Patrick Gannon, S.J. had written a vigorous defence of the censorship policy in the Jesuit periodical, *Studies*, in 1942.

finely describes in his famous 'Speech for the Liberty of Unlicensed Printing.'[31] We visioned fresh and eager life sloughing its old skin. Those things I poked fun at in the beginning of this article are not young and eager. They are very old, and very silly, and very cowardly. I do not believe that they are in the least characteristic of our people, or of the kind of world our people will ultimately make.

But wishful thinking will not make it, and as to how it will come nobody knows. It will probably come very slowly — unless, by chance, some other Man of the People, like O'Connell, should rise to lead us, or some circumstance re-enliven the old spirit. All intelligent men can do is to cast scorn on the fake thing wherever it shows itself, and try to save, in every small way, the unspoiled living People. It was all summed up for me a few years ago in a picture of the old President of Finland in his home — a simple, graceful, modest, original, Finnish house: and then I consider why we should not find a more fitting setting for our own old Gaelic Leaguer President than the aspidistras and tawdry bamboos of the former Viceregal Lodge.[32]

That is what our middle-classes have done for us. That is what we must, with patience, work to undo.

31. The speech is taken from Milton's *Areopagitica* (1644).
32. Douglas Hyde, the first President of Ireland (1937-45), had his official residence in the former Viceregal Lodge in Dublin's Phoenix Park.

from: A PURSE OF COPPERS (1937)

[In this story, first published in 1936, Seán O'Faoláin uses the expedient of a train journey to bring together a group of Irish people to discuss the social reality of the new state.]

A BROKEN WORLD

'That's a lonely place!' said the priest suddenly. He was rubbing the carriage window with his little finger. He pointed with the stem of his pipe through the window, and the flutter of snow and the blown steam of the engine, at the mountainy farm to his right. He might have been talking to himself, for he did not stir his head or remove his elbow from its rest. He was a skeleton of a man, and the veins of his temples bulged out like nerves. Peering I could barely see, below the pine forest of 'The Department,'[1] through the fog of the storm, a lone chapel and a farmhouse, now a tangle of black and white. Although it was the middle of the day a light shone yellow in a byre. Then the buildings swivelled and were left behind. The land was blinding.

'Aye!' I said. 'It is lonely. But,' I said easily, 'sure every parish is a world in itself.'

He grunted and pulled at his cherrywood pipe and kept looking out the window at the whirling dots of white.

Then, without looking at me — looking down at the flap of my trousers, instead — he leaned forward, one bony hand gripping his left knee, and his elbow resting on the other knee so that he might still hold and smoke his pipe in comfort. I could see that he spoke less for the sake of conversation than from a desire to instruct me, for he seemed to get no other pleasure out of his talk.

'That used to be a credo with me, too,' he said, 'that every parish is a world in itself. But where there is no moral unity there is no life.'

'Moral unity?'

There were ten notes in the wind, boom and whistle and groan and sigh. Listening to them I hardly heard him. The snow had stopped.

'Yes.' He was cock-assuredly positive. 'Life is a moral unity with a common thought. The *compositum* of one's being, emerging from the Divine Essence, which is harmony itself, cannot, unless it abdicates its own intelligence and lives in chaos, that is to say, in sin, be in disunity with itself. Since society, however, is an entity composed of many members, life becomes a moral unity with a common thought. You can see that?'

'Yes.'

He went on, while I wondered if he was a professor in some seminary trying out something he had been studying. He enunciated his ideas with indrawn lips. That gave him a hellish, pedagogic look. The glare outside turned him into marble.

'In places like that you have a broken world, and there is no unity.'

In spite of this abstract way of talking the next thing he said showed me that he was not a professor.

'Let me give you an example of what life is like in those isolated places,' jerking his head. 'When I was ordained my first parish was a lonely parish in the

1. The Department of Agriculture, which had planted forests as a national investment.

County Wicklow. From my presbytery window I could see the entire coast, a long straight beach, miles to the north, miles to the south, with a headland at each end stuck out into the sea. By the sea it is marsh. Then comes the first wave of highland around villages like Newtownmount-kennedy. The land isn't bad on those hills, though it isn't what you would call really good land. They grow good turnips and potatoes and mangolds; the greens are not bad; but they cannot grow wheat. You need a good marl bottom for wheat. I was a young man then, and keen, so I studied these questions.'[2]

(Whatever else you were, I said to myself, you must have been a bloody bore.)

'Look'! he said pointing through the opposite window.

A vast white plain, level as a sea, mapped with black hedgerows, all diminishing in size, spread away and away, maybe twenty miles, to a much lower range of mountains.

'My parish was in the same relation to that good land as these mountains here' — nodding over his shoulder — 'in relation to that plain. That is to say, it was mountain bog, reclaimed by much labour, but always badly drained. Last of all, beyond me, was the utterly, miserably' — his voice was almost oratorical here — 'wretched moor. Miles and miles of it on the plateau of the mountaintops. The native tribes lived as freebooters up there as late as the end of the eighteenth century. It was wooded then, and untouched by any road. Then, in ninety-eight,[3] two so-called military roads cut it across and across like a scissors. They were fifty miles long, and straight as rulers. By the way,' he asked suddenly, catching me looking idly out through the window, 'were you ever in County Wicklow?'

'Oh, no, Father,' I replied, as suddenly. I forced myself to attend. Just then my eye caught the eye of an old farmer seated opposite me in the carriage; he was midway on the same seat as the priest, and, so, near enough to hear everything. A pool of water had gathered around each boot. Spits starred the dry patch between. Seeing me look at him he took from his mouth, with his entire fist, a bit of a cigarette he was smoking, and winked at me. Then he put back the cigarette and contemplated the priest's face with an air of childlike wonderment. At that wink I began to listen more carefully. Evidently my priest was a local 'character.'

'They are remarkable roads,' went on the priest. 'Well, the people of my parish were all poor. The interesting thing about them is that there were two sets of names — either the old tribal names, like O'Toole or O'Byrne or Doyle, or foreign names like Ryder, Nash, Greene, Pugh, Spink, Empie, Gascon, Latour.'

A little smile took the corners of his mouth as he said those names; but he never raised his eyes.

'The Greenes and Ryders and Pughs, and the rest of them, were soldiers who long ago trickled down into the houses of the poor, intermarried there, and became poor themselves as a result. However, they brought the people respect for law and order. Or, if you like, they knocked the last bit of rebel spirit out of them.'

'Interesting!' I said, politely. I was beginning to enjoy the joke, for I could see the old farmer getting cross, and at the end of that last bit he had spat out his butt end of cigarette.

'But the middle land, the good land, remained in the possession of the big people who never inter-married. When I went there to take over my duties I looked up the history of these wealthy people in *Debrett* and *Who's Who*, and *Burke's Landed Gentry*.'[4]

His palm became an imaginary book, and with his pipestem he followed the lines and pretended to read:

'"Lord Blank, family name of Baron Blank. Fifth baron. Created in eighteen hundred and one. Lieu-tenant of the Seventeenth Hussars. Married Dorothy, oldest daughter of, let's say something like James Whipple Teaman of Grange House, Dilworth, Dorsetshire, you know the kind of thing. Succeeded his father in nineteen-eighteen. Educated at Eton and Sandhurst. Address, Gros-venor Square, London. Club — Travellers' or Brooks's. Recreation? Oh, as usual, hunting, shooting, fishing, racquets, riding."'

Again the thin smile. The farmer was gob-open.

'My parishioners were their stableboys, gate-lodge keepers, woodmen, beaters, farmhands, lady's maids, et cetera. *They* were always inter-

2. Mangolds, or mangold-wurzels, are a variety of beet, cultivated as cattle food. Marl is a limey clay, used as fertilizer.
3. The reference is to the Rebellion of 1798, during which military roads were laid in strategic areas.
4. Gazetteers of the aristocracy and important personages.

marrying. *Their* bits of farms, reclaimed from the furze, were always being divided. I've seen people live on a bit of land about twice the size of this carriage.'

The farmer leaned forward, listening now with great interest. Our three heads nodded with the jolt of the train.

'Then there was emigration. In the five years I spent there I had one solitary marriage. I had sixty schoolchildren on roll when I went there. I had thirty-five when I left. Last year I heard they were reduced to eleven, and five of those were all one family. No wonder the county is full of ruins. You come on them in scores on scores, with, maybe, a tree growing out of the hearth, and the marks of the ridges they plowed still there, now smooth with grass.'

'Begobs, then, they're here too, Father,' said the old farmer. The priest nodded sideways to him and proceeded:

'I liked the people. They were clean, hard-working, respectful. Too respectful — tipping their hats to everybody. They were always making what we call "the poor mouth" — a mendicant habit of centuries, I suppose. They gave me no trouble, except for two things. They had a habit of writing anonymous letters, and I couldn't stop it. They were at it all the time. They wrote them to one another.'

He paused. I prompted him.

'The other thing?' I asked.

The farmer leaned closer and closer.

'The other thing?' he said irritably to his pipe bowl. 'In every one of these cabins they earned money by taking in boarded-out children — children unwanted by poor parents, or simply illegitimates. There was hardly a cottage without one, two, or three of these stranger children. They were well looked after, and the people often grew so fond of them they wouldn't part with them; and, I suppose, that was a nice trait too. But the point is that the only fresh blood coming into the county was .... Well — a curious county, as you can see, and the morals were a bit curious too. However, that's enough about them.'

And he had at least enough sense to go no further with that.

'Well, there you are. That was my parish, and you can't say it was a world in itself. It was too incomplete. Too many things left out. The human dignity of men is always impaired when, like that, they're depending on other people who can make or break them. They weren't men. They were servants. That's the whole of it.'

'But did that make their lives lonely? You said they were lonely?'

For the first time he looked up at me. The veins on his temples, swollen from holding his head down, throbbed with relief.

'I didn't say *they* were lonely.'

His eyes wavered sideways to the farmer. I easily followed him over the hiatus when he jumped to —

'One day, after three years without stepping out of the parish, I decided to see if the neighbouring parish was any better.' (When I heard the personal note come into his voice I wished the farmer was not there; as it was he kept to his cold, factual description.)

'Do you know, the contrast was amazing! When I climbed down to the valley and the good land! And it was the trees that made me realize it. Beeches instead of pines. Great, old beeches with roots like claws on the double ditches. The farmhouses, too. They were large and prosperous with everything you might expect to find in a sturdy English farm — barns, ducks in the pond, thick-packed granaries, airy lofts, a pigeon croft, a seat under an arbour, fruit gardens.

'All that was good. But it was those beeches that really impressed me. They were so clean and old, not like the quick-growing pines of the mountains — dirty trees that scatter their needles into the shoots[5] of the houses and block them up three times every winter.'

'Oh, they're buggers, Father!' agreed the farmer earnestly.

'I climbed lower still and came to the gates of the houses where the gentry used to live.'

'Used to?'

'Used to. I should have expected it, but somehow it hadn't occurred to me. It's funny how we all forget how times passes. But there they were — the gateposts falling. The lodges boarded up. Notices, *For Sale*. Fifteen years of grass on the avenues. You see? "Owns tens thousand acres in Ireland. Address, Grosvenor Square, London." '

The pipestem travelled across the palm.

'I met an old man who took me down one of those avenues to see the ruins of a big house burned out during the troubled times. It was a lovely spring

5. gutters.

evening. The sky was like milk. The rooks were cawing about the roofless chimneys just like the flakes of soot come to life again. I spotted a queer little building at the end of a cypress avenue. The old man called it "the oftaphone". He meant octagon. It was a kind of peristyle.[6] He said, "The Lord" — just like that — "The Lord used to have tea parties and dances there long ago." I went into it and it had a magnificent view, a powerful view, across the valley over at my mountainy parish, yes, and beyond it to the ridges of the mountains, and even beyond that again to the very moors behind with their last little flecks and drifts of snow. They could have sat there and drunk their tea and seen my people — the poor Ryders, and Greenes, and O'Tooles — making little brown lines in the far-off fields in the plowing time.'

'They could! Oh, begobs, Father, so they could!' — and a mighty spit.

'Or at night, of summer evenings, they could have sipped their brandy and coffee and seen the little yellow lights of our cabin windows, and said, "How pretty it is!" '

'Begobs, yes! That's true!'

If anyone entered the carriage then he would have taken us for three friends, we were huddled together so eagerly. The priest went on:

' "They must have had good times here, once?" I said to the man who was with me. "The best Father!" says he. "Oh, the best out. The best while they lasted. And there were never any times like the old times. But they're scattered now, Father," says he, "to the four winds. And they'll never come back." "Who owns the land now?" I asked him. "They own it always, but who wants it?" says he. "The people here don't want it. They'd rather live in the towns and cities and work for wages." '

'That's right,' said the farmer, as if we were really discussing his own county. 'Begobs, you're talking sense now, Father!'

' "The land was kept from them too long," says he. "And now they have lost the knack of it. I have two grown sons of my own," says he, "and they're after joining the British Army." '

'Begobs, yes!' said the farmer, leaning to catch every word; but the priest stopped and leaned back.

The white, cold fields were singing by us. The cabins so still they might be rocks clung to the earth. The priest was looking at them and we were all looking at them, and at the flooded and frozen pools of water divided by the hedgerows. By his talk he had evoked a most powerful sense of comradeship in that carriage, whether he meant to or not: we felt one. Then, as quickly, he proceeded to break it.

'Well?' I asked eagerly. 'Well?'

'Why, that's all!' said the priest. 'I came back from my voyage of exploration much refreshed. Much improved in spirits. You see, I had extended the pattern of life of my own poor parish. I saw how, how — I mean, how the whole thing had worked, hung together, made up a real unity. It was like putting two halves of a broken plate together. As I walked up another one of those hill roads on my way home I passed more prosperous houses — smaller houses this time, what you would call private houses. They had neat, green curtains with fine, polished brassware inside on the polished mahogany. And through another window three aluminium hot-water bottles shining on a dark hall table, signs of comfort, as you might say. . . . Yes! I had completed the pattern. That parish and my parish made up a world, as neither did by itself, rich and poor, culture and . . . .'

'But,' I cried angrily, 'where's your moral unity? Your common thought? It's absurd.'

'Oh, yes! I realized that even before I got home. I just tell you the thing as it happened. But they in their octagon and we in our lighted cabins, I mean to say, it was two halves of a world. . . .'

The farmer was looking at us both with dull, stupid eyes. He had lost the thread of the talk.

'Yes, I suppose so,' I agreed, just as lightly. 'But now that the gentry are gone, won't the people, the mountainy people, and so on, begin to make a complete world of their own?'

He shook his head. The farmer listened again.

'I refuse to believe they won't,' I said.

He shrugged his shoulders.

'And is there no possible solution, then?' I asked him.

He was looking out of the window, his poll[7] to the farmer. He rolled up his eyes under his brows — a warning look — and faintly indicated the man behind him. Then he actually began to laugh, a cold, cackling laugh, an extraordinary, inhuman kind of laugh that ended in a noise like a little groan.

The train slowed up, and we were in a station,

6. A system of roof-supporting columns on all sides of a court or building.

7. head.

and he was gathering his bags. He got out without even saying 'Good day' to us, and his face was coldly composed. A manservant, touching his cap, took the bags. The stationmaster touched his cap to him. The jarvey,[8] who was waiting for him, bowed as he received the bags from the manservant. Black, tall, thin, and straight as a lamp post, he left the lit, snow-bright station with every downlooking lounger there bowing and hat touching as he passed. When I turned away, the train was moving out, and the old farmer, in his own place, had lit another cigarette.

'Do you know his Reverence?' I asked — as irritated as somebody from whom a book has been snatched before the end of the tale.

'Oh, aye!' said the old man, and he added, without interest, 'He's silenced.'

There was a touch of dread in that word, *silenced*.

'What did they silence him for?'

'Politics.'

'Oh? He was too extreme?'

'Aye!' Still without interest.

'A clever man?'

No answer. His mind had gone to sleep. I looked at him in annoyance.

'What kind of ideas had he? I mean, what did he want?'

'Begobs, I dunno.'

Then he added, as if it was a matter of no importance:

'He wanted the people to have the land.'

'What land?'

'The land. The gentry's land.'

I leaned to him eagerly —

'But isn't that what ye want? Isn't that what the whole trouble is? Isn't that what the government wants?'

'Aye. I suppose it is, you know. But he wanted it to be a sudden business.'

'They didn't silence him for that?'

'Maybe they didn't. Ach, he's odd. Sure, he took ten or twenty foolish young lads and, one night, he thrun down[9] the walls of Lord Milltown's estate. He started some sort of a league, too. He's odd. God help him.'

'What did he want to do with this league of his?'

'I dunno. It was some kind of faddy business. He wanted halls . . . and . . . some kind of halls he wanted. Halls. I dunno what he wanted 'em for. Ah, he's a decent poor man.'

I tried another line.

'I suppose it's true for his Reverence — ye have a hard time of it up here on the poor land?'

Puffing at his ease he was looking idly at the passing fields. A woman and two small boys, crushed into the doorway of a cabin, waved to us. He looked, and when they were gone his eyes were still fixed, seeing whatever passed beneath them with equal interest — or disinterest?

He tilted his head, but he said nothing. I made one last effort to shake him from his lethargic mood — possibly, most likely indeed, the mood in which he spent the greater part of his life.

'You know,' I said, warmly, 'I think I'd die in this lonely place. That priest is right!'

He looked at it, and scratched his ear, and said:

'Aye!' And then, suddenly, he added a second 'Aye!' — and then, when I thought he was finished, he actually added, 'I suppose 'tis quiet,' and relapsed into indifference.

Angrily I burst out at him:

'But, damn it all, don't you mind, or is it that ye don't want to stir, ye're too damn lazy to stir?'

He took the butt end from his mouth, and he looked at me, and by the way he looked up and down at me, I was hoping he would say something bitter and strong. But his stare was childish, and the eyes wavered, as if he was very tired. He just dropped one last, vast spit on the wet floor, snuggled into his corner, and went to sleep under his hat.

In his sleep he was a motionless as a rock; but you could not say he was 'like a rock' because he was like nothing on earth but himself, everything about him was so personal to him. Unless, because he was so much a random accumulation of work and season and all that belongs to the first human that was ever made, I chose to say, as I glared at him snoring in his corner, that time and nature had engendered something no more human than a rock. So I thought, as the dusk drew down, and the wind moaned in many keys, and the snow blew horizontally and stuck to the edges of the window. It was as if we two might have been jolting into a blank, beyond either sleep or night, and I wanted to get up and kick him. I felt that if I did he would only moo.

We halted at several stations, with their one or

8. The driver of a hackney coach or Irish jaunting car.
9. threw down, dismantled.

two silent white-shouldered figures. He slept on. I was just wondering if I should wake him when suddenly, at a station, identical with every other station, as if some animal magnetism in the place stirred him, he rose and stumbled out. He did not speak. He did not raise his head to see if it was his station. He saluted no one. Anyway, there was no one there but a muffled porter who silently waved a lantern over his head. As we moved off he was trudging in the middle of a road that glimmered with its own strange afterglow, passing between a row of pines whose sheltered sides were red and raw as with the cold. He was exactly like an old black mongrel loping home.

So I was left with the pool of water on the floor, dark under the carriage light, and the snow crumbling into the corners of the windows outside, and beyond that only the light leaping and falling along the hedges. And in another two hours or so, when I got out, the carriage would be racing along, empty, through the night — three bits of separateness, the priest and the farmer and myself, flung off it like bits of the *disjecta membra*[10] of the wheel of life.

For those two hours I tried to refute the talk of that priest, thinking that he had merely spoken out of the snowy landscape, which above all other conditions of nature is so powerful to make life seem lonely, and all work futile, and time itself a form of decay; or thinking that, had it been the green-dripping spring or the hot summer, we might all have shown different and more happy sides of our worlds; or thinking that the thin cheeks and the throbbing nerves of the man were nothing but the sign of twenty years of self-corrosion, and that even when he was a young man in his first parish, his heart must have been so bitter and vain that, like a leech, it began to destroy everything to preserve itself; or thinking that because of it he had joined us for a few moments until we seemed to crouch over a fire, and then deliberately scattered us and left us with his pox. But, though that might be all true, I could not deny to the wintry moment its own truth, and that under that white shroud, covering the whole of Ireland, life was lying broken and hardly breathing. His impress remained even when the train swished slowly into the city, where the arc lamps sizzled in the snow, and the sounds were muffled, and through every street a sharp, pure wind blew down from the Wicklow hills. Once their distant convex gleamed, far away, beyond the vista of a street. There were few people abroad, and as they walked against the wind with huddled backs they, too, seemed to be shrouding something within them that slept, and barely palpitated, and was hurt by the cold. What image, I wondered, as I passed through them, could warm them as the Wicklow priest had warmed us for a few minutes in that carriage now chugging around the edge of the city to the sea? What image of life that would fire and fuse us all, what music bursting like the spring, what triumph, what engendering love, so that those breasting mountains that now looked cold should appear brilliant and gay, the white land that seemed to sleep should appear to smile, and these people who huddled over the embers of their lives should become like the peasants who held the hand of Faust with their singing one Easter morning?[11] Perhaps it was foolish to wish for such an image — so magnificent that it would have the power of a resurrection call? Yet, there are times, as when we hear the percussion of some great music, or when we feel the shrivelling effect of the cold wind and snow, that leave us no other choice but to live splendidly, or gather up at least enough grace for a quick remove.

The train could be heard easily, in the rarefied air, chugging across the bridges that span the city, bearing with it an empty coach. In the morning, Ireland, under its snow, would be silent as a perpetual dawn.

10. scattered parts or limbs.

11. Goethe's *Faust*, Part I (1808), lines 903-1,010.

FRANK O'CONNOR

(1903-66)

from: BONES OF CONTENTION (1936)

[In this short story, first published in 1935, Frank O'Connor dramatizes an encounter between the new state's representative and older forms of social awareness.]

THE MAJESTY OF THE LAW

Old Dan Bride was breaking brosna[1] for the fire when he heard a step on the path. He paused, a bundle of saplings on his knee.

Dan had looked after his mother while the life was in her, and after her death no other woman had crossed his threshold. Signs on it, his house had that look. Almost everything in it he had made with his own hands in his own way. The seats of the chairs were only slices of log, rough and round and thick as the saw had left them, and with the rings still plainly visible through the grime and polish that coarse trouser-bottoms had in the course of long years imparted. Into these Dan had rammed stout knotted ash-boughs that served alike for legs and back. The deal table, bought in a shop, was an inheritance from his mother and a great pride and joy to him though it rocked whenever he touched it. On the wall, unglazed and fly-spotted, hung in mysterious isolation a Marcus Stone[2] print, and beside the door was a calendar with a picture of a racehorse. Over the door hung a gun, old but good, and in excellent condition, and before the fire was stretched an old setter who raised his head expectantly whenever Dan rose or even stirred.

He raised it now as the steps came nearer and when Dan, laying down the bundle of saplings, cleaned his hands thoughtfully on the seat of his trousers, he gave a loud bark, but this expressed no more than a desire to show off his own watchfulness. He was half human and knew people thought he was old and past his prime.

A man's shadow fell across the oblong of dusty light thrown over the half-door before Dan looked round.

1. firewood.
2. Marcus Stone (1840-1921), English historical genre painter and illustrator.

'Are you alone, Dan?' asked an apologetic voice.

'Oh, come in, come in, sergeant, come in and welcome,' exclaimed the old man, hurrying on rather uncertain feet to the door which the tall policeman opened and pushed in. He stood there, half in sunlight, half in shadow, and seeing him so, you would have realized how dark the interior of the house really was. One side of his red face was turned so as to catch the light, and behind it an ash tree raised its boughs of airy green against the sky. Green fields, broken here and there by clumps of red-brown rock, flowed downhill, and beyond them, stretched all across the horizon, was the sea, flooded and almost transparent with light. The sergeant's face was fat and fresh, the old man's face, emerging from the twilight of the kitchen, had the colour of wind and sun, while the features had been so shaped by the struggle with time and the elements that they might as easily have been found impressed upon the surface of a rock.

'Begor, Dan,' said the sergeant, ''tis younger you're getting.'

'Middling I am, sergeant, middling,' agreed the old man in a voice which seemed to accept the remark as a compliment of which politeness would not allow him to take too much advantage. 'No complaints.'

'Begor, 'tis as well because no one would believe them. And the old dog doesn't look a day older.'

The dog gave a low growl as though to show the sergeant that he would remember this unmannerly reference to his age, but indeed he growled every time he was mentioned, under the impression that people had nothing but ill to say of him.

'And how's yourself, sergeant?'

'Well, now, like the most of us, Dan, neither too good nor too bad. We have our own little worries, but, thanks be to God, we have our compensations.'

'And the wife and family?'

'Good, praise be to God, good. They were away from me for a month, the lot of them, at the mother-in-law's place in Clare.'

'In Clare, do you tell me?'

'In Clare. I had a fine quiet time.'

The old man looked about him and then retired to the bedroom, from which he returned a moment later with an old shirt. With this he solemnly wiped the seat and back of the log-chair nearest the fire.

'Sit down now, sergeant. You must be tired after the journey. 'Tis a long old road. How did you come?'

'Teigue Leary gave me the lift. Wisha now, Dan, don't be putting yourself out. I won't be stopping. I promised them I'd be back inside an hour.'

'What hurry is on you?' asked Dan. 'Look, your foot was only on the path when I made up the fire.'

'Arrah, Dan, you're not making tea for me?'

'I am not making it for you, indeed; I'm making it for myself, and I'll take it very bad of you if you won't have a cup.'

'Dan, Dan, that I mightn't stir, but 'tisn't an hour since I had it at the barracks!'

'Ah, whisht,[3] now, whisht! Whisht, will you! I have something here to give you an appetite.'

The old man swung the heavy kettle on to the chain over the open fire, and the dog sat up, shaking his ears with an expression of the deepest interest. The policeman unbuttoned his tunic, opened his belt, took a pipe and a plug of tobacco from his breast pocket, and, crossing his legs in an easy posture, began to cut the tobacco slowly and carefully with his pocket knife. The old man went to the dresser and took down two handsomely decorated cups, the only cups he had, which, though chipped and handleless, were used at all only on very rare occasions; for himself he preferred his tea from a basin. Happening to glance into them, he noticed that they bore signs of disuse and had collected a lot of the fine white turf-dust that always circulated in the little smoky cottage. Again he thought of the shirt, and, rolling up his sleeves with a stately gesture, he wiped them inside and out till they shone. Then he bent and opened the cupboard. Inside was a quart bottle of pale liquid, obviously untouched. He removed the cork and smelt the contents, pausing for a moment in the act as though to recollect where exactly he had noticed that particular smoky smell before. Then, reassured, he stood up and poured out with a liberal hand.

'Try that now, sergeant,' he said with quiet pride.

The sergeant, concealing whatever qualms he might have felt at the idea of drinking illegal whisky, looked carefully into the cup, sniffed, and glanced up at old Dan.

'It looks good,' he commented.

'It should be good,' replied Dan with no mock modesty.

'It tastes good too,' said the sergeant.

'Ah, sha,' said Dan, not wishing to praise his own hospitality in his own house, ''tis of no great excellence.'

'You'd be a good judge, I'd say,' said the sergeant without irony.

'Ever since things became what they are,'[4] said Dan, carefully guarding himself against a too-direct reference to the peculiarities of the law administered by his guest, 'liquor isn't what it used to be.'

'I've heard that remark made before now, Dan,' said the sergeant thoughtfully. 'I've heard it said by men of wide experience that it used to be better in the old days.'

'Liquor,' said the old man, 'is a thing that takes time. There was never a good job done in a hurry.'

''Tis an art in itself.'

'Just so.'

'And an art takes time.'

'And knowledge,' added Dan with emphasis. 'Every art has its secrets, and the secrets of distilling are being lost the way the old songs were lost. When I was a boy there wasn't a man in the barony but had a hundred songs in his head, but with people running here, there, and everywhere, the songs were lost.... Ever since things became what they are,' he repeated on the same guarded note, 'there's so much running about the secrets are lost.'

'There must have been a power of them.'

'There was. Ask any man today that makes whisky do he know how to make it out of heather.'

'And was it made of heather?' asked the policeman.

'It was.'

'You never drank it yourself?'

'I didn't, but I knew old men that did, and they told me that no whisky that's made nowadays could compare with it.'

'Musha,[5] Dan, I think sometimes 'twas a great mistake of the law to set its hand against it.'

Dan shook his head. His eyes answered for him, but it was not in nature for a man to criticize the occupation of a guest in his own home.

'Maybe so, maybe not,' he said noncommittally.

3. 'Be silent! Hush!'

4. The reference is to the establishment of the Irish Free State with its constabulary, the Garda Síochána.

5. Indeed.

'But sure, what else have the poor people?'

'Them that makes the laws have their own good reasons.'

'All the same, Dan, all the same, 'tis a hard law.'

The sergeant would not be outdone in generosity. Politeness required him not to yield to the old man's defence of his superiors and their mysterious ways.

'It is the secrets I'd be sorry for,' said Dan, summing up. 'Men die and men are born, and where one man drained another will plough, but a secret lost is lost forever.'

'True,' said the sergeant mournfully. 'Lost forever.'

Dan took his cup, rinsed it in a bucket of clear water by the door and cleaned it again with the shirt. Then he placed it carefully at the sergeant's elbow. From the dresser he took a jug of milk and a blue bag containing sugar; this he followed up with a slab of country butter and — a sure sign that he had been expecting a visitor — a round cake of home-made bread, fresh and uncut. The kettle sang and spat and the dog, shaking his ears, barked at it angrily.

'Go away, you brute!' growled Dan, kicking him out of his way.

He made the tea and filled the two cups. The sergeant cut himself a large slice of bread and buttered it thickly.

'It is just like medicines,' said the old man, resuming his theme with the imperturbability of age. 'Every secret there was is lost. And leave no one tell me that a doctor is as good a man as one that had the secrets of old times.'

'How could he be?' asked the sergeant with his mouth full.

'The proof of that was seen when there were doctors and wise people there together.'

'It wasn't to the doctors the people went, I'll engage?'

'It was not. And why?' With a sweeping gesture the old man took in the whole world outside his cabin. 'Out there on the hillsides is the sure cure for every disease. Because it is written' — he tapped the table with his thumb — 'it is written by the poets "wherever you find the disease you will find the cure". But people walk up the hills and down the hills and all they see is flowers. Flowers! As if God Almighty — honour and praise to Him! — had nothing better to do with His time than be to making old flowers!'

'Things no doctor could cure the wise people cured,' agreed the sergeant.

'Ah, musha, 'tis I know it,' said Dan bitterly. 'I know it, not in my mind but in my own four bones.'

'Have you the rheumatics at you still?' the sergeant asked in a shocked tone.

'I have. Ah, if you were alive, Kitty O'Hara, or you, Nora Malley of the Glen, 'tisn't I'd be dreading the mountain wind or the sea wind; 'tisn't I'd be creeping down with my misfortunate red ticket for the blue and pink and yellow dribble-drabble of their ignorant dispensary.'

'Why then indeed,' said the sergeant, 'I'll get you a bottle for that.'

'Ah, there's no bottle ever made will cure it.'

'That's where you're wrong, Dan. Don't talk now till you try it. It cured my own uncle when he was that bad he was shouting for the carpenter to cut the two legs off him with a handsaw.'

'I'd give fifty pounds to get rid of it,' said Dan magniloquently. 'I would and five hundred.'

The sergeant finished his tea in a gulp, blessed himself, and struck a match which he then allowed to go out as he answered some question of the old man. He did the same with a second and third, as though titillating his appetite with delay. Finally he succeeded in getting his pipe alight and the two men pulled round their chairs, placed their toes side by side in the ashes, and in deep puffs, lively bursts of conversation, and long, long silences enjoyed their smoke.

'I hope I'm not keeping you?' said the sergeant, as though struck by the length of his visit.

'Ah, what would you keep me from?'

'Tell me if I am. The last thing I'd like to do is waste another man's time.'

'Begor, you wouldn't waste my time if you stopped all night.'

'I like a little chat myself,' confessed the policeman.

And again they became lost in conversation. The light grew thick and coloured and, wheeling about the kitchen before it disappeared, became tinged with gold; the kitchen itself sank into cool greyness with cold light on the cups and basins and plates of the dresser. From the ash tree a thrush began to sing. The open hearth gathered brightness till its light was a warm, even splash of crimson in the twilight.

Twilight was also descending outside when the sergeant rose to go. He fastened his belt and tunic and carefully brushed his clothes. Then he put on his cap, tilted a little to side and back.

'Well, that was a great talk,' he said.

''Tis a pleasure,' said Dan, 'a real pleasure.'

'And I won't forget the bottle for you.'

'Heavy handling from God to you!'

'Good-bye now, Dan.'

'Good-bye, sergeant, and good luck.'

Dan didn't offer to accompany the sergeant beyond the door. He sat in his old place by the fire, took out his pipe once more, blew through it thoughtfully, and just as he leaned forward for a twig to kindle it, heard the steps returning. It was the sergeant. He put his head a little way over the half-door.

'Oh, Dan!' he called softly.

'Ay, sergeant?' replied Dan, looking round, but with one hand still reaching for the twig. He couldn't see the sergeant's face, only hear his voice.

'I suppose you're not thinking of paying that little fine, Dan?'

There was a brief silence. Dan pulled out the lighted twig, rose slowly, and shambled towards the door, stuffing it down in the almost empty bowl of the pipe. He leaned over the half-door while the sergeant with hands in the pockets of his trousers gazed rather in the direction of the laneway, yet taking in a considerable portion of the sea line.

'The way it is with me, sergeant,' replied Dan unemotionally, 'I am not.'

'I was thinking that, Dan; I was thinking you wouldn't.'

There was a long silence during which the voice of the thrush grew shriller and merrier. The sunken sun lit up rafts of purple cloud moored high above the wind.

'In a way,' said the sergeant, 'that was what brought me.'

'I was just thinking so, sergeant, it only struck me and you going out the door.'

'If 'twas only the money, Dan, I'm sure there's many would be glad to oblige you.'

'I know that, sergeant. No, 'tisn't the money so much as giving that fellow the satisfaction of paying. Because he angered me, sergeant.'

The sergeant made no comment on this and another long silence ensued.

'They gave me the warrant,' the sergeant said at last, in a tone which dissociated him from all connexion with such an unneighbourly document.

'Did they so?' exclaimed Dan, as if he was shocked by the thoughtlessness of the authorities.

'So whenever 'twould be convenient for you —'

'Well, now you mention it,' said Dan, by way of throwing out a suggestion for debate, 'I could go with you now.'

'Ah, sha, what do you want going at this hour for?' protested the sergeant with a wave of his hand, dismissing the notion as the tone required.

'Or I could go tomorrow,' added Dan, warming to the issue.

'Would it be suitable for you now?' asked the sergeant, scaling up his voice accordingly.

'But, as a matter of fact,' said the old man emphatically, 'the day that would be most convenient to me would be Friday after dinner, because I have some messages to do in town, and I wouldn't have the journey for nothing.'

'Friday will do grand,' said the sergeant with relief that this delicate matter was now practically disposed of. 'If it doesn't they can damn well wait. You could walk in there yourself when it suits you and tell them I sent you.'

'I'd rather have yourself there, sergeant, if it would be no inconvenience. As it is, I'd feel a bit shy.'

'Why then, you needn't feel shy at all. There's a man from my own parish there, a warder; one Whelan. Ask for him; I'll tell him you're coming, and I'll guarantee when he knows you're a friend of mine he'll make you as comfortable as if you were at home.'

'I'd like that fine,' Dan said with profound satisfaction. 'I'd like to be with friends, sergeant.'

'You will be, never fear. Good-bye again now, Dan. I'll have to hurry.'

'Wait now, wait till I see you to the road.'

Together the two men strolled down the laneway while Dan explained how it was that he, a respectable old man, had had the grave misfortune to open the head of another old man in such a way as to require his removal to hospital, and why it was that he couldn't give the old man in question the satisfaction of paying in cash for an injury brought about through the victim's own unmannerly method of argument.

'You see, sergeant,' Dan said, looking at another little cottage up the hill, 'the way it is, he's there now, and he's looking at us as sure as there's a glimmer of sight in his weak, wandering, watery eyes, and nothing would give him more gratification than for me to pay. But I'll punish him. I'll lie on bare boards for him. I'll suffer for him, sergeant, so that neither he nor any of his children after him will be able to raise their heads for the shame of it.'

On the following Friday he made ready his donkey and butt[6] and set out. On his way he collected a number of neighbours who wished to bid him farewell. At the top of the hill he stopped to send them back. An old man, sitting in the sunlight, hastily made his way indoors, and a moment later the door of his cottage was quietly closed.

Having shaken all his friends by the hand, Dan lashed the old donkey, shouted: 'Hup there!' and set out alone along the road to prison.

6. pannier, large basket.

LIAM O'FLAHERTY

(1896-1984)

from: SPRING SOWING (1924)

[In this short story, first published in 1924, Liam O'Flaherty confronts the experience of emigration, which remained a chronic problem in rural Ireland until the 1960s.]

GOING INTO EXILE

Patrick Feeney's cabin was crowded with people. In the large kitchen men, women and children lined the walls, three deep in places, sitting on forms, chairs, stools, and on one another's knees. On the cement floor three couples were dancing a jig and raising a quantity of dust, which was, however, soon sucked up the chimney by the huge turf fire that blazed on the hearth. The only clear space in the kitchen was the corner to the left of the fireplace, where Pat Mullaney sat on a yellow chair, with his right ankle resting on his left knee, a spotted red handkerchief on his head that reeked with perspiration, and his red face contorting as he played a tattered old accordian. One door was shut and the tins hanging on it gleamed in the firelight. The opposite door was open and over the heads of the small boys that crowded in it and outside it, peering in at the dancing couples in the kitchen, a starry June sky was visible and, beneath the sky, shadowy grey crags and misty, whitish fields lay motionless, still and sombre. There was a deep, calm silence outside the cabin and within the cabin, in spite of the music and dancing in the kitchen, and the singing in the little room to the left, where Patrick Feeney's eldest son Michael sat on the bed with three other young men, there was a haunting melancholy in the air.

The people were dancing, laughing and singing with a certain forced and boisterous gaiety that failed to hide from them the real cause of their being there, dancing singing and laughing. For the dance was on account of Patrick Feeney's two children, Mary and Michael, who were going to the United States on the following morning.

Feeney himself, a black-bearded, red-faced, middle-aged peasant, with white ivory buttons on his blue frieze shirt and his hands stuck in his leather waist belt, wandered restlessly about the kitchen, urging the people to sing and dance, while his mind was in agony all the time, thinking that on the following day he would lose his two eldest children, never to see them again perhaps. He kept talking to everybody about amusing things, shouted at the dancers and behaved in a boisterous and abandoned manner. But every now and then he had to leave the kitchen, under the pretence of going to the pigsty to look at a young pig that was supposed to be ill. He would stand, however, upright against his gable and look gloomily at some star or other, while his mind struggled with vague and peculiar ideas that wandered about in it. He could make nothing at all of his thoughts, but a lump always came up his throat, and he shivered, although the night was warm.

Then he would sigh and say with a contraction of his neck: 'Oh, it's a queer world this and no doubt about it. So it is.' Then he would go back to the cabin again and begin to urge on the dance, laughing, shouting and stamping on the floor.

Towards dawn, when the floor was crowded with couples, arranged in fours, stamping on the floor and going to and fro, dancing the 'Walls of Limerick',[1] Feeney was going out to the gable when his son Michael followed him out. The two of them walked side by side about the yard over the grey sea pebbles that had been strewn there the previous day. They walked in silence and yawned without need, pretending to be taking the air. But each of them was very excited, Michael was taller than his father and not so thickly built, but the shabby blue serge suit that he had bought for going to America was too narrow for his broad shoulders and the coat was too wide around the waist. He moved clumsily in it and his hands appeared altogether too bony and big and red, and he didn't know what to do with them. During his twenty-one years of life he had never worn anything other than the homespun clothes of Inverara,[2] and the shop-made clothes appeared as strange to him and as uncomfortable as a dress suit worn by a man working in a sewer. His face was flushed a bright red and his blue eyes shone with excitement. Now and again he wiped the perspiration from his forehead with the lining of his grey tweed cap.

At last Patrick Feeney reached his usual position at the gable end. He halted, balanced himself on his heels with his hands in his waist belt, coughed and said, 'It's going to be a warm day.' The son came up beside him, folded his arms and leaned his right shoulder against the gable.

'It was kind of Uncle Ned to lend the money for the dance, father', he said. 'I'd hate to think that we'd have to go without something or other, just the same as everybody else has. I'll send you that money the very first money I earn, father ... even before I pay Aunt Mary for my passage money. I should have all that money paid off in four months, and then I'll have some more money to send you by Christmas.'

And Michael felt very strong and manly recounting what he was going to do when he got to Boston, Massachusetts. He told himself that with his great strength he would earn a great deal of money. Conscious of his youth and his strength and lusting for adventurous life, for the moment he forgot the ache in his heart that the thought of leaving his father inspired in him.

The father was silent for some time. He was looking at the sky with his lower lip hanging, thinking of nothing. At last he sighed as a memory struck him. 'What is it?' said the son. 'Don't weaken, for God's sake. You will only make it hard for me.' 'Fooh!' said the father suddenly with pretended gruffness. 'Who is weakening? I'm afraid that your new clothes make you impudent.' Then he was silent for a moment and continued in a low voice: 'I was thinking of that potato field you sowed alone last spring the time I had influenza. I never set eyes on the man that could do it better. It's a cruel world that takes you away from the land that God made for you.'

'Oh, what are you talking about, father?' said Michael irritably. 'Sure what did anybody every get out of the land but poverty and hard work and potatoes and salt?'

'Ah yes', said the father with a sigh, 'but it's your own, the land, and over there' — he waved his hand at the western sky — 'you'll be giving your sweat to some other man's land, or what's equal to it.'

'Indeed', muttered Michael, looking at the ground with a melancholy expression in his eyes, 'it's poor encouragement you are giving me.'

They stood in silence fully five minutes. Each hungered to embrace the other, to cry, to beat the air, to scream with excess of sorrow. But they stood silent and sombre, like nature about them, hugging their woe. Then they went back to the cabin. Michael went into the little room to the left of the kitchen, to the three young men who fished in the same curragh[3] with him and were his bosom friends. The father walked into the large bedroom to the right of the kitchen.

The large bedroom was also crowded with people. A large table was laid for tea in the centre of the room and about a dozen young men were sitting at it, drinking tea and eating buttered raisin cake. Mrs Feeney was bustling about the table, serving the food and urging them to eat. She was assisted by her two younger daughters and by another woman, a relative of her own. Her eldest daughter Mary, who was going to the United States that day, was sitting on the edge of the bed with several other young women. The bed was a large four poster bed with a deal canopy over it, painted red, and the young

1. An Irish set dance.
2. A fictitious island off the west coast of Ireland where O'Flaherty sets his story.
3. coracle.

women were huddled together on it. So that there must have been about a dozen of them there. They were Mary Feeney's particular friends, and they stayed with her in that uncomfortable position just to show how much they liked her. It was a custom.

Mary herself sat on the edge of the bed with her legs dangling. She was a pretty, dark-haired girl of nineteen, with dimpled, plump, red cheeks and ruminative brown eyes that seemed to cause little wrinkles to come and go in her little low forehead. Her nose was soft and small and rounded. Her mouth was small and the lips were red and open. Beneath her white blouse that was frilled at the neck and her navy blue skirt that outlined her limbs as she sat on the edge of the bed, her body was plump, soft, well-moulded and in some manner exuded a feeling of freshness and innocence. So that she seemed to have been born to be fondled and admired in luxurious surroundings instead of having been born a peasant's daughter, who had to go to the United States that day to work as a servant or maybe in a factory.

And as she sat on the edge of the bed crushing her little handkerchief between her palms, she kept thinking feverishly of the United States, at one moment with fear and loathing, at the next with desire and longing. Unlike her brother she did not think of the work she was going to do or the money that she was going to earn. Other things troubled her, things of which she was half ashamed, half afraid, thoughts of love and of foreign men and of clothes and of houses where there were more than three rooms and where people ate meat every day. She was fond of life, and several young men among the local gentry had admired her in Inverara. But . . . .

She happened to look up and she caught her father's eyes as he stood silently by the window with his hands stuck in his waist belt. His eyes rested on hers for a moment and then he dropped them without smiling, and with his lips compressed he walked down into the kitchen. She shuddered slightly. She was a little afraid of her father, although she knew that he loved her very much and he was very kind to her. But the winter before he had whipped her with a dried willow rod, when he caught her one evening behind Tim Hernon's cabin after nightfall, with Tim Hernon's son Bartly's arms around her waist and he kissing her. Ever since, she always shivered slightly when her father touched her or spoke to her.

'Oho!' said an old peasant who sat at the table with a saucer full of tea in his hand and his grey flannel shirt open at his thin, hairy, wrinkled neck. 'Oho! indeed, but it's a disgrace to the island of Inverara to let such a beautiful woman as your daughter go away, Mrs Feeney. If I were a young man, I'd be flayed alive if I'd let her go.'

There was a laugh and some of the women on the bed said: 'Bad cess to you,[4] Patsy Coyne, if you haven't too much impudence, it's a caution.' But the laugh soon died. The young men sitting at the table felt embarrassed and kept looking at one another sheepishly, as if each tried to find out if the others were in love with Mary Feeney.

'Oh, well, God is good', said Mrs Feeney, as she wiped her lips with the tip of her bright, clean, check apron. 'What will be must be, and sure there is hope from the sea, but there is no hope from the grave. It is sad and the poor have to suffer, but . . . .' Mrs Feeney stopped suddenly, aware that all these platitudes meant nothing whatsoever. Like her husband she was unable to think intelligently about her two children going away. Whenever the reality of their going away, maybe for ever, three thousand miles into a vast unknown world, came before her mind, it seemed that a thin bar of some hard metal thrust itself forward from her brain and rested behind the wall of her forehead. So that almost immediately she became stupidly conscious of the pain caused by the imaginary bar of metal and she forgot the dread prospect of her children going away. But her mind grappled with the things about her busily and efficiently, with the preparation of food, with the entertaining of her guests, with the numerous little things that have to be done in a house where there is a party and which only a woman can do properly. These little things, in a manner, saved her, for the moment at least, from bursting into tears whenever she looked at her daughter and whenever she thought of her son, whom she loved most of all her children, because perhaps she nearly died giving birth to him and he had been very delicate until he was twelve years old. So she laughed down in her breast a funny laugh she had that made her heave where her check apron rose out from the waist band in a deep curve. 'A

4. Bad luck to you. The term 'cess' actually means an assessment, a tax or a levy. In Ireland it often meant a military exaction — i.e. an obligation to supply soldiers of the lord deputy's household. It is, therefore, an expression of considerable force.

person begins to talk', she said with a shrug of her shoulders sideways, 'and then a person says foolish things.'

'That's true', said the old peasant, noisily pouring more tea from his cup to his saucer.

But Mary knew by her mother laughing that way that she was very near being hysterical. She always laughed that way before she had one of her fits of hysterics. And Mary's heart stopped beating suddenly and then began again at an awful rate as her eyes became acutely conscious of her mother's body, the rotund, short body with the wonderful mass of fair hair growing grey at the temples and the fair face with the soft liquid brown eyes, that grew hard and piercing for a moment as they looked at a thing and then grew soft and liquid again, and the thin-lipped small mouth with the beautiful white teeth and the deep perpendicular grooves in the upper lip and the tremor that always came in the corner of the mouth, with love, when she looked at her children. Mary became acutely conscious of all these little points, as well as of the little black spot that was on her left breast below the nipple and the swelling that came now and again in her legs and caused her to have hysterics and would one day cause her death. And she was stricken with horror at the thought of leaving her mother and at the selfishness of her thoughts. She had never been prone to thinking of anything important but now, somehow for a moment, she had a glimpse of her mother's life that made her shiver and hate herself as a cruel, heartless, lazy, selfish wretch. Her mother's life loomed up before her eyes, a life of continual misery and suffering, hard work, birth pangs, sickness and again hard work and hunger and anxiety. It loomed up and then it fled again, a little mist came before her eyes and she jumped down from the bed, with the jaunty twirl of her head that was her habit when she set her body in motion.

'Sit down for a while, mother', she whispered, toying with one of the black ivory buttons on her mother's brown bodice. 'I'll look after the table.'

'No, no', murmured the mother with a shake of her whole body, 'I'm not a bit tired. Sit down, my treasure. You have a long way to travel today.'

And Mary sighed and went back to the bed again.

At last somebody said: 'It's broad daylight.' And immediately everybody looked out and said: 'So it is, and may God be praised.' The change from the starry night to the grey, sharp dawn was hard to notice until it had arrived. People looked out and saw the morning light sneaking over the crags silently, along the ground, pushing the mist banks upwards. The stars were growing dim. A long way off invisible sparrows were chirping in their ivied perch in some distant hill or other. Another day had arrived and even as the people looked at it, yawned and began to search for their hats, caps and shawls preparing to go home, the day grew and spread its light and made things move and give voice. Cocks crew, blackbirds carolled, a dog let loose from a cabin by an early riser chased madly after an imaginary robber, barking as if his tail were on fire. The people said goodbye and began to stream forth from Feeney's cabin. They were going to their homes to see to the morning's work before going to Kilmurrage to see the emigrants off on the steamer to the mainland. Soon the cabin was empty except for the family.

All the family gathered into the kitchen and stood about for some minutes talking sleepily of the dance and of the people who had been present. Mrs Feeney tried to persuade everybody to go to bed, but everybody refused. It was four o'clock and Michael and Mary would have to set out for Kilmurrage at nine. So tea was made and they all sat about for an hour drinking it and eating raisin cake and talking. They only talked of the dance and of the people who had been present.

There were eight of them there, the father and mother and six children. The youngest child was Thomas, a thin boy of twelve, whose lungs made a singing sound every time he breathed. The next was Bridget, a girl of fourteen, with dancing eyes and a habit of shaking her short golden curls every now and then for no apparent reason. Then there were the twins, Julia and Margaret, quiet, rather stupid, flat-faced girls of sixteen. Both their upper front teeth protruded slightly and they were both great workers and very obedient to their mother. They were all sitting at the table, having just finished a third large pot of tea, when suddenly the mother hastily gulped down the remainder of the tea in her cup, dropped the cup with a clatter to her saucer and sobbed once through her nose.

'Now mother', said Michael sternly, 'what's the good of this work?'

'No, you are right, my pulse', she replied quietly. 'Only I was just thinking how nice it is to sit here surrounded by all my children, all my little birds in my nest, and then two of them going to fly away made me sad.' And she laughed, pretending to treat it as a foolish joke.

'Oh, that be damned for a story', said the father, wiping his mouth on his sleeve; 'there's work to be done. You Julia, go and get the horse. Margaret, you milk the cow and see that you give enough milk to the calf this morning.' And he ordered everybody about as if it were an ordinary day of work.

But Michael and Mary had nothing to do and they sat about miserably conscious that they had cut adrift from the routine of their home life. They no longer had any place in it. In a few hours they would be homeless wanderers. Now that they were cut adrift from it, the poverty and sordidness of their home life appeared to them under the aspect of comfort and plenty.

So the morning passed until breakfast time at seven o'clock. The morning's work was finished and the family was gathered together again. The meal passed in a dead silence. Drowsy after the sleepless night and conscious that the parting would come in a few hours, nobody wanted to talk. Everybody had an egg for breakfast in honour of the occasion. Mrs Feeney, after her usual habit, tried to give her egg first to Michael, then to Mary, and as each refused it, she ate a little herself and gave the remainder to little Thomas who had the singing in his chest. Then the breakfast was cleared away. The father went to put the creels[5] on the mare so as to take the luggage into Kilmurrage. Michael and Mary got the luggage ready and began to get dressed. The mother and the other children tidied up the house. People from the village began to come into the kitchen, as was customary, in order to accompany the emigrants from their home to Kilmurrage.

At last everything was ready. Mrs Feeney had exhausted all excuses for moving about, engaged on trivial tasks. She had to go into the big bedroom where Mary was putting on her new hat. The mother sat on a chair by the window, her face contorting on account of the flood of tears she was keeping back. Michael moved about the room uneasily, his two hands knotting a big red handkerchief behind his back. Mary twisted about in front of the mirror that hung over the black wooden mantelpiece. She was spending a long time with the hat. It was the first one she had ever worn, but it fitted her beautifully, and it was in excellent taste. It was given to her by the schoolmistress, who was very fond of her, and she herself had taken it in a little. She had an instinct for beauty in dress and deportment.

But the mother, looking at how well her daughter wore the cheap navy blue costume and the white frilled blouse, and the little round black hat with a fat, fluffy, glossy curl covering each ear, and the black silk stockings with blue clocks in them, and the little black shoes that had laces of three colours in them, got suddenly enraged with.... She didn't know with what she got enraged. But for the moment she hated her daughter's beauty, and she remembered all the anguish of giving birth to her and nursing her and toiling for her, for no other purpose than to lose her now and let her go away, maybe to be ravished wantonly because of her beauty and her love of gaiety. A cloud of mad jealousy and hatred against this impersonal beauty that she saw in her daughter almost suffocated the mother, and she stretched out her hands in front of her unconsciously and then just as suddenly her anger vanished like a puff of smoke, and she burst into wild tears, wailing: 'My children, oh, my children, far over the sea you will be carried from me, your mother.' And she began to rock herself and she threw her apron over her head.

Immediately the cabin was full of the sound of bitter wailing. A dismal cry rose from the women gathered in the kitchen. 'Far over the sea they will be carried', began woman after woman, and they all rocked themselves and hid their heads in their aprons. Michael's mongrel dog began to howl on the hearth. Little Thomas sat down on the hearth beside the dog and, putting his arms around him, he began to cry, although he didn't know exactly why he was crying, but he felt melancholy on account of the dog howling and so many people being about.

In the bedroom the son and daughter, on their knees, clung to their mother, who held their heads between her hands and rained kisses on both heads ravenously. After the first wave of tears she had stopped weeping. The tears still ran down her cheeks, but her eyes gleamed and they were dry. There was a fierce look in them as she searched all over the heads of her two children with them, with her brows contracted, searching with a fierce terror-stricken expression, as if by intensity of her stare she hoped to keep a living photograph of them before her mind. With her quivering lips she made a queer sound like 'im-m-m-m' and she kept

5. Wickerwork baskets for carrying turf.

kissing. Her right hand clutched at Mary's left shoulder and with her left she fondled the back of Michael's neck. The two children were sobbing freely. They must have stayed that way a quarter of an hour.

Then the father came into the room, dressed in his best clothes. He wore a new frieze[6] waistcoat, with a grey and black front and a white back. He held his soft black felt hat in one hand and in the other hand he had a bottle of holy water. He coughed and said in a weak gentle voice that was strange to him, as he touched his son: 'Come now, it is time.'

Mary and Michael got to their feet. The father sprinkled them with holy water and they crossed themselves. Then, without looking at their mother, who lay in the chair with her hands clasped on her lap, looking at the ground in a silent tearless stupor, they left the room. Each hurriedly kissed little Thomas, who was not going to Kilmurrage, and then, hand in hand, they left the house. As Michael was going out the door he picked a piece of loose whitewash from the wall and put it in his pocket. The people filed out after them, down the yard and on to the road, like a funeral procession. The mother was left in the house with little Thomas and two old peasant women from the village. Nobody spoke in the cabin for a long time.

Then the mother rose and came into the kitchen. She looked at the two women, at her little son and at the hearth, as if she were looking for something she had lost. Then she threw her hands into the air and ran out into the yard.

'Come back', she screamed; 'come back to me.'

She looked wildly down the road with dilated nostrils, her bosom heaving. But there was nobody in sight. Nobody replied. There was a crooked stretch of limestone road, surrounded by grey crags that were scorched by the sun. The road ended in a hill and then dropped out of sight. The hot June day was silent. Listening foolishly for an answering cry, the mother imagined she could hear the crags simmering under the hot rays of the sun. It was something in her head that was singing.

The two old women led her back into the kitchen. 'There is nothing that time will not cure', said one. 'Yes. Time and patience', said the other.

6. Coarse woollen cloth, traditional in Ireland.

FLANN O'BRIEN (BRIAN O'NOLAN)

(1911-66)

from: AT SWIM-TWO-BIRDS (1939)

[In this extract from *At Swim-Two-Birds*, Flann O'Brien (a pseudonym of Brian O'Nolan) satirizes as he delights in the perennial Irish preoccupation with grandiose anecdote, since it sets the legend of Sweeny (a Gaelic king, who in his madness travelled the country, sojourning in the trees) against the exploits of a present-day hero. Modern English versions of Gaelic source material and cliché-ridden dialogue are each skilfully rendered ridiculous.]

After a prolonged travel and a searching in the skies, Sweeny arrived at nightfall at the shore of the widespread Loch Ree,[1] his resting-place being the fork of the tree of Tiobradan for that night. It snowed on his tree that night, the snow being the worst of all the other snows he had endured since the feather grew on his body, and he was constrained to the recital of these following verses.

Terrible is my plight this night
the pure air has pierced my body,
lacerated feet, my cheek is green —
O Mighty God, it is my due.

1. A lough, or lake, in the Irish midlands.

It is bad living without a house,
Peerless Christ, it is a piteous life!
a filling of green-tufted fine cresses
a drink of cold water from a clear rill.

Stumbling out of the withered tree-tops
walking the furze — it is truth —
wolves for company, man-shunning,
running with the red stag through fields.

If the evil hag had not invoked Christ against me that I should perform leaps for her amusement, I would not have relapsed into madness, said Sweeny.

Come here, said Lamont, what's this about jumps?

Hopping around, you know, said Furriskey.

The story, said learned Shanahan in a learned explanatory manner, is about this fellow Sweeny that argued the toss with the clergy and came off second-best at the wind-up. There was a curse — a malediction — put down in the book against him. The upshot is that your man becomes a bloody bird.

I see, said Lamont.

Do you see it, Mr Furriskey, said Shanahan. What happens? He is changed into a bird for his pains and he could go from here to Carlow in one hop. Do you see it, Mr Lamont?

Oh I see that much all right, said Lamont, but the man that I'm thinking of is a man by the name of Sergeant Craddock, the first man in Ireland at the long jump in the time that's gone.

Craddock?

That was always one thing, said Shanahan wisely, that the Irish race was always noted for, one place where the world had to give us best. With all his faults and by God he has plenty, the Irishman can jump. By God he can jump. That's one thing the Irish race is honoured for no matter where it goes or where you find it — jumping. The world looks up to us there.

We were good jumpers from the start, said Furriskey.

It was in the early days of the Gaelic League, said Lamont. This Sergeant Craddock was an ordinary bloody bobby[2] on the beat, down the country somewhere. A bit of a bags,[3] too, from what I heard. One fine morning he wakes up and is ordered to proceed if you don't mind to the Gaelic League Sports or whatever it was that was being held in the town that fine spring Sunday. To keep his eye open for sedition do you know and all the rest of it. All right. In he marches to do his duty, getting the back of the bloody hand from the women and plenty of guff from the young fellows. Maybe he was poking around too much and sticking his nose where it wasn't wanted . . . .

I know what you mean, said Shanahan.

Anyway, didn't he raise the dander of the head of the house, the big man, the head bottle-washer. Up he came to my cool sergeant with his feathers ruffled and his comb as red as a turkeycock and read out a long rigmarole in Irish to your man's face.

That'll do you, said the sergeant, keep that stuff for them that wants it. I don't know what you're saying, man.

So you don't know your own language, says the head man.

I do, says the sergeant, I know plenty of English.

Your man then asks the sergeant his business in Irish and what he's doing there in the field at all.

Speak English, says the sergeant.

So be damned but your man gets his rag out and calls the sergeant a bloody English spy.

Well maybe he was right, said Furriskey.

Shh, said Shanahan.

But wait till I tell you. The sergeant just looked at him as cool as blazes.

You're wrong, says he, *and I'm as good a man as you or any other man*, says he.

You're a bloody English bags, says your man in Irish.

And I'll prove it, says the sergeant.

And with that your man gets black in the face and turns his back and walks to the bloody platform where all the lads were doing the Irish dancing with their girls, competitions of one kind and another, you know. Oh it was all the fashion at one time, you were bloody nothing if you couldn't do your Walls of Limerick. And here too were my men with the fiddles and the pipes playing away there at the reels and jigs for further orders. Do you know what I mean?

Oh I know what you're talking about all right,

2. police constable.

3. A jocular, although pejorative, term, meaning 'an incompetent person'.

said Shanahan, the national music of our country, Rodney's Glory, the Star of Munster and the Rights of Man.

The Flogging Reel and Drive the Donkey,[4] you can't beat them, said Furriskey.

That's the ticket, said Lamont. Anyway, didn't your man get into a dark corner with his butties till they hatched out a plan to best the sergeant. All right. Back went your man to the sergeant, who was taking it easy in the shade of a tree.

You said a while ago, says your man, that you were a better man than any man here. Can you jump?

I can not, says the sergeant, but I'm no worse than the next man.

We'll see, says your man.

Now be damned but hadn't they a man in the tent there from the county Cork, a bloody dandy at the long jump, a man that had a name, a man that was known in the whole country. A party by the name of Bagenal, the champion of all Ireland.

Gob that was a cute one, said Furriskey.

A very cute one. But wait till I tell you. The two of them lined up and a hell of a big crowd gathering there to watch. Here was my nice Bagenal as proud as a bloody turkey in his green pants, showing off the legs. Beside him stands another man, a man called Craddock, a member of the polis.[5] His tunic is off him on the grass but the rest of his clothes is still on. He is standing as you find him with his blue pants and his big canal-barges on his two feet. I'm telling you it was something to look at. It was a sight to see.

I don't doubt it, said Shanahan.

Yes. Well Bagenal is the first off, sailing through the air like a bird and down in a shower of sand. What was the score?

Eighteen feet, said Furriskey.

Not at all man, twenty-two. Twenty-two feet was the jump of Bagenal there and then and by God the shout the people gave was enough to make the sergeant puke what was inside him and plenty more that he never swallowed.

Twenty-two feet is a good jump any day, said Shanahan.

After the cheering had died down, said Lamont, my man Bagenal strolls around and turns his back on the sergeant and asks for a cigarette and starts to blather out of him to his friends. What does my sergeant do, do you think, Mr Shanahan.

I'm saying nothing, said knowing Shanahan.

By God you're a wise man. Sergeant Craddock keeps his mouth shut, takes a little run and jumps twenty-four feet six.

Do you tell me that! cried Furriskey.

Twenty-four feet six.

I'm not surprised, said Shanahan in his amazement, I'm not surprised. Go where you like in the wide world, you will always find that the Irishman is looked up to for his jumping.

Right enough, said Furriskey, the name of Ireland is honoured for that.

Go to Russia, said Shanahan, go to China, go to France. Everywhere and all the time it is hats off and a gra-ma-cree[6] to the Jumping Irishman. Ask who you like they'll all tell you that. The Jumping Irishman.

It's a thing, said Furriskey, that will always stand to us — jumping.

When everything's said, said Lamont, the Irishman has his points. He's not the last man that was made now.

He is not, said Furriskey.

When everything had been said by Sweeny, said droning dark-voiced Finn,[7] a glimmering of reason assailed the madman till it turned his steps in the direction of his people that he might dwell with them and trust them. But holy Ronan[8] in his cell was acquainted by angels of the intention of Sweeny and prayed God that he should not be loosed from his frenzy until his soul had been first loosed from his body and here is a summary of the result. When the madman reached the middle of Slieve Fuaid,[9] there were strange apparitions before him there, red headless trunks and trunkless heads and five stubbly rough grey heads without trunk or body between them, screaming and squealing and bounding hither and thither about the dark road beleaguering and besetting him and shouting their mad abuse, until he soared in his fright aloft in front of them. Piteous was the terror and the wailing

4. Irish set dances, with some of their characteristic names parodied.

5. police.

6. Literally, 'love of my heart'; used jocularly here.

7. Finn MacCumhaill, the hero of the Fenian Cycle of heroic stories. They tell of the adventures of Finn and the hunter warriors of the Fianna, a military brotherhood that was active in the third century, during the high-kingship of Cormac Macairt. Finn is one of the central figures in *At Swim-Two-Birds*.

8. St Ronan was abbot of Drumiskin, Co. Louth. He died of the plague in 664.

9. The Fews mountains, in south-east Ulster.

cries, and the din and the harsh-screaming tumult of the heads and the dogsheads and the goatsheads in his pursuit, thudding on his thighs and his calves and on the nape of his neck and knocking against trees and the butts of rocks — a wild torrent of villainy from the breast of a high mountain, not enough resting for a drink of water for mad Sweeny till he finally achieved his peace in the tree on the summit of Slieve Eichneach. Here he devoted his time to the composition and recital of melodious staves on the subject of his evil plight.

After that he went on his career of wild folly from Luachair Dheaghaidh to Fiodh Gaibhle[10] of the clean streams and the elegant branches, remaining there for one year on the sustenance of saffron heart-red holly-berries and black-brown oak-acorns, with draughts of water from the Gabhal,[11] concluding there with the fashioning of this lay.

Ululation, I am Sweeny,
my body is a corpse;
sleeping or music nevermore —
only the soughing of the storm-wind.

I have journeyed from Luachair Dheaghaidh
to the edge of Fiodh Gaibhle,
this is my fare — I conceal it not —
ivy-berries, oak-mast.

10. Luachair Dheaghaidh is Slieve Lougher, near Castleisland, Co. Kerry. Fiodh Gaibhle is a wood in County Kildare.

11. Gabhal is the Feegile, a river that joins the River Barrow in County Kildare.

MYLES NA gCOPALEEN (BRIAN O'NOLAN)

[Myles na gCopaleen (another pseudonym of Brian O'Nolan) responds to an ill-informed editorial in *The Irish Times* (where in fact his humorous column the 'Cruiskeen Lawn', appeared regularly), which referred slightingly to the Irish language. Beneath its droll tone and whimsy, Brian O'Nolan's concern for the language is clearly evident, as is his discriminating understanding of socio-linguistics.]

from: THE BEST OF MYLES (1968)

Last week we had a rather stern address over here ——[1] regarding the inadmissibility of the Irish language and although it is almost a *gaffe* for anybody who is qualified to speak on this subject to express opinions on it in the public prints, I feel I must speak out; otherwise there is the danger that the lying rumour will be spread by my enemies that I am silent because once again money has changed hands. (It cannot be too often repeated that I am not for sale. I was bought in 1921 and the transaction was final and conclusive.)

In my lordship's view the movement to revive the Irish language should be persisted in. I hold that it is fallacious to offer the Irish people a simple choice between slums and Gaelic. (Indeed, it is hardly an adult attitude and is known in hibernian philosophy as the *Ignoratio MacGlinchy*.)[2] If this doctrine of bread alone were followed, we would have (for one thing) to divert the revenues of Trinity College to slum clearance, and Alton[3] and I simply will not have this. The horrible charge is made that Mr de Valera is spending half a million a year on reviving Irish. I may be a wild paddy but I take the view that the free expenditure of public money on a cultural pursuit is one of the few boasts this country can make. Whether we get value for all the money spent on Irish, higher learning and on our university establishments is one question but that we spend liberally on these things is to our credit and when the great nations of the earth (whose civilisations we are so often asked to admire) are spending up to £100,000,000 (roughly) per day

1. i.e. in the editorial of *The Irish Times*.

2. Mock Irish form of the Latin phrase 'Ignoratio elenchi', meaning a logical fallacy, an argument irrelevant to the given subject.

3. Ernest Henry Alton (1873-1952), provost of Trinity College, Dublin 1942-52.

on destruction, it is surely no shame for our humble community of peasants to spend about £2,000 per day on trying to revive a language. It is the more urbane occupation. And what is half a million in relation to slum clearance? Faith now, could we be honest enough (for one moment) to admit to ourselves (in our heart of hearts) that there is another sort of Irish, and forced down people's throats, too, and that we spend enough on it every year to re-build all Dublin.

Irish has an intrinsic significance which (naturally enough) must be unknown to those who condemn the language. It provides through its literature and dialects a great field for the pursuit of problems philological, historical and ethnological, an activity agreeable to all men of education and good-will. Moreover, the language itself is ingratiating by reason of its remoteness from European tongues and moulds of thought, its precision, elegance and capacity for the subtler literary nuances; it attracts even by its surpassing difficulty, for scarcely anybody living today can write or speak Irish correctly and exactly in the fashion of 300 years ago (and it may have been noticed that the one person qualified to attempt the feat has been too tired to try for the past two or three weeks). True Irish prose has a steely latinistic line that does not exist in the fragmented English patois. Here is a literal translation of a letter addressed by Hugh O'Neill[4] to a hostile captain:

> Our blessing to ye, O Mac Coghlin: we received your letter and what we understand from her is that what you are at the doing of is but sweetness of word and spinning out of time. For our part of the subject, whatever person is not with us and will not wear himself out in the interest of justice, that person we understand to be a person against us. For that reason, in each place in which ye do your own good, pray do also our ill to the fullest extent ye can and we will do your ill to the absolute utmost of our ability, with God's will. We being at Knockdoney Hill, 6 februarii, 1600.

That seems to me to be an exceptional achievement in the sphere of written nastiness and the original exudes the charm attaching to all instances of complete precision in the use of words.

There is probably no basis at all for the theory that a people cannot preserve a separate national entity without a distinct language but it is beyond dispute that Irish enshrines the national ethos and in a subtle way Irish persists very vigorously in English. In advocating the preservation of Irish culture, it is not to be inferred *that this culture* is superior to the English or any other but simply that certain Irish modes are *more comfortable and suitable* for Irish people; otherwise these modes simply would not exist. It is therefore dangerous to discourage the use of Irish because the revival movement, even if completely ineffective, is a valuable preservative of certain native virtues and it is worth remembering that if Irish were to die completely, the standard of English here, both in the spoken and written word, would sink to a level probably as low as that obtaining in England and it would stop there only because it could go no lower. Not even the Editor of the *Irish Times* is an authority on the hidden wells which sustain the ageless western Irishman, and cannot have considered the vast ethnogenic problems inherent in a proposal to deprive him of one of his essential chattels. I admire Liverpool but if Cork is to become another Liverpool by reason of stupid admiration for the least worthy things in the English civilisation, then I can only say that the Corkmen will not live there any more, the mysterious language they speak, which is not Irish and certainly not English will be heard no more, and a race of harmless, charming and amusing people will have been extirpated.

There is another aspect to this question. Even if Irish had no value at all, the whole bustle of reviving it, the rows, the antagonisms, and the clashes surrounding the revival are interesting and amusing. There is a profusion of unconscious humour on both sides. The solemn humbugs who pronounce weightily on the Irish language while knowing absolutely nothing about it I hold to be no less valuable than monetary reformers in the business of entertaining the nation. The lads who believe that in slip-jigs we have a national prophylaxis makes life less stark. And the public-spirited parties who write letters to the papers in illiterate English expressing concern at the harm the revival movement is doing to the standard of education

4. Hugh O'Neill (1550-1616), 3rd baron Dungannon and 2nd earl of Tyrone. He was one of the most important Irish leaders in the Elizabethan wars.

generally are also of clownish significance. They all combine to make colour and to amuse.

To one and all I would say this, my hand upon my heart: Go your ways, build and take down, capture and set free, gather in conclave and debate ... but ... do not tamper with the Irishman, touch not his sacred belongings, be solicitous that thy tongue contemneth not the smallest thing he may prize or the least thing he may love. For he is unique; if you kill him he cannot be replaced, and the world is poorer.

Biographies/Bibliographies

George Russell (AE)

For biography and bibliography, see Volume II, p. 560.

George Bernard Shaw

For biography and bibliography, see Volume II, p. 514.

Daniel Corkery

LIFE. Born in Cork in 1878, Corkery spent his entire life in that city and its environs, except for a year when he trained as a teacher at St Patrick's College, Dublin. Until 1931 he was a school teacher, whose literary interests expressed themselves in amateur theatricals and writings of a very varied standard. Only his collection of short stories, *A Munster Twilight* (1916), achieves real literary power, although his novel, *The Threshold of Quiet* (1917), has a thoughtful sombreness of tone. Corkery published his widely influential study of the Gaelic poets of eighteenth-century Munster, *The Hidden Ireland,* in 1925 and received the Master of Arts degree for a study of J. M. Synge from the National University of Ireland in 1929. He was appointed professor of English in University College, Cork in 1931, in which office he served until his retirement in 1947. He published his contentious nationalistic study of Synge, *Synge and Anglo-Irish Literature,* in 1931. It is as a polemicist and nationalist that Corkery is remembered. He was a Senator in Seanad Eireann from 1951 to 1954. He died in 1964.

CHIEF WRITINGS. *A Munster Twilight* (Dublin and Cork: The Talbot Press; New York: Stokes, 1916); *The Threshold of Quiet* (Dublin and Cork: The Talbot Press; London: Unwin, 1917); *The Hounds of Banba* (Dublin and Cork: The Talbot Press, 1920; New York: Huebsch, 1922); *The Hidden Ireland: A Study of Gaelic Munster in the Eighteenth Century* (Dublin: Gill, 1925); *The Stormy Hills* (Dublin: The Talbot Press; London: Jonathan Cape, 1929); *Synge and Anglo-Irish Literature* (Cork: Cork University Press; London: Longmans, Green, 1931); *Earth Out of Earth* (Dublin and Cork: The Talbot Press, 1939); *The Fortunes of the Irish Language* (Dublin: Fallon, 1954).

BIOGRAPHY AND CRITICISM. George Brandon Saul, *Daniel Corkery* (Lewisburg, Pennsylvania: Bucknell University Press, 1973); Seán O'Faoláin, 'Daniel Corkery', *Dublin Magazine* 11 (April-June 1936), 49-61.

Seán O'Faoláin

LIFE. Born John Whelan in Cork in 1900. Educated University College, Cork, where he became involved with the Republican movement. Took A.M. in English at Harvard University in 1929 where he had studied for three years. From 1929 to 1933 he taught in a secondary school in the south of England, but in 1933 he returned to Ireland where he has lived subsequently. His first collection of stories, *Midsummer Night Madness* (1932), was banned in Ireland, as was his second novel, *Bird Alone* (1936). Since 1933 O'Faoláin, apart from the period when he edited *The Bell* (1940-46), has lived the life of a professional writer. He has produced short stories, novels, plays, criticism, biographies, an autobiography (*Vive Moi!*), numerous essays, travel books and broadcasts, and has occasionally accepted temporary lectureships at universities in the United States. It is as a distinguished practitioner of the short-story form that he has achieved his greatest reputation.

CHIEF WRITINGS. *Midsummer Night Madness and Other Stories* (London: Jonathan Cape, 1932); *A Nest of Simple Folk* (New York: Viking, 1934); *Bird Alone* (London: Jonathan Cape, 1936); *A Purse of Coppers: Short Stories* (London: Jonathan Cape, 1937); *King of the Beggars* (London: Thomas Nelson and Sons; New York: Viking, 1938); *The Great O'Neill, A Biography of Hugh O'Neill, Earl of Tyrone* (New York: Duell, Sloan and Pearce; London: Longmans, Green, 1942); *Teresa and Other Stories* (London: Jonathan Cape, 1947); *The Irish* (London: Penguin; New York: Devin-Adair, 1948); *The Short Story* (London: William Collins, 1948); *The Man Who Invented Sin and Other Stories* (New York: Devin-Adair, 1948); *The Vanishing Hero, Studies in Novelists of the Twenties* (London: Eyre and Spottiswoode, 1956); *I Remember! I Remember!* (Boston: Little, Brown, 1961); *Vive Moi!* (Boston: Little, Brown, 1963); *The Heat of the Sun, Stories and Tales* (London: Rupert Hart-Davis; Boston: Little, Brown, 1966); *The Talking Trees and Other Stories* (London: Jonathan Cape, 1971); *Foreign Affairs and Other Stories* (London: Constable, 1976); *And Again?* (London: Constable, 1979); *The Collected Stories of Seán O'Faoláin*, Vols 1-3 (London: Constable, 1980, 1981 and 1982).

BIOGRAPHY AND CRITICISM. Paul A. Doyle, *Seán O'Faoláin* (New York: Twayne, 1968); Maurice Harmon, *Seán O'Faoláin: A Critical Introduction* (South Bend, Indiana: University of Notre Dame Press, 1966); Maurice Harmon (ed.), *The Irish University Review*, Vol. 6, No. 1 (Spring 1976), Seán O'Faoláin Special Issue. (This issue contains much excellent biographical and critical material.) A brilliant essay on O'Faoláin's politics is Donat O'Donnell (Conor Cruise O'Brien), 'The Parnellism of Seán O'Faoláin' in *Maria Cross* (London: Burns and Oates, 1963), pp. 87-105.

Frank O'Connor

LIFE. Born Michael O'Donovan in Cork in 1903, O'Connor grew up in poor circumstances and received little formal schooling. One teacher, however, Daniel Corkery, fired him with a love of the Irish language and with the political ideals which led to his involvement with the Republican movement. During the Civil War he was interned with other Republicans. His first collection of stories, *Guests of the Nation* (1931), reflected on the idealism and betrayals of the revolutionary period and suggested O'Connor's intense disillusionment with the Irish Free State. This was to find expression in many of his activities in the next twenty years, when he lived by his writing in Dublin and acted as a director of the Abbey Theatre from 1935 to 1939. From this period came some of his most famous short stories and the three excellent volumes of verse translations from the Irish. O'Connor, like O'Faoláin, suffered the Censor's interdiction. His novel, *Dutch Interior* (1940), was banned, as was his version of Merriman's 'The Midnight Court'.

O'Connor's outspoken criticism of social and moral hypocrisy in Ireland and his own tempestuous personal life made his position difficult in Dublin and in 1951 he left for a teaching post in the United States, where he spent much of the rest of his life. A frequent contributor of stories to *The New Yorker*, the work of this period often seemed conventional and formulaic. However, his translations from the Irish in *Kings, Lords and Commons* (1959) make for a vigorous, effective book, while his study of Ireland's literary inheritance, *The Backward Look* (1967), is a powerful personal statement. His study of the short-story form,

The Lonely Voice (1962), is a suggestive essay, helpful in a reading of his own stories, while volume one of his autobiography, *An Only Child* (1961), is a minor classic. O'Connor died in Dublin in 1966. In about a dozen short stories he makes a claim to be considered a modern master of the form.

CHIEF WRITINGS. *Guests of the Nation* (London: Macmillan, 1931); *The Saint and Mary Kate* (London: Macmillan, 1932); *Bones of Contention and Other Stories* (London: Macmillan, 1936); *Dutch Interior* (London: Macmillan, 1940); *Crab Apple Jelly* (London: Macmillan, 1944); *The Common Chord* (London: Macmillan, 1947); *The Stories of Frank O'Connor* (New York: Alfred A. Knopf, 1952; London: Hamish Hamilton, 1953); *More Stories by Frank O'Connor* (New York: Alfred A. Knopf, 1954, 1967); *Kings, Lords and Commons* (New York: Alfred A. Knopf, 1959); *An Only Child* (New York: Alfred A. Knopf, 1961; London: Macmillan, 1962); *The Lonely Voice* (Cleveland: World, 1962; London: Macmillan, 1963); *The Backward Look* (London: Macmillan, 1967), published in the United States as *A Short History of Irish Literature* (New York: Putnam, 1967); *My Father's Son* (London: Macmillan, 1968; New York: Alfred A. Knopf, 1969).

BIOGRAPHY AND CRITICISM. James H. Matthews, *Frank O'Connor* (Lewisburg, Pennsylvania: Bucknell University Press, 1976); Maurice Sheehy (ed.), *Michael/Frank: Studies on Frank O'Connor* (Dublin: Gill and Macmillan, 1969), a useful collection of reminiscences and critical and biographical essays; Maurice Wohlgelernter, *Frank O'Connor: An Introduction* (New York: Columbia University Press, 1977); James Matthews, *Voices: A Life of Frank O'Connor* (Dublin: Gill and Macmillan; New York: Atheneum, 1983); but see review of this biography by Ruth Sherry in *Irish University Review*, Vol. 14, No. 2 (Autumn 1984), 290-99.

Liam O'Flaherty

LIFE. Born on Inishmore on the Aran Islands, off the coast of County Galway, in 1896, and spent his childhood there. Educated at Rockwell College, Co. Tipperary and at Blackrock College, Co. Dublin. Spent one year at University College, Dublin, intending to take holy orders, but left and joined the Irish Guards (a regiment of the British army) in 1915. Saw action at the Somme and was discharged, following shell-shock, in 1917. Wandered for several years until, in 1921, he seized the Rotunda in Dublin with a group of the unemployed and raised the red flag of revolution. Took the Republican side in the Civil War, but left for London in 1922 where he began his writing career. In the next two decades, amid much travel and emotional trauma, he wrote his best short stories and novels. Most of his work was banned in Ireland. During World War II he lived in the United States, but he returned to Europe in 1946. Spent most of his later life in Dublin, although his writing activities declined after the early 1960s. He died in 1984. Remembered as the author of strong, simple short stories of natural life and rural mores, but his historical novels, particularly *Famine* (1937), remain powerful statements. His novel, *The Informer* (1925) (which was the basis of a successful film by John Ford), is a memorable psychological thriller.

CHIEF WRITINGS. *Thy Neighbour's Wife* (London: Jonathan Cape, 1923; New York: Boni and Liveright, 1924); *Spring Sowing* (London: Jonathan Cape, 1924); *The Black Soul* (London: Jonathan Cape, 1924; New York: Boni and Liveright, 1925); *The Informer* (London: Jonathan Cape; New York: Alfred A. Knopf, 1925); *The Assassin* (London: Jonathan Cape; New York: Harcourt, Brace, 1928); *The Mountain Tavern and Other Stories* (London: Jonathan Cape, 1929); *Skerrett* (London: Gollancz; New York: Long and Smith, 1932); *Shame the Devil* (London: Grayson and Grayson, 1934); *Famine* (London: Gollancz; New York: Random House, 1937); *The Short Stories of Liam O'Flaherty* (London: Jonathan Cape, 1937); *Land* (London: Gollancz; New York: Random House, 1946); *Two Lovely Beasts* (London: Gollancz, 1948; New York: Devin-Adair, 1950); *Insurrection* (London: Gollancz, 1950; Boston: Little, Brown, 1951); *The Stories of Liam O'Flaherty* (New York: Devin-Adair, 1956); *The Pedlar's Revenge* (Dublin: Wolfhound, 1976).

BIOGRAPHY AND CRITICISM. Paul A. Doyle, *Liam O'Flaherty: An Annotated Bibliography* (New York: Whitston Publishing, 1972); A. A. Kelly, *Liam O'Flaherty, the Storyteller* (London: Macmillan, 1976); Brendan Kennelly, 'Liam O'Flaherty: The Unchained Storm. A View of His Short Stories', in P. Rafroidi and T. Brown (eds), *The Irish Short Story* (Lille: publications de l'université de Lille III, 1979, pp. 175-87; Patrick Sheeran, *The Novels of Liam O'Flaherty* (Dublin: Wolfhound, 1976); John N. Zneimer, *The Literary Vision of Liam O'Flaherty* (Syracuse, N.Y.: Syracuse University Press, 1970).

Brian O'Nolan

LIFE. Born in Strabane, Co. Tyrone in 1911. O'Nolan's family settled in Dublin in 1923, where he was educated at Blackrock College and University College, Dublin. He entered the Irish civil service in 1935 and was employed in the Department of Local Government until his retirement in 1953. *At Swim-Two-Birds* was published in 1939, but his second novel, *The Third Policeman* (completed in 1940), did not find a publisher until after his death. Between 1940 and 1966 O'Nolan (under the pseudonym of Myles na gCopaleen) contributed a humorous column, 'Cruiskeen Lawn', to *The Irish Times*. His satiric novel, *An Béal Bocht* (The Poor Mouth), was published in Irish in 1941. *At Swim-Two-Birds* was reissued to greater notice in 1960 and before his death in 1966 O'Nolan saw two further novels in print. Since his death, O'Nolan's reputation as an experimental writer has grown steadily, *At Swim-Two-Birds* and *The Third Policeman* attracting particular acclaim.

CHIEF WRITINGS: *At Swim-Two-Birds* (London: Longmans, Green, 1939; Harmondsworth: Penguin, 1967, 1977); *An Béal Bocht* (Dublin: An Press Naisiúnta, 1941; Dolmen Press, 1964); *Faustus Kelly: a play in three acts* (Dublin: Cahill, 1943); *The Hard Life* (London: MacGibbon and Kee, 1961; Four Square Books, 1964; Picador, 1976); *The Dalkey Archive* (London: MacGibbon and Kee, 1964); *The Third Policeman* (London: MacGibbon and Kee, 1968); Kevin O'Nolan (ed.), *The Best of Myles: A Selection from 'Cruiskeen Lawn'* (London: MacGibbon and Kee, 1968; Grafton, 1987); *Stories and Plays* (London: Hart-Davis, MacGibbon, 1973); B. Kiely (ed.), *The Various Lives of Keats and Chapman and The Brother* (London: Hart-Davis, MacGibbon, 1976); K. O'Nolan (ed.), *Further Cuttings from Cruiskeen Lawn* (London: Hart-Davis, MacGibbon, 1976); *The Hair of the Dogma: A Further Selection from 'Cruiskeen Lawn'* (London: Hart-Davis, MacGibbon, 1977); M. Green (ed.), *Myles Away From Dublin* (London: Granada, 1985).

BIOGRAPHY AND CRITICISM. *Journal of Irish Literature*, A Flann O'Brien: Myles na gCopaleen Number, Vol. 3, No. 1 (January 1974), with bibliography on pp. 104-12; Anne Clissmann, *Flann O'Brien: A Critical Introduction* (Dublin: Gill and Macmillan, 1975); Anthony Cronin, *Dead As Doornails* (Dublin: The Dolmen Press, 1975), a brilliant portrait of literary Dublin in the 1950s, contains a sharp cameo impression of O'Nolan; T. O'Keeffe (ed.), *Myles* (London: Martin Brian and O'Keeffe, 1973); E. Wäppling, *Four Irish Legendary Figures in 'At Swim-Two-Birds'* (Uppsala: Almqvist and Wiksell, 1984); R. Imhof (ed.), *Alive-alive O! Flann O'Brien's At Swim-Two-Birds* (Dublin: Wolfhound; Totowa, New Jersey: Barnes & Noble, 1985); B. Ó Conaire, *Myles na Gaeilge* (Dublin: An Clóchomhar, 1986); P. Costello and P. Van de Kamp, *Flann O'Brien: An Illustrated Biography* (London: Bloomsbury, 1987); Anthony Cronin, *No Laughing Matter: The Life and Times of Flann O'Brien* (London: Grafton Books, 1989).

TERENCE BROWN, *Editor*

The Counter-Revival 1930-65: Poetry

In the late 1920s and the 1930s W. B. Yeats dominated the Irish poetic firmament as he did that of the literary world in general. His international reputation, recognized in the award of the Nobel Prize for Literature in 1923, his continued poetic creativity — manifested in the publication of perhaps his finest single collection of poems, *The Tower and Other Poems*, in 1928, and his intimidating presence as a Senator in the Irish Free State Parliament and as literary public man all made him a force to be reckoned with by his immediate successors.

Yeats's challenging legacy to those successors was a body of verse and a literary career charged with both a sense of the heroic and the romantic. For Yeats gave exemplary witness to the rhetorical powers of poetry, to its historical significance in an era of cultural nationalism and to the privileged role it could play in a period of political revolution. However, the poets who began their work in the 1920s and the next decade were inheritors of an altogether less exhilarating social climate than that in which Yeats had established his poetic reputation. The disillusionment of the immediate aftermath of the Civil War (1922-23) had given way to a period of sober reconstruction, in which a pragmatic realism governed social and artistic aspiration alike. In such a context, it could not be assumed that poetry would be able to maintain the kind of privileged status that it had enjoyed when cultural and revolutionary nationalism had invested a whole era with a sense of spiritual possibilities. Accordingly, the work of most of the post-Yeats generation of Irish poets gives evidence that they endured a sense of cultural belatedness *vis à vis* both Yeats and the Literary Revival as a whole. Yeats and his fellow Revivalists had set the pace, had defined the Irish poetic as heroic and romantic in a period when that had seemed appropriate. What role might poetry play in the diminished circumstances in which the young poets of the 1920s and 1930s found themselves?

The career of Austin Clarke (1896-1974) gives ample opportunity for the critic to observe how profoundly Yeats's achievements influenced the work of his successors and how difficult it was for them to make their own poetic way.

Austin Clarke began his poetic career as a devoted child of the Revival. His earliest works were epic attempts, in the Revival mode, to realize the matter of Ireland in English verse. Douglas Hyde's example and teaching, as Clarke tells us in his autobiography, had inspired him: 'The hands of our lost despised centuries were laid on me.' Clarke was never quite to lose this first enthusiasm, nor indeed his respect for the Yeats who had so successfully exploited the Celtic past in his poetry, even when that poet treated him shabbily (excluding him, for example, from *The Oxford Book of Modern Verse* in 1936). But in the late 1920s, Clarke's relationship with the Irish past began to alter in ways that were to distinguish his writings from those of the Revivalists.

The Revival writers had almost without exception directed their attention to the pre-Christian centuries of Ireland's Celtic past. There they had found images of the heroic and an endorsement for romantic and even occult conceptions of Ireland's essence. In the disillusioned, puritanical, censorious social climate of the 1920s (Clarke vigorously opposed the Censorship Act of 1929) he began to reflect poetically on the high period of Irish Christianity in the Middle Ages. His source books for this imaginative preoccupation were George T. Stokes's *Ireland and the Celtic Church* (1886) and Margaret Stokes's *Early Christian Art in Ireland* (1887). Clarke's interest in what he termed the Celtic-Romanesque (identified in terms of its artistic and architectural styles) stimulated his personal sense of an Irish tradition to which he had access as a student of the Irish language (he had been taught English at University College, Dublin by the 1916 martyr, Thomas MacDonagh, and Irish by Douglas Hyde). His volume of poems, *Pilgrimage and Other Poems* (1929), provides a distinct impression of a young poet laying claim to his own territory in the Irish past, one on which the Revival had no title deed. In this volume Clarke celebrates a world of a medieval monasticism, which represents a sane balance between imagination, piety, scholarship and the sexual impulse. It is a world of fresh beauty, aesthetic ambition and clerkly duty. In publishing such a work in the year in which a Censorship Bill was enacted in the newly independent Irish Free State, Clarke implied that a more wholesome relationship between the pagan and the Christian, the aesthetic and the moral, had been achieved in the Irish past than that which obtained in his own Ireland.

In so employing the past to write of the present, Clarke was of course engaging in the kind of cultural dialectics that had characterized the Revival. He was developing a personal myth of the past by which the present might be measured and challenged, in just the way Yeats had done in his celebration of the exploits of Cuchulain in pagan antiquity. And like Yeats's mythologizing, Clarke's assumed a continuing, privileged role for poetry (the poet as interpreter of the past's admonition of the present). But Clarke's version of the past differed from the Yeatsian in significant ways. Yeats's vision of the Irish past was mediated through a profound nostalgia; pagan Irish antiquity was shrouded in the mist of ages (its presence, appropriately, to be discerned in the Celtic Twilight). Clarke's version of the Celtic-Romanesque is of a period authenticated by scholarship. Where Yeats's Celticism partakes fully of myth, Clarke's myth of the Celtic-Romanesque is involved significantly with history. Accordingly, the past in Clarke's work is not a heroic ideal, glimpsed in a symbolic and mythological dimension, but a social norm, evidence of an actual human achievement that may serve as an ethical stimulus. As such, Clarke's sense of the past is more that of a classicist than that of a romantic, one for whom the past supplies a necessary measure of daily experience.

It was the classic society of a Celtic-Romanesque Ireland and its humane attitudes to creativity and the sexual impulse that Austin Clarke especially admired. He believed, too, that the Gaelic strand in Irish life had retained some of this free-thinking good sense and throughout his career he sought to identify with an authentic Gaelic tradition. However, his own psyche had been disturbed by the darker energies of modern Irish puritanism. In his volume of poetry, *Night and Morning* (1938), he wrestled with catholic guilt and neurosis — disabling forces that he confronted with controlled, clinical objectivity in his poem of breakdown and recovery, *Mnemosyne Lay in Dust* (published in 1966). Out of these struggles Clarke emerged in the mid-1950s as a satiric, learned poet, whose verse, emulating the prosodic features of the Gaelic poetic tradition in assonantal patterns and internal rhyming, expressed a quietly insistent, wholly serious humanism. The absurdities and crippling repressions of Irish life are subjected to a closely crafted satiric critique. Underlying this mature achievement is a hard-won materialist vision (even when the work is at its most realistic and even tiresomely local), which celebrates the ordinary even as it reckons Irish life to be subject to universal laws exacting their own punishments and rewards. Clarke's late poems were works of frank eroticism — playful, worldly, exuberantly explicit — as if to bear witness to the earthy satisfactions of achieved psychological health and to deny the religious implications of the tragic sense of life. Where Yeats at the last lay down in 'the foul rag-and-bone shop of the heart' ('The Circus Animals' Desertion') in an attitude of tragic despair, Clarke in such a poem as 'The Healing of Mis' rededicated poetry to the celebration of the flesh.

If Austin Clarke, Dublin-born, middle-class, university-educated, felt the anxiety of influence in relation to Yeats and the Revival, for Patrick Kavanagh (1904-67), small-farmer son of a County Monaghan cobbler, that condition amounted nearly to a phobia.

When Kavanagh began writing, he knew almost

no modern English and Irish poetry, and drew his inspiration from the school anthologies. His earliest verses are naïve pastorals touched with a mystical catholic piety. His work came to the attention of AE, who published an early poem in one of the final issues of *The Irish Statesman*. Kavanagh had been discovered and in the process became conscious of a literary environment in which he felt profoundly ill-at-ease. He thought the Revival's aristocratic vision of the heroic Irish peasant an impertinent absurdity, believing that the whole enterprise involved a profound misrepresentation of the local, intimate truths of Irish life. The dramatist John Synge especially drew his ire: 'His peasants are picturesque conventions; the language he invented for them did a disservice to letters in this country by drawing our attention away from the common speech whose delightfulness comes from its very ordinariness.' As late as 1964, when his own successes as a poet might have been expected to induce a more mellow estimate, Kavanagh claimed that the Revival was a 'thoroughgoing English-bred lie.' About Yeats in particular he was capable of a respectful wariness, although he denied Irish authenticity to him too. And he saw in Yeats's work a fabricated Irish spiritual essence that took almost no account of the country's social and religious realities: 'For all his burden of his native country in his work no poet could be more outside what we may call the Irish consciousness . . . .'

Kavanagh's *The Great Hunger* (1942) can be read at one level as a fiercely realistic riposte to the Revival's romantic pastoralism. This bleak, uncompromising report from the heart of rural Ireland uncovers no hint of the idyllic: rather, it reveals how emotional and sexual poverty are the inevitable concomitants of grinding economic deprivation. Paddy Maguire is seen in this starkly analytic work as the victim of economic, religious and familial forces, mercilessly crushing the life instinct. The natural life of the body, the fully human engagement in the earth's fertile cycle of birth, procreation and death are denied to this martyr to economic necessity. Raw, angry and pained, *The Great Hunger* achieves a compelling power in the almost unrelieved realism of its vision. Flesh becomes clay, spirit becomes matter in this *tour de force* of disillusionment. The work's only relaxation from a tone of inexorable, almost forensic, reductionism comes at those moments when the poet raises his eyes from the clay to discern in the natural world fleeting suggestions of a spiritual presence.

The catholic church in *The Great Hunger* is complicit with the forces of darkness, its message shaped to the conditions of small-farm life. But Kavanagh was imaginatively possessed by the symbols, rituals and festivals of a rural catholicism and he could not easily or unambiguously reject a faith that in its more malign forms was in part responsible for the sufferings of a Paddy Maguire. Indeed the catholicism that Kavanagh believed had helped to form the Irish consciousness was something that Yeats might never comprehend. Much of Kavanagh's work is therefore a troubled attempt to come to terms with the ambivalence of his own religious awareness. 'Lough Derg', almost a companion poem to *The Great Hunger*, is another long poem written in the 1940s, in which Kavanagh confronts the varying expressions of catholicism in Irish life. In this study of the practice of pilgrimage to the penitential island in County Donegal, the poet seeks in the catholicism of his fellow-countrymen and of his own sensibility some principle of vitality and spiritual worth.

As he matured as an artist, Kavanagh increasingly began to trust his own secure poetic hold on local aspects of his Irish experience. He developed, in an influential distinction, a faith in the parochial as a mode of transcendence of the merely provincial. And in the 1950s, following a life-threatening illness, he produced a small body of verse that takes for granted the spiritual worth of the daily and the banal, celebrating these in an artfully casual poetic. At their best, these poems suggest a religious calm (the fruit of Kavanagh's mature philosophy of 'not caring'), a poise and emotional urbanity that imply spiritual achievements even amid the tawdry failures of nerve and faith, the pragmatic realism that characterized independent Ireland's social climate.

For Kavanagh, Joyce rather than Yeats had been the artist who in the recent past had come nearest to expressing the Irish consciousness (in the nineteenth century it had been William Carleton). There were other poets of the 1930s and 1940s who saw in Joyce's fully European imagination a more enabling example than the romantic idealism of a Yeats. The varying careers of Denis Devlin, Thomas MacGreevy and Brian Coffey all suggest that the lessons of Joycean modernism had been absorbed, the philosophic self-consciousness of the

Modernist enterprise admitted to Irish poetic activity. Each of these poets is as aware of the weight of Irish history as any nationalist *pur sang*, but is concerned to bear witness more to crises of individual consciousness, metaphysically conceived, than to collective distresses. In their work, poetry reveals itself as a privileged form of discourse in the intensity of its private soundings of human consciousness during a bleak period of history.

In both Devlin and Coffey, the problematic aspects of the Christian tradition are matter for recondite, often obscure, poetic reflection. How it is possible to be a Christian in a century of metaphysical anxiety troubles these almost uniquely earnest Irish poets. Devlin seeks to reconcile flesh and spirit in an understanding of sexual love and thereby to sustain a Christian tradition profoundly under threat in a modern world of political and philosophical nihilism. Coffey, with a Kierkegaardian attention to the movements of the ethical self, seeks personal authenticity in a knowledge of judgment; all the fictive definitions of self — national, political, personal — are a distraction from the painful, absolute encounter with one's moral being.

Both Devlin and Coffey were poets of exile, and that geographic fact is emblematic of the deep psychic dislocation that their work records. MacGreevey settled in Ireland, but not before he had almost completed his poetic career with a small body of verse that takes seriously the fragmentation of modern consciousness. In his poetry, the art of perception itself endures a subversive reordering. A sense of mystical otherness is the only metaphysical consolation afforded in the multiple perspectives of present. As the manifesto he jointly signed in 1932 proclaimed: 'In a world ruled by the hypnosis of positivism, we proclaim the autonomy of the poetic vision, the hegemony of the inner life over the outer life. . . . Poetry builds a nexus between the "I" and the "you", by leading the emotions of the sunken, telluric depths upwards towards the illumination of a collective reality and a totalistic universe.'[1]

In contrast to these sombre exiles, Louis MacNeice (1907-63), by reason of his English public school education and Oxford University classical training, was able to begin his career with a suave flourish of cosmopolitan disdain and repugnance for his native city. His poem, 'Belfast', not only is an indictment of a city, but is also a declaration of personal independence. His early work is marked by a modish, sequined elegance and *déraciné* disillusionment. The multiple perspectives of a precociously contemporary consciousness are celebrated in a verse that assumes a world of the 'incorrigibly plural'. But a strain of constitutional unease saves these early poems from a superficial, journalistic fashionability. The sense of doom conveyed is not merely that of the left-wing social critic, but of a sensibility that melancholy early marked for its own.

Ireland remained for Louis MacNeice a stratum of consciousness, laid down in a grim and death-haunted Northern Irish childhood, which the experience of metropolitan English social and literary life could not completely overlay. It was both an oppressive condition, in which an obsessional sense of historical disaster inhibited free thought and action, and a tantalizing, imaginative alternative to the empirical certainties of daily life in the twentieth century. For MacNeice, the poetry of Yeats represented the point where that ambiguity made itself most resonantly present. In his study of Yeats (published in 1941, two years after the poet's death, it was the first book-length estimate of Yeats's poetic *oeuvre*), MacNeice wrestled with both his own response to the Yeatsian achievement and to the Ireland in which it had its sources.

MacNeice's encounter with Yeats, during the early years of World War II, when he was reassessing his own view of the world, stimulated his innate interest in dreams, myth and folklore. Accordingly, his later work reckons with metaphysical possibilities in a characteristically wry, sceptical fashion. However, he does not allow these fully to enter the world of his poems. There, parable rather than symbol is employed to mediate between the private world of nightmare and a social world of failed opportunities and vanished hopes. MacNeice's late work achieves its most compelling effects in the apparently casual deployment of cliché and catch-phrase in a poetry of bleak, sardonic desperation. The poet's ambivalence about the status of the poetic act itself — in part attracted by the visionary Yeatsian mode and in part ironically dismissive of it as an archaic grandeur — gives way to a compulsive, zestful gloom, a Beckettian last throw of the linguistic dice. Poetic belatedness

1. This manifesto, *Poetry is Vertical*, was published in Paris in the magazine *transition* in 1932. It is reprinted in Thomas MacGreevy, *Collected Poems* (Dublin: New Writers' Press, 1971), pp. 73-74.

is transformed into a kind of uncomfortable virtue. The mood is one of stoical élan, the language that of a lethal insouciance.

Compared with their fellow Ulsterman's troubled sense of poetry's precarious existence and dubious worth, the work of both John Hewitt (1907-87) and W. R. Rodgers (1909-69) is marked by a shared conviction that the poet's role remains a significant one. In Hewitt there is an evident seriousness of purpose, which results from a conviction that the poet can serve as a social and moral critic. In Rodgers's work, a romantic's belief that the poet is endowed with a distinctive vision occasions much verbal display and emotional excess. To varying degrees, they both accept the burden of a historically charged local history, which invests their writing with a certain air of anachronism. For they do not share their Irish contemporaries' uncertainties, in a less starkly composed society, about the social significance of poetic endeavour. Indeed, there is a quaint innocence in the work of both poets. But in their attempts to come to terms with the society in which they found themselves (the Northern Ireland of unionist misrule, British misgovernment and sectarian division), they were without much in the way of a contemporary poetic model or truly enabling ideological resource. The Yeatsian stance of aristocratic, passionate disdain and dramatic involvement was an inappropriate archaism; the current English mode of Audenesque social engagement lacked full Irish credibility and authenticity.

In this context, Hewitt composed his earnest reflections on his Northern Irish dissenter and planter identity, providing in 'The Colony' the most convincing poetic analysis of the fraught history of his native province to appear before the present Northern Irish crisis erupted in 1968. Its success is that of the parable, the dogged moralizing of some of his less successful work mythologized in the fiction of Roman civic virtue and made universal by historical perspective. It was through his regional commitment that Hewitt achieved his most consistently secure if somewhat limiting poetic identity, which allowed him to write poems of quiet, sane reflectiveness on the natural world.

W. R. Rodgers's successes were those of momentary lyric intensity, as when the forces of puritanical religion and social convention provoke a sense of illicit celebration. In such poems ('The Net', 'Lent') his linguistic experimentalism (elsewhere the self-defeating stratagem of an inadequately grounded or realized poetic) becomes expressive of an exuberant sensuousness. But a romantic regard for sensation rather than thought vitiates Rodgers's more public poems, rendering even such a socially attentive and acidulous piece as 'White Christmas' oddly fey and archly spry. Such poems seem curiously archaic even as they announce their modish contemporaneity in clever effect and glib verbal associations.

The difficulties for the Irish poet of the post-Yeats generation were compounded by the fact that there was no Irish publishing house (for much of the period) through which they might have sought a national audience. Between 1926, when the company of Maunsel and Roberts (which had published much of the literature of the Literary Revival) closed, and 1951 when Liam Miller founded the Dolmen Press (through which Austin Clarke achieved his later fame), the Irish poet either sought British publication or published his work at his own expense. The differing careers of Clarke, Kavanagh, Devlin and Hewitt in various ways show the effects of this dismal situation. In a period when public life seemed to have endured a kind of spiritual retraction from the heady days of the movement for national independence, when a poet might only with unusual difficulty see his work in print, and when the literary pace seemed to be set by the realistic short story, it does not surprise that the dominant poetic form became the lyric of private disengagement.

At the heart of poetic endeavour in the four decades following Irish independence is an assumption that poetry represents a withdrawal to the lyric possibilities of true feeling, in an era of unsympathetic and inauthentic social experience. There was, however, a concurrent interest in the powers of the poetic sequence to transcend the social atomism of the purely lyric moment; it was as if the poetry of the period was seeking to renegotiate an entry to the public domain. Poems such as MacNeice's 'Autumn Journal', Kavanagh's 'The Great Hunger' and 'Lough Derg', Clarke's 'Mnemosyne Lay in Dust' and even Hewitt's 'The Colony' (although the latter is not properly a sequence; it moves from lyric resolution to lyric resolution) constitute a body of longer poems that seek to re-establish the rights of poetry in the larger arenas of twentieth-century historical experience. Their example was to prove enabling and artistically propitious when the general Irish crisis of the late 1960s and 1970s laid new personal and public demands on the poet, which could not easily be met in the predominantly lyric terms that recent Irish poetry had established as normative in the context of the post-Yeats period.

AUSTIN CLARKE

(1896-1974)

from: THE CATTLEDRIVE IN CONNAUGHT (1925)

[In the late 1920s and 1930s Austin Clarke established in his poetry a personal myth of the Gaelic and Celtic-Romanesque traditions in Irish cultural history, against which he measured the inadequacies of life in a newly independent Ireland.]

The Lost Heifer[1]

When the black herds of the rain were grazing
In the gap of the pure cold wind
And the watery hazes of the hazel
Brought her into my mind,
I thought of the last honey by the water
That no hive can find.

Brightness was drenching through the branches
When she wandered again,
Turning the silver out of dark grasses
Where the skylark had lain,
And her voice coming softly over the meadow
Was the mist becoming rain.

1. Clarke gives the following note to this poem: 'This is in the mode of the Jacobite Songs. The lines were written during a period when our national idealism suffered eclipse. The Heifer or Silk of the Kine is a secret name used by the Jacobite poets for Ireland.'

from: PILGRIMAGE AND OTHER POEMS (1929)

Pilgrimage

When the far south glittered
Behind the grey beaded plains,[1]
And cloudier ships were bitted
Along the pale waves,
The showery breeze — that plies
A mile from Ara[2] — stood
And took our boat on sand:
There by dim wells the women tied
A wish on thorn,[3] while rainfall
Was quiet as the turning of books
In the holy schools at dawn.

Grey holdings of rain
Had grown less with the fields,
As we came to that blessed place
Where hail and honey meet.
O Clonmacnoise[4] was crossed
With light: those cloistered scholars,
Whose knowledge of the gospel
Is cast as metal in pure voices,
Were all rejoicing daily,
And cunning hands with cold and jewels
Brought chalices to flame.

Loud above the grassland,
In Cashel[5] of the towers,
We heard with the yellow candles
The chanting of the hours,
White clergy saying High Mass,
A fasting crowd at prayer,
A choir that sang before them;
And in stained glass the holy day
Was sainted as we passed
Beyond that chancel where the dragons
Are carved upon the arch.

1. Clarke provides the following note: 'The plains of Galway are covered with countless field-walls of loose stone and boulders forming a strange pre-historic landscape, fascinating when the light of day is seen through the myriad chinks.'
2. The Aran Islands.
3. Superstitious remnants of old pagan rituals.
4. One of Ireland's principal monastic sites, in County Offaly.
5. A monastery in County Tipperary.

Treasured with chasuble,
Sun-braided, rich cloak'd wine-cup,
We saw, there, iron handbells,
Great annals in the shrine
A high-king bore to battle:
Where, from the branch of Adam,
The noble forms of language —
Brighter than green or blue enamels
Burned in white bronze — embodied
The wings and fiery animals
Which veil the chair of God.

Beyond a rocky townland
And that last tower where ocean
Is dim as haze, a sound
Of wild confession rose:
Black congregations moved
Around the booths of prayer
To hear a saint reprove them;
And from his boat he raised a blessing
To souls that had come down
The holy mountain of the west
Or wailed still in the cloud.

Light in the tide of Shannon
May ride at anchor half
The day and, high in spar-top
Or leather sails of their craft,
Wine merchants will have sleep;
But on a barren isle,
Where Paradise is praised
At daycome, smaller than the sea-gulls,
We heard white Culdees[6] pray
Until our hollow ship was kneeling
Over the longer waves.

6. A monastic order.

The Scholar[1]

Summer delights the scholar
With knowledge and reason.
Who is happy in hedgerow
Or meadow as he is?

Paying no dues to the parish,
He argues in logic
And has no care of cattle
But a satchel and stick.

The showery airs grow softer,
He profits from his ploughland
For the share of the schoolmen
Is a pen in hand.

When midday hides the reaping,
He sleeps by a river
Or comes to the stone plain
Where the saints live.

But in winter by the big fires,
The ignorant hear his fiddle,
And he battles on the chessboard,
As the land lords bid him.

1. Clarke gives the following note to this poem: 'A free paraphrase of an anonymous poem, "Dán Mac Leighinn", discovered at Maynooth Library.'

from:
NIGHT AND MORNING (1938)

[In 'Tenebrae', Clarke confronts the conflict in his psyche between a rational conscience and the residual power of religious faith.]

Tenebrae[1]

This is the hour that we must mourn
With tallows on the black triangle,
Night has a napkin deep in fold
To keep the cup;[2] yet who dare pray
If all in reason should be lost,
The agony of man betrayed
At every station of the cross?[3]

O when the forehead is too young,
Those centuries of mortal anguish,
Dabbed by a consecrated thumb[4]
That crumbles into dust, will bring
Despair with all that we can know;

1. The Roman catholic Holy Week ritual, when all the lights in the church are extinguished to symbolize both Christ's passion and death and the disciples' desertion, the world left dark.
2. The allusion is to Christ's prayer in the Garden of Gethsemane — 'remove this cup from me: nevertheless not my will, but thine, be done' — and to the chalice used in Holy Communion.
3. Refers to the various stages of Christ's passion, represented in Roman catholic churches by fourteen tableaux.
4. The ritual of baptism.

And there is nothing left to sing,
Remembering our innocence.

I hammer on that common door,
Too frantic in my superstition,
Transfix with nails that I have broken,
The angry notice of the mind.[5]
Close as the thought that suffers him,
The habit every man in time
Must wear beneath his ironed shirt.

An open mind disturbs the soul,
And in disdain I turn my back
Upon the sun that makes a show
Of half the world, yet still deny
The pain that lives within the past,
The flame sinking upon the spike,
Darkness that man must dread at last.

5. A passage with Lutheran connotations. Martin Luther nailed ninety-five theses to the door of the Castle Church in Wittenberg in 1517, an act associated with the beginning of the protestant Reformation.

from:
ANCIENT LIGHTS (1955)

[In 'Ancient Lights' Clarke celebrated a moment of personal liberation. It is an irony typical of Clarke's work that this poem in praise of illumination requires extensive annotation of its manifold obscurities.]

Ancient Lights[1]

When all of us wore smaller shoes
And knew the next world better than
The knots we broke, I used to hurry
On missions of my own to Capel
Street, Bolton Street and Granby Row[2]
To see what man has made. But darkness
Was roomed with fears. Sleep, stripped by woes
I had been taught, beat door, leaped landing,
Lied down the bannisters of naught.

1. In England and the Ireland of Clarke's boyhood, the inscription 'Ancient Lights' was sometimes put on the face or side of a house adjacent to a site on which lofty buildings could be erected; the object being to give warning that the owner would have grounds for action against any person who obstructed the access of light to his windows. Clarke accordingly serves notice in this poem that the dark forces in religion will not in the future be allowed to obstruct the light of personal liberation, which is celebrated here.
2. Streets in Dublin near Clarke's childhood home.

Being sent to penance,[3] come Saturday,
I shuffled slower than my sins should.
My fears were candle-spiked at side-shrines,
Rays lengthened them in stained-glass. Confided
To night again, my grief bowed down,
Heard hand on shutter-knob.[4] Did I
Take pleasure, when alone — how much —
In a bad thought, immodest look
Or worse, unnecessary touch?

Closeted in the confessional,
I put on flesh, so many years
Were added to my own, attempted
In vain to keep Dominican[5]
As much i' the dark as I was, mixing
Whispered replies with his low words;
Then shuddered past the crucifix,
The feet so hammered, daubed-on
  blood-drip,
Black with lip-scrimmage[6] of the damned.

Once as I crept from the church-steps,
Beside myself, the air opened
On purpose. Nature read in a flutter
An evening lesson above my head.
Atwirl beyond the leadings,[7] corbels,[8]
A cage-bird came among sparrows
(The moral inescapable)
Plucked, roof-mired, all in mad bits. O
The pizzicato of its wires!

Goodness of air can be proverbial:
That day, by the kerb at Rutland Square,[9]
A bronze bird fabled out of trees,
Mailing the spearheads of the railings,
Sparrow at nails, I hailed the skies
To save the tiny dropper, found
Appetite gone. A child of clay
Has blustered it away. Pity
Could raise some littleness from dust.

3. A reference to confession, the sacrament that in the catholic rite is by private verbal admission of sin to a priest, who prescribes certain religious obligations as mortification as he grants forgiveness.
4. An allusion to the confessional box in a catholic church.
5. A priest of the Dominican order.
6. In his autobiographical work, *Twice Round the Black Church* (1962), Clarke records how in the church where he made his regular childhood confession, the nailed feet of Jesus on a crucifix had been made black by the kisses of the faithful.
7. i.e. the lead of roofs.
8. Projections from the faces of walls which support weights.
9. A Dublin square on the northside of the river Liffey, now called Parnell Square.

What Sunday clothes can change us now
Or humble orders in black and white?[10]
Stinking with centuries the act
Of thought. So think, man, as Augustine[11]
Did, dread the ink-bespattered ex-monk,[12]
And keep your name. No, let me abandon
Night's jakes.[13] Self-persecuted of late
Among the hatreds of rent Europe,
Poetry burns at a different stake.

Still, still I remember awful downpour
Cabbing[14] Mountjoy Street, spun loneliness
Veiling almost the Protestant church,
Two backyards from my very home,
I dared to shelter at locked door.
There, walled by heresy, my fears
Were solved. I had absolved myself:
Feast-day effulgence, as though I gained
For life a plenary indulgence.[15]

The sun came out, new smoke flew up,
The gutters of the Black Church[16] rang
With services. Waste water mocked
The ballcocks: down-pipes sparrowing,
And all around the spires of Dublin
Such swallowing in the air, such cowling[17]
To keep high offices pure: I heard
From shore to shore, the iron gratings
Take half our heavens with a roar.

10. Priests of the Dominican order wear a white cassock (a full-length garment) and a black scapular (a dress-like garment covering the shoulders and descending front and back, usually open at the sides).
11. St Augustine, bishop of Hippo (A.D. 353-430), here identified with what Clarke believed were life-denying aspects of catholicism.
12. A reference to the protestant reformer Martin Luther (1483-1546), who once threw an inkhorn at an apparition he believed to be the devil.
13. A privy.
14. i.e. making muddy or dirty (dialect).
15. In catholic teaching, the remission in full of the temporal punishment due to sin that has already been forgiven.
16. A Church of Ireland (protestant) church on Dublin's northside, near Clarke's childhood home.
17. The covering of chimney pots, which improves the drafts and enables noxious fumes to escape more quickly.

from: FLIGHT TO AFRICA (1963)

['The Last Republicans' is a poem in tribute to the die-hard Republicans who remained militarily active after Eamon de Valera's conversion to constitutional politics in 1927. They all suffered for their idealism.]

The Last Republicans

Because their fathers had been drilled,
Formed fours among the Dublin hills,
They marched together, countermarched
Along the Liffey valley, by larch-wood,
Spruce, pine road. Now, what living shout
Can halt them? Nothing of their faces
Is left, the breath has been blown out
Of them into far lonely places.
Seán Glynn pined sadly in prison. Seán
McNeela, Tony Darcy, John
McGaughey died on hunger-strike,
Wasting in the ribbed light of dawn.
They'd been on the run, but every dyke
Was spy. We shame them all. George Plant,
Quick fighter and a Protestant,
Patrick McGrath and Richard Goss,
Maurice O'Neill with Thomas Harte
Were executed when Dev's party
Had won the country pitch-and-toss,[1]
Pat Dermody, John Kavanagh,
John Griffith, John Casey, black-and-tanned[2]
At Mountjoy Gaol, young Charlie Kerins
Was roped; we paid five pounds to Pierpont,[3]
The Special Branch[4] castled their plans,
Quicklimed the last Republicans.

1. A game in which coins are thrown at a mark or pitched in the air. The winning combination is usually a pair of coins that fall head up.
2. A punning reference to a notorious auxiliary force that committed many atrocities in Ireland during the War of Independence.
3. The English hangman imported to perform executions by the Irish Free State in the absence of any local occupant of the position of official hangman.
4. The state security branch of the police force who worked out of Dublin Castle.

[In 'Martha Blake At Fifty-One' the poet draws a poignant sketch of a sexually repressed catholic spinster, with an exacting realism that reminds one of the Joyce of *Dubliners*. The poem, in fact, is set mainly in Rathgar, a Dublin suburb.]

Martha Blake at Fifty-One

Early, each morning, Martha Blake
  Walked, angeling the road,
To Mass in the Church of the Three Patrons.
  Sanctuary lamp glowed

And the clerk halo'ed the candles
  On the High Altar. She knelt
Illumined. In gold-hemmed alb,[1]
  The priest intoned. Wax melted.

Waiting for daily Communion, bowed head
  At rail, she hears a murmur.
Latin is near. In a sweet cloud
  That cherub'd, all occurred.
The voice went by. To her pure thought,
  Body was a distress
And soul, a sigh. Behind her denture,
  Love lay, a helplessness.

Then, slowly walking after Mass
  Down Rathgar Road, she took out
Her Yale key, put a match to gas-ring,
  Half filled a saucepan, cooked
A fresh egg lightly, with tea, brown bread,
  Soon, taking off her blouse
And skirt, she rested, pressing the Crown
  Of Thorns[2] until she drowsed.

In her black hat, stockings, she passed
  Nylons to a nearby shop
And purchased, daily, with downcast eyes,
  Fillet of steak or a chop.
She simmered it on a low jet,
  Having a poor appetite,
Yet never for an hour felt better
  From dilatation, tightness.

She suffered from dropped stomach, heartburn
  Scalding, water-brash[3]
And when she brought her wind up, turning
  Red with the weight of mashed
Potato, mint could not relieve her.
  In vain her many belches,
For all below was swelling, heaving
  Wamble,[4] gurgle, squelch.

She lay on the sofa with legs up,
  A decade[5] on her lip,
At four o'clock, taking a cup
  Of lukewarm water, sip

By sip, but still her daily food
  Repeated and the bile
Tormented her. In a blue hood,
  The Virgin sadly smiled.

When she looked up, the Saviour showed
  His Heart, daggered with flame
And, from the mantel-shelf, St. Joseph
  Bent, disapproving. Vainly
She prayed for in the whatnot corner,
  The new Pope was frowning. Night
And day, dull pain, as in her corns,
  Recounted every bite.

She thought of St. Teresa,[6] floating
  On motes of a sunbeam,
Carmelite[7] with scatterful robes,
  Surrounded by demons,
Small black boys in their skin. She gaped
  At Hell: a muddy passage
That led to nothing, queer in shape,
  A cupboard closely fastened.

Sometimes, the walls of the parlour
  Would fade away. No plod
Of feet, rattle of van, in Garville
  Road. Soul now gone abroad
Where saints, like medieval serfs,
  Had laboured. Great sun-flower shone.
Our Lady's Chapel was borne by seraphs,
  Three leagues beyond Ancona.[8]

High towns of Italy, the plain
  Of France, were known to Martha
As she read in a holy book. The sky-blaze
  Nooned at Padua,[9]
Marble grotto of Bernadette.[10]
  Rose-scatterers. New saints
In tropical Africa where the tsetse
  Fly probes, the forest taints.

1. A full-length, white linen vestment, worn by the priest at Mass.
2. An iconographic representation of the crucified Christ.
3. An eructation or belching of water from the stomach.
4. nausea.
5. A decade of the rosary — in catholic practice, the *Our Father,* followed by the prayer *Hail Mary,* repeated ten times, itself followed by the prayer *Glory Be to the Father.*
6. St Teresa of Avila (1515-82) was a Spanish conventual reformer and mystic. References in this stanza are to St Teresa's visions of the Devil as a black man and of the entrance to Hell.
7. An order of Roman catholic mendicant friars. St Teresa entered the Carmelite convent at Avila; she had many visions and trances, which she believed were caused by the devil, and she tried to exorcize them by penitential exercises, including flagellation.
8. An Italian coastal city visited by St Thérèse of Lisieux (1873-97), a French Carmelite, who also experienced visions.
9. A university city, twenty miles west of Venice.
10. St Bernadette (1844-79) claimed to have seen a vision of the Virgin Mary in Lourdes, France.

Teresa had heard the Lutherans
  Howling on red-hot spit,
And grill, men who had searched for truth
  Alone in Holy Writ.
So Martha, fearful of flame lashing
  Those heretics, each instant,
Never dealt in the haberdashery
  Shop, owned by two Protestants.

In ambush of night, an angel wounded
  The Spaniard to the heart
With iron tip on fire. Swooning
  With pain and bliss as a dart
Moved up and down within her bowels
  Quicker, quicker, each cell
Sweating as if rubbed up with towels,
  Her spirit rose and fell.

St. John of the Cross,[11] her friend, in prison
  Awaits the bridal night,
Paler than lilies, his wizened skin
  Flowers. In fifths of flight,
Senses beyond seraphic thought,
  In that divinest clasp,
Enfolding of kisses that cauterize,
  Yield to the soul-spasm.

Cunning in body had come to hate
  All this and stirred by mischief
Haled Martha from heaven. Heart palpitates
  And terror in her stiffens.
Heart misses one beat, two . . . flutters . . . stops.
  Her ears are full of sound.
Half fainting, she stares at the grandfather clock
  As if it were overwound.

The fit had come. Ill-natured flesh
  Despised her soul. No bending
Could ease rib. Around her heart, pressure
  Of wind grew worse. Again,
Again, armchaired without relief,
  She eructated, phlegm
In mouth, forgot the woe, the grief,
  Foretold at Bethlehem.[12]

11. St John of the Cross, San Juan de la Cruz (1542-91), a Carmelite monk and one of the greatest of all mystic poets. His major poem *Cántico espiritual (Spiritual Canticle)* is an allegory of the soul's mystic love for God, expressed in erotic terms; it is drawn from the biblical Song of Solomon. The subsequent references to *bridal night*, *Paler than lilies*, are taken from the *Spiritual Canticle*.
12. Possibly a reference to Luke 11. 17-20.

Tired of the same faces, side-altars,
  She went to the Carmelite Church
At Johnson's Court, confessed her faults,
  There, once a week, purchased
Tea, butter in Chatham St. The pond
  In St. Stephen's Green was grand.
She watched the seagulls, ducks, black swan,
  Went home by the 15 tram.

Her beads in hand, Martha became
  A member of the Third Order,[13]
Saved from long purgatorial pain,
  Brown habit and white cord
Her own when cerges[14] had been lit
  Around her coffin. She got
Ninety-five pounds on loan for her bit
  Of clay in the common plot.

Often she thought of a quiet sick-ward,
  Nuns, with delicious ways,
Consoling the miserable: quick
  Tea, toast on trays. Wishing
To rid themselves of her, kind neighbours
  Sent for the ambulance,
Before her brother and sister could hurry
  To help her. Big gate clanged.

No medical examination
  For the new patient. Doctor
Had gone to Cork on holidays.
  Telephone sprang. Hall-clock
Proclaimed the quarters. Clatter of heels
  On tiles. Corridor, ward,
A-whirr with the electric cleaner,
  The creak of window cord.

She could not sleep at night. Feeble
  And old, two women raved
And cried to God. She held her beads.
  O how could she be saved?
The hospital had this and that rule.
  Day-chill unshuttered. Nun, with
Thermometer in reticule,[15]
  Went by. The women mumbled.

Mother Superior believed
  That she was obstinate, self-willed.

13. A religious order for lay persons.
14. tapers.
15. A small bag, made of woven material.

Sisters ignored her, hands-in-sleeves,
  Beside a pantry shelf
Or counting pillow-case, soiled sheet.
  They gave her purgatives.
Soul-less, she tottered to the toilet.
  Only her body lived.

Wasted by colitis, refused
  The daily sacrament
By regulation, forbidden use
  Of bed-pan, when meals were sent up,
Behind a screen, she lay, shivering,
  Unable to eat. The soup
Was greasy, mutton, beef or liver,
  Cold. Kitchen has no scruples.

The Nuns had let the field in front
  As an Amusement Park,
Merry-go-round, a noisy month, all
  Heltering-skeltering at darkfall,
Mechanical music, dipper, hold-tights,
  Rifle-crack, crash of dodgems.
The ward, godless with shadow, lights,
  How could she pray to God?

Unpitied, wasting with diarrhea
  And the constant strain,
Poor Child of Mary[16] with one idea,
  She ruptured a small vein,
Bled inwardly to jazz. No priest
  Came. She had been anointed
Two days before, yet knew no peace:
  Her last breath, disappointed.

16. A catholic women's sodality.

[*Flight to Africa* also contained this poem, one of a series described by Clarke as 'free variations on Gaelic songs by Turlough O'Carolan (1670-1738), poet, harpist, composer.' In these poems Clarke identified with the more sexually uninhibited traditions of an authentic Gaelic Ireland, in contrast to the puritanism, which he believed had deformed modern expressions of a Gaelic identity.]

Eighteenth Century Harp Songs

I: MABEL KELLY

  Lucky the husband
Who puts his hand beneath her head.
  They kiss without scandal
Happiest two near feather-bed.
He sees the tumble of brown hair
Unplait, the breasts, pointed and bare
  When nightdress shows
  From dimple to toe-nail,
And Mabel glowing in it, here, there, everywhere.

  Music might listen
  To her least whisper,
Learn every note, for all are true.
  While she is speaking,
  Her voice goes sweetly
To charm the herons in their musing.
Her eyes are modest, blue, their darkness
Small rooms of thought, but when they sparkle
  Upon a feast-day,
  Glasses are meeting,
Each raised to Mabel Kelly, our toast and darling.

Gone now are many Irish ladies
Who kissed and fondled, their very pet-names
Forgotten, their tibia[1] degraded.
She takes their sky. Her smile is famed.
Her praise is scored by quill and pencil.
  Harp and spinet
  Are in her debt
And when she plays or sings, melody is content.

  No man who sees her
  Will feel uneasy.
He goes his way, head high, however tired.
  Lamp loses light
  When placed beside her.
She is the pearl and being of all Ireland
Foot, hand, eye, mouth, breast, thigh and instep,
    all that we desire.
Tresses that pass small curls as if to touch the
    ground:
  So many prizes
  Are not divided
Her beauty is her own and she is not proud.

1. Possibly refers here to an ancient kind of flute.

from:
MNEMOSYNE LAY IN DUST (1966)

[In *Mnemosyne Lay in Dust,* Clarke described the experience of mental breakdown and the slow process of recovery in St Patrick's Hospital in Dublin. Section VIII confronts the despair of madness.]

VIII

The heavens opened. With a scream
The blackman at his night-prayers
Had disappeared in blasphemy,
And irons beds were bared;
Day was unshuttered again,
The elements had lied,
Ashing the faces of madmen
Until God's likeness died.

Napoleon took his glittering vault
To be a looking-glass.
Lord Mitchell, pale and suffering,
Fell to the ground in halves.
The cells were filling. Christopher
O'Brien, strapped in pain,
For all the rage of syphilis,
Had millions in his brain.

James Dunn leaped down the dormitory,
Thought has no stopping-place,
His bright bed was a corner shop,
Opening, closing, late.
Behind a grille, the unfrocked priest
Had told his own confession:
Accidents in every street
Rang the Angelus.[1]

Flight beyond flight, new stories flashed
Or darkened with affliction
Until the sweet choir of Mount Argus[2]
Was heard at every window,
Was seen in every wing. The blackman
Kept laughing at his night-prayers
For somebody in white had taken
His photograph downstairs.

When sleep has shot the bolt and bar,
And reason fails at midnight
Dreading that every thought at last
Must stand in our own light
Forever, sinning without end:
O pity in their pride
And agony of wrong, the men
In whom God's image died.

1. A church bell, rung twice daily to remind the faithful of the Virgin Mary's submission to the will of God.
2. A Dublin church, in Harold's Cross.

from: ORPHIDE AND OTHER POEMS (1970)

['The Healing of Mis' employs a Celtic myth to celebrate the healing powers of sexuality.]

The Healing of Mis[1]

Along that mountain in the south named after
her, Mis,
The only daughter of Dáire Mor, the King
Of Munster, escaped after the battle near
Cahirconlish
Hurled by Fionn and the Fianna[2] from shingle
To rock against the invaders who had sailed out
of Greece
And Spain. Her fingers a-drip with a father's
blood, she
Fled up a forest, echoing foreign cries. Streams
That passed her ran down to faster flood.

Fear put her in caverns, in greenth of fern, on
branches that grieved
About her and for three centuries her mind
Was lost. A raggedness in thorn-set bramble, in
greed
Of gorse, she sprang from gorge to cave-mouth,
hind
Or hare in her claws, devoured it raw. A
nakedness
Blue'd by the sea-gales that blew from
Dursey,[3] on freezing
Ridges, she lanked her lengthening hair, a
mantle that guarded
The bushiness above her knees.

In winter when turf was raked under the
household cauldron,

1. Clarke based this poem on an ancient Irish tale, *The Romance of Mis and Dubh Ruis*. The Irish text has been edited by Brian Ó Cúiv, but Clarke worked from a translation by his friend David Greene. In a note to the poem, Clarke tells us: 'This ancient story seems to anticipate the curative methods of Freud. . . . I have ventured to add a few stanzas about dream-analysis.'

The tale tells of the daughter of the King of Munster in the time of Fionn during the sixth century. Mis goes mad when, in grief, she drinks the blood of her slaughtered father. She flees to the mountains and wildness of remote County Kerry, where she remains for three centuries, crazed and wild on Slieve Mish mountain. In the ninth century, a successor to her father on the throne of Munster invites a harpist, Dubh Ruis, to reclaim her. He does this by seducing her.
2. The Fianna were the warrior brotherhood of the Fenian Cycle, led by Finn MacCumhaill (McCool).
3. Dursey is an island off the coast of West Cork.

Stories were told of a Geilt[4] that flew over forest top and
Cliff to pray from the sky. Sometimes a shepherd, hatted
By crack of twig, had a glimpse of hairiness
Crawling from filth and hurried back to safe pasturage.
Those cloudy cantreds were dreaded and accursed
For a legend endured from the Paps of Dana to Mount Brandon[5]
Of a lonely sorrow time could not cure.

It happened in the third century that word was brought to Felim,
The King of Munster, as he came from the boar-hunt in a local
Forest. Riding thoughtfully back to Cashel, he felt
Such pity that when brands flickered in the banquet-hall,
He offered tribute and tax to any man there who could cure
The Woe of Mis. 'Greatness, your wish will be fulfilled.'
A harper called, braving from a corner. 'Who's that?' 'Duv Ruis.
She'll listen to strings, but I need a fistful

Of gold and silver coins.' 'Harper, take as much
As back can carry.' 'And a farl[6] from the royal griddle,
Your Grace?' 'It's yours. What else?' 'Nothing. All can touch
The bottom of female complaint.' 'Hard to unriddle.
Faith-healers like to darken their say. But mine is plain. Let
My steward be summoned to give this man the sum on credit.
If he fails to perform the feat in three months, he has little to gain,
For he will pay the debt with his head.'

Laughter unbarred the door: the harper went into the night-rain,
Journeyed by dysart[7] and dyke, strummed for half-loaf
And the yellowness of ale, sheltered in house or hidy-
Hole, came to a white battle of waves that broke
Along four promontories. In a sombre glen
Between the uphills, he stole into the forest of
Slieve Mis. At times a lonely bird-cry vaulted the silence.
He stopped, listened from a dry course.

When young beaks had been filled and pickaback insects were safe
As air, Duv Ruis rested awhile in a sun-scented
Vale, then hastened to spread his travelling cloak in the shade
Of a blossoming quicken-tree, tossed his ring-coins up,
A silver and golden frolic of profit-making pelf,
Then arranged them carefully in emblems
Along the cloth-edge, lay on his back to greet the Geilt
Opened his flap, exposed himself.

Holding his harp, the consolation of his bosom,
He played a suantree[8] with grace-notes that enspelled
Traditional tunes and, smiling quietly at his ruse,
Waited. Soon his senses knew that loneliness
Stood by, a bareness modestly draped in tangle-black hair,
With timeless hands, listening to the special
Melling[9] that drew and soothed her mind as she stared
In surmise at his rising flesh.

'Are you a man?' she asked. 'I am.' 'What's that you are holding?'
'A harp.' 'I remember the triangle.' 'Pluck it.'
'You will not harm me?' 'I won't.' She tapped the sounding-board,
Laughed as it answered her. 'What's this I'm touching

4. A mad person (from the Irish).
5. Cantreds are districts. The Paps of Dana are mountains in County Kerry. Mount Brandon is a famous mountain in the same county.
6. A flour or oatmeal cake.
7. A deserted place.
8. A soothing song.
9. Blending and mixing; in this instance, of musical notes.

Below?' 'A couple of pouched eggs I like to
carry.'
'Can you lay them as the poult-hen?' 'Only
the glair.'[10]
'What's this so high and mighty?' 'Marry-come-
up, my dear:
The wand of the feat as scholars declare!'

He spun the gold and silver pieces into a reel
Around her temples, an oriental garland,
Faster, faster they went. She clapped. 'I know
that gleam
For I recall the cargoes of bullion from the
harbours
Of Tyre and Gaza.'[11] Eyes cannot gaze at the
feat for it closes
The lids in bliss.' 'Like this?' She palmed the
sun. 'Yes.'
'Perform the feat,' she commanded. Powerfulness
held him closely.
'I cannot. I'm much too hungry.'

'Wait here. I'll bring you venison.' She leaped
over
The quicken-tree with lifted head. He hurried
To pick up kindling in the forest, gather arm-
loads
Of withered branches, fanned them into up-
rushers,
Cracklers, with a flick of his flint, set large
stones
For a nearby cooking-pit the Fianna
Had used, then waited, uneasy as his shoes. At
last
She rose above the rowan[12] branches,
Lightly bearing a buck on her shoulder. 'Here's
a meal
For both our bellies . . . Look, day is aflame
on the edge
Of night. Run, run!' 'It's only faggots turned
into heat.'
He poked the stones from the ash and the
slope sent them,
Red-hot, into the paven[13] pit. He coiled up
Each sweeping tress from her filthy body, saw
Her nipples harden into blackberries. 'Bogholes
have spoiled them.
But soon that pair will be redder than haws . . .

I stumbled on a helmet in sand near to washed-
in wreckage,
Brimmed it from a high cascade, going
And coming patiently to fill your bath.' He
sloshed
Himself as he lathered her down, soaped her
skin of her back
With a lump of deer-fat, washed the crack
between the slurried
Cheeks, like a mother, turned her round,
picked crabs[14] from
Her sporran, nit-nurseries hidden in tiny flurries
Through tangled tresses, then began
All over again. He soaped her body, washed it
down,
Drawing the wad of deer-skin to-and-fro
Softly between her glossing thighs, turned her
around
And frizzled her neglected faddle,[15] noticed
It needed a thorough-going cleansing inside and
out, scrubbed
And douched it, cursing her ignorance, lack of
care,

Then coiled her tresses neatly after he
currycombed them
As if she was a gainly mare.

'Now canter into dryness, my filly.' She
galloped, instead, up
The smooth slope, became a momentary
Speck on the summit, then flew down again into
his arms —
The favourite no ostler had led across the
Curragh[16]
Or mounted yet. 'Lie down with me under the
blossoms.'
He entered so quietly she never felt it
Until a pang shook her. Fearing involuntary loss,
He waited, obedient as she helped
His through the hymen. Then at the thrusting of
the wand,
Her eyelids closed in bliss. The flowers of the
quicken-tree

10. The white of an egg; thence, semen.
11. Tyre, in the Lebanon, and Gaza, in Palestine, were important trading centres in the ancient world.
12. The mountain ash.
13. A poetic form of paved.
14. crab-lice, parasitic insects.
15. To 'faddle' is to fondle or caress. Clarke here is using the word for the pudendum.
16. A broad, grassy plain in County Kildare, famous for its horses.

Were poppies. Both drowsed but how could they stop fingers that wandered
Until their passion was no longer tender?
'Buck, buck me,' she cried, 'as the stag in rut.' Wildly crouping
Herself while he husbanded roughly, she spent with him in the spasm
That blurs the sight. They lay without words. Soon limbs drooped
Towards sleep in the deepening grass.

They woke for late supper. He cut and crusted two fillets in dampish
Clay, left them to bake until the savour
Called to their mouths. He gave her thick slices of bannock.[17] When
The hot meal was over, she said: 'Why do you delay
The feat of the wand again?' 'We must prepare the bridal
Bed.' Waist-deep in ferns, he gathered sunny swathes.
She ran to pull the fennel bloom, wildering woodbine
And made a border of braided daisies.

She did not wake until the sun-god had gone by
Next day. Hidden in foliage, he could hear
Her lamenting: 'Ba, be, ba, pleasant the gold and silver on
Our double bed. Pleasant the grace-notes that appeared
Above his breast. But better than money in a ring
Coining more bright ones, better than skiddle,'[18] she desponded,
As she searched around in vain, hair mantling her from the mist,
'His pouched eggs and the feat of the wand.'

Climbing down from the leaves to comfort her, he thought:[19] 'I must trim it
Tomorrow.' He held her a minute then led her to the glowing
Branches that waited for her beyond the forest dimness,
While steaks were broiling, he showed her the honeycomb,
The goat-cheese, the heather-ale, he had bought for the feast at
A farm near Ventry.[20] After they had eaten, idled
And ale'd, he murmured: 'Tell me about those curious dreams.'

'How did you guess?' 'From stir and dire cry.'
'High tiers of oars from the Mediterranean were dipping whiteness
In blueness. Ships swept from archipelagoes
Into surds[21] of sound. Hundreds of bucklers[22] lightened
Through a conflagratory storm: "Stromboli!" "Stromboli!"[23]
Look-outs were calling down from a red hail of cinders. Main-sails
Were furling as keels hurtled from fumeroles.[24]
Finger-tips of diluvian fire were piling their rains
On temple, ziggurat.[25] I ziggzagged, stole

In another dream through labyrinthine corridors
Where serpentries of momentary flashes
Revealed the figurative walls, as iron doors
Clanged at my heels. Clueless in a subterranean
Maze, I reached a hall where darkness was worshipping
Itself. The unseen, the unheard-of, moved in self-horror
Around me. Yielding to the force of writhesome limbs,
Unvirgined by the Minotaur [26]—

17. A round flat bread, made from wheat or barley.
18. A contemptuous term for tea or any insipid liquid.
19. The next three stanzas introduce the 'dream analysis' to the tale.
20. A town on the Dingle peninsula in County Kerry.
21. Voiceless sounds, but also suggesting the mathematical surds — i.e. not expressible in rational numbers.
22. arm shields.
23. A Mediterranean island, off north-eastern Sicily, where there is an active volcano.
24. Or fumaroles; holes or orifices in volcanic regions, from which gases and vapours issue.
25. A temple tower of the Babylonians; also a pinnacle, the top of a mountain. Both senses apply here.
26. The legendary monster with the body of a man and the head of a bull, shut into the labyrinth built for King Minos of Crete by the Athenian architect, Daedalus. Minos fed the monster annually with seven young men and seven young women. Theseus volunteered as one of the victims and, with the help of Ariadne, slew the Minotaur and found his way out of the labyrinth.

I knew my father.' 'Wrong dreams are dispelled with the help of music
And the wand.' Soon Nature showed them more delightful
Ways as they heaved under the mantle. How could he refuse
The interplay of limbs that orientalised them?
Daily he scrutinised, scrubbed her, rosied all her skin.
They stayed in the mountain forest twelve weeks or more
Hugging his harp at night he lulled her to sleep. Then, thinly,
Tried to serve the longing that woke her.

So Mis was healed. Often she hunted in the forest depths
While he kept house, moss lodge. When rain-clouds hid
All Ireland, and waters ran down their tumultuous steps,
Unseen, they warmed themselves in a cave by crowdering
Flame. O she might have come from a Sidhe-mound[27] for the gods
Had made her a mortal. 'I'll examine her future dreams,
Interpret them, find in chance word much she has forgotten;
Signs and symbols are underneath.'

Early one morning they came down by the turns of a dry course
And coombe[28] to the highway. Gaily she wore the blue gown,
Shoes and Tyrian cloak he had brought her. A roan horse
Waited, a servant at the bridle. Her arms were around him
As he rode by ford, rath,[29] to be invested. Goodness
Blared from the trumpets faring them to the high door
That had laughed him one night from the feast. Blessing,
Victory, to him who relates this story!

27. A fairy mound.

28. A small valley.

29. A circular mound or earthworks.

PATRICK KAVANAGH

(1904-67)

from:
THE GREAT HUNGER (1942)

[Patrick Kavanagh's long poem, *The Great Hunger*, explores in fourteen sections the depressed life of a bachelor farmer in County Monaghan. Section III sets the repressed miseries of the poem's central persona against a vision of the mystical presence of nature.]

III

Poor Paddy Maguire, a fourteen-hour day
He worked for years. It was he that lit the fire
And boiled the kettle and gave the cows their hay.
His mother tall hard as a Protestant spire
Came down the stairs barefoot at the kettle-call
And talked to her son sharply: 'Did you let
The hens out, you?' She had a venomous drawl
And a wizened face like moth-eaten leatherette.
Two black cats peeped between the banisters
And gloated over the bacon-fizzling pan.
Outside the window showed tin canisters.
The snipe of Dawn fell like a whirring stone
And Patrick on a headland stood alone.

The pull is on the traces, it is March
And a cold old black wind is blowing from Dundalk.
The twisting sod rolls over on her back —
The virgin screams before the irresistible sock.
No worry on Maguire's mind this day
Except that he forgot to bring his matches.
'Hop back there Polly, hoy back, woa, wae,'

From every second hill a neighbour watches
With all the sharpened interest of rivalry.
Yet sometimes when the sun comes through a gap
These men know God the Father in a tree:
The Holy Spirit is the rising sap,
And Christ will be the green leaves that will come
At Easter from the sealed and guarded tomb.

Primroses and the unearthly start of ferns
Among the blackthorn shadows in the ditch,
A dead sparrow and an old waistcoat. Maguire
learns
As the horses turn slowly round the which is
which
Of love and fear and things half born to mind.
He stands between the plough-handles and he sees
At the end of a long furrow his name signed
Among the poets, prostitutes. With all miseries
He is one. Here with the unfortunate
Who for half-moments of paradise
Pay out good days and wait and wait
For sunlight-woven cloaks. O to be wise
As Respectability that knows the price of all things
And marks God's truth in pounds and pence
and farthings.

from:
A SOUL FOR SALE (1947)

Advent[1]

We have tested and tasted too much, lover—
Through a chink too wide there comes in no
wonder.
But here in the Advent-darkened room
Where the dry black bread and the sugarless tea
Of penance will charm back the luxury
Of a child's soul, we'll return to Doom
The knowledge we stole but could not use.

And the newness that was in every stale thing
When we looked at it as children: the
spirit-shocking
Wonder in a black slanting Ulster hill
Or the prophetic astonishment in the tedious
talking
Of an old fool will awake for us and bring
You and me to the yard gate to watch the
whins[2]
And the bog-holes, cart-tracks, old stables
where Time begins.

O after Christmas we'll have no need to go
searching
For the difference that sets an old phrase
burning—
We'll hear it in the whispered argument of a
churning
Or in the streets where the village boys are
lurching.
And we'll hear it among decent men too
Who barrow dung in gardens under trees,
Wherever life pours ordinary plenty.
Won't we be rich, my love and I, and please
God we shall not ask for reason's payment,
The why of heart-breaking strangeness in
dreeping hedges
Nor analyse God's breath in common statement.
We have thrown into the dust-bin the clay-
minted wages
Of pleasure, knowledge and the conscious
hour—
And Christ comes with a January flower.

1942

1. The period including the four Sundays before Christmas in the Christian liturgical year.

2. gorse.

from:
COME DANCE WITH KITTY STOBLING (1960)

[Throughout his career, Kavanagh achieved his surest poetic success as a celebrant of the ordinary and the everyday. The following poems declare his faith in Irish life as poetic matter and discern lyric potential within it. The dates given for these poems are those of first publication.]

Shancoduff

My black hills have never seen the sun rising,
Eternally they look north towards Armagh.
Lot's wife would not be salt[1] if she had been
Incurious as my black hills that are happy
When dawn whitens Glassdrummond chapel.

1. Lot's wife was turned to salt when she turned to look at the doomed cities of the plain, Sodom and Gomorrah. See Genesis 19.26.

My hills hoard the bright shillings of March
While the sun searches in every pocket.
They are my Alps and I have climbed the
  Matterhorn[2]
With a sheaf of hay for three perishing calves
In the field under the Big Forth of
  Rocksavage.

The sleety winds fondle the rushy beards of
  Shancoduff
While the cattle-drovers sheltering in the
  Featherna Bush
Look up and say: 'Who owns them hungry hills
That the water-hen and snipe must have
  forsaken?
A poet? Then by heavens he must be poor'
I hear and is my heart not badly shaken?

1938

2. A mountain in the Swiss Alps.

In Memory of My Mother

I do not think of you lying in the wet clay
Of a Monaghan graveyard; I see
You walking down a lane among the poplars
On your way to the station, or happily

Going to second Mass on a summer Sunday—
You meet me and you say:
'Don't forget to see about the cattle—'
Among your earthiest words the angels stray.

And I think of you walking along a headland
Of green oats in June,
So full of repose, so rich with life—
And I see us meeting at the end of a town

On a fair day by accident, after
The bargains are all made and we can walk
Together through the shops and stalls and markets
Free in the oriental streets of thought.

O you are not lying in the wet clay,
For it is a harvest evening now and we
Are piling up the ricks against the moonlight
And you smile up at us — eternally.

1945

Epic

I have lived in important places, times
When great events were decided, who owned
That half a rood of rock, a no-man's land
Surrounded by our pitchfork-armed claims.
I heard the Duffys shouting 'Damn your soul'
And old McCabe stripped to the waist, seen
Step the plot defying blue cast-steel—
'Here is the march along these iron stones'
That was the year of the Munich bother.[1] Which
Was more important? I inclined
To lose my faith in Ballyrush and Gortin[2]
Till Homer's ghost came whispering to my mind
He said: I made the Iliad from such
A local row. Gods make their own importance.

1951

1. The meeting at Munich between Adolf Hitler and Neville Chamberlain (prime minister of Britain) in September 1938, following the Nazi invasion of Czechoslovakia.
2. Townlands in County Monaghan.

If Ever You Go To Dublin Town

If ever you go to Dublin town
In a hundred years or so
Inquire for me in Baggot Street
And what I was like to know.
O he was a queer one,
Fol dol the di do,
He was a queer one
I tell you.

My great-grandmother knew him well,
He asked her to come and call
On him in his flat and she giggled at the thought
Of a young girl's lovely fall.
O he was dangerous,
Fol dol the di do,
He was dangerous
I tell you.

On Pembroke Road look out for my ghost,
Dishevelled with shoes untied,
Playing through the railings with little children.
Whose children have long since died.
O he was a nice man,
Fol dol the di do,
He was a nice man
I tell you.

Go into a pub and listen well
If my voice still echoes there,
Ask the men what their grandsires thought
And tell them to answer fair.
O he was eccentric,
Fol dol the di do,
He was eccentric
I tell you.

He had the knack of making men feel
As small as they really were
Which meant as great as God had made them
But as males they disliked his air.
O he was a proud one,
Fol dol the di do,
He was a proud one
I tell you.

If ever you go to Dublin town
In a hundred years or so
Sniff for my personality,
Is it Vanity's vapour now?
O he was a vain one,
Fol dol the di do,
He was a vain one
I tell you.

I saw his name with a hundred others
In a book in a library,
It said he had never fully achieved
His potentiality.
O he was slothful,
Fol dol the di do,
He was slothful
I tell you.

He knew that posterity has no use
For anything but the soul,
The lines that speak the passionate heart,
The spirit that lives alone.
O he was a lone one,
Fol dol the di do
Yet he lived happily
I tell you.

1953

The Hospital

A year ago I fell in love with the functional ward
Of a chest hospital: square cubicles in a row
Plain concrete, wash basins — an art lover's woe,
Not counting how the fellow in the next bed
  snored.
But nothing whatever is by love debarred,
The common and banal her heat can know.
The corridor led to a stairway and below
Was the inexhaustible adventure of a gravelled
  yard.

This is what love does to things: the Rialto Bridge,
The main gate that was bent by a heavy lorry,
The seat at the back of a shed that was a suntrap.
Naming these things is the love-act and its pledge;
For we must record love's mystery without
  claptrap,
Snatch out of time the passionate transitory.

1956

October

O leafy yellowness you create for me
A world that was and now is poised above time,
I do not need to puzzle out Eternity
As I walk this arboreal street on the edge of a town.
The breeze too, even the temperature
And pattern of movement is precisely the same
As broke my heart for youth passing. Now I am
  sure
Of something. Something will be mine wherever I
  am.
I want to throw myself on the public street without
  caring
For anything but the prayering that the earth
  offers.
It is October over all my life and the light is staring
As it caught me once in a plantation by the fox
  coverts.
A man is ploughing ground for winter wheat
And my nineteen years weigh heavily on my feet.

1958

from: COLLECTED POEMS (1964)

Innocence

They laughed at one I loved—
The triangular hill that hung
Under the Big Forth. They said
That I was bounded by the whitethorn hedges

Of the little farm and did not know the world.
But I knew that love's doorway to life
Is the same doorway everywhere.

Ashamed of what I loved
I flung her from me and called her a ditch
Although she was smiling at me with violets.

But now I am back in her briary arms
The dew of an Indian Summer morning lies
On bleached potato-stalks—
What age am I?

I do not know what age I am,
I am no mortal age;
I know nothing of women,
Nothing of cities,
I cannot die
Unless I walk outside these whitethorn hedges.

1951

from: NOVEMBER HAGGARD (1971)

[In 1942 Patrick Kavanagh completed a long poem, 'Lough Derg', in which he described the annual pilgrimage to Lough Derg, Co. Donegal, striving to come to terms with his own ambiguous feelings about Irish catholicism. The following extract seeks to discover a mystical significance in the medieval ritual.]

Lough Derg

Over the black waves of the lake trip the last
echoes
Of the bell that has shooed through the chapel
door
The last pilgrims, like hens to roost.
The sun through Fermanagh's[1] furze fingers
Looks now on the deserted penance rings of
stone
Where only John Flood on St Kevin's Bed[2]
lingers
With the sexton's heaven-sure stance, the man
who knows
The ins and outs of religion . . . .
'Hail glorious St Patrick' a girl sings above
The old-man drone of the harmonium.
The Rosary is said and Benediction.[3]
The sacramental sun turns round and 'Holy,
Holy, Holy'
The pilgrims cry, striking their breasts in
Purgatory.
The same routine and ritual now
As serves for street processions or congresses
That take all shapes of souls as a living theme
In a novel refuses nothing. No truth oppresses.

Women and men in bare feet turn again
To the iron crosses and the rutted Beds,
Their feet are swollen and their bellies empty —
But something that is Ireland's secret leads
These petty mean people
For here's the day of a poor soul freed
To a marvellous beauty above its head.
The Castleblaney[4] grocer trapped in the
moment's need
Puts out a hand and writes what he cannot read,
A wisdom astonished at every turn
By some angel that writes in the oddest words.
When he will walk again in Muckno street
He'll hear from the kitchens of fair-day eating
houses
In the after-bargain carouses
News from a country beyond the range of birds.

The lake waves caught the concrete stilts of the
Basilica
That spread like a bullfrog's hind paws. A
Leitrim man
With a face as sad as a flooded hay-field,
Leaned in an angle of the walls with his rosary
beads in his hands,
Beside St Brigid's Cross[5] — an ancient relic
A fragment of the Middle Ages set
Into the modern masonry of the conventional
Basilica
Where everything is ordered and correct —
A queue of pilgrims waiting to renounce
The World, the Flesh, the Devil and all his
house.

1. County Fermanagh, one of the six counties of Northern Ireland, borders on County Donegal.
2. One of the stations (or stages) of the penitential itinerary at Lough Derg, named after a sacred site in Glendalough, Co. Wicklow.
3. The rosary is a prayer traditionally popular in Irish catholicism. Benediction consists of canticles and antiphons, followed by the blessing of the congregation by the priest, who makes the sign of the cross with the blessed sacrament, usually displayed in the centre of a monstrance.
4. A town in County Monaghan.
5. In legend, St Brigid shaped a crucifix from rushes for a poor man. This popular symbol is replicated in stone in the Basilica at Lough Derg.

DENIS DEVLIN

(1908-59)

from:
LOUGH DERG AND OTHER POEMS (1946)

['Lough Derg' attempts to consider Irish catholicism in the context of European expressions of the Roman catholic faith. The following extract, the work's opening section, sees in the penitential excesses of the Lough Derg pilgrimage an Irish manifestation of ascetic tendencies in the universal church and in religion in general. This excerpt also suggests the poet's sense of a European crisis generated by the world war.]

Lough Derg

The poor in spirit on their rosary rounds,[1]
The jobbers with their whiskey-angered eyes,
The pink bank clerks, the tip-hat papal counts,
And drab, kind women their tonsured mockery
tries,
Glad invalids on penitential feet
Walk the Lord's majesty like their village street.

With mullioned Europe shattered, this Northwest,
Rude-sainted isle would pray it whole again:
(Peasant Apollo![2] Troy is worn to rest.)
Europe that humanized the sacred bane
Of God's chance who yet laughed in his mind
And balanced thief and saint: were they this kind?

Low rocks, a few weasels, lake
Like a field of burnt gorse; the rooks caw;
Ours, passive, for man's gradual wisdom take
Firefly instinct dreamed out into law;
The prophets' jewelled kingdom down at heel
Fires no Augustine[3] here. Inert, they kneel;

All is simple and symbol in their world,
The incomprehended rendered fabulous.
Sin teases life whose natural fruits withheld
Sour the deprived nor bloom for timely loss:
Clan Jansen![4] less what magnanimity leavens
Man's wept-out, fitful, magniloquent heavens

Where prayer was praise, O Lord! the Temple
trumpets
Cascaded down Thy sunny pavilions of air,
The scroll-tongued priests, the galvanic strumpets,
All clash and stridency gloomed upon Thy stair;
The pharisees, the exalted boy their power
Sensually psalmed in Thee, their coming hour!

And to the sun, earth turned her flower of sex,
Acanthus[5] in the architects' limpid angles;
Close priests allegorized the Orphic egg's
Brood,[6] and from the Academy,[7] tolerant
wranglers
Could hear the contemplatives of the Tragic
Choir[8]
Drain off man's sanguine, pastoral death-desire.

It was said stone dreams and animal sleeps and
man
Is awake; but sleep with its drama on us bred
Animal articulate, only somnabulist can
Conscience like Cawdor[9] give the blood its head
For the dim moors to reign through druids again.
O first geometer! tangent-feelered brain

Clearing by inches the encircled eyes,
Bolder than the peasant tiger whose autumn
beauty
Sags in the expletive kill, or the sacrifice
Of dearth puffed positive in the stance of duty

1. The pilgrims said the rosary as they made their way round the penitential stations.
2. A Greek god often associated with the higher developments of civilization, inculcating high moral and religious principles.
3. Saint Augustine (A.D. 354-430).
4. Cornelius Otto Jansen (1585-1638), a French bishop and founder of the religious movement known as Jansenism, which is believed to have influenced Irish catholicism in puritan directions. Jansenism stresses in Augustinian terms the fallen nature of man, particularly as it is expressed in aberrant sexuality.
5. An architectural ornamentation patterned after leaves of the acanthus, as in the Corinthian capital.
6. In Greek Orphic religion, Chronus gave birth to Aether, Chaos and Erebus. Chronus found an egg in the Aether from which Phones, the creator and first king of the gods, sprang forth. Orphism was marked by other-worldliness and a mental attitude of self-denial and seriousness.
7. The school or college established by Plato *c.* 385 B.C. on the outskirts of Athens.
8. The Greek tragedians.
9. Macbeth is thane of Cawdor before he becomes king in Shakespeare's play. He abandons conscience for ambition.

With which these pilgrims would propitiate
Their fears; no leafy, medieval state

Of paschal cathedrals backed on earthy hooves
Against the craftsmen's primary-coloured skies
Whose gold was Gabriel[10] on the patient roofs,
The parabled windows taught the dead to rise,
And Christ the Centaur[11] in two natures whole,
With fable and proverb joinered body and soul.

Water withers from the oars. The pilgrims blacken
Out of the boats to masticate their sin
Where Dante smelled among the stones and bracken
The door to Hell[12] (O harder Hell where pain
Is earthed, a casuist sanctuary of guilt!).
Spirit bureaucracy on a bet built

Part by this race when monks in convents of coracles
For the Merovingian centuries[13] left their land,
Belled, fragrant; and honest in their oracles
Bespoke the grace to give without demand,
Martyrs Heaven winged nor tempted with reward,
And not ours, doughed in dogma, who never have dared

Will with surrogate palm distribute hope:
No better nor worse than I who, in my books,
Have angered at the stake with Bruno[14] and, by the rope
Watt Tyler[15] swung from, leagued with shifty looks
To fuse the next rebellion with the desperate
Serfs in the same need to eat and get;

Have praised, on its thunderous canvas, the Florentine smile
As man took to wearing his death, his own
Sapped crisis through cathedral branches (while
Flesh groped loud round dissenting skeleton)
In soul, reborn as body's appetite:
Now languisht back in body's amber light,

Now is consumed. O earthly paradise!
Hell is to know our natural empire used
Wrong, by mind's moulting, brute divinities.
The vanishing tiger's saved, his blood transfused.
Kent is for Jutes[16] again and Glasgow town
Burns high enough to screen the stars and moon.

Well may they cry who have been robbed, their wasting
Shares in justice legally lowered until
Man his own actor, matrix, mould and casting,
Or man, God's image, sees his idol spill.
Say it was pride that did it, or virtue's brief:
To them that suffer it is no relief.

All indiscriminate, man, stone, animal
Are woken up in nightmare. What John the Blind
From Patmos saw[17] works and we speak it. Not all
The men of God nor the priests of mankind
Can mend or explain the good and broke, not one
Generous with love prove communion.

Behind the eyes the winged ascension flags,
For want of spirit by the market blurbed,
And if hands touch, such fraternity sags
Frightened this side the dykes of death disturbed
Like Aran Islands' bibulous, unclean seas:
Pietà:[18] but the limbs ache; it is not peace.

Then to see less, look little, let hearts' hunger
Feed on water and berries. The pilgrims sing:
Life will fare well from elder to younger,
Though courage fail in a world-end, rosary ring.
Courage kills its practitioners and we live,
Nothing forgotten, nothing to forgive,

We pray to ourself. The metal moon, unspent
Virgin eternity sleeping in the mind,
Excites the form of prayer without content;
Whitethorn lightens, delicate and blind,
The negro mountain, and so, knelt on her sod,
This woman beside me murmuring *My God! My God!*

10. One of the Archangels.
11. The fabled beast of Greek legend, half-man, half-horse.
12. It is possible that Dante based his vision of hell in the *Inferno* on reports of St Patrick's purgatory at Lough Derg.
13. The Frankish dynasty of the Merovingians is thought to be the first race of the kings of France. They reigned from the fifth to the eighth centuries.
14. Giordano Bruno, Italian renaissance thinker and heretic, who was burned at the stake by the Inquisition in 1600.
15. Wat Tyler was one of the leaders of the Peasants' Revolt in England in 1381. He was in fact beheaded.
16. Early settlers in the south of England.
17. St John is believed to have seen the visions that constitute the Book of Revelation in the New Testament while in exile on the Aegean island of Patmos.
18. An allusion to Michelangelo's sculpture, which depicts Jesus lying dead in his mother's arms.

[In 'Encounter', Devlin dramatizes a moment of racial tension in a cosmopolitan milieu.]

Encounter

'Our saints are poets, Milton and Blake,[1]
Who would rib men with pride against the spite
Of God,' the Englishman said, and in the silence
Hatred sparkled along our bones. He said:
'Celt, your saints adorn the poor with roses
And praise God for standing still.'

Between the two of us, François from Touraine,
Where women and the wheat ripen and fall due
Suavely at evening, smiled, teasing the breadcrumbs.
He whispered: 'Patience; listen to the world's
Growth, rustling in fire and childlike water!'

And I: 'Milton and Marvell,[2] like the toady, Horace,[3]
Praised the men of power for the good
They happened on, with bible and sword; the
 wretched
Hold out their begging-bowls at the wooden gates,
Too poor to weep, too poor to weep with tears.'

Boxflower scent. Fumes of burgundy.
Nagging children at the tables
A dream's remove from their fathers smoking
Along the boulevard laid with yellow evening.

1. John Milton (1608-74) and William Blake (1757-1827), whose epic and visionary works challenged the established systems of political and religious belief.
2. Andrew Marvell (1621-78), friend and assistant to Milton, who praised Cromwell in several poems, including the famous 'An Horatian Ode upon Cromwell's Return from Ireland' (1650). Milton was Latin Secretary to the Council of State under Cromwell.
3. Roman poet and satirist (65-8 B.C.), who, under the influence of his patron, Maecenas, gave his support to the cause and later to the regime of the Emperor Augustus.

from: LATER POEMS (1946-59)

[As a troubled Christian in a metaphysically nihilistic age, Devlin found in the experience of sexual love a reflection of the doctrine of the Incarnation, which speaks of the spirit made flesh. The opening stanzas of his poem 'The Colours of Love' (1952) are a religio-erotic celebration of love's redemptive powers.]

The Colours of Love

to my wife Caren

Women that are loved are more than loveable,
 Their beauty absolute blows:
But little, like the urgent, carnal soul,
 More than its leaves so mortal in the rose.

O rose! O more than red mortality!
 What can my love have said
That made me her imagine more than be?
 Her mind more than mind, blood more
 than red?

As the noise of cars and chariots fades,
 And the empire of the stars
Reconquers with its bright and lusty[1] blades
 My room, and heals my scars,

I raise my arms to that mistress planet,
 Venus, whose hunting priests explain
My heart and the rush of legend on it,
 Making me man again! . . . .

1. The most recent edition of Devlin's poetry, edited by J. C. C. Mays, gives 'dusty'.

[In 'The Tomb of Michael Collins', Devlin composes an elegy for the hero of the War of Independence, who was killed in action in August 1922 as commander-in-chief of the government forces during the Civil War.]

The Tomb of Michael Collins

to Ignazio Silone[1]

Much I remember of the death of men,
But his I most remember, most of all,
More than the familiar and forgetful
Ghosts who leave our memory too soon —
Oh, what voracious fathers bore him down!

It was all sky and heather, wet and rock,
No one was there[2] but larks and stiff-legged hares
And flowers bloodstained. Then, Oh, our shame so
 massive
Only a God embraced it and the angel
Whose hurt and misty rifle shot him down.

1. Ignazio Silone was the pseudonym of Secondo Tranquilli (1900-86), the Italian novelist whose most famous work is *Fontamara* (1933). Like his other writings, this manifests his hatred of fascism. He was a friend of Devlin.
2. Béal na Bláth, the place in County Cork where Michael Collins was killed in an ambush.

One by one the enemy dies off;
As the sun grows old, the dead increase,
We love the more the further from we're born!
The bullet found him where the bullet ceased,
And Gael and Gall went inconspicuous down.

II

There are the Four Green Fields[3] we loved in boyhood,
There are some reasons it's no loss to die for:
Even it's no loss to die for having lived;
It is inside our life the angel happens
Life, the gift that God accepts or not,

Which Michael took with hand, with harsh, grey eyes,
He was loved by women and by men,
He fought a week of Sundays and by night
He asked what happened and he knew what was —
O Lord! how right that them you love die young!

He's what I was when by the chiming river
Two loyal children long ago embraced —
But what I was is one thing, what remember
Another thing, how memory becomes knowledge —
Most I remember him, how man is courage.

And sad, Oh sad, that glen with one thin stream
He met his death in; and a farmer told me
There was but one small bird to shoot: it sang
'Better Beast and know your end, and die
Than Man with murderous angels in his head.'

3. A traditional description of the four provinces of Ireland.

III

I tell these tales — I was twelve years old that time.
Those of the past were heroes in my mind:
Edward the Bruce whose brother Robert made him
Of Ireland, King;[4] Wolfe Tone and Silken Thomas[5]
And Prince Red Hugh O'Donnell[6] most of all.

The newsboys knew and the apple and orange women
Where was his shifty lodging Tuesday night;
No one betrayed him to the foreigner,
No Protestant or Catholic broke and ran
But murmured in their heart: here was a man!

Then came that mortal day he lost and laughed at,
He knew it as he left the armoured car;
The sky held in its rain and kept its breath;
Over the Liffey and the Lee,[7] the gulls,
They told his fortune which he knew, his death.

Walking to Vespers[8] in my Jesuit school,
The sky was come and gone: 'O Captain, my Captain!'[9]
Walt Whitman was the lesson that afternoon —
How sometimes death magnifies him who dies,
And some, though mortal, have achieved their race.

4. Edward the Bruce (*c.*1276-1318), Scottish king, crowned King of Ireland in 1316, but defeated and killed at Dundalk.

5. Thomas Lord Offaly, son of the earl of Kildare, known to the Irish as Tomás an tSioda, Silken Thomas, because of the silken garments worn by him and his bodyguard. He repudiated his allegiance to Henry VIII in 1534 and besieged Dublin. After the siege of Maynooth, he was sent to London and was executed, along with five of his uncles, at Tyburn in 1537.

6. The exiled 'Red' Hugh O'Donnell (*c.*1571-1602), chief of the O'Donnells, fled to Spain after the battle of Kinsale (1601). He was poisoned and buried in Valladolid, in an unknown grave.

7. The rivers of Dublin and of Cork city.

8. Evening prayers in church; the seventh or evening hour of the Divine Office.

9. The reference is to one of Walt Whitman's elegies for the assassinated Abraham Lincoln, 'O Captain! My Captain!' (1865-66).

THOMAS MacGREEVY

(1893-1967)

from:
POEMS (1934)

[The following poems by Thomas MacGreevy, in their allusiveness, free verse and fragmentation, show the influence of T. S. Eliot, about whom MacGreevy published a book in 1931.]

De Civitate Hominum[1]

To A.S.F.R.

The morning sky glitters
Winter blue.
The earth is snow-white,
With the gleam snow-white answers to sunlight,
Save where shell-holes are new,
Black spots in the whiteness —

A Matisse[2] ensemble.

The shadows of whitened tree stumps
Are another white.

And there are white bones.

Zillebeke Lake[3] and Hooge,[4]
Ice gray, gleam differently,

Like the silver shoes of the model.

The model is our world,
Our bitch of a world.
Those who live between wars may not know
But we who die between peaces
Whether we die or not.

It is very cold
And, what with my sensations
And my spick and span subaltern's uniform,
I might be the famous brass monkey,
The *nature morte*[5] accessory.

Morte . . . !
'Tis still life that lives,
Not quick life —
There are fleece-white flowers of death
That unfold themselves prettily
About an airman

Who, high over Gheluvelt,[6]
Is taking a morning look around,
All silk and silver
Up in the blue.

I hear the drone of an engine
And soft pounding puffs in the air
As the fleece-white flowers unfold.

I cannot tell which flower he has accepted
But suddenly there is a tremor,
A zigzag of lines against the blue
And he streams down
Into the white,
A delicate flame,

A stroke of orange in the morning's dress.

My sergeant says, very low, 'Holy God!
'Tis a fearful death.'

Holy God makes no reply
Yet.

1. 'On the government of men'; from St Augustine's *The City of God (De Civitate Dei)*.
2. Henri Matisse (1869-1954), French painter.
3. A lake in Flanders, in north-west Belgium.
4. A chateau in Flanders, scene of several battles in World War I.
5. still life. The reference in the line above to the well-known effect of extreme cold on the balls of a brass monkey derives from the naval name for the metal fixture that carried cannonballs.
6. A town in Flanders, north-east of Zillebeke Lake, where battles were fought in 1914 and 1917.

[MacGreevy supplied the following note to this poem: 'Aodh Ruadh O Domhnaill, 'Red' Hugh O Donnell, Prince of Tirconaill, went to Spain to consult with King Philip III after the defeat of the Irish and Spanish at Kinsale in 1601. He was lodged in the castle of Simancas during the negotiations but, poisoned by a certain James Blake, a Norman-Irish creature of the Queen of England (Elizabeth Tudor), he died there. As a member of the Third Order of Saint Francis, he was buried in the church of San Francisco at Valladolid. This Church was destroyed during the nineteenth century and none of the tombs that were in it seems to have been preserved.']

Aodh Ruadh O Domhnaill

To Stiefán MacEnna[1]

Juan de Juni[2] the priest said,
Each J becoming H;

Berruguete,[3] he said,
And the G was aspirate;

Ximenez,[4] he said then
An aspirated first and last.

But he never said
And — it seemed odd — he
Never had heard
The aspirated name
Of the centuries-dead
Bright-haired young man
Whose grave I sought.

All day I passed
In greatly built gloom
From dusty gilt tomb
Marvellously wrought
To tomb
Rubbing
At mouldy inscriptions
With fingers wetted with spit
And asking
Where I might find it
And failing.

Yet when
Unhurried —
    Not as at home
    Where heroes, hanged, are buried
    With non-commissioned officers' bored
        maledictions
    Quickly in the gaol yard —
They brought
His blackening body
Here
To rest

1. Stiefán MacEnna = Stephen MacKenna (1872-1934), Irish scholar and journalist who covered the Russian Revolution. MacGreevy and he met at Trinity College, Dublin and corresponded for many years.
2. Juan de Juni (1507-77), a French sculptor who worked in Valladolid.
3. Alonso Berruguete (1488-1561), Spanish painter and sculptor, worked at Valladolid, where he completed his masterpiece — the altarpiece of Saint Benito.
4. Donoso Jimenez (1628-90), Spanish painter and architect.

Princes came
Walking
Behind it

And all Valladolid knew
And out to Simancas[5] all knew
Where they buried Red Hugh.

5. Simancas, a Moorish castle seven miles from Valladolid.

Nocturne of the Self-Evident Presence

Fortunate,
Being inarticulate,
The alps
Rise
In ice
To heights
Of large stars
And little;
To courts
Beneath other courts
With walls of white starlight.
They have stars for pavements,
The valley is an area,
And I a servant,
A servant of servants,
Of metaphysical bereavements,
Staring up
Out of the gloom.

I see no immaculate feet on those pavements,
No winged forms,
Foreshortened,
As by Reubens[1] or Domenichino,[2]
Plashing the silvery air,
Hear no cars,

Elijah's[3] or Apollo's[4]
Dashing about
Up there.
I see alps, ice, stars and white starlight
In a dry, high silence.

1. Peter Paul Rubens (1577-1640), the great Flemish painter.
2. Probably Feti Domenichino (*c.*1589-1624), who was closely associated with the works of Rubens. Possibly the more famous Domenico Zampieri (1581-1641), called Domenichino, one of the most important artists of the Bolognese School.
3. The Old Testament prophet lofted by a whirlwind into heaven on a fiery chariot. See II Kings 2.11-12.
4. The Greek god who drew the sun across the heavens in his chariot.

BRIAN COFFEY

(1905-)

from:
SELECTED POEMS (1971)

[In 'Missouri Sequence', first published in 1962, Brian Coffey explored, at a crisis in his own life, the springs of human action and the nature of personal freedom. In the opening poem, a free verse letter to his friend and fellow poet, Thomas MacGreevy, Coffey reflects on his complex relationship with Ireland. When this poem appeared in the *University Review* (1962) in Dublin, Coffey had published no full collection of his poetry. 'Missouri Sequence' inaugurated a period of increased productivity.]

Missouri Sequence

I

NIGHTFALL, MIDWINTER, MISSOURI

To Thomas MacGreevy

Our children have eaten supper,
play Follow-my-Leader,
make songs from room to room
around and around;
once each minute
past my desk they go.

Inside the house is warm.
Winter outside blows from Canada
freezing rain to ice our trees
branch by branch, leaf by leaf.
The mare shelters in the barn.

On the impassable road no movement.
Nothing stirs in the sky against the black.
If memory were an ice-field
quiet as all outside!
Tonight the poetry is in the children's game:
I am distracted by comparisons,
Ireland across the grey ocean,
here, across the wide river.

* * *

We live far from where
my mother grows very old.
Five miles away, at Byrnesville,
the cemetery is filled with Irish graves,
the priest an old man born near Cork,
his bloss[1] like the day he left the land.

1. From the Irish *blás*, meaning a correct or rich accent.

People drifted in here from the river,
Irish, German, Bohemians,
more than one hundred years ago,
come to make homes.

Many Irish souls have gone back to God from
Byrnesville,
many are Irish here today
where cedars stand like milestones
on worn Ozark hills
and houses white on bluegrass lawns
house people honest, practical and kind.

All shows to a long love
yet I am charmed
by the hills behind Dublin,
those white stone cottages,
grass green as no other green is green,
my mother's people, their ways.

France one loves with a love apart
like the love of wisdom;
Of England everyday love is the true love;
there is a love of Ireland
withering for Irishmen.

Does it matter where one dies,
supposing one knows how?

Dear Tom, in Ireland,
you have known
the pain between
its fruiting and the early dream
and you will hear me out.

* * *

Our children have ended play,
have gone to bed,
left me to face
what I had rather not.

They know nothing of Ireland,
they grow American.
They have chased snakes through the couch-grass
in summer, caught butterflies and beetles
we did not know existed,

fished for the catfish,
slept on an open porch
when Whip-poor-Will and tree-frog
work all night,
observed the pupa of the shrill cicada
surface on dry clay,
disrobe for the short ruinous day.
The older ones have helped a neighbour, farmer,
raise his field of ripe corn
in heat that hurt us to the bone,
paid homage to dead men
with fire-crackers in July,
eaten the turkey in November.[2]
Here now they make their friendships,
learn to love God.

Yet we must leave America,
bitter necessity no monopoly
of Irish soil.
It was pain once to come,
it is pain now to go.

How the will shifts from goal to goal
for who does not freely choose.
Some choose, some are chosen
to go their separate paths.
I would choose, I suppose, yet would be chosen
in some equation between God's will and mine,
rejecting prudence to make of conflict
a monument to celtic self-importance.

The truth is, where the cross is not
the Christian does not go.

* * *

Return home takes on while I dream it
the fictive form of heaven on earth,
the child's return to motherly arms
for fright at frogs disturbed among iris leaves.

One poet I admire has written:
wherever the soul gives in to flesh
without a struggle is home.[3]

Would one want home like that,
rest, supine surrender
to oneself alone,
flight from where one is?

There is no heaven on earth,
no facile choice for one
charged with care of others,
none for one like me
for whom no prospect opens
fairly on clear skies.

It grows late and winter
lays its numbing pall.
Doubts restless like what you see
when you lift a flat damp stone
exasperate my warring wishes
until wrenched apart by desperate extremes
I am back where I started.

Pain it was to come,
Pain it will be to go.

* * *

Not just to go,
not just to stay,
but the act done in wisdom's way —
not impossible
if one is wise.

Our William Butler Yeats
made island flowers grow
that need as much
the local rain
as wind from overseas
to reach their prime.
He struggled towards the exact muse
through a sunless day.

No servant, the muse
abides in truth,
permits the use of protest
as a second best
to make clean fields,
exults only in the actual
expression of a love,
love all problem,
wisdom lacking.

* * *

2. The poet here refers to the feast of Thanksgiving, celebrated annually in the United States to re-enact the feast of thanksgiving with which the Pilgrim Fathers marked the gathering of the first harvest after their arrival in North America.
3. The quotation is from a poem by Laura Riding (born 1901), entitled 'Laura and Francisca'. See Laura Riding, *Collected Poems* (1938), p. 399.

How near the surface of the pool
sunfish play, distract
us from where down deep
real reasons impose their rule.

The room is filled with children's lives
that fill my cares who turn again
to sudden starting words
like birds in cages.
Without all is silent,
within I have no peace at all,
having failed to choose
with loving-wise choice.

Midnight now.
Deepest winter perfect now.
Tomorrow early we shall make lunches
for the children to take to school,
forgetting while working out the week
our wrestling with the sad flesh
and the only Ireland we love
where in Achill[4] still
the poor praise Christ aloud
when the priest elevates
the Saviour of the world.

4. Achill Island, Co. Mayo, the largest island off the Irish coast.

LOUIS MacNEICE
(1907-63)

from: POEMS (1935)

Belfast

[In the 1930s, when he was associated with the left-wing poets of the Auden group in England, Louis MacNeice expressed his alienation from an Ireland for which he felt little sympathy. An epicurean delight in the surfaces of life, however, could not banish his constitutional melancholy, which, in a decade of international foreboding, made him a compelling prophet of doom. Only the transitory experience of love redeems the time.]

The hard cold fire of the northerner
Frozen into his blood from the fire in his basalt
Glares from behind the mica of his eyes
And the salt carrion water brings him wealth.

Down there at the end of the melancholy lough
Against the lurid sky over the stained water
Where hammers clang murderously on the girders
Like crucifixes the gantries stand.

And in the marble stores rubber gloves like polyps
Cluster; celluloid, painted ware, glaring
Metal patents, parchment lampshades, harsh
Attempts at buyable beauty.

In the porch of the chapel before the garish Virgin
A shawled factory-woman as if shipwrecked there
Lies a bunch of limbs glimpsed in the cave of gloom
By us who walk in the street so buoyantly and glib.

Over which country of cowled and haunted faces
The sun goes down with a banging of Orange drums
While the male kind murders each its woman
To whose prayer for oblivion answers no Madonna.

September 1931

Snow

The room was suddenly rich and the great
  bay-window was
Spawning snow and pink roses against it
Soundlessly collateral and incompatible:
World is suddener than we fancy it.

World is crazier and more of it than we think,
Incorrigibly plural. I peel and portion
A tangerine and spit the pips and feel
The drunkenness of things being various.

And the fire flames with a bubbling sound for world
Is more spiteful and gay than one supposes —
On the tongue on the eyes on the ears in the palms
  of one's hands —

There is more than glass between the snow and the
huge roses.

January 1935

from:
POEMS (1937)

The Sunlight on the Garden

The sunlight on the garden
Hardens and grows cold,
We cannot cage the minute
Within its nets of gold,
When all is told
We cannot beg for pardon.

Our freedom as free lances
Advances towards its end;
The earth compels, upon it
Sonnets and birds descend;
And soon, my friend,
We shall have no time for dances.

The sky was good for flying
Defying the church bells
And every evil iron
Siren and what it tells:
The earth compels,
We are dying, Egypt, dying[1]

And not expecting pardon,
Hardened in heart anew,
But glad to have sat under
Thunder and rain with you,
And grateful too
For sunlight on the garden.

1937

1. cf. Mark Antony to Cleopatra in Shakespeare's *Antony and Cleopatra*, IV. 15. 18.

Bagpipe Music

It's no go the merrygoround, it's no go the
rickshaw,
All we want is a limousine and a ticket for the
peepshow.
Their knickers are made of crêpe-de-chine, their
shoes are made of python,
Their halls are lined with tiger rugs and their walls
with heads of bison.

John MacDonald found a corpse, put it under the
sofa,
Waited till it came to life and hit it with a poker,
Sold its eyes for souvenirs, sold its blood for whisky,
Kept its bones for dumb-bells to use when he was
fifty.

It's no go the Yogi-Man, it's no go Blavatsky,[1]
All we want is a bank balance and a bit of skirt in a
taxi.

Annie MacDougall went to milk, caught her foot in
the heather,
Woke to hear a dance record playing of Old Vienna.
It's no go your maidenheads, it's no go your culture,
All we want is a Dunlop tyre and the devil mend the
puncture.

The Laird o' Phelps spent Hogmanay[2] declaring he
was sober,
Counted his feet to prove the fact and found he had
one foot over.
Mrs. Carmichael had her fifth, looked at the job
with repulsion,
Said to the midwife 'Take it away; I'm through with
over-production'.

It's no go the gossip column, it's no go the Ceilidh,[3]
All we want is a mother's help and a sugar-stick for
the baby.

Willie Murray cut his thumb, couldn't count the
damage,
Took the hide of an Ayrshire cow and used it for a
bandage.
His brother caught three hundred cran[4] when the
seas were lavish,
Threw the bleeders back in the sea and went upon
the parish.[5]

It's no go the Herring Board, it's no go the Bible,
All we want is a packet of fags when our hands are
idle.

1. Madame Helena Petrovna Blavatsky (1831-91), a famous medium and theosophist, once fashionable in literary circles. W. B. Yeats took instruction from her and she was satirized as Madame Sosostris in T. S. Eliot's *The Waste Land* (1922).
2. Scottish New Year festival.
3. Irish: an informal evening of song, dance, story and conversation.
4. A measure of capacity for herrings just landed. It comprises about one thousand fish.
5. i.e. received parochial relief.

It's no go the picture palace, it's no go the stadium,
It's no go the country cot with a pot of pink
  geraniums,
It's no go the Government grants, it's no go the
  elections,
Sit on your arse for fifty years and hang your hat on
  a pension.

It's no go my honey love, it's no go my poppet;
Work your hands from day to day, the winds will
  blow the profit.
The glass is falling hour by hour, the glass will fall
  for ever,
But if you break the bloody glass you won't hold up
  the weather.

1937

from: AUTUMN JOURNAL (1939)

[In 1939 MacNeice published his long autobiographical poem, *Autumn Journal*, in which, addressing the political crisis of 1938 provoked by Nazi military adventure, he reflected on his own political commitments. Section XVI, a powerful indictment of political intransigence, which he associates especially with his native Northern Ireland, serves to give weight throughout the poem to the poet's liberal stance, which might otherwise have seemed an inadequate response to the challenge posed to civilized values by the rise of fascism.]

XVI

Nightmare leaves fatigue:
  We envy men of action
Who sleep and wake, murder and intrigue
  Without being doubtful, without being haunted.
And I envy the intransigence of my own
  Countrymen who shoot to kill and never
See the victim's face become their own
  Or find his motive sabotage their motives.
So reading the memoirs of Maud Gonne,[1]
  Daughter of an English mother and a soldier father,
I note how a single purpose can be founded on
  A jumble of opposites:
Dublin Castle, the vice-regal ball,
  The embassies of Europe,
Hatred scribbled on a wall,
  Gaols and revolvers.
And I remember, when I was little, the fear
  Bandied among the servants
That Casement would land at the pier
  With a sword and a horde of rebels;
And how we used to expect, at a later date,
  When the wind blew from the west, the noise of
    shooting
Starting in the evening at eight
  In Belfast in the York Street district;
And the voodoo of the Orange bands
  Drawing an iron net through darkest Ulster,
Flailing the limbo lands —
  The linen mills, the long wet grass, the ragged
    hawthorn.
And one read black where the other read white, his
    hope
  The other man's damnation:
Up the Rebels, To Hell with the Pope,
  And God Save — as you prefer — the King or
    Ireland.
The land of scholars and saints:
  Scholars and saints my eye, the land of ambush,
Purblind manifestoes, never-ending complaints,
  The born martyr and the gallant ninny;
The grocer drunk with the drum,
  The land-owner shot in his bed, the angry voices
Piercing the broken fanlight in the slum,

1. The historical and legendary personages mentioned in the poem are: Maud Gonne MacBride (1866-1953), Irish revolutionary. Courted in vain by W. B. Yeats and celebrated successfully in his poetry, she married Major John MacBride, one of the martyrs of the 1916 Easter Rising, in 1903.
Sir Roger Casement (1864-1916), Irish revolutionary, formerly employed in the British consular service. An Ulster protestant, Casement gave himself to the nationalist cause, and smuggled guns from Germany to Ireland in 1916 for use in the Rising of that year. He was arrested, tried in England and hanged for high treason.
Kathleen ni Houlihan (Kathleen, daughter of Houlihan), a traditional personification of Ireland, much favoured by nationalists.
William, Prince of Orange and King of England, defeated James Stuart (James II of England) at the battle of the Boyne in 1690. This decisive victory is celebrated by the Orange Order, a militant protestant organization founded to defend the protestant heritage, on 12 July, the modern equivalent of the date of the battle. William ('King Billy') is the folk hero of Ulster loyalism.
Arthur Griffith (1871-1922), political leader and journalist, who edited the periodicals *The United Irishman* and *Sinn Féin*. He founded the Sinn Féin (We Ourselves) movement in Dublin in 1905, to encourage national self-reliance in political and economic affairs.
James Connolly (1868-1916), socialist and revolutionary, founded the Irish Citizen Army in 1913, to protect workers against police brutality, manifested in the great strike of that year. Along with Pearse, he led the 1916 Rising. After the surrender, he was executed.
Michael Collins (1890-1922), Irish revolutionary. He was a member of the Irish delegation to London which negotiated the Treaty to end the War of Independence in 1921. He was killed in an ambush by republicans during the Irish Civil War.

The shawled woman weeping at the garish altar.
Kathaleen ni Houlihan! Why
Must a country, like a ship or a car, be always female,
Mother or sweetheart? A woman passing by,
We did but see her passing.
Passing like a patch of sun on the rainy hill
And yet we love her for ever[2] and hate our neighbour
And each one in his will
Binds his heirs to continuance of hatred.
Drums on the haycock, drums on the harvest, black
Drums in the night shaking the windows:
King William is riding his white horse back
To the Boyne on a banner.
Thousands of banners, thousands of white
Horses, thousands of Williams
Waving thousands of swords and ready to fight
Till the blue sea turns to orange.
Such was my country and I thought I was well
Out of it, educated and domiciled in England,
Though yet her name keeps ringing like a bell
In an under-water belfry.
Why do we like being Irish? Partly because
It gives us a hold on the sentimental English
As members of a world that never was,
Baptised with fairy water;
And partly because Ireland is small enough
To be still thought of with a family feeling,
And because the waves are rough
That split her from a more commercial culture;
And because one feels that here at least one can
Do local work which is not at the world's mercy
And that on this tiny stage with luck a man
Might see the end of one particular action.
It is self-deception of course;
There is no immunity in this island either;
A cart that is drawn by somebody else's horse
And carrying goods to somebody else's market.
The bombs in the turnip sack, the sniper from the roof,
Griffith, Connolly, Collins, where have they brought us?
Ourselves alone![3] Let the round tower stand aloof
In a world of bursting mortar!
Let the school-children fumble their sums
In a half-dead language;
Let the censor be busy on the books; pull down the Georgian slums;
Let the games be played in Gaelic.
Let them grow beet-sugar; let them build
A factory in every hamlet;
Let them pigeon-hole the souls of the killed
Into sheep and goats, patriots and traitors.
And the North, where I was a boy,
Is still the North, veneered with the grime of Glasgow,
Thousands of men whom nobody will employ
Standing at the corners, coughing.
And the street-children play on the wet
Pavement — hopscotch or marbles;
And each rich family boasts a sagging tennis-net
On a spongy lawn beside a dripping shrubbery.
The smoking chimneys hint
At prosperity round the corner
But they make their Ulster linen from foreign lint
And the money that comes in goes out to make more money.
A city built upon mud;
A culture built upon profit;
Free speech nipped in the bud,
The minority always guilty.
Why should I want to go back
To you, Ireland, my Ireland?[4]
The blots on the page are so black
That they cannot be covered with shamrock.
I hate your grandiose airs,
Your sob-stuff, your laugh and your swagger,
Your assumption that everyone cares
Who is the king of your castle.
Castles are out of date,
The tide flows round the children's sandy fancy;
Put up what flag you like, it is too late
To save your soul with bunting.
Odi atque amo:[5]
Shall we cut this name on trees with a rusty dagger?
Her mountains are still blue, her rivers flow
Bubbling over the boulders.
She is both a bore and a bitch;
Better close the horizon,

2. cf. ballad collected in Thomas Ford, *Music of Sundry Kinds* (1607):
There is a lady sweet and kind,
Was never face so pleased my mind;
I did but see her passing by,
And yet I love her till I die.
3. A frequent mistranslation of Sinn Féin (We Ourselves).
4. cf. William Ernest Henley. 'For England's Sake':
What have I done for you,
England, my England?
5. Catullus, *Carmina*, lxxxv: 'I hate and love'.

Send her no more fantasy, no more longings which
  Are under a fatal tariff.
For common sense is the vogue
  And she gives her children neither sense nor money
Who slouch around the world with a gesture and a brogue
  And a faggot of useless memories.

from:
THE LAST DITCH (1940)

Meeting Point

Time was away and somewhere else,
There were two glasses and two chairs
And two people with the one pulse
(Somebody stopped the moving stairs):
Time was away and somewhere else.

And they were neither up nor down;
The stream's music did not stop
Flowing through heather, limpid brown,
Although they sat in a coffee shop
And they were neither up nor down.

The bell was silent in the air
Holding its inverted poise —
Between the clang and clang a flower,
A brazen calyx of no noise:
The bell was silent in the air.

The camels crossed the miles of sand
That stretched around the cups and plates;
The desert was their own, they planned
To portion out the stars and dates:
The camels crossed the miles of sand.

Time was away and somewhere else.
The waiter did not come, the clock
Forgot them and the radio waltz
Came out like water from a rock:
Time was away and somewhere else.

Her fingers flicked away the ash
That bloomed again in tropic trees:
Not caring if the markets crash
When they had forests such as these,
Her fingers flicked away the ash.

God or whatever means the Good
Be praised that time can stop like this,
That what the heart has understood
Can verify in the body's peace
God or whatever means the Good.

Time was away and she was here
And life no longer what it was,
The bell was silent in the air
And all the room one glow because
Time was away and she was here.

April 1939

from:
HOLES IN THE SKY (1948)

[In the post-war period, MacNeice's poetry became more and more concerned with exploring the problematic nature of human identity. Consciousness in time and place seemed to find its most appropriate expression in poems of a parable-like obliquity. The tone became more desperate as it grew more savagely sardonic.]

The Strand

White Tintoretto[1] clouds beneath my naked feet,
This mirror of wet sand imputes a lasting mood
To island truancies; my steps repeat

Someone's who now has left such strands for good
Carrying his boots and paddling like a child,
A square black figure whom the horizon understood —

My father. Who for all his responsibly compiled
Account books of a devout, precise routine
Kept something in him solitary and wild,

So loved the western sea and no tree's green
Fulfilled him like these contours of Slievemore
Menaun and Croaghaun[2] and the bogs between.

1. Tintoretto, the nickname of Jacopo Robusti (1518-94), an Italian painter. He was called Tintoretto (little dyer) after his father's trade. Famed for his treatment of the effects of light and shade and for unusual, tilted angles of vision, he is an appropriate presence here.
2. Cliffs in County Mayo.

Sixty-odd years behind him and twelve before,
Eyeing the flange of steel in the turning belt of brine
It was sixteen years ago he walked this shore

And the mirror caught his shape which catches mine
But then as now the floor-mop of the foam
Blotted the bright reflections — and no sign

Remains of face or feet when visitors have gone home.

1945

from: VISITATIONS (1957)

House on a Cliff

Indoors the tang of a tiny oil lamp. Outdoors
The winking signal on the waste of sea.
Indoors the sound of the wind. Outdoors the wind.
Indoors the locked heart and the lost key.

Outdoors the chill, the void, the siren. Indoors
The strong man pained to find his red blood cools,
While the blind clock grows louder, faster. Outdoors
The silent moon, the garrulous tides she rules.

Indoors ancestral curse-cum-blessing. Outdoors
The empty bowl of heaven, the empty deep.
Indoors a purposeful man who talks at cross
Purposes, to himself, in a broken sleep.

1955

Charon[1]

The conductor's hands were black with money.
Hold on to your ticket, he said, the inspector's
Mind is black with suspicion, and hold on to
That dissolving map. We moved through London,
We could see the pigeons through the glass but failed
To hear their rumours of wars, we could see
The lost dog barking but never knew
That his bark was as shrill as a cock crowing,
We just jogged on, at each request
Stop there was a crowd of aggressively vacant
Faces, we just jogged on, eternity
Gave itself airs in revolving lights
And then we came to the Thames and all
The bridges were down, the further shore
Was lost in fog, so we asked the conductor
What we should do. He said: Take the ferry
Faute de mieux.[2] We flicked the flashlight
And there was the ferryman just as Virgil[3]
And Dante[4] had seen him. He looked at us coldly
And his eyes were dead and his hands on the oar
Were black with obols[5] and varicose veins
Marbled his calves and he said to us coldly:
If you want to die you will have to pay for it.

1962

1. In Greek mythology, the aged ferryman in Hades, the underworld, who conveyed the dead across the rivers of the lower world, including the Styx, the river of death.
2. For want of anything better.
3. Virgil (70-19 B.C.), the great Roman poet, who gives a famous description of Charon in the *Aeneid*, 6.298-315.
4. Dante Alighieri (1265-1321), the greatest of Italian poets, who gives a description of Charon in the *Inferno*, Canto III.
5. Ancient Greek coins. An obolus was the fee charged by Charon for ferrying the dead. The Greeks used to put an obolus in the mouth of the dead person as a fee for Charon.

JOHN HEWITT
(1907-87)

from: NO REBEL WORD (1968)

[In the 1930s and 1940s John Hewitt explored his relationship with his native region and pondered the ambiguities of his Northern Irish identity. The poet's pastoral sense of the Ulster landscape, however, could not fully resolve his troubled awareness of a problematic historical inheritance.]

Frost

With frost again the thought is clear and wise
that rain made dismal with a mist's despair,

the raw bleak earth beneath cloud-narrowed skies
finds new horizons in the naked air.
Light leaps along the lashes of the eyes;
a tree is truer for its being bare.

So must the world seem keen and very bright
to one whose gaze is on the end of things,
who knows, past summer lush, brimmed autumn's
height,
no promise in the inevitable springs,
all stripped of shadow down to bone of light,
the false songs gone and gone the restless wings.

Once Alien Here

Once alien here my fathers built their house,
claimed, drained, and gave the land the shapes of
use,
and for their urgent labour grudged no more
than shuffled pennies from the hoarded store
of well rubbed words that had left their overtones
in the ripe England of the mounded downs.

The sullen Irish limping to the hills
bore with them the enchantment and the spells
that in the clans' free days hung gay and rich
on every twig of every thorny hedge,
and gave the rain-pocked stone a meaning past
the blurred engraving of the fibrous frost.

So I, because of all the buried men
in Ulster clay, because of rock and glen
and mist and cloud and quality of air
as native in my thought as any here,
who now would seek a native mode to tell
our stubborn wisdom individual,
yet lacking skill in either scale of song,
the graver English, lyric Irish tongue,
must let this rich earth so enhance the blood
with steady pulse where now is plunging mood
till thought and image may, identified,
find easy voice to utter each aright.

The Swathe Uncut[1]

As the brown mowers strode across the field
shapes fled before them thrusting back the grain,
till in a shrinking angle unrevealed
the frightened hare crouched back, the last at bay,
for even the corncrake, blind in his dismay,
had found the narrow safety of the drain.

And so of old the country folk declared
the last swathe holds a wayward fugitive,
uncaught, moth-gentle, tremulously scared,
that must be, by the nature of all grain,
the spirit of the corn that should be slain
if the saved seed will have the strength to live.

Then by their ancient ritual they sought
to kill the queen, the goddess, and ensure
that her spent husk and shell be safely brought
to some known corner of beneficence,
lest her desired and lively influence
be left to mock the next plough's signature.

So I have figured in my crazy wit
is this flat island sundered to the west
the last swathe left uncut, the blessed wheat
wherein still free the gentle creatures go
instinctively erratic, rash or slow,
unregimented, never yet possessed.

1. In Irish folklore, when the harvest was gathered in, the last swathe was plaited into a harvest knot. This knot was believed to possess magical powers and may have been seen as possessing the spirit of the harvest. In the north of Ireland, the last sheaf was frequently known as the 'hare'. In some places, the harvest knot was employed in a ritual, which suggests a fertility cult. See Elizabeth Andrews, *Ulster Folklore* (1913), pp. 17-21. This book was probably the source for Hewitt's poem.

from:
COLLECTED POEMS 1932-67 (1968)

Because I Paced My Thought

Because I paced my thought by the natural world,
the earth organic, renewed with the palpable
seasons,
rather than the city falling ruinous, slowly
by weather and use, swiftly by bomb and argument,

I found myself alone who had hoped for attention.
If one listened a moment he murmured his dissent:
this is an idle game for a cowardly mind.
The day is urgent. The sun is not on the agenda.

And some who hated the city and man's
unreasoning acts
remarked: He is no ally. He does not say that
Power and Hate are the engines of human treason.
There is no answering love in the yellowing leaf.

I should have made it plain that I stake my future
on birds flying in and out of the schoolroom-window,
on the council of sunburnt comrades in the sun,
and the picture carried with singing into the temple.

The Colony

First came the legions, then the colonists,
provincials, landless citizens, and some
camp-followers of restless generals
content now only with the least of wars.
Among this rabble, some to feel more free
beyond the ready whim of Caesar's fist;
for conscience' sake the best of these, but others
because their debts had tongues, one reckless man,
a tax absconder with a sack of coin.

With these, young lawclerks skilled with chart and
stylus,
their boxes crammed with lease-scrolls duly marked
with distances and names, to be defined
when all was mapped.
When they'd surveyed the land,
they gave the richer tillage, tract by tract,
from the great captains down to men-at-arms,
some of the sprawling rents to be retained
by Caesar's mistresses in their far villas.

We planted little towns to garrison
the heaving country, heaping walls of earth
and keeping all our cattle close at hand;
then, thrusting north and west, we felled the trees,
selling them off the foot hills, at a stroke
making quick profits, smoking out the nests
of the barbarian tribesmen, clan by clan,
who hunkered in their blankets, biding chance,
till, unobserved, they slither down and run
with torch and blade among the frontier huts
when guards were nodding, or when shining corn
bade sword-hand grip the sickle. There was once
a terrible year when, huddled in our towns,
my people trembled as the beacons ran
from hill to hill across the countryside,
calling the dispossessed to lift their standards.
There was great slaughter then, man, woman, child,
with fire and pillage of our timbered houses;
we had to build in stone for ever after.

That terror dogs us; back of all our thought
the threat behind the dream, those beacons flare,
and we run headlong screaming in our fear;
fear quickened by the memory of guilt
for we began the plunder — naked men
still have their household gods and holy places,
and what a people loves it will defend.
We took their temples from them and forbade them,
for many years, to worship their strange idols.
They gathered secret, deep in the dripping glens,
chanting their prayers before a lichened rock.

We took the kindlier soils. It had been theirs,
this patient, temperate, slow, indifferent,
crop-yielding, crop-denying, in-neglect-
quickly-returning-to-the-nettle-and-bracken,
sodden and friendly land. We took it from them.
We laboured hard and stubborn, draining, planting,
till half the country took its shape from us.

Only among the hills with hare and kestrel,
will you observe what once this land was like
before we made it fat for human use —
all but the forests, all but the tall trees —
I could invent a legend of those trees,
and how their creatures, dryads, hamadryads,[1]
fled from the copses, hid in thorny bushes,
and grew a crooked and malignant folk,
plotting and waiting for a bitter revenge
on their despoilers. So our troubled thought
is from enchantments of the old tree magic,
but I am not a sick and haunted man ....

Teams of the tamer natives we employed
to hew and draw, but did not call them slaves.
Some say this was our error. Others claim
we were too slow to make them citizens;
we might have made them Caesar's bravest legions.
This is a matter for historians,
or old beards in the Senate to wag over,
not pertinent to us these many years.

But here and there the land was poor and starved,
which, though we mapped, we did not occupy,

1. Wood nymphs, fabled to die with the trees they inhabited.

leaving the natives, out of laziness
in our demanding it, to hold unleased
the marshy quarters, fens, the broken hills,
and all the rougher places where the whin
still thrust from limestone with its cracking pods.

They multiplied and came with open hands,
begging a crust because their land was poor,
and they were many; squatting at our gates,
till our towns grew and threw them hovelled lanes
which they inhabit still. You may distinguish,
if you were schooled with us, by pigmentation,
by cast of features or by turn of phrase,
or by the clan-names on them which are they,
among the faces moving in the street.

They worship Heaven strangely, having rites
we snigger at, are known as superstitious,
cunning by nature, never to be trusted,
given to dancing and a kind of song
seductive to the ear, a whining sorrow.
Also they breed like flies. The danger's there;
when Caesar's old and lays his sceptre down,
we'll be a little people, well-outnumbered.

Some of us think our leases have run out
but dig square heels in, keep the roads repaired;
and one or two loud voices would restore
the rack, the yellow patch, the curfewed ghetto.
Most try to ignore the question, going their way,
glad to be living, sure that Caesar's word
is Caesar's bond for legions in our need.
Among us, some, beguiled by their sad music,
make common cause with the natives, in their hearts
hoping to win a truce when the tribes assert
their ancient right and take what once was theirs.
Already from other lands the legions ebb
and men no longer know the Roman peace.

Alone, I have a harder row to hoe:
I think these natives human, think their code,
though strange to us, and farther from the truth,
only a little so, — to be redeemed
if they themselves rise up against the spells
and fears their celibates surround them with.
I find their symbols good, as such, for me,
when I walk in dark places of the heart;
but name them not to be misunderstood.
I know no vices they monopolise,
if we allow the forms by hunger bred,
the sores of old oppression, the deep skill
in all evasive acts, the swaddled minds,
admit our load of guilt — I mourn the trees
more than as symbol — and would make amends
by fraternising, by small friendly gestures,
hoping by patient words I may convince
my people and this people we are changed
from the raw levies which usurped the land,
if not to kin, to co-inhabitants,
as goat and ox may graze in the same field
and each gain something from proximity;
for we have rights drawn from the soil and sky;
the use, the pace, the patient years of labour,
the rain against the lips, the changing light,
the heavy clay-sucked stride, have altered us;
we would be strangers in the Capitol;
this is our country also, no-where else;
and we shall not be outcast on the world.

W. R. RODGERS

(1909-69)

from:
AWAKE! AND OTHER POEMS
(1941)

White Christmas

Punctually at Christmas the soft plush
Of sentiment snows down, embosoms all
The sharp and pointed shapes of venoms, shawls
The hills and hides the shocking holes of this
Uneven world of want and wealth, cushions
With cosy wish like cotton-wool the cool
Arm's length interstices of caste and class,
And into obese folds subtracts from sight
All truculent acts, bleeding the world white.

Punctually that glib pair, Peace and Goodwill,
Emerges royally to take the air,

Collect the bows, assimilate the smiles,
Of waiting men. It is genial time.
Angels, like stalactites, descend from heaven,
Bishops distribute their own weight in words,
Congratulate the poor on Christlike lack,
And the member for the constituency
Feeds the five thousand, and has plenty back.

Punctually tonight, in old stone circles
Of set reunion, families stiffly sit
And listen; this is the night, and this the happy time
When the tinned milk of human kindness is
Upheld and holed by radio-appeal.
Hushed are hurrying heels on hard roads,
And every parlour's a pink pond of light
To the cold and travelling man going by
In the dark, without a bark or a bite.

But punctually tomorrow you will see
All this silent and dissembling world
Of silted sentiment suddenly melt
Into mush and watery welter of words
Beneath the warm and moving traffic of
Feet and actual fact. Over the stark plain
The stilted mill-chimneys once again spread
Their sackcloth and ashes, a flowing mane
Of repentance for the false day that's fled.

from: EUROPA AND THE BULL (1952)

[In W. R. Rodgers's best poems a sense of illicit celebration or of moral outrage finds expression in convincing verbal experiment. The impression is of puritan morality and feeling breaking their bonds in unexpected displays of energy. The linguistic ostentation seems momentarily appropriate to its occasion.]

Lent[1]

Mary Magdalene,[2] that easy woman,
Saw, from the shore, the seas
Beat against the hard stone of Lent,
Crying, 'Weep, seas, weep
For yourselves that cannot dent me more.

1. A period of penance and fasting in the Christian liturgical year between Ash Wednesday and the Feast of the Resurrection on Easter Sunday.
2. One of Jesus's followers, traditionally believed to have been a prostitute. See Matthew 28. 1-2.

O more than all these, more crabbed than all stones,
And cold, make me, who once
Could leap like water, Lord. Take me
As one who owes
Nothing to what she was. Ah, naked.

My waves of scent, my petticoats of foam
Put from me and rebut;
Disown. And that salt lust stave off
That slavered me — O
Let it whiten in grief against the stones

And outer reefs of me. Utterly doff,
Nor leave the lightest veil
Of feeling to heave or soften.
Nothing cares this heart
What hardness crates it now or coffins.

Over the balconies of these curved breasts
I'll no more peep to see
The light procession of my loves
Surf-riding in to me
Who now have eyes and alcove, Lord, for Thee.'

'Room, Mary', said He, 'ah make room for me
Who am come so cold now
To my tomb.' So, on Good Friday,
Under a frosty moon
They carried Him and laid Him in her womb.

A grave and icy mask her heart wore twice,
But on the third day it thawed,
And only a stone's-flow away
Mary saw her God.
Did you hear me? Mary saw her God!

Dance, Mary Magdalene, dance, dance and sing,
For unto you is born
This day a King.[3] 'Lady', said He,
'To you who relent
I bring back the petticoat and the bottle of scent.'

3. cf. Luke 2.11.

The Net

Quick, woman, in your net
Catch the silver I fling!
O I am deep in your debt,
Draw tight, skin-tight, the string,

And rake the silver in.
No fisher ever yet
Drew such a cunning ring.

Ah, shifty as the fin
Of any fish this flesh
That, shaken to the shin,
Now shoals into your mesh,
Bursting to be held in;
Purse-proud and pebble-hard,
Its pence like shingle showered.

Open the haul, and shake
The fill of shillings free,
Let all the satchels break
And leap about the knee
In shoals of ecstasy.
Guineas and gills will flake
At each gull-plunge of me.

Though all the Angels, and
Saint Michael at their head,
Nightly contrive to stand
On guard about your bed,
Yet none dare take a hand,
But each can only spread
His eagle-eye instead.

But I, being man, can kiss
And bed-spread-eagle too;
All flesh shall come to this,
Being less than angel is,
Yet higher far in bliss
As it entwines with you.

Come, make no sound, my sweet;
Turn down the candid lamp
And draw the equal quilt
Over our naked guilt.

Biographies/Bibliographies

Austin Clarke

LIFE. Born in Dublin in 1896, Clarke was educated at Belvedere College and at University College, Dublin, where his teachers included Douglas Hyde and Thomas MacDonagh. He succeeded to MacDonagh's post in University College when that 1916 leader was executed by the British. In 1920 he married in a registry office and was dismissed from his post the next year, probably because of his civil marriage. Between 1922 and 1937 Clarke spent much time in England, attempting to support his art by literary journalism. He also wrote verse drama at this time and two novels, *The Bright Temptation* (1932) and *The Singing Men at Cashel* (1936), both of which were banned in Ireland. In 1936 W. B. Yeats omitted Clarke from the *Oxford Book of Modern Verse*. The first phase of Clarke's poetic career was completed by the publication of *Night and Morning* in 1938, the year following his permanent return to Ireland. Between 1938 and 1955 Clarke published no book of poetry, but he was active in the writing and encouragement of verse drama. In 1955, with *Ancient Lights*, he entered a new phase of creativity, which would complete his poetic *oeuvre* with the publication of his *Collected Poems* in 1974, the year of his death. In this period Clarke published five full-length collections and the long poem, *Mnemosyne Lay in Dust* (1966), which greatly increased his readership and reputation. His association with the Dolmen Press gave him an international readership for the first time and at his death he was recognized as a distinctive twentieth-century poetic voice.

CHIEF WRITINGS. *The Vengeance of Fionn* (Dublin and London: Maunsel, 1918); *The Fires of Baal* (Dublin and London: Maunsel and Roberts, 1921); *The Sword of the West* (Dublin and London: Maunsel and Roberts, 1921); *The Cattledrive in Connaught* (London: Allen and Unwin, 1925); *The Son of Learning* (London: Allen and Unwin, 1927); *Pilgrimage and Other Poems* (London: Allen and Unwin, 1929); *The Bright Temptation* (London: Allen and Unwin, 1932); *Collected Poems* (London: Allen and Unwin, 1936); *The Singing Men at Cashel* (London: Allen and Unwin, 1936); *Night and Morning* (Dublin: Orwell, 1938); *The Sun Dances at Easter* (London: Andrew Melrose, 1952); *Ancient Lights* (Dublin: Bridge Press, 1955); *Later Poems* (Dublin: The Dolmen Press, 1961); *Twice Round the Black Church* (autobiography) (London: Routledge & Kegan Paul, 1962); *Poetry in Modern Ireland* (Cork: Mercier Press, 1962); *Collected Plays* (Dublin: The Dolmen Press, 1963); *Flight to Africa* (Dublin: The Dolmen Press, 1963); *Mnemosyne Lay in Dust* (Dublin: The Dolmen Press, 1966); *Old-Fashioned Pilgrimage* (Dublin: The Dolmen Press, 1967); *A Penny in the Clouds* (autobiography) (London: Routledge & Kegan Paul, 1968); *The Echo at Coole and Other Poems* (Dublin: The Dolmen Press, 1968); *Orphide and Other Poems* (Dublin: The Dolmen Press, 1970); *Collected Poems* (Dublin: The Dolmen Press, 1974).

BIOGRAPHY AND CRITICISM. Susan Halpern, *Austlin Clarke, His Life and Works* (Dublin: The Dolmen Press, 1974); *Irish University Review*, Austin Clarke Special Issue, Maurice Harmon (ed.), Vol. 4, No. 1 (Spring 1974) (very useful, with biographical notes, critical essays by various hands and a bibliography); Craig Tapping, *Austlin Clarke: A Study of his Writings* (Dublin: The Academy Press, 1981); Gregory A. Schirmer, *The Poetry of Austin Clarke* (Mountrath: The Dolmen Press; Notre Dame, Indiana: University of Notre Dame Press, 1983); Maurice Harmon, *Austin Clarke: A Critical Introduction* (Dublin: Wolfhound Press, 1989).

Patrick Kavanagh

LIFE. Born in 1904 at Iniskeen, Co. Monaghan, Kavanagh worked as a cobbler and small farmer until 1939 when he moved to Dublin to try to make his way as a poet. His first book of poems *(Ploughman and Other Poems)* had been published in 1936 and his autobiography, *The Green Fool*, appeared in 1938. Through these, Kavanagh had achieved a minor reputation as a peasant poet, but his autobiography was suppressed by a libel action and the Dublin literary world offered few opportunities for the professional writer in the war years. Kavanagh survived as a hack reviewer and journalist for many years, during which he attempted realistic fiction and even in 1952, with his brother Peter, launched a political and cultural journal, *Kavanagh's Weekly*, which lasted for several controversial months.

In 1942 Kavanagh published his major long poem, *The Great Hunger*, the work on which, although he later repudiated its angry satiric stance, his reputation was largely to depend. In 1952 he took an action for libel against the *Leader* newspaper (which had published an unflattering profile of him); this failed, but not before Kavanagh had been publicly humiliated in court. In the same year he survived an operation for lung cancer. For a few years following these traumata, Kavanagh experienced a poetic renewal and from this period came the poems of casual, mature celebration that have seemed exemplary to subsequent Irish poets. Kavanagh's *Collected Poems* were published in 1964. He married in 1967, the year of his death in Dublin.

CHIEF WRITINGS. *Ploughman and Other Poems* (London: Macmillan, 1936); *The Green Fool* (London: Michael Joseph, 1938); *The Great Hunger* (Dublin: The Cuala Press, 1942); *A Soul for Sale* (London: Macmillan, 1947); *Tarry Flynn* (London: The Pilot Press, 1948); *Come Dance With Kitty Stobling* (London: Longmans, Green and Co. Ltd., 1960); *Self Portrait* (Dublin: The Dolmen Press, 1964); *Collected Poems* (MacGibbon and Kee, 1964); *Collected Prose* (London: MacGibbon and Kee, 1967); *November Haggard* (New York: The Peter Kavanagh Hand Press, 1971); *The Complete Poems of Patrick Kavanagh* (New York: The Peter Kavanagh Hand Press, 1972).

BIOGRAPHY AND CRITICISM. Brendan Kennelly, 'Patrick Kavanagh' in Séan Lucy (ed.), *Irish Poems in English* (Cork and Dublin: The Mercier Press, 1972), pp. 159-84. Alan Warner, *Clay Is The Word* (Dublin: The Dolmen Press, 1973); Seamus Heaney, 'The Poetry of Patrick Kavanagh: From Monaghan to the Grand Canal' in Douglas Dunn (ed.), *Two Decades of Irish Writing* (Cheadle Hulme: Carcanet Press, 1975), pp. 105-17; Darcy O'Brien, *Patrick Kavanagh* (Lewisburg, Pennsylvania: Bucknell University Press, 1975); John Wilson Foster, 'The Poetry of Patrick Kavanagh: A Reappraisal' in *Mosaic*, XII, 3 (1979), 139-52; John Nemo, *Patrick Kavanagh* (Boston: Twayne, 1979); Seamus Heaney, 'The Placeless Heaven: Another Look at Kavanagh' in *The Government of the Tongue* (London: Faber, 1988), pp. 3-14.

Denis Devlin

LIFE. Born in Greenock, Scotland in 1908, Devlin was educated at Belvedere College in Dublin, at University College, Dublin, at Munich University and at the Sorbonne in Paris. He joined the Department of External Affairs in 1935, in whose service he remained until his death in Dublin in 1959. Served as diplomat in Rome, New York, Washington (where he spent the years 1940-47), London and Turkey. He was Ireland's first ambassador to Italy in the last year of his life. Widely read in European poetry, Devlin was a skilled translator, particularly of the French poet St-John Perse. His work never achieved a wide readership, but was respected by his literary contemporaries. It still awaits its definitive critic.

CHIEF WRITINGS. *Intercessions* (London: Europa, 1937); *Lough Derg and Other Poems* (New York: Reynal and Hitchcock, 1946); trans., *Exile and Other Poems* by St John Perse (New York: Pantheon Books, 1949); Brian Coffey (ed.), *Collected Poems* (Dublin: The Dolmen Press, 1964); *The Heavenly Foreigner* (Dublin: The Dolmen Press, 1967); *Collected Poems of Denis Devlin*, edited by J. C. C. Mays (Dublin: Dedalus Press, 1989).

BIOGRAPHY AND CRITICISM. Brian Coffey, 'Of Denis Devlin: Vestige, Sentences, Presages', *University Review* 2, No. 10 (1965), 3-18; Mary Salmon, 'Modern Pilgrimage: Denis Devlin's "Lough Derg"', *Studies* (Spring 1973), 75-83; *Advent VI*, Denis Devlin Special Issue (Southampton: Advent Books, 1976).

Thomas MacGreevy

LIFE. Born in Tarbert, Co. Kerry in 1893. Fought in the British army in World War I at Ypres salient and the Somme, Educated subsequently at Trinity College, Dublin, MacGreevy lived in Paris from 1927 to 1933 where he involved himself in the avant-garde movement in the arts. Among his friends, acquaintances and correspondents were James Joyce, Wallace Stevens and Samuel Beckett (with whom he conducted an extensive correspondence). He returned to Dublin in 1941 and was appointed director of the National Gallery nine years later. He retired from this post in 1963 and died in Dublin in 1967.

CHIEF WRITINGS. *Collected Poems*, edited by Thomas Dillon Redshaw, with a foreword by Samuel Beckett (Dublin: New Writers' Press, 1971); *Collected Poems of Thomas MacGreevy: An Annotated Edition*, edited by Susan Schreibman (Dublin: Anna Livia Press; Washington, D.C.: The Catholic University of America Press, 1991).

BIOGRAPHY AND CRITICISM. Stan Smith, 'From a Great Distance: Thomas MacGreevy's "Frames of Reference"', *The Lace Curtain*, No. 6 (Autumn 1978), 47-55; Anthony Cronin, 'Thomas MacGreevy: Modernism Not Triumphant', in *Heritage Now* (Dingle: Brandon Press, 1982), pp. 155-60.

Brian Coffey

LIFE. Born in Dun Laoghaire, Co. Dublin in 1905, Coffey was educated at University College, Dublin and in Paris, where he studied with the French catholic philosopher, Jacques Maritain. He was awarded a doctoral degree from Institut Catholique in Paris in 1947. Coffey has made his living as a teacher and as a professor of philosophy in St Louis University, Missouri, from which post he resigned in 1952. He has lived in London and Southampton since this date. His consistently experimental and avant-garde work has had a dedicated, if small, readership.

CHIEF WRITINGS. *Selected Poems* (Dublin: New Writers' Press, 1971); *Advent*, in *Irish University Review*, Vol. 5, No. 1 (Spring 1975); *Death of Hektor* (Guildford: Circle Press, 1979) (limited edition); London: Menard Press, 1982); *Chanterelles* (Cork: The Melmoth Press, 1985).

BIOGRAPHY AND CRITICISM. Stan Smith, 'On Other Grounds: The Poetry of Brian Coffey', in Douglas Dunn (ed.), *Two Decades of Irish Writing* (Cheadle Hulme: Carcanet, 1975), pp. 59-80; *Irish University Review*, Brian Coffey Special Issue, Vol. 5, No. 1 (Spring 1975) — as well as works by Coffey (including 'Advent'), contains 'Biographical Note and Introductory Essay' by James Mays; James Mays, 'Passivity and Openness in Two Long Poems by Brian Coffey', *Irish University Review*, Vol. 13, No. 1 (Spring 1983), 67-82.

Louis MacNeice

LIFE. Born in Belfast in 1907, MacNeice spent his childhood in Carrickfergus, Co. Antrim. He was educated in England at Marlborough and Oxford, where he studied Classics. In 1929 he was appointed to a lectureship in Classics at Birmingham University, where he remained until 1936 when he accepted a post as lecturer in Greek at Bedford College, University of London. In the 1930s MacNeice was associated with the Auden group of left-wing English poets. He visited the United States in 1939 and again in 1940, but returned at the end of that year, intending to enlist in the British armed forces in the war against Hitler; his application was rejected on health grounds. He joined the British Broadcasting Corporation in 1941 and remained as a producer there until 1961. He wrote many radio plays and features during those two decades, and also travelled frequently. In his final phase of poetic activity, which culminated in the posthumous volume, *The Burning Perch* (1963), he confirmed a reputation as one of the most accomplished lyric poets of the period. He died in Shoreditch, London in 1963.

CHIEF WRITINGS. *Poems* (London: Faber; New York: Random House, 1935); *Modern Poetry: a personal essay* (London and New York: Oxford University Press, 1938); *The Earth Compels* (London: Faber, 1938); *Autumn Journal* (London: Faber; New York: Random House, 1939); *Selected Poems* (London: Faber, 1940); *Poems 1925-40* (New York: Random House, 1940); *Plant and Phantom* (London: Faber, 1941); *The Poetry of W. B. Yeats* (London and New York: Oxford University Press, 1941); *Springboard* (London: Faber; New York: Random House, 1944); *The Dark Tower and Other Radio Scripts* (London: Faber, 1947); *Holes in the Sky* (London: Faber; New York: Random House, 1948); *Collected Poems* (London: Faber; New York: Oxford University Press, 1949); *Ten*

Burnt Offerings (London: Faber; New York: Oxford University Press, 1953); *Autumn Sequel* (London: Faber; 1954); *Visitations* (London: Faber; New York: Oxford University Press, 1957); *Eighty-Five Poems* (London: Faber; New York: Oxford University Press, 1959); *Solstices* (London: Faber; New York: Oxford University Press, 1961); *The Burning Perch* (London: Faber; New York: Oxford University Press, 1963); *The Strings Are False* (autobiography) (London: Faber, 1965); *Varieties of Parable* (Cambridge: Cambridge University Press, 1965); *Collected Poems* (London: Faber, New York: Oxford University Press, 1966); *Selected Poems*, edited by Michael Longley (London and Boston: Faber, 1989).

BIOGRAPHY AND CRITICISM. Elton Edward Smith, *Louis MacNeice* (New York: Twayne, 1970); William T. McKinnon, *Apollo's Blended Dream* (London: Oxford University Press, 1971) (a detailed study of MacNeice as a philosophic poet); D. B. Moore, *The Poetry of Louis MacNeice* (Leicester: Leicester University Press, 1972); T. Brown and A. Reid, *Time Was Away: The World of Louis MacNeice* (Dublin: The Dolmen Press, 1974); Terence Brown, *Louis MacNeice: Sceptical Vision* (Dublin: Gill and Macmillan, 1975); Barbara Coulton, *MacNeice in the BBC* (London and Boston: Faber, 1980); Robyn Marsack, *The Cave of Making: The Poetry of Louis MacNeice* (Oxford: Clarendon Press, 1982); see also C. M. Armitage and Neil Clark, *A Bibliography of the Works of Louis MacNeice* (London: Kaye and Ward, 1973); Edna Longley, *Louis MacNeice: A Study* (London and Boston: Faber, 1989).

John Hewitt

LIFE. Born in Belfast in 1907, Hewitt was educated at Methodist College and at Queen's University, Belfast. Between 1930 and 1957 he worked in the Belfast Museum and Art Gallery. In 1957 he became director of the Herbert Art Gallery and Museum in Coventry, England, where he remained until his retirement in 1972. Since that time until his death in 1987, he lived in Belfast. After the publication of his *Collected Poems* in 1968, Hewitt maintained a steady flow of verse, which now constitutes a very considerable body of work. He also published art history and criticism.

CHIEF WRITINGS. *No Rebel Word* (London: Frederick Muller, 1948); *Collected Poems 1932-67* (London: MacGibbon and Kee, 1968); *Out of My Time* (Belfast: Blackstaff Press, 1974); *Time Enough* (Belfast: Blackstaff Press, 1976); *The Rain Dance* (Belfast: Blackstaff Press, 1978); *Kites in Spring* (Belfast: Blackstaff Press, 1980); Alan Warner (ed.), *The Selected John Hewitt* (Belfast: Blackstaff Press, 1981); *Mosaic* (Belfast: Blackstaff Press, 1981); *Loose Ends* (Belfast: Blackstaff Press, 1985); *Freehold* (Belfast: Blackstaff Press, 1986).

BIOGRAPHY AND CRITICISM. John Montague, 'Regionalism into Reconciliation', *Poetry Ireland*, 3 (Spring 1964), 113-18; Seamus Heaney, 'The Poetry of John Hewitt', *Threshold*, 22 (Summer 1969), 73-77 (reprinted in Seamus Heaney, *Preoccupations* (London and Boston: Faber and Faber, 1980), pp. 207-10; Douglas Sealy, 'An Individual Flavour: *The Collected Poems of John Hewitt*', *The Dublin Magazine*, 8 (Spring/Summer 1969), 19-24; Terence Brown, *Northern Voices: Poets from Ulster* (Dublin: Gill and Macmillan, 1975), pp. 86-87; John Wilson Foster, 'The Landscape of Planter and Gael in the Poetry of John Hewitt and John Montague', *The Canadian Journal of Irish Studies*, 1 (November 1973), 1733; T. Clyde (ed.), *Ancestral Voices: The Selected Prose of John Hewitt* (Belfast: Blackstaff Press, 1987).

W. R. Rodgers

LIFE. Born in Belfast in 1909 and educated there, W. R. Rodgers graduated from Queen's University, Belfast and entered the Presbyterian Theological College in that city. He was ordained as a presbyterian minister in 1935 and served at Loughgall, Co. Armagh from 1935 to 1946. In 1946 Rodgers resigned from the ministry and settled in London where he made many contributions to the BBC as a member of the Third Programme Features Department. In 1966 he accepted a post as a writer in residence at Pitzer College, Claremont, California. He died in Los Angeles in 1969.

CHIEF WRITINGS. *Awake! and Other Poems* (London: Secker and Warburg, 1941); *Europa and the Bull* (London: Secker and Warburg, 1952); *Collected Poems* (London: Oxford University Press, 1971).

BIOGRAPHY AND CRITICISM. Darcy O'Brien, *W. R. Rodgers* (Lewisburg, Pennsylvania: Bucknell University Press, 1970); Terence Brown, 'The Poetry of W. R. Rodgers and John Hewitt' in Douglas Dunn (ed.), *Two Decades of Irish Writing* (Cheadle Hulme: Carcanet Press, 1975), pp. 81-97; Terence Brown, *Northern Voices: Poets from Ulster* (Dublin: Gill and Macmillan, 1975), pp. 114-27.

TERENCE BROWN, *Editor*

The Counter-Revival 1930-60: Drama

It is one of the ironies of W.B. Yeats's career that an artist who proposed for the Irish nation a theatre of high idealism and poetic intensity in fact presided over an actual theatre company, The Abbey, whose staple was a dogged realism lit only momentarily by flashes of symbolic possibility. That an artist of indisputable cosmopolitanism should have acquiesced for so many years in a repertoire both resolutely local in theme and staunchly national in outlook compounds the sense of irony.

In the heady days of its inception, the Abbey had not espoused a nativist outlook in any dogmatic rejection of European or world drama. Rather, Yeats's instinct for the poetic in the theatre made him apathetic at best about the dominant Ibsenism of the early years of the century. Had the drama of Europe been mounted under the aegis of Maurice Maeterlinck (one of Yeats's symbolist heroes) in the first two decades of the century, then the history of the Irish national theatre, one supposes, would have been altogether different. As it was, Yeats's idealistic disregard of Ibsenism, again ironically, allowed less exalted souls in the Abbey company to mount a steady diet of local plays, whose realism paid modest respects to the dramatic spirit of the age, but whose general complacency of vision owed little to the author of *The Doll's House* and *An Enemy of the People*.

In 1919 the Abbey at last gave way to the demand of some of its younger actors and writers that the recent upsurge of experimental drama in Europe should find expression on a Dublin stage. In that year Lennox Robinson founded the Dublin Drama League and with Yeats's (if not Lady Gregory's) approval, this group was allowed to present international drama at the Abbey on Sundays and Mondays when the theatre was normally closed for business. Therefore in the 1920s it was possible to see in Dublin the experimental plays of such writers as Benevente, Strindberg, O'Neill and Pirandello, and to become aware of how Expressionism threatened to supersede Ibsenism as the quintessence of the modern. It was undoubtedly this slight change in Dublin's dramatic climate in the 1920s, whereby the steady prevailing winds of Abbey realism were met by more exotic, if fitful, Expressionist breezes from Europe and America, which inspired the young Denis Johnston, who, with *The Old Lady Says 'No!'*, was to produce an Irish Expressionist *tour de force* in 1929. This climatic alteration also meant that when the Abbey rejected the play, in legend because Lady Gregory said no (so *Shadowdance*, the play's original title, was replaced by the satiric masterstroke), a new professional theatre existed in Dublin willing and able to give it dramatic life.

The Gate Theatre was founded in 1928 by Hilton Edwards and Micheál MacLiammóir to perform the best of the modern classics and to provide an imaginative counterweight to the Abbey's naturalism. Where the Abbey was realistic and rural, the Gate would be stylized and urban and would experiment visually and choreographically. It would be cosmopolitan, presenting 'ancient and modern plays from all sorts of places'. Johnston's play might have been written to order, easily finding its place among such works as Wilde's *Salomé*, Evreinov's *The Theatre of the Soul*, Tolstoy's *The Power of Darkness*, and O'Neill's *The Hairy Ape* and *Anna Christie*.

The Old Lady Says 'No!' was first presented by the Gate on 3 July 1929, immediately attracting public attention to its astringent critique of popular Irish national sentiment and quickly establishing itself as an addition to the Irish dramatic heritage (it was revived by the Gate in 1931, 1934 and 1938 and was performed in the Gaiety in Dublin in 1941 and 1947).

The Old Lady Says 'No!' opens with a dramatic prologue in which we eavesdrop on a scene from some melodramatic recreation of Robert Emmet's arrest after his failed rebellion in 1803. The elements familiar from legend and from frequent dramatization are present — the speech from the dock, the love affair with Sarah Curran — but all are rendered ridiculous in a high-flown rhetoric, drawn as Johnston himself later advised us 'almost entirely from lines from Mangan, Moore, Ferguson, Kickham, Todhunter, and the romantic school of nineteenth-century Irish poets'. Many in Johnston's Dublin audience would have been familiar with these sources and with the tones of nationalist piety with which they were customarily recited. Johnston's irreverent and absurdly disrespectful theatrical cocktail would have been instantly offensive where it was not found a cause of modish hilarity.

The playlet swiftly forsakes mock-heroic melodrama for Expressionist experiment when Major Sirr arrests Robert Emmet and accidentally knocks the hero unconscious. And it is the contents of that unconscious mind that we eavesdrop upon in the play's main scenes as a bemused Speaker (half actor playing Emmet, half Emmet himself) is set abroad in a twentieth-century Dublin unable to cope with the reality of a heroic ideal it so hypocritically espouses.

The play's technique, in which past and present are elided in a kind of dramatic kaleidoscope — where dream and reality intertwine, where mental states and physical locations can be juxtaposed by tricks of lighting — creates a world of parodic subversion. But the victim of this subversion is not just the contemporary social world, with, for example, its pretentious literary salon. The play's message is not simply that, in the light of an Emmet's idealism, the present is a sad spectacle. Rather, the play dramatizes in its spritely pessimistic fashion the ways in which sentimentalities, whether of idealism or of cynical despair, betray life to death, action to fatuity. So, near the play's final curtain, the crowd, who have been the Speaker's antagonists throughout the action, join with him in a litany of savage nihilism:

SPEAKER: Cursed be he who values the life above the dream.

VOICES: Amen.

SPEAKER: Cursed be he who builds but does not destroy.

VOICES: Amen.

SPEAKER: Cursed be he who honours the wisdom of the wise.

VOICES: Amen.

SPEAKER: Cursed be the ear that heeds the prayer of the dead.

VOICES: Amen.

The Old Lady Says 'No!', appearing as it did at the end of the 1920s, might have proved a watershed in the history of Irish theatre. Dublin had been introduced to Expressionism and the modern European drama through the work of the Dublin Drama League. The hesitant experimentalism of a decade had borne fruit, it must have seemed, in the establishment of a new Irish theatre company, The Gate, and in the discovery of a truly modern talent. The aesthetic hegemony of the Abbey tradition must have seemed in jeopardy, especially when one remembers that in 1928 Seán O'Casey, who had reinvigorated that tradition with his great trilogy, severed his connection with the Abbey theatre. That he did so following the rejection of his play of World War I, *The Silver Tassie*, with its Expressionist second act, might have intensified a sense that the Abbey had missed a turning tide. The 1930s proved otherwise.

As it happened, the Gate, which found itself a permanent theatrical home in 1930, experienced grave financial difficulties. The capital city of a country where there was almost no audience for symphonic music, for ballet, for the opera, and where the National Gallery was almost empty of modern painting and sculpture, also could not sustain a professional theatre company dedicated to 'the production of plays of unusual interest, and to experiment in methods of presentation free from the conventional limitations of the commercial theatre.' Dependent on patronage, the company became prey to fractious disputation, its major contribution resting not on a consistent repertoire but on the brilliant theatricality of Hilton Edwards's direction and of MacLiammóir's stage design and acting.

The Abbey in fact retained its hold on the national consciousness in the 1930s and 1940s, with its realistic portrayal of rural and small town life. Its concerns remained local and its style unadventurous. When this is reflected upon, it should be remembered that not only was such a repertoire a prudent response to the period's prevailing conservatism, but a consequence of a developing Irish interest in amateur dramatics. During the war years especially (with their markedly restricted social opportunities), this movement amounted almost to an obsession. And it was 'the Abbey play', with its recognizable domestic regimes, its familial concerns and local vision, which proved most readily assimilable to the parish halls and school rooms of provincial Ireland. In such a climate the Abbey received numerous new plays in this successful and saleable mode. Even Denis Johnston's second play, *The Moon in the Yellow River*, produced by the Abbey in 1931, forsook experiment for a realism that the Abbey directors indeed could welcome (despite the fact that the play had its origins in Johnston's intention to parody 'the Abbey play'). Its focus on precise political issues in the Irish Free State (although the work achieves a universal statement on the paradoxes of conflicting ideals) prompts the recognition that much of the success of even *The Old Lady Says 'No!'* had depended on a sure local knowledge. That had been a quintessentially Dublin play, an extravaganza of local lore, legend and feeling (it has never travelled well). The universalizing theatrical impulses of Expressionism were held in check by a Dublinman's ambiguous feelings for his native place, the metaphysical solemnity of much contemporaneous European and American drama, happily dispelled by a characteristic Anglo-Irish *sprezzatura*, a wit bred of excruciatingly complex loyalties:

> Strumpet city in the sunset
> Suckling the bastard brats of Scot, of
> Englishry, of Huguenot
> Brave sons breaking from the womb,
> wild sons fleeing from their Mother
> Wilful city of savage dreamers,
> So old, so rich with memories!

So the play concludes, identifying Emmet's terminal condition with a malaise symptomatic of a city's experience.

It was the experience of the small towns of provincial Ireland that most frequently occupied the Irish dramatic imagination in the 1930s and 1940s. Well-constructed plays about local dilemmas and crises attracted audiences to the Abbey Theatre, which, despite a general sense of decline, managed to produce 104 new plays by recognized and new dramatists between 1930 and 1940. Some of these attempted an Ibsen-like social critique, but in a fashion that seemed to satisfy audiences rather than to disturb them. The dramatist Hugh Leonard has characterized the period as one of parish-pump Ibsenism, and has wittily supplied an identikit sketch of a typical Abbey play's *dramatis personae* in those depressed years:

> . . . a living room setting behind a general store in a provincial town; a middle-aged protagonist, who was a guerrilla fighter in the Civil War and is now a publican or merchant of substance with political aspirations; his wife, a drab creature worn out by her husband's ruthlessness and insatiable ambition; and their children: a young man who has been forced against his will to enter a seminary, and a daughter who, to further her father's designs, is being compelled into an arranged marriage with the weakling son of a local politician. Among the supporting cast are the father's old comrade in arms, now his chief clerk, whose dramatic function is that of comic relief and chorus combined; the daughter's preferred suitor, an idealistic young schoolteacher; and the parish priest, venal and tyrannical, who has the schoolteacher dismissed from his post and hounded from the town on a trumped-up charge of moral turpitude.[1]

Unsurprisingly then, one of the most popular plays of the 1930s was Lennox Robinson's *Drama at Inish* (1933). Set in an Irish seaside resort, it has its complement of stock characters — the genially despotic proprietor of the one hotel and his fashion-conscious wife; the young woman who has departed the town for a job in the capital city, leaving behind a fond admirer; the local, almost inarticulate, member of parliament; a Civic Guard. But where the play differs from many of the works of the period is that its tone is engagingly lighthearted. The drab, provincial facts of Irish local life are taken for granted and made the stuff of a nicely concocted comic trifle. Robinson, whose early dramatic attempts had been marked by an Ibsenite intensity

1. Hugh Leonard, 'Drama, the Turning Point' in P. Rafroidi and P. Joannon (eds), *Ireland at the Crossroads* (Lille: Publications de l'université de Lille III, 1978), pp. 80-81.

of moral feeling, and who contributed much to the enlargement of the Irish dramatic imagination in his work with the Dublin Drama League in the 1920s, in fact found his métier in such well-made comedies.

Drama at Inish indeed finds its comedy in a gently preposterous portrayal of the deleterious effects on a local community of an overly theatrical and serious dramaturgy. A theatre company has been booked to play a season in the seaside town, the comic turns of the previous summer having proved less than successful. Hector de la Mare and his wife, Constance Constantia, have been engaged to fill the bill. In Act I Hector announces his dramatic policy: 'I now confine myself entirely — with the co-operation of Miss Constantia — to psychological and introspective drama. The great plays of Russia, an Ibsen or two, a Strindberg . . . .' By the end of the second act, the reverberations (to employ his own pretentious term) of this policy, have made themselves felt in the town in suicide pacts, incendiarism and personal disruptions of various kinds. Helena, the servant girl, has accused the boot-boy Michael of fathering her illegitimate child (who had died at birth two years earlier); John Twohig, the hotel's owner, has quarrelled with his wife, Annie, about her extravagance; Lizzie, Twohig's sister, has declared that she had been jilted by Peter Hurley, the local parliamentary representative; Eddie Twohig, John's son, has fallen into a metaphysical melancholy; Michael wants to forsake cleaning boots for the stage. And all because of the plays produced at the Pavilion through a wet three weeks of summer.

In the final act, Inish is allowed to return to the even tenor of its ways. Beneath the near-farcical comedy of the play, Robinson implies, in an almost patronizing if affectionate manner, that provincial Irish life does not need its Ibsens or Chekhovs. Hector's mission, announced in Act I, is unnecessary. There he had pompously declared that he performed his plays so that 'they may revolutionize some person's soul'. He is engaged on 'a tremendous mission where the pulpit is the stage and the great dramatists preach the sermon'. Inish, Robinson is saying, can do very well without such elevated instruction. For life there, as the final act indicates, is well worth the living. So Robinson's play, in its artful and knowing way, with its *fausse naiveté* and its acute ear for dialogue and provincial Irish speech patterns, is a suavely managed endorsement of a conservative society's self-satisfaction. Its popularity is all too readily explicable. In a pleasingly light comic mode, Robinson offered his audiences images of a life they knew, a range of almost stock characters, and sent them away secure in the knowledge that all was fundamentally well in the lives they were living.

There was one dramatist who in the 1930s made of the well-constructed realistic play of Ibsenite social concern something more than local dramatics. In two plays, *Things That Are Caesar's* (1932) and *Shadow and Substance* (1937), Paul Vincent Carroll came close to charging provincial Irish life with universal significance, vitalized as they are by a rebellious if not wholly consistent current of feeling. *Things That Are Caesar's* is an Irish *A Doll's House*, where the heroine is trapped in an arranged marriage that has the approval of the church and its representative, the local parish priest. The play dramatizes a conflict between the need for order, with its attendant hypocrisies, and the human instinct for freedom, with its dangers and inevitable costs. Carroll wrote of his own dramaturgy: 'Ibsen took a sure and disciplined hand in my development and with the addition of Synge, whose work taught me colour and rhythm, I began to visualize more sanely the strengths and weaknesses of human characters.'[2] It is Carroll's ability to present on his stage a range of characters and render them comprehensible in their social context that makes *Shadow and Substance* so theatrically powerful. What might have remained a rather unconvincing Ibsenite problem play about aspects of Roman catholic spirituality begins to touch on a more fundamentally human conflict between intellect and vision, authority and rebellion. For in *Shadow and Substance* we see Irish provincial life in all its narrow-minded pettiness, stimulated, by familiar conflicts between conventional character types, into true dramatic intensity.

In the play, Canon Skerritt is an intellectual, urbane, ironic and self-controlled parish priest. He is also a social snob, consoling himself in the less than fashionable Ardmahone, one of 'the small towns lying round the feet of the Mourne hills in County Louth', with visions of the broad vistas of European catholic civilization. Improbably enough, the character of Skerritt was based on the

2. Cited in Paul A. Doyle, *Paul Vincent Carroll* (Lewisburg, Pennsylvania: Bucknell University Press, 1971), p. 19.

personality of Jonathan Swift. Carroll wished to make Swift 'not only a Catholic but a learned interpreter of Catholicism, and throw him into the modern mental turmoil in Ireland'. Skerritt suggests the great Dean's social discomfiture in Dublin when he aspired to a bishopric in England, as well as his sardonic rigour of mind; but sadly the parish priest of Ardmahone lacks the Swiftian grandeur. Indeed he can seem merely ridiculous in his lofty disdain for common humanity (something Swift never evinced).

The play's action concerns a quarrel between the Canon and the local schoolmaster, Dermot Francis O'Flingsley. The thirty-two-year-old O'Flingsley (in a play strongly influenced by religious symbolism, the fact that Christ was crucified at about that age should not pass unnoticed) is the pseudonymous author of an anti-clerical book, which arouses much local pietistic passion. The Canon is not inclined to make much of O'Flingsley's rebellion, treating it with a proud indifference. But the Canon's step-niece, Thomasina Concannon, is a newly trained teacher with her eye on a job in O'Flingsley's school. Add a local spinster, Miss Jemima Cooney, and her nephew, Francis Ignatius O'Connor, also with a brand new teaching certificate and a need for a job, two dim-witted curates, a social climbing publican and his wife, and the Ibsenite brew is complete. But Carroll complicates the ingredients by the inclusion of the saintly servant girl, Brigid, who has frequent conversations with Saint Brigid, herself an Irish saint associated in legend particularly with the Louth area. Brigid is a foil both to the narrow-minded piety of the parish and to its priest's pretentious pride. Carroll has his plot proceed in predictable ways. The Canon decides to dismiss O'Flingsley and put his step-niece, who will marry Francis Ignatius, in position together as his schoolteachers. But the play takes an unusual turn when Brigid's visionary religious experience challenges the Canon's righteous self-possession. She sacrifices herself in an attempt to protect O'Flingsley, whom a mob wishes to drive from the parish. Throughout the play Brigid has stood simply for love and understanding and at the end she dies for these values. In so doing, she induces a traumatic disturbance of spirit in a community that has known little of such values. Skerritt and O'Flingsley are at the last companions in grief and guilt. Neither authority nor rebellion are adequate in the face of a simple yet mystical faith — the play's epigraph is Keats's 'Oh, what a power has white Simplicity.'

In Carroll's *Shadow and Substance* one senses realism discovering its own limitations. The play's central weakness is an unsettling tendency to lapse into near melodrama when matters of spiritual import arise. It is as if Carroll's realism can handle issues of social and moral significance but finds itself embarrassed before those things — such as sainthood and vision — that concern the religious imagination. In the final two acts, therefore, one is not clear whether Brigid is mad or inspired, whether the dramatic occasion is one merely of psychological insight or that of true religious revelation. The play therefore gestures impressively at universality of theme, but achieves no convincingly universal dramatic existence as symbolic action.

D.E.S. Maxwell has written of the modern Irish drama:

> The work of the Abbey Theatre, of Irish drama, is a long experiment, sometimes descending to stretches of mechanical self-duplication, with the boundaries of realist theatre. On its heights it engages realist theatre in poetic transformation . . . beyond the mere traffic with, in Yeats's phrase 'the sensation of an external reality'.[3]

The 1930s and 1940s saw much of that mechanical self-duplication, although Johnston, Robinson and Carroll in their various ways suggested how the mere traffic with Yeats's 'external reality' might be transcended. However, only Johnston, with his Anglo-Irish blend of tragic feeling and patrician wit, came close to what might be deemed the characteristic mode of the greatest Irish drama of the twentieth century, the tragi-comic. Synge's *The Playboy of the Western World* and O'Casey's *Juno and the Paycock* can each be classed as tragi-comedies that verge on farce or melodrama. In these plays, a vision of the world as chaotically absurd is complicated and enriched by a sense of the eruptive, grotesque, comic energies of life and language.

It was in fact the most inexorably realistic play of this period, Brendan Behan's *The Quare Fellow* (1954), which most closely approximated to this form (if we except Samuel Beckett's *Waiting for*

3. D.E.S. Maxwell, *A Critical History of Irish Drama 1891-1980* (Cambridge: Cambridge University Press, 1984), pp. 6-7.

Godot, which was first performed in Dublin in 1955, having been initially produced in France in 1953).

Behan's play is a grindingly realistic dramatization of prison life on the day and night preceding an execution by hanging. But the play's almost documentary naturalism of dialogue and action is enlarged into compelling theatrical metaphor by elements of music hall routines and songs, and by swift juxtapositions of mood and dramatic tone. Throughout there is a contrast between the formal, even scientific, correctness of the warders and the demotic, unsentimental irreverence of the prisoners, which reaches its climax in Act III, Scene II with Mickser's savagely black comic commentary on the preparations for the hanging as if it were the start of a horse race. But each response seems a way of coping with the appalling fact that a man's life is being ended. *The Quare Fellow* is at the centre of a vision of life as atrocity, which finds expression in a play that blends precise documentary with compulsive ritual, cruel humour with sardonic and poignant song and with solemn hymn.

DENIS JOHNSTON

(1901-84)

from: THE OLD LADY SAYS 'NO!' (1929)

[In the opening scene of the second part of *The Old Lady Says 'No!'*, Denis Johnston satirizes the provincial pretentiousness of a middle-class Dublin soirée. Robert Emmet is an unlikely and unwelcome intruder.]

PART TWO

Through the Curtain, amidst a hearty round of applause, comes the MINISTER'S *talented daughter,* MAEVE. *She has on a nice white dress with a white bow to match in her long, loose, black hair which reaches quite to her waist. Around her neck on a simple gold chain hangs a religious medal. She curtsies in charming embarrassment and commences to recite.*

MAEVE:

Kingth Bweakfatht.
The King athed de Queen
And de Queen athed de Dar-med
Could — I (*a little breathlessly*) — se — butter
For-de-roy —— thlaice — a — bwead?
Queen athed de Dar-med
De Dar-med thed Thertinley
Ah goan tell — Cow now
Fore the goeth tebed . . .

She continues this amusing piece to the very end, when the Curtain parts amid general applause disclosing a fantastically respectable drawing-room loud with the clatter of tea things. A party is in progress under the aegis of the MINISTER FOR ARTS AND CRAFTS *and his nice little* WIFE. *The guests consist of one of the* REDCOATS, *now a* GENERAL *in a green uniform, the Statue of* GRATTAN,[1] *rather a nice woman called* LADY TRIMMER — *one of those people whose expression of pleased expectancy never for a moment varies, the old* FLOWER WOMAN *who is seated unobtrusively in the background eating an orange, and a small but enthusiastic* CHORUS. *Side by side upon the sofa reading from right to left are* O'COONEY *the well-known dramatist,* O'MOONEY *the rising portrait painter, and* O'ROONEY *the famous novelist.* O'COONEY *wears a cloth cap, blue sweater and a tweed coat.* O'MOONEY *has a red shirt and horn-rimmed spectacles, while* O'ROONEY *is dressed in full saffron kilt together with Russian boots. The* MINISTER *himself bears a strange resemblance to the* STAGE HAND. *It is all very nice indeed.*

CHORUS:

Oh very nice nice
Oh very nice nice nice
How old how nice how very nice don't you think so
Oh yes indeed yes very nice indeed I do think so indeed don't you indeed. (*Teaspoons clink*)

LADY TRIMMER: What was that one, my dear?

MAEVE: Kingth Bweakfatht pleathe.

LADY TRIMMER: Very nice indeed, Maeve. I

1. Henry Grattan (1746-1820), orator, politician and lawyer, was the dominant figure in the Irish parliament between 1782 and 1800, so much so that it is commonly known as 'Grattan's parliament'. His statue stands in College Green, Dublin, outside the former parliament building.

must teach that one to my two chicks. Where do you learn, my dear?

MAEVE: The Banba Thcool of Acting, Lower Abbey Thweet.

CHORUS: The Banba School of Acting, Lower Abbey Street.

O'COONEY: Wasn't that bloody awful?

O'MOONEY: The question is, is she an aartist? A real aartist?

O'ROONEY: O'Mooney sounds better with his mouth shut.

WIFE: Of course, she hasn't been learning very long. But she has the language, and that's half the battle these days. Show them, Maeve.

MAEVE: *Caed mile failte.*[2]

LADY TRIMMER: Oh very good indeed. But of course, she has her father's talent.

MINISTER: Ah, well, now . . .

WIFE: *(Pleased)* Oh, Lady Trimmer!

MINISTER: Well, now, all the same I don't know about that. But mind you I do say this, Talent is what the country wants. Politics may be all O.K. in their way, but what I say to *An Taoischach*[3] is this, until we have Talent and Art in the country we have no National Dignity. We must have Talent and Art. Isn't that right?

CHORUS: We must have Art have Talent and Art.

LADY TRIMMER: Quite. And cultivated people of taste. You mustn't forget them, Mr Minister. Art cannot live you know by taking in its own washing — if I may put it that way.

O'COONEY: Aw Holy God!

O'MOONEY: *(Ruminatively)* The reel aartist must be fundamental. Like Beethoven. Now, *I'm* fundamental.

O'ROONEY: Fundament, all right.

MINISTER: Now see here. I'm Minister for Arts and Crafts, you see. Well, a young fellow comes along to me and he says, Now look, Liam, here's some Art I'm after doing . . . it might be a book you see, or a drawing, or even a poem . . . and can you do anything for me, he says? Well, with that, I do . . . if he deserves it, mind you, only if he deserves it, under Section 15 of the Deserving Artists' (Support) Act, No. 65 of 1926. And there's none of this favouritism at all.

CHORUS: The State supports the Artist.

GRATTAN: And the Artist supports the State.

CHORUS: Very satisfactory for everybody and no favouritism at all.

MINISTER: *(Confidentially)* And of course, then you see, it helps us to keep an eye on the sort of stuff that's turned out, you understand.

CHORUS: Clean and pure Art for clean and pure people.

LADY TRIMMER: What we need most is a small Salon.

GENERAL: That's right. A small Art Saloon.

WIFE: We often have people in on Sunday evenings for music and things. Won't you sing something now, General?

GENERAL: Aw, I have no voice at all.

O'COONEY: He's bloody well right there.

O'MOONEY: The question is . . . .

LADY TRIMMER: Just somewhere where the nicest people . . . the people one wants to meet . . . like Mr O'Cooney and Mr O'Mooney . . .

O'ROONEY: *(Suspiciously)* And Mr O'Rooney.

LADY TRIMMER: *And* Mr O'Rooney, can get together quietly and discuss Art and common interests.

WIFE: Haven't you brought your music?

CHORUS: You must have brought your music.

GENERAL: Well now . . . if you insist. Maybe I might find something.

O'COONEY: *(To* O'MOONEY*)* Ay, have *you* put my cap somewhere?

WIFE: Do, General.

GENERAL: I don't know for sure, mind you. I might . . . just happen to have something on me. *(He produces a roll of music from inside his tunic)*

CHORUS: The General's going to sing.

GENERAL: Ah, but . . . sure there's no one to play th' accompanyment.

WIFE: Maeve will play. Won't you, darling?

MAEVE: Yeth mammy.

Signs of distress from the sofa.

WIFE: Of course you will dear. Give her the music, General.

CHORUS: Ssssh! *(The* GENERAL *gives her the music rather doubtfully and they are opening the performance, when there comes a loud, peremptory knock at the door. General surprise)*

WIFE: *(Bravely but apprehensively)* What can that be?

LADY TRIMMER: Strange!

MINISTER: A knock at the door?

GENERAL: Ah now, isn't that too bad!

LIZZIE: *(Entering)* There's a gentleman at the

2. Irish: 'a hundred thousand welcomes.' The proper spelling is *cead*.
3. The chief, i.e. the prime minister of the Irish government, although it is usually spelled *Taoiseach*.

door, ma'am, looking for the Rathfarnham bus.

WIFE: What kind of a gentleman, Lizzie?

LIZZIE: A gentleman in a uniform, ma'am.

MINISTER: A uniform? Tell me, does he look like the start of a Daring Outrage?

CHORUS: Possibly the Garda Síothchána.[4]

LIZZIE: He has a sword, sir.

MINISTER: A sword?

LIZZIE: (*Primly*) And a pair of slippers.

WIFE: Slippers?

GENERAL: I don't think I know that unyform.

CHORUS: Can't be the Garda Síothchána after all.

WIFE: Did he give any name, Lizzie?

LIZZIE: Yes, ma'am. A Mr Emmet.

LADY TRIMMER: Not *the* Mr Emmet?

LIZZIE: I don't know I'm sure, ma'am.

MINISTER: Ah, yes I remember. That's him all right.

GENERAL: Aw, the hard Emmet.

MINISTER: The old Scout.

WIFE: The gentleman who is far from the land.[5] Show him up at once, Lizzie.

LIZZIE: Yes, ma'am. (*She goes, muttering*) Doesn't look like a sailor to me.

LADY TRIMMER: How nice of him to call.

WIFE: Yes, indeed, but you know we can't be too careful since the Trouble.[6]

MINISTER: Emmet's all right. I know him well. Used to work with him in the old days.

GENERAL: Aw, the rare old Emmet.

LADY TRIMMER: You know I've wanted to meet him for such a long time. My husband always says that we of the old regime ought to get into touch with those sort of people as much as possible. We can assist each other in so many ways.

MINISTER: That's right. We must all get together for the good of the country.

WIFE: I wonder has he brought his music too?

GRATTAN: I expect he has.

LIZZIE *enters, cocking her head contemptuously towards the* SPEAKER, *who follows her with a strange, hunted look in his eye. He glances round apprehensively as though prepared for the worst and yet hoping against hope.*

CHORUS: Oh how do you how do you how do you how do you how . . . .

WIFE: How do you do? Bring another cup, Lizzie.

LIZZIE: Yes, ma'am. (*She goes, muttering*) I'll have to wash one first.

SPEAKER: Excuse . . . me.

WIFE: Come and sit down and let me introduce you to everybody. It was so nice of you to call. Liam has just been speaking about your work.

SPEAKER: I only came in to ask . . . .

CHORUS: Have you brought your music?

WIFE: This is Lady Trimmer, Mr Emmet.

CHORUS: Of the old regime.

LADY TRIMMER: Dee do.

SPEAKER: (*After peering closely into her face*) No, ah, no.

LADY TRIMMER: You must come and visit us too, Mr Emmet. First Fridays. Now promise.

WIFE: And General O'Smith of the *Oglaigh na h-Eireann*.[7]

GENERAL: (*Affably*) And many of them.

SPEAKER: It was you who hit me.

WIFE: And of course you know my husband, the Minister for Arts and Crafts.

CHORUS: Vote *Fianna na Poblacht*.[8]

MINISTER: *A chara*.[9]

The SPEAKER *tries to remonstrate but is hurried on.*

WIFE: And Mr Grattan's statue from College Green.

GRATTAN: Welcome Don Quixote Alighieri.[10] Did I speak the truth?

The SPEAKER's *head goes up.*

WIFE: And this is Mr O'Cooney, the great dramatist.

SPEAKER: Cap?

WIFE: Oh, Mr O'Cooney always wears his cap in the drawing-room.

O'COONEY: And why the bloody hell shouldn't I wear my cap in the drawing-room?

General laughter.

SPEAKER: I see.

O'MOONEY: Now me.

WIFE: This is Mr O'Mooney, the artist, if you can

4. The Garda Síochána are the Irish police force.
5. A satiric allusion to Thomas Moore's lament for Robert Emmet, the song 'She is far from the land'. Emmet, a friend of Moore's at Trinity College, led an abortive rebellion against British rule, in Dublin in 1803. He was executed after a famous trial.
6. The War of Independence and the Civil War, 1919-23.
7. The Irish army.
8. Band, or Warriors, of the People. A satiric allusion to the names adopted by Irish political parties after Independence.
9. Means 'Sir', as in 'Dear Sir' in an official communication.
10. Emmet is here identified with Dante, poet of the *Inferno*, and with the hero of Cervantes's novel. The implication is that he, a tilter at windmills, is being led, like Dante before him, through a personal hell.

remember everybody.

O'MOONEY: The reel Aartist.

O'COONEY: The owl cod.[11]

WIFE: Oh, please, Mr O'Cooney!

CHORUS: I love the way he talks, don't you?

O'MOONEY: Oh, don't mind O'Cooney. He's a great friend of mine, really.

O'COONEY: He is not!

WIFE: And this is Mr O'Rooney, the well-known novelist. Now I think you know everybody.

SPEAKER: (*Indicating the costume*) You play the pipes?

O'MOONEY *laughs shrilly*.

O'ROONEY: I do not. I do not believe in political Nationalism. Do you not see my Russian boots?

WIFE: Mr O'Rooney believes in the workers.

O'ROONEY: I do not believe in the workers. Nor do I believe in the Upper Classes nor in the Bourgeoisie. It should be perfectly clear by now what I do not believe in, unless you wish me to go over it again?

LADY TRIMMER: (*Archly*) Mr O'Rooney, you dreadful man!

SPEAKER: I'm sorry.

WIFE: Sit down now and have a nice cup of tea.

LIZZIE *meanwhile has been back with a dirty cup*.

CHORUS: I do like a nice cup of tea.

SPEAKER: So she is here, too!

WIFE: What's that?

SPEAKER: That damned old flower woman who turned them all against me!

WOMAN: Ay, mister, have ye e'er an old hempen rope for a neckcloth?

WIFE: You're joking, Mr Emmet. There's no old flower woman.

SPEAKER: I mean . . . look there.

WIFE: Have some tea, Mr Emmet. You're a little tired, no doubt.

SEMICHORUS: Delightful drink.

SEMICHORUS: Pity it tans the stomach.

WIFE: You'll feel much the better of it. And we'll have a little music afterwards. We often have music in the evenings.

MINISTER: Are you interested in Art, Mr Emmet?

LADY TRIMMER: I suppose you're a member of the Nine Arts Club?

WIFE: And the Royal Automobile Academy?

CHORUS: Celebrity Concerts. The Literary Literaries.

11. A common expression in Ireland, meaning 'old fool, idiot'.

SPEAKER: I don't feel very . . . Did you say that statue of Grattan was there?

WIFE: Oh yes, that's Mr Grattan's statue from College Green. We always have a few of the nicest statues in on Sunday evening. My husband is Minister for Arts and Crafts, you know.

LADY TRIMMER: Just to form a little group you know. A few people of taste.

WIFE: Of course we're only amateurs, but we're doing our best. (*Pause*)

SPEAKER: (*Suddenly*) Let me be persuaded that my springing soul may meet the . . . . (*Pause*)

LADY TRIMMER: I beg your pardon?

SPEAKER: Let me be per— (*He shakes his head hopelessly*) I am Robert Emmet.

GRATTAN: You are not.

SPEAKER: Who are you to question me?

GRATTAN: You are only a play-actor.

SPEAKER: Look well to your own soul, Major Sirr![12]

GRATTAN: Have you found your Holy Curran, Galahad?[13]

WIFE: I always say to Liam, Liam you really *must* get a nice statue of Mr Emmet. It's positively disgraceful that we haven't got one, don't you think?

MINISTER: Ah, well, dear, you know, expense, expense.

LADY TRIMMER: What a nice uniform! Tell me, do you admire the plays of Chekhov?

WIFE: Perhaps he acts for the Civil Service Dramatics.

SPEAKER: Act? . . . No. No cake, thank you.

CHORUS: Benevente Strindberg Toller Euripides Pirandello Tolstoy Calderon O'Neill.[14]

LADY TRIMMER: I'm sure you'd be good.

CHORUS: An annual subscription of one guinea admits a member to all productions and to all At Homes.

MINISTER: (*Confidentially*) Say the word and I'll get you into the Rathmines and Rathmines. I know the man below.[15]

12. The town-major who organized the arrest of Emmet in 1803.
13. Sarah Curran was the beloved of Robert Emmet. Sir Galahad, in Malory's *Morte d'Arthur* (1485), is predestined by his immaculate purity to achieve the quest of the Holy Grail, the vessel used by Christ at the Last Supper in which his blood was received at the Crucifixion.
14. A cosmopolitan roll-call of eight dramatists, many of whose plays were presented by the Dublin Drama League.
15. The reference is to the Rathmines and Rathgar Musical Society, an amateur group in the inner suburbs of Dublin. 'The man below' is a popular expression meaning 'the man in charge at the place referred to.'

LADY TRIMMER: Now do tell us, Mr Emmet, about your wonderful experiences in the Trouble.

The SPEAKER *spills his tea and looks around wild-eyed.*

SPEAKER: What do you mean?

GRATTAN: Ah — ha!

WIFE: Never mind. It's quite all right. I'll pour you out another cup.

LADY TRIMMER: (*Hastily*) You must have had such interesting times all through the fighting.

SPEAKER: I shall never fight again! (*He buries his face in his hands*)

MINISTER: Oh come, Mr Emmet! What's the matter!

WIFE: Are you not feeling well?

LADY TRIMMER: (*Aside*) Ssssh! Don't pay any attention. I understand. Do tell us about it, Mr Emmet. Talk. Talk someone.

SPEAKER: God have pity on me.

CHORUS: Oh the fighting everyone talk don't pay any attention wonderful experiences those were the attention fighting days how wonderful do tell us about the fighting days interesting and wonderful.

SPEAKER: It was I who shot him and you all know it! You all know! Isn't it enough for you? Haven't I suffered enough?

CHORUS: (*Louder*) Oh tuttut poor man don't talk do talk as hard as you can fighting wonderful pay no attention shellshock probably to have seen it all wonderful is he better yet poor man everybody pretend not to fighting notice.

SPEAKER: They trapped me! A good man . . . a true man . . . and I did it!

WIFE: Well what if you did shoot somebody? Everybody's shot somebody nowadays. That's all over now.

LADY TRIMMER: Yes, yes; of course we didn't approve of it at the time, but it's all so interesting now.

SPEAKER: Interesting!

MAEVE: (*Plaintively*) You never let me —

GENERAL: Ah, go on when I tell you!

MAEVE *commences the introduction to 'She is Far from the Land'.*

SPEAKER:

The air is rich and soft — the air is mild and
 bland.
Her woods are tall and straight, grove rising
 over grove.
Trees flourish in her glens below and on her
 heights above,
Oh, the fair hills of Eire, oh.[16]

O'ROONEY: Will you move up on the sofa and breathe into yourself.

O'MOONEY: We'd be better off if your hips were as soft as your head.

(*Simultaneously*)

SPEAKER:

Down from the high
 cliffs the rivulet is
 teeming
To wind around the
 willow banks that
 lure me from above;
Ah, where the
 woodbines with
 sleepy arms have
 wound me.[17]

GENERAL: (*Singing*)

She is far from the
 land where her
 young hero sleeps
And lovers around her
 are sighing:
But coldly she turns
 from their gaze and
 weeps
For her heart in his
 grave is lying.

MINISTER: (*Solo*) And do you remember the day, Seamus, of the big round-up in Moore Street when the 'G' man[18] tried to plug me getting out of the skylight?

SPEAKER, GENERAL *and* O'COONEY
(*Simultaneously*)

SPEAKER: (*Louder*)

But there is lightning in my blood;[19] red lightning tightening in my blood. Oh! if there was a sword in every Irish hand! If there was a flame in every Irish heart to put an end to slavery and shame! Oh, I would end these things!

GENERAL:

She sings the wild
 songs of her dear
 native plains,
Every note which he
 loved awaking.
Ah! little they think,
 who delight in her
 strains,
How the heart of the
 ministrel is
 breaking.

O'COONEY:

Aw, Jesus, and the evenings down in the
old I.R.B. in Talbot Street, picking out the
'Soldiers' Song' on the blackboard.[20]

16. The speaker is slightly misquoting James Clarence Mangan's poem 'The Fair Hills of Eire, O!' This poem has been associated with Robert Emmet's sweetheart, Sarah Curran, from the opening playlet.

17. The speaker is quoting George Darley's poem, 'Serenade of a Loyal Martyr', written sometime in the 1830s. The General is singing the Tom Moore song referred to earlier, from *Irish Melodies* (1808-34).

18. A member of the British plain-clothes police unit that fought the IRA during the War of Independence.

19. An allusion to Mangan's famous poem 'Dark Rosaleen'.

20. The IRB is the Irish Republican Brotherhood, the revolutionary group that plotted the 1916 Rising. The 'Soldier's Song' became the Irish national anthem.

SPEAKER, MINISTER *and* GENERAL
(*Simultaneously*)

SPEAKER:

I have written my name in letters of fire across the page of history. I have unfurled the green flag in the streets and cried aloud from the high places to the people of the Five Kingdoms: Men of Eire, awake to be blest! to be blest!

GENERAL:

He had lived for his love, for his country he died,
They were all that to life had entwined him;
Nor soon shall the tears of his country be dried,
Nor long will his love stay behind him.

MINISTER:

Sometimes I wish I was back again on the run with the old flying column out by the Glen of Aherlow.

O'MOONEY *and* O'ROONEY *join in low undertones.*

O'ROONEY:

My good woman, I said, I'll tell you what's wrong with you. Virginity, my good woman, that's all. And believe me, it's nothing to be proud of.

O'MOONEY:

Saint Peetric d'ye see because Saint Peter was the rock and Saint Patrick was the seed. That makes Saint Peetric, d'ye see. For the rock is underneath and the seed lies above, so Saint Peter and Saint Patrick are Saint Peetric.

(*At the same time*)
O'COONEY:

And that night waiting up on the North Circular[21] for word of the executions. Ah, not for all the wealth of the world would I give up the maddenin' minglin' memories of the past . . . .

SPEAKER:

Rise, Arch of the Ocean and Queen of the West! I have dared all for Ireland, I will dare all again for Sarah Curran. Their graves are red. O make her a maddening mingling glorious morrow . . .

GENERAL:

O! make her a grave where the sunbeams rest
When they promise a glorious morrow . . .

The black curtain closes behind the SPEAKER, *blotting out the room, and the voices fade away. The* SPEAKER *himself has somehow chimed in upon the last few lines of the song, and is left singing it by himself.*

21. A ring road in Dublin.

LENNOX ROBINSON
(1886-1958)

from: DRAMA AT INISH (1933)

[In the final act of Lennox Robinson's *Drama at Inish: An Exaggeration in Three Acts*, the town, disturbed out of recognition by the arrival of the players for a summer season, comes to its senses. Things get back to normal.]

JOHN TWOHIG, *proprietor of the Seaview Hotel, Inish*
ANNIE TWOHIG, *his wife*
LIZZIE, *his sister*
EDDIE TWOHIG, *his son*
PETER HURLEY, *the local TD*
CHRISTINE LAMBERT
HECTOR DE LA MARE, *an actor*
CONSTANCE CONSTANTIA, *an actress, his wife*
JOHN HEGARTY, *a reporter*
TOM MOONEY, *a Civic Guard*
WILLIAM SLATTERY, *P.S.I.*

ACT III

Scene: The same, a week later. Morning; dull, raining slightly. LIZZIE *comes in, ushering* MR HEGARTY, *a young man.*

LIZZIE: Will you come in here, Mr ——, Mr ——

HEGARTY: Hegarty, John Hegarty.

LIZZIE: Oh, yes, you told me, of course. Will you

sit down Mr Hegarty? I'm afraid my brother is out and my sister-in-law too; they went out after breakfast and I haven't seen them since.

HEGARTY: That doesn't matter at all, Miss Twohig. I am sure you can give me all the information I want.

LIZZIE: Well, of course I can tell you about the hotel, seeing that I more or less run it. I can let you have a very nice room from about —

HEGARTY: No, no. I'm afraid I'm not staying. I just want a little information.

LIZZIE: Information?

HEGARTY: I always think that in these little country towns there's no place like the hotel for gathering news. The hotel is the hub of the town, so to speak.

LIZZIE: Maybe.

HEGARTY: (*Suddenly and dramatically*) Miss Twohig, why has Inish suddenly put itself on the map of Ireland?

LIZZIE: Sure it was always there — on big maps, anyway.

HEGARTY: Why has Inish suddenly become news? Not yet front-page news, but front-page news maybe tomorrow.

LIZZIE: Front-page? Oh, you're from a newspaper?

HEGARTY: I thought I had explained that. I'm not from any particular paper, I'm free lance. It's part of my business to read all the Irish papers every day, and during the last two weeks one word has caught my eye again and again. Inish! Attempted suicide at Inish. Boy breaks open till in Inish. Respectable butcher called McClusky beats up his wife at Inish. Young couple attempt suicide pact, couple employed at Inish. Now I happen to know Inish. My sister and I spent a month here two summers ago, for our sins. It was very expensive and it was deadly dull.

LIZZIE: Where did you stay?

HEGARTY: Not here. You were even more expensive. But that's not the point. The point is that during that month nothing happened. There wasn't even a decent dog-fight, and now all these things happen — in ten days. An outbreak of this kind doesn't come by chance. I've been putting two and two together — I believe I'm the first journalist in Ireland to put this particular two and two together, and I'm here this morning to try and find out what they make.

LIZZIE: I don't understand all you say, but sure there was nothing at the back of that boy breaking into McGarry's till except that he wanted money to go to the theatre. McGarry let him off, and Mr de la Mare gave him a season ticket, and there's been no more about it.

HEGARTY: Yes, I hardly expected there was anything in that particular incident, but I've been all round the town this morning — I came from Dublin by the early train — I've been into shops and pubs, and I notice the strangest kind of attitude in the people. Everyone seems suspicious, watching everyone else, expecting something strange to happen. If you mention anyone to anyone else, you're met with a kind of veiled suggestion that they are not what they seem to be; that they have a shady past and are likely to have a blacker future. I hasten to add that no one has had a word to say against you, Miss Twohig.

LIZZIE: Did you mention my name?

HEGARTY: I don't think I did.

LIZZIE: Well, let you try mentioning it and see what happens. You're right, Mr Hegarty; this town is full of gossipers and slanderers, and I could tell you things about some of them that would make your hair stand on end.

HEGARTY: But they weren't like this two years ago. They just seemed nice, ordinary people, a little on the dull side. Come, Miss Twohig, there's something at the back of it all. What is it?

LIZZIE: Indeed, I couldn't tell you — unless it would be the weather. Rain every day for a fortnight.

HEGARTY: If rain were accountable for crime, all Ireland would have murdered itself long ago. No, no, it can't be the weather.

LIZZIE: Maybe it's politics. Them and the weather are about the only things we think of outside our own business.

HEGARTY: Yes, I hadn't thought of politics. It might be a curious result of recent legislation. Perhaps your local T.D.[1] could help to elucidate this point.

LIZZIE: Is it Peter Hurley?

HEGARTY: Yes.

LIZZIE: You'd do well not to go near Peter Hurley; he's the deceiver if ever there was one.

HEGARTY: In what way?

LIZZIE: I'd rather not say; it's a personal matter.

1. T.D. = teachta Dála, i.e. a Dáil deputy, a member of the lower house of the Irish legislature.

But be deceitful in one way and you'll be deceitful in every way. Isn't that right, Mr Hegarty?

HEGARTY: I suppose so.

LIZZIE: Anyway, you can't see him today because he's away in Dublin at the Dáil.[2]

HEGARTY: Oh, yes, of course. They were having a very important all-night sitting last night.

LIZZIE: (*Laughing*) Imagine poor old Ireland depending on the votes of men like Peter Hurley. I have to laugh.

HEGARTY: The division was likely to be very close, I believe.

LIZZIE: Oh, they can depend on Peter. Peter'll vote the way he is told to vote. The creature hasn't the courage of a mouse. (HECTOR *and* CONSTANCE *come in. They look rather gloomy*) Oh, come in, come in; this is a young gentleman from a newspaper — Mr de la Mare and Miss Constantia — Mr Hegarty.

Mutual greetings. Everyone sits down.

HECTOR: You wanted to interview me?

HEGARTY: Well — er — I'm not sure.

HECTOR: Or perhaps it was Miss Constantia you wanted to talk to?

CONSTANCE: No, please, Hector; you know how I hate publicity and all my pictures are at the theatre.

HECTOR: There are times, darling, when one must sacrifice oneself to the great hungry public.

HEGARTY: I am just looking for general information.

HECTOR: Well, we opened our season here nearly three weeks ago, and we have had the most — I won't say astonishing, because I have always believed that the public at heart — *au fond*, as the French say — is quite sound and wants the best. Fine plays, well presented, mind you, and with suitable *décor*. I admit that our *décor* is not at present all it might be. You can understand, Mr Hegarty, how the exigencies of continual touring —

HEGARTY: (*Light breaking on him*) Oh, you're actors?

HECTOR: (*With exaggerated humility*) Well, I hope we are actors. Are we, Constance, my love?

LIZZIE: The De la Mare Repertory Company, Mr Hegarty. (*To* HECTOR) Mr Hegarty is from Dublin, and he's maybe a bit out of touch with things, you must forgive him.

HECTOR: I quite understand and there is nothing to forgive. We have not played Dublin for years. When were we there last, darling?

CONSTANCE: I really can't remember.

HEGARTY: What theatre did you play in?

HECTOR: One of the big ones, of course; I can't remember which.

HEGARTY: And you're doing well here?

HECTOR: We have been doing extraordinarily well — up to this week. Miss Twohig, can you explain the curious falling off in the audiences this week?

LIZZIE: I can not. And I don't know why everyone this morning is asking me to explain everything.

HECTOR: I'm sure the repertory was varied enough — some new plays and some old favourites, but no one comes — at least only a handful. Things seem to be happening in the town all the time, and everybody is so busy talking about what has just happened or waiting for the next thing to happen to have any inclination or time to come to the Pavilion.

HEGARTY: Ah, so you've noticed it too?

HECTOR: Noticed what?

HEGARTY: The accumulation of incidents of a mildly criminal nature.

HECTOR: Oh, there have been many strange things which have not got into the papers.

HEGARTY: It's extraordinarily interesting.

CONSTANCE: It's extraordinarily distressing, Mr Hegarty, when as a consequence we play to empty houses.

HECTOR: Never mind, dearest. We've learned to take the rough with the smooth.

CONSTANCE: We have. ''Tis not in mortals to command success, but we'll do more, Sempronius, we'll deserve it.'[3]

HECTOR: (*Chiming in*) 'We'll deserve it.'

HEGARTY: Bravo!

LIZZIE: I wish you could see some of their plays, Mr Hegarty. They're gorgeous — though sometimes it's a bit hard to get to sleep after them. That one, Mr de la Mare, where you throw the lamp at Miss Constantia and are then put in a strait-waistcoat — that was a very good one, but of course my favourite is where the baby is murdered in the cellar.

HECTOR: Perhaps you will come to the theatre tonight, Mr Hegarty? Any representative of the

2. The lower house of the Irish legislature.

3. The quotation is from *Cato* (1713) I.2.43-44, by Joseph Addison (1672-1719), dramatist, poet and essayist.

press is, of course, more than welcome.

HEGARTY: I am afraid I have to get back to Dublin.

HECTOR: Well, shall you be here for a little time?

HEGARTY: I think so. At any rate I'll be knocking around the town until the afternoon train.

HECTOR: I see . . . I thought, Constance, we might stroll to the Pavilion and look for letters, and if we chanced to come on any photographs, Mr Hegarty might like to have them. Just as a little souvenir, Mr Hegarty; just as a little souvenir.

HEGARTY: Thank you very much.

HECTOR: (*Rising*) We won't be more than a few minutes. The Pavilion is just round the corner. Will you come, Constance?

CONSTANCE: (*Rising*) Yes, I should like a walk. I want to feel the sea-spray beating on my face.

LIZZIE: I'm afraid it's quite calm this morning, dear. The sun was trying to come out a little while ago.

CONSTANCE: What matter? I shall at least get a breath of ozone.

HECTOR: Shall I reserve your seat as usual, Miss Twohig?

LIZZIE: (*Sadly*) No, I can't come tonight.

HECTOR: You've missed every night this week. Fie, fie!

LIZZIE: No one is sorrier than myself. But I don't like the way Eddie is going on at all and I want to keep an eye on him.

HECTOR: Dear, dear!

CONSTANCE: What's the matter with Eddie, Miss Twohig?

LIZZIE: Haven't you noticed him yourself? So dark and shut up in himself. And, worse than that, he's broken his pledge.

CONSTANCE: Oh, Miss Twohig!

LIZZIE: Yes, dear, never took a drop in his life till now. I feel quite frightened.

HECTOR: Where is he?

LIZZIE: I don't know. He's not around the house. I'm sorry, Mr de la Mare, but I must stay at home tonight.

HECTOR: That's quite all right, Miss Twohig, quite all right. Constance, let us go. (*They go out*)

HEGARTY: (*Very keen*) Who is 'Eddie', Miss Twohig?

LIZZIE: My brother's only child.

HEGARTY: And he's behaving queerly?

LIZZIE: He is indeed.

HEGARTY: I'd like to speak to him.

LIZZIE: He's out, as you heard me say; but indeed you'll get nothing from him. I'm the only one he speaks to — whenever he does speak — I'm the only one knows what's preying on his mind.

HEGARTY: And what is that?

LIZZIE: The old story, Mr Hegarty, the old, old story — love's young dream, as Thomas Moore[4] said long ago . . . Are you married, Mr Hegarty?

HEGARTY: (*Rather taken aback*) Why — yes.

LIZZIE: And happy?

HEGARTY: Very happy.

LIZZIE: (*Disappointed, but making the best of it*) Ah, you're one of the few lucky ones so. (*A tap at the door*) Come in. (*Enter* SLATTERY *furtive and poorly dressed*) Oh, good morning, Mr Slattery.

SLATTERY: Good morning, Miss Twohig.

LIZZIE: My brother is out, but can I do anything for you?

SLATTERY: You're just the one that can. (*From under his coat he produces a large tin.*) D'ye see that?

LIZZIE: I do.

SLATTERY: 'Tis a grand weed killer you sold to Mick Tobin a few years back. I want one the like of it, and they told me below in the shop it's you had the key of all the poisons.

LIZZIE: (*Taking tin and looking at it*) So I have . . . 'Kill-em-Quick' — ah, Mr Slattery, isn't it a pity, we're not allowed to stock that any longer; 'twas too poisonous altogether.

SLATTERY: (*Very dejected*) Is that so? Well, have you anything in the nature of rat poison?

LIZZIE: I have, to be sure.

SLATTERY: Can I buy some?

LIZZIE: Lashin's of it. Wait till I get me keys.

HEGARTY: Just a minute; Mr Slattery — pardon my butting in — but what do you want the weed killer for?

SLATTERY: For me weeds.

LIZZIE: Of course.

HEGARTY: And, failing the weed killer, you want rat poison?

SLATTERY: For me rats.

LIZZIE: Of course.

HEGARTY: I see . . . (*He takes up the tin and examines it thoughtfully*) I imagine, Mr Slattery, that you are very unhappily married.

SLATTERY *gapes.*

LIZZIE: Sure the poor man's not married at all.

4. Thomas Moore (1779-1852), Irish poet and author of *Irish Melodies*. The lines come from the opening stanza of 'Love's Young Dream'.

HEGARTY: (*Taken aback*) Oh!

LIZZIE: He lives with an old termagant of an aunt who is rotten with money and won't let him have more than sixpence a week in his pocket — pardon me saying so, Mr Slattery.

SLATTERY: It's no more than the truth.

HEGARTY: But you'll come into all her money when she dies?

SLATTERY: I suppose I will.

HEGARTY: Hm. Very interesting.

LIZZIE: I'll have me keys in a minute.

SLATTERY: (*Trying to take back the tin*) Maybe I won't mind today. I'll get a few penn'orth of sweets instead.

LIZZIE: No trouble at all.

HEGARTY: (*Holding on to the tin*) I think I'll keep this.

SLATTERY: (*Snatching it from him*) You will not. (*Very rapidly and noiselessly he leaves the room*)

LIZZIE: (*Turning; she hadn't seen him go*) I can't find — oh! he's gone! Isn't that very queer now?

HEGARTY: Very queer, Miss Twohig. I think I've put that two and two together anyhow. This may be a case for the police.

LIZZIE: The police? (*And immediately the door opens and* MOONEY, *a Civic Guard, appears*) Oh! heaven protect us!

MOONEY: 'Morning, Miss Twohig. Is your brother about?

LIZZIE: He's not.

MOONEY: Or the mistress?

LIZZIE: She's out too. Why do you want them? Can I do anything for you?

MOONEY: Well — I wanted to prepare them like.

LIZZIE: Prepare them?

MOONEY: Break the news, as you might say.

LIZZIE: Merciful heavens, what's happened?

MOONEY: It's Master Eddie.

LIZZIE: Eddie! Eddie! He's dead?

MOONEY: No, no, miss. But he's terrible wet.

LIZZIE: Wet?

MOONEY: Yes, miss. He was in the sea.

LIZZIE: Bathing?

MOONEY: No, miss. In his clothes.

LIZZIE: Is he after falling in? Poor little Eddie!

MOONEY: No one knows rightly how he got into the sea, miss.

LIZZIE: And who rescued him?

MOONEY: He rescued himself, miss. It seems he got out of the sea at the White Rocks. Maybe he fell in, or maybe he — no matter. Anyway, he walked out of the sea himself, and then he hid among the rocks because he was ashamed-like to walk through the town dripping wet; but a lad came on him and brought him back, and he's having a sup of whiskey at Breen's, so I thought I'd just come ahead and give you all the bend.[5]

LIZZIE: I'm sure it's very kind of you, Tom. Oh! I wish Annie was here, or Helena — I haven't seen her all the morning either. I'd better get a cup of tea for him, anyway.

MOONEY: Don't bother about the tea, miss. Put him to bed the minute he comes in.

LIZZIE: Yes, that's a good idea.

MOONEY: And have a couple of hot-water bottles ready.

LIZZIE: Yes.

MOONEY: And give him two aspirins.

LIZZIE: Two? Yes.

MOONEY: And tell the master I'll be back in a little while as soon as Master Eddie is dried off. I'm afraid there'll be a few questions I'll have to put to him.

LIZZIE: (*Fussing about the room*) What an upset it all is — poor Eddie — aspirin and hot-water bottles — where are my keys? Tom, do you see my keys anywhere?

MOONEY: (*Starting to look*) What class of keys?

LIZZIE: Oh, just a bunch of keys. Oh, Eddie, Eddie! Mr Hegarty, for goodness' sake have a look round for a bunch of keys. (*They all start looking*) The kettle's sure to be off the boil — 'twould be bound to happen. If Helena was here itself —

MOONEY: I have them here, miss, here on the writing table.

LIZZIE; (*Taking them*) Thank you, Tom. I won't be two minutes now. (*She goes out*)

HEGARTY: Is there any statement you'd like to make?

MOONEY: About what?

HEGARTY: Master Eddie.

MOONEY: Who the devil are you?

HEGARTY: I write for the papers, and —

MOONEY: Ah! go to blazes.

HEGARTY: There is nothing you want to say?

MOONEY: There is not.

HEGARTY: I see. It's a pity. It might have got your name before the public.

MOONEY: I don't want my name before the

5. 'Give you the advantage of being forewarned' — letting someone have priority at the bend in a road.

public. I want to live quiet. Here, out with you.

HEGARTY: Before I go I have a statement to make in connection with poisons.

MOONEY: I won't hear it. I'm bothered out of my life with people coming to me with statements about attempted murders and suicides and God knows what. I'll hear no more of them.

CHRISTINE *comes in, in evident distress*

CHRISTINE: Is Eddie —? Oh! I beg your pardon.

MOONEY: That's all right, Miss Lambert. (*To* HEGARTY) Out of this, you.

HEGARTY: But really —

MOONEY: No more talk. (*He pushes him out*) Master Eddie's as right as rain and will be here in a minute.

CHRISTINE: They told me at the factory he was drowned.

MOONEY: Wisha,[6] bad luck to them for story-tellers.

CHRISTINE: Then in the street they said he had only got a ducking.

MOONEY: Let you sit down. You're all of a tremble.

CHRISTINE: Thank you, Mr Mooney.

MOONEY: (*Moving to the door*) I'll see that they send Eddie home; he should get out of his wet clothes and not be drinking at Breen's. (*He hesitates: he comes back to her*) Miss Lambert, if you'll excuse the intrusion, we've all a great respect for John Twohig and the family and I'd be sorry anything to happen Eddie.

CHRISTINE: Happen Eddie? But he's safe, isn't he?

MOONEY: He is in one way, and he isn't in another. It'll be my business, I'm afraid, to find out what brought him into the water today, and, begging your pardon, it'll be a little bit your business too.

CHRISTINE: (*Getting up indignantly*) I had nothing to do with it. What do you mean? What are you accusing me of?

MOONEY: (*Soothingly*) Now, there's no use flying out at me. I'm too old, and I'm married; that makes me patient. Everyone in town knows you and Master Eddie. Everyone likes the two of you; and that's a sweet little place John has outside the town.

CHRISTINE: I don't know it.

MOONEY: 'Tis well you know it. The last time you were down here, didn't I see you and Eddie walking the land? Good land and a smart, tidy little garden all going to waste because John's too busy to live out there. A doaty little house[7] — a woman living out there would be crowned. However, I won't go into all that. I'll just hint that, under certain circumstances (*Voice of* EDDIE, *off*), I might overlook any charges I might have to bring against the young gentleman in question. I think I hear him coming. (*He goes to the door and looks out*) Come in here, Eddie, for a minute before you go to your room. There's someone wants to see you.

EDDIE: (*Heard off*) Who is it?

MOONEY: 'Tis Miss Lambert.

EDDIE: (*Heard off*) No, no, I can't come in.

MOONEY: (*Going outside the door*) In with you and no nonsense. (*There is a bit of a scuffle outside and* MOONEY *shoots in* EDDIE. EDDIE *looks very woe-begone; he has no hat and his hair is tousled and wet. Someone has lent him an overcoat, old and too big for him. Below it are seen two wet flannel-trousered legs*) Here he is for you, Miss Lambert.

CHRISTINE: (*Rushing to him*) Eddie, darling!

MOONEY: Exactly. (*He goes softly out*)

CHRISTINE: My darling, what happened to you?

EDDIE: (*Rather stiffly*) Let me go, Christine. I'm not — I want to change, I'm dripping.

CHRISTINE: I know, darling. But what happened?

EDDIE: Oh, nothing.

CHRISTINE: Nothing? Nonsense. What did you do?

EDDIE: (*Glibly*) Well, I was on a rock and I got giddy and fell into the sea.

CHRISTINE: That may be a good enough story to tell round the town but it's not good enough for me. (*Softly*) Won't you tell me, Eddie?

EDDIE: (*Sniffing*) I was so miserable, Christine.

CHRISTINE: I know, darling.

EDDIE: It didn't seem worth going on with.

CHRISTINE: I know.

EDDIE: And there seemed no hope things would ever come right.

CHRISTINE: I know.

EDDIE: So — so I tried to make an end of it all.

CHRISTINE: My poor darling.

EDDIE: I'm no good at living, Christine.

CHRISTINE: Hush, hush.

EDDIE: But if I'm no good at living, I'm as bad at

6. A variant form of the Hiberno-English expression 'Musha', from the Irish *muise* or *Mhuise*, meaning 'Indeed!'. Generally, an exclamation of strong feeling.

7. A darling little house, one that would make you dote on it.

dying. For the minute I felt the cold of the water I wanted to get out of it quick and go on living and unfortunately I'm an awfully strong swimmer so — so I just swam ashore and — and that's all.

CHRISTINE: Darling!

EDDIE: Wasn't I the fool to try and destroy myself by drowning? I should have tried any other way but that.

CHRISTINE: Darling! . . . Eddie, do you know I've called you 'darling' about a dozen times in the last two minutes?

EDDIE: (*Quite dumb*) Have you, Christine?

CHRISTINE: Yes, darling.

EDDIE: Well?

CHRISTINE: Oh, you donkey?

EDDIE: You don't mean —? Oh, Christine!

CHRISTINE: (*In his arms*) Of course I mean. If you'd been drowned, Eddie, I'd have been the next off that rock, and I can't swim.

ANNIE *appears. She is in outdoor clothes. She takes in the situation at a glance.*

ANNIE: (*A little stern*) Hm! Upstairs with you, Eddie, and get out of your wet things.

EDDIE: Yes, Mammy. But Christine says she'll —

ANNIE: I think I know quite well what Christine says, but off with you. Do you want to get your death of cold?

EDDIE: No, Mammy. Very well, Mammy. I won't be five minutes changing, Christine.

ANNIE: You'll have a hot bath and you'll go to bed. Your Aunt Lizzie has everything ready for you.

EDDIE: Very well, Mammy. But I'm not going to bed. (*He dashes out*)

ANNIE: (*Softening*) I had to hunt him, Miss Lambert. I don't want him down on our hands with pneumonia.

CHRISTINE: Do you mind, Mrs Twohig?

ANNIE: Mind?

CHRISTINE: Eddie and me —?

ANNIE: Sure my dear, it's what I've been wanting ever since I set eyes on you. Eddie's foolish in some ways and a bit young, but he's as good as gold and I know you'll make a fine man of him.

CHRISTINE: Eddie's splendid, Mrs Twohig, splendid.

ANNIE: We'll talk it all out by and by. I've a lot of things on my mind this morning. You'll stay, won't you? It's not worth going back to the factory before dinner.

CHRISTINE: Yes, I'll stay. I'll just run upstairs and tidy myself. I rushed out of the factory without so much as a hat — and I think I've been crying.

ANNIE: Well, off with you. (CHRISTINE *goes out.* ANNIE *goes to the door and calls*) Helena! Helena! Bad luck to that girl; there's no getting any good out of her these days. (*She goes out*)

There is a little pause. JOHN *comes in, pushing* PETER *in front of him.* JOHN *looks very stern;* PETER *very frightened and small.* JOHN *locks the door.*

JOHN: Tell it to me again. I want to know are me ears mad or what.

PETER: (*In a tiny voice*) Well, 'twas an all-night sitting, as you know, and the late Minister for Agriculture made a terrible powerful speech and —

JOHN: To hell with the late Minister for Agriculture. Why did you listen to him?

PETER: I couldn't sort of help it. He made a terrible powerful speech and —

JOHN: And you let yourself be swayed by a bit of mob oratory?

PETER: It was not mob oratory, John, it was not. It was facts and figures and —

JOHN: Facts and figures! What the hell business have you with facts and figures? Your business is to vote with the Government.

PETER: I know. But —

JOHN: But?

PETER: It was that play, 'An Enemy of the People'[8] — do you remember it, John? I couldn't get it out of my head.

JOHN: Oh, those bloody plays!

PETER: Do you remember when the doctor in the play said that nobody should act so that he'd have to spit in his own face? I felt I sort of had to tell the truth, and the only way I could tell the truth — I'm no speechifier — was by my vote.

JOHN: So you voted against the Government?

PETER: I did.

JOHN: And defeated the bill?

PETER: Yes.

JOHN: And now the Government has to go to the country?

PETER: I suppose so.

JOHN: Suppose so? Don't you know? And don't you know that this place is disgraced for ever in the eyes of the world? Why, thunder and turf, man, what's going to become of public life at all if

8. Henrik Ibsen (1828-96), the great Norwegian dramatist, wrote *An Enemy of the People* (*En folkefiende*) (1882) as a satire on those who did not want to listen to truth that conflicted with their personal interests.

members of Parliament start being swayed this way and that by speeches and arguments, facts and figures, moryah?[9] There's an end to all stability in public affairs; nobody will know where they stand; no party will know from day to day whether it has a majority or not; it's chaos, man, pure chaos.

PETER: I know, I know. I'll never do it again.

JOHN: You'll never have the chance to do it again, me bucko. Do you think you're going to be a candidate at the next election?

PETER: I suppose I won't.

JOHN: I know you won't.

PETER: It was that play — 'An Enemy of the People'.

JOHN: 'An Enemy of the People.' Faith, that's you; that's your name from this out.

PETER: I nearly cried in the car coming down — I got a lift as far as Shangarry Strand and I kem on by bus. I'm afraid to face the wife, though she herself was mad about that same play.

JOHN: Ah, don't talk to me about those plays, they have been the ruination of this place. However, thanks to Annie, I have already made up my mind how to deal with them. (*He goes to the door and unlocks it*) You'd better be off home, Peter, and get over it. We'll be friends again one of these days, but for the next week for God's sake keep out of my sight.

PETER: (*Meekly*) Very well, John. (*He goes out*)

JOHN: (*Calling from the door*) Annie! Annie!

ANNIE: (*Heard off*) Yes, John.

JOHN: Come here. (ANNIE *comes in*) It's even worse than you thought.

ANNIE: What is?

JOHN: That play business. Peter Hurley's put out the Government on the head of some blasted play.

ANNIE: In heaven's name! That's awful, John.

JOHN: 'Tis a national tragedy — and to think that we're to blame for it all. Are they upstairs? Fetch them down. The sooner the whole thing is settled the better.

ANNIE: I think they're just after coming in from the Pavilion. I'll get them.

JOHN: Do so. And, Annie, come back yourself. You'll be a great help in case they turn nasty.

ANNIE: Very well. There's one thing, John. Eddie had a little accident this morning; he got a wetting. Say nothing to him about it, and if you hear any gossip in the town pay no heed to it.

JOHN: What do you mean? What's all this about?

ANNIE: Nothing at all. Pay no heed to anything but what I tell you. All's turned out for the best, and Eddie's going to marry Miss Lambert.

JOHN: The devil he is! Well, I'm delighted. Me bold Eddie!

ANNIE: I knew you would be. I'll go call Mr de la Mare. (*She goes out*)

JOHN *sits at the writing table, takes out a cheque book and writes a cheque.* HECTOR *and* CONSTANCE *come in.* HECTOR *has a large envelope in his hand.* ANNIE *follows them.*

HECTOR: You wanted to see us, Mr Twohig?

JOHN: I did. Will you sit down? (*The three sit.* JOHN *stands*) It's a bit hard for me to say what I have to say. Maybe I'd better begin by giving you this. (*He hands him the cheque*)

HECTOR: (*Looking at it*) Fifty pounds? What is this for?

JOHN: Maybe you don't remember that it was in our agreement that the contract at the Pavilion could be terminated on either side without notice on payment of fifty pounds?

HECTOR: Oh . . . . But — I do not understand. I admit that the audiences this week have been a disappointment, a sore disappointment, but I am confident that they will improve as the week goes on.

CONSTANCE: Miss Joyce bought three seats while we were there just now.

JOHN: It's got nothing to do with the audiences.

HECTOR: You can't have any complaint about the acting, I'm sure.

JOHN: I've nothing against the acting — 'tis very good.

ANNIE: Too good.

HECTOR: Or the conduct of the company?

JOHN: No. Decent people, every one of them.

HECTOR: Then, I repeat, I do not understand.

JOHN: Well, it's this way. Queer things have started to happen here, things that never happened in fifty years, and it was Annie who put her finger on the root of the trouble.

CONSTANCE: What sort of things do you refer to, Mr Twohig?

JOHN: You know very well, Miss Constantia. Nasty things that were getting Inish into the paper.

CONSTANCE: And what have we to do with such things?

JOHN: Annie, maybe you could explain better

9. From the Irish, *mar deadh*, an interjection implying doubt and irony — 'I don't think!'.

than I can.

ANNIE: In a word, it's all you and your plays, Mr de la Mare; and mind, I'm not saying a word against you personally or Miss Constantia either, but maybe they're too good for the like of us or we're too simple for them. I remember saying the morning you came — God forgive me — that we were blue-mouldy here for want of a good scandal or two; well, it seems there were lots of scandalous things going on in the town that no one knew anything of except the parties concerned. We were all more or less happy and comfortable, good tempered and jolly — until these plays began to put ideas into our heads. We got suspicious of our neighbours and of our own families. The young people got asking themselves 'Is life worth living?' If I've heard that question asked once in the last week I've heard it asked a dozen times. My own boy asked it of me! Sure never before did we think of asking ourselves such a ridiculous question.

HECTOR: It is far from ridiculous, Mrs Twohig. *Is* it worth living? I often wonder.

ANNIE: Ah, don't talk nonsense, man. Of course it is.

CONSTANCE: You have faith, Mrs Twohig.

ANNIE: I have my religion, Miss Constantia. Did you ever see a big stone in a field, Mr de la Mare?

HECTOR: Of course I did.

ANNIE: You might be sitting by it, idle-like, some sunny afternoon, and then for no reason at all you'd turn it over. And what would you see? Worms. Little beetles that'd run this way and that, horrible little creepies that'd make your stomach turn, and you'd put the stone back as quick as you could, or you'd run away.

HECTOR: I see, I see! A splendid simile, Mrs Twohig. We have lifted the stone, we have exposed Inish. Constance, it's wonderful. We have a mission here, a great duty.

JOHN: Oh no, sir, you haven't. Your duty is to get yourself and your traps[10] out of the hall as quick as you can. Annie and myself saw the Monsignor early this morning and he agrees with the course I'm taking.

ANNIE: He agrees that there must be a stop put to people going into suicide pacts on the head of 'Is life worth living?'

CONSTANCE: What nonsense. It shows great moral courage.

10. Luggage and theatrical gear.

ANNIE: Whining and running away? A thing we never did before in Ireland.

HECTOR: You know you really can't turn us out like this at a moment's notice.

JOHN: The agreement says I can, and things is so desperate that I have to stick by that agreement even if it seems a bit hard on you. Do you know that we'd have a murder on our consciences only by the good luck that McCluskey the butcher is such a bad shot with a hatchet?

CONSTANCE: I don't believe that had anything to do with our plays.

JOHN: And Tommy McCluskey in the front row every night? Of course, we all knew he fought now and again with Julia, but the night he threw the hatchet was the night he came home after seeing Mr de la Mare throw the lamp at you.

HECTOR: But there are quite a number of seats booked for tonight, Mr Twohig. Are you going to disappoint those people?

JOHN: (*With a confident smile*) They'll get their money's worth.

HECTOR: In what way?

JOHN: I was on the 'phone this morning to Shangarry Strand. I'm having the circus over.

HECTOR: (*Really pained*) A circus!

JOHN: It's on the road now. It will be in the town any minute.

CONSTANCE: (*Outraged*) This is an insult, a deliberate insult.

JOHN: It's nothing of the kind.

CONSTANCE: You are a narrow, bigoted man; you are afraid of the truth, and your wife is worse; she is an ignorant provincial. She has only seen our work twice —

ANNIE: Twice was enough.

CONSTANCE: We were giving you great art. I have played here as I have never played before. Mr de la Mare has given himself — all of himself — night after night to an audience of — clodhoppers. And now, when we stir something in these clods, waken them to some spark of life, you say they must go to sleep again, and you rock them to sleep with a circus! It's an insult to them and to us.

ANNIE: I don't know what you mean by awakening them to life, Miss Constantia. It seems to me you were awakening them to kill each other or themselves, and to say mean, slanderous things of each other and —

JOHN: And to put out the Government. Oh! when I think of that Peter Hurley —

ANNIE: The long and the short of it is, you were doing no good here and you must be gone.

HECTOR: You really mean this?

JOHN: I do.

HECTOR: I can only say that I am sorry. I think you are mistaken — tragically mistaken — in your attitude, but you have treated us fairly all along and I am not going to stoop to a sordid quarrel. (*He puts the cheque in his pocket*) My wife has said some things she should not have said, but I know that you'll forgive her.

ANNIE: Of course. Sure, dear, I'm sorry for you.

CONSTANCE: (*Sitting down and crying a little*) We were so happy here; you were all so kind to us, I thought we were fixed for the whole summer. I'm so tired of dragging from place to place.

ANNIE: (*Going to her with lovely sympathy*) I know, dear, I know. But you mustn't think of going away, not until you've settled where you can go. This is your home for as long as you care to stay. Isn't that so, John?

JOHN: To be sure it is. I'll take it badly if you go away in a huff.

CONSTANCE: (*Sniffing*) Thank you, Mrs Twohig.

ANNIE: Ah sure, call me Annie.

HECTOR: I appreciate your attitude Mrs Twohig, and I am very grateful for your offer of hospitality. We shall probably avail ourselves of it for a few days. I think it will be only for a few days, because our success here has had reverberations elsewhere and I have at least two very good offers in my pocket.

JOHN: I'm more than delighted to hear that.

HECTOR: Let us go to the Pavilion, darling, and start to pack.

CONSTANCE: (*Rising*) Very well. (*As they reach the door* CONSTANCE *whispers something to* HECTOR)

HECTOR: Oh, yes . . . . Mrs Twohig, if that young newspaper man comes back you might give him this envelope; it contains some photographs he particularly asked for.

ANNIE: (*Taking the envelope*) Certainly.

HECTOR: (*To* JOHN) And keep a couple of seats for us tonight, please; it's twenty years since I've seen a circus. (*They go out*)

JOHN: Well, that's over. They took it very nicely.

ANNIE: They did, the creatures.

JOHN: (*Crossing to the sideboard*) I think I deserve a little drink after that.

ANNIE: You do, to be sure.

JOHN: You ought to make a cup of tea for yourself.

ANNIE: I'll have a glass of port instead.

JOHN: (*Astonished*) Annie, what's come to you?

ANNIE: I don't know, but I feel so light in the heart, as if a big cloud was gone.

JOHN: Faith, you're welcome to a bucket of port, but here's a wineglassfull to begin with.

As he is pouring it out, HELENA *comes in. She is in outdoor clothes.*

ANNIE: Helena, where were you? I was looking everywhere for you.

HELENA: I know, ma'am. I was at the chapel, ma'am.

ANNIE: And what were you doing at the chapel this hour of the morning?

HELENA: I was getting married, ma'am.

ANNIE: Merciful heaven! Who to?

HELENA: Michael, of course. Who else?

ANNIE: Oh, my poor girl, is this what has come of all that nasty talk? Why didn't you tell me? I'd have told you not to mind a thing they said and not to tie yourself up for life with a man who's no more to you than the next.

HELENA: It's not that way at all, ma'am. Michael and me have been promised to each other for the last two months, only I could never bring myself to tell him about — you know what. I was delighted it slipped out of me that morning. Anyway, to stop tongues wagging, we thought we might as well be married at once.

JOHN: Well, thunder and turf! That's one good thing the plays did, anyhow. Where's Michael?

HELENA: Outside the door, listening. (*Raising her voice*) You can come in, Michael, they're not mad at all.

MICHAEL *comes in a little sheepish.*

JOHN: Oh, there's the bold bridegroom. Hold up your head, Michael. Here, put the hand there and I wish you the best of luck.

MICHAEL: Thank you, sir.

ANNIE: And I wish you the same, and the best of luck to you, Helena, and years of happiness.

HELENA: Thank you, ma'am, you've always been the good friend to me.

LIZZIE *hurries in.*

LIZZIE: A band, John, a band!

ANNIE: Where?

LIZZIE: Coming up the street, I think. I heard it from the upper window.

JOHN: (*Coolly*) Did you ever hear of a circus without a band?

LIZZIE:
HELENA: } A circus?
MICHAEL:

JOHN: In the Pavilion tonight, and free seats for all the town. (*Music is heard*)

LIZZIE: Glory!

MICHAEL: I hear the band myself. Come out to the door, Helena. (*He and* HELENA *rush out*)

LIZZIE: And look, there's the sun bursting out.

ANNIE: My heart's lepping with joy.

It is quite true; the room is flooded with sunshine. CHRISTINE *and* EDDIE *rush in and make for the window.* EDDIE *is dressed in his nicest suit.*

EDDIE: A band, Pappy, a band!

CHRISTINE: Eddie, am I mad or do I see a clown?

LIZZIE: (*Crowding to the window*) A clown? Clowns are my joy.

EDDIE: (*With a shout*) Two clowns!

CHRISTINE: (*Topping him*) Three!

LIZZIE: And a doaty little girl in spangles on a piebald pony. John, what's the meaning of it all?

JOHN: We've put back the old stone, Lizzie, thank God.

LIZZIE: I don't know what you mean. Anyhow, it sounds grand.

The music has swelled near. The band is playing 'Stars and Stripes For Ever', EDDIE *and* CHRISTINE *can't resist it. They must do a little dance together in the background.* LIZZIE, *staring out the window, is softly clapping her hands and smiling.* JOHN *and* ANNIE *are near the front.*

JOHN: Annie, get on the telephone to Dublin.

ANNIE: Why so?

JOHN: Get on to the best shop in the city. I think I owe you a new dress.

ANNIE: Maybe you do . . . . Have you got six coppers?[11]

He fingers for them. The music fills the room. The CURTAIN *falls.*

11. Copper pennies for the telephone coin-box.

PAUL VINCENT CARROLL
(1900-68)

from:
SHADOW AND SUBSTANCE
(1937)

[In the second act of Paul Vincent Carroll's *Shadow and Substance*, the venal affairs of the parish are conducted in an atmosphere of subservient piety, even as hysteria about offensive literature reaches a crescendo. Only Brigid, the servant girl, seems touched by a genuine religious spirit.].

VERY REV. THOMAS CANON SKERRITT
BRIGID, *his servant, about eighteen*
FATHER CORR } *two curates, in their twenties*
FATHER KIRWAN
MISS JEMIMA COONEY, *a local spinster*
FRANCIS IGNATIUS O'CONNOR, *her nephew*
MARTIN MULLAHONE, *middle-aged*
ROSEY VIOLET, *in her thirties*

ACT TWO

SCENE: *Following day*

The CANON *is discovered reading the castigated novel,* I Am Sir Oracle. *Now and again he smiles sardonically, and sips from a glass of wine.*

The picture of the Sacred Heart[1] *is removed.* BRIGID *knocks and enters. Lays evening paper on table.*

BRIGID: That's the *Evenin' Herald*, Canon.

CANON: Very good, Brigid. (*He reads on*)

BRIGID: And if you please, Canon, are ye not forgettin' about them two in the waitin' room?

CANON: (*Tolerantly*) Which two, Brigid? You are always a little vague lately.

BRIGID: The two I told you about, after dinner. Miss Cooney and her nephew with his new

1. In Act One, Canon Skerritt objected to a vulgar picture of the Sacred Heart of Jesus displayed in the presbytery's dining-room.

teacher's certificate. I told them you'd see them after you were done readin' the Bishop's Pastoral.

CANON: (*Remembering*) Of course, of course, Brigid. I remember now. I distinctly remember saying to you, 'Brigid, I'll see them presently.'

BRIGID: That's just what you said, Canon.

CANON: To be sure it was. Tell them, Brigid — tell them to come back tomorrow.

BRIGID: But they've spent the whole day between waitin' on you here, Canon, and follyin' ye about the streets.

CANON: But my dear child, they like doing that. It is a corporate part of our national life. Tell them, Brigid, that the Canon — no, no — say, 'His reverence presents his compliments to Miss Cooney and his heartiest congratulations to Francis Xavier —'

BRIGID: Francis Ignatius, Canon.

CANON: Thank you, Brigid. Let us have accuracy at all costs in these important matters. But be careful of the exact wording. Wording, Brigid, is an art. (*Repeating*) 'His reverence presents his compliments.' (*He reads on*)

BRIGID: Yis, Canon, but sure they're in and out o' the kitchen every minute pesterin' me. Is the Canon here? Is the Canon there? Where is the Canon? What hat has he on? Sure you could get rid of them in a minute, Canon, with a grand word and a clap on the back.

CANON: (*Rising*) Excellent, Brigid. An answer and a suggestion at once plausible and philosophic. The Canon, Brigid — the Canon shall do exactly as you say.

BRIGID: Will I show them in then, Canon?

CANON: By all means, Brigid. And Brigid, if by any ill chance, they weary me beyond their time — (*He raises a finger meaningly*)

BRIGID: Sure, you needn't tell me, Canon. (*She goes.* CANON *lays down the book resignedly, and mutters in Latin.* BRIGID *re-enters followed by* MISS JEMIMA COONEY *and her nephew* FRANCIS O'CONNOR. FRANCIS *is a sheepish, obsequious youth, his whole being in the grip of an inferiority complex. He is awkward and without confidence.* JEMIMA *is a thin, gaunt spinster, secretly vicious but very virtuous before the* CANON. *The storm of 'Yis, Canons' and 'No, Canons' should be played very rapidly*) This is them, Canon. (*She goes*)

JEMIMA *and* FRANCIS *advance awkwardly gesticulating and very obsequious. The* CANON *rises with calm dignity, embraces his nose with a silk handkerchief, and gives them a curt bow, tempered with a quite unreadable smile.*

JEMIMA: Sure, Lord, Canon, are we disturbin' ye?

FRANCIS: Sure, now, Canon, anny time would do!

JEMIMA: Sure, now, Canon, are ye after leavin' off sayin' your office for us?

FRANCIS: Sure, Lord, Canon, we could have come back anny time at all.

JEMIMA: Sure, Heavens, Canon, Francis is that up in the air about his new certificate!

FRANCIS: Sure, Canon, you'll be thinkin' me a nuisance!

CANON: (*In a lull, dignified*) You may be seated. (*Silence while they sit.* CANON *heroically contains himself, again embraces his nose, and seats himself opposite them. With scoundrel grace*) And now, Miss Cooney, I hope I see you well. And you too, Francis, none the less, mark! In short, I hope I see you *both* well. (*He smiles sardonically*)

JEMIMA: Sure, Lord, Canon, I'm lovely now. Sure I never felt so well since I came home from the hospital.

FRANCIS: And I'm like a two-year-old, Canon, ready to attack me work.

CANON: (*With bow*) Excellent. I assure you this news is a *great* satisfaction to me.

JEMIMA: (*Exploding*) Sure, you're too good, Canon. Run, Francis now, and show His Reverence your teacher's certificate.

FRANCIS: (*Opening scroll, and going awkwardly to* CANON) I just got it from the college yisterday mornin', Canon.

CANON: (*Viewing the certificate without touching it*) Creditable, Francis. Very creditable. I see in this the seal of — of scholarship, and the beginning of attainment. I congratulate you, Francis.

JEMIMA *beams*

FRANCIS: (*Explosively*) Canon, will you please do all you can for me about the school?

JEMIMA: (*Irascibly*) Francis, will you mind your manners now? Sure don't you know you don't need to ask the Canon that! (*To the* CANON, *apologetically*) Sure he — he's over-exuberant, Canon.

CANON: (*With bow to* JEMIMA) As your aunt Jemima so wisely observes, Francis, your request is superfluous, since I *must* do my best for you. Is it not written, Francis, in your Penny Catechism that we must all of us come to the aid of each other?

JEMIMA: There now, Francis.

FRANCIS: (*Backing awkwardly to seat*) Sure, I'm a — a — an ass, Canon.

CANON: Not a bit, Francis. *Quandoque bonus dormitat Homerus.*[2]

JEMIMA: (*Impulsively running to the* CANON *with photograph of* FRANCIS) Look, Canon. A wee surprise. I got it taken in Dublin before we left, in a grand place in Talbot Street. (*Pointing*) That's Francis's certificate in his hand, and the wee book in his waistcoat pocket is the prayer book you gave him yourself for servin' Mass for eight years.

CANON: (*Benignly regarding photograph as if it were a new uncategorised animal*) Very good! Uncommonly good! And very farseeing of you, Miss Cooney, to — to have Francis's scholarly achievement — er — permanently recorded.

JEMIMA: (*Driveling*) Wouldn't his ma, God rest her, be proud of him there, Canon.

FRANCIS: (*Blushing and smirking*) Sure, I'm nothin' at all, Canon.

CANON: (*With preliminary grave bow to* JEMIMA) Your mother, Francis, was a good woman. (*With great gravity*) In fact, a very good woman.

FRANCIS: Thank ye, Canon.

CANON: (*Gravely*) In fact, Francis, in the light of my home and foreign experience, I might even say — an excellent woman.

JEMIMA: There now is news for you, Francis!

FRANCIS: It's awful kind of you to say the like of that, Canon.

CANON: (*Handing back photograph to* JEMIMA) Very creditable, Miss Cooney. And now, Francis, you must be a little patient. We must *all* be a little patient. Your Aunt Jemima with her invaluable experience of life, as we live it, and of the — the idiosyncrasies of our checkered existence, will have impressed *that* upon you, I feel sure.

JEMIMA: Sure, Lord, Canon, isn't it all now in the will o' God!

CANON: (*Bowing delightfully*) Excellent, Miss Cooney. Your Aunt Jemima, Francis, has just made a very wise observation. It is — if I may repeat, Miss Cooney? — in the will of God. Did I say, Francis, that your mother was a good woman?

FRANCIS: You did, indeed, Canon. A very good woman, you said.

CANON: So I did, Francis. I distinctly remember the remark now. I want to add to it, Francis. (*With great gravity*) I want to observe that your Aunt Jemima is a woman, to my knowledge, of incomparable wisdom, piety and virtue.

JEMIMA: (*Head down, blushing*) Sure, I'm not worth that, Canon.

FRANCIS: Indeed she's the best in the world, Canon. Sure, I'd be nothin' only for *her*.

CANON: As you say, Francis, you might be nothing but for *her*. And look what you are! *Hoc opus! hic labor est!*[3] (CANON *smiles delightfully*)

FRANCIS: (*Blushing and confused*) Yis, Canon. Indeed yis. I owe her everythin'.

JEMIMA: You didn't happen to see, Canon, the piece in the *Dundalk Sentinel* about him? Sure, the editor was a great college friend of Francis's brother before he failed for the teachin' and fell back on bein' an editor.

CANON: I regret, Miss Cooney, I missed it. I must inquire from Father Corr. I believe *he* buys the — the *Dundalk Semaphore*.

FRANCIS: *Sentinel*, Canon.

CANON: *Sentinel*, Francis. *Sentinel*, to be sure. Accuracy, Francis, accuracy always.

BRIGID: (*Entering*) If you please, Canon, there's a gentleman waitin' with a soft hat and an umbrella.

CANON: Ah, yes, Brigid. Presently, my child, presently. Francis and his aunt are just going. (*They take the tip and rise to go.* CANON *claps* FRANCIS *on back*) And now, Francis, I hope to have excellent news for you shortly. I can say nothing further now. The tongues of none of us are free. But keep within easy call, and employ your waiting time properly.

JEMIMA: Indeed, Canon, he'll spend his time of waitin' your command in makin' a novena.

FRANCIS: (*Outrageously*) Sure, Canon, *orare est vigilare.*[4]

JEMIMA: Well, will you listen to that, Canon. And him only a child.

CANON: (*Beaming*) Excellent, Francis. I can see you are deeply versed in the profundities of the classics.

JEMIMA: Come on now, Francis, we're keepin' the Canon. And he'll pray for you, Canon. We'll both pray for you.

CANON: (*Bowing repeatedly as they go out*)

2. The full quotation is *'Indignor quandoque bonus dormitat Homerus'* (Horace, *Ars Poetica*, 359); 'But if Homer, usually good, nods for a moment, I think it shame.'

3. Vergil, *Aeneid* VI.129: 'There is the toil and there the task!'

4. 'To pray is to be vigilant'; a variation on the traditional phrase, *Orare est laborare*, 'To pray is to work'.

Excellent . . . (*They go. He sinks wearily into chair*)

BRIGID *comes in quickly and opens up window.*

BRIGID: I knew you'd want the window open, Canon.

CANON: You are a very understanding child, Brigid. The law of Nature's compensation is not after all a myth. (*He looks up at her as she stands solicitously watching him*) Brigid, promise me you'll never leave me.

BRIGID: (*Shrinking*) I — I couldn't do that, Canon.

CANON: (*Startled*) What? ... What is this, Brigid? Are you not happy here?

BRIGID: Oh, yis, Canon. It's not that. I'm always happy.

CANON: Well? . . .

BRIGID: I might want to go away in a little while, Canon.

CANON: For what purpose, Brigid?

BRIGID: I — I don't know how to say it, Canon . . .. It's the way I feel.

CANON: You are not well, child. You must take a good rest.

BRIGID: It's not that, Canon.

CANON: Nonsense! It *must* be that. Listen, Brigid. When I die, you will get every penny I have. There now! There's a secret out. Don't breathe it!

BRIGID: But Canon, it's not money I'll be wantin' where I — I think I'm goin'.

CANON: What talk is this? Where are you going?

BRIGID: (*Falteringly*) Please, Canon, I want to be a nun.

CANON: (*Flabbergasted*) Eh? You — you want to be a nun, eh? My God, am I not sufficiently stocked with boobs that *you*, Brigid, *you* must add the final straw.

BRIGID: You're vexed with me, Canon.

CANON: Displeased, Brigid . . . . Displeased that you would go and leave me here alone. And you my friend! You the — the Canon's friend.

BRIGID: It's not just *you*, Canon, but everythin' I'd be leavin'.

CANON: (*Clapping her affectionately*) Brigid, you have been doing too much lately, and you are overwrought. Excess in anything is bad, Brigid — in work, in play, in religion — it is not — classical. I am going to send you away for a holiday. And you must have a new hat too — a new hat with — with a feather in it. There now!

BRIGID: (*Amused*) But sure, Canon, feathers is not worn anywhere now.

CANON: Do you tell me that, Brigid? That — that — that's astonishing — astonishing, Brigid.

BRIGID: It's a wee white dog at the side they have now and a nose veil.

CANON: (*Gravely*) A — a white dog and a nose veil, Brigid? I — I must make a careful note of that, and you must certainly have them both. And it must be size six or seven or whatever you want.

BRIGID: Sure, Canon, with them shallow crowns that's out now, you can't depend on sizes. I'd need a fit-on.

CANON: (*Gravely*) You'd need a fit-on, Brigid. So you would. These shallow — shallow crowns are certainly a bit of a problem. We'll arrange that too.

BRIGID: Thank you, Canon.

CANON: There now, you've forgotten already. When you get your holiday you will be again classically simple and quiescent. (*Pause*) Brigid, do you know where we keep the Baptismal Registers in the Cloak Room?

BRIGID: Yis, Canon. In the cupboard behind the door.

CANON: Go, Brigid, and bring me the Register for the year nineteen — nineteen and eight.

BRIGID: Yis, Canon. Nineteen and eight. (*She goes*)

CANON *lifts the book again, and looks at the page he left open. He smiles sardonically. He then begins to read aloud. It is near the end of the book.*

CANON: (*Reading*) 'The Canon lay dying. The mists came white and wraith-like from the bogs to tell him so . . .' (*Puts down book*) Not a bit. On the contrary, the Canon feels well — feels in fact very well. (*As* BRIGID *comes in and hands him Register*) It may interest you to know, Brigid, that the Canon feels — excellently. (*He smiles sardonically*)

BRIGID: Sure, thanks be to God, Canon.

CANON: (*As he opens Register*) Amen, Brigid, amen . . . Let me see now. (*Turns pages rapidly*) Mallin, Melling, Nagle, Nolan, O'Brien, O'Connell, O'Kelly . . . ah, here we are, — O'Flingsley. (*He moves his finger along a line of data*) June 8th, 1908, Dermot Francis O'Flingsley.

BRIGID: (*Looking*) Is that the Master's birthday, Canon?

CANON: That's it, Brigid. (*Gleefully as he reads on*) His father's name was Francis Eugene O'Flingsley. Mark the princely name, Eugene. Ah, and his mother bore the — storied name of Gibney. Could you credit that now? . . . Incomprehensible in fact. . . . Let me introduce you, Brigid, to Mr

Eugene Gibney, — er — author, amateur theologian, Catholic reformer, public moralist, student of Northern apologetics, erstwhile schoolmaster, ex-peasant and — gentleman.

BRIGID: (*Sensing fear*) What does that mean, Canon?

CANON: To you, Brigid, it shall mean — *nothing*. Put that Register back, Brigid, and not a word to any one. (*As she goes*) Did I say a *word*, Brigid?

BRIGID: Yis, Canon.

CANON: (*Gravely*) I meant a syllable, Brigid.

BRIGID: Sure, I won't even breathe, Canon.

CANON: Excellent, Brigid.

BRIGID: (*Turning as she crosses with Register*) Please, Canon, is there anythin' wrong with the Master?

CANON: You're *breathing*, Brigid.

BRIGID: Yis, Canon. . . .No, Canon. . . . (*She crosses disconsolately*)

CANON: And Brigid. Send Dave Dooley down to the school to tell Mr O'Flingsley that I wish to see him in the morning.

BRIGID: (*Almost in tears*) Y-yis, Canon. (*She looks at him for a moment, as if wishing to speak, then goes off sadly with Register*)

FATHER CORR *and* FATHER KIRWAN *enter from the window, carrying their hats.*

FATHER CORR: Father Kirwan and meself, Canon, would like a word with you, if you're not busy.

CANON: I *am* busy.

FATHER CORR: It's about a meeting we've just had of the Confraternity over that scurrilous book. A — a resolution was passed, Canon.

FATHER KIRWAN: Unanimously, Canon.

CANON: Well, what of it? It's a national pastime, isn't it?

FATHER KIRWAN: The members of the Football Club, Canon, are very excited. (*Worriedly*) *They're* the worst. They're gettin' out of hand.

CANON: No doubt, it's the warm weather, Father Kirwan. (*He crosses*) And I note you haven't as yet found time, even between resolutions, to shave. (CANON *goes out slowly*)

CURATES *look after him perplexed.*

FATHER CORR: For Heaven's sake, can you not go and shave and not be makin' things harder for us?

FATHER KIRWAN: Ach, can a man not get wearin' his own hair if he wants to! Sure he's so contrary if I shaved every day, he'd grumble because I hadn't a beard like Don-the-Divil's-Father! Is he an Irishman at all?

FATHER CORR: His father was Irish. It's his mother was the Spaniard. They met in Brussels.

FATHER KIRWAN: It's a pity she didn't stay at home instead of gallivantin' about the continent. Sure you'd think he hadn't a drop of Irish Ireland blood in his veins. I'll bet me boots he'll side with that book agin the Confraternity and the Football Club.

FATHER CORR: With a book like that! My God, at least he's a priest.

FATHER KIRWAN: Did you see the schoolmaster?

FATHER CORR: I did, and he was worth seein'. He's all for us burnin' the book in public, and he thinks that the Canon is the proper one to do the actual casting into the flames.

FATHER KIRWAN: (*Noticing open book*) Great Scott! Will you look at what's here!

FATHER CORR: (*With a start*) The book!

FATHER KIRWAN: It's open at the last chapter where the P.P. dies miserably. He must have been readin' it.

FATHER CORR: (*With passionate aversion*) I loathe the thing. It's accursed and vile. (*He flings it venomously on the floor*)

FATHER KIRWAN: (*'Dribbling'*[5] *with the book with both feet*) He was certainly no lover of clean sport and the team spirit. (*Still dribbling*) Suppose now yon door was the net. Wait till you see a grand penalty from the touch line. (*He kicks with judgment, and it is hurled against the doorway just as the* CANON *re-enters. He suddenly sees the* CANON *and sinks visibly into himself*)

FATHER CORR *is very confused. The* CANON *regards them with extreme frigidity. A definite pause.*

CANON: (*Tensely*) You may both be seated. (*They obey silently. With cold hauteur*) My property, Father Corr.

FATHER CORR: (*Defiantly*) I — I refuse to touch it. It's — vile.

CANON: My property, Father Corr. (FATHER CORR *is defiant for a definite moment, then emotionally lifts the book and hands it to* CANON. *He then reseats himself. The* CANON *lays the mutilated book on table*) I suppose I am to regard this outbreak of hooliganism in my study, as a typical spasm of — Catholic action.

5. Controlling an object with the feet at a run, as a ball is controlled in soccer.

FATHER CORR: (*Flashing out*) Canon, that book is a disgrace and a shame. The Irish Press in Dublin says it's an insult to the Catholic nation.

CANON: (*Courteously*) Didn't catch that word, Father Corr. (*Hand to ear*) The Irish what?

FATHER CORR: The Irish Press, Canon.

CANON: Never heard of it. (*He pours out a small glass of golden-coloured wine at sideboard, and examines it.*)

FATHER KIRWAN: Sure, the *Ballyedminstown Courier* quotes whole columns from it every Saturday, Canon.

CANON: (*Sipping wine*) In that case, Father Kirwan, I must concede it has a definite claim to our attention.

BRIGID: (*Entering*) If you please, Canon, there's four o' the parishioners here wearin' badges, and they'd like a talk with you.

FATHER CORR: I'd like very much, Canon, if you'd receive them. They're a deputation.

FATHER KIRWAN: Sure the whole country's takin' action, Canon.

CANON: Mm . . . I am presumably to agree to a — a descent into Lutheranism and a sort of Kirk Session. Say, Brigid, the Canon says No.

BRIGID: (*Repeating*) The Canon says No. (*She makes to go*)

FATHER CORR: Sure, after all if it was only for appearances' sake.

BRIGID: Canon, would you not just give another clap on the back and a grand word?

CANON: What *are* we come to? (*Pause*) Very well then, very well, let the — the neo-theologians come in, but let it be at their peril. I shall ring, Brigid.

BRIGID: Yis, Canon. I'll keep them in the waitin' room. (*She goes*)

CANON: Who are these people, Father Corr?

FATHER CORR: They're all strong confraternity and football club members, Canon. There's Miss Cooney and her nephew Francis —

CANON: Is *he* here? Who are the other two?

FATHER KIRWAN: Martin Mullahone, Canon, the referee of our football team, that has the public house and farm on the Dublin Road, and his wife, Rosey Violet.

CANON: His wife who?

FATHER KIRWAN: He calls her Rosey Violet, Canon.

CANON: I think I recall her, but if my recollection is correct, she was neither rosey nor a violet. (*He rings the bell*) Be seated, Fathers, and offer no comments until these people are gone.

FATHER CORR *and* FATHER KIRWAN *sit at either end of the empty chairs for the deputation. The* CANON *sits magisterially at the large writing desk.* BRIGID *enters with a deputation behind her.* MISS COONEY *and* FRANCIS O'CONNOR *are as obsequious as usual.* MARTIN MULLAHONE, *a large awkward man, with a large stomach and a red nose, is followed by his wife who is typical in dress and voice of the 'social status' aspirants in rural Ireland.*

BRIGID: This is them, Canon.

CANON (*Curtly*) Good afternoon, all. You may be seated. (BRIGID *goes. All sit in chairs opposite the* CANON. *They smirk and bow to the* CANON *and look as virtuous as possible. The* CANON*'s sardonic eye surveys them pitilessly. They wilt and shift uneasily. His eye on* MARTIN.) Are you the man, Martin Mullahone?

MARTIN: I — I am then, Canon.

ROSEY VIOLET: (*Chipping in sweetly*) And I'm his wife, Canon.

CANON: Martin Mullahone, where are your hands?

MARTIN *whips them violently out of his pockets.*

MARTIN: Sure, I — I never thought, Canon. Sure, God's —

ROSEY VIOLET: Sure, I'm always tellin' him, Canon.

CANON: Sit erect and don't loll or sag. Decorum and personal dignity are not by any means the least of the Christian virtues. (*All sit fearfully erect*) And now to the point. You have come — or should I say you have taken it upon yourselves to come — about a certain book.

MARTIN: (*Explosively*) Sure, it's a — a terror, Canon. A — a terror and a fright to the world, Canon.

CANON: (*With suave irony*) Having learned from your husband, Mrs Mullahone, that this book is a — a terror and a fright — two quite incomprehensible epithets to me — do you wish to — er — supplement his observation?

ROSEY VIOLET: If you please, Canon, I agree with what Father Kirwan said when he thumped the table at the meetin', that no clean sportin' man with the team spirit in him could write such a book.

FATHER KIRWAN *is confused.*

CANON: (*Ironic, with side glance at* FATHER KIRWAN) An *excellent* observation, Mrs Mullahone.

ROSEY VIOLET: Sure, if you please, Canon, me eldest son, Dan, is the fullback in Father Kirwan's team.

CANON: (*Cruelly*) Didn't catch that word, Mrs Mullahone. (*Hand to ear*) The — the what?

FATHER KIRWAN *is very confused.*

ROSEY VIOLET: The fullback, Canon.

CANON: Ah! of course. The — the fullback. I must ask Father Kirwan for a glossary of these terms. (*Side glance at* FATHER KIRWAN) And you, Miss Cooney, have *you* any observation?

JEMIMA: Sure, Canon, I only came because Father Corr told me it was me duty to God and Ireland. (*Grasping* FRANCIS's *arm*) Say it in Irish for the Canon, Francis. Go on now!

FATHER CORR *is confused.*

FRANCIS: (*Rising awkwardly*) *Do cum gloire De, agus onora na h-Eireann.*[6]

CANON: (*Hand to ear*) Didn't catch that Francis. Cum — cum what?

FRANCIS: (*Unconscious of cruelty*) *Do cum gloire De, agus onora na h-Eireann.*

CANON: (*scoundrelishly*) Excellent, Francis. Excellent! You may be seated. Any other observation, Miss Cooney?

JEMIMA: Sure, I'll just listen now to you, and learn, Canon. Isn't that me duty?

CANON: Very creditable, Miss Cooney. An attitude at once wise, womanly and prudent. And you, Francis?

JEMIMA: (*Hurriedly*) He'll just do the same as meself, Canon. Not a word now, Francis, before his reverence.

FRANCIS: Sure, it's for *you* to say, Canon.

CANON: Commendable, Francis. You have a good — a very good counsellor.

ROSEY VIOLET: (*Not to be outdone*) Sure, if you please, Canon, me brother, Father Jamsie, says it was no one but the divil guided the hand that wrote that book.

CANON: (*Startled*) Your who — the what? Speak up, Mrs Mullahone.

ROSEY VIOLET: (*exuberantly*) Why, me brother, Father Jamsie, Canon, that's up in Dunaree with Father Crone. Sure, Canon, it was Father Jamsie that anointed your sister, Thomasina's mother, when she near died and didn't, last Christmas.

CANON: (*Shaking head*) Never heard of him.

ROSEY VIOLET: (*Sentimentally*) Ah, sure poor wee Father Jamsie, Canon. Sure, God help him.

6. 'To the glory of God and the honour of Ireland.'

CANON: What's the matter with him?

ROSEY VIOLET: (*Surprised*) Sure, nothin' at all, Canon. Sure, Lord, what would be the matter with him?

CANON: (*With an effort*) Very well then.

ROSEY VIOLET: Sure, he's happy and lovely in Dunaree, Canon.

CANON: (*Heroically*) Very well then.

MARTIN: (*Blunderingly interposing*) Sure, will you not be sickenin' the Canon, bargin' in every minute about Father Jamsie because he's your brother.

ROSEY VIOLET: (*Bursting into tears*) If you please, Canon, Martin's always insultin' and belittlin' me in public.

CANON: (*With great gravity, eyeing* MARTIN *who quails and shifts about*) Martin Mullahone, what *grave* charge is this I hear as to your conduct and public morals?

MARTIN: Sure — sure, Canon, you'd think by the talk of her mornin' and night that he was a Canon like yourself, and him with the — the cloth on him only a month.

ROSEY VIOLET: (*Crying*) Me heart's broke with him, Canon.

CANON: You are a good woman, Mrs Mullahone, and you have pleased me considerably.

ROSEY VIOLET: Sure, everyone loves me, Canon.

CANON: As for you, Martin Mullahone, I am gravely incensed (MARTIN *squirms*) and not a little pained.

ROSEY VIOLET: Oh, thank you, Canon. Martin badly needed that talkin' to.

CANON: Very well then. We digress. How many of you have read this book?

Negative murmurs and shaking of heads.

ROSEY VIOLET: Sure, what Catholic could read a book like that, Canon?

CANON: I take it then that none of you has read this book?

ALL: (*Shaking heads, murmurs*) Not a one, Canon.

CANON: And you come here to condemn a book you have not read! What nonsense is this? (*Taps desk*) Preposterous and ridiculous! The deputation is dismissed. (*The* CANON *is just rising when* FATHER CORR *jumps up*)

FATHER CORR: If I may say a word, Canon —

CANON: Be seated, Father Corr.

FATHER CORR *sits.*

FRANCIS: (*Rising*) If you please, Canon —

JEMIMA: (*Seizing him and flinging him down*) That's enough, you pup! Sit down!

CANON: (*Sitting back, eyeing* FRANCIS *benignly*) We shall allow him the privilege on this occasion, Miss Cooney. Proceed, Francis.

FRANCIS: (*Awkwardly*) I was just goin' to say, Canon, that is, as a — a certified teacher, I — I read the book — judiciously.

CANON: (*Hand to ear, cruelly luring him on*) What — what word was that, Francis?

FRANCIS: Judiciously, Canon.

CANON: Ah! Enlarge upon that, Francis. It is a little vague.

FRANCIS: Well, Canon, if I — I felt a part was gettin' bad, I skipped.

CANON: You — you skipped, Francis. (*He smiles*)

ROSEY VIOLET: (*Interposing*) I done that too, Canon.

JEMIMA: If you please, Canon, when I saw that Francis was determined to — to study it, I felt it me duty to read it before him and turn down some of the pages.

CANON: (*Face masklike*) I understand — exactly. And you, Martin Mullahone?

MARIN: (*Hoarsely*) I can't read, Canon. It's me wife is the scholar in our family.

ROSEY VIOLET: (*Interposing, gushingly*) I was three years in the convent, Canon, before Martin won me.

MARTIN: (*Hoarsely*) It was the little fella that has the bike shop, Canon — wee Joey Hardy, that was readin' out bits of it at the counter on Friday, and I — I couldn't help hearin' them, Canon. Out — outrageous and terrible, Canon! A fright to the world!

CANON: (*Rounding on them*) I am to take it then that four of my parishioners, deliberately — I might even say, wantonly — and without right or lawful authority from me either in person or by proxy, committed themselves to the reading of a book gravely alleged to be pernicious, immoral and — subversive. (*He sizes up the four, severely*) Of these, one is the sister of a priest (ROSEY VIOLET *sobs*) another presumptuously aspires to the position of teacher of the young (JEMIMA *gives* FRANCIS *a vicious elbow big in the ribs*), a third, is or should be a father and a husband (MARTIN *sags visibly*), and a fourth — (JEMIMA *bows her head and sniffs*) — I can find no words to castigate the curiosity that tempted the fourth to this grave indiscretion. (*He rings the bell*) I shall deliver my directions to the two Fathers here who will communicate them to you for your unswerving acceptance. You will leave immediately. I shall contemplate whether it is humanly possible to pardon any or all of you. (CANON *rises, as* BRIGID *appears. The deputation also rises. The* CANON *waves. They go out in confusion following* BRIGID. *The two* CURATES *turn nervously to the* CANON. *Curtly*) Be seated. (*They sit.* CANON *resumes his seat*) I may take it, I suppose, that you two have also presumed to read this book.

FATHER CORR: I frankly considered it my duty, Canon.

FATHER KIRWAN: So did I, Canon.

CANON: Bad theology, Fathers, bad theology. And equally bad theology of course to have any — er — unofficial conflagrations on the public street without my express approval. (*Pause*) The author of this book which I have read, Fathers, is obviously a very young man. I fear his education cannot be more — adequate than that of the average young man of the present, either lay or — er — clerical. (*He coughs*) The theme I take to mean that Ireland has dangerously materialized the outlook of the Church, and that its profound spiritual essence has been stolen by a small band of learned men whom it does not even recognize. A dangerous theme, Fathers, I grant you.

FATHER CORR: (*Blazing out*) A blasphemous lie on Catholic Ireland!

CANON: (*Calmly*) A theme, Fathers, that in the hands of an abler controversialist with a claim to scholarship or a classic status, might possibly cause alarm amongst us, especially when we have presently no known Irish Catholic scholar with that delicacy of touch, subtlety of culture and profundity of classical knowledge to defend and even rescue the Church intellectually. Coming in contact with such an immaturity as this the insufficiently scholared mind, fed mostly on sentimentalisms in the form of learning, is often shocked, and — vulgarly agitated. Violent emotionalism results, followed by a quite ridiculous hubbub, tawdry heroics, even bigoted physical violence under holy names, and generally a quite ludicrous procedure that the classic dignity of the mind of the Church recoils from. As I have no desire, Fathers, to make a presumptuous young man bogusly important in an age that is itself bogusly important, or to condone a procedure too undignified to be Catholic, I therefore decree that no action of any sort be taken in the case of this book, except such action as I, in my official capacity, shall think fit to perform. (*Pause*) That, I think, Fathers, will be all.

FATHER CORR: (*Livid*) Are we then actually to take it that our efforts to deal with this disgraceful libel are banned?

CANON: You are!

FATHER KIRWAN: (*Touching* FATHER CORR, *as he is about to burst out*) That's enough now. You'll only be sayin' things you'll be sorry for.

FATHER CORR: (*In a temper*) I'll say what I like.

FATHER KIRWAN: Now, can't you see that's wild talk?

FATHER CORR: (*Cooling*) I suppose it is. But he's never done belittlin' and humblin' me. But I'll try not to mind. It's in my nature to be humble.

CANON: Inoculated would be a better word. Inoculated with the prevalent deluge of sentimentalism.

FATHER CORR: I'm afraid, Canon, there's nothin' for me to do but ask the Bishop for a shift and to give my reasons.

CANON: And in spite of your impertinences, Father, I shall be prepared to give his Grace an — adequate report on your work. (FATHER CORR *abruptly leaves the room, left. The* CANON *looks after him quietly and then turns to* FATHER KIRWAN) And you, Father Kirwan? Are you also going to the Bishop?

FATHER KIRWAN: (*Confused, and crossing*) I'm goin' for a — for a shave, Canon.

CANON: Dear me! We — progress! (FATHER KIRWAN *goes awkwardly, left*)

The CANON *turns away tiredly, goes to the leaded bookcase, unlocks it and extracts a volume. He settles with it in an armchair. But the dusk is falling fast, and in a moment he looks up towards the lamp. He reaches for the bell, and is about to shake it when, with a cry,* BRIGID *runs in.*

BRIGID: Canon! Canon! (*He rises rapidly and goes to her. She tries to recover and looks up at him pathetically*)

CANON: What on earth is the matter, child?

BRIGID: (*Breathing hard, but trying to recover*) It's nothin', Canon, nothin' at all. I — I'm all right now.

CANON: Did something frighten you?

BRIGID: Y-yis, Canon. But it's nothin'.

CANON: You should have the lamp lighted in there at this time. There, you are tired and overwrought.

BRIGID: Canon, may I — ask you somethin'?

CANON: Certainly, Brigid.

BRIGID: Do you — do you love St Brigid?

CANON: (*Looking at her uncertainly*) Why, of course I do, child. Sure we *all* love St Brigid.

BRIGID: (*Happy*) Yes . . . I'm glad you do. She'll be pleased.

CANON: (*Solicitously*) Brigid, you are ill. You are not well.

BRIGID: Yis, Canon, I'm well.

CANON: I'm afraid not, child.

BRIGID: It's just, Canon, that I — I still want to be a nun.

CANON: There now! I *knew* you weren't well.

BRIGID: (*Pleadingly*) But if I could just be a nun, Canon.

CANON: Don't you know, Brigid, that nuns must be very, very strong and brave? They must be cruel to themselves and they must give all.

BRIGID: (*Tensely*) I will give all, Canon. I will! I promised her.

CANON: What nonsense is this? Promised whom, child?

BRIGID: (*Her eyes aglow*) St Brigid, Canon. I — I was dryin' the cups in the kitchen when she touched me on the shoulder and says she, 'You're holdin' the dish-towel wrong, Brigid.' And when I held it right, she whispered to me, 'Ask him if he loves me more than the rest.'

The CANON *stares at her, walks irascibly away, and then returns to her, collected.*

CANON: (*Gravely*) Brigid, you are, I fear, stubborn, disobedient, and even defiant, and — I am seriously annoyed and displeased with you.

BRIGID: (*Simply*) I — I knew you would, Canon.

CANON: If you were a boob, Brigid, or a footling trifler, I should expel you from my presence. But you are my friend, and I try to bear with you.

BRIGID: (*Sadly*) Yis, Canon.

CANON: I have borne all day with fools, Brigid, knowing that at the end you would come to me, and ask my wants and find no fault in me. There now. You see how it is with me.

BRIGID: Yis, Canon. (*Sadly*) I'm a wretch and a villain.

CANON: On the contrary, child, you are a good girl, and you have wisdom and grace. God, Brigid, is not *always* pleased with girls who want to be nuns. Sometimes He expects them to remain at their posts as His soldiers.

BRIGID: (*Pathetically persistent*) If only I could just be a nun instead of a soldier! Soldiers make so much noise.

CANON: Brigid, I am afraid your nerves are all shaken. You must go to bed now and on Friday I shall send you to Bray to a friend of mine for a holiday. Miss Cooney will take your place for a few weeks. You must get plenty of sleep and rest. Rest to the body, Brigid, is like prayer to the soul. And you will then forget these imaginings of yours.

BRIGID: But in bed, how can I forget, if her face is there in the curtains and the mark on her cheek where she struck the loveliness out of her face.[7]

CANON: (*Irascibly*) Now, now, now! I am trying not to be angry. There is no historical authority for that at all. The Church in its wisdom does not confirm it. It is probably just a myth. A myth, Brigid. Doesn't that show you!

BRIGID: (*Pathetically*) What is a myth, Canon?

CANON: A legend, child. (*Pause*)

BRIGID: (*Venturing*) And what is a — a legend, Canon?

CANON: Brigid, this is very trying! An old tale, that may or may not be true.

BRIGID: Then — it *could* be true, Canon?

CANON: Now which of us knows best about these things, Brigid?

BRIGID: You, Canon.

CANON: Well now, I say this thing you foolishly think you see is not — not of God. Dismiss it!

BRIGID: (*In pain, her head in her hands*) Canon! . . . oh, Canon! . . . how — how could you be sayin' that?

CANON: (*Sympathetically*) There, there! God tempts most those whom He loves best. You should be proud. The soul's great battles are not fought by common boobs. The great Ignatius[8] was tempted like this, and so were Theresa[9] and Augustine[10] and Dominic,[11] but they were not deceived. They rose up and conquered the tempter. So must you conquer this, Brigid.

7. In legend Saint Brigid disfigured her face in order to escape the attentions of persistent suitors.
8. St Ignatius Loyola (1491-1556), Spanish founder of the Society of Jesus.
9. St Teresa of Avila (1515-82), Spanish Carmelite nun and mystic.
10. St Augustine of Hippo (354-430), the greatest doctor of the early Latin Church, whose *Confessions* is regarded as a classic of Christian mysticism.
11. St Dominic, Confessor (1170-1221), Castilian founder of the Order of Friar Preachers, the Dominicans.

BRIGID: (*Tearfully*) But I — I love her so much. She is so lovely and beautiful.

CANON: Not more beautiful, Brigid, than the demon that twisted himself round the crucifix St Ignatius prayed before. He had to lie on his face to save himself. You too, Brigid, must turn away from this thing you think you see. You must be wise. Wise, Brigid, and brave. Promise me, Brigid.

BRIGID: (*Sobbing*) I want to die, Canon . . . . I want to — to die. . . .

CANON: (*Softly*) Come now, Brigid. That is not being brave! That is being merely heroic, like these modern vulgarians. Say, Brigid, 'I want to live and conquer.' (*She is silent*) Say it, Brigid. Be proud like a soldier and say it.

BRIGID: (*Sadly*) I want to live and — conquer . . . .

CANON: (*Clapping her on back*) Ah, Brigid, excellent! Go now, Brigid, to bed and sleep. And none of these dreams, remember, or foolishness. To sleep is safe, to dream is dangerous. I shall go out and send Dave Dooley for Miss Cooney to take your place.

BRIGID: (*Emotionally*) Yis, Canon. (*He crosses to window, opens it and passes out, into the garden*)

CANON: (*Without*) Dooley! Are you there! Come here, Dooley!

BRIGID's *emotional stress now visibly shakes here, as she stands undecided and forlorn in the deepening shadows. She sobs pathetically, her head down, like a child. She gives the impression of having lost someone very beloved. She lifts her head suddenly, and stares stealthily over her own shoulders at the slightly swaying curtains, that reach to the ground. Her body shudders, and she covers her face with her hands.*

BRIGID: (*Sobbing*) I'm not to look at you . . . . I — I promised him . . . . I'm not to see your face . . . . No, no. I — I mustn't . . . I daren't . . . I must keep my eyes covered from you . . . I must be — be wise and brave . . . I must sleep but not dream . . . but I — I . . . (*She draws her hands from her eyes, shakingly, stretches out her two arms to the curtains, and with a sob, rushes to them as to a loved one*) But I — I love you . . . I love you . . . I love you . . . . (*Her face is buried sobbingly in the great curtains, and her arms are about them pathetically, as the curtain falls slowly*)

BRENDAN BEHAN

(1923-64)

THE QUARE FELLOW

A COMEDY-DRAMA (1954)

[In Brendan Behan's play *The Quare Fellow* (first performed in the Pike Theatre in Dublin in 1954) a prison prepares itself for the execution of one of its inmates. Prisoner and warder alike participate in the preparations for the quare fellow's death as they take part in a grisly ritual. Despite the play's inexorable realism, the overall effect is of a near-symbolic statement about the impersonal and dehumanizing power of legal authority, and an anarchic, black-comic spirit saves the work from complete pessimism.

The text reprinted here is that of the first London production (a Theatre Workshop production at the Theatre Royal, London in 1956). There were differences between this version and the text used for the first Dublin production. Peter René Gerdes, in his book *The Major Works of Brendan Behan*, gives a useful summary of the changes made in the Dublin version for the London production. The principal change is that in the Pike production the Other Fellow hangs himself in his cell at the end of Act I. The London version is the one customarily performed.]

PRISONERS

Dunlavin
Neighbour
Prisoner A. (Hard Case)
Prisoner B. (The Man of Thirty)
Lifer
The Other Fellow
Mickser
English Voice
Scholara } *(Young Prisoners)*
Shaybo }
Prisoner C. (The Boy from the Island)
Prisoner D. (The Embezzler)
Prisoner E. (The Bookie)

WARDERS

Chief Warder
Regan
Crimmin
Donelly (Warder 1)
The New One (Warder 2)
The Prison Governor
Holy Healey
The Hangman
Jenkinson

ACT I

A prisoner sings: he is in one of the punishment cells.

A hungry feeling came o'er me stealing
And the mice were squealing in my prison cell,
And that old triangle
Went jingle jangle,
Along the banks of the Royal Canal.[1]

The curtain rises.

The scene is the bottom floor or landing of a wing in a city prison, 'B.1'. The cell doors are of metal with a card giving the name, age and religion of the occupant. Two of the cells have no cards. The left of the stage leads to the circle, the administrative heart of the prison, and on the right, in the wall and at right angles to the audience, is a window, from which a view may be had of the laundry yard of the women's prison. On the wall and facing the audience is printed in large block shaded Victorian lettering the word 'SILENCE'.

PRISONER:
To begin the morning
The warder bawling
Get out of bed and clean up your cell,
And that old triangle
Went jingle jangle,
Along the banks of the Royal Canal.

A triangle is beaten, loudly and raucously. A WARDER *comes briskly and, swinging a bunch of keys, goes to the vacant cells, looks in the spyholes, takes two white cards from his pocket, and puts one on each door. Then he goes to the other doors, looks in the spyholes and unlocks them.*

Meanwhile the singer in the base punishment cells is on his third verse:

The screw[2] was peeping
And the lag[3] was weeping ....

1. A canal in Dublin, which runs nearby Mountjoy Jail.
2. warder.
3. long-term prisoner.

But this only gets as far as the second line, for the warder leans over the stairs and shouts down ....

WARDER: The screw is listening as well as peeping, and you'll be bloody well weeping if you don't give over your moaning. We might go down there and give you something to moan about. (*The singing stops and he turns and shouts up and down the landing*) B. Wings: two, three and one. Stand to your doors. Come on, clean up your cells there. (*He goes off* R.)

PRISONERS A *and* B *come out of their cells, collect buckets and brushes, and start the morning's chores.* A. *is a man of 40, he has done two 'laggings', a sentence of five years or more, and some preventive detention.* B. *is a gentle-looking man and easy-going.*

PRISONER A: Nice day for the races.

PRISONER B: Don't think I can make it today. Too much to do in the office. Did you hear the commotion last night round in D. Wing? A reprieve must have come through.

PRISONER A: Aye, but there's two for a haircut and shave, I wonder which one's been chucked?[4]

PRISONER B: Dunlavin might know; give him a call there.

PRISONER A: Dunlavin!

VOICE: (*From cell*)

There are hands that will welcome you in
There are lips that I am burning to kiss
There are two eyes that shine ....

PRISONER A: Hey, Dunlavin, are you going to scrub that place of yours away?

VOICE:

Far away where the blue shadows fall
I will come to contentment and rest,
And the toils of the day
Will be all charmed away ....

PRISONER A: Hey, Dunlavin.

DUNLAVIN *appears in the door of the cell polishing a large enamel chamber pot with a cloth. An old man, he has spent most of his life in jail. Unlike most old lags he has not become absolutely dulled from imprisonment.*

DUNLAVIN: . . . In my little grey home in the West.

PRISONER A: What do you think that is you're polishing — the Railway Cup?[5]

DUNLAVIN: I'm shining this up for a special visitor. Healey of the Department of Justice[6] is coming up today to inspect the cells.

PRISONER A: Will he be round again so soon?

DUNLAVIN: He's always round the day before an execution. I think he must be in the hanging and flogging section.

PRISONER B: Dunlavin, there you are, at the corner of the wing, with the joints in the hot-water pipes bringing you news from every art and part, any time you put your ear to it.

DUNLAVIN: Well? Well?

PRISONER B: Well, what was the commotion last night round in D. Wing? Did the quare fellow get a reprieve?

DUNLAVIN: Just a minute till I put back me little bit of china, and I'll return and tell all. Now which quare fellow do you mean? The fellow beat his wife to death with the silver-topped cane, that was a presentation to him from the Combined Staffs, Excess and Refunds[7] branch of the late Great Southern Railways, was reprieved, though why him any more than the other fellow is more nor I can tell.

PRISONER A: Well, I suppose they looked at it, he only killed her and left it at that. He didn't cut the corpse up afterwards with a butcher's knife.

DUNLAVIN: Yes, and then of course the other fellow used a meat-chopper. Real bog-man act. Nearly as bad as a shotgun, or getting the weed-killer mixed up in the stirabout.[8] But a man with a silver-topped cane, that's a man that's a cut above meat-choppers whichever way you look at it.

PRISONER A: Well, I suppose we can expect Silver-top round soon to start his life.

PRISONER B: Aye, we've a couple of vacancies.

PRISONER A: There's a new card up here already.

DUNLAVIN: I declare to God you're right. (*Goes to read one of the cards*) It's not him at all, it's another fellow, doing two year, for ... oh, the dirty beast, look what the dirty man-beast is in for. 'Clare to God, putting the likes of that beside me. They must think this is the bloody sloblands.

PRISONER B: There's another fellow here.

DUNLAVIN: I hope it's not another of that persuasion. (*Reads the card*) Ah, no, it's only the murderer, thanks be to God.

The others have a read of the card and skip back to their own cells.

DUNLAVIN: You wouldn't mind old Silver-top.

4. refused.
5. A cup awarded to the winning provincial team in the annual Gaelic football competition.
6. The government department responsible for Ireland's prisons.
7. A railway workers' association.
8. porridge.

Killing your wife is a natural class of a thing could happen to the best of us. But this other dirty animal on me left . . . .

PRISONER B: Ah well, now he's here he'll just have to do his birdlime[9] like anyone else.

DUNLAVIN: That doesn't say that he should do it in the next flowery dell[10] to me. Robbers, thieves and murderers I can abide, but when it comes to that class of carry-on — Good night, Joe Doyle.[11]

PRISONER A: (*Indicates 22*) This fellow was dead lucky.

PRISONER B: Live lucky.

PRISONER A: Two fellows waiting to be topped[12] and he's the one that gets away. As a general rule they don't like reprieving one and topping the other.

DUNLAVIN: So as to be on the safe side, and not to be making fish of one and flesh of the other, they usually top both. Then, of course, the Minister might have said, enough is as good as a feast.

They rest on their brooms.

PRISONER B: It must be a great thing to be told at the last minute that you're not going to be topped after all. To be lying there sweating and watching. The two screws for the death watch coming on at twelve o'clock and the two going off shaking hands with you, and you go to bed, and stare up at the ceiling.

DUNLAVIN: And the two screws nod to each other across the fire to make a sup of tea, but to do it easy in case they wake you, and you turn round in the bed towards the fire and you say 'I'll take a sup as you're at it' and one of the screws says 'Ah, so you're awake, Mick. We were just wetting it; isn't it a good job you spoke up in time.'

PRISONER A: And after that, the tea is drunk and they offer you cigarettes, though the mouth is burned off you from smoking and anyway you've more than they have, you've got that many you'll be leaving them after you, and you lie down and get up, and get up and lie down, and the two screws not letting on to be minding you and not taking their eyes off you for one half-minute, and you walk up and down a little bit more . . . .

PRISONER B: And they ask you would you like another game of draughts or would you sooner write a letter, and getting on to morning you hear a bell out in the city, and you ask them the time, but they won't tell you.

DUNLAVIN: But they put a good face on it, and one says 'There's that old watch stopped again' and he says to the other screw 'Have you your watch, Jack?' and the other fellow makes a great joke of it, 'I'll have to take a run up as far as the North City Pawn shop and ask them to let me have a look at it.' And then the door is unlocked and everyone sweats blood, and they come in and ask your man to stand up a minute, that's if he's able, while they read him something: 'I am instructed to inform you that the Minister has, he hasn't, he has, he hasn't recommended to the President, that . . . .'

PRISONER A: And the quare fellow says 'Did you say "has recommended or has not recommended . . .?" I didn't quite catch that.'

DUNLAVIN: My bloody oath but he catches it. Although I remember once in a case like now when there were two fellows to be topped over two different jobs, didn't the bloody fellow from the Prison Board, as it was then, in old Max Greeb's time, didn't he tell the wrong man he was reprieved? Your man was delighted for a few hours and then they had to go back and tell him 'Sorry, my mistake, but you're to be topped after all'.

PRISONER B: And the fellow that was reprieved, I bet he was glad.

DUNLAVIN: Of course he was glad, anyone that says that a condemned man would be better off hung than doing life, let them leave it to his own discretion. Do you know who feels it worse going out to be topped?

PRISONER A: Corkmen and Northerners . . . they've such bloody hard necks.

DUNLAVIN: I have to do me funny half-hour for Holy Healey. I'm talking serious now.

PRISONER A: All right, come on, let's have it —

DUNLAVIN: The man that feels it worst, going into that little house with the red door and the silver painted gates at the bottom of D. Wing, is a man that has been in the nick[13] before, when some other merchant was topped; or he's heard screws or old lags in the bag shop or at exercise talking about it. A new chap that's never done anything but murder, and that only once, is usually a respectable man, such as this Silver-top here. He knows nothing about it, except the few lines that he'd see in the

9. Cockney rhyming slang for time, i.e. a jail sentence.
10. Cockney rhyming slang for cell.
11. Roughly means 'Count me out'.
12. hanged.
13. jail.

papers. 'Condemned man entered the hang-house at seven fifty-nine. At eight three the doctor pronounced life extinct.'

PRISONER B: That's a lot of mullarkey.[14] In the first place the doctor has his back turned after the trap goes down, and doesn't turn and face it until a screw has caught the rope and stopped it wriggling. Then they go out and lock up the shop and have their breakfast and don't come back for an hour. Then they cut your man down and the doctor slits the back of his neck to see if the bones are broken. Who's to know what happens in the hour your man is swinging there, maybe wriggling to himself in the pit.

PRISONER A: You're right there. When I was in the nick in England, there was a screw doing time, he'd been smuggling out medical reports on hangings and selling them to the Sunday papers, and he told me that one bloke had lived seventeen minutes at the end of a rope.

DUNLAVIN: I don't believe that! Seventeen minutes is a bloody long time to be hanging on the end of a rope.

PRISONER A: It was their own medical report.

PRISONER B: I'll lay odds to a make[15] that Silver-top isn't half charmed with himself he's not going with the meat-chopper in the morning.

DUNLAVIN: You could sing that if you had an air to it.

PRISONER A: They'll have him down to reception, changed into Fry's[16] and over here any time now.

DUNLAVIN: Him and this other jewel here. Bad an' all as Silver-top was to beat his wife's brains out, I'd as lief have him near to me as this article. Dirty beast! I won't have an hour's luck for the rest of me six months, and me hoping to touch Uncle Healey today for a letter to the Room-Keepers[17] for when I'd go out.

PRISONER B: Eh, Dunlavin, is the Department trying to reform, reconstruct and rehabilitate you in your old age?

DUNLAVIN: Ah no, it's nothing to do with the Department. Outside his job in the Department, Uncle Healey's in some holy crowd, that does good be stealth. They never let the right hand know what the left hand doeth, as the man said.[18] Of course they never put either hand in their pocket, so you'd never get money off them, but they can give letters to the Prisoners' Aid[19] and the Room-Keepers. Mind you, Healey's not here today as a holy man. He'll just be fixing up the man that's getting hung in the morning, but if I can get on the right side of him, he might mix business with pleasure and give me a letter for when I get out.

PRISONER B: Now we know the cause of all the spring-cleaning.

DUNLAVIN: And a fellow in the kitchen told us they're doing a special dinner for us on account of Uncle Healey's visit.

PRISONER A: Do you mean we're getting food with our meals today?

DUNLAVIN: That's right, and I can't be standing yapping to youse. I've to hang up my holy pictures and think up a few funny remarks for him. God, what Jimmie O'Dea[20] is getting thousands for I've to do for a pair of old socks and a ticket for the Prisoners' Aid.

DUNLAVIN *goes into his cell. Two* YOUNG PRISONERS *aged about seventeen go past with sweeping brushes in front of them, singing softly and in unison.*

YOUNG PRISONERS:

Only one more cell inspection
We go out next Saturday,
Only one more cell inspection
And we go far, far away.

PRISONER A: What brings you fellows round here this morning?

YOUNG PRISONER 1: Our screw told us to sweep all round the Juvenile Wing and then to come round here and give it a bit of a going over.

PRISONER B: And have you your own wing done?

YOUNG PRISONER 2: No, but if we did our wing first, we'd miss the mots[21] hanging out the laundry. You can't see them from our wing.

PRISONER A: Just as well, maybe; you're bad enough as it is.

YOUNG PRISONER 1: But I tell you what you will see from our wing this morning. It's the carpenter bringing up the coffin for the quare fellow and leaving it over in the mortuary to have it handy for the morning. There's two orderlies besides us over

14. foolish nonsense. Usually spelled malarkey.
15. Slang for a halfpenny.
16. prison clothes. Named after the English prison reformer Elizabeth Fry (1780-1845).
17. A charitable organization that helps the homeless.
18. An irreverent allusion to the Gospel teaching on charity. See Matthew 6.3.
19. A charitable organization that aids prisoners.
20. A well-known Dublin comedian, 1899-1965.
21. women.

in the Juveniles, and we were going to toss up who'd come over here, but they're country fellows and they'd said they'd sooner see the coffin. I'd sooner a pike[22] at a good-looking mot than the best coffin in Ireland, wouldn't you, Shaybo?

YOUNG PRISONER 2: Certainly I would, and outside that, when you're over here, there's always a chance of getting a bit of education about screwing jobs, and suchlike, from experienced men. Do you think Triplex or celluloid is the best for Yale locks, sir?[23]

YOUNG PRISONER 1: Do you carry the stick all the time, sir?

PRISONER A: If I had a stick I'd know where to put it, across your bloody . . . .

YOUNG PRISONER 2: Scholara, get sweeping, here's the screw.

They drift off sweeping and singing softly.

PRISONER B: He's bringing one of 'em. Is it Silver-top or the other fellow?

PRISONER A: Silver-top. I remember him being half carried into the circle[24] the night he was sentenced to death.

PRISONER B: He has a right spring in his step this morning then.

PRISONER A: He's not looking all that happy. Still, I suppose he hasn't got over the shock yet.

WARDER *and a* PRISONER *come on* L. *The* PRISONER *is in early middle age; when he speaks he has a 'good accent'. He is carrying a pillow slip which contains his sheets and other kit. The* WARDER *halts him.*

WARDER REGAN: Stand by the door with your name on it. Later on when you've seen the doctor these fellows will show you how to lay your kit. Stand there now, till the doctor is ready to see you. (*He goes*)

There is a pause, while the PRISONERS *survey the newcomer.*

PRISONER B: He'll bloody well cheer the place up, won't he?

LIFER: Have any of you got a cigarette?

PRISONER A: That's a good one. You're not in the condemned cell now, you know. No snout[25] allowed here.

PRISONER B: Unless you manage to scrounge a dog-end off the remands.

PRISONER A: Or pick one up in the exercise yard after a man the like of yourself that's allowed them as a special concession. Not, by God, that we picked up much after you. What did you do with your dog-ends?

LIFER: Threw them in the fire.

PRISONER B: You what!

PRISONER A: How was it the other poor bastard, that's got no reprieve and is to be topped in the morning — how was it he was always able to leave a trail of butts behind him when he went off exercise?

LIFER: I've never been in prison before; how was I to know?

PRISONER A: You're a curse of God liar, my friend, you did know; for it was whispered to him by the fellows from the hospital bringing over the grub to the condemned cell. He never gave them as much as a match! And he couldn't even bring his dog-ends to the exercise yard and drop them behind for us to pick up when we came out later.

PRISONER B: I bet you're charmed with yourself that you're not going through the iron door tomorrow morning.

The LIFER *doesn't speak, but looks down at his suit.*

PRISONER A: Aye, you're better off in that old suit, bad as it is, than the wooden overcoat the quare fellow is going to get tomorrow morning.

PRISONER B: The longest you could do would be twenty years. More than likely you'll get out in half of that. Last man to finish up in the Bog,[26] he done eleven.

LIFER: Eleven. How do you live through it?

PRISONER A: A minute at a time.

PRISONER B: You haven't got a bit of snout for him, have you? (PRISONER A *shakes his head*) Maybe Dunlavin has. Hey, Dunlavin, have you e'er a smoke you'd give this chap? Hey, Dunlavin.

DUNLAVIN: (*Coming from his cell*) Yes, what is it? Anyone there the name of headache?

PRISONER B: Could you manage to give this chap something to smoke? E'er a bit of snout at all.

DUNLAVIN: There's only one brand of tobacco allowed here — 'Three Nuns'. None today, none tomorrow, and none the day after. (*He goes back into his cell*)

PRISONER B: Eh, Dunlavin, come back to hell out of that.

DUNLAVIN: Well, what?

22. look.
23. The young prisoner is inquiring about the best kind of plastic-like material to use in picking Yale locks.
24. The prison's main entrance, onto which the various wings give.
25. tobacco.
26. A slang reference to a maximum security prison in Portlaoise, Co. Laois, in the Irish midlands.

PRISONER B: This poor chap after being smoking about sixty a day . . . .

DUNLAVIN: Where?

PRISONER B: In the condemned cell — where else?

DUNLAVIN: Now I have you. Sure I thought you were the other fellow, and you're not, you're only the murderer. God comfort you. (*Shakes hands*) Certainly so. (*Takes off his jacket, looks up and down the wing, undoes his trousers and from the depths of his combinations*[27] *he produces a cigarette end, and a match, and presents them to the* LIFER) Reprieved in the small hours of the morning. Certainly so. The dead arose and appeared to many, as the man said,[28] but you'll be getting yourself a bad name standing near that other fellow's door. This is your flowery dell, see? It has your name there on that little card. And all your particulars. Age forty-three. Religion R.C.

LIFER: (*Reads*) Life.

DUNLAVIN: And a bloody sight better than death any day of the week.

PRISONER B: It always says that. The Governor will explain it all to you later this morning.

DUNLAVIN: Or maybe they'll get holy Uncle Healey to do it.

PRISONER B: Go into your cell and have a smoke for yourself. Bring in your kit bag. (*Passes in kit to* LIFER) Have a quiet burn[29] there before the screw comes round; we'll keep nick.

LIFER *closes the door of his cell*

DUNLAVIN: God knows I got the pick of good neighbours. Lovely people. Give me a decent murderer though, rather than the likes of this other fellow. Well, I'll go into me little place and get on with me bit of dobying[30] so as to have it all nice for Healey when he comes round. (*He goes back to his cell*)

PRISONER B: (*To* LIFER) Don't light up yet! Here's the screw coming.

PRISONER A: With the other fellow.

WARDER REGAN *and another prisoner, 'the* OTHER FELLOW*', an anxious-faced man, wearing prison clothes and carrying a kit bag, come on* L.

WARDER REGAN: Yes, this is your flowery dell. Leave in your kitbag and stand at your door and wait for the doctor. These other fellows will show you where to go when he comes.

OTHER FELLOW: Right, sir. Very good, sir.

WARDER REGAN *goes, the* OTHER FELLOW *has a look round.*

PRISONER B: There's a bloke in the end cell getting himself a quiet burn. Why don't you join him before the screws get back?

The OTHER FELLOW *notices the card on* LIFER's *cell.*

OTHER FELLOW: My God! Is this what I've come to, mixing with murderers! I'd rather not, thank you, though I could do with a smoke. I'll have to spend long months here, even if I get my remission, with murderers and thieves and God knows what! You're not all murderers are you? You haven't killed anyone, have you?

PRISONER B: Not for a while, I haven't.

OTHER FELLOW: I cannot imagine any worse crime than taking a life, can you?

PRISONER B: It'd depend whose life.

OTHER FELLOW: Of course. I mean, a murderer would be justified in taking his own life, wouldn't he? 'We send him forth' says Carlisle — you've heard of Carlisle haven't you? — 'We send him forth, back to the void, back to the darkness, far out beyond the stars. Let him go from us.'

DUNLAVIN: (*Head out of door of cell*) Oh. (*Looks at* OTHER FELLOW) I thought it was Healey from the Department or someone giving it out of them.

PRISONER A: Looks like this man is a bit of an intellectual.

DUNLAVIN: Is that what they call it now?

LIFER: Thanks for the smoke, Mr. Dunlavin.

DUNLAVIN: Not at all, sure, you're welcome, call again when you're passing. But remember the next wife you kill and you getting forty fags[31] a day in the condemned cell, think of them as is not so fortunate as yourself and leave a few dog-ends around the exercise yard after you. Here's these noisy little gets[32] again.

The two YOUNG PRISONERS *come round from the left, their sweeping brushes in front of them and singing their song. The* OTHER FELLOW *stands quite still at his door.*

YOUNG PRISONERS:

Only one more cell inspection
We go out next Saturday
Only one more cell inspection
Then we go far far away.

27. An undergarment comprising a vest and drawers.
28. See Matthew 27.51-53, in the Douai-Rheims version.
29. smoke.
30. clothes-washing (from the Anglo-Indian *dhobi*, a washerman).
31. cigarettes.
32. ill-begotten creatures.

(*They are sweeping near the* LIFER)
Only one more cell inspection
We go out next Saturday
Only one more cell . . . .

LIFER: For God's sake shut up that squeaking . . .

YOUNG PRISONER 1: We've as much right to open our mouth as what you have, and you only a wet day in the place.

PRISONER B: Leave the kids alone. You don't own the place, you know. They're doing no harm. (*To the* YOUNG PRISONERS) You want to sweep this bit of floor away?

DUNLAVIN: What brings you round here so often? If you went over to the remand wings you might pick up a bit of snout or a look at the paper.

YOUNG PRISONER 1: We get a smoke and the *Mail* every day off a limey[33] on our road that's on remand. He's in over the car smuggling. But round here this morning you can see the mots from the laundry over on the female side hanging out the washing in the exercise yard. Do youse look at them? I suppose when you get old, though, you don't much bother about women.

PRISONER B: I'm thirty-six, mac.

YOUNG PRISONER 1: Ah, I thought that. Don't suppose you care if you never see a mot. There's Shaybo there and he never thinks of anything else. Do you think of anything else but women, Shaybo?

YOUNG PRISONER 2: Yes. Robbing and stealing, Scholara. You go to the window and keep an eye out for them and I'll sweep on round here till you give us a call.

YOUNG PRISONER 1: Right, Shaybo, they should be nearly out now. (*Goes up and stands by window*)

PRISONER B: I forgot about the women.

DUNLAVIN: I didn't. It's a great bit of a treat today — that and having me leg rubbed. Neighbour and I wait in for it.

YOUNG PRISONER 1: (*From the window, in a coarse whisper*) Shaybo, you can see them now.

YOUNG PRISONER 2: The blondy one from North Crumlin?[34]

YOUNG PRISONER 1: Yes, and there's another one with her. I don't know her.

YOUNG PRISONER 2: Must be a country mot. Scholara doesn't know her. Women.

DUNLAVIN: Women.

PRISONER A: I see the blondy one waving.

YOUNG PRISONER 1: If it's all the one to you, I'd like you to know that's my mot and it's me she's waving at.

PRISONER A: I'll wave you a thick ear.

DUNLAVIN: Hey, Neighbour! Where the hell is he this morning? Neighbour!

AN OLD MAN'S CREAKING VOICE: Here I am, Neighbour, here I am.

NEIGHBOUR, *a bent old man, comes on from* L., *hobbling as quickly as he can on a stick.*

DUNLAVIN: Ah, you lost mass.[35]

NEIGHBOUR: What, are they gone in already?

DUNLAVIN: No, but they're finished hanging up the top row of clothes. There'll be no stretching or reaching off chairs.

NEIGHBOUR: Still, thanks be to God for small mercies. They'll be out again this day week.

PRISONER A: If you lives to see it.

NEIGHBOUR: Why wouldn't I live to see it as well as what you would? This is not the nearest I was to fine women, nor are they the first good-looking ones I saw.

PRISONER A: With that old cough of yours they could easy be the last.

NEIGHBOUR: God, you're a desperate old gas bag. We remember better-looking women than ever they were, don't we, Dunlavin? Meena La Bloom, do you remember her?

DUNLAVIN: Indeed and I do; many's the seaman myself and Meena gave the hey and a do, and Mickey Finn to.[36]

NEIGHBOUR: And poor May Oblong.

DUNLAVIN: Ah, where do you leave poor May? The Lord have mercy on her, wasn't I with her one night in the digs,[37] and there was a Member of Parliament there, and May after locking him in the back room and taking away his trousers, with him going over the north wall that morning to vote for Home Rule. 'For the love of your country and mine,' he shouts under the door to May, 'give me back me trousers.' 'So I will,' says May, 'if you shove a fiver out under the door.'

NEIGHBOUR: He had the wad hid? Dirty suspicious old beast.

DUNLAVIN: That's right. He was cute enough to hide his wad somewhere, drunk and all as he was

33. An Englishman.
34. A district of Dublin.
35. i.e. missed Mass — the ritual of the women hanging out their laundry.
36. Dunlavin is describing in colourful terms how he and a prostitute entrapped and robbed unwary seamen with the help of drugged drinks.
37. lodgings.

the previous night. All we got in his trousers was a locket of hair of the patriotic plumber of Dolphin's barn that swore to let his hair grow till Ireland was free.

NEIGHBOUR: Ah, poor May, God help her, she was the heart of the roll.[38]

DUNLAVIN: And when she was arrested for carrying on after the curfew, the time of the trouble,[39] she was fined for having concealed about her person two Thompson sub-machine guns, 1921 pattern, three Mills bombs, and a stick of dynamite.

NEIGHBOUR: And will you ever forget poor Lottie L'Estrange, that got had up for pushing the soldier into Spencer Dock?[40]

DUNLAVIN: Ah, God be with the youth of us.

NEIGHBOUR: And Cork Annie, and Lady Limerick.

DUNLAVIN: And Julia Rice and the Goofy One.

NEIGHBOUR: (*Turns towards window*) Hey, you, move out of the way there and give us a look. Dunlavin, come up here before they go, and have a look at the blondy one.

YOUNG PRISONER 1: Go 'long, you dirty old dog. That's my mot you're speaking about. (*Shoves* NEIGHBOUR) You old heap of dirt, to wave at a decent girl.

PRISONER A: Hey, snots,[41] d'you think you own the bloody place?

YOUNG PRISONER 1: Would you like it, to have that dirty old eyebox looking at your mot?

PRISONER B: He's not going to eat her.

DUNLAVIN: (*From behind*) No, but he'd like to.

YOUNG PRISONER 2: That's right, and Scholara is nearly married to her. At least she had a squealer[42] for him and he has to pay her money every week. Any week he's outside like, to give it, or her to get it.

YOUNG PRISONER 1: (*Blows a kiss*) That's right, and I have him putting his rotten old eye on her.

OTHER FELLOW (*At his doorway*) God preserve us.

PRISONER A: Well, you don't own the bloody window. (*Shoves* YOUNG PRISONER 1 *out of way and brings over* NEIGHBOUR) Come on, you, if you want to see the May procession.

NEIGHBOUR: Ah, thanks, butty, your blood's worth bottling.

38. i.e. one of the best. From 'Dicey Reilly', a popular Dublin ballad.
39. During the War of Independence.
40. One of Dublin's sea docks.
41. A term of abuse, from snot, mucus from the nose.
42. baby.

PRISONER A: I didn't do it on account of you, but if you let them young pups get away with too much they'd be running the place.

YOUNG PRISONER 2: Come on, Scholara, we'll mosey back. The screw will think we're lost.

They go back down the stairs, pick up their brushes, and start sweeping again and singing . . . .

YOUNG PRISONER 1:

Only one more cell inspection
We go out next Saturday

YOUNG PRISONER 2:

Only one more cell inspection . . . .

LIFER: Shut your bloody row, can't you?

DUNLAVIN: Shut up yourself; you're making more noise than any of them.

YOUNG PRISONER 1: Don't tell us to shut up, you bastard.

PRISONER B: Ah leave him alone; he started life this morning.

YOUNG PRISONER 1: Ah we're sorry, mister, ain't we, Shaybo?

YOUNG PRISONER 2: God, we are. Go over and take a pike at the female yard. They hang up the clothes now and Scholara's mot is over there. You can have a look at her. Scholara won't mind, will you, Schol?

YOUNG PRISONER 1: Certainly and I won't. Not with you going to the Bog to start life in a couple of days, where you won't see a woman.

YOUNG PRISONER 2: A child.

YOUNG PRISONER 1: A dog.

YOUNG PRISONER 2: A fire.

PRISONER A: Get to hell out of that round to your own wing. Wouldn't you think a man would know all that forbye you telling it to him?

YOUNG PRISONER 2: We were going anyway. We've seen all we wanted to see. It wasn't to look at a lot of old men we came here, but to see mots hanging out the washing.

YOUNG PRISONER 1: And eitherways, we'll be a lot nearer the women than you'll be next Saturday night. Think of us when you're sitting locked up in the old flowery, studying the Bible, Chapter 1, verse 2, and we trucking round in chase of charver.[43]

They samba out with their brushes for partners, humming the Wedding Samba.

PRISONER A: Them young gets have too much

43. i.e. looking for sexual adventure. Charver — woman, or sexual embrace.

old gab out of them altogether. I was a Y.P.[44] in Walton[45] before the war and I can tell you they'd be quiet boys if they got the larrying[46] we used to get.

OTHER FELLOW: And talking so disrespectfully about the Bible.

NEIGHBOUR: Belied and they needn't; many's the time the Bible was a consolation to a fellow all alone in the old cell. The lovely thin paper with a bit of mattress coir in it, if you could get a match or a bit of tinder or any class of light, was as good a smoke as ever I tasted. Am I right, Dunlavin?

DUNLAVIN: Damn the lie, Neighbour. The first twelve months I done, I smoked my way half-way through the book of Genesis and three inches of my mattress. When the Free State[47] came in we were afraid of our life they were going to change the mattresses for feather beds. And you couldn't smoke feathers, not, be God, if they were rolled in the Song of Solomon itself. But sure, thanks to God, the Free State didn't change anything more than the badge on the warders' caps.

OTHER FELLOW: Can I be into my cell for a while?

PRISONER B: Until the doctor calls you. (*Goes into his cell*)

PRISONER A: Well, I'm going to have a rest. It's hard work doing a lagging.

LIFER: A lagging? That's penal servitude, isn't it?

DUNLAVIN: Three years or anything over.

LIFER: Three years is a long time.

DUNLAVIN: I wouldn't like to be that long hanging.

NEIGHBOUR: Is he the . . . .

DUNLAVIN: (*Sotto voce*) Silver-top! (*Aloud*) Started life this morning.

NEIGHBOUR: So they're not going to top you after all? Well, you're a lucky man. I worked one time in the hospital, helping the screw there, and the morning of the execution he gave me two bottles of stout to take the hood off the fellow was after being topped. I wouldn't have done it a second time for two glasses of malt, no, nor a bottle of it. I cut the hood away; his head was all twisted and his face black, but the two eyes were the worst; like a rabbit's; it was fear that had done it.

LIFER: Perhaps he didn't feel anything. How do you know?

NEIGHBOUR: I only seen him. I never had a chance of asking him. (NEIGHBOUR *goes to the murderer's door*) Date of expiration of sentence, life. In some ways I wouldn't mind if that was my lot. What do you say?

DUNLAVIN: I don't know; it's true we're too old and bet for lobbywatching and shaking down anywhere, so that you'd fall down and sleep on the pavement of a winter's night and not know but you were lying snug and comfortable in the Shelbourne.[48]

NEIGHBOUR: Only then to wake up on some lobby and the hard floorboards under you, and a lump of hard filth for your pillow, and the cold and the drink shaking you, wishing it was morning for the market pubs[49] to open, where if you had the price of a drink you could sit in the warm anyway. Except, God look down on you, if it was Sunday.[50]

DUNLAVIN: Ah, there's the agony. No pub open, but the bells battering your bared nerves and all you could do with the cold and the sickness was to lean over on your side and wish that God would call you.

LIFER: If I was outside my life wouldn't be like that.

NEIGHBOUR: No, but ours would.

DUNLAVIN: (*Quietly*) See, we're selfish, mister, like everyone else.

WARDER: (*Shouts off*) Medical applications and receptions. Fall in for the doctor.

LIFER *looks lost*.

DUNLAVIN: Yes, that's you. Go up there to the top of the wing and wait there till the screw tells you to go in. Neighbour, call them other fellows.

Exit LIFER.

NEIGHBOUR: Come on — the vet's here.

DUNLAVIN: (*Calling in to the* OTHER FELLOW) Hey, come out and get gelded.

OTHER FELLOW *and* PRISONERS A *and* B *come out of cells*.

NEIGHBOUR: You're for the doctor. Go on up there with the rest of them. Me and Dunlavin don't go up. We only wait to be rubbed.

DUNLAVIN: Don't have any chat at all with that fellow. D'you see what he's in for?

NEIGHBOUR *goes and looks. Exit* OTHER FELLOW *and* PRISONERS A *and* B.

NEIGHBOUR: What the hell does that mean?

44. Young Prisoner.
45. A jail in Liverpool, England. See Brendan Behan's *Borstal Boy*.
46. severe beating.
47. The foundation of the Irish Free State in 1922.
48. Well-known, luxurious hotel on St Stephen's Green in Dublin.
49. Public houses in Dublin in which alcohol is available from an early hour.
50. On Sunday mornings, even the early pubs are closed.

DUNLAVIN: A bloody sex mechanic.[51]

NEIGHBOUR: I didn't know.

DUNLAVIN: Well, you know now. I'll go in and get me chair. You can sit on it after me. It'll save you bringing yours out.

NEIGHBOUR: Well, if you go first and you have a chance of a go at the spirit bottle, don't swig the bloody lot. Remember I'm for treatment too.

DUNLAVIN: Don't be such an old begrudger. He'll bring a quart bottle of it, and who could swallow that much methylated spirit in the few drops you'd get at it?

NEIGHBOUR: You could, or a bucket of it, if it was lying anywhere handy. I seen you do it, bluestone and all, only buns to a bear as far as you were concerned.

DUNLAVIN: Do you remember the old doctor they had here years ago?

NEIGHBOUR: The one they used to call Crippen.[52]

DUNLAVIN: The very man. There was one day I was brought in for drinking the chat[53] and I went to court that morning and was here in the afternoon still as drunk as Pontius Pilate.[54] Crippen was examining me. 'When I put me hand there you cough,' and all to that effect. 'Did you ever have V.D.?'[55] says he. 'I haven't got your habits,' says I to him. These fellows weren't long.

Re-enter PRISONERS A *and* B.

NEIGHBOUR: What did he give youse?

PRISONER B: (*Passing into cell*) Extra six ounces of bread. Says we're undernourished.

PRISONER A: Is the bar open yet?

NEIGHBOUR: Never you mind the bar. I've cruel pains in my leg that I want rubbed to take out the rheumatics, not to be jeered at, and I've had them genuine since the war.

PRISONER A: What war? The economic war?[56]

NEIGHBOUR: Ah, you maggot. It's all your fault, Dunlavin, telling them fellows we do get an odd sup out of the spirit bottle. Letting everyone know our business.

PRISONERS A *and* B *go into cells and shut the doors.*

DUNLAVIN: No sign of Holy Healey yet.

NEIGHBOUR: You're wasting your time chasing after old Healey. He told me here one day, and I trying to get myself an old overcoat out of him, that he was here only as a head man of the Department of Justice, and he couldn't do other business of any other sort or size whatever, good, bad or indifferent. It's my opinion that old Healey does be half-jarred[57] a deal of the time anyway.

DUNLAVIN: The likes of Healey would take a sup all right, but being a high-up civil servant, he wouldn't drink under his own name. You'd see the likes of Healey nourishing themselves with balls of malt,[58] at eleven in the morning, in little back snugs round Merrion Row. The barman would lose his job if he so much as breathed their name. It'd be 'Mr. H. wants a drop of water but not too much.' 'Yes, Mr. O.' 'No, Sir, Mr. Mac wasn't in this morning.' 'Yes, Mr. D. Fine morning; it will be a lovely day if it doesn't snow.' Educated drinking, you know. Even a bit of chat about God at an odd time, so as you'd think God was in another department, but not long off the Bog,[59] and they was doing Him a good turn to be talking well about Him.

NEIGHBOUR: Here's the other two back. The M.O.[60] will be down to us soon.

LIFER *and* OTHER FELLOW *go into cells and shut the doors.*

DUNLAVIN: That other fellow's not looking as if this place is agreeing with him.

NEIGHBOUR: You told me a minute ago that I wasn't even to speak to him.

DUNLAVIN: Ah, when all is said and done, he's someone's rearing after all, he could be worse, he could be a screw or an official from the Department.

WARDER REGAN *comes on with a bottle marked 'methylated spirit'.*

WARDER REGAN: You're the two for rubs, for your rheumatism.

DUNLAVIN: That's right, Mr. Regan, sir, old and bet, sir, that's us. And the old pains is very bad with us these times, sir.

WARDER REGAN: Not so much lip, and sit down

51. A Malapropism: a sex maniac.
52. A notorious wife poisoner, Dr H. H. Crippen (1862-1910).
53. i.e. drinking methylated spirits, which is an illegal act.
54. Satiric reference to the Roman prefect of Judaea, before whom Jesus stood trial.
55. Venereal Disease.
56. In the 1930s the Irish government withheld payments to the British government which were due under the terms of the Treaty of 1922. The British responded by imposing tariffs on Irish imports to Britain in a process that was known in Ireland as the economic war.
57. half-drunk.
58. Glasses of Irish whiskey.
59. i.e. not long away from the manual labourer of cutting turf on the Irish bogs — hence one from a provincial rural background.
60. Medical Officer.

whoever is first for treatment.

DUNLAVIN: That's me, sir. Age before ignorance, as the man said. (*Sits in the chair*)

WARDER REGAN: Rise the leg of your trousers. Which leg is it?

DUNLAVIN: The left, sir.

WARDER REGAN: That's the right leg you're showing me.

DUNLAVIN: That's what I was saying, sir. The left is worst one day and the right is bad the next. To be on the safe side, you'd have to do two of them. It's only the mercy of God I'm not a centipede, sir, with the weather that's in it.

WARDER REGAN: Is that where the pain is?

DUNLAVIN: (*Bending down slowly towards the bottle*) A little lower down, sir, if you please. (*Grabs the bottle and raises it to his mouth*) Just a little lower down, sir, if it's all equal to you.

REGAN *rubs, head well bent, and* DUNLAVIN *drinks long and deeply and as quickly lowers the bottle on to the floor again, wiping his mouth and making the most frightful grimaces, for the stuff doesn't go down easy at first. He goes through the pantomime of being burnt inside for* NEIGHBOUR's *benefit and rubs his mouth with the back of his hand.*

DUNLAVIN: Ah, that's massive, sir. 'Tis you that has the healing hand. You must have desperate luck at the horses; I'd only love to be with you copying your dockets.[61] (REGAN *turns and pours more spirit on his hands*) Ah, that's it, sir, well into me I can feel it going. (*Reaches forward towards the bottle again, drinks*) Ah, that's it, I can feel it going right into me. And doing me all the good in the world. (REGAN *reaches and puts more spirit on his hand and sets to rubbing again*) That's it, sir, thorough does it; if you're going to do a thing at all you might as well do it well. (*Reaches forward for the bottle again and raises it.* NEIGHBOUR *looks across in piteous appeal to him not to drink so much, but he merely waves the bottle in elegant salute, as if to wish him good health, and takes another drink*) May God reward you, sir, you must be the seventh son of the seventh son or one of the Lees from Limerick[62] on your mother's side maybe. (*Drinks again*) Ah, that's the cure for the cold of the wind and the world's neglectment.

WARDER REGAN: Right, now you.

61. Betting slips used when wagering on horse races.

62. In folklore the seventh son of a seventh son is gifted with special powers. Such magical good fortune is here humorously associated with the mythical standing of a Limerick family.

NEIGHBOUR *comes forward.*

WARDER DONELLY: (*Offstage*) All present and correct, Mr. Healey, sir.

DUNLAVIN: Holy Healey!

Enter WARDER DONELLY.

WARDER DONELLY: This way, Mr. Healey.

WARDER REGAN: Attention! Stand by your doors.

DUNLAVIN: By the left, laugh.

WARDER DONELLY: This way.

Enter MR. HEALEY, *an elegantly dressed gentleman.*

HEALEY: Good morning.

WARDER DONELLY: Any complaints?

PRISONER A: No, sir.

HEALEY: Good morning!

WARDER DONELLY: Any complaints?

OTHER FELLOW: }
PRISONER B: } No, sir.

HEALEY: Good morning all! Well, now, I'm here representing the Department of Justice, if there are any complaints now is the time to make them.

SEVERAL PRISONERS: No complaints, sir.

WARDER REGAN: All correct, sir. Two receiving medical treatment here, sir.

DUNLAVIN: Just getting the old legs rubbed, sir, Mr. Healey.

HEALEY: Well, well, it almost smells like a bar.

DUNLAVIN: I'm near drunk myself on the smell of it, sir.

HEALEY: Don't let me interrupt the good work.

DUNLAVIN: Ah, the old legs. It's being out in all weathers that does it, sir. Of course we don't have that to contend with while we're here, sir.

HEALEY: Out in all weathers, I should think not indeed. Well, my man, I will be inspecting your cell amongst others in due course.

DUNLAVIN: Yes, sir.

HEALEY: It's always a credit to you, I must say that. (*He turns to* REGAN) Incorrigible, some of these old fellows, but rather amusing.

WARDER REGAN: Yes, sir.

HEALEY: It's Regan, isn't it?

WARDER REGAN: Yes, sir.

HEALEY: Ah yes, you're helping the Canon at the execution tomorrow morning, I understand.

WARDER REGAN: Well, I shall be with the condemned man sir, seeing that he doesn't do away with himself during the night and that he goes down the hole with his neck properly broken in the morning, without making too much fuss about it.

HEALEY: A sad duty.

WARDER REGAN: Neck breaking and throttling, sir? (HEALEY *gives him a sharp look*) You must excuse me, sir. I've seen rather a lot of it. They say familiarity breeds contempt.

HEALEY: Well, we have one consolation, Regan, the condemned man gets the priest and the sacraments, more than his victim got maybe. I venture to suggest that some of them die holier deaths than if they had finished their natural span.

WARDER REGAN: We can't advertise 'Commit a murder and die a happy death,' sir. We'd have them all at it. They take religion very seriously in this country.

HEALEY: Quite, quite so! Now, I understand you have the reprieved man over here, Regan.

WARDER REGAN: No. Twenty-six sir.

DUNLAVIN: Just beside me, sir.

HEALEY: Ah, yes! So here we are! Here's the lucky man, eh? Well, now, the Governor will explain your position to you later in the day. Your case will be examined every five years. Meanwhile I thought you might like a holy picture to hang up in your cell. Keep a cheerful countenance, my friend. God gave you back your life and the least you can do is to thank him with every breath you draw! Right? Well, be of good heart. I will call in and see you again, that is, if duty permits. (*He moves to* DUNLAVIN'S *cell*)

HEALEY: (*At* DUNLAVIN'S *cell*) Very creditable. Hm.

DUNLAVIN: Well, to tell you the truth, sir, it's a bit extra special today. You see, we heard you was here.

HEALEY: Very nice.

DUNLAVIN: Of course I do like to keep my little place as homely as I can with the little holy pictures you gave me of Blessed Martin,[63] sir.

HEALEY: I see you don't recognize the colour bar.[64]

DUNLAVIN: The only bar I recognize, sir, is the Bridge Bar or the Beamish House the corner of Thomas Street.[65]

HEALEY: Well, I must be off now, and I'm glad to see you're being well looked after.

DUNLAVIN: It's neither this nor that, but if you could spare a minute, sir?

HEALEY: Yes, what is it? But hurry; remember I've a lot to do today.

DUNLAVIN: It's like this, sir. I won't always be here, sir, having me leg rubbed and me bit of grub brought to me. As it says in the Bible, sir, have it yourself or be without it and put ye by for the rainy day, for thou knowest not the night thou mayest be sleeping in a lobby.[66]

HEALEY: Yes, yes, but what is it you want?

DUNLAVIN: I've the chance of a little room up round Buckingham Street,[67] sir, if you could only give me a letter to the Room-Keepers after I go out, for a bit of help with the rent.

HEALEY: Well, you know, when I visit the prison, I'm not here as a member of any outside organization of which I may be a member but simply as an official of the Department of Justice.

DUNLAVIN: Yes, but where else would I be likely to meet you, sir? I'd hardly bump into you in the Bridge Bar when I'd be outside, would I, sir?

HEALEY: No, no, certainly not. But you know the Society offices in the Square. See me there any Friday night, between eight and nine.

DUNLAVIN: Thank you, sir, and a bed in heaven to you, sir.

HEALEY: And the same to you. (*Goes to next cell*)

DUNLAVIN: And many of them, and I hope we're all here this time next year (*venomously after* MR. HEALEY) that it may choke you.

WARDER DONELLY *bangs on* LIFER'S *closed door, then looks in.*

WARDER DONELLY: Jesus Christ, sir. He's put the sheet up! Quick.

REGAN *and* DONNELLY *go into* LIFER'S *cell. He is hanging. They cut him down.*

WARDER REGAN: Gently does it.

They lay him down in the passage and try to restore him.

HEALEY: What a dreadful business, and with this other coming off tomorrow.

THE PRISONERS *crowd out of line.*

WARDER DONELLY: Get back to your cells!

HEALEY: Is he still with us?

WARDER REGAN: He'll be all right in an hour or two. Better get the M.O., Mr. Donelly.

The triangle sounds.

WARDER DONELLY: B.Wing, two, three and one. Stand by your doors. Right, lead on. Now come on,

63. Blessed Martin de Porres (1579-1639), Peruvian Dominican. The son of a Spanish soldier and a black Panamanian, he devoted himself to the sick and forlorn, building an orphanage and living an ascetic life.

64. i.e. practise race discrimination.

65. A Dublin street.

66. An irreverent parody of Gospel injunctions.

67. A Dublin street.

come on, this is no holiday. Right sir, over to you. Lead on, B.I.

WARDER REGAN *and* HEALEY *are left with the unconscious* LIFER.

HEALEY: Dear, dear. The Canon will be very upset about this.

WARDER REGAN: There's not much harm done, thank God. They don't have to put a death certificate against the receipt for his live body.

HEALEY: That doesn't seem a very nice way of looking at it, Regan.

WARDER REGAN: A lot of people mightn't consider ours a very nice job, sir.

HEALEY: Ours?

WARDER REGAN: Yes, ours, sir. Mine, the Canon's, the hangman's, and if you don't mind my saying so, yours, sir.

HEALEY: Society cannot exist without prisons, Regan. My job is to bring what help and comfort I can to these unfortunates. Really, a man with your outlook, I cannot see why you stay in the service.

WARDER REGAN: It's a soft job, sir, between hangings.

The triangle is heard. The M.O. *comes on with two stretcher-bearers.*

The curtain falls.

ACT II

The curtain rises.

The prison yard, a fine evening.

VOICE OF PRISONER: (*Off-stage, singing*):

A hungry feeling came o'er me stealing
And the mice were squealing in my prison cell
And the old triangle
Went jingle jangle
Along the banks of the Royal Canal.

WARDER DONELLY: B.1. B.2. B.3. Head on for exercise, right! Lead on, B.1. All one, away to exercise.

The prisoners file out, WARDER DONELLY *with them.*

On a fine spring evening,
The lag lay dreaming
The seagulls wheeling high above the wall,
And the old triangle
Went jingle jangle
Along the banks of the Royal Canal.
The screw was peeping
The lag was sleeping,

The prisoners wander where they will; most go and take a glance at the half-dug grave.

While he lay weeping for the girl Sal,

WARDER DONELLY: Who's the bloody baritone? Shut up that noise, you. Where do you think you are?

NEIGHBOUR: It's not up here, sir; it's one of the fellows in the basement, sir, in the solitary.

WARDER DONELLY: He must be getting birdseed with his bread and water. I'll bloody well show him he's not in a singing house. (*Song is still going on*) Hey, shut up that noise! Shut up there or I'll leave you weeping. Where do you think you are? (*Song stops*) You can get sitting down any of you that wants it. (DUNLAVIN *sits*)

NEIGHBOUR: (*At the grave*) They'll have to bottom out another couple of feet before morning.

PRISONER B: They! Us you mean; they've got four of us in a working party after tea.

NEIGHBOUR: You want to get that clay nice and neat for filling in. (*He spits and wanders away*)

PRISONER B: We'll get a couple of smokes for the job at least.

They wander.

NEIGHBOUR: How are you, Neighbour?

DUNLAVIN: Dying.

NEIGHBOUR: If you are itself, it's greed that's killing you. I only got a sup of what was left.

DUNLAVIN: I saved your life then; it was very bad meths.

PRISONER B: What did Regan say when he caught youse lying in the cell?

NEIGHBOUR: He wanted to take us up for drinking it on him, but Dunlavin said we were distracted with the events of the morning and didn't know what we were doing. So he just told us to get to hell out of it and he hoped it would destroy us for life.

DUNLAVIN: May God forgive him.

NEIGHBOUR: I thought it was as good a drop of meths as ever I tasted. It would never come up to the pre-war article, but between the spring-time and the warmth of it, it would put new life into you. Oh, it's a grand evening and another day's work behind us.

PRISONER B: With the winter over, Neighbour, I suppose you don't feel a day over ninety.

NEIGHBOUR: If you'd have done all the time I have you wouldn't look so young.

PRISONER A: What time? Sure, you never done a lagging in your life. A month here and a week there for lifting the collection box out of a chapel or running out of a chemist's with a bottle of cheap wine. Anything over six months would be the death of you.

NEIGHBOUR: Oh, you're the hard chaw.[1]

PRISONER A: Two laggings, I've done. Five year and seven, and a bit of Preventive Detention, on the Moor and at Parkhurst.[2]

NEIGHBOUR: What for? Ferocious begging?

PRISONER A: I've never been a grasshopper or a nark[3] for the screws anyway, wherever I was; and if you were in a lagging station I know what they'd give you, shopping the poor bastard that was singing in the chokey.[4] He was only trying to be company for himself down there all alone and not knowing whether it was day or night.

NEIGHBOUR: I only did it for his own good. If the screw hadn't checked him the Principal might have been coming out and giving him an extra few days down there.

DUNLAVIN: Will youse give over the pair of youse for God's sake. The noise of youse battering me bared nerves is unhuman. Begod, an Englishman would have more nature[5] to a fellow lying with a sick head. A methylated martyr, that's what I am.

NEIGHBOUR: (*To* PRISONER A) Meself and that man sitting there, we done time before you came up. In Kilmainham,[6] and that's where you never were. First fourteen days without a mattress, skilly[7] three times a day. None of your sitting out in the yard like nowadays. I got my toe amputated by one of the old lags so I could get into hospital for a feed.

DUNLAVIN: (*Looks up and feebly moans*) A pity you didn't get your head amputated as you were at it. It would have kept you quiet for a bit.

NEIGHBOUR: I got me mouth to talk, the same as the next man. Maybe we're not all that well up, that we get up at the Christmas concert and do the electrocutionist performance, like some I could mention.

DUNLAVIN: It's neither this nor that, Neighbour, but if you would only give over arguing the toss about nothing and change over to a friendly subject of mutual interest — like the quare fellow that's to be topped in the morning.

NEIGHBOUR: True, true, Dunlavin, and a comfortable old flowery dell he'll have down there. (*He prods the grave with his stick*) We'll be eating the cabbages off that one in a month or two.

PRISONER A: You're in a terrible hurry to get the poor scut[8] under the cabbages. How do you know he won't get a reprieve, like old Silver-top?

LIFER: Jesus, Mary and Joseph, you'd like to see me in there, wouldn't you! (*He moves violently away from them*)

NEIGHBOUR: Your man doesn't like any talk about hanging.

PRISONER A: No more would you, if you'd tried to top yourself this morning.

NEIGHBOUR: Anyway he's gone now and we can have a chat about it in peace. Sure we must be saying something and it's better than scandalizing our neighbours.

PRISONER B: You never know what might happen to the quare fellow. God is good.

PRISONER C: And has a good mother.

They look in surprise at the young person who has quietly joined them.

DUNLAVIN: No, no, it's too late now for him to be chucked.

PRISONER A: It has been known, a last-minute reprieve, you know.

NEIGH NEIGHBOUR: (*Stands and calls loudly after* didn't he, that had been set aside for the pig-slaughtering and mangled the remains beyond all hope of identification.

PRISONER C: Go bfoiridh Dia reinn.[10]

NEIGHBOUR: He hasn't got a chance, never in a race of cats. He'll be hung as high as Guilderoy.[11]

PRISONER A: You're the life of the party, aren't you? You put me in mind of the little girl who was sent in to cheer her father up. She was so good at it that he cut his throat.

PRISONER E: Ah, sure he was only computing the odds to it. He'll be topped.

NEIGHBOUR: I'd lay me Sunday bacon on it if anyone would be idiot enough to take me up.

PRISONER E, *a bookie, has been listening.*

PRISONER E: I wouldn't take your bacon, but I'll lay it off for you if you like.

1. tough individual.
2. English jails; the Moor is Dartmoor.
3. Slang terms for informer.
4. punishment cell.
5. i.e. would be more considerate.
6. A Dublin jail.
7. gruel.
8. Jocular, but pejorative, for 'person'.
9. A pot or jar.
10. Irish: God look down on us.
11. A Scottish highwayman, whose real name was Patrick Macgregor. He was hanged in Edinburgh in 1636 and is the subject of one of the ballads in Thomas Percy's *Reliques of Ancient English Poetry* (1765).

Another prisoner watches for the screws. PRISONER E *acts as if he were a tick-tack man*[12] *at the races.*

PRISONER E: The old firm. Here we are again. Neighbour lays his Sunday bacon the quare fellow will be topped tomorrow morning. Any takers?

PRISONER D: Five snout.

PRISONER E: Away home to your mother.

MICKSER: Half a bacon.

PRISONER E: Half a . . . .

NEIGHBOUR: Even bacons.

PRISONER E: Even bacons. Even bacons any takers? Yourself, sir, come on now, you look like a sportsman.

PRISONER A: I wouldn't eat anything after he'd touched it, not if I were starving.

NEIGHBOUR: Is that so . . . .

PRISONER E: Now, now, now, don't interrupt the betting. Any takers?

DUNLAVIN: I'll take him up if only to shut his greedy gob.

NEIGHBOUR: You won't! You're having me on!

DUNLAVIN: No, I'll bet you my Sunday bacon that a reprieve will come through before morning. I feel it in my bones.

NEIGHBOUR: That's the rheumatics.

PRISONER E: Is he on, Neighbour?

NEIGHBOUR: He is.

PRISONER E: Shake on it, the two of youse!

DUNLAVIN: How d'ye do, Lord Lonsdale![13]

NEIGHBOUR: Never mind all that. The minute the trap goes down tomorrow morning your Sunday bacon is mine.

PRISONER A: God leave you health to enjoy it.

NEIGHBOUR: He'll be topped all right.

PRISONER A: And if he isn't, I'm the very man will tell him you bet your bacon on his life.

NEIGHBOUR: You never would.

PRISONER A: Wouldn't I?

NEIGHBOUR: You'd never be bad enough.

PRISONER A: And what would be bad about it?

NEIGHBOUR: Causing a dissension and a disturbance.

The two YOUNG PRISONERS *enter.*

PRISONER A: You mean he mightn't take it for a joke.

NEIGHBOUR: Here's them two young prisoners; they've the life of Reilly,[14] rambling round the place. Where youse wandering off to now?

SCHOLARA: We came over here to see a chiner[15] of ours. He turned twenty the day before yesterday, so they shifted him away from the Juveniles to here. *(He sees* PRISONER C) Ah, there you are. We were over in the hospital being examined for going out on Saturday and we had a bit of snout to give you. (*Takes out a Woodbine package, extracts a cigarette from it and gives it to* PRISONER C, *who shyly stands and takes it.*)

PRISONER C: (*Quietly*) Thanks.

SCHOLARA: Gurra morra gut,[16] you mean.

PRISONER C: (*Smiles faintly*) Go raibh maith agat.[17]

SCHOLARA: (*Grandly*) Na bac leis.[18] (*To the other prisoners*) Talks Irish to beat the band. Comes from an island between here and America.[19] And Shaybo will give you a couple of strikers.

SHAYBO: (*Reaches in the seams of his coat and takes out a match which he presents to* PRISONER C.) Here you are. It's a bloody shame to shove you over here among all these old men even if you are twenty itself, but maybe you won't be long after us, and you going home.

PRISONER C: (*Kerry accent*) I will, please God. It will be summer-time and where I come from is lovely when the sun is shining.

They stand there, looking embarrassed for a moment.

DUNLAVIN: Go on, why don't you kiss him good-bye.

SHAYBO: Eh, Schol, let's have a pike at the grave before the screw comes out.

SCHOLARA: Ah, yes, we must have a look at the grave.

They dive into the grave, the old men shout at them, but WARDER DONELLY *comes to the door of the hospital.*

WARDER DONELLY: Get up to hell out of that and back to your own wing, youse two. (*Shouts to the warders in the prison wing*) Two on you there, pass them fellows into the Juveniles. Get to hell out of that!

SCHOLARA *and* SHAYBO *samba off, give the so-called V-sign, slap the right biceps with the left palm, and*

12. A person who signals the betting odds at a horse race.
13. Lord Lonsdale was an English aristocrat who established a prize for British boxing in 1909. He encouraged sportsmanship in boxing matches.
14. The mythical Reilly leads a life of fabled pleasure and ease.
15. mate. From cockney rhyming slang: china plate.
16. 'Thank you', in a heavily Dublin accent.
17. 'Thank you', in correct Irish.
18. It's no trouble.
19. Satiric reference to one of the islands off County Kerry.

turning lightly, run in through the door.

NEIGHBOUR: Aren't they the impudent pups? Too easy a time they have of it. I'd tan their pink backsides for them. That'd leave them fresh and easy. Impudent young curs is going these days. No respect for God nor man, pinch anything that wasn't nailed down.

PRISONER B: Neighbour, the meths is rising in you.

DUNLAVIN: He might as well rave there as in bed.

ENGLISH VOICE: (*From one of the cell windows*) I say, I say, down there in the yard.

DUNLAVIN: The voice of the Lord!

PRISONER A: That's the geezer[20] from London that's in over the car smuggling.

ENGLISH VOICE: I say, down there.

PRISONER B: Hello, up there.

NEIGHBOUR: How are you fixed for fillet?[21]

PRISONER B: Shut up a minute. Wait till we hear what is it he wants.

ENGLISH VOICE: Is there any bloke down there going out this week?

PRISONER B: Mickser is going out tomorrow. He's on this exercise. (*Shouts*) Hold on a minute. (*Looks round*) Hey, Mickser.

MICKSER: What's up?

PRISONER B: That English fellow that's on remand over the cars, he wants to know if there's anyone going out this week. You're going out tomorrow, ain't you?

MICKSER: Yes, I am. I'm going out in the morning. (*To* ENGLISH PRISONER) What do you want?

ENGLISH VOICE: I want you to go up and contact my mate. He's in Dublin. It's about bail for me. I can write his name and address here and let it down to you on my string. I didn't want the law to get his address in Dublin, so I can't write to him. I got a quid[22] in with me, without the screw finding it, and I'll let it down with the address if you'll do it.

MICKSER: Good enough. Let down the address and the quid.

ENGLISH VOICE: My mate will give you some more when you see him.

MICKSER: That's all right. Let the quid down now and the address before the screw comes out of the hospital. I'm going out tomorrow and I'll see him for you, soon as we get out of the market pubs at half two.

PRISONER B: He's letting it down now.

MICKSER: There's the quid anyway. (*Reading the note.* NEIGHBOUR *gets to his feet and goes behind and peers over his shoulder.* MICKSER *see him*) Get to hell out of it, you.

NEIGHBOUR: I only just wanted to have a look at what he wrote.

MICKSER: And have his mate in the Bridewell,[23] before the days was out. I know you, you bloody old stag.[24]

NEIGHBOUR: I saw the day you wouldn't say the like of that.

MICKSER: (*Proffering him the pound*) Here, get a mass said for yourself.

NEIGHBOUR: It wouldn't do you much harm to put yourself under the hand of a priest either.

MICKSER: (*Laughs at him*) That's for sinners. Only dirty people has to wash.

NEIGHBOUR: A man of your talent and wasting your time here.

MICKSER: (*Going back to walk with the prisoners behind*) Good luck now, Neighbour. I'll call up and see you in the hospice for the dying.

NEIGHBOUR: (*stands and calls loudly after him*) You watch yourself. I saw the quare fellow in here a couple of years ago. He was a young hard chaw like you in all the pride of his strength and impudence. He was kicking a ball about over in A yard and I was walking around with poor old Mockridge, neither of us minding no one. All of a sudden I gets such a wallop on the head it knocks the legs from under me and very nigh cuts off my ear. 'You headed that well,' says he, and I deaf for three days after it! Who's got the best of it now, young as he is and strong as he is? How will his own ear feel tomorrow morning, with the washer under it, and whose legs will be the weakest when the trap goes down and he's slung into the pit? And what use is the young heart?

Some of the prisoners walking round stop and listen to him, but MICKSER *gives him a contemptuous look and walks on, shouting at him in passing.*

MICKSER: Get along with you, you dirty half animal.

A WARDER *passes, sounds of the town heard, factory*

20. An English colloquialism for 'man'.
21. Perhaps a sarcastic reference to prison cuisine.
22. A bill worth one pound sterling.
23. A Dublin jail.
24. informer.

sirens, distant ships. Some of the prisoners pace up and down like caged animals.

NEIGHBOUR: Dunlavin, have you the loan of a pencil for a minute?

DUNLAVIN: What do you want it for?

NEIGHBOUR: I just want to write something to that English fellow about his bail.

DUNLAVIN: You'd better hurry, before the screw comes back out.

NEIGHBOUR *writes.*

NEIGHBOUR: Hey, you up there that's looking for the bail.

ENGLISH VOICE: Hello, you got the quid and the address?

PRISONER A: What's the old dog up to?

DUNLAVIN: Ah, leave him alone. He's a bit hasty, but poor old Neighbour has good turns in him.

PRISONER A: So has a corkscrew.

NEIGHBOUR: Let down your string and I'll send you up this bit of a message.

ENGLISH VOICE: (*His hands can be seen at the window holding the note*) 'Get a bucket and bail yourself out.' (*Shouts in rage*) You dirty bastard bleeder to take my quid and I'll tell the bloody screw I will; I'll shop you,[25] you bleeding . . . .

MICKSER: What's up with you?

NEIGHBOUR: Get a bucket and bail yourself out. (*Laughing an old man's cackle*)

ENGLISH VOICE: You told me to get a bucket and bail my bleeding self out, but I'll tell the screw; I'll shop you about that quid.

MICKSER: (*Shouts up to the window*) Shut your bloody big mouth for a minute. I told you nothing.

PRISONER A: It was this old get here.

MICKSER: I sent you no message; it was this old pox bottle.

NEIGHBOUR: (*Ceases to laugh, is alarmed at the approach of* MICKSER) Now, now, Mickser, take a joke, can't you, it was only a bit of gas.[26]

MICKSER: (*Advancing*) I'll give you gas.

MICKSER *advances on* NEIGHBOUR. *The lags stop and look — suddenly* MICKSER *seizes the old man and, yelling with delight, carries* NEIGHBOUR *over to the grave and thrusts him into it. The prisoners all crowd around kicking dirt on to the old man and shouting 'Get a bucket and bail yourself out.'*

PRISONER B: Nick, Mickser, nick, nick, here's the screw.

25. i.e. inform on you.

26. i.e. a jape. A very common Irish idiom.

PRISONER A: It's only the cook with the quare fellow's tea.

A PRISONER *comes through the hospital gate and down the steps. He wears a white apron, carries a tray and is surrounded by an interested band, except for the* LIFER, *who stands apart, and* DUNLAVIN, *who lies prone on the front asleep. From the prisoners around the food rises an excited chorus:*

PRISONER A: Rashers and eggs.

PRISONER B: He got that last night.

MICKSER: Chicken.

NEIGHBOUR: He had that for dinner.

PRISONER B: Sweet cake.

PRISONER A: It's getting hung he is, not married.

NEIGHBOUR: Steak and onions.

MICKSER: Sausages and bacon.

PRISONER B: And liver.

PRISONER A: Pork chops.

PRISONER B: Pig's feet.

PRISONER A: Salmon.

NEIGHBOUR: Fish and chips.

MICKSER: Jelly and custard.

NEIGHBOUR: Roast lamb.

PRISONER A: Plum pudding.

PRISONER B: Turkey.

NEIGHBOUR: Goose.

PRISONER A, PRISONER B, NEIGHBOUR: Rashers and eggs.

ALL: Rashers and eggs, rashers and eggs, and eggs and rashers and eggs and rashers it is.

COOK: (*Desperate*) Ah, here, lads.

PRISONERS: Here, give us a look, lift up the lid, eh, here, I never seen it.

The COOK *struggles to protect his cargo, the* PRISONERS *mill round in a loose scrum of excitement and greed, their nostrils mad almost to the point of snatching a bit. There is a roar from the gate.*

WARDER DONELLY: (*From inside the hospital gate*) Get to hell out of that. What do youse think you are on?

The PRISONERS *scatter in a rush.*

The COOK *with great dignity carries on.*

NEIGHBOUR: (*Sitting down*) Oh, the two eggs, the yolk in the middle like . . . a bride's eye under a pink veil, and the grease of the rashers . . . pale and pure like melted gold.

DUNLAVIN: Oh, may God forgive you, as if a body wasn't sick enough as it is.

NEIGHBOUR: And the two big back rashers.

PRISONER A: Go along, you begrudging old dog. Maybe when you go back the standard of living in your town residence, No. 1 St. James Street, might be gone up. And they'll be serving rashers and eggs. You'd do a lot for them, when you'd begrudge them to a man for his last meal on this earth.

NEIGHBOUR: Well, it's not his last meal if you want to know. He'll get a supper tonight and a breakfast in the morning, and I don't begrudge him the little he'll eat of that, seeing the rope stew to follow, and lever pudding and trap door doddle[27] for dessert. And anyway didn't you run over the same as the rest of us to see what he was getting?

PRISONER A: And if I did, it wasn't to begrudge it to the man.

PRISONER B: Sure we all ran over, anything to break the monotony in a kip[28] like this.

The triangle is heard.

PRISONER A: (*Gloomily*) I suppose you're right. In Strangeways, Manchester,[29] and I in it during the war, we used to wish for an air-raid. We had one and we were left locked up in our cells. We stood up on our tables and took the blackouts off the windows and had a grand-stand view of the whole city burning away under us. The screws were running round shouting in the spy-holes at us to get down from the windows, but they soon ran off down the shelters. We had a great view of the whole thing till a bomb landed on the Assize Court next door, and the blast killed twenty of the lags. They were left standing on their tables without a mark on them, stone dead. Sure anyway, we all agreed it broke the monotony.

Enter WARDER DONELLY.

WARDER DONELLY: Right, fall in there!

PRISONER B: Don't forget the bet, Neighbour.

WARDER DONELLY: Come on, get in line there.

PRISONER A: And don't forget what I'm going to tell the quare fellow.

WARDER DONELLY: Silence there. (*Search begins*) What's this you've got in your pocket? A file? Scissors out of the bag shop? No? A bit of rope? Oh, your handkerchief, so it is. (*Searching next* PRISONER) You here, what's this? A bit of wax end, you forgot to leave in the bag shop? Well, don't forget the next time. What's this? (MAN *takes out two inches of rope*) What's this for? You were roping mail bags today, and after all they don't rope themselves. Ah, you forgot to leave it behind? Well, go easy, save as much as that each time and in five years' time you'd have enough to make a rope ladder. Oh, you're only doing six months? Well maybe you want to save the taxpayers a few quid and hang yourself. Sorrow the loss if you did, but they'd want to know where you got the rope from. (PRISONERS *laugh as they are expected to do*) Come on, next man. (*He hurries along now*) Come along now, no mailbags, scissors, needles, knives, razor blades, guns, hatchets or empty porter bottles. No? (*To the last* PRISONER) Well, will you buy a ticket to the Police Ball?

PRISONERS *laugh dutifully.*

WARDER REGAN: (*Voice from prison wing*) All done, sir?

PRISONER A: Don't forget, Neighbour.

WARDER DONELLY: Right, sir, on to you, sir. (*Gate swings open*) Right, lead on, B.1.

NEIGHBOUR: Anyway, his grave's dug and the hangman's on his way.

PRISONER A: That doesn't mean a thing, they always dig the grave, just to put the wind up them—

WARDER DONELLY: Silence!

The prisoners march, the gate clangs behind them; the tramp of their feet is heard as they mark time inside.

WARDER REGAN: (*Voice from the prison wing*) Right, B. Wing, bang out your doors. B.1, get in off your steps and bang out your doors, into your cells and bang out your doors. Get locked up. BANG THEM DOORS! GET INSIDE AND BANG OUT THEM DOORS!

The last door bangs lonely on its own and then there is silence.

VOICE FROM BELOW: (*Singing*).

The wind was rising,
And the day declining
As I lay pining in my prison cell
And that old triangle
Went jingle jangle

The triangle is beaten, the gate of the prison wing opens and the CHIEF *and* WARDER DONELLY *come down the steps and approach the grave.*

Along the banks of the Royal Canal.

CHIEF: (*Resplendent in silver braid*) Who's that singing?

WARDER DONELLY: I think it's one of the prisoners in the chokey, sir.

CHIEF: Where?

27. Possibly a misprint for 'coddle', a Dublin dish made from rashers, sausages, tripe, vegetables, milk and seasonings. The prompt copy of the Pike production gives 'doddle' — something easily accomplished or swallowed.
28. A mean lodging or doss-house.
29. An English jail.

WARDER DONELLY: In the punishment cells, sir.

CHIEF: That's more like it. Well, tell him to cut it out.

SONG:

In the female prison
There are seventy women . . .

WARDER DONELLY: (*Goes down to the area and leans and shouts*) Hey, you down there, cut it out, or I'll give you jingle jangle.

The song stops. WARDER DONELLY *walks back.*

CHIEF: Is the quare fellow finished his tea?

WARDER DONELLY: He is. He is just ready to come out for exercise, now. The wings are all clear. They're locked up having their tea. He'll be along any minute.

CHIEF: He's coming out here?

WARDER DONELLY: Yes, sir.

CHIEF: (*Exasperated*) Do you want him to see his grave, bloody well half dug? Run in quick and tell those bloody idiots to take him out the side door, and exercise him over the far side of the stokehold,[30] and tell them to keep him well into the wall where he'll be out of sight of the cell windows. Hurry and don't let him hear you. Let on it's something about another duty. Warders! You'd get better in Woolworths.[31]

He goes to the area and shouts down.

Hey, you down there. You in the cell under the steps. You do be singing there to keep yourself company? You needn't be afraid, it's only the Chief. How long you doing down there? Seven days No. 1 and twenty-one days No. 2. God bless us and love us, you must have done something desperate. I may be able to do something for you, though God knows you needn't count on it, I don't own the place. You what? With who? Ah sure, I often have a bit of a tiff with the same man myself. We'll see what we can do for you. It's a long time to be stuck down there, no matter who you had the tiff with.

Enter WARDER DONELLY.

CHIEF: Well?

WARDER DONELLY: It's all right, they've brought him out the other way.

They look out beyond the stage.

CHIEF: Looks as if they're arguing the toss about something.

WARDER DONELLY: Football.

CHIEF: Begod, look at them stopping while the quare fellow hammers his point home.

WARDER DONELLY: I was down in the condemned cell while he was getting his tea. I asked him if it was all right. He said it was, and 'Aren't the evenings getting a grand stretch?'[32] he says.

CHIEF: Look at him now, putting his nose to the air.

WARDER DONELLY: He's a grand evening for his last.

CHIEF: I took the name of the fellow giving the concert in the punishment cells. In the morning when we get this over, see he's shifted to Hell's gates[33] over the far side. He can serenade the stokehold wall for a change if he's light enough to make out his music.

WARDER DONELLY *copies the name and number.*

CHIEF: I have to attend to every mortal thing in this place. None of youse seem to want to do a hand's turn, bar draw your money — you're quick enough at that. Well, come on, let's get down to business.

WARDER DONELLY *goes and uncovers the grave.*

CHIEF: (*Looking off*) Just a minute. It's all right. They've taken him round the back of the stokehold. (*Looking at the grave*) Not so bad, another couple of feet out of the bottom and we're elected. Regan should be down with the working party any minute, as soon as the quare fellow's finished his exercise.

WARDER DONELLY: There, he's away in now, sir. See him looking at the sky?

CHIEF: You'd think he was trying to kiss it goodbye. Well, that's the last he'll see of it.

WARDER DONELLY: No chance of a reprieve, sir?

CHIEF: Not a chance. Healey never even mentioned fixing up a line with the Post Office. If there'd been any chance of developments he'd have asked us to put a man on all night. All he said was 'The Governor will get the last word before the night's out.' That means only one thing. Go ahead.

WARDER REGAN *and* CRIMMIN *comes out with* PRISONERS A, B, C *and* D

WARDER REGAN: Working party all correct, sir. Come on, get those boards off. Bottom out a couple more feet and leave the clay at the top, nice and neat.

CHIEF: Oh, Mr Regan.

WARDER REGAN: Take over, Mr. Crimmin.

CHIEF: Mr. Regan. All I was going to say was —

30. The boiler-room.
31. A cut-price department store.
32. A reference to the lengthening daylight of spring.
33. i.e. completely out of the way.

why don't you take yourself a bit of a rest while these fellows are at work on the grave. It's a long old pull till eight tomorrow morning.

WARDER REGAN: Thank you, sir.

CHIEF: Don't mention it. I'll see you before you go down to the cell. Get yourself a bit of a smoke, in the hospital. Don't forget now.

He and WARDER DONELLY *go back in.*

WARDER REGAN: Mr. Crimmin. The Chief, a decent man, he's after giving us his kind permission to go into hospital and have a sit down and a smoke for ourselves when these fellows have the work started. He knew we'd go in anyway, so he saw the chance of being floochalach,[34] at no expense to the management. Here (*takes out a packet of cigarettes, and takes some from it*), here's a few fags for the lads.

CRIMMIN: I'll give them some of mine too.

WARDER REGAN: Don't do anything of the sort. One each is enough, you can slip them a couple when they're going to be locked up, if you like, but if these fellows had two fags each, they'd not work at all but spend the time out here blowing smoke rings in the evening air like lords. I'll slip in now, you come in after me. Tell them not to have them in their mouths if the Chief or the Governor comes out. (*He goes up the steps to the hospital*)

CRIMMIN: (*Calls* PRISONER C) Hey!

PRISONER C: (*Comes to him*) Seadh a Thomais?

CRIMMIN: (*Gives him cigarettes and matches*) Seo, cupla toitin. Taim fhein is an scew eile ag dul isteach chuig an oispeadeal, noimeat. Roinn amach na toitini siud, is glacfhaidh sibh gal. Mathagann an Governor no'n Chief no an Principal, na biodh in bhur moeil agaibh iad. A' tuigeann tu?

PRISONER C: Tuigim, a Thomais, go raibh maith agat.[35]

CRIMMIN: (*Officially*) Right, now get back to your work.

PRISONER C: Yes, sir.

CRIMMIN *goes up the hospital steps.*

PRISONER C: He gave me some cigarettes.

PRISONER D *has gone straight to the grave,* PRISONER B *is near it.*

PRISONER A: May I never dig a grave for less! You two get on and do a bit of digging while we have a quiet burn, then we'll take over.

PRISONER C: He said to watch out for the chief and them.

PRISONER B: Pass down a light to your man. He says he'd enjoy it better down there, where he can't be seen! Decent of him and Regan wasn't it?

PRISONER A: They'd have you dead from decency. That same Regan was like a savage in the bag shop today, you couldn't get a word to the fellow next to you.

PRISONER C: I never saw him like that before.

PRISONER B: He's always the same at a time like this, hanging seems to get on his nerves.

PRISONER A: Why should he worry, he won't feel it.

PRISONER B: He's on the last watch. Twelve till eight.

PRISONER A: Till death do us part.

PRISONER C: The quare fellow asked for him, didn't he?

PRISONER A: They all do.

PRISONER C: He asked to have Mr. Crimmin too.

PRISONER A: It'll break that young screw up, and him only a wet day in the place.

PRISONER B: Funny the way they all ask for Regan. Perhaps they think he'll bring them good luck, him being good living.[36]

PRISONER A: Good living! Whoever heard of a good living screw? Did you never hear of the screw, married the prostitute?

PRISONER B: No, what happened to him?

PRISONER A: He dragged her down to his own level.

PRISONER B: He told me once that if I kept off the beer I need never come back here. I asked him what about himself, and he told me he was terrible hardened to it and would I pray for him.

PRISONER C: When I was over in the Juveniles he used to talk like that to us. He said that the Blessed Virgin knew us better than the police or the judges — or ourselves even. We might think we were terrible sinners but she knew we were good boys only a bit wild . . . .

PRISONER A: Bloody mad he is.

PRISONER C: And that we were doing penance here for the men who took us up, especially the judges, they being mostly rich old men with great opportunity for vice.

34. generous. From Irish *flaithiúil.*

35. Prisoner C: (*Comes to him*) Yes, Thomas?
Crimmin: (*Gives him cigarettes and matches*). Here, a couple of cigarettes. Myself and the other screw are going into the hospital for a moment. Divide these cigarettes and let you take a smoke. If the Governor or the Chief or the Principal come, don't have them in your mouths. Do you understand?
Prisoner C: I understand, Thomas, thanks.

36. i.e. living according to a strict moral and religious code.

PRISONER D *appears from the grave.*

PRISONER A: The dead arose and appeared to many.

PRISONER A *goes and rearranges the work which* PRISONER D *has upset.*

PRISONER B: What's brought you out of your fox hole?

PRISONER D: I thought it more discreet to remain in concealment while I smoked but I could not stop down there listening to talk like that, as a ratepayer,[37] I couldn't stand for it, especially those libellous remarks about the judiciary. (*He looks accusingly at the boy*)

PRISONER C: I was only repeating what Mr. Regan said, sir.

PRISONER D: He could be taken up for it. According to that man, there should be no such thing as law and order. We could all be murdered in our beds, the innocent prey of every ruffian that took it into his head to appropriate our goods, our lives even. Property must have security! What do you think society would come to without police and judges and suitable punishments? Chaos! In my opinion hanging's too good for 'em.

PRISONER C: Oh, Mr. Regan doesn't believe in capital punishment, sir.

PRISONER D: My God, the man's an atheist! He should be dismissed from the public service. I shall take it up with the Minister when I get out of here. I went to school with his cousin.

PRISONER A: Who the hell does he think he is, a bloody high court judge?

PRISONER D: Chaos!

PRISONER B: He's in for embezzlement, there were two suicides and a bye-election over him.

PRISONER D: There are still a few of us who care about the state of the country, you know. My family's national tradition goes back to the Land War.[38] Grandfather did four weeks for incitement to mutiny — and we've never looked back since. One of my young nephews, as a matter of fact, has just gone over to Sandhurst.[39]

PRISONER B: Isn't that where you done your four years?

PRISONER A: No, that was Parkhurst.

PRISONER C: (*To others*) A college educated man in here, funny, isn't it?

PRISONER D: I shall certainly bring all my influence to bear to settle this Regan fellow.

PRISONER C: You must be a very important man, sir.

PRISONER D: I am one of the Cashel Carrolls, my boy, related on my mother's side to the Killens of Killcock.[40]

PRISONER B: Used to wash for our family.

PRISONER C: Go bhfoiridh Dia 'rainn.[41]

PRISONER D: Irish speaking?

PRISONER C: Yes, sir.

PRISONER D: Then it might interest you to know that I took my gold medal in Irish.

PRISONER C: Does that mean he speaks Irish?

PRISONER D: Of course.

PRISONER C: Oh sir. Ta Gaeilge go leor agamsa. O'n gcliabhain amach, sir.[42]

PRISONER B: That's fixed you.

PRISONER D: Quite. Tuigim tu.[43]

PRISONER B: The young lad's from Kerry, from an island where they don't speak much else.

PRISONER D: Kerry? Well of course you speak with a different dialect to the one I was taught.

PRISONER B: The young screw Crimmin's from the same place. He sneaks up to the landing sometimes when the other screws aren't watching and there they are for hours talking through the spy hole, all in Irish.

PRISONER D: Most irregular.

PRISONER B: There's not much harm in it.

PRISONER D: How can there be proper discipline between warder and prisoner with that kind of familiarity?

PRISONER C: He does only be giving me the news from home and who's gone to America or England; he's not long up here and neither am I . . . the two of us do each be as lonely as the other.

PRISONER B: The lad here sings an old song betimes. It's very nice. It makes the night less lonely, each man alone and sad maybe in the old cell. The quare fellow heard him singing and after he was sentenced to death he sent over word he'd be listening every night around midnight for him.

PRISONER A: You'd better make a big effort tonight, kid, for his last concert.

PRISONER C: Ah, God help him! Sure, you'd pity

37. One who pays house tax on his or her property. Such a person is usually assumed to be a respectable member of society.
38. Irish movement for land reform led by Michael Davitt in the 1880s.
39. British army military academy in England. Parkhurst is a high-security prison in England.
40. Imaginary country families of substance and social distinction.
41. God look down on us.
42. Oh sir, I have Irish galore. From the cradle up, sir.
43. I understand you.

him all the same. It must be awful to die at the end of a swinging rope and a black hood over his poor face.

PRISONER A: Begod, he's not being topped for nothing — to cut his own brother up and butcher him like a pig.

PRISONER D: I must heartily agree with you sir, a barbarian if ever there was one.

PRISONER C: Maybe he did those things, but God help him this minute and he knowing this night his last on earth. Waiting over there he is, to be shaken out of his sleep and rushed to the rope.

PRISONER A: What sleep will he take? They won't have to set the alarm clock for a quarter to eight, you can bet your life on that.

PRISONER C: May he find peace on the other side.

PRISONER A: Or his brother waiting to have a word with him about being quartered in such an unmannerly fashion.

PRISONER C: None of us can know for certain.

PRISONER D: It was proved in a court of law that this man had experience as a pork butcher and put his expert knowledge to use by killing his brother with an axe and dismembering the body, the better to dispose of it.

PRISONER C: Go bhfoiridh Dia 'rainn.

PRISONER A: I wouldn't put much to the court of law part of it, but I heard about it myself from a fellow in from his part of the country. He said he had the brother strung up in an outhouse like a pig.

PRISONER D: Actually he was bleeding him into a farmhouse vessel according to the evidence. He should be hung three or four times over.

PRISONER A: Seeing your uncle was at school with the President's granny, perhaps he could fix it up for you.

PRISONER C: I don't believe he is a bad man. When I was on remand he used to walk around with me at exercise every day and he was sad when I told him about my brother, who died in the Yank's army, and my father, who was buried alive at the demolition of Manchester . . . . He was great company for me who knew no one, only jackeens[44] would be making game of me, and I'm sorry for him.

PRISONER A: Sure, it's a terrible pity about you and him. Maybe the jackeens should spread out the red carpet for you and every other bog barbarian that comes into the place. (*He moves away irritably*) Let's get a bit more off this bloody hole.

44. Dubliners.

PRISONER B: Nick. Nick.

WARDER REGAN: (*Entering with* CRIMMIN) I've been watching you for the last ten minutes and damn the thing you've done except yap, yap, yap the whole time. The Chief or the Governor or any of them could have been watching you. They'd have thought it was a bloody mothers' meeting. What with you and my other bald mahogany gas pipe[45] here.

PRISONER D: We were merely exchanging a few comments, sir.

WARDER REGAN: That's a lie and it's not worth a lie.

PRISONER A: All right! So we were caught talking at labour. I didn't ask to be an undertaker's assistant. Go on, bang me inside and case me in the morning! Let the Governor give me three days of No. 1.[46]

WARDER REGAN: Much that'd worry you.

PRISONER A: You're dead right.

WARDER REGAN: Don't be such a bloody big baby. We all know you're a hard case. Where did you do your lagging? On the bog?

PRISONER A: I did not. Two laggings I done! At Parkhurst and on the Moor.

WARDER REGAN: There's the national inferiority complex for you. Our own Irish cat-o'-nine-tails and the batons of the warders loaded with lead from Carrick mines aren't good enough for him. He has to go Dartmooring and Parkhursting it. It's a wonder you didn't go further while you were at it, to Sing Sing[47] or Devil's Island.[48]

PRISONER A: (*Stung*) I'm not here to be made a mock of, whether I done a lagging in England or not.

WARDER REGAN: Who said a word about it, only yourself — doing the returned Yank in front of these other fellows? Look, the quare fellow's got to be buried in the morning, whether we like it or not so cut the mullarkey and get back to work.

PRISONER A: I don't let anyone make game of me!

WARDER REGAN: Well, what are you going to do about it? Complain to Holy Healey's department? He's a fine bloody imposter, isn't he? Like an old

45. A red-haired (though bald) overly talkative individual.
46. solitary confinement.
47. A state penitentiary outside New York city, notorious for its extreme discipline. It is situated in the town of Ossining.
48. French prison colony in French Guiana.

I.R.A. man with a good agency in the Sweep now.[49] Recommend me to the respectable people! Drop it for Christ's sake, man. It's a bad night for all of us. Fine job, isn't it, for a young fellow like him, fresh from his mother's apron strings. You haven't forgotten what it's like to come from a decent home, have you, with the family rosary said every night?

PRISONER A: I haven't any time for that kind of gab. I never saw religion do anything but back up the screws. I was in Walton last Christmas Eve, when the clergyman came to visit a young lad that had been given eighteen strokes of the cat that morning. When the kid stopped moaning long enough to hear what he had to say, he was told to think on the Lord's sufferings, then the cell door closed with a bang, leaving a smell of booze that would have tripped you up. (*He takes a look at the quare fellow's side of the stage and, muttering to himself, goes back to work*)

WARDER REGAN: You should pray for a man hardened in drink. Get back to it, all of you, and get that work a bit more advanced. Myself and Crimmin here have a long night ahead of us; we don't want to be finishing off your jobs for you.

They get into the grave.

PRISONER A: I never seen a screw like that before.

PRISONER B: Neither did anyone else.

They work.

CRIMMIN: What time is it, sir?

WARDER REGAN: Ten to seven.

CRIMMIN: Is himself here yet?

WARDER REGAN: Yes, he came by last night's boat. He's nervous of the 'plane, says it isn't natural. He'll be about soon. He's been having a sleep after the trip. We'll have to wait till he's measured the quare fellow for the drop, then we can go off till twelve.

CRIMMIN: Good.

WARDER REGAN: And for Christ's sake try to look a bit more cheerful when you come back on.

CRIMMIN: I've never seen anyone die, Mr. Regan.

WARDER REGAN: Of course, I'm a callous savage that's used to it.

CRIMMIN: I didn't mean that.

WARDER REGAN: I don't like it now any more than I did the first time.

CRIMMIN: No sir.

WARDER REGAN: It was a little Protestant lad, the first time; he asked if he could be walked backwards into the hanghouse so as he wouldn't see the rope.

CRIMMIN: God forgive them.

WARDER REGAN: May He forgive us all. The young clergyman that was on asked if the prison chaplain could accompany him; it was his first hanging too. I went to the Canon to ask him, a fine big man he was. 'Regan,' he says, 'I thought I was going to escape it this time, but you never escape. I don't suppose neither of us ever will. Ah well,' he says, 'maybe being hung twenty times will get me out of purgatory a minute or two sooner.'

CRIMMIN: Amen, a Thighearna Dhia.[50]

WARDER REGAN: The young clergyman was great; he read a bit of the Bible to the little Protestant lad while they waited and he came in with him, holding his hand and telling him, in their way, to lean on God's mercy that was stronger than the power of men. I walked beside them and guided the boy on to the trap and under the beam. The rope was put round him and the washer under his ear and the hood pulled over his face. And still the young clergyman called out to him, in a grand steady voice, in through the hood: 'I declare to you, my living Christ this night . . .' and he stroked his head till we went down. Then he fainted; the Canon and myself had to carry him out to the Governor's office.

A pause. We are aware of the men working at the grave.

WARDER REGAN: The quare fellow asked for you especially, Crimmin; he wanted you because you're a young lad, not yet practised in badness. You'll be a consolation to him in the morning when he's surrounded by a crowd of bigger bloody ruffians than himself, if the truth were but told. He's depending on you, and you're going to do your best for him.

CRIMMIN: Yes, Mr. Regan.

REGAN *walks to the grave.*

WARDER REGAN: How's it going?

PRISONER A: Just about done, sir.

WARDER REGAN: All right, you can leave it.

They get up.

WARDER REGAN: Leave your shovels; you'll be wanting them in the morning. Go and tell the

49. i.e. a lucrative agency as ticket seller in the lottery held on the result of the Irish Sweeps handicap chase, a horse race. It was not uncommon for Irish Republican Army veterans to be awarded such sinecures.

50. My Lord God.

warder they've finished, Mr. Crimmin. I'll turn them over.

He searches the PRISONERS, *finds a cigarette end on A. and sniffs it.*

Coffin nail. Most appropriate. (*He goes towards exit and calls*) You needn't bother searching them, sir. I've turned them over.

PRISONER A: (*Aside*) He's as mad as a coot.

PRISONER C: But charitable.

WARDER REGAN: Right, lead on there!

PRISONER D: This is no place for charity, on the taxpayers' money.

PRISONER A: Take it up with your uncle when you get back into your stockbroker's trousers.

WARDER REGAN: Silence. Right, sir, working party off.

As the PRISONERS *march off, the* HANGMAN *comes slowly down the steps.*

CRIMMIN: Is this . . . .

WARDER REGAN: Himself.

HANGMAN: It's Mr. Regan, isn't it? Well, as the girl said to the soldier 'Here we are again.'

WARDER REGAN: Nice evening. I hope you had a good crossing.

HANGMAN: Not bad. It's nice to get over to old Ireland you know, a nice bit of steak and a couple of pints as soon as you get off the boat. Well, you'll be wanting to knock off, won't you? I'll just pop down and have a look, then you can knock off.

WARDER REGAN: We were just waiting for you.

HANGMAN: This young man coming with us in the morning?

CRIMMIN: Yes, sir.

HANGMAN: Lend us your cap a minute, lad.

CRIMMIN: I don't think it would fit you, sir.

HANGMAN: We don't have to be so particular. Mr. Regan's will do. It ought to fit me by this time, and he won't catch cold the time I'll be away. (*He goes out*)

CRIMMIN: What does he want the cap for?

WARDER REGAN: He gets the quare fellow's weight from the doctor so as he'll know what drop to give him, but he likes to have a look at him as well, to see what build he is, how thick his neck is, and so on. He says he can judge better with the eye. If he gave him too much one way he'd strangle him instead of breaking his neck, and too much the other way he'd pull the head clean off his shoulders.

CRIMMIN: Go bhfoiridh Dia 'rainn.

WARDER REGAN: You should have lent him your cap. When he lifts the corner of the spy-hole all the quare fellow can see is the peak of a warder's cap. It could be you or me or anyone looking at him. Himself has no more to do with it than you or I or the people that pay us, and that's every man or woman that pays taxes or votes in elections. If they don't like it, they needn't have it.

The HANGMAN *comes back.*

HANGMAN: Well set up lad. Twelve stone, fine pair of shoulders on him. Well, I expect you'll give us a call this evening over at the hospital. I'm in my usual apartments. This young man is very welcome, too, if he wants to join the company.

WARDER REGAN: Right, sir.

HANGMAN: See you later. (*He goes out*)

WARDER REGAN: Right, Crimmin. Twelve o'clock and look lively. The quare fellow's got enough on his plate without putting him in the blue jigs[51] altogether. As the old Home Office[52] memorandum says 'An air of cheerful decorum is indicated, as a readiness to play such games as draughts,[53] ludo, or snakes and ladders; a readiness to enter into conversations on sporting topics will also be appreciated.'

CRIMMIN: Yes, sir.

WARDER REGAN: (*As they go*) And, Crimmin . . . .

CRIMMIN: Yes, sir?

WARDER REGAN: Take off your watch.

They go out.

NEIGHBOUR: (*From his cell*) Hey, Dunlavin, Don't forget that Sunday bacon. The bet stands. They're after being at the grave. I just heard them. Dunlavin, do you hear me?

PRISONER A: Get down on your bed, you old Anti-Christ. You sound like something in a week-end pass out of Hell.

ENGLISH PRISONER: Hey, you bloke that's going out in the morning. Don't forget to see my chiner and get him to bail me out.

NEIGHBOUR: Get a bucket and bail yourself out.

SONG:

The day was dying and the wind was sighing,
As I lay crying in my prison cell,
And the old triangle
Went jingle jangle
Along the banks of the Royal Canal.

The curtain falls.

51. A state of fearful anxiety.
52. The British ministry of justice.
53. British name for checkers.

ACT III

Scene One

Later the same night. Cell windows lit. A blue lamp in the courtyard. A faint tapping is heard intermittently. As the curtain rises, two WARDERS *are seen. One is* DONELLY, *the other a fellow new to the job.*

WARDER 1: Watch the match.

WARDER 2: Sorry.

WARDER 1: We're all right for a couple of minutes, the Chief'll have plenty to worry him tonight; he's not likely to be prowling about.

WARDER 2: Hell of a job, night patrol, at any time.

WARDER 1: We're supposed to pass each cell every half-hour tonight, but what's the use? Listen to 'em.

The tapping can be distinctly heard.

WARDER 2: Yap, yap, yap. It's a wonder the bloody old hot-water pipes aren't worn through.

Tapping.

WARDER 1: Damn it all, they've been yapping in association since seven o'clock.

Tapping.

WARDER 2: Will I go round the landings and see who it is?

WARDER 1: See who it is? Listen!

WARDER 2: Do you think I should go?

WARDER 1: Stay where you are and get yourself a bit of a burn. Devil a bit of use it'd be anyway. As soon as you lifted the first spy-hole, the next fellow would have heard you and passed it on to the whole landing. Mind the cigarette, keep it covered. Have you ever been in one of these before?

WARDER 2: No.

WARDER 1: They'll be at it from six o'clock tomorrow morning, and when it comes a quarter to eight it'll be like a running commentary in the Grand National.[1]

Tapping.

WARDER 1: (*Quietly*) Shut your bloody row! And then the screeches and roars of them when his time comes. They say it's the last thing the fellow hears.

Tapping dies down.

WARDER 2: Talk about something else.

Tapping.

WARDER 1: They're quietening down a bit. You'd think they'd be in the humour for a read or a sleep, wouldn't you?

WARDER 2: It's a hell of a job.

WARDER 1: We're in it for the three Ps, boy, pay, promotion and pension, that's all that should bother civil servants like us.

WARDER 2: You're quite right.

WARDER 1: And without doing the sergeant major on you, I'm senior man of us two, isn't that right, now?

WARDER 2: I know what you mean.

WARDER 1: Well, neither bragging nor boasting — God gives us the brains and no credit to ourselves — I think I might speak to you as a senior man, if you didn't mind.

WARDER 2: Not at all. Any tip you could give me I'd be only too grateful for it. Sure it'd only be a thick wouldn't improve his knowledge when an older man would be willing to tell him something that would be of benefit to him in his career.

WARDER 1: Well now, would I be right in saying that you've no landing of your own?

WARDER 2: Quite right, quite right. I'm only on here, there or any old where when you or any other senior man is wanting me.

WARDER 1: Well, facts is facts and must be faced. We must all creep before we can walk, as the man said; but I may as well tell you straight, what I told the Principal about you.

WARDER 2: Tell me face to face. If it's fault you found in me I'd as lief hear it from me friend as from me enemy.

WARDER 1: It was no fault I found in you. If I couldn't do a man a good turn — I'd be sorry to do him a bad one.

WARDER 2: Ah, sure I know that.

WARDER 1: What I said to the Principal about you was: that you could easily handle a landing of your own. If it happened that one was left vacant. And I don't think I'm giving official information away, when I say that such a vacancy may occur in the near future. Before the month is out. Have you me?

WARDER 2: I have you, and I'm more than grateful to you. But sure I'd expect no less from you. You're all nature.

WARDER 1: It might happen that our Principal was going to the Bog on promotion, and it might happen that a certain senior officer would be promoted in his place.

WARDER 2: Ah, no.

WARDER 1: But ah, yes.

WARDER 2: But there's no one in the prison but'd

1. Annual steeplechase horse race at Aintree, near Liverpool, England.

be delighted to serve under you. You've such a way with you. Even with the prisoners.

WARDER 1: Well, I hope I can do my best by me fellow men, and that's the most any can hope to do, barring a double-dyed bloody hypocrite like a certain party we needn't mention. Well, him and me have equal service and it's only the one of us can be made Principal, and I'm damn sure they're not going to appoint a half-lunatic that goes round asking murderers to pray for him.

WARDER 2: Certainly they're not, unless they're bloody-well half-mad themselves.

WARDER 1: And I think they know him as well as we do.

WARDER 2: Except the Canon, poor man; he has him well recommended.

WARDER 1: You can leave out the 'poor man' part of it. God forgive me and I renounce the sin of it, the Lord says 'touch not my anointed', but the Canon is a bloody sight worse than himself, if you knew only the half of it.

WARDER 2: Go to God.

WARDER 1: Right, I'll tell you now. He was silenced for something before he came here and this is the *only* job he can get. Something terrible he did, though God forgive us, maybe it's not right to talk of it.

WARDER 2: You might sing it.

WARDER 1: I hear it was the way that he made the housekeeper take a girl into the house, the priest's house, to have a baby, an illegitimate!

WARDER 2: And could a man like that be fit to be a priest!

WARDER 1: He'd hardly be fit to be a prison chaplain, even. Here's the Chief or one of them coming. Get inside quick and let on you're looking for them fellows talking on the hot-water pipes, and not a word about what I said. That's between ourselves.

WARDER 2: Ah sure I know that's under foot. Thanks anyway.

WARDER 1: You're more than welcome. Don't be surprised if you get your landing sooner than you expected. Thirty cells all to yourself before you're fifty.

WARDER 2: I'll have the sister's children pray for you.

Enter CHIEF WARDER.

WARDER 1: All correct, sir.

CHIEF: What the hell do you mean, 'All correct, sir'? I've been watching you this half-hour yapping away to that other fellow.

WARDER 1: There were men communicating on the hot-water pipes, sir, and I told him ten times if I told him once to go inside the landing and see who it was; it's my opinion, sir, the man is a bit thick.

CHIEF: It's your opinion. Well, you're that thick yourself you ought to be a fair judge. And who the bloody hell are you to tell anyone to do anything? You're on night patrol the same as what he is.

WARDER 1: I thought, sir, on account of the night that's in it.

CHIEF: Why, is it Christmas? Listen here, that there is an execution in the morning is nothing to do with you. It's not your job to care, and a good job too, or you'd probably trip over the rope and fall through the bloody trap. What business have you out here, anyway?

WARDER 1: I thought I had to patrol by the grave, sir.

CHIEF: Afraid somebody might pinch it? True enough, this place is that full of thieves, you can leave nothing out of your hand. Get inside and resume your patrol. If you weren't one of the old hands I'd report you to the Governor. Get along with you and we'll forget about it.

WARDER 1: Very good, sir, and thank you, sir.

Tapping.

CHIEF: And stop that tapping on the pipes.

WARDER 1: I will, sir, and thanks again, sir.

FIRST WARDER *salutes, goes up the steps to the prison gates, which open. The* GOVERNOR *comes in in evening dress. The* FIRST WARDER *comes sharply to attention, salutes and goes off. The* GOVERNOR *continues down the steps and over to the* CHIEF WARDER.

CHIEF: All correct, sir.

GOVERNOR: Good. We had final word about the reprieve this afternoon. But you know how these things are, Chief, hoping for last-minute developments. I must say I should have been more than surprised had the Minister[2] made a recommendation. I'll go down and see him before the Canon comes in. It makes them more settled for confession when they know there is absolutely no hope. How is he?

CHIEF: Very well, sir. Sitting by the fire and chatting to the warders. He says he might go to bed

2. The Minister for Justice, who has the responsibility for penal affairs in Ireland.

after he sees the priest.

GOVERNOR: You'll see that there's a good breakfast for himself and the two assistants?

CHIEF: Oh, yes, sir, he's very particular about having two rashers and eggs. Last time they were here, some hungry pig ate half his breakfast and he kicked up murder.

GOVERNOR: See it doesn't happen this time.

CHIEF: No indeed. There's a fellow under sentence of death next week in the Crumlin;[3] we don't want him going up to Belfast and saying we starved him.

GOVERNOR: Have they come back from town yet?

CHIEF: (*Looks at his watch*) It's after closing time. I don't expect they'll be long now. I put Clancy on the side gate to let them in. After he took the quare fellow's measurements he went over to the place he drinks in. Some pub at the top of Grafton Street.[4] I believe he's the life of the bar there, Sir; the customers think he's an English traveller. The publican knows who he is, but then they're both in the pub business, and sure that's as tight a trade as hanging.

GOVERNOR: I suppose his work here makes him philosophical, and they say that drink is the comfort of the philosophers.

CHIEF: I wouldn't doubt but you'd be right there, sir. But he told me himself he only takes a drink when he's on a job. The rest of the time he's serving behind his own bar.

GOVERNOR: Is Jenkinson with him?

CHIEF: Yes, sir. He likes to have him with him, in case he gets a bit jarred. Once he went straight from the boat to the pubs and spent the day in them, and when he got here wasn't he after leaving the black box with his rope and his washers and his other little odds and ends behind him in a pub and forgot which one it was he left them in.

GOVERNOR: Really.

CHIEF: You could sing it. You were in Limerick at the time, sir, but here we were, in a desperate state. An execution coming off in the morning and we without the black box that had all his tools in it. The Governor we had then, he promised a novena to St Anthony and two insertions in the *Messenger*[5] if they were found in time. And sure enough after squad cars were all over in the city, the box was got in a pub down the North Wall,[6] the first one he went into. It shows you the power of prayer, sir.

GOVERNOR: Yes, I see what you mean.

CHIEF: So now he always brings Jenkinson with him. You see Jenkinson takes nothing, being very good living. A street preacher he is, for the Methodists or something. Himself prefers T.T.s.[7] He had an Irishman from Clare helping one time, but he sacked him over the drink. In this Circus, he said, there's only one allowed to drink and that's the Ringmaster.

GOVERNOR: We advertised for a native hangman during the Economic War. Must be fluent Irish speaker. Cailioctai de reir Meamram V. a seacht.[8] There were no suitable applicants.

CHIEF: By the way, sir, I must tell you that the warders on night patrol were out here conversing, instead of going round the landings.

GOVERNOR: Remind me to make a note of it tomorrow.

CHIEF: I will, sir, and I think I ought to tell you that I heard the principal warder make a joke about the execution.

GOVERNOR: Good God, this sort of thing is getting out of hand. I was at my School Union this evening. I had to leave in sheer embarrassment; supposedly witty remarks made to me at my own table. My eldest son was furious with me for going at all. He was at a table with a crowd from the University. They were even worse. One young pup went so far as to ask him if he thought I would oblige with a rendering of 'The night before Larry was stretched'.[9] I shall certainly tell the Principal that there's at least one place in this city where an execution is taken very seriously indeed. Good night to you.

CHIEF: Good night, sir.

Tapping. The CHIEF WARDER *walks up and down.* REGAN *enters.*

Ah, Mr. Regan, the other man coming along?

WARDER REGAN: He'll be along in a minute.

CHIEF: I don't know what we'd do without you, Regan, on these jobs. Is there anything the Governor or I could do to make things easier?

3. Crumlin Road jail in Belfast.
4. Dublin's main shopping street.
5. The *Sacred Heart Messenger*, a catholic magazine, which printed testimonies of favours received from various saints. These were often accompanied by the detail of the prayers promised in advance of the favour — as in this case.
6. An area in the Dublin docks.
7. Tee-totallers — total abstainers from alcohol.
8. 'Qualifications in accordance with memorandum V, seven . . . .'
9. A popular nineteenth-century ballad about a hanging, a fine example of gallows humour. See Volume II, p. 99.

WARDER REGAN: You could say a decade of the rosary.

CHIEF: I could hardly ask the Governor to do that.

WARDER REGAN: His prayers would be as good as anyone else's.

CHIEF: Is there anything on the practical side we could send down?

WARDER REGAN: A bottle of malt.

CHIEF: Do you think he'd drink it?

WARDER REGAN: No, but I would.

CHIEF: Regan, I'm surprised at you.

WARDER REGAN: I was reared among people that drank at a death or prayed. Some did both. You think the law makes this man's death someway different, not like anyone else's. Your own, for instance.

CHIEF: I wasn't found guilty of murder.

WARDER REGAN: No, nor no one is going to jump on you in the morning and throttle the life out of you, but it's not him I'm thinking of. It's myself. And you're not going to give me that stuff about just shoving over the lever and bob's your uncle. You forget the times the fellow gets caught and has to be kicked off the edge of the trap hole. You never heard of the warders down below swinging on his legs the better to break his neck, or jumping on his back when the drop was too short.

CHIEF: Mr. Regan, I'm surprised at you.

WARDER REGAN: That's the second time tonight.

Tapping. Enter CRIMMIN.

CRIMMIN: All correct, sir.

CHIEF: Regan, I hope you'll forget those things you mentioned just now. If talk the like of that got outside the prison . . . .

WARDER REGAN: (*Almost shouts*) I think the whole show should be put on in Croke Park;[10] after all, it's at the public expense and they let it go on. They should have something more for their money than a bit of paper stuck up on the gate.

CHIEF: Good night, Regan. If I didn't know you, I'd report what you said to the Governor.

WARDER REGAN: You will anyway.

CHIEF: Good night, Regan.

WARDER REGAN: (*To* CRIMMIN) Crimmin, there you are. I'm going into the hospital to fix up some supper for us. An empty sack won't stand, as the man said, nor a full one won't bend.

He goes. CRIMMIN *strolls. Traffic is heard in the distance, drowning the tapping. A drunken crowd are heard singing.* DONELLY *and the* NEW WARDER *appear in the darkness.*

WARDER 1: Is that young Mr. Crimmin?

CRIMMIN: Yes, it's me.

WARDER 1: You've a desperate job for a young warder this night. But I'll tell you one thing, you've a great man with you. Myself and this other man here are only after being talking about him.

WARDER 2: That's right, so we were. A grand man and very good living.

WARDER 1: There's someone coming. Too fine a night to be indoors. Good night, Mr. Crimmin.

CRIMMIN: Good night, sir.

WARDER 1: (*As they go off*) Come on, let's get a sup of tea.

CRIMMIN *waits. Tapping heard.* WARDER REGAN *re-enters.*

WARDER REGAN: Supper's fixed. It's a fine clear night. Do you hear the buses? Fellows leaving their mots home, after the pictures or coming from dances, and a few old fellows well jarred but half sober for fear of what herself will say when they get in the door. Only a hundred yards up there on the bridge, and it might as well be a hundred miles away. Here they are back from the pub.

Voices are heard in the dark approaching. Enter HANGMAN *and* JENKINSON.

HANGMAN: (*Sings*)

'She was lovely and fair like the rose of the summer,
Though 'twas not her beauty alone that won me,
Oh, no, 'twas the truth in her eyes ever shining,
That made me love Mary the Rose of Tralee.'

Don't see any signs of Regan.

JENKINSON: He's probably had to go on duty. You've left it too late.

HANGMAN: Well, if the mountain won't come to M'ammed then the M'ammed must go to the mountain.

WARDER REGAN: (*From the darkness*) As the girl said to the soldier.

HANGMAN: As the girl said to the soldier. Oh, it's you, Regan. Will you have a drink?

WARDER REGAN: I'm afraid we've got to be off now.

HANGMAN: Never mind off now. Have one with me. It's a pleasure to see you again. We meet all too seldom. You have one with me. Adam, give him a bottle of stout.

He sings again.

10. A large stadium in Dublin, headquarters of the Gaelic Athletic Association.

'Oh, no, 'twas the truth in her eyes ever shining,
That made me love Mary the Rose of Tralee.'

Not bad for an old 'un. Lovely song, in't it? Very religious though. 'The Poor Christian Fountain.'[11] I'm very fond of the old Irish songs; we get a lot of Irish in our place on a Saturday night, you know.

WARDER REGAN: Is it what they call a sporting pub?

HANGMAN: That's just what it is, and an old sport behind the bar counter an' all. All the Irish come in, don't they, Adam?

JENKINSON: (*Gloomily*) Reckon they do. Perhaps because no one else would go in it.

HANGMAN: What do you mean? It's best beer in the district. Not that you could tell the difference.

WARDER REGAN: Good health.

HANGMAN: May we never do worse. (*To* JENKINSON) You're in a right cut,[12] aren't you, making out there's nobody but Irish coming into my pub? I've never wanted for friends. Do you know why? Because I'd go a 'undred mile to do a man a good turn. I've always tried to do my duty.

JENKINSON: And so have I.

HANGMAN: Do you remember the time I got out from a sickbed to 'ang a soldier at Strangeways, when I thought you and Christmas 'adn't had enough experience?

JENKINSON: Aye, that's right enough.

HANGMAN: I'm not going to quarrel with you. Here, go and fetch your concertina and sing 'em that hymn you composed.

JENKINSON *hesitates.*

HANGMAN: Go on. It's a grand tune, a real credit to you. Go on, lad.

JENKINSON: Well, only for the hymn, mind. (*He goes off to fetch it*)

WARDER REGAN: Sure, that's right.

HANGMAN: 'E's a good lad is our Adam, but 'e's down in the dumps at the moment. 'Im and Christmas, they used to sing on street corners with the Band of Holy Joy, every Saturday night, concertina and all. But some of the lads found out who they were and started putting bits of rope in collection boxes; it's put them off outdoor testimony. But this 'ymn's very moving about hanging and mercy and so forth. Brings tears to your eyes to 'ear Adam and Christmas singing it.

JENKINSON *returns.*

JENKINSON: Right?

HANGMAN: Right!

JENKINSON: (*Sings*)

My brother, sit and think.
While yet some time is left to thee
Kneel to thy God who from thee does not shrink
And lay thy sins on Him who died for thee.

HANGMAN: Take a fourteen-stone man as a basis and giving him a drop of eight foot . . . .

JENKINSON:

Men shrink from thee but not I,
Come close to me I love my erring sheep.
My blood can cleanse thy sins of blackest dye,
I understand if thou canst only weep.[13]

HANGMAN: Every half-stone lighter would require a two-inch longer drop, so for weight thirteen and a half stone — drop eight feet two inches, and for weight thirteen stone — drop eight feet four inches.

JENKINSON:

Though thou hast grieved me sore,
My arms of mercy still are open wide,
I still hold open Heaven's shining door
Come then, take refuge in my wounded side.

HANGMAN: Now he's only twelve stone so he should have eight foot eight, but he's got a thick neck on him so I'd better give him another couple of inches. Yes, eight foot ten.

JENKINSON:

Come now, the time is short.
Longing to pardon and bless I wait.
Look up to me, my sheep so dearly bought
And say, forgive me, ere it is too late.

HANGMAN: Divide 412 by the weight of the body in stones, multiply by two gives the length of the drop in inches. (*He looks up and seems sobered*) 'E's an R.C., I suppose, Mr. Regan? (*Puts book in his pocket*)

WARDER REGAN: That's right.

HANGMAN: That's all, then. Good night.

JENKINSON: Good night.

WARDER REGAN: Good night. (*The* HANGMAN *and* JENKINSON *go off*) Thanks for the hymn. Great night for stars. If there's life on any of them, I wonder do the same things happen up there? Maybe some warders on a planet are walking across a prison yard this minute and some fellow up there

11. The line from the song is, in fact, 'When I stray'd with my love to the pure crystal fountain.' The lines sung here are the closing lines of the original poem by William P. Mulchinock (*c.* 1820-64). See Volume II, p. 102.
12. i.e. in a bad humour.

13. A revivalist hymn in the manner of Moody and Sankey, the American evangelists.

waiting on the rope in the morning, and looking out through the bars, for a last look at our earth and the moon for the last time. Though I never saw them to bother much about things like that. It's nearly always letters to their wives or mothers, and then we don't send them — only throw them into the grave after them. What'd be the sense of broadcasting such distressful rubbish?

PRISONER C: (*Sings from his cell window*) Is é fath mo bhuartha na bhfaghaim cead chuarta.[14]

WARDER REGAN: Regular choir practice going on round here tonight.

CRIMMIN: He's singing for . . . for . . . .

WARDER REGAN: For the quare fellow.

CRIMMIN: Yes. Why did the Englishman ask if he was a Catholic?

WARDER REGAN: So as they'd know to have the hood slit to anoint him on the rope, and so as the fellows below would know to take off his boots and socks for the holy oil on his feet when he goes down.

PRISONER C: (*Sings*) Ni'l gaoth adthuaidh ann, ni'l sneachta cruaidh ann . . . .

WARDER REGAN: We'd better be getting in. The other screws will be hopping mad to get out; they've been there since four o'clock today.

PRISONER C: (*Sings*) Mo mhuirnin bhan . . . .

His song dies away and the empty stage is gradually lightened for

14. The lines are a variation on those of an anonymous Gaelic love song. The plaint in the song is that the lover is banished from his beloved; were he able to visit her, there, in an idealized landscape, all would be well. The lines translate: 'It is the cause of my sorrow that I have not permission to visit.' 'There is no north wind there, there is no drear snow there . . . .' 'My fair-haired darling . . . .'

Scene Two

The prison yard. It is morning.

WARDER 1: How's the time?

WARDER 2: Seven minutes.

WARDER 1: As soon as it goes five to eight they'll start. You'd think they were working with stop watches. I wish I was at home having my breakfast. How's the time?

WARDER 2: Just past six minutes.

MICKSER'S VOICE: Baíl o Dhia orribh go léir a chairde.[1]

WARDER 1: I knew it. That's that bloody Mickser. I'll fix him this time.

MICKSER'S VOICE: And we take you to the bottom of D. Wing.

WARDER 1: You bastard, I'll give you D. Wing.

MICKSER'S VOICE: We're ready for the start, and in good time, and who do I see lined up for the off but the High Sheriff of this ancient city of ours, famous in song and story as the place where the pig ate the whitewash brushes and — (*The* WARDERS *remove their caps*) We're off, in this order: the Governor, the Chief, two screws Regan and Crimmin, the quare fellow between them, two more screws and three runners from across the Channel, getting well in front, now the Canon. He's making a big effort for the last two furlongs. He's got the white pudding bag on his head, just a short distance to go. He's in. (*A clock begins to chime the hour. Each quarter sounds louder*) His feet to the chalk line. He'll be pinioned, his feet together. The bag will be pulled down over his face. The screws come off the trap and steady him. Himself goes to the lever and . . . .

The hour strikes. The WARDERS *cross themselves and put on their caps. From the* PRISONERS *comes a ferocious howling.*

PRISONERS: One off, one away, one off, one away.

WARDER 1: Shut up there.

WARDER 2: Shut up, shut up.

WARDER 1: I know your windows, I'll get you. Shut up.

The noise dies down and at last ceases altogether.

Now we'll go in and get that Mickser. (*Grimly*) *I'll* soften his cough. Come on . . . .

WARDER REGAN *comes out.*

WARDER REGAN: Give us a hand with this fellow.

WARDER 1: We're going after that Mickser.

WARDER REGAN: Never mind that now, give us a hand. He fainted when the trap was sprung.

WARDER 1: These young screws, not worth a light.

They carry CRIMMIN *across the yard.*

NEIGHBOUR'S VOICE: Dunlavin, that's a Sunday

1. 'God bless all of you, my friends.' These were commonly the opening words of sports commentators of Gaelic games on Radio Éireann, the Irish state broadcasting service.

bacon you owe me. Your man was topped, wasn't he?

PRISONER A'S VOICE: You won't be long after him.

DUNLAVIN'S VOICE: Don't mind him, Neighbour.

NEIGHBOUR'S VOICE: Don't you forget that bacon, Dunlavin.

DUNLAVIN'S VOICE: I forgot to tell you, Neighbour.

NEIGHBOUR'S VOICE: What did you forget to tell me?

ENGLISH VOICE: Where's the bloke what's going out this morning?

NEIGHBOUR'S VOICE: He's up in Nelly's room behind the clock. What about that bacon, Dunlavin?

ENGLISH VOICE: You bloke that's going out this morning, remember to see my chiner and tell him to 'ave me bailed out.

NEIGHBOUR'S VOICE: Get a bucket and bail yourself out. What about me bacon, Dunlavin?

ENGLISH VOICE: Sod you and your bleeding bacon.

DUNLAVIN'S VOICE: Shut up a minute about your bail, till I tell Neighbour about his bet.

NEIGHBOUR'S VOICE: You lost it, that's all I know.

DUNLAVIN'S VOICE: Yes, but the doctor told me that me stomach was out of order; he's put me on a milk diet.

CHIEF (*Comes through prison gates and looks up*) Get down from those windows. Get down at once. (*He beckons inside and* PRISONERS A, B, C *and* D *file past him and go down on the steps.* PRISONER B *is carrying a cold hammer and chisel*) Hey, you there in front, have you the cold chisel and hammer?

PRISONER B: Yes, sir.

CHIEF: You other three, the shovels are where you left them; get to work there and clear the top and have it ready for filling in.

They go on to the canvas, take up the shovels from behind and begin work. PRISONER B *stands on the foot of the steps with his cold chisel while the* CHIEF *studies his paper to give final instructions.*

CHIEF: Yes, that's it. You're to carve E.777. Got that?

PRISONER B: Yes, sir. E.777.

CHIEF: That's it. It should be E.779 according to the book, but a '7' is easier for you to do than a '9'. Right, the stone in the wall that's nearest to the spot. Go ahead now. (*Raising his voice*) There's the usual bottles of stout a man, but only if you work fast.

WARDER 1: I know the worst fellow was making this noise, sir. It was Mickser, sir. I'm going in to case[2] him now. I'll take an hour's overtime to do it, sir.

CHIEF: You're a bit late. He was going out this morning and had his civilian clothing on in the cell. We were only waiting for this to be over to let him out.

WARDER 1: But . . . Sir, he was the whole cause.

CHIEF: Well, what do you want me to do, run down the Circular Road after him? He went out on remission. We could have stopped him. But you were too bloody slow for that.

WARDER 1: I was helping to carry . . . .

CHIEF: You were helping to carry . . . . Warders! I'd get better in Woolworths.

WARDER 2: To think of that dirty savage getting away like that. Shouting and a man going to his God.

WARDER 1: Never mind that part of it. He gave me lip in the woodyard in '42, and I couldn't do anything because he was only on remand. I've been waiting years to get that fellow.

WARDER 2: Ah, well, you've one consolation. He'll be back.

At the grave PRISONER A *is the only one visible over the canvas.*

PRISONER B: Would you say that this was the stone in the wall nearest to it?

PRISONER A: It'll do well enough. It's only for the records. They're not likely to be digging him up to canonize him.

PRISONER B: Fair enough. E.777.

REGAN *drops the letters into the grave, and goes.*

PRISONER A: Give us them bloody letters. They're worth money to one of the Sunday papers.

PRISONER B: So I understood you to say yesterday.

PRISONER A: Well, give us them.

PRISONER D: They're not exclusively your property any more than anyone else's.

PRISONER B: There's no need to have a battle over them. Divide them. Anyone that likes can have my share and I suppose the same goes for the kid.

PRISONER D: Yes, we can act like businessmen.

2. To 'case' means to commit to a punishment cell, usually in solitary confinement.

There are three. One each and toss for the third. I'm a businessman.

PRISONER A: Fair enough. Amn't I a business-man myself? For what's a crook, only a business-man without a shop.

PRISONER D: What side are you on? The blank side or the side with the address?

VOICE OF PRISONER BELOW: (*Singing*)

In the female prison
There are seventy women
I wish it was with them that I did dwell,
Then that old triangle
Could jingle jangle
Along the banks of the Royal Canal.

The curtain falls.

Biographies/Bibliographies

Denis Johnston

LIFE. Born in Dublin in 1901, educated St Andrew's College, Dublin, Merchiston, Edinburgh, Cambridge University and Harvard University Law School. Wrote *The Old Lady Says 'No!'* in his twenties. Worked as a director with the Gate Theatre in the early 1930s, when his second play, *The Moon in the Yellow River*, had a considerable success at the Abbey. He was a war correspondent for the BBC in various parts of the world. Spent much of his later life as a professor at various American universities. Died in 1984 in Dublin.

CHIEF WRITINGS. *Nine Rivers from Jordan* (autobiography) (London: Derek Verschoyle, 1953); *In Search of Swift* (Dublin: Allen Figgis, 1959); *The Brazen Horn* (autobiography) (Dublin: The Dolmen Press, 1977); *Collected Plays Vols. I and II* (London: Jonathan Cape, 1960); *Collected Plays Vol. 1* (Gerrards Cross: Colin Smythe, 1977); *Collected Plays Vol. 2* (Gerrards Cross: Colin Smythe, 1979).

BIOGRAPHY AND CRITICISM. A. Gene Barnett, *Denis Johnston* (New York: Twayne, 1978); Harold Farrar, *Denis Johnston's Irish Theatre* (Dublin: The Dolmen Press, 1973); Joseph Ronsley (ed.), *Denis Johnston: A Retrospective* (Gerrards Cross: Colin Smythe; Totowa, New Jersey: Barnes and Noble, 1981) a useful collection of essays.

Lennox Robinson

LIFE. Born in Douglas, Co. Cork, in 1886, the son of a Church of Ireland clergyman. Because of poor health, Robinson had little formal schooling. After the success of his early play, *The Clancy Name* (1908), he was invited by Yeats and Lady Gregory to become manager of the Abbey Theatre and to direct plays. Resigned in 1914 but returned as manager five years later. Became a member of the Abbey's board of directors in 1923 in which post he remained until his death in 1958. Made his dramatic reputation with his comedy *The Whiteheaded Boy* in 1916. In the 1930s his well-made comedies were a commercial resource of the Abbey Theatre Company. He died in Monkstown, Co. Dublin in 1958 and is buried in St Patrick's Cathedral.

CHIEF WRITINGS. *The Whiteheaded Boy: A Comedy in Three Acts* (London: Putnam, 1921); *Crabbed Youth and Age: A Little Comedy* (London: Putnam, 1924); *The Big House: Four Scenes in its Life* (London: Macmillan, 1928); *Plays* (London: Macmillan, 1928); *The Far-Off Hills: A Comedy in Three Acts* (London: Chatto and Windus, 1931); *Drama at Inish: An Exaggeration in Three Acts* (retitled *Is Life Worth Living?*) (London: Macmillan, 1933); *Ireland's Abbey Theatre: A History, 1899-1951* (London: Sidgwick and Jackson, 1951); *Selected Plays of Lennox Robinson*, chosen and with an introduction by Christopher Murray (Gerrards Cross: Colin Smythe; Washington, D.C.: The Catholic University Press of America, 1982) (contains *Patriots*, *The Whiteheaded Boy*, *Crabbed Youth and Age*, *The Big House*, *Drama at Inish* and *Church Street* and a selected checklist compiled by Frances-Jane French).

BIOGRAPHY AND CRITICISM. Michael J. O'Neill, *Lennox Robinson* (New York: Twayne, 1964).

Paul Vincent Carroll

LIFE. Born near Dundalk, Co. Louth, in 1900. Educated at St Mary's College, Dundalk, and at St Patrick's Training College, Dublin. Settled in Glasgow, Scotland in 1921 where he remained as a schoolteacher for sixteen years. Retired from school teaching in 1937 following the success of *Shadow and Substance*. From 1945 lived in England, where he wrote for television and the cinema. He died in Bromley, Kent in 1968.

CHIEF WRITINGS. *Things That Are Caesar's* (London: Rich and Cowan, 1934); *Shadow and Substance* (New York: Random House, 1937; (London: Macmillan, 1938); *The White Steed and Coggerers* (New York: Random House, 1939).

BIOGRAPHY AND CRITICISM. Paul A. Doyle, *Paul Vincent Carroll* (Lewisburg, Pennsylvania: Bucknell University Press, 1971).

Brendan Behan

LIFE. Born in Dublin in 1923. As a teenager, he joined the republican movement, with which his family was associated. Arrested on bombing mission in Liverpool in 1939. Spent two years in a juvenile detention centre in England. Deported to Ireland in 1941, where he was arrested several months later and charged with shooting at a detective. He spent five years (of a fourteen-year sentence) in jail and was released under a general amnesty at the end of 1946. These experiences bore literary fruit in *Borstal Boy* (1958), his finest work. Wrote poems, stories and plays in English and Irish. In 1954 *The Quare Fellow* was performed at the Pike Theatre in Dublin and in 1956 a Theatre Workshop production in London brought him international critical success. An Irish-language play, *An Giall*, realized in English by Joan Littlewood in a London production in 1958 as *The Hostage*, brought its author even greater fame. He died, a victim of alcohol and adulation in 1964, without producing further work of real merit, but by then he was firmly ensconced as a Dublin folk-hero.

CHIEF WRITINGS. *An Giall* (Dublin: An Chomhairle Naisiúnta Dramaíochta, n.d.); *Borstal Boy* (autobiography) (London: Hutchinson, 1958); *Brendan Behan's Island* (London: Hutchinson, 1962); *The Complete Plays of Brendan Behan* (London: Eyre Methuen, 1978).

BIOGRAPHY AND CRITICISM. Ulick O'Connor, *Brendan* (London: Hamish Hamilton; Englewood Cliffs, N.J.: Prentice Hall, 1970); Colbert Kearney, *The Writings of Brendan Behan* (Dublin: Gill and Macmillan, 1977), an acute and sympathetic study; Ted E. Boyle, *Brendan Behan* (New York: Twayne, 1969); Peter René Gerdes, *The Major Works of Brendan Behan* (European University Papers, Bern: Herbert Lang; Frankfurt: Peter Lang, 1973); Alan Simpson, *Beckett and Behan and a Theatre in Dublin* (London: Routledge and Kegan Paul, 1962); Anthony Cronin, *Dead As Doornails* (Dublin: The Dolmen Press, 1975); E. H. Mikhail, *The Art of Brendan Behan* (London: Vision, 1979), a useful collection of reviews of *The Quare Fellow*, including an excellent one by Kenneth Tynan; E. H. Mikhail, *Brendan Behan: An Annotated Bibliography of Criticism* (London: Macmillan, 1980).

J. C. C. MAYS, *Editor*

Samuel Beckett

(1907-89)

Beckett's writing, and responses to it, are enveloped in contradictions. He has a reputation for not having written very much — for wordless three-minute statements, like *Breath* — yet his writing fills more than twenty separate volumes. He has a reputation for misanthropy and gloom — placing his characters in dustbins or up to their necks in sand — yet he is cherished as a great humourist. His attitude towards readers and audiences has been more or less to disregard them, yet he has evoked an enormous body of criticism and exegesis, and affection as well as respect. He is a totem of bourgeois intellectuals, yet he has been taken up by life-term prisoners and by the politically unfree behind the Iron Curtain and in South Africa. The world thinks of him as an Irish writer, when it thinks in such categories, yet he himself said that the Irish public does not care 'a fart in its corduroys for any kind of art whatsoever,' and he preferred to live in France.

The contradictions are severe and bewildering, but the way to understand why Beckett is an important and an exciting writer is not by way of the Nobel Prize citation ('sounding liberation to the oppressed and comfort to those in need'), nor by way of his academic reputation, nor by way of popular preconceptions. It is more profitable to begin at the beginning, with a recognition of what he thought he was writing about, and why.

Beckett identified his subject matter at the moment he committed himself fully to being a writer, in the early 1930s. He was always concerned with a sense of the unreality of life on the surface, of 'existence by proxy' or 'being absent'; an intuition of 'a presence, embryonic, undeveloped, of a self that might have been but never got born, an *être manqué*.' He was well aware of the connections between this exacerbated self-consciousness on his part and several dualistic, sceptical and pessimistic traditions at large, but the intellectual backgrounds served only to clarify or extend the terms of the problem. This scepticism in the face of what we might naturally accept as the actual world is complicated by his scepticism about the perceiving self. This is the problem with which his writing attempts to come to terms. He felt the problem not merely as a matter of academic philosophy: it got him in the solar plexus to the extent that he referred to it as a disaster: 'If you really get down to the disaster, the slightest eloquence becomes unbearable.'

Writing is a paradigm. It is only through writing that the problem can be known and solutions can be temporarily arrived at or shown to be impossible; or arrived at and shown to be impossible in the same process. 'Whatever is said is so far from experience.' 'Painting and music have so much better a chance.' At the same time, because writing contains the problem, to cease from writing or even to commit suicide do not afford solutions. 'What do you do when "I can't" meets "I must"?'

Samuel Beckett's earliest writing was primarily in criticism and verse. It wears mannerisms like a carapace, and hides behind display. Allusions and references glitter and distract, the pace is nervous, the tone is detached yet defensive. The larger part of his early verse remains uncollected, and the criticism was collected only in 1983 by Ruby Cohn. The extent to which Beckett's style was contaminated by Joyce's can be exaggerated; in fact, Beckett began to define his distance from

Joyce's ideas almost from the moment he found himself in Joyce's personal orbit. The mannerisms that inhibited his writing through the 1930s were instead prompted by feelings that had drawn him to writing in the first place.

In verse — the mode that reflects Beckett's personal concerns most transparently — he discovered coherence at the cost of emotional range. His only volume of poetry (other than the late collections), which was published in 1935, is distinguished by relative abstraction. The abstraction enabled him to distance contradictions that were intrinsically confusing. The poems are buoyed up by urgency, but the condition of their success is to set emotion under severe constraint. As Beckett's later verse shows, the mode can restate conclusions, but cannot extend the terms on which they are founded. The successful poems are rammed full of life, in Ben Jonson's phrase, but in ways that communicate the cost as forcefully as the containment.

In an important sense, Beckett is primarily a poet. Yet even his most successful verse contains only shards, literally 'echo's bones', and he was able to give expression to a wider emotional range in fiction. Attitudes whose contradictions choke the poems become creative opposites when deployed at a distance in dramatic scenes. The detachment generated by the distance between the author and his characters allows the display of what is characteristic of the best of Beckett's writing — the mobile, sensitive point of view, the fluid turns and reversals of emotion, the interpenetration of ordinarily contradictory attitudes offering a new insight into the way the mind responds, particularly instances of comic deflation and inflation.

There is a quality in Beckett's writing that makes it instantly recognizable. 'All I know is what the words know, and the dead things, and that makes a handsome little sum, with a beginning, a middle and an end as in the well-built phrase and the long sonata of the dead' (*Molloy*). His detachment gives it qualities of elegance, humour and precision: 'For in me there have always been two fools, among others, one asking nothing better than to stay where he is and the other imagining that life might be slightly less horrible further on' (*Molloy*). The writing is nuanced in particular instances towards elegy or despair or absurdity or apothegm ('Birth was the death of him,' *A Piece of Monologue*), but most characteristically it combines such qualities. Take for instance the closing sentences of *Krapp's Last Tape*:

> Perhaps my best years are gone. When there was a chance of happiness. But I wouldn't want them back. Not with the fire in me now. No, I wouldn't want them back.

Do the words contain resentment or regret? Are they meant to convey anger or pathos? Of course they embrace both qualities, and more. Such elusive combinations, held in phrasing that is scrupulously exact ('a bow tie about a throat cancer'), are utterly distinctive. John Russell Brown has called it the art of nonplus.

'Dante and the Lobster' was one of two stories from the collection that Beckett was happy to see republished, and his subsequent writing might be said to develop from here. *Murphy*, which was written not long afterwards, extends the same method to an entirely recast version of the same sequence. It is the most successfully entertaining of Beckett's early pieces of fiction, yet in one sense it is too entertaining. As Dylan Thomas said in a review, while praising the book's energy, hilarity, irony and comic invention (to which he might have added its tenderness and lyricism), it tries to sell its bluffs over a double counter. It explores in a clear and subtle way the dualistic themes that were Beckett's continuing concern, but it is not consistently serious about them; that is, it hesitates to adopt a consistent attitude or to bring conflicts into resolution.

The way in which the success of *Murphy* might be construed as its fault is the basis for the next direction taken by Beckett after the war. *Watt* was written in difficult conditions, as he said 'to keep [his] hand in', but when he returned to his Paris apartment in 1946 he began writing in an entirely different mode. He shifted to first-person narrative, thus closing the gap between author and protagonist. He shifted into French in a conscious effort to reduce the area in which he could be led astray by his facility as a writer. Characters who had existed simply in and for themselves were replaced by motifs that were closer to the new protagonist's commitments (a maternal presence, objects, natural things, a sense of order and of the past). The constraints of the foreign language were paradoxically liberating and enabled him to bring into focus the themes of all his writing in English up to that time.

The trilogy of novels written in the period 1947-50 — *Molloy*, *Malone Dies*, *The Unnamable* —

makes up the centre of Beckett's *oeuvre*, at least as he saw it. The first two are a pair, and constituted his most serious attempt to define his subject matter, without distraction and having regard to its social and other consequences. Their starting-point is close to the nineteenth-century alienation expressed by Rimbaud's phrase, 'Je est un autre,' but the first two novels pursue the theme in characteristically Beckettian directions. The third novel repeats the pattern of the second, in an attempt to cut deeper and so test the limits of form and language. It drives to a conclusion that is an impasse. 'No "I", no "have", no "being." No nominative, no accusative, no verb. There's no way to go on.'

Beckett did find a way to go on, in drama. *Waiting for Godot* was written between the first two novels of the trilogy, quickly, for relaxation and for clarification. *Endgame*, on the other hand, was written after *The Unnamable* and the success of *Godot*, with difficulty and partly in order to restate the conclusions of the trilogy in a way that audiences could not misunderstand. *Godot* made Beckett famous, but he himself described it as 'messy' and 'not well thought out'. 'I loathe it. It's a great struggle for me even to have to listen to it. I can't bear to think that it's what I'm most associated with.' *Endgame* is more inhuman and more difficult, elliptic and more under control; it is the play Beckett preferred above all others he wrote.

The naturalness of Beckett's transition to the stage is worth remark, and offers an instructive contrast to the Joyce of *Exiles*. It has to do with the different kind of self-consciousness that led Beckett away from lyric poetry in the first place. Emotions in his writing expand and relax as action and character establish themselves at a distance from the lyric self. Beckett's writing is more theatrical than dramatic, in that it is essentially performative. In *Exiles*, the silences between Bertha and Richard Rowan and Robert Hand make the audience aware of what is unspoken between them. We supply a dialogue that is too deep for their words, and which their words too easily distort into melodrama. The danger in any performance of *Exiles* is that the unspoken dialogue will upstage the action, and that social and psychological echoes will multiply and drown out the intended meaning. By contrast, the silences between Vladimir and Estragon in *Waiting for Godot* evacuate meaning; the dialogue that had seemed funny or tense comes to seem frail and inadequate; the echoes do not accumulate unwanted noise but become hollow.

If we identify with Beckett's speakers, it is not as social characters, but with their metaphysical predicament. Whereas the means for an actor to realize his part in *Exiles* is to identify with a character as a person, and whereas in performance he will attempt to share that sense of identification with an audience, *Godot* is destroyed by this approach. The only kinship to be discovered and shared is by the display of a situation on stage; the first duty of an actor to his audience is to make the situation clear, not to look for sympathy. The Beckett actor never quite loses himself in the part, which is what makes the part distinctively theatrical.

Beckett is often identified with protagonists like Belacqua, Murphy, Molloy and Krapp. There is a direct line of succession from book to book, from the novels to the plays and from the plays to the novels. There are properties that solo performers can employ that identify them as 'Beckett characters' — a ruined hat, unkempt hair, a long, torn coat, clownish trousers held up with string and braces, or a long dressing gown-like cloak. The highly formalized speech, with its Irish mannerisms and its shards of half-forgotten learning, is as characteristic as the near-empty stage, with its sharply divided light and dark areas.

Nonetheless, these conventions are no less artificial for being readily acceptable. No one who lives in Paris or Dublin looks or speaks like Jack MacGowran or Billie Whitelaw performing Beckett. The persona and the voice is a creation that draws on a number of backgrounds, and develops towards what Beckett in *How It Is* called 'the voice of us all'. It never represents Beckett in the way that Stephen or Bloom might be held to be versions of Joyce, or pretends to the kind of representative status possessed by the language of *Finnegans Wake*. Its relation to Beckett's own self is complicated because, although it is the voice he heard or the persona he saw when he wrote, it lives at an uncertain distance from his writing self. The novels and plays cohere as a connected fiction, but the speaking subject is dispersed among them in continually different ways.

Beckett's method in drama, as in fiction, depends on a sense of formal limits, so that his use of theatre has been an investigation of its nature. The method is again exhaustive or, literally, evacuative. When an essay in a genre is a critique of the potentialities of that genre, and meaning expresses itself against boundaries, bridges are burnt behind the writing as it advances. The method opens onto a disturbing freedom and has been widely influential. As Peter Hall said at the Lyttleton Theatre in 1977: 'Beckett has changed the way we do Shakespeare, the way we act, the way we write and the way we direct in the theatre.'

Beckett's only full-length fiction after the trilogy was *How It Is*, originally written in French. But following *Godot* and *Endgame*, which were also written in French, he wrote, in French and in English, plays for stage, radio, television, film and mime. It is noticeable that the exigencies of form brought with them a sense of shape, a recognition of companionship, a degree of lyricism. In retrospect, what began as a restatement of the conclusions reached by the trilogy came to appear as a restatement of the problem itself, and thereby as a way of resolving the Unnamable's impasse of 'complete disintegration'.

Beckett spoke of writing a novel as like 'entering a jungle, an area of utter lawlessness,' and of plays as being like 'coming into the light' — relaxation. For him, drama changed the order of things as they appear or are apprehended. It re-established the physical existence of his characters and relocated them in time. Coincidentally and contemporaneously, some of the pressures on his private life eased, and with this alleviation many of the qualities that the trilogy had pushed to one side returned. What began as simple transposition from fiction to drama changed Beckett's understanding of both.

The short prose texts he began to write in the later 1950s and throughout the 1960s have a firmness of outline unlike anything he had attempted before. Their analysis of the human condition is not less rigorous, nor was Beckett any the more willing to admit palliatives born of human need. But in a situation that derives pictorially from *Endgame*, texts like *Ping* and *Lessness* return to explore qualities Beckett appeared to have jettisoned after the portrayal of Celia and the last chapter of *Murphy*. The basis of the writing is often patterned, sometimes elaborately mathematical, yet the rhythms are complicated by more feelings than merely the willed obligation to express.

At the same time, during the 1960s, Beckett became extensively involved in productions of his own plays, mainly for the Schiller Theater in Berlin. He exercised strict control, as far as possible, over all productions everywhere. For example, he withheld permission for Sir Laurence Olivier and Joan Plowright to do a stage-version of *All That Fall*, and he intervened to have a production of *Endgame* by the distinguished American Repertory Company closed down because it departed from the stage directions and instructions, concerning set-design, lighting and the movement of performers. In his own productions he evolved a style of production that is a logical extension of his kind of drama; indeed it could have been predicted on the basis of its personal origins. Actors play against their idea of the text as if to a fourth wall. The dramatic tension is all between the actors and their impossible task, the audience participating as spectators, but not to alter the rules of the game.

Rick Cluchey has described the experience of being directed by Beckett as follows:

> To evoke the echo from the printed page to the dramatic stage requires a knowledge of the exact space between the words; so, tonally, he becomes a musician. The linear possibility begins to evoke musical beats.
>
> He arrives at the point where he can tell you instantly if you've gone off the tonal property, if the musicalization is incorrect, and tell you why certain tensions are in your body because of it. He is a master of this form now.

The resultant kind of theatre is disciplined and formalized. It has drawn inspired performances from some and has antagonized others — Sir John Gielgud, among the latter.

Some of the plays might almost have been conceived as balanced pairs — *Krapp's Last Tape* and *Happy Days*, for instance (although Beckett would not allow these two to be performed as a double-bill, perhaps because the pairing is trite). Again, there is a considerable overlapping of types of character between radio and stage plays and other kinds — for example, Mrs Rooney in *All That Fall* has much in common with Winnie in *Happy Days*. In a slightly different way, a number of prose texts group themselves round *The Lost Ones* during the 1960s as miniaturizations of and variations on the same theme, which Beckett found problematic.

During the 1970s, the interrelation between the drama and fiction Beckett was writing led to modifications of each in the light of the other, and experiments in the different way each could realize a shared theme. The relationship between plays like *That Time*, *Footfalls* and *Ohio Impromptu*, on the one hand, and *Company*, *Ill Seen Ill Said* and *Worstward Ho*, on the other, is apparent at the level of form and rhythm as well as at the level of character and theme. Theatre and fiction explore different modes of presentation that are symbiotically related. They draw on autobiographical material in their different ways, sometimes in surprising detail, yet their concern is with the way memory distorts and creates 'reality' as it presents it to the mind.

I have said that writing is the paradigm of the problem that Beckett's writing attempts to solve. In his later writing, words are often less important than the image they accompany — images of a stage shaped like the inside of a skull in *Endgame*, or of a moving mouth and someone listening in *Not I*. The television play *Eh Joe* was the first in which the character we see listens but does not speak, as in *That Time*. And in another sequence of dramatic writings, which extends from the beginnings of Beckett's writing for theatre — from *Act Without Words I and II*, to *Film*, to finally *Quad* — words do not even accompany images; they only describe them.

The art in such extreme cases as the last is still literary, but it attempts to use words to go behind words, as Beckett described in his 1937 letter to Axel Kaun. The same method also carries over to texts like *Company*. Robert Creeley said of a conversation with Beckett: 'It was his dream to realize one word that was absolutely self-created. And he said it's about this big [indicating a height of about seven inches, both laughing] and it has the situation of stone.' (Creeley points out the connection with Jung's phallic stone.) These late texts — fiction, theatre — are the nearest Beckett came to realizing a word that is autonomous in its creation and existence, that has no other cause but itself.

In this introduction, I have deliberately concentrated on the coherence of Beckett's writing at the expense of its context. Because he was so wholly inside his writing, it moves forward as a whole. *Enough* for a long while appeared anomalous, until Billie Whitelaw included it in a performance also comprising *Footfalls* and *Rockaby*. The same consideration applies to *Eh Joe* and *How It Is*. Beckett's inspiration was constantly recuperative and interrelated.

Selection is unusually problematic because, since Beckett was not interested in repeating himself, each piece of writing attempts something different. I am particularly aware of not being able to include one or more parts of the trilogy, for which *Endgame* will have to stand as a summary. It marks the end of a phase in which he confronted the problems that had first drawn him to writing, without evasion, but that also appeared as a cul de sac. The early story, the poems and the chapters from *Murphy* make clear the cost at which this clarification was achieved. I also regret not being able to include *Waiting for Godot*, with which Beckett's name is indelibly associated, for better or worse, and which marked a turning-point in his career and fortunes. But again, the late plays and fiction demonstrate how the qualities that found expression in *Godot* could be incorporated in more characteristic forms.

Beckett's career as a writer rested on a narrow basis, but the life within the writing showed variety and change. He wrote for himself alone, but as the agent, not the victim, of the dilemma he described. He thereby almost accidentally expressed the concerns of several, different generations — of Irish expatriate writers in the 1930s, French existentialists in the 1940s, absurdists and angry young men in the 1950s, postmodernists in the 1960s, deconstructionists in the 1970s. His writing rests on assumptions that are twentieth-century commonplaces. 'In the "search for oneself" ... one says "I am" this, that or the other, and with the words scarcely uttered one ceases to be that thing' (Ezra Pound, 1916); 'The point of view which I am struggling to attack is perhaps related to the metaphysical theory of the substantial unity of the soul' (T. S. Eliot, 1919). Pound and Eliot anticipate precisely the kinds of distinctions to be found in Jacques Lacan's *Four Fundamental Concepts of Psychoanalysis* (1973) and other versions of contemporary theorizing. Yet Beckett conducted his dialogue about the limits and ends of art as a writer and as a person, not as a theorist. His writing reflects concerns that are deeply private. It makes up an *oeuvre* very different from Pound's or Eliot's, and even further removed from Lacan's.

It is difficult to speculate where posterity will judge his achievement to lie. At the present time, I think, there is a tendency for his verse to be undervalued. There is also a lack of discrimination between those of his later plays that succeed and those that do not. But whether the trilogy is his central achievement or only works out his private needs, and whether one has to accept his correspondingly dim view of *Godot*, I do not know. He is certainly an exemplary and inspiring figure in modern writing. Whether the Irish tradition can assimilate his example remains to be seen.

The texts are taken from the most recent printings by John Calder (Publishers) and by Faber and Faber. A few, minor, typographical errors have been silently corrected.

from:
MORE PRICKS THAN KICKS (1934)

[The first, longer version of 'Dante and the Lobster' was published in *This Quarter* (Paris) V (December 1932). The present, revised version was published as the first of the ten stories that make up *More Pricks Than Kicks*. The protagonist, Belacqua, is a continuing presence, and the sequence describes his life, loves and demise. He is also the hero of Beckett's earlier, unpublished novel, *Dream of Fair to Middling Women*, and reappears in *Murphy* (p. 254) and *Company* (p. 311) below.

Beckett borrowed the central character from Dante's *Purgatorio*, and the present story is loaded with Dantean motifs, echoes and allusions. For example, Belacqua's Italian lesson with Signorina Ottolenghi parallels Dante's lesson with Beatrice about the spots on the moon in *Paradiso* II. Thematically the most important reference is contained in the phrase Belacqua quotes to his Italian teacher, '*qui vive la pietà quando è ben morta*' (*Inferno*, XX, 28). It may be translated as 'Here lives pity when it should be dead', but with connotations here that may be paraphrased as 'What kind of piety is this?'

Again, the incident in the hallway that so alarms Mlle. Glain while Belacqua is having his Italian lesson alludes to an incident in which James Joyce alarmed the sister and mother of the Ottolenghi's original in a Dublin hallway in 1904 and about which Joyce wrote a poem (see Richard Ellmann, *James Joyce* (New York: Oxford University Press, 1982), pp. 160-61. The allusion is the first of several more or less obvious allusions to Joyce in Beckett's collection of stories, and they serve to counterpoint the allusions to Dante.

The story is about the disjunctions between piety and pity, form and feeling, order and chaos. Belacqua witnesses the violent baptism of the cruciform lobster in boiling water, and only then, momentarily, do his compulsive habits fail to protect him against the truth. It draws together a wide range of heterogeneous material — literary, moral and autobiographical — and brings the elements into a significant relationship with each other. A certain dislocation is the point: to communicate contradiction as well as equivocation.

The reference to the hanging of Henry McCabe, the Malahide Murderer, fixes the action of the story on 10 December 1926, during Beckett's final year as an undergraduate at Trinity College, Dublin.]

DANTE AND THE LOBSTER

It was morning and Belacqua[1] was stuck in the first of the canti in the moon.[2] He was so bogged that he could move neither backward nor forward. Blissful Beatrice was there, Dante also, and she explained the spots on the moon to him. She showed him in the first place where he was at fault, then she put up her own explanation. She had it from God, therefore he could rely on its being accurate in every particular. All he had to do was to follow her step by step. Part one, the refutation, was plain sailing. She made her point clearly, she said what she had to say without fuss or loss of time. But part two, the demonstration, was so dense that Belacqua could not make head or tail of it. The disproof, the reproof, that was patent. But then came the proof, a rapid shorthand of the real facts, and Belacqua was bogged indeed. Bored also, impatient to get on to Piccarda.[3] Still he pored over the enigma, he would not concede himself conquered, he would understand at least the meanings of the words, the order in which they were spoken and the nature of the satisfaction that they conferred on the misinformed poet, so that when they were ended he was refreshed and could raise his heavy head, intending to return thanks and make formal retraction of his old opinion.

He was still running his brain against this impenetrable passage when he heard midday strike. At once he switched his mind off its task. He scooped his fingers under the book and shovelled it back till it lay wholly on his palms. The Divine Comedy face upward on the lectern of his palms. Thus disposed he raised it under his nose and there he slammed it shut. He held it aloft for a time,

1. Belacqua is a slothful lute-maker in Dante, *Purgatorio* IV, 97-139. He was condemned to wait in Antepurgatory for a period equal to his lifespan before being admitted to Purgatory proper, and several details of Beckett's description echo Dante's in the poem. The literal meaning of the name — beautiful water — is ironically appropriate for the baptism of the lobster.
2. *Paradiso* II-IV. Subsequent sentences in this paragraph summarize the stages of *Paradiso* II.
3. Piccarda Donati, in *Paradiso* III, 46-123.

squinting at it angrily, pressing the boards inwards with the heels of his hands. Then he laid it aside.

He leaned back in his chair to feel his mind subside and the itch of this mean quodlibet[4] die down. Nothing could be done until his mind got better and was still, which gradually it did. Then he ventured to consider what he had to do next. There was always something that one had to do next. Three large obligations presented themselves. First lunch, then the lobster, then the Italian lesson. That would do to be going on with. After the Italian lesson he had no very clear idea. No doubt some niggling curriculum had been drawn up by someone for the late afternoon and evening, but he did not know what. In any case it did not matter. What did matter was: one, lunch; two, the lobster; three, the Italian lesson.[5] That was more than enough to be going on with.

Lunch, to come off at all, was a very nice affair. If his lunch was to be enjoyable, and it could be very enjoyable indeed, he must be left in absolute tranquillity to prepare it. But if he were disturbed now, if some brisk tattler were to come bouncing in now with a big idea or a petition, he might just as well not eat at all, for the food would turn to bitterness on his palate or, worse again, taste of nothing. He must be left strictly alone, he must have complete quiet and privacy, to prepare the food for his lunch.

The first thing to do was to lock the door. Now nobody could come at him. He deployed an old Herald and smoothed it out on the table. The rather handsome face of McCabe the assassin stared up at him. Then he lit the gas-ring and unhooked the square flat toaster, asbestos grill, from its nail and set it precisely on the flame. He found he had to lower the flame. Toast must not on any account be done too rapidly. For bread to be toasted as it ought, through and through, it must be done on a mild steady flame. Otherwise you only charred the outsides and left the pith as sodden as before. If there was one thing he abominated more than another it was to feel his teeth meet in a bathos of pith and dough. And it was so easy to do the thing properly. So, he thought, having regulated the flow and adjusted the grill, by the time I have the bread cut that will be just right. Now the long barrel-loaf came out of its biscuit-tin and had its end evened off on the face of McCabe. Two inexorable drives with the bread-saw and a pair of neat rounds of raw bread, the main elements of his meal, lay before him, awaiting his pleasure. The stump of the loaf went back into prison, the crumbs, as though there were no such thing as a sparrow in the wide world, were swept in a fever away, and the slices snatched up and carried to the grill. All these preliminaries were very hasty and impersonal.

It was now that real skill began to be required, it was at this point that the average person began to make a hash of the entire proceedings. He laid his cheek against the soft of the bread, it was spongy and warm, alive. But he would very soon take that plush feel off it, by God but he would very quickly take that fat white look off its face. He lowered the gas a suspicion and plaqued one flabby slab plump down on the glowing fabric, but very pat and precise, so that the whole resembled the Japanese flag. Then on top, there not being room for the two to do evenly side by side, and if you did not do them evenly you might just as well save yourself the trouble of doing them at all, the other round was set to warm. When the first candidate was done, which was only when it was black through and through, it changed places with its comrade, so that now it in its turn lay on top, done to a dead end, black and smoking, waiting till as much could be said of the other.

For the tiller of the field the thing was simple, he had it from his mother. The spots were Cain with his truss of thorns, dispossessed, cursed from the earth, fugitive and vagabond.[6] The moon was that countenance fallen and branded, seared with the first stigma of God's pity, that an outcast might not die quickly. It was a mix-up in the mind of the tiller, but that did not matter. It had been good enough for his mother, it was good enough for him.

Belacqua on his knees before the flame, poring over the grill, controlled every phase of the broiling. It took time, but if a thing was worth doing at all it was worth doing well, that was a true saying. Long before the end the room was full of smoke and the reek of burning. He switched off the gas, when all that human care and skill could do had been done, and restored the toaster to its nail. This was an act of

4. Exercise in disputation.
5. Beckett returns again and again to such tripartite divisions in his writing (e.g., *Murphy*, Chapter 6 and the three 'acts' of *Come and Go*). They mimic and parody the tripartite structure and patterning of the *Divine Comedy*.

6. Referring to *Paradiso* II, 49-51 and *Inferno* XX, 124-26.

dilapidation, for it seared a great weal in the paper. This was hooliganism pure and simple. What the hell did he care? Was it his wall?[7] The same hopeless paper had been there fifty years. It was livid with age. It could not be disimproved.

Next a thick paste of Savora, salt and Cayenne[8] on each round, well worked in while the pores were still open with the heat. No butter, God forbid, just a good forment of mustard and salt and pepper on each round. Butter was a blunder, it made the toast soggy. Buttered toast was all right for Senior Fellows and Salvationists, for such as had nothing but false teeth in their heads. It was no good at all to a fairly strong young rose like Belacqua. This meal that he was at such pains to make ready, he would devour it with a sense of rapture and victory, it would be like smiting the sledded Polacks on the ice.[9] He would snap at it with closed eyes, he would gnash it into a pulp, he would vanquish it utterly with his fangs. Then the anguish of pungency, the pang of the spices, as each mouthful died, scorching his palate, bringing tears.

But he was not yet all set, there was yet much to be done. He had burnt his offering, he had not fully dressed it. Yes, he had put the horse behind the tumbrel.

He clapped the toasted rounds together, he brought them smartly together like cymbals, they clave the one to the other on the viscid salve of Savora. Then he wrapped them up for the time being in any old sheet of paper. Then he made himself ready for the road.

Now the great thing was to avoid being accosted. To be stopped at this stage and have conversational nuisance committed all over him would be a disaster. His whole being was straining forward towards the joy in store. If he were accosted now he might just as well fling his lunch into the gutter and walk straight back home. Sometimes his hunger, more of mind, I need scarcely say, than of body, for this meal amounted to such a frenzy that he would not have hesitated to strike any man rash enough to buttenhole and baulk him, he would have shouldered him out of his path without ceremony. Woe betide the meddler who crossed him when his mind was really set on this meal.

He threaded his way rapidly, his head bowed, through a familiar labyrinth of lanes and suddenly dived into a little family grocery. In the shop they were not surprised. Most days, about this hour, he shot in off the street in this way.

The slab of cheese was prepared. Separated since morning from the piece, it was only waiting for Belacqua to call and take it. Gorgonzola cheese. He knew a man who came from Gorgonzola, his name was Angelo.[10] He had been born in Nice but all his youth had been spent in Gorgonzola. He knew where to look for it. Every day it was there, in the same corner, waiting to be called for. They were very decent obliging people.

He looked sceptically at the cut of cheese. He turned it over on its back to see was the other side any better. The other side was worse. They had laid it better side up, they had practised that little deception. Who shall blame them? He rubbed it. It was sweating. That was something. He stooped and smelt it. A faint fragrance of corruption. What good was that? He didn't want fragrance, he wasn't a bloody gourmet, he wanted a good stench. What he wanted was a good green stenching rotten lump of Gorgonzola cheese, alive, and by God he would have it.

He looked fiercely at the grocer.

'What's that?' he demanded.

The grocer writhed.

'Well?' demanded Belacqua, he was without fear when roused, 'is that the best you can do?'

'In the length and breadth of Dublin' said the grocer 'you won't find a rottener bit this minute.'

Belacqua was furious. The impudent dogsbody, for two pins he would assault him.

'It won't do' he cried, 'do you hear me, it won't do at all. I won't have it.' He ground his teeth.

The grocer, instead of simply washing his hands like Pilate, flung out his arms in a wild crucified gesture of supplication. Sullenly Belacqua undid his packet and slipped the cadaverous tablet of cheese between the hard cold black boards of the toast. He stumped to the door where he whirled round however.

'You heard me?' he cried.

'Sir' said the grocer. This was not a question, nor

7. Probably 39 New Square, Trinity College, Dublin where Beckett roomed during his last two years as an undergraduate.

8. Savora was a proprietary flavouring, Cayenne is a particularly pungent spice.

9. From *Hamlet*, I.1.63.

10. It is not clear if Beckett intends more than a punning overlap of gorgons and angels and the adjective 'nice'. The Gorgonzola cheese establishes connections with Bloom's lunch, in the Lestrygonians episode of *Ulysses*.

yet an expression of acquiescence. The tone in which it was let fall made it quite impossible to know what was in the man's mind. It was a most ingenious riposte.

'I tell you' said Belacqua with great heat 'this won't do at all. If you can't do better than this' he raised the hand that held the packet 'I shall be obliged to go for my cheese elsewhere. Do you mark me?'

'Sir' said the grocer.

He came to the threshold of his store and watched the indignant customer hobble away. Belacqua had a spavined gait, his feet were in ruins, he suffered with them almost continuously. Even in the night they took over from the corns and hammer-toes, and carried on. So that he would press the fringes of his feet desperately against the end-rail of the bed or better again, reach down with his hand and drag them up and back towards the instep. Skill and patience could disperse the pain, but there it was, complicating his night's rest.

The grocer, without closing his eyes or taking them off the receding figure, blew his nose in the skirt of his apron. Being a warm-hearted human man he felt sympathy and pity for this queer customer who always looked ill and dejected. But at the same time he was a small tradesman, don't forget that, with a small tradesman's sense of personal dignity and what was what. Thruppence, he cast it up, thruppence worth of cheese per day, one and a tanner[11] per week. No, he would fawn on no man for that, no, not on the best in the land. He had his pride.

Stumbling along by devious ways towards the lowly public where he was expected, in the sense that the entry of his grotesque person would provoke no comment or laughter, Belacqua gradually got the upper hand of his choler. Now that lunch was as good as a fait accompli, because the incontinent bosthoons[12] of his own class, itching to pass on a big idea or inflict an appointment, were seldom at large in this shabby quarter of the city, he was free to consider items two and three, the lobster and the lesson, in closer detail.

At a quarter to three he was due at the School.[13] Say five to three. The public closed, the fishmonger reopened, at half-past two. Assuming then that his lousy old bitch of an aunt had given her order in good time that morning, with strict injunctions that it should be ready and waiting so that her blackguard boy should on no account be delayed when he called for it first thing in the afternoon, it would be time enough if he left the public as it closed, he could remain on till the last moment. Benissimo. He had half-a-crown. That was two pints of draught anyway and perhaps a bottle to wind up with. Their bottled stout was particularly excellent and well up. And he would still be left with enough coppers to buy a Herald and take a tram if he felt tired or was pinched for time. Always assuming, of course, that the lobster was all ready to be handed over. God damn these tradesmen, he thought, you can never rely on them. He had not done an exercise but that did not matter. His Professoressa was so charming and remarkable. Signorina Adriana Ottolenghi! He did not believe it possible for a woman to be more intelligent or better informed than the little Ottolenghi. So he had set her on a pedestal in his mind, apart from other women. She had said last day that they would read Il Cinque Maggio together. But she would not mind if he told her, as he proposed to, in Italian, he would frame a shining phrase on his way from the public, that he would prefer to postpone the Cinque Maggio to another occasion. Manzoni was an old woman, Napoleon was another. Napoleone di mezza calzetta, fa l'amore a Giacominetta.[14] Why did he think of Manzoni as an old woman? Why did he do him that injustice? Pellico[15] was another. They were all old maids, suffragettes. He must ask his Signorina where he could have received that impression, that the nineteenth century in Italy was full of old hens trying to cluck like Pindar.[16] Carducci was another. Also about the spots on the moon. If she could not tell him there and then she would make it up, only too gladly, against the next time. Everything was all set now and in order. Bating, of course, the lobster, which had to remain

11. An informal word for six (old) pence.
12. Awkward fellows, spiritless, senseless persons (from Irish *bastún*).
13. Beckett took extra Italian lessons at the Berlitz School of Languages, situated at 4-5 Grafton Stret, while he was a student at Trinity College. His teacher was Signora Bianca Esposito, of whom the portrait of Ottolenghi is a Beatrice-tinged but accurate depiction.
14. Beckett studied Manzoni, Carducci and other nineteenth-century writers in his first and third years at Trinity College (1923-24, 1925-26). The Italian quotation appears to be Beckett's invention, and may be translated 'Napoleon in short pants makes love to Giacominetta.' In *This Quarter,* it is printed as two lines of verse, with a full stop for the comma.
15. Silvio Pellico (1789-1854), Italian dramatic poet and author of *Francesca da Rimini* (1815).
16. Greek lyric poet, famous for the boldness and elevation of his odes.

an incalculable factor. He must just hope for the best. And expect the worst, he thought gaily, diving into the public, as usual.

Belacqua drew near to the school, quite happy, for all had gone swimmingly. The lunch had been a notable success, it would abide as a standard in his mind. Indeed he could not imagine its ever being superseded. And such a pale soapy piece of cheese to prove so strong! He must only conclude that he had been abusing himself all these years in relating the strength of cheese directly to its greenness. We live and learn, that was a true saying. Also his teeth and jaws had been in heaven, splinters of vanquished toast spraying forth at each gnash. It was like eating glass. His mouth burned and ached with the exploit. Then the food had been further spiced by the intelligence, transmitted in a low tragic voice across the counter by Oliver the improver,[17] that the Malahide murderer's petition for mercy, signed by half the land, having been rejected, the man must swing at dawn in Mountjoy and nothing could save him. Ellis the hangman was even now on his way. Belacqua, tearing at the sandwich and swilling the precious stout, pondered on McCabe in his cell.

The lobster was ready after all, the man handed it over instanter, and with such a pleasant smile. Really a little bit of courtesy and goodwill went a long way in this world. A smile and a cheerful word from a common working-man and the face of the world was brightened. And it was so easy, a mere question of muscular control.

'Lepping' he said cheerfully, handing it over.

'Lepping?' said Belacqua. What on earth was that?[18]

'Lepping fresh, sir' said the man, 'fresh in this morning.'

Now Belacqua, on the analogy of mackerel and other fish that he had heard described as lepping fresh when they had been taken but an hour or two previously, supposed the man to mean that the lobster had very recently been killed.

Signorina Adriana Ottolenghi was waiting in the little front room off the hall, which Belacqua was naturally inclined to think of rather as the vestibule. That was her room, the Italian room. On the same side, but at the back, was the French room. God knows where the German room was. Who cared about the German room anyway?

He hung up his coat and hat, laid the long knobby brown-paper parcel on the hall-table, and went prestly in to the Ottolenghi.

After about half-an-hour of this and that obiter, she complimented him on his grasp of the language.

'You make rapid progress' she said in her ruined voice.

There subsisted as much of the Ottolenghi as might be expected to of the person of a lady of a certain age who had found being young and beautiful and pure more of a bore than anything else.

Belacqua, dissembling his great pleasure, laid open the moon enigma.

'Yes' she said 'I know the passage. It is a famous teaser. Off-hand I cannot tell you, but I will look it up when I get home.'

The sweet creature! She would look it up in her big Dante when she got home. What a woman!

'It occurred to me' she said 'apropos of I don't know what, that you might do worse than make up Dante's rare movements of compassion in Hell. That used to be' her past tenses were always sorrowful 'a favourite question.'

He assumed an expression of profundity.

'In that connexion' he said 'I recall one superb pun anyway: "qui vive la pietà quando è ben morta . . ."'[19]

She said nothing.

'Is it not a great phrase?' he gushed.

She said nothing.

'Now' he said like a fool 'I wonder how you could translate that?'

Still she said nothing. Then:

'Do you think' she murmured 'it is absolutely necessary to translate it?'

Sounds as of conflict were borne in from the hall. Then silence. A knuckle tambourined on the door, it flew open and lo it was Mlle Glain, the French instructress, clutching her cat, her eyes out on stalks, in a state of the greatest agitation.

'Oh' she gasped 'forgive me. I intrude, but what was in the bag?'

'The bag?' said the Ottolenghi.

17. The earlier version of the story in *This Quarter* makes clear that Beckett means the barman. The petition for mercy is not reported in the newspapers, and appears to be Beckett's invention.

18. A variant of leaping, common enough in Ireland. Compare *prestly* (=promptly) and *instanter* (=forthwith), both before; and *flitters* (=torn pieces) later in the piece, which are obsolete or rare in England, but less surprising in an Irish context.

19. See headnote p. 238.

Mlle Glain took a French step forward.

'The parcel' she buried her face in the cat 'the parcel in the hall.'

Belacqua spoke up composedly.

'Mine' he said, 'a fish.'

He did not know the French for lobster. Fish would do very well. Fish had been good enough for Jesus Christ, Son of God, Saviour.[20] It was good enough for Mlle Glain.

'Oh' said Mlle Glain, inexpressibly relieved, 'I caught him in the nick of time.' She administered a tap to the cat. 'He would have tore it to flitters.'

Belacqua began to feel a little anxious.

'Did he actually get at it?' he said.

'No no' said Mlle Glain 'I caught him just in time. But I did not know' with a bluestocking snigger 'what it might be, so I thought I had better come and ask.'

Base prying bitch.

The Ottolenghi was faintly amused.

'Puisqu'il n'y a pas de mal . . .' she said with great fatigue and elegance.

'Heureusement' it was clear at once that Mlle Glain was devout 'heureusement'.[21]

Chastening the cat with little skelps she took herself off. The grey hairs of her maidenhead screamed at Belacqua. A devout, virginal bluestocking, honing after a penny's worth of scandal.

'Where were we?' said Belacqua.

But Neapolitan patience has its limits.

'Where are we ever?' cried the Ottolenghi, 'where we were, as we were.'

Belacqua drew near to the house of his aunt. Let us call it Winter, that dusk may fall now and a moon rise. At the corner of the street a horse was down and a man sat on its head. I know, thought Belacqua, that that is considered the right thing to do. But why? A lamplighter flew by on his bike, tilting with his pole at the standards, jousting a little yellow light into the evening. A poorly-dressed couple stood in the bay of a pretentious gateway, she sagging against the railings, her head lowered, he standing facing her. He stood up close to her, his hands dangled by his sides. Where we were, thought Belacqua, as we were. He walked on, gripping his parcel. Why not piety and pity both, even down below? Why not mercy and Godliness together? A little mercy in the stress of sacrifice, a little mercy to rejoice against judgment. He thought of Jonah and the gourd and the pity of a jealous God on Nineveh.[22] And poor McCabe, he would get it in the neck at dawn. What was he doing now, how was he feeling? He would relish one more meal, one more night.

His aunt was in the garden, tending whatever flowers die at that time of year. She embraced him and together they went down into the bowels of the earth, into the kitchen in the basement. She took the parcel and undid it and abruptly the lobster[23] was on the table, on the oilcloth, discovered.

'They assured me it was fresh' said Belacqua.

Suddenly he saw the creature move, this neuter creature. Definitely it changed its position. His hand flew to his mouth.

'Christ!' he said 'it's alive.'

His aunt looked at the lobster. It moved again. It made a faint nervous act of life on the oilcloth. They stood above it, looking down on it, exposed cruciform on the oilcloth. It shuddered again. Belacqua felt he would be sick.

'My God' he whined 'it's alive, what'll we do?'

The aunt simply had to laugh. She bustled off to the pantry to fetch her smart apron, leaving him goggling down at the lobster, and came back with it on and her sleeves rolled up, all business.

'Well' she said 'it is to be hoped so, indeed.'

'All this time' muttered Belacqua. Then, suddenly aware of her hideous equipment: 'What are you going to do?' he cried.

'Boil the beast' she said, 'what else?'

'But it's not dead' protested Belacqua 'you can't boil it like that.'

She looked at him in astonishment. Had he taken leave of his senses.

'Have sense' she said sharply, 'lobsters are always boiled alive. They must be.' She caught up the lobster and laid it on its back. It trembled. 'They feel nothing' she said.

In the depths of the sea it had crept into the cruel pot. For hours, in the midst of its enemies, it had breathed secretly. It had survived the Frenchwoman's cat and his witless clutch. Now it was going alive into scalding water. It had to. Take into the air my quiet breath.[24]

20. The traditional play on Christ's name in Greek being an anagram of the word for fish, IXOYE.

21. Since there's no harm done . . . . Thank goodness . . . . successfully.

22. Alluding to Jonah 4.4-11; 3.10.

23. Interestingly, in *This Quarter* the text reads 'the red lobster'.

24. Keats, *Ode to a Nightingale,* line 54.

Belacqua looked at the old parchment of her face, grey in the dim kitchen.

'You make a fuss' she said angrily 'and upset me and then lash into it for your dinner.'

She lifted the lobster clear of the table. It had about thirty seconds to live.

Well, thought Belacqua, it's a quick death, God help us all.

It is not.

RECENT IRISH POETRY (1934)

[This essay was published in *The Bookman* for August 1934 under the pseudonym Andrew Belis. It had very little influence, although a similar analysis was attempted by A. Rivallan, *Littérature irlandaise contemporaine* (Paris: Hachette, 1939), and was forgotten by Beckett until it was discovered and reprinted nearly forty years later.

Beckett wrote separately on Thomas MacGreevy (who had introduced him to Joyce in 1928) and on Denis Devlin, as well as on O'Casey, Jack B. Yeats and, of course, on Joyce. But the present essay constitutes his most comprehensive description of how he understood his relationship to Irish literature when he himself began to write. His preferences are clarified by a useful selection edited by Michael Smith, *Irish Poetry. The Thirties Generation* (Dublin: Raven Arts, 1983). MacGreevy's *Collected Poems* were edited by Thomas Dillon Redshaw (Dublin: New Writers' Press, 1971; Dublin: Raven Arts, 1983); Devlin's by Brian Coffey (Dublin: The Dolmen Press, 1964); and Coffey himself is still writing, his latest publications being *Death of Hektor* (London: Menard Press, 1982) and *Chanterelles* (Cork: The Melmoth Press, 1985). Most of the lesser figures and 'antiquarians', and their publications, can be traced through Robert Hogan (ed.), *Dictionary of Irish Literature* (Westport, Connecticut: Greenwood Press, 1979; Dublin: Gill and Macmillan, 1980).

Beckett's attitude towards W. B. Yeats as a historical influence should not obscure such coincidences as exist, as with Yeats's ideas of selfhood and purgatory. The text *Lessness* (p. 290 below) might be understood as an extended meditation on the line from Yeats's poem, *The Black Tower*: 'There in the tomb stand the dead upright.' Beckett's feelings of kinship with other figures of the Revival, such as Synge and George Moore, should also not be obscured by his commitment to the alternative role exemplified by Joyce.]

I propose, as rough principle of individuation in this essay, the degree in which the younger Irish poets evince awareness of the new thing that has happened, or the old thing that has happened again, namely the breakdown of the object, whether current, historical, mythical or spook. The thermolaters — and they pullulate in Ireland — adoring the stuff of song as incorruptible, uninjurable and unchangeable, never at a loss to know when they are in the Presence, would no doubt like this amended to breakdown of the subject. It comes to the same thing — rupture of the lines of communication.

The artist who is aware of this may state the space that intervenes between him and the world of objects; he may state it as no-man's-land, Hellespont or vacuum, according as he happens to be feeling resentful, nostalgic or merely depressed. A picture by Mr Jack Yeats,[1] Mr Eliot's 'Waste Land', are notable statements of this kind. Or he may celebrate the cold comforts of apperception. He may even record his findings, if he is a man of great personal courage. Those who are not aware of the rupture, or in whom the velleity of becoming so was suppressed as a nuisance at its inception, will continue to purvey those articles which, in Ireland at least, had ceased to be valid even before the literary advisers to J. M. Synge found themselves prematurely obliged to look elsewhere for a creative hack. These are the antiquarians, delivering with the altitudinous complacency of the Victorian Gael the Ossianic goods.[2]

Thus contemporary Irish poets may be divided into antiquarians and others, the former in the majority, the latter kindly noticed by Mr W. B. Yeats as 'the fish that lie gasping on the shore',[3] suggesting that they might at least learn to expire with an air. This position, needless to say, is not peculiar to Ireland or anywhere else. The issue between the conventional and the actual never lapses, not even when the conventional and the actual are most congruent. But it is especially acute

1. Jack B. Yeats (1871-1957), Ireland's foremost painter and brother of the poet. Beckett made his acquaintance through Thomas MacGreevy, and greatly admired his work (see *Disjecta* — London: Calder, 1983 — pp. 89-90, 95-97, 148-49; Deirdre Bair, *Samuel Beckett. A Biography* — London: Picador, 1980 — pp. 107-09, 173, 335).
2. James Macpherson (1736-96) published the work by which he is best known in the guise of translations from the Scots Gaelic of Ossian, son of Fingal, a bard of the third century — heroic narratives that mingle nationalistic, antiquarian and romantic interests.
3. The last line of Yeats's 'Three Movements' (*The Winding Stair*, 1933) is 'What are all those fish that lie gasping on the strand?'

in Ireland, thanks to the technique of our leading twilighters.

The device common to the poets of the Revival and after, in the use of which even beyond the jewels of language they are at one, is that of flight from self-awareness, and as such might perhaps be described as a convenience. At the centre there is no theme. Why not? Because the centre is simply not that kind of girl, and no more about it. And without a theme there can be no poem, as witness the exclamation of Mr Yeats's 'fánatic heart':[4] 'What, be a singer born and lack a theme!'[5] ('The Winding Stair'). But the circumference is an iridescence of themes — Oisin, Cuchulain, Maeve, Tir-nanog, the Táin Bo Cuailgne [*sic*], Yoga, the Crone of Beare[6] — segment after segment of cut-and-dried sanctity and loveliness. There are the specialists, but no monopolies, each poet being left perfect liberty to make his selection. The poem of poems would embrace the sense of confinement, the getaway, the vicissitudes of the road, the wan bliss on the rim. But a large degree of freedom may enter into the montage of these components, and it is very often in virtue of this, when the tics of mere form are in abeyance, that attributions are to be made. Thus typically the first may be scarcely perceptible in Mr Colum and even less so in Mr Stephens, the second predominate in Mr Yeats, the third be acutely dilated by Miss Pamela Travers or the Rev. Monk Gibbon, and the fourth to all intents and purposes discarded by George Russell[7] who, when thoroughly galvanized by the protracted apathies, rigidities and abstractions, enters his heart's desire with such precipitation as positively to protrude into the void.

What further interest can attach to such assumptions as those on which the convention has for so long taken its ease, namely, that the first condition of any poem is an accredited theme, and that in self-perception there is no theme, but at best sufficient *vis a tergo*[8] to land the practitioner into the correct scenery, where the self is either most happily obliterated or else so improved and enlarged that it can be mistaken for part of the *décor*? None but the academic. And it is in this connection that our lately founded Academy[9] may be said to meet a need and enjoy a function.

Mr W. B. Yeats, as he wove the best embroideries, so he is more alive than any of his contemporaries or scholars to the superannuation of these, and to the virtues of a verse that shall be nudist. 'There's more enterprise in going naked.'[10] It eliminates swank — unless of course the song has something to swank about. His bequest in 'The Tower' of his pride and faith to the 'young upstanding men'[11] has something almost second-best bed, as though he knew that they would be embarrassed to find an application for those dispositions. Yet when he speaks, in his preface to Senator Gogarty's 'Wild Apples',[12] of the 'sense of hardship borne and chosen out of pride' as the ultimate theme of the Irish writer, it is as though he were to derive in direct descent the very latest prize canary from that fabulous bird, the mesozoic pelican, addicted, though childless, to self-eviscerations.

Mr James Stephens in 'Theme and Variation' (1930) and 'Strict Joy' (1931), remains in his annexe of the tradition, where the poet appears as beauty expert:

> Yea, wonder is that he has done,
> For all that is beneath the sun
> By magic he transfigures to
> A better sound, a finer view.
>
> ('Theme and Variations')

4. The phrase recurs in the refrain of Yeats's 'Remorse for Intemperate Speech' (*The Winding Stair*), to which Yeats added a note explaining that he pronounced the word in 'the older and more Irish way'.
5. From 'Vacillation', Part VII, though the original line ends in a question mark.
6. Oisin, Cuchulain and Maeve are figures from the Irish legendary past, part of the Fenian cycle. Tir-nanog is literally 'Land of the Ever-Young'. *Táin Bo Cuailnge* is the ancient Irish prose epic from the Ulster cycle, in which Cuchulain and Maeve are characters. Yoga is the odd one out in this list, unless one considers all the ingredients as odd. The Crone of Beare is the protagonist of a number of early Irish poems, quite separate from the Ulster and Fenian cycles.
7. Padraic Colum (1881-1972), whose emergence was fostered by W. B. Yeats and Lady Gregory, presents an idyllic picture-book Ireland in a simple narrative style. James Stephens (1880 or 1882-1950) is best-known for his tales based on Irish folklore and folklife, characterized by fantasy and charm. Pamela Travers was a friend and assistant to AE, among other things. Monk Gibbon (1896-1987), like Miss Travers, wrote as much for an English as for an Irish audience, in a rather conventionally poetic way. George Russell (1867-1935), better-known as AE, whose paintings, poetry and prose all tend to the mystically vague.
8. A force operating from behind, a propulsive force.
9. Yeats and Shaw founded the Irish Academy of Letters in 1932.
10. The close of Yeats's 'A Coat' (*Responsibilities*, 1914), though Yeats wrote 'walking naked'.
11. 'The Tower', Part III (in the eponymous volume, 1928). The same poem provides the title and some of the text of Beckett's late television play, '*. . . but the clouds . . .*'
12. Oliver St John Gogarty's collection was published in 1928.

Then follows the psychometricization of Plotinus, rather less of a success than that practised on Descartes by La Fontaine.[13] When the theme, without which there can be no poem, is in itself presentable, then its transmission is a mere question of metrical adjustments; but when it is not, when it is a mournful or a miserable thing, then it must be smartened up:

> . . . Because all things transfer
> From what they seem to what they truly are
> When they are innocently brooded on —
> And so the poet makes grief beautiful.
>
> ('Strict Joy')

'Reverie on a Rose' is a good sample of this process — and a gloss on its innocency.

Mr Austin Clarke, having declared himself, in his 'Cattle-drive in Connaught' (1925), a follower of 'that most famous juggler, Mannanaun', continues in 'The Pilgrimage' (1920) to display the 'trick of tongue or two' and to remove, by means of ingenious metrical operations, 'the clapper from the bell of rhyme.'[14] The fully licensed stock-in-trade from Aisling to Red Branch Bundling,[15] is his to command. Here the need for formal justifications, more acute in Mr Clarke than in Mr Higgins,[16] serves to screen the deeper need that must not be avowed.

Though in his 'Island Blood' (1925), 'The Dark Breed' (1927) and 'Arable Holdings' (1933) Mr Higgins has accumulated a greater number of 'By Gods' than all the other antiquarians put together, though he is less of the 'glimmering fawn' than Mr Russell and less of the lilter and lisper than Mr Colum or Mr Stephens, yet he is still victim of the centrifugal daemon:

> Come away to this holy air . . .
> Come away to this simple lake
> And learn at the voice of a bird
> To view with their music and make
> New worlds in a word.
>
> ('Island Blood')

It is agreeable, if unreasonable, to connect this impulse, the entire Celtic drill of extraversion, with Mr Higgins's blackthorn stick, thus addressed:

> And here, as in green days you were the perch,
> You're now the prop of song . . .
>
> ('Arable Holdings')

His verses have what Ledwidge's[17] had, what all modern nature poetry excepting Wordsworth's has, a good smell of dung, most refreshing after all the attar of far off, most secret and inviolate rose.[18] And surely it is a great pity that the discernment enabling Mr Higgins to see his native land as 'an Easter Island in the Western Sea' should be so intolerant of its own company. It is symptomatic that both Mr Clarke and Mr Higgins are now taking up prose.

In 'For Daws to Peck At' (1929) and 'Seventeen Sonnets' (1932), the Rev. Monk Gibbon follows his secret heart from the 'lack-luck lot'. He is the poet of children ('Chacun Son Goût'), and as such is bound to consider thought a microbe:

> And, though the tune's of little count
> And knowledge more than all to me,
> Who knows what music may have died
> When that small seed fell silently?
>
> ('For Daws To Peck At')

The sonnets, with so many definite and indefinite articles excised, recall the succinctness of the Cambridge Experimenters.[19]

These, to whom Mr Brian O'Higgins, An Philibin and Miss Large[20] may conveniently be annexed, are the chief of the younger antiquarians.

13. Plotinus (205-70), Greek philosopher and founder of Neoplatonism. Jean de la Fontaine (1621-95), French poet, famous for his *Fables* (1668-94). La Fontaine combatted the Cartesian doctrine of *bêtes-machines* — that animals are merely automata, acting mechanically without volition or reasoning powers — implicity throughout his *Fables* and explicitly in his *Discourses à Mme de la Sablière* (1679).
14. The first two quotations are *variatim* from the 'Induction' to Clarke's *The Cattledrive in Connaught* (1925), p. 9; the third is from the 'Commentary' to Clarke's *Pilgrimage* (1929 [*sic*]), p. 43, which Beckett parodied in his comments on Ticklepenny's prosodoturfy (*Murphy* — London: Picador, 1973 — p. 53).
15. i.e. from the vision-poem (a dominant form in Munster in the eighteenth century) to Ulster cycle 'couplings'.
16. F. R. Higgins (1896-1941), whose earlier poetry reflects his passionate interest in Irish folk tradition.
17. Francis Ledwidge (1887-1917), a self-educated Irish Georgian poet from County Meath; he died at Ypres.
18. From the opening line of W. B. Yeats's 'The Secret Rose' in *The Wind Among the Reeds* (1899).
19. Jacob Bronowski, William Empson, Humphry Jennings, George Reavey, Hugh Sykes-Davies, Julian Trevelyan and others associated with the Cambridge magazine, *Experiment*, and also published alongside Beckett in *The European Caravan* and *This Quarter*. (Monk Gibbon was educated at Oxford; the appellation 'Rev.' is jocular.)
20. Brian O'Higgins was best-known for his verses on 'Celtic' Christmas cards. An Philibin was the pen-name of John Pollock (1887-1964), a Dublin doctor, who wrote novels and plays, as well as poetry, under this pseudonym which means 'The Lapwing'. Miss Large cannot be traced, although 'she' is said to appear as a sexual double-entendre in Austin Clarke's papers.

Mr Thomas MacGreevy[21] is best described as an independent, occupying a position intermediate between the above and the poor fish, in the sense that he neither excludes self-perception from his work nor postulates the object as inaccessible. But he knows how to wait for the thing to happen, how not to beg the fact of this 'bitch of a world' — inarticulate earth and inscrutable heaven:

I labour in a barren place,
Alone, self-conscious, frightened, blundering;
Far away, stars wheeling in space,
About my feet, earth voices whispering.
('Poems, 1934')

And when it does happen and he sees, 'far as sensitive eyesight could see', whatever happens to be dispensed, *gile na gile* or empty hearths, it is the act and not the object of perception that matters. Mr MacGreevy is an existentialist in verse, the Titchener[22] of the modern lyric. It is in virtue of this quality of inevitable unveiling that his poems may be called elucidations, the vision without the dip, and probably the most important contribution to post-War Irish poetry.

There is much in Mrs Blanaid Salkeld's[23] 'Hello Eternity' (1933) that is personal and moving, when not rendered blue in the face by the sonnet form. What is badly needed at the present moment is some small Malherbe[24] of free verse to sit on the sonnet and put it out of action for two hundred years at least. Perhaps Mr Pound . . .? Other Irish sonneteers are Mr Erik [*sic*] Dodds ('Thirty-two poems', 1929) and Mr Francis Macnamara ('Marionettes', 1909),[25] but only in the leisure moments of a university professor and a student of social theory respectively. The influence of Rossetti is strong in Mr Macnamara. The Oxford Georgians have left their mark on Mr Dodds.

In 'Man Poem' (1919) Mr Percy Usher,[26] [*sic*] best known as translator of Merriman's 'Midnight Court', deals with himself and the vacuum in a manner that abides no question. One would like to see this work, before it is improved out of existence, safely between the boards.

Mr Francis Stuart[27] is of course best known as a novelist, but he writes verse. So does Mr R. N. D. Wilson. So does Mr Leslie Yodaiken[28] when his politics let him. So I am sure do Mr Frank O'Connor and Mr Seán O'Faoláin — also best known as novelists of course. And I know that Mr Seán O'Casey does, having read a poem of his in *Time and Tide.*[29]

In 'Primordia Caeca' (1927) Mr Lyle Donaghy[30] undertook a regular *Saison en Enfer*:

Enter again into the womb;
  be saturate with night;
  let the vain soul be satisfied,
Descend into the dark cell;
  look on the unnatured, undistinguished pulp;
  peruse the incipient page.
Retrace the way come blindly;
  from centre and cause revisited,
  draw the pure being up.

It is drawn up, but in the unfinished condition made manifest in his 'Flute Over the Valley' (1931), which contains however a fine poem about a steam-roller. Some years ago Mr Donaghy published an admirable 'objectless' poem — 'The Fort' — in the *Criterion.* Another volume, 'Into the Light', is announced as impending. May it be down into the light.

Mr Geoffrey Taylor,[31] in his 'Withering of the

21. Beckett's quotations are from MacGreevy's 'De Civitate Hominum', 'Nocturne' (complete), 'Gioconda' and *'Crón Tráth Na nDeíthe'* (*Poems* — 1934 — pp. 4, 3, 52, 21). *Gile na gile,* 'brightness most bright,' is itself the title of a famous eighteenth-century poem by Aogán Ó Rathaille. MacGreevy's poems, 'Fragments' and 'Sour Swan' (ibid., pp. 40, 56-57), turn on the same line from *Inferno* XX, 28 as 'Dante and the Lobster'. For later comments by Beckett on MacGreevy (1893-1967), see *Disjecta,* pp. 68-69, 95-97, and Bair index, s.v.
22. E. B. Titchener (1867-1927) was instrumental in introducing the new, experimental German psychology (Külpe and Wundt) to English-speaking students.
23. Blanaid Salkeld (1880-1959), poet and actress. Her grand-daughter, Beatrice, married Brendan Behan.
24. François de Malherbe (1555-1628), French poet, literary legislator, architect of Classicism.
25. E. R. Dodds (1893-1979), born in Northern Ireland and educated at Oxford, published *Thirty-two poems* in 1929 while he was professor of Greek at Birmingham University.
26. Percival Arland Ussher (1899-1980), self-taught Irish scholar and philosophical belle-lettrist.
27. Francis Stuart (born 1902), whose first volume was a collection of verse, *We Have Kept the Faith* (1923), but thereafter he turned increasingly to prose fiction.
28. R. N. D. Wilson was a friend of Austin Clarke. Leslie Yodaiken (1912-64) was a freelance writer and anthologist, and politically radical.
29. O'Casey published two poems in *Time and Tide* in 1933-34: 'Wisdom and Life' (23 June 1934) and 'She will give me rest' (7 July 1934), both collected in *Windfalls,* which Beckett reviewed (*Disjecta,* pp. 82-83).
30. Lyle Donaghy (1902-47) whose *Into the Light* was published by The Cuala Press in 1934.
31. Geoffrey Taylor (1900-56), author of *A Dash of Garlic* (1933) and later literary editor of *The Bell.*

Fig-leaf' and 'It Was Not Jones', performed a very diverting ballet away from the pundits. But I do not know that he has done anything since.

Mr Denis Devlin and Mr Brian Coffey are without question the most interesting of the youngest generation of Irish poets, but I do not propose to disoblige them by quoting from the volume of verse which they published jointly in 1930. Since then they have submitted themselves to the influences of those poets least concerned with evading the bankrupt relationship referred to at the opening of this essay — Corbière, Rimbaud, Laforgue, the *surréalistes* and Mr Eliot, perhaps also to those of Mr Pound — with results that constitute already the nucleus of a living poetic in Ireland:

Phrases twisted through other
Reasons reasons disproofs
Phrases lying low
Proving invalid that reason
With which I prove its truth
Identity obscured
Like the reflections of
One mirror in another
Reasons reasons disproofs.[32]

It is no disparagement of Mr Devlin to observe that this is still too much by the grace of Eluard.[33] What matters is that it does not proceed from the *Gossoons Wunderhorn*[34] of that Irish Romantic Arnim-Brentano combination, Sir Samuel Ferguson[35] and Standish O'Grady,[36] and that it admits — stupendous innovation — the existence of the author. *Es wandelt niemand ungestraft unter Palmen* is peculiarly applicable to these islands, where pigeons meet with such encouragements. But it is preferable to dying of mirage.

Of Mr Niall Sheridan and Mr Donagh MacDonagh[37] I know nothing, except that they have just published 'Twenty Poems' between them; of Miss Irene Haugh, nothing, except that she has just published 'The Valley of the Bells', and that her chief concern, in the words of her *Dublin Magazine* reviewer, is God; of Mr Niall Montgomery's poetry, nothing at all.[38]

32. From Devlin's 'Est Prodest', collected in his *Intercessions* (1937), pp. 52 and later revised. Beckett's review of *Intercessions* is included in *Disjecta*, pp. 91-94. It should be compared with MacGreevy's review, which sets Devlin's volume against Beckett's *Echo's Bones*, in *Ireland Today* II (October 1937), 81-82.
33. Paul Eluard (1895-1952), a leader of the *Surréalistes*, whom Beckett, Devlin and Coffey translated.
34. A play on words involving the Anglo-Irish word *gossoon* (lackey or servant-boy) and *Das Knaben Wunderhorn* (1806-08), a collection of German folk songs by Arnim and Brentano. The German sentence derives from Ottilie's diary in Goethe's *Die Wahlverwandtschaften* (1809) Part 2, Chapter 7, made famous by its use as a leitmotiv in Fontane's novel *L'Adultera* (1882) Chapter 12, 'Unter Palmen'. It might be translated here: 'No one walks under a palm tree with impunity.'
35. Sir Samuel Ferguson (1810-86), best-known for his work putting legends into Irish verse.
36. Standish O'Grady (1846-1928), author of *History of Ireland* (1878, 1880) and numerous adventure novels based on early Irish sources, which made him, in the eyes of Yeats and AE, 'the father of the Irish Renaissance'.
37. Niall Sheridan (born 1912), a UCD contemporary of Denis Devlin and Brian Coffey. In 1934 he published *20 Poems* with Donagh MacDonagh (1912-68), the son of Thomas MacDonagh, one of the 1916 martyrs.
38. Niall Montgomery (1914-87), a school and college contemporary of Denis Devlin, who never published as much as his abilities might have led one to hope.

from:
COLLECTED POEMS 1930-1978 (1984)

['Gnome' (inspired, Beckett has said, by Goethe's *Xenien*) was written after his resignation from Trinity College, Dublin in January 1932 and was published in the *Dublin Magazine* for July-September 1934. The title connects the Greek word *gnosis,* knowledge, with the sense of a diminished, shrivelled being. In earlier versions, 'a' in the third line read 'the'; the change was made when the poem was collected in 1977.]

Gnome

Spend the years of learning squandering
Courage for the years of wandering
Through a world politely turning
From the loutishness of learning

1934

[The next poem stands last in the eponymous collection, *Echo's Bones*, published in Paris in 1935. The story of Echo and Narcissus comes originally from Ovid's *Metamorphoses* III, 341-401, and images a dualistic theme that threads Beckett's previous poems. In line 3, compare Prospero in *The Tempest*, IV.1.147; in line 4, 'gantelope' is an archaic form of 'gauntlet' ('running the gauntlet'), which contains the image of an antelope.]

Echo's Bones

asylum under my tread all this day
their muffled revels as the flesh falls
breaking without fear or favour wind
the gantelope of sense and nonsense run
taken by the maggots for what they are

1935

['Dieppe', composed in French in 1937, was suggested by a passage in Hölderlin's *Der Spaziergang.* The English translation was first published in *The Irish Times,* 9 June 1945, and was collected along with the French original in *Poems in English* (1961). In the version published in 1945 and 1961, 'lights of old' read 'lighted town'. The revision was made for *Collected Poems in English and French* (1977).]

Dieppe

encore le dernier reflux
le galet mort
le demi-tour puis les pas
vers les vieilles lumières

Dieppe

again the last ebb
the dead shingle
the turning then the steps
towards the lights of old

['Saint-Lô' commemorates the period Beckett spent working with the Red Cross at this devastated town in Normandy, on the river Vire (French *virer,* to turn, Latin *vitrare,* to tremble, gleam), in 1945-46. He described his experiences at greater length in a radio talk (published in Eoin O'Brien, *The Beckett Country* — Dublin: Black Cat, 1986 — Chapter 10, with photographs), and in John Calder (ed.), *As No Other Dare Fail* — London: Calder, 1986 — pp. 71-76). The poem was first published in *The Irish Times,* 24 June 1946, where line 3 reads 'and the old mind/ghost-abandoned'. The present version was arrived at when the poem was collected in *Poems in English* (1961).]

Saint-Lô

Vire will wind in other shadows
unborn through the bright ways tremble
and the old mind ghost-forsaken
sink into its havoc

1946

[The French original of the next poem is reported to have been written by Beckett on Killiney Strand, Co. Dublin, during a summer visit to his mother. The threshold image recurs throughout the later pages of *The Unnamable,* the novel he was writing at the time. The French and English versions were first published in *transition 48* (1948) and were first collected in *Poems in English* (1961).]

je suis ce cours de sable qui glisse
entre le galet et la dune
la pluie d'été pleut sur ma vie
sur moi ma vie qui me fuit me poursuit
et finira le jour de son commencement

cher instant je te vois
dans ce rideau de brume qui recule
où je n'aurai plus à fouler ces longs seuils mouvants
et vivrai le temps d'une porte
qui s'ouvre et se referme

---

my way is in the sand flowing
between the shingle and the dune
the summer rain rains on my life
on me my life harrying fleeing
to its beginning to its end

my peace is there in the receding mist
when I may cease from treading these long shifting
  thresholds
and live the space of a door
that opens and shuts

['I would like my love to die' was first published in *transition 48* in French, with facing English translation. In that version, the last two lines of the French read 'et dans les rues/pleurant la seule qui m'ait aimé'; and the last line of the English reads 'mourning the first and last to love me'. When the poem was collected in *Poems in English* (1961), the French version was changed to its present form and the English version was left as first published. Raymond Federman and John Fletcher (eds), *Samuel Beckett: His Works and His Critics* (Berkeley: University of California Press, 1970), p. 52, record variants introduced by Beckett into a broadcast made in 1966. When *Poems in English* was reprinted in 1971, Beckett supplied an alternative last line, 'mourning she who sought to love me'. The final version given here was arrived at in *Collected Poems* (1977). Compare Yeats's poem, 'He wishes his Beloved were Dead' in *The Wind Among the Reeds* (1899).]

je voudrais que mon amour meure
qu'il pleuve sur le cimetière
et les ruelles où je vais
pleurant celle qui crut m'aimer

I would like my love to die
and the rain to be raining on the graveyard
and on me walking the streets
mourning her who thought she loved me

from:
MURPHY (1938)

[*Murphy* is the most consistently successful example of Beckett's pre-war writing, and the most consistently entertaining. It was never published in trial-sections before publication in book form and it was turned down by a good many publishers before being accepted at Routledge, through the good offices of Herbert Read. Beckett began translating it into French, with Alfred Péron, as early as 1938-39. Joyce paired the English original with Flann O'Brien's *At Swim-Two-Birds*, as *Jean qui pleure* with *Jean qui ri*, and was able to quote sections of it from memory.

The three chapters given here are selected to illustrate: (Chapter 1) the volatility of Beckett's point of view, as he contemplates first his protagonist alone, then some 'puppets' from a distance, and finally Murphy's tug towards Celia; (Chapter 6) Murphy's intellectual ambition to attain to a 'matrix of surds', which, the narrative demonstrates, comically and tragically, he cannot attain; (Chapter 13) a scene of kite-flying in a London park, with which Beckett always planned to end the novel. It incorporates several deliberate parallels with Chapter 1 and at the same time supplies a kind of coda. It embodies the feelings that obstruct Murphy's ambitions, set out in Chapter 6, in a particularly pure form and only partly sentimentally.

Most surveys of Beckett's early fiction devote a chapter or more to discussing the novel, and two monographs — Robert Harrison, *Samuel Beckett's 'Murphy': A Critical Excursion* (Athens, Georgia: University of Georgia Press, 1968) and Rubin Rabinovitz, *The Development of Samuel Beckett's Fiction* (Urbana: University of Illinois Press, 1984) — supply useful annotations.]

One

The sun shone, having no alternative, on the nothing new. Murphy sat out of it, as though he were free, in a mew in West Brompton. Here for what might have been six months he had eaten, drunk, slept, and put his clothes on and off, in a medium-sized cage of north-western aspect commanding an unbroken view of medium-sized cages of south-eastern aspect. Soon he would have to make other arrangements, for the mew had been condemned. Soon he would have to buckle to and start eating, drinking, sleeping, and putting his clothes on and off, in quite alien surroundings.

He sat naked in his rocking-chair of undressed teak, guaranteed not to crack, warp, shrink, corrode, or creak at night. It was his own, it never left him. The corner in which he sat was curtained off from the sun, the poor old sun in the Virgin[1] again for the billionth time. Seven scarves held him in position. Two fastened his shins to the rockers, one his thighs to the seat, two his breast and belly to the back, one his wrists to the strut behind. Only the most local movements were possible. Sweat poured off him, tightened the thongs. The breath was not perceptible. The eyes, cold and unwavering as a gull's, stared up at an iridescence splashed over the cornice moulding, shrinking and fading. Somewhere a cuckoo-clock, having struck between twenty and thirty, became the echo of a street-cry, which now entering the mew gave *Quid pro quo! Quid pro quo!* directly.

These were sights and sounds that he did not like. They detained him in the world to which they belonged, but not he, as he fondly hoped. He wondered dimly what was breaking up his sunlight, what wares were being cried. Dimly, very dimly.

He sat in his chair in this way because it gave him pleasure! First it gave his body pleasure, it appeased his body. Then it set him free in his mind. For it was not until his body was appeased that he could come alive in his mind, as described in section six. And life in his mind gave him pleasure, such pleasure that pleasure was not the word.

Murphy had lately studied under a man in Cork called Neary.[2] This man, at that time, could stop his

1. The sun enters the constellation Virgo about 20-23 August. The main action takes place between Thursday, 12 September 1935 and the late afternoon of Saturday, 26 October. Calendar time is exactly calculated, and hitched to zodiacal time, with parodic punctilio.
2. Based in part on the great Trinity College Hegelian, H. S. Macran, who spent much of his time in Neary's public house. ('Perhaps you hadn't heard, said Neary, Hegel arrested his development,' p. 124) Beckett appears to have worked up the pre-Socratic vocabulary

heart more or less whenever he liked and keep it stopped, within reasonable limits, for as long as he liked. This rare faculty, acquired after years of application somewhere north of the Nerbudda,[3] he exercised frugally, reserving it for situations irksome beyond endurance, as when he wanted a drink and could not get one, or fell among Gaels and could not escape, or felt the pangs of hopeless sexual inclination.

Murphy's purpose in going to sit at Neary's feet was not to develop the Neary heart, which he thought would quickly prove fatal to a man of his temper, but simply to invest his own with a little of what Neary, at that time a Pythagorean, called the Apmonia. For Murphy had such an irrational heart that no physician could get to the root of it. Inspected, palpated, auscultated, percussed, radiographed and cardiographed, it was all that a heart should be. Buttoned up and left to perform, it was like Petrushka in his box.[4] One moment in such labour that it seemed on the point of seizing, the next in such ebullition that it seemed on the point of bursting. It was the mediation between these extremes that Neary called the Apmonia. When he got tired of calling it the Apmonia he called it the Isonomy. When he got sick of the sound of Isonomy he called it the Attunement. But he might call it what he liked, into Murphy's heart it would not enter. Neary could not blend the opposites in Murphy's heart.

Their farewell was memorable. Neary came out of one of his dead sleeps and said:

'Murphy, all life is figure and ground.'

'But a wandering to find home,' said Murphy.

'The face,' said Neary, 'or system of faces, against the big blooming buzzing confusion.[5] I think of Miss Dwyer.'

Murphy could have thought of a Miss Counihan. Neary clenched his fists and raised them before his face.

'To gain the affections of Miss Dwyer,' he said, 'even for one short hour, would benefit me no end.'

The knuckles stood out white under the skin in the usual way — that was the position. The hands then opened quite correctly to the utmost limit of their compass — that was the negation. It now seemed to Murphy that there were two equally legitimate ways in which the gesture might be concluded, and the sublation effected. The hands might be clapped to the head in a smart gesture of despair, or let fall limply to the seams of the trousers, supposing that to have been their point of departure. Judge then of his annoyance when Neary clenched them again more violently than before and dashed them against his breast-bone.

'Half an hour,' he said, 'fifteen minutes.'

'And then?' said Murphy. 'Back to Teneriffe and the apes?'[6]

'You may sneer,' said Neary, 'and you may scoff, but the fact remains that all is dross, for the moment at any rate, that is not Miss Dwyer. The one closed figure in the waste without form, and void! My tetrakyt!'

Of such was Neary's love for Miss Dwyer, who loved a Flight-Lieutenant Elliman, who loved a Miss Farren of Ringsakiddy [*sic*], who loved a Father Fitt of Ballinclashet, who in all sincerity was bound to acknowledge a certain vocation for a Mrs West of Passage,[7] who loved Neary.

'Love requited,' said Neary, 'is a short circuit,' a ball that gave rise to a sparkling rally.

'The love that lifts up its eyes,' said Neary, 'being in torment; that craves for the tip of her little finger, dipped in lacquer, to cool its tongue[8] — is foreign to you, Murphy, I take it.'

'Greek,' said Murphy.

'Or put it another way,' said Neary; 'the single, brilliant, organized, compact blotch in the tumult of heterogeneous stimulation.'

'Blotch is the word,' said Murphy.

'Just so,' said Neary. 'Now pay attention to this. For whatever reason you cannot love — But there is a Miss Counihan, Murphy, is there not?'

(Isonomy, Attunement, *tetrakyt*) from the then standard textbook, John Burnet's *Greek Philosophy: Thales to Plato* (1924). 'Apmonia' is a joke transliteration of the Pythagorean term αρμόνια — 'harmony' —, which indeed appears as APMONIA in the capital letters of Burnett's running-head (p. 45).

3. A river in west-central India.
4. The puppet-hero of Stravinsky's ballet *Petrushka* (1911), who suffers constant wrong and unjust persecution.
5. Neary actually repeats the phrase from William James's: compare Horace M. Kallen (ed.), *The Philosophy of William James* (New York: Modern Library, 1953), p. 76. It crops up again later in the novel (Picador: pp. 21, 138).
6. Wolfgang Köhler's celebrated *The Mentality of Apes* (1917; trans. 1925) was based on researches at the Anthropoid Research Station on Tenerife, where he was interned during World War I. The form of Murphy's question matches Neary's description of his love for Miss Dwyer in terms of Gestalt psychology.
7. Ringaskiddy, Ballinclasket and Passage West are all within a sixteen-mile radius of Cork City, to the south and east.
8. Based on Luke 16.24.

There was indeed a Miss Counihan.[9]

'Now say you were invited to define let us say your commerce with this Miss Counihan, Murphy,' said Neary. 'Come now, Murphy.'

'Precordial,'[10] said Murphy, 'rather than cordial. Tired. Cork County. Depraved.'

'Just so,' said Neary. 'Now then. For whatever reason you cannot love in my way, and believe me there is no other, for that same reason, whatever it may be, your heart is as it is. And again for that same reason — '

'Whatever it may be,' said Murphy.

'I can do nothing for you,' said Neary.

'God bless my soul,' said Murphy.

'Just so,' said Neary. 'I should say your conarium[11] has shrunk to nothing.'

He worked up the chair to its maximum rock, then relaxed. Slowly the world died down, the big world where *Quid pro quo* was cried as wares and the light never waned the same way twice; in favour of the little, as described in section six, where he could love himself.

A foot from his ear the telephone burst into its rail. He had neglected to take down the receiver. If he did not answer it at once his landlady would come running to do so, or some other lodger. Then he would be discovered, for his door was not locked. There was no means of locking his door. It was a strange room, the door hanging off its hinges, and yet a telephone. But its last occupant had been a harlot, long past her best, which had been scarlet. The telephone that she had found useful in her prime, in her decline she found indispensable. For the only money she made was when a client from the old days rang her up. Then she was indemnified for having been put to unnecessary inconvenience.

Murphy could not free his hand. Every moment he expected to hear the urgent step of his landlady on the stairs, or of some other lodger. The loud calm crake of the telephone mocked him. At last he freed a hand and seized the receiver, which in his agitation he clapped to his head instead of dashing to the ground.

'God blast you,' he said.

'He is doing so,' she replied. Celia.[12]

He laid the receiver hastily in his lap. The part of him that he hated craved for Celia, the part that he loved shrivelled up at the thought of her. The voice lamented faintly against his flesh. He bore it for a little, then took up the receiver and said:

'Are you never coming back?'

'I have it,' she said.[13]

'Don't I know,' said Murphy.

'I don't mean that,' she said, 'I mean what you told me — '

'I know what you mean,' said Murphy.

'Meet me at the usual at the usual,' she said. 'I'll have it with me.'

'That is not possible,' said Murphy. 'I expect a friend.'

'You have no friends,' said Celia.

'Well,' said Murphy, 'not exactly a friend, a funny old chap I ran into.'

'You can get rid of him before then,' said Celia.

'That is not possible,' said Murphy.

'Then I'll bring it round,' said Celia.

'You mustn't do that,' said Murphy.

'Why don't you want to see me?' said Celia.

'How often have I to tell you,' said Murphy, 'I—'

'Listen to me,' said Celia. 'I don't believe in your funny old chap. There isn't any such animal.'

Murphy said nothing. The self that he tried to love was tired.

'I'll be with you at nine,' said Celia, 'and I'll have it with me. If you're not there —'

'Yes,' said Murphy. 'Suppose I have to go out?'

'Goodbye.'

He listened for a little to the dead line, he dropped the receiver on the floor, he fastened his hand back to the strut, he worked up the chair.

9. A character who preceded Celia for Murphy's affections, and is pursued by the supporting cast throughout the book. Her name prompts associations with Kathleen Ní Houlihan, a figure who embodies much nationalist feeling about Ireland.

10. In the original sense — situated in the stomach or midriff, sexual — rather than the ordinary sense of extra-cordial, situated near the heart.

11. In Descartes' philosophy, the soul is brought into contact with the body by the pineal gland or conarium. Murphy's soul and body are discordant, and allusions to Cartesian dualism pervade Beckett's writing.

12. A prostitute with whom Murphy is in love, and in a sense his muse (*s'il y a*). The intellectual action of the novel describes Murphy caught between Celia and a Mr Endon (Greek 'within'), who embodies a state of complete withdrawal.

13. A horoscope prepared by a swami named Suk, given in full in Chapter 3, and which bears intermittently on the action. The horoscopical theme should be compared with Beckett's earlier 'Whoroscope' (in *Collected Poems 1930-1978* — Calder, 1984 — pp. 1-6) and the allusions to Dante's soothsayers (*Inferno* XX) which recur throughout his writing. It is possible that Beckett's interest was stimulated through his friendship with Joyce, who was vividly superstitious about dates and anniversaries; and the theme in *Murphy* is thereby a comment on Joycean values.

Slowly he felt better, astir in his mind, in the freedom of that light and dark that did not clash, nor alternate, nor fade nor lighten except to their communion, as described in section six. The rock got faster and faster, shorter and shorter, the iridescence was gone, the cry in the mew was gone, soon his body would be quiet. Most things under the moon got slower and slower and then stopped, a rock got faster and faster and then stopped. Soon his body would be quiet, soon he would be free.[14]

14. Echoed at the end of Chapter 11, just before the accident that causes Murphy's death — as well as in situational terms in Chapters 6 and 13 (below).

Six

Amor intellectualis quo Murphy se ipsum amat.[1]

It is most unfortunate, but the point of this story has been reached where a justification of the expression 'Murphy's mind' has to be attempted. Happily we need not concern ourselves with this apparatus as it really was — that would be an extravagance and an impertinence — but solely with what it felt and pictured itself to be. Murphy's mind is after all the gravamen of these informations. A short section to itself at this stage will relieve us from the necessity of apologizing for it further.

Murphy's mind pictured itself as a large hollow sphere, hermetically closed to the universe without. This was not an impoverishment, for it excluded nothing that it did not itself contain. Nothing ever had been, was or would be in the universe outside it but was already present as virtual, or actual, or virtual rising into actual, or actual falling into virtual, in the universe inside it.

This did not involve Murphy in the idealist tar.[2] There was the mental fact and there was the physical fact, equally real if not equally pleasant.

He distinguished between the actual and the virtual of his mind, not as between form and the formless yearning for form, but as between that of which he had both mental and physical experience and that of which he had mental experience only. Thus the form of kick was actual, that of caress virtual.

The mind felt its actual part to be above and bright, its virtual beneath and fading into dark, without however connecting this with the ethical yoyo. The mental experience was cut off from the physical experience, its criteria were not those of the physical experience, the agreement of part of its content with physical fact did not confer worth on that part. It did not function and could not be disposed according to a principle of worth. It was made up of light fading into dark, of above and beneath, but not of good and bad. It contained forms with parallel in another mode and forms without, but not right forms and wrong forms. It felt no issue between its light and dark, no need for its light to devour its dark. The need was now to be in the light, now in the half light, now in the dark. That was all.

Thus Murphy felt himself split in two, a body and a mind. They had intercourse apparently, otherwise he could not have known that they had anything in common. But he felt his mind to be bodytight and did not understand through what channel the intercourse was effected nor how the two experiences came to overlap. He was satisifed that neither followed from the other. He neither thought a kick because he felt one nor felt a kick because he thought one. Perhaps the knowledge was related to the fact of the kick as two magnitudes to a third. Perhaps there was, outside space and time, a non-mental non-physical Kick from all eternity, dimly revealed to Murphy in its correlated modes of consciousness and extension, the kick *in intellectu* and the kick *in re*. But where then was the supreme Caress?

However that might be, Murphy was content to accept this partial congruence of the world of his mind with the world of his body as due to some such process of supernatural determination. The problem was of little interest. Any solution would do that did not clash with the feeling, growing stronger as Murphy grew older, that his mind was a closed system, subject to no principle of change but its own, self-sufficient and impermeable to the vicissitudes of the body. Of infinitely more interest than how this came to be so was the manner in which it might be exploited.

He was split, one part of him never left this mental chamber that pictured itself as a sphere full

1. 'The intellectual love with which Murphy loves himself.' The epigraph is a twisted quotation from Spinoza, *Ethics* V, 35 (substituting Murphy for Spinoza's God).
2. *Siris* (1744), the most popular work of the Irish idealist philosopher, George Berkeley (1685-1753), was subtitled *Philosophical Reflections Concerning the Virtues of Tar-Water.*

of light fading into dark, because there was no way out. But motion in this world depended on rest in the world outside. A man is in bed, wanting to sleep. A rat is behind the wall at his head, wanting to move. The man hears the rat fidget and cannot sleep, the rat hears the man fidget and dares not move. They are both unhappy, one fidgeting and the other waiting, or both happy, the rat moving and the man sleeping.

Murphy could think and know after a fashion with his body up (so to speak) and about, with a kind of mental *tic douloureux*[3] sufficient for his parody of rational behaviour. But that was not what he understood by consciousness.

His body lay down more and more in a less precarious abeyance than that of sleep, for its own convenience and so that the mind might move. There seemed little left of this body that was not privy to this mind, and that little was usually tired on its own account. The development of what looked like collusion between such utter strangers remained to Murphy as unintelligible as telekinesis or the Leyden Jar,[4] and of as little interest. He noted with satisfaction that it existed, that his bodily need ran more and more with his mental.

As he lapsed in body he felt himself coming alive in mind, set free to move among its treasures. The body has it stock, the mind its treasures.

There were the three zones, light, half light, dark, each with its speciality.[5]

In the first were the forms with parallel, a radiant abstract of the dog's life, the elements of physical experience available for a new arrangement. Here the pleasure was reprisal, the pleasure of reversing the physical experience. Here the kick that the physical Murphy received, the mental Murphy gave. It was the same kick, but corrected as to direction. Here the chandlers were available for slow depilation, Miss Carridge for rape by Ticklepenny,[6] and so on. Here the whole physical fiasco became a howling success.

In the second were the forms without parallel. Here the pleasure was contemplation. This system had no other mode in which to be out of joint and therefore did not need to be put right in this. Here was the Belacqua bliss and others scarcely less precise.

In both these zones of his private world Murphy felt sovereign and free, in the one to requite himself, in the other to move as he pleased from one unparalleled beatitude to another. There was no rival initiative.

The third, the dark, was a flux of forms, a perpetual coming together and falling asunder of forms. The light contained the docile elements of a new manifold, the world of the body broken up into the pieces of a toy; the half light, states of peace. But the dark neither elements nor states, nothing but forms becoming and crumbling into the fragments of a new becoming, without love or hate or any intelligible principle of change. Here there was nothing but commotion and the pure forms of commotion. Here he was not free, but a mote in the dark of absolute freedom. He did not move, he was a point in the ceaseless unconditioned generation and passing away of line.

Matrix of surds.

It was pleasant to kick the Ticklepennies and Miss Carridges simultaneously together into ghastly acts of love. It was pleasant to lie dreaming on the shelf beside Belacqua, watching the dawn break crooked.[7] But how much more pleasant was the sensation of being a missile without provenance or target, caught up in a tumult of non-Newtonian motion.[8] So pleasant that pleasant was not the word.

Thus as his body set him free more and more in his mind, he took to spending less and less time in the light, spitting at the breakers of the world; and less in the half light, where the choice of bliss introduced an element of effort; and more and more and more in the dark, in the will-lessness, a mote in its absolute freedom.

3. i.e. nervous (literally painful) twitch.
4. A kind of electrical condenser.
5. Murphy's three zones correspond to Dante's Paradiso, Purgatorio and Inferno. They also invert Descartes' dream of 10 November 1619, when Descartes felt himself pulled down into the darkness of chaotic forms before being restored to the light where certainty of knowledge reigns. Murphy's will-less ideal owes something to Schopenhauer's *The World as Will and Idea*.
6. Miss Carridge is a mendacious landlady who presides over Murphy and Celia when they move in together on Brewery Road. Austin Ticklepenny is an Irish pot poet who also works at the Magdalen Mental Mercyseat, where Murphy comes into contact with Mr Endon. The fictional portrait is based on the Irish poet Austin Clarke, and is oddly obvious and uncharacteristically ungenerous. Indeed, when the novel first appeared, Clarke was urged by Dublin friends to take a libel action against Beckett (which he declined to do).
7. The dawn breaks crooked for Belacqua because he watches it sideways, with his head resting on his knee (*Purgatorio* IV, 106-08).
8. The other characters, caught in a parodied nexus of cause and effect, are elsewhere described as Newtonians.

This painful duty having now been discharged, no further bulletins will be issued.

Thirteen[1]

Late afternoon, Saturday, October the 26th. A mild, clear, sunless day, sudden gentle eddies of rotting leaves, branches still against the still sky, from a chimney a pine of smoke.

Celia wheeled Mr Willoughby Kelly[2] south along the Broad Walk. He wore his kiting costume, a glistening slicker many sizes too large for him and a yachting-cap many sizes too small, though the smallest and largest of their kind obtainable. He sat bolt upright, with one gloved hand clutching the winch, with the other the kite furled and in its sheath, and his blue eyes blazed in the depths of their sockets. To either side of him the levers flailed the air with heavy strokes, causing a light draught that he found not unpleasant, for he burned with excitement.

At the top of the incline he laid the winch and kite in his lap and seized the pulls. It was the signal for Celia to let go. His arms flashed back and forth, faster and faster as the chair gathered speed, until he was rocking crazily along at a good 12 mph, a danger to himself and to others. Then resisting with one hand the pull, with the other the thrust of the levers, he brought himself smoothly to rest level with the statue of Queen Victoria, whom he greatly admired, as a woman and as a queen.

It was only in the legs and face that Mr Kelly was badly gone, he still had plenty of vigour in his arms and torso.

He was as fond of his chair in his own way as Murphy had been of his.

Celia was a long time coming. He unwrapped the old silk kite, stained and faded hexagon of crimson, stretched it on its asterisk of sticks, made fast the tail and line, tested the tassels one by one. One just such milky Saturday afternoon many years previously a regular had said: 'Silk ain't worth a b—. Give me nainsook.'[3] To which Mr Kelly recalled with satisfaction the exact terms of his rejoiner, which had been loudly applauded: 'Nainsook my rump.'

Celia touched the back of his chair and he said: 'You were a long time.'

'Business,' said Celia.

The leaves began to lift and scatter, the higher branches to complain, the sky broke and curdled over flecks of skim blue, the pine of smoke toppled into the east and vanished, the pond was suddenly a little panic of grey and white, of water and gulls and sails.

It was as though Time suddenly lost patience, or had an anxiety attack.

Beyond the Long Water Rosie Dew and Nelly,[4] the worst of her heat behind her, turned their faces to the rising wind and home. A pair of socks was waiting from Lord Gall. He had written: 'If this pair of socks does not prove more productive, I shall have to try a new control.'

Celia wheeled Mr Kelly into position, at the north-east corner of the plot between the Round Pond and the Broad Walk, the prow of his chair wedged against the railing. She took the assembled kite gently from his hands, backed along the path until she stood on the margin of the water, held up the kite as high as her arms would reach and waited for the glove to fall. The wind blew her skirt against her legs, her jacket back from her breasts. A weekend lecher well advanced in years, sprawling on his sacrum (which was a mass of eczema) in a chair directly before her, discomposed his features in what he had good reason to suppose was the smile obscene, and jingled his change, his very small change. Celia smiled back, strained upward with her arms, settled herself more firmly on the ground.

Mr Kelly's hand felt the wind he wanted, the glove fell, Celia threw up the kite. And so great was his skill that in five minutes he was lying back, breathing hard and short, his eyes closed of

1. The number recurs like a signature through Beckett's earlier writing, probably because he was born on the thirteenth day of the month (a Good Friday). Murphy's name — like Mercier's, Molloy's, Moran's and Malone's after him — begins with the thirteenth letter of the alphabet. For Beckett's comment on the importance of the chapter, which is set in Hyde Park, see *Disjecta*, p. 102.
2. Celia's grandfather and Murphy's rival for her affections. His action in the wheel chair is carefully counterpointed with Murphy's in the rocking chair in Chapter 1; his attempt to join seen and unseen is the opposite of Murphy's ideal set out in Chapter 6; his first name is an imperative of the will, and sets him off from the will-less ideal of 'a mote in its absolute freedom'; he sails under blue skies, the colour of hope, whereas Murphy's colour is yellow, the colour of cowardice and evasion; he is always called Mr, the title which in real life Joyce and Beckett always used when addressing one another.
3. A kind of muslin or jaconet, of Indian origin.
4. Rosie Dew is a middle-aged spiritual medium who accosted Murphy in Hyde Park and whose dog, Nelly, ate Murphy's biscuits (Chapter 5). Lord Gall is her benefactor, and she plans to use his socks to establish contact with his father.

necessity but in ecstasy as it happened, half his line paid out, sailing by feel.

Celia paused for a second to clinch the client, then rejoined Mr Kelly. The cord wormed slowly off the winch — out, back a little, stop; out, back a little, stop. The historical process of the hardened optimists. With still a quarter of the line to go the kite rode without a flicker high above the Dell, a speck in the glades that this wind always opened in the east. The chair drove against the railing, Mr Kelly wished his bottom were more prehensile. Without opening his eyes he said:

'You did that very nicely.'

Celia did not choose to misunderstand him.

'And yesterday?' said Mr Kelly.

'A kid and a drunk,' said Celia.

Mr Kelly let out a wild rush of line, say the industrial revolution, then without recoil or stop, gingerly, the last few feet. The kite being now absolutely at the end of its tether, he sat up and opened his eyes, hypermetropic in the extreme, to admire the effect.

Except for the sagging soar of line, undoubtedly superb so far as it went, there was nothing to be seen, for the kite had disappeared from view. Mr Kelly was enraptured. Now he could measure the distance from the unseen to the seen, now he was in a position to determine the point at which seen and unseen met. It would be an unscientific observation, so many and so fitful were the imponderables involved. But the pleasure accruing to Mr Kelly would be in no way inferior to that conferred (presumably) on Mr Adams by his beautiful deduction of Neptune from Uranus.[5] He fixed with his eagle eyes a point in the empty sky where he fancied the kite to swim into view, and wound carefully in.

Moving away a little Celia also looked at the sky, not with the same purpose as Mr Kelly, for she knew that he would see it long before she could, but simply to have that unction of soft sunless light on her eyes that was all she remembered of Ireland. Gradually she saw other kites, but above all the tandem of the child that had not answered her good night, because he had been singing.[6] She recognized the unusual coupling, not in file but abreast.

The ludicrous fever of toys struggling skyward, the sky itself more and more remote, the wind tearing the awning of cloud to tatters, pale limitless blue and green recessions laced with strands of scud, the light failing — once she would have noticed these things. She watched the tandem coming shakily down from the turmoil, the child running forward to break its fall, his trouble when he failed, his absorbed kneeling over the damage. He did not sing as he departed, nor did she hail him.

The wail of the rangers came faintly out of the east against the wind. *All out. All out. All out.* Celia turned and looked at Mr Kelly. He lay sideways in the chair, his cheek on his shoulder, a fold of the slicker lifting his lip in a mild snarl, not dying but dozing. As she watched the winch sprang from his fingers, struck violently against the railing, the string snapped, the winch fell to the ground, Mr Kelly awoke.

All out. All out.

Mr Kelly tottered to his feet, tossed up his arms high and wide and quavered away down the path that led to the water, a ghastly, lamentable figure. The slicker trailed along the ground, the skull gushed from under the cap like a dome from under its lantern, the ravaged face was a cramp of bones, throttled sounds jostled in his throat.

Celia caught him on the margin of the pond. The end of the line skimmed the water, jerked upward in a wild whirl, vanished joyfully in the dusk. Mr Kelly went limp in her arms. Someone fetched the chair and helped to get him aboard. Celia toiled along the narrow path into the teeth of the wind, then faced north up the wide hill. There was no shorter way home. The yellow hair fell across her face. The yachting-cap clung like a clam to the skull. The levers were the tired heart. She closed her eyes.

All out.[7]

5. John Couch Adams (1819-92) predicted the existence of Neptune on the basis of the irregular motion of Uranus. Neptune and Uranus are mentioned in Suk's horoscope in Chapter 3, and are connected with the astronomical/astrological motif.

6. A reference to a boy with a pair of kites flown in tandem from a double winch in Chapter 8, also at the Round Pond in Hyde Park.

7. The triplicated motif owes something to Dante; the diminishing intrusion, which is like a knell, to Eliot's *The Waste Land* (the close of Part II, 'A Game of Chess').

from:
LETTER TO AXEL KAUN (1937)

[Beckett made the acquaintance of Axel Kaun (b. 1912, now a translator living in San Francisco) in 1936; the letter was written in German, dated 9 July 1937. Beckett later dismissed it as 'German bilge'; it was collected by Ruby Cohn in *Disjecta* and the English translation is by Martin Esslin. The earlier part of the letter, omitted here, describes Beckett's reading of Joachim Ringelnatz (pseud. Hans Bötticher, 1883-1934), whom Kaun had suggested that Beckett might translate. Beckett explains why he thinks Ringelnatz is not worth the effort, describing him as a 'Rhyme Coolie'. In a postscript to the same letter, offering to return the Ringelnatz, Beckett asks if there is an English translation of Trakl.

The fact that the letter was written in German might bear on why it is so unusually explicit. Beckett's general remarks on the limitations of art are more often to be found in his essays on painters and painting. Compare his essay 'Peintres de l'Empêchement', written at the time of *Molloy* and *Malone Dies*, and his *Three Dialogues*, contemporary with *The Unnamable*. The interviews with Israel Shenker (1956) and with Tom Driver (1961), conveniently reprinted in Lawrence Graver and Raymond Federman (eds), *Samuel Beckett: The Critical Heritage* (London: Routledge & Kegan Paul, 1979), pp. 146-49, 217-23, cover some of the same ground and extend it to different areas.]

. . . Es freut mich immer, einen Brief von Ihnen zu bekommen. Schreiben Sie also möglichst häufig und ausführlich. Wollen Sie unbedingt, dass ich Ihnen auf Englisch das gleiche tue? Werden Sie beim Lesen meiner deutschen Brief ebenso gelangweilt, wie ich beim Verfassen eines englischen? Es täte mir Leid, wenn Sie das Gefühl hätten, es handele sich etwa um einen Kontrakt, dem ich nicht nachkomme. Um Antwort wird gebeten.

Es wird mir tatsächlich immer schwieriger, ja sinnloser, ein offizielles Englisch zu schrieben. Und immer mehr wie ein Schleier kommt mir meine Sprache vor, den man zerreissen muss, um an die dahinterliegenden Dinge (oder das dahinterliegende Nichts) zu kommen. Grammatik und Stil. Mir scheinen sie ebenso hinfällig geworden zu sein wie ein Biedermeier Badeanzug oder die Unerschüttlichkeit eines Gentlemans. Eine Larve. Hoffentlich kommt die Zeit, sie ist ja Gott sei Dank in gewissen Kreisen schon da, wo die Sprache da am besten gebraucht wird, wo sie am tüchtigsten missbraucht wird. Da wir sie so mit einem Male nicht ausschalten können, wollen wir wenigstens nichts versäumen, was zu ihrem Verruf beitragen mag. Ein Loch nach dem andern in ihr zu bohren, bis das Dahinterkauernde, sei es etwas oder nichts, durchzusickern anfängt — ich kann mir für den heutigen Schriftsteller kein höheres Ziel vorstellen.

Oder soll die Literatur auf jenem alten faulen von Musik und Malerei längst verlassenen Wege allein hinterbleiben? Steckt etwas lähmend Heiliges in der Unnatur des Wortes, was zu den Elementen der anderen Künste nicht gehört? Gibt es irgendeinen Grund, warum jene fürchterlich willkürliche Materialität der Wortfläche nicht aufgelöst werden sollte, wie z.B die von grossen schwarzen Pausen gefressene Tonfläche in der siebten Symphonie von Beethoven, so dass wir sie ganze Seiten durch nicht anders wahrnehmen können als etwa einen schwindelnden unergründliche Schlünde von Stillschweigen verknüpfenden Pfad von Lauten? Um Antwort wird gebeten.

Ich weiss, es gibt Leute, empfindsame und intelligente Leute, für die es an Stillschweigen gar nicht fehlt. Ich kann nicht umhin anzunehmen, dass sie schwerhörig sind. Denn im Walde der Symbole, die keine sind, schweigen die Vöglein der Deutung, die keine ist, nie.

Selbstverständlich muss man sich vorläufig mit Wenigem begnünen. Zuerst kann es nur darauf ankommen, irgendwie eine Methode zu erfinden, um diese höhnische Haltung dem Worte gegenüber wörtlich darzustellen. In dieser Dissonanz von Mitteln und Gebrauch wird man schon vielleicht ein Geflüster der Endmusik oder des Allem zu Grunde liegenden Schweigens spüren können.

Mit einem solchen Programm hat meiner Absicht nach die allerletzte Arbeit von Joyce gar nichts zu tun. Dort scheint es sich vielmehr um eine Apotheose des Wortes zu handeln. Es sei denn, Himmelfahrt und Höllensturz sind eins und dasselbe. Wie schön wäre es, glauben zu können, es sei in der Tat so. Wir wollen uns aber vorläufig auf die Absicht beschränken.

Vielleicht liegen die Logographen von Gertrude Stein dem näher was ich im Sinne habe. Das Sprachgewebe ist wenigstens porös geworden, wenn nur leider ganz zufälligerweise, und zwar als Folge eines etwa der Technik von Feininger ähnlichen Verfahrens. Die unglückliche Dame (lebt sie noch?) ist ja ohne Zweifel immer noch in ihr Vehikel verliebt, wenn freilich nur wie ein Mathematiker in seine Ziffern, für den die Lösung des Problems von ganz sekundärem Interesse ist, ja ihm als Tod der Ziffern direkt schrecklich vorkommen muss. Diese Methode mit der von Joyce in Zusammenhang zu bringen, wie es die Mode ist, kommt mir genau so sinnlos vor wie der mir noch nicht bekannte Versuch den Nominalismus (im Sinne der Scholastiker) mit dem Realismus zu vergleichen. Auf dem Wege nach dieser für mich sehr wünschenswerten Literatur des Unworts, kann freilich irgendeine Form der nominalistischen Ironie ein notwendiges Stadium sein. Es genügt aber nicht, wenn das Spiel etwas von seinem heiligen Ernst verliert. Aufhören soll es. Machen wir es also wie jener verrückte (?) Mathematiker, der auf jeder einzelnen Stufe des Kalküls ein neues Messprinzip anzuwenden pflegte. Eine Wörterstürmerei im Namen der Schönheit.

Inzwischen mache ich gar nichts. Nur von Zeit zu Zeit habe ich wie jetzt den Trost, mich so gegen eine fremde Sprache unwillkürlich vergehen zu dürfen, wie ich es mit Wissen und Willen gegen meine eigene machen möchte und — Deo juvante — werde.

TRANSLATION

I am always glad to receive a letter from you. So please write as frequently and fully as possible. Do you insist that I should do likewise in English? Are you are bored by reading my Geman letters as I am in writing one in English? I should be sorry if you felt that there might be something like a contract between us that I fail to fulfil. An answer is requested.

It is indeed becoming more and more difficult, even senseless, for me to write an official English. And more and more my own language appears to me like a veil that must be torn apart in order to get at the things (or the Nothingness) behind it. Grammar and Style. To me they seem to have become as irrelevant as a Victorian bathing suit or the imperturbability of a true gentleman. A mask. Let us hope the time will come, thank God that in certain circles it has already come, when language is most efficiently used where it is being most efficiently misused. As we cannot eliminate language all at once, we should at least leave nothing undone that might contribute to its falling into disrepute. To bore one hole after another in it, until what lurks behind it — be it something or nothing — begins to seep through; I cannot imagine a higher goal for a writer today.

Or is literature alone to remain behind in the old lazy ways that have been so long ago abandoned by music and painting? Is there something paralysingly holy in the vicious nature of the word that is not found in the elements of the other arts? Is there any reason why that terrible materiality of the word surface should not be capable of being dissolved, like for example the sound surface, torn by enormous pauses, of Beethoven's seventh Symphony, so that through whole pages we can perceive nothing but a path of sounds suspended in giddy heights, linking unfathomable abysses of silence?[1] An answer is requested.

I know there are people, sensitive and intelligent people, for whom there is no lack of silence. I cannot but assume that they are hard of hearing. For in the forest of symbols,[2] which aren't any, the little birds of interpretation, which isn't any, are never silent.

Of course, for the time being we must be satisfied with little. At first it can only be a matter of somehow finding a method by which we can represent this mocking attitude towards the word, through words. In this dissonance between the means and their use it will perhaps become possible to feel a whisper of that final music or that silence that underlies All.

With such a program, in my opinion, the latest work of Joyce[3] has nothing whatever to do. There it seems rather to be a matter of an apotheosis of the word. Unless perhaps Ascension to Heaven and Descent to Hell are somehow one and the same. How beautiful it would be to be able to believe that that indeed was the case. But for the time being we want to confine ourselves to the mere intention.

Perhaps the logographs of Gertrude Stein[4] are nearer to what I have in mind. At least the texture of language has become porous, if only, alas, quite by chance, and as a consequence of a technique similar

1. Beckett expressed the same view of Beethoven's 'punctuation of dehiscence' as early as the 1932 *Dream of Fair to Middling Women* (*Disjecta*, pp. 49-50). Compare his post-war analysis of Bram Van Velde's painting in *Disjecta*, pp. 118 ff.
2. Alluding to the 'forêts de symboles' in Baudelaire's sonnet 'Correspondances'.
3. *Work in Progress/Finnegans Wake*. Beckett commented on the vertical oppositions in Joyce's writing in his essay, 'Dante . . . Bruno. Vico . . Joyce' (*Disjecta*, pp. 21, 33, etc.), and announced his alienation from the Joycean coincidence of opposites in the 1934 poem, 'Home Olga' (*Collected Poems 1930-1978*, p. 8).
4. Gertrude Stein (1874-1946), American expatriate writer, had lived in Paris since 1903. Her literary experiments, many of which remained unpublished until after her death, were often conscious attempts to find an equivalent for Cubist techniques in painting.

to that of Feininger.[5] The unfortunate lady (is she still alive?) is doubtlessly still in love with her vehicle, albeit only in the way in which a mathematician is in love with his figures; a mathematician for whom the solution of the problem is of entirely secondary interest, indeed to whom must the death of his figures appear quite dreadful. To bring this method into relation with that of Joyce, as is the fashion,[6] strikes me as senseless as the attempt, of which I know nothing as yet, to compare Nominalism (in the sense of the Scholastics) with Realism. On the way to this literature of the unword, which is so desirable to me, some form of Nominalist irony might be a necessary stage. But it is not enough for the game to lose some of its sacred seriousness. It should stop. Let us therefore act like that mad (?) mathematician who used a different principle of measurement at each step of his calculation. An assault against words in the name of beauty.

In the meantime I am doing nothing at all. Only from time to time I have the consolation, as now, of sinning willy-nilly against a foreign language, as I should love to do with full knowledge and intent against my own — and as I shall do — Deo juvante.[7]

5. Lyonel Feininger (1871-1956), Cubist painter, lived, was trained and worked in Germany until he returned to New York in 1937. He was particularly close to Klee and Kandinsky, and taught at the Bauhaus.
6. The fashion Beckett complains of appears to have been encouraged by Wyndham Lewis (*Time and Western Man*, 1927, p. 397), followed by Frank Swinnerton, Edith Sitwell, Henry Beardsley, and so on.
7. God willing.

ENDGAME (1958)

For Roger Blin[1]

[The original French version, *Fin de Partie* (1957), has been edited for Methuen's Twentieth-Century Texts by Beryl S. Fletcher and John Fletcher (1970). Their introduction describes how the manuscript evolved from a two-act version, and how changes arrived at in production were incorporated in Beckett's English translation, published in the following year (for instance, at pp. 276-77 of the text below: see note 29). The published English text has remained unchanged in successive printings, and has undergone much less revision in Beckett's own productions than *Krapp's Last Tape, Happy Days* and *Waiting for Godot*.

Beckett has, however, amended details such as Hamm's 'very red face' and the blood stains on the handkerchief covering it, at the beginning, and by adding an extra 'No! Clov.' to Hamm's 'No? Good.' at the end (p. 278). The text ideally should be read alongside the photographic record of his (German) production, *Samuel Beckett inszeniert das 'Endspiel'* (Frankfurt/Main: Suhrkamp, 1967). Beckett made further changes for the production he directed for Rick Cluchey (see *Journal of Beckett Studies*, No. 8, Autumn 1982).

When Beckett rehearsed *Endgame* in Berlin, he told Hamm and Clov, 'Your war is the heart of the play.' Hamm longs to bring the whole pointless farce to an end, but fears what lies beyond. His assurance and self-possession alternate with panic. Clov's distress is more constant; he wishes only to return to his kitchen and to be left alone. Hamm communicates violence and variability, Clov is elegaic. Their relationship is reflected, in muted form, in the mordant humour of Nagg and in the reflective pathos of Nell. The action is threaded by allusions to biblical and theatrical motifs (Ham and Noah, Hamlet and Prospero) and by references to chess, Zeno's paradox and the like.

The action divides into sixteen scenes. Three introductory scenes are followed by the main business of the first half; then Hamm's story (below pp. 270-71) takes the audience out of the action for a moment and serves as a rest or interval; then the main business is repeated, and is followed by three valedictory scenes that match the three opening scenes. The second half lacks the diversion of Nagg and Nell, and centres on Hamm and Clov alone. The dialogue becomes more urgent, the situation that was ending as the play began intensifies and becomes desperate, the sense of obligation becomes more cruel, since it is not able to unburden itself. There is no slack, no alleviation, as there is in *Waiting for Godot*. As Beckett told Alan Schneider, the effect depends on 'the power of the text to claw'.

Surveys of Beckett's drama all include a chapter on the play, and see Bell Gale Chevigny (ed.), *Twentieth-Century Interpretations of 'Endgame'* (Englewood Cliffs, New Jersey: Prentice Hall, 1969). The collection *Materialen zu Becketts 'Endspiel'* (Frankfurt/Main: Suhrkamp, 1968) complements the Suhrkamp photographic record, and there are three other anthologies of criticism in German.]

1. Blin directed the première of *En attendant Godot* (in which he played Pozzo) and also of *Fin de Partie* (in which he played Hamm). He died on 20 January 1984.

THE CHARACTERS[2]

HAMM
CLOV
NAGG
NELL

Bare interior.
Grey light.
Left and right back, high up, two small windows, curtains drawn.
Front right, a door. Hanging near door, its face to wall, a picture.
Front left, touching each other, covered with an old sheet, two ashbins.
Centre, in an armchair on castors, covered with an old sheet, HAMM.
Motionless by the door, his eyes fixed on HAMM, CLOV.
Very red face.
Brief tableau.

CLOV *goes and stands under window left. Stiff, staggering walk. He looks up at window left. He turns and looks at window right. He goes and stands under window right. He looks up at window right. He turns and looks at window left. He goes out, comes back immediately with a small step-ladder, carries it over and sets it down under window left, gets up on it, draws back curtain. He gets down, takes six steps (for example) towards window right, goes back for ladder, carries it over and sets it down under window right, gets up on it, draws back curtain. He gets down, takes three steps towards window left, goes back for ladder, carries it over and sets it down under window left, gets up on it, looks out of window. Brief laugh. He gets down, takes one step towards window right, goes back for ladder, carries it over and sets it down under window right, gets up on it, looks out of window. Brief laugh. He gets down, goes with ladder towards ashbins, halts, turns, carries back ladder and sets it down under window right, goes to ashbins, removes sheet covering them, folds it over his arm. He raises one lid, stoops and looks into bin. Brief laugh. He closes lid. Same with other bin. He goes to* HAMM, *removes sheet covering him, folds it over his arm. In a dressing-gown, a stiff toque on his head, a large blood-stained handkerchief over his face, a whistle hanging from his neck, a rug over his knees, thick socks on his feet,* HAMM *seems to be asleep.* CLOV *looks him over. Brief laugh. He goes to door, halts, turns towards auditorium.*

CLOV: (*Fixed gaze, tonelessly*) Finished, it's finished, nearly finished, it must be nearly finished.[3] (*Pause*) Grain upon grain, one by one, and one day, suddenly, there's a heap, a little heap, the impossible heap.[4] (*Pause*) I can't be punished any more. (*Pause*) I'll go now to my kitchen, ten feet by ten feet by ten feet, and wait for him to whistle me. (*Pause*) Nice dimensions, nice proportions, I'll lean on the table, and look at the wall, and wait for him to whistle me.

He remains a moment motionless, then goes out. He comes back immediately, goes to window right, takes up the ladder and carries it out. Pause. HAMM *stirs. He yawns under the handkerchief. He removes the handkerchief from his face. Very red face.*[5] *Black glasses.*

HAMM: Me — (*he yawns*) — to play. (*He holds the handkerchief spread out before him*) Old stancher! (*He takes off his glasses, wipes his eyes, his face, the glasses, puts them on again, folds the handkerchief and puts it neatly in the breast-pocket of his dressing-gown. He clears his throat, joins the tips of his fingers*) Can there be misery — (*he yawns*) — loftier than mine? No doubt. Formerly. But now? (*Pause*) My father? (*Pause*) My mother? (*Pause*) My . . . dog? (*Pause*) Oh I am willing to believe they suffer as much as such creatures can suffer. But does that mean their sufferings equal mine? No doubt. (*Pause*) No, all is a — (*he yawns*) — bsolute, (*proudly*) the bigger a man is the fuller he is. (*Pause. Gloomily*) And the emptier. (*He sniffs*) Clov! (*Pause*) No, alone. (*Pause*) What dreams! Those forests! (*Pause*) Enough, it's time it ended, in the refuge too. (*Pause*) And yet I hesitate, I hesitate to . . . to end. Yes, there it is, it's time it ended and yet I hesitate to — (*he yawns*) — to end. (*Yawns*) God, I'm tired, I'd be better off in bed. (*He whistles. Enter* CLOV *immediately. He halts beside the chair*) You pollute the air! (*Pause*) Get me ready, I'm going to bed.

CLOV: I've just got you up.

2. Note the associations with hammer and French *clou*/German *nagel*, both meaning nail (as well as with ham/pork and clove/herb). Compare Mother Pegg on pp. 269 and 276 below.

3. Echoes the last words of the dying Jesus (John 19.30) — what in *Murphy* is called 'Christ's parthian shaft' (Picador, p. 44).

4. A reference to Zeno's paradox, which denies that it is possible to reach the end of an infinite series in a finite time. Compare *Company*, p. 309 below.

5. Beckett had been told that incarceration makes people red in the face. The reference is now dropped in productions with which he is associated because he judges the notion to be clownish and the contrast with the white faces of Nagg and Nell 'too manichean'.

HAMM: And what of it?

CLOV: I can't be getting you up and putting you to bed every five minutes, I have things to do.

(Pause)

HAMM: Did you ever see my eyes?

CLOV: No.

HAMM: Did you never have the curiosity, while I was sleeping, to take off my glasses and look at my eyes?

CLOV: Pulling back the lids? *(Pause)* No.

HAMM: One of these days I'll show them to you. *(Pause)* It seems they've gone all white. *(Pause)* What time is it?

CLOV: The same as usual.

HAMM: *(Gesture towards window right)* Have you looked?

CLOV: Yes.

HAMM: Well?

CLOV: Zero.

HAMM: It'd need to rain.

CLOV: It won't rain. *(Pause)*

HAMM: Apart from that, how do you feel?

CLOV: I don't complain.

HAMM: You feel normal?

CLOV: *(Irritably)* I tell you I don't complain!

HAMM: I feel a little queer. *(Pause)* Clov!

CLOV: Yes.

HAMM: Have you not had enough?

CLOV: Yes! *(Pause)* Of what?

HAMM: Of this . . . this . . . thing.

CLOV: I always had. *(Pause)* Not you?

HAMM: *(Gloomily)* Then there's no reason for it to change.

CLOV: It may end. *(Pause)* All life long the same questions, the same answers.

HAMM: Get me ready. (CLOV *does not move)* Go and get the sheet. (CLOV *does not move)* Clov!

CLOV: Yes.

HAMM: I'll give you nothing more to eat.

CLOV: Then we'll die.

HAMM: I'll give you just enough to keep you from dying. You'll be hungry all the time.

CLOV: Then we shan't die. *(Pause)* I'll go and get the sheet. *(He goes towards the door)*

HAMM: No! (CLOV *halts)* I'll give you one biscuit per day. *(Pause)* One and a half. *(Pause)* Why do you stay with me?

CLOV: Why do you keep me?

HAMM: There's no one else.

CLOV: There's nowhere else.

(Pause)

HAMM: You're leaving me all the same.

CLOV: I'm trying.

HAMM: You don't love me.

CLOV: No.

HAMM: You loved me once.

CLOV: Once!

HAMM: I've made you suffer too much. *(Pause)* Haven't I?

CLOV: It's not that.

HAMM: *(Shocked)* I haven't made you suffer too much?

CLOV: Yes!

HAMM: *(Relieved)* Ah you gave me a fright! *(Pause. Coldly)* Forgive me. *(Pause. Louder)* I said, Forgive me.

CLOV: I heard you. *(Pause)* Have you bled?

HAMM: Less. *(Pause)* Is it not time for my pain-killer?

CLOV: No. *(Pause)*

HAMM: How are your eyes?

CLOV: Bad.

HAMM: How are your legs?

CLOV: Bad.

HAMM: But you can move.

CLOV: Yes.

HAMM: *(Violently)* Then move! (CLOV *goes to back wall, leans against it with his forehead and hands)* Where are you?

CLOV: Here.

HAMM: Come back! (CLOV *returns to his place beside the chair)* Where are you?

CLOV: Here.

HAMM: Why don't you kill me?

CLOV: I don't know the combination of the larder.

(Pause)

HAMM: Go and get two bicycle-wheels.

CLOV: There are no more bicycle-wheels.

HAMM: What have you done with your bicycle?

CLOV: I never had a bicycle.

HAMM: The thing is impossible.

CLOV: When there were still bicycles I wept to have one. I crawled at your feet. You told me to get out to hell. Now there are none.

HAMM: And your rounds? When you inspected my paupers. Always on foot?

CLOV: Sometimes on horse. *(The lid of one of the bins lifts and the hands of* NAGG *appear, gripping the rim. Then his head emerges. Nightcap. Very white face.* NAGG *yawns, then listens)* I'll leave you, I have things to do.

HAMM: In your kitchen?

CLOV: Yes.

HAMM: Outside of here it's death. (*Pause*) All right, be off. (*Exit* CLOV. *Pause*) We're getting on.

NAGG: Me pap!

HAMM: Accursed progenitor!

NAGG: Me pap!

HAMM: The old folks at home![6] No decency left! Guzzle, guzzle, that's all they think of. (*He whistles. Enter* CLOV. *He halts beside the chair*) Well! I thought you were leaving me.

CLOV: Oh not just yet, not just yet.

NAGG: Me pap!

HAMM: Give him his pap.

CLOV: There's no more pap.

HAMM: (*To* NAGG) Do you hear that? There's no more pap. You'll never get any more pap.

NAGG: I want me pap!

HAMM: Give him a biscuit. (*Exit* CLOV). Accursed fornicator! How are your stumps?

NAGG: Never mind me stumps.

Enter CLOV *with biscuit.*

CLOV: I'm back again, with the biscuit. (*He gives the biscuit to* NAGG *who fingers it, sniffs it*)

NAGG: (*Plaintively*) What is it?

CLOV: Spratt's medium.[7]

NAGG: (*As before*) It's hard! I can't!

HAMM: Bottle him!

CLOV *pushes* NAGG *back into the bin, closes the lid.*

CLOV: (*Returning to his place beside the chair*) If age but knew![8]

HAMM: Sit on him!

CLOV: I can't sit.

HAMM: True. And I can't stand.

CLOV: So it is.

HAMM: Every man his speciality. (*Pause*) No phone calls? (*Pause*) Don't we laugh?

CLOV: (*After reflection*) I don't feel like it.

HAMM: (*After reflection*) Nor I. (*Pause*) Clov!

CLOV: Yes.

HAMM: Nature has forgotten us.

CLOV: There's no more nature.

HAMM: No more nature! You exaggerate.

CLOV: In the vicinity.

HAMM: But we breathe, we change! We lose our hair, our teeth! Our bloom! Our ideals!

CLOV: Then she hasn't forgotten us.

HAMM: But you say there is none.

CLOV: (*Sadly*) No one that ever lived ever thought so crooked as we.

HAMM: We do what we can.

CLOV: We shouldn't.

(*Pause*)

HAMM: You're a bit of all right, aren't you?

CLOV: A smithereen.[9]

(*Pause*)

HAMM: This is slow work. (*Pause*) Is it not time for my pain-killer?

CLOV: No. (*Pause*) I'll leave you, I have things to do.

HAMM: In your kitchen?

CLOV: Yes.

HAMM: What, I'd like to know.

CLOV: I look at the wall.

HAMM: The wall! And what do you see on your wall? Mene, mene?[10] Naked bodies?

CLOV: I see my light dying.

HAMM: Your light dying! Listen to that! Well, it can die just as well here, *your* light. Take a look at me and then come back and tell me what you think of *your* light.

(*Pause*)

CLOV: You shouldn't speak to me like that.

(*Pause*)

HAMM: (*Coldly*) Forgive me. (*Pause. Louder*) I said, Forgive me.

CLOV: I heard you.

The lid of NAGG's *bin lifts. His hands appear, gripping the rim. Then his head emerges. In his mouth the biscuit. He listens.*

HAMM: Did your seeds come up?

CLOV: No.

HAMM: Did you scratch round them to see if they had sprouted?

CLOV: They haven't sprouted.

HAMM: Perhaps it's still too early.

CLOV: If they were going to sprout they would have sprouted. (*Violently*) They'll never sprout.[11] (*Pause*)

NAGG *takes biscuit in his hand.*

HAMM: This is not much fun. (*Pause*) But that's always the way at the end of the day, isn't it, Clov?

6. The title of a once-popular ballad by Stephen C. Foster.
7. A brand of dog biscuit.
8. Compare the saying, 'If youth but knew, if age but could!'
9. From Irish *smidirín*: a bit, indeed, a fragmentary bit.
10. Alluding to the ominous warning that appeared on Belshazzar's wall in Daniel 5.26.
11. Reminiscent of Eliot's *The Waste Land*, lines 71-72 — the one poem by Eliot that Beckett admires (compare note 7 on *Murphy*, p. 256 above).

CLOV: Always.

HAMM: It's the end of the day like any other day, isn't it, Clov?

CLOV: Always.

HAMM: It's the end of the day like any other day, isn't it, Clov?

CLOV: Looks like it.

(Pause)

HAMM: *(Anguished)* What's happening, what's happening?

CLOV: Something is taking its course.

(Pause)

HAMM: All right, be off. *(He leans back in his chair, remains motionless.* CLOV *does not move, heaves a great groaning sigh.* HAMM *sits up)* I thought I told you to be off.

CLOV: I'm trying. *(He goes to door, halts)* Ever since I was whelped.

Exit CLOV

HAMM: We're getting on. *(He leans back in his chair, remains motionless)*

NAGG *knocks on the lid of the other bin. (Pause) He knocks harder. The lid lifts and the hands of* NELL *appear, gripping the rim. Then her head emerges. Lace cap. Very white face.*

NELL: What is it, my pet? *(Pause)* Time for love?

NAGG: Were you asleep?

NELL: Oh no!

NAGG: Kiss me.

NELL: We can't.

NAGG: Try.

Their heads strain towards each other, fail to meet, fall apart again.

NELL: Why this farce, day after day? *(Pause)*

NAGG: I've lost me tooth.

NELL: When?

NAGG: I had it yesterday.

NELL: *(Elegiac)* Ah yesterday!

They turn painfully towards each other.

NAGG: Can you see me?

NELL: Hardly. And you?

NAGG: What?

NELL: Can you see me?

NAGG: Hardly.

NELL: So much the better, so much the better.

NAGG: Don't say that. *(Pause)* Our sight has failed.

NELL: Yes. *(Pause)*

They turn away from each other.

NAGG: Can you hear me?

NELL: Yes. And you?

NAGG: Yes. *(Pause)* Our hearing hasn't failed.

NELL: Our what?

NAGG: Our hearing.

NELL: No. *(Pause)* Have you anything else to say to me?

NAGG: Do you remember ——

NELL: No.

NAGG: When we crashed on our tandem and lost our shanks.

They laugh heartily.

NELL: It was in the Ardennes.

They laugh less heartily.

NAGG: On the road to Sedan. *(They laugh still less heartily)* Are you cold?

NELL: Yes, perished. And you?

NAGG: I'm freezing. *(Pause)* Do you want to go in?

NELL: Yes.

NAGG: Then go in. (NELL *does not move)* Why don't you go in?

NELL: I don't know.

(Pause)

NAGG: Has he changed your sawdust?

NELL: It isn't sawdust. *(Pause. Wearily)* Can you not be a little accurate, Nagg?

NAGG: Your sand then. It's not important.

NELL: It is important. *(Pause)*

NAGG: It was sawdust once.

NELL: Once!

NAGG: And now it's sand. *(Pause)* From the shore. *(Pause. Impatiently)* Now it's sand he fetches from the shore.

NELL: Now it's sand.

NAGG: Has he changed yours?

NELL: No.

NAGG: Nor mine. *(Pause)* I won't have it! *(Pause. Holding up the biscuit)* Do you want a bit?

NELL: No. *(Pause)* Of what?

NAGG: Biscuit. I've kept you half. *(He looks at the biscuit. Proudly)* Three quarters. For you. Here. *(He proffers the biscuit).* No? *(Pause)* Do you not feel well?

HAMM: *(Wearily)* Quiet, quiet, you're keeping me awake. *(Pause)* Talk softer. *(Pause)* If I could sleep I might make love. I'd go into the woods. My eyes would see . . . the sky, the earth. I'd run, run, they wouldn't catch me. *(Pause)* Nature! *(Pause)* There's something dripping in my head.[12] *(Pause)* A heart, a heart in my head. *(Pause)*

12. Compare below p. 270 and *Embers*, p. 279.

NAGG: (*Soft*) Do you hear him? A heart in his head! (*He chuckles cautiously*)

NELL: One mustn't laugh at those things, Nagg. Why must you always laugh at them?

NAGG: Not so loud!

NELL: (*Without lowering her voice*) Nothing is funnier than unhappiness, I grant you that. But ——

NAGG: (*Shocked*) Oh!

NELL: Yes, yes, it's the most comical thing in the world. And we laugh, we laugh, with a will, in the beginning. But it's always the same thing. Yes, it's like the funny story we have heard too often, we still find it funny, but we don't laugh any more. (*Pause*) Have you anything else to say to me?

NAGG: No.

NELL: Are you quite sure? (*Pause*) Then I'll leave you.

NAGG: Do you not want your biscuit? (*Pause*) I'll keep it for you. (*Pause*) I thought you were going to leave me.

NELL: I am going to leave you.

NAGG: Could you give me a scratch before you go?

NELL: No. (*Pause*) Where?

NAGG: In the back.

NELL: No. (*Pause*) Rub yourself against the rim.

NAGG: It's lower down. In the hollow.

NELL: What hollow?

NAGG: The hollow! (*Pause*) Could you not? (*Pause*) Yesterday you scratched me there.

NELL: (*Elegiac*) Ah yesterday!

NAGG: Could you not? (*Pause*) Would you like me to scratch you? (*Pause*) Are you crying again?

NELL: I was trying.

(*Pause*)

HAMM: Perhaps it's a little vein.

(*Pause*)

NAGG: What was that he said?

NELL: Perhaps it's a little vein.

NAGG: What does that mean? (*Pause*) That means nothing. (*Pause*) Will I tell you the story of the tailor?[13]

NELL: No. (*Pause*) What for?

NAGG: To cheer you up.

NELL: It's not funny.

NAGG: It always made you laugh. (*Pause*) The first time I thought you'd die.

NELL: It was on Lake Como. (*Pause*) One April afternoon. (*Pause*) Can you believe it?

NAGG: What?

NELL: That we once went out rowing on Lake Como. (*Pause*) One April afternoon.

NAGG: We had got engaged the day before.

NELL: Engaged!

NAGG: You were in such fits that we capsized. By rights we should have been drowned.

NELL: It was because I felt happy.

NAGG: (*Indignant*) It was not, it was not, it was my story and nothing else. Happy! Don't you laugh at it still? Every time I tell it. Happy!

NELL: It was deep, deep. And you could see down to the bottom. So white. So clean.

NAGG: Let me tell it again. (*Raconteur's voice*) An Englishman, needing a pair of striped trousers in a hurry for the New Year festivities, goes to his tailor who takes his measurements. (*Tailor's voice*) 'That's the lot, come back in four days, I'll have it ready.' Good. Four days later. (*Tailor's voice*) 'So sorry, come back in a week, I've made a mess of the seat.' Good, that's all right, a neat seat can be very ticklish. A week later. (*Tailor's voice*) 'Frightfully sorry, come back in ten days, I've made a hash of the crutch.' Good, can't be helped, a snug crutch is always a teaser. Ten days later. (*Tailor's voice*) 'Dreadfully sorry, come back in a fortnight, I've made a balls of the fly.' Good, at a pinch, a smart fly is a stiff proposition. (*Pause. Normal voice*) I never told it worse. (*Pause. Gloomy*) I tell this story worse and worse. (*Pause. Raconteur's voice*) Well, to make it short, the bluebells are blowing and he ballockses the buttonholes. (*Customer's voice*) 'God damn you to hell, Sir, no, it's indecent, there are limits! In six days, do you hear me, six days, God made the world. Yes Sir, no less Sir, the WORLD! And you are not bloody well capable of making me a pair of trousers in three months!' (*Tailor's voice, scandalized*) 'But my dear Sir, my dear Sir, look — (*disdainful gesture, disgustedly*) — at the world — (*pause*) — and look — (*loving gesture, proudly*) — at my TROUSERS!' (*Pause. He looks at* NELL *who has remained impassive, her eyes unseeing, breaks into a high forced laugh, cuts it short, pokes his head towards* NELL, *launches his laugh again*)

HAMM: Silence!

NAGG *starts, cuts short his laugh.*

NELL: You could see down to the bottom.

HAMM: (*Exasperated*) Have you not finished? Will you never finish? (*With sudden fury*) Will this

13. Beckett used the same story as epigraph to an essay on the Van Velde brothers (*Disjecta*, p. 118).

never finish? (NAGG *disappears into his bin, closes the lid behind him.* NELL *does not move. Frenziedly*) My kingdom for a nightman![14] (*He whistles. Enter* CLOV) Clear away this muck! Chuck it in the sea!

CLOV *goes to bins, halts.*

NELL: So white.

HAMM: What? What's she blathering about?

CLOV *stoops, takes* NELL's *hand, feels her pulse.*

NELL: (*To* CLOV). Desert!

CLOV *lets go her hand, pushes her back in the bin, closes the lid.*

CLOV: (*Returning to his place beside the chair*) She has no pulse.

HAMM: What was she drivelling about?

CLOV: She told me to go away, into the desert.

HAMM: Damn busybody! Is that all?

CLOV: No.

HAMM: What else?

CLOV: I didn't understand.

HAMM: Have you bottled her?

CLOV: Yes.

HAMM: Are they both bottled?

CLOV: Yes.

HAMM: Screw down the lids. (CLOV *goes towards door*) Time enough. (CLOV *halts*) My anger subsides, I'd like to pee.

CLOV: (*With alacrity*) I'll go and get the catheter. (*He goes towards the door*)

HAMM: Time enough. (CLOV *halts*) Give me my pain-killer.

CLOV: It's too soon. (*Pause*) It's too soon on top of your tonic, it wouldn't act.

HAMM: In the morning they brace you up and in the evening they calm you down. Unless it's the other way round. (*Pause*) That old doctor, he's dead, naturally?

CLOV: He wasn't old.

HAMM: But he's dead?

CLOV: Naturally. (*Pause*) You ask *me* that? (*Pause*)

HAMM: Take me for a little turn. (CLOV *goes behind the chair and pushes it forward*) Not too fast! (CLOV *pushes chair*) Right round the world! (CLOV *pushes chair*) Hug the walls, then back to the centre again. (CLOV *pushes chair*) I was right in the centre, wasn't I?

CLOV: (*Pushing*) Yes.

HAMM: We'd need a proper wheel-chair. With big wheels. Bicycle wheels! (*Pause*) Are you hugging?

CLOV: (*Pushing*) Yes.

HAMM: (*Groping for wall*) It's a lie! Why do you lie to me?

CLOV: (*Bearing closer to wall*) There! There!

HAMM: Stop! (CLOV *stops chair close to back wall.* HAMM *lays his hand against wall*) Old wall! (*Pause*) Beyond is the … other hell. (*Pause. Violently*) Closer! Closer! Up against!

CLOV: Take away your hand. (HAMM *withdraws his hand.* CLOV *rams chair against wall*) There!

HAMM *leans towards wall, applies his ear to it.*

HAMM: Do you hear! (*He strikes the wall with his knuckles*) Do you hear? Hollow bricks! (*He strikes again*) All that's hollow! (*Pause. He straightens up. Violently*) That's enough. Back!

CLOV: We haven't done the round.

HAMM: Back to my place! (CLOV *pushes chair back to centre*) Is that my place?

CLOV: Yes, that's your place.

HAMM: Am I right in the centre?

CLOV: I'll measure it.

HAMM: More or less! More or less!

CLOV: (*Moving chair slightly*) There!

HAMM: I'm more or less in the centre?

CLOV: I'd say so.

HAMM: You'd say so! Put me right in the centre!

CLOV: I'll go and get the tape.

HAMM: Roughly! Roughly! (CLOV *moves chair slightly*) Bang in the centre!

CLOV: There! (*Pause*)

HAMM: I feel a little too far to the left. (CLOV *moves chair slightly*) Now I feel a little too far to the right. (CLOV *moves chair slightly*) I feel a little too far forward. (CLOV *moves chair slightly*) Now I feel a little too far back. (CLOV *moves chair slightly*) Don't stay there (*i.e. behind the chair*), you give me the shivers.

CLOV *returns to his place beside the chair.*

CLOV: If I could kill him I'd die happy. (*Pause*)

HAMM: What's the weather like?

CLOV: The same as usual.

HAMM: Look at the earth.

CLOV: I've looked.

HAMM: With the glass?

CLOV: No need of the glass.

HAMM: Look at it with the glass.

CLOV: I'll go and get the glass.

Exit CLOV.

14. Echoing Shakespeare, *Richard III*, V.4. 7.

HAMM: No need of the glass!

Enter CLOV *with telescope.*

CLOV: I'm back again, with the glass. (*He goes to window right, looks up at it*). I need the steps.

HAMM: Why? Have you shrunk? (*Exit* CLOV *with telescope*) I don't like that, I don't like that.

Enter CLOV *with ladder, but without telescope.*

CLOV: I'm back again, with the steps. (*He sets down ladder under window right, gets up on it, realizes he has not the telescope, gets down*) I need the glass. (*He goes towards the door*)

HAMM: (*Violently*) But you have the glass!

CLOV: (*Halting, violently*) No I haven't the glass!

Exit CLOV.

HAMM: This is deadly.

Enter CLOV *with telescope. He goes towards ladder.*

CLOV: Things are livening up. (*He gets up on ladder, raises the telescope, lets it fall*) I did it on purpose. (*He gets down, picks up the telescope, turns it on auditorium*) I see . . . a multitude . . . in transports . . . of joy. (*Pause*) That's what I call a magnifier. (*He lowers the telescope, turns towards* HAMM) Well? Don't we laugh?

HAMM: (*After reflection*) I don't.

CLOV: (*After reflection*) Nor I. (*He gets up on ladder, turns the telescope on the without*) Let's see. (*He looks, moving the telescope*) Zero . . . (*he looks*) . . . zero . . . (*he looks*) . . . and zero.

HAMM: Nothing stirs. All is ——

CLOV: Zer ——

HAMM: (*Violently*) Wait till you're spoken to! (*Normal voice*) All is . . . all is . . . all is what? (*Violently*) All is what?

CLOV: What all is? In a word? Is that what you want to know? Just a moment. (*He turns the telescope on the without, looks, lowers the telescope, turns towards* HAMM) Corpsed.[15] (*Pause*) Well? Content?

HAMM: Look at the sea.

CLOV: It's the same.

HAMM: Look at the ocean!

CLOV *gets down, takes a few steps towards window left, goes back for ladder, carries it over and sets it down under window left, gets up on it, turns the telescope on the without, looks at length. He starts, lowers the telescope, examines it, turns it again on the without.*

CLOV: Never seen anything like that!

HAMM: (*Anxious*) What? A sail? A fin? Smoke?

CLOV: (*Looking*) The light is sunk.

HAMM: (*Relieved*) Pah! We all knew that.

CLOV: (*Looking*) There was a bit left.

HAMM: The base.

CLOV: (*Looking*) Yes.

HAMM: And now?

CLOV: (*Looking*) All gone.

HAMM: No gulls?

CLOV: (*Looking*) Gulls!

HAMM: And the horizon? Nothing on the horizon?

CLOV: (*Lowering the telescope, turning towards* HAMM, *exasperated*) What in God's name could there be on the horizon?

(*Pause*)

HAMM: The waves, how are the waves?

CLOV: The waves? (*He turns the telescope on the waves*) Lead.

HAMM: And the sun?

CLOV: (*Looking*) Zero.

HAMM: But it should be sinking. Look again.

CLOV: (*Looking*) Damn the sun.

HAMM: Is it night already then?

CLOV: (*Looking*) No.

HAMM: Then what is it?

CLOV: (*Looking*) Grey. (*Lowering the telescope, turning towards* HAMM, *louder*) Grey! (*Pause. Still louder*) GRREY! (*Pause. He gets down, approaches* HAMM *from behind, whispers in his ear*)

HAMM: (*Starting*) Grey! Did I hear you say grey?

CLOV: Light black. From pole to pole.

HAMM: You exaggerate. (*Pause*) Don't stay there, you give me the shivers.

CLOV *returns to his place beside the chair.*

CLOV: Why this farce, day after day?

HAMM: Routine. One never knows. (*Pause*) Last night I saw inside my breast. There was a big sore.

CLOV: Pah! You saw your heart.

HAMM: No, it was living. (*Pause. Anguished*) Clov!

CLOV: Yes.

HAMM: What's happening?

CLOV: Something is taking its course.

(*Pause*)

HAMM: Clov!

CLOV: (*Impatiently*) What is it?

HAMM: We're not beginning to . . . to . . . mean something?

CLOV: Mean something! You and I, mean

15. In actors' jargon, left without a cue and therefore unable to continue the action.

something! (*Brief laugh*) Ah that's a good one!

HAMM: I wonder. (*Pause*) Imagine if a rational being came back to earth, wouldn't he be liable to get ideas into his head if he observed us long enough. (*Voice of rational being*) Ah, good, now I see what it is, yes, now I understand what they're at! (CLOV *starts, drops the telescope and begins to scratch his belly with both hands. Normal voice*) And without going so far as that, we ourselves ... (*with emotion*) ... we ourselves ... at certain moments ... (*Vehemently*) To think perhaps it won't all have been for nothing!

CLOV: (*Anguished, scratching himself*) I have a flea!

HAMM: A flea! Are there still fleas?

CLOV: On me there's one. (*Scratching*) Unless it's a crablouse.

HAMM: (*Very perturbed*) But humanity might start from there all over again! Catch him, for the love of God!

CLOV: I'll go and get the powder.

Exit CLOV.

HAMM: A flea! This is awful! What a day!

Enter CLOV *with a sprinkling-tin.*

CLOV: I'm back again, with the insecticide.

HAMM: Let him have it!

CLOV *loosens the top of his trousers, pulls it forward and shakes powder into the aperture. He stoops, looks, waits, starts, frenziedly shakes more powder, stoops, looks, waits.*

CLOV: The bastard!

HAMM: Did you get him?

CLOV: Looks like it. (*He drops the tin and adjusts his trousers*) Unless he's laying doggo.

HAMM: Laying! Lying you mean. Unless he's *lying* doggo.

CLOV: Ah? One says lying? One doesn't say laying?

HAMM: Use your head, can't you. If he was laying we'd be bitched.

CLOV: Ah. (*Pause*) What about that pee?

HAMM: I'm having it.

CLOV: Ah that's the spirit, that's the spirit!

(*Pause*)

HAMM: (*With ardour*) Let's go from here, the two of us! South! You can make a raft and the currents will carry us away, far away, to other ... mammals!

CLOV: God forbid!

HAMM: Alone, I'll embark alone! Get working on that raft immediately. Tomorrow I'll be gone for ever.

CLOV: (*Hastening towards door*) I'll start straight away.

HAMM: Wait! (CLOV *halts*) Will there be sharks, do you think?

CLOV: Sharks? I don't know. If there are there will be. (*He goes towards door*)

HAMM: Wait! (CLOV *halts*) Is it not yet time for my pain-killer?

CLOV: (*Violently*) No! (*He goes towards door*)

HAMM: Wait! (CLOV *halts*) How are your eyes?

CLOV: Bad.

HAMM: But you can see.

CLOV: All I want.

HAMM: How are your legs?

CLOV: Bad.

HAMM: But you can walk.

CLOV: I come ... and go.

HAMM: In my house. (*Pause. With prophetic relish*) One day you'll be blind, like me. You'll be sitting there, a speck in the void, in the dark, for ever, like me. (*Pause*) One day you'll say to yourself, I'm tired, I'll sit down, and you'll go and sit down. Then you'll say, I'm hungry, I'll get up and get something to eat. But you won't get up. You'll say, I shouldn't have sat down, but since I have I'll sit on a little longer, then I'll get up and get something to eat. But you won't get up and you won't get anything to eat. (*Pause*) You'll look at the wall a while, then you'll say, I'll close my eyes, perhaps have a little sleep, after that I'll feel better, and you'll close them. And when you open them again there'll be no wall any more. (*Pause*) Infinite emptiness will be all around you, all the resurrected dead of all the ages wouldn't fill it, and there you'll be like a little bit of grit in the middle of the steppe. (*Pause*) Yes, one day you'll know what it is, you'll be like me, except that you won't have anyone with you, because you won't have had pity on anyone and because there won't be anyone left to have pity on.

(*Pause*)

CLOV: It's not certain. (*Pause*) And there's one thing you forget.

HAMM: Ah?

CLOV: I can't sit down.

HAMM: (*Impatiently*) Well, you'll lie down then, what the hell! Or you'll come to a standstill, simply stop and stand still, the way you are now. One day you'll say, I'm tired, I'll stop. What does the attitude matter?

(*Pause*)

CLOV: So you all want me to leave you.

HAMM: Naturally.

CLOV: Then I'll leave you.

HAMM: You can't leave us.

CLOV: Then I shan't leave you.

(*Pause*)

HAMM: Why don't you finish us? (*Pause*) I'll tell you the combination of the larder if you promise to finish me.

CLOV: I couldn't finish you.

HAMM: Then you shan't finish me.

(*Pause*)

CLOV: I'll leave you, I have things to do.

HAMM: Do you remember when you came here?

CLOV: No. Too small, you told me.

HAMM: Do you remember your father?

CLOV: (*Wearily*) Same answer. (*Pause*) You've asked me these questions millions of times.

HAMM: I love the old questions. (*With fervour*) Ah the old questions, the old answers, there's nothing like them! (*Pause*) It was I was a father to you.

CLOV: Yes. (*He looks at* HAMM *fixedly*) You were that to me.

HAMM: My house a home for you.

CLOV: Yes. (*He looks about him*) This was that for me.

HAMM: (*Proudly*) But for me (*gesture towards himself*) no father. But for Hamm (*gesture towards surroundings*) no home.

(*Pause*)

CLOV: I'll leave you.

HAMM: Did you ever think of one thing?

CLOV: Never.

HAMM: That here we're down in a hole. (*Pause*) But beyond the hills? Eh? Perhaps it's still green. Eh? (*Pause*) Flora! Pomona! (*Ecstatically*) Ceres![16] (*Pause*) Perhaps you won't need to go very far.

CLOV: I can't go very far. (*Pause*) I'll leave you.

HAMM: Is my dog ready?

CLOV: He lacks a leg.

CLOV: Is he silky?

CLOV: He's a kind of Pomeranian.[17]

HAMM: Go and get him.

CLOV: He lacks a leg.

HAMM: Go and get him! (*Exit* CLOV) We're getting on.

Enter CLOV *holding by one of its three legs a black toy dog.*

CLOV: Your dogs are here.

He hands the dog to HAMM *who feels it, fondles it.*

HAMM: He's white, isn't he?

CLOV: Nearly.

HAMM: What do you mean, nearly? Is he white or isn't he?

CLOV: He isn't.

(*Pause*)

HAMM: You've forgotten the sex.

CLOV: (*Vexed*) But he isn't finished. The sex goes on at the end.

(*Pause*)

HAMM: You haven't put on his ribbon.

CLOV: (*Angrily*) But he isn't finished, I tell you! First you finish your dog and then you put on his ribbon!

(*Pause*)

HAMM: Can he stand?

CLOV: I don't know.

HAMM: Try. (*He hands the dog to* CLOV *who places it on the ground*) Well?

CLOV: Wait! (*He squats down and tries to get the dog to stand on its three legs, fails, lets it go. The dog falls on its side*)

HAMM: (*Impatiently*) Well?

CLOV: He's standing.

HAMM: (*Groping for the dog*) Where? Where is he?

CLOV *holds up the dog in a standing position.*

CLOV: There. (*He takes* HAMM's *hand and guides it towards the dog's head*)

HAMM: (*His hand on the dog's head*) Is he gazing at me?

CLOV: Yes.

HAMM: (*Proudly*) As if he were asking me to take him for a walk?

CLOV: If you like.

HAMM: (*As before*) Or as if he were begging me for a bone. (*He withdraws his hand*) Leave him like that, standing there imploring me.

CLOV *straightens up. The dog falls on its side.*

CLOV: I'll leave you.

16. Flora was the Roman goddess of flowers and Pomona of fruits and fruit trees; Ceres was the protectress of agriculture and the fruits of the earth at large — Mother Earth. Hamm's classical references are another point of similarity with the character of Pozzo in *Godot*. Note also their blindness and Hamm's once having had retainers (above p. 261).

17. A breed of dog that gains Beckett's attention in *Molloy* (Picador, p. 12), and which his mother favoured at the time (Bair, illustration facing p. 192). In the Berlin production, Beckett changed the breed to poodle, in homage to Schopenhauer, who owned one.

HAMM: Have you had your visions?

CLOV: Less.

HAMM: Is Mother Pegg's light on?

CLOV: Light! How could anyone's light be on?

HAMM: Extinguished!

CLOV: Naturally it's extinguished. If it's not on it's extinguished.

HAMM: No, I mean Mother Pegg.

CLOV: But naturally she's extinguished! (*Pause*) What's the matter with you today?

HAMM: I'm taking my course. (*Pause*) Is she buried?

CLOV: Buried! Who would have buried her?

HAMM: You.

CLOV: Me! Haven't I enough to do without burying people?

HAMM: But you'll bury me.

CLOV: No I shan't bury you.

(*Pause*)

HAMM: She was bonny once, like a flower of the field.[18] (*With reminiscent leer*) And a great one for the men!

CLOV: We too were bonny — once. It's a rare thing not to have been bonny — once.

(*Pause*)

HAMM: Go and get the gaff.[19]

CLOV *goes to door, halts.*

CLOV: Do this, do that, and I do it. I never refuse. Why?

HAMM: You're not able to.

CLOV: Soon I won't do it any more.

HAMM: You won't be able to any more. (*Exit* CLOV) Ah the creatures, the creatures, everything has to be explained to them.

Enter CLOV *with gaff.*

CLOV: Here's your gaff. Stick it up.

He gives the gaff to HAMM *who, wielding it like a punt-pole, tries to move his chair.*

HAMM: Did I move?

CLOV: No.

HAMM *throws down the gaff.*

HAMM: Go and get the oilcan.

CLOV: What for?

HAMM: To oil the castors.

CLOV: I oiled them yesterday.

HAMM: Yesterday! What does that mean? Yesterday!

CLOV: (*Violently*) That means that bloody awful day, long ago, before this bloody awful day. I use the words you taught me. If they don't mean anything any more, teach me others. Or let me be silent.

(*Pause*)

HAMM: I once knew a madman who thought the end of the world had come. He was a painter — and engraver. I had a great fondness for him. I used to go and see him, in the asylum. I'd take him by the hand and drag him to the window. Look! There! All that rising corn! And there! Look! The sails of the herring fleet! All that loveliness! (*Pause*) He'd snatch away his hand and go back into his corner. Appalled. All he had seen was ashes. (*Pause*) He alone had been spared. (*Pause*) Forgotten. (*Pause*) It appears the case is . . . was not so . . . so unusual.

CLOV: A madman? When was that?

HAMM: Oh way back, way back, you weren't in the land of the living.

CLOV: God be with the days!

(*Pause.* HAMM *raises his toque*)

HAMM: I had a great fondness for him. (*Pause. He puts on his toque again*) He was a painter — and engraver.

CLOV: There are so many terrible things.

HAMM: No, no, there are not so many now. (*Pause*) Clov!

CLOV: Yes.

HAMM: Do you not think this has gone on long enough?

CLOV: Yes! (*Pause*) What?

HAMM: This . . . this . . . thing.

CLOV: I've always thought so. (*Pause*) You not?

HAMM: (*Gloomily*) Then it's a day like any other day.

CLOV: As long as it lasts. (*Pause*) All life long the same inanities.

(*Pause*)

HAMM: I can't leave you.

CLOV: I know. And you can't follow me.

(*Pause*)

HAMM: If you leave me how shall I know?

CLOV: (*Briskly*) Well you simply whistle me and if I don't come running it means I've left you.

(*Pause*)

HAMM: You won't come and kiss me good-bye?

CLOV: Oh I shouldn't think so.

(*Pause*)

HAMM: But you might be merely dead in your kitchen.

CLOV: The result would be the same.

18. Echoing Psalms 103.15.
19. A stick armed with an iron hook.

HAMM: Yes, but how would I know, if you were merely dead in your kitchen?

CLOV: Well . . . sooner or later I'd start to stink.

HAMM: You stink already. The whole place stinks of corpses.

CLOV: The whole universe.

HAMM: *(Angrily)* To hell with the universe! *(Pause)* Think of something.

CLOV: What?

HAMM: An idea, have an idea. *(Angrily)* A bright idea!

CLOV: Ah good. *(He starts pacing to and fro, his eyes fixed on the ground, his hands behind his back. He halts)* The pains in my legs! It's unbelievable! Soon I won't be able to think any more.

HAMM: You won't be able to leave me. (CLOV *resumes his pacing)* What are you doing?

CLOV: Having an idea. *(He paces)* Ah! *(He halts)*

HAMM: What a brain! *(Pause)* Well?

CLOV: Wait! *(He meditates. Not very convinced)* Yes . . . *(Pause. More convinced)* Yes! *(He raises his head)* I have it! I set the alarm.

(Pause)

HAMM: This is perhaps not one of my bright days, but frankly —

CLOV: You whistle me. I don't come. The alarm rings. I'm gone. It doesn't ring. I'm dead.

(Pause)

HAMM: Is it working? *(Pause. Impatiently)* The alarm, is it working?

CLOV: Why wouldn't it be working?

HAMM: Because it's worked too much.

CLOV: But it's hardly worked at all.

HAMM: *(angrily)* Then because it's worked too little!

CLOV: I'll go and see. *(Exit* CLOV. *Brief ring of alarm off. Enter* CLOV *with alarm-clock. He holds it against* HAMM*'s ear and releases alarm. They listen to it ringing to the end. Pause)* Fit to wake the dead! Did you hear it?

HAMM: Vaguely.

CLOV: The end is terrific!

HAMM: I prefer the middle. *(Pause)* Is it not time for my pain-killer?

CLOV: No! *(He goes to the door, turns)* I'll leave you.

HAMM: It's time for my story. Do you want to listen to my story.

CLOV: No.

HAMM: Ask my father if he wants to listen to my story.

CLOV *goes to bins, raises the lid of* NAGG'S, *stoops, looks into it. Pause. He straightens up.*

CLOV: He's asleep.

HAMM: Wake him.

CLOV *stoops, wakes* NAGG *with the alarm. Unintelligible words.* CLOV *straightens up.*

CLOV: He doesn't want to listen to your story.

HAMM: I'll give him a bon-bon.

CLOV *stoops. As before.*

CLOV: He wants a sugar-plum.

HAMM: He'll get a sugar-plum.

CLOV *stoops. As before.*

CLOV: It's a deal. *(He goes towards door.* NAGG*'s hands appear, gripping the rim. Then the head emerges.* CLOV *reaches door, turns)* Do you believe in the life to come?

HAMM: Mine was always that. *(Exit* CLOV*)* Got him that time!

NAGG: I'm listening.

HAMM: Scoundrel! Why did you engender me?

NAGG: I didn't know.

HAMM: What? What didn't you know?

NAGG: That it'd be you. *(Pause)* You'll give me a sugar-plum?

HAMM: After the audition.

NAGG: You swear?

HAMM: Yes.

NAGG: On what?

HAMM: My honour.

(Pause. They laugh heartily)

NAGG: Two.

HAMM: One.

NAGG: One for me and one for —

HAMM: One! Silence! *(Pause)* Where was I? *(Pause. Gloomily)* It's finished, we're finished. *(Pause)* Nearly finished. *(Pause)* There'll be no more speech. *(Pause)* Something dripping in my head, ever since the fontanelles.[20] *(Stifled hilarity of* NAGG*)* Splash, splash, always on the same spot. *(Pause)* Perhaps it's a little vein. *(Pause)* A little artery. *(Pause. More animated)* Enough of that, it's story time, where was I? *(Pause. Narrative tone)* The man came crawling towards me, on his belly. Pale, wonderfully pale and thin, he seemed on the point of — *(Pause. Normal tone)* No, I've done that bit. *(Pause. Narrative tone)* I calmly filled my pipe — the meerschaum, lit it with . . . let us say a vesta, drew a few puffs. Aah! *(Pause)* Well, what is it *you*

20. A membraneous space in the head of children.

want? (*Pause*) It was an extra-ordinarily bitter day, I remember, zero by the thermometer. But considering it was Christmas Eve there was nothing ... extra-ordinary about that. Seasonable weather, for once in a way. (*Pause*) what ill wind blows you my way? He raised his face to me, black with mingled dirt and tears. (*Pause. Normal tone*) That should do it. (*Narrative tone*) No, no, don't look at me, don't look at me. He dropped his eyes and mumbled something, apologies I presume. (*Pause*) I'm a busy man, you know, the final touches, before the festivities, you know what it is. (*Pause. Forcibly*) Come on now, what is the object of this invasion? (*Pause*) It was a glorious bright day, I remember, fifty by the heliometer, but already the sun was sinking down into the ... down among the dead. (*Normal tone*) Nicely put, that. (*Narrative tone*) Come on now, come on, present your petition and let me resume my labours. (*Pause. Normal tone*) There's English for you. Ah well ... (*Narrative tone*) It was then he took the plunge. It's my little one, he said. Tsstss, a little one, that's bad. My little boy, he said, as if the sex mattered. Where did he come from? He named the hole. A good half-day, on horse. What are you insinuating? That the place is still inhabited? No no, not a soul, except himself and the child — assuming he existed. Good. I inquired about the situation at Kov, beyond the gulf. Not a sinner. Good. And you expect me to believe you have left your little one back there, all alone, and alive into the bargain? Come now! (*Pause*) It was a howling wild day, I remember, a hundred by the anemometer. The wind was tearing up the dead pines and sweeping them ... away. (*Pause. Normal tone*) A bit feeble, that. (*Narrative tone*) Come on, man, speak up, what is it you want from me, I have to put up my holly. (*Pause*) Well to make it short it finally transpired that what he wanted from me was ... bread for his brat. Bread? But I have no bread, it doesn't agree with me. Good. Then perhaps a little corn? (*Pause. Normal tone*) That should do it. (*Narrative tone*) Corn, yes, I have corn, it's true, in my granaries. But use your head. I give you some corn, a pound, a pound and a half, you bring it back to your child and you make him — if he's still alive — a nice pot of porridge (NAGG *reacts*), a nice pot and a half of porridge, full of nourishment. Good. The colours come back into his little cheeks — perhaps. And then? (*Pause*) I lost patience. (*Violently*) Use your head, can't you, use your head, you're on earth, there's no cure for that! (*Pause*) It was an exceedingly dry day, I remember, zero by the hygrometer. Ideal weather, for my lumbago. (*Pause. Violently*) But what in God's name do you imagine? That the earth will awake in spring? That the rivers and seas will run with fish again? That there's manna in heaven still for imbeciles like you? (*Pause*) Gradually I cooled down, sufficiently at least to ask him how long he had taken on the way. Three whole days. Good. In what condition he had left the child. Deep in sleep. (*Forcibly*) But deep in what sleep, deep in what sleep already? (*Pause*) Well to make it short I finally offered to take him into my service. He had touched a chord. And then I imagined already that I wasn't much longer for this world. (*He laughs. Pause*) Well? (*Pause*) Well? Here if you were careful you might die a nice natural death, in peace and comfort. (*Pause*) Well? (*Pause*) In the end he asked me would I consent to take in the child as well — if he were still alive. (*Pause*) It was the moment I was waiting for. (*Pause*) Would I consent to take in the child ...[21] (*Pause*) I can see him still, down on his knees, his hands flat on the ground, glaring at me with his mad eyes, in defiance of my wishes. (*Pause. Normal tone*) I'll soon have finished with this story. (*Pause*) Unless I bring in other characters. (*Pause*) But where would I find them? (*Pause*) Where would I look for them? (*Pause. He whistles. Enter* CLOV) Let us pray to God.

NAGG: Me sugar-plum!

CLOV: There's a rat in the kitchen!

HAMM: A rat! Are there still rats?

CLOV: In the kitchen there's one.

HAMM: And you haven't exterminated him?

CLOV: Half. You disturbed us.

HAMM: He can't get away?

CLOV: No.

HAMM: You'll finish him later. Let us pray to God.

CLOV: Again!

NAGG: Me sugar-plum!

HAMM: God first! (*Pause*) Are you right?

CLOV: (*Resigned*) Off we go.

HAMM: (*To* NAGG) And you?

NAGG: (*Clasping his hands, closing his eyes, in a gabble*). Our Father which art ——[22]

21. Compare Hamm's 'I was a father to you' (p. 268 above). Various passages in the MS versions of the play make clear that the child was indeed Clov.

22. Beginning the Lord's Prayer.

HAMM: Silence! In silence! Where are your manners? (*Pause*) Off we go. (*Attitudes of prayer. Silence. Abandoning his attitude, discouraged*) Well?

CLOV: (*Abandoning his attitude*). What a hope! And you?

HAMM: Sweet damn all! (*To* NAGG) And you?

NAGG: Wait! (*Pause. Abandoning his attitude*) Nothing doing!

HAMM: The bastard! He doesn't exist!

CLOV: Not yet.

NAGG: Me sugar-plum!

HAMM: There are no more sugar-plums!

(*Pause*)

NAGG: It's natural. After all I'm your father. It's true if it hadn't been me it would have been someone else. But that's no excuse. (*Pause*) Turkish Delight, for example, which no longer exists, we all know that, there is nothing in the world I love more. And one day I'll ask you for some, in return for a kindness, and you'll promise it to me. One must live with the times. (*Pause*) Whom did you call when you were a tiny boy, and were frightened, in the dark? Your mother? No. Me. We let you cry. Then we moved you out of earshot, so that we might sleep in peace. (*Pause*) I was asleep, as happy as a king, and you woke me up to have me listen to you. It wasn't indispensable, you didn't really need to have me listen to you. Besides I didn't listen to you. (*Pause*) I hope the day will come when you'll really need to have me listen to you, and need to hear my voice, any voice. (*Pause*) Yes, I hope I'll live till then, to hear you calling me like when you were a tiny boy, and were frightened, in the dark, and I was your only hope. (*Pause.* NAGG *knocks on lid of* NELL'*s bin. Pause*) Nell! (*Pause. He knocks louder. Pause. Louder*) Nell! (*Pause.* NAGG *sinks back into his bin, closes the lid behind him. Pause*)

HAMM: Our revels now are ended.[23] (*He gropes for the dog*) The dog's gone.

CLOV: He's not a real dog, he can't go.

HAMM: (*Groping*) He's not there.

CLOV: He's lain down.

HAMM: Give him up to me. (CLOV *picks up the dog and gives it to* HAMM. HAMM *holds it in his arms. Pause.* HAMM *throws away the dog*) Dirty brute! (CLOV *begins to pick up the objects lying on the ground*) What are you doing?

CLOV: Putting things in order. (*He straightens up. Fervently*) I'm going to clear everything away! (*He starts picking up again*)

HAMM: Order!

CLOV: (*Straightening up*) I love order. It's my dream. A world where all would be silent and still and each thing in its last place, under the last dust. (*He starts picking up again*)

HAMM: (*Exasperated*) What in God's name do you think you are doing?

CLOV: (*Straightening up*) I'm doing my best to create a little order.

HAMM: Drop it!

CLOV *drops the objects he has picked up.*

CLOV: After all, there or elsewhere. (*He goes towards door*)

HAMM: (*Irritably*) What's wrong with your feet?

CLOV: My feet?

HAMM: Tramp! Tramp!

CLOV: I must have put on my boots.

HAMM: Your slippers were hurting you?

(*Pause*)

CLOV: I'll leave you.

HAMM: No!

CLOV: What is there to keep me here?

HAMM: The dialogue. (*Pause*) I've got on with my story. (*Pause*) I've got on with it well. (*Pause. Irritably*) Ask me where I've got to.

CLOV: Oh, by the way, your story?

HAMM: (*Surprised*) What story?

CLOV: The one you've been telling yourself all your . . . days.

HAMM: Ah you mean my chronicle?

CLOV: That's the one.

(*Pause*)

HAMM: (*Angrily*) Keep going, can't you, keep going!

CLOV: You've got on with it, I hope.

HAMM: (*Modestly*) Oh not very far, not very far. (*He sighs*) There are days like that, one isn't inspired. (*Pause*) Nothing you can do about it, just wait for it to come. (*Pause*) No forcing, no forcing, it's fatal. (*Pause*) I've got on with it a little all the same. (*Pause*) Technique, you know. (*Pause. Irritably*) I say I've got on with it a little all the same.

CLOV: (*Admiringly*) Well I never! In spite of everything you were able to get on with it!

HAMM: (*Modestly*) Oh not very far, you know, not very far, but nevertheless, better than nothing.

CLOV: Better than nothing! Is it possible?

23. Compare *The Tempest*, IV.1.148. The second act, in the original MS version of the play, began here. Clov's 'I use the words you taught me' (above p. 269) echoes Caliban's 'You taught me language' in *The Tempest*, I.2.363.

HAMM: I'll tell you how it goes. He comes crawling on his belly ——

CLOV: Who?

HAMM: What?

CLOV: What do you mean, he?

HAMM: Who do I mean! Yet another.

CLOV: Ah him! I wasn't sure.

HAMM: Crawling on his belly, whining for bread for his brat. He's offered a job as gardener. Before — (CLOV *bursts out laughing*) What is there so funny about that?

CLOV: A job as gardener!

HAMM: Is that what tickles you?

CLOV: It must be that.

HAMM: It wouldn't be the bread?

CLOV: Or the brat.

(Pause)

HAMM: The whole thing is comical, I grant you that. What about having a good guffaw the two of us together?

CLOV: (*After reflection*) I couldn't guffaw again today.

HAMM: (*After reflection*) Nor I. (*Pause*) I continue then. Before accepting with gratitude he asks if he may have his little boy with him.

CLOV: What age?

HAMM: Oh tiny.

CLOV: He would have climbed the trees.

HAMM: All the little odd jobs.

CLOV: And then he would have grown up.

HAMM: Very likely.

(Pause)

CLOV: Keep going, can't you, keep going!

HAMM: That's all. I stopped there.

(Pause)

CLOV: Do you see how it goes on.

HAMM: More or less.

CLOV: Will it not soon be the end?

HAMM: I'm afraid it will.

CLOV: Pah! You'll make up another.

HAMM: I don't know. (*Pause*) I feel rather drained. (*Pause*) The prolonged creative effort. (*Pause*) If I could drag myself down to the sea! I'd make a pillow of sand for my head and the tide would come.

CLOV: There's no more tide.

(Pause)

HAMM: Go and see is she dead.

CLOV *goes to bins, raises the lid of* NELL's, *stoops, looks into it.*

(Pause)

CLOV: Looks like it.

He closes the lid, straightens up. HAMM *raises his toque. Pause. He puts it on again.*

HAMM: (*With his hand to his toque*) And Nagg?

CLOV *raises lid of* NAGG's *bin, stoops, looks into it.*

(Pause)

CLOV: Doesn't look like it. (*He closes the lid, straightens up*)

HAMM: (*Letting go his toque*) What's he doing?

CLOV *raises lid of* NAGG's *bin, stoops, looks into it.*

(Pause)

CLOV: He's crying. (*He closes the lid, straightens up*)

HAMM: Then he's living. (*Pause*) Did you ever have an instant of happiness?

CLOV: Not to my knowledge.

(Pause)

HAMM: Bring me under the window. (CLOV *goes towards chair*) I want to feel the light on my face. (CLOV *pushes chair*) Do you remember, in the beginning, when you took me for a turn? You used to hold the chair too high. At every step you nearly tipped me out. (*With senile quaver*) Ah great fun, we had, the two of us, great fun! (*Gloomily*) And then we got into the way of it. (CLOV *stops the chair under window right*) There already? (*Pause. He tilts back his head*) Is it light?

CLOV: It isn't dark.

HAMM: (*Angrily*) I'm asking you is it light.

CLOV: Yes.

(Pause)

HAMM: The curtain isn't closed?

CLOV: No.

HAMM: What window is it?

CLOV: The earth.

HAMM: I knew it! (*Angrily*) But there's no light there! The other! (CLOV *pushes chair towards window left*) The earth! (CLOV *stops the chair under window left.* HAMM *tilts back his head*) That's what I call light! (*Pause*) Feels like a ray of sunshine. (*Pause*) No?

CLOV: No.

HAMM: It isn't a ray of sunshine I feel on my face?

CLOV: No.

(Pause)

HAMM: Am I very white? (*Pause. Angrily*) I'm asking you am I very white!

CLOV: Not more so than usual.

(Pause)

HAMM: Open the window.

CLOV: What for?

HAMM: I want to hear the sea.

CLOV: You wouldn't hear it.

HAMM: Even if you opened the window?

CLOV: No.

HAMM: Then it's not worth while opening it?

CLOV: No.

HAMM: (*Violently*) Then open it! (CLOV *gets up on the ladder, opens the window. Pause*) Have you opened it?

CLOV: Yes.

(*Pause*)

HAMM: You swear you've opened it?

CLOV: Yes.

(*Pause*)

HAMM: Well . . .! (*Pause*) It must be very calm. (*Pause. Violently*) I'm asking you is it very calm?

CLOV: Yes.

HAMM: It's because there are no more navigators. (*Pause*) You haven't much conversation all of a sudden. Do you not feel well?

CLOV: I'm cold.

HAMM: What month are we? (*Pause*) Close the window, we're going back. (CLOV *closes the window, gets down, pushes the chair back to its place, remains standing behind it, head bowed*) Don't stay there, you give me the shivers! (CLOV *returns to his place beside the chair*) Father! (*Pause. Louder*) Father! (*Pause*) Go and see did he hear me.

CLOV *goes to* NAGG's *bin, raises the lid, stoops. Unintelligible words.* CLOV *straightens up.*

CLOV: Yes.

HAMM: Both times?

CLOV *stoops. As before.*

CLOV: Once only.

HAMM: The first time or the second?

CLOV *stoops. As before.*

CLOV: He doesn't know.

HAMM: It must have been the second.

CLOV: We'll never know. (*He closes lid*)

HAMM: Is he still crying?

CLOV: No.

HAMM: The dead go fast. (*Pause*) What's he doing?

CLOV: Sucking his biscuit.

HAMM: Life goes on. (CLOV *returns to his place beside the chair*) Give me a rug, I'm freezing.

CLOV: There are no more rugs.

(*Pause*)

HAMM: Kiss me. (*Pause*) Will you not kiss me?

CLOV: No.

CLOV: On the forehead.

CLOV: I won't kiss you anywhere.

(*Pause*)

HAMM: (*Holding out his hand*) Give me your hand at least. (*Pause*) Will you not give me your hand?

CLOV: I won't touch you.

(*Pause*)

HAMM: Give me the dog. (CLOV *looks round for the dog*) No!

CLOV: Do you not want your dog?

HAMM: No.

CLOV: Then I'll leave you.

HAMM: (*Head bowed, absently*) That's right.

CLOV *goes to door, turns.*

CLOV: If I don't kill that rat he'll die.

HAMM: (*As before*) That's right. (*Exit* CLOV. *Pause*) Me to play.[24] (*He takes out his handkerchief, unfolds it, holds it spread out before him*) We're getting on. (*Pause*) You weep, and weep, for nothing, so as not to laugh, and little by little . . . you begin to grieve. (*He folds the handkerchief, puts it back in his pocket, raises his head*) All those I might have helped. (*Pause*) Helped! (*Pause*) Saved. (*Pause*) Saved! (*Pause*) The place was crawling with them! (*Pause. Violently*) Use your head, can't you, use your head, you're on earth, there's no cure for that! (*Pause*) Get out of here and love one another! Lick your neighbour as yourself![25] (*Pause. Calmer*) When it wasn't bread they wanted it was crumpets. (*Pause. Violently*) Out of my sight and back to your petting parties! (*Pause*) All that, all that! (*Pause*) Not even a real dog! (*Calmer*) The end is in the beginning and yet you go on.[26] (*Pause*) Perhaps I could go on with my story, end it and begin another. (*Pause*) Perhaps I could throw myself out on the floor. (*He pushes himself painfully off his seat, falls back again*) Dig my nails into the cracks and drag myself forward with my fingers. (*Pause*) It will be the end and there I'll be, wondering what can have brought it on and wondering what can have . . . (*he hesitates*) . . . why it was so long coming. (*Pause*) There I'll be, in the old refuge, alone against the silence and . . . (*he hesitates*) . . . the stillness. If I can

24. As at the opening, Hamm sees himself as a chess player called upon to make a move. A game of chess occupies a prominent position in *Murphy* (Chapter 10), and Beckett indeed hoped that two chimpanzees playing chess might illustrate the dustjacket of the novel (Bair, pp. 192-93).
25. A bitter variant of Christ's commandment in Matthew 19.19.
26. A version of a Heraclitan fragment, which is also quoted by T. S. Eliot as an epigraph to *Four Quartets* (1944).

hold my peace, and sit quiet, it will be all over with sound, and motion, all over and done with. (*Pause*) I'll have called my father and I'll have called my . . . (*he hesitates*) . . . my son. And even twice, or three times, in case they shouldn't have heard me, the first time, or the second. (*Pause*) I'll say to myself, He'll come back. (*Pause*) And then? (*Pause*) And then? (*Pause*) He couldn't, he has gone too far. (*Pause*) And then? (*Pause. Very agitated*) All kinds of fantasies! That I'm being watched! A rat! Steps! Breath held and then . . . (*he breathes out*) Then babble, babble, words, like the solitary child who turns himself into children, two, three, so as to be together, and whisper together, in the dark.[27] (*Pause*) Moment upon moment, pattering down, like the millet grains of . . . (*he hesitates*) . . . that old Greek,[28] and all life long you wait for that to mount up to a life. (*Pause. He opens his mouth to continue, renounces*) Ah let's get it over! (*He whistles. Enter* CLOV *with alarm-clock. He halts beside the chair*) What? Neither gone nor dead?

CLOV: In spirit only.

HAMM: Which?

CLOV: Both.

HAMM: Gone from me you'd be dead.

CLOV: And *vice versa.*

HAMM: Outside of here it's death! (*Pause*) And the rat?

CLOV: He's got away.

HAMM: He can't go far. (*Pause. Anxious*) Eh?

CLOV: He doesn't need to go far.

(*Pause*)

HAMM: Is it not time for my pain-killer?

CLOV: Yes.

HAMM: Ah! At last! Give it to me! Quick!

(*Pause*)

CLOV: There's no more pain-killer.

(*Pause*)

HAMM: (*Appalled*) Good . . .! (*Pause*) No more pain-killer!

CLOV: No more pain-killer. You'll never get any more pain-killer.

(*Pause*)

HAMM: But the little round box. It was full!

CLOV: Yes. But now it's empty.

Pause. CLOV *starts to move about the room. He is looking for a place to put down the alarm-clock.*

HAMM: (*Soft*) What'll I do? (*Pause. In a scream*) What'll I do? (CLOV *sees the picture, takes it down, stands it on the floor with its face to wall, hangs up the alarm-clock in its place*) What are you doing?

CLOV: Winding up.

HAMM: Look at the earth.

CLOV: Again!

HAMM: Since it's calling to you.

CLOV: Is your throat sore? (*Pause*) Would you like a lozenge? (*Pause*) No? (*Pause*) Pity.

CLOV *goes, humming, towards window right, halts before it, looks up at it.*

HAMM: Don't sing.

CLOV: (*Turning towards* HAMM) One hasn't the right to sing any more?

HAMM: No.

CLOV: Then how can it end?

HAMM: You want it to end?

CLOV: I want to sing.

HAMM: I can't prevent you.

Pause. CLOV *turns towards window right.*

CLOV: What did I do with that steps? (*He looks round for ladder*) You didn't see that steps? (*He sees it*) Ah, about time. (*He goes towards window left*) Sometimes I wonder if I'm in my right mind. Then it passes over and I'm as lucid as before. (*He gets up on ladder, looks out of window*) Christ, she's under water! (*He looks*) How can that be? (*He pokes forward his head, his hand above his eyes*) It hasn't rained. (*He wipes the pane, looks. Pause*) Ah what a mug I am! I'm on the wrong side! (*He gets down, takes a few steps towards window right*) Under water! (*He goes back for ladder*) What a mug I am! (*He carries ladder towards window right*) Sometimes I wonder if I'm in my right senses. Then it passes off and I'm as intelligent as ever. (*He sets down ladder under window right, gets up on it, looks out of window. He turns towards* HAMM) Any particular sector you fancy? Or merely the whole thing?

HAMM: Whole thing.

CLOV: The general effect? Just a moment. (*He looks out of window*)

(*Pause*)

HAMM: Clov.

CLOV: (*Absorbed*) Mmm.

HAMM: Do you know what it is?

CLOV: (*As before*) Mmm.

HAMM: I was never there. (*Pause*) Clov!

CLOV: (*Turning towards* HAMM, *exasperated*) What is it?

HAMM: I was never there.

CLOV: Lucky for you. (*He looks out of window*)

27. Compare *That Time*, p. 297 below.

28. Zeno. Compare p. 260 above and p. 309 below.

HAMM: Absent, always. It all happened without me. I don't know what's happened. (*Pause*) Do you know what's happened? (*Pause*) Clov!

CLOV: (*Turning towards* HAMM, *exasperated*) Do you want me to look at this muckheap, yes or no?

HAMM: Answer me first.

CLOV: What?

HAMM: Do you know what's happened?

CLOV: When? Where?

HAMM: (*Violently*) When! What's happened! Use your head, can't you! What has happened?

CLOV: What for Christ's sake does it matter? (*He looks out of window*)

HAMM: I don't know.

Pause. CLOV *turns towards* HAMM.

CLOV: (*Harshly*) When old Mother Pegg asked you for oil for her lamp and you told her to get out to hell, you knew what was happening then, no? (*Pause*) You know what she died of, Mother Pegg? Of darkness.

HAMM: (*Feebly*) I hadn't any.

CLOV: (*As before*) Yes, you had.

(*Pause*)

HAMM: Have you the glass?

CLOV: No, it's clear enough as it is.

HAMM: Go and get it.

Pause. CLOV *casts up his eyes, brandishes his fists. He loses balance, clutches on to the ladder. He starts to get down, halts.*

CLOV: There's one thing I'll never understand. (*He gets down*) Why I always obey you. Can you explain that to me?

HAMM: No . . . Perhaps it's compassion. (*Pause*) A kind of great compassion. (*Pause*) Oh you won't find it easy, you won't find it easy.

Pause. CLOV *begins to move about the room in search of the telescope.*

CLOV: I'm tired of our goings on, very tired. (*He searches*) You're not sitting on it? (*He moves the chair, looks at the place where it stood, resumes his search*)

HAMM: (*Anguished*) Don't leave me there! (*Angrily* CLOV *restores the chair to its place*) Am I right in the centre?

CLOV: You'd need a microscope to find this — (*He sees the telescope*) Ah, about time. (*He picks up the telescope, gets up on the ladder, turns the telescope on the without*)

HAMM: Give me the dog.

CLOV: (*Looking*) Quiet!

HAMM: (*Angrily*) Give me the dog!

CLOV *drops the telescope, clasps his hands to his head. Pause. He gets down precipitately, looks for the dog, see it, picks it up, hastens towards* HAMM *and strikes him on the head violently with the dog.*

CLOV: There's your dog for you!

The dog falls to the ground.

(*Pause*)

HAMM: He hit me!

CLOV: You drive me mad, I'm mad!

HAMM: If you must hit me, hit me with the axe. (*Pause*) Or with the gaff, hit me with the gaff. Not with the dog. With the gaff. Or with the axe.

CLOV *picks up the dog and gives it to* HAMM *who takes it in his arms.*

CLOV: (*Imploringly*) Let's stop playing!

HAMM: Never! (*Pause*) Put me in my coffin.

CLOV: There are no more coffins.

HAMM: Then let it end! (CLOV *goes towards ladder*) With a bang! (CLOV *gets up on ladder, gets down again, looks for telescope, sees it, picks it up, gets up ladder, raises telescope*) Of darkness! And me? Did anyone ever have pity on me?

CLOV: (*Lowering the telescope, turning towards* HAMM) What? (*Pause*) Is it me you're referring to?

HAMM: (*Angrily*) An aside, ape! Did you never hear an aside before? (*Pause*) I'm warming up for my last soliloquy.

CLOV: I warn you. I'm going to look at this filth since it's an order. But it's the last time. (*He turns the telescope on the without*) Let's see. (*He moves the telescope*) Nothing . . . nothing . . . good . . . good . . . nothing . . . goo — (*He starts, lowers the telescope, examines it, turns it again on the without. Pause*) Bad luck to it!

HAMM: More complications! (CLOV *gets down*) Not an underplot, I trust.

CLOV *moves ladder nearer window, gets up on it, turns telescope on the without.*

CLOV: (*Dismayed*) Looks like a small boy![29]

HAMM: (*Sarcastic*). A small . . . boy!

CLOV: I'll go and see. (*He gets down, drops the telescope, goes towards door, turns*) I'll take the gaff. (*He looks for the gaff, sees it, picks it up, hastens towards door*)

HAMM: No!

CLOV *halts.*

CLOV: No? A potential procreator?

HAMM: If he exists he'll die there or he'll come

29. The French text enlarges on the description of the boy, and Hamm suggests that he might be looking at the house with the eyes of the dying Moses.

here. And if he doesn't ...

(*Pause*)

CLOV: You don't believe me? You think I'm inventing?

(*Pause*)

HAMM: It's the end, Clov, we've come to the end. I don't need you any more.

(*Pause*)

CLOV: Lucky for you. (*He goes towards door*)

HAMM: Leave me the gaff.

CLOV *gives him the gaff, goes towards door, halts, looks at alarm-clock, takes it down, looks round for a better place to put it, goes to bins, puts it on lid of* NAGG's *bin.*

(*Pause*)

CLOV: I'll leave you. (*He goes towards door*)

HAMM: Before you go . . . (CLOV *halts near door*) . . . say something.

CLOV: There is nothing to say.

HAMM: A few words ... to ponder ... in my heart.

CLOV: Your heart!

HAMM: Yes. (*Pause. Forcibly*) Yes! (*Pause*) With the rest, in the end, the shadows, the murmurs, all the trouble, to end up with. (*Pause*) Clov ... He never spoke to me. Then, in the end, before he went, without my having asked him, he spoke to me. He said ...

CLOV: (*Despairingly*). Ah ...!

HAMM: Something . . . from your heart.

CLOV: My heart!

HAMM: A few words ... from your heart.

(*Pause*)

CLOV: (*Fixed gaze, tonelessly, towards auditorium*) They said to me, That's love, yes yes, not a doubt, now you see how ——

HAMM: Articulate!

CLOV: (*As before*) How easy it is. They said to me, That's friendship, yes yes, no question, you've found it. They said to me, Here's the place, stop, raise your head and look at all that beauty. That order! They said to me, Come now, you're not a brute beast, think upon these things and you'll see how all becomes clear. And simple! They said to me, What skilled attention they get, all these dying of their wounds.

HAMM: Enough!

CLOV: (*As before*) I say to myself — sometimes, Clov, you must learn to suffer better than that if you want them to weary of punishing you — one day. I say to myself — sometimes, Clov, you must be there better than that if you want them to let you go — one day. But I feel too old, and too far, to form new habits. Good, it'll never end, I'll never go. (*Pause*) Then one day, suddenly, it ends, it changes, I don't understand, it dies, or it's me, I don't understand that either. I ask the words that remain — sleeping, waking, morning, evening. They have nothing to say. (*Pause*) I open the door of the cell and go. I am so bowed I only see my feet, if I open my eyes, and between my legs a little trail of black dust. I say to myself that the earth is extinguished, though I never saw it lit. (*Pause*) It's easy going. (*Pause*) When I fall I'll weep for happiness. (*Pause. He goes towards door*)

HAMM: Clov! (CLOV *halts, without turning*) Nothing. (CLOV *moves on*) Clov!

CLOV *halts, without turning.*

CLOV: This is what we call making an exit.

HAMM: I'm obliged to you, Clov. For your services.

CLOV: (*Turning, sharply*) Ah pardon, it's I am obliged to you.

HAMM: It's we are obliged to each other. (*Pause.* CLOV *goes towards door*) One thing more. (CLOV *halts*) A last favour. (*Exit* CLOV) Cover me with the sheet. (*Long pause*) No? Good. (*Pause*) Me to play. (*Pause. Wearily*) Old endgame lost of old, play and lose and have done with losing. (*Pause. More animated*) Let me see. (*Pause*) Ah yes! (*He tries to move the chair, using the gaff as before. Enter* CLOV, *dressed for the road. Panama hat, tweed coat, raincoat over his arm, umbrella, bag. He halts by the door and stands there, impassive and motionless, his eyes fixed on* HAMM, *till the end.* HAMM *gives up*) Good. (*Pause*) Discard. (*He throws away the gaff, makes to throw away the dog, thinks better of it*) Take it easy. (*Pause*) And now? (*Pause*) Raise hat. (*He raises his toque*) Peace to our ... arses (*Pause*) And put on again. (*He puts on his toque*) Deuce. (*Pause. He takes off his glasses*) Wipe. (*He takes out his handkerchief and, without unfolding it, wipes his glasses*) And put on again. (*He puts on his glasses, puts back the handkerchief in his pocket*) We're coming. A few more squirms like that and I'll call. (*Pause*) A little poetry.[30] (*Pause*) You prayed — (*Pause. He*

30. Hamm half-translates the first stanza of Baudelaire's sonnet, *Receuillement*:

Sois sage, ô ma Douleur, et tiens-toi plus tranquille.
Tu réclamais le Soir; il descend; le voici:
Une atmosphère obscure enveloppe la ville,
Aux uns portant la paix, aux autres le souci.

corrects himself) You CRIED for night; it comes — (*Pause. He corrects himself*) It FALLS: now cry in darkness. (*He repeats, chanting*) You cried for night; it falls: now cry in darkness. (*Pause*) Nicely put, that. (*Pause*) And now? (*Pause*) Moments for nothing, now as always, time was never and time is over, reckoning closed and story ended. (*Pause. Narrative tone*) If he could have his child with him . . . (*Pause*). It was the moment I was waiting for. (*Pause*). You don't want to abandon him? You want him to bloom while you are withering? Be there to solace your last million last moments? (*Pause*) He doesn't realize, all he knows is hunger, and cold, and death to crown it all. But you! You ought to know what the earth is like, nowadays. Oh, I put him before his responsibilities! (*Pause. Normal tone*) Well, there we are, there I am, that's enough. (*He raises the whistle to his lips, hesitates, drops it. Pause*) Yes, truly! (*He whistles. Pause. Louder. Pause*) Good. (*Pause*) Father! (*Pause. Louder*) Father! (*Pause*) Good. (*Pause*) We're coming. (*Pause*) And to end up with? (*Pause*) Discard. (*He throws away the dog. He tears the whistle from his neck*) With my compliments. (*He throws whistle towards auditorium. Pause. He sniffs. Soft*) Clov! (*Long pause*) No? Good. (*He takes out the handkerchief*) Since that's the way we're playing it . . . (*he unfolds handkerchief*) . . . let's play it that way . . . (*he unfolds*) . . . and speak no more about it . . . (*he finishes unfolding*) . . . speak no more. (*He holds the handkerchief spread out before him*) Old stancher! (*Pause*). You . . . remain. (*Pause. He covers his face with handkerchief, lowers his arms to armrests, remains motionless*)

Brief tableau.

CURTAIN

EMBERS
(1959)

[*Embers* is the second of Beckett's plays for radio. It was written in English under the provisional title *Ebb*, completed at the beginning of 1959, and was broadcast that June. Published later in the same year, it was collected and reprinted with only very minor changes. Although it is probably less well-known than *All That Fall,* it is less imperfect, being wholly conceived 'to come out of the dark'.

The confusion of voices that succeed one another in Henry's mind is deliberate, and could not exist in a stage presentation. Similarly the artificiality of the sound-effects is emphasized, so that it is not certain whether Henry is 'really' by the sea-shore or has something 'wrong with [his] brain'. The whole play, indeed, might be a figment of Henry's imagination. He might be trapped inside what he hears, even though listening to what he hears gives him involuntary respite. The play arranges the possibilities, and works to resolve rather than to oppose them.

Comparisons with *Endgame* (the son's need, in the dark, for the listening presence of his father; Hamm's and Henry's storytelling; the dripping they hear in their heads; their need for pain-killers) provide a measure of the different effect, at once more recognizable and at the same time more ventriloquial, that *Embers* works towards. Details of the BBC production are given by Clas Zilliacus, *Beckett and Broadcasting: A Study of the Works of Samuel Beckett for and in Radio and Television* (Åbo, Finland: Åbo Akademi, 1976), pp. 76-99.]

HENRY
ADA
MUSIC MASTER
ADDIE
RIDING MASTER

Sea scarcely audible. HENRY'S *boots on shingle. He halts. Sea a little louder.*

HENRY: On. (*Sea. Voice louder*) On! (*He moves on. Boots on shingle. As he goes*) Stop. (*Boots on shingle. As he goes, louder*). Stop! (*He halts. Sea a little louder*) Down. (*Sea. Voice louder*) Down! (*Slither of shingle as he sits. Sea, still faint, audible throughout what follows whenever pause indicated*) Who is beside me now? (*Pause*) An old man, blind and foolish. (*Pause*) My father, back from the dead, to be with me. (*Pause*) As if he hadn't died. (*Pause*) No, simply back from the dead, to be with me, in this strange place. (*Pause*) Can he hear me? (*Pause*). Yes, he must hear me. (*Pause*) To answer me? (*Pause*) No, he doesn't answer me. (*Pause*) Just be with me. (*Pause*) That sound you hear is the sea. (*Pause. Louder*) I say that sound you hear is the sea, we are sitting on the strand. (*Pause*) I mention it because the sound is so strange, so unlike the sound of the sea, that if you didn't see what it was you wouldn't know what it was. (*Pause*) Hooves! (*Pause. Louder*) Hooves! (*Sound of hooves walking on hard road. They die rapidly away. Pause*) Again! (*Hooves as before. Pause. Excitedly*) Train it to mark time! Shoe it with steel and tie it up in the yard, have it stamp all day! (*Pause*) A ten-ton mammoth back from the dead, shoe it with steel and have it tramp the world down! Listen to it! (*Pause*) Listen to the light now, you always loved light, not long past noon and all the shore in shadow and the sea out as far as the island.[1] (*Pause*) You would never live this side of the bay, you wanted the sun on the water for that evening bathe you took once too often. But when I got your money I moved across, as perhaps you may know. (*Pause*) We never found your body, you know that held up probate an unconscionable time, they said there was nothing to prove you hadn't run away from us all and alive and well under a false name in the Argentine for example, that grieved mother greatly. (*Pause*) I'm like you in that, can't stay away from it, but I never go in, no, I think the last time I went in was with you. (*Pause*) Just be near it. (*Pause*) Today it's calm, but I often hear it above in the house and walking the roads and start talking, oh just loud enough to drown it, nobody notices. (*Pause*) But I'd be talking now no matter where I was, I once went to Switzerland to get away from the cursed thing and never stopped all the time I was there. (*Pause*) I usen't to need anyone, just to myself, stories, there was a great one about an old fellow called Bolton, I never finished it, I never finished any of them, I never finished anything, everything always went on for ever. (*Pause*) Bolton (*Pause. Louder*) Bolton! (*Pause*) There before the fire. (*Pause*) Before the fire with all the shutters . . . no, hangings, hangings, all the hangings drawn and the light, no light, only the light of the fire, sitting there in the . . . no, standing, standing there on the hearthrug in the dark before the fire with his arms on the chimney-piece and his head on his arms, standing there waiting in the dark before the fire in his old red dressing-gown and no sound in the house of any kind, only the sound of the fire. (*Pause*) Standing there in his old red dressing-gown might go on fire any minute like when he was a child, no, that was his pyjamas, standing there waiting in the dark, no light, only the light of the fire, and no sound of any kind, only the fire, an old man in great trouble. (*Pause*) Ring then at the door and over he goes to the window and looks out between the hangings, fine old chap, very big and strong, bright winter's night, snow everywhere, bitter cold, white world, cedar boughs bending under load and then as the arm goes up to ring again recognizes . . . Holloway . . . (*Long pause*) . . . yes, Holloway, recognizes Holloway, goes down and opens. (*Pause*) Outside all still, not a sound, dog's chain maybe or a bough groaning if you stood there listening long enough, white world, Holloway with his little black bag, not a sound, bitter cold, full moon small and white, crooked trail of Holloway's galoshes, Vega in the Lyre[2] very green. (*Pause*) Vega in the Lyre very green. (*Pause*) Following conversation then on the step, no, in the room, back in the room, following conversation then back in the room, Holloway: 'My dear Bolton, it is now past midnight, if you would be good enough —', gets no further, Bolton: 'Please! PLEASE!' Dead silence then, not a sound, only the fire, all coal, burning down now, Holloway on the hearthrug trying to toast his arse, Bolton, where's Bolton, no light, only the fire, Bolton at the window his back to the hangings, holding them a little apart with his hand looking out, white world, even the spire, white to the vane, most unusual, silence in the house, not a sound, only the fire, no flames now, embers. (*Pause*) Embers. (*Pause*) Shifting, lapsing, furtive like, dreadful sound, Holloway on the rug, fine old chap, six foot, burly, legs apart, hands behind his back holding up the tails of his old macfarlane,[3] Bolton at the window, grand old figure in his old red dressing-gown, back against the hangings, hand stretched out widening the chink, looking out, white world, great trouble, not a sound, only the embers, sound of dying, dying glow, Holloway, Bolton, Bolton, Holloway, old men, great trouble, white world, not a sound. (*Pause*) Listen to it! (*Pause*) Close your eyes and listen to it, what would you think it was? (*Pause. Vehement*) A drip! A drip![4] (*Sound of drip, rapidly amplified, suddenly cut off*) Again! (*Drip again. Amplification begins*) No! (*Drip cut off. Pause*) Father! (*Pause. Agitated*) Stories, stories, years and years of stories, till the need came on me, for someone, to be with me, anyone, a stranger, to talk to, imagine he hears me, years of that, and then, now, for someone who . . . knew me, in the old days, anyone, to be with me, imagine he hears me, what I am, now. (*Pause*) No good either. (*Pause*) Not there

1. Beckett has identified the setting as the Whiterock end of Killiney Strand, near where his brother Frank had a house and which is in shadow by evening. The island is therefore Dalkey Island, where Lady Pedal, Lemuel and Macmann picnic at the close of *Malone Dies*.

2. Vega is the chief star in the constellation Lyra, as Joyce notes in the Ithaca chapter of *Ulysses*.

3. A man's sleeveless cloak, apparently, incorporating a cape to cover the shoulders.

4. Compare Hamm in *Endgame*, pp. 263, 270 above.

either. (*Pause*) Try again. (*Pause*) White world, not a sound. (*Pause*) Holloway. (*Pause*) Holloway says he'll go, damned if he'll sit up all night before a black grate, doesn't understand, call a man out, an old friend, in the cold and dark, an old friend, urgent need, bring the bag, then not a word, no explanation, no heat, no light, Bolton: 'Please! PLEASE!' Holloway, no refreshment, no welcome, chilled to the medulla, catch his death, can't understand, strange treatment, old friend, says he'll go, doesn't move, not a sound, fire dying, white beam from window, ghastly scene, wishes to God he hadn't come, no good, fire out, bitter cold, great trouble, white world, not a sound, no good. (*Pause*) No good. (*Pause*) Can't do it. (*Pause*) Listen to it! (*Pause*) Father! (*Pause*) You wouldn't know me now, you'd be sorry you ever had me, but you were that already, a washout, that's the last I heard from you, a washout. (*Pause. Imitating father's voice*) 'Are you coming for a dip?' 'No.' 'Come on, come on.' 'No.' Glare, stump to door, turn, glare. 'A washout, that's all you are, a washout!'[5] (*Violent slam of door. Pause*) Again! (*Slam. Pause*) Slam life shut like that! (*Pause*) Washout. (*Pause*) Wish to Christ she had. (*Pause*) Never met Ada, did you, or did you, I can't remember, no matter, no one'd know her now. (*Pause*) What turned her against me do you think, the child I suppose, horrid little creature, wish to God we'd never had her, I use to walk with her in the fields, Jesus that was awful, she wouldn't let go my hand and I mad to talk. 'Run along now, Addie, and look at the lambs.' (*Imitating* ADDIE's *voice*) 'No papa.' 'Go on now, go on.' (*Plaintive*). 'No papa.' (*Violent*) 'Go on with you when you're told and look at the lambs!' (ADDIE's *loud wail. Pause*) Ada too, conversation with her, that was something, that's what hell will be like, small chat to the babbling of Lethe about the good old days when we wished we were dead. (*Pause*) Price of margarine fifty years ago. (*Pause*) And now. (*Pause. With solemn indignation*) Price of blueband[6] now! (*Pause*) Father! (*Pause*) Tired of talking to you. (*Pause*) That was always the way, walk all over the mountains with you talking and talking and then suddenly mum and home in misery and not a word to a soul for weeks, sulky little bastard, better off dead. (*Long pause*) Ada. (*Pause. Louder*) Ada!

ADA: (*Low remote voice throughout*) Yes.

HENRY: Have you been there long?

ADA: Some little time. (*Pause*) Why do you stop, don't mind me. (*Pause*) Do you want me to go away? (*Pause*) Where is Addie? (*Pause*)

HENRY: With her music master. (*Pause*) Are you going to answer me today?

ADA: You shouldn't be sitting on the cold stones, they're bad for your growths. Raise yourself up till I slip my shawl under you. (*Pause*) Is that better?

HENRY: No comparison, no comparison. (*Pause*) Are you going to sit down beside me?

ADA: Yes. (*No sound as she sits*) Like that? (*Pause*) Or do you prefer like that? (*Pause*) You don't care. (*Pause*) Chilly enough I imagine, I hope you put on your jaegers.[7] (*Pause*) Did you put on your jaegers, Henry?

HENRY: What happened was this, I put them on and then I took them off again and then I put them on again and then I took them off again and then I took them on again and then I —

ADA: Have you them on now?

HENRY: I don't know. (*Pause*) Hooves! (*Pause. Louder*) Hooves! (*Sound of hooves walking on hard road. They die rapidly away*) Again!

(*Hooves as before. Pause*)

ADA: Did you hear them?

HENRY: Not well.

ADA: Galloping?

HENRY: No. (*Pause*) Could a horse mark time? (*Pause*)

ADA: I'm not sure that I know what you mean.

HENRY: (*Irritably*) Could a horse be trained to stand still and mark time with its four legs?

ADA: Oh. (*Pause*) The ones I used to fancy all did. (*She laughs. Pause*) Laugh, Henry, it's not every day I crack a joke. (*Pause*) Laugh, Henry do that for me.

HENRY: You wish *me* to laugh?

ADA: You laughed so charmingly once, I think that's what first attracted me to you. That and your smile. (*Pause*) Come on, it will be like old times. (*Pause. He tries to laugh, fails*)

HENRY: Perhaps I should begin with the smile. (*Pause for smile*) Did that attract you? (*Pause*) Now

5. Compare note 8 on *Company* (p. 302 below).
6. A modern brand of margarine. The incongruity of the brand name points up the distinctive character of the play as a whole. The proper names, social ambience and formal syntax of Henry's monologue possess a period remoteness and fictive quality that, it should be stressed, is at some distance from Beckett's own social and biographical background. *Embers* makes very different use of biographical material from Beckett's previous radio play, *All That Fall* (as does, in a different way again, *That Time* compared with *Company*).

7. Woollen underclothing.

I'll try again. (*Long horrible laugh*) Any of the old charm there?

ADA: Oh Henry! (*Pause*)

HENRY: Listen to it! (*Pause*) Lips and claws! (*Pause*) Get away from it! Where it couldn't get at me! The Pampas! What?

ADA: Calm yourself.

HENRY: And I live on the brink of it! Why? Professional obligations? (*Brief laugh*) Reasons of health? (*Brief laugh*) Family ties? (*Brief laugh*) A woman? (*Laugh in which she joins*) Some old grave I cannot tear myself away from? (*Pause*) Listen to it! What is it like?

ADA: It is like an old sound I used to hear. (*Pause*) It is like another time, in the same place. (*Pause*) It was rough, the spray came flying over us. (*Pause*) Strange it should have been rough then. (*Pause*) And calm now. (*Pause*)

HENRY: Let us get up and go.

ADA: Go? Where? And Addie? She would be very distressed if she came and found you had gone without her. (*Pause*) What do you suppose is keeping her?

Smart blow of cylindrical ruler on piano case. Unsteadily, ascending and descending, ADDIE *plays scale of A Flat Major, hands first together, then reversed. Pause.*

MUSIC MASTER: (*Italian accent*) Santa Cecilia! (*Pause*)

ADDIE: Will I play my piece now please?

Pause. MUSIC MASTER *beats two bars of waltz time with ruler on piano case.* ADDIE *plays opening bars of Chopin's 5th Waltz in A Flat Major,* MUSIC MASTER *beating time lightly with ruler as she plays. In first chord of bass, bar 5, she plays E instead of F. Resounding blow of ruler on piano case.* ADDIE *stops playing.*

MUSIC MASTER: (*Violently*) Fa![8]

ADDIE: (*Tearfully*) What?

MUSIC MASTER: (*Violently*) Eff! Eff!

ADDIE: (*Tearfully*) Where?

MUSIC MASTER: (*Violently*) Qua! (*He thumps note*) Fa!

Pause. ADDIE *begins again,* MUSIC MASTER *beating time lightly with ruler. When she comes to bar 5 she makes same mistake. Tremendous blow of ruler on piano case.* ADDIE *stops playing, begins to wail.*

MUSIC MASTER: (*Frenziedly*) Eff! Eff! (*He hammers note*) Eff! (*He hammers note*) Eff! (*Hammered note, 'Eff!' and* ADDIE'*s wail amplified to paroxysm, then suddenly cut off. Pause*)

ADA: You are silent today.

HENRY: It was not enough to drag her into the world, now she must play the piano.

ADA: She must learn. She shall learn. That — and riding.

(*Hooves walking*)

RIDING MASTER: Now Miss! Elbows in Miss! Hands down Miss! (*Hooves trotting*) Now Miss! Back straight Miss! Knees in Miss! (*Hooves cantering*) Now Miss! Tummy in Miss! Chin up Miss! (*Hooves galloping*) Now Miss! Eyes front Miss! (ADDIE *begins to wail*) Now Miss! Now Miss! (*Galloping hooves, 'Now Miss!' and* ADDIE'*s wail amplified to paroxysm, then suddenly cut off. Pause*)

ADA: What are you thinking of? (*Pause*) I was never taught, until it was too late. All my life I regretted it.

HENRY: What was your strong point, I forget.

ADA: Oh . . . geometry I suppose, plane and solid. (*Pause*) First plane, then solid. (*Shingle as he gets up*) Why do you get up?

HENRY: I thought I might try and get as far as the water's edge. (*Pause. With a sigh*) And back. (*Pause*) Stretch my old bones.

(*Pause*)

ADA: Well, why don't you. Don't stand there thinking about it. (*Pause*) Don't stand there staring. (*Pause. He goes towards sea. Boots on shingle, say ten steps. He halts at water's edge. Pause. Sea a little louder. Distant*) Don't wet your good boots. (*Pause*)

HENRY: Don't, don't . . .

(*Sea suddenly rough*)

ADA: (*Twenty years earlier, imploring*) Don't! Don't!

HENRY: (*Ditto, urgent*) Darling!

ADA: (*Ditto, more feebly*) Don't!

HENRY: (*Ditto, exultantly*) Darling!

(*Rough sea.* ADA *cries out. Cry and sea amplified, cut off. End of evocation. Pause. Sea calm. He goes back up deeply shelving beach. Boots laborious on shingle. He halts. Pause. He moves on. He halts. Pause. Sea calm and faint*)

ADA: Don't stand there gaping. Sit down. (*Pause. Shingle as he sits*). On the shawl. (*Pause*) Are you afraid we might touch? (*Pause*) Henry.

HENRY: Yes.

ADA: You should see a doctor about your talking, it's worse, what must it be like for Addie? (*Pause*)

8. *Fa* is Italian for F, and *Qua* for Here. Santa Cecilia (above) is the patron saint of music.

Do you know what she said to me once, when she was still quite small, she said, Mummy, why does Daddy keep on talking all the time? She heard you in the lavatory. I didn't know what to answer.

HENRY: Daddy! Addie! (*Pause*) I told you to tell her I was praying. (*Pause*) Roaring prayers at God and his saints.

ADA: It's very bad for the child. (*Pause*) It's silly to say it keeps you from hearing it, it doesn't keep you from hearing it and even if it does you shouldn't be hearing it, there must be something wrong with your brain.

(*Pause*)

HENRY: That! I shouldn't be hearing that!

ADA: I don't think you are hearing it. And if you are what's wrong with it, it's a lovely peaceful gentle soothing sound, why do you hate it? (*Pause*) And if you hate it why don't you keep away from it? Why are you always coming down here? (*Pause*) There's something wrong with your brain, you ought to see Holloway, he's alive still, isn't he?

(*Pause*)

HENRY: (*Wildly*) Thuds, I want thuds! Like this! (*He fumbles in the shingle, catches up two big stones and starts dashing them together*) Stone! (*Clash*) Stone! (*Clash. 'Stone!' and clash amplified, cut off. Pause. He throws one stone away. Sound of its fall*) That's life. (*He throws the other stone away. Sound of its fall*) Not this . . . (*Pause*) . . . sucking!

ADA: And why life? (*Pause*) Why life, Henry? (*Pause*) Is there anyone about?

HENRY: Not a living soul.

ADA: I thought as much. (*Pause*) When we longed to have it to ourselves there was always someone. Now that it does not matter the place is deserted.

HENRY: Yes, you were always very sensitive to being seen in gallant conversation. The least feather of smoke on the horizon and you adjusted your dress and became immersed in the *Manchester Guardian*. (*Pause*) The hole is still there, after all these years. (*Pause. Louder*) The hole is still there.

ADA: What hole? The earth is full of holes.

HENRY: Where we did it at last for the first time.

ADA: Ah yes, I think I remember. (*Pause*) The place has not changed.

HENRY: Oh yes it has, *I* can see it. (*Confidentially*) There is a levelling going on! (*Pause*) What age is she now?

ADA: I have lost count of time.

HENRY: Twelve? Thirteen? (*Pause*) Fourteen?

ADA: I really could not tell you, Henry.

HENRY: It took us a long time to have her. (*Pause*) Years we kept hammering away at it. (*Pause*) But we did it in the end. (*Pause. Sigh*) We had her in the end. (*Pause*) Listen to it! (*Pause*) It's not so bad when you get out on it. (*Pause*) Perhaps I should have gone into the merchant navy.

ADA: It's only on the surface, you know. Underneath all is as quiet as the grave. Not a sound. All day, all night, not a sound. (*Pause*)

HENRY: Now I walk about with the gramophone. But I forgot it today.

ADA: There is no sense in that. (*Pause*) There is no sense in trying to drown it. (*Pause*) See Holloway. (*Pause*)

HENRY: Let us go for a row.

ADA: A row? And Addie? She would be very distressed if she came and found you had gone for a row without her. (*Pause*) Who were you with just now? (*Pause*) Before you spoke to me.

HENRY: I was trying to be with my father.

ADA: Oh. (*Pause*) No difficulty about that.

HENRY: I mean I was trying to get him to be with me. (*Pause*) You seem a little cruder than usual today, Ada. (*Pause*) I was asking him if he had ever met you, I couldn't remember.

ADA: Well?

HENRY: He doesn't answer any more.

ADA: I suppose you have worn him out. (*Pause*) You wore him out living and now you are wearing him out dead. (*Pause*) The time comes when one cannot speak to you any more. (*Pause*) The time will come when no one will speak to you at all, not even complete strangers. (*Pause*) You will be quite alone with your voice, there will be no other voice in the world but yours. (*Pause*) Do you hear me? (*Pause*)

HENRY: I can't remember if he met you.

ADA: You know he met me.

HENRY: No, Ada, I don't know, I'm sorry, I have forgotten almost everything connected with you.

ADA: You weren't there. Just your mother and sister. I had called to fetch you, as arranged. We were to go bathing together. (*Pause*)

HENRY: (*Irritably*) Drive on, drive on! Why do people always stop in the middle of what they are saying?

ADA: None of them knew where you were. Your bed had not been slept in. They were all shouting at one another. Your sister said she would throw herself off the cliff. Your father got up and went out, slamming the door. I left soon afterwards and passed him on the road. He did not see me. He was sitting on a rock looking out to sea. I never forgot his posture. And yet it was a common one. You used to have it sometimes. Perhaps just the stillness, as if he had been turned to stone. I could never make it out. (*Pause*)

HENRY: Keep on, keep on! (*Imploringly*). Keep it going, Ada, every syllable is a second gained.

ADA: That's all, I'm afraid. (*Pause*) Go on now with your father or your stories or whatever you were doing, don't mind me any more.

HENRY: I can't! (*Pause*) I can't do it any more!

ADA: You were doing it a moment ago, before you spoke to me.

HENRY: (*Angrily*) I can't do it any more now! (*Pause*) Christ! (*Pause*)

ADA: Yes, you know what I mean, there are attitudes remain in one's mind for reasons that are clear, the carriage of a head for example, bowed when one would have thought it should be lifted, and vice versa, or a hand suspended in mid-air, as if unowned. That kind of thing. But with your father sitting on the rock that day nothing of the kind, no detail you could put your finger on and say, How very peculiar! No, I could never make it out. Perhaps, as I said, just the great stillness of the whole body, as if all the breath had left it. (*Pause*) Is this rubbish a help to you, Henry? (*Pause*) I can try and go on a little if you wish. (*Pause*) No? (*Pause*) Then I think I'll be getting back.

HENRY: Not yet! You needn't speak. Just listen. Not even. Be with me. (*Pause*) Ada! (*Pause. Louder*) Ada! (*Pause*) Christ! (*Pause*) Hooves! (*Pause. Louder*) Hooves! (*Pause*) Christ! (*Long pause*) Left soon afterwards, passed you on the road, didn't see her, looking out to . . . (*Pause*) Can't have been looking out to *sea*. (*Pause*) Unless you had gone round the other side. (*Pause*) Had you gone round the cliff side? (*Pause*) Father! (*Pause*) Must have I suppose. (*Pause*) Stands watching you a moment, then on down path to tram, up on open top and sits down in front. (*Pause*) Sits down in front. (*Pause*) Suddenly feels uneasy and gets down again, conductor: 'Changed your mind, Miss?', goes back up path, no sign of you. (*Pause*) Very unhappy and uneasy, hangs round a bit, not a soul about, cold wind coming in off sea, goes back down path and takes tram home. (*Pause*) Takes tram home. (*Pause*) Christ! (*Pause*) 'My dear Bolton . . .' (*Pause*) 'If it's an injection you want, Bolton, let down your trousers and I'll give you one, I have a panhysterectomy at nine,' meaning of course the anaesthetic. (*Pause*) Fire out, bitter cold, white world, great trouble, not a sound. (*Pause*) Bolton starts playing with the curtain, no, hanging, difficult to describe, draws it back no, kind of gathers it towards him and the moon comes flooding in, then lets it fall back, heavy velvet affair, and pitch black in the room, then towards him again, white, black, white, black, Holloway: 'Stop that for the love of God, Bolton, do you want to finish me?' (*Pause*) Black, white, black, white, maddening thing. (*Pause*) Then he suddenly strikes a match, Bolton does, lights a candle, catches it up above his head, walks over and looks Holloway full in the eye. (*Pause*) Not a word, just the look, the old blue eye, very glassy, lids worn thin, lashes gone, whole thing swimming, and the candle shaking over his head. (*Pause*) Tears? (*Pause. Long laugh*) Good God no! (*Pause*) Not a word, just the look, the old blue eye, Holloway: 'If you want a shot say so and let me get to hell out of here.' (*Pause*) 'We've had this before, Bolton, don't ask me to go through it again.' (*Pause*) Bolton: 'Please!' (*Pause*) 'Please!' (*Pause*) 'Please, Holloway!' (*Pause*) Candle shaking and guttering all over the place, lower now, old arm tired, takes it in the other hand and holds it high again, that's it, that was always it, night, and the embers cold, and the glim shaking in your old fist,[9] saying, Please! Please! (*Pause*) Begging. (*Pause*) Of the poor. (*Pause*) Ada! (*Pause*) Father! (*Pause*) Christ! (*Pause*) Holds it high again, naughty world,[10] fixes Holloway, eyes drowned, won't ask again, just the look, Holloway covers his face, not a sound, white world, bitter cold, ghastly scene, old men, great trouble, no good. (*Pause*) No good. (*Pause*) Christ! (*Pause. Shingle as he gets up. He goes towards sea. Boots on shingle. He halts. Pause. Sea a little louder*). On. (*Pause. He moves on. Boots on shingle. He halts at water's edge. Pause. Sea a little louder*) Little book. (*Pause*) This evening . . . (*Pause*) Nothing this evening. (*Pause*) Tomorrow . . . tomorrow . . . plumber at nine,[11] then nothing. (*Pause. Puzzled*) Plumber at nine? (*Pause*) Ah yes,

9. The Bolton story is elsewhere told in the third person, and the second person refers to Henry's father. The slip, in which Henry confuses the story with reality, shows how he is contained within his own fiction.
10. Compare *The Merchant of Venice,* V.1.91, 'So shines a good deed in a naughty world.' Henry varies the phrasing later in the sentence, presumably because he notices the echo.
11. See the earlier references to 'drips', as well as Holloway's 'panhysterectomy at nine'.

the waste. (*Pause*) Words. (*Pause*) Saturday ... nothing. Sunday ... Sunday ... nothing all day. (*Pause*) Nothing, all day nothing. (*Pause*) All day all night nothing. (*Pause*) Not a sound.

ENOUGH (1967)

[The piece was written in French, as *Assez,* in 1965-66; Beckett's English translation (published in 1967) omits one paragraph of the French text after the nineteenth, and makes other changes too. The piece describes a relationship between a subservient, loving 'I' and a dominant, eccentric, older 'He'. In the first printed edition in French, there are clues that the 'I' is masculine. Beckett eliminated them when the piece was revised for the collected French edition, and of course the 'I' of the English version is of indeterminate sex.

The point of the story lies not in the characters themselves, but in their role in the story as it is told. The relatively coherent tale of romance told by 'I' is pretence and self-delusion, posturing to satisfy the other self that hears. The piece has little in common with others written about the same time (for instance, *Ping* and *Lessness*). It instead looks back to *From an Abandoned Work* (1955) — which is literally 'abandoned', in excess of 'enough' — and forward to texts like *Company*.

Another way to understand the story is in relation to texts that Beckett wrote immediately afterwards, represented here by *Ping* and *Lessness*. It bears the same relation to them as Beckett's novellas do to his trilogy. That is, it is a propaedeutic exercise in adequate style. It formulates a manner of proceeding which rests deliberately on balance, equivalence, 'endless equinox'.]

All that goes before forget. Too much at a time is too much. That gives the pen time to note. I don't see it but I hear it there behind me. Such is the silence. When the pen stops I go on. Sometimes it refuses. When it refuses I go on. Too much silence is too much. Or it's my voice too weak at times. The one that comes out of me. So much for the art and craft.

I did all he desired. I desired it too. For him. Whenever he desired something so did I. He only had to say what thing. When he didn't desire anything neither did I. In this way I didn't live without desires. If he had desired something for me I would have desired it too. Happiness for example or fame. I only had the desires he manifested. But he must have manifested them all. All his desires and needs. When he was silent he must have been like me. When he told me to lick his penis I hastened to do so. I drew satisfaction from it. We must have had the same satisfactions. The same needs and the same satisfactions.

One day he told me to leave him. It's the verb he used. He must have been on his last legs. I don't know if by that he meant me to leave him for good or only to step aside a moment. I never asked myself the question. I never asked myself any questions but his. Whatever it was he meant I made off without looking back. Gone from reach of his voice I was gone from his life. Perhaps it was that he desired. There are questions you see and don't ask yourself. He must have been on his last legs. I on the contrary was far from on my last legs. I belonged to an entirely different generation. It didn't last. Now that I'm entering night I have kinds of gleams in my skull. Stony ground but not entirely. Given three or four lives I might have accomplished something.

I cannot have been more than six when he took me by the hand. Barely emerging from childhood. But it didn't take me long to emerge altogether. It was the left hand. To be on the right was more than he could bear. We advanced side by side hand in hand. One pair of gloves was enough. The free or outer hands hung bare. He did not like to feel against his skin the skin of another. Mucous membrane is a different matter. Yet he sometimes took off his glove. Then I had to take off mine. We would cover in this way a hundred yards or so linked by our bare extremities. Seldom more. That was enough for him. If the question were put to me I would say that odd hands are ill-fitted for intimacy. Mine never felt at home in his. Sometimes they let each other go. The clasp loosened and they fell apart. Whole minutes often passed before they clasped again. Before his clasped mine again.

They were cotton gloves rather tight. Far from blunting the shapes they sharpened them by simplifying. Mine was naturally too loose for years. But it didn't take me long to fill it. He said I had Aquarius hands.[1] It's a mansion above.

All I know comes from him. I won't repeat this apropos of all my bits of knowledge. The art of combining is not my fault. It's a curse from above. For the rest I would suggest not guilty.

1. The eleventh of the twelve zodiacal constellations, not visible north of the equator. Here because the constellation figures a water-bearer, his left hand raised (like the speaker's) and his right hand pouring from a ewer (filling!).

Our meeting. Though very bowed already he looked a giant to me. In the end his trunk ran parallel with the ground. To counterbalance this anomaly he held his legs apart and sagged at the knees. His feet grew more and more flat and splay. His horizon was the ground they trod. Tiny moving carpet of turf and trampled flowers. He gave me his hand like a tired old ape with the elbow lifted as high as it would go. I had only to straighten up to be head and shoulders above him. One day he halted and fumbling for his words explained to me that anatomy is a whole.

In the beginning he always spoke walking. So it seems to me now. Then sometimes walking and sometimes still. In the end still only. And the voice getting fainter all the time. To save him having to say the same thing twice running I bowed right down. He halted and waited for me to get into position. As soon as out of the corner of his eye he glimpsed my head alongside his the murmurs came. Nine times out of ten they did not concern me. But he wished everything to be heard including the ejaculations and broken pasternosters that he poured out to the flowers at his feet.

He halted then and waited for my head to arrive before telling me to leave him. I snatched away my hand and made off without looking back. Two steps and I was lost to him for ever. We were severed if that is what he desired.

His talk was seldom of geodesy. But we must have covered several times the equivalent of the terrestrial equator. At an average speed of roughly three miles per day and night. We took flight in arithmetic. What mental calculations bent double hand in hand! Whole ternary numbers we raised in this way to the third power sometimes in downpours of rain. Graving themselves in his memory as best they could the ensuing cubes accumulated. In view of the converse operation at a later stage. When time would have done its work.

If the question were put to me suitably framed I would say yes indeed the end of this long outing was my life. Say about the last seven thousand miles. Counting from the day when alluding for the first time to his infirmity he said he thought it had reached its peak. The future proved him right. That part of it at least we were to make past of together.

I see the flowers at my feet and it's the others I see. Those we trod down with equal step. It is true they are the same.

Contrary to what I had long been pleased to imagine he was not blind. Merely indolent. One day he halted and fumbling for his words described his vision. He concluded by saying he thought it would get no worse. How far this was not a delusion I cannot say. I never asked myself the question. When I bowed down to receive his communications I felt on my eye a glint of blue bloodshot apparently affected.

He sometimes halted without saying anything. Either he had finally nothing to say or while having something to say he finally decided not to say it. I bowed down as usual to save him having to repeat himself and we remained in this position. Bent double heads touching silent hand in hand. While all about us fast on one another the minutes flew. Sooner or later his foot broke away from the flowers and we moved on. Perhaps only to halt again after a few steps. So that he might say at last what was in his heart or decide not to say it again.

Other main examples suggest themselves to the mind. Immediate continuous communication with immediate redeparture. Same thing with delayed redeparture. Delayed continuous communication with immediate redeparture. Same thing with delayed redeparture. Immediate discontinuous communication with delayed redeparture. Same thing with delayed redeparture. Delayed discontinuous communication with immediate redeparture. Same thing with delayed redeparture.

It is then I shall have lived then or never. Ten years at the very least. From the day he drew the back of his left hand lingeringly over his sacral ruins and launched his prognostic. To the day of my supposed disgrace. I can see the place a step short of the crest. Two steps forward and I was descending the other slope. If I had looked back I would not have seen him.

He loved to climb and therefore I too. He clamoured for the steepest slopes. His human frame broke down into two equal segments. This thanks to the shortening of the lower by the sagging knees. On a gradient of one in one his head swept the ground. To what this taste was due I cannot say. To love of the earth and the flowers' thousand scents and hues. Or to cruder imperatives of an anatomical order. He never raised the question. The crest once reached alas the going down again.

In order from time to time to enjoy the sky he resorted to a little round mirror. Having misted it with his breath and polished it on his calf he looked in it for the constellations. I have it! he exclaimed referring to the Lyre or the Swan. And often he added that the sky seemed much the same.

We were not in the mountains however. There were times I discerned on the horizon a sea whose level seemed higher than ours. Could it be the bed of some vast evaporated lake or drained of its waters from below? I never asked myself the question.

The fact remains we often came upon this sort of mound some three hundred feet in height. Reluctantly I raised my eyes and discerned the nearest often on the horizon. Or instead of moving on from the one we had just descended we ascended it again.

I am speaking of our last decade comprised between the two events described. It veils those that went before and must have resembled it like blades of grass. To those engulfed years it is reasonable to impute my education. For I don't remember having learnt anything in those I remember. It is with this reasoning I calm myself when brought up short by all I know.

I set the scene of my disgrace just short of a crest. On the contrary it was on the flat in a great calm. If I had looked back I would have seen him in the place where I had left him. Some trifle would have shown me my mistake if mistake there had been. In the years that followed I did not exclude the possibility of finding him again. In the place where I had left him if not elsewhere. Or of hearing him call me. At the same time telling myself he was on his last legs. But I did not count on it unduly. For I hardly raised my eyes from the flowers. And his voice was spent. And as if that were not enough I kept telling myself he was on his last legs. So it did not take me long to stop counting on it altogether.

I don't know what the weather is now. But in my life it was eternally mild. As if the earth had come to rest in spring. I am thinking of our hemisphere. Sudden pelting downpours overtook us. Without noticeable darkening of the sky. I would not have noticed the windlessness if he had not spoken of it. Of the wind that was no more. Of the storms he had ridden out. It is only fair to say there was nothing to sweep away. The very flowers were stemless and flush with the ground like water-lilies. No brightening our buttonholes with these.

We did not keep tally of the days. If I arrived at ten years it is thanks to our pedometer. Total mileage divided by average daily mileage. So many days. Divide. Such a figure the night before the sacrum. Such another the eve of my disgrace. Daily average always up to date. Subtract. Divide.

Night. As long as day in this endless equinox. It falls and we go on. Before dawn we are gone.

Attitude at rest. Wedged together bent in three. Second right angle at the knees. I on the inside. We turn over as one man when he manifests the desire. I can feel him at night pressed against me with all his twisted length. It was less a matter of sleeping than of lying down. For we walked in a half sleep. With his upper hand he held and touched me where he wished. Up to a certain point. The other was twined in my hair. He murmured of things that for him were no more and for me could not have been. The wind in the overground stems. The shade and shelter of the forests.

He was not given to talk. An average of a hundred words per day and night. Spaced out. A bare million in all. Numerous repeats. Ejaculations. Too few for even a cursory survey. What do I know of man's destiny? I could tell you more about radishes. For them he had a fondness. If I saw one I would name it without hesitation.

We lived on flowers. So much for sustenance. He halted and without having to stoop caught up a handful of petals. Then moved munching on. They had on the whole a calming action. We were on the whole calm. More and more. All was. This notion of calm comes from him. Without him I would not have had it. Now I'll wipe out everything but the flowers. No more rain. No more mounds. Nothing but the two of us dragging through the flowers. Enough my old breasts feel his old hand.

PING (1967)

[The piece was written in French, as *Ping*, after *Enough* in 1965-66, and Beckett's English translation was published in 1967. The earlier French drafts are published in Federman and Fletcher (1970), Appendix II, pp. 325-43, and in Richard L. Admussen, *The Samuel Beckett Manuscripts. A Study* (Boston, Massachusetts: G. K. Hall, 1979), Appendix C, pp. 131-48.

The word *ping* (which translates two words in the French version, *hop* and *bing*) is defined only by its context. It marks intervals of consciousness during the time that an almost blank, constrained situation is described, and it comes to accumulate such an amount of meaning in the course of its thirty-four appearances that one could say it indicates a 'plot'.

The place described is clear enough: it is a small, bare, white and symmetrical room. All that can be seen is whiteness, although there are vague traces of colour (of grey and blue). All that can be heard is silence, although there are 'murmurs'. All that can be felt is a constant temperature. In every way — visually, aurally, tactually — dimensions are fused into a continuous present, or nearly. No purchase is offered to the mind, or very little. The qualifications are important because the traces of colour, hints of sound, suggestions of shape, appear to offer some minimal hope, although so minimal that hope is not really the word.

Once introduced, the piece swells and modulates into a passage that hints bleakly at redemption, that is, at some hope of meaning within this solitude, thus breaking out of it. But the hope is illusory, and the meanings that had accrued to the word *ping* are thereafter shed. Fragmentarily at the close, another human presence is hinted at, but no more. Such a hint of a trace of a proof of a vestige of life is conjured out of need. It is not a discovery that gives the situation an outcome.

The statement made by the single voice, which returns again and again to the single punctuating word, is quite distinct from *Lessness* and other related texts. Each fresh formal projection of a similar situation describes different thematic values. They are miniaturizations of a predicament described in *The Lost Ones*, which Beckett had abandoned in 1966 and was not able to complete until 1970.]

All known all white bare white body fixed one yard legs joined like sewn. Light heat white floor one square yard never seen. White walls one yard by two white ceiling one square yard never seen. Bare white body fixed only the eyes only just. Traces blurs light grey almost white on white. Hands hanging palms front white feet heels together right angle. Light heat white planes shining white bare white body fixed ping fixed elsewhere. Traces blurs signs no meaning light grey almost white. Bare white body fixed white on white invisible. Only the eyes only just light blue almost white. Head haught[1] eyes light blue almost white silence within. Brief murmurs only just almost never all known. Traces blurs signs no meaning light grey almost white. Legs joined like sewn heels together right angle. Traces alone unover given black light grey almost white on white. Light heat white walls shining white one yard by two. Bare white body fixed one yard ping fixed elsewhere. Traces blurs signs no meaning light grey almost white. White feet toes joined like sewn heels together right angle invisible. Eyes alone unover given blue light blue almost white. Murmur only just almost never one second perhaps not alone. Given rose only just bare white body fixed one yard white on white invisible. All white all known murmurs only just almost never always the same all known. Light heat hands hanging palms front white on white invisible. Bare white body fixed ping fixed elsewhere. Only the eyes only just light blue almost white fixed front. Ping murmur only just almost never one second perhaps a way out. Head haught eyes light blue almost white fixed front ping murmur ping silence. Eyes holes light blue almost white mouth white seam like sewn invisible. Ping murmur perhaps a nature one second almost never that much memory almost never. White walls each its trace grey blur signs no meaning light grey almost white. Light heat all known all white planes meeting invisible. Ping murmur only just almost never one second perhaps a meaning that much memory almost never. White feet toes joined like sewn heels together right angle ping elsewhere no sound. Hands hanging palms front legs joined like sewn. Head haught eyes holes light blue almost white fixed front silence within. Ping elsewhere always there but that known not. Eyes holes light blue alone unover given blue light blue almost white only colour fixed front. All white all known white planes shining white ping murmur only just almost never one second light time that much memory almost never. Bare white body fixed one yard ping fixed elsewhere white on white invisible heart breath no sound. Only the eyes given blue light blue almost white fixed front only colour alone unover. Planes meeting invisible one only shining white infinite but that known not. Nose ears white holes mouth white seam like sewn invisible. Ping murmurs only just almost never one second always the same all known. Given rose only just bare white body fixed one yard invisible all known without within. Ping perhaps a nature one second with image same time a little less blue and white in the wind. White ceiling shining white one square yard never seen ping perhaps a way out there one second ping silence. Traces alone unover given black grey blurs signs no meaning light grey almost white always the same. Ping perhaps not alone one second with image always the same same time a little less that much memory almost never ping silence. Given rose only just nails fallen white over. Long hair fallen white invisible over. White scars invisible same white as flesh torn of old given rose

1. high, in a moral as well as a physical sense — though not in a pejorative sense, as in the modern usages of 'haughty'.

only just. Ping image only just almost never one second light time blue and white in the wind. Head haught nose ears white holes mouth white seam like sewn invisible over. Only the eyes given blue fixed front light blue almost white only colour alone unover. Light heat white planes shining white one only shining white infinite but that known not. Ping a nature only just almost never one second with image same time a little less blue and white in the wind. Traces blurs light grey eyes holes light blue almost white fixed front ping a meaning only just almost never ping silence. Bare white one yard fixed ping fixed elsewhere no sound legs joined like sewn heels together right angle hands hanging palms front. Head haught eyes holes light blue almost white fixed front silence within. Ping elsewhere always there but that known not. Ping perhaps not alone one second with image same time a little less dim eye black and white half closed long lashes imploring that much memory almost never. Afar flash of time all white all over all of old ping flash white walls shining white no trace eyes holes light blue almost white last colour ping white over. Ping fixed last elsewhere legs joined like sewn heels together right angle hands hanging palms front head haught eyes white invisible fixed front over. Given rose only just one yard invisible bare white all known without within over. White ceiling never seen ping of old only just almost never one second light time white floor never seen ping of old perhaps there. Ping of old only just perhaps a meaning a nature one second almost never blue and white in the wind that much memory henceforth never. White planes no trace shining white one only shining white infinite but that known not. Light heat all known all white heart breath no sound. Head haught eyes white fixed front old ping last murmur one second perhaps not alone eye unlustrous black and white half closed long lashes imploring ping silence ping over.

COME AND GO (1968)
A dramaticule
for John Calder[1]

[This play, written in English early in 1965, was based on an earlier draft called *Good Heavens*. It was performed in German and was published in a French version before being first performed in English (in Dublin) in 1968. The first, separate publication (London: Calder, 1967) incorporates photographs of the German production. The American, Grove Press edition incorporates some but not all of the improvements arrived at in the French, Minuit text. A reconstructed text of the improved English version is given by Breon Mitchell, 'Art in Microcosm: The Manuscript Stages of Beckett's *Come and Go*,' *Modern Drama*, XIX: 3 (September 1976), 245-60.

It is important to understand how 121 words, which take a few minutes to read, fill seven minutes in performance. Timed intervals between the words surround them with silence. The action returns to ground-level zero three times, as each character appeals differently to God. The three women immerse themselves in trivial gossip, while their cries go unanswered. It is also important to understand how the situation should be seen. Two areas impress themselves on our understanding, where the characters are together in the light and the dark to which they are exiled. Their eyes are in shadow, and their conventionally dressed figures are similar yet distinct. Their hands are displayed so that we can measure what they say about their rings against what we can (cannot) see. The play is literally about its tableau of a love-knot —— happiness in defiance of what is visibly not there.]

THE CHARACTERS[2]

FLO
VI
RU

(Ages undeterminable)

Sitting centre side by side stage right to left FLO, VI *and* RU. *Very erect, facing front, hands clasped in laps. Silence.*

VI: When did we three last meet?[3]

RU: Let us not speak.

(*Silence*)

Exit VI *right.*

1. Compare *King Lear,* V. 2. 9-10: 'Men must endure/ Their going hence, even as their coming hither.' 'Dramaticule' is a Beckettian coinage, meaning small play. John Calder has been Beckett's British publisher for many years.
2. Abbreviated forms of Flora/Florence, Violet and Ruby (in the original MS: Poppy, Violet and Rose). Violet and Rue connect with the mad Ophelia in *Hamlet,* IV. 5. 180-86. It has been suggested that their appearance resembles the three mothers in Fritz Lang's *'M'*, a film Beckett admired.
3. Recalls the opening of *Macbeth,* where the First Witch asks, 'When shall we three meet again?' Nonetheless, the three women just as much resemble the Three Graces, linked hand in hand, or the Three Sisters in Chekhov's play of that name.

   Beckett revised the American and French texts, adding four word/lines before the present opening, as follows: 'VI: Ru./ RU: Yes./ VI: Flo./ FLO: Yes.' The added lines transform those which open each of the later whispered exchanges into echoes of the first.

(*Silence*)

FLO: Ru.

RU: Yes.

FLO: What do you think of Vi?

RU: I see little change. (FLO *moves to centre seat, whispers in* RU's *ear. Appalled*)[4] Oh! (*They look at each other.* FLO *puts her finger to her lips*) Does she not realize?

FLO: God grant not.

Enter VI. FLO *and* RU *turn back front, resume pose.* VI *sits right. Silence.* Just sit together as we used to, in the playground at Miss Wade's.[5]

RU: On the log. (*Silence*) Exit FLO *left.* (*Silence*) Vi.

VI: Yes.

RU: How do you find Flo?

VI: She seems much the same. (RU *moves to centre seat, whispers in* VI's *ear. Appalled*) Oh! (*They look at each other.* RU *puts her finger to her lips*) Has she not been told?

RU: God forbid. (*Enter* FLO,[6] RU *and* VI *turn back front, resume pose.* FLO *sits left*) Holdings hands . . . that way.

FLO: Dreaming of . . . love.[7]

(*Silence*)

Exit RU *right.*

(*Silence*)

VI: Flo.

FLO: Yes.

VI: How do you think Ru is looking?

FLO: One sees little in this light. (VI *moves to centre seat, whispers in* FLO's *ear. Appalled*) Oh! (*They look at each other.* VI *puts her finger to her lips*) Does she not know?

VI: Please God not. (*Enter* RU, VI *and* FLO *turn back front, resume pose.* RU *sits right. Silence*) May we not speak of the old days? (*Silence*) Of what came after? (*Silence*) Shall we hold hands in the old way?[8] *After a moment they join hands as follows:* VI's *right hand with* RU's *right hand.* VI's *left hand with* FLO's *left hand.* FLO's *right hand with* RU's *left hand,* VI's *arms being above* RU's *left arm and* FLO's *right arm. The three pairs of clasped hands rest on the three laps.*

Silence.

FLO: I can feel the rings.[9]

(*Silence*)

CURTAIN

4. The longer, MS version of the play, entitled *Good Heavens*, makes clear that each woman has an incurable illness. The revised, published version shifts the emphasis away from such sensational revelation towards the way each woman differently reacts (God grant not, God forbid, Please God not).
5. A select school for young ladies, in Beckett's childhood, at Morehampton House, 78 Morehampton Road, Donnybrook, Dublin. It was in fact run by two sisters.
6. Notice that silence does not break up the conversation on Flo's return. Each of the three 'acts' has individual character.
7. In *Good Heavens*, each of the women seeks to avoid her fate by adulterous sexual activity.
8. Notice that Vi is in the middle at the beginning and end, although Flo has the final words. Each character has a different kind of centrality.
9. In the French version, and the text reconstituted by Breon Mitchell, Flo's speech begins: 'Ru. (*Silence*) Vi. (*Silence*)' — which brings the play full circle with its revised opening (see note 3 above).

NOTES

Successive positions

1	FLO	VI	RU
2	[FLO		RU
		FLO	RU
3	VI	FLO	RU
4	[VI		RU
	VI	RU	
5	VI	RU	FLO
6	[VI		FLO
		VI	FLO
7	RU	VI	FLO

Hands

RU VI FLO

Lighting

Soft, from above only and concentrated on playing area. Rest of stage as dark as possible.

Costume

Full-length coats, buttoned high, dull violet (Ru), dull red (Vi), dull yellow (Flo). Drab nondescript hats with enough brim to shade faces. Apart from colour differentiation three figures as alike as possible. Light shoes with rubber soles. Hands made up to be as visible as possible. No rings apparent.

Seat

Narrow benchlike seat, without back, just long enough to accommodate three figures almost touching. As little visible as possible. It should not be clear what they are sitting on.

Exits

The figures are not seen to go off stage. They should disappear a few steps from lit area. If dark not sufficient to allow this, recourse should be had to screens or drapes as little visible as possible. Exits and entrances slow, without sound of feet.

Ohs

Three very different sounds.

Voices
As low as compatible with audibility. Colourless except for three 'ohs' and two lines following.

LESSNESS (1970)

[The piece proceeds directly from *Ping*. It was written in French, as *Sans*, and Beckett's English translation was published in 1970. The first English separate publication was accompanied by a publisher's blurb based on Beckett's own notes. These are now at Yale University, and explain even more clearly how the piece is composed of six groups of statements, each containing ten sentences, i.e. sixty sentences. These sixty are given in a certain order and paragraph structure, then repeated in a different order and different paragraph structure. The whole consists therefore of two times sixty — 120 sentences — arranged and rearranged in two times twelve (twenty-four) paragraphs. Each statement group is formally differentiated, and the ten sentences composing it are 'signed' by certain elements common to them all. Thus:

Group A — Collapse of refuge — Sign: 'true refuge'
Group B — Outer world — Sign: 'earth .. sky', juxtaposed or apart
Group C — Body exposed — Sign: 'little body'
Group D — Refuge forgotten — Sign: 'all gone from mind'
Group E — Past and future denied — Sign: 'never —' except in the one sentence, 'figment dawn . . .'
Group F — Past and future affirmed — Sign: future tense.

Rhythms are set up, which quiver across the surface of the fixed situation. This motion without movement both encourages and disappoints our expectancy, as readers, of release. The situation is one in which no change is observable but in which traumatic eddies can be sensed, so that the piece enacts a process that can be measured only in comparative terms — hence the title. Both the situation and the theme are close to *Ping*. The fact that *Lessness* is scored for six separate voices, in a peculiar, random combination, is the measure of its different, shifting, eddying movement.

One might compare the patterning of the three voices in *Come and Go*, and the more complicated arrangement of voices in *That Time*. Beckett was dissatisfied with the way a BBC reading of *Lessness*, in which the six groups of sentences were given to six different actors, made the six voices sharply different; and perhaps this lies behind his emphasis, in the prefatory note to *That Time*, that all three voices should clearly sound like aspects of one voice.]

Ruins true refuge long last towards which so many false time out of mind. All sides endlessness earth sky as one no sound no stir. Grey face two pale blue little body heart beating only upright. Blacked out fallen open four walls over backwards true refuge issueless.

Scattered ruins same grey as the sand ash grey true refuge. Four square all light sheer white blank planes all gone from mind. Never was but grey air timeless no sound figment the passing light. No sound no stir ash grey sky mirrored earth mirrored sky. Never but this changelessness dream the passing hour.

He will curse God again as in the blessed days face to the open sky the passing deluge. Little body grey face features crack and little holes two pale blue. Blank planes sheer white eye calm long last all gone from mind.

Figment light never was but grey air timeless no sound. Blank planes touch close sheer white all gone from mind. Little body ash grey locked rigid heart beating face to endlessness. On him will rain again as in the blessed days of blue the passing cloud. Four square true refuge long last four walls over backwards no sound.

Grey sky no cloud no sound no stir earth ash grey sand. Little body same grey as the earth sky ruins only upright. Ash grey all sides earth sky as one all sides endlessness.

He will stir in the sand there will be stir in the sky the air the sand. Never but in dream the happy dream only one time to serve. Little body little block heart beating ash grey only upright. Earth sky as one all sides endlessness little body only upright. In the sand no hold one step more in the endlessness he will make it. No sound not a breath same grey all sides earth sky body ruins.

Slow black with ruin true refuge four walls over backwards no sound. Legs a single block arms fast to sides little body face to endlessness. Never but in vanished dream the passing hour long short. Only upright little body grey smooth no relief a few holes. One step in the ruins in the sand on his back in the endlessness he will make it. Never but dream the days and nights made of dreams of other nights better days. He will live again the space of a step it will be day and night again over him the endlessness.

In four split asunder over backwards true refuge issueless scattered ruins. Little body little block genitals overrun arse a single block grey crack overrun. True refuge long last issueless scattered down four walls over backwards no sound. All sides endlessness earth sky as one no stir not a breath. Blank planes sheer white calm eye light of reason all gone from mind. Scattered ruins ash grey all sides true refuge long last issueless.

Ash grey little body only upright heart beating face to endlessness. Old love new love as in the blessed days unhappiness will reign again. Earth sand same grey as the air sky ruins body fine ash grey sand. Light refuge sheer white blank planes all gone from mind. Flatness endless little body only upright same grey all sides earth sky body ruins. Face to white calm touch close eye calm long last all gone from mind. One step more one alone all alone in the sand no hold he will make it.

Blacked out fallen open true refuge issueless towards which so many false time out of mind. Never but silence such that in imagination this wild laughter these cries. Head through calm eye all light white calm all gone from mind. Figment dawn dispeller of figments and the other called dusk.

He will go on his back face to the sky open again over him the ruins the sand the endlessness. Grey air timeless earth sky as one same grey as the ruins flatness endless. It will be day and night again over him the endlessness the air heart will beat again. True refuge long last scattered ruins same grey as the sand.

Face to calm eye touch close all calm all white all gone from mind. Never but imagined the blue in a wild imagining the blue celeste of poesy.[1] Little void mighty light four square all white blank planes all gone from mind. Never was but grey air timeless no stir not a breath. Heart beating little body only upright grey face features overrun two pale blue. Light white touch close head through calm eye light of reason all gone from mind.

Little body same grey as the earth sky ruins only upright. No sound not a breath same grey all sides earth sky body ruins. Blacked out fallen open four walls over backwards true refuge issueless.

No sound no stir ash grey sky mirrored earth mirrored sky. Grey air timeless earth sky as one same grey as the ruins flatness endless. In the sand no hold one step more in the endlessness he will make it. It will be day and night again over him the endlessness the air heart will beat again.

Figment light never was but grey air timeless no sound. All sides endlessness earth sky as one no stir not a breath. On him will rain again as in the blessed days of blue the passing cloud. Grey sky no cloud no sound no stir earth ash grey sand.

Little void mighty light four square all white blank planes all gone from mind. Flatness endless little body only upright same grey all sides earth sky body ruins. Scattered ruins same grey as the sand ash grey true refuge. Four square true refuge long last four walls over backwards no sound. Never but this changelessness dream the passing hour. Never was but grey air timeless no sound figment the passing light.

In four split asunder over backwards true refuge issueless scattered ruins. He will live again the space of a step it will be day and night again over him the endlessness. Face to white calm touch close eye calm long last all gone from mind. Grey face two pale blue little body heart beating only upright. He will go on his back face to the sky open again over him the ruins the sand the endlessness. Earth sand same grey as the air sky ruins body fine ash grey sand. Blank planes touch close sheer white all gone from mind.

Heart beating little body only upright grey face features overrun two pale blue. Only upright little body grey smooth no relief a few holes. Never but dream the days and nights made of dreams of other nights better days. He will stir in the sand there will be stir in the sky the air the sand. One step in the ruins in the sand on his back in the endlessness he will make it. Never but silence such that in imagination this wild laughter these cries.

True refuge long last scattered ruins same grey as the sand. Never was but grey air timeless no stir not a breath. Blank planes sheet white calm eye light of reason all gone from mind. Never but in vanished dream the passing hour long short. Four square all light sheer white blank planes all gone from mind.

Blacked out fallen open true refuge issueless towards which so many false time out of mind. Head through calm eye all light white calm all gone from mind. Old love new love as in the blessed days unhappiness will reign again. Ash grey all sides earth sky as one all sides endlessness. Scattered ruins ash grey all sides true refuge long last issueless. Never but in dream the happy dream only one time to serve. Little body grey face features

1. The phrase suggests the *azur*, which is almost a signature of Mallarmé and the symbolist ideal of pure poetry. But it is not a quotation and, curiously, the suggestion is less obvious in Beckett's French original. Compare the use of the colour blue in *Ping*.

crack[2] and little holes two pale blue.

Ruins true refuge long last towards which so many false time out of mind. Never but imagined the blue in a wild imagining the blue celeste of poesy. Light white touch close head through calm eye light of reason all gone from mind.

Slow black with ruin true refuge four walls over backwards no sound. Earth sky as one all sides endlessness little body only upright. One step more one alone all alone in the sand no hold he will make it. Ash grey little body only upright heart beating face to endlessness. Light refuge sheer white blank planes all gone from mind. All sides endlessness earth sky as one no sound no stir.

Legs a single block arms fast to sides little body face to endlessness. True refuge long last issueless scattered down four walls over backwards no sound. Blank planes sheer white eye calm long last all gone from mind. He will curse God again as in the blessed days face to the open sky the passing deluge. Face to calm eye touch close all calm all white all gone from mind.

Little body little block heart beating ash grey only upright. Little body ash grey locked rigid heart beating face to endlessness. Little body little block genitals overrun arse a single block grey crack overrun. Figment dawn dispeller of figments and the other called dusk.

2. Beckett's earlier translation into English, published in *New Statesman*, 1 May 1970, reads 'slit'. This is the only difference between the two versions.

NOT I (1972)

[This play was written quickly in English in the spring of 1972 with, Beckett has said, Billie Whitelaw's voice in mind. It was first performed in New York in November 1972 and in London in January 1973. Beckett's manuscript and typescript analyses at Reading University make clear how a number of statements and themes are interwoven in the body of the text, and reappear all together in the last page or so. It is nonetheless not necessary for the words to be intelligible at first hearing. Beckett told the American actress, Jessica Tandy, before the first production in New York, to 'work on the nerves of the audience, not its intellect.'

The torrent of words contains the speaker's vehement refusal to relinquish the third person, to acknowledge that 'she' is 'I'. The utterance of a particular phrase triggers five pauses in which the lips cease to move, and the hitherto motionless figure of the auditor, dimly lit at the side of the stage, stretches out his arms, but more and more feebly. By the fifth pause, he ceases to respond.

There are problems in producing the play: the luminous moving mouth is such a powerful image that it has proved difficult to transfer attention across the width of the stage to the auditor. Some stage productions have therefore dispensed with Auditor, as the television version must, but it should be noted that the change affects the meaning significantly. In the French production of 1975, Beckett eliminated Auditor; when he directed the play a second time, in 1978, he gave Auditor greater prominence.]

Note

Movement: this consists in simple sideways raising of arms from sides and their falling back, in a gesture of helpless compassion. It lessens with each recurrence till scarcely perceptible at third. There is just enough pause to contain it as MOUTH recovers from vehement refusal to relinquish third person.

Stage in darkness but for MOUTH, *upstage audience right, about 8 feet above stage level, faintly lit from close-up and below, rest of face in shadow. Invisible microphone.*

AUDITOR[1], *downstage audience left, tall standing figure, sex undeterminable, enveloped from head to foot in loose black djellaba, with hood, fully faintly lit, standing on invisible podium about 4 feet high shown by attitude alone to be facing diagonally across stage intent on* MOUTH, *dead still throughout but for four brief movements where indicated. See Note.*

As house lights down MOUTH's *voice unintelligible behind curtain. House lights out. Voice continues unintelligible behind curtain, 10 seconds. With rise of curtain ad-libbing from text as required leading when curtain fully up and attention sufficient into:*

MOUTH: . . . . out . . . into this world . . . this world . . . tiny little thing . . . before its time . . . in a godfor— . . . what? . . girl? . . yes . . . tiny little girl . . . into this . . . out into this . . . before her time . . . godforsaken hole called . . . called . . . no matter . . .

1. Beckett said that Auditor was inspired by a painting of Caravaggio's in Valletta Cathedral, in which the beheading of St John the Baptist is witnessed by a group of shadowy observers, and which struck him as 'a voice crying in the wilderness'. The *djellaba* comes from an Arab woman he saw in Morocco, 'crouched in an attitude of intense waiting' (Bair, p. 524).

parents unknown . . . unheard of . . . he having vanished . . . thin air . . . no sooner buttoned up his breeches . . . she similarly . . . eight months later . . . almost to the tick . . . so no love . . . spared that . . . no love such as normally vented on the . . . speechless infant . . . in the home . . . no . . . nor indeed for that matter any of any kind . . . no love of any kind . . . at any subsequent stage . . . so typical affair . . . nothing of any note till coming up to sixty when— . . . what? . . seventy? . . good God! . . coming up to seventy . . . wandering in a field . . . looking aimlessly for cowslips . . . to make a ball . . . a few steps then stop . . . stare into space . . . then on . . . a few more . . . stop and stare again . . . so on . . . drifting around . . . when suddenly . . . gradually . . . all went out . . . all that early April morning light . . . and she found herself in the— . . . what? . . who? . . no! . . she! . . (*Pause and movement 1*) . . . found herself in the dark . . . and if not exactly . . . insentient . . . insentient . . . for she could still hear the buzzing . . . so-called . . . in the ears . . . and a ray of light came and went . . . came and went . . . such as the moon might cast . . . drifting . . . in and out of cloud . . . but so dulled . . . feeling . . . feeling so dulled . . . she did not know . . . what position she was in . . . imagine! . . what position she was in! . . whether standing . . . or sitting . . . but the brain— . . . what? . . kneeling? . . yes . . . whether standing . . . or sitting . . . or kneeling . . . but the brain— . . . what? . . lying? . . yes . . . whether standing . . . or sitting . . . or kneeling . . . or lying . . . but the brain still . . . still . . . in a way . . . for her first thought was . . . oh long after . . . sudden flash . . . brought up as she had been to believe . . . with the other waifs . . . in a merciful . . . (*Brief laugh*) . . . God . . . (*Good laugh*) . . . first thought was . . . oh long after . . . sudden flash . . . she was being punished . . . for her sins . . . a number of which then . . . further proof if proof were needed . . . flashed through her mind . . . one after another . . . then dismissed as foolish . . . oh long after . . . this thought dismissed . . . as she suddenly realized . . . gradually realized . . . she was not suffering . . . imagine! . . not suffering! . . indeed could not remember . . . off-hand . . . when she had suffered less . . . unless of course she was . . . *meant* to be suffering . . . ha! . . *thought* to be suffering . . . just as the odd time . . . in her life . . . when clearly intended to be having pleasure . . . she was in fact . . . having none . . . not the slightest . . . in which case of course . . . that notion of punishment . . . for some sin or other . . . or for the lot . . . or no particular reason . . . for its own sake . . . thing she understood perfectly . . . that notion of punishment . . . which had first occurred to her . . . brought up as she had been to believe . . . with the other waifs . . . in a merciful . . . (*Brief laugh*) . . . God . . . (*Good laugh*) . . . first occurred to her . . . then dismissed . . . as foolish . . . was perhaps not so foolish . . . after all . . . so on . . . all that . . . vain reasonings . . . till another thought . . . oh long after . . . sudden flash . . . very foolish really but— . . . what? . . the buzzing? . . yes . . . all the time the buzzing . . . so-called . . . in the ears . . . though of course actually . . . not in the ears at all . . . in the skull . . . dull roar in the skull . . . and all the time this ray or beam . . . like moonbeam . . . but probably not . . . certainly not . . . always the same spot . . . now bright . . . now shrouded . . . but always the same spot . . . as no moon could . . . no . . . no moon . . . just all part of the same wish to . . . torment . . . though actually in point of fact . . . not in the least . . . not a twinge . . . so far . . . ha! . . so far . . . this other thought then . . . oh long after . . . sudden flash . . . very foolish really but so like her . . . in a way . . . that she might do well to . . . groan . . . on and off . . . writhe she could not . . . as if in actual agony . . . but could not . . . could not bring herself . . . some flaw in her make-up . . . incapable of deceit . . . or the machine . . . more likely the machine . . . so disconnected . . . never got the message . . . or powerless to respond . . . like numbed . . . couldn't make the sound . . . not any sound . . . no sound of any kind . . . no screaming for help for example . . . should she feel so inclined . . . scream . . . (*Screams*) . . . then listen . . . (*Silence*) . . . scream again . . . (*Screams again*) . . . then listen again . . . (*Silence*) . . . no . . . spared that . . . all silent as the grave . . . no part— . . . what? . . the buzzing? . . yes . . . all silent but for the buzzing . . . so-called . . . no part of her moving . . . that she could feel . . . just the eyelids . . . presumably . . . on and off . . . shut out the light . . . reflex they call it . . . no feeling of any kind . . . but the lids . . . even best of times . . . who feels them? . . opening . . . shutting . . . all that moisture . . . but the brain still . . . still sufficiently . . . oh very much so! . . at this stage . . . in control . . . under control . . . to question even this . . . for on that April morning . . . so it reasoned . . . that April morning . . . she fixing with her eye . . . a distant bell . . . as she hastened towards it . . . fixing it with her eye . . . lest it elude her . . . had not all gone out . . . all that light . . . of itself . . . without any . . . any . . . on her part . . . so on . . . so on it reasoned . . . vain questionings . . . and all dead still ... sweet silent as the grave ... when suddenly ... gradually ... she realiz— ... what? .. the buzzing? .. yes ... all dead still but for the buzzing ... when suddenly she realized ... words were— ... what? .. who? .. no! .. she! .. (*Pause and movement 2*) ... realized ... words were coming ... imagine! .. words were coming ... a voice she did not recognize ... at first ... so long since it had sounded ... then finally had to admit ... could be none other ... than her own ... certain vowel sounds ... she had never heard ... elsewhere ... so that people would stare ... the rare occasions ... once or twice a year ... always winter some strange reason ... stare at her uncomprehending ... and now this stream ... steady stream ... she who had never ... on the contrary ... practically speechless ... all her days ... how she survived! .. even shopping ... out shopping ... busy shopping centre ... supermart ... just hand in the list ... with the bag ... old black shopping bag ... then stand there waiting ... any length of time ... middle of the throng ... motionless ... staring into space ... mouth half open as usual ... till it was back in her hand ... the bag back in her hand ... then pay and go ... not as much as good-bye ... how she survived! .. and now this stream ... not catching the half of it ... not the quarter ... no idea ... what she was saying ... imagine! .. no idea what she was saying! .. till she began trying to ... delude herself ... it was not hers at all ... not her voice at all ... and no doubt would have ... vital she should ... was on the point ... after long efforts ... when suddenly she felt ... gradually she felt ... her lips moving ... imagine! .. her lips moving! .. as of course till then she had not ... and not alone the lips ... the cheeks ... the jaws ... the whole face ... all those— ... what? .. the tongue? .. yes ... the tongue in the mouth ... all those contortions without which ... no speech possible ... and yet in the ordinary way ... not felt at all ... so intent one is ... on what one is saying ... the whole being ... hanging on its words ... so that not only she had ... had she ... not only had she ... to give up ... admit hers alone ... her voice alone ... but this other awful thought ... oh long after ... sudden flash ... even more awful if possible ... that feeling was coming back ... imagine! .. feeling coming back! .. starting at the top ... then working down ... the whole machine ... but no ... spared that ... the mouth alone ... so far ... ha! .. so far ... then thinking ... oh long after ... sudden flash ... it can't go on ... all this ... all that ... steady stream ... straining to hear ... make something of it ... and her own thoughts ... make something of them ... all— ... what? .. the buzzing? .. yes ... all the time the buzzing ... so-called ... all that together ... imagine! .. whole body like gone ... just the mouth ... lips ... cheeks ... jaws ... never— ... what? .. tongue? .. yes ... lips ... cheeks ... jaws ... tongue ... never still a second ... mouth on fire ... stream of words ... in her ear ... practically in her ear ... not catching the half ... not the quarter ... no idea what she's saying ... imagine! .. no idea what she's saying! .. and can't stop ... no stopping it ... she who but a moment before ... but a moment! .. could not make a sound ... no sound of any kind ... now can't stop ... imagine! .. can't stop the stream ... and the whole brain begging ... something begging in the brain ... begging the mouth to stop ... pause a moment ... if only for a moment ... and no response ... as if it hadn't heard ... or couldn't ... couldn't pause a second ... like maddened ... all that together ... straining to hear ... piece it together ... and the brain ... raving away on its own ... trying to make sense of it ... or make it stop ... or in the past ... dragging up the past ... flashes from all over ... walks mostly ... walking all her days ... day after day ... a few steps then stop ... stare into space ... then on ... a few more ... stop and stare again ... so on ... drifting around ... day after day ... or that time she cried ... the one time she could remember ... since she was a baby ... must have cried as a baby ... perhaps not ... not essential to life ... just the birth cry to get her going ... breathing ... then no more till this ... old hag already ... sitting staring at her hand ... where was it? .. Croker's Acres[2] ... one evening on the way home ... home! .. a little mound in Croker's Acres ... dusk ... sitting staring at her hand ... there in her lap ... palm upward ... suddenly saw it wet ... the palm ... tears presumably ... hers presumably ... no one else for miles ... no sound ... just the tears ... sat and watched them dry ... all over in a second ... or grabbing at straw ... the brain ... flickering away on its own ... quick grab and on ... nothing there ... on to the next ... bad as the voice ... worse ... as little sense ... all that together ... can't— ... what? .. the buzzing? .. yes ... all the

2. A property next to Leopardstown Racecourse, Dublin, once used by Boss Croker, a Tammany Hall millionaire, to train horses. Compare *Company* (p. 303 below).

time the buzzing ... dull roar like falls ... and the beam ... flickering on and off ... starting to move around ... like moonbeam but not ... all part of the same ... keep an eye on that too ... corner of the eye ... all that together ... can't go on ... God is love ... she'll be purged ... back in the field ... morning sun ... April ... sink face down in the grass ... nothing but the larks ... so on ... grabbing at the straw ... straining to hear ... the odd word ... make some sense of it ... whole body like gone ... just the mouth ... like maddened ... and can't stop ... no stopping it ... something she— ... something she had to— ... what? .. who? .. no! .. she! .. (*Pause and movement 3*) ... something she had to— ... what? .. the buzzing? .. yes ... all the time the buzzing ... dull roar ... in the skull ... and the beam ... ferreting around ... painless ... so far ... ha! .. so far ... then thinking ... oh long after ... sudden flash ... perhaps something she had to ... had to ... tell ... could that be it? .. something she had to ... tell ... tiny little thing ... before its time ... godforsaken hole ... no love ... spared that ... speechless all her days ... practically speechless ... how she survived! .. that time in court ... what had she to say for herself ... guilty or not guilty ... stand up woman ... speak up woman ... stood there staring into space ... mouth half open as usual ... waiting to be led away ... glad of the hand on her arm ... now this ... something she had to tell ... could that be it? .. something that would tell ... how it was ... how she— ... what? .. had been? .. yes ... something that would tell how it had been ... how she had lived ... lived on and on ... guilty or not ... on and on ... to be sixty ... something she— ... what? .. seventy? .. good God! .. on and on to be seventy ... something she didn't know herself ... wouldn't know if she heard ... then forgiven ... God is love ... tender mercies ... new every morning[3] ... back in the field ... April morning ... face in the grass ... nothing but the larks ... pick it up there ... get on with it from there ... another few— ... what? .. not that? .. nothing to do with that? .. nothing she could tell? .. all right ... nothing she could tell ... try something else ... think of something else ... oh long after ... sudden flash ... not that either ... all right ... something else again ... so on ... hit on it in the end ... think everything keep on long enough ... then forgiven ... back in the— ... what? .. not that either? .. nothing to do with that either? .. nothing she could think? .. all right ... nothing she could tell ... nothing she could think ... nothing she— ... what? .. who? .. no! .. she! .. (*Pause and movement 4*) ... tiny little thing ... out before its time ... godforsaken hole ... no love ... spared that ... speechless all her days ... practically speechless ... even to herself ... never out loud ... but not completely ... sometimes sudden urge ... once or twice a year ... always winter some strange reason ... the long evenings ... hours of darkness ... sudden urge to ... tell ... then rush out stop the first she saw ... nearest lavatory ... start pouring it out ... steady stream ... mad stuff ... half the vowels wrong ... no one could follow ... till she saw the stare she was getting ... then die of shame ... crawl back in ... once or twice a year ... always winter some strange reason ... long hours of darkness ... now this ... this ... quicker and quicker ... the words ... the brain ... flickering away like mad ... quick grab and on ... nothing there ... on somewhere else ... try somewhere else ... all the time something begging ... something in her begging ... begging it all to stop ... unanswered ... prayer unanswered ... or unheard ... too faint ... so on ... keep on ... trying ... not knowing what ... what she was trying ... what to try ... whole body like gone ... just the mouth ... like maddened ... so on ... keep— ... what? .. the buzzing? .. yes ... all the time the buzzing ... dull roar like falls ... in the skull ... and the beam ... poking around ... painless ... so far ... ha! .. so far ... all that ... keep on ... not knowing what ... what she was— ... what? .. who? .. no! .. she! .. SHE! .. (*Pause*) ... what she was trying ... what to try ... no matter ... keep on ... (*Curtain starts down*) ... hit on it in the end ... then back ... God is love ... tender mercies ... new every morning ... back in the field ... April morning .... face in the grass ... nothing but the larks ... pick it up—[4]

Curtain fully down. House dark. Voice continues behind curtain, unintelligible, 10 seconds, ceases as house lights up.

3. 'God is love' is frequently advertised in protestant contexts; 'tender mercies' is from Psalms 12.10; 'New every morning is the love' is the first line of John Keble's well-known matins hymn.

4. At the end of Beckett's 1978 production, Auditor was made to cover head with hands, as if unable to register Mouth's suffering any longer. The moral ambivalence of the witness-artist's role is portrayed specifically in *Catastrophe* (1982).

THAT TIME (1976)

[The play was written in English between June 1974 and August 1975, and was first performed in London in 1976 by Patrick Magee. When Beckett wrote to James Knowlson that the play was 'a brother to *Not I*,' he meant that it was complementary. The three voices that the old man hears express different stages of an ordinary lifespan: childhood, adulthood and old age. They are associated with different images and are punctuated by moments when the old man's memory flags and when the light on his face intensifies. The voices are combined with each other and with the three pauses in an exact pattern, which Beckett's letter to Knowlson sets out clearly. Thus (reading down each column in succession, and where S stands for silence):

	I			II				III			
A	A	A	C	C	C	C	B	B	B	B	B
C	C	C	A	B	B	B	C	A	A	A	A
B	B	B	B	A	A	A	A	C	C	C	C

------ 12 ----->S ------ 12 ----->S ------ 12 ----->S

The light on the face is brought up after B4, A8 and C12, and is faded back to normal as the voices resume. The effect at the end, after C12, is no different from the preceding, except that the 'fade back' is continued to 'fade out'. No particular significance is intended by the combinations, except that Beckett wished to make each passage verbally interesting and to provide it with some associative connection with the next.

Observed and invented details coexist and combine here in ways quite different from Beckett's other texts. They are commented upon in the footnotes.]

Note

Moments of one and the same voice A B C relay one another without solution of continuity — apart from the two 10-second breaks. Yet the switch from one to another must be clearly faintly perceptible. If threefold source and context prove insufficient to produce this effect it should be assisted mechanically (e.g. threefold pitch).

Curtain. Stage in darkness. Fade up to LISTENER'S FACE *about 10 feet above stage level midstage off centre.*

Old white face, long flaring white hair as if seen from above outspread.

Voices A B C *are his own coming to him from both sides and above. They modulate back and forth without any break in general flow except where silence indicated. See note.*

Silence 7 seconds. LISTENER'S EYES *are open. His breath audible, slow and regular.*

A: that time you went back that last time to look was the ruin still there where you hid as a child when was that (*Eyes close*) grey day took the eleven to the end of the line[1] and on from there no no trams then all gone long ago that time you went back to look was the ruin still there where you hid as a child that last time not a tram left in the place only the old rails when was that

C: when you went in out of the rain always winter then always raining that time in the Portrait Gallery[2] in off the street out of the cold and rain slipped in when no one was looking and through the rooms shivering and dripping till you found a seat marble slab and sat down to rest and dry off and on to hell out of there when was that

B: on the stone together in the sun on the stone at the edge of the little wood and as far as eye could see the wheat turning yellow vowing every now and then you loved each other just a murmur not touching or anything of that nature you one end of the stone she the other long low stone like millstone no looks just there on the stone in the sun with the

1. The eleven tram in Dublin ran from Drumcondra to the Nelson Pillar, and then via Dawson Street, St Stephen's Green and Leeson Street to a terminus at Eglinton Road, Clonskeagh. It would be the natural tram to catch from the North Wall ferry, if a passenger was not daunted by the five- or six-mile walk from the end of the line in Clonskeagh to Foxrock. (Most passengers would have alighted from the eleven at the corner of St Stephen's Green, and walked the few hundred yards to the Harcourt Street railway station.) The eleven tram ceased to operate in 1939, ten years before the last trams in Dublin. Although the wires were removed fairly soon afterwards, the tracks were taken up piecemeal, and rusting sections were still in place until the mid-1950s.
2. Beckett told Beryl and John Fletcher that he had no particular gallery in mind, but that it could be the London one (*A Student's Guide to the Plays of Samuel Beckett* — Faber, second ed., 1985 — p. 222). C's contribution suggests that this might be the case, his experience being described as taking place 'far from home'. There is, however, no record of either marble benches or shufflers being used in the Portrait Gallery in London, whereas they were both to be found in Ireland's National Gallery on Merrion Square in the 1920s and 1930s. The prominence and proximity of Post Office and Library is also suggestive of central Dublin, and Beckett's early writing shows that he spent a good deal of time in Ireland's National Gallery (of which his friend, Thomas MacGreevy, became Director). At the same time, the marble benches in the Dublin Gallery were in the then-sculpture room and a 'big round table' was not (is not) a prominent feature in the National Library. It is as if the National Gallery of Ireland has become the British Portrait Gallery, and the Irish National Library has become a London Public Library, memory being both definite and reconstitutive.

little wood behind gazing at the wheat or eyes closed all still no sign of life not a soul abroad no sound

A: straight off the ferry and up with the nightbag to the high street[3] neither right nor left not a curse for the old scenes the old names straight up the rise from the wharf to the high street and there not a wire to be seen only the old rails all rust when was that was your mother ah for God's sake all gone long ago that time you went back that last time to look was the ruin still there where you hid as a child someone's folly

C: was your mother ah for God's sake all gone long ago all dust the lot you you last huddled up on the slab in the old green greatcoat with your arms round you whose else hugging you for a bit of warmth to dry off and on to hell out of there and on to the next not a living soul in the place only yourself and the odd attendant drowsing around in his felt shufflers not a sound to be heard only every now and then a shuffle of felt drawing near then dying away

B: all still just the leaves and ears and you too still on the stone in a daze no sound not a word only every now and then to vow you loved each other just a murmur one thing could ever bring tears till they dried up altogether that thought when it came up among the others floated up that scene

A: Foley was it Foley's Folly[4] bit of a tower still standing all the rest rubble and nettles where did you sleep no friend all the homes gone was it that kip on the front where you no she was with you then still with you then just the one night in any case off the ferry one morning and back on her the next to look was the ruin still there where none ever came where you hid as a child slip off when no one was looking and hide there all day long on a stone among the nettles with your picture-book

C: till you hoisted your head and there before your eyes when they opened a vast oil black with age and dirt someone famous in his time some famous man or woman or even child such as a young prince or princess some young prince or princess of the blood black with age behind the glass where gradually as you peered trying to make it out gradually of all things a face appeared had you swivel on the slab to see who it was there at your elbow

B: on the stone in the sun gazing at the wheat or the sky or the eyes closed nothing to be seen but the wheat turning yellow and the blue sky vowing every now and then you loved each other just a murmur tears without fail till they dried up altogether suddenly there in whatever thoughts you might be having whatever scenes perhaps way back in childhood or the womb worst of all or that old Chinaman long before Christ born with long white hair[5]

C: never the same after that never quite the same but that was nothing new if it wasn't this it was that common occurrence something you could never be the same after crawling about year after year sunk in your lifelong mess muttering to yourself who else you'll never be the same after this you were never the same after that

A: or talking to yourself who else out loud imaginary conversations there was childhood for you ten or eleven on a stone among the giant nettles making it up now one voice now another[6] till you were hoarse and they all sounded the same well on into the night some moods in the black dark or moonlight and they all out on the roads looking for you

B: or by the window in the dark harking to the owl not a thought in your head till hard to believe harder and harder to believe you ever told anyone you loved them or anyone you till just one of those things you kept making up to keep the void out just another of those old tales to keep the void from pouring in on top of you the shroud.

(*Silence 10 seconds. Breath audible. After 3 seconds eyes open*)

C: never the same but the same as what for God's sake did you ever say I to yourself in your life come on now (*Eyes close*) could you ever say I to yourself in your life turning-point that was a great word with you before they dried up altogether always having turning-points and never but the one the first and

3. Another instance where the impression of verisimilitude mixes with invention. A ferry docking at a wharf from which passengers walk uphill to 'the high street', near to bed-and-breakfast kips 'on the front', gives a picture of Dún Laoghaire rather than of the North Wall ('the high street' corresponding to George's Street). But the Dún Laoghaire trams were numbers six, seven and eight, and Dún Laoghaire is a very long way from the Harcourt Street train terminus in central Dublin. It would be quicker to walk directly inland to Foxrock.

4. 'Barrington's Tower' in the original MS. Barrington's Tower still stands near Beckett's childhood home, off the Brenanstown Road in Carrickmines, Co. Dublin.

5. According to legend, Lao Tse or Tzu (6th century B.C., the father of Taoism) was born with long white hair and a beard.

6. Compare above *Endgame* (p. 275) and *Embers* (p. 279).

last that time curled up worm in slime when they lugged you out and wiped you off and straightened you up never another after that never looked back after that was that the time or was that another time

B: muttering that time altogether on the stone in the sun or that time together on the towpath[7] or that time together in the sand that time that time making it up from there as best you could always together somewhere in the sun on the towpath facing downstream into the sun sinking and the bits of flotsam coming from behind and drifting on or caught in the reeds the dead rat it looked like came on you from behind and went drifting on till you could see it no more[8]

A: that time you went back to look was the ruin still there where you hid as a child that last time straight off the ferry and up the rise to the high street to catch the eleven neither right nor left only one thought in your head not a curse for the old scenes the old names just head down press on up the rise to the top and there stood waiting with the nightbag till the truth began to dawn

C: when you started not knowing who you were from Adam trying how that would work for a change not knowing who you were from Adam no notion who it was saying what you were saying whose skull you were clapped up in whose moan had you the way you were was that the time or was that another time there alone with the portraits of the dead black with dirt and antiquity and the dates on the frames in case you might get the century wrong not believing it could be you till they put you out in the rain at closing-time

B: no sight of the face or any other part never turned to her nor she to you always parallel like on an axle-tree never turned to each other just blurs on the fringes of the field no touching or anything of that nature always space between if only an inch no pawing in the manner of flesh and blood no better than shades no worse if it wasn't for the vows

A: no getting out to it that way so what next no question of asking not another word to the living as long as you lived so foot it up in the end to the station bowed half double get out to it that way all closed down and boarded up Doric terminus of the Great Southern and Eastern all closed down and the colonnade crumbling away[9] so what next

C: the rain and the old rounds trying making it up that way as you went along how it would work that way for a change never having been how never having been would work the old rounds trying to wangle you into it tottering and muttering all over the parish till the words dried up and the head dried up and the legs dried up whoever they were or it gave up whoever it was

B: stock still always stock still like that time on the stone or that time in the sand stretched out parallel in the sand in the sun gazing up at the blue or eyes closed blue dark blue dark stock still side by side scene float up and there you were wherever it was

A: gave it up gave up and sat down on the steps in the pale morning sun no those steps got no sun somewhere else then gave up and off somewhere else and down on a step in the pale sun a doorstep say someone's doorstep for it to be time to get on the night ferry and out to hell out of there no need sleep anywhere not a curse for the old scenes the old names the passers pausing to gape at you quick gape then pass pass on pass by on the other side[10]

B: stock still side by side in the sun then sink and vanish without your having stirred any more than the two knobs on a dumbbell except the lids and every now and then the lips to vow and all around all still all sides wherever it might be no stir or sound only faintly the leaves in the little wood behind or the ears or the bent[11] or the reeds as the case might be of man no sight of man or beast no sight or sound

C: always winter then always raining always slipping in somewhere when no one would be looking in off the street out of the cold and rain in the old green holeproof coat your father left you places you hadn't to pay to get in like the Public Library that was another great thing free culture far from home or the Post Office that was another another place another time

A: huddled on the doorstep in the old green

7. Of the Dublin Grand Canal, in an earlier MS version.
8. Compare the scene in *Company* (p. 304 below) and also *Krapp's Last Tape* (in *Complete Dramatic Works* — Faber, 1986, pp. 220-21, 223).
9. Harcourt Street Station, the terminus of the line linking central Dublin with Foxrock and beyond, which closed on 1 January 1959. Described again in *Texts for Nothing* VII (*Collected Shorter Prose 1945-1980* — Calder, 1984 — p. 94). However, the colonnade has always been in good repair, and is not crumbling even in 1990.
10. Alluding to Jesus's being stared at on the cross (Matthew 27.39, Mark 15.29, Luke 23) — as Beckett admitted to the German actor, Klaus Herm. Compare Psalms 22.13 and also the parable of the Good Samaritan in Luke 10.30-35.
11. A name given to grass of a reedy habit; also to various grass-like reeds and sedges.

greatcoat in the pale sun with the nightbag needless on your knees not knowing where you were little by little not knowing where you were or when you were or what for place might have been uninhabited for all you knew like that time on the stone the child on the stone where none ever came

(*Silence 10 seconds. Breath audible. After 3 seconds eyes open*)

B: or alone in the same the same scenes making it up that way to keep it going keep it out on the stone (*Eyes close*) alone on the end of the stone with the wheat and blue or the towpath alone on the towpath with the ghosts of the mules the drowned rat or bird or whatever it was floating off into the sunset till you could see it no more nothing stirring only the water and the sun going down till it went down and you vanished all vanished

A: none ever came but the child on the stone among the giant nettles with the light coming in where the wall had crumbled away poring on his book well on into the night some moods the moonlight and they all out on the roads looking for him or making up talk breaking up two or more talking to himself being together that way where none ever came

C: always winter then endless winter year after year as if it couldn't end the old year never end like time could go no further that time in the Post Office all bustle Christmas bustle in off the street when no one was looking out of the cold and rain pushed open the door like anyone else and straight for the table neither right nor left with all the forms and the pens on their chains sat down first vacant seat and were taking a look round for a change before drowsing away

B: or that time alone on your back in the sand and no vows to break the peace when was that an earlier time a later time before she came after she went or both before she came after she was gone and you back in the old scene wherever it might be might have been the same old scene before as then then as after with the rat or the wheat the yellowing ears or that time in the sand the glider passing over that time you went back soon after long after

A: eleven or twelve in the ruin on the flat stone among the nettles in the dark or moonlight muttering away now one voice now another there was childhood for you till there on the step in the pale sun you heard yourself at it again not a curse for the passers pausing to gape at the scandal huddled there in the sun where it had no warrant clutching the nightbag drooling away out loud eyes closed and the white hair pouring out down from under the hat and so sat on in that pale sun forgetting it all

C: perhaps fear of ejection having clearly no warrant in the place to say nothing of the loathsome appearance so this look round for once at your fellow bastards thanking God for once bad and all as you were you were not as they till it dawned that for all the loathing you were getting you might as well not have been there at all the eyes passing over you and through you like so much thin air was that the time or was that another time another place another time

B: the glider passing over never any change same blue skies nothing ever changed but she with you there or not on your right hand always the right hand on the fringe of the field and every now and then in the great peace like a whisper so faint she loved you hard to believe you even you made up that bit till the time came in the end

A: making it all up on the doorstep as you went along making yourself all up again for the millionth time forgetting it all where you were and what for Foley's Folly and the lot the child's ruin you came to look was it still to hide in again till it was night and time to go till that time came

C: the Library that was another place another time that time you slipped in off the street out of the cold and rain when no one was looking what was it then you were never the same after never again after something to do with dust something the dust said sitting at the big round table with a bevy of old ones poring on the page and not a sound

B: that time in the end when you tried and couldn't by the window in the dark and the owl flown to hoot at someone else or back with a shrew to its hollow tree and not another sound hour after hour hour after hour not a sound when you tried and tried and couldn't any more no words left to keep it out so gave it up gave up there by the window in the dark or moonlight gave up for good and let it in and nothing the worse a great shroud billowing in all over you on top of you and little or nothing the worse little or nothing

A: back down to the wharf with the nightbag and the old green greatcoat your father left you trailing the ground and the white hair pouring out down from under the hat till that time came on down neither right nor left not a curse for the old scenes the old names not a thought in your head only get back on board and away to hell out of it and never come back or was that another time all that another time was there ever any other time but that time away to hell out of it all and never come back

C: not a sound only the old breath and the leaves turning and then suddenly this dust whole place suddenly full of dust when you opened your eyes from floor to ceiling nothing only dust and not a sound only what was it it said come and gone was that it something like that come and gone come and gone no one come and gone in no time gone in no time

(*Silence 10 seconds. Breath audible. After 3 seconds eyes open. After 5 seconds smile, toothless for preference. Hold 5 seconds till fade out and curtain*)

COMPANY (1980)

[The original English version was written between May 1977 and August 1979, at intervals in various places. The French version, *Compagnie*, was made quickly during August 1979, and the English was revised in the light of it before either was published. The text is to be read alongside two subsequent ones of similar length and format, *Ill Seen Ill Said* and *Worstward Ho*, as well as Beckett's late plays.

To one lying in the dark, a voice tells the story of his life. The voice is repetitious, breathless, faint, estranged, flat, yet it summons up memories of a different quality, luminous, as if lit from behind, and still. Faint mental activity and feeling is provoked by the voice, and without it there is none, even as if it shed a faint light. Meanings and values are established between the voice of the story and the ear of the listener, who is telling the story, in complicated rhythms dictated by need and necessity. 'Old scenes' return with a sense of great exactitude, but they are simultaneously called into question, as invented details combine with present need.

The piece includes elements that will appear familiar to the reader of the present selection, and memories of a south County Dublin landscape and childhood provide the substance of many scenes. What makes the piece new and original is the way such company is drawn upon so fully yet, finally, is dispensed with. The analogies between hearer-creator, devised-deviser and voice are orchestrated in ways not heard before in Beckett's fiction. It is simple in the manner one expects from the late writing of a master, that is, in a manner difficult to grasp because it is so simple.]

A voice comes to one in the dark. Imagine.

To one on his back in the dark. This he can tell by the pressure on his hind parts and by how the dark changes when he shuts his eyes and again when he opens them again. Only a small part of what is said can be verified. As for example when he hears, You are on your back in the dark. Then he must acknowledge the truth of what is said. But by far the greater part of what is said cannot be verified. As for example when he hears, You first saw the light on such and such a day. Sometimes the two are combined as for example, You first saw the light on such and such a day and now you are on your back in the dark. A device perhaps from the incontrovertibility of the one to win credence for the other. That then is the proposition. To one on his back in the dark a voice tells of a past. With occasional allusion to a present and more rarely to a future as for example, You will end as you now are. And in another dark or in the same another devising it all for company. Quick leave him.

Use of the second person marks the voice. That of the third that cankerous other. Could he speak to and of whom the voice speaks there would be a first. But he cannot. He shall not. You cannot. You shall not.

Apart from the voice and the faint sound of his breath there is no sound. None at least that he can hear. This he can tell by the faint sound of his breath.

Though now even less than ever given to wonder he cannot but sometimes wonder if it is indeed to and of him the voice is speaking. May not there be another with him in the dark to and of whom the voice is speaking? Is he not perhaps overhearing a communication not intended for him? If he is alone on his back in the dark why does the voice not say so? Why does it never say for example, You saw the light on such and such a day and now you are alone on your back in the dark? Why? Perhaps for no other reason than to kindle in his mind this faint uncertainty and embarrassment.

Your mind never active at any time is now even less than ever so. This is the type of assertion he does not question. You saw the light on such and such a day and your mind never active at any time is now even less than ever so. Yet a certain activity of mind however slight is a necessary complement of company. That is why the voice does not say, You are on your back in the dark and have no mental activity of any kind. The voice alone is company but not enough. Its effect on the hearer is a necessary complement. Were it only to kindle in his mind the state of faint uncertainty and embarrassment mentioned above. But company apart this effect is clearly necessary. For were he merely to hear the voice and it to have no more effect on him than speech in Bantu or in Erse[1] then might it not as well cease? Unless its object be by mere sound to plague one in need of silence. Or of course unless as above surmised directed at another.

A small boy you come out of Connolly's Stores holding your mother by the hand.[2] You turn right and advance in silence southward along the highway. After some hundred paces you head inland and broach the long steep homeward. You make ground in silence hand in hand through the warm still summer air. It is late afternoon and after some hundred paces the sun appears above the crest of the rise. Looking up at the blue sky and then at your mother's face you break the silence asking her if it is not in reality much more distant than it appears. The sky that is. The blue sky. Receiving no answer you mentally reframe your question and some hundred paces later look up at her face again and ask her if it does not appear much less distant than in reality it is. For some reason you could never fathom this question must have angered her exceedingly. For she shook off your little hand and made you a cutting retort you have never forgotten.

If the voice is not speaking to him it must be speaking to another. So with what reason remains he reasons. To another of that other. Or of him. Or of another still. To another of that other or of him or of another still. To one on his back in the dark in any case. Of one on his back in the dark whether the same or another. So with what reason remains he reasons and reasons ill. For were the voice speaking not to him but to another then it must be of that other it is speaking and not of him or of another still. Since it speaks in the second person. Were it not of him to whom it is speaking speaking but of another it would not speak in the second person but in the third. For example, He first saw the light on such and such a day and now he is on his back in the dark. It is clear therefore that if it is not to him the voice is speaking but to another it is not of him either but of that other and none other to that other. So with what reason remains he reasons ill. In order to be company he must display a certain mental activity. But it need not be of a high order. Indeed it might be argued the lower the better. Up to a point. The lower the order of mental activity the better the company. Up to a point.

You first saw the light in the room you most likely were conceived in. The big bow window looked west to the mountains.[3] Mainly west. For being bow it looked also a little south and a little north. Necessarily. A little south to more mountain and a little north to foothill and plain. The midwife was none other than a Dr Hadden or Haddon. Straggling grey moustache and hunted look. It being a public holiday[4] your father left the house soon after his breakfast with a flask and a package of his favourite egg sandwiches for a tramp in the mountains. There was nothing unusual in this. But on that particular morning his love of walking and wild scenery was not the only mover. But he was moved also to take himself off and out of the way by his aversion to the pains and general unpleasantness of labour and delivery. Hence the sandwiches which he relished at noon looking out to sea from the lee of a great rock on the first summit scaled. You may imagine his thoughts before and after as he strode through the gorse and heather. When he returned at nightfall he learned to his dismay from the maid at the back door that labour was still in swing. Despite its having begun before he left the house full ten hours earlier. He at once hastened to the coachhouse some twenty years distant where he housed his De Dion Bouton.[5] He shut the doors behind him and climbed into the driver's seat. You may imagine his thoughts as he sat there in the dark not knowing what to think. Though footsore and weary he was on the point of setting out anew across the fields in the young moonlight when the maid came running to tell him it was over at last. Over!

1. Irish Gaelic, though the word is not preferred by Irish speakers.
2. The first of fifteen scenes from the past, which draw to varying extents on memories and actual events. The same incident as the one here is described towards the end of *Malone Dies* (Picador — 1979, p. 246) and compare *The End* (*Collected Shorter Prose*, p. 53). A note accompanying the Reading University MS confirms the scene is what is now called Cornelscourt Hill, although Connolly's Stores (William Connolly, Grocer, Tea, Wine and Provision Merchant) did not open in their new premises until 1920, when Beckett was past holding his mother's hand. Connolly's van makes a sound-appearance in *All That Fall* (*Complete Dramatic Works*, p. 175).
3. Compare the photograph of the house in which Beckett was born (taken from the west) in Ruby Cohn, *Back to Beckett* (Princeton: Princeton University Press, 1973), facing p. 108.
4. Beckett was born on Good Friday, a public holiday. Compare the several references to Good Friday below and also Beckett's interest in Dante's soothsayers (*Murphy*, note 13, p. 252 above).
5. Beckett's father is reputed to have been one of the first owners of a De Dion Bouton in Ireland (and he passed on an enthusiasm for performance cars to his son).

You are an old man plodding along a narrow country road. You have been out since break of day and now it is evening. Sole sound in the silence your footfalls. Rather sole sounds for they vary from one to the next. You listen to each one and add it in your mind to the growing sum of those that went before. You halt with bowed head on the verge of the ditch and convert into yards. On the basis now of two steps per yard. So many since dawn to add to yesterday's. To yesteryear's. To yesteryear's. Days other than today and so akin. The giant tot in miles. In leagues. How often round the earth already. Halted too at your elbow during these computations your father's shade. In his old tramping rags. Finally on side by side from nought anew.[6]

The voice comes to him now from one quarter and now from another. Now faint from afar and now a murmur in his ear. In the course of a single sentence it may change place and tone. Thus for example clear from above his upturned face, You first saw the light at Easter and now. Then a murmur in his ear. You are on your back in the dark. Or of course vice versa. Another trait its long silences when he dare almost hope it is at an end. Thus to take the same example clear from above his upturned face, You first saw the light of day the day Christ died and now. Then long after on his nascent hope the murmur, You are on your back in the dark. Or of course vice versa.

Another trait its repetitiousness. Repeatedly with only minor variants the same bygone. As if willing him by this dint to make it his. To confess, Yes I remember. Perhaps even to have a voice. To murmur, Yes I remember. What an addition to company that would be! A voice in the first person singular. Murmuring now and then, Yes I remember.

An old beggar woman is fumbling at a big garden gate.[7] Half blind. You know the place well. Stone deaf and not in her right mind the woman of the house is a crony of your mother. She was sure she could fly once in the air. So one day she launched herself from a first floor window. On the way home from kindergarten on your tiny cycle you see the poor old beggar woman trying to get in. You dismount and open the gate for her. She blesses you. What were her words? God reward you little master. Some such words. God save you little master.

A faint voice at loudest. It slowly ebbs till almost out of hearing. Then slowly back to faint full. At each slow ebb hope slowly dawns that it is dying. He must know it will flow again. And yet at each slow ebb hope slowly dawns that it is dying.

Slowly he entered dark and silence and lay there for so long that with what judgement remained he judged them to be final. Till one day the voice. One day! Till in the end the voice saying, You are on your back in the dark. Those its first words. Long pause for him to believe his ears and then from another quarter the same. Next the vow not to cease till hearing cease. You are on your back in the dark and not till hearing cease will this voice cease. Or another way. As in shadow he lay and only the odd sound slowly silence fell and darkness gathered. That were perhaps better company. For what odd sound? Whence the shadowy light?

You stand at the tip of the high board.[8] High above the sea. In it your father's upturned face. Upturned to you. You look down to the loved trusted face. He calls to you to jump. He calls, Be a brave boy. The red round face. The thick moustache. The greying hair. The swell sways it under and sways it up again. The far call again, Be a brave boy. Many eyes upon you. From the water and from the bathing place.

The odd sound. What a mercy to have that to turn to. Now and then. In dark and silence to close as if to light the eyes and hear a sound. Some object moving from its place to its last place. Some soft thing softly stirring soon to stir no more. To darkness visible[9] to close the eyes and hear if only that. Some soft thing softly stirring soon to stir no more.

6. The computations and the companionship recall *Enough*, and compare elsewhere (pp. 285, 310, etc.). The phrase is an alliterative inversion of Ann Livia Plurabelle's 'seim anew' (*Finnegans Wake*, 215.23). The same section of Joyce's book contains references to Beckett, and Beckett helped to translate it into French.

7. A note accompanying the Reading MS locates the scene at Elvery's Gate, that is, 'Rothbury' on Torquay Road. The 'woman of the house' was Mrs Theresa Elvery, though her attempt to fly from a first-floor window is not recorded. (Her daughter, Beatrice, Lady Glenavy, does however record that Hamm in *Endgame* struck her as based on Beckett's Aunt Cissie: *'Today We Will Only Gossip'* (London: Constable, 1964), pp. 178-79.)

8. Beckett's traumatic memory of diving lessons at the Forty Foot swimming place at Sandycove recurs in the jettisoned poem 'For Future Reference' and in *Watt* (see Laurence Harvey, *Samuel Beckett Poet and Critic* — Princeton: Princeton University Press, 1970 — pp. 298-301, and Bair, p. 24). Also compare the scene in *Embers* (p. 280 above), 'Are you coming for a dip?'

9. From *Paradise Lost*, I. 63.

By the voice a faint light is shed. Dark lightens while it sounds. Deepens when it ebbs. Lightens with flow back to faint full. Is whole again when it ceases.[10] You are on your back in the dark. Had the eyes been open then they would have marked a change.

Whence the shadowy light? What company in the dark! To close the eyes and try to imagine that. Whence once the shadowy light. No source. As if faintly luminous all his little void. What can he have seen then above his upturned face. To close the eyes in the dark and try to imagine that.

Another trait the flat tone. No life. Same flat tone at all times. For its affirmations. For its negations. For its interrogations. For its exclamations. For its imperations. Same flat tone. You were once. You were never. Were you ever? Oh never to have been! Be again. Same flat tone.

Can he move? Does he move? Should he move? What a help that would be. When the voice fails. Some movement however small. Were it but of a hand closing. Or opening if closed to begin. What a help that would be in the dark! To close the eyes and see that hand. Palm upward filling the whole field. The lines. The fingers slowly down. Or up if down to begin. The lines of that old palm.

There is of course the eye. Filling the whole field. The hood slowly down. Or up if down to begin. The globe. All pupil. Staring up. Hooded. Bared. Hooded again. Bared again.[11]

If he were to utter after all? However feebly. What an addition to company that would be! You are on your back in the dark and one day you will utter again. One day! In the end. In the end you will utter again. Yes I remember. That was I. That was I then.

You are alone in the garden. Your mother is in the kitchen making ready for afternoon tea with Mrs Coote.[12] Making the wafer-thin bread and butter. From behind a bush you watch Mrs Coote arrive. A small thin sour woman. Your mother answers her saying, He is playing in the garden. You climb to near the top of a great fir. You sit a little listening to all the sounds. Then throw yourself off.[13] The great boughs break your fall. The needles. You lie a little with your face to the ground. Then climb the tree again. Your mother answers Mrs Coote again saying, He has been a very naughty boy.

What with what feeling remains does he feel about now as compared to then? When with what judgement remained he judged his condition final. As well inquire what he felt then about then as compared to before. When he still moved or tarried in remains of light. As then there was no then so there is none now.

In another dark or in the same another devising it all for company. This at first sight seems clear. But as the eye dwells it grows obscure. Indeed the longer the eye dwells the obscurer it grows. Till the eye closes and freed from pore the mind inquires, What does this mean? What finally does this mean that at first sight seemed clear? Till it the mind too closes as it were. As the window might close of a dark empty room. The single window giving on outer dark. Then nothing more. No. Unhappily no. Pangs of faint light and stirrings still. Unformulable gropings of the mind. Unstillable.

Nowhere in particular on the way from A to Z. Or say for verisimilitude the Ballyogan Road.[14] That dear old back road. Somewhere on the Ballyogan Road in lieu of nowhere in particular. Where no truck any more. Somewhere on the Ballyogan Road on the way from A to Z. Head sunk totting up the tally on the verge of the ditch. Foothills to left. Croker's Acres ahead. Father's shade to right and a little to the rear. So many times already round the earth. Topcoat once green stiff with age and grime from chin to insteps. Battered once buff block hat and quarter boots still a match. No other garments if any to be seen. Out since break of day and night now falling. Reckoning ended on together from nought anew. As if bound for Stepaside. When suddenly you cut through the

10. Compare the rhythmic alternation of sourceless light and dark in *Imagination Dead Imagine* and *The Lost Ones* (both in *Collected Shorter Prose*). However, the light of memory and the aspects of a shadow self are more various in the present piece: the lighting in the scenes from the past embraces evening and afternoon, azure and sunless skies, rainbow light and trembling shade, moonlight and illumination from below, lamplight and shadow.

11. Compare the description of Mr Endon's eyes in *Murphy* (Picador, pp. 139-40) and the hooded and bared eyes ('over', 'unover') of *Ping*.

12. A real neighbour, who lived at 'Mountrath' on Kerrymount Avenue. Recollections of Beckett's Foxrock childhood by Mrs Coote's daughter, Dorothy, have been published by Colin Duckworth, 'Beckett's Early Background: A New Zealand Biographical Appendix', *New Zealand Journal of French Studies*, I (1980), 57-67.

13. Something the young Beckett liked to do, apparently (Harvey, p. 298; Bair, p. 23).

14. The Ballyogan Road, Croker's Acres, Stepaside, The Gallops are all real places on the way from Foxrock towards the Dublin Mountains. Compare *Not I* (p. 294 above) for Croker's Acres.

hedge and vanish hobbling east across the gallops.

For why or? Why in another dark or in the same? And whose voice asking this? Who asks, Whose voice asking this? And answers, His soever who devises it all. In the same dark as his creature or in another. For company. Who asks in the end, Who asks? And in the end answers as above? And adds long after to himself, Unless another still. Nowhere to be found. Nowhere to be sought. The unthinkable last of all. Unnamable. Last person. I. Quick leave him.[15]

The light there was then. On your back in the dark the light there was then. Sunless cloudless brightness. You slip away at break of day and climb to your hiding place on the hillside. A nook in the gorse.[16] East beyond the sea the faint shape of high mountain. Seventy miles away according to your Longman. For the third or fourth time in your life. The first time you told them and were derided. All you had seen was cloud. So now you hoard it in your heart with the rest. Back home at nightfall supperless to bed. You lie in the dark and are back in that light. Straining out from your nest in the gorse with your eyes across the water till they ache. You close them while you count a hundred. Then open and strain again. Again and again. Till in the end it is there. Palest blue against the pale sky. You lie in the dark and are back in that light. Fall asleep in that sunless cloudless light. Sleep till morning light.

Deviser of the voice and of its hearer and of himself. Deviser of himself for company. Leave it at that. He speaks of himself as of another. He says speaking of himself, He speaks of himself as of another. Himself he devises too for company. Leave it at that. Confusion too is company up to a point. Better hope deferred than none. Up to a point. Till the heart starts to sicken.[17] Company too up to a point. Better a sick heart than none. Till it starts to break. So speaking of himself he concludes for the time being, For the time being leave it at that.

In the same dark as his creature or in another not yet imagined. Nor in what position. Whether standing or sitting or lying or in some other position in the dark. These are among the matters yet to be imagined. Matters of which as yet no inkling. The test is company. Which of the two darks is the better company. Which of all imaginable positions has the most to offer in the way of company. And similarly for the other matters yet to be imagined. Such as if such decisions irreversible. Let him for example after due imagination decide in favour of the supine position or prone and this in practice prove less companionable than anticipated. May he then or may he not replace it by another? Such as huddled with his legs drawn up within the semicircle of his arms and his head on his knees. Or in motion. Crawling on all fours. Another in another dark or in the same crawling on all fours devising it all for company. Or some other form of motion. The possible encounters. A dead rat.[18] What an addition to company that would be! A rat long dead.

Might not the hearer be improved? Made more companionable if not downright human. Mentally perhaps there is room for enlivenment. An attempt at reflexion at least. At recall. At speech even. Conation[19] of some kind however feeble. A trace of emotion. Signs of distress. A sense of failure. Without loss of character. Delicate ground. But physically? Must he lie inert to the end? Only the eyelids stirring on and off since technically they must. To let in and shut out the dark. Might he not cross his feet? On and off. Now left on right and now a little later the reverse. No. Quite out of keeping. He lie with crossed feet? One glance dispels. Some movement of the hands? A hand. A clenching and unclenching. Difficult to justify. Or raised to brush away a fly. But there are no flies. Then why not let there be? The temptation is great. Let there be a fly. For him to brush away. A live fly mistaking him for dead. Made aware of its error and renewing it incontinent. What an addition to company that would be! A live fly mistaking him for dead. But no. He would not brush away a fly.

You take pity on a hedgehog out in the cold and put it in an old hatbox with some worms.[20] This box

15. The syntax of Beckett's sentences has analogies with the opening of *The Unnamable*.
16. Resembles the 'book read in a nook when a boy' of *From an Abandoned Work* (*Collected Shorter Prose*, p. 134). The 'faint shape of high mountain' to the east is in Wales, which is visible in exceptional circumstances from the hills behind Foxrock. Longman publishes atlases.
17. 'Hope deferred maketh the heart sick', Proverbs 13.12. Also quoted (imperfectly) by Vladimir in *Waiting for Godot* (*Complete Dramatic Works*, p. 11).
18. Compare *Endgame* (p. 271 above).
19. See note 11 on *conarium* in *Murphy* (p. 252 above).
20. Several analogous episodes in Beckett's writing comment on the futility of 'charitable gestures' — for example, *Molloy* (Picador, 1979), pp. 23-24.

with the hog inside you then place in a disused hutch wedging the door open for the poor creature to come and go at will. To go in search of food and having eaten to regain the warmth and security of its box in the hutch. There then is the hedgehog in its box in the hutch with enough worms to tide it over. A last look to make sure all is as it should be before taking yourself off to look for something else to pass the time heavy already on your hands at that tender age. The glow at your good deed is slower than usual to cool and fade. You glowed readily in those days but seldom for long. Hardly had the glow been kindled by some good deed on your part or by some little triumph over your rivals or by a word of praise from your parents or mentors when it would begin to cool and fade leaving you in a very short time as chill and dim as before. Even in those days. But not this day. It was on an autumn afternoon you found the hedgehog and took pity on it in the way described and you were still the better for it when your bedtime came. Kneeling at your bedside you included it the hedgehog in your detailed prayer to God to bless all you loved. And tossing in your warm bed waiting for sleep to come you were still faintly glowing at the thought of what a fortunate hedgehog it was to have crossed your path as it did. A narrow clay path edged with sere box edging. As you stood there wondering how best to pass the time till bedtime it parted the edging on the one side and was making straight for the edging on the other when you entered its life. Now the next morning not only was the glow spent but a great uneasiness had taken its place. A suspicion that all was perhaps not as it should be. That rather than do as you did had perhaps better let good alone and the hedgehog pursue its way. Days if not weeks passed before you could bring yourself to return to the hutch. You have never forgotten what you found then. You are on your back in the dark and have never forgotten what you found then. The mush. The stench.

Impending for some time the following. Need for company not continuous. Moments when his own unrelieved a relief. Intrusion of voice at such. Similarly image of hearer. Similarly his own. Regret then at having brought them about and problem how dispel them. Finally what meant by his own unrelieved? What possible relief? Leave it at that for the moment.

Let the hearer be named H. Aspirate. Haitch. You Haitch are on your back in the dark. And let him know his name. No longer any question of his overhearing. Of his not being meant. Though logically none in any case. Of words murmured in his ear to wonder if to him! So he is. So that faint uneasiness lost. That faint hope. To one with so few occasions to feel. So inapt to feel. Asking nothing better in so far as he can ask anything than to feel nothing. Is it desirable? No. Would he gain thereby in companionability? No. Then let him not be named H. Let him be again as he was. The hearer. Unnamable. You.

Imagine closer the place where he lies. Within reason. To its form and dimensions a clue is given by the voice afar. Receding afar or there with abrupt saltation or resuming there after pause. From above and from all sides and levels with equal remoteness at its most remote. At no time from below. So far. Suggesting one lying on the floor of a hemispherical chamber of generous diameter with ear dead centre. How generous? Given faintness of voice at its least faint some sixty feet should suffice or thirty from ear to any given point of encompassing surface. So much for form and dimensions. And composition? What and where clue to that if any anywhere. Reserve for the moment. Basalt is tempting. Black basalt. But reserve for the moment. So he imagines to himself as voice and hearer pall. But further imagination shows him to have imagined ill. For with what right affirm of a faint sound that it is a less faint made fainter by farness and not a true faint near at hand? Or of a faint fading to fainter that it recedes and not in situ decreases. If with none then no light from the voice on the place where our old hearer lies. In immeasurable dark. Contourless. Leave it at that for the moment. Adding only, What kind of imagination is this so reason-ridden? A kind of its own.

Another devising it all for company. In the same dark as his creature or in another. Quick imagine. The same.

Might not the voice be improved? Made more companionable. Say changing now for some time past though no tense in the dark in that dim mind. All at once over and in train and to come. But for the other say for some time past some improvement. Same flat tone as initially imagined and same repetitiousness. No improving those. But less mobility. Less variety of faintness. As if seeking optimum position. From which to discharge with greatest effect. The ideal amplitude for effortless audition. Neither offending the ear with loudness nor through converse excess constraining it to strain. How far more companionable such an organ than it initially in haste imagined. How far more likely to achieve its object. To have the hearer have a past and acknowledge it. You were born on an Easter Friday after long labour. Yes I remember. The sun had not long sunk behind the larches. Yes I remember. As best to erode the drop must strike unwavering. Upon the place beneath.[22]

The last time you went out the snow lay on the ground.[21] You now on your back in the dark stand that morning on the sill having pulled the door gently to behind you. You lean back against the door with bowed head making ready to set out. By the time you open your eyes your feet have disappeared and the skirts of your greatcoat come to rest on the surface of the snow. The dark scene seems lit from below. You see yourself at that last outset leaning against the door with closed eyes waiting for the word from you to go. To be gone. Then the snowlit scene. You lie in the dark with closed eyes and see yourself there as described making ready to strike out and away across the expanse of light. You hear again the click of the door pulled gently to and the silence before the steps can start. Next thing you are on your way across the white pasture afrolic with lambs in spring and strewn with red placentae.[23] You take the course you always take which is a beeline for the gap or ragged point in the quickset that forms the western fringe. Thither from your entering the pasture you need normally from eighteen hundred to two thousand paces depending on your humour and the state of the ground. But on this last morning many more will be required. Many many more. The beeline is so familar to your feet that if necessary they could keep to it and you sightless with error on arrival of not more than a few feet north or south. And indeed without any such necessity unless from within this is what they normally do and not only here. For you advance if not with closed eyes though this as often as not at least with them fixed on the momentary ground before your feet. That is all of nature you have seen. Since finally you bowed your head. The fleeting ground before your feet. From time to time. You do not count your steps any more. For the simple reason they number each day the same. Average day in day out the same. The way being always the same. You keep count of the days and every tenth day multiply. And add. Your father's shade is not with you any more. It fell out long ago. You do not hear your footfalls any more. Unhearing unseeing you go your way. Day after day. The same way. As if there were no other any more. For you there is no other any more. You used never to halt except to make your reckoning. So as to plod on from nought anew. This need removed as we have seen there is none in theory to halt any more. Save perhaps a moment at the outermost point. To gather yourself together for the return. And yet you do. As never before. Not for tiredness. You are no more tired now than you always were. Not because of age. You are no older now than you always were. And yet you halt as never before. So that the same hundred yards you used to cover in a matter of three to four minutes may now take you anything from fifteen to twenty. The foot falls unbidden in midstep or next for lift cleaves to the ground bringing the body to a stand. Then a speechlessness whereof the gist, Can they go on? Or better, Shall they go on? The barest gist. Stilled when finally as always hitherto they do. You lie in the dark with closed eyes and see the scene. As you could not at the time. The dark cope of sky. The dazzling land. You at a standstill in the midst. The quarter boots sunk to the tops. The skirts of the greatcoat resting on the snow. In the old bowed head in the old block hat speechless misgiving. Halfway across the pasture on your beeline to the gap. The unerring feet fast. You look behind you as you could not then and see their trail. A great swerve. Withershins.[24] Almost as if all at once the heart too heavy. In the end too heavy.

Bloom of adulthood.[25] Imagine a whiff of that. On your back in the dark you remember. Ah you you remember. Cloudless May day. She joins you in the little summerhouse. A rustic hexahedron. Entirely of logs. Both larch and fir. Six feet across. Eight from floor to vertex. Area twenty-four square

21. The whole paragraph was published separately as *Heard in the Dark 1* (*Collected Shorter Prose*, pp. 203-04).
22. What Portia says in *The Merchant of Venice*, IV.1.186.
23. Recalls a scene in *Watt* (Calder, 1976 — p. 45) chosen for Jack MacGowran's selection.
24. Contrary to the direction of the sun (and so, traditionally, unlucky or associated with disaster).
25. The whole paragraph (down to p. 308) was published separately as *Heard in the Dark 2* (*Collected Shorter Prose*, pp. 205-07). For the summer house, compare *Still* (ibid., pp. 183-85) and *As the Story Was Told* (ibid., pp. 211-12).

feet to furthest decimal. Two small multicoloured lights vis-à-vis. Small stained diamond panes. Under each a ledge. There on summer Sundays after his midday meal your father loved to retreat with Punch and a cushion. The waist of his trousers unbuttoned he sat on the one ledge turning the pages. You on the other with your feet dangling. When he chuckled you tried to chuckle too. When his chuckle died yours too. That you should try to imitate his chuckle pleased and tickled him greatly and sometimes he would chuckle for no other reason than to hear you try to chuckle too. Sometimes you turn your head and look out through a rose-red pane. You press your little nose against the pane and all without is rosy. The years have flown and there at the same place as then you sit in the bloom of adulthood bathed in rainbow light gazing before you. She is late. You close your eyes and try to calculate the volume. Simple sums you find a help in times of trouble. A haven. You arrive in the end at seven cubic yards approximately. Even still in the timeless dark you find figures a comfort. You assume a certain heart rate and reckon how many thumps a day. A week. A month. A year. And assuming a certain lifetime a lifetime. Till the last thump. But for the moment with hardly more than seventy American billion behind you you sit in the little summerhouse working out the volume. Seven cubic yards approximately. This strikes you for some reason as improbable and you set about your sum anew. But you have not made much headway when her light step is heard. Light for a woman of her size. You open with quickening pulse your eyes and a moment later that seems an eternity her face appears at the window. Mainly blue in this position the natural pallor you so admire as indeed from it no doubt wholly blue your own. For natural pallor is a property you have in common. The violet lips do not return your smile. Now this window being flush with your eyes from where you sit and the floor as near as no matter with the outer ground you cannot but wonder if she has not sunk to her knees. Knowing from experience that the height or length you have in common is the sum of equal segments.[26] For when bolt upright or lying at full stretch you cleave face to face then your knees meet and your pubes and the hairs of your heads mingle. Does it follow from this that the loss of height for the body that sits is the same as for it that kneels? At this point assuming height of seat adjustable as in the case of certain piano stools you close your eyes the better with mental measure to measure and compare the first and second segments namely from sole to kneepad and thence to pelvic girdle. How given you were both moving and at rest to the closed eye in your waking hours! By day and by night. To that perfect dark. That shadowless light. Simply to be gone. Or for affair as now. A single leg appears. Seen from above. You separate the segments and lay them side by side. It is as you half surmised. The upper is the longer and the sitter's loss the greater when seat at knee level. You leave the pieces lying there and open your eyes to find her sitting before you. All dead still. The ruby lips do not return your smile. Your gaze descends to the breasts. You do not remember them so big. To the abdomen. Same impression. Dissolve to your father's straining against the unbuttoned waistband. Can it be she is with child without your having asked for as much as her hand? You go back into your mind. She too did you but know has closed her eyes. So you sit face to face in the little summerhouse. With eyes closed and your hands on your pubes. In that rainbow light. That dead still.

Wearied by such stretch of imagining he ceases and all ceases. Till feeling the need for company again he tells himself to call the hearer M at least. For readier reference. Himself some other character. W. Devising it all himself included for company. In the same dark as M when last heard of. In what posture and whether fixed or mobile left open. He says further to himself referring to himself, When last he referred to himself it was to say he was in the same dark as his creature. Not in another as once seemed possible. The same. As more companionable. And that his posture there remained to be devised. And to be decided whether fast or mobile. Which of all imaginable postures least liable to pall? Which of motion or of rest the more entertaining in the long run? And in the same breath too soon to say and why after all not say without further ado what can later be unsaid and what if it could not? What then? Could he now if he chose move out of the dark he chose when last heard of and away from his creature into another? Should he now decide to lie and come later to regret it could he then rise to his feet for example and lean against a wall or pace to and fro? Could M be reimagined in

26. Beckett has drawn a diagram of the two positions in the Reading MS.

an easy chair? With hands free to go to his assistance? There in the same dark as his creature he leaves himself to these perplexities while wondering as every now and then he wonders in the back of his mind if the woes of the world are all they used to be. In his day.

M so far as follows. On his back in a dark place form and dimensions yet to be devised. Hearing on and off a voice of which uncertain whether addressed to him or to another sharing his situation. There being nothing to show when it describes correctly his situation that the description is not for the benefit of another in the same situation. Vague distress at the vague thought of his perhaps overhearing a confidence when he hears for example, You are on your back in the dark. Doubts gradually dashed as voice from questing far and wide closes in upon him. When it ceases no other sound than his breath. When it ceases long enough vague hope it may have said its last. Mental activity of a low order. Rare flickers of reasoning of no avail. Hope and despair and suchlike barely felt. How current situation arrived at unclear. No that then to compare to this now. Only eyelids move. When for relief from outer and inner dark they close and open respectively. Other small local movements eventually within moderation not to be despaired of. But no improvement by means of such achieved so far. Or on a higher plane by such addition to company as a movement of sustained sorrow or desire or remorse or curiosity or anger and so on. Or by some successful act of intellection as were he to think to himself referring to himself, Since he cannot think he will give up trying. Is there anything to add to this esquisse?[27] His unnamability. Even M must go. So W reminds himself of his creature as so far created. W? But W too is creature. Figment.[28]

Yet another then. Of whom nothing. Devising figments to temper his nothingness. Quick leave him. Pause and again in panic to himself, Quick leave him.

Devised deviser[29] devising it all for company. In the same figment dark as his figments. In what posture and if or not as hearer in his for good not yet devised. Is not one immovable enough? Why duplicate this particular solace? Then let him move. Within reason. On all fours. A moderate crawl torso well clear of the ground eyes front alert. If this no better than nothing cancel. If possible. And in the void regained another motion. Or none. Leaving only the most helpful posture to be devised. But to be going on with let him crawl. Crawl and fall. Crawl again and fall again. In the same figment dark as his other figments.

From ranging far and wide as if in quest the voice comes to rest and constant faintness. To rest where? Imagine warily.

Above the upturned face. Falling tangent to the crown. So that in the faint light it sheds were there a mouth to be seen he would not see it. Roll as he might his eyes. Height from the ground?

Arm's length. Force? Low. A mother's stooping over cradle from behind. She moves aside to let the father look. In his turn he murmurs to the newborn. Flat tone unchanged. No trace of love.

You are on your back at the foot of an aspen. In its trembling shade. She at right angles propped on her elbows head between her hands. Your eyes opened and closed have looked in hers looking in yours.[30] In your dark you look in them again. Still. You feel on your face the fringe of her long black hair stirring in the still air. Within the tent of hair your faces are hidden from view. She murmurs, Listen to the leaves. Eyes in each other's eyes you listen to the leaves. In their trembling shade.

Crawling and falling then.[31] Crawling again and falling again. If this finally no improvement on nothing he can always fall for good. Or have never risen to his knees. Contrive how such crawl unlike the voice may serve to chart the area. However roughly. First what is the unit of crawl? Corresponding to the footstep of erect locomotion. He rises to all fours and makes ready to set out. Hands and knees angles of an oblong two foot long width irrelevant. Finally say left knee moves forward six inches thus half halving distance between it and homologous hand. Which then in due course in its turn moves forward by as much. Oblong now rhomboid. But for no longer than it takes right knee and hand to follow suit. Oblong restored. So on till he drops. Of all modes of crawl this the repent

27. First rough sketch.
28. The word recurs on this page and on p. 310 and its peculiar force might derive from recollections of the part it plays in the concluding sentence of *Lessness* (p. 292 above).
29. Suggests Aristotle's description of God as the unmoved mover (*Metaphysics*, 1073).
30. Compare the scene in *Krapp's Last Tape* (*Complete Dramatic Works*, pp. 220-21, 223) and, differently, in *That Time* (above, p. 297).
31. The mechanism of crawling recalls similar detailed descriptions in *How It Is*.

amble possibly the least common. And so possibly of all the most diverting.

So as he crawls the mute count. Grain by grain[32] in the mind. One two three four one. Knee hand knee hand two. One foot. Till say after five he falls. Then sooner or later on from nought anew. One two three four one. Knee hand knee hand two. Six. So on. In what he wills a beeline. Till having encountered no obstacle discouraged he heads back the way he came. From nought anew. Or in some quite different direction. In what he hopes a beeline. Till again with no dead end for his pains he renounces and embarks on yet another course. From nought anew. Well aware or little doubting how darkness may deflect. Withershins on account of the heart. Or conversely to shortest path convert deliberate veer.[33] Be that as it may and crawl as he will no bourne as yet. As yet imaginable. Hand knee hand knee as he will. Bourneless dark.[34]

Would it be reasonable to imagine the hearer as mentally quite inert? Except when he hears. That is when the voice sounds. For what if not it and his breath is there for him to hear? Aha! The crawl. Does he hear the crawl? The fall? What an addition to company were he but to hear the crawl. The fall. The rising to all fours again. The crawl resumed. And wonder to himself what in the world such sounds might signify. Reserve for a duller moment. What if not sound could set his mind in motion? Sight? The temptation is strong to decree there is nothing to see. But too late for the moment. For he sees a change of dark when he opens or shuts his eyes. And he may see the faint light the voice imagined to shed. Rashly imagined. Light infinitely faint it is true since now no more than a mere murmur. Here suddenly seen how his eyes close as soon as the voice sounds. Should they happen to be open at the time. So light as let be faintest light no longer perceived than the time it takes the lid to fall. Taste? The taste in his mouth? Long since dulled. Touch? The thrust of the ground against his bones. All the way from calcaneum to bump of philogenitiveness. Might not a notion to stir ruffle his apathy? To turn on his side. On his face. For a change. Let that much of want be conceded. With attendant relief that the days are no more when he could writhe in vain. Smell? His own? Long since dulled. And a barrier to others if any. Such as might have once emitted a rat long dead. Or some other carrion. Yet to be imagined. Unless the crawler smell. Aha! The crawling creator. Might the crawling creator be reasonably imagined to smell? Even fouler than his creature. Stirring now and then to wonder that mind so lost to wonder. To wonder what in the world can be making that alien smell. Whence in the world those wafts of villainous smell. How much more companionable could his creator but smell. Could he but smell his creator. Some sixth sense? Inexplicable premonition of impending ill? Yes or no? No. Pure reason? Beyond experience. God is love.[35] Yes or no? No.

Can the crawling creator crawling in the same create dark as his creature create while crawling? One of the questions he put to himself as between two crawls he lay. And if the obvious answer were not far to seek the most helpful was another matter. And many crawls were necessary and the like number of prostrations before he could finally make up his imagination on this score. Adding to himself without conviction in the same breath as always that no answer of his was sacred. Come what might the answer he hazarded in the end was no he could not. Crawling in the dark in the way described was too serious a matter and too all-engrossing to permit of any other business were it only the conjuring of something out of nothing. For he had not only as perhaps too hastily imagined to cover the ground in this special way but rectigrade into the bargain to the best of his ability. And furthermore to count as he went adding half foot to half foot and retain in his memory the ever-changing sum of those gone before. And finally to maintain eyes and ears at a high level of alertness for any clue however small to the nature of the place to which imagination perhaps unadvisedly had consigned him. So while in the same breath deploring a fancy so reason-ridden and observing how revocable its flights he could not but answer finally no he could not. Could not conceivably create while crawling in the same create dark as his creature.

A strand. Evening. Light dying. Soon none left to die. No. No such thing then as no light. Died on to dawn and never died. You stand with your back to the wash. No sound but its. Ever fainter as it

32. Compare *Endgame* (p. 260 above).
33. Compare above, and Molloy's attempt to correct involuntary veer in the penultimate stage of his journey (*Molloy*, p. 83).
34. A recollection of *Hamlet*, III.1.79-80?
35. A Sunday School emblem that also appears in *Not I* (p. 295 above).

slowly ebbs. Till it slowly flows again. You lean on a long staff. Your hands rest on the knob and on them your head. Were your eyes to open they would first see far below in the last rays the skirt of your greatcoat and the uppers of your boots emerging from the sand. Then and it alone till it vanishes the shadow of the staff on the sand. Vanishes from your sight. Moonless starless night. Were your eyes to open dark would lighten.

Crawls and falls. Lies. Lies in the dark with closed eyes resting from his crawl. Recovering. Physically and from his disappointment at having crawled again in vain. Perhaps saying to himself, Why crawl at all? Why not just lie in the dark with closed eyes and give up? Give up all. Have done with all. With bootless crawl and figments comfortless. But if on occasion so disheartened it is seldom for long. For little by little as he lies the craving for company revives. In which to escape from his own. The need to hear that voice again. If only saying again, You are on your back in the dark. Or if only, You first saw the light and cried at the close of the day when in darkness Christ at the ninth hour cried and died. The need eyes closed the better to hear to see that glimmer shed. Or with adjunction of some human weakness to improve the hearer. For example an itch beyond reach of the hand or better still within while the hand immovable. An unscratchable itch.[36] What an addition to company that would be! Or last if not least resort to ask himself what precisely he means when he speaks of himself loosely as lying. Which in other words of all the innumerable ways of lying is likely to prove in the long run the most endearing. If having crawled in the way described he falls it would normally be on his face. Indeed given the degree of his fatigue and discouragement at this point it is hard to see how he could do otherwise. But once fallen and lying on his face there is no reason why he should not turn over on one or other of his sides or on his only back and so lie should any of these three postures offer better company than any of the other three. The supine though most tempting he must finally disallow as being already supplied by the hearer. With regard to the sidelong one glance is enough to dispel them both. Leaving him with no other choice than the prone. But how prone? Prone how? How disposed the legs? The arms? The head? Prone in the dark he strains to see how best he may lie prone. How most companionably.

See hearer clearer. Which of all the ways of lying supine the least likely in the long run to pall? After long straining eyes closed prone in the dark the following. But first naked or covered? If only with a sheet. Naked. Ghostly in the voice's glimmer that bonewhite flesh for company. Head resting mainly on occipital bump aforesaid. Legs joined at attention. Feet splayed ninety degrees.[37] Hands invisibly manacled crossed on pubis. Other details as need felt. Leave him at that for the moment.

Numb with the woes of your kind you raise none the less your head from off your hands and open your eyes. You turn on without moving from your place the light above you. Your eyes light on the watch lying beneath it. But instead of reading the hour of night they follow round and round the second hand now followed and now preceded by its shadow.[38] Hours later it seems to you as follows. At 60 seconds and 30 seconds shadow hidden by hand. From 60 to 30 shadow precedes hand at a distance increasing from zero at 60 to maximum at 15 and thence decreasing to new zero at 30. From 30 to 60 shadow follows hand at a distance increasing from zero at 30 to maximum at 45 and thence decreasing to new zero at 60. Slant light now to dial by moving either to either side and hand hides shadow at two quite different points as for example 50 and 20. Indeed at any two quite different points whatever depending on degree of slant. But however great or small the slant and more or less remote from initial 60 and 30 the new points of zero shadow the space between the two remains one of 30 seconds. The shadow emerges from under hand at any point whatever of its circuit to follow or precede it for the space of 30 seconds. Then disappears infinitely briefly before emerging again to precede or follow it for the space of 30 seconds again. And so on and on. This would seem to be the one constant. For the very distance itself between hand and shadow varies as the degree of slant. But however great or small this distance it invariably waxes and wanes from nothing to a maximum 15 seconds later and to

36. Like Nagg's in *Endgame* (p. 264 above).

37. Compare the position in *Ping*, p. 287.

38. The episode, at first puzzling in its circumstantiality and length, has a paradigmatic importance in the piece as a whole. See the note on light and shadow re. p. 303 above. Krapp (in *Krapp's Last Tape*) is similarly preoccupied with an equinoctial balance of light and dark.

nothing again 15 seconds later again respectively. And so on and on. This would seem to be a second constant. More might have been observed on the subject of this second hand and its shadow in their seemingly endless parallel rotation round and round the dial and other variables and constants brought to light and errors if any corrected in what had seemed so far. But unable to continue you bow your head back to where it was and with closed eyes return to the woes of your kind. Dawn finds you still in this position. The low sun shines on you through the eastern window and flings all along the floor your shadow and that of the lamp left lit above you. And those of other objects also.

What visions in the dark of light! Who exclaims thus? Who asks who exclaims, What visions in the shadeless dark of light and shade! Yet another still? Devising it all for company. What a further addition to company that would be! Yet another still devising it all for company. Quick leave him.

Somehow at any price to make an end when you could go out no more you sat huddled in the dark. Having covered in your day some twenty-five thousand leagues or roughly thrice the girdle. And never once overstepped a radius of one from home. Home! So sat waiting to be purged the old lutist cause of Dante's first quarter-smile[39] and now perhaps singing praises with some section of the blest at last. To whom here in any case farewell. The place is windowless. When as you sometimes do to void the fluid you open your eyes dark lessens. Thus you now on your back in the dark once sat huddled there your body having shown you it could go out no more. Out no more to walk the little winding back roads and interjacent pastures now alive with flocks and now deserted. With at your elbow for long years your father's shade in his old tramping rags and then for long years alone. Adding step after step to the ever mounting sum of those already accomplished. Halting now and then with bowed head to fix the score. Then on from nought anew. Huddled thus you find yourself imagining you are not alone while knowing full well that nothing has occurred to make this possible. The process continues none the less lapped as it were in its meaninglessness. You do not murmur in so many words, I know this doomed to fail and yet persist. No. For the first personal and a fortiori plural pronoun had never any place in your vocabulary. But without a word you view yourself to this effect as you would a stranger suffering say from Hodgkin's disease or if you prefer Percival Pott's surprised at prayer. From time to time with unexpected grace you lie. Simultaneously the various parts set out. The arms unclasp the knees. The head lifts. The legs start to straighten. The trunk tilts backward. And together these and countless others continue on their respective ways till they can go no further and together come to rest. Supine now you resume your fable where the act of lying cut it short. And persist till the converse operation cuts it short again. So in the dark now huddled and now supine you toil in vain. And just as from the former position to the latter the shift grows easier in time and more alacrious so from the latter to the former the reverse is true. Till from the occasional relief it was supineness becomes habitual and finally the rule. You now on your back in the dark shall not rise again to clasp your legs in your arms and bow down your head till it can bow down no further.[40] But with face upturned for good labour in vain at your fable. Till finally you hear how words are coming to an end. With every inane word a little nearer to the last. And how the fable too. The fable of one with you in the dark. The fable of one fabling of one with you in the dark. And how better in the end labour lost[41] and silence. And you as you always were.

Alone.

39. Belacqua. See note 1 on 'Dante and the Lobster' (p. 238 above).

40. That is, in an embryonic, Belacquan repose adopted by many Beckett characters. Compare above pp. 250, 255, 260.

41. A Beckettian restatement of Shakespeare's title, *Love's Labour's Lost.*

Biography/Bibliography

LIFE. Samuel Beckett was born on Good Friday, 13 April 1906, in a prosperous suburb of south County Dublin, to a protestant professional family. He was the younger of two brothers. His mother, an odd mixture of the conventional and the eccentric, was a strong and frequently painful presence behind Beckett's life and writing. His father enjoyed outdoor recreations.

After local schools, Beckett attended Portora Royal School, in what is now Northern Ireland. Oscar Wilde had also been a pupil, although the school is better known for its athletic tradition, and Beckett excelled at rugby and cricket. He went on to Trinity College, Dublin to study Modern Languages, specializing in French and Italian. His academic interest intensified in the second part of his course, and he graduated in 1927 at the head of his year. After two terms teaching in a Belfast school, he took up an appointment as exchange-lecturer at the Ecole Normale Supérieure in Paris.

Beckett met Joyce soon after he arrived in Paris, as a result of which his interests veered towards writing. His first published piece was an essay on

Finnegans Wake, and his first separately published work, the poem *Whoroscope,* won a competition in 1930. He also completed a short monograph on Proust before returning to Trinity as assistant lecturer in French, where he remained unhappily until he resigned in 1932. The following years were spent restlessly divided between Dublin, London, Germany and France. His father died in 1933. He published a volume of short stories, a volume of poems and a novel, but none of them was well received. The stories were banned in Ireland, and his personal life, as well as his career, seemed stifled. Towards the end of the decade, he settled permanently in Paris, began to write in French, and met the woman he was eventually to marry. He was a member of Joyce's circle (although he was never Joyce's secretary, as is sometimes reported) and enjoyed the friendship of a number of other writers, painters and musicians.

Beckett remained in Paris and later the unoccupied zone during the war, and his work for the Resistance was afterwards awarded the Croix de Guerre. When he picked up his career again in1946, he began the series of writings in French, which includes the trilogy of novels, *Waiting for Godot* and much else besides. As they appeared, the novels attracted the attention of discerning French critics, but *Godot* made him famous when it was produced in Paris (1953) and London (1955), so that his earlier writings also began to be sought out. He meanwhile received requests for plays from the BBC and elsewhere, and from the mid-1950s onwards he wrote for stage, radio, film and television, as well as translating his work from French to English and English to French. He also returned to fiction.

The subsequent story of Beckett's life has been told in the introduction. He was involved in the production of his own plays from the beginning, and came to accept more and more direct responsibility for them. His fiction changed under the influence of values discovered and rediscovered by his plays. The forms of his writing became shorter (he called the late pieces 'chamber music') and at the same time more resonant and pictorial. He was awarded the Nobel Prize for Literature in 1969, and a full-length biography was published in 1978. He divided his time between Paris and a cottage in the Marne, with visits to London, Berlin and elsewhere. He carried an Irish passport, but did not visit Ireland regularly after his mother died in 1951. He died on 22 December 1989, and is buried in Montparnasse cemetery alongside his wife.

CHIEF WRITINGS. The standard bibliography is by Raymond Federman and John Fletcher (eds), *Samuel Beckett: His Works and His Critics* (Berkeley: University of California Press, 1970). It should be supplemented — for books by Beckett — by Robin J. Davis, *Samuel Beckett: Checklist and Index of his Published Works 1967-1976* (The Library, University of Stirling: for the author, 1979) and by Breon Mitchell, 'A Beckett Bibliography: New Works 1976-1982,' *Modern Fiction Studies,* XXIX:1 (Spring 1983), 131-51. Richard L. Admussen, *The Samuel Beckett Manuscripts. A Study* (Boston, Massachusetts: G. K. Hall, 1979) is also relevant, as are the published catalogues of Beckett material at the University of Reading and at the University of Texas at Austin (1978 and 1984 respectively) and the catalogue of the Reading exhibition, James Knowlson (ed.) (London: Turret Books, 1971).

Beckett's bibliography is complicated because he has published in English and French, translating himself from one to the other — the texts in each language constituting separate entities; also because the English and American texts and collections are often not identical, despite their having identical titles; furthermore, because he has allowed to be reprinted texts of plays that have been superseded by different versions of the same plays that have evolved in production. In Britain, Beckett's texts are published in London by John Calder (fiction, and also verse and criticism), Picador (selected paperback fiction) and Faber and Faber (plays); in the United States everything is published in New York by Grove Press. All Beckett titles are in print in one collection or another, this on both sides of the Atlantic. The French titles are published in Paris by Editions de Minuit.

Beckett committed himself to writing with a critical work on Joyce's work in progress: *Our Exagmination round his Factification for Incamination of Work in Progress* (Paris: Shakespeare and Company, 1929; London: Faber, 1936; New York: New Directions, 1939, 1962).

The verse — comprising *Whoroscope* (1930) and *Echo's Bones* (1935), with selected other poems and translations — is gathered in *Collected Poems 1930-1978* (Calder, 1984); and more of Beckett's translations are included in *Anthology of Mexican Poetry* (Bloomington: Indiana University Press, 1958; Calder, 1970). A useful supplement is Lawrence Harvey, *Samuel Beckett: Poet and Critic* (Princeton, New Jersey: Princeton University Press, 1970), which includes early poems that Beckett himself declined to collect and which provides necessary annotation. A number of Beckett's translations — for instance, of Alain Bosquet — also remain uncollected.

The criticism is to be found in two volumes — *Proust* (1931; Grove, 1957; Calder, 1965) and *Disjecta,* Ruby Cohn (ed.) (Grove/Calder, 1983). The latter volume collects Beckett's essay on *Finnegans Wake,* 'Dante... Bruno. Vico .. Joyce', journalism and reviews dating mainly from the 1930s, and essays and dialogues on painters. Brief but discerning comments on other writers and artists (G. B. Shaw, the Marquis de Sade, Irish culture, etc.) have been published in interviews, letters, publishers' blurbs, memoirs, *festschrifts.* At least three series of notes, recording Beckett's lectures at Trinity, are extant and have been published in part.

The fiction comprises *More Pricks Than Kicks* (1934), *Murphy* (1938); written 1934-35), *Watt* (1953; written 1941-44), *Mercier and Camier* (1970; written 1946; English translation 1974), *Molloy, Malone Dies, The Unnamable* (collected by Grove as *Three Novels* and by Picador as *The Beckett Trilogy*), *How It Is* (1961; English translation 1964). *Collected Shorter Prose 1945-1980* (1984). *Nohow On* (1989). *Collected Shorter Prose* gathers texts related to the trilogy ('First Love', 'The Expelled', 'The Calmative', 'The End', 'Texts for Nothing'), as well as groups of texts written in the three following decades. Several of them have been published in groupings with different collective titles, before this most comprehensive collection. *Nohow On* gathers *Company* (1980); English translation 1980), *Ill Seen Ill Said* (1981; English translation 1982), *Worstward Ho* (1983). Beckett's first novel, from which he constructed the stories *More Pricks Than Kicks,* remains unpublished (though extracts are included in *Disjecta*). His last-written prose work, *Stirrings Still,* was published first in an expensive limited edition (New York: Blue Moon; London: Calder, 1988).

Collected Plays (Faber, 1986) is what it says, and gathers thirty-two plays between its covers. That it reprints the expurgated and superseded text of *Godot* is unfortunate. The more important titles are as follows (the dates are of first performances, not of publication): *Waiting for Godot* (Paris 1953; London 1955; Miami 1956); *All That Fall* (radio play, BBC 1957); *Endgame* (London 1957 in French; New York and London 1958 in English); *Act Without Words I* (London 1957); *Act Without Words II* (published 1959, performed London 1960); *Krapp's Last Tape* (London 1958); *Embers* (radio play, BBC 1959); *Happy Days* (New York 1961; London 1962); *Words and Music* (radio play, BBC 1962); *Cascando* (radio play, Paris 1963; London 1964); *Play* (Ulm 1963 in German; London 1964); *Film* (New York 1965); *Come and Go* (Berlin 1966 in German; Dublin and London 1968); *Eh Joe* (television play, Süddeutscher Rundfunk 1966 in German; BBC 1966); *Breath* (New York and Glasgow 1969); *Not I* (New York 1972, London 1973); *That Time* (London 1976); *Footfalls* (London 1976); *Ghost Trio* (television play, published 1976; BBC 1977); *... but the clouds ...* (television play, BBC 1977); *A Piece of Monologue* (New York 1979; Edinburgh 1984); *Rockaby* (Buffalo 1981; London 1982); *Ohio Impromptu* (Columbus 1981; Edinburgh 1984); *Quad* (television mime, Süddeutscher Rundfunk 1981; BBC 1982); *Catastrophe* (Avignon 1982 in French; Paris 1983 in French; Edinburgh 1984); *Nacht und Träume* (television mime, Süddeutscher Rundfunk 1983); *What Where* (Graz 1983 in German; Edinburgh 1984).

No text survives of Beckett's first dramatic work, *Le Kid,* a parody-sketch after Corneille, performed at Trinity College, Dublin in February 1931. The single extant scene from his play about Dr Johnson and Mrs Thrale, *Human Wishes,* begun and abandoned in 1937, is included in *Disjecta. Eleuthéria,* which precedes *Molloy* and therefore *Godot,* remains unpublished. It was announced for publication by Editions de Minuit in 1951, but Beckett subsequently changed his mind about issuing it.

BIOGRAPHY AND CRITICISM. The biography by Deirdre Bair (New York: Harcourt Brace Jovanovich; London: Cape, 1978) has been criticized for its journalistic approach and lack of literary understanding, but it is the only one there is on a comprehensive scale. A new biography is in preparation by James Knowlson. Eoin O'Brien, *The Beckett Country.*

Samuel Beckett's Ireland (Dublin: Black Cat; London: Faber, 1986) identifies local references and is richly illustrated. Beckett's developing reputation among reviewers can be followed in Lawrence Graver and Raymond Federman (eds), *Samuel Beckett: The Critical Heritage* (London: Routledge, 1979). Hugh Kenner, *Samuel Beckett: A Critical Study* (New York: Grove, 1961; London: Calder, 1962) set the tone of much earlier Beckett criticism; as did Martin Esslin, *The Theatre of the Absurd* (New York: Anchor, 1962; revised Harmondsworth: Penguin, 1968). For a full list of books and writing about Beckett, see Federman and Fletcher (1970) and also Cathleen Culotta Ándonian, *Samuel Beckett: A Reference Guide* (Boston, Massachusetts: G. K. Hall, 1989).

Good one-volume surveys of the whole of Beckett's task are by Ruby Cohn, *Back to Beckett* (Princeton, New Jersey: Princeton University Press, 1975) and John Pilling, *Samuel Beckett* (London: Routledge, 1976). John Fletcher, *Samuel Beckett's Art* (London: Chatto and Windus, 1967) might also be mentioned as a helpful starting-point for anyone feeling ignorant about Beckett's backgrounds (Dante, Geulincx, etc.). Less interpretive and historical, more theoretical readings are suggested by Floyd Merreu, *Deconstruction Reframed* (West Lafayette, Indiana: Purdue University Press, 1985); Peter Gidal, *Understanding Beckett: A Study of Monologue and Gesture in the Works of Samuel Beckett* (London: Macmillan, 1986); Steven Connor, *Samuel Beckett: Repetition, Theory and Text* (Oxford: Blackwell, 1988).

In a different medium, *MacGowran Speaking Beckett* (Dublin: Claddagh Records, CCT3) and *A Tribute to Beckett: Barry McGovern Reads 'Dante and the Lobster' and 'From an Abandoned Work'* (Dublin: Abbey Cassettes, ABB 013) give direct access to two very sympathetic interpreters. Other recordings have been made, in English, French and German, on disk, tape, film and video. National Public Radio (Washington, D.C.) published audiocassettes of new productions of five radio plays — including *Embers* — in 1989.

Criticism in English of Beckett's fiction is plentiful, but it tends to be unfocussed, compared to criticism in French (although this has been on the wane in recent years) and in German (which is on the increase). There are several surveys of Beckett's earlier fiction in particular, and monographs on individual novels, but the following anthologies contain material that is in general more thought-provoking: Martin Esslin (ed.), *Samuel Beckett. A Collection of Critical Essays* (Englewood Cliffs, New Jersey: Prentice Hall, 1965); Melvin J. Friedman (ed.), *Samuel Beckett Now* (Chicago: University of Chicago Press, 1970); Ruby Cohn (ed.), *Samuel Beckett: A Collection of Criticism* (New York: McGraw-Hill, 1975); Edouard Morot-Sir, Howard Harper and Dougald McMillan (eds), *Samuel Beckett: The Art of Rhetoric* (Chapel Hill:University of North Carolina Press, 1976); Morris Beja, S. E. Gontarski and Pierre Astier (eds), *Samuel Beckett: Humanistic Perspectives* (Columbus: Ohio State University Press, 1983); S. E. Gontarski (ed.), *On Beckett: Essays and Criticism* (New York: Grove, 1986); Patrick A. McCarthy (ed.), *Critical Essays on Samuel Beckett* (Boston, Massachusetts: G. K. Hall, 1986).

The following special issues of journals also contain useful essays on aspects of Beckett's fiction: *James Joyce Quarterly,* VIII:4 (Summer 1971); *L'Esprit Créatur,* XI:3 (Fall 1971); *L'Herne,* No. 31 (1976); *Journal of Modern Literature,* VI:1 (February 1977); *AUMLA,* No. 55 (May 1981); *College Literature,* VIII:3 (Fall 1981); *Modern Fiction Studies,* XXIX:1 (Spring 1983); *Irish University Review,* XIV:1 (Spring 1984). *Hermathena* No. CXLI (Winter 1986); *The Review of Contemporary Fiction,* VII: 2 (Summer 1987).

Criticism and scholarship surrounding the plays is on a more satisfactory footing, that is, better able to combine research and criticism. Beryl S. Fletcher and John Fletcher, *A Student's Guide to the Plays of Samuel Beckett* (London: Faber, 2nd ed., 1985) supplies annotation and lists essays and casebooks on particular plays. The following studies exemplify what seems to me the most rewarding approach: S. E. Gontarski, *Beckett's 'Happy Days': A Manuscript Study* (Columbus: Ohio State University Libraries, 1977); James Knowlson, *Theatre Workbook I: 'Krapp's Last Tape'* (London: Brutus Books, 1980); James Knowlson, *'Happy Days': Samuel Beckett's Production Notebook* (London: Faber; New York: Grove, 1985); S. E. Gontarski, *The Intent of Undoing in Samuel Beckett's Dramatic Texts* (Bloomington: Indiana University Press, 1985); Enoch Brater (ed.), *Beckett at 80/Beckett in Context* (New York: Oxford University Press, 1986); Dougald McMillan and Martha Fehsenfeld, *Beckett in the Theatre* (Calder, forthcoming). *Beckett in the Theatre* (London: Calder, 1988); Jonathan Kalb, *Beckett in Performance* (Cambridge: Cambridge University Press, 1989).

The following also contain material of value: James Knowlson and John Pilling, *Frescoes of the Skull: The Later Prose and Drama of Samuel Beckett* (London: Calder, 1979; New York: Grove, 1980); Ruby Cohn, *Just Play: Beckett's Theatre* (Princeton: Princeton University Press, 1986); Enoch Brater, *Beyond Minimalism: Beckett's Late Style in the Theater* (New York: Oxford University Press, 1987); James Acheson and Kateryna Arthur (eds), *Beckett's Later Fiction and Drama: Texts for Company* (London: Macmillan, 1987); Susan D. Brienza, *Samuel Beckett's New Worlds: Style in Metafiction* (Norman, Oklahoma: University of Oklahoma Press, 1987); Alan Warren Friedman et al (eds), *Beckett Translating/Translating Beckett* (University Park, Pennsylvania: Pennsylvania State University Press, 1987); Brian T. Fitch, *Beckett and Babel: An Investigation into the Status of the Bilingual Work* (Toronto: University of Toronto Press, 1988); Robin J. Davis and Lance St J. Butler (eds), *Make Sense Who May: Essays on Samuel Beckett's Later Works* (Gerrards Cross: Colin Smythe, 1988). Two periodicals, in particular, have published special issues or part-special issues devoted to Beckett's drama: *Cahiers Renaud Barrault,* No. 44 (November 1966), No. 93 (1976), No. 102 (1981); and *Modern Drama,* IX:3 (December 1966), XIX:3 (September 1976), XXV:3 (September 1982), XXVIII:1 (March 1985).

Finally, *Journal of Beckett Studies* (1976 onwards, ten issues to date) contains essays, reviews and photographs of productions; and, in news-sheet format, *The Beckett Circle* carries short notices and announcements of recent and forthcoming events and publications.

TOM PAULIN, *Editor*

Northern Protestant Oratory and Writing 1791-1985

In his maiden speech in the House of Lords, Edward Carson attacked the Anglo-Irish Treaty of 1921 and warned British politicians not to turn Ulster 'against the British connection'. With characteristic hyperbole, he urged them to remember that when 'through your laws, Ulstermen were driven out of Ireland and went to America, it was thirty-six Ulstermen, smarting under a grievance, who signed the Declaration of Independence.' More than fifty years later, in a short book entitled *America's Debt to Ulster*, the Rev. Ian Paisley described how 'Ulster men and men of Ulster stock' had a 'leading hand' in framing the Declaration of Independence. This pride in the Ulster presbyterian contribution to the American Revolution was echoed during the 1980s in publications associated with the Ulster Defence Association, the chief loyalist paramilitary organization, and it issues from those contradictory emotions and beliefs that form the basis of 'loyalist' culture. Distrusting traditional definitions of Irish identity, that culture often aggressively presents itself as being simultaneously British and anti-British.

In order to establish the distinctive characteristics and values of Ulster loyalist or protestant culture, it is necessary to abandon conventional ideas of the literary and the aesthetic and consider forms of writing that are often dismissed as ephemeral or non-canonical — familiar letters, political speeches, oaths and toasts, sermons, pieces of journalism, overtured addresses, the minutes of synodical and other meetings. All these texts are forms of cultural production which for a variety of reasons have remained unexamined for many generations. The consciously modulated and often passionate voices that speak out of these printed texts have not so far attracted that critical appraisal to which self-evidently literary texts are submitted, nor have they yet been gathered and reproduced by cultural historians; but they stand nevertheless as the distinctive achievements of a community.

From William Drennan's seminal letter of 21 May 1791, with its idea of a new republican society, to Carson's threatened Ulster independence, there is a curiously syncopated continuity of attitude, which cannot be subsumed under that overworked and misleading term 'tradition'. The eighteenth-century Belfast republican, Drennan, writes with a dissenting enthusiasm about the idea of independence, while the late-Victorian Dublin unionist, Carson, speaks for his adopted province's grievances with a punitive earnestness. Separated by ideology and history, they share a passionate seriousness about politics and a self-justifying energy and sense of personal integrity that seem strangely innocent.

Drennan's symbol for an organized international republican movement — a 'caisson' — is ambiguous and revealing, and it may be read as articulating that type of protestant imagination which he and Carson shared. A caisson is a large water-tight chest, used in laying the foundations of bridges in deep water, and for Drennan the term represents the idea of stability, secrecy, political and intellectual power, a new enlightened international order. However, the term also means an explosive device, a mine, and in that sense it is a highly unstable power, the embodiment of active revolutionary energy and enthusiasm. Drennan's imagination wants to destroy the old order and create a new society, an idea that derives ultimately from Pauline theology ('Therefore if any man be in Christ, he is a new creature: old things are passed away; behold, all things are become new', II Corinthians 5. 17). At the root of Drennan's imagination is this idea of being born again, an idea that fuses the personal life with the civic life; and, like St Paul, he sees epistolary communication as the essential medium for his ideas.

Commenting on Paul's statement in his Epistle to the Romans that the gospel of Christ 'is the power of God' (1. 16), Ian Paisley states that gospel preaching 'is charged with the dynamic of heaven. Dynamite to be displayed in all its mighty potency must have the fuse and the fire.' He imagines the 'strongholds of Satan' toppling and the 'bulwarks of idolatry' collapsing. For Paisley, as for Drennan, ideas are a form of high explosive and both writers share a detestation of 'torpid acquiescence', a fundamental hostility to Roman catholicism, an intense commitment to the right of private judgment and a belief in a value they term 'energy' or 'the dynamic of heaven'. Like 'honest', 'independent' and 'pure', such terms represent key concepts in protestant discourse and may be set against terms such as 'organic' or 'balanced', which feature so strongly in certain forms of British literary criticism and conservative argument. In essence, they express a constantly challenging or polemical 'mind-set' and this is one result of a belief in the right of private judgment.

That belief also stimulates the frequent protestations of personal integrity that can disfigure protestant discourse — in his 'Intended Defence', Drennan often insists on his 'pure intentions and honest principles', while Henry Montgomery speaks of himself as being 'an honourable and irreproachable man, who has raised himself to a station of honest independence by his *own exertions*'. Protestantism can protest its integrity too much and mask an argument with a series of self-images and personal testimonies. One result, though, of such self-addressed character references is to foreground consciousness as the subject of both writing and oratory and, by breaking down the barriers between printed text and speech act, impart a free-flowing, improvisatory texture to what is being said.

In 'The Intended Defence', Drennan speaks of 'that conscious mind, which is its own awful world', and although he is referring specifically to the burdens of the individual conscience — its solitary sense of guilt and damnation — there are moments in protestant discourse when consciousness for its own sake, consciousness as subject, erupts and dominates. This sense of consciousness as process, as an end in itself, can be observed in much American writing, and it is rooted in puritan ideas of private judgment and personal testimony. Its effect is sometimes circular and narcissistic — Drennan, Montgomery and Henry Cooke can base arguments on their own affirmations of personal worth. This presbyterian habit of insisting on one's integrity finds a philosophical justification in the work of Frances Hutcheson, but it can appear to be an over-personal and personalized method of argument. That enduring presbyterian preference for the direct testimony of consciousness over formal argument creates a solipsistic universe gnawed at its edges by anger and incoherence. Such powerful frustrations can be observed in Paisley's discourse and in Harold McCusker's heartfelt manner of testifying against the 1985 Anglo-Irish Agreement.

This type of urgent, declamatory, polemical anger fuels the Rev. James Carlile's attack on 'an individual, styling himself Lord Castlereagh', an attack that is egalitarian in outlook and sometimes populist in expression ('Who or what was this Lord Castlereagh . . .?'). Insisting on the right of private judgment and the principle of non-interference by the state, Carlile describes the manner in which the Synod of Ulster has reacted to Castlereagh's threat of withdrawing the *regium donum*:

> . . . here we are gravely deliberating whether we shall suffer the civil Government to interfere in our spiritual concerns — whether we shall barter what we believe, and what we have declared again and again to be, the spiritual interests of our people, for money — I say to barter them for money. O fatal day for the independence of the Synod of Ulster! O miserable degeneracy from the spirit of our forefathers! There was a time when, if the Sovereign himself, in all the pomp of royalty, attended by an armed force, had appeared within these walls, and held out such a threat,

> and had added to it the threat of fire and faggot, he would have met with a unanimous opposition to his interference, and not one of our number would have been found base enough to justify it, or to insinuate that we ought to yield to his requisition.

The appeal to 'the spirit of our forefathers' is one of the hallmarks of presbyterian oratory (there is a similar reference in the Solemn League and Covenant of 1912), and the exclamatory, dramatic style of Carlile's speech has all the appearance of being sudden and extempore and therefore passionately sincere. This is an eruptive moment which begins with the recapitulatory emphasis *I say to barter them for money*. From this point, a volatile consciousness — that of the speaker fused with his audience — expands moment by moment and pushes far beyond conventional and restraining notions of decorum, propriety and 'gentlemanly civility'. Such an ethic is hostile to hierarchical codes of manners and expresses itself in a free unpolished vernacular. Its equivalent in the visual arts is action painting, and it is no accident that Jackson Pollock was of Scotch-Irish descent. (Elizabeth Frank notes in her study of the painter, that the Scotch-Irish were 'historically dispossessed, rootless, and deeply presbyterian'.) Pollock's father's credo — 'I think every person should think, act and believe according to the dictates of his own conscience without to [*sic*] much pressure from the outside' — is characteristically presbyterian.

The puritan aesthetic that shapes vernacular discourse is founded on an anti-aesthetic of 'truth' or immediate divine inspiration. On the surface there is usually an appearance of directness and informality, but it is a carefully calculated illusion which can make the preacher resemble a method actor in his urgent authenticity and professions of personal sincerity. The church becomes a theatre where we witness an intense drama of consciousness and where a powerful sense of the absolute importance of the present moment — the urgent *now* of utterance — springs from the fusion of audience attention with the preacher's voice and gestures. The frequent dashes and exclamation marks that appear in printed texts signal an impatience with the fixity of print and a liberating ambition to make a primal reality of the spoken word. Like Emily Dickinson, the puritan writer wishes to substitute a series of exclamatory speech moments for the codified formality of print. This vocal aesthetic is a version of the argument in the third chapter of the second epistle to the Corinthians where Paul rejects actual inscribed letters through an imaginative assertion, which abolishes the distinction between readers of written texts or 'epistles of commendation' and the writers of such texts. He asserts that 'ye' — the Corinthians he is addressing — are 'our epistle written in our hearts', and then draws a distinction between letters written with ink or 'in tables of stone' and those letters written 'with the Spirit of the living God . . . in fleshy tables of the heart.' This is an antinomian, born-again attitude which dedicates itself to 'the new testament; not of the letter, but of the spirit: for the letter killeth, but the spirit giveth life.' Paul contrasts this new spiritual text with the 'ministration of death, written and engraven in stones' (i.e. the Mosaic Law). This inscribed law is a veil that remains 'untaken away in the reading of the old testament'. Paul abolishes it and offers instead a new libertarian speech, 'great plainness of speech' as he terms it. Carlile's plea for 'very strong language' similarly insists on the necessity of a direct plain style, and he also follows Paul in his rejection of a formal, codified discourse. Like Drennan, Carlile is an enthusiast who wants to make everything new.

The published writings of the Rev. Henry Montgomery articulate a firm belief in civil and religious liberty and a liberal dislike of rigid official modes of faith. Montgomery delights in human diversity, loves natural scenery, respects other people's opinions and believes absolutely in the right of private judgment. He fears that Cooke and his supporters would create a 'dead sea' of presbyterian conformity, and his legendary controversy with Cooke is a version of the battle fought in the 1790s between republicanism and loyalism. For all his professed belief in the British Empire and the Union with Britain, Montgomery's imagination appears to have a secret lien to the world of republican dissent that Drennan speaks for. He was professor of English at the Belfast Academical Institution, which Drennan founded, and was closely linked to the liberal middle-class of Belfast.

Contemporary witnesses noted that Montgomery's oratory was more polished than Cooke's, but that he lacked his opponent's ability to sway a large crowd. Persuasion rather than vivid rhetorical effect was a leading feature of his oratory and he left audiences feeling 'not so much delighted as improved'. Montgomery's biographer and son-in-law, J.A. Crozier, notes that Cooke spoke with a 'slow and rather provincial and drawling accent', and we may assume that Montgomery's speaking voice reflected his yeoman background and middle-class connections. It would not be stretching a point to see his quarrel with Cooke as anticipating Paisley's struggle with Captain Terence O'Neill, the Ulster prime minister (1963-69) whose 'nasal tones' the Antrim preacher-politician defied.

Montgomery's beliefs are defined by invoking what he terms the 'native purity and simplicity' of the early Christian church. For Montgomery, primitive Christianity knew 'no creed but that which came from on high', and his benign rejection of narrow systems of belief means that he places little emphasis on sin and damnation. Unlike Calvinist thinkers, he does not dismiss sense experience as irredeemably evil and is appreciative of natural beauty, preferring a fluid variousness to 'one unnatural and unwholesome calm'. This element of sensuous responsiveness in Montgomery's thinking is a significant feature of puritan libertarianism and finds its classic expression in Milton's evocation of Eden before the Fall. D.H. Lawrence's writings offer a romantic version of this type of primitivism, and the paintings of Edward Hicks and other early American artists also embody this puritan belief in a primally innocent world where human beings and animals live in harmony with nature and each other.

Like all presbyterians, Montgomery repeatedly insists that he can never be a time-server and submit to human authority. It could be that Daniel O'Connell's attack on him as a 'fawning, cringing sycophant' touched this sensitive nerve and thus provoked the unusual vehemence of his reply to O'Connell. On the other hand, Montgomery's hostility to O'Connell can be seen as the frightened response of the liberal protestant bourgeoisie to the threat posed to their property by O'Connell's mass political movement. As in his earlier 'Letter to Henry Cooke', where he identifies with Joseph Priestley against 'an infuriated multitude', Montgomery is affirming a liberal position midway between 'arbitrary power' and 'wild democratical theories'. If Montgomery's thinking is rooted in the Volunteer Movement and the United Irishmen, it also looks toward the liberal Unionist position now represented politically by the Alliance Party. In opposing Cooke's drive to consolidate and unify protestant power in Ulster, and in opposing O'Connell's agitation for the repeal of the Union, Montgomery occupies a position that is exposed to attack by both romantic nationalism and populist unionism. In this changed political climate, the late eighteenth-century values articulated by both Drennan and Montgomery appear stranded and inert, accessible only to sentimental recuperation by literary antiquarians.

Where Montgomery's suasive style is scrupulous and decorous, Henry Cooke often resorts to hyperbole, brutal simplification and sensational imagery. Part stand-up comic, part atavistic Covenanter, part Wellington look-a-like, he impressed contemporary observers with his visceral powers of argument and his ability to move huge popular audiences. Attacking O'Connell during the Liberator's famous visit to Belfast in 1841, Cooke used the date to invoke atavistic memories of 1641 and remind his audience of the massacres of protestants that took place in that year. This type of headline-grabbing opportunism is also apparent in Cooke's attack on Arianism, where he seizes on the birthplace of Arius in order to dismiss his ascetic theology as a 'sickly exotic', bred like Cleopatra in the warm mud of the Nile. Here Cooke's thinking is based on a form of racial exclusivism that is as central to orthodox Ulster protestant thinking as the idea of the pure Gael is to the ideology of Irish nationalism. (In 1985, for example, the leader of the Official Unionist Party, James Molyneaux, opposed Irish unity by arguing that protestants and catholics are racially different.)

Cooke followed traditional British protestant thinking in viewing the catholic Irish as barbarians and the Ulster protestants as civilizers. In his private letters he refers to the 'great unwashed' who attended O'Connell's meeting in Belfast, exults at the eviction of 'savages' from their cabins on an improving landlord's estate, and distinguishes between the 'cool, logical' northern protestants and the 'excitable Celts' of the south. Developing the image of floodwaters as a metaphor for sin, Cooke exclaims:

> It comes! — The flood! — dark, deep, and sudden. Merciful Heaven hath given it a voice: but the warning uttered, there remains not an instant for delay. He that flees may escape; but he that deliberates is lost.

Cooke's image is not simply religious in its application; it represents the gathering force of O'Connellite nationalism, and Cooke's hysterical, distinctly uncool, development of the flood image articulates the most profound social fear in his audience, the fear of being forced off the land:

> In lands exposed to frequent inundations, experience teaches to guard against their inroads. But, if the flood rise far above its ordinary level; or, if it descend with unusual violence, it overtops or bears away the mounds or barriers erected for its confinement: and, the destructive element once let loose, it sweeps away property and life . . . .

Cooke then cites the twelfth chapter of Revelation, the New Testament book traditionally interpreted by protestants as a prophecy of the rise of Roman catholicism; this underlines the anti-catholic significance of the flood image.

For all his proud provincialism ('Look at the town of Belfast'), Cooke also aims to create an international protestant identity in which Hus, Luther, Milton, Ridley, Latimer and the Scottish Covenanters are ranged against the power of Rome. The concept of heroic martyrdom is as deeply ingrained in Ulster loyalism as it is in the discourse of Irish nationalism. Ian Paisley has published a number of sermons on the Scottish Covenanters, who were, he states, 'bold, courageous, strong men . . . these were not the putty paper men of the twentieth century — these were the rugged men of the Reformation.'

If Cooke helped to lay the foundations for that failed polity, the State of Northern Ireland, it is not difficult to admire the gruelling and aggrieved search for identity that his long career embodies. He speaks for the moral north, and his attitudes and values are firmly rooted in Ulster. Craigavon's proud reference in his speech, 'We Are King's Men', to 'our rock-bound and turbulent coast' shows a similar form of regional nationalism, and both Cooke and James Craig (Viscount Craigavon) share a modernizing energy and belief in economic development. For them, Ulster is a paradisal garden occupied solely by hardworking Bible-reading protestants. Craigavon's remark, 'Britain's difficulty is Northern Ireland's opportunity', inverts a standard nationalist shibboleth and implicitly links the Nazi threat with the bombing campaign that the IRA had recently mounted in Britain. It exemplifies the dialogical or polemical nature of the protestant imagination, an imagination that sees itself dramatically as pitched against certain powerful ideas that threaten its existence and values. Feisty, restless, argumentative, never quite at home in this world, that imagination has seldom shaped itself in traditionally aesthetic form in the North of Ireland. There, its characteristic forms of cultural production are the religious sermon, the pamphlet, the political speech; and it is because those forms have received such little attention that this selection of protestant *écriture* is intended as an enabling initiative, rather than as a canonical gathering of isolated texts.

WILLIAM DRENNAN

(1754-1820)

A STABLE UNSEEN POWER (1791)

[On 21 May 1791, William Drennan wrote from Dublin to his brother-in-law, Samuel McTier, in Belfast, outlining his plan for a new reform organization which was to become the Society of United Irishmen.]

I should much desire that a Society were instituted in this city having much of the secrecy and somewhat of the ceremonial of Freemasonry, so much secrecy as might communicate curiosity, uncertainty, expectation to the minds of surrounding men, so much impressive and affecting ceremony in its internal economy as without impeding real business might strike the soul through the senses. A benevolent conspiracy — a plot for the people — no *Whig* Club — no party title — the Brotherhood its name — the Rights of Men and the Greatest Happiness of the Greatest Number its end — its general end Real Independence to Ireland, and Republicanism its particular purpose — its business every means to accomplish these ends as speedily as the prejudices and bigotry of the land we live in would permit, as speedily as to give us some enjoyment and not to protract anything too long in this short span of life. The means are manifold, publication always coming from one of the Brotherhood, and no other designation. Declaration, a solemn and religious compact with each other to be signed by every member, and its chief and leading principles to be conveyed into a symbol worn by every of them round their body next the heart. Communication with leading men in France, in England and in America so as to cement the scattered and shifting sand of republicanism into a body (as well as those malignant conspiracies which courts and classes of men have formed) and when thus cemented to sink it like a caisson[1] in the dark and troubled waters, a stable unseen power. Why should secrecy be necessary? For many reasons. It gives greater energy within, greater influence abroad. It conceals members whose professions, etc., would make concealment expedient until the trial comes, etc., etc. I therefore think and insist on your not even mentioning it, nor do not imagine I shall neglect my profession or injure my character by keeping bad company. You are not, I believe, a republican, but not many years will elapse till this persuasion will prevail, for nothing else but the public happiness as an end, and the public will as the power and means of obtaining it, is good in politics and all else is job.[2] Such schemes are not to be laughed at as romantic, for without enthusiasm nothing great was done, or will be done.

1. A large water-tight chest, used in laying the foundations of bridges; a chest containing explosives to be buried and fired as a mine.
2. A public service turned to private or party advantage.

THE UNITED IRISH DECLARATION (1791)

[In early November 1791, Drennan again wrote to McTier, enclosing a 'solemn Declaration or Test' which was to be read to every member of the Society of United Irishmen upon his being admitted and then repeated by him after the president.]

I, A.B., in the presence of God, do pledge myself to my country, that I will use all my abilities and influence in the attainment of an impartial and adequate representation of the Irish nation in Parliament and as a means of absolute and immediate necessity in accomplishing this chief good of Ireland, I shall do whatever lies in my power to forward a brotherhood of affection, an identity of interests, a communion of rights, and an union of power among Irishmen of all religious persuasions without which every reform must be partial, not national, inadequate to the wants, delusive to the wishes and insufficient for the freedom and happiness of this country.

THE INTENDED DEFENCE (1794)

[Drennan was tried for sedition, but was acquitted on 29 June 1794, after a powerful defence by John Philpot Curran. Drennan was advised, presumably by Curran, not to present his defence in court, and instead it was 'communicated in such a way as to contribute to the acquittal'. After his acquittal, Drennan appears to have withdrawn from active involvement in political conspiracy.]

I am the son of an honest man; a minister of that gospel which breathes peace and good will among men; a Protestant Dissenting minister, in the town of Belfast; whose spirit I am accustomed to look up, in every trying situation, as my mediator and intercessor with Heaven. He was the friend and associate of good, I may say, great men; of Abernethy,[1] of Bruce,[2] of Duchal,[3] and of Hutcheson;[4] and his character of mild and tender benevolence is still remembered by many in the North of Ireland, and by not a few in this city.

I may be imprudent in mentioning, that he was, and that I glory to be, a Protestant Dissenter,

1. John Abernethy (1680-1740), a distinguished presbyterian clergyman in the north of Ireland, who refused to recognize 'the tyrannical exercise of ecclesiastical power' and became head of the non-subscribing presbyterians.
2. James Bruce (*c.*1660-1730), northern Irish presbyterian minister who sided with the subscribers in the non-subscription controversy (1720-26).
3. James Duchal (1697-1761), northern Irish presbyterian clergyman. The leading intellectual among the Irish non-subscribers.
4. Frances Hutcheson (1694-1746) was the son of a northern Irish presbyterian minister. An influential philosopher, he argued that human beings have an innate moral faculty and referred disputed questions in philosophy to the testimony of consciousness and natural instincts rather than to formal argument. He maintained a 'benevolence theory' of ethics.

obnoxious as this appellation is at present, in both countries; but my future life would appear to me one continued lie, were I not on this occasion to profess myself one of that division of Protestants who regard no authority on earth, in matters of religion, save the words and the works of its author, and whose fundamental principle it is, that every person has a right, and in proportion to his abilities, is under an obligation, to judge for himself in matters of religion; a right, subservient to God alone, not a favour to be derived from the gratuitous lenity of government; a right, the resignation of which produces slavery on the one hand, persecution on the other; and of consequence that disturbance of the public peace, which has so much, and so long distinguished the Christian world.

Such religious principles, founded as they are on the right of private judgment, to be accounted as sacred in others as in ourselves, naturally produce that independence of mind, which is the buckler[5] of political as well as private virtue, and has made the Protestant Dissenters, in all critical times, the active defenders and guardians of the British constitution; and to the best of fathers, the best of religions, and the best, as I think, of persuasions included in that religion, am I indebted for that veneration of the rights of mankind, which I find to be the true source of personal happiness, because the violation of any right must be the transgression of a duty, and so far must make a man miserable. From the earliest of my school-boy days, from the delightful hours in which I voyaged with the patient, persevering Ulysses, and made *his* country the Ithaca of my wishes, in which I panted through the Greek and Roman story; from those days, the love of my country has been in my breast, not merely a classical image, or a cold principle, but an animating spring of action; and surely, our ancient poets, orators, and historians, would have been long ago placed by some inquisitorial committee in a political 'index expurgatorius,' and prohibited from the use of youth, were it not hoped, that the bustle of a selfish world would soon brush off such childish ideas, and that the prudence, and caution, and moderation of a premature old age, would keep down, even in manhood, the propensities of nature, and the instinct of liberty.

I have heard, that the first address which Sir Robert Walpole, (he who deflowered the British constitution,) was accustomed to make to the young men who were sent for to his closet, was, 'Well, sir, are you really resolved to continue an old Roman?'[6] and on hearing it, I have cursed the public bawd, whose aim it was to blast the blossoming virtues of the heart; and have blessed my own good fortune, that education, habit, small ability, and simple integrity, would always shield me from such seducing connections.

In the year 1778, when the people of Ireland took up arms through necessity, but through public spirit retained them: when the public peace was undisturbed, because the people were armed; when common danger united all ranks whom the feeling of a common country could not unite before, I entered, with ardent zeal, and feeble frame, into the first Volunteer association made in this kingdom, and was among the first and among the last in that ever memorable institution which saved the island from invasion, secured domestic tranquillity, advanced civil liberty, laid the foundation of national independence, and by their liberal resolutions, showed toleration to be but a mitigated persecution; and taught administration a lesson, which they were soon after obliged to put into practice, viz. that the surest way of guarding the constitution, is to interest as many of all descriptions of religion as is possible, in its preservation. Indeed, I associated every thing great and good, every thing most auspicious to the hopes, most connected with the best interests of the country, to an institution which raised every man in it to a higher value, and I wished it to be perpetual, with an ardour which he that has been a Volunteer, might imagine would suggest such an address, (as is the present subject of prosecution), on the supposed extinction of that body, and which he that has not felt, might excuse in an enthusiastic, but not ill-intentioned mind.

From the year 1778 to that of 1782,[7] I observed such a line of conduct as might be expected from one who has ever most justly looked on himself most humbly as an individual, but most proudly as an Irishman; and, as an Irishman, I added one particle to that mass of public spirit which then

5. defence, protection.

6. Sir Robert Walpole (1676-1745), generally regarded as the first British prime minister, and notorious for patronage and corruption. To be an 'old Roman' is to be strictly honest in the public service.

7. From the formation of the Irish Volunteers to the achievement of parliamentary independence.

asserted the exclusive rights, and legislative competency of this imperial island; its distinct dominion, and independent parliament: and I was one of the millions who *then* thought that the truest way of honouring Britain for renouncing her assumption of right, was to proceed in reforming every *internal* abuse that corrupted our constitution. I then thought, and I ever will think, that a more equal representation of the people, was absolutely necessary for their freedom, their virtue, their happiness, and their *peace*; and by exerting myself in my little sphere, by rallying all the powers I possessed, round this central point, I thought that I was practising the doctrine of him who went about doing good continually to the poor people, himself poor and lowly; and that I was copying the example of a father who felt for all that lived, particularly for the living mass of humanity.

I thought that the truest way of promoting civil war, was to put the people out of conceit with the constitution, by hearing always of its perfections, and feeling only its abuses, until they might come to confound the excellencies of the government with the errors of its mal-administration; and that the truest way for promoting peace was, as in the case of the Volunteers, to arm the people for their liberties, so now, to arm them — with their rights, which is the first step in giving them a knowledge of their duties: for until they enjoy the one, they will remain ignorant of the other, and the exclusion which first made, will support the incapacity. The enjoyment of rights implies the performance of duties: and the unequal distribution of the former prevents the discharge of the latter; so that the freedom of the public is necessarily connected with their virtue as well as their happiness. An arbitrary, irregular, and undetermined subordination, not only checks and destroys industry, but is a provocative on the one part to every excess which is natural to the abuse of power without right; and on the other part, to those crimes, and that disturbance of the public peace, which the hopelessness of redressing their wrongs begets in ferocious and savage natures: and thus, to the corruptions of our constitution are traceable all the crime as well as misery of *our* civil society. I thought I should become an accessory in that crime, as well as a promoter of that misery, if I did not act as a zealous advocate for a reform in parliament; and, as such, fervently desire, that the Volunteers should retain the possession of those arms which are the prime distinction of freemen; that this energetic establishment, arising from the innate vigour of the citizens, should perpetually exist, as being necessarily connected with that public spirit, in which alone I saw reason to hope for ultimate attainment of the great object — an adequate and impartial representation.

As my principles in religion were brought from nature and the New Testament, and as my reasons for being a Protestant Dissenter were early drawn from a book named 'The Dissenting Gentleman's Answer to White';[8] and afterwards from Blackburne,[9] Furneaux,[10] Priestley,[11] and Price,[12] so my prime authority in politics was 'Locke's Essay on Government';[13] and my authorities for the justice, the expediency, and the necessity of a parliamentary reform, were drawn from the general, I may say, the universal opinion of the deepest reasoners, the most splendid orators, and the best men; from the petitions of twenty-eight out of thirty-two counties in Ireland; from the concurrent opinion of two meetings, the nature and name of which are now under legal interdiction, the one a delegation of citizen-soldiers, sanctioned by Lord Charlemont,[14] the other a delegation purely civil, where Mr. Sharman[15] presided, both equally inefficacious; from the authorities of persons, in other respects most opposite; from Flood[16] and Grattan;[17] from Fox[18] and Pitt;[19] from the first peers, and the lowest peasants; from the early

8. Michaijah Towgood's classic compendium of English nonconformist argument was published in 1746.
9. Francis Blackburne (1705-87), liberal anglican divine.
10. Philip Furneaux (1726-83), British independent minister.
11. Joseph Priestley (1733-1804), radical British political theorist, scientist and dissenter. He was one of the most prominent opponents of Burke in the pamphlet war of the 1790s.
12. Richard Price (1723-91), British moral philosopher and radical dissenter. His famous eulogy on the French Revolution, *Discourse on the Love of our Country* (1789) prompted Burke's reply, *Reflections on the Revolution in France*.
13. John Locke (1632-1704) published his two *Treatises of Government* (1690) to combat the theory of the divine right of kings.
14. James Caulfeild (1728-99), earl of Charlemont, a leader of the Irish Volunteer movement.
15. William Sharman Crawford (1781-1861), Irish radical politician and colonel of a Volunteer regiment.
16. Henry Flood (1732-91), Irish statesman and founder of the Patriot Party, a group of Irish Whigs who aimed to win for Ireland a real parliament and a 'free constitution'.
17. Henry Grattan (1746-1820), leader of the movement that forced Britain to grant legislative independence to Ireland in 1782.
18. Charles James Fox (1749-1806), British Whig politician who opposed the policies of George III and helped to abolish the British slave trade.
19. William Pitt the Younger (1759-1806), British prime minister during the French revolutionary wars.

principles of Richmond,[20] and the purer practice of Burke. At this flame I lighted my taper; it illumined my understanding, warmed my heart, and influenced my conduct; and from 1783 to 1790, during those seven years, I continued to act, from principle and from passion, for a reform; not deeming that the duties of a good citizen, and a good physician, were at all incompatible; not believing that so liberal a profession should act in this country, as they might have been forced to have done at Rome, where they were chosen from the class and condition of slaves. Were the duties of the profession in all cases to obliterate those of the citizen, there could be no public, but at the moment of election; and however good the rule is, to mind our own business, there are times, when the business of the public is every man's own business, and the personal and general weal are the same.

On coming to this city, in the year 1790, I did not relinquish those principles, nor alter that mode of conduct, which I thought best suited the character of a good citizen. Sensible that Catholics and Protestants agreed in the essential articles of religious duty, and that though the form and ceremonial may vary, as the features of the face, the substance, like the construction of the heart, was in all, alike; I co-operated in an union of sects, for the interest of the whole society, and against the dominancy, the political dominancy, of any religious persuasion. I believed the general character of mankind to be less influenced by the excellencies of religion, or injured by its abuses, than the mutual crimination of sects would lead us to imagine — a crimination often built on surmise and conjecture, or on a logic equally disgraceful, which builds the rule upon the exception, and poisons the judgment by preconceived impressions. I therefore entered into a society, of which this union of Catholic and Protestant Irishmen was the first stone and base, and a parliamentary reform the sole object and end. Nothing, surely, but the most intimate and heartfelt conviction of right intention, could have kept me attached to a society, which, during all its political life, has been the object of so much obloquy. Nothing could have supported me under the effects of professional injury, of the desertion of once valued friends, of being deemed an agent in the worst designs, and marked out by the eyes of those whom I met in the streets, as a dark and malignant conspirator; nothing, I say, could have supported me, but that conscious mind, which is its own awful world; and which, I trust in God, will, at this hour, support me, even under the sentence of professional and personal ruin!

I thought it the duty of every good citizen who regarded the peace of Ireland, to cling to the people the more strongly, on the very account, that the panic of French principles and French practices, had made not only the upper ranks, but even the men of middling property, who had been accustomed to assimilate with the mass, now forsake and abandon the people, and the cause of the people — a PARLIAMENTARY REFORM. I thought it the very time for men to *popularise* themselves; and that it was most dangerous for men of rank, fortune, and connexions, to stand off, in sullen and suspicious sequestration, and thus make themselves be considered in no other light than as a political party, and a large predominating association, who have been so long accustomed to enjoy the whole constituent, as well as representative power, that their 'scorn and horror' is readily excited at 'the frenzy, folly, and wickedness' of those who desire any share in the legislation, or in the common rights of humanity. I did not think that it was the charity of individuals, or the munificence of the great, which could make the people happy, or keep them in peace. The social intercourse of the higher and lower orders ought not to be sustained solely by charity on the one hand, and blessings on the other, but by an adequate equivalent, given and received, that might make the poor and rich reciprocally *dependent*; and thus endowing every individual, however low, with an exchangeable value, must make the happiness of the community depend, not on inadequate and intermitting benevolence, but on the action and re-action of self-interest; a principle constant and universal. I thought, (and acted from the thought,) that the enjoyment of the elective right, could alone give this value to every man; and that, without it, there may be parties, and classes, and sects, and ascendancies — but there can be no people.

The great object of that society was, UNIVERSAL SUFFRAGE, and ANNUAL PARLIAMENTS; and their plan of reform was founded upon the eternal and immutable principle of justice. In repeating and justifying my political creed, I think I am defending

20. Charles Lennox (1735-1806), 3rd duke of Richmond and Lennox, leading British Whig politician and champion of American and Irish grievances.

myself from the imputation of sedition, by showing, as I can do, that none of these principles travel out of the constitution, but are justified by its philosophy, its practice, and the best authorities; and that all of these principles converge towards the permanent peace and happiness of my country — *for*, until there be an equality of rights, which it is the end of the social union to realize, and substantiate, there must be smothered *war* in civil society. I have appealed to the best constitutional *authorities*. 'To be taxed without being represented,' said Lord Chatham,[21] with the energy of justice, 'is contrary to the maxims of the law, and the first principles of the constitution.' As all are taxed, all ought to be represented; and none can be represented, who has no power to vote. 'Taxation and representation are inseparable,' said Lord Camden.[22] 'In a free state,' says Judge Blackstone,[23] 'every man who is a free agent, ought to be, in some measure, his own governor; and, therefore, a branch at least of the legislative power should reside *in the whole body of the people*.' Thus, it is a vital *principle* of the constitution, that the property of the people cannot be granted, but by their own consent, in person, or by representative; and until the reign of Henry VI and the act of disfranchisement, which then dispossessed persons, and as it were appropriated the constitution, its PRACTICE also was built upon personal representation.

The British constitution is a conquest made, at different times, over the feudal system imposed by the first William;[24] but the powers that made this conquest, were actuated by party interest, which accidentally, rather than intentionally, co-operated for the public good. The clergy and the barons combated and repressed the inordinate power of the monarch. But was it done for the good of the people? No! It was for the privileges of their noble rank, or for the safety of their sacred order. When commerce diffused property, a new resistance rose to the accumulation of power, made by the clerical and aristocratical factions. But was this resistance less selfish, though equally successful? No! The victories of these commons were the victories of sectaries,[25] not of society; of parties, not of the people; of the proprietary interest, rather than of the general weal. Looking upward, the party is always for the people. Looking downward, they begin to vilify and abuse them. They are 'the refuse and scum of the earth — mob — swine — sturdy beggars — of no value in the eye of God'; and any society who defends their cause is denominated 'a blasted Jacobin society — wicked and vicious — the advocates of white-boys,[26] — scavengers, defenders, felons, paupers, and of Channel-row.' The clergy maintained their order against the King: the nobles their rank against the clergy and King: the commons, their privileges against the clergy, nobles, and King: and the people are now to maintain their personal rights against the propertied and privileged community, including commons, clergy, nobles, and King.

The *philosophy* of the constitution, which is nothing else than the improvement of human reason, concurs in proving that men alone can be represented, but not land nor money; that property does not confer any exclusive right to be represented; and that poor men, with an equal right, have more need to be represented than the rich. Those rights which the social union confirms and substantiates, are founded on *personality* alone; and since they are inherent in the nature of man, as man, they can never yield to, nor be extinguished by any acquired rights, such as property; which is a thing not natural, but incidental; which may or may not belong to a man; and which has no necessary connexion with either a good conscience, or a good understanding. When the right of property, which was comparatively late in its establishment, no longer confines itself to its own security, but lays a claim to dominion and ascendancy over the *anterior* rights of nature, converts persons into things, and men into cattle; the intention of the social union seems to be defeated, and the land subjugates the inhabitants. Even on the supposition, that property is the rule of representation, the mass of property, the great fund of productive taxation, rests with the

21. William Pitt the Elder (1708-88), earl of Chatham. Known as the 'Great Commoner', Pitt championed the cause of the American colonies.
22. John Pratt (1759-1840), 2nd earl and marquess of Camden, lord lieutenant of Ireland 1795-98. His repressive measures sparked the 1798 Rebellion.
23. Sir William Blackstone (1723-80), famous British jurist, best known for his *Commentaries on the Laws of England* (1765-69).
24. William I (1028-87), the conqueror of England.
25. Members of a sect, particularly a religious sect that is regarded as heretical.
26. Members of a secret society, formed about 1760, given to violent agrarian protest. They wore white shirts over their other clothes to identify each other at night.

mass of the people; and though scattered into minute portions, is not less real, and ought to be as really represented as when cumulated in the hands of the comparative few.

'To give the mass of property, commercial and landed, the whole of the return of members to serve in parliament,' is, in effect, to form the propertied community into one great corporation, whose end it may be, to league together, and combine their whole influence, against the population of the country; 'a proprietary influence,' which, however applauded, is, *at best*, but a conspiracy between two classes of people — the landholders and tenantry against the intendment of the constitution; a collusive traffic of franchise and private judgment, which the rich buy, and the poor sell. It appears to me, that the fluctuation which attends property is, of itself, a proof, how absurd it is to base the rights of man on a bottom so unstable; and still more so to draw circles around places, as if to encompass or confine a quality so fugitive, and to seat the genius of the constitution on the still revolving wheel of blind and capricious fortune; and hence, proceeding as far with a good principle as it would lead me, I thought it my duty, as a man, to advocate the equality of rights, a political equality, perfectly consistent with civil distinctions; and to reprobate any plan of reform which pets and cherishes portions of the community, to interest them in abuses; and to irritate the remainder by invidious comparison, which, by attaching the oldest inheritance of the *whole* people to certain round spots of earth, gives a locality to liberty, inconsistent with its nature: turns legislators into land-measurers, and land-measurers into legislators; extending lines of demarcation, on one side of which, privilege is heaped up, and on the other, common right trodden down: paling in with pieces of pack-thread, the liberality of the constitution, and circumscribing, with boroughmonger-authority,[27] the principles of eternal justice.

This outline of my life, made up, as I presume to think, of pure intentions, and honest principles, tending to maintain the rights of man, his dignity, his tranquillity, and his happiness, appears to me as a volume of circumstantial evidence against the charge, however positive, of having written or published a single paper with seditious intention; and in acknowledging, that as a citizen, I wish to strengthen the popular order of the government, the democratic or republican part of the constitution; actively persevering in a pursuit, which most of the choice and master spirits of the age have, I think, shamefully abandoned, seized with a panic that has congealed their principles; I do not think it any sign of sedition to have been proof against that panic — and to have felt the influence of what I should call a rational panic, a panic which leads me to dread the *Jacobin* more than the *Jacobite*,[28] and the revival of those doctrines of passive obedience, non-resistance, and epidemic Toryism, which produced one revolution, and may provoke another. If *that* panic be not accounted seditious, which drives men, not only to abandon all exertions to rectify those abuses by which the constitution may have been perverted, but to countenance and connive at the violations it may have suffered, by their torpid acquiescence, passive concurrence, and strenuous inactivity; if *that* panic be founded on legal and constitutional principles, which has led these men to outrage the wretchedness of the people, (who, though decried as dirt, are yet, like the earth on which they tread, the great pabulum[29] of luxury and enjoyment,) by base allusions, and contumelious appellations, and by the low estimation thus set upon them, to sink them still lower in self-estimation, and drive them to abandonment and despair; is not *that* opposite panic as well founded, and as little allied to sedition, which makes me dread the effects of this terrible estrangement taking place between the upper and lower orders of society; which makes the wish of arbitrating and mediating between them, of averting their rude and revolutionary collision, by a reform of reason and accomodation; and of holding out that torch of instruction which may guide the infatuated rich, as well as the uninformed poor, in the just medium between their rights and their duties? Or is it to be construed into any intention of disturbing the public peace, if, on beholding the approaching extinction of an institution, which had raised this country from a state of brutal ferocity,

27. A boroughmonger traded in parliamentary seats for boroughs.

28. A Jacobin was a member of a radical club founded during the French Revolution. It overthrew the Girondists in 1793 and, led by Robespierre, instituted the Reign of Terror. A Jacobite was a supporter of the deposed James II and his heirs. Jacobites were active for almost sixty years after the Glorious Revolution of 1688. Their name derives from the Latin Jacobus (James).

29. food.

and was advancing it to a perfect civilization, I should have addressed the Volunteers, in the fervour and in emphasis of the heart, and in terms, the mere shade or faint reflexion of what had been said by the most illustrious men? O memory of Grattan! let those words that made our hearts burn within us at the time, shield us now from the charge of sedition!

'The Irish constitution, commerce, and power, with you began, and with you they would vanish. You are the great charter of the nation, our efficient cause, and our final hope. Obnoxious for your virtue, you are to confirm your advocates, and to preserve your associations, the dreadful instrument of national deliverance. Believe me, you have many enemies; and you are to guard against false friends, and national foes; against the weakness of human nature, and the depravity of man, against sloth, against security, against administration, against a *militia*. I have heard your legality disputed. Conscious as I am that no law prohibits the subject to arm, convinced as I am, of your legality, I conceive that question to be lost in the immensity of your numbers; and with the pomp, and power, and trade, and all that train which await your progress, I shall not stop your army to ask what law has made you; — sufficient, that there is no law against you — sufficient, that without you, there could be neither law nor liberty! *Go on*, and prosper, thou sword of justice, and shield of Freedom — the living source of an ancient flame — the foundation of our pride — a providential interposition — an army, enriching the land with industry, costing the state nothing, adequate to all her enemies, and greater than all her revenues could pay. Awful! indeed, to the tyrant, but to the just prince unconquerable strength. The custody of the nation's character is in your hands — Go on, and multiply, and add immortal security to the cause of your country.'[30]

Are not such awakening words hallowed in our remembrance? and is the faint echo of such sentiments to be now hallooed at as the rankest sedition? once rewarded with a popular pension, and now punished with fine and a prison? But the times are changed; alas! it is very true. Yet what are the times? The sun still makes the seasons, and the earth produces the harvest; but it is the change in *men's* dispositions which *unmake* the times; for truth is still the same, and rests on the base of its own immutability. Because men of station and abilities fell, at one time, into the ranks of the people, from mere panic, and in order to preserve their 'proprietary influence', and, at another time, from another panic, have forsaken that very institution which they had so warmly patronized, and reproach and vilify it for the very effects which their own abandonment had occasioned, was it sedition in a man to stand undisturbed by panic of the one kind, or panic of the other, on a firm and sound-set principle, that in an armed people lies the best security for public peace? — and does he deserve a jail for reverencing and thinking well of, and hoping much from the people in their lowest abasement — still recognizing in the tenant of the meanest hovel, the capability of human nature, and in the veriest wretch over whom he stumbles in the streets, deploring the victim of a corrupted public constitution?

With respect to this address to the Volunteers of Ireland, a paper raised from its intrinsic insignificance, *by serving as a plausible pretext for repeated prosecutions*, I do think there is an honest physiognomy, which indicates on its face the simple sincerity of the heart which dictated it. Let any man place himself, if he can, at an impartial distance from the paper, and he would characterize it as the hurried effusion of an enthusiastic mind, the general tenor of which was well-intentioned, but with some rash and imprudent expressions, probably arising from the difficulty of separating what was meant to be energetic, from what was really inflammatory; a composition which was easily pervertible to purposes unthought of by the author; a perversion which might be made by opposite parties, the one to obtain an instrument for sedition, the other to find a subject for prosecution; and thus the innocent author might become the dupe of inconsiderate friends, or the prey of watchful enemies. Though the paper may have been adjudged a libel, it may have been written without any libellous or seditious intention, and that may have been distributed with an intention of exciting commotion, which the writer certainly meant as a preservative of the public peace. The best intentions are liable to be abused; the best purposes perverted; and things written with the most pure and sincere heart, have been conjoined with the worst actions. Men have taken the Gospel in one hand, and the sword in another; and the word of the

30. The source of this quotation from Grattan cannot be found.

Scottish rebels, under Montrose,[31] was, '*Jesus, and no quarter!*'

The subject matter of this prosecution is now a year and a half old. I will not presume to ascribe any improper designs in bringing it forward so long after the publication, and at this very invidious time, when plot and treason is so much talked of, that an innocent man may be prejudged, even by a supposed implication in crimes of which others have been accused; but if I, as the supposed author of this paper, had any designs of disturbing the public peace, it is strange, that they should not, in all this time, have manifested themselves in some other *overt acts*; that sedition did not go on into treason; and as there has been nothing of that kind produced by the ingenuity and vigilance of the crown lawyers, it is to me a strong presumptive proof, that I was as little seditious at the period of the publication, as I appear to have been both before and after it; and thus my whole life (a parte-post, as well as a parte-ante)[32] seems to me a cumulation of evidence against the individual charge of sedition.

With respect to the informer in this prosecution, I can scarcely think it possible that conviction could be grounded on a *single* evidence, so notoriously influenced by a malicious mind, with vengeance on his tongue on all occasions, and virulence distilling from his pen, even *during* the pendency of the prosecution; but I have a pride in hating personalities; and leaving the commentary on such a character to others, I can only exclaim with Brasidas,[33] when a rat seized him by the hand, that the most contemptible creatures acquire a portion of respect from their danger. 'Although I have not the power to shake off the viper which comes out of the heat, and to remain free from harm,' I am able, thank God, so far to overcome an instinctive moral antipathy, as to acquiesce in the philosophical opinion, that such creatures, however odious to sense, are in the order of nature; and that there is a use in all things most venomous, though we are not able to find it out. But though I can view this being, swollen into dangerous significance, as a philosopher contemplates some reptile, magnified in the field of his microscope, yet I cannot help lamenting, that it should ever be necessary in any government, to foster a set of informers, and to place them, as Locusta[34] was in the days of Tiberius,[35] 'inter instrumenta regni.'[36] I should have thought, that an argument very commonly adduced by modern as well as ancient Italian policy, would never have found an advocate in this land. 'Egli e un huomo honesto, ma *La Ragiona di Stato*' raichiede che sia punito.'[37]

My Lords, I have spoken with the assurance of innocence, and, I hope, without audacity. My defence rests on the *purity of motive*; and that purity may be deduced from the character of my conduct, and the consistency of my life. That little life has been rounded by a single benevolent principle, the object of which was to serve my country as far as *I* could serve her, in promoting a reform in parliament; and, as a means for this object, to elevate the public to a knowledge of their rights and their duties, and to perpetuate an institution which contributed to this high information. That the constitution was imperfect, as all the works of man are, it cannot be seditious to suppose; but that it can reform *itself*, or contains in *itself* a principle of rejuvenescence, I do not believe; or that those will ever contribute to its rectification, who are most interested in its abuses. The wish of every lover of peace, and his country, is not to rend, but to renovate; not to ruin, but to restore; not to anarchize, but to cement and consolidate — and that wish must look for its completion, not to this or that individual, not to a propertied community, not to a pusillanimous gentry, not to an interested opposition, not to a venal city, not to the rashness of a mob, but to the CONSTITUTIONAL INTERPOSITION OF THE WHOLE PEOPLE.

If I am to suffer, I hope to do it with patient equanimity; not the less sensibly feeling the horror of imprisonment, and the prospect of professional, and most probably personal ruin.

Dublin, 25th June, 1794.

31. James Graham (1612-50), 5th earl and 1st marquess of Montrose, a general who won a series of victories in Scotland for Charles I during the English Civil War.
32. from the part after; from the part before.
33. Brasidas (died 422 B.C.), a Spartan general in the Peloponnesian War. In 424 B.C. he saved Megara from Athenian attack. In 422 he routed an Athenian army, under Cleon, which was storming Amphipolis, but both he and Cleon were killed. The incident with the rat is recounted in Thucydides, *History*, Book 4.
34. Locusta was a noted poisoner employed by the Emperor Nero to poison Britannicus.
35. Tiberius Claudius Nero Caesar Augustus (42 B.C.-37 A.D.).
36. among the instruments of domination.
37. 'He is an honest man, but reason of state requires him to be punished.'

WHEN ERIN FIRST ROSE (1795)

[In his song 'Erin', composed in 1795, Drennan invented the name 'the Emerald Isle'. Reflecting on the popularity of the name twenty years later, he expressed the hope that it would gradually become associated with the name of the country 'as descriptive of its prime natural beauty, and its inestimable value'.]

When Erin first rose from the dark-swelling flood,
God bless'd the green island, He saw it was good:[1]
The Emerald of Europe, it sparkled, it shone,
In the ring of this world the most precious stone!

In her sun, in her soil, in her station, thrice blest,
With back turn'd to Britain, her face to the West,
Erin stands proudly insular, on her steep shore,
And strikes her high harp to the ocean's deep roar.

But when its soft tones seem to mourn and to weep,
The dark chain of silence is cast o'er the deep;
At the thought of the past, tears gush from her eyes,
And the pulse of the heart makes her white bosom rise:—

'O, sons of green Erin! lament o'er the time
When religion was — war, and our country — a crime;[2]
When men, in God's image, inverted his plan,
And moulded their God in the image of man.

'When int'rest of state wrought the general woe;
The stranger — a friend, and the native — a foe;
While the mother rejoic'd o'er her children distress'd,
And clasp'd the invader more close to her breast.

'When with pale[3] for the body, and pale for the soul,
Church[4] and state join'd in compact to conquer the whole;
And while Shannon ran red with Milesian[5] blood,
Ey'd each other askance, and pronounc'd it was good!

'By the groans that ascend from your forefathers' grave,
For their country thus left to the brute and the slave,
Drive the Demon of Bigotry home to his den,
And where Britain made brutes, now let Erin make men!

'Let my sons, like the leaves of their shamrock, unite,[6]
A partition of sects from one footstalk of right;
Give each his full share of this earth, and yon sky,
Nor fatten the slave, where the serpent would die![7]

'Alas, for poor Erin! that some still are seen,
Who would dye the grass red, in their hatred to green!
Yet, oh! when you're up, and they down, let them live,
Then, yield them that mercy which they did not give.

'Arm of Erin! prove strong; but be gentle as brave,
And, uplifted to strike, still be ready to save;
Nor one feeling of vengeance presume to defile
The cause, or the men, of the EMERALD ISLE.[8]

'The cause it is good, and the men they are true;
And the green shall outlive both the orange and blue;[9]
And the daughters of Erin her triumph shall share,
With their full-swelling chest, and their fair-flowing hair.

'Their bosoms heave high for the worthy and brave,
But no coward shall rest on that soft swelling wave;
Men of Erin! awake, and make haste to be blest!
Rise, arch of the ocean! rise, queen of the West!'

1. Recalling Genesis 1.4: 'And God saw the light, that it was good.'
2. Referring particularly to the religious warfare of the seventeenth century.
3. The Pale was the chief area of English control in Ireland. It radiated to the north, west and south of Dublin, but varied in area throughout the period of English domination.
4. The established Church of Ireland.
5. Milesian = Irish. In Irish mythology, the Milesians were the ancestors of the present inhabitants of Ireland. Milesius was a fabulous Spanish king whose sons are said to have conquered Ireland *c.* 1300 B.C.
6. Echoing the traditional story of St Patrick's use of the shamrock as an emblem of the Holy Trinity, and referring to the late eighteenth-century identification of the plant with Irish patriotism.
7. i.e. Do not let those who accept the yoke of English domination to prosper in the land from which even snakes have been banished (by St Patrick, according to legend).
8. The first recorded use of the phrase.
9. The Orange Order, which came into being in 1795 after a battle between catholics and protestants in County Armagh, became a powerful force in northern Irish protestantism. Blue is the colour of St Andrew's Cross, which represents Scotland in the Union Jack and thereby becomes a symbolic colour in Ulster.

ORANGE TOASTS

(1795-)

[On 21 September 1795, armed protestant Peep o'Day Boys and catholic Defenders clashed in Armagh. Known as 'the Battle of the Diamond', this sectarian encounter led to the founding later that day of the Orange Order. The Order aimed to maintain the protestant constitution and to defend the king and his heirs 'as long as they shall maintain the protestant ascendancy'. Rooted in a long tradition of agrarian and sectarian violence, the Orange Toast is infinitely variable.]

1. To the glorious, pious and immortal memory of King William III, who saved us from rogues and roguery, slaves and slavery, knaves and knavery, from brass money and wooden shoes: and whoever denies this toast may he be slammed, crammed and jammed into the muzzle of the great gun of Athlone,[1] and the gun fired into the Pope's belly, and the Pope into the devil's belly, and the devil into hell, and the door locked, and the key forever in an Orangeman's pocket.

2. To the glorious, pious and immortal memory of the great and good King William, who saved us from popery, slavery, priestcraft and knavery, brass money, and wooden shoes, and who allowed a debtor to walk on Sunday,[2] and he who will not drink this toast shall be rammed, crammed and jammed down the Big Gun of Athlone, and shot up against the Rock of Gibraltar, and his bones made into sparables[3] to make boots for decent protestants, and a fig for the Bishop of Cork.

1. General Ginkel (1644-1703), 1st earl of Athlone, captured Athlone on 30 June 1691. The town had earlier withstood a siege by William III.

2. An edict of William III allowed imprisoned debtors to go out on parole every Sunday.

3. A sparable is a small, headless, wedge-shaped iron nail used in the soles and heels of boots and shoes.

BENDING THE KNEE: PRESBYTERIAN ADDRESSES

(1798)

[The outbreak of the 1798 Rebellion forced the Synod of Ulster to postpone its annual meetings until August of that year. In a loyal address to the king, the Synod offered a fulsome profession of absolute loyalty to the crown and constitution.]

TO THE KING'S MOST EXCELLENT MAJESTY

THE HUMBLE ADDRESS OF THE MINISTERS & ELDERS OF THE GENERAL SYNOD OF ULSTER ASSEMBLED AT LURGAN ON THE 28TH DAY OF AUGUST 1798

Most Gracious Sovereign

We your Majesty's Dutiful & Loyal Subjects the Ministers & Elders of the General Synod of Ulster, though prevented by a Daring & Flagitious[1] Rebellion raging in two Counties of this Province, from assembling at our stated season, eagerly embrace the first Opportunity afforded by the return of Tranquility to lay our Sentiments of Loyalty to your Majesty, and of sorrow & shame for the Calamities & Crimes of our Country, at the foot of the Throne.

We cheerfully renew those Declarations of Fidelity to the Crown & Attachment to the Constitution, from which we have never swerved. We can confidently assure your Majesty that these have been the Invariable Principles, & Professions of this Body; and we appeal to History to attest the Inviolable Attachment of the Presbyterians of Ireland to Monarchy, Counselled by an Hereditary Nobility, & supported & limited by an Elective Representative of the Commons.

But while we dwell with Exultation on those

1. heinous, villainous.

Periods of our Annals in which our Ancestors firmly resisted the Usurption [*sic*] of Cromwell, vigorously supported the Exertions of King William, & strenuously defended your Majesty's Illustrious Progenitors from the repeated attempts of a Desperate Pretender to the British Throne, and this Kingdom against the restless Ambition of France; we are constrained to lament, with the deepest Humiliation, that the most Stable & Sacred Principles of many of our People & of some of our members, have been shaken by the Convulsions of this Sceptical & Revolutionary aera.

Though we cannot presume to suggest the general Infatuation of a great part of Europe, nor the incessant & deceitful artifices employed in this country to seduce our People, as Apologies for crimes which we ourselves deem inexcusable, much less for those few unworthy members of our Body,[2] whose conduct we can only view with grief & Indignation, yet we venture to entreat your Majesty not to impute to the Whole the Transgressions of a part, nor to believe that the Synod of Ulster has fallen off from that line of Conduct which it heretofore uniformly maintained, nor from those Principles which it has often so solemnly avowed.

We Beseech your Majesty to accept the faithful Exertions of those who have withstood the torrent of Popular fury, & the Seductions of Sophistical Philosophy, as an atonement for their deluded Brethren. Let the madness of the Multitude be hidden from your eyes, by the courage, & sufferings of those of our Communion who have fought & died in defence of their King & Country, their Liberty, & Religion, and deign to harken to our Solemn Engagement, to do our utmost to recall the deluded from their Errors & Crimes, to make a strict Inquiry into the Conduct of our delinquent members; and to withstand to the best of our Abilities those pernicious foreign Principles which threaten alike the Temporal and Eternal Interests of Mankind.

Finally, we Beseech the King of Kings, who stilleth the madness of the People, and maketh the Wrath of men to praise him, & their vices to redound to His Glory, to Bless & Protect your Majesty, to preserve your Subjects from every fatal Delusion & to convert our follies, Crimes, & Miseries, into Instruments of Wisdom, Piety, & happiness both now & for ever.

Signed in our name & by our appointment,

THOMAS CUMING, Mod^{r}.

2. The Reverend James Porter of Greyabbey was hanged for alleged complicity during the Rebellion. Other presbyterian ministers were arrested and imprisoned.

TO HIS EXCELLENCY THE MOST NOBLE CHARLES MARQUIS CORNWALLIS, LORD LIEUTENANT GENERAL, AND GENERAL GOVERNOR OF IRELAND[1]

May it please your Excellency

We his Majesty's Dutiful & Loyal Subjects, the Presbyterian Ministers, & Elders of the General Synod of Ulster embrace this our earliest opportunity of expressing our Congratulations on your Excellency's arrival in this Kingdom.

Though the Reasons of our meeting do not lead to the Investigation of Political Subjects, yet we feel ourselves irresistibly called on at this important Period, rendered still more Interesting[2] by the actual landing of a foreign Enemy on our shores, to declare our unfeigned attachment to the Laws & Constitution of our Country, a Constitution in behalf of which our Fathers suffered & bled, & in defence of which we, their Descendants, are also willing to risk everything that is valuable & dear to us.

As we abjure every Idea of foreign Interference[3] in the affairs of this Kingdom, so we view with Sorrow and Indignation the late Attempts which have been made at Home to subvert our Government, under the specious pretext of Reforming it: Attempts, originating with the Crafty & Ambitious, seconded by the Ignorant & Credulous; and in too many Instances reduced to practice by the abandoned & Licentious. And we fondly trust that the Firm, Wise & Healing Measures pursued by your Excellency will be the Happy Means, as well of preventing such Attempts in future, as of calming that anxiety & Apprehension with which the Popular mind has been so long agitated.

Our fellow Subjects in far distant Lands, have born ample Testimony to that wisdom & virtue which form most striking features in your

1. Charles Cornwallis (1738-1805), 1st marquess Cornwallis, British soldier and statesman, was defeated at Yorktown in the last campaign of the American War of Independence.
2. That which concerns, touches or affects; important.
3. General Humbert's three French frigates landed at Killala in Connacht on 23 August 1798.

Excellency's Character; and we anticipate with pleasure the Period when we also shall have learned by happy Experience how eminently qualified your Excellency, is to restore Harmony, & Comfort to a distracted Land.

We entreat your Excellency to lay before our Gracious Sovereign our Humble & Dutiful Address, which we herewith deliver to your Excellency, and we rely on your Goodness for a favourable Representation of our Principles & Conduct.

Signed,
THOS. CUMING, Moderator.

OVERTURED ADDRESSES
(1798)

[The Synod also unanimously agreed an Overtured Address[1] to the people under its pastoral care. The Address was ordered to be read from the pulpit and copies of it were printed for distribution among church members.]

Christian Brethren
Influenced by a sincere and Affectionate regard for your Happiness, Temporal and Eternal, and by a sense of the Obligations we are under to promote, as far as in our Power, the Welfare of our Country, we feel it our Duty to address you, on the present deeply Interesting Occasion. Whilst we lament the late Disturbance of the public Peace, we derive no small satisfaction, from the Conviction, that the great Body of the People with whom we are connected have given by their Conduct the most decisive Proof how greatly they condemned all acts of Violence.

With respect to those of our Communion who unhappily have been led into open Outrage and Rebellion, we entreat them to reflect dispassionately on their Conduct; and to Place before their view, the melancholy consequences by which it has been followed. On making an appeal to their own Hearts, they must see, & feel, that it cannot be justified. So many of their fellow creatures deprived of life & hurried into Eternity; Numbers driven from their Habitations without knowing where to seek for Refuge; So much property destroyed, and the Commerce of the Country in so many Respects injured. These are Evils of such magnitude, as we are confident, must make upon their minds a very deep Impression. Men may violate the Duty which they owe to themselves, and to their King, to their country, and to their God, from Error or from Passion, but to persist in doing wrong, where the wrong is so apparent would testify a Depravity of mind, with which we hope they will not be chargeable.

With respect to all of you under our Care, the great Object of our Ambition is that you should maintain that Loyalty to the King & Attachment to the Constitution combined with those Virtuous, Honourable & Pious Principles which distinguished your forefathers, and which have rendered their memories dear to their Posterity.

Here is an Example which we earnestly recommend to your Imitation, an example equally distinguished by Loyalty & by a Veneration for those Rights of the Governed, the securing of which is alike the Duty & the Interest of the Crown.

We beseech you to look back to the Period when these Disputes commenced which have involved this Country in its present Calamities, and say whether in matters of a Political nature on wheighing [*sic*] their Blessings, with the evils of which they complained, the People of Ireland could be Justified in rising in Opposition to Government & disturbing the Public Peace. Did not Christians of every Denomination enjoy perfect liberty of conscience? Were not the shackels broken which had confined our Trade? Was not private property secure, and the land every day becoming more prosperous? Can a wise or a virtuous man be found who would not wish to see us brought back to the same comfortable Situation? The accomplishment of this most desirable Object, will be greatly forwarded, by your acting under the influence of a steady regard to the Laws & to the Constitution, by

1. A motion introduced in the supreme court of a presbyterian church.

your avowed and manly Opposition to every species of Insurrection, and by those exertions to restore the public Tranquility, which at this critical and important Period, will be the best proof of your regard to your own Interest, of your Loyalty to your King, and your love to your Country.

Thus co-operating with the efforts in behalf of Ireland of our excellent chief Governor, whose name for Dignity of Principle, for Benevolence & true Wisdom, is so eminently distinguished, you will evince, That you know & feel what you owe to your own Character, testifying in the most effectual manner that you reprobate the views of those who would involve this country in the incalculable Horrors of a Revolution, and aid in restoring to it the enjoyment of its former Blessings.

In your endeavours to restore Order & the Public Peace, it is necessary for us to observe how much it is your Duty, on every Occasion to place in the strongest point of view to every one with whom you can have Influence the Danger, and pernicious Consequences of a foreign Connexion. Here in respect to France your argument is simple, it is plain, and not to be resisted. It is the Fact that this nation has exercised a Despotic Power, over every country, which has had the misfortune to apply to it for assistance, or to be conquered by its arms. As a strong additional Motive to excite you to oppose any attempt against this country, of this restless ambitious People, we beseech you to consider how unfriendly their Declarations, & Conduct have been, to those Principles of Religion, which are the support of our present comfort, and the sure foundation of our Eternal Happiness.

Permit us likewise to entreat you to guard against a Party Spirit & to cultivate goodwill towards your fellow-subjects of every Religious Description. Everything contrary to this would be hostile to that Christian Temper, by which you should be animated, would be inconsistent with your Principles as Protestant Dissenters, and a reproach to your Character. Brethren deeply concerned in what respects your Duty & Happiness, & as ministers of the Gospel of Peace, we Beseech you to attend to, & to practice the things that make for Peace. And we offer up our fervent Prayers to the Almighty, that you may conduct yourselves, in the manner, in which your own Hearts will approve, on Reflection, which will give you Comfort at the hour of Death, and which will be approved at the Great Day when you shall stand before the Tribunal of your Judge.

Signed by order
THOS. CUMING, Moderator.

[The Synod further unanimously agreed a brief Overture which repudiated the actions of those presbyterian ministers who had supported the rebellion.]

The Synod reflecting with grief & Indignation on the Conduct of some members of this Body, and of the Licentiates under their Care who have been lately implicated in Seditious & Treasonable Practices, do hereby declare their most pointed abhorrence of a Deportment so inconsistent with the Character of a minister of Religion. And they do strictly enjoin the several Presbyteries within their Bounds, to Institute a Solemn Inquiry into the Conduct and Conversation of their respective members and Probationers, to distinguish impartially between the Innocent & the Guilty, that the ministry may be Blameless, and to make a faithful report of their Procedure at next meeting of Synod, under Penalty of severe Censure.

THE SYNOD OF ULSTER VERSUS VISCOUNT CASTLEREAGH

(1802-17)

In 1802 the Irish chief secretary, Viscount Castlereagh,[1] expressed concern at the existence of a 'democratic party' in the Synod of Ulster and remarked that several presbyterian ministers were 'deeply infected' by the principles of the 1798 Rebellion. Castlereagh noted that the presbyterians of Ireland 'have partaken so deeply first of the popular and since of the democratic politics of the country as to be an object much more of jealousy than of support to Government.' He expressed the view that only through a 'considerable internal fermentation' of the body of Irish presbyterians, coupled with 'some change of system', could Irish presbyterians put on a different temper and acquire 'better habits'.

Castlereagh aimed to bind the presbyterians to the British government and hoped to secure their loyalty by making a huge increase in the *regium donum*[2] and offering it on new terms. Instead of being paid as a block grant to the Synod, the grant was to be paid to ministers as individuals. The agent responsible for the distribution of the individual grants would no longer be chosen by the Synod, nor would he be responsible to it. Instead, the *regium donum* agent would be appointed by the government. Significantly, the office went to Robert Black[3] of Derry, a presbyterian minister who corresponded closely with Castlereagh and gave him information about the democratic party in the Ulster Synod. Another of Castlereagh's correspondents, Alexander Knox,[4] expressed the hope that the qualifying terms of the grant would turn the Synod's ministers into a 'subordinate ecclesiastical aristocracy' (the terms were that a minister would have to acquire a certificate, signed by two magistrates, which proved that he had taken and subscribed an oath of allegiance). Knox argued that the members of an ecclesiastic aristocracy would be actuated by feelings of 'zealous loyalty' and would communicate those feelings to their congregations. The moment was favourable, Knox insisted, because the 'republicanism of that part of Ireland (i.e. Ulster) is checked and repressed by the cruelties of Roman Catholics in the late rebellion and by the despotism of Bonaparte.' The presbyterians were therefore 'in a humour for acquiescing in the views of government beyond which they ever were or (should the opportunity be missed) may be hereafter.' Knox also pointed out that the improved financial status of presbyterian clergy would assist their 'future respectability' by helping them to marry into families 'of repute and influence'.

The clash between presbyterian libertarianism and subservience to the state can be observed in a controversy that followed Castlereagh's use of the *regium donum* as a means of buying presbyterian loyalty. Castlereagh attempted to interfere in the internal workings of the Belfast Academical Institution, founded in 1814 by William Drennan, which fulfilled the presbyterian demand for a college in Ireland where ministerial students could be trained. The Institution was established on unambiguously non-sectarian principles and it refused to agree to the Synod's request that teaching in divinity should be provided. Instead, the college authorities invited the Synod to appoint its own divinity professors and those professors would then be given accommodation for their classes in the Institution. This arrangement would enable students for the ministry to take their entire training in Belfast.

This proposal was opposed by Castlereagh, who believed that it was part of a 'deep laid scheme again to bring the Presbyterian synod within the ranks of democracy'. He perceived that the Institution was the creation of the liberal Belfast business community and the intelligentsia (William

1. Robert Stewart (1769-1822), viscount Castlereagh, Anglo-Irish politician and statesman who was British foreign secretary 1812-22.
2. 'royal gift'. In 1690 William of Orange made a grant to presbyterian ministers in Ulster as a reward for their support during his struggles with James II. The grant was made annually from public funds and was discontinued in 1869.
3. Robert Black (1752-1817), an influential presbyterian minister who was a friend and correspondent of Castlereagh.
4. Alexander Knox (1757-1831), an important theological writer who was private secretary to Castlereagh during the 1798 Rebellion and afterwards.

Drennan was a member of its governing body), and he knew that members of that community had been United Irishmen or had United Irish sympathies. Castlereagh was particularly antagonistic to Drennan, who had given an address at the opening ceremony of the Institution in 1814 in which he expressed the hope that the educational process would unite students of all denominations. Two years later, on the eve of St Patrick's Day, some members of the college's governing body and staff allegedly drank disloyal toasts at a dinner. Castlereagh responded by threatening that the Institution might lose its annual government grant of £1,500. He also threatened that if the plan to educate ministerial students in the college was implemented, the presbyterian ministers might lose their increased *regium donum*.

In a letter to Sir Robert Peel, then Irish chief secretary, Castlereagh noted that the protestant body was 'the sheet anchor and bulwark of the British connection in this country'. As one half of that body was 'materially' influenced by the Synod of Ulster, it was of 'incalculable importance' not to allow Drennan and his associates the power of granting or withholding certificates of qualification for the presbyterian ministry. However, Peel's proposed strategy was to make the governing body and staff of the Institution 'stipendaries', and he was prepared to withhold the annual grant unless the college authorities gave the government a controlling interest in its management. Ignoring Castlereagh's threat, the Synod went ahead with its decision to appoint a divinity professor and complete the arrangements with the Institution. In the final debate in the Synod on the Institution question, a young Scottish presbyterian minister, James Carlile, stated the presbyterian principle of the church's independence of the state and attacked Castlereagh.

JAMES CARLILE
(1784-1854)

ATTACK ON CASTLEREAGH (1817)

Rev. Mr. Carlile requested that the report of the deputation to Lord Castlereagh might be read, with the additions made to it, as he intended to found a motion on it: which was agreed to.[1]

Mr. Carlile then begged to call the attention of the house to a part of the conversation between Lord Castlereagh and the deputation. The deputation reminded his Lordship that the Government stood pledged not to interfere in the discipline of the Synod: on which his Lordship asked if the Synod regarded the education of their students as a matter of discipline. The deputation answered that they conceived so; but his Lordship could not agree with them. It is necessary therefore, said Mr. Carlile, to set this matter at rest, and by an explicit declaration either to confirm or disavow the sentiment expressed by the deputation. It is evident that the sentiment expressed by Lord Castlereagh has run through all his proceedings, and the proceedings of Government, respecting our proposed change in the education of our students; we see it in his Lordship's message to us at Cookstown; we see it in his conversation with our deputation; and we see it in Mr. Peel's official letter to the Managers of the Academical Institution, which has been laid before us. The sooner, therefore, that the Synod declares its mind on this subject, the better; and before he sat down, he would propose a resolution to that effect. It was surely unnecessary to take up the time of the Synod in proving that the education of their students was strictly a matter of internal arrangement. Nothing was more nearly connected with the spiritual interests of their people. They did not educate their students to make them respectable in the eyes of the world, or of Government, but to make them able ministers of the gospel; and, although in point of worldly respectability, they were sunk as low as our

1. Report in *The Newsletter*, 1 July 1817.

Lord and his Apostles, who went about as itinerant preachers, despised by the Government and by the noble and powerful of their country, it would be of little moment, provided they stood high in the only scale which the Synod ought to recognise — the approbation of God. The education of the students did not consist merely in their learning Greek, Latin and Philosophy, nor even Theology, it included their moral education, and in all the decisions of the Synod respecting a home education, they were swayed chiefly by the moral effect that would be produced on the young men, by their being brought under the inspection of those among whom they were to exercise their office, and of their natural guardians, the Presbyteries. He begged therefore that the Synod would recollect that this was the nature of that education in which they were required to permit the Government to interfere in return for his Majesty's bounty. There are some proposals that may be made to individuals or to public bodies, on which it is infamous even to deliberate. If a man be asked to rob or steal, and a bribe be offered to him to induce him to comply, it would betray dishonesty in him to hesitate for a moment in his decision. In such cases, men feel it to be necessary to decide at once to treat the proposal as a subject on which they are not to be tampered with. [Here he referred to the practice of the House of Commons, in throwing out money bills coming from the House of Lords, without deliberating upon them.] Just such seemed to me, said he, the nature of the proposal that was made to us at Cookstown, when by a verbal message from an individual, styling himself Lord Castlereagh, we were informed that Government might regard our electing a Professor for educating our students in theology, as an act of hostility to them, and we were required to desist from our purpose. Who or what was this Lord Castlereagh, that he should send such a message to the Synod of Ulster? Who called for him? Was he an elder? Had he his credentials with him? What right had he to obtrude himself officiously on our deliberations?

[Here Mr. Carlile was called to order by Dr. Black, who thought the manner in which Lord Castlereagh was spoken of indecorous, and put it to the Moderator whether Lord Castlereagh had *officiously obtruded* himself on the Synod. The Moderator objected to the word *officiously*, but certainly thought he had obtruded himself.

Mr. W. Boyd stated that Lord Castlereagh authorized him to deliver the message to the Synod at Cookstown. Rev. Mr. Carlile went on.] He advised us, it is said, as one of his Majesty's Government. This, however, he himself denied, and said expressly that he spoke only as Lord Castlereagh, although every one knew that had he not been in the administration, he never would have thought of favouring us with his advice. But what right have Government to interfere in such a question? Who qualified Ministers to tell us where and how we should educate our students, or what measure will promote the spiritual interests of our people? I revere the Government of my country. I pay it a willing obedience in civil matters. I am no cavilling politician. I do not remember uttering, in the whole course of my life, a discontented word at the measures of Government. But I protest against their prying into our private concerns, and giving their opinion on the measures that we may think fit to adopt for the interests of religion. As long as I can raise my voice I will raise it against the principle of admitting civil governors, as such, to be heard in our deliberations. It is a breach of privilege, it is a dereliction of principle, it is permitting secular interests to weigh with us in determining on spiritual concerns, and it is setting up another authority than the authority of God in the regulation of his Church. But this was not all. There was not merely interference, there was a threat that if we did not submit to that interference, nay and obey the injunction of Government, they might visit us with a pecuniary penalty. Yes, we heard a verbal message delivered to us threatening us with the loss of the *regium donum* if we proceeded to the election of a Professor of Theology according to our declared resolution. Was ever a public body so insulted? Yet we did not spurn the proposal away from us. We deliberated, and after deliberating for several hours, we resolved to send a respectful deputation to the Nobleman who sent the message, and then to deliberate again; and accordingly here we are gravely deliberating whether we shall suffer the civil Government to interfere in our spiritual concerns — whether we shall barter what we believe, and what we have declared again and again to be, the spiritual interests of our people, for money — I say to barter them for money. O fatal day for the independence of the Synod of Ulster! O miserable degeneracy from the spirit of our forefathers! There was a time when, if the Sovereign himself, in all the pomp of royalty, attended by an armed force, had appeared within these walls, and held out such a threat, and had added to it the threat of fire and faggot, he would have met with a unanimous opposition to his interference, and not one of our number would have been found base enough to justify it, or to insinuate that we ought to yield to his requisition. But now, if it be but one of his servants who happens to come into the neighbourhood of our assembly, and sends to us a verbal message, threatening us with punishment if we refuse to comply with his wishes, we are panic struck. A kind of thing in the form of a verbal message, which no man till this day can tell what it was, whether official or demi-official, or not official at all, makes us waver and swerve from our purpose. A spectre stood before us in all the terror of indistinctness — we could not discern the form of it, but it whispered something mysterious about the *regium donum* — our ear received a little thereof,[2] and fear came upon us, and the hair of our flesh stood up,[3] and we were frightened from our post — (*No, no*) — I have said, and I maintain that it was a desertion of our post to deliberate for a moment on the subject. O shame upon us! Where was fled the high spirit of independence, the stern integrity of our ancestors, that would have made them walk steadily to the stake or to the gibbet before they would have suffered any civil governor, any man or body of men, without the pale of their own Church, to dictate to them where their students should be educated. We are imperiously called upon to do what is yet in our power towards wiping off the aspersion that has already been cast upon our character in the eyes of the public. Let us tell the civil Government that while we cheerfully submit to it in civil matters, we cannot, consistently with the duty that we owe to God and to our people, permit them to dictate to us in spiritual affairs, and that we are ready to part not only with money but with life itself, if it were required, rather than submit to such interference. Let us tell our people, and it will require very strong language, and very decisive measures to convince them, that we will never permit his Majesty's bounty to operate as a bribe to induce us to desert what we believe to be for their spiritual welfare. You are this day put on your trial for your integrity — the eyes of Ulster are upon you — the eyes of the kingdom will soon be upon you — the eyes of God are observing your motions and purposes — the eyes of him who, although he was rich, for our sakes became poor, are watching our determination. This day's decision will tell whether we deserve to rank as an independent, upright, conscientious body, who have no other end in view than the glory of God, and the welfare of his church; or whether we deserve that Lord Castlereagh should drive his chariot into the midst of us and tread us down like the offal of the streets. The best mode of bringing this to an issue, in my opinion, is to pass a declaratory act, stating that we regard the education of our students as strictly a matter of discipline, in which we are determined to admit of no interference whatever, and then to follow it up by distinct overt acts, to shew that we have made up our minds to act on that principle.

[Mr. Carlile then proposed a motion to that effect, in which there was reference to Lord Castlereagh's interference, but on the suggestion of friends, and seemingly the feeling of the House, the reference to that subject was omitted, and the motion was put generally, that the education of our students is strictly a matter of ecclesiastical discipline.

Rev. Mr. Wright was decidedly of opinion that they should not give up their independence, but here it was not called in question; nothing official had been communicated on the subject, and if no interference had taken place, there could be no propriety in calling to the contest a government that had been so liberal to the Presbyterians of Ulster. He suggested that they should proceed to the plain question — shall we proceed to the appointment of a Professor or not? . . . .

Rev. Mr. Blakely said, that he considered it unnecessary to state, that he was friendly to the Belfast Academical Institution, and to the Presbyterian interest. He thought the motion was uncalled for and superfluous. The Synod of Ulster, he said, had given countenance to the Institution, not because Government had established it by act of Parliament, but because it was likely to be permanent in consequence of the act of incorporation. The communication from the managers and visitors, the verbal statement given by a respectable elder at Cookstown in November, and the deputation appointed to wait upon Lord Castlereagh, he looked upon as extraordinary and inconsiderate. So far from attaching any blame to the

2. Job 4. 12-16.
3. ibid.

deputation, he considered them as worthy of the highest approbation; but the Synod had surely gone out of their way in appointing them. The present civil Constitution he admired, it was entitled to loyalty and affection, in consequence of the religious liberty which the subject enjoyed. But from the very spirit and nature of our excellent Constitution, no man had a right, however exalted, to dictate to the Synod of Ulster, how they were to educate the students under their care. Have Government a right to tell us how many sessions our young men are to attend any University? No. Have they a right to interfere as to the *place* of education? No. Have they a right to dictate as to the candidates, who shall be licensed by *us*, or called by the people? No. He would pay no attention to the opinion of any individuals on this subject, or to the surmises of the people. The Government have never directly or indirectly attempted to encroach upon the rights and privileges of the Presbyterians of this country. If they had, *then* the motion might be necessary, and if they would, Mr. Carlile would not stand alone, as the only advocate of so serious a cause. . . .

Rev. Mr. Horner did not speak till he found two motions of quite a contrary nature before the Synod. He considered that it would have been more proper merely to move that we are Presbyterians, which implied, that we, as a Church, legislated for ourselves, without the interference of any power whatever. It shewed the principle upon which our forefathers had acted, and on which we shall act; and, said Mr. H. I insist upon it, that we at no time have submitted to interference. I call upon them to put their hand on any instance where the Synod of Ulster acted either under the fear or influence of Government. Respecting the measure proposed, there may exist ground for his Lordship, as a friend, recommending delay. Negotiations are even now pending between the Government and the Institution respecting its constitution, and it is very natural for his Lordship to recommend us not to proceed in the appointment till they are finished. I have no apprehensions that Government will interfere in our internal arrangements; we should, therefore, go on to the motion. . . .

Rev. Mr. Blakely said in reply, let us suppose that the motion *now* before the house shall pass, and that it be laid before his Majesty's Ministers, will they not ask what is the cause of all this? Who has been attempting to abridge the liberty of the General Synod of Ulster. Has the Government of France or Spain been interfering in the discipline of their church? Surely *we* have never dictated to them on *that or any other* ecclesiastical subject. Let us suppose, said he, that the Government had interfered in these things. By appointing a Professor of Divinity and Church History, we will more simply publish and declare our rights as Presbyterians, than by any written declaration that could be made. This would go *further* than his friend's measure on the other side, and would be *acting* in place of *speaking*.

Rev. Mr. Stewart was against the declaration, as inconsistent with the modesty and temperance which should characterise their proceedings. No message had been sent in writing to the Synod, and Government had not interfered, nor said they would interfere; the subject ought therefore to be passed by, as unnecessary and uncalled for. Perhaps there was a fear from another and an opposite quarter — that of public opinion; but such an apprehension could never influence the conduct of the Synod of Ulster. . . .

Rev. Dr. Black thought the subject would not be settled by the previous question. The education of students for the Ministry was no doubt a matter of discipline in the abstract; but he would candidly state it as a question of fair discussion, when Government gave so large a bounty, whether they should not be considered as having some natural right of interference as to their mode of education adopted for the Ministry. In 1803, when the augmentation took place, a connection existed between the Synod and a known public body, by the education of their students at a University connected with the Church of Scotland, and a question may arise how far the Synod is exclusively authorised to alter the arrangements then made. It was a serious business — he was sorry it had been discussed, and he would greatly lament if it should tend in its consequences to any unpleasant misunderstanding between the Government of the country and the Synod.

After some further observations by other members, Mr. Carlile, after all he had heard, urged the necessity of his motion. Dr. Black,[4] he said, had

4. The Synod's decision was a defeat for Black and marked the end of his dominance of its proceedings. Embarrassed by deficiencies in the widows' fund, which he administered as part of his duties as *regium donum* agent, and humiliated by his defeat in Synod, Black committed suicide in 1817.

set the matter on its right footing; all doubts upon the subject should now be removed. Government had a right to interfere when disaffection was threatened, but it was another thing as to the literary and theological education of their students.

The motion was passed by a great majority.

The Rev. Samuel Hanna[5] was then chosen Professor of Divinity and Church History.]

5. Rev. Samuel Hanna (c. 1772-1852), Irish presbyterian minister and noted preacher.

HENRY MONTGOMERY

(1788-1865)

from: THE COOKSTOWN SPEECH (1828)

[At the meeting of the Synod of Ulster held in Cookstown, Co. Tyrone in 1828, James Morell, minister of Ballybay, Co. Monaghan, carried a resolution for the appointment of a committee for the theological examination of all candidates for the ministry. The intention was to block the liberal presbyteries and stop the appointment of Arian clergy. Montgomery's speech in support of religious liberty at the Synod caught the attention of the public and copies of it were circulated throughout Ireland.]

I shall set out upon a principle which I consider to be unassailable — viz., that religion is entirely a matter between man and his Creator, excepting so far as one human being may lawfully endeavour to influence another by friendly counsel and instruction. Farther than this no earthly power has a right to extend; to one Master alone all are accountable; and as no man can stand in my place to answer for my principles and conduct before the tribunal of my Judge, I shall never regulate my views of Divine truth by the opinions of fallible mortals, nor permit them to interfere with that faith which is to direct my conduct and to hallow my heart. For instruction, if I be in error, I would be grateful; with courteous admonition I would not be offended; but to authoritative decisions I never shall submit, for I should thereby renounce the unalterable allegiance which I owe to the sole King and Head of the Church. . . .

The fact is, it was this ignorant vanity of man which first led to human interference in matters of faith, obscured the lustre of Divine truth, and paved the way for all subsequent corruptions. In the apostolic ages, when there was no creed but that which came from on high, when there was no interference with opinions save 'the counsels of love,' Christianity went forth in its native purity and simplicity, captivating the hearts and adorning the lives of men. But the moment that earth attempted to patronise the religion of Heaven — the moment that the Empire of Rome took Christianity under its protection — that moment corruptions commenced, 'the fine gold became dim.'[1] Priests and governors dictated modes of faith and forms of worship; and, in order to sanction the assumption, laid claim to infallibility in determining the counsels of Heaven. Under this pretence arose a power more extensive and more terrible than any that ever influenced the destinies of the world — a power that equally held in thraldom the cottage and the palace; that almost extinguished the light of literature and science; that took away much of the genuine substance of religion, and left but shadowy forms and ceremonies in its room. The argument of the *majority* having a right to coerce the *minority* was urged with equal justice then, as it is now; might constituted right; whilst racks and dungeons and flames confirmed her decisions and preserved uniformity.

Upon what principle was it first attempted to change this scene of things! Why, upon the simple and rational and Scriptural principle, that every man has an inalienable right to take up his Bible, and to form his own conclusions regarding the things which belong to his duty here and his

1. Lamentations 4. 1.

prospects hereafter. Upon this immutable principle the Reformation commenced; and happy would it have been for the world had it continued as it began. But, alas! the leaven of Popery has been more or less infused into every Church. No sooner did Protestants acquire power, than they began to trench[2] upon Christian liberty; they wrested the scourge from the Church of Rome, in order to apply it to the backs of their brethren; they wrote creeds, appointed ceremonies, and connected civil interests with religious professions, until every division of the Protestant Church exhibited a miniature of the great establishment from which it had dissented. The right of private judgment, indeed, was still talked of, and even praised, as I have heard done in this house, by those that are treading it in the dust; but with such persons it consisted then, as it does now, in exercising the right to judge both for *themselves* and for *others*. . . .

I am not much inclined to submit to human authority; but were I compelled to do so, I should much prefer placing myself under the power of the Pope, to coming under the control of your projected Committee. I might study the character, and accommodate myself, in due time, to the caprices of an individual; but to the ever-changing medley of passions and prejudices and opinions of which your Committee must necessarily be composed, no man could ever be conformed. The only consolation which I enjoy in contemplating this ecclesiastical monster is, that as it is not similar to anything that ever existed in air, or earth, or sea, I am fully convinced that, in its own turbid and jarring elements, it will carry the seeds of its dissolution, and speedily pass away from the world.

One argument much relied upon by our opponents is, that every society has a right to make laws for the government of its own members, and for the admission of others to its privileges. There is some plausibility, but no solidity in this. No society has any right to make a subsequent law in violation of a previous compact. Now the projected Overture would be a direct infringement of those liberal regulations under which we entered the Synod of Ulster; and if you take from us any power or privilege which we then enjoyed, you are guilty of a gross breach of faith. So much for your power of making laws affecting those already in your body; and now a few words respecting those who claim admission. On this point I assert that you have no power to make any laws but such as are in accordance with the clear and express Word of God. The Lord Jesus Christ is the King of His Church, the Bible is its constitution, and we are subjects bound to obey the laws of His kingdom. Our sole business, therefore, is to regulate our conduct by the laws contained in the statute-book; for it is evident that we have no right to alter any law, either to benefit ourselves or to injure others. . . .

Mr. Cooke says that 'we should all wear the same livery.' Now I hate livery, because it is a badge of subjection to man. The livery of sects creates as much disturbance as the livery of parties. And, after all, outward conformity by no means implies internal resemblance. Even externally, however, Mr. Cooke's friends will wear but a motley aspect; the collar, and perhaps the sleeves of their livery, may be the same, but the body and the skirts will be as patched and diversified as the pantaloons of Harlequin. Stern Calvinism, moderate Calvinism, Arianism,[3] and many fainter shades of difference, never can present a uniform appearance. Variety, indeed, is the immutable law of nature. If we cast our eyes over this fair earth which we inhabit, how beautifully is it diversified with hill and dale, with lakes and plains, with oceans and continents, with woods and rivers, with the wildness of nature and the richness of cultivation! In all the extended surface presented to the eye, we cannot find two trees, two animals, nor even two blades of grass exactly alike. And if we turn to the beautiful canopy of heaven, we perceive that 'one star differeth from another star in glory.'[4] When I look around upon this assembly, and contemplate 'the human face divine,'[5] I see the same principle amply recognised in the infinite diversity of feature, expression, and intelligence presented to my view. And could I penetrate the hearts, and enter the secret recesses of the minds by which I am surrounded, what an endless variety of emotions, and passions, and opinions would I behold! To attempt, therefore, by human legislation to produce an absolute agreement in religious sentiments, would be to rise in

2. encroach.

3. The doctrine of Arius (*c.* 250-336), a Greek Christian theologian, who maintained that Jesus Christ was a supernatural creature, not quite human and not quite divine; more like a demigod. It was declared heretical at the Council of Nicaea in 325, which asserted that Christ was not of one substance with the Father, but a person raised by the Father to the dignity of Son of God.

4. I Corinthians 15. 41.

5. cf. William Blake, 'A Divine Image': 'the human form divine'.

rebellion against nature, and consequently against 'nature's God.' Wherever such attempts have been made, and just in proportion as they have succeeded, the beauty and the power of religion have declined. In turning the eye back upon the course of time, what a deep and melancholy gloom broods over those ages, in which the power of man imposed creeds and confessions, and daringly interfered with the prerogatives of Heaven! The state of our Church before our late contentions has been compared to the Dead Sea. The comparison will not stand examination. There was no deadness or stagnation amongst us; there was diversity of mind, but unity of heart; there was an honourable maintenance of our own opinions, and an equally creditable forbearance with regard to the conscientious convictions of others: we met and parted like men and Christians! But if the proposed measures could succeed, then there would, indeed, be a dead sea of Presbyterianism: inquiry would cease; the salutary agitation of conflicting opinions would be done away; and one unnatural and unwholesome calm would reign over the whole extent of your Church. But I rejoice in the certainty that this cannot be: there are conflicting elements amongst yourselves; and the various sects with which you are intermingled will not permit you to stagnate in heartless inactivity.

LETTER TO HENRY COOKE (1829)

[On 16 October 1828, Henry Montgomery and his friends adopted a 'remonstrance' at a presbyterian meeting in Belfast, which was attended by Cooke. Montgomery gave his last speech to the Synod of Ulster on 3 July 1829, and the remonstrance was presented at a special meeting of the Synod, held at Cookstown on 18 August. The terms of the separation were arranged at a conference on 8 September.]

Weak and degraded as human beings are, there is still remaining a sufficient impress of the divine image, to make them abhor open villainy and undisguised persecution. No man would dare boldly to say, here is a neighbour whose prosperity I envy — whose reputation I would wither — whose influence I would destroy; or, here is another upon whom I would be revenged for a number of private disputes, who stands in the way of my interest and ambition, or who does not choose to take *my meaning* of the Bible. No; bad as human nature is, such an avowal would not be tolerated: but the very same sentiments, cloaked under the guise of religion, sent up the mingled shrieks and burnings of human victims from the bloody altars of Paganism, and tarnished the bright and glorious name of Christianity, by the smoke of ten thousand Christian martyrs; whilst the deluded multitude were taught to believe that a God of mercy was gratified by the miseries of His creatures. The same sentiments, in the progress of ages, developed themselves, under the milder name of Protestantism, in fines and imprisonments, in confiscations and banishments, in civil penalties and social degradations. The same principles, in the end of the last century, in the very heart of Protestant England, roused an infuriated multitude to burn the dwelling, the valuable apparatus and library, and the meeting-house of the Christian philosopher of Birmingham[1] — yea, and his very life would have fallen a sacrifice to their bigoted fury, had he not, with extreme difficulty, effected his escape. Such sentiments, in latter times, have disorganised the frame of society in our native land — converted the salutary emulation of sects into the bitterness of anti-Christian hatred — divided happy religious communities, and even invaded the peace of the domestic circle. . . .

Oh, with what enthusiasm he [Cooke] shouted forth his indignation against those dastardly men, who refused to profess their belief in the creed which he chose to impute to them — how he 'gloried in proclaiming *his* opinions to the world' — how little *he* valued the smiles or the frowns of men — and how joyfully *he* would come 'even to the stake in defence of the truth!' And firm determination sat upon his open brow, and 'a love of complacency' dwelt upon his benevolent countenance, and his hands were clasped and elevated, and he seemed undaunted by the discordant shouts of those around him; and I could almost have fancied that the flames were beginning to ascend, and

1. Joseph Priestley (1733-1804), English theologian and chemist. He served as a presbyterian clergyman in several churches in England, but gradually rejected orthodox Calvinism and adopted unitarian views. His *History of the Corruptions of Christianity* (1782) was officially burned in 1785. His sympathy with the French Revolution aroused popular prejudice against him and in 1791 his house was wrecked and his library and scientific equipment (Priestley discovered oxygen) were destroyed.

that a Latimer or a Ridley[2] was before me! But just at that moment, an intelligent elder in the seat beside me exclaimed, 'Well, that is too bad; to hear a man boasting of his courage, in avowing popular and patronised opinions; of his integrity, in professing what is conducive to his interest and gratifying to his ambition; and of his willingness to become a martyr, with three-fourths of the people, and all the power of Church and State, at his back!' The scene instantly changed, without the aid of 'Aladdin's wonderful lamp,' and I saw but an ambitious actor, 'tearing nature to tatters,'[3] and reaping the merited applause of a set of turbulent boys in the gallery.

Mr. Cooke grievously complains that notwithstanding his disinterested support of profitable opinions, and the hazards which he has run in openly avowing them, with power at his back, and promotion in his front, some persons have called him 'fanatic and enthusiast.' If any persons accused him of being either the one or the other, they did him great injustice; but no such accusation, I am convinced, was ever brought. Both his partisans and opponents know him too well to prefer any such charge. His entire proceedings have manifested far too much calculation and prudent arrangement, to afford even the shadow of a plea for such a groundless imputation. I certainly have heard his name occasionally coupled with no very complimentary epithets; but the man who would venture to call him either fanatic or enthusiast, would justly become the object of universal derision....

But we are told over and over again, 'surely the Church has a right to tell the *meaning* which it attaches to Scripture, and to require its members to declare the meaning which *they* hold to be true.' The former I admit; the latter I deny. Every minister is certainly bound to give to the members of his own congregration the most explicit statement of his views of the Bible; but as he is neither the teacher of his brother ministers nor their flocks, he lies under no obligation to satisfy them. To the Head of the Church and to his own people alone he is responsible. The root of the error into which these fall, who advocate the power of Ecclesiastical Courts, lies in mistaking the meaning of the word *Church*, as it is used in the New Testament. They seem to think that it was some kind of clerical conclave or synod; whereas it never has any such meaning, but either signifies the whole body of believers, or a particular congregation. Whatever power therefore originally rested in the Church 'to try spirits,'[4] or in other words, to judge of the doctrines of teachers, is now solely vested in distinct worshipping societies, and not in presbyteries or synods. To the Synod of Ulster I owe no allegiance in matters of faith; their meaning of Scripture may be true, or it may be false; and if they lay any penalty upon me for not adopting their views in opposition to my own, they are guilty of an act of tyranny, by requiring blind submission to their own fallible interpretation of the Sacred Records. It is only 'throwing dust into men's eyes,' therefore, for Mr. Cooke to say that demanding an assent to the Church's *meaning* of the Bible is different from subscribing a written creed. The only difference between them is that a written creed is much less exceptionable than the changing, capricious, and prejudiced meaning of a variable public body....

I proceed, therefore, to animadvert upon another grand fallacy of Mr. Cooke's — viz., that human creeds and explanations enable men more clearly both to understand the Word of God and each other's views of its meaning than the language of Scripture itself. Now this position I consider utterly untenable; for it alleges that a perfect standard may be measured and regulated by an imperfect one. The creed is a thousand times more likely to misrepresent the Scriptures, by leading men blindly to acquiesce in human interpretations, than the Scriptures are likely to be elucidated by the creed. In fact, creeds and confessions have been the great bulwarks of error and superstition in all ages. They have sanctified every corruption; they have been the chief instruments of all sectarian and political persecutions; they have prostrated the energies of the human mind before the vain idol of human authority; and they have led deluded mortals 'to forsake the fountain of living waters, and to hew themselves out cisterns, broken cisterns, that can hold no water.'[5] Had it not been for them, Christendom would have been spared ten thousand

2. Hugh Latimer (1485-1555) and Nicholas Ridley (*c.* 1500-55), English protestant reformers, were burned at the stake for heresy during the reign of Mary Tudor.
3. *Hamlet*, III. 3. 1.
4. I. John 4. 1.: 'Beloved, believe not every spirit, but try the spirits whether they are of God: because many false prophets are gone out into the world.'
5. Jeremiah 2. 13.

scenes of horror; and were it not for their baleful influence, our own wretched country would not at this moment, from the centre to the circumference, exhibit nothing but one wide prospect of hatred and contention. Were it not for them, the children of the same Father and the disciples of the same Master would not be separated from each other by barriers and enclosures 'of men's device';[6] but, merging all human distinctions in the one glorious appellation of Christians, would live together as one great family of brethren. How any man, therefore, can say that those things which have defaced the simple beauty of the Gospel, and so materially impeded its blessed influence, have been friendly to the cause of truth, is quite amazing; nor is it almost less wonderful that they should be said to enable men to know each other's opinions. Some satirist, reprobating human disingenuousness, has said that 'words are intended to conceal our thoughts';[7] and this is pre-eminently true with regard to the language of creeds. Under the mask of a uniform confession, with worldly fame and emolument attached to insincerity, and temporal odium and loss standing forth as the consequences of integrity, all possible varieties of Christian doctrine, and even rank infidelity itself, may securely lurk in the very bosom of the same Church. A creed may go a considerable way to show the opinions of an honest man; but just in the same proportion it acts as a screen for the hypocrite. Were men left free, without the influence of interest or penalty, to express their sincere views of evangelical truth, we might sometimes feel compelled to dissent from their opinions; but we could never doubt that they were teaching what they firmly believed. Under present circumstances, however, there are many men of whose real sentiments I know no more from the creeds which they have subscribed than I should from the fashion of their coats. Do I by these observations intend to cast any reproach upon the honest professors of what are called Orthodox opinions? By no means; for I freely admit that there are very many such in the world — men of apostolic zeal and purity, whose indefatigable exertions and exemplary lives justly entitle them to universal praise and respect. But even those excellent men are rendered liable to the suspicion of insincerity by the uses to which human formularies of faith have been too frequently applied. With regard to Mr. Cooke's oracular maxim — 'that men are infallible interpreters of their own opinions' — it has not the slightest foundation in fact. To say that they are, would be to give them a power which he seems to deny to the Spirit of Truth, when he insinuates that the Word of God is 'equivocal,' even on fundamental doctrines. But the truth is, human beings, from the poverty of language, and the imperfection of their powers, are very frequently unable 'to interpret their own opinions.' Hence, although 'without equivocation or mental reservation,' the ministers of the Established Church all subscribe the same articles and canons, yet they are almost equally divided into two conflicting parties of Calvinists and Arminians.[8]

6. Acts 17. 29.
7. Oliver Goldsmith, *The Use of Language.*

8. The protestant doctrines of Jacobus Arminius (1560-1609), a Dutch theologian. They rejected absolute predestination and contended that the sovereignty of God is compatible with free will in man. These beliefs greatly influenced methodist and Wesleyan theology.

LETTER TO DANIEL O'CONNELL (1831)

[Henry Montgomery published three long articles in a Belfast daily newspaper, the *Northern Whig* (December 1829-January 1830), attacking the condition and management of the Marquis of Hertford's estates in County Antrim. The articles were unsigned but Montgomery's authorship was an open secret. When the Marquis of Hertford (1777-1842), an English Tory politician, entered a libel action against the proprietor of the *Northern Whig*, O'Connell offered his services for the defence and the action was quickly withdrawn.

Montgomery and O'Connell's political friendship soon disintegrated. On 1 February 1831 Montgomery published an attack on O'Connell which had a great effect on public opinion and helped alienate many liberals from O'Connell's cause.]

Sir, — Many of my friends can testify how intensely mortified I felt a few weeks ago by your fulsome panegyrics. Smarting under your degrading adulation, I was disposed to exclaim with Phocion,[1] 'What foolish thing have I said, what

1. An Athenian general, statesman and orator (*c.*402-318 B.C.). He served successfully against the forces of Philip of Macedon, but later became the leader of the peace party and urged conciliation with Alexander and the Macedonians.

wicked thing have I done, that *he* should praise me!' Last week, however, you washed away the stain of your approbation by a torrent of abuse; and my character has regained that station which, I am proud to think, it long held in public estimation. For almost twenty years I have been the consistent, uncompromising enemy of arbitrary power and exclusive laws upon the one hand, and of wild democratical theories and anarchical projects on the other. The supercilious tyranny of an aristocracy is hateful; but the ignorant, heartless despotism of a mob is a thousand times more appalling. In consequence of my unconcealed sentiments upon these subjects, I have neither been a favourite with aristocrats nor demagogues; but I thank God that I have lived to obtain the approbation of a numerous and influential class of my countrymen who are equally removed from both extremes — men who have been the unswerving advocates of equal rights and honest laws; men who, in the worst of times, discreetly preserved themselves from the contamination of faction, whilst, by the powerful moral influence of their wisdom and their virtues, they restrained the unhallowed fury of parties; men who, in co-operation with others of similar sentiments and character throughout the empire, will press onward the great cause of national regeneration, to the equal discomfiture of those worthless beings that would perpetuate abuses for the benefit of the few, and of those still more unprincipled wretches who, to gratify their own malignity or ambition, would, without cause, involve their unfortunate country in all the horrors of a sanguinary revolution. It was, sir, from your intimate knowledge of the fact that my name is associated with the sentiments of the enlightened and influential body of men to whom I have referred — the consistent, temperate, and patriotic reformers of Ulster[2] — that you meanly stooped to the lowest, fawning sycophancy, in order to avert the indignant expression of the opinions of independent Irishmen with regard to your wild and criminal schemes of agitation, and falsely to impress upon the minds of the people of Great Britain and the South of Ireland, that the liberal reformers of this Province were ready to follow the wheels of your triumphant chariot. This despicable trick only hastened the catastrophe which you dreaded. The liberal Dissenters of Ireland, from North to South, who to a man had been the zealous advocates of Catholic Emancipation, and who are at present no less united in the great cause of rational and effectual reform, promptly threw off the incubus of your praise, and amply proved that, whilst they are the uncompromising friends of liberty, they are equally the determined enemies of anarchy and confusion. Their Address[3] to the Lord-Lieutenant, coming from men of intelligence, property, and moral respectability — from men who have ever been equally distinguished by their sincere regard for the just prerogatives of the Crown, and their strenuous maintenance of the indefeasible rights of the people — from men who have never fawned or crouched; who have never concealed one opinion, religious or political, which they truly entertained, or feigned one sentiment which they did not feel — such an Address, at such a time, gave the first death-wound to your destructive projects. Had it emanated from Orangemen, it might have been regarded as the offspring of party hatred; had it proceeded from members of the Established Church, it might have been represented as the work of those who desired to perpetuate a selfish monopoly; but coming from the liberal Dissenters of Ireland, the hereditary and proverbial assertors of freedom, whom you had endeavoured to represent as participating in your sentiments, it operated like a talisman upon your chimerical scheme of agitation, and dissolved the charm by which so many of the people had been held in delusion. Were anything wanting to prove that our Address was both well-timed and efficacious, it would be found in the ungoverned, ridiculous, and malignant fury into which it has driven yourself and your myrmidons[4] of the press. You know, you feel that it materially tended to turn the tide of popular opinion; and the current is now running against you with a rapidity and a force which you have no power to stem.

At this moment you afford a melancholy but instructive lesson to all who would gratify a depraved ambition, or advance their selfish interests, by sacrificing the peace and prosperity of

2. On 18 June 1828, members of various religious denominations presented Montgomery with a service of plate in recognition of his defence of religious liberty.

3. Montgomery and a group of remonstrant and non-subscribing clergymen presented an address to the lord lieutenant. This secured them formal and financial recognition. On 26 January 1831, O'Connell attacked Montgomery for his part in presenting the address and called him 'a fawning, cringing sycophant'.

4. followers, henchmen.

their native land. Although you have lauded me with a disgusting meanness in order to involve me in your snares, and abused me with a reckless malignity to gratify a disappointed resentment, I can assure you that I entertain towards you, at this moment, no sentiment but a feeling of compassion, mingled with irrepressible contempt. It is impossible to consider what you *might* have been, and to behold what you *are*, without almost forgetting your follies and offences in contemplating the deplorable effects of your fatuity. Sir, you *might* have been a respectable, useful, and influential man. The circumstances of the times, the anomalous condition of your native land, and the peculiar tendencies of your own mind, all conspired to raise you above the crowd of ordinary men. Although nature had not bestowed upon you an understanding of the highest order, you were gifted with a tact, an address, and, above all, an unbounded self-confidence, which enabled you to display to the greatest advantage whatever talents you possessed, and frequently to take the lead of abler men. Hence you were placed — by popular opinion at least, if not by your brother barristers — in the first class of the legal profession. With such a reputation and such qualifications, you were eminently calculated to become a popular leader, and to rally round you the affections of an injured and degraded people. Even when you went astray (and your aberrations were not few), every generous mind was disposed to put a charitable construction upon the actions of a man smarting under unmerited privations, and struggling for the attainment of his natural rights. Whilst several of your schemes were so wild and injudicious that many of the best friends of Emancipation frequently doubted your sincerity, *you* still retained your pre-eminence, although much wiser and better men were cast into the shade. Finally, when that great act of national justice was consummated, which restored the Catholic to his inalienable rights in his native land, you were hailed with almost universal acclaim as the sole instrument of the great deliverance. Had you then manifested a conciliatory disposition — had you been inclined to forget and to forgive — you would have entered Parliament with the amazing moral power of public opinion at your back; and although your mind is essentially unstatesmanlike, and utterly incapable of taking enlarged views of national policy or the general interests of the world, you might have rendered essential service to your country in the minor details of business and reforms of law. In due time you might have worn with honour the peaceful robes of a Baron — perhaps the *Chief Baron* — of the Exchequer, by the side of your old friend, Mr. Leslie Foster;[5] and, dying in honoured age, there might have been inscribed upon your tomb — 'THE BENEFACTOR OF HIS COUNTRY.'. . .

I shall place your praise and reprobation in the form of a regular Dr. and Cr. Account; although I am duly sensible that the balance of censure is greatly in my favour.

DANIEL O'CONNELL, ESQ., M.P., SPEAKETH.

Dr.

Dec. 21, 1830. — 'The North is arousing itself. The Belfast meeting was transcendently splendid.[6] There never was anything which I read with greater pleasure than the speech of my *excellent* and *respected* friend, the Rev. Mr. Montgomery. He is a Unitarian clergyman; he and I differ widely as human beings can do in religious belief; but that never can produce dissension between us — he is answerable for his belief, as I am for mine. (Hear.) I know his *excellence*, his *charity*, and his *purity of conduct*; may God in heaven bless him! And never yet did I read a speech so good for the purpose for which it was intended as that delivered by my *excellent* friend, and never was an abler one pronounced at a public meeting.' (Loud and continued cheering.)

January 15, 1831. — 'The ever patriotic George Ensor will respond to your call; the brilliant light of the genius of the Montgomery of Belfast may then shine on the route that leads to the legislative independence of Ireland.' (Cheers.)

Cr.

Jan. 21, 1831. — 'What do these Presbyterians expect to *gain* by their address? Oh! they want *Regium Donum!*'

Jan. 26, 1831. — 'For the honest Presbyterians I entertain the greatest respect; but for

5. John Leslie Foster (*c.*1781-1842), Irish judge and politician.

6. Montgomery advocated catholic emanipation at public dinners in Manchester and London. At a meeting in Belfast in 1829, presided over by William Crolly, the catholic bishop of Down and Connor, Montgomery again spoke in favour of emancipation.

those — for that man whom I once called my friend — for the Rev. Henry Montgomery, I entertain the most sovereign contempt. I called him my friend; he is no longer a friend of mine. I boasted of his friendship in public and private, but I arraign him now as a paltry and pitiful slave, for his conduct towards me while a prosecution was still pending over me. But he is a reformer — a Belfast reformer; and this is his love of liberty! Henry Montgomery, you are no friend of mine. I despise you, fawning, cringing sycophant.' (Loud cheers.)

Now, Mr. O'Connell, 'look upon *this* picture and upon *this*.'[7] Why, sir, Hamlet's mother was not more capricious than you are. '*A little month!*'[8] 'Your bosom friend a bright genius, and a paltry, pitiful slave!' I was totally unconscious of any change in myself; nay, I verily believe that I did not lose my personal identity between the 21st of December and the 21st of January; and I am perfectly certain that, during the whole of that time, and up to the present moment, I never altered my mind with respect to you and your measures of agitation. Many persons can testify that there are two celebrated characters of whom I have never changed my opinion — William Cobbett[9] and Daniel O'Connell. In the *zenith of your glory* I thought, I spoke of you precisely as I do now. It required no penetration to estimate your character. A good cause, for a short period, threw its brightness around you, and dazzled many eyes; but to any man accustomed to look deeper than the surface, a dark *nucleus* of selfishness and vanity was distinctly visible. And why, sir, did such an amazing revolution take place in your sentiments with regard to me in the brief space of one month, nay, of six days? Why? Solely because, in the exercise of my free judgment and natural rights, I ventured to express my opposition to your wild schemes of anarchy and national ruin. 'This was the head and front of my offending,'[10] and for this I am no longer a 'bright genius,' but merely a 'fawning, cringing sycophant!' *You* dare to talk of liberty of conscience and of speech! Are you not ashamed! Has not Henry Montgomery as good a right to deprecate a Repeal of the Union as Daniel O'Connell has to advocate the dissolution of that connexion? Sir, your wild and wicked denunciations of every man who has the honesty to oppose your revolutionary projects have eminently tended to strengthen the hands of wholesome government, and to consolidate the national connexion between Great Britain and Ireland. The striking exhibitions which you have given of your temper and designs, even in the midst of your impotency, amply prove what you would be capable of executing had we 'a domestic Legislature,' with Daniel O'Connell as 'the *bully* of the bad house,' and a Dublin mob and armed soldiery to enforce his decrees! You would not then rant and rave and gnash your teeth in impotent fury; the honest men whom you now denounce as 'paltry, pitiful slaves' would be speedily converted into 'traitors'; and the bare whisper of opposition to your brutal tyranny would be the prelude of confiscations, dungeons, and scaffolds. I solemnly declare that if I could anticipate the probability of a domestic Government composed of men like-minded with yourself, or subject to your control, I would prepare to fly with my family to the deepest wilds of America, rather than submit to the galling yoke of a heartless, profligate, iron despotism.

I shall not stoop, sir, nor do I require, in this country, to repel your infamous accusation of my being 'a sycophant and a slave.' You have, with your characteristic fatuity and want of honour, selected a charge the farthest possible from TRUTH. If I have been remarkable for anything in life, it has been for a spirit and demeanour which rather braved the frowns than courted the smiles of earthly power. In the very Address which has evoked your spleen, we stood in the firm attitude of free-born men and Christians before the representative of a temporal monarch. We [never] compromised, we kept back no sentiment, religious or political, which we ever entertained; and I have good reason to believe that our tribute of respect and confidence was the more graciously received by a generous nobleman, because it emanated from men who did not forget the respect due to themselves. I tell you more, sir; I never was the bond slave of my own degrading passions, nor the contemptible sycophant of a mob! Are you not ashamed to apply the words 'paltry and pitiful' to an honourable and irreproachable man, who has raised himself to a station of honest independence by his *own exertions?* — you, who are at this moment lying

7. *Hamlet*, III. 4. 53: 'Look here, upon this picture, and on this.'
8. *Hamlet*, I. 2. 47.
9. William Cobbett (1763-1835), English journalist and social reformer.
10. *Othello*, I. 3. 80: 'The very head and front of my offending.'

under the unequalled degradation of supporting a disgraceful splendour by 'paltry' pence extorted from the starving paupers of your native land! Whether you may be 'unable to *dig*,' I cannot pretend to say; but I am certain that 'to *beg* you are NOT ashamed.'[11] 'Paltry and pitiful!' Why, sir, such epithets are your own peculiar property; and even the meanest agitator in your train will never dispute your title to their sole enjoyment.

But it seems, according to your own allegation, and that of your satellite 'Argus' in the 'Freeman's Journal,' that I went to Dublin with an Address 'in order to crush you while a prosecution was hanging over your head.' Now, sir, this is a pretty, mawkish appeal to public sympathy; but it happens to be of the O'Connell school — utterly destitute of foundation! The Address was drawn up by the Northern Synod and Presbytery ten days before your arrest; sent up to Dublin for revision by the Synod of Munster; and a copy of it placed in the hands of the Lord-Lieutenant four days previously to your being taken into custody! I did not even hear of your arrest until I arrived in Dublin, in company with several of my brother deputies from this Province. I did not go to 'crush you' in the hour of your misfortune; I went to state that the liberal Dissenters of Ireland abhorred your proceedings, even whilst you were in the plenitude of your power, at the very time when you had, with *Bobadil*[12] courage, 'defied Lord Grey,'[13] insulted Lord Anglesey,[14] and exhausted the vocabulary of Billingsgate[15] in abusing the young and talented Secretary for Ireland.[16] 'A prosecution pending over you!' No, sir, we went 'to brave the lion in his den,'[17] when you seemed more like the Autocrat of the Empire than a peaceable and loyal subject — when, from the appalling rumours that reached the North, we should not have been surprised had the entrance to Dublin been barricaded ere we approached the city. You well knew, when you uttered the calumny, that we were incapable of acting from the motives which you ascribed to us.

But this, sir, is not the only slander invented by yourself and your myrmidons of the incendiary press. In one of your own speeches, in the editorial remarks of the 'Freeman's Journal,' in the letter of 'Argus,' and in a Northern print, which I shall not condescend to name, we are repeatedly and distinctly charged with acting from venal and corrupt motives, in order to advance our own pecuniary interests, by obtaining Royal Bounty. Whatever injury this accusation may inflict upon us, it gives a deeper wound to the characters of those that have preferred it. The man who, without evidence, impeaches the motives of his brother, proves that he is himself capable of acting upon the principles which he imputes. I never knew a man who talked of all the world as rogues that was not himself 'an arrant knave.'[18] The insinuation of base motives is the vilest of all slanders, because it is the most unmanly, and the most difficult of refutation. The sincerest worshipper might be branded as a hypocrite, and the purest patriot condemned as an interested speculator. Some have been malicious enough to aver that *you* have set the country in an uproar merely to collect *the farthings of the poor*, and to give a fresh impulse to the 'O'Connell Fund'; and you well know how difficult a thing it would be for you to wipe away the gross imputation, although your patriotism may be as pure as the untrodden snow! The Remonstrant Presbyterians,[19] however, are more fortunately circumstanced. Although you and your retainers take it for granted, as an axiomatic truth, that none but 'villains' can oppose your projects, there are still some persons in the world who will look a little into evidence before they bring in their verdict. To such individuals, not to you, I appeal in vindication of myself and my ungratefully calumniated brethren. . . .

So far from being a body of avowed Arians, we have constantly *disavowed* any such bond of union; and we were *not* expelled from the Synod of Ulster. Many ministers, holding our religious views, are still members of that body; and had we been so inclined, we could have remained in it until this hour. The simple facts of the case are these. In the years 1827 and 1828, the majority of the Synod of Ulster violated their own solemn laws, trampled upon their own established usages, broke the

11. Luke 16.3.
12. A boastful character in Ben Jonson's *Every Man in his Humour* (1601).
13. Charles Grey (1764-1854), 2nd earl Grey, English Whig politician, prime minister 1830-34.
14. Henry William Paget (1768-1854), 1st marquis of Anglesey, lord lieutenant of Ireland.
15. The largest London fish market was notorious for its obscene and abusive language.
16. Edward Stanley (1779-1849), English Whig politician.
17. See Daniel. 7.
18. cf. *Hamlet*, III. 1. 131: 'We are arrant knaves all; believe none of us.'
19. See headnote to 'Letter to Henry Cooke' (p. 339).

compact under which we entered the body, and departed from the fundamental principles of Presbyterianism, by erecting human standards of faith. Against these encroachments upon our Christian rights and liberties we contended, we remonstrated, we appealed. During those conflicts, our opponents raised against us the cry of *heresy*; and when this unjust accusation failed in its intended effect, they truly and more injuriously branded us with the epithet of Catholic Emancipators. Certain fanatics had the ingenuity to identify *Orthodoxy and Orangeism*, and thus to array against us two of the most powerful engines of hostility — religious bigotry and political intolerance. Thus encompassed with difficulties, without the least prospect of being able to remain in the Synod of Ulster, some of our own hearers discontented, and the Duke of Wellington,[20] who held in his hand the disposal of the largest portion of our earthly support, apparently irreconcilable to Emancipation — how did we act? Did we shrink from the open and manly avowal of our religious and political opinions in the face of peril? No, sir; we trusted in God, and in the strength of a righteous cause; and every Remonstrant minister in Ulster was a fearless emancipator, although many of them had their congregations rent in twain by the intrigues of a political faction, and all of them had their Royal Bounty placed in jeopardy by their faithful adherence to the dictates of conscience. And these are the men upon whom you, a Catholic, and your slanderous co-agitators, now turn round and brand them as time-servers and sycophants! As I have been specially singled out for abuse, I am compelled, even at the risk of being called an egotist, to enter upon a special vindication. You will recollect the commencement of the year 1829. From the effects of your agitation, the zeal of the Orange and fanatical party, and various other causes, your prospects were involved in midnight darkness. Lord Wellington had almost insulted the Duke of Leinster,[21] and the Marquis of Anglesey (your idol *then*) was about to be recalled on account of his conversion to your cause. At that very period I had occasion to visit some of the principal towns in England. Did I forget my country? Did I fail to proclaim your injuries and vindicate your rights? No, sir; identified as I then was with the Remonstrant cause in its hour of greatest peril, and well knowing that my name was familiar to some in power, 'I cried aloud and spared not,'[22] in vindication of your natural and Christian privileges. When I returned to Belfast, there was a meeting of the Catholics of the County Antrim to petition for Emancipation. I shall never forget that day; I looked around for the crowds of Presbyterians who had formerly cheered such assemblies. I saw a few honoured and venerable faces, but there was a melancholy defalcation;[23] and the spirit of despondency brooded over the meeting. Did I, too, sail away upon the ebbing tide of desertion? Did I listen to the prudent counsels of those who told me 'that if I raised my voice in that assembly I would ruin the interests of the Remonstrants'? Did I attend to the admonitions of friends who told me truly of the *hundreds I had lost*, and the *thousands I would lose*, as a public teacher, by arraying against myself the power, the fashion, and the opulence of Protestant Ulster? No; Unitarian and Presbyterian though I am, I ascended the steps of a Catholic altar; I had brought cheering tidings across the channel for my Catholic countrymen; I poured forth my whole heart and spirit in their cause, and drove away the demon of despondency that had frowned upon their assembly. For that and many similar exertions I obtained all that I desired — their cordial affection and esteem: I lost but what I expected — a considerable portion of worldly patronage and worldly pelf.[24] And yet, sir, you and your abettors have the baseness and audacity to accuse a man of sacrificing his conscience, in the midst of security, for some paltry 'prospective gain,' who, in the midst of perils, cheerfully surrendered the almost certainty of thousands in vindication of your rights. I blush to be *compelled* to speak thus of myself and my concerns; but it is notorious that I suffered greater pecuniary loss than any other Protestant in Ireland by my uncompromising advocacy of Catholic Emancipation. Yet you, sir, because I have been honest enough to join in reprobation of your follies, have had the black ingratitude to raise against me the war-whoop of

20. Arthur Wellesley (1769-1852), 1st duke of Wellington, soldier and politician and British prime minister 1828-30. He was the son of an Irish peer.
21. Augustus Fitzgerald (1791-1874), 3rd duke of Leinster, Irish Whig politician.
22. Isaiah 58.1.
23. diminution.
24. money, wealth.

faction in a Catholic assembly — ay, and it was answered with *cheers!* I will venture to assert that the cry found no responsive echo amongst the Catholics of Ulster; and, unless I greatly err in my estimate of their hearts, your assault upon me has been chiefly injurious to yourself.

HENRY COOKE

(1788-1868)

'THE COLD AIR OF THE NORTH' (1828)

[In a speech at the 1828 meeting of the Synod of Ulster in Cookstown, Co. Tyrone, Cooke replied to Montgomery's defence of religious liberty. Cooke had described the Belfast Academical Institution as 'a seminary of Arianism' in 1824 and in his speech he glances at the controversy over the merits of Glasgow and Belfast as places of education for the presbyterian ministry.]

Mr. Montgomery says I endeavoured to show that our students would be safer in Glasgow than in Belfast. I never endeavoured to do any such thing. Every time I was examined I testified in favour of a home education. The book he holds in his hand, and which he has flaunted before you, proves it. I pointed out, indeed, some advantages which Glasgow possesses over Belfast. I thought, and I still think, that there is a want of congeniality with Arian sentiment in Glasgow. The cold air of the north is not congenial to Arianism. Its germ arose out of the mud of the Nile.[1] It cannot bear the healthy soil and keen air of a northern clime. Orthodoxy is the hardy mountain heath, which flourishes on bare hill-side and exposed upland. It courts the light of day. It bids defiance to the storm. It sports with the tempest, and it smiles upon the sunbeam. Arianism is the sickly exotic. It can only be forced by artificial heat. It takes root in the mud of intellectual and moral stagnation. It grows up among the seething population of a neglected city. But it droops and dies when exposed to the free blast of scriptural inquiry.

1. Arius (*c.*250-336) was an ascetic Christian priest in Alexandria, Egypt. Arianism, the most famous of Christian heresies, held that Christ was not co-eternal with God the Father, but was begotten by him. Condemned at the Councils of Nicaea (325) and Constantinople (381), Arianism ceased to exist within the catholic church. A number of presbyterian congregrations in the eighteenth century moved from Calvinism to Arianism and thence to unitarianism, the most politically radical of the protestant churches. Joseph Priestley was the outstanding unitarian of late eighteenth-century England.

from: 'OUR CULTIVATED FIELDS' (1833)

[Cooke believed that the British government intended to remove the Bible from the curriculum of the national schools. He regarded this policy as showing undue deference to catholic opinion and in 1833 made a speech on the subject to the Educational Society for Ireland.]

I do not approve of everything in the society; but I do approve of its uncompromising adherence to Scripture education . . . . So far as it honestly and simply acts upon this principle, I would call upon every one who loves the Bible to give to the society his countenance and his prayers. We should recommend its claims to the attention of the Legislature; and in the cause of education the voice of Ulster deserves to be heard . . . . Let us call upon them by our cultivated fields. Our fathers found the hills a succession of barren heaths; their religion and their toil clothed them with verdure. They found the country covered with unprofitable woods, and intersected with impassable morasses; their industry and their education have rendered it a productive garden. The cause of education may be retarded by the withdrawal of public patronage; but the plant can never be blighted by the frowns of modern Liberalism. It has struck its root deep into the principles and habits of the people; and, by the blessing of Providence, it will spread and flourish with increasing fruitfulness, till the wish of the pious monarch shall be realised, and every child in these realms shall be able to read his Bible.

from: 'THE HILLSBOROUGH SPEECH' (1834)

[At the Hillsborough meeting (30 October 1834) Cooke published the banns of marriage between the presbyterian and the established church of Ireland. The union was to be a political, rather than an ecclesiastical merger, and aimed to consolidate protestant conservative interests against liberalism and the threat of the repeal of the Union. The meeting was attended by over 40,000 people and Cooke's speech had a powerful effect.]

As this is a meeting where great political questions are discussed, the interference of ministers of the Gospel will by some be condemned. I must, therefore, vindicate myself from such shallow and hypocritical cavils. Shallow cavils I call them, and shallow they are; for there is not a prophet in the Old Testament, nor an apostle in the New, that ever evaded a political question — that ever tamely surrendered a political right, or shrunk from teaching rulers, as well as subjects, their various and reciprocal duties. Hypocritical cavils, I call them, and hypocritical they are; for never are they adduced except when the Christian politics of ministers condemn the time-serving expediencies of the world; and then, forsooth, there arises a cry deprecating all clerical interference with politics as a descent from a higher office, or an unwarranted intrusion into forbidden ground. Such shallow, hypocritical cavils I shall ever treat with the contempt they deserve. I am, nevertheless, most willing to admit, that there are departments of politics with which ministers of the Gospel should never interfere; to the politics of mere partizanship, the strivings of worldly men for place, and not for principle — to these they should never descend. 'Touch not, taste not, handle not,'[1] should be their motto and their practice.

But there are two departments of politics where I hold it to be the bounden duty of every minister to interfere. The first department embraces the teaching of the relative duties of rulers and subjects. This is well defined and permanent. It forms an integral part of the Gospel commission, and has equally been discharged by prophets and apostles. The second is of a more indefinite and uncertain character, and I endeavour to explain it thus: a minister may, and must, interfere with politics whenever politics interfere with religion. Such a crisis, I believe, has now arisen; and I pity the faithless watchman who sees the enemy coming in like a flood, and will not blow the trumpet and rouse the sleeping garrison. The thoughtless may wonder, the incredulous may deny, the bold may disregard, and the abettors of anarchy may affect to despise, when I declare it to be my deliberate and fixed opinion, that never, in the history of Ireland, was Protestantism in greater danger than at this hour.

I have made my election to serve under the banners of our common Protestantism; and this declaration will require me to explain how I, as a Presbyterian, and standing by all the religious and political principles of my Puritan fathers, can in anywise undertake the defence of a Church not governed by presbyters, but by prelates. I know it is possible that by some my attempt at explanation, or, if you will, vindication, will be supposed hopeless. Let me bespeak their candour and their patience; and, above all, I entreat them to open that old almanac, history, and read to learn, and wait to judge, before they pronounce sentence.

First, then, allow me to state, that I stand here as a Presbyterian, supporting and adhering to every principle of Presbyterianism, in doctrine and Church government. Were my appearance here to imply my surrender of one jot or tittle of the doctrines of the Church of Scotland, I should hold myself unworthy to be called her son. Did my appearance here imply that I surrendered the humble temple of Presbyterianism to ruinous dilapidation, or more splendid reconstruction, I should hold myself unworthy of a sentinel's post upon the lowest of her venerable watch-towers.[2] But I surrender not my own post, I betray not my own charge, while I cheer forward another column of our noble Protestant army, who, though differently officered and differently dressed, yet wield the same weapons of truth, and serve under the same banners. (*Cheers*) And if any one condemn me for affording them that cheer; if any one think I should leave them to their fate, without sympathy for their sufferings, or encouragement in

1. Colossians, 2.21.

2. See Isaiah 21.8.

their conflict, I would again entreat such an one to recur to the old almanac of history; and, before he condemn me for uniting in defence of our general and common Protestantism, ask himself would he condemn our Presbyterian forefathers for uniting in a similar defence within the walls of Derry, or at the passes of Enniskillen? Common danger produced that union. . . . Presbyterians, I speak to you. The days are gone by when in Ireland Wentworth[3] unleashed his bloodhounds on the track of your fathers; when Laud,[4] papist at heart, forged chains at once for their consciences and their liberties. The days are gone by when a Lauderdale[5] plotted, and, upon the mountains of Scotland, a Dundee[6] executed, the purposes of a bloody and heartless tyranny. Let us thank God that these days are gone by; and let us not stand, like moody magicians, conjuring up the ghosts of departed jealousies or injuries; but let our common faith, and our common dangers, unite us for common protection; and, united thus, though the powers of earth, and the powers of darkness, frown with equal hate upon our compacted ranks, they will never make a breach in our array; but they will flit around us as fierce, yet as innocuous, as the Chasseurs[7] of Napoleon galloped round the irongirt squares of Wellington upon the memorable field of Waterloo.

3. Thomas Wentworth (1593-1641), 1st earl of Strafford, leading adviser to Charles I, impeached by the Long Parliament in November 1640 and executed.
4. William Laud (1573-1645), archbishop of Canterbury and religious adviser to Charles I, tried by the Long Parliament and executed.
5. John Maitland (1616-82), 1st duke of Lauderdale, one of Charles II's chief ministers. He was widely disliked for his enforcement of royal and episcopal power.
6. John Graham of Claverhouse (1648-89), 1st viscount Dundee, who led a Highland rising in 1689 in support of the deposed James II.
7. Members of a unit in the French army who were specially trained and equipped for swift deployment.

from:
THE SINS OF THE TIMES (1837)

[On 20 August 1837, Cooke preached this sermon to his congregation. It was printed and, according to Cooke's biographer, his son-in-law J. L. Porter, it roused the 'slumbering energies' of the Ulster protestants and made Cooke a recognized political leader.]

... And, shall we then continue our survey [of Church history] through the ten first persecutions, when the might of Imperial Rome seemed to concentrate all its energies to one single point — the extirpation of the faith of Christ? Or, shall we survey Rome Papal, when she blows the trumpet of war, and summons her deadly crusaders to invade the peaceful homes of the Waldenses[1] — 'those slaughtered Saints, whose bones lie buried on the Alpine mountains cold'?[2] Or, shall we descend the stream of time, and mark how the era of the blessed Reformation is registered in the blood of Hus, and Jerome, and Hamilton, and Ridley;[3] and a glorious host of Martyrs and Confessors, who did not count their lives of any worth, but as testimonies to the Gospel of grace and truth? Nor do we require to cull out our examples in peculiar times, or amongst elevated characters. Down till this hour, every one, however humble his lot, — every one 'that will live godly in Christ Jesus, shall suffer persecution.'[4] The world hateth God; and, from the very instinct of its nature, hateth all that is 'born of God.'[5] Of the ancient Church it was testified, 'He that was born of the flesh, persecuted him that was born of the spirit';[6] and of the Church of our own days, it must be added, 'even so is it now'.

The experience of every private Christian will respond to the statement; and, were a modern evidence required to attest a fact which all ancient history has already confirmed, we have it in the persecutions of the godly and devoted men, who, taking their lives in their hands, have carried the Gospel into the wilds and fastnesses of our Western islands, and there lifted up the standard of 'the Gospel of the grace of God,'[7] and sustained the assaults of the flood of papal enmity, as fearlessly and unflinchingly as their rocks repel the waves. . . .

There are times when the enemy, either through restraint or cunning, intermits his assaults; there are times, again, 'when he cometh in like a flood.'[8] Indeed, in all human affairs, temporal as well as spiritual, there are ebbs and tides. One time, as it were, the water retires, and seems to surrender its

1. A protestant sect centred on the Franco-Italian border.
2. John Milton, 'On the Late Massacre in Piedmont'.
3. Jan Hus (1372-1415), Czech religious reformer who was burned at the stake for heresy; Jerome of Prague (1365-1416), Czech reformer burned at the stake for heresy; Patrick Hamilton (*c.* 1504-28), Scottish protestant martyr; Nicholas Ridley (*c.* 1500-55), protestant bishop of London, burned at the stake for heresy.
4. II Timothy 3. 12.
5. I John 3. 9.
6. Galatians 4. 29.
7. Acts 20. 24.
8. Isaiah 59. 19.

bed, for a residence to man; but scarcely hath he taken possession of the ceded territory, when the waters return, reassert their violated rights, and sweep away in their fury his mounds and embankments.

And so undoubtedly it is with the incoming of our cunning and inveterate enemy. At times, he seems utterly foiled, and trampled under our feet: at other times, he seems to retire from the hopeless contest, and to leave God in the peaceable possession of his own world; but, during this period of apparent submission, he is but collecting his strength for a new effort, — and during this retirement, he is but accumulating the waters for a new flood of temptation.

Perhaps, it may tend to give us clearer views of the devices of our enemy, if we consider, for a little, some of the various circumstances attendant on 'the incoming of a flood.'

The origin of the mightiest floods, may generally be traced to small and inconsiderable beginnings. A few heavy drops of rain, falling singly and distant, slight showers, and fleecy clouds, form the disregarded portents of the coming storm. The thirsty earth, at first, drinks up the falling waters; and when, at last, the saturated soil begins to be channeled by the infant rivulet, still the foot of the traveller can bridge it over, nor can his eye discover in it the most distant probability of danger. But let him follow the stream, — it is soon joined by another; and their united waters are rapidly receiving additional tributes: the rivulet is now swollen into a mountain torrent, disdaining the limits of its former bed, overwhelming, as it descends, the cultivation of its banks, and hurrying resistlessly to the ocean.

At other times, and especially amid mountain regions, a flood comes on sudden and unexpected. This moment, the deep-worn channel of some lowland stream is almost dry; the sun shines bright; no shower has fallen to indicate a change. But the distant mountain clouds have poured down their avalanche of waters. It comes! — The flood! — dark, deep, and sudden. Merciful Heaven hath given it a voice: but the warning uttered, there remains not an instant for delay. He that flees may escape; but he that deliberates is lost.

In lands exposed to frequent inundations, experience teaches to guard against their inroads. But, if the flood rise far above its ordinary level; or, if it descend with unusual violence, it overtops or bears away the mounds or barriers erected for its confinement: and, the destructive element once let loose, it sweeps away property and life, — spreads misery and dismay during the hour of its terrible supremacy; and, when its fatal hour is past — for the hour of all evil things is brief — we may read the history of its might and destructiveness, in the ruin and desolation left behind.

Under this emblem of a FLOOD, we find set forth all the malicious efforts of Satan, against the Church of Christ, in the twelfth chapter of the Revelation. There we are told, 'There appeared a great wonder (or sign) in Heaven: a woman clothed with the sun'[9] — the light of Christ, the 'sun of righteousness,' 'and the moon' — the time-keeper of Heaven, ever marking the growths and decreasings of this changeful world — 'under her feet,' indicating her supremacy over all that is changeable; 'and upon her head a crown of twelve stars' — the twelve inestimable apostolic gems, the brightest in the diadem of the King of Kings. — 'And she being with child, cried, travailing in birth, and pained to be delivered. And there appeared another wonder in Heaven; and behold, a great red dragon, having seven heads' — a multiplicity and completeness of supremacy in thought, opinion, and sovereignty, 'and ten horns' — a multiplicity and completeness of power for aggression or defence, 'and seven crowns upon his head' — a multiplicity and completeness of acknowledged right from conquest or hereditary descent. 'And his tail drew the *third part* of the stars of heaven.' The 'heaven' is the emblem of the Church of Christ, raised by the power of God from, and above, the world, *to give light to the world*. Now, through all her history, the Church hath been separated into *three* great divisions. First, the Eastern, or Greek; second, the Western, or Roman; and third, the true Catholic, Apostolic, and Protestant Church, — for the Protestant Church is no novelty set up by the glorious Reformers; but a Church, ever visibly existing in all Christian countries, and through all ages, — which never hath for a moment, like the others, described herself, or been described, by any geographical bearings; for she embraceth alike all quarters of the universe, in the arms of that freedom, 'wherewith Christ hath made her free.'[10] We are not, therefore, ignorant of what is meant by

9. Revelation, chapter 12.
10. Galatians 5. 1.

drawing the '*third* part of the stars of heaven,' for it is the third division of the lights of the Christian Church; and, to identify them beyond question, we are told, the dragon 'did cast them to the earth' — that is, the territory of the Roman empire, to which the Clergy of the Church of Rome, — being subject themselves thereto, — ever labour to subject all other Churches, instead of to Christ, their only King and Head. 'And the dragon,' we are told, 'stood before the woman which was ready to be delivered, for to devour her child as soon as it was born.' So sought Rome Pagan to devour the Church of Christ in all the helplessness of its infancy. So sought Rome Papal to devour every solitary witness, that from time to time arose within her immediate presence, and every Church that she discovered amongst the recesses of the Alps or Appenines, bearing a combined testimony to Scripture liberty and Scripture truth. And so sought she to devour the Reformation, at the moment of its birth; and, with an appetite still equally voracious and insatiable, she still 'raveneth after the prey';[11] and, whether it be the temporalities of the Churches on the earth, or the spiritualities of the Churches in the Bible, she equally longeth to appropriate the one to her own uses, and imprison the other in her own shackles.

But, on returning from this brief and cursory view of the cunning and malice of the serpent, we discover him as a persecutor in the thirteenth, and the first act of his persecution is thus recorded in the fifteenth verse: 'And the serpent cast out of his mouth water as a FLOOD after the woman, that he might cause her to be carried away of THE FLOOD. And the earth helped the woman; and the earth opened her mouth, and swallowed up the flood which the dragon cast out of his mouth.'. . . .

Remember, also, we beseech you, that in the hour of the 'flood,' the surest place of escape is always the highest ground. Let us not timidly shrink from the avowal of high scriptural principles. The avowal may expose us to the shafts of calumny; but why should a Christian dread them? They are the same arrows that pierced his Lord. Rather let us stir up our energies, rouse our sleeping associates, and unite to *stem the torrent*. And, ye Ministers of the Gospel, a word more especially to you. In these days, when men seem as ignorant of the contents of civil history as of the policy of the Bible, you will be told you are neither called nor competent to expound political principles, or defend political rights. But we tell these ignorant men, that the Ministers of the Gospel have been the real liberators of Europe. Who freed Saxony and the other members of the Smalkaldic league[12] from the iron fangs of the Pope and the Emperor? The gentle Melancthon,[13] the unbending Luther![14] Who freed Scotland? Was it the chivalry of her nobles — the hardihood of her peasantry? No; but the learning of her Melville[15] and the thunder of her Knox.[16] Who created the imperishable fortress of England's liberties? Not the patriotism of her Commons, nor the power of her nobility, but the patience and boldness of her Puritan Fathers. These mighty men were not enchained by the puling sentimentalism of these days, or by that 'fear of men which ever bringeth a snare.'[17] Remember ye, that your commission is, as theirs, not from men, but from God; that it is not narrowed by any authority, but extends, like theirs, over the wide dominions of your Lord and Master. Remember how your Lord conjoined in the same rebuke every religious error, and every political error, when he charged his disciples, saying, 'Take heed, beware of the leaven of the *Pharisees*, and of the leaven of *Herod*.'[18] So charge upon this generation, to beware of the leaven of Rome ecclesiastical, which teacheth self-righteousness, as the Pharisees; and to beware of the leaven of Rome political, which enforceth a yoke as Herod. And, whether these things be introduced under a Protestant name and disguise, or whether in their own proper Romish name and garb, describe with equal truth, warn with equal faithfulness, and denounce them with equal authority — if ye would be faithful witnesses for the crown and kingdom of your only Lord and Saviour.

And, when all has been done that man can do, to meet the 'flood' of 'the enemy,' remember he 'cometh in' but as a judgment against our individual, ecclesiastical, or national sins; and cannot be repelled but by co-extensive repentance. Hear, then, every man that loves either the land or the

11. Ezekiel 22. 25.

12. A politico-religious alliance formally concluded on 27 February 1531, at Smalkalden in Hesse-Nassau, among German protestant princes and cities for their mutual defence.
13. Philipp Melancthon (1497-1560), German protestant reformer.
14. Martin Luther (1483-1546), founder of the protestant Reformation.
15. Andrew Melville (1545-1622), Scottish presbyterian reformer.
16. John Knox (*c.* 1505-72), leader of the Scottish Reformation.
17. Proverbs 29. 25.
18. Mark 8. 15.

Church of his fathers, and adopt the language of a scriptural statesman, conjoining his own salvation with the welfare of his country. 'I acknowledged my sin unto thee and mine iniquity have I not hid. I said I will confess my transgressions unto the Lord; and thou forgavest the iniquity of my sin. For this shall every one that is godly pray unto thee in a time when thou mayest be found: surely in the *floods of great waters* they shall not come nigh unto him. Thou art my hiding place; thou shalt preserve me from trouble; thou shalt compass me about with songs of deliverance. Many sorrows shall be to the wicked; but he that trusteth in the Lord mercy shall compass him about. Be glad in the Lord, and rejoice, ye righteous; and shout for joy, all ye that are upright in heart.'[19]

Now unto the Father, the Son, and the Holy Spirit, be undivided kingdom, power, and glory. Amen.

19. Psalms 32. 5-11.

from: 'THE REPEALED REPULSED' (1841)

[In January 1841, when Daniel O'Connell visited Belfast, Cooke issued a challenge to a public debate. O'Connell refused on the grounds that if he was to argue politics with a presbyterian clergyman, this would be tantamount to admitting that he was a political antagonist of presbyterianism. Cooke's speech was delivered at a large anti-Repeal meeting in Belfast on 21 January.]

The moment his portentous visit was threatened, my duty became matter of solemn prayer to Him who can employ the 'weak to confound the mighty.'[1] . . . I did believe that in 1841 I saw the fearful shadow of 1641.[2] I saw the circumstances merely so far changed, that, in 1641, physical force marched in the van of rebellion and massacre; but in 1841 intellect and eloquence, enlisting argument, prejudice and passion, advanced in the front, to mask and to cover the array of physical force that fearfully gathered behind. I judged the spirit of the terrible movement to lie in pretended appeals to reason, interest, and facts. And I said in my heart, Shall we see the sword coming, and will no man give warning, and grapple with it, ere it come too nigh? I did believe, and I do still believe, that this mighty conspiracy may, under Providence, be met and averted: therefore did I take one step in advance to meet it. I did not miscalculate when I counted on Mr. O'Connell's abuse — nay, I did know I was taking my life in my hand; but I did also calculate that my life was in the hands of Him who gave it, and that if one hair of my head were molested, or one drop of my blood spilled, yet would the event be overruled to unite still more closely all true Protestant hearts, and that the loss of one humble man might be the salvation of our Churches and our country. I may not overlook the newspaper statement, that Mr. O'Connell has challenged me to twenty-six hours of a discussion upon civil and religious liberty. I take him at his word. The time, the place, I leave to himself, but London and Exeter Hall I take to be the best; and I claim but one conditon — the issue of half the tickets. And never since truth tore the cloak off hypocrisy, did man stand for such a stripping as awaits you, Daniel O'Connell. . . . There should I exhibit him, sitting this moment in the councils of the land, as the transformed hero of Milton sat at the ear of the sleeping Eve.[3] So sits he whispering his dreams of Repeal into the ear of the people, and infusing the poison of his Popery into the vitals of the Constitution. But as the spear of Ithuriel[4] compelled the foul toad to start into his native Satanic form, so shall the history of the past, and the condition of the present, compel O'Connell to appear in form, what he is in heart — the genius of knavery, the apostle of rebellion. . . .

You [Mr. O'Connell] have said, there is no hope of the Presbyterian youth of Ulster so long as 'that loathsome theologue, Dr. Cooke, has influence over them.' Now, that there is no hope of their becoming Repealers is, happily, one truth; but that I have influence over them, such as you would indicate, is utterly untrue. No! I will tell you what and who has influence over them. The Bible and its principles have influence over them. The Spirit that descended upon John Knox, who never feared the face of man, has influence over them. His mantle has fallen around their manly shoulders, and they will never exchange it for the frieze coat of Repeal

1. I Corinthians 1.27.
2. A reference to the massacres of English and Scottish planters during the rebellion led by Sir Phelim O'Neill (1604-53).
3. John Milton, *Paradise Lost*, IV. 800-09.
4. John Milton, *Paradise Lost*, IV. 810.

. . . . Look at the town of Belfast. When I was a youth it was almost a village. But what a glorious sight does it now present? The masted grove within our harbour — our mighty warehouses teeming with the wealth of every clime — our giant manufactories lifting themselves on every side — our streets marching on, as it were, with such rapidity, that an absence of a few weeks makes us strangers in the outskirts of our town. And all this we owe to the Union. No, not all — for throned above our fair town, and looking serenely from our mountain's brow, I beheld the genii of Protestantism and Liberty, sitting inseparable in their power, while the genius of Industry which nightly reclines at their feet, starts with every morning in renovated might, and puts forth his energies, and showers down his blessings, on the fair and smiling lands of a Chichester, a Conway, and a Hill.[5] Yes, we will guard the Union, as we will guard our liberties, and advance and secure the prosperity of our country.

5. Arthur Chichester (1563-1625), lord Chichester of Belfast, English soldier and politician who became lord deputy of Ireland. Francis Conway (1719-94), lord lieutenant of Ireland 1765. Arthur Hill (1601-63), son of an English soldier, Moyses Hill, he built Hillsborough Fort.

ULSTER'S SOLEMN LEAGUE AND COVENANT (1912)

[In April 1912, the leader of the British Conservative Party, Andrew Bonar Law, travelled to Belfast with seventy British unionist MPs to take part in a mass demonstration at Balmoral Show Grounds against Asquith's Home Rule Bill. At the demonstration, Sir Edward Carson and Bonar Law clasped hands as though ratifying a public compact before a battle. The crowd then uncovered their heads, raised their hands and solemnly repeated after Carson words abjuring Home Rule. This ceremony inspired Ulster unionist leaders to draw up a more formal bond in which Ulster protestants could affirm their mutual obligation. Modelled on the Scottish Covenant of 1581, but dropping its anti-catholic abuse out of sensitivity to English opinion, the Ulster Covenant was drafted by Sir James Craig. It was signed by a total of 218,206 men (a separate declaration was signed by nearly 230,000 women).]

Being convinced in our consciences that Home Rule would be disastrous to the material well-being of Ulster as well as of the whole of Ireland, subversive of our civil and religious freedom, destructive of our citizenship and perilous to the unity of the Empire, we, whose names are underwritten, men of Ulster, loyal subjects of His Gracious Majesty King George V, humbly relying on the God whom our fathers in days of stress and trial confidently trusted, do hereby pledge ourselves in solemn Covenant throughout this our time of threatened calamity to stand by one another in defending for ourselves and our children our cherished position of equal citizenship in the United Kingdom and in using all means which may be found necessary to defeat the present conspiracy to set up a Home Rule Parliament in Ireland. And in the event of such a Parliament being forced upon us we further solemnly and mutually pledge ourselves to refuse to recognise its authority. In sure confidence that God will defend the right we hereto subscribe our names. And further, we individually declare that we have not already signed this Covenant. God Save the King.

EDWARD CARSON

(1854-1935)

'I WAS IN EARNEST' (1921)

[On 14 December 1921, the House of Lords debated the terms of the Anglo-Irish Treaty. In his maiden speech, Carson attacked Lord Curzon, the British foreign secretary, and Viscount Birkenhead, the lord chancellor, in an attempt to break up Lloyd George's coalition government and form a new Conservative Party.]

My Lords, in venturing to address your Lordships' House for the first time I am bound to admit that the only pleasure I find in such an operation is in having to welcome here the mover of this Address, Lord Morley.[1] I cannot but recollect that it was his speech in the House of Commons just thirty years ago which, when I first spoke there, I had to answer. I think it is befitting that he should attend here at these splendid obsequies of the Unionist Party. I think he is a very proper person to pronounce the funeral oration over all that has been said and done by that misguided Party (as we have just learnt from the noble Marquess)[2] for the last thirty-five years, dead and buried from today, with all this engineered splendour to cover up the defeat and humiliation you have had in Ireland; dead and buried, strangled, without consultation with their followers, by the leaders and trustees who were sent into the Government to protect them.

The seconder of the Address is a brother Irishman.[3] I have known him many years. His one great characteristic has always been that he never could agree with anybody on any subject, and I cannot but congratulate him that this evening he has at last found peace and understanding in the knowledge that he will now be under that perfect Government which will be evolved out of the murder gang in Ireland. I wish him every success and every happiness in the future of his country and of his own life there.

But, after all, we must come down to the realities of the situation. I wish I had something of the eloquence of the noble Marquess in advocating his new-found faith. I wonder when it came to him. It would be worth inquiring. Was it yesterday, or was it the day before? Why, it is not very long ago that he used to tell us that black was very black, just with as great eloquence as he has assured us that it is very white. He has what they call in boys' slang 'gone the whole hog.' It is always the way with a man who has a newly-found faith. I believe in religion they call him a pervert, but I should be sorry to apply an epithet of that kind to so great, so eloquent, and so superior a man as the noble Marquess.

It is a curious thing. I once heard the late Duke of Devonshire.[4] It was one of the earliest political meetings I ever attended and it was in Dublin, and he was commenting upon the then recent change of Mr. Gladstone on this very question. Having quoted some of his previous utterances, the noble Duke made this remark, which I commend, if I may most humbly, to the noble Marquess. He said:

> Is it necessary that because a man turns his coat he should divest himself of every particle of his raiment?

I suggest to the noble Marquess that it was not in the least necessary, because he came down here with his coat turned, that he should have tried to picture himself in such a state of absolute nudity as his speech appeared to indicate.

I read a statement in an essay in a paper a few weeks ago by that great statesman, so intimately connected with Ireland, Mr. Birrell.[5] He said this, and I never knew it was true till I heard the noble Marquess speak this evening —

> It is a British characteristic, though not an amiable one, that once we are beaten we go over in a body to the successful enemy, and too often abandon and cold-shoulder and snub, both in action and writing, the suffering few who adhere to our cause in evil and difficult times.

I am one of the suffering few. I speak for a good many. I speak — I can hardly speak — for all those who, relying on British honour and British justice, have in giving their best to the service of the State seen them now deserted and cast aside without one single line of recollection or recognition in the whole of what you call peace terms in Ireland. The noble Marquess paid a generous and eloquent tribute to Michael Collins,[6] the head of the murder gang, as Sir Hamar Greenwood[7] described him only a few months ago in the House of Commons.

1. John Morley (1838-1923), 1st viscount Morley, British politician and writer. He proposed the motion to confirm and ratify the Articles of Agreement.
2. George Curzon (1859-1925), marquess Curzon, British statesman and foreign secretary 1919-24.
3. Windham Thomas Wyndham-Quin (1841-1926), 4th earl of Dunraven, Irish politician whose Wyndham Land Act of 1903 enabled tenants to own land.
4. William Cavendish (1808-91), 7th duke of Devonshire, British politician who supported Gladstone until the secession of the Liberal Unionists on the question of Home Rule in 1885.
5. Augustine Birrell (1850-1933), British politician and man of letters whose policies while chief secretary for Ireland (1907-16) contributed to the Easter Rising.
6. Michael Collins (1890-1922), Irish nationalist. On 6 December 1921 he signed the Anglo-Irish Treaty, which was repudiated by many republicans and led to civil war. After taking over the leadership of the transitional government, he was killed in an ambush by republicans.
7. Sir Hamar Greenwood (1870-1948), 1st viscount Greenwood, a Canadian-born British politician who became the last chief secretary for Ireland in April 1920.

THE MARQUESS CURZON OF KEDLESTON: I never mentioned him.

LORD CARSON: You mentioned the delegates. Perhaps you did not know he was one of them. I do not know if you were ever there, but he was. He committed many murders with his own hands — the hand that you have now so willingly grasped. But I heard nothing said of a case that I saw in the newspapers only two days ago — a letter written by a broken-hearted mother, whose son had been through the whole war and won honour and distinction for himself, and safety and security for you. The recompense he got was that when he went to see his mother in Ireland he was foully murdered, and the next night her house was burned down, and, while you and your colleagues were carrying on all these negotiations in Downing Street, without remonstrance or interference every single article that this broken-hearted woman had was being auctioned off in the light of day.

THE MARQUESS OF LONDONDERRY:[8] During the truce?

LORD CARSON: Yes, during the truce, and while the negotiations were going on in Downing Street, and you, the Government, are proud of the results that you have brought about. Well might Lord Crewe[9] ask, as he did ask, why, if you are so certain of all this peace being gained by the abandonment of Ulster, did you go on for a year or two years sacrificing these precious lives, and rendering desolate households whose only crime was that they thought you were going to back them up. In that same letter I saw it stated that this young officer was murdered solely because he dared to refuse to subscribe to Sinn Fein,[10] because he thought it was dishonourable; and all the time you were plotting to throw him over and to give to Sinn Fein what you had denied to him — namely, the honour and the glory of having beaten this terrible organisation of crime and assassination which existed in Ireland.

I would like to know where we stand at the present moment. I notice in the Resolution moved by the noble Viscount for an Address in reply to His Majesty's gracious Speech that we are asked to confirm and ratify what you are pleased to call these Articles of Agreement for a Treaty between Great Britain and Ireland. Was ever a House of Lords or House of Commons put into such an extraordinary position? Just see what it is. For thirty years or more the late Unionist Party has been fighting the question of modified Home Rule — as I think the noble Marquess called it, a 'milk-and-watery Home Rule,' or something of that kind. All of a sudden they say that that Home Rule is not good enough; you must have the real thing; the country must abandon Ireland at the very heart of the Empire to independence, with an Army, with a Navy, with separate Customs, with Ministers at foreign Courts, and delegates to the League of Nations, where they can vote against you.

And how is it presented to the country? I do not believe, in the whole of the history of our Constitution, anything approaching it has ever been attempted. It is brought out one morning cut and dried, signed, sealed, and delivered; and before making this great act of constitutional change, which is to break up the United Kingdom and, in the words of Sir Hamar Greenwood, to smash the British Empire, you are not to present this to Parliament or to the country, but you are to advise His Majesty to give his consent. I say there never was a greater outrage attempted upon constitutional liberty than this Coalition Government have attempted at the present time.

I should like to ask you this. If Mr. Gladstone[11] or Mr. Asquith[12] had attempted to do what you are attempting to do in this case, what would be the speech that the noble Marquess would have made in those circumstances? It would repay the noble Marquess to see what the leader of the Party in the House of Commons said in 1914, when the milk-and-watery Home Rule Bill was put upon the Statute Book. Why, I was ordered to walk out of the House of Commons with indignation — which I did. And now not only am I to have no indignation at the grant of what they are pleased to call Dominion Home Rule to Ireland — and I will show

8. Charles Vane-Tempest-Stewart (1878-1949), 7th marquess of Londonderry, Irish politician.
9. Robert Crewe-Milnes (1858-1945), marquess of Crewe, British politician and lord lieutenant of Ireland 1892-95.
10. Irish: We Ourselves. A nationalist political party founded by Arthur Griffith in 1905. In the 1918 general election, under Eamon de Valera, Sinn Féin won an overwhelming majority in Ireland, except in the north-east. The Sinn Féin MPs refused to sit in Westminster, proclaimed a parliament in Ireland in 1919 and set up an alternative administration.
11. William Ewart Gladstone (1809-98), four times prime minister of Britain. He devoted most of his later career to achieving a Home Rule bill for Ireland, but without success.
12. Herbert Asquith (1852-1928), 1st earl of Oxford and British prime minister 1908-16.

you what they said about it themselves two or three months ago — but I get a long lecture from the noble Marquess which, may I say, I hope in the future he will spare me; because the man (let me speak plainly) who, in my opinion at all events, has betrayed me, has no right afterwards to lecture me.

There you get it all cut and dried, like an Act of Parliament signed by the King. I saw the other day that Mr. Asquith, with whom I never have much sympathy, and never have had, made a speech and said an unusual thing had happened, that when all this came out, of which he entirely approved — indeed, I think he claimed to be the author of it — he felt an unaccustomed moisture coming down his cheeks. I do not wonder.

And how beautifully it has all been managed! The stage management is one of the most perfect things I ever recollect. The chorus in the papers, frantic telegrams to every Prime Minister to send back another telegram in order that we might have it published here. I know the Prime Minister[13] so well, for I served under him. Make no mistake, I am grateful for all that he did in the war; but I know his methods. 'Now I give *The Times* into your charge; I give the *Daily News* into your charge; and the *Daily Chronicle* into your charge; you see that they are all in a chorus tomorrow.' And so they are. And do you think either we or the country are going to be taken in by this manufactured glorification of what you are pleased to call the Treaty between Great Britain and Ireland? No, we are not. We tell you, if you want to pass it, go and ask the country, but you will not dare. That is the last thing you will do, or the last thing you care about. And all this comes from the long continuance in office of a Coalition Government which was formed for entirely different objects and entirely different purposes.

One thing the noble Marquess entirely forgot to tell us was how the Government came to the conclusion that these Articles of Treaty were so much for the benefit of the country. The difficulty I have in commenting upon them at all is that, unless as a matter of mere pretence, when we are seeming to be very dignified and concerned, there is not a noble Lord in this House who believes for a moment that these terms were passed upon the merits. Not at all. They were passed with a revolver pointed at your head. And you know it. You know you passed them because you were beaten. You know you passed them because Sinn Fein with its Army in Ireland has beaten you. Why do you not say so? Your Press says so, and you may as well confess it. There may be nothing dishonourable in it.

But when we are told that the reason why they had to pass these terms of Treaty, and the reason why they could not put down crime in Ireland was because they had neither the men nor the money, nor the backing, let me say that that is an awful confession to make to the British Empire. If you tell your Empire in India, in Egypt, and all over the world that you have not got the men, the money, the pluck, the inclination, and the backing to restore law and order in a country within twenty miles of your own shore, you may as well begin to abandon the attempt to make British rule prevail throughout the Empire at all.

How did this new-born faith come into existence? I have here a speech of the noble Marquess's leader, which I have no doubt he has read over and over again out of loyalty. This speech was made on October 9 of last year. I am sorry that I shall have to inflict upon the House a certain number of quotations, because I want to show the House the unreality of the pretext put forward for these Articles of Treaty. Here is a speech made on October 9 of last year at Carnarvon by the Prime Minister, and I might mention before I read the passage, in order that you may thoroughly understand what happened, that Mr. Lloyd George, upon rising, was vociferously cheered. Now listen to it:

> Mr. Gladstone went to what he considered to be the safe limit in his concessions to Ireland. There were many who thought he went too far. He went as far as he could consistent with the security of the United Kingdom and of the Empire, and consistent with supremacy in Ireland. The same applied to Mr. Asquith in 1912. But there are men, and responsible men, who would go far beyond anything Mr. Gladstone ever thought safe —

that was the noble Marquess tonight!

> far beyond that which Mr. Asquith himself thought safe in 1912, and I have got to deal with these appeals which have been made.

Now mark this —

> Why are we asked to go further? I protest against

13. David Lloyd George (1863-1945), British prime minister 1916-22 who negotiated the establishment of the Irish Free State.

the doctrine that you should go further and give more, not because Ireland needs it, not because it is fair to the United Kingdom, but because crime has been more successful. It is a fatal doctrine for any Government in any country (*Loud cheers*). Give it because it is right. Give it because it is just. Give it because it is good for Ireland and good for the United Kingdom. Give it because it brings peace and good will, but do not give it because you are bullied by assassins.

And that is what you did, or are trying to do.

We have heard a great deal about delivering the goods. 'Only show me somebody,' said the Prime Minister, 'who can deliver the goods.' What goods has anyone delivered? I know of no goods that have been delivered as a consideration for these concessions, but five hundred or six hundred bleeding corpses of men who have tried to do their duty and have lost their lives in the service of their country.

Look at the document! I defy anybody to show me anything in that document but one provision, and that is that Great Britain should scuttle out of Ireland. You may talk of a Free State. You may put in window-dressing about the *status* of the Colonies and everything else, but from the beginning to the end of this document there is nothing you will find except that England, beaten to her knees by the gun of the assassin, says: 'We are willing to scuttle out of Ireland and to leave to the tender mercies of the assassins everybody who has supported us in the past.' I noticed this as I looked through these provisions, and I looked through them with anxiety. I know that since the truce was entered into and while you were parleying in Downing Street with, and making up your minds as to the sincerity of, these men, they were taking possession of the lands and properties of men in Ireland by force and without any interference upon the part of our splendid Coalition Government. What provision is there about that in this document? Not one word. You leave them in undisturbed possession. You know well that you have not even the courage to tell them that they ought to have the externals of decency in the pretence of carrying out what is supposed to be a peace charter for Ireland.

But let me not be mistaken. It may be that you have to start in a consideration of this question upon the basis that this country was not strong enough to put down crime in Ireland. It may be that that is so. I do not know; I have not the means of judging. I regret it and I feel humiliated by it. But I know that we have gone through a great and terrible war, and it may be that by reason of the expense or of the slaughter that would occur either to your own men or to the people in Ireland, you were bound to abandon Unionist policy and to give up Ireland, which you had tried for so long to retain as a constituent part of the United Kingdom. It may be that that would become necessary. But I ask your Lordships, ought Unionist leaders to have been parties to that — Unionist leaders who had undertaken to defend Unionist policy? At least, they might have said what Peel[14] said and, unfortunately, did not do: 'I was elected for another purpose; I was put into office by those who were my followers for another purpose. If there is to be a change of policy it is not for me to carry it out.' That, I think, would have been a more honourable position to take up in public life, but the truth of the matter is that if you go on like this, if you have men in high positions stating today that A. is white, and tomorrow arguing that it is certainly black, you will destroy the confidence of the democracy of this country in its rulers and in its institutions. I believe that is what has happened in this case, and it will make public life and politics stink in the nostrils of the country for the next twenty years.

When I took up this document involving independence, finance, and the granting of an Army and a Navy, I thought that I recollected a good deal that was said by the Prime Minister during the past year in the House of Commons and elsewhere about the impossibility of granting these things. Here is what he said on February 8, 1921, in very welcome surroundings no doubt, at the meeting of the executive of the Welsh National Liberals at the Central Hall, Westminster.

> They must have an Irish Republic, an Irish Army, an Irish Navy. They won't get it.

But you have given it. Will it be given to them by this new Party? If it will, we ought to know.

> It is the most dangerous menace to the life of this country that there ever was. If they do not get it they will kill our policemen and our soldiers, not in open fighting but in hiding, in houses, walking

14. Sir Robert Peel (1788-1850), British prime minister 1834-35, 1841-46. He was chief secretary for Ireland 1812-18 and preserved protestant ascendancy by opposing demands for catholic emancipation.

about as respectable tenant farmers, swaggering along the road until they come to their hiding place, where they find rifles ready placed for them, passing perhaps on the way the very policeman they are about to murder, as if they were innocent men. They are not open, straightforward fighters.

If I had the time, and if you, my Lords, had the patience, I could trace through the utterances of this great statesman and you would find that his enthusiasm for the preservation of the *status quo* has cooled as the number of murders multiplied in Ireland. Later, on June 15, 1921, he said at a semi-religious ceremony, the General Assembly of the Calvinistic Methodist Church of Wales, speaking there, no doubt, as a man of peace —

> There can be no doubt in the mind of any reasonable man that if Ireland were given complete independence, with its own Army, and control of its own ports, and powers to enter into Treaties with foreign countries, whether they were friendly or hostile to us, that would place Britain in a position of such peril that I should hesitate to think what might befall in the event of a repetition of either the great struggle with Napoleon or the struggle with Germany.

Now, however, that is all put down, cut and dried, with the King's assent, without the country having the slightest opportunity of passing a verdict upon it, and without the terms being even examined in the way that we were accustomed in the old days to examine proposals of political Parties when they were brought forward.

There are other utterances of the Prime Minister which, I think, will repay a perusal. Here is one where he tackles poor Mr. Asquith. This is what he said in a speech at Carnarvon —

> I put to Mr. Asquith a question in the House of Commons —

I remember the scene perfectly well. I think I was rather exuberant over the way the Prime Minister dealt with Mr. Asquith, but at that time I did not know, as I know now, that I was a mere puppet in a political game. I was in earnest. I was not playing politics. I believed all this. I thought of the last thirty years, during which I was fighting with others whose friendship and comradeship I hope I will lose from tonight, because I do not value any friendship that is not founded upon confidence and trust. I was in earnest. What a fool I was. I was only a puppet, and so was Ulster, and so was Ireland, in the political game that was to get the Conservative Party into power. And of all the men in my experience that I think are the most loathsome it is those who will sell their friends for the purpose of conciliating their enemies, and, perhaps, still worse, the men who climb up a ladder into power of which even I may have been part of a humble rung, and then, when they have got into power, kick the ladder away without any concern for the pain, or injury, or mischief, or damage that they do to those who have helped them to gain power.

This is what the Prime Minister said in October last year —

> I put to Mr. Asquith a question in the House of Commons. I said you are talking about Dominion Home Rule —

The noble Marquess told us tonight that that is exactly what they are giving. The Prime Minister spoke of it as if it were a ridiculous idea —

> You are talking about Dominion Home Rule, but the Dominions have got Armies and Navies of their own —

A terrible point that against Mr. Asquith.

> Their ports are entirely in their control. They can shut their ports against British ships, and we know perfectly well that we could not interfere —

No more than you could interfere with Ireland.

> I ask, would you give the same rights to Ireland? If not, it is no use talking about Dominion Home Rule.

And yet every word of that the Cabinet have now agreed to, without consulting, so far as the Unionist members were concerned, the Party, and without consulting the country. They have agreed to pass into law all that. It may be right or it may be wrong, but I say, if that is the way measures are going to be allowed to be passed in this country, then set up an autocracy in Downing Street and get rid both of the House of Lords and of the House of Commons.

But that is not all. There is another quotation —

> Nobody wishes to manage Ireland's domestic affairs, but dangerous weapons like Armies and Navies I think we had better not trust them with. It would hurt them to grasp weapons of that

kind, and for the sake of Ireland they had better not have them. As far as I am concerned, and I speak on behalf of the Government, we shall certainly resist out and out any demand for an Army or Navy to be set up in Ireland at our doors to menace the existence of the United Kingdom.

And you, my Lords, are expected to be the complaisant puppets of His Majesty's Government, and without demur and with extreme politeness, such as we heard in all the speeches which went before mine, to take off your hats and say: 'Thank God for our Prime Minister and our Foreign Secretary and all the rest of them. They have done everything which they told us would ruin the United Kingdom, and with the open minds they have, and great hearts, are prepared even to risk that for the sake of putting down assassination in Ireland.'

But that is not all. Upon what issue did you go to the country? You went to the country upon the issue setting up the Home Rule Act, which was on the Statute Book; which retained the Army and Navy here, which retained all finance here, which provided that Ireland was to have only a subordinate Parliament and which preserved the supremacy of the Crown. The noble Marquess and I used to go down to platforms together and tell the people that the Act would be absolute ruin to this country and mean the break-up of the United Kingdom and the Empire. I suppose you were humbugging all the time and had your tongue in your cheek. I was not. I was taking risks, right or wrong; and you were encouraging me all you knew. Many a man who is now party to all this treason and treachery has come up to me time after time in the House of Commons and elsewhere, and said, 'For God's sake do not give way an inch, and we will win the next Election.'

I hope you are proud of your Treaty. Let me say this, and it is the last word so far as this point is concerned. I think it is an innovation which this House ought very carefully to consider — namely, the entry into a Treaty between different parts of one Kingdom. Was such a thing ever heard of before? The next time you have a dispute in the coal fields of this country you will find suddenly coming down here, with the King's Assent to it beforehand, a Treaty between England and the coal-owners and coal-miners of Yorkshire, Derbyshire and elsewhere.

A Treaty! On the very face of the document itself it is false. It says: 'A Treaty between Great Britain and Ireland,' and before you signed it you never even asked Ulster. Nor is her signature necessary. It is only to be signed in the House of Commons of Southern Ireland and by this House, and your Lordships, who only last year set up a separate entity in the six counties consisting of 1,200,000 people, disregard that as part of Ireland. But when you come to ask for contributions and taxes then you say: 'Small patch as you are' (to use Mr. Asquith's phrase) 'you must pay 44 per cent. of the contribution.' I say the document has a lie on the face of it. And it is put there purposely. It is put there for this reason — that you wish to admit in the presence of those men, because you were afraid of them, that they were representative of the whole of Ireland. They are not, and please God they never will be.

Let me say before I sit down — I deeply apologise to the House for the time I have taken — a word about Ulster. Like everybody else, you have betrayed Ulster. The noble Marquess, in his lecture to me, hoped that I would advance opinions that Ulster should come in. This constant preaching at Ulster is nauseating. The other evening I saw with disgust that Mr. Austen Chamberlain,[15] the son of Mr. Joseph Chamberlain,[16] having agreed to put Ulster into these terms, then said he made an appeal to the comradeship of his old friend Sir James Craig[17] to come in and submit to the domination of Sinn Fein. I could not help thinking that it was very like, after having shot a man in the back, going over to him and patting him on the shoulder and saying: 'Old man, die as quickly as you can, and do not make any noise.'

Your Lordships, I have no doubt, read the papers. I hope you read more of them than I do. For the last three or six months the whole vitriolic power of the Press, inspired by No. 10, Downing Street and their able propaganda department, have been carrying on week after week and day after day a campaign of falsehood and misrepresentation

15. Sir Austen Chamberlain (1863-1937), leader of the Conservative Party 1921-22.
16. Joseph Chamberlain (1836-1914), British politician opposed to Irish home rule, who led the Liberal Unionists into an alliance with the Conservatives in 1886.
17. James Craig (1871-1940), viscount Craigavon. A strong supporter of Carson, Craig became prime minister of the newly established government of Northern Ireland in 1921, a position he held until his death.

against Ulster, bellowing, bullying and blustering as if Ulster cared one farthing about it. But why is all this attack made upon Ulster? What has Ulster done? I will tell you what Ulster has done. She has stuck too well to you, and you believe that because she is loyal you can kick her as you like.

In 1914 the whole Conservative Party, headed by the noble Marquess, had pledged the whole force and power of the Party and, if they got into the Government, of this country, to maintain and keep Ulster outside the modified Home Rule Bill of 1914. What has happened since to change your attitude? When the war came on and you were in want of men, just at the point when you were turning Ulster (as she thought, at all events) out of the United Kingdom, I was asked to go over and try to raise a division. I had to go to the men who were smarting under the fact that you were trying to turn them out of the heritage of citizenship to which they were loyal and devoted, and I had to say to them: 'Never mind; that is merely an act of the Government and not an act of the people; the people are all right, and, after all, our union and the United Kingdom are all wrapped up in the success of this war.' I said to them: 'Go and enlist, go and bring glory to Ulster and safety to the Empire; that is your first duty.' And they went, and they suffered, and they lost thousands and thousands of men, while your new-found friends were murdering your troops in the city of Dublin. Is it that which has turned you from your desire to help Ulster?

And then, in 1916, after the Rebellion, I was asked by the present Prime Minister, at the instigation of Mr. Asquith, who was then his chief, to go to Ireland and to try to induce the Ulster people to agree to the setting up of the Act of 1914 in the south and west on the condition that the Six Counties should be left out. I knew they would hate it, but I cared more about the success of the war than I did even about Ulster. I am not ashamed to say it, because I thought the one involved the other. I went over, and I had as a guarantee a letter from the present Prime Minister, which I shall always keep as a precious possession, guaranteeing me that the Six Counties would be left out, and that they never could be put back again without an Act of Parliament. Was it my action on that account which has turned you to take a different attitude towards Ulster?

Again, conscription was brought in for Ireland — in my opinion far too late, and at a very fatal moment, as I advised at the time — and Ulster was willing to be conscripted. But all your friends, your new-found friends in Ireland, went down and met together in solemn conclave with the Catholic hierarchy, and determined to send to perdition anybody that dared even to advocate and allow it. And there again they beat you. Was it that which turned you against Ulster? And in 1920, when this Government came into power and you brought in your Home Rule Bill of 1920, was that your policy? Did it represent your policy, or was it a sham? Do any of your Bills ever represent your policy, or do you mean to correct them the moment the ink is dry upon His Majesty's signature? Was it your policy? All I can say, as I said in the House of Commons at the time, is that I refused absolutely to go over and ask Ulster, which loathed and detested it, to accept a Parliament there unless I had the most solemn assurances from the Prime Minister that that was to be a settlement of the case, and a permanent one, so that Ulster might proceed, after being threatened for thirty years, to the natural development of her resources and to the progress of the great democratic community over which she presides.

I got those solemn assurances over and over again from the Prime Minister. I went there, and I lost many friends. Lord Farnham[18] can tell you something of what I went through at the time, because he was there. I am not sure he did not very nearly fall out with me himself, only he is far too good a fellow. I went through all that, and I came back and supported it, and did what I could to support it in this House. I was not a member, but many members asked me about it, because they knew I was interested in it, and I think they believed I was sincere.

Then the Bill was passed; and you advised His Majesty to open this new Parliament, with all the paraphernalia and splendour of a new-born Parliament in the Empire. He did so, with great success, and he met with a loyalty that he himself declared had never been exceeded in any part of His Majesty's Dominions. And then what happens? The murders go on, and you forget all your pledges. What a splendid thing a statesman's conscience is in modern times! It is becoming nearly as elastic as the conscience of the Press, and I do not know which of them I have insulted more in saying that.

Next you enter into your parleys with the Sinn

18. Arthur Kenlis (1879-1957), 11th baron Farnham, Irish soldier.

Feiners. I want to be perfectly frank about that. I do not see any reason why the Prime Minister should not enter into parleys with these gentlemen if he thought he could save bloodshed, or get such modifications of the Act of 1920 as would make a real settlement. But what happened? Without one word of warning to Ulster, without one single communication to the Prime Minister or Government of Ulster — which, after all, you cannot altogether despise, as you are the parents of it — that would be an unnatural thing of which I would never accuse the noble Marquess — without one word of warning there is sprung upon them this: 'We have arranged with the Sinn Feiners that there is to be a Parliament for the whole of Ireland, that the six counties are to go in, and if you go in here is good news for you, because you are not to pay a 6*s.* Income Tax, but probably only a 1*s.* 6*d.* one, and now how happy you ought to be.' Ulster is not for sale. Her loyalty does not depend upon taxes. Ulster values her heritage as citizens of the United Kingdom, and neither you nor the Press, nor your friends in the south of Ireland, need try to terrorise her by the bogey of her having to pay more. At the same time, I make this observation in passing, that it does seem an extraordinary idea of British justice that because Ulster will not join the enemies of this country, and will not go under the murder gang in Dublin, therefore she must pay higher taxation. However, I merely make that observation in passing.

When Ulster refuses to accept these terms, you proceed behind her back, having promised to submit new proposals to her which you never did until they were signed — you proceed to pass the Treaty, as you call it, which is now under discussion. Even then you must outrage her sentiments by putting her, without her consent, into what they call the Free State of Ireland. Why should you do that? Do you not know perfectly well that the way she takes that is this, and I am sure she is right — that you are throwing the whole weight of the British Government into the policy of compelling her to go under the Sinn Fein Parliament in Dublin? Why else did you put her in that way, and how have you framed your Bill if she comes out? And I promise you she will come out. I promise you that she will come out within ten minutes of her hearing of the King's Assent being given to a Bill putting her in.

Then, how does she stand? You have tried to make — and I charge you that you have done it wilfully and deliberately — you have tried to make her position impossible, and, what is more, I believe you have told the Sinn Fein delegates so. What have you done? You give these people power to have an Army and to pay for it out of the taxes which they collect. You give them the free Customs, which enables them to bring in arms, ammunition and all the weapons of war, as they like. What do they want an Army for unless it be to invade Ulster? What do you give them the Army for? What is your plan? Is it to invade America, or the Isle of Man, or the Channel Islands? You know well that you want to strengthen her against Ulster, and that Ulster will have standing on her frontier, a difficult frontier always, a standing Army supported out of the taxes of the south and west of Ireland.

Ulster has no provision for raising an Army. That you have reserved for yourselves. Of course you may answer me: 'You need have no fear, because the British Army will be at Ulster's disposal.' Do you think, after what has happened, that we can trust any Government that it will be so, and, above all, that we can trust a Government who have shown by their framing of the Bill that their policy is to drive us under? No! we will have to trust our own right arm, and we will trust our own right arm. But what a message of peace to send to Ireland, to tell the south and west: 'You can maintain an Army and all the accoutrements of war for the purpose, if you like, of invading Ulster and of compelling Ulster to come under you. You can commence with an Army, and also, if you like, with some naval ships.' Peace! What is the good of pretence? You are crying peace when there is no peace.

But that is not all. What more have you done? You have given free Customs to the south and west, and you have retained Ulster under your own powers of taxation here. When Ulster goes out, what does that mean? At the present moment, and for some months past, a vigorous boycotting of Ulster goods, or goods that come into Ireland through Ulster, has been going on by the south and west, and not merely Ulster goods but also English goods, for I am told that you cannot buy any Ulster or any English goods anywhere in the south and west at the present moment. You have that boycotting going on, and you have trains stopped daily and the goods of loyal merchants pitched upon the ground, or into rivers, or burnt, merely as a coercive policy towards Northern Ireland; and of course without any interference — for how could you interfere after the character you have given them tonight? — by the British Government.

What will it be when the Act passes? Why, you will have legitimised all this, because you will have given power to the Sinn Fein Parliament in the south and west, by prohibition or tariffs, just as they please, to prevent anything coming into Ireland through Ulster, or anything being sent from Ulster to the south and west. Therefore, I say that you have given into their hands the power of actual physical coercion, and also the power of economic coercion. Is it any wonder that Ulster has, I regret to say, begun to break away from you. You have been preaching at her day after day and beseeching her to become Sinn Fein, and what is the result? That for the first time the people are wavering towards you. I have had many letters and many communications. Perhaps you will allow me to read a passage from one. That is not from a politician; it is from an official —

'The feeling here —'

that is, Londonderry —

> is very bitter, and a strong feeling exists that if solid, reliable guarantees could be got, Ulster should join in with a Republican Ireland and wash its hands from all connection with such a perfidious people. In my opinion all faith of the Ulster Protestants in Englishmen's honesty or capacity has been wrecked.'

That is the record of your message of peace.

But I say to my Ulster friends, and I say it with all sincerity and solemnity: 'Do not be led into any such false line. Stick to your old ideals of closer and closer connection with this country. The Coalition Government, after all, is not the British nation, and the British nation will certainly see you righted. Your interests lie with Great Britain. You have helped her, and you have helped her Empire, and her Empire belongs just as much to you as it does to England. Stick to it, and trust the British people.' But I warn the Government of this tendency, because do not imagine that, if any such thing happens, it would be merely that you had achieved your ambition to turn the people of the North of Ireland into Sinn Feiners and assassins. Not at all. Out through the whole Empire — Canada, Australia, New Zealand — Ulstermen are strong and powerful. Toronto is an Ulster city. Do not do something which, throughout the length and breadth of our Empire, will turn Ulster against the British connection. God forbid! And do remember that when, through your laws, Ulstermen were driven out of Ireland and went to America, it was thirty-six Ulstermen, smarting under a grievance, who signed the Declaration of Independence.[19]

Loyalty is a strange thing. It is something which you cannot get by merely sitting round a table and trying to find a formula for an Oath of Allegiance which means nothing. It is something born and bred in you. I have often — I admit it — when we have been threatened because we were loyal in Ulster in times past, threatened day after day and night after night, for no crime except that we were loyal — I have often said to myself: 'Well, why don't you give it up and join the others?' And I never did, because I know I could not, because I know that it is something that is born in you, inherited in you, and that is the safety of the State. But do not try us too high. Do recognise that we have tried to help you, as you have helped us, and do not, when we want to stay with you, do anything to turn us out.

19. A gross exaggeration. Five Ulstermen signed the American Declaration of Independence.

JAMES CRAIG
(1871-1940)

'WE ARE KING'S MEN' (1940)

[This speech was broadcast on 5 February 1940.]

It is a high privilege for me to be afforded an opportunity of explaining briefly something of the part which is being played by this outpost of the Empire in the great struggle in which the United Kingdom and her gallant Allies are engaged.

Before doing so, however, let me say with what profound admiration we here have observed the almost miraculous way in which, under the wise and courageous leadership of Mr. Chamberlain,[1] the British Government has achieved in a few months what took so long to accomplish in the last great war; unity of command on the Western front, close economic alliance with France, the swift mobilisation of our man power, the rapid dispatch of the expeditonary force, the instant action of the Royal Navy in taking command of the seas and of the Royal Air Force in taking command of the air. This has been achieved with a speed, a smoothness and a precision beyond praise, and all that despite the gigantic problems of home defence, the organisation of supply and the control and equitable distribution of foodstuffs which had to be dealt with at the same time. Is it to be wondered at, our attachment to the Mother Country — our pride in Britain's might?

In this stronghold of the United Kingdom of Great Britain and Northern Ireland we have been thrilled, just as you must have been, by the moving accounts of heroic deeds on sea, on land, and in the air, and have been stirred by the news of war activities from the more distant parts of the Empire — New Zealand, Australia, Canada, South Africa, India, Newfoundland,[2] and, indeed, from all those far-flung lands which owe allegiance to the British Crown, and which manifest such impressive unity of purpose in the prosecution of the war. We like to hear how they are getting on.

It may, therefore, be of interest to my listeners across the Channel — that narrow strait which lies between us, but does not separate us — to hear something of Ulster's contribution to the common cause.

Prior to the outbreak of hostilities, when international affairs had reached a critical stage, each House of our local Parliament on March 22, 1938, passed a resolution which I should like to read to you, as an illustration of our early determination to give such support, as lies in our power, to those who guide the destinies of the British people. It was in these terms: 'That this House, fully realising the anxieties besetting his Majesty's Government of the United Kingdom at the present time, and praying that its efforts to attain and preserve peace throughout the world will be completely successful, assures the Prime Minister of that Government that, should any crisis arise, he can confidently rely upon the people of loyal Ulster to share the responsibilities and burdens with their kith and kin in other parts of the United Kingdom and the Empire, to the utmost of her resources.'

That undertaking we shall honour. Britain's difficulty is Northern Ireland's opportunity to place all her resources, both human and material, at the disposal of the United Kingdom in this hour of crisis. It is our desire also that this determination should be expressed to the full in terms of practical service and personal sacrifice.

In Great Britain it has been agreed to refrain from party controversy during the period of the war. It is our wish, too, that the voice of controversy should be stilled, and that, as a united people, we should bend all our energies towards the completion of the one supreme task confronting us. We cherish with you those traditions of democracy and freedom which alone make political controversy possible, and we should feel that we were acting a coward's part if, instead of taking an active share in safeguarding our common heritage, and preserving it for generations yet to be, we were to allow our attention to be diverted to less urgent questions.

I have spoken of our resources. What are these resources, and what contribution are we making

1. Neville Chamberlain (1869-1940), was British prime minister from 28 May 1937 to 10 May 1940.
2. Newfoundland was to become the tenth province of Canada after a referendum in 1949.

towards the national effort? Pride of place must be given to all those who have gone forth to serve in the Forces of the Crown. Northern Ireland has in the past always been to the forefront as a recruiting ground for the British Army, to which she has given many famous regiments, such as the Royal Inniskilling Fusiliers, the Royal Ulster Rifles, the Royal Irish Fusiliers, the North Irish Horse, and many others whose exploits are recorded on the scroll of history. Since the outbreak of war there has been a steady response to the call for volunteers; countless numbers of our young men have enlisted in the regiments to which I have just made reference and in other Army units, as well as in the Navy and in the Air Force. We have given, also, many men to the Mercantile Marine, for around our rock-bound and turbulent coast some of the finest seamen in the Kingdom have been born and bred. Those at home are, of course, engaged in some form of national service — in a host of important though less spectacular roles. Large numbers of our women, too, are employed in the women's auxiliary services, or are engaged in war hospital supply work or other useful activities on the 'home front.'

Secondly, I would mention the part being played by our farmers and farm labourers, whose skill in husbandry enables them to make a contribution of the greatest value at the present time. We are largely an agricultural community of small farmers cultivating nearly 100,000 holdings of which over 65 per cent. do not exceed 30 acres in extent. We have had, therefore, to build up and organise an agricultural system suitable for our peculiar local conditions. In recent years by education, by research, and, above all, by the improvement of marketing methods, we have been able to raise the standard of our agricultural produce and to increase the productivity of our farms. In peace time we send to Great Britain not only cattle, sheep, and pigs, but also such commodities as eggs, bacon, and potatoes.

It is now our aim to increase our contribution to the common larder and to render the greatest possible assistance within our power in augmenting the Nation's food production. We plan, for example, to plough a quarter of a million additional acres of land this year. On any of these wintry days — snow permitting — one may see all over the Ulster countryside the most modern type of tractor as well as horse-drawn ploughs passing to and fro across green fields, some of which have not been broken up within living memory.

In addition to an increase in our production of food and feeding stuffs, we are planning a substantially larger acreage of flax — a crop for the growing of which our land is suitable and in the handling of which our people are skilled. In these times, when imported supplies of flax are difficult to come by, it is important that our linen manufacturers should be in a position to obtain a supply of the raw material which will enable them not only to meet the needs of the Fighting Services, but also to maintain and expand the overseas trade of the United Kingdom — a vital consideration, as you all know, when enormous sums must be spent abroad in purchasing supplies essential for military purposes.

It is not generally known that in point of value linen goods constitute the second largest item in the export trade of the United Kingdom to the USA, and that the bulk of these goods come from Northern Ireland.

In the sphere of industry, too, we have at hand an unrivalled reservoir of technical skill and adaptability in the ranks of our artisans. We have a living tradition of craftsmanship which is being utilised to the full in many forms of specialised work which it would not be proper for me to reveal. All however — employers and employees — are concentrating their combined energies on the allotted tasks.

We have not lost sight, either, of the contribution our people can make in the financial field, and Northern Ireland has entered with enthusiasm into the National Savings campaign. Sales of Savings Certificates and Defence Bonds have been maintained at the rate of £100,000 per week. Perhaps I might also add that we bear exactly the same heavy burden of taxation as our fellow-citizens in Great Britain, and we are glad to be able this year to hand over to the British Treasury an Imperial contribution of £2,000,000.

So much for our positive efforts. On the home front we have accepted without question every restriction which the Imperial Government has deemed it necessary in the national interest to impose — the black-out, petrol, and food rationing, and all the other 'controls,' and we gladly recognise that it is one of the obligations of our common citizenship that we should endure them with good humour and a stout heart.

Our resources are by no means exhausted. We have an understanding with British Ministers that they will let us know from time to time of any requirements which it may be within our power to supply. It will be our proud ambition to meet such demands with energy and despatch.

I have tried to indicate very briefly a few of the ways in which we are endeavouring to pull our weight in the present struggle. But neither material resources nor human skill and ingenuity can by themselves ensure the victory of our cause. There must also be a deep-rooted conviction that those things for which we have taken up arms are dearer than life itself, an unflinching resolve on the part of our people not to cease from the fight until our purpose has been fully accomplished and a real and lasting victory achieved. It is this spirit which today animates Ulstermen and Ulsterwomen, as it does their fellow citizens in the rest of the United Kingdom and the Empire, and it is this spirit which, as in the past, will ensure the ultimate triumph of liberty, freedom, and justice.

We make no claim to having done anything more than our duty, nor do we claim superiority in patriotism over other parts of the United Kingdom, but I am anxious that all my listeners across the Channel should realise that though Ulster be but a small link in the chain which encircles and binds the Empire, she is, by virtue of her strategical position and her hardy Northern stock, a strong link — a link that will neither break nor bend before the King's enemies. We are King's men. We will be with you to the end.

IAN PAISLEY

(1926-)

GOSPEL POWER

THREE MEN GOING TO HELL, ALL LIVING IN BALLYMENA, THEIR NAMES SHALL BE GIVEN (1976)

[Ian Paisley's preaching is strongly influenced by the life and work of John Bunyan. In a lecture celebrating Bunyan, he calls him a 'dreamer and penman' and remarks that this 'poor unschooled tinker' became a prominent man of letters. Bunyan was able to draw enormous crowds, he suggests, because he had 'the tinker's power of reaching the heart'.]

'Woe unto you scribes, Pharisees, hypocrites!'
Matthew 23.15

Some people say 'What right has Ian Paisley to come to the Ballymena Town Hall and talk about three men going to hell?'

First of all, *let me say that there is a hell* and the hell which I preach is the hell which Jesus preached, the hell which the Bible speaks of, and the hell which is revealed in all its terror and torment, in the Word of God.

So if you are one of those people who with a shrug of your shoulders, can put away the thought of hell, then you are a fool because at the end of every life there is either Heaven with Christ or Hell without Him.

The second thing I want to say, by way of preface, is *that it would be a very happy thing if there were only three men in this town going to hell.* But the great tragedy is this that passing onward, quickly passing throughout this town, district and neighbourhood there are many scores of hundreds of precious souls, aye, thousands and ten thousands of men and women in this North Antrim constituency, and if this Bible is the Word of God (and it is), if Jesus Christ is the Son of God (and He is), if the gospel is God's Truth (and it is), then those scores of hundreds, those tens of thousands of men and women are going to a lost sinner's hell. That is why we are concerned. That is why we are praying. That is why, on Friday night, men give up their sleep to intercede before Almighty God for their fellows, their brothers, their sisters, their fathers, their mothers, their neighbours and their relations. They were praying in that prayer-meeting 'Lord, save them from hell.'

I trust that the reality of a lost eternity, I trust that the eternal verity of hell fire will be impressed in your heart this afternoon and that you will realise that we are handling things which are true, things which are eternal, and things which are established and cannot be altered.

This message which I am going to preach was prompted by a reading of that great immortal dream of John Bunyan's, the 'Pilgrim's Progress.'[1] No doubt, you will recognise some of Bunyan's characters as I proceed with my message. . . .

The first man in this town who is headed out for hell is Mr. Obstinate.

Now the Bible has many things to say about obstinacy of heart and mind and soul.

How many people in the Town Hall today are not saved just because they are obstinate? Just because of that stubbornness of sin, that iron brass neck which they have developed through sinning and wilful and continual sinning. When I press upon you the claims of the gospel, when I urge you to repent and believe the Word of God, when you feel the conviction of the Spirit, in the service, on your life and heart, what is it that keeps you from Jesus Christ? Obstinacy of will! Obstinacy of heart! Obstinacy of habit!

I want to show you from God's Word what God says about the obstinate man.

I Samuel chapter fifteen. This is a tremendous scripture. I would not have time this afternoon to plumb its depth, examine its truth or expound its great implications and ramifications. This is what God says about obstinacy. Verse twenty-three of this fifteenth chapter of I Samuel, *'For rebellion is as the sin of witchcraft, and stubbornness is as iniquity and idolatry.'* Do you hear it? 'Stubbornness is as iniquity and idolatry.'

You stubborn, obstinate, hard-willed, hard-hearted sinners, brought up in the evangelical tradition, brought up in the evangelical Protestant tradition, God says you are just as filthy and iniquitous in your sin as a pagan idolator who bows down to wood and stone. Stubbornness is as iniquity and idolatry.

Oh, stubborn sinner today, let me remind you that one day God will break that stubborn neck of yours. It will be broken in the day of death, and it will be broken in the day of judgment.

Listen to what the Book says over in Proverbs, *'He that being often reproved hardeneth his neck, shall suddenly be destroyed, and that without remedy.'* (Proverbs chapter twenty-nine and verse one). Let me repeat it friend, 'He that being often reproved hardeneth his neck, shall suddenly be destroyed, and that without remedy.'

Many years ago, with the Rev. John Wylie,[2] I erected a tent in the village of Dundonald in the outskirts of Belfast, and had a great Old Time Gospel Campaign. Five young men attended the mission services there night after night, and then one of them came to Christ. They continued to attend until four of them were redeemed and saved and one of them was still out of Christ. One night at the end of the meeting, standing in the doorway of the tent, the four men were round their companion. I can see them now, and they were pleading with him to make the great decision, to trust Christ, to be saved and complete the circle of five. They called me down to the door and they said 'Mr. Paisley, we all came together to the meetings. Four of us are saved, and our friend here has not come to Christ' and those young men wept for their companion. I opened the Word of God and I showed him the way of salvation as plainly as I could put it, as simple as the Book says it. That young man looked at me and he said 'I am not coming to Christ.' I can hear his words in my ear at this moment, 'I am not coming to Christ.' His companions cried out in utter despair. I told them to continue to pray — and the five of them went down the Comber Road. That young man went home. Some days later when he awoke one morning he was mentally deranged. He could not understand a thing. They had to take him to a mental hospital and there, as far as I am aware, he is to this day.

'He that being often reproved hardeneth his neck, shall suddenly be destroyed, and that without remedy.'[3] *'Because there is wrath beware, lest He take thee away with his stroke, then a great ransom cannot deliver thee.'*[4] Do not be playing with your soul friend. Do not be gambling with time that is not yours. Do not be treating eternal things as trivialities. Obstinate sinner, today I command you in the Name of Jesus Christ, repent and believe the gospel. Turn to Christ and seek the meekness which comes through the Blood of the Lamb.

1. John Bunyan (1628-88), English puritan preacher and writer, imprisoned for twelve years during the reign of Charles II. *The Pilgrim's Progress, from This World to That Which is to Come* was published in 1678.

2. A close associate of Ian Paisley during the 1950s and 1960s.
3. Proverbs 29.1.
4. Job 36.18.

I want to turn now to the second man in Ballymena. He is a man you will find in every church in this town. He is a good church attender and he is a good mission hall attender. You will always find him among the people of God.

His father was *Mr. Sham.* And I am sure you have met that man about this town. His mother was *Miss Deceit*. Now if you marry Sham to Deceit, the result is *Hypocrisy*.

The second man I want to talk about is the hypocrite. The man that pretends to be what he is not. The man who gives an outward appearance, but inside he is the very opposite to that outward appearance.

I want to say something to the hypocrite in this meeting. I know there are such hypocrites here. There are people who go to church on the Sabbath Day, who sing in the choir, who teach in the Sabbath School, who hold office in the church but they never have been born again. They have never been saved and washed in the Blood of Christ, and yet they pretend to be children of God. They go and come from the place of the holy. They stand and sit with God's people. They stand and sing the songs of Zion. They handle the sacred things of God, but their hearts have never been changed by God's Sovereign Grace.

I want to tell you, Mr. Hypocrite, three things.

Number one, God knows you. Now I do not know you. You could pull the wool over my eyes. You could pull the wool over Mr. Begg's eyes, over Mr. Cooke's eyes. You could pull the wool over the eyes of the best good-living man in this town who knows his God and walks with Christ. My friend, you do not deceive God Almighty. *God knows you!* He knows the hypocrisy of your heart. He knows how you are covering up your old iniquitous living. He knows how deceitful, how two-faced and what a sham and a liar you are. *God knows you.* You can deceive your friends. You can deceive your wife. Is there some man living a double life here today? His wife thinks he is straight up and down, but he is a snivelling hypocrite. He is playing around with the affections of another woman. He is trying to tell his wife that he is faithful to his marriage vows. I tell you man, God sees you and God knows all about you.

Is there someone here today in this service and they are not right with their God? Let me say to you, *God knows you.* It is simple, but how true it is. Yes, and I could go on and talk about people living double lives, pretending one thing and doing the opposite.

Secondly, that Life will prove you. You can put on a fair show in the flesh for a time. You can cover it up for a time. You can conceal it for a time. You can bury it for a time. But I want to tell you, woman, some day your sins will rise up and confront you. Be sure your sin will find you out. Oh, yes, man, your sins will find you out.

I could tell you story after story about men and women whose sins found them out. To the surprise of their neighbours, to the surprise of their wives, to the surprise of their husbands, and to the surprise of their family, their sin was uncovered.

'Be not deceived, God is not mocked, whatsoever a man soweth that shall he also reap.'[5]

Sir, you will reap what you are sowing. Madam, you will reap what you are sowing. The harvest will certainly come, and you will reap whatsoever you sow.

One final word. *Death will unmask you.*

Oh, there is an unmasking day coming for the hypocrite. My, when the cold river of death flows at our feet, when the great summons to meet God reaches us, when the curtains of that great corridor of death are drawn aside, when a hand greater than eternity seizes us and urges along that dark lonely journey through the waters of death, out into the great eternity, I tell you, all your hypocrisy will be unmasked then. Unconverted communicant member of the church, how will you do when you come to die? Passing yourself off as a Christian will not help you then. All that will be torn from you, and you will be portrayed in the nakedness of your sin, in the shame of your hypocrisy before the God Whose eyes will search you through and through.

The saddest death, the most tragic death is the death of the hypocrite. It was to the hypocrites Jesus said 'Ye serpents, ye generation of vipers, how can ye escape the damnation of hell?'[6]

Have done with hypocrisy. Have done with sham. Have done with the lie. Get right with God. Really get converted. Really get saved. Really get washed in the Blood of the Lamb. Go out with the full assurance of faith, having your heart sprinkled with the precious pardoning Blood of Christ.

The last man I want to speak about is a man who is found in every locality and district. He comes of

5. Galatians 6.7.
6. Matthew 12.34.

the *Sloth* family. And his mother was a *Miss Take-it-easy*. His name is *Presumption*. He is not in any hurry. I need to be saved, but I am not getting saved today. I know those men down in the Waveney Road were praying on Friday night. I know I need to be saved, but I am not getting saved today. I know there is a Heaven to be gained and a Hell to be shunned. I know that. I know that Jesus died for my sin, He shed His Blood to pardon me. I know if I trusted Christ and came to Him, He would receive me, 'For him that cometh unto me I will in no wise cast out,'[7] He says.

But I am not coming today. I have no intention of being saved today. I have no intention of trusting Christ today. Some more convenient day I will call on you, but not today. I have plenty of time. I am going to enjoy life. I am going to have my pleasure. I am going to spend my youth in comfort, then maybe I will come to Christ, and trust Him. I have plenty of time.

That is the greatest lie the devil ever whispered in your ear. You have not got plenty of time. The only time you have is now. 'Now is the accepted time, (says the infallible Book) now is the day of salvation.'[8]

I want to finish this message with a story which is very appropriate.

There was a prominent man who lived in this locality of Ballymena. He was in the grocery business. I had a friend of mine worked for him. It was from this friend I got the story. This businessman was not a Christian. Two Faith Mission pilgrims came to a certain mission hall near to where this man had his business. This friend of mine who worked for him asked him to go to the mission and he went. He came under conviction of sin, and he realised that he had a decision to make. He needed to trust Christ and be saved. But he resisted the Spirit of God. In his resistance he was miserable, as a convicted, undecided sinner always is. Now he went on for some time in this misery. He could not eat, he could not sleep, he could not attend to his business.

One day a traveller came in and said to him 'You do not look well.' He replied 'I am not well.' The traveller said, 'What is wrong with you?' He responded, 'I do not know. There were two Faith Mission pilgrims who came and preached the gospel. I attended the meetings.' The traveller said, 'Did you get saved?' He said 'No, I did not get saved. I would not accept Christ. I was not going to get converted but ever since I have been miserable. I can neither sleep nor eat, nor attend to my business.' The man was an emissary of hell sent to that man. Do you know what he said? He said 'You have plenty of time. As long as the candle holds out to burn, the greatest sinner may return. Your candle is burning, brightly, you have years before you. Do not trouble about it any more.'

That little couplet became a deception and a deceit to that man. My friend who worked for him told him to get saved, to get right with God, and when the mission came to an end he pleaded with him to go and settle the matter. The man only laughed and said 'As long as the candle holds out to burn, Tom, the greatest sinner may return. There is no need for me to be in a hurry.'

That man did well in business. He wanted to do better and he sold his grocery establishment and bought a well-known pub. If he did well in groceries, he did better still in the devil's butter-milk, in liquor. He was well received. He was a prominent free mason. One night there was a Masonic Lodge meeting and dinner in Brough-shane. He was the guest of honour. He made a brilliant speech and his masonic brethren hailed him for an up and coming man. He was just in his early forties.

He came back home. He drove up the drive into his house, but he did not know he was driving up the drive for the last time. He thought as long as the candle held out to burn, the greatest sinner may return. He put his latch key in the front door. He did not know he was opening his own front door for the last time. He stepped into the hall. His wife met him and she asked, 'How did your dinner go?' He said 'It was great. I delivered the speech of the evening. My masonic brethren cheered until the rafters of the hall rang!' He added 'I am a bit tired. I will see you upstairs dear.' He climbed the stairs, but he did not know he was climbing the stairs for the last time. 'As long as the candle holds out to burn, the greatest sinner may return.' He opened the door of his bedroom. He did not know he was opening it for the last time. He went in and shut that door and shut himself in with death. His wife came up the stairs five minutes later, he was lying across the bed and his body was lifeless, and his soul was in a lost eternity.

7. John 6.37.
8. II Corinthians 6.2.

Do you know what that man did? He presumed on Almighty God. He thought he had plenty of time. 'As long as the candle holds out to burn, the greatest sinner may return.'

Friend, the candle of your life could be almost out. This may be the last hour you will live. The car could be on the road that is going to knock you into eternity. The shroud could be woven that will wrap your lifeless body, the wood cut and the coffin made that will encase your corpse. Ah friend, do not be a fool. In God's Name with God's Bible in my hand let me give you this text of scripture, 'Boast not thyself of tomorrow, for thou knowest not what a day may bring forth.'[9]

O come sinner, come,
O why do you delay?
The striking invitation is
That you should come today,
Tomorrow has no promise,
That it can give to you,
Tomorrow is Eternity
Just hidden from your view,
O come sinner come,
Accept the proffered grace,
For death may soon be calling you
Into her cold embrace.
The harvest will be ended,
The summer will be past,
Your lamentation then will be,
My soul is lost at last.

Lost at last! Lost at last! Lost at last!
God forbid that should ever be *your* lamentation.

AMEN AND AMEN!

9. Proverbs 27.1.

from:
WHAT THINK YE OF CHRIST? (1976)

[Puritan preaching is remarkable for its habit of autobiographical witness. In the introduction to this sermon Paisley recalls his student days at the Barry School of Evangelism in South Wales.]

I served my apprenticeship in preaching in the open air. I had a great tutor. My tutor in open-air preaching was a man that had been saved from the very depths of sin and from the dark dungeons of evil habit and polluting vice. His name was Teddy Sherwood. Once he was the champion welterweight boxer of Southern England. He had his prize gold belt always at the gospel meetings. He used to swing that great gold belt, which he won as the welterweight for the South of England, around his head and shout as only Ted Sherwood could shout. He had a voice like a trumpet. People had to heed and listen to him. When he got tired and husky, he used to say, 'Go on Ian, you have a go.' So he drew the crowd, and so I served my apprenticeship, preaching when his voice was gone, his throat husky and his powerful frame exhausted.

I remember very well, one Lord's Day afternoon during the war on Barry Island in South Wales. There was a tremendous gathering of servicemen and women at the amusements in that great amusement centre. I remember Teddy taking his gold belt and swinging it round his head as hard as he could, and shouting for the crowd to come. They gathered in their hundreds to hear that man preach. He threw down the belt, pulled off his coat, and rolled up his sleeves. When Teddy preached, you would have thought he was back in the boxing ring. I used to say 'Teddy, you are taking on the devil.' He used to reply, 'Hallelujah! brother, I will give him a cauliflower ear tonight.' He would set about preaching like an old boxer would set about boxing in the ring.

After he had finished preaching one evening he said 'Ian, come on, get into the ring.' I was only a stripling lad of sixteen. I stood there with a Bible in my hand. As best as I could I followed that great open-air preacher. The crowd stayed, and a young woman started to heckle me. Of course, in those days I was a foolish young man. I thought that I could talk a woman down. I have more sense now. I know you could not talk any woman down. I talked on, and the crowd cried out, 'Come on and answer her question. Come on, answer her question.' I stopped and I said, 'What is your question?' She said 'How do you know there is a Jesus Christ? How do you know there is a Jesus Christ?' And oh, a great shout of derision went up from the ungodly in that crowd.

Here was I, a mere stripling with little experience, faced with a hostile crowd. I sent a prayer to Heaven. I said, 'Lord, give me an answer. Turn this weapon as a boomerang in the face of the devil.' God gave me the answer. I said, 'Young woman, I come from Ireland, and an Irishman always answers a question by asking another. I will answer your question, if you will answer me a question?' 'What is your question?' she replied. I said, 'Could you tell me what day it is?' The crowd laughed. She said, 'It is Sunday.' I said, 'Could you tell me what *month* it is?' She said, 'It is the month of August.' I said, 'Now I have only one more question. Could you tell me what *year* it is?' The crowd saw what I was getting at now. They started to laugh and sneer at her. She said, 'It is nineteen hundred and forty-two.' I cried. 'Where did you get that from? Nineteen hundred and forty-two years from where?' She mumbled and stuttered. I said, 'I will help you out. It is A.D., it is the year of our Lord, after the death of Christ. There is a Christ and young woman, when you take your Diary out and look at the year, that number stands as a living testimony that there is a Christ.'

Oh, friend, the best established fact in history is the Person of Jesus Christ. Let me talk about that Person tonight. Who would deny the Person of Jesus? Only a fool would shut his eyes to the reality of Christ. Christ divides men. Christ divides people. Christ divides history. Jesus Christ!

from:
AN EXPOSITION OF THE EPISTLE TO THE ROMANS (1966)

[In 1966 Paisley was imprisoned for three months for demonstrating against the Unionist government outside the General Assembly of the presbyterian church. In a statement he attacked the prime minister, Terence O'Neill, saying: 'It will take more than Captain O'Neill's nasal twang to defy us.' O'Neill replied with a warning against alienating 'our British friends' and referred to Northern Ireland as 'this small corner of the British Commonwealth'. Angered by O'Neill's patronizing view of the province, Paisley replied: 'To Our Lord, puppet politicians are but grasshoppers with portfolios.' While in jail in July 1966, Paisley wrote an exposition of St Paul's *Epistle to the Romans*.]

The Desire of Preaching

'I am ready to preach,' v. 15.[1]

'So, as much as in me is, I am ready to preach the gospel to you that are at Rome also,' v. 15.

Paul was a true preacher. He must preach, yea, woe was unto him if he preached not the gospel.

He was ready to preach to everybody in every place, at every opportunity and under every circumstance.

He could do nothing else but preach. When in prison he could not be silenced but through his pen he preached the gospel round the world and to all generations.

In the days of the great evangelical awakening a prominent Church of England clergyman was reported to his bishop for preaching at times other than those recognized by the laws of the established Church. Summoned before the bishop the clergyman was asked, 'How many times do you preach?' 'Only two times your lordship,' was the quick reply. 'When is that?' questioned the bishop, 'for I hear you are always preaching.' 'In season and out of season,' retorted the preacher.

Yes indeed, in season and out of season, that is when the true preacher is at his business.

These silent sabbaths troubled the imprisoned Rutherford[2] and they most certainly trouble, at this very moment, the writer of these lines. Loyalty to Christ, even if it entails silence, however, is far more important than the liberty of the preacher. What we cannot preach we can nevertheless pen. For this we are indeed more than grateful to God and to the prison governor. In the vast majority of countries no such privilege would be ours.

The Defence of Preaching

'I am not ashamed of the gospel of Christ,' v. 16.

Paul was a defender both of the gospel and of the pulpit. He was unashamedly a preacher. He stood up for both his message and the means by which it was delivered. The message was divine and dynamic and the means of its delivery were also divine and dynamic.

Paul calls the message, 'the power of God' in this first chapter of Romans and in the first chapter of First Corinthians he calls the means 'The power of God'.

'For the preaching of the cross is to them that perish foolishness; but unto us which are saved it is the power of God' (I Cor. 1:18).

1. The verses are all from Romans, chapter 1.

2. Samuel Rutherford (1600-61), Scottish presbyterian clergyman. His *Lex, Rex* (1644) gained him wide attention as a political theorist. The book was ordered to be burned after the Restoration when he was removed from his official positions and summoned by parliament on a charge of treason. He died before his trial.

He also maintains in this verse (verse 16) that the end of the gospel is the salvation of both Jew and Greek. In the first chapter of First Corinthians he maintains the very same of the preaching of the gospel. 'It pleased God by the foolishness of preaching to save them that believe. For the Jews require a sign and the Greeks seek after wisdom: But we preach Christ crucified, unto the Jews a stumbling block, and unto the Greeks foolishness: But unto them which are called, both Jews and Greeks, Christ the power of God, and the wisdom of God' (I Cor. 1:24). With Paul the gospel and its preaching could not be divorced. They were eternally united. The attempt to divorce them has wrought havoc with Twentieth Century Christianity. Today the pulpit is weak. Its authority is usurped. Consequently the church is paralysed. Ministers are good executives rather than good expositors. They do not give themselves to prayer and the ministry of the word like the early apostles. Preaching, the divinely appointed means, is discountenanced and the tragic results are evident. The church needs to return to preaching, old-fashioned, heaven-blessed, soul-stirring, sin-slaying preaching. The greatest need of the hour is a band of prophets with flaming message to set the land on fire.

The church's ministers today are mere clerical puppets on wire.

God's ministers are flames of fire.

The Reformation came through preaching. In Protestantism, apostolic and pure, the preacher displaced the priest. Today in Protestantism, apostate and corrupt, the priest has displaced the preacher. The Reformation is in reverse. Such Protestantism falls an easy prey to the wolf of popery. This displacing of the preacher is manifested in modern church architecture. The pulpit no longer dominates for the modern cleric cannot preach. The central position is occupied by what is called the altar. The pulpit is pushed aside for the Word of God is rejected and a self-styled priest capable only of essay reading has taken the place of the preacher.

All true revivals are revivals of great preaching. When the trumpet of God really sounds then do sinners awaken from their slumbers of death. Oh for strength to blow the gospel trumpet!

The Dynamic of Preaching
'for it is the power of God', v. 16.

Gospel preaching is charged with the dynamic of heaven. Dynamite to be displayed in all its mighty potency must have the fuse and the fire. When the fuse of true prayer is set alight with the fire of the Holy Ghost and thus the gospel dynamite is exploded, what tremendous results occur. Then do the strongholds of Satan topple. Then do the bulwarks of idolatry collapse. Then do the towering walls of sin suddenly fall. Then is the enemy dislodged. Then is all opposition blasted and the power of truth is proved to be more than a conqueror. Oh for a day of real gospel preaching and gospel power! Lord let me witness such a day.

Human power stands impotent in the presence of the sins of our age. Divine power stands omnipotent over the sins of all ages. Oh for its mighty manifestation!

THE THREE HEBREW CHILDREN (1985)

[On 14 November 1985, Paisley denounced the Anglo-Irish Agreement, which was signed the following day in Hillsborough Castle, Co. Down.]

Having failed to defeat the IRA you now have capitulated and are prepared to set in motion machinery which will achieve the IRA goal — a united Ireland. We now know that you have prepared the Ulster unionists for sacrifice on the altar of political expediency.

They are to be the sacrificial lambs to appease the Dublin wolves. You can build your altar: you can use bent and corrupted law to ignite the fire; you can prepare to stifle truth with a propaganda of lies paid for out of the taxpayers' pocket; you can bring into Northern Ireland those who illegally and unconstitutionally claim jurisdiction over this part of the Queen's dominions; you can wine and dine them on Ulster's soil and in the Queen's residence; you can offer bribes to the Iscariots who in their day of betrayal always surface with hands outstretched for the blood money — but you can never break the spirit of Ulster unionism.

Like the three Hebrew children,[1] we will not budge, we will not bend and we will not burn. This simple sum you will have to learn the hard way — six into 26 will never go.

1. Daniel, chapter 3.

HAROLD J. McCUSKER

(1940-90)

'WAITING LIKE A DOG: THE GATES OF HILLSBOROUGH' (1985)

[On 27 November 1985, the British House of Commons debated the Anglo-Irish Agreement which had been signed on 15 November by the British prime minister, Margaret Thatcher, and the Taoiseach of the Irish Republic, Dr Garret FitzGerald. In the debate, the Official Unionist MP, Harold McCusker, gave personal witness to his feelings about the Agreement.]

When a journalist described my reaction to the Prime Minister's statement on 18 November, he said that it was the most bitter of all. I should like to believe that, while it might have been the most bitter of all, the bitterness was conveyed with dignity. As I try to explain that bitterness, I hope that I shall also conduct myself with dignity.

The agreement deals with my most cherished ideals and aspirations. On three occasions in the week prior to the signing of the agreement, on the Tuesday, Wednesday, and Thursday, I stood in the House, having been told in essence by foreign journals what the agreement contained, and it was denied to me that an agreement existed or had even been reached.

I went to Hillsborough[1] on the Friday morning, despite the obstacles put in my way by the Northern Ireland Office, the headquarters of the RUC, the divisional commander in Lisburn and the police commander in Hillsborough. I stood outside Hillsborough, not waving a Union flag — I doubt whether I will ever wave one again — not singing hymns, saying prayers or protesting, but like a dog and asked the Government to put in my hand the document that sold my birthright. They told me that they would give it to me as soon as possible. Having never consulted me, never sought my opinion or asked my advice, they told the rest of the world what was in store for me.

I stood in the cold outside the gates of Hillsborough castle and waited for them to come out and give me the agreement second hand. It is even more despicable that they could not even send one of their servants to give it to me. I had been told three hours before that it would be brought out to me. At 2.45 pm, 15 minutes after the press conference had begun, I asked a policeman whether he would bring me the declaration that betrayed everything that I had ever stood for. A senior police officer went into Hillsborough castle, asked for the document and brought it out to me.

I felt desolate because as I stood in the cold outside Hillsborough castle everything that I held dear turned to ashes in my mouth. Even in my most pessimistic moments, reading the precise detail in the Irish press on the Wednesday before, I never believed that the agreement would deliver me, in the context that it has, into the hands of those who for 15 years have murdered personal friends, political associates and hundreds of my constituents. I hope that no one else in the House ever has to stand outside the gates of anywhere and see his most cherished privileges and ideals turn to dust and ashes in his mouth. That is what it felt like to me.

For 12 years I have asked for only one thing in the House. I believed voices on this Bench, no doubt well-intentioned but foolish, telling me that the House of Commons would one day treat me in the same way as my fellow citizens. I listened to people from other parties telling me the same thing. I am glad to report that even Labour Members were telling me the same thing — if I asked the House to treat me like my fellow citizens, conferring no special privileges or benefits, and I would simply meet my obligations, one day I hoped they would treat me like my fellow citizens.

I pursued that and I told the people of Northern Ireland that. When I walked behind nine funerals in one day and could not console the people, I told them that. When we buried Sir Norman Stronge,[2] Her Majesty's lieutenant in county Armagh, and his son on the same day, I told them, 'Don't worry;

1. The Anglo-Irish Agreement was signed in Hillsborough Castle, Co. Down.

2. Sir Norman Stronge (1895-1981), speaker of the Stormont parliament (1944-69), was shot dead, along with his son, James, by the Provisional IRA on 21 January 1981.

the House of Commons is above party. It has a responsibility to cherish all the children of the nation'. That was said in the proclamation of 1916.[3] I thought that I belonged to the nation, and I thought that the House had an obligation to cherish me as it cherished the rest. When I read the agreement, I realised that that would never be the case.

I have lost 12 years. I have only one complaint. Why was I not told 12 years ago? There are one or two honourable exceptions. The right hon. Member for Waveney (Mr. Prior)[4] told me four or five years ago as precisely as he could. Another prominent member of the Government Front Bench, a very gentle man whose integrity would be accepted by everyone in the House, tried to nudge me towards that realisation nine years ago. I was not prepared to believe it. I thought that one day I would gain equality. Why did not successive Governments tell me that I would never be treated with equality? If I had been told, my attitude over the past 12 years would have been different. I would have looked at political developments in Northern Ireland differently.

The right hon. Member for Old Bexley and Sidcup (Mr. Heath)[5] talked about unscrupulous misrepresentation. I have three children in Northern Ireland as well as my constituents, so what have I to gain by unscrupulously misrepresenting my position?

I had to go home on the Friday night after the Hillsborough agreement and tell my wife that I regretted bringing up our children to believe what hon. Members have brought their children up to believe because they will have to live with the legacy that I have to live with. It would have been better if they had never looked at the Union flag or thought that they were British or put their trust in the House of Commons than spending the rest of their lives knowing that they are now some sort of semi-British citizen.

I shall not argue with the Secretary of State[6] about sovereignty because the House can change what it means by that. That came out in the debate yesterday. Sovereignty is what the Government decide it is. The one thing that the right hon. Gentleman cannot deny, and that the right hon. Member for Waveney (Mr. Prior) did not deny, is that the way in which Northern Ireland is now governed has changed fundamentally. I am being told that I should be prepared to accept this fundamental change in the way in which Northern Ireland is governed because of article 1.[7]

The Secretary of State accused me of parroting. I wonder what he would consider this to be. In one hour during the statement on the agreement the Prime Minister said 15 times that Northern Ireland would remain part of the United Kingdom. As well as repeating that 15 times, she assured us eight times that there was no derogation of responsibility for Northern Ireland from the Government of the United Kingdom.

On those 23 occasions, the right hon. Lady felt compelled to garnish those statements with all sorts of high-falutin' language, such as:

> the most formal commitment made by any Irish Government .... For the first time, the Republic has recognised the legitimacy of the Unionist cause .... the best guarantee from the Republic that the people of Northern Ireland have ever had .... This is the first time that we have had a recognition of that in writing from the Republic of Ireland .... I believe that this is the first time in a formal international agreement that the Republic has recognised this position in Northern Ireland.— [*Official Report*, 18 November 1985; Vol. 87, c. 19-31.]

I went to the Public Record Office in Northern Ireland and got a copy of another internationally binding agreement, signed by Stanley Baldwin[8] on behalf of the British Government, by Liam

3. The 1937 Constitution of Ireland, largely drafted by Eamon de Valera, contains a commitment to 'cherish all the children of the nation equally.'
4. James Prior (b. 1927), a British Conservative MP, was secretary of state for Northern Ireland 1981-84.
5. Edward Heath (b. 1916), a British Conservative MP and prime minister 1970-74.
6. Tom King (b. 1933) was the secretary of state for Northern Ireland at the institution of the Anglo-Irish Agreement.
7. Article 1 of the Anglo-Irish Agreement states: 'Status of Northern Ireland. The two Governments (a) affirm that any change in the status of Northern Ireland would only come about with the consent of a majority of the people of Northern Ireland; (b) recognize that the present wish of a majority of the people of Northern Ireland is for no change in the status of Northern Ireland; (c) declare that, if in the future a majority of the people of Northern Ireland clearly wish for and formally consent to the establishment of a united Ireland, they will introduce and support in the respective Parliaments legislation to give effect to that wish.'
8. Stanley Baldwin (1867-1947), British prime minister 1923-24, 1924-29, 1935-37.

Cosgrave[9] and Kevin O'Higgins[10] on behalf of the Government of the Irish Free State and by James Craig[11] on behalf of the Government of Northern Ireland. It was signed on 3 December 1925 and lodged in the League of Nations on 8 February 1926. If hon. Members are interested, it is registration No. 1088, page 263, of the 'League of Nations Treaty Series'.

That agreement recognised the legitimacy of the state of Northern Ireland. It recognised the international frontier of Northern Ireland. Of course, five or six years later, De Valera said that it was extracted under duress. That was about four years after he had had Kevin O'Higgins murdered,[12] who, after he had signed that agreement, described it as the best day's work that he had ever done for Ireland.

It was easy for De Valera to tear up the agreement and say that it had been extracted under duress when Kevin O'Higgins had been murdered some years previously.

Those are the people I am expected to believe and to put my trust in. Those are the people who will deliver the measures that will save my constituents. Why did they not save the people to whom I have just referred? Why did they not save the 230 of my constituents who have been murdered over the past 12 years? I have listened to Secretary of State after Secretary of State telling me that there is nothing more they can do. Secretaries of State have said, 'Co-operation is so good that it cannot be improved.' But now things can be done. If one pays the right price, people are prepared to stop killing unionists and those who put their trust in the British House of Commons, which itself cannot protect them.

If hon. Members are wondering why I was angry about having to stand like a dog outside Hillsborough, let me bring this document to their attention. It is produced by the Irish Labour party, entitled 'Anglo-Irish Agreement', and has the photograph of Dick Spring[13] on it. It is the party's official response to the agreement. It was issued with a covering letter by Dick Spring, dated 15 November. That was the day when the agreement was signed. Is any one suggesting to me that Dick Spring ran home to Cork[14] immediately after signing the agreement and had this document with his photograph published and sent out to his constituents to tell them what he was doing? The document was printed perhaps two or three days before the agreement was signed, when I was being told in the House, 'There is no agreement. We might not even reach an agreement.'

Mr. Spring refers to other things in the document, such as the signing of the European convention. I have been told that the first benefit of the agreement is that my constitutional position is now more secure than ever. The second is supposed to be the convention. Mr. Spring says:

> When this Convention was first introduced in 1977 it was believed we could not sign it because of the particular interpretation of our High Court of 'political offences' for extradition purposes. But in the light of the fact that our Courts now make a distinction between terrorist offences and truly political offences this obstacle has been removed. The form of any legislation giving effect to our accession to the Convention would be designed to ensure that the final decision as to whether a particular offence is political or terrorist will continue to be determined by the Courts.

The constitutional position has not changed one iota. According to the constitution, the Republic could not sign the convention. It is now able to sign the agreement because the court has moved from A to B. If the court can move from A to B, what assurance do Her Majesty's Government have that it cannot move from B to A? The decision that was taken by the High court, which is now considered to be so significant, was on whether the gunning down of a 73-year-old widow — a non-combatant, an ordinary elderly rural widow — was a political offence. Even the High court in Dublin could not bring itself to admit that murdering a 73-year-old widow could be construed as a political offence. That is what the decision is based on.

I wonder whether the same High court would make the same decision if it were confronted with

9. William T. Cosgrave (1880-1965), Irish nationalist politician and first president of the executive council of the Irish Free State 1922-32.
10. Kevin O'Higgins (1892-1927), minister for justice and external affairs after the establishment of the Irish Free State.
11. James Craig (1871-1940), first prime minister of Northern Ireland 1921-40.
12. Kevin O'Higgins was shot dead by an unknown gunman on 10 July 1927 while he was on his way to Mass in Booterstown, Co. Dublin.
13. Dick Spring (b. 1950), leader of Ireland's Labour Party since 1982 and Tánaiste (deputy prime minister) of the Irish Republic 1982-87.

14. Dick Spring's home is, in fact, in Tralee, Co. Kerry.

an extradition request for a young man who confronted an Army or police patrol and shot a member of the Regular Army or the UDR,[15] or a policeman, escaped across the border and was arrested. I wonder whether the High court would say that it was not a political offence when that man stood in the court and said, 'As a soldier in the Irish Republican Army I killed that British invading soldier in pursuit of my political objectives.' That is when the test will come. The Government have been given no assurance. Today, we are making a case on the basis that the High court in Dublin will find that to be a criminal rather than a political offence. I wish that I could trust the Republic more on that one than on the declaration of my constitutional position.

Article 1 of the agreement is a statement of fact. The fact that two and two make four does not have to be lodged at the United Nations. I know that two and two make four. There is no definition of the status of Northern Ireland. The Sunningdale agreement[16] has been mentioned. From our point of view, it was much better than this agreement. What does Dick Spring say? What does the deputy Prime Minister of the Government who signed the agreement say? He has an interesting observation. He also mentions the 'first time'. We have been told for a week now that this is the first time for us — a big benefit for us. It is also the first time for Dick Spring, who says:

> But this Agreement for the first time commits the British Government to introducing and supporting legislation for the reunification of Ireland if and when the consent emerges. This commitment settles once and for all the argument about whether Britain wants to stay in the North.

That is why they could not say that Northern Ireland is part of the United Kingdom.

Hon. Members can rest assured of this. I shall never have to explain to my constituents again why the Prime Minister believes that they are as British as the people of Finchley.[17] I shall never have to listen to people telling me that Northern Ireland is an integral part of the United Kingdom. We shall never hear those words. They will be removed from the political dictionary of Northern Ireland.

This is where we come to the crunch because it is where misrepresentation will occur. In return a commitment has been given to the Irish Government that they can interfere with every aspect of life in Northern Ireland.

MR. TOM KING *indicated dissent*.

MR. McCUSKER: The right hon. Gentleman need not shake his head. This is more than a consultative role. He said that. If he wants to deny it, he can intervene. He said that on a BBC radio programme. When pushed to say why it was more than a consultative role, he said, 'It has to be more than a consultative role because if it was not Dr. FitzGerald[18] would have no power. Oh sorry, I did not mean to use that word.' [*Interruption*] We can get out the transcript and look at it. I challenge the right hon. Gentleman to say that. Garret FitzGerald says that it is more than a consultative role. The right hon. Gentleman also said it.

I am sorry to take so much time on this, but it is important. It is more important to me and the people of Northern Ireland than to anyone else. The right hon. Gentleman has accused me of lying and misrepresenting the agreement. Let me take him through it. Is the conference concerned with every aspect of life in Northern Ireland? Can this conference discuss every aspect of the life of the people of Northern Ireland? If it cannot, will the right hon. Gentleman please stand up and tell me that it cannot? When he does not take that opportunity, I presume that that it is a reasonable statement.

The conference will be chaired by joint chairmen when it meets on its most important occasions. The right hon. Gentleman is not the chairman and his junior partner the deputy chairman. There will be joint chairmen. The joint chairman from the Republic will be a permanent Minister from the Government of the Republic. He will be joined on occasions by other Ministers from the Republic and from the Northern Ireland Office. They will be

15. Ulster Defence Regiment.
16. Representatives of the three parties participating in the Northern Ireland Executive met representatives of the British and Irish governments in December 1973 at Sunningdale near London. On 9 December an agreement was reached on the future establishment of a Council of Ireland with some loosely defined executive power to be shared equally by North and South. Direct rule from Westminster ended on 31 December 1973.
17. Margaret Thatcher (b. 1925), leader of the Conservative Party since 1975 and British prime minister since 1979, is MP for Finchley.
18. Garret FitzGerald (b. 1926), Taoiseach (prime minister) of the Irish Republic June 1981-March 1982 and December 1982-March 1987.

joined by advisers and others. At that conference, where they are able to discuss every aspect of life in Northern Ireland, the Government of the Republic can put forward ideas and proposals for the better government of Northern Ireland.

Therefore, we have the meeting convened with its joint chairmen, able to put on the table views and ideas about the Government of my Province. Both parties can do that, but it is the fact of a foreign Government doing that which concerns me. Not only will those views and ideas be put on the table, but the British Government have entered into an international binding agreement that they will seek to remove any obstacles and reach agreement on the various ideas and proposals. The right hon. Gentleman says that that is not the case, but this international declaration states:

> In the interest of promoting peace and stability, determined efforts shall be made through the Conference to resolve any differences.

The Prime Minister of the Irish Republic, the other partner in this deal, has said that the conference could fail only if there were a series of disagreements which would show bad faith on the side of either party. He went on, when pressed, to say that many of the proposals that they would make would be taken on board.

We are told today that matters will not all be secret and that efforts will be made to tell the people of Northern Ireland what it is all about. But in essence, irrespective of whether we argue about sovereignty, a coalition will govern Northern Ireland. On one side of that coalition will be Her Majesty's Government and on the other side will be the Government of the Irish Republic. They will have all their Ministers and advisers with them. Proposals will be put on the table by both parties concerning every aspect of life in Northern Ireland. Determined efforts will be made to reach agreements, and that means that on most occasions agreements will be reached. When those agreements are reached, that will be the decision that is taken. If that is not the case, will the right hon. Gentleman please stand up and tell me that I am wrong? I presume that he will tell me later that I am wrong and I look forward to that.

Will the right hon. Gentleman also answer the point that I put to the Leader of the House last Thursday when I said that this agreement renders me redundant? I honestly do not know any longer what role I have as a Member of Parliament. If every aspect of life in Northern Ireland will be dealt with under the auspices of this conference — that is the case — I presume that proposals for draft orders will be considered by the conference. When they come to this House, they will do so with the approval of the conference. If that is the case, what role have I? If I manage to convince the right hon. Gentleman that there is something wrong in his proposals for a draft order, he cannot stand at the Dispatch Box and say that he will change them. That would be an act of bad faith vis-à-vis his partners in the coaliton. He will have to go back to them and say that there is new information and ask that the matter be reconsidered. If that is wrong, will the right hon. Gentleman please tell me?

I have suffered the systematic humiliation of being excluded from the government of the part of the country to which I belong because I thought that price was worth paying to be a British citizen. I will not suffer this humiliation. I will not come along here as a self-seeking time server and pretend that I am a Member of Parliament when I am not. That is what the people of Northern Ireland will think that I am if I do.

I said at the start that I wished that the House had been honest with me. The right hon. Member for Old Bexley and Sidcup (Mr. Heath) said that most hon. Members could not understand the people of Northern Ireland because somehow we are different but he could not explain what that difference was. He described how the Prime Minister of the Irish Republic and the Prime Minister of Northern Ireland could relate to each other because they both respected each other's position. I can relate to the leader of the SDLP[19] without any problem because I respect his position and he respects mine. If I had known that this was the proposition that would be put to me; if I had realised that direct rule, which has been so offensive, would be made this offensive; if I had realised that the government of the Province to which I belong would be put to a large extent into the hands of a foreign Government, I would have viewed my political relationships in Northern Ireland very differently.

The people of Northern Ireland whom I represent would prefer to be governed by a Catholic

19. John Hume (b. 1937), a founder of the Social Democratic and Labour Party and its leader since 1979.

nationalist in Northern Ireland than a Minister from the Irish Republic who lives in Cork and who did not know where Northern Ireland was until five years ago. If I had known that those were the terms for my continued membership of the House of Commons, I would have considered other options. I did not consider other options because my first option was simply to be an ordinary British citizen. But, as the hon. Member for Antrim, North (Rev. Ian Paisley) has confirmed, I cannot consider that now. I am not prepared to consider a sharing of power or the governing of Northern Ireland with the SDLP with the threat that every time they do not get their way they will run down to their nursemaid in Dublin to take it up with the Secretary of State in the Anglo-Irish conference.

That is the position in which the unionists are being put. They are being told that they will not be citizens of the nation to which they belong on the basis that they want but that they will be governed within the framework of an Anglo-Irish conference and that if, within that framework, they want devolution it will be on the basis that they virtually concede equality of power to their political opponents in Northern Ireland and, at the same time, give the Irish Government a direct influence on every other aspect of life in Northern Ireland. That is too high a price for me to pay.

I say in all sincerity, and I mean it, that I will never accept this agreement as the means whereby I will be governed in Northern Ireland. Tens and tens and tens of thousands of people in Northern Ireland share that view. If that is construed as me flying in the face of the sovereignty of this Parliament, so be it. I have heard the threats over the past two days. Let us have a referendum in the United Kingdom and let Northern Ireland accept the result. I will accept the judgment. If the people of the United Kingdom say to me that they no longer want me, it will simply be echoing what the Government are saying anyway and they will have to live with the consequences of that decision. That referendum cannot deliver me against my will into an Irish Republic. I will not go to the Irish Republic and what might flow from whatever the developments might be would be something with which everybody in the United Kingdom would have to live. I am not scared of a referendum. I am prepared to live with its consequences.

I have heard variations on the sponger theme. It is said that we are given £1.5 billion each year and we had better be careful or it will be taken from us. As I said last night, I can accept money from the richer parts of the United Kingdom being given to Northern Ireland if it is the decision of the parliament of the United Kingdom to redistribute the United Kingdom's wealth to the poorer parts. However, I cannot accept, and I do not want United Kingdom charity. I do not want money to be offered to me to buy my acquiescence. That is the view of the majority of the people in Northern Ireland. Do not threaten me with a referendum or with turning off the financial tap. We are proud people. When we say what we mean, we mean what we say. I wish that that standard could be adopted by all right hon. and hon. Members.

Biographies/Bibliographies

William Drennan

LIFE. Born in Belfast in 1754, the son of the radical presbyterian minister, Thomas Drennan. He was educated at Glasgow University and studied medicine at the University of Edinburgh. A friend and pupil of the philosopher, Dugald Stewart, he took his medical degree in 1778. He practised medicine in Belfast, Newry and Dublin and during the 1780s his 'Irish Helot' letters to the press attracted great attention. A founding member of the Society of United Irishmen, he was tried for sedition in 1794, but was acquitted after a powerful defence by John Philpot Curran.

Drennan appears to have withdrawn from politics after 1794. He published poems and lyrics, some of which — 'The Wail of the Women after the Battle' and 'The Wake of William Orr' — became famous. He founded the Belfast Academical Institution in 1814 and started the *Belfast Magazine*. He died in Belfast in 1820. In accordance with his egalitarian republican principles, his coffin was carried by six catholics and six protestants.

CHIEF WRITINGS. *Letters of an Irish Helot*, signed Orellana (Dublin, 1785); *A Letter to the Right Honourable William Pitt* (Dublin, 1799); *A Second Letter to the Right Honourable William Pitt* (1799); *A Letter to Charles James Fox* (Dublin, 1806); *Fugitive Pieces in Verse and Prose* (Belfast, 1815); *Glendalloch and other poems, with a life of the author by his sons, J.S. and William Drennan* (Dublin, 1859); D.A. Chart (ed.), *The Drennan Letters* (Belfast: HMSO, 1931).

BIOGRAPHY AND CRITICISM. A.T.Q. Stewart, '"A Stable Unseen Power", Dr. William Drennan and the Origins of the United Irishmen', in J. Bossy (ed.), *Essays Presented to Michael Roberts* (Belfast: Blackstaff Press, 1976).

James Carlile

LIFE. Carlile was born in Paisley, Scotland in 1784 and was educated at Glasgow University. He became minister at Mary's Abbey, Dublin in 1813. An educationalist and theologian, he helped prepare and edit many school textbooks. As resident commissioner to the Irish board of education, he helped organize the school system. He opposed sectarianism in education, but his liberal policies were opposed by Cardinal Cullen. He died in 1854.

CHIEF WRITINGS. *Examination of Arguments for Roman Catholic Episcopacy* (Dublin, 1815); *Sermons on Faith and Repentance* (London, 1821); *The Old Doctrine of Faith Asserted* (London, 1823); *The Apocryphal Controversy Summed Up* (Glasgow, 1827); *On the Constitution of the Primitive Churches* (Dublin, 1831); *Letters on the Divine Origin and Authority of Scripture* (Edinburgh, 1837); *On the First and Second Advents* (Edinburgh, 1848); *Fruit Gathered from Among Roman Catholics in Ireland* (London, 1848); *The Papal Invasion: How to Repel It* (London, 1850); *Manual of the Anatomy and Physiology of the Human Mind* (London, 1851); *Station and Occupation of Saints in Final Glory* (London, 1854).

Henry Montgomery

LIFE. Henry Montgomery was born in 1788 in Killead, Co. Antrim. His mother and father were of Scottish descent. His father, Archibald Montgomery, was a lieutenant in the Irish Volunteers and his elder brothers, William and John, joined the United Irishmen and fought in the battle of Antrim (1798). The ten-year-old Henry observed the battle from a hill and, after the defeat of the rebels, William was captured. The Montgomery farmhouse was ransacked and set on fire by local yeomanry.

Montgomery matriculated at Glasgow College in 1804 and graduated in 1808. In 1809 he became minister at Dunmurry, Co. Antrim, a post he held until his death. In 1817 he became headmaster of the English school at the Belfast Academical Institution and in 1818 was elected moderator of the Synod of Ulster. In the 1820s, as Henry Cooke worked to reshape the synod and make it orthodox and conservative, Montgomery opposed him in a series of powerful speeches which articulate the liberal presbyterian position. Montgomery was a professed Arian and he set out his beliefs in an essay, *The Creed of an Arian* (1830). (Arianism is a Christian doctrine first proposed in the 4th century by the Alexandrian presbyter, Arius. It affirms that Christ is a created being and therefore is not truly divine. Although it was suppressed as a heresy, it survives in modified form in unitarianism.)

Montgomery and his followers were defeated in synod by Cooke and his party. They withdrew in 1829 and set up a remonstrant synod that met on 25 May 1830. Montgomery had close links with English unitarians and was a passionate advocate of catholic emancipation and of civil liberties. He opposed O'Connell's agitation for the repeal of the Union and in later life became more politically conservative. He died in 1865.

CHIEF WRITINGS. *The Creed of an Arian* (Belfast, 1830); *Letter to Daniel O'Connell* (Cork, 1831); *We Persuade Men* (Belfast, 1845).

BIOGRAPHY AND CRITICISM. J.A. Crozier, *The Life of the Rev. Henry Montgomery* (Belfast, 1875) Vol. I only.

Henry Cooke

LIFE. Henry Cooke was born on his father's farm near Maghera, Co. Derry, in 1788. His father, John Cooke, was descended from a family of Devon puritans; his mother, Jane Howie, was of Scottish descent. The 1798 Rebellion made a deep impression on the young Cooke, whose family was loyalist. He remembered that for weeks during the summer of 1798 they had to sleep in the fields for fear of assassination.

Cooke attended Glasgow University and was ordained in 1808. In 1818 he was installed at Killyleagh, Co. Down. The lord of the manor and leading presbyterian at Killyleagh was the United Irishman, Archibald Hamilton Rowan. Rowan's younger son, Sidney Hamilton Rowan, who was an elder of Killyleagh and a Calvinist, secured Cooke's election. Cooke did not appear to hold bigoted opinions at this time and had joined in Arian ordinations during his previous ministry at Donegore. However, influenced by Captain Rowan, he soon began to make a reputation as an enemy of liberal theologians — the Arian or New Light ministers. In 1821 he and Rowan helped destroy a mission led by the English unitarian, John Smethhurst.

Cooke was elected moderator of the Synod of Ulster in 1824 and he began to mobilize protestant opinion against catholic emancipation. He also moved to impose a narrow standard of orthodoxy on the synod members and forced the Arians to secede. From 1829 until the close of his active ministry in 1867, Cooke was minister at May Street Church, Belfast. He became the presiding spirit of Irish presbyterianism and also a leading protestant political force. He joined evangelicism to Orangeism and built bridges between the aristocracy (who were members of the established church) and the common people. He died in Belfast in 1868.

CHIEF WRITINGS. *A Letter to the Rev. Dr. Ritchie* (Edinburgh, 1836); *A Second Letter to the Rev. John Ritchie* (Edinburgh, 1837); *Sins of the Times* (Belfast, 1837); *A Lecture on Popery* (London, 1851); *The Self-Interpreting Bible* (Glasgow, 1855).

BIOGRAPHY AND CRITICISM. J.L. Porter, *The Life and Times of Henry Cooke* (Belfast, 1871); Finlay Holmes, *Henry Cooke* (Belfast: Christian Science Journals, 1981).

Edward Carson

LIFE. Edward Carson, baron Carson of Duncairn, was born in 1854 into a southern Irish protestant family and became known as the 'uncrowned king of Ulster' through his leadership of Northern Irish unionist resistance to Home Rule. A successful barrister, he became a Unionist member of the House of Commons in 1892 and was British solicitor general from 1900 to 1905. His notorious cross-examination of Oscar Wilde at the trial of the Marquis of Queensberry helped to secure Wilde's subsequent trial and conviction for homosexual offences.

In 1910, Carson accepted the parliamentary leadership of the Irish Unionists and so gave up the chance of becoming leader of the British Conservative Party. He set up a provisional government in Belfast in 1913 and helped organize the landing of a large arms shipment at Larne, Co. Antrim on 24 April 1914. The British government conceded to the demands of the Unionists and in July 1914 Carson agreed to Home Rule for Ireland apart from Ulster. He served in Asquith's and Lloyd George's coalition ministries during World War I and was given a life peerage in 1921. He died in Kent in 1935 and was given a state funeral in Belfast.

BIOGRAPHY AND CRITICISM. Edward Marjoribanks and Ian Colvin, *The Life of Lord Carson* (London: Victor Gollancz, 1932-36); H. Montgomery Hyde, *Carson* (London: Heinemann, 1953; reissued by Constable in 1974); R.B. McDowell, 'Edward Carson' in Conor Cruise O'Brien (ed.), *The Shaping of Modern Ireland* (London: Routledge & Kegan Paul, 1960); A.T.Q. Stewart, *Edward Carson* (Dublin: Gill and Macmillan, 1981).

James Craig

LIFE. James Craig, 1st viscount Craigavon, was born in Belfast in 1871. He fought on the British side during the Boer War and entered the House of Commons as a Unionist in 1906. He worked with Sir Edward Carson to oppose Home Rule and served in the British government during World War I, recruiting and organizing the 36th (Ulster) Division. In June 1921 he became the first prime minister of Northern Ireland and served in that office from the creation of the state until his death at Glencarrig, Co. Down in November 1940.

BIOGRAPHY AND CRITICISM. Hugh Shearman, *Not an Inch: A Study of Northern Ireland and Lord Craigavon* (London: Faber and Faber, 1942); St. John Ervine, *Craigavon, Ulsterman* (London: Allen & Unwin, 1948); Patrick Buckland, *James Craig* (Dublin: Gill and Macmillan, 1982).

Ian Paisley

LIFE. Ian Paisley was born in Armagh in 1926. He was ordained in 1946 and has been moderator of the Free Presbyterian Church of Ulster since its foundation in 1951. He was imprisoned for three months in 1966 after leading a protest march to the presbyterian General Assembly in Belfast. He took a prominent part in loyalist counter-demonstrations at the time of the Civil Rights campaign in Northern Ireland 1968-72. In 1970 he gained a seat at Stormont and later that year a seat at Westminster as the MP for North Antrim. In 1971, with Desmond Boal, he set up the Democratic Unionist Party. With other unionist politicians he sat on the strike committee which brought down the power-sharing Executive at Stormont in 1974. In 1979 he gained a seat in the European Assembly at Strasbourg.

CHIEF WRITINGS. *The Fifty-Nine Revival* (Belfast: Martyrs Memorial Free Presbyterian Church, 1958); *Christian Foundations* (Belfast: Martyrs Memorial Publications, 1960); *An Exposition of the Epistle to the Romans* (London: Marshall, Morgan and Scott, 1968); *The Massacre of St. Bartholomew* (Belfast: Martyrs Memorial Publications, 1972); *Paisley: The Man and His Message* (Belfast: Martyrs Memorial Publications, 1976); *America's Debt to Ulster* (Belfast: Martyrs Memorial Publications, 1976). Paisley has also published numerous sermons and pamphlets.

BIOGRAPHY AND CRITICISM. Ed Moloney and Andy Pollak, *Paisley* (Swords, Co. Dublin: Poolbeg Press, 1986); Steve Bruce, *God Save Ulster: The Religion and Politics of Paisleyism* (Oxford: Oxford University Press, 1986); Tom Paulin, 'Paisley's Progress' in *Ireland and the English Crisis* (Newcastle-upon-Tyne: Bloodaxe Books, 1984).

Harold McCusker

LIFE. Harold McCusker was born in 1940. He became MP for Armagh in the 1974 general election. He became deputy leader of the Official Unionist Party in 1982. He pressed for tougher security measures in south Armagh and voted with the Labour government in the crucial vote of confidence that led to the defeat of James Callaghan's government and the 1979 general election. He died in 1990.

SEAMUS DEANE, *Editor*

Autobiography and Memoirs 1890-1988

Autobiography is not just concerned with the self; it is also concerned with the 'other', the person or persons, events or places, that have helped to give the self definition. The selection of pieces presented here, although drawn from a diversity of sources, has at least this feature in common. All the authors included are seeking, through personal experience, self-examination, reconsideration of historical events and circumstances, to identify the other force, the hostile or liberating energy, which made the self come into consciousness and thereby give to existence a pattern or the beginnings of a pattern of explanation. Inevitably, in a colonial or neo-colonial country like Ireland, the forms of 'otherness' available are multiple and blatant, so much so that they rarely escape stereotyping. An idea of Ireland has to be fashioned, discovered, recreated over and against that which threatens to disallow it. These oppressive agencies are often institutional; sometimes they are embodied in a person. So, in William Carleton's case, one of the agencies of oppression is the Orange Order; this can quickly change into the Orange Order's enemy, Ribbonism; in W. B. Yeats's case, the agency involved is his version of the modern spirit, which is identified first in the new drama and embodied in George Bernard Shaw. The maimed spirit Shaw represents is then extended to Wilde, Parnell and various others until a whole 'tragic generation' stands for the modern world against which the new idea of Ireland and of Irish theatre and of Yeats has contrastingly to assert itself. Synge, too, is full of subtle mutations: from illness to health, from decadence to vigour, from protestant unionism to Celtic nationalism. Events such as the Easter Rising, the Civil War, the Northern crisis, are read — by Seán O'Casey, Bulmer Hobson, Austin Clarke, Ernie O'Malley and others — as bright moments of liberation that have within them the darker moments of oppression, radical revelations of the ceaseless discovery and loss of identity and freedom, which is one of the obsessive marks of cultures that have been compelled to inquire into the legitimacy of their own existence by the presence of another culture that is forever foreign and forever intimate. In such circumstances, autobiography, or the writing of a memoir, or the analysis of a political situation, is always going to reproduce, in some variation, those ultimately disturbing queries about the issue of identity, national or personal. Does it have anything other than a fictive existence? Is it a necessary fiction? Can it not be more securely anchored? Best of all, can it not be forgotten, ignored, so that life might be lived without this endless truffling for the questionable source of its originating moment? Police and priests, soldiers and assassins, invaders and natives, Gaels and Galls, revolutionaries and reactionaries, dominate in these worlds, where the only freedom from social and political pressures is in the writing about its elusiveness.

One of the advantages gained from this self-reflexive meditation is that the writers are compelled, in their confrontation with the obduracy of existing conditions, to create alternatives to them. Some alternatives are more suasive than others, but they all have their attractions, no matter where they are situated in space and time. The most exploited alternative is the Edenic one, the imagined time in which present strife and rupture did not exist and the question of the self's relationship to the society was not even at issue. This demands a reading of history that is, of course, open to dispute, but the reading is a heuristic manoeuvre rather than a scientific analysis, and should be so understood in these autobiographical contexts.

When W. R. Le Fanu speaks of the period before the tithe war of the 1830s, before alienation set in, he is not wholly vulnerable to the charge that he is fantasizing, distorting the terrible realities of eighteenth-century Ireland. By exploring his memory of the peace that predated 1830, he is sharpening our sense of the difference, for the protestant ruling class, of the relationship between authority and disaffection as it had developed in the nineteenth century. (His memoir was published in the last decade of the century.) The tithe war was a traumatic experience for Le Fanu and his family. Sixty years later, in post-Parnellite Ireland, we can see — as he does — that the psychological shock of that period is one shared by his class and co-religionists. It is the more profound for having become an increasingly prominent political reality. The protestant church, which took the assault in the 1830s, was disestablished in 1869; by the 1890s the landlords who abandoned it in those early years had themselves been reduced. This is the story of an individual experience that is also a group experience. It achieves its prominence because it is set against the earlier, nostalgically remembered era when the protestant sense of alienation did not exist, when power and authority were one and the threat of protestant exclusion from Ireland was unimaginable.

The benign vision of the other place and time is a necessary counterbalance to the recognition of the malign 'other' which dominates the present. Daniel O'Connell's catholic hordes, led by the priests, is one of those images of the 'other'; later, it is Victorian, industrial England with its utilitarian ethos and its commercial theatre; later again, it is the Fenian brotherhood, plotting destruction and the downfall of civilization; or it is the Orange faction, organized into a powerful political movement by Edward Carson; or it is the pro-Treaty faction, betraying the Republic; or it is the men of Easter week betraying the Empire. Events provide the material, but the categories of comprehension and apprehension remain remarkably in place. When Hubert Butler laments the destruction of the big houses in Kilkenny during the Civil War, and associates this with the destruction of the Public Records Office in the Four Courts, and, as in other instances, the destruction of the Custom House in the War of Independence, he is lamenting two things at once: the self-destructiveness of the revolutionaries who destroy their own history and culture in the name of liberation, and the self-extermination of the landowning class, who have brought so much of this upon their own heads by their failures in generosity and leadership. All those ruins dotting the Irish landscape also populate Irish writing. The great buildings destroyed — monasteries, churches, libraries, public buildings, big houses, cottages, even whole villages and city centres — and the cultures they represented are the relics of both external and internal oppression. The security and peace of Augustan Ireland, of Celtic-Romanesque Ireland, of Gaelic Ireland, are not just historical fantasies. They are part of the countering energy of the self in the face of circumstances that threaten to dismiss it. The dismissal of a religious group, a class, a sect, from the prevailing idea of what constitutes the culture is a governing theme, especially when the nationalisms of the Irish and British varieties collide in the nineteenth and twentieth centuries.

Ruined buildings are evidence of how drastic that dismissal can be. To repudiate the dismissal, the building must, so to speak, be reconstituted in the political and social setting that produced it and in the contemporary setting in which it stands, needlessly and suicidally, destroyed. A ruin may be 'romantic' in the sense that it has become so embedded in the landscape that it bespeaks not only loss but also the native endurance that will prevail even over and through the destruction of the buildings it once created. Conversely, the ruin of a fort, keep, castle or barrack can be understood as the symbolic failure of coercion to survive resistance to it. But time and again we see that the shadow that falls across these Edens is the original sin of self-destructiveness, the ruination of a group, race or class by its own internalized desire for extinction. This is the final, but bitter triumph of oppression. It teaches the oppressed to oppress themselves more effectively than any external agency could do. The catalogue of self-destructive acts is not confined to buildings or cultural artifacts; it also includes the language, the so-called Gaelic or Celtic spirit, the Anglo-Irish drive towards domination. Such self-destructiveness takes many forms. One is desertion, the desertion of the people by their 'natural' leaders, whether they be seventeenth-century catholic aristocrats or twentieth-century protestant landowners. As in all such accounts, desertion, which is self-willed, has its opposite, which is imposed. The opposite here is emigration, but emigration too reconverts itself eventually back into a form of desertion, for it includes many who emigrate out of disillusion with Ireland, and seek economic security elsewhere, or those who, like the republicans mentioned by C. S. Andrews, desert post-Treaty Ireland and leave it in the hands of the Free Staters. Even the great leaders are deserted or deserters — Young Ireland deserts O'Connell, the Irish Party deserts Parnell, de Valera deserts the republicans, and, with a variation, the British government deserts the landlords, then the northern unionists. Thus, there are ruined political causes and political heroes as well as buildings, each a reminder of the failure of any political cause to achieve an enduring stability.

The Edenic resource is one alternative; the utopian is another. They can be simply distinguished by saying that one looks backwards with a longing as fierce as the hope with which the other looks forward. The utopian possibility is quite as complex as its opposite, although it might seem more susceptible to a rigid and doctrinaire formulation than any reading of the complicated past could offer. Most utopian visions are, naturally enough, modes of remembering the future. They are projections of the past thrown against an ideological screen. One strange version, emergent in poetry from the early years of the nineteenth century, is the idea of a utopian language in which the Gaelic and the English are so imbued with one another that they produce a new harmonics (Gaelic metres, assonance and English verse forms), a new 'Elizabethan' vigour and, ultimately, a new kind of literature. This is one of the utopias of the Literary Revival, but it is not confined to that grouping or period. Another utopian form is the secular republican vision promoted by men like Bulmer Hobson, or the Gaelic-catholic vision, or the Anglo-Irish version espoused by Yeats and others. All these have a strange, flawed recognition at their heart. They know what they are struggling for, but they do not know for whom they are struggling. Even a revolutionary soldier like Ernie O'Malley finds the country people for whom he is fighting strange to him. The people, spoken of as an entity, are liable to be estranged from the utopian because they always seem to be unregenerate, retarded in their catholicism, their unionism or whatever it may be. But that itself is analogous to the writer's struggle to 'universalize the data I had experienced in my body locally', as Seán O'Faoláin puts it in *Vive Moi!* The local drags, in its retarding fashion, on the aspiration to transcend it. Once it is abandoned, the transcendence becomes a pure abstraction of the sort experienced by republicans after the Treaty, when they fought for the principle the people had abandoned, or, at a personal level, the theological abstractions George Tyrrell had fed to him when he converted to catholicism and found that he still could not appease the protestant longing for a religion of evangelical fervour and warmth.

The struggle between the sense of the 'other' and the wish to find a way of including the other in some unified version both of self and culture is one of the motive forces behind most of the writings included here. It produces strange and memorable images. Bernadette Devlin fights in the Bogside for a socialist vision even as the fight itself intensifies the sectarian feeling she wants to appease. Austin Clarke sits in a coffee-shop with F. R. Higgins and finds his hidden Ireland in a passing mention of the Celtic-Romanesque centuries. Oliver Gogarty attends upon the dying Griffith, meets the coffin of Collins and understands, while repudiating it, the self-destructiveness of the republicans. Patrick Kavanagh, defending his image of himself as a poet in open court, against a former Taoiseach, is apparently betrayed by a Brendan Behan, who was himself taken by the spectacle of Wilde in court, bringing on the punishment that would confirm his myth. Ernie O'Malley, the most literary of the republican soldiers, precipitates the Civil War by capturing General Ginger O'Connell and waits in the Four Courts to the end for the explosion that will destroy 800 years of records and documents. This is amputating the past with a vengeance. Hubert Butler laments the passing of the Anglo-Irish while lauding the Wolfe Tone who predicted their fate and said how richly they deserved it. Yeats completes himself by brooding on the incompleteness of others. O'Casey repudiates 1916 while admiring it; Eamon McCann calls for intervention from the south while promising to resist it; Bulmer Hobson criticizes a secret organization — the IRB — for acting in a clandestine fashion; Shaw displays his Fabian philosophy as a release from a city and childhood of which it is no more than a therapeutic reordering; George O'Brien thinks of his generation as the first to be free even as he invokes, in that freedom, the whole history of subjugation in Lismore.

The element of contradiction in these images is one of the sources of their power. The self is reaffirmed through its cancellation. There is, in all this, a radical privation. None of these autobiographies or memoirs can avoid the sense of a missing feature or energy. What they indicate is that there is no substitution for this missing agency; there is nothing that can compensate. To the extent that the world, especially the world of childhood and youth, is restored in writing to its full presence, there is a corresponding sense of its inadequacy. It is always something to escape from. There is always a provincial Cork, like the city of O'Connor or O'Faoláin, or a provincial Belfast, like that of Robert Harbinson, which must be left. But there is no other place that can be as fully realized, most especially no other place in which the self and the other can be met so frontally. This incapacity to accept origin, this need to seek an alternative to it, is one of the symptoms of a culture that believes itself always to be provincial, always to be in need of a metropolitan world elsewhere. It is, in a curious way, an emigrant literature, always dependent for its sense of emigrant freedom on a vision of the home from which it escaped and inclined to see the escape as a loss and as a gain. The profound contradictions of Irish experience are registered in such seemingly conflicting impulses. Ireland exports its writers; Irish writers import their Irelands. This is as true of the internal emigrés as of those who actually leave. It is a place that takes precedence over all others and is, at the same time, a nowhere, a utopia inverted and perverted.

It was a 'Mother's Help' called Miss Craig 'who brought Hell home to me' wrote Louis MacNeice in his autobiography, *The Strings Are False*. His sister appended a note to this remark, absolving Miss Craig and explaining that it was the shock of his mother's illness and her death 'which caused Louis's memories of childhood to be so sad and sometimes so bitter. He was too young to have any real understanding of what had happened'. If this is so, what are we to make of what MacNeice actually wrote? It is obvious from the excerpt given here that Miss Craig is a protestant and a fierce contrast to the charming and content Annie, the catholic who came to cook for them, and that both women perhaps manifest certain aspects of MacNeice's reaction to his mother. But if these are her two faces for him as a writer, we are seeing him transmute her into an emblem of his reaction to the North of Ireland. His sister is too condescending when she says he did not understand. He understood the personal in terms provided by the culture and then reconverted the cultural back into the personal. In that small instance we may see how a memory, even when not ratified by someone who 'was there', apprehends a personal experience socially and, further, understand how the trauma of the personal translates easily into the trauma of the social. When that translation is made, we sense in autobiography the whole society's conflict with the 'other', with the manner in which it deals with the experience of a country in which Hell is brought home and experienced and, on rare occasions like this, understood. MacNeice is one of those writers who helps us to understand the conflicts that exist within the North; he also helps us to understand much other writing about the North because he creates the self through that conflict rather than by an avoidance or an overcoming of it. It is parental, original. It comes shockingly upon a childhood Eden; and the subsequent expulsion and emigration from that Edenic moment is a narrative pattern in which much of Irish history and experience has been written and rewritten.

WILLIAM RICHARD LE FANU

(1816-94)

from: SEVENTY YEARS OF IRISH LIFE (1893)

[The tithe war of the 1830s, following upon catholic emancipation in 1829, emphasized the continuing sectarian basis of Irish life. Catholics objected to paying tithes to the established church; their opposition, led by the priests, and inflamed by economic hardship, became organized to such a degree in the 1830s that the British government was forced to pass the Tithe Commutation Act in 1838, making the tithe a part of the rent charge. But the effect of the war, in which some hundreds of people were killed, was enduring. The alienation between the catholic people and the protestant establishment was thereafter more pronounced and, after the Famine, the agitation spread to the question of the land system itself.

Le Fanu was the younger brother of the novelist, Joseph Sheridan Le Fanu. The incidents described here, which took place in Doon, Co. Limerick, were among the most publicized, if by no means the most bloody, of the tithe war in the years between 1830-38.]

CHAPTER V

In 1831 came the tithe war, and with it our friendly relations with the priests and people ceased. The former, not unnaturally, threw themselves heart and soul into the agitation. The Protestant clergy were denounced by agitators and priests from platform and from altar, and branded as the worst enemies of the people, who were told to hunt them like mad dogs from the country; they were insulted wherever they went, many were attacked, some were murdered. It is hard now to realize the suddenness with which kindness and good-will were changed to insult and hate; for a short time we were not so badly treated as some of the neighbouring clergy, but the people would not speak to us, and scowled at us as we passed.

Of Doon, a parish which adjoined Abington, our cousin, the Rev. Charles Coote, was rector. At the very commencement of the agitation he had given much offence by taking active measures to enforce the payment of his tithes. It was thus his fight began. He had for years been on the most intimate and friendly terms with Father H[ickey], the parish priest, who held a considerable farm, for which Mr. Coote would never allow him to pay tithe. When the agitation against tithes began, Father H[ickey] preached a fierce sermon against them, denouncing Mr. Coote from the altar, telling the people that any man who paid one farthing of that 'blood-stained impost' was a traitor to his country and his God. 'Take example by me, boys,' he said; 'I'd let my last cow be seized and sold before I'd pay a farthing to that scoundrel Coote.' On hearing of this, Mr. Coote wrote to ask him whether the report he had heard was true; he replied that he was proud to say that it was true, adding, 'You may seize and sell my cattle if you can, but I'd like to see the man that would buy them.' Coote, who was a brave and determined man, was so indignant that he resolved to fight it out with the priest. He gave orders to his bailiff, and next morning at break of day, before any one dreamt that he would make the attempt, one of the priest's cows was taken and impounded. Public notice was given that, on a day and hour named, the cow would be sold in Doon; counter notices were posted through the country telling the people to assemble in their thousands to see Father H[ickey]'s cow sold. Mr. Coote went to Dublin to consult the authorities at the Castle, and returned next day, with a promise from the Government that they would support him.

Early on the morning fixed for the sale I was sitting at an open window in our breakfast-room, when my attention was roused by the sound of bagpipes playing 'The Campbells are Coming.' On looking in the direction whence the sound came, I saw four companies of Highlanders, headed by their pipers, marching down the road, followed by a troop of lancers and artillery with two guns.

On this little army went to Doon, where many thousands of the country people were assembled. At the appointed hour the cow was put up for sale. There was a belief then prevalent among the people that at a sale unless there were at least three bidders, nothing could be sold; under this mistaken idea, a friend of the priest bid a sum, much beyond her value, for the cow; she was knocked down to him, he was obliged to hand the money to the auctioneer, and the tithe was paid. During all this time, except shouting, hooting at the soldiers, and 'groans for Coote', nothing was done; but when the main body of the troops had left the village shots were fired, and volleys of stones were thrown at four of the lancers who had remained after the others as a rear guard. They fired their pistols at their assailants, one of whom was wounded. The rest of the lancers, hearing the shots, galloped back and quickly dispersed the crowd. It was weary work for the troops, as the day was very hot and bright, and their march to and from Doon was a long one, that village being certainly not less than fifteen miles from Limerick. On their return they bivouacked and dined in a field close to us, surrounded by crowds of the peasantry, many of whom had never seen a soldier before; after a brief rest the pipes struck up, 'The Campbells are Coming,' and they were on their march again. So ended this, to us, memorable day.

The next morning, as we were at breakfast, the room door opened; an old man came in; he fell on his knees and cried, 'Oh, wirasthru,[1] my little boy is killed, my boy is shot! Sure the craythur was doin' nothing out of the way when the sogers[2] shot him. Oh, Vo! Vo! What will I ever do widout my little boy!' 'What can I do for you, my poor man?' said my father. 'Ah! then it's what I want your honour to give me a bit of note that'll get him into the hospital in Limerick.'

My father at once gave him the order for his son's admission. He departed invoking blessings on us, and shedding tears of gratitude.

As we afterwards found, the 'little boy' was a youth of six and twenty, who had got a slight flesh wound in the leg. They never brought him to the hospital, but they paraded him, all day, through the streets of Limerick, lying in a cart, covered with a blood-stained sheet; to the back of the cart a board was fixed, on which, in large letters, was this inscription, 'THESE ARE THE BLESSINGS OF TITHES.' From that day Mr. Coote was a marked man.

Wherever he or any of his family were seen they were received with shouts and yells, and cries of 'Mad dog! mad dog! To hell with the tithes! Down with the tithes!' One afternoon, when we returned from a visit to the rectory at Doon, we received a message from our parish priest to say that if we went there any more we should be treated as the Cootes were. Accordingly on our return from our next visit to them, shouts and curses followed us all the way home; from that day forward, when any of us (or even our carriage or car) was seen, the same shouts and cursing were heard in all directions....

At this time none of us went out alone, and we were always well armed. This the people knew, and did not actually attack any of us except on two occasions. On one of these my sister, who till a few months before had been idolized by the people for her goodness to them and untiring work amongst them, thought that if she and two girls, cousins, who were with us at the time, drove out by themselves, they would not be molested, especially as she had recently been in very delicate health. So taking advantage of an hour when the rest of the family were out, they went for a drive, when not only were they received with the usual hooting, but were pelted with mud and stone. One of the girls had a front tooth broken and they were glad to get home without further injury, and never again ventured to go out without protection.

The other attack happened thus. My father had been persuaded by some friends to try whether offering a large abatement, and giving time, might induce some of the farmers to pay at least some part of the tithes then due. A number of circulars offering such terms were prepared. These my cousin, Robert Flemyng, and I (little more than boys at the time) undertook to distribute, and to explain the terms to the farmers whose houses we proposed to visit. On our first day's ride nothing worth mentioning beyond the usual hooting occurred. Some of the houses were shut against us as the inmates saw us approach; at some few we were not uncivilly received, but were distinctly told that under no circumstances would one farthing of tithes ever be paid again.

On the following day we rode to a different part of the parish, to visit some farmers in the direction of Limerick. As we turned off the main road down a by-road leading to the village of Kishiquirk, we saw a man standing on a hillock holding in his hands a spade, high in air, then lowering the spade and giving a shrill whistle, then holding up the spade again. We knew this must be a signal, but for what we couldn't think. When we reached the village, a considerable and very threatening crowd was collected there, who saluted us with 'Down with the Orangemen! Down with the tithes!' As this looked

1. A corrupt rendering of the Irish expression *A Mhuire is trua*! (Mary, alas!)
2. soldiers.

like mischief, we drew our pistols from our pockets, and each holding one in his right hand, we rode slowly through the throng. As we got near the end of the village a woman called to us, 'What are ye riding so slow for? Push on, I tell you; they are going to kill ye!' We did push on, and with some difficulty, by riding one after the other, got past a cart which was hastily drawn across the road to stop us. On we galloped, showers of stones after us as we went. About a quarter of a mile further on another but smaller crowd awaited us; they were not on the road, but just inside the mound fence which bordered it. On this mound they had made ready a good supply of stones for our reception, but, seeing us hold our pistols towards them, they did not venture to throw the stones till just as we had passed them, when they came after us volley after volley. Many a blow we and our horses got, but none that stunned. One man only was on the road, and, as we got near him, I saw him settling his spade in his hand as if to be ready to strike a blow. I presented my pistol at him. 'Don't shoot me,' he called out; 'I'm only working here.' But just as I passed him he made a tremendous blow at me; it missed me, but struck the horse just behind the saddle. The spade was broken by the violence of the blow. Down went the horse on his haunches, but was quickly up again, and on we went. Had he fallen, I should not have been alive many minutes; he brought me bravely home, but never recovered, and died soon afterwards.

As we neared our house we met a funeral, headed by the Roman Catholic curate of the parish. We rode up to him, covered as we and our horses were with mud and blood, in the vain hope that he would say some words of exhortation to the people. 'See,' we said, 'Father M——, how we have been treated when we were on a peaceful and friendly mission to some of your flock.' 'I suppose,' said he, 'ye were unwelcome visitors.' 'Is that any reason,' said I, 'that they should try to murder us?' 'It's no business of mine,' said he, and passed on.

A proclamation, as fruitless as such proclamations then were, and now are, was issued by the Government offering a reward to any one who would give such information as would lead to the conviction of any of the men who had attacked us. It was well we had not gone that day to visit a farmer in another direction, where, as we afterwards learned, four armed men lay in wait, in a plantation by the road, to shoot us.

Mr. Coote was much surprised when he heard all this. He had always said, 'Let them shout and hoot as they will, in their hearts they like us too well to shoot either you or me, or any one belonging to us.' A few weeks later he was painfully undeceived. As he rode home from church he stopped his horse, as he had often done before, to let him take a mouthful of water from a little stream which crossed the road; he had scarcely stopped when a thundering report, which nearly deafened him, and a cloud of smoke came from a little grove close beside him. The blunderbuss which had been aimed at him had burst: its shattered remains, a half-emptied bottle of whisky, and a quantity of blood were found in the grove. Hearing of this, I went next day to see him. Never did I see a man more saddened and disappointed. He said, 'I would not have believed it would ever come to this.'

Boycotting, supposed to be a recent invention (in reality only new in name),[3] was put in force against the clergy, to whom the people were forbidden to speak. Placards were posted all through the neighbourhood ordering that no one should work for Mr. Coote on pain of death.

There lived near Doon six stalwart young fellows, brothers, named Lysaght, whom some years previously Mr. Coote, being fully convinced of their innocence, had by his exertions saved from transportation, to which, on perjured evidence, they had been sentenced. The real culprits were afterwards arrested and convicted. These six fellows were determined to work for their benefactor, so they, with some Protestant parishioners of his, assembled one fine morning on the bog of Doon, to cut his turf. Suddenly about midday crowds of men appeared crossing the bog from all sides towards the workmen, shouting and firing shots. The turf-cutters ran for their lives to the rectory, not waiting to put on their coats. The mob came on, tore up the clothes, destroyed the turf that had been cut, smashed the turf-cutting implements, and then retired as they came, with shouts and shots.

We were not 'boycotted' to the same extent, and were allowed to cut our turf and save our crops. One morning we heard a rumour that our labourers,

3. Boycotting — refusing to have dealings with a person or organisation — was named after Captain C.C. Boycott (1832-97), the land agent for the Earl of Erne, Co. Mayo. He was ostracized for refusing to reduce rents. Parnell's phrase for boycotting was 'moral Coventry'.

who were saving our hay, were to be stopped, and we were preparing for an attack, when our steward said, 'You needn't be a morsel uneasy, for it would be *illegal* for them to come to annoy us without giving us regular proper notice.'...

During all these troublous times the landlords looked on with indifference, and showed little sympathy with the clergy in their difficulties. My brother used to say, 'Never mind, their time will come; rents will be attacked, as tithes are now, with the same machinery, and with like success.' His prophecy was laughed at. Long after, one who had heard him said to him, 'Well, Le Fanu, your rent war hasn't come.' All he said was, ''Twill come, and soon too.' And, as we know, come it did with a vengeance.

In 1832 Lord Stanley (afterwards Lord Derby), then Chief Secretary for Ireland,[4] who was a friend of my father's, placed him on a commission, appointed by the Government to make inquiries and investigations respecting tithes with a view to legislation. This necessitated his residence in or near Dublin for a considerable time, so we left Abington and all our troubles there, and did not return till nearly three years later. Meantime, the tithe question having been settled by Parliament, the country had settled down into its normal state; and though the old cordial relations with the peasantry never could be quite restored, still we lived on friendly terms with them till my father's death, in 1845.

4. E. G. G. Stanley (1799-1869), 14th earl Derby, chief secretary for Ireland 1830-33, introduced a Tithe Commutation Bill in 1833, but it had little effect on the crisis.

CHAPTER XXX

As I have passed a long life, well over seventy years, almost altogether in Ireland, and have constantly come in contact with every class in the country, and as I may, I think, fairly claim to have a considerable knowledge of its people, I trust I shall be excused for making a few remarks, before I conclude this book, on the present state of affairs, as seen by one who has personally observed the many agitations and the many changes in the condition of the country, which have occurred since the early part of the century.

The first great agitation which I remember was that for Catholic Emancipation, which was granted in 1829 under the pressure of a fear of an Irish rebellion. The great meetings and marchings to which I have already referred, had led the Duke of Wellington, then Prime Minister, to fear that Ireland was ripe for a rebellion, more serious than that of '98, the danger and bloodshed of which he was unwilling to face. I can well remember the exaggerated notions the peasantry had of all the benefits they were to derive from the measure. Wages were at once to be doubled, and constant, well-paid employment to be given to every man.[1]

My father and mother had been always ardently in favour of Catholic Emancipation, and were delighted when the Act was passed. On the night when the news that the bill had become law reached our part of the country, we were all assembled to see the bonfires which blazed on all the mountains and hills around us, and I well remember the shouting and rejoicings on the road that passed our gate, and the hearty cheers given for us. I specially recollect one man, a farmer named James Fleming, generally known as Shamus Oge (Young James), being asked by some one in the crowd what emancipation meant. 'It means,' said he, 'a shilling a day for every man as long as he lives, whatever he does.' The ordinary wages of the labourers were then sixpence a day.

We little thought on that night how soon we should see the same fires lighted all around us, when any of the clergy near us had suffered outrage, or how soon, without any change on our part, we should be hooted and shouted at whenever we appeared.

It is now nearly forgotten that in 1825, four years earlier, a bill for Catholic Emancipation was passed in the House of Commons, and at the same time a bill by virtue of which the Roman Catholic priests would have received payment from the State, and been made entirely independent of the voluntary contributions of their congregations.[2] One of the

1. The Irish peasantry had long believed in an ultimate deliverance. In the early nineteenth century, many maintained that protestantism would be extinguished in 1825 — according to a prophecy — and many more thought that, in a general sense, emancipation would lead to a restructuring of society as a whole.
2. Sir Francis Burdett introduced a Catholic Relief Bill, providing for state payment of the clergy, in Westminster in 1824. It passed the Commons, but was thrown out by the Lords.

main facts that has to be borne in mind by any one who desires to judge fairly of the influence exercised by the Roman Catholic priesthood over their people in any great crisis, is this, that they are so entirely dependent for their sole means of support on the goodwill of the people, that they must always to a greater extent than is desirable follow, instead of lead, those over whom they are placed. If this bill had passed into law, there can be little doubt that the whole influence of the Roman Catholic priesthood would have been thrown into the opposite scale from that in which it has been during the last fifty years, and that the whole course of events in Ireland would have been very different. The bills were, however, unfortunately thrown out by the House of Lords, and when emancipation was granted, it was not accompanied by the other measure which had in 1825 been joined to it.

After the passing of the Emancipation Act comparative quiet reigned in the country till 1832, when the tithe war, with all its outrages, began. This agitation was carried out by O'Connell, on nearly the same lines as that for emancipation, and was crowned with like success. But the abolition of tithes did not bring to the peasantry all the benefits they expected; it merely changed the tithe into a rent-charge payable to the landlords, who were made liable for the payment of the clergy.

The success which attended the agitations for Catholic Emancipation and for the abolition of tithes — which success was in large measure due to the fear the English people entertained of an Irish rebellion — led O'Connell to commence his agitation for the repeal of the Union. This, however, failed, and its failure resulted in O'Connell's fall.

Great meetings had been held all through the country, at which O'Connell and others had used language more threatening than had been ventured on in the former agitations. Encouraged by the non-interference of the Government, O'Connell announced that a monster meeting would be held at Clontarf, close to Dublin, on Sunday, the 8th of September, 1843.

The Government determined that the meeting should not take place; a proclamation was issued forbidding it, and it was arranged that all the leaders of the agitation should be arrested. The duty of arresting O'Connell himself was assigned to Colonel Brown, the Chief Commissioner of Police, whom I have already mentioned in connection with my only attempt to enlist in that force. The excitement was intense; but at the last moment O'Connell struck his colours, and issued a second proclamation forbidding the people to meet. I was at Clontarf on the day fixed for a meeting. Nearly the whole of the garrison of Dublin — horse, foot, and artillery — was there, but no meeting was held. The subsequent prosecution and imprisonment of O'Connell and the other principal leaders put a complete stop to the agitation; and although it is true that their conviction was shortly afterwards quashed, after an appeal to the House of Lords, O'Connell's power was gone for ever.

Before the next agitation of any moment, the great famine of 1846-7 occurred. Up to that time the number of the people, and their poverty, steadily increased, and the first change for the better in their condition, within my memory, was subsequent, and in a great measure due, to that terrible affliction. It put a stop in some degree to the subdivision of holdings, which had been carried on to such an extent that, in many parts of the country, the holdings were so small that even had they been rent free they would have been insufficient for the maintenance of their occupiers. It forced the people not to depend in future on the potatoes as their staple food, and it led to some extent to better cultivation of the soil. The famine had hardly ended when Smith O'Brien's abortive rebellion occurred. Although earnest and able men — such as O'Brien himself, Tom Davies [*sic*], Meagher, Mitchell [*sic*], and others — were the leaders in the movement, it was an almost ludicrous failure; the hearts of the people were not in it, and the Roman Catholic priesthood were opposed to it.

For seventeen years after this time no agitation worth recording arose, and, with the exception of some isolated outrages, peace prevailed in the country, and the prosperity of all classes increased. Then in 1865 the Fenian Society came into existence, and continued to increase in power and in the number of members enrolled, until in February, 1866, the Habeas Corpus Act was suspended. Immediately before this a large number of Americans or Irish-Americans, easily recognizable by their dress and appearance, were to be met walking about the streets of Dublin. These gentlemen must somehow have got a hint of what was about to happen, for, on the day before the suspension of the Act, their sudden disappearance from the city was as remarkable as their previous appearance there had been.[3] This conspiracy was not completely put down till March, 1867, when the principal Fenian army succumbed at Tallaght, a few miles from Dublin, to twelve men of the Royal Irish Constabulary, and smaller risings in other parts of Ireland at the same time were easily suppressed.

What I have called the principal Fenian army was in reality only a mob of half-armed and utterly undisciplined Dublin youths, who had assembled near this village of Tallaght. When opposed by the small force of constabulary, who fired a few shots, they retired to a neighbouring hill. Many of them dispersed during the night, but a considerable number remained till the morning, when they surrendered to a military force, and were marched into Dublin. I did not myself see the prisoners, but I remember my brother telling me how he had seen them, so tired out that, wet as it was, they were lying about on the ground, in the Castle yard. My brother's pantry-boy had joined the army, but was one of those who escaped being made prisoner, and he used to give a most interesting account of the Battle of Tallaght.

The agitation for Home Rule, begun by Isaac Butt, never appeared to me to have any reality in it until Parnell became the leader of the movement.

Looking back on these various agitations to which I have briefly referred, it appears to me that none of those which appealed merely to the anti-English sentiment of the people, ever obtained any real hold of the peasantry. Those which did succeed appealed to feelings of an entirely different nature, and aimed at the abolition of some religious inequality or some pecuniary burden, and there are few who would now deny the justice of Catholic Emancipation and of the abolition of the tithe system in Ireland.

I do not mean to suggest, by what I have just written, that the anti-English feeling is not a real thing. It is, on the contrary, as far as my observation goes, a very deep and far-reaching sentiment; and I have had opportunities of forming an opinion, from conversations with many of the peasantry in different parts of the country, whom I have known from their early youth, and who have not been afraid, as they generally are, to tell the real feelings entertained by themselves and their neighbours.

Their chief hope has always appeared to lie in a successful rebellion, by the aid of America, or, possibly, of France. Many of them have looked forward all their lives to 'the War,' as they call it. It is not long since a tenant of my brother-in-law, when on his death-bed, said to him, 'Ah, yer honour, isn't it too bad entirely that I'd be dying now, and the War that I always thought I'd live to see coming so near?' The strength of the feeling was shown by the wild burst of enthusiasm in favour of the French at the beginning of the Franco-Prussian War, when processions marched through Dublin and other towns in Ireland, with tricolor banners, and led by bands playing the 'Marseillaise.' This sympathy with the French was undoubtedly due to the tradition of the help that had been expected from France in 1798, and to the hope that, if necessary, help against England might again be obtained from the same quarter.

But, strong as this anti-English feeling is, it is not in it, as I think, that the real strength of the agitation of the last fifteen years has lain. If it had been founded on this alone, or even mainly on this, it would never have obtained the support it has obtained from the people. It was the uniting of the Land Question with the agitation for Home Rule which really roused the peasantry. It is impossible for any one who has not resided in Ireland, and been on intimate terms with the people, to realize the intense longing which animates them for the possession of land, no matter how small or how bad the holding may be. If a farm was vacant owing to eviction of the tenant or otherwise, there were always numbers ready to compete for it, and willing to pay the landlord a fine for its possession, far beyond its value. They would often borrow the money to pay this fine at high interest, and, in most cases, left themselves without sufficient means to cultivate the land properly. To this land-hunger was also due, to a great extent, the subdivision of farms, which was so ruinous to the country; for in former days the father of the family thought the best way he could provide for his younger sons was to give each of them some portion of his land. I remember numbers of instances in our own immediate neighbourhood where farms, originally large, were divided among the sons of the tenants, and subsequently subdivided again and again, until

3. The Fenian Society actually dates from 1858. The arrests of many of the Fenian leaders, after the suppression of their newspaper *The Irish People*, occurred in 1865. Captain Thomas J. Kelly and a number of American Fenians were sent to Ireland in January 1867 to plan a rising. This ill-fated venture took place in March 1867.

some of the holdings became quite too small to support a family. In the neighbourhood of bogs these subdivisions were more numerous than in other places, the reason being that fuel was more easily and cheaply obtained there; in most cases, indeed, there were rights of turbary[4] attached to the holdings.

This anxiety for the possession of land is no doubt, as has often been pointed out, largely due to the fact that Ireland is so destitute of mineral wealth, that there has been comparatively little industrial development, and that the land has been the only resource for the people; but I am sure that it is also an innate sentiment. Any one who once grasps the fact that this land-hunger does exist, and realizes at all what a passion it is, will easily see what an attraction there was for the peasantry in the hopes held out to them, that by joining this agitation they would ultimately get their land for little or nothing. These hopes were undoubtedly fostered by the Land Act of 1881, which, though it may have been unavoidable, certainly struck a fatal blow at the obligation of contract between landlord and tenant.[5]

Hopes of this kind appeal with an especial force to an excitable and highly imaginative people like the Irish. It is scarcely possible to believe how extravagant are the hopes entertained by many of the peasantry of the benefits which they would derive from the establishment of an Irish Parliament. Not only do they expect that after a short time rent would be enormously reduced, or that they would become proprietors of their holdings at a very small price; but many of them have the most fanciful ideas as to the immediate advantages that would arise. Many believe that there are numerous mines and coal-fields which the English Government has never allowed to be worked, and that these would greatly enrich the country; while others suppose that wages would be at least trebled, and abundance of work afforded everywhere. In Dublin, too, there is a widespread idea that the city would be greatly benefited, as all the nobility and gentry would again reside there, as they did before the Union. In fact, it is no exaggeration to say that the peasantry at least expect that there would be 'a plethora of wealth,' and that 'a pauper population would roll in riches.' No reasonable man can doubt that all these hopes would be disappointed, except possibly that as to the land, which might indeed be realized, but only by a shameful and cruel injustice to the landlords; and the inevitable disappointment would, it can hardly be doubted, lead to a condition of discontent greater than any that has heretofore existed. I have always believed that it is the Land Question which is really at the root of the whole matter, and that it should be settled by some system of compulsory purchase to be determined upon and carried out by the Imperial Parliament, for it is difficult to imagine that such a question could be really fairly dealt with by a body of men elected almost entirely by the votes of one of the parties to the dispute.

Whatever may be said of the effect of the Union and of subsequent legislation, there is no doubt that the general condition of the country and the peasantry has improved in every respect during my lifetime. I cannot speak of the earlier days immediately following the Union; but I can clearly recollect what the country was over sixty years ago as compared with what it is now, and the improvement has been quite as great as the most sanguine could have expected.

I have already spoken of the faction fights which were common when I was a boy, and which have since entirely died out, although in some few places the recollection of the former feuds still exists, and is occasionally the cause of an isolated crime. . . .

There have also, unfortunately, from time to time been serious outbreaks of crime, and there are some parts of the south where lawlessness still prevails to a lamentable extent; but, taking Ireland as a whole, there is no doubt that the peasantry have a greater respect for the law than they had in my early days, and that the country is more peaceful and quiet. One feature which distinguished the outbreak of crime during the late land agitation from any that I remember, was that the outrages and intimidation were mainly directed, not against the landlords and agents as heretofore, but against any of the peasantry who broke or evaded the unwritten law of the Land League. It was marked by a far greater amount of combination than ever existed before, and it was by this combination that the taking of farms, from which tenants had for any cause been evicted, was so effectually prevented. It is not that the desire to take such farms is less than it

4. That is, rights to cut turf.
5. The Act of 1881 established the principle of dual ownership by landlord and tenant. In Gladstone's words, the aim was not to destroy landlordism, but to make it impossible.

ever was, but that no man dare take one, as he does so at the risk of his life. . . .

The drainage and cultivation of land have certainly greatly improved during my lifetime; and so have the dwellings of the peasantry. Large numbers of loans for drainage and other land improvements have been made by the Treasury through the Board of Public Works, and it is satisfactory to know that these loans have, on the whole, been advantageously expended and are being honestly repaid.

It is unfortunately true that considerable religious animosity still exists, which, though dormant, is ready to break out on any provocation; but I cannot see how these feelings would be at all mitigated by the proposed change in the government of this country; in fact, it appears to me that they would undoubtedly be intensified.

Looking back on the last seventy years, and remembering the progress that Ireland has made, I see no reason to despair of the future of my country. Although, during the first five and thirty years of my life, there was comparatively little change for the better in the condition of the people, since the year 1850 it has vastly improved. Wages have more than doubled; the people are better housed, better clad, and better fed. In recent years this improvement has been even more marked, and, if nothing untoward arises to retard its progress, if (is the hope too sanguine?) Ireland can cease to be 'the battle-field of English parties,' it will, I trust, ere many years, be as happy and contented as any part of our good Queen's dominions.

WILLIAM CARLETON

(1794-1869)

from: AUTOBIOGRAPHY in THE LIFE OF WILLIAM CARLETON (1896)

[William Carleton's fragment of *Autobiography* was incorporated into D. J. O'Donoghue's *The Life of William Carleton.* The excerpt printed here is taken from that text.

Carleton's struggle for an education in the midst of the political strife in the north of Ireland in the years after 1798 is in itself an important historical document, revealing, as does all his best work, the hitherto submerged life of the Irish peasantry. The vestigial remains of the old Gaelic culture — the hedge-school, the ramshackle church, the Irish language — are barely surviving the long war of attrition which 1798 had once more intensified. Orange and Ribbon factions are locked in a struggle — one for supremacy, the other for existence — in a world that was to disappear with the Great Famine of 1845.]

CHAPTER III

I cannot distinctly remember how long I remained with Pat.[1] My brother John made a first-rate arithmetician; but Pat never could succeed in that direction with me. I had no genius for science, nor was I ever able to work out a proposition of Euclid during my life. The terms were perfectly unintelligible to me. The only thing then remarkable about me was my distinction in the spelling lessons. These lessons always closed the business of the school, and all the boys capable of spelling were put into the class. Each boy put down a pin, which the master placed in the spelling book, and then they all took their places — forming a circle that almost went round the whole school. The head of the class was

1. Pat Frayne, the 'poor scholar' who returned to take over the local hedge-school that Carleton attended. A poor scholar was one who wandered, looking for the education he could not receive in his local area. The hedge-school was an unofficial, clandestine establishment, where the rudiments of a classical and scientific education were provided, depending upon the expertise of the teacher. Carleton modelled Matt Kavanagh, the hedge-school master of his story 'The Hedge-School', on Frayne.

called King — the second Queen — and the third Prince. In that class I held the first place, nor do I recollect that I was ever dethroned. I went home every day with the coat sleeve of my left arm shining with the signals of my triumph from my shoulder to my wrist.

About this time a classical school was opened in the upper part of Aughentain,[2] and as my father, in accordance with the humble ambition which then prevailed and still prevails among persons of his class, had taken it into his head to make one of his sons a priest, he sent my brother John to that school, with a hope that he might live to see him 'with robes upon him.' John, however, had an aversion to the classics as unconquerable as mine to science. He sulked, and refused to go to school, and by the advice of Pat Frayne my father gave the matter up. I was then pitched upon for the priesthood, but when I was prepared to go, and nicely smoothed up by a new suit of clothes, it was found that the classical master had vanished.

Here, then, was another obstruction to my advance in education. Still, I returned to Pat Frayne, with whom I accomplished little good. I did not at all relish arithmetic, and I consequently made but little progress in it. I was principally engaged in hunting through the neighbours' houses for books of some or any description to read. Sometimes I happened upon an odd volume of a novel, and literally felt entranced by the perusal of it.

At this period, when I was about nine years of age, an extraordinary exhibition of political enthusiasm was made by the Protestant and Catholic young men in this remote district of the north — principally among the Protestants. If I had not been myself an eye-witness of the movement and a participator in it, I really would have imagined that the whole progress of the principle by which the people were actuated was an idle dream. Such, however, it was not, and no man ought to be a better judge of its reality than myself — because, young as I was, I became an active and a prominent character in it. It is unnecessary to say that for some years after the Rebellion of '98 a bitter political resentment subsisted between Protestants and Catholics. Well do I remember it. The party fights at that time were frequent and in many instances fatal. This, indeed, was the period which I selected for my 'Party Fight and Funeral'.[3] In this instance the political rancour became dramatic. The plays of 'The Siege of Londonderry', and 'The Battle of Aughrim' were acted in barns and waste houses[4] night after night, and were attended by multitudes, both Catholic and Protestant. 'The Battle of Aughrim', however, was the favourite, and the acting play. I heard that 'The Siege of Londonderry' had been also acted, but I never saw it. This feeling of political enthusiasm directed my attention to the plays, which in their printed shape were school-books at the time. In fact I had 'The Battle of Aughrim' off by heart, from beginning to ending. This came to be known, and the consequence was that, though not more than ten years of age, I became stage director and prompter both to the Catholic and Protestant amateurs. In the mornings and in the evenings such of them — and there were not a few on both sides — as could not read, spent hours with me in attempting to make themselves perfect in their parts. It is astonishing, however, what force and impetus such an enthusiastic desire to learn and recollect bestows upon the memory. I had here an opportunity of witnessing this, for the quickness and accuracy with which they prepared themselves was astonishing.

The play selected for action on this occasion was, of course, 'The Battle of Aughrim', and the theatre the identical barn belonging to Jack Stuart which I have already described.[5] The crowds that flocked to it, both Catholics and Protestants, would, if admitted, have overcrowded the largest theatre in Europe. One element of their great curiosity, independently of the political feeling, was simply the novelty of seeing a play. On the right hand side of the lofted floor which constituted the barn, and

2. Carleton was born in the parish of Clogher in south County Tyrone. His local townland was called Prillisk. The places named here — Aughentain, Nurchasy, Towney and Findramore — are all in that area.

3. A story first published in *Traits and Stories of the Irish Peasantry*, First Series (Dublin, 1830).

4. *The Siege of Londonderry* (1705) was written by Colonel John Mitchelburne, governor of Derry during the famous siege of 1689; *The Battle of Aughrim*, first printed in 1756, written *c.*1727, is by Robert Ashton. Both these events at Derry and Aughrim are legendary and triumphant moments of protestant history, appreciated with renewed relish after 1798. See G. C. Duggan, *The Stage Irishman* (Dublin: The Talbot Press, 1937), pp. 30-37, 84-102. 'Waste houses' were formerly inhabited buildings that had fallen into disrepair.

5. Described in Chapter II: '. . . the barn was a loft over the cowhouse and stable, and the door of it on a level with the hay yard, which was about thirty feet above the road that passed.'

under which, as I have said, were the cowhouse and stable, was a range of chairs and forms for the audience to sit upon; on the left was a range of sacks filled with barley, the heaviest grain that grows; on these the other portion of the spectators were placed. It was summer, and the heat was suffocating. I was on the left side, standing behind those who sat upon the sacks, and with my feet upon them. In order to keep myself at ease and steady, I held by a wattle in the roof above me, and in that position enjoyed the play. When it had reached the scene in which the ghost makes its appearance, or rather a little before it, I felt something like a descent of that part of the floor on which the sacks had been stretched. In about a quarter of a minute there was another descent of the sacks, and I shouted out 'the floor is going to fall.' Such, however, was the attention of the audience, that my warning had no effect. The ghost came forward, when a tremendous crash took place, and the last thing I saw was his heels in the air, as he and that portion of the audience with whom I stood, sacks and all, went down together. Fortunately, there was a large beam which ran longitudinally through the barn — by which I mean from end to end. The barn was an old one, and its timbers, as was found afterwards, quite decayed with age. The weight of the sacks, and the crowded audience on the left hand side, was more than the rotten rafters could bear, and the consequence was that one half the barn floor with its weighty burthen was precipitated into the cowhouse and stable. I dropped down upon those who fell, and scrambled over their heads towards those who were on the safe side, by whom I was pulled up without having received any injury.

In this case the force of instinct was exhibited in a remarkable manner. The animals beneath the loft must have heard the sharp jerking noise of the rafters as they gave symptoms of being about to fall, because it was found that they had broken the ropes which held them, and taken shelter under that part of the loft which did not fall. I saw them there with my own eyes, as did every other person, and I need not describe the wonder it occasioned. As it was, scarcely any injury resulted from the descent of the loft, if I except that which was sustained by the ghost, who had his arm broken.

These senseless exhibitions inflamed political feeling very much. In the town of Augher,[6] this stupid play was acted by Catholics and Protestants, each party of course sustaining their own principles. The consequence was, that when they came to the conflict with which the play is made to close, armed as they were on both sides with real swords, political and religious resentment could not be restrained, and they would have hacked each other's souls out had not the audience interfered and prevented them. As it was, some of them were severely if not dangerously wounded.

During the period of which I now write, the country was in a state sufficient, in the mind of every liberal and thinking man, to fling back disgrace and infamy upon the successive administrations which permitted it. This was the period of Protestant, or rather of Orange, ascendancy. There were at that time regular corps of yeomen, who were drilled and exercised on the usual stated occasions. There were also corps of cavalry who were subjected to the same discipline. Now all this was right and proper, and I remember when a review day was looked forward to as we used to look for Christmas or Easter. On those occasions there were thousands of spectators, and it would have been well if matters had ended there. Every yeoman with his red coat on was an Orangeman. Every cavalryman mounted upon his own horse and dressed in blue was an Orangeman; and to do both foot and cavalry justice, I do not think that a finer body of men could be found in Europe. Roman Catholics were not admitted into either service. I think I may say that I knew almost every yeoman in the parish, but I never knew of a Roman Catholic to be admitted into either force, with one exception — his name was William Kelly, a cousin of my own.

Merciful God! In what a frightful condition was the country at that time. I speak now of the North of Ireland. It was then, indeed, the seat of Orange ascendancy and irresponsible power. To find a justice of the peace *not* an Orangeman would have been an impossibility. The grand jury room was little less than an Orange lodge. There was then no law *against* an Orangeman, and no law *for* a Papist. I am now writing not only that which is well known to be historical truth, but that which I have witnessed with my own eyes.

These yeomen were in the habit — especially when primed with whisky, or on their way from an Orange lodge — of putting on their uniform, getting their guns and bayonets, and going out at night to pay domiciliary visits to Catholic families

6. The town of the parish of Clogher.

under the pretence of searching for firearms; and it is painful to reflect upon, or even to recollect, the violence and outrage with which these illegal excursions were conducted. Take an instance.

I have mentioned Sam Nelson as one of Pat Frayne's scholars, and of course the schoolfellow of myself and my brother; and I have said, I think, that his father's house was next to ours — in fact it was not ten yards from us; in truth we were in daily intercourse of the most neighbourly and friendly character. We were perpetually in each other's houses, lending and borrowing, and discharging all those duties towards each other which constitute friendly neighbourhood. Sam Nelson was what is termed a humorous or droll kind of good-natured 'slob', and evidently fond of me and my brother. On one occasion he made us a present of a little tin gun or cannon about four or five inches in length, of which we were naturally very proud. Before I proceed farther in this reminiscence I think it necessary to say that my father was one of the quietest and most highly respected men in the parish, considering his position in life. Neither he nor any of his family were ever known to give utterance to an offensive word. They took no part whatsoever in politics, neither did they ever engage in those senseless party or faction fights which were so disgraceful to the country, or give expression to any political opinion that could be construed into offence. Having made these observations, I now proceed with my reminiscence.

One night, about two or three o'clock, in the middle of winter, a violent bellowing took place at our door, and loud voices were heard outside. My father got up, alarmed, and asked who was there.

'Open the door, your rebellious old dog, or we will smash it in.'

'Give me time to get on my clothes,' replied my father.

'Not a minute, you old rebel; you want to hide your arms — open or we smash the door,' and the door was struck violently with the butts of guns. My father, having hurried on his small clothes and lit a candle, opened the door, when in an instant the house was filled with armed yeomen in their uniform.

'Come, you traitorous old scoundrel, deliver up your d—d rebelly gun.'

'My good friends,' replied my father, 'I have no gun.'

'It's a lie, you rebel, it's well known you have a gun. Produce it, or I put the contents of this through you.' And as he spoke the man cocked and deliberately aimed the gun at my father. (I forgot to state that the men appeared with screwed bayonets.) When my mother saw my father covered by the ruffian's gun, she placed herself with a shawl about her between them, and corroborated what my father said, that we had no gun. She was called a liar; it was notorious we had a gun. In the meantime, some others of them began to institute a search. Two of them went into my sister's bedroom, a third man holding the candle.

'Who is this?' said one scoundrel.

'It's my daughter,' replied my mother, trembling and in tears.

'Well,' he returned, 'let her get up until we have a look at her; it's likely she has the gun in the bed; at all events we'll rouse her a bit—' and as he spoke, he put the point of the bayonet to her side, which he pressed until she screamed with pain. At this moment his companion pulled him back with something of indignant violence, exclaiming:

'D—n your soul, you cowardly scoundrel, why do you do that?'

At this moment my mother, with the ready recollection and presence of mind of her sex, exclaimed:

'I think it likely that all this trouble has come from the little tin gun that Sam Nelson gave the children — here it is,' she proceeded — 'here is the only gun that ever was under this roof. If it's treason to keep *that*, we are rebels' — and as she spoke she handed them the gun. They looked at it, and after some ruffianly grumbling they retired. My sister was slightly wounded in the side. My readers will be surprised to learn that one of Sam Nelson's brothers was among this scoundrelly gang, and never once interfered in our behalf. No man knew better than he did that my father had no gun. No man knew better than he that this midnight and drunken visit was a mere pretence, deliberately founded upon the history of the tin gun which his brother Sam had given to me and my brother John. My readers may form an opinion of the state of society, when they hear that there was not an individual present that night in this gross and lawless outrage with whom we were not acquainted, nor a man among them who did not know everyone of us intimately.

Such was the outrageous and licentious conduct of the Orangemen of that day, and of many a day long before and afterwards. As a public writer, guided by a sense of truth and justice, I could not allow such a system as that which Orangeism then was to remain without exposure, and I did not. It is to that midnight visit that they owe 'Valentine McClutchy'.[7] Little they dreamt that there was a boy present, not more than ten years of age, who would live to punish them with a terrible but truthful retaliation.

Soon after this event my father began to think of leaving Towney. A farm of eighteen acres was vacant in a townland called Nurchasy, about two miles towards the south. Hugh Traynor, a very respectable man, although an extensive and notorious private distiller, was the under-landlord, or middleman. From him my father took the farm, and we removed to it without loss of time. I will never forget that removal. All our furniture had been taken to the new place, which I had not yet seen, and every member of our family had gone with it, I alone excepted. In fact my father did not wish me to come until everything should be settled, and I accordingly remained with a married sister of mine, who also lived in Towney, until my father should call in the evening to bring me home. This he did, but not until after night, and many a time since have I thanked God that he did not. The season was summer, and such an exquisitely beautiful night I have never recollected since.

The moon was in the full, and the sky so perfectly clear and cloudless as to present the idea of nothing but that blue void which is so full of poetry and beauty. My father, for what purpose I know not, unless it was to give me a surprise, brought me to the farm by a way quite circuitous, but a way which to me was beautiful beyond the power of language to express. It was the first time I experienced the delight of travelling through new and beautiful scenery by moonlight.

Nurchasy to me was paradise. The view from it of Fardress Glen, so beautifully wooded, and of Fardress grazing-fields, so green and extensive, together with the effect of those small circular grove, peculiar to some portions of the north, absolutely enchanted me. Nothing, in fact, could surpass my happiness. I frequently dreamt of the scenery about me, although I had it before my eyes every day in the week. It was while we were in Nurchasy, which was not more than half a mile from Findramore, that a classical school was opened in the townland of Tulnavert, the property of John Birney, now of Oakley Park, in the county of Down. Like most Irish schools, it also was held in a barn, which belonged to Tom Hall and his brothers, three wealthy old bachelors, who have long disappeared. The man who taught this school was an individual who should have been kept closely confined in a lunatic asylum during his life. He had been one of the earliest students of Maynooth on its first establishment;[8] there he remained until he became insane — a calamity which necessarily caused his removal. The slavish, ill-tempered scoundrel never raised his hand to a Protestant boy, no matter how insolent or provoking his conduct, but if one of his own creed only broke a straw he would chastise him most severely. It was he who sat for the heartless tyrant in 'The Poor Scholar'.[9] By the way, talking of a poor scholar, we had an unfortunate wretch of that description in our school at Tulnavert. His name was John Quin, and indeed I may add that he was the scapegoat of the school. It was not he, however, who sat for the character of the poor scholar whom I have made the hero in my tale of that name. There was a man in our Parish called Dominick Donnelly, who was and had been for many years the Mass-server to the successive Catholic clergymen who came to the parish. I believe in my soul the man could not read, but it was not at all extraordinary during my early life to meet persons capable of serving Mass, that is, acting as clerk, who did not know a letter in the alphabet. The memory of some men is perfectly astonishing. When you think, however, of a totally illiterate man giving the Latin responses to the priest during Mass, I will give you leave to entertain some doubts as to the purity of his latinity. . . .

7. *Valentine McClutchy, the Irish Agent*: *or*, *The Chronicles of the Castle Cumber Property* (Dublin, 1845), a ferocious attack upon the injustice and corruption of the established system in Ireland.

8. In 1795.

9. In Vol. II of *Traits and Stories of the Irish Peasantry*, Second Series, 3 vols (Dublin, 1833).

CHAPTER VII

. . . I now began to look out for books of fiction and entertainment. It is true I had read all those cheap amusing little works which were at that time the only reading books in the common schools, from *The Arabian Nights* downwards. Need I say with what an enthusiastic delight I read them — but they only stimulated the taste for fiction by which I was then absorbed. I had now little on my hands to do as a student, but so anxious was I for this sort of amusement, that I went throughout the greater part of the parish hunting for books of entertainment.

Although the state of education was, at the period of which I write, very low, and knowledge scanty among the people, yet it is surprising what a number of books, pamphlets and odd volumes, many of these works of fiction, I found among them. If you examined the number of Catholic families in the parish, you would find that one half of them could not read; yet several of these utterly illiterate persons had many of the works I have alluded to, most carefully laid up, under the hope that some young relation might be able to read them. I remember two, by which I was much struck — *The Life of Edward, Lord Herbert*, and Defoe's *History of the Devil*.[1]

After having ransacked almost all the old cupboards and boxes in the parish, I accidentally heard of a relative of mine who, I was told, was curate of a place called Glennon, in the parish of Donagh, county Monaghan. What was most agreeable to me, and least expected, was that he kept a classical school. On making further inquiry among my family, and having consulted my uncle — brother to my father — I discovered that Mr Keenan (for such was his name) and I were second cousins. This information afforded me great satisfaction. I accordingly went to a family named McCarron, who held a fine farm in the townland of Derrygola, in the adjoining parish of Truagh. The wife of Patrick McCarron was my mother's niece. Here I stayed for a few days, and then proceeded to the house of a man named Traynor, with whom I understood my cousin Keenan lodged. Traynor's house was immediately beside the chapel, and a comfortable one it was. Fortunately I found my reverend cousin at home, and on making myself known to him I was very kindly received. His family and ours lived at least thirty miles from each other, so that except in blood relationship were utter strangers. I gave him a history of my past life and education, and mentioned the declining circumstances of the family, expressing deep regret that I had not had an opportunity of completing my classical education. The man saw at once the object of my visit, and asked me could I not attend his school.

'If I had a house of my own,' said he, 'I could with pleasure afford you a place of residence, but as it is I am only a lodger here.'

I told him that I had relations in the neighbouring parish of Truagh, about five miles distant, with whom I could live.

'Well, in that case,' he replied, 'the sooner you come the bettter; whatever I can do for you I will feel very happy in doing. I only hope,' he added, smiling 'that you are not a better scholar than myself. Before you go, you must take a drop of dram,' and in a couple of minutes I got a bumper of as good poteen[2] as ever ran through the eye of a still, as the phrase is. I went to Keenan in the year 1814 and remained with him until the year 1816. I lived at Derrygola for some time with my relations the McCarrons, who were wealthy people, and most affectionate to me. My residence with them was the most delightful period of my youth. Keenan, as I said, was only the curate of the parish of Donagh. Glasslough was the next town to his residence, that is to say, about three-quarters of a mile from it. The parish priest of Donagh was the Rev. Mr McMullan. The parish was not a large one, and Keenan's salary was so small that he was unable to live without the assistance he derived from the profits of his school. He collected oats besides from the parishioners, both Catholic and Protestant, and indeed I may affirm with truth that he was treated with more liberality by the latter class than by the former. The Protestants, however, could well afford to be liberal, as they were by far the more wealthy.

While I was with Keenan a brother of his returned from the Peninsular War,[3] accompanied by a Portuguese wife. I remember bringing a common low-wheeled car for them, covered with a feather bed and quilt, to the 'Westenra Arms' in

1. Edward Herbert (1583-1648), 1st baron Herbert of Cherbury, elder brother of the poet George Herbert, wrote his *Autobiography c.*1625. It was first printed in 1764. Herbert genially boasts of his valour, success with women and his amazing adventures. The book was popular, but its reprint history is complex. Perhaps Carleton found an abridged version.

Daniel Defoe's *The Political History of the Devil* (1726) was much reprinted.

2. From Irish *poitín* (little pot): an illicit spirit.
3. The Peninsular War (1808-14) was fought between the Napoleonic armies and an alliance of British forces under the Duke of Wellington and Spanish insurgents.

Monaghan, where they stopped the night before. Paddy Traynor, with whom Keenan lodged, contrived to make room for them in his house. Here, however, they did not remain long. Keenan's brother had either saved money in the army or got it with his wife: be this as it may, he was able to open the largest grocery and liquor establishment that ever was seen in Glasslough.

There were then at Keenan's school three individuals whom I will mention. Two of these were full-grown young men. One of them was Mr Peter McPhillips, who afterwards kept the 'Westenra Arms' Hotel in Monaghan for many years; the others were Frank McGough and John McNally. When Keenan's brother opened the grocery establishment in Glasslough, his brother the priest went to reside with him, and honest Peter McPhillips, one of the full-grown pupils just mentioned, and than whom a man of more sterling integrity never lived, gave up all notions of the priesthood, and went to conduct the peninsular hero's establishment as a grocer. In the meantime I had removed during the winter from McCarron's of Derrygola to Traynor's, with whom Keenan had lodged. From Traynor's I went for some months to the house of a man named Moynagh, whose residence was in Donagh, that being the name of the town from which the parish itself is named.

Of course it must not be supposed that I neglected to visit my mother and family during this period of absence. So far from that, I went home, I think, at least once a month, if not oftener. These visits sometimes lasted three or four days, and I not unfrequently went to Clogher market on these occasions — feeling naturally anxious to see and meet many of my young friends, who were also as anxious to see me. I may add here for once that there never was in that part of the country a young fellow more popular or better loved by persons of all creeds and classes — by the Protestants as well as by the Catholics. On such occasions, however, my associates were generally of my own religion. During those reunions I was struck with one fact, for which I could not by any means account. These young fellows, and others, frequently looked with a very mysterious kind of inquiry into my face, and occasionally asked me what age I was. I generally replied, 'I'm in my nineteenth year,' upon which the expression of their faces became lengthened and indicative of disappointment. This puzzled me very much: I could not by any train of reasoning understand it. I now return to a particular visit I made to see my mother and other relations at Springtown. The day was Saturday, and the month either June or July, when, having started for home from Glasslough, a distance of at least sixteen miles across the country, which to me was nothing, I had arrived at the townland next to Springtown, named Cargah, immediately above which was a very pretty smooth eminence ending in a flat greensward. On this table-land I found there was a dance, in which was engaged a number of young men and women, with nearly every one of whom I was acquainted. It was not, I soon found, an ordinary dance, but what they call in the north an *infare*,[4] or the haling home of a newly-married bride to the house of her husband, of which she is to be the future mistress. At these *infares*, there was generally such a dance as I found on the table on Cargah Hill, animated to a greater sense of enjoyment by plenty of excellent poteen whisky. Here I danced with the bride, whom I looked upon for the first time, and several other girls with whom I was intimately acquainted. Even at this time I was celebrated as a dancer. After my last dance was concluded, I stood to observe the progress of the general amusement, when I observed the young fellows getting together into knots and looking at me as if I had been the subject of their conversation. Before this period the bridegroom had forced me to take two glasses of the poteen, which, as I was not in the habit of drinking anything in the shape of spirits, had got a very little into my head. They offered me a third glass, which I refused, lest my mother might observe the signs of drink upon me. After some time, about half a dozen of them were led behind a dry green ditch by a red-haired fellow named Hugh Roe McCahy, who lived in the townland of Cloghleim, not half a mile distant. He was one of those important individuals who make themselves active and prominent among their fellows, attend dances and wakes, are seldom absent in fair or market from a fight, and, I may add, lose no opportunity of giving rise to one when everything else fails them.

'William,' said he, 'aren't you ashamed to be ignorant of what is going on about you over the whole country?' He had a prayerbook, or what is

4. A dialect word, of Old English and Middle English origin, literally meaning the act of going in, but, as here, referring to an entertainment given at the reception of a bride to her new home, on her first 'going in'.

called a *manual*, a book of Roman Catholic devotion, in his hand as he spoke — a fact which greatly puzzled me, as I was perfectly aware that he could not read. I had once before this, while book-hunting throughout the neighbourhood, called upon him and found in his house an odd volume of Catholic theology in Latin. The fellow was rapid in his language as well as in his personal motions.

'Why,' said I, 'what is going on in the country?'

'I will tell you,' he replied; 'but first take this *manual* in your hand, and repeat after me what I will say.'

He then went over the oath of Ribbonism, which he had got by heart, until he concluded it; after this he made me kiss the book.

'Now,' said he, 'you're *up* — you're a Ribbonman; all you want is the words and signs — and here they are.'

He then communicated them to me, and, although but a schoolboy, I went home a Ribbonman.

Here was a new view of life opened to me, and that with such dexterous rapidity, that I found myself made a member of a secret and illegal society by this adroit scoundrel, before I had time to pause or reflect upon the consequences. In like manner were hundreds, nay thousands, of unreflecting youths seduced into this senseless but most mischievous system.

I now discovered that the whole Catholic population, with the exception of the aged heads of families, was affiliated to Ribbonism. In fact it was not only almost impossible, but dangerous, to avoid being involved in the system. If a young man happened to possess the sense and spirit to resist the Ribbonmen's importunities to join them, he would probably be waylaid and beaten by persons of whom he knew nothing.

The following is the Ribbon oath, a curiosity in its way:

'I A.B., with the sign of the Cross do declare and promise, in the name and through the assistance of the Blessed Trinity, that I will keep inviolate all secrets of this Fraternal Society from all but those whom I know to be regular members of the same, and bound by the same solemn oath and fraternal ties:

'1st. I declare and profess, without any compulsion, allegiance to his present Majesty, George the Third, King of Great Britain and Ireland.

'2nd. That I will be true to the principles of this Society, dedicated to St Patrick, the Holy Patron of Ireland, in all things lawful and not otherwise.

'3rd. That I will duly and regularly attend on the shortest possible notice, at any hour, whether by night or by day, to perform, *without fail or inquiry*, such commands as my superior or superiors may lay upon me, under whatever penalty he or they may inflict for neglecting the same.

'4th. I will not deliberately or willingly provoke, challenge or strike any of my brothers, knowing him to be such. If he or they should be ill spoken of, ill-used, or otherwise treated unjustly, I will, according to circumstances and the best of my judgment, espouse his cause, give him the earliest information, and aid him with my friendship when in distress as a Ribbonman.

'5th. I also declare and promise that, I will not admit or propose a Protestant or heretic of any description as a member of our Fraternal Society, knowing him to be such.

'6th. That, whether in fair or market, in town or country, I will always give the preference in dealing to those who are attached to our national cause, and that I will not deal with a Protestant or heretic — but above all with an Orangeman — so long as I can deal with one of my own faith upon equal terms.

'7th. That I will not withdraw myself from this Society without stating my reasons for the same, and giving due notice to my superior or superiors; and that I will not without permission join any other society of different principles or denominations, under penalty of God's judgment, and whatever penalty may be inflicted on me — not including in these the Masonic Institution, Trade Societies, or the profession of soldier or sailor.

'8th. That I will always aid a brother in distress or danger by my person, purse, and counsel so far as in me lies; and that I will not refuse to subscribe money, according to my means, for the general or particular purposes of this our Fraternal Society.

'9th. That I will not, under the penalty inflicted by my superiors, give evidence in any Court of Law or Justice against a brother, when prosecuted by an Orangeman or heretic; and that I will aid him in his defence by any means in my power.

'10th. That when forced to take refuge from the law in the house of a brother or of any person friendly to our national cause, I will not have any improper intercourse or foul freedom with his sister, daughter, wife or cousin, and thus give cause of scandal to our Society.

'Having made the above solemn declaration and promise of my own free will and accord, I swear true and real allegiance to the cause of Ireland only, and no longer to be true as a subject nor to bear allegiance to George the Third, King of Britain and Ireland; and I now pray that God may assist me in my endeavours to fulfil the same; that He may protect me and prosper our Society, and grant us to live and die in a state of grace! — Amen.'

I may as well give what were then the 'Words' and the 'Grip', as I am on this subject. The words were as follows: — '*What age are we in?*' Answer. '*The end of the fifth.*' '*What's the hour?*' Answer. '*Very near the right one.*' '*Isn't it come yet?*' Answer. '*The hour is come, but not the man.*' '*When will he come?*' Answer. '*He is within sight.*'[5]

The grip was, when shaking hands, to press the point of the thumb on the second joint of the forefinger, and if the person with whom you shook hands was a brother, he was to press upon the middle joint of your little finger. Such were the words and grip of Ribbonism about the year 1814.

The reader will observe that there was a vagueness and a want of object in this ridiculous oath which gave conclusive evidence that it must have proceeded from a very ignorant source. I subsequently made inquiries into its origin, but could never ascertain the name of any man possessed of the slightest claim to respectability in connection with it. It originated with, and was confined to, the very lowest dregs of the people. That some scheming vagabonds must have been at the head of it, or the bottom of it is evident enough. Money was subscribed for fictitious objects, but where it went to no one could tell. In the county Louth it was set going by an Orangeman called Gubby (evidently an assumed name), and I think it was afterwards discovered that he was a native of Middleton, in that part of the county Tyrone which projects into the county of Armagh. This discovery, however, was made too late — for he had left the country.

I am not a friend to any of these secret societies, because they were nothing but curses to the country. The Orange system is a curse to the country, and will be so as long as it exists. It is now comparatively harmless, but at the period of which I write it was in the very height of its ascendancy, and seemed to live only as if its great object were to trample upon 'Popery'. The truth, however, is, if there can be an apology for Ribbonism, that it was nothing more nor less than a reactive principle against Orangeism, of whose outrages it was the result. In my works I have depicted both systems to the marrow, without either favour or affection, as the phrase has it. I never entertained any ill feeling against the people on either side; it is their accursed systems which I detest.

5. The wording of the oath is deeply influenced by the millenarian prophecies of Pastorini (Charles Walsmley), published in 1771, which foretold the extinction of protestantism in Ireland in 1825.

JOHN MILLINGTON SYNGE

(1871-1909)

from: AUTOBIOGRAPHY (1896-1907)

[The text is taken from Alan Price (ed.), *Synge: Collected Works* II (1962), which is itself constructed from three sources, manuscript and typewritten, dating from 1896-1907. It is useful to compare this with the biography of Synge by his nephew Edward Stephens, which fills out some of the detail given here (see A. Carpenter (ed.), *My Uncle John. Edward Stephens's Life of J.M. Synge* (London: Oxford University Press, 1974)).

The *Autobiography* reveals something of the nervous intensity with which Synge encountered the governing experiences of his childhood and youth — the loss of religious belief, first love, natural landscape, and the transfiguring conversion to 'Ireland'.]

Every life is a symphony, and the translation of this life into music, and from music back to literature or sculpture or painting is the real effort of the artist. The emotions which pass through us have neither end nor beginning — are a part of the sequence of existence — and as the laws of the world are in harmony it is this almost cosmic element in the person which gives great art, as that of Michelangelo or Beethoven, the dignity of nature.

I do not think biography — even autobiography — can give this revelation. But while the thoughts and deeds of a lifetime are impersonal and concrete — might have been done by anyone — art is the expression of the essential or abstract beauty of the person. . . . If by the study of an adult who is before his time we can preconstruct the tendency of life and if — as I believe — we find in childhood perfect traces of the savage, the expression of a personality will reveal evolution from before history to beyond the science of our epoque. . . .

For three days a south wind has been blowing over Paris. I have put syringa and white lilac in green vases round my room and left my windows open so that I can hear the crowds passing under them. This contact of perfume and sound recalls my childhood with peculiar surety.

The first moment that I remember I was sitting upon my nurse's knee while she arranged my clothes. I do not think I can have been more than two years old. Then I remember walking in under some shelves in the corner of my nursery and looking up at them with a vague curiosity how long it would take my head to reach them.

My promotion to knickerbockers and a severe cough or croup came about the time that I began to remember coherently. If I could know the dates of my nurses I could trace the whole course of my opening memory, but they are lost. I remember old Maria, Liz, squatty Kate, Agnes, a handsome girl that I admired who was soon sent away, a girl who cried in the evenings when I was in bed, and red-haired Sarah who still starts up [in my mind] when people talk of red hair. In all I remember eight or nine nurses, and as I was rid of them when I was eight years old my memory goes back a good way.

My childhood was a long series of coughs and colds, with plenty of amusement in the intervals and summer visits to the sea-side which were delightful. I have a vivid recollection of being caught in a heavy shower in the ladies' bathing place and bundled into a bathing-box that was not empty! Little boys are rightly considered inoffensive but some of them who have unusual memories grow up with souvenirs that illustrate a celebrated line in Dante.

I was painfully timid, and while still very young the idea of Hell took a fearful hold on me. One night I thought I was irretrievably damned and cried myself to sleep in vain yet terrified efforts to form a conception of eternal pain. In the morning I renewed my lamentations and my mother was sent for. She comforted me with the assurance that the Holy Ghost was convicting me of sin and thus preparing me for ultimate salvation. This was a new idea, and I rather approved. Later in the day while I was playing in the drawing-room I overheard my mother telling my aunt about my experience. While I gave no sign of attention I was inwardly flattered that I had caused this excitement and that the Holy Ghost should single me out so distinctively. I must have been quite young as my mother would not have talked about me in my presence for she was always judicious — except perhaps in her portrayal of Hell.

Religion remained a difficulty and occasioned terror to me for many years, though I do not think the brand I was brought up on was peculiarly Calvinistic. When I went to church I remember wondering whether it might not all be a fraud got together to aid the bringing-up of children which I believed to be arduous. Later in my early teens I think I had moments of great fervour and thought myself saved, but never for long at a time. [Still] the well-meant but extraordinary cruelty of introducing the idea of Hell into the imagination of a nervous child has probably caused more misery than many customs that the same people send missionaries to eradicate.

Before I went to school I used to go out to walk every day with my maid or my relations. Even at this time I was a worshipper of nature. I remember that I would not allow my nurses to sit down on the seats by the [River] Dodder because they were [man-]made. If they wished to sit down they had to find a low branch of a tree or a bit of rock or bank. I do not seem to have lacked a certain authority for they all obeyed. My brother also had this idea about 'made' things, perhaps he gave it to me. I had a very strong feeling for the colour of locality which I expressed in syllables of no meaning, but my elders checked me for talking gibberish when I was heard practising them. . . .

I studied the arabs of the streets. . . . I remember coming out of St. Patrick's, Sunday after Sunday, strained almost to torture by the music, and walking out through the slums of Harold's Cross as the lamps were being lit.[1] Hordes of wild children used to play round the cathedral of St. Patrick and I remember there was something appalling — a proximity of emotions as conflicting as the perversions of the Black Mass — in coming out suddenly from the white harmonies of the Passion according to St. Matthew among this blasphemy of childhood. The boys and girls were always in groups by themselves, for the utterly wild boy seems to regard a woman with the instinct of barbarians. I often stood for hours in a shadow to watch their manoeuvres and extraordinarily passionate quarrels. . . .

If we find in Bach an agreeable vibration of some portion of the brain and in the study of these children the vibration of another portion a little inferior — the attitude of science — we loose in the music our transcendent admiration, and in the slums the ecstasy of pity and with it the thin relish of delightful sympathy with the wildness of evil which all feel but few acknowledge even to themselves. The man who feels most exquisitely the joy of contact with what is perfect in art and nature is the man who from the width and power of his thought hides the greatest number of Satanic or barbarous sympathies. His opposite is the narrow churchman or reformer who knows no ecstasy and is shocked chiefly by the material discomforts of earth or Hell. . . .

Although I had the usual affection for my near relations I began while still very young to live in my imagination in enchanted premises that had high walls with glass upon the top where I sat and drank ginger-beer in a sort of perpetual summer with one companion, usually some small school-fellow I hardly knew. One day the course of my class put me for a moment beside my temporary god, and before I could find a fit term of adulation he whispered an obscene banality which shattered my illusions.

Soon afterwards — when I was about ten — my real affections and imagination acted together in a friendship with a girl of my own age[2] who was our neighbour. . . . We had a large establishment of pets — rabbits, pigeons, guinea pigs, canaries, dogs — which we looked after together. I was now going to school, but I had many holidays from ill health — six months about this time especially which were recommended on account of continual head-aches that I suffered from which gave us a great deal of time to wander about among the fields near our houses. We were left in complete liberty and never abused it. . . . She was, I think, a very pleasant-featured child and must have had an excellent character as for years I do not remember a single quarrel — with brothers, of course, I had plenty, sometimes of considerable violence. She was handy with her pencil and on wet days we used to draw animals from Vere Foster's copy books with great assiduity. . . .

About this same time an aunt of mine died in our own house. My mother asked me the day after if I was not sorry. I answered with some hesitation — at this time I was truthful to an almost morbid degree — that I feared not. My mother was much shocked and began telling me little things about my aunt till I wept copiously. In reality the death impressed with a sort of awe and wonder, but although I was fond of my aunt [it] did not grieve me — I suppose I did not realize what death meant. The days when the house was darkened — it was August — I spent in some woods near Rathfarnham with my little friend. They were wonderfully delightful, though I hardly remember what we did or talked of. The sense of death seems to have been only strong enough to evoke the full luxury of the woods. I had never been so happy. It is a feeling like this makes all primitive people inclined to merry making at a funeral.

We were always primitive. We both understood all the facts of life and spoke of them without much hesitation but a certain propriety that was decidedly wholesome. We talked of sexual matters with an indifferent and sometimes amused frankness that was identical with the attitude of folk-tales. We were both superstitious, and if we had been allowed . . . we would have evolved a pantheistic scheme like that of all barbarians. . . . I never spoke of religion with my companion, although we were both well-versed in Christianity. The monotheistic doctrines seem foreign to the real genius of childhood in spite of the rather maudlin appeal Christianity makes to little children. . . .

As I grew older I became more interested in

1. St Patrick's Cathedral in Dublin, where Swift was once dean. The protestant cathedral is in a predominantly catholic working-class area. In *My Uncle John*, this incident is cited with the accompanying note by Synge: 'With the same presumption that we show in forcing civilization on the savage, we teach the child how to be childlike, and for this reason the most interesting type of childhood is perhaps the uncultivated arab of the streets.' (p. 58).
2. Florence Ross, herself a friend of Cherrie Matheson, to whom Synge later, and vainly, transferred his affections.

definite life, and I used to hide in bushes to watch with amorous fellowship the mere movements of the birds. People said I had an interesting taste for natural history and gave me books. [My girl friend] took fire at my enthusiasm and we devoted a great deal of our spare time to observation and reading books on ornithology. Further we clubbed our resources and bought a ten-shilling telescope, which led to trouble afterwards. This period was probably the happiest of my life. It was admirable in every way.

The following summer, however, I had a horrible awakening. Our two families joined in a large country house in June where some Indian cousins of mine[3] were coming to spend the later months with us. This June was absolutely delightful. I had my friend now under the same roof, and we were inseparable. In the day-time we played tennis or watched the birds . . . and we wandered arm in arm about among the odours of the old-fashioned garden till it was quite dark watching the bats and moths. I loved her with a curious affection that I cannot pretend to analyse and I told her, with more virile authority than I since possess, that she was to be my wife. She was not displeased. My cousins arrived, a small boy and a girl of my own age. My friend threw [me] over completely, apparently without a shadow of regret, and became the bosom friend of her new companion, my accursed cousin. I was stunned with horror. I complained to no-one, but I fretted myself ill in lonely corners whistling 'Down in Alabama', the only love-song I knew. My mother knew what was in my mind, and contrived occasionally to get me a walk with my old comrade but our old friendship was at an end, for the time at any rate. Thus I learned very young the weakness of the false gods we are obliged to worship.

The following winter I do not recollect very clearly. I had a tutor, and a dog, and devoted myself to birds and Euclid with a good deal of success. When the spring returned I began a collection of birds' eggs, in finding which I was remarkably fortunate, far more so than my cousin or brother who sometimes [searched] with me. I kept careful notes of all that I thought interesting, with the intention of publishing a book on birds when old enough. I used to rise at six in the morning and slip out to a quiet corner in the woods or fields near our house and watch for birds building. In this way I found water ouzels and other nests by the Dodder that no ordinary search could have revealed. My friend was still absorbed by her new companion yet we were again on good terms. I remember telling — or intending to tell her — that each egg I found gave three distinct moments of rapture: the finding of the nest, the insertion of [the] egg successfully blown in my collection, and, lastly, the greatest, exhibiting it to her. I still believed that she was a naturalist, though her interest in birds — at least in wild birds — had been only a development of her friendship for myself. The following summer my cousins went abroad. My affection was again [freely accepted.] Now, however, it took a different shade, it was less a steady liking than a curious form of being in love. I used to kiss the chair she had sat on and kiss the little notes she sometimes sent me till I blotted the ink. Formerly we had always walked arm in arm but now we never touched each other even to shake hands. I had moved into long trousers, begun to read Scott and felt myself a man.

I was now at school again, but ill continually. This ill health led to a curious resolution which has explained in some measure all my subsequent evolution. Without knowing, or, as far as I can remember, hearing anything about doctrines of heredity I surmised that unhealthy parents should have unhealthy children — my rabbit breeding may have put the idea into my head. Therefore, I said, I am unhealthy, and if I marry I will have unhealthy children. But I will never create beings to suffer as I am suffering, so I will never marry. I do not know how old I was when I came to this decision, but I was between thirteen and fifteen and it caused me horrible misery.

The following spring I had measles and gave up school finally. When I recovered I began to collect moths and butterflies and other insects, a pursuit which kept me engrossed for several years. It gave me a great fondness for the eerie and night and encouraged a lonely temperament which was beginning to take possession of me. My girl friend was now absent a good deal so that our childish intimacy was no longer possible. I had realized too that though we were excellent companions we knew each other too well and were both eager for more exciting flirtations.

In my sixteenth year everything changed. I took to the violin and the study of literature with wild excitement and lost almost completely my

3. Dr Alan Price notes that the cousins in fact came from South America.

interest in natural science although the beauty of nature influenced me more than ever. I had a tutor three times a week, for the rest I was alone. I began taking very long walks among the Dublin mountains, of which I soon knew every turn and crevice. Natural history did [much] for me. . . . To wander as I did for years through the dawn of night with every nerve stiff and strained with expectation gives one a singular acquaintance with the essences of the world. The obscure noises of the owls and rabbits, the heavy scent of the hemlock and the flowers of the elder, the silent flight of the moths I was in search of gave me a passionate and receptive mood like that of early [man]. The hunter, poacher and painter are the only men who know nature. The poet too often lets his intellect draw the curtain of connected thought between him and the glory that is round him. The forces which rid me of theological mysticism reinforced my innate feeling for the profound mysteries of life. I had even psychical adventures which throw perhaps an interesting light on some of the data of folklore.

One evening when I was collecting on the brow of a long valley in County Wicklow wreaths of white mist began to rise from the narrow bogs beside the river. Before it was quite dark I looked round the edge of the field and saw two immense luminous eyes looking at me from the base of the valley. I dropped my net and caught hold of a gate in front of me. Behind the eyes there rose a black sinister forehead. I was fascinated. For a moment the eyes seemed to consume my personality, then the whole valley became filled with a pageant of movement and colour, and the opposite hillside covered itself with ancient doorways and spires and high turrets. I did not know where or when I was existing. At last someone spoke in the lane behind me — it was a man going home — and I came back to myself. The night had become quite dark and the eyes were no longer visible, yet I recognized in a moment what had caused the apparition — two clearings in a wood lined with white mist divided again by a few trees which formed the eye-balls. For many days afterwards I could not look on these fields even in daylight without terror. It would not be easy to find a better instance of the origin of local superstitions, which have their origin not in some trivial accident of colour but in the fearful and genuine hypnotic influence such things possess upon the prepared personality.

Before I abandoned science it rendered me an important service. When I was about fourteen I obtained a book of Darwin's. It opened in my hands at a passage where he asks how can we explain the similarity between a man's hand and a bird's or bat's wings except by evolution.[4] I flung the book aside and rushed out into the open air — it was summer and we were in the country — the sky seemed to have lost its blue and the grass its green. I lay down and writhed in an agony of doubt. My studies showed me the force of what I read, [and] the more I put it from me the more it rushed back with new instances and power. Till then I had never doubted and never conceived that a sane and wise man or boy could doubt. I had of course heard of atheists but as vague monsters that I was unable to realize. It seemed that I was become in a moment the playfellow of Judas. Incest and parricide were but a consequence of the idea that possessed me. My memory does not record how I returned home nor how long my misery lasted. I know only that I got the book out of the house as soon as possible and kept it out of sight, saying to myself logically enough that I was not yet sufficiently advanced in science to weigh his arguments, so I would do better to reserve his work for future study. In a few weeks or days I regained my composure, but this was the beginning. Soon afterwards I turned my attention to works of Christian evidence, reading them at first with pleasure, soon with doubt, and at last in some cases with derision.

My study of insects had given me a scientific attitude — probably a crude one — which did not and could not interpret life and nature as I heard it interpreted from the pulpit. By the time I was sixteen or seventeen I had renounced Christianity after a good deal of wobbling, although I do not think I avowed my decision quite so soon. I felt a sort of shame in being thought an infidel, a term which I have always used as a reproach. For a while I denied everything, then I took to reading Carlyle, [Leslie] Stephen[5] and Matthew Arnold, and made myself a sort of incredulous belief that illuminated nature and lent an object to life without hampering the intellect. This story is easily told, but it was a terrible experience. By it I laid a chasm between my

4. Charles Darwin, *On the Origin of Species by Means of Natural Selection* (1859), p. 479. See *My Uncle John*, p. 36.
5. Leslie Stephen (1832-1904) wrote several essays defending his agnosticism, notably *Essays on Free Thinking and Plain Speaking* (1873).

present and my past and between myself and my kindred and friends. Till I was twenty-three I never met or at least knew a man or woman who shared my opinions. Compared with the people about me, compared with the Fellows of Trinity, I seemed a presumptuous boy yet I felt that the views which I had arrived at after sincere efforts to find what was true represented, in spite of my immediate surroundings, the real opinion of the world.

Sometimes I was absorbed by the ideas that beset men at this period and thought myself a low miscreant because I had a tendency which was really natural and healthy. Often, however, I worked myself into a sort of mystical ecstasy with music and the works of Carlyle and Wordsworth which usually ended by throwing me back into all manner of forebodings. I began to write verses and compose. I wished to be at once Shakespeare, Beethoven and Darwin; my ambition was boundless and amounted to a real torture in my life. I would go down on my knees at times with my music paper on a chair before me and cry to God for a melody. I lay awake whole nights planning poems or struggling with geometrical problems — which I was now studying for my entrance to Trinity — creeping downstairs at daybreak for a piece of bread or if it was fine slipping out to watch the sun-rise, and then going back to bed for a couple of hours' sleep. When I was fiddling[6] I mourned over the books I wished to read; when I was reading I yearned for all manner of adventures. Vulgar sensuality did not attract me but I was haunted by dreams of the verdant liberty that seemed to reign in pagan forests of the south. Often I threw my books or music aside and darted off on my bicycle among the loneliest hollows of the hills in vain hopes of an adventure.

In my childhood the presence of furze bushes and rocks and flooded streams and strange mountain fogs and sunshine gave me a strange sense of enchantment and delight but I think when I [rested] on a mountain I sat quite as gladly looking on the face of a boulder as at the finest view of glen and river. My wish was that nature should be untouched by man, whether the view was beautiful or not did not interest me. A wood near Rathfarnham represented my idea of bliss until someone told me it was a piece of artificially arranged planting on an artificial hillock. I hated the neighbourhood from that day. This feeling has never entirely left me, and I remember fifteen years later after a long afternoon in a French forest that I enquired in the evening with real anxiety whether or not this forest was a mere recent plantation. It was the same with the people who were round me. There is no doubt that I was sensible to beauty but I distinguished only forces that attracted or repelled me. I remember when I was very young, watching a lady in the pew before me [in church] and wishing vaguely to stroke her cheek, but I did not know for years that she was considered singularly beautiful. About puberty when the boy begins to look out with an uneasy awakened gaze that lingers because it is not satisfied, I saw in one hour that both nature and women were alive with indescribable radiance — with beauty. Even when the animal feelings were at their height a beautiful woman seemed an always intangible glory. All earth [was] transfigured in a moment. I became a pilgrim to the sun and used to arrange my excursions to reach a certain corner where there was [a] fine outlook of hill and sky half an hour before twilight. . . .

I think the consciousness of beauty is awakened in persons as in peoples by a prolonged unsatisfied desire. . . . Perhaps the modern feeling for the beauty of nature as a particular quality — an expression of divine ecstasy rather than a mere decoration of the world — arose when men began to look on everything about them with the unsatisfied longing which has its proper analogue in puberty . . . . The feeling of primitive people is still everywhere the feeling of the child; an adoration that has never learned or wished to admire its divinity. This feeling everyone will recognize in Wordsworth's *Ode*,[7] though he does not seem perhaps to give it its truest interpretation.

When I realized that the life about could not give me any real satisfaction my desire for study came on me again. I ran through history, chemistry, physics, botany, Hebrew, Irish, Latin, Greek, something of French and German and made a really serious study of the history and theory of music. English literature also I read with much care though I was painfully conscious of my uncertain judgement and formed my opinions reluctantly for fear a blunder

6. Synge was an accomplished vilionist.

7. Wordsworth's ode, 'Intimations of Immortality from Recollections of Early Childhood', was first published in *Poems in Two Volumes* (1807).

might lower me in my proper estimation. I believe I never allowed myself to like a book that was not famous, though there were many famous books, such as Tennyson's poems, that I did not care for. The Irish ballad poetry of 'The Spirit of the Nation' school[8] engrossed me for a while and made [me] commit my most serious literary error; I thought it excellent for a considerable time and then repented bitterly.

Soon after I had relinquished the Kingdom of God I began to take a real interest in the kingdom of Ireland. My politics went round from a vigorous and unreasoning loyalty to a temperate Nationalism. Everything Irish became sacred ... and had a charm that was neither quite human nor divine, rather perhaps as if I had fallen in love with a goddess, although I had still sense enough not to personify Erin in the patriotic verse I now sought to fabricate. Patriotism gratifies Man's need for adoration and has therefore a peculiar power upon the imaginative sceptic, as we see in France at the present time.

About this time I entered Trinity, but did not gain much after the first emotion had gone over. All my time was given to the violin and vague private reading, and the work for my examinations received just enough attention to attain a pass standard. I joined an amateur orchestra, which gave me unusual pleasure. The collective passion produced by a band working together with one will and ideal is unlike any other exaltation.... We played the *Jupiter Symphony* of Mozart. It was in an academy and a Jewess was playing at the desk before me. No other emotion that I have received was quite so puissant or complete. A slight and altogether subconscious avidity of sex wound and wreathed itself in the extraordinary beauty of the movement, not unlike the sexual element that exists in all really fervent ecstasies of faith.... I found the mysterious mansion I had dreamed, [and] I played with morbid assiduity. I remember particularly the long blue days of a June that I spent looking out over the four strings of my violin into the filling leaves and white erect florescence of a chestnut and a wilderness of plants beneath it that crushed and strangled each other in a green and silent frenzy of expression.... One is lost in a blind tempest [of music] that wails round one with always beautiful passion, the identity is merged in a ... symmetrical joy, cathedrals build themselves about one with the waves of purple storm, yet one remains sane and a man. Then there were the slow movements which perhaps fulfil more exactly the peculiar mission of harmony. This sigh of beautiful relief which comes as an explanation rather than as a mere cessation of an excitement near to pain is perhaps the greatest utterance of man. [It resembles] the assuagement of morning and spring which follows feverish nights and desolate winters, and the assuagement of autumn and evening which follows the passions of summer and sultry days, the first depending on the cessation of pain, the other on the cessation of indulgence. A cycle of experience is the only definite unity, and when all has been passed through, and every joy and pain has been resolved in one passion of relief, the only rest that can follow is in the dissolution of the person.

This extraordinary instinct of music which leads to such ecstasy, the suave balm that draws out intricate characteristics from places not open to the world [helped me] to realize that all emotions depend upon and answer the abstractions of ideal form and that humanity as God is but the first step toward a full comprehension of this art. For the hypersensitive organization the musical excitement is perhaps too powerful, too nearly a physical intoxication, but it is not surprising that when I found in the orchestra the world of magical beauty I dreamed of, I threw aside all reasonable counsel and declared myself a professional musician.[9]

8. *The Spirit of the Nation*, a collection of ballads and songs from *The Nation* newspaper, published in 1843 with several reprints thereafter. A further collection, *The New Spirit of the Nation*, appeared in 1894; another enlarged edition, *Songs and Ballads of Young Ireland*, came out in 1896.

9. Synge went to Germany to study music from 1892 to 1894.

from:
THE ARAN ISLANDS (1907)

[Synge completed *The Aran Islands* in 1901. Urged on by Yeats, he first visited Aran in May 1898. On his annual returns from Paris, he spent part of each summer on the islands over a four-year period. This brief extract has an obvious bearing on *The Playboy of the Western World*, staged in the year the book was published. The attitude of the islanders to the law and its officers was more pronounced than in most parts of Ireland, but the resentment and suspicion of the law was — quite understandably — widespread.]

. . . Another old man, the oldest on the island, is fond of telling me anecdotes — not folk-tales — of things that have happened here in his lifetime.

He often tells me about a Connaught man who killed his father with the blow of a spade when he was in passion, and then fled to this island and threw himself on the mercy of some of the natives with whom he was said to be related. They hid him in a hole — which the old man has shown me — and kept him safe for weeks, though the police came and searched for him, and he could hear their boots grinding on the stones over his head. In spite of a reward which was offered, the island was incorruptible, and after much trouble the man was safely shipped to America.

This impulse to protect the criminal is universal in the west. It seems partly due to the association between justice and the hated English jurisdiction, but more directly to the primitive feeling of these people, who are never criminals yet always capable of crime, that a man will not do wrong unless he is under the influence of a passion which is as irresponsible as a storm on the sea. If a man has killed his father, and is already sick and broken with remorse, they can see no reason why he should be dragged away and killed by the law.

Such a man, they say, will be quiet all the rest of his life, and if you suggest that punishment is needed as an example, they ask, 'Would any one kill his father if he was able to help it?'

Some time ago, before the introduction of police, all the people of the islands were as innocent as the people here remain to this day. I have heard that at that time the ruling proprietor and magistrate of the north island[1] used to give any man who had done wrong a letter to a jailer in Galway, and send him off by himself to serve a term of imprisonment.

As there was no steamer, the ill-doer was given a passage in some chance hooker[2] to the nearest point on the mainland. Then he walked for many miles along a desolate shore till he reached the town. When his time had been put through, he crawled back along the same route, feeble and emaciated, and had often to wait many weeks before he could regain the island. Such at least is the story.

It seems absurd to apply the same laws to these people and to the criminal classes of a city. The most intelligent man on Inishmaan[3] has often spoken to me of his contempt of the law, and of the increase of crime the police have brought to Aranmore. On this island, he says, if men have a little difference, or a little fight, their friends take care it does not go too far, and in a little time it is forgotten. In Kilronan[4] there is a band of men paid to make out cases for themselves; the moment a blow is struck they come down and arrest the man who gave it. The other man he quarrelled with has to give evidence against him; whole families come down to the court and swear against each other till they become bitter enemies. If there is a conviction the man who is convicted never forgives. He waits his time, and before the year is out there is a cross summons, which the other man in turn never forgives. The feud continues to grow, till a dispute about the colour of a man's hair may end in a murder, after a year's forcing by the law. The mere fact that it is impossible to get reliable evidence in the island — not because the people are dishonest, but because they think the claim of kinship more sacred than the claims of abstract truth — turns the whole system of sworn evidence into a demoralising farce, and it is easy to believe that law dealings on this false basis must lead to every sort of injustice. . . .

1. Inishmore, the largest of three Aran Islands, lying north-west of the others.

2. A commercial fishing boat.

3. The second largest of the Aran islands.

4. On Inishmore, the largest island. Synge refers to it as 'Aranmor'.

GEORGE TYRRELL

(1861-1909)

from: AUTOBIOGRAPHY AND LIFE OF GEORGE TYRRELL (1912)

[Tyrrell's stormy career saw him convert to catholicism from his protestant faith, join the Jesuit order, be expelled from it and feud with the church in which he had sought consolation and peace. Tyrrell came from a fervently protestant-Irish background. His family was middle-class, and his conversion to catholicism came as a profound shock to them. In the Supplement to the chapter from which the following excerpt is taken, the Rev. Dr Newport White, regius professor of divinity at Trinity College, Dublin, gives an indication of how serious a matter such a conversion was in 1878: 'We never met or exchanged letters after he became a Roman Catholic. Tyrrell's change of religion was to me a far greater severance than his death would have been. Those who know Ireland need not be told that, thirty years ago, the feeling of the average Irish Protestant towards Irish Romans Catholics was a repugnance, instinctive rather than reasoned, based on racial and social as much as on religious antipathies.' This atmosphere in part explains the intensity of Tyrrell's experience of conversion and the even greater intensity of his disappointment in the church, for the sake of which he had broken so many familial and social bonds.]

CHAPTER V

. . . A grain of dust, blown into a man's eye at a certain moment, may change the course of the world's history, still more easily the course of his own history; so I must be excused for recording similar trifles that shunted my destiny on to new lines. At Peter Place[1] there was a Roman Catholic maid-of-all-work, whose bright cheery ways made her attractive to me as a companion, and I used to slip down to the kitchen more frequently than was ever my custom before. She abounded in stories and songs, and was persistently good-tempered and jolly. At the same time she was a good practising Catholic, and if she was on handkerchief-waving terms with most of the engine-drivers who sped past the end of our garden on the Dublin, Wicklow and Wexford Railway line, it was part of her general buoyancy and gaiety, and quite remote from any sort of impropriety or flightiness. My mother, always inclined to treat servants as distinct personalities, was also much interested in the same Anne Kelly, and used to drift into controversy with her. In my early days, far more than now, all my geese were swans, and if I admired anything I admired everything. Hence in these controversies, which in themselves were absolutely uninteresting to me, I rejoiced when it seemed to me that the weaker party had triumphed, and my sympathies were all with Rome, or, rather, with Anne Kelly.

I think the love of paradox, both now and long after, mingled with my anxiety to say something in favour of so preposterous a religion as Popery; while my secret unbelief made me find little objection to the gnats of Romanism after the camels of Christianity. I used to get hold of R.C. prayer-books and manuals, and if much that I saw there seemed silly and unintelligent, much also surprised me as being the same sort of Christianity I had imagined to be an exclusively Protestant heritage. Indeed my mother, who was too kindly and sensible to be very bigoted, and had, moroever, been much disgusted with the fanatical and venomous anti-Romanism of her own mother, was quite prepared to allow that Roman Catholics were Christians, and that salvation was possible inside that Church for those whose ignorance was invincible. She was once much amused, and, I think, slightly piqued, when one of our R.C. servants extended an analogous toleration to Protestants; but we never see the absurdity of our own position till we stand outside it.

What I learned of Roman Catholicism at this time left me at least with a sort of interest in that religion; there was so much more to know about it than about bald, Low-Church Protestantism; it was so much more complex and mysterious, and had moreover, for me, the spell of being not only novel and paradoxical, but even dangerous, wicked and forbidden. But when the house in Peter Place broke up and we flitted to Clanbrassil St. off the South Circular Road, the interest in Popery fell asleep. It was in no sense an interest in religion as such, but simply in a paradox and a novelty. . . .

1. In Rathmines, then a newly developed suburb of Dublin.

[Tyrrell enters the Jesuit novitiate and recounts his experience therein, especially his disappointment with the quality of the teaching, the nervelessness of the Christianity and the low intellectual level of his companions. This is part of the story of what he calls the 'growth, decline and fall of the Jesuitism with which Father Morris [a teacher] succeeded in impressing me.']

CHAPTER XIII

. . . In the main I think I was liked — at least not disliked, by my companions. I fancy they looked on me as much older than I was; and certainly as more learned and mature. Perhaps, in the occasional sermons and catechisms which one had to give in public, I betrayed an easy familiarity in regions strange to most of them. Also, there was an hour of Latin schools every morning for the second year novices, over which I was set to preside, and my treatment of Cicero's 'De Senectute,'[1] if not on Stonyhurst lines, was perhaps sufficiently mature to silence unfavourable criticism.

I never fell a victim to scruples during this time, or even later, though the whole system made for scrupulosity; for the usual occasion (not cause) of scrupulosity is a paralysing terror of mortal sin, and the belief that one can slip into hell by a mere inadvertence of thought. It is the parasite of a much more vivid faith than I ever possessed in the conclusions of moral theology; and as such it has no place in Protestant piety, though the same mental disease may break out in other matters connected with religion. With me it took the form of a certain fidgetiness of mind, endeavouring to reduce to a single formula the life of sanctity or perfection — the search for some brief golden rule, applicable to every action of life, internal or external. Plainly such a quest is chimerical; for the 'self' to be governed is never twice the same, and needs now one, now another aspect of right to be emphasised. Still the search for this panacea got hold of me, like that for the philosopher's stone — no inept symbol of it — and wore out my brain and broke my rest. The craze wakes up at times even still, in full vigour, and can only be banished by some healthy distraction. The more universally applicable such a principle is, the less is its helpfulness and the more barren will it be of content. 'Do the right' is the most universal of all; but what one seeks is just the determination, and therefore the limitation, of the right. Hence a perpetual see-saw of the mind, quite analogous to that occasioned by a scruple. Only God can combine the universal and particular in one thought; with us they vary inversely.

Father Morris put me through a course of what he called 'solid' spiritual reading: Jerome Platus; Scaramelli; Lancicius; Druzbicki; Le Gaudier,[2] and other Jesuit ascetics; in order to create in me the 'spirit of the Society.' I found them dreary and uninspiring to the last degree, with their scholastic analysis of virtues into *genus* and *species*; their lists of motives, causes, effects and the rest — as if method could coerce the Holy Ghost. The last named went so far as to follow the scheme of theological treatises with *Thesis-Probatur-Objicitur-Respondetur*[3] and the rest.

Father Gaspar Druzbicki has two chapters, applying the theory that 'to will to love is the same as to love' — as grotesque a fallacy as ever was fabricated. Hence, says this ingenious fabricator of merit, if I say 'I want to love God with an act equal to that of the Blessed Virgin and all the angels put together and multiplied by 1,000,' I do, *ipso facto*, elicit such an act. Therefore I will take my beads, and on each bead I will renew this act. But, happy thought! I may proceed by geometrical as well as by arithmetical progression, and on the second bead square the act on the first, cube it on the third, and so forth, till the very angels reel at the contemplation of acts so exceeding their own.

This drivel seems incredible in one who writes otherwise sanely, and even shrewdly, for the most part. But practical minds are often intoxicated, in the rarefied atmosphere of speculation, more easily than others, just as speculative minds are easily bewildered in concrete affairs. It was, however, an unusually startling application of arithmetic to grace; and though this was after my surrender of arms, I ventured to show the chapters to Father Morris, and ask him demurely if he would advise me to adopt that particular form of devotion. He read them without a smile and said: 'No, brother; perhaps you've read enough of Druzbicki and had

1. Cicero's treatise 'On Old Age'. Stonyhurst is a Jesuit school in the north of England.

2. Gaspar Druzbicki (1589-1662), a Polish Jesuit, was a prolific writer; his *Tribunal of Conscience* was translated into English in 1885. Jerome Platus (1365-1416), G.B. Scaramelli (1687-1752), N. Lancicius (1574-1652) and H. Le Gaudier (1692-1770) were all Jesuits and writers in the ascetic tradition.

3. Thesis — Proof — Objections — Responses: a conventional technique in Jesuit apologetics.

better try Le Gaudier for a change'; and so I went to Le Gaudier and his sanctity in syllogisms.

Most of the novices read endless Saints' Lives, of the usual unhealthy type. It was the nearest thing to a story-book they could find. I tried one or two, but could not get on. I am thankful that I was made to read À Kempis[4] for a quarter of an hour daily; and not at all thankful for the daily half hour wasted over the banalities and fallacies of Rodriguez's mischievous and much overrated book.[5] Our rule orders a few verses of Scripture to be read at table daily; but as this is usually in Latin, and read in fixed lengths, irrespective of connection, and during the noise and clatter of the soup plates, no one pays the least attention to it. In the theologate[6] there are some fugitive lectures on some portions of Scripture during the last two years; but as they do not form matter for the final, or for any, examination, they are not much heeded. A priest, with his Breviary office, would roughly cover the Scriptures each year, were not the ferial lessons[7] cancelled three or four times a week by feasts, and the connection thus hopelessly broken; and even then the lessons are mostly to be 'got through,' and not read or pondered. So that, taking it all together, it is not wonderful if most priests are grossly ignorant of the very text of most of the Bible — a feature that distinguishes the modern Church from the medieval very unfavourably, and explains the poverty of religious imagination characteristic of minds fed solely on abstract theology, and not on the strong meat of the word of God. Surely things were different when the homilies of the Fathers represented the ordinary preaching, and men's minds were filled with the words, and therefore in some measure with the very inspiration, of the words of Scripture.

One book I read, which left a deep mark on me — Lacordaire's 'Conferences on God.'[8] It was like meeting a cool spring in the arid waste of scholastic asceticism in which I had been wandering. Had he known its speculative trend, and the secret of its fascination for me, Father Morris would not have allowed me to read it; but he was not personally familiar with it, and he gave me permission, with a shrug of the shoulders, which meant that a Dominican could not foster the spirit of the Society — for each Order glories that its spirit is as unlike as possible to that of other Orders, and loves to accentuate differences and ignore similarities; to preserve and deepen its own type, and impose it as widely as possible.

Here I found the theism of Aquinas set forth with all the elegance and fire of Lacordaire's imagination. Here I realised that devotion and personal religion could find food and an object in the pure deity, released from the figures and idols of the imagination. Truly, it was an external God still, not the God Who is the centre and light of the heart and mind; still it set my confused conceptions in some sort of order, and quieted my mind, which had been dulled, but never satisfied, as to the difficulties of my earliest childhood. I had learned, in my own vague way, that though the God of the imagination was absurd, yet there was an unimaginable but conceivable God; and now this conception was first given a definite shape, and shown, moreover, to be harmonious with reason. It was an immense relief to me, and broke open the door into a new world of thought. For, after all, my theistic doubts had never been quite slain. If I now believed in God without admitting my doubts to audience, it was not but I knew they were waiting outside the door. I had, by wilful and repeated practical assumption of the truth of theism, made it a habit of my mind — a necessity of my life. From a mere wish to believe I had passed to a will to believe in defiance of felt doubts, which I did not think imprudent. It was not bare theism and morality that thus biassed my mind through my affection, but Catholicism — *the religion as a whole* — depending, indeed, on theism as its root, but attracting rather in virtue of its fruit and flower. I had, then, allowed Catholicism (including theism) to absorb my interest in the way I have already tried to describe, and at every step my practical grasp on theism was tightened; but in my mind there had been really no advance, only a smothering of ghosts that would arise again if ever my will should alter and my interest in Catholicism grow cold. If the will is, in this matter, a protection

4. Thomas À. Kempis (*c.* 1379-1471), contemplative monk and mystic, whose *The Imitation of Christ* is a devotional classic.
5. Alonso Rodriguez (1526-1616), a Spanish Jesuit, whose *The Practice of Christian and Religious Perfection* (Seville, 1609) was translated into English in the seventeenth century and also in 1878.
6. The course in theology prescribed for candidates for the priesthood.
7. The weekday, regular lkessons, part of the compulsory reading for a priest; these were altered for readings appropriate to whatever feast days occurred.
8. Jean Baptiste Henri Lacordaire (1802-61) was the greatest pulpit orator of the nineteenth century. He gave the first of his famous conferences (or lectures) at Notre Dame in 1835-36, and resumed them 1843-52. His *Conferences de Notre Dame de Paris* were published in London in 1852.

against the feebleness of the mind, the mind is also a protection against that of the will; the two are co-operant and complementary principles of solid faith. This book, then, took me back to the root-problem, and reawakened an interest that had been locked away from my direct consideration, partly through wilfulness, partly in despair; it took my mind out of the narrow grooves of ecclesiastical and ascetical thought, into which I had been so long constraining it, and allowed it to stretch its cramped limbs and inhale fresh air. I read it once or twice afterwards, but doubt if it would appeal to me now; and I will not spoil my memory of it by trying. Nor was it merely speculative, but an appeal through the intellect to the heart; and it did more to give me a personal love of the Pure Divinity than any other book I have ever read, except St. Augustine's 'Confessions.' To it, and to the personal elevation of Father Morris's character, I owe any lasting good I received during my noviceship. All that was wrought laboriously, and against the grain, and in conformity with a system that was essentially uncongenial, had to be undone bit by bit, till not a thread remained. A man can absolutely stand on his head, but not easily or for long.

In short, if I had a vocation to follow St. Ignatius, and to that Society which exists in the pages of Paul Féval,[9] I had none whatever to the Society that exists here and now; and Father Morris was right instinctively, though wrong in his reasons. He himself was one who, by his intensity and narrowness, could — more effectually and stably than I — read his own ideal into the most flagrant contradictions of them. The 'Society' that he believed in, and even 'Holy Mother Church,' were figments of his brain, and determined his faculty of vision to see just what accorded with his ideals, and to miss all else. Except for that, he was as little a typical Jesuit as myself — as the common consent among us allows. Had he seen the facts as I saw them, he would have felt as I felt — but perhaps this is a barren truism; yet I think the typical Jesuit sees the facts and is content with them; he is not sufficiently interested in the ideals to care to distort the facts; and thus extremes meet.

After I left home, in 1879, my mother and Louy stayed on with Miss Lynch for some time; then I think they went to live in Wexford for some reason or other. While there my mother developed a cancer in the breast, and went up to Dublin, ostensibly on some mysterious business, which she concealed from Louy and myself. She took a private ward, in I forget what hospital, and was operated on, with temporary success. During her convalescence she went, as was her way, among the patients in the public wards, and chatted with them, most of them being Roman Catholics, and was profoundly impressed by the simple faith and happy resignation of the suffering poor to the 'holy will of God,' as they call it. I had kept up regular and frequent correspondence with her since my departure, always carefully avoiding any controversy, and making it clear that my change had in no way weakened, but rather strengthened, the bonds of affection — as indeed is true of more kinds of distance than that which is local. I never, of course, had the least uneasiness about her salvation — that would have supposed a much more vivid faith than I ever had; but naturally I wished her to be where I was, and the sense of any separation was painful. She, too, was drawn after me with the cords of a mother's love — the most imperious of all influences. And then there was that quiet pressure of little Miss Lynch's personality. Hence when they migrated to London, professedly to live with my uncle Arthur Chamney, but really to be near me, I was not surprised when my mother told me one day, at Manresa,[10] that she had determined to follow me.

She was received by Father Arthur Devine, C.P., at Highgate, some time in 1881. I do not think it made much difference in her spiritual life, for better or for worse, apart from mystical and sacramental benefits, though perhaps it added a sense of rest and finality, which had been lacking in regard to dogmatic questions. She was too old to change her habits of thought, and carried her Bible-reading and extempore prayer on to the end. In the wanderings of her last illness, in 1884, she prayed much and spoke much of religion, but it was always the simple old evangelical faith of former years, untouched by Romanism — Christ crucified and nothing more.

9. Paul Féval (1817-87) was a novelist, best-known for his *Étapes d'une conversion* (Paris, 1877) and *Les Mystères de Londres* (Paris, 1844). Between 1877-82 he published a revised edition of all his numerous books to bring them into conformity with catholic teaching.

10. Manresa House, Roehampton, England, named after a town in Catalonia, north-west of Barcelona. Beneath one of its churches is a cave that served as a spiritual retreat for St Ignatius of Loyola (1491-1556), the founder of the Society of Jesus (1534).

At the time this worried me; but of course it only meant that, in her state, her mind was governed by former strata of consciousness, and all her thoughts belonged to some eight years previously — Willie had recently died and I was still at school. She often came to see me at Manresa, and those visits are among the tenderest of my memories.

They at last settled to go to Bonn, that Louy might perfect her German; and came to pay a farewell visit. On parting, near the gate of Manresa — I often stop on the spot to recall it — my mother suddenly saddened and said: 'I have a presentiment I shall never see you again.' I said: 'Your presentiments were always wrong, and I am perfectly certain I shall see you again.' We were both right!

Perhaps had I lived at home, instead of going on this wild-goose chase after abstractions and ideals, I might have made common what has remained sacred; I might have worn down an affection which separation fomented; I might have broken those hearts whose love was everything to me, and to which my love was everything. That is my faint hope, and the salve of my conscience, when I think, with bitterness, how I abandoned the life of affection for the service of so barren a mistress as truth, and let the substance of life escape me in the pursuit of shadows. And here, once more, I draw a line.

GEORGE A. BIRMINGHAM

(1865-1950)

from: IRISHMEN ALL (1913)

[George Birmingham, the pseudonym of Canon James O. Hannay, made his reputation as a popular novelist, but he was also an acute commentator on public affairs. *Irishmen All* is a series of portraits of representative types and their social and political condition in the early years of the twentieth century. In this portrait of the country gentleman, Birmingham broaches a theme that had been the subject of much speculation since the beginning of the decline of landlordism in the 1880s and was taken up by various writers — Standish O'Grady, Yeats, Horace Plunkett, Parnell, Griffith, Redmond, and many others. The loss of power and status — often exaggerated — suffered by the landowning aristocracy, and its subsequent withdrawal from public affairs, had deprived Ireland of seasoned leadership at a crucial period. How that leadership could be renewed and a contribution made to the changed Ireland of the time is Birmingham's theme here. It was to become an even more vexed question within the next decade and, in effect, the contribution from the landlord class to the new state was to be minimal. The exile of this class from Ireland in the twentieth century is interestingly paralleled with the exile of the catholic aristocracy in the seventeenth century. It is characteristic of Birmingham that he seeks the ultimate explanation for these exiles in economic and political rather than sectarian-religious terms, although his genial view may be thought to be more hopeful than the situation warranted.]

CHAPTER SIXTH

THE COUNTRY GENTLEMAN

The more popular a proverb is, the less likely it is to be true. When we get one which is repeated every day in newspaper articles and many times every day in conversation, we feel confident that it must be a lie. 'History repeats itself' is such a saying. It is so popular that we feel it must be quite indispensable. Neither the leader-writer nor the prosy old gentleman who bores the members of his family at breakfast-time by commenting on the foreign intelligence could get on comfortably without saying that history repeats itself. As a matter of fact, the same thing never happens twice. But the proverb has this much justification: things are constantly happening which are a little like things which happened before, and the facile essayist of shallow mind and small real knowledge exaggerates the likeness and tries to gain a reputation as a philosophic historian by pretending to observe that human affairs run round and round in circles.

I am a facile essayist. I here point out that Ireland

has seen the decay and failure of two aristocracies, and that the circumstances which attended the collapse were to some extent the same in both cases. We lost one aristocracy at the end of the seventeenth century, when Lying Dick Talbot died in Limerick, and Patrick Sarsfield, with the Wild Geese in his train, crossed the seas to France.[1] That was a very nice, picturesque aristocracy with a lot of fine qualities, especially good at fighting, which is indeed a characteristic of all aristocracies worthy of the name. Poets sang songs about it, most beautiful songs, and we have all sentimentalised about it ever since. The other aristocracy went under two hundred years later. We have not yet discovered that it was picturesque — our children will probably find that out — and nobody has as yet sung a single song about it; but it too was a fine fighting stock.

Now we come to the points of resemblance, the points in which the later muse of history plagiarised the work of her elder sister.

Both aristocracies were loyal in a stupid, unselfish way. Our seventeenth-century Jacobites were loyal to James II, who never cared anything about them, but used their loyalty as long as he thought it profitable to do so. Our nineteenth-century gentlemen were loyal to England, which was quite as stupid a thing to be, for Englishmen cared just as little for them as the Stewarts did for their predecessors. As long as they could be serviceable to England as a garrison to hold Ireland down, England used them. As soon as English statesmen discovered that they could govern Ireland more easily in other ways they surrendered their 'faithful garrison,' and the Irish aristocracy was forced to act the uncomfortable part of Jonah in the ship of State.[2]

That is one point of resemblance; but it by no means exhausts the possibilities of the comparison. The seventeenth-century aristocracy was predominatingly [*sic*] Roman Catholic in religion, and their struggles partook of the nature of a religious war. Their nineteenth-century successors were quite as predominatingly Protestant, and they too succeeded in mixing their cause up with their religion. The Church of England appears to have succeeded in keeping James I loyal to it by teaching him to say 'No Bishop, no King'; and there was a good deal of truth in that, as Charles I found when the Puritans triumphed at Naseby.[3] The Irish gentry kept the Church of Ireland in order by saying 'No landlord, no rector,' and it may perhaps turn out that there was a small element of truth in that. At all events, the landlords did very sincerely believe that the faith of Protestantism throughout three-fourths of Ireland was bound up with that of their order. We cannot blame either aristocracy for acting as it did in this matter. Religion is always a respectable sanction for conduct, and there are many men who will not do their best for any cause without it.

But neither loyalty nor religion was the real reason for the fall of these two aristocracies. The Irish Jacobites might have gone on, as the Scottish Jacobites did, making themselves objectionable to the Government for a century or so, and nothing worse would have happened than the cutting off of the heads of a few of them. The survivors might today be enrolling themselves in the Leagues of the White Rose,[4] and nobody would mind. The nineteenth-century gentlemen might have fallen down and worshipped the English flag. The bulk of the Irish people would not have objected in the least, and the handful of genuine Nationalists would have raged against them in vain. The Irish Jacobites did not have to go away to France because they were Roman Catholics, any more than the gentry today are forced to desert their country because they are Protestants. We Irish are, after all, sane, and we do not object to any kind of religion so violently as to want to suppress it unless it has got itself mixed up with some other matter of a more

1. Richard Talbot (1630-91), the earl of Tyrconnel, was lord deputy of Ireland under James II 1687-89 and 1690-91. He was one of the commanders of the Irish forces at the battle of Aughrim in 1691 and died in August of that year. Birmingham's description of him as 'Lying Dick Talbot' may refer to his abortive attempts and promises to restore catholic power in Ireland.

   Patrick Sarsfield succeeded Talbot as Irish commander. He signed the Treaty of Limerick after the defeat at Aughrim and led his commanders into exile, an exodus known as the Flight of the Wild Geese. The Wild Geese enrolled in the continental armies of France and Spain. A glamorous myth had grown up around them since the days of Young Ireland. Sarsfield died at the battle of Landen in 1693.
2. Jonah, the Old Testament prophet, was thrown overboard when the sailors discovered, by casting lots, that a storm had been sent because of his presence on board.
3. The battle of Naseby (1645), an engagement in the English civil war, in which the Cromwell's parliamentarians defeated the royalists, commanded by Charles I and Prince Rupert.
4. The White Rose was adopted by the Jacobites as an emblem of the Old Pretender, James Stuart (1688-1766), because his adherents were obliged to abet him sub rosa (in secret).

practical kind. All religions teach that malefactors will suffer hereafter, and we are most of us content to wait till the proper time for the punishment of heretics. But there are some things which cannot very well be put off till after death, and one of them is the land question. If we do not settle here and now who is to own the land, there is no use settling it at all. Some people may conceivably want water in the next world. No creed suggests that anyone will want land.

And it is just over this land question that both our aristocracies have been broken. The seventeenth-century Jacobites look very fine and romantic in the pages of the poetry books, with their loyalty and their Catholicism, standing out against the commonsense compromise of Hanoverian kingship, and the Penal Laws looming on the horizon. But what these gentlemen wanted most was their estates and the upsetting of the Act of Settlement.[5] The estates were theirs by all kinds of rights, but a new set of men had them and were disinclined to give them up. Irish history during the reigns of Charles II and James II is a welter of intrigues, law proceedings, petitions, fraud, bullying and fighting, all about land. English adventurers and Cromwellian soldiers had dispossessed the Irish proprietors. They held the reins of the Irish government. English public opinion was all on their side. Charles and James could do little in the way of restoring estates to their original owners. Dick Talbot was a good political advocate, for he had brains and few scruples, but he failed in his pleading. He failed again when he took to fighting, and the Irish gentry then became 'Wild Geese,' having been 'worsted in the game.'

The history of the fall of the nineteenth-century aristocracy is far less romantic. But the essential thing is the same. It was for their estates they struggled, not indeed against the original proprietors, for *they* had long ago become dukes in Spain, counts in Austria, generals in France, or else disappeared. The new claimants for the soil of Ireland were the tenants, men whose ancestors had laboured for the advantage of both aristocracies, and never been treated with very much consideration by either. The story of this land war need not be retold. It is for the most part sordid and unpleasant. But it is interesting to speculate on the position and prospects of the now dispossessed gentlemen of Ireland.

They come of a fine stock, though they get little credit from anyone for the part they played in the past, and are even inclined, with a curious modesty, to ignore their own greatness. They, for instance, invented Irish Nationalism. Before their time there were Ulstermen, Munstermen, Geraldines, and Jacobites. But until the statesmen of Grattan's Parliament conceived it there was no idea of an Irish nation. They were good fighters, captains of men. A long list might be made of the great fighting men who sprang from this stock, with the name of Wellington[6] at the head of it. I prefer to mention specially two men who seem typical, Beresford and Gough. Beresford raided Buenos Ayres with a handful of men, a buccaneering exploit which the Government had not the nerve to support. He organised the Portuguese army before Wellington took over the command. He blundered and won at Albuera. Gough fought the Sikhs, and few commanders have to their credit such a list of victories as his, won under the most amazing difficulties against overwhelming odds. These two men may stand as examples of the finest qualities of their race.[7] Theirs was a toughness of fibre, a supreme daring, and a joy in desperate adventure.

The older Irish aristocracy, the Jacobites whom the Cromwellians ousted, did not perish off the earth or sink into insignificance because they lost their estates. Their names go sounding through European history. It is not likely that the men of the other breed will vanish either. At present they are puzzled, inclined to bewilderment, a little sore. The changes of the last thirty years have come very quickly, very unexpectedly, and they have not yet adjusted themselves to their new circumstances. Parnell's brilliant plan of combining agrarian agitation with nationalism deprived the landlords of their political power. There are men still living who

5. There were three Acts of Settlement, in 1652, 1662 and 1701, all of which confirmed the confiscation of Irish land and its retention by the new settlers.

6. Arthur Wellesley (1769-1852), the duke of Wellington, was born in Dublin and was MP for Trim in the Irish House of Commons 1790-95.

7. William Carr Beresford (1768-1854), 1st marquess of Waterford, was a general in the British army. He took Buenos Aires in a surprise attack in 1806; he was in charge of the Portuguese Brigade in the Peninsular War and fought with Marshal Soult in the bloody battle of Albuera in Spain in 1811.

General Sir Hubert De La Poer Gough (1870-1963) fought in India and South Africa. He led the mutiny of officers at the Curragh in March 1914 — the year after this essay was published.

remember bonfires blazing in honour of the victory of a landlord at the polls, who have seen in Connacht the brothers or cousins of great lords drawn home from the hustings by crowds of cheering people. No such scenes are possible now. The people have chosen other representatives, and, if the old tales are true, display considerably less enthusiasm for them. Since Parnell's time the Irish landlords have ceased to count with the English party managers. They command no votes in elections and therefore cannot make themselves really unpleasant to any party. Their position is not unlike that of a small nation with no army in a congress of the representatives of the European Powers. They are listened to politely and then ignored. They do not really matter, unless it suits someone, for strategic reasons, to pretend to exploit their grievances. It is not easy, it is certainly not pleasant, to recognise this kind of sudden impotence. It is perhaps impossible for men like the Irish gentry to realise all at once that in the whirling gamble of democratic politics things like friendship and loyalty are of no value or importance whatever. In time, no doubt, they will understand. In the meanwhile, with a pathetic faith in the existence of some kind of principle somewhere, they keep asking, 'But what is to happen to our demesnes? How are we to live if you take our incomes from us?' Just as if anyone in the whole of England, Scotland, or Wales ever thinks about their demesnes or cares whether men with no voting power succeed in living or not!

For indeed their political power, their weight in the councils of State, is not the only thing the Irish gentry have lost. In what Michael Davitt called 'The Fall of Feudalism'[8] they have lost their land, and the revolution which changed the ownership of the soil of Ireland was brought about with great bitterness of spirit. It might indeed have been bloodier — many revolutions are. There never were any actual battles; but battles are not the worst things in the world. Assassinations and hangings — even when they go on for years — do not result in as much loss of life as a couple of well-fought battles; but they leave much more ill-feeling behind. It is not easy for the men who lived through the 'bad times' in Ireland to pass a damp sponge over the records of the past. The iron has entered into the soul of the men who took willing or unwilling part in our land war. And perhaps magnanimity is a harder virtue for the conquered than the conqueror to attain. The Irish gentry of the older generation still regard agrarian Nationalists as 'blackguards.' It is easy to blame them for a stubborn refusal to see any point of view but their own, but for men with their experience many excuses must be made. And, after all, the attitude of the older generation of Irish landlords towards Ireland is not nearly so astonishing a thing as their attitude towards England. That they should distrust their own fellow-countrymen is comprehensible. That they should go on trusting the English and continue loyal is amazing. For the English had quite as much to do with taking away their land from them as the Irish agitators. Act after Act was passed by Parliament, sometimes by one party, sometimes by the other, which diminished the power of landlords over what they regarded as their absolute property; until at last there was no way out of the hopeless tangle except the final abdication of sale.

Things might of course have been much worse. Many landlords have little to complain of in the price they got for their estates, and even those who are most unfortunate in this respect are getting money, the most manageable of all forms of property, instead of land, which in Ireland, at all events, has of late years been an investment which no prudent capitalist would touch. The thought of an income, diminished but secure, accruing regularly though well-secured debentures, ought to, and no doubt does, take a good deal of the bitterness out of a sentimental grievance. But there remains a sadness. We picture an elderly gentleman viewing from the windows of his stately home the broad stretch of some pleasant countryside. 'This,' he reflects, 'was mine once, was my father's before me and his father's before his day. The woods which cluster on the hills, the river with its pleasant fishing pools, the fields where oxen graze, the ploughed land and the bogs, were mine. The houses where the people live, even in a sense the people themselves, were mine. I rode among them a veritable lord, master of men and things with undisputed power. It is mine no more.' He sees — and I cannot suppose the sight a pleasant one — the official surveyor making maps, the engineer following hard on his steps, cutting the old fields into strangely regular new shapes, making a chessboard of the countryside, erecting everywhere

8. The reference is to Davitt's *The Fall of Feudalism in Ireland* (1904).

houses so ugly that the devil himself will not be able to devise uglier when he arranges accommodation in hell for impenitent artists.

Along with the loss of political power and the loss of landed property must be reckoned another loss still, and perhaps the most galling of the three. The Irish gentleman has lost his influence in local affairs. Once as a member of the Grand Jury[9] he levied the local taxes, appointed the nephews of his old friends to collect them, and spent them when they were gathered in. He controlled the Boards of Guardians,[10] appointed dispensary doctors, regulated the diet of paupers, inflicted fines and administered the law at Petty Sessions. Of all this power hardly a vestige now remains to him. Taxes are levied by County Councils, and he, somehow, is not a member of these bodies. The nephews of County Councillors, men strange to him, go round with demand notes and extract cash from the pockets of unwilling citizens. The roads are mended, and he reflects, not with entire satisfaction, that they are no worse than when he managed the mending of them. Even in the Petty Sessions Court he no longer holds his old pride of place. Magistrates — *ex officio* magistrates, who are only magistrates because people elected them to be something else — sit side by side with him, and the law, though slightly altered in its tendencies, is quite as erratic a thing in these new hands as it was when he had it entirely in his.

The Irish gentleman, bereft of his chance of going to Parliament, cut off from the interest of managing an estate, denied the control of local affairs, considerably poorer than he used to be, is apparently condemned to a life of idleness. Men of an outworn stock might be content to fold their hands and rail at destiny. But the Irish gentleman, for all he has been through, has blood in his veins yet. He feels that he has it in him to play some part in life, and is dimly aware that the old tradition of his order, the *noblesse oblige* which moves all true aristocracies, is of value even in the modern democratic state. The days of fighting on Landlord Defence Committees[11] are nearly over, for year by year there are fewer landlords to defend. The solace of bold speaking in the House of Lords, his by virtue of election by his peers or the possession of some forgotten English title, ceases to be comforting, since it is obviously of no great moment what the House of Lords says or does. The maintenance of the Union still has a certain attraction as as a field for activity; but it is not to be supposed that a man can occupy his whole time and energy in writing cheques for a party organisation, and it is only occasionally that the General Synod of the Church of Ireland gives the Irish landlords an opportunity for declaring that they are Unionists for the good of their country. What remains for him? Along what lines is he to work? What chance has he, a man of energy and a certain knowledge of the world, with a high tradition behind him and a good heart in him — what chance has he of doing something?

Things are certainly confusing, and our Irish gentleman is not the most clear-sighted of men. He belongs to a class which, taken as a whole, has better hearts and principles than brains. There are in Ireland today a dozen or so minor forms of social service, lace-making industries for peasant girls, knitting industries, the embroidery of the corners of pocket-handkerchiefs, and so forth. But a grown man can hardly find his life's work in the promotion of lace-making, or direct his whole energies to selling tweeds. These are more properly work for his wife, and she, in the intervals of other duties, does them admirably. There are crusades against consumption, desperate struggles to get windows open, and the foundation of sanatoria. But — it is singularly unfortunate — the tone of the philanthropists who go forth with banners against the Great White Plague is unattractive to the Irish gentleman. He has, in spite of his misfortunes, a sense of humour. It is almost the only one of his old possessions which has survived the *débâcle*, and no man with a sense of humour can be the apostle of a cause exploited as this one is. He always fails at critical moments to take himself quite seriously.

There is the economic gospel of Sir Horace Plunkett,[12] and this, at first sight, has much to

9. The grand jury was the body responsible for the county unit. The members were landowners, but peers could not serve. They struck the rate for the county. The Local Government Act of 1898 replaced them with a system of elected county and district councils.
10. Boards of Guardians were set up to administer the workhouses under the Poor Law Act of 1837. The system was revised during the Famine.
11. A landlords' syndicate to resist tenants' demands for rent reduction was formed in 1889. Horace Plunkett's autobiographical work, *Noblesse Oblige* (1908), may have been in Birmingham's mind, given the reference to Plunkett below.
12. Sir Horace Plunkett (1854-1932), one of the founder-members of the

commend it. The official Nationalists, the men of a pledge-bound Parliamentary party, hate it heartily. The Irish gentleman hates them, and is therefore predisposed to find some good in anything which they detest. It is also, like most economic movements, an affair of common sense. In a country where every sane man is sick to death of flights of oratory and great sentiments of every kind the cold water of common sense is a singularly attractive thing. Yet the Irish gentry, as a class, have hitherto held aloof from the co-operative movement. There is a remnant of old prejudice to be got rid of; for it is not many years since the founder of the movement was suspected of sympathy with Land Leaguers. There is a deep-rooted distrust of all new things, partly instinctive, partly the consequence of having seen a number of new things all of which turned out in the end to be either futile or objectionable. There is a certain fastidious timidity, a dislike of going down into the dusty highways where the pedestrians are, a doubt about the welcome which awaits men of another class. Yet it seems that our disinherited class of country gentlemen are getting over their difficulties. One and another and another have grasped at the opportunity for useful service which the co-operative movement offers them.

It is perhaps not altogether vain to look forward to a time when Irish farmers, tired of the cant of political publicans, will seek for disinterested leaders from a class which they have no longer any reason to distrust when the Irish gentleman, tired of sulking in his tent, realising again his capacity for public work, will accept the new conditions and be ready to be greatest among us because he is one that serveth, not his own interests only, but those of others.

Irish Co-operative Movement, which numbered George Russell and Father Thomas Finlay among its supporters. Plunkett alienated many by his lack of political tact.

KATHARINE TYNAN

(1861-1931)

from:
TWENTY-FIVE YEARS (1913)

[Katharine Tynan is one of the most prolific of all Irish writers. Her four autobiographical volumes, of which this is the first — the others are *The Middle Years* (1916), *The Years of the Shadow* (1919), *The Wandering Years* (1922) — have more enduring interest than the scores of novels and volumes of poetry and essays she published in a writing life of forty-five years. Although her memory is not always reliable, as in the reference here to the Maamtrasna murders of 1882, she does describe in this account of the Ladies' Land League, how middle-class women gradually and even reluctantly, as in her own case, came to participate in public affairs. Interesting too is the distinction she makes between the Fenians and the Land League. It is a class distinction which had then and was later to continue to have important political implications; because of it, one can readily see at this stage how shocking the Easter Rising was to be for her. Whatever else may be said of the Ladies' Land League, it brought Katharine Tynan out of the social purdah of her father's house into the public world and provided her with the opportunity of becoming a professional writer. Her career is anticipatory of that of many women in the next half-century — Maud Gonne, Constance Markievicz, Susan Mitchell, Nora Connolly and others.]

CHAPTER VII

THE LAND LEAGUE

. . . However, some time following the eighties I was taken up with a new interest in the shape of active politics. At least they became active after the arrest of the Irish leaders towards the end of 1881, with the formation of the Ladies' Land League.[1] I may as well confess that the Land League in itself did not greatly interest me. Nor did it interest my father, who belonged to the old '48 party, and was

1. The Ladies' Land League, more properly the Central Land League of the Ladies of Ireland, was founded in 1881 by Anna Parnell, the sister of Charles Stewart Parnell, when Davitt, Parnell and others were arrested and the state trials of 1880 began.

more in sympathy with Isaac Butt's movement than with anything agrarian. To be sure he owned his land for the greater part, and so the shoe did not pinch him as it pinched the tenant-farmers. But I think, in any case, the movement would not have attracted him, nor did it attract me, in itself. It brought for the first time a certain Americanism into Irish politics which was altogether opposed to sentiment and romance, unless one finds romantic the enormous sums poured week by week from Irish America into the Land League coffers; and that, I think, belonged more to the realm of the fairy-story than to anything of actual life.

The romantic force that did attract one, beyond an agitation which had largely a material aspect, was the personality of the leaders. In 1874 Mr. Parnell had made his first appearance in Irish public life when he contested County Dublin as a Home Ruler. In Mr. Barry O'Brien's *Life of Parnell* you will read about the impression he created.[2] Handsome, refined, distinguished, he was painfully shy, and broke down after a single sentence in his first speech. None of the experienced politicians who listened to him saw anything in him but a gentle, well-mannered young man. No one imagined his greatness or forecasted his fortune, except perhaps the car-driver who drove him from Rathdrum station to Avondale,[3] after the declaration of the poll which left him a badly defeated candidate. 'That's a regular devil,' he said. 'He talked about nothing all the way from the station but fighting again and smashing them all, and he looked wild and fierce.'

I can remember a day in 1874 when Mr. A. M. Sullivan,[4] for whom my father had a great admiration and respect, who was occasionally our honoured guest, told us about that appearance of Mr. Parnell's. I was quite a little girl then, but I think an intelligent one. We must have been sitting about the fire in the dining-room of my old home, where afterwards many politicians and interesting people of all sorts were to sit, for I remember the cold glimmer of a white marble mantelpiece while A. M., as we called him, talked of the gentle brown eyes of the young Wicklow squire, and his shyness in face of a crowd.

And that brings me to another reminiscence in what must be a very discursive narrative. It is again A. M. Sullivan, and the year is 1880, the year of the great Tory *débâcle*.[5] He is telling of Lord Beaconsfield's remark when he realised the ruin of his party. It is not, 'This year I shall see the roses blow at Hughenden'; but, 'There has been nothing like it since Overend and Gurney,' referring to the great bank smash of some years earlier.[6]

Mr. Parnell's was a romantic personality, and so was Michael Davitt's.[7] There were a number of interesting personalities among the younger men. One was able to see them more clearly because at the time there was no towering personality. We did not yet know what Mr. Parnell was. And that brings me to the thought of how he was, and is, and shall be *Mr.* Parnell. There are certain men to whom the 'Mr.' belongs — Mr. Pitt, Mr. Fox, Mr. Disraeli, Mr. Gladstone, Mr. Balfour, Mr. Parnell. The 'Mr.' in these cases is prouder than any title. Occasionally you will hear a former colleague of Mr. Parnell's refer to him as 'Parnell' — even as 'poor Parnell.' At which one is repelled, as though by an irreverence.

Michael Davitt had urged the formation of the Ladies' Land League, foreseeing the time when the men would be in prison and there would be need for someone to look after the evicted tenants. I was present at the first meeting, when Mr. Davitt and Mr. Andrew Kettle[8] saw us started. I stood and talked with them afterwards by the fire. It was on a later Sunday that we met in an upper room of the Land League Offices at 39 Upper Sackville Street. I cannot remember that any men were present, nor indeed anything of the proceedings, except an inflammatory speech from a woman organiser,

2. R. B. O'Brien, *The Life of Charles Stewart Parnell* (1898).
3. Avondale, outside Rathdrum, Co. Wicklow, was Parnell's birthplace and home.
4. Alexander Martin Sullivan (1830-84), journalist and politician. He was MP for Louth 1874-80, and owner editor of *The Nation* newspaper until 1876. Sullivan was an enemy of the Fenians, who passed a death-sentence on him in 1865.

5. In the general election of 1880, the second Tory administration of Benjamin Disraeli, lord Beaconsfield, suffered a crushing defeat.
6. Hughenden Manor, near High Wycombe in Buckinghamshire, was bought by Disraeli in 1848.
   The disastrous failure of the great banking house of Overend and Gurney in May 1866 was followed by a crash on the Stock Exchange and a rise in the bank rate to 10 per cent. At the time Disraeli was chancellor of the exchequer.
7. Michael Davitt (1846-1906), founder of the Land League and ally of Parnell in the New Departure of 1879 — the alliance of the Land League, the Fenians and the Irish Parliamentary Party.
8. Andrew Kettle (1833-1916), a close associate of Parnell and one of the founders of the Land League. At this time, he had just been released from prison for organizing resistance to coercion. His son was the nationalist Thomas Kettle (1880-1916).

which rather frightened some of us who were not extremists.

I believe Mr. Parnell disliked the women's organisation from the beginning, as he certainly detested it in the end.[9] It was carried forward by the compelling force of the sister who in every way so strongly resembled him, who had his mystery, his strangeness, his aloofness, his extraordinary charm in great measure.

I cannot remember Miss Anna Parnell[10] at those early meetings, which have a somewhat dull, somewhat crude feeling in my memory of them. I think if she had been there she must have illumined them. I remember so strongly the extraordinarily compelling force of her personality, so that later on, when the Ladies' Land League was in full work — everyone as busy as bees — that one always knew, without seeing or hearing her, when she had entered the room. Crowds of people, most interesting for one reason or another, came to those offices. You might not lift your eyes from your letter-writing for Members of Parliament, country priests, released suspects, American journalists, revolutionary leaders, but you would certainly lift them and turn about when the little lady, whose very atmosphere was quietness, glided gently into her place.

I had been leading a singularly dull life for some years previous to the Ladies' Land League.... If I had not the cause very much at heart, at least I had enough inspiration from the leaders to keep me going.

I do not know who was responsible for the alliterative title. If it was Miss Parnell, it was a part of the simplicity which marked both her and Mr. Parnell. Perhaps she allowed someone else to make the title for her. Perhaps it was Michael Davitt's choice. At one of the first meetings I said: 'Why not Women's Land League?' and was told that I was too democratic.

It was such a title as gives the scoffer his opportunity, and no doubt he took it. But, looking back and recalling the big room with its desks and tables, I see a group of singularly interesting women. Of course there were a number of rustics, but these were of the rank and file, the ones who wrote dictated letters; it was not yet the day of the typewriter. Miss Parnell, having the elements of greatness, had attracted to her a group of women and girls who fitted easily into her *entourage.* Ireland is the place for the unexpected. Few fashionable gatherings could furnish forth such a group of faces as I remember — not merely pretty, but faces with soul and intelligence bright in them....

I dare not say that this family group of girls — there were others, younger sisters, younger cousins, all beautiful and young — I dare not say it was typical. That would be too much.

The one I knew best, Bee Walshe, was steeped to the lips in an ideal patriotism, which had very little to do with a movement *à servir*,[11] such as the Land League was. She had read much poetry. I can remember her, in the dusk, reading English ballad-poetry to me with an ecstasy which forgot the flight of time. She was very religious, yet she had endured what was to happen to many Parnellite women later — the denunciations of the priests. The old parish priests, at least, Conservatives at heart and friends with the gentry, being men who had received a continental education and naturally gravitated towards the gentlefolk, were as bitter in denunciation of the Land League at the start as later priests were of Parnellism. It was some time before the priests were compelled to come into line, or to seem to acquiesce if they did not. At that time the difference between the priest who had been educated abroad and the Maynooth priest was very marked. There has been very much more of a levelling up in our own days.

In the Ladies' Land League I found a whole new world of interests. For one thing, I found there my first real touch with literature. There was another group of sisters as remarkable in their way as the Walshes and Nallys. In their house I really entered the literary atmosphere. One of them was Hannah Lynch, whose novels appealed to the discriminating.[12] She was one of the few people I have known who eat, drink and dream books, and not many can

9. Parnell was hostile to the activities of the Ladies' Land League, even though it had kept party organization going during his and Davitt's imprisonment. He suppressed it in 1882. This caused a breach with his sister that was never healed.

10. Anna Catherine Parnell (1852-1911), the first woman agitator of importance in modern Irish history. She founded the Ladies' Land League on the promptings of her sister, Frances ('Fanny') Parnell, and addressed its first public meeting at Claremorris, Co. Mayo on 31 January 1881. See A. Parnell, *The Tale of a Great Sham*, ed. D. Hearne (Dublin: Arlen House, 1986).

11. i.e. a practical movement.

12. Among her best-known books are *Through Troubled Waters* (1885) and *Autobiography of a Child* (1899).

have given to literature a more passionate delight and devotion. They were all literary in so far as a devotion to literature goes; and the well-packed bookcases of the house filled with the great things were a wonder-world to me after my miscellaneous and very odd reading.

These sisters, with their mother, were quite at home amid the alarums and excursions of the Land League. Their father had been a Fenian, one of those useful ones who stood a little outside the danger zone, so to speak, and were in the counsels and confidence of the leaders. John O'Leary[13] used to say of the Fenians: 'We are not a transacting party.' Still, a party, even of Fenians, must transact sometimes; and there are men still living in Dublin who, I think, were the safe depositories of Fenian transactions, and were free to transact, standing just outside the fighting line. This may or may not have been true of the father of my early friends. I do not remember that in their conversations they ever spoke of him as having been imprisoned; but he may have been. It was a commonplace at the time.

These girls grew up among the writers, thinkers, orators, politicians, conspirators of their day. The names that dropped from their tongues with an easy intimacy opened the doors of a wonder-world for me. They had grown up in the midst of affairs. Not only the men of the Irish movements were familiar to them from babyhood, but men of another reputation. Edmond O'Donovan, who had not so long before ridden to Merv, had grown up with them like a brother.[14] They knew the whole brilliant Irish group of war-correspondents of those days. One feels now that there must have been a certain Parisian atmosphere in the Dublin of that time, so brilliant was its Bohemia. In Dublin the *Vie de Bohème* was quite in its place. In Fleet Street it could never have been so much at home, although John Augustus O'Shea[15] and other Irish journalists kept the traditions of it there. One has to go back to the Elizabethans for the English *Vie de Bohème*. But in our own day and an earlier one, the influence of the ever-growing and expanding middle-class has made the Bohemian spirit outcast even from Fleet Street, into which frock-coated, top-hatted respectability has overflowed from the City.

This family opened to me its hospitable doors. I learnt much from them. The mother was a woman of spirit and cleverness. She was very bookish: full of personality, and a perfect mine of stories about the men of the Forty-Eight, of the Fifties and Sixties.[16] She used to drop words of wisdom into my receptive ears. From her I heard for the first time of the magnificences of the Old Testament in the Authorised Version. I heard from her that the translation was made by some great group of poets and scholars, whose names are unknown to us; that Shakespeare might have had a hand in it; that we Catholics were at a sad loss in not having been nourished on those Noble Numbers.[17] She pointed out to me how much the great English writers derived from the Bible. All trite and commonplace, perhaps, to people concerned with literature; but to me it was a light. Not that it set me to reading the Bible; that was reserved for my maturer years. I believe I made one or two excursions into the Family Bible about this period, and was driven back by the terrible plain-speaking I chanced upon. . . .

Of the books I was introduced to by these early friends two or three stand out. Two were the *Anatomy of Melancholy* and the *Religio Medici*.[18] I envied them reading George Sand[19] in the French as easily as I could in the English. I had just enough French dimly to apprehend something I thought evil in a book by Michelet — *La Femme*, was it?[20] I had taken it to bed with me one night, and coming upon a passage I did not like I got up very quietly,

13. John O'Leary (1830-1907), one of the most respected of the Fenian leaders. He was president of the supreme council of the IRB 1885-1907 and spent nine years (1865-74) in English jails.
14. Edmond O'Donovan (1844-83), Irish war-correspondent who made a journey to Merv in Central Asia in 1879. He was imprisoned by the Turks for several months, on suspicion of being an agent for the Russians. On his release, he wrote a book, *The Merv Oasis* (1882). He died in a battle in the Sudan in 1883.
15. John Augustus O'Shea (1839-1905), Irish journalist, published *An Iron-Bound City* (2 vols, 1886) and *Roundabout Recollections* (2 vols, 1892).
16. The Young Irelanders, the Fenians, and perhaps the men of the Tenant League of 1850 and the Independent Irish Party.
17. The Authorized Version of the Bible appeared in 1611. Forty-seven revisers were employed in the task of revision and retranslation. The catholic translation, the Rheims and Douai version, appeared in 1582 (New Testament) and 1609-10 (Old Testament).
18. Robert Burton's *Anatomy of Melancholy* (1621) is a learned and affectionate commentary on the inefficacy of human learning and endeavour; Sir Thomas Browne's *Religio Medici* (1642) is famous for its wit, learning and eccentricity, as well as its essentially Christian spirit.
19. George Sand (1804-76), French novelist, whose early works portrayed the struggles of the individual woman against social constraints.
20. Jules Michelet (1798-1874), French historian, was the author of *La Femme* (1860).

opened the door gently, and deposited the book in the passage. I had an idea that there was not room for my angel and Michelet in the little chamber where I slept. I told my hosts the next day, and I remember how they laughed at me.

In that same little narrow room in the kind hospitable house over against the Jesuits' Church in Upper Gardiner Street, Dublin, I lay the night before the execution of Myles Joyce for a murder of which the popular opinion of the day acquitted him, and heard in the darkness the short strokes of a spade all night as though someone dug a grave.[21] It was not likely that anyone should be digging all night in Upper Gardiner Street, Dublin. But there it was all the same.

In the daytime at the League offices I was of those who addressed envelopes and wrote letters. After the 'No Rent Manifesto' had been issued, grants were made to evicted tenants.[22] I think they were sometimes allowed to pay and not be evicted if they paid 'at the point of the bayonet'[23] — that was the phrase: the Irish love a military phrase. In saying this I am ready to be corrected. I was only one of the rank and file, and a frivolous one. After thirty years my memory is not very sure.

I was present that winter at the trial of the men who were accused of murdering the Huddys, Lord Ardilaun's bailiffs, who were found in Lough Corrib, tied up in sacks.[24] An Irish Judge has told me since that the elder Huddy was the bailiff. He was feared of delivering his notices to quit to the wild people and took his young grandson of twelve with him to soften their hearts. Both were murdered. An anonymous letter came to the police telling the exact spot where the bodies would be found. He described for me the strange wildness of the scene when the police-boats went out at night dragging the Lough for the dead bodies. We went to the trial. I wonder now how I endured it. For some reason or other while we waited we were put in the waiting-room with the wives and families of the accused men, Irish-speaking peasants of the Western seaboard — dark, tragic, handsome, the whole sorrow of the world in their desolate faces.

I don't thinking anyone wanted to be jurymen in those wild times, more especially when the outrages began in Dublin — the work of the Invicibles. So well was the secret of the Invincibles kept that at that time no one suspected the existence of a secret society in Dublin — other than the Fenianism which was always going on; but Fenianism was a high-minded, clean-handed Quixotism, very unlike the conspiracy hatched by James Carey.[25] Indeed, the Fenians more than looked askance at the Land League. They looked on it as a demoralising, debasing agitation; and doubtless in many ways it did not make for high-mindedness. I cannot imagine that Mr. Parnell was ever much in love with it, except as a weapon to his hand — the matter that must be settled before the country could set out on a higher adventure. No one, at least no one I knew at the time, suspected the Invincibles. Indeed, I had been assured by these who ought to know — it was a commonplace of the time — that the Land League had killed the secret societies, the evil having come to the surface healthily. Therefore when the outrages began in Dublin, when a man was murdered under the railway arch in Seville Place, when there was another murder or attempted murder at the corner of Abbey Street at the busiest hour of the winter afternoon, when Mr. Field, a juryman, was stabbed as he went home to his house in North Frederick Street, peaceful citizens might well begin to be afraid. There was a horrible series of murders and hangings in that first year of the eighties. There were many winter mornings when one awoke to the horrible thought that there was a

21. Myles Joyce was one of three men executed for the Maamtrasna Murders (or Massacre) of 1882, in which five members of a family named Joyce protested his innocence to the end; he could speak only Irish, so could not understand the court proceedings. James Joyce commemorated this event in *Finnegans Wake*. Since Myles Joyce was executed in Galway in December 1882, Tynan is clearly mistaken here.

22. The No Rent Manifesto, drawn up by William O'Brien (1852-1928), was issued from Kilmainham Jail by the leaders of the Irish Parliamentary Party in October 1881. It called on supporters of the Land League to withhold payment of rent. O'Brien became editor of the Land League journal, *United Ireland*, in 1881.

23. That was not the phrase. The sentence in the No Rent Manifesto read: 'The landlord who evicts will be a ruined pauper and the government who supports him with its bayonets will learn in a single winter how powerless its armed force is against the will of a united and self-reliant nation.'

24. The Land War was at its height between October 1881 and the middle of 1882. The number of evictions in this period was the worst since the Famine clearances; agrarian crime also increased.

25. James Carey (1845-83), one of the leaders of the Irish national Invincibles, a breakaway group from the Fenians. They planned and executed the Phoenix Park murders of 1882. Carey turned informer and his evidence led to the execution of five of his associates. The British authorities sent him and his family to South Africa. There, he was himself assassinated by another Invincible on board a ship off Cape Town.

hanging at Kilmainham Jail. Once I had the misfortune on the night before a hanging to sleep at a friend's house, and being insufficiently provided with bed-clothes and the night cold as it seldom is in Ireland, to lie awake all night shivering before the thought of the dawn and the condemned wretch in his cell.

I saw more than one murder trial in Green Street.[26] I suppose it was the psychology of the crowd that carried me thither and kept me there. I remember those Irish-speaking prisoners who stood in the dock, their arms outstretched in the form of a cross, while the sentence was passed in a tongue of which they did not understand a word, after a trial in the same strange speech.

Once I met my father on the stairs of Green Street Courthouse. He had escaped serving as a jury-man by urging a conscientious objection to hanging. 'It seems to me, my Lord,' he said, 'that you could not make a worse use of a man than to hang him.' He was triumphant as he went down the stairs. Another time he was not so fortunate. Someone was being tried for murder, and he was on the jury. The conscientious man's mind was unsettled in those days by the rumours that flew about of the innocence of prisoners who seemed to have so little chance for their lives, seeing that only through an interpreter could they know the evidence against them or realise the sentence of death except by the judge's black cap. On this second occasion the trial fell through because of the disinclination of a humane Conservative to hang a man, which was so violent that he fell in a dead faint. There was a new jury to try the case, on which my father was not empanelled.

How glad I was on that first occasion to see him going out to his little pony and trap from the courthouse, back to his country life and pursuits. I was dreadfully afraid of danger for him: and he had nothing to do with the air of the shambles which rested upon Green Street at the time.

The Land League in those days was the expression of the Nationalist spirit in Ireland. I think a good many of us felt the uninspiringness of it, but there it was! And there was always Mr. Parnell and the other leaders to inspire us. Had not Mr. Parnell said in one of his public speeches that if it was only the land he would never have taken off his coat for this. I imagine a good many people besides my father and myself looked beyond the Land League to that for which Mr. Parnell had taken off his coat. . . .

26. The site of a courthouse in central Dublin.

WILLIAM BUTLER YEATS

(1865-1939)

from: THE TREMBLING OF THE VEIL (1922)

[Yeats's hostility to the theatre of Ibsen and Shaw and his contrasting idea of the Irish theatre is one of the subsidiary themes in 'The Tragic Generation'. Yeats saw Shaw and Wilde as writers who were in some sense victims of the era in which they lived. They embodied the modern spirit in different ways but in each case there was something maimed or fatally flawed in their work. By making them representative in this fashion, Yeats enhances the version of himself and the vision of the Irish theatre that he wishes to promote against the modern trend.

Florence Farr (1860-1917) was a gifted actress who took over the Avenue Theatre in London in 1894. She acted in Yeats's play, *The Land of Heart's Desire* (1894), which Yeats dedicated to her, as well as in plays by Shaw (*Arms and the Man* was staged in 1894). John Todhunter's play, *The Comedy of Sighs*, put on with *The Land of Heart's Desire* in March 1894, had a disastrous reception and had to be taken off. Florence Farr, who never fully realized her gifts as an actress, is another exemplary figure of the 'tragic generation'. Shaw's success and Wilde's disgrace are, of course, the most remarkable instances. By portraying them in this manner, Yeats displaces the two great contemporary Irish dramatists and leaves himself and Dublin in the spotlight.]

BOOK IV

THE TRAGIC GENERATION

... When Florence Farr opened her theatre she had to meet a hostile audience, almost as violent as that Synge met in January 1907, and certainly more brutal, for the Abbey audience had no hatred for the players, and I think but little for Synge himself. Nor had she the certainty of final victory to give her courage, for *The Comedy of Sighs* was a rambling story told with a little paradoxical wit. She had brought the trouble upon herself perhaps, for always in revolt against her own poetical gifts, which now seemed obsolete, and against her own Demeter-like[1] face in the mirror, she had tried when interviewed by the Press to shock and startle; and yet, unsure of her own judgment, being out of her own trade, had feared to begin with Shaw's athletic wit; and now outraged convention saw its chance. For two hours and a half, pit and gallery drowned the voices of the players with boos and jeers that were meant to be bitter to the author who sat visible to all in his box surrounded by his family, and to the actress struggling bravely through her weary part; and then pit and gallery went home to spread their lying story that the actress had a fit of hysterics in her dressing-room.

Todhunter had sat on to the end, and there were, I think, four acts of it, listening to the howling of his enemies, while his friends slipped out one by one, till one saw everywhere their empty seats, but nothing could arouse the fighting instincts of that melancholy man. Next day I tried to get him to publish his book of words with satirical designs and illustrations by Beardsley,[2] who was just rising into fame, and an introduction attacking the public, but though petulant and irascible he was incapable of any emotion that could give life to a cause. He shared the superstition still current in the theatre, that the public wants sincere drama, but is kept from it by some conspiracy of managers or newspapers, and could not get out of his head that the actors were to blame. Shaw, whose turn came next, had foreseen all months before, and had planned an opening that would confound his enemies. For the first few minutes *Arms and the Man* is crude melodrama and then just when the audience are thinking how crude it is, it turns into excellent farce. At the dress rehearsal, a dramatist who had his own quarrel with the public, was taken in the noose; at the first laugh he stood up, turned his back on the stage, scowled at the audience, and even when everybody else knew what turn the play had taken, continued to scowl, and order those nearest to be silent.

On the first night the whole pit and gallery, except certain members of the Fabian Society,[3] started to laugh at the author, and then, discovering that they themselves were being laughed at, sat there not converted — their hatred was too bitter for that — but dumbfounded, while the rest of the house cheered and laughed. In the silence that greeted the author after the cry for a speech one man did indeed get his courage and boo loudly. 'I assure the gentleman in the gallery', was Shaw's answer, 'that he and I are of exactly the same opinion, but what can we do against a whole house who are of the contrary opinion?' And from that moment Bernard Shaw became the most formidable man in modern letters, and even the most drunken of medical students knew it. My own play, which had been played with *The Comedy of Sighs*, had roused no passions, but had pleased a sufficient minority for Florence Farr to keep it upon the stage with *Arms and the Man*, and I was in the theatre almost every night for some weeks. 'O yes, the people seem to like *Arms and the Man*', said one of Mr. Shaw's players to me, 'but we have just found out that we are all wrong. Mr. Shaw did really mean it quite seriously, for he has written a letter to say so, and we must not play for laughs any more.' Another night I found the manager triumphant and excited, the Prince of Wales and the Duke of Edinburgh had been there, and the Duke of Edinburgh had spoken his dislike out loud so that the whole stalls could hear, but the Prince of Wales had been 'very pleasant' and 'got the Duke of Edinburgh away as soon as possible'. 'They asked for me', he went on,

1. Demeter, the corn goddess of Greek legend and protector of women. In works of art she is represented often with a garland of corn-ears or a riband around her head.
2. Aubrey Beardsley (1872-98), illustrator and writer, and art editor of the *Yellow Book* (1894-96).
3. The Fabian Society was an organization, founded in 1884, to achieve socialism through gradual and democratic means.

'and the Duke of Edinburgh kept on repeating, "The man is mad", meaning Mr. Shaw, and the Prince of Wales asked who Mr. Shaw was, and what he meant by it.' I myself was almost as bewildered, for though I came mainly to see how my own play went, and for the first fortnight to vex my most patient actors with new lines, I listened to *Arms and the Man* with admiration and hatred. It seemed to me inorganic, logical straightness and not the crooked road of life, yet I stood aghast before its energy as today before that of the *Stone Drill* by Mr. Epstein[4] or of some design by Mr. Wyndham Lewis.[5] Shaw was right to claim Samuel Butler[6] for his master, for Butler was the first Englishman to make the discovery that it is possible to write with great effect without music, without style, either good or bad, to eliminate from the mind all emotional implication and to prefer plain water to every vintage, so much metropolitan lead and solder to any tendril of the vine. Presently I had a nightmare that I was haunted by a sewing-machine, that clicked and shone, but the incredible thing was that the machine smiled, smiled perpetually. Yet I delighted in Shaw, the formidable man. He could hit my enemies and the enemies of all I loved, as I could never hit, as no living author that was dear to me could ever hit.

Florence Farr's way home was mine also for a part of the way, and it was often of this that we talked, and sometimes, though not always, she would share my hesitations, and for years to come I was to wonder, whenever Shaw became my topic, whether the cock crowed for my blame or for my praise.

Shaw and Wilde, had no catastrophe come, would have long divided the stage between them, though they were most unlike — for Wilde believed himself to value nothing but words in their emotional associations, and he had turned his style to a parade as though it were his show, and he Lord Mayor.

I was at Sligo again and I saw the announcement of his action against Lord Queensberry, when starting from my uncle's house to walk to Knocknarea to dine with Cochrane of the Glen, as he was called, to distinguish him from others of that name, an able old man. He had a relation, a poor mad girl, who shared our meals, and at whom I shuddered. She would take a flower from the vase in front of her and push it along the tablecloth towards any male guest who sat near. The old man himself had strange opinions, born not from any mental eccentricity, but from the solitude of his life; and a freedom from all prejudices that were not of his own discovery. 'The world is getting more manly,' he would say, 'it has begun to drink port again', or 'Ireland is going to become prosperous. Divorced couples now choose Ireland for a retreat, just as before Scotland became prosperous they began to go there. There are a divorced wife and her lover living at the other side of the mountain.' I remember that I spoke that night of Wilde's kindness to myself, said I did not believe him guilty, quoted the psychologist Bain,[7] who has attributed to every sensualist 'a voluminous tenderness', and described Wilde's hard brilliance, his dominating self-possession. I considered him essentially a man of action, that he was a writer by perversity and accident, and would have been more important as soldier or politician; and I was certain that, guilty or not guilty, he would prove himself a man. I was probably excited, and did most of the talking, for if Cochrane had talked, I would have remembered an amusing sentence or two; but he was certainly sympathetic. A couple of days later I received a letter from Lionel Johnson, denouncing Wilde with great bitterness. He had 'a cold scientific intellect'; he got a 'sense of triumph and power, at every dinner-table he dominated, from the knowledge that he was guilty of that sin which, more than any other possible to man, would turn all those people against him if they but knew'. He wrote in the mood of his poem, *To the Destroyer of a Soul*, addressed to

4. Jacob Epstein (1880-1959), monumental and portrait sculptor, regarded as the greatest of his day. His work had the angularity and mechanical impersonality that Yeats detested. Epstein carved the Oscar Wilde memorial at Père Lachaise cemetery in Paris.
5. Wyndham Lewis (1884-1957), chief figure in the foundation of Vorticism, his work has been likened to Cubism and Futurism. Like Epstein, Lewis represented Yeats's conception of all that was 'mechanical'.
6. Samuel Butler (1835-1902), best-known for his posthumously published autobiography, *The Way of All Flesh* (1903), and his utopian satire *Erewhon* (1872), also wrote extensively on scientific topics. Shaw wrote admiringly of Butler on a number of occasions, most particularly in the Preface to *Major Barbara* (1905), in which he called him 'in his own department the greatest English writer of the second half of the XIX century' and admits that Butler's suggestions 'have an obvious share' in his own plays.
7. Alexander Bain (1818-1903), Scottish psychologist and associate of John Stuart Mill. His books include *The Senses and the Intellect* (1855) and *The Emotions and the Will* (1859). He founded the first psychological journal, *Mind*, in 1886.

Wilde, as I have always believed, though I know nothing of the circumstance that made him write it.[8]

I might have known that Wilde's fantasy had taken some tragic turn, and that he was meditating upon possible disaster, but one took all his words for play — had he not called insincerity 'a mere multiplication of the personality'[9] or some such words? . . . .

8. Johnson's poem 'To the Destroyer of a Soul' appeared in *Poems* (1895). It is presumed to be dedicated to Wilde and indicates that Johnson felt that Wilde had replaced him in the affections of Lord Alfred Douglas.
9. In *Intentions, The Critic As Artist*, Part II (1891): 'What people call insincerity is simply a method by which we can multiply our personalities.'

from:
AUTOBIOGRAPHY (1938)

[Yeats's autobiographical writings are complex in intention and in the history of their passage from manuscript to print. The volume *Autobiographies* (London, 1955, 1961) gathered various fragments into one. These were *Reveries over Childhood and Youth* (1915), *Four Years: 1887-1891* (1921), *The Trembling of the Veil* (1922), *Estrangement* (1926), *The Death of Synge, and Other Passages from an Old Diary* (1928) and *Dramatis Personae 1896-1902* (1935). The *Autobiography* (1938) and the *Journal*, parts of which were published in some of the volumes mentioned, were finally published in the original text under the title *W. B. Yeats Memoirs* ed. D. Donoghue (London: Macmillan, 1972). This is the text used here.

Had there not been an Irish Revival, Yeats would have invented it. Indeed, perhaps he did. The people he commemorates — Maud Gonne, John O'Leary, Wilde, Lionel Johnson, Synge, Shaw, and scores of others — all belong within an unfolding and enfolding theme. In part, that theme is the growth of Yeats to his full dimensions, a process in which many fellow labourers were unwittingly employed. In part, it is the creation of a great historical moment which has Ireland as its arena. The complicated relationship between these two parts of a single theme informs Yeats's recording of remembered events.]

CHAPTER X

I was twenty-three years old when the troubling of my life began. I had heard from time to time in letters from Miss O'Leary,[1] John O'Leary's old sister, of a beautiful girl[2] who had left the society of the Viceregal Court for Dublin nationalism. In after years I persuaded myself that I felt premonitory excitement at the first reading of her name. Presently she drove up to our house in Bedford Park with an introduction from John O'Leary to my father.[3] I had never thought to see in a living woman so great beauty. It belonged to famous pictures, to poetry, to some legendary past. A complexion like the blossom of apples, and yet face and body had the beauty of lineaments which Blake calls the highest beauty because it changes least from youth to age, and a stature so great that she seemed of a divine race. Her movements were worthy of her form, and I understood at last why the poet of antiquity, where we would but speak of face and form, sings, loving some lady, that she paces like a goddess. I remember nothing of her speech that day except that she vexed my father by praise of war, for she too was of the Romantic movement and found those uncontrovertible Victorian reasons, that seemed to announce so prosperous a future, a little grey. As I look backward, it seems to me that she brought into my life in those days — for as yet I saw only what lay upon the surface — the middle of the tint, a sound as of a Burmese gong, an overpowering tumult that had yet many pleasant secondary notes.

She asked [me] to dine with her that evening in her rooms in Ebury Street, and I think that I dined with her all but every day during her stay in London of perhaps nine days, and there was something so exuberant in her ways that it seemed natural she should give her hours in overflowing abundance. She had heard of me from O'Leary; he had praised me, and it was natural that she should give and take without stint. She lived surrounded by cages of innumerable singing birds and with these she always travelled, it seemed, taking them even upon short journeys, and they and she were now returning to Paris where their home was.

She spoke to me of her wish for a play that she could act in Dublin. Somebody had suggested

1. Ellen O'Leary (1831-89). Yeats wrote an Introduction to a selection of her poems, edited by T. W. Rolleston, *Lays of Country, Home and Fireside* (1891); it is reprinted in J. P. Frayne (ed.), *Uncollected Prose by W. B. Yeats* I (London: Macmillan, 1970), pp. 256-58.
2. Maud Gonne (1865-1953) had, by the time she met Yeats, fallen in love with Lucien Millevoye, a French politician and journalist.
3. 30 January 1889. John O'Leary (1830-1907) returned to Dublin in 1885, after spending nine years in prison and eleven years in exile, most of them in Paris.

Todhunter's *Helena in Troas*,[4] but he had refused. I told her of a story I had found when compiling my *Fairy and Folk Tales of the Irish Peasantry*,[5] and offered to write for her the play I have called *The Countess Cathleen*.[6] When I told her I wished to become an Irish Victor Hugo, was I wholly sincere? — for though a volume of bad verse translations from Hugo had been my companion at school, I had begun to simplify myself with great toil. I had seen upon her table *Tristram of Lyonesse*[7] and *Les Contemplations*,[8] and besides it was natural to commend myself by claiming a very public talent, for her beauty as I saw it in those days seemed incompatible with private, intimate life.

She, like myself, had received the political tradition of Davis[9] with an added touch of hardness and heroism from the hand of O'Leary, and when she spoke of William O'Brien,[10] [who] was in jail making a prolonged struggle against putting on the prison clothes, she said, 'There was a time when men sacrificed their lives for their country, but now they sacrifice their dignity.' But mixed with this feeling for what is permanent in human life there was something declamatory, Latin in a bad sense, and perhaps even unscrupulous. She spoke of her desire for power, apparently for its own sake, and when we talked of politics spoke much of mere effectiveness, or the mere winning of this or that election. Her two and twenty years had taken some colour, I thought, from French Boulangist adventurers and journalist *arrivistes* of whom she had seen too much,[11] and [she] already had made some political journey into Russia in their interest.[12] I was full of that thought of the 'Animula Vagula' chapter, I had heard it at the feet of a young Brahmin in Dublin, 'Only the means can justify the end.'[13] She meant her ends to be unselfish, but she thought almost any means justified in their success. We were seeking different things: she, some memorable action for final consecration of her youth, and I, after all, but to discover and communicate a state of being. Perhaps even in politics it would in the end be enough to have lived and thought passionately and have, like O'Leary, a head worthy of a Roman coin.

I spoke much of my spiritual philosophy. How important it all seemed to me; what would I not have given that she might think exactly right on all those great questions of the day? All is but faint to me beside a moment when she passed before a window, dressed in white, and rearranged a spray of flowers in a vase. Twelve years afterwards I put that impression into verse: ('she pulled down the pale blossom'. Quote):

> [Blossom pale, she pulled down the pale blossom
> At the moth hour and hid it in her bosom.][14]

I felt in the presence of a great generosity and courage, and of a mind without peace, and when she and all her singing birds had gone my melancholy was not the mere melancholy of love. I had what I thought was a 'clairvoyant' perception but was, I can see now, but an obvious deduction of an

4. John Todhunter (1839-1916). *Helena in Troas* was produced in 1886 in London and published the same year. In the preceding excerpt, we read of the fate of his play, *A Comedy of Sighs* (1894).
5. Published in London in 1888 (reprinted Gerrards Cross: Colin Smythe, 1977). The story is 'The Countess Kathleen O'Shea'.
6. It was Florence Farr who acted in *The Countess Cathleen* in 1899; Maud Gonne appeared, with sensational effect, in *Cathleen ni Houlihan* (1902).
7. Algernon Charles Swinburne's *Tristram of Lyonesse, and Other Poems* (1882) included the poem 'The Statue of Victor Hugo', one of Swinburne's many tributes to Hugo.
8. Hugo's *Les Contemplations* (1856).
9. Thomas Davis (1814-45), leader of the Young Ireland movement, and one of the founders of *The Nation* in 1842.
10. Not one of Maud Gonne's more perceptive remarks. William O'Brien (1852-1928), journalist, MP and land agitator, had refused to wear prison clothes after his arrest in 1887 over a rent-strike he had organized in Tipperary. Wilfrid Scawen Blunt (1840-1922) had been the first to refuse to wear prison garb, on the grounds that he was a political prisoner (he spent two months in prison for speaking at a meeting in favour of Irish nationalism). These actions were to have wide repercussions later. Further, the MP arrested with O'Brien, John Mandeville, died shortly after his release because of the hardship he had suffered in prison on account of his refusal to wear prison clothes.
11. General Boulanger, minister of war in a number of coalition cabinets during the Third Republic in France, was put forward in 1888 as the leader of a new national party by conservatives anxious to win back ground lost by the church in the previous decade. The chamber of deputies forestalled this attempt to transform the régime, and impeached Boulanger, who immediately and ingloriously fled to Brussels. The Republic survived and the extreme right, backed by the church, was left in disarray. An *arriviste* is a recent and vulgar recruit to a powerful position. Lucien Millevoye, Maud Gonne's lover by whom she had two children between 1893 and 1895, edited a right-wing journal, *La Patrie*.
12. This was in 1888. Tzar Alexander III was an ally of the Boulangist faction.
13. Mohini Chatterjee, an Indian theosophist and ally of Madame Blavatsky (1831-91), visited Dublin in 1885. The most memorable result of this meeting was Yeats's poem of 1929, 'Mohini Chatterjee'. The 'Anima Vagula' seems to be a reference to the Anima Isvara (ceative potency) mentioned in Madame Blavatsky's *Isis Unveiled* (1887).
14. From 'The Arrow', in the version which appeared in *In the Seven Woods* (1903).

awaiting immediate disaster. I was compiling for an American publisher a selection from the Irish novelists,[15] and I can remember that all the tribulations of their heroes but reminded me of that dread. They too, according to a fashion of the writers of early Victoria, had been so often thrown without father or mother or guardian amid a world of deception, and they too, in their different way, were incurably romantic. I was in love but had not spoken of love and never meant to speak, and as the months passed I grew master of myself again. 'What wife could she make,' I thought, 'what share could she have in the life of a student?'

On some journey to Sligo I must have lingered in Dublin; my old circle of friends and acquaintances, once flattered by her descent among them, had begun to criticize. Even old John O'Leary[16] was angry. William O'Brien and John Dillon had just persuaded the townsmen of Tipperary, who had a quarrel with the landlord,[17] to build a new town on a neighbouring plot of land, and it had been discovered that the old landlord by some grip over the new one in some forgotten clause in a lease could turn them out of the new town also. O'Leary himself owned property in the old town, but if he had not he would certainly have disliked the adventure as much, for he hated those two politicians above others. 'They want to influence English opinion at the moment, and they think a Home Rule Bill will come before they are found out. They are gambling with other people's lives,' he would say, or some such phrases. Maud Gonne had been to some formal opening of the new town. 'She is no disciple of mine,' he said, 'she went there to show off her new bonnets.' Somebody else had some tale of her going to the Parnell Commission[18] like some sentimental English sympathizer, in a green dress covered with shamrocks. Somebody else, a Unionist, had another tale, not less fabulous as I discovered in my anger, of her going to an otter hunt in a muslin dress that was soon covered with mud. . . .

15. *Representative Irish Tales, compiled by W. B. Yeats* (New York: Putnam, 1891).
16. Yeats had written here, then deleted, 'refused now to consider her among his disciples'.
17. John Dillon (1851-1927), MP for Tipperary 1880-83 and for East Mayo 1885-1918. In a clash between a landlord syndicate led by Arthur Smith-Barry (1843-1925), and tenants in Tipperary in 1889, evictions and boycotts led to the construction of a shanty town, called New Tipperary, which was supported by the Tenant Defence League founded by Dillon and William O'Brien.
18. A special parliamentary commission established by a select committee of the House of Commons to investigate charges by *The Times* newspaper that Parnell and his associates had supported conspiracy and murder during the Land War of 1879-82.

GEORGE BERNARD SHAW

(1856-1950)

from: IMMATURITY (1930)

[Shaw wrote five novels between 1879 and 1883, *Immaturity* being the first. The other four were published serially in socialist periodicals, but *Immaturity* had to wait until 1930 before it appeared in print. Shaw's Preface to the 1930 edition is, in effect, an autobiographical essay in which he handles with comic expertise the pain of his growing up in Dublin. To him, as to Joyce, it was indeed the deposed capital, a place to escape from but impossible to leave imaginatively.

Joyce's *Ulysses*, to which Shaw famously refers here, had appeared eight years earlier and the distance between him and Shaw as writers could hardly be more tellingly displayed than by a comparison between it and Shaw's well-named effort of 1879. Yet the great novelist and the great playwright had in common the experience of Dublin, social humiliation, poverty and the determination to expose the conventions that underpinned the middle-class world in work that would be revolutionary in its anti-heroic subversion of the forces enslaving mankind. Shaw left Ireland before the Revival began, yet his contribution, as artist and as commentator, is integral to our understanding of what the Revival was.]

... I came to London from Dublin in the spring of 1876, and found my mother and my one surviving sister (I had no brothers) established in No. 13 Victoria Grove, trying to turn their musical accomplishments to account: my mother by teaching, my sister by singing. My father, left in Dublin, spared us a pound a week from his slender resources; and by getting into debt and occasionally extracting ourselves by drawing on a maternal inheritance of £4000 over which my mother had a power of appointment, and which therefore could be realized bit by bit as her three children came of age, we managed to keep going somehow.

Impecuniosity was necessarily chronic in the household. And here let me distinguish between this sort of poverty and that which furnishes an element of romance in the early lives of many famous men. I am almost tempted to say that it is the only sort of poverty that counts, short of the privations that make success impossible. We all know the man whose mother brought him up with nineteen brothers and sisters on an income of eighteen shillings a week earned by her own labor. The road from the log cabin to the White House, from the bench in the factory to the Treasury Bench, from the hovel to the mansion in Park Lane, if not exactly a crowded road, always has a few well fed figures at the end of it to tell us all about it. I always assure these gentlemen that they do not know what poverty and failure is. Beginning with as much as they expected or were accustomed to, they have known nothing but promotion. At each step they have had the income of the society in which they moved, and been able to afford its clothes, its food, its habits, its rents and rates. What more has any prince? If you would know what real poverty is, ask the younger son of a younger son of a younger son. To understand his plight you must start at the top without the income of the top, and curse your stars that you were not lucky enough to start at the bottom. . . .

My able and flourishing friend A tells me that he knows what poverty is and what drink is: was he not brought up in the Borough by a drunken mother? B, rolling in wealth, tells me that when he was a boy he had meat only twice a year. C, wallowing in fame, calls me a snob, after gleefully narrating his experiences in the kitchen of his father's small shop, and how he was enabled to study country house society by a childish privilege of visiting the servants' hall. How easily I cap these zests to success by the simple statement that my father was second cousin to a baronet, and my mother the daughter of a country gentleman whose rule was, when in difficulties, mortgage. That was my sort of poverty. The Shaws were younger sons from the beginning, as I shall shew when I reveal my full pedigree. Even the baronetcy was founded on the fortunes of a fifth son who came to Dublin and made that city his oyster. Let who will preen himself on his Mother Hubbard's bare cupboard, and play for sympathy as an upstart: I was a downstart and the son of a downstart. But for the accident of a lucrative talent I should today be poorer than Spinoza; for he at least knew how to grind lenses, whereas I could not afford to learn any art. Luckily Nature taught me one.

This social *degringolade*[1] never stops in these islands. It produces a class which deserves a history all to itself. Do not talk of the middle class: the expression is meaningless except when it is used by an economist to denote the man of business who stands in the middle between land and capital on the one hand, and labor on the other, and organizes business for both. I sing my own class: the Shabby Genteel, the Poor Relations, the Gentlemen who are No Gentlemen. If you want to know exactly where I came in, you will get at such facts as that of my many uncles only one, the eldest, contrived to snatch a university education. The rest shifted as best they could without it (rather better than he, mostly). . . .

On the whole, they held their cherished respectability in the world in spite of their lack of opportunity. They owed something perhaps, to the confidence given them by their sense of family. In Irish fashion they talked of themselves as the Shaws, as who should say the Valois, the Bourbons, the Hohenzollerns, the Hapsburgs, or the Romanoffs; and their world conceded the point to them. I had an enormous contempt for this family snobbery, as I called it, until I was completely reconciled to it by a certain Mr Alexander Mackintosh Shaw, a clansman who, instead of taking his pedigree for granted in the usual Shaw manner, hunted it up, and published 100 copies privately in 1877. Somebody sent me a copy; and my gratification was unbounded when I read the first sentence of the first chapter, which ran: 'It is the general tradition, says the Rev. Lachlan Shaw

1. tumble, fall.

[bless him!], that the Shaws are descended of McDuff, Earl of Fife.' I hastily skipped to the chapter about the Irish Shaws to make sure that they were my people; and there they were, baronet and all, duly traced to the third son of that immortalized yet unborn Thane of Fife who, invulnerable to normally accouched swordsmen, laid on and slew Macbeth. It was as good as being descended from Shakespear, whom I had been unconsciously resolved to reincarnate from my cradle. . . .

And now you will ask why, with such unexceptional antecedents and social openings, was I not respectably brought up? Unfortunately or fortunately (it all depends on how you look at it) my father had a habit which eventually closed all doors to him, and consequently to my mother, who could not very well be invited without him. If you asked him to dinner or to a party, he was not always quite sober when he arrived; and he was invariably scandalously drunk when he left. Now a convivial drunkard may be exhilarating in convivial company. Even a quarrelsome or boastful drunkard may be found entertaining by people who are not particular. But a miserable drunkard — and my father, in theory a teetotaller, was racked with shame and remorse even in his cups — is unbearable. We were finally dropped socially. After my early childhood I cannot remember ever paying a visit at a relative's house. If my mother and father had dined out, or gone to a party, their children would have been much more astonished than if the house had caught fire.

How my mother rescued herself from this predicament by her musical talent I will tell elsewhere. My father reduced his teetotalism from theory to practice when a mild fit, which felled him on our doorstep one Sunday afternoon, convinced him that he must stop drinking or perish. It had no worse effect; but his reform, though complete and permanent, came too late to save the social situation; and I, cut off from the social drill which puts one at one's ease in private society, grew up frightfully shy and utterly ignorant of social routine. My mother, who had been as carefully brought up as Queen Victoria, was too humane to inflict what she had suffered on any child; besides, I think she imagined that correct behavior is inborn, and that much of what she had been taught was natural to her. Anyhow, she never taught it to us, leaving us wholly to the promptings of our blood's blueness, with results which may be imagined. . . .

The truth is that all men are in a false position in society until they have realized their possibilities, and imposed them on their neighbors. They are tormented by a continual shortcoming in themselves; yet they irritate others by a continual overweening. This discord can be resolved by acknowledged success or failure only: everyone is ill at ease until he has found his natural place, whether it be above or below his birthplace. The overrated inheritor of a position for which he has no capacity, and the underrated nobody who is a born genius, are alike shy because they are alike out of place. Besides, this finding of one's place may be made very puzzling by the fact that there is no place in ordinary society for extraordinary individuals. For the worldly wiseman, with common ambitions, the matter is simple enough; money, title, precedence, a seat in parliament, a portfolio in the cabinet, will mean success both to him and his circle. But what about people like St Francis and St Clare? Of what use to them are the means to live the life of the country house and the west end mansion? They have literally no business in them, and must necessarily cut an unhappy and ridiculous figure there. They have to make a society of Franciscans and Poor Clares for themselves before they can work or live socially. It is true that those who are called saints are not saintly all the time and in everything. In eating and drinking, lodging and sleeping, chatting and playing: in short, in everything but working out their destiny as saints, what is good enough for a ploughman is good enough for a poet, a philosopher, a saint, or a higher mathematician. But Hodge's work is not good enough for Newton, nor Falstaff's conversation holy enough for Shelley. Christ adapted himself so amiably to the fashionable life of his time in his leisure that he was reproached for being a gluttonous man and a winebibber, and for frequenting frivolous and worthless sets. But he did not work where he feasted, nor flatter the Pharisees, nor ask the Romans to buy him with a sinecure. He knew when he was being entertained, well treated, lionized: not an unpleasant adventure for once in a way; and he did not quarrel with the people who were so nice to him. Besides, to sample society is part of a prophet's business: he must sample the governing class above all, because his inborn knowledge of human nature will not explain the anomalies produced in it by Capitalism and Sacerdotalism. But he can never feel at home in it. The born Communist, before he knows what he is, and understands why, is always awkward and unhappy in plutocratic society and in the poorer societies which ape it to the extent of their little means; in short, wherever spiritual values are assessed like Income Tax. In his nonage he is imposed on by the prestige which the propertied classes have conferred on themselves and inculcated in the schools, and by the comfort and refinement and splendor of their equipment in contrast to the squalor of the proletariat. If he has been brought up to regard himself as one of the propertied classes, and has its whole equipment of false standards of worth, lacking nothing but the indispensable pecuniary equipment without which his education is utterly meaningless, his embarrassment and bewilderment are pitiable, and his isolation often complete; for he is left alone between the poor whom he regards as beneath him and the rich whose standards of expenditure are beyond his means. He is ashamed of his poverty, in continual dread of doing the wrong thing, resentfully insubordinate and seditious in a social order which he not only accepts but in which he actually claims a privileged part.

As I write, there is a craze for what is called psycho-analysis, or the cure of diseases by explaining to the patient what is the matter with him: an excellent plan if you happen to know what is the matter with him, especially when the explanation is that there is nothing the matter with him. Thus a bee, desperately trying to reach a flower bed through a window pane, concludes that he is the victim of evil spirits or that he is mad, his end being exhaustion, despair, and death. Yet, if he only knew, there is nothing wrong with him: all he has to do is go out as he came in, through open window or door. Your born Communist begins like the bee on the pane. He worries himself and everybody else until he dies of peevishness, or, else is led by some propagandist pamphlet, or by his own intellectual impulses (if he has any), to investigate the economic structure of our society.

Immediately everything becomes clear to him. Property is theft:[2] respectability founded on poverty is blasphemy: marriage founded on property is prostitution: it is easier for a camel to go through the eye of a needle than for a rich man to enter the kingdom of heaven.[3] He now knows where he is, and where this society which has so intimidated him is. . . .

If he be not a born Communist, but a predatory combative man, eager to do the other fellow down, and happy in a contrast between his prosperity and the indigence of others, happy also in a robust contempt for cowards and weaklings, the very same discovery of the nature of our Capitalism will nerve him to play the Capitalist game for all it and he are worth. But for the most part men drift with the society into which they are born, and make the best of its accidents without changing its morals or understanding its principles.

As it happens, I was a born Communist and Iconoclast (or Quaker) without knowing it; and I never got on easy terms with plutocracy and snobbery until I took to the study of economics, beginning with Henry George and Karl Marx.[4] . . . When, at a public meeting of the Shelley Society, I scandalized many of the members by saying that I had joined because, like Shelley, I was a Socialist, an atheist, and a vegetarian,[5] I did not know that I could have expressed my position more accurately by simply saying that my conception of God was that insisted on in the first Article of the Church of England,[6] then as now vehemently repudiated by all pious persons, who will have it that God is a substantial gentleman of uncertain and occasionally savage temper, and a spirit only in the sense in which an archbishop is a spirit. . . .

It may be asked here how I came by my heterodox opinions, seeing that my father's alcoholic neurosis, though it accounts for my not going into society, does not account for my not going to church. My reply, if put in the conventional terms

2. 'La propriété c'est le vol', a famous quotation from the French social philosopher Pierre Joseph Proudhon (1809-65), cited in the opening chapter of his work *Qu'est-ce que la Propriété?* (1840).

3. Matthew 19.24.

4. In 1882 Shaw heard the American economist Henry George (1839-97) lecture in London and bought his famous book *Progress and Poverty* (1879) on his way out of the lecture hall. George remained an important influence on his thinking. In 1881, George wrote an interesting pamphlet, *The Irish Land Question*. It was in the winter of 1882-83 that Shaw began his reading of Marx's *Das Kapital* (1867).

5. Shelley was indeed an atheist and vegetarian, but it is less certain that he could be called a socialist.

6. The first of the 39 Articles of Religion in the *Book of Common Prayer* of the Church of England states: 'There is but one living and true God, everlasting, without body, parts, or passions; of infinite power, wisdom and goodness; the Maker, and Preserver of all things both visible and invisible. And in unity of this Godhead there be three Persons, of one substance, power and eternity: the Father, the Son, and the Holy Ghost.'

of that day, would be that I was badly brought up because my mother was so well brought up. Her character reacted so strongly against her strict and loveless training that churchgoing was completely dropped in our family before I was ten years old. In my childhood I exercised my literary genius by composing my own prayers. I cannot recall the words of the final form I adopted; but I remember that it was in three movements, like a sonata, and in the best Church of Ireland style. It ended with the Lord's Prayer; and I repeated it every night in bed. I had been warned by my nurse that warm prayers were no use, and that only by kneeling by my bedside in the cold could I hope for a hearing; but I criticised this admonition unfavorably on various grounds, the real one being my preference for warmth and comfort. I did not disparage my nurse's authority in these matters because she was a Roman Catholic: I even tolerated her practice of sprinkling me with holy water occasionally. But her asceticism did not fit the essentially artistic and luxurious character of my devotional exploits. Besides, the penalty did not apply to my prayer; for it was not a petition. I had too much sense to risk my faith by begging for things I knew very well I should not get; so I did not care whether my prayers were answered or not: they were a literary performance for the entertainment and propitiation of the Almighty; and though I should not have dreamt of daring to say that if He did not like them He might lump them (perhaps I was too confident of their quality to apprehend such a rebuff), I certainly behaved as if my comfort were an indispensable condition of the performance taking place at all. . . .

My father disapproved of the detachment of his family from the conventional observances that were associated with the standing of the Shaw family. But he was in the grip of a humorous sense of anticlimax which I inherited from him and used with much effect when I became a writer of comedy. The more sacred an idea or a situation was by convention, the more irresistible was it to him as the jumping-off place for a plunge into laughter. Thus, when I scoffed at the Bible he would instantly and quite sincerely rebuke me, telling me, with what little sternness was in his nature, that I should not speak so; that no educated man would make such a display of ignorance; that the Bible was universally recognized as a literary and historical masterpiece; and as much more to the same effect as he could muster. But when he had reached the point of feeling really impressive, a convulsion of internal chuckling would wrinkle up his eyes; and (I knowing all the time quite well what was coming) would cap his eulogy by assuring me, with an air of perfect fairness, that even the worst enemy of religion could say no worse of the Bible than that it was the damndest parcel of lies ever written. He would then rub his eyes and chuckle for quite a long time. It became an unacknowledged game between us that I should provoke him to exhibitions of this kind.

With such a father my condition was clearly hopeless as far as the conventions of religion were concerned. In essential matters his influence was as good as his culture permitted. One of my very earliest recollections is reading the Pilgrim's Progress[7] to him, and being corrected by him for saying grievious instead of grievous. I never saw him, as far as I can remember, reading anything but the newspaper; but he had read Sir Walter Scott and other popular classics; and he always encouraged me to do the same, and to frequent the National Gallery,[8] and to go to the theatre and the opera when I could afford it. His anticlimaxes depended for their effect on our sense of the sacredness he was reacting against: there would have been no fun whatever in saying that the Adventures of Munchausen[9] (known to us as Baron Mun Chawzon) were a parcel of lies. If my mother's pastors and masters had had a little of his humor, she would not simply have dropped the subject of religion with her children in silent but implacable dislike of what had helped to make her childhood miserable, and resolved that it should not do the same to them. The vacuum she left by this policy had, I think, serious disadvantages for my two sisters (the younger of whom died just before I came to London); but in my case it only made a clear space for positive beliefs later on.

My mother, I may say here, had no comedic impulses, and never uttered an epigram in her life: all my comedy is a Shavian inheritance. She had plenty of imagination, and really lived in it and on

7. John Bunyan's *The Pilgrim's Progress* (1678), the most popular of all English religious classics.
8. The National Gallery of Ireland is one of the beneficiaries of Shaw's will.
9. *Baron Munchausen, the Narrative of his Marvellous Travels* by Rudolphe Eric Raspe, published in an English translation in 1785, is a collection of fantastic tales.

it. Her brother, my uncle Walter, who stayed with us from time to time in the intervals of his trips across the Atlantic as a surgeon on the Inman Liners, had an extraordinary command of picturesque language, partly derived by memory from the Bible and Prayer Book, and partly natural. The conversation of the navigating staffs and pursers of our ocean services was at that time (whatever it may be today) extremely Rabelaisian and profane. Falstaff himself could not have held his own with my uncle in obscene anecdotes, unprintable limericks, and fantastic profanity; and it mattered nothing to him whether his audience consisted of his messmates on board ship or his schoolboy nephew: he performed before each with equal gusto. To do him justice, he was always an artist in his obscenity and blasphemy, and therefore never sank to the level of incontinent blackguardism. His efforts were controlled, deliberate, fastidiously chosen and worded. But they were all the more effective in destroying all my inculcated childish reverence for the verbiage of religion, for its legends and personifications and parables. In view of my subsequent work in the world it seems providential that I was driven to the essentials of religion by the reduction of every factitious or fictitious element in it to the most irreverent absurdity.

It would be the greatest mistake to conclude that this shocking state of affairs was bad for my soul. In so far as the process of destroying reverence for the inessential trappings of religion was indecent, it was deplorable; and I wish my first steps to grace had been lighted by my uncle's wit and style without his obscenity. My father's comedy was entirely decent. But that the process was necessary to my salvation I have no doubt whatever. A popular book in my youth was Mark Twain's New Pilgrim's Progress,[10] which horrified the thoughtlessly pious by making fun of what they called sacred things. Yet Mark Twain was really a religious force in the world: his Yankee at the Court of King Arthur[11] was his nearest approach to genuine blasphemy; and that came from want of culture, not from perversity of soul. His training as a Mississippi pilot must have been, as to religion, very like my training as the nephew of a Transatlantic surgeon. . . .

The institution of the family, which is the centre of reverence for carefully brought-up children, was just the opposite for me. In a large family there are always a few skeletons in the cupboard; and in my father's clan there were many uncles and aunts and cousins, consequently many cupboards, consequently some skeletons. Our own particular skeleton was my father's drunkenness. It was combined with a harmlessness and humaneness which made him the least formidable of men; so that it was impossible for him to impress his children in the manner that makes awe and dread almost an instinct with some children. It is much to his credit that he was incapable of deliberately practising any such impressiveness, drunk or sober; but unfortunately the drunkenness was so humiliating that it would have been unendurable if we had not taken refuge in laughter. It had to be either a family tragedy or a family joke; and it was on the whole a healthy instinct that decided us to get what ribald fun was possible out of it, which, however, was very little indeed. If Noah had made a habit of drinking, his sons would soon have worn out the pious solicitude which they displayed on the occasion of his single lapse from sobriety. A boy who has seen 'the governor,' with an imperfectly wrapped-up goose under one arm and a ham in the same condition under the other (both purchased under heaven knows what delusion of festivity), butting at the garden wall in the belief that he was pushing open the gate, and transforming his tall hat to a concertina in the process, and who, instead of being overwhelmed with shame and anxiety at the spectacle, has been so disabled by merriment (uproariously shared by the maternal uncle) that he has hardly been able to rush to the rescue of the hat and pilot its wearer to safety, is clearly not a boy who will make tragedies of trifles instead of making trifles of tragedies. If you cannot get rid of the family skeleton, you may as well make it dance. . . .

Though the neurosis which produced my father's joyless craving for alcohol had the same effect, with the same curious recalcitrance and final impermanence, in one or two other cases, and was perhaps connected with occasional family paroxysms of Evangelical piety, and some share of my father's comedic love of anticlimax, yet on the whole our collection of skeletons was not exceptionally large. But as, compared with similar English

10. *The Innocents Abroad; or, The New Pilgrim's Progress* (1869), an account of Twain's journey through Europe and the Holy Land. Twain satirizes foreign sights and manners from the point of view of an American democrat.

11. *A Connecticut Yankee in King Arthur's Court* (1889), a realistic-satirical fantasy of Arthurian England.

families, we had a power of derisive dramatization that made the bones of the Shavian skeletons rattle more loudly; and as I possessed this power in an abnormal degree, and frequently entertained my friends with stories of my uncles (so effectively, by the way, that nobody ever believed them), the family, far from being a school of reverence for me, was rather a mine from which I could dig highly amusing material without the trouble of inventing a single incident. What idle fancy of mine could have improved on the hard facts of the Life and Death of Uncle William?[12]

Thus the immediate result of my family training in my Victoria Grove days was that I presented myself to the unprepared stranger as a most irreverent young man. My Mephistophelean moustache and eyebrows had not yet grown; and there was nothing in my aspect to break the shock of my diabolical opinions. Later on, when I had made a public reputation as an iconoclast, people who met me in private were surprised at my mildness and sociability. But I had no public reputation then: consequently expectation in my regard was normal. And I was not at all reticent of the diabolical opinions. I felt them to be advantageous, just as I felt that I was in a superior position as an Irishman, without a shadow of any justification for that patriotic arrogance. As it never occurred to me to conceal my opinions any more than my nationality, and as I had, besides, an unpleasant trick of contradicting everyone from whom I thought I could learn anything in order to draw him out and enable me to pick his brains, I think I must have impressed many amiable persons as an extremely disagreeable and undesirable young man. . . .

I cannot learn anything that does not interest me. My memory is not indiscriminate: it rejects and selects; and its selections are not academic. I have no competitive instinct; nor do I crave for prizes and distinctions: consequently I have no interest in competitive examinations: if I won, the disappointment of my competitors would distress me instead of gratifying me: if I lost, my self-esteem would suffer. Besides, I have far too great a sense of my own importance to feel that it could be influenced by a degree or a gold medal or what not. There is only one sort of school that could have qualified me for academic success; and that is the sort in which the teachers take care that the pupils shall be either memorizing their lessons continuously, with all the desperate strenuousness that terror can inspire, or else crying with severe physical pain. I was never in a school where the teachers cared enough about me, or about their ostensible profession, or had enough conviction and cruelty, to take any such trouble; so I learnt nothing at school, not even what I could and would have learned if any attempt had been made to interest me. I congratulate myself on this; for I am firmly persuaded that every unnatural activity of the brain is as mischievous as any unnatural activity of the body, and that pressing people to learn things they do not want to know is as unwholesome and disastrous as feeding them on sawdust. Civilization is always wrecked by giving the governing classes what is called secondary education, which produces invincible ignorance and intellectual and moral imbecility as a result of unnatural abuse of the apprehensive faculty. No child would ever learn to walk or dress itself if its hands and feet were kept in irons and allowed to move only when and as its guardians pulled and pushed them.

I somehow knew this when I began, as a boy entering on my teens, to think about such things. I remember saying, in some discussion that arose on the subject of my education, that T.C.D.[13] men were all alike (by which I meant all wrong), and that I did not want to go through college. I was entirely untouched by university idealism. When it reached me later on, I recognized how ignorantly I had spoken in my boyhood; but when I went still further and learnt that this idealism is never realized in our schools and universities, and operates only as a mask and a decoy for our system of impressing and enslaving children and stultifying adults, I concluded that my ignorance had been inspired, and had served me very well. I have not since changed my mind.

However that may be, I decided, at thirteen or thereabouts, that for the moment I must go into business and earn some money and begin to be a grown-up man. . . .

Behold me therefore in my twentieth year, with a

12. In the preceding paragraph, here omitted, Shaw had described the development of Uncle William's religious mania and his suicide, achieved by giving himself heart-failure in an attempt to strangle himself by putting his head in a carpet bag.

13. Trinity College, Dublin.

business training, in an occupation which I detested as cordially as any sane person lets himself detest anything he cannot escape from. In March 1876 I broke loose. I gave a month's notice. My employers naturally thought I was discontented with my salary (£84, I think, by that time), and explained to me quietly that they hoped to make my position more eligible. My only fear was that they should make it so eligible that all excuse for throwing it up would be taken from me. I thanked them and said I was resolved to go; and I had, of course, no reason in the world to give them for my resolution. They were a little hurt, and explained to my uncle that they had done their best, but that I seemed to have made up my mind. I had. After enjoying for a few days the luxury of not having to go to the office, and being, if not my own master, at least not anyone else's slave, I packed a carpet bag; boarded the North Wall boat; and left the train next morning at Euston, where, on hearing a porter cry, in an accent quite strange to me (I had hardly ever heard an h dropped before), 'Ensm' faw weel?' which I rightly interpreted as 'Hansom or four wheel?' I was afraid to say hansom, because I had never been in one and was not sure that I should know how to get in. So I solemnly drove in a growler[14] through streets whose names Dickens had made familiar to me, London being at its spring best, which is its very best, to Victoria Grove, where the driver accepted four shillings as a reasonable fare for the journey.

I did not set foot in Ireland again until 1905, and not then on my own initiative. I went back to please my wife; and a curious reluctance to retrace my steps made me land in the south and enter Dublin through the backdoor from Meath rather than return as I came, through the front door on the sea. In 1876 I had had enough of Dublin. James Joyce in his Ulysses has described, with a fidelity so ruthless that the book is hardly bearable, the life that Dublin offers to its young men, or, if you prefer to put it the other way, that its young men offer to Dublin. No doubt it is much like the life of young men everywhere in modern urban civilization. A certain flippant futile derision and belittlement that confuses the noble and serious with the base and ludicrous seems to me peculiar to Dublin; but I suppose that is because my only personal experience of that phase of youth was a Dublin experience; for when I left my native city I left that phase behind me, and associated no more with men of my age until, after about eight years of solitude in this respect, I was drawn into the Socialist revival of the early eighties,[15] among Englishmen intensely serious and burning with indignation at very real and very fundamental evils that affected all the world; so that the reaction against them bound the finer spirits of all the nations together instead of making them cherish hatred of one another as a national virtue. Thus, when I left Dublin I left (a few private friendships apart) no society that did not disgust me. To this day my sentimental regard for Ireland does not include the capital. I am not enamored of failure, of poverty, of obscurity, and of the ostracism and contempt which these imply; and these were all that Dublin offered to the enormity of my unconscious ambition. The cities a man likes are the cities he has conquered. Napoleon did not turn from Paris to sentimentalize over Ajaccio, nor Catherine from St Petersburg to Stettin as the centre of her universe.[16]

On this question of ambition let me say a word. In the ordinary connotation of the word I am the least ambitious of men. I have said, and I confirm it here, that I am so poor a hand at pushing and struggling, and so little interested in their rewards, that I have risen by sheer gravitation, too industrious by acquired habit to stop working (I work as

14. A colloquial name for the four-wheeled, horse-drawn cab, popular since the mid-1860s. The name derived from the surly attitude of their drivers.

15. Shaw was a founder-member of the Fabian Society in 1884. His response to Joyce's view of Dublin was the same in 1921; then he wrote to Sylvia Beach: 'Dear Madam, I have read several fragments of *Ulysses* in its serial form. It is a revolting record of a disgusting phase of civilisation; but it is a truthful one; and I should like to put a cordon round Dublin; round up every male person in it between the ages of 15 and 30; force them to read it; and ask them whether on reflection they could see anything amusing in all that foul mouthed, foul minded derision and obscenity. To you, possibly, it may appeal as art: you are probably (you see I don't know you) a young barbarian beglamoured by the excitements and enthusiasms that art stirs up in passionate material; but to me it is all hideously real: I have walked those streets and known those shops and have heard and taken part in those conversations. I escaped from them to England at the age of twenty; and forty years later have learnt from the books of Mr. Joyce that Dublin is still what it was, and young men are still drivelling in slackjawed blackguardism just as they were in 1870. It is, however, some consolation to find that at last somebody has felt deeply enough about it to face the horror of writing it all down and using his literary genius to force people to face it. In Ireland they try to make a cat cleanly by rubbing its nose in its own filth. Mr. Joyce has tried the same treatment on the human subject. I hope it may prove successful. . . .'

16. The birth-places of these two world-historical figures.

my father drank), and too lazy and timid by nature to lay hold of half the opportunities or a tenth of the money that a conventionally ambitious man would have grasped strenuously. I never thought of myself as destined to become what is called a great man: indeed I was diffident to the most distressing degree; and I was ridiculously credulous as to the claims of others to superior knowledge and authority. But one day in the office I had a shock. One of the apprentices, by name C. J. Smyth, older than I and more a man of the world, remarked that every young chap thought he was going to be a great man. On a really modest youth this commonplace would have had no effect. It gave me so perceptible a jar that I suddenly became aware that I had never thought I was to be a great man simply because I had always taken it as a matter of course. The incident passed without leaving any preoccupation with it to hamper me; and I remained as diffident as ever because I was still as incompetent as ever. But I doubt whether I ever recovered my former complete innocence of subconscious intention to devote myself to the class of work that only a few men excel in, and to accept the responsibilities that attach to its dignity.

Now this bore directly on my abandonment of Dublin, for which many young Irishmen of today find it impossible to forgive me. My business in life could not be transacted in Dublin out of an experience confined to Ireland. I had to go to London just as my father had to go to the Corn Exchange. London was the literary centre for the English language, and for such artistic culture as the realm of the English language (in which I proposed to be king) could afford. There was no Gaelic League in those days, nor any sense that Ireland had in herself the seed of culture.[17] Every Irishman who felt that his business in life was on the higher planes of the cultural professions felt that he must have a metropolitan domicile and an international culture: that is, he felt that his first business was to get out of Ireland. I had the same feeling. For London as London, or England as England, I cared nothing. If my subject had been science or music I should have made for Berlin or Leipsic. If painting, I should have made for Paris: indeed many of the Irish writers who have made a name in literature escaped to Paris with the intention of becoming painters. For theology I should have gone to Rome, and for Protestant philosophy to Weimar. But as the English language was my weapon, there was nothing for it but London. In 1914 the Germans, resenting my description of their Imperial political situation as Potsdamnation,[18] denounced me as a fatherlandless fellow. They were quite right. I was no more offended than if they had called me unparochial. They had never reproached me for making pilgrimages to Bayreuth[19] when I could as easily have made them to the Hill of Tara. . . .

It was not until I went back to Ireland as a tourist that I perceived that the charm of my country was quite independent of the accident of my having been born in it, and that it could fascinate a Spaniard or an Englishman more powerfully than an Irishman, in whose feeling for it there must always be a strange anguish, because it is the country where he has been unhappy and where vulgarity is vulgar to him. And so I am a tolerably good European in the Nietzschean sense,[20] but a very bad Irishman in the Sinn Fein or Chosen People sense.

17. The Gaelic League was founded in 1893.

18. Potsdam, once the residence of Prussian kings and German emperors, became the centre of Prussian militarism. Shaw's *Common Sense About the War* (1914) aroused a storm of protest in Britain. The Berlin *Vorvarts* described Shaw as 'a man without a Fatherland'. The remark was not offensively meant; it merely indicated that Shaw was not pro-British.

19. As a disciple of Richard Wagner, Shaw was a frequent visitor to Bayreuth in Bavaria, where an annual festival of the composer's works is held.

20. In his *Untimely Meditations* (1876), Friedrich Neitzsche attacked the German nationalism associated with the Franco-Prussian War and its identification with German culture, as represented by Wagner.

EARNÁN O'MALLEY
(1898-1957)

from: ON ANOTHER MAN'S WOUND (1936)

[O'Malley's account of the period from 1916 to the end of the War of Independence some five years later is the best memoir of the fighting in that period. It was 1978 before the companion volume, *The Singing Flame*, which dealt with the Civil War period, was published. *On Another Man's Wound* was first serialized in *The Irish Press* newspaper. O'Malley fought in 1916, in the War of Independence and in the Civil War. He was tortured during the War of Independence, severely wounded and sentenced to death during the Civil War, was present when an explosion destroyed the Public Records Office in the Four Courts in 1922, went on hunger-strike in 1923, was elected to Dáil Éireann, and in 1947 to the Irish Academy of Letters. No other soldier of the time could write with his cool economy and power of observation.]

CHAPTER TEN

[Sent out by Michael Collins to organize a county or a brigade, O'Malley found that he did not understand the people among whom he had to operate. (Although born in Castlebar, Co. Mayo, his family had moved to Dublin when O'Malley was a boy.) This excerpt records his observation of the country life he found so strange.]

. . . The house that took in a daily paper would be the teacher's — the Master's, Mr. So-and-so, or the Big House; mostly the people were content with the *Weekly Freeman*, or the weekly local papers from the nearest big town. Around the fire the people talked of daily events, the weather, crops, letters from friends and relations in America or foreign parts; here was their paper; a living warp and weft spun of their own thoughts, fancies and doings. Now and again a biting turn of phrase for in their nature was the old Gaelic satire; sharp and direct or twisted endlessly like a súgán[1] being made across the door into the cobbled street. Malice and spleen might burst forth suddenly or heavy hearty cursing. Words were often used as a club, a means, not an end in themselves.

There was a love of discussion and argument that would take up a subject casually without belief and in a searching way develop it. That might mean a pleasant joking or an ornate, shrewd and enjoyable development for him who sustained his unbelief and heated words from his opponents; or anger from all in the end as the baiter was drawn into the net of his own words. Anger they played on often as on fiddle strings. Deferential to a stranger, they evoked in themselves a sympathetic mood, changing gears in conversation to suit his beliefs and half believing then through sympathy whilst he was present. Afterwards when they checked up on themselves it might be different; they would laugh at the stranger's outlandish opinions when their mood had hardened.

Always for me there was the relish of a phrase; they were conscious of it also. Acute, natural observation was converted into shades of meaning; some improvised as they talked, they became more extravagant, and delighted listeners helped them over appreciative stiles. Proverbs were many, even in the English-speaking districts, but the Gaeltacht alone kept the richer anthology, remembered from old literature; quotations from poets and stories, sayings of ollaimh,[2] and their apt use.

At a wake, turf spreading, hay gathering, threshing or a *meitheal*[3] to help a widow woman or neighbour in difficulties, I could enjoy their co-operative sense; hard work together was a relaxation; bantering jokes, songs, a racing competition in individual work and a natural place for match-making.

The weekly market was a break in routine. The men were able to drink double or triple porter to their hearts' content. Then the boisterous drive home, often without lights, careering along the country roads in a bone-shaking cart.

The countryman to himself was worth what he had in his pocket at any given moment. The land was his wealth; unlike the townsman, he had few ornate possessions. He would look with envy at the many knick-knacks and furniture of town house.

1. rope.

2. Irish: learned men, experts.
3. Irish: a working party, a combined community effort.

His total wealth would be greater, but his living was simpler. He had no useless possessions. He had not to keep up appearances like the townsfolk, he had not their mannerisms, fashions, or interest in superficial values. Yet the countryman would think of the townsman in terms of the prosperity that his own sons might strive for.

The boys worked into manhood without pay. If they were given a sixpence or a shilling on a fair day it would mean a deal, but the sons of a house had their own means of getting money. A bag of 'praties[4] sold on the sly, the hansel money[5] when a beast was sold and the readjusted sales price, or a gathered dozen of eggs. The girls had less say. Even their marriages were arranged. The parish matchmaker, I often listened to, as he wound his sinuous conversational way amongst the tussocks of the parental bog: 'A fine upstanding man with five milch cows, two springers[6] and ten fine head of cattle.' The parish priest might carry out the deal: 'It's well to have the children settled early.' From the fortune that came in with a girl, the husband would be able to have his next eldest sister married off. If there was not enough to fortune her to the satisfaction of her boy's parents, it meant a runaway match, if she had spirit — and America.

The Jansenistic older priests, hard, austere, some more human as they grew into age bore on the people: sermons, advice and the-to-be-feared calling from the altar submerged them in a facile but unreal submission. Some priests were hostile to dancing and gatherings; they interfered in every aspect of life. The lack of organized social intercourse made the young discontented, especially in the towns. The wise domination of age, to some hard and harsh in the soul as the cancer of foreign rule, made volunteering an adventure and a relief. Parish priests were managers of national schools. They had the power to appoint and remove teachers. Some, hostile to the movement, dismissed young men and women who were separatists. They found work in England or turned their hand to anything they could find or joined our export of youth to America. We had other exports: priests to the mission fields of the British Empire, artists and writers to London because our nation did not support them.

4. potatoes.
5. Money given as a first instalment or as a mark of luck and goodwill.
6. A cow or heifer that is about to calve.

There were certain hide-bound conventions within which the people moved and solved problems by formula. To them there was a normal in life and in individual human conduct. Life was simple, as it were, between good and bad, easy to classify, accept or reject: anything outside of this was not to be tolerated, sympathised with or understood. Life was to be lived in compartments, but some disputed in their hearts though they accepted the outward interpretation. Advice on life, action and procedure in terms of observed normality was always forthcoming.

The movement had created for me as for others a code of ethics that disciplined. There were no affairs; the nearest approach to them were the furtive hole-and-corner meetings that took place. I did not drink now because I was too active, and partly because it was easy to slip into heavy drinking in the country. Drink meant an open mouth, talk and rumour. It was easier to discourage drink among the men if one did not drink oneself.

The people were conservative; they had a hatred of change. They had been driven in on themselves too long, clinging for centuries to Gaelic usage in land and law, and suspicious of changes that had been forced on them by the conquerors. What was good enough for their fathers would be good enough for them.

I had left home with suits neatly pressed and cleansed, an ample supply of ties, collars and shirts. In time my store disappeared. A spare shirt and a few socks were all the clothes I needed. I was glad to leave aside a collar. It was a badge of distinction seldom worn by countrymen save on Sunday and Fair days. At night the shirt and socks or suit beside my bed would be taken away to be sewn, darned or washed, and clean clothes left in their place; if I stayed two nights my socks and shirt would be back at my bedside. All this often without a word.

My clothes were now a composite collection from many counties. I had my coat from Donegal, my waistcoat from Dublin, my trousers, very voluminous, formerly belonged to Michael Murray of Newmarket-on-Fergus,[7] and he was somewhat rotund; my shirts and socks generally belonged to the county I happened to be in at the time. My trousers billowed around my legs in folds, the waist had to be folded and refolded beneath a belt. Michael Murray had girth.

7. A town in County Clare.

My hat I seldom wore when passing through towns and villages; when I was given it I do not remember; it was a faded green. Sun and rain had each in turn touched it strongly. There was a bullet hole on either side of the crown near the top. Once in Clare, Peadar, Maurteen and myself were cycling from Ennis to Kilfenora. At a cross road we saw police with carbines; at the same time came a command 'Halt there!' We drew our revolvers and fired, running for cover. The police used their carbines. It was near sunset. We had carried our bicycles over the ditch. When twilight came Peadar brought our bicycles across the next field whilst we replied slowly to the ragged police firing. Then we crawled away, reached our bicycles and cycled into the welcome friendly darkness. When I arrived at Maurteen's house I found the bullet hole in the hat. The most obvious sign of my light-headedness in the eyes of the old people was my not wearing a cap or hat; the men usually wore their hats, even in the house, and they always thought I would catch cold in my bare head.

My boots reaching to the knees were my own; they were heavy, but being well oiled, kept out rain. They were conspicuous, however, and when worn about Dublin must have attracted some comment for few, save the Plunketts, wore them. At night when moving across country and jumping ditches filled with water my long boots brought me into difficulties. I had not the agility of the countrymen in jumping with heavy kit. When we crossed country at night with a local guard we endeavoured to avoid the honour of taking the lead, for one profited by the leader's stumbles and splashes. We made use of a long length of stick to probe our way when the darkness was intense. I had a good sense of direction and was able to retrace my way at night after I had once crossed country, but I went astray occasionally and blundered around. Fixing a landscape was often like remembering a face.

I was on the outside. I felt it in many ways by a diffidence, by an extra courtesy, by a silence. Some were hostile in their minds; others in speech; often the mother would think I was leading her son astray or the father would not approve of what the boys were doing. We of the Volunteers were talked of at first: 'Musha, God help them, but they haven't a stim[8] of sinse'. Yet there was a tradition of armed resistance, dimly felt; it would flare up when we carried out some small successful raid or made a capture. Around the fire it would be discussed; it would heighten the imagination of those who were hostile. In their minds a simple thing became heroic and epical. Perhaps the sense of glory in the people was stirred, and the legend that had been created about myself, whom they did not know, helped them to accept me as part of it.

I felt that I should be able to fuse with my material, the people, so that I could make better use of it; yet look at them dispassionately, as if from a distance. My approach to teaching and training of the men was impersonal; they would have to learn to do without me, to depend on themselves and avoid too much trust in what they considered leadership. This often meant a cold quality creeping in, but few could mingle with them without gaining warmth.

At the beginning it was the poor who stood by us in the country, and with them mostly I stayed; in some parts the standard of comfort was better, as in North Tipp, or when I was in a town house; but food, irregular meals or conditions did not matter to me whilst I was busy trying to improve a command. The life of the people was hard enough, but money or comfort were not standards that interrupted their content; above all they were alive and personal. The struggle with the soil rarely ground them down.

At home gatherings I sometimes felt the people withdraw their already partly granted family intimacy; the eddy that had taken me in would fling me out again. I would be like a hole in the wall then. That was all right, I thought later. They had their own dignity and aloofness; there was a seemingly unconscious boundary beyond which I could not get.

In time I learned to judge men by a look, bearing, intensity or deliberateness of speech. I had to make quick decisions about them for the time I remained in any area was short. Each county was different; the very map boundaries in many places seemed to make a distinction. The land seemed to determine the nature of the people often enough; whether pasture, grazing, tillage; good or bad; nearness to the sea; whether remote from towns and cities; hilly, mountainous, or undulating. Sometimes I came to a townland where there was a company of twenty or thirty men and boys. Tall, well set up or lanky, eager, lithe, willing to learn and anxious to

8. a trace.

take risks. Six miles away across the barony the people were cowed; the men had no initiative. They were irresolute. The Captain of the Company sometimes made the difference, sometimes the men themselves, but in parts it was the nature of the land and the long struggle against odds that had told.

Areas of country had a habit of going to sleep. They would wake up after a century or more and step into a gap. This unexpected quality was there in what I knew to be a bad area. It might awaken of itself: the times and situation might start the spark.

The selection of their own officers by the men was a difficulty. Election was traditional. Had they not elected their Tanists?[9] but then the selection had been limited to a caste. Often at first I felt the choice was faulty; the men must know in their hearts that the new commander was no bloody good. He was chosen because he was from the town, a strong farmer, or a neat hurler. I knew that another candidate would not be put forward when a name had been proposed. After the meeting men would speak their thoughts on the way home. It would be too late then. A disposition to please rather than to be direct; a desire of not wishing to start ill-feeling or to begin trouble; irresoluteness, or not thinking things through were at the root of it; a moral cowardice with extenuating undercurrents of a candidate's influence, position or power.

The clan spirit as such, deeper than the isolation and accent of individual counties, had to be overcome or switched to rivalry in organisation and action with those across the border. Distrust and jealousy had to be fought by fostering their own development in command; the dead weight of tradition grinding us between millstones had to be diverted to a new outlook and in a new hold on the present.

I grew a moustache to change my appearance in the towns. Some of the officers were elderly as judged by my age. They might be 35 or 40, and I felt a diffidence in giving orders. In a short time this wore off. The men had learned to judge of themselves. Hard work, zeal, ability, driving force, eagerness and enthusiasm; all these in their eyes contributed. Sometimes the man who would have made a good Volunteer, if left in the ranks, was now neither a good officer nor a good Volunteer. The responsibility of fighting the empire with his untrained men must have changed him. Later I set the election system aside. I picked an eager boy and appointed him captain.

I was lonely. It was hard work, this constant supervision, insisting on work being done. Often in an area where the spirit was poor one seldom or ever met with boys who could influence the others or whose eagerness would give warmth and cheer. Then life seemed as if I was wearing damp clothes on my skin, and the light and colour went out of the landscape; yet I would be caught up by a silver mercurial sun-glint on water or by the peace of twilight.

That was heartbreaking when I felt I had to keep driving; but when I met a keen boy or man the day became brighter; I could lift my mind from drudgery and responsibility. In bad areas senior officers did not come round with me. As they did not know even the physical nature of their command they would have to rely on me for information. They would have very little personal contact outside of their headquarters town or battalion. I felt then more than ever isolated. I could not do much good. I knew the random threads of my work would not be gathered up; in time the instructions, orders, notes would be forgotten. I felt that I was a burden imposing on the people's hospitality. The people would be indifferent if the officers were dispirited. Conversation would become hushed when I appeared. Often I slept out under a hedge or rolled up in hay which I had pulled down from a rick or cock. On rainy nights I was wet through.

I ate hedgehog in late winter or stewed hare with wind red tinkers in their camp on the sheltered side of a hedge. They accepted the length of strong cut plug I usually carried with me for other people's emergency smokes. They were curious for they knew there was something strange; but I would lead their few questions away to their own activities and likings. Many of the men had been reservists, but their great foes were the police who interfered with their frenzy of drink and stick-walloping in the towns.

There was always the solace of the men in the ranks; why did they turn up week after week for the same monotonous minor movements? They must have felt the lack of imagination of their officers. They were not being trained in the use of arms; two or three men in a company would have held a rifle in

9. The tanist was the heir apparent of a Celtic chieftain, chosen by election during the chief's lifetime. From the Irish *tánaiste* (the second person).

their hands, and their drill was too ragged to give them a composite sense so that in danger they would feel each other and act together. Anyhow they would seldom have to fight in large bodies, but they were not being trained to any decent squad or section sense. Yet there was a certain co-operative value in meeting boys who thought as they did. During the European War the English found that the platoons of a company had to be self-contained for trench warfare. We would have to think in terms of the quarter company, the section.

To effect any change I would have to remain four months in an area and insist that some of the senior officers remain with me. My temper was ready to fly when I found that men had shirked duties and responsibilities. I did not remember that they had been working hard all day. Only for a short time in the day could they think in terms of military work. On parade I would curse, tell off sharply the absent ones, but that lash-stinging would affect the relations between myself and the individual men in front of me. Before council meetings or parades I lectured myself, composed my mind and was perfectly at peace. Then I would go up in smoke at some unexpected stupidity, prevarication or neglect and time passed before harmony was restored. They might get a certain satisfaction when I sprawled over a rabbit hole, tripped in a hedge, or fell in a dyke of water weighed down by heavy knee-boots when jumping in the dark, or when after long shouting my crisp-enough voice broke and trailed to a falsetto squeak.

By degrees the stern parental discipline was broken, and youth learned a certain independence. Dispatch riders had to leave their work, ride off on horseback, bicycle, or walk on foot across the fields. A raid by police or soldiers on a house meant the threat of another raid, and arrests broke up the family circle. In gaol, boys learned to carry on a gaol war; they mixed with men from other provinces and widened their national horizon. Men had to leave home to avoid arrest, then they were 'on the run.' Girls in Cumann na mBan[10] had First Aid Classes and weekly meetings to attend; their officers had to cycle to meet others at the District Council. Gradually sons and daughters built up a small life of their own. Now fathers might attend the village Sinn Féin Clubs to discuss the situation or to debate and carry out instructions forwarded by the County Secretaries.

One had to fight against unpunctuality, lack of method, carelessness. Time did not matter to a countryman who judged time by the sun or his stomach. Dawn, breakfast, noon, dinner, after-noon, tea. One tried to make them appear neat on parade; boots brushed, coats buttoned up, but the outward discipline would be nullified at home. Inward discipline, the urge from men themselves to do what each considered his duty, was hard to build up. That was a thing of the spirit.

There were so many shades and half shades. The force of a flame like spirit; the owner had never to be reprimanded. One knew that he would always do more than he should; with him one was at once closely knit. Something jumped across the gap of personality and made a contact. He was indeed a friend; a comrade with whom one could travel at ease. Talk was not necessary; an understanding had been firmly set. There were others whose spirit was not strong; they joined from mixed motives, or because their girls egged them on. It was hard for them. They created their own difficulties. They saw the land ahead too much; they questioned them-selves at every new departure; they were inclined to count the cost. Talking to some made me feel how inadequate speech could be: you said things that meant nothing unless a man was attuned, and in the conversation there would be two languages. I would fence for an opening, slowly or quickly follow with words that might or might not have a common value. At times one came across a man who had been born free. There was no explaining it. One just accepted and thanked God in wonder.

It had been difficult to avoid comment and observation moving from one place to another. I had to remain in a town or scattered village in bad areas. Any gossip would be sure to get to the police barracks. I had to study the layout of the town or village closely, its streets, by-paths and back gardens. The neighbours would not know that a stranger was near them; often the children of the house did not know I was living with them, or they had to be kept from school whilst I remained. It was hard to sneak about from place to place, but as part of the game it was interesting. It would keep the eyes and ears alert. I had to learn to efface myself, to merge into the customs, speech and dress; to with-draw myself from my own work in such a way that my movements and talk would seem natural.

10. The Women's Division of the Irish Volunteers, founded in 1913.

Almost by steady ignoring of the fact that I had to move cautiously was I able to make others think that my movements were not out of the way.

This alertness could be annoying. I felt that it might undermine courage and interfere with outlook. I would like to stride down the town street rattling my hob nails knowing that my gun could be quickly pulled if challenged by the police; sometimes I did rattle past the open door of the barracks. Perhaps the strain told in time; there was a constant watchfulness, a training in observation and minute detail, but also, at times, was the sense of being pursued. My first few fights left me unafraid, anxious to close at once, less inclined to carry out our plan of running to fight another day. Later we avoided towns and villages altogether; avoided the danger without making it the less. . . .

CHAPTER FIFTEEN
(October-November 1920)

[Dublin was under curfew during this period. O'Malley went to the National Gallery or to read in the National Library and watched the city fill with the newly arrived auxiliary forces from England, drafted in to support the police and other army units in the war against the IRA. On 21 November, Michael Collins's special intelligence unit killed eleven British intelligence agents, known as the Cairo Gang. Black and Tans retaliated that afternoon by opening fire on a Gaelic football crowd in Dublin's Croke Park, killing twelve and injuring sixty. The British officer, General Crozier, coined the phrase 'Bloody Sunday' for this event, the first of the three Bloody Sundays of modern Irish history. (The other two were 10 July 1921, when fifteen catholics were killed in a pogrom in Belfast; and 30 January 1972, when British paratroopers murdered fourteen civil rights marchers in Derry City.) O'Malley watches the consequences of these events with a dispassionate interest.]

. . . Wind was dull in the city; it was more like a draught save when a gale swept in. The night sky and the moving moon had nothing to do with city life. I had the taste of the country firmly in my teeth. There was a definite friendliness and ease about Dublin, but also an air of polite helplessness. It was more tolerant. A quiet aloofness lingered round the mellow austerity of its eighteenth-century houses in a number of large squares, but the mood became strident and frowsy in the blight of the slums. Dignified wealth and open-mouthed poverty alternated their strophe and antistrophe in the capital.

The city's breweries, distilleries and biscuits were not much of an economic asset; unskilled labour predominated, and was quickly affected by trade conditions. A walk through by-streets to St. Patrick's Cathedral and the Coombe, by Thomas Street to the duplicated forms in Guinness's Brewery brought one more in touch with the haphazard life and trade of Dublin.

The new Cadet Force could be seen, moving swiftly in open Crossley tenders, seated on each side with rifles held across their knees. Wearing officers' khaki tunics, Glengarry bonnets angled, they had a dashing neat appearance. They were conscious of their power and soldierly snap. They felt impressive. People stopped to look at them. 'Why aren't they attacked?' I asked Diarmuid O Hegarty; 'it would be easy to lob an egg.'[1]

'That will come, don't fear,' he said.

Four months ago cadets had been sent out as defence officers to instruct the R.I.C.[2] in the defence of barracks and to strengthen *morale*. Then they had been formed into an Auxiliary Police Division, commanded by a divisional staff. Individual companies were moved from place to place throughout Ireland and were controlled directly by the Police Adviser through their divisional staff.

In the evening time I did Grafton Street between four and six. Cadets and officers were in mufti or uniform; it was easy to pick them out when they wore civies. We passed each other or sat drinking tea at nearby tables in Mitchell's café or the Grafton Street Picture House. That was stupid, I would admit to myself, as I drank my solitary tea, for a cup of tea was not worth fighting for; but Dublin was my city and I would not admit the right of foreign troops to deprive me of a habit.

Some of their hip pockets jutted out in rigid lines; all would be armed. I carried a Smith and Wesson forty-five and a Parabellum[3] underneath my coat; the revolver seemed to follow the contour of my iliac bone, the automatic was strapped over my heart. I could reach it in a quick draw as if I were fixing my tie. Daily I practised quick draws so that there would be no fumbling when I was in trouble. Weapons were now an undisturbing part of us, they

1. That is, 'throw a hand-grenade'.
2. Royal Irish Constabulary.
3. An automatic pistol much-favoured by the IRA.

could not be noticed even by one of ourselves. Before I left home my brother's service Webley had been sent back from Greece. Then it had looked like a small piece of artillery. It was heavy, awkward, my hand shook when I tried to hold it steady, now it seemed to be as relative and as indispensable as a fountain pen.

Terence McSwiney's hunger strike in an English prison was coming to an end.[4] The result was inevitable; we hoped he would not be released when his body was almost used up. Feeling at home seemed to have sent impulses abroad to the European Press. It seemed the most important event that had occurred in Ireland. In Washington women picketed the British Embassy, longshoremen walked off British boats. Ireland went into mourning when he died on the seventy-fourth day of his fast. He had become a symbol of part of a new nation; disciplined, hard, clear, unsentimental, uncompromising, a conscious using of vigour to build up strength.

Kevin Barry, a young medical student, was court-martialled in Dublin. He had taken part in an attack on a military lorry. A young English soldier had been killed. After dawn on the morning of the hanging crowds walked along the streets to Mountjoy under a cold November sky. Outside the jail gate armoured cars moved through the kneeling people who said the Rosary aloud. Tin-hatted Tommies with fixed bayonets stood in rows on the sides of armoured lorries. A quiet crowd, tense with emotion, hardly speaking to each other. 'The poor boy, the poor boy,' a woman cried, 'God help us all.' Tears came as she swayed on her knees, both hands held up; those near her began to cry, some could not stop, gulping noises continued for a long time. A girl kept saying aloud: 'Mother of Perpetual Succour, help us; Mother of Perpetual Succour, help us.' Aeroplanes circled; with a metallic beat the noise crashed above the rise and fall of Hail Marys. 'Bad luck to ye, wouldn't less than that do ye,' shouted a man who straightened a fist at the sky. Kevin Barry was a symbol of the enthusiasm of youth; resolute in giving, he, for the people, was the nation, which, however warped, futile and misdirected, had youth, life and a spirit of sacrifice.[5]

It had been intended to rescue him by blowing in part of the gaol wall. Rory O Connor[6] was to be in charge of the demolition party, but the British, alarmed at the gathering crowds, had strongly reinforced the gaol garrison.

Our Headquarter's Staff had become more organized. Throughout the city were their offices and duplicate offices, and those of government departments of Dáil Éireann, houses where ministers and staff officers could be met; others in which they ate and slept. They carried on their work as if they controlled the city. Dublin for over seven hundred years had been held by the British. It was their sea-opening to the plains and their principal base; for the past hundred years it had been the centre of separatist Ireland. Hidden meshes of either government stretched in tenuous nets below the everyday life, but the enemy web was now nearer to the surface. Dublin Castle, the great symbol of misgovernment in the people's minds, was again a fortress which higher officials seldom left openly. Towns built around a King John's keep or a Tudor castle were again garrisons; their influence varying between their armed strength and the people's resistance. The gap between the two was becoming more impenetrable; it was deepened by a steady withdrawal of the factors in which a joint life once met.

I saw Mulcahy,[7] the Chief of Staff, to discuss the situation in Munster, talk of operations and read reports. He would spread out a number of half-inch maps as he talked, and point a pencil at barracks or battalion headquarters. He said, 'I see,' at intervals when I answered questions about relative strength of our men and the British.

In general, the Staff were too absorbed in routine to dissect minor points in tactical evolution. Rory O Connor, Director of Engineering, had not yet

4. Terence MacSwiney, lord mayor of Cork, embarked on his 74-day hunger-strike on 12 August 1920, in Brixton Prison in London.

5. Kevin Barry, an eighteen-year-old medical student at University College, Dublin, was hanged in Mountjoy Jail on 1 November 1920 for his part in an attack on a British army bread van in Dublin, in which six soldiers were killed. Barry's interrogation and execution became the subject of the ballad named after him.

6. Rory O'Connor (1883-1922), director of engineering of the IRA during the War of Independence. During the Civil War he was executed along with three others in reprisal for the assassination of a deputy of the provisional government. O'Connor had been best man at the wedding of Kevin O'Higgins, the minister who ordered the execution.

7. General Richard Mulcahy (1886-1971), chief-of-staff of the IRA at this period, was later to be leader of the fight against the IRA in the Civil War. He was a founder-member of Fine Gael, prominent in the neo-fascist Blueshirt movement in the 1930s and later held various ministries in the inter-party governments.

devised a simple container for throwing petrol or inflammatory material under pressure from a distance; the blowing up of some men who had been experimenting with a Stokes' trench mortar had deprived us of a useful weapon against posts and barracks. We had no armour-piercing bullets. Munitions Department had few hand grenades, there were no rifle grenades, no explosives worth talking about. There was no standard land mine for dealing with armoured cars or steel-coated lorries on the roads. A man was lucky if he had two fills for his automatic or revolver; no brigade had more than forty or fifty rounds for each rifle; there was not much shot-gun stuff, and it was useful only when it had been refilled with buckshot pellets. It was hard to keep our weapons in repair, harder still to keep arms and stuff dry and clean. Police and military raids were becoming more thorough; they tapped walls, tore up floors, dug up backyards, measured heights and lengths of rooms to try to ferret out hiding places.

Headquarters staff officers were always spoken of by their initials: C.S., Chief of Staff; A.C.S., Assistant Chief; M.D., Minister of Defence; D.O., Director of Organization; D.I., Director of Intelligence; D.T., Director of Training; A.G., Adjutant-General. They signed their names in different ways. Mulcahy used a hieroglyph; some of the others used their ranks without names. Michael Collins in clear writing always signed his name in full. A hand grenade was now an 'egg,' an ambush was a 'job', a 'hit-up,' or a 'bush'; papers might be spoken of as 'dope,' and explosives made by our Director of Chemicals, Jim O Donovan, were 'war flour' or 'Irish cheddar.'

O Connell, known as Ginger, was Assistant Director of Training. Ginger was willing to discuss Foch's principles or Henderson's essays, call down the weighty Clausewitz, or suddenly illustrate a point from a text book or from wide browsing.[8] He quoted precedents from the guerilla tactics of the Boer War or Cuban fight. Von Lettow Vorbeck, he spoke of with admiration; we had read of his campaign in German East Africa, cut off for years from Germany and supplies, against the British. He could deal with training in a mildly scientific way though he smacked of the text book. It was always easy to talk to him. Owing to lack of arms, however, we could only dribble at fighting; precedents gained in other countries as a result of hard fighting might be stimulating to talk about, or to be proved possible, but we could only muck around. The other members of the staff knew little or nothing about training and operations, their strong points were organization and administration. The training staff, as far as the country was concerned, dealt with training through short notes in the monthly issues of *An t-Óglach*,[9] which was smuggled to all brigades.

Ginger was of medium height and portly. He had a rather heavy red moustache, was inclined to baldness, about which he laughed but with apprehension. He had a slow reflective manner of speech and when he talked he stroked his moustache and plucked his upper lip. He made puns; in an evangelistic manner he laughed at his own jokes, an expectant chuckle, dry at the base. Energetic men were 'thrusters' and 'stout' fellows; there were others who 'saw the other side of the hill.' He savoured the detailed circumstances of the plugging of a detective or the bloody mess of a successful ambush. His knowledge of strategy and general line of thought in terms of our fight evidently made contribution to the C.S. who now referred to men 'who saw the other side of the hill.'

Staff officers and Dáil officials changed their offices to avoid suspicion. There was a constant movement, an unceasing watchfulness, but small sign of tension. Communications were carried by special messengers as telephones could not be used. The Post Office was used only for correspondence sent to people who were not associated with the movement, or suspect. They would then pass on the letters to our officers. This made for extra clerical work and paper records; or made meetings of individuals more necessary to relieve the load on, and the danger run by, dispatch carriers.

With Desmond Fitzgerald,[10] Director of

8. Lieutenant-general 'Ginger' O'Connell (1887-1944) was kidnapped by O'Malley in June 1922 and held with the Four Courts garrison. This precipitated the outbreak of the Civil War. He was well-versed in the literature of military strategy.

Marshal Ferdinand Foch (1851-1929) was commander-in-chief of the allied armies on the western front in 1918.

Karl von Clausewitz (1780-1831), the Prussian general, was noted for his works on military strategy, especially *Vom Kriege* (1833).

9. First published by the Irish Volunteers in 1918, this periodical was declared illegal and appeared intermittently. Seventeen numbers appeared in 1920.

10. Desmond FitzGerald (*c.* 1888-1947), later a minister in the Free State governments 1922-32.

Publicity, I met foreign journalists and labour men who were getting angles from either side. It was a mild adventure for some, an exciting thrill for others, to talk to men of the hidden government, for whom castle officials, seen earlier in the day, were hunting. Mick Collins was busy as Minister of Finance and as D.I. His armed intelligence squad moved about looking for enemy officials, secret service men and detectives. Collins was often with Arthur Griffith, Vice-President of the Ministry. Griffith had seen the development of the military aspect with misgiving; since the German Plot arrests of 1918 the I.R.B. had gained more control in all organizations.[11] Griffith had hoped to build up a constitutional movement, Sinn Féin, and through it slowly to absorb the power and control of the British. Some of us thought that he was not a separatist, and I did not like to see Collins become more friendly with him. My doubts voiced the pseudo-military mind of the I.R.A. and its fear of constitutional respectability.

One Saturday Collins said, 'Mind yourself tomorrow, Earnán.' No other explanation. Probably there was to be some kind of a general round-up. The last time he had told me to watch out had been on Armistice Day, 1919, when men from the Dublin Brigade had been mobilised to wipe out Lord French[12] and his staff as they took the salute during the march past. Volunteers, who had lined the streets, and their concentration at the saluting base outside the Bank of Ireland, had been demobilised as they were ready to hit up the well-drilled lines of chest medals.

That night I went to a *céilidhe*[13] run by a literary society, actually by a company of the Fourth. An excited captain from the University whispered to me in the dressing room: 'My God, it's awful, a H.Q. job, damned awful.' He cracked the joints of his fingers with loud snaps. He laughed with a nervous whinny as he pressed back his hair, then his hand pressed tightly and grasped the other till the tendons were white. At the college I had heard him talk of footling military details amongst girls and non-volunteers with pauses and chuckles as he covered his mouth with his hand. Once he had been a legend, now I thought him windy. He had been out in '16. I did not know what all this talk of his meant. Later I gathered tags[14] from two others who talked as if I knew what was to happen. Next day British secret service officers, who had steadily improved their system until it now overshadowed ours, were to be shot in Dublin. 'The other battalions are on the job,' said a law student, 'all attacks are to be timed, but I have my doubts. Won't you come with my bunch? It will be tough. Maybe it's a no-come-back job.'

I went home to Sears'[15] house in Terenure. He was a member of the Dáil and thought it too risky to sleep at home as he was well known. I had not many houses I could change about to; I was unattached to a unit and made my own arrangements. I lay awake for a long time. I found it hard to sleep, thinking of what would happen; how many people besides myself knew about it, who should not? I tried to read bits about headstrong Bhima and the hero Arjuna in the Mahabharata,[16] but sleeping officers and Volunteers overhauling guns jumped into the pages. Dublin would no longer be a picnic.

Next day a stop press: thirteen officers scattered through the city and suburbs had been shot dead, three had been wounded, others had escaped. Some had been killed in their beds beside their wives. Dublin was jumpy, passersby were nervous; they spoke less as they walked, and groups at street corners took on a new significance. Something would happen, but what? The British would not take that lying down. The city had been safe enough so far. City people had not experienced the desolate remoteness of the country during the raids of threatening soldiers, drunken Tans and fiercely arrogant Auxies. Dublin had not felt the loneliness and awed night of a country town or small city controlled by its garrison.

Soldiers held up men walking in threes or fours.

11. The British authorities claimed in 1918 that they had evidence of treasonable communications between the Germans and Irish people. The leadership of Sinn Féin was arrested. The aim was to discredit Sinn Féin at the height of the anti-conscription campaign of that year, but the plot backfired. Sinn Féin won more support; no evidence for the German plot ever came to light.
12. J. D. French, Lord French of Ypres (1852-1925), was commander-in-chief of the British expeditionary force to France in 1914. He became lord lieutenant of Ireland in May 1918, with emergency powers provided by the Defence of the Realm Act. He arrested many Sinn Féin leaders on charges of involvement in a so-called German Plot. From December 1920, when martial law was declared, French became an effective dictator. The IRA tried to kill him on a dozen occasions and he mainly confined himself to the Vice-Regal Lodge.
13. An informal gathering with folk music, singing and dancing.
14. Bits and pieces of information.
15. Tom Sears, a Sinn Féin TD.
16. The Mahabarata is one of the great Hindu epics. It contains the Bhagavad Gita.

Crossley tenders nosed up and down as if the Auxiliaries did not know what to do next. Heavy lorries stopped outside flats and private houses; soldiers hurriedly helped to move the belongings of other intelligence officers, and those who might be open to attack, to the Castle or to an hotel which was heavily guarded. In the afternoon the crowd at a Gaelic football match in Croke Park had been surrounded by soldiers, police and Auxiliaries: twelve killed, eleven seriously wounded, fifty slightly wounded by machine guns and rifles. I had heard the distant rattling.

Steel plated Lancias and armoured cars with swinging turrets dashed through the streets; they curved in towards the footpaths, people scurried. The troops had blood in their eyes. Streets were suddenly held up by soldiers and men in plain clothes; at the top of Dawson Street I saw two lorries spill out Auxies who snapped on bayonets as they ran out to cut off a part of the street. They hit men with the butts of their rifles. I was told at McGilligans in Leeson Street where I often slept that it would not be safe for me to stay the night. Kathleen McGilligan was worried: 'Seán MacBride[17] will find you a place, and get there as soon as you can; what's that?' A sound of shooting. Seán MacBride was the son of Major John MacBride who had been executed after Easter Week. We voiced our fears as we walked.

It was seven o'clock. Soldiers and Auxiliaries were firing over the heads of the moving people shouting 'Go home, you bastards, go home.' Curfew should begin at twelve o'clock. Seán MacBride brought me to the flat of an Abbey Theatre dramatist. It was on the top floor of a four-storey house. 'I have two guns and an egg,' I said. 'I'll fight if there's a raid.'

'I'll take one.' But he did not know how to work a Parabellum.[18] Sitting on the stairs I showed him the action, the use of the safety catch and how to clear a jam. We were welcomed. I was introduced to Lennox Robinson, whom I had often seen at the Abbey and to Thomas McGreevy.[19] They did not object to us remaining there the night. It was risky to be outside now. Robinson played Beethoven on a pianola; McGreevy took his turn to press on the wide wooden pedals. The instruments coughed and wheezed when the movement of the feet was irregular, or the music came in pauses. Robinson pedalled furiously, his long body bent itself as the notes jerked out. 'Should I tell him we'll fight?' I whispered.

'No, better not,' said Seán, 'there's not much chance of a raid anyhow.' I got drawn into the music and I felt still inside, but squeaking wood or a cluster of shots would enter as a motif. He was trying to take his mind away from the brooding horror of the day and the outside street.

Our attempts to talk had been short meaningless sentences. McGreevy clicked the switch. 'It's better to put it out; nearly all the other houses are without light.' Robinson closed the pianola. We sat in front of the fire. McGreevy talked. He had been a gunner officer in France. He had a sensitive face; he must have suffered in the hell of the World War. I ate hazel nuts out of a red bowl. The others said 'Good-night,' and went into the next room. We, watching the twisting yellow of the flames, sat on the floor. 'It will go hard with any prisoners taken tonight,' I said.

There was a feeling of uncertainty as if something was going to happen. We talked in whispers as if afraid of the sound of our own voices; outside in the street the noise of heavy cars and sharp commands. Later, as we looked out a window, we saw an armoured car stop below close to the curb under an arc lamp. Men with dark bonnets jumped down; they were joined by others from a tender which pulled in. There were few people on the street. Three men walking on the footpath were held up. They were backed against a shop window. They held their hands over their heads. I saw an Auxiliary hit one of the men in the face with his fist. The three were searched, something was brought over to the lamp post, the armed men crowded around whilst it was being looked at. I heard a voice shout: 'Run for it.' The three ran towards the corner of Clare Street, spreading out. A tearing smash of rifle fire, the metal snap of bolts throwing out cartridges. One man twisted and sprawled forward out of sight. The rifles flared again.

17. Seán MacBride (1904-88), later a prominent politician in Ireland and winner of the Nobel and Lenin Peace Prizes for his work with Amnesty International. Patrick McGilligan (1889-1979), secretary to Kevin O'Higgins in the first Dáil, later held several ministries in Irish governments. He joined Sinn Féin in 1915.
18. A heavy pistol favoured by the IRA.
19. Lennox Robinson (1886-1958), dramatist and at this time manager of the Abbey Theatre; Thomas McGreevy (1893-1967), poet and critic, close friend of Joyce and Beckett, later director of the National Gallery of Ireland 1950-64.

We went away from the window thinking we might be seen. We ate nuts. In the darkness the crash of the nut shells boomed up and down the room. Heavy cars, armoured evidently, from the vibration, rattled; soft gliding noises of tenders, revolver shots in the dull distance, close by the jerky beat of a Vicker's gun. From the next room came low voices whenever a loud burst of shooting woke us up. The others could not sleep. 'Do you think we have their beds?' I asked.

Troops drove through the street at a more rapid rate. Shops were raided at all hours of the day, and streets held up; in the dark, houses were searched, often half a street at a time. At night I could see soldiers moving quietly on rubber soles as patrols, or in extended order, followed, perhaps, by the cobbled bumps of a steel-plated Lancia, or I watched the shafts from a movable search light turned on houses. A wreck of a car might noise along, followed at a short distance by a strong smooth engine without lights. That was a night trap for those who might attempt to tackle the first one, or who would be off their guard when it passed. One night the house opposite to me was raided. I saw figures outside my gate as I laid out automatic magazines on a chair. A search light swept on to the fronts of the nearby houses and picked out a swarm of soldiers, trailing rifles as they left the house without prisoners. A week after 'Bloody Sunday' sixteen cadets were killed in an ambush by the West Corkmen in the mountainy pass of Kilmichael. They had killed some of the men who went out to take their surrender, and the column men wiped out the rest of them.

In two recent raids the British had found papers of Mulcahy, Chief of Staff, whom they had nearly captured. That captured information seemed to be the most reliable insight their Secret Service could get of the movement. Amongst the papers were plans for a systematic destruction of docks, warehouses and technical plant in England. Touts, spies, and secret servicemen were thick in Dublin, but they worked too much in the dark of faulty psychology.

I was given a message by word. The C.S. wished to see me urgently that night in Ranelagh on the south side. I met him with Ginger and Emmet Dalton. Ginger was now D.T. Dick McKee, who had been brigadier of Dublin and Director of Training, had been murdered at the Castle with his Vice-Com., Peadar Clancy, on the morning after 'Bloody Sunday.'[20]

Mulcahy had a thick fair moustache, although his hair was dark. It looked out of place in relation to the moustache, but I suppressed my smile. He was more than usually serious. On the table was large scale map of the South of Ireland. 'We intend to give you command of the Martial Law area,' he said. 'You can move around selecting your staff as you go through the brigades.' The Martial Law area comprised five counties. 'I would suggest Liam Lynch,'[21] I said, 'he is a good officer; he has his command well organized; he could use that as a basis from which to work outwards.'

'You know Limerick, Tipperary and part of Cork,' Mulcahy said. 'You will soon become familiar with the remainder of Cork and with County Kerry.' We discussed likely staff officers for the new command. Organizing and training an area was one thing, I thought; taking command of a province with twelve brigades was a big responsibility. Would I meet with hostility? How would the other brigades take the appointment? Cork County had no great love for G.H.Q. officers. Its brigades had developed of themselves; within the past three months the concentration of British had intensified. In their new development they might not be willing to be dictated to. I was younger than any of the officers. They would probably like someone with the weight of years and gravity. Of course, I could grow a moustache, but many of them knew me. Aloud I said, 'All right, sir. I will do my best.'

'Before you go to the South there is an operation the Staff would like to to undertake. What do you think of the Auxiliaries?'

'They are a fine body of men and a tough problem.'

'We must tackle them at once. The adjoining Cork Brigades will co-operate in taking Macroom Castle where there's an Auxiliary Company. I want

20. Emmet Dalton (1898-1978), close friend of Michael Collins, accompanied him to London for the Treaty negotiations and was with him when he was killed in an ambush in 1922. Dalton later became a film producer in Hollywood and founded Ardmore Studios in Ireland. McKee and Clancy had been captured the day before Bloody Sunday; they and a third prisoner, Conor Clune, were shot 'while trying to escape', according to the official explanation.

21. Liam Lynch (1890-1923), commander of the Cork no. 2 brigade during the War of Independence, chief-of-staff of the anti-Treaty IRA during the Civil War, killed by Free State forces in April 1923.

you to capture Inistiogue, the headquarters of the Auxiliaries in County Kilkenny.'

'Kilkenny County has done little fighting.'

'You will have help from the Waterford men.'

'Waterford hasn't done much either and I don't know any of the officers in Kilkenny.'

'You can summon a Brigade Staff meeting and meet them.'

'Are there any flying columns in Kilkenny?'

'No, I don't think so,' said Mulcahy. 'Are you prepared to undertake the job?'

I hesitated. Operating with men whom I did not know in an area that I had never previously visited, and which had not seen much fighting, did not appeal to me. Besides I had been directly ordered to capture a post which our best command would not undertake.

'This is your last independent operation. When it is over you will command the Martial Law area.'

'Yes, sir,' I said, 'I'll take Inistiogue.'

It was easy to say, 'I'll take Inistiogue.' That night I thought over the problem. I had no information about the strength of the Auxiliaries or of the British in the County, or even of our men there. It was hard enough to capture a small police barracks. Why didn't the Staff supply us with small artillery, trench mortars, Stokes guns, machine guns, or rifle grenades, even with decent land mines? We had not anything like a good supply of ammunition for our rifles. Why didn't the Staff pay attention to pure Staff work, leaving the political field to the others? The Chief of Staff was a member of Dáil Éireann, the Director of Intelligence was a Minister of Finance, the Director of Organization was a Secretary to the Dáil, the Director of Engineering was the Secretary of the Local Government Board.

Next day I met Mulcahy in Parnell Square, in Banba Hall.

'Have you any plan of action to outline?'

'We might attack a barracks near their headquarters and wait for their reinforcements, then Inistiogue might be tackled while its garrison was weakened.'

'Well, you'll see the situation for yourself when you reach Kilkenny.' We shook hands. 'Good luck now, Earnán.' I saluted and was walking out the door when he called me back.

'Is there any activity down town?' he asked. 'I'm going to Brunswick Street Technical Schools.'

'No, I've just come across the Liffey and through O'Connell Street; no hold-ups and not much activity. I'll scout the way for you.'

'And what about yourself?'

'I'm armed.'

'No, you could not be replaced either,' he said, smiling slowly as he gripped my arm. 'Don't you know that? Take care of yourself and good luck.'

That was the first sign of personal regard I had received from him. I was happy as I walked across town, whistling.

Lloyd George yet had faith in unofficial reprisals: burning of creameries, factories, shops, town halls, private houses, went on. Towns showed jagged stumps of broken teeth where fire had spread; raiding parties smashed property and looted. Perhaps the Premier thought the destruction of the economic life would cow the people and turn them against the Dáil and the I.R.A.; but it irritated neutrals and made our friends more bitterly staunch. The American elections would soon be due; if reprisals wore out weak links in the separatist chain, martial law, which admitted serious trouble, would not be necessary.

Rory O'Connor, D.E., went to England on a tour of inspection. He was responsible for operations there. Irishmen and men of Irish descent in the cities had been organized in units on the lines of the Irish Volunteers. They could destroy power plants, warehouses and supplies, and burn the houses of Tans, Auxiliaries and officers. The counter demonstration would throw light on the destruction in Ireland and possibly slow it down. At the end of November fires burst out in English warehouses and docks.

I left my papers in a concealed cupboard. There was no sense in risking my notes and papers in a county like Kilkenny. I left my two guns in another dump. I felt I had a tough job before me, and I knew nothing about the type of men there. A friendly checker brought me through a side door at the Kingsbridge station, which was carefully watched by enemy intelligence. Seated in a carriage, I waited impatiently for the train to pull out.

Passersby scanned the windows in a casual way or glanced sharply with well-trained eyes. I tried to read a magazine; but always behind the page was a sense of being cornered in a carriage, open to a stray memoried snapshot. At a junction police and Tans came on board, but they did not search. The engine driver walked off the train; he would not drive armed police. The Tans threatened him. Two pulled guns and one said, tapping his ribs with a Webley: 'Do you know what this is?' An hour later a new driver who was willing to drive armed police was found; but they remained behind on the platform when the train started. The new driver had been threatened by railway workers as to what would happen to him when he came back.

I passed by the police on the platform on Kilkenny station, outwardly calm, but confused enough in my mind on the difficulties I sensed would lie before me.

THE BOLD BLACK AND TAN

The town of Balbriggan they burnt to the ground
The bullets like hail were all whizzing around.
Lloyd George said to Greenwood, 'Now this is our plan,
We'll conquer Ireland with the bold Black and Tan.'

From Cork on to Limerick, Clare and Mayo.
Lies a trail of destruction wherever they go.
We'll shoulder our rifles, we'll fight to a man
And we'll humble the pride of the bold Black and Tan.

CHAPTER TWENTY-TWO
(May-July 1921)

[This episode, describing the execution of three British officers, is like Frank O'Connor's short story 'Guests of the Nation' (see Volume II, p. 1192), only less sentimental.]

I slept out with men from Rosegreen company at the Centre under a tent which had once been a hay rick cover; some had hammocks which they slung in the hedge from tree branches. I was working in 47 when a scout came to see me. Three men had been captured on the hillside; they were British officers, and the Rosegreen men had them in a dug-out lower down. I met the two boys who had captured them. One had a rifle and two rounds of ammunition, the other an empty bandolier, when they saw the three men coming across the fields. The boy with the rifle halted them; the men began to run. He fired. One of the men was wounded slightly; the others came back and all three surrendered. Each had an automatic in his pocket and an identification card. Two were gunner officers from Fethard[1] Artillery Barracks, five miles across the hill. I sent two boys up the hill to find out where the officers had stopped and what they had been doing. Later one came back. The officers had been searching hedges; at a house on the slope, they had asked about dug-outs. They had questioned the young man of the house.

I brought them up one by one. They gave me their names, ranks, the name of their commanding officer. They had been out for a walk, they said.

'Any officers we capture in this area are to be shot until such time as you cease shooting your prisoners.'

'We have nothing to do with the shooting of prisoners,' one said.

'This is not a personal question. Our men whom your men may capture and later shoot will have nothing to do with your being shot. My mind is made up about it. You will be shot at dawn tomorrow.'

'Can't you consider the matter?' one asked.

'You will have to consult your officers,' another said, 'you can't do it without authority.'

'I happen to be in command of this area. This is my authority. It would be better to prepare your minds. I will get food ready for you.' I gave them cigarettes. A boy with a rifle lay near the entrance to the dug-out.

A scout rushed down to where I sat. Beside me were six riflemen who had been mobilized in the meantime.

'Soldiers with a machine gun. They've just come over the brow of the hill and they're searching.'

'Easy,' I said, 'the officers will hear you.' The scouring soldiers came from Fethard. Other sections of troops would possibly be making their way in our direction.

I blindfolded the officers so that they could not see where they were going. The covering on their eyes made them helpless; their hands were free, but tying a man's hands was not a job we liked. Men held them by the sleeves so that they could walk more easily. One of them limped. He had a slight flesh wound. I put him on a cart.

'If we are surrounded,' I said to the one whose face I liked best, 'I'll let you go. I'm not going to shoot you like dogs.' The guard of riflemen grumbled.

1. In County Tipperary.

'But you'll shoot them tomorrow anyhow,' said the Brigade Q.M. 'Where's the difference?'

The Q.M. was right, but it was tough to have to turn on them suddenly when we were hard put in a fight to shoot them like injured beasts.

One of the officers said, 'We can do first-aid for your wounded if there's a fight.'

A sloe-skin dusk came slowly down on the steep western slopes of Slievenamon and across the woods there. It blurred the valley of the Suir below the Comeraghs; hedges of tangled hawthorn with fresh leaves, in amongst the neat stems of spruce, stood out against the rise of hills. There was a strong, spicy smell carried across from the bright pink blossoms of a corner hedge of wild crab.

We halted at a gateway. A horse and trap came up. The officers got up into the seats. A young girl came out from a house. She peered at the men in the half light. 'Who are they?' she asked.

'English officers,' said a guard.

'Shooting's too good for them,' she said, bitterly, as she looked up at them. They looked down at her with set faces.

'Oh, leave them alone,' I said.

'God help the poor boys,' said a woman beside her, 'perhaps they'd like a sup of milk.' She came back with a large jug and three delph[2] mugs. The officers drank. They thanked her.

We walked into the closing-in darkness, riflemen in front and behind the trap, until we were a distance from where the officers had been captured. I expected a big round-up in which the countryside would be combed by troops from Cahir and Clonmel — both strong military posts. They would probably converge in the triangular area of which Fethard was the apex. We came to a farmhouse up in the fields some way off the main Clonmel road. Sentries were posted. The girls and women of the house got ready supper; they did not ask any questions. A fire was lighted in the room where the officers were. After supper I went into the room. The blinds were drawn so that they could not look out. It was a large room. They were seated at a table. One had his head in his hands.

'Would you like to see a clergyman of your own religion?'

'No,' said one. The others shook their heads.

'Would you like a civilian, an Imperialist, to stay with you?'

'No.' They did not need any one.

'Here's writing paper and envelopes. You can write to anyone you wish. If you give me your words of honour that you won't mention anything of military importance, you can seal the envelopes yourselves.'

Each gave me his word. There were beds for them to sleep on.

I sat in the kitchen by the fire. The women of the house had gone to bed quietly. None of us spoke for a long time. I was putting myself in the place of the men inside. My turn might come, too, and soon. It seemed easier to face one's own execution than to have to shoot others. 'It's very dark outside,' said the Quartermaster. 'I hope the boys are keeping a good look out.' He strode into the darkness.

He was an elderly man. Freckles showed through a wind-red face. There were thin folds in his neck. He had a long skillet of a jaw, he showed the wide gaps between his teeth when he smiled. His step was as deliberate as a gander's. He would have his say no matter what happened; he was accustomed to jump objections — for that was a quartermaster's offensive. He could advise about a round of ammunition as seriously as we would discuss or draw up a plan of operations. He was the oldest of us, about thirty-five years. He spoke slowly and carefully, toothing his words in a dry humour.

None of us was twenty-four; the youngest officer inside was about that age. One was tall and dark with brown eyes. He had illtreated prisoners in Tipperary, one of the Rosegreen men said. He had been insulting when on raids. One was stout with a thick neck, his hair was a little thin. He had been more anxious to talk and to remonstrate than the others. The third was quiet and reserved. He had a sensitive face and he did not talk. I liked him best. I was worried about him because he was wounded. It was an accepted convention that a wounded man should not be shot until he was able to walk. I did not bother about the convention, only the presence of the wounded man made its own conditions. I did not see any sense in keeping him for a few days longer. It would be harder on him if his companions went first.

'I wish it were over,' I said to the Q.M. There were two other men seated on chairs making a round of the fire.

'It'll be over soon enough,' he said. He was calm enough about it. I knew that I would continue to shoot their officers. Of that, there would be no

2. earthenware; from Delft.

doubt, but this kind of work was hard enough. If we shot enough of them it would make the others think a little. I don't know what we talked about. Odds and rags of conversation about men in other battalions, the relative merits of different kinds of explosives, the making of improvised Stokes guns and the history of this part of Desmond.[3] Two men went out to relieve their comrades. I walked outside in the darkness. The night was misty, the moon shone softly through cloud veils. Sounds carried well, away through the distance came the lonely bray of an ass; it was answered in sardonic harshness near by. Sheep coughed drily in the shelter of a hedge and a cow chewed loudly.

'It'll soon be dawn,' said the Q.M. I knocked at the door. They were seated around the table. Their faces looked worn and drawn. None of them had slept.

'Have you written your letters?'

'Yes,' said the thin swarthy one, 'here they are.'

'If you would like to send your money or valuables to your friends or relatives I will forward them for you.'

'We would like to send them with a note to our C.O., Major King, in Fethard,' the quiet one said.

I found an empty Fry's chocolate box on a side table. They put their watches, money and rings inside.

'Would you like some tea? It'll soon be dawn and we'll have to be on our way.'

'No thanks, we don't want anything.'

We walked down the sloping fields towards the roadway. The sky was clouded with heavy grey. The light was dim, a cold dawn wind blew across the thick hedges. It ruffled the grass which was shiny with dew drops. Men with rifles formed an extended five-pointed figure. An officer walked on each side of the Q.M. I was behind with the third. 'It's a mistake,' he said. 'It won't do any good. We could be good to prisoners.'

'None of us want to do it,' I said, 'but I must think of our men.' I could not see the ultimate implications of our proposed action. The sky lighted silvery grey, the wind dropped. We caught up with the three in front. 'Stiff banks those for hunting,' said the tall, swarthy officer. They smiled as if they had thought of horses and the sight of a red-brown fox. 'There's not much hunting now,' I said. We had stopped hunting through the Martial Law area.

We reached the roadway. There was a wall in front of a church. The three officers were placed on the green grass edge of the dusty road.

'Do you mind?' I said, as I placed their handkerchiefs around their eyes. One handkerchief was of silk and claret coloured.

'No.'

'This is good-bye,' I said.

They shook hands with the Q.M. and myself. Their hands were cold and limp. They shook hands with each other.

The six men of the firing squad stood near the other side of the road. One of the men fumbled for a while with his magazine. He could not click it into place. An officer pulled down his handkerchief and looked at us, then he put it back over his eyes. Perhaps he thought we were trying to frighten and test them and that we did not intend to shoot. 'Ram in the magazine,' I whispered to the Q.M.

'Are you ready?' asked the Q.M.

One of the officers nodded. They joined hands, 'Good-bye, old boy,' they said, inclining their heads.

'Squad.' . . . 'Ready' . . . 'Fire.'

The volley crashed sharply. The three fell to the ground; their arms twitched. The Q.M. put his revolver to each of their foreheads in turn and fired. The bodies lay still on the green grass. We stood to attention. Then slowly we went up the hill across country making for the Centre. None of us spoke till we had crossed a good many fields where wind had snaked the rye grass. . . .

3. An old name for that part of Tipperary that once belonged to the earls of Desmond.

OLIVER ST JOHN GOGARTY

(1878-1957)

from: AS I WAS GOING DOWN SACKVILLE STREET (1937)

[The deaths of Arthur Griffith and Michael Collins within eight days of one another in 1922 made the August of that year one of the bitterest and saddest months of the Civil War. Gogarty was a close friend of Griffith and attended him in his last illness, when Griffith lived in a state of semi-siege in Government Buildings in Merrion Street, Dublin. Gogarty had Griffith, then president, moved to a private nursing home in Lower Leeson Street, where he died on 12 August. On 20 August, Michael Collins, who had walked before Griffith's coffin, was killed in an ambush in County Cork. Since all communications with Cork were cut off by the war, his body had to be taken by sea to Dublin, on board the *S.S. Classic*. Gogarty carried out a post-mortem and embalmed the body.

In this excerpt from Chapter 12, the story of the death of Collins is told first, although he died after Griffith.]

. . . By the quay-side we waited: midnight and as yet no ship. All communications with Cork had been destroyed. Only by sea was there a way to Dublin. The corpse of Collins, the vital, the mighty, was being borne by a boat long overdue. I stood for hours at the North Wall. Drizzling rain added to our gloom. I stood by the river-side hour after hour with the officers in their uniforms blackened by rain — officers of an Irish National Army that Griffith created by a stroke of his courageous pen.

At last in the silence of the dark a moving light appeared, coming slowly up an invisible stream. The death-ship carrying the mortal remains of the most rapid and bright soul that alien envy in Ireland ever quenched. Troops formed up. A gun-carriage received the coffin. It was bound for the City Hall.

I reached home in the early hours. I had to make provision for embalming the body.

Never in our life cycle shall we see the like of Mick Collins. He dwelt among us as our equal. Now that he is dead, we find that we were the familiars of a Napoleon who knew no Waterloo.

No matter how it may be diminished, the fact is that Michael Collins beat the English in the guise they chose to adopt at a time of great stress: England's extremity was his opportunity. He kicked it hard. Opportunity brings more than opportunists to the front. Ireland's struggle was old and long sustained tenaciously through the years, opportunities or no opportunities. Hundreds of Irishmen in every age were glad to put their necks in risk of England's halter and quick-lime. Collins alone pulled his generation out.

My guest was coming home to me to be embalmed. Not England, but his fellow-countrymen murdered him.

What an unlucky shake-hands De Valera gives! He shakes hands to speed Collins and Griffith to London. They are dead within a year.

I had to be up betimes if the embalming was to be completed before noon. Hardly had I slept when a loud knocking summoned me. Desmond Fitzgerald, Minister for Defence,[1] to keep me company. It was 4.30 a.m. As he knew little of such processes as embalming, he was anxious that no time should be lost. In my bedroom slippers, I walked him round through the empty streets to awaken the porter of the College of Surgeons. No answer. We went round to the great gate at the back of the dissecting-room. Loudly we knocked, hammering with the flat of our hands to make the greater noise. A bullet embedded itself above our hands. Hastily I kicked the door. Oh, my slippers! I had forgotten. But the invisible sniper guessed what we were about. Another plunge of lead in pine. We must get out of this.

'Leave it to me,' I assured the Minister. 'The job is not a lengthy one. I will come back at six o'clock. Meanwhile, I will try the Anatomy School of Trinity College.'

Arthur Griffith lay on a small mattress in a room off the Ministry for Justice high up in the Government

1. Desmond FitzGerald (*c.* 1888-1947) fought in the GPO during the Easter Rising, for which he was court-martialled and sentenced to life imprisonment. Elected Sinn Féin MP for Pembroke, Dublin in 1918 and released later that year. Supported the Treaty and was minister for external affairs 1922-27 and minister for defence 1927-32. Gogarty here identifies the wrong portfolio.

Buildings, as the place intended for a College of Science in the days of the British Administration was now called. He was besieged by a large part of the 'Irish People' in whom he believed. He could not leave the building without risking his life. His guards were troops drawn from as distant places as possible. They spoke like Scotsmen. If you wished to see him as a medical attendant, you had to put your face into a large letter-box-like grille and hold it against the revolver of the sentry on duty, before the door was opened. When you were admitted into the Hall you found yourself in a small chamber, walled by bullet-proof sheets of steel. Search and interrogation preceded your admittance. The lift was not working, neither were the charwomen. Through dirty marble halls and up dirty staircases of a building never designed for dwellings, at last you reached the fourth storey. A long corridor led to the Ministry. Past both, you reached the small closet where Arthur Griffith lay. At a glance you recognized a man who was very ill. He had a solicitor administering to him. The hour was nine o'clock of a morning. My mind was made up at once. Out of this he must be taken. But before removing him him permission had to be got from command. I drove without loss of time to Portobello Barracks. There was no nonsense, no red or, what is worse, green tape about these men.

'Griffith is ill and I want him to have adequate nursing and attention, which is impossible in a building designed for offices, not for homes.'

'Certainly. But we must know where you intend to take him so that we can provide the necessary guard.'

Griffith has to be guarded from the Irish people! I suppressed the chain of thought for my patient's sake. No. 96 Lower Leeson Street recommended itself to me because, being as it was the private hospital of the Mercy nuns, I hoped that their sacred character would prove a bulwark against the assassination of the man who believed in his fellow-countrymen.

With military formalities complete and adequate guards, the Father of the Free State was taken secretly from the Government Building and as far as possible from De Valera and his besieging Irregulars. I could never countenance this euphemism 'Irregulars'. They were mostly town riff-raff misled, or country dupes and discontents whom De Valera aroused when he found that his methods had landed him in a minority.

'I see you have Arthur in the front drawing-room of 96,' one of the hard political women said to me with a knowing smirk, an hour later. She had seen Griffith from the top of a tram as he moved restlessly to and fro in front of his windows.

Knowing that there was not a moment to be lost before she would spread the news amongst the gang that aimed at breaking his heart, I ordered that Griffith be removed from the first to the fourth floor.

'There is the fireplace and there is your armchair, Arthur, and don't expect a single visitor until I come again this afternoon.'

Arthur grunted. 'What's wrong with me?'

'You've had a hard life for fifty years and you think ease is a disease. But you have got to resign yourself to rest, and even to comfort, for the first time in your life, and to obey your doctor when you would resist a friend.'

That he did not 'stay put' in his armchair was only too evident. I was returning with shaving tackle and pyjamas for the suddenly removed President, when I found him sitting crosswise from the fire with a chair on each side, on which he placed the daily papers as he read them. He could read print as easily upside down as upright, for he was at one time a compositor.

I moved and turned his chair with him in it to the fire, saying, 'No Irishman ever sits across his hearth. For God's sake, Ireland's sake, and all our sakes, give yourself a little relaxation and behave as if you had escaped from 17 Crow Street for a day or two.'

'What do you mean?'

'I mean . . .'

'I'm all right!'

'I'm not; for I have to look after the worst and most fatal kind of patient — the healthy snob who will not look after himself.'

'There's nothing wrong with me.'

'That's one of your symptoms. But I am carrying your complaint. It's up to me to get myself right with you.'

'Ugh!'

'All the newspapers! No visitors. No telephoning. Me thrice daily. And all the Cabinet stuff can wait. You are going to be decorated for the first time in your life with carpet slippers.'

'I must keep on the telephone.'

'No. Unless it is laid on to this room.'

He took his pince-nez off and polished them

resentfully. I knew that so much depended on his complete removal from affairs that I was anxious to remove myself before he could formulate objections to his isolation. You are handicapped as a medical man when it comes to making an invalid believe in his illness. An Englishman likes to be invalided with his back to the wall so that he may summon to his aid his *vis medicatrix*.[2] He fights best in a tight corner. A man like Arthur Griffith looks upon disease or illness as a nuisance and something to be shaken off as we shake off an importunate bore. He cannot react to that which he will not recognize.

'Try to think you are taking a holiday.'

'I never had a holiday in my life, and I don't want an artificial one. I'll go back to the Building. Kindly send for my clothes.'

'Do you really imagine or think that I am keeping you here in order to provide myself with a patient? I want to provide you with regular meals and rest. Consider yourself a "nudist" meanwhile. If in three weeks . . .'

A nurse brought in a large envelope containing reports from the Cabinet. Knowing that these would make him restless and increase the irascibility which was manifest of late, I said that I would permit his secretary to see him or allow him one or two of his colleagues in.

Not for a moment did he refer to the report. He kept his troubles to himself and his responsibilities unshared.

Next morning nurse telephoned: 'You are wanted at once, Mr Griffith is very bad.' He is fighting hard against my orders, I thought. But I went round without hurry, thinking that he had been enraged at my restrictions on the visits of his secretaries and friends. Sir Thomas Myles laid it down that a doctor should never hurry. No Athenian gentleman did. If the condition be fatal, what can you do? If it be not, the probabilities are that a minute or two will make no difference. But what you can do in the first instance is to avoid arriving at the critical moments. Callous philosophy, were it meant to be taken seriously!

I was at the nursing home within four minutes. This absolved me. At the stairs' head President Griffith, the man who believed in the Irish people, lay on his back. His left arm was outstretched and bloody. A long incision of our four inches gaped where his pulse was. It was not bleeding, though the artery had been severed by Mr Meade, who was on the spot, the only attempt that could be made to counteract cerebral haemorrhage. Nurses and porters were fussing about asking each other if it were not terrible. Did they think he was really dead?

'Take up that corpse at once,' I said, letting something of the bitterness of my spirit escape into that harsh word. A moment after, I regretted it. 'Take the President's body into the bedroom.'

'I perish by this people which I made' — KING ARTHUR[3]

Rumours take the place of prodigies in Ireland. Instead of risen corpses in the Forum and chickens with three legs which would have satisfied ancient Rome's superstition, it was given out that poison slew Arthur Griffith. Much as I hate the 'Republicans' and their spurious pretensions, I will affirm that the only poison about them is turned against themselves. They are poisoned by false doctrines. But they do not poison their enemies, only themselves. It would have been a simple thing for me to order an inquest and to have the viscera examined for poison. But the poison that slew Griffith was envy and jealousy and calumny, which can be deadlier than prussic acid, and, what is more mortal to a martyr, ingratitude.

2. medical strength.

3. Tennyson, *Morte D'Arthur* (1842), line 22.

ELIZABETH BOWEN

(1899-1973)

from: SEVEN WINTERS: MEMORIES OF A DUBLIN CHILDHOOD (1942)

[Elizabeth Bowen's other autobiographical work, *Bowen's Court* (1942), is better known than this short memoir of the winters she spent as a child in Dublin. Although she is writing of the early years of the twentieth century, she remembers a Dublin in which the after-effects of the Act of Union were still felt, in which protestant and catholic were still separated by a yawning social divide and in which the middle classes were still in the process of moving in to the places vacated by the eighteenth-century gentry. Her visual sense of that one part of south Dublin, extending from the Liffey — which she rarely crossed — to the area around Baggot Street confirms the impression, now almost entirely faded, of an eighteenth-century city that slowly and reluctantly had become a Victorian town.]

BRASS PLATES

Between the middle of Dublin and Herbert Place lies a tract of Georgian streets and squares. We had a choice of two routes into the city. From the foot of our steps we could turn right, then go along Lower Baggot Street; or we could turn left, take the curve round St. Stephen's Church and after that go along Upper Mount Street and the south side of Merrion square; to this route was added the charm of going through Leinster Lawn, between the Museum and the National Gallery; one then followed that secretive passage, under the high flank of Leinster House, through to the circular lawn on the other side and the gates opening on to Kildare Street. . . .

The perspectives of this quarter of Dublin are to any eye, at any time, very long. In those first winters they were endless to me. The tense distances that one only slowly demolished gave a feeling of undertaking to any walk. Everything in this quarter seemed outside. The width of the streets, the stretch of the squares, the unbroken cliff-like height of the houses made the human idea look to me superhuman. And there was something abstract about this idea, with its built-up planes of shadow and light.

At the same time, the complexion of these façades humanly altered from day to day. The neighbourhood seemed infused with a temper or temperament of its own, and my spirits, on morning or afternoon walks, corresponded with this in their rise and fall. . . . Some days, a pinkish sun-charged gauze hung even over the houses that were in shadow; sunlight marked with its blades the intersections of streets and dissolved over the mews that I saw through archways. On such days, Dublin appeared to seal up sunshine as an unopened orange seals up juice. The most implacable buildings were lanced with light; the glass half-moons over the darkest front doors glowed with sun that, let in by a staircase window, fell like a cascade down flights of stairs.

But as often I felt a malign temper at work. Stories of gloom would add themselves to the houses, till these shut out the sky. The streets tautened and the distances frowned. Walking down Upper Mount Street or Lower Baggot Street I at once had the feeling of being in the wrong, and Leeson Street became a definite threat. Any human movement about the pavements showed signs of infection by nervous moodiness. But there never was much movement: though I took this for granted (as being the rule of cities) I saw too few people in view of the height and space. The tyrannical grandness of this quarter seemed to exist for itself alone. Perhaps a child smells history without knowing it — I did not *know* I looked at the tomb of fashion.

Even so, this quarter had declined, since the Union, to nothing worse than a sombre, solid propriety. This was not really a case of bared ruined choirs.[1] The houses in which my Anglo-Irish progenitors, gathering round their Parliament, had made merry with a stylish half-savagery were the homes of professional people now. I know now it did mark the end of an epoch when the first brass

1. Shakespeare, Sonnet 73: 'Bare ruined choirs, where late the sweet birds sang.'

plate appeared in Merrion Square. The original lordly plan had been dedicated to Society; it commemorated the migration southwards across the river after the Duke of Leinster had taken his bold decision to sink the foundations of his great new house in a snipe bog. The original is never alone for long, and society took chances after the Duke.

The post-Union exodus of the bright-plumaged people had not (as I saw) been followed by real decay. The Irish Bar and the eminent Dublin doctors kept South Dublin witty and sociable. Judges and specialists now lived round Merrion Square. The front doors were painted, the fanlights and windows polished, the great staircases possibly better swept and the high-ceilinged double drawing-rooms heated and lit for *conversazioni.* In the winters of my childhood this second society was still in full, if not at its fullest, force. The twentieth century governed only in name; the nineteenth was still a powerful dowager. Between England and Anglo-Ireland a time-lag is, I think, always perceptible. Any transition into Edwardian dashingness would have been seen in the Castle set. But the Castle seasons left my father and mother cold. The world my parents inhabited, and the subworld of its children, was still late-Victorian. Their friends were drawn from the Bar, from Trinity College, from among the prelates of the Church of Ireland or landed people quietly living in town.

In fact, the climatic moodiness of South Dublin (a bold Italianate town-plan in tricky Celtic light) must have existed only in my eye. All here stood for stability. The front doors were, as I say, fresh painted — crimson, chocolate, chestnut, ink-blue or olive-green. One barrister friend of my father's had a chalk-white front door I found beautiful. And each door — to this my memory finds no single exception — bore its polished brass plate. Daughter of a professional neighbourhood, I took this brass plate announcing its owner's name to be the *sine qua non* of any gentleman's house. Just as the tombstone says '*Here Lies*' the plate on the front door (in my view) said '*Here Lives.*' Failure to write one's name on one's door seemed to me the admission of nonentity. The householder with the anonymous door must resign himself to being overlooked by the world — to being passed by by the postman, unfed by tradesmen, guestless, unsought by friends — and his family dwelt in the shadow of this disgrace.

The fact that I could not read made these plates with writing still more significant. The first time I did see a town front door of unmistakable standing *without* a plate, I remember being not only scornful but hostile. Why should the dweller here envelop himself in mystery? On that occasion, my mother explained to me that plates were not, after all, the rule. If not, why not? I said hotly: how very silly. How else was one to know who lived in a house? In the light of this fixed idea (which I still think a good one) I remember my first view of London — street after street of triste anonymity. So no one cares who lives in London, I thought. No wonder London is so large; all the nonentities settle here. Dublin has chosen to be smaller than London because she is grander and more exclusive. All the important people live in Dublin, near me.

At the top of the Herbert Place front steps, waiting for the front door to be opened (for my governess never carried a latchkey) I would trace with my finger my father's name. This was not an act of filial piety only; it gave him an objective reality, which I shared.

SUNDAYS

On Sundays we went to St. Stephen's, our parish church, a few minutes' walk along the canal. St. Stephen's Georgian façade, with its pillars and steps, crowns the Upper Mount Street perspective, and looks down it into the airy distance of Merrion Square. To the ascending sound of bells we went up the steps — my mother with a fine-meshed veil drawn over her features, my father already removing his top-hat, I in my white coat. The Sunday had opened with mysterious movements about the staircase of Herbert Place — my mother's and father's departure to 'early church.'

About this Matins *I* went to there was no mystery. I could be aware that this was only an outer court. None the less, I must not talk or look behind me or fidget, and I must attempt to think about God. The church, heart of and key to this Protestant quarter, was now, at mid-morning, packed: crosswise above the pews allotted to each worshipping family ran galleries, with, I suppose more people up there. The round-topped windows let in on us wintry, varying but always unmistakably Sunday light, and gas burned where day did not penetrate far enough. The interior, with its clear sombreness, sane proportions, polished woodwork and brasswork and aisles upon which confident feet rang, had authority — here one could feel a

Presence, were it only the presence of an idea. It emphasized what was at once august and rational in man's relations with God. Nowhere was there any intensity of darkness, nowhere the point of a small flame. There was an honourable frankness in the tone in which we rolled out the General Confession — indeed, sin was most felt by me, in St. Stephen's, as any divagation from the social idea. There was an ample confidence in the singing, borne up by the organ's controlled swell.

Bookless (because I could not read) I mouthed my way through the verses of hymns I knew. Standing packed among the towering bodies, I enjoyed the feeling that something was going on. During prayers I kneeled balanced on two hassocks, and secretly bit, like a puppy sharpening its teeth, into the waxed prayer-book ledge of our pew. Though my inner ear was already quick and suspicious, I detected, in the course of that morning service, no hypocritical or untrue note. If I did nothing more, I conformed. I only did not care for the Psalms, which struck me as savage, discordant, complaining — or, sometimes, boastful. They outraged all the manners I had been taught, and I did not care for this chanted airing of troubles.

My mother attended St. Stephen's out of respect for my father's feeling that one should not depart from one's parish church. He mistrusted, in religion as in other matters, behaviour that was at all erratic or moody; he had a philosophic feeling for observance and form. But she liked St. Bartholomew's better because it was 'higher,' and once or twice in the course of every winter she would escape and take me there. Archbishop Trench[2] and his daughters were her cousins; the happiest days of her girlhood had been spent at the Palace, and for the rest of her days she remained High Church. She spoke of 'Prods' (or, extreme, unctuous Protestants) with a flighty detachment that might have offended many. I was taught to say 'Church of Ireland,' not 'Protestant,' and 'Roman Catholic,' not simply 'Catholic.'

It was not until after the end of those seven winters that I understood that we Protestants were a minority, and that the unquestioned rules of our being came, in fact, from the closeness of a minority world. Roman Catholics were spoken of by my father and mother with a courteous detachment that gave them, even, no myth. I took the existence of Roman Catholics for granted but met few and was not interested in them. They were, simply 'the others,' whose world lay alongside ours but never touched. As to the difference between the two religions, I was too discreet to ask questions — if I wanted to know. This appeared to share a delicate, awkward aura with those two other differences — of sex, of class. So quickly, in a child's mind, does prudery seed itself and make growth that I remember, even, an almost sexual shyness on the subject of Roman Catholics. I walked with hurried step and averted cheek past porticos of churches that were 'not ours,' uncomfortably registering in my nostrils the pungent, unlikely smell that came round curtains, through swinging doors. On Sundays, the sounds of the bells of all kinds of churches rolled in a sort of unison round the Dublin sky, and the currents of people quitting their homes to worship seemed to be made alike by one human habit, such as of going to dinner. But on weekdays the 'other' bells, with their (to my ear) alien, searching insistence had the sky and the Dublin echoes all to themselves. This predisposition to frequent prayer bespoke, to me, some incontinence of the soul. . . .

2. Rt Rev. Richard Trench (1807-86) was consecrated archbishop of Dublin on 1 January 1864. Earlier (1846-58), he had been dean of Westminster.

SEÁN O'CASEY

(1880-1964)

from: DRUMS UNDER THE WINDOW (1945)

[O'Casey's six volumes of autobiography were published between 1939 and 1954. They were published collectively in New York under the title *Mirror in My House: The Autobiographies of Seán O'Casey* (1956) and in London as *Autobiographies* (1963), with a new edition in 1981.

A number of reviewers objected to *Drums Under the Window*. St John Ervine impugned its accuracy; George Orwell found it distressingly anti-English, although it must be said that O'Casey's irony and anger at Easter Week escaped Orwell entirely. O'Casey admired the heroism of the people involved, but he thought their tactics foolish and their nationalism provincial. O'Casey's style was, and remains, distasteful to many. Ervine called it 'a mixture of Jimmy O'Dea and Tommy Handley'; Seán O'Faoláin thought it indulgent and uncontrolled. Despite these faults, O'Casey's *Autobiographies*, or at least the first four volumes, are probably surpassed only by his 'Dublin' plays. His histrionic method is often embarrassingly unsuccessful; but there are times when it achieves unexpectedly moving effects.

The six volumes of *Autobiographies* are: *I Knock at the Door* (1939), *Pictures in the Hallway* (1942), *Drums Under the Window* (1945), *Inishfallen, Fare Thee Well* (1949), *Rose and Crown* (1952), *Sunset and Evening Star* (1954).

The extract below is from the end of the third volume.]

THE BOLD FENIAN MEN

Larkin was gone, and Connolly was going, to the great joy of some of the labour leaders whose harts panteth after a cushy job as a deer's panteth after the water brooks.[1] They were never at heart's ease while either of these leaders was near; but now, like wise and sensible men, they could, thank God, set about knocking fighting Unions into safe, pruden-tial enterprises. Larkin had gone to America, and Connolly had left his Union to give all he had to the Citizen Army. He began to write patriotic verse that shivered with wretchedness. His fine eyes saw red no longer, but stared into the sky for a green dawn. A play of his called *Under Which Flag?* blundered a sentimental way over a stage in the Hall in a green limelight, shot with tinsel stars.[2] All the old-age punchioners of commonplace outcries were poured into the pages of *The Workers' Republic*[3] week by week; legions of words, each the same in stature and appearance, mob-capped and mock-cussined, dumbly plodded over the paper, unled by a single officer-word in sword and sash to justify the long, swing-song, dull purrade.

The world war was waxing over Europe, and Ireland was enjoying the hardships suffered by her enemy.... But all the time, the stoutest men from hill, valley, and town were pressing into the British Army, and long columns of armed Irishmen, singing Ireland's latest love-song, *It's a long way to Tipperary*, went swinging by Liberty Hall down to the quays to the ships waiting to bring them to a poppy-mobbed grave in Flanders. The I.R.B. worked hard sticking up fly-by-night posters calling on Irishmen to keep out of the British Army, while the journals *Sinn Fein* and *Irish Freedom* warned them that the coming fight must be, not for Catholic Belgium, but for Catholic Ireland; but the swinging columns went on marching down to the quays to the ships that go down to the sea. H. H. Asquith, Prime Minister, stood side by side with John Redmond at a recruiting meeting in the house of Dublin's Lord Mayor, but the forest of British guns and bayonets round the building kept his voice from travelling; and Dublin roared out her contempt for the pair of political brokers, but still the swinging columns of Kellys, Burkes, and Sheas tramped to the quays, and, singing, went forth to battle for England, little nations, and homes unfit

1. James Larkin (1876-1947), the labour leader, left Dublin for the United States in 1914. James Connolly (1868-1916), leader of the Transport Workers Union, reorganized the Irish Citizen Army after the end of the Lockout in 1914. The biblical phrase is a conflation of Psalms 42.1 — 'Like as the hart desireth the water brooks' — and Nahum Tate's *New Version of the Psalms* (1696), 'As pants the hart for cooling streams'.

2. The script of *Under Which Flag?*, performed at Liberty Hall, Dublin on 26 March 1916, just before the Easter Rising, has been lost.

3. *The Workers' Republic*, originally founded by James Connolly in 1898 as the newspaper of the Irish Socialist Republican Party, was revived again, for the sixth time, in May 1915, after the collapse of James Larkin's weekly newspaper, *The Irish Worker*.

for humans to live in; for while the sky was green for some, for many more it turned to the solid and salutary buff colour of a ring-paper.

Connolly determined to try to damn the stream of men flowing out of Ireland, and was seized with the idea that he could turn the sky green for all to see by hoisting a flag of the same colour over Liberty Hall. He had banished the Committee, and now ruled alone; so, after being thoroughly rehearsed, the Citizen Army, numbering about one hundred and seventy men, paraded outside, and Connolly, followed a pace behind by Madame Markievicz,[4] inspected them. Connolly wore his new dark-green uniform for the first time, and didn't look too well in it, for he had a rather awkward carriage; and bow-legs, partly ensnared in rich, red-brown, leather leggings, added to the waddle in his walk. He carried an automatic gun in his left hand, the barrel resting in the crook of his arm. Madame having dressed herself in man's attire to fight for liberty, was in full green uniform too, and carried a big automatic pistol on her thin hip.

There was a dire sparkle of vanity lighting this little group of armed men: it sparkled from Connolly's waddle, from the uniformed men stiff to attention, and from the bunch of cock-feathers fluttering in the cap of the Countess. But it was a vanity that none could challenge, for it came from a group that was willing to sprinkle itself into oblivion that a change might be born in the long-settled thought of the people. There they stood — a tiny speck of green among a wide surge of muddily-garbed watchers, still and silent too, as if from their listlessness they were draining out their last drop of energy and hope into this tiny goblet-group of men so that they might go forth and make a last short fight for them. Here was the purple heart of Ireland.

Now the escort marched with the flag, carried by a young girl, and not a murmur broke from the big crowd watching, Sean, a little loose on his legs, and nursing a septic neck-wound, among those in the front rank. Not a cheer went up when Connolly declared to his men that as soon as the old Green Flag flew from the roof, the Irish soldiers passing by would swing left, assemble before the Hall, and vow that they served neither Kaiser nor King, but Ireland. The flag was borne to the roof, fixed to the traces, and as it broke out on the breeze, the men of the army presented arms, and the great crowd cheered as if the breaking of the flag meant the ending of time for England.

Not an Irish soldier passing by to the quay, led by bands playing *Garryowen* or *Let Erin Remember*, turned aside; not one of them turned a head to glance at the lonely banner flying from the roof-top, lonelier now that the crowd had gone, pathetically flapping a call no-one heard; loneliest at night waving, seemingly, among the stars, tired and drooping, but still fluttering a faint message to those tough men of Dublin City who now slept, waiting for the dawn to come to go in full marching kit down to the ships, and set their sails for Flanders. It was a childish thought for Connolly to harbour: it was a fiery-tale, a die-dream showing a false dawn that no soul saw.

But Sean knew that Connolly's men would fight, and the Irish Volunteers would stand by them; but he knew in his soul that they were going the wrong way about it. Their methods were those of the days of the red-coats, busby, and plume; salute your superior officers, fix bayonets, and charge, boys. These uniformed batches of men attacking, holding, and defending particular positions couldn't hope to measure themselves against the heavy forces that would be sent out to down them. Once they were cut off, they were as good as gone. The arrangements were too open, and the idea that the British wouldn't use cannon, vouched for by Connolly, Pearse, and others, maddened Sean. Capitalists of England won't destroy capitalist property here, said Connolly, and so said Pearse, and so say all of us. I tell you they will, shouted Sean; And I tell you they won't, shouted back those who heard him. They used artillery in the streets during the Franco-Prussian War, said Sean, and at the siege of Paris the French soldiers battered their way over the Communard barricades with cannon-fire, careless of what property the bursting shells destroyed.[5] . . .

Connolly began his madnight route marches, sometimes ending with a furiosius attack on Dublin Castle. He seemed to see the beautiful Cathleen ni Houlihan immured within, pining away, chained

4. Constance Markievicz (1868-1927), whose involvement in the Citizen Army was one of the circumstances that prompted O'Casey's resignation from it. She fought in the 1916 Rising.

5. In the battles between the National Guard and the Communards in the Commune of Paris in 1871.

hand and foot with ring-papers. The capture of the Castle would mean nothing, for shortly afterwards the fighters would find that in taking the Castle they had but been taken themselves. Behind this romantic façade Connolly was shoving the Volunteers forward, quicker than they wanted to go. His men were kibing their heels.[6] Quicker, quicker, and Volunteers crossed and recrossed Citizen Army men, route-marching, drilling, raising the wind of war. In between this criss-cross of armed Irishmen wove the sparkling, half-galloping equipage of the Viceroy, drawn by four silky-skinned animals ridden by outriders in velvet coats, white breeches, and long-peaked jockey caps; followed by red-breasted lancers, brass-helmeted dragoons, or plumed hussars trying to weave an elegant binding embroidery through the more rough-and-ready pattern with which Ireland was busy, determined to cover up for ever every sign and thread in it of coloured conquest.

The Easter vigil was nearly over. Thousands were crumbling tobacco in the palms of their hands, preparing for the first smoke in seven long Lenten weeks of abstinence; the time had passed for forcing oneself (if you were lucky) to swallow sharply-tasting potted herrings, leathery strips of salted ling, and tea without milk.[7] Steak and onions, bacon and cabbage, with pig's cheek as a variation, would again glorify the white-scrubbed kitchen tables of the Dublin workers. Dancing for the young; the rollicking call into Eden would again swing into life to the tune of *Hoosh the Cat from under the Table* or *Lift the Roof Higher*; older ones, thinking of their children, would be getting ready for a trip to Portmarnock's Velvet Strand, or Malahide's silver one; and those who weren't would be poring over the names of horses booked to run at Fairyhouse on Easter Monday. The danger aglow in an All-Ireland Parade of the Volunteers had passed. It had been whispered, only whispered, mind you, that it had been planned by a few of remember-for-ever boys to suddenly change the parade from a quiet walk into an armed revolt. A near thing. Only for God's gillie, Eoin Mac Neill, Chief of Stuff, and Bulmer Hobson, God's gillie's gillie, the Volunteer Sacredary, neither of whom had been told about the plan, but who caught the wisp of a whisper, the deadly dreama would have been on top of the people.[8] But these two sent out couriers in trains, on horseback, on bicycles, in donkey-carts, and on roller-skates, running, galloping, and puffing all over the country, to countermind the whole thing, and so muted the silver trumpets that had lifted themselves up to call to the great race that was to come. So the country stretched itself before the fire, examined the form of the horses, filled its pipe, and watched the pig's cheek simmering on the fire for the morrow's dinner, thanking God that the long threatening hadn't come at last.

And on Easter Monday, off they went to the races, to their velvet strands, or got out their pretty frocks for the night dancing, all in a state of grace after the Easter devotions, full up of the blessed *joie deo feevre*; part of the country coming to the city to see the Museum, the Four Courts, the Custom House, and the Pro-Cathedral; while up one street Roger Casement, surrounded by armed detectives, was being taken to a boat chartered to land him at the nearest point to Tyburn; and down another street Bulmer Hobson, in the midst of armed I.R.B. men, was being taken to where he could do no good.[9] All was quiet as a none breathless in madoration.[10] Then down the centre of O'Connell Street, silent but for the tramp of their feet, came hundreds of armed Volunteers and Irish Citizen Army, led by Pearse, Connolly, and Tom Clarke,[11] to halt, wheel, and face the General Post Office.

—There go the go-boys! muttered an old man, half to himself and half to an elderly, thin lady beside him who had stopped to help him stare at the Volunteers. Well, Mac Neill put a stop to their gallop! What th' hell are th' up to now? They seem to be bent on disturbin' th' whoremony of the sacred day. Goin' in, eh? What' for, I wondher? Can't be wantin' postage stamps. Can't be to get th'

6. treading on one another's heels.
7. Standard penitential gestures observed during the Lenten fast.

8. 'gillie' is servant, from the Irish *giolla*. MacNeill, chairman of the committee of the Irish Volunteers, and Bulmer Hobson, the secretary, were both excluded from the arrangements for the Rising. They tried to countermand the orders for rebellion.
9. Roger Casement, arrested in County Kerry while trying to land arms from a German submarine, was arrested, taken to Dublin and then to London, where he was executed on 3 August 1916. Bulmer Hobson was taken into unofficial 'custody' on Good Friday by an IRB unit.
10. Mock version of the line in Wordsworth's sonnet ' It is a Beauteous Evening': 'The holy time is quiet as a nun,
Breathless with adoration.'
11. Tom Clarke (1858-1916), a member of the military council set up to plan the Rising. At the request of the other leaders, he was the first to sign the proclamation of the Republic. He was executed for his part in the Rising.

right time, for there's a clock in th' window. What'r they doin, ma'am? I dunno. Somethin' brewin'? Ma'am, there's always somethin' brewin'. I'm seventy, an' I've never known an hour that I didn't hear tell of somethin' brewin'. Be God, they're takin' th' clock outa th' window! That's odd, now. Looka, they're smashin' out th' windows with their rifles! There's a shower o' glass — right over th' passers-by! That's goin' beyond th' beyond. Tha's, tha's just hooliganism. We betther be gettin' outa here — th' police'll be here any minute! Didn' I tell you before, ma'am, I dunno! They're shovin' out the Post Office workers; pointin' their guns at them. We betther be gettin' outa here while we're safe. Houl' on a second — here's someone out to read a paper. What's he sayin'? I dunno. How th' hell can you expect a fella to hear from here? Oh! pushin' th' people off th' streets, now. Eh? G'on home, is it? An' who are you t'ordher me about? Takin' over th' city? D'ye tell me that? Well, you're not goin' to take over me! I'm a peaceful man out on a peaceful sthroll on a peaceful day, an' I stand be me constitutional rights. Gunfire here soon? Arrah, from where? From where, ma'am? I dunno, I'm tellin' you! He says he's speakin' in th' name of th' Irish Republic, so now you're as wise as I am meself. Th' police'll soon explain matthers. Don't be talkin', looka what's comin' up O'Connell Street! A company o' throttin' lancers — full regalia with carbines, lances, an' all! Comin' to clear th' Post Office. Don't be pushin' me ribs in, ma'am! Hear th' jingle of them! This looks like business. Here we see, ma'am, the Irish Republic endin' quicker'n it began. Jasus, Mary, an' Joseph! th' fools are firin' on them! Here, get outa th' way, ma'am, an' let a man move! Near knocked you down? Why th' hell are you clingin' on me tail for, then? Didn' I tell you hours ago that it was dangerous dawdlin' here? D'ye hear that volley! Looka th' police runnin' for their lives! Here, let's get outa this; we've dilly-dallied too long where we've no real business to be!

—Oh, looka them breakin' into the shops! Isn't that provokin', ma'am? After all, th' boys are out for somethin' higher. Looka this fella comin' along with a gramophone. Eh, sonny boy, where'd you get that? Didja hear that answer? Go an' find out! Uncivilised lot. Looka these comin' with a piano, no less! Didja hear that? Give them a shove! Cheek, wha'? Look, they're bringin' out hand-carts an' prams. A sad day for Dublin's fair name. What's that fella in beard an' knickerbockers doin'? Pastin' up bills. Willya read that — callin' on the citizens to do nothin' to dishonour the boys. Why doesn't he mind his own business? Sheehy-Skeffington?[12] Never heard of him. One o' Ireland's noblest sons? Is it on for coddin' me y'are? If he was less noble an' less unselfish, I'd ha' heard a lot of him? Maybe; but he's not goin' to be let dictate to me. It's none o' his business if I want to rifle, rob, an' plundher. Looka! There he goes, now, with two others, in a web o' soldiers! That doesn't look like he was noble. What was that, now, went whizzin' by me? A bullet? You're jokin'! I can tell them, if they harm me, there'll be more about it!

The tinkle of breaking glass wandered down the whole street, and people were pushing and pulling each other, till through broken windows all the treasures of India, Arabia, and Samarkand were open before them. Sean watched them as they pulled boxes down on top of themselves, flung clothing all over the place; tried to pull new garments over their old ones; while one woman, stripped naked, was trying on camisole after camisole, ending with calm touches that smoothed out the light-blue one that satisfied her at last. All who were underdressed before, were overdressed now, and for the first time in their frosty lives the heat of good warm things encircled them.

He heard the humming zipzz of bullets flying a little way overhead, and guessed someone was firing to frighten the looters; so he dodged into the doorway of a shop to put a protection between him and them. A solidly-built man came trotting along carrying a large jar by the handle against his right thigh, while from his left hung a pair of vividly yellow boots. A sharp ping sounded, and the jar separated into halves, letting a golden stream of liquor honour the road. The man stopped, and gazed at the jagged neck of the jar left in his hand.

—Jasus! he said, not a dhrop of it left — the wasteful bastards!

Sean squirmed round an angle of the doorway to get a look into the shop. Through the great jagged

12. Francis Sheehy-Skeffington (1878-1916), a friend of some of the leaders of the Rising, had tried to dissuade them from fighting and, instead, to organize a body 'armed and equipped with the weapons of the intellect and will'. His only part in the Rising was to stop citizens looting, yet on 25 April 1916 he was arrested and taken to Portobello Barracks in Dublin. Later, as a hostage, he witnessed the shooting of an unarmed boy by Captain Bowen-Colthurst, the officer who had arrested him. The next day, Bowen-Colthurst ordered Sheehy-Skeffington and two other prisoners to be taken to the yard and shot dead.

hole in the window he saw the inside was a litter of tossed clothing, caps, shoes, collars, and ties on which people were trampling, and over which they were jostling each other; ignoring the value of what lay on the floor or what was spread over the counter, for the hidden value of what lay neatly folded in the still unopened boxes. One man, alone, was rooting among a heap of caps on the floor, feverishly planting one after the other on his head, and flinging to the far end of the shop those which didn't seem to fit. Another, trying by main force to pull a delicate-looking pair of tweed trousers over a pair of big thick boots, was cursing loudly when he discovered they wouldn't go, and cursing louder still when he found he couldn't get them off again. A third was holding his old coat tightly between his legs while he excitedly thrust raggedly-shirted arms through the sleeves of a bran-new one; while yet another was calling out that if anyone came across a seven-size in socks, they might let him know. And there, too, was the old man, leaning on the counter directing with his stick a younger man on a ladder, busy searching among the boxes on the higher shelves.

—What's in that one to your left? he shouted to the man on the ladder; to your left, man! Shirts? What kinda shirts? Ordinary cotton ones? Aw, don't waste time clawin' them things! They can be picked up anywhere. That box to your right — to your right! Good God, man! D'ye know your right from your left? De Luxe written on them? Throw them down, throw them down! Where'r you pushin', want to do business here. Wha'? How th' hell do I know where to direct you to the ladies' department! One, two, three, four, five, six, an' one for Sunday — they'll be about enough for the time bein'. Have a look for a box marked pyjamas — I always had a notion of wantin' to feel how they felt on a fella. Wha's that? What do they want th' ambulance for? A woman's been shot? Wha', just outside? Who done it? A sniper, or somebody? God Almighty, where's our boasted law an' ordher!

Sean watched their wonderful activity, and couldn't desecrate their disorder with dishonour. All these are they who go to Mass every Sunday and holy day of obligation; whose noses are ground down by the clergy on the grindstone of eternal destiny; who go in mortal fear of the threat of a priest, he thought; but now he was glad to see they hadn't lost their taste for things material. In spite of the clergy's fifing and drumming about venial and mortal sin, they were stretching out their hands for food, for raiment, for colour, and for life. If the lilies of the field, that neither toiled nor spun,[13] could be lovely, how much more that these whose lives were a ceaseless labour should be lovely too? The time would come when they would no longer need to take their kingdom of heaven by violence, for they would build it themselves, and warmth, adornment, and satisfaction in the midst of fair sounds and bright colours would be their own.

When the shooting seemed to have got less, Sean slid cautiously out of his shelter and, keeping close to the walls of shop and house, made his way home. Darkness had fallen, and his near-sighted eyes could see but a few feet in front of them. Coming to the bridge across the canal at Spencer Dock, his semi-consciousness heard a calm, tired voice say somewhere, Halt! Who goes there? A few steps farther, and the voice, tired no longer, terse and threatening, said again, Who goes there! In the hesitating shock of seeing nothing, he managed to say, Friend, and a moment after, passed by the dim form of a soldier with the rifle at the ready, who passed him by with the advice of, Answer quicker, next time, friend. A narrow squeak, that! A few seconds more of hesitation and he'd have been high among the stars. Watch your steps, Sean. A little farther on, his breast almost touched a bayonet as another voice said, Who goes there? Murmuring, Friend, the bayonet was lowered, and a soldier's voice said, Pass on, friend. They were dotted along the road up to the corner of the street that held his home. Pouring in by the North Wall,[14] and no-one here to stop them. Poor ould Ireland!

He halted at the doorway thrust through with the knowledge that it was dangerous for him to be abroad at night. His eyes were blank in the darkness. He thought of the things that had happened, and wondered how it would all end. It was a deserted city now, but for those who fought each other. The pubs had emptied, the trams had jingled back to their sheds, the shops were shut. Lansdowne Road, Rathmines, and Rathgar gathered up their fine clothes and ran home; the janitors of the Bank of Ireland came rushing out to slam-to the great iron gates with a clang, turning the thick lips of the lock with hurried hands, and the sentries rushed into the guardroom; those coming

13. cf. Matthew 6.28.
14. In the port of Dublin.

home from Fairyhouse[15] had been stopped by British barricades, and choruses of How th' hell am I goin' to get home ascended to God and His blessed saints. And Sean, standing in the doorway of his house, gazed back towards the centre of the city and saw a great plume of flame rising high into the sky: the first passion-flower had blossomed. . . .

In the sky the flames were soaring higher, till the heavens looked like a great ruby hanging from God's ear. It was tinging the buildings with a scarlet glow, while the saints stretched their ears to catch the tenour of the Irish prayers going up, for each paterroster and ave maria mingled with the biting snarl from the Howth guns, and the answering roar from Saxon rifle, machine-gun, and cannon, that were weaving a closer cordon of fire round the Sinn Feiners, the fire creeping towards the group of innocents blessed with arms in their hands for the first time. Now it was above them, licking away the roof from over their heads, and they were too weary to go on trying to put it out. Their haggard faces were chipped into bleeding jaggedness of splinters flying from shattered stones and brick; the wounded were in a corner making their moan to themselves, while a few men and women were risking their lives to get the seriously hurt away to some hospital, wending through falling walls, fire and brimstone, and gauntlets of burning buildings. The grey-green Volunteer uniforms now no longer looked neat; they were ragged, and powdered thick with the pulverised mortar clouding from the walls. The fighters now looked like automatons moving unsteadily about, encased tightly in a fog of dust and acrid ashes. They were silent, unshaven, maybe muttering an act of contrition for things done before they went to war; wan-eyed, they persuaded their drooping lids to lift again, for drowsiness might mean a sudden and silent death to them. Those handiest with a rifle kept firing into the flames coming closer; a few, hoarse and parched, still tried to control the flames with tiny buckets of water, their leaders, before a wall of flame, standing dignified among them, already garlanded for death; gay outwardly, and satisfied, their inner wakefulness wondering how they'd fare when the world faded. They had helped God to rouse up Ireland: let the whole people answer for them now! For them, now, tired and worn, there was but a long, long sleep; a thin ribbon of flame from a line of levelled muskets, and then a long sleep. For evermore, Ireland's Easter lilies would have a crimson streak through them.

The thyme had turned to rue. And through the ring of fire and smoke, passing by the flying bullets, went the brown-robed Capuchins, bending over the wounded, unable to do much, but standing by their people and the danger. Father Aloysius, with a white apron on a broomstick, hurries to the British barricade to ask for a surgeon, but an elegant Colonel Taylor turns his back on him and leaves him there alone with the Tommies[16] and with God; and later on an equally elegant Captain does all a man can do to help the minister with humane thoughts and a courteous address. . . .

A rare time for death in Ireland; and in the battle's prologue many a common man, woman, and child had said goodbye to work and love and play; and many more in an hour or so would receive a terse message that life no longer needed them. There they are, lying so quiet — a child surprised in the doorway; an old man stretched in the street; a young man near a lamp-post which he had clutched when the bullet struck him, and down which he had slid when he died, his curiously white face containing wide eyes staring upwards, as if asking the sky why this had happened, a stiff arm still half-encircling the lamp standard; a young lassie in holiday attire, lying on her face, maybe hurrying home when she heard the uproar, but going too slow, for on the brilliant white blouse a purple patch of death was spreading over the middle of the back; an old woman on the floor of her tenement room, alone, her blood seeping through the ceiling below: all of the goodly company of the dead who died for Ireland. Jesu, have pity! Quiet, comrades, quiet. It was necessary that you should die for Ireland too. You didn't want to die. I know, I know. You signed no proclamation; you invaded no building; you pulled no trigger; I know, I know. But Ireland needed you all the same. Many will die like that before Ireland can go free. They must put up with it. You will be unknown for ever; you died without a word of praise; you will be buried without even a shadowy ceremony; no bugle will call your name; no gunshot will let loose brave echoes over your

15. The racecourse to the north of Dublin where the Irish Grand National had been run on Easter Monday afternoon.

16. Privates in the British army.

grave; you will not be numbered among the accepted slain. But listen, comrades, listen: Whitman[17] will be there to meet you; he will marshal you into the march-past with the greater dead; on the cornet he will give you a shrill salute. Listen — there it goes! Forward! March!

Here comes Paudrig Pearse[18] down the silent street, two elegant British officers waiting for him. He comes steadily, in no hurry; unafraid, to where two elegant British officers are waiting to meet him. His men have been beaten; the cordon of flame has burnt out their last fading hope. *The struggle is over; our boys are defeated; and Ireland's surrounded with silence and gloom*: the old ballad is singing in his ears. He wears a topcoat, for the Easter sun has gone west, and a nipping breeze blows. It is the wind of death blowing keenly on this brave man's pure face. His eyes droop, for he hasn't slept for days. He has lain down, but not to sleep. Soon he will sleep long and well. He feels this is no defeat; that to stand up in an armed fight against subjection is a victory for Ireland. So he stands silently, and listens to the elegant British officer demanding unconditional surrender. The fools, the fools! So he agrees, and hands over his sword; bows, and returns to marshal his men for a general surrender. . . .

The listening people hear the quick, short, sharp steps of Tom Clarke over the stony square of Kilmainham.[19] There is the squad waiting, khaki-clad, motionless, not knowing the argument. Here, in front, halt! A brown-robed friar stands aside, hurrying prayers over his rosary beads. There is no bravery here save in the thin figure with its arms bound tight; a cloth over the gleaming eyes. The guns suddenly give forth a jet of flame, the figure jerks rhythmically, slides awkwardly to the ground, twitches for a second, then lies for ever still. Ireland has scored another victory over England, for the people begin to ponder over what this man has done, and search for everything he has said, that what was spoken by the prophets might be fulfilled — he will be remembered for ever.

Then another came forth to die, with head, usually bent, now held high, for Pearse has bidden farewell to the world, though he still holds Ireland by her rough and graceful hand, loth to let it go: farewell to St. Enda's,[20] its toil, its joy, its golden brood of boys; farewell to Emmet's Fort, to the Hermitage, the lake in the woods, the scented hayfield; farewell to the azure sky, the brown bog, the purple heather of Connemara; farewell the pageants that wheeled broad palaces into simple places and turned greyness into magic colours; farewell the jewelled quaintness in the thoughts and play of children. — Oh, farewell! The moments have grown bigger than the years.

The face of Ireland twitches when the guns again sing, but she stands steady, waiting to fasten around her white neck this jewelled string of death, for these are they who shall speak to her people for ever; the spirit that had gone from her bosom returns to it again to breathe out hope once more, and soon to sing.

Ere the tiny curl from the gun-muzzles has hid in the upper air, the flames lash out again, and Connolly,[21] last of the lost leaders, loses his place in life, and becomes a marbled memory.

Black prison vans, packed with prisoners, cavalry with naked swords before an behind them, move swift through the streets. Crowds, silent and sullen, watch them go by at the street corners, and stare at white faces pressed against the tiny grating at the back of the van, striving for a last glimpse of Erin ere they walk the decks of the ship that will carry them to the prisons of England. And the Castle[22] is alert and confident; files all correct, and dossiers signed and sealed for the last time. Now the Irish may be quiet, and quit their moan, for nothing is whole that could be broken. And the glasses are full of wine, and cigar-smoke incenses the satisfaction.

But Cathleen, the daughter of Houlihan, walks firm now, a flush on her haughty cheek. She hears the murmur in the people's hearts. Her lovers are gathering around her, for things are changing, changed utterly:

A terrible beauty is born.[23]

Poor, dear, dead men; poor W. B. Yeats.

17. Walt Whitman (1819-92), American poet.
18. Patrick Pearse (1879-1916), teacher, writer and revolutionary, executed for his part in the Rising.
19. Kilmainham Jail, where many Irish patriots had been held and where the leaders of the Rising were shot.
20. The school where Pearse had taught.
21. James Connolly (1868-1916).
22. Dublin Castle was the administrative centre of British rule in Ireland.
23. The famous refrain from Yeats's poem 'Easter 1916'.

ROBERT HARBINSON

(1928-)

from: NO SURRENDER: AN ULSTER CHILDHOOD (1960)

[In this excerpt, Harbinson describes the northern protestant fixation with the pope and its fear and loathing of catholicism. This is a cultural and political reality often underestimated. Almost thirty years after Harbinson wrote, the reality is as pronounced as ever. It is also important to note that this phenomenon is to be found in its fullblown form in the protestant working class. Sandy Row is a street in the heartland of Orange Belfast and has almost legendary associations for those who know what it represents. The sense of solidarity provided by the Orange Order, the annual celebrations of the Twelfth of July, the forever present enemy, give a political coloration to neighbourliness and explain the inner warmth of a community that is outwardly hostile. This is the incubator in which sectarianism and loyalty are nourished.]

THE BOYS OF SANDY ROW

'No Pope here', 'Not an inch', 'God save the King', and 'Remember 1690' were signs we saw every day. They appeared in huge permanently painted letters on the gable ends of the streets round about. Although our street lay midway between Falls Road, the centre of everything Catholic in Belfast, and Sandy Row, the strongest Orange quarter, we were staunchly Protestant. Even ruder slogans against His Holiness decorated some gables; together with elaborate paintings, some twenty feet or more high, of coronation scenes complete with flowering robes, regalia, and recognizable portraits of King George V and Queen Mary. The crossing of Boyne Water by King Billy, with flying banners and flashing swords, was, however, the favourite topic for these vast outdoor murals.

We had a mural too in the backyard of our house, but only a painted crown on the whitewash under the window-sill. Higher up, only just visible, remained the fragments of King Billy's charger, the open Bible, a lurid eye through the clouds, Jacob's ladder, the rainbow, and Noah's ark, painted years before by my father while in a mood of patriotism. Whatever they represented religiously and politically, the pictures added a dash of colour and life to the drab mien of the streets.

We tried to reckon how much an ordinary Mickey[1] would have to pay at confession for a week's sins. It was our firm belief that every sin had to be paid for in hard cash, and that was why so many Catholics were publicans — unlike so many others their tills were always full of cash.

For one particular crime we could never forgive the Mickeys; their hatred of the Bible. All Catholics were under orders, we were told, to burn any scripture they found, especially New Testaments. The old song supported us,

The intriguing Paypishes surround this loyal and
ancient town
They tried you know not long ago to pull the
Bible down
And to destroy it root and branch they often
have combined
But from Sandy Row we made them fly like
chaff before the wind.

What pride we enjoyed for living so near to Sandy Row — the Boys of Sandy Row, stalwarts of our Orange Order.

We imagined also that newly dead popes were embalmed like Takabuti in the museum, and then put on display as human money-boxes; and that when they were stuffed so full that not another penny would go in, they were canonized and became saints.

Takabuti, the Egyptian mummy, a house-mistress of a priest of Amunre, reclined in a case at the museum not altogether without a vestige of former dignity. She could never have imagined, three thousand years before, the tiny faces that would press so often against the glass of her exhibition table. Her hair and teeth, whole though shrivelled and discoloured, and her delicate foot complete with flesh and toenails, attracted as much attention as perhaps they had so long ago. Certainly the priest of Amunre could not have paid her more

1. A colloquialism for a catholic.

attention than we did. However, much as we loved Takabuti and her wimple of blue beads, other kinds of priests occupied our minds — those of Rome.

Crowding out any other aspects of history, our schools dinned into us over and over again the Protestant story. On leaving school, and that none too early for my liking, I had no notion of the world's past other than a few prehistoric tales and dreary details concerning our Protestant faith and the unrelieved darkness of Rome. The particular rack on which they tortured us appeared in the form of a small, buff covered booklet entitled *How we differ from Rome*.

With what surprising, singeing pains my hands and fingers often smarted when a cane or strap was administered because on being asked 'How does Pope Honorius, writing in 1221, refer to the entry of the English into Ireland?' I could not furnish the correct answer. 'Pope Honorius[2] states that "the English entered Ireland by the authority of the Apostolic See and made it obedient to the Church of Rome".' Really! No excuse could be offered, they told me so frequently, probably every day, certainly every week; I had no reason, on being asked to 'Quote from Pope Adrian's letter to Henry II', for failing to report that 'Pope Adrian states: "While as a Catholic prince you intend to widen the bounds of the Church we are anxious to introduce a faithful plantation in that land" (of Ireland).'[3] The complete horrid booklet had to be learnt by heart, before we could be upgraded to commit the Prayer Book catechism to memory, and finally present ourselves, suitably primed, for confirmation.

This picture appears black, but a lighter side did exist, a comic-relief provided by intimate details of the popes' private lives. Before we tumbled out of our cradles, we knew of the unspeakable behaviour by the pontiffs and their courts. The goings-on of the Borgias[4] were as familiar as the affairs of the next-door neighbour.

2. Pope Honorius III made this statement to remind the English king, Henry III, that the papacy would not tolerate independent action on his part — for example, the declaration that no Irishman could be a bishop.
3. Nicholas Breakspear, the only Englishman to occupy the papal chair, ruled as Adrian IV 1154-59. In 1155 he issued the papal bull, *Laudabiliter*, authorizing Henry II of England to enter Ireland and cleanse the Irish church of its abuses. It was in effect permission to invade the country.
4. Cesare and Lucrezia Borgia were children of Rodrigo Borgia, Pope Alexander VI (1475-1507). Cesare was the model for Machiavelli's *The Prince*; Lucrezia was said to have committed incest with her father and brother.

Even proper history books, we were assured, disclosed the antics at the papal court, with Roman strumpets running round and burning their bare bottoms on the great lighted candles of the Vatican. Nuns underdoing initiation were sometimes forced to play the part of these naked shepherdesses — until too old for orgies. Then they were given the flowing habits to cover up the singe marks on their buttocks and legs, and sent back to Ireland or wherever they came from. No wonder our preachers referred in horror to Rome as the Scarlet Woman! And little wonder amongst our first nursery rhymes was,

If I had a penny
Do you know what I would do?
I would buy a rope
And hang the pope
And let King Billy through.

After all, our unswerving loyalty to the British crown was through King Billy — William of Orange, the man who defeated the Catholic Stuarts, the Irish and French, in the famous battle at the Boyne river.

From these allegiances the greatest spectacular event of the Ulster year took place on the twelfth of July. How wise of William to win his battle at the height of summer, so that festivities in its honour through the centuries after could be held in sunshine and fine weather! How we children waited for that day, and for the day preceding, when the riot of decorations received finishing touches in the streets. A Union Jack hung from every house, and masses of bunting criss-crossed the street from upper windows; crowns and mystical triangles; crescent moons each with seven stars, and flaming suns with faces; the burning bush and David's sling and five stones; streamers; red, white and blue rosettes bloomed in a profuse garden of paper and linen.

Each street vied with the next in the splendour of the main piece, its triumphal arch. Spanning between two houses, bedizened with orange and purple streamers, the arch was studded with pictures of British royalty. The climax of these preliminaries to the Twelfth was the lighting of bonfires. In the manner of the English November Fifth,[5] we had effigies of Catholic leaders, that had

5. Guy Fawkes day, celebrating the discovery of the Gunpowder Plot on 5 November 1605.

sat for weeks on street corners collecting pennies, and which were solemnly consigned to the flames like Guy Fawkes.

Before the ashes had lost their red hearts, the drums of Lambeg[6] rolled like thunder through the summer night and ushered in our Glorious Twelfth. Day dawned; everyone was up early, ready to go out and see the sights and watch the traditional 'walk to the field'. It was a public holiday, as important to us as the Fourth of July in the U.S.A.

For miles along the Lisburn Road, thousands waited to see the Orangemen walk in procession behind elaborate banners painted with symbols of their secret society. To us Belfast boys, the Black men we looked for in the procession were not negroes, but the most respected holders of the highest rank within the hierarchy of the Order. Purple men followed them in precedence and lastly the ordinary Orangemen, all three wearing sashes coloured after their rank and bordered with a heavy gold fringe.

Everywhere orange colour flamed in sash and banner, and in the lily which people wore. They twined in bunches with sweet-williams on top of the standards, for the orange-lily was as sacred to us as the shamrock was to the Mickeys or Fenians.

Do you think that I would let
A dirty Fenian cat
Destroy the leaf of a lily-o,
For there's not a flower in Ireland,
Like King Billy's orange-lily-o.

Such sights! Such music, churning the Protestant blood in our veins! For my first eight Twelfths I had needs be content with trailing through the crowds, craning for a glimpse of glory, straining to see the cymbals flashing as zing-zing-zing they crashed in a flash of sun, pushing my way through a forest of arms and legs to catch the dozens of pipe-bands, the flutists, and the drummers. The drummers came between each Lodge, flaying the hides of the big bass drums from Lambeg, where, naturally, they made the finest drums in the world. The huge cylinders were painted and decorated in gold, red, and orange with figures and patterns, crests and royal coats-of-arms in a whirligig of colour and line. It was considered a point of honour by some Lambeggers to beat the great drums so hard, and for so long, that wrists chafed the drum's edge until the skin became sore or even until cuts and bleeding resulted.

As expression of loyalty to a Protestant throne it would have been hard to find anything finer. But as music the effect was open to question. Whether of pipes or flutes or brass, or simply four of the gigantic Lambeg drums, each band felt that responsibility for the day's music rested solely, and by no means lightly, on their shoulders. Consequently they blew, blasted, and banged as heartily as wind and muscle knew how. For a single band in isolation this would have been admirable, but since one band succeded another long before the first one was out of earshot, closely followed by yet more, and all playing different music, the total effect was overwhelming.

Unsurpassable day! In the pomp's midst, we tried to see friends from our neighbourhood's Lodges, and waited especially for Nodding Will to come. He lived two doors away from us, was old and had a twitching, shell-shocked head. But he was also a Black man[7] and because of this rode in state in an open landau, clad in his best dickie[8] and Sunday bowler.

The very first time my mother allowed me to follow the Orange procession to Finaghy Field,[9] where the brave followers of King Billy met, I lost myself. Holiday mood had seized everyone, money went like water, and so many lemonades and iced cakes were given to the lost boy that he was ill. But not so ill that he could not hear his name called over the loudspeakers, a thrill with an exquisite edge, the climax of climaxes, the gilding indeed of the orange-lily. The Field was Elysian for me on that first day, for I went round collecting hundreds of coloured bottle-tops, which I fastened to my jersey, so that by the time I arrived home, exhausted with excitement, I was as scaly as a crocodile.

But Orange celebrations did not occur only on the Twelfth, for later in the year children sat out on the backyard walls, singing Orange ballads as the trains went by crammed with Black men going to

6. A village in County Antrim.

7. Founded in 1796, associated with the Orange Order.
8. A false shirt front, worn with formal dress. Also the name of a bow tie.
9. A field outside Belfast where the Twelfth of July Parade traditionally ends with a series of speeches.

the traditional closing of the gates of Derry. Although we enjoyed these celebrations as much as the grown-ups, we knew that serious feelings underlay the festivities. We had odd ideas on many things, but not about the reasons for these demonstrations.

In school nobody ever told us about Marie Antoinette or Marshal Foch, but we knew Louis XIV and Robert Lundy the treacherous governor of Derry.[10] We might not know the date of the French Revolution but we did know that in 1688, thirteen young men, apprentices in the city, closed the gates of Derry in the face of the Catholic soldiers. We would forget our avoirdupois tables, but we remembered well enough that during the famous siege a dog's head cost two-and-six-pence, a rat or a quart of horse blood one shilling, and a handful of chickweed one penny. Dogs were fattened on the dead, and sold for five-and-sixpence per quarter carcass. Our greatest bed-time story was of the fat gentleman who hid himself for three days because several of the garrison troops had looked on him with greedy eyes. It was our heritage, and we were proud of it.

Confident of the city's surrender, James II himself went outside the walls of Derry to receive it. Instead, the beleaguered Protestants lined the walls and shouted 'No Surrender', which we fancied still resounded in our own breast as we watched the Black men go off to the famous scene. On the gable walls, along with the murals of coronations and anti-papal slogans, 'No Surrender' was also painted. When we drank our lemonade we toasted,

To the goose that grew the feather,
To the hand that wrote No Surrender.

The passing of the years, which swept the heroic 17th century further and further away, also brought nearer the time when I could graduate from being a thrilled bystander to an actual member of the Orange Order. I joined a junior Lodge, a proud day indeed for it was the 'Loyal Sons of William', whose headquarters were in Sandy Row itself. To be reckoned amongst the Boys of Sandy Row who had made the Mickeys go 'like chaff before the wind', was high honour and laid grave claims on my own courage. And now I would most certainly get a good place in heaven and be able to see King Billy and the Protestant martyrs. Our Bible spoke of four-and-twenty elders before the great white throne, and we deduced that this meant King Billy and company, to whom also were given the key to the bottomless pit where the Mickeys would go.

At my Lodge enrolment ceremony I had to stand outside the sacred locked doors of the inner chamber, trembling and waiting in a gloomy passage. Then before the whole assembly wearing its glittering regalia my name was put forward and approved. The doors opened and my sponsors emerged to lead me in, keeping position on both sides of me. I was marched through the columns of Loyal Sons. I was now shaking physically and almost incoherent as I swore to keep the Lodge password.

A concert took place afterwards, and I won first prize for declaiming the tale of the boy who stood on the burning deck.[11] The Lodge wanted threepence for enlisting me, and I had only a penny. A bad beginning, to fall into arrears, but nevertheless I left the hall with an impressive penknife loaded with unusual blades and gadgets which must have cost at least two-and-sixpence. Such a possession had no appeal for me, and I gave it to Gandhi[12] in exchange for a tin of condensed milk.

Such a careless attitude could not be adopted towards the secret password. This frightened me very much, for I reputedly talked in my sleep. And my fear of divulging the special word was not because of loyalty to the Lodge, but rather fear that my sisters, or people in the hospital when I went in, would hear it, and tell it to their friends. And eventually Catholic ears would hear it and this would bring catastrophe on us, and we would be hounded from Belfast for breaking so solemn a vow. The Order's shadow fell everywhere in the city, and I kept the wretched word and felt separated from my family by the Lodge.

When I got home from my enrolment, little Helen wanted to know everything that happened, especially if I had had to ride the goat. Until then we had been as thick as inkle-weavers.[13] But now the hocus-pocus of secret societies inserted a wedge

10. Lundy opened the gates of the protestant garrison for the besieging Jacobite forces. He is still burned in effigy in Derry every December.

11. The opening line of the poem 'Casabianca' in *The Forest Sanctuary* (1829) by Felicia Dorothea Hemans (1793-1835).

12. The name of the boy's closest friend.

13. Weavers of linen. He and his sister were very close to one another.

between us. Big 'Ina overheard us and gave me a meaning look to keep silence, and I knew the Lodge doings must burn unrelieved in my breast, and Helen be content with a slap for presuming to enquire into such things.

Junior Lodges had their big parade on a different day from the elders, normally on Easter Tuesday; and we made an excursion by train, assembling again at the other end. Nothing could quieten us as we waited at the station, milling chaotically in orange sashes, dashing madly all over the place, mixing ourselves up with banner-bearers and bandsmen, and finally falling into the train as the whistle blew. There were always saucy girls on the train encouraging us to go with them to the carriages where the 'big kilties' from the pipe-bands sat, to find out how many of them were wearing trews[14] under their kilts.

Over the years, the riotous outings merged into a general blur without detail except for a few occasions, such as when I could hardly walk in the procession. On the previous day I had been surprised taking flowers from a preparatory school garden, and a master had chased me for the best part of a mile. He never caught up, but the flowers cost me dear in the form of terrible blisters on my feet. For the outing I could not wear shoes, and set out in white plimsolls.[15] In the train, someone took my overcoat by mistake and left me theirs which was too big for me. When we reached our destination I joined the march in a garment that came down to meet my plimsolls. The onlookers laughed as I trudged along in the pelting rain, holding on to a thick orange rope to steady our banner of King Billy on his white charger.

A sneaking feeling began inside, that perhaps the crowd's derision was well-deserved, for my odd appearance could hardly do credit to our cause. I tried to take my mind off it by concentrating on holding the banner steady, and listening to the band in front as it changed from *The Sash my Father wore* to *Dolly's Brae*,[16] while the band behind bombarded us with:

On the green grassy slopes of the Boyne,
Where King Billy and his men they did join,
And they fought for our glorious deliverance
On the green grassy slopes of the Boyne.

The parade always included some Orange champion dressed in 17th-century clothes and riding on a white horse to conjure before our very eyes a vision of King Billy himself. But on the Easter Tuesday when I limped along in plimsolls the day's rewarding feature was to see the white horse rear up on his hind legs and throw the rider. He was a little, wide-moustached man, rather like the one in the famous 19th-century cartoon of Lord Randolph Churchill as 'King Randolph crossing the Boyne'.[17] Off he went tumbling to the ground, his elaborate peruke[18] flying. While two St. John's Ambulance nurses rushed to gather him up, we speculated on the certainty that the Mickeys had attempted an assassination.

Only one real assassination took place before my eyes on an Orange Easter outing. Some of my fellow Lodgemen from Sandy Row set fire to a hayrick and out of the holocaust dashed a rabbit. Better sport than hay-burning ensued, and in a few minutes the poor creature was dead, wounded from the things thrown at it and from the pursuers' boots. When the warm, furry football was left to go cold, and the louts went off in search of other fun, I gathered the rabbit up, happy to be alone so that I could bury it in a wood. I took the red-white-and-blue rosette from my lapel and gave the rabbit a good Protestant funeral. And in my heart I could not forgive the boys of Sandy Row for killing it.

Part of the day's thrill included leaning out of the train window to pick out which of the houses speeding by belonged to the Catholics. We could spot them easily enough for their gables, like ours, were painted. But the Mickeys' walls bore different signs — 'Up the I.R.A.', 'Remember 1916', 'Silence is Golden'. The sign of the cross would appear on any blank space, and worse than any of them, 'God bless the Pope'.

The Pope! How we feared and hated him, we thought the Pope more terrible than Hitler when that German came to our notice, and certainly a greater evil than his disciple, Mr. de Valera. From the safety of the passing train we could boldly hurl abuse at the Mickeys' houses and their papish murals. Pushing to get a space at the compartment window we shouted 'To Hell with the Pope', a

14. Close-fitting trousers, originally of tartan.
15. Light, rubber-soled canvas shoes, worn for playing sports.
16. Famous Orange songs from the nineteenth century.
17. Lord Randolph Churchill (1849-95) opposed Home Rule and made a speech in Belfast in which he used the slogan 'Ulster will fight; Ulster will be right' — thereafter a loyalist watchword.
18. wig.

devout prayer on Ulster lips and favourite one. As late as 1951 a member of parliament built a climax into an election speech with 'God save the King, and to Hell with the Pope'.

But God had not left us defenceless against the dreaded Roman Pontiff. He had sent us Lord Carson to secure our Ulster freedom. Lord Carson was dead, and when the C.L.B. parade brought me to St. Anne's Cathedral, I sat with great awe near the new tomb.[19] He was another of the four-and-twenty elders mentioned in the *Book of Revelation*, and would be found sitting on God's right hand at the Judgement Day. The least religiously or politically minded knew about Lord Carson as did the fervent, and all knew the song,

Edward Carson had a cat,
He sat it by the fender,
And every time it caught a mouse,
It shouted, 'No Surrender'.

Our rhymes were like calypsos, endless, ingenious if monotonous, and dealing with everyday events whether political or not. Whenever anything new happened, then we found doggerel for the occasion. Mr. Baldwin and an urging on to fight in Abyssinia appeared at one time.[20] Mrs. Simpson[21] became the theme of endless variations. How our mothers had idolized the Prince of Wales! And although pictures of the Princesses, Elizabeth and Margaret Rose, with their corgies in 'Y Bwthyn Bach', the Welsh cottage,[22] now filled the photograph frames in the parlour, we could sense the survival of the liking for Prince Eddie. Often the only contact maintained with the exile was through the medium of the Sunday papers. We scanned the pages for scandal or pictures.

Reaction to any incident concerning Protestant or Roman Catholic was always violent, nothing escaped notice and comment. When the new king ascended the throne his was our forsworn loyalty. And yet, in spite of such entrenched opinion, our ignorance of the Catholic world was profound. I for instance, believed that Mickeys existed only in parts of Belfast and nowhere else except the Free State and Rome itself.

That many Catholics were living in London, or were allowed to live in London with our Protestant king, seemed impossible. The idea of a papist cathedral near the gates of Buckingham Palace would have been laughed at with scorn. So thought I, until Coronation year.[23] The celebrations burst over the city like a great coloured rocket, exploding in the drabness of our lives with a million sparks, a spectrum of excitement. Belfast went mad with patriotism. Even the Plymouth Brethren[24] so immured to anything but 'the word', published a coronation photograph on their Sunday tract.

Then we were presented with a magnificent coronation book, with close details of the ceremony, as well as pictures and diagrams of the important personages and Westminster Abbey, where it had all taken place. We prized the rare possession, and why not — for apart from religious story-books won as Sunday School prizes, hymn-books, and a vast collection of Bibles, New Testaments and Books of Common Prayer, it was the only real book in the house.

But through the coronation book I learned of what seemed a terrible betrayal. Included in the pictures of the royalty involved was one of the Duke of Norfolk greeting the two princesses.[25] In a blood-curdling Orange sermon we heard about the subtleties of Catholic scheming, and the preacher had included Norfolk by implication. And there he was, a Mickey, shaking the hand of the heir to the Protestant throne, King Billy's successor!

But there were other, worse things of sinister import. Not only did he hold the office of Earl Marshal (we did not know what this was, but no matter) but he was head of the nobility. If all the House of Windsor died, or were deliberately got out of the way, the Duke would be king, and the glorious freedom of Boyne Water would indeed be lost!

19. Sir Edward Carson (1854-1935), leader of the unionists against Home Rule from 1910. CLB is an acronym for Church Lads' Brigade.
20. Stanley Baldwin (1867-1947), English prime minister in 1936 at the time of the abdication crisis and the Abyssinian War, which led to the annexation of Abyssinia by Italy.
21. King Edward VIII of England abdicated in December 1936 and married Mrs Wallis Simpson, an American divorcee, the following June. He was succeeded by his brother, George VI, and took the title of the Duke of Windsor.
22. The daughters of George VI, Elizabeth (now Elizabeth II) and Princess Margaret. Their corgi dogs and Welsh cottage were part of the royal family image.
23. Elizabeth II came to the throne in 1952 but her coronation was in June 1953.
24. A calvinistic, millenarian sect, founded in Dublin in 1827.
25. The Duke of Norfolk, a catholic, was in charge of administrative and ceremonial arrangements of Queen Elizabeth II's coronation.

How I imagined Norfolk to be scheming and counter-scheming to win the crown, and send the country back to the days of Bloody Mary,[26] whose history besides that of Protestant martyrs we had heard in school. Perhaps Norfolk would one day buy the confidence of a Buckingham Palace servant, who guarded the King night and day, and persuade him to steal the crown. I could see the vast, richly draped bedchamber, the Yeomen of the Guard,[27] and tall plumed soldiers standing round the sleeping monarch, and his crown hanging on the end of his bed, next to his long underpants. The crown gone, life for us would be over. Was not that the reason why my mother, every year when the backyard was whitewashed, got a neighbour to freshen up the painted crown on the wall?

Such a pity for the lovely book to be spoilt like this. We would have liked to rip out Norfolk's picture and burn it, but this could not be done for the Princesses were on the same page and the King on the other side, and to remove them would be disrespectful. In fact, reflection showed it would have been disloyal, just as disloyal as the Mickeys putting their postage stamps on letters upside down as an insult to the Protestant throne. Instead, we gave the Duke a pair of horns and a nice tail with an arrow point sticking outside his rich coronation robes.

26. Mary (1542-87), queen of Scots, scourge of protestants during her reign (1542-67).
27. The bodyguard of the British monarch. Founded in 1485 and now retained for ceremonial functions.

FRANK O'CONNOR

(1903-66)

from: AN ONLY CHILD (1961)

[O'Connor's account of his youth in Cork is memorable for its portrayal of the wild and amateurish spirit that informed the country before the new state quenched it with the assault on the Four Courts that began the bitter Civil War. He blends this narrative with the story of his own growth as a writer under the tutelage of Daniel Corkery, the formidably impressive figure who presided over the emergence of the new regional literature that O'Connor and Seán O Faoláin were to dominate.]

AFTER AUGHRIM'S GREAT DISASTER

15

Once again I was without a job. Like the old men whose landladies and daughters-in-law turned them out in the mornings, I made the Public Library my headquarters, and continued to read through the advertisements for a smart boy, though I realized that I was ceasing to be a boy and would probably never be smart. Then I went out and wandered aimlessly about the town in hope of meeting someone who would talk to me, and even maybe give me a cigarette. It was a dreary existence, because Father kept on asking what I was going to do with myself, and I had no notion. It was no use telling him that eventually I hoped to find a job that would suit my peculiar brand of education or meet some rich girl who would recognize my talents and keep me in decent comfort till I established myself. She didn't have to be *very* rich; my needs were simple; only a trousers without a patch on the seat of it, so that I could be seen with her without embarrassment, and an occasional packet of cigarettes. Father, having returned from the War with a disability pension to add to his service pension, was past arguing with — a man who had really set himself up for life!

It was a period of political unrest, and, in a way, this was a relief, because it acted as a safety valve for my own angry emotions. Indeed, it would be truer to say that the Irish nation and myself were both engaged in an elaborate process of improvization. I was improvizing an education I could not afford, and the country was improvizing a revolution it could not afford. In 1916 it had risen to a small, real revolution with uniforms and rifles, but the English had brought up artillery that had blown the centre of Dublin flat, and shot down the men in uniform. It was all very like myself and the Christian Brothers. After that, the country had to content itself with a make-believe revolution, and I had to content myself with a make-believe education, and the curious thing is that it was the make-believe that succeeded.

The elected representatives of the Irish people (those who managed to stay out of gaol) elected what they called a government, with a Ministry of Foreign Affairs that tried in vain to get Woodrow Wilson[1] to see it, a Ministry of Finance that exacted five to ten pounds from small shopkeepers who could ill afford it, a Ministry of Defence that tried to buy old-fashioned weapons at outrageous prices from shady characters, and a Ministry of Home Affairs that established courts of justice with part-time Volunteer policemen and no gaols at all.

It all began innocently enough. People took to attending Gaelic League concerts at which performers sang *She Is Far from the Land*, recited *Let Me Carry Your Cross for Ireland, Lord*, or played *The Fox Chase* on the elbow pipes, and armed police broke them up. I remember one that I attended in the town park. When I arrived, the park was already occupied by police, so after a while the crowd began to drift away towards the open country up the river. A mile or so up it reassembled on the river-bank, but by this time most of the artistes had disappeared. Somebody who knew me asked for a song. At fourteen or fifteen I was delighted by the honour and tried to sing in Irish a seventeenth-century outlaw song about 'Sean O'Dwyer of the Valley'.[2] I broke down after the first verse — I always did break down whenever I had to make any sort of public appearance because the contrast between what was going on in my head and what was going on in the real world was too much for me — but it didn't matter much. At any moment the police might appear, and this time there could be real bloodshed. It was sheer obstinacy that had driven respectable people to walk miles just to attend a concert they were not very interested in, and they paid their sixpences and went home, rightly feeling that they were the real performers.

It was the same at Mass on Sunday. The bishop, Daniel Coholan[3] — locally known as 'Danny Boy' — was a bitter enemy of all this pretence, and every Sunday we had to be ready for a diatribe at Mass. It was as upsetting as discovering that the Invisible Presences still regarded us as traitors, for, though I knew that Ellen Farrell and her husband had defied the Church in Parnell's day, I had had no expectation of ever having to do so. The priest would turn on the altar or ascend the pulpit and start the familiar rigmarole about 'defiance of lawful government', and some young man would rise from his seat and move into the nave, genuflect and leave the church. Suddenly every eye would be turned on him, and even the priest would fall silent and wait for the interruption to end. Then there would be a shuffling of feet in one of the aisles, and a girl would rise, genuflect and leave as well. Sometimes this went on for minutes till a considerable group had left. They stood and talked earnestly in the chapel yard, all of them declared rebels, some perhaps marked down for assassination, till the priest finished his harangue and they went back. Naturally, I always joined them, hoping for a nod or a smile from one of them.

It was childish, of course, but so was everything else about the period, like the little grocery shop you saw being repainted and the name on the fascia board changed from 'J. Murphy' to 'Sean O'Murchadha'. One can still almost date that generation by its Liams, Seans, and Peadars. I suspect that in those few years more books were published in Ireland than in any succeeding twenty years. Not good books, God knows, any more than the little papers that kept on appearing and being suppressed were good papers. But they expressed the mind of the time. One paper I still remember fondly because it proposed that English as a 'secondary' language be dropped in favour of French. In those days it struck me as an excellent idea. The impossible, and only the impossible, was law. It was in one way a perfect background for someone like myself who had only the impossible to hope for.

1. It was, in fact, Irish-American pressure that forced the question to Wilson's reluctant attention. See A. Ward, *Ireland and Anglo-American Relations 1899-1921* (London: Weidenfeld and Nicolson, 1961).
2. A popular rebel song, translated in the nineteenth century by Thomas Furlong, more generally known as 'Sean O'Dwyer of the Glen'.
3. Daniel Cohalan (or Coholan) (1859-1952), catholic bishop of Cork 1916-52, was an outspoken critic of the policy of reprisal, carried out by both sides, during the War of Independence. He declared that anyone killing from ambush would be excommunicated, and his life was threatened by the IRA. He also condemned the British government for allowing Terence MacSwiney to die on hunger-strike, although the condemnation came eight years after the event.

Then the real world began to catch up with the fantasy. The Lord Mayor, Thomas MacCurtain, was murdered by English police in his own home before the eyes of his wife; another Lord Mayor, Terence MacSwiney, was elected in his place and promptly arrested.[4] He went on hunger strike and died in Brixton Gaol. Mother and I were among those who filed past his coffin as he lay in state in the City Hall in his volunteer uniform; the long, dark, masochistic face I had seen only a few months before as he chatted with Corkery by the New Bridge. Years later I talked with a little country shopkeeper from North Cork who had organized a company of Volunteers in his home town, and been so overawed by the tall, dark young man who cycled out from the city to inspect them that he was too shy to ask where MacSwiney was spending the night. Long after, cycling home himself, he saw someone lying in a field by the roadside, and, getting off, found MacSwiney asleep in the wet grass with nothing but an old raincoat round him. That vision of MacSwiney had haunted him through the years of disillusionment.

Curfew was imposed, first at ten, then at five in the afternoon. The bishop excommunicated everyone who supported the use of physical force, but it went on just the same. One night shots were fired on our road and a lorry halted at the top of the square. An English voice kept on screaming hysterically 'Oh, my back! my back!' but no one could go out through the wild shooting of panic-stricken men. Soon afterwards the military came in force, and from our back door we saw a red glare mount over the valley of the city. For hours Father, Mother, and I took turns at standing on a chair in the attic, listening to the shooting and watching the whole heart of the city burn.[5] Father was the most upset of us, for he was full of local pride, and ready to take on any misguided foreigner or Dublin jackeen who was not prepared to admit the superiority of Cork over all other cities. Next morning, when I wandered among the ruins, it was not the business district or the municipal buildings that I mourned for, but the handsome red-brick library that had been so much a part of my life from the time when as a small boy I brought back my first Western adventure story over the railway bridges. Later I stood at the corner by Dillon's Cross where the ambush had been and saw a whole block of little houses demolished by a British tank. One had been the home of an old patriot whom my grandparents called 'Brienie Dill'. A small, silent crowd was held back by soldiers as the tank lumbered across the pavement and thrust at the wall until at last it broke like pie crust and rubble and rafters tumbled. It made a deep impression on me. Always it seemed to be the same thing: the dark, shrunken face of MacSwiney in the candle-light and the wall that burst at the thrust of the tank; 'the splendour falls'[6] and 'There is no such thing in business as an out-and-out free gift'. It was like a symbolic representation of what was always happening to myself, and it seemed as though Ireland did not stand a much better chance. The material world was too strong for both of us.

All the same I could not keep away from Ireland, and I was involved in most of the activities of that imaginative revolution — at a considerable distance, of course, because I was too young, and anyway, I had Father all the time breathing down my neck. In the absence of proper uniform our Army tended to wear riding breeches, gaiters, a trench coat, and a soft hat usually pulled low over one eye, and I managed to scrape up most of the essential equipment, even when I had to beg it, as I begged the pair of broken gaiters from Tom MacKernan. I conducted a complicated deal for the Ministry of Defence and bought a French rifle from a man who lived close to Cork Barrack, though, when I had risked a heavy sentence by bringing it home down my trouser leg, all the time pretending I had just met with a serious accident, it turned out that there wasn't a round of ammunition in Ireland to fit it. When the British burned and looted Cork and encouraged the slum-dwellers to join in the looting, I was transferred to the police and put to searching slums in Blarney Lane for jewellery and furs. In a back room in Blarney Lane we located a

4. Thomas MacCurtain (1884-1920), first republican lord mayor of Cork, was murdered on 20 March 1920 by members of the Royal Irish Constabulary. Five months later one of the officers charged with the murder was shot dead in Lisburn, Co. Antrim.

Terence MacSwiney, MacCurtain's successor, was arrested and embarked on a 74-day hunger-strike in Brixton Prison in London. His hunger-strike and death attracted international attention and the condemnation of the British government.

5. British forces burned down and looted the central part of Cork in December 1920, shortly after suffering a severe reversal at an IRA ambush in Kilmichael.

6. Tennyson, from the Introductory Song to *The Princess* (3rd ed. 1850): 'The splendour falls on castle walls'.

mink coat which the woman who lived there said had just been sent her by her sister in America. Being a polite and unworldly boy of seventeen, I was quite prepared to take her word for it, but my companion said she hadn't a sister in America, and, shocked by her untruthfulness, I brought the coat back to its rightful owners. That she might have needed it more than they didn't occur to me; I remembered only that I was now a real policeman, and acted as I felt a good policeman should act. When Belfast was boycotted during the anti-Catholic pogroms,[7] I was sent with one or two others to seize a load of Belfast goods at the station where I had worked a year before. The Belfast goods mysteriously turned out to be a furniture van, but you couldn't take me in like that. Belfast businessmen were very cunning and besides I had my orders. So we made the poor van driver and his horse trudge all the way to Glanmire, miles down the river, and only when he opened it up did we realize that it contained nothing but the furniture of some Catholic family flying from the pogroms.

It was in this atmosphere that I produced my second work, which — as may be understood — was a translation into Irish of Du Bellay's sonnet, *'Heureux Qui Comme Ulysse'*, well spoken of in George Wyndham's chatty book on the Pleiade.[8] I was probably deeply moved by Du Bellay's sentiments, for, being a great wanderer in my own imagination, I took a deep interest in the feelings of returned travellers. It is probably a recurring fantasy of the provincial, for one friend whom I made later — the most conscientious of officials — never read anything but sea stories, and from Corkery's novel, *The Threshold of Quiet*[9] — itself full of sailors and ships — I can still quote his excellent translation of an inferior French sonnet: 'Returned at last from lands we yearn to know.'

But this sonnet of mine is another triumph of mind over matter, and, so far as I know, unique in literature, because it is a translation from one language the author didn't know into another that he didn't know — or at best, knew most imperfectly. This was obscured when the poem was published in one of the political weeklies that were always appearing and disappearing as the English caught up with them because *both* languages were even more unknown to editor and printer; and the only thing that could be perceived from the resulting mess was that, whatever the damn thing meant, it must be a sonnet; octet and sestet were unmistakably distinguished. However, a journalist in the *Sunday Independent*, mad with patriotic and linguistic enthusiasm, hailed it as a 'perfect translation'. It was a period when journalists could improvize a literature as lightly as country clerks improvized government departments. The occasion brought forth the man — a view of history I have always been rather doubtful of.

I haunted the streets for Corkery till I finally trapped him one day by the Scots Church at the foot of Summerhill and casually showed him the cutting from the *Sunday Independent*. He asked if I had the translation with me, and curiously I had that too. He read it carefully with one eye half closed, not commenting too much on the grammar, which was probably invisible through the typographical errors, and said judicially that it *was* a beautiful translation. At any rate, he apparently decided that, since what could not be cured must be endured, he had to admit me to his own little group. After all, I was now a published author.

He lived in a small suburban house on Gardiner's Hill with his mother and sister, surrounded by books and pictures. Over the mantelpiece was a large water colour of his own of a man with a scythe on Fair Hill, overlooking the great panorama of the river valley. Inside the door of the living room was a bust of him by his friend, Joe Higgins, which — if my memory of it is correct — is the only likeness of him that captures all his charm. He presided over his little group from a huge Morris chair with a detachable desk that he had made for himself (he was an excellent craftsman, having been brought up to the trade, and once told me in his oracular way that 'nobody had ever met a stupid carpenter', which I later found to be untrue).

He had a good deal of the harshness and puritanism of the provincial intellectual which I share. As those brought up to wealth and rank tend to under-rate them, people accustomed from childhood to an intellectual atmosphere can take classical

7. As a reaction to the anti-catholic pogroms in Belfast in 1920, goods from the North were boycotted in the South from 1920 to 1922.
8. Joachim du Bellay (1522-60) produced the first sonnet sequence in French — *L'Olive* — in 1549-50. La Pléiade was a group of seven French writers, named after the constellation of the Pleiades, and led by Ronsard. The group sought to promote the French language to a status equal to that of the classical languages and wrote poetry in the metres and style of the ancient Greeks and Romans. George Wyndham (1863-1913), chief secretary for Ireland 1900-05, published *Ronsard and La Pléiade* in 1906.
9. *The Threshold of Quiet* (1917) was Corkery's second book.

standards lightly and permit themselves to be entertained by mere facility; not those who have had to buy them dear. Once, when I was working on the railway, and had spent a whole week's pocket money on Wilde's *Intentions*, I met Corkery and he glanced at the book and shook his head. 'It'll ruin whatever style you have,' he said, and even the suggestion that I might have a style did not make up to me for the realization that once again I had backed the wrong horse.

Most of his friends belonged to a little group that had worked with him when he ran a tiny theatre in Queen Street. The most faithful visitor was Denis Breen, a schoolteacher like himself, who had provided the music and married one of the actresses. He was a big, emotional man with a fat, sun-coloured face, clear, childish blue eyes, and a red moustache that he apparently cultivated for the sole purpose of eating it — a face Franz Hals would have loved. At Gaelic League meetings he roared down patriotic souls who decried English music and talked of the greatness of Byrd, Dowland, and Purcell,[10] whom none of us had ever heard of. He also professed to be an atheist, which was rather like proclaiming yourself a Christian in modern China, and the defensiveness this had induced in him was reflected in everything he did and said. He had a great contempt for our little colony of German musicians, whom he spoke of as though they were Catholic priests, as 'bleddy eejits'. They, more objectively, spoke of him as a genius without musical training. It might be fairer to say that his temperament was too immoderate for the precise and delicate work of the artist — the very opposite of Corkery's. The two men were always arguing, Corkery gently and inquiringly, Breen uproariously and authoritatively, something like this. 'Well, on the other hand, would it not be possible to say . . .?' 'Me dear man, it's possible to say anything, if you're fool enough.' I listened in shame for the whole human race to think that anyone could be so presumptuous as to disagree with Corkery.

I did not like Breen. I was connected with him through two coincidences: one that he had taught me for a couple of days before I left Blarney Lane for good, and even in that short time he had beaten me (Irish teachers, like American policemen, never having learned that to go about armed is not the best way of securing obedience and respect); the other was that my mother and his mother, who kept a little sweet shop at the gate of the University, had been friends. *His* mother had told *my* mother that even when he was a small boy no one could control him. He would get hungry at night, go down to the shop for biscuits, sample every tin and leave them all open, so that by morning her stock was ruined. Even when I knew him he would begin his tea by eating all the sweet cakes in case anyone else took a fancy to them. He was greedy with a child's greed, shouted everyone down with what he thought 'funny' stories or denunciations of the 'bleddy eejits' who ran the country or its music, and battered a Beethoven sonata to death with his red eyebrows reverently raised, believing himself to be a man of perfect manners, liberal ideas, and perfect taste. All of which, of course, he was, as I learned later when we became friends, for though his wife and my mother would look blank while he ate all the confectionery and then shouted for more; and though afterwards he hammered Wolf's *An Die Geliebte*[11] unconscious; he struck out the last chords as only a man who loved music could do it, scowling and muttering: 'Now listen to the bloody stars!' He quarrelled bitterly with me after the first performance of a play called *The Invincibles*[12] because he had convinced himself that I had caricatured him in the part of Joe Brady, the leader of the assassins — a brave and simple man driven mad by injustice — and though at the time I was disturbed because such an idea had never occurred to me, it seems to me now that the characters in whom we think we recognize ourselves are infinitely more revealing of our real personalities than those in which someone actually attempts to portray us.

But Corkery's greatest friend was Sean O'Faolain,[13] who was three years older than I and all the things I should have wished to be — handsome, brilliant, and, above all, industrious. For Corkery, who loved application, kept on rubbing it in that I didn't work as O'Faolain did. Once the three of us met on Patrick's Bridge after Corkery and O'Faolain had attended a service at the

10. William Byrd (1543-1623), John Dowland (*c.* 1563-1626) and Henry Purcell (*c.* 1659-95). Dowland, the greatest lutenist of his age, was born in Dalkey, Co. Dublin.

11. Hugo Wolf (1860-1903), Austrian composer, the last great exponent of German *lieder*. *An Die Geliebte* is a setting of a poem by Eduard Friedrich Mörike (1804-75).

12. *The Invincibles* (1828), a play by Thomas Morton. O'Connor and Hugh Hunt together wrote a play, *The Invincibles*, produced at the Abbey Theatre in 1937.

13. Seán O'Faoláin (b. 1900) changed his name, John Whelan, to the Irish form. He was influenced in this by Corkery.

cathedral, and when O'Faolain went off in his home-spun suit, swinging his ash-plant, Corkery looked after him as I had once seen him look after Terence MacSwiney and said: 'There goes a born literary man!' For months I was mad with jealousy.

The first book I took from Corkery's bookcase was a Browning. It was characteristic of my topsy-turvy self-education that I knew by heart thousands of lines in German and Irish, without really knowing either language, but had never heard of Browning, or indeed of any other English poet but Shakespeare, whom I didn't think much of. But my trouble with poetry was that of most auto-didacts. I could not afford books, so I copied and memorized like mad. It is a theory among scholars that all great periods of manuscript activity coincide with some impending social disaster and that scribes are like poor Jews in the midst of a hostile community, gathering up their few little treasures in the most portable form before the next pogrom. Obviously I anticipated the disaster of the Irish Civil War, because I never seemed to possess anything unless I had written it down and learned it by heart, and though I scorned what I thought mediocre verse, and never bothered to acquire anything that had not been approved by the best authorities, the authorities themselves proved most unreliable, and for every good poem I learned, I learned six bad ones. Unlike the poor Jew, I could not throw away the imitation pearls,[14] so, though my taste in poetry improved, my memory refused to adapt itself, and when it should have been producing masterpieces, it would suddenly take things into its own hands and produce something frightful by some minor Georgian poet like Drinkwater.[15] Describing the death of a neighbour, a small boy in our locality drew his hand across his throat and said darkly: 'De woman went before her God full up to *dat* in whisky.' I shall go before mine full up to *that* of bad poetry.

Music was different and much more difficult because I had no standards at all. When people played or sang music-hall songs I behaved as I did when they told dirty stories and either left the room or read a book, but I could not go out in the evening without passing a neighbour's house where an old-fashioned horn-gramophone bellowed songs from *The Arcadians*[16] and, in spite of the fact that the Christian Brothers thought I had a defective ear, I picked them up and — like the bad poetry — I have them still. When I became friends with a young fellow called Tom MacKernan, who drilled beside me in the Volunteers and played the fiddle, I got him to play me certified classical tunes from his violin book. I even got him to lend me an old fiddle and a tutor, but I could not make head or tail of staff notation. When I met Jack Hendrick, whose brother was a singer, I got him to teach me the songs his brother sang at musical competitions like *Where'er You Walk* and *Am Stillen Herd*,[17] though I still could not understand key changes and thought he was probably singing out of tune. Corkery took me a couple of times to real piano recitals by Tilly Fleischmann and Geraldine Sullivan, but, though I read the programme notes like mad — they were usually by Corkery's friend, Father Pat MacSwiney — and pretended to myself that I could recognize the moment when 'the dawn wind wakes and sleeping leaves, and these, tapping at the window pane, rouse the joyous maiden who has been dreaming of her secret lover', it always turned out that I had just been listening to the climax in which 'Smiling, she leans through the window and plucks a rose for her hair'. It mortified me to see all those educated people who had no difficulty in distinguishing the dawn wind rising from a girl plucking a rose for her hair and made me feel that life was really unfair.

I had no luck with music till Corkery bought a gramophone from Germany immediately after the 1914-18 War, when the rate of exchange was favourable, and with it a selection of records that included Bach's Sixth Cello Sonata, a couple of Beethoven symphonies, Mozart's Violin Concerto in A, Schubert's 'Unfinished' and Strauss's *Till Eulenspiegel*. I gave Strauss up as a bad job because it would clearly not be portable in any future pogrom, but I practically learned the Seventh Symphony[18] and the Mozart Concerto by heart, and for years judged everything by them. I can now

14. A confused memory, perhaps of the lines from *Othello*, V. 5.46-47:
'Like the base Indian, threw a pearl away
Richer than all his tribe;'
15. John Drinkwater (1882-1937), whose work appeared in all five volumes of the famous anthology, *Georgian Poetry* (1912-22).
16. An Edwardian musical comedy by Lionel Monckton (1861-1924).
17. 'Where'er You Walk' is from Handel's musical drama *The Story of Semele* (now usually called *Semele*), set to a text by William Congreve (1743). The words are by Alexander Pope. 'Am Stillen Herd' is from Act I, Scene 3 of Wagner's *Die Meistersinger*.
18. Presumably Beethoven's.

read second-rate books without getting sick, but I still cannot listen to mediocre music. I had too much trouble escaping from it.

Corkery took me sketching with him as well, but I was never much good at that; 'it's like me with my game leg entering for the hundred yards,' he said kindly, blaming it on my sight, but it wasn't my sight. It was my undeveloped visual sense. The imagination, because it is by its nature subjective, pitches first on the area of the intimate arts — poetry and music. Painting, which is more objective and critical, comes later. Still, that did not keep him from getting me into the School of Art, where I spent my time copying casts, drawing from the male model, and arguing like mad with my teacher, who said that Michelangelo was 'very coarse'. Apparently, Corkery's idea was that since I could never get into a university, I should become an art teacher, and he even arranged a scholarship in London for me. But I was in a frenzy to earn a little money, and, instead, like a fool, I applied for a scholarship to a Gaelic League Summer School in Dublin that had been formed to train teachers of Irish, who would later cycle about the country from village to village, teaching in schools and parish halls. It sounded exactly the sort of life for an aspiring young writer who wanted to know Ireland as Gorky[19] had known Russia.

The Summer School was held in the Gaelic League headquarters in Parnell Square, and the head of it was a sly, fat rogue of a West Cork man called Hurley, who was later Quarter-Master General of the Free State Army. I did not like Dublin, probably because most of the time I was light-headed with hunger. I lodged in a Georgian house on the Pembroke Road, and, having rarely eaten in any house other than my own, I contented myself with a cup of tea and a slice of bread for breakfast. I decided that the chamber pot in my bedroom was for ornament rather than use. I was even more scared of restaurants than of strange houses. I had never eaten in one except when Mother took me to Thompson's café in Patrick Street for a cup of coffee — her notion of high life — so I lived entirely on coffee and buns in Bewley's. It was to be years before I worked up the courage to go into a real restaurant. Besides, the scholarship did not amount to more than the price of modest lodgings, and I needed every penny I could spare for the books I could pick up cheap at the stalls on the quays. I could not keep away from them. There were books there the like of which one never saw in a Cork bookstore. It was there that I picked up for a few pence the little *Selected Poems of Browning* published by Smith, Elder, which for me has always been one of the great books of the world, and when the hunger got too much for me I would recite to myself: 'Heap cassia, sandal-buds and stripes of labdanum and aloeballs'[20] as though it were a spell.

Far from being recognized as a genius at the school, I was obviously regarded as a complete dud. The reason for this did not dawn on me till years had gone by. All the other students had had a good general education, some a university education. I talked Irish copiously, but nobody had explained to me the difference between a masculine and feminine noun, or a nominative and dative case. Nobody explained to me then either, probably because the problem of a completely uneducated boy masquerading as a well-educated one was outside everyone's experience.

And yet, the whole country was doing the same, and Hurley, who gave the impression of having served his time in a West Cork drapery store, was on his way to one of the highest ranks in the army. My friends in the school were a Dubliner called Byrne and a Kerryman called Kavanagh. Byrne was doubly endeared to me because, though only a boy scout, he had already been involved in a pistol fight with a police patrol. Some hunger striker had died in prison and was being given a public funeral, so the three of us demanded the afternoon off to attend it, and fell foul of Hurley, who objected to what he called 'politics' in the school. When the time for the funeral came the three of us got up to leave the class, and Hurley, in a rage, dismissed it. We were expecting trouble, and Byrne had a revolver. The imaginary revolution was taking shape as well.

I was lucky to return to Cork with a certificate that made me a qualified teacher of Irish — which I was not — and for a few weeks I cycled eight or ten

19. Maxim Gorky (1868-1936), Russian novelist, dramatist and short-story writer, known for his depiction of the outcasts of society. His sympathy for Russia and the 1917 Revolution is manifest in all his writings.

20. Browning's *Paracelsus* (1835) Part IV. The Smith, Elder edition was published in 1895.

miles out of the city in the evenings to teach in country schools by lamp-light. But already even this was becoming dangerous, and soon curfew put an end to my new career as well. I seemed to be very unlucky with my jobs.

At the same time I was making friends of a different type. One evening a pale, thin-lipped young clerk, in an insurance office, called Jack Hendrick came to see me with an introduction from Corkery and proposed that the two of us should start a literary and debating society. Our conversation was rather at cross-purposes, for he did not seem to have read anything but d'Israeli's *Curiosities of Literature*[21] and he continued to quote this to me as I quoted Turgenev and Dostoevsky to him. He didn't seem to know about them, and I had never heard of d'Israeli, so I agreed to borrow it from him and meanwhile lent him Turgenev's *Virgin Soil* and Gogol's *Taras Bulba*.[22] When we met again I admitted that I was bored with d'Israeli, and he said he thought Turgenev was 'cold'. We didn't seem to be getting anywhere, but I needed a friend too badly to reject one merely because he said outrageous things about Turgenev, and Hendrick was exactly the sort of friend I needed because he had every virtue that I lacked and was well-mannered, methodical, cool, and thoughtful. He had a neat, square, erect handwriting that I greatly admired for its legibility, and I set out to imitate it as I had imitated Corkery's monosyllabic articulation, but I was too restive to do anything that required exacting labour, and Hendrick's handwriting was a career in itself.

I explained to him that I now had a chance of a teaching job, but it meant I would have to ride a bicycle, and I had been assured by the man who had tried to teach me that I had no sense of balance and would never be able to ride. I had accepted this without question because it was only one of the dozen things I had been told I couldn't do. I couldn't sing; I couldn't pass an examination; I couldn't persevere at a task — naturally I couldn't ride a bicycle. That evening Hendrick brought his sister's bicycle out the Ballyvolane Road, put me up on it, unclenched my fists on the handlebars, and when we came to the first long hill, gave me a push that sent me flying. I was a mass of bruises when I picked myself up at the foot of the hill, but when I had wheeled back the bicycle, Hendrick, who by this time was sitting on the grass by the roadside, smoking, took out his cigarettes and said with a pale smile: 'Now you know how to ride a bicycle.'

But even this was of less importance to me than the fact that I was beginning to make friends away from my own gas-lamp. It was probably this that Blake had in mind when he said that if only a fool would persevere in his folly he would become a wise man, because sooner or later the imaginative improvization imposes itself on reality. But it is only then that its real troubles begin, when it must learn to restrain itself from imposing too far, and acquire a smattering of the practical sense it has rejected. That, I think, is where the Irish Revolution broke down. The imagination is a refrigerator, not an incubator; it preserves the personality intact through disaster after disaster, but even when it has changed the whole world it has still changed nothing in itself and emerges as a sort of Rip Van Winkle, older in years but not in experience. This sets up a time lag that can never be really overcome.

Friendship did not make me wiser or happier, for years of lonely daydreaming had left me emotionally at the age of ten. I was ashamed to admit that there was anything I didn't know, and one evening when Corkery talked to me about a story of Gorky's in which there was a eunuch, I was too mortified to admit that I didn't know what a eunuch was. I was morbidly sensitive, jealous, exacting, and terrified of strangers. I did not merely make friends; I fell in love, and even the suspicion of a slight left me as frantic as a neurotic schoolgirl. The attitudes of the ghetto survive emancipation, and I had only to enter a strange house or talk to a stranger to make a complete fool of myself. From excessive shyness I always talked too much, usually lost control of myself, and heard myself say things that were ridiculous, false, or base, and afterwards remained awake, raging and sobbing by turns as I remembered every detail of my own awkwardness, lying, and treachery. Years later, when I was earning money, I never went to a strange house without first taking a drink or two to brace me for the ordeal. Whether that was much help or not I do not know. It is enough that the things I said when I was slightly intoxicated were never quite as bad as the things I said when I wasn't.

21. Isaac D'Israeli (1766-1848) published his collections *Curiosities of Literature* in six volumes between 1791 and 1834.
22. Ivan S. Turgenev (1818-83). His novel *Virgin Soil* was published in 1877. Nikolai Gogol (1809-52). His story 'Taras Bulba' was published in *Mirgovod* (1835). Corkery introduced O'Connor and O'Faoláin to the great Russian tradition of the short story.

As if this weren't enough, I was also going through the usual adolescent phase of snobbery and was ashamed of my parents, ashamed of the little house where we lived, and when people called for me, I grabbed my cap and dragged them out anywhere, for fear Father should start telling funny stories about his army days or Mother reveal that she was only a charwoman. With me, of course, this was also complicated by the number of things that really humiliated me, like my clothes, which were decent but patched, and the fact that I could never get on a tram without first scanning the passengers to make sure there was no girl aboard whose fare I should not be able to pay. As a result I never got on a tram at all until the moment it started to move, and tried to find a seat where no one could come and sit beside me. Then if I continued to look out at the street till the conductor had gone by, I was safe.

My fight for Irish freedom was of the same order as my fight for other sorts of freedom. Still like Dolan's ass, I went a bit of the way with everybody, and in those days everybody was moving in the same direction. Hendrick did not get me to join a debating society, but I got him to join the Volunteers. If it was nothing else, it was a brief escape from tedium and frustration to go out the country roads on summer evenings, slouching along in knee breeches and gaiters, hands in the pockets of one's trenchcoat and hat pulled over one's right eye. Usually it was only to a parade in some field with high fences off the Rathcooney Road, but sometimes it was a barrack that was being attacked, and we trenched roads and felled trees, and then went home through the wet fields over the hills, listening for distant explosions and scanning the horizon for fires. It was all too much for poor Father, who had already seen me waste my time making toy theatres when I should have been playing football, and drawing naked men when I should have been earning my living. And this time he did at least know what he was talking about. For all he knew I might have the makings of a painter or writer in me, but, as an old soldier himself, he knew that I would never draw even a disability pension. No good could come of such foolishness, and it would only be the mercy of God if the police at St Luke's didn't blame him for my conduct and write to the War Office to get his pensions stopped. The old trouble about locking the door at night became acute. Ten o'clock was when he went to bed — earlier when curfew was on — and the door had to be fastened for the night: the latch, the lock, the big bolt, and the little bolt. When I knocked, Mother got out of bed to open it, Father shouted at her, and she called back indignantly to him not to wake the neighbours, and whispered in anguish to me: 'Don't answer him whatever he says!' But stung in my pride as a soldier of Ireland, I often did answer back, and then he roared louder than ever that I was 'better fed than taught'. Mother's sympathies were entirely with the revolution, and he would have been more furious still if he had known that not long after she was doing odd errands herself, carrying revolvers and despatches. Or maybe he did know, and, like many another husband, decided to ignore her minor infidelities.

I was changing, but though I did not realize it till much later, Corkery was changing, too, in an infinitely subtler and more significant way, and the man I loved was turning into someone I should not even be able to understand. I was merely puzzled and hurt when one night he said: 'You must remember there are more important things in life than literature.' I knew there weren't, because if there were I should be doing them. That change goes farther back than the period I am writing of, and was not perceptible until years later. It is not in his novel, *The Threshold of Quiet*, but it is already adumbrated in the first story of *A Munster Twilight*.[23] In this a worldly farmer wishes to plough the Ridge of the Saints — sanctified ground — but his old farmhand, steeped in traditional pieties, refuses to do it. He taunts his employer by offering to plough the Ridge if the farmer will put his great sire-horse, Ember, to the plough. At the end of the story the old farmhand yokes the sire-horse and the mare, whose name is Beauty, and goes out at nightfall to plough the Ridge, the horses quarrel and horses and man are hurled together over the cliff.

This is a typical bit of symbolism that seems to sum up a deep personal conflict. It describes the suicidal destruction of the creative faculty as an act of revolt against the worldliness of everyday life. 'There are more important things in life than literature.' Scores of other modern writers like Ibsen and James have used such symbolic equations as a way of trying out their personal problems, but this one seems to me to describe what really

23. The first story of *A Munster Twilight* (1916) is 'The Ploughing of Leaca-na-Naomh'.

happened. It is as though the imaginative improvization of the community had begun to dominate the imaginative improvization of the artist and make its fires seem dim by comparison. Of course there must have been some more immediate cause, and I sometimes wonder whether it was not Corkery's friendship with Thomas MacCurtain and Terence MacSwiney. MacCurtain's murder aroused the country and MacSwiney's death on hunger-strike was watched by the whole world and cost the British Government more than a major military defeat. It seems to me now that Corkery's admiration for the two men may have made him feel that men of action had more to give than the mere artist like himself. His admiration for the men of action is in *The Hounds of Banba*,[24] the book of stories he was writing at the time, and there are stories in this that repeat the symbolic equation of the horses. One, for instance, describes how a jockey, who is also a traditionalist, takes up a bet made by his half-witted employer, rides a famous horse along the cliffs, and then wrestles with the horse and throws him bodily over the edge into the sea. Even in the stories where there is no symbolism there is a celebration of imaginary heroes and an attack on imaginary enemies who are not far removed from windmills. And Corkery knew his windmill-fighters, for once when we were looking at a picture called *Don Quixote* he said sharply: 'Those eyes are wrong. They're looking out. Quixote's eyes looked inward.'

I do not blame myself for not understanding and sympathizing with what was happening to him, because it was precisely the opposite of what was happening to me. He was a man who, by force of character, had dominated physical difficulties, family circumstances, and a provincial environment that would have broken down anyone but a great man. Breen, who gave the impression of being opposed to him, cursed and raged whenever he described Corkery's suffering in the teachers' training college they had attended together, and I am certain that this sprang from Breen's own clear eye and passionate heart rather than from any self-pity on Corkery's part. Nowadays I remember how his mind seemed always to brood on self-control, as when he described how he had written his novel, getting up each morning at six, or wrote to me when I was in prison, quoting Keats on the beneficial effect of a shave and wash-up when one's spirits were low,[25] or praised Michael Collins,[26] who had made himself leader of the whole revolutionary movement because he was up answering letters when everyone else was in bed. He was as shy and reserved as Chekhov and never asked for sympathy, but behind words like these one could detect a whole lifetime of self-control. Yet he did not, as a lesser man might have done, lose generosity in speaking of an enemy or gentleness in rebuking a friend. He would gaze at me gloomily, and predict in his harsh, unmodulated voice that I would go through life without ever finishing anything, and then add 'like Coleridge', awarding me a valuable second prize. I have described how he ticked me off for reading Wilde, because it would injure whatever style I had. Yeats had exactly the same trick. When he was forming his Academy,[27] even before I had published a book, he and I quarrelled about the constitution of the Academy and he muttered: 'Why worry about literary eminence? You and I will provide that.' Of course it was guileful, and in a lesser man it might have been the basest flattery, but I understood it in him as in Corkery as the desperate attempt of the elderly and eminent man to break down the barriers that separated him from youth and awkwardness. Because of that Corkery developed an authority that was like Yeats's. If, as I now fancy, he was impressed by MacSwiney's sacrifice, it was probably because MacSwiney's remarkable self-control and self-denial had given him an authority beyond his intellect and gifts, but Corkery's self-control was of a rarer kind. However little he said, and however insipid what he said might seem, it was on his judgement that we all relied, and I think that in the way of those who combine self-control and humanity, austerity and sweetness, he was full of a consciousness of his own power he would have been much too shy to reveal. Only once did he let anything drop that suggested it, and that was one evening when I suggested that great writers might

24. *The Hounds of Banba* (1920) is a collection of stories about guerrilla activities.

25. Letter 17 September 1819.

26. Michael Collins (1890-1922), president of the supreme council of the IRA during the War of Independence and coordinator of the campaign.

27. The Irish Academy of Letters was founded in 1932 by Yeats and Shaw.

be more careful of what they did and said if only they remembered the sort of people who would write their lives, and he shrugged and replied: 'Well, I know people will write my life ...'

That is the period when I best like to remember him. After a cruel day's teaching he would take his paints and sketchbook and trudge miles into the country with me at his heels. I would quote a line or two of Omar Khayyám, and at once he would take alarm lest any fledgeling of his should be taken in by something less than a masterpiece. 'What *is* it about Fitzgerald[28] that's not quite right?' he would ask, and I, as well-skilled in the responses as any acolyte, would reply: 'Well, it is a bit sugary, isn't it?' 'It is on the sweet side,' he would say thoughtfully, as though the idea had only just occurred to him, and then, seeing the gable of a cottage in the evening light, he would climb laboriously over a stone wall and search for a dry stone to sit on, cracking jokes about his own softness. 'Turner, of course, sat in a wet ditch to paint.' Then, in the late evening he stood at the door of his little house, leaning against the jamb to take the weight from off his bad foot, his hands in his trousers pockets and his small, dark, handsome head thrown lazily back as he talked endlessly about writers and writing, lost to everything else, a man mad on literature. And remembering him like this I find myself humming the song I made Hendrick teach me: *Herr Walther von der Vogelweid, der ist mein Meister gewesen.*[29]

But self-control like his exacts a terrible price from the artist, and already, like the king in his own play, weary of struggle with the world, he must have been brooding on abdication before those who seemed to exercise real authority, even though it could never be more than a shadow of his own.

16

Then came the Truce. It was an extraordinary event that deserves a whole book to itself, though, so far as I know, no one has even tried to describe it. It had all been announced and prepared for, but it was quite impossible to believe it would really happen. Then, a little before noon on Monday, July 11, 1921, when I was still a few months short of eighteen, a slow procession of armoured cars, tanks, and patrols began to move back on Cork Barracks, and I walked along beside it. There were little crowds in every street, all watchful and silent, since everyone realized that anything might yet happen. Then, as the Angelus rang out from the city churches, the barrack gates were thrown open and tanks, armoured cars, officers, and men filed in. Here and there a man would turn and give a derisive hoot at the silent crowd. Then the barrack gates closed, and the crowd began to move away quietly with bewildered looks. Did it really mean that it was all over? That there would be no more five o'clock curfew and that one could walk that night as late as one pleased without being shot? That one could sleep in one's own bed? That it really represented the end of seven hundred years of military occupation, the triumph of the imagination over material power, the impossible become law?

All that perfect summer young men who had been for years in hiding drove about the country in commandeered cars, drinking, dancing, brandishing their guns. In the evening the local Volunteers, their numbers vastly increased by careful young men who were now beginning to think that after all there be something in this for them, drilled openly and learned how to use rifles and machine guns.

And then, in the depth of winter, came the Treaty with England, which granted us everything we had ever sought except an independent republican government and control of the loyalist province of Ulster. The withholding of these precipitated a Civil War, which, in the light of what we know now, might have been anticipated by anyone with sense, for it was merely an extension into the fourth dimension of the improvization that had begun after the crushing of the insurrection in 1916. The Nationalist movement had split up into the Free State Party, who accepted the treaty with England, and the Republicans who opposed it by force of arms, as the Irgun[30] was to do much later in Israel. Ireland had improvized a government, and clearly no government that claimed even a fraction less than the imaginary government had claimed could attract the loyalty of young men and women with imagination. They were like a theatre audience that, having learned to dispense with fortuitous properties, lighting, and scenery and begun to

28. Edward Fitzgerald (1809-73), translator of *The Rubaiyat of Omar Khayyam* (1859).
29. Hans Sachs's song from Wagner's *Die Meistersinger von Nürnberg* (1868).

30. The Irgun Zvai Leumi was the chief guerrilla organization of the Zionist movement under the British mandate in Palestine.

appreciate theatre in the raw, were being asked to content themselves with cardboard and canvas. Where there is nothing, there is reality.

But meanwhile the improvization had cracked: the English could have cracked it much sooner merely by yielding a little to it. When, after election results had shown that a majority of the people wanted the compromise — and when would *they* not have accepted a compromise? — our side continued to maintain that the only real government was the imaginary one, or the few shadowy figures that remained of it, we were acting on the unimpeachable logic of the imagination, that only what exists in the mind is real. What we ignored was that a whole section of the improvization had cut itself adrift and become a new and more menacing reality. The explosion of the dialectic, the sudden violent emergence of thesis and antithesis from the old synthesis, had occurred under our very noses and we could not see it or control it. Rory O'Connor and Melowes [*sic*] in seizing the Four Courts were merely echoing Patrick Pearse and the seizure of the Post Office, and Michael Collins, who could so easily have starved them out with a few pickets, imitated the English pattern by blasting the Four Courts with borrowed artillery.[31] And what neither group saw was that every word we said, every act we committed, was a destruction of the improvization and what we were bringing about was a new Establishment of Church and State in which imagination would play no part, and young men and women would emigrate to the ends of the earth, not because the country was poor, but because it was mediocre. . . .

31. Collins shelled the Four Courts with artillery borrowed from the British, who themselves had shelled the General Post Office six years before.

SEÁN O'FAOLÁIN
(1900-)

from: VIVE MOI! (1964)

[In describing Yeats, O'Faoláin is describing the triumph of a personality who shadowed his whole generation. Yeats was a great founder of organizations and societies that never lived with the same vigour after he had gone. O'Faoláin is fascinated by Yeats's creation of a persona (not to mention the work) and by the manner in which he dominated the literary world.

The passage below occurs towards the end of the work.]

. . . He [Yeats] had been our inspiration and our justification in the sense that all the rest of us younger men and women could not, between us, represent literature with anything like his achievement and authority in the eyes of the public. When he retired to Rapallo to die,[1] and most of his generation had passed away or gone into exile one by one — George Moore, Russell, Forrest Reid, Robert Lynd, Gwynn, Gogarty, Shaw, Desmond McCarthy, Hone, Seumas O'Sullivan — the vitality of the Academy[2] oozed away and, as Lennox Robinson used to say — he was one of the longest-lived of that remarkable generation — there was nothing to do but wait until Time, if it ever did, created new reputations of equal authority.

Time did not and could not. It was not a matter alone of literary achievement. Had, for example, Joyce returned to live in Dublin his presence would have made no difference. For the source of Yeats's authority, like the source of his poetry, was the extraordinary union in his nature of a powerful imagination, the will to enforce it, and a persistent dramatic self-image of himself as seer and leader. It

1. Yeats in fact died in Roquebrune in France.

2. Yeats and Shaw founded the Irish Academy of Letters in 1932. Those in the list who are not represented elsewhere in the anthology are R.W. Lynd (1879-1949), Belfast-born essayist and journalist; S. L. Gwynn (1864-1950), poet, politician and journalist; Desmond McCarthy (1877-1952), literary journalist; Joseph Hone (1882-1959), biographer and critic.

was his plasma, nobody else's. It was the blend that at once bestowed greatness on him and condemned him to loneliness. At this point I have arrested my pen as it was about to write that few knew him as a man; it is more likely that nobody did; indeed, it is unlikely that there was, in the common implication of the word, a man to know. His intimates may have known him as a poet, or a colleague in the theatre, or in the Senate, but it can only have been very much as they might have known a prime minister or a cardinal who, to use a crude phrase, never came off it, never unbuttoned. As there are priests who move, who live within the aura of *l'esprit ecclésiastique,* Yeats moved and lived within *l'esprit poétique*. He had created a mask and had become it, in his every nerve and artery, thought and mood. He was writing an autobiographical testimony, not merely making a poetic flourish, when in 'The Tower', in 1926, he declared his faith, that

Death and life were not
Till man made up the whole,
Made lock, stock and barrel
Out of his bitter soul,
Aye, sun and moon and star, all,
And further add to that
That, being dead, we rise,
Dream and so create
Translunar Paradise.[3]

This is not solipsism, though it is extravagantly near it. He did truly believe that man can not only make 'a superhuman, mirror-resembling dream' but can make it come to pass as reality, if he has the accompanying will. He imagined a theatre, and it grew, not quite his dream yet one that without his dream would not have come to pass at all, and that now, when there is nobody like him to keep on imagining it into life, has virtually passed out. He imagined his Academy, and it became. The strange thing is that he never seemed to realize that his mirror and his dream were indivisible, so that when he was about to leave the fray he could say to Frank O'Connor, 'You will save the Abbey Theatre, and O'Faolain will save the Academy,' as if we could dream his dreams as passionately as he did. We might dream some other dreams but not his. Does this make him a bad builder? I think so. He left no Peter and Paul behind him. He prepared no disciples. He was too aloof....

Yeats loved Ireland, and [in] a sense knew Ireland better than most people, but I do not believe he knew people in Ireland. MacCartan[4] once said an odd but true thing: 'Yeats is much more of a nationalist than Gogarty, but Gogarty is much more Irish.' Meaning that Yeats had Ireland in his soul, but that Gogarty had it in his body. Here is the great Yeats, during the riots over Sean O'Casey's play, coming to the footlights and declaring to the audience with all the magnificence of poet to peasant: 'You have disgraced yourselves again! You have rocked the cradle of a new genius.'[5]

But how else could he rule them, how else preserve his soul in their 'rude, unmannerly town,'[6] except by refusing to know them other than in his imagination of them? As in his 'Easter 1916', where he recalls how he used to meet some of those sixteen executed rebels in the streets before the Rising, and pass on with a nod of the head, or 'polite meaningless words', or think of them as a mocking story to be told at the club:

Being certain that they and I
But lived where motley is worn:
All changed, changed utterly,
A terrible beauty is born.

I have said poet to peasant, reverting to an odd phrase in his 1937 speech[7] describing an I.R.A. ambush as 'a peasant ambush'. It is an old-fashioned word, and the wrong word — there are no peasants in Ireland; there are small tenant farmers — and it is a revealing use of [the] word. I, as I have recounted, once took part, in the hills, in something remotely like an ambush. Many of my friends took part in serious ambushes. Ministers of state, friends of MacCartan, had taken part in ambushes. All peasants? It was not, of course, that Yeats looked down on peasants, of whom, as a boy, he had known many, and been inspired by many, as

3. From Part III of 'The Tower' in the volume *The Tower* (1928).

4. Dr Patrick McCartan (1878-1966), republican, member of the first Dáil Éireann, friend of de Valera, accompanying him on his first trip to the United States.

5. This occurred during the riots at O'Casey's *The Plough and the Stars* at the Abbey Theatre in 1926.

6. A misquote from Yeats's poem 'The People' in *The Wild Swans At Coole* (1919): 'The daily spite of this unmannerly town'.

7. At the Irish Academy's fourth dinner in August 1937, Yeats made a speech in which he used the phrase 'a peasant ambush'.

a poet. It was his way, his poet's way, wise for him, necessary for him, of holding every common fact at a slight distance. It has been observed by critics that he would even, for this, deliberately make some slight, seeming mistake of nomenclature when writing about Irish things, which other readers have too readily ascribed to ignorance; as when the Hag of Beare — in Gaelic, as he must have known well, An Cailleach Beire — is called Clooth-na-Bare,[8] because he preferred the sound of it that way, or the Fianna, or even the Fenians, are called Finians, or the place name Doona is altered to suit his ear in 'The Fiddler of Dooney'. It is interesting to go from that poem which accompanied his last speech, 'The Municipal Gallery Revisited', to the actual pictures he saw and slightly reconstituted. That peasant ambush is not an ambush at all: it is a studio painting of three west-of-Irelanders provided with rifles. Casement is not, in the painting referred to in his poem, half hidden by the bars.[9] He speaks of 'an Abbot or Archbishop with upraised hand blessing the Tricolor'. Why an Abbot? I am not carping about a fine, warm, passionate poem. All I am saying is that this way of moving all things a little out of focus into a slight distance was part of his art of living as well as of writing. It was his need of his nature, as poet and man, to live a foot off the ground, a foot or two, or more, away from common life.

Dear fellow-artist, why so free
With every sort of company,
With every Jack and Jill?
Choose your companions from the best;
Who draws a bucket with the rest
Soon topples down the hill.[10]

But we had marched with Sheila and Sean, taken refuge with them, gone to jail with them, been poor with them, bitter with them, fought with them, toppled with them at times very far down the hill. We had known nobody else but them. We could not walk away from them in his aerial footsteps. We must, at times, have bristled at this withdrawal of his. In those days, heaven help us, we thought of ourselves as the new realists, which we certainly were not in comparison with any other writer in the world, apart from him. We had to deal with much more intractable material than he. His fiddler of Dooney was, for us, at every street corner, in every shop, every office, not at all larger than life, just irreducibly life-size. We knew too damned much about the Jacks and Jills of Ireland.

I would like to have known him, but for all the times we met and worked together I never did know him. I suppose his oldest friend was George Russell (AE). I knew Russell, in the common, intimate, unbuttoned sense in which men know men, and it was apparent that Russell never knew him in that way. One of his latest close companions in Dublin was F. R. Higgins, a good poet and one-time manager of the Abbey Theatre. Fred, a fat, amiable, nerve-ridden, devious, earthy man, and a fine poet, had many puckish stories about their encounters; but they were all those little sidelights with which the favored companion of a great man tries, without much success, to suggest humanity behind greatness. As when he recalled how, while he, Yeats and a third man were discussing some problem, perhaps of the theatre, or of poetry, two Persian cats kept frolicking in heat with one another in a corner of the room, quite unobserved, it seemed, by Yeats, but much to the amusement of Fred; yet when the deep discussion ended and Yeats and he were in the taxi driving away, Yeats murmured as if to himself: 'Yes, Higgins! Cats *are* very interesting creatures,' and resumed the discussion where it had left off. For that matter, I feel sure that Yeats also knew Higgins only in his imagination of him, as when he once said of Fred's frequent visits to his home, 'He comes to me here sweating from his whore!' — a fantasy-image that gave much amusement to the good and most uxorious Higgins when it was repeated back to him; as every such remark made in Dublin is always repeated back to its victim.

He lived on a peak: but there was no pose about him, although he did sometimes act his play and the Dublin gossips always said he was a poseur. Garnett, who met him often in his young London days, was quite certain that he was just a natural dreamer. 'No pose at all!' he once said to me. 'The first time he came to stay with us at the Cearne he had no luggage whatever. I asked him about it. He put his hand absently into his pocket and produced

8. In 'The Hosting of the Sidhe', the first poem in *The Wind Among the Reeds* (1899), Yeats has:
'The host is riding from Knocknarea
And over the grave of Clooth-na-Bare.'
9. The painting is Seán Keating's 'The Men of the West'; the Casement painting is Sir John Lavery's 'The Court of Criminal Appeal'.
10. 'To A Young Beauty' from *The Wild Swans at Coole* (1919).

and gazed at a toothbrush. He had no sense of place or time. I have walked from my place in London to his late at night; he returned with me; I saw him home again; he returned again, talking, talking, completely lost.'

Other poets descend from their peaks to common earth; he never. Even as a critic he was best when to the point, the word, the line, the phrase, the image. Other poets can be men of the reason and the intelligence; he never, except when he unwillingly had to for the purposes of the theatre or to make some philosophical statement, pronouncement or hazard pertinent to the course of his thinking as a poet. Apart from that he loathed, and rightly loathed, the reason, that generalizing, abstracting power that takes from the object its intimate particularity by relegating it to its dull social purpose and category; as was plain also to men like T. E. Hulme, Flint, Bergson, Ezra Pound[11] and all the imagist poets who must have influenced him, also, in the early 1900s; and as is plain, in practice, to every artist. It is something every artist recognizes instinctively: not to see a 'priest' or a 'soldier' or a 'dustman', but to see the faces of Thomas, Richard and Henry; to concentrate on the particular until it becomes almost hallucinatory, to avoid at all costs the purely rational, which turns the hallucination into an essay. (As I, writing like this — inescapably in this kind of book — know that it would be much more interesting to try to describe the peculiar, slanting shape of his eyes, or the long droop of his fingers so well observed by O'Sullivan in the portrait that used to hang in the foyer of the Abbey Theatre.)[12] Yeats, protecting his hallucinations, would never wish, or be able, to communicate with intellectual, organizing men whose role and habit is to turn everything into a generalization, into the sort of blueprint picture of life that, of its nature, obliterates that most interesting part of experience, the particular and the exceptional. He was a poet, for poets, about poetry, a Blakeian creation of his own imagination. I think he probably communicated best with his own like, poets and contemplatives. And yet he might, I have often thought, he just might be a good man to live with marooned on a desert island. Or would I prefer old dirty Jack or sweaty Jill?

11. Ezra Pound (1885-1972), T.E. Hulme (1883-1917) and F.S. Flint (1885-1960) were among the best-known Imagist poets, a group formed before World War I. Pound's anthology *Des Imagistes* (1914) was their manifesto. Henri Bergson (1859-1941) was an influential French philosopher.

12. Seán O'Sullivan's portrait of Yeats still hangs in the foyer of the Abbey.

PATRICK KAVANAGH

(1904-67)

from:
SELF PORTRAIT (1964)

[Kavanagh's repudiation of the Irish Revival was part of his general repudiation of the inauthentic and almost wholly literary versions of Ireland that had become commonplace by mid-century. The adversarial stance, which he so carefully adopted and developed, was the outward aspect of his inner strength as a poet — a strength that had its source in 'learning how not to care'. Kavanagh repudiates a great deal of his own work — the poem *The Great Hunger*, the novel *The Green Fool* — in the course of repudiating the narcissistic idea of the self as such. He saw poetry as a way of discovering the miracle in the ordinary. To do so, he had to travel light — without the Irish Revival baggage, without his own misdirected early work, without the desire to be literary. Then he could be humorous, weightless, free.]

I dislike talking about myself in a direct way. The self is only interesting as an illustration. For some reason, whenever we talk about our personal lives they turn out to be both irrelevant and untrue — even when the facts are right, the mood is wrong.

English publishers and newspapers are mad for personal data, especially about people from Ireland. They love Irishmen. America is now even worse. And the unfortunate peoples of my island home lap up all that vulgarity when it is dished out to them.

The quality that most simple people fear — and by simple people I mean terrified, ignorant people — is the comic spirit, for the comic spirit is the ultimate sophistication which they do not understand and therefore fear.

When, under the evil aegis of the so-called Irish literary movement, I wrote a dreadful stage-Irish, so-called autobiography called *The Green Fool*, the common people of this country gobbled up this stage-Irish lie.[1] When, years later, I wrote *Tarry Flynn*[2] which I am humble enough to claim is not only the best but the only *authentic* account of life as it was lived in Ireland this century (a man shouldn't be afraid to tell the truth even when it is in favour of himself), the principal people who enjoyed this novel were literary sophisticates; its uproarious comedy was too much for the uneducated reader.

I am not trying to boost my wares. I am merely trying to illustrate a position. And I would say now that that so-called Irish Literary Movement which purported to be frightfully Irish and racy of the Celtic soil[3] was a thoroughgoing English-bred lie. Anybody can write tragedy. The English reviewers went crazy about the poetry of O'Casey's *Juno*, whereas in fact we only endure that embarrassment for the laughs in Captain Boyle.

I am supposed to be self-portraying myself and I hope I am so doing. I can tell all about my background and upbringing without being very original. And it is there the lie comes in. I would have to show that my background and my childhood adventures were out of the common, just as journalists do when they report on foreign countries. I remember reading a journalist on a visit to Greece who made the illuminating disclosure that the Greeks were very fond of conversation. But if the place and the experience weren't different what the devil was he doing out there?

My childhood experience was the usual barbaric life of the Irish country poor. I have never seen poverty properly analysed. Poverty is a mental condition. You hear of men and women who have chosen poverty, but you cannot choose poverty. Poverty has nothing to do with eating your fill today; it is anxiety about what's going to happen next week. The cliché poverty that you get in the working-class novel or play is a formula.

My father, being a shoemaker, was probably less poor than the small farmer classes. What was called the 'dropping shilling' kept coming in. But as for the *scraidíns*[4] of farmers with their watery little hills that would physic a snipe, I don't know where they got any money. But the real poverty was the lack of enlightenment to get out and get under the moon.

I am afraid this fog of unknowing affected me dreadfully. But, as I have suggested earlier, all this is of little importance.

Round about the late nineteen-thirties, a certain prosperity came through and foolishly enough that was the time I chose to leave my native fields. I had no messianic impulse to leave. I was happy. I went against my will. A lot of our actions are like that. We miss the big emotional gesture and drift away. Is it possible to achieve our potential grand passion? I believe so. Perhaps that has been my weakness.

I came to Dublin in nineteen-thirty-nine. It was the worst mistake of my life. The Hitler war had started. I had my comfortable little holding of watery hills beside the Border. What was to bate it for a life? And yet I wasted what could have been my four glorious years, begging and scrambling around the streets of malignant Dublin. I could have done my smuggling stint. I could never see my own interest. I could never see love on bended knees begging me to come. I was always in the fog.

When I came to Dublin the Irish Literary affair was still booming. It was the notion that Dublin was a literary metropolis and Ireland, as invented and patented by Yeats, Lady Gregory and Synge, a spiritual entity. It was full of writers and poets and I am afraid I thought their work had the Irish quality.

The conversation in Poets' Pub had the richness and copiosity that H. W. Nevinson said all Dublin conversation had.[5] To me, even then, it was tiresome drivel between journalists and civil servants. No humour at all. And, of course, they thought so much of poetry they didn't believe in the poet ating.[6] I am not, I assure you, complaining, merely

1. *The Green Fool*, an account of Kavanagh's early years, was published in 1938.
2. *Tarry Flynn* was published in 1948.
3. 'racy of the soil' had been a standard phrase since it was used as part of the epigraph for *The Nation* newspaper in 1843.
4. From the Irish word meaning 'small, a small amount of, diminutive'. In the north of Ireland, the word is almost always used with intent to injure.
5. H. W. Nevinson (1856-1941), essayist and war correspondent. The remark is in his autobiographical volume, *Running Accompaniments* (1936).
6. eating.

stating a few ridiculous facts. It was all my fault. What was I doing there? Wasn't I old enough to know the differ? Shouldn't I have cottoned on? Ah well, we live and we sometimes learn.

Now, part of my poverty-stricken upbringing was my belief in respectability — a steady job, decency. The bohemian rascals living it up in basements and in mountain hideouts horrified me. If I had joined them and endured them they'd have taken me to their bosoms. But I couldn't do it. Instinctively I realized that they were embittered people worshipping the poor man's poet. Their left-wingery was defeat. But the key to prosperity was with that sort of enemy and still is.

When I think of the indignities I endured in the cause of respectability I can kick myself. And me with health and strength to dig ditches, or to leap them anyway with a sack of white flour on me back. The Monaghan-Armagh-Louth border was not a severe test for a true stayer carrying top weight. I can kick myself for all the people I didn't kick then. Sometimes, when walking along a Dublin street, I might well be noticed making wild, vicious kicks at emptiness and scringing[7] my teeth at the same time. Thinking over the matter in the light of hindsight, I realize it would not have been easy for a man of sensibility to survive in the society of my birth, but it could have been done had I been trained in the technique of reserve and restraint.

A poet is never one of the people. He is detached, remote, and the life of small-time dances and talk about football would not be for him. He might take part but could not belong.

A poet has to have an audience — half a dozen or so. Landor, who said he esteemed ten a sufficient audience,[8] was very optimistic. I know about half a dozen and these are mainly London-based. It may be possible to live in total isolation but I don't understand how. The audience is as important as the poet. There is no audience in Ireland, though I have managed to build up out of my need a little audience for myself.

The real problem is the scarcity of a right audience which draws out of a poet what is best in him. The Irish audience that I came into contact with tried to draw out of me everything that was loud, journalistic and untrue. Such as:

My soul was an old horse
Offered for sale in twenty fairs.[9]

Anthologists everywhere keep asking for this. Also asked for is another dreadful job about Mother Ireland:

It would never be summer
always autumn
After a harvest always lost.[10]

Thank God, I control the copyrights in these poems and nobody can use them. What the alleged poetry-lover loved was the Irishness of a thing. Irishness is a form of anti-art. A way of posing as a poet without actually being one. The New Lines poets[11] of today have invented a similar system.

They are also sympathetic to the Irish thing.

No young person today would think of coming to live in Dublin as a metropolis. A new awareness is in the air. A couple of years ago I remember a young chap accosting me in a Dublin street. He was from the southern part of Ireland and he was on his way to Rome — to take up the poetry trade. He was right too. At least something might happen to him there, a rich woman might take a fancy to his poetry and keep him in the decency and comfort which are a necessity of the poet.

I pause here to emphasize that I have no belief in the virtue of a place. Many misguided persons imagine that living in France or Italy is the equivalent of a liberal education. French in particular is the language of art. Still, Dublin hasn't the possibilities for getting hitched up to a rich woman, and this is about the only way a true poet can remain true and keep up an adequate supply of good whiskey.

I am wandering around Dublin when I run into a poetry lover.

'How are you getting on at all?' says he with much pity.

The instinct to do a day's good deed has always

7. grinding.
8. Walter Savage Landor (1775-1864), English poet and essayist.

9. The opening lines of 'Pegasus' in *A Soul for Sale* (1947).
10. From 'Memory of Brother Michael' in the same volume. The *Collected Poems* has 'It would never be spring, always autumn'.
11. *New Lines* (1956) was the title of an anthology edited by Robert Conquest and containing poems by the poets of the 'Movement' — Philip Larkin, Thom Gunn, Kingsley Amis, D. J. Enright, Donald Davie, John Wain. *New Lines Volume Two* (1963) included a number of others.

been a weakness with me, so I reply:

'Terrible.'

'Poor fella.'

'Sure what can I do?'

'And you're not writing any poetry these times. I never see anything by you in the *Irish Times*. The flash is gone. I say, the flash is gone.'

'I suppose so.'

'A terrible scandal that the Government doesn't do something for our Irish poets. There's forty or fifty major poets in this country today and if I had me way they'd all have a civil list pension. Is the health all right again?'

I cough hard and send him away happy. I won't be long in it and that City Hall booking for my lying-in-state can be taken up. And that was interesting too. When I was above in the Rialto Hospital,[12] and the report of my impending demise spread, two well-wishers decided to do me proud in death: they would have me waked in the City Hall. A journalist friend of mine brought me the news as I lay in hospital at the end of a real tether, which was attached to the bottom of the bed and to rise sitting you pulled on the rope. It must have been disappointing that I didn't oblige.

I fear that the mood I have been evoking may give the impression that what happened to me is important and that I am important. Nobody is important. Nobody is major. We get to our destiny in the end. I am not in the least bitter over all this. In fact I am always in danger of bursting out laughing.

I merely state the facts. Of course I do not blame some of these people. I had been assailing the myth of Ireland by which they were managing to beat the artistic rap. I had seen and shewn that this Ireland thing was an undignified business — the trade of enemies and failures.

The English lower orders and their voices, the popular journalists, wanted a certain image of the Irishman, one that would make them feel better, but of recent years a small group of Irishmen in London founded an enclave which did not tolerate such blackguardism. Some of those newspapermen were very humble if they happened to be allowed into that company, and they knew their place better than to write about them. That is indeed one thing to be said for English newspapers, they hardly ever gossip about poets — only actors and film and telly stars. I love reading that stuff, the handouts telling us of the stars and their affairs off the set. All supposed to be real life stuff.

For a number of years I was a film critic. I attended the Irish Film Society shows of a Saturday and wrote as enthusiastically as the next man about the marvellous Italian film — the photography, the direction and the director, a man of superb genius. That was before I learned the difficult art of not caring, of having the courage of one's feelings. But it did take me quite a while before I came out with the terrible disclosure that I thought of most of these foreign films what George the Third thought of Shakespeare — poor stuff, but one mustn't say so.[13]

I burned my way through the film critics' world till in the end I was unable to say another word. If I had been able to stick it out I would probably today be a maker of films or a director of telly shows, or even one of those suave chaps who talk on telly and who are all noted for an excellent head of hair and who all have the same smiling face, the same age too, frozen at thirty-nine. See what I missed and see what the public missed.

Among the other things I missed, one I regret was refusing the offer of Reuters to go in as a reporter with the Second Front. And look at the fellow who wrote *The Longest Day*.[14]

Once again and as always, I was showing my cautious, respectable mentality. Instead of letting it rip. This has been a great defect in my nature. On the other hand I know of a couple of very fine poets in England who avoided the draft, one by pretending to be bonkers. But every man to his fancy. I was a different class of animal. I should have done something.

Another great experience I had was my law case, hereinafter to be known as The Trial or Trial and Error, mostly error.[15] Curious thing is that an event

12. Kavanagh went into the Rialto Hospital in Dublin with cancer of the lung. He recovered and afterwards referred to his convalescence, 1955-56, as his 'rebirth'. See 'The Hospital' on p. 148.

13. George III to Fanny Burney, as recorded in her *Diary* for 19 December 1785: 'Was there ever', cried he, 'such stuff as great part of Shakespeare? Only one must not say so! But what think you? — what? — Is there not sad stuff? what? — what?'

14. Cornelius Ryan (1920-74), war correspondent and the author of three bestsellers: *The Longest Day* (1959), *The Last Battle* and *A Bridge Too Far*. He was born and educated in Dublin.

15. Kavanagh sued the newspaper *The Leader* for libel after it published an unsigned 'Profile' of him in October 1952. He lost his case, was granted a new trial on appeal, but had to go into hospital before it could be brought to court.

so seemingly large at the time disappears in the perspective of a few years. What seems of public importance is never of any importance. Stupid poets and artists think that by taking subjects of public importance it will help their work to survive. There is nothing as dead and damned as an important thing. The things that really matter are casual, insignificant little things, things you would be ashamed to talk of publicly. You are ashamed and then after years someone blabs and you find that you are in the secret majority. Such is fame.

Of my early Dublin experiences I have little of value to offer. In the frosty winter of 1946 I went around trying to sell a contraption for attaching to furnaces to conserve the heat which was scarce those days. I spent a fortnight tramping the frozen streets, my contraption rejected and denounced by all sorts of janitors. Eventually, in the furnace (not the bargain) basement of a Grafton Street store, the boss foreman made a complimentary remark about my article as shown in the illustrated folder. I couldn't carry the machine, which was a hundredweight. Twenty-five pounds was the price, but he said there wasn't a whit the matter with the idea if it came at a fiver. 'Worth about a fiver for a trial,' he said. Morality triumphed over commerce. I said, 'It's not worth five shillings never mind five pounds; it's a complete fraud.'

In those days in Dublin the big thing besides being Irish was peasant quality. They were all trying to be peasants. They had been at it for years but I hadn't heard. And I was installed as the authentic peasant, and what an idea that was among rascals pretending to have an interest in poetry. Although the literal idea of the peasant is of a farm labouring person, in fact a peasant is all that mass of mankind which lives below a certain level of consciousness. They live in the dark cave of the unconscious and they scream when they see the light. They take offence easily, their degree of insultability is very great. I have written:

But I, trained in the slum pubs of Dublin
Among the most offensive class of all
The artisans — am equal to the problem;
I let it ride and there is nothing over.
I understand through all these years
That my difference in their company is an intrusion
That tears at the sentimental clichés.
They can see my heart squirm when their star rendites
The topmost twenty in the lowered lights.
No sir, I did not come unprepared.[16]

Which brings me to something that I might say is the very heart of the matter of human contentment or as near as we can get. This is the secret of learning how not to care. Not caring is really a sense of values and feeling of confidence. A man who cares is not the master. And one can observe this in the matter of simple singing in the rain or in a pub. The fellows who around Christmas sing in pubs are not just chaps enjoying themselves. Enjoying themselves has nothing to do with it. They are *expressing* themselves. This is their art, their reason for existence. And they are usually very humble and ashamed of their own selves, for they always assume the part of some singing star or other. No wonder I squirm. I do not blame them; few people have the courage to be themselves. And when they do appear themselves it is all put on with spade-fulls of bravado. It took me many years to learn or relearn not to care. The heart of a song singing it, or a poem writing it, is not caring. I will sing now and give the poems later:

On Raglan Road on an autumn day
I met her first and knew
That her dark hair could weave a snare
that I might one day rue.
I saw the danger yet I walked
upon the enchanted way
And I said let grief be a fallen leaf
at the dawning of the day.[17]

In the beginning of my versing career I had hit on the no-caring jag but there was nobody to tell me that I was on the right track:

My black hills have never seen the sun rising
Eternally they look north to Armagh.[18]

There are two kinds of simplicity, the simplicity of going away and the simplicity of return. The last is the ultimate in sophistication. In the final simplicity we don't care whether we appear foolish or not. We talk of things that earlier would embarrass. We are satisfied with being ourselves,

16. From 'The Main Body' in the sequence 'Living in the Country'.
17. 'On Raglan Road'.
18. 'Shancoduff' from *The Great Hunger and Other Poems* (1942).

however small. So it was that on the banks of the Grand Canal between Baggot and Leeson Street bridges in the warm summer of 1955, I lay and watched the green waters of the canal. I had just come out of hospital. I wrote:

Leafy-with-love banks and the green waters of the
canal
Pouring redemption for me, that I do
The will of God, wallow in the habitual, the banal
Grow with nature again as before I grew.[19]

And so in this moment of great daring I became a poet. Except for brief moments in my very early years I had not been a poet. The poems in *A Soul for Sale* are not poetry and neither is *The Great Hunger*. There are some queer and terrible things in *The Great Hunger*, but it lacks the nobility and repose of poetry. The trouble is that there are so few who would know a poem from a hole in the ground.

It is possible on the other hand to recognize a poet, for the animal is recognizable. The main feature about a poet, if you ever happen to meet one — and that's a remote chance, for I can't be everywhere at the one time — the main feature is his humorosity. Any touch of boringness and you are in the wrong shop.

Beautiful women, I am glad to say, are capable of recognizing the baste. Recently a man was presented to me as being a great poet. He wrote in Irish. I expressed me doubts and the introducer said: 'How can you tell when you don't know the language?' That was a sore one, but I was able for it. I said, 'I can't bawl like a cow but I'd know a cow if I saw one.'

That a poet is born, not made, is well known. But this does not mean that he was a poet the day he was physically born. For many a good-looking year I wrought hard at versing but I would say that, as a poet, I was born in or about nineteen-fifty-five, the place of my birth being the banks of the Grand Canal.

Thirty years earlier Shancoduff's watery hills could have done the trick, but I was too thick to take the hint. Curious this, how I had started off with the right simplicity, indifferent to crude reason and then ploughed my way through complexities and anger, hatred and ill-will towards the faults of man, and came back to where I started. For one of the very earliest things I wrote, even pre-dating Shancoduff, started this way:

Child do not go
Into the dark places of soul
For there the grey wolves whine,
The lean grey wolves[20]

In that little thing I had become airborne and more; I had achieved weightlessness. And then I heard about having one's roots in the soil, of being a peasant. And I raged at Monaghan and the clay and all to that. But poetry has to do with the reality of the spirit, of faith and hope and sometimes even charity. It is a point of view. A poet is a theologian.

Arts councils and the like love to believe in the poet as a simple singer piping down the valleys wild.[21] When Shelley said that poets were the real legislators of the world he was right, although he may not have fully understood his rightness. A poet is an original who inspires millions of copies. That's all education consists of — the copying of a good model.

Reverting at that to my public career, I must mention that adventure when I edited and wrote *Kavanagh's Weekly* in 1952.[22] We had no ads. — a distinction that looks like overtaking many other papers before the century is out. I wrote almost the whole paper including the poems, letters to the editor, etc. Why do people engage in such madness?

But recently looking up the files I read something that has relevance here. On 'School Book Poetry' I wrote — quoting Longfellow:

There are things of which I may not speak,
How strange things happen to a man.
He dabbles in something and does
Not realize that it is his life.[23]

That was what I wrote then. And yet I had not yet been born, as I believe I afterwards was, though perhaps some folks may not agree. It doesn't matter. Anyhow, I did arrive at complete casualness, at being able to play a true note on a dead slack string.

19. 'Canal Bank Walk' from *Come Dance with Kitty Stobling and Other Poems* (1960).

20. 'To A Child' from *Ploughman and Other Poems* (1936).
21. William Blake, Introduction to *Songs of Innocence* (1789-90).
22. *Kavanagh's Weekly* appeared from 12 April to 5 July 1952.
23. *Kavanagh's Weekly,* 10 May 1952, p.8

LOUIS MACNEICE

(1907-63)

from: THE STRINGS ARE FALSE: AN UNFINISHED AUTOBIOGRAPHY (1965)

[This episode in MacNeice's autobiography describes his first great loss — the effect of his mother's death and the ending of the happiness he had earlier known. The footnotes (E.N.) to the text are by MacNeice's sister, Lady Nicholson, and the page references are to his *Collected Poems* (1966).]

V

The cook Annie, who was a buxom rosy girl from a farm in County Tyrone, was the only Catholic I knew and therefore my only proof that Catholics were human. She worked very well and fast and filled in her spare time doing Irish crochet work. We would watch the shamrocks and roses growing from her crochet hooks while in a gay warm voice she would tell us about Fivemiletown where she came from and the banshees[1] and fairies and cows of the Clogher valley. They had nice rhymes out there — Lisnaskea for drinking tea, Maguire's Bridge for whisky — and County Tyrone sounded like a land of content. Annie in fact was always contentful except when she had palpitations. And we were content with Annie.

One day, however, my mother engaged what was called a Mother's Help. My brother and I were busy laying pebbles along a little ledge outside the conservatory porch when the Mother's Help came up the drive. She was small and lean and scrawny, quite unlike Annie, her face was sour and die-hard Puritanical, she had a rasping Northern accent. The daughter of a farmer in County Armagh, she knew all there was to be known about bringing up children; keep them conscious of sin, learn them their sums, keep all the windows shut tight and don't let them run for it is bad for their hearts.

It was the end of *laissez-faire*. Miss Craig nearly pulled your ears off when she cleaned them and she always got the soap in your eyes. When she carried you off in disgrace your face would be scratched by the buckle on her thick leather belt. Though small she was strong as leather and we soon developed new reflexes when we saw the slaps coming. Believing in economy she made dresses for my sister out of the funeral scarves with which my father was presented at funerals. Obsessed by a righteous hatred of the Common Cold she loaded us down with perspiring layers of clothing. In spite of this my sister kept catching cold and Miss Craig would jeer at her bitterly, say she would never live to grow up and they would write on her tombstone 'Here lies Old Snivelly'.

It was Miss Craig who brought Hell home to me.[2] Being one of a rector's family I had heard it mentioned before but it had never been cardinal; Miss Craig made it almost the Alpha and Omega, hell-flames embroidered her words like Victorian texts. I realised now that I was always doing wrong. Wrong was showing-off, being disobedient, being rude, telling stories, doing weekday things — or thinking weekday thoughts — on Sundays. I had done so much wrong I knew I must end in Hell and, what was worse, I could imagine it. Sometimes when Miss Craig had jerked me and thumped me into bed she would look at me grimly and say: 'Aye, you're here now but you don't know where you'll be when you wake up.'[3]

Miss Craig, however, had her glamour. County Armagh was not so romantic as County Tyrone but it was also somewhere unseen and Miss Craig told us of the will-o'-the-wisps that went skipping around in the bogs. Also she had a trunk which she would unpack for us sometimes for a treat; the

1. A banshee (Irish *bean sidhe*, fairy woman) is said to be a premonition of death in a family. She cries and wails before the death occurs.

2. Louis's picture of Miss Craig is, I think, rather misleading. She was an eccentric person, and after our mother left she found herself in a position of responsibility for which she was perhaps unfitted. But in spite of her sharp tongue she had a kind heart and gave us many little pleasures. I am doubtful about the authenticity of the 'hell-fire' remarks attributed to her; I think that Louis may have heard or read these elsewhere and unconsciously projected them on to his memory of her. My father disapproved strongly of 'hell-fire religion', but it would have been hard for an imaginative child to escape some knowledge of it in the Ulster of fifty years ago. [E.N.]

3. Cf. *Autumn Sequel*, canto xvii (p. 399). [E.N.]

contents were always the same but we always looked forward to seeing them. There was a photograph album — yellow snaps of gaitered and whiskered farmers — and a heavy Bible with a brown binding (always a novelty, for the Bibles we knew were all black) and at the bottom of all was a little parasol which took to pieces. We never even wondered what Miss Craig was doing with a parasol, Miss Craig who had hair on her face and whose style of dress was not only plain but repulsive.

My mother became steadily more ill and at last she went away; the last I can remember of her at home was her walking up and down the bottom path of the garden, the path under the hedge that was always in shadow, talking to my sister and weeping. I had no part in this, I did not know what it was all about.[4] Later I visited my mother in hospital and she offered me a box of chocolates. Something evil came up in me — I knew it to be evil, although it was quite different from the wrongdoings for which I was going to Hell — and I refused to take the box. I wanted the chocolates very much and also I wanted to be gracious to my mother, but something or other made me spite myself and her and stand there surly and refuse. When I got home the box was there (someone had brought it back furtively) and I was filled with remorse and remembered the other time with the poplar twigs. That had been a fresh spring morning and everyone well and gay and my father was perched on a ladder clipping the arbour which was made of little trees we called poplars. The long sprays fell on the ground with light green lively leaves and I gathered some of them up to arrange in a jam-jar. But one of my twigs was too long, whenever I put it in the jar the jar fell over. My mother came up smiling, folded the twig double, put it in the jar and the jar stayed upright. And I was outraged, went off in a sulk.

At the age of five, while my mother was away, I made my first rebellion. Thursday was Mrs. M'Quitty's Day and we always had stewed steak. Mrs. M'Quitty, the charwoman, was very stout and friendly, she had a son who was a fisherman and she had given us our cat but she had to have stewed steak. I could not bear stewed steak, I found it too tough to swallow, had to keep the pieces in my cheek till after dinner, then spit them out in the shrubbery. So one spring Thursday, as we were spending the morning with Annie raking up new-cut grass, I planned that, when the gong went, I would hang behind and hide and have no steak. So the gong went and I hung behind, crawled in under some laurel bushes at the side of the lawn. In a few minutes they came out and called for me but I did not answer. This was achievement, I felt, something entirely new, I had planned to do something outrageous and the outrage was working. The steak too must be getting cold.

There was a great hue and cry, Miss Craig and Annie and Mrs. M'Quitty screaming all over the garden but they never looked under the laurels; I was proud to be so clever. 'There he is now,' Miss Craig cried suddenly, 'I see the red cap on him in the cemetery.' So they all stampeded to the cemetery hedge but, whatever it was red, it was not my cap. I could feel ripples of delight going over my face as I lay snug under the laurels drawing patterns with my finger in the dried crumbly soil. Dinner-time — steak-time — was past but I was not in the least hungry, would lie there all afternoon; the experience was too precious not to exploit to the full. Mrs. M'Quitty and Annie brought out a carpet on to the lawn right in front of me and began to beat it, with great wicker bats; the thud of their strokes

4. In 1910 our mother developed a gynaecological complaint which occasioned intermittent attacks of illness, but these did not become frequent or serious until late in 1912. In March 1913 she had an operation which completely cured her former malady, but at the same time she quite suddenly developed an agitated melancholia. Louis and I saw her change almost overnight from a mother who had always been the mainstay of the household — serene and comforting, apparently the very essence of stability — into someone who was deeply unhappy and no longer able to make decisions. Louis in particular, as the youngest, was greatly attached to his mother, and before her illness I remember him as being with her a very great deal. Through the early summer of 1913 she was still at home and Louis was still constantly with her. She always remained gentle and loving, but as she became more and more sad and restless Louis, who was only five and a half, must have been completely bewildered and greatly disturbed. His last memory-picture of her walking up and down the garden path in tears seems to have haunted him for the rest of his life.

In August 1913 she left the rectory for a nursing-home in Dublin. In the children's eyes (and I think this is important) she did not appear ill in the ordinary sense of the word, only inexplicably sad. Louis and I never saw her again (the chocolate-box episode took place on a visit paid to her by Louis after her operation six months earlier). For a long time after her departure both Louis and I waited for and expected her return; Louis has expressed his own feelings at this period in his poem 'Autobiography' (p. 183). She died in December 1914 of tuberculosis, presumably contracted in the hospital where she then was.

I think that the shock of seeing the sudden change in the mother whom he loved so much, followed by the uncertainty of her return, may have been the chief factor which caused Louis's memories of childhood to be so sad and sometimes so bitter. He was too young to have any real understanding of what had happened. [E.N.]

reiterated around me and the dust rose up in the sunshine. A terrible thing, Mrs. M'Quitty kept saying, me to be lost and my mother ill and away. Sure he may be killed on the roads; the master has the polis out looking for him.

I was a little scared to think that the polis were after me; maybe, I thought, I am in for a lot of trouble. I lay very quiet and left it to fate. I might not have come out for a long time had there not been a scratching and a blustering behind me in the nettles and there, broken out from the henyard, were the hens led by the rooster. The rooster looked like the Devil with his great scarlet wattles and crest and he was leading his hens straight into my hideout. It was too much for me, I scrambled out on to the lawn and was caught. Miss Craig told me I was bound for Hell and my father told me it was very wrong to make everyone so frightened and I ought to think of my mother.

Adventure did not pay and life settled into routine. In the morning I would have my lessons from Miss Craig in a small nursery with the window shut tight. On the walls there hung a multiplication table and a calendar with a picture of John Peel and a coloured picture from the *Sphere* of Queen Mary dressed for her Coronation; I liked Queen Mary very much because of her jewellery and I liked John Peel for the names of his dogs. Sometimes Miss Craig would put a new nail in the walls and the plaster would drop out. One day I picked up what looked like a piece of sugar and ate it and Miss Craig said at once it was plaster, I was a bad wicked child and would die. She was always talking of dying, and in winter, when the trees in between were not in leaf, would marshal us at the window to watch the funeral processions on their way to the cemetery next door.

In the afternoon when it was not raining too hard (which it often was) we would walk with Miss Craig up the road up the hill behind our house to a point called Mile Bush and back again. Always — or nearly always — the same walk because Miss Craig disliked going through the town; you never know [*sic*] what you might catch. We walked very slowly because of my brother and Miss Craig kept saying 'Don't drag.' My sister and I were agog to see something new, if only a horse drinking at the water-trough, but everything was usually just the same except that the hawthorn hedges which were flaming green in spring were jaded by autumn and in winter were barren black with raindrops ricocheting from twig to twig. Miss Craig, however, would tell us stories, always on the pattern of *Jungle Jinks*, the children's comic section in *Home Chat*; my brother was Jacko and I was Tiger Tim and my sister (Miss Craig's one original contribution) was Careless.

When we got home we would have tea in the nursery, strong tea thick with sugar, and sometimes before we went to bed Miss Craig, for a treat, would give us thick beef sandwiches with mustard or a cold drink made from cream of tartar. Possibly our diet, though it was not the cause, was one of the conditions of my dreams. These got worse and worse. Where earlier I had had dreams of being chased by mowing-machines or falling into machinery or arguing with tigers who wanted to eat me I now was tormented by something much less definite, much more serious. There was a kind of a noise that I felt rather than heard, 'ah . . . ah . . . ah', a grey monotonous rhythm which drew me in towards a centre as if there were a spider at the centre drawing in his thread and everything else were unreal.

'Oh God, I do not want to have any dreams. If I am going to go to sleep, do not let me have any dreams. And if I am going to have dreams, do not let me go to sleep, God, please I will do anything if only You keep me awake.' But I always went to sleep all the same. One night I woke up and yelled, my father came up from downstairs, there was light and his voice, he told me nothing would hurt me.[5] I felt quite safe when he had gone but next morning Miss Craig was very angry; my father had forgotten to go down again to the study and had left the lamp burning there all night. I was a very wicked boy and might have burnt the house down.

There were also the terrors of Church. The church was cruciform, and the rectory pew, being the front pew of the nave, looked out on to the space where the chancel and the nave and the two transepts met. The transept on our left was on a higher level and was reached by a short flight of steps; the end wall of it was occupied by a huge Elizabethan monument to the Chichester family who had then been the power in the land. The father and mother, who were each very large, knelt each under an arch, opposite each other, praying; below them, much smaller, was a Chichester

5. cf. MacNeice's poems 'Intimations of Mortality' (p. 28) and 'Autobiography' (p. 183). [E.N.]

brother who had been beheaded by the rebels, and between them, like a roll of suet pudding, on a little marble cushion was a little marble baby. None of these marble people worried me at all; what I disliked were the things that hung high up on the wall on either side of the monument's narrower top. A decayed coat of mail, a couple of old weapons, a helmet. I could not see the coat of mail when I was sitting, thanks to the solid front of the first pew in the transept, but, whenever I had to get up, there it would be, older and older and deader and deader, yet somehow not quite dead enough.

On the other hand if I looked down the chancel there was a rich old widow who always wore black and whom therefore I took to be blind. And blindness was not a misfortune, blindness was evil magic. When I was sitting down I could not see her either as she was hidden by the reading-desk, so the morning service became an alternation of agony and relief, but the relief itself shadowed with the knowledge that soon we should have to stand up again and there I should be, exposed to the blind old lady on the one hand and the coat-of-mail man on the other. . . .

AUSTIN CLARKE

(1896-1974)

from: A PENNY IN THE CLOUDS (1968)

[Clarke's first volume of autobiography, *Twice Round the Black Church* (1962), appears, like its successor, to be little more than a series of interlinked reminiscences. In fact, Clarke details both his own career and part of the internal history of the literature of the period in a highly organized narrative. The following excerpts do more than tell of his friendships with F. R. Higgins, Stephen MacKenna, and Thomas MacDonagh. They give an indication of the existence of a literary world in Dublin that was influenced by, but not strictly part of, the Revival and demonstrate the relationship between it and the political world which produced the Easter rebellion. Figures like MacKenna and MacDonagh were involved in the creation of an Ireland other than that of Yeats and his colleagues at the Abbey Theatre. MacDonagh tried to formulate a description of it in his work on Thomas Campion and in his book *Literature in Ireland*, both of which had their ultimate impact on Clarke's own work. MacDonagh's search for an 'Irish mode' is different from Yeats's search for the Irish essence. It was a quest for an accommodation between what has been called, in the introduction to the Poetry and Song 1800-1890 section in Volume II, 'Irish Elizabethanism' with elements from the Gaelic traditon in poetry. By introducing Clarke to the history of Celtic-Romanesque Ireland, Stephen MacKenna gave Clarke's poetry a focus that MacDonagh's never achieved; yet Clarke's work carries with it echoes of the 1890s, of its studied 'Elizabethan' elegances as well as a great deal from that Gaelic poetic tradition about which Yeats was so ignorant and eloquent.

Clarke's relationship to Yeats has frequently been considered, but it is his relationship to the poets and writers mentioned here that more fruitfully establishes for us the literary matrix out of which his work grew. It is ironic and proper that his version of the Revival should emerge in the 1930s as a counter-revival, as a rebuke to what Yeats and others had achieved. It would be truer to see it as an alternative, as the deferred achievement of the 'other' revival which, like the first, had its origins in the late eighties and nineties of the previous century. For this other revival, the Easter Rising was an inaugurating event, quickly aborted by the Treaty of 1921-22 and the subsequent reduction of the revolutionary dream to the philistine oppressiveness of the new state.]

CHAPTER TWO

One evening, early in 1915, if I remember rightly, I went to a public lecture given by St. John Irvine[1] in the Vegetarian Restaurant, a pleasant place near College Green in Dublin, long since vanished. Mr. Irvine was Manager of the Abbey Theatre at the time and, in speaking of drama, dealt with the

1. St John Greer Irvine (more usually 'Ervine') (1883-1971) was appointed manager of the Abbey (to which he had earlier contributed four plays) in 1915. He tried to turn it into a standard repertory theatre and so alienated audiences and players that he had to be replaced.

touchiness of our audiences and compared us unfavourably with our countrymen in the north. I was a Second Year Arts student at University College and that day, the Assistant Lecturer in English, Thomas MacDonagh, who was afterwards one of the poet-leaders of the Easter Week Rising, had lent me a slim volume of verse. It was one of the Poetry Book Shop publications, either *The Old Ships* by James Elroy Flecker or, as I think, a reprint of his earlier poem *The Bridge of Fire*.[2] At the time I knew scarcely anything about contemporary poetry and was very pleased to have a loan of this brand new chapbook with its bold lettering on the title page. I suspect that I carried it rather ostentatiously for, as the crowd was leaving after the lecture, a tall young man, round-faced, and with rimless glasses, stopped me and said in a polite, Protestant voice: 'Excuse me, is that Elroy Flecker's *Bridge of Fire* you have?' That was how I met the future Manager of the Abbey Theatre. We walked part of the way home together and I learned that he wrote poetry and was a clerk in the office of Brooks Thomas, a large building firm. His name was F. R. Higgins.[3]

F. R. Higgins and I became close friends and went for long walks at night time along the Green Lanes of Clontarf, now a residential area, or chatted in small Italian cafes over Camp coffee and penny cakes. We were both eighteen, but I was awed by his knowledge of the 'Nineties, the Celtic Twilight, Symbolism, and Maeterlinck[4] for at that time he was still known as the Celtic Maeterlinck. He discoursed on Chinese poetry; lent me Victor Plarr's little book on Ernest Dowson.[5] It was all confusing, exciting and stimulating to me for I had only a knowledge of academic literature and had not got much farther than Tennyson. I had also some academic knowledge of Gaelic poetry and for that reason was all the more puzzled by Celtic Twilight Impressionism. I do not think Higgins ever asked me about the poems which I was trying to write: they were too bad to show to anyone and so I listened reverently as, along the dark hedgerows, he walked with me intoning some of his earliest delicate lyrics. Even then he was constantly reshaping and rewriting them.

On one memorable occasion Higgins decided to share a secret with me. He would show me a wonderful pool, which was to him a symbol of Immortal Beauty, for in those years beauty was not, as we say, a dirty word. I was thrilled for now at last the perplexities of Symbolism would be made clear to me. It was a misty night. Suddenly the young poet stopped and pointed out to me near the roadside his symbol. I saw in the fitful light of the moon, beneath a few bare trees, a muddy hollow. I said nothing but to that sudden shock I trace back my dislike for the Symbolist movement.

Higgins composed even his early poems to the rhythm of Irish airs and ballad tunes. Like Colum, Campbell[6] and the poets of the previous generation, he was much influenced by the delicate Love Songs of Connaught, collected and translated by Douglas Hyde.[7] He had spent his childhood in Foxford, County Mayo and spoke often of the little river-gardens along the Moy and of gathering wild strawberries at Ballivor, County Meath, where he stayed at times with his father's relatives. His early poems were based on those memories, in the city, of a country childhood. . . .

Higgins told me little of his home life but I knew there was strain. His father, a railway employee, was a strict Unionist, but Fred had been swept into the nationalism of the literary movement. Indeed shortly after we met, his father turned him out because he refused to join up and fight for King and Country and so he had to live in lodgings. Thus one of his finest poems 'Father and Son' written long afterwards, came from a deep conflict of emotion over the years. The quiet of its delicate speech-rhythm prepares us for its mood of reunion.

Only last week, walking the hushed fields
Of our most lovely Meath, now thinned by
　November,
I came to where the road from Laracor leads

2. James Elroy Flecker (1884-1915), English poet, published *The Old Ships* in 1915 and *The Bridge of Fire* in 1907.
3. F. R. Higgins (1896-1941) became a director of the Abbey in 1936 and managed the company during its American tour the next year. He later became the company's business director.
4. Maurice Maeterlinck (1862-1949), the Belgian poetic dramatist and essayist, won great fame with his Symbolist plays *La Princesse Maleine* (1889) and *L'Oiseau Bleu* (1908). He drew on traditions of folk-tale and romance; hence his early reputation as a 'Celtic' writer.
5. Ernest Dowson (1867-1900), one of the 'decadents' and a friend of Wilde, Lionel Johnson and others. His poems appeared in *Verses* (1896) and *Decorations* (1899). His friend and fellow-poet Victor Plarr wrote *Ernest Dowson 1888-97: Reminiscences* (London, 1914).
6. Padraic Colum (1881-1972) was already established at this time as a poet and dramatist. Joseph Campbell (1879-1944) had published seven volumes of poetry by 1913.
7. In 1893.

To the Boyne river — that seemed more lake
than river,
Stretched in uneasy light and stript of reeds.[8]

Anger is good. I think discipline, meditation, may be better.

Differing in our religious upbringing, Higgins and I learned from one another. One summer's evening, we went to see the great rhododendron display open to the public at the Howth Demesne.[9] We lingered on in that Caucasian sunset of blossom. In a quiet spot, Higgins climbed up until he was hidden and read out the Song of Songs, while I lay luxuriously on the ground under the petals. I had known only the Douai version and the notes that assured readers that this voluptuous poem was really an allegory of the future Church.[10] But as that voice rang out from the blossoms, I knew indeed that it was the poetry of polygamy and written by a poet who had a hundred wives.

Thy lips are like a thread of scarlet,
And thy speech is comely
Thy temples are like a piece of a pomegranate
Within thy locks.
Thy neck is like the tower of David builded
For an armoury
Whereon there hung a thousand bucklers,
All shields of mighty men.[11]

Higgins was not only a poet and convert to the Sinn Fein movement, he was also a pioneer of the Labour movement. As a student I had been only dimly aware of the grim conditions when the Lock Out of 1913 happened and the employers, led by William Martin Murphy, supported by the Church, endeavoured to starve out the workers.[12] Soon after I knew him, Higgins founded the Clerical Workers' Union; he told me that he was instantly dismissed from his employment. He was given a small salary as secretary of the Union, but funds were low — clerks were still timid — and so, for all his dream-life of the country, the poet had to face the problem of earning his living. He showed much practicality, ingenuity and cheerfulness. He was the first to found a woman's magazine in Ireland.[13] It lasted about a year. Then with the same genial hope, he persuaded our printing firms to produce trade journals and when one failed, he started another.

One evening, over our Camp coffee and our cake, Higgins explained to me that the disestablished Church of Ireland still kept the tradition and simple services of the early Celtic Church. As I knew little about ecclesiastical history, I was impressed by his knowledge and the powerful arguments which he had been taught. To that talk behind a wooden partition in a plain Café, I owed my later interest in the neglected Celtic-Romanesque centuries.[14]

Both of us longed to meet a real poet and we took a tram several times to the Rathmines Town Hall, near which was the small chemist's shop owned by James Starkey, better known to us as the poet, Seumas O'Sullivan.[15] We bought a tin of Zambuk, another of Vaseline, a box of Beecham's Pills, in the hope that the poet would be behind the counter or dispensing at the back of the shop. But he was never there.

So, in desperation, we made our way one afternoon, when Fred was on holiday, to the public-house in Patrick Street, owned by P. J. McCall, who had written 'Follow me up to Carlow' and other rousing ballads.[16] There were no drinkers in the bar, when we came in. He ordered two small ports, and we stole admiring glances at the poet, who was about forty years of age, curly-headed, handsome as John MacCormack, the great tenor.[17] Fred, in his manly way, talked about racing and sport to the poet, as he dried tumblers expertly and

8. From *The Gap of Brightness* (1940). Higgins's adaptation of the rhythms of traditional music to what Clarke called 'the patterns for his lyrics' and, indeed, all his technical innovations, had a deep influence on Clarke's own verse. See Clarke's *Poetry in Modern Ireland* (Cork: Mercier Press, 1951), pp. 42-47.
9. The prominent Hill of Howth forms the northern horn of the crescent of Dublin Bay. The demesne of Howth Castle is renowned for its rhododendrons, azaleas, and Ireland's first elm tree, planted in 1585.
10. The catholic translation of the Old Testament, the Rheims and Douai version, appeared in 1609-10. According to the traditional allegorical reading, the church is the bride of Christ.
11. Song of Solomon, 4.1-4.8.
12. William Martin Murphy (1844-1919), businessman and newspaper proprietor, president of the Employers' Federation which collided with the trade union, led by Jim Larkin, in the Great Lockout of 1913. Clarke's later poem, 'Inscription for a Headstone', commemorates Larkin.
13. The first was called *Welfare* (one issue), the second *Farewell* (one issue).
14. In effect, Christian Ireland before the Norman Conquest of 1172, with especial emphasis on the seventh to ninth centuries.
15. Seumas O'Sullivan, pseudonym of James Starkey (1879-1958), poet and small-scale publisher.
16. Patrick Joseph McCall (1861-1919), poet and humourist, best-known for the song 'Boulavogue' from *Irish Fireside Songs* (1911).
17. John McCormack (1884-1945), midway through his distinguished operatic career in 1915.

then mentioned casually a Wexford ballad. The poet modestly changed the conversation. Fred was not to be deterred, so he talked of the Love Songs of Connaught, which had been collected by Douglas Hyde. Again, the poet dodged us and talked of the Irish favourite for the Grand National. After a while, he happened to remark that the Boss was at home in Clontarf with a bad cold. We realized that we were talking to the barman.

Hastily, we left that public-house.

II

Often F. R. Higgins and I went to Artane where Mrs. Reddin held a *salon* every Sunday. I had been to school with two of her sons, Norman and Kenneth. Their mother had made a happy discovery in Armagh of an old ballad with a pretty refrain:

> The lambs on the green hills
> Stood gazing at me
> And many's the ship on the ocean
> And strawberries grow by the salt sea.[18]

At nine o'clock, guests trooped into the dining room where an ample cold supper was laid on the long table. At one end was an enormous baron of beef, at the other end an equally enormous one of corned beef. There, I met Edward Martyn,[19] whom I had often seen near the Kildare Street Club, dressed in a reefer, with jaunty sea-cap, looking as if he had left his yacht around the corner. One evening a guest at supper boldly asked him whether he had ever read *Hail and Farewell* in which his great friend, George Moore, had depicted him as an absurdly comical character. 'Good heavens!' he exclaimed, 'I wouldn't dream of doing so.' Cardinal Logue[20] had replied with similar surprise, when asked if he had read *The Countess Cathleen* before damning that play in public.

On a showery Sunday afternoon in May, I went with the Reddins on a pleasant drive through North County Dublin where Nathaniel Hone[21] had painted wide skies, that seemed to spread beyond his canvasses. We stopped at a roadside cottage, and I turned to a youth of eighteen called Michael Willmore, who had come with us. He was a promising artist and had already illustrated two books, one by Padraic O'Conaire, the other by Daniel Corkery.[22] To my astonishment, he was radiant in sunlight. I remembered, then, that he lived at Howth, where Diarmuid and Grainne, in the old legend, had hidden in a sea-cave from the pursuit of the Fianna. Diarmuid of the Love Spot had been blessed in the same way when Aonghus, the God, appeared to him.[23]

Later, that raysome youth won fame as an actor, under the Irish form of his name, Michael MacLiammoir.[24]

18. See Volume II, p. 101. This is a variation on the usual version.
19. Edward Martyn (1859-1923), dramatist, co-founder of the Irish Literary Theatre and, in 1914, of the Irish Theatre. He had rooms in Nassau Street, Dublin, near the Kildare Street Club.
    A 'reefer' is a man's short double-breasted jacket, made of wool.
20. Michael, Cardinal Logue (1839-1924), archbishop of Armagh and catholic primate of all Ireland 1887-1924. Logue had read only a pamphlet attacking the play.
21. Nathaniel Hone (1831-1917), painter in oils and water-colours; his 'Pastures at Malahide' (an area in north County Dublin) is one of his best-known works.
22. Pádraic Ó Conaire (1882-1928), writer in Irish; Daniel Corkery (1878-1964), writer, critic and powerful influence on Seán O'Faoláin and Frank O'Connor.
23. Diarmuid and Grainne, legendary lovers, eloped and were pursued by the Fianna, the warriors of Fionn to whom Grainne had been bethrothed. The god Aonghus occasionally intervened to help them escape.
24. Mícheál MacLiammóir (1889-1978), born Michael Willmore, famous actor and founder, with Hilton Edwards, of the Gate Theatre in Dublin in 1928. There he became a director, author, set designer and costume designer. He wrote several plays, including *Diarmuid agus Gráinne* (1935).

CHAPTER THREE

I

Strangely enough, I cannot remember how I first met Stephen MacKenna.[1] He was not widely known in his own lifetime, although scholars and literary critics acclaimed his rendering of the *Enneoads* [*sic*] of Plotinus into English as one of the great translations of our age. When he started his task, which took him twenty years, many had avoided the reediting and translating of the philosophic work, because they did not wish to risk their reputations, owing to the grammatical difficulties and obscurities. The adventure was undertaken by an ex-clerk and struggling Irish

1. Stephen MacKenna (1872-1934), a friend of J. M. Synge. His translation of Plotinus's *Enneads* appeared in five volumes between 1917 and 1930.

journalist, who had forgotten his school Greek. 'In the army of scholarship MacKenna was destined to fight to the end as an irregular,' wrote E. R. Dodds,[2] Regius Professor of Greek at Oxford, in a Memoir of his friend. Lacking a University degree, he was forced to complete his labours against hardship and poverty.

In his translation, he set himself against what he called wittily 'the-Verral-Jebb-pesudo-grand-days-of-yore-is-a-sham'.[3] His Journal written in the peaceful days of 1908 shows how worthily he prepared himself:

> For years I played foolishly with 'The Phrase', seeking the bubble 'self esteem' even in the canon's teeth, defying all the sanctities if only I might anyhow please myself with a yell and a flare and a fit of ribald glee: now only I begin to know that it is not 'The Phrase' that counts to any good, it is 'La Phrase'. Hence, the orderly suave and gracious setting of the true mood is the clear meaning. This is the anatomy of style as anatomy is the beginning of medicine and of surgery, of painting and of sculpture. The glory is to come later, if it ever comes: as a man must first be sober before he can be a saint, and learn to behave himself before he climbs into the pulpit.

Stephen MacKenna was an almost legendary figure in the literary circles of Dublin. He had shared scanty meals with Synge in Paris, fought for the sacred soil of Greece in the Turkish War of 1897,[4] swept out a restaurant for a livelihood in New York. As a journalist he caught the eye of Pulitzer,[5] the newspaper magnate, and had been appointed Continental correspondent in Paris with a staff of assistants and a large salary. He cast the post aside with a magnificent gesture and returned to Dublin to pursue his studies in Greek and Irish. More than all this, in a city where conversation was still recognized as an art, this moody scholar was an incomparable talker, astonishing all with his imaginative eloquence.

He had some amusing oddities and was not always aware of the noisy outside world. Robert Donovan,[6] my professor of English at University College, who had been a Leader writer on *The Freeman's Journal*, told me of a characteristic example of MacKenna's absent-mindedness, when he was on the staff of that paper. News had just come in that the missing Dr. Crippen[7] had been arrested on a charge of murder on his way to the United States, and a radio message — the first of its kind — had been relayed to the Liner. MacKenna was asked to write a leaderette on the subject. He went over to the reference shelf to look up the name Crippen in an Encyclopaedia.

George Moore shocked his conservative neighbours in Ely Place by having his hall door painted a patriotic green. MacKenna offended a highly respectable suburb by his queer taste in music. I called to his house in Anglesea Road once and was told in awed tone, that Mr. MacKenna could not possibly be disturbed. It was the sacred Thursday evening when his concertina teacher gave him and James Stephens[8] an hour's lesson in the attic.

Once, in writing a letter to him, I addressed it to Stephen McKenna, Esq. In reply I got an indignant postcard informing me that he spelled his name with a 'Mac' not with the Kaffir 'M' or 'M.K.' From its rhythmic sentence-run, it was clear that the same postcard had been dashed off and dropped into a pillarbox many times.

When I met MacKenna, he seemed to be in easy circumstances, and I assumed that his American wife, Marie, had an income. Often in the afternoon, I went to see him and he would rouse himself from his melancholic mood and start talking in his impassioned way on many subjects, snatching up whatever book he was reading at the time. He defended, for example, the complimentary songs of the eighteenth-century Gaelic poet, Carolan,

2. In *Stephen MacKenna: Journal and Letters*, edited with a memoir by E. R. Dodds and a preface by Patrick Colum (New York: W. Morrow, 1936).
3. R. C. Jebb (1841-1905), professor of Greek at Glasgow and later regius professor at Cambridge. He was a diligent and prolific scholar.
4. After Crete proclaimed union with Greece, Turkey declared war, but was defeated at Thessaly. The war was concluded by the Peace of Constantinople (1897).
5. Joseph Pulitzer (1847-1911), owner of the New York *World* 1866-1931, for which MacKenna worked as a European representative and for which he covered the Russian Revolution and visited Tolstoy.
6. Robert Donovan (1852-1934), journalist, university lecturer and advocate of censorship in the late 1920s.
7. Hawley Harvey Crippen (1862-1910), called Dr Crippen, an American doctor living in England, who was executed for poisoning his wife. He was the first criminal to be apprehended by the use of radio-telegraphy.
8. James Stephens (1882-1950), poet and a man of letters, one of MacKenna's closest friends.

showing me how the occasional, irregular rhythms were due to his improvisations on the harp. He declaimed passages from Rabelais so powerfully that the onomatopoeic effect of the monkish compounds and nonsense words in the mighty parody were clear to me.

He spoke Irish fluently and in a Dublin way. Once I listened for half an hour while Mrs. Alice Stopford Green,[9] the historian, and he conversed so eagerly that it became a living language to me. Later he taught Irish to James Stephens, and to his enthusiasm and help, we owe *Reincarnations*.[10]

Stephen MacKenna, who suffered from ill-health, was tall, black-haired, languid in his movements. Nevertheless, his deep musical voice became vibrant as it moved onward in sombre eloquence. I asked him once about his experiences in London during the 'Nineties, but he disliked the great city and dismissed it in one of his vivid sentences: 'In the middle of Piccadilly Circus, a navvy would get down from a cart, open his trousers, take out an organ as large as that of an elephant, and proceed to piddle against the back-wheel.'

I regarded Stephen MacKenna as my literary father, but he was a difficult parent and I did not always venture to visit him, for his moods were uncertain. He had praised excessively my first book. So when my third book was published, I went to see him at Bray where he was staying to recuperate. 'I've a golden boil on my bottom,' he exclaimed, rising painfully from the cushion on an armchair. He pushed aside *The Sword of the West*[11] with an impatient gesture, 'I couldn't get through it.' He talked of other subjects, with sore halts, his first alliterative exclamation coming as a refrain, much to my confusion for I was young and outwardly modest.

II

After the Irish Treaty was signed in 1921 and a Provisional Government set up, Stephen MacKenna, who remained a Republican, was so indignant that he left the country at once. At the same time, that caustic critic and Unionist, John Eglington [*sic*],[12] left for contrary reasons. Both settled down, sharing their grievances, in Bournemouth.

At the first Tailteann Games in 1924,[13] a prize was awarded to him, which he refused to accept in a violent letter. But the wily promoters of culture suppressed the letter and got that 'innocent essayist', G. K. Chesterton, who was over for the occasion, to present the prize *in absentia* to the unwilling translator of Plotinus.

I met Stephen MacKenna by chance one morning in the tea-room at Victoria Station. He had come up from Bournemouth to see the wealthy patron, who subsidized the translation, and was having breakfast, of tea, toast and boiled egg. He was dressed for the great occasion in a suit of dark blue, with a nice new tie. Unfortunately, in the middle of the tie was a blob of yolk. Such was my awe of him, that I did not dare to tell him. He seemed incapable of finding his way to Addison Road, and so I brought him there on the bus. Still worrying over that yellow blob and my lack of courage, I left him at the gate of the lordly mansion. That was the last time I met Stephen MacKenna.

III

On a sunny afternoon in the Spring of 1915, I ventured hesitantly along Oakley Road, in Ranelagh, and found after a brief search the address for which I was looking. The front garden of the small Georgian house was gay with daffodils between the ornamental shrubs. The door was opened by a tall young women, pale, red-lipped, with heavy black hair and languorous movements. In a Rossettian dream, I waited for a few moments in the drawing-room, until her husband, Thomas MacDonagh, came in and greeted me.

I had met the poet once or twice in College, although I was not as yet in his class. I saw him often making his way happily among the throng of students in the hall, small as Thomas Moore, and as curly-headed, speaking vivaciously with quick

9. Alice Stopford Green (1847-1929), historian and senator of the Free State. Among her best-known works are *The Making of Ireland and Its Undoing* (1908) and the pamphlet *Ourselves Alone and Ulster* (1918).
10. A collection of poems adapted from the writings of several Gaelic poets, published in 1918.
11. Clarke's third book was published in 1921, preceded by *The Vengeance of Fionn* (1918) and *The Fires of Baal* (1921).
12. John Eglinton (1868-1961), pseudonym of William Kirkpatrick Magee, best remembered for his *Anglo-Irish Essays* (1917) and for his appearance in the 'Scylla and Charybdis' chapter of *Ulysses*.
13. The Tailteann Games were held in Croke Park, Dublin on 2 August 1924. They were named after the ancient Irish festival, Aonach Tailteann of 716 A.D.

gestures. He dressed in light grey, wore a brown bow, a round hat clapped back.

He was Assistant to Professor Robert Donovan, a white-haired, fatherly man who explained Bradley's Theory of Tragedy[14] to us and portrayed Shakespeare as the great Moral Teacher recognized by the Victorian age. He read from the plays, modestly skipping the coarser passages which we enjoyed secretly at our desks. Fr. George O'Neill, our Professor of Philology and Language gave us on one occasion the practical task of writing a Petrarchan sonnet, a Spenserian stanza and a short lyric. Thomas MacDonagh liked the lyric which I wrote about a green fantastic valley, and so he invited me to his house.

'A lyric comes suddenly with a lilt or a verbal tune,' he exclaimed that day, as soon as we sat down. 'But you may often have to wait for months until the words come.'

Much to my delight he treated me already as a fellow poet. He talked to me of his favourite lyric writer, Thomas Campion, who was a contemporary of Shakespeare. He was certain that Campion was of Irish descent, for he was described in the minutes of the Parliament held in the Middle Temple in 1565 as 'son and heir of John Campion of Dublin, Ireland, deceased'. The name, formerly pronounced 'Champion' in Ireland and England, was one of the anglicized forms of O'Crowley, in Gaelic, O'Cruaidhlaoch, the grandson of the Head Warrior, or Champion. It is quite common to the present day in Kilkenny and Offaly. Thomas MacDonagh[15] explained to me his own theory of song-verse and speech-verse, quoted from the songs which Campion wrote and set to music, read out a passage from his rich, elaborate prose:

'The Apothecaries have Books of Gold, whose leaves, being opened, are so light, that they are subject to be shaken with the least breath; yet rightly handled, they serve both for ornament and use'.[16]

The small drawing-room was pleasant that afternoon with the fancied sound of lute notes, catches and glees.

As I was leaving, the poet's son, aged about two, toddled out beside us to the kerb. While his father was still talking to me about Tudor lyrics, the child called out as a horse and cart went by, 'Look Daddy, at the *capall*!'[17] This was my first experience of the hoped-for bilingual age.

While I was reading for an M.A. Degree, I attended the voluntary lectures given by Thomas MacDonagh on Anglo-Irish literature. In these lectures, he explained to us his theory of the Irish Mode, drawing on his study, *Literature in Ireland*, which was published after his execution a year later. As a lecturer he spoke in the easy, lucid, conversational way that shaped the prose of his book. Most of the writers he discussed were new to us and he held us by his enthusiasm. He showed us how translation of poems from Gaelic had led to a new, wavering, delayed rhythm. Thomas Moore had discovered this rhythm when setting words to some Irish folk tunes, as in the lyric which begins:

'At the mid hour of night when stars are weeping
I fly'[18]

Callanan[19] used it also in a few of his translations and it was further developed by Samuel Ferguson, for example, in *Cashel of Munster*:[20]

I'd wed you without herds, without money, or rich array,
And I'd wed you on a dewy morning at day-dawn grey.
My bitter woe it is, love, that we are not far away
In Cashel town, though the bare deal board were our marriage bed this day!

As a young man, Yeats had, with much perception, brought this delayed rhythm back into use:

I will arise and go now, and go to Innisfree.[21]

At a time when many poets still used a stilted diction, Yeats found in native ballads a simple natural speech. MacDonagh was fond of quoting that fascinating lyric from the play *Deirdre*:

'Why is it', Queen Edain said,
'If I do but climb the stair
To the tower overhead,

14. A. C. Bradley (1851-1935), whose *Shakespearean Tragedy* (1904) became a standard item in university reading lists.
15. MacDonagh developed this theory in his *Literature in Ireland* (1916).
16. Thomas Campion (1567-1619), author of four *Books of Ayres* (1610-12) and of *Observations in the Art of English Poesie* (1602), from which the quotation is taken.
17. Irish for 'horse'. The son was Donagh MacDonagh (1912-68), later to become poet, dramatist and lawyer.
18. From Moore's *Irish Melodies*.
19. J. J. Callanan (1795-1829); some of his best translations are in *The Recluse of Inchidony* (1830).
20. In *Lays of the Western Gael* (1867).
21. 'The Lake Isle of Innisfree' in *The Rose* (1893).

When the winds are calling there,
Or the gannets calling out
In waste places of the sky,
There's so much to think about
That I cry, that I cry?'[22]

Thomas MacDonagh suggested that I should write a thesis on the influence of lute-music in the shaping of the Tudor lyric. For months I picked out Elizabethan tunes on the piano at home, pursued delicate shifts of accent, cunning pauses, wandering, entranced and bewildered, in a region where all was evasive and tantalizingly beyond grasp. As my difficulties increased, I hurried for advice to my tutor and always his enthusiasm sent me away in hope. But when I thought over his words, they were as elusive as the long and short syllables, heavy and light stresses, which tormented my ear.

Once as we were crossing St. Stephen's Green together, MacDonagh mentioned A.E. 'His mysticism is too vague,' he remarked, comparing it with that of St. John of the Cross. Secretly, I resented what he said, for I admired the poems of A.E., but I kept a respectful silence. On another occasion, thinking of some of my less serious companions in class, I began, with youthful pomposity 'Mr. MacDonagh, why do you cast ...' Before I could finish, he glanced at me sharply 'Who are the swine?' I was abashed for I realized at that moment how deep was his feeling for our country.

One of Thomas MacDonagh's early books had the Whitmanesque title *Songs of Myself*,[23] but his vanity was so innocent and gay, that it was inoffensive. He told us how he had often gone into the book-shops to enquire about the sales of his books.

'Publish here,' he advised me, great was still the reputation of Dublin since the Revival.

Students watch their lecturers with close attention, so it was that late in the Spring of 1916, I began to realize, with a feeling of foreboding, that something was about to happen for I noticed at times, though only for a few seconds, how abstracted and worried Thomas MacDonagh looked. Suddenly, one day, during a lecture on the Young Ireland Poets, he took a large revolver from his pocket and laid it on the desk, 'Ireland can only win freedom by force' he remarked, as if to himself.

22. Yeats's *Deirdre* (1906); song of the First Musician.
23. Published in 1910.

The young are conventional and so I was shocked by what he had done. I remembered a story about Edmund Burke, which Professor Donovan had read to us in our First Arts Class when we were studying *Reflections on the French Revolution*, a book kept on the course in order, no doubt, that all undergraduates should become Constitutionalists and faithful followers of the Irish Party at Westminster. During a speech the great orator had flourished and flung a dagger on the floor of the House of Commons, offending members by that histrionic gesture.[24]

Shortly after I had discovered the Abbey, a small theatre was founded in Hardwick Street by Edward Martyn, for the production of realistic and Continental plays.[25] On my first visit to the hall, I saw MacDonagh and Joseph Plunkett,[26] his fellow-poet, in the front row, watching a play by Ibsen. Plunkett, thin, bespectacled, looked as emaciated as the Spanish Saint in his prison cell at Toledo. I longed so much to be in their company that I followed vaguely what was afoot on the stage....

24. This scene took place on 28 December 1792, during a speech on a government bill for the restriction of aliens, as England moved towards a declaration of war with revolutionary France.
25. The Irish Theatre (1914-20) founded by Edward Martyn, Thomas MacDonagh and Joseph Plunkett as an alternative to the Abbey and the commercial theatre. It concentrated on contemporary continental drama.
26. Joseph Mary Plunkett (1887-1916), one of the executed leaders of the 1916 Rising. He had been editor of *The Irish Review* 1913-14 and a founder of the Irish Theatre (see preceding note). He published one volume of poems in his lifetime, *The Circle and the Sword* (1911); his *Poems* appeared in 1916, after his death.

CHAPTER FOUR

I

On the morning of Easter Monday, the road outside our terrace was quiet. Thousands had already left the city on their way to the Fairyhouse Races by train, on outside cars, in traps, wagonettes, and even in Ford cars. My eldest sister, Doto, and I were busy in the sunny breakfast room. She was playing a tune by John Dowland on the piano for me, which I had copied out in the National Library from an old Book of Ayres.[1] Suddenly, the side-

1. John Dowland (1563-1626), born in Dalkey, Co. Dublin, published his *The First Booke of Songes or Ayres* in 1597, *The Second Booke of Songs or Ayres* 1600, *The Third and Last Booke of Songs* 1603.

door bell rang urgently. She hurried to answer the ringing and in less than a minute, my father, mother and Eileen were with us, listening in astonishment as an excited neighbour told us the news.

'The G.P.O. has been occupied by the Volunteers.... The tricolour of the Irish Republic is flying above it.... Jacob's factory ... Boland's Mill have also been occupied.... Some say there has been an attack on Dublin Castle.... The O.T.C.[2] are guarding Trinity College ... others say all the country is rising ... the No. 10 trams have stopped. ... The Railway Bridge down the road is barricaded'.

We went out to the front gate. A quarter of a mile down the road, we could see a double-decker tram on the Bridge, over the railway line, with upturned carts piled on each side of it.

Another neighbour came to the gate to tell us that a regiment of Lancers had been scattered near Nelson Pillar.

In a couple of minutes, I was among the sightseers at the barricade, my bicycle against the nearby railings. Five or six Volunteers, a couple of them in green uniforms, were on guard, while others were at their posts in the upper windows of several houses on each side of the road, with rifles ready. I noticed with surprise when I looked down the railway line towards Cabra, that the other bridge had not been barricaded. This seemed odd planning and I wondered whether the Lancers had trotted down the Cabra Road to the City.

One of the Volunteers was a medical student from our College, whom I knew well, a large earnest fellow with a slow stammer. He had been called up that morning, but would tell me nothing of what had happened. He was in his ordinary clothes and wore a bandolier. I did not mention anything to him about the other unguarded bridge.

I cycled home to report, and at about half-past twelve passed the barricade again, pedalling as fast as I could by Doyle's Corner, over the Canal Bridge, by Goldsmith Street, the Mater Hospital, down Blessington Street to Rutland Square.

Lower O'Connell Street, to my surprise, was silent and without people. On the left near Nelson Pillar, a dead horse lay on the road — a melancholy sight. When I came nearer, I saw a little crowd outside the General Post Office and the tricolour — green, white and yellow — fluttering above the great building. Inside the sand-bagged windows were armed men, silent, watchful.

I turned to read the printed proclamation on an electric standard at the corner:

> The Republic guarantees religious and civil liberty, equal rights and equal opportunities to all [its] citizens and declares its resolve to pursue the happiness and prosperity of the whole nation and of all its parts, cherishing all the children of the nation equally. . . .

I crossed the street and wheeled my bicycle slowly by the kerb. Within a shop doorway, near the D.B.C.,[3] I was alarmed to see a workman, bristled, unshaven, smoking a clay pipe contentedly, as he sat, rifle on knee, I guessed that he was a member of the Citizen Army. Carlyle's description of the Reign of Terror came into my mind: I heard the creaking of the tumbrils, the shouts of the sans-culottes.[4] I went past the O'Connell Monument, feeling ashamed of the middle-class snobbery which had disturbed my patriotic emotion for I thought I had rid myself of it when I left school.

Soon I was among the crowd outside the College of Surgeons in St. Stephen's Green. Behind the sandbagged windows were armed men, silent, watchful. A few people were peering between the railings of the Park and I hurried over to join them. Volunteers were digging trenches across the path inside and I wondered why they were doing so, for it was obvious that they could be shot down mercilessly from the high houses around the Green.

Puzzled and bewildered, I cycled down Grafton Street, past the G.P.O., up Rutland Square, to Phibsborough Church, and soon was at the barricade again. My student friend was not there, and one of the Volunteers told me that he had been sent for, as his father had been taken ill and was dying. He would be back shortly. I wondered why this officer had given him leave. Later I heard what happened. When he got home to Drumcondra, he found that his father was quite well. He was angry at the trick which had been played on him. His mother, however, persuaded him to change into an older suit and while he was doing so, his father locked the bed-room door. After the Rebellion was

2. Officer Training Corps (for the British army).

3. Dublin Bakery Company.

4. The French revolutionary mob. Thomas Carlyle's *French Revolution* was published in three volumes in 1837.

over, he gave himself up and was interned in the camp at Frongach in Wales.[5]

II

It was about five o'clock in the afternoon when I met Stephen MacKenna in the middle of O'Connell Street, directly opposite the G.P.O. A restless, difficult crowd was gathered at the corner of Earl Street, while a few Volunteers armed with rifles and in full green uniform were endeavouring to keep order. As I made my way here and there through the scattered groups, I saw Stephen MacKenna alone in a little space, lost in thought, indifferent to those about him. He was leaning weakly against a tram standard, but he greeted me in his quick melancholy way. He told me that he had hurried down that morning as soon as he heard the news. He had been there all day. He looked pale and ill: it was obvious that only the intensity of his own feelings and of the event itself had sustained him. The G.P.O. was already cold grey in the shadow and beyond passing heads I could see again, almost obscured by the great pillars, the watchful figures of armed men behind the sand-bagged windows. Clearly against the blue sky above the roof waved the flag of the Irish Republic declared that morning.

Stephen MacKenna said little to me. Thought, emotion, could find no other end for themselves than the words 'At Last'. Certainly, neither of us mentioned any of those friends who, as we knew, must be at their posts, so near to us or somewhere else in the city. The historic hour existed with all its secret, countless memories of the past, in and of itself, so that even the feeling of suspense and of coming disaster seemed to belong to a lesser experience of reality. It is difficult now to recapture that emotion, that thought, from which even the crowd, dimly hostile or, perhaps, taken by total surprise, was scarcely a distraction. It has become quite easy to forget how completely the country had turned away from its own individual, national life, to forget how bitterly the few awakeners and poets who revived pride, were hated and abused.

As I stood silently beside Stephen MacKenna, I was increasingly aware, not only of a supreme event but of the painful emotion in his few broken words from time to time. I was still a student, with a healthy respect both for his Greek scholarship and for the wilful anger which I had once innocently drawn upon myself. His tormented exaltation — which I secretly understood — filled me with a superstitious alarm for him. I wanted to be alone, even to be rid of him, that I might think of Wolfe Tone, Robert Emmet, and the hosts of the dead.

Realising that his wife and others might be already searching for him, and calling to mind the imminent danger in the City, I tried vaguely to persuade him to leave. By then, he had almost forgotten my presence — perhaps, he too, wished to be rid of me. After a few timid, futile efforts, I went away, full of compunction, leaving him to his thoughts. . . .

IV

During the struggle for independence, hasty encounters between a score of British soldiers and hedge-hidden guerrilla-fighters were always described largely in the newspapers as battles. So I record now the forgotten Battle of the North Circular Road, in which a regiment fought alone.

On the third sunny day of the Rising, at two o'clock in the afternoon, I was sitting in a deck-chair in the front garden, when I heard a rattle around the bend near our house. I got up and saw the muzzle of a field-gun protruding around the corner. A few soldiers in war-time khaki, accompanied by an Officer, were pushing it forward. As they crouched behind its low shield, the gunner took aim. I heard the bang as the shell went by and a few seconds later the crash of it into the tram a quarter of a mile away. Then like the last feeble reverberations of its echo came the crackle of a volley from the houses beside the barricade. Half a dozen shells hurtled by in rapid succession. The carts were blown to smithereens. The tram was still there, gaunt and shattered.

Mr. Bergin, the corn-factor who lived next door and his sister, Mrs. Maughan, a widow with seven annoying cats, were in their front garden like us. No one was alarmed, for in those days of British Rule, we were used to the sight of soldiers. Every evening, Tommies in their smart red tunics and dark blue trousers, silver knobbed canes under their arm, strutted towards the City to flirt with girls in Lower O'Connell Street. In the house on our left, the two

5. An internment camp for Irish prisoners, near Bala, Merioneth. The men, including Michael Collins, were held in a huge distillery that once had produced Welsh whiskey.

spinsters were watching from one of the top windows.

Then, around the corner, a regiment of soldiers came, pressing against the wall. Some crept along by the garden railings, others stooped by the flower-beds, and dropped quickly over the low walls. As they filed slowly through our garden, a young soldier stopped to ask Doto for a drink of water. He was trembling, and pitying him she hurried in to get a tumbler-full. As he gulped the water down, I glared at her as boldly as I could, in patriotic indignation. Slowly the soldiers moved from garden to garden or crouched by the railings, then darted from gate to gate. In the silence, there was only the clump of their boots on the pavement, the rattle of their gun-butts. It seemed like a mock advance in manoeuvres. We watched, keeping our secret from the enemy. As there had been only one round of rifle shots from the Bridge, we knew that the Volunteers, acting under orders — or frightened by the shelling — had skipped over the backgarden walls and fled along the railway embankment.

Soon most of our neighbours left the doorsteps and went back to their sitting rooms. Even the two old maids had retired from their favourite window. I waited on, watching caps bobbing up and down quickly, bodies slumping over the walls between flowering shrubs, or hunkering along the pavement. The twenty minutes of advance seemed as slow as an hour.

At last, the entire regiment seemed to have vanished. There was a long pause, but I knew that at any moment the attack would start. Suddenly, there was volley after volley. Then a detachment of the infantry charged past the broken barricade. In a few moments, the empty houses had been captured.

The Battle of the North Circular Road was over.

Rumours had ceased. The sunny weather continued and in a few days another leaf would be pulled from the Almanac. Fear was everywhere. All were aware of the approaching might of Great Britain, terrible as that of the Kaiser.[6] Some were waiting for the sea-rumble when our ancient City would be bombarded by warships.

V

Something strange was going on in our house, but I did not pretend to notice it. Then, one night, as I sat in my small study in the return,[7] the door opened. My father brought someone in with him and quickly left us to talk. I was much surprised to find myself greeting an old family friend, an engineer in the Dublin Corporation, for I thought that he was in the Pigeon House, the electric power station near Ringsend. I had understood that he was Commandant of the small force that had occupied it on Easter Monday morning.

He was a middle-sized man, about forty years of age, with a dark pointed beard, always full of high spirits, always ready to play another practical joke. Once, when I was much younger, he had given me a fright. The downstairs bell rang at twilight and when I opened the side-door, a dwarf rushed past me along the passage. The next moment, I saw the engineer leaning against the wall, laughing at me after his acrobatic act.

But, this night, he was pale, agitated, I guessed that he had failed to turn up at his post. He talked awkwardly to me about my studies, took several books from the shelves and put them back. Every quarter of an hour he left the room hurriedly and went upstairs. While he was in the bathroom I thought of him with contempt, for the young are harsh in their judgement. While I smoked my pipe, poked the fire in the small grate, I wondered what had happened at the Pigeon House.

On the next night, he was back again in my room and, as before, neither of us mentioned the events of the week. Every quarter of an hour, he left the room restlessly and I could hear him going upstairs. I did not see him again after the second night.

At last, rumours came back. Smoke was rising from the centre of the city. The G.P.O., the Gresham Hotel and several large buildings in O'Connell Street were ablaze. Padraic Pearse and the other leaders had surrendered unconditionally. Hundreds of Volunteers were prisoners in the Military barracks. Only Eamonn [*sic*] De Valera was holding out with his riflemen in Boland's Mill.

The newspapers were on sale again. Aghast, day after day, we read of the execution of the signatories of the Proclamation, one by one. In the British House of Commons, John Dillon, one of the leading Members of the Irish Parliamentary Party, pleaded in vain for clemency.

The *Irish Independent*, the clericalist newspaper owned by William Martin Murphy, the formidable

6. Kaiser Wilhelm II (1888-1918), German emperor.

7. A part of a house that forms an angle with the façade.

magnate of the Lock-Out three years previously, demanded the blood of the Socialist leader, James Connolly, who had been badly wounded.

General Maxwell obeyed what was claimed to be the will of the people. James Connolly was carried out in a chair and shot.

My father had disappeared from the house on a secret journey. Later, I learned that he had smuggled his old friend out of the country to Liverpool. Then, in his affable way, with the help of some bribing, he had got the Commandant, disguised as a stoker, on board a liner leaving for New York.

Exhausted by work in the furnace room, fear and remorse, the unfortunate fugitive died a few weeks later of double pneumonia in an American hospital, leaving, penniless in Dublin, his wife and two small children.

BULMER HOBSON

(1883-1969)

from: IRELAND YESTERDAY AND TOMORROW (1968)

[Between 1913 and 1915 the Irish Volunteers grew in strength and organization. Bulmer Hobson was the most energetic member of the provisional committee that arranged the two conventions of 1914 and 1915 and did most of the editorial work for the movement's newspaper, *The Irish Volunteer*, in which he and others advocated the military strategy of guerrilla warfare that later would be practised in 1919-21. Hobson had been a member of the Irish Revolutionary Brotherhood since 1904 and he was determined to use the Volunteer organization to further the IRB's aims. But he found himself to be the victim of a more deeply sown IRB conspiracy which produced the 1916 Rising, an action that Hobson thought foolish in itself and in contravention of the IRB constitution. His version of the events leading to the Rising demonstrates the difference between the secular, pragmatic republicanism of one wing of the IRB and the sacrificial and religious zealotry of the faction that Pearse came, very suddenly, to dominate.]

CHAPTER VIII

THE IRISH VOLUNTEERS AND THE RISING

. . . It was the generally accepted aim of the Irish Volunteers, first to build up their strength both as regards men and arms in order to become a real power; that if they were attacked, or if an attempt was made to disarm them, they would resist such an attempt by every means open to them. The military instruction which was given in their paper, *The Irish Volunteer*, was all directed to this end. Guerilla fighting was inevitably the method to be adopted, as the Volunteers could never hope, with their resources of men and equipment, to place an army in the field, and with our resources it was the only method by which resistance could be maintained over any length of time or with any prospect of success.

The training notes in the paper, such as the notable series written by O'Connell entitled 'Hedge Fighting,' were all calculated to turn the men's minds to the possibilities of putting up a resistance which could be prolonged and would be very difficult for a foreign force to suppress. On the political side it was hoped, as we became stronger, to start a policy of complete non-co-operation with the Castle Government, a passive resistance which would clog all its machinery and by degrees make its operation impossible. In short, it was the policy outlined by Fintan Lalor in 1847, advocated by Griffith in the *United Irishman*, by the Dungannon Clubs in *The Republic*, by the IRB in *Irish Freedom* and which was subsequently put into operation in the period before the Treaty of 11 July 1921.[1]

1. In Chapter V of this book, Hobson describes how he had discovered Lalor's writings of 1847 and his theory of 'moral insurrection', based on a distinction between the defensive and aggressive use of physical force. Lalor, in effect, was describing the tactics of guerrilla warfare. Hobson published a pamphlet, *Defensive Warfare*, in 1909 in which his debt to Lalor is evident. Arthur Griffith was much more given to

Soon after the war started in August 1914, there was constant talk of the British Government bringing in a measure of military conscription. Sections of the British press were clamouring for such action and some influential people were calling for it. We hoped that before any such development could take place we would have at least the nucleus of a force to resist it effectively. It was clear that if conscription was seriously threatened the great mass of Redmond's supporters would come flocking back into the Irish Volunteers as they had done in 1913, and that our problem would be one of armaments and organisation, and not one of winning popular support.

Out of many discussions a general plan began to emerge. In the event of conscription being imposed on the country, it was intended that men drafted for the army should join small flying columns in various parts of the country, defend themselves from being captured, with whatever arms we could obtain, and conduct a guerilla war against the forces sent to draft them into the British armies.

It was intended that only those men whom the authorities were immediately attempting to press into their army should take this action, as it was very important to keep the numbers of men on active service as small as possible relative to the civilian population which would support them, conceal them and assist them to avoid capture.

We, on the Volunteer Executive, knew that if it was attempted to impose conscription almost the entire population would actively support our resistance to it, and we were confident that we could defeat it. We believed that not only could we make conscription unworkable, but that, in the ensuing struggle, we could make a continuance of the British government of Ireland impossible also. That in general terms was the policy.

Behind the scenes other events were taking place. I was well aware when I resigned from the Supreme Council of the IRB that I was leaving the direction of the organisation largely in the hands of Sean McDermott.[2] This was inevitable unless I was prepared to engage in a struggle for power which would have split the movement, and I was not prepared to do this. I had many reasons. Apart from a natural distaste for such a contest, I was over-burdened with work for the Irish Volunteers, and I felt that policies of which I might not approve could hardly be as disastrous as a conflict which might well leave the movement incapable of pursuing any policy at all.

I had other difficulties as well. The work I had been doing for many years to further the national movement was entirely unpaid, and it took up nearly all my time. I was Honorary Secretary of the Irish Volunteers and spent ten or twelve hours a day in their office. I had been the unpaid editor of *Irish Freedom*[3] for several years, and I had to try to make a living in odd moments of ill-paid journalism. A situation like this sets a limit to what one can undertake, and I had about reached my limit at that moment.

McDermott and I had been on friendly terms in the Dungannon Club days in Belfast, and I had been responsible for his appointment as our full-time organiser in the country. But we had been drifting apart for some time, though the bitterness of his antagonism took me quite by surprise. I had no such feelings towards him. Differences of background and education and a different set of values were partly responsible, but since by the greatest of ill-fortune he had become permanently crippled (after an attack of poliomyelitis I think) he had, unawares, become resentful of my greater activity. He was a man completely devoted to the cause of Irish freedom, a man of deep sincerity, but I had come to distrust his judgement and to dislike his methods. After his very hostile attitude at the time of the admission of Redmond's nominees, the breach between us was complete.[4]

the doctrine of passive resistance than to the use of physical force, but the IRB tactic was to recruit his opinions and prestige to their own interpretation of Lalor. *The Republic* was the organ of the Dungannon Clubs, founded in 1905 by Hobson and Denis McCullough in commemoration of the 1782 Volunteer Convention at Dungannon, Co. Tyrone. The Clubs were absorbed into Sinn Féin between 1906 and 1908. *Irish Freedom* was the IRB newspaper, managed by Seán MacDiarmada and in effect edited by Hobson for a time between 1910 and 1914.

2. Seán McDermott (MacDiarmada) (1884-1916), was estranged from Hobson because the latter agreed to John Redmond's request for a preponderant representation of the Irish Parliamentary Party on the executive committee of the Irish Volunteers.
3. *Irish Freedom*, founded in 1910, was suppressed by government order in 1914.
4. Hobson admitted Redmond's nominees 'because I knew that a split at that time would end volunteering in Ireland'. But when Redmond, without consulting the Volunteers, urged the members to fight on Britain's side in World War I, Hobson and MacNeill decided that 'the time for a break had come'. The bitterness of the dispute with McDermott and Tom Clarke was compounded by the fact that they had accused Hobson of treachery in admitting Redmond's nominees.

In the autumn of 1914, under the influence of McDermott, the Supreme Council of the IRB decided they would embark on an insurrection against the British Government before the European War came to an end. Some members of the Council demurred at this, but ceased to oppose it when they saw they were outnumbered. None of them apparently remembered that such action was forbidden by the Constitution they had all sworn to obey.[5] No time was fixed; just a decision to act before the end of the war.

A small committee, of which McDermott and Clarke[6] were the effective members, was appointed with instructions to examine the project, and to report back to the Supreme Council. They never reported back. The Supreme Council met seldom after this and they were never informed what their committee was doing. The Supreme Council was, in effect, superseded and ceased to count. The committee proceeded to co-opt whom they pleased and to consult whom they pleased, and they were very careful to conceal their proceedings from any members of the Supreme Council who could not be counted on to approve of their actions.

Even the President of the Supreme Council, Denis McCullough,[7] was not allowed to know of their proceedings and the fact that he did not then live in Dublin made it easier to keep him in the dark. This secrecy was maintained until a few days before the insurrection.

Just a week before the insurrection was planned to take place McCullough came to Dublin to try to find out what was happening. Tom Clarke denied all knowledge and McDermott tried to avoid meeting him. Only when it was no longer possible to conceal the situation from him did McCullough learn that a rising was to take place in a few days' time.

I occupied a key position as Dublin Centre of the IRB and Secretary of the Volunteers, and great care was taken to ensure that no information should reach me. Those who were made privy to McDermott's plans were warned that no one outside their small close circle must know anything. It was, in effect, a secret society organised within a secret society, much as the Invincibles[8] had been organised in the 1880s, only this time the chief organiser was Secretary of the Supreme Council and in a unique position to carry out his plans.

Quite independently of all this, James Connolly let it be known that he was contemplating an insurrection all on his own, with his Citizen Army.[9] There was no secrecy about this; in fact it became a subject of general conversation in the IRB and the Volunteers. Connolly's weekly paper was full of abuse of leading members of the Irish Volunteers, who were supposed to be 'bourgeois' or anti-labour, or generally not revolutionary enough.[10] The position would have been ridiculous if it were not so dangerous.

This was very embarrassing for the secret Military Committee who had not yet made their plans, and they could not be sure that Connolly did not mean what he said. Connolly had only a handful of men and very few arms, but that did not seem to matter. The action Connolly threatened, if he took it, would forestall the Military Committee, take the initiative from them and leave them in the position of falling in behind Connolly which they were very reluctant to do, or of abandoning all hope of completing their own plans for an insurrection.

It was in these circumstances that the mysterious disappearance or kidnapping of Connolly took place on 19-22 January 1916. He certainly disappeared suddenly and without explanation for several days, and the Citizen Army threatened to start their insurrection if he did not return within a few days. He did reappear in time, but would not give any explanations of where he had been or why he had vanished without a word to any of his friends.

I believe that what happened was that the Military Committee asked Connolly to come to a conference. They sent two men in a car, who were armed, to convey the invitation, but with instructions to bring him anyway if he did not accept. He went and was away for several days, and in the

5. Hobson quotes the passage below; it is part of the constitution of the IRB, adopted in 1873.
6. Thomas Clarke (1858-1916), a Fenian and one of the leaders of the 1916 Rising.
7. Denis McCullough (1883-1968), director of the IRB in Ulster, then president of its supreme council. He supported the 1916 Rising, but was not informed of the final preparations.
8. The Invincibles, the terrorist group founded in 1881 as a breakaway from the Fenians.
9. James Connolly (1868-1916) became involved with the workers' defence force, the Irish Citizen Army, after the Great Lockout of 1913.
10. Connolly's paper *The Workers' Republic* (suppressed in February 1915) attacked the Volunteers for their middle-class attitudes and for their inactivity.

course of discussions they reached agreement. The Military Committee agreed to fix the date for the insurrection at Easter 1916, and Connolly agreed to wait till then and to join with them and abandon his threat of independent action. It was heroic, and in the Irish tradition. 'The Celts always marched forth to battle — and always fell.' There was not the slightest chance of any other outcome. I had hoped with Fintan Lalor's policy to change that — and to win. I believed that, as Lalor had said, our fight, to be successful, must be a defensive one, never to risk a decisive defeat, to paralyse the Administration with passive resistance and to restrict active resistance to a guerilla war. These were, I thought, the essential conditions for success.

While I had little specific knowledge of what was taking place, I had a good deal of suspicion, and, very early in 1916, O'Connell, Fitzgibbon[11] and I demanded a special all-day meeting of the Executive Committee of the Volunteers in order to make a final effort to arrive at a clear understanding as to the policy which was to be pursued by the Irish Volunteers. At our request, McNeill prepared a clear statement on Volunteer policy, which it was proposed to ask everybody present either to assent to or dissent from. The original of that document, in McNeill's handwriting, is among my papers in the National Library.

The meeting was held at Woodtown Park, Rathfarnham, where McNeill was then living, in order that we might have uninterrupted discussion for as long as was necessary. Pearse and McDermott at this meeting denied in the most explicit terms having any intention to land the Volunteers in an insurrection, and reproached the rest of us for our suspicious natures. McNeill, who always tried to avoid conflict, did not press the matter. Shortly after the discussion began I saw him slip his document into a drawer. There was no subscription to his memorandum, and the discussion ended with a complete denial on the part of Pearse and McDermott that they had ever contemplated committing the Volunteers to any policy not decided on by the Executive Committee. With this assurance we had to be content, little as some of us believed their protestations.

I remember having a discussion with Pearse in a Dublin restaurant about this time, which ended with him saying as he rose from the table: 'I cannot answer your arguments, but I *feel* that we must have an insurrection.' About the same time, in another Dublin restaurant, I had a similar conversation with James Connolly. His conversation was full of clichés derived from the earlier days of the socialist movement in Europe. He told me that the working class was always revolutionary and that Ireland was a powder magazine, and that all that was necessary was for someone to apply the match.

I thought of this later as I watched the Dublin mob, not joining Connolly in the Post Office, but looting the shops in O'Connell Street. I thought of it again when I read in the Press how the British soldiers, after the surrender, had to protect their prisoners from the violence of the Dublin populace.

In the early months of 1916 there was a feeling of growing tension, and, as far as I was concerned, of growing disbelief in the protestations of Pearse and McDermott. This was greatly heightened when, about a week before the insurrection, McNeill brought me a document, which purported to be secret orders issued by the British authorities for the suppression of the Irish Volunteers, and desired me to have it circulated throughout the country.

I read this document with considerable doubt and asked McNeill where he got it. He said that he was not at liberty to tell me. The document did not appear to me to be genuine on the face of it, and, unable to get any information as to where it came from, I finally said to McNeill: 'Are you completely and absolutely satisfied as to its authenticity?' 'I am,' he said, and on that assurance I circulated it all over the country.

As a result of subsequent investigations in 1917, I discovered that McNeill had got the document from P. J. Little, who had got it from Rory O'Connor, who had got it from James Plunkett, a member of our Executive Committee, who was actively associated with Pearse and who had taken elaborate precautions to plant the document on McNeill.[12] The document was written by Plunkett

11. J. J. O'Connell (1887-1944), later General 'Ginger' O'Connell of the Irish Army, had written on military tactics in the *Irish Volunteer*; his kidnapping in 1922 precipitated the Civil War. Seán Fitzgibbon (MacGiobuin) supported Hobson on the executive committee of the Volunteers.

12. Joseph Plunkett (1887-1916) and Seán MacDermott forged the 'Castle Document' with the intent that it would incite more Volunteers to join the 1916 Rising. Published on 19 April 1916, it called for the arrest of specific individuals, the occupation of key areas and the suppression of the Irish Volunteers.

and printed for Plunkett by Colm O'Loughlin. Most of us were hoping to outwit the common enemy, but Plunkett devoted his talents to outwitting his friends.

There was a concert organised by Cumann na mBan[13] and held at 41 Parnell Square on Palm Sunday 16 April. Someone, whose name I do not remember, was to have given an address but did not turn up, and I was asked to fill the gap. On the spur of the moment I made a speech in very guarded language, so as not to excite the suspicions of the authorities, and yet sufficiently definite to be intelligible to the many Volunteers who were in the hall. I warned them of the extreme danger of being drawn into precipitate action, which could only have the effect of bringing the Volunteer movement to an end, and I said that no man had a right to risk the fortunes of the country in order to create for himself a niche in history. The great majority of the audience appeared to be in agreement with what I had said.

P. H. Pearse, whom I had sworn into the IRB at the end of 1913, once he had started moving to the left in Irish politics, moved so rapidly that six months later he was writing to people to whom I had introduced him in America casting doubts about my reliability as an Irish revolutionary. He had evolved a strange theory that to keep the national spirit alive it was necessary that there should be a blood sacrifice in every generation. He had visions of himself as the scapegoat for the people. I do not know if Connolly shared these views, but he is quoted in Nevinson's *Recollections* as having said to William O'Brien 'We are going out to be slaughtered.'[14]

The majority of the Executive Committee of the Irish Volunteers did not share this passion for self-immolation. They had no use for it as a political policy. They wanted to build up a real strength in Ireland, which would be sufficiently powerful to defend the country against conscription and wrest control of the administration from the British Government. We fully expected that the British Government would take the opportunity of dragooning the country and enforcing conscription if they were given the excuse of an abortive rising in Dublin.

13. The Women's Division of the Irish Volunteers, founded in 1913.
14. H. R. Nevinson (1856-1941). The remark is quoted in *Between the Wars* (1936); Nevinson has no volume entitled *Recollections*.

There were no plans, and in the circumstances there could not have been plans, which could seriously be called military. There was no military objective, no remotest possibility of military success. The tactic of locking bodies of men up in a number of buildings to stay there until they were shot or burned out of them was a demonstration in force, a revolt, a protest, and one which might well have been disastrous had it not been saved by the subsequent mishandling by the British Government, the unity of the people in face of the threat of conscription, the paralysis of the Administration by the polices adopted under the guidance of Dail Eireann, the magnificent courage and devotion of the flying columns in the guerilla war, and finally developments outside Ireland which could not have been foreseen. The disasters and follies of four years of war had left Britain dependent on American aid, and without an Irish settlement the American Government could not help.

The first definite information I had that an insurrection was to occur in the immediate future was late in the evening of Holy Thursday 1916, when J. J. O'Connell and Eimar O'Duffy[15] came into my office and told me that an insurrection had been planned for the following Sunday. With them I went immediately to McNeill's house at Rathfarnham, arriving a considerable time after he had gone to bed. We got McNeill up and with him we went to St Enda's to see Pearse, arriving about 2 a.m., knocking Pearse up.

McNeill, O'Connell and I went in to see Pearse, leaving O'Duffy, who was not a member of the Executive, outside. Pearse then admitted what he had so often denied, that an insurrection was to take place, and told us that nothing we could do could prevent it. This was in striking contrast to the assurances which he had so recently and so frequently given, that he was acting loyally and in good faith with his colleagues on the Executive Committee.

McNeill, O'Connell and I then returned to McNeill's house, where McNeill, as Chief-of-Staff, wrote an order instructing me to take complete charge in Dublin, and to take all necessary steps to

15. Eimar O'Duffy (1893-1935) wrote on military tactics for *The Irish Volunteer*; disillusioned with the Rising, he turned to writing. His novel *The Wasted Island* (1919) is one of the darkest accounts of the events of this period.

prevent the Volunteers being drawn into taking the initiative in an offensive action against the Government. McNeill also wrote a second order, directing O'Connell to proceed to Cork, and to take complete charge there, with the same object in view.

I arrived early on Good Friday at the Volunteer office after the night-long activity, and, immediately the office staff arrived, I set them to work burning correspondence and lists of names, so that, whatever happened, the authorities should not come into possession of the names of our members throughout the country. Before I had time to do anything else I received a note from McNeill: 'Take no action till I see you. Am coming in.' I waited till morning, but he did not come! I spent the time hurrying on the destruction of our papers.

Apparently, after we had left him, Pearse had communicated with some of his friends, because quite early on Good Friday morning, McDermott and MacDonagh[16] went to McNeill's house. They appear to have told him that the rising was inevitable, and to have convinced him that he could do nothing. It was often easier to convince McNeill that nothing could be done than it was to spur him into positive action. I realised, by this vacillation on McNeill's part, that it was impossible for me to take any further action, and, at any rate, events had by then got completely out of our control.

That afternoon I was asked by Sean Tobin, who had succeeded me as Chairman, to attend a meeting of the Leinster Executive of the IRB at Martin Conlon's house in Phibsboro. I was reluctant to go, and did not see any purpose to be served. At the same time I wondered if this was a ruse to get me out of the way. I yielded to the importunities of Sean Tobin to attend, and was not greatly surprised when, as I entered the house, a number of IRB men who were armed with revolvers, told me that I was a prisoner and could not leave the house. I felt that I had done all I could to keep the Volunteers on the course which I believed essential for their success, and that there was nothing further I could do.

My principal feeling was one of relief. I had been working under great pressure for a long time and was very tired. Now events were out of my hands.

On Easter Saturday, while I was still detained in Martin Conlon's house, McNeill was again galvanized into action by Sean Fitzgibbon and Colm O'Loughlin. Both had been induced to go on journeys to Kerry in connection with the projected landing of arms from Germany,[17] and Fitzgibbon had gone only after he had received the most explicit assurances from Eamonn Ceannt[18] that McNeill and I were enthusiastically participating in the venture. This roused McNeill into sending his countermanding order to the newspaper, in a last hopeless attempt to prevent the insurrection.

I was released from Martin Conlon's house on Easter Monday evening about six or seven o'clock, and my first object was to get in touch with McNeill and find out what the position was. I passed down O'Connell Street and saw Volunteers standing on guard at the Post Office, and on the other side of the street the Dublin mob, not joining Connolly but systematically looting the shops.

I stayed in Dublin on Monday night, and on Tuesday went out to Rathfarnham, where I got in touch with McNeill at his home in Woodtown Park. I had a long talk with him that night, but there did not seem to be anything that we could do at the moment. I stayed with him for the rest of the week.

On Wednesday of Easter week, Arthur Griffith and Patrick Bradley came to Woodtown Park to discuss the situation. They had cycled from Clontarf, keeping on the outskirts of the city. Griffith had received a mobilisation order on Easter Monday and had ignored it, as he shared our view as to the danger and the futility of the insurrection.

Towards the end of the week, when the surrender had taken place and most of the fighting had ceased, McNeill drafted a letter addressed to General Maxwell.[19] In it he asked for an interview with the object of preventing further bloodshed. He wanted me to sign it, too, but I refused, because I regarded it as a mere invitation to Maxwell to have us arrested by disclosing where we were. McNeill told me that we would have no political future if we were not arrested, but I replied that while I probably would be arrested, I was not going to ask for it.

16. Thomas MacDonagh (1878-1916), the university lecturer and poet.

17. The arms that were to be brought from Germany by Roger Casement.

18. Eamonn Ceannt (1881-1916) was elected to the provisional committee of the Irish Volunteers on their formation in November 1913. He was one of the seven signatories of the Proclamation of the Republic and was executed by firing squad in Kilmainham Jail, Dublin on 8 May 1916.

19. Commander of the British forces in Ireland in 1916.

The letter was taken into the British Military Headquarters by McNeill's eldest son, Niall, and very soon after an officer in uniform came out in a car, ostensibly to take McNeill in to see Maxwell. But when McNeill arrived, instead of meeting Maxwell he was confronted with Major Price, the head of the Dublin political police, who placed him under arrest. The officer who came out to bring McNeill in was a Belfast man called McCammond, whom I had known fairly well. He saw me at McNeill's but made no sign of recognition.

An overwhelming majority of the Irish Volunteer Executive supported McNeill and I [*sic*] in our design to build up the Volunteers into a powerful organisation, and to resort to guerilla tactics if and when we were attacked. The 1916 men were unable to challenge this policy successfully in the Executive Committee and were, therefore, driven to deceive their colleagues and to misuse their position as officers in the Volunteers to order men into action in pursuance of a policy different from the one they were publicly pledged to maintain.

After the pitiful demonstration in 1867, when a handful of Fenians were marched out to Tallaght and Stepaside, the IRB had to reorganize in 1873 and specifically inserted a clause in the new Constitution designed to prevent a recurrence of the futile demonstrations of the kind they had seen. They, therefore, inserted in the IRB Constitution the following sentence:

> The I.R.B. shall await the decision of the Irish Nation as expressed by a majority of the Irish People as to the fit hour of inaugurating a war against England. . . .

It was not the Supreme Council of the IRB who organized the insurrection, but a small junta inside the IRB, acting with the utmost secrecy and without the knowledge of the President and most other members of the Supreme Council.

After the insurrection I remained in Dublin for several months and then went to Belfast for a time. I took the necessary precautions to evade arrest. So, not having been in jail, as McNeill had said, I had no political future. But the policies I had advocated through arduous years had a political future — they led to the downfall of British power in Ireland.

BERNADETTE DEVLIN

(1947-)

THE PRICE OF MY SOUL (1969)

[Bernadette Devlin was elected to Westminster as MP for Mid-Ulster in April 1969. At that time, she was a member of the Peoples' Democracy Movement, founded in Belfast in October 1968, and the organizing body behind the Belfast-Derry protest march of 1 January 1969, which had been ambushed at Burntollet Bridge outside Derry by a motley band of B-Specials and loyalists. That incident, and a subsequent assault by the Royal Ulster Constabulary, the police force, on the catholic area of the Bogside in Derry, led to the consolidation of the catholic vote which gave Bernadette Devlin her electoral victory.

She was the youngest women MP ever elected to the House of Commons and the youngest MP elected there on universal suffrage. The publicity attending her arrival at Westminster turned into notoriety when she participated in the so-called 'Battle of the Bogside' in August 1969, when civilians and police engaged in a long battle that ended with the calling in of British troops.

The extract below is the book's last chapter.]

CHAPTER FOURTEEN

Both inside and outside Parliament I'd lost a great deal of popularity by the time my first session at Westminster ended in the summer of 1969. To begin with I was the greatest publicity gimmick since Kraft cheese slices, but it wasn't long before people discovered the final horrors of letting an urchin into Parliament. The British had shown what grand democrats they were: anybody — even a Northern Ireland brat of twenty-two — was allowed to sit in their House of Commons. And what did these ungrateful Irish peasants do, when you made them Members of Parliament and gave them £3,250 a year? They simply went off home and threw stones at you.

But I decided other people's attitudes didn't really matter and I left London to settle down to work in the constituency. I'd a number of things on my programme. I wanted to go to America to collect money for the civil rights movement. More particularly, I wanted to campaign for funds to start self-help schemes in the constituency, especially among the farmers. I was also going to do a lot of hard study and turn up in Parliament in October having read all their books and beat them at the parliamentary game as well.

Such were my intentions. Events were to prove that I might as well not have bothered to plan.

Ever since Major Chichester-Clark's election as Prime Minister,[1] a sort of false calm had prevailed in Northern Ireland, but below the surface the whole situation was becoming more and more tense. The 12th of July, the great Protestant celebration of King Billy's victory over James II and his Fenian hordes, was a curtain-raiser for the violence to come. In Derry the tension exploded in riots during which the Bogside took most of its own area apart. It was the first occasion on which there was massive looting in Derry, and all the respectable leaders of the community condemned it, failing to realize that the 'hooligans' were quite simply frustrated people wrecking everything because they couldn't find any other way of expressing their discontent. Once again the trouble in Derry spread across the country. In Dungiven — a town which is almost ninety per cent Roman Catholic — the Catholics burned the Orange Hall to the ground and tried to take the burnt stone apart with their hands. But there was no immediate sequel: tempers were calmed on the surface, the hooligans were put back in their cages and their ghettoes, and the country settled down to wait in some suspense for August 12th.

August 12th is the day of the Apprentice Boys' Procession in Londonderry, which celebrates the defence of the besieged city by the apprentices in 1689. These young boys, against the orders of their betters and wisers, closed the city gates and encouraged the population to fight off the besiegers, many of them dying at their posts, until the relief ships reached Derry 105 days later. So every year a procession some twenty to thirty thousand strong processes round the walls of Derry to ensure they've not been breached since last year, and normally no one pays any attention to it — it's just part of Northern Ireland's pageantry, one which, ironically enough, celebrates a struggle for civil and religious liberty. But by August 1969, the procession could be seen only as a provocative political act, and leaders of many sections of the community, Protestant and Catholic, asked the Government to put a blanket ban on marching until feelings cooled and reforms could be brought in which would create better relations between the townspeople in any given area. But the Government, which by this time had totally abdicated its responsibility to govern, refused to stop the procession on the grounds that it was traditional, and the pomp and ceremony for August 12th continued.

It led to further disorders. An Orangemen's parade in Belfast stopped outside a Catholic block of flats and doused the Papishes with 'God save the Queen' and a volley of stones. In return a bottle was hurled at the bandleader, and the resulting scuffle quickly escalated into general wrecking and rioting, but with a new twist: the people in the Protestant slum area began looting and ravaging their own district, just as the Catholics had done in Bogside, and from equally irrational motives. They felt their whole heritage was being threatened and the Government whose power base they were was doing nothing for them, so in the traditional pattern, they vented their frustration on their own property. Completely failing to understand all this, the Unionists turned round and called their own supporters hooligans. It was a great blow to the Protestant working class: after all they had done for the Unionists, in return for the little the Unionists had done for them, they were being classed as anti-social elements. Their allegiance began to slip. Knowing they were losing contact with their grass-roots, Major Chichester-Clark and his ministers didn't dare to ban the Apprentice Boys' Procession. It would have seemed the final sell-out. So it went ahead.

Remembering what the police action had been on every other public occasion in Derry over the

1. Prime minister of Northern Ireland 1969-71.

past twelve months, the people of the Bogside decided that, for their own safety, they would ignore the procession, mind their own business, and stay in the Catholic area outside the city walls with their heads down until it was all over. But if the twenty thousand marchers came down to attack them, after a day's celebration and drinking, they would defend their homes. The Bogsiders' gesture towards peace was met with provocation. From the walls overlooking the Catholic slum, the marchers and their supporters hurled taunts about keeping Catholics shut up in rabbit hutches. 'All Fenians ought to be penned in, anyway,' they yelled. Finally, the attempts to goad the Catholics out succeeded in a small way and a few squabbles broke out between the marchers and the Bogsiders. Rather than sort the squabblers out and send them on their separate ways, the police decided a baton-charge was in order and made a run into the Bogside. Promptly the barricades went up, but this time the police decided they were not going to tolerate the Bogside's resistance to being beaten into the ground. 'We've got to beat them this time, miss, or we're done for,' they told Mary Holland of *The Observer*.[2]

And so the Battle of the Bogside began. It was then about four o'clock in the afternoon of August 12th. Not for another fifty hours did the day-and-night fighting stop, and when it was over, it was the police who retreated. The Bogside was still unbreached, and the Unionist Government was a great stride nearer its downfall.

The Battle of the Bogside, according to Major Chichester-Clark, was part of a planned conspiracy to overthrow the Government. If the Major had been inside the barricades he would have found something much stronger and more terrifying than the plots of any organization. What was happening there was that ordinary, peaceful people, who had no desire to spend fifty hours throwing stones and petrol bombs, had realized the harm that had been done to them for half a century and were learning how to fight in self-defence. We threw up barricades of rubble, pipe, and paving stones — anything we could get our hands on — to prevent the police coming straight into the area and, in their own words, 'settling the Bogside once and for all'. Within the first half-hour eight police tenders were trapped in our barricades and if only we'd had the means to destroy them we would have burned those tenders out.

It was at that point that the manufacture of petrol bombs began. The petrol bombs were made, literally, by pregnant women and children. Kids of seven and eight who couldn't fight made the petrol bombs, and they made them pretty well. The kids of nine and ten carried them in crates to the front lines. The young girls collected stones and built the barricades, and the girls, the boys, and the men fought on the front line against the police. The police answered our stones and petrol bombs with stones of their own, and with ever-increasing supplies of tear-gas. The whole air was saturated with it, and we had not a gas-mask between us. I telephoned the Southern Ireland Minister of Defence to beg him to send us a thousand gas-masks for the children at least. I was willing to claim I'd stolen them, I said, if he didn't want us to have them openly. But he wouldn't co-operate. Jack Lynch, the Premier, was making grand-sounding statements from Dublin about his readiness to march to our defence.[3] But he was only playing politics: such a march would have been tantamount to a declaration of war on England, and Mr Lynch is economically tied to Mother England's apron-strings and his army is no match for the British. In any case, in the middle of the twentieth century no two Western European powers, however unimportant, are going to declare war because everybody is frightened of what the Russians would do when their backs were turned. We got medical supplies from the South, but gas-masks we had to go without. So we made do with wet blankets, with cotton wool steeped in vinegar, with handkerchiefs soaked in sodium bicarbonate, and we fought on through the night, all through the next day and the following night, and into the third day, and we showed the police that nothing they did was going to beat us.

Meanwhile, what was left of my reputation was taking a beating in the newspapers. All the papers were carrying photographs of Bernadette Devlin,

2. Mary Holland, Irish journalist, noted for her coverage of the Irish situation since the beginning of the present crisis.

3. On 13 August 1969, in a broadcast to the nation, Jack Lynch promised that the Irish government 'can no longer stand by and see innocent people injured and perhaps worse'. There is dispute about the phrase; perhaps he said 'stand by', perhaps 'stand idly by'. In the event, it did not matter. He stood by.

bejeaned, besweatered, and besieged in the Bogside, leading people on and organizing the manufacture of petrol bombs and hollering at people through loudhailers to 'throw them hard and throw them straight'; or organizing little guerrilla troops of a hundred men, in ten rows of ten men, to run like hell down side-streets and catch the police in the middle, making sure that everybody had two petrol bombs and somebody got a copper. But what the Press said about me didn't have the effect they intended. I didn't have time to read the papers myself — I was always on the barricades; and other people in Northern Ireland, who had begun to take the discrediting line fed them by the British Press, could see that what I was doing was necessary. 'If they come in here to get Bernadette Devlin, we'll slaughter them all,' they said.

While we fought on, the Civil Rights Association organized demonstrations in ten other towns, hoping this would take police pressure off Derry and allow us a certain amount of relaxation in the struggle. These demonstrations were held in defiance of the Government's ban, imposed as soon as the Apprentice Boys had stopped marching, but they failed in their object. Instead of withdrawing policemen from Derry, the Government called out the B-Specials.[4] Three hours later Harold Wilson sent the British Army into Derry,[5] and the B-Specials were switched to Belfast to wreak havoc on the citizens. There are no regulation tests to get into the B-Specials. You don't have to do an eye-test; you don't have to have a minimum or a maximum height; there are no weight restrictions and no intelligence qualifications. All you've got to be is a supporter of the Government, but once you're in you are entitled to service pay, to a gun, to all the ammunition you want, and to a uniform which is usually either two sizes too big or three sizes too small.

In Belfast the B-Specials, alongside the police, fought the demonstrators. They did more. With small arms, machine guns, and armoured cars, they launched a vicious, well-planned attack on Catholic areas. They burned down row upon row of houses. Only the arrival of the British Army brought their destructive progress to a halt, and I have no doubt myself that the army came, not because Major Chichester-Clark asked for help, but because Harold Wilson wasn't prepared to tolerate the Unionist Party's private army of reserve police. The soldiers got an ironic reception: while the Unionists, who have always been the Union Jack wavers, stayed cool, Republicans and Nationalists cheered the arrival of British troops on Irish soil.

But the barricades stayed up. The fighting was over, for the moment at any rate, but our demands had still to be met. One of these was an amnesty for every civilian in Northern Ireland, Catholic or Protestant, who had been forced into illegality. We leafleted the Free State Army, asking them to desert and come to our aid. We campaigned among the British troops, asking them to do the same thing. I believe they call it sedition. There was some doubt whether I personally was guilty of treason or not. I'd thrown stones at policemen (unfortunately, I can't throw straight, and they missed). According to Major Chichester-Clark, I'd incited Bogsiders to rebellion and plotted the overthrow of the State. But the situation in Northern Ireland was such that nobody cared. It was the Government who interned, without trial, people whose only crime was their political viewpoint. It was their men who set up kangaroo courts, murdered children, burned families out. Our sin was the lesser, and we will win in the long term, or the short.

Derry suddenly found itself the centre of revolutionary Europe, setting a pattern which revolutionaries the world over will never forget. It was very interesting to note that in Czechoslovakia in August 1969 they followed our pattern, perhaps unconsciously. As soon as the troops came in, the people raced down side-streets and put up barricades. Demonstrators in Dublin did exactly the same thing when they protested at the British Embassy. And they did it in London. It became the fashion to throw up barricades between yourself and the forces of the law and pelt them with petrol bombs from the other side. We had an influx of foreign revolutionary journalists searching for illumination on the Theory of Petrol Bomb Fighting. The people of the Bogside thought it was fantastic: they didn't know how to spell revolution, never mind work it out, but they were really

4. The Ulster Special Constabulary, established in 1921, to support the Royal Ulster Constabulary, a notoriously sectarian force, was disbanded on 30 April 1970 on the recommendation of a British government commission. However, most of its members were thereafter recruited into the Ulster Defence Regiment, established in January 1970.

5. Harold Wilson, prime minister of the Labour government in Britain 1964-70, 1974-76. The first British troops, 300 men of the Prince of Wales' Own Regiment, moved into Derry on the afternoon of 14 August 1970.

delighted with themselves, that people should come from the Sorbonne to ask the unemployed of Bogside where they learned to fight so well.

But behind the farcical aspects of the whole affair lay a serious problem: these people, out of fear, could never go back to the situation before August 12th, 1969. We reached then a turning-point in Irish history, and we reached it because of the determination of one group of people in a Catholic slum area in Derry. In fifty hours we brought a government to its knees, and we gave back to a downtrodden people their pride and the strength of their convictions.

It is very difficult to forecast what will happen next. For fifty years things have been static in Northern Ireland, and we are catching up on fifty years' history in the period of a year. Every day means a new chapter in a book and a new chapter in the life of a person. But whatever happens, never again will the Unionist Government be able to govern Northern Ireland as it has done since the country was created by Act of Parliament. The people have made their situation clear. We will fight for justice. We will try to achieve it by peaceful means. But if it becomes necessary we will simply make it impossible for any unjust government to govern us. We will refuse to have anything to do with it. We will build our own houses and refuse to pay rent on those houses to the Government. We will take control of our own areas and we will run them. We'll build our own factories, we'll pay taxes to our own people, and the Government can sit in Stormont and govern whoever will put up with it, for more and more people will stand by a fair system, however illegal, than will stand by a discredited government. The Unionists can struggle as much as they like to get back the support of the Protestant working class, but we shall get through to the Protestants in the end. Some of them have burned down Catholic homes, but we will not allow our forces to terrorize the ordinary Protestant population. One day they will realize we have no more quarrel with people who happen to be Protestant than with people who happen to be Catholic. They will see that our only quarrel is with the Unionist Party Government.

For half a century it has misgoverned us, but it is on the way out. Now we are witnessing its dying convulsions. And with traditional Irish mercy, when we've got it down we will kick it into the ground.

EAMON McCANN

(1943-)

from: WAR AND AN IRISH TOWN (1974)

[Eamon McCann, a native of Derry City, was involved in the formation of the Civil Rights movement which began the assault on unionist prejudice and injustice in 1968. One of the clichés of British and Irish Republic propaganda since the emergence of the IRA has been that the provisional IRA (the Provos) was formed as part of a general conspiracy, either against the northern state and/or the southern state, or against the cause of human happiness and peace, as is the way of all modern terrorist organizations. McCann's account of what actually happened in Derry, although by no means exhaustive, gives a saner and more truthful impression of how and why the IRA became active again in the catholic ghetto districts of Belfast and Derry. McCann is also important because his was one of the few revolutionary, left-wing voices to be heard at the time. There were others, but they tended to be more muted.

The Bogside is that part of the catholic ghetto in Derry closest to the old city walls and to the city centre. The Falls, in Belfast, is the name of the catholic area in the west of the city, which has the Falls Road as its main artery.]

PART 5

. . . Much has been written about the emergence of the Provos, almost all of it silly moralizing. The Provisional IRA was not created by a section of the Fianna Fail Party, although some money from

Fianna Fail sources did ensure that it was better financed at the outset than would otherwise have been the case.[1] Nor was it the creation of a few blood-lusting Catholic Nationalists in the North. Nor, despite the paranoiac ramblings of churchmen and contributors to the *Daily Telegraph*, is it part of an international terrorist conspiracy to destroy civilization as we know it.[2]

The machinery of government could not operate democratically. It was not designed for the job. So the fight for a democratic Northern Ireland was always likely to become a fight against the state itself. The 'national issue' was going to be posed. The only question left open was: by whom and in what form?

When, in January 1969, Johnnie McMenamin saw a crowd of men in his street in the middle of the night smashing up houses and beating up his neighbours and rushed to the telephone to dial 999 he was reacting as any working-class person in an 'ordinary' society would to such a spectacle. But what does one do when it is the police themselves who are doing the marauding? Who then does one call in?

A few months later that question would have been answered in the Bogside with: 'the British Army'. And when the army begins to behave exactly as the police had done, what then?

One turns to oneself, there being no one else, and tries to put together an organization as capable as possible of repelling the assaults. In the short term the politics of the defence group is irrelevant. It is irrelevant whether it has any politics at all. The long term is different. On a day-to-day basis defence groups can prevent random arrests, assaults and worse in an area simply by refusing admission to forces so intentioned. But tiny enclaves cannot exist in isolation for ever.

In 1970 the poster most frequently to be seen in windows and on gable walls in the Bogside and the Falls depicted a clenched fist and the words: 'Never Again!' Never again were mobs, whether in uniform or not, going to be allowed to rampage through the streets shooting and petrol bombing. The logic of that demanded that an offensive military campaign be launched against the state. When it is the state itself which threatens to destroy you it is necessary to attack the state, not just to defend oneself against *its* attacks, to try to ensure that there will be no repetition.

The trajectory of events led inevitably to a military campaign against the existence of Northern Ireland. The responsibility for the launching of the campaign rests entirely with those who created the situation which made that inevitable; that is, with the British ruling class and its agents in Ireland. That said, one can analyse why the campaign took the form that it did, how the politics of the activists involved developed and what, in the light of that, ought now to be done.

In 1968 and 1969 the left and the right, the 'militants' and the 'moderates' in the civil rights movement, were united on one point: that partition was irrelevant. No meeting was complete without at least one speaker declaring that we wished to make it clear that we were not setting out to unite Ireland, rather to achieve change within Northern Ireland — the extent of the change desired varying according to the tendency to which the speaker adhered. This was in line with the general drift of Catholic politics for the previous decade.

The left was, if anything, even more determined than other anti-Unionist groups to 'keep partition out of it'; and for reasons which were not ignoble. The partition issue had for so long been the 'property' of what we regarded as contending Tory factions that the mere mention of it smacked of jingoism. The result was that when, in 1969-70, Catholics in Belfast and Derry were, in the literal sense of the word, forced to raise partition there was no existing organization for them to turn to naturally. So they created one. The Provisional IRA — notwithstanding allegations to the contrary from various 'leftists' in Ireland and Britain — did not 'bring partition into it'. The Provisional IRA exists because partition was going to come into it whether or not the right, the left, or anyone else thought this advisable.

The one organization which might have been expected to have preserved its anti-partitionist credentials in the period before 1969 was the Republican movement, which traditionally had offered little other than a '32-County Republic'

1. Such speculations were fed by the sacking of two senior ministers by Jack Lynch, the Taoiseach, in Dublin in May 1970. Subsequently, the former minister for finance, Charles Haughey, was tried on a charge of importing arms, but was found not guilty. The Fianna Fáil party traditionally leans towards sympathy for republicans, provided the definition of republicanism remains the property of the party.
2. The *Daily Telegraph* is strongly supportive of English Toryism in almost all its more extreme manifestations. These are often stimulated to articulacy by the Irish situation.

as a remedy for all Irish ills. After the débâcle of the 1956-62 border campaign,[3] however, the Republican leadership had turned away from their traditional politics — or lack of them. Realizing that their emphasis on purely military activity had played no small part in rendering them politically irrelevant, they sought to make an analysis which would enable them to build a firm political base for the future. Assisted by products of the British Communist Party such as Dr Roy Johnston — the Number One Republican ideologue of the middle and late sixties[4] — they finally adopted a crudely updated version of Joseph Stalin's 'Stages Theory of Revolution'.[5] This laid down that there were predetermined stages through which 'the Revolution' must pass, that it was not possible to skip stages, and that therefore it would be a tactical mistake to make demands designed to achieve, say, stage three before stage two had been reached. As Dr Johnston explained it to us in Derry in 1969, stage one in the Irish Revolution would be the winning of 'bourgeois democracy' in the North; stage two would be the achievement of an 'independent capitalist Ireland'; stage three would be 'socialism in Ireland'. In an effort to achieve stage one the Republicans had helped to found the Northern Ireland Civil Rights Association and had directed the energies of its members in the North towards the building of the NICRA as a 'broad-based movement for reform'.

Stated briefly the theory sounds crazy; and indeed it is. Still, in the mid-sixties it represented a genuine attempt by the leadership and the remaining rank and file of the Republican movement to escape from the narrow nationalism and gun-fetishism of the past and to lay the basis for a socialist republican organization. One of the effects of the adoption of the theory was that in 1968 and 1969 some Republicans were among those most vehemently opposed to mention of partition (that had to wait for stage two) and equally strongly opposed to attempts to argue socialist politics from civil rights platforms (that was stage three).

When after 1969 Northern Catholics began to raise the question of partition without waiting for the culmination of stage one the Republican perspective became irrelevant.

The non-Republican left failed to understand the importance of the national question because it had no coherent analysis of the situation. The Republican left failed to understand it because its coherent analysis turned out to be wrong. Morever, the left as a whole had not managed by August 1969 clearly to demonstrate the difference which *did* exist between itself and the 'moderates'. And it was largely as a result of *that* failure that when the national question was posed anyway it was posed in stark and increasingly sectarian, for-or-against-partition terms.

Lacking any clear, common programme the original detonating group in Derry all but disappeared into the Citizens Action Committee. After that, left-wingers directed attention and hopes towards the People's Democracy.[6] But while maintaining a separate existence the PD too was for a long time effectively submerged in the mainstream of civil rights agitation, establishing itself not as an organization with a programme qualitatively different from that of the 'moderates', but as a lively and aggressive ginger-group within the same broad movement. To the mass of the people it was clear that the PD in Belfast and White, Finbar Doherty, myself, and others in Derry were more militant than the NICRA or the Derry Citizens Action Committee.[7] But it was not clear what we were being militant about. This meant that Unionist spokesmen were able plausibly to suggest that the difference was this: that the moderates were anti-Protestant — and the militants even more anti-Protestant.

This was plausible because it contained a tiny kernel of truth. There was one sense in which the civil rights movement was 'anti-Protestant'. The movement was demanding an end to discrimination. Its leading moderate spokesmen, such as John Hume and Gerry Fitt,[8] insisted endlessly

3. The IRA's campaign in this period was restricted to a few attacks on police stations, some arms smuggling and the blowing-up of customs huts along the border. It withered for lack of public support.
4. Scientist, member of the Official IRA, Wolfe Tone Clubs and various other republican organizations.
5. In Stalin's work, *On Dialectical Materialism and Historical Materialism.*
6. McCann, Bernadette Devlin and Michael Farrell were among the founders of the socialist Peoples' Democracy movement, founded on 9 October 1968 in Queen's University, Belfast.
7. A committee formed in October 1968 to co-ordinate defensive measures for the community. One of the founders was John Hume.
8. John Hume (born 1937), co-founder and since 1979 leader of the Social Democratic and Labour Party, has represented Derry as MP in Westminster and in Northern Ireland. He is a member of the European Parliament and is the most influential politician in Anglo-Irish affairs. Gerard Fitt (born 1926), Republican Labour MP at

that this was all they were demanding. In a situation in which Protestant workers had more than their 'fair' share of jobs, houses and voting power the demand for an end to discrimination was a demand that Catholics should get more jobs, houses and voting power than they had at present — *and Protestants less*. This simple calculation seemed to occur to very few leading civil rights 'moderates', but five minutes talk with a Paisleyite[9] counter-demonstrator in 1968 or 1969 would have left one in no doubt that it was not missed by the Protestant working class. There never was the slightest possibility of a movement demanding 'fair play' in Northern Ireland engaging the support, or even securing the neutrality, of Protestant workers. In terms of strict economics the only programme with any potential to undercut sectarianism would have been one which linked the demand for fair distribution of the relevant commodities to demands designed to increase absolutely the number of jobs and houses available for distribution. This would have involved campaigning for an end to the system of grants and inducements to private industry, a ban on the export of profits from Northern Ireland, direct state investment in areas of high unemployment. With regard to housing it would have meant demanding the cessation of repayments and interest payments by the Housing Trust and the local authorities to the London banks — payments which were and are crippling the housing programme in the North. In a phrase, it would have involved the elaboration of a comprehensive anti-capitalist, not just anti-Unionist, programme.

If any group had fought consistently — from within or without the civil rights movement — or both — for such a programme, the all-class Catholic alliance, which is what the civil rights movement became, could not have held together. And such a programme, hardly the normal stuff of Northern Irish politics, would not have attracted immediate mass support; but it might have enabled those of us in Derry at least to go on *talking* to Protestants in the Fountain[10] in 1969. At any rate the matter was never put to the test. No such group existed or emerged.

By the middle of 1969 'the left' was established as those who were most important and most willing to run risks, who wanted to go along the same road as the moderates, but further, faster. It was not at all established that the left wanted to go along a different road. Thus, when the explosion came in August we were still imprisoned within the sectarian strait-jacket, forced to operate almost exclusively within the Catholic community but quite unable in doing so to give any clear lead to the Catholic masses. When the raging bitterness of Catholics in Belfast and Derry swamped Fitt and Hume and carried the partition issue on to the centre of the political stage, support did not pass over into the socialist camp. There was no socialist camp there to receive it. The politics of the Provisionals was predetermined by that fact, and it is bottomless hypocrisy for 'leftists' in Ireland, including and especially those who held leadership positions in the Official Republic movement before 1969, now to attribute the reactionary social attitudes of a part of the Provisional movement to the malign influence of agents of Fianna Fail or some other suggested *diabolus ex machina*. The primary reason why the Provisionals *exist* is that 'socialism' as we presented it was shown to be irrelevant. The Provisionals are the inrush which filled the vacuum left by the *absence* of a socialist option.

That the national question was going to be posed in non-socialist terms, that it was going to be posed as a straight, sectarian choice between the maintenance of the border and the incorporation of the Six into the 26 Counties, was further guaranteed by the fact that the 'struggle' had been confined to the North. Since 1922 the majority of Protestants had understood and had been encouraged by their leaders to understand that any attack on Unionism was an attempt to extend the rule of the Dublin government of the day over them. For very sound reasons the Protestants were against that. Every self-respecting left-winger was against it too. At all times we were opposed to the low wages, the bad housing, the pathetic level of welfare benefits and Rome-rule in the schools in the South, and we were never done saying so. (In the period before August 1969 this indeed was one of the reasons why we were against raising partition at all — that Dublin had nothing to offer.) Thereafter, when we found

Stormont in Belfast from 1962; Westminster MP for Belfast in 1966 and 1970. In 1979 he resigned from the SDLP, of which he had been leader since its foundation in 1970 and has since been translated to the House of Lords.

9. An adherent of the unionist views of the Rev. Ian Paisley (born 1926).
10. The Fountain area in Derry is a protestant working-class neighbourhood, adjacent to the city centre and close to the Bogside.

that we *had* to deal with partition, we continued to make it clear that in supporting a fight to end the Northern state we were not advocating its absorption into the South as it stood.

But these unimpeachable sentiments had no convincing practical expression. We were not part of a fight *in* the South against the set-up there, and one cannot expect acceptance as an opponent of bourgeois nationalism if one is not seen to be part of a struggle against that section of the national bourgeoisie which is actually in power.

The point was illustrated by one early elaborate attempt to 'extend the fight to the South'. In April 1969 the People's Democracy organized a march from Belfast to Dublin. The marchers swung into O'Connell Street after four days on the road chanting, pithily enough, 'Lynch, Lynch, lynch O'Neill'.[11] What we meant was that Lynch and O'Neill represented two equally oppressive Tory régimes and that the working class in each area ought to rise up and eject them from power. There was a difference, however. We had been involved in a well-publicized campaign to bring O'Neill down. We had not been involved in any similar movement against Lynch. So what the people standing in O'Connell Street understood us to mean was that O'Neill, as a Unionist, would have to go, and that Lynch would have to go because he was insufficiently militant in pursuing this same objective. The difference between Fianna Fail and the revolutionary left was seen, not in terms of the social content of the societies they aimed at, but almost exclusively in terms of the intensity with which they were willing to attack the régime in the North.

That is how the Protestants in the North saw it: not that we were opposed to Catholic bourgeois-nationalist rule in any part of Ireland, but that we were in favour of its extension to every part of Ireland — even more strongly than the bourgeois-nationalists. And that was some difference.

All this resulted in confusion so total as almost to defy description. At one of our meetings at the bottom of Westland Street in the summer of 1969 I recall making a ten-minute speech which included the following two points: (1) that Lynch was a traitor because he had not sent his troops over the border when we needed them, and (2) that if he had sent them we would have opened up a 'second front' to drive them out again. Looking back, I find it difficult to know what the listeners can have made of this.

The absence of a movement in the South allowed the establishment there much room for manoeuvre, and they certainly needed it. And it gave the Provos, with their lack of any analysis of the South and therefore of any basis on which they *could* oppose it, an almost clear field in the North. It was they and their politics which began to dictate the course of events. What most significantly they dictated was the final destruction of the Orange machine as a ruling institution.

By the time the Provo campaign got into gear all tenuous links between Catholic radicals and Protestant workers had been broken. The mass of the Protestant population reacted to the campaign by demanding ever more stringent measures to smash the culprits down and made no distinction between Provos and Officials[12] once the Officials joined in. That, after all, was the way such affairs had always been managed in the past. For a long time the British government tried to accede to the demand. The British strategy from mid-1970 until March 1972 was militarily to defeat the IRA and to hope that the Protestant population would be so cheered by this victory that they might readily accept a reformed Stormont. The Catholics, suitably demoralized by the IRA's defeat, would thankfully accept the reforms and wait quietly for them to have some effect. That is what the Falls curfew, the 'arms searches', the murder of Cusack and Beattie and internment were all about.[13] It failed totally. The reason why it failed was that the Catholic guerrilla forces were not defeated. As long as they held out the strategy could not work. Bloody Sunday was the last desperate effort to make it

11. Jack (John) Lynch (born 1917), Taoiseach 1966-73, 1977-79, best remembered for the size of the majority he won in 1977; he initially spoke, in 1968, of not standing by while the minority in the north was under attack. Terence O'Neill (1914-90), prime minister of Northern Ireland, MP for Bannside from 1946, whose seat was taken on his resignation by Ian Paisley. O'Neill's attempt to introduce moderate reforms created consternation within the Unionist Party; the opposition he encountered led to his resignation.

12. The Provisional IRA split from the Official IRA in 1971.

13. The Falls Road was subjected to a British army curfew in July 1970; Seamus Cusack and Desmond Beattie, unarmed civilians, were murdered by British soldiers in Derry in July 1971; Brian Faulkner (1921-77), prime minister of Northern Ireland 1971-72, introduced internment without trial on 9 August 1971. It was directed at the catholic population, particularly in Belfast.

work, and it was the most disastrous failure to date. Catholic intransigence increased tenfold. Once that became apparent, Stormont was doomed and the stage set for direct rule.[14]

Direct rule presaged a new British strategy. But it did not connote any change in the overall British objective. Britain was still seeking to achieve a reformed 'democratic' Northern Ireland. That had been the central thrust of British policy in Ireland for a decade. Direct rule meant merely that Heath's[15] government had realised that buying off the Protestants by publicly brutalizing the Catholics was not going to achieve it.

When Stormont was prorogued a shudder went through the Orange machine of such violence that it began to fall apart. Unionism had always meant two things: Protestant power and the link with Britain. Direct rule made it dramatically clear that the Unionists now could choose one or the other — but not both. And they could only choose the former *in opposition* to Britain.

That had always been on the cards. That is what the Downing Street Declaration had meant, although Wilson was too cowardly a bourgeois leader to face up to it.[16]

While the strategy of repressing the Catholics had been open and unashamed it had been possible for Unionist leaders to maintain or to pretend that the choice need never be made. Not any longer. What has happened to the Unionist Party since March 1972 is that the various elements within it have made their choice — always excepting Mr Faulkner, who has never been a one for making choices while there remains a sliver of a chance of having it both ways. Mr Faulkner has been impaled for so long on the fence that he could be torn neatly in half along the perforations.[17]

Those, like Mr Craig,[18] whose political careers had been entirely within the Orange-Unionist complex and who represented, objectively, small local business threatened by the expanding operations of outside monopolies, went so far as to contemplate cutting the link with Britain if that was the price to be paid for clamping the machine back on to the state. More sensitive to the overall needs of big business were men such as Roy Bradford[19] who had achieved political eminence other than by threading their way up through the various Orange and Unionist institutions. They had no real commitment to Orangeism and in the year after direct rule they scuttled out of it, most of them issuing press statements drawing attention to that passionate commitment to common decency which had always characterized their public lives. Some of them joined the 'moderate' Alliance Party;[20] others waited, refusing to place bets until the likely winner emerged more clearly.

Dr Paisley[21] was the one significant Protestant leader who had been outside the apparatus from the start. He was a member neither of the Unionist Party nor of the Orange Order. It was for that reason that immediately after direct rule he plumped more quickly and decisively than any official Unionist for the maintenance of the British link. UDI,[22] which Mr Craig was wont to canvass in his more flamboyant moments — that is, the machine back in place as the effective state apparatus and this time with no 'outside' supervision — would have denied Dr Paisley, as surely as his erstwhile enemies Bradford and Faulkner, any position in the power structure. For a time Dr Paisley therefore advocated the total integration of Northern Ireland into the United Kingdom and began to adopt the required 'British' attitudes to Southern Ireland, community relations, and so on. British commentators, rather charmingly,

14. Stormont, the seat of regional government in Northern Ireland, was prorogued after Bloody Sunday (30 January) on 30 March 1972. It was replaced by direct rule from Westminster, under a secretary of state.
15. Edward Heath (born 1916), British prime minister 1970-74.
16. The Downing Street declaration of 19 August 1969, was issued by the Labour home secretary, James Callaghan, promising reforms in the police force, local government, housing and various other places where discrimination had taken place.
17. Brian Faulkner first opposed concessions to the Civil Rights movement; later he supported them. He pursued a mixture of hard-line and reformist policies for the remainder of his career, aiming at all times to gain or to retain power.
18. William Craig (born 1924), minister for home affairs in the unionist government 1966-68, founded the Ulster Vanguard movement in February 1972 and in 1973 the Vanguard Unionist Party, a quasi-military group that wanted to restore the pre-1968 state of affairs, by force if necessary.
19. R. H. Bradford, minister of commerce in Northern Ireland 1969-71 and minister of development 1971-72.
20. The Alliance Party, which favoured power-sharing in Northern Ireland, was founded in April 1970.
21. Rev. Ian Paisley, a clergyman of the Free Presbyterian Church of Ulster, founded in 1951, founder and leader of the Democratic Unionist Party in 1971, has represented North Antrim at Westminster since 1970 and is a member of the European Parliament. He is the leader of all the extreme varieties of unionism in Northern Ireland.
22. Unilateral Declaration of Independence (of Ulster from Britain), a manoeuvre favoured by Craig, the Ulster Defence Association and other unionist groups at different times since 1970.

attributed Dr Paisley's new moderation to the civilizing effects of membership of the Westminster Parliament.

Direct rule lifted racks of Catholic politicians off the hooks on which they had been dangling. Mr Lynch, for example, had not had an easy time. Each British outrage against the Northern Catholic community had sent a gust of Republicanism across the border, and he had spent the previous three years frantically trimming his sails to suit the prevailing wind, all the time hampered by the fact that some of his crew were intent on making the craft capsize. Every time the British army killed a Catholic he would essay a Republican phrase. A few days after the funeral he would make the point that of course he and his government were firmly committed to a moderate course. After Bloody Sunday he sent a car-load of cabinet ministers to the requiem mass. A fortnight later, the furore having slightly calmed, his Minister of Justice, Donagh [*sic*] O'Malley,[23] announced the introduction, 'if necessary', of 'military or special courts' to deal with Republicans. With Stormont gone Mr Lynch was able to make much less erratic progress towards an Anglo-Irish consensus. With only an occasional judicious genuflexion towards a Republican past, he was able gradually to tighten the screw of repression.

Direct rule forced the Protestant workers to realize that Britain cared little for them and their 'loyalty'. At the same time Catholic workers were being made to see that the South cared just as little for them and their 'Republicanism'.

This realization drained from the Catholic ghettoes some of the fierce passion for a united Ireland which twelve months previously had provided an emotional dynamic seeming to carry the community forward towards the achievement of the old goal. Coupled with the welcome given anyway to the end of Stormont and the fragmenting effect of incidents like the Best killing,[24] it created in the Bogside and like places emotional and political confusion which led in turn to a degree of passivity. By the end of 1972 the Bogside was more ready than it had been for two years to accept whatever package the British government wrapped up in its White Paper. The fact that Catholic acceptance was not certain, the fact that there remains considerable doubt whether the collection of plastic conventionalities issued on 20 March 1973 will work at all in the long run, is attributable in large part to the factor which had removed Stormont in the first place — the dogged refusal of the Provos to give up.

If the Provos had heeded the chorus of advice to call a halt when Stormont was prorogued, support in the Catholic ghettoes would have flowed rapidly to the SDLP. The Provos did not have a *political* base from which they could have counteracted this swing. The Nationalist Party was withering away. The Officials and other leftists had solidified their organizations in some places but did not wield decisive influence in the crucial areas, Belfast and Derry. Once established as the sole authentic voice of the Catholic masses the SDLP's team of quick-change artists — perhaps with an occasional dissenting voice from within — would have worked energetically to deliver their constituents up to the settlement Whitelaw[25] was attempting to dictate, and, being proficient in such things, they might well have succeeded.

At first sight the SDLP is a curious party. Of the six members of the Stormont Parliament who came together to form it in the summer of 1970 three had been elected as Independents, one as a member of the Republican Labour Party, one as a Nationalist and one as a member of the Northern Ireland Labour Party. Mr Gerry Fitt was selected as leader because he was, on aggregate, the least unacceptable to all the others. Mr Fitt is one of those people whose personalities seem to create a particular atmosphere, no matter where they be.

Since it was formed by the coming-together of six individuals elected on four different platforms, each of whom had his own local power-base, the SDLP was riven with contradictions. But underlying all the contradictions there has been a basic consistency, the significance of which far outweighs that of various internal squabbles. In the period after August 1969 it was, from the British point of view, necessary to have an organization which could

23. Desmond, not Donogh, O'Malley, minister of justice in the Fianna Fáil government 1970-73. McCann confuses his name with that of his uncle, Donogh O'Malley, minister for education 1966-68.
24. Ranger William Best, a Derry youth who had joined the British army, was murdered by the Official IRA while he was on home leave from Germany on 21 May 1972. There was an enormous public protest by people from the Bogside and Creggan areas of Derry.
25. William Whitelaw, a senior Tory minister, was secretary of state for Northern Ireland 1972-73. He was one of the architects of the abortive Sunningdale Agreement of 9 December 1973.

speak plausibly for the Catholic community in the North, which would be willing to accept, and capable of leading the community as a whole to accept, a reformist solution in the British interest. No such organization existed. The SDLP emerged to take on the role, and it is not without significance that members of the Labour Party front bench at Westminster were active in promoting its formation.

Since then it has striven manfully to coax the Catholics towards acceptance of the British objective. It has not been easy. The SDLP has not always been helped by the means the British government has used to attain its objective. Military assaults tended to stiffen the resistance and boost the Republicanism of Catholic areas and on occasion this carried the SDLP, conscious of the necessity not to lose contact with its base, outside the pale of consensus politics — for example after the murder of Cusack and Beattie. In the six months after internment, particularly in the period immediately after Bloody Sunday when it appeared that Catholic rage might not be assuaged by any British reforms, a few of them took the precaution of hedging their bets — driving Provo leaders around for all to see or trying to break into the gelignite-trafficking business. But always the overriding aim was to find a way back into the bourgeois consensus. Mr Fitt never lost sight of this. During the period when the SDLP was pledging daily that it would not ever, under any possible circumstances, etc. talk to British ministers while a single man remained 'behind the wire',[26] Mr Fitt's chatter was such as to lead a junior minister in Whitelaw's administration to lament to a political correspondent on a weekly paper: 'if this is what he is like when he is refusing to talk to us, God help our eardrums when he changes his mind.' As change his mind he did, of course.

At the beginning of 1973, as Whitelaw prepared to announce the Tory blueprint for the future, Provo persistence remained the single most formidable stumbling-block: because whether or not the Catholic community as a whole now adjudged attacks on the army to serve any worthwhile purpose, the mere fact that the attacks continued forced Catholics to take sides. And when it came to the sticking point there was still no doubt which side most of them would take.

Whitelaw's White Paper[27] and the Bills based on it set out the framework within which British capitalism wanted Irish politics to be conducted. What, in summary, they said was this: the contradictions between the two sections of Irish capitalism have all but disappeared. A new relationship between the political representatives of these interests must therefore be found. At present this requires political office to be shared between the Catholic and Protestant middle classes. Under an executive so constituted Catholic workers will not and must not be exploited more than Protestant workers. Once an assembly is elected we shall look at its composition. If it appears likely to be able to work towards such a situation it will be allowed powers to do so. If it appears unlikely to be able, or willing, to achieve this, we will intervene directly to impose the structure we wish to see.

The White Paper was issued to the accompaniment of a massive propaganda effort. On the Sunday before its publication Cardinal Conway[28] delivered a 'sermon' in Armagh Cathedral which came close to suggesting that it would be a sin to reject it. (It is to be noted that in the nineteenth century Catholic prelates in Ireland retained a certain regard for public decency and a modicum of self-respect; they waited until British governments had actually announced their plans for Ireland before issuing endorsements.)

In the months before and after the publication of the White Paper other stratagems, less public and innocent than the employment of pliant clerics, were used to maximize its chances of popular acceptance. British Army murder squads were sent out in Belfast to shoot up Catholic areas, hoping so to terrorize the inhabitants that they would accept whatever was offered. It was very difficult to distinguish between the activities of these units, who operated in civilian clothes from unmarked cars, and the parallel activities of right-wing Protestant assassins. Probably it will never be known what percentage of the 'unexplained'

26. That is, interned without trial.

27. In a White Paper published on 20 March 1973, the British government proposed the abolition of Stormont and its replacement by an 80-seat Assembly, elected by proportional representation, that would govern the region through a power-sharing executive. Its nominated executive would contain members of the catholic community.

28. William Conway (1913-77), catholic archbishop of Armagh and primate of All Ireland 1963-77.

murders in Belfast since mid-1972 each can claim.[29]

In the 26 Counties at the same time British agents were at work petrol-bombing police stations, suborning members of the Irish security services and, almost certainly, planting bombs and killing people. There was later to be some dispute between two of these agents, Kenneth and Keith Littlejohn, and British ministers about whether the Littlejohns had been in breach of orders when they robbed a Dublin bank;[30] what was not in dispute was that the British government was sending criminals into the 26 Counties to make mayhem, in the hope of engendering a law-and-order atmosphere conducive to an anti-IRA crackdown. The most dramatic piece of such mayhem occurred on 1 December 1972, when two bombs exploded in Dublin while the Dail was debating the Offences against the State (Amendment) Bill.[31] This lays down that if a senior police officer says that you did it, you did it.

The Bill was opposed by the opposition parties, Fine Gael and Labour, not because they were hostile to law-and-order, but because they saw no reason to help Mr Lynch out of difficulties which, they reckoned, were of his own making. Some dissident members of Mr Lynch's own party were also pledged to oppose the measure. It seemed certain, therefore, to be defeated. Then the bombs exploded outside, killing two and injuring more than a hundred. With the dead and the maimed strewn all around, concern for civil liberty quickly disappeared. A few Labour Party mavericks did hold on to the stubborn belief that to send a man to jail on the unsupported say-so of a policeman was going a bit far. But the main Party spokesman on such matters was Dr O'Brien.[32]

The fact that some members of Mr Lynch's party were not enthusiastic about the bill — or about law-and-order generally — had much to do with the defeat of Fianna Fail in the General Election of February 1973 and its replacement by the coalition of former fascists and reformed radicals led by Messrs Cosgrave, Corish, Fitzgerald and O'Brien.[33]

With both the Protestant and the Catholic communities in the North divided and confused, with a more-than-friendly government in the South and a blank-cheque endorsement from the leader of the Catholic Church, hopes for the success of the White Paper plan were high indeed. Elections for the 'Northern Ireland Assembly' were held in June. On the Catholic side, only the SDLP offered candidates in all constituencies and they swept the board. (The Provisionals, as an illegal organization, could not of course put candidates forward.) Before the election Mr Craig, having despaired of taking the Orange machine with him in a piece, had left to form the 'Vanguard Unionist Progressive Party' from as many of the components as he could get. He made an electoral alliance with Dr Paisley and they, together with various other dissident loyalists, won rather more Protestant votes than Mr Faulkner's Official Unionists. The Alliance Party did poorly, the Northern Ireland Labour Party disastrously.[34]

After the election a protracted period of wheeling and dealing between these parties commenced in an attempt to form a 'power-sharing' executive. How far, if at all, the RUC should be reformed, and what powers, if any, a Council of Ireland should possess were notable stumbling-blocks. Formulas and counter-formulas were produced. Mr Whitelaw held meeting after meeting with representatives of the various parties. In August Mr Heath went to Belfast to express irritation that more rapid progress was not being made. In the same month the Provos started bombing Britain.

Since the publication of the White Paper, and presumably in order to assist in its implementation, claims that the Provisionals had finally been smashed multiplied. Such claims were compounded of — in about equal measures — fact, wishful thinking and misunderstanding.

29. Evidence shows that the British Army participated in undercover sectarian assassinations in Northern Ireland. The year 1972 was the bloodiest so far in the history of the 'troubles'; most of the dead were victims of assassination squads.
30. The Littlejohn brothers, Kenneth and Keith, were convicted of armed bank robbery in Dublin in August 1972. In March 1974 they escaped from Mountjoy Jail. At his trial at the Special Criminal Court, Kenneth Littlejohn admitted spying on the IRA for British military intelligence.
31. The bombs killed two people and injured 127 others. On hearing about the bombs, most Fine Gael deputies joined their leader, Liam Cosgrave, and abstained in the vote. The bill passed all its stages by 69 votes to 22. The 'no's comprised the Labour Party, some members of Fine Gael, and dissident Fianna Fáil deputies.
32. Conor Cruise O'Brien (born 1917).
33. Liam Cosgrave (born 1920) Taoiseach 1973-77, Brendan Corish (1918-90), leader of The Labour Party and Garret FitzGerald (born 1926), minister for foreign affairs in the Fine Gael/Labour coalition.
34. The Alliance Party won 8 and the NILP 3 seats out of a total of 78.

The British tactic of directing both open and covert military operations, not at the Provisionals as such, but more generally at any community which might be tempted to give the Provos support, had met some success. It had made things very difficult for Provo activists; it had not made them impossible. In Belfast, where the pressure was strongest, the campaign continued, albeit at a reduced level. In Derry there was a bombing or a shooting weekly. Activity in the countryside was stepped up. In South Armagh particularly, Provo units fought and seemed to win a series of set-piece battles.

The decision to launch a campaign in Britain was taken after much heartsearching. The fact that the British had taken the war to the people in the North removed any quasi-moral inhibition Republicans felt about involving British civilians. The new campaign was directly in support of what had become the Provo's central, short-term demand — that the British set a time-limit for the withdrawal of their troops.

Support for withdrawal among British people had been growing for some time. It had manifested itself in a 'bring the boys home' campaign among service families, in the speeches of various Labour politicians and in a general weariness with the whole question of Ireland. Mr Heath was quite explicit that the bombing campaign would not lead to the growth of this movement, nor would it direct the thinking of any British government along such lines. Rather would it stiffen the will of the British people to see the Northern Ireland operation through. Editorials in all major British newspapers made the same point. Time will tell. And, contrary to the assertion that the Provos are on the verge of defeat, time is something they believe they have in abundance.

The Provisionals are very young. Most of them were at school when the 'troubles' began on 5 October 1968. Since then, trouble is the only life they have known. They are very, very determined. If the Irish conflict could be settled by determination, by unconcern for personal aggrandizement, by an ability and a willingness to fight on against overwhelming disadvantageous odds, the Republicans would be assured of victory. On their own, however, such qualities are not decisive.

The Provos, in the North especially, are almost entirely working-class; but for the reasons outlined earlier many of them have little understanding of the need for working-class politics. At leadership level they are shot through with Catholic Nationalism. Their ideologists tend frequently towards a mystical conception of Nationhood and are, therefore, sometimes more concerned to re-enact scenarios from the past than to deal with present reality. Between 1971 and 1973, as the Provos developed into the most effective urban guerrilla army of the twentieth century, they managed marvellously to frustrate the designs of British governments. But finally to frustrate such designs it is necessary to have a coherent, class-based programme. Thus far, the only detailed programme the Provisionals have produced is the document *Eire Nua*, the centrepiece of which is a hare-brained scheme for four regional parliaments in Ireland. (This idea was first mooted by Brian ua Dubhghaill in the columns of *An Phoblacht*[35] in 1934.) As an alternative to British plans it is quite unreal and despite energetic promotion it has excited little interest, much less gathered support.

Only the revolutionary left could offer the programme which is needed. If it is to do that it must quickly learn the lessons of the last five years. The left failed in Ireland. There is nothing to despair about in that. Even Trotsky made mistakes. Mistakes are disastrous only when one fails or refuses to recognize that they were mistakes and fails thereby to learn from them.

We have learned that mass 'influence' or prominent involvement in mass agitation is, despite sometime appearances to the contrary, meaningless and fruitless unless one is in the process of forging the political instrument necessary to lead such agitation to victory over the opposing force. We have learned that it is impossible to do that if one is not forearmed with a coherent class analysis of the situation and a clear programme based on it.

We need a movement without illusions in any section of the bourgeois class, which understands that the interests of all sections of the ruling class in Ireland, Orange, Green and pastel-pink, are now identical and that to attempt to ally with one section against another is to become the plaything of the enemy.

35. The newspaper of the Provisional IRA. It first appeared in May 1970, resuming the title of the first *An Phoblacht*, the repulican newspaper founded in 1925, banned in 1931, active from 1933 until 1937 when it ceased publication. It was traditionally a newspaper of the left-wing of the IRA.

We need a movement which will deal with sectarianism by fighting all its manifestations. That means, among other things, confronting the power of the Catholic church in the South.

We need a movement which understands the continuing importance of the national question — that it cannot be avoided; and which will seek to show to those, like the Provos, who are tempted therefore to concentrate on it exclusively that to demand a 'united Ireland' in the 1970s without reference to its social content is to demand something which imperialism, in the long term, has no essential interest in denying and which a large section of the working class in the short term, has no essential interest in achieving.

In a phrase, we need to build a mass, revolutionary Marxist party. The opportunity to do it will present itself. In the Catholic community in the North, particularly among the rank and file of both Republican movements, there are many who seek for an analysis which will enable them to carry the struggle on to a new phase.

The apparatus of discrimination, the mechanism whereby Protestant workers had been given an illusory sense of privilege, has been wrecked beyond repair. Placed in the same social situation as their Catholic counterparts many Protestant workers will react — as they have done — by moving to the right. Others will recognize that the ferocious loyalty they gave to Orange leaders was never really reciprocated. They will recognize more quickly their identity of interest with Catholic workers if there emerges an organization with roots in the Catholic working class which is seen to be opposing the conservatism and clericalism which has shrouded that community for so long.

Either British imperialism or the Irish working class will win. There is no other social force in Ireland with a potential for power. In the end, the only thing which can prevent William Whitelaw putting his priorities into operation is the revolutionary overthrow of his parasite class. The future in Ireland lies with the small, but at last steadily growing, forces of Marxism. To make the revolution we need a revolutionary party. This book is intended as a contribution to discussion of how best to build it.

ANTHONY CRONIN

(1926-)

from:
DEAD AS DOORNAILS (1975)

[Anthony Cronin's memoir of literary life in Dublin in the 1940s and 50s is on a par with those by George Moore and Oliver St John Gogarty which memorialized earlier decades. There is a good deal of humour in the portrayal of what was, in effect, a tragic group of men, including Patrick Kavanagh, Brendan Behan and Flann O'Brien. Cronin gives us an insight into the individuals while also providing us with a sense of the state of Irish society at that time. While not an autobiography — as he himself insists — it has the intimacy of an autobiographical work and the objectivity of a chronicle.]

CHAPTER 1

. . . The Irish for a musical gathering, a concert, is *cuirm cheoil*, the combination of words indicating a necessary connection between song and drink. That is what we had in the Catacombs.[1] Nearly every regular frequenter had a party piece. One had thousands. This was Brendan Behan.

When I first went to McDaid's and took up residence in the Catacombs, Brendan was in Paris, whither he had gone with Gainor Crist[2] and a Limerick man who had come into a small legacy and was disposed to spend it, if such can be imagined. His doings there were much storied and talked about and his return was much heralded. It was a wet Sunday morning when he eventually

1. A basement area in a decayed Georgian mansion, divided into various dark little rooms. It became the gathering place, and lodgings, of this Dublin Bohemia.
2. Gainor Crist is one of the seven people whose lives are presented to us in the memoir. He provided the original for J. P. Donleavy's novel, *The Ginger Man* (1956): in Cronin's words, 'a curiously transformed and lessened portrait'.

arrived in the pub. He had his father, mother and brothers with him and there was a large company assembled, but as we walked up Leeson Street towards the Catacombs at three o'clock closing, he fell back deliberately so that we walked together. Friendship, like other forms of love, takes immediately or not at all. In the course of that otherwise dismal Sunday afternoon we became friends and discovered we were confreres.

Brendan in those days was far from being the gross ogre whose picture became so familiar years later in the English newspapers. He was fat, it is true, for his height and age, but his girth combined with his personality gave the impression that he was somehow merely bursting at the seams. Nor was the porcine effect, to be produced later on by the contrast between his general grossness and his tiny hands and feet, apparent: one was struck instead by the sort of expansive and inflationary possibilities he managed to extract from the contrast, like an operatic tenor who can seemingly expand parts of his anatomy at will.

At this time he worked, when it suited him, and when he was not on his travels, at the house-painting which was his father's trade, but he had published a few poems in Irish and a documentary piece about one of his terms of imprisonment in *The Bell* — he belonged, he said, to 'that large and respectable body in the community that had once had an article in that magazine'. Both then and later he would pose when it suited him as much more of an orthodox working-class product than he really was. In fact there were currents of literacy, liberalism and unconventionality on both sides of his family which many a product of the lower middle-classes like myself might have had cause to envy. And on one side there was a strong theatrical tradition. (His uncle was a music-hall song-writer who had written the national anthem.)[3] If the realities of working-class life were known to him it was also true that he had never been among the great unacquainted submerged; there was plenty of acquaintance and tradition about in his growing-up; and indeed it was, to some extent at least, the show business element in him that contributed to his destruction in the end.

He lived for the most part in his parents' house, out in the grey spaces of Crumlin, a working-class housing estate dating from the 'thirties, better than some of the more recent experiments in ghettoisation, but not a very cheerful place all the same. However, he was nomadic by nature and it was frequently too far for him to go in the small hours, so he stayed wherever he was welcome, and often in the Catacombs. Sometimes in the days to come he would share my palliasse in the wine-cellar and on these occasions we would talk long in the mornings, and then when the pubs were open venture forth into the streets, in search of company, drink and diversion. These days became more frequent as my resolution, such as it ever had been, weakened, my new acquaintance developed, and my hold on the job loosened in the clouds of hangover. Eventually I gave it up altogether and became fairly happily jobless, though beginning to publish poems and ill-informed critical comment in the backs of such magazines as there were.

You could not in fact have a better companion in a day's idleness than Brendan. He was a kaleidoscopic entertainment, but he was also fecund in serious ideas. He had a line in bemused wonderment about the activities of the world which was only partly an affectation, for he was genuinely naïve in certain ways and genuinely full of questionings. And he knew too when to drop the act and show himself capable of intimacy. The salt which makes penury palatable, ironic comment on all forms of possession and ownership, sometimes quite savage, he had in abundance. He had also in those days the remarkable gift of being able to realise and humorously illuminate the other person's circumstance while comically examining his own; and he was a good ally, fiercely contemptuous of all who disapproved of one's way of life. 'Fuck the begrudgers', he used to say, the implication being that envy lay at the root of most such disapproval.

He talked a lot in those days about his homosexuality, though I have since met others who knew him then and who claim they never heard of the matter. Mostly when he spoke of it, it was not as a difficulty but as a distinction. Sometimes he averted to it simply to shock. In the presence of a bishop and a curate for example, if that unlikely eventuality can be imagined, he would declare that he fancied the curate, or perhaps even the bishop, in order to shock the one and embarrass the other. He

3. Peadar Kearney (1883-1942) wrote the words of 'A Soldier's Song' in 1907. It was published by Bulmer Hobson in *Irish Freedom* in 1912 and became the marching-song of the Irish Volunteers. Subsequently it became Ireland's national anthem.

used to say wryly that De Valera's housing reforms had ruined his ordinary sexual development; that the move from the cosy slums out to the windy spaces and semi-detached houses of Crumlin had come at a crucial age and had been disastrous. On the landings and in the dark hallways of the tenements you could always get a grope or a squeeze and at fourteen he was just getting the hang of things and acquiring the necessary casualness of approach when the move came along, the casual courting opportunities among childhood acquaintances vanished and the elaborate approaches and settings-up which all sensitive, shy adolescents find difficult became the order of the day. This history was not advanced as a justification or a pathology nor, to do him credit, were his prison experiences. 'No worse than boarding school', he said he supposed, and in terms of my own experience, we agreed he was right.

It was agreed also that whatever the accidents or the latent tendencies involved one would probably have suffered in any case from the Irish syndrome. Apart altogether from prisons or boarding schools, 'life' would not have lived up to certain literary notions. 'Normal' adolescent development, 'normal' adolescent ecstasies were a myth. Something had gone wrong somewhere along the line, as it was pretty well bound to: though you could of course be cheerful about your flaws or your freedoms and suggest that it had gone right. This feeling was perhaps particularly strong in our generation. You could, and most people did, blame the Catholic religion, of which, incidentally, in the early days — he was to become rather maudlin about the matter later — Brendan had a ferocious hatred. The war, with its impediments to ordinary living, had something to do with it. So had boarding schools. And prisons. Indeed perhaps government housing estates.

It is almost impossible for sensitive, intelligent, over-imaginative people not to make a hames[4] of their development anyway and then only two responses are really open to them; they can believe themselves the ultimate oddity, or they can suggest that everybody else is lying. There are always those of course who lay claim both to sensitivity and simplicity of development; who allege that in spite or because of their poetic imaginations they slipped into life and cunts as to the manner born. Patrick Kavanagh was later to invent a word to cover this sort of literary pretence along with other related ones: 'bucklepping'. As far as we were concerned the buckleppers were liars.

In public Brendan's manner was rabelaisian, jocose, knowledgeable. In private he would admit to difficulties and bewilderments about which he was in fact much funnier. Unfortunately for him, his writing — with the possible exception of *Borstal Boy* — when he eventually got round to it, was a public matter also, and as a way of sorting himself out through the rigours, honesties and ironies of art, it was largely useless to him. That was part of the debacle.

Whatever the truth of his assertions about his basic homosexuality may have been, I do not ever remember him striking up any sort of a liaison, and though there were considerably less admitted homosexuals around in our age-group in those days, there were enough. Nor did he give any surface impression of being queer: of course, contrary to popular belief, most people who are do not: the word covers a multitude of sins and states anyway.

Apart from being queer, he claimed that he suffered from what he called 'a Herod complex', a preference for youth, named so after Herod's fancying the daughter rather than the mother. He fancied only boys of about fourteen to eighteen, he would say; and in the right circumstances these declarations were usually made publicly, humorously and loudly enough to destroy any prospect of success. Once when we were sharing the wine-cellar together he made advances to myself: perhaps he felt he had to. The matter being cheerfully disposed of was never heard of again, through all our wanderings and bunkings.

He complained, however, of strange ignorances and naïveties where 'ordinary' sex and the female were concerned; and was bitter about those who, not being privy to his real preferences, prescribed more orthodox sex as a corrective to our way of life. When reproached once by a progressive lady we knew for not having a regular girl-friend, Brendan replied that it was every bit as un-Marxist to reproach a man for not having a fancy woman as it would be to reproach him for not having a motorcar. For a long time afterwards he used to refer to her suggestion that all his ills and malaises would disappear if he had more sex as 'Dr. so-and-so's

4. i.e. make a botch.

remedy for the human condition'.

But even about the physical side of homosexual relationships he would admit to bewilderments. He came across something in Enid Starkie's biography of Rimbaud[5] which apparently bothered him and led to much speculation; and he spent days in the National Library reading various accounts of the trial of Oscar Wilde to find out precisely what practices Oscar had engaged in — the only time I can remember him going near the place.

In saying all this I do not mean to suggest that Brendan was more than ordinarily ignorant, naïve or innocent about sex. Quite the contrary in fact. And if one were to take some of his boastings for gospel one would have to assume heights — or depths — of sophistication rather rare at the time. These boastings were not of the ordinary kind, however, suggesting mere conquest and procured licence. There was in them an element of picaresque braggadocio which was meant to suggest cynicism and villainy on his part. He did, at one time, have a penchant for such boastings and surprised me by asserting that he got money from a woman I knew for performing what was to him a particularly onerous, not to say unpleasant, sexual service for her.

However that may be, and behind all the boastings and the jokes, what is certain to me is this: Brendan, when I knew him first, had a much more complex awareness of himself, his diffidences, failures and complications than he chose to present even then, and more especially later, to the outside world. He knew he was complicated and he chose to deal with the complications in the best way possible: ironic confession, humorous self-disparagement, mock surprise, combined of course with a satiric savagery about the pretensions of other people. Unfortunately very little of this appears later on in his work or his alleged work, whichever it happens to be. Here the complications and their confessional shadows are constantly at the mercy of bravado, show, pretence. And in the public figure as well as in the writer, for the two are now inseparable, it is the same. He is the great liver, who has drunk it to the lees[6] at all stages of the game, the great avatar of booze and sex and 'life'. Fatal of course, the more so because part of our nature impels us to try 'to become what we sing'; even though, the more our pretences take over, the more we secretly know how much we need 'the deep counter-minings of art'.

In public, comic drama was Brendan's primary mode of being and his enormous talent for it was constantly employed in enactments of one kind or another, created anywhere there was an audience, from the cold morning kitchen of the Catacombs to the partially empty McDaid's[7] of the mid-afternoon. Some of these were merely satirical in intent and involved imaginary scenes between people we knew; but he had too a strangely coherent if very mixed mythology, peopled by miscellaneous patriotic and literary figures, and in the miniature dramas involving these an extraordinary talent for the grotesque took over, so that the originals attained a new surrealist dimension.

'The childhood of D. H. Lawrence' was a very elaborate performance, often repeated with many variations, in which Lawrence's drunken father comes home to find the boy reading a book and keeps up a running stream of monstrous abuse of the child while getting into the bath and having his back scrubbed, Brendan playing scurrilous father, anxious mother and patronising little boy in various postures and with accents varying from broad Yorkshire to badly cultivated middle-class English. 'The boyhood of John Ruskin' was created as a sort of companion piece one winter night in the Catacombs when there was very little to drink, and it took the sensitive Ruskin, and his doting parents on a tour of Europe in which sulkings and reconciliations, aesthetic wonderments, raptures and incomprehensions alternated. How Ruskin came to find a place in his mythology I do not know, but his reading, being a matter of chance, was strangely various. 'Maud Gonne at the Microphone' was usually performed with a towel over the head by way of a veil and it consisted of fruity recollections of Yeats in a quavering, aged, but, of certain undertones, deeply expressive voice. 'Mr Cosgrave's Visit to Mountjoy' involved the former President of the Free State in a scene with a patriotic lady who to her chagrin is not arrested in a general swoop. She puts a camp bed outside the gates of the prison, gets into

5. Enid Starkie (*c.* 1899-1970), born in Killiney, Co. Dublin, spent most of her life teaching at Somerville College, Oxford. She wrote biographies of Rimbaud (1947), Baudelaire (1957) and Flaubert (1967).

6. i.e. to the dregs. 'Lees' is the sediment of an alcoholic drink.

7. A pub in Harry Street, Dublin, where Behan, Patrick Kavanagh and Flann O'Brien drank.

it and goes on hunger strike. Goaded by questions in the Dail about the ill-treatment of other republican lady prisoners who are on hunger strike within, Mr Cosgrave arrives at the prison in a motor-car to see for himself. The disappointed lady rises up in her camp bed and calls after him: 'Imperialist! Lackey! West Briton![8] Liar! Arrest me! Arrest me!' To which Mr Cosgrave turns round and replies: 'Madame. Imperialist I may be. Lackey I may be. Liar I may even be. But I am not a collector of curiosities.' The rich part of the performance consisted of the lady attiring herself suitably for her vigil, setting up the camp bed, composing herself on it, and refusing all offers of refreshment.

These vignettes were, where possible, embellished and illustrated by song; but he loved song anyway and was happy to sing anywhere and in almost any circumstance. He had a resonant baritone, perfect pitch, and, again, an enormous theatrical sense, whether for the rendition of scurrilous comic pieces or passionate patriotic and left-wing ballads — often the two merged into one. According to what was needed by the song, the lips would curl, the eyes flash and roll and the tiny, sensitive hands clench or unclench in passion, or reach out in mock unavailing yearning and despair.

It was, in all its elements, an original form of *cabaret intime* and it was a highly developed art. Given the proper circumstances he might have used it to feed the exhibitionist in himself that eventually devoured him and the unsatisfied actor who interrupted his own plays, desperate to appear on stage himself and be, for every moment of the performance, the centre of love and attention. It was not an ignoble art — far from it. It was spontaneous, and as his later addiction to the tape-recorder apart from anything else shows, he was an essentially spontaneous creator, who needed company in the act. It drew from its audience and depended on a confidence in affection given and received which might have been the ultimate reassurance for one who so feared to go it alone. It might certainly, ephemeral or otherwise, have been a better outlet for him than the tape-recorder. Perhaps there was a better, and certainly a happier artist of another kind lost in Brendan.

8. A derogatory term for an Irish person who apes British customs. It was coined by D.P. Moran of *The Leader* to describe anglophilic Irish Parliamentary Party members.

CHAPTER 5

. . . But whatever my own fortunes and misfortunes in those years, I do not think that they were happy ones for Brendan Behan. The figure I remember in the two or three years immediately preceding his marriage and his fame was in truth more that of a repetitive performer who had already shot his bolt than that of a brilliant young writer on the verge of great success. One of his tragedies when success overtook him was to be the knowledge that those who knew him in the days of fame scarcely knew him at all. He was giving only repeat performances, ever more tired, desperate and confused, and needing larger and larger amounts of alcohol to keep them up. The impresarios of the London antics of which the world was now shortly to read had only a dummy figure to manipulate. They benefited from the fact that most of those with whom Brendan came in contact had never seen or heard him before, but they would have done even better had they had the true star that some of us remembered on their hands, bursting at the seams, with his initial sensitivity, his scurrilous comic inventiveness and his peculiar comic grace.

But Brendan was over thirty by the time that anybody paid any real attention to him as anything but a performer, and even then it was as a performer that the larger audience really wanted him. He had therefore a long, too long, experience of the gap that some people feel more acutely than others between their capabilities and their recognised achievement, too long that is for his inner resources. Some people's inner resources are inexhaustible: they go on working away in some hole or corner whether the world wants the product or not. Brendan's inner resources were small, even in the early days. On one of the first occasions he stayed in the wine-cellar he talked of someone who had offered him the loan of a cottage in the Wicklow Mountains. 'But the trouble with this fucking writing', he said, 'is that you have to be by yourself while you're doing it. And that's hard.'

Sometime in the early nineteen-fifties he began to write a twice-weekly column in the *Irish Press*. Since nobody in intellectual Dublin in those days ever saw anything but the *Irish Times*, this was simply not read by most of those he wanted to impress. I was not even aware of it until after he had been at it for more than a year. In fact the very people he cared most for had by then given him up as a bad job.

Brendan carried, therefore, into the broad plains and possibilities of fame, an especially onerous burden: the bitterness of what he felt to be an unwarranted neglect. When fame eventually came to him he was like the Imperial candidate who has waited so long that his dreams of power have turned into dreams of revenge, and who has thought of the prerogatives that will ensue so often and with such intensity that the reality can never provide the expected sensation. When at least he became famous, he had to prove it to himself every day, and others had to repeat continually that it was so. Of course the people from whom such recognitions could never be extracted were those from whom he most wanted them. The possibilities of fame as an instrument of power over others are limited to those who admit its importance, which serious fellow-artists rarely do.

Meanwhile [Patrick] Kavanagh's hostility was implacable and, instead of accepting this, Brendan went about the town creating a sort of intimacy with him by abuse, constantly talking in abusive terms about anybody to third parties being of course one of the best known means of remaining close to them that there is. Now to add to his troubles came the Kavanagh libel action, which, even if it provided him with an obscure and unsatisfactory sort of revenge, reduced his stock still further among the two or three whose respect he most wanted.

Like all Irish countrymen, Kavanagh was highly litigious. He had a great respect for legal forms and phrases and he would often use them in ordinary conversation, accurately or inaccurately, in or out of context. If you taught him a new one, or he picked one up, he would use it for weeks. Worse still, he had the Irish countryman's dream of a bonanza thrown up by an action. In the case of simple folk this takes the form of dreams about damages for personal injury, breach of promise, trespass and whatnot. Kavanagh, being a literary man, dreamed of libel. And, unfortunately for himself, he was libelled. An old-established but attenuated weekly called *The Leader* was rouging its aged cheeks and decided to do a series of sophisticated profiles of contemporary personalities. Among them was Kavanagh.

The piece itself was a typical example of a certain kind of Dublin bad manners, but it was scarcely any more. Dublin is the administrative capital of a small country with a swollen civil service. It is also a University city twice over. Academics and civil servants are frequently of a literary bent, but they are rarely real writers. Dublin therefore contains some hundreds of uncreative literary men, most of them recruited from the provinces and liberated from provincial backgrounds of varying remoteness. To be able to exchange literary gossip, to be 'in' becomes essential for them. The piece complained of was an exercise in a sort of 'innishness' that is highly offensive, but, *sub specie aeternitatis*, not very important.

Unfortunately, besides being litigious by nature, Paddy had a well-sharpened appetite for martyrdom. I understood why in part even then, but I understand better now. There is in every human being a desire for the explainable, clear-cut, black and white circumstance on which we can bring the more obvious emotions about justice and injustice to bear. Paddy was, in a very real sense, the victim of society, but, apart from the suppression of *The Great Hunger* many years before, it was hard to point to any overt act of persecution.[1]

He was largely derided and certainly unsupported, but this, unless in a reasoned indictment of society for its sins of omission, did not amount to a crime against him. His circumstances were almost as bad as were those of many who suffered overt persecution in Russia and elsewhere; indeed, as a consequence, he used to speak with scorn of such writers and their fashionable sympathisers; yet, in his case, there was no actual persecution or dramatic martyrdom to point to. Without perhaps realising it therefore, he decided to bring all his inchoate feelings about this to a head through the medium of a libel action. He decided in fact to achieve martyrdom, and, up to a point, he succeeded brilliantly. By the time he was in the witness box being cross-examined about his character, general reputation and way of life, by the former Prime Minister, John A. Costello,[2] it had been largely forgotten by himself, by his supporters and by the general public that he was the instigator of the action. With a sort of subliminal strategic genius he had succeeded in bringing the whole

1. *The Great Hunger* was never banned, but it was thought it might be. Mrs Yeats sent copies of the Cuala edition to a London bookseller, who held stock and filled the orders from there.
2. John A. Costello (1891-1976), Taoiseach of the first inter-party government 1948-51.

thing full circle. Like Oscar before him — who of course was also the instigator of the original action[3] — he had become the persecuted one, and before it was over hung high on his cross for all to see, answering his persecutors disdainfully through bleeding lips.

There was one further aspect of the affair, small in itself, which was made to serve the persecution complex brilliantly also. The article was anonymous. This did not seem to me to matter very greatly unless on a personal level, or unless the lawyers could succeed in proving malice, but it was all Paddy needed to link whole segments of the town in a conspiracy against him. It gradually began to be borne in on me that as far as persecution feelings were concerned he was pretty far gone. Aided by whiskey, of which he was now drinking large quantities, and an illness, cancer of the lung, which was as yet undiagnosed, the imaginings of persecution flourished.

For weeks preliminary to the trial one was compelled to engage in speculation as to who had written the offending piece. He would ring me up at *The Bell*,[4] which, bound by some unalterable law of return, I was now editing yet again, and, dropping his voice to the hoarse bellow that passed for conspiratorial tones, begin.

'I say. You know that piece.'

One did of course.

'I've been thinking it over. I was thinking about it all night. I've been putting two and two together.'

There would be a pause here during which one had to make some sound, for he was the most demanding of interlocutors on the telephone, requiring responses even to his silences.

'Do you know what my opinion is, my considered opinion?'

Since he had had several over the last forty-eight hours one could only say something weak like, 'No, what is it?'

'My opinion is that that blackguard so-and-so wrote it.'

This was very likely a name that had already been discussed at length so you could only repeat what you had said the night before. Of course if it was a new name, it was easier to comment; but some of the suggested names were simply beyond discussion.

At length Paddy decided that the piece had been written by *(a)* a University College Dublin historian or *(b)* a well-known civil servant poet or *(c)* both of them together.

But something else suggesting conspiracy was necessary and this was found. The piece was mainly concerned with the *persona* Paddy presented to the world in McDaid's and it had occasional gleams of accuracy as to his line of chat and general demeanour. Therefore a McDaid's informant was postulated. This role was alloted to Behan. Whichever of them had written it, if either of them had written it, or if it had been written by them both jointly, Behan had been the 'informer'. Further Behan was being paid by the opposition to follow him round at a distance and spy on him. Why particularly an informant or 'informer' had been necessary to help in the concocting of a piece which even the most amateur of journalists could have managed if its owner had put his head round the back door of McDaid's for five minutes, or what such an informer could hope to gain from cocking his ear to Paddy's conversation in Ryan's or Mooney's[5] that would be of assistance to anybody in a libel action in a court of law, was never clear, but such questions no longer arose. He was now on trial for a nameless offence, in the realms of literature, philosophy and politics all at once, in fact, one might say, for mere being, and his enemies had of course to be credited with employing the traditional Irish weapons of persecution, including spies and informers. The objection, if any had the temerity to make it, that shouting inchoate abuse at a man was a funny way of spying on him was answered by the theory that Behan was also employed to upset him and make him do something foolish which could be brought out in court. The sum which Behan received was even named: ten shillings a day.

As the time of the hearing came nearer his nervousness naturally increased, as would anyone's with any temperament whatever. He asked me whether they could 'bring out' things in his past life

3. Wilde brought a case against the Marquess of Queensbury, who had publicly insulted him. This led to his own trial and imprisonment.
4. *The Bell* (1940-54) was the best literary-political magazine of the period. Cronin was assistant editor on several occasions.
5. Well-known Dublin pubs. The owner of Ryan's, John Ryan (born 1925), founder and editor of the magazine *Envoy* (1949-51) and of the *Dublin Magazine*, published a memoir of this period, including many of the figures mentioned by Cronin. Entitled *Remembering How We Stood*, it was published in 1975 and reprinted in 1987.

against him. I thought this meant some unnamed foolishness or misdemeanour in his past. It turned out that to make himself slightly younger he had been giving the wrong year of birth in biographical notes for books and the occasional anthology. He had been worrying about this as well as a multiplicity of other things. Nobody with a highly developed sense of privacy or with more than the usual number of secrets to guard should ever engage in legal action. Unfortunately they are the very people who do.

As a means of raising money the trial was certainly a flop, since the jury found that there was no libel at all. However, as an exercise in martyrdom it was, up to a certain point anyway, a superb success. In this respect the other side played into Paddy's hands by engaging John A. Costello as senior counsel. Costello was a forceful, occasionally rather savage lawyer of the old school, dating back to O'Connell, a great juryman who on this occasion pretended, if that were possible, to be more ignorant of art and letters than the jury themselves, while concealing behind his pretended bafflement a mind as sharp as a knife. For Paddy's subconscious purposes he was therefore the ideal instrument and there took place between them an extraordinary dance of opposites. One was the poet, high style. The other was the plain citizen who knew nothing about such matters and was inclined to be distrustful of them. Costello could not pronounce the names of certain writers; indeed he affected to find them somehow funny; and he had never heard of *Moby Dick*. Paddy, in spite of his alleged peasant cunning and his indubitable desire for the spoils, was a vatic figure who made sometimes obscure but occasionally profound pronouncements much more suited to the bar of history than the tribunal in question. Costello kept turning to the jury with a mixture of sarcasm, condescension to 'the quare poet' and occasional winks of heavy understanding. Paddy leaned wearily down from the slopes of Parnassus to deliver his ultimate aesthetic. It was Mammon and Spirit, Philistine and Poet, even Marsyas and Apollo.[6]

The purposes of both parties, overt or subconscious, were further served by a judge who allowed Costello to get away with what was in effect a plea of justification without actually introducing one and taking the consequences, that is to say he allowed him to cross-examine Paddy on the truth of the article's general picture of his way of life without specifically pleading that the article was true. There thus emerged a portrait which was in one light that of a 'character' who never paid for his own drink: in another that of The Poet and His Poverty-stricken Way. Both parties were happy with this. The only difference was that Costello was winning the verdict of the jury and he knew it, while Paddy was in all innocence asking for that of posterity.

Unfortunately the tone of the proceedings was somewhat lowered when he agreed that his work had been praised by Sir Desmond MacCarthy[7] and that he was highly regarded as a Catholic journalist. It did not help either that he should reply when Costello asserted that Austin Clarke was equally highly regarded in the world of poetry: 'He's not in *The Faber Book of Twentieth Century Verse*.'[8]

Yet by and large he maintained his role while Costello gleefully played the heavy straight man opposite him. Histrionically both parties were superb: Costello comically sharing his incomprehension with the jury; Paddy dropping pearls before swine in prolonged, nasal Monaghan vowels which gave an impression of the utmost distaste. Then across this masterly dialectic, subtle and self-contained, fell the outrageous shadow of Brendan. The gods had decided to turn high comedy into low farce.

On the fourth day Costello quietly and without apparent relevance asked him if he was a friend of Brendan Behan's. The object at that stage may only have been to associate him with somebody disreputable. No harm would have been done if Paddy had replied non-committally, or casually, or even declared that he was unfortunately acquainted with the said party. Instead he grew almost hysterical. In high and passionate tones he described Behan as a low blackguard who followed him about, shouting after him in the streets and forcing him to run away. Anybody who knew Paddy and the relationship such as it was could have testified to the truth of this picture. Unfor-

6. Marsyas, the satyr, challenged Apollo to a contest in music. He lost and Apollo flayed him alive.

7. Sir Desmond MacCarthy (1877-1952), literary journalist, editor and theatre critic.

8. The *Faber Book of Modern Twentieth Century Verse* was edited by M. Roberts (1936).

tunately the protest was too shrill. The jury were sharp fellows. They exercised their intelligences in the only way common humanity knows how. They looked for the motive.

When I came out of the packed courtroom Brendan was, oddly enough, in the hallway. He had a heavy growth of beard, the blue suit was even more crumpled and stained than usual and the open-necked shirt was torn down the front. Whatever this role was, that of despised proletarian writer or rough diamond among the dishonest sophisticates, he was got up for it. He was also evidently drunk.

It was a surprise to see him there, for this was the first time he had been anywhere near the proceedings. He shouldered his way through a knot of people towards the outer door and towards where I was standing. I thought he was going to speak to me but he did no more than mutter something about the Monaghan bogman as he passed. I didn't want a scene, but I had hoped for more.

On the next day, early in the proceedings, Costello produced his secret weapon, his Zinoviev letter.[9] Amid the sort of hush which pervades a courtroom when the audience realises that here at last is what it came to witness, he handed Paddy a copy of his own book *Tarry Flynn* and asked him to read the inscription on the flyleaf. It said: 'To my friend Brendan Behan on the day he painted my flat.' The effect was calamitous. The jury now had something they could understand, and they were no longer afraid. Up to that point they had been to some degree intimidated by attitudes they could no more comprehend than they could the mysteries of their own religion, but which a good deal of their conditioning had led them in some obscure way to respect. Now the god had died. Kavanagh was like themselves, a fallible mortal who tried to get away with it when he could. The broad smiles with which they witnessed his discomfiture were those of fellowship and understanding.

The book had of course no relevance whatever to the issues of the trial, but it finished Kavanagh off with the good men and true. What was worse from his own point of view was that it made him uncertain and affected adversely the Parnassian way in which he had hitherto conducted his own part of the proceedings. It was not just that he had been found out, it was that his obsession with Behan and with plots and counter-plots took over. To be too much concerned with anybody, whether through love or hate or fear, or even merely an ungovernable distaste, is to give them power over you.

In fact the moment Costello sprung his trap I had remembered the strange freak of chance that gave him the opportunity. Paddy had been destroyed by the one and only occasion, certainly more than two years before, on which he had ever allowed himself to talk to Brendan in amity. One Sunday night, towards the ultimate end of the Catacombs as a gathering place, there had been a rather nondescript party with a good deal of tuneless song and repetitive argument. At the height of the proceedings, such as they were, in came Brendan, and, to my extreme surprise, Kavanagh. That Kavanagh should have come there was strange enough; that he should have come with Brendan was incredible.

He had a way when entering any gathering of announcing his presence immediately. His was a speaking part, and everybody should know it. Immediately on entering a room or a pub he would deliver himself of his thought of the moment as if it was so exciting that he could wait no longer. On this occasion he came straight over to where I stood and said: 'I've discovered another fallacy. They were telling us lies. It's not true about oil and water. Not true at all. They do mix.' At first I thought he was talking metaphorically about himself and his companion, but it turned out that he meant literally oil and water. The discovery had been made when Behan, who was painting his flat preparatory to the arrival from America of a rich woman in whom he reposed some hopes, had used water instead of turpentine to thin out the paint. How it came about that the same fellow was allowed inside the door I could only guess. In this enthusiasm about the prospect of entertaining the lady, Paddy had evidently assented to the proposition of some third party that Behan was the very man for the job, being in the trade and able to knock off some paint — an important consideration — and Behan of course had leaped at the chance. The day was one of those islands of amity which occur when the stronger, or at least the besieged, party in such a relationship weakens for the moment, nearly always

9. On 24 October 1924 the Foreign Office in London produced a letter purportedly from Grigori Zinoviev, chairman of the Comintern (Third International), inciting British communists to sedition. The letter was almost certainly a forgery, intended to discredit the British Labour Party.

to his subsequent regret. The *rapprochement*, if it can be called such, lasted for that Sunday only, but it was a Sunday which was to rise again above the waters of time, to Kavanagh's amazement and dismay. On that far away day had occurred, all unbeknownst to him, The Convergence of the Twain.[10]

Of course the event served to increase his belief in the prevalence of plots of all descriptions and for the first time — or at least the first time of which I was aware — I fell under suspicion. In the immediate aftermath I suggested that if it was possible, or the lawyers thought it advisable, I should be called to testify to the uniqueness of the occasion on which the book was presented. This was decided against, but not before Paddy had expressed his suspicions to one of the lawyers. 'I don't know who I can trust any longer', he said. 'I'm not even sure if I can trust Cronin.' As it turned out, my father had worked for years for the solicitor in question. 'If he's anything like his father you can trust him with your life', he said, a reply which Paddy had the grace to tell me of immediately.

On the night it all ended he and I and his brother went to the nearby Ormond Hotel. At least four of Paddy's women friends were in and about the place, hoping to be the chosen sympathiser, but we secluded ourselves in an inner room, and there we attempted a statement. When we failed to make much fist of a joint attempt the brother suggested that we should sit down separately, make drafts and then compare and combine them. 'After all, we're all writers here', he said. To which Paddy replied with comic resignation, 'Ay, ay. All brothers of the pen.'

The lawyers countermanded the issue of a statement because an appeal had been decided on. Then the question of costs was discussed between the brothers. Fearing secrets, I attempted to leave, but was told peremptorily to stay. I learned at least a good deal about Paddy's circumstances that I had not known before, including the fact that he was not as badly off as he had led us all to believe. He had at least a proprietory interest in the farm and throughout all the years in Dublin he was in receipt of money from it. Thus, although frequently without cash, he may be regarded as a man with a small private income which, of course, was utterly inadequate to his needs. In the event the question of his having to pay costs never arose. His lawyers appealed; after prolonged argument before the Supreme Court a retrial was ordered; the ancient weekly journal which had published the article was of course utterly unable to sustain further legal action; a small settlement was accordingly arranged; and there the matter died.

There had been no bonanza, but in the aftermath the trial had one important financial consequence for Paddy. When, shortly afterwards, he fell ill, a consortium which included the Archbishop of Dublin, John Charles McQuaid[11] (an old friend), John A. Costello (now Prime Minister again[12] and making generous and gratuitous amends for his role in the proceedings) and Professor Michael Tierney[13] arranged that he should receive an annual stipend for delivering some lectures annually in U.C.D. It was not a princely sum, but it was the long awaited pension and it was to have curious consequences.

In the aftermath of the Kavanagh 'trial' (which of course it was not, but which was how he and I and others now thought of it) I refused to speak to Brendan at all. The handing over of the book seemed to me to have been a particularly shabby and, indeed, a particularly Irish act. It might almost indeed have been part of Kavanagh's scenario for martyrdom, for no matter what he had said about Brendan in the witness box, it savoured of King's evidence. I was a prig of course, indulging myself in a little bit of drama in which I was the haughty incorruptible and Brendan the indubitable villain. I was to pay a penalty. We should beware of the grand gestures which it costs us nothing to make.

Further, I believe now that I was wrong about the facts. He did not give the lawyers the book at all. It was a member of the family in whose house he had left it who, incensed by what Kavanagh had said, handed it over to the defence.

Brendan took the refusal hard. Several times in McDaid's and elsewhere he attempted to speak to me, whether to explain or not I don't know. He was

10. Reference to Thomas Hardy's poem of that title on the loss of the *Titanic*.

11. John Charles McQuaid (1895-1973), catholic archbishop of Dublin and primate of All Ireland 1940-72.

12. Costello was Taoiseach of the second inter-party government 1954-57.

13. Michael Tierney (1894-1975), president of University College, Dublin 1947-64.

usually drunk and not very coherent, but in any case I would not listen. On one occasion he even embarrassingly went on his knees, begging me to come and have a drink with him. Prig that I was, I refused, and soon the pleadings turned not unnaturally to mutterings, which I ignored also. Finally the mutterings and the occasional bit of abuse flung at me from the middle distance turned to physical assault.

I was sitting by the counter in Davy Byrne's one evening when he came in. He stood a few yards away in the middle of the floor and delivered himself hoarsely of some well thought out if somewhat monotonous remarks about bogmen, kulchies[14] and the like. After a while I had had enough and stood up. What ineffectual form, physical or otherwise, my attempts to shut him up would have taken I do not know, but anyway at that moment the barmen decided, somewhat reluctantly, to do their duty and he was shoohed and persuaded off the premises, though such was their evident nervousness that it became a sort of whistle-stop tour, with Brendan making farewell addresses every few yards of the way.

I stayed till closing time, a matter of a good two hours, and emerged alone. As I came out of the door, adjusting myself to the night, a stertorous being suddenly flung itself out of the darkness, grabbed me by the top of the lapels, behind the neck, and using my own momentum, ran my head forward against the lamp post on the edge of the pavement. Even while I saw stars I knew from the 'fuck you' it was Brendan. Hitting a metal lamp post with the top of your head at six or seven miles an hour is a trying experience, but fortunately I was not knocked out, and fortunately also Brendan made the mistake of releasing his grip.

What followed was certainly not a fight, but neither, as 'the brides in the bath' murderer is reported to have said, was it fun. I staggered backwards into the middle of the road and Brendan charged after me. Like most dirty fighters he was fond of leading with his head and this was his undoing. I had the old duffle coat that I then wore over my left arm and each time he charged I used it to baffle him. After a while the thing began to become like a bullfight, with Brendan repeatedly rushing and snorting, only to get enveloped every time in the folds of the cape. Luckily for me he had been hanging round for two hours brooding on the wrongs and injustices that were being done to him, so he was by now berserk with rage, while my only thought was self-preservation and I had the icy calmness of fear; but in fact it was his usual insatiable desire for the favour of the generality, that, penetrating even through his rage, turned out his Achilles heel, and saved me in the end.

There had been the normal knot of people in the street at closing time and they were all watching. Brendan had incurred a lot of opprobrium by his initial tactic and now he was being made to look ridiculous as well. Every bull-like rush that he made only to get entangled in the coat was greeted with an ironic cheer and, if the occasional blows that I was able to get in at the top of his head over the coat while I circled away were not very effectual, they were at least crowd-pleasers. When all this began to penetrate to him his dominant passion began to prevail even over his rage, as dominant passions always will, and eventually he rushed no more, but stood still, looked around and delivered himself a few words of abuse to the crowd in general. It was, it seemed, composed of kulchies and bogmen too. It was no use. They were the audience and there was no other and ultimate one before whom they could be made to feel embarrassed or ridiculous. In fact they cheered each remark as they had cheered each rush and so eventually, after standing for a moment in the middle of the road, muttering and evidently at a loss, he gave up and walked away. If to be left in possession of the field was victory, I had it.

A man with an English accent came over and asked me if I was all right. Then he very decently said he was going to Matt Smith's and would I like a lift. I needed a drink and I accepted. We had to walk a bit to his car so when we got out to the bona fide[15] rumours were already circulating which suggested that I had met my end in Duke Street. I was therefore able to fulfil a common ambition by echoing Mark Twain's remark about the rumours of his death being greatly exaggerated, but Kavanagh, who was there with John Ryan, went one better.

14. A 'kulchie' is a term of urban contempt for a country person. The name derives from the village of Kiltimagh in County Mayo, pronounced to sound like 'Kulchie-ma'.

15. A pub outside the city limits where genuine (bona fide) travellers could drink after hours.

'Didn't I tell you the bacon would be no match for the slicer?' he demanded, turning to John.

Next day I found out something about Brendan as a politician. There were at that time two famous Dublin characters who hung about the Duke Street-Grafton Street area pretending to sell newspapers, in fact begging and running occasional small errands for people. As I walked up Grafton Street towards McDaid's that evening one of them accosted me.

'I want to tell yew somethin' about Be'in, Mister Cronin, Jimser an' me saw the fight las' night, ef fight ye choose te call it, an' we did'n like what he done to yew at the kick-off. That was a durty trick, Mister Cronin, a very durty trick, an I did'n scruple to tell annywan I was talkin' to today what a durty trick it was. Well Be'in comes up to me an' Jimser after the holy hour an' he asks us to have a drink with em. I did'n mind. I'll have a drink with annywan until he proves his sincerity. So we went into Ryan's with em an' he buys us gargle[16] and buys us gargle until it's comin' out our ears, wherever he got the money.

'Now, I don't want annything from yew, Mister Cronin. I'm only tellin' ye in case yew heard we was drinkin' with Be'in an' might come to the wrong construction. Of course what Be'in wanted was for me an' Jimser to forget what we seen las' night an' have seen somethin' else entirely. Well, I'll tell ye this much, Mister Cronin. It was too obvious for my taste. Too obvious entirely. An' I don' like the obvious. No I certainly don' like things bein' made too obvious.'

Here, to tell truth, I did the obvious thing myself and offered him one of my last three half-crowns to have a pint. With a pained but kindly look he replied: 'Keep yer money, Mister Cronin. I don't want annything from yew. Yew an' me will have a jar some other day. I'm ony tellin' yew so that yew'll know what a blackguard Be'in is an' that Jimser an' me were ony drinkin' with him for the gargle.'

Of course he was the smartest politician of the three.

Unfortunately, however, the fight, if fight it was, was only the beginning of a prolonged nightmare. Brendan was adept at using the hysteric's weapon and he calculated its many advantages to a nicety. The principal one is that it attracts public attention, from which only the other party suffers, the hysteric having made up his or her mind that he or she is beyond considerations of shame or personal dignity and that so long as the other party retains the capacity to feel either, suffering can be inflicted. Any attempt to reason only brings further indignity with it, for the reasoner is rightly regarded by the bystanders as being somehow hangdog and in need of justification. The striking of women only adds zest to their performance, not to mention bringing other consequences down on the poor consort's head, including the risk of being lynched by the same moralising bystanders. And if the poor fellow actually suffers at the spectacle of the hysteric's own lack of dignity, the victory is complete.

Brendan was neither a woman nor a hysteric, but he constantly used the hysteric's weapon of a public scene from which only one party could be the gainer. If you scarpered, which of course was the sensible thing to do, you would be pursued to the door, if not further, with allegations of cowardice calculated to delight the crowd. On the other hand if you struck him, you would certainly not be the gainer either, for a good messy fight with both parties afterwards barred from the pub — where very likely he was barred already — would bring you right down to his level. You couldn't shout back, for he could outshout Vesuvius. And you most certainly could not reason with him, even if you were talking to him, which I was not.

At the same time his apparent size — when he was in a rage or assumed rage he swelled out, so that he looked enormous; ferocity — all red face and chest — and strength made barmen reluctant to intervene when he pushed open the door of a pub, peered blearily round the interior of the premises, spotted one already cowering in one's corner, advanced with that rolling assertive gait which was perhaps meant to combine the distressed British seaman with a few other *personae*, and began the abuse. I have said shouting, but it would perhaps be wrong to think of him as shouting on these occasions. What he adopted was more the steady, level, hoarse, stentorian tone of the public orator who is intent on drowning out all opposition. Indeed, now that I think of it, drowning out is not a bad metaphor, for the amount of moisture he emitted was considerable and could be felt at a considerable distance.

To make matters worse I was courting a girl. I took her to the pubs I knew because there are

16. Common Dublin idiom for alcoholic drink.

advantages to be gained by playing on the home pitch and a bit of capital to be extracted out of the attention you are paid by barmen and even gurrierdom[17] in the places where you are known. At least there should be. In this case the advantages were rather inclined to be outweighed by the omnipresence of Brendan. Besides being beautiful, the girl concerned was literate, and she knew a lot of the people I knew, but all the same she was young, she knew nothing about bohemia and had hitherto heard of McDaid's only by reputation. In this situation the value of the cards that Brendan held was doubled, and he knew it. We would be quietly ensconced in a corner of Davy Byrne's or Neary's[18] when the door would open and with a sinking of the heart I would see the well-known figure poised to roll forward. He would usually stand some yards away, to ensure the maximum of attention from the other people in the pub, and then he would begin. The performance was orotund, more in the style of a labour leader of the old school than of the sharp-witted politicians of today; indeed, passionate as it appeared to be, there was even a touch of leisureliness about it, as if the meeting was scheduled to go on for quite some time. To the girl concerned everything he said was incomprehensible, but the spectacle was frightening all the same; and to me, with my mixture of emotions, the whole thing was agonising. Also, I knew that there was damn-all to be done about it.

I would therefore take her by the hand and flee through the nearest available door. She did not expect, I am glad to say, as other, more orthodox, girls might have done, the prescribed male reactions. Ten or twenty minutes later, in another pub, there would be another performance. Sometimes we were pursued into the alleyway, only Brendan's general lack of locomotion preventing further chase, and as we vanished down a neighbouring street we would hear his voice still grinding and booming away, as one hears the voice of the orator at the public meeting one has left, receding gradually into the distance, until one comes to a place where the traffic noises take over and it is an ordinary summer twilight again.

17. A gurrier in Dublin slang is a n'er-do-well.
18. Well-known pubs in the Grafton Street area.

PATRICK SHEA

(1908-)

from:
VOICES AND THE SOUND OF DRUMS: AN IRISH AUTOBIOGRAPHY (1981)

[Patrick Shea's father was a member of the Royal Irish Constabulary, which was disbanded when the Anglo-Irish Treaty of 1921 had brought to a close hostilities between the IRA and the forces of the British Crown. Partition followed, and Shea's family moved to the North where he found employment in the Northern Ireland civil service in 1926. He remained in the service until 1973, eventually becoming permanent secretary to the Public Building and Works Department. He was only the second catholic in the history of the state to reach that level of seniority. One of the reasons for his appointment was the change in the political climate which came in 1968, the year the Civil Rights marches began in Northern Ireland and the liberal reforms of Captain Terence O'Neill, prime minister since 1963, began to accelerate.

Shea grew up in Athlone, Co. Westmeath, during the years of violence that led to the partitioning of the island. His father was in the firing line against the IRA and his defence of the RIC contrasts remarkably with the attacks on the force that were orchestrated into a policy of ostracization in the proceedings of Dáil Eireann in 1919. Shea's autobiography is important because it represents one aspect of the Irish catholic readiness to trust to constitutional reform rather than to violence for the solution of the country's abiding political problems. Nevertheless, Shea's account of the northern administration, of the influence of the Orange Order and of the failure of the British government to stand up to loyalist violence in 1974, as it had failed to do over sixty years before, shows just how deeply embedded the political problems are. His account of Easter Week and the subsequent developments contrasts with the other accounts given in this section; but it has the added advantage of being included in a story that also embraces the onset of the Northern crisis, one of the long-term consequences of the events Shea witnessed as a child.]

CHAPTER 2

. . . I have a clear memory of the Easter Week Rebellion of 1916. Mother had gone to Dublin for a surgical operation and on the day on which news of the Rising reached us Father told us that he was going off to try and see her because she was very ill. From what we overheard of his conversation with people who called to enquire about her we knew that he had been told that she was critically ill. I remember his distracted face as he left his four sons, the eldest less than nine years of age, to stay with friends and the sick feeling that came over me when I overheard a passer-by on the street referring to us as the 'poor little orphans'. Fortunately Mother recovered and lived to a great age.

During that Easter week, when there was no news either of Father's whereabouts or Mother's condition, we went to the Square every day and watched the lorries carrying armed soldiers and policemen racing through on their way to Dublin. The townspeople cheered them as they passed and, when a lorry stopped for a few minutes, brought them refreshments. In that week Yeats's 'terrible beauty' was born but its birth was not celebrated by the people of Ireland. There was only anger at the wild, foolhardy men who had been responsible for many deaths and the destruction of much property in Dublin.

When Mother came home she told us of returning to consciousness to the sound of a machine-gun operating from the roof of the hospital, of seeing from her window horse-drawn breadvans being set upon by crowds of hungry people and emptied of their loads in seconds. We had a visit from a big ruddy-complexioned sergeant in the police whose brother, also a policeman, had been killed at Ashbourne[1] where a party of police reinforcements had been attacked. I had to leave the room because he was crying and the sight of an adult shedding tears was too much for me.

After the execution of the leaders of the Rising, pictures of them and ballads about their exploits began to appear but only one or two shops in Athlone stocked them. But opinion was changing. Sympathy for the dead leaders was growing as people began to learn more about the kind of men they were; the idea of a republic rather than the 1914 proposition of a subordinate Irish parliament was being thought about. But this was still a minority movement; the revolutionary implications of republicanism were unwelcome to God-fearing people who were making money as never before. Besides, Athlone had long been a garrison town, the young men of the district had gone to the war in large numbers and the big army training camp which had been established early in the war had brought new business to the town and new diversions for the townspeople. From most of them the appeal to participation in a hazardous form of extreme patriotism met with little response.

There was a fierce earnestness about those who were preaching the doctrine of complete separation. Their flag, the green, white and orange tricolour, began to be seen more often. They organised public meetings which were addressed by articulate young men from Dublin and fiery old men who had taken part in the land agitation of the nineteenth century. Every Sunday afternoon they gathered in Mardyke Street and if the meeting was to be held in a neighbouring village they went off in horse-drawn brakes with a tricolour hoisted over the leading vehicle. Police were required to attend the meetings and at first they went in the brakes with the organisers but this handy arrangement came to an end when the letters 'IRA' began to appear on the flags, for the Irish Republican Army, of which people had first heard in 1916, was a proscribed organisation.

Early in 1918 the announcement of the British Government's intention to impose military conscription on Ireland sent the temperature of the country soaring. It aroused anger and dismay everywhere; mass meetings and petitions were organised, resolutions of protest were passed by public bodies, cries of condemnation came from the press and the pulpit, men wore green, white and orange badges inscribed 'Death Before Conscription'. Although the Parliamentary Party's members

1. During the Easter Rising, Irish Volunteers ambushed forty men of the Royal Irish Constabulary at Ashbourne, Co. Meath, 12 miles north of Dublin. Eight policemen were killed and twice as many injured; the police had to surrender when they ran out of ammunition. The incident is sometimes known as the battle of Ashbourne (28 April 1916).

at Westminster bitterly opposed the proposal to conscript Irishmen, the Government's declaration came powerfully to the aid of those who had been crying out about the futility of trying to achieve anything by negotiation with England and advocating abstention from the British Parliament. Reasonable people thought the Government's announcement was an ungracious affront to a country which had contributed so many thousands of volunteers to fight in the British forces. The Constitutional party, with the promise of Home Rule when peace came, had, at least until the 1916 Rising hardened many British hearts, collaborated with the Government in the prosecution of the war effort. Now they were discredited. The separatists reminded their listeners that the men who died in the Rising had declared an Irish Republic and sanctified the declaration with their blood. If further Irish blood was to be shed, let it be for Ireland, they said.

In the face of opposition both in Great Britain and in Ireland, the conscription proposal was dropped. But a body blow had been dealt the Irish Parliamentary Party. John Redmond, its leader, had urged his followers to join in the fight for the freedom of small nations; he had lost his brother at the battle of the Somme.[2] The conscription threat had brushed aside the helping hand of the parliamentarians and the Sinn Fein party had benefited enormously. Sinn Fein leaders had taken a prominent part in the expression of the people's anger and when the argument was over their weekly gatherings were seen to gather larger crowds than ever before. The newspapers gave more space to what they had to say and in parts of the country meetings ended in clashes with the police who were under instructions to seize flags bearing the letters 'IRA'.

My brothers and I were in the crowds watching the parades and the torchlight processions and we went to the open-air meetings. We saw Maud Gonne MacBride, Countess Markiewicz and red-bearded Darrel [*sic*] Figgis; de Valera, Harry Boland, Father O'Flanagan, then the leading orator of the movement, Laurence Ginnell and many others.[3] Like the military displays and the picnics on the river and the pilgrimages to Clonmacnoise, it was all part of a very busy boyhood; there was no feeling of involvement in the controversy in which so many earnest words were being used. But on the morning on which we were first attacked by our schoolmates, everything changed; whether or not we wished it, we were involved in a conflict of loyalties and we were on the side that, although not yet a minority, was losing support. The beatings were to continue but we were sturdy and not excessively put out by our experiences. The Master was on our side and if danger threatened he made an excuse to walk home with us. But these juvenile outbursts were spasmodic. For much of the time our relations with the other pupils were, with one or two exceptions, normal.

The possibility of violence was being talked about; there were convictions of men who had publicly called for the use of arms against the oppressor; it was known that young men were acquiring arms. The police had some knowledge of what was going on and it became their duty to seek out and enforce the law against those found with arms or other evidence of association with seditious intentions.

My first sight of political prisoners was when half a dozen young men, most of them farmers' sons, were brought into Fry Place Barrack. They were cheerful, friendly men and during their four or five days in the barrack they sang Irish songs, played handball or sat about in the yard talking with the

2. William Redmond (1861-1917), younger brother of John, leader of the Irish Parliamentary Party who had encouraged the Irish Volunteers to fight on the British side in World War I. He was MP for East Clare when he was killed; his seat was won by Eamon de Valera in the same year.

3. Maud Gonne MacBride (1866-1953), republican, advocate of physical force, also remembered for her relationship with Yeats. Countess Markievicz (1868-1927), republican, officer in the Irish Citizen Army, fought in 1916, later opposed the Treaty. Darrell Figgis (1892-1925), member of Sinn Féin and the Irish Volunteers, involved in the Howth gun-running incident in 1914, Sinn Féin representative in the first Dáil and supporter of the Treaty; he committed suicide in 1925. Eamon de Valera (1882-1975), the dominant figure in Irish political life from 1927 to 1959. Harry Boland (1887-1922), member of the IRB and the Irish Volunteers, fought in 1916, represented Dáil Éireann in the United States in 1919, rejected the Treaty and was shot dead during the Civil War. Rev. Michael O'Flanagan (1876-1942), a catholic priest who became deeply involved in the land agitation in the West 1912-14, then became an ardent supporter of Sinn Féin. He split with de Valera on the founding of Fianna Fáil in 1927, was silenced by his bishop in 1932, supported the republican cause during the Spanish Civil War and retired to devote himself to the study of literature. He edited 50 volumes of the *Letters* of John O'Donovan, the great Gaelic scholar. Lawrence Ginnell (1854-1923), MP at Westminster for Westmeath 1906-18, joined Sinn Féin after 1916 and was director of publicity for the movement 1919-21. He was known for his impassioned oratory and for his deep involvement in the land question.

police. On one night a ceilidh[4] was held; musicians were brought in, girl friends of the arrested men were invited and the young constables and their prisoners danced Irish dances in the big, tiled kitchen.

In the more southerly parts of the country there were occasional skirmishes between the police and Sinn Fein supporters; stones were thrown and batons were drawn. It was a time of great emotional verbiage. There was talk of the resumption of the fight for freedom, of throwing off the yoke of England; Thomas Francis Meagher's 'Stigmatise the sword' speech was the text of many an oration;[5] Patrick Pearse, the executed 1916 leader, was much quoted: 'Ireland unfree can never be at peace'.[6] There were new patriotic songs. 'Who Fears to Speak of Easter Week' was a re-write of a song about the 'Ninety-Eight' but the 'Soldiers' Song' was new and stirring and quickly became the theme song of Republicanism.[7] The oddest composition for a Republican movement must have been 'We'll Crown de Valera King of Ireland'. The clergy were divided. Some of the priests spoke out against the violent implications of Sinn Fein, others used their pulpits to rouse their parishioners to support of the ideals of the militant Republicans. And Father Michael O'Flanagan was addressing meetings here there and everywhere so that people wondered if his parishioners ever saw him at all.

On 11 November 1918 as I crossed the town Square, the big gates of the military barrack swung open and the entire garrison came running out in one great, disorderly crowd. The war in Europe had ended. For the rest of the day there was drinking and music and dancing. There was a sports meeting and band parade in the field in which the Gaelic Football team played. Many of the townspeople put red, white and blue ribbons in their buttonholes; everyone was out celebrating.

In December 1918 there was a General Election. Except in the northern counties the Sinn Fein party had a big victory. It won seventy-three seats and the once great Parliamentary Party's representation shrank to six members. Some said that a good many voters had changed their allegiance through fear of the young men in trench coats who were on the move wherever political arguments arose but there could be no doubt that public opinion had changed dramatically. The men who had died in 1916 were becoming the inspiration of the new generation.

The Sinn Fein candidates had taken a pledge not to claim their seats in the British Parliament. The Irish Republican Army was being talked about in school. In secret, it was swearing in new members whose oath, it was said, bound them to pursue the ideal of a free Irish Republic even at the risk of their lives. Arms and explosives and books on military training and operations were being acquired and by unseen means distributed to the underground army. The St Patrick's Day parade of the Irish National Foresters became a small procession of old men in fancy dress.

There were more and more police raids, arrests and prison sentences, more meetings and angry, defiant words, seizures of privately-owned arms and explosive materials by groups of masked men, the burning of houses regarded as possible accommodation for Crown Forces.

The political atmosphere was tense; the Sinn Fein party, triumphant at the polls, was becoming increasingly defiant; the existence of an armed organisation was undeniable; magistrates concerned with the trials of political prisoners were getting threatening letters; men sent to gaol for preaching sedition were the heroes of the hour. The question on many minds was whether all the threats and the secret plotting and the wild words would lead to bloodshed. A repeat of the 1916 Rising was improbable; the precaution of locking up possible leaders of a rebellion had been taken. Nevertheless, the frequency of lawless acts was on the increase, the shooting of the enforcers of British law had openly been advocated by some of the more fanatical leaders. But one was reassured by the thought that Ireland was a Catholic country with a long Christian tradition and although its history contained many instances of hot-blooded violence under the stress of oppressive laws, peace-loving people felt that, in the conditions then prevailing, a planned campaign of calculated killing was, despite what was being said by the hotheads, unlikely.

4. A social gathering with singing, dancing and story-telling.
5. Thomas Francis Meagher (1822-67), the Young Irelander, whose 1848 speech in Conciliation Hall, in which he refused to 'stigmatize the sword' (renounce violence), led to the break between Young Ireland and O'Connell. (See Volume II, pp. 121-24.)
6. The quotation is from Pearse's speech of 1915 at the grave of Jeremiah O'Donovan Rossa.
7. 'Who Fears to Speak of Ninety-Eight?' by John Kells Ingram, first published in 1843, was rewritten to celebrate the Easter Rising. 'The Soldier's Song' was written in 1907 (words by Peadar Kearney, music by Patrick Heeney). It became the national anthem of the new state.

CHAPTER 8

. . . At last the time came when the arrangements for the disbandment of the Royal Irish Constabulary were completed. They were to go to the big Depot at Gormanston where each man would be given his discharge and a warrant entitling him to a pension for life.

The Black and Tans were first to go. Seeing them in civilian clothes, carrying their shabby luggage to the station, one was struck by their very ordinariness. The name Black and Tan had aroused fear and hatred throughout the country but, stripped of their uniforms and fearsome trappings, they seemed insignificant little men on their way back to their working-class homes in the industrial towns and cities of Britain. There was a great, curious crowd at the station when the train, which had been gathering unfrocked Black and Tans along its journey, came steaming into the station with its occupants crowding the windows, cheering and singing. From one carriage an Irish tricolour fluttered. I had never seen so many drunk men. They got a boisterous, good-humoured send-off.

A little later the remainder of the force went away and after a few days Father came home. He was now a civilian and the Royal Irish Constabulary was no more.

My judgement of the Royal Irish Constabulary must be a very subjective one. I was thirteen years old when the force was disbanded. Those years which were, more than any time in my life, full of exciting and often entertaining happenings, had been spent in the company of these men. My earliest memories are of endless happy days in the barrack in Athlone with large men in uniform always on hand to help solve the immense problems of childhood, to provide interest and entertainment and friendship and to open doors into the exciting and often eccentric world of adults. When the cold wind of hostility began to blow and the new Republicans tried to brand them as enemies of the Irish people, I wanted to cry out for justice for they were my friends. Throughout the campaign of shooting many influential voices were raised in sympathy with them. When the fierce retaliation of the Black and Tans added a new dimension to terrorism men of courage did not exempt one side more than the other from their expressions of disapproval.

The men of the Royal Irish Constabulary had not the background or the disposition or the training which produces heroes; they were quite unfitted for the part which they were called upon to fill by those who saw a resort to violence as the way to the attainment of the Ireland they wanted. The designers of the campaign of killing thought that once they had claimed a few unwary victims the Royal Irish Constabulary would disintegrate, but they knew nothing of the deep loyalty of those simple men one towards another. Because they believed that they belonged to a unique police force with proud traditions, they grew angry at the vituperation of the extremists and they were sustained by the sympathy of responsible opinion. When shootings, following the unheroic pattern of Soloheadbeg, became daily happenings, a small number left the force but the majority remained to serve not (as Tom Kettle put it) for King or Crown or Empire[1] but out of the comradeship which bound them together. Some to whom the events of those years are part of history may say that they were wrong but I can think of them only as I knew them. It would be idle to pretend that in the heat of the conflict there were no instances of men who behaved unworthily. I knew one such man; I knew also of the contempt in which he was held by his colleagues. But I am quite sure that there were in the Royal Irish Constabulary more good men than my children or my children's children will meet in any company, anywhere.

1. Thomas Kettle (1880-1916), a close friend of James Joyce and Francis Sheehy-Skeffington, was nationalist MP for East Tyrone 1906-10, and was appointed first professor of economics of the National University of Ireland in 1908. He volunteered for active service on the Western front and was killed during the battle of the Somme. The last four lines of his poem 'To My Daughter Betty, the Gift of God' read:
   'Know that we fools, now with the foolish dead,
   Died not for flag, nor King, nor Emperor —
   But for a dream, born in a herdsman's shed,
   And for the secret Scripture of the poor.'

CHAPTER 18

[Shea wrote a memorandum setting out the main issues between the two communities in the North. He reproduces it in this chapter, saying 'If it does no more than reveal the prejudices of one Irishman, perhaps its composition has not been a waste of time.']

. . . In the twenty years after the 1939-45 War the Northern Ireland Government and the

Unionist Party, by failing to build on the growth of goodwill, missed an opportunity of winning the trust of a large section of the Catholic community. A little magnanimity (for example some concern about the more blatant discriminatory practices in local government; more just electoral arrangements in Derry)[1] would have gone a long way.

The close association between the Orange Order and the Unionist Party made it virtually impossible for a Catholic to be a member of the Party. Some years ago when a leading Unionist was quoted as saying that Catholics could be members of the Party, the Orange Order immediately said 'No'. After lengthy cogitation the Party announced that Roman Catholics could be considered for membership 'provided they are found to be suitable people'. Needless to say, the Party's Headquarters in Glengall Street was not embarrassed by any rush of applicants anxious to be adjudged 'suitable people'.

Despite efforts by liberal-minded men (Terence O'Neill notably) to change its image, the Unionist Party was seen to be a party established by Protestants for Protestants and too few of its leaders showed any real concern for this being so.

The Catholics of Northern Ireland did, of course, benefit in many ways from the Government's progressive legislation; any fair-minded person would be bound to admit that in material things they would not have fared so well in a united Irish Republic. But when Unionists point to these benefits and ask why Catholics did not more actively support the Government, they talk as though the Protestant community has been sharing its wealth with the less well-deserving. (This attitude was outrageously typified by the comment of a schoolmaster in my presence: 'We should never have given them Maynooth'.)

It is probably inevitable that any group or class which has controlled government continuously for more than fifty years, which has had a specially privileged position in the country for centuries, should feel endowed with a divine right to govern and should resent any suggestion that the power and the privileges which have been at their exclusive disposal for so long should be shared with those who have been outside and often resentful of their special position.

It would however be wrong to leave the impression that over the past sixty years one-third of the people of Northern Ireland have spent their time brooding on these matters. Many, many people on either side of the 'religious divide' have, without any inhibitions or reservations, established the most cordial (what in other places would be called 'normal') relationships with their neighbours. If divisive issues impinged on their thinking, they managed to shut their minds to allegations of past wrongs and to discard inherited prejudices.

Unhappily recent events have revived mistrust and hostility. Now, when solutions are being sought, it is as well to understand that the roots of the evils that beset us lie deep in history.

When I joined the Civil Service in 1926, I did not do so out of any burning desire to serve the Union. (Who did?) Nor did it occur to me that by entering the service of the Government of Northern Ireland I was being in any way disloyal to my co-religionists. I wanted a job at a time when jobs were hard to get and I was appointed as a result of a competitive examination. And yet, particularly in those early years, I sometimes felt rather like a cuckoo in the nest. Protestants would ask me how I had 'got in'. And Catholics, particularly in Belfast, looked on me with suspicion. I must have 'influence'; I was probably a 'bad Catholic', perhaps secretly a Freemason or the son of a Freemason. Until quite recent times members of my own Church, including politicians and clerics, showed little interest in the welfare of Catholics in the Northern Ireland Civil Service. We had gone over to the 'other side' and if we thought we were not getting fair play, what did we expect? It should be emphasised that this attitude was particularly a Belfast one.

I believe that there have been serious dis-

1. The gerrymandering of the Derry city corporation was one of the more blatant examples of anti-catholic discrimination before 1969.

criminatory practices operating to the disadvantage of Catholics in parts of the public service and particularly in the local government services. At the same time I regret that, until rather late in the day, Catholics failed to make full use of the opportunities which were there; too often they accepted second-class citizenship as their lot and they got little help from their political representatives. Generations of Nationalist politicians were miserably resourceless in finding ways of drawing attention to the more scandalous allegations of unfair practices.

Throughout my service I never found in a civil servant or a Minister any curiosity about my political opinions and I have made a point of not telling anyone how I vote. But I cannot say that I did not encounter evidence of prejudice against Catholics. My colleagues in the Civil Service I acquit of any such charge but I believe that, until very late in the life of the Northern Ireland Parliament, Catholics were seriously at a disadvantage in those grades in which advancement was subject to the approval of Ministers. That is not to say that all Ministers would have approved such attitudes; there were honourable exceptions.

That paper was written in 1972, a year before I retired from the Civil Service. Although from the outside, things do not look quite as they then did, I don't think I would wish to change it except to suggest that the time has come for someone to tell us more than has yet been revealed about the extent to which the Orange Order influenced not just the organisation and the thinking of the Unionist Party but the policies and the actions of the Government. Evidence of the Order's considerable association with the Party can be seen in the fact that over the life of the Northern Ireland Parliament, Unionist Members who were not Orangemen were rare exceptions. Membership of the Order seemed to be a prerequisite for nomination.

The Cabinet Ministers with whom I came into contact were, almost without exception, kind to me, conscientious in their attitude to the public services, anxious to manage their departments efficiently. In private conversation many of them showed a liberality of mind pleasantly at variance with the accepted public image of Unionist politicians. One wondered how men for whom one could feel genuine respect could have acquiesced, even participated in, illiberal practices which, in the end, brought discredit on fifty years of government. I believe the answer lies in the relationship between the Orange Order and the Unionist Party; the influence of Orangeism was, I believe, considerable, often malevolent, and always an impediment to good government. But my impressions come from sounds emanating from behind doors which were closed to me. Someone who was in those locked rooms should tell us about what went on there.

CHAPTER 19

During my last months in the Government service I participated with colleagues in examining aspects of devolved government on which administrators as well as politicians were expected to have something to say. The decision to work towards a 'power sharing' administration had been settled in the Cabinet in London. We were invited to examine and comment on various matters related to a settlement of that sort; how such a government might be shaped, how the public services could be affected, what difficulties or problems might arise in the reallocation of departmental functions, the effects of withholding certain services, such as law and order, from the new administration. Those deliberations took us into some quite new places. I believe that it was around that table that the term 'Irish Dimension', about which much has since been heard, was first used.[1]

I had ceased to frequent the 'corridors of power' when, following the 'Sunningdale Agreement',[2] a new form of multi-party government came into being. Moderate people (a head count of whom, in our community, even Solomon would not be capable) hoped that at last we had found a formula which would lead to the banishment of sectarianism from our political life. The failure of that experiment is now a matter of history. In a society in which democracy normally means rule by the elected majority, perhaps it was an artificial creation

1. The phrase, used in different circumstances but to the same end since then, refers to the acknowledgement that the Republic of Ireland has a role to play in the solution to the problems of Northern Ireland.
2. The Sunningdale Agreement of December 1973 was reached after talks between the British and Irish governments and the executive of Northern Ireland. It was brought down by the loyalist Ulster Workers' Council strike of May 1974.

doomed to failure in any case but the event which brought it to an end, the so-called Ulster Workers' Council Strike, was the most bewildering and in some respects the most frightening experience of my life.

Our home was then in a suburb in south Belfast; our neighbours were, in the main, business and professional people with a sprinkling of academics and public service employees. We had the good fortune to be in an area which had remained virtually undisturbed by civil strife, amongst many kind people. When the Workers' Council strike began and the shops and business premises were closed under threats of violence we were, as all around us were, discommoded and not a little annoyed. Mr Merlyn Rees,[3] the Secretary of State, with advice from his security chiefs, decided to adopt a 'low profile' which meant that the bully-boys who were on the move, closing shops and offices, halting traffic, ordering people off the streets, searching inoffensive citizens, went unchecked. No names were taken, no attempt made to send the gangs home or to remove the obstructions which had been placed across the Queen's highway.

I watched a group of club-carrying youths stopping and searching cars within sight of a large police station and a military check-point and I began to feel what life must have been like in Nazi Germany. During those days we were in the presence of raw Nazism.

It was a time of rumours and one which swept through our area and indeed, much of Belfast, was that the Catholics were in danger; people told us that lists of all the Catholic households, which were not very numerous where we lived, had been circulated so that, on an agreed signal, action could be taken to 'clear them out'. I don't think I believed that there was any real danger of a pogrom but with the atmosphere more tense every day, the forces of law and order apparently standing by, and all too many signs of lack of discipline amongst those who had been allowed to take charge, it was not easy for any household to remain calm. However unfounded the rumours might have been, many people were afraid; we knew families who went to bed with suitcases packed.

Merlyn Rees cannot look back on his handling of the UWC strike with any pride. In at least one household in Belfast he got no marks at all for judgement or courage or concern for the fears of law-abiding citizens.

Although the rumours and inconveniences and the strutting cornerboys brought moments of concern, I went about my business more or less as usual, albeit on foot, and was never molested. For me the most bewildering aspect of the whole business was the extent to which the stoppage had the acquiescence, too often the active support, of what might be called the middle and upper middle classes; the people of means and property, professional people, industrialists, the directorial classes, some of the teachers of our youth, one or two highly-placed civil servants. Their sympathy and co-operation, in substantial numbers, ensured the effectiveness of the stoppage. Their response was, with undoubted exceptions, surprisingly and depressingly strong; it was astonishing that so many apparently intelligent, educated people could, in the presence of open anarchy, feel anything but revulsion and fearful concern for the future of their community.

Those events confirmed my opinion that centuries of privileged treatment created in Ireland a governing class of which, after the partitioning of the country, the Northern Ireland Unionists remain a residue; a possessive, unbending remnant of a powerful ruling class. The principal demands of the strikers were forgotten when the power-sharing Executive was forced to resign. Middle-class support evaporated overnight once power had been taken from the hands of the non-Unionists (which, sadly, means the Catholics).

The notes which have gone to the making of this book were begun some years ago when I realised that I have lived in a generation in which there have been a great many social changes, two World Wars and, in my own country, more attempts than ever before to settle a centuries-old problem. In the cradle I heard of Home Rule. Attempts at Irish Home Rule in various forms seem to stand as milestones over the years and the sound of political controversy has always been there. I have heard men preach revolution, seen men of peace condemned as traitors, witnessed the cruel manifestations of sectarian hatred; on occasions I have been close to scenes of violence and death; I have seen its ugliness and its cruelty and listened to the

3. Merlyn Rees was secretary of state for Northern Ireland in the Labour government in 1974. His mishandling of the strike was only the most notable of the blunders that marked his incumbency.

unbalanced fanaticism of some of its advocates. My present political views are different from those of my prejudiced youth, but I am totally convinced that whatever may be said about the righting of past wrongs or the maintenance of inherited power and privilege, there has been no moral justification for violence or the threat of violence for political ends in Ireland at any time in the present century. . . .

C. S. ANDREWS

(1901-88)

from: MAN OF NO PROPERTY (1982)

[This is one of the best accounts of the disillusion of republicans after the Civil War and the turn from militant republicanism to constitutional politics under the aegis of de Valera. Andrews was one of the senior civil servants who presided over some of the state-run enterprises that played a central role in economic development in the Republic. His first volume of autobiography, *Dublin Made Me* (1980), dealt with his childhood and early years; this second volume begins with the ending of the Civil War. Released from internment, he enters the newly established and, as far as republicans were concerned, triumphant Free State.]

CHAPTER I

. . . The defeat of the Republic had been a matter of great disappointment to me. As the climax of the Civil War was reached I had been close to the events associated with it. I saw all the devotion to the ideal of the Republic, supported by bravery, endurance and an indifference to self-interest, crumble through lack of political expertise. The leadership of the IRA (and of course its enthusiastic members like me) had become largely the victims of shibboleths of their own creation. They turned too late to de Valera, the one man who could have led them out of the political morass where they had got bogged down at the time of the 1922 Army Convention.[1] Eventually he did succeed in using to advantage the stepping stones embedded in the Treaty settlement to open up the way for re-establishing the Republic. But from the time of his release in July 1924 until he came to power in the Twenty-six counties there was a lapse of eight years.[2] It seemed to me and my like an interminable period. Eaten up by bitterness and adhering to 'principle' — that fatuous word so all-pervasive and such a darkener of counsel in the story of the Republic — we wasted valuable years giving allegiance to an ineffective, and largely imaginary, underground government and army before de Valera and Seán Lemass broke with Sinn Féin and the Second Dáil to form Fianna Fáil.[3]

During those eight years we saw the Free State administration entrenching itself and showing all signs of retaining power for ever. A mutiny in the army might have dislodged them but the government bought it off successfully. They had learned the truism that there are few problems that money will not solve. They accepted the theory that whatever economic prosperity the nation might achieve could only result from its capacity to sell our agricultural products in the British market; hence the catch cry; 'one more cow, one more sow, one more acre under the plough'. Our role in the world was to be an agricultural annex of Britain or, as some of them referred to it, the 'mainland'.

They had adopted without noticeable change the governmental institutions of Britain. The procedure in the Dáil and the processing of legislation were identical to those operating in the House

1. There were two Army Conventions in 1922, on 26 March and 9 April. The anti-Treaty IRA attended and confirmed its allegiance to the Irish Republic, repudiated the authority of the provisional government and drafted a new constitution for the army. By the end of April, republicans had seized the Four Courts in Dublin and the course for civil war was set.

2. Eamon de Valera (1882-1975) came to power in 1932. One of his first acts was to use the Statute of Westminster to remove the oath of allegiance to the British Crown, demanded by the Treaty.

3. Seán Lemass (1900-71), later minister of industry and commerce for a total of almost sixteen years, and Taoiseach in succession to de Valera 1959-66. Fianna Fáil was founded in 1926.

of Commons, leaving aside a few details such as Black Rod.[4] The Courts followed the same judicial practices, wigs and all. Poyning's [*sic*] Law[5] was refurbished in the shape of an appeal to the Privy Council. The civil service as it existed before the Treaty had been kept undisturbed in structure and nearly intact in personnel.

Although the *Freeman's Journal* ceased publication at the end of 1924, to the satisfaction of us Republicans, the remaining Dublin dailies continued to publish the British Court Circular and as late as September 1927 the *Irish Independent* gave the Irish public the interesting information that: 'Queen Mary, who has been staying with Princess Mary and Viscount Lascelles at Goldsborough Hall since last Friday, leaves for Balmoral today. The Duke of York will leave Balmoral tomorrow when he will re-join the Duchess of York and Princess Elizabeth at Glamis Castle. The Duke and Duchess are expected to visit Edinburgh next Wednesday for the unveiling of the Scots-American War Memorial'. It also told us that 'Lord Decies is taking the waters at Vichy'[6] — thus providing the Irish dimension.

Implicit in all this was the assumption that we were still part of the Empire. That, too, was the assumption clearly exemplified in the composition of the Senate. In fact not merely had the Free Staters adopted the British system of government but they accepted and proceeded to imitate the British social system having at its pinnacle a governor-general in lieu of a king and a senate in lieu of a house of lords. The first governor-general, Tim Healy,[7] did not fill the role successfully. He was too old and too thoroughly despised and disliked by the mass of the people to be a centre of social attraction. Not even the most ambitious social climber would want to be 'received' by him. It was the common belief that the government had been persuaded by Lord Beaverbrook[8] to appoint him. The vice-regal lodge was a generous reward for the man who had wrecked Parnell.

A fair argument in favour of the acceptance of the Treaty was that it would provide stepping stones to the Republic. When Michael Collins died that possibility was no longer realistic as those like Liam Tobin and Frank Thornton, his closest military collaborators, found out to their cost. Tobin was relegated to the post of aide-de-camp to Tim Healy and Thornton was eased out of the army. Fortunately Thornton, unlike Tobin, had somewhere to go and he went.[9]

The Senate consisted of sixty members, thirty of whom were to be nominated by the President of the Executive Council, W. T. Cosgrave.[10] Cosgrave had been selected for the post for no better reason than that he was the senior survivor amongst the Free Staters of the old pre-Treaty cabinet. He had the additional cachet of having been 'out' in 1916. Cosgrave had been a publican and, like every successful Dublin publican, he had yearnings towards respectability. Ordinarily, however successful a publican had been, he could never have hoped for upper class social acceptance. But now he had arrived. Not merely was he accepted by what remained of the ascendancy but he became their well-respected patron. He had joined what Brendan Behan called 'the horse Protestants'. In his nominations to the Senate he stated without equivocation that the government 'stood absolutely on class'. His nominations, with few exceptions, consisted of members of the landed gentry or of wealthy unionists. It would have been difficult to imagine them using the stepping stones said to be embodied in the Free State charter to achieve a Republic.

The ethos of the Republican Movement before the Treaty had been egalitarian. We assumed that except for the usual tendency of tuppence-halfpenny to look down on tuppence the Irish nation in the mass was a classless society. There was no social immobility based on birth or inherited wealth. To us the make-up of the Senate was just one example of the extent the Free Staters were prepared to go to keep in step with the manners, customs and values of the British. Some of the senators were men of distinction by any standards;

4. 'Gentleman Usher of the Black Rod' carries a black wand. He keeps order in the House of Lords.
5. The law of 1495 that asserted England's right to legislate for Ireland.
6. A landowner with estates in County Wexford.
7. T. M. Healy (1855-1931), first governor general of the Irish Free State 1922-28, one of the leaders of the anti-Parnellite faction in 1890.
8. W. Maxwell Aitken (1879-1964), 1st baron Beaverbrook, British newspaper proprietor, including the *Daily Express*. He was born in Canada, but became minister of information 1918 and minister of aircraft production 1941-42.
9. Liam Tobin and Frank Thornton were members of Michael Collins's special intelligence squad.
10. William T. Cosgrave (1880-1965), president of the executive council of the Irish Free State 1922-32, founder and leader of the Cumann na nGaedheal party in 1923.

some had little to recommend them except wealth and the Protestant religion. Neither wealth nor religion seemed good reasons for their selection. It was wrong-headed policy to treat Protestant Irishmen differently from their fellow citizens in any circumstances. It was part of the Republican ethic that all Irishmen were equal and should be treated equally by the organs of state.

The senators, distinguished or not, had one thing in common: they were strong supporters of the Treaty and had a bitter hatred of us Republicans. The Clerk of the Senate, Donal O'Sullivan, a scholarly and priggish socialite, who refused to hang the ritual portrait of Collins in his home because Collins used bad language, wrote a well-researched history of the Senate disfigured by the partisanship of the time.[11] Over the years Republicans of whatever kind have acquired the image of being anti-intellectual; they live, it is said, on their ignorant emotions. O'Sullivan's book, scholar though he was, is a clear statement of that point of view. As a nasty polemic directed against de Valera and all he stood for it encapsulated all the contempt for Republicans felt by him and his kind. It is not to be wondered at that Republicans were short on intellectualism since the bulk of the professional and literary class was solidly behind the Free State.

The Free Staters plunged deeper and deeper into the mire created by the Treaty. Having been outmanoeuvred by the British in the matter of the Boundary Commission[12] they represented the betrayal as 'a damn good bargain'. Except for the damming of the Shannon and the foundation of the Electricity Supply Board[13] — no small achievement it must be admitted — and a half-hearted attempt to start a sugar beet industry, they contributed nothing to the economic development of the country. An intense and expensive effort was made to revive the Irish language; through pedagogic inexperience the campaign had little success. It was dominated on the one hand by pedants and on the other by native speakers of rural origin and background. If in Ireland the word peasant could be used without offence the bulk of native speakers could be classified as peasants. They hardly provided the best foundation on which to base the revival of the language. Furthermore the revival effort relied too much on money and material rewards; dispensing money was not a good way to evoke patriotic enthusiasm. Nor was the effort assisted by us Republicans. As in every other project initiated by the Free Staters we opted out. Unfortunately we did nothing to promote the language ourselves. My belief is that from the time the Volunteers took the Oath of Allegiance to Dáil Éireann and became the IRA, interest in the language movement among Republicans began to decline. Certainly at the end of the Civil War it scarcely existed.

Economic depression had begun to take effect after the relative prosperity of the Great War years. What jobs the government could create, such as public works on roads and drainage schemes, went to demobilised soldiers and supporters of the Free State regime — not an unreasonable policy to be expected from the government. There was a mini-diaspora of Republicans; it is estimated that 100,000 emigrated between 1924 and 1927 — principally to the USA. It is probably from that nucleus, or their descendants, that succour has been coming to the Provos in our day.

Even though military activities had ceased the IRA organisation had not yet disintegrated and when they were released from jail many of the Army Executive went underground. On the political scene Sinn Féin — the political wing of the Republican party — continued to exist with some semblance of reality. It is true that the great Sinn Féin party taken over from Arthur Griffith had come apart after the Treaty and only a rump of the organisation remained faithful to the Republican cause, but it was a rump sufficiently strong to have ensured a surprising measure of success in the election of 1923. The party workers in that election were all older men — most of the younger members were in jail or on the run — but in the face of threats, harassments and actual physical assault, often by trigger-happy CID men,[14] their efforts

11. Donal O'Sullivan, *The Irish Free State and Its Senate* (London: Faber and Faber, 1940).

12. The Boundary Commission was established in 1924 to determine the boundary between Northern Ireland and the Free State. In 1925 the governments involved agreed that the border should remain as fixed by the Government of Ireland Act of 1920.

13. The Shannon hydroelectric scheme was completed between 1925 and 1929. The Electricity Supply Board, established in 1927, was made responsible for the national network of generating stations.

14. Criminal Investigation Department, the detective division of the police force.

ensured that the ideals of the Republican movement did not go by default and were openly proclaimed.

Unfortunately, and contrary to what might have been expected, the return of the prisoners from the jails and internment camps did not accelerate the growth of the Republican Party, the nucleus of which had successfully survived the Civil War. In fact, there was a decline in numbers and financial resources. It became increasingly evident to the Republican leadership, and more evident to the rank and file members of the organisation, that there was no hope of attaining power and undoing the Treaty debacle while abstention from the Dáil was part of policy. In addition the Party made no effort to deal with the economic and social problems which at the time offered a fertile ground from which to draw mass support. Hence between 1924 and 1926 there was a general sense of depression among Republicans. In Dublin especially the problems of purely personal survival of those IRA men who did not emigrate left them with very little heart or enthusiasm for 'the cause'. The first evidence of a recognition of the realities came from Seán Lemass in the columns of *An Phoblacht*.[15] He had stood as a candidate for a by-election in 1925. To everyone's surprise — that is to say to the surprise of all us Republicans — he was elected. We regarded the election as an event of no significance. We didn't dream that any consequence would flow from it nor, I think, did Seán Lemass. He was Minister for Defence in the Republican Dáil. He owed no allegiance to the Free State and, like the other members of Sinn Féin, he had no intention of taking his seat in the Dáil. In a series of articles published about this time he analysed the shortcomings of the party, the futility of pursuing its current policies and the need to concentrate on politically realisable objectives. The Lemass initiative, which later became known as the 'New Departure', caused a major furore in Sinn Féin circles. It also marked him out as a future leader and maker of party policy. . . .

15. *An Phoblacht*, published by the IRA, first appeared in 1925. It was banned in 1931, resumed publication in 1933 and ceased in 1937. Its successor was begun in 1970 by the Provisional IRA.

HUBERT BUTLER

(1900-)

from: ESCAPE FROM THE ANTHILL (1985)

[Hubert Butler, of the ancient Butler family of Kilkenny, is one of the rare examples of what Irish nationalism and protestant ascendancy could have produced had they blended their respective traditions after 1916. The separation between them and their consequent mutual impoverishment has been one of the themes of the essays he has written over the last forty years. The alliance which men like AE and Count Plunkett represented earlier in the century has almost disappeared from Irish life. Butler, therefore, has been a minority, but never a marginal, voice in the years since the end of World War II. Although the destruction of the Anglo-Irish houses during the Civil War has been much commented upon and written about — especially in novels — it is in Butler's essays that we sense the real pathos of those actions, both for the destroyers and the destroyed. His sense of the culture that was destroyed in Ireland and in Europe at that time is the more vigorous because it is not an exclusively literary sense. It is rooted in actualities — landscape, houses, habits, memories and people. This imparts to his writing a solidity and an assurance, which are enhanced by the modesty of his tone.]

CHAPTER 9

DIVIDED LOYALTIES

In 1984 Ireland is so deeply divided that few now talk of a *modus vivendi* between Unionist and Nationalist, between Catholic and Protestant. You never read that ancient newspaper cliché about a 'Union of Hearts', or think as I did when I was a boy, and read AE's *Irish Statesman*,[1] that Ireland might become the central focus of our love and loyalty.

Nobody ever investigates how these ethnic and religious love-affairs, which occasionally occur, are conducted. It is obvious though that while they can be easily frustrated, they can only very warily and deviously be promoted.

Opposites often attract each other but the attraction seldom lasts if the full extent of the opposition is ignored. It is as neighbours, full of ineradicable prejudices, that we must love each other, not as fortuitously 'separated brethren'.

I became an Irish nationalist when I was very young. I had to return to school at Charterhouse[2] some days after the Easter week rebellion and to pass barricades near O'Connell Bridge. I had to show a pass signed by the sergeant of the RIC in Kilkenny. There were still wisps of smoke coming from Sackville Street,[3] the names of Pearse and Connolly meant nothing to me but I felt it was my war in a way that the war in which I was prepared to fight in the Charterhouse OTC[4] was not. When I came home for the holidays I argued ignorantly with my parents about it. Most of our Protestant neighbours, diminished in numbers and in spirit by the everlasting brain-drain to England, were solidly Unionist. They got their little jokes about Ireland from *Punch* and *The Morning Post*.

As far as I was concerned, the first crucial discussion occurred when my slightly older cousin, Theobald Butler, came to stay. He had been head boy at Charterhouse but had become an Irish nationalist and, refusing to fight in an imperialist war, had taken a job in a school in Co. Down. He had first done relief work in Serbia with a friend, Eric Dodds, who, for the same reason, was teaching at Kilkenny College. Dodds had won the famous Craven Scholarship at Oxford. There were heated arguments when they came to lunch. Sometimes after this, if I made a nationalist remark, my mother said, 'Oh, you got that off Theo and Dodds. They'll scuttle back to England the moment the war is over.' And that indeed is what they did, for England has a magnetism for the Anglo-Irish intellectual that very few can resist. Sometimes even a few acres of Irish soil can give us an unreasoning obstinacy and the illusion of security, but Theo and Dodds had not an acre between them. Before he died Theo had a full inch of London legal achievements after his name in *Burke's Peerage*, and Dodds became Regius Professor of Greek at Oxford. In his autobiography, *Missing Persons* (1977), he has described the missing person, the Irish nationalist he once was, and the disillusionment endured by all Anglo-Irishmen who had given their first love to Ireland. 'The birth of a terrible beauty has ended with the establishment of a grocers' republic,' he wrote.[5]

But, if you are heir to some trees and fields and buildings and a river bank, your love for your country can be more enduring. It is a not too blameworthy extension of self-love; you feel qualified to influence its destiny on a small scale and you are not content, as so many of the Irish are, to radiate goodwill to Ireland from across the sea. We were minor gentry and our activities were all minor, but my father had brought the village creamery to Bennettsbridge and was the committee's president, and my mother ran a Boot-and-Coal Fund and a committee connected with tuberculosis, both subsidized by annual jumble sales and concerts. My aunt had founded the Kilkenny Horticultural Society and used to drive a fat pony round the country judging cottage gardens; I used to think she judged the cottages as well as their gardens. She had a bossy manner and this seemed to me suitable enough.

AE had believed that, as the co-operative movement developed in Ireland, a real village community would grow round every creamery and that the principle of sharing would extend into every branch of life, spiritual, economic, cultural. The communal marketing of eggs and butter would lead to more intimate and domestic forms of sharing. AE saw the hedges planted with apple trees and gooseberry bushes, as in Germany, and gymnasiums and libraries, picture galleries and village halls, to which each man or woman made his contribution according to his powers, so that each village became a focus of activity and debate. Sixty years ago, an ingenuous young person could really believe this

1. AE's weekly review, *The Irish Statesman*, was revived in 1923, after a three-year gap, by Sir Horace Plunkett and was edited by AE from that date until 1930, when it ceased publication.
2. An English public school.
3. Now O'Connell Street.
4. Officer Training Corps.

5. E. R. Dodds (1893-1979) was asked to leave Oxford because of his support for the 1916 Rebellion. He was a close friend of Louis MacNeice and edited his *Collected Poems* (1966).

would happen. There, anyway, was the new creamery on the edge of the village and it stood till 1983 when it was bulldozed away. To make all these creameries AE had travelled hundreds of miles on his bicycle and Plunkett, a sick man kept alive by his burning zeal, had made these long journeys which he records in his diaries: 'A two hours crawl in the Major's brougham to Longford. Did good I think but, oh, how boring and tiring! Two long speeches to two small meetings. My thoughts germinate in other brains and when the brains are attached to the proper physique the enthusiasm works.'[6]

When I told my mother about the gooseberry bushes, she said, 'Stuff and nonsense! Those trees that the Kilkenny Corporation planted along the canal-walk were all slashed down in a week. When O'Grady and Otway Cuffe gave that Irish play at Sheestown[7] the crowds all strolled out from Kilkenny and pulled up all the shrubs and broke the tea cups.'

When I suggested to my sister, who organized the village concerts, that they should do a Synge play or a Lady Gregory or at least a George Shiels,[8] she said, 'Oh they'd hate that sentimental Irish stuff,' and as usual, she sent for a bunch of one-act farces from Messrs French in London, and she was quite right. They vastly preferred them.

And it always happened like that. When it was rumoured in the Kildare Street Club that the creameries had become social centres where the farmers discussed sedition over their milk-churns, and when the Black and Tans started burning them, many members congratulated themselves on the hostility they had shown to Plunkett.[9] The rest of the story runs along familiar lines.

AE and Plunkett died disillusioned, in England. Kilteragh, Plunkett's house in Foxrock, which had been the meeting-place for the Anglo-Irish who were concerned about their country, was burned to the ground in the civil war, because he had become a Senator.

I was young at the time and did not realize that I was living at the end of a relatively humane and sensible era and at the beginning of a cruel and chaotic one. Ireland had her freedom and Europe had her League of Nations. I enjoyed my holidays at home, the raids and rumours, the 'battle of Kilkenny' and the three-day siege of Kilkenny Castle, and I believe there were many young people as silly as myself.[10]

Compared to other counties, Kilkenny was peaceful and gentle. Apart from the burning of three famous and beautiful houses, Woodstock, Desart Court and Bessborough,[11] life went on as usual with rare interruptions.

One night, at 3 a.m., we were woken by loud knocking at the front door. My sister and I went down and found two unknown men there. We were elated rather than scared. Here was real life at last. One of the men said they wanted money for the 'dependents of the Irish Republic'. I said, 'We've no guns in the house; if you're just common thieves we can't stop you taking what you want.' He replied, 'Ah we're not that sort of chap at all,' and they went away.

Another afternoon two of them came again, asking as before for money. My mother and I were in the porch and she danced about with fury. 'I know who you are,' she said to one of them. 'You're Jim Connell. Take your cigarette out of your mouth when you're talking to me.' He took it out and I began to scold my mother for interrupting what might have been a revealing conversation. It was only the second time I had seen a Republican, and when I went back to Oxford I wanted at least to say what they were like and what their plans were. My mother answered me sharply and we started an angry argument. The two men looked at each other in embarrassment and slunk politely away.

The third occasion was an episode that found its way into J. G. Farrell's *Troubles*.[12] My sisters and I were on our way with two friends to the St George's

6. Sir Horace Plunkett (1854-1932), one of the founders of the Co-operative Movement, chairman of the Irish Convention 1917-18, author of *Ireland in the New Century* (1904) and an autobiographical work, *Noblesse Oblige* (1908).
7. Standish O'Grady (1846-1928), a seminal figure for the Irish Revival and a spokesman for the ascendancy tradition, although he despaired of its survival. The play was possibly *In the Gates of the North* (1901). Otway Cuffe (1853-1912) was a captain in the British army.
8. George Shiels (1886-1949), one or more of whose plays was staged by the Abbey almost every year between 1921 and 1948.
9. Plunkett was disliked or distrusted by many members of his own class because of his involvement in the Co-operative Movement. The Kildare Street Club in Dublin was a social centre for the gentry.
10. In May 1922, anti-Treaty forces in Kilkenny took over Ormond Castle, the City Hall and several other buildings. The provisional government in Dublin sent 200 men to Kilkenny and, after a gun-battle, they retook the buildings. See M. Hopkinson, *Green against Green: The Irish Civil War* (Dublin: Gill and Macmillan, 1988), p. 75.
11. Three great houses in County Kilkenny.
12. J. G. Farrell (1935-74), whose novel *Troubles* (1970) is set in 1919 in a decaying Big House in County Wexford.

dance at Kilrush, seven or eight miles beyond Kilkenny. It was a period when everyone had to have a permit signed by the police for his car, and all those who were legally on the road could be thought of as the enemy. When we got to Troyeswood, a mile outside Kilkenny, we found a wall built across the road. In front of it stood two men with long white beards, which proved, when we got closer, to be white scarves veiling their faces; they had revolvers. Behind them lay three or four cars turned upside down in the middle of the road. They turned us out of the car and led us across the hedge into the field where already a dozen of our friends were grouped with another muffled figure guarding them. When three or four more cars had been turned over and their occupants ushered into the field, we were told: 'At the expiration of half an hour you may proceed to your destinations.'

We walked back in our evening clothes across Kilkenny. Some stayed at the Club House Hotel. I tramped back home to tell my family.

Far worse things happened in Tipperary. One night in March 1923 Graiguenoe Park, my mother's home at Holycross, was burnt. We shared her sadness for we had spent many happy days with our cousins there. It was between thirty and forty miles away, but when we were children we thought of it as in another country, much wilder, less ordinary. My sister and I used to get up early and start off with our night things on our bicycle carriers and the dew still on the grass. As soon as we crossed the Tipperary border the smell of turf, unknown to us in Kilkenny, prepared us to expect everything strange and new. Leaving behind us the familiar woods of Farmley and Desart Court, we crossed Slieveardagh and turning aside after Littleton bog, we made for Killough hill and, when it came in sight, we knew we had arrived. . . .

Even Graiguenoe itself, a large early Victorian house built by my great grandfather beyond the ruins of Holycross Abbey, had romance and mystery for us. My uncle had been boycotted in 1910 and there was a police barracks on his property and for a time a general store. His farm workers had stood by him and could buy their food there when the shopkeepers in Thurles, intimidated by the Land Leaguers, refused to supply them.

Some years ago there was a dramatic dynamiting of the ruins of Graiguenoe in the presence of a photographer from *The Tipperary Star*, and the stones were used in the reconstruction of Holycross Abbey. When I went there soon after, there was no trace of the house except for a broad band of daisies that wound through the field where the avenue had been. Tom Nolan, the coachman's grandson, still lived in the lodge and I found that the new proprietor farmed a thousand acres more than Uncle Charlie had done.

Some twenty houses of the Anglo-Irish were burnt at this time in Tipperary. . . .

Did the Anglo-Irish deserve the fate which was so often predicted for them? Wolfe Tone had written, 'They have disdained to occupy the station they might have held among the people and which the people would have been glad to see them fill. They see Ireland only in their rent-rolls, their places, their patronage, their pensions. They shall perish like their own dung. Those that have seen them will say, "Where are they?"'[13]

The Anglo-Irish could have dodged their fate if their interest in Ireland, let alone their love, had been more than marginal. They recognized a duty certainly to their neighbourhood and this duty was usually intelligently fulfilled, but it only rarely happened that, like Plunkett and a few of their contemporaries, they could give their first love to their country. I believe that in a generation or two, had there been no 1914 war, no rebellion and no civil war, this duty might have turned itself into love as it often had in the eighteenth century.

Then, for a brief period, they had been able to represent something very precious. Only they could give Irishmen a sense of historical continuity and of identity. It was to be found in their bookshelves, when those who remained no longer read books, in their estate maps when they no longer had estates, in their memories when they no longer had the leisure or literary skill to write them down. The Irishmen who burnt down those Tipperary houses were sawing away the branch on which they were sitting. Clamouring that they were a distinctive people, they obliterated much of the heritage that distinguished them. The burning of the Four Courts, which swept away the records of eight centuries, was only one episode in this tale of self-destruction.[14]

13. *Argument on Behalf of the Catholics of Ireland* (1791), p. 69.
14. On 28 June 1922, government forces shelled the Four Courts, the centre of the Irish judiciary, which was being held by the anti-Treaty IRA forces. The garrison surrendered two days later, but not before mining and destroying the Public Records Office.

A new and more suffocating ascendancy, that of international commerce, was on the way; many of those ruined houses would have been strongholds of resistance to it, and the Anglo-Irish, with their easy-going pragmatic Christianity, would certainly have tempered the religious and political passions of our northern countrymen.

NOEL BROWNE

(1915-)

from: AGAINST THE TIDE (1986)

[Noel Browne became minister of health in the first inter-party government of 1948-51. The Taoiseach was J. A. Costello and the minister of external affairs and leader of Clann na Poblachta, one of the constituent parties of the coalition, was Seán MacBride, son of Maud Gonne and John MacBride. Browne's main achievements were the launching of a building programme to provide the sanatoria needed to control and finally almost extinguish tuberculosis; and the collision between church and state, which he unwittingly brought about by reintroducing the 1947 Health Scheme that Fianna Fáil had first introduced. Although the bishops won this battle, they lost the war. The relationship between church and state came under scrutiny and the issue of the confessional state was raised in such a form that it did not, despite changes in circumstances over the subsequent years, entirely go away.

Browne's autobiography is a candid account of early hardship, political triumph and political isolation; it is also an exemplary history of the achievement of personal integrity in almost impossible circumstances. The excerpt given here is an account of a meeting between Dr Browne and an episcopal commission, consisting of Dr McQuaid, archbishop of Dublin, Dr Michael Browne, bishop of Galway, and Dr Staunton, bishop of Ferns. The bishops have read to the minister a letter they had sent to the Taoiseach the day before, describing their objections to the proposed Health Service. 'It is not', the letter stated, 'sound social policy to impose a medical service on the whole community on the pretext of relieving the necessitous 10% from the so-called indignity of a means test.' It should also be said that the Irish Medical Association was hostile to the proposed bill and that it, like the episcopate, wanted a means test. At the crunch, Noel Browne found that his colleagues were against him, his resignation was demanded and he resigned in April 1951. The new Fianna Fáil government, which replaced the Inter-Party coalition, introduced a public health scheme with a means test.]

CHAPTER 10

CRISIS

. . . Dr. McQuaid asked why it was necessary to go to so much trouble and expense simply to provide a free health service for the 10% necessitous poor. This comment was not only wrong, since the percentage involved was thirty and not ten, but surely represented a strange attitude from a powerful prelate of a Christian church towards the life and death of the 'necessitous poor' and their children. I replied that if I were an ordinary member of the public, then such a position was possible through ignorance. As a doctor, I believed that a free health service was an essential prerequisite to an effective and a just health service. As Minister for Health the necessitous poor, a considerable sector of our society, were my special responsibility. I was implementing a Cabinet decision, in accordance with the law passed by the Oireachtas.[1]

Bishop Browne[2] then took up a question dear to his heart, that of the burden of rates and taxation. He claimed that it was unfair to tax the rest of the community in order to give the poor a free health service. I pointed out that taxation was surely not a matter of morality; as far as I was concerned, it was a problem for the government, the Minister for Finance and myself.

So far their concern had been strictly with temporal issues. There was a distinct cooling in the

1. The legislature of the Republic of Ireland, consisting of Dáil Éireann (the Lower House), Seanad Éireann (the Senate) and the Presidency.
2. Bishop of Galway.

previously warm manner of the Archbishop. He questioned the right of the state to assume the responsibility of 'the education of mothers in motherhood', or to provide a maternity and gynaecological service for women, and claimed that these were dangerous powers for the state to arrogate to itself. He mentioned possibilities which in those days were quite unthinkable, even in many of the advanced western European countries. He postulated the inevitability of contraception and abortion.

During the subsequent general election in 1951, these two forbidden subjects were to become examples of clerically-inspired 'black propaganda' and were frequently claimed to be part of my health proposals. So also was euthanasia for the aged and sterilisation for the unit [*sic*]. Quickly forgotten was the fact that I was the first Cabinet minister seriously to concern myself with doing something for the sick and aged. At An Cnoc parish church in Connemara, where I spent weekends learning Irish, I was referred to during a sermon in Irish as being one of those people who 'come amongst us disguised as friends, when meanwhile their real work is to poison the wells, and so kill off our stock'. This was clever and damaging imagery. How I valued the courage of my good friends Seosamh O Cadhain, Seán O Conghaile and others who, under such pressure, refused to disown or repudiate me.

I reminded Dr McQuaid that 95% of our doctors, nurses and patients were Catholic. Could he not depend on his flock to obey the teachings of their church? Seemingly not. Listening to this kind of insidious and damaging innuendo, I began to realise the possibilities for misrepresentation by the hierarchy at any subsequent election. I quickly decided that with a Cabinet which was already frightened of the hierarchy and anxious to scrap the scheme, damage could be done to the no-means-test ideal if I were simply to ignore all the fears, real or imagined, of the hierarchy.

Contrary to the image widely fostered about me as an obstinate, doctrinaire and uncompromising person, I compromised on the offending clauses. In respect of 'the education of mothers', I would reconsider these clauses and submit them to the hierarchy. Alternatively the hierarchy could consider the offending clauses and submit them to the Department of Health for improvement. Finally, since these provisions were not the most important section of the scheme, we would agree, regretfully, to withdraw the section completely if it were found impossible to agree.

The Archbishop of Dublin is said to have described this meeting as having been 'incredible' during his later discussions with John Costello.[3] He claimed that I had brushed aside all suggestions about the means test: 'the Minister himself terminated the meeting, and walked out'. What a dilemma faces the student of history, deciding which of two bishops was lying about this meeting According to Dr. Michael Browne, while he agreed that the meeting was contentious, his phrase was that I was truculent, and he concludes his recollection of the meeting with the words, 'the interview ended amicably'.

As far as I was concerned the meeting was open and frank. While having no wish to make concessions, I knew of my weak position in a wavering Cabinet, and felt that I must at least save the no-means-test principle. It was clear that the bishops would support the wealthy consultants. I felt not anger but simply astonishment that men of their profession should so blatantly side with the rich against the poor. A reasoned discussion had taken place and I had made important concessions.

As to the charge that I left the room and slammed the door, the driver of my car could verify this to be untrue. A courteous host, Dr McQuaid left the room with me. He walked the length of the hall to the front door, enquiring for the welfare of my wife and family. Finally he bade farewell at the door of the palace. By order of the bishops I had been deprived of a witness on my side, but having met their proposals where possible, I was convinced that I had satisfied them. As far as I was concerned the matter was at an end.

I am convinced that such would have been the case if only my Cabinet colleagues, and in particular my party leader Seán MacBride,[4] had not wilted under the medical propaganda hostile to the health scheme. Above all, the subsequent misrepresentation from beginning to end of this whole affair emphasised the wisdom of the advice given to me

3. The bishops provided John Costello, the Taoiseach, with a copy of the correspondence between them and Dr Browne.
4. Seán MacBride (1904-88), then founder and leader of the political party Clann na Poblachta. He was later a founder-member and chairman of Amnesty International and winner of the Nobel Peace Prize in 1976 and of the Lenin Peace Prize in 1977.

by my departmental secretary, Mr. Kennedy. Long experienced in these matters, he had advised me to insist on bringing a witness on my side to any negotiations.

I outlined the events of the afternoon to Mr. Kennedy, the concessions we should make, the reaction of the bishops and my clarification of their confused misunderstanding of the scheme. We decided that we would prepare a memorandum for submission to the hierarchy, which would be of paramount importance in the struggle to come, and include a full résumé of that meeting.

Within days of the meeting, the memorandum was sent to the Taoiseach as a matter of courtesy, for his information. Protocol insisted that a mere Cabinet minister had no direct access to an Archbishop's office; it was my intention that with its compromise proposals, the memorandum should and would be transmitted to the hierarchy for their detailed study. For some unexplained reason the Taoiseach did not send this document, either as a courtesy or for their information, to the hierarchy. Cabinet records show that we in the Department of Health had no difficulty either in refuting the bishops' arguments or in correcting the errors of fact in their understanding of the scheme. The memorandum also included the significant concessions reluctantly made by my department to the objections made by the hierarchy.

The memorandum went on: 'The Minister respectfully desires to draw attention to the fact that, in introducing the Mother and Child scheme, the government was simply implementing the law . . . the government is merely giving effect to an act of the Oireachtas passed in 1947. To remove any possible misunderstanding about the basis of the scheme, the Minister desires to emphasise that part three of the Health Act of 1947, which became law on 13 August 1947, provided for the introduction of a mother and child health service, and determines the broad outline of such a service. Our draft scheme has been prepared to conform with, and in fact does conform with, the provisions of that 1947 Health Act.' In order to clarify the doubts about the voluntary nature of the health service, the memorandum went on, 'in view of the fact that the mother and child health scheme is in no sense compulsory, and that whatever guarantees the hierarchy wish in the matter of "instruction of mothers" would be unreservedly given, the Minister respectfully asks whether the Hierarchy consider the Mother and Child scheme to be contrary to Catholic moral teaching'.

Our memorandum, sent to the Taoiseach within days of the meeting at the Archbishop's palace, did not reach the hierarchy until after a delay of several months, on 28 March 1951. Yet is is clear from statements made by him in the Dáil that Mr. Costello was in constant verbal contact with the Archbishop during that time.

Significance must attach to one word in my concluding request for clarification to the hierarchy. Despite the fact that I was the product of four Catholic schools, my knowledge of Catholic theology was vague and unreliable. For this reason I sought the advice of a theologian who had been recommended to me by a lawyer, Brian Walsh, who lectured at Maynooth briefly and subsequently became a member of the Supreme Court. Aware of the implications and dangers for the theologian, we took special precautions to safeguard his identity at all times. Meetings were held under the most stringent security precautions, not in the Department of Health but in Brian Walsh's home.

Surprisingly, still fearful of the consequences though in retirement, and having only fulfilled his duty to offer moral advice to a member of his own church, my theological adviser requested that secrecy be maintained and he continues to request anonymity to this day.

As Bevan's socialist national health service[5] was freely used by Catholics in the North of Ireland without either public or private protest by the teaching authority of the church, I asked the theologian why our much less extensive mother and child health scheme was condemned by the same hierarchy in the Republic, but he could not answer my question. He was as puzzled as we were. However, he pointed out that there was an important distinction between Catholic 'social' and Catholic 'moral' teaching. The conscientious Catholic sins if he transgresses against Catholic moral teaching. There is no such sanction attached to Catholic social teaching, which varies from one period in history to another. The theologian noted that the hierarchy had carefully declined to claim that the scheme was contrary to Catholic moral teaching; there seemed to be no reason why our

5. Aneurin Bevan (1897-1960), as minister of health, introduced the National Health Service in Britain in 1948.

politicians could not, as Catholics, conscientiously agree to implement it.

The theologian was disturbed by the position taken by certain members of the hierarchy. He was compelled to assume either that the hierarchy were uninformed on this relatively simple matter of Catholic moral teaching or, alternatively, that they were deliberately taking sides against the new health scheme. Since the hierarchy dared not publicly claim that the scheme was contrary to Catholic *moral* teaching, we had removed the one valid objection on religious grounds which could be held against it.

It is now widely acknowledged that the condemnation by the bishops of the health scheme was crudely political. Unashamedly the church was 'playing politics' even to the point of bringing down a properly elected representative government on the issue.

Having considered the theologian's advice, my final memorandum was drawn up. It made significant concessions on a number of points so as to remove all possible sources for deliberate mistakes or calculated misrepresentation by the hierarchy. It then went on to challenge the hierarchy about the morality of the scheme.

Finally, I asked the theologian a question concerning my personal position. Since I wished to survive in the years ahead in order to continue the struggle for a socially just order in the Republic, I asked what my position would be if I were to tell the bishops bluntly that I rejected their objections, as being politically motivated. Having thought carefully, he replied: 'The Roman Catholic hierarchy must denounce you as a Catholic who no longer accepts the teaching authority of the Roman Catholic church'. I was grateful for that advice.

I also discussed my problems with my political colleagues. Having given me their best advice, they told me that any future decisions about my personal religious or political beliefs and actions were decisions that only I could take. Undoubtedly the episcopal opposition and my condemnation by them woud be exploited by my political opponents before the 95% Catholic electorate. I decided that for the present, I would try to survive.

John Whyte, in his *Church and State in Modern Ireland 1923-1979*,[6] has suggested that I seriously limited my scope for action by agreeing in advance to the bishops' ruling. This is not true, and for this reason. The bishops are the teaching authority of the Catholic Church. The teachers or leaders of any religious group must decide on matters where their religion is concerned. Because of this, 'I accept your ruling without question' became an inevitable part of my letter to the hierarchy.

Next, my question was 'Is the scheme contrary to Catholic moral teaching?' Inevitably the bishops' reply was that the scheme was contrary not to Catholic 'moral' teaching, but to Catholic 'social' teaching. As already explained by my theological advisor such a decision is not binding on a conscientious Catholic under pain of sin. On the authority of the bishops I could now claim that the scheme was not immoral and that the ruling of the bishops against the scheme could be ignored by the Cabinet. My theologian had assured me that the health scheme could not be publicly condemned by even the most obscurantist bishops as contrary to Catholic moral teaching. The question was put by me so as to make that clear to both public and politicians.

The Bishops were conceded the right to come to any conclusion they chose, but denied the right to dictate to an elected government the kind of health service that it must implement. The theologian's advice to me was fully vindicated by subsequent events when the hierarchy would not dare put in writing whatever they might say individually and privately in order to frighten politicians in both government and opposition at all levels. The very existence of the existing free no-means-test schemes within our own social, education and health services, as well as the British national health scheme in the North, patently gave the lie to the bishops' condemnation of the scheme.

There are those who would say that my behaviour throughout was mildly Jesuitical. In all the circumstances of the powerful forces arraigned against me and of the grave issues of an important health service, as well as the fundamental question of 'Who Rules?', I felt justified.

6. Published in 1971. A second edition was issued in 1980.

GEORGE O'BRIEN

(1945-)

from:
THE VILLAGE OF LONGING (1987)

[Childhood in Lismore, Co. Waterford, dominated by its castle, as the country is still dominated by its neo-colonial past, is the subject of George O'Brien's lucid autobiography. The period is the 1950s. The British Empire is giving way to the Roman Catholic Empire, but with reluctance. On the day of the point-to-point race meeting, the gentry of the old empire appear and dominate the scene again. The Duke of Devonshire in his castle is no longer a conqueror, but his inheritance is that of the conquerors of the Elizabethan days when the south-east of Ireland opened to the great piratical penetration.

The extracts are from Chapters 2 and 3 of Part III of the book, entitled 'The Duchy'.]

2

. . . The racing itself was terrible. Mutinous animals being flogged over hedges and ditches: that's all it amounted to, as far as I could see. I much preferred the bookies, the syntax of their sign language, their outsized doctors' bags, their strange, energetic cries, 'Three-to-one, bar one! Five-to-one the field.'

I was too small to see much. And in any case the races took place mainly out in the country; most of the time all anyone could see were figures flitting beyond the branches of the naked trees. Still, it was possible to get a taste of the race if you stood by a jump. There one caught the sensational urgency of approaching hoofs and the moments of strained silence as, with a sound like fibre tearing, the snorting, airborne steeds had their bellies struck by the jump's mane of brushwood.

Standing by a jump had a couple of drawbacks, however. One was that it was impossible to get back to see the finish in time. The other was that every so often a horse fell and, as the official phrase went, had to be destroyed. The poor thing would strive to right itself, wild-eyed, frothing, whinnying with terror and pain. But all its efforts only made a shallow grave in the moist, spring earth. The vet went to his case. The slim, brass-barrelled humane-killer was applied to the temple. A last lurch and —.

Finishes frightened me too, though. Not the desperate striving of the hacks to be past the post and out of this; not the giant, bony figure of the great McLernan (champion jockey of all east Munster) stretched taut in the stirrups, welting his mount to glory; not the clash of rival tributes in the turbulent crowd. What frightened me, and forcefully reminded me that the gentry were no mere presence, but power, was the whipper-in. He too went on horseback and wore an official colour, though not the gay silks of jockeys, but the blood-red blazer of the huntsman (and, as I thought, the soldier). His job was to clear the way along the run-in to the winning-post, and he managed to press the crowd back quite simply: by riding as close to it as he possibly could and waving aloft, in threat, his riding-crop. 'Get back!' he barked. 'Make way!'

In his reckless policing and scarlet coat and horrid unenjoyment on his face, he seemed a hellish figure. He'd run you down as quick as he'd look at you. He's brute force, I thought, he doesn't give a damn; he's everything I heard about the English in the terrible days gone by. His presence suggested that I was quite wrong to think that race-day was all looseness, all squandering, all pleasure. He was purpose and order. He was alien, hostile. He charged at us with the force of a law, terrifying us for our own good.

I ran from him like a chastised whelp, and although he was especially careful not to touch anyone and I realized, however inarticulately, that he was not a throw-back, not a symbol, not a force of destiny, but really only a jacket on a horse, my mind was turned into a tissue of painful smouldering, as though a branding-iron had touched it. I saw power without substance, force without salience, form without tact. For maybe twenty seconds I felt spurned and trodden down. Twenty seconds was plenty.

3

The whipper-in put the heart crossways on me, yet I felt free to repudiate him. His behaviour was hateful: I hated him right back. I don't think older people were quite able, or willing, to be so cut-and-dried in their reactions — and I mean not only in their reactions to the whipper-in, whose mode of discipline they seemed to approve, shouting commands of their own to support his, but also to the gentry at large. They seemed in some way tied psychologically to the gentry's presence.

The tie took various forms. For one thing, the valley had no history of rebelliousness: poaching was about the only form of local deviance — by no means a trivial one, to my mind, but one which has no place in the legends of the national struggle that were handed down to us (which may be unfortunate). And then when I saw those old lads admiring Royal Tan, or when I noticed Moss and his cronies doffing their caps as an elegant black roadster swished by, or even at the races looking at gaggles of elderly labourers leaning on the paddock fence and gazing in deep amaze at the steaming, exemplary creature now being fussed by the foulard fraternity (I wonder where they got those neckerchiefs, the ones with the pattern of amoeba swimming on a piss-yellow field) — simply being present in the particular theatre of gestures suggested to me that some principle of unity, or at least of implication, was at work.

I even saw it at home. Staunch though Mam was in her nationalist affections — none stauncher: she'd bite the head off anyone who dared murmur a demurral — she still bought a Poppy every year. There weren't many in the town who were invited to, either. But Miss Anson always came to our house and received a half-crown to remember the fallen of Flanders by. And if Geo objected he was soon made to desist. Of course, Mam had her own memories of the Great War, of the boys she knew who never came back from it (quite a number volunteered to go from loyal Lismore). Her first daughter was born on Armistice Day; she was christened Mary but known forever as Peace. And what did Georgie know?

It must have been hard for his generation. The patterns of close attachment between master and man had loosened considerably by the time George came into his manhood, and responsibility for moral exemplification had passed entirely to the officers of another empire, the clergy. No wonder he, my father and father's Dublin friends had no time for priests. Yet there were elements of the whipper-in about Geo too, in his fiery temper, his unpredictable vitality, his ability to make me fear him. But it was all unwitting. The instrument on horseback acted deliberately, secure in his power for the time being. George struck out blindly, innocently, as though through the bars of a cage, as though to snap for good his real and imagined bands.

My generation, perhaps, is the first to be in a position to disregard loyalty either to Christ or to Caesar. It is tempting to think so — since I'd like to be proud of my generation. Besides, it makes excellent cultural sense to take the gentry's invisibility at face value, and to regard priests as simply religious functionaries. But I'm not in sufficiently close contact with my generation to know if it thinks along these lines. Maybe it's tempting to hope for the best, for a set of liberating loyalties, because it seems to me now that such a possibility existed when I was growing up. Though, of course, I may be able to say that only because possibility exalts every childhood; it's the hallmark of the child's openness and ignorance.

The vestiges of loyalty that I observed around me were hard to understand. I took them to be reminders of continuity, but the continuum to which the village's star had been hitched was, as far as I could see, going nowhere. Yet, I suppose when centuries of continuity stall, the mechanisms which kept it running smoothly for so long are bound to run on a little, fuelled by compulsiveness and uncertainty. No generation should ever take upon itself the task of undoing the work of a few hundred predecessors, though in order to achieve anything at all it probably has to believe it can. In Lismore, however, there was nobody equal to the job, no heroic consciousness to facilitate a return to the days before the Duchy.[1]

Just as well, no doubt; complexity is more nourishing to the spirit than reverie. There was no concept of complexity, either, though. There was a landscape — a mindless, enduring litter of evidence.

Even before King John was a twinkle in his daddy's

1. That is, before the days of King John, who built Lismore Castle in 1185.

eye, the valley had been settled by monks and monastery.[2] And even before that there must have been something going on at the Round Hill, a mound two miles east of town overlooking the river, from which the town takes its name. God only knows what such a druidic remnant really represents.

We know that Edmund Spenser knew the valley. So did Sir Walter Ralegh, and an impoverished Robert Boyle, afterwards Earl of Cork, and who knows who else of their contemporaries besides.[3] The valley was a natural attraction for coast-hugging, westward-tending adventurers — I assume they hugged the coast as long as they could, for protection. And the Blackwater estuary was the first major one they would have come to without a sizeable fortified town at its mouth.

There is a town there now, of course, Youghal, but I don't think it was there to any extent before Ralegh came in from the ocean and built a jail on the site. The town in those parts long ago was Ardmore, home of a celebrated round tower, a much more impressive and more mystical edifice than Lismore Castle. It's easier for me to appreciate the tower for what it is, rather than for what it represents. Of course, it can be made to stand for the solitary, embattled and enduring Church, beacon of the Dark Ages when only Irish monasticism stood between the Northmen and the lights going out all over Europe. But it's a strain to employ such terms; the struggle against darkness is no longer being waged on remote beach-heads in County Waterford. Unlike the Castle, the tower is historically complete: its meaning is bounded by the era of its service. And although still intact, in every other respect it's like all the other ruined abbeys and disused graveyards that dot the country from top to bottom — a placid, assimilated shell. An icon, the invisibility of whose inner life is entirely appropriate. But it wasn't on an estuary, and so Youghal was an ideal point of entry, wide, welcoming waterway. To express a thought too sacrilegious for nationalists, once again — in the wake of King John — nature was not on the side of the natives. The river was tidal. So, up came Gloriana's crew: nothing to stop them.[4]

What did they see, those *conquistadores*, stealing up that still, accommodating river? Green slopes on either bank, rising gently, densely, as though they were the dark waters reproduced in an even more permanent form. Penumbrous, impenetrable. They met the river's unexpected, right-angle sweep west at Cappoquin, where there was nothing, nothing to attack or appropriate. Then, at last, Lismore, the Castle — the relief of seeing in that fastness something recognizably their own.

They sailed in clear and free. No people. If the forests harboured natives, they showed no sign. The land existed in a state of perfect integrity: aqueous, unmoving, arboreal, silent. A cathedral, a queen, a virgin. Like the James River, the Charles River, Potomac, Hudson — the penetrations without number later on. And it so little resembled property, being undefended. The urge to possess it, to seize it like a treasure, to treasure it so jealously that power became the sole metaphysic of occupancy .... That urge must have been as irresistible as an event in the subconscious. To pitch picturesquely, to shed blood, burn and starve in honour of possessions .... That lust to grasp this peace at all costs, this unmanned world, this kingdom without factions .... From what did such unstaunchable desire arise, this sacrilege-sized need to rupture the chaste greenery and husband it, this immense impulse to settle, as though the object of adventuring were anchorage, refuge, port after stormy sea?

And out of the husbandry grew a mind. The ardour of their lordships' eyes perceived the valley in a wholly new way. Their longing was secular, material. They freely thought the world their plaything; there was nobody to put a check on their avarice. The mind they fostered was called 'property'. Once mindfulness was installed, once a scale of values was introduced (whether consciously as an intellectual habit or just as a means of attempting to calibrate lust), once ownership became a synonym for living — then the beauty turned terrible. The place could never be just a place again. In addition, making immodest the whole accident of locality, there would be somebody's sense of it to cope with. The valley lost its nature and entered history. The appropriators,

2. St Carthach founded a monastery at Lismore in the seventh century. Despite Viking attacks, it retained its pre-eminence in the area until the twelfth century.
3. Sir Walter Ralegh (*c.* 1554-1618) got to know Spenser (*c.* 1552-99) in Ireland in 1580 and sold the castle, which had been presented to him in 1589, to Richard Boyle, 1st earl of Cork, in 1602. Spenser married Elizabeth Boyle, daughter of a kinsman of Sir Richard.
4. One of the poetic names attributed to Elizabeth I of England.

who retained the freedom of mind to do whatever they pleased, pretended that this didn't happen, or behaved as though history meant green reverie. Which was their undoing, requiring more freedom than they knew how to contain, eliminating challenge, corrupted by absolute power, their aftermath the mock-heroic present of my childhood with its stagnation, emigration and the new invaders, tourists . . . .

Biographies/Bibliographies

William Richard Le Fanu

LIFE. Born in Dublin in 1816, young brother of Joseph Sheridan Le Fanu. The family moved to County Limerick in 1826 on the appointment of their father as dean of Emly and rector of Abington. There they experienced the hardships of the tithe war 1831-38. Le Fanu was educated as an engineer at Trinity College, Dublin and became engineer for railways and other works in 1859. In 1848 he moved to Rathporeen House in County Cork, where he met Anthony Trollope, then employed in the General Post Office. He died in 1894.

CHIEF WRITINGS. *Seventy Years of Irish Life* (London: Arnold, 1893).

William Carleton

For biography and bibliography, see Volume II, p. 205.

John Millington Synge

For biography and bibliography, see Volume II, p. 717.

George Tyrrell

LIFE. Born in Dorset Street, Dublin in 1861, posthumous son of the Dublin journalist, W. H. Tyrrell. Robert Yelverton Tyrrell, the classical scholar, was his first cousin. He was received into the catholic church in 1879 and, in preparation for his entry to the Jesuits, spent a year's probation in the Jesuit college at Malta, before entering the novitiate at Manresa House, Roehampton, England in 1880. Tyrell took his first vows in 1882, studied scholastic philosophy at Stonyhurst College, emerged an ardent Thomist and returned to the college at Malta where he was employed as a schoolmaster. On his return from Malta, he spent four years theological training at St Beuno's College in north Wales and was ordained in 1891. After mission work in various English cities, he lectured at Stonyhurst and in 1896 was transferred to the literary staff at the Jesuit House in Farm Street, London. In 1899 he was forced to retire to the Jesuit Mission House at Richmond, Yorkshire after the publication of an article that displeased the church authorities. His *A Confidential Letter to a . . . Professor of Anthropology* (1906) acknowledged the untenability of the catholic conservative position, even though the point of the letter was to persuade its recipient not to leave the church. When it was published as *A Much Abused Letter* in the same year, the estrangement between Tyrrell and his order was complete. He was expelled from the order and in 1907 brought upon himself minor excommunication from the church because of letters to *The Times* newspaper, in which he opposed recent papal decrees (1907) against modernism. In the following year, Cardinal Mercier, archbishop of Malines, in his Lenten Letter, attacked modernism and Tyrrell as its embodiment. Tyrrell replied, with vigour, in *Medievalism* (1908). He died at Storrington, Surrey in 1909.

CHIEF WRITINGS. *Nova et Vetera* (London: Longmans, 1897); *Hard Sayings* (London: Longmans, 1898); *External Religion* (London: Sands & Co., 1899); *The Faith of the Millions*, 1st and 2nd Series (London: Longmans & Co., 1901-02); *Oil and Wine* (London: Longmans & Co., 1902); *Lex Orandi* (London: Longmans & Co., 1903); *Lex Credendi* (London: Longmans, 1906); *A Confidential Letter to a friend who is a Professor of Anthropology*, later *A Much Abused Letter* (London: Longmans, 1906); *Through Scylla and Charybdis* (London, Longmans, 1907); *Medievalism* (London: Longmans & Co., 1908); *Christianity at the Crossroads* (London: Longmans, 1909); *Essays on Faith and Immortality* (London: Arnold, 1914).

BIOGRAPHY AND CRITICISM. M. D. Petre (ed.), *Autobiography and Life* 2 vols I. *Autobiography, 1861-84*; II. *Life, 1884-1909* by M. D. Petre (London: Arnold, 1912); A. Loisy, *Memoires pour servir à l'histoire religieuse de notre temps* 3 vols (Paris: Table Rond, 1930-31); J. L. May, *Father Tyrrell and the Modernist Movement* (London: Eyre and Spottiswoode, 1932); M. D. Petre, *Von Hugel and Tyrrell: The Story of a Friendship* (London: Dent, 1937); M. Ward, *The Wilfrid Wards and the Transition* (London: Sheed and Ward, 1937); C. Dawson, *Prophets of Past Time* (Baltimore: Johns Hopkins University Press, 1988), pp. 25-69.

George A. Birmingham (James O. Hannay)

LIFE. Born James Owen Hannay in Belfast in 1865. Educated at Trinity College, Dublin, Birmingham was ordained a deacon of the Church of Ireland in 1888, a priest in 1889 and was appointed rector of the parish of Westport, Co. Mayo, in 1892. He remained there until 1913. He was involved in the Gaelic League and was much influenced by Douglas Hyde, Horace Plunkett and Standish O'Grady. He wrote prolifically and from 1908 commanded a large audience for his novels. His play *General John Regan* caused a riot when it was performed by a touring company in Westport in 1914. In 1916-17, Birmingham served as a chaplain in France. He was rector of a parish in Kildare 1918-20 and chaplain to the lord lieutenant of Ireland. In 1922, he resigned and went to Budapest for two years as chaplain to the British legation. On his return, he accepted a living in Mells, Somerset where he lived until his wife died. In 1934, he moved to London where he died in 1950.

CHIEF WRITINGS. As George Birmingham: *The Seething Pot* (London: Edward Arnold, 1905); *Hyacinth* (London: Edward Arnold, 1906); *Benedict Kavanagh* (London: Edward Arnold, 1907); *The Northern Iron* (Dublin: Maunsel, 1907); *Spanish Gold* (London: Methuen, 1908); *The Bad Times* (London: Methuen, 1908); *The Search Party* (London: Methuen, 1909); *Lalage's Lovers* (London: Methuen, 1911); *The Inviolable Sanctuary* (London: Nelson, 1911); *The Lighter Side of Irish Life* (London and Edinburgh: T. N. Foulis, 1911); *The Red Hand of Ulster* (London: Smith, Elder, 1912); *General John Regan* (London: Hodder and Stoughton, 1913); *The Adventures of Dr. Whitty* (London: Hodder and Stoughton, 1913); *Irishmen All* (London Hodder and Stoughton, 1919); *A Padre in France* (London: Hodder and Stoughton, 1919); *An Irishman Looks at His World* (London: Hodder and Stoughton, 1923); *Send for Dr O'Grady* (London: Hodder and Stoughton, 1923); *The Grand Duchess* (London: Hodder and Stoughton, 1924); *General John Regan* (play) (London: Allen and Unwin, 1933); *Pleasant Places* (London: Heinemann, 1934); *Appeasement* (London: Methuen, 1938); *Over the Border* (London: Methuen, 1944).

As J. O. Hannay: *The Life of Frederick Richard Wynne* (London: Hodder and Stoughton, 1897); *The Spirit and Origin of Christian Monasticism* (London: Methuen, 1903); *The Wisdom of the Desert* (London: Methuen, 1904); *Is the Gaelic League Political?* (pamphlet) (Dublin, 1906).

Katharine Tynan

LIFE. Born in Dublin in 1861. She attended convent school in Drogheda for six years. During the 1880s, she was hostess of a literary salon, befriended W. B. Yeats and quickly established a reputation as a promising poet. After her marriage in 1893 to Henry Hinkson, she moved to England and embarked on a journalistic career. This, along with a series of novels of social protest, won her a wide audience. In 1911, she and her family returned to Ireland. Her husband was a resident magistrate in Mayo from 1914 until his death in 1919. Katharine Tynan regarded the insurrection as a terrible and mistaken event. When her husband died, she was forced to make a living by writing. For ten years she travelled in war-torn Europe and wrote extensively on the countries she visited. Her output was astonishing. In all, she published 161 books, as well as innumerable articles, essays, and stories. An eye infection, which had troubled her since childhood, got worse and for many years she was almost blind. She died in Wimbledon, England in 1931.

CHIEF WRITINGS.
Poetry. *Louis de la Valliere* (London: Kegan Paul, 1885); *Shamrocks* (London: Kegan Paul, 1887); *Ballads and Lyrics* (London: Kegan Paul, 1891); *Cuckoo Songs* (London: E. Mathews and J. Lane, 1894); *The Wind in the Trees* (London: G. Richards, 1898); *Innocencies* (London: A. H. Bullen, 1905); *Twenty-One Poems* (Dundrum: Dun Emer, 1907); *New Poems* (London: Sidgwick and Jackson, 1911); *Irish Poems* (London: Sidgwick and Jackson, 1913); *The Holy War* (London: Sidgwick and Jackson, 1916); *Twilight Songs* (Oxford: Basil Blackwell, 1927); *Collected Poems* (London: Macmillan, 1930).

Novels. *The Way of a Maid* (London: Lawrence & Bullen, 1895); *A Daughter of Kings* (London: Smith, Elder and Co., 1904); *The Sweet Enemy* (London: Archibald Constable and Co., 1901); *Julia* (London: Smith, Elder and Co., 1904); *Her Ladyship* (London: Smith, Elder and Co., 1907); *Peggy the Daughter* (London: Cassell and Co., 1909); *Freda* (London: Cassell and Co., 1910); *The Story of Celia* (London: Smith, Elder and Co., 1911); *The House* (London: W. Collins Sons and Co., 1920); *The Rich Man* (London: W. Collins Sons and Co., 1929); *Her Father's Daughter* (London: W. Collins Sons and Co., 1930).

Memoirs. *Twenty-Five Years* (London: Smith, Elder and Co., 1913); *The Middle Years* (London: Constable and Co., 1916); *The Years of the Shadow* (London: Constable and Co., 1919); *The Wandering Years* (London: Constable and Co., 1922).

BIOGRAPHY AND CRITICISM. E. Boyd, in *Ireland's Literary Renaissance* (New York: Alfred A. Knopf, 1916); K. R. Alspach, 'The Poetry of Katharine Tynan Hinkson', *The Ireland America Review* 4 (1940), 121-26; M. G. Rose, *Katharine Tynan* (Lewisburg, Pennsylvania: Bucknell University Press, 1973).

William Butler Yeats

For biography, see Volume II, p. 830. The following select list of Yeats's prose works can be supplemented by the poetry and drama bibliographies in Volume II, on pages 830 and 717 respectively.

A Vision (London: T. Werner Laurie, 1925; 2nd edition London: Macmillan, 1937; reprinted with corrections 1961, 1962); G. Mills Harper and W. K. Hood (eds), *A Critical Edition of Yeats's A Vision (1925)* (London: Macmillan, 1978); *Autobiographies* (London: Macmillan, 1926; expanded edition, 1955); *Mythologies* (London and New York: Macmillan, 1959); *Essays and Introductions* (London and New York: Macmillan, 1961); D. R. Pearce (ed.), *The Senate Speeches of William Butler Yeats* (London: Faber and Faber, 1961); *Explorations*, selected by Mrs W. B. Yeats (London: Macmillan, 1962; New York: Macmillan, 1963); J. P. Frayne (ed.), *Uncollected Prose by W. B. Yeats*, Vol. I (London: Macmillan; New York: Columbia University Press, 1970); J. P. Frayne and C. Johnson (eds), *Uncollected Prose by W. B. Yeats* Vol. II (London: Macmillan, 1975; New York: Columbia University Press, 1976); D. Donoghue (ed.), *Memoirs* (London: Macmillan, 1972; New York: Macmillan, 1973).

Stories. The Tables of the Law. The Adoration of the Magi (Dublin: privately printed, 1897; London: Elkin Mathews, 1904; Stratford-upon-Avon: Shakespeare Head Press, 1914); *Stories of Red Hanrahan* (Dundrum: Dun Emer Press, 1904; reprinted Shannon: Irish University Press, 1971); *Stories of Michael Robartes and his Friends* (Dublin: Cuala Press, 1931; Shannon: Irish University Press, 1970); R. J. Finneran (ed.), *John Sherman and Dhoya* (Detroit: Wayne State University Press, 1969); W. H. O'Donnell (ed.), *The Speckled Bird, With Variant Versions* (Toronto: McClelland and Stewart, 1976); P. L. Marcus, W. Gould, and M. J. Sidnell (eds), *The Secret Rose: Stories by W. B. Yeats: A Variorum Edition* (Ithaca, New York: Cornell University Press, 1981).

Letters. H. Reynolds (ed.), *Letters to the New Island* (Cambridge, Massachusetts: Harvard University Press, 1934); U. Bridge (ed.), *W. B. Yeats and Sturge Moore: Their Correspondence 1901-1937* (London: Routledge and Kegan Paul; New York: Oxford University Press, 1953); A. Wade (ed.), *The Letters of W. B. Yeats* (London: Rupert Hart-Davis, 1954; New York: Macmillan, 1955); *Letters on Poetry from W. B. Yeats to Dorothy Wellesley* introduction by Kathleen Raine (London and New York: Oxford University Press 1964); R. McHugh (ed.), *'Ah, Sweet Dancer': W. B. Yeats/Margot Ruddock, a Correspondence* (London and New York: Macmillan, 1970); R. J. Finneran, G. M. Harper and W. M. Murphy (eds), *Letters to W. B. Yeats* 2 vols (London: Macmillan; New York: Columbia University Press, 1973); R. J. Finneran (ed.), *The Correspondence of Robert Bridges and W. B. Yeats* (London: Macmillan, 1977; Toronto: Macmillan of Canada, 1978); J. Kelly and E. Domville (eds), *The Collected Letters of W. B. Yeats, Vol. I 1865-95* (Oxford: Clarendon Press, 1986).

See also A. Wade, *A Bibliography of the Writings of W. B. Yeats* 3rd revised edition R. K. Alspach (London: Rupert Hart-Davis, 1968); K. P. S. Jochum, *W. B. Yeats: A Classified Bibliography of Criticism* (Folkestone: Dawson, 1978); and the journals *Yeats Annual*, edited by W. Gould (London, Macmillan, 1982–) and *Yeats: An Annual of Critical and Textual Studies* edited by R. J. Finneran (Ann Arbor: UMI Research Press, 1983–).

George Bernard Shaw

For biography and bibliography, see Volume II, p. 514.

Earnán ('Ernie') O'Malley

LIFE. Born in Castlebar, Co. Mayo in 1898. His family moved to Dublin in 1906. He was educated at O'Connell Schools and University College, Dublin, where he studied medicine. O'Malley was a member of the Irish Volunteers, took part in the Easter Rising of 1916 and was a military organizer for Michael Collins during the War of Independence. He was wounded in action in 1920, later captured and tortured, but escaped in 1921. He rejected the Treaty, was a member of the Four Courts garrison during the shelling that destroyed the Public Records Office. He fought in the Civil War, was badly wounded and arrested in 1922 and imprisoned under sentence of death until 1924. He went on hunger-strike in 1923 for forty-one days, was elected Sinn Féin representative to the Dáil in the same year, but refused to take the mandatory oath of allegiance after his release in 1924. He left Ireland for Spain and was involved with the Basque separatist movement. Later he went to the United States where he lived for several years, settling finally in New York, where he married. In 1935 he returned to Ireland, was elected to the Irish Academy of Letters in 1947 and worked on his memoirs, the second volume of which was published posthumously. He died in Howth, Co. Dublin in 1957.

CHIEF WRITINGS. *On Another Man's Wound* (Dublin: Three Candles; London: Rich and Cowan, 1936; Tralee: Anvil Books, 1979); published under the title *Army Without Banners; Adventures of an Irish Volunteer* (Boston: Houghton Mifflin, 1937); F.-M. Blake (ed.), *The Singing Flame* (Tralee: Anvil Books, 1978).

Oliver St John Gogarty

For biography and bibliography, see p. 779.

Elizabeth Bowen

For biography and bibliography, see Volume II, p. 949.

Sean O'Casey

For biography and bibliography, see Volume II, p. 718.

Robert Harbinson

For biography and bibliography, see p. 1133.

Frank O'Connor

For biography and bibliography, see p. 127.

Seán O'Faoláin

For biography and bibliography, see p. 127.

Patrick Kavanagh

For biography and bibliography, see p. 168.

Louis MacNeice

For biography and bibliography, see p. 169.

Austin Clarke

For biography and bibliography, see p. 168.

Bulmer Hobson

LIFE. Born in Holywood, Co. Down in 1883, of Quaker stock, and educated at the Friends' School, Lisburn. He founded the Fianna Éireann, a local boys' organization, in Belfast in 1903, was recruited into the IRB in 1904 and, with Denis McCullough, founded the Dungannon Clubs in 1905. Hobson became vice-president of Sinn Féin in 1907. He founded a weekly journal, *The Republic* (1906-07), and worked on *The Peasant* (1908). The IRB paper, *Irish Freedom*, was founded at his suggestion in 1910 and he bore the brunt of the editorial work for it. He became chairman of the Dublin Centre of the IRB, was a member of the Leinster executive and then a member of the supreme council. He played a prominent role in establishing the Irish Volunteers in 1913, took part in the Howth gun-running incident, but lost influence with other IRB members in a dispute over the representation of the Irish Parliamentary Party on the board of the Volunteers. In 1915 he resigned from the supreme council and from his position in *Irish Freedom.* On discovering the secret plans for the Easter Rising, he informed Eóin MacNeill and both tried to prevent its taking place. He was taken prisoner by the IRB until the Rising had begun. After 1916, he went to Belfast and then withdrew from active politics altogether. Hobson worked as a civil servant in the Free State and retired to Connemara. He died in 1969.

CHIEF WRITINGS. *The Creed of the Republic* (Belfast: Republican Press, 1907); ed. (with P. S. O'Hegarty), *The Voice of Freedom: A Selection from 'Irish Freedom' 1910-1913* (Dublin: Freedom Office, 1913); *Ireland Yesterday and Tomorrow* (Tralee: Anvil Books, 1968).

Bernadette McAliskey (Devlin)

LIFE. Born in Cookstown, Co. Tyrone, in 1947, and educated at St Patrick's Girls Academy, Dungannon, and Queen's University, Belfast, where she became a founder-member of the People's Democracy movement in 1968 and participated in the Civil Rights march of January 1969. She stood for election to Westminster in February 1969 in South Derry and in April won the Mid-Ulster seat as an Independent Unity candidate in a by-election. She played a prominent role in the 'Battle of the Bogside' in August 1969, when the citizens defended the area against the assaults of the police. In February 1972 she physically attacked the British home secretary, Reginald Maudling, in the House of Commons during an emergency debate on the killings of Bloody Sunday of January 1972. Bernadette Devlin lost her seat in the general election of 1974. That same year she was a founder member of the Irish Republican Socialist Party. She married Michael McAliskey in 1978. They and their children barely survived an assassination attempt by protestant paramilitaries in 1981. She failed to win a seat in the European Parliament in 1979 and was twice unsuccessful in general elections in the Republic in 1982.

CHIEF WRITINGS. *The Price of My Soul* (London: André Deutsch, 1969).

BIOGRAPHY AND CRITICISM. G.W. Target, *Bernadette: The Story of Bernadette Devlin* (London: Hodder & Stoughton, 1975).

Eamon McCann

LIFE. Born in Derry in 1943 and educated at St Columb's College and Queen's University. He left Queen's in 1965 without a degree and worked in London until 1968, when he returned to Derry and became involved in local radical politics. McCann helped to organize the first civil rights march in Derry in October 1968. He was a Labour candidate in the February 1969 Stormont election and stood as an Independent Socialist in the Westminster general election of 1970. He is a member of International Socialists and a regular contributor to the *Socialist Worker*. He lived and worked in Dublin in the 1980s as a journalist and broadcaster, but now lives in Derry.

CHIEF WRITINGS. *War and an Irish Town* (Harmondsworth: Penguin, 1974; 2nd revised edition London: Pluto Press, 1980).

Anthony Cronin

LIFE. Born in County Wexford in 1926. In a varied literary career in Dublin and London, he has been associate editor of *The Bell* and literary editor of *Time and Tide*, a member of the editorial board of the quarterly *X*, a columnist for *The Irish Times*, broadcaster, chairman and founder of Aosdana, cultural adviser to the Taoiseach, Charles Haughey, and visiting professor in the United States.

CHIEF WRITINGS. *Poems* (London: Cresset, 1957); *The Life of Riley* (London: Secker and Warburg, 1964); *A Question of Modernity* (London: Secker and Warburg, 1966); *Collected Poems 1950-1973* (Dublin: New Writers' Press, 1973); *Dead as Doornails* (Dublin: Dolmen Press, 1975); *Identity Papers* (Dublin: Co-op Books, 1979); *Reductionist Poem* (Dublin: Raven Arts, 1980); *R.M.S. Titanic* (Dublin: Raven Arts, 1981); *New and Selected Poems* (Dublin: Raven Arts; Manchester: Carcarnet Press, 1982); *Heritage Now: Irish Literature in the English Language* (Dingle: Brandon, 1982); *Letter to An Englishman* (Dublin: Raven Arts, 1985); *An Irish Eye: Viewpoints* (Dingle: Brandon, 1985); *The End of the Modern World* (Raven Arts, 1989); *No Laughing Matter. The Life and Times of Flann O'Brien* (London: Grafton, 1989).

Patrick Shea

LIFE. Born in Delvin, Co. Westmeath in 1908. His father was a member of the Royal Irish Constabulary, stationed first at Athlone, then Rathfriland, Co. Down and Clones, Co. Monaghan. Shea entered the Northern Ireland civil service in 1926 and remained there until his retirement in 1973. In 1969 he was promoted to the rank of departmental permanent secretary. In this position he observed the opening years of the northern crisis.

CHIEF WRITINGS. *Voices and the Sound of Drums: An Irish Autobiography* (Belfast: Blackstaff Press, 1981).

BIOGRAPHY AND CRITICISM. D. Donoghue, 'Castle Catholic' in *We Irish. Essays on Irish Literature and Society* (New York: Knopf, 1986), pp. 165-68.

C. S. Andrews

LIFE. Born in Summerhill, Dublin in 1901, Christopher (Tod) Andrews was educated at Synge Street school and at University College, Dublin. He took part in the War of Independence and in the Civil War, during which he was adjutant to Liam Lynch, chief of staff of the IRA. On his release from internment after the Civil War, he became involved in the new Fianna Fáil party under Eamon de Valera and was a member of the party's executive. He worked for the Irish Tourist Association and the Electricity Supply Board before joining the Turf Development Board. This he transformed into Bord na Móna, one of the most successful of the many semi-state bodies developed by the government at that time in its attempt to accelerate the industrialization of the country. He was also chairman of the national transport company, Córas Iompair Éireann. After fifty years in public service, he was appointed chairman of the national broadcasting station, Radio Telefís Éireann. His contribution to the development of the new state was remarkable both in its range and in its selflessness. He died in 1988.

CHIEF WRITINGS. *Dublin Made Me* (Cork: Mercier Press, 1980); *Man of No Property* (Cork: Mercier Press, 1982).

Hubert Butler

LIFE. Born at Maidenhall, Bennetsbridge, Co. Kilkenny in 1900. He was educated at Charterhouse and St John's College, Oxford. Butler worked with the Irish County Libraries in the mid-1920s, travelled in Europe and taught English in Alexandria and Leningrad. In 1934, he went to Yugoslavia for three years on a scholarship from the School of Slavonic Studies in London. Since 1941, he has lived in Kilkenny, where he revived the Kilkenny Archaeological Society (1944), organized a controversial series of Kilkenny Debates (1962-67) and founded the Butler Society, whose *Journal* he edits. He has broadcast for Radio Eireann and the BBC and has written for many journals and periodicals, including *The Bell, The Dublin Magazine, Twentieth Century* and *New Blackfriars.*

CHIEF WRITINGS. Translations: *The Thief* by Leonid Leonov (London: Martin Secker, 1931); *The Cherry Orchard* by Chekhov (London: W. H. Deane, 1934). *Ten Thousand Saints: A Study in Irish and European Origins* (Kilkenny: Wellbrook Press, 1972); *Escape from the Anthill* (Mullingar: The Lilliput Press, 1985); *The Children of Drancy* (Dublin: The Lilliput Press, 1988); *Grandmother and Wolfe Tone* (Dublin: The Lilliput Press, 1990).

Noel Browne

LIFE. Born in Waterford in 1915. He was educated at various schools in Ireland and England before going to Trinity College, Dublin, where he qualified as a doctor. Browne contracted tuberculosis, a disease that had killed his parents. He thereafter became a leading campaigner for the eradication of the disease, which caused many deaths in Ireland at the time. In 1948 he was elected to the Dáil as Clann na Poblachta member for Dublin South-East and became a government minister on the day he entered the Dáil: minister for health in the Inter-Party government 1948-51. Browne was successful in his campaign against tuberculosis, but his confrontation with the catholic hierarchy over his Mother and Child Scheme led to his resignation and was a factor in the government's downfall in 1951. He held his seat as an Independent 1951-53, joined Fianna Fáil 1953-57, regained his seat as an Independent in 1957 and was co-founder of the National Progressive Democratic Party, which he represented from 1958 to 1963. He joined the Labour Party in 1963 and was elected to the Dáil, holding his seat 1969-73. He became a Senator in 1973, stood for election as an Independent in 1977 and was elected. He then helped form the Socialist Labour Party. He retired from active politics in 1983.

CHIEF WRITINGS. *Against the Tide* (Dublin: Gill and Macmillan, 1986).

George O'Brien

LIFE. Born in Enniscorthy, Co. Wexford in 1945, he was raised in Lismore, Co. Waterford, and educated at St Augustine's College, Dungarvan, at Ruskin College, Oxford and at Warwick University, where he lectured in English 1976-80. He became assistant professor of English at Vassar College, New York in 1980 and since 1984 has lectured in English at Georgetown University, Washington. In 1973 he won the Hennessy New Irish Writing Award and in 1977 the Ulster Tatler Story Prize. He is married and has two sons.

CHIEF WRITINGS. *The Village of Longing* (Mullingar: The Lilliput Press, 1987); *Dancehall Days* (Dublin: The Lilliput Press, 1988). Both books were published in a single edition by Penguin Books in 1990.

LUKE GIBBONS, *Editor*

Challenging the Canon: Revisionism and Cultural Criticism

Writing in 1944 about the 'cult of the Gael' in Irish society, Seán O'Faoláin observed mordantly that the Gaelic mystique is 'the opponent of all modernisations and improvisations — being by nature, in its constant reference to the middle-ages — terrified of the modern world, afraid of modern life, inbred in thought, and, so, utterly narrow in outlook'.[1] Its enervating effects extended to politics, where the backward look of nationalism had all but cut off Ireland from invigorating contacts with the rest of the world. O'Faoláin, however, was careful to exempt one politician from the terms of his critique. That politician was Seán Lemass, and for the next generation, Lemass became the person who laid to rest the myth of the Gaelic past.

Seán Lemass's appointment as Taoiseach in 1959 is generally credited — or blamed, depending on one's standpoint — with ushering in the 'revisionist' turn in Irish history and culture. The opening up of the Irish economy to international investment in the early 1960s, the application for membership of the European Community (1961), the reforms of the second Vatican Council (1962-65), the advent of Irish television and other social changes — all these were considered to have brought with them a new liberalization of Irish society which questioned the religious and national consensus of what was called 'the age of de Valera'. The celebrations attending the golden jubilee of the Easter Rising in 1966 marked a watershed in this process of re-evaluation and self-questioning, acting both as an apotheosis and as a purging of the memory of dead generations.

Towards the end of the decade, the eruption of civil strife in Northern Ireland added a new political urgency to the task of redefining the relationship of a modernizing society to the legacy of the past. In 1972, the publication of two important revisionist texts set the agenda for many of the intellectual debates that were to dominate the next two decades.[2] The first was Father Francis Shaw's article 'The Canon of Irish History — A Challenge', a hostile analysis of Patrick Pearse and the 1916 Rising, originally written in 1966 but withheld from publication until 1972. The second was *States of Ireland*, a polemical, critical study of

1. See p. 573 below.

2. This was also the year in which Garret FitzGerald published his influential, liberal reappraisal of nationalism, *Towards a New Ireland.* These were the first significant publications to make a popular impact, but they were preceded by numerous scholarly revisions of nationalist historiography, particularly in the fields of economic and cultural history. See, for example, Louis Cullen (ed.), *The Formation of the Irish Economy* (Cork: Mercier Press, 1966), and his wide-ranging reappraisal of Daniel Corkery, 'The Hidden Ireland: Re-assessment of a Concept', *Studia Hibernica*, No. 9 (1969), now available as a pamphlet (Gigginstown, Co. Westmeath: The Lilliput Press, 1988). Much of the new scholarship was incorporated into F.S.L. Lyons, *Ireland Since the Famine* (London: Collins, 1971), which quickly became the standard account of the period. It was Lyons, apparently, who first made explicit use of the term 'historical revision' in an 1957 article on the Famine (see Terence Brown, *Ireland: A Social and Cultural History, 1922-79*, London: Fontana, 1981, p. 228).

nationalism by Conor Cruise O'Brien, the intellectual figure who, in the popular imagination at any rate, came to represent the cutting edge of the new iconoclasm in Irish culture and politics.

While it is true that revisionism had to await the 1970s to make a popular impact on Irish life, the first direct challenges to the orthodoxies of the national revival date not from the 1960s, but from the 1930s and 1940s, from, in fact, the writings of O'Faoláin and others associated with *The Bell* magazine (founded in 1940), and the publication of *Irish Historical Studies* (1938), a journal that strove to bring international standards of academic rigour to bear on Irish history. Revisionism, in this early sense, meant a parting of ways between those brought up in the shadow of the revolution: while the Anglo-Irish were having difficulties being accepted as integral to the Irish nation, others who had 'inherited' it as part of their birthright grew disillusioned with the failure to fulfil the promise of a new beginning. It was to be expected that an element of recrimination and self-reproach would make its appearance in the works of disaffected nationalists, who were looking at the past more in anger than with nostalgia. An early expression of this is found in O'Faoláin's strategic shift of the blame for the ultimate failure of the revolution from *external sources* — British imperialism — to inherent deficiencies in the native tradition. In the opening chapter of his dissident biography of Daniel O'Connell, *King of the Beggars* (1938), O'Faoláin argued that, contrary to Daniel Corkery, the demise of the 'hidden Ireland' in the eighteenth century had less to do with colonial oppression than with its own incapacity, as an anachronistic social order, to face up to the advent of democracy and modernization.

With the publication of *The Bell* in October 1940, the sounding of the Celtic note became increasingly discordant. Many of the disparate strands in the magazine's critique of nationalism come together in O'Faoláin's editorial on 'The Gaelic Cult', but this article is also of interest because it illustrates many of the underlying critical stratagems in the revisionist approach to history. O'Faoláin's initial procedure is to deprive 'the Gaelic cult' of its mystique by undermining its basis in tradition. So far from attesting to the continuity of a cultural heritage, he argues that it is of quite recent origin, not appearing on the centre of the nationalist stage until the writings of James Connolly. O'Faoláin then attempts to establish a link between the Gaelic ideal and racialism, equating it with the doctrines of racial purity promulgated in Nazi Germany. This is said more in the way of an aside, but it was precisely in this parenthetical fashion that the association between nationalism and racialism became part of the repertoire of revisionism. Thus we find Conor Cruise O'Brien, almost thirty years later, taking the nationalist tradition to task for its use of the term 'race', and then making the fateful German connection in the throwaway remark that 'the popularity of the term "race" came, I think, partly from the Zeitgeist'.[3] O'Brien proceeds to single out the poet and critic Thomas MacDonagh, one of the executed leaders of the Rising, as a writer whose views on race are representative of nationalist thinking on the subject. The problem here is that while MacDonagh is certainly a representative figure, he is part of a critical current in nationalism that sought to *distance* itself from racial distinctions:

> I have little sympathy [wrote MacDonagh] with the criticism that marks off subtle qualities in literature as altogether racial, that refuses to admit natural exceptions in such a naturally exceptional thing as high literature, attributing only the central body to the national genius, the marginal portions to this alien strain or that.[4]

MacDonagh stated the obvious in arguing that the main contribution to an anti-colonial literature must come from the colonized themselves — 'the Irish people, *mainly* of Gaelic stock'. But, as his careful choice of words indicates, there is nothing exclusive about this. MacDonagh has no difficulty including in the cultural canon many Anglo-Irish figures who were later to be the subjects of 'exclusionary orders' in Daniel Corkery's writings: Charles Lever, Samuel Lover, the gothic novelists Charles Maturin and Sheridan Le Fanu, and even Corkery's *bête noire* — the historian W. E. H. Lecky. At a time when J. M. Synge was incurring the wrath of the Sinn Féin movement, MacDonagh was commending him for his love of the Irish language. Unlike those who wanted to de-anglicize

3. Conor Cruise O'Brien, *States of Ireland* (London: Panther, 1974), p. 49. O'Brien exempts protestant nationalists from charges of racialism; it was, he contends, catholic nationalists such as Thomas MacDonagh who placed a harder, more explicit emphasis on race.
4. See Volume II, p. 989.

Ireland, and purify it of 'alien influences', MacDonagh sought an accommodation with the English language and literature, and was the first to propose systematically that Irish literature in the English language was no less authentic than the native Gaelic mode. 'Irishness' for him was not a genetic or racial inheritance: it was something to be achieved as part of a concerted, cultural effort. The poet Lionel Johnson, an Englishman, was more Irish in MacDonagh's eyes than many writers whose claim to be Irish extended no further than the biological fact of having been born in the country.[5]

MacDonagh's replacement of Matthew Arnold's 'Celtic note' by what he called 'the Irish mode' derived partly from his distrust of racial theories of national identity. Celticism is precisely an attempt to construe a native culture as a manifestation of an underlying racial or national 'character', and not the least of the ironies of this form of cultural exclusivity is that it is itself largely an import into Irish culture. Whether in the cultural nationalist form that emanated from the writings of Johann Gottfried von Herder and German Romanticism, the racialism of Ernest Renan or the benevolent colonialism of Matthew Arnold, Celticism sought to impose a racial uniformity on the state of flux that was Irish culture.[6] Celticism, then, was a means of stabilizing and hence controlling the vagaries of Irish experience from *the outside*, but the idea of an underlying Irish 'essence' proved equally attractive to native revivalists intent on furnishing Irish identity with a distinctive cultural pedigree. That the notion of race calcified a dynamic cultural identity, thereby playing into the hands of the colonial régime, escaped the notice of all but the more astute nationalist writers.

Thus in the first decade of the Revival, the term 'race' was appended indiscriminately to the terms 'Celtic', 'Gaelic' and 'Irish', but by the turn of the century a subtle shift in terminology had emerged, motivated as much by a realignment in politics as by the need for a greater linguistic precision. The change in title of the Celtic Literary Society to Cumann na nGaedheal (later to become Sinn Féin) was symptomatic of this change, and in trenchant cultural polemics such as F. H. O'Donnell's *The Stage Irishman of the Pseudo-Celtic Drama* (1904), and the writings of the Irish Ireland movement led by D. P. Moran, Celticism was disowned as an alien Anglo-Irish imposition onto what was essentially a Gaelic, catholic tradition. The non-Irish connotations of Celticism were dispensed with (for the Celtic fringe, after all, included Scotland, Wales and Brittany), but its essentialist dimension was retained by conservative nationalists to allow for a more purified and streamlined version of Irishness. Although Moran was at pains to dissociate himself from the crudities of racial hatred, he was a strong believer in racial pride and baulked at Thomas Davis's notion that a composite race represented the only genuine form of Irish unity. Yet Moran, at least, was rigorously consistent in espousing the cause of Irish Ireland, and was prepared to exclude 'non-Gaels' such as Wolfe Tone, Robert Emmet and Thomas Davis from pride of place in the nationalist canon.[7] Whatever the limitations of his views, he cannot be seconded into the company of those, excoriated by O'Faoláin, who mythologized 'the dead generations' of 1798 and 1848 to legitimize their own nationalist aspirations.

It is this strand of thought that has been taken, with revisionist hindsight, as characteristic of all nationalist thinking, and that has been used as a foil to throw into relief the more enlightened, liberal contribution made by the Anglo-Irish to the Revival.[8] Yet there was an important countercurrent *within* the nationalist tradition which, in marked contrast to the Irish Ireland movement, rejected Celticism precisely because its racial provenance carried with it a narrow, exclusivist interpretation of Irishness. The first influential exponent of this view was the antiquarian and translator Dr George Sigerson, who, because of his own Nordic background, had a personal interest in arguing that Irishness was not the sole preserve of those with a pure Celtic filiation. Sigerson had argued for a syncretic form of Irishness as early as 1868, and developed this approach in a lecture in

5. MacDonagh's critical writings have been badly served by his commentators. For two perceptive discussions, see Robert Lynd, *Ireland A Nation* (London: Grant Richards Ltd, 1919), pp. 164-70, and Declan Kiberd, 'Writers in Quarantine?: The Case for Irish Studies', *The Crane Bag*, Vol. 3, No. 1 (1979), 16-17.
6. For a wide-ranging discussion of the emergence of Celticism, see W. J. Mc Cormack, *Ascendancy and Tradition* (Oxford: Clarendon Press, 1985), chapter 6.
7. D. P. Moran, *The Philosophy of Irish Ireland* (Dublin: James Duffy & Co, 1904 (first published in 1898-1900)), pp. 36-37.
8. See F. S. L. Lyons, *Culture and Anarchy in Ireland 1890-1939* (Oxford: Clarendon Press, 1979), chapters 3 and 4.

1893, 'Irish Literature: Its Origin, Environment', which accompanied, and indeed was overshadowed by, Douglas Hyde's famous address on 'The Necessity for De-Anglicizing Ireland'.[9] He returned to this theme in his pioneering book of translations, *Bards of the Gael and Gall*, first published in 1897:

> Though it is now common to apply the epithet 'Celtic' to the old inhabitants of Ireland, I have preferred to write of them as the 'ancient Irish', that being a term less exclusive and more exact.... The Milesian [i.e. Celtic] invaders are now generally supposed to have superseded completely the former owners of the island. This is essentially a modern fancy, founded on ignorance; for the elder Irish historians — often Milesians themselves — not only admit but emphasize the fact that the population of the country was composed of different races.[10]

Thomas MacDonagh's greatest intellectual debt was to Sigerson, as is clear from the dedication to his book *Literature in Ireland* (1916), a disjointed but remarkably perceptive study of the problems involved in establishing, or even identifying, a distinctive Irish literature. MacDonagh was indebted to Sigerson not only for his rejection of the Celtic note, but also for his attitude to the controversial role of *translation* — from the original Irish to the English — in maintaining a cultural heritage. Sigerson's approach to translation clearly marked him out as a cultural latitudinarian. One of the standard criticisms levelled at the medium of translation by Celtic fundamentalists was that it acted as a kind of Trojan horse, smuggling into Irish literature values and sentiments that were alien to the native tradition. In an acerbic attack on the Celtic posturing of Anglo-Irish writers during the Revival, Father Francis Shaw argued in 1934 that 'the Celtic Twilight' was not indigenous to Irish culture but was in fact 'a product of the exaggerated Romanticism of the eighteenth century' which 'has drawn much of its force from untrustworthy and highly coloured translations, in which the subjective contribution of the translator and not the original has been the chief source of inspiration'.[11] The spectre of James Macpherson, the forger of the Ossian poems of the 1760s, haunted Gaelic revivalists, for the possibility of a 'translation' without an original struck at the very basis of restoring an ancient culture, the original native voice, to its pre-eminent place in the canon.

It is interesting then to find both Sigerson and MacDonagh praising Macpherson's contribution to the eighteenth-century Celtic Revival, and even more vigorously defending the role of translation as a literary device. Translation was important not only as a means of maintaining contact with other cultures; it also raised far-reaching questions about the writer's relationship to the past. For Sigerson, the recourse to translation was not a fall from grace, an abandonment of the original Gaelic order, for there was no original or 'pure' Irish race there in the first place, only a conglomeration of different cultural influences. Instead of subscribing to the authenticity of the original, MacDonagh made the almost heretical suggestion that, in many cases, the English translations improved on the original Irish poems. The transition from the Irish to the English language became, in his writings, a metaphor for a complex renegotiation of the past, a means of extending cultural debates beyond the simple alternatives of either abolishing or restoring a native tradition. In recent years the philosopher Richard Kearney, following the lead of Brian Friel's play *Translations* (1981), has looked to translation as a paradigm for a *post*-nationalist approach to history, as if it is somehow incompatible with the type of nationalism espoused by MacDonagh.[12] Ironically, Kearney sees in translation a form of continuity with the past, whereas MacDonagh was more aware of its capacity to disrupt the continuum of tradition.

MacDonagh was under no illusion about restoring an ancient civilization to its original pristine condition: the most that could be hoped for was to 'resume a broken tradition and make a literature in consonance with our past'. Recovering a Gaelic golden age was not possible or even

9. George Sigerson, *Modern Ireland* (London: Longmans, Green, Reader and Dyer, 1868); 'Irish Literature: Its Origin, Environment' in *The Revival of Irish Literature* (London: T. Fisher Unwin, 1894).
10. George Sigerson, *Bards of the Gael and Gall*, first published in 1897 (London: Unwin, 1925), p. 377.
11. Father Francis Shaw, 'The Celtic Twilight', *Studies*, Vol. XXIII, No. 89 (March 1934), 25. It is interesting to note in passing that the fundamentalist Father Shaw of the 1930s was to become the revisionist of the 1970s.
12. See Kearney below, pp. 632.

desirable in view of the fossilized state into which the Gaelic order had fallen during centuries of English rule:

> A language that transmits its literature mainly by oral tradition cannot, if spoken only by thousands, bequeath as much to posterity as if spoken by millions. The loss of idiom and of literature is a disaster. But, on the other hand, the abandonment has broken a tradition of pedantry and barren conventions; and sincerity gains thereby.[13]

Preserving a native heritage is not an act of embalming: it is often a matter of revitalizing a moribund tradition, opening it up to new cultural energies and influences. For MacDonagh, the continuity between the Celtic Revival and early Irish literature was even less than that between the Italian Renaissance and classical antiquity. Interestingly, this chasm between the past and the present led him to quote with approval John Eglinton's early strictures on the use of Celtic mythology and similar archaic subject-matter in modern literature:

> These subjects [Eglinton wrote], much as we may admire them and regret that we have nothing equivalent to them in the modern world, obstinately refuse to be taken up out of their old environment, and be transplanted into the world of modern sympathies. The proper mode of treating them is a secret lost with the subjects themselves.[14]

In this reading, a dynamic sense of history is less preoccupied with the recovery of the past and is more concerned with the discontinuities and changes visited upon the cultural canon. 'History is between us and our heroes,' wrote MacDonagh: it is not a mysterious form of communion with the dead but a reminder that there is no direct access to the past, no way of resurrecting a vanished Gaelic order.

The reason for drawing attention to MacDonagh's writings is to highlight the complex relationship to the past in certain strands of cultural nationalism with the often simple-minded historical pieties that revisionist critics and historians attribute to nationalism. Part of the animus in O'Faoláin's critique of the Gaelic cult derives from his conviction that nationalism is trapped in the past, in a time warp that refuses to acknowledge the modern world. James Connolly is singled out as the first modern politician who seized on 'Gaelic Ireland *as a prototype*, or model, to be *reincarnated* in a politically free Ireland', but in fact Connolly's views resisted such simple formulas. 'The clans are now no more,' he wrote, 'and could not be revived, even if it were desirable to do so, which is more than questionable.'[15] The complexity of MacDonagh's ideas was also overlooked when critics and historians in the 1960s and 1970s got around to demythologizing his contribution to the national revival. MacDonagh was conscripted into the ranks of those nationalists who, under the inspiration of Patrick Pearse, looked to messianism and a sacrificial cult of violence as a rationale for political insurrection.

It was the messianism of Pearse's politics of redemption, the idea that out of death comes life and out of defeat victory, that drew the wrath of Father Shaw in his canonical revisionist article in 1972, though it is worth remembering, in view of the ready association between liberalism and revisionism, that the main thrust of Father Shaw's analysis was that Pearse had blasphemed religion, reducing it from the sacred to the profane world of politics. MacDonagh, however, as his most perceptive critics have shown, was ill-at-ease with such messianic sentiments, a point that was evident even to some of his contemporaries. In December 1914 he was the principal speaker at a pacifist meeting on 'Ireland, Women and the War', and in the course of his talk expressed the hope that the Volunteer Movement would never have to use arms, and admitted that he found his own duty as instructor of bayonet-fighting 'disgusting'. This led Francis Sheehy-Skeffington, the ardent pacifist, to publish an open letter in reply, in which he stated that, while he did not doubt MacDonagh's sincerity, his views stood in stark contrast to those of another Volunteer (presumably Pearse) whom he had heard recently 'win plaudits by saying that the hills of Ireland would be crimsoned with blood rather than that the partition of Ireland should be

13. See Volume II, pp. 994.
14. See Volume II, pp. 993.
15. See *Workers' Republic*, 23 September 1899. Connolly's article also explicitly criticizes those who look to history in order to turn back the clock and restore a vanished social order.

allowed'.[16] During MacDonagh's own lifetime, therefore, his views on violence were clearly distinguishable from those of Pearse.[17] Yet by the late 1970s the most popular reappraisal of the Literary Revival by a revisionist historian, F. S. L. Lyons's *Culture and Anarchy in Ireland 1890-1939*, could state unambiguously that there was 'a clear indication that both Plunkett [i.e. Joseph Mary Plunkett] and MacDonagh were already imbued with the doctrine of the blood-sacrifice'[18] before the Rising. How can we account for such divergent interpretations?

One of the attractions of blood-sacrifice and messianic themes for revisionist critics and historians is that they clearly establish myth, violence and catholicism as the coordinates of militant nationalism. The task of forging a new set of cultural values for a liberal, modernizing society is easier if the ideology it is trying to replace is shown to be insular, illogical and narrow-minded. The combustible fusion of mysticism and militarism, catholicism and violence in the figure of Pearse was not only taken as representative of the 1916 Rising, but was read back into history as the driving force of nationalism over the centuries. Though D. P. Moran could argue from an 'Irish Ireland' position in the early days of the Revival that the periodic rebellions against British rule — 1798, 1803, 1848 — were organized over the heads of the native catholic population, by the early 1970s even the romantic violence espoused by the liberal, protestant-affiliated Young Ireland movement in the 1840s was construed as an expression of catholic — and by implication, sectarian — nationalism.[19] The most influential exponent of this view has been Conor Cruise O'Brien, and it is interesting that for the purposes of securing his argument he considers it necessary to posit an unbroken tradition linking catholicism and nationalism since the seventeenth century:

> There is a real continuity of Irish nationalism: not an ideological continuity, but a continuity of the traditions and feelings of a people. That people sees itself as the people of Ireland, and that perception is a large part of the problem. For these are not *all* the people of Ireland. They are the Catholic people of Ireland, formerly Gaelic-speaking.[20]

The advantages in this mode of argument are obvious, for the need to make a break with a dominant ideology such as cultural nationalism is much more desirable if it is shown to be a rigid, continuous tradition, unable to register difference or social change. The task of a new critical departure, then, is to introduce discontinuity and diversity into the cultural equivalent of an enclosed religious order, opening it up to the ways of the world in the late twentieth century. Thomas Kinsella's influential essays 'The Irish Writer' (1966) and 'The Divided Mind' (1972),[21] which acknowledged that discontinuity was the norm in the Irish cultural experience and that a 'great rift' separated the old from the new order, became something of a manifesto for a new generation of writers wishing to free themselves from the shackles of faith and fatherland. The exposure to cosmopolitan and international influences initiated by magazines such as *The Bell* and *Studies*[22] in the 1940s, and by *Envoy* and *Irish Writing* in the 1950s, was expected to facilitate the process of modernization, bringing Irish society into line with the rest of the advanced industrial nations. As David Thornley wrote in the optimistic atmosphere of the 1960s:

> It seems certain that our island will become affected increasingly by the spread of European social and philosophical ideas, strongly tinged with Catholicism ... and that our social habits and our politics will take on

16. F. Sheehy-Skeffington, 'Open Letter to Thomas MacDonagh', *Irish Citizen*, 22 May 1915. The letter was reprinted in Owen Dudley Edwards and Fergus Pyle (eds), *1916: The Easter Rising* (London: MacGibbon & Kee, 1968).
17. The best discussions of MacDonagh's ambivalent attitude to violence, as expressed through his poetry, are in William Irwin Thompson, *The Imagination of an Insurrection* (Oxford: Oxford University Press, 1967), pp. 124-31; Richard J. Loftus, *Nationalism in Modern Anglo-Irish Poetry* (Madison and Milwaukee: University of Wisconsin Press, 1964), chapter 6; Johann Norstedt, *Thomas MacDonagh: A Critical Biography* (Charlottesville: University Press of Virginia, 1980).
18. Lyons, ibid., p. 89.
19. Patrick O'Farrell, *Ireland's English Question* (New York: Schocken Books, 1971), pp. 136-37.
20. See Cruise O'Brien below, p. 595.
21. 'The Divided Mind' (see below pp. 625ff) develops some of the arguments that appeared first in 'The Irish Writer', later published in W. B. Yeats and Thomas Kinsella, *Davis, Mangan, Ferguson? Tradition and the Irish Writer* (Dublin: Dolmen Press, 1970).
22. Although magazines such as *The Bell* and *Envoy* are often credited with introducing into Ireland modern currents in European philosophy, it was in fact the Jesuit magazine, *Studies*, that first introduced existentialism into cultural debates as early as 1946.

> the flavour that is ever more urban and, as a consequence, ever more cosmopolitan. And this in turn will sound the death-knell of the attempt to preserve any kind of indigenous Gaelic folk culture in these islands.[23]

It seemed as if liberal humanism and the philosophical legacy of the Enlightenment, with its emphasis on progress and universal values, were about to make a belated entry into Irish cultural life, albeit initially in a post-Vatican II guise.

But like the foreign aid that was expected to deliver Ireland from the yoke of oppression in the past, it was too little, too late. Irish society had hardly embarked on full-scale modernization than the storm clouds of recession, and the world economic crisis of the 1970s, appeared on the horizon. With an even greater irony, the *rapprochement* with more radical European ideas, in journals such as *Atlantis* (1970-74) and *The Crane Bag* (1977-85), had no sooner become integral to Irish cultural debates than European philosophy set about undermining — deconstructing — humanism and the entire legacy of the Enlightenment. While liberals of a secular persuasion were announcing the death of God in Ireland, philosophers on the Continent such as Michel Foucault and Jacques Derrida were proclaiming the death of man.[24] The revisionist enterprise in Ireland, based as it is on a liberal-humanist ethic, was faced with an intractable dilemma as it gradually became apparent that a belief in a human condition, transcending all historical and political divisions, belonged to the kind of cultural fantasy that Seán O'Faoláin associated with nationalism, except that it was now a humanist rather than a Gaelic mystique. 'The autonomous individual may be a bourgeois humanist fantasy,' John Wilson Foster writes, 'but many of us in Ireland would like to enjoy that fantasy, thank you very much.'[25] Not least of the anomalies in this situation is that it is now revisionist critics who are keen to insulate Irish society against the shock of present-day European and Anglo-American ideas. Exposed to the theoretical voltage of Marxism, psychoanalysis and post-structuralism, they have advocated a new form of intellectual protectionism, thereby emulating the most conservative strands of cultural nationalism of the past. It is not just the rearguard but the avant-garde that threatens their critical composure, the fusion of 'Derry with Derrida' which Edna Longley discerns in the work of Seamus Deane, among others.

The fact that the modernization project has lost its way in Ireland is clear to all who are willing to disengage themselves from fantasy, 'bourgeois humanist' or otherwise. The crisis in the balance of payments in the 1980s, the break-up of the welfare consensus, and the dismantling of the public sector, dispelled any illusion that the industrialization of Irish society would mean lasting, or even minimal, prosperity for all. The increasing intensification of the conflict in Northern Ireland, following the H-Block struggle in 1981, put paid to the widely held view that nationalism was the relic of a bygone era which would be rendered obsolete by European integration and the levelling operations of the world economy. The secularization of Irish society was checked by two controversial referenda on abortion (1983) and divorce (1986), and the resurgence of a new catholic fundamentalism. It could be argued from an international perspective that these reversals were part of a general offensive in Western societies against the social-democratic advances of the post-war years, and that the incorporation of Ireland into the European Community in 1973 and the Anglo-American cultural complex left it with no defences against this backlash. Revisionist commentators in Ireland, however, preferred to look for an internal cause, and the 'explanation' lay conveniently to hand.

Writing in 1985, Conor Cruise O'Brien observed ruefully:

> It would be wrong to conclude that all Ireland has fallen victim to Enlightenment values. In rural Ireland, throughout the last summer, and into this summer, numerous statues of the Blessed Virgin were seen to move, and thousands of people came, by car and minibus, to see them move.[26]

23. David Thornley, *Ireland: The End of an Era?* Tuairim pamphlet, No. 12, 1965, p. 12 (cited in T. Brown, *Ireland: A Social and Cultural History, 1922-79*, p. 243).
24. For a good introduction to the critique of humanism in modern European philosophy, see Kate Soper, *Humanism and Anti-Humanism* (London: Hutchinson, 1986).
25. John Wilson Foster, 'The Critical Condition of Ulster', *The Honest Ulsterman*, No. 79 (Autumn 1985), 53.
26. Conor Cruise O'Brien, 'The Nationalist Trend', *The Times Literary Supplement*, 1 November 1985, p. 1,230.

In the persistence of rural ideology and the tenacity of traditional values in the face of external material change, disillusioned liberal commentators found what they were looking for. The failure of the modernization process was not attributed to an unequal relationship with the metropolitan centre, nor to the problems of introducing Enlightenment ideals of progress and equality to a newly industrialized country in an era of late capitalism. Rather, it was attributed to the rural hinterland and outlying regions — the heartlands of the moving statues — which had refused to participate in the transformation of Irish society. Modernization, it was argued, had not made the desired impact on society because of the residual power of an anachronistic agricultural sector, and genuine urbanization had not got off the ground, literally speaking, because the city in Ireland is simply the country at one remove. In the parlance of political science, Ireland was described as a 'periphery-dominated centre',[27] a country in which social progress was burdened by the accumulated weight of tradition and a lingering peasant society.

In this retrospective consolidation — or invention — of tradition, the revisionist thesis has travelled full circle. The underlying strategy of O'Faoláin's attack on the Gaelic mystique in the 1940s was to *deny* the continuity that cultural nationalists sought, in order to establish a cultural lineage for the nation. Forty years later, however, it is deemed essential for revisionist purposes to argue that there was indeed such an enduring tradition, and that the past throws a long shadow over the present. It is at this point that we see the rationale for reading back from the 1916 Rising, or present-day events in Northern Ireland, a one-dimensional catholic nationalist tradition, immune to cross-cultural influences and social change.

This becomes the burden of history, the source of all our present discontents. Part of the problem with 'Celticism', as we have seen, was that it was an attempt by a colonial power to hypostatize an alien, refractory culture in order to define it within its own controlling terms. By the same token, the spectre of nationalism conjured up by revisionism is largely of its own making, a spirit of the nation whose very lack of substance makes it all the more easy to exorcise. It is as if Pearse's and Corkery's belief in an enduring spiritual nation had to await a negative critique to achieve its full affirmation. The fact that the 'nationalist martyr' Thomas MacDonagh shared many of the critical positions of an opponent of the Revival, such as John Eglinton, or that writers as diverse as George Sigerson, Arthur Clery, Tom Kettle, Aodh de Blacam, W. P. Ryan, James Connolly and Frederick Ryan had a complex understanding of the relationship between past and present, 'Gael' and 'Gall', was overlooked in the interests of fixing an essential nationalist idea, a static monolithic tradition.

By denying the variegated pattern of nationalism, the fissures and tensions in a disparate set of responses to colonial domination, the revisionist enterprise gave back to the most conservative strands in nationalism the unity and cohesion they found so difficult to attain on their own terms. There is even a sense in which traditionalists and revisionists may have unwittingly collaborated in upholding the myth that to be Irish is to be beyond self-criticism, as if it is the sole prerogative of the outsider to cast a suspecting glance on Irish society. The myth of the nation as an 'imagined community', in Benedict Anderson's apt phrase,[28] devoid of the internal conflicts produced by class, gender and cultural divisions, is under greater attack from its own hidden history than from any 'post-nationalist' criticism. Ernest Boyd's answer to those who attempted to disenfranchize John Eglinton of his Irish identity, stands as an eloquent tribute to those who took the most difficult rather than the least line of resistance against colonial domination:

> There seems to be a tacit understanding that all criticism of national aspirations must come from the side of the enemy, for whom a reply is usually ready. But when the critic cannot be stigmatised as hostile to nationalist ideals, the problem of silencing him becomes more difficult.[29]

27. See Tom Garvin, *The Evolution of Irish Nationalist Politics* (Dublin: Gill and Macmillan, 1981), p. 217.
28. Benedict Anderson, *Imagined Communities* (London: Verso, 1983).
29. Ernest A. Boyd, 'An Irish Essayist: John Eglinton', in *Appreciations and Depreciations* (Dublin: The Talbot Press Ltd; London: T. Fisher Unwin Ltd, 1917), p. 61.

I. THE REVISIONIST TURN

SEÁN O'FAOLÁIN

(1900-)

from: THE BELL (1944)

[This lively editorial in *The Bell* (Vol. 9, No. 3, December 1944) is an early example of a revisionist approach to Ireland's Gaelic past. O'Faoláin develops some of the criticisms that he had levelled at Daniel Corkery's views on nationalism in the 1930s, and clearly aligns himself with an industrializing, cosmopolitan outlook. This commitment to modernization did not become public policy until Seán Lemass came to power in 1959 — and Lemass, interestingly, is the one politician exempted from criticism in O'Faoláin's article.]

THE GAELIC CULT

To the historian few spectacles are so fascinating as mass-delusions. For, as we all know, and nowadays more than ever, it is quite possible to delude whole peoples into believing that they are living, or dying for causes that are not the really effective causes, and which are in effect forms of the imagination. One of the commonest and simplest exercises of the imagination, for example, is the attempt to unify those scattered incidents and accidents, those various and often conflicting human urges and ambitions which we call a country's story, into a neatly bounded stream of purely local event, flowing from start to finish to one single sea — as if they were not all, rather, streams of the many tributaries of the great river which is the story of the world. Thus there is no such thing, in this sense, as the History of Ireland. You might as well say there could be such a thing as the History of Yeats, or the History of the Liffey. You could, it is true, as Croce[1] distinguishes, tell the Chronicle of Ireland or the Chronicle of Yeats — born, worked, married, wrote, died. But once you tackle the essential thing, *i.e.*, the problems of Ireland or of Yeats, then the whole world and all time float in. Yet people do commonly think and feel about Ireland as if they were thinking of a personal demi-goddess, and one may agree that it is a noble fancy, and even an inspiring fancy, to speak of 'her' as a beautiful queen, or as a poor little woman. It is nevertheless a fancy and not a fact, and it is well to keep that in mind because the great danger of this sort of thing is that while it often inspires noble deeds it can also end up in a complete mystification of the mind and a stultification of the heart and of all human feeling, and make men act very stupidly. For one certain effect of these efforts to unify and localise and simplify is to produce what is called Nationalist, and, if you choose, also Imperialist histories, which are inevitably and invariably a pack of lies, because they inevitably and invariably produce wildly passionate exhalations that obfuscate and madden like a drug — cults and myths and mystiques in the adoration of which all rational thought and all pity for human life is forgotten. We have seen many examples in contemporary Europe — indeed there is scarcely a country in Europe that has not, at some period of its history, succumbed in this way: Spain, France, England, Austria, Germany, Italy, and let us add Ireland. It must be one of the greatest attractions of America that she is still too young to have developed a historical cult.

In our own small way we have, in recent times, created one such very wonderful delusion. It is variously called the Gaelic Tradition, or the Gaelic Nation, or simply The Gael. It is a mystique, and like all mystiques it has a basis in fact, or rather an impossible bundling together of disparate facts. In sum the mystique has tried to discover in the old Gaelic world a model, or master-type — rather like the National Socialist mythology of the Pure Aryan — to which we must all conform. Now, this imagination of an Avatar, or incarnation of race or nationality at its purest, almost in its divine perfection, is a natural poetic flight, and all peoples indulge in it in moments of ecstasy: but they do not really believe in it, and they do not keep it up, and they certainly are not so foolish as to try to *live* according to it. On the contrary, they usually have

1. Benedetto Croce (1866-1952), the great Italian idealist philosopher, argued in his *Theory and History of Historiography* (1917) that whereas science deals with general laws, history is solely concerned with particular details and unique events.

a second and more homely image of themselves for the purposes of day-to-day existence. Thus 'Britannia' sits nobly on the coins of Britain: but it is 'John Bull' who pockets her. Even America, like France, has her goddess of Liberty but it was an inspector of food named Sam Wilson who created for her the practical image of Uncle Sam. What one might call the iconography of Irish symbolism is various, chiefly women, mainly unrepublican queens, but we have yet to find a really homely effigy — having long discarded the one which the 18th century foisted on us, Paddy with the pig. But, whatever he may turn out to be when we begin to see ourselves sanely enough to define him, a Gaelic avatar will certainly never appear in homely caricature: for the very solid reason that he has not even yet appeared in apotheosis. The attempt to conceive the master-type as 'Gaelic' could not succeed since it is, as we will see, based on a fundamental delusion.

This history of the Gaelic mystique is fascinating. It is really dual, partly cultural and partly political. For that reason it will be simplest to speak of it in the bivalvular term — 'The Gaelic Nation'. The story of its gradual arrival is likewise dual, partly a matter of politics and partly of literature, and it is comparatively recent. For if we cast our minds back over any distance — say over a couple of centuries — we do not find any of our political leaders or observers aware of it at all. I do not think that you will even as much as find the word 'Gael' in Swift, Molyneux, Grattan, Wolfe Tone, Lord Edward, Robert Emmet, Dan O'Connell (except when he said that he had no use for the Gaelic language), nor is it in John Mitchel, Michael Doheny, Fintan Lalor, Michael Davitt, Parnell, John Redmond,[2] or, though this may surprise some, even in our *pater patriæ*, the founder of Sinn Fein, Arthur Griffith. He, like all those others before him, is content to speak of 'Ireland' and 'Irishmen'. Some of them, of course, speak in favour of the Irish language — but that has nothing to do with the political cult, or the imaginary master-type of the 'Gael'. Thus, Davitt, for example, presented Parnell in 1882 with a political programme whose ninth point advocated 'the cultivation of national literature and the encouragement of the Irish language', and we can well believe, too, that all our political leaders were naturally inspired by a knowledge of the past.

There was only one man who, it might be argued — though I think, after reading his essays, not very convincingly — did make some small effort to make some sort of actual link between contemporary politics and the old Gaelic world. That was Thomas Davis.[3] Even his essay on the language would have to be carefully edited by any modern enthusiast hopeful of using it today. And it might be noted, in passing, that several of his colleagues on his paper *The Nation* opposed his revivalist ideas — even the antiquary, John O'Donovan[4] — being eager, instead, for a modern cosmopolitan culture. In any case, on all political matters, Davis was overshadowed by the colossus from Kerry[5] whose defined policy, and whose clear contribution to the development of native political thought — agree or disagree with it now as one chooses — was to say, in sum, to his ragged army, 'Start afresh. Modernise.' As we know, they did, throwing overboard every scrap of the past that had not already, like The Wild Geese,[6] abandoned the sinking ship. Davis and we might bewail the harsh necessity, but he had no political alternative to O'Connell's modernisations. So far, then, the Gaelic Nation as a political theory has no pedigree.

Some may here say: 'But what about what Professor Corkery called "The Hidden Ireland"? Maybe the inarticulate people held to it in secret?'

2. Jonathan Swift, William Molyneux and Henry Grattan were the leading figures in late seventeenth- and eighteenth-century protestant (or 'colonial') nationalism; Wolfe Tone, Lord Edward Fitzgerald and Robert Emmet are representatives of the republican tradition associated with the United Irishmen (founded in 1791); Daniel O'Connell was the leader of the catholic emancipation movement in the 1820s, and John Mitchel, James Fintan Lalor and Michael Doheny were associated with the Young Ireland movement of the 1840s. Michael Davitt and Charles Stewart Parnell were leading organizers of the Land League, and John Redmond took over leadership of the Home Rule Party when it reunited after the Parnell split.

3. Thomas Davis (1814-45) was the first influential exponent of cultural nationalism in Ireland, and popularized his views through the columns of *The Nation* newspaper. O'Faoláin's own note here reads: 'Possibly one might base the argument for Davis as a pro-Gael on his essay, "Udalism and Feudalism". By Udalism he meant a form of titular peasant proprietorship with an over-riding State Control. We have something very like it now and I do not see anything particularly Gaelic about it. His ideas there, of course, all went out of date with the Land Acts.'

4. Charles Gavan Duffy (1816-1903), founder and editor of *The Nation*, did not share Davis's revivalist ideals, but John O'Donovan (1809-61), the great scholar and antiquarian, did express an interest in reviving the Irish language and, on occasion, even declared his support for militant nationalism.

5. i.e. Daniel O'Connell.

6. The popular name for those catholics associated with the Stuart cause who left Ireland after the Williamite wars to fight on the Continent.

They did not. The 'inarticulate' people found a voice in O'Connell (1775-1847). If anybody wants a line on the political theory of the last of the Gaelic poets, from the ruin of the old Gaelic society to his day, I venture to suggest that he might read the Preface to my biography of O'Connell, *King of the Beggars*.[7] In sum, all the poor devils could think of was the return of the Stuarts, and, presumably, some kind of Anglo-Irish monarchy to patronise poetry.

Neither had the militant separatists any alternative to O'Connell's ideas, though they had, of course, to his methods. That was natural: the rebels of '48 and '67[8] were insurrectionists, not revolutionaries. All they knew was that they craved something that would satisfy racial pride. (Nationalism and racialism was [*sic*] in the air of Europe, it was part of the Romantic movement, winging westward on the words of Herder, Lessing, young Wordsworth, Shelley, Mazzini, Garibaldi, Hugo, Lamartine.)[9] But what that *something* was the '48 and '67 men could not define, and all that emerges from them is the craving to be 'different', to 'separate'. They had no more idea of what they meant by that — in terms of life, of human beings, of social order — than the kids who used to chant at school in my young days 'A Nation Once Again.'[10]

But the Romantic movement was now about to satisfy the craving that it had thus helped to create. That same romantic urge that had in England produced Percy's *'Reliques of Ancient English Poetry'* in 1765, had produced Charlotte Brooke's *'Reliques of Irish Poetry'* in 1789, as it had Walker's *'Memoirs of the Irish Bards'* in 1786: two literary landmarks. There followed many little societies interested in antiquities and the Gaelic language; local archæological societies; more and more publications; scholars native and foreign; until by about 1900, there began to emerge — almost wholly in English, it may be said — a vivid awareness of the existence of an Ireland that had been completely forgotten. That was Gaelic Ireland. What was even more wonderful and exciting, there were still places where men and women told ancient folktales by the fireside, believed in the *sidhe*,[11] held in their rude hands the thin thread of Ariadne back to the forgotten labyrinth.[12] All one needed to get back to that wonder-world was to be able to speak Irish. One could even touch that world without it. Yeats, Lady Gregory, Synge, Colum, all the poets of the Anglo-Irish Revival drank eagerly at the fountain, and handed the winy goblets back to such of the populace as had the wit and heart to gather around them. No young man reading these lines — not even young Gaelic enthusiasts of today — can realise what that discovery of the 'ancient mother' meant. Its outward signs were Anglo-Irish Literature and the founding of the Gaelic League in 1893. But let us keep our eyes on the point — there is still no mention of the 'Gaelic Nation' as a political ideal.

So far, then, we see the three elements: constitutional politics, in pretty low water after the fall of Parnell, the Separatists now burrowing underground, and this new Gaelic inspiration. Arthur Griffith established Sinn Fein in 1905-1906. (I repeat that there is, so far as I have been able to see, no mention in all his writings of the 'Gael.')[13] The first modern politician after Parnell whom I have found seizing on Gaelic Ireland *as a prototype*, or model, to be reincarnated in a politically free Ireland is, of all people, the Socialist Jim Connolly in his *'Labour in Irish History'* (1910). Whether it is with him or with somebody else that the grand delusion begins he had it badly. He was apparently under the impression that the antique social order enshrined for those whom he called 'our Gaelic forefathers' certain nobly desirable democratic rights and institutions, and that the modern, debased commercialised Irish stood between the people and these admirable traditions. Alas for the glory of Tara's Hall,[14] nothing could have been

7. Published in 1938.
8. The Young Ireland and Fenian rebellions, respectively.
9. Johann Gottfried von Herder (1744-1803) was the main inspiration behind folk ideals of cultural nationalism in Germany. The writings of Gotthold Lessing (1729-81), as both dramatist and critic, helped to break the grip of classicism on European thought. The young William Wordsworth and Percy Bysshe Shelley fused Romanticism with radical politics, as did Alphonse de Lamartine (1790-1869) and Victor Hugo (1802-85), two of the central figures of French Romanticism. Giuseppe Mazzini (1805-72), the leading exponent of Italian romantic nationalism, exercised a profound influence on Giuseppe Garibaldi (1807-82), the military leader who achieved the unification of Italy in 1860.
10. Written by Thomas Davis and first published in *The Nation*.
11. The fairy folk.
12. In Greek mythology. Ariadne supplied Theseus with a thread that enabled him to escape from the labyrinth after he had slain the minotaur.
13. As is clear from his obituary of Frederick Ryan (see Volume II, p. 1002), Griffith in fact did subscribe to the Gaelic cult.
14. Tara in County Meath was the seat of the ancient high kings of Ireland, and was immortalized in Thomas Moore's poem 'The harp that once through Tara's halls'.

farther from the truth. He could have saved himself and thousands of others much disappointment and more folly had he done no more than look at the Gaelic preface to the great collection of Gaelic Laws known as the 'Senchus Mor,'[15] which lists all the awful things that existed before these laws were codified — plagues and disorders of every kind, and, as the crowning worst, such general anarchy that 'even the churl's son dared to consider himself the equal of the son of a king.'

Whoever began it, there it is, in one example, already at work: and if some student of our universities should make the whole question a subject of research he would find other examples. I seem to remember that Mr. Sean Milroy (Heaven forgive him) wrote a book, also in praise of the Brehon Laws. Constance Markievicz[16] gave lectures about the subject — an extraordinary medley of Marx, Republicanism, and Gaeldom. The general idea of the 'Gaelic Nation' is implicit in the very title of Mr. P. S. O'Hegarty's interesting book '*The Indestructible Nation*' which, note, was originally given as a series of lectures to the London Gaelic League 'in (I quote the author's own words) the first and best decade of Sinn Fein, in 1911-1913.'

There one can see the idea of a Revival shake hands with the idea of Revolution. As we know, the Gaelic League was shattered by that hand-shake. The first President and founder, Dr. Douglas Hyde, now President of Ireland, resigned from it in 1915 when the militant separatists inside the League — they had deliberately gone into it in order to control it politically — insisted on making Independence one of its avowed objects. From that day onward politics infected Gaelic; and the idea of the 'Gael' and the 'Gaelic Nation' infected politics. It is all summed up in a well-known phrase of Pearse — 'Not merely free but Gaelic as well, not merely Gaelic but free as well.'[17]

I am afraid that we have become so accustomed to the jargon of this mystique that some, reading that phrase again, will dumbly react to it in a reflex now almost mechanically conditioned by twenty years of propaganda. They may say, 'A Gaelic Nation? Well — why not? It sounds all right.' It sounds all right. But let us shake off the drug and ask: What did Connolly and Pearse mean? They refer to a period when the people of Ireland possessed and lived by an indigenous culture of their very own — laws, dress, language, social order, and so on: and they refer, simultaneously, to later periods when various Irishmen, finding themselves misgoverned by the British people, propounded the solution of the absolute and unqualified separation of Ireland from Britain as a modern Republic. Two entirely different ideas are there thrown together — one cannot say 'mixed' together because they are immiscible. For the antique Gaels never heard of and would have fought to the death against the idea of a Republic and all it connotes, and the men who first initiated the idea of Republicanism — Tone onward — knew nothing about the antique Gaels[18] and would, whether Davis, Lalor or Jim Connolly, have been appalled by the reality of those days and conditions. If anything other than common-sense were needed to prove that the men of 1916 were, like the men of '48 and '67, not social revolutionaries but romantic insurrectionists, this idea of an Ancient - Modern - Republican - Gaelic - Nation should suffice. It is obvious that nobody could base anything like a social revolution on the lines of this fairy-tale fantasy.

Actually long before 1916 a very real revolution in Ireland had been brought about by the pressure of the Irish Parliamentary Party, or really by Davitt[19] — a true and genuine social reform of the largest kind — when they won the land for the people: so that the most serious social gravamen had

15. The *Seanchus Mór*, the great compendium of ancient Irish law, resisted all scholarly and antiquarian investigations until it was finally deciphered and translated by Eugene O'Curry and John O'Donovan, whose edition was published in 1865 by W. N. Hancock.
16. Seán Milroy (1877-1946), a leading republican activist, published one book of historical interest, *The Case of Ulster* (1922), but it does not contain any account of the Brehon laws, the ancient Irish legal system. Constance Markievicz (1868-1927), republican activist, was the first woman to be elected an MP (1918) and was Minister for Labour in the First and Second Dáil assemblies.
17. Pearse expressed this vision of Ireland in his graveside oration on O'Donovan Rossa in 1915: 'not free merely, but Gaelic as well; not Gaelic merely, but free as well.' ('O'Donovan Rossa — Graveside Oration' in *The Collected Works of Padraic H. Pearse: Political Writings and Speeches* (Dublin: Phoenix Publishing Co, 1929, p. 135.)
18. O'Faoláin overlooks the role of Henry Joy McCracken (1767-98), one of the leading United Irishmen, in organizing The Belfast Harpers' Festival in 1792, commonly seen as one of the last celebrations of the old Gaelic order. Other prominent United Irishmen, such as William Drennan and Thomas Russell, took an active interest in the Gaelic past.
19. Michael Davitt (1846-1906) founded the Land League in 1879, and later joined the Irish Parliamentary Party, which campaigned for Home Rule.

already been removed before the political change-over occurred. That marks off Davitt as a man apart in Irish history: one of our very few real revolutionaries, perhaps our only one. It shows us, too, how revolutions occur, on the pressure of actual not imaginary circumstances. The only other big thing waiting to be done after that was perceived clearly by another realistic man, Griffith — the need for autonomy in order to make possible an industrial revolution. So that what is needed, and perhaps alone needed today is not so much a further revolution as a revolutionary *approach* to both land and industry to set the dynamo going full-blast.

We can see, now, why the insurrectionists seized on the Gaelic Nation ideal, absurd and impossible as it was: their hearts were full, but their minds were vacant: into the vacuum there swept the first exciting idea to hand. Far be it from me to assail the memory of brave and noble-hearted men whose courage and idealism we will for ever honour. But we must not imagine that they had all the virtues; and the virtue of political thought they had not. Yet, to this day, their dual theory dominates the minds of our legislators, or of most of them — I find it hard to think that men like Mr. Sean Lemass, for instance, is [*sic*] thus affected — so that all you have to say to them is 'Not merely free but Gaelic as well, not merely Gaelic but free as well,' and their mouths will begin to water like Pavlov's dogs.

It is an amazing hypnosis. But still more amazing is the manner in which it affects the minds it dominates. For it produces nothing positive. On the contrary its effect is wholly negative and inhibitory; as with some mumbo-jumbo that is feared for its destructive powers and given mere lip-service to keep it quiet. Anything that has been done has been done without reference to it or without any assistance from it — whether it be the Shannon Scheme,[20] or improved rural housing, or the growing of wheat, or migratory schemes to lessen unemployment, or the efficiency of the Army, or the development of Air Transport, or Tourism, etc. Thus all that the more perfervid Gaelic addicts have ever contributed to any of these things is a nark.[21]

20. The Shannon electricity scheme, completed in 1929 under the aegis of the state-owned Electricity Supply Board, was the showpiece of industrialization policy in the 1920s and 1930s.

21. An irritating complaint.

Why should the Army play rugby! Tourism will ruin the West! Keep the Gaelic migrants inside a kind of Red Indian reservation — as was proposed last month by the Gaelic League at its Annual Conference. This is natural because the mystique is the opponent of all modernisations and improvisations — being by nature, in its constant reference to the middle-ages — terrified of the modern world, afraid of modern life, inbred in thought, and, so, utterly narrow in outlook. All its ideas of life are mediæval. Take even industry which might be thought safe from it. Can we seriously hope to develop a dynamic industrial future with a system of education which is based on an uncritical adoration for Finn MacCool (or Thomas Davis) and which has no interest in encouraging, let alone in producing, young technicians? Look even at the school-readers in *English*. For all the reference they make to the world of science or industry they might have been prepared for Ancient Britons. And does the mystique not affect politics — its politics are shiveringly isolationist; and is not our industrial future close bound to politics, seeing that we can have no large commercial future unless we look to the wide world as our market? In culture the mystique is equally fearful and inbred. That should be evident in our literary censorship alone which strives to keep out anything that savours of a bold facing-up to modern problems — banning even books by reputable Catholics abroad, books and pamphlets sanctioned by the most reputable members of all churches. How utterly different all that is to the magnificent courage of O'Connell, who said to our people. 'There is another world outside. Follow me. I will lead you into it.'

But we are not yet finished with the wonders of this hypnosis. We know, as I have said, the many good things our legislators have done without thanks to it. That means that when they do anything effective they are, for that time, free of the Cult and do not really, in their clearer brains, then dream any longer of harking back to the mediæval myth. Yet, not one single man of them will admit it. They still imagine that they are carrying out the Gaelic gospel. They are thus in the delightfully befuddled condition, and this is the most wonderful wonder of all, of being under the delusion that they are under a delusion....

T. W. MOODY

(1907-84)

from: HERMATHENA (1977)

[This article is one of the standard expositions of the revisionist approach to history. Although he is careful to demythologize loyalist as well as nationalist myths, Moody reserves the main thrust of his admonitions regarding present-day purveyors of mythology to the nationalist side, and specifically to the Provisional IRA. In fact, revisionism as practised by historians has come to be identified more with setting a new agenda for nationalist rather than for loyalist history. Central to Moody's argument is the assumption that myth and ideological agenda-setting are found only in popular history, as against the 'scientific' history practised by professional historians.

The paper was given as a presidential address to the Dublin University History Society in May 1977. It was subsequently published in *Hermathena*, No. CXXIV (Summer 1978). T. W. Moody's own notes are indicated by alphabetical letters.]

IRISH HISTORY AND IRISH MYTHOLOGY

The past is dead. Nothing, for good or ill, can change it; nothing can revive it. Yet there is a sense in which the past lives on: in works of human hands and minds, in beliefs, institutions, and values, and in us all, who are its living extension. It lives on in us, both for good and ill, shaping our lives and helping to determine our action, whether or not we know how our present is related to our past. But just as individuals cannot exist as complete persons without knowledge of their past, so human societies must have their self-knowledge if they are to preserve their corporate identity and their distinctive patterns of living. To supply this knowledge is one of the primary functions of the history of nations. But nations derive their consciousness of their past not only — and not mainly — from historians. They also derive it from popular traditions, transmitted orally, in writing, and through institutions. I am using the word myth to signify received views of this kind as contrasted with the knowledge that the historian seeks to extract by the application of scientific methods to his evidence. Myths as I define them combine elements of fact and of fiction; they are a part of the dead past that historians study, as well as being part of the living present in which we all, historians included, are involved.

All nations have their myths, which affect their corporate lives and do so most strongly in times of strain or crisis or unresolved conflict. Such myths can be sustaining or destroying, benign or malignant, influences, a stimulus to effort or an encouragement to resignation, a source of harmless amusement or an incitement to malice and hatred — or they can be a mixture of such elements. The myth-system or mythology of Ireland exemplifies all this in confusing abundance, and I want to consider some illustrative examples. Myth-making is an ancient Irish industry, of which the origin-legends and heroic tales of early and medieval Ireland are a characteristic product. But the myths I have in mind all took shape within the past four centuries, and are still more or less current. . . .

I turn now to a rich and many-sided mythology, that of orangeism. A quasi-official history of orangeism, by R. M. Sibbert, published in 1914-15, opens with the following:

> An orangeman who was asked how long his order had been in existence answered offhand that orangeism could be traced back to the Garden of Eden. He simply meant to convey that all the essentials of a perfect nature and of an exalted religion were to be found associated in the primal day of our race.[a]

The fall of man destroyed all this perfection but in the fullness of time man's relationship with God was renewed through Christ. 'While we maintained that relationship, by faith and obedience, no one could take away our inheritance. That was protestantism and that was orangeism.' Popery, however, obscured the truth until it was challenged and its dominion in part overthrown by the reformation. Though wounded, Rome remained a powerful and vigilant enemy of the reformed religion. The orange institution, which was the means of placing the prince of Orange on the throne of England, was

a. R. M. Sibbert, *Orangeism in Ireland and Throughout the Empire*, 2 vols (Belfast 1914-15), i, iii-iv; and see Hereward Senior, *Orangeism in Ireland and Britain, 1795-1836* (London, 1966), pp. 288-9.

simply protestantism alive to its own interests and organised for its own defence.

In a less rhapsodical spirit orangeism was characterised in 1967 by the Imperial Grand Master of the Imperial Grand Orange Council of the World, Captain L. P. S. Orr, M.P. for South Down, as follows:

> No great historical movement has been more misunderstood .... Yet it is to this movement that the world owes the establishment of the concept of civil and religious liberty....
>
> The famous struggle for liberty in Europe against the concept of the dictatorship of kings can be traced back to the ... rise of the Dutch Republic against the tyranny of the Spanish sovereigns.... Throughout this famous story runs the continuous thread of the leadership of the house of Orange from William the Silent to our own King William III. The principles of this movement (which we call orangeism because of this leadership) were constant throughout the struggle. They were to establish and protect the protestant religion (by which general terms was understood not any particular sect, but the general concept of freedom of conscience in religion), and to establish civil and religious liberty.
>
> The destruction of the doctrine of the divine right of kings and the establishment in England of constitutional monarchy, while its roots in English history may in fact go very deep, was none the less accomplished by orangeism; and the tradition of opposition to European dictatorship can fairly be claimed to have started with the same movement.[b]

This, I think, may be taken as an authoritative and up-to-date statement of the myth of orangeism. In its engaging mixture of fact and fantasy, of history and mythology, it admirably illustrates my theme.

William, prince of Orange, and stadtholder of Holland, who became King William III of England in 1689, certainly was a champion — tolerant, stoical, large-minded — of human liberty in a European context. He was the central figure in a European coalition, the 'grand alliance', formed to resist the aggressions of France under Louis XIV; and in accepting the crown of England offered by a parliament that had deposed the catholic King James II, William combined this role with that of defender of English constitutional liberties, including the protestant succession. But the European war in which he was the leading spirit was not a protestant-catholic struggle; for his allies included the Holy Roman Emperor and the Most Catholic King (that is, the king of Spain), and the pope himself, Innocent XI, was no less hostile than William to Louis XIV, who made the cause of James II his own. The war of the two kings in Ireland (1689-91) was a conflation of three issues: between William and James as the new and the deposed king of England; between the grand alliance and France; and between the protestants and the catholics of Ireland. For William it was, as Dr Simms has put it, a 'fringe event' in the European war.[c] The battle of the Boyne (1 July 1690), in which William showed exemplary courage and dash, though it was far from ending the war in Ireland, was seen in contemporary Europe as a victory not only for William but also for the grand alliance. In Ireland, where William had tried to avoid the image of a protestant partisan, the battle soon came to be commemorated by protestants as the symbol of a great deliverance. And well it might, because the outcome of the war between Ri Liam and Ri Séamus[1] was to establish protestant ascendancy more securely than ever, and to confirm protestants in the ownership of nearly all the land in Ireland. The 'glorious, pious and immortal memory of the great and good King William', who 'freed us from pope and popery, knavery and slavery, brass money and wooden shoes', was an ascendancy cult during the eighteenth century, and was even invoked by the Volunteers, the embodiment of colonial nationalism in the age of the American revolution....

At the opposite pole to orangeism and 'loyalism', modern Irish nationalism, as formulated with conspicuous literary ability and missionary ardour by Thomas Davis and the Young Ireland group in the 1840s, has its own rich mythology. Among its myths was that of an ancient Irish nation struggling for seven centuries to recover its independence from the domination of England. Young Ireland

b. M. W. Dewar, John Brown and S. E. Long, *Orangeism: A New Historical Appreciation* (Belfast: Grand Orange Lodge of Ireland, 1967), pp. 9-10.

c. J. G. Simms, 'Remembering 1690' in *Studies* (Autumn 1974), p. 231.

1. i.e. King William and King James.

dreamed of 'a nation once again', but it was in fact to be a new creation, a self-reliant, self-respecting community, in which all Irishmen, whatever their religion, class, or origin, would have their place, to live and work together in freedom for the common good. To promote such a union among Irishmen was the daunting task to which the Young Irelanders addressed themselves, as Tone and the United Irishmen had done half a century before. They failed to make any significant change in the divisions, above all the sectarian division, in Irish life, but they founded a myth, both magnanimous and misleading, that has never died out of Irish nationalism. It is crystallised in a characteristic poem of Davis's:

What matter that at different shrines
  We pray unto one God?
What matter that at different times
  Our fathers won this sod?
In fortune and in name we're bound
  By stronger links than steel;
And neither can be safe nor sound
  But in the other's weal.

And oh! it were a gallant dead
  To show before mankind,
How every race and every creed
  Might be by love combined—
Might be combined, yet not forget
  The fountains whence they rose,
As, filled by many a rivulet,
  The stately Shannon flows.[2]

But the hard historical fact is that it has mattered, and still matters, enormously in Ireland to which religion a man belongs. Davis, a protestant liberal, knew from painful experience that it mattered. But he shared a vision with both catholic and protestant friends in Young Ireland which the harsh realities of sectarian conflict have never extinguished. The Irish nation of the late eighteenth century, the nation of Grattan and Flood, of Charlemont, of Tone, the Emmets, Fitzgerald, and Henry Joy McCracken, to which Davis and his friends looked back with pride, was a protestant nation, and it had perished in the horrors of the 1798 rebellion. The Irish nation that was roused to self-consciousness by the gigantic personality of Daniel O'Connell in the 1820s was overwhelmingly a catholic nation, closely identified with the catholic church and its clergy. As the catholic church emerged out of the shadows of the penal laws to become the strongest social institution in Ireland, Irish protestants were haunted by the spectre of a catholic ascendancy replacing protestant ascendancy. They closed their divided ranks: episcopalians and presbyterians composed their differences, and joined forces in fervent support of the union and in implacable hostility to nationalism. A protestant element remained in the national movement; and in the early 1870s conservative protestants expressed their resentment against Gladstone for disestablishing the anglican church by helping to start the Home Government Association. But within a few years the broad correlation of protestants with unionists and of catholics with nationalists was reestablished, and was to be reflected in the partition of Ireland in 1920-21.

The great famine (1845-50) and the land war (1879-82) together produced a crop of strong and bitter myths. As seen by nationalists at the time and subsequently the famine was 'a fearful murder committed on the mass of the people'[d] by a heartless British government and its no less heartless adherents in Ireland, the landlords. Historical research has drawn a very different picture. The famine was too monstrous and impersonal to be the mere product of individual ill-will, or 'the fiendish outcome of a well-planned conspiracy.[e]

> Human limitations and timidity dominate the story of the great famine, but of great and deliberately imposed evil in high positions of responsibility there is little evidence. The really great evil lay in the totality of the social order which made such a famine possible, and which could tolerate, to the extent it did, the sufferings and hardships caused by the failure of the potato crops.[f]

No doubt had Ireland had a parliament of its own, government would have been more immediately responsive to the needs of the situation. Dr P. M. Austin Bourke has shown that if all the grain crop of

2. From Davis's 'Celts and Saxons', a poem written in order to depreciate Celticism and make the case that 'Irish Saxons' (i.e. the Anglo-Irish) were as Irish and national as 'Irish Celts'.

d. R. D. Edwards and T. D. Williams (eds), *The Great Famine* (Dublin, 1956), p. vii.

e. ibid., p. xiii.

f. ibid., pp. xiv-xv.

1846 had been retained in Ireland, instead of only part of it, an appreciable contribution would have been made 'to bridging the starvation gap between the destruction of the potato crop in August and the arrival of the first maize cargoes [from America] in the following winter'.[g] But it remains true that the total food deficiency resulting from the potato failure in 1846 could not have been met by prohibiting the export of grain from Ireland, even if problems of acquisition, storage, milling, and distribution could have been solved at short notice.

Michael Davitt and other leaders of the Land League saw the great famine primarily as the monstrous and inevitable outcome of an evil land system. In 1879 an agrarian crisis, the product of three years of exceptionally bad weather, crop disasters, falling prices, and rural unemployment, seemed to threaten a new catastrophe of the same kind. That this did not happen was due partly to improved economic conditions in Ireland since the famine, partly to the timely and realistic efforts of voluntary relief-organisations facilitated by government, and partly to the achievement of the Land League in organising a great popular agitation of tenant farmers and townspeople, relying on methods technically legal but revolutionary in spirit, to resist eviction and put pressure on the government to transform the land system on a basis of peasant proprietorship. Not only was actual starvation averted, evictions limited, and a new fighting spirit infused into the farmers, in dramatic contrast with their mood of resignation in the great famine, but Gladstone was convinced that only a radical change in landlord-tenant relations would restore social order. The land act that he carried through parliament in 1881 was a far-reaching victory for the farmers, enabling them to become joint owners with the landlords and preparing the way for their eventual conversion into full owner-occupiers through state-aided land purchase.

This, the greatest social revolution in modern Ireland, was associated with a mythology that has only recently begun to be examined in the cold light of history. The crisis of 1879-80 was presented by Davitt and other spokesmen of the Land League as the culmination of deep-seated evils arising out of an intolerable land system that in the famine decade had reduced Ireland's population by two millions. Landlordism was a system of legalised robbery, under which a few thousand unproductive and alien owners pocketed the lion's share of the product of 600,000 hard-working tenant farmers, the great bulk of whom paid excessive rents and, as tenants from year to year, lived under the constant shadow of the landlord's power to evict. This parasitic landlord class owed its privileged position to its historic role as the 'English garrison' in Ireland, endowed with the spoils of centuries of land-confiscation inflicted on the native Irish by the conquering English. Before this 'feudal' regime was imposed on Ireland by its conquerors the Irish knew nothing of absolute property in land, which was under 'tribal' ownership, each man having his fair share. The establishment of 'feudalism' in Ireland on the ruins of an ancient Irish social order was thus rooted in English conquest. The feudal principle had never been recognised by the moral sentiments of the Irish people, whose claim to an indefeasible interest in their holdings was therefore a claim to restitution of rights of which their ancestors had been wrongfully deprived. To replace feudal landlordism by peasant proprietorship would not only remedy a monstrous social injustice, and remove the greatest obstacle to social peace and progress in Ireland, but would prepare the way for the undoing of the English conquest itself.

One fallacy in this argument is what Dr W. E. Vaughan, a pioneer in the critical investigation of estate records of the period 1830-78, calls 'the myth of the predatory landlord'.[3] The landlords as a class were not characteristically predatory nor the tenants as a class characteristically victimised. The period between the great famine and the land war was in general marked not by worsening but by improving rural conditions, and the tenants as a whole shared more fully in the increasing profits of agriculture than did the landlords. The worst faults of the landlords appear to have been not heartlessness or heavyhandedness but rather apathy and neglect, bred by encumbrances on their estates, traditions of extravagance, and the impossibility of taking a benevolent and constructive interest in a myriad of very small holdings.

The crisis of 1879-80 was not the climax of a

g. 'The Irish Grain Trade 1839-48' in *Irish Historical Studies*, Vol. XIX, No. 78 (September 1976).

3. See W. E. Vaughan, *Landlords and Tenants in Ireland 1848-1904* (Dublin: The Economic and Social History Society of Ireland, 1984) for a summary of this thesis.

long ferment of bitterness between landlords and tenants but the product of a combination of economic difficulties peculiar to those years, which created a situation favourable to a mass demand for 'the abolition of landlordism'. There seems no evidence of any long-standing tradition among the farmers of regarding the landlords as aliens, with no moral right to their property. On the contrary, the authority most frequently invoked for this view during the land war was not Irish but was the English liberal economist, John Stuart Mill. And as to feudalism, the total absence of it from pre-conquest Ireland is a myth partly due to the publication, under the auspices of the British government, of ancient Irish law texts in translation. Popular misconceptions derived from such sources and from historical works did much to mislead the reading public about the character of early Irish society, which Mr Donnchadh Ó Corráin has shown in a recent study[4] to have strong resemblances to the general European pattern.

My final example of mythology is what may be called the 'predestinate nation' myth. This myth identifies the democratic Irish nation of the nineteenth century with pre-conquest Ireland, incorporates the concept of a seven (now an eight) centuries' struggle with England as the central theme of Irish history, and sees the achievement of independence in 1922 as the partial fulfilment of a destiny that requires the extinction of British authority in Northern Ireland to complete itself. Modern Irish history thus becomes, in the words of P. S. O'Hegarty, 'the story of a people coming out of captivity, out of underground, finding every artery of national life occupied by her enemy, recovering them one by one, and coming out at last in the full blaze of the sun'.[h]

This myth is incompatible with the history of social living in modern Ireland, which is far from being coextensive with a struggle for national independence; and nationalist politics have not generally been dominated by the idea of unending war with Britain until complete separation is achieved. Revolutionary nationalism as it established itself after the great famine, in the secret Irish Republican Brotherhood or fenian organisation, though professing to be democratic and though recruited principally from the working-class, never comprehended more than a small minority of Ireland's population. The movement had no social programme, and its whole political thinking was focused on a single object, absolute independence, to be achieved by physical force. It claimed that this was the real will of the Irish people, and that the I.R.B. was the infallible interpreter of that will. Yet the mainstream of Irish nationalism in the later nineteenth century ran in the moderate and constitutional channel of home rule, to be achieved by act of the United Kingdom parliament. In the first general election, that of 1885, to be held in Ireland under a relatively democratic franchise, the home rule party under Parnell won 85 of the 103 Irish seats in the United Kingdom parliament, and this pattern continued until the triumph of Sinn Féin in the general election of 1918. In 1886, when Gladstone committed the liberal party to the home rule cause, Parnell accepted his home rule scheme as a final settlement of the Irish question, and did so with overwhelming support from Irish nationalists in Ireland, Great Britain, America, and elsewhere. It was not till the home rule movement had been reduced to utter frustration by the failure of the British government to cope with Ulster unionist preparations to resist the home rule bill of 1912 by armed force that the majority of nationalists eventually transferred their support from the parliamentary party to revolutionary nationalism, which came to be symbolized by the Easter rising of 1916. And in the new twenty-six county state that emerged from the war of independence (1919-21), the tradition of parliamentary nationalism at once reasserted itself.

On the other hand the tradition of absolute predestinarian nationalism has been continued, and has been revived by the Provisional I.R.A. in its irredentist[5] war to abolish partition. Like the fenians, they have no doubt of their moral right to wage war, in the name of the Irish people, against Britain, though they have no popular mandate to do so and though the situation has been fundamentally changed by the existence since 1922 of an independent Irish state, to which a majority of the people of Ireland belong. Whatever the cost in

h. *A History of Ireland Under the Union* (London, 1952), p. vii.

4. Donnchadh Ó Corráin, *Ireland before the Vikings* (Dublin: Gill and Macmillan, 1972).

5. 'Irredentism' is the name given to national movements that seek to reclaim from foreign rule neighbouring areas or regions of their own nationality.

human suffering, demoralisation, and destruction, and in material damage, they see their campaign in Northern Ireland as justified by their own infallible interpretation of Ireland's past. When Britain has been forced to acknowledge Ireland's right to national self-determination and has withdrawn her army from Northern Ireland, the various elements making up the Irish people will settle their differences and establish a new, democratic, independent republic of thirty-two counties. And so Ireland's national destiny will at last be fulfilled. Perhaps the most fantastic element in the Provisionals' mythology is their theory that they are waging war not on the protestant people of Northern Ireland but only on Great Britain. It is a theory for which the ground was prepared by the myth, widely cherished in the Republic till recently, that partition was wholly the creation of Great Britain and that only a British army of occupation prevented the fraternal reunion of the six separated counties with the rest of Ireland.

There has been a recent televised debate in Northern Ireland on the theme that 'Irish history will be the death of us'. If 'history' is here used as meaning the past itself, it can well be argued that the consequences of long-standing bitterness and violence will destroy us. But if 'history' is used in its proper sense of a continuing, probing, critical search for truth about the past, my argument would be that it is not Irish history but Irish mythology that has been ruinous to us and may prove even more lethal. History is a matter of facing the facts of the Irish past, however painful some of them may be; mythology is a way or refusing to face the historical facts. The study of history not only enlarges truth about our past, but opens the mind to the reception of ever new accessions of truth. On the other hand the obsession with myths, and especially the more destructive myths, perpetuates the closed mind. Irish history is far from being wholly a history of conflict, but in so far as it is so it provides little comfort for those who today identify themselves with one side or another in the great conflicts of the past. Even the perennial Irish-English dichotomy repeatedly breaks down as a principle of interpretation, from the days of the first Anglo-Norman invaders to the last hundred years, in which British people have been almost as deeply divided over the Irish question as the people of Ireland itself. Irish history has made great and unprecedented advances during the past forty years, but the effect on the public mind appears to be disappointingly slow. The business of demythologizing is not the same thing as the revisionism of historians, but the two are connected. You cannot argue with a myth, but historians can, and do, argue with one another, and the result usually is that knowledge is extended and understanding deepened. The new historiography of Ireland has been making its impact on the teaching of history in the schools all too slowly, but there has been significant progress in both parts of Ireland. It is encouraging that the department of education in Dublin has significantly altered its notes for history teachers in the primary schools since the early days of the state, when it was firmly laid down that Irish history should be an instrument of national edification. The mental war of liberation from servitude to the myth is an endless, and it may be an agonizing, process. It is, I believe, one in which Irish historians are called on to take an active part. We are called, if I may draw from a saying of Sir Herbert Butterfield's, to 'fight against principalities and powers, but not against flesh and blood. And ours is the work of the leaven which gradually leavens the whole lump.'[i]

i. 'Tendencies in Historical Study in England' in *Irish Historical Studies*, Vol. IV, No. 15 (March 1945), p. 223. cf. Ephesians 6.12.

F. S. L. LYONS

(1923-83)

from: THE BURDEN OF OUR HISTORY (1978)

[In this lecture, delivered in Belfast in 1978, Lyons argues that the revisionist revolution in Irish historiography has not been sufficiently thorough-going, and needs to be extended from conventional political history to the more diffuse fields of economic history, social history, cultural history and the history of ideas. In so doing, he prepares the ground for his influential survey of Irish cultural development, *Culture and Anarchy in Ireland 1890-1939* (1979).]

... I shall be asking two questions, both more closely linked to our contemporary predicament than might at first appear.

One concerns the past itself, the other concerns the study of the past as we have engaged in it hitherto. The question about the past is simply this — have we in our entanglement with history locked ourselves into a hall of distorting mirrors so grotesque that we can no longer distinguish the realities of what has happened in this island from the myths we have chosen to weave about certain symbolic events? And my question about our study of the past is best expressed by rephrasing that question W. B. Yeats asked himself in old age about his early nationalist play, Cathleen ni Houlihan — 'Did that play [or book] of mine send out certain men the English shot?'[1] Or, to put it less emotively, have historians, in their preoccupation with particular themes, helped to shape modern attitudes and do they therefore incur a responsibility, beyond the responsibility which we all as individuals share, for the present condition of Ireland?...

It has always been our besetting sin, north and south, to be so obsessed by the London-Belfast-Dublin triangle as to be often incapable of measuring our internal relationships against the broad movement of history elsewhere, or of profiting from the experience of others in not always dissimilar circumstances. Membership of the E.E.C. has already begun to widen our horizons and more perhaps may be expected from this in the future.[2] But apart altogether from that enlargement, an increasing awareness that terrorism is an international phenomenon and that anti-terrorist techniques are developing as a result of international experience is not without relevance for Northern Ireland. To have been, as it were, an experimental laboratory in this operation is, God knows, no comfort for the dead and the maimed, but if in due course it leads to more effective measures against this unmitigated evil, then we may feel that to belong to the wider world may have its compensations as well as its stresses.

Yet whether the international factor works for or against us will ultimately depend upon ourselves. Essentially, as I believe, it will depend upon all of us in this island gaining a clearer view of our history and a greater understanding of the burden that history has bequeathed to us. This may seem a rather self-indulgent assertion. Do we not suffer from a surfeit of history, you may ask, and should we not forget the whole tedious, sordid story? But that evasion is not open to us or to anyone else. We are all what we have become and what we have become is what past circumstances have made of us. Nor, it must be said, is there the slightest sign among those who aspire to be responsible for our destiny that they intend to omit those past circumstances from their present calculations, so we had better be aware of them too.

There is, of course, another sense in which we may legitimately pray for deliverance — from the false history that has for too long masqueraded as the real thing. It has become fashionable recently to speak much of the contrast between myth and history and there have even been some gestures towards demythologising certain aspects of our past. There is now, for example, a more balanced view of what the battle of the Boyne was really about, the romantic nationalism of Patrick Pearse has come in for some fairly disenchanted criticism, and the Easter Rising of 1916 itself has begun to be

1. W. B. Yeats, 'The Man and the Echo' in Richard J. Finneran (ed.), *The Poems: A New Edition* (London: Macmillan, 1983), p. 345.

2. Ireland entered the European Community in January 1973.

seen in a colder and one hopes more objective light. These are welcome developments provided that they do not lead to the opposite extreme. What historians call revisionism is not only reasonable but necessary if it is done in the right way and for the right reasons. These are not subjectively arrived at by the light of the individual conscience, receiving from some private source a special infusion of grace. Revisionism is proper revisionism if it is a response to new evidence which, after being duly tested, brings us nearer to a truth independent of the wishes and aspirations of those for whom truth consists solely of what happens to coincide with those wishes and aspirations.

But why lecture us about the perils of revisionism, you may object, when we are living in the midst of what you yourself were among the first to call an historiographical revolution? Given that the study of our history is now on a far firmer professional base than ever before, may we not assume that the processes of revision and demythologising are in perfectly safe hands? Of course I agree, and speaking in the Queen's University it would be strange if I did not. For it was here some forty years ago that the modern movement in Irish history began and it was your own distinguished graduate and my beloved teacher, T. W. Moody, who was the mainspring of that movement as he has ever since remained.

All this I gladly concede, and yet ... and yet ... while agreeing that the whole subject has been marvellously transformed, I still have two serious reservations. One is that the historiographical revolution has been slow in reaching the schools. According to a survey of 1971, textbooks were still often being used in Northern Ireland which had been written thirty or forty years previously.[3] The situation, indeed, has much improved since then and there is now available a far wider range of modern, attractively produced and reasonably objective books which should in time produce a more balanced view of the past in both parts of Ireland. But I have to add that time will be much longer than it need be if different versions of Irish history continue to be taught in different kinds of schools.

My other reservation is more far-reaching. There can be no denying that for much of the past forty years the main emphasis has been upon the rewriting of Irish political history; necessarily so, because it was around politics that the myths clustered most thickly. And of course this rewriting will continue as the opening of the archives brings the more recent past within our scope. Yet this emphasis on political history has often led to serious neglect of other kinds of history. It is still the case, for example, a generation after Kenneth Connell pioneered Irish economic history in this university,[4] that the number of reputable economic historians in the whole island could be numbered on the fingers of two hands. But when we look beyond that — to social history, cultural history, the history of ideas — the poverty of what we have to offer is deeply disturbing. It is not long since Professor Estyn Evans, in his Wiles Lectures, castigated Irish historians *en masse* for their neglect, not only of these matters, but of the physical environment within which our past has been lived. 'It has been my contention,' he said, '... that historical studies would be enriched if they paid more attention to habitat and heritage and that closer co-operation with geography and anthropology would be fruitful.... To the specialist in the history of restricted periods it may well appear that the most powerful forces in history are individual personality and free will.' 'On the larger view,' he added, 'I believe that the personality of society is a powerful motive force and that it finds expression in the cultural landscape.'[5]

Unfortunately, the case is much worse than Professor Evans imagined. Not only have historians too often disregarded the physical evidence around them, they have not even fully explored their literary evidence to give us a rounded view of our society. I do not want to overstate the case, for research is now going forward on a much wider front than formerly, but many years of specialisation are required before a more general public will get the books it so urgently needs. That is why, if for a moment we take a restricted view of cultural history as the history of the arts, we still have no comprehensive works on any major art with the

3. See, for example, Lorna Hadkins, 'Textbooks', *Community Forum*, 1/1, 1971. See also John Magee, *The Teaching of Irish History in Irish Schools* (Belfast: Irish National Teachers' Organisation, 1970).

4. K. H. Connell's *The Population of Ireland 1756-1845* (Oxford: Oxford University Press, 1950) was a pioneering study in Irish demographic and economic history.

5. Estyn Evans, *The Personality of Ireland: Habitat, Heritage and History* (Belfast: Blackstaff Press, 1981), pp. 87-88.

possible exception of architecture. Even in literature, though it attracts a great deal of attention, there is no adequate historical survey of Irish writing. But perhaps that is not really so surprising, since we apparently can't agree on what Irish literature consists of, or in what language it should be written. Nor is this all. If we broaden our definition of culture, as we surely must, to include the whole mode of life of a community, we shall find, with some honourable exceptions, that our histories do not tell us much about many things which make up such a mode of life. And these deficiencies are equally glaring, whether we are thinking about day-to-day details of existence, or about patterns of belief, or about intellectual influences, both internal and external.

In short, though our days are filled with the actualities of communal strife, how much do we really know, in historical terms, about how a community evolves and how it interacts with, or reacts against, another community? Oh, we know about community politics all right, we know about parties and elections, about caucuses and manifestoes, and the rest of the democratic or pseudo-democratic paraphernalia. But about the essence of a community we know, I repeat, all too little outside our immediate, personal and highly fallible experience. And to cross the barriers imaginatively between one community and another is given as yet only to that small compassionate minority of whom Brian Rankin[6] was one of the foremost in our day.

If I seem vehement in this matter, it is not that I want to belittle the valuable work already done, especially in this university and particularly in its Institute of Irish Studies, though even that has to be measured against the vast amount that has still to be achieved. Nor do I wish to take a pharisee's view of my fellow-historians. I, too, have been seduced by political history, only to find when I moved on to other fields that the foundations were often lacking and that significant generalisation was virtually impossible. But this, you may say, is for the historians to settle among themselves. Let them get on with their history of culture and not bother us until they have something to show for their labours. Fair enough, I reply, if it were only a problem for the historians. That, however, is just what it is not. For the fact that historians are inarticulate about the different cultures which collide with each other in this island is merely a symptom of a more profound ignorance which runs right through our society and is exhibited *in excelsis* on the other side of the Irish Sea.

This leads me straight to the main thrust of my argument, which is about what I shall call the disconnection in our history between politics and culture. Whether one looks at the nineteenth century arguments about Home Rule, or at the twentieth century arguments about devolution or about republicanism, the crucial questions have tended to be posed primarily in political terms. Will there be self-government for the whole of Ireland? Once partitioned, will Ireland be reunited and if so, how and when? What should be the relations of Dublin and Belfast with each other and of both with London? So the questions go on and on, and the political solutions, which are in fact no solutions, go round and round in a vacuum that seems increasingly unreal. Why is the unreal vacuum there? Why do the questions and the answers seem in the end so inane? Very largely, in my view, because over the last hundred years few people have tried to relate political solutions to cultural realities. Here in Northern Ireland, under the pressure of horrendous events, you have begun to come to terms with this problem. Indeed, a longer perspective than any we can envisage now may yet reveal that out of all the suffering of the past decade has come a far more sympathetic response to the sensitivities of the different cultures than was evident before the troubles began, or has been evident in the south at any time....

6. 'The Burden of Our History' was delivered as part of the Brian Rankin Memorial Lectures at Queen's University, Belfast in 1978. Brian Rankin (1915-76) was official solicitor to the Supreme Court of the Judicature of Northern Ireland, and played a prominent part in public life in Northern Ireland, particularly in community relations and human rights.

ROY FOSTER

(1949-)

from:
THE IRISH REVIEW (1986)

[In this astringent polemic against the detractors of revisionism, Roy Foster seeks to rebut the charge that revisionism is an ideological endorsement of British rule in Ireland. He reserves his harshest criticisms for those who persist in depicting Anglo-Irish relations in black and white, although it is not always clear that Irish nationalists have a monopoly on this 'Manichean logic'. The extent to which revisionism has become the new orthodoxy is clear from the title and final sentence of his article, and raises the interesting possibility that, according to its own dictates, revisionism itself may now stand in need of revision.

The article was published in *The Irish Review*, No. 1 (1986).]

WE ARE ALL REVISIONISTS NOW

The last generation to learn Irish history only from the old nationalist textbooks will soon be middle-aged men and women; most of the pioneers of the 'new' history in university teaching and research have died, deservedly full of years and honours. For the last twenty years, academic audiences settling down before a historical lecture have muttered wearily to each other 'Oh god, not *more* revisionism'. Scholars have learned to appreciate half-tones, to be sceptical about imputing praise or blame, to separate contemporary intentions from historical effects. By exploring nineteenth- and twentieth-century Irish politics in all their density, sophistication and ramifications, scholars like David Fitzpatrick and Theo Hoppen have made it impossible to interpret Irish history in the rousing terms of P. S. O'Hegarty: 'the story of a people coming out of captivity'.[1] It is occasionally tempting to feel that something has been lost as well as gained; to miss the compelling Manichean logic of the old 'Story of Ireland' view,[2] with a beginning, a middle and what appeared (up to about 1968) to be a triumphant end. But this dangerous nostalgia makes it all the more necessary to look at the state of affairs now.

Those outside the profession are always telling historians that impartiality is a myth, and 'history' is a construct formed by the times in which it is written. More yawns from the historians; this insight is nothing new, and the proliferation of 'historiography' courses on university syllabuses shows that they are almost too conscious of it. The swift progress of 'revisionism' in Irish academe demonstrates it yet again. Twenty years ago, Father Francis Shaw's swingeing exposé of lacunae in Pearse's ideology was seen as too hot for *Studies* to handle (it was nervously let out of the bag after his death six years later); but nowadays the most robust scepticism about the pieties of Irish nationalism can issue forth from a historian who teaches in Maynooth:

> The creators and custodians of mainstream Irish mythology have succeeded over a period of generations in blurring a salient fact about Irish nationalism, namely, that since the early nineteenth century at least it has been essentially an expression of the felt needs, social and psychological, of the Irish Catholic body, including their apparent need to challenge other Christians on the island in various ways (R. V. Comerford, *The Fenians in Context* (Dublin, 1984), p. 30).

This bracing wind has blown through the schools, in the Republic at least. At the point when old moulds were being broken in terms of Unionist dominance up north, the straitjacket of historiographical piety was loosened in the south. And over the intervening years, commentary on the part played by myth in Irish history has become as

1. See David Fitzpatrick, *The Politics of Irish Life 1913-21* (Dublin: Gill and Macmillan, 1977); K. Theodore Hoppen, *Elections, Politics and Society in Ireland 1832-1885* (Oxford: Oxford University Press, 1984). O'Hegarty's statement is taken from a standard nationalist history of the period: *A History of Ireland Under the Union 1801 to 1922* (London: Methuen, 1952), p. vii.

2. Manichean logic, based on an early Christian heresy, taught that the cosmos was a site of struggle between the conflicting powers of Good and Evil, with no middle ground. *The Story of Ireland* (Dublin, 1867) was the name of perhaps the most influential popular nationalist history. It was written by A. M. Sullivan (1830-84), assistant editor of *The Nation* newspaper.

profuse as research into actual historical problems.

To wonder why this process has not had a more obvious effect on public opinion is legitimate; but the question demands one or two clarifications. What, after all, *is* historical 'revisionism'? To the scholars, it is quite simply a desire to eliminate as much as possible of the retrospectively 'Whig' view of history which sees every event and process in the light of what followed it rather than what went before: the effort to get behind hindsight.[3] Along the way, many simple assumptons need to be questioned. The thinking behind the Act of Union, or the relief measures in the first years of the Famine, or the concept of Home Rule, are more profitably interpreted in terms of what people knew or assumed at the time, rather than what we know (or assume) to have happened subsequently. Culpability may still be apportioned, for those with an Actonian desire to hand down judgment; but it will necessarily be tempered. On another level, the shift in the use of economic 'evidence', preferring statistical reconstruction to contemporary impressions, has enforced a reconsideration of how policy-making related to actual economic effects. As D. P. Moran — of all people — remarked long ago, there is a great deal of nonsense in whining about 'how England stole our woollen industries some hundreds of years ago'.[4] To blame every unwelcome development in Irish history on British malevolence, disallowing economic, social and political forces within Ireland, is an attractively easy option; it also implies an Irish moral superiority which leads too easily to self-righteous whingeing.

To oppose this view of historical study, however, is not the same thing as an endorsement of British influence in Ireland; it is merely adopting a different focus. Anyone who knows a few Irish historians will have realised that 'revisionism' in scholarship is perfectly compatible with 'nationalism' in politics. It may seem odd that the point needs making. But the trouble is that 'revisionist' has come to be used as a smear-word for those supposedly unsound on the national question. Thus in his introduction to *The Faber Book of Political Verse*, Tom Paulin identifies 'the revisionist school of Irish history' as 'a school hostile to Irish nationalism'.[5] But revisionist historians are not a 'school', nor are they 'hostile to Irish nationalism' (or not necessarily). The term has become so abused that, as Ronan Fanning has recently and trenchantly said, it may as well be abandoned — having simply turned into 'a term of abuse for defenders of the republican ideological commitment to physical force to use about those nationalists who seek to undermine that tradition.... It carries, and is intended to carry, pejorative connotations which are designed to erode his professional authority in the popular mind' ('The great enchantment: uses and abuses of modern Irish history' in James Dooge (ed.), *Ireland in the contemporary world: essays in honour of Garret FitzGerald* (Dublin, 1986), p. 143). The notion should be thankfully abandoned that historians need to apologise for querying 'truths' that are by no means self-evident.

But such intellectual latitude is still unallowed in some circles; and it is often unacceptable outside Ireland. The slightly *blasé* and sceptical way in which many Irish people view the institutionalized pieties of Irish history is not echoed in Irish communities abroad; nor does it appear in influential popular histories written by zealous converts like Cecil Woodham-Smith.[6] A desire to expiate what are seen as past sins, and a genuine surprise at the appalling record of much of British government in Ireland, is understandable; it is probably good for the English soul; but it must be questioned whether it gets us any nearer understanding. Innocent and sometimes naively hilarious works of piety about the Fenians or Young Irelanders, written by amateur historians on the British left, fall into a much cruder category. They are joined by the half-baked 'sociologists' employed on profitably never-ending research into 'anti-Irish racism', determined to prove what they have already decided to be the case.[7] Historians like Sheridan Gilley may have scrupulously and sympathetically explored the definitions of historical 'racism' and rejected

3. See Herbert Butterfield, *The Whig Interpretation of History* (London: Bell, 1931). Lord Acton (1834-1902), professor of modern history at Cambridge, formulated the principles of the Whig interpretation of history in his *Lectures on Modern History* (1906).
4. D. P. Moran, *The Philosophy of Ireland* (Dublin: James Duffy & Co., 1904), pp. 2, 99.
5. Tom Paulin (ed.), *The Faber Book of Political Verse* (London: Faber and Faber, 1985).
6. Cecil Woodham-Smith, *The Great Hunger: Ireland 1845-9* (London: Hamish Hamilton, 1962).
7. The reference here, presumably, is to works such as Liz Curtis, *Nothing But the Same Old Story* (London: Information on Ireland Publications, 1984), a popular expositon of English racist attitudes to Ireland.

them for the Irish case,[8] but this matters to such zealots as little as the fact that the 'Great Starvation' as a synonym for the Famine is a concept long exploded by economic historians.

They can, of course, dismiss those historians as an elite of collaborators, which saves having to read them. The abrasive queries of Raymond Crotty, Joseph Lee, Vincent Comerford or Paul Bew carry little resonance in Camden Town — where one is told that the only work of 'real history' to have come out of Ireland is Gerry Adams's *Falls Memories*,[9] and where any discussion of the (largely unknown and unwritten) history of 1916-1922 will be deflected into sentimental reminiscences of 'the songs we sang in my auntie's front room'. It is from this side of the water too that the most violent vituperation was heaped on Michael Laffan and other distinguished Irish academics for their annoyance when a series of lectures they had been engaged to give was christened, as a *fait accompli*, in memory of a republican martyr.[10] Perhaps the most hysterical attack was launched by an incoherent 'scholar on the subject of conflict and revolution' from the University of Toledo, Ohio, who — after referring intriguingly to 'the *obscene* socio-economic status of nationalists in the Six Counties' — issued an open invitation to Laffan and his UCD colleagues. 'When you've finished rewriting Irish history you can start on the rest of the world. You then may use your limited literary skills to convince us that Dachau, Hiroshima, My Lai, Sharpeville, Shattila and Selma, Alabama, were not so bad either.'

'Revisionists!' In Toledo and London, growing up, working and living in Ireland are apparently considered disqualifications for thinking about Irish history; distance, especially transatlantic distance, lends a storybook enchantment to the historical view. The late F. S. L. Lyons, doyen of modern Irish historians, was once told by a friend that his *Ireland since the Famine* was written with a bias in favour of 'sentimental nationalism'; to which he replied 'Yes, but you must remember I was living in England then.'

Thus, connoisseurs of crossed lines may enjoy social incidents like the agonised irritation of the Irish Ambassador to Great Britain when addressed by the Director of a London polytechnic on the assumption that he is a fellow Troops Out fanatic. On another level, there is innocent diversion to be had in observing the various attempts to square old-fashioned Marxism and nationalism (often rechristened 'anti-imperialism' for the purpose). These usually end up by implying that capitalism in Ireland is British and that Irish capitalists are somehow *de facto* British too (a variant of the old Corkery idea that Catholic and Gaelic were morally congruent with 'Irish'). The logical result of this argument is to Anglicise, not only William Martin Murphy,[11] but also the majority of the post-Famine farming classes. Meanwhile, the intellectual Left in Ireland have long deserted these unprofitable pastures and are browsing among the more congenial theories of Gramsci. But to expatriate commentators on Irish history, 'oppression' is a far easier concept than 'hegemony'.[12]

Yet back home in Irish academe the old battles are so long forgotten that those once called 'revisionists' are now being themselves revised (*quis revidebit ipsos revisores?*). Thanks to the work of Crotty and others, it is now axiomatic that the

8. Sheridan Gilley, 'English Attitudes to the Irish in England 1789-1900', in C. Holmes (ed.), *Immigrants and Minorities in British Society* (London: Croom Helm, 1978). Gilley's article is a valuable corrective to overschematic accounts of English radical prejudice against the Irish, but is hampered by an assumption that racial stereotyping necessarily entails hostility and repulsion: 'benevolent' stereotypes that depicted 'the imaginative Celt' as *complementary* to Anglo-Saxon rationality served colonial domination far more effectively than crude forms of debasement, since they justified the continuation of 'the Union' between Britain and Ireland. Gilley's argument that British concepts of race did not always entail biological exclusivism, however, could be usefully applied to the Irish context by those revisionist critics who are disposed to equate Irish nationalists' use of the term 'race' with proto-fascist sentiments.
9. Raymond Crotty, *Ireland in Crisis: A Study in Colonial Development* (Dingle: Brandon Books, 1986); Joseph Lee, *The Modernization of Irish Society* (Dublin: Gill and Macmillan, 1973); Vincent Comerford *The Fenians in Context* (Dublin: Wolfhound Press, 1985); Paul Bew, *Land and the National Question in Ireland 1858-82* (Dublin: Gill and Macmillan, 1978). Gerry Adams, *Falls Memories* (Dingle: Brandon Books, 1982) is a book of reminiscences by the president of Sinn Féin.
10. In 1985, the historian Michael Laffan and a number of others withdrew from a series of lectures in London arranged for early the following year, when it was revealed that the lecture series would be named after Terence MacSwiney (1879-1920), the republican Lord Mayor of Cork who died on hunger strike.
11. William Martin Murphy (1844-1919), one of the most successful Irish capitalists at the turn of the century, led the 1913 lock-out against the Irish Transport and General Workers' Union. He was the founder of *The Irish Catholic* newspaper. His highly conservative version of catholic nationalism has yet to attract revisionist scrutiny.
12. The Italian Marxist Antonio Gramsci (1891-1937) developed the concept of 'hegemony' to explain how class rule and social control could continue in Western societies under the guise of 'consensus politics' rather than through state coercion. The achievement of an internal parliamentary consensus as a means of resolving the Northern conflict could, on Gramscian terms, constitute a more effective, because more 'invisible', form of British rule.

Famine did not begin the processes of decline in population growth, consolidation of farms, and the shift to grazing; with the aid of econometrics, the case has even been advanced that overpopulation and subsistence farming were not the causes of poverty in the pre-Famine age. But there has been something of a tendency to throw the baby out with the bathwater, in claiming that the Famine was not a turning point at all; and the result is that the latest work tends to come back to the old question of the shortcomings of British government policy. Having elucidated at least some of the economic complexities, we may return to the basic question of 'why Ireland starved' (the title of a major study of Joel Mokyr).[13] Similarly, it has long been accepted, since the path-breaking work of Maureen Wall,[14] that the eighteenth-century Penal Laws against Catholics were primarily intended as a campaign against the possession of landed and political power; when that had succeeded, the establishment was happy to let Catholics carry on their religion. But recent work by Sean Connolly, in interpreting the rationale of the Laws as a proselytising offensive, restores a religious motivation to the centre of the picture once more.[15] The best history arouses argument without end; and Ireland has for decades produced an almost embarrassing quantity of the very best historians.

13. Joel Mokyr, *Why Ireland Starved* (London: Allen and Unwin, 1983).
14. Maureen Wall, *The Penal Laws 1691-1760* (Dublin: Dublin Historical Association, 1961).
15. S. J. Connolly, 'Religion and History', *Irish Economic and Social History*, Vol. X (1983).

But whether they speak loudly enough to those outside the profession is another matter. The judicious reassessments of the vast volumes of the *New History of Ireland*[16] barely penetrate to the popular audience; still less do the pioneering monographs from the university presses, or the articles in *Irish Economic and Social History*. Efforts have been made to serve up the new history in palatable form, like the attractive pamphlets published by the Economic and Social History Society in Ireland. But as regards political history, the old pieties have it their own way and historians tread carefully for fear of the 'anti-nationalist' smear. Irish cultural self-confidence should surely have reached the stage where this can be questioned. Need 'nationalism', defined as a commitment to Irishness, presuppose obsessive Anglophobia and a dedication to the mentality of the conspiracy theory? A historical habit of mind has been the mark of the Irish since such things began to be noticed; this establishes a ready-made audience for Irish historians, but at the same time ensures that the audience will be *parti pris*.[17] The sceptical strengths of the Irish mind should be capable of taking this on, and questioning everything that needs questioning. In a country that has come of age, history need no longer be a matter of guarding sacred mysteries. And to say 'revisionist' should just be another way of saying 'historian'.

16. *A New History of Ireland* (Oxford: Oxford University Press), under the general editorship of T. W. Moody, F. X. Martin and F. J. Byrne, commenced publication in 1976.
17. i.e. that the audience will have preconceived views.

DESMOND FENNELL

(1929-)

from: THE IRISH REVIEW (1988)

[In this riposte to revisionism, Desmond Fennell challenges the view that revisionism consists in establishing 'the facts' behind various nationalist myths, and argues that its intellectual force derives from its being a new moral interpretation of the facts — or in Roy Foster's words, 'merely adopting a different focus'. Unlike Foster, however, Fennell aligns revisionism to a process of foreign cultural domination, centring on the Anglo-American axis. Significantly, he does not contest the revisionist image of nationalism as a closed, continuous, hero-worshipping tradition: he simply disagrees with the negative evaluation of this tradition.

The article was published in *The Irish Review*, No. 4 (1988) and subsequently formed the second chapter of the author's *The Revision of Irish Nationalism* (1989).]

AGAINST REVISIONISM

... What is the popular image of historical revisionism in Ireland today? A retelling of Irish history which seeks to show that British rule of Ireland was not, as we have believed, a *bad* thing, but a mixture of necessity, good intentions and bungling; and that Irish resistance to it was not, as we have believed, a *good* thing, but a mixture of wrong-headed idealism and unnecessary, often cruel, violence. The underlying message is that in our relations with Britain on the Irish question we Irish have been very much at fault. This is the popular image of historical revisionism, but it will be evident, when I quote you a passage from the mild revisionist — mild at the time at least — F. S. L. Lyons, that it is not far from the reality.... In a radio lecture in 1971 Professor Lyons said:

> In the present situation, with the dire past still overhanging the dire present, the need to go back to fundamentals, and consider once more the meaning of independence, asserts itself with almost intolerable urgency. The theories of revolution, the theories of nationality, the theories of history, which have brought Ireland to its present pass, cry out for re-examination, and the time is ripe to break with the great enchantment which for too long has made myth so much more congenial than reality.[1]

Leave aside that political call 'to break with the great enchantment' meaning presumably the Irish revolution's dream of a prosperous independent Ireland and a recreated Irish mind and culture. That dream of becoming a normal European nation had, in Lyons' view, addled our minds and rationality. Note, rather, his theory of historical causation, his moralising interpretation of cause and effect in recent Irish history. Ireland has been brought to its present pass (that is, the violent chaos in Northern Ireland and its spillovers), not by Britain's conniving with the Ulster unionist rebellion of 1912 and ignoring the will of most of the people of Ireland, but particularly of the nationalist Irish in the Six Counties; nor by the scandalous 50 years of British rule in Northern Ireland; nor again by the continuing refusal of Britain, even in 1971, to recognise the Irish nation and its rights there. No, we are told, Ireland had been brought to its present pass in the North by theories of revolution, of nationality, and of history, which we Irish had entertained and must now reexamine; the present dire situation had been caused, in other words, by *ourselves*, by the ideas and convictions inspiring our freedom struggle, by our nationalism. The cause of the present evil was not the wrong mind and action of British imperialist nationalism, but the wrong ideas and action of our liberationist nationalism.

This example of historical revisionism illustrates its key features well. It is not, primarily, the presentation of new facts, nor again, as some revisionists would have us believe, the refutation of factually false historical 'myths'. Primarily, it is a *new moral interpretation* of the known major facts, and the general course of events, especially in the last century and a half — with the help occasionally of new minor facts, or a new treatment of already known minor facts. More precisely, it is a new allocation, with regard to the known major facts and the general course of events, or *rightness* and *wrongness*, as between the ideas and actions of the Irish and the intentions and actions of the British (or Ulster British). The net tendency of this reallocation is a threefold discrediting. It tends to discredit, in the first instance, the basic, motivating tenet of historical Irish nationalism, namely that British rule of Ireland (or of part of it) was — regardless of exonerating factors — morally wrong, and that the Irish resistance to it was — regardless of blemishes — morally right; in the second instance, and thereby, the Irish nationalist tradition, and particularly what was by European and world standards its *genuinely* nationalist wing, the republican tradition ('genuinely' nationalist because it sought a nation-state rather than regional self-government); and finally, then, the main achievement of that republican nationalist tradition, the Irish revolution. Revisionism, both in its ultimate thrust, and as a matter of objective fact, is the historiography of the Irish counter-revolution.

I am suggesting, in other words, that it is untrue to regard it simply as a rewriting of history in reaction to the events in Northern Ireland after 1969, and with the aim of depriving the republican rebellion there of moral legitimacy. In the Republic, from the early 60s onwards, with British,

1. F. S. L. Lyons, 'The Meaning of Independence' in Brian Farrell (ed.), *The Irish Parliamentary Tradition* (Dublin: Gill and Macmillan, 1973), p. 223.

American and German capital providing the wealth which Sinn Féin economics had failed to provide, and the rise to power in Dublin of a new elite of businessmen, bureaucrats, media people and politicians who adopted swinging London as their cultural and moral lodestar, a journalistic campaign got underway against everything which de Valera and his era stood for, from the Constitution back to and including 1916. This reflected and expressed the new elite's scepticism about the value of the revolution and of the Irish nation-state itself, and its growing hostility to both of them. When, accordingly, in 1970-71, the Irish Government, faced with open warfare in the North, decided to treat, not Britain, but the IRA as the malign factor, this Dublin counter-revolutionary movement saw its opportunity and seized it. By fomenting revulsion against the republican rebellion, and representing it, simultaneously, as the outcome of the nationalist ideology which had inspired the revolution and was incarnate in the Republic, it persuaded many and confused many more. It was at this stage, and objectively therefore as servants of the counter-revolution, that some professional historians, within the universities and outside them, began to formalise what had existed previously largely in journalism and chat-shows.[2]

When I said earlier that I was opposed to revisionism, I was exaggerating somewhat. I am not opposed to the *writing* of such history, as I am not opposed to the writing of any kind of history, if its factual narrative is substantially true, and its interpretation, moral or otherwise, clearly argued. But I reject the pretension of revisionist history to be a value for the nation. I oppose its recommending itself, or its being accepted, as the proper or true history of modern Ireland. First, because I believe that its moral interpretation is not correct; second, because such history does not serve the wellbeing of the nation. The first of those reasons is, by its nature, open to debate — I have stated my position, which, as it happens, accords with that of the world in general with regard to Irish-British relations up to and beyond the revolution. My second reason, however, is not debatable.

Every nation in its here and now, the people who make up the nation now, have needs with respect to their national history. They need for their collective wellbeing an image of their national past which sustains and energises them personally, and which bonds them together by making their inherited nation seem a value worth adhering to and working for. (Of course, for their national wellbeing, they need to have this complemented by a similarly fortifying image of the present; but my point is that they need in the first place that kind of image from their history.) The modern Irish nation — the new Irish nation formed from the late eighteenth century onwards — was provided with such a history by scholars whose aim was, often explicitly, to supply it with such a history in place of the nationally useless and undermining histories (or pseudo-histories) of Ireland written by Englishmen. And this new Irish nation would not have [been] formed, and made the very notable mark which it did make on the world, without that history-writing.

The kind of history-writing and history-telling which sustains, energises and bonds a nation, and thus serves its wellbeing, can be briefly described. It shows the nation, in its past, involved in a continuous or near-continuous pattern of meaning[3] in which the nation, represented by its state (if it had one), and/or by great men, women and movements, brave soldiers, righteous civilian insurgents perhaps, was always, in some sense, right-minded and right-acting, and occasionally morally splendid. (I say 'in some sense', for the designated mode of right-mindedness and right action varies from nation to nation and, often enough, between an earlier and later period of a national history.) Within that general framework of meaning and moral interpretation, historians of successive generations, or of the same one, differ; revision succeeds revision, new facts are integrated, perspectives changed, images of outstanding historical figures or movements transformed. Many particular moral interpretations alter. Factual truth is pursued scrupulously — and the more factually true the history, the better for the nation. But always, in the end, if the history is to serve the nation's wellbeing, the framework of meaning and

2. This argument is developed in greater detail in Fennell's *The State of the Nation: Ireland since the Sixties* (Dublin: Ward River Press, 1983), chapters 1 and 2.

3. Compare this emphasis on continuity with the acknowledgement of the fragmented nature of Irish cultural traditions by nationalists such as George Sigerson and Thomas MacDonagh, who saw in discontinuity a dynamic form of cultural change, often incorporating external or even colonial influences.

of moral interpretation which I have sketched above are maintained and renewed.

Obviously, I am talking about a science of history which is also an art: an art like that of those composers or musicians who, in successive generations, with meticulous dedication, and each differently than [*sic*] his contemporaries, rearrange, or make striking variations on, an old tune or song. But this art comes easily, and without betrayal of self, but rather with affirmation and satisfaction of self, to those historians whose passion for factual truth, and for conscientious moral judgment, is equalled by their piety for their nation's pattern of historical meaning, and their regard for what their fellowcountrymen, and they themselves, need from their national history for their minds and hearts — being, as they are, ineluctably, English, Irish, French or Egyptian human beings.

Mark well, I am not saying that historians *must* have this disposition, and *must* practise this art of reconciling their concern for factual truth and correct moral judgment with the pattern of meaning and moral interpretation which their predecessors and the people, working together, have established. I am saying simply that historians so disposed, who practise this art, contribute to the wellbeing of the nation, and that those not so disposed, and who therefore do not practise this art, do not. Fortunate the nation whose historians are mainly of the former kind, unfortunate the nation in which historians of the latter kind predominate.

The Irish nation, as it moved into the 1960s and 70s, possessed an established framework of historical meaning and moral interpretation. Its continuous pattern of meaning from the eighteenth century onwards — the only thread of *national political* expression running through this period — was its liberationist nationalism. This, along with its poverty and its Catholicism, had given Ireland its character in the world. In the eyes of the great majority of people, South and North, it was this historic nationalism which had brought the nation to where it was and which pointed towards its future political completion. Two main strands ran through it up to the Treaty of 1921: nation-state or republican nationalism, which organised for armed insurrection, and a nationalism of less than that — Repeal, Home Rule — which we can call devolution nationalism, and which pursued parliamentary methods. Both strands were motivated by the same objective conditions of the nation, and the same moral convictions about the wrongness of English rule and the right of Ireland to freedom — though they defined 'freedom' differently. The two strands bickered; they also intermingled and overlapped, in sentiment and song and literary sustenance. They joined in Parnell's New Departure,[4] commemorated the '98 Rising together, and, after 1916, fought electorally for the nation's soul. Out of the victory of republicanism came a revolutionary combination of parliamentary and physical force methods which led to the establishment of the Irish nation-state; and in that state, under the aegis of mainstream republican nationalism, parliamentary democracy triumphed and endured, and diehard republicanism was outlawed.

That was the pattern of meaning leading from the past to the present which most Irish people saw, vaguely or clearly, in their history. In that continuous pattern they saw the nation, represented by great men, women and movements, righteous insurgents, and brave soldiers, inspired by right ideas and acting rightly. They saw this with pride. They cherished songs, poems and other writings emanating from this inheritance, and they revered countless places, buildings and relics which it had imbued with value. The revisionist historians, instead of maintaining this framework of meaning, moral interpretation, and anchored value, and renewing it through industrious and creative revision, set about demolishing it. Their articles, books, radio talks and speeches represented the Irish nationalist tradition, and in particular its revolution, as radically flawed by wrong ideas and wrong action, to such a degree as to make it something we should be ashamed of. 'Forget,' they told the Irish and the world of Africa, Asia and beyond, 'that you saw in the Irish revolution one of the great liberating landmarks of this century, and treasured the names of MacSwiney[5] and de Valera. It was all a mistake, a huge blunder, something we should not have done, or at least not that way.' In short, the revisionists provided a history which, far from

4. 'The New Departure' was the name for the coalition of Fenians and parliamentarians, Land League activists, priests, peasants and farmers during the Land War (1879-82). The name was first proposed by John Devoy, the American-based Fenian leader, in 1878.

5. Terence MacSwiney (1879-1920), Lord Mayor of Cork, died in August 1920 after being on hunger strike for seventy-four days. His was the first republican hunger strike to gain wide international attention.

sustaining, energising and bonding the nation, tended to cripple, disintegrate and paralyse it. It was as if a counter-revolution, come to power in Moscow, should rewrite Russian history so as to denigrate the October revolution, all that led to it, and all that flowed from it. Just as such a history would not serve the wellbeing of the Russian nation, so this Irish revisionist history has not served the wellbeing of the Irish nation, but has served and promoted its illbeing, and the illbeing of its nation-state, which we are all experiencing and which many of our educated young people are fleeing from in disgust.

The best defence of their history-writing which the revisionists can offer is that its moral judgments of historical Irish nationalism are correct, and that, in the exceptional circumstances of recent years, history-writing could best serve the nation and the state by undermining the moral legitimacy which the Northern rebels against British rule might draw, or seem to draw, from history. But this is an absurd argument; for, leaving aside whether the revisionists' historical moral judgments are correct, it says, in effect, that a history (theirs, namely) which undermines the moral legitimacy of the national revolution, and of the state which emerged from it, is at present the best way history can serve the national interest! Quite apart from its intrinsic absurdity, however, such a defence raises many questions. Questions about the revisionists' common sense and knowledge. Do they really imagine that the IRA in the North sit cowering in their burrows and trenches fearful of some new blast of revisionist history from UCD?[6] Are they not aware that the principal motivation of these Irish men and women is drawn, not from history, but from the national and social circumstances in which they live — and that their rebellion could have been ended long ago simply by changing *those*? Questions about moral legitimacy. Is it morally legitimate for Irishmen who are living in freedom to try to undermine the rebellion of Irishmen and women who are not? Was it, in the 70s, morally legitimate to try to undermine a rebellion which, in the 80s, has led to an Anglo-Irish Agreement that some revisionists, like most people, regard as a good thing? Is it morally legitimate for historians to use history-writing for dabbling, amateurishly, in contemporary politics, and that at the cost of offering their nation a meaningless and disabling past, such as English historians, hostile to Ireland, once offered it?

There, I believe, lies the nub of the matter.

6. University College, Dublin. Fennell's article was a response to an elaboration of revisionism by the UCD historian Ronan Fanning, 'The Meaning of Revisionism', in the same issue of *The Irish Review*.

II. ASPECTS OF REVISIONISM

FATHER FRANCIS SHAW

(1908-70)

from: STUDIES (1972)

[In this controversial article, written in 1966 for the fiftieth anniversary of the Easter Rising, but withheld from publication until 1972, when it was published in the summer number of *Studies* (Vol. LXI), Father Francis Shaw attempted to dispel the aura that surrounded the figure of Patrick Pearse in modern nationalism. To understand the force of Father Shaw's polemic, it is necessary to recall that the devotion to Pearse was such that the most comprehensive biography of him written up to then, by Louis Le Roux in 1932, ended with an earnest plea for his canonization. It was this blend of catholicism and nationalism that Father Shaw deemed sacrilegious, and he traced the mystical strain in militant nationalism back to Pearse's own writings. Father Shaw did not object to the fusion of catholicism and nationalism as such, but only to those occasions on which nationalists gained the upper hand, appropriating religious imagery for their own ends. Similarly, the cult of violence itself did not repel him, as is clear from his endorsement of those nationalists who joined the British forces in World War I. His objection was to the glorification of violence in religious terms.]

THE CANON OF IRISH HISTORY — A CHALLENGE

... One of the commonest occupations in the Ireland of today is the plying of sleeping dogs with tranquillizers. In this study of the Easter Rising in relation to Irish history an accepted view is challenged, a canon of history which has come into being, has been carefully fostered and was newly consecrated in the massive State-inspired and State-assisted Commemoration in 1966. The final seal on the Easter Rising is to be seen today on the walls of our schools in which the proclamation of Easter Monday is presented as the charter of our freedom and of our State.[1]

The canon of history of which I speak stamps the generation of 1916 as nationally degenerate, a generation in need of redemption by the shedding of blood. It honours one group of Irishmen by denying honour to others whose merit is not less. In effect it teaches that only the Fenians and the separatists had the good of their country at heart, that all others were either deluded or in one degree or another sold to the enemy. This canon moulds the broad course of Irish history to a narrow preconceived pattern; it tells a story which is false and without foundation. It asks us to praise in others what we do not esteem or accept in ourselves. It condemns as being anti-Irish all who did not profess extremist nationalist doctrine, though it never explains how it is possible to be judged to be against your own people when the views you hold are those which they overwhelmingly support. This canon is more concerned with the labels and trappings of national politics than with the substance which wisely-used political action can bring. It sets more store on [*sic*] what people profess themselves to be than on what they are.

It is urged here that Irishmen of today owe it to their fathers and grandfathers to think again before accepting a facile judgment which charges a whole people with national apostasy. Pearse may have been entitled to judge as he did because he took his stand on the infallible teaching of Wolfe Tone, but those who do not admit Pearse's premisses should not endorse his conclusion. Further, Irishmen of today owe it to many generations of their countrymen to reject the myth in accordance with which the Rising of 1916 was, as it were, the beginning and the end of Ireland's struggle for freedom. And those who will allow no credit for any achievement to the constitutionalists, but who insist that every good that was achieved was won by force of arms, are inclined to overlook the inconvenient truth that militarily the Rising was a complete failure, that all the arms and ammunition of the Volunteers throughout the whole country, which had been obtained with such difficulty, were handed over to the British authorities, and that when the fighting started again it had militarily to start from scratch.

In the commonly accepted view of Irish history the Irishman of today is asked to disown his own past. He is expected to censure as unpatriotic the common Irishmen who were not attracted by the new revolutionary ideas, but who adhered to an ancient tradition. Irishmen of today are invited at least implicitly to apologize for their fellow-countrymen who accepted loyally the serious guidance of the Church to which they belonged. Irishmen of today must despise as unmanly those of their own countrymen who preferred to solve problems, if possible, by peaceful rather than by violent means.[2]

It is my contention that some attempt should be made to challenge this chain of error in Ireland's history. The views expressed here may surprise many readers; I hope they will offend none. It is no tribute of honour to the brave men of 1916 to accept their words and their works in an unthinking and uncritical spirit. They were men who differed very widely from the vast majority of their own people, and they did not fear either controversy or contradiction. Sentiment is a poor substitute for intellectual honesty and sincerity. To examine and to re-examine the foundations of our political and national institutions is a duty never to be shirked. The 'troubles' of the decade which followed 1916

1. Copies of the 1916 proclamation were hung prominently on the walls of all primary schools in Ireland during the celebrations for the fiftieth anniversary of the Rising in 1966.

2. The reference in these paragraphs is to the Home Rule (or Nationalist) Party, which had been removed from the mainstream of nationalist politics by the insurgent republican movement. It is open to question whether the Home Rule Party's support for the carnage of World War I could be construed as the pursuit of politics through peaceful rather than through violent means.

may be in part at least responsible for the fact that today, over fifty years after the Rising, there is no mature, comprehensive, objective study of the political philosophy and the ideals of the men of 1916. . . .

'To break the connection with England, the never-failing source of all our political evils.'[3] More than once Pearse declared that these words of Tone said all that needed to be said about the national objective. Though he said that nothing needed to be added to them, in fact Pearse did add two important themes. The first was the sanctity of nationalism, especially of Irish nationalism; with this may be joined the notion of the sacredness of warfare and blood-shedding. The second theme is that the new Ireland should be separated from England, not only politically and economically, but also culturally and linguistically: the new Ireland should be Gaelic as well as free.

The idea that dedication to one's country is a good thing, a Christian duty, is a commonplace, but Pearse introduced a new idea, a startling one: the idea that patriotism and holiness are the same, that they are convertible concepts. This idea is most unambiguously expressed by Pearse in the oration at the grave of Tone in Bodenstown in 1913:[4]

> We have come to the holiest place in Ireland; holier to us even than the place where Patrick sleeps in Down.[5] Patrick brought us life, but this man died for us . . . He was the greatest of Irish Nationalists; I believe he was the greatest of Irish men. And if I am right in this I am right in saying that we stand in the holiest place in Ireland, for it must be that the holiest sod of a nation's soil is the sod where the greatest of her dead lies buried.
>
> *How Does She Stand*, pp. 53-4.

There is no ambiguity here; nationalism and holiness are identical.

Pearse's solemn and alarming words at Bodenstown were not due to oratorical exaggeration. We find the same sentiment again and again in his writings. I do not know whether Davis is considered to be a holy man in the conventional sense, but Pearse says: 'The highest form of genius is the genius for sanctity, the genius for noble life and thought. That genius was Davis's.' (*The Spiritual Nation*, p. 328).

But it is even more disturbing to find that consistently and deliberately and without reservation Pearse equates the patriot and the patriot-people with Christ. I accept without question the sincerity and the subjective reverence of Pearse in this matter, but one has to say that objectively this equation of the patriot with Christ is in conflict with the whole Christian tradition and, indeed, with the explicit teaching of Christ.[6] The prayer of Pearse:

> O King that was born
> To set bondsmen free,
> In the coming battle,
> Help the Gael!
>
> *Christmas 1915*, Plays etc. p. 340.

is aggressively unorthodox. In the sense in which Pearse uses the words they are false. Christ was not born to set bondsmen free from any chains other than those of sin. In the Judea of his day, Christ was set down in a situation comparable to that of the Ireland of 1916. Christ made it unmistakably plain that he was not a national saviour, and his words to his disciplines on the day of the Ascension expressed his sorrow that those who knew him and

3. Wolfe Tone's statement, made in his *Journal* in 1796, was a retrospective clarification of the motives that had led him to write his pioneering pamphlet, *An Argument on Behalf of the Catholics of Ireland*, in 1791.
4. The author's own note reads: 'The page references to Pearse's writings throughout are to the *Collected Works of Padraic H. Pearse*, 5 Volumes: *St Enda's and its Founder* (including 'The Story of a Success'); *Political Writings and Speeches* (including 'The Murder Machine'); *Songs of the Irish Rebels etc.* (including 'Some Aspects of Irish Literature' and 'Three Lectures on Gaelic Topics'); *Plays, Stories, Poems* (including 'The Singer') and *Schríbhinní Phádraig Mhic Phiarais*. The Phoenix Publishing Co., Dublin, Cork, Belfast. Numerous editions from 1917 onwards, which appear to be re-impressions with the same pagination. The earlier editions bear the imprint of Maunsell [*sic*] & Roberts, Dublin and London. The title on the spine is *The Complete Works of P. H. Pearse*. In references here the titles of the original pamphlets, etc., are retained, as they are (with dates of first publication) in the collection. Later editions have the imprint of The Talbot Press, Dublin.'
5. St Patrick died *c.* 492 and is reputed to be buried at Saul, near Downpatrick, Co. Down. Father Shaw is not slow to point out the irony in Pearse's appropriation of Wolfe Tone as a holy martyr, and later in his lengthy article he dwells on Tone's contemptuous dismissal of catholicism as 'priestcraft and superstition' and his reference to the archbishop of Dublin and the catholic primate of Ireland as 'ignorant bigots'.
6. Father Shaw was not the first to break ranks with the consensus that identified Pearse's nationalism with catholicism. In 1948, John J. Horgan, a prominent figure in the constitutional Nationalist Party until 1918, wrote in his memoirs of the conspiracy behind the Easter Rising that 'It is hard to conceive a procedure more cynical or undemocratic, or, from a Catholic point of view, more wicked' (*Parnell to Pearse*, Dublin: Browne and Nolan, 1948, p. 286, cited in F. X. Martin's valuable account of the literature of the Rising '1916 — Myth, Fact and Mystery', *Studia Hibernica*, No. 7 (1961)).

who loved him could continue so long in error.

Pearse had no misgivings. In *The Singer* the patriot-martyr explicitly professes the doctrine of the blood sacrifice in terms of the Gospel.

> You should have kept all back but one. One man can free a people as one Man redeemed the world. I will take no pike, I will go into battle with bare hands. I will stand up before the Gall[7] as Christ hung naked before men on the tree!

For Pearse, Tone is the prophet of the Lord: 'God spoke to Ireland through Tone' (*The Separatist Idea*, p. 293); and of Emmet's death Pearse says: 'It is the memory of a sacrifice Christ-like in its perfection. . . . This man was faithful even unto the ignominy of the gallows, dying that his people might live, even as Christ died.' (*How Does She Stand*, p. 69 and 71). When he speaks of war and blood-shedding (against a tradition as old as Christianity), Pearse applies the words of Our Lord thus: 'The Christ that said: "My peace I leave you, My peace I give you," is the same Christ that said: "I bring not peace but a sword"' (loc. cit., p. 77); in another place he says: 'Ireland will not find Christ's peace until she has taken Christ's sword.' (*Peace and the Gael*, p. 218). He never cited the words of Christ to Peter: 'Put up thy sword; he who takes the sword will perish by the sword.' The doctrine of separatism is 'the New Testament of Irish nationality'. Incidentally there are many things in the writings of Tone and his fellow-evangelists other than their doctrine of separatism, but it is to that doctrine, almost exclusively and *par excellence*, that Pearse gives the name of gospel. 'John Mitchel's *Jail Journal* [is] the last gospel of the New Testament of Irish Nationality, as Wolfe Tone's *Autobiography* is the first.' (*From a Hermitage*, p. 168); 'This gospel of the Sovereign People that Fintan Lalor delivered is the shortest of the gospels.' (*The Sovereign People*, p. 346). The notion of expressing politico-national ideas in terms of the Christian faith became an obsession with Pearse, as when he writes: 'Like a divine religion, national freedom bears the marks of unity, of sanctity, of catholicity, of apostolic succession.' (*Ghosts*, p. 226).

Possibly the most extreme example of this obsession is the extraordinary idea which Pearse expresses in his lecture entitled 'Aspects of Irish literature', given in 1912. Pearse is speaking of the old Irish epic the *Táin Bó Cúailnge* and of its hero Cú Chulainn, whom he always looked on as the great prototype of the Irish patriot-martyr:

> The story of Cuchulainn I take to be the finest epic stuff in the world . . . the story itself is greater than any Greek story . . . the theme is as great as Milton's in *Paradise Lost*: Milton's theme is a fall, but the Irish theme is a redemption. For the story of Cuchulainn symbolizes the redemption of man by a sinless God . . . it is like a retelling (or is it a foretelling?) of the story of Calvary.
>
> op. cit, p. 156.

But it is when Pearse comes to speak of the nation rather than of the individual patriot that he seems to abandon all reserve and all restraint:

> The people itself will perhaps be its own Messiah, the people labouring, scourged, crowned with thorns, agonizing and dying, to rise again immortal and impassible. For peoples are divine and are the only things that can properly be spoken of under figures drawn from the divine epos.
>
> *The Coming Revolution* (November 1913), p. 91-2

> The people who wept in Gethsemane, who trod the sorrowful way, who died naked on a cross, who went down into hell, will rise again glorious and immortal, will sit on the right hand of God, and will come in the end to give judgment, a judge just and terrible.
>
> *The Sovereign People*, p. 345.

It is hard to imagine anyone reading those words today without a shudder.

With the Messianic view of nationalism is connected the unqualified glorification of blood-shedding and war. In reading Pearse's words about this, however, we should keep in mind the enormous change which has taken place in the world in the last half-century in regard to war.[8] Nonetheless,

7. i.e. stranger or member of a foreign country — in this case, England.

8. Terence Brown and Seamus Deane have argued that Pearse's sentiments must be placed in the wider context of the blood-sacrifice ideals that presided over World War I in Britain and the Continent — a cult of violence to which the constitutional Nationalist or Home Rule party lent its support: Terence Brown, *Ireland: A Social and Cultural History 1922-79* (London: Fontana, 1981), p. 81; Seamus Deane, *Celtic Revivals* (London: Faber and Faber, 1985), chapter 5.

one must admit that, for a man of obviously gentle and sensitive disposition, the writer Pearse is very bloody-minded. He does 'not know how nationhood is achieved except by armed men,' (*How Does She Stand*, p. 75); and 'When war comes to Ireland, she must welcome it as she would welcome the Angel of God,' (*Peace and the Gael*, p. 217). The famous essay *Ghosts* ends with the grim application of scripture taken from Mitchel: '"That thy foot may be dipped in the blood of thine enemies, and that the tongue of thy dogs may be read through the same."' (p. 255). At times Pearse seems to hold human life cheaply as when he says: 'We may make mistakes in the beginning and shoot the wrong people; but bloodshed is a cleansing and a sanctifying thing ...' (*The Coming Revolution*, p. 98). In Easter Week, 1916, fifty-six Volunteers were killed in action. The number of civilian non-combatants killed was over two hundred.

The most frightening passage is in *Peace and the Gael* (p. 216); it was written in December 1915; it says:

> The last sixteen months have been the most glorious in the history of Europe. Heroism has come back to the earth.... It is good for the world that such things should be done. The old heart of the earth needed to be warmed with the red wine of the battlefields. Such august homage was never offered to God as this, the homage of millions of lives given gladly for love of country....

and to this is added the relevant gloss:

> Ireland has not known the exhilaration of war for over a hundred years.
>
> *Peace and the Gael*, pp. 216 and 217.

I refrain from any comment on these passages. They speak for themselves. About this time, it is of interest to note, Casement was recording his horror at the suffering caused by the war.[9]

It would be dishonest on my part if I were to pass from this subject without stating that the most potent ingredient in the separatism which Pearse adopted was hatred of England. In three of the four 'gospels' it is as assuredly the motive force as love is that of the Gospel of Christ. Tone's hatred of England was implacable. He says himself, 'I was led by a hatred of England so deeply rooted in my nature that it was rather an instinct than a principle.' Tone preached an undying hatred. 'The truth is, I hate the very name of England; I hated her before my exile; I hate her since; and I will hate her always.' (*Autobiography*, edited by R. Barry O'Brien, ii, 146). England, 'the never failing source of all our political evils', must be hated always even after Ireland has achieved her complete freedom. Tone looked to 'the pleasure of revenge in humbling a haughty and implacable rival'. These words are cited by Pearse, and it is in this place that Pearse says that 'God spoke to Ireland through Tone' (*The Separatist Idea*, p. 293).

'Irish hate of the English,' Pearse tells us in 'Songs of the Irish Rebels', is a 'holy passion'. In *O'Donovan Rossa: A Character Study*, Pearse writes: 'O'Donovan Rossa[10] was not the greatest man of the Fenian generation, but he was its most typical man.' In his eulogy of Rossa, Pearse then says:

> To him the Gael and the Gaelic ways were splendid and holy, worthy of all homage and all service; for the English he had a hatred that was tinctured with contempt. He looked upon them as an inferior race, morally and intellectually; he despised their civilization; he mocked at their institutions and made them look ridiculous.
>
> op. cit., pp. 127-8.

Speaking in praise of Davis, Pearse wrote: 'To him the English language was "a mongrel of a thousand breeds"', and Pearse blesses Davis for the petty observation that 'modern English literature was "surpassed" by French literature' (*The Spiritual Nation*, p. 317). Pearse must have been a little unhappy in this commendation of Davis, for not many writers of his time showed forth so splendidly in

9. At the end of 1915, while based in Germany, Roger Casement wrote in his diary: 'I very much hope that peace would come ... it is dreadful to think of all the world beginning the New Year with nothing but death — killing and murdering wholesale, and destroying all that makes life happy....' (quoted in Brian Inglis, *Roger Casement* (London: Hodder and Stoughton, 1973), p. 305). Yet Inglis also notes that Casement anticipated Pearse's oration at the graveside of O'Donovan Rossa. In a letter to the *Irish Independent* in 1914, Casement wrote: 'If Irish blood is to be "the seal that will bring all Ireland together in one nation and in liberties equal and common to all", then let that blood be shed in Ireland, where alone it can be righteously shed to secure those liberties ... let our graves be that patriot grass where alone the corpse of Irish nationality can spring to life.' (Inglis, op. cit., p. 299).

10. The funeral of the Fenian organizer Jeremiah O'Donovan Rossa (1831-1915) at Glasnevin cemetery provided Patrick Pearse with an opportunity to make a dramatic oration, in which he invoked O'Donovan Rossa's spirit to renew the nationalist call to arms.

writing the power of the English tongue, and these sentiments about the English language and English literature are different from the views which Pearse expresses in *The Story of a Success*.

It is true that nowhere does Pearse teach as explicitly as Tone the duty of hate, and it is true that Pearse follows Mitchel in the classical (but usually ineffective) distinction between hating the person and hating the evil done — nonetheless it is regrettably evident that 'the gospel of the New Testament of Irish nationality' was essentially a gospel of hate....

CONOR CRUISE O'BRIEN

(1917-)

from: PASSION AND CUNNING (1988)

[In this article, Conor Cruise O'Brien seeks to establish a catholic pedigree for nationalism since the seventeenth century, particularly in its militant forms. There is some difficulty in doing this since republicanism, the main conduit for insurrectionary ideas, was a secular, Enlightenment ideology, and the various movements that relied on physical force had either strong protestant affiliations (the United Irishmen in 1798, the Young Irelanders in 1848) or were execrated by the catholic church (the Fenian movement in 1867, and the Irish Republican Brotherhood after the Parnell split in 1890). Cruise O'Brien resolves this problem by arguing that an enduring catholic substratum or tradition has underpinned militant nationalism throughout, despite its widely divergent manifestations in ideology or leadership. With its marginalization of the protestant contribution to nationalism, this argument seems to reinstate a version of Daniel Corkery's or D. P. Moran's idea of an essentially catholic, nationalist tradition, albeit from a position of disapproval rather than approval.

The article was first published in *The New York Review of Books*, 29 April 1985.]

IRELAND: THE SHIRT OF NESSUS

... There is a real continuity of Irish nationalism: not an ideological continuity, but a continuity of the traditions and feelings of a people. That people sees itself as the people of Ireland, and that perception is a large part of the problem. For these are not *all* the people of Ireland. They are the Catholic people of Ireland, formerly Gaelic-speaking. These were the losers in the seventeenth-century wars — wars that were dynastic, social, cultural, national and religious, all at the same time. The forms of oppression which this people suffered — as a result of their decisive defeat — throughout the eighteenth century and into the nineteenth, were economic, social and cultural, but justified by a politico-religious criterion: the presumed disloyalty of Irish Catholics to the British Protestant Crown. This presumption of disloyalty was generally well founded.

The main theme of Irish history, for nearly three centuries now, has been the recovery of the Irish Catholics: the Catholics getting their own back, in more senses than one. Throughout this long period, the Catholic clergy have been at or near the centre of the process of recovery. It was a struggle, after all, not only against alien domination but against domination — until the process of recovery was already well advanced — in the name of an alien and false religion.

The tactics of recovery shifted widely: hence the impossibility of identifying any continuity of their ideology. At the time of the American Revolution, for example, the tactic pursued in the interests of Catholic recovery was demonstration of loyalty to the British Crown.[1] By this tactic, Catholic leaders wrong-footed the Irish Protestant community — whose more radical members supported the American colonists — and at the same time sought to establish that Britain could now safely remove Catholic disabilities. That was the strategy of the

1. In 1759, the Catholic Committee was formed under the stewardship of leading catholic figures such as Charles O'Conor (1710-91). They disowned the Jacobite cause espoused by previous generations of catholics, and in the 1770s their pledges of loyalty to the crown intensified after the passing of the Relief Act of 1778 led to expectations of the total repeal of the Penal Laws. In the early 1790s, the association of the catholic cause with the radical republicanism of the United Irishmen placed catholic loyalty to the crown under considerable strain.

leaders. What the mass of the Catholic people — then mainly Gaelic-speaking — thought about this matter, or whether they thought about it at all, we have no means of knowing. Gaelic literature of the period contains hardly any reference to the American Revolution. Contrary to assumptions that later became general among Irish-American Catholics, enthusiasm in Ireland for the American revolutionary cause was exclusively a Protestant affair, at the time.

If the American Revolution left Irish Catholics cold, the French Revolution was very different. Only at this point does it become meaningful to talk about an Irish nationalist ideology, because up to this point no ideology distinguishable from Irish Catholicism exists among Irish Catholics. From the sixteenth century well into the eighteenth, the Faith and the Nation were one. The people are oppressed for their loyalty to their Faith: the people of Israel enchained by infidels — the parallel is explicit in Gaelic literature. The people had looked for deliverance to the Catholic powers of Europe: to the Pope and the emperor, the king of Spain, the king of France; or in practice to whichever of these happened to be at loggerheads with England at any particular time.

Long before the French Revolution, however, it had become clear to educated Catholics that no deliverance was at hand, from any Catholic power. The best hope seemed to lie in dropping all that, and pursuing equal rights for Catholics under the British Crown: in effect dropping what had been up to then the political aspect of Irish Catholicism. This was pragmatically sound, but psychologically difficult and divisive. The people's songs were telling them quite different things from what their bishops were telling them. The old unity of Irish Catholicism was under stress.

The French Revolution not only vastly increased that stress; it created new and complex stresses and syntheses of its own. For Irish Catholics, the French Revolution was a wildly confusing and intoxicating phenomenon: anti-English and anti-landlord, and powerful; all that was great, but was it anti-*Catholic* as well?

The confusion was greatly increased by the blazing simplifications of the revolutionary idea itself. There was to be an Irish nation modelled on *la Grande Nation* itself. Irish revolutionaries, Catholic and Protestant together, transcending the outmoded superstitious animosities that monarchy, aristocracy and the English had created, would make the new Ireland, of free, equal, fraternal citizens — 'United Irishmen', as the revolutionaries called themselves.

French revolutionary ideas, more or less in their original form, caught on among radical, educated Irish Protestants — mostly in what is now Northern Ireland — and among a few Catholics of the same class. But where it caught on in rural Catholic Ireland, as in Wexford, it caught on as an opportunity to overthrow Protestant landlords and their Protestant hangers-on, and the English power behind them. The story of the 'United Irish' Risings of 1798 is covered in two splendid modern books which complement each other: Thomas Pakenham's *The Year of Liberty* and Thomas Flanagan's novel *The Year of the French*.[2]

What is relevant to look at here is the condition of Irish nationalism and ideology as these developed in the period following the bloody and comprehensive repression of the 1798 Risings. One should note first the disappearance of Protestants from an Irish nationalism whose 'French revolutionary' manifestations they had done so much to stimulate. Eastern Ulster, the only area where Protestants are in a majority, was henceforward committed, as it is today, to being no part of any united Ireland separate from Britain, or of any political union with Catholics. The course of the Rising (and particularly the massacres of Protestants in Wexford)[3] convinced Protestants generally that 'United Irish' ideas had been a disastrous illusion. Henceforward there would be isolated Protestant adherents to Irish nationalism but they would be adhering, in practice though not in rhetoric, to an Irish Catholic nation.

Some Protestant intellectuals — Thomas Davis, John Mitchel in the early nineteenth century, and later W. B. Yeats — played an important part in keeping 'United Irish' ideas alive among Catholics. Charles Stewart Parnell, at the end of the nineteenth century, was a Protestant leader of Catholic people, on their terms.

2. Thomas Pakenham, *The Year of Liberty* (London: Hodder and Stoughton, 1969); Thomas Flanagan, *The Year of the French* (London: Hutchinson, 1979).
3. On 5 June 1798, Wexford insurgents, prompted by rumours that government forces were butchering rebels in New Ross, massacred over 100 defenceless protestants at Scullabogue. Recent research by historians such as Louis Cullen and Kevin Whelan has underlined the very distinctive local conditions that heightened sectarian animosities in Wexford in the late eighteenth century.

Among Catholics, the primary effect of the Rising and its suppression was to reinforce the authority of the Catholic hierarchy, and the more conservative elements generally. The year 1798 was to look romantic in a far later retrospect, but in its immediate aftermath it had to be seen for the bloody disaster it actually was. The bishops, who had warned of the ruin attendant on monkeying around with French revolutionary ideas, were felt to have been proved right: no more of that, was a general feeling. Few Catholics seem to have thought any the worse of Daniel O'Connell for helping to crush the Protestant Robert Emmet's hopeless United-Irish-type rising in 1803. O'Connell, as leader of the Irish Catholic people, pursued, in essentials, the course set by the Irish bishops in the eighteenth century: removal of Catholic disabilities, improvement of conditions for Catholics, under the British Crown. This was the general strategy of Irish nationalism, with mass support, throughout the nineteenth century. As democracy in the United Kingdom developed — Ireland's separate (and Protestant) parliament was abolished in the aftermath of the 1798 Rising — political autonomy for Ireland under the Crown ('Repeal of the Union', 'Home Rule') came to appear an essential goal.

That was the mainstream of Irish nationalism: pragmatic, Church-conditioned. But there was an undercurrent, and this took the form of a distinct ideology: Irish Republicanism. Republicanism, defying the bishops, took its inspiration from 1798 and the United Irishmen and especially from the teaching of Theobald Wolfe Tone, the United Irish leader and martyr. The goal was Tone's: 'To break the connection with England, the never-failing source of all our political evils.' The connection, of course, included the Crown, and this was what made the central formal distinction between the Republicans and the mainstream 'constitutional' nationalists, who were willing to accept autonomous national status under the British Constitution and Crown. The Republican objective could only be attained, if at all, by physical force, and Irish Republicanism was and is a physical-force movement.

After yet another hopeless insurrection, in 1848, the Republican movement, like others of its kind in Europe, became embodied in a secret, oath-taking society. This was the Irish Republican Brotherhood, founded in 1858, begetter of the Irish Republican Army. The IRB had strong Irish-American links and its members were known as the Fenians.

The Church, or at least the bishops, condemned the Fenians: as carriers of the alien godless ideology of the French Revolution, as bound by a forbidden oath, and — above all — as inciting people into a hopeless, and therefore by Catholic teaching immoral, insurrection. After the Fenian Rising of 1867, one bishop proclaimed that hell was not hot enough nor eternity long enough to punish the Fenian leaders.[4]

The mass of the people remained loyal to the Church, and supported the constitutional nationalists. But they also admired the Fenians, for their courage, their tenacity and their uncontaminated continuity of Irish Catholic feeling. For what the Fenians were doing, and what the IRA is now doing (in practice, as distinct from rhetoric), was carrying on the *political aspect of the Irish Catholic tradition, as it had existed in the Counter-Reformation times*: root-and-branch hostility to the British Crown and all it stood for. The bishops, with their — relatively — novel doctrine of loyalty to the British Crown (and therefore the Protestant succession!) were on slippery ground, emotionally speaking.

Intellectually, it was the Fenians who were, and are, on slippery ground. Formally the Republican ideology is a modern, secular, post-Enlightenment affair. It preaches, in theory, union between the Irish people of all religious denominations, transcending the tragic sectarian divisions of the past, and so on. It all sounds very nice. At a distance and in a poor light, it is possible to mistake an Irish Republican for some kind of liberal.

But there is a catch, and the catch is that, as well as preaching non-sectarian unity among the Irish people, Republicans have as their prime objective the breaking of the connection with England. So what happens if — as is actually the case — a community of Irish people, the Protestants of Northern Ireland, refuse to break that connection, but on the contrary are determined to defend it?

In that case, with respect to Republican doctrine, the relevant characteristic of these people is not that

4. These sentiments were expressed in 1867 by Bishop Moriarty of Kerry, one of the most bitter opponents of Fenianism among the Hierarchy: 'Hell is not hot enough, nor eternity long enough, to punish these miscreants.'

they are Protestants — in which capacity Republicans, theoretically, welcome them with open arms — but that they are Unionists. Unionists can be regarded either as British, part of the occupying forces, or as Irish traitors. In either case Republicans have warrant from their ideology to shoot these people down, whenever opportunity offers.

So when, in our time, Catholic Republican gunmen systematically pick off Protestant farmers and shopkeepers in the border areas, they are not carrying on a sectarian civil war, as you might imagine, and as Protestants in their ignorance believe. No, they are breaking the connection with England, by killing the people who form that connection.

'We have nothing against Protestants *as such*,' the executioners explain.

You see the importance of ideology.

Sectarian — that is politico-sectarian — civil war in Ireland was always *latent* in Republican ideology. It did not, however, come to the point of actual Catholic-Protestant (Republican-Unionist) civil war until as late as 1971,[5] after the emergence of the Provisional IRA, the heirs to the ideology in its purest, perfected and most deadly form.

So let us look back at some of the stages in the maturing of that ideology.

By the late nineteenth century, what looked like a rather stable symbiosis had been achieved in the political culture of the Irish Catholic community (or nation). The people went to Mass, and voted for constitutional nationalists. The Church, through the bishops, condemned the Republicans, and so sometimes did the constitutional nationalists, but not so loudly or so often as the bishops. The constitutional nationalists, unlike the bishops, depended on popular suffrage, and they knew that the people had a 'weakness' for the Republicans. They wouldn't follow them, or swallow their ideology, and they felt uneasy about them, but at the same time they liked to feel that deep down they were on the side of these patriotic men, up to a point and in a way.[6] Under these conditions the Republicans could ignore the Church leaders. A Republican leader knew that, while he would have little visible following in life, there would be a marvellous turnout at his funeral.

So this bloody subcult firmly established itself within an otherwise exceptionally docile body of religious people whose religious leaders fiercely condemned the subcult. Religion is a bit like that: compare non-violent Hinduism, with its subcult of the Goddess Kali, and her strings of human heads.[7]

A hundred years ago, however, the subcult didn't look serious. The Republicans very seldom actually killed anyone in those days. 'The Church versus the Fenians' was a kind of standing political and cultural Punch-and-Judy show, adding to the fun and colour of life. You knew the Church wasn't *really* all that down on the Fenians. And you also knew that most of the Fenians were really good Catholics, and would probably make their peace with the Church before they died — and there would be a lovely funeral. It was all very cozy. But then around the turn of the century, a number of things happened to dispel the coziness.

The first of these events was the downfall of Charles Stewart Parnell in 1891. Parnell in that year [*sic*] was co-respondent in an undefended divorce suit. In no part of the Victorian United Kingdom, including Ireland, could a political leader expect to retain his leadership under those conditions. Parnell, nonetheless, attempted to hold on. In this way, he created an extraordinary coalition against himself. The coalition consisted of his former allies, the British Liberal Party, headed by Gladstone; the Catholic hierarchy in Ireland; and a majority of the constitutional nationalists, his own party.

This situation presented the Republicans with a truly wonderful opportunity to reshape the whole political culture of Ireland to their own advantage. In their version of history, the English had decreed the fall of the greatest of Irish leaders, and the fawning bishops and fawning constitutional nationalists had hastened to do their bidding. As the writings of W. B. Yeats and James Joyce reflect, this scenario had a powerful appeal to the young, making them at the same time more refractory to Church control and more anti-English: two key points as far as the expansion of Republican influence was concerned.

As far as the young were concerned, the channel

5. The Provisonal IRA was formed after a split with the Official IRA, and its political wing, Official Sinn Féin (now The Workers' Party), in 1970–71.
6. See, for example, constitutional nationalists such as A. M. and T. D. Sullivan, the latter of whom attempted to fuse religious and Fenian sentiments in his patriotic ballad, 'God Save Ireland', written on the execution of the Manchester Martyrs in 1867.

7. Kali was the cult name of a Hindu goddess to whom the Thugs sacrificed their victims.

of Irish nationalism began to shift its course at this time: away from its tamer shore of Church approval and compromise with Britain and nearer to its wilder shore of Republicanism and human sacrifice. Kali had assumed a higher place in the pantheon.

The post-Parnell period — the last decade of the nineteenth century and the first decade of this one — was a period of apparent political quiet. In fact it was a period of major politico-cultural change. A cultural nationalism grew up — especially among the middle classes and in the cities — highly charged with romantic Republicanism, and resistant to the influence of the Church. W. B. Yeats of course — a Fenian of sorts himself at the time — played a notable part in all that, especially through his play *Cathleen ni Houlihan* (1902), with its mystical glorification of the blood sacrifice of 1798, and its evocation of further blood sacrifice to come. By this time, a great deal of explosive emotional material had accumulated.

Ironically, it was the triumph of the constitutional nationalists that supplied the detonator. Their triumph, followed by their undoing. For nearly forty years, since Parnell's day, it had been the strategy of the constitutional nationalists to win Home Rule — devolved autonomy — by parliamentary action: in practice by controlling the balance of power in the House of Commons and enacting Home Rule through an alliance with a British party, the Liberals. In 1912, Asquith's Liberals[8] and the Irish nationalists together made up a Home Rule majority in Parliament. The House of Lords, which had vetoed the last Home Rule Bill, no longer had a veto. To Irish nationalists of all descriptions, Home Rule seemed home and dry.

The whole thing then struck a rock, in Ulster. Ulster Protestants first by mass demonstrations, then by arming and drilling, showed their implacable refusal to be incorporated in a Catholic-majority Home Rule State. They were supported by the British Tories. Asquith realized that there was no way by which he could compel Ulster Protestants to accept Home Rule. If Irish Catholics wanted Home Rule, they could have it for themselves, but they would have to do without Protestant-majority eastern Ulster. Rather than get no Home Rule at all, the constitutional nationalists agreed, with bitter reluctance, to a formula of 'temporary exclusion' of eastern Ulster. Everybody knew 'temporary' meant 'permanent'.

The best-known account of these transactions is contained in George Dangerfield's spirited and entertaining *The Strange Death of Liberal England.*[9] The reader should be warned, however, that this account suffers from an underestimation of the autochthonous component in the Ulster crisis. As its title implies, Mr Dangerfield's book is an Anglo-centric account, with its emphasis on the amusing and unedifying gyrations of the English parties. The author assumes, without proving his case, that the English Government both could and should have transferred a million Ulster Protestants out of the jurisdiction under which their ancestors had lived for centuries and in which they insisted on remaining, into a new jurisdiction which they passionately refused. This seems a large assumption, and I for one refuse to make it.

It was, however, and is, the almost universal assumption among Irish Catholic nationalists, and these generally regarded the partitionist outcome of the Home Rule crisis with deep shock and disappointment.

One group, however, that did not share the disappointment was the Republican hard core. For them the Home Rule debacle — as they saw it — provided an even more favourable conjuncture than the downfall of Parnell had done. That debacle did two things, both of them satisfactory to the Republican ideologues. First of all, it comprehensively discredited the constitutional nationalists. Second — and even more vital — it reaccredited physical force. Republicans had always said that the only argument England paid any attention to was the gun. The Ulster Volunteers had proved that this was true.[10] In fact it would have been impossible for Britain to force a million refractory Ulster Protestants into Home Rule, even if they had had no guns, but it suited the Republicans to put the emphasis on the guns.

So the Irish Volunteers were founded in response to the Ulster Volunteers. (In reality Irish *Catholic* volunteers, but the religious labels are un-

8. Herbert Asquith (1852-1928) was British prime minister from 1908 until 1916.

9. George Dangerfield, *The Strange Death of Liberal England* (first published in 1935; reprinted London: MacGibbon & Kee, 1966).

10. The Ulster Volunteer Force was formed in January 1913 to resist Home Rule and within a short period had 100,000 members.

necessary; everybody knows, without saying, what the realities are).

The Irish Volunteers were nationalists of all descriptions, many still adhering to the constitutional nationalist leaders who, though shaken and demoralized, still at this stage held much of their former respect. But then the First World War broke out and the constitutionally minded among the Irish Volunteers went off to fight the Germans.[11] The Volunteers who remained in Ireland were heavily under the Republican influence; the controlling element among the Republicans was the Irish Republican Brotherhood: and the Brotherhood had decided on insurrection. The Easter Rising of 1916 was in preparation.

The IRB, on the outbreak of the First World War, decided, in principle, in accordance with its historic doctrine 'England's difficulty is Ireland's opportunity', to bring about an insurrection at some time during the war. The timing and methods were left to a kind of subcommittee: the Military Council of the IRB. By 1916, the Military Council consisted of seven members, including Patrick Pearse and James Connolly. The members of the Military Council became the signers of the Proclamation of the Republic. When the insurrection had been crushed, within a week, the British executed the members of the Military Council, along with others.

While the insurrection was unpopular in Catholic Ireland when it was actually happening, the executions of the leaders and other events brought about widespread revulsion against the British and the constitutional nationalists, and a corresponding retrospective glorification of the men of 1916. By 1917 this swing to the Republic dominated most of the political life of Catholic Ireland.

It is at this point that the decisive event occurred for nationalism and for ideology. The old antagonists, the Church and the Fenians, now tacitly came to terms. The interlocutors were two exceptionally able and pragmatic men: Eamon de Valera, the senior survivor of 1916, and Archbishop Walsh, of Dublin.[12]

Each had something to gain by coming to terms. De Valera intended to fight the post-war elections through an appeal to the mystique of 1916. Such an appeal was highly vulnerable, from the side of the Church; for according to the traditional teaching of the Irish Church, the enterprise of 1916 was literally damnable: it was a hopeless insurrection irresponsibly precipitated by a secret and oath-bound society, many times condemned by the Church. De Valera did not need the Church's blessing for his political movement (now called Sinn Fein). What he did need was the Church's neutrality: to be able to get on with the political sanctification of 1916 Republicanism, without awkward episcopal interventions reminding the faithful of the traditional theology.

The archbishop and his colleagues, for their part, had some strong reasons for according neutrality, at least. The constitutional nationalists were going downhill rather fast.[13] The Church's interest had to be protected in the event of the disapperance of these politicians. De Valera and his friends showed themselves respectful to the Church, and churchmen. With regard to 1916, there was the traditional teaching of course, and that could not be set aside, but there were other considerations too. The signers of the proclamation may have been secret and oath-bound, but they died exemplary Catholic deaths. Indeed all these people in their ordinary lives seemed to be exemplary Catholics;[14] much better than the constitutional nationalists, many of whom had been contaminated by too much living in London, rubbing shoulders with godless English Liberals.

What exactly happened will probably always remain unknown. Irish historians have generally not looked very hard at this crucial transaction in the history of Republicanism, the Church and Irish ideology. By far the fullest exploration of this is

11. In the split over recruitment for the war effort, approximately 150,000 members of the nationalist Irish Volunteers joined the British army, and 10,000 remained in Ireland, where they gradually came under the control of the IRB.
12. Eamon de Valera (1882-1975) was a commandent during the 1916 Rising and went on to become the leading political figure in Ireland in the twentieth century, coming to power in 1932 and becoming president in 1959. Archbishop William J. Walsh (1841-1921) was archbishop of Dublin from 1885 to 1921.
13. On the dissolution of the British Parliament in 1918, Sinn Féin had only 7 seats, while the constitutional Nationalist Party had 78 seats. After the general election, the situation was reversed: Sinn Féin won 73 seats, while the Nationalist Party retained only 6 seats.
14. But see, for example, James Connolly's frank admission that 'though I have usually posed as a Catholic, I have not gone to my duty for fifteen years, and I have not the slightest tincture of faith left' (Bernard Ransom, *Connolly's Marxism*, London: Pluto Press, 1980, p. 100). According to Ruth Dudley Edwards, moreover, Thomas MacDonagh was a Freethinker (Ruth Dudley Edwards, *Patrick Pearse: The Triumph of Failure*, London: Gollancz, 1977, p. 262).

contained in an admirable book by an American historian: David W. Miller's *Church, State and Nation in Ireland*.[15] From Miller's account, it looks as if de Valera convinced the Archbishop of the essential point: that in a Sinn Fein Republican Ireland, the Catholic Church would be left with the same tight control over Catholic education as it had achieved under the British. And so indeed it worked out.

In any case, the Church refrained from intruding any awkward theological points into the election campaign of November 1918 — and also generally refrained from warning that a Sinn Fein victory would lead to further violence. (They did not of course know that it would, but as prudent men they ought to have been aware of the danger and warned against it. Archbishop Walsh voted for Sinn Fein himself, and announced the fact.) Sinn Fein, in the name of the Republic proclaimed in 1916, won an overwhelming victory in Catholic Ireland. Republicanism became, and still is, the official political ideology of Catholic Ireland.

Pearse's Republic did not, however, arrive and has not arrived yet. Three years of guerrilla war and reprisals, following Sinn Fein's victory, ended in a treaty with Britain in 1921. That treaty accepted what all Republicans had contemptuously rejected in 1914: autonomy for the homogeneously Catholic part of Ireland, while the Protestant part (with some Catholic areas attached) remained in the United Kingdom. And this of course is still the case today.

The Irish (Catholic) people electorally endorsed the treaty. They had not known what they were letting themselves in for when they voted Sinn Fein, and they were only too happy to let themselves out again. A minority of Republicans, however, opposed the treaty by arms. These were excommunicated by the Church and crushed militarily by the pro-treaty forces.

Ten years later, however, the most eminent of the excommunicated, Eamon de Valera, came to power through free elections, in the state that the treaty had established.[16] In substance, but not in form, de Valera now accepted the treaty arrangements. But even while doing so he insisted that what he represented was the 1916 tradition. Nineteen-sixteen Republicanism was now tightly fastened as the official ideology of the Irish state, now known as the Republic.

In today's Republic the schools of the Catholic people are controlled by the Catholic Church. And in many such schools there hangs a copy of the Proclamation of the Republic, with the portraits of the seven men who made up the Military Council of a secret and oath-bound society many times anathematized by the Church. The Church acquiesces in the enthronement of the Fenianism that it had so long condemned, as today the official ideology of the state.

The contemporary IRA, however, rejects that state quite consistently, precisely in the name of its own official ideology. They point out that this Republic, not being all Ireland, is not Pearse's Republic; and it is not. They quote, to deadly effect, Pearse's statement, 'Ireland unfree shall never be at peace.'[17] They show from Tone that an Ireland still politically connected with Britain — through Northern Ireland — is unfree. They claim the right to use violence, as Pearse and Tone did, to achieve the objective of Pearse and Tone. If they are told they have no democratic mandate, they ask what democratic mandate did Pearse and Tone have? To which the only honest answer has to be: none whatever.

The official ideology of the Republic fully legitimizes the IRA's 'war' in Northern Ireland and so helps that 'war' go on and on. The people of the Republic do not endorse that war, very far from it. We are nationalists in the sense of wanting to run our own affairs, not in the sense of wanting to annex territory and crush other people. We dislike the IRA, most of us, and fear it. We are a peaceful and democratic people. But our history, our 'idealistic' pretensions and our fatal ambivalence have stuck us with an ideology that is warlike and anti-democratic, and calls increasingly for further human sacrifice.

Our ideology, in relation to what we actually are and want, is a lie. It is a lie that clings to us and burns, like the shirt of Nessus.[18]

15. David W. Miller, *Church, State and Nation in Ireland 1898-1921* (Dublin: Gill and Macmillan, 1973).
16. In 1926, de Valera broke with Sinn Féin and established the Fianna Fáil party. It came to power in February 1932.
17. Pearse's statement was made in his funeral oration at the grave of the Fenian leader, Jeremiah O'Donovan Rossa, in 1915: 'The fools, the fools, the fools! — they have left us our Fenian dead, and while Ireland holds these graves, Ireland unfree shall never be at peace.' (O'Donovan Rossa — Graveside Oration' in *The Collected Works of Padraic H. Pearse: Political Writings and Speeches* (Dublin: Phoenix Publishing Co., 1929, p. 137).
18. In Greek mythology, the shirt of Nessus, the centaur, killed Hercules.

Postcript, November, 1987

This month, more than two years after the original essay, that 'Shirt of Nessus' has been clinging and burning, even more grievously than it was then.

On 8 November, Remembrance Sunday, the Provisional IRA detonated a bomb in Enniskillen along the route of the town's Remembrance parade. The bomb killed eleven people and wounded many others. Those killed were all civilians. They were also all Protestants. Although Catholics as well as Protestants fought in both world wars with the British forces, in Ireland it is only Protestants — with very few exceptions — who keep Remembrance Day. In Northern Ireland, in particular, when you see a person wearing a poppy, you assume automatically that that person is a Protestant.

'The Poppy Day Massacre', as it came to be called, was the IRA's most spectacular act of war to date against the Protestant population. While murdering and maiming a random sample of that population, the IRA was simultaneously desecrating their sacred day.

The place chosen for the massacre was also significant. Enniskillen is the principal town of Co. Fermanagh. Fermanagh is a border county, and in the districts of the county which are closest to the border, all the Republic Protestants are in a rather small minority. Or rather they were in a minority; now they are gone altogether from those districts. Over more than ten years, the Provisionals have been systematically picking off isolated Protestants — farmers and shopkeepers — along the Fermanagh border. As the pattern became clear, the surviving isolated Protestants left the deadly border districts, often for Enniskillen (which is half and half Catholic and Protestant). And the IRA pursued them there.

The Nazis used to make regions and countries *Jadenrein*: clean from Jews. The IRA is out to make Fermanagh clean from Protestants, and then the rest of Northern Ireland, though that will take longer.

The Poppy Day Massacre was designed to cause the maximum outrage in the Protestant community. But it also brought about a revulsion against the IRA in the *Catholic* community, on a scale never known before. Responding to that mood and participating in it, the Catholic clergy throughout Ireland, on the Sunday following the massacre, denounced the IRA and its accomplices, without the customary ambivalence, and with unaccustomed specifics. People who provided 'safe houses' for IRA fugitives were warned that they were guilty of grave sin as accomplices in murder. Cardinal Tomas O'Fiaich, Archbishop of Armagh and Primate of All Ireland, apologized, on behalf of his community, to the Protestants of Northern Ireland.

In the past, the Cardinal has often seemed ambivalence incarnate in these matters. He has denounced the violence of the IRA but declined to condemn Provisional Sinn Fein, which is nothing more than the political and propaganda arm of the Provisional IRA. But the Cardinal now seems to be troubled by a realization that our ambivalence — not just *his*, but that of the whole Catholic community — has been feeding a monster.

Will Enniskillen prove a turning point? There is some reason to hope that it may. Certainly, I cannot remember a time when the ambivalence count has been as low as it was at the middle of this month. It is as if that single spectacular explosion so lit up the landscape that people suddenly became aware of what the IRA is about, and what helping it means.

Whether that change of mood can be relied on is another matter. It needs to be translated into a determined effort to isolate and defeat the IRA. Personally I do not think that can be done without the introduction of internment without trial *on both sides of the border*. The Anglo-Irish Agreement[19] has not produced any improvement where violence is concerned. Violence has been rising steadily since the Agreement even before Enniskillen, and Protestant rejection of the Agreement remains solid. But if the Agreement were used for the joint implementation of internment, then the Agreement could become acceptable to Protestants. Nothing less will do it. But we are nowhere near that point this November. And as I write, in late November, with the memory of Enniskillen receding, the ambivalence count seems once more to be rising. We have not yet done with that shirt.

19. The Anglo-Irish Agreement was signed in November 1985, giving official recognition to the Irish government's involvement in Northern affairs, while, at the same time, underpinning the right of the Unionist population to remain in the United Kingdom while they were in a majority in Northern Ireland (see below, p. 803).

MARIANNE ELLIOTT

(1948-)

from: WATCHMEN IN ZION: THE PROTESTANT IDEA OF LIBERTY (1985)

[In this extract, Marianne Elliott seeks to establish the distinctively protestant contribution to the development of militant nationalism in Ireland by associating it with a radical republican tradition which justified the recourse to arms in the face of unrepresentative government. This early Irish republicanism had its basis in libertarian presbyterian thinking, and influenced both American revolutionary thought and the United Irishmen, founded in 1791. Her demonstration of the links between this form of republicanism and cultural nationalism contrasts with Seán O'Faoláin's claim that 'the Gaelic cult' and democratic ideals were incompatible, and with the widely accepted view that the rediscovery of the Gaelic past was the preserve of catholic nationalism.]

... In a culture where the past is so much part of the present, a protestant who opposes perceived threats to his freedom and his religion is acting radically, in the same tradition as the Covenanters, the Commonwealthmen and the 'real Whigs'[1] of the seventeenth and eighteenth centuries, who made 1688 and the protestant succession fundamental to the British tradition of liberty. Behind the seemingly antiquated bigotry, there is a dynamic libertarianism, at times a millenarianism, which still finds its inspiration in Old Testament imagery of the Israelites fighting their way to possess the promised land. It is, however, a brand of libertarianism ill-attuned to modern secular thinking which accepts nationality, rather than religion, as a badge of identity.

There is a tendency to see the problem of Northern Ireland simplistically in terms of a protestant/catholic conflict. But protestantism is not a monolith, and it is the failure to recognise the libertarian tradition, particularly in presbyterianism, which causes many commentators to dismiss such appeals to freedom as either rhetoric or pure hypocrisy. Yet the presbyterians' heightened sense of persecution is as old as that of the Irish catholics and the Irish problem is as much one of conflicting ideas of liberty as anything else....

The most important aspect of early presbyterianism — the notion of a church as a covenant between God and man — was ... reflected in the political sphere in the contractarian thinking[2] which came to dominate British political thought in the era of the Glorious Revolution and which, through Locke, became part of the Enlightenment. The Scottish universities — where the Ulster presbyterian clergy was trained — became the centres for the most advanced contractarian ideas in the age of the Enlightenment. This nonconformist tradition of contract, rooted in the republican thought of Milton, Harrington and Sidney,[3] was to inspire the eighteenth-century reform campaign in Britain which attacked corruption, placemen, excessive executive influence and unrepresentative government. But it was in Ireland, Scotland and colonial America that it retained its dogged purity, and the most lasting testimony to presbyterian libertarianism is the American Constitution. In explaining the foundations of civil society, the contract theory assumes the surrender of individual liberty, by mutual consent of a community, to a government which in return undertakes to act for the general good. The contract assumes mutual obligation; but in its more radical form of government as a trust, the obligations are one-sided and the government can be rejected when that trust is seen to have been

1. This phrase refers to the radical, or republican, factions in seventeenth- and eighteenth-century English politics who sought the transfer of power from the monarch to parliament. James Harrington's *The Commonwealth of Oceana* (1656), a depiction of an ideal republican state, was the founding text for this tradition, and exerted a considerable influence on the formation of the American constitution.

2. Political philosophy identified with John Locke's *Two Treatises of Civil Government* (1690). As against the theory of the divine right of kings, it held that government derives its legitimacy from an agreement or 'contract' between members of society, who mutually forego certain freedoms in exchange for the benefits and security provided by the state.

3. John Milton's *Areopagitica* (1644) and other pamphlets, James Harrington's *The Commonwealth of Oceana* (1656) and Algernon Sidney's *Discourses Concerning Government* (1698) played a central role in shaping English republican thought.

betrayed. It was this more radical form which reached Irish dissent from Scotland, especially from Glasgow University, where the influence of the Armagh-born presbyterian, Francis Hutcheson, continued long after his death in 1746.[4]

Hutcheson had already made an impact on Dublin reform politics before becoming professor of law at Glasgow. In Dublin he was particularly associated with a number of advanced presbyterian thinkers, including Thomas Drennan, William Bruce and Samuel Haliday,[5] whose descendants would provide the lead in the advanced reformism of Ulster in the 1780s and 1790s and who proudly paraded their dissent as a bastion against tyranny. Hutcheson carried the idea of a contract between governor and governed much further than Locke; he was quite explicit about the right of resistance in the event of a betrayal of trust, and through the writings of Richard Price and Joseph Priestley, his ideas were carried into American revolutionary thinking. Hutcheson also expounded that doctrine of religious toleration which was to become part of the platform of New Light presbyterianism,[6] and he deeply admired the tradition of armed militias for the protection of civil rights which was to produce the Volunteers at a later date. Given such influences and existing presbyterian consciousness, there is nothing inherently implausible about the promotion of early Irish republicanism in presbyterian Belfast. Presbyterian radicalism could be, and at times was, profoundly revolutionary, and in the latter part of the eighteenth century there was a marked sense of pride among Ulster presbyterians in their reputation as advanced thinkers. United Irish thinking was steeped in the presbyterian contractual tradition, and it was this old, yet deeply revolutionary tradition, which was behind their reluctant resort to arms after 1795.

There was, however, a fundamental dilemma within the theory of contract: what of those who had played no part in making the original compact? Locke had assumed that majority rule would prevail, and his notional minority consisted of a few individuals only. The problem with Ireland lay in the non-involvement of the majority, and the unsatisfactory nature of the contract theory to explain civil society was already recognised by the closing decades of the eighteenth century. It was then that Thomas Paine[7] made the sovereignty of the people the basis of modern democracy, and today popular sovereignty is seen to be vested in parliament. But the Ulster presbyterians have continued to argue in contractarian and increasingly archaic terminology and their refusal to accept parliamentary sovereignty and their appeal instead to the sovereignty of the monarch, demonstrates the difficulty they now experience in finding any convincing justification for their own privileged position within the political community of Great Britain....

With considerable justification, the Irish protestants felt that their stand at Derry and the Boyne[8] had played a major role in securing the protestant succession and certain fundamental liberties, and they were bitterly disillusioned when the gains of 1688 were not also extended to Ireland. After the struggles and insecurity of the seventeenth century, and the overwhelming defeat of the catholic cause in 1690, the Irish parliament became the seat of the new-found protestant supremacy and Irish protestants expected it to be elevated to equal partnership with the English parliament. Instead, the Irish parliament was left in the same inferior position as before and that inferior status was further confirmed by the Declaratory Act of 1720 and a host of

4. Francis Hutcheson (1694-1746) was born in Armagh and educated at Glasgow University. His *An Inquiry into the Original of our Ideas of Beauty and Virtue* (1725), perhaps the first modern treatise on aesthetic theory, was written in Dublin, as was his *An Essay on the Nature and Conduct of the Passions and Affections* (1728). He was appointed professor of moral philosophy at Glasgow University in 1729, where he trained some of the founding fathers of the Scottish Enlightenment such as Adam Smith. His *A System of Moral Philosophy* (1755), which justifies the right of revolution against unrepresentative government, helped to provide the rationale for the American War of Independence.
5. Thomas Drennan (1696-1768), a libertarian presbyterian clergyman, was a close friend of Hutcheson, and was the father of the United Irishman William Drennan. Samuel Haliday (1685-1739) became one of the leaders of the dissident presbyterian campaign against the anti-catholic tenets of the Westminster confession. William Bruce (1702-55) was a cousin of Francis Hutcheson and co-authored, with John Abernethy, one of the key texts in the libertarian presbyterian 'New Light' movement.
6. 'New Light' presbyterians were those who refused to subscribe to the sectarian tenets of the Westminster confession which enjoined presbyterians to 'extirpate' popery. The 'New Light' movement was founded in 1719 by the Rev. John Abernethy in Belfast and numbered Frances Hutcheson, Thomas Drennan, Samuel Haliday and William Bruce among its adherents.
7. Thomas Paine (1737-1809), political theorist and writer. His *Common Sense* (1776) popularized many of the ideas that inspired the American War of Independence, and his *The Rights of Man* (1791), a riposte to Edmund Burke, was taken as a manifesto for the French Revolution in the English-speaking world.
8. In 1689, beleaguered protestants lifted the siege of Derry; in 1690, William of Orange defeated the catholic Stuart forces at the battle of the Boyne, securing the 1688 'Glorious Revolution'.

other restrictive measures. Nor did the sequel to the Williamite victory in Ireland bring about any closer association between presbyterians and episcopalians against the common enemy. General protestant dissatisfaction at England's treatment after 1688 was further aggravated among the presbyterians by the non-extension of the 1719 Toleration Act to Ireland and their further exclusion from political life under the Test Act of 1704. Whereas the catholics had submitted to the Penal Code,[9] the presbyterians, conscious of their own loyalty and with a greater sense of injustice at exclusion, had little cause to respect the authorities. Moreover, the factor which kept Irish protestants tied to an increasingly degrading connection — the expectation of English military protection against internal and external enemies — proved non-existent more often than not, and the century after the Glorious Revolution witnessed repeated incidences of Irish protestants taking their own defence initiatives. Why then did they insist on maintaining the connection, while taking their dispute for greater independence from England to the very brink of separation? The answer lies in that deep-seated fear of the catholics, which had already been considerably eroded in England in the eighteenth century but which was intensified in Ireland by its peculiar historic situation.

The sense of historic wrong felt by the catholic populace existed in protestant imagination long before it did so in reality. Given the voluntary exile of the bulk of catholic leaders after the Williamite victory and the progressive erosion under the Penal Code of the power of those who remained, protestant fear of a catholic populace poised to take revenge on protestants at their first sign of weakness, was unrealistic, if not entirely unreasonable. Indeed the overwhelming identification of catholicism with nationalism is a relatively recent development, as is the image of Ireland as a devoutly catholic country. Until the nineteenth century there was scant regard for the dictates of the catholic church among a populace only nominally catholic, and while there was a vague sense of grievance common to poor rural populaces everywhere in pre-industrial Europe, the object of that discontent in Ireland was not yet the English connection or even the protestant government in Dublin. In fact the Irish peasantry shared with the protestants both their faith in the monarch and a tendency to attribute their ills to his evil advisers.

That Ireland became such an intensely catholic nation was due to protestant fears. No real effort was made to win the Irish people to the Reformation, and Ireland might just as easily have become a protestant as a catholic nation had the effort been made. That it was not made was the product of that invidious association between politics and religion which Ireland has never lost. 'Popery in the gross', was not seen simply as a religion, but as 'a dangerous and untrustworthy political system, biding its time for another attempt to overthrow the settlement by force.' The struggle for political dominance between the Old English and the New English had revolved around religion, and, with the former's defeat, around confiscations.

The Penal Laws of the eighteenth century were designed to exclude catholics from the political power which any reacquisition of landed property would bring. As a result three-quarters of Ireland's population became the victims of a strategy which aimed simply at excluding a political élite. The catholic religion on the whole was left undisturbed and religious tolerance grew apace from the 1730s onwards. But the net effect of the Penal Laws was to teach the catholics a sense of separate and aggrieved identity, and when the Irish economy began to prosper in the second half of the eighteenth century, they became increasingly conscious of their exclusion from a proper share in it. Most importantly, this legal exclusion bred an exaggerated sense of insecurity within a protestant ascendancy conscious that much of its power rested on recent confiscation and plantation. The examples of the 1641 catholic rebellion and James II's last parliament were frequently evoked as deterrents to protestant liberalism and there was a deep-seated fear that sheer numbers would mean domination by catholics if they were ever re-admitted to equal rights with protestants. The catholics were to be kept in their place, and the long absence of leadership after the Williamite victory ensured that they would remain there if reform did not come from outside elements such as the London government and, latterly, the protestants themselves.

The result was a catholic quiescence (or apathy)

9. The first of the Penal Laws was enacted in 1695. They were designed to prohibit catholics from participating in the political, economic and ecclesiastical life of the country. Presbyterians were also subject to some of the penal codes but were allowed, for example, to participate fully in economic activities.

which lasted for most of the eighteenth century, and the insulation of the protestant ascendancy which permitted it to campaign for greater autonomy under the British crown, without much reference to the rest of the Irish population. That campaign, whose origins were co-terminous with the very establishment of protestant supremacy in the 1690s, was to see the full application of the contract theory, leading eventually to the question: who are the ruled? and the inevitable answer: three million unrepresented catholics, as well as the million protestants. It was, when it came, in the 1780s and 1790s, a disturbing recognition that their own campaign for greater independence from England, a campaign based on fundamental liberties and the notion of a contract between ruler and ruled, made nonsense if three-quarters of the Irish populace was excluded from political life.

The campaign had impeccable roots within the protestant ascendancy, its earliest and most influential spokesman being the Dublin M.P. and close friend of Locke, William Molyneux.[10] Molyneux's *The Case of Ireland's being bound by Acts of Parliament in England, stated* (1698), portrayed the bitter protestant disappointment at the outcome of the Glorious Revolution for Ireland and became one of the key documents in the protestant 'patriot' campaign, culminating in the grant of legislative independence to Ireland in 1782-3. Molyneux had argued that the original compact had been made between the Irish people and the English king at the time of Henry II's 'conquest' of Ireland in the twelfth century. Consequently they owed no allegiance to any intermediary bodies and the English parliament had no right to bind Ireland by its statutes because no man could submit to laws to which he had not consented. The argument was potentially profoundly revolutionary and was to prove so when writers who had read Molyneux applied the concept of no taxation without representation to the similar American situation. But the full implications for Ireland only emerged when the protestant political nation came to develop a sense of pride in its own Irishness in that golden age of confident protestant liberalism, the 1770s and 1780s.

This movement within the protestant ascendancy for greater independence from England combined with the romantic Ossianic folk revival,[11] which was then sweeping Europe, to send these 'settlers' turned 'patriots' in search of their Irish heritage. In the latter part of the eighteenth century this rationalisation by the protestant 'patriots' of their own libertarian traditions seemed about to resolve that identity crisis which had situated them as foreign conquerors among hostile natives. That cultural nationalism which in the 1890s the second gaelic revival laid claim to for the Irish catholics, was deployed during the first gaelic revival in the 1780s and 1790s to promote the kind of secular unitary state which the Enlightenment was attempting to bring about elsewhere. Bardic poems were collected and translated; in 1786 the Royal Irish Academy was established in Dublin, with the Ulster Volunteer earl, Charlemont,[12] as its first president, while Belfast sponsored the revival of traditional music, the Harpers' Festival and the first magazine and dictionaries in the Irish language.[13] Although it was a 'self-conscious attempt' on the part of an élite to establish 'contact with a newly rediscovered indigenous popular culture', this sudden interest in gaelic culture was both produced by the campaign for greater autonomy from England and an influence which further radicalised that campaign, by highlighting the exclusion of its historic inhabitants from the evolving concept of an Irish nation.

The new interest in the native (and by the same token) the catholic heritage, made nonsense of any push for greater independence which did not also involve the catholics in the political nation, and in the reluctance of the protestants to allow catholic

10. William Molyneux's *The Case of Ireland Stated* (1698) instigated the development of 'colonial' or Anglo-Irish nationalism in the eighteenth century. It inspired the patriotic writings of Swift, Charles Lucas (1713-71) and, later, Grattan's parliament.

11. The Ossianic folk revival, which promoted romantic interest in the Celtic periphery of Europe and in cultural nationalism, was prompted by the publication of James Macpherson's forged translations from Scots Gaelic sources, *Fragments of Ancient Poetry* (1760), *Fingal* (1702) and *Temora* (1763). The eagerness displayed by both Anglo-Irish and native Irish historians in establishing Ossian's Irish credentials was an important contributory factor in the growth of cultural nationalism in Ireland.

12. James Caulfeild (1728-99), the earl of Charlemont, was commander-in-chief of the Irish Volunteers (1780) and was a leading supporter of Grattan's parliament, though he opposed catholic emancipation.

13. The Harpers' Festival, timed to coincide with the Fall of the Bastille celebrations in Belfast in 1792, was organized by (among others) the United Irishman Henry Joy McCracken, and the young music collector Edward Bunting, who lived with the McCrackens. In 1795 the United Irishmen in Belfast published *Bolg an tSolair*, the first Irish-language magazine.

involvement lay the ultimate explanation for their long acceptance of the more disadvantageous aspects of English rule. Later reformers in the Volunteers and United Irishmen recognised only too well this correlation between the protestants' fear of the catholics and their reluctance to push the attack on English rule too far....

The Volunteers were a northern phenomenon. Originating in Belfast in 1778, they were the product of Ulster's impatient independence, distrust for politicians, and glorification of the right of every citizen to arm in his own defence. Though they originated as Ulster's solution to the defenceless state of Ireland during Britain's war with America, they nevertheless embodied the central tenets of protestant libertarianism, and with their conventions of 1782-93 and their advanced programme for parliamentary reform, the Volunteers became the most effective extra-parliamentary pressure-group of the age. Tom Paine regarded them as the only truly revolutionary body in the country, and it was the Volunteers which produced the most radical of the reform groups to emerge in Britain in the dramatic decade of the 1790s — the United Irishmen. It is a reflection of the 'loyalist' and 'nationalist' misrepresentation of Irish history that the United Irishmen are traditionally considered part of catholic nationalist heritage. In reality they were a further manifestation of protestant — largely presbyterian — libertarianism, and non-presbyterian United Irishmen fully recognised their debt to that tradition.

But that libertarianism could display quite opposing characteristics depending on local circumstances. Thus in prosperous, New Light-dominated Belfast, with its sprinkling of catholics, Volunteering developed along more radical and pro-catholic lines; while in neighbouring Armagh, heavily populated by catholics who threatened lower-class protestant supremacy in the new and militantly catholic Defender movement,[14] the Volunteering tradition narrowed into the bitter sectarian channels which were to produce Orangeism. Even the more advanced Volunteer leaders, clearly disturbed by the logical conclusions of their own reformist philosophy, reined in before the spectre of 'popery in the gross', and reflected the bulk of protestant opinion in the North by their preference for gradual emancipation. But while they drew back, presbyterian libertarianism pushed the north-east in the other direction. The decaying Volunteering tradition was infused with the new militancy coming out of Belfast and with Thomas Drennan's son, Dr. William Drennan,[15] and a number of other Glasgow-educated presbyterians taking the lead, Belfast defiantly opened Volunteer ranks to catholics in May 1784. On 12-13 July the same Volunteers assembled for review in the plain of Falls on the outskirts of Belfast and voted an address to Lord Charlemont, their commander, expressing their 'satisfaction at the decay of those prejudices which have long involved us in feud and disunion — a disunion which ... has ... tended to create and foster that *aristocratic tyranny*, which is the foundation of every Irish grievance.'

Charlemont declined to accept the address. An arch-gradualist on the catholic emancipation issue, he and many more among the landed classes were already expressing traditional fears for the land settlement in the event of catholics regaining political rights. That class antagonism which has always suffused presbyterianism and which still deeply divides Ulster Unionism, now came to the fore in one of those remarkable periods in Irish history when the two persecuted sects, catholic and dissenter, joined together.

It was these middle-class presbyterians who took the decision to found a new movement which would reflect the impatient demand for reform coming out of Belfast, and they called on the most prominent protestant apologist for catholic emancipation, Theobald Wolfe Tone, to join them.[16] Tone had come to despise everything which his own episcopalian class stood for and he regarded himself as an honorary presbyterian in politics, if not in religion. Indeed right up to 1798, particularly after the republicanisation of the United Irish movement in 1795-6, the United executive and its French revolutionary ally regarded the real strength of the movement as lying in Ulster. The

14. The Defenders were a highly politicized catholic agrarian movement of the 1780s and 1790s. It was based in Ulster, North Connacht and North Leinster and established close links with the United Irishmen.

15. Dr William Drennan (1754-1820) proposed the founding of a subversive secret organization within the Irish Volunteers as early as 1784. Under the guiding hand of Drennan and Wolfe Tone, it eventually took the form of the United Irishmen, founded in October 1791.

16. In August 1791, Wolfe Tone published his *An Argument on Behalf of the Catholics of Ireland*, which acted as a catalyst for the founding of the United Irishmen.

founders of the United Irishmen clearly sensed the contradiction of seeking further political reform without also restoring political status to the catholics. But the tendency to evade this logical conclusion to their own rhetoric was even symptomatic of advanced presbyterian thinking and Tone gives a vivid account of the heated debates in Belfast on the catholic issue in the days prior to the inauguration of the new society....

But the transformation of Ulster from the heartland of early Irish republicansim in the 1790s to the later centre of bitterly anti-catholic loyalism was not such a dramatic reversal as it may appear. The strange combination of radicalism and reaction at the heart of presbyterianism can produce quite divergent responses depending on the level of insecurity at the given moment. Nor was that radicalism entirely destroyed by the shock of the sectarian nature of the 1798 rebellion in the south. It continued well into the nineteenth century and beyond, though it was severely muted by the impact of fundamentalist evangelicalism and by the Home Rule crisis after the 1880s. Moreover, the United Irish takeover of Ulster was never as complete as has been supposed. It was confined to areas of presbyterian domination and low incidence of catholic settlement, like Antrim and Down, and even here the process of early industrialisation was already starting to bring the hitherto largely rural sectarian conflict between protestant and catholic into the towns....

The traditional notion of popery as enslaving its adherents revealed itself in a certain contempt for the catholic intellect. Protestant radicals looked to the failure of the eighteenth-century catholic leaders to improve the lot of their co-religionists, and saw in that failure an inherent political conservatism, an obsequiousness and tendency to conform, so distasteful to presbyterian thinking which glorified in the freedom of the individual. Whatever conclusions future commentators will draw from current IRA activities in Ireland, the Irish catholic populace has never been naturally rebellious and the entire experience of modern Irish rebellion, from 1798, 1848, 1867 through to 1916[17] has shown the error of identifying the physical force tradition of Irish nationalism with catholicism in general. It was the conservative influence of the catholic leaders in the United Irish executive after 1797 which reactivated the latent mistrust of the Ulster protestants for catholicism — and indeed for 'southerners' in general — and caused a bitter and ultimately crippling split between the Ulster and Dublin leaders....

17. This refers to the United Irishman Rebellion of 1798, the Young Ireland Rebellion of 1848, the Fenian Rebellion of 1867, and the IRB-led Rising of 1916.

SEAMUS DEANE

(1940-)

from: CELTIC REVIVALS (1985)

[In this article, a reworking of his influential earlier paper 'The Literary Myths of the Revival: A Case for their Abandonment' (1977), Seamus Deane redirects the critical focus on revisionism from the catholic or Gaelic tradition to the Anglo-Irish Ascendancy. While historians such as F. S. L. Lyons have presented the Anglo-Irish as a constraining influence on the myth-makers of the Revival, Deane argues that many of the most pervasive myths of the Revival are, in fact, of Anglo-Irish origin. Cultural fictions of tradition and continuity, the importance of the heroic gesture and the desire for community, were important assets in the struggle waged by a declining ruling caste to maintain its cultural dominance in a period of transition and political upheaval. As the abiding preoccupation with the 'Big House' in Irish literature shows, this tradition is by no means obsolete and is, in fact, one of the main sources for the obfuscation of social realities that vitiated so much of literature after the Irish Renaissance.

The author's own notes are indicated by alphabetical letters.]

Perhaps the most seductive of all Yeats's historical fictions is his gift of dignity and coherence to the

Irish Protestant Ascendancy tradition. This was, in itself, a considerable achievement on behalf of a group which Standish O'Grady described in 1901 as 'rotting from the land in the most dismal farce-tragedy of all time, without one brave deed, without one brave word'.[a] We tend perhaps to forget just how much retrospective glamour the Ascendancy has gained from the Yeatsian version of its achievement in literature. The literary tradition has absorbed this fiction as a vital and even unquestionable imaginative truth. As a consequence, we fail to see that the heroic impulse which rather ambiguously transforms the physical-force tradition in politics (as in 'Easter 1916' or in 'The Statues') also produces the intellectual chauvinism of that Yeatsian recitation of the great eighteenth-century names — Berkeley, Burke, Swift, Goldsmith and Sheridan.

Briefly, Yeats claims that the eighteenth-century Irish writers have in common a specifically anti-modernist outlook. Berkeley's refutation of Locke, Swift's attacks on the Royal Society and on the mercantile system, Goldsmith's lament for the old way of life destroyed by 'luxury' and the agrarian revolution and, above all, Burke's great tirade against the French Revolution,[1] were all, in his view, attempts to stem the 'filthy modern tide' for which empiricism, science and parliamentary democracy were responsible. It had been a standard charge since the first generation of Romantic writers, that Locke and/or Newton were to blame for the afflictions of modernism. This was as much a stock response for literary men as was the attribution of Europe's political problems to Voltaire and Rousseau by political commentators. 'C'est la faute à Voltaire, c'est la faute à Rousseau' was a refrain adaptable to almost any persuasion. Yeat's selectivity is revealed in his omission from the Anglo-Irish pantheon of John Wilson Croker[2] — the outstanding Government spokesman against the revolution, France and the new 'Jacobinical' world.[b] Croker's hostility to the new literature (especially towards Shelley) probably disqualified him in Yeats's eyes. But this one example reveals what an oddly construed Anglo-Irish tradition we are offered. It is more comprehensible as a version of the Romantic polemic against the Enlightenment than as an account of Irish intellectual history in the eighteenth century.

Yeats, however, was unique in attributing the shared anti-modernism of his eighteenth-century heroes to their Irishness. The Irishness is, for him, partly genetic, partly environmental:

> Born in such a community, Berkeley with his belief in perception, that abstract ideas are mere words, Swift with his love of perfect nature, of the Houyhnhnms, his disbelief in Newton's system, and every sort of machine, Goldsmith and his delight in the particulars of common life that shocked his contemporaries, Burke with his conviction that all States not grown slowly like a forest tree are tyrannies, found in England the opposite that stung their own thought into expression and made it lucid.[c]

This particular version of eighteenth-century literary and intellectual history is manifestly absurd. In that short paragraph, Yeats misreads Berkeley and Swift, makes Goldsmith appear far more eccentric and controversial than he actually was, attributes to England a role in Burke's thought which really belongs to France — and yet he manages to escape derision. This is because he provides himself with the exit much favoured by poets since the Romantic revival, especially by those irresistibly drawn to the mythologizing of history. Very simply, we are told not to take such myths *as* history: they are myths *of* history. In *A Vision*, speaking of his 'circuits of sun and moon', Yeats asks that we learn to regard them as 'stylistic

a. Standish O'Grady, *Selected Essays and Passages* (Dublin, 1918), p. 180.

b. Myron F. Brightfield, *John Wilson Croker* (London, 1940). See also Croker's *Essays on the Early Period of the French Revolution* (London, 1857), and L. J. Jennings (ed.), *The Correspondence and Diaries of the late Right Honourable John Wilson Croker*, 3 vols (London, 1884).

c. *Essays and Introductions* (London, 1961), p. 25.

1. Yeats believed that Bishop Berkeley's philosophical idealism had refuted John Locke's belief in an underlying material reality as the sources of our ideas and sensations. Swift satirized the linguistic reforms of the Royal Society (founded by Charles II in 1660) in his *Gulliver's Travels* (1726) and the mercantilist monetary theories of the English government in *The Drapier's Letters* (1724-25). Goldsmith's nostalgia for a vanishing rural world is the theme of 'The Deserted Village' (1770). Burke's *Reflections on the Revolution in France* (1790) brought him to prominence as a bitter opponent of the French Revolution.

2. John Wilson Croker (1780-1857), conservative Irish politician and essayist, enjoys the dubious distinction of being one of the writers associated with *The Quarterly Review*, whose savage criticism devastated the young John Keats. He was a vitriolic adversary of the Irish novelist Lady Morgan, on account of her Whig sympathies. His critique of the French Revolution was contained in *Military Events of the French Revolution* (1830), and *Essays on the Early Period of the French Revolution* (1857).

arrangements of experience'.[d] On that level, the hermeneutic[3] value for Yeats of his circuits and of his version of the Protestant Ascendancy is undeniable. But it should be very clearly recognized that, in relation to history, these things are metaphors, lending to widely dispersed materials a provisional coherence.

This part of Yeats's writings does not then, in any serious sense, constitute a reading of history, even though the first to be so fooled was Yeats himself. When he told the Irish Senate that the Anglo-Irish were 'no petty people',[4] he was evidently not thinking of the John Wilson Croker type. He was translating into a proud assertion an almost comically absurd historical fiction. Unfortunately, the fiction has been believed. Yet its absurdity does not render it futile. It may not be a very persuasive reading of history but it is fascinating in the manner of Romantic aesthetics. In Coleridge, in Blake, in Carlyle, in William Morris, history is essentially engaged with the fortunes of the Imagination and, therefore, almost indistinguishable from aesthetics. The various histories we have inherited from the *Prophetic Books* or the *Philosophical Lectures*[5] or, indeed, from the essays of T. S. Eliot as well as Yeats, are at root theories of the imagination expressed in historical terms. More simply, they are aesthetic theories rendered as stories of which Yeats's Ascendancy is one of the more notable examples. This particular story has won a measure of acceptance equal to Arnold's story of the Celt.[6] One flatters the Protestant, the other the Catholic and both depend upon the notion that there is an identifiable and commonly shared racial component — Irishness — which expresses itself in hostility towards the modern world.

Yeats's account of the Anglo-Irish tradition blurs an important distinction between the terms 'aristocracy' and 'Ascendancy'. Had he known a little more about the eighteenth century, he would have recognized that the Protestant Ascendancy was, then and since, a predominantly bourgeois social formation. The Anglo-Irish were held in contempt by the Irish-speaking masses as people of no blood, without lineage and with nothing to recommend them other than the success of their Hanoverian cause over that of the Jacobites. This is evident in the poetry of men such as Daithi O'Bruadair and Aodagain O Rathaille[7] who lived through the first and most painful phase of the Whig Settlement in Ireland. But much later in the century Burke also went to great lengths to distinguish what Yeats ignored. Ireland, Burke claimed in his *Letter to a Peer of Ireland on the Penal Laws against Irish Catholics* (1782), had an oligarchy without an aristocracy. The Protestants in Ireland are, he claims, plebeian. And:

> A plebeian oligarchy is a monster: and no people, not absolutely domestic or predial slaves, will long endure it. The Protestants of Ireland are not *alone* sufficiently the people to form a democracy; and they are *too numerous* to answer the ends and purposes of *an aristocracy*. Admiration, the first source of obedience, can only be the claim or the imposture of the few. I hold it to be absolutely impossible for two millions of plebeians, composing certainly a very clear and decided majority in that class, to become so far in love with six or seven hundred thousand of their fellow citizens, (to all outward appearance plebeians like themselves, and many of them tradesmen, servants, and otherwise inferior to some of them,) as to see with satisfaction, or even with patience, an exclusive power vested in them, by which *constitutionally* they become the absolute masters; and, by the manners derived from their circumstances, must be capable of exercising upon them, daily and hourly, an insulting and vexatious superiority.[e]

d. *A Vision* (New York, 1961), p. 25.

3. Hermeneutics is the science of understanding and is based on the belief that events in the human world have *meaning* and stand in need of interpretation as well as causal or physical explanation.
4. In his famous speech on divorce delivered in the Irish Senate on 11 June 1925, Yeats argued that its prohibition treated the protestant population of the Free State as second-class citizens: 'We against whom you have done this thing are no petty people. We are one of the great stocks of Europe....'
5. William Blake's *Prophetic Books* (1792-1820) constitute the main bulk of his writing. Samuel Taylor Coleridge's *Philosophical Lectures* were delivered in 1818-19.
6. Matthew Arnold's *On the Study of Celtic Literature* (1867) popularized the image of the imaginative, impractical Celt and, notwithstanding its role as a colonial stereotype, exerted a considerable influence on the Literary (Celtic) Revival. Yeats praised Arnold in his essay 'The Celtic Element in Literature' (1898).

e. 'A Letter to Sir Hercules Langrishe', in *The Works of the Right Honourable Edmund Burke*, 8 vols (London, 1877), vol. 3, pp. 304-5.

7. Dáibhí Ó Bruadair (*c.* 1625-98) was the first great scholar/scribe poet in the Irish language. Aogán Ó Rathaille (*c.* 1670-1726) was another scribe and poet; he is credited with the composition of the first political *aisling* or vision poem.

Nevertheless, it is this group which Yeats refers to as an aristocracy and it is to Burke and others he looks for an intellectual justification for this description. It may be argued that he had more grounds for his view of the Ascendancy by the twentieth century. Yet Yeats's defence of this 'aristocracy' is developed in the twenties and thirties, after its defeat and, as O'Grady had pointed out, its rather ignoble demise. Since the death of Parnell, modern Irish writing has been fond of providing us with the image of the hero as artist surrounded by the philistine or clerically-dominated mob. This is a transposition of the political theory of aristocracy into the realm of literature and it has had, since Yeats, a very long run in Irish writing. The Big House surrounded by the unruly tenantry, Culture besieged by barbarity, a refined aristocracy beset by a vulgar middle class — all of these are recurrent images in twentieth-century Irish fiction which draws heavily on Yeats's poetry for them. Since Elizabeth Bowen's *The Last September* (1929) to more recent novels such as Aidan Higgins's *Langrishe, Go Down* (1966), Thomas Kilroy's *The Big Chapel* (1971), John Banville's *Birchwood* (1973) and Jennifer Johnston's *How Many Miles to Babylon?* (1976), the image and its accompanying themes have been repeated in a variety of forms. The power of this tradition is reflected in the work of English writers who set their novels in Ireland. Two remarkable examples here would be Henry Green's *Loving* (1933) and J. G. Farrell's *Troubles* (1972). The irony is that the Yeatsian view of the Irish Catholic middle classes is so similar to the Irish Catholic view of the eighteenth-century Protestant Ascendancy. Yeats was so eager to discover an aristocratic element within the Protestant tradition and to associate this with the spiritual aristocracy of the Catholic and Celtic peasantry — defining aristocracy in each case as a mark of Irishness and Irishness as a mark of anti-modernism — that he distorted history in the service of myth. This myth of history, the bequest of some of his greatest poems and of his highly eccentric essays, is a subtle and adaptable figure of thought, as a careful reading of 'Nineteen Hundred and Nineteen' or of 'Meditations in Time of Civil War' reveals. Yeats's poetry constitutes the real link between the Irish nineteenth-century novel and its twentieth-century counterpart. The experimental tradition which includes Joyce, Flann O'Brien and Beckett is clearly distinct in many ways from this Yeatsian inheritance. But in John Banville's fiction we can see how the traditional imageries of the Irish novel can be wedded to the experimental tradition.[f] The survival of the Big House novel, with all its implicit assumptions, is a tribute to the influence of Yeats and a criticism of the poverty of the Irish novelistic tradition. In fact the Big House is now more concerned with tourism and tax concessions, with the preservation of the artifacts of 'culture', than with power or value. In fiction, it is an anachronism. The over-extension of the Yeatsian myth of history into fiction helps us to see what an odd and protean thing it is and how far removed it has become from contemporary reality. In seeing this, we might finally decide to seek our intellectual allegiances and our understanding of our history elsewhere.

Yeats is not the only example of a writer making history palatable by imaging it as a version of the personality. Synge and Austin Clarke also come to mind. Synge's West, and Clarke's medieval, monastic, Ireland are not historically accurate so much as imaginatively useful in yielding a sense of the artist's enterprise in a world which, without these metaphorical suasions, would remain implacably hostile. The sweet-tongued vagrants of Synge's world are memorable Irish versions of the Baudelairean *poète maudit*[8] — healthier and folksier no doubt, but estranged in a similar way. Equally, we can see that the randy clerics of Clarke's beehive-hut civilization[9] signal a reconciliation between religion and sexuality, Clarke's most obsessive concerns, which twentieth-century Ireland had, in his view, failed to achieve. These images do not operate as ideals, nor do I insinuate that they are to be deplored because they distort social and historical fact. But it is surely remarkable that the treatment of history as metaphor by these writers enables them to mount an attack upon the small and squalid soul of the modern bourgeois by glamorizing either the Ascendancy, the peasantry or the medieval clergy. In other words, the desire to see Ireland as 'a country of the imagination' led to a conclusion that was identical with its premise. And

f. See especially *Birchwood* (London, 1973).

8. For Charles Baudelaire (1821-67), the poet's fascination with evil aligns him with the damned rather than with those who are saved.
9. See Austin Clarke's novel *The Bright Temptation* (1932), a risqué medieval romance.

that was the old Romantic premise that the world could be seen, falsely, in a bleak Newtonian light or, truly, in a pre-Newtonian aura. The destruction of aura, the argument runs, has been brought about by the development of modern science and its evolution into philosophies such as dialectical materialism which Yeats, in an astonishing and garbled paragraph, claims 'works all the mischief Berkeley foretold'.[g] This Romantic-aesthetic heritage, with which we still struggle, clearly harbours the desire to obliterate or reduce the problems of class, economic development, bureaucratic organization and the like, concentrating instead upon the essences of self, community, nationhood, racial theory, Zeitgeist.[10] Yeats had demonstrated throughout his long career that the conversion of politics and history into aesthetics carries with it the obligation to despise the modern world and to seek rescue from it. His sympathy for fascism is consistent with his other opinions, although he is, in the end, loyal to his early conception of an aristocratic society dominated by 'some company of governing men'.[h]

O'Connell and Parnell had mobilized Irish political energies into national movements. Yeats mobilized Irish cultural energies in a similar way, enhancing the distinction between Irish and English culture and providing the leadership to make this institutionally effective. The élite company which he envisaged would govern a community rather than represent a public. Therefore his aristocratic views needed reinforcement from the belief in the possibility of such a community in Ireland and, of course, the peasantry were there to supply it. The astonishingly swift decline of the Irish language in the years after the Famine and the increasing prominence of shopkeepers, publicans and innkeepers in the Land League and Home Rule movements were clear indications that Yeats's view of the peasantry was outmoded by the 1870s.[i] Their language was dying, their social formation had been drastically altered, their nationalism was fed on the Young Ireland diet of Thomas Moore, James Clarence Mangan and the pervasive emblems of harp, wolfhound and round tower. In addition, the literature of the Gaelic civilization was making its way into Yeats's and indeed into the national consciousness in the form of translation, most of it inept. Yeats came at the end of a long line of amateur antiquarians, most of whom regarded the translation of Gaelic poetry into English as a contribution to the enlightenment of an English (or English-speaking) audience on the nature of the Irish Question. Charlotte Brooke's *Reliques of Irish Poetry* (1789), James Hardiman's *Irish Minstrelsy* (1831), Samuel Ferguson's *Lays of the Western Gael* (1867) and even Douglas Hyde's *Love Songs of Connacht* (1894) helped to consign Gaelic poetry to the bookshelf, transforming it into one of the curiosities of English literature.[j] They were little more than obituary notices in which the poetry of a ruined civilization was accorded a sympathy which had been notably absent when it was alive. The same can be said for Standish O'Grady's *History of Ireland: Heroic Period* (1878-80), the work which so coloured Yeats's mind that he believed all modern Irish writing owed part of its distinctive tincture to that source. Much of what Yeats believed about the Irish peasantry, its past and its native literature, was formed by the literature produced by the more cultivated sections of the nineteenth-century landlord class. The paradox does not seem to have troubled him unduly.

Nevertheless, it might trouble his readers. The flimsy basis upon which Yeats built his conception of the Ascendancy and of the peasantry ultimately affects his poetry and drama. All his ideas and images of tradition and communion are predicated on the idea of spiritual loneliness. Even when he sees himself as being in some sense the inheritor of Young Ireland,[11] he envisages the crisis of his own times as one in which the individual is liberated from conformity, in which the lonely aristocratic spirit can survive only because it lives within an organic community:

g. *Essays and Introductions*, p. 401.

h. 'Michael Robartes: Two Occult Manuscripts', ed. W. K. Hood, in *Yeats and the Occult*, ed. George Mills Harper (London, 1976), p. 219.

i. K. Theodore Hoppen, 'Politics in Mid-Nineteenth-Century Ireland', in *Studies in Irish History*, eds. A. Cosgrove and D. McCartney (Dublin, 1979), p. 222.

j. See Cathal G. O Hainle, 'Towards the Revival: Some Translations of Irish Poetry 1789-1897', in *Literature and the Changing Ireland*, ed. Peter Connolly (London, 1982), pp. 37-58.

10. The spirit of genius that prevails in a given age. It has taken on ominous connotations since its association with national aggrandizement in German idealist philosophy.

11. Young Ireland, the political group in the 1840s associated with Thomas Davis and *The Nation* newspaper, was a cultural nationalist movement that ended in the abortive rising of 1848.

> Ireland is passing through a crisis in the life of the mind greater than any she has known since the rise of the Young Ireland party, and based upon a principle which sets many in opposition to the habits of thought and feeling come down from that party, for the seasons change, and need and occupation with them. Many are beginning to recognise the right of the individual mind to see the world in its own way, to cherish the thoughts which separate men from one another, and that are the creators of distinguished life, instead of those thoughts that had made one man like another if they could, and have but succeeded in setting hysteria and insincerity in place of confidence and self-possession.[k]

His heroes — Parnell, John O'Leary, Synge and Hugh Lane[12] — were all men whose aloofness and loneliness were a product of their immersion in some aspect of the national consciousness. They were embodiments of individuality, enemies of individualism; aristocrats, not democrats. Three of them, Parnell, Synge and Lane, were at the centre of three great controversies — the O'Shea divorce case, the *Playboy* riots and the Lane bequest. In each instance, Yeats viewed them as heroic and aristocratic figures attacked by the plebeian mob. Events like these, and the carnage of the First World War and of the revolutionary period in Ireland 1916-22, deprived them of that sanguine spirit which had informed his early writings, especially those essays in which he declared his faith in the sense of a beginning which the revived Ireland of his youth provided. Thereafter, from about 1913 onwards, he is, like so many of his Edwardian contemporaries, preoccupied with gloomy predictions and fears of the end of civilization.[l] Perhaps Yeats had a more pronounced sense of disappointment than Wells, Conrad, Forster, Shaw or Galsworthy precisely because he had so recently entertained such high hopes for his country. The frailty of his conception of the Irish tradition and community made its collapse inevitable. Yet, in Auden's famous phrase, Ireland did 'hurt' him 'into poetry',[13] not by being mad but simply by being other than he had imagined. After the death of Swinburne in 1909 Yeats, with the Bullen edition of his *Collected Works* published in 1908, was the senior poet of the English-speaking world. At the age of 43 he already appeared to be 'one of that generation of massive late Victorians who were to dominate our literature.'[m] At the age of 50 he had become one of the great modernists. It is in 1915 that his poem 'Scholars' opens Pound's *Catholic Anthology*, followed by 'The Love Song of J. Alfred Prufrock'; it is in 1922, the *annus mirabilis* of the modern movement,[14] that his *Later Poems* appeared. With an almost inexhaustible resourcefulness, he maintains the privileged role for Ireland in his thought, contrasting the self-sacrifice of Easter Week with the mindless slaughter of the trenches, using the bitterness of the Civil War as the ground for a great threnody on the disappearance of the civilization of the Big House, the Anglo-Irish spirit and, by extension, of Western Christendom itself. But in the thirties Yeats's fidelity to his governing ideas of aristocracy and community was to betray him into absurdity through his association with the fascist Blueshirt movement.[15] Romantic Ireland was dead and gone but Yeats seemed to be less ready to believe this in 1933 than he had been in 1913.

Still, the power and influence of Yeats's versions of Irish community and tradition remain, no matter how insubstantial their basis in our contemporary understanding of history. They retain their life because they are rooted in his poems and plays although our inclination is to think of the poems and plays as rooted in them. The principle of continuity which he established in literature, stretching from Swift to the Revival, and that which Pearse established in politics, stretching from Wolfe Tone to the men of 1916, are both exemplary instances of

k. *Plays and Controversies* (London, 1923), p. 198.
l. Samuel Hynes, *Edwardian Occasions* (London, 1972), pp. 1-12.
m. Cyril Connolly, *Previous Convictions* (London, 1967), p. 252.

12. John O'Leary (1830-1907), the Fenian leader, was one of Yeats's early mentors. Hugh Lane (1875-1915), the art collector, became a subject of controversy when a proposal to build an art gallery in Dublin to house his modern art collection, mainly French Impressionists, was turned down by Dublin Corporation. The attack on the proposal was spearheaded by the businessman William Martin Murphy through his newspapers, the *Irish Independent* and the *Evening Herald*.
13. W. H. Auden's famous line is taken from his poem 'In Memory of W. B. Yeats' (1940).
14. James Joyce's *Ulysses* and T. S. Eliot's 'The Waste Land' were published in 1922.
15. The Blueshirt movement, founded by supporters of the Cumann na nGaedheal (later Fine Gael) party in 1933, was a right-wing paramilitary group modelled on fascist lines.

the manner in which tradition becomes an instrument for the present. Without such a tradition, or the idea of it, history appears gapped, discontinuous, unmanageably complex. The period between 1880 and 1940 made a fetish of continuity in part because the generation before had witnessed the final rupturing of the Gaelic civilization. The glamorization of the Celt and of the Ascendancy was an attempt to reconcile on the level of myth what could not be reconciled at the level of politics. It was, in effect, an Arnoldian 'healing measure' which failed. It offered the Irish the opportunity to be unique but refused them the right to be independent on the grounds that independence would lead to a loss of their uniqueness. Yeats's unhappiness with the new Irish state stemmed from this. In refusing to accept an Ascendancy-led cultural nationalism of Yeats's sort, with its aristocratic claims, post-Treaty Ireland effectively put an end to the Revival, a fact for which many of its writers and artists have not forgiven it. The great myths had gone. The best of the poets after Yeats quickly learned that the local and the ordinary defined the horizon for literature as it did for politics. With the emergence of Patrick Kavanagh, the new state found its characteristic, if adversary, voice. The day of the literary peasant and of the aristocratic hero was over. It was not Emain Macha[16] but Armagh which the dawn light revealed to the poet from County Monaghan. Moreover, there was a political border between them.

16. The old Gaelic name for Armagh. It was the most important political centre in ancient Ulster, and in 444 was established by St Patrick as the ecclesiastical capital of Ireland.

TERENCE BROWN

(1944-)

from: IRELAND'S LITERATURE (1988)

[Terence Brown's 1985 Field Day pamphlet, from which this extract is taken, is one of the few attempts from outside conventional nationalist critiques to examine the gap between the rhetoric and the historical realities of the protestant community in Northern Ireland, particularly the Presbyterian Church. Like its traditional nationalist counterparts, the protestant community is in the grip of the past (albeit of a more recent vintage). It is also immobilized by irrational strains, such as millenarianism (the cult of the leader/prophet who promises deliverance from a state of siege) and the religious hysteria of evangelical revivalism, both representing a substantial departure from Max Weber's association of a legal-rational mentality with protestantism in his classic work, *The Protestant Ethic and the Spirit of Capitalism* (1905). Revisionist glosses on the Northern loyalist tradition however, are confined largely to academic or cultural criticism and, in marked contrast to the waning of nationalism in political practice in the Republic, have yet to become part of a major realignment in unionist politics.]

THE WHOLE PROTESTANT COMMUNITY: THE MAKING OF A HISTORICAL MYTH

In his poem 'After the Summit' in *Liberty Tree* (1983) Tom Paulin reflects plaintively on the northern protestant's contemporary lack of a significant historical inheritance:

> Boot polish and the Bible,
> the Boys' Brigade is arming.
> This is the album you found
> in your grandmother's sideboard,
> the deedbox with her burial papers,
> a humped ledger and a lock
> of that dead uncle's hair.
> There is so little history
> we must remember who we are.

In view of the recurrent complaint, usually voiced by impatient British commentators on Irish affairs, that Irishmen of all persuasions are invincibly attached to an all-too-palpable historical legacy, Paulin's sense of deprivation might strike one as beside the point. It isn't — rather, it's a perception of poverty grounded in an accurate reading of the northern protestant's historical imagination.

That imagination is one that has in modern times (at least since 1886)[1] had recourse to a vision of the protestant community's history which is starkly simple in outline and depressingly lacking in emotional range and complexity. In that sense, a community that superficially might appear to be burdened by historical awareness can accurately be said to possess 'so little history'....

The contemporary northern protestant's sense of history is, I would argue, markedly similar to that of the catholic nationalist. That his history seems impoverished by comparison with nationalist historical awareness is because that history has had to perform fewer functions and is necessarily simpler. By its nature, it is bound to comprehend imaginatively much less of the human condition. Northern protestants, as inheritors of those who have prosecuted the political cause of the protestants of Ireland have in the last analysis only the one historical requirement — to uphold the Settlement of 1689[2] and to try to ensure that the principle of protestant hegemony is recognised and supported. Accordingly, in MacDonagh's words 'The siege of Derry in 1689 is their original and most powerful myth. They seem to see themselves in that, and since then, as an embattled and enduring people. Their historical self-vision is of endless repetition of repelled assaults, without hope of absolute finality or fundamental change in their relationship to their surrounding and surrounded neighbours.'[3] To this one would only wish to add that this primal sense of siege has, like nationalist historiography, been infused with millenialism (the assaults may be endless but faith must recurrently be placed in the powers of some eschatalogically prescient prophet). And it draws also on a dour blend of the Calvinistic doctrine of election with a Whiggish commitment to a liberty which can only be enjoyed by those possessed of the true faith. As an interpretation of human experience such a historical myth is not without some merit; tenacity, acceptance of suffering, will, are the emotional registers of which it can take account. But there is little else to recommend it for it is disabled by an imaginative exclusiveness which many find repellent. Indeed that the siege was, in the telling of the tale, self-imposed by the Apprentice boys, the temporizing Lundy forced to flee the city,[4] seems metaphorically appropriate to the emotionally exclusive quality of the northern protestant's historical self-vision. And it may be this emotional narrowness in the northern protestant's basic self-vision that has led to the literary trope of 'the Black North', with its sense of restriction, bleakness, and atrophied possibility which is employed in dozens of poems, novels and plays,[5] and representatively in a poem by Patrick Williams, 'Cage Under Siege' (published in Padraic Fiacc's anthology of 1974, *The Wearing of the Black*).

This is home. This is the Irish North.
Where we endure the earth's falling away
Rivets an iron sky to north and west.
Where the covetous South darkens, granite
Rears a grave wall. Eastward the sea recoils
Toward England, breathless with horror, sobs back.

On our borders the known world ends sheer.
We've pulled the sea around us like a shawl
And heaved the mountains higher. The waiting
South's bog-barbarians starve against a grand
Squiggle on our map. The sky is closed.
This is home. This is the Irish North.

Writing in 1969 of the established church in Ireland, Sir Robert Southwell (the diplomat and principal Secretary of State for Ireland) referred to 'those English protestants who have nothing on this side of paradise to adhere to but old England'.[6] For most of the time since the Settlement of 1689 northern protestants have not been forced to place their trust in heaven alone. This is because British power has in varying degrees and for varying reasons sought to protect their position, allowing them the dubious luxury of permanent dependency

1. In 1886, William Ewart Gladstone introduced the first Home Rule Bill, provoking intense opposition from protestants in Northern Ireland. This hostility culminated in the founding of the forerunner of the Unionist Party.
2. In 1689, William of Orange and Mary became monarchs of England, Scotland and Ireland in the wake of the 1688 Glorious Revolution, which removed James II from the throne.
3. Oliver MacDonagh, 'Time's Revenge and Revenge's Time: A View of Anglo-Irish Relations', *Anglo-Irish Studies*, Vol. IV (1979), 17.
4. The siege of Derry began in April 1689 when the Apprentice Boys locked the gates of the city against King James II, forcing the 'traitor' Colonel Lundy, the leader of the city garrison, to flee. They were relieved after 105 days.
5. Terence Brown's own footnote reads: 'For an excellent discussion of some of these works, see Edna Longley, 'The Writer and Belfast' in *The Irish Writer And The City*, ed. M. Harmon, Gerrards Cross, 1984, pp. 66-70.'
6. Cited in J. C. Beckett, *Confrontations: Studies in Irish History* (London: Faber and Faber, 1972), p. 98.

in a country where, had such support been definitively withdrawn, they would have been forced to develop a different, ultimately more truly serviceable self-understanding and historiographical consciousness. And British policy in Ireland has accordingly been able to depend for its needs upon one apparent constant in Irish affairs: that whatever internal differences there may have been within the northern protestant community — for example, between episcopalians and presbyterians — that community will unite in opposition to any threat of domination by catholic Ireland. With one exception — the years leading to the '98 rebellion — this has always been the case.[7] And it has been especially apparent since 1886. Indeed, it was the prospect of Home Rule which in the years between 1886 and the Great War forged the modern Ulster Unionist identity, an identity which subsumed manifold differences within northern protestant society in a fundamental, all-embracing opposition to the proposed constitutional change. Since that time, the historical myth of siege has had its greatest social utility as the expression of a primary solidarity of purpose within a community principally defined by a determination to resist.

Yet any detailed consideration of northern Irish protestantism since the seventeenth century would, of course, easily destroy the myth of perpetual united solidarity. The northern protestant community has recurrently been riven by contentious disputes, oppositions of class and creed, and theological schisms to a degree which is remarkable, given the almost total contemporary silence on the matter. Only a community with very simple historical needs could maintain such an extraordinary, near-unanimous reticence about the complications of its past. Individual academic historians have, it is true, produced monographs on aspects of history that touch on the protestant experience in the north of Ireland (an example is J. C. Beckett's lucid, coolly analytic *Protestant Dissent in Ireland*),[8] but almost no awareness exists in the general community of how such works might challenge the dominant self-consciousness of contemporary northern protestantism. It is only when we consider the works of certain protestant church historians that we can find traces of a more general awareness of how complex the north's past has been. There the piously inspired exercises of presbyterian historians have had to reckon with a social history which is not conducive to a vision of the northern protestant experience as one of continuous, unified, lawful, rational, disciplined resistance to a papally dominated, terrifyingly irrational nationalism.

In terms of modern historical studies the church historian is in a somewhat anomalous position. He may choose to study the history of a church or a sect as one phenomenon among many, and to employ that emotionally and intellectually neutral manner which is currently respected in the academy. He is more likely, however, to be drawn to his subject, as a nationalist is to the study of his nation, or a Marxist to the history of a working class, by reason of faith and creed. The story of the trials and tribulations of those whom he must consider his brethren in the faith is hardly then merely matter for disinterested enquiry, since that historical suffering touches the historian's personal sense of religious values as a living part of the community. For such a historian the study of, for example, the presbyterian church in Ireland will, inevitably, involve value judgments and personal commitments in a way which draws historical research out of the library and lecture-hall into the meeting-house and manse where it must more readily affect contemporary attitudes and assumptions.

At least five aspects of the history of the presbyterian church in Ireland present the contemporary presbyterian historian with severe problems because they do not co-exist easily with the dominant Unionist ideological framework which conditions most protestant thinking. Such historians must frankly face these truths about their church: the church had its origins in the crucible of dissent from established authority; it has been involved in direct ways with sedition and revolutionary action; it has traditions of conflict on issues of conscience and has endured schism; it has had an ambivalent and not always mutually accommodating relationship with the Orange Order,[9] and it has been profoundly affected by the dangerously uncontrollable

7. Northern presbyterians were prominent among the leaders of the United Irishmen (founded in 1791).

8. J. C. Beckett, *Protestant Dissent in Ireland* (London: Faber and Faber, 1948).

9. The protestant Orange Order was founded in County Armagh in 1795 to counter the agrarian agitation of the catholic Defenders, and to offset the demand for catholic emancipation by the radical protestant leadership of the United Irishmen.

forces of evangelical revivalism. Each of these in obvious ways can be seen to disturb the vision of the northern protestant as having always belonged to a homogeneous, ideologically monolithic, social group which stands for authority, law, order, loyalty, conformity, social cohesion and reason. . . .

. . . [W]hat strikes . . . the cultural historian as he reflects on the history of Irish presbyterianism is the contrast between the energy expended, polemical skill employed and quality of mind displayed in church matters and the extraordinarily debased level of political consciousness expressed by the Unionist Party since the foundation of the northern Irish state until very recent times. How individuals nurtured in the disputatious atmosphere of presbyterian life have so readily acquiesced in the monolithic political simplicities of Northern Ireland is surprising — especially if church conflicts have indeed possessed political significance. For political life is conducted within a rarely challenged homogeneous ideological monolith, while theological and ecclesiastical life (often bearing on political matters) displays vigorous heterogeneity. If the presbyterian respect for dissent, individual conscience and personal commitment were to be translated into the political dimension one could at the least expect a toughening and sharpening in northern Irish political discourse, and to see the dominant historical myth of Ulster protestantism subjected to some characteristically cantankerous disrespect. Similarly, the frequently effete and condescending utterances of Official Unionists and of British Secretaries of State on the Union would not be so often accepted without demur as reflecting a regrettable historical necessity. Facing the uncharacteristically timorous political engagement of many of his fellow presbyterians, the Reverend Fulton suggests that the rise of Ian Paisley has inhibited them from expressing political dissent:

> Political and ecclesiastical leaders glance carefully over their shoulders before committing themselves publicly on issues in which Paisley is involved. The Roman catholic Bishop of Derry is reported in the Belfast Telegraph for 21 March 1981, saying: 'Any protestant churchman or politician who shows any sense of rapproachment [*sic*] or willingness to come closer or work closer with members of the catholic church will usually find that is prelude to the end of his career.' If that statement exaggerates, it is only slightly. Paisley's followers seem to invest him with an almost messianic destiny: the defender of the Faith, the champion of true protestantism, the guarantor of civil and religious liberty. Others may fear that here is a dangerous threat to the freedoms of Democracy; but their fears are usually muted.[10]

What Fulton doesn't care to reflect on is how presbyterianism, in the period before Paisley's emergence, allowed its political commitments to become predictably uniform, so that there is no twentieth century Montgomery to oppose the twentieth century Cooke.[11]

If Fulton ignores this particular challenge, there is yet another challenge which the presbyterian historian has to face, because the protestant who identifies his creed with order, law, stability and rationality must consider the deep presbyterian involvement with evangelical revival.

During the nineteenth century, an evangelical awakening swept through much of the protestant world — it affected Scandinavia, Germany, Switzerland, France, Holland, England, Scotland, the United States — and this phenomenon took a particularly bizarre and unnerving form in the north of Ireland. In 1859 a wave of religious enthusiasm spread from Connor in Co. Antrim to inspire thousands of rural protestants. The Revival often affected the poorest sections of the community and was marked by symptoms of violent hysteria which terrified spectators. It stimulated many in their religious enthusiasm and clearly remains an important, if unacknowledged, influence on the northern psyche. Its monuments are the innumerable mission halls and tents, evangelistic crusades, and evangelical associations that make Northern Ireland an Irish extension of the Bible belt.

Revivalism challenges the Ulster historical myth in two ways — it suggests that an ordered, dignified, disciplined vision of life is no match for the excitements of religious ecstasy and that the

10. The Very Reverend Dr A. A. Fulton, 'Church in Tension' in *Challenge and Conflict: Essays in Irish Presbyterian History and Doctrine* (Belfast: W. G. Baird, 1981), p. 188.

11. Rev. Henry Cooke (1788-1868), a fiery presbyterian preacher, orator and avid opponent of catholicism, is often seen as a precursor of Ian Paisley. Cooke was forcefully challenged from within presbyterianism by the liberal Rev. Henry Montgomery (1788-1865), who supported catholic emancipation (see above pp. 339-40).

northern protestant is no more immune to irrational forces than the Irish catholic. A presbyterian historian whose work on the subject is cited with approval in *Challenge and Conflict* reveals a characteristic unease before the emotional violence that was released by the Year of Grace:

> There were elements which shocked and puzzled, as in so many similar movements found in the States at the same period; but many strange and objectionable features presented themselves. After all, the movement was a tremendous stimulus to the nervous system of those brought under its power, and, whatever the source of the manifestations might be thought or claimed to be, the overwrought system of many people played them strange tricks in those involuntary phenomena which are today known as automatism, such as trances, kicking, screaming and the like; hysterical evidence of the coming of great and unaccustomed emotion into channels as yet ill-adapted to contain or control it in normal ways.[12]

What precisely such channels might be is not clear, but the fear of abnormality is noticeably present.

The phenomenon of revivalist fundamentalism in present-day Northern Ireland therefore raises doubts in sensitive minds as to how 'normal' their society is. This is because so many of its members seem to require emotional outlets that combine extremes of individualism with the gratification of a mass movement. And for the presbyterian intellectual there is no ready mechanism whereby he may dissociate himself from a disturbing, threatening awareness. The atavistic celebrations of the Orange Lodges can be held at a distance in the knowledge that presbyterians were in general not responsible for their foundation. But Revivalism arose in the very heart of presbyterianism. Accordingly presbyterian historians tread uneasily between the religious interpretation of revivalism as the outpouring of the Holy Spirit and sociological explanations which regard it as the inevitable outcome of a process of modernisation which has created a class of deracinated, lonely, frightened people, ready prey for the exotic emotional appeal of a millenialist eschatology.[13] Neither is supportive of a sense of northern protestant identity as characterised by a resolute, stable attachment to civic virtue.

Most presbyterians who know something of the history of their church and the enduring tensions within it are able to ignore the ways in which that rich and complex tradition challenges the dominant historical myth of the whole protestant community. That this myth is a disabling one I have suggested earlier, for it excludes a great deal of human experience, so that a lot of life must be lived without communal imaginative support.[14] It is also crucially disabling in the political sphere since all political possibilities are subordinated to the basic determination to maintain the historically authenticated resistance. Temporizers who dally with political revisionism are made immediate victims by appeal to the historical myth. . . .

One last reflection may be in order. A people without much history, or which feels the need for no very complex historical self-awareness, is homeless in a particularly special way. The visual constituents of the past (within which it makes a home) are all around it, and no matter how indifferent individuals may profess themselves to be they cannot fail to be aware of them, if only subliminally. Indeed, the spate of books of photographs published in recent years on Victorian and Edwardian Ulster bear a kind of mute testimony to the power the past holds even over a people who have suffered a kind of collective amnesia about so much of their experience. But for so historically bereft a people as the northern protestant community, what the past cannot vouchsafe is the language in which their predecessors expressed their public experience. Consequently the northern protestant lives without much sense of the modes of thought and feeling that the written records of his ancestors represent. What T. S. Eliot in *Four*

12. Fulton, p. 152.
13. Terence Brown's own note reads: 'No full-scale history of the Revival as yet exists. John T. Carson's *God's River In Spate* (1959) is an evangelical's centenary celebration. Interestingly Ian Paisley has written on the Revival in one of his historical soundings. Peter Gibbon, in *The Origins of Ulster Unionism* (Manchester, 1975) attempts a brief assessment of the phenomenon in Marxist terms while David Miller has examined it as a product of the process of modernisation. See David W. Miller, 'Presbyterians and "Modernization" in Ulster', *Past and Present*, No. 80, August, 1978, pp. 66-90. It would be fascinating to read a historical recreation of the events of 1859 in the manner of such a writer as Le Roy Ladurie. It is also a strange fact that the world of northern protestant revivalism has scarcely been explored by Irish writers. Sam Thompson's play *The Evangelist* was a rare attempt to address the topic directly.'
14. Terence Brown's own note reads: 'Though individual writers can exploit this lack as a kind of liberal freedom, often in a highly engaging fashion, as in the poetry of James Simmons.'

Quartets termed 'the communication/Of the dead ... tongued with fire beyond the language of the living'[15] is simply not heard in Ulster. With its messages of social complexity, that communication hints at a richer kind of cultural inclusiveness than the myth of besieged solidarity can possibly allow....

15. The lines occur in 'Little Gidding' (1942), the last 'Quartet'.

III. TRADITION AND DISCONTINUITY

OLIVER MacDONAGH

(1925-)

from: STATES OF MIND .... (1983)

[The pervasive role of history in the legitimation of political aspirations in Ireland is the subject of the opening chapter of Oliver MacDonagh's book *States of Mind: A Study in Anglo-Irish Conflict 1780-1980*. Whereas English historiography is marked by a belief in progress and a sense of historical development ('the Whig interpretation of history'), Irish history, whether in its nationalist or unionist form, is characterized by the contemporaneity of the past, the view that history is condemned to repeat itself.

In an important gloss on received views of the Irish preoccupation with the past, MacDonagh shows that the concern with what has gone before does not necessarily entail a desire to restore a vanished order, or even to establish a link with a continuous tradition, but may often look to the past as simply a model, or a precedent, for present-day political initiatives.]

I

After Lloyd George's first meeting with de Valera on 14 July 1921 to negotiate a peace treaty between Great Britain and Ireland, he told his secretary, 'I made no impression. I listened to a long lecture on the wrong done to Ireland ... [by] Cromwell, and when[ever] I tried to bring him [de Valera] to the present day, back he went to Cromwell again'.[a] The trouble, as Lloyd George was saying in effect, was that while the English do not remember any history, the Irish forget none. Behind this familiar facetiousness lies a profound truth. To Lloyd George, the seventeenth century was dead, irrelevant to current difficulties, except perhaps in helping to explain how they might, remotely, have come into being. To de Valera, the seventeenth century lived on in that it had generated still unexpiated and irredeemed injustices; the mere intervention of years, however many, could do nothing whatever to change the ethical reality. When and how did this Irish habit of historical thought arise?

a. E. Holt, *Present under Arms: The Irish Troubles, 1916-23* (London, 1960), p. 258.

II

Modern Irish historiography was born in 1790 with the publication of the Revd Edward Ledwich's *Antiquities of Ireland*. Ostensibly, Ledwich wrote as an enlightenment man, bent on dissipating by eighteenth-century sunlight what he called the bardic fictions which had enveloped early Irish history. In fact, as the subsequent controversy about his work revealed, he was signalling the fact that the Irish past had become an additional arena for current Irish political conflict. His real target was rising papists like Charles O'Connor [*sic*] and Thomas Wyse, founders of the Catholic Committee in 1760,[1] who had combined agitation for Catholic relief with attempts to preserve the traditional Gaelic culture. The Celtic revival had been common ground between the new Catholic

1. The Catholic Committee was founded in 1760 with a view to repealing the Penal Laws against catholics. Charles O'Conor (1710-91), the intellectual force on the Committee, pioneered the study of Irish history and antiquarianism among native catholics, publishing his *Dissertations on the Antient History of Ireland* in 1753.

intelligentsia and many of the Anglo-Irish liberals in the 1770s and 1780s, as the very warm encouragement of Celtic studies by the Royal Irish Academy in the latter decade testifies.[2] But, consciously or unconsciously, men like O'Connor and Wyse had further ends in view than mere scholarship and the classification of antiquities. They were using the remote past to support their claims to social and civic parity. As with so many anti-colonialists of the twentieth century, they were pressing the fact and character of a pre-conquestal native civilisation into service as a means of establishing their equality of footing with their overlords. Part of the conquerors' claim to superiority rested on their supposedly more advanced culture. In so far as the gap between this and the social forms it attempted to supersede could be narrowed, *pro tanto*[3] their ascendancy was weakened. Ledwich, however, thought that he had seen through the upstarts' design in canvassing pre-conquest Ireland. He was not deceived as to their ulterior purpose. He had discerned a dangerous association of Gaelic, Catholic and radical political views, and was proceeding to take his counter-measures. The *Antiquities of Ireland* was the opening shot of a campaign.

During the next three decades the lines of division became quite clear. After 1800 Protestant and unionist antiquarians and historians worked, almost without exception, to undermine romantic or glorious conceptions of pre-Norman or pre-Danish Ireland, while their nationalist and Catholic counterparts strove to sustain and develop them. This polarisation had various interesting implications. We might draw attention again to the fact that Protestant denigration of the ancient Celtic culture was a new phenomenon. Before 1790 Irish Protestant scholarship had often seen in early Irish history purer and less adulterated social forms. We might note, for future reference, that this was to prove the case once more especially *after* 1870. Then, Anglo-Irish intellectuals, faced with an ebullient Home Rule (and, as they would generally have added, Rome Rule) movement, sought to trump it by playing the card of a Gaelic civilization which predated the Christian bifurcation by a millenium or more.[4] Again — to take another example of the curiosity of the affair — it is remarkable that although most of the historical protagonists of 1790-1820 were in holy orders (of one sort or another) it was the character of pre-Christian Ireland which was being contested.

But what I especially wish to emphasise in the scholarly warfare over the resuscitated body of the Celtic past is the elision of time common to all the combatants. Time was being so foreshortened that the character of druidical Ireland was being treated as validating or invalidating, in some significant fashion, the early-nineteenth-century political and social order. In part, this use of antiquity as a touchstone of the present resembled the use made of the early Church by the religious reformers and counter-reformers in the theological disputations of the sixteenth century; but with the roles reversed. The nationalist-Catholic school saw the course of Irish history in terms of degeneration from an initial purity, whereas the unionist-Protestants presented it in terms of a triumphant, if lengthy and incomplete, emergence from barbarism.

A more directly political foreshortening of time rapidly succeeded the controversy on the sophistication of Celtic culture. The 1798 rebellion in Leinster was as stunning an event to contemporaries in Ireland as 1789 had been to French men and women in France. The floor of organised society had collapsed — albeit momentarily — and the established classes suddenly awoke to the existence of passions and hatred which they had hitherto relegated comfortably to a primeval phase in Britain's conquest of Ireland. . . .

. . . [B]y the middle 1820s, the 1798 rising began to appear in nationalist historiography in its own right, paraded as the latest chapter of an age-old but unvarying struggle against English oppression. Characteristic of the new mood, tone and subject matter was the observation, in 1825, of Thomas McNeven, one of the earliest historians of the Leinster rising, that 'the present recollection of past events, if properly applied, would emancipate the catholics, or, better still, emancipate the Irish'.[b] Simultaneously, the

2. The Royal Irish Academy was founded in 1785 to foster, among other pursuits, the cultivation of native antiquarian and linguistic studies.
3. i.e. to such an extent.

b. Meeting of Irishmen in New York (New York, 1825), pp. 9-11, quoted in D. McCartney, 'The Writing of History in Ireland, 1800-1830', *Irish Historical Studies*, Vol. x, 1957, p. 358.

4. Among the prominent leaders of this protestant antiquarianism was the poet Samuel Ferguson (1810-86), who saw in pre-Christian

concept of a golden *Christian* age which invasion from Britain had abruptly ended was taking shape and finding voice. As O'Connell expressed it in 1827:

> Accursed be the day . . . when the invaders first touched our shores. They came to a nation famous for its love of learning, its piety, its heroism [and] . . . doomed Ireland to seven centuries of oppression.[c]

Two years later, in a private letter, O'Connell stressed the spiritual facet of this particular vision of the past more heavily:

> Ireland seems to me to be the most proper nursery for spiritual needs — Irish priests are in *demand* all over the Christian world and in my day dreams I revive the brighter period of Irish history where Erin was the cradle of saints and science.[d]

Each of these developments of the 1820s was met antiphonally by a Protestant-unionist counterview. Each was also in itself portentous. For the two myths of repetitive heroic violence and of an early Christian Elysium of saints and scholars were to form staples of Irish nationalist culture for the next century or more. *Pari passu*,[5] they reinforced a national feeling for the timeless. For 1798 was presented from the outset as but the latest item in an essentially undifferentiated series, while the age of spiritual empire was seen as merely overlaid by seven hundred years of English domination, ready to spring back in its original glory once the terrible weight of suppression had been removed.

III

In one sense, of course, the successive and overlapping historical debates of the late eighteenth and early nineteenth centuries in Ireland were ahistorical. It would be difficult to deny that all of them were politics by other means, although it is also true that somewhere amidst the heat and dust the foundations of modern historical scholarship in Ireland were being laid. But if change is the 'objective' historian's point of concern, time is the coinage in which he deals; and if this early phase of history-writing is remarkable for its imperception of change, it is no less remarkable for its concept of time. This is relevant to us today because the early history-writing both shaped and solidified what was to prove an enduring characteristic in Irish political attitudes. Negatively, it may be described as an absence of a developmental or sequential view of past events. Positively, it implies a mode or habit of judgment and apprehension outside a chronologically calibrated, or indeed any, time scale. It may be no coincidence that the society in which this mode or habit prevailed was deeply Christian. Ranke's celebrated phrase, 'Every generation is equidistant from eternity',[6] was doubtless meant as a corrective to the Whig interpretation of history, that which follows the furrow of progress to the present and praises the dead ploughman who deviated least from the appointed line. But the phrase can also be usefully appropriated by the Christian — at any rate, by those Christians who sheer off from the idea of predestination. However dimly it may be perceived, however brokenly it may be expressed, the collision between God's foreknowledge of events and human choice is a matter of profound concern to them; and precisely the same applies to their obvious route of escape from this dilemma — the Christian view of God as standing outside time entirely, without yesterdays or tomorrows, omnipresent in an ever-present.

Such a view appears to me to approximate to the concept of the past which infused Irish historiography at its modern commencement and which still infuses the historical assumptions of most ordinary Irish people. Of course, this rendered and renders the past an arsenal of weapons with which to defend both inveterate prejudice and that ignorance which wishes only to remain invincible. But it also implies historical interpretations in terms of law and morals. In such a view, no statute of limitations softens the judgment to be made upon past events, however distant. In such a view, no prescriptive rights can be established by the passage of time, however lengthy. . . .

But timelessness might also have a most practical and literal meaning for those looking back upon

c. W. Phelan, *The History of the Policy of the Church of Rome in Ireland* (London, 1827), quoted in ibid., p. 361.
d. M. O'Connell (ed.), *The Correspondence of Daniel O'Connell* (Dublin, 1974), Vol. iv, pp. 87-8.

Ireland a form of Gaelic identity that transcended sectarian divisions, and hence provided a basis for protestant claims to be truly Irish.
5. i.e. simultaneously and equally.

6. Leopold von Ranke (1795-1886), *On the Epoch of Modern History* (1854). Ranke's statement was made in the context of an argument that moral judgments be excised from history and that each epoch be judged on its own terms.

the Irish past. Let me take as one example O'Connell's reflections of 1828 upon his failure to secure Catholic Emancipation three years before, despite his concession to the British government of the two so-called 'wings' or securities — one, state payment of the Catholic clergy, and the other, the disenfranchisement of the almost exclusively Catholic 40s[hilling] freehold voters. Because he was determining parliamentary strategy on the eve of its first application by Irish nationalists in the House of Commons, O'Connell's reading of history may well have been a fateful one, casting shadows ahead for the subsequent ninety years. 'In fact', O'Connell wrote, shortly before the famous Clare election of 1828,

> we were carrying the Emancipation bill [in 1825] not by reason of the political wisdom of the Ministry but from the apprehension [it] entertained of the resentment of the Irish nation.... The course I should have taken was to have kept up that salutary apprehension and I could easily have done so but, instead of that I listened in an evil hour to the suggestion of Mr. Plunket, etc., who said that if we conceded 'the Wings' by way of security, we should certainly carry the bill ... I procured for this purpose public tranquillity. The Ministry saw that I had appeased the storm, they considered that the danger was passed and the House of Lords scouted our Emancipation bill. Nay, Peel ... actually taunted me with having betrayed popular rights in order to attain the objects of my personal ambition. I was deceived once but I should indeed be ... 'a knave or a fool' if [I] were to be deceived ... again. We shall never be emancipated but as we were relieved in 1778, 1782 and 1793,[7] that is, when it becomes necessary for the English Government to do something for Ireland.[e]

O'Connell is presenting here a pragmatic or experiential, rather than a moral or legal, historical judgment. But in the essential matter of the time-frame, he is at one with the other strand in Irish historical thought. He assumes an absolute repetitive form to lie at the heart of Anglo-Irish dealings. Whether it is 1778, 1782, 1793 or 1825 the same forces operate in the same fashion. There is a constant relationship between the oscillation of coercion and conciliation on the part of the overlord and the oscillation of negotiation and the threat of violence upon the part of the subjected. *Mutatis mutandis*,[8] Butt, Parnell and Redmond, or for that matter O'Neill, Faulkner and John Hume in Northern Ireland in recent years,[9] have analysed their various predicaments in substantially the same terms and with substantially the same assumptions about the repetitiveness of the historical process.

e. M. O'Connell (ed.), *O'Connell Correspondence*, Vol. iii, p. 30.

7. In 1778 the Volunteer Movement was founded under the leadership of the Duke of Leinster and Lord Charlemont as a means of protection against foreign invasion; in 1782 Grattan's parliament was established; in 1793 the Penal Laws against catholics were relaxed following an initial Catholic Relief Bill in 1792.

IV

In *Viewless Winds* a Sydney surgeon, Herbert Moran, describes the reactions of his father, an Irish-Australian, to the Civil War in Ireland when he returned to his homeland for the last time in 1922:

> For him this was the first stage of his disillusionment. He could not understand it. So back he turned gladly to Australia. Between him and Ireland there was now more than a world of miles. There were centuries, aeons, the span of a man's struggle and triumph in a new land.[f]

We may take this peculiarly dramatic conversion from one temporal framework to its opposite as a text for the consideration of the British counterpart of what we have been discussing. As the concept of the contemporiety of the past came to dominate popular historical thought in Ireland in the late eighteenth and early nineteenth century, a counter-concept of history, that of beneficial development, was gradually triumphing in Britain. It was fitting that congratulatory history should have come to predominate there through the work of the master-celebrator, Macaulay.[10] Let me attempt, by way of

f. H. M. Moran, *Viewless Winds: Being the Recollections and Digressions of an Australian Surgeon* (London, 1939), pp. 407-8.

8. i.e. taking into account the necessary changes.
9. Isaac Butt (1813-79), Charles Stewart Parnell (1846-91), and John Redmond (1856-1918) were the leading Home Rule leaders. Terence O'Neill (1914-90) and Brian Faulkner (1921-77) were prime ministers of Northern Ireland during the present Northern conflict. John Hume (born 1937) is leader of the Social Democratic and Labour Party in Northern Ireland.
10. Thomas Babington Macaulay (1800-59), English politician, poet and historian, best-known for his five-volume *History of England* (1849-61) which enshrines Whig ideals of progress.

the single example of the master, to indicate certain of the characteristics of this chronological outlook.

First, Macaulay's iron faith in progress embraced the moral as well as the material. Faced with the discovery of double-dealing by his seventeenth-century hero, Sidney, he found it

> some consolation to reflect that in our time, a public man would be lost to all sense of duty and of shame, who would not spurn from him a temptation which conquered the virtue and the pride of Algernon Sydney.[g]

But the moral and the material were ultimately commingled in the grand advance. Complacently, Macaulay described the supersession, from one century to the next, of 'the savage tragedy of the Argyll rebellion' by the commercial prosperity of modern Greenock; and this 'was, of course, pointing a moral by contrast, fulfilling the pledge at the opening of the *History* to refute those who sighed for a past superior to the present'.[h] Nor did he reserve his strenuous optimism for his books. His tergiversations and rationalisations on the contemporary issue of child employment neatly illustrate its uses in his own conduct. Between 1830 and 1845 Macaulay had been a leading opponent of factory reform in the interests of children and women. But in 1847 he, like many other Liberal members of the House of Commons, changed his mind. Characteristically, he then struck the note of progress which the mass of his educated compatriots wished to hear:

> the practice of setting children prematurely to work, a practice which the state, the legitimate protector of those who cannot protect themselves, has, in our time, wisely and humanely interdicted, prevailed in the seventeenth century to an extent which, when compared to the extent of the manufacturing system, seems almost incredible.... The more carefully we examine the history of the past, the more reason shall we find to dissent from those who imagine that our age has been fruitful of new social evils. The truth is that the evils are, with scarcely an exception, old. That which is new is the intelligence which discerns and the humanity which remedies them.[i]

Here was a view of time in which past evils were weighted according to the lesser potentiality for evil which existed in simpler circumstances. Here was a view of time in which the march of reason, of knowledge and of compassion was steadily diminishing the relative power and extent of immorality. All the judgments and estimates were, so to speak, calibrated for amelioration on a measure marked off by half-centuries or even decades; and, in such a framework, a sudden turnabout in attitude, such as his own on the factory question, might be a matter not for apology but for satisfaction. The corollary of such moral expansionism was a corresponding diminution of any sense of responsibility for the past. It even declined steadily in significance as it receded.

High Whig history has not of course survived in England — at any rate, not wholly or in its first crude colours. But the two truly essential elements of its conception of time, relativism and steadily declining responsibility for, and interest in, the receding past, have outlived the death of Macaulayism in the general historical thinking of its birthplace. Complacency about the present and abounding faith in the future may have disappeared; but these were mere ornamental features of this cast of mind. The cast itself could and did, and perhaps still does, endure in England, long after their disappearance.

I do not mean, of course, to suggest that the respective common historical assumptions of the two peoples were, or are, either innate or universal. As we have seen, mid-eighteenth-century Ireland was conventionally 'enlightened' in its view of the earlier past. Conversely, there were bodies in Victorian England whose historical view was timeless and moral, at least upon religious subjects: the fires of Smithfield and the braziers on the Devon headlands burned as if it were yesterday in the imagination of millions of Evangelicals.[11] None the

g. Lady Trevelyan (ed.), *The Complete Works of Lord Macaulay* (London, 1875), Vol. i, p. 180, [Algernon Sidney (1622-83), one of the seventeenth-century architects of modern republicanism, was believed to have accepted bribes from the French court to overthrow the Stuart monarchy. He was executed following his alleged involvement in a plot to assassinate Charles II and his catholic brother James. (Ed.)]

h. J. W. Burrow, *A Liberal Descent* (London, 1981), p. 65.

i. Trevelyan (ed.), *Macaulay Works*, Vol. i, p. 327.

11. Smithfield in London was a site for executions during the Reformation. 'The braziers' of Devon refers to the welcome that greeted the Duke of Monmouth's invasion of the south-west of England in 1685 in his ill-fated attempt to remove the catholic King James II from the throne.

less the contrast stood and stands as generally valid. In terms of norms and masses, it *is* true that the Irish do not forget and that the English do not remember.

Given these crosspurposes of historical thought and impressions, one of the leading tasks in almost any Anglo-Irish analysis — and not least the analysis of the imbroglio of the last decade and a half — is to search out and fix the different sets of assumptions and the different meanings attached to words and symbols by the generality of people in each tradition. The failure of mutual comprehension has sometimes been very plain, and the consequences have often been of first importance. Take, as an instance of both together, John Redmond's speech as leader of the Irish Nationalist Party, to the House of Commons on 3 August 1914, as war with the German empire was almost upon them:

> The House will remember that in 1778, at the end of the disastrous American War, when . . . the military power of this country was almost at its lowest ebb, and when the shores of Ireland were threatened with foreign invasion, a body of 100,000 Irish Volunteers sprang into existence for the purpose of defending her shores . . . from the very first day, the Catholics of the South and West subscribed money and sent it toward the arming of their Protestant fellow-countrymen . . . in the North. May history repeat itself today? There are in Ireland two large bodies of Volunteers [the Ulster Volunteer Force (UVF) and National Volunteers] . . . I say to the [British] Government that they may tomorrow withdraw every one of their troops from Ireland. I say that the coast of Ireland will be defended from foreign invasion by her armed sons, and for this purpose armed Nationalist Catholics in the South will be only too glad to join arms with the armed Protestant Ulstermen in the North . . . .[j]

Redmond's meaning, to all Irish auditors, whether they heard him with horror or delight, was that 'Grattan's Parliament' should be reinaugurated in the same fashion and by the same means as in 1782, and that sectarian conflict in Ireland should be overridden in the same fashion as the Patriot movement of the 1780s was supposed at the time to have overridden the religious polarisation obtaining there since 1691. But to British auditors, Redmond's speech simply signified Irish support for the imminent war effort. Doubtless a whiff or two of patriotic-sentimental rodomontade were necessary for him to draw quietly the surviving stumps of any dragon's teeth which their ancestors might inadvertently have sown. But what a bagatelle was this in the general state of things! The consequences of the gross, almost comic, divergence in interpretation cannot be calculated exactly. But it seems to me quite an arguable proposition that without its occurrence and the subsequent crosspurposes, the Easter Rising of 1916 might have proved impossible to mount. . . .

But what of those other Irishmen, the northern Protestants, whose corporate principle of being rests upon the success of the Boyne in 1690? Are they truly different from the remainder? The siege of Derry of 1689 is their original and most powerful myth. They see themselves in that, and since then, as an embattled and enduring people. Their historical self-vision is one of an endless repetition of repelled assaults, without hope of absolute finality or of fundamental change in their relationship to their surrounding and surrounded neighbours. In the last analysis they share the historical cyclicalism of nationalist Ireland, or at least the two mental habits tend to converge. The one may take shape as insurgent and degenerative successively, the other as beleaguerment. But their rhythms, their ultimate world-views, are extraordinarily similar. This being so, such a phrase as 'the solution' or 'a solution' to the Northern Ireland question has little meaning or promise for either. They are committed too deeply to ancient roles and modes of interpreting the historical flow, and the patterns they perceive in — or, if you will, impose upon — the past, are at once a cause of the present crisis, and a force making for its continuance. Each would add, of course, that the present crisis is also an effect of many past crises which conformed to and which in retrospect constitute the fatal pattern.

j. *Hansard*, 5th series, lxv, cols 1828-9, 3 August 1914. Redmond prefaced these remarks with, 'There is a possibility, at any rate, of history repeating itself'.

THOMAS KINSELLA

(1929-)

from: THE IRISH WRITER (1966)

[Thomas Kinsella's influential article 'The Irish Writer', delivered to a meeting of the Modern Languages Association in New York in 1966, the year of the fiftieth anniversary of the Easter Rising, marks a final break with the legacy of the Revival. In keeping with the modernizing ethos of Ireland in the 1960s, Kinsella suggests that a sense of tradition and cultural continuity are no longer adequate for a creative imagination disturbed by the complexities of the self and the wider human predicament. Interestingly, Kinsella does not rule out the possibility of renewing contact with tradition altogether, for it was precisely by poring over the humdrum exigencies of the modern world that Joyce became 'the first major Irish voice to speak for Irish reality since the death of the Irish language'. In this sense, Joyce resolved the antimony between modernity and tradition that had presided over cultural debates in Ireland since the Yeats/Eglinton controversy at the beginning of the Revival.

The paper was later published in *Mangan, Davis, Ferguson?* (Dublin: Dolmen Press, 1969).]

A writer who cares who he is and where he comes from looks about him and begins by examining his colleagues. In that very act a writer in Ireland must make a basic choice: do I include writers in Irish among my colleagues? Or am I to write them off as a minor and embattled group, keeping loyal — for the best of reasons — to a dead or dying language? Some of the best writers in Irish already believe that their language is doomed, rejected by its people. They are pessimistic, but my instinct tells me they are right. So I turn only toward those who are writing in English. And, to speak only of the poets, the word 'colleague' fades on the lips before the reality: a scattering of incoherent lives. It will seem on a bad day that they are a few madmen and hermits, and nothing more. I can learn nothing from them except that I am isolated.

So I begin again, and look for the past in myself. An English poet would have an easier time of it. His course is clear. No matter what his preoccupations may be, he will find his forebears in English poetry; as inheritor of the parent language he is free to 'repatriate' a great American poet or a great Irish poet. As he looks backward, the line might begin with Yeats and T. S. Eliot and continue with Matthew Arnold and Wordsworth and Keats and Pope — and so on through the mainstream of a tradition. An Irish poet will have only the first point in common with this. Or so I find in my own case, when I try to identify my forebears. Who are those whose lives in some sense belong to me, and whose force is there for me to use if I can, if I am good enough, as I try to write my own poetry?

The line begins, again, with Yeats. Then, for more than a hundred years, there is almost total silence. I believe that silence, on the whole, is the real condition of Irish literature in the nineteenth century — certainly of poetry. There are enough hideous anthologies to bear me out: collections in which one falls with relief on anything that shows mere competence — say, John Todhunter's lyrics or Robert Dwyer Joyce's political ballads — not to speak only of Ferguson and Mangan and Allingham and Moore.[1] But there is nothing that approaches the full literary achievement of an age. It is all tentative, or displaced.

If I look deeper still, further back, in the need to identify myself, what I meet beyond the nineteenth century is a great cultural blur. I must exchange one language for another, my native English for eighteenth century Irish. After the dullness of the nineteenth century, eighteenth century Irish poetry seems to me suddenly full of life: expertise in the service of real feeling — hatred for the foreign landowner; fantasies and longings rising from the loss of an Irish civilisation (the poets putting their trust in the Stuarts[2] or the Spanish fleet or even the Pope of Rome); satires, love-songs, lamentations; outcries of religious fervour or repentance. And all of this in

1. John Todhunter (1839-1916) was a leading figure in the early period of the Literary Revival, and his poems on Irish subjects, *The Banshee and other Poems* (1888), were highly praised by Yeats. Robert Dwyer Joyce (1830-83) wrote for *The Nation* newspaper, and is best known for his ballads 'The Boys of Wexford', 'The Wind that Shakes the Barley' and 'The Leprechaun'. Samuel Ferguson, James Clarence Mangan, William Allingham, and Thomas Moore were the leading Irish poets of the nineteenth century.
2. The Stuarts were the catholic dynasty that was forced off the throne of England by the Williamite Wars (1689-91). Thereafter they found political expression in the Jacobite cause.

full voices, the voices of poets who expect to be heard and understood, and memorised — Eoghan Ruadh O Súilleabháin, Donnchadh Ruadh Mac Connmara, Seán Clárach Mac Domhnaill, Tadhg Gealach O Súilleabháin;[3] they are the tragic, almost-doggerel end of Gaelic literature — but they have no more need to question the medium they write in than, say, John Clare writing in English.

Beyond them is the poet Aogán O Rathaille[4] writing at the end of the seventeenth century and the beginning of the eighteenth. I am sure he is a major poet: the last great poet in Irish, and the last Irish poet, until Yeats, whose life can be seen as a true poetic career. It is a career that begins in the full light of Gaelic culture and ends in darkness, with the Gaelic aristocracy ruined and the death-blow already delivered to the Irish language.

Then beyond O Rathaille, the course of Irish poetry stretching back for more than a thousand years, full of riches and variety: poetry as mystery and magic, in the earliest fragments and interpolated in the early sagas; poetry as instant, crystalline response to the world, in a unique body of nature lyrics; poetry as a useful profession — the repository of historical information and topography and custom; love poems and devotional poems of high dignity and technique; conventional bardic poetry stiff with tradition and craft. Here, in all this, I recognise simultaneously a great inheritance and a great loss. The inheritance is mine, but only at two enormous removes — across a century's silence, and through an exchange of worlds. The greatness of the loss is measured not only by the substance of Irish literature itself, but also by the intensity with which we know it was shared; it has an air of continuity and shared history which is precisely what is missing from Irish literature, in English or Irish, in the nineteenth century and today.

Why can I not make living contact with that inheritance, my own past? Others have. It is because I believe I would have to make a commitment to the Irish language; to write in Irish instead of English. And that would mean loss of contact with my own present — abandonment of the language I was bred in for one which I believe to be dying. It would also mean forfeiting a certain possible scope of language: English has a greater scope, if I can make use of it, than an Irish which is not able to handle all the affairs of my life. So that even with a commitment to the Irish language, a full contact with the old tradition — a contact between two whole entities — is, I believe, impossible. But in the end it is really not a matter of choice; for my own part I simply recognise that I stand on one side of a great rift, and can feel the discontinuity in myself. It is a matter of people and place as well as writing — of coming, so to speak, from a broken and uprooted family, of being drawn to those who share my origins and finding that we cannot share our lives.

I wish it were otherwise. And with that wish, I have the impulse to make an offering to the past from which I feel separated. I suppose that is the reason for my few laborious translations from the early Irish; the two or three that have been published and the *Táin Bó Cuailnge* which I have been translating for years, off and on.[5] It is not one of the greatest things in world literature, perhaps; in its later form, which is complete, it has an overblown decadence; in its earlier form, which is good stylistically, it is unfinished and mutilated. But it seems extraordinary to me that, with all the fairy tale versions of the story, the romantic, the dramatised and the bowdlerised, there has never been an acceptable translation of the better version — the earlier one — tidied a little and completed from other sources; nothing to give an idea of the story as we first have it. So I grind on with the work — a labour of some kind of love.

The death of a language . . . it is a calamity. And its effects are at work everywhere in the present, reducing energies of every kind, undermining individual confidence, lessening the quality of thought. Daniel Corkery has written very well, I think, about this in his book *Synge and Anglo-Irish Literature*. We know that he has some special convictions about nationality and literature — a strident pessimism that frequently amounts to distortion — but in this passage his emotion seems very much in place:

3. Eoghan Rua O Súilleabháin (*c.* 1748-84), a Kerry poet who supported the Jacobite cause; Donnchadh Ruadh Mac Connmara (1715-1810), a Waterford-based poet and author of the well-known 'Bán-Chnoic Eireann Oigh' (The Fair Hills of Ireland); Seán Clárach Mac Domhnaill (1691-1754), the chief Jacobite poet in Ireland; Tadhg Gealach O Súilleabháin (1715-95), a devotional poet from Waterford.

4. Aogán Ó Rathaille (*c.* 1670-1726), one of the major Irish poets, lived in Killarney, Co. Kerry and wrote highly politicized *aisling*, or visionary poems, supporting the Jacobite cause.

5. Thomas Kinsella's acclaimed translation of the *Táin Bó Cuailnge*, the most celebrated tale from the early Irish mythological cycle, was published in 1969.

> Everywhere in the mentality of the Irish people are flux and uncertainty. Our national consciousness may be described, in a native phrase, as a quaking sod. It gives no footing. It is not English, nor Irish, nor Anglo-Irish; as will be understood if one think awhile on the thwarting it undergoes in each individual child of the race as he grows to manhood.... For practically all that he reads is English;* what he reads in Irish is not yet worth taking account of. It does not therefore focus the mind of his own people, teaching him the better to look about him, to understand both himself and his surroundings. It focuses instead the life of another people. Instead of sharpening his gaze on his own neighbourhood, his reading distracts it, for he cannot find in these surroundings what his reading has taught him is the matter worth coming upon. His surroundings begin to seem unvital.... At the least his education sets up a dispute between his intellect and his emotions.... What happens in the neighbourhood of an Irish boy's home — the fair, the hurling match, the land grabbing, the *priesting*,[6] the mission, the Mass — he never comes on in literature, that is, in such literature as he is told to respect and learn.... In his riper years he may come to see the crassness of his own upbringing ... but of course the damage is done....[7]

Corkery is not writing about Dublin, where the hurling match and the land grabbing and the priesting are all foreign games. But to have been born in Dublin, as I was, of people whose families came from the country a hundred years ago, is not to escape the deprivation, nor even to feel it less sharply once the process of self-search has begun.

The only semblance of an escape — consonant with integrity — is into a greater isolation still, as Yeats's career shows. Yeats looks back over the course of literature in Ireland and sees it very differently. He values what he can in Gaelic literature, and uses it, as we know; but his living tradition is solely in English. And it has its high point, not its almost-doggerel last gasp, in the eighteenth century. Its literature and its human beings are specialised and cut off, an Anglo-Irish annex to the history of Ireland. He yokes together Swift and Burke and Berkeley and Goldsmith for his writers, and for his chosen people finds a race of 'swashbucklers, horsemen, swift indifferent men'.[8] It is English literature, not Irish, that lies behind them, and their line — as he sees it — is ending in his own time. You might feel that Yeats created this brief Anglo-Irish tradition for himself, by special selection, and then projected his own values into it. But it is still a coherent entity, at a graceful elegiac height above the filthy modern tide.[9] Yeats is isolated to begin with, like Aogán O Rathaille, at a turning point in history — there is a notable similarity in the way these poets regard their times: turning away from a miserable present and a terrible future to lament and celebrate an old nobility at the end of the line. But I believe that Yeats's isolation is at least partly a matter of choice. He refuses to come to terms with the real shaping vitality of Ireland where he sees it exists; to take the tradition in any other way would have been to write for Daniel O'Connell's children, for De Valera and Paudeen at his greasy till;[10] to recognise these as the heirs of Anglo-Ireland's glory, and of the fruits of the 1916 Rising (which — for its 'gallantry' — Yeats is almost tempted to include in his Anglo-Irish system).

Yeats is of course *in* the tradition of Irish

* He is of course writing some years ago, and about something that has now changed, or begun to change. Recent changes in the school text books have brought contemporary Irish writers into the curriculum and lessened the curious reliance on eighteenth and nineteenth century English journalism. Important and widespread changes in attitude seem to underlie this reform. The effect, however slight it must remain without matching reforms in the training (and payment) of teachers, can only be for the good. But for us it is still in the future. For the Irish writer today — all but the very youngest, who may now be making the first moves toward dedication — the conditions described by Corkery still matter: we have come out of what he describes.

6. Priesting refers to the rituals attending ordination to the priesthood.
7. Daniel Corkery, *Synge and Anglo-Irish Literature* (Cork: Cork University Press, 1931).
8. W. B. Yeats, 'Introduction' to *The Oxford Book of Modern Verse* (Oxford: Clarendon Press, 1936), p. xv.
9. See Yeats's poem 'The Statues': 'We Irish, born into that ancient sect/But thrown upon this filthy modern tide'.
10. Refers to Yeats's indictment of the avaricious catholic middle classes in his poems 'To a Wealthy Man who promised a Second Subscription to the Dublin Municipal Gallery if it were proved the People wanted Pictures' and 'September 1913'. The reference to 'Daniel O'Connell's children' is a sly, humorous allusion to the popular belief that O'Connell fathered numerous illegitimate offspring.

literature; he gives it body and — in many ways — meaning. But he is isolated in the tradition. That isolation is the substance of his life. Early in his career, in an essay in 'Ideas of Good and Evil', he remembers standing on the side of Sliabh Echtge,[11] looking out over the Galway plains. He thinks of the continuing generations of poetry and poetical life:

> There is still in truth upon those great level plains a people, a community bound together by imaginative possessions, by stories and poems which have grown out of its own life, and by a past of great passions which can still waken the heart to imaginative action. One could still, if one had the genius, and had been born to Irish, write for these people plays and poems like those of Greece. Does not the greatest poetry always require a people to listen to it?[12]

There is the isolation: from a people whose language is not his own and whose lives, therefore, he cannot touch. At the end of his life, in 'A General Introduction for my Work', written in 1937, he returns to the same fact. He recalls that he had found in the poetry of Thomas Davis and others on the *Nation* newspaper (though it was not good poetry) 'one quality I admired and admire: they were not separated individual men: they spoke or tried to speak out of a people to a people'. Then he dramatises his isolation remembering the past persecutions of the Irish people:

> No people hate as we do in whom that past is always alive, there are moments when hatred poisons my life and I accuse myself of effeminacy because I have not given it adequate expression. It is not enough to have put it into the mouth of a rambling peasant poet. Then I remind myself that though mine is the first English marriage I know of in the direct line, all my family names are English, and that I owe my soul to Shakespeare, to Spenser and to Blake, perhaps to William Morris,[13] and to the English language in which I think, speak, and write, that everything I love has come to me through English; my hatred tortures me with love, my love with hate.'[14]

But Yeats is a great artist, and it is clear that this passionate frustration, though deep, did not take over his soul. Sanity is embodied in his career, in his final rejection of politics and its shrieking women, and his rejection of the people as an audience for his work. He writes: 'I am no Nationalist, except in Ireland for passing reasons; State and Nation are the work of intellect, and when you consider what comes before and after them they are, as Victor Hugo said of something or other, not worth the blade of grass God gives for the nest of the linnet.'[15]

As poet he is preoccupied with the leading work of the imagination which renders demagoguery — and all the doings of history that are not embodied in his own imagining self — of no account. The continuity or the mutilation of traditions becomes, in itself, irrelevant as the artist steps back from his entire world, mutilations and all, and absorbs it.

Yeats bestrides the categories. He had a greatness capable, perhaps, of integrating a modern Anglo-Irish culture, and which chose to make this impossible by separating out a special Anglo-Irish culture from the main unwashed body.

Joyce, with a greatness like Yeats's, was able to reject (that is, accept) the whole tradition as he found it — as it lay in stunned silence, still recovering from the death of its old language. Joyce's isolation is a mask. His relationship with the modern world is direct and intimate. He knows the filthy modern tide, and he immerses himself in it to do his work. His relationship with Ireland is also direct and intimate. In rejecting Ireland he does so on its own terms. Turning to *Synge and Anglo-Irish Literature* again, we find Corkery looking for the forces which give the Irish national being its Irishness. He finds three: (1) The Religious Consciousness of the People, (2) Irish Nationalism, (3) The Land. The things Stephen Dedalus refuses to serve, the things in which he no longer believes, are Home, Fatherland and Church; the nets he escapes from are Nationality, Language and Religion. Religion, Church: Fatherland, Nationalism, Language — these are two of Corkery's forces. The third, the Land, is not a force

11. A range of hills near Gort, Co. Galway. Lady Gregory lived in Coole Park, not far from the town.
12. 'The Galway Plains', reprinted in A. Norman Jeffares (ed.), *W. B. Yeats: Selected Criticism* (London: Pan Books, 1976), p. 129.
13. The English poet William Morris (1834-96) exercised a strong influence on the young Yeats. Yeats attended his socialist lectures in Hampstead in 1881.
14. 'A General Introduction for my Work', reprinted in A. Norman Jeffares (ed.), *W. B. Yeats: Selected Criticism*, op. cit., p. 267.
15. ibid., p. 269.

in Stephen's world, Dublin. Although he rejects them and escapes from them, he cannot forget them. His stomach, unlike Yeats's, is not turned by what he sees shaping the new Ireland: the shamrock lumpenproletariat, the eloquent and conniving and mean-spirited tribe of Dan.† Daniel O'Connell or de Valera or Paudeen do not deter him from his work; they are his subjects. He is the first major Irish voice to speak for Irish reality since the death of the Irish language.

The filthy modern tide does not run only in Ireland, of course, and Joyce's act of continuity is done with a difference: he simultaneously revives the Irish tradition and admits the modern world. It is symptomatic that for Corkery's third force, the Land, Joyce substitutes the City. He makes up all the arrears at once.

So, the Irish writer, if he cares who he is and where he comes from, finds that Joyce and Yeats are the two main objects in view; and I think he finds that Joyce is the true father. I will risk putting it diagrammatically, and say that Yeats stands for the Irish tradition as broken; Joyce stands for it as continuous, or healed — or healing — from its mutilation.

Which brings us only to the beginning. Relationship to tradition, whether broken or not, is only part of the story. For any writer there is also the relationship with other literatures, with the present, with the 'human predicament', with the self. This last may be the most important of all, for certain gaps in ourselves can swallow up all the potentiality in the world. Say that we are not crippled in this way, then we all inherit all the past, one way or another. A writer, according to his personal scope, stands in relation to what he can use of man's total literary tradition. Eliot or Joyce can use much, Dylan Thomas[16] very little. But Thomas's relationship with the self was — or was beginning to be — adequate for great poems. A man in his life shares more with all men than he does with any class of men — in eating, sleeping, loving, fighting, dying; he may lack the sense of tradition and still have most of human experience.

Is there then any virtue, for literature, for poetry, in the simple continuity of a tradition? I believe there is not. A relatively steady tradition, like English or French, accumulates a distinctive quality and tends to impose this on each new member. Does this give him a deeper feeling for the experience gathered up in the tradition, or a better understanding of it? I doubt it. It is not as though literature, or national life, were a corporate, national investigation of a corporate, national experience — as though a nation were a single animal, with one complex artistic feeler. This may be true for brief great periods that have 'unity of being', like those that produced Greek and Elizabethan tragedy; there is probably some truth in it, ultimately, for mankind as a whole. But for the present — especially in this present — it seems that every writer has to make the imaginative grasp at identity for himself; and if he can find no means in his inheritance to suit him, he will have to start from scratch.

To look at it more remotely still: pending the achievement of some total human unity of being, every writer in the modern world — since he can't be in all the literary traditions at once — is the inheritor of a gapped, discontinuous, polyglot tradition. Nevertheless, if the function of tradition is to link us living with the significant past, this is done as well by a broken tradition as by a whole one — however painful it may be humanly speaking. I am certain that a great part of the significance of my own past, as I try to write my poetry, is that that past *is* mutilated.

† It has been suggested to me that an historian might more suitably label this phenomenon 'the rise of the Catholic Bourgeoisie'; but I find the suggestion unhelpful. My words would read strangely perhaps on a label, but they are trying to enact what I mean. (And what I mean can't all be pinned on the Bourgeoisie, or even on Irish Catholicism.)

16. Kinsella is making the point that Dylan Thomas (1914-53), who knew no Welsh, did not require a tradition to sustain his own creative (or even distinctively Welsh) vision.

RICHARD KEARNEY

(1954-)

from: TRANSITIONS (1987)

[In this extract from the introduction to his collection of essays, *Transitions*, Richard Kearney maps out the influence of modernism on Irish culture. Although essentially an ideology of discontinuity, the emphasis on *language* in modernism offers a way of negotiating between the divisions or 'hateful contraries' at the heart of Irish culture. Basing his argument on an extended interpretation of Brian Friel's play *Translations* (1981), Kearney argues that the process of translation can be seen as a mediating influence, a means of securing continuity amidst discontinuity and fragmentation. Translation, then, offers a *transitional* paradigm for understanding cultural change, rather than a model based on disruption.]

... Modernism rejects both the aims and idioms of revivalism. It affirms a radical break with tradition and endorses a practice of cultural self-reflection where inherited concepts of identity are subjected to question. Modernism is essentially a 'critical' movement in the philosophical sense of questioning the very notion or *origins*. And as such it challenges the *ideology of identity* which revivalism presupposes. The modernist mind prefers discontinuity to continuity, diversity to unity, conflict to harmony, novelty to heritage. Rimbaud offers one of the earliest manifestos of this modernist attitude in his *Lettre du Voyant*: 'Newcomers are free to condemn their ancestors.... The poet makes himself a seer by a long, gigantic and rational derangement of all the senses ... he leaps through unheard of and unnameable things. ... Let us ask the poet for the *new*'.[1]

Modernism is, consequently, suspicious of attempts to re-establish national literatures or resurrect cultural traditions. And most of those we might call Irish modernists deny the possibility of sustaining a continuous link between past and present. The contemporary crisis of culture is, as it were, their point of departure, their *raison d'être*. It is something to be exploited, not resolved.

The modernist tendency in Irish culture is characterized by a determination to *demythologize* the orthodox heritage of tradition in so far as it lays constraints upon the openness and plurality of experience. Joyce's Stephen Dedalus exemplifies this impulse when he speaks of trying to awaken from the 'nightmare of history'. He refuses to serve that in which he no longer believes, whether it call itself 'home, fatherland or church'. The revivalist credos of 'nationality, language and religion' are derided as nets which hold the creative spirit back from flight. For Stephen the 'conscience of his race' is not something inherited from the past but something still 'uncreated' and therefore, by definition, still to be invented. Repudiating revivalist nationalism as a 'pale afterthought of Europe,' Joyce went into exile and chose an experimental aesthetic. Beckett too rejected the myths of the Irish Literary Revival concentrating instead on the modernist problematic of language itself — what he termed 'the breakdown of the lines of communication.[2] The privileged province of his exploration was to be the no-man's-land of the author's own interior existence: an existence condemned to perpetual disorientation.

For Joyce and Beckett — and the Irish modernists who succeeded them — it is not what one writes about that is of primary importance but the process of writing itself. Or as Beckett said of Joyce, 'his writing is not *about* something, it *is* that something'.[3] What matters, in other words, is less the content than the form of language. The modes of communication are more significant than the message communicated, since there no longer exists any inherited reservoir of meaning which can be taken for granted. Not surprisingly then, the very

1. Arthur Rimbaud's *Lettres du Voyant* were written to his friends Georges Izambard and Paul Demery in May 1871.

2. See Samuel Beckett's 1934 essay 'Recent Irish Poetry' in *Disjecta: Miscellaneous Writings and a Dramatic Fragment* (London: Calder, 1983), where he writes that the breakdown of the artistic subject and object 'comes to the same thing — rupture of the lines of communication' (p. 70).

3. See Samuel Beckett, 'Dante ... Bruno, Vico, Joyce' in Samuel Beckett et al, *Our examination round his factification for incamination of work in progress* (London: Faber and Faber, 1972), p. 14. This work was first published in 1929.

notion of culture as a transmission of collective experience is itself at issue. Language becomes self-conscious, reflexive; it begins to question its own conditions of possibility. It is in this context that we may best understand John Banville's recent claim that there is no such thing as an Irish national literature, only Irish writers engaged in the practice of writing.[4] We might say that the modernist tendency of certain Irish writers, artists and intellectuals generally represents a shift away from the cultural nationalism of the Revival to a cultural internationalism committed to formal and critical experimentation. Turning its back on the political agenda of national revival, modernism espouses an aesthetic 'revolution of the word'. Seamus Deane puts this point well: 'In the place of political ideology we discover a whole series of ideologies of writing — those of Joyce, Beckett, Francis Stuart ... and others — in which politics is regarded as a threat to artistic integrity; the heroics of the spirit which formerly were indulged for the sake of the Yeatsian "Unity of Being" become a doctrinaire aesthetic of privacy, insulation, isolation and exile'.

Instead of attempting to rekindle tradition, the modernist movement in Irish culture disassembles it by critically exploring language itself as the privileged site of innovation and difference. The contemporary sense of 'homelessness' which revivalism sought to remedy by the reinstatement of a lost homeland, becomes for modernism the irrevocable condition not only of Irish culture but of world culture. The 'filthy modern tide' is here to stay. At worst, one must attest to its divisive ravages, without alibi or illusion. At best, one might discover in the flotsam and jetsam of its wake, the still floating possibilities of other, postmodern, modes of consciousness. Either way, the modernist prefers, as Brecht put it, to begin with 'the bad new things' rather than the 'good old ones'.[5]

Most of the narratives analysed in this book bear witness to a tension between revivalism and modernism. There are, of course, different degrees of attraction towards either pole. Some narratives largely gravitate towards tradition and the past: an attitude that might be described, paradoxically, as 'revivalist modernism'. Others veer in the opposite direction, resisting the pull of tradition and its attendant idioms of national revival: this attitude may be described as 'radicalist modernism'. Others again comprise a third set of narratives occupying a middle position in the transitional compass: a position which we might call 'mediational modernism' — or perhaps 'postmodernism'. But whatever their individual leanings, all of the narratives examined in this work reflect, to one degree or another, a *transitional crisis*.[a]

The transitional paradigm exemplifies the essentially conflictual nature of contemporary Irish experience; it expresses the multiple complexities and paradoxes which inform our sense of history. It is striking how many modern Irish authors have spoken of being in transit between two worlds, divided between opposing allegiances. They often write as *émigrés* of the imagination, conveying the feeling of being both part and not part of their culture, of being estranged from the very traditions to which they belong, of being in exile even while at home. Joyce described his own work as a dual fidelity to the 'familiar' and the 'foreign', inhabiting a sort of liminal space between 'twosome twiminds'. And Heaney defines his poetry as 'journeywork' — a migrant preoccupation with threshold and transit, passage and pilgrimage, with the crossing over of frontiers and divisions. The chosen emblems of his work are, accordingly, Terminus (the god of boundaries), Sweeney Astray (the displaced, wandering king)[6] and Janus (the double-faced god who looks simultaneously backward to the myths of indigenous culture and forward to the horizons of the future). But Heaney's journeywork is nowhere more evident than in his relentless probings of the hidden ambiguities and duplicities which enseam the very language he writes. While this preoccupation with language is a common feature of international modernism in general, it carries a

4. See John Banville's statement: 'There is an Irish writing, but there isn't an Irish literature' in 'Novelists on the Novels: Ronan Sheehan talks to John Banville and Francis Stuart', *The Crane Bag*, Vol. 3, No. 1 (1979), 78.
5. See Walter Benjamin, 'Conversations with Brecht' in *Understanding Brecht*, translated by Anna Bostok (London: New Left Books, 1973), p. 121: 'Don't start from the good old things but the bad new ones.'

a. Precisely as a *collage* of modern and traditional motifs, this third narrative tendency cannot strictly be confined to either modernist or revivalist categories. It may be termed postmodern to the extent that it borrows freely from the idioms of both modernity and tradition, one moment endorsing a deconstruction of tradition, another reinventing and rewriting the stories of the past transmitted by cultural memory.

6. See Seamus Heaney's poems 'Terminus' in *The Haw Lantern* (London: Faber and Faber, 1987) and *Sweeney Astray: A Version from the Irish* (Derry: Field Day Theatre Company Ltd, 1983).

singular resonance for those Irish writers who remain aware of their dual linguistic heritage.[7] Modern Irish literature often dwells on the medium in which it is written because 'it is difficult not [to] be self-conscious about a language which has become simultaneously native and foreign'.

Brian Friel marks yets another inflection in the transitional paradigm when he affirms that his plays are concerned with 'man in society, in conflict with community, government, academy, church, family — and essentially in conflict with himself'.[8] A consequence of this recognition of conflict is the impulse to negotiate between the terms of the opposition, to mediate between the split selves — in short, the need for translation. The problem of transition thus becomes a problem of *translation* (*transferere-translatum,* meaning to carry over or across). The schoolmaster of Friel's play *Translations* recognizes the necessity of transition, poised as he is between the vanishing ancestral order and the emerging new one. 'It is not the literal past, the "facts" of history, that shape us', he acknowledges, 'but the images of the past embodied in language. We must never cease renewing those images because once we do we fossilize'.[9] But Friel is aware that one does not cross the frontiers dividing cultures with ease or impunity. The translation from the old set of images to the new is frequently seen as a *transgression* — even as betrayal. As another of Friel's characters observes: 'You don't cross those borders casually — both sides get very angry'. Our transitional culture has its share of victims as well as its survivors. While some manage a successful translation from the traditional to the modern order of images, there are many who fail to do so. In one 'Diary Entry' on *Translations* (18 June, 1979), Friel describes the casualties of transition as follows: 'The cultural climate is a dying climate — no longer quickened by its past, about to be plunged almost overnight into an alien future. The victims in this situation are the transitional generation. The old can retreat into and find immunity in the past. The young acquire some facility with the new cultural implements. The in-between ages become lost, wandering around in a strange land. Strays.[10] The winners and the losers of the transitional crisis are, as it were, two sides of the same dialectic, siamese twins of the migratory imagination.

A central problem facing contemporary Irish culture is how to mediate between the images of past and future; how to avoid the petrification of tradition and the alienation of modernity; how, in short, to obviate the extremes of either a reactionary Re-Evangelization or a multi-national Los-Angelisation of society. In a study entitled 'Universal Civilisation and National Cultures', the French philosopher, Paul Ricoeur, provides a relevant account of this dilemma facing many post-colonial societies. Acknowledging that the contemporary phenomenon of universalization generally represents an advancement for mankind, he notes how it sometimes constitutes a subtle attrition not only of traditional cultures — which he admits might not be an irreparable loss — but also of what he calls 'the creative, mythical and ethical nucleus of all great cultures': the nucleus on the basis of which we interpret our history and make sense of our lives. Ricoeur describes the resulting conflict of conscience:

> In order to get onto the road towards modernisation, is it necessary to jettison the old cultural past which has been the *raison d'être* of a nation? . . . Whence, the paradox: on the one hand, it has to root itself in the soil of its past, forge a national spirit and unfurl this spiritual and cultural revindication before the colonialist's personality. But in order to take part in modern civilization, it is necessary to take part in scientific, technical and political rationality, something which very often requires the pure and simple abandonment of a whole cultural past. There is the paradox: how to become modern and return to sources; how to respect an old dormant civilization and take part in universal civilization.[11]

. . . Considered as a whole, there is much evidence here to counter the received wisdom that Irish culture constitutes a single entity. These texts [i.e. in *Translations*] suggest, on the contrary, that our

7. The modernist aspects of Heaney's use of language are explored in Blake Morrison, *Seamus Heaney* (London: Methuen, 1982).
8. Brian Friel, 'The Theatre of Culture and Despair', *Everyman*, No. 1, 1968, p. 20 (first published in *The Critic*, 26 (August-September 1967)).
9. Brian Friel, *Translations* (London: Faber and Faber, 1981), p. 66.
10. Brian Friel, 'Extracts from a Sporadic Diary' in Tim Pat Coogan (ed.), *Ireland and The Arts*, a special issue of *The Literary Review*.
11. Paul Ricoeur, 'Universal Civilization and National Cultures' in *History and Truth* translated by Charles A. Kebley (Evanston, Illinois: Northwestern University Press, 1965), pp. 276-77.

culture may be more properly understood as a manifold of narratives which resist the uniformity of a closed system. There is no unitary master narrative of Irish cultural history, but a plurality of transitions between different perspectives. Moreover, this very plurality is perhaps our greatest cultural asset; something to be celebrated rather than censored.

As I have suggested elsewhere, the notion of an 'Irish mind' should be comprehended in terms of a multiplicity of Irish minds. This tension between unity and difference is crucial. And it must be preserved in the face of ideological reductionism. Modern Irish culture is larger than the distinct ideological traditions — nationalist, unionist or otherwise — from which it derives and which it critically reinterprets.[b] And it is this *surplus* of cultural meaning which makes it possible for contemporary Irish minds to engage in a dialogue which resists both the tyranny of a single dominant identity and the sectarianism of embattled tribes. Such dialogue has the beneficial effect of encouraging us to reinvent the past as a living transmission of meaning rather than revere it as a deposit of unchangeable truth. It is only when we abandon what AE called the 'infantile simplicity of a single idea' that we can properly affirm cultural diversity.

The commitment to a transitional model of open-endedness has meant, furthermore, that the narratives analyzed in this collection not only attest to an interplay between familiar (national) and foreign (international) ideas, but also lend themselves to the kinds of reading I have attempted here. I see no good reason why the critical methods of contemporary European thought — hermeneutics, existentialism, structuralism, psychoanalysis, dialectics or deconstruction — cannot be usefully employed in the interpretation of the texts of Irish culture. And so I have not hesitated to read Joyce and Beckett, for example, in the light of Derrida or the structuralists; Heaney in the light of Heidegger and Freud; Friel and Jordan in the light of Lévi-Strauss or Saussure; le Brocquy in the light of Marcuse; or the ideology of Irish Republicanism in the light of Ricoeur or Sartre.[12] These readings stem from the conviction that it is neither necessary nor always illuminating to interpret Irish culture exclusively in terms of Ireland, literary works exclusively in terms of literature, political ideologies exclusively in terms of politics. The interdisciplinary character of this work is intended to resist the academic habit of consigning the multiple and cross-referential discourses of intellectual life to ghettoes of specialization. Against such academic apartheid, I have sought to inscribe a series of transitions between Irish and European culture, between thinking and writing, between politics and art. Such boundaries, I believe, cannot be sustained in any absolute fashion without leading to cultural indifference, or worse, dogmatism. And if the crossing of boundaries causes some degree of interference, maybe it is an interference worth experiencing.

b. . . . Most of our discussion of the transitional paradigm concentrates on texts engaged, directly or indirectly, in the debate concerning Irish 'nationalist' culture — in the broadest sense of the phrase. However critical Joyce, Flann O'Brien, Heaney, Friel, Jordan or Murphy may be apropos of tradition, it is largely the nationalist tradition that is in question. I have no doubt that similar tensions between tradition and modernity exist for those contemporary Irish writers who seek to revoke or revise what we might term, by way of distinction, Irish unionist culture. Some obvious examples would be the work of Hewitt, Mahon, Longley, Paulin, Simmons, Parker and Reid. Transitional paradigms are also at work here; though admittedly the opposition between revivalist and modernist tendencies has not been as explicit. And this for the reason, perhaps, that the mythological past of the 'planter' (to borrow Hewitt's term) has rarely been invoked by Ulster poets to compensate at a *cultural* level for the historical experience of *political* failure or dispossession. Nevertheless, both traditions of Irish culture, nationalist and unionist (in the sense of traditions which the modernist impulse interrogates, demythologizes or rewrites), have produced literary works preoccupied with the transition from the past to present. And at times, of course, these two traditions have overlapped and complemented each other.

One must be wary, too, of hasty oppositions. For just as it is a mistake to conceive of Irish culture as a seamless continuum, it would be equally erroneous to posit two or more Irish cultures which are absolutely polarized or mutually exclusive by virtue of their differences. Here again, Irish culture is best conceived as a complex web of interweaving narratives which refuses the facility of an homogeneous totality.

12. This refers to the essays in *Transitions* in which Kearney draws on developments in contemporary philosophy and cultural criticism in his readings of various Irish writers and artists and in his explorations of key issues in Irish cultural life.

DAVID LLOYD

(1955-)

from:
THE IRISH REVIEW (1988)

[In this extract, Lloyd suggests that expatriation, in the sense of being sundered from one's native culture, is a permanent condition which affects Irish writers at home as well as those who go abroad. Cultural nationalism owes its origin to a fundamental dislocation in Irish experience in that its emergence coincided with the eclipse of the Irish language and the culture it purported to represent. The insistence on wholeness and continuity in the dominant strands in Irish nationalism can be seen as an attempt to mask the fragmentation of Irish culture. Ironically, the belief that the 'spirit' of the Irish language is carried over unaltered into a new English-speaking order facilitates imperial expansion since, by suppressing cultural dissonance, it integrates a refractory native culture into a narrative of universal civilization.

The first seven notes and note 13 are by David Lloyd. An expanded version appeared in *Modern Fiction Studies* Vol 35, No. 1 (Spring 1989), under the title *Writing in the Shit: Beckett, Nationalism and the Colonial Subject.*]

THE COLONIAL SUBJECT

... 'What goes by the name of love is banishment, with now and then a postcard from the homeland', declares the narrator of *First Love*.[1] His remark scrupulously disdains a western tradition for which, from the *Odyssey* to *Ulysses*, love is the figure simultaneously for homecoming and for truth. We are, of course, left in the dark as to whether banishment is the condition of love, or love that of banishment, nor are we offered the surety that through banishment home truths will lapse forever into love's oblivion; postcards maintain some kind of sporadic connection, if only a dim reminder of origins and dependence. Both aspects of this love are written into its original title: if *Premier Amour* speaks of a first love, it does so in the language of exile itself. The original language of first love is adoptive, not natural, and as such constitutes a provocative refusal of the naturalization and the nationalization of language as the ground of a proper subjectivity. The text, the first work which Beckett wrote and published in French, raises at the level of the most primary decision, the language of 'self-expression', the questions of exile and translation in their relation to the formation of the subject.

Both questions are the troublesome but constitutive matter of Irish nationalism wherever it touches on the crucial question of national culture. According to Daniel Corkery, writing on John Millington Synge less than a decade after the founding of the Irish Free State, the perpetual condition of 'expatriation' that Irish writers accept has produced a virtually pathological absence of national culture in Ireland.[2] Though Corkery accepts that this expatriation is primarily due to 'the proximity of the English market' (p. 26), the acquiescence of the Irish writer in the economy of imperialism has its psychic effects. On the one hand, a writing directed towards an English market serves to perpetuate the alien stereotypes of the Irish: it is a 'Colonial literature, written to explain the quaintness of the humankind of this land, especially the native humankind, to another humankind that was not quaint, that was standard'. (7-8). On the other hand, and more significantly, it is not simply that their presentation as alien to an English market is a misrepresentation, but that in the dissymmetry of representation what is left in Ireland is not the true identity of the Irish, unmasked and intact, but rather its absence. Into the cultural vacuum left by the export trade in Irish writers rushes an English culture, which, being alien, deforms where it is intended to form harmonious subjects:

> Everywhere in the mentality of Irish people are flux and uncertainty. Our national consciousness may be described, in a native phrase, as a quaking sod. It gives no footing. It is not English, nor Irish, nor Anglo-Irish; as will be understood if one think a while on the thwarting it undergoes in each individual child of the race as he grows into manhood .... His

1. Samuel Beckett, *First Love and Other Shorts* (New York: Grove Press, 1974), p. 18. Page references cited in the text hereafter.

2. Daniel Corkery, *Synge and Anglo-Irish Literature* (Cork: Cork University Press, 1931), pp. 2-4. Page references cited in the text hereafter.

> education, instead of buttressing and refining his emotional nature, teaches him the rather to despise it, inasmuch as it teaches him not to see the surroundings out of which he is sprung, as they are in themselves, but as compared with alien surroundings: his education provides him with an alien medium through which he is henceforth to look at his native land. (pp. 14-15)

The proper function of the Irish writer would accordingly be to *represent* the people, in every sense of that word. If at one level, this involves the demand to *depict* Irish people and their ways, it is intrinsic to Corkery's argument that proper depiction is a function of the representativeness of the writer as Irish. In a sense of the word quite strictly analogous to its usage in democratic political theory, the writer is the people's representative. Accordingly, the concept of representation here involves an implicit narrative of development: by representing in himself the common identity of the Irish people, by canalizing 'some share of Irish consciousness so that that consciousness would better know itself' (p. 6) the writer produces the national and subjective unity which is as yet only a latent potential. Corkery thus insists upon a continuity between individual and national identity which is borne by literature, and insists, moreover, that *only* a national literature can be considered literature at all, since only such a literature is representative: 'Is the writer the people's voice? has there ever been, can there be, a distinctive literature that is not a national literature?' (p. 2)

We will pass over momentarily the *normalizing* function which national literature performs for Corkery — 'normal and national are synonymous in literary criticism' (p. 3) — to address rather the question which is critical but constantly displaced in this essay on Anglo-Irish literature, namely the very presence of the prefix 'Anglo-'. Though in later writings, Corkery vehemently espouses the gaelicization of Irish culture, in *Synge and Anglo-Irish Literature* the problem of the predominant anglicization of Irish culture is largely elided.[3] What might seem at first a strange displacement is in fact intrinsic to, even constitutive of, Corkery's essay and of the nationalist discourse to which it belongs. Indeed, Corkery's sketchy treatment of the matter is allowed by the previous writings of Irish nationalists who seek to resolve the founding contradiction of their political culture. For Irish nationalism emerges in consequence of a relatively rapid though uneven modernization of parts of Irish society in the early nineteenth century which produced an expanding middle class along with the technical and administrative apparatus capable of producing and disseminating the concept of the nation as a whole.[4] By virtue, however, of the commercial and bureaucratic activities which produced and occupied this class, all necessarily transacted primarily if not exclusively in English, the political doctrines of nationalism are conceived and propagated in English. Simultaneously, the emergence of an increasingly politically conscious middle class coincides with the critical decline of the Irish language as the medium of daily life for the people, a decline that has already passed the 50% mark by the mid-1840s.[5] Irish nationalism thus emerges at the moment of virtual eclipse of what would have been its 'natural' language and primarily among a class which was already, necessarily, estranged from that language. The peculiar forms taken by Irish nationalism develop from this vividly apprehended dislocation and from the consequent absence of the political legitimation available to other European nationalisms through the putatively *a priori* transcendent unity of a national language.[6]

In an article written in 1843 for the English-language nationalist newspaper, *The Nation*, Thomas Davis gave vivid expression to the problem caused by the loss of a national language to a nationalism predicated on European models:

> To impose another language on such a people is to send their history adrift among the

3. For a discussion of Corkery's shift in attitude, see Declan Kiberd, 'Writers in Quarantine? The Case for Irish Studies', in *The Crane Bag*, 3.1 (1979), p. 348.

4. On the background to administrative modernization in nineteenth century Ireland generally, see F. S. L. Lyons, *Ireland Since the Famine* (Weidenfeld and Nicolson, 1971), Chap. 3. Jacqueline Hill, 'The Intelligentsia and Irish Nationalism in the 1840s', *Studia Hibernica* 20 (1980), p. 94, argues for the impact of the British state in Ireland on the integration of the population as well as on the centralization of its apparatuses. She also shows, passim, the primarily middle class composition of the Young Ireland movement.
5. The best general survey of the linguistic orientation of European nationalisms is still Elie Kedourie, *Nationalism* (London: Hutchinson, 1961).
6. See Donald Akenson, *The Irish Educational Experiment: the National System of Education in Nineteenth Century Ireland* (London: Routledge and Kegan Paul, 1970), pp. 379-380, for statistical deductions relating to the decline of Irish.

> accidents of translation — 'tis to tear their identity from all places — 'tis to substitute arbitrary signs or picturesque and suggestive names — 'tis to cut off the entail of feeling, and separate the people from their forefathers by a deep gulf — 'tis to corrupt their very organs, and abridge their power of expression.[7]

To take on another language is already to live as an exile, to lose one's identity with one's paternity, to be condemned to translate. But we should note that the paternity to which Davis lays claim is a family romance: his case, as with most of his Young Ireland collaborators, is absolutely not that of a Gaelic speaker forced to abandon the language of his literal father and to speak or write in English. On the contrary, Davis and the Young Irelanders were mostly raised and educated in English and were hence obliged to graft themselves back on to a Gaelic past in order to claim it as their proper heritage. This backward movement has double-edged consequences: on the one hand, the paternal language, like the paternal heritage which it represents, becomes a sublimated ideal;[8] on the other, the actual Gaelic language, still current even if culturally embattled, is projected as a lost mother-tongue which is at once natural and in need of supplementation.[9] Irish nationalist writings inaugurate a subtle but decisive shift from the recognition of the economic and political threat which Gaelic culture faced from British imperialism to its representation as lost, past, primitive, fragmented and, indeed, feminine. This shift is inseparable from the specific project of bourgeois nationalism in Ireland, namely, the forging of a sense of Irish *identity* that would transcend historically determined cultural and political differences and form the reconciliatory centre of national unity. This project is engaged at the level of the culture as a whole, through the various research and propaganda activities which nineteenth century nationalists carried out and encouraged, and equally significantly at the level of the individual, whose ethical development was prerequisite to his integration with a still-to-be-realized fatherland. The future-oriented project of Irish nationalism, devoted to the ethical formation of Irish subjects through powerful sublimated identifications, ironically supplants the Gaelic culture in whose name it speaks, furthering its transformation into a primitive or undeveloped substrate of nationalist culture.

In the field of language-politics, it could be argued that the obsession with national identity, conceived as an ideal to be forged rather than an actual set of cultural and historical determinants, contributes to the decay of the Irish language. For the reconciliation which the Young Irelanders pursue, given that they regard any attempt to promote a national linguistic revival as impractical, calls for a work of translation, of translation redefined so that Davis's 'accidents' are replaced by principles. Since the Gaelic culture which is the sign of a separate political identity will have in any case to be mediated to an already anglicized people by translation, the theory of translation adopted proclaims the possibility of transmitting entirely the generative *spirit* (the 'genius') of the Irish language into the English. This act can, however, only be performed by writers who are representative of, already integrated spiritually with, the racial spirit and who, accordingly, prefigure for the fragmentary actual population the unity which is to come. The gulf which separates us from our putative forefathers on the material level is sutured[10] by a second level identification with the paternal spirit of the nation, assuring the reproduction of an identity and unity of the people that supposedly pre-existed the shattering invasion of an alien power.

Paradoxically, in adopting such a model of cultural identification, whose complement is the development through literature of a feeling of nationality in the citizen, Irish nationalists reproduce in their very opposition to the Empire a narrative of universal development which is funda-

7. Thomas Davis, 'Our National Language', *The Nation*, 1 April 1843, p. 304.
8. In his *Three Lectures on Sexuality* (1905), Freud introduced the concept of sublimation, to signify the process whereby (natural) sexual instinctual forces are diverted into the more 'psychically effective' ends of culture, and the civilizing of the individual subject.
9. Supplementation here is used in Jacques Derrida's sense of something (e.g. translation in English) that appears to be optional but that, in fact, is indispensable, indicating a lack or absence in the supposedly complete pre-existing state of things (e.g. The Old Gaelic Order). (See Jacques Derrida, *Of Grammatology*, translated by Gayatri Chavravorty Spivak (Baltimore and London: Johns Hopkins University Press, 1976), pp. 141-64.
10. Suture, the process of stitching or tying in surgical joining, was appropriated by psychoanalytic film theory to signify the process whereby the cuts and gaps in a film are seamlessly edited to give the impression of a coherent, totalizing narrative.

mental to the legitimation of imperialism.[11] What we apprehend actually as difference and fragmentation is no more than the process of differentiation or individuation by which what was an original, unreflective unity progresses to an identity which sublates[12] difference into self-conscious unity. This ethical metaphysics finds its practical realization in the gradual assimilation of subjected peoples into the more advanced civilization of the Empire whose temporal position within the universal narrative guarantees its greater proximity to that normative humanity which is our collective goal. Within this schema, it is constantly the ethical function of the aesthetic work to furnish representative instances of this narrative, as it is the function of aesthetic history, the history of aesthetic forms, to demonstrate the congruity of aesthetic forms of increasing self-reflexive complexity with the preordained stages of humankind's development. Hence the importance for aesthetic thought of the notion of the aesthetic work as arousing a contemplative desire which reconciles subject and object, and, complementary to this notion, of the stress it lays upon the formal identity of the human which resides in the formative capacity of human being in general.[13]

Hence, from Young Ireland through to Corkery, a *normal* literature is a national literature, and the function of a national literature is normalizing. Conceived in terms entirely congruent with the aesthetic and developmental theories current in the major European imperial states, the aesthetics of Irish nationalism similarly espouses a literature which will develop from its primitive, native incoherence to the status of a representative national institution and which will operate, at the individual as at the national level, to develop ethical identity.

11. This point is developed in David Lloyd, *Nationalism and Minor Literature: James Clarence Mangan and the Emergence of Irish Cultural Nationalism* (Berkeley: University of California Press, 1987).
12. 'Sublate' in the Hegelian sense means to abolish something in order to reconstitute it at a higher level.
13. On these two aspects of aesthetic culture and their relation to a quasi-political theory of representation, see David Lloyd, 'Arnold, Ferguson, Schiller: Aesthetic Culture and the Politics of Aesthetics', *Cultural Critique*, No. 2 (Winter 1985-86), 163-69.

IV. CULTURE AND CONFLICT

DECLAN KIBERD

(1951-)

from: ANGLO-IRISH ATTITUDES (1984)

[In this Field Day pamphlet, Declan Kiberd argues that many of the dominant myths and idealized (self-) images of Ireland are not truly indigenous but are partly of colonial origin. The fact that they appear to be authentic native expressions only adds to the subtlety of colonial domination. In recent times, some of these stereotypes have surfaced in critical writings, as in the attempt to attribute the present conflict in Ireland primarily to cultural factors, the 'Celtic' disposition towards myth and imagination. Kiberd instead calls for an examination of the material forces that underpin the various manifestations of cultural conflict.]

'Every power in nature must evolve its opposite in order to realise itself,' wrote Giordano Bruno, 'and opposition brings reunion'.[1] What is true of nature may also be true of nations. The English did not invade Ireland — rather, they seized a neighbouring island and invented the idea of Ireland. The notion 'Ireland' is largely a fiction created by the rulers of England in response to specific needs at a precise moment in British history. The English have always presented themselves to the world as a cold, refined and urbane race, so it suited them to see the Irish as hot-headed, rude and garrulous —

1. See James Joyce's summary of Bruno's philosophy: 'Every power in nature must evolve an opposite in order to realise itself and opposition brings revision etc etc . . . .' Stuart Gilbert (ed.), *Letters of James Joyce* (London: Faber and Faber, 1957), p. 224.

the perfect foil to set off British virtues.[a] The corollary of this is also true. The Irish notion of 'England' is a fiction created and inhabited by the Irish for their own pragmatic purposes. Coming from an almost neolithic community on wind-swept seashores, the Irish immigrants in British cities had no understanding of life in the anonymous workplaces into which they were plunged. They found it easier to don the mask of the garrulous Paddy than to reshape a complex urban identity of their own. As early as 1818, John Keats described the Irish as cunning blusterers and gallous fellows who were 'sensible of the Character they hold in England and act accordingly to Englishmen'.[b] Within their tightly-knit communities, these immigrants continued to subscribe to their ancient pieties, while happily conforming to the folk image of the stage Irishman in affairs of business and politics. Acting the buffoon, they seemed harmless and lovable adults to those Englishmen who might otherwise have resented their competition for jobs in a contracting work-force. An art of fawning duplicity was perfected by the most successful Irish businessmen, who acted the buffoon while making shrewd deals which outsmarted their English rivals.

For almost two centuries, both the Irish and the English have been using each other's territory as a gigantic laboratory in which to conduct experiments which would be unthinkable in the domestic context.[c] In recent years, for example, thousands of Irish girls have travelled to London, Manchester and Birmingham in order to procure the abortions which are still illegal in their native land. In the same period, crowds in Belfast and Derry have been fired on by a British Army employing those plastic bullets which the Home Secretary still prohibits from use on domestic rioters in such trouble-spots as Southall and Toxteth. Lest these seem depressing examples, it should be added that the manifestations of the 'laboratory theory' can be positive and encouraging. Because Ireland was a testing-ground for the new educational theories of the 1830s, her people had the benefits of efficient, nationalised schools long before their counterparts in Britain itself. Equally, it has often been argued that the cultural life of England has been immensely enriched by many Irish writers, artists, actors and teachers who have chosen that country as the prime location for what Yeats once called 'an experiment in living'. The entire tradition of Anglo-Irish comedy seems to be based on the conviction that each country is an experimental laboratory, to be used at will by the neighbouring people. George Bernard Shaw once described Ireland as an open-air sanitorium to which all Englishmen should be sent for a time in order to learn flexibility of mind.[2] But the attitude is reciprocal. Yeats said that to an Irishman England is fairyland. . . .

Faced with these realities, the British intelligentsia of the nineteenth century came up with its notion of an antithesis between all things English and Irish. For some, this expressed their revulsion at the spectacle of the neighbouring barbarians. For others, Ireland seemed to embody valuable qualities such as pastoral beauty, emotional spontaneity and spiritual idealism which had slowly disappeared from the British way of life. British literary figures began to find in Ireland all those traits which they feared they were losing in themselves. Inevitably, there was much that was sentimental, and even patronising, in their view. They gave the Irish a reputation for colourful speech which did not always square with the facts, a reputation so powerful that it still clings to those Irish writers who have done most to repudiate it. The 'scrupulous meanness' of the opening paragraphs of *Dubliners*; the attack on 'poetry talk' as a substitute for action in the plays of Synge; the attempt by Kavanagh to write a poetry that flirts with the possibility of becoming prose; the success of Beckett's translation to French, a language in which it is 'plus facile d'écrire sans style' — all betoken a critique of Irish wit and wordplay. Joyce turns his suspecting glance onto the English liberal Haines,[3] his phrase-book at the ready for those wisecracks and witticisms that refuse to come;

a. See Declan Kiberd, 'The Fall of the Stage Irishman', *The Genres of the Irish Literary Revival*, ed. R. Schleifer (Dublin, 1980), 39-60. Some of these opening points recapitulate the main thesis of that essay.

b. John Keats, *Letters of John Keats*, selected by Frederick Page (Oxford University Press, London, 1954), 149.

c. For historical applications of the 'laboratory theory', see Patrick O'Farrell, *Ireland's English Question* (New York, 1971) and *England and Ireland since 1800* (Oxford, 1975); Joseph Lee, *The Modernisation of Irish Society 1848-1918* (Dublin, 1975); and Oliver MacDonagh, *Ireland: The Union and Its Aftermath* (London, 1973).

2. Cited in M. Holroyd, 'G. B. S. and Ireland', *Sewanee Review*, Vol. LXXXIV, No. 1 (Winter 1976), p. 54.

3. Haines, 'a ponderous Saxon', shares the Martello Tower with Stephen Dedalus and Buck Mulligan in the opening scene of James Joyce's *Ulysses*.

Kavanagh repents of the paddy-whackery of *The Green Fool*[4] with a lifetime of linguistic self-denial; Beckett is so ashamed of his early versions of 'Sodom and Begorrah' that he changes language rather than risk repeating the mistake. Even Yeats, aware of his own fatal propensity for eloquence, resolved to take rhetoric and wring its neck, and if he did not always succeed, then at least he pointed the way.[5] A poem like 'Easter 1916' is a highly ironic catalogue of cliché, done with only part of the tongue in the cheek. By the time Flann O'Brien emerges with his resuscitated banalities, the tongue will be wholly lodged in the side of the mouth. The Irish revival, seen in this light, may be less an explosion of verbal colour, than a dignified assertion of a people's right to be colourless. To give this thesis the extended consideration it deserves would be to risk dismantling one of the most potent myths in the history of Anglo-American criticism of Irish writing.[d]

Confronted with a set of clichés which compound insult ('violent') and patronisation ('eloquent') in equal measure, it is not surprising that Irish writers and critics often bite the liberal English hand that feeds them. But the sole alternative is to be told by the High Tories that West Belfast is like East Finchley. For better or worse, the audience of British liberals and leftists remains Ireland's most firm hope. (The notion that the Tories will initiate the final withdrawal, just as the Republicans and not the Democrats extricated America from Vietnam, is probably wishful thinking). Irish writers, political and literary, have for more than a hundred years addressed themselves to that modest but influential constituency, often with painful results for both sides. Those Englishmen who take an interest in Irish affairs often feel that rejection and contempt are their only thanks. Their interest often seems incomprehensibly quixotic to their fellow-countrymen who know just how often Ireland has been the graveyard of English political hopes. These English students of the Irish situation see themselves as conscience-stricken idealists, reaching across the divide of centuries, only to be accused by a new generation of Irishmen of repressive tolerance, of being the subtlest exploiters of all, of being the reincarnation of Broadbent[6] and Haines. It was in such a mood that Donald Davie wrote 'Ireland of the Bombers'.[7] It was, doubtless, in such a mood that Robert Kee read many of the Irish responses to his *Ireland: A Television History*. Here, he must have felt, was a decent English liberal, scrupulously telling both sides of the tragic story in a helpful and level-headed way. Here, many Irish felt, was another liberal posing as a moderate and factual Englishman between warring Irish extremists — and thereby perpetuating the greatest single illusion that underlies the British presence in Ireland. Mr. Kee's series did immense good in Ireland as well as in England. There can hardly have been a single citizen who did not learn something new, and often uncomfortable, about his own past. But the more skilled it was in demolishing all the minor myths, the more successful it became in renovating the greatest myth of all. In marked contrast, the ITV series entitled *The Troubles*[8] employed no 'impartial' British front-man and resorted to a flat, descriptive script read in clipped, impersonal tones by a hired actress. It was considerably more radical in its interpretation of events than the BBC Series, and, of course, no less 'loaded' or prejudged. But it had the merit of allowing the Irish realities to speak for themselves.

What all this demonstrates is simple enough — the power of an ancient myth to reappear in a new guise even when men think that it has been exploded forever. The well-intentioned Englishman who thinks that he might be part of the solution turns out to be part of the problem; and the dispassionate Irishman who sets out to question British clichés often finds himself forced covertly to appeal to them, if only to initiate a dialogue. Those who refuse this compromise are thrown out of court; those who accept the constraints are often forced to betray the cause they love. The forces which neutralised the subversive paradoxes of Wilde and Shaw are no less potent in the 1980s than they were in the 1880s. The attempts to explain Ireland to the English are scarcely more advanced.

d. For further comments on this, see S. Deane, 'Heroic Styles: The Tradition of an Idea', Field Day Pamphlet No. 4 (Derry, 1984).

4. Patrick Kavanagh's early autobiographical novel, *The Green Fool*, was published in 1938, much to his subsequent regret.
5. Yeats cited Verlaine's injunction, 'wring the neck of rhetoric', in his introduction to *The Oxford Book of Modern Verse* (1936).
6. Broadbent is the gullible English visitor to Ireland in Shaw's play *John Bull's Other Island* (1904).
7. Donald Davie, 'Ireland of the Bombers' in *Collected Poems 1971-83* (Manchester: Carcanet New Press, 1983), pp. 130-31.
8. The BBC/RTE series *Ireland: A Television History*, written and presented by Robert Kee, and the ITV series on Northern Ireland, *The Troubles*, were first screened in 1980.

Just as the English took the traditionalist Yeats to their hearts and shunned the modernist Joyce, so now they shower praise the prizes on those analysts of the Irish imbroglio who offer culture rather than cash by way of explanation.

The reception accorded to the late F. S. L. Lyons's Ford Lectures at Oxford University in 1978 is a case in point. These were published in the following year by the Clarendon Press under the title *Culture and Anarchy in Ireland: 1890-1939*. Professor Lyons's thesis was that 'the essence of the Irish situation is the collision of a variety of cultures, Gaelic, English, Anglo-Irish and Ulster Protestant'. He argued that no political solution will be successful unless it is based on an understanding of the intricacies of this interlocking pattern. In seeking to provide the historical basis for such an understanding, he was at pains to reject the more fashionable Marxist analysis of men like Michael Farrell and Eamonn McCann.[9]

> The ancient quarrel is, of course, about power [wrote Lyons], and about its economic base, as well as about its economic manifestations. But such clichés can hardly satisfy us. If we ask further what are the ends for which the possession of power is coveted, we may perhaps come closer to the truth about Ulster. In that small and beautiful region different cultures have collided, because each has a view of life which it deems to be threatened by its opponents; and power is the means by which a particular view of life can be maintained against all rivals. These views of life are founded upon religion, because this is a region where religion is still considered as a vital determinant of everything important in the human condition.[e]

Professor Lyons demonstrated that sectarian rioting began in 1813, long before Catholics were numerous enough in cities to constitute an economic threat to the employment of Protestants. Furthermore, he documented with rare descriptive power that curious blend of resolution and hysteria, of barbarous vulgarity and boot-faced sobriety, which lies beneath the emotions of Ulster Protestantism. An evangelical religion which demanded that the Lambeg drum[10] should be beaten 'until the knuckles of the drummers ran with blood' has clearly more than an economic motivation.

Such cultural history offers a timely antidote to those who have held that the sectarian conflict was always and only about jobs; but this book does not necessarily explode the Marxist claim that the current war is primarily economic in its underlying motivations. 1813 is not 1969, much less 1984. While Professor Lyons was right to suggest that the problem 'can only be understood in its historical context', he would have been wiser to add that the past decade provides many more telling insights into the roots of the current strife. As a contribution to cultural history, his book stops quite reasonably at 1939 with the outbreak of world war and the death of Yeats. But, as an attempt to explain the current conflict, this work is seriously marred by that terminal date. A great deal has happened in the intervening decades which Lyons could not discuss — the coming of the welfare state in the 1940s embraced with marked reluctance by the Unionists, the consequent emergence of articulate Catholic graduates in the 1960s, the failure of the Belfast régime to respond intelligently to their demands, and the ensuing violence of the 1970s. The overthrow of an upperclass Unionism (in the person of O'Neill), followed by the removal of mercantile Unionism (in the person of Faulkner),[11] cleared the way for a proletarian leadership. The working-class leaders of militant Unionism in the 1980s bear scant resemblance to the Carsons and Craigs of previous decades. Similarly, the contemporary IRA is filled with unemployed radicals and leftist revolutionaries, quite unlike the puritanical schoolmasters and idealistic civil servants satirised by Brendan Behan in the 1950s and 1960s. These changes are fundamentally economic in nature, just as the very emergence of the civil rights movement was chiefly made possible by the welfare state.

e. F. S. L. Lyons, *Culture and Anarchy in Ireland: 1890-1939* (Clarendon Press, Oxford, 1979), 144.

9. See Michael Farrell, *The Orange State* (London: Pluto Press, 1976) and Eamonn McCann, *War and an Irish Town* (Harmondsworth: Penguin Books, 1974).

10. The Lambeg drum, called after a district in County Antrim, is the centrepiece of the marching bands associated with the Orange Order, which commemorate key events in the Loyalist calender such as the 12 July celebration of the battle of the Boyne.

11. Terence O'Neill was prime minister of Northern Ireland when the present conflict broke out in 1968; Brian Faulkner was the prime minister who fell from power after the Sunningdale agreement in December 1974.

Professor Lyons, in his anxiety to prove that culture makes things happen, chose to end his book with a date which allowed him to neglect these salient points. If his thesis were explained to some of the current protagonists in the conflict, it would doubtless evoke bizarre responses. Is it really true that the difference between Glenn [*sic*] Barr and John Hume is attributable to a clash of cultures?[12] How vital is the Gaelic tradition to a Dublin Government whose Minister for Education cannot even speak the Irish language?[13] How deep is the loyalty of insurgent Unionism to the Anglo-Irish tradition? And to England, for that matter? 'For the Lenox-Conynghams of Ulster', remarked Lyons, 'service in the British Army was as inevitable as breathing'.[f] It was not quite so inevitable for many current Unionist leaders, whose 'loyalism' did not extend to enlisting in his majesty's forces to safeguard the world from the fascists. Mina Lenox-Conyngham's charming memoir of an ascendancy Big House is quoted by the author, who sees the following scene as quintessentially Anglo-Irish:

> ... we like to remember the evening sunlight slanting through tall trees where jackdaws chatter, and making flickering patterns on walls hung with portraits, from which many a former occupant looks mysteriously down.[g]

Whatever else this represents, it is certainly *not* what the UDA[14] is fighting for.

The trouble with Lyons's exhilarating book is that its thesis works fairly well in its earlier nineteenth-century settings, but in modern Ulster men's emotions have been ruled not so much by culture as by cash. In a city of chronic unemployment such as Derry, money doesn't talk — it swears. In his zeal to prove that culture motivates political action, Lyons quoted those lines in which Yeats wondered if his play had sent out certain men the English shot. But poets are not the unacknowledged legislators of the world. As W. H. Auden observed with bitter resignation, such a description better fits the secret police. The denizens of Ballymurphy and the Shankill[15] will hardly argue with that.

Conor Cruise O'Brien's *States of Ireland*[16] confronts very squarely those decades of change which are unrecorded by F. S. L. Lyons and his stance, though polemical at the time of writing, has already become the orthodoxy in Dublin government circles. Yet his account of events contains scant reference to the economic factors which played such a part in the current phase of the struggle. The works of Lyons and O'Brien have been massively influential on British politicians of all parties and on British journalists of all papers, while books like Michael Farrell's *Northern Ireland: The Orange State* and Eamonn McCann's *War and an Irish Town* have not. The socialist analysts may be somewhat cavalier in their dismissal of culture as a potent source of distinctive symbols — symbols which reinforce and seem to legitimise the economic aspirations of the various Ulster factions. But it is at least arguable that they are a good deal nearer to the facts of the matter. An Irish reviewer of the texts spawned by the current crisis might wonder why they must turn exclusively to culture *or* to economics by way of explanation, when it is clear that the two go hand-in-hand, even if economics is leading the way. But he might also ask why the British intelligentsia choose to believe one set of explanations rather than the other. Is it because middle-class liberals are too cushioned by affluence to notice the way in which the world actually works? Is it that they fear to admit the reality of imperialist plunder which was the economic basis for that most admirable of systems, the welfare state? Is it that an audience of academics, journalists and politicians has a vested interest in the thesis that culture, and culture alone, makes things happen? Or could it be that Ireland is still deemed 'interesting and different', a place where the unexpected always happens, where men kill and die for abstract images and evocative symbols? This reading of the Irish as martyrs to abstraction — a reading sponsored most notoriously in the poetry of Yeats — is the greatest single obstacle to a full understanding of the situation in Ireland today. It

f. Ibid., 119.
g. Quoted ibid., 120.

12. Glen Barr was one of the prominent protestant leaders in the Ulster Workers' Council strike which brought down the power-sharing executive established by the Sunningdale agreement in 1974. John Hume has been leader of the Social and Democratic Labour Party since 1979.
13. This refers to Gemma Hussey, minister for education in the coalition government 1982-86.
14. The Ulster Defence Association, a broadly based loyalist paramilitary organization, was founded in 1971.
15. Two working-class areas of Belfast, inhabited respectively by catholics and protestants.
16. Conor Cruise O'Brien, *States of Ireland* (London: Hutchinson, 1972).

bedevils attempts by students, both native and foreign, to understand the masterpieces of Irish literature; but it bedevils also the attempts by British well-wishers to understand John Bull's Other Island. . . .

British commentators are rightly outraged whenever London is bombed by the IRA, and they ask 'What kind of people could do such a thing?' But they never ask an equally pressing question — 'What kind of people are we supporting in Ulster?' The ignorance of Ireland among English people is considerable, but the ignorance of Ulster Unionism among English liberals is almost total. The current crisis has promoted most Irish people to re-examine some of their deepest historical assumptions, but it has as yet given rise to no similar self-questioning in England. On the contrary, a bomb in Harrod's[17] gives all the hoariest anti-Irish clichés a new lease of life. If British writers are serious in their attempts to contribute to a solution, they must break out of the current impasse. To do that, they must cure themselves of their longstanding fixation on Irish nationalism and apply themselves to the study of Ulster Unionism. For most English liberals, this is a disagreeable prospect. The anonymous reviewer of Robert Kee's *The Green Flag* in the *Times Literary Supplement* of 26 May 1972 spoke for them all when he invoked

> . . . the superior attraction for the cultivated mind of the winding caravan of Irish nationalism with its poets, assassins, scholars, crackpots, parlour revolutionaries, windbags, mythopoeic essayists, traitors, orators from the scaffold, men of action, emerging from so long and so great suffering of the people to impart an almost mythic quality to their often futile and often brutal deeds — the superior attraction of that to the hard, assertive, obsessive, successful self-reliance of the Ulster Protestant which has about it as much imagination as is contained in a bowler hat.[h]

Because they are so sympathetic to the green flag, English intellectuals have focussed on its tradition to the virtual exclusion of any informed assessment of the deeper meanings of Ulster Unionism. But, by their obsession with Irish nationalism, they have jeopardised its long-term prospects and the hopes of all Ireland and English for a solution. Since the time of Matthew Arnold, they have offered countless mythological analyses of the culture which England is nominally opposing. It is now time for them to conduct a pragmatic analysis of the Unionist culture which England is still actually supporting.

17. Harrods, the exclusive department store in London, was bombed by the Provisional IRA in 1983.

h. Quoted by Tom Nairn, *The Break-Up of Britain: Crisis and Neo-Nationalism* (New Left Books, London, 1977), 230. This book contains one of the few attempts by British Marxists to offer a sympathetic analysis of Ulster Unionism, but the author's information is obviously sparse and often inaccurate.

DENIS DONOGHUE

(1928-)

from: WE IRISH (1986)

[In this essay, first published in *Hibernia* (1978), Donoghue rejects the view that politics has a corrosive effect on Irish poetry, and argues instead that it is an invigorating influence on the work of poets such as Yeats and Seamus Heaney. Donoghue insists, however, that a genuine poetic response to 'The Troubles' is not raw or unmediated but takes the form of a complex articulation alive to competing perspectives on both art and politics. By subjecting history to the multi-layered operation of language, or the stratified deposits of the landscape, for example, Heaney's poetry critically engages the past rather than succumbs to it. The recourse to an imaginative landscape predating the troubles, which Edna Longley (see p. 648) considers a baneful form of nostalgia in Brian Friel's *Translations*, is interpreted by Donoghue as a liberating device in the context of Heaney's work.]

. . . It is well known that much of modern Irish literature has been provoked by violence, and that images of war soon acquire a symbolic aura in this country. Our traditions are histrionic and oratorical. The themes of Irish literature are few: if we list childhood, isolation, religion, and politics, we come nearly to the end of them. R. P. Blackmur once argued that 'the politics of existing states is always too simple for literature; it is good only to aggravate literature.'[1] The institutions of a state, of any state we think of, are never sufficiently complex to animate the difficult purposes of literature. But when he allows that the politics of existing states is good only to aggravate literature, he makes an allowance good enough for Irish writers. It is simple fact that Yeats, O'Casey, and a dozen writers up to Francis Stuart, Brian Friel, Thomas Kinsella, and Seamus Heaney have been aggravated by Irish politics to the point of turning their aggravation into verse and prose.

In August 1915, Yeats told Henry James that he did not feel inclined to write a war poem, even on Edith Wharton's invitation, and he sent James a few verses in that spirit, including the famous disclaimer, 'We have no gift to set a statesman right'.[2] The plain fact is that Yeats did not feel inclined to put his genius to work in England's cause; but he never thought himself incapable of setting statesmen right if he felt sufficiently exasperated by their follies. A few months later the Easter Rising set his verses astir; he saw no reason to silence himself on that occasion.

Walter Benjamin once wrote that 'all efforts to render politics aesthetic culminate in one thing: war.'[3] The remark occurs in an essay of 1936 when Benjamin was pondering the Fascist way of organising the proletarian masses without affecting the property structure which the masses, in principle, strive to eliminate. Fascism saw its salvation, according to Benjamin, in giving these masses not their right, but merely a chance to express themselves. Hence the rigmarole of public displays, marches, celebrations, anniversaries, those secular rituals by which thousands of men are given the illusion of living a dramatic life in common.

The introduction of aesthetics into politics is a perennial theme; to consider politics as entertainment, or to ponder the aesthetic aspects of war, blood, and death, is not necessarily self-indulgence, it may be a crucial aspect of modern society. Indeed, modern Irish literature has often been animated by the aesthetic aspect of violence. Padraic Fiacc's recent anthology *The Wearing of the Black* contains many poems, most of them bad in nearly every respect, which testify to the thrill of blood and sacrifice.[4] But it also contains a few poems in which the transfiguring power of violence is recognised, its way of turning boredom into drama; and in one of these poems the poet is tender toward the desire and the need. He virtually withholds his irony from it, while allowing the reader's irony to assert itself. The poet sees how naturally a young man wants to become a dramatic figure in an otherwise wearisome and characterless time. The poem is 'Bogside, Derry, 1971':

Shielded, vague soldiers, visored, crouch alert:
between tall houses down the blackened street;
the hurled stones pour, hurt-instinct aims to hurt,
frustration spurts in flame about their feet.

Lads who at ease had tossed a laughing ball,
or, ganged in teams, pursued some shouting game,
beat angry fists against that stubborn wall
of faceless fears which now at last they name.

Night after dark this city yields a stage
with peak of drama for the pointless day,
where shadows offer stature, roles to play,
urging the gestures which might purge in rage
the slights, the wrongs, the long indignities
the stubborn core within each heart defies.

It is common for war correspondents to speak of a theatre of war. The aesthetic form most pertinent to war is theatre with its terminology of action, gesture, role-playing. John Hewitt's poem is perceptive in recognising the fact that people can deal with nameless fears only by finding a name for them and objectifying them in a hostile presence; in this case the British Army. He comes close to sentimentalising those stone-throwing youths, I suppose, but he narrowly avoids the temptation.

1. R. P. Blackmur, 'The Politics of Human Power' in *The Lion and The Honeycomb* (New York: Harcourt, Brace 1955), p. 41.
2. 'On being asked for a War Poem', in Richard Finneran (ed.), *W. B. Yeats: The Poems* (London: Macmillan, 1983), p. 155.
3. Walter Benjamin, 'The Work of Art in the Age of Mechanical Reproduction', in *Illuminations*, translated by Harry Zohn (London: Fontana, 1974), p. 243.
4. Padraic Fiacc, *The Wearing of the Black* (Belfast: Blackstaff Press, 1974).

There are many poems which do not scruple to avoid it.

Some poems, like Thomas Kinsella's 'Butcher's Dozen', and some plays, like Brian Friel's *The Freedom of the City*, have emerged far too readily from the events that provoked them. It is hard to deny a poet the right to cry and rant and rage when an act strikes him as peculiarly outrageous, as the events of 'Bloody Sunday' struck Kinsella and Friel.[5] Yeats spoke of the will trying to do the work of the imagination, and he thought the effort misplaced; but it is hard to be patient.

There is further exorbitance: that of direct, apparently unmediated feeling which has not reached the stage of being either will or imagination; demanding to leap into expression without any mediation. We are told, and we believe, that there is no such thing as unmediated feeling, that the feeling is already inscribed, as if in invisible ink, and that we are never spontaneous. But it is a hard linguistics to act upon. Kinsella's poem and Friel's play come from the primitive demand, the insistence upon unmediated rage. The crudity of these works is not the price these writers willingly pay for the semblance of spontaneity, it is a sign of their rage with everything that stands between them and the feeling of the moment, everything that offers itself as form but could as well offer itself as delay or patience. It is natural for a writer to resent, on such a violent occasion, the admonition that his art is bound to be indirect in its effect and slow to act upon its cause. That poetry makes nothing happen is normally a tolerable fact; but there are occasions on which a poet feels that he must respond to one act with another similar in character and force.

Even in a quieter poet, like Heaney, there are moments of impatience. One of his Northern poems is called 'Whatever you say, say nothing,'[6] a satirical piece, not one of his better poems but a minor essay in observation. His theme is the Northern habit of keeping one's counsel, saying nothing, intoning the clichés of communication for safety's sake. Heaney recites many of the currencies of such conversation, but at one point he breaks through them into an apparently direct speech of his own:

Christ, it's near time that some small leak was sprung

In the great dykes the Dutchman made
To dam the dangerous tide that followed Seamus[7]
Yet for all this art and sedentary trade
I am incapable.

'This sedentary trade' is a phrase from Yeats's poem 'The Tower', and Heaney's use of it brings him in under Yeats's shadow for the moment, the theme being the poet's general predicament, the gap between writing and action. But the reference to incapacity comes immediately after an outburst of political rhetoric; it's nearly time, Heaney says, the Unionist structures were undermined, and he goes back to the Dutchman William's victory over James at the Boyne in 1690 and the Orange Ascendancy in force in the North since that day. Heaney is more patient than Kinsella and Friel, but there are moments in him, too, when he chafes under the constraints of his trade. Not surprising in an Irish poet. Is it not significant, for instance, that Yeats normally used 'violent' as a word of praise, especially when he surrounded it with words of strong heroic cast? 'Some violent bitter man, some powerful man': the power takes the harm out of the violence and the bitterness. 'To show how violent great hearts can lose . . .'; greatness and violence are kin.[8] And in 'Cuchulain Comforted' there is that line, 'Violent and famous, strode among the dead.' Indeed, I can recall only one line in Yeats's poems in which violence is repudiated: in 'No Second Troy' where Maud Gonne's intentions include teaching 'to ignorant men most violent ways,' and even in that case it is the ignorance of her pupils that drags the violent ways down to commonplace.

The troubles in the North have been with us now for ten years. Everything that can be said has been said, though much of it has then been forgotten or ignored. So long as the present balance of forces continues, there is no clear reason why the troubles should ever stop. I have long thought that the British Government should make a declaration of intent to withdraw, and ease the transition to the next phase of Irish history. That would mean an end to the British guarantee, regularly given to the

5. On Sunday, 30 January 1972, the British army shot dead thirteen civilians in Derry during a peaceful demonstration. Both Kinsella's poem and Friel's play were written in response to 'Bloody Sunday'.
6. In *North* (London: Faber and Faber, 1975), p. 57.
7. 'Seamus' refers to the Irish name for King James II — and, of course, to Heaney's own Christian name.
8. The lines quoted are from, respectively, 'Ancestral Houses' and 'The Gift of Harun Al-Rashid', *The Poems*, pp. 200, 443.

Unionists, that the position of Northern Ireland within the United Kingdom will remain intact unless and until a majority of the people in the North want a change.[9] It would also mean either the unification of Ireland or the establishment of an independent Northern Ireland, independent of Britain and of Dublin alike. It is hard to say whether the majority of us in the South genuinely want the country to be united or not; a referendum would return a loud 'yes', but in the meantime a common sentiment in the South would say, 'Lord, let us be united . . . but not yet.'

I have implied that Yeats was not alone in Irish poetry in his ambivalence toward acts of violence. Conflict as such was dear to Yeats because it was the readiest form of his energy: he was more in need of conflict than of the peace that brings it to an end. He feared peace because he feared inertia. I do not mean that he was a propagandist for murder or that he condoned the Civil War; but he was afraid his poetry would stop if conflict stopped within himself; the grappling of opposites kept his art in force. This motive is still active in Irish poetry, but on the whole our poets have been turning their rhymes toward some form of transcendence.

Heaney is the most telling poet in this respect, and the success of *North* makes his case exemplary; it is clear that thousands of readers have found their feelings defined in that volume more than in any other. I shall maintain that Heaney's readers do not see themselves as lords of counter-positions, commanding a perspective in which all forms of conflict are held in poise. Rather, they find release in an area of feeling somehow beneath the field of violence and ideology; or imaginatively prior to such a moment. Heaney's poems in *North* point to such an area. The dominant analogy for his verses is archaeology, not history; his sense of time circumvents the immediacies of historical event by recourse to several different levels of experience, the accretion of cultures. He is, in *North*, a poet 'after Foucault', his knowledge archaeological rather than linear or sequential.[10] In the poem 'Belderg' he writes of quernstones, millstones discovered in a bog, the hole in the middle of the stone like an eye, a pupil:

To lift the lid of the peat
And find this pupil dreaming
Of neolithic wheat!
When he stripped off blanket bog
The soft-piled centuries

Fell open like a glib:

A glib is a thick mass of matted hair, as the *Oxford Dictionary* reports, 'formerly worn by the Irish'. It is typical of Heaney to represent the experience of the archaeologist as a human discovery arising from a discovery of earth. Archaeology represents for him, paradoxically, the dream of full and immediate presence, time at once historical and perennial, in which the dichotomy between self and other is obliterated. The reconciliation which other poets represent as a vision of landscape is available to Heaney as meaning and value lying under the skin of the earth, waiting to be discovered. Heaney's desire is predicated upon the depth of earth, the levels and sites waiting, like the eye of the quernstone, to be found and seen. And the feeling goes both ways. In 'The Digging Skeleton', pictures in medical textbooks are called

Mysterious candid studies
Of red slobland around the bones.

presumably because the tissue seems alluvial. And generally Heaney's imagination turns toward the bogland which contains and preserves the human past in forms deeper and more secret than history.

The word 'bog', Heaney has remarked, is one of the few English borrowings from the Irish language. In Irish, the word means soft and wet, and survives in Hiberno-English in the phrase 'a soft day', meaning a wet day, gentle, not cold. He has also reported that in Derry they call a bog a 'moss', a word of Norse origin probably carried to the North of Ireland by planters in the early seventeenth century. So he finds in the two words the record of invasion, colonisation, and shift of language in which the Irish word, for once, has held its place. There is a poem, 'Kinship', which ponders these affinities. But I think the pondering might go further. It strikes me that bogland, for Heaney, is the meeting-place between mineral and vegetable

9. The British guarantee was given to unionists after the official declaration of an Irish Republic in 1949.

10. In his *Archaeology of Knowledge* (London: Tavistock, 1972), Michel Foucault attacked linear theories of historical or intellectual development. Heaney alludes to the aversion of English critics such as Donald Davie to Foucaultian theories of discourse in his *An Open Letter* (Derry: Field Day Pamphlet, 1983).

life, a state of nature which is soft, yielding, maternal, and full of secret lore. He has referred to 'images drawn from Anglo-Saxon kennings,[11] Icelandic sagas, Viking excavations, and Danish and Irish bogs.' In 'Viking Dublin', he says:

a worm of thought

I follow into the mud.

As a motto for the procedures of *North*, the lines would answer very well. Many of the poems in that volume follow those worms of thought into soft bogland. In the poem 'Belderg', talking to the archaeologist:

So I talked of Mossbawn,
A bogland name, 'But moss?'
He crossed my old home's music
With older strains of Norse.
I'd told how its foundation

Was mutable as sound
And how I could derive
A forked root from that ground
And make bawn *an English fort,*
A planter's walled-in mound,

Or else find sanctuary
And think of it as Irish,
Persistent if outworn.

Bawn can indeed mean a walled-in fort, if you take its meaning from the English or Scots planter; or it can mean a place for milking cows, if you leave its meaning in Ireland, especially the South. Heaney takes pleasure in these matters, as a poet should.

He also likes to think of his language as issuing from the accretion of centuries. In the poem 'Bone Dreams' he writes:

I push back
through dictions,
Elizabethan canopies.
Norman devices,
the erotic mayflowers
of Provence
and the ivied latins
of churchmen

to the scop's
twang, the iron
flash of consonants
cleaving the line.

'Scop' means a poet, minstrel, or satirist in Old English, so Heaney is invoking the two strongest traditions in the forked tongue of English: the Anglo-Saxon and the Latin. He puts the two dictions side by side in the poem 'Kinship':

This is the vowel of earth
dreaming its root
in flowers and snow,

mutation of weathers
and seasons,
a windfall composing
the floor it rots into.

I grew out of all this
like a weeping willow
inclined to
the appetites of gravity.

It is common to think of vowels as the pleasure principle of language, and of consonants as the reality principle; a thought congenial to Heaney, who writes in the poem 'Aisling':[12]

He courted her
With a decadent sweet art
Like the wind's vowel
Blowing through the hazels:

But Heaney likes to play off vowel against consonant, Latin pleasure against Anglo-Saxon reality, within the grand allowance which is Language itself, a concessive, permeable medium. So the topics or commonplaces on which his language relies are those in which nature and culture meet so harmoniously that we are not aware of a distinction between them.

I think this goes some way to account for the appeal of Heaney's poems. His poetry as a whole gives the reader the satisfaction of believing that nature and culture are not, as he feared, split apart once for all, or that one term has overwhelmed the other. Make a short list of Heaney's themes: salmon-fishing, the blacksmith's craft, the eel's journey, the thatcher's art, threshing corn, pumping water, digging potatoes, water divining. Think of water divining; an ancient skill, beneath or beyond explanation, requiring nothing but a forked stick, two hands, and the gift of divination. As a

11. Kennings, descriptive word clusters that function as names ('storm of swords' for 'battle'), are a distinctive feature of Anglo-Saxon poetry.

12. The Irish word for dream, in the political, visionary sense.

parable of the still vivid relation between man and nature, it is complete. Writing a poem about it is hardly necessary, since it is already a form of poetry, at once craft and gift. These motifs in Heaney's poetry make a natural symbolism; or rather, testify to the continuing life of such processes. He turns to them as Yeats turned from the reality of civil war to the honey-bees of generation and creative force.

The bees build in the crevices
Of loosening masonry, and there
The mother birds bring grubs and flies.
My wall is loosening; honey-bees,
Come build in the empty house of the stare.[13]

The sweetness of the honey-bees represents everything in Yeats's feeling that longs to move beyond the arguments and counter-arguments that make civil wars and keep them brutal. They speak of a natural world prior to history and culture and indifferent to their terrible possibility. Heaney's version is an appeal to those parts of human life which are still parts of natural life. In the poem 'At a Potato Digging', from *Death of a Naturalist*, the gestures of the potato-diggers are assimilated to the seasons:

Processional stooping through the turf

Recurs mindlessly as autumn.

'Mindlessly' is a word of ease and satisfaction in this poem because it points to a custom, a way of work and life, so deeply grained in the lives of farmers that it does not need to be enforced by mind; the 'thinking of the body' is enough.

The welcome extended to Heaney's *North* has been remarkably profuse. Part of the explanation is probably the consolation of hearing that there is a deeper, truer life going on beneath the bombings and torture. There are levels of action and responsiveness deeper than those occupied by Protestants and Catholics; there are archaic processes still alive despite times and technologies.

It is a comfort to receive such news, especially in poems such as Heaney's. The outrage of an obscene act such as the bombing of the La Mon Hotel is indeed the denial of humanity which it entails, but it is also its immediacy.[14] What the act gives, without our asking, is immediacy, a quality which we are ready to accept when it comes as an attribute of chance and misfortune but which leaves us baffled when it comes with human motive. This outrage is not diminished by anything we can say of it. Heaney's poems are as hapless in this respect as any editorial after the event in a newspaper or the standard expressions of sympathy from politicians and bishops. But the archives presented as an archaeological site in Heaney's poems offer a perspective of depth upon local and terrible events. Precisely because he does not present history in linear terms, Heaney offers the reader not a teleology[15] implicit in historical interpretation but a present moment still in touch with its depth. The procedure has the effect of releasing the reader — for the moment, God knows, and only for that — from the fatality which otherwise seems inscribed in the spirit of the age. There is little point in fancying ourselves free in space if we are imprisoned in time, but there are signs that poets and readers are turning away from time, having made such a mess of it, and seen such a mess made of it.

The immediate source of Heaney's bog-poems is P. V. Glob's book, *The Bog People*,[16] which contains descriptions and photographs of the Tullund man, who died 2,000 years ago, hanged in Tollund Fen in Denmark; his body was thrown into a bog and it has been preserved to this day by some chemical quality in the bog water. There is little consolation to be found in these facts, but Heaney's poems invoke them, I think, to release the reader's mind from the immediacy of his experience. I find the same motive in many of Donald Davie's[17] poems, and in the poets he especially admires: poets of place and space rather than of time; or poets who find time resumed in space. Davie has argued that modern poets have made a mess of their politics because they have misunderstood their history; history and time have formed an extremely dangerous element which they could not negotiate. Davie has turned from history to geography, to the history that extends from the geographer-historian Herodotus to the geographer-morphologist Carl Sauer and the 'archaeologist of morning', Charles Olson, who

13. W. B. Yeats, 'The Stare's Nest by My Window', *The Poems*, p. 230.
14. On 17 February 1978, the Provisional IRA placed a bomb at the La Mon Hotel, Cumber, Co. Down. It killed sixteen people and injured many others.
15. The idea that history is developing towards a predetermined goal.
16. P. V. Glob, *The Bog People: Iron Age Man Preserved* (London: Faber and Faber, 1969).
17. See Donald Davie, *The Shires: Poems* (London: Routledge & Kegan Paul, 1974).

wrote as the first sentence of his famous meditation on Melville, *Call Me Ishmael*, 'I take Space to be the central fact to man born in America from Folsom cave to now.'[18]

So what am I saying? Only this: that Heaney is the first of the poets of the North who are turning away from the terminology of time, with its claim to recognise the spirit of the age and to see a divinely inscribed teleology written in what they say is the past. I think I understand the motives at work, and some of their probable consequences. A vision founded on space, depth, archives, levels of soil is likely to emphasise continuity rather than change, and therefore the universality of human life. What his poems mainly give is the sentiment of that universality. But they do not guarantee that we will get our politics right, when it comes to the time in which we have to get them right or wrong. It means that the relationship between history and politics can be disconnected for a while and that this may be a prudent as well as a consoling thing to do. But beyond that, I am not sure. The evidence is not decisive.

18. Charles Olson, *Call Me Ishmael* (San Francisco: City Lights, 1967), p. 11.

EDNA LONGLEY

(1940-)

from: POETRY IN THE WARS (1986)

[In this extract from *Poetry in the Wars*, Edna Longley argues that the recourse to translation as a model for renegotiating the relationship between past and present is flawed, at least in the formulation adopted in Brian Friel's play *Translations* and, by extension, in Richard Kearney's interpretation of Friel's play. Language, instead of affording a form of transition or common ground, becomes a site of conflict, a source of 'the excessive awareness of linguistic difference' that she discerns in the writing of Friel, Seamus Deane and Tom Paulin. It is only by restoring language to its proper role as a mediating influence that literature and art can escape the contaminating effects of politics in a divided society, and resume its true humanistic vocation in the search for common ground.

The essay was published first in *The Crane Bag*, Vol. 9, No. 1 (1985).]

POETRY AND POLITICS IN NORTHERN IRELAND

'The antagonist of imaginative writing in Ireland is not a habit of scientific observation but our interest in matters of opinion. . . . All fine literature is the disinterested contemplation or expression of life, but hardly any Irish writer can liberate his mind sufficiently from questions of practical reform for this contemplation. Art for art's sake, as he understands it, whether it be the art of the Ode on a Grecian Urn *or of the imaginer of Falstaff, seems to him a neglect of public duty. It is as though the telegraph-boys botanised among the hedges with the undelivered envelopes in their pockets. . . .'*

—W. B. Yeats, *Explorations*

'A good poem is a paradigm of good politics'

— Derek Mahon

1.

Poetry and politics, like church and state, should be separated. And for the same reasons: mysteries distort the rational processes which ideally prevail in social relations; while ideologies confiscate the poet's special passport to *terra incognita*. Its literary streak, indeed, helps to make Irish Nationalism more a theology than an ideology. Conor Cruise O'Brien calls 'the area where literature and politics overlap' an 'unhealthy intersection';[1] because, 'suffused with romanticism', it breeds bad politics — Fascism and Nationalism.[a] But it also breeds bad literature, particularly, bad poetry, which in a vicious circle breeds — or inbreeds — bad politics.

a. 'An Unhealthy Intersection', *Irish Times*, 21 August 1975. See also 'An Unhealthy Intersection', *New Review*, 2 no. 16 (July 1975), pp. 3-8.

1. In a series of articles, 'Politics and the Poet' (*The Irish Times*, 21 August 1975) and 'Eradicating the Tragic Mode' (*The Irish Times*, 22 August 1975), Conor Cruise O'Brien took issue with what he termed the 'unhealthy intersection' between culture and politics, particularly in Ireland.

As Yeats says: 'We call certain minds creative because they are among the moulders of their nation and are not made upon its mould, and they resemble one another in this only — they have never been foreknown or fulfilled an expectation.'[b] Ulster poets today are sometimes the victims of improper expectations. Whatever causes they may support as citizens, their imaginations cannot be asked to settle for less than full human truth. And no cause in Ireland (unlike, say, opposition to Adolf Hitler) carries such an *imprimatur*. This does not let the poet off the hook of general or particular 'responsibility' towards political events. The price of imaginative liberty is eternal vigilance.

Yet Yeats's very formulation gives the poet a national if not a Nationalist role. And in the early years of the century creating literature and creating a nation could validly be seen as concentric labours....

2.

The literary intellectual too assumes (or assumes that he has) more prominence in Irish than in British life. Seamus Deane explains: 'in literature at least Ireland has sometimes overcome the severe limitations of its geography and of the catastrophic burden of its history'.[c] Despite (or because of) Joyce, Faustian overcompensations beckon. Deane makes this claim in a retrospect on *Crane Bag*, a journal which has often hovered over O'Brien's 'unhealthy intersection',[2] In the first issue Richard Kearney's 'Beyond Art and Politics' begins: 'Politics is far too grave a matter for the politician. Art is far too potent a medium for the artist.'[d] What is already powerful should not be encouraged to covet art's 'potency', and vice versa. In the same issue, Deane's interview with Heaney (see page 168) introduces a key *Crane Bag* word, 'atavism',[3] another intersection of literary and political emotion. With regard to O'Brien's demythologising of Republicanism, he asks: 'is not his humanism ... being used as an excuse to rid Ireland of the atavisms which gave it life even though the life itself may be in some ways brutal?'[e] Despite the plural, 'atavism' is *never* applied favourably to Ulster Protestant gut-feelings. Try this triad: 'I'm atavistic; you're bigoted; he's a terrorist.' In *Crane Bag*'s New Ireland Forum[4] issue Kearney's study of similar Irish journals approves those that 'refused the polarisation of literature and politics into opposed discourses'[f]....

However, the editorial, while stating that Ireland stands at a 'cultural crossroads', also offers this sophistication of the backward look:

> we might take our cue from Brian Friel when he writes in *Translations*[5] that 'it is not the literal past, the "facts" of history that shape us, but images of the past embodied in language'. A central preoccupation of this *Crane Bag* is the problem of how, if at all, the inherited 'images of the past' may be translated into idioms for a new society.[g]

A cue from *Translations*? Does *Translations* itself renew 'images of the past', or does it recycle a familiar perspective? Is it an aisling? *Translations* has its context in the poetic and political nexus of the Field Day theatre company, whose directors include Seamus Heaney, Seamus Deane and Tom Paulin. The Forum *Crane Bag* juxtaposes Friel's account of translating 'history' (a word which has replaced 'atavism' as flavour of the month, though it means much the same) with the reactions of John Andrews who wrote *A Paper Landscape*, the history of the nineteenth-century Irish Ordnance Survey that gave Friel ideas. Kevin Barry's introduction to their dialogue gilds the backward look with forward-looking terminology:

> It is certain that both history and fiction imagine and structure a past which neither could make known without sharing the images and structures of narrative. Both discourses enable the entry of what has been lost into a society's understanding of its present.[h]

b. *Explorations* (Macmillan, 1962), pp. 158-9.
c. 'Postscript' *Crane Bag*, 3 no. 2 (1979), p. 93.
d. *Crane Bag*, 1 no. 1 (1977), p. 8.
e. *Crane Bag*, 1 no. 1 (1977), p. 64.

2. *The Crane Bag*, edited by Mark Hederman and Richard Kearney, was founded in 1977 and until its demise in 1985 was the leading forum for cultural debate in Ireland.
3. Tribal or collective memory.

f. *Crane Bag*, 7 no. 2 (1983), p. 160.
g. *Crane Bag*, 7 no. 2 (1983), p. 3.
h. *Crane Bag*, 7 no. 2 (1983), p. 119.

4. The New Ireland Forum was convened in 1983 by the government of the Republic of Ireland to act as a discussion forum for constitutional settlements to the conflict in Northern Ireland. It issued a report at the end of its proceedings, which paved the way for the Anglo-Irish Agreement of November 1985.
5. *Translations*, Brian Friel's highly acclaimed play about the confrontation between the old Gaelic order and colonial representations of Ireland (in the form of a military Ordnance Survey expedition) on the eve of the Famine, was first performed in Derry in 1980 by the Field Day Company.

In fact his description of *Translations* assumes more than 'imaginative' accuracy: 'The "hidden Ireland" emerges from Friel's play.... By imagining an unwritten past Friel translates a defeated community into the narrative of history.'[i] Has it never been so translated before? As O'Brien asks, 'if Ireland were ever to cease to be oppressed, what would happen to "history", how would one get into it?'[j] Andrews the historian gets nearer the mark when he reads *Translations* as 'a play about late twentieth-century Ireland' whose 'real subject.... is the relation between authority and alienation'.[k] They play does not so much *examine* myths of dispossession and oppression as repeat them.

When Friel's soldier-researchers deploy unhistorical bayonets after Lieutenant Yolland goes missing, his subject is the behaviour of British troops in the Catholic ghettoes of Belfast and Derry during the 1970s. At the end of the play Owen, who has 'collaborated' with the Survey, perceives the middle ground as a premature illusion and reverts to potentially violent tribal loyalty. He rejects the translated names as 'A mistake, my mistake — nothing to do with us.' Owen's final adherence to 'fact' ('if Yolland is not found, we are all going to be evicted') contrasts with the concluding attitudes of Hugh, his drunken hedge-schoolmaster father. Hugh accepts linguistic change, and advises: 'Take care Owen. To remember everything is a form of madness.' In one sense, then, Hugh has taken his other advice: 'we must never cease renewing [the images of the past] because once we do, we fossilise'. But the 'language' here appears theoretic, chosen with *Crane Bag* already in mind. And Owen is the doer, Hugh the dreamer who turned back on the road to '98. Hugh himself embodies the play's pervasive nostalgia for 'what has been lost': for the hedge-school era, for a land of saints and scholars, for Ballybeg as a kind of Eden. In his last speech, Aeneas making good the fall of Troy stands in for another restored civilisation: 'a race was springing from Trojan blood to overthrow some day these Tyrian towers'. Friel, then, translates contemporary Northern Catholic feeling into historical terms. He does this very well. But the play is partly 'fossilised' because he explores the ethos of a particular community exclusively in relation to British dominion over the native Irish. No perspective discriminates between past and present, nineteenth-century Ireland and twentieth-century Northern Ireland. There is simply equation (as in Heaney's *North*). *Translations* refurbishes an old myth. Its imagery, structure of feeling, and cultural vision correspond to John Wilson Foster's account of Montague's *The Rough Field* (if we substitute culture for agriculture), itself perhaps a seminal work behind both *Translations* and Heaney's *Wintering Out*:

> The Ulster Catholic writer has lived so long with the imagery of land-decay and land-loss that he has become addicted to it.... What he wants is not progress, a forward-looking reversal of decay through agricultural improvement, but rather a return, the recovery of a politico-spiritual impossibility — a mythic landscape of beauty and plenitude that is pre-Partition, pre-Civil War, pre-Famine, pre-Plantation and pre-Tudor.[l]

Field Day, like Hugh, 'dreams of a perfect city' as well as a promised land. Hence Tom Paulin's romantic programme-note to Friel's later play *The Communication Cord*, a farce which comfortably fails in its intention to subvert the pieties of *Translations*:

> anyone who looks at the Hobbesian[6] civic wilderness which is Derry now is likely to nourish a similar dream. Nevertheless, they can also perceive that there is in Derry an effort at civil definition which appears to be absent, or at least less keenly felt, in Belfast and Dublin. Imaginatively, Derry is the most advanced city in Ireland and the Guildhall is a temple which joins the stained, bright images of empire to the idea of a new *res publica*.

The projection on to 'history' of contemporary aspirations accords with the Republican viewpoint from which history stands still: an attitude that refuses to accept the internal Northern vendetta as at least a variation on the old colonial theme, that

i. ibid.
j. 'An Unhealthy Intersection', *The New Review*, 2 no. 16 (July 1975), p. 7.
k. *Crane Bag*, 7 no. 2 (1983), pp. 120-1.

l. 'The Landscape of the Planter and the Gael in the Poetry of John Hewitt and John Montague', *Canadian Journal of Irish Studies*, 1 no. 2 (November 1975). Quoted by Aidan Mathews, 'Affirmations and Motifs in the Work of Six Contemporary Northern Poets', unpublished thesis, Trinity College, Dublin, 1983.

6. A reference to the grim view of human life as 'nasty, brutish and short... the war of all against all', disseminated by the English political philosopher Thomas Hobbes (1588-1679).

writes Northern Protestants out of history unless prepared to go back and start again in 1798. . . .

Deane, Paulin and Friel (in Heaney's wake) are highly conscious of the political role of language. They rebel against name-calling and name-changing. Paulin's pamphlet *A New Look at the Language Question*[7] begins: 'The history of a language is often a story of possession and dispossession, territorial struggle and the establishment or imposition of a culture'.[m] Yet Field Day's resistance to linguistic colonialism (which logically requires the revival of Irish) must remain even more of a rearguard action than the liberation-struggles of Feminist and working-class writers. Meanwhile, their ability to use the English language contradicts their inclination to abuse it. Friel's clever device in *Translations* of making the audience believe that English *is* Irish may imply more irrevocable loss than he intended. At the period of the Irish Literary Revival it seemed at least conceivable that a 'Battle of Two Civilisations' might result in victory for the Gaelic League and the Irish language. But although 'Irish Ireland'[8] won the social and political battle in the Free State/ Republic, it lost the language battle, making literary partition and apartheid forever impossible (surely a source of hope as well as regret). In default of Gaelic, Paulin opts for local English speech as the linguistic arm of his new *Res Publica*:

> Many words which now appear simply gnarled, or which 'make strange' or seem opaque to most readers would be released into the shaped flow of a new public language. Thus in Ireland there would exist three fully-fledged languages — Irish, Ulster Scots and Irish English. Irish and Ulster Scots would be preserved and nourished, while Irish English would be a form of modern English which draws on Irish, the Yola and Fingallian dialects, Ulster Scots, Elizabethan English, Hiberno-English, British English and American English. A confident concept of Irish English would substantially increase the vocabulary and this would invigorate the written language. A language that lives lithely on the tongue ought to be capable of becoming the flexible written instrument of a complete cultural idea.[n]

In fact since Yeats, such an idea, shorn of Paulin's totalitarianism, has informed the practice of the best poets. Nor can Ulster Scots, either for conversational or literary purposes, be cordoned off in some linguistic zoo-park as a backward species whose robust primitivism may one day contribute to the national bloodstock. The natural spectrum of Seamus Heaney's vocabulary shows the way that Paulin would harshly floodlight with academy or dictionary. Moreover, Paulin has invented a new form of poetic diction by sprinkling his poems with dialect, or would-be dialect, words (in Edward Thomas's phrase) 'like the raisins that will get burnt on an ill-made cake':[o] scuffy, choggy, glooby, claggy, biffy, keeks, glup, boke. If that's meant to be Ulster-Scots idiom, the implications are almost racist. As Thomas maintained: 'Only when a word has become necessary to him can a man use it safely; if he try to impress words by force on a sudden occasion, they will either perish of his violence or betray him.'[p] Even Synge went a bit far in the matter of idiomatic vitamin-injections. And prose-writers, particularising character and scene, can perhaps do more than poets to preserve local words. Lallans poetry, in the mouth of Hugh MacDiarmid, was virtually a one-man show.[9] On the political front, Paulin's advocacy of a 'confident concept of Irish English' has met with some amazement among Nationalist Irish-language enthusiasts, who refer scornfully to 'the creole dialects of English'.

Paulin creates division where unities already exist. And his own writing proves that excessive awareness of linguistic difference, of 'competing discourses', the loss of creative innocence once language is comprehended as political, can damage your style. Propaganda breeds antithesis: black-and-white readings, black-and-white writings.

m. *A New Look at the Language Question*, Field Day Pamphlet no. 1 (1983), p. 5, reprinted in *Ireland & the English Crisis* (Bloodaxe Books, 1984), p. 178.

7. Tom Paulin, *A New Look at the Language Question* (Derry: Field Day Pamphlet, 1983).
8. A phrase associated with D. P. Moran (1871-1936), journalist and leader of the advanced nationalist Irish Ireland movement.

n. *A New Look*, p. 17; *Ireland & the English Crisis*, p. 191.
o. For Edward Thomas on the 'self-conscious' diction of Walter Pater, see E. Longley (ed.), *A Language Not to be Betrayed: Selected Prose of Edward Thomas* (Carcanet Press, 1981), p. 159.
p. Longley, p. 160.

9. Hugh McDiarmid (1892-1978), the leading Scottish poet in the twentieth century, wrote much of his poetry in a synthetic Scots language called Lallans.

Deane structures the past as two 'symbolic' cathedrals, the present as 'the new security barracks, and, confronting them, the new and increasingly violent housing estates'.[q] He sees civilians and barbarians,[10] cops and robbers, wherever he goes, no inbetweeners. The same polarity shapes 'The Longing for Modernity', his editorial in the Winter 1982 issue of *Threshold*. Here 'modernity' replaces 'humanism' as the wolf in sheep's clothing eager to devour that harmless lamb, atavism. Responding to the secular assault on religion (mainly Catholic, since he insults Irish Protestantism as 'essentially a negative religion, more accurately defined as being anti-catholic on principle than anything else'), Deane offers 'an equally polemical account of modernism and its triumph in a century of almost unbroken disasters ... global war, threat of holocaust, concentration camps, wastelands, alienation, cancer, bureaucracy, mock-religious cults, crime waves, propaganda, the creation of plenty by the starvation of millions — and so on. Rationality, it appears, needs no encouragement to compete with atavism in the production of misery.'[r] Polemical indeed! Did rationality or atavism, in its nationalist guise, set up the concentration camps? Rationalised atavism, perhaps. Deane's own atavised rationalism betrays more clearly than usual the strains of reconciling Derry with Derrida. Even Heaney (in prose) occasionally succumbs to easy and false antithesis:

> far from the elegances of Oscar Wilde and the profundities of Shakespeare, I was acting with the Bellaghy Dramatic Society in plays about 1798, now playing a United Irishman ... now playing Robert Emmet .... Far from discussing the Victorian loss of faith, I was driving my mother to evening devotions in the 'chapel' .... Far from the melodies of courtly love, I was acting as *fear a' tigh*[11] at the GAA ceilidh. ...[s]

Since Heaney, Deane and Paulin no longer live in Northern Ireland, it may be inevitable that they should fall into the tropes of stylised retrospect. ...

q. 'Another Ulster', *Fortnight*, no. 198 (October 1983), p. 18-19.
r. *Threshold*, no. 32 (Winter 1982), p. 4.
s. 'Forked Tongues, Ceilis and Incubators', *Fortnight*, no. 197 (September 1983), p. 18.

10. See Seamus Deane's Field Day Pamphlet, *Civilians and Barbarians* (Derry: Field Day, 1983).
11. Master of ceremonies, literally 'Man of the House'.

3.

After 1939 Louis MacNeice wrote:

> If the war made nonsense of Yeats's poetry and of all works that are called 'escapist', it also made nonsense of poetry that professes to be 'realist'. My friends had been writing for years about guns and frontiers and factories, about the 'facts' of psychology, politics, science, economics, but the fact of war made their writing seem as remote as the pleasure dome in Xanadu. For war spares neither the poetry of Xanadu nor the poetry of pylons.[t]

Since 1969 all Northern Irish poetry has shared the same bunker. Thus what Derek Mahon calls 'An eddy of semantic scruple/In an unstructurable sea'[u] might as well concentrate on 'semantic scruple'. Nevertheless MacNeice, knowing Yeats and Ireland, did not follow Auden into his post-Marxist conviction that 'poetry makes nothing happen': 'The fallacy lies in thinking that it is the *function* of art to make things happen and that the effect of art upon actions is something either direct or calculable.'[v] Yet Auden's own phrase in his Yeats elegy — 'A way of happening' — defines the only social and political role available to poetry *as* poetry. In my view the emergence of something recognised and recognisable as 'Ulster poetry' out of the experience of the North — from 'that once birdless, if still benighted province'[w] — marks an irreversible shift of sensibility, if slow as a glacier.

Now the term 'Ulster' or 'Northern Irish' poetry may itself bring me into conflict with a third Field Day pamphlet, Heaney's *Open Letter*, in which he objects to the ethno-political heading under which his poems appear in *The Penguin Book of Contemporary British Poetry*.[12] Eavan Boland's *Irish Times* review queried the necessity for a statement so mild ('Don't be surprised/If I demur'), and so unlike the polemics of Deane and Paulin, that it seems to realise its own superfluousness: 'Poetry is defined by its energies and its eloquence, not by the

t. Louis MacNeice, *The Poetry of W.B. Yeats* (London: Oxford University Press, 1941), p. 2.
u. 'Rage for Order', *Lives* (OUP, 1972), p. 22.
v. MacNeice, p. 192. [p. 225, 1941 edition — Ed.]
w. Derek Mahon, Introduction to *The Sphere Book of Modern Irish Poetry* (Sphere, 1972), p. 14.

12. Seamus Heaney, *An Open Letter* (Derry: Field Day, 1983), a satirical poem questioning his inclusion in Blake Morrison and Andrew Motion (eds), *The Penguin Book of Contemporary British Poetry* (Harmondsworth: Penguin Books, 1982).

passport of the poet or the editor; or the name of the nationality. That way lie all the categories, the separations, the censorships that poetry exists to dispel.'[x] Nobody doubts Heaney's Irishness. But his or Field Day's exclusive insistence, like the triumphalism which wants Londonderry to obliterate Derry and now vice versa, denies other contexts which his poetry nourishes and which nourish it. Ulster poets have been appearing for years in anthologies of English, Irish and British poetry. The confusion is perhaps more accurate than any attempt to tidy it up. (Frank Ormsby succeeded with the elegant diplomacy of *Poets from the North of Ireland*,[13] itself a history-making anthology.) That notorious Penguin generously represents no less than five Northerners besides Heaney, to the point where *English* poets complain of colonisation. And younger poets in both England and the South of Ireland look North, not only to Heaney. On the other hand, the historian A. T. Q. Stewart tried in a TV talk to familiarise and normalise Belfast for British viewers, by informing them that 'Philip Larkin wrote many of his early poems there'. This does not make Belfast Hull.[14] Larkin's retrospect begins: 'Lonely in Ireland, since it was not home', and refers to 'The salt rebuff of speech, /Insisting so on difference.'[y] Yet like Mahon, just then starting to write, his voice flavoured by that speech, Larkin owes a profound debt to Yeats. None of the lines of creative energy runs straight.

Nor do they run straight within Ulster itself. Zigzags of energy are not picked up by receiving apparatus tuned to 'two traditions'. Ulster people hug wonderfully 'fossilised' versions of their own or someone else's Irishness/Britishness, which retards newer definition in the Republic and Britain. Yet one of the junctures where the North may harbour a cultural vanguard as well as a rearguard is the point where traditions meet and fuse in poetry. Early in the 1960s, not for the first time though more intensely than before, political confrontation — as during the Irish Literary Revival — turned into cultural encounter. Contraries no longer found in the South became progressive instead of regressive, and even adumbrated genuine unity. Within that space, for instance, the 'slightly aggravated young Catholic male' in Seamus Heaney was submerged by his urge to express 'the private country Derry childhood part of myself'.[z] Besides the local Muse, Heaney's early influences include Robert Frost, Patrick Kavanagh, Ted Hughes,[15] and the stimulus of his Belfast contemporaries. His poetic landscape receives a particular assent from all kinds of Ulster readers as an authentic common ground; almost, despite subterranean tensions, as a *de facto* imaginative recognition of the whole terrain. Although Heaney saw himself as 'politicising' Moss-bawn[aa] in *Wintering Out* (1972), the poems respect dialect more than dialectic. 'The Other Side' characterizes the distances between Catholic speaker and Protestant farmer in simultaneous terms of land, religion and language:

> For days we would rehearse
> each patriarchal dictum:
> Lazarus, the Pharaoh, Solomon
>
> and David and Goliath rolled
> magnificently, like loads of hay
> too big for our small lanes,
>
> or faltered on a rut—
> 'Your side of the house, I believe,
> hardly rule by the book at all.'
>
> His brain was a whitewashed kitchen
> hung with texts, swept tidy
> as the body o' the kirk.

The point of the poem is Heaney's imaginative entry into the mind and idiom of the other side, into the 'other', beyond psychic hinterlands, across psychic frontiers. 'Rehearse' suggests how childhood mimicry (an articulation of the peculiar Northern intimacy, commoner in rural areas, that knows if not loves its neighbour) has nurtured the poet's ear and negative capability. Although the poem does not minimise difference, its cultural vision, much more humanly sedimented than the coy polarity between Wilde and Emmet, spans two

x. *Irish Times*, 1 October 1983.
y. 'The Importance of Elsewhere', *The Whitsun Weddings* (Faber, 1964), p. 34.

13. Frank Ormsby, *Poets from the North of Ireland* (Belfast: Blackstaff Press, 1979).
14. Philip Larkin (1922-85), the major British poet of the post-war era, worked for a time in Belfast before moving to Hull.

z. *Crane Bag*, no. 1 (1977), p. 61.
aa. Interview with James Randall, *Ploughshares*, 5 no. 3 (1979), p. 18.

15. Although the popularity of the American poet Robert Frost (1874-1963), the Irish poet Patrick Kavanagh (1905-67) and the English poet Ted Hughes (born 1930) derives partly from their rural themes, their evocations of the countryside possess a hard edge from a common awareness of the harsher aspects of rural life, and the darker forces at work in nature.

languages to create a third. As throughout his work, Heaney relishes the whole heritage of Ulster English, graces with equal humorous affection Graeco-Latin 'patriarchal dictum' and Scots 'body o' the kirk'. (Contrast Paulin's autarkic boke.) 'The Other Side' stresses its own language to raise the language question at another level: not as power-struggle but as a struggle towards expression. Can there be communication, community, even communion founded on a shared landscape?

> Should I slip away, I wonder,
> or go up and touch his shoulder
> and talk about the weather
>
> or the price of grass-seed?

This is the question on which Ulster, let alone Anglo-Irish, agreement depends. 'The price of grass-seed' symbolises the cost of fundamental growth and change. However, the poem itself symbolises the cross-fertilisation between poets and traditions in Ulster. Language which crosses rather than takes sides is not merely the poetic wing of wet Alliance Party[16] liberalism, of middle-class middle ground. 'The Other Side' stretches Heaney to full emotional and verbal sensitivity. I have already noted the absence of mediating language, complicating language, in the antithetical word-worlds of Deane and Paulin. *Translations* too may fall short of complete human complexity, as in the rather stereotyped renderings of Irish peasant girl and English soldier, because Friel simplifies the concept of translation itself....

16. The Alliance Party is a moderate unionist party on the fringes of Northern politics.

V. MODERNIZATION AND MODERNISM

FINTAN O'TOOLE

(1958-)

from: THE CRANE BAG (1985)

[Fintan O'Toole here examines the extent to which modernization in Ireland is impeded by the persistence of an anachronistic rural ideology. At one level, he appears to reject the view that rural ideology represents a genuine case of the 'periphery dominating the centre', but rather sees it as emanating from the metropolitan centre, a projection of an idealized community onto the rural hinterland. However, this tendency to sentimentalize the countryside itself can be attributed to the survival of rural values in an urban context, to the fact that the city in Ireland is simply the country at one remove. Until it throws off the shackles of a residual rural tradition, O'Toole contends, urban culture — and by extension modernization — will not come into its own in Ireland.

The article was first published in *The Crane Bag*, Vol. 9, No. 2 (1985).]

GOING WEST: THE COUNTRY VERSUS THE CITY IN IRISH WRITING

On 2 July 1963, *Time* Magazine carried a cover which tried to sum up the new Ireland that was then being born. Under the banner 'Ireland: New Spirit in the Ould Sod' there was a portrait of the Taoiseach Sean Lemass, who had begun the process of opening up the country to foreign investment which would amount to nearly £6,000 million pounds over the next twenty years. Behind Mr Lemass was drawn a spanking new high tech factory complex. But this factory was draped in green shamrock-spangled curtains, and the curtains were being held aside by a little Irish leprechaun in a red nightcap and big buckled shoes. It was in many ways a perfect image of modern Irish culture: an increasingly urban and industrialised reality made palatable, both to ourselves and to those whom we wish to attract, by being wrapped up in harmless rural folksy images. For the last hundred years, Irish culture and in particular Irish writing has been marked by this dominance of the rural over the urban, a dominance based on a false opposition of the country to the city which has been vital to the maintenance of a conservative political culture in the country.

The Irish literary revival of the turn of the century was not a rural phenomenon. It was created in a metropolitan context for a metropolitan audience. Yet it helped to create and sustain an image of rural Ireland as an ideal which fed into the emergent political culture of Irish nationalism. In that political culture, a sense of the nobility of the land and of the hardy peasants who worked it had a crucial place. As the revival was getting underway, Ireland had experienced a revolution in rural property relations in which the property rights of the landlords had come under sustained and successful attack, and in which the ownership of the land had finally come into the hands of the small tenant farmers. After such an upheaval, a notion of the sacredness of the land, a mystical sense of place, could serve at once to give the landlord class a sense of spurious continuity by 'aristocratising' the peasantry and on the other hand, by postulating an immanent and 'natural' link between the peasantry and the land, to confer the sanction of time and place on a new and raw arrangement of property. Added to this was the fact that the nationalist revolt, even when conducted from Boston or New York, always had the character of a revolt against the metropolis London, and its satellite as the centre of British domination in Dublin....

In their 1906 pamphlet *Irish Plays*, Yeats, Synge and Lady Gregory were quick to see Irish life as the life of the peasants. They had, they wrote, 'taken their types and scenes direct from Irish life itself. This life is rich in dramatic materials while the Irish peasantry of the hills and coast speak an exuberant language and have a primitive grace and wildness due to the wild country they live in, which gives their most ordinary life a vividness and colour unknown in more civilised places.'[1] Irish life equals the peasant, and the peasant equals the landscape. By being identified with the landscape, the peasant becomes a primaeval and uncomplicated figure, free from the complications of social and commercial relations. And already the language is the language of colonial paternalism, of 'primitive grace and wildness' and 'more civilised places'. The contrast implied in these two terms, the contrast between city and country, is already cast in a late colonial mould, in which the object of attention — in this case the peasant of the west, in others the noble savage of the jungle — is at once patronised and idealised....

1. W. B. Yeats, J. M. Synge, William Boyle and Lady Gregory, *Irish Plays*, Summer 1906, p. 6.

This notion of the peasant and of the country which the peasant embodied was not a reflection of Irish reality but an artificial literary creation, largely made in Dublin, for Dubliners. It was a political image of the countryside which helped to create a sense of social cohesion in a country which was trying to define itself over against England. Since the revival centred around the Abbey Theatre it was not enough to simply create peasants of the mind, creatures of the imagination. The Abbey had to literally create a company of peasants to act the peasant plays which made up two thirds of its early repertoire. It had to create an imagined country in the heart of the city. It had to turn Dublin clerks and civil servants into western peasants. Willie Fay, the director of the original Abbey acting company, took as his first task the job of beating the Dublin accents out of his players. They had to learn to talk like peasants and to act like peasants, to remember back a few generations to their country ancestors. Sara Allgood, the working-class Dubliner who was one of the first great actors of the Abbey company, recalled that when she created the role of Maura in *Riders to the Sea* she tried to copy her grandmother's mannerisms. In presenting revolutionary new plays, the Abbey players were already presenting an image of their own collective past, already in a sense disowning the present. The second of the Fay Brothers who formed the company, Frank, in a letter of 1908 referred to 'the slovenly movement and speech of the class of Dublin man and girl out of whom the company was and must be formed.'[2] What would save them, he wrote elsewhere, would be their collective past, their ancestry in the peasantry. 'The actors have most of them peasant blood, if they are not the children of peasants, and instinctively talk, move and act as peasants would , and are familiar with the habits of the country folk.[3] The contradiction between Fay's contempt for the speech and mannerisms of Dublin people of the working-class and his contention that they 'instinctively' act like peasants and talk like peasants points to an underlying belief that Dubliners are really unspoilt peasants encrusted in a mire of urban decadence which can be washed away by

2. Frank Fay to W. J. Lawrence, 7 April 1908, cited in Brenna Katz Clarke, *The Emergence of the Irish Peasant Play at the Abbey Theatre* (Epping, Essex: Bowker Publishing Company, 1982), p. 39.
3. Frank Fay, 'Some Account of the Early Days of the Irish National Theatre Society' in R. Hogan (ed.), Frank J. Fay, *Towards A National Theatre* (Dublin: Dolmen Press, 1970).

contact with the mountain streams of the real Ireland. The existence in the Abbey of an ideology of acting which saw Dubliners as peasants manqués would have its effect later on, particularly in the early work of Sean O'Casey.

The need to convince Dubliners that they were witnessing real peasants on the stage led to the development of super-naturalistic scenery in the Abbey style. They scoured the West for *real* three-legged stools to place beside the fireside, *real* creels of turf, genuine spinning wheels, and guaranteed Aran cowskin pampooties.[4] The combination of museum-piece sets and props with the learned mannerisms of peasant speech and movement meant that for a Dublin audience which was often no more than a generation removed from the countryside, a visit to the Abbey was a travelogue into its collective past. And the pretence that the Abbey was a theatre of peasants in the heart of the city seems to have worked. An early reviewer claimed that 'the men and women who play the parts live for the most part lives not dissimilar from those they play', a claim which was patently false. The effect was heightened when the company played in London, where its alignment with the Irish nationalist movement was rendered harmless by the fact that it fitted so well the Victoria stereotype of the charming, childish native. The English critics took what was often incompetence for simple, naive charm. In 1903 the London *Times* was praising the Abbey players for their 'little natural clumsiness', and a few years later Max Beerbohm, reviewing their performances at the Court Theatre wrote: 'They certainly are charming, these Irish players; charming in their remoteness from ourselves and from any other players that we know.... Part of their charm is the naivete of their method.... they are producing just their own selves as they are at ordinary times.'[5] The charm and naturalness seen by the writers in the Irish west is in its turn reproduced as a literary creation and is recognised at the heart of the Empire as the genuine essence of Ireland. The Irish identity which had been 'revived' over and against England is an identity which fits in well with one aspect of colonial paternalism. The Abbey presented itself in such a way as to allow it to be patronised, creating a strong identification between the peasant and childishness, and, for England, an identification between Ireland and childishness....

The persistence of the literature of the Golden Age, drawing its poetry from the past, as the dominant mode of Irish writing has affected urban literature as much as rural. If the salient features of the domination of the rural over the urban in Irish writing have been: (a) The pull of the past, the movement in the direction of the world of a previous generation, (b) the impulse towards a knowable community in which the individual has an identifiable place and (c) in the theatre, the need to convince the audience that what they are seeing is real, a need which arises out of the fact that it is patently unreal, a literary creation, then all three features can be seen to apply in the work of major Dublin writers like Sean O'Casey and Brendan Behan. Both worked primarily in the theatre and in both the forms and the structures evolved through the myth of the country were so powerful in a political culture dominated by rural values that they took precedence over the development of specifically urban forms.

The classic location for Irish urban writing has been the tenement building. If the characteristics of rural forms in Irish writing are the pull to the past, the attraction of a knowable and self-contained community and in the theatre a tendency to super-naturalism, then the use of the tenement as the typical urban setting clearly allows for all three of these characteristics to come into play. The tenement is essentially an urban version of the rural setting. In the first place the pull of the past is present in the fact that the Dublin tenements are immediately associated with the fall from the Golden Age, being the elegant homes of the ascendancy fallen into the hands of the poor. They are a physical embodiment of a decline, imposing a sense that the city is not the ground of the future but a place fallen into decadence from a glorious past. In the second place, the tenement allows for the presentation of a self-contained community in the theatre. It is, of its nature, an enclosed world where everything is known about everybody. It thus simulates a rural community as opposed to the displaced sense of being constantly in collision with unknown people which stems from the city. And thirdly, it is an *indoor* community, a way of bringing people into contact in their own homes, thus

4. Creels are baskets used to carry turf; pampooties are soft cowskin boots worn by Aran Islanders.
5. Max Beerbohm, 'Irish Players after a Performance at the Court Theatre', *The Saturday Review*, 12 June 1909.

allowing for the continuance of super-naturalistic sets and props. In urban plays it was still possible to have the creel of turf and the kitchen table and the cups of tea, giving point to Behan's remark that the Abbey company was the best fed group of actors in the world since the natural reaction at a crisis point in an Irish play was to put on a pan of rashers or make a cup of tea.

To bear out the belief that the Dublin stage tenement is a rural setting in urban guise, it is worth looking at a rural playwright trying his hand at a play set in Dublin. In 1949, George Fitzmaurice, the Kerry playwright who had written some of the Abbey's best peasant drama, wrote *One Evening Gleam*, setting what was essentially a Kerry folk-play of magic and mystery in a Dublin tenement. The extraordinary thing is that he had no problem in doing this. The Dublin tenement play had such an affinity to the rural peasant play that Fitzmaurice was able to make his old peasant women into Dublin oul' wans with little in the way of a jarring effect. The one male character — and since urban men do substantially different work from rural men, a male character might have been more difficult — is blind, lies on the bed and has one line: 'Mother, I see the moon, I see the moon,' before he quietly expires.

If O'Casey's early plays are urban drama in a rural form, what tensions does this create? In the first place the tenement setting excludes the world of the streets and the world of work, the two crucial elements of urban experience. The only people who manage to do any work in O'Casey's early plays and in Behan's *The Hostage* are whores, barmen and soldiers. When Denis Johnston wanted to attack the nascent Free state, in *The Old Lady Says 'No'!* he had to reject the tenement play in favour of a play of the streets.[6] As O'Casey began to attend to large-scale statements of urban socialist politics, beginning with the second last act of *The Plough and the Stars*, he too began to move out of the tenement and onto the streets. That move allowed for a vision of the city as the Holy City, the New Jerusalem, a place transformed. *The Plough and the Stars*, having moved out onto the streets moves back in again to the tenement, precisely because that transformation is a failure. It is no accident that in his search for a transformation, in his move away from the tenement, he was forced away from the Abbey.

Like the early O'Casey, Brendan Behan stuck closely to the search for knowable communities. Although he moved with his family out to the new working-class suburb of Kimmage while still young, his writing returns constantly to childhood, the past, the world of the tenements and to knowable communities. The pattern of opposition of country to city is so strong that Behan simply reverses it, making the new city of the suburbs into a country, a wild place, and keeping the old city of the tenements as a place of family and community ties. Behan's one attempt to write for a new suburb where he lived is a radio play called *Moving Out*, rather than *Moving In*, where the hero complains of being 'shoved out to Siberia'. Dominic Behan mirrors this sense of the inner city tenements as a knowable community compared to the wastelands of Kimmage. In his autobiographical book, *Teems of Times and Happy Returns* he has his father crossing Sean O'Casey's famous Mountjoy Square: 'Slowly, Frank made his unsteady way across Mountjoy Square .... A small cart passed, laden heavily with scraps of furniture of a Kimmage-bound family. "Poor bastards," he thought, "Don't know what they're in for".'[7]

Even those Dublin writers who sought to glorify the city above the country often found themselves drawing on the sense of the city as a landscape of the past, drawing again on the rural mode of the Golden Age. Donagh MacDonagh's famous poem *Dublin Made Me*,[8] after attacking the country with great passion — 'the jobbers, the gombeenmen and the cheats' of 'the raw and hungry hills of the west' and 'the soft and dreary midlands with their tame canals' — finds that the only image of the city which he can counterpose to the country and give his loyalty to is 'the Dublin of old statues', the rich man's tenements. Or Louis McNiece [*sic*] in his encomium on the city *Dublin*, finds himself claiming that 'she is not an Irish town', thus accepting the cultural distinction between what is urban and what is Irish.[9]

6. Denis Johnston's experimental play, *The Old Lady Says 'No!'*, a critical dramatic treatment of nationalism, was first performed at the Gate Theatre, Dublin in 1928.

7. Dominic Behan, *Teems of Times and Happy Returns* (London: Heinemann, 1961), p. 165.
8. Donagh MacDonagh, 'Dublin Made Me', in *The Hungry Grass* (London: Faber and Faber, 1947), p. 19. A 'gombeen-man' is a usurer. The word is often associated with an influential shopkeeper in a local community.
9. Louis MacNeice, 'Dublin', in *Collected Poems* (London: Faber and Faber, 1966), pp. 163-64.

The contrast between the city and the country, the fictional division of the nation into a place of primaeval innocence and a fallen place, is a division which has served ideologically to obscure the change that has taken place in the countryside, making it economically more like the city, and at the same time to make the Irish countryside more susceptible to a peculiar process of modernisation and Americanisation. By retaining a notion of a real, true Ireland of nature and landscape and sturdy peasantry, it has been possible to modernise the countryside, to turn it into a profitable base for American multinational industry and EEC capitalist farming, while still believing that the heart of the nation remains pure. And the maintenance of that ideal has prevented a defence against Americanisation, so that the thatched cottage has become a hacienda with Spanish arches and Mexican walls, the three-legged stool has become the corner seat in the lounge bar and Pegeen Mike has become Sierra Sue, making the notion of a Gaelic peasant paradise merely laughable.[10]

The counter-tradition in Irish writing has not been an urban one, but a series of attacks on the synthetic notions of the country in the name of genuine rural experience. Patrick Kavanagh's bitter epic on the nature of peasant life *The Great Hunger*, Flann O'Brien's satire on the absurdity of Gaelic nationalist rural pieties in *The Poor Mouth*,[11] where it is explained that the inventors of the myth of the Irish countryside choose not to live there because '1. The tempest of the countryside was too tempestuous. 2. The putridity of the countryside was too putrid. 3. The poverty of the countryside was too poor. 4. The Gaelicism of the countryside was too Gaelic. 5. The tradition of the countryside was too traditional', and the plays of Tom Murphy, including, *On the Outside*, *Famine*, *A Whistle in the Dark* and *Conversations on a Homecoming*, have attempted to destroy the illusions from within.[12]

What has been missing has been a Utopian tradition, drawing its poetry from the future, taking the city as the ground of transformation to set against the tradition of the Golden Age which draws its poetry from the past, taking the country as the ground of timeless, ahistorical innocence. For it is in the nature of the city that it cannot be merely represented without being transformed. The later O'Casey tried to show the city by transforming it, viewing its daily realities from the point of view of the future, of a radically altered Holy City. Joyce, having named the city and informed its daily realities with new dimensions of symbol and myth in *Ulysses*, went on to the Utopian geography of *Finnegans Wake* in which the city achieves a new unity by absorbing the country, history and the world. But these attempts to make Dublin a new Jerusalem, the stirrings of a genuinely urban literature do not amount to a tradition.

It is only now that an urban literature from within the modern city is beginning to develop, perhaps most clearly in the work of the Finglas writers Dermot Bolger and Michael O'Loughlin. It is no accident that the first task that they set themselves is the reclaiming of modern Irish history by those who have been written out of it. In that re-reading of modern Ireland, there is a legacy of broken dreams and false promises. In his poem *Dublin After the Civil War*, for instance, Michael O'Loughlin sees Dublin after independence as like Russia after the Revolution had turned to Stalinism:

> Here it was hunger, there it was murder
> De Valera, Stalin, Free State and Soviet
> The grotesque reality of an aborted ideal
> Where we talked like kings in a p[a]lace of
> dreams
> And lived like dogs in the rains of the city.[13]

Now that the palace of dreams has become a hacienda bungalow, it is time that the dogs of the city began to bark.

10. Fintan O'Toole has developed this point in his accompanying text to Martin Parr, *A Fair Day* (Wallasey: Promenade Press, 1985).
11. Flann O'Brien, *The Poor Mouth*, translated by Patrick C. Power (London: Hart-Davis, MacGibbon Ltd, 1973).
12. See Fintan O'Toole, *The Politics of Magic: The Work and Times of Tom Murphy* (Dublin: Raven Arts Press, 1987).
13. Michael O'Loughlin, 'Dublin after the Civil War', in *Stalingrad: The Street Directory* (Dublin: Raven Arts Press, 1980).

LIAM DE PAOR

(1926-)

from: THE CRANE BAG (1979)

[In this article, first published in *The Crane Bag* (Vol. 3, No. 1), Liam de Paor focusses on the problem of the break-up of traditional values in Ireland, and argues that often what is taken as tradition is of quite recent origins, dating from the social crisis in mid-nineteenth-century Ireland after the Famine. National identity — the 'Irish Nation' — was not something inherited from time immemorial but was a cultural project that required completion with the attainment of political independence. The leaders of the new Ireland lacked this cultural vision, however, and concentrated their energies on the state rather than on the nation. As against Eoin MacNeill's idea that the nation sustains the state, it is now the state that sustains a fragile, attenuated sense of national identity in Ireland.]

IRELAND'S IDENTITIES

Arland Ussher printed on the title page of his essay, *The Face and Mind of Ireland*, a quotation from Emile Montégut:

> This race is at the same time inferior and superior to the rest of humanity. One might say of the Irish that they find themselves in a false situation here below. Placed between memory and hope, the race will never conquer what it desires, and it will never discover what it regrets.[1]

A romanticised view. But, even if it seems very dated, it has some validity, expressing one reaction to an Irish characteristic often, if variously, noticed: ambiguity; distancing from reality. When we ask if there has been a continuous and literally *identifiable* Irish identity, we confront this ambiguity — this evasiveness, this insistence by many Irish writers and nationalistic leaders that we in Ireland are not what we seem on the surface to be, but something else, older, wiser, truer; to be found not here and now but only in the past and in the future. As Ussher put it:

> The Irishman is a bohemian and a *j'm' enfoutiste*[2] in his way of living, somewhat of a play-actor (or 'playboy') alike in action and passion, seeing existence as a *show* — while remaining as far as possible uninvolved.

In his heyday of power, Eamon de Valera, then Taoiseach, gave a famous radio address[3] in which he spoke of what he called 'the Ireland we dream of'. It was rural idyll that he described — 'the contests of athletic youth . . . the laughter of comely maidens . . . the wisdom of old age in the chimney corner . . .' and so on. This was a more or less self-contained Ireland, with a decent way of life deeply rooted in a rural past and in a frugal sufficiency. In the extended version of the vision, equalitarianism and personal independence appear — the offshoot of the republican tradition — the equalitarianism deriving not merely from the equality of citizens before the law but also from a levelling of incomes by means of differential taxation and other financial devices to an approximation of equality, in which no one was destitute and no one earned or received more than was necessary for modest comfort. This was an ideal, vision, or image shared by quite a few of those who fought for independence and steered the course of the infant Irish state. It is a version of the Jeffersonian ideal, with precedents in the stern political philosophy of the early Roman Republic as this was imagined by the Enlightenment: the ideal of a republic of small property-holders, personally and economically independent, with therefore a minimum need for dependence on governmental institutions. It is not an ignoble ideal, and it must further be said that some limited progress towards its achievement was, briefly, made by the early leaders of the State. . . .

What has been described is familiar enough, and to recount it may be to labour the obvious. But in the area of ideas where mystification prevails, there may be some virtue in the obvious. In particular it is

1. Arland Ussher, *The Face and Mind of Ireland* (London: Victor Gollancz, 1949).

2. i.e. a feckless individual, one with a 'couldn't care less' attitude.

3. See Eamon de Valera's famous St Patrick Day broadcast 1943, in commemoration of the fiftieth anniversary of the Gaelic League: Maurice Moynihan (ed.), *Speeches and Statements of Eamon de Valera 1917-73* (Dublin: Gill and Macmillan, 1980), p. 466, See below, p. 747.

worth emphasising that we are not now passing but we have *already* passed from the kind of society that is traditional to another kind of society altogether — the urbanised industrialised society which has emerged from the several technological revolutions that have transformed large parts of the earth in the past two centuries and have affected every corner of the globe.

Looking back, we can now see that de Valera's 'Ireland that we dream of' was quite impossible of fulfilment, because the world's technological and other revolutions simply will not permit the necessary measure of isolation. It is not possible to build a wall, paper or otherwise, around Ireland and to maintain here a kind of frugal republican virtue, while the outside world indulges in an orgy of greedy affluence.

Besides, there are flaws in the vision itself, both as a perception of what (if anything) is essentially Irish about Ireland and as the objective of political action. It is the kind of vision or ideal which tends to produce the kind of political ideology and movement loosely called populist, and such movements in turn tend to foster prejudice, obscurantism and in particular a suspicious hostility between town and country. The vision came to grief politically in Ireland largely on the simple failure to provide employment and on the consequent scandal of mass emigration. Isolationism was abandoned ultimately: Sean Lemass, who succeeded de Valera in 1959, told us to forget the Poor Old Woman lamenting over her fourth green field[4] and to look to the bright future offered by the modern world. This was making a virtue of necessity. Catastrophe, in the fifties, had befallen the vision of Arthur Griffith, Eamon de Valera (and the younger Lemass) of an independent Ireland. Did a lusty baby go out with the mystical bath-water?

The change, at any rate, has now happened. Our traditional society has come to an end, and tradition has been relegated, as long since in the urbanised parts of Britain and America, to sentiment and fragmentary memories. The Irish 'tradition' has been displaced from being the cultural matrix to being merely an embellishment to a culture which is essentially different, and non-Irish. The shift happens in various ways. To take an . . . illustration from County Clare — . . . from the west of the county: it is only a few years since traditional music there *was* traditional. A man like Willie Clancy or Jimmy Ward would play to please himself and his friends or to conform to long-standing customs. Now, the traditional musicians who survive are fully professional. The tradition has been commercialised and absorbed into the all-embracing international culture, so that what was a fiddler in the corner of a farmhouse or a pub is now a member of a 'group', travelling on a kind of international nightclub circuit, modifying his skill to accommodate electronic amplification and the tastes of a wider — and shallower — audience. This is not a plea for retaining the 'purity' of traditional Irish music: it is an attempt to record a fact: that the change of context marks a radical change of culture.

Figures give some measure of the change. Only a little over a fifth of the people of the Republic now live directly on agriculture. The Dublin-east-coast conurbation amounts to about a million people, a third of the population of the State; and virtually all the larger towns have been increasing in numbers. If we look at the population pattern of the east and south coasts, from Larne around to Cork, we can see a shift taking place, representing to a large extent an integration into what is now the world of the European Common Market. This shift may prove in time to be as significant as that caused by the first Industrial Revolution, which similarly brought about a concentration of population in the north-east of the island and the integration of Belfast into the commercial and industrial world of north-west England and south-west Scotland — the now moribund but then highly active centres of economic development. This effect of the Industrial Revolution was probably far more important than the seventeenth-century plantations in sowing the seeds of Ulster's political troubles of today.

The Irish diaspora have been urbanised for a century or more, and founded overseas the distinctive displacement culture which is at odds in some respects with the culture of the homeland. Now, even at home, the Irish are chiefly, and increasingly, an urban people: but a rural background continues for the moment to dominate many aspects of Irish culture. In the early fifties, when I

4. The 'fourth green field' is a euphemism for Northern Ireland. The action of W. B. Yeats's play *Cathleen Ni Houlihan* (1902) centres on the siren-like appeal of an old woman who lures young men to join her on her quest to regain her 'four green fields', i.e. the four provinces of Ireland then under British rule. See also George O'Brien, *The Four Green Fields* (Dublin: The Talbot Press, 1936).

was doing a great deal of field-work in rural Ireland, I remember watching with dismay the great exodus of those years, which brought so many country parishes to the point of no return. The emigrants left in ones and twos and threes; then suddenly, in a single season, all the remaining young people would go from a village or district.

This was true even of the east and south, of the pleasant valleys of Barrow and Nore. But in 1956, for example, the trains from the west each Friday afternoon had coach-loads of Irish-speakers drowning their sorrows in the bar and emptying the Gaeltacht[5] into the work-camps and industrial towns of Britain. Except for those going to isolated work-camps, the sorrow was mitigated; sizeable Irish emigrant communities had already built up in the British cities to provide a receptive environment. The emigrants of the fifties did not have to travel with quite the same lonely dismay as was the lot of many who thronged to the factories of war-time Britain ten or fifteen years earlier when the great emigration was in its early stages.

All this of course repeated an old experience. It happened in the thirties, forties, fifties, sixties, seventies, eighties and nineties of the last century, in other ways. That great outflow only slackened in the second decade of this century. It was young men who, a few decades earlier, would have emigrated who fought the War of Independence of 1919-21.

The modern emigration has been documented in part. Domhnall Mac Amhlaigh has told us vividly about one end of the process in his *Dialann Deoraí*,[6] and John Healy about the other end in his *Death of an Irish Town*.[7] The failure marked by this emigration was a profound one; for the very people who flocked from the country in such numbers were the sons and daughters of those who had fought a revolutionary war (although not to a finish) in the early part of the century, and on whose behalf the revolutionary war had been fought. Their going made nonsense of the official ideology of the twenty-six-county State, of what was taught in the schools and preached from pulpits and platforms. As surely as we have witnessed in recent years the breakdown of the British province in the north-eastern part of the island, we have seen over a longer period the slow failure of the other province — a failure, at the very least, in respect of the intentions of its founders.

Some recent studies give us glimpses of parts of the problems of breakdown. For example, Hugh Brody, who previously collaborated with F. H. A. Aalen in producing *Gola: the Life and Last Days of an Island Community*, — which was the obituary of one of our most recently depopulated Atlantic islands, in the Donegal Gaeltacht — published in 1973 a work to which he gave the fictitious place-name *Inishkillane*.[8] This was not a work of fiction, but a study of an isolated parish on the west coast, in County Clare, with some misdirection merely to conceal the identity of the people whose lives are discussed. 'Strictly speaking,' as the author says, 'Inishkillane does not exist. Unfortunately many hundreds of parishes like it do.'

While this book is about one parish on the west coast, it tells us much about Ireland as a whole, and suggests much more. Romantic nationalism and impatient anti-nationalism, in their various forms, have made it difficult for us to see Ireland as a whole, and we need to get down more and more to local detail in order to understand the present direction of our society. *Inishkillane*, for example, makes plain (as in its different way did *Death of an Irish Town*) that the 'traditional' life of rural Ireland *has* come to an end. The frugal, self-sufficient, arcadian Ireland that Mr de Valera dreamed of is now less than a dream.

This traditional life, in turn, however, had quite a brief history, dating only from the Famine. Before that, the tradition was very different, and in *Inishkillane* Mr Brody draws on the work of Kenneth Connell, George O'Brien[9] and other scholars to demonstrate just how profound the change of the early nineteenth century was. Late marriages, the consolidation of holdings with inheritance by the eldest son, the movement away from the co-operation and communal work in favour of household self-sufficiency: these are among the most significant new developments which gave a distinctive character to western rural life of the past hundred and twenty-five years. The large question

5. Those districts of Ireland that contain the last native speakers of Irish.
6. Translated as *An Irish Navvy: The Diary of an Exile*, by Valentine Iremonger (London: Routledge & Kegan Paul, 1964).
7. John Healy, *The Death of an Irish Town* (Cork: Mercier Press, 1968).
8. Hugh Brody, *Inishkillane* (Harmondsworth: Penguin Books, 1973).
9. K. H. Connell, *The Population of Ireland 1750-1845* (Oxford: Oxford University Press, 1950); George O'Brien, *An Economic History of Ireland in the Eighteenth Century* (Dublin: Maunsel & Co., 1918).

of the change of language, discussed by Seán de Fréine in his book *The Great Silence*[10] and the late Maureen Wall in a brilliant essay in *A View of the Irish Language*[11] is one which requires much further investigation, involving as it does a major trauma in the Irish psyche.

The influence of developed capitalism has now destroyed the possibility of survival of the traditional culture, and for a long time emigration to urban centres has been one of the chief media of transmission of such influence. . . .

The moment when emigration ceases to be reluctant — the emigrant being driven out by economic necessity from a valued way of life — and becomes almost eager — the emigrants hastening to a valued culture from one they have come to despise — this moment marks the turning-point, and it has long since occurred over much of western Ireland.

The point of breakdown came, according to Mr Brody's book, about thirty-five years ago. This, I believe, would accord with the experience and general observation of anyone who has been at all in touch with rural Ireland in general in these decades. The traditional way of life established after the Famine had many contradictions which weakened its capacity for resistance or adaptation to change. Its resilience, in spite of these, was considerable, but perhaps the sexual isolation imposed by post-Famine marriage-patterns on so large a proportion of the population was bound sooner or later to lead to breakdown. At any rate, in the kind of society which was once the paradigm for 'Irishness' demoralisation and breakdown are now widespread . . . .

In many ways the Irish crisis (it continues in new forms) is responding to situations which already belong to the past. The breakdown of the nineteenth-century tradition was apparent by the nineteen-fifties in the Republic, and the Republic, having through the achievement of independence solved *some* of the perennial problems of Irish society, was flexible enough (for a while) to begin adapting. New economic programmes brought some prosperity for a while; ideology began to loosen up; emigration overseas fell away, and rapid urbanisation began.[12] The population, falling from the Famine to the beginning of this century, then declining very slowly, has been rising for two decades. All the towns of any size have grown fast. The old picture of an industrial north and a rural south is out of date: the contrast, in both Northern Ireland and the Republic, is between east and west, and, British subventions aside, until the present depression, the southern economy for some time has possibly been a shade stronger than the northern. The problem here does not lie in contrasts which no longer have meaning, but in the difficulty which over-rigid political, social and *imaginative* structures have had in accommodating change. In particular, the Stormont system, hastily but rigidly constructed on a basis which was already out of date in 1920, broke rather than bent under the stresses of the post-war world. It simply could not adapt to a combination of Welfare State policies, imposed by Westminster, and the demands of the multinational corporations of advanced capitalism.

But in many areas there has been slowness to accommodate, comparable to the fatal slowness of the British to realise, in the world after 1945, how very diminished in reality were their power and influence. The crisis of identity in Ireland is most acute among the Ulster loyalists, but it exists elsewhere as well.

In the past few generations at least, a majority in Ireland has been obsessed with the need to appear before the world distinguished by a certain kind of national identity. The efforts to cultivate such a national identity constitute the last phase in a process which has been going on for three hundred years and are the outcome of the destruction of an old culture in circumstances in which it was not possible, and indeed not intended, that another culture — that is, a genuine integrated culture — could take its place without serious interruption.

The conquest of Ireland, as envisaged, for example, by Sir John Davies in 1603,[13] was intended to ensure that the whole Irish people would, in a relatively short time, become in every way a part of English civilisation. But this did not happen. What happened was a different kind of

10. Seán de Fréine, *The Great Silence* (Cork: Mercier Press, 1969).
11. Maureen Wall, 'The Decline of the Irish Language' in Brian Ó Cúiv (ed.), *A View of the Irish Language* (Dublin: Stationery Office, 1969).
12. Over 200,000 people emigrated between 1954 and 1956, but following the new economic policies introduced by *The First Programme for Economic Expansion* (1958), the figure dropped to 80,000 from 1961 to 1966.
13. In 1603, Sir John Davies (1569-1626), solicitor general for Ireland, proposed the establishment of a parliament in Ireland to mark the replacement of the old Gaelic order by a new English political system.

conquest: the confiscation and the exploitation of the sources of wealth and power by adventurers who became, and long remained, an alien ruling minority, without thought for the good government or the spiritual or the material condition of the Irish masses. As Dr. R. B. Walsh put it in a lecture a few years ago:

> There was no question of the ancient Gaelic world — which as an economic and social system had long outlived its time — being modernised, or its language and institutions being superseded by a more advanced language and more advanced institutions: it was simply condemned to economic and social inferiority, degraded and left to disintegrate and to rot away slowly. The religious conflict was a very significant complication of the cultural conflict which developed: Irish and Catholic came to mean virtually the same thing, namely, the designation of the majority of the people, consigned to social and economic inferiority. In these circumstances, what gradually succeeded Gaelic Ireland was a cultural desert, which in time became the habitat of the majority of the Irish people.[14]

... Dr Walsh, in his lecture, 'Aspects of Irishness', distinguishes three groups of nineteenth-century Ireland: the remnants of Gaelic Ireland, already in wreck, but still with a vigorous *oral* tradition reflecting an older world, long vanished from western Europe, the world of which Yeats wrote in 1906, 'In Ireland today the old world that sang and listened is, it may be for the last time in Europe, face to face with the world that reads and writes, and their antagonism is always present under some name or other in Irish imagination and intellect';[15] the Anglo-Irish; and, thirdly, the group now dominant in the Republic, the people who, as he put it, have 'proliferated in a cultural desert', quasi-anglicised Irish, growing as Gaelic Ireland shrank, inheritors neither of the Gaelic nor of the English cultural tradition.

We acquired, with our 'revolution' of more than half a century ago, a generation of people who were pious, verbally skilled, capable of handling the lower offices of an imperial administrative machine, and for the most part deaf and blind to the higher achievements of western civilisation. This did not greatly affect the effectiveness of the first generation of administrators of the new state. They came from the background of the world-wide empire on which, in those days, the sun never set, and had some sense of the values of a larger world. They were conscious, in taking over their tasks, of being in a big competition, and they did reasonably well.

But the rather stodgy and uninspired Protestant middle class which had long had control of the comfortable end of the business of Ireland, was replaced in the revolution by what proved to be a rootless Catholic middle class, which had only a tenuous verbal ideology to sustain it — neither a peasant culture nor a bourgeois culture going back into the past. The great ideological struggle which engaged the masses of the Irish people at the beginning of the century, the struggle to discover, to revive, to create and sustain a distinctive cultural and political nationhood, as the people of the time understood it (or the contrary struggle to preserve the British heritage against this nationhood) had inevitably to give way gradually to the business of building and sustaining the States whose crude outlines were marked out in Ireland after the First World War. Only in the North did the intolerable pressures of the procrustean six-county enclave maintain the fervour of the opposed ideologies. The twenty-six-county State soon made an identity for itself through the working-out of the practice of government and politics, through its 1937 Constitution, which was only nominally for all Ireland, and above all, perhaps, through the experience of the Second World War, when the twenty-six-county State was on its own.

The collapse of Northern Ireland has in the long run strengthened that isolation. 'Old moulds are broken in the North'[16] wrote the poet John Montague a few years ago. They are broken in the South too. The Southern State struggles with sudden and overwhelming economic problems. It has, to sustain it, a good infrastructure, built up in the years of independence, and the habit, formed over sixty years even if now diminishing, of self-reliance. It is physically and visibly changing at an

14. R. B. Walsh, 'Aspects of Irishness' in A. Feder and B. Schrank (eds), *Literature and Folk Culture: Ireland and Newfoundland* (St Johns, Newfoundland: Memorial University of Newfoundland, 1977), pp. 7-31.
15. W. B. Yeats, 'Literature and the Living Voice' in *Explorations* (New York: Collier Books, 1962), p. 206.
16. Epigraph to *The New Siege* (Dublin: Dolmen Press, Poet Card I, 1970).

alarming pace, and the spectacle in the early seventies of gathering chaos north of the Border diminished greatly the old rhetoric of the nationalist revolution. In a time, not of revolutionary, but of rapid and bewildering change, it is not a sense of identity which sustains the State but the State, for the moment, which sustains a sense of national identity.

W. J. Mc CORMACK

(1947-)

from: ASCENDANCY AND TRADITION IN ANGLO-IRISH LITERARY HISTORY FROM 1789 TO 1939 (1985)

[In this extract, W. J. Mc Cormack takes Thomas Kinsella's argument (in *The Irish Writer*) a stage further by emphasizing the radical break that both Yeats and Joyce effected with the tradition out of which they emerged. The existing body of native literature, he argues, is too frail a base to encompass their achievements, and only by relating their work to modernism in its more general European context can the full measure of their respective breakthroughs be appreciated. Modernism, in this sense, must be seen not only as a literary movement but in wider social and economic terms, having to do in particular with the uneven integration of a late developing country such as Ireland into the global economy of capitalism in its imperialist phase.]

ENTR'ACTE: MODERNISM, HISTORY, AND IRELAND

It is a cramped little state with no foreign policy,
Save to be thought inoffensive. The grammar of the language
Has never been fathomed . . .

(Richard Wilbur)[a]

The history of Marxist approaches to culture in recent years has seen a marked reluctance to endorse any single or universal theoretical perspective on the relation between literature and society, and this is indeed but a specific example of the re-examination of the much-abused model of base/superstructure which had dominated official pronouncements in this area.[b] The new interest in the work of the Frankfurt school, and that of Walter Benjamin, has provided a more penetrating and sophisticated account of the problem of historical necessity, and of the relationship of continuity to radical change.[c] Benjamin, in particular, stresses in 'Theses on the Philosophy of History' that 'thinking involves not only the flow of thoughts, but their arrest as well.'[d] For a historical materialist such as Benjamin it follows that the same is true of history itself. Far from constituting an uninterrupted flow of events, history for him is conceptualized as specific and concrete movements, and discontinuities between these provide the opportunities for revolutionary intervention. The classic instance of such an opportunity is the year 1848.

Nineteenth-century Irish history — within the context of the United Kingdom — appears to break

a. Richard Wilbur, 'Shame', *Advice to a Prophet* (London: Faber, 1962), p. 33.

b. The British discussion of the base/superstructure metaphor, while it has been invigorated recently by the work of Raymond Williams, was effectively initiated by E. P. Thompson in 'Socialist Humanism', *New Reasoner* (1957), vol. 1.

c. The Frankfurt School is known in the English-speaking world principally through the work of Theodor Adorno, Max Horkheimer, Jurgen Habermas, Herbert Marcuse, and (more marginally) Walter Benjamin. Two anthologies are available — *The Essential Frankfurt School Reader*, edd. Andrew Arato and Eike Gebhardt (Oxford: Blackwell, 1978); *Critical Sociology*, ed. Paul Connerton (Harmondsworth: Penguin, 1976). The best critical account of the movement is Martin Jay, *The Dialectical Imagination: A History of the Frankfurt School and the Institute of Social Research 1923-50* (London: Heinemann, 1973). In addition to the various books by Adorno, Benjamin, and Habermas quoted elsewhere in this study, Adorno's essay on Arnold Schoenberg in *Philosophy of Modern Music*, trans. Anne G. Mitchell and Wesley V. Blomster (New York: Seabury Press, 1973), is most useful. The impact of Frankfurt on intellectual discussion in Ireland has been slight, though some traces of recent interest may be found in the various numbers of the Dublin-based journal *Crane Bag*.

d. Walter Benjamin, 'Theses on the Philosophy of History', *Illuminations*, ed. and intro. Hannah Arendt, trans. Harry Zohn [n.p.]: (Fontana/Collins, 1973), p. 264.

neatly into two such movements, with the Famine of the 1840s and its attendant political aspects acting as a demarcation line between the old and the new. Language change, emigration, and so forth are indicators of the contrast. Yet the younger Irish historians today are busy arguing for a recognition of the *modernization* of Irish society even before the Famine.[e] While this argument is ostensibly directed against an older, nationalist view that nothing flourished under the foreign yoke, it should be noted that the new historiography also serves to conceal the 'arrest' of history which Benjamin for one would require. Literary modernism, which follows so promptly in Ireland upon the heels of those modernizing developments documented by the historians, acts with a similar masking effect upon our engagement with the past. Yet it is characteristic of literature (and other forms of cultural production also) that, when subjected to a thorough critique, it manifests both its own strategies and the past it seeks to represent. In Ireland, where literature is pre-eminent among forms of cultural production and where literature has been long attuned to a so-called national psyche, the demarcation lines and discontinuities can be conveniently traced in psychological terms.

One of the central experiences of Anglo-Irish literature is embarrassment. In narrative terms this may be traced in fictions of shame such as *Castle Rackrent*, *Uncle Silas*, or, later, Somerville and Ross's *Big House of Inver*.[1] As one advances through the nineteenth century and into the twentieth, sectarianism translated into quasi-racial terms, provides a vocabulary for this theme. But, in a more basic sense, embarrassment characterizes that advance itself — embarrassment at the nearness of Yeats to Aubrey de Vere or William Larminie.[2] So great a poet, so merely competent his precursors. Whether one focuses on Yeats or Joyce, poetry or prose or drama, the sequential history of Anglo-Irish literature reproduces these embarrassing antecedents. George Moore, in whom competence and greatness compete for attention, made such *frissons* the material of *Hail and Farewell* — 'dear Edward' Martyn,[3] with his sublime folly, is truly a central idol in the Anglo-Irish pantheon. But for Yeats and Joyce a history of embarrassment became a matter of artistic pride, the pride of heroic overcoming in Yeats, of devious transfiguration in Joyce. This is not to deny the persistence of a problematic history in the work of both authors, but rather to emphasize the manner in which the two, considered as a binary and mutually dependent cultural production, confront the totality of history.

Taking up, say, McHugh and Harmon's *Short History of Anglo-Irish Literature from its Origins to the Present Day*, one encounters a sequence of discontinuities — the 'older civilization and its literature' (in Gaelic) . . . 'the Irish Literary Revival' (in English) . . . 'Contemporary Writing' (in English . . . .[f] When literary history accepts chronology as its model, unspoken and unanswered questions necessarily proliferate. Eighteenth-century antiquarianism, vigorously employed to bridge some of these discontinuities — is it not as much a German or British phenomenon as a 'Celtic' one? And beyond this particular issue, perhaps the most accessible general assumption is the unchallenged nationalism of such chronologies. Yet in noting the dislocation of Yeats and Joyce from Irish chronology we are really acknowledging their place in European modernism. To move from a discussion of Charles Lever[4] to the work of Joyce, or from a discussion of early Irish lyrics to the poetry of Yeats, is to cross seismic lines of demarcation.

Modernism — the term is misleadingly unified. While it has its eighteenth-century usage, 'modernism' is decisively altered by the controversy within Catholicism which led in 1907 to *Pascendi gregis*, Pope Pius X's encyclical 'de modernistarum

e. A useful introduction to this area is Joseph Lee, *The Modernisation of Irish Society 1848-1918* (Dublin: Gill and Macmillan, 1973). But compare the concept of modernization employed in Marshall Berman, *All that is Solid Melts into Air: The Experience of Modernity* (London: Verso, 1982).

1. Maria Edgeworth, *Castle Rackrent* (1800); Joseph Sheridan Le Fanu, *Uncle Silas* (1864); Edith Somerville and Martin Ross, *The Big House of Inver* (1925).
2. Aubrey de Vere (1814-1902) made considerable use of Irish history and legends in his poetry, and is best known for his poem 'The Little Black Rose'. William Larminie (1849-1900), poet and folklorist, was one of the participants in the Eglinton/Yeats controversy on 'Literary Ideals in Ireland'.

f. Roger McHugh and Maurice Harmon, *Short History of Anglo-Irish Literature from its Origins to the Present Day* (Dublin: Wolfhound Press, 1982).

3. George Moore's three-volume *Hail and Farewell* (1911-14) is a lively panoramic survey of his association with the Literary Revival. The playwright Edward Martyn (1859-1924) was a central figure in *Hail and Farewell*.
4. Charles Lever (1806-72), a popular Victorian novelist, was frequently charged by cultural nationalists with popularizing the stage Irishman in his fiction.

doctrinis'. Modernism, here, is a mode of theological inquiry according to which the Bible and the doctrines of the Church are examined in the light of modern thought. Far from being a unified philosophy or even a single attitude, modernism challenged such unities in a spirit of inquiry and disclosure. Marx, Nietzsche, and Freud were not so much advocates of modernist approaches as they were channels through which the historical moment of modernism was variously defined. The eclipse of the human individual as conscious and self-regulating shaper of his existence was a common element among these contending reinterpretations of human society. Literary modernism, it need hardly be remarked, manifested itself in different ways in Germany, Austro-Hungary, Italy, Britain, and America, and this largely in relation to the differing forms of individual consciousness in these societies.

Yeats and Joyce are exemplary in this multifarious context in that each denies his inherited orthodoxy and strives to recreate a specifically literary heterodoxy. But the orthodoxy they had lost was itself radically fractured, and fractured in a manner increasingly articulated as a sectarian sociology. A disproportionately large Irish contribution to English-language modernism is central to the elaboration in the nineteenth century of Protestant Ascendancy as ideology. In addition to the imperfect schism achieved by Yeats and Joyce in their rejection of (an already shattered) orthodoxy, it is worth noting that both were sons of men who had in their generation distanced themselves from the conventions and loyalties of their churches. Yeats and Joyce are not primary rebels in any simplistic Oedipal pattern, and when we come to study the father/son bond in Yeats's drama this factor should be recollected.

To return to broader matters, the comparison with English modernism is illuminating. Recognizing that Henry James, T. S. Eliot, and Ezra Pound remain essentially American figures (at least up to the moment of Christian conversion in Eliot's case), and recognizing that Conrad cannot be domesticated without great difficulty, and that E. M. Forster and Ford Madox Ford were never really modernist in their practice (whatever their sensibility) — recognizing all that, we are left with D. H. Lawrence and Virginia Woolf as English modernists. Now, the important point relates not to their marginal or exposed position within the dominant British system (Lawrence as border-line lower middle-class, Woolf as woman) but rather to the contrasting literary histories into which English and Irish modernists might be placed. Lawrence had Hardy and Dickens to look back to; and beyond that, Blake and even Milton provided lines of legitimate descent, Virginia Woolf could cite Jane Austen, in addition to her own family network. They had, in other words, various means of disguising their exposed position even if these did not soothe the wounds inflicted upon them by the bourgeois suburbia of Edwardian Britain. In contrast, Yeats and Joyce found the drafting of a literary pedigree highly taxing. Joyce, in his early days, acknowledged debts to Defoe and Blake, but his place in English literature can scarcely be defined in terms of lineage.[g] Yeats, it is true, came to a striking statement of the complexities of 'lineage' seen as the symbol of literary tradition:

> The 'Irishry' have preserved their ancient 'deposit' through wars which, during the sixteenth and seventeenth centuries, became wars of extermination. No people, Lecky said at the opening of his *Ireland in the Eighteenth Century*, have undergone greater persecution. Nor did that persecution altogether cease up to our own day. No people hate as we do in whom that past is always alive. There are moments when hatred poisons my life and I accuse myself of effeminacy because I have not given it adequate expression. It is not enough to have put it into the mouth of a rambling peasant poet:
>
> You ask what I have found, and far and wide; I go:
> Nothing but Cromwell's house and Cromwell's murderous crew,
> The lovers and the dancers are beaten into clay,
> And the tall men and the swordsmen and the horsemen, where are they?
> And there is an old beggar wandering in his pride—
> His fathers served their fathers before Christ was crucified.

g. For treatment of this question of Joyce's place in English literature see the contributions of Philip Brockbank (pp. 166-84) and Timothy Webb (pp. 30-55), in W. J. Mc Cormack and Alistair Stead, edd. *James Joyce and Modern Literature* (London: Routledge and Kegan Paul, 1982).

> *O what of that, O what of that,*
> *What is there left to say?*

> Then I remind myself that though mine is the first English marriage I know of in the direct line, all my family names are English, and that I owe my soul to Shakespeare, to Spenser and to Blake, perhaps to William Morris, and to the English language in which I think, speak, and write, that everything I love has come to me through English; my hatred tortures me with love, my love with hate.[h]

The manner in which Yeats advances from the notion of a historical memory to details of his own family tree, and from that to a literary tradition incorporating Shakespeare and Blake is a graph of specific conceptual shifts in the background to Anglo-Irish literature and its emergent definition. The romantic organicism of the first stage (history to pedigree) is followed by the elaboration of a sequential literary chronology of the classic nineteenth-century kind, and this finally elevated in the passionate, Yeatsian antinomy of love and hate. The interpolated verse from 'The Curse of Cromwell' contributes far more than a mere illustration of hatred, or reason for hatred: being a imaginary translation from Gaelic it reflects with venom upon its own linguistic status as English. Moreover, the title of the poem also enacts a drastic transference — the dramatic speech which follows is *not* the curse but the words of one who is victim of Cromwell's curse. In all this we see the degree to which Yeats's employment of his own verse adds complexity to what is on the surface a casual commentary on the relation between art and history. The pseudo-translation, which is victim to its own title, encapsulates Yeats's own entanglement in the history he aspires to summarize.

While Yeats became increasingly articulate on the topic of his own relation to Ireland as he advanced in years, Joyce's comments on such matters nearly all date from his apprenticeship as an author. Yet even a passage from 'Ireland, Island of Saints and Sages' (1907) can establish Joyce's antithetical relation to Yeats:

> to exclude from the present nation all who are descended from foreign families would be impossible, and to deny the name of patriot to all those who are not of Irish stock would be to deny it to almost all the heroes of the modern movement — Lord Edward Fitzgerald, Robert Emmet, Theobald Wolfe Tone and Napper Tandy, leaders of the uprising of 1798, Thomas Davis and John Mitchel, leaders of the Young Ireland movement, Isaac Butt, Joseph Biggar, the inventor of parliamentary obstructionism, many of the anticlerical Fenians, and finally, Charles Stewart Parnell.[i]

In due course these names will undergo different metamorphoses in Yeats's poetry (e.g. 'September 1913') and in *Finnegans Wake*. But whereas Yeats's citations are predominantly liturgical in form or intention, Joyce's historical allusions from 'Ivy Day in the Committee Room', The 'Cyclops' episode of *Ulysses*, to the *Wake* itself deliberately act upon the reader to demand of him that he relate once again the elements of his knowledge. This courteous insistence on the reader's active participation in the *work* of art generates a serene absence of kinetic anxiety in the prose — nothing is at risk in Joyce's prose. In *A Portrait of the Artist as a Young Man* the famous disquisition on 'funnel' and 'tundish' shows Joyce's fictional representative calmly acknowledging — in English — that the language belonged to the English Dean of Studies *before* it belonged to the Irish undergraduate. If this repeats the Yeatsian concern with the chronology of Irish history and the place of language displacement in that chronology, Joyce's fiction takes us further in highlighting some of the crucial strategies of Anglo-Irish modernism — its recourse to a 'primitive past' and a primitive hinterland, its invention of/dependence on a vestigial, other culture in the west. In this, as in many other respects, Joyce appears as a critical modernist, embodying in his own work a critique of the larger movement within which that work takes on its local significance.

h. W. B. Yeats, 'A General Introduction for my Work', in Edward Callan, *Yeats on Yeats: The last Introductions and the 'Dublin' Edition* (Mountrath: Dolmen Press, 1981), New Yeats Papers, XX, p. 59-63. Callan's editing of the General Introduction is important in that he demonstrates Yeats's intention to include the lines from 'The Curse of Cromwell' (omitted in the standard text): unfortunately he misquotes the poem, which is rendered here in its canonical form.

i. James Joyce, 'Ireland, Island of Saints and Sages', in *Critical Writings*, eds. Ellsworth Mason and Richard Ellmann (New York: Viking Press, 1959), pp. 161-2. Dominic Manganiello, *Joyce's Politics* (London: Routledge and Kegan Paul, 1980) and Colin MacCabe, *James Joyce and the Revolution of the Word* (London: Macmillan, 1978), are the two most influential treatments of this topic: Manganiello concentrates on political attitude as announced by Joyce and his characters, while MacCabe is concerned with a post-modernist politics of writing. Neither pays much attention to the question of history.

This sense of modern embarrassment in the face of a nobler past is closely linked to Ireland's closely administered ability to give evidence of a primitive *ur*-culture within the United Kingdom. The Scottish clearances had too thoroughly affected the Gaels of North Briton, while the perseverence of the Welsh language was linked to 'progressive' features such as mining and Methodism. Only in Ireland did the demographic and economic developments of the nineteenth century permit the recognition of an endangered (and hence valorized) older culture open to aesthetic rather than industrial investment and exploitation. The Famine, far from paralleling the clearances, had the effect of rendering Irish linguistic change traumatic, and that will be shown to have immense repercussions within Joyce's prose. ('Uneven development' provides a classic Marxist account of the Irish question, and much could be said along these lines in relation to the economics of the United Kingdom: the transference of this dynamic into the cultural arena has been neglected however.) In relation to development and retardation, Ireland exemplified at many levels the identity of opposites, the paradox of the 'disunited kingdom', the sociology of Protestant Ascendancy. Pursuing an exhaustive account of the political unconscious in Conrad and others, Fredric Jameson has pointed to an uneven development, a non-synchronous overlap in Conrad's own values and experience (feudal Poland, capitalist England); and a reading of *Lord Jim*, *Heart of Darkness*, and *Nostromo* (fictions of colonial and imperial activity *par excellence*) would acknowledge that overlap.[j] Where Conrad is a special case, a unique biographical dossier, the Anglo-Irish modernists constitute a socially extensive and interrelated structure of cultural productions emanating from a far more central and crucial overlap within the terms of the most advanced capitalist and imperialist economy on the globe. In its very incompleteness, its inability to clothe the fissures in its ideological claims, Protestant Ascendancy is both the political and the unconscious element in this uneven development within the United Kingdom in the period leading up to High Capitalism's crisis in 1914-18, the period of modernist efflorescence. . . .

j. Fredric Jameson, *The Political Unconscious: Narrative as a Socially Symbolic Act* (London: Methuen, 1981), esp. pp. 206-80.

The over-simplified identification of industry with capitalist advance and of agriculture with an underdeveloped economy dogs Marxist commentary on Ireland as surely as the nineteenth-century denial of industrial activity itself. Birmingham and Ballyporeen[5] existed together within the economy of the United Kingdom: and if Birmingham displayed industrial advance, Ballyporeen saw alterations in landownership which were deliberately limited to the smaller island. From the 1850s onwards, the reform of the Irish landlord system posed a threat to landed estate which British spokesmen for property in great masses of accumulation were not slow to resist.[k] And in the west of Ireland, the establishment of the Congested Districts Board introduced a degree of state participation in the local economy without parallel elsewhere in the Kingdom. Synge's Aran Islands, for example, had a fishing industry using large trawlers from the east coast and linked directly to the London markets. As in Conrad's non-metropolitan world, it is the transitional status of 'the west of Ireland', the tangible insecurity of its vestigial pre-capitalist social relations, already shot through with practices deriving from the metropolis and the developed world, which is significant. One might say that for the full operation of industrial capitalism in the United Kingdom, it was necessary for one sector of its society to be non-industrialized, and only subliminally capitalized. It was Ireland's historical destiny to fulfil this aesthetic function.

The Ireland of C. S. Parnell and Michael Davitt, of the Land War and the Home Rule campaign, was not the abject primitive outback occasionally advanced for propagandist purposes. It had a sizeable industrial sector, and an extensive middle class — though both were hidden in part by the heavy tapestry of Protestant Ascendancy ideologies. The social composition of the Land League was petit-bourgeois rather than peasant-based, and the very terminology of *Home* Rule loudly proclaimed a domestic metaphor in keeping with bourgeois attitudes. Moreover, the labour movement had active links with Scotland, with the English ports and great cities. In America, the ex-

k. See John W. Mason, 'The Duke of Argyll and the Land Question in Late Nineteenth-Century Britain', *Victorian Studies*, vol. 21, No. 2 (Winter 1978), pp. 149-70.

5. Ballyporeen, Co. Tipperary is the ancestral home of former American President, Ronald Reagan.

perience of Fenian exiles and other emigrants was — unlike the Germans of the mid-west for example — primarily urban and industrial. Ireland indeed had its place in the industrialized world, but it was a place conditioned in the consciousness of native and outsider alike by the contradictions of its role as a metropolitan colony....

The entire conjunction of High Capitalism in its imperial phase, Ireland in its complex social development within the leading capitalist economy, literature in Ireland shifting qualitatively from the provincial margins to the centre of Anglophone culture, the entire conjunction gives rise to concepts and questions rarely aired in literary criticism of the Revival. After so many pages hunting historical allusion amid the tasteless productions of minor authors, or exploring dark metaphors in obscure political pronouncements, may we not now relax into the familiar attitudes of Practical Criticism applied to familiar texts by undisputed genius? Having sketched the background can we now sit upon the verandah of our culture and contemplate equally dislocated, autonomous poems and stories? Much could be written on the violence implicit in such contemplation, its violation of relation and reflection, its self-mutilating projections. And the truth is that Practical Criticism — as distinct from close reading within a larger interpretive strategy — is the logical extension of that epistemology by which text is taken as an unchanging object of contemplation.[6] If Leavis is introduced to counter the sterility of Practical Criticism in its post-war seminar, we should recall Leavis's own historically significant impatience with Joyce and the striking inability of Leavisite critics to come to terms with the Irish modernists.[7] It is too late to re-integrate Yeats and Joyce to the curriculum of English letters, except in the most obscurantist denial of the European context in which the academic discipline itself might be ultimately judged. It is with Joyce that we can look for the first comprehensive attempt to 'write through' the historical experience of modernism, with a critical dimension which will subsequently inform our several approaches to the poetry and drama of Yeats.

6. Practical criticism was a form of close reading of literary texts pioneered by I. A. Richards (1893-1979). Under the influence of the American New Criticism, it sought to treat literary texts as autonomous works, disengaged from their social or political contexts.
7. F. R. Leavis's critique of Joyce is in his article 'James Joyce and the Revolution of the Word', *Scrutiny*, Vol. 2, No. 2 (1933), 193-201.

SEÁN GOLDEN

(1948-)

from: THE CRANE BAG (1979)

[In Seán Golden's article, the absence of an overpowering tradition is again cited as a positive asset, except that in this case it is the distance between Irish writers and the 'great tradition' of English literature which is considered to have brought about the modernist breakthrough in twentieth-century Irish literature. The displacement of creative energies from the metropolitan centre to the periphery was not necessarily an extension of colonial domination, but represented a genuine weakness, a crisis in an English literary tradition collapsing under its own complacency. So far from being an expression of a residual or anachronistic ideology (e.g. traditional nationalism), anti-colonial currents in Irish literature were the cutting edge of modernism. As against the Enlightenment view that cosmopolitanism is a precondition of progress, Golden contends that it is now *resistance* to absorption by the metropolitan centre that brings peripheral cultures into the modern world.

The article was first published in *The Crane Bag*, Vol. 3, No. 2.]

POST-TRADITIONAL ENGLISH LITERATURE: A POLEMIC

In his discussion of *Hugh Selwyn Mauberly* as Ezra Pound's epitaph for the English literary tradition, Donald Davie, referring to the poem's 'Envoi' writes that

> It is impossible to read this, if one is an Englishman, without real distress. Only

> Lawrence, in letters written about this time, registers the death of England as a live cultural tradition with such sorrow and with the added poignancy of being English.[a]

The literary tradition native to England to which I will refer in this essay is Davie's; it is that which many contemporary English writers (e.g. contributors to *PN Review*) wish to canonize as the only legitimate English literary tradition. Their attempts to rewrite modern literary history are symptomatic of the post-imperial condition of contemporary English culture. They are highbrow Little Englanders. The term 'native', once condescendingly assigned to the colonized, is now clung to and honoured by English writers in their steeply declining present circumstances. There is also, of course, another tradition of English literature, or of literature written in English. This second tradition has come to dominate twentieth-century writing in the English language. Its exponents are colonial or, at least, not English. I would suggest that the invocation of the native English tradition, so loudly voiced today, is essentially nostalgic, is an anti-Modernism disguised as traditionalism and constitutes a reactionary trend. Nowadays English writers face the same problems of insular self-definition in the face of developed and formerly colonial literatures which English imperialism and cultural oppression formerly imposed on much of the rest of the world.

Thus it is not coincidental that the demise of the native tradition as a live cultural tradition occurs contemporaneously with what literary critics have been calling Modernism, nor that the great Modernist masters do not in fact belong, as natives, to the native tradition. The great prose masters were James Joyce, a native Catholic Irishman, Joseph Conrad, natively Polish, and D. H. Lawrence, a coalminer's son, and if not totally proletarian, certainly non-U, or at least non-Bloomsbury. Ford Madox Ford modelled his prose on French masters (John Rodker called *The Good Soldier* the best French novel in the English language). This pattern holds true in poetry as well. W. B. Yeats was Irish, Pound and T. S. Eliot American. Oscar Wilde, G. B. Shaw, J. M. Synge, and Sean O'Casey were Irish masters of modern 'British' drama. Historically, the advent of Modernism as a literary trend characterized by radical formal innovation coincides with the beginning of the end of the British Empire. This is not insignificant. The non-English, or formerly colonial, Modernists consistently lacked the vested emotional interest in a native English literary tradition which hamstrung (and hamstrings) native English writers, for that tradition represents far more than literary conventions or styles, and a vested interest in its conventions and styles reflects a vested interest in its more extensive and pervasive cultural and socioeconomic connotations.

The English literary tradition developed contemporaneously with England's establishment, first of nationhood, then of empire, and is necessarily implicated in the ramifications of this historical process. Non-native literature in the English language developed under different historical circumstances in the colonies, and reflects those facts. Colonials and former colonials had (and have) a different stance, a more detached, objective one, toward the native English tradition than native English writers. With this detached stance comes a different perspective, and freedom in handling the tradition not available to native English writers. The development of twentieth century writing in English and the shift of its creative centres away from England proper to America and the Celtic countries are symptoms of this process.

I will interweave descriptions of the native English tradition and colonial reactions to it in order to develop a portrait of the issue. Stanislaus Joyce indicated what being Irish meant in terms of his brother's art.

> In *A Portrait of the Artist*, Dedalus speaks of a certain disadvantage at which Irish writers find themselves in using the English language. The very slight differences in the shades of meaning which English words may have for Englishmen can give pause, I fancy, only to Irishmen like Yeats or my brother, whose sensibility to words applies extreme tests.... In Ireland, a country which has seen revolutions in every generation, there is properly speaking no national tradition. Nothing is stable in the country; nothing is stable in the minds of the people. When the Irish writer begins to write, he has to create his moral world from chaos by himself, for himself. Yet, though this is an

a. Donald Davie, 'Ezra Pound's *Hugh Selwyn Mauberley*,' *The Modern Age*, ed. Boris Ford. Harmondsworth: Penguin Books, 1961, p. 326.

enormous disadvantage for a host of writers of average talent, it proves to be an enormous advantage for men of original genius, such as Shaw, Yeats or my brother.... When an English writer — Wells or Galsworthy or Huxley or Aldington — deals with social, religious, or intellectual problems, one has the impression that even though the problems are real and the writer is striving to be sincere, the life that produced him is in general stable and balanced. It has been lived for centuries against a Constable background. And if he poses as an extremist, it is merely a picturesque attitude like Count Tolstoy's donning of his Russian smock-frock, over trousers cut by the most expensive tailor in Petersburg, to play at being a peasant saint. The characters whom these writers create to voice conflicts of opinion are people of ease and culture.... Their brilliant chatter gives the impression of purely academic after-dinner discussions. In Ireland, on the other hand, the dinner itself is often lacking, and in consequence the discussions assume a different tone. The bread and butter test is not irrelevant. For my brother life was not an interesting subject for discussion; it was a passion.[b]

I would extend Stanislaus Joyce's depiction of particular English writers and a particular tone in their work to the native English tradition in general: its literature is an extension of the generally stable and balanced life lived against a Constable background which represents in some way the English ideal. Not they but the wind that blows through them. This is natural enough. Cultures reflect and are informed by hegemonies of social ideas and ideals, though the concrete particulars which constitute cultural expression vary according to time and place. The instability of the Modern period disrupted and displaced that generally stable and balanced life permanently.

One of the many peculiarities of the English imperial adventure and its aftermath is Ireland's anomalous role. Australia, Canada, New Zealand, and the United States are all English-speaking former colonies where English and other European settlers totally overwhelmed and replaced the native population. Ireland/*Eire*, Rhodesia/*Zimbabwe*, and South Africa are English-speaking former's colonies where the settlers did not replace the native population, and they remain a minority. This is less obvious in the case of Ireland, which was the only European country to undergo total colonization on the English model, but it is a fundamental fact of Irish life and culture. Literature written in English outside of the native English tradition falls into three categories as a result: the literature of settlers who took over completely (America for instance), literature of colonized natives (like Joyce), and the literature of minority control. Concrete particulars will change, but this fundamentally colonial relationship between native English literature and other literatures in English has a major structural impact on twentieth century writing in English.

Early critical reactions to Joyce's *Portrait* reveal how deeply the imperial/colonial element was felt on all sides. From the native Irish side John Eglinton (W. K. Magee) wrote:

> Joyce is ... a champion spirit in the new national situation. In him, for the first time, the mind of Catholic Ireland triumphs over the Anglicism of the English language, and expatiates freely in the element of a universal language: an important achievement, for what has driven Catholic Ireland back upon the Irish language is the ascendancy in the English language of English literature, which, as a Catholic clergyman once truly asserted, is 'saturated with Protestantism'. In Joyce, perhaps for the first time in an Irish writer, there is no faintest trace of Protestantism, that is, of the English spirit.... We are obliged to admit that in Joyce literature has reached for the first time in Ireland a complete emancipation from Anglo-Saxon ideals.[c]

H. G. Wells, on the other hand (or opposite side), sounded the alarm:

> *A Portrait of the Artist as a Young Man*, by James Joyce ... is a book to buy and read and lock up ... of immense significance is the fact that everyone in this Dublin story, every

b. Stanislaus Joyce, *My Brother's Keeper*. New York: Viking Press, 1958, p. 185-186.

c. Cf. Robert H. Deming, ed. *James Joyce: The Critical Heritage*. New York: Barnes & Noble, 1970, Vol. ii, p. 459.

> human being, accepts as a matter of course, as a thing in nature like the sky and the sea, that the English are to be hated. There is no discrimination in that hatred, there is no gleam of recognition that a considerable number of Englishmen have displayed a very earnest disposition to put matters right with Ireland, there is an absolute absence of any idea of a discussed settlement, any notion of helping the slow-witted Englishman in his three-cornered puzzle between North and South. It is just hate, a cant cultivated to the pitch of monomania, an ungenerous violent direction of the mind. That is the political atmosphere in which Stephen Dedalus grows up, and in which his essentially responsive mind orients itself....[The extreme Irish 'patriot'] will play into the hands of the Tories by threatening an outbreak and providing the excuse for a militarist reaction in England.... No reason in that why England should not do justice to Ireland, but excellent reason for bearing in mind that these bright-green young people across the Channel are something quite different from the liberal English in training and tradition, and absolutely set against helping them. No single book has ever shown how different they are....[d]

Wells also comments on the Catholicism of the book, and the poverty of the world it depicts, though from exactly those Protestant and stable perspectives noticed by Eglinton and Stanislaus Joyce. The horror and incomprehension of the English liberal evident in Wells's review is reproduced in Joyce's portrayal of the character Haines in *Ulysses*, whom Stephen rejects as totally as any Irishman he rejects in the course of eluding his nets.

James Joyce was quite clear about his personal stance toward the English tradition. 'And in spite of everything, Ireland remains the brain of the United Kingdom. The English, judiciously practical and ponderous, furnish the overstuffed stomach of humanity with a perfect gadget — the water closet. The Irish, condemned to express themselves in a language not their own, have stamped on it the mark of their genius and compete for glory with the civilized nations. This is then called English literature.'[e] He told Arthur Power, 'It is my revolt against the English conventions, literary and otherwise that is the main source of my talent.'[f] And he told Padraic and Mary Colum, 'I have great difficulty in coming to any understanding with the English. I don't understand them no more than they understand me.'[g] ('But I don't write in English,' he used to say.)[h]

I think Joyce represents the first great attempt by a colonized native culture to break through the cultural oppression and internalization of the oppressor's culture to produce a native statement free of the trappings and prevalent ideological assumptions of the colonizer, and that his *Portrait* illustrates vividly the problem a colonized writer faces when he seeks to express himself in the language and tradition which have supplanted his own. ('The advent of an overcoming power may be attested by the crippled diction, or by the complete disuse of the original tongue, save in solitary dear phrases, spontaneous in grief or gladness,' he wrote in an undergraduate essay, 'The Study of Languages.')[i] American writers also (and earlier) freed themselves from the yoke of the Mother Country's tongue and traditions, but as conquerors themselves, not as colonized natives. Joyce grew up amid the revolutionary ferment Wells singled out in his review (a prescient one as it turned out — the Easter Rising occurred the same year.) Writers like Wilde and Shaw (from the Protestant tradition of the settler minority) infiltrated the English tradition and made their careers in England. Douglas Hyde and others atavistically advocated the de-Anglicization of Ireland and a return to the pre-colonial native culture.[1] Yeats was consciously attempting to fashion an Irish literary tradition in English ('Nor may I less be counted one/ With Davis, Mangan, Ferguson').[2]

d. Cf. James Joyce, *A Portrait of the Artist as a Young Man: Text, Criticism, and Notes*. New York: Viking Press, 1968, pp. 329-333.

e. Cf. Richard Ellmann, *James Joyce*. New York: Oxford University Press, 1959, p. 226.

f. Cf. Ulick O'Connor, ed. *The James Joyce We Knew*. Cork: Mercier Press, 1967.

g. Padraic & Mary Colum, *Our Friend James Joyce*. New York: Doubleday, 1958, p. 18.

h. ibid.

i. James Joyce, 'The Study of Languages', *Critical Writings of James Joyce*, ed. Ellsworth Mason & Richard Ellmann. New York: Viking Press, 1959, p. 28.

1. See Douglas Hyde, 'The Necessity for De-anglicizing Ireland', in *The Revival of Irish Literature* (London: Fisher Unwin, 1894).
2. W. B. Yeats, 'To Ireland in the Coming Times' in Richard J. Finneran (ed.), *W. B. Yeats: The Poems* (London: Macmillan, 1983), p. 50.

> I could not endure ... an international art, picking stories and symbols where it pleased. Might I not, with health and good luck to aid me, create some new *Prometheus Unbound*; Patrick or Columbkil, Oisin or Fion, in Prometheus' stead; and, instead of Caucasus, Cro-Patric or Ben Bulben.[3] Have not all races had their first unity from a mythology that marries them to rock and hill? We had in Ireland imaginative stories, which the uneducated classes knew and even sang, and might we not make those stories current among the educated classes ... and at last, it might be, so deepen the political passion of the nation that all, artist and poet, craftsman and day-labourer would accept a common design?[j]

Joyce and his comperes had many alternatives to choose from. In the *Portrait* he puts Stephen through the full range, taking great pains to illustrate the difficulty which the English language and literary tradition represented for the Irish writer-to-be. A proper understanding of this dilemma is crucial. It centres on Stephen's love of Elizabethan songs and literature, elements of the native English tradition associated historically with both the fulfilment of the English Renaissance (the Shakespearean apotheosis of the tradition) and the first successful imposition of the English language on Ireland (with a consequent perpetuation of Elizabethan terminology and pronunciation in Irish-English).

Stephen waits in an empty classroom, remembering a story told him by Davin, a native Irish speaker, a close friend, the only character who calls Dedalus by his christian name, whom Stephen admires for his quaint turns of Elizabethan speech, a story in response to Stephen's lyrical effusions which Davin cannot understand, which disturb him.

> His nurse had taught him Irish and shaped his rude imagination by the broken lights of Irish myth. He stood towards this myth upon which no individual mind had ever drawn out a line of beauty and to its unwieldy tales that divided themselves as they moved down the cycles in the same attitude as towards the Roman catholic religion, the attitude of a dull-witted loyal serf. Whatsoever of thought or feeling came to him from England or by way of English culture his mind stood armed against in obedience to a password ... (p. 181).

Yet Davin tells a story, a very Irish story, in Joyce's meticulously accurate Irish-English, which is more powerful for Stephen than his own quasi-Elizabethan lyrics. Stephen cannot share the older native culture and will not artificially cultivate it, a still unconscious culture. He turns toward English literary culture. Stephen has arrived at the classroom after a walk through Dublin in which he quotes to himself a line of Ben Jonson's and notes, in passing, the statue of Tom Moore, 'the droll statue of the national poet in Ireland', poised appropriately, between Trinity College and what had been Grattan's Parliament: twin bastions of Irish Ascendancy culture. He imagines the statue covered in symbolic vermin, characterizing it as 'a Firbolg in the borrowed cloak of a Milesian,'[4] i.e., as a native adopting the manner of his conqueror. Moore diluted songs from the Irish language into English drawing room ditties, and made his bid for fame and fortune within the English tradition (though his English words for Irish airs introduced a new, non-English prosody), symbolizing part of the colonized writer's dilemma. Davin's story provides an authentic but unconscious instance of the native culture. Stephen then engages in a discussion with the dean of studies, an English convert to Catholicism, like John Henry Cardinal Newman, whom Stephen quotes to illustrate a point about language usage.

> —One difficulty, said Stephen, in aesthetic discussion is to know whether words are being used according to the literary tradition or according to the tradition of the marketplace. I remember a sentence of Newman's in which he says of the Blessed Virgin that she was detained in the full company of the saints. The use of the word in the marketplace is quite different. *I hope I am not detaining you.*
> —Not in the least, said the dean politely.
> —No, no, said Stephen, smiling, I mean ...

j. W. B. Yeats, *The Autobiography of William Butler Yeats*. New York: Collier, 1965, p. 131.

3. In the original myth, Prometheus is chained to a rock in the Caucasus mountains in South-West Asia. Yeats is suggesting that famous Irish mountains, such as Ben Bulben in Sligo or Croagh Patrick in Mayo, may be equally suitable as mythological material.

4. The Firbolgs were the mythological race who were supplanted in Ireland by the Milesians or Celts.

—Yes, yes: I see, said the dean quickly, I quite catch the point: *detain*.

He thrust forward his underjaw and uttered a dry short cough. (p. 188)

The dean attempts to regain his composure by instructing Stephen in the lighting of a lamp (Stephen had used the lamp metaphorically in his discussion, the dean literalized it).

—To return to the lamp, he said, the feeding of it is also a nice problem. You must choose the pure oil and you must be careful when you pour it in not to overflow it, not to pour in more than the funnel can hold.

—What funnel? asked Stephen.

—The funnel through which you pour the oil into the lamp.

—That? said Stephen. Is that called a funnel? Is it not a tundish?

—What is a tundish?

—That. The ... the funnel.

—Is that called a funnel in Ireland? asked the dean. I never heard the word in my life.

—It is called a tundish in Lower Drumcondra, said Stephen laughing, where they speak the best English.

—A tundish, said the dean reflectively. That is a most interesting word. I must look that word up. Upon my word I must. (p. 188)

This is a crucial passage in the *Portrait*. Besides illustrating Stephen's point about literary and marketplace word usage, it also brings to a head the mutual attitudes and relationships between the English language and literary tradition and the Irish use of them. Stephen, who prides himself on his literary knowledge, has been caught not knowing a common English word. The dean has never heard the word still commonly used in Ireland. (Later Stephen looks it up. '13 *April*: That tundish has been on my mind for a long time. I looked it up and find it English and good old blunt English too. Damn the dean of studies and his funnel. What did he come here for to teach us his own language or to learn it from us? Damn him one way or the other!' (p. 251) (When he looked it up, Stephen would have found a reference to *Measure for Measure* where an act of fornication is described as filling a bottle with a tundish). *Funnel* is a loan word from Old French (*founil*) carrying overtones of the Norman invasion. *Tundish* is an Elizabethan word which illustrates the archaicism of some aspects of the Irish-English language and recalls the Elizabethan conquest of Ireland. To complicate things further, *tun* derives from a Gaelic word, and *tundish* is a loan word in English from Irish. Stephen is forced to use the dean's vocabulary to define the Irish-English word. The quaint Elizabethan turns of phrase which Stephen admires in Davin's speech, and the Elizabethan literature he loves, are bound up in the Elizabethan conquest, a little emphasized sidelight of the English literary tradition. Stephen's affection for that tradition complicates his feelings about the historical relationship between colonized and colonizer. This episode begins to crystallize his understanding of that point.

The little word seemed to have turned a rapier point of his sensitiveness against this courteous and vigilant foe. He felt with a smart of dejection that the man to whom he was speaking was a countryman of Ben Jonson. He thought:

—The language in which we are speaking is his before it is mine. How different are the words *home, Christ, ale, master*, on his lips and on mine! I cannot speak or write these words without unrest of spirit. His language, so familiar and so foreign, will always be for me an acquired speech. I have not made or accepted its words. My voice holds them at bay. My soul frets in the shadow of his language. (p. 189)

... Stephen cannot divorce the literary tradition from its historical and cultural context, nor can he ignore his own context as an Irishman and its historical relationship to the historical context of English literature. If he is to be a writer he must forge a new way to write, and he wrestles symbolically at the end of the book, not with an angel, but with an old man from the west of Ireland: the recalcitrant, stubborn, stunted and maimed native tradition he has inherited.[k] And this is the dilemma of the colonized writer. Yeats and the other Ascendancy writers found themselves in the peculiar position of being neither native Irish nor native

k. The issue of Stephen's relationship to the English tradition is treated more complexly and at greater length in the 'Scylla and Charybdis' chapter of *Ulysses*, where Stephen sees himself steering a dangerous path between the 'Saxon smile' and the 'barbaric yawp' — i.e. between the English and American literary traditions.

English, but heirs to an Anglo-Irish experience and tradition (Congreve, Farquhar, Swift, Sterne, Burke, Goldsmith, Sheridan, Davis, Mangan, Ferguson). They came from minority settler stock and held sway over the native majority and found themselves caught somewhere in limbo between mother country and colony. The native Irish writer was traditionless in the English language, had to create his own tradition. The native Irish culture never developed those monuments of unageing intellect manifest in the English literary tradition precisely because that same English tradition destroyed the Irish cultural tradition before it had a chance to develop such monuments. There is inherent in this dilemma a painful alienation and disaffection which can also liberate: like Joyce or Beckett, the colonized or colonial writer is free of tradition, free to create as he pleases, choosing the language and form he pleases since he has none of his own (though contemporary Irish writers inherit the tradition of Yeats, Joyce, Beckett, *et al.*). One natural consequence of this will be freedom in handling the language and forms of the tradition of literature in English, a freedom far more manifest in the work of colonial writers than in the work of native English writers who manipulate their tradition subtly, sophisticatedly, but within its bonds.

Part of the pain of this dilemma is the realization that the English tradition *has* produced monuments of unageing intellect worthy of emulation, but not only have they been achieved at the expense of other cultures, their very authors have wrought the destruction of other cultures. Herein lies a key example of how the colonized views the colonizer. . . .

England's Renaissance poets were mercenaries. The architecture runs with blood. The ruins of Boyle Abbey are another example. What remains indicates splendour and dignity. The Abbey had been given to Sir Henry King, who promptly destroyed it. King had a son named Edward, better known to the rest of the world as Lycidas, but in that part of Ireland the name King recalls Boyle Abbey, not Milton.[5] Cromwell's name is still a curse in Ireland, whatever his role as a Republican hero in English eyes, and Milton was his propagandist. While Spenser wrote *The Faerie Queene*, an unageing monument, on a confiscated estate in Kilcolman, he also wrote *A View of the Present State of Ireland*, advocating genocide as official state policy to subdue the Irish, whose country he would depopulate more easily to appropriate 'his' landscape. Modern critics may question Pound's Fascism, treason, and anti-Semitism, or the authoritarian tendencies of Yeats, Eliot or Lawrence, but the genocidal Spenser? Royalist Shakespeare? Milton's praise of Cromwell's Irish massacres? Pound at least remained a poet, not a politician. Yeats became an ineffectual *Seanador*.[6] Spenser and Raleigh were the Queen's agents, actively subduing and colonizing Ireland. The native Irish look upon Spenser's work with a remnant of the reservations about his worth which may have smouldered in the eyes of Red Hugh's guerillas as they burned him out of Kilcolman, chasing him away from his spare time literary activities.[7] Raleigh crucified a priest and slaughtered five hundred Spaniards who surrendered to him at *Dun an Oir*.[8] Examples accumulate. The Irish writer casts a cold eye on all the monuments of the English tradition or their remains. The point is that the colonized native *cannot* have the same relationship with the English tradition that the native Englishman has (without deluding himself into thinking he is English). The English tradition is more than its masterworks, it is also the context which produced them, a context which differs when you are on the receiving end of colonization, not one who benefits. If the colonized bear scars, the colonizer bears a burden of guilt.

When the colonized writer attempts to deal impartially with the colonizer's tradition, problems develop. Having no native culture left, he internalizes the culture of his oppressor. Often the process goes no further. But once his consciousness is raised to see this process of internalization he

5. Boyle Abbey, one of the finest Cistercian abbeys in Ireland, was built in 1198. It was desecrated by Cromwellian troops in 1659. The family of Edward King, Milton's close friend and the subject of the elegy *Lycidas*, lived at Rockingham, near Boyle. King is buried in the grounds of Boyle Abbey.

6. That is, a member of the Irish Senate.

7. After the battle of the Yellow Ford in 1598, the victorious army of the Northern chieftains Hugh O'Neill and Red Hugh O'Donnell swept through Munster, evicting the poet Edmund Spenser from his castle at Kilcolman, Co. Cork, in the process.

8. At Dun-an-Oir (Fort of Gold), Smerwick, Co. Kerry in 1580, over 700 Spaniards and Italians, who had landed to aid the Munster rising against Elizabethan rule, were massacred by the forces of the lord deputy. Edmund Spenser was also present at the massacre.

cannot remain totally impartial. Stephen Dedalus has to learn this. So, in another time, in another part of the empire, in more obvious ways, but within the same structure, does Obi Okonkwo in Chinua Achebe's *No Longer At Ease*,[9] which portrays the dilemma of the native African writer who has learned English, been schooled in English schools, trained in the English literary tradition, only to discover, when he tries to write himself, how inimical to his circumstances is the English tradition he has acquired. . . .

The emergence of non-native writers in English in the Modernist period of the first quarter century as the major literary figures of the period signals the end of the native English literary tradition as the major force in writing in English. Non-English writers used the native tradition and its forms in new ways and integrated them with cosmopolitan traditions precisely because it was an object to them, not a vested interest. Once the tradition was recognized as a 'tradition', once it was capable of definition, it became historical, not living, so that any 'return' to it is reactionary, deliberately atavistic, a conscious choice, not an unconscious working of the same vein but the reopening of a closed mine, a deliberate anti-Modernism. The key here is the idea of an historical period earlier in the century which is post traditional English literature. Modernism is one of its symptoms. The poetry of the trenches is another. The fundamental changes in English society which accompany the demise of the Empire and the working classes' acquisition of literacy and education fundamentally change the literature England produces. World War I changed things utterly. *Mauberley* registers the death of England as a live cultural tradition. What remains? Fossil? Skeleton? Wounded fisher king? The Irish, Americans, and others writing in English forge their own traditions, increasingly independent of England's. English writers are faced with developing a post-traditional English literature, no longer metropolitan and tolerant of provincial, i.e. colonial, upstart crows, but itself provincial, measuring and defining itself in light of American and other literatures. What now is the state of contemporary writing in English? The attempt to be contemporary versus the attempt to be traditional . . . .

9. Chinua Achebe, *No Longer at Ease* (London: Heinemann, 1960).

Is contemporary English writing rooted in a hoary tradition or stumped, sending out stray shoots? American writers are moving in many directions. Irish writers are increasingly turning to America for models (as in the cases of Tom Kinsella and John Montague), or creating their own personal tradition, like Richard Murphy, or liberating themselves and Irish verse from the English mode through ironic traditionalism, ironic Irish manipulations of the well made poem which turn that tradition inside out, and here Derek Mahon is paramount, or writing naturally and unselfconsciously as Irish poets, like Paul Muldoon or John Ennis or Eilean Ni Chuilleanain, or as novelists, like Dermot Healy, Neil Jordan, John Banville, John McGahern or Aidan Higgins, or saying farewell to English and writing in Irish, like Michael Hartnett, or reconstructing literary history and criticism like Seamus Deane. But Ireland now has the advantage of being small and unpretentious and, free of vested interests, free to choose without fear of losing identity. Our traumas still lie in heaps about us but we no longer go into exile: as Kinsella has said, we only commute.

Biographies/Bibliographies

Seán O'Faoláin

For biography and bibliography, see p. 127.

T. W. Moody

LIFE. Theodore William Moody was born in Belfast in 1907. He was professor of modern history at Trinity College, Dublin 1939-77 and as dean of the faculty of arts did much to bring the college into the mainstream of Irish life. In 1938, with Robin Dudley Edwards, he founded the academic journal *Irish Historical Studies*, which introduced new standards of rigour into Irish historical research. Moody initiated the Thomas Davis lectures on Radio Éireann in 1953 and subsequently was appointed to the Authority of Radio Telefís Éireann. In 1972 he and the rest of the Authority were sacked by the government following a radio interview with an IRA spokesman (a breach of Section 31 of the Broadcasting Authority Act). In 1966, Moody devised the television series, *The Course of Irish History*, and his energies throughout the 1970s were devoted to planning and publishing the multi-volume *A New History of Ireland*. He died in 1984, having seen his monumental biography of Michael Davitt through the press in 1981.

CHIEF WRITINGS. *The Londonderry Plantations, 1609-41: The City of London and the Plantations of Ulster* (Belfast: William Mullan & Son, 1939); *Thomas Davis, 1814-45* (Dublin: Hodges Figgis, 1945); (ed., with H. A. Crone and D. B. Quinn) *Essays on British and Irish History in Honour of James Eadie Todd* (London: Muller, 1949); (ed., with J. C. Beckett) *Ulster since 1800: A Political and Economic Survey* (London: BBC, 1954); (with J. C. Beckett) *Queen's, Belfast 1845-1949: The History of a University* (London: Faber and Faber, 1959); (ed., with F. X. Martin) *The*

Course of Irish History (Cork: Mercier Press, 1967; New York: Weybright and Talley, 1967); (ed.) *Historical Studies: Papers read before the Irish Conference of Historians* (London: Routledge & Kegan Paul, 1968); (ed.) *The Fenian Movement* (Cork: Mercier Press, 1968); *The Ulster Question 1603-1973* (Dublin and Cork: Mercier Press, 1974); (ed., with F. X. Martin and F. J. Byrne) *A New History of Ireland*, Vols III, VIII and IX (Oxford: Clarendon Press, 1976); (ed.) *Nationality and the Pursuit of National Independence* (Belfast: Appletree Press, 1978); *Davitt and Irish Revolution 1846-82* (Oxford: Oxford University Press, 1981).

F. S. L. Lyons

LIFE. Francis Steward Leland Lyons was born in Derry in 1923. He lectured in Hull and at Trinity College, Dublin and from 1964 to 1974 was professor of modern history at the University of Kent at Canterbury. Subsequently he was appointed provost of Trinity College, Dublin. His books include a history of the Irish Parliamentary Party and a biography of one of its major figures, John Dillon. Lyons published two studies of Parnell, including the standard biography. His *Ireland Since the Famine* was published in 1971 and became the standard study of the period. In 1978 he delivered the W. B. Rankin Memorial Lecture, 'The Burden of Our History', at Queen's University, Belfast, and the Ford Lectures at the University of Oxford, later published as *Culture and Anarchy in Ireland 1890-1939*. He was working on the authorized biography of W. B. Yeats at the time of his death in 1983.

CHIEF WRITINGS. *The Irish Parliamentary Party 1890-1910* (London: Faber and Faber, 1951; Westport, Connecticut: Greenwood Press, 1975); *The Fall of Parnell 1890-91* (London: Routledge & Kegan Paul, 1960); *Internationalism in Europe 1815-1914* (Leyden: A. W. Scytoff, 1963); *John Dillon: A Biography* (London: Routledge & Kegan Paul, 1968); *Ireland Since the Famine* (London: Weidenfeld and Nicolson, 1971); *Charles Stewart Parnell* (London: Collins, 1977); *The Burden of our History* (Belfast: Queen's University, 1978); *Culture and Anarchy in Ireland 1890-1939* (Oxford: Oxford University Press, 1979); (ed., with R. J. Hawkins) *Ireland Under the Union: Varieties of Tension. Essays in Honour of T. W. Moody* (Oxford: Clarendon Press, 1980).

BIOGRAPHY AND CRITICISM. Roy Foster, *F. S. L. Lyons 1923-1983* (London: British Academy; Wolfeboro, New Hampshire: Longwood Publishing Group, 1986).

Roy Foster

LIFE. Robert Fitzroy Foster was born in Waterford in 1949. Educated at Trinity College, Dublin, he held a visiting fellowship at St Antony's College, Oxford. He is now professor of modern British history at Birkbeck College, University of London and is a specialist in nineteenth-century history. In 1988 his panoramic survey of modern Irish history was published. He currently holds a British Academy research readership to work on the authorized biography of W. B. Yeats and was a visiting fellow at the Institute of Advanced Study, Princeton University 1988-89.

CHIEF WRITINGS. *Charles Stewart Parnell: The Man and his Family* (Hassocks, Sussex: Harvester Press, 1976); *Political Novels and Nineteenth Century History* (Winchester: King Alfred's College, 1981); *Lord Randolph Churchill: A Political LIfe* (Oxford and New York: Oxford University Press, 1982); *F. S. L. Lyons 1923-1983* (London: British Academy; Wolfeboro, New Hampshire: Longwood Publishing Group, 1986); *Modern Ireland 1600-1972* (Harmondsworth: Penguin Books, 1988; New York: Viking Penguin, 1988); (ed.) *The Oxford Illustrated History of Ireland* (Oxford/New York: Oxford University Press, 1989).

Desmond Fennell

LIFE. Desmond Fennell was born in Belfast in 1929. He received an MA in modern history at University College, Dublin, studied at Bonn University and travelled widely, pursuing a career in journalism. He edited the influential theological review, *Herder Correspondence*, from 1964 to 1968. Fennell subsequently returned to Ireland to live in Connemara, where he was involved in launching the Gaeltacht civil rights movement. In 1972 he contributed to the *Eire Nua* (New Ireland) federal policy that was adopted as a political programme by Provisional Sinn Féin. Between 1976 and 1982, he lectured in politics and history at University College, Galway, and since 1982 has lectured in communications at the College of Commerce in Rathmines, Dublin, as well as writing numerous books.

CHIEF WRITINGS. *The Northern Catholics: An Inquiry* (Blackrock: Mount Salus Press, 1959); *Mainly in Wonder* (London: Hutchinson, 1959); *Art for the Irish* (Blackrock: Mount Salus Press, 1962); *The British Problem* (Dublin: Sceptick Press, 1963); (ed.) *The Changing Face of Catholic Ireland* (London: G. Chapman, 1968); *A New Nationalism for the New Ireland* (Monaghan: Comhairle Uladh, 1972); *Take the Faroes for Example* (Dublin: Pobal, 1972); *Build The Third Republic* (Carna: Foilseacháin Mhaoinse, 1972); *Towards a Greater Ulster 1969-72* (Indreabhán: Comharchumann Chois Fharraige, 1973); *Sketches of the New Ireland* (Galway: Association for the Advancement of Self-Government, 1973); *The State of the Nation: Ireland since the Sixties* (Swords, Co. Dublin: Ward River Press, 1984); *Irish Catholics and Freedom since 1916: A Humanist Essay* (Dublin: Dominican Publications, 1984); *Beyond Nationalism* (Swords, Co. Dublin: Ward River Press, 1985); *Nice People and Rednecks: Ireland in the 1980s* (Dublin: Gill and Macmillan, 1986); *A Connacht Journey* (Dublin: Gill and Macmillan, 1987); *The Revision of Irish Nationalism* (Dublin: Open Air, 1989); *Bloomsway* (Swords, Co. Dublin: Poolbeg Press, 1990).

Francis Shaw

LIFE. Francis Shaw was born in Mullingar, Co. Westmeath in 1907. He entered the Society of Jesus in 1924. From 1941 to 1970 he was professor of early and medieval Irish at University College, Dublin. He was a member of the editorial board of *Studies*, the Jesuit quarterly review. An eminent scholar, he made contributions to linguistic, historical, literary and hagiographical studies. He died in Dublin in 1970.

CHIEF WRITINGS. *The Real St Patrick* (Dublin: Messenger Office, 1931); (ed.) *Aislinge Oenguso* 'The Celtic Twilight', *Studies*, Vol. XXXIII (1934), 25-41, 260-78; 'Medieval Medico-philosophical Treatises in the Irish Language', in Reverend John Ryan S.J. (ed.), *Feil-sgribhinn Eoin Mhic Neill* (Dublin: At the Sign of the Three Candles, 1940); *Gone with the Wind* (Dublin: Messenger Office, 1942); 'Irish Medical Men and Philosophers in Brian O Cúiv (ed.), *Seven Centuries of Irish Learning 1000-1700* (Dublin: Institute for Advanced Studies, 1961); 'Mac Neill the Person' in F. X. Martin and F. J. Byrne (eds), *The Scholar Revolutionary: Eoin MacNeill, 1867-1945, and the Making of the New Ireland* (Shannon: Irish University Press, 1973).

Conor Cruise O'Brien

LIFE. Conor Cruise O'Brien was born in Dublin in 1917. He entered the Department of External Affairs in 1944 and was appointed assistant secretary general of the department in 1960. From 1956 to 1960, he was head of the United Nations section and a member of the Irish delegation to the UN. In 1961, he came to international attention as representative of the secretary general of the UN in Katanga during the Congo crisis, events related in his book *To Katanga and Back*. In the 1960s, he pursued a university career as vice-chancellor of the University of Ghana (1962-65) and professor of humanities, New York University. A notable critic of US policy in Vietnam, he entered Irish politics as a TD (Member of Parliament) for the Labour Party in 1969, at a time when the party promised that 'the seventies would be socialist' in Ireland. In fact, nationalism rather than socialism became his abiding concern in the 1970s, and in 1972 he published a wide-ranging critique of Irish nationalism, *States of Ireland*. In 1973, he became minister for posts and telegraphs in a coalition government and in 1976 extended the controversial Section 31 of the Broadcasting Authority Act to prohibit Provisional Sinn Féin, as well as the IRA, from the airwaves. He lost his parliamentary seat in the 1977 general election, and since then has pursued an international career as a lecturer, journalist and author, taking up an appointment as editor-in-chief of *The Observer* (London) 1979-81, and contributing editor to *The Atlantic* (Boston). He is married to the poet Máire Mhac an tSaoi.

CHIEF WRITINGS. Donat O'Donnell (pseudonym), *Maria Cross: Imaginative Patterns in a Group of Modern Catholic Writers* (New York: Oxford University Press, 1952; London: Chatto and Windus, 1953); *Parnell and his Party 1880-1890* (Oxford: Oxford University Press, 1957); (ed.) *The Shaping of Modern Ireland* (London: Routledge & Kegan Paul, 1960); *To Katanga and Back: A U.N. Case History* (London: Hutchinson, 1962; New York: Simon and Schuster, 1962); *Writers and Politics* (London: Chatto and Windus, 1965; New York: Pantheon Books, 1965); *The United Nations: Sacred Drama* (with Felix Topolski) (London: Hutchinson, 1967; New York: Simon and Schuster, 1968); *Murderous Angels* (play) (Boston: Little, Brown, 1968; London: Hutchinson, 1969); (ed.) Edmund Burke, *Reflections on the Revolution in France* (Harmondsworth: Penguin Books, 1969); (ed., with William Dean Varech) *Power and Consciousness* (London: University of London Press, 1969; New York: New York University Press, 1969); *Conor Cruise O'Brien Introduces Ireland* (London: André Deutsch, 1969); *Camus* (London: Fontana, 1969 (published in the United States as *Albert Camus of Europe and Africa*, New York: Viking Press, 1970)); *A Concise History of Ireland* (with Maire Cruise O'Brien) (London: Thames and Hudson, 1972); *The Suspecting Glance* (London: Faber and Faber, 1972): *States of Ireland* (London: Hutchinson, 1972; New York: Vintage Books, 1973): *Herod: Reflections on Political Violence* (London: Hutchinson, 1978); *Neighbours: Four Lectures* (London: Faber and Faber, 1980); *The Siege* (London: Weidenfeld and Nicolson, 1986; New York: Simon and Schuster, 1987); *Passion and Cunning: Essays* (London: Weidenfeld and Nicolson, 1988); *God Land: Reflections on Religion and Nationalism* (Cambridge, Massachusetts: Harvard University Press, 1988).

Marianne Elliott

LIFE. Marianne Elliott was born in Belfast in 1948 and educated at Queen's University, Belfast and Oxford University. She taught at the West London Institute of Higher Education, at the University of Swansea and at the University of Liverpool, and has been a visiting professor to the Universities of Iowa and South Carolina. At present she is on a research fellowship to the University of Liverpool.

CHIEF WRITINGS. *Partners in Revolution: The United Irishmen and France* (New Haven: Yale University Press, 1982); *Watchmen in Zion: The Protestant Concept of Liberty* (Derry: Field Day, 1985); (translation) Richard Cobb, *People's Armies* (New Haven, Connecticut: Yale University Press, 1987); *Wolfe Tone: Prophet of Irish Independence* (New Haven, Connecticut: Yale University Press, 1989).

Seamus Deane

For biography and bibliography, see p. 1434.

Terence Brown

LIFE. Terence Brown was born in Loping, China in 1944 but was raised in Holywood, Co. Down. He was educated at Magee University College, Derry and at Trinity College, Dublin. He joined the Department of English at Trinity College in 1968 and was appointed associate professor of English in 1982. In 1975 he was visiting associate professor of English at the University of Vermont. He acted as director of modern English at Trinity College 1976-84 and 1988-89.

CHIEF WRITINGS. ed. (with Alec Reid), *Time Was Away: The World of Louis MacNeice* (Dublin: Dolmen Press, 1974); *Northern Voices: Poets from Ulster* (Dublin: Gill and Macmillan; New Jersey: Rowman and Littlefield, 1975); *Louis MacNeice: Sceptical Vision* (Dublin: Gill and Macmillan; New York: Barnes & Noble, 1975); *The Selected Padraic Fiacc*, Introduction by Terence Brown (Belfast: Blackstaff Press, 1979); ed. (with Patrick Rafroidi) *The Irish Short Story* (Gerrards Cross, Bucks: Colin Smythe, 1979; New Jersey: Humanities Press, 1980); *Ireland: A Social and Cultural History, 1922-1979* (London: Fontana, 1981); *Ireland: A Social and Cultural History, 1922-the Present* (Ithaca, New York: Cornell University Press, 1985); *The Whole Protestant Community: The Making of a Historical Myth* (Derry: Field Day, 1985); ed. (with Barbara Hayley) *Samuel Ferguson: A Centenary Tribute* (Dublin: Royal Irish Academy, 1987); *Ireland's Literature: Selected Essays* (Mullingar, Co. Westmeath: The Lilliput Press; Totowa, New Jersey: Barnes & Noble, 1988); ed. (with Nicholas Grene) *Tradition and Influence in Anglo-Irish Poetry* (London: Macmillan Press, 1989).

Oliver MacDonagh

LIFE. Oliver MacDonagh was born in Carlow in 1925. He was educated at University College, Dublin, King's Inns Dublin, and Cambridge University. He was lecturer (1950-55) and fellow (1952-64) of St Catharine's College, Cambridge, foundation professor of history, Flinders University, South Australia (1964-68), professor of modern history, University College, Cork (1968-72), and visiting professor at Yale University (1970-71). He has published works on Victorian government, Irish history, and the relationship between literature, ideas and history, and has completed a two-volume biography of Daniel O'Connell. He holds the W. K. Hancock chair of history and is head of the department of history at the Institute of Advanced Studies in the Australian National University, Canberra.

CHIEF WRITINGS. *A Pattern of Government Growth 1800-1860: The Passenger Acts and their Enforcement* (London: MacGibbon and Kee, 1961); *Ireland: The Union and its Aftermath* (Englewood Cliffs, New Jersey: Prentice Hall, 1968; London: Allen and Unwin, 1977); *The Nineteenth Century Novel and Irish Social History* (Dublin: National University of Ireland, 1970); *Early Victorian Government 1830-1870* (London: Weidenfeld and Nicolson, 1977; New York: Holmes and Maeir Publishers, 1977); *The Inspector General: Sir Jeremiah Fitzpatrick and the Politics of Social Reform 1783-1802* (London: Croom Helm, 1981; New York: Routledge, Chapman Hall, 1981); *States of Mind: A Study of Anglo-Irish Conflict 1780-1980* (London: Allen and Unwin, 1983; Winchester: Unwin Hyman, 1983); (ed., with W. K. Mandle and P. Travers) *Irish Culture and Nationalism 1750-1950* (London: Macmillan, 1983; New York: St Martin's Press, 1983); (ed. with W. K. Mandle) *Ireland and Irish Australia* (London: Croom Helm, 1986; New York: Routledge, Chapman Hall, 1986); *The Hereditary Bondsman* (London: Weidenfeld and Nicolson, 1988; New York: St Martin's Press, 1988); *The Emancipist* (London: Weidenfeld and Nicolson, 1990).

Thomas Kinsella

For biography and bibliography, see p. 1432.

Richard Kearney

LIFE. Richard Kearney was born in Cork in 1954. He was educated at University College, Dublin, McGill University, Montreal, and at the Sorbonne. Kearney was a co-founder/editor of the influential cultural journal *The Crane Bag* (1977-85) and *The Irish Review* since its founding in 1986. A prominent figure in intellectual and cultural debates in Ireland, he has presented arts and book programmes on Irish television. In 1989 he became a member of the Arts Council and was appointed chairperson of the Irish Film Centre. He has edited and published widely in philosophy, literature and cultural theory, has been a visiting professor to Boston College and is at present associate professor in philosophy, University College, Dublin.

CHIEF WRITINGS. (ed.) *The Black Book: An Analysis of Third Level Education* (Dublin: Denam Press, 1975); (ed.) *Heidegger et la Question de Dieu* (Paris: Grasset, 1981); *The Crane Bag Book of Irish Studies 1977-81* (Dublin: Blackwater Press, 1982); *Dialogues with Contemporary Continental Thinkers* (Manchester: Manchester University Press, 1984; New York: St Martin's Press, 1984); *Poètique du Possible* (Paris: Beauchesnes, 1984); *Myth and Motherland* (Derry: Field Day Publications, 1984); (ed.) *The Irish Mind: Exploring Intellectual Traditions* (Dublin: Wolfhound Press, 1985; Atlantic Highlands, New Jersey: Humanities Press, 1985); *Modern Movements in European Philosophy* (Manchester: Manchester University Press, 1986; New York: St Martin's Press, 1986); (ed.) *The Crane Bag Book of Irish Studies 1982-85* (Dublin: Wolfhound Press, 1987; St Paul, Minnesota: Irish Books and Media, 1987); *The Wake of Imagination* (London: Hutchinson, 1987; Minneapolis: University of Minnesota Press, 1987); *Transitions: Narratives in Modern Irish Culture* (Dublin: Wolfhound Press, 1988; New York: St Martin's Press, 1988); (ed.) *Across the Frontiers: Ireland in the 1990s* (Dublin: Wolfhound Press, 1988).

David Lloyd

LIFE. David Lloyd was born in Dublin in 1955 and educated at Cambridge University. In 1983 he was appointed assistant professor of English at the University of California in Berkeley, and is now associate professor of English there. His book on James Clarence Mangan is the first sustained attempt to apply modern critical theory in a rigorous fashion to the study of Irish cultural nationalism.

CHIEF WRITINGS. *Nationalism and Minor Literature: James Clarence Mangan and the Emergence of Irish Cultural Nationalism* (Berkeley: University of California Press, 1987).

Declan Kiberd

LIFE. Declan Kiberd was born in Dublin in 1951. He was educated at St Paul's College, Raheny, Trinity College Dublin and Oxford University. He was lecturer in English and American Literature at the University of Kent at Canterbury 1976-77; lecturer in Irish at Trinity College, Dublin 1977-79; and has been lecturer in English at University College, Dublin since 1979. He was visiting professor in Irish Studies at the University of Minnesota 1986, and visiting professor of English at the University of California, Santa Barbara 1987-88. He has lectured on Irish writing and politics in many countries, including Japan, Mexico, Canada, Sweden, France, Italy, Spain, Portugal, England, Switzerland, Venezuela and the USSR. Between 1985 and 1987 he was director of the Yeats International Summer School in Sligo. From 1984 to 1986 he was co-presenter of an arts programme on RTE television; and from 1986 to 1988 he wrote a weekly column for *The Irish Times*.

CHIEF WRITINGS. *Synge and the Irish Language* (London: Macmillan, 1979; Totowa, New Jersey: Barnes and Noble, 1979); *Anglo-Irish Attitudes* (Derry: Field Day, 1984); *Men and Feminism in Modern Literature* (London: Macmillan, 1985; New York: St Martin's Press, 1985). Co-editor of *Omnium Gatherum: Essays for Richard Ellmann* (Gerrards Cross, Bucks: Colin Smythe, 1989; Montreal: McGill University Press, 1989) and of *An Crann Faoi Bhlath: The Flowering Tree — Gaelic Poetry and Translations 1940-1989* (Dublin: Wolfhound Press, 1990).

Denis Donoghue

LIFE. Born in Tullow, Co. Carlow in 1928, Denis Donoghue grew up in Newry, Co. Down, the son of a catholic member of the predominantly protestant police force, the Royal Ulster Constabulary. He was educated at University College, Dublin and spent some time as a civil servant in the Department of Finance in Dublin before his appointment to an assistant lectureship in the English department at University College, Dublin, in 1953. He spent a year as visiting professor at King's College, Cambridge (1966-67) before returning to University College, Dublin as professor of modern English and American literature. He retained that post until 1980 when he resigned to become Henry James professor at the University of New York, where he still teaches. He is one of the best-known academics in the English-speaking world, an accomplished critic and a brilliant lecturer. He received an honorary doctorate from University College in 1989.

CHIEF WRITINGS. *The Third Voice. Modern British and American Verse Drama* (Princeton, New Jersey: Princeton University Press, 1959); (ed.) *The Integrity of Yeats* (Cork: Mercier Press, 1964; Philadelphia: R. West, 1976); (ed., with J. R. Mulryne) *An Honoured Guest: New Essays on W. B. Yeats* (London: Edward Arnold, 1965); *Connoisseurs of Chaos: Ideas of Order in Modern American Poetry* (London: Faber and Faber, 1966; New York: Columbia University Press, 1984); *The Ordinary Universe: Soundings in Modern Literature* (London: Faber and Faber, 1968); (ed.) *Swift Revisited* (Cork: Mercier Press, 1968); *Emily Dickinson* (Minneapolis: University of Minnesota Press, 1969); *Jonathan Swift: A Critical Introduction* (Cambridge: Cambridge University Press, 1969); *Yeats* (London: Fontana, 1971); (ed.) *Jonathan Swift: A Critical Anthology* (Harmondsworth: Penguin Books, 1971); (ed.) *W. B. Yeats Memoirs: Autobiography and First Draft Journal* (London: Macmillan, 1972); *Thieves of Fire* (London: Faber and Faber, 1973; New York: Oxford University Press, 1974); (ed.) *Seven American Poets from MacLeish to Nemerov* (Minneapolis: University of Minnesota Press, 1975); *The Sovereign Ghost: Studies in Imagination* (Berkeley: University of California Press, 1976; London: Faber and Faber, 1978); (ed.) *Poems of R. P. Blackmur* (Princeton: Princeton University Press, 1977); *Ferocious Alphabets* (London: Faber and Faber, 1981; New York: Columbia University Press, 1984); *The Arts Without Mystery: Reith Lectures (London: BBC, 1983); We Irish* (Brighton: Harvester Press, 1986; Berkeley: University of California Press, 1988); *Reading America: Essays on American Literature* (New York: Knopf, 1987); *England, Their England: Commentaries on English Language & Literature* (New York: Knopf, 1988); *Warrenpoint* (New York: Braziller, 1990).

Edna Longley

LIFE. Edna Longley was born in Cork in 1940. She has written extensively on Irish and English poetry, taking a particular interest in the poetry of Louis MacNeice and Edward Thomas. Longley has edited the works of several modern Irish poets, and in her recent critical writings has explored the relationship between the protestant tradition in Northern Ireland and literature. She is a senior lecturer at Queen's University, Belfast.

CHIEF WRITINGS. (ed.) *Edward Thomas: Poems and Lost Poems* (London: Collins, 1973); (ed.) *The Selected James Simmons* (Belfast: Blackstaff Pres, 1978); (ed.) *A Language Not to be Betrayed; Selected Prose of Edward Thomas* (Manchester: Carcanet Press, 1981); (ed.) *The Selected Paul Durcan* (Belfast: Blackstaff Press, 1982; Wolfeboro, New Hampshire: Longwood Publishing Group, 1986); (ed., with Gerald Dawe) *Across a Roaring Hill: The Protestant Imagination in Modern Ireland* (Belfast: Blackstaff Press, 1985); *Poetry in the Wars* (Newcastle-upon-Tyne: Bloodaxe, 1986; Cranbury, New Jersey: University of Delaware Press, 1987); *Louis MacNeice* (London: Faber and Faber, 1988); *From Cathleen to Anorexia: The Breakdown of Ireland* (Dublin: Attic Press, 1990).

Fintan O'Toole

LIFE. Fintan O'Toole was born in Dublin in 1958 and was educated at University College, Dublin. He was Young Journalist of the Year in 1982. From 1983 to 1985 he was arts editor of the *Sunday Tribune*; he was editor of *Magill* current affairs magazine 1985-86. His writing for the *Sunday Tribune* established him as one of the leading theatre critics in Ireland. In 1988 O'Toole joined *The Irish Times* as a columnist and feature writer. He has written extensively on drama, cultural issues and current affairs. He is working on a full-length study of the country and the city in Irish writing.

CHIEF WRITINGS. *The Southern Question* (Dublin: Raven Arts Press, 1987); *The Politics of Magic: The Work and Times of Tom Murphy* (Dublin: Raven Arts Press, 1988); *No More Heroes: A Guide to Shakespearean Tragedies* (Dublin: Raven Arts Press, 1990).

Liam de Paor

LIFE. Liam de Paor was born in Dublin in 1926. A graduate of University College, Dublin, in archaeology and early Irish history, he has worked on the excavation of historical and archaeological sites in Ireland and central Europe. He acted as UNESCO advisor to the government of Nepal. In 1964 he was appointed lecturer in history at University College, Dublin, and has held professorships in New York, Pittsburgh and Toronto. Liam de Paor has published widely on archaeology, the Northern Ireland conflict and on Irish history.

CHIEF WRITINGS. (with Maire de Paor) *Early Christian Ireland* (London: Thames and Hudson, 1958); *Archaeology: An Illustrated Introduction* (Harmondsworth: Penguin Books, 1967); *Divided Ulster* (Harmondsworth: Penguin Books, 1970); *Portrait of Ireland: Ireland Past and Present* (Bray: Rainbow House, 1985; New York: St Martin's Press, 1986); (ed.) *Milestones in Irish History* (Cork: Mercier Press/RTE, 1986); *The Peoples of Ireland: From Prehistory to Modern Times* (London: Hutchinson, 1986; Notre Dame, Indiana: University of Notre Dame Press, 1986); *Unfinished Business* (London: Radius Hutchinson, 1990).

W. J. Mc Cormack

For biography and bibliography, see under Hugh Maxton on p. 1435.

Seán Golden

LIFE. Born in London of Irish parents in 1948, Golden spent part of his childhoood in the West of Ireland before the family emigrated to the United States. He took his doctorate from the University of Connecticut where he also taught. He has also taught English at the University of Notre Dame, Indiana, and at the Foreign Languages Institute and Beijing University in China. He now lives in Barcelona, although his home is in Ballaghderreen, Co. Mayo.

CHIEF WRITINGS. (ed., with Peter Fallon) *Soft Day: A Miscellany of Contemporary Irish Writing* (Notre Dame and London: Notre Dame University Press, 1980).

SEAMUS DEANE, *Editor*

Political Writings and Speeches 1900–1988

This section is primarily given over to the political events and crises that have wrought such a profound alteration in Ireland over the past ninety years. Violence has been one of the determining factors in these alterations; the 1916 Easter Rising, the War of Independence, the Civil War, the pogroms in the North of the 1920s, the effects of the two World Wars and the twenty-two years of violence in Northern Ireland since 1968 have all brought constitutional change in their wake. The confetti of documents, treaties, position papers and constitutional treatises that has been showered on the political marriages, christenings and rechristenings of these years has been, for the most part, provided by the shredding of the Act of Union of 1800. In the process, Ireland's relationship with the United Kingdom, the British Empire and the Commonwealth has been transformed and the internal relationships within Ireland, north and south, have been dramatically readjusted. The connections between Ireland and Europe have also by turns faded and strengthened as a result of the state's policy of neutrality in World War II and by its membership of the European Community since 1973. By 1992, the integration of Ireland within the new European super-power structure will be almost complete, save for the policy of neutrality which has so far kept the Republic out of NATO and stimulated it into playing an active part in the various United Nations peace-keeping ventures in the Congo, Lebanon and Namibia.

Yet, for all the changes in structure and name that it has undergone, Ireland has remained steadfastly imprisoned within its colonial past. The most remarkable and rancid symptom of that long, half-cherished, half-repellent bondage is religious sectarianism and its tenacious embrace with political loyalties. It seemed proper, in the light of that, to open the section with the once-famous dispute between Sir Horace Plunkett and Father Michael O'Riordan. There we see, in an almost naive and open display, the contrasting protestant/catholic versions of the Irish 'national character' and its presumed fitness for independence. By now, we have witnessed that kind of dispute taking place all over the world, as the European empires withdraw — from Africa, Asia and the Middle East — amid a chorus of speculation about the capacity of the respective liberated races to 'run' a society. There the problem of 'national character' takes a racial rather than, as in Ireland, a religious/sectarian form, although there is an obvious homology between the two. But it is not sufficient to indicate that the Irish sectarian divide conceals (if not very effectively) a racial divide and to show that such categorizing of peoples is, in itself, one of the standard cultural weapons of any imperial or colonial system. For it is often the case that the deformations that imperialism produces as a policy — lack of education, cultural humiliation, poverty, an enslaving meekness — are indeed disabling and that communities long subject to them do have to undergo a long and painful recovery before they can learn to take effective control of their own destiny. In a sense, both Plunkett and O'Riordan are right. It is true that the Irish catholics were (are?) the less capable of independence and co-operation because of the authoritarian nature of the church to which they had given their loyalty and which had remained the only institution they could call their own. It is also true, as O'Riordan claims, that their capacity to endure indicated that they were not disabled because of their catholicism; they were disabled as catholics in a series of specific political situations. Both men are, in fact, looking to history and to institutions to explain the qualities of a national character that, by its very nature, must be independent of these. National character, so understood, is a concept that supports racial and sectarian convictions. Neither seems to see that it is itself a product of such convictions, whether that character be seen in a kindly or an unkindly light. But no critique of Plunkett and O'Riordan can deny the historical importance of their dispute. Their terms survive to the present day, most especially in Northern Ireland, as part of the vocabulary of politics, while also being part of the powerful folklore of imperialism.

Nationalism both breeds and is bred by sectarianism, in its British and its Irish forms. When a culture is politically homogeneous, like that of Britain, the sectarianism is directed externally rather than internally and is usually xenophobic in character. When, as in Ireland's case, the culture is politically divided, the sectarianism is largely internally directed. The only escape from this inbred infestation is provided by a vision of the human community at large, rather than by a version of the local community at home. At the beginning of this century, socialism was the most attractive and available of the more hospitable and enlightened visions. It offered a systematic analysis of imperialism at home and abroad; it provided a critique of capitalism, although this was indebted for most of its penetration to Marxism; and it seemed to have the intellectual strength to incorporate nationalism and disengage it from its local and provincial origins and aims. Frederick Ryan, Francis Sheehy-Skeffington and, above all, James Connolly, are exemplary instances of this movement. Ryan and Sheehy-Skeffington were both analysts of oppressive systems — Ryan seeing in Egypt, Iran (then Persia), and in the Middle East in general, resemblances between British rule there and British rule in Ireland, Sheehy-Skeffington seeing violence as the ultimate form of oppression and the subjection of women as one of its engendering causes. It is a bitter irony that Sheehy-Skeffington, of all people, should have been murdered during the 1916 Rising by an Anglo-Irish officer of the British army, who had an insane evangelical conviction that his violent actions were directed by God. Captain Colthurst's background, religious fanaticism and position in the army weirdly represented some of the singular forces in Irish history which were locked in combat on that date.

In James Connolly's life and writings the political history of twentieth-century Ireland achieves a lucid and tragic form. He, more than any other, tried to blend nationalism and socialism into republicanism and, more than any other, had to choose to give priority to one (nationalism) in the hope that it would further the cause of the other (socialism). It did not. In addition, having seen the official violence of the Lockout in 1913 and of the outbreak of World War I, he had to decide if insurrectionary violence against the established powers would reveal to the Irish, many of whom had already died in the war, the true nature of the state which treated the workers so brutally (as in the 1907 strike in Belfast as well as in 1913 in Dublin) and brainwashed them so effectively that they gave their lives for the sake of its survival. It is in Connolly even more than in Patrick Pearse that we see the force of the argument that a violent and effective system can be altered only by violent action. In this belief he was, no doubt, influenced by the spectacular Dublin career of James Larkin, who had made it clear that a native capitalist class was as savage towards the mass of the people as the imperial power itself. It was the co-operation between these men that made nationalism suspect as an ideology; but it was the need to defeat or challenge the imperial power, having lost the first battle to the native capitalists in 1913, which made nationalism a necessary ally in the socialist-republican programme.

It has often been said in recent years that 1916 gave to violent rebellion a deathly and legitimizing glamour that has not yet faded away. But it was the executions of the 1916 leaders that gave them a retrospective heroism. It was the violence of the state which legitimized 1916. Equally, in the War of Independence, Black-and-Tan atrocities gave additional moral authority to the IRA. The position in the Civil War was more complex, but the actions of the national army of the Free State did cast doubt on the authority of the new state to claim moral supremacy for the system of law and order, even though the catholic church did all it could to bolster that claim. In the 1930s, Eamon de Valera used the IRA to help him defeat the fascist Blueshirts, and then, once that threat had been removed, outlawed the organization. Since 1968, in Northern Ireland, the demonising of the 'men of violence' has been only partially effective because of the unpunished violence of the police and army, the obvious suppression of damning information on all sorts of issues — the Stalker affair, the Kincora scandal, the Widgery Tribunal, the Compton Report — and the corruption of the legal system by the introduction of various forms of emergency legislation and by the discriminatory sentencing-policies of carefully chosen judges. The sorry history of emergency legislation north and south, under British and under Irish rule, is a testimony to the difficulty of concealing the iron hand of power inside the velvet glove of the law. A colonizing power has a peremptory way with the law, and a community acclimatized to the law's peremptory way with them has, as part of its memory and heritage, a scepticism about its moralizing claims. It is true that there is in Ireland a species of double-think about violence; but it has been learned from harsh experience of the link between political power and the manipulation of the legal system for the sake of retaining power in the name of justice. The critical years 1916–22 and 1968 to the present day reinforced that scepticism.

Therefore, when Connolly joined with Pearse in 1916, it seemed that socialism had sacrificed its international ideals to a local, Gaelic nationalism and that the Left and the Right had combined to give to violent rebellion a do-or-die glamour, which made constitutional nationalism seem pallid and ineffective. The failure of the Irish Parliamentary Party, from the death of Parnell in 1891 to the recruiting speech by his successor John Redmond at Woodenbridge in 1914, committing Irish volunteers to the blood-bath of the trenches, was a crucial moulding factor in the emergence of the gunman as hero. The man who epitomized that heroism was Michael Collins. Yet his career itself displays the subtle and treacherous interplay between the guerrilla or freedom-fighter (who is also seen as a gunman and murderer by his opponents) and the statesman. To become a statesman is, as the name implies, to settle finally for the legitimacy of a state; in effect, in doing so, the statesman forgoes all the questioning of what constitutes legitimacy which had been central to his previous career as guerrilla. Those who do not so settle see him as a traitor to the cause of the 'republic', the unrealized and perhaps unrealizable entity in which power and authority will be as one, in which everything that smacks of compromise and negotiation will be forgotten and the false status of the Pharisee will be exposed before the true worth of the Publican (or re-Publican). This desperate search for purity, for the political thing-in-itself, was focused by the Treaty (1921) and by the earlier Government of Ireland Act (1920). de Valera was its metaphysician-in-chief; Collins was his alter ego, the swashbuckling guerrilla and pragmatic statesman. The metaphysician won. The pure idea of the Republic survived, and the long and tortuous process of fumigating it of any connection with Britain began — through the trade war of the 1930s with Britain, the repudiation of the land annuities, the 1936 External Relations Act, the 1937 Constitution and the policy of neutrality in World War II. Yet, when the climax came, it was John A. Costello and the Inter-Party government which brought it on. Costello finally gave the Republic its name in 1949; the moment he did so, the British government replied with the Ireland Act of 1949, which ratified partition more emphatically than ever before (or since) and left the Republic to ponder the difference between its rhetorical vision of itself and the actuality of the divide between itself and Northern Ireland.

The Irish Free State, Eire, the Twenty-Six Counties (with its opposing Six Counties, Ulster, Northern Ireland) was, in one sense, a stable, because homogeneous, political entity. But it was also, in another sense, as uncertain about its status as it was about its name(s). de Valera's reply to Churchill's post-war attack on Irish neutrality is a notable and dignified rebuke. Churchill's ballooning rhetoric was always vulnerable to a deflationary response; de Valera delivered it with a nicely judged mildness. But his own version of the ideal Ireland, broadcast in a speech in 1934, is imbued with a Fenian pastoralism of the sort made popular by Charles Kickham's novel, *Knocknagow*, in 1873. The comely youths of that vision belong to the pure republic. They are figures in a literary landscape and, oddly enough, by the 1930s they have become, in their idealized forms, ideological realities.

In the meantime, Connolly's embattled dispute between nationalism and socialism was resumed by those radical members of the IRA who had been marginalized by de Valera's decision to enter Dáil Éireann and, thereby to betray the Republic, which had announced its plans in the Democratic

Programme of the First Dáil in 1919. It is a well-known but not sufficiently repeated fact that Ireland, between 1916 and 1930, lost a whole generation of potential leaders. Those executed in 1916, killed in the War of Independence, killed in action, executed or assassinated in the Civil War and after, those who emigrated in disillusion or under political pressure in the 1920s, constituted a desolate loss. Michael Collins, Liam Mellowes, Kevin O'Higgins, Sir Horace Plunkett, Liam Lynch and Arthur Griffith make a list of those who died or emigrated that may be taken to represent the range of the random casualties among the political leadership. Others suffered a form of exile-at-home. Many writers — Austin Clarke, Flann O'Brien, Samuel Beckett — have borne witness to this. It also affected politically dedicated people like George Gilmore, Peadar O'Donnell and Frank Ryan, all of whom founded Saor Éire in 1931, organized the Republican Congress of 1934 and consistently attempted to revive republicanism by reminding it of the importance of its socialist and internationalist component, more vital than ever after the triumph of a church-directed provincial nationalism and during the rise of fascism in Europe. Although the Republican Congress had no immediate, substantial effect, it remained as an important moment and its charter survived as a decisive document for the future development of the left-wing of the IRA in the 1960s and its initial association with the Northern Ireland Civil Rights Movement. Just as the rump of the IRA moved leftwards, so did an important section of the Cumann na nGaedhal party move right. Its attraction to Italian fascism (represented below by an excerpt from an article by Michael Tierney, later president of University College, Dublin) interlinked with its anxiety to effect an intellectual revival in catholicism. The result was a brief flare of popularity for the idea of the corporate state and a flurry of paramilitary activity by the Army Comrades Association, better-known as the Blueshirts. But these movements were ultimately only reflections of the European crisis of the 1930s. They gave an added sharpness to the internecine political divisions within the country, but the circumstances in which fascism and international Marxism could flourish did not then obtain.

The economic revival of the 1960s was led by Seán Lemass. It was his visit to Captain Terence O'Neill in Stormont in 1965 which, together with the 1966 celebrations of the fiftieth anniversary of 1916, precipitated the crisis in Northern Ireland and the emergence of Ian Paisley and John Hume as the predominant political figures on the island for the next twenty years. With the outbreak of violence in the North, sectarianism returns as the most intractable and characteristic feature of a colonial system. Practised as a policy by the Tory and Unionist Party since the late nineteenth century, protestant sectarianism was effective in preventing the granting of Home Rule to Ireland before World War I, in preventing any consolidated opposition between catholic and protestant workers, particularly in the 1930s, and in sustaining a system of political, social and economic discrimination against the catholic minority from 1922 onwards. The Orange Order, the Unionist Party and the protestant churches formed a solid alliance which, supported by Britain and intensified by World War II and, later, by the IRA border campaign of 1956–62, successfully maintained protestant hegemony until 1968. When the collapse came, it was initially swift and bloody. By 1972, the local (Home Rule) government at Stormont had gone, new anti-discriminatory legislation was beginning to appear on the statute book (though rarely getting much farther than that) and the war between the IRA and the security forces (British army, Royal Ulster Constabulary, Ulster Defence Regiment) was on. In addition, a sectarian campaign of assassination, initially favoured by protestant paramilitaries (who to date have killed 650 catholics) had begun. The spasmodic violence, so far more than five times bloodier than the Irish Civil War, could continue for the foreseeable future. It is in this context that the excerpts from Garret FitzGerald, Charles J. Haughey, John Hume and Gerry Adams should be read.

FitzGerald tried to change the political game by switching the usual charge of sectarianism from the protestant north to the catholic south and its 1937 Constitution. His northern policy was predicated on the belief that changes in the Republic on issues like the position of the catholic church, divorce, contraception, abortion, along with increased social welfare benefits, would clear the way for an amicable conjuncture between the partitioned states. Central to this policy was the assumption that the British would be glad to leave Northern Ireland if Northern Ireland avowed that it would be glad to leave them. Not only was such an avowal not forthcoming then or likely ever to be, the assumption had little to support it other than the vaguest of assurances by the British government. When the assurances were less vague, as in the case of the Labour Party in opposition, they nevertheless became meaningless when the Labour Party gained power. FitzGerald's 'constitutional crusade' of 1981 and his constant advocacy of a 'pluralist' culture finally took a specific, if merely consultative, form in the New Ireland Forum of 1983. Its proposals were so bluntly repudiated by the British premier, Margaret Thatcher, that all the assumptions of the FitzGerald policy seemed to lie in ruins. Apparently Britain wanted to stay after all; all the pluralism in the world would not make the Republic more endearing. To help the British defend the Northern Irish border against the IRA (itself largely a Northern organisation) seemed to be the Republic's only useful purpose. A year later, the Anglo-Irish Agreement appeared to have altered that. The Republic recognized Northern Ireland as a separate state and in return had a consultative and advisory role in Northern affairs. This infuriated both unionists and republicans and so far has led to no visible substantial change in the situation.

Charles Haughey, perhaps the most resourceful politician in Ireland, has repeatedly called Northern Ireland 'a failed entity' and seeks negotiation about its future on that basis. There is, in his policy and in the attitudes of his party, Fianna Fáil, a recognition that a political crisis is not susceptible to genial gestures, like those of FitzGerald. It is a matter of interest and power, and most of the power is in the hands of the British. Haughey has still to show that he knows where the British see their interest to lie. But, in the interval, he skilfully combines de Valera's meticulously crafted republicanism with Seán Lemass's best possible blend of cosmopolitan modernity and ancestral loyalty for present-day Ireland.

John Hume, leader of the (catholic) Social and Democratic Labour Party (SDLP), sees the central issue in Northern Ireland as what it has been since the Ireland Act of 1949 and in subsequent assurances by the British to the unionists — that their constitutional position within the United Kingdom is guaranteed. Given that, why should they negotiate with anyone who wishes to see that position weakened or broken? As a consequence, there is no constitutional air to breathe; thus the militants, especially the IRA, are given their opportunity to make the running. By immense efforts abroad in the European Community, the USA and in Britain, Hume has succeeded in making himself the spokesman for rational and peaceful change in Northern Ireland, thereby making a sharp contrast with Ian Paisley, whose powerful, narrow evangelicalism has earned him an international reputation as a bigot and a demagogue.

The republican view, here represented in two different forms by Seán MacBride and Gerry Adams, the leader of Provisional Sinn Féin, is rooted in one central conviction — that the British system in Ireland is now, always has been and always will be dependent for its survival on the maintenance of injustice and division. For Adams, but not for MacBride, that legitimizes violent rebellion against it, especially because that system is in itself violent to a far greater extent than any resistance ever brought against it. However, all wars are propaganda as well as military exercises and Adams shows, with a plain force, what a creation of propaganda systems the Peace Movement in Northern Ireland was.

It is now fashionable to discuss as too simple-minded any 'colonial' analysis of the existing crisis in Ireland. This derives, in part, from an assumption of what is still sometimes called 'revisionist' history — that is to say that a recognition of the unique complexities of a specific situation precludes the possibility of interpreting it satisfactorily in the light of an 'ideology'. Ideology is something abstract, schematic, biased and is an illness to which revisionist historians are themselves immune, even though they sing in chorus, if not in unison, against anything that threatens to upset the established structures. What is most interesting is the relationship between the new history and the development of the Northern crisis. As they become more strained, as interpretation increasingly has to interpret its own action in order to accommodate political developments, we may see the spectral colonialism of the Northern Irish situation finally exorcised by those who at the moment fail to see it because they have been taught not to believe in the ghosts of ideology.

HORACE PLUNKETT

(1854–1932)

from: IRELAND IN THE NEW CENTURY (1904)

[Plunkett, as well-known for his lack of tact as for his energy and dedication, wrote and said many things others would have preferred not to hear. In a period when the so-called national character was being assiduously burnished for the purposes of self-admiration, Plunkett pointed out that catholicism might not be the most enabling of religions for the spirit of independence and enterprise he was so anxious to promote. This involved him in a dispute, part of which is pursued in the next item in this section. Plunkett went to some pains to give a historical explanation for his diagnosis. His participation in the Co-operative Movement was in itself sufficient testimony to his good faith. Nevertheless, Irish catholicism was increasingly becoming integrated with the notion of Irish 'Celticism'. Plunkett's commentary has similarities with the critique of Ireland that is found in Synge's *The Playboy of the Western World* and in the work of James Joyce. It was no more welcome from them than from him. The importance of what he writes is not to be denied, even though the categorical stereotypes of protestant and catholic, Irish and Celt, English and Anglo-Saxon are in themselves suspect.]

CHAPTER IV

THE INFLUENCE OF RELIGION UPON SECULAR LIFE IN IRELAND

In the preceding chapter I attempted to estimate the influence of our political leaders as a potential and as an actual force. I come now to the second great influence upon the thought and action of the Irish people, the influence of religion, especially the power exercised by the priests and by the unrivalled organisation of the Roman Catholic Church. I do not share the pessimism which sees in this potent influence nothing but the shackles of mediævalism restraining its adherents from falling into line with the progress of the age. I shall, indeed, have to admit much of what is charged against the clerical leaders of popular thought in Ireland, but I shall be able to show, I hope, that these leaders are largely the product of a situation which they themselves did not create, and that not only are they as susceptible as are the political leaders to the influences of progressive movements, but that they can be more readily induced to take part in their promotion. In no other country in the world, probably, is religion so dominant an element in the daily life of the people as in Ireland, and certainly nowhere else has the minister of religion so wide and undisputed an authority. It is obvious, therefore, that, however foreign such a theme may *prima facie* appear to the scope and aim of the present volume, I have no choice but to analyse frankly and as fully as my personal experience justifies, what I conceive to be the true nature, the salutary limits, and the actual scope of clerical influence in this country.

But before I can discuss what I may call the religious situation, there is one fundamental question — a question which will appear somewhat strange to anyone not in touch with Irish life — which I must, with a view to a general agreement on essentials, submit to some of my co-religionists. In all seriousness I would ask, whether in their opinion the Roman Catholic Church in Ireland is to be tolerated. If the answer be in the negative, I can only reply that any efforts to stamp out the Roman Catholic faith would fail as they did in the past; and the practical minds among those I am now addressing must admit that in toleration alone is to be found the solution of that part of the Irish difficulty which is due to sectarian animosities.

This brings us face to face with the question, What is religious toleration — I do not mean as a pious sentiment which we are all conscious of ourselves possessing in a truer sense than that in which it is possessed by others, but rather toleration as an essential of the liberty which we Protestants enjoy under the British Constitution, and boast that all other creeds equally enjoy? Perhaps I had better state simply how I answer this question in my own mind. Toleration by the Irish minority, in regard to the religious faith and ecclesiastical system of the

Irish majority, implies that we admit the right of Rome to say what Roman Catholics shall believe and what outward forms they shall observe, and that they shall not suffer before the State for these beliefs and observances. I do not think exception can be taken to the statement that toleration in this narrow sense cannot be refused consistently with the fundamental principles of British government.

Now, however, comes a less obvious, but, as I think, no less essential condition of toleration in the sense above indicated. The Roman Catholic Hierarchy claim the right to exercise such supervision and control over the education of their flock as will enable them to safeguard faith and morals as preached and practised by their Church. I concede this second claim as a necessary corollary of the first. Having lived most of my life among Roman Catholics — two branches of my own family belonging to that religion — I am aware that this control is an essential part of the whole fabric of Roman Catholicism. Whether the basis of authority upon which that system is founded be in its origin divine or human is beside the point. If we profess to tolerate the faith and religious system of the majority of our countrymen we must at least concede the conditions essential to the maintenance of both the one and the other, unless our tolerance is to be a sham . . . .

I need hardly say that in criticising religious systems and their ministers I have not the faintest intention of entering on the discussion of doctrinal issues. I am, of course, here concerned with only those aspects of the religious situation which bear directly on secular life. I am endeavouring, it must be remembered, to arrive at a comprehensive and accurate appreciation of the chief influences which mould the character, guide the thought, and, therefore, direct the action of the Irish people as citizens of this world and of their own country. From this standpoint let us try to make a dispassionate survey of Protestantism and Roman Catholicism in Ireland, and see wherein their votaries fulfil, or fail to fulfil, their mission in advancing our common civilisation. Let us examine, in a word, not merely the direct influence which the creed of each of the two sections of Irishmen produces on the industrial character of its adherents, but also its indirect effects upon the mutual relations and regard for each other of Protestants and Roman Catholics.

Protestantism has its stronghold in the great industrial centres of the North and among the Presbyterian farmers of five or six Ulster counties. These communities, it is significant to note, have developed the essentially strenuous qualities which, no doubt, they brought from England and Scotland. In city life their thrift, industry, and enterprise, unsurpassed in the United Kingdom, have built up a world-wide commerce. In rural life they have drawn the largest yield from relatively infertile soil. Such, in brief, is the achievement of Ulster Protestantism in the realm of industry. It is a story of which, when a united Ireland becomes more than a dream, all Irishmen will be proud.

But there is, unhappily, another side to the picture. This industrial life, otherwise so worthily cultivated, is disturbed by manifestations of religious bigotry which sadly tarnish the glory of the really heroic deeds they are intended to commemorate. It is impossible for any close observer of these deplorable exhibitions to avoid the conclusion that the embers of the old fires are too often fanned by men who are actuated by motives, which, when not other than religious, are certainly based upon an unworthy conception of religion. I am quite aware that it is only a small and decreasing minority of my co-religionists who are open to the charge of intolerance, and that the former extravagances of the July celebrations are now less frequent.[1] But this bigotry is so notorious, as for instance in the exclusion of Roman Catholics from many responsible positions, that it unquestionably reacts most unfavourably upon the general relations between the two creeds throughout the whole of Ireland. The existence of such a spirit of suspicion and hatred, from whatever motive it emanates, is bound to retard our progress as a people towards the development of a healthy and balanced national life . . . .

It is, however, with the religion of the majority of the Irish people and with its influence upon the industrial character of its adherents that I am chiefly concerned. Roman Catholicism strikes an outsider as being in some of its tendencies non-economic, if not actually anti-economic. These tendencies have, of course, much fuller play when they act on a people whose education has (through no fault of their own) been retarded or stunted. The fact is not in dispute,

1. Ulster protestants annually celebrate the battle of the Boyne on 12 July. The marches and processions, dominated by the Orange Order, are exercises in triumphalism and provocation – more so now than when Plunkett wrote.

but the difficulty arises when we come to apportion the blame between ignorance on the part of the people and a somewhat one-sided religious zeal on the part of large numbers of their clergy. I do not seek to do so with any precision here. I am simply adverting to what has appeared to me, in the course of my experience in Ireland, to be a defect in the industrial character of Roman Catholics which, however caused, seems to me to have been intensified by their religion. The reliance of that religion on authority, its repression of individuality, and its complete shifting of what I may call the moral centre of gravity to a future existence — to mention no other characteristics — appear to be calculated, unless supplemented by other influences, to check the growth of the qualities of initiative and self-reliance, especially amongst a people whose lack of education unfits them for resisting the influence of what may present itself to such minds as a kind of fatalism with resignation as its paramount virtue.

It is true that one cannot expect of any church or religion, as a condition of its acceptance, that it will furnish an economic theory; and it is also true that Roman Catholicism has, at different periods of history, advantageously affected economic conditions, even if it did not act from distinctively economic motives — for example, by its direct influence in the suppression of slavery* and its creation of the mediæval craft guilds. It may, too, be admitted that during the Middle Ages, when Roman Catholicism was freer than now to manifest its influence in many directions, owing to its practically unchallenged supremacy, it favoured, when it did not originate, many forms of sound economic activity, and was, to say the least, abreast of the time in its conception of the working of economic causes. But from the time when the Reformation, by its demand for what we Protestants conceive to be a simpler Christianity, drove Roman Catholicism back, if I may use the expression, on its first line of defence, and constrained it to look to its distinctively spiritual heritage, down to the present day, it has seemed to stand strangely aloof from any contact with individual and economic issues. When we consider that in this period Adam Smith[2] lived and died, the industrial revolution was effected, and the world-market opened, it is not surprising that we do not find Roman Catholic countries in the van of economic progress, or even the Roman Catholic element in Protestant countries, as a rule, abreast of their fellow countrymen. It would, however, be an error to ignore some notable exceptions to this generalisation. In Belgium, in France, in parts of Germany and Austria, and in the north of Italy economic thought is making headway amongst Roman Catholics, and the solution of social problems is being advanced by Roman Catholic laymen and clergymen. Even in these countries, however, much remains to be done. The revolution in the industrial order, and its consequences, such as the concentration of immense populations within restricted areas, have brought with them social and moral evils that must be met with new weapons. In the interests of religion itself, principles first expounded to a Syrian community with the most elementary physical needs and the simplest of avocations, have to be taught in their application to the conditions of the most complex social organisation and economic life. Taking people as we find them, it may be said with truth that their lives must be wholesome before they can be holy, and while a voluntary asceticism may have its justification, it behoves a Church to see that its members, while fully acknowledging the claims of another life, should develop the qualities which make for well-being in this life. In fact, I believe that the influence of Christianity upon social progress will be best maintained by co-ordinating these spiritual and economic ideals in a philosophy of life broader and truer than any to which the nations have yet attained.

What I have just been saying with regard to Roman Catholicism generally, in relation to economic doctrines and industrial progress, applies, of course, with a hundred fold pertinence to the case of Ireland. Between the enactment of the first Penal Laws and the date of Roman Catholic Emancipation,[3] Irish Roman Catholics were, to put it mildly, afforded scant opportunity, in their own country, of developing economic virtues or achieving industrial success. Ruthlessly deprived of education, are they to be blamed if they did not use the newly acquired

* *'Pro salute animae meae'* was, I am reminded, the consideration usually expressed in the old charters of manumission.

2. Adam Smith (1723–90), Scottish economist and philosopher, whose book *An Inquiry into the Nature and Causes of the Wealth of Nations* (1776) advocated a system of 'natural liberty' based on the free division of labour and largely unimpeded by state intervention.
3. i.e. from 1691 to 1829.

facilities to the best advantage? With their religion looked on as the badge of legal and social inferiority, was it any wonder that priests and people alike, while clinging with unexampled fidelity to their creed, remained altogether cut off from the current of material prosperity? Excluded, as they were, not merely from social and political privileges, but from the most ordinary civil rights, denied altogether the right of ownership of real property, and restricted in the possession of personality, is it any wonder that they are not today in the van of industrial and commercial progress? Nay, more, was it to have been expected that the character of a people so persecuted and ostracised should have come out of the ordeal of centuries with its adaptability and elasticity unimpaired? That would have been impossible. Those who are intimate with the Roman Catholic people of Ireland, and at the same time familiar with their history, will recognise in their character and mental outlook many an inheritance of that epoch of serfdom. I speak, of course, of the mass, for I am not unmindful of many exceptions to this generalisation.

But I must now pass on to a more definite consideration of the present action and attitude of the Irish Roman Catholic clergy towards the economic, educational, and other issues discussed in this book. The reasons which render such a consideration necessary are obvious. Even if we include Ulster, three quarters of the Irish people are Roman Catholics, while, excluding the Northern province, quite nine-tenths of the population belong to that religion. Again, the three thousand clergymen of that denomination exercise an influence over their flocks not merely in regard to religious matters, but in almost every phase of their lives and conduct, which is, in its extent and character, quite unique, even, I should say, amongst Roman Catholic communities. To a Protestant, this authority seems to be carried very far beyond what the legitimate influence of any clergy over the lay members of their congregation should be. We are, however, dealing with a national life explicable only by reference to a very exceptional and gloomy history of religious persecution. What I may call the secular shortcomings of the Roman Catholics in Ireland cannot be fairly judged except as the results of a series of enactments by which they were successively denied almost all means of succeeding as citizens of this world.

From such study as I have been able to give to the history of their Church, I have come to the conclusion that the immense power of the Irish Roman Catholic clergy has been singularly little abused. I think it must be admitted that they have not exhibited in any marked degree bigotry towards Protestants. They have not put obstacles in the way of the Roman Catholic majority choosing Protestants for political leaders, and it is significant that refugees, such as the Palatines, from Catholic persecutions in Europe, found at different times a home amongst the Roman Catholic people of Ireland.[4] My own experience, too, if I may again refer to that, distinctly proves that it is no disadvantage to a man to be a Protestant in Irish political life, and that where opposition is shown to him by Roman Catholics it is almost invariably on political, social, or agrarian, but not on religious grounds.

A charge of another kind has of late been often brought against the Roman Catholic clergy, which has a direct bearing upon the economic aspect of this question. Although, as I read Irish history, the Roman Catholic priesthood have, in the main, used their authority with personal disinterestedness, if not always with prudence or discretion, their undoubted zeal for religion has, on occasion, assumed forms which enlightened Roman Catholics, including high dignitaries of that Church, think unjustifiable on economic grounds, and discourage even from a religious standpoint. Excessive and extravagant church-building in the heart and at the expense of poor communities has been objected to on the surely not irreligious ground that the best monument of any clergyman's influence and earnestness must always be found in the moral character and the spiritual fibre of his flock, and not in the marbles and mosaics of a gaudy edifice. If, however, in some cases the sense of proportion has been obscured by a misdirected zeal, the excesses complained of cannot be fairly judged without some reference to the past. They may be regarded as an extreme reaction from the penal times, when the hunted *soggarth*[5] had to celebrate the Mass in cabins and caves on the mountain side — a reaction the converse of which was witnessed in Protestant England when Puritanism rose up against Anglicanism in the seventeenth century . . . .

4. An ecclesiastical palatinate was established in Tipperary in 1328.
5. Irish, *sagart*: priest.

But it is not alone extravagant church building which in a country so backward as Ireland, shocks the economic sense. The multiplication — in inverse ratio to a declining population — of costly and elaborate monastic and conventual institutions involving what in the aggregate must be an enormous annual expenditure for maintenance, is difficult to reconcile with the known conditions of the country. Most of these institutions, it is true, carry on educational work, often, as in the case of the Christian Brothers[6] and some colleges and convents, of an excellent kind. Many of them render great services to the poor, and especially to the sick poor. But, none the less, it seems to me, their growth in number and size is anomalous. I cannot believe that so large an addition to the classes, technically called unproductive, is economically sound, and I have no doubt at all that the competition with lay teachers of celibates 'living in community' is excessive and educationally injurious. Fully admitting the importance of religion in education, I still hold that teachers who have renounced the world and withdrawn from contact with its stress and strain are at a great disadvantage in moulding the characters of youths who will have to take their part in the hard struggle of modern industrial life . . . .

But, after all, these criticisms are, for the purposes of my argument, of minor relevance and importance. The real matter in which the direct and personal responsibility of the Roman Catholic clergy seems to me to be involved, is the character and *morale* (still using the terms in the restricted sense which I have, I hope, made sufficiently clear) of the people of this country. No reader of this book will accuse me of attaching too little weight to the influence of historical causes on the present state, social, economic and political, of Ireland, but even when I have given full consideration to all such influences I still think that, with their unquestioned authority in religion, and their almost equally undisputed influence in education, the Roman Catholic clergy cannot be exonerated from some responsibility in regard to Irish character as we find it today. Are they, I would ask, satisfied with that character? I cannot think so. The impartial observer will, I fear, find amongst a majority of our people a striking absence of self-reliance and moral courage; an entire lack of serious thought on public questions; a listlessness and apathy in regard to economic improvement which amount to a form of fatalism; and, in backward districts, a survival of superstition, which saps all strength of will and purpose — and all this, too, amongst a people singularly gifted by nature with good qualities of mind and heart . . . .

The methods by which clerical influence is wielded in the inculcation of chastity may be criticised from exactly the same standpoint as that from which I have found it necessary to deal with the question of temperance. Here the success of the Irish priesthood is, considering the conditions of peasant life, and the fire of the Celtic temperament, absolutely unique. No one can deny that almost the entire credit of this moral achievement belongs to the Roman Catholic clergy. It may be said that the practice of a virtue, even if the motive be of an emotional kind, becomes a habit, and that habit proverbially develops into a second nature. With this view of moral evolution I am in entire accord; but I would ask whether the evolution has not reached a stage where a gradual relaxation of the disciplinary measures by which chastity is insured might be safely allowed without any danger of lowering the high standard of continence which is general in Ireland and which of course it is of supreme importance to maintain . . . .

My position, then, towards the influence of the Roman Catholic clergy — and this influence is a matter of vital importance to the understanding of Irish problems — may now be clearly defined. While recognising to the full that large numbers of the Irish Roman Catholic clergy have in the past exercised undue influence in purely political questions, and, in many other matters, social, educational, and economic, have not, as I see things, been on the side of progress, I hold that their influence is now, more than ever before, essential for improving the condition of the most backward section of the population. Therefore I feel it to be both the duty and the strong interest of my Protestant fellow-countrymen to think much less of the religious differences which divide them from Roman Catholics, and much more of their common citizenship and their common cause. I also hold with equal strength and sincerity

6. The Irish Christian Brothers, a catholic teaching order, was founded in 1802 by Edmund Ignatius Rice. They provided elementary education for the poor and remained outside the state-run National Schools system. In the twentieth century they expanded into secondary education and have communities in various parts of the world. The Brothers are not priests; they take vows of chastity, poverty and obedience and wear a religious habit.

to the belief, which I have already expressed, that the shortcomings of the Roman Catholic clergy are largely to be accounted for, not by any innate tendency on their part towards obscurantism, but by the sad history of Ireland in the past. I would appeal to those of my co-religionists who think otherwise to suspend their judgement for a time. That Roman Catholicism is firmly established in Ireland is a fact of the situation which they must admit, and as this involves the continued powerful influence of the priesthood upon the character of the people, it is surely good policy by liberality and fair dealing, especially in the matter of education, to turn this influence towards the upbuilding of our national life.

To sum up the influence of religion and religious controversy in Ireland, as it presents itself from the only standpoint from which I have approached the matter in this chapter, namely, that of material, social, and intellectual progress, I find that while the Protestants have given, and continue to give, a fine example of thrift and industry to the rest of the nation, the attitude of a section of them towards the majority of their fellow-countrymen has been a bigoted and unintelligent one. On the other hand, I have learned from practical experience amongst the Roman Catholic people of Ireland that, while more free from bigotry, in the sense in which that word is usually applied, they are apathetic, thriftless, and almost non-industrial, and that they especially require the exercise of strengthening influences on their moral fibre. I have dealt with their shortcomings at much greater length than with those of Protestants, because they have much more bearing on the subject matter of this book. North and South have each virtues which the other lacks; each has much to learn from the other; but the home of the strictly civic virtues and efficiencies is in Protestant Ireland. The work of the future in Ireland will be to break down in social intercourse the barriers of creed as well as those of race, politics, and class, and thus to promote the fruitful contact of North and South, and the concentration of both on the welfare of their common country. In the case of those of us, of whatever religious belief, who look to a future for our country commensurate with the promise of her undeveloped resources both of intellect and soil, it is of the essence of our hope that the qualities which are in great measure accountable for the actual economic and educational backwardness of so many of our fellow-countrymen, and for the intolerance of too many who are not backward in either respect, are not purely racial or sectarian, but are the transitory growth of days and deeds which we must all try to forget if our work for Ireland is to endure.

[Plunkett, like many liberal unionists, welcomes what he here calls 'the Gaelic Revival' — i.e. the Gaelic League, founded in 1893 for the revival and preservation of Irish as a spoken language. Like Douglas Hyde, one of its co-founders, Plunkett hoped that a non-political and non-sectarian movement would offer common cultural ground to all Irish people. The League expanded rapidly, had 600 branches by 1908, taught evening classes, held social functions and generally gave a stimulus to the country's social and cultural life. By 1915, the League had become a political force, dedicated to the independence of Ireland. Plunkett is naive to hope that the animosities of Irish life could be dissolved in a co-operative cultural programme. Still, the urge to find some means of overcoming these animosities is, in itself, part of the intellectual and political history of this period. The League remains alive to the present day.]

CHAPTER VI

THROUGH THOUGHT TO ACTION

. . . Among these new forces in Irish life there is one which has been greatly misunderstood; and yet to its influence during the last few years much of the 'transformation scene' in the drama of the Irish Question is really due. It deserves more than a passing notice here, because, while its aims as formulated appear somewhat restricted, it unquestionably tends in practice towards that national object of paramount importance, the strengthening of character. I refer to the movement known as the Gaelic Revival. Of this movement I am myself but an outside observer, having been forced to devote nearly all my time and energies to a variety of attempts which aim at the doing in the industrial sphere of very much the same work as that which the Gaelic movement attempts in the intellectual sphere — the rehabilitation of Ireland from within. But in the course of my work of agricultural and industrial development I naturally came across this new intellectual force and found that when it began to take effect, so far from diverting the minds of the peasantry from the practical affairs of life, it made them distinctly more amenable to the teaching of the dry economic doctrine of which I was an apostle. The reason for this is plain enough to me now, though, like all my theories about Ireland, the truth came to me from observation and practical experience rather than as the result of philosophic speculation. For the co-operative movement depended for its success upon a two-fold achievement. In order to get it started at all, its principles and working details had to be grasped by the Irish peasant mind and commended to his intelligence. Its further development and its hopes of permanence depend upon the strengthening of character, which, I must repeat, is the foundation of all Irish progress.

The Irish Agricultural Organisation Society[1] exerts its influence — a now established and rapidly-growing influence — mainly through the medium of associations. The Gaelic movement, on the other hand, acts more directly upon the individual, and the two forces are therefore in a sense complementary to each other. Both will be seen to be playing an important part — I should say a necessary part — in the reconstruction of our national life. At any rate, I feel that it is necessary to my argument that I should explain to those who are as ill-informed about the Gaelic revival as I was myself until its practical usefulness was demonstrated to me, what exactly seems to be the most important outcome of the work of that movement.

The Gaelic League, which defines its objects as 'The preservation of Irish as the national language of Ireland and the extension of its use as a spoken tongue; the study and publication of existing Irish literature and the cultivation of a modern literature in Irish,' was formed in 1893. Like the Agricultural Organisation Society, the Gaelic League is declared by its constitution to be 'strictly non-political and non-sectarian,' and, like it, has been the object of much suspicion, because severance from politics in Ireland has always seemed to the politician the most active form of enmity. . . . It resembled the agricultural movement also in the fact that it made very little headway during the first few years of its existence. But it had a nucleus of workers with new ideas for the intellectual regeneration of Ireland. In face of much apathy they persisted with their propaganda, and they have at last succeeded in making their ideas understood. So much is evident from the rapidly-increasing number of affiliated branches of the League, which in March, 1903, amounted to 600, almost treble the number registered two years before. But even this does not convey any idea of the influence which the movement exerts. Within the past year the teaching of the Irish language has been introduced into no less than 1,300 National Schools. In 1900 the number of schools in which Irish was taught was only about 140. The statement that our people do not read books is generally accepted as true, yet the sale of the League publications during one year reached nearly a quarter of a million copies. These results cannot be left unconsidered by anybody who wishes to understand the psychology of the Irish mind. The movement can truly claim to have effected the conversion of a large amount of intellectual apathy into genuine intellectual activity.

The declared objects of the League — the popularising of the national language and literature — do not convey, perhaps, an adequate conception of its actual work, or of the causes of its popularity. It seeks to develop the intellectual, moral, and social life of the Irish people from within, and it is doing excellent work in the cause of temperance. Its president, Dr. Douglas Hyde, in his evidence given before the University Commission, pointed out that the success of the League was due to its meeting the people half way; that it educated them by giving them something which they could appreciate and assimilate; and that it afforded a proof that people who would not respond to alien educational systems, will respond with eagerness to something they can call their own. The national factor in Ireland has been studiously eliminated from national education, and Ireland is perhaps the only country in Europe where it was part of the settled policy of those who had the guidance of education to ignore the literature, history, arts, and traditions of the people. It was a fatal policy, for it obviously tended to stamp their native country in the eyes of Irishmen with the badge of inferiority and to extinguish the sense of healthy self-respect which comes from the con-

1. Plunkett was the first president of the Irish Agricultural Organization Society, formed in Dublin in 1894. It established its own newspaper, *The Irish Homestead*, in 1895 and successfully spread the ideals of the co-operative movement under the energetic editorship of George Russell (AE).

sciousness of high national ancestry and traditions. This policy, rigidly adhered to for many years, almost extinguished native culture among Irishmen, but it did not succeed in making another form of culture acceptable to them. It dulled the intelligence of the people, impaired their interest in their own surroundings, stimulated emigration by teaching them to look on other countries as more agreeable places to live in, and made Ireland almost a social desert. Men and women without culture or knowledge of literature or of music have succeeded a former generation who were passionately interested in these things, an interest which extended down even to the wayside cabin. The loss of these elevating influences in Irish society probably accounts for much of the arid nature of Irish controversies, while the reaction against their suppression has given rise to those displays of rhetorical patriotism for which the Irish language has found the expressive term *raimeis*,[2] and which (thanks largely to the Gaelic movement) most people now listen to with a painful and half-ashamed sense of their unreality.

The Gaelic movement has brought to the surface sentiments and thoughts which had been developed in Gaelic Ireland through hundreds of years, and which no repression had been able to obliterate altogether, but which still remained as a latent spiritual inheritance in the mind. And now this stream, which has long run underground, has again emerged even stronger than before, because an element of national self-consciousness has been added at its re-emergence. A passionate conviction is gaining ground that if Irish traditions, literature, language, art, music, and culture are allowed to disappear, it will mean the disappearance of the race; and that the education of the country must be nationalised if our social, intellectual, or even our economic position is to be permanently improved.

With this view of the Gaelic movement my own thoughts are in complete accord. It is undeniable that the pride in country justly felt by Englishmen, a pride developed by education and a knowledge of their history, has had much to do with the industrial pre-eminence of England; for the pioneers of its commerce have been often actuated as much by patriotic motives as by the desire for gain. The education of the Irish people has ignored the need for any such historical basis for pride or love of country, and, for my part, I feel sure that the Gaelic League is acting wisely in seeking to arouse such a sentiment, and to found it mainly upon the ages of Ireland's story when Ireland was most Irish.

It is this expansion of the sentiment of nationality outside the domain of party politics — the distinction, so to speak, between nationality and nationalism — which is the chief characteristic of the Gaelic movement. Nationality had come to have no meaning other than a political one, any broader national sentiment having had little or nothing to feed upon. During the last century the spirit of nationality has found no unworthy expression in literature, in the writings of Ferguson, Standish O'Grady and Yeats, which, however, have not been even remotely comparable in popularity with the political journalism in prose and rhyme in which the age has been so fruitful. It has never expressed itself in the arts, and not only has Ireland no representative names in the higher regions of art, but the national deficiency has been felt in every department of industry into which design enters, and where national art-characteristics have a commercial value. The national customs, culture, and recreations which made the country a pleasant place to live in, have almost disappeared, and with them one of the strongest ties which bind people to the country of their birth. The Gaelic revival, as I understand it, is an attempt to supply these deficiencies, to give to Irish people a culture of their own; and I believe that by awakening the feelings of pride, self-respect, and love of country, based on knowledge, every department of Irish life will be invigorated.

Thus it is that the elevating influence upon the individual is exerted. Politics have never awakened initiative among the mass of the people, because there was no programme of action for the individual. Perhaps it is as well for Ireland that such should have been the case, for, as it has been shown, we have had little of the political thought which should be at the back of political action. Political action under present conditions must necessarily be deputed to a few representatives, and after the vote is given, or the cheering at a meeting has ceased, the individual can do nothing but wait, and his lethargy tends to become still deeper. In the Gaelic revival there is a programme of work for the individual; his mind is engaged, thought begets energy, and this energy

2. Irish for 'nonsense'. The journalist D. P. Moran, editor of *The Leader*, popularized the term.

vitalises every part of his nature. This makes for the strengthening of character, and so far from any harm being done to the practical movement, to which I have so often referred, the testimony of my fellow-workers, as well as my own observation, is unanimous in affirming that the influence of the branches of the Gaelic League is distinctly useful whenever it is sought to move the people to industrial or commercial activity.

Many of my political friends cannot believe — and I am afraid that nothing that I can say will make them believe — that the movement is not necessarily, in the political sense, separatist in its sentiment. This impression is, in my opinion, founded on a complete misunderstanding of Anglo-Irish history. Those who look askance at the rise of the Gaelic movement ignore the important fact that there has never been any essential opposition between the English connection and Irish nationality. The Elizabethan chiefs of the sixteenth and the Gaelic poets of the seventeenth and eighteenth centuries, when the relations between the two countries were far worse than they are today, knew nothing of this opposition. The true sentiment of nationality is a priceless heritage of every small nation which has done great things, and had it not largely perished in Ireland, separatist sentiment, the offspring, not of Irish nationality, but of Irish political nationalism, could hardly have survived until today.

But undoubtedly we strike here on a danger to the Gaelic movement, so far at least as that movement is bound up with the future of the Gaelic League; a danger which cannot be left out of account in any estimate of this new force in Irish life. The continuance of the League as a beneficent force, or indeed a force at all, seems to me, as in the case of the co-operative organisation to which I have compared it, to be vitally dependent on a scrupulous observance of that part of its constitution which keeps the door open to Irishmen of every creed or political party. Only thus can the League remain a truly national body, and attract from all classes Irishmen who are capable of forwarding its true policy. I do not think there is much danger of a spirit of sectarian exclusiveness developing itself in a body mainly composed of Roman Catholics whose President is a Protestant.[3] But it cannot be denied that there has been an occasional tendency to interpret the 'no politics' clause of the constitution in a manner which seems hardly fair to Unionists or even to constitutional Home Rulers who may have joined the organisation on the strength of its declaration of political neutrality. If this is not a mere transitory phenomenon its effect will be serious. As a political body the League would immediately sink into insignificance and probably disappear amid a crowd of contending factions. It would certainly cease to fulfil its great function of creating a nationality of the thought and spirit, in which all Irishmen who wish to be anything else than English colonists might aspire to share. . . .

It is, however, on more general grounds that I have, albeit as an outside observer, watched with some anxiety and much gratification the progress of the Gaelic Revival. In the historical evolution of the Irish mind we find certain qualities atrophied, so to speak, by disuse; and to this cause I attribute the past failures of the race in practical life at home. I have shown how politics, religion, and our systems of education have all, in their respective influences upon the people, missed to a large extent, the effect upon character which they should have made it their paramount duty to produce. Nevertheless, whenever the intellect of the people is appealed to by those who know its past, a recuperative power is manifested which shows that its vitality has not been irredeemably impaired. It is because I believe that, on the whole, a right appeal has been made by the Gaelic League that I have borne testimony to its patriotic endeavours.

The question of the Gaelic Revival seems to be really a form of the eternal question of the interdependence of the practical and the ideal in Ireland. Their true relation to each other is one of the hardest lessons the student of our problems has to learn. . . .

I now come to the principles which, it appears to me, must underlie the solution of this problem. The narrative contained in the second part of this book is a record of the efforts made during the last decade of the nineteenth and the first two years of the twentieth century by a small, but now rapidly augmenting group of Irishmen, to pluck the brand of Irish intellect from the burning of the Irish Question. The problem before us was, my readers will now understand, how to make headway in view of the weakness of character to which I have had to attribute

3. Douglas Hyde was a protestant.

the paralysis of our activities in the past. We were quite aware that our progress would at first be slow. But as we were satisfied that the defects of character which stood in the way of economic advancement were due to causes which need no longer be operative, and that the intellect of the people was unimpaired, we faced the problem with confidence.

The practical form which our work took was the launching upon Irish life of a movement of organised self-help, and the subsequent grafting upon this movement of a system of State-aid to the agriculture and industries of the country. I need not here further elaborate this programme, for the steps by which it has been and is being adopted will be presently described in detail. But there is one aspect of the new movement in Ireland which must be understood by those who would grasp the true significance and the human interest of an evolution in our national life, the only recent parallel for which, as far as I am aware, is to be found in Japan: though to my mind the conscious attempt of the Irish people to develop a civilisation of their own is far more interesting than the recent efforts of the Japanese to westernise their institutions.

The problem of mind and character with which we had to deal in Ireland presented this central and somewhat discouraging fact. In practical life the Irish had failed where the English had succeeded, and this was attributed to the lack of certain English qualities which have been undoubtedly essential to success in commerce and in industry from the days of the industrial revolution until a comparatively recent date. It was the individualism of the English economic system during this period which made these qualities indispensable. The lack of these qualities in Irishmen today may be admitted, and the cause of the deficiency has been adequately explained. But those who regard the Irish situation as industrially hopeless probably ignore the fact that there are other qualities, of great and growing importance under modern economic conditions, which can be developed in Irishmen and may form the basis of an industrial system. I refer to the range of qualities which come into play rather in association than in the individual, and to which the term 'associative' is applied. So that although much disparaging criticism of Irish character is based upon the survival in the Celt of the tribal instincts, it is gratifying to be able to show that even from the practical English point of view, our preference for thinking and working in groups may not be altogether a *damnosa hereditas*.[4] If, owing to our deficiency in the individualistic qualities of the English, we cannot at this stage hope to produce many types of the 'economic man' of the economists, we think we see our way to provide, as a substitute, the economic association. If the association succeeds, and by virtue of its financial success becomes permanent, a great change will, in our opinion, be produced on the character of its members. The reflex action upon the individual mind of the habit of doing, in association with others, things which were formerly left undone, or badly done, may be relied upon to have a tonic effect upon the character of the individual. This is, I suppose, the secret of discipline, which, though apparently eliminating volition, seems in weak characters to strengthen the will . . . .

4. 'blighting inheritance'.

MICHAEL O'RIORDAN

(1857–1919)

from: CATHOLICITY AND PROGRESS IN IRELAND (1905)

[Father Michael O'Riordan's reply to Plunkett is effective in one essential respect; it shows that there is no natural link between protestantism and liberty either in Ireland or in the Empire. He gives his own version of Irish history, similar to Plunkett's, but designed to produce a quite different conclusion. Plunkett's linking of progress with material prosperity and with protestantism allows O'Riordan to take the higher spiritual ground, claiming for catholicism all those virtues that are not 'material' and relegating protestantism to the role of maidservant to imperial rapacity. O'Riordan also insinuates a deep affinity between catholic spirituality and the Irish or Celtic spirit. The elements of his response remain, in different combinations, as part of the catholic and nationalist critique of protestantism and colonialism.]

CHAPTER 3

THE CATHOLIC CHURCH AND PROGRESS

. . . This, then, is the process of his [Plunkett's] reasoning. Individuality and self-reliance are necessary for industrial progress. But the reliance of Catholics on authority represses individuality, and checks self-reliance. Therefore, the religion of Roman Catholics is essentially an impediment to industrial progress. Moreover, industrial progress demands the development of the qualities of this life. But Catholicism completely shifts the moral centre of gravity to the other life. Hence the absence of those qualities in Catholics which make for industrial progress.

Now, I might admit all that, and pass it by as being outside the business of the Catholic Church. Even though I granted that Catholicism is an obstacle to industrial progress, there would be no ground for complaint unless it professed, or ought to have professed, to promote the temporal interests of man . . . .

The want which Sir Horace Plunkett finds in Catholicism, any Roman citizen would have found in the teaching of Christ. Any economist of old Rome might object that He made no provision for commercial enterprise, said nothing about the copper or corn trade in the Sermon on the Mount, in fact that His principles tended to tear up by the roots the very idea of Roman citizenship . . . .

The Christian is not obliged to forego wealth, but is warned of its dangers; the Pagan man of material progress must look on wealth as the one thing it behoves him to have, and must try to have it anyhow. To the mind of the Roman Imperialists, the early Christians no doubt wanted that individuality which, we are told, is wanting in Catholics today. Like the Catholicism of today, they placed their centre of gravity in another life. Yet, Roman society contained the germs of decay, and soon fell of its own weight and through its own rottenness. To Christianity fell the task of building up society again, and Christianity succeeded in the task.

Here, then, we have a people, great in peace and war, whose works of art we contemplate with admiration, in whose writers we still study literature, whose orators are models for us, on the writings of whose jurists the laws of modern Europe are based both as to principles and as to procedure. They had not the disadvantage of fixing their centre of gravity in the other life; their thoughts were entirely centred in the concerns of this. They had their agrarian and commercial quarrels as we have now, and able and ardent men amongst them studied the economic systems according to which the issues should be decided, without any reference whatever to the interests of any other life than this. Sir Horace Plunkett, or a man of his temper of mind and bent of will, visiting Rome in those times, would at once discern those 'strenuous qualities,' those 'civic virtues and efficiencies'[1] which make for progress . . . .

1. The phrases are from Plunkett's *Ireland in the New Century* (see above p. 691).

Now, the end of these conquerors, economists, orators, artists, poets, and jurists, whose centre of gravity was quite *in terra firma*, came suddenly and soon; and these uneconomic Glabrios and Clemens and Domitillas whose 'conversation was in heaven,'[2] fostered a new race of manhood out of their dissolution, just as new corn comes up when new elements bring back life to the elements into which the old seed had been corrupted. I set out from that time of social dissolution when Imperial Rome became the easy prey of the Northern Barbarians. Roman civilisation was crushed; society had gone into its primitive elements; ignorance, selfishness, passions supported by brute force tore amongst them all that was left of humanity and whatever relics remained of pagan progress. I begin at that time, because the only form of Christianity which then existed was Roman Catholicism, and because its field of labour was a human wilderness, vast and wild. Catholicism had, at that time, if ever it had, its Mass-idolatry, Image-worship, monkish ignorance, priestly domination, and a rich array of all those Romish superstitions which have been driven into their dark dens of ignorance by the meridian light which the Reformers brought — superstitions such as, we are told, are to be found 'in backward districts' of Ireland today 'sapping all strength of will and purpose.'[3]

Here, then, we can fairly test the tendency of Catholicism in relation to human progress. Popery could do what it pleased in those days; and let the history of Europe for the next thousand years bear witness to its deeds. Civilisations unquestionably revived, human progress went on, and what power or influence under heaven but the Catholic Church was there to create the one and to foster the other? Amidst the mingling of races, and the formation of nations; without a remnant of the old civilisation, or any other rival to stir her energy; whilst the world assailed her from without and intrigued against her from within; many of her own, both clergy and laity, led on through human weakness by the lawless passions of their time; wealth lying at her feet tempting her to subside into the animal indolence which became the ruin of old Rome — in spite of all these she instilled into society those principles of human progress on which modern civilisation is founded. The seeds of all that is really great and enduring in our modern civilisation — the abolition of slavery, the Republics of Italy, and the *Magna Charta* of England, municipal liberties, commerce, distributive justice, hospitals, literature and art, agriculture, geographical discoveries, ancient literature guarded and saved — were then sown and cultivated, from generation to generation, when priests and monks had undisputed intellectual sway over the mind of Europe.

Modern times can show nothing to compare with the social work which Catholicism did in those days. Protestant nations started with the capital which Catholicism had made. No non-Catholic nation — neither of Protestantism which took its share and went its own way, like the Prodigal Son; nor of naturalism which is begotten of it, with the 'pig philosophy'[4] which it picked up in its wanderings — has ever civilised itself from within, as the Christian Commonwealth of Europe arose from the bosom of the Catholic Church. How can any man, with such a history before him, think of doubting that the tendency of Catholicism is to human progress? No modern instances of national decadence can disprove the evidence of a thousand years. I am now neither admitting nor denying that decadence; but, in any case, the social structure which Catholicism had raised out of ruins and rubbish is a *fact* which should make us seek some other cause than Catholicism of that decadence . . . .

And if we acknowledge the soul to be a substantial element of man's nature at all, and the future life to be a reality in man's existence, is not the philosophy of the Church the philosophy also of common sense? And is not the 'economic sense' which is shocked by that philosophy, the plainest common nonsense? Philosophers of naturalism! tell me straight out that what I call my soul is only phosphorous, or merely the result of molecular forces; assure me that what I call my future life is only my fancy projected beyond the grave, and I will make short work of each by ignoring both. But if the former is a reality of my being, and the latter a reality in my existence, I must in consistency give them their due place. At the cost of disgracing my reason as well as of damning

2. Glabrio, Clemens and Domitilla were Christian converts of the Roman imperial household. The phrase 'our conversation is in heaven' is from St Paul.

3. *Ireland in the New Century* (see above, p. 690).

4. Thomas Carlyle's phrase for the philosophy of utilitarianism as expounded by Jeremy Bentham and John Stuart Mill.

my soul, I dare not tinker with their claims. It provokes one's common sense, almost irritates one's nerves, to hear of these awful things dealt with, trifled with, as if they were chattels of man's absolute ownership, which one may beg, borrow, buy, or steal, at one's pleasure. In the last analysis, naturalistic economics are reducible to mere gastronomics; the concerns of the soul and of the future life fall to the same level with the concerns of a creamery, the Vatican Council should have consulted the House of Commons, and the Synod of Maynooth should become a section of the Department.[5]

It may be said to me that the moral and divine law, or the Catholic Church which I suppose to be their official interpreter, have nothing to do with politics or economics; I reply — with politics or economics as such, certainly not. But, may Parliament then justly revive the Penal Laws, make laws of distributive injustice, legalise a system of slavery by which human beings may be bought and sold and become the property of their purchaser? Is an economic system right which sanctions usury, or finds a place for trusts and monopolies which place the public at the mercy of a grinding industrialism? If not, why not? What is the criterion according to which they are wrong? Not surely the politics or the economics which sanction them. Then we must seek the source of their injustice in a higher law, namely, the moral and the divine, whose official interpreter is the Church of Christ. It will be asked, what has the Gospel of Christ to do with factories or the Stock Exchange? I reply, no more than a professor of mathematics has to do with the building of railway bridges, or a professor of chemistry with the sowing of potatoes or oats; and yet, let a railway bridge be built irrespective of the principles taught in mathematics, and it will be shattered and broken down by the first goods train that passes over it; let potatoes or oats be sown in a soil not suited to them, and the crop will be a failure. In like manner, society, either in its political or economic action, cannot go on irrespective of the moral and divine law. It was tried in old Rome by the wisest and the ablest men the world has ever know, and we have seen what came of it. As Lecky pointed out,[6] the Catholic Church simply taught the doctrines of the equality of men, the sacredness of marriage, the rights of woman, the spirit of sacrifice, the duty and dignity of labour — none of them directly economic, but all bound up with the mystery of the Incarnation — and selfishness, slavery, divorce, luxury, and the other social evils which began in naturalism and finally ruined Roman society, had no part in the new civilisation, as far as the Church could prevent it, or human passion yielded to its principles.

We must not identify human or social progress with mere material or industrial progress. They are quite separable, and are often found apart. They are neither necessarily opposed nor necessarily united. One is found without the other, for instance, in the millionaire who has no higher notion than making money, and he makes it; whose highest aspirations are on a level with the luxury which wealth can minister. Old Rome was in a state of national decadence at the time when its literature, art, and wealth were at their highest. A man may subdue the forces of nature and turn them to his use by the application of science, and when he has made himself most the master of matter may have become most its slave. It can be so with a nation also.

Human progress and civilisation then must not be identified with material progress; with gas, electricity, railroads and factories . . . .

Industrialism is not civilisation; industrial progress is undoubtedly both a law and a duty for a people, but it is not their highest law, nor their first duty.

> But sometimes virtue starves, while vice is fed,
> What then? Is the reward of virtue bread?[7]

I have now pointed out the wide difference there is between human progress and mere material progress . . . Human progress or civilisation implies improvement and expansion in all the elements which make up man's nature, in all the human interests of a people. The will and the heart are the great motive forces in human activity, and if due attention is not given to the proper cultivation of those, the attempt to build a truly prosperous nation is as vain as the task of the fool in the Gospel who tried to build his house on sand. The old Romans tried it, and they ended in miserable failure; and no people of today are more worldly wise than they

5. The ruling body of the catholic seminary at Maynooth, Co. Kildare should become a part of the Department of Agriculture.

6. Earlier O'Riordan had quoted from W.E.H. Lecky's *History of the Rise and Influence of Rationalism in Europe* 2 vols (1865), I, pp. 234, 236, 237, 245. This is a paraphrase of those quotations.

7. Alexander Pope, *The Essay on Man* (1733–34), lines 149–50.

were. By the most natural process they passed from comfort to wealth, from wealth to luxury, from luxury to indolence, from indolence to selfishness, and thence through 'the survival of the fittest'[8] to the distinction between the few masters who alone were citizens of the great Republic, and the multitudes who were their slaves and chattels.

It was the Catholic Church built up civilization again, and led men along the way of human progress.

I have already pointed out the mistake which Sir Horace Plunkett has made in representing the Catholic Church as 'completely shifting the moral centre of gravity to the future existence.' I now recall his argument, that its reliance on authority is an impediment to progress, inasmuch as it checks initiative and self-reliance.

If reliance on authority be a check to individual initiative and an obstacle to progress, how is progress possible at all? Authority is an essential element in every society. It is authority which gives unity and stability to society and is the safeguard of the liberty of its members. Society is the offspring of human intelligence and liberty. Civil authority unifies millions of individuals of different personal interests and passions, and makes them act with common national interest and purpose. It guards the rights and liberties of each, protecting each from the injustice or the despotism of the selfish and strong. Any society, from a municipal corporation to a nation, is simply inconceivable without an authority to rule it. Authority, so far from lessening individual liberty was conceived by human intelligence and established by human liberty for its own safeguard; and thus it is not an obstacle, but a help to initiative, and is a necessary condition of human progress. If anyone complain that his liberty is restricted in not being allowed to invade the rights of others, he has to explain how he came by the right to invade their rights and thus to restrict the liberty of his neighbour. For his complaint implies simply that others have no rights or liberties in the presence of his, that he has unlimited liberty, and even the right to do wrong. We thus alight on the difference on the one hand between authority which secures liberty and despotism which restrains it; and on the other hand, the difference between liberty which is the birthright of everybody, and license — the abuse of liberty — which is the right of nobody. The truth is, authority and liberty are two phases of one and the same principle.

Sir Horace will remind me that he was not speaking of civil, but of religious authority. But, then, how is it that authority which secures individual liberty in the State, restrains it in the Church? Authority is the safeguard of liberty also in religion, he will reply, except in the Catholic Church. It is reliance on that authority which 'represses individuality,' 'checks the growth of the qualities of initiative and self-reliance,'[9] and is for that reason an impediment to progress. But how would he explain, then, the genesis of liberty, the impulse to enterprise, the birth, growth, and the vast strides of human progress which began at the dawn of the Middle Ages, when there was no power but Catholicism to create them, and whilst it was in the power of the Catholic Church to check their growth or to nip them in the bud if it chose? . . .

Every Catholic knows, unless those 'Catholics' who are outside everything Catholic except the name, that he is as free as air in all his political and economic, in his temporal activities and relations of all sorts, as long as he does not run counter to the teaching or discipline of that Church which he believes to have been instituted by Christ to expound the moral and divine Law, and to guard their observance by the necessary discipline of life. And the doctrine and discipline of the Catholic Church gives every member of it plenty of scope for all the economic activity he wishes to put forth. I know that Catholics may not lawfully believe or do some things as to which non-Catholics enjoy untrammelled scope for thought and action. But, if those things are false it is not liberty of thought to assent to them; if those things are wrong it is not liberty of action to do them. It is not liberty of thought or of action, but license in both, that lets a man think what is false and do what is wrong. If I do my neighbour an injustice I do not use my liberty; I abuse it. It is an act, not of liberty, but of license. In truth, there is no such thing in nature as free-thought. It is a chimera; a crude expression without a meaning.

Authority in society is for the sake of and is the safeguard of the liberty of the subject. But what is the safeguard of authority? Force may make it feared; only religion inspires the sense of duty which

8. Charles Darwin used the phrase in *The Descent of Man* (1871), although he attributed it to the English philosopher Herbert Spencer (1820–1903).

9. *Ireland in the New Century* (see above, p. 688).

respects it. But it must be a religion which does not owe its power to the individuals whom it is supposed to guide. If it depends on the people to determine what doctrines it shall teach, what discipline it shall order, it is only a religion of their own making which they may shape or discard at their will. Made by the people they can unmake it with equal right; it is a function of the State; nothing more than the concrete manifestation of what happens to be the trend of public opinion for the time being. To subject oneself to a religion of human manufacture like that is to bear a yoke of religious despotism which a people can never venerate, and which they will not long endure at an inconvenience. Well, that is Protestantism precisely; for it assumes that God has ordered a religion; but instead of having to take charge of anybody, everybody has to take charge of it. Protestantism is essentially of home manufacture; each person makes his own according to his conviction or fancy. I apprehend that Sir Horace Plunkett will not approve that exposition of it. I set it forth as what I think to be a plain corollary from what he will of course avow. Because Protestantism was inaugurated on the supposition that Catholicism had grown so corrupt that the Church of Christ had long ceased to be. But they assumed that individuals may succeed where a whole Church failed, and each one thought himself commissioned by God to construct the real article at least for his own use.

The Reformers, therefore, considered religion as a thing which was not to teach or to take care of them, but as a thing to be taught and taken care of by them. I will be reminded that Protestants are bound by the Thirty-nine Articles;[10] but I remind whoever reminds me that if I were a Protestant I would, on the principle of my divine right of private judgment, resent the impertinence of any person or institution that would ask me to subscribe to any number of them more or less than I thought well to accept. May not Parliament in the morning change the number to thirty-eight? May not any Member bring in a bill to enlarge or lessen their number, or to modify them, side by side with a bill to fix a duty on tea or tobacco? It may be said that I am now casting ridicule; it may be ridicule, but it is reason. Nay, it is fact. The Act of Union decreed that in future the Protestant Church in Ireland should hold the same articles of belief as the Protestant Church in England. The 5th Article of the Act provided 'that the Churches of England and Ireland, as now by law established, be united into one Protestant Episcopal Church, to be called the United Church of England and Ireland; and that the doctrine, worship, discipline, and government of the said United Church shall be, and shall remain in full force for ever, as the same one now by law established for the Church of England.' However, they did not remain *the same for ever*, but only for 70 years; for in 1871 the chief legislative power in the Irish Protestant Church was transferred to a General Synod consisting of clergy and laity in Ireland, who, in spite of the natural variations of private judgment, as if by the inspiration of a *Deus ex machina*, have happened upon the usual creed of thirty-nine articles and other formularies, 'subject to such alterations only as may be made therein from time to time by the lawful authority of the Church.'* I have no intention to make Protestantism look ridiculous; my purpose is to make plain that it is part and parcel of the State; pure naturalism in principle. It is simply the conviction, feeling, or fancy which actuates each individual for the time being. In other words, it leaves each one in the condition in which it found him; it gives a glow to noble instincts if he happen to have such; it bends to baser passions if such be his; in a word, it satisfies his selfishness, whatever form his selfishness assumes.

Such is Protestantism in principle; let us see what it is in practice. We have seen on the avowal of non-Catholic writers, what Catholicism did in the ages of faith. Protestantism began its work with the accumulated capital of civilisation which Catholicism had created; nevertheless, during the three centuries of its existence, it has not Christianized or civilised a single barbarian or pagan people. Let us take England as a type. What is the result of the civilising influence of English rule in India? That influence began in the middle of the 18th century, when the Mogul power had been crushed by Clive.[11] How did it set about civilising the natives? They were subjected to a systematic oppression, under the name of government, which is one of the blackest

**The Constitution of the Church of Ireland*. — Preamble and Declaration, adopted by the General Convention in the year 1870.

10. These were drawn up in the sixteenth century to define the doctrinal position of the Church of England.

11. Robert Clive (1725–74), architect of British rule in India through his campaigns of 1756–60 and his governorship of Bengal (1758).

blots on the pages of human history. They, as well as their country, which they no longer dared to call their own, were made mere instruments of wealth for the relays of English adventurers who went there to make money and came home when they had it made . . . . Whilst Protestantism was forcing itself down our throats here in Ireland, it let the Hindoos hug their idols and worship their gods, provided they peacefully gave up their treasures, and paid the taxes imposed on them. We find the 'economic sense' asserting itself also in this fact, that Protestantism had held sway over India for more than half-a-century before it thought of building a church for itself.

Let us pass to Australasia, and a similar history meets us. A century and a-half ago, Australia, New Zealand, and Tasmania, were inhabited solely by barbarian natives. It was a fruitful field from which a rich harvest of civilisation and Christianity might have been reaped. Protestantism had the field to itself; because Catholic influence, for good or evil, was for long kept away by the Penal Laws. How did it civilise the natives? By a simple process — it exterminated them. They were chased to death as the beasts that roamed through their forests; they were betrayed and butchered, and that under protection of government. In twenty years the Tasmanians were extinguished; the Australians are almost gone; and the Maories [*sic*] of New Zealand, whose bravery and natural ability deserve a better fate, are fast disappearing.

The same method of civilisation has done its work on those native tribes of Africa whose natural right to live where they got life English Protestantism found obstructing the march of its industrial progress. And here I am reminded to ask: — which shows more proof of human civilisation, the honest industry, the frugal comfort, the heroic bravery of the Boers, or the aggressiveness of British commercialism which only, from a confusion of ideas and by a misuse of words, could be called human progress? It may be called material progress . . . .

Chapter 5

CHARACTER IN IRISH CATHOLICS

. . . Character is the moral texture or disposition which is formed in a person as the result of repeated action and of habitual thought. We say that one is a man of character if we find him showing persistent activity in striving after some purpose which he has set before himself, or in suffering trial and loss for a principle. For character is proved in passivity as well as and even more than in activity. The early Christian martyrs proved themselves men and women of character by sacrificing their lives for their principles. I do not now consider whether those principles were true or false. Our fathers who gave up their lives as well as their lands in Ireland for their principles proved themselves thereby to be men of character; otherwise they would have kept their lands and saved their lives, as they might easily have done by turning their backs on their principles and by lying to themselves . . . .

Sir Horace Plunkett links character with the industrial spirit, but in that he is plainly wrong. To identify with one thing a quality which many things have in common is a pitfall into which hobby-jockies[1] invariably and unthinkingly tumble. Sir Horace is possessed of the industrial spirit, and he easily takes for granted that there is no such thing as character unless that which spends itself in industry. On the other hand, a Quietist who seeks rest for his soul, a Mahatma awaiting the Nirvana, the modern Christian scientist, or others cast in a like mould would call themselves men of character. But a philosopher would open his eyes and look without prejudice before and around him over the whole field of human activity where every human energy is exercised and every human activity is pursued. As a Catholic I must look at life in that way, and if I narrow my reason exclusively within a spiritual sphere, in so far do I turn off at a tangent from the Catholic ideal. The spirit of Catholicism is opposed both to the spirit of industrialism and to the spirit of esoteric Buddhism. Industrialism and experimentalism are like a magpie's nest; everything on which their votaries can lay their minds or hands goes into it. Those who are led on by that spirit want to gather into their own narrow corner of interest every human activity, as if men were made to live either in a laboratory or in a factory, or at least should have their highest interest there. Those who are possessed by the industrial spirit, and those who call themselves 'men of science' are ever boasting of their breadth of view, whilst they are amongst the most

1. Those who are on a hobbyhorse — obsessed by a fixed idea.

narrow-minded of mankind. The consumptive talks of health, because he has it not, and the men of fallen fortune talk of wealth, for they feel the need of make-believe. So with many who affect enlightenment beyond their kind. . . .

But, let us examine the relation of Irish Catholics to character in the sense in which Sir Horace uses it.

The first condition that is necessary for the exertion of human activity is liberty. I refer to character as it manifests itself in activity, and which is impossible without liberty; but I do not forget that the strongest character might be proved in the sacrifice of liberty for principle, and in such case slavery would be the result and the proof of character. I have already recalled the sacrifices made by our forefathers under the Penal Laws in proof of their character; because only a strong character could suffer so much for a principle. Many of the Young Irelanders and Fenians were men of strong character . . . .

The Irish Catholics who did those deeds and bore those consequences in their struggle for their civil and religious rights unquestionably proved themselves to be men of strong character. Or, what better evidence of their strength of character should anyone want? Should we expect them to inaugurate industrial movements or form co-operative societies? Such things were not thought of, or if thought of, only thought of as Utopian in those days. The Catholics of Ireland were then struggling to secure such a condition of affairs as would make industry possible or profitable. 'Self-reliance and moral courage' were necessary for such a purpose, and the Catholics of Ireland proved their character in striving for and achieving it. It was the only kind of opportunity they then had of proving that they were men of character, and they proved it.

The history of Irish Catholics for the last hundred years has this thread running through it — a denial of existing grievances; a partial redress of those same grievances; that partial redress made with a bad grace and unwillingly; when made, a boasting of the fairmindedness of those who yielded up those rights; the admission that such grievances had existed, together with expressions of regret that they should ever have been, and a demand on the gratitude of the people for the pretended liberality that lessened those wrongs, and an acknowledgement of the magnanimity which now acknowledged and regretted them; a denial that any more grievances remained to be redressed — reprobation and imprisonment to any who pointed out to the people that more remained, or who dared to urge the people to another struggle to take those also away; again, an unwilling and partial redress of those — then the same staging of magnanimity, justice, contrition, and tears — then the further demand for the removal of remaining wrongs — the denial of any more — then another struggle — more turmoil and trial — then unwilling and partial redress — and so, denial, assertion, demand, struggle, and success, have followed one another by rotation in the political life of Ireland during the past century. That has been the web of our history in every department of Irish Catholic life. And if those long withheld rights have been yielded to the people only after struggle, strife, and suffering in every case, how have those measures of justice been effected? Only by the persistent fight for principle on the part of the people, in spite of misrepresentation, obloquy, imprisonment, exile and death. And they have never considered the creed or even the country of those who championed their cause. They followed Butt and Parnell as they had followed O'Connell, Gavan Duffy and Frederick Lucas.[2] Sir Horace Plunkett acknowledges that he himself has secured a following beyond all his expectation, and notwithstanding personal disadvantages of more than one kind. In fact he says that the priests 'have put no obstacle in the way of the Roman Catholic majority choosing Protestants for political leaders'; that 'it is no disadvantage to a man to be a Protestant in Irish political life, and that where opposition is shown to him by Roman Catholics it is almost invariably on political, social, or agrarian, but not on religious grounds.'[3]

The history of Irish Catholics for the past century, then, shows not only character, but character of a very enlightened kind. That century has been spent in political strife, because it was the only path, although a thorny one, open to them for the enjoyment of those civil rights which are a necessary basis of any industrial life or success.

2. Isaac Butt (1813–79) was the early leader of the Home Rule movement; he was succeeded by Charles Stewart Parnell (1846–91), who led the movement until 1890. Daniel O'Connell (1775–1847) was the great leader of catholic Ireland from 1814 to 1845. Charles Gavan Duffy (1816–1903) was a prominent Young Irelander and founder, with his colleague, Frederick Lucas (1812–55), of the Tenant League and the Irish Independent Party. Clerical opposition disillusioned Duffy and hastened Lucas's death. They are not the happiest examples to cite in this context.

3. *Ireland in the New Century* (see above, p. 689).

FREDERICK RYAN

(1874–1913)

from: CRITICISM AND COURAGE AND OTHER ESSAYS (1906)

[Frederick Ryan, founder and first secretary of the Socialist Party of Ireland, consistently argues that there was no point in arguing, as Plunkett, Hyde and others had done, for the necessity of finding a non-political ground for national regeneration. Sectarianism and injustice were integral to the Irish situation; they could not be extracted so that something benign could be made of the remainder. Writing in 1904, during the disputes surrounding the issue of devolution, a modified version of Home Rule, Ryan refers to the resurgence of Orangeism, forever alert to any reappearance of the Home Rule threat, and the unionist boycott of any discussions designed to secure devolved powers of self-government. Ryan, like most socialist thinkers after him — with the notable exception of the present-day Workers' Party and Labour Party — believed that sectarianism could be defeated only by the achievement of independence.

The article was first published in the magazine *Dana*, No. 1 (May 1904).]

POLITICAL AND INTELLECTUAL FREEDOM

More than one recent incident has set up the fear in many minds that Ireland is about to experience another attack of that religious fever which has so often afflicted her in the past, at a time when other indications went to show that saner and more pacific ideals were gaining in strength. We continually suffer in Ireland from rival bigotries which, so far from injuring, positively help one another and stimulate each other. There is, firstly, the Orange and ascendancy party, continually waging a political war against the people and against the policy of self-government which is the chief cure for Orange and Catholic bigotry alike. That Orange party, with the vices which peculiarly attach to every such faction, maintained by outside political support and kept in countenance by outside authority, actuated by base and bigoted ideas, has the strength which all such minorities possess. It is comparatively compact, unimaginative, self-centred. Its boycott, of course, is chiefly political, but it also serves to set up a counter bigotry on the other side. That is the fate of all countries so situated as Ireland. The vices of the dominant faction, ruling without consent and without sympathy, corrupt the whole body politic, so that in such a soil, race and religious passion waxes strong, and political science is at a discount.

This seems to me the simple explanation of such incidents as the campaign started a year or so ago by a weekly Dublin journal to accentuate and embitter Catholic feeling, to make Catholics particularly sensitive as to their Catholicism, and to urge them to demand rights, not as citizens, nor in the interests of national well-being, but to demand them as Catholics in the interests of Catholicity.[1] This campaign, it is true, was carried on at a level of vulgarity and with a wealth of epithet that would have excited the envy of Mr. Chamberlain,[2] and was of that 'will-you-take-it-lying-down' order which peculiarly appeals to the uneducated and semi-educated mob, since it touches that natural and even healthy egoism which lies so near the surface in any crowd. The formula of that mob-appeal is now fairly familiar to most of us. When England with a quarter of a million of men set out to conquer two little peasant states in Africa, the English Jingo politicians and journals appealed to the English mob in a fashion that would lead an observer to imagine that they were fighting a desperate battle for their very existence against tremendous odds.[3] The race or religious bigot generally paints the conditions of those whom he is addressing in the worst colours, tells them they are in a very perilous state, and that they are being trampled upon by a wily and treacherous enemy,

1. The reference is probably to *The Irish Catholic*, a weekly paper owned by William Martin Murphy, which supported the Dublin Catholic Association, founded in 1902, in its campaign to highlight discrimination in employment.
2. Joseph Chamberlain (1836–1914), Liberal and Liberal Unionist, a leading opponent of Home Rule and a rabid imperialist. His vituperative gifts were considerable.
3. The reference is to the Boer War, 1899–1902; the 'two little peasant states' were the Transvaal and the Orange Free State.

against whom any and every means of defence is permissible. The 'enemy' — or the worst elements on its side — may easily be trusted to better the example, and, if all goes well, the bigot will soon be at the summit of his ambition; rival mobs will glare at each other, mob-newspapers will hurl abuse at one another, and every member of the community will have a keen consciousness of every other member's sins.

A case by which the ethical standard of the leaders of this Catholic campaign might be tested arose in the matter of the anti-Jewish outburst in Limerick.[4] An ignorant priest in Limerick preached a sermon retailing old and exploded libels against Jews in general and urging the people to boycott the Jews in Limerick, a sermon which, by the way, evoked a humane and admirable protest from Mr. Michael Davitt, which justifies the high place he holds in the esteem of Irish democrats. What was the conduct of those who are so loud in their demands for 'justice' to Catholics? They supported the priest. When Catholics are boycotted it is an outrageous injustice; when Catholics boycott others it is all right and proper, being merely a process of recovering their own. On many to whom this conduct appears defensible, probably nothing that is here written will have any effect. But to others the question may be put: on what principle is any lawless egoism to be condemned, if this be justified?

Let us, however, seek a clear intellectual outlook. Philosophically, of course, the conduct of the religionists all round is absurd. According to the Christian view, this world is a 'vale of tears', a vestibule of eternity, a mere halting place on a road that stretches into the illimitable future. Yet amongst the people who profess this belief, the fight is waged with a bitterness which seems to suggest that the combatants are determined to stay in the 'vestibule' as long as they can, and are determined to make it as comfortable, in the meantime, as possible.

The contrast between Christian precept and practice is certainly amusing. Yet far be it from me to press the precepts mentioned on the various combatants. The only modern Christian to profess the doctrine of non-resistance is Count Tolstoy, and even with him it is only a profession since he maintains a continuous and vigorous propaganda against what he considers the evils of modern society.[5] Indeed his English admirers keep up a supply of books, pamphlets and leaflets from his pen in such bewildering profusion that one never knows exactly whether one is reading a new pronouncement or merely a new edition of an old one.

Yet Tolstoy's example surely sets us on the right path. The method of redressing the sectarian bitterness in Ireland is not by counter bitterness. We shall never cure matters by boycotting, or intimidation, or abuse. It is by science and by moral appeal that progress is always to be permanently won. The first and absolutely necessary step is the winning of self-government. And it is the failure to recognise this that vitiates otherwise capable surveys like Mr. Filson Young's[6] and Sir Horace Plunkett's. Indeed the latter book, in this respect, considering its title and pretensions, is almost rendered worthless. A man sets out to describe the condition of a patient suffering from cancer, and the one thing he will not discuss is — cancer. He will dispassionately and even illuminatingly discuss every by-effect of the malady, but he is ignorant of the fact of the malady itself, or else is professionally precluded from dealing with it. For many of the evils that many recent writers discuss have their proximate cause in the lack of political wisdom. And the only road to political wisdom is by way of political responsibility. A people long suffering from political servitude have the vices of slavery, lack of constructive political faculty, lack of initiative, lack of the wise compromise that comes of action; though notwithstanding these defects the Irish people, on the whole, have shown at the least as much political sagacity as the English.

But to recognise and proclaim these things does not by any means preclude the right or the propriety of internal criticism. Rather does that criticism come the more appropriately from those who are alive to the main political evil. And whilst demanding the redress of that evil, it becomes necessary, concurrently, to raise our own canons of conduct and

4. In early 1904 in Limerick, a local catholic priest stirred up anti-semitic feelings in his sermons; this led to a series of violent incidents, directed against the small Jewish community, most of whom left the city.

5. Leo Tolstoy set out his conversion to the doctrine of Christian love and acceptance of the principle of non-resistance to evil in his *Confession* (1879) and subsequently expounded his views in a series of works.

6. Filson Young, *Ireland at the Crossroads; An Essay in Explanation* (London: Richards, 1903).

scrutinise our own standards of thinking. Sir Horace Plunkett in one passage in his book observes:

> The revolution in the industrial order, and its consequences, such as the concentration of immense populations within restricted areas, have brought with them social and moral evils that must be met with new weapons. In the interests of religion itself, principles first expounded to a Syrian community with the most elementary physical needs and the simplest of avocations, have to be taught in their application to the conditions of the most complex social organisation and economic life. Taking people as we find them, it may be said with truth that their lives must be wholesome before they can be holy; and while a voluntary asceticism may have its justification, it behoves a Church to see that its members, while fully acknowledging the claims of another life, should develop the qualities which make for well-being in this life.[7]

Some of us, of course, might cavil at Sir Horace's implication that it is possible to really combine concern for 'another life' with effective regard for the well-being of this. The essential business of the Churches all round and the essence of the Church ideal is to prepare men for the 'hereafter'; and the affairs of this world are only treated as incidental to such preparation. The true logical antithesis of this view is the positivist and scientific ideal which, taking humanity as the highest we know, regards the well-being of humanity here as the greatest end for which we can work, and frankly accepting the fact that this life is the only one of which we have real knowledge, ignores all distracting hypothesis.

None the less, however, is it well and courageous for Sir Horace Plunkett to put the secular ideal in his own words and fashion. It is easy for the popular press to sneer at him on this score, for it is sure of a response from the religious multitude. But it is precisely in a country where the 'principles' of 'Syria', to use Sir Horace Plunkett's euphemism, are professed on all sides with a heartiness almost unknown elsewhere, that we have the eternal sectarian wrangles, here over the creed of a dispensary doctor or an inspector of schools, there over the religion of an unfortunate foundling who may be 'damned' without its knowledge by the votes of a Board of Guardians consisting for the most part of publicans and slum-owners.

One would on first thoughts conclude that the spectacle of such sectarian squabbling would perforce raise in an ordinarily intelligent people doubts of the genuineness of the creeds that could stimulate it. But such is not the case; it seems to require a definitely humanist philosophy and a humanitarian enthusiasm to realise that the welfare of humanity as such is the greatest and noblest end for which humanity can work. But humanity in Ireland has not yet come into its inheritance. In a recent review of Mr. Filson Young's book *Ireland at the Cross Roads*, the Rev. Dr. McDonald[8] in an article in the *Freeman's Journal* wrote: 'Consider the real Ireland too. In that sad country one thing only has prospered, as Mr Young admits, the Church; and she is based on a system of almost absolute self-government'. So far as Dr. McDonald intended this as an argument for self-government, as against Mr. Young, I am with him. But he does not seem to have realised the ominous significance of his analogy. The Church has flourished amidst universal decay. Precisely. In a country warped and injured by lack of political freedom, it would be curious if intellectual freedom prospered. The Irish people, trampled by alien and unsympathetic rule, have looked with aching eyes to a heaven of bliss, and they have, more or less contentedly, lain down in their chains soothed by the hope of after-reward. If Ireland is to be saved we must surely change all that; the people must turn their energies from dreaming of another world to the task of bettering and beautifying the things of this. It is nobler to make a happy human home than to raise a dozen granite temples for a worship which does not need them; it is a greater thing to rescue one human heart from despair than to have kept every letter of the religious law. We need in Ireland a spirit of intellectual freedom, and a recognition of the supremacy of humanity. And so far from this prescription being offered as a substitute for national freedom it is urged as a necessity of a true national ideal. For the synthesis of much recent criticism is this: intellectual freedom and political freedom are not opposites. Rightly understood, intellectual freedom and political freedom are one.

7. *Ireland in the New Century* (see above, p. 688).

8. Dr Walter McDonald (1854–1920), professor of dogmatic theology at St Patrick's College, Maynooth and a leading opponent of autocratic episcopal behaviour.

from: THE SPOIL OF EGYPT: A SORDID STORY OF MODERN EMPIRE-BUILDING (1910)

[This review of Theodore Rothstein's book *Egypt's Ruin* reminds us of the fact that Irish nationalists saw parallels between the Irish situation and the British imperial system in India, Egypt and Persia. Wilfrid Scawen Blunt, the Englishman who was perhaps the most acute observer of the analogies between Ireland and the eastern empire, wrote an introduction to Rothstein's book. Along with W. P. Ryan, George Bernard Shaw and many other commentators in magazines and journals, Frederick Ryan contributed to an analysis of imperialism in its most advanced and bureaucratic form, as perfected by Lord Cromer in Egypt.

The review was published in W. P. Ryan's *The Irish Nation* on 10 December 1910.]

AN EXPOSURE OF LORD CROMER

. . . Such were the sordid and treacherous origins of British rule in Egypt and the different stages of the transaction are set out in this remarkable book[1] with a lucidity and thoroughness that make it indispensable to anyone who desires to get at the real facts of the case. The author lays bare the hypocrisies, the subterfuges, the diplomatic tricks, with a ruthlessness that must startle the self-complacency of the ordinary British Imperialist. Mr. Rothstein gives his references for every single statement, and his pages teem with footnotes. He has ransacked the pages of official Blue Books, the files of the *Times*, the records of Parliament, the writings of English apologists, of foreign critics, of Egyptian patriots. The amount of reading that has gone to the production of this volume is enormous. Incidentally it is a crushing exposure of Lord Cromer, the like of which has not hitherto appeared in English. His work, *Modern Egypt*, which he issued a couple of years ago to slander the Egyptians and justify himself, and which was received by the whole tribe of British jingoes as a positively inspired production, is here turned inside out.[2] Its half-truths, its whole suppressions, its smooth glosses are mercilessly laid bare. In several places Mr. Rothstein is able to give the text of documents, available in old newspapers or forgotten Blue Books, which Cromer, professing elaborately to tell the whole story, has adroitly suppressed. In all probability Lord Cromer will ignore this indictment; it is his way in such cases. His 'dignity' will be above taking note of such criticism. But Mr. Rothstein's work remains for all that, and cannot be set aside by any serious student of modern Egyptian affairs.

We have sketched the malodorous intrigue in which the present British Occupation of Egypt began. Mr. Wilfred [*sic*] Blunt, the most weighty friend that the cause of Egyptian liberty has in England today,[3] contributes a preface to the present volume in which he dwells on the ignorance of the circumstances of that intrigue on the part of English publicists of the present day. Most of the public men who were then alive have passed away. He says, indeed, that the only competent and courageous speaker on Egyptian questions heard any longer in the House of Commons is Mr. John Dillon.[4] Mr. Blunt ably sets out the fallacies and the pseudo-history now current in England. The first is that Egypt, before the intervention of England, was a barbarous land, where universal ignorance prevailed, and where there were neither law nor order, nor the common safeguards of life and property. Another statement to be found repeated by various writers is that England did not desire to go to Egypt, that the intervention was not of her choice, but was forced upon by her by circumstances she could not avoid. Another is that Egypt owes all her present material prosperity to England. And so on. We could easily forecast the sort of arguments that Imperialists indulge in with regard to Egypt by just remembering the arguments they employ with regard to Ireland. Mr. Blunt easily exposes these absurdities, and supplies a damning record of England's broken pledges with reference to Egypt, stretching from Lord Granville's dispatch of November 4th, 1881,

1. Theodore Rothstein, *Egypt's Ruin: A Financial and Administrative Record* with an introduction by W. S. Blunt (London: A. C. Fifield, 1910).

2. Evelyn Baring, Lord Cromer (1841–1917), was British consul-general and effective ruler of Egypt from 1883 to 1907.
3. Wilfrid Scawen Blunt (1840–1922), English diplomat and author, whose extensive travels in North Africa and Asia made him a vigorous opponent of British imperialism. He strongly supported the Irish Home Rule campaign.
4. John Dillon (1851–1927) was MP for East Mayo 1885–1918.

to Sir Edward Gorst's Consular Report of 1910.[5] Mr. Blunt simply sets out these quotations, and adds: 'Surely never were such pledges given, to be afterwards broken, in the whole history of England's imperial dealings'. Whether there is any parallel to the Egyptian case in British Imperial history we need not here discuss, but certainly the British breach of faith in that case is one of the blackest. The moral collapse, that open and shameless disregard to solemn pledges, has done more to sap British moral prestige, and with it general European prestige, in the East, than any other episode. Educated Egyptians, who have followed the recent history of their own country, and know of these broken pledges, which, by the way, the National Press there takes care to blazon forth, such Egyptians simply receive with mocking laughter the high and mighty certificates of honesty and disinterestedness which the British Imperialist Press gives to British policy. Some politicians in England who recognise the blackness of the moral record are inclined to appeal to results. 'Granted', they say, 'we did not arrive at our position in Egypt by fair means. But look at the results . . . what matters it, after all, how we came to be in Egypt so long as our stay there has been of immense benefit to the Egyptian people?' This attitude is dealt with in Part III of Mr. Rothstein's work, and it is a powerful criticism. He shows the extravagance of the British claims, the mismanagement of finance, the absolute neglect of education, so that Egypt has scarcely advanced a step in that direction during the whole thirty years of British rule, the growth of crime, the exhaustion of the soil owing to the excessive forcing of the cotton crop, and the persistent denial of the chance of Egyptians acquiring a knowledge of the administration of their own country by the way in which all the higher posts of government are packed with foreigners. Certainly Mr. Rothstein makes a tremendous case, and, so far from being a rhetorical case, it is one that is backed throughout by facts and figures. I can only conclude by saying that anyone who desires to get a serious view of the Egyptian problem, and there are many reasons why Irishmen should be interested in that problem, cannot neglect Mr. Rothstein's book. Neither can they neglect it who, though not particularly interested in Egypt, yet desire to study a typical and glaring case of the fashion in which modern capitalism and finance pulls [*sic*] the wires of government today, and uses the machinery of international diplomacy to protect even its most shady and illicit schemes.

5. George Granville (1828–92), who was present at the opening of the Suez Canal, urged a more complete takeover of Egypt in a dispatch of 1881. Sir John Eldon Gorst (1861–1911), successor to Lord Cromer as consul-general in Egypt (1907–10), recorded the failure of British-style institutions in Egypt and advised against conceding self-government to the Egyptians in his final consular report of 1910.

JAMES LARKIN

(1876–1947)

from: LARKIN'S SCATHING INDICTMENT OF DUBLIN SWEATERS (1913)

[Between 1911 and 1913, James Larkin, aided by James Connolly, tried to organize workers in various industries into an effective trade union structure. In 1913, a series of strikes and lockouts culminated in the confrontation between William Martin Murphy's Dublin United Tramways Company and Larkin's Irish Transport and General Workers' Union. Those who wanted to unionise were locked out by the Company. Street violence ensued; the police were brutal and the workers were defeated. An inquiry was held into workers' conditions in the Tramways Company. Larkin was called to give evidence at this court of industrial commissioners. He addressed the court on behalf of the workers on 4 October 1913.

The text is from a pamphlet entitled *Larkin's Scathing Indictment of Dublin Sweaters* (Manchester and London: The National Labour Press Ltd., n.d. (1920?).]

[Mr. Larkin, addressing the Court, said:]

I hope the Court will bear with me during the short time now at my disposal while I put before it a reply, somewhat of a personal character, but which, at the same time, will cover the matters dealt with during the past few days. The first point I wish to make is that the employers in this city, and throughout Ireland generally, think they have a right to deal with their own as they please, and to use and exploit the workers as they please. They assume all the rights and deny any to the men who make their wealth. They are men who say they are of paramount intelligence; they say they are able in organising abilities as 'captains of industry'; that they can always carry out their business in their own way. They deny the right of the men and women who work for them to combine and try and assist one another to improve their conditions of life. While denying the men and women who work for them the right to combine, these men not only take unto themselves this right, but they also intimidate the men — a matter upon which I shall enlarge later on.

The employers have failed everywhere. They claim to have the fullest capacity for carrying on business, and as they stand between the consumer and producer, they also claim the right to control production. But we deny that. We say they are not fitted to carry on industry. Business in this city and country is carried on in a chaotic manner. There is no system. This want of system we want to prove and will prove by the appearance of the men themselves in the witness-box. The employers were invited to meet the representatives of the working classes, men denied access to education and the assistance it might have been to them. Their claim is that as they have the means, they have the right to do as they like with their employees. The working classes deny the right of the masters to lock out their employees. The masters violate all laws, even the laws of Nature. The employers have shown their incapacity during the inquiry. These gallant gentlemen, who claimed to have a capacity for organising and conducting business, and most of whom had had a public school education, these men have had to employ men to explain their case to the Court for them. They have to call upon the Irish Bar for three of the most brilliant men who ever spoke or worked at that Bar — and yet these men, able men, eloquent men, have made a most unholy hash of the whole business. The employers have proved the case for the workers. They have demonstrated individually and collectively that they cannot carry on business properly. The employers claim that they have the law on their side, but their counsel, Mr. Healy,[1] says there is no law in Ireland, and I agree with him. The masters assert their right to combine. I claim that the same right should be given to the workers. There should be equal rights for both sides in the contest. The employers claim that there should be rights only on one side. The employers are the dominant power in this country and they are going to dominate our lives. As Shakespeare says, 'The man who holds the means whereby I live holds and controls my life.'[2] That is not the correct version — I could give it — but I want to put the quotation in my own way.

For fifty years the employers have controlled the lives of workers. Now, when the workers are trying to get some of their rights, the employers deny the right of their men to combine. Man cannot live without intercourse with his fellow beings. Man is, as has been said by an eminent authority,[3] a social animal. But these men — these 'captains of industry' — draw a circle round themselves and say, 'No one must touch me.' But they have no right to a monopoly. The workers desire that the picture should be drawn fairly. But these able gentlemen who have painted the picture for the employers have found that they could not do it. They have got the technique, the craftsmanship, but they have not got the soul. No man can paint a picture without seeing the subject for himself. I will try to assist our friends who have failed. As I say, they have the pigments and the craftsmanship, but they have not been able to paint a picture of life in the industrial world of Ireland.

Let us take the statement made by their own apologist. Let us take the statement by Sir Charles Cameron.[4] There are, he says, 21,000 families, averaging 4½ to each family, living in single rooms in this city. Will these gentlemen opposite accept responsibility? They say they have the right to control the means by which the workers live. They

1. Timothy Healy (1855–1931), Parnell's most notorious opponent after the famous 'split', was engaged as counsel for the employers at the Inquiry of the Industrial Commissioners, September-October 1913, after the Lockout.
2. *The Merchant of Venice*, IV.1. 377–78: '. . . you take my life/ When you do take the means whereby I live.'
3. Probably a reference to Aristotle's definition of man as a political animal.
4. Sir Charles Cameron, a senior civil servant and, later, a judge.

must, therefore, accept responsibility for the conditions under which the workers live. Twenty-one thousand families living in the dirty slums of Dublin, five persons in each room, with, I suppose, less than one thousand cubic feet. Yet it was laid down that each sleeping room should at least have 300 cubic feet space. In Mountjoy Gaol — where I have had the honour to reside on more than one occasion — criminals (but I am inclined to believe that most of the criminals were outside and innocent men inside) were allowed 400 cubic feet. Yet men who slave and work, and their women — those beautiful women we have among the working classes — are compelled to live, many of them, five in a room, with less than 300 cubic feet. They are taken from their mother's breasts at an early age and are used up as material is used up in a fire. These are some of the conditions that obtain in this Catholic city of Dublin, the most church-going city, I believe, in the world.

The workers are determined that this state of affairs must cease. Christ will not be crucified any longer in Dublin by these men. I, and those who think with me, want to show the employers that the workers will have to get the same opportunities of enjoying a civilised life as they themselves have. Mr. Waldron, the Chairman of the Canal Company, on the previous day admitted that right. There is one phase in the present condition of affairs which I will not put before a mixed audience such as this, but of which you are all aware. One of the chief arguments used against Larkin is that he came from Liverpool, but I claim to have as much right to speak in Dublin as Mr. Healy, although I did not come from Bantry. But wherever he came from it is time that someone came from somewhere to teach the employers Christianity. Will the gentlemen on the other side show me that they have a right to speak in the name of the Irish people? The majority of the employers in Dublin have no associations by birth with Ireland: they have no interest in Dublin; they have come here simply to grind wealth out of the bodies and souls of the workers, their wives, and their children. My claim to speak is a human claim, a universal claim, one not limited by geographical boundaries. Mr. Healy has drawn a picture from the employers' viewpoint. I want to show the other side, the true side. I will use other pigments and more vivid colours. Go to some of the factories in Dublin. See some of the maimed men, maimed girls, with hands cut off, eyes knocked out, eyes punctured, bodies and souls seared, and think of the time when they are no longer useful to come up to the £1 a week or some other standard. Then they are thrown on the human scrapheap.

See at every street corner the mass of degradation controlled by the employers, and due to the existing system. Their only thought was the public-house, and, driven to death, they made their way thither to poison their bodies and get a false stimulant to enable them, for a time, to give something more back to the employer for the few paltry shillings thrown at them. These are the men whom the employers called loafers. Mr. Murphy[5] has agreed with me that in the main the Dublin worker is a good, decent chap; but Mr. Murphy and others of his class deny the Dublin men the right to work on the Dublin trams, on the Dublin quays, and in the Dublin factories. They deny Dublin men the right to enjoy the full fruit of their activities. Why? Because they want to bring up in their place poor, uncultured serfs from the country, who knew nothing of Dublin or city life — to bring these men into a congested area, so that they would bring down the wages of the men already here. The employers do this because their souls are steeped in grime and actuated only by the hope of profit-making, and because they have no social conscience. But this lock-out will arouse a social conscience in Dublin and in Ireland generally. I am out to help to arouse that social conscience and to lift up and better the lot of those who are sweated and exploited. But I am also out to save the employers from themselves, to save them from degradation and damnation.

Take Mr. Murphy. I do not mean in any personal sense. I know that Mr. Murphy is imbued with strong views of the rights of property, and on the right to use workers as he pleases. Mr. Murphy is one of the strongest men in the capitalist class of this country, in the Kingdom, on the Continent, or even in America. But the day of the capitalist class is rapidly passing. Mr. Murphy believes in Trade Unionism, but he must make his own Trade Union. Mr. Murphy says that Larkin's Union is not a Trade Union, but is Anarchy. But what is Anarchy? Anarchy means the highest form of love. It means that a man must trust himself and live on himself.

5. William Martin Murphy (1844–1919), Irish Parliamentary MP 1885–92, owned the *Irish Catholic* and the *Irish Independent* newspapers and led the Dublin Employers' Federation during the 1913 Lockout.

We cannot do that yet. We are all set out to injure one another. The present system and policy of those opposed to us is to pull down, but our Anarchism means universal brotherhood. Mr. Murphy, though he is one of the ablest exponents of capitalism, admitted that he did not know the details of his own business, and claimed that I had no right to interfere with it.

Fortified by a wage slave, he was absolutely unable to state his own case. He admitted he had no knowledge of the facts put before him of the details of his own business. He said he had had no strikes of any moment during his connection with industrial concerns, but I have proved that his life has been one continuous struggle against the working classes. I give him credit that in a great many cases he came out on top. Why? Because he has never been faced by men who were able to deal with him, because he has never been faced by a social conscience such as has now been aroused, and, according to which the working classes could combine to alter the present conditions of Labour. He had said he would drive 'Larkinism' headlong into the sea — I evidently have the honour of coining a new word. But there is such a thing as human thought — and nobody has killed it yet, or driven it into the sea, or kept it from making progress.

A very able theologian of the Church, with whom I am supposed to have some association, said, 'That a wall should be built around Ireland so high that the thought of modern Europe could not get over it.' But nobody can build such a wall or kill human thought, not even the theologians, the police, or the politicians — corrupt as they are. Mr. Murphy ought to realise in the later hours of his life, and before he passes hence, that he ought to give something back to the men who made his wealth for him and raised him to the plane of the capitalist, that they deserved something to encourage them from the lower plane on which they existed to a higher plane on which they might live. . . .

It is thought by some that no one should be allowed to live in Ireland except those born on Irish soil. Well, that would be a bad thing for some of those on the other side of the Channel. There is no sense in such an argument as that. The Irish workmen are out to work for a living, and to get access to the means of life. They are not going to be slaves; they are not going to allow their women to be the slaves of a brutal capitalistic system which has neither a soul to be saved nor a soft place to be kicked. Owing to chronic unemployment, and to the misgovernment of the country, there is a state of things in Ireland that has no parallel anywhere. Home Rule is essential to the class to which I belong. We are born Home Rulers. We want a true Home Rule and we want proper people to govern the country — not in the interests of a few individuals, who care not for the country, but in the interests of the whole of the people.

I am engaged in holy work. . . . I have not had the opportunities of the men opposite, but I have made the best use of my opportunities. I have been called anti-Christ. I have been called an Atheist. Well, if I were an Atheist I would not deny it. I am a Socialist. I believe in a co-operative commonwealth, but that is far ahead in Ireland. But why should not a man be allowed to improve the condition of things as they exist? The farmers say they have always treated the men with justice and kindness, but that is not so. I was sorry to hear Mr. Healy express the view that the farmers' case of the labourers in the country, and the case of the toilers in the city, should be split up. The farmers' problem and the merchants' problem are the same. The agricultural industry, and the urban industry are bulked, and you have got to settle both problems at the one time, and if you do not attempt to settle it then yours will be the responsibility. The working classes will not accept the responsibility, but they will do their utmost on all occasions to get over difficulties. We cannot trust the farmers to carry out any arrangement they enter into. . . .

Let Mr. Healy ask Shaw's opinion of Ireland. Shaw would tell him that when he got out of Ireland he did not want to come back because of the hellish conditions of life here. If we had a few more Shaws, and a few less Healys it would be the better for Ireland. Lawyers and politicians, and the people misled by them, are the cause of all the troubles in Ireland. The workers are now getting rid of the old, slothful drunken fellows who pose as their leaders. The men who are responsible for the present chaotic condition of thing are the men who would not pay fair wages, or give fair conditions, and the other employers, who are willing to give these things, are victimised by unscrupulous men. The employers have combined, but the right of combination must be recognised on both sides. If an employer is a member of an association and does not pay a decent wage, he should be socially ostracised, and if the workers do not carry out an arrangement they should be dealt with by their associations. Sauce for the goose should be sauce for the gander. I have put forward that long since, but the reply is 'No, we will have nothing but a strike or a lock-out; we will have constant dislocation of trade; and we are going to beat you down to the gutter so that there will not be a strike for twenty years.' Has there been a reason why there were not strikes long ago? Is the reason not to be found in the fact that the men have been so brutally treated that they had not had the strength to raise their heads? When I came to Dublin I found that the men on the quays had been paid their wages in public-houses, and if they did not waste most of their money there they would not get work the next time. Every stevedore was getting 10 per cent of the money taken by the publican from the worker, and the man who would not spend his money across the counter was not wanted. Men are not allowed to go to their duties on Sunday morning. After a long day's work they get home tired and half drunk. No man would work under the old conditions except he was half drunk. I have tried to lift men up out of that state of degradation. No monetary benefit has accrued to me. I have taken up the task through intense love of my class. I have given the men a stimulus, heart, and hope which they have never had before. I have made men out of drunken gaol-birds. The employers may now drive them over the precipice; they may compel them, after a long a weary struggle, to recognise the document submitted to them not to belong to the Irish Transport Workers' Union, but it will only be for a time. The day will come when they will break their bonds, and give back blow for blow. They may bring to their aid men like Father Hughes, of Lowtown, who went round in a motor-car and used the power of the Church against the poor to induce them to sell their bodies and souls to capitalists, like Mr. Waldron.[6] Father Hughes has got men to sign a document that they would not belong to the Union. There were men in the pulpits of all denominations getting up and denouncing Larkinism, but can any of them say anything against me or my private life? Yet, having taken upon themselves high office and sacred calling, they denounce Larkin — said he was making £18 a week and had a mansion in Dublin, and was gulling the working men.

I am told I am an Atheist. Why, it is the clergy who are making the people Atheists, making them Godless, making them brutes! The people are going to stop that and are going to be allowed a chance of exercising their religion. Mr. Waldron, a member of the Privy Council and an ex-M.P., would not allow his slaves to bow down to the Creator on Sundays because he wanted to make a profit out of their bodies. Mr. Waldron has admitted that his men went to bed in their boots. What else could he expect? After walking 30 miles along a canal bank, foodless, but always having the enemy, Drink, waiting for them, foul alcohol to poison and chloroform them, quarts of porter on credit! leg-tired, soul-tired, they lay down in their dirt. I have seen 13 men in one room and 17 lying round a big coke fire, heads to feet, in an establishment owned and controlled by this Privy Councillor. That was the man talking of Christianity! That was the man sent from Stephen's Green to ask for Home Rule for Ireland!

Is it any wonder a Larkin arose? Was there not need for a Larkin? I have proved out of the mouth of an alleged Catholic that workmen were brutalised and denied the right to worship their God on Sunday, Catholic and Protestant employers have been equally guilty in this matter. There are conditions of the same kind in Ulster, Munster, Leinster, and Connaught — and then Ireland sent 103 men to the House of Commons, all speaking as in the Tower of Babel. But the workers speak with one voice, and will stop this damnable hypocrisy. We want neither Redmond nor Carson, neither O'Brien nor Healy. We want men of our own class to go there and tell the truth. We want to tell Carson that he is preaching rapine, slaughter, and disorder. Yet nobody interferes with him. Why? Because the Government know it is all gas — all froth. But they know that the workers mean business and are going to unite in one field of economic activity and abolish all racial and sectarian differences. It will be a good day for Ireland when the Carson's [*sic*] of all classes are cleared out of the country. Mr. Healy, with all his eloquence, could not preach what I have preached because it would not pay. The politicians dine and wine together. The workers neither dine nor wine, but they suffer and starve together. If the employers want peace they can have peace, but if they want war they will get war.

6. Luke Waldron had extensive shareholdings in warehousing and department stores in Dublin.

FRANCIS SHEEHY-SKEFFINGTON

(1878–1916)

WAR AND FEMINISM (1914)

[Francis Sheehy-Skeffington, known to literature as the model for McCann in Joyce's *A Portrait of the Artist as a Young Man*, is also remembered for his pacifism, his campaign for women's rights and for the fact that he was murdered by a British officer, Captain J. C. Bowen-Colthurst, in 1916.

This article first appeared in *The Irish Citizen*, the official organ of the Irish Women's Suffrage Movement, on 12 September 1914. It, and the following item, *Speech from the Dock*, are reprinted as appendices in L. Levenson, *With Wooden Sword: A Portrait of Francis Sheehy-Skeffington, Militant Pacifist* (Boston and Dublin, 1983).]

That the logical and necessary antithesis between War and the Woman's Movement is not clearly recognised is due to a want of consistent and penetrative thought as to the bases of these two antipodal factors in human affairs.

I propose to demonstrate, first, that war is necessarily bound up with the destruction of Feminism; secondly, that Feminism is necessarily bound up with the abolition of war.

I

In the course of the evolution of Life on this planet, we observe a steady replacement of the ideal of quantity of life by that of quality.

The lowest forms of life spawn freely, produce an enormous number of seeds or eggs. Concurrently with this stage, we find that the progeny thus prolifically produced are subject to wholesale destruction from co-existing natural causes. The individual life has very small chances of survival; it is only by producing it in overwhelming quantities that the low-grade animal or plant can hope to escape the entire destruction of the species.

As we proceed up the line of evolution, we find this prolific spawning and wholesale destruction gradually giving way to a life-cycle in which less fertility, with increased chance of survival, is the rule. It is generally true that, the higher an organism is in the evolutionary scale, the fewer individuals of the species are born, and the greater proportion of these survive to complete the full life-cycle.

Mankind, at the top of the scale relatively to other living forms, repeats within its own evolutionary ascent the features of biological evolution in general. Lower races of mankind — and lower types among the higher races — are very prolific; but only a small proportion of the progeny survives. The others are weeded out by the natural forces co-existent with a low state of civilisation; by famine, by pestilence, and above all by war.

Following the analogy of other forms of life, we might expect two related phenomena to present themselves in the evolution of human society — a greatly reduced fertility, and a greatly increased chance of survival.

The diseased state of modern civilisation arises mainly from the fact that the latter phenomenon has presented itself without the former. Pestilence and famine are of increasingly rare occurrence; the progress of science makes life day by day easier, lessens hardship, lengthens the average duration of the individual life. The result is that the world is 'filling up.' Mankind, having become the dominant form of life on the earth, finds itself confronted with a condition of affairs — not too remote for the earth as a whole, and immediately pressing for certain portions of its surface — in which the resources of the planet may prove insufficient to nourish its human colony. It is this fact, the despair of believers in human perfectibility, which has hitherto proved an insuperable stumbling block in the way of the creators of utopias.

They, and other philosophic and scientific minds, have wrestled with this problem and attempted its solution along many different lines. Crude theorists have advocated infanticide as a solution — only a few months ago a bulky volume, seriously propounding this 'solution,' appeared from the London press. Devotees of science, agriculture and land reform point with enthusiasm to the as yet unexhausted possibilities of the earth. But to these there must be some limit; postponement, not solution, is the most that is to be looked for in that direction. Certain misusers of the name of Malthus[1] advocate artificial restrictions on population. But the instinctive aesthetic repugnance which these evoke in normal minds is shown by experience to be justified by the grave physical and moral evils which they bring in their train. No healthy solution can be found in that direction.

There are two methods, and two only, of solving the difficulty. One is War; the other is the Emancipation of Women.

II

The systematic upholders of war as a beneficent factor in human affairs (and they are not by any means confined to Germany) declare that not only is war a tonic to prevent mankind from growing torpid and slothful, not only is it valuable as a 'shaker-up,' but that it presents the only practicable solution of the population question. Like the older school of surgeons, they think occasional blood-letting, as a matter of deliberate policy, is the proper cure for the congested social system. Whenever the pressure of excessive population becomes too great, war will automatically reduce the numbers of mankind, and at the same time — so say the war-mongers — provide for the survival and dominance of the 'fittest' race.

This is a simple, blunt, and logical theory. But it is based on the logic of barbarism. It implies that war is to be retained as a permanent factor while its old co-partners, pestilence and famine, have been weeded out by science — except in so far as they are again and inevitably brought back in the train of war itself. It implies that the qualities which lead to success in war are those which ought to be perpetuated in the race. With the present revelation of what success in war means before our eyes, the falsity of this theory needs no demonstration.

This theory implies that, ever and anon, the fabric of civilisation, so painfully built up by generations, is to be overturned in catastrophe, and a fresh start made. It condemns mankind, at best, to a wearisome treadmill; at worst, to the total decay and disappearance of civilisation and human society. For in every such outbreak of barbarism something is lost; mankind is left several steps nearer to the primeval beast at its conclusion than at its commencement.

This theory renders impossible the emancipation of women. By the war-maker, woman is, and must be, regarded merely as a breeding machine. No escape is possible along the line of 'quality rather than quantity'; in war it is the quantity that counts, the overwhelming numbers of human beings wantonly flung to slaughter. Moreover, the increasing destructiveness of modern weapons renders this slaughter greater in every war than in the preceding one.

Men, and more men, is the cry of the war-lords. Women count only as producers of men. Woman must remain, as one writer of this school has coarsely put it, 'an appendage of the uterus.' We should be thankful to him for his bluntness. Woman as a human being disappears; she is of value but to reproduce 'food for powder.'

III

Start now from the other theory — the antipodes of the war-theory of society; start by assuming the emancipation of women. This, in its broadest aspect, means that woman must cease to be 'an appendage of the uterus.' Woman must count in and for herself, as a human being, with the human rights of an individual. Woman's vital energy, hitherto dammed up into one channel — that of reproduction — will be spread over all the fields of constructive human thought and action. And automatically, by the quiet action of the conservative processes of nature, the amount of woman's vital energy available for reproduction will diminish. The ideal of 'quality, not quantity,' will prevail; the nightmare of over-population will disappear. Humanity — man and woman — can proceed to construct its Utopias, to organise a social system based on peace and cooperation, without being haunted by the dread of an overcrowded and starving world. War, which is in ultimate analysis the expression of the savage competition of the hungry for food — 'commercial competition' is the polite term — will be generally recognised as the crime and madness it always is, and will cease to trouble the earth.

This is the line of true human progress — the only

1. Thomas Malthus (1766–1834) whose famous *An Essay on the Principle of Population* (1798) proposed that, since population increases in geometric ratio and subsistence in arithmetic ratio, population is necessarily limited by the checks of vice and misery.

possible line of human progress. The Emancipation of Woman is the essential condition of progress in that direction. That is why the Emancipation of Woman is incomparably the greatest World-Question for Humanity.

IV

So much for general principles. In the application of them to contemporary circumstances, one runs some risk of provoking disagreement among those who have followed the argument thus far. Nevertheless, I shall proceed to show how, in my opinion, these principles ought to be applied at the present moment by those who accept them.

If we want to stop war, we must begin *now*. This war is the product of a system — a system for which every statesman in Europe must bear his share of the blame. All deliberately accepted war as a permanent factor in the adjustment of international relations. All prepared to be as strong as possible against the day of the 'inevitable' war. None took any sincere or effective steps to make *Peace* inevitable.

Pacifists were fooled by the pretence that great armaments would maintain the peace. We now know the folly, or the hypocrisy, or both, of that pretence. But we are insensibly yielding to a new cant, preached by Mr. H. G. Wells[2] and others of his school — that this war will make an end of war. It is false. War can breed nothing but a fresh crop of wars.

By accepting this war, in any degree whatever, we are helping to perpetuate war. If we want to stop war, we must begin by stopping this war. The only way we can do that is to hamper as far as possible the conduct of it. The best way to do that is to *stop recruiting*.

We shall be told, of course, that 'the country is in danger.' What is in danger is the governing bureaucracy, which tries to identify itself with the nation. *No conquest could possibly be so disastrous as the continuance of war.* We cannot admit that 'now we are in it, we must go through with it.' That is the argument of all tyrants and evil-doers. We must simply say to the governing bureaucracy, 'You have brought on this war. If you say you could not have prevented it, you stand condemned as incompetent. If was your business to prevent it. We cannot allow you to use the weapon of war, any more than we could allow you to use the weapon of forcible feeding, under plea of necessity. Stand aside, and let us start afresh on a better path.'

Nothing that has been alleged of 'German atrocities' in the hot blood of war exceeds in horror the callous brutality of forcible feeding, in cold blood. And the man that is guilty of that crime is on a recruiting mission — to get more men to strengthen his hold on power.

The woman who does not, in the measure of her opportunities, discourage recruiting, has an imperfect understanding of the basis of the feminist movement. The woman who deliberately encourages recruiting is betraying that movement — though her name be Christabel Pankhurst.[3]

2. H. G. Wells (1866–1946) published a pamphlet *The War That Will End War* in 1914.

3. Christabel Pankhurst (1880–1958), daughter of the suffragette leader Emmeline Pankhurst, spoke at many recruiting meetings in England.

SPEECH FROM THE DOCK (1915)

[Skeffington's crusade against the war led to his arrest on 23 May 1915 under the notorious Defence of the Realm Act (DORA), which suspended trial by jury and allowed for summary jurisdiction. On being sentenced by Magistrate Mahoney, Skeffington went on hunger-strike for seven days. He was released under the so-called Cat and Mouse Act, which permitted the authorities to rearrest him once the effects of the hunger-strike had worn off. This they did not do.]

MR. SHEEHY-SKEFFINGTON: I do not think it will be necessary for me to detain you very long in my defence. I do not propose to call any witnesses, for, though there are certain textual errors that do not materially affect the case, the police report is a very fair one of what I said, apart from some small details. I shall not have to detain you very long and I am sure you will understand that I do not intend any personal discourtesy if I begin by complaining against the form of this trial — of having been deprived of the right to appear before a jury. I perfectly understand why the military authorities, who, in pursuance of their war against German militarism are exercising an absolute military despotism in this country, did not choose to bring a case of this kind before a jury. They have recognised that it is not possible to get a jury, in Dublin at all events, to make themselves the amenable instruments for the enforcement of this most iniquitous of the Coercion Acts — the Act known as the Defence of the Realm Act[1] — and they have decided, perhaps mistakenly, that they will have a better chance before a tribunal less amenable and responsible to public opinion. That action of theirs is a confession of defeat. It is an admission that they have not got the popular sentiment behind them in this country.

Whatever may be said with regard to the motives actuating me — I do not expect you will look on them favourably — but, whether you agree or not with the views I put forward, I claim *as an elementary right of a citizen in a free state* the right to put forward those opinions. It is clearly a matter of constitutional right to tell the people of Ireland that they had a right to take no part in a war as to which they were not consulted. When I say the people of Ireland were not consulted, I do not wish to imply that the peoples of other countries under the same rulers were consulted. It is notorious they were not. To take that portion of the population which suffers most in war time — the women — no pretence ever was made of consulting them. As regards the men who do the actual fighting, there is a pretence that they were consulted; but that it is merely a pretence is proved by the action of the Government. They found themselves quite unable to face an election in their own constituencies and, have passed a special Indemnity Bill absolving Members of Parliament who have been appointed to the Cabinet from facing their electors. So evident is it that the war was brought on by oligarchs that even in Great Britain the cry has gone out for the impeachment of Mr. Asquith and Sir Edward Grey.[2] In England a 'Stop-the-War Society' has been formed for the purpose of getting the people of England to bring pressure to bear on the oligarchs to stop the War. If I lived in England I should still deem it my duty to join such a society and to insist on the propaganda to stop the war in the only way in which the people can stop the war, namely by stopping recruiting, by ceasing to provide the food for powder. It is true that some friends of mine, both in England and in Ireland, say that while opposed to enlistment in the Army, they prefer to leave it to the free decision of individuals whether they should join or not. I should agree, if it were really left to the free decision of individuals; but in a time like this, when every force and influence both in the Press and on the platform, and every kind of social and economic pressure is being brought to bear upon men of military age to join the Army, it is the right and duty of every person of articulate speech to do what he can to produce the contrary pressure so as to give real freedom of decision to the people on the question. So much is true even of England, and of Ireland it is strengthened and intensified. Whatever may be said of the English people, the Irish people never at any time gave the slightest mandate of authority to their leaders, or representatives to commit them to a European war. No leader has any right to pledge the Irish people without such a mandate.

Everything I have said at these meetings fits in with what I consider my constitutional right and moral duty. It was necessary. In order to prevent the pressure being brought to bear on the weaker and more cowardly section and individuals being coerced, it was necessary to go into such questions as the origin of the war. Here I have based myself largely upon the literature published by the Independent Labour Party in England. I have shown, by quoting from a pamphlet entitled 'How the War Came About,' how the war was forced on by Russia against the wishes of Germany. I have also had to go into the causes of the war (going further back than the immediate year) and have based myself here largely on a book published in England 'Ten Years of Secret Diplomacy' by E. D. Morel,[3] in which the whole of the plot by which the war was brought about is laid bare — the plot for the encirclement and final crushing of Germany. It was necessary for me to go into the question of the progress and conduct of the war for the benefit of those weak

1. The Defence of the Realm Act, emergency legislation, was passed in November 1914 to prevent collaboration between Irish revolutionaries and Germany. It was used after 1916 to suppress all suspect organizations. It ceased to function in 1921.
2. Herbert Asquith (1852–1928) was prime minister of Britain 1908–16. Sir Edward Grey (1862–1933) was British foreign secretary 1905–16.
3. E. D. Morel (1873–1924) was a prolific anti-imperialist writer. His *Ten Years of Secret Diplomacy* (1910) dealt for the most part with Morocco.

individuals who are liable to be attracted by success, and to show that there was no prospect, no probability — one might even say, possibility — of England winning a decisive victory. It was necessary to expose (as was done by *Forward* in Glasgow)[4] the infamous cascade of lies poured forth in the papers of so-called German atrocities in Belgium and elsewhere.[5] It was also necessary for me to expose the humbug of the saying that Ireland had a special right to fight for Catholic Belgium. If it is true that Ireland had a right to fight for Catholic Belgium then it is true that Ireland had a right to fight for Catholic Galicia[6] against the Russians —

MR. REARDON: I am most unwilling to interfere, having regard to the fact that Mr. Sheehy-Skeffington is defending himself, but I think a great many things he is referring to are irrelevant.

MR. MAHONEY: I think it is better not to intervene. (*Inaudible*)

MR. SHEEHY-SKEFFINGTON: I have lastly dealt with the special Irish case: that Ireland has no direct quarrel with Germany. Ireland, from its depopulation, from its impoverishment, requires peace more than any other nation in Europe. That is one of the strongest points in the case I present.

On the basis of that claim for 'small nationalities,' which is assumedly the basis of this war, it is now taken for granted that it is right and rational for the people of Bohemia and Transylvania to rejoice in the defeats and break-up of the Austrian Empire; that it is right and rational for the people of Alsace-Lorraine and of Posen to rejoice in the break-up of the German Empire. It used to be taken for granted that the people of Poland had a right to rejoice in the break-up of the Russian Empire, but that opinion is no longer —

MR. MAHONEY: You are wandering very far away. You must be brief. The only point I have to consider is whether you spoke against recruiting in His Majesty's Army, and I know nothing about Irish politics, or Austrian politics, or Transylvanian politics.

MR. SHEEHY-SKEFFINGTON: I claim that to put this argument before the Irish people in the form which I have shown, and to tell them that it was just as right and natural for them to rejoice in the danger of the British Empire was a constitutional right.

MR. MAHONEY: I cannot allow you to go on in this way.

MR SHEEHY-SKEFFINGTON: You will say that is a breach of the law. What of it? We have had distinguished law-breakers before in Ireland. I am sure you will not prevent me referring to them, as you allowed Mr. Healy to do in a previous case.

MR. MAHONEY: I did not wish him to do so.

MR. SHEEHY-SKEFFINGTON: It is not necessary for me to refer to the cases of passive resisters in England, who refused to obey the law at the dictates of their consciences. It is not necessary for me to refer to the imprisonment of Mr. Redmond and Mr. Dillon on behalf of the welfare of the people.[7] It is only necessary for me to refer to Sir Edward Carson —

MR. MAHONEY: It will do you no good to talk about that. It will not affect your position.

MR. SHEEHY-SKEFFINGTON: It may not affect my position as regards Your Worship, but it may have a great effect on my position as regards the people. If Sir Edward Carson, as a reward for saying that he would break every law possible, gets a Cabinet appointment, what is the logical position as regards myself?[8] (*Laughter and applause in Court*) Your Worship cannot make me Attorney-General for England, nor even Lord Chancellor for Ireland, and it may even happen that Your Worship may

4. *Forward* was published in Glasgow between 1910 and 1915.
5. British World War I propaganda scored one of its great successes in persuading the world to believe the lies and exaggerations about the atrocities of the 'Hun' in Belgium.
6. A region of east-central Europe, now in south-east Poland and the south-west of the Soviet Union.
7. Redmond was imprisoned in 1888 and Dillon in 1881.
8. Sir Edward Carson (1854–1935), the unionist leader, threatened to break every rule possible in 1911 during his campaign against Home Rule; he later became a member of the war cabinet.

think it necessary to send me to prison for a small breach of an infamous law —

MR. MAHONEY: Strike out the word 'infamous' and I accept your description as accurate.

MR. SHEEHY-SKEFFINGTON: I think the word 'infamous' adds to the accuracy of the description. You may think it necessary to add to the eleven days I have spent in prison a few days more. If so I will serve them, provided I can do so under conditions suitable to political offenders, but I wish it clearly understood that I will serve no long sentence under any conditions, and I will serve no sentence whatever which does not recognise my rights as a political prisoner.

I am prosecuted, not for the attacks on recruiting, on voluntary enlistment in the Army — but for my attacks on Conscription. In attacking Conscription not only were my moral duty and my constitutional right equally strong, but here there was no breach of law whatever. To say that 'if Conscription comes we will not have it' is no more a breach of law than it was treason for Sir Edward Carson to say that 'if Home rule comes we will not have it.' In England an anti-Conscription League has been formed whose members declare their intention to resist to the death. In this case you will not find it possible to condemn me for breaking the law. I have only advocated passive resistance, because I believe that that form of resistance is sufficient to smash any Compulsory Military Service Act that may be put in force. It is because I have advocated passive resistance and because as Conscription came nearer, I have pledged an increasing number every Sunday to resist Conscription, it is because of this that this prosecution is brought against me, after holding similar meetings for forty weeks. For twenty or thirty weeks I have pledged audiences of from 500 to 1,000 that they would passively resist Conscription. That does not mean that 30,000 were pledged. No doubt many of them were the same each Sunday; but take it at the lowest figure, suppose it was 500, suppose there were only 100 who will keep the pledge to resist Conscription to the death, that 100 is enough to kill Conscription in Ireland. Whatever happens to me today, the work is done. If those men keep their pledges the enforcement of Conscription becomes impossible in Ireland.

In doing this, I have done what I regarded both as a duty and a right, both in opposing recruiting and conscription, and in the latter case I have broken no law. This prosecution would be intelligible in a country ruled by an autocrat, in a country under the iron heel of military despotism, in a country ruled by a narrow oligarchy fearing the smallest breath of criticism. It would be intelligible above all in a country held by force by another country, the rulers of which would fear to allow any expression of opinion amongst the subject people. If you condemn me, you condemn the system you represent as being some or all of these things. Any sentence you may pass on me is a sentence upon British rule in Ireland.

MR. MAHONEY: Mr. Skeffington admits the offence and glories in it. The chances are that he will repeat the offence when he gets his liberty. I know nothing of political offences. I am a long time here, but I do not know what a political offence is. The only offence I know is an offence against the law, and this is a grave offence. I will sentence him to six months' imprisonment with hard labour; and, at the expiration of that period, he will have to find bail in £50 or, in default, go to prison for another period of six months.

MR. SHEEHY-SKEFFINGTON: I will serve no such sentence. I will eat no food from this moment, and long before the expiration of the sentence I shall be out of prison, alive or dead! (*Loud cheering in Court*)

JAMES CONNOLLY

(1868–1916)

from: SOCIALISM AND NATIONALISM (1897)

[Here Connolly argues that, without nationalism, socialism cannot be realized in Ireland; without socialism, nationalism merely leads to an exchange of masters.]

In Ireland at the present time there are at work a variety of agencies seeking to preserve the national sentiment in the hearts of the people.

These agencies, whether Irish Language movements, Literary Societies or Commemoration Committees, are undoubtedly doing a work of lasting benefit to this country in helping to save from extinction the precious racial and national history, language and characteristics of our people.

Nevertheless, there is a danger that by too strict an adherence to their present methods of propaganda, and consequent neglect of vital living issues, they may only succeed in stereotyping our historical studies into a worship of the past, or crystallizing nationalism into a tradition – glorious and heroic indeed, but still only a tradition.

Now traditions may, and frequently do, provide materials for a glorious martyrdom, but can never be strong enough to ride the storm of a successful revolution.

If the national movement of our day is not merely to re-enact the old sad tragedies of our past history, it must show itself capable of rising to the exigencies of the moment.

It must demonstrate to the people of Ireland that our nationalism is not merely a morbid idealising of the past, but is also capable of formulating a distinct and definite answer to the problems of the present and a political and economic creed capable of adjustment to the wants of the future.

This concrete political and social ideal will best be supplied, I believe, by the frank acceptance on the part of all earnest nationalists of the Republic as their goal.

Not a Republic, as in France, where a capitalist monarchy with an elective head parodies the constitutional abortions of England, and in open alliance with the Muscovite despotism brazenly flaunts its apostacy [*sic*] to the traditions of the Revolution.[1]

Not a Republic as in the United States, where the power of the purse has established a new tyranny under the forms of freedom; where, one hundred years after the feet of the last British red-coat polluted the streets of Boston, British landlords and financiers impose upon American citizens a servitude compared with which the tax of pre-Revolution days was a mere trifle.[2]

No! the Republic I would wish our fellow-countrymen to set before them as their ideal should be of such a character that the mere mention of its name would at all times serve as a beacon-light to the oppressed of every land, at all times holding forth promise of freedom and plenteousness as the reward of their efforts on its behalf.

To the tenant farmer, ground between landlordism on the one hand and American competition on the other, as between the upper and the nether millstone; to the wage-workers in the towns, suffering from the exactions of the slave-driving capitalist to the agricultural labourer, toiling away his life for a wage barely sufficient to keep body and soul together; in fact to every one of the toiling millions upon whose misery the outwardly-splendid fabric of our modern civilisation is reared, the Irish Republic might be made a word to conjure with — a rallying point for the disaffected, a haven for the oppressed, a point of departure for the Socialist, enthusiastic in the cause of human freedom.

This linking together of our national aspirations with the hopes of the men and women who have raised the standard of revolt against that system of capitalism and landlordism, of which the British

1. The reference is to the dual alliance between Russia and France, formally signed in late 1895.
2. Connolly may be referring here to the catastrophic fall in American stocks which followed upon President Grover Cleveland's aggressive declaration of the Monroe doctrine in 1895 on the issue of the border between British Guiana and Venezuela. The dispute was settled through the Treaty of Washington (1897).

Empire is the most aggressive type and resolute defender, should not, in any sense, import an element of discord into the ranks of earnest nationalists, and would serve to place us in touch with fresh reservoirs of moral and physical strength sufficient to lift the cause of Ireland to a more commanding position than it has occupied since the day of Benburb.[3]

It may be pleaded that the ideal of a Socialist Republic, implying, as it does, a complete political and economic revolution would be sure to alienate all our middle-class and aristocratic supporters, who would dread the loss of their property and privileges.

What does this objection mean? That we must conciliate the privileged classes in Ireland!

But you can only disarm their hostility by assuring them that in a *free* Ireland their 'privileges' will not be interfered with. That is to say; you must guarantee that when Ireland is free of foreign domination, the green-coated Irish soldiers will guard the fraudulent gains of capitalist and landlord from 'the thin hands of the poor'[4] just as remorselessly and just as effectually as the scarlet-coated emissaries of England do today.

On no other basis will the classes unite with you. Do you expect the masses to fight for this ideal?

When you talk of freeing Ireland, do you only mean the chemical elements which compose the soil of Ireland? Or is it the Irish people you mean? If the latter, from what do you propose to free them? From the rule of England?

But all systems of political administration or governmental machinery are but the reflex of the economic forms which underlie them.

English rule in England is but the symbol of the fact that English conquerors in the past forced upon this country a property system founded upon spoliation, fraud and murder: that, as the present-day exercise of the 'rights of property' so originated involves the continual practice of legalised spoliation and fraud, English rule is found to be the most suitable form of government by which the spoliation can be protected, and an English army the most pliant tool with which to execute judicial murder when the fears of the propertied classes demand it.

3. Owen Roe O'Neill won a striking victory over an army of Ulster Scots in 1646. It was hailed in Ireland and abroad as a decisive victory for the Catholic Confederation.

4. Untraced.

The Socialist who would destroy, root and branch, the whole brutally materialistic system of civilisation, which like the English language we have adopted as our own, is, I hold, a far more deadly foe to English rule and tutelage, than the superficial thinker who imagines it possible to reconcile Irish freedom with those insidious but disastrous forms of economic subjection — landlord tyranny, capitalist fraud and unclean usury; baneful fruits of the Norman Conquest, the unholy trinity, of which Strongbow and Diarmuid MacMurchadha — Norman thief and Irish traitor — were the fitting precursors and apostles.[5]

If you remove the English army tomorrow and hoist the green flag over Dublin Castle, unless you set about the organisation of the Socialist Republic your efforts would be in vain.

England would still rule you. She would rule you through her capitalists, through her landlords, through her financiers, through the whole array of commercial and individualist institutions she has planted in this country and watered with the tears of our mothers and the blood of our martyrs.

England would still rule you to your ruin, even while your lips offered hypocritical homage at the shrine of that Freedom whose cause you had betrayed.

Nationalism without Socialism — without a reorganisation of society on the basis of a broader and more developed form of that common property which underlay the social structure of Ancient Erin — is only national recreancy.

It would be tantamount to a public declaration that our oppressors had, so far, succeeded in inoculating us with their perverted conceptions of justice and morality that we had finally decided to accept those conceptions as our own, and no longer needed an alien army to force them upon us . . . .

5. McMurchadha, king of Leinster *c.* 1126–71, requested support from the Normans and it came with Strongbow's army in 1170.

PARNELLISM AND LABOUR (1898)

[First published on 8 October 1898 in *The Workers' Republic*, the paper founded by Connolly earlier that year as the organ of the Irish Socialist Republican Party, this article was designed to coincide as far as possible with the seventh anniversary of Parnell's death. Connolly makes it clear that the Irish Parliamentary Party is not even notionally friendly to Labour or mildly threatening to the English government. This was one of many attacks on the party which emphasized its profound disarray and futility in this, the centenary year of the rebellion of 1798.]

So long as they seek for Home Rule — for mere changes within the Constitution — our Irish parties at Westminster are, and must ever be, in the position of political hucksters seeking a good price for the votes they offer as wares. Their 'independence' is only the fraudulent cloak with which they strive to cover their venality and lack of spirit.

We must not omit to specify one other cause of the decay of the official Parnellite party, viz., their unsatisfactory attitude towards labour. When Charles Stewart Parnell was basely deserted in Committee Room 15 by the crowd of adventurers and hack journalists out of whom he had constructed a formidable political party; when he was attacked in Ireland by the tenant farmers who owed much of whatever security they possessed to his skilful leadership; when the priesthood, whom he had elevated to power in the branches of the National League, turned to rend the man under whose firm guidance their influence might have become a power for freedom; when he was, in fact, deserted by the men who had ever been most loud-mouthed in their adulation of his person, it was the leal and true-hearted workingmen of Ireland who sprang to his side and fought his battles. They had never gained, but ever lost by his agitation, but in the supreme crisis of his destinies they rose superior to all considerations and fought for the man battling against an insulting form of foreign dictation. They asked no reward — and got none. During the early days of the split Mr. Parnell did, indeed, adopt a programme laid before him by Dublin workingmen[1] — a programme embodying nearly every measure advocated as palliative measures by the Socialist parties, but with his untimely death disappeared every hope of seeing that programme adhered to by any Home Rule party. Every succeeding year has seen the Parnellite party become more and more conservative and reactionary. Today, in direct opposition to the policy of their great leader, we find the Parnellite chiefs seeking every opportunity to hob-nob with the representatives of Irish landlordism; hailing their feeblest utterances upon a financial question as the brightest scintillations of wisdom; and not scrupling to tell at Cambridge an audience, composed of the young fledglings of English aristocracy, that the realisation of Ireland's independence was neither possible nor desirable.[2]

Followers of Parnell they are indeed, but they follow at such a respectable distance they have lost sight not only of the leader but of his principles.

Meanwhile, the manhood of Ireland, no longer dazzled by the glare of a great personality, have had time to more closely examine their position, social and political. As a result they turn alike from the men who sold their leader at the bidding of an unscrupulous politician; from the incapable gang whose only hope of existence is to live like political cannibals upon the reputation of the dead; and from the pitiful compromise of the National Demand[3] which scarce even the genius of Parnell could make appear respectable.

The working class of Ireland trusts no more the charming of the middle-class politician, charm he never so plausibly; strong in its own power it marches irresistibly forward to its destiny, the Socialist Republic.

1. In March 1891, Parnell gave his 'general and practical agreement' to a programme of reform presented by a conference of trade unionists, presided over by Fred Allen, then prominent in the Irish Republican Brotherhood.

2. This refers to a statement made at the Cambridge Union in 1897 by the Irish Parliamentary Party member, Frank Hugh O'Donnell (1848–1916).

3. Home Rule was the National Demand, although in 1898 it had lost much of its peremptory quality.

SINN FEIN, SOCIALISM AND THE NATION (1909)

[Connolly's anxiety to distinguish between socialism and the economic doctrines of Sinn Féin is as manifest here as his determination to show that the socialist position is also nationalist but not sectarian.

The article first appeared in W. P. Ryan's *The Irish Nation* on 23 January 1909.]

In a recent issue of *The Peasant*,[1] a correspondent, 'Cairbre,' in the midst of a very fair and reasonable article on 'Sinn Fein and Socialism,' says: 'A rapprochement between Sinn Feinism and Socialism is highly desirable.' To this I desire to say a fervent 'Amen,' and to follow up in my prayer with a suggestion which may help in realising such a desirable consummation. Always presupposing that the rapprochement is desired between Sinn Feiners who sympathise with Socialism and not merely with those who see no further than 'the Constitution of '82,'[2] on the one hand, and Socialists who realise that a Socialist movement must rest upon and draw its inspiration from the historical and actual conditions of the country in which it functions and not merely lose themselves in an abstract 'internationalism' (which has no relation to the real internationalism of the Socialist movement), on the other.

But, first, it would be as well to state some of the difficulties in the way in order that we may shape our course in order to avoid them.

Sinn Fein has two sides — its economic teaching and its philosophy of self-reliance. With its economic teaching, as expounded by my friend Mr. Arthur Griffith in his adoption of the doctrines of Frederick List,[3] Socialists have no sympathy, as it appeals only to those who measure a nation's prosperity by the volume of wealth produced in a country, instead of by the distribution of that wealth amongst the inhabitants. According to that definition, Ireland in 1847 was a prosperous country because it exported food, whereas Denmark was comparatively unprosperous because it exported little. But with that part of Sinn Fein which teaches that Ireland must rely upon itself, respect her own traditions, know her own history, preserve her own language and literature without prejudice to, or denial of, the worth in the language or literature or other people, stand erect in her own worth and claim to be appraised for her own intrinsic value, and not as part of the wheels and cogs of the imperial system of another people — with that side of Sinn Fein Socialists may sympathise; and, indeed, as a cold matter of fact, those doctrines were preached in Dublin by the Irish Socialist Republican Party from 1896 onward,[4] before the Sinn Fein movement was founded.

The first side of Sinn Fein necessarily excludes the Socialists; the second does not. The first rests upon a capitalist conception of progress; the second is a gateway by which Ireland may enter into the intellectual domain which Socialism has made its own — by its spiritual affinity with all the world-wide forces making for social freedom.

Socialists are also somewhat divided in their ideas as to what is a proper course in a country like Ireland. One set, observing that those who talk loudest about 'Ireland a Nation' are often the most merciless grinders of the faces of the poor, fly off to the extremest limit of hostility to Nationalism and, whilst opposed to oppression at all times, are also opposed to national revolt for national independence.

Another, principally recruited amongst the workers in the towns of North-East Ulster have been weaned by Socialist ideas and industrial disputes from the leadership of Tory and Orange landlords and capitalists; but as they are offered practical measures of relief from capitalist oppression by the English Independent Labour Party, and offered nothing but a green flag by Irish Nationalism, they naturally go where they imagine relief will come from. Thus their social discontent is lost to the Irish cause. These men see that the workers shot down last winter in Belfast were not shot down in the interests of the Legislative Union; they were shot down in the interests of Irish capitalists.[5] Hence, when a Sinn Feiner waxes eloquent about restoring the Constitution of '82, but remains silent about the increasing industrial despotism of the capitalist; when the Sinn Feiner speaks to men who are fighting against low wages and tells them that the Sinn Fein body has promised lots of Irish labour at low wages

1. *The Irish Peasant* (1905–06) was edited by W. P. Ryan (1867–1942), a socialist and sharp opponent of clerical opposition to nationalism.
2. The 'constitution' granted in 1782 when Ireland won a measure of legislative independence from England.
3. In 1905 Griffith outlined his economic ideas to the National Council, an ad hoc nationalist grouping. He followed the German economist Friedrich List (1789–1846) in supporting protective tariffs that would allow home-based light industry to develop.
4. Connolly was himself the founder of the ISRP, which came into being on 29 May 1896. In 1903 the party was reorganised by William O'Brien (1881–1968) as the Socialist Party of Ireland. In 1921, it became the Communist Party of Ireland. Sinn Féin dates, as a movement, from 1905.
5. During the Belfast strike of 1907, the police fired on the strikers, killing two and wounding several others. James Larkin organized the strike, with the support of catholic and protestant workers.

to any foreign capitalist who wishes to establish in Ireland, what wonder if they come to believe that a change from Toryism to Sinn Feinism would simply be a change from the devil they do know to the devil they do not know!

The other section of Socialists in Ireland are those who inscribe their banners with the watchword 'Irish Socialist Republic,' who teach that Socialism will mean in Ireland the common ownership by Irish people of the land and everything else necessary to feed, clothe, house and maintain life in Ireland, and that therefore Socialism in its application to Ireland means and requires the fullest trust of the Irish people as the arbiters of their own destinies in conformity with the laws of progress and humanity.

This section of Socialists were so Irish that they organised and led the great anti-Jubilee procession of 1897 in Dublin,[6] which completely destroyed all the carefully-prepared British preparations to represent Irish as loyal; and yet their position was so correct from their standpoint that at the International Congress of 1900 at Paris they were granted, in the name of Ireland, separate representation from England and treated and acted as a separate nation.[7]

Now the problem is to find a basis of union on which all these sections who owe allegiance to one or other conception of Socialism may unite. My position is that this union, or rapprochement, cannot be arrived at by discussing our differences. Let us rather find out and unite upon the things upon which we agree. Once we get together, we will find that our differences are not so insuperable as they appear whilst we are separated. What is necessary first is a simple platform around which to gather, with the understanding that as much as possible shall be left to future conditions to dictate and as little as possible settled now by rules or theories. As each section has complete confidence in their own doctrines, let them show their confidence by entering an organisation with those who differ from them in methods, and depend upon the development of events to prove the correctness of their position. Each person to have complete freedom of speech in conformity with the common object; the lecture platform to be common to all, and every lecture to be followed by questions and discussion. With mutual toleration on both sides, the Protestant worker may learn that the cooperation of the Catholic who works, suffers, votes and fights alongside him is more immediately vital to his cause and victory day by day than the co-operation or workers on the other side of the Channel; and that Socialists outside of Ireland are all in favour of that national independence which he rejects for the sake of a few worthless votes.

And the Catholic Sinn Feiners may learn that love of freedom beats strongly in the breasts of Protestant peasants and workmen who, because they have approached it from a different historical standpoint, regard the Nationalist conception with suspicion or even hostility.

6. The celebration of the sixtieth anniversary of Queen Victoria's accession to the throne was countered by anti-processional groups, of which the socialists were the most prominent.

7. The International Socialist Congress of 1900 recognized the Irish Socialist Party and the British Independent Labour Party.

from: NORTH-EAST ULSTER (1913)

[Connolly published the first part of this article in *Forward* on 7 June 1913; two other parts followed, in August of that year. The later parts are reprinted here.

Connolly wants to make a number of important distinctions here: between Belfast and Dublin, between the British and the Irish Labour Parties, and between the situation of the new Irish Labour Party and that of the traditional Irish Parliamentary Party. Most of all, he emphasizes the basic feature of the Ulster situation — industrial progress linked to political backwardness. This seemed a rare phenomenon to English socialists, who knew little of the influence in Ulster of the Orange Order.]

II

According to all socialist theories North-East Ulster, being the most developed industrially, ought to be the quarter in which class lines of cleavage, politically and industrially, should be the most pronounced and class-rebellion the most common.

As a cold matter of fact, it is the happy hunting ground of the slave-driver and the home of the least rebellious slaves in the industrial world.

Dublin, on the other hand, has more strongly developed working-class feeling, more strongly accentuated instincts of loyalty to the working class than any city of its size in the globe.

I have explained before how the perfectly devilish ingenuity of the master class had sought its ends in North-East Ulster. How the land were [*sic*] stolen from Catholics, given to Episcopalians, but planted by Presbyterians; how the latter were persecuted by the Government, but could not avoid the necessity of defending it against the Catholics, and how out of this complicated situation there inevitably grew up a feeling of common interests between the slaves and the slave-drivers.

As the march of the Irish towards emancipation developed, as step by step they secured more and more political rights and greater and greater recognition, so in like ratio the disabilities of the Presbyterians and other dissenters were abolished.

For a brief period during the closing years of the eighteenth century, it did indeed seem probable that the common disabilities of Presbyterians and Catholics would unite them all under the common name of Irishmen. Hence the rebel society of that time took the significant name of 'United Irishmen.'

But the removal of the religious disabilities from the dissenting community had, as its effect, the obliteration of all political difference between the sects and their practical political unity under the common designation of Protestants, as against the Catholics, upon whom the fetters of religious disability still clung.

Humanly speaking, one would have confidently predicted that as the Presbyterians and Dissenters were emancipated as a result of a clamorous agitation against religious inequality, and as that agitation derived its chief force and menace from the power of Catholic numbers in Ireland, then the members of these sects would unite with the agitators to win for all an enjoyment of these rights the agitators and rebels had won for them.

But the prediction would have missed the mark by several million miles. Instead, the Protestants who had been persecuted joined with the Protestants who had persecuted them against the menace of an intrusion by the Catholics into the fold of political and religious freedom — 'Civil and religious liberty.'

There is no use blaming them. It is common experience in history that as each order fought its way upward into the circle of governing classes, it joined with its former tyrants in an endeavour to curb the aspirations of these orders still unfree.

That in Ireland religious sects played the same game as elsewhere was played by economic or social classes does not prove the wickedness of the Irish players, but does serve to illustrate the universality of the passions that operate upon the stage of the world's history.

It also serves to illustrate the wisdom of the Socialist contention that as the working class has no subject class beneath it, therefore, to the working class of necessity belongs the honour of being the class destined to put an end to class rule, since, in emancipating itself, it cannot help emancipating all other classes.

Individuals out of other classes must and will help as individual Protestants have helped in the fight for Catholic emancipation in Ireland; but on the whole, the burden must rest upon the shoulders of the most subject class.

If the North-East corner of Ireland is, therefore, the home of a people whose minds are saturated with conceptions of political activity fit only for the atmosphere of the seventeenth century, if the sublime ideas of an all-embracing democracy equally as insistent upon its duties as upon its rights have as yet found poor lodgment here, the fault lies not with this generation of toilers, but with those pastors and masters who deceived it and enslaved it in the past — and deceived it in order that they might enslave it.

But as no good can come of blaming it, so also no good, but infinite evil, can come of truckling to it. Let the truth be told, however ugly. Here, the Orange working class are slaves in spirit because they have been reared up among a people whose conditions of servitude were more slavish than their own. In Catholic Ireland the working class are rebels in spirit and democratic in feeling because for hundreds of years they have found no class as lowly paid or as hardly treated as themselves.

At one time in the industrial world of Great Britain and Ireland the skilled labourer looked down with contempt upon the unskilled and bitterly resented his attempt to get his children taught any of the skilled trades; the feeling of the Orangemen of Ireland towards the Catholics is but a glorified representation on a big stage of the same passions inspired by the same unworthy motives.

An atavistic survival of a dark and ignorant past!

Viewing Irish politics in the light of this analysis, one can see how futile and vain are the criticisms of the Labour Party in Parliament which are based upon a comparison of what was done by the Nationalist group in the past and what is being left undone by the Labour Group today. I am neither criticising nor defending the Labour Group in Parliament; I am simply pointing out that any criticism based upon an analogy with the actions, past or present, of the Irish party, is necessarily faulty and misleading.

The Irish party had all the political traditions and prejudices of centuries to reinforce its attitude of hostility to the Government, nay, more, its only serious rival among its own constituents was a party more uncompromisingly hostile to the Government than itself – the republican or physical force party.

The Labour party, on the other hand, has had to meet and overcome all the political traditions and prejudices of its supporters in order to win their votes, and knows that at any time it may lose these suffrages so tardily given.

The Irish party never needed to let the question of retaining the suffrages of the Irish electors enter into their calculations. They were almost always returned unopposed. The Labour party knows that a forward move on the part of either Liberal or Tory will always endanger a certain portion of Labour votes.

In other words, the Irish group was a party to whose aid the mental habits formed by centuries of struggle came as a reinforcement among its constituents at every stage of the struggle. But the Labour party is a party which, in order to progress, must be continually breaking with and outraging institutions which the mental habits of its supporters had for centuries accustomed them to venerate.

I have written in vain if I have not helped the reader to realise that the historical backgrounds of the movement in England and Ireland are so essentially different that the Irish Socialist movement can only be truly served by a party indigenous to the soil, and explained by a literature having the same source: that the phrases and watchwords which might serve to express the soul of the movement in one country may possibly stifle its soul and suffocate its expression in the other.

One great need of the movement in Ireland is a literature of its very own. When that is written people will begin to understand why it is that the Irish Catholic worker is a good democrat and a revolutionist, though he knows nothing of the fine spun theories of democracy or revolution; and how and why it is that the doctrine that because the workers of Belfast live under the same industrial conditions as do those of Great Britain, they are therefore subject to the same passions and to be influenced by the same methods of propaganda, is a doctrine almost screamingly funny in its absurdity.

III

A correspondent of *Forward* in a recent edition asked how it was that if the Orangemen were so bad they allowed Mr. Connolly to hold meetings in the principal streets of Belfast? Our answer to that is that neither Mr. Connolly nor any other Socialist can now hold outdoor meetings in an exclusively Orange district, even those Belfast Socialists who 'will not have Home Rule' in their programme, cannot hold open-air meetings in any exclusively Orange district. Socialist meetings in Belfast can only be held in the business centre of the town where the passing crowd is of a mixed or uncertain nature.

All this demonstrates how immensely difficult is the task at present in Belfast. No part of these countries has a part more difficult. It means the propagation of twentieth century revolutionism amidst the mental atmosphere of the early seventeenth century.

When striving to induce my Belfast comrades to adopt this policy we are now propagating in our meetings, I was asked did I think it would make our propaganda easier. I answered that I did not, that on the contrary it would arouse passions immensely more bitter than had even been met here by the Socialist movement in the past, but that it would make our propaganda more fruitful and our organisation more enduring.

To this I still adhere. A real Socialist movement cannot be built by temporising in front of a dying cause such as that of the Orange ascendancy, even although in the paroxysms of its death struggle it assumes the appearance of an energy like unto that of health. A real Socialist movement can only be born of struggle, of uncompromising affirmation of the faith that is in us. Such a movement infallibly gathers to it every element of rebellion and of progress, and in the midst of the storm and stress of the struggle solidifies into a real revolutionary force.

Therefore, we declare to the Orange workers of Belfast that we stand for the right of the people in Ireland to rule as well as to own Ireland, and cannot conceive of a separation of the two ideas, and to all and sundry we announce that as Socialists we are Home Rulers, but that on the day the Home Rule Government goes into power the Socialist movement in Ireland will go into opposition.

from: SOCIALISM AND NATIONALISM (1914)

[The third Home Rule Bill was introduced by the British prime minister Herbert Asquith in April 1911. The House of Lords used its veto to delay the passage of the bill and Asquith tried to reach a compromise between the Irish Parliamentary Party leader John Redmond, his fellow MP and supporter from Belfast, Joseph Devlin (1872–1934), and the leader of unionist opposition to the Bill, Sir Edward Carson. This involved consideration of the exclusion of Ulster or part of Ulster from the Bill. The Home Rule Bill was signed into law by King George V in September 1914, but was suspended for the duration of World War I, without the exclusionary problem being fully resolved. However, both Redmond and Devlin were willing to accept a form of partition, at least as a temporary measure. Connolly's fears of their behaviour and of the effects of partition were well-founded. Redmond and Devlin also encouraged Irishmen to enlist in the British army during the Great War. To Connolly, this was a slavish and stupid action, of a piece with the acceptance of partition.

The following articles are taken respectively from *The Irish Worker*, 14 March 1914; *Forward*, 11 April 1914; *The Irish Worker*, 8 August 1914. They were collected and edited by D. Ryan and published under the title *Socialism and Nationalism: A Selection from the Writings of James Connolly* in 1948.]

LABOUR AND THE PROPOSED PARTITION OF IRELAND

The recent proposals of Messrs. Asquith, Devlin, Redmond[1] and Co. for the settlement of the Home Rule question deserve the earnest attention of the working class democracy of this country. They reveal in a most striking and unmistakeable manner the depths of betrayal to which the so-called Nationalist politicians are willing to sink. For generations the conscience of the civilised world has been shocked by the historical record of the partition of Poland; publicists, poets, humanitarians, patriots, all lovers of their kind and of progress have wept over the unhappy lot of a country torn asunder by the brute force of their alien oppressors, its unity ruthlessly destroyed and its traditions trampled into the dust.

But Poland was disrupted by outside forces, its enemies were the mercenaries of the tyrant kingdoms and empires of Europe; its sons and daughters died in the trenches and on the battlefields by the thousand rather than submit to their beloved country being annihilated as a nation. But Ireland, what of Ireland? It is the trusted leaders of Ireland that in secret conclave with the enemies of Ireland have agreed to see Ireland as a nation disrupted politically and her children divided under separate political governments with warring interests.

Now, what is the position of Labour towards it all? Let us remember that the Orange aristocracy now fighting for its supremacy in Ireland has at all times been based upon a denial of the common human rights of the Irish people; that the Orange Order was not founded to safeguard religious freedom, but to deny religious freedom, and that it raised this religious question, not for the sake of any religion, but in order to use religious zeal in the interests of the oppressive property rights of rack-renting landlords and sweating capitalists. That the Irish people might be kept asunder and robbed whilst so sundered and divided, the Orange aristocracy went down to the lowest depths and out of the lowest pits of hell brought up the abominations of sectarian feuds to stir the passions of the ignorant mob. No crime was too brutal or cowardly; no lie too base; no slander too ghastly, as long as they served to keep the democracy asunder.

And now that the progress of democracy elsewhere has somewhat muzzled the dogs of aristocratic power, now that in England as well as in Ireland the forces of labour are stirring and making for freedom and light, this same gang of well-fed plunderers of the people, secure in Union held upon their own dupes, seek by threats of force to arrest the march of ideas and stifle the light of civilisation and liberty. And, lo and behold, the trusted guardians of the people, the vaunted saviours of the Irish race, agree in front of the enemy and in face of the world to

1. Joseph Devlin (1871–1934) played a prominent part in organizing the National Volunteers in opposition to Carson's Ulster Volunteers. John Redmond (1856–1918) secured the introduction of the third Home Rule Bill in 1912.

sacrifice to the bigoted enemy the unity of the nation and along with it the lives, liberties and hopes of that portion of the nation which in the midst of the most hostile surroundings have fought to keep the faith in things national and progressive.

Such a scheme as that agreed to by Redmond and Devlin, the betrayal of the national democracy of industrial Ulster would mean a carnival of reaction both North and South, would set back the wheels of progress, would destroy the oncoming unity of the Irish Labour movement and paralyse all advanced movements whilst it endured.

To it Labour should give the bitterest opposition, against it Labour in Ulster should fight even to the death, if necessary, as our fathers fought before us.

THE EXCLUSION OF ULSTER

Socialists and Labour people generally in Great Britain have had good reason to deplore the existence of the Irish question and to realise how disastrous upon the chances of their candidates has been the fact of the existence in the constituencies of a large mass of organised voters whose political activities were not influenced solely or even largely by the domestic issues before the electors. Our British comrades have had long and sore experience of contests in which all the arguments and all the local feeling were on the side of the Socialist or Labour candidate, and yet that local candidate was ignominiously defeated because there existed in the constituency a large Irish vote — a large mass of voters who supported the Liberal, not because they were opposed to Labour, but because they wanted Ireland to have Home Rule.

Our British comrades have learned that the existence of that Irish vote and the knowledge that it would be cast for the Home Rule official candidate, irrespective of his record on or his stand upon Labour matters, caused hundreds of thousands who otherwise would have voted Labour to vote Liberal in dread that the Irish defection would 'let the Tory in'. For a generation now the Labour movement in Great Britain has been paralysed politically by this fear; and all hands have looked forward eagerly to the time when the granting of Home Rule would remove their fear and allow free expression to all the forces that make for a political Labour movement in that country. Even many of the actions and votes of the Labour party in the House of Commons which have been strenuously complained of have been justified by that Party on the plea that it was necessary to keep in power the government that would get Home Rule out of the way. Now, in view of this experience of the Socialist movement in Great Britain, we can surely not view with any complacency a proposal that will keep that question to the front as a live issue at British elections for six years longer or rather for a totally indefinite period. We know that this 'six years period' so glibly spoken of by politicians has no background of reality to justify the belief that that term can be considered as more than a mere figure of speech . . . .

Thus we have it clearly foreshadowed that there is no such thing as a six years' limit which can be binding upon future Parliaments and that therefore the question of Home Rule for the Ulster Counties will be a test question at future elections in Great Britain, and will then play there the same disastrous role for the Labour movement as the question of Home Rule does now. The political organisation of the Home Rule party will be kept alive in every industrial constituency on the pretext of working for a 'United Ireland,' and in the same manner the Unionist Party will also keep up its special organisations, Orange Lodges, etc., in order to keep alive the sectarian appeal to the voters from Ireland who will be asked to 'vote against driving Ulster under the heels of the Papish Dublin Parliament.'

Labour men in and out of Ireland have often declared that if Home Rule was wanted for no other purpose, it was necessary in order to allow of the solidifying the Labour vote in Great Britain, and the rescue of the Irish voters in that country from their thraldom to the Liberal caucus. It might not be far from the truth to surmise that the Liberal Party managers have seen the same point as clearly as we did ourselves, and have quietly resolved that such a good weapon as the Nationalist Party sentiment should not be entirely withdrawn from their armoury. The reader will also see that with a perfectly Mephistophelian subtlety the question of exclusion is not suggested to be voted upon by any large area where the chances for or against might be fairly equal, where exclusion might be defeated as it might be if all Ulster were the venue of the poll, and all Ulster had to stay out or come in as a result of the verdict of the ballot box. No, the counties to be voted on the question are the counties where the

Unionists are in an overwhelming majority, and where therefore the vote is a mere farce — a subterfuge to hide the grossness of the betrayal of the Home Rule electors. Then again each county or borough enters or remains outside according to its own vote, and quite independent of the vote of its neighbours in Ulster. Thus the Home Rule question as far as Ulster is concerned, may be indefinitely prolonged and kept alive as an issue to divide and disrupt the Labour vote in Great Britain.

The effect of such exclusion upon Labour in Ireland will be at least equally, and probably more, disastrous. All hopes of uniting the workers, irrespective of religion or old political battle cries will be shattered, and through North and South the issue of Home Rule will be still used to cover the iniquities of the capitalist and landlord class. I am not speaking without due knowledge of the sentiments of the organised Labour movement in Ireland when I say that we would much rather see the Home Rule Bill defeated than see it carried with Ulster or any part of Ulster left out . . . .

Meanwhile, as a study in political disparity, watch the manoeuvres of the Home Rule Party on this question. The deal is already, I believe, framed up, but when the actual vote is to be taken in the Counties of Down, Antrim, Derry and Armagh and the Boroughs of Belfast and Derry, Messrs Redmond, Devlin and Co. will tour these counties and boroughs letting loose floods of oratory asking for votes against exclusion and thus will delude the workers into forgetting the real crime, viz., consenting to make the unity of the Irish Nation a subject to be decided by the votes of the most bigoted and passion-blinded reactionaries in these four counties where such reactionaries are in the majority. The betrayal is agreed upon, I repeat, the vote is only a subterfuge to hide the grossness of the betrayal.

It still remains to be seen whether the working class agitation cannot succeed in frightening these vampires from the feast they are promising themselves upon the corpse of a dismembered Ireland . . . .

OUR DUTY IN THIS CRISIS

What should be the attitude to the working-class democracy of Ireland in face of the present crisis? I wish to emphasise the fact that the question is addressed to the 'working-class democracy' because I believe that it would be worse than foolish — it would be a crime against all our hopes and aspirations — to take counsel in this matter from any other source.

Mr. John E. Redmond has just earned the plaudits of all the bitterest enemies of Ireland and slanderers of the Irish race by declaring, in the name of Ireland, that the British Government can now safely withdraw all its garrisons from Ireland, and that the Irish slaves will guarantee to protect the Irish estate of England until their masters come back to take possession[1] — a statement that announces to all the world that Ireland has at last accepted as permanent this status of a British province. Surely no inspiration can be sought from that source.

The advanced Nationalists have neither a policy nor a leader. During the Russian Revolution such of their Press as existed in and out of Ireland, as well as their spokesmen, orators and writers vied with each other in laudation of Russian and vilification of all the Russian enemies of Czardom. It was freely asserted that Russia was the natural enemy of England; that the heroic revolutionalists were in the pay of the English Government and that every true Irish patriot ought to pray for the success of the armies of the Czar. Now, as I, amongst other Irish Socialists, predicted all along, when the exigencies of diplomacy makes it suitable, the Russian bear and the English lion are hunting together and every victory for the Czar's Cossacks is a victory for the paymasters of those King's Own Scottish Borderers who, but the other day, murdered the people of Dublin in cold blood.[2] Surely the childish intellects that conceived of the pro-Russian campaign of nine years ago cannot give us light and leading in any campaign for freedom from the British allies of Russia today? It is well to remember also that in this connection since 1909 the enthusiasm for the Russians was replaced in the same quarter by as blatant a propaganda in favour of the German War Lord. But since the guns did begin to speak in reality this propaganda had died out in whispers, whilst without a protest, the manhood of Ireland was

1. Redmond made this statement in the House of Commons in August 1914.
2. On 26 July 1914, after the Howth gun-running incident, a regiment of the King's Own Scottish Borderers opened fire on civilians at Bachelor's Walk, Dublin, killing three and injuring at least thirty-eight.

pledged to armed warfare against the very power our advanced Nationalist friends have wasted so much good ink in acclaiming.

Of late, sections of the advanced Nationalist press have lent themselves to a desperate effort to misrepresent the position of the Carsonites, and to claim for them the admiration of Irish Nationalists on the grounds that these Carsonites were fearless Irishmen who had refused to take dictation from England. A more devilishly mischievous and lying doctrine was never preached in Ireland. The Carsonite position is indeed plain — so plain that nothing but sheer perversity of purpose can misunderstand it, or cloak it with a resemblance to Irish patriotism. The Carsonites say that their fathers were planted in this country to assist in keeping the natives down in subjection that this country might be held for England. That this was God's will because the Catholic Irish were not fit for responsibilities and powers of free men and that they are not fit for the exercise of these responsibilities and powers till this day. Therefore, say the Carsonites, we have kept our side of the bargain; we have refused to admit the Catholics to power and responsibility; we have manned the government of this country for England, we propose to continue to do so, and rather than admit that these Catholics — these 'mickies and teagues' — are our equals, we will fight, in the hope that our fighting will cause the English people to revolt against their government and re-establish us in our historic position as an English colony in Ireland, superior to, and unhampered by, the political institutions of the Irish natives.

How this can be represented as the case of Irishmen refusing to take dictation from England passeth all comprehension. It is rather the case of a community in Poland, after 250 years colonisation, still refusing to adopt the title of natives, and obstinately clinging to the position and privileges of a dominant colony. Their programme is summed up in the expression which forms the dominant note of all their speeches, sermons and literature:

> We are loyal British subjects. We hold this country for England. England cannot desert us.

What light or leading then can Ireland get from the hysterical patriots who so egregiously misrepresent this fierce contempt for Ireland as something that ought to win the esteem of Irishmen?

What ought to be the attitude of the working-class democracy of Ireland in face of the present crisis?

In the first place, then, we ought to clear our minds of all the political cant which would tell us that we have either 'natural enemies' or 'natural allies' in any of the powers now warring. When it is said that we ought to unite to protect our shores against the 'foreign enemy' I confess to be unable to follow that line of reasoning, as I know of no foreign enemy of this country except the British Government and know that it is not the British Government that is meant.

In the second place we ought to seriously consider that the evil effects of this war upon Ireland will be simply incalculable, that it will cause untold suffering and misery amongst the people, and that as this misery and suffering have been brought upon us because of our enforced partisanship with a nation whose government never consulted us in the matter, we are therefore perfectly at liberty morally to make any bargain we may see fit, or that may present itself in the course of events.

Should a German army land in Ireland tomorrow we should be perfectly justified in joining it if by doing so we could rid this country once and for all from its connection with the Brigand Empire that drags us unwillingly into this war.

Should the working class of Europe, rather than slaughter each other for the benefit of kings and financiers, proceed tomorrow to erect barricades all over Europe, to break up bridges and destroy the transport service that war might be abolished, we should be perfectly justified in following such a glorious example and contributing our aid to the final dethronement of the vulture classes that rule and rob the world.

But pending either of these consummations it is our manifest duty to take all possible action to save the poor from the horrors this war has in store.

Let it be remembered that there is no natural scarcity of food in Ireland. Ireland is an agricultural country, and can normally feed all her people under any sane system of things. But prices are going up in England and hence there will be an immense demand for Irish produce. To meet that demand all nerves will be strained on this side, the food that ought to feed the people of Ireland will be sent out of Ireland in greater quantities than ever and *famine prices will come in Ireland to be immediately followed by famine itself*. Ireland will starve, or rather the townspeople of Ireland will starve, that the British army and navy and jingoes may be fed. Remember, the Irish farmer like all other farmers will benefit by the high prices of the war, but these high prices will mean starvation to the labourers in the towns. But without these labourers the farmers' produce cannot leave Ireland without the help of a garrison that England cannot now spare. We must consider at once whether it will not be our duty to refuse to allow agricultural produce to leave Ireland until provision is made for the Irish working class.

Let us not shrink from the consequences. This may mean more than a transport strike, it may mean armed battling in the streets to keep in this country the food for our people. But whatever it may mean it must not be shrunk from. It is the immediately feasible policy of the working-class democracy, the answer to all weaklings who in this crisis of our country's history stand helpless and bewildered crying for guidance, when they are not hastening to betray her.

Starting thus, Ireland may yet set the torch to a European conflagration that will not burn out until the last throne and the last capitalist bond and debenture will be shrivelled on the funeral pyre of the last war lord.

from: A CONTINENTAL REVOLUTION (1914)

[The outbreak of World War I was a blow to international socialism. In Ireland, those who went to fight for Britain seemed to Connolly to be misguided men who were fighting for their own worst enemies and against their own best interests. The official propaganda presented the war on the British side as a battle for civilization and, under that slogan, concealed its true purposes and its complex causes. Connolly only could appeal, at this stage, to the socialist and nationalist spirit to resist the war fever in Britain. The effect of the war on his thinking may have been to bring him closer to the belief that only a nationalist and socialist alliance could have any effect on the prevailing situation.

This article first appeared in *Forward* on 15 August 1914.]

. . . But why go on? Is it not as clear as the fact of life itself that no insurrection of the working class; no general strike; no general uprising of the forces of Labour in Europe, could possibly carry with it, or entail a greater slaughter of socialists, than will their participation as soldiers in the campaigns of the armies of their respective countries? Every shell which explodes in the midst of a German battalion will slaughter some socialists; every Austrian cavalry charge will leave the gashed and hacked bodies of Serbian or Russian socialists squirming and twisting in agony upon the ground; every Russian, Austrian, or German ship sent to the bottom or blown sky-high will mean sorrow and mourning in the homes of some socialist comrades of ours. If these men must die, would it not be better to die in their own country fighting for freedom for their class, and for the abolition of war, than to go forth to strange countries and die slaughtering and slaughtered by their brothers that tyrants and profiteers might live?

Civilisation is being destroyed before our eyes; the results of generations of propaganda and patient heroic plodding and self-sacrifice are being blown into annihilation from a hundred cannon mouths; thousands of comrades with whose souls we have lived in fraternal communion are about to be done to death; they whose one hope it was to be spared to co-operate in building the perfect society of the future are being driven to fratricidal slaughter in shambles where that hope will be buried under a sea of blood.

I am not writing in captious criticism of my continental comrades. We know too little about what is happening on the continent, and events have moved too quickly for any of us to be in a position to criticise at all. But believing as I do that any action would be justified which would put a stop to this colossal crime now being perpetrated, I feel compelled to express the hope that ere long we may read of the paralysing of the internal transport service on the continent, even should the act of paralysing necessitate the erection of socialist barricades and acts of rioting by socialist soldiers and sailors, as happened in Russia in 1905. Even an unsuccessful attempt at social revolution by force of arms, following the paralysis of the economic life of militarism, would be less disastrous to the socialist cause than the act of socialists allowing themselves to be used in the slaughter of their brothers in the cause.

A great continental uprising of the working class would stop the war; a universal protest at public meetings will not save a single life from being wantonly slaughtered.

I make no war upon patriotism; never have done.

But against the patriotism of capitalism — the patriotism which makes the interest of the capitalist class the supreme test of duty and right — I place the patriotism of the working class, the patriotism which judges every public act by its effect upon the fortunes of those who toil. That which is good for the working class I esteem patriotic, but that party or movement is the most perfect embodiment of patriotism which most successfully works for the conquest by the working class of the control of the destinies of the land wherein they labour.

To me, therefore, the socialist of another country is a fellow-patriot, as the capitalist of my own country is a natural enemy. I regard each nation as the possessor of a definite contribution to the common stock of civilisation, and I regard the capitalist class of each nation as being the logical and natural enemy of the national culture which constitutes that definite contribution.

Therefore, the stronger I am in my affection for national tradition, literature, language, and sympathies, the more firmly rooted I am in my opposition to that capitalist class which in its soulless lust for power and gold would bray the nations as in a mortar.[1]

Reasoning from such premises, therefore, this war appears to me as the most fearful crime of the centuries. In it the working class are to be sacrificed that a small clique of rulers and armament makers may sate their lust for power and their greed for wealth. Nations are to be obliterated, progress stopped, and international hatreds erected into deities to be worshipped.

1. i.e. pound or crush to a paste.

A WAR FOR CIVILISATION (1915)

[In this article, published in *The Workers' Republic* (30 October 1915), Connolly's bitterness against the war is further sharpened by the realization that it is the workers who are not only fighting, but also dying, in appalling numbers for their enslavers.]

We are hearing and reading a lot just now about a war for civilisation. In some vague, ill-defined manner we are led to believe that the great empires of Europe have suddenly been seized with a chivalrous desire to right the wrongs of mankind, and have sallied forth to war, giving their noblest blood and greatest measures to the task of furthering the cause of civilisation.

It seems unreal, but it may be possible. Great emotions sometimes master the most cold and calculating individuals, pushing them on to do that which in their colder moments they would have sneered at. In like manner great emotions sometimes master whole communities of men and women, and nations have gone mad, as in the Crusades, over matters that did not enter into any scheme of selfish calculation.

But in such cases the great emotions manifested themselves in at least an appropriate manner. Their actions under the influence of great emotions had a relation to the cause or the ideal for which they were ostensibly warring.

In the case of the war for civilisation, however, we look in vain for any action which in itself bears the mark of civilisation. As we count civilisation it means the ascendancy of industry and the arts of industry over the reign of violence and pillage. Civilisation means the conquest by ordered law and peaceful discussion of the forces of evil, it means the exaltation of those whose strength is only in the righteousness of their cause over those whose power is gained by a ruthless seizing of domination founded on force.

Civilisation necessarily connotes the gradual supplanting of the reign of chance and muddling by the forces of order and careful provision for the future; it means the levelling up of classes, and the initiation of the people into a knowledge and enjoyment of all that tends to soften the natural hardships of life and to make that life refined and beautiful.

But the war for civilisation has done none of those things — aspires to do none of these things. It is primarily a war upon a nation whose chief crime is that it refuses to accept a position of dependence, but insists instead upon organising its forces so that its people can co-operate with nature in making their lives independent of chance, and independent of the goodwill of others.

The war for civilisation is a war upon a nation which insists upon organising its intellect so as to produce the highest and best in science, in art, in music, in industry; and insists moreover upon so co-ordinating and linking up all these that the final result shall be a perfectly educated nation of men and women.

In the past civilisation has been a heritage enjoyed by a few upon a basis of the brutalisation of the vast multitude; that nation aims at a civilisation of the whole resting upon the whole, and only made possible by the educated co-operation of an educated whole.

The war for civilisation is waged by a nation like Russia, which has the greatest proportion of illiterates of any European power, and which strives sedulously to prevent education where it is possible, and to poison it where prohibition is impossible.

The war for civilisation is waged by a nation like Britain which holds in thrall a sixth of the human race, and holds as a cardinal doctrine of its faith that none of its subject races may, under penalty of imprisonment and death, dream of ruling their own territories. A nation which believes that all races are subject to purchase, and which brands as perfidy the act of any nation which, like Bulgaria, chooses to carry its wares and its arms to any other than a British market.

This war for civilisation in the name of neutrality and small nationalities invades Persia and Greece, and in the name of the interests of commerce seizes the cargo of neutral ships, and flaunts its defiance of neutral flags.

In the name of freedom from militarism it establishes military rule in Ireland, battling for progress it abolishes trial by jury, and waging war for enlightened rule it tramples the freedom of the press under the heel of a military despot.

Is it any wonder then that that particular war for civilisation arouses no enthusiasm in the ranks of the toiling masses of the Irish nation?

But there is another war for civilisation in which these masses are interested. That war is being waged by the forces of organised labour.

Civilisation cannot be built upon slaves; civilisation cannot be secured if the producers are sinking into misery; civilisation is lost if they whose labour makes it possible share so little of its fruits that its fall can leave them no worse than its security.

The workers are at the bottom of civilised society. That civilisation may endure they ought to push upward from their poverty and misery until they emerge into the full sunlight of freedom. When the fruits of civilisation, created by all, are enjoyed in common by all, then civilisation is secure. Not till then.

Since this European war started the workers as a whole have been sinking. It is not merely that they have lost in comfort — have lost a certain standard of food and clothing by reason of the increase of prices — but they have lost in a great measure, in Britain at least, all those hard won rights of combination and freedom of action, the possession of which was the foundation upon which they hoped to build the greater freedom of the future.

From being citizens with rights the workers were being driven and betrayed into the position of slaves with duties. Some of them may have been well-paid slaves, but slavery is not measured by the amount of oats in the feeding trough to which the slave is tied. It is measured by his loss of control of the conditions under which he labours.

We here in Ireland, particularly those who follow the example of the Irish Transport and General Workers' Union, have been battling to preserve those rights which others have surrendered; we have fought to keep up our standards of life, to force up our wages, to better our conditions.

To that extent we have been truly engaged in a war for civilisation. Every victory we have gained has gone to increase the security of life amongst our class, has gone to put bread on the tables, coals in the fires, clothes on the backs of those to whom food and warmth and clothing are things of ever pressing moment.

Some of our class have fought in Flanders and the Dardanelles; the greatest achievement of them all combined will weigh but a feather in the balance for good compared with the achievements of those who stayed at home and fought to secure the rights of the working class against invasion.

The carnival of murder on the continent will be remembered as a nightmare in the future, will not have the slightest effect in deciding for good the fate of our homes, our wages, our hours, our conditions. But the victories of labour in Ireland will be as footholds, secure and firm, in the upward climb of our class to the fullness and enjoyment of all that labour creates, and organised society can provide.

Truly, labour alone in these days is fighting the real *war for civilisation*.

THE IRISH FLAG (1916)

[This is Connolly's final statement on his decision to ally the cause of socialism with militant nationalism.

The flag was hoisted over Liberty Hall in Dublin, the headquarters of the Irish Citizen Army, on Sunday, 16 April 1916; the Easter Rising began on 24 April. The act is a declaration of war against the British Empire and its appalling record in Ireland and in the world at large.

This article was published in *The Workers' Republic* on 8 April 1916. The newspaper was suppressed a month later.]

The Council of the Irish Citizen Army has resolved after grave and earnest deliberation, to hoist the green flag of Ireland over Liberty Hall, as over a fortress held for Ireland by the arms of Irishmen.

This is a momentous decision in the most serious crisis Ireland has witnessed in our day and generation. It will, we are sure, send a thrill through the hearts of every true Irish man and woman, and send the red blood coursing fiercely along the veins of every lover of the race.

It means that in the midst of and despite the treasons and backslidings of leaders and guides, in the midst of and despite all the weaknesses, corruption and moral cowardice of a section of the people, in the midst of and despite all this there still remains in Ireland a spot where a body of true men and women are ready to hoist, gather round, and defend the flag made sacred by all the sufferings of all the martyrs of the past.

Since this unholy war first started we have seen every symbol of Irish freedom desecrated to the purposes of the enemy, we have witnessed the prostitution of every holy Irish tradition. That the young men of Ireland might be seduced into the service of the nation that denies every national power to their country, we have seen appeals made to our love of freedom, to our religious instincts, to our sympathy for the oppressed, to our kinship with suffering.

The power that for seven hundred years has waged bitter and unrelenting war upon the freedom of Ireland, and that still declares that the rights of Ireland must forever remain subordinate to the interests of the British Empire, hypocritically appealed to our young men to enlist under her banner and shed their blood 'in the interests of freedom.'

The power whose reign in Ireland has been one long carnival of corruption and debauchery of civic virtue, and which has rioted in the debasement and degradation of everything Irish men and women hold sacred, appealed to us in the name of religion to fight for her as the champion of christendom.

The power which holds in subjection more of the world's population than any other power on the globe, and holds them in subjection as slaves without any guarantee of freedom or power of self-government, this power that sets Catholic against Protestant, the Hindu against the Mohammedan, the yellow man against the brown, and keeps them quarrelling with each other whilst she robs and murders them all — this power appeals to Ireland to send her sons to fight under England's banner for the cause of the oppressed. The power whose rule in Ireland has made of Ireland a desert, and made the history of our race read like the records of a shambles, as she plans for the annihilation of another race appeals to our manhood to fight for her because of our sympathy for the suffering, and of our hatred of oppression.

For generations the shamrock was banned as a national emblem of Ireland, but in her extremity England uses the shamrock as a means for exciting in foolish Irishmen loyalty to England. For centuries the green flag of Ireland was a thing accurst and hated by the English garrison in Ireland, as it is still in their inmost hearts. But in India, in Egypt, in Flanders, in Gallipoli, the green flag is used by our rulers to encourage Irish soldiers of England to give up their lives for the power that denies their country the right of nationhood. Green flags wave over recruiting offices in Ireland and England as a bait to lure on poor fools to dishonourable deaths in England's uniform.

The national press of Ireland, the true national press, uncorrupted and unterrified, has largely succeeded in turning back the tide of demoralisation, and opening up the minds of the Irish public to a realisation of the truth about the position of their country in the war. The national press of Ireland is a real flag of freedom flying for Ireland despite the enemy, but it is well that also there should fly in Dublin the green flag of this country as a rallying point of our forces and embodiment of all our hopes. Where better could that flag fly than over the unconquered citadel of the Irish working class, Liberty Hall, the fortress of the militant working class of Ireland.

We are out for Ireland for the Irish. But who are the Irish? Not the rack-renting, slum-owning landlord; not the sweating, profit-grinding capitalist; not the sleek and oily lawyer; not the prostitute pressman — the hired liars of the enemy. Not these are the Irish upon whom the future depends. Not these, but the Irish working class, the only secure foundation upon which a free nation can be reared.

The cause of labour is the cause of Ireland, the cause of Ireland is the cause of labour. They cannot be dissevered. Ireland seeks freedom. Labour seeks that an Ireland free should be the sole mistress of her own destiny, supreme owner of all material things within and upon her soil. Labour seeks to make the free Irish nation the guardian of the interests of the people of Ireland, and to secure that end would vest in that free Irish nation all property rights as against the claims of the individual, with the end in view that the individual may be enriched by the nation, and not by the spoiling of his fellows.

Having in view such a high and holy function for the nation to perform, is it not well and fitting that we of the working class should fight for the freedom of the nation from foreign rule, as the first requisite for the free development of the national powers needed for our class? It is so fitting. Therefore on Sunday, April 16th, 1916, the green flag of Ireland will be solemnly hoisted over Liberty Hall as the symbol of our faith in freedom, and as a token to all the world that the working class of Dublin stands for the cause of Ireland, and the cause of Ireland is the cause of a separate and distinct nationality.

In these days of doubt, despair, and resurgent hope we fling our banner to the breeze, the flag of our fathers, the symbol of our national redemption, the sunburst shining over an Ireland re-born.

PROCLAMATION OF THE REPUBLIC (1916)

Poblacht na hÉireann

The Provisional Government of the Irish Republic to the People of Ireland

[The proclamation was issued on 24 April 1916. The text is from E. Curtis and R. B. McDowell (eds), *Irish Historical Documents 1172–1922* (1943).]

Irishmen and Irishwomen: In the name of God and of the dead generations from which she receives her old tradition of nationhood, Ireland, through us, summons her children to her flag and strikes for her freedom.

Having organized and trained her manhood through her secret revolutionary organizations, the Irish Republican Brotherhood, and through her open military organizations, the Irish Volunteers, and the Irish Citizen Army,[1] having patiently perfected her discipline, having resolutely waited for the right moment to reveal itself, she now seizes that moment, and, supported by her exiled children in America and by gallant allies in Europe, but relying in the first on her own strength, she strikes in full confidence of victory.

We declare the right of the people of Ireland to the ownership of Ireland, and to the unfettered control of Irish destinies, to be sovereign and indefeasible. The long usurpation of that right by a foreign people and government has not extinguished the right, nor can it ever be extinguished except by the destruction of the Irish people. In every generation the Irish people have asserted their right to national freedom and sovereignty; six times during the past three hundred years they have asserted it in arms.[2] Standing on that fundamental right and again asserting it in arms in the face of the world, we hereby proclaim the Irish republic as a sovereign independent state, and we pledge our lives and the lives of our comrades-in-arms to the cause of its freedom, of its welfare, and of its exaltation among the nations.

The Irish republic is entitled to, and hereby claims, the allegiance of every Irishman and Irishwoman. The republic guarantees religious and civil liberty, equal rights and equal opportunities to all its citizens, and declares its resolve to pursue the happiness and prosperity of the whole nation and of all its parts, cherishing all the children of the nation

1. Irish Republican Brotherhood, founded in 1858; it played a leading role in the founding of the Irish Volunteers in 1913. The Irish Citizen Army was founded by Connolly and James Larkin as a defence force for the unemployed against the attacks of the police.
2. Presumably in the rebellions of 1601, 1640, 1798, 1803, 1848, and 1867.

equally, and oblivious of the differences carefully fostered by an alien government, which have divided a minority from the majority in the past.

Until our arms have brought the opportune moment for the establishment of a permanent national government, representative of the whole people of Ireland, and elected by the suffrages of all her men and women, the Provisional Government, hereby constituted, will administer the civil and military affairs of the republic in trust for the people. We place the cause of the Irish republic under the protection of the Most High God, whose blessing we invoke upon our arms, and we pray that no one who serves that cause will dishonour it by cowardice, inhumanity, or rapine. In this supreme hour the Irish nation must, by its valour and discipline, and by the readiness of its children to sacrifice themselves for the common good, prove itself worthy of the august destiny to which it is called.

Signed on behalf of the provisional government,

Thomas J. Clarke, Sean MacDiarmada, Thomas MacDonagh, P. H. Pearse, Eamonn Ceannt, James Connolly, Joseph Plunkett.

THE DEMOCRATIC PROGRAMME OF THE FIRST DÁIL (1919)

[This statement provides a basis for all future declarations of republican principle. It clearly influenced the Constitution of 1937 and remains an embarrassing reminder to all subsequent meetings of the Dáil of what the struggle for independence was supposed to achieve. The text is from Dáil Éireann proceedings, 1919–21, 1922–23.]

We declare in the words of the Irish Republican Proclamation the right of the people of Ireland to the ownership of Ireland, and to the unfettered control of Irish destinies to be indefeasible, and in the language of our first president, Pádraig Mac Phiarais,[1] we declare that the Nation's sovereignty extends not only to all men and women of the Nation, but to all its material possessions, the Nation's soil and all its resources, all the wealth and all the wealth-producing processes within the Nation, and with him we reaffirm that all right to private property must be subordinated to the public right and welfare.

We declare that we desire our country to be ruled in accordance with the principles of Liberty, Equality, and Justice for all, which alone can secure permanence of Government in the willing adhesion of the people.

We affirm the duty of every man and woman to give allegiance and service to the Commonwealth, and declare it is the duty of the Nation to assure that every citizen shall have opportunity to spend his or her strength and faculties in the service of the people. In return for willing service, we, in the name of the Republic, declare the right of every citizen to an adequate share of the produce of the Nation's labour.

It shall be the first duty of the Government of the Republic to make provision for the physical, mental and spiritual well-being of the children, to secure that no child shall suffer hunger or cold from lack of food, clothing, or shelter, but that all shall be provided with the means and facilities requisite for their proper education and training as Citizens of a Free and Gaelic Ireland.

The Irish Republic fully realises the necessity of abolishing the present odious, degrading and foreign Poor Law System,[2] substituting therefor a sympathetic native scheme for the care of the Nation's aged and infirm, who shall not be regarded as a burden, but rather entitled to the Nation's gratitude and consideration. Likewise it shall be the duty of the Republic to take such measures as will safeguard the health of the people and ensure the physical as well as the moral well-being of the Nation.

It shall be our duty to promote the development of the Nation's resources, to increase the productivity of its soil, to exploit its mineral deposits,

1. Patrick Pearse (1879–1916).

2. The Poor Law System, introduced in 1838, revised in 1847, was abolished upon the establishment of the Free State. The workhouses it instituted were detested symbols of poverty and oppression.

peat bogs, and fisheries, its waterways and harbours, in the interests and for the benefit of the Irish people.

It shall be the duty of the Republic to adopt all measures necessary for the recreation and invigoration of our Industries, and to ensure their being developed on the most beneficial and progressive co-operative and industrial lines. With the adoption of an extensive Irish Consular Service, trade with foreign Nations shall be revived on terms of mutual advantage and goodwill, and while undertaking the organisation of the Nation's trade, import and export, it shall be the duty of the Republic to prevent the shipment from Ireland of food and other necessaries until the wants of the Irish people are fully satisfied and the future provided for.

It shall also devolve upon the National Government to seek co-operation of the Governments of other countries in determining a standard of Social and Industrial Legislation with a view to a general and lasting improvement in the conditions under which the working classes live and labour.

MICHAEL COLLINS

(1890–1922)

from: ARGUMENTS FOR THE TREATY (1922)

[The following address is compiled from reports of what Collins said at a public meeting on 5 March 1922. He began his speech in Irish, claiming that the recently signed Treaty with Britain had won Ireland a measure of independence greater than that achieved under Grattan's leadership in 1782 and more secure, since it was ratified by an international agreement. The battle of words between Collins and Eamon de Valera, who was leading the campaign against the Treaty, was a prelude to the Civil War. 'The Republic' is the real issue, perhaps because of its phantasmal character.]

THE SUBSTANCE OF FREEDOM

. . . We gather here today to uphold and to expound the Treaty. It was not our intention to hold any meetings until the issue was definitely before the electorate. But as a campaign has been begun in the country by Mr. de Valera and his followers we cannot afford to wait longer.

Mr. de Valera's campaign is spoken of as a campaign against the Treaty. It is not really that.

The Irish people have already ratified the Treaty through their elected representatives. And the people of Ireland will stand by that ratification. The weekly paper of our opponents, which they call *The Republic of Ireland*, admits that ratification. Document No. 2[1] lapsed with the approval by the Dail of the Treaty, they said in a leading article in the issue of February 21st; and in the issue of February 28th it is said 'alternative documents are no longer in question.'

No, it is not a campaign against the Treaty.

Nothing would disconcert Mr. de Valera and his followers more than the wrecking of the Treaty, than the loss of what has been secured by the Treaty.

It is a campaign, not against the Treaty, but against the Free State. And not only against the Free State, but still more against those who stand for the Free State. 'Please God we will win,' said Mr. de Valera last Sunday at Ennis, 'and then there will be an end to the Free State.' And if there were an end to the Free State, what then? What is the object of our opponents? I will tell you what it is.

In the same leading article of February 28th (in the *Republic of Ireland*) they say: 'The Republican position is clear,' and 'We stand against the Treaty for the maintenance of the Republic.'

The maintenance of the Republic, [exclaimed Mr. Collins.] That is very curious. Because in the previous week's issue we were told by a member of the Dail Cabinet that before the Truce of July last it

1. Document No. 2 was a document containing alternative proposals for a treaty between Britain and Ireland. de Valera first put it forward at a private session of Dáil Éireann on 14 December 1921. The main points of difference were proposals to create a form of external association with Britain and the Commonwealth and a different formal relationship with north-east Ulster.

had become plain that it was physically impossible to secure Ireland's ideal of a completely isolated Republic in the immediate future, otherwise than by driving the overwhelmingly superior British forces out of the country.

The Republic was an ideal which it was physically impossible to secure last July. By February it has become their policy to maintain the Republic.

In his speech at Ennis last Sunday Mr. de Valera repeated that he was not a Republican doctrinaire. He said that it was as a symbol, an expression of the democratic right of the people of Ireland to rule themselves without interference from any outside power, that they had raised the banner of the Republic! I do not quarrel with that description. The Republic was a symbol, an expression of our right to freedom. But at Limerick Mr. de Valera speaks of the possible disestablishment of the Republic.

These appear to be contradictory views, but the object of our opponents is becoming plain.

The ideal of a Republic was physically impossible in July, and it was dropped by Mr. de Valera in favour of Document No. 2. But now alternative documents are no longer in question, and Mr. de Valera and his supporters once more stand for the Republic. What has happened since to account for the burial of the Republican ideal and its subsequent resurrection?

I will tell you what has happened since.

The Treaty has been brought back. It has brought and is bringing such freedom to Ireland in the transference to us of all governmental powers, but, above all, in the departure of the British armed forces, that it has become safe, and simple, and easy, and courageous to stand now for what was surrendered in July, because the British armed forces were still here.

We could not beat the British out by force, so the Republican ideal was surrendered. But when we have beaten them out by the Treaty the Republican ideal, which was surrendered in July, is restored.

The object of Mr. de Valera and his party emerges. They are stealing our clothes.

We have beaten out the British by means of the Treaty. While damning the Treaty, and us with it, they are taking advantage of the evacuation which the Treaty secures.

After the surrender of the Republican ideal in July we were sent over to make a Treaty with England.

Some of us were sent very much against our wishes. That is well-known to our opponents. Everyone knew then, and it is idle and dishonest to deny now, that in the event of a settlement some postponement of the realisation of our full national sentiment would have to be agreed to.

We were not strong enough to realise the full Republican ideal. In addition, we must remember that there is a strong minority in our country up in the North-East that does not yet share our national views, but has to be reckoned with. In view of these things I claim that we brought back the fullest measure of freedom obtainable — the solid substance of independence.

We signed the Treaty believing it gave us such freedom. Our opponents make use of the advantage of the Treaty while they vilify it and us. The position gained by the Treaty provides them with a jumping off ground. After dropping the Republic while the British were still here, they shout bravely for it now from the safe foothold provided for them by means of the Treaty.

It is a mean campaign.

We were left with the Herculean labour and the heavy responsibility of taking over a Government. This would be a colossal task for the most experienced men of any nation. And we are young and not experienced. While we are thus engaged our former comrades go about the country talking. They tell the people to think of their own strength and the weakness of the enemy. Yes! and what is it that has made us strong and the enemy weak in the last few months? Yes, the enemy becomes weaker every day as his numbers grow less. And as they grow less, louder and louder do our opponents shout for the Republic which they surrendered in July last.

What has made the enemy weaker? The enemy that was then too strong for us? Is it the division in our ranks, which is Mr. de Valera's achievement, and which is already threatening a suspension of the evacuation? Or is it the Treaty which is our achievement?

Mr. de Valera, in Limerick last Sunday, compared Ireland to a party that had set out to cross a desert, and they had come to a green spot, he said, and there were some who came along to tell them to lie down and stay there, and be satisfied and not go on.

Yes, we had come by means of the Treaty to a green oasis, the last in the long weary desert over which the Irish nation has been travelling. Oases are the resting-places of the desert, and unless the traveller finds them and refreshes himself he never reaches his destination.

Ireland has been brought to the last one, beyond which there is but a little and an easy stretch to go. The nation has earned the right to rest for a little while we renew our strength, and restore somewhat our earlier vigour.

But there are some amongst us who, while they take full advantage of the oasis — only a fool or a madman would fail to do that — complain of those who have led them to it. They find fault with it. They do nothing to help. They are poisoning the wells, wanting now to hurry on, seeing the road ahead short and straight, wanting the glory for themselves of leading the Irish nation over it, while unwilling to fill and shoulder the pack.

We are getting the British armed forces out of Ireland. Because of that evacuation our opponents are strong enough and brave enough now to say: 'They are traitors who got you this. We are men of principle. We stand for the Republic' — that Republic which it was physically impossible to secure until the traitors had betrayed you.

Have we betrayed you?

I claim that we have got in the Treaty the strongest guarantee of freedom and security that we could have got on paper. We have got the strongest guarantees that we could have got in a written Treaty between ourselves and England. We have got the greatest amount of real practical freedom in the evacuation of their troops. In their place we have the right to have our own troops, our own army. This is the proof, the making good — the proof that the status we have secured in the Treaty is what we claim it to be — something which gives us independence and the right and power to maintain it.

The status we accepted, which we forced the British to define, was the constitutional status of Canada. Constitutionally all the British nations of the Commonwealth have full freedom, and the same equality, one with the other: Canada equal to England, South Africa equal to Canada.

We have secured by the Treaty this constitutional position. That is the substance of the Treaty — a position of freedom and equality with all the other nations — and we can, and will take full advantage of that position.

Legally, and absolutely, the Dominions are in subjection to the British Parliament. Constitutionally, actually, they are completely free. They have the advantage over us of great distance. We have the advantage over them of having the position they hold assured to us by a treaty. We have annulled our disadvantage of nearness by securing that advantage.

We have the signed agreement with England, defining our status. We have the free nations of the Commonwealth as witnesses to England's signature.

Our position cannot be challenged by England. Were she to challenge it she would challenge the position of Canada, Australia, and South Africa. Such a challenge would disrupt her Empire at once.

The occupation of the six ports is said to derogate from our status.[2] It does not, any more than it does under Document No.2. No arrangements afterwards mentioned in the Treaty can effect the status of freedom and equality defined in the Treaty.

As a result of the war Britain made peace with us as with an equal nation, and a Treaty was drawn up and signed to establish the peace.

By that Treaty we agree to certain arrangements between the two countries. The agreement was made as freely as any peace could be made between two belligerents, one of whom was weaker in a military sense.

The naval facilities are *granted* by us to Britain, and are occupied by Britain under the Treaty as by one independent nation from another, by international agreement. For any purpose of interference with our freedom these facilities can never be used.

The arrangement in regard to North-East Ulster is not ideal. But then the position in North-East Ulster is not ideal.

If the Free State is established, however, union is certain. Forces of persuasion and pressure are embodied in the Treaty which will bring the North-East into a united Ireland. If they join us they can have control in their own area. If they stay outside Ireland, then they can only have their own corner, and cannot, and will not, have the counties and areas which belong to Ireland and to the Irish people, according to the wishes of the inhabitants.

Then upon the area remaining outside will fall the burdens and restrictions of the 1920 Partition Act. These disabilities cannot be removed without our consent. If the North-East does not come in, then they are deciding upon bankruptcy for themselves

2. The Treaty specified harbour and port facilities which would be afforded to Britain in times of peace or war. The six ports were Berehaven, Queenstown (now Cobh), Belfast, Lough Swilly, Haulbowline and Rathmullan.

and, remember, this is not our wish but their own.

We must not, however, take a gloomy view of this situation, for, with the British gone, the incentive to partition is gone; but the evacuation is held up by our own disunion — if the Free State is threatened, as long as there is any hope of seeing it destroyed, the North-East will remain apart. Partition will remain.

Destroy the Free State, and you perpetuate Partition. You destroy all hopes of union.

It is best to speak out plainly.

Destroy the Free State now and you destroy more even than the hope, the certainty of union. You destroy our hopes of national freedom, all realisation in our generation of the democratic right of the people of Ireland to rule themselves without interference from any outside power.

Let us look things straight in the face. Unless we are careful, says Dr. Fogarty,[3] we may find ourselves one day without either Treaty or Republic. Make no mistake; we are not going to get both the Free State and the Republic at once — nor yet the Republic by means of the Treaty at once, nor by destroying the Free State.

Britain is in a stronger position than she was in July. She has offered us, and agreed with us, on a peace which the world considers a fair peace. In July world opinion was against her. World opinion is no longer against her. Somebody has said that it was the signing of the Treaty put world opinion on her side.

That is nonsense. Any offer from Britain which the world considered a generous offer would do that. The offer of July 20th last would do that. Britain knows well that she can keep world opinion without conceding a Republic.

She believes now, as she believed in July last, that she cannot afford to concede it. That it would break up her Commonwealth — that it would destroy her security and prestige if she were to acquiesce in a forcible breaking away, which would show her so-called Empire to be so intolerable, or herself so feeble as to be unable to prevent it.

But she will acquiesce in the ultimate separation of the units, we amongst them, by evolution, which will not expose her and not endanger her.

3. Michael Fogarty (1859–1955), catholic bishop of Killaloe 1904–53. Up to 1922 he had been a strong supporter of Sinn Féin and de Valera, but he was in favour of the Treaty.

We must have a little patience. Have we not gained great things for our country?

We believe that the Treaty gives us the substance of independence, said the resolution of the Co. Council of Clare sent to Mr. de Valera, and that it will lead inevitably and in a short period to the complete fulfilment of our national aspirations.

It gives us scope for all, and more than we can achieve by the most strenuous united effort of the present generation to rebuild Ireland.

Do not believe those who tell you that under the Free State the British Government will be still here, that the British King has any power over you, or that you owe any subservience to him; that your soldiers will be the soldiers of the British Crown.

It is an infamous and deliberate misrepresentation. It is not so under the Treaty. And it will not be so in fact.

How can there be a British Government in Ireland, how can they tyrannise over us, how can they legislate for us, if they are not here. When were they, in their whole history, ever able to legislate for us without a pistol at our heads? Is the claim that, by some magic, they will now be able to legislate for us when the pistol is removed? Would they have kept their forces here, with the trouble and expenditure it involved, with the loss of prestige it involved, if they could have held us in subjection by the reading, or misreading, of a document, or by the presence of a figurehead with or without his ear to the telephone?

The real point on which the plenipotentiaries had to decide, on which the Dail had to decide, on which the Ard Fheis[4] had to decide, and on which the nation will have to decide at the election, was and is, whether the Treaty really frees us from British control.

That it does so can be proved, and is being proved. The question is not whether the Treaty gives everything that everybody would like, and in the form and words which everyone would prefer. That, indeed, is not possible, because even the absolute Republican form would have been disliked by and would have alienated many Irishmen, probably as many as the Treaty form does.

The Unionists would say that they had sacrificed something in accepting the Free State. North-East Irishmen will think they have sacrificed a great deal when they accept it.

4. Party convention. In Irish, the phase means 'high gathering'.

But the aim of all of us can be for unity and independence. In public matters it must be realised that we cannot get all each one wants. We have to agree to get what is essential.

We have to agree to sink individual differences or only to work for them on legitimate lines which do not undermine and destroy the basis on which all rests and which alone makes it possible for us all, as Irishmen and women, to pursue our own aims freely in Ireland, namely, the union and independence of the nation as a whole.

We must be Irish first and last, and must be Republicans or Document Two-ites, or Free Staters, only within the limits which leave Ireland strong, united and free.

Would any other form of freedom which was obtainable now, which would have been acquiesced in by so large a body of our countrymen, have fulfilled the objects of Sinn Fein better, have put us in such a strong position to secure any that are yet unfulfilled?

We claim that the solid substance of freedom has been won, and that full powers are in the hands of the nation to mould its own life, quite as full for that purpose as if we had already our freedom in the Republican form.

Any difficulties will not be of our own making. There is no enemy nor any foreign Government here any longer to hinder us. Will we not take the fruits of victory, or do we mean to let them decay in our hands, while we wrangle as to whether they are ripe or whether they have exactly the bloom and shape we dreamed of before they had ripened?

No freedom when realised has quite the glory dreamed of by the captive.

The bargain has been struck and the goods are being delivered. You may think a better bargain could have been made, but can we not stand together, accept delivery of the goods, and make use of the unquestionable value they contain?

Are our opponents going to go on making difficulties — to stand aside when the help of every Irishman and woman is needed for the colossal task which is before us? Think of the burden of building up the nation materially, one of our chief objects — Sinn Fein — and now capable of realisation. The Labour Party told us the other day that there were probably 130,000 men and women unemployed in Ireland, and thousands of children are hungry and naked, huddled together like swine in so-called houses; that from all parts of the country were cries of desperation. 'These murmurings,' said Mr. Johnson,[5] 'presage something in our minds very like the rumblings of an earthquake.' Unless something is done rapidly, unless something effective is done, a grave situation will develop in this country which will be a problem for an old-established government, let alone a new one.

Will our opponents help us so that something effective may be done? How long must the children remain hungry while you argue whether common citizenship, a British King, a Governor-General has or has not the power still to prevent us from feeding and clothing them? Isn't it time to stop Nero's fiddling?

How can you reconcile it with the objects of Sinn Fein to stand aside, to give no hand, when from our country are going up these cries of desperation, when it is in our power now to silence those cries, in your power, you who are opposing us, who are putting thorns in the path of your own people at the moment when they are ridding themselves of the thorns the enemy put there — you, who keep crying out freedom, a Republic, and are ready to destroy your nation for a name at such a moment? Those who are not with their own people are against them.

That is the question. Are our opponents going to keep on making difficulties? At this serious crisis in our national history what is their policy? What do they mean to do? Will they tell us what they mean to do? We have heard what they had to say, but what do they mean to do?

What line of action do they propose to take? Are they going to continue to give support to the indisciplined units which shoot enemy agents when we are not at war, and seize their arms when we are not at war? What is the object of this? The one object I can see, the one object anybody can see, is that those arms are to be used either against the people or to force the British to return.

Why are our opponents conniving at these things? At the close of the Dail debates on Thursday last Mr. de Valera warned the Provisional Government that they must do nothing towards establishing a new police force — this challenge at a time when robbery is rife in the land, when human life is not safe, when the forces of disorder that always follow

5. Thomas Johnson (1872–1963), Labour politician, co-author of the Democratic Programme of the first Dáil.

war are operating without check. It is the duty of any Government to stop these things. It will fail in its duty to the people if it does not stop them, and although we have agreed not to seek the support of the electorate for three months we want the support of the people now. We want your support for the police force which we are forming. It will be a People's Guard for the protection of all parties and classes.[6]

Will our opponents hinder and obstruct that course? Will they go on making difficulties? We have a right to hear the answers to these questions. Let the people hear the answers. Above all, let us hear their policy and their programme.

We have a definite programme which we can expound and justify — which indeed is being justified daily. It may not be perfect, but what is the alternative?

The question before the people of Ireland is, do they approve of the Treaty or do they not approve of it? The Treaty has been signed by the plenipotentiaries of both countries, and it has been ratified by the Parliaments of both countries. To return to power representatives to carry the Treaty into effect and to take full advantage of it, to reap the fruits of evacuation, to establish an Irish Free State, in accordance with the national character, so that the British forces which have abandoned Ireland may never be able to return to Ireland, and the liberties of our own people may be definitely secured; or the return to power of representatives whose policy is to use the position gained by the Treaty to destroy the Irish Free State and take the certain risks involved in such a betrayal.

And if they succeed, and if, and when, the British forces return, what will happen? Will the idea of a Republic be put back into its pigeon-hole; will the abandoned little orphan, Document No. 2, be re-adopted, and will that, too, be a second time abandoned in the chaos and loss which will ensue?

War, though necessary and noble, for necessary and noble ends, has terrible effects incidental to it, not only material ruin, but moral effects when prolonged unrighteously; a tendency to lose balance and judgment, to forget or misinterpret the real object of the national struggle, to grow to believe that strife, even fratricidal strife, is noble in itself. Such things must cease as soon as freedom is secured, or the nation will perish.

6. The Garda Síochána (Guardians of the Peace) was established as an unarmed police force under the title 'Civic Guards' in 1922.

THE TREATY

(1921)

[The text of the Treaty, as the 'Articles of Agreement for a Treaty between Great Britain and Ireland, 6 December 1921' became more popularly known, was as follows.]

1. Ireland shall have the same constitutional status in the community of Nations known as the British Empire as the Dominion of Canada, the Commonwealth of Australia, the Dominion of New Zealand, and the Union of South Africa, with the parliament having powers to make laws for the peace, order and good government of Ireland and an Executive responsible to that parliament, and shall be styled and known as the Irish Free State.

2. Subject to the provisions hereinafter set out, the position of the Irish Free State in relation to the Imperial parliament and government and otherwise shall be that of the Dominion of Canada, and the law, practice and constitutional usage governing the relationship of the Crown or the representative of the Crown and of the Imperial parliament to the Dominion of Canada shall govern their relationship to the Irish Free State.

3. The representative of the Crown in Ireland shall be appointed in like manner as the Governor-General of Canada, and in accordance with the practice observed in the making of such appointments.

4. The oath to be taken by members of the parliament of the Irish Free State shall be in the following form:

I . . . do solemnly swear true faith and allegiance to the Constitution of the Irish Free State as by law established and that I will be faithful to H.M. King George V, his heirs and successors by law, in virtue of the common citizenship of Ireland with Great Britain and her adherence to and membership of the group of nations forming the British Commonwealth of Nations.

5. The Irish Free State shall assume liability for the service of the Public Debt of the United Kingdom as existing at the date hereof and toward the payment of War Pensions as existing at that date in such proportion as may be fair and equitable, having regard to any just claims on the part of Ireland by way of set-off or counter-claim, the amount of such sums being determined in default of agreement by the arbitration of one or more independent persons being citizens of the British Empire.

6. Until an arrangement has been made between the British and Irish governments whereby the Irish Free State undertakes her own coastal defence, the defence by sea of Great Britain and Ireland shall be undertaken by His Majesty's Imperial Forces. But this shall not prevent the construction or maintenance by the government of the Irish Free State of such vessels as are necessary for the protection of the Revenue or the Fisheries. The foregoing provisions of this Article shall be reviewed at a conference of Representatives of the British and Irish governments, to be held at the expiration of five years from the date hereof with a view to the undertaking by Ireland of a share in her own coastal defence.

7. The government of the Irish Free State shall afford to His Majesty's Imperial Forces:

(*a*) In time of peace such harbour and other facilities as are indicated in the Annex hereto, or such other facilities as may from time to time be agreed between the British government and the government of the Irish Free State; and

(*b*) In time of war or of strained relations with a Foreign Power, such harbour and other facilities as the British government may require for the purposes of such defence as aforesaid.

8. With a view to securing the observance of the principle of international limitation of armaments, if the government of the Irish Free State establishes and maintains a military defence force, the establishments thereof shall not exceed in size such proportion of the military establishments maintained in Great Britain as that which the population of Ireland bears to the population of Great Britain.

9. The ports of Great Britain and the Irish Free State shall be freely open to the ships of the other country on payment of the customary port and other duties.

10. The government of the Irish Free State agrees to pay fair compensation on terms not less favourable than those accorded by the Act of 1920 to judges, officials, members of Police Forces, and other Public Servants who are discharged by it or who retire in consequence of the change of government effected in pursuance hereof. Provided that this agreement shall not apply to members of the Auxiliary Police Force or to persons recruited in Great Britain for the Royal Irish Constabulary during the two years next preceding the date hereof. The British government will assume responsibility for such compensation or pensions as may be payable to any of these excepted persons.

11. Until the expiration of one month from the passing of the Act of Parliament for the ratification of this instrument, the powers of the parliament and the government of the Irish Free State shall not be exercisable as respects Northern Ireland, and the provisions of the Government of Ireland Act, 1920, shall, so far as they relate to Northern Ireland, remain in full force and effect, and no election shall be held for the return of members to serve in the parliament of the Irish Free State for constituencies in Northern Ireland, unless a resolution is passed by both houses of the parliament of Northern Ireland in favour of holding such election before the end of the said month.

12. If, before the expiration of the said month, an address is presented to His Majesty by both houses of parliament of Northern Ireland to that effect, the powers of the parliament and government of the Irish Free State shall no longer extend to Northern Ireland, and the provisions of the Government of Ireland Act, 1920 (including those relating to the Council of Ireland) shall, so far as they relate to Northern Ireland, continue to be of full force and effect, and this instrument shall have effect subject to the necessary modifications.

Provided that if such an address is so presented a Commission consisting of three persons, one to be appointed by the government of the Irish Free State, one to be appointed by the government of Northern Ireland and one who shall be Chairman to be appointed by the British government shall determine in accordance with the wishes of the inhabitants, so far as may be compatible with economic and geographic conditions, the boundaries between Northern Ireland and the rest of Ireland, and for purposes of the Government of Ireland Act, 1920, and of this instrument, the boundary of Northern Ireland shall be such as may be determined by such Commission.[1]

13. For the purpose of the last foregoing article, the powers of the parliament of Southern Ireland under the Government of Ireland Act, 1920, to elect members of the Council of Ireland shall, after the parliament of the Irish Free State is constituted, be exercised by that parliament.

14. After the expiration of the said month, if no such address as is mentioned in Article 12 hereof is presented, the parliament and government of Northern Ireland shall continue to exercise as respects Northern Ireland the powers conferred on them by the Government of Ireland Act, 1920, but the parliament and government of the Irish Free State shall in Northern Ireland have in relation to matters in respect of which the parliament of Northern Ireland has not powers to make laws under that Act (including matters which under the said Act are within the jurisdiction of the Council of Ireland) the same powers as in the rest of Ireland, subject to such other provisions as may be agreed in manner hereinafter appearing.

15. At any time after the date hereof the government of Northern Ireland and the Provisional Government of Southern Ireland hereinafter constituted may meet for the purpose of discussing the provisions subject to which the last foregoing article is to operate in the event of no such address as is therein mentioned being presented and those provisions may include:

(*a*) Safeguards with regard to patronage in Northern Ireland:

(*b*) Safeguards with regard to the collection of revenue in Northern Ireland:

(*c*) Safeguards with regard to import and export duties affecting the trade or industry of Northern Ireland:

(*d*) Safeguards for minorities in Northern Ireland:

(*e*) The settlement of the financial relations between Northern Ireland and the Irish Free State:

(*f*) The establishment and powers of a local militia in Northern Ireland and the relations of the Defence Forces of the Irish Free State and of Northern Ireland respectively:

and if at any such meeting provisions are agreed to, the same shall have effect as if they were included amongst the provisions subject to which the powers of the parliament and government of the Irish Free State are to be exercisable in Northern Ireland under Article 14 hereof.

16. Neither the parliament of the Irish Free State nor the parliament of Northern Ireland shall make any law so as either directly or indirectly to endow any religion or prohibit or restrict the free exercise thereof or give any preference or impose any disability on account of religious belief or religious status or affect prejudicially the right of any child to attend a school receiving public money without attending the religious instruction at the school or make any discrimination as respects State aid between schools under the management of different religious denominations or divert from any religious denomination or any educational institution any of its property except for public utility purposes and on payment of compensation.

17. By way of provisional arrangement for the administration of Southern Ireland during the interval which must elapse between the date hereof and the constitution of a parliament and government of the Irish Free State in accordance therewith, steps shall be taken forthwith for summoning a meeting of members of parliament elected for constituencies in Southern Ireland since the passing of the Government of Ireland Act, 1920, and for constituting a Provisional Government, and the British Government shall take the steps necessary to transfer to such Provisional Government the powers and machinery requisite for the discharge of its duties, provided that every member of such Provisional Government shall have signified in writing his or her acceptance of this instrument. But this arrangement shall not continue in force beyond the expiration of twelve months from the date hereof.

18. This instrument shall be submitted forthwith by His Majesty's Government for the approval of parliament and by the Irish signatories to a meeting summoned for the purpose of the members elected to sit in the House of Commons of Southern Ireland,

1. The Boundary Commission was established in 1924 to determine the boundary between Northern Ireland and the Free State. Its report was not published until 1969 because no agreement on a joint report could be found. In December 1925, it was agreed that the border should remain as fixed by the Government of Ireland Act 1920 and the Treaty.

and if approved shall be ratified by the necessary legislation.

On behalf of the Irish Delegation
Signed
Art Ó Gríobhtha
Micheál Ó Coileáin
Riobárd Bartún
Eadhmonn S. Ó Dúgáin
Seórsa Ghabháin Uí Dhubhthaigh[2]

2. Arthur Griffith, Michael Collins, Robert Barton, Eamon Duggan, George Gavan Duffy.

On behalf of the British Delegation
Signed
D. Lloyd George.
Austen Chamberlain
Birkenhead
Winston S. Churchill
L. Worthington-Evans
Hamar Greenwood
Gordon Hewart

6th December 1921

EAMON DE VALERA

(1882–1975)

from: SPEECHES AND STATEMENTS OF EAMON DE VALERA 1917–1973 (1980)

[An order to cease fire and dump arms was issued on 22 May 1922, accompanied by the following message from de Valera. The text of this and other speeches by de Valera is from M. Moynihan (ed.), *Speeches and Statements of Eamon de Valera 1917–1973* (Dublin: Gill and Macmillan, 1980).]

Soldiers of the Republic, Legion of the Rearguard:

The Republic can no longer be defended successfully by your arms. Further sacrifice of life would now be vain and continuance of the struggle in arms unwise in the national interest and prejudicial to the future of our cause. Military victory must be allowed to rest for the moment with those who have destroyed the Republic. Other means must be sought to safeguard the nation's right.

Do not let sorrow overwhelm you. Your efforts and the sacrifices of your dead comrades in this forlorn hope will surely bear fruit. They have even already borne fruit. Much that you set out to accomplish is achieved. You have saved the nation's honour, preserved the sacred national tradition, and kept open the road of independence. You have demonstrated in a way there is no mistaking that we are not a nation of willing bondslaves.

Seven years of intense effort have exhausted our people. Their sacrifices and their sorrows have been many. If they have turned aside and have not given you the active support which alone could bring you victory in this last year, it is because they saw overwhelming forces against them, and they are weary and need a rest. A little time and you will see them recover and rally again to the standard. They will then quickly discover who have been selfless and who selfish — who have spoken truth and who falsehood. When they are ready, you will be, and your place will be again as of old with the vanguard.

The sufferings which you must now face unarmed you will bear in a manner worthy of men who were ready to give their lives for their cause. The thought that you have still to suffer for your devotion will lighten your present sorrow, and what you endure will keep you in communion with your dead comrades, who gave their lives, and all these lives promised, for Ireland.

May God guard every one of you and give to our country in all times of need sons who will love her as dearly and devotedly as you.

AFTER THE CIVIL WAR

[After the Civil War ended in May 1923, a general election was declared for 27 August. On 15 August, de Valera went to County Clare, where he had first been elected, to address his constituents. This was his first public appearance in over a year. He had scarcely begun when Free State troops appeared, firing over the heads of the crowd. de Valera was arrested and imprisoned for eleven months. Exactly one year later, he again faced a County Clare audience, at Ennis.]

I am afraid I would disappoint a number here if I were not to start by saying, 'Well, as I was saying to you when we were interrupted,' but a year has passed since then and in that year Ireland has once again recovered her soul. I, for one, had never any doubt that she would do it, but I feared she could not do it in the short space in which I find it has been accomplished. Here in 1917 Clare led the way, and a year ago Clare led the way and sent a message to the Irish race all over the world just when they wanted it, telling them that we were not finished yet.[1] There are a number of pressmen here today waiting to hear, I suppose, some new policy. We need no new policy. The policy of 1917, the policy of 1918, the policy of 1921 is still good. They ought to have no trouble in knowing where Republicans stand. Today the aims of Irish Republicans, in Ireland and out of Ireland, could be expressed in Wolfe Tone's words, to assert the independence of our country, to unite the whole people of Ireland, to abolish the memory of our past dissensions, and to substitute the common name of Irishmen in place of all sectional denominations.[2] That is what Irish Republicans stand for; that is our goal; and our means are every available means by which determined men can win their freedom.

These aims preclude, very definitely, first of all any possible assent by us to the dismemberment of our country. You cannot have a sovereign Ireland if you have Ireland cut in two. Therefore when we put to the unity of Ireland the sovereignty of Ireland we are in a sense not adding much. We want the sovereignty of Ireland too. As I have said, that sovereignty would be impossible without the unity of our country. There are no two Irelands, there are no Northern or Southern Irelands for us. Every Irishman, be he Sir James Craig[3] or the bravest and most extreme man here in the South — they are for us all comprised in the common name of Irishmen, and we will never own that there are two motherlands for us.

The sovereignty of Ireland, then, cannot possibly be given away by Irish Republicans. We can never give allegiance to any foreign power or to any foreign people. These are the basic principles on which we stand. Things may be forced upon us, we may have temporarily to submit to certain things, but our assent they can never have. You know the old proverb 'You can bring a horse to the water but you cannot make him drink.' We are never going to drink of the pool they have brought us to. Do not forget for a moment that there is a vast difference between patiently submitting, when you have to for a time, and putting your signature to a consent or assent to these conditions. That is where we draw the line. We are not — I hope we have never shown ourselves to be — fools. Lloyd George said on one occasion — at least it was reported to me he said so — that dealing with me was like trying to take up mercury with a fork. I daresay he wanted to lay the blame on the mercury, but if he thought a little of the instrument he was using, a fork, he might have thought that there was a little blame attached to the person who tried the foolish task of using a fork to take up mercury. If the interstices in the fork had not been there, if it had been something solid, he would have had no difficulty in taking up the mercury. . . .

My task and the task of my colleagues in the past was to bring you together, to make of you a united body, and I repeat now what I was saying when the interruption of a year ago occurred — this nation united cannot be denied freedom. The practical question is: how can we be united? There is only one way, and before I started on this course seven years ago I proved it clearly, to my own satisfaction in any case, that if we wanted unity, that is a unity which could secure freedom, we could only get it on the one basis — the basis of the Irish Republic. As an instrument to secure that unity we devised in 1917 the Sinn Féin constitution. Now, if it was necessary to state in explicit terms the words of Tone, we have them in that Sinn Féin constitution. I have got the exact words here:

> Sinn Féin aims at securing the international recognition of Ireland as an independent Irish Repub-

1. de Valera was elected Sinn Féin MP for East Clare in 1917. In 1918, as president of Sinn Féin, he drafted the anti-conscription pledge.
2. T. W. Tone (ed.), *The Life of Theobold Wolfe Tone* (Washington, 1826), Vol. I, p. 69.
3. James Craig (1871–1940), 1st viscount Craigavon, succeeded Carson as leader of the Northern unionists in February 1921 and four months later became first prime minister of Northern Ireland.

lic. Having achieved that status the Irish people may by referendum freely choose their own form of government.†

Let no one, then, taunt us with being undemocratic. We realise the difficulties of uniting in the cause of freedom. We know that in such a fight there has to be a vanguard, and we know that very often it is only a few choice spirits can form that vanguard. It was a recognition of that that made us stand out in denial of the fact [proposition?] that elections held as these past elections were held could determine the form of government or the freedom that the Irish people wanted. When you are free to determine that without any pressure from England, or from any outside power, when the form you choose will be the expression truly of your own free will, then we are certainly ready to bow down our heads before it. That constitution, then, of Sinn Féin guards these essentials — the sovereignty of our nation, the unity of our nation, and the democratic right of the people of this free nation to choose for themselves how they shall be governed. For my part, I have always accepted that constitution. I have always done my utmost to live up to it. I believed that I had no right in public to speak as a representative of the people if I departed from that, because it is owing to the fact that I subscribed to that constitution that I was put in a position to represent or speak for the nation. . . .

Remember that for years — for three or four years in particular — we told everyone who listened to us what the demand of the Irish people was. We told them they wanted complete freedom, freedom to choose their own government, freedom to choose their political relations with other peoples. Now, what happened, the moment the signatures of Irishmen were forced by threats to that fatal treaty, is this: British propaganda throughout the world made itself busy in trying to get all who were interested in the Irish cause to imagine that Ireland's full claim had been granted. The extent and power of that deception, and the danger to Ireland, may easily be illustrated by hundreds of incidents. . . . We have got to make it clear that we cannot yet dispense with the aid of our friends throughout the world, that we have not yet reached the goal, and I want you to join with me in sending this message . . . :

> A so-called treaty that has been imposed upon them by threats of force, that purports to deny their sovereignty and dismember their country, is not accepted by the Irish people and is not regarded, and never will be regarded, by them as binding either on their honour or on their conscience.

No, my friends, do not imagine because I have not touched upon them here that I have not clearly in mind the difficulties under which our country labours at present. If only we would judge in the terms 'by their fruits you shall know them',[4] we can judge by the fruits of that so-called treaty that was signed in 1921. We see throughout the country what we have seen for the past couple of years, what we never thought in our lifetimes to see in Ireland. The bright dreams we cherished in 1921, when we were planning for the immediate future of this country, have all been shattered. The prosperous Ireland, the Ireland which we honestly would have tried to make a nation fit for heroes to live in — not in mockery, but in truth — we have seen our hopes of it for the moment dashed to the ground. But if Ireland becomes as Clare is, we can easily remedy the mischief. Why cannot Ireland become as Clare is? That is the question.

We shall have an Ard-Fheis[5] of our organisation in a couple of months' time. In the organisation of Sinn Féin we never regarded Sinn Féin as a political machine. Sinn Féin was, to us, the Irish people organised for all purposes, not merely narrow political ends. We never thought of it as a political machine to get men into power or positions or jobs. We thought of it as an organisation in which we would have the value of decentralisation and centralisation all combined. You in your local branches felt you had your own little community organised. In these branches, and through them, you were able to have your Arbitration Courts, you were able to take cognizance of local needs and provide for them in every way. We want you to go back to that organisation again. Let it be once more the organised

†In fact only a close approximation to the 'exact words' are given in the text found among Mr de Valera's papers. This has been replaced above by the wording given in printed versions of the Sinn Féin constitution of 1917. [M. Moynihan]

4. Matthew 7.20.
5. A party convention; from the Irish : 'high gathering'.

citizenry of the Irish Republic. O'Connell in 1843, I think it was, asked for three million Repealers.[6] We want three million Irish Republicans registered. Give us three million registered voluntary citizens of the Irish Republic and then we will tell you what we will do. That is what we are out for today. Get ready, then, for it by organising locally, get ready for the great Ard-Fheis of this year, which will, I hope, begin again for Ireland a glorious term, a term which, remember, brought us actually to the threshold — if there had not been a stumble on the threshold — actually to the threshold of freedom.

Let no man say that we are afraid to go back to 1917 because of the years 1917 to 1921. We are not going to get off the track. We are going to move along the straight road. I remember telling you long ago that if you keep the straight road, no matter how difficult it may be, every inch you go is an inch of progress. If you get off that straight road and go on to the bypaths, take care that it is not backwards you are going. The whole history of Ireland — the political history of Ireland anyhow — has been a record of going off the track and going backwards — going off the track and pretending, or believing, they were going to get a short cut. The history of nations proves there are very few short cuts to freedom. The one short cut is the short cut of unity and determination. That is the history — it is the shortest way, it is the best way, it is the most honest way, and it is certainly the most victorious.

6. Daniel O'Connell's Repeal Association, founded in 1840, reached its zenith in the 'Year of Repeal', 1843.

SIMPLY FAITHFUL

Bodenstown, 21 June 1925

[The editorial title to this speech, the headnote below and its accompanying footnotes, are from M. Moynihan, *Speeches and Statements of Eamon de Valera 1917–1973*.

When, in October 1922, de Valera acceded to the request of the Republican armed forces that he should form an emergency government, he was, no doubt, influenced to some extent by the hope that this would supply a degree of civilian control over the activities of those forces. A further step towards political, rather than military, control of the opposition to the Treaty settlement was his announcement in January 1923 of the reorganisation of Sinn Féin. On 7 February 1923 he stated, in a letter to Liam Lynch, the Republican Chief of Staff, his belief that 'We can best serve the nation at this moment by trying to get the constitutional way adopted.' A few weeks later he was deploring the fact that 'our country has been placed in a cruel dilemma, out of which she could be rescued only by gentleness, skill, and patience, and on all sides a desire for justice and fair dealing' and that he personally had 'been condemned to view the tragedy here for the last year as through a wall of glass, powerless to intervene effectively' — but he had 'still the hope that an opportunity may come my way'.[1] When eventually he had succeeded in bringing about a cease-fire, and the general election of August 1923 was approaching, he declared that 'the war, so far as we are concerned, is finished' and that the 'present purpose' of the Republicans was 'to work through the Sinn Féin political organisation'.[2] In June 1925, speaking beside the grave of Wolfe Tone in Bodenstown churchyard, he expressed the resolve of the Republicans to see to it, so far as they could, that 'the ancient enemy of our nation . . . will not divert against any section of our people the attacks that are meant for him'; but otherwise they were 'content to rest for the moment, if it must be so, simply faithful'.

The text of the Bodenstown speech was published in *An Phoblacht*, 26 June 1925.]

1. Letter to Edith M. Ellis, 26 February 1923.
2. Interview to Associated Press of America, published in *The Irish Times*, 23 July 1923.

Republicans, you have come here today to the tomb of Wolfe Tone on a pilgrimage of loyalty! By your presence you proclaim your undiminished attachment to the ideals of Tone, and your unaltered devotion to the cause for which he gave his life. It is your answer to those who would have it believed that the Republic of Ireland is dead and its cause abandoned.

Republicans — you who were privileged to repeat your vows at this shrine in the company of Clarke and Pearse and Connolly, of Cathal Brugha and Liam Mellows[1] — you who were admitted to the comradeship of heroes, and have drunk of the same draughts of freedom, and caught the same glimpses of the Land of Promise, you are not here in hypocrisy or in an idle demonstration of a lifeless faith! You

1. Pearse and Connolly were among the executed leaders of 1916. Cathal Brugha (1874–1922) died in the Civil War. Liam Mellowes (1892–1922) was executed by the Provisional Government.

are here to bear witness to that which is living and true — immortal and secure above every chance of fortune — to the aspirations of the Irish people for freedom, and you are here to pledge your sincerity and your constancy, your toil and your sacrifice, until these aspirations be achieved.

Yes, the achievement of these aspirations to the full — that is the task which you, Republicans, have consciously set yourselves.

How can you accomplish it? Only with the greatest difficulty, most surely, if you remain unassisted by the rest of the Irish people who hold these aspirations in common with you. Scarcely at all if you are actively opposed by them.

It is by divisions amongst the conquered that conquests have ever been best secured. 'Divide and conquer' was a motto of empire long before the wily Louis XI chose it for his.[2]

A nation united no tyrant could resist. A people broken and distracted with divisions is incapable of progress in any direction, though half the intensity of their factions would carry them to freedom.

Wolfe Tone realised that the masters of empire knew their craft. His keen vision cut down to the bedrock of human passions and weaknesses on which the principles of that craft were founded. He saw these principles being applied to the Ireland of his day, as we see them being applied to the Ireland of ours. He knew that honest differences, as they are called, were no less useful for the purposes of the tyrant, and no less fatal to the people among whom they existed, than differences purely factious and artificial. And so, when he set himself as objects to assert the independence of Ireland, to subvert its execrable government, and to break the connection with England, the never-failing source of all Ireland's political evils, he prescribed, as his means, to unite the whole people of Ireland, to abolish the memory of all past dissensions, and to substitute the common name of Irishman in the place of the denominations (of the day) of Protestant, Catholic and Dissenter.[3]

He who would take up Tone's task today must, if he would foil the enemies of his country, also adopt the means that Tone chose. He who would be the liberator of his country must, as a preliminary, earnestly seek a basis on which to secure a unification of the people. He must win them to acceptance of, first, an agreed objective, and secondly, and equally important, and vastly more difficult, as you know, an agreed policy towards attaining it.

How do we stand with respect to these? What is our objective? Is it one on which we can hope to unite the people of Ireland? I say not only is it so, but it is the only possible basis on which they can be united.

> Ireland her own — Ireland her own, and all therein, from the sod to the sky. The soil of Ireland for the people of Ireland, to have and hold from God alone who gave it — to have and to hold to them and their heirs forever, without suit or service, faith or fealty, rent or render, to any power under heaven.[4]

2. More often ascribed to an earlier (Roman) source: 'Divide et impera'.
3. T. W. Tone (ed.), *The Life of Theobold Wolfe Tone* (Washington, 1826), Vol. I, p. 69.
4. James Fintan Lalor, *The Irish Felon* (1848). See Volume II, p. 172.

THE UNDESERTED VILLAGE IRELAND

[On St Patrick's Day 1943, in celebration of the fiftieth anniversary of the founding of the Gaelic League, de Valera's radio broadcast address to the Irish people began with an urgent appeal, in Irish, for the revival of the language. He then continued to elaborate in English his vision of the Ireland that could be attained, an ideal that is a mix of Thomas Davis, Patrick Pearse and de Valera himself. It has since been an occasion of some amusement and bitterness, since, subsequently to this, the great tide of emigration began, the Irish language continued to wither and 'the unity of the national territory' became even more improbable. Nevertheless, it is a version of Ireland for which de Valera was the most appropriate and important spokesman.]

Before the present war began I was accustomed on St Patrick's Day to speak to our kinsfolk in foreign lands, particularly those in the United States, and to tell them year by year of the progress being made towards building up the Ireland of their dreams and ours — the Ireland that we believe is destined to play, by its example and its inspiration, a great part as a nation among the nations.

Acutely conscious though we all are of the misery

and desolation in which the greater part of the world is plunged, let us turn aside for a moment to that ideal Ireland that we would have. That Ireland which we dreamed of would be the home of a people who valued material wealth only as the basis of right living, of a people who were satisfied with frugal comfort and devoted their leisure to the things of the spirit — a land whose countryside would be bright with cosy homesteads, whose fields and villages would be joyous with the sounds of industry, with the romping of sturdy children, the contests of athletic youths and the laughter of comely maidens, whose firesides would be forums for the wisdom of serene old age. It would, in a word, be the home of a people living the life that God desires that man should live.

With the tidings that make such an Ireland possible, St Patrick came to our ancestors 1,500 years ago, promising happiness here as well as happiness hereafter. It was the pursuit of such an Ireland that later made our country worthy to be called the Island of Saints and Scholars. It was the idea of such an Ireland, happy, vigorous, spiritual, that fired the imagination of our poets, that made successive generations of patriotic men give their lives to win religious and political liberty, and that will urge men in our own and future generations to die, if need be, so that these liberties may be preserved.

One hundred years ago the Young Irelanders, by holding up the vision of such an Ireland before the people, inspired our nation and moved it spiritually as it had hardly been moved since the golden age of Irish civilisation. Fifty years after the Young Irelanders, the founders of the Gaelic League similarly inspired and moved the people of their day, as did later the leaders of the Volunteers. We of this time, if we have the will and the active enthusiasm, have the opportunity to inspire and move our generation in like manner. We can do so by keeping this thought of a noble future for our country constantly before our minds, ever seeking in action to bring that future into being, and ever remembering that it is to our nation as a whole that future must apply.

Thomas Davis, laying down the national programme for his generation, spoke first of the development of our material resources as he saw them, of the wealth that lay in our harbours, our rivers, our bogs and our mines. Characteristically, however, he passed on to emphasise the still more important development of the resources of the spirit:

> Our young artisans must be familiar with the arts of design and the natural sciences connected with their trade; and so of our farmers; and both should, beside, have that general information which refines and expands the mind, that knowledge of Irish history and statistics that makes it national and those accomplishments and sports which make leisure profitable and home joyous.
>
> Our cities must be stately with sculpture, pictures and buildings, and our fields glorious with peaceful abundance.

'But this is an utopia!' he exclaimed, but then questioned, 'Is it?' He answered:

> No; but the practicable (that is, the attainable) object of those who know our resources. To seek it is the solemn, unavoidable duty of every Irishman.[1]

Davis's answer should be our answer also. We are aware that Davis was mistaken in the extent of some of the material resources which he catalogued, but we know, none the less, that our material resources are sufficient for a population much larger than we have at present, if we consider their use with a due appreciation of their value in a right philosophy of life. And we know also that the spiritual resources which Davis asked the nation to cultivate are inexhaustible.

For many the pursuit of the material is a necessity. Man, to express himself fully and to make the best use of the talents God has given him, needs a certain minimum of comfort and leisure. A section of our people have not yet this minimum. They rightly strive to secure it, and it must be our aim and the aim of all who are just and wise to assist in the effort. But many have got more than is required and are free, if they choose, to devote themselves more completely to cultivating the things of the mind, and in particular those which mark us out as a distinct nation.

The first of these latter is the national language. It is for us what no other language can be. It is our very own. It is more than a symbol; it is an essential

1. 'Foreign Travel', *The Nation*, 17 August 1844.

part of our nationhood. It has been moulded by the thought of a hundred generations of our forebears. In it is stored the accumulated experience of a people, our people, who even before Christianity was brought to them were already cultured and living in a well-ordered society. The Irish language spoken in Ireland today is the direct descendant without break of the language our ancestors spoke in those far-off days.

As a vehicle of three thousand years of our history, the language is for us precious beyond measure. As the bearer to us of a philosophy, of an outlook on life deeply Christian and rich in practical wisdom, the language today is worth far too much to dream of letting it go. To part with it would be to abandon a great part of ourselves, to lose the key of our past, to cut away the roots from the tree. With the language gone we could never aspire again to being more than half a nation.

For my part, I believe that this outstanding mark of our nationhood can be preserved and made forever safe by this generation. I am indeed certain of it, but I know that it cannot be saved without understanding and co-operation and effort and sacrifice. It would be wrong to minimise the difficulties. They are not slight. The task of restoring the language as the everyday speech of our people is a task as great as any nation ever undertook. But it is a noble task. Other nations have succeeded in it, though in their case, when the effort was begun, their national language was probably more widely spoken among their people than is ours with us. As long as the language lives, however, on the lips of the people as their natural speech in any substantial part of this land we are assured of success if — *if* we are in earnest.

It is a task in which the attitude of the individual is what counts most. It is upon the individual citizen, upon you who are listening to me, that the restoration of the language finally depends. The State and public institutions can do much to assist, but if the individual has not the inclination or the will-power to make the serious efforts initially required or to persevere till reasonable fluency is attained, outside aids will be of little use. The individual citizen must desire actively to restore the language and be prepared to take the pains to learn it and to use it, else real progress cannot be made.

Today there is no dearth of books and reading matter and other facilities for those who wish to begin their study or to improve their knowledge. Twenty years of work in the schools has brought some knowledge of the language to hundreds of thousands of our young people. If these make it a practice to read and to speak it to one another, even a little at the beginning, particularly in the case of those living in the same house, they will add to their store continually through conversation until all sense of effort has disappeared and the words and phrases come naturally and correctly as they are needed. Each additional person who speaks the language makes the task of all the others easier. Each one who opposes the language and each one who knowing it fails to use it makes the task of those striving to restore it more difficult. For those who can speak it, to neglect doing so, whenever and wherever it can be understood, is a betrayal of those who gave their lives so that not merely a free but an Irish-speaking nation might be possible. Were all those who now have a knowledge of the language to speak it consistently on all occasions when it could reasonably be spoken, our task would be easy.

Let us all, then, do our part this year. The restoration of the unity of the national territory and the restoration of the language are the greatest of our uncompleted national tasks. Let us devote this year especially to the restoration of the language; let the year be one in which the need for this restoration will be constantly in our thoughts and the language itself as much as possible on our lips.

The physical dangers that threaten, and the need for unceasing vigilance in the matters of defence as well as unremitting attention to the serious day-to-day problems that the war has brought upon us, should not cause us to neglect our duty to the language. Time is running against us in this matter of the language. We cannot afford to postpone our effort. We should remember also that the more we preserve and develop our individuality and our characteristics as a distinct nation, the more secure will be our freedom and the more valuable our contribution to humanity when this war is over.

Bail ó Dhia oraibh agus bail go gcuire Sé ar an obair atá romhainn. Go gcumhdai Dia sinn agus gur fiú sinn choíche, mar náisiún, na tíolacaí a thug Pádraig chugainn. Go dtuga an tUilechumhachtach, A thug slán sinn go dtí seo ón anachain is ón mí-ádh atá ar oiread sin náisiún eile de bharr an chogaidh seo, scáth agus dídean dúinn go dtí an deireadh, agus go ndeonaí Sé gur fiú sinn cion uasal a dhéanamh sa saol nua atá romhainn.[2]

2. 'God bless you and bless the work that lies before us. May God protect us, and may we always, as a nation, be worthy of the gifts that St Patrick brought us. May the Almighty, Who has brought us safe until now from the calamity and misfortune that have befallen so many other nations in consequence of this war, grant us shelter and protection to the end and make us worthy to play a noble part in the new world of the future.'

from: NATIONAL THANKSGIVING

[The following headnote is from M. Moynihan:
On 13 May 1945, when the war in Europe had come to an end, Winston Churchill included in a broadcast address a passage referring to the policy of neutrality which had been observed by Ireland. He blamed de Valera for having denied the use of Irish ports and airfields and took credit for the 'restraint and poise' of the British Government in refraining from laying 'a violent hand' upon them. While acknowledging the part which thousands of Irishmen had played as members of the British forces, Churchill used expressions regarding Ireland's official neutrality so offensive as to arouse deep and widespread resentment among the people of Ireland. It was confidently expected that de Valera would reply, and rarely were his words awaited with such tense eagerness as when it was announced that he would broadcast on Wednesday 16 May.

In the earlier — and longer — part of his address, including the opening passage in Irish, the Taoiseach devoted himself to matters which, in the ordinary course, even if Churchill had not spoken about Ireland, would have been the natural subjects for him to choose at such a time. He thanked God for the preservation of the people from the horrors of the war and recognised their duty to assist in succouring those who had been less fortunate. He recalled that at the beginning of the war he had declared that in the circumstances of Ireland — with its history, its experience after the war of 1914–18 and the unjust partition which still existed — no policy other than neutrality was possible. He thanked the members of the various services and voluntary bodies who had helped in the national effort, and he pointed out that certain restrictions and controls, such as rationing, would have to be continued for a time. In the course of his opening remarks in Irish he declared that he had been confident that the Irish speakers, and others who shared their special attachment to Gaelic traditions, would be foremost among those who would form a protecting shield for Ireland; and he added that they, the Gaels, had not failed him, that they had done their share of the work which had brought the nation safely through the five preceding years.

It was not until he had said these things that de Valera turned to Churchill's remarks about Irish neutrality. There is some reason to believe that Churchill himself was impressed by the dignity and strength of the reply.

The following text of de Valera's statement has been copied from a reprint which was issued by Irish Press Ltd in 1945.]

. . . The long and fearful war which has devastated Europe has at last, mercifully, come to an end. And my first object in speaking to you tonight must be to try to express in words the gratitude to Almighty God with which all our hearts are full. I am assured that we shall be able to arrange for a day of national thanksgiving on which we may publicly express due gratitude to God for His immense mercy in our regard.

To the people of all the nations which have been directly involved in the war our thoughts go out in sympathy on their deliverance from the daily terrors in which they lived, and in sorrow that they must still endure the inevitable suffering of the aftermath. We have been spared what so many nations have had to undergo, and there lies upon us, accordingly, a duty, within our limited power, to assist in succouring those who have been less fortunate than we have been.

I have here before me the pencilled notes from which I broadcast to you on September 3, 1939. I had so many other things to do on that day that I could not find time to piece them together into a connected statement. From these notes I see that I said that, noting the march of events, your Government had decided its policy the previous spring and had announced its decision to the world.

The aim of our policy, I said, would be to keep our people out of the war. I reminded you of what I had said in the Dáil, that in our circumstances, with our history and our experience after the last war and with a part of our country still unjustly severed from us, no other policy was possible.

I did not have to go into any details then as to what precisely were the circumstances to which I referred, nor had I to go into detail as to what were our experiences after the last war, nor had I to point out what a vital factor in our situation was the partition of our country. I had merely to refer to them and I felt sure you would understand. Similarly, I do not think it necessary to dwell upon them tonight.

I pointed out then that the policy adopted had the backing of practically the entire Dáil and the entire community, irrespective of any personal views which citizens held on the merits of the cause which occasioned the conflict.

The national policy then announced was thus supported by a unity rare to find amongst democratic peoples, a unity tested through two free general elections in 1943 and 1944, a unity which happily survived with us to the end. All political parties and all sections are entitled to their share of credit for what that unity has achieved. It has been a triumph of national understanding and good sense.

There were times when we stood in the gravest danger. But we have been preserved from the calamity of invasion, and such privations as we have suffered in our economic life have been by comparison very slight indeed.

The dire economic consequences which might have been anticipated were prevented by the united efforts of our people, by the co-operation of the public representatives of all parties, by hard work, by careful organisation, and by being enabled to obtain supplies from other countries, particularly Britain, the United States and Canada. . . .

Certain newspapers have been very persistent in looking for my answer to Mr Churchill's recent broadcast. I know the kind of answer I am expected to make. I know the answer that first springs to the lips of every man of Irish blood who heard or read that speech, no matter in what circumstances or in what part of the world he found himself.

I know the reply I would have given a quarter of a century ago. But I have deliberately decided that that is not the reply I shall make tonight. I shall strive not to be guilty of adding any fuel to the flames of hatred and passion which, if continued to be fed, promise to burn up whatever is left by the war of decent human feeling in Europe.

Allowances can be made for Mr Churchill's statement, however unworthy, in the first flush of his victory. No such excuse could be found for me in this quieter atmosphere. There are, however, some things which it is my duty to say, some things which it is essential to say. I shall try to say them as dispassionately as I can.

Mr Churchill makes it clear that, in certain circumstances, he would have violated our neutrality and that he would justify his action by Britain's necessity. It seems strange to me that Mr Churchill does not see that this, if accepted, would mean that Britain's necessity would become a moral code and that when this necessity became sufficiently great, other people's rights were not to count.

It is quite true that other great powers believe in this same code — in their own regard — and have behaved in accordance with it. That is precisely why we have the disastrous succession of wars — World War No. 1 and World War No. 2 — and shall it be World War No. 3?

Surely Mr Churchill must see that, if his contention be admitted in our regard, a like justification can be framed for similar acts of aggression elsewhere and no small nation adjoining a great power could ever hope to be permitted to go its own way in peace.

It is, indeed, fortunate that Britain's necessity did not reach the point when [*sic*] Mr Churchill would have acted. All credit to him that he successfully resisted the temptation which, I have no doubt, many times assailed him in his difficulties and to which I freely admit many leaders might have easily succumbed. It is, indeed, hard for the strong to be just to the weak, but acting justly always has its rewards.

By resisting his temptation in this instance, Mr Churchill, instead of adding another horrid chapter to the already bloodstained record of the relations between England and this country, has advanced the cause of international morality an important step — one of the most important, indeed, that can be taken on the road to the establishment of any sure basis for peace.

As far as the peoples of these two islands are concerned, it may, perhaps, mark a fresh beginning towards the realisation of that mutual comprehension to which Mr Churchill has referred and for which he has prayed and for which, I hope, he will not merely pray but work, also, as did his predecessor[1] who will yet, I believe, find the honoured place in British history which is due to him, as certainly he will find it in any fair record of the relations between Britain and ourselves.

That Mr Churchill should be irritated when our

1. Neville Chamberlain (1869–1940), British prime minister 1937–40.

neutrality stood in the way of what he thought he vitally needed, I understand, but that he or any thinking person in Britain or elsewhere should fail to see the reason for our neutrality, I find it hard to conceive.

I would like to put a hypothetical question — it is a question I have put to many Englishmen since the last war. Suppose Germany had won the war, had invaded and occupied England, and that after a long lapse of time and many bitter struggles she was finally brought to acquiesce in admitting England's right to freedom, and let England go, but not the whole of England, all but, let us say, the six southern counties.

These six southern counties, those, let us suppose, commanding the entrance to the narrow seas, Germany had singled out and insisted on holding herself with a view to weakening England as a whole and maintaining the security of her own communications through the Straits of Dover.

Let us suppose, further, that after all this had happened Germany was engaged in a great war in which she could show that she was on the side of the freedom of a number of small nations. Would Mr Churchill as an Englishman who believed that his own nation had as good a right to freedom as any other — not freedom for a part merely, but freedom for the whole — would he, whilst Germany still maintained the partition of his country and occupied six counties of it, would he lead this partitioned England to join with Germany in a crusade? I do not think Mr Churchill would.

Would he think the people of partitioned England an object of shame if they stood neutral in such circumstances? I do not think Mr Churchill would.

Mr Churchill is proud of Britain's stand alone, after France had fallen and before America entered the war.

Could he not find in his heart the generosity to acknowledge that there is a small nation that stood alone, not for one year or two, but for several hundred years against aggression; that endured spoliations, famines, massacres in endless succession; that was clubbed many times into insensibility, but that each time, on returning consciousness, took up the fight anew; a small nation that could never be got to accept defeat and has never surrendered her soul?

Mr Churchill is justly proud of his nation's perseverance against heavy odds. But we in this island are still prouder of our people's perseverance for freedom through all the centuries. We of our time have played our part in that perseverance, and we have pledged ourselves to the dead generations who have preserved intact for us this glorious heritage, that we too will strive to be faithful to the end, and pass on this tradition unblemished.

Many a time in the past there appeared little hope except that hope to which Mr Churchill referred, that by standing fast a time would come when, to quote his own words, 'the tyrant would make some ghastly mistake which would alter the whole balance of the struggle'.

I sincerely trust, however, that it is not thus our ultimate unity and freedom will be achieved, though as a younger man I confess I prayed even for that, and indeed at times saw no other.

In latter years I have had a vision of a nobler and better ending, better for both our peoples and for the future of mankind. For that I have now been long working. I regret that it is not to this nobler purpose that Mr Churchill is lending his hand rather than, by the abuse of a people who have done him no wrong, trying to find in a crisis like the present excuse for continuing the injustice of the mutilation of our country.

I sincerely hope that Mr Churchill has not deliberately chosen the latter course but, if he has, however regretfully we may say it, we can only say, be it so.

Meanwhile, even as a partitioned small nation, we shall go on and strive to play our part in the world, continuing unswervingly to work for the cause of true freedom and for peace and understanding between all nations.

As a community which has been mercifully spared from all the major sufferings, as well as from the blinding hates and rancours engendered by the present war, we shall endeavour to render thanks to God by playing a Christian part in helping, so far as a small nation can, to bind up some of the gaping wounds of suffering humanity.

BRITISH GUARANTEE TO NORTHERN IRELAND

[The following headnote is from M. Moynihan: In October and November 1948 Clement Attlee, the

British Prime Minister, made statements in the House of Commons guaranteeing that Northern Ireland would not cease to be a part of the United Kingdom without the consent of its Parliament. He also announced that the twenty-six county State, now preparing to sever its last link with the British Commonwealth, would not be regarded by Britain as a foreign country and that its people would not be treated as aliens.

The assurance to Northern Ireland was strongly resented in nationalist Ireland and was the subject of protests by [John] Costello's Government. The British Government nevertheless proceeded to give legislative effect to the assurance (and to its decision in favour of non-alien status for Irish citizens). The Republic of Ireland Act, passed by the Irish Parliament in December 1948, came into operation on Easter Monday, 18 April 1949; and two weeks later the House of Commons at Westminster gave a first reading to the Ireland Bill, 1949, which, among other things, declared that in no event would Northern Ireland or any part of it cease to be a part of the United Kingdom without the consent of the Parliament of Northern Ireland. On 10 May Costello moved for the adoption by Dáil Éireann of a statement — which was unanimously approved by the House — protesting against the British Government's action and calling upon that Government and the British people 'to end the present occupation of our six north-eastern counties and thereby enable the unity of Ireland to be restored and the age-long differences between the two nations brought to an end'. The motion was seconded by de Valera, at that time the leader of the Opposition.]

I think most deputies in the House have seen that, when I first heard of this proposal and the rumour that a Bill would be introduced in the British Parliament purporting to confirm the partition of our country, I took the earliest opportunity to warn everybody concerned that the introduction of such a Bill would sow anew the seeds of enmity between the two peoples. I was amazed when I heard the rumour. I was more amazed when I found that it was based on substance. As I said then, I could not understand how something so unnecessary as to seem gratuitous and even wanton could be introduced at this time.

The Taoiseach[1] has told us today that, from the first moment he saw the communiqué he referred to, our Government has been active in bringing to the attention of the British Governemt the consequences that would flow from the introduction of this measure. He has told us — and I thought myself beforehand that this must be the case — that it would not be possible for a measure of this sort to be introduced without the strongest representations being made from the Government here. I felt that it was equally certain that the representatives of the British Government here could hardly have failed to apprise their own Government of the feelings that would be aroused in this country if such a measure were introduced. I can see no reason for the measure. As the Taoiseach has said, it did not seem to be in any way necessary. To me it does not even seem to be effective, on the supposition that at a later stage the majority of a British Parliament, with the majority of the British people, should desire to abrogate it. What then could be its purpose? It seems to me it can only have been designed by somebody who deliberately wished to give our people 'a slap in the face'. Why should that have been done? How can anybody imagine people in responsible positions acting like that? Was it due to resentment because the people of this country decided, through their elected representatives and by a majority, that the form of government they wanted to preserve — and, in my opinion, that is all that was in it — was the republican form of government and that they wanted that fact to be generally known and recognised? I myself had declared the position in 1945. If it was desired, as the majority of the representatives here seemed to think that it was desired, that there should be formal expression given to that fact — in my opinion an existing fact — why should that engender resentment on the part of any British Ministers?

Surely it is the right of our people to choose for themselves their own form of government, whatever that may be, and to choose in a democratic way also the relationships which they wish to have with other nations. We have laid that down as fundamental during the whole of the time in which the Irish people, in the present generation anyhow, have been struggling for independence. We have laid it down as a fundamental right, the claim of our people to choose their own form of government and to choose whether they will have certain relationships with other people or not. The people of this country know that they are entitled to claim as the national territory the whole of Ireland and not a part of it. We

1. John Costello (1891–1970) became Taoiseach of the inter-party government in February 1948. See pp. 762–64 below for his statement on the Republic of Ireland Bill of 1948.

have never surrendered that claim. Why should the British Parliament at this time, in the wanton way it is being done, try to assert a claim which they know will be resisted always as long as this nation exists? As I have said, the whole thing seemed almost incredible to me. It seemed to me as if a malignant spirit were at work attempting to discover by what means it could best arouse old animosities. A more effective way could hardly be devised. I am amazed at it, but the fact is there.

I have been hoping, though I must say with not a great deal of feeling that my hope will ever be realised, that even at this last moment this thing would not be done. I can say that at no time did the Fianna Fáil Government — we were in office for a long time, including a very critical period in the world's history — fail to do what apparently the present Government has been doing, namely, on every single occasion on which we met British Ministers, to point out to them that the basis of good relations between our two countries was the unity of our country. The Taoiseach found that some of these Ministers did not know the facts. I can say I had the same experience in my time, that some of them did not know the facts. That is not surprising in one way, when you remember that, from the time Mr Lloyd George brought the Partition Bill[2] before the British House of Commons, it has been the constant aim of British propaganda to misrepresent the situation, and those who were not brought directly into contact with the problem had not the ordinary way of learning the facts. One would imagine, I will admit, that a Minister of State should know them, but I can assure the House that my experience has been the same as the Taoiseach's experience — that I did meet in my time English Ministers who clearly did not know the facts or else wanted to pretend to me they did not know the facts.

What is proposed in this Bill that is being introduced into the British House of Commons? It proposes, in so far as it can, to perpetuate the present division of our country. The Taoiseach has already pointed out, and every deputy here, of course, knows it, that these six counties were cut off arbitrarily from the rest of the country, that they were cut off despite the expressed will of the vast majority of the Irish people, that the area cut off did not correspond to any local majority that was in favour of the cutting off, that the only portion of the country where there is a local majority in favour of the cutting off is in the area around Belfast — an area that does not amount to one-half of the total area of the six counties that have been cut off.

The Taoiseach has reminded the House that the majority of the people in County Tyrone do not want to be cut off, that the majority of the people in County Fermanagh do not want to be cut off, that the majority of the people in the city of Derry do not want to be cut off, that the majority in the old constituencies of South Armagh, South Down and East Down do not want to be cut off. On what principle, we ask, can it be justified that an area including these people should be cut off and put under the heel of the ascendancy concentrated in the neighbourhood of Belfast?

The suggestion, of course, at the time of the cutting off, was that there was a majority in that area whose political outlook was not that of the majority of the Irish people. That general statement concealed a falsehood. It is true that, if you take the area as a whole, you will find in that area a majority who are against unity with the rest of the country, due to the concentration around Belfast. The Taoiseach has already indicated here that, if you take a bloc of four of these counties, there is a majority who want to be with us. If they can cut off six of the thirty-two counties on such a principle as has been indicated, why should we not be allowed, under the same principle, to cut off four out of the six? They pretend it is to prevent coercion, but they are coercing, and everybody knows it. They are coercing into the present six-county arrangement the majority of the people in the city of Derry, in the counties of Tyrone and Fermanagh, in South Down, South Armagh and in what used to be East Down. What do they mean, then, when they say that the people of Ulster must not be coerced? We deny, of course, that a local majority in any part of our country, against the will of the majority of the people as a whole, have any right to cut themselves off, because if that were permitted, it would mean an end to democracy, which can only exist by the application of majority rule. We must have some natural unit for the application of self-determination. The natural unit for the application of self-determination is the nation. The demand was not for self-determination for a county or for a parish — it was self-determination

2. The Government of Ireland Bill 1920.

for the nation. We demand the application of that principle to ourselves.

This resolution asserts our national right to the whole of our territory, and it pledges the nation to do everything in its power to see that that right is asserted. It is true, as the Taoiseach has said, that we are a small nation and that we have not the means physically to make our will effective. We have to resolve to resort to other means. We have now the leadership for the nation in this House. We have represented in this House all sections of our people as far as the Twenty-six Counties are concerned, and we have to take upon ourselves the leadership for the nation as a whole. We have here, therefore, the national directing centre for the nation, and the efforts that have to be made to assert our rights, if they are to be disciplined and effective, will have to be exercised through the leadership of this House. We ask the people to work with their elected representatives to see that our claim is understood throughout the world. Propaganda for nearly thirty years has been directed to misrepresent the situation. The first thing that is necessary is to bring the facts to fair-minded people to enable them to judge. That was the purpose, for instance, for which I went to Britain.[3] I went to Britain because I wanted to point out, first of all, that this division of our country was perpetrated by Britain — that Britain was responsible, that it was maintained by British power and by British influence.

I had hoped that there were sufficient fair-minded people in Britain who, when the facts were known to them, would be able to influence their Government to do justice to Ireland. If this thing is to be ended peacefully, it should be ended by British action to start with. Britain has done this thing, and Britain ought to undo it. They have the power to do it. If they really want to, they can tell this minority in our country, that is not a fifth of the population of this country and not a fiftieth of the population of Britain, 'We are not going to support you in your claim for privilege. We are not going to permit this small minority of the two peoples to continue to set the two peoples by the ears and to stir up and continue the old antagonisms between them.' My belief was that, if you had properly informed public opinion in Britain and a Parliament and a Government that responded to the feelings of the fair-minded people in Britain, we would have reached the stage when this would be done.

I tried in my time to secure from a British Prime Minister, speaking for the British Government and the British people, a declaration to the effect that they wanted this partition of our country to end, that they desired it to end, that they would use all their good offices to bring it to an end and that they would use their influence to bring it to an end.[4] If they were sincere, a declaration of that sort would not be too much to expect. We have never got that. Instead we have got the contrary assertion now. We have got the suggestion through this Bill that it is a British interest to keep our country cut in two, that Britain does not want us united, that Britain wants still to help this minority to maintain their position of ascendancy and privilege against the expressed will of the majority of the Irish people.

I hoped for the ending of partition in the interests of good relations between the two peoples. I can honestly say that I have worked for that, whilst at every stage maintaining the rights of our people. I felt that the rights of our people were more than consistent, that they were the source of good relations between the two peoples. I felt that in an independent Ireland an Irishman would have an interest in seeing a strong Britain. I knew that these good relations could not be established so long as Britain tried to interfere in our affairs, and, as a basis for good relations, I worked constantly over the whole period of time during which I was Minister for External Affairs[5] — I can say I worked even at an earlier period — to try to get this fundamental point of difference ended and to get the whole question of partition settled. It is we, through all these times, who have been trying to make suggestions for the settlement of partition, but we were

3. de Valera was referring here to the campaign in favour of Irish territorial unity which he initiated in Britain after the conclusion of the Anglo-Irish economic dispute and the transfer to Ireland of the disputed harbour defences in 1938. This effort to enlist the sympathy of British public opinion was frustrated by the 'I.R.A.', who started a bombing campaign in England in January 1939 [M. Moynihan].

4. During the negotiations which led to the Anglo-Irish agreements [*sic*] of 25 April 1938 de Valera did his utmost to secure from the British Prime Minister, Neville Chamberlain, a declaration of the nature described here [M. Moynihan].

5. Eamon de Valera was minister for external affairs from 1932 to December 1937, when he was also president of the executive council of the Irish Free State, and from December 1937 to February 1948 when he was Taoiseach.

met at every stage and every step with 'Not an inch'.

The British have the responsibility for ending this. Now they want to pretend that they have not the responsibility and to pass it off and to hand over to us a task which they themselves have practically made impossible. They have put in this position of dominance in the Six Counties a group to whom they have assured a majority, practically a perpetual majority. That majority was designed to be a lasting majority. Political opinion has changed in other countries. There has been no change of political opinion there, and every time — as you see by looking back on the history — this question of the partition of our country loomed up as a question to be considered between the Irish and British Governments, you had immediately an election call to pretend that the people in the Six Counties were democratically supported in their attitude. They told us that it is only by the will of this Northern Ireland Parliament that we can ever hope to get our unity — through the will of a Parliament that is specially designed to deny it! We are told that no part of that territory can be taken from them except by the will of that Parliament — a Parliament that is empowered to gerrymander, as they have done in many cases, to any extent they wish. We do not admit that the majority in that area have a right to cut themselves off from the country. The Taoiseach has said what every one of us feels in this matter. I believe that every party and every individual in this part of Ireland will agree that what the Taoiseach has said about our feelings represents our feelings.

By this resolution we assert the right of our nation to its unity and independence. By it we promise that we will do everything we can do to maintain that right. If I were in office at this time — and I suppose the present Government have done it also — I would have tried at a time like this to get people who understand the situation and get them to use their good offices to stop, even at the eleventh hour, this Bill. I was in Australia. I spoke there to members of the Australian legislature and of the Australian Government. I was similarly in New Zealand. I found in all the places an understanding of the Irish national position and a desire that this partition of our country should be ended. Before this position gets still more embittered I would ask that the statesmen in those countries would intervene and try to get the British Government to see sense. As I have already said, a minority that is only one-fifth of the population of this country and one-fiftieth of the population of the other country ought not to be permitted to put these two peoples perpetually at each other's throats. It is quite wrong that that should be done. There are solutions that could be offered. We offered a solution in the past, and we were prepared to go to our people on it. I do not believe that it would have got universal support, but it would have got majority support and it would have laid the foundation for good relations, which could develop to meet the wishes of our people at any time. Surely there ought to be enough statesmanship at present to get a solution. A solution has been possible with other countries, and why should a solution not be possible with ours?

There can be no solution, however, so long as those who are in a privileged position can say, 'We will not touch you unless you are prepared to agree with us.' They have only to say 'No'. Bring them into a conference, it has been suggested; I have heard it suggested even in this House, when I was in charge of External Affairs, that the representatives of the Government of Ireland, of the British Government and of the Six Counties should get together and sit down at a table and try to work out a solution. Surely everybody knows what would be the result of that. As long as one member of the conference is going to say, 'No, I will not accept that,' the result would obviously be that there could be no agreement, and the end of such a conference would obviously be worse than the beginning. You cannot do it like that. The British Government has the responsibility and has the power — this Bill is showing it. The British Government has responsibility at the present moment to exercise that statesmanship which should bring about the ending of this intolerable situation. My appeal, as one who has been trying for these good relations while in office, my appeal now, as a member of the Opposition, is that the statesmen of the British Commonwealth, the statesmen abroad, who are desirous of seeing good relations established between Ireland and Britain, the Irish people and the British people throughout the world, should intervene in this critical situation and try to prevent this position from developing. I believe that it can be done. I believe that goodwill can do it. I believe that there is goodwill. Here, on both sides of this House, goodwill has been shown in the past. Goodwill has been shown, I know, by us. I believe that it has been shown in the past by members on the opposite benches; and why should not this goodwill show itself in exercise — by responsible people sitting down together and trying to work out a solution?

I, for one, would promise, as far as I personally am concerned — I cannot promise for anybody else — that the days that may be left to me in my life will be devoted to the duties of cementing good relations, on the basis of Irish rights being respected, as I have devoted my life up to the present time to securing Irish rights. I believe too that what I can say of myself is something that can be said for every member of our party, for every person in public life in this country and for every Irishman abroad. We are at the crossroads, in my opinion, at a point where Britain, if she is wise enough, can take the hand of friendship which is offered or spurn that hand of friendship again. If she spurns it, she will do something for which nobody but the enemies of England will be glad. We will not be glad, because it means a good deal of suffering, perhaps, ahead for us. If we were free, we would not want to see Britain's downfall, as I said somewhere else, but by doing this, by continuing to hold a portion of our country against the will of our people, Britain is giving us an interest in her downfall. Why does she do that? Is it statesmanship on the part of her Ministers to do it? Why does she do something that will only please the people who want to see Britain's downfall? If I were one of those who believed in certain continental theories and ideologies, I would welcome this Bill because I would see one state that was going to be weakened by the fact that the Irish people were dissatisfied and inimical to it.

The people who will be pleased with this are neither the friends of Ireland nor the friends of Britain, and those who wish well to both Ireland and Britain would want to see the end of this source of antagonism and bitterness. Instead of this Bill they would want to see the opportunity taken to bring about arrangements whereby a solution of partition would be got. Perhaps, if that line were taken, out of what is at the moment an evil and a danger good may come. I pray that it may, and I pray that the animosities between the two peoples, which were dying down, may not be revived.

FRANK RYAN and GEORGE GILMORE

(1902–44) (1898–1985)

from: THE IRISH REPUBLICAN CONGRESS (1934–35)

[Frank Ryan, George Gilmore and Peadar O'Donnell led a socialist-republican splinter group of the Irish Republican Army. In 1931 they founded Saor Éire, and appealed for working-class support against the urban middle classes and the big farmers who, in their view, had hijacked the republican ideal. Saor Éire was proscribed in 1931 and the catholic hierarchy condemned it as communist and as a 'sinful and irreligious' organization. The movement was reconstituted as the Republican Congress in 1934. Its charter was the 'Athlone Manifesto' of that year, largely the work of George Gilmore.

The text given here is the foreword to the second edition (1935) of the charter document, co-written by Gilmore and Frank Ryan.]

The first session of the Republican Congress held at Rathmines in the autumn of 1934 had to overcome some mistakes which were being made by a section of the delegates as to the stage of struggle in which the independence movement finds itself. There was a section which held the opinion that the Congress ought to differentiate its policy from those of the Fianna Fail and I. R. A. leaderships according to the kind of Republic they wished to establish. That section wished to adopt the slogan of 'The Workers' Republic' as opposed to 'The Republic.' It wished to form a new party instead of working for a united front movement.

The Congress decided that that was an incorrect approach to the present political situation. It held that the correct line of approach for Republicans, no matter what form of Republic they visualized as their ultimate objective, was a united front of Republican and Labor organizations for the breaking of the connection with the British Empire and the re-establishment of an independent Republic for a united Ireland. It realized that only that association of forces could raise the Republican struggle clear of the dwarfed formulae in which it was being stated and mobilize sufficient revolutionary power to sever the connection with the Empire. And it realized that only that association of forces could set the masses on the march for their emancipation by breaking them clear of the middle-class leaders who were blocking the road to the Republic.

The best proof of how correct the Congress decisions were is to be found in the process of clarification which has gone on within the different political bodies since that session.

It is becoming every day more apparent that the middle class leadership of Fianna Fail, in pursuance of its policy of protecting Capitalism in Ireland, is not attempting to sever the connection with the British Empire but is negotiating with a view to altering the form of association. And it is worthy of note that the principal advocates of the 'Workers' Republic' slogan who broke with the Republican Congress on that issue have merged into the reformist Labor Party which, while claiming to be actuated by the ideals of James Connolly, supported the Free State against the Republic in 1922.

It is no exaggeration to say that the Rathmines meeting raised the Republican struggle on to a new high plane. It will be agreed that the demand for complete national independence does now, in the words of the Athlone Manifesto, dominate the whole political field.

The Congress declared the necessity for the workers and small farmers of Ireland winning to the leadership of the national struggle. And here again considerable success was effected. Through the team work made possible within the Congress the working class was able to take the lead in anti-fascist, anti-imperialist demonstrations. But we have not done all that we ought to have done. We talk of the working class coming into the leadership of the Republican movement without realizing that the way to do that is just to do it. Republican demonstrations organized around militant workers rousing all the Republican passion in an area have not been carried out as they should.

This must now be remedied. There is really no unsurmountable obstacle preventing us from getting up meetings where workers who are pivotal in Fianna Fail, I. R. A. and Trades Union bodies would be present and where the demand would be raised and enthusiastically backed to have British overlordship completely uprooted.

We need now the campaign for the Republic to rally the working-class factors within the Republican organizations behind their own militants. And this will only be done by doing it!

We have weaknesses to overcome in other parts of the Congress work, too. The Agricultural Resolution adopted by the Congress in Rathmines expressed the view that 'The heaviest share of today's bad times falls on the agricultural community,' and that 'The heaviest share of the agricultural crisis falls on the agricultural wage earners and small farmers.'

It demanded, amongst other things, 'That ranch lands be distributed, without compensation to the ranchers, to landless and small farmer youth, with the State provision of the necessary credits, machinery and housing.' . . . 'That agricultural wage earners be guaranteed a wage which, in cash and perquisites, shall not be less than 40s. per week, out of work benefit; and adequate housing.' . . . 'That, as an immediate relief, all holdings under twenty-five acres be relieved of land annuities.'

Here is sketched a view of a tremendously important section of Irish life; and behind these demands a tremendous campaign can be waged. This is work upon which the Congress has only made a beginning.

In the carrying out of the tasks visualized in the Congress Industrial Resolution there is also a vast field for effort. It was a long resolution. A few of its most important points dealt with: 'Development of workers' councils in every town as fighting organs to co-ordinate and direct the struggles of the different Unions; these councils to include representatives of the unemployed.' . . . 'Struggle to organize the presently unorganized workers; to minimize the falling away from Unions due to inter-Union disputes.' . . . 'To favor and agitate for the reorganization of the Trades Unions on the basis of one Union for each industry, to be formed, with the consent of the Unions concerned, by the amalgamation of members in several Unions catering for the industry; such Union to be organized on an All-Irish basis, with headquarters in Ireland, North or South.' . . . 'Wages for women workers in industry to be equal to that of men employed in similar capacities.'

The need for effort on the lines of all of those clauses of the resolution has been demonstrated in the various strikes and lockouts that have taken place since its adoption by the Congress. The urgency of the last has been made especially apparent by the attack upon the status of women workers in the 'Conditions of Employment Bill' sponsored by the Fianna Fail Government.

Unemployment is increasing both in Northern and Southern Ireland, but still the Unemployed are largely unorganized.

Included in the Unemployed Resolution of the Congress is the clause 'That the Unemployed should be aided by all Congress supporters and Trades Unionists to develop a nation-wide organization, and that they be given representation on the Workers' Councils in every town'; and a demand for 'Abolition of all task work; all work done under relief schemes to be at Trades Union rates of pay and under Trades Union conditions.' It cannot be claimed that in this work we have done more than make a good beginning.

The resistance to the Congress idea from the leaders of organizations — Fianna Fail, I. R. A., and Labor Party — is being weakened under the pressure of a rising appreciation of the need for team work — for united action. In this connection it would be impossible to overestimate the value of the Call from the different Republican organizations in America for unified action in Ireland for the re-establishment of the Republic.

'We believe that Ireland has reached the critical stage when the Republican enthusiasm of the people can be used to re-establish the Republic or may be dissipated in civil strife. In this serious situation we urge the Irish people to insist that representatives of all Republican thought in Ireland must meet in conference to find a means of reconciling their various differences, uniting on unswerving principle, presenting a solid front to the common enemy and re-establishing the independence of the country as a Republic.' This appeal, issued jointly by the A. A. R. I. R., the Clan na Gael[1] and I. R. A., and the Irish Republican Congress League of America, expresses so truly — both in its warning against the danger of the present situation, and in its recognition of the one basis upon which unity can be achieved — the fears and hopes of the Irish people that the response to it must be immense.

Already it has been endorsed by several of the County Councils, and in the voting upon it it is noticeable that the only opposition has come from members — Cosgravite[2] and Unionist — who are definitely opposed to the Republic.

Old I. R. A. associations in various parts of the country are also beginning to speak in support of the Call, and the fact that it has struck a deep note amongst the Republican population generally is proved by the many letters which have appeared in the press in support of it from people of various different Republican groupings as well as from people of no Republican affiliations. One of the most interesting was from Capt. Denis Ireland[3] of Belfast, suggesting that the proposed conferences should include representatives of sections of the Protestant population of the North of Ireland who, while still unwilling to commit themselves to a campaign for the re-establishment of the Republic for all Ireland, are sufficiently interested in the proposal to wish to explore its possibilities.

Our exiles have done their part in creating a situation pregnant with wonderful possibilities for the development of an irresistible Republican movement. The next step remains with the leaders of Republican organizations at home. So far they have hesitated about assuming the responsibilities pertaining to a great forward movement such as the exiles have called for. Surely they will see that the time is ripe for it now!

FRANK RYAN
GEORGE GILMORE,
Hon. Secs.

Republican Congress,
57 Middle Abbey St.,
Dublin, Ireland.

1. The American Association for the Recognition of the Irish Republic was founded by de Valera in 1920. Clan na Gael (Family of the Gael) was an Irish-American republican revolutionary organization, founded in 1867. The organization split over the War of Independence and the Treaty.

2. W. T. Cosgrave (1880–1965), first president of the executive council of the Irish Free State 1922–32 and founder of the Cumann na nGaedheal political party.

3. Denis Ireland (1894–1974) was a freelance writer and broadcaster. Much of his writing set forth his ideal of a united and sovereign Ireland. In 1948, when he was appointed to the Irish Senate, he became the first resident of Northern Ireland to become a member of one of the Houses of the Oireachtas.

MICHAEL TIERNEY

(1894–1975)

IRELAND AND THE CORPORATE STATE (1933)

[Fascism is properly associated in its origins with a crisis in Italian parliamentary institutions, exploited by Mussolini from 1922. By 1930/31, Italian fascism was seeking some intellectual defence of its actions and beliefs. Central to this defence was the notion of the corporate state. A number of ideas were involved. Briefly, they were that (a) the community alone had the right to determine what the national interest required; (b) the conflicting interests of owners, workers and the state were to be harmonized within a single unit, the corporation, operating under public control; (c) strikes and lockouts were to be forbidden; (d) the doctrine of the primacy of the politician over the expert was to be abandoned. The divisiveness of politics was to be eliminated by the unity of expertise. (See Mario Einaudi, 'Fascism' in the *International Encyclopaedia of the Social Sciences*.)

The papal document, *Quadragesimo Anno*, was entirely in line with fascist thinking, except that it gave a Christian coloration to the corporate idea. Michael Tierney was one of those who attempted to apply these notions to Irish conditions. The only political movement that emerged to lay claim to these doctrines was the squalid Blueshirt movement under General Eoin O'Duffy and with the support of some sections of the Cumann na nGaedheal party, only recently (1932) removed from power. It is in these same years that the IRA, which helped to destroy the Blueshirt movement, began its move to the left, under the influence of Frank Ryan, Peadar O'Donnell and George Gilmore. This right/left polarization remained important but muted for the next twenty-five years.

The article was first published in *United Ireland* (16 December 1933).]

It is a very significant fact that since the Fianna Fáil Government took up office practically nothing has been heard of the movement, so loudly propagated two years ago, for the reform of our social and even our political organisation along lines more Christian than at present. There are two very good and closely-related reasons for this fact. One is that the 'movement,' in the form it then took, was almost entirely Fianna Fáil propaganda. Its initiators and supporters were practically to a man more interested in securing the defeat of the then Government, and in revenge for the events of 1922–3, than in Christian social principles. The other reason is a corollary to the first. It lies in the fact that not a single one of these Christian champions ever got within shouting distance of any kind of real social programme whatsoever. They contented themselves with vague generalities or else with irrelevant denunciations of imagined or exaggerated grievances. Their utterances contained a great deal of criticism of 'urbanism,' of Freemasonry, and of emigration, which had almost ceased at the time. These were all handy bricks to throw at the Cosgrave Government, but they were more fitted for smashing political windows than for building intellectual habitations.

In reality, the problem of reorganising our social and political institutions, while it exists here as elsewhere, is one very little susceptible of solution by mere propagandist methods. In the first place, even its very formulation, and in the second place the proposing of means by which it can be solved, require a great deal of hard work and hard thinking. It is not merely a question, for instance, of alleviating the hardships of poverty. There is, in fact, grave danger that by stating it in such terms the utopian-revolutionary tendency which has been one curse of modern times may be strengthened and the evil thereby more increased than lessened.

Neither is it by any means solely a religious question; and one of the dangers of stating it in religious terms is the confusion of politics with religion, a confusion that generally eventuates in putting politics on top.

Nor is it again by any means solely an economic or financial question. Bankers have at least as much right to blame statesmen for the evils of the times as statesmen have to blame bankers. The defects of our social system have, in fact, a strangely multiple origin in diametrically opposite causes: the religious fanaticism which divided Europe, the irreligious rationalism which succeeded it and added confusion to division, the preoccupation with economics and the universal concentration by poor and rich alike on the good things of this world to the exclusion of everything else.

These varying factors have fundamentally altered the character of the State twice in modern times. From the hierarchic State of the Middle Ages there developed the anarchic State of the eighteenth and nineteenth centuries, the State of the industrial revolution. From this again there has developed or is developing the totalitarian State, the all-competent machine of the present period. First the State was stripped of all its natural organs and then expected to undertake the ownership and management of all property and means of production.

From the philosophic standpoint there could be nothing funnier than the spectacle of a piebald and, in general, unintelligent and uneducated assembly of public representatives, chosen by most defective methods, claiming, or having thrust upon it, the whole enormously complicated and very subtle task of conducting the march of a complicated and subtle civilisation. Yet that is the exact spectacle with which philosophical observers of politics are presented in the countries which yesterday were regarded as the leaders in political wisdom. Other countries have substituted, as Russia has done, the control of political parties for that of Parliament.

Only in one country, Italy, is there any sign of an attempt to create out of the wreckage both of parliament and party a really well-designed and complex machinery for dealing with a complex situation. It is a complete mistake to suppose that Italian Fascism is merely a crude individual or party dictatorship. It is a product of peculiar Italian conditions, unknown elsewhere, but it has gradually evolved a scheme of social and political organisation which is quite certain as time goes on to be adapted to the needs of every civilised country. In that scheme, dictatorship has more and more given place to a new and more intelligent, because more subtly organised, kind of democracy. Mussolini, when his time comes to retire, will be succeeded, not by another dictator, but by a new entity suited to the needs of modern civilisation — the Corporate State.

In the great Encyclical, *Quadragesimo Anno*,[1] promulgated two years ago, Pope Pius XI briefly stated the problem and its solution in words which strangely enough have received little attention among the spokesmen of the Christian State in this country. 'Things have come to such a pass,' says the Pope, 'that the highly-developed social life, which once flourished in a variety of prosperous institutions organically linked with each other, has been damaged and all but ruined, leaving thus virtually only individuals and the State.' (English Translation, p.36). He goes on to say (p.37):

> The primary duty of the State and of all good citizens is to abolish conflict between classes with divergent interests and thus foster and promote harmony between various ranks of society. The aim of social legislation must, therefore, be the re-establishment of vocational groups.

This is the aim which has been set before itself by Italian Fascism. It can be reached, under different historical and political conditions, without necessarily having recourse to all the accidentals of Italian dictatorship. However it may be reached in differing circumstances, these two sentences of the Pope's deserve to be thoroughly studied, commented on, and understood, by every intelligent citizen in Ireland as elsewhere.

We are not freer than any other country from the present evils and future menaces that a defective social organisation entails. That something like the Pope's solution of the gravest problem of our time is envisaged even in England may be seen by many signs. Even so experienced and highly-placed an administrator as Sir Arthur Salter[2] has suggested for Great Britain a tentative scheme of reform along the lines of what he calls 'institutional self-discipline' — in other words something very like the Corporate State. All who need the encouragement of authority such as his will find it in a series of three lectures published for him this year for half-a-crown by the Cambridge University Press, and called *The Framework of an Ordered Society*. More interesting still in this connection is the benediction given by the Right Hon Walter Elliott, British Minister for

1. *Quadragesimo Anno* was the name of a famous encyclical by Pope Pius XI on the relations between workers and employers and on the function of the state in society.

2. James Arthur, Baron Salter (1881–1975), was a senior civil servant before becoming Gladstone professor of political theory at Oxford in 1934. The book referred to here, *The Framework of an Ordered Society* (London, 1933) was a published version of the Alfred Marshall lectures, delivered at Cambridge University in 1932.

Agriculture, to an admirable little survey of the Italian system . . . .[3]

There are signs of a very powerful similar tendency not only in Germany and Austria, where Hitler and Dollfuss[4] have drawn the attention of the world, but also in France. In the latter country the movement has taken a very strong Catholic turn, and its periodical, *Esprit*,[5] is a remarkable record of a quite extraordinary ferment of ideas.

The whole civilised world is being driven to face the necessity of some third course between the individualism which produces Kruegers[6] and the Communism which produces Lenins. America is at the present moment attempting, probably after inadequate thought and over-hastily, the sort of reform that is demanded everywhere. Here in Ireland we seem still strangely wedded to a mystic belief in unconsidered tariffs as a means to an industrial utopia on the one hand, and a belated and insincere lip-service to 'democracy,' accompanied by carefully fostered disorder, on the other. If we wish to build up a really just and Christian social system we must go deeper than either. The Corporate State must come in the end, in Ireland as elsewhere. Its inauguration need not be the work of any one political party, but the future is with those who honestly, intelligently and fearlessly will undertake its cause.

3. Walter Elliott (1888–1958) was a Conservative MP and Britain's minister for agriculture 1932–36. He was closely identified with Neville Chamberlain's policy of appeasement towards Hitler.
4. Englebert Dollfuss (1892–1934), Austrian chancellor, suspended parliament in 1933 and, supported by Mussolini, ruled by emergency decree. He broke the Austrian socialist party by main force and in 1934 promulgated a new constitution based on *Quadragesimo Anno*. In July of that year he was murdered by Nazis who were trying to organize a putsch.
5. *Esprit* was a right-wing catholic journal which flourished in France between 1930 and 1938.
6. Paul Krueger (1825–1904), South African statesman and soldier, leader of the Boer Rebellion in 1880, president of the Transvaal 1883–1900.

JOHN A. COSTELLO
(1891–1976)

THE REPUBLIC OF IRELAND BILL (1948)

[During a visit to Ottawa in September 1948, John A. Costello, Taoiseach of the inter-party government of the time, surprised everyone by suddenly declaring Ireland a Republic, thereby stealing a march on the opposition party, Fianna Fáil, which had always championed the republican cause with greater vigour. It was a sudden but not a masterly stroke. Britain retaliated by passing the Ireland Act of 1949, which confirmed the status of Northern Ireland as part of the United Kingdom and declared that it would never cease to be so unless by consent. The Republic was given constitutional embodiment but at the price of deepening the partition to which all theories of the republic had previously objected or denied legitimacy.

The text below is from *Dáil Eireann Debates*, Vol. 113, cols 394–98, 24 November 1948.]

. . . The Bill is a simple Bill but it has tremendous and, I believe and hope, very beneficial results. The first section repeals the External Relations Act.[1] I have dealt fully with that. Section Two provides: 'It is hereby declared that the description of the State shall be the Republic of Ireland'. That section is so obviously necessary that it requires no advocacy on my part to commend it to the Dáil. Deputies will recall that under the Constitution the name of the State is Éire or, in the English language, Ireland. Now, this section does not purport, as it could not, to repeal the Constitution. There is the name of the State and there is the description of the State. The name of the State is Ireland and the description of the State is the Republic of Ireland. That is the description of its constitutional and international status. Deputies are probably aware of the fact that tremendous confusion has been caused by the use of that word 'Éire' in Article 4. By a misuse by malicious

1. The External Relations Act, introduced by de Valera in 1936 during the abdication crisis in Britain, delimited the functions of the British crown in the field of external relations of the Irish Free State.

people of that word, 'Éire', they have identified it with the Twenty-Six Counties and not with the State that was set up under this Constitution of 1937.[2]

In documents of a legal character, such as, for instance, policies of insurance, there is always difficulty in putting in what word one wants to describe the State referred to. Section 2 provides a solution for these difficulties, and those malicious newspapers who want to refer in derogatory tones to this country as 'Éire' and who have coined these contemptuous adjectives about it, such as 'Eireannish' and 'Eirish', and all the rest of it, will have to conform to the legal direction here in this Bill.

Section 2 does these subsidiary things but it does more than that. It does something fundamental. It declares to the world that when this Bill is passed this State is unequivocally a republic. It states that as something that cannot be controverted or argued about and we can rely, I think and I hope, on international courtesy to prevent in future this contemptuous reference to us and the name of our State being used for contemptuous purposes, as it has been, by some people and by some organs in the last few years.

Section 3 merely provides that the President, on the authority and on the advice of the Government, may exercise the executive power or any executive function of the State in or in connection with its external relations. We now, and we will under this clause and under this Bill, have clarified our international position. No longer will there be letters of credence sent furtively across to Buckingham Palace. Diplomatic representatives will be received by the President of Ireland, the head of the State. We now have the unambiguous position that the President is head of the State and, if there are heads of State treaties to be entered into, if he goes abroad, he will go abroad as the head of this State, the head of the Republic of Ireland.

Section 4 says:

'This Act shall come into operation on such day as the Government may by Order appoint.'

When this Bill is enacted there will be no reason for those fears, those apprehensions which have been so assiduously set abroad by the poisonous sections of the Press, but there will be certain difficulties though not of a major character. I can hardly call them difficulties because they are not difficulties but merely legal matters that have to be cleared up and which may necessitate legislation here perhaps or perhaps in Canada, Australia, or Great Britain and we must provide a time limit, a breathing space within which these matters of detail can be carried out in concord and agreement. There are no very important matters; they are matters of detail, legal technicalities, not matters of difficulty or controversy. They will take some little time. I cannot say how long it will take to have these details brought into operation and accordingly, however much we would like to see this Bill come into immediate operation, we will have to have a breathing space for the various Parliaments to settle up the details which require to be settled up. They are not matters of difficulty.

As I said before and now repeat, I recommend this Bill to the Dáil and ask for its unanimous acceptance by the Dáil. It will, I believe, if it is passed in a spirit of goodwill, if it is passed unanimously, do and achieve what its primary purpose hopes for: to bring peace here in this part of our country and by bringing this country well on to the international stage, by lifting this problem of Partition from the domestic arena and putting it on the international scene, give us not a faint hope but a clear prospect of bringing about the unity of Ireland.

I should like to say one more thing in conclusion. There have been sometimes smug, sometimes fearsome declarations by British Ministers or British Governments that the problem of Partition is an Irish problem, that must be settled between Irishmen. That Pilate-like attitude can no longer be held by statesmen with the courage and decency to look facts in the face. This problem was created by an Act of the British Parliament, the Government of Ireland Act, 1920. It may be insisting on the obvious, but I have had occasion to insist very strongly on the obvious in recent months. That Act of 1920 was passed before the Treaty of 1921 and it is surprising how many people think that the Partition of our country was effected by the Treaty of 1921.[3] The

2. de Valera's Constitution of 1937 rechristened the Irish Free State 'Eire' (Article 4) and affirmed the essential unity of the country, stating that 'the national territory consists of the whole island of Ireland, its islands and the territorial seas' (Article 2).

3. The Government of Ireland Act of 1920 repealed the 1914 Home Rule Act and granted a large measure of Home Rule to the 'southern' twenty-

problem was created by the British Government and the British Parliament and it is for them to solve the problem. They cannot wash their hands of it and clear themselves of responsibility for it. The Act of 1920 is a very poor title for a claim which is not based upon morality and justice. The Government of the six north-eastern counties claim[s] that and assert it by virtue of a majority, a statutorily created majority, a majority created deliberately under the Act of 1920 to coerce and keep within the bounds of their so-called State masses of our Catholic people and fellow Irishmen who do not want to be there. That Act of 1920 was put on the Statute Book and brought into operation without a single vote cast in its favour by any Irish representative in the British Parliament or without anybody North or South wanting it. Therefore the problem of undoing that wrong devolves upon the British Government. We are doing our part down here. We are doing our part by this Bill.

The whole basis of the case I make for this Bill is founded on goodwill, is founded on the end of bitterness. It is founded on a sincere desire to have greater goodwill with Great Britain. We hope through the creation of that goodwill, through fostering further goodwill, that that will help materially to induce the British Government and Great Britain to take a hand in the undoing of the wrong for which their predecessors were responsible in 1920. We believe that this Bill, by creating conditions on which that goodwill can increase, will help towards the solution of the problem of Partition. We hold out, as I said here earlier today, the hand of friendship to the decent people of Northern Ireland and they can be assured if they come in here, end this great wrong and come into a unified Ireland, they will be doing good work for themselves, for the whole of Ireland and for that country to which they proclaim their intense loyalty, Great Britain, and the Commonwealth of Nations and be giving a lasting contribution to the peace of the world.[4]

six counties while making the six northern counties a separate state of Northern Ireland within the United Kingdom. At the time of its passage, the War of Independence had begun; the Act was largely ignored in the twenty-six counties. In the Treaty of 1921, Article 11 states that 'the provisions of the Government of Ireland Act, 1920, shall, so far as they relate to Northern Ireland, remain in full force and effect . . . .' (see above, p. 741).

4. For a full discussion of this act, see J. I. McCabe, *The Republic of Ireland: The Formulation and Consequences of the Republic of Ireland Act 1948–1949* (Dublin: Irish Academic Press, 1990).

GARRET FITZGERALD

(1926–)

from: TOWARDS A NEW IRELAND (1972)

[Garret FitzGerald here anticipates the policies he would follow or try to follow in relation to Northern Ireland during his two future terms of office as Taoiseach (1981–82 and 1982–87). The year 1972 was not an auspicious one for such conciliatory gestures. It began with the murder of fourteen civil rights marchers in Derry by British paratroopers, continued with the proroguing of the Stormont regime in Northern Ireland and its replacement by a system of direct rule and, thereafter, an organized assassination campaign, directed for the most part against Roman Catholics by protestant paramilitary organizations, and an IRA car-bomb offensive, carried out in crowded city areas. Nevertheless, FitzGerald persisted with his conciliatory policies, the culmination of which was the New Ireland Forum of 1983–84.]

CHAPTER 9

TOWARDS CHANGES IN THE REPUBLIC

Throughout most of the past half-century the issue of Irish reunification was debated in somewhat simplistic terms. Because to both sides it appeared at first a temporary arrangement (although of course this was not publicly admitted by leaders of the majority in the North), relatively little thought was given to how it could be brought to an end, or even as to how the divergence between the two parts of Ireland could be prevented from widening. Northern Unionists were content with a 'no surrender' attitude, which some of them in their hearts did not take too seriously, and the Northern minority and the bulk of the people in the rest of the country were equally content to assert a claim to unity without pursuing very far the question of how this ambition might be realised. As the years passed the attitude of many supporters of Irish reunification imperceptibly and unconsciously changed from a presumption that Partition was temporary and would be brought to an early end, to an equally unconscious acceptance of it as an indefinitely continuing feature on the Irish landscape, but this underlying change of private attitudes brought no change in public policies. From time to time politicians in the Republic were moved to public statements of abhorrence of the political division of the island and at certain periods this sporadic competition in oratory developed into a campaign against Partition; most notably, perhaps, in the period 1948–1949, when Mr. De Valera took advantage of a spell in Opposition after sixteen years of government to launch a world-wide campaign on the subject. This campaign continued into the early 1950s, aided by a fund collected, rather tactlessly from the point of view of Northern Unionist sentiment, at the gates of Catholic churches, and punctuated by the declaration of the Republic in 1949, and by the British guarantee in the consequential Ireland Act, 1949, of the Northern Ireland Parliament's right to decide the reunification issue.[1]

The IRA border raid campaign of the years from 1956 onwards introduced a new element into the controversy, which, however, had no lasting effects, except on Northern Unionist attitudes.[2] By the early 1960s the whole question seemed to be back where it had started, except that opinion had become accustomed to the fact of Partition, and pessimistic about prospects for its disappearance in the forseeable future.

Within Northern Ireland these decades saw many fluctuations in the attitude of the minority, ranging from abstentionism to limited participation in the governmental system, and even, at certain periods, an abdication by the constitutional Nationalist Party of its role in the face of Republican determination to contest seats at elections. (Fearing that to put forward candidates as it had done for decades previously would 'split the vote' and let the seats concerned go to the Unionists, the Nationalists temporarily ceded the ground to abstentionist Republicans, possibly believing that this threat to their political control of the minority would go away if left to blow itself out, as in fact eventually happened.)

The 1960s saw the emergence of a new attitude amongst the Northern minority, however. In the aftermath of the border raids and the temporary takeover of parliamentary representation by abstentionist Republicans, the mood of the minority switched back towards acceptance of a measure of involvement with the system; a willingness to try co-operation. One of the earliest protagonists of this policy was Mr. G. B. Newe, later, towards the end of 1971, to be appointed a member of the Northern Ireland Cabinet in a belated effort by Mr. Brian Faulkner to lend credibility to his government.[3] But it received a measure of support as time went on from Nationalist politicians also, amongst them Mr. Paddy Gormley, MP, brother of Mr. Tom Gormley, who in early 1972, with two Unionist MPs, joined the Alliance Party.[4]

1. The Anti-Partition League was established in 1947 to protest against the partitioning of Ireland. In Northern Ireland it was supported by the Nationalist Party. In January 1949 the Irish inter-party government and the leaders of the main opposition parties organized an All-Party Anti-Partition Committee, also known as the Mansion House Committee, to finance the peaceful reunification of Ireland. Anti-partition propaganda was issued and a diplomatic offensive was lauched; anti-partition candidates in Northern Ireland were financially supported and an Anti-Partition League was set up in England.

   The 1949 Ireland Act, passed by the Labour government in Britain, declared that 'Northern Ireland remains part of His Majesty's Dominions and of the United Kingdom and it is hereby affirmed that in no event will Northern Ireland or any part thereof cease to be part of His Majesty's Dominions and of the United Kingdom without the consent of the Parliament of Northern Ireland.'

2. The IRA border campaign of 1956–62 was a small-scale affair which won little support from the catholic minority in Northern Ireland and even less in the Republic.
3. Brian Faulkner (1921–77) became prime minister of Northern Ireland in March 1971. In August he introduced an internment policy entirely directed against the catholic minority. On 27 October 1971 he appointed Dr Gerard B. Newe, a catholic but not an MP, as a minister of state in Northern Ireland, to give the impression that his hard-line reputation was ill-deserved.
4. The Alliance Party was founded in April 1970 in an attempt to provide a middle ground between catholics and protestants. Tom and Paddy

It is against this background that one must see the analysis of minority attitudes in the Rose Survey, carried out in 1968 and briefly summarised in Chapter 5.[5] This Survey was undertaken just at the end of this 'honeymoon' period, which had also been marked by the exchange of visits at Prime Minister level initiated by Mr. Sean Lemass in 1965.

But it is also against this background that one must see the emergence of the Civil Rights Movement. The tactical approach of this Movement reflected the shift in minority attitudes during the 1960s towards an attempt to work the system by concentrating on a political evolution within Northern Ireland as a preliminary to, and indeed a condition precedent of, any move towards seeking reunification by consent. Of course the Civil Rights Movement did not accept the rather formless drift towards co-operation that had marked the years before 1968; it adopted a positive policy of non-violent demonstration in pursuit of its aims, conscious, no doubt, of the strong possibility that such a show of independence and self-confidence by those who had suffered from the system of government in Northern Ireland since 1920 would be likely to arouse opposition and even physical resistance by supporters of the regime.

But although its tactics were aggressive rather than passive, its strategy was similar to that which had emerged more or less haphazardly amongst the minority during the immediately preceding years: tackle the internal problems of Northern Ireland in the first instance, and leave the issue of reunification on one side for the time being, to be settled later by agreement in the light of the new and, hopefully, saner situation that would emerge following the battle for reforms.

Despite the fact that the conservatism of most Northern Protestants, and their suspicion of Republican influences in the Civil Rights Movement, prevented that Movement from mobilising significant support from the Protestant community (although many Protestants did, of course, support the reforms when they were introduced), this development nevertheless changed the character of the Northern problem. Because the Civil Rights Movement was content to leave the Partition issue to be decided at a later stage, in a, hopefully, different atmosphere created by reforms, its reform programme was much more difficult to resist than any previous Opposition movement to the Northern Government. The Northern Government might convince a high proportion of its own supporters that the Civil Rights Movement was, despite its new policies, only anti-partitionism under another guise; it could not so easily persuade opinion outside Northern Ireland of this thesis. Moreover because civil rights had become a fashionable issue in other countries during the 1960s, and because the campaign — and any attempt to repress it — was transmitted with all the instantaneity and impact of television, the effect of the Civil Rights Movement on opinion outside Northern Ireland was greater than, perhaps, even its organisers had ever conceived possible. Had it been merely another stage in a long-drawn out campaign against Partition, it is doubtful whether, even with the aid of television, it could have had the same effect on opinion in Britain and elsewhere. The reaction to this campaign culminated in the violence of August, 1969, the intervention of the British Army to prevent a pogrom, and the granting of the reforms — subject to a certain amount of subsequent delay and whittling down, referred to earlier.[6] In retrospect one is forced to wonder whether the Civil Rights Movement, and the politicians associated with it who later formed the Social Democratic and Labour Party, were prepared for the measure of success they achieved, and for the speed with which it was secured. The logical corollary of the anti-discrimination reform programme would have been a demand for a right on the part of the minority to participate in government, yet this demand was not made until much later, long after the minority in Belfast and Derry had come into conflict with the British Army.

The extent to which the new approach — concentrating on internal changes within Northern Ireland and leaving the Partition issue for later settlement — had taken deep root amongst the minority became

Gormley, nationalist MPs, and Phelim O'Neill and Robert McConnell, unionist MPs, defected to the Alliance Party in February 1972.

5. Richard Rose, *Governing Without Consensus: An Irish Perspective* (London: Faber and Faber, 1971).

6. Police violence in Derry in August 1969 began the 'Battle of the Bogside' which ended with the arrival of the British army to keep the peace and with the withdrawal of the police. Police and protestant paramilitaries killed several people in Belfast before the army came in. Reforms in relation to discrimination in housing and in jobs and a reformed local government franchise were conceded, but they were not executed with any enthusiasm.

evident during the period from August, 1969, until August, 1971, when internment was introduced. Throughout this period the Partition issue remained in the background, despite the increasing polarisation between Protestants and Catholics. It was only after the introduction of internment that the emphasis of minority attitudes began to switch back from internal change within the North to national reunification as an immediate aim. This reversal of emphasis in the autumn of 1971 was encouraged by the Wilson proposals, which envisaged an agreement on ultimate reunification, followed by a fifteen-year transitional period.[7] It was given further impetus by the radio and newspaper interviews with Rev. Ian Paisley towards the end of 1971, when his proposals for constitutional change in the Republic, and deliberate side-stepping of questions about his attitude to reunification if these changes were effected, hinted at a possible change of attitude on this issue.

By the beginning of 1972 there was, moreover, evidence of similar stirrings in non-Paisleyite Northern Protestant opinion. The sense of insecurity of the Northern majority, and their fear that even if this crisis were overcome, the whole cycle of violence could start again in the future, seemed to be beginning to lead some more thoughtful members of the Protestant community to ask themselves whether there might not be something to be gained by examining the question of the kind of Ireland that might emerge if the two parts of the country were eventually to be reunited. Speeches by Richard Ferguson, a former Unionist MP,[8] from December, 1971, onwards in which he addressed himself to the need to consider the possibility of a new non-sectarian united Ireland, underlined this new mood.

Thus, the failure to find a solution within the context of Northern Ireland based on the willingness of the minority in the late 1960s to leave the reunification issue on one side for the time being and to concentrate rather on internal reforms, had created by the start of 1972 a situation in which the whole question of a united Ireland had again become a live issue. Now, however, reunification seemed to have rather more prospect of realisation within a reasonable period than had seemed to exist at any time during the first forty years of the existence of Northern Ireland, when a sporadic campaign was being waged against Partition. Historians will, no doubt, debate the relative contributions to this new situation of a multiplicity of factors at work during the period from 1969 onwards, and especially in the closing months of 1971. These factors will probably include the following:

1. The policy vacuum on the side of the minority after the concession of the reform programme in August and October, 1969, which in retrospect, can be seen to have inhibited change in the political structure of the North during this period.
2. The intransigence of the Unionist Government and Party when the proposals for minority participation in government in Northern Ireland emerged during the course of 1971.
3. The British Government's internment decision and that Government's failure, influenced, no doubt, by repeated Army promises of imminent victory over the IRA, to take any initiative in the closing months of 1971 to recover the ground thus lost.
4. The brutality associated with internment, and the failure of the British Army authorities to prevent some of its units from behaving in a manner that alienated the goodwill of even the most moderate members of the minority.
5. The disturbing effect on Northern Protestant opinion of the IRA campaign in the period after internment, and the growing belief amongst Protestants in Northern Ireland that the British Government, politicians and people neither understood their situation nor cared enough about it to sustain a prolonged campaign.
6. The reintroduction of the reunification issue into the sphere of practical politics by the Harold Wilson initiative of late 1971.
7. The emergence in the Republic of a movement favouring a more liberal and pluralist society, which for the first time offered Northern Protestants some hope that a united Ireland would not necessarily be simply an enlarged version of what they had always seen as a Republic dominated by Roman Catholic teaching and influence.

All of these factors, and perhaps others besides that

7. In the aftermath of internment in 1971, Harold Wilson, the British leader of the opposition, made a series of proposals for Irish reunification which seemed to be the kernel of Labour Party policy on Northern Ireland.
8. Richard Ferguson, unionist MP for South Antrim 1970–72.

may not be evident to an observer writing early in 1972, myopically close to the events in question, no doubt played their part, for nothing less than a complex combination of many causes could account for the emergence of a willingness on the part even of a thinking minority of Northern Protestants to start giving serious consideration to a solution involving eventual reunification in some form.

The ultimate significance of this shift in opinion is unknowable in early 1972; but enough has happened to make it worth considering seriously ways in which it might prove possible to overcome the obstacles to reunification that have been strengthened in the past half-century, reinforcing the basic inter-community hostility that initially led to Partition. The shape of an eventual solution, rather than the practical path towards its negotiation, will be the theme of the concluding pages of this book. How and whether it might be possible to secure the consent, or at any rate, acquiescence, of the Northern majority to a peaceful evolution towards national unity remains an uncertain question — and reunification achieved other than peacefully would ensure lasting discord affecting the whole of Ireland, rather than anything that could properly be called national unity. All that can be said is that the prospect of reunification without violence had by the start of 1972 emerged as a possibility strong enough to warrant practical consideration and to call for serious study.

First of all, some 'non-starter' solutions should, perhaps, be ruled out. Thus the proposal sometimes canvassed in Britain, and occasionally even in Ireland, for a re-partitioning of Northern Ireland should be excluded. The politico-religious geography of Northern Ireland is much too complex to make any such solution worth considering. While there is a rather higher proportion of Catholics in the West and South of Northern Ireland, than in the North and East of the area, there are, nevertheless, about 200,000 Catholics in the North-East corner of Northern Ireland — Antrim, North Down, Belfast and North Armagh. Thus even if the boundary were re-drawn to include only those parts of Northern Ireland in which there is an overwhelming Protestant majority, less than 10% of the land area of Ireland, there would remain within this enclave 200,000 Catholic hostages — well over half of them in Belfast itself. This problem could no doubt be overcome by a transfer of populations, but the hardship this would entail would be immense and the resultant all-Protestant enclave would by the standards of modern European civilisation be a political monstrosity. This kind of solution assumes that the differences between Protestants and Catholics are of a permanently irreconcilable character; that these two communities of Ulster people are so inherently different and mutually hostile that it is hopeless to conceive of their *ever* living together in peace. Even the events of the years from 1969 to 1972 do not warrant such a deeply pessimistic conclusion.

Another proposal for a boundary change — the inclusion within Northern Ireland of the three Ulster counties now in the Republic — has been put forward by the Provisional Sinn Fein organisation as a means of persuading Unionists to accept reunification.[9] This solution would, however, be highly unlikely to prove acceptable to the majority of people in the three Ulster counties in the Republic, and it is, of course, specifically designed to threaten the position of the Protestant community within the area of Northern Ireland. Protestants who might accept participation in a United Ireland if they retained their own provincial autonomy within the present territory of Northern Ireland, where they have a clear domestic majority, would not be attracted by a proposal which with the faster growth of the Catholic population of these areas, would threaten at a fairly early date their submergence as a minority in an overwhelmingly Catholic Ireland. Moreover, as the Provisional Sinn Fein proposal envisages four provincial parliaments within a federal Ireland, the Ulster province, within which the Protestants would have a tenuous and impermanent majority, would at the level of the federal institutions find itself in a minority of one-in-four — whereas if the existing Northern Ireland State federated with the Republic, the balance in population terms would be only two-to-one against Northern Ireland, and Northern Ireland might reasonably hope within such a twin-State system to be accorded equal representation at, say, the level of the Upper House, as is accorded in certain other federations (e.g. the United States of America) where the lower house of parliament is constituted on the one-man-one-vote principle.

9. Provisional Sinn Féin, the political wing of the Provisional IRA, put forward a series of devolutionary proposals in which Ulster would constitute one of the four administrative units of a federalist Ireland.

Thus there seems to be nothing to be gained by playing around with the existing boundary; for good or ill, it exists, and if a federal system is to be created, it is more likely that agreement can be reached on the basis that this boundary would be let stand, than on a basis that involved a radical change in it.

The concept of a federation of the two existing Irish political entities has its difficulties, of course. There appears to be a general sentiment in the Republic in favour of such a solution, however — at any rate, no voices have been raised to protest that a united Ireland must be a unitary State, and most discussion has either explicitly or implicitly been based on the concept of an autonomous Northern Ireland region within a unified but not unitary 32-county Irish State.

This general acceptance of the concept of an autonomous Northern Ireland region depends, however, upon agreement on a reconstitution of the system of government within that region along lines that would be acceptable to the minority and would guarantee human rights, viz. on the pattern suggested in the immediately preceding chapter. This would leave the following questions to be settled:

1. The nature of the special relationship, if any, that would exist between a united Ireland and Great Britain.
2. The guarantees that the Northern Protestant community would have for their rights within a united Ireland.
3. The kind of Constitution required for a United Ireland.
4. The steps to be taken to ensure that the ending of Northern Ireland's present relationship with the United Kingdom, and its participation in a United Ireland, would not adversely affect agricultural incomes, employment in industries such as shipbuilding, social welfare benefits, or living standards generally.
5. The changes that would, in the meantime, be required within the Republic to persuade Northern Protestants that an association with the Republic within an Irish Federal State could be acceptable . . . .

A clear distinction must be made here between more immediate changes required within the Republic to create a favourable atmosphere for future discussions, and the eventual changes in the present Constitution of the Republic that would be required to make it acceptable as the Constitution of a federal Irish State. While some matters will come up for consideration under both headings, this distinction is an important one, which emerged clearly towards the end of 1971, in the limited public debate that surrounded the decision to establish an all-party Committee in the Republic to discuss Northern Ireland policy and possible relevant constitutional changes.

The sensitivities of Northern Protestant opinion with respect to laws and practices in the Republic have been outlined earlier. At this stage the only issue is what changes are necessary to prepare the way for constructive discussions on eventual reunification. The central problem here is the influence of the Catholic Church in the Republic on social and legal issues within the political forum. This is only minimally a matter of constitutional and legal provisions: much more important to the Northern Protestant is the evidence of indirect influence wielded by the authorities of the Catholic Church, either in preventing laws being enacted, or in securing the administration of laws in a manner favourable to what its authorities regard as the interests of the Catholic religion.

The formal constitutional and legal changes called for are, indeed, relatively few. The provisions of Articles 44.1.2 — 'The State recognises the special position of the Holy Catholic Apostolic and Roman Church as the guardian of the Faith professed by the great majority of the citizens' — would clearly have to be repealed, but as Cardinal Conway[10] has said that he would not shed a tear at its deletion from the Constitution, and as only one member of the Dail — a rural Labour Deputy — has criticized its proposed repeal, this creates no problem.

Secondly, it would be desirable as an indication of goodwill towards the Northern Ireland legal position on divorce, to delete also the provision of Article 41.3.2 of the Constitution — which forbids the enactment of any law granting a dissolution of marriage. The making of such a constitutional change *might* suffice to meet Northern Protestant opinions on this matter, without going beyond this to

10. Cardinal William Conway (1913–77), archbishop of Armagh and Roman catholic primate of All Ireland 1963–77. The article referred to was repealed in December 1972.

introduce actual divorce legislation in the Republic, for divorce is a matter of jurisdiction and, as is evident from the legal position with respect to divorce in England and Wales and in Scotland, different divorce laws can exist within a non-federal State, and all the more so within a federal State, as Ireland on this hypothesis might in time become.

There will be those who argue that divorce is a human right, and that failure by the Republic to make provision for this 'right' would make more difficult reunification on a federal basis, even if Northern Ireland could retain its own divorce law, and power to modify this law in future. But the concept of divorce as an absolute human right is an arguable one, if for no other reason than because the divorce laws of every State are different, allowing the dissolution of marriage for widely differing reasons, and with widely different conditions attached. A human right must surely be something more precise than a vague provision of this kind, differently interpreted from State to State. Moreover, although the question of divorce is frequently raised in connection with the question of reunification, divorce is in fact disapproved of in varying degrees by all the Protestant Churches in Ireland, and is frowned on by a high proportion, possibly a substantial majority, of their members; although, of course, this does not mean that they would wish their view to have the force of law. The introduction of divorce in Northern Ireland is of relatively recent origin; apart from the traditional system of divorce by Act of Parliament, which applied to the whole of Ireland up to and after the division of the country and the establishment of the Irish Free State, it was only in 1939 that divorce through the Courts was introduced in Northern Ireland. In these circumstances it is possible that the genuine feelings of Northern Ireland people on this matter would be met if pending reunification a change in the Republic's Constitution were effected that made it clear that reunion would not interfere with Northern Ireland's freedom of action in relation to divorce laws, although some will feel that the Republic should go further in this matter.[11]

Abortion, an issue sometimes raised by British commentators, and rather oddly included in Mr. Wilson's late 1971 proposals for a solution to the Irish problem, is not an issue with the bulk of Northern Protestant opinion, although there is some sensitivity about differences in obstetrical practice between Catholic and Protestant or public authority hospitals. Easier abortion has not hitherto been a significant issue within Northern Ireland, and accordingly should not create a serious problem in relation to proposals for reunification.[12]

The Republic's laws on censorship and contraception are highly contentious issues with Northern Protestant opinion. Moreover, since unlike divorce, what is involved here is the movement of goods rather than legal jurisdiction, and as, presumably, in a united federal Ireland it would be proposed to eliminate customs controls between the two parts of the country, some solutions must in any event be found to divergences in practice in these matters when a negotiated settlement is sought. It seems sensible, therefore, to initiate changes in the Republic in advance of such a settlement, as part of a programme designed to show Northern Protestant opinion that the will to reunification on an acceptable basis is genuine.

The scale of minority support in the Republic for changes in the law on contraception, demonstrated by a public opinion poll in April, 1971, which posed the issue in the context of the Republic alone, without reference to the question of reunification, suggests that if the issue were re-posed as part of a 'package' designed to create a favourable climate for reunification, it would have the assent of a majority; especially if safeguards and limitations on free sale, not adverted to the poll, were spelt out.[13]

In the case of obscene literature the contentious issue is the method of control rather than any disagreement on the need for some form of control. Perhaps because the censorship system of the Republic has applied not only to obscene printed matter but also to works 'advocating' artificial methods of birth control, thus enforcing what Protestants regard as Catholic morality on this issue, it has got a bad name in Northern Ireland. It may also

11. On 26 June 1986, Garret FitzGerald's coalition government held a referendum on the proposed introduction of divorce in the Republic. The proposal was overwhelmingly defeated, 63% to 36%.

12. On 7 September 1983, an anti-abortion amendment to the constitution was carried in a referendum by a little more than two to one.

13. A family planning scheme, permitting the import and use of contraceptives, subject to a number of restrictions, was passed in 198?.

be that the mere fact that the system of control in the Republic is different from that in the North, and is called 'censorship', has helped to make it a bone of contention.

The removal of the control over books advocating artificial forms of birth control would go some way to meet Northern objections, but it may be worth considering whether the Republic's pre-censorship system is worth maintaining, in view of its controversial character, now that it is in practice virtually limited in application to books which, by reasonable standards — such as may be shared by many Protestants in Northern Ireland — could be regarded as pornographic and thus amenable to a normal legal process. Such a process could be implemented in accordance with regional norms, but subject to some overall supervision to prevent local outbursts of excessive illiberalism from interfering with the sale of works which by the general standards of the time in Ireland, or in the relevant part of Ireland, would not be regarded as obscene.

In other words the real issue is not now so much a divergence of view between North and South as to what kind of books should be banned — local divergences of this kind can and do exist within the legal systems of unitary States such as Great Britain — but rather the method of control. A national pre-censorship system is objectionable in principle to many Northern Protestants, for reasons that are not necessarily entirely logical, and raises issues as between North and South which a normal police-type control on a regional or local basis would not raise. As this latter type of control could well yield similar results in the Republic to those at present achieved through pre-censorship a reversion to this latter system, employed in the independent Irish State during its early years, could well provide a solution to this problem — if accompanied by provisions to eliminate the ban on books advocating certain methods of birth control. In considering such an arrangement it must be borne in mind that the attitudes of many Northern Protestants to pornography is as close to that of Irish Catholics as to that of British public opinion, so that the problem of divergence of standards in this matter is probably less acute than the controversy over the *method* of censorship might suggest.

It is in the educational sphere, however, that the influence of the Roman Catholic Church is seen by Northern Protestants as most pervasive. At the same time the educational systems of the two parts of Ireland, despite the differences that have grown up between them in the past half-century, retain basic similarities; both have post-primary public schools operating in parallel with denominational post-primary schools; and in both areas primary education is denominational. In Northern Ireland, however, the acceptance by the Roman Catholic Hierarchy of the principle that one-third of the members of the management boards of Catholic post-primary schools in receipt of 80% capital grants should be representatives of the relevant Local Education Authority to be nominated by the Minister for Education, has created a situation very different from that in the Republic.

But although Protestant fears of Roman Catholic ecclesiastical influence in education are real and run very deep, the concern of the Church of Ireland in particular, especially in the Republic, to retain its own denominational schools at both primary and post-primary level has meant that there has been relatively little pressure for a diminution of the denominational element in education. In these circumstances, it is not easy to see what precise changes in the educational system in the Republic could be initiated, or are required, in order to offer reassurance to Protestant opinion in Northern Ireland.

The other important area where a change in the present arrangements in the Republic would be regarded as an earnest of the sincerity of its people's wish for a reunited Ireland acceptable to the Protestants of Northern Ireland is that concerning the Irish language. To Protestants in Northern Ireland the refusal to grant School Leaving Certificates to those who do not pass in Irish, the Irish language requirement for entry to the Colleges of the National University of Ireland, and the Irish language requirements in relation to recruitment into and promotion within the public service of the Republic, appear discriminatory against people of their tradition, few of whom in past generations were Irish speaking. It can, of course, be argued (in this as in every other instance where changes are proposed in the Republic as an indication of willingness to meet the point of view of the majority in Northern Ireland) that the present arrangements in the Republic are without prejudice to quite different arrangements that might apply in the examination system or public service of a federal Irish State. But this will not appear convincing to Northern Protestants, even those with goodwill towards an eventual reunification of the country, for they see their co-religionists in the Republic as being adversely affected by these language requirements, and regard the provisions under which these requirements are imposed as penal in character vis-à-vis people who do not belong to the native Gaelic tradition, and as indicating an attitude of mind opposed to the kind of pluralist society that they would expect to find in a united Ireland.

A change of policy in this matter, as in the others referred to above, seems desirable, therefore, if the Republic is to show itself to the Protestant people of Northern Ireland as liberal and open-minded, concerned to meet their reasonable requirements, and determined to treat the existing small Protestant minority in the Republic in a manner satisfactory to Protestants of the North. It is worth noting that the principal Opposition party in the Republic, Fine Gael, is in fact committed to these reforms affecting the Irish language.

Summing up the specific steps that might usefully be taken in the Republic at this stage as an earnest wish of its people to seek a reunification of the country in terms that could be acceptable to Northern Protestants, the changes that seem to be most needed are the repeal by referendum of the constitutional provisions on the special position of the Catholic Church and divorce; amendment of the law banning the import and sale of contraceptives; a modification of the system of dealing with obscene printed matter, substituting a new version of the older system of control by prosecution for the existing censorship system and the removal of Irish language requirements in examinations and in recruitment for, and promotion within, the public service.

Consideration should also be given to implementing in the Republic reforms introduced in Northern Ireland since 1969. Some of these reforms may be less necessary in the Republic than in Northern Ireland, but they nevertheless could have a useful part to play, and Northern Catholics and Protestants alike would be reassured to know that the Republic was keeping in step with Northern Ireland in this respect. The matters concerned include the appointment of a Commissioner for Complaints and a Parliamentary Commissioner for Administration; the appointment also of a Police Authority; and steps to extend the impartial system of public appointments in the Republic to posts not now covered, e.g. rate collectors, sub-postmasters, etc. In these and other reforms the guiding principle should be the provision of absolute guarantees of fair and equal treatment for all citizens regardless of religion, or politics.

Finally, in all legislation dealing with matters that may be at issue between the two religious communities, the guiding principle should be the general welfare of all, rather than the moral consensus of the majority community. If that principle is followed then the problems hitherto created both North and South as a result of legislation influenced by the views of the predominant group in the area concerned, will be avoided in future.

Such a programme, if implemented generously, and if accompanied by an evident willingness on the part of the Catholic Church authorities and the political parties in the Republic to offer concrete reassurance to Northern Protestants that a united Ireland would not, as they fear, be dominated by the Church authorities, or by the teaching and influence of the Church, would create conditions favourable to an eventual serious discussion of a programme of reunification. Some kind of declaration of intent by churchmen and politicians could make a great contribution here.

Pressures favouring a development of this kind have been the impact in the Republic of the implication by Rev. Ian Paisley in his December, 1971, radio and newspaper interviews that changes in the Republic might affect the attitude of Northern Protestants towards the North-South relationship, and the proposals by Richard Ferguson, the former Unionist MP who since his resignation has joined the Alliance Party, for a new, non-sectarian Ireland, which in the spring of 1972 began to make a significant impact in the Republic. The refusal of the Fianna Fail Party Conference early in 1972 to accept a proposal to postpone constitutional reform until negotiations started for a united Ireland reflected the growing willingness of public opinion in the Republic to seek a solution in the form of a new kind of society, rather than by an attempt to impose the Republic's cultural values and Catholic ethos on Northern Ireland. Up to May, 1972, however, this approach was still being resisted by the Fianna Fail Government which appeared, however, to be swimming increasingly against the tide of public opinion on this issue. Even if the all-party committee of the Dail announced in December, 1971, but not set up until May, 1972, was envisaged by the Government as a body that should concern itself with changes to be made as part of an eventual negotiation, it is quite possible that its work will lead to proposals for interim changes in the Republic along the lines suggested above. Fresh pressure in favour of such changes will come from the proposal in the British initiative of March 24, 1972,[14] to have regular plebiscites in Northern Ireland on the reunification issue.

14. On this day Brian Faulkner and his cabinet refused to accept the transfer of security to Whitehall. From 30 March Stormont was prorogued for a year, and direct rule from Westminster was imposed on Northern Ireland.

CHARLES J. HAUGHEY

(1925–)

from: THE SPIRIT OF THE NATION: THE SPEECHES AND STATEMENTS OF C. J. HAUGHEY 1957–1986 (1986)

[In September 1981, the then Taoiseach, Dr Garret FitzGerald, launched his 'constitutional crusade' against sectarianism in the Republic, most especially in its 1937 Constitution. He sought modification of Articles 2 and 3 of the Constitution which claim the whole territory of Ireland as the possession of the Republic. Charles Haughey responded to the crusade with anger at what he claimed were its unjustified premises and with near-disbelief at the naiveté with which the Taoiseach had presented the unionists and the British with a propaganda weapon against the Irish Republic.

In Ennis, Co. Clare, Haughey took the opportunity to give a full reply when he was asked to unveil a memorial to Eamon de Valera on 11 October 1981.]

EAMON DE VALERA AND THE COLONIAL MENTALITY — A REPLY TO THE CONSTITUTIONAL CRUSADE (1981)

We are all privileged that it falls to us to have the honour of erecting the first major memorial to the memory of one of the greatest Irishmen of all time, Eamon de Valera.

This is a historic place: the place which Eamon de Valera chose as the venue for many of his famous political pronouncements in the sure knowledge that, here in Clare, he would receive generous and unstinted support for his national endeavours.

Throughout his unparalleled political life, this historic town of Ennis was the scene of the great landmarks in Eamon de Valera's political life. It was here he came in days of victory to celebrate with the people he loved and it was to here he returned in days of defeat, to find new encouragement and inspiration. It was here he could be certain that he would receive that warm enthusiasm and revered affection which have not been afforded in such generous measure to any other Irish political leader in modern times. Is it any wonder then that the people of Clare held such a special place in the heart of Eamon de Valera? From the day he was first elected for East Clare, in the historic by-election of 1917, the people of Clare claimed him as their own. From that day onward, in good days and bad, they never wavered in their loyalty to the Chief; sharing his ideals and his hopes, his aspirations and his dreams. With him they sought the full independence and sovereignty of Ireland and the freedom and well-being of all her people.

Eamon de Valera was not alone one of the great central figures and rallying points in the fight for independence. He was also a source of inspiration for the sort of Ireland that afterwards emerged. He and his comrades set out to achieve a great deal and they achieved a great deal. The economic, social and cultural progress that Ireland has won was largely the result of their vision and their endeavours. It is to Eamon de Valera and his colleagues that we are indebted for the fact that we live under a democratic constitution in this part of Ireland, a Constitution that guarantees our fundamental rights as individual citizens. We are the only people in these islands who have a democratic constitution adopted by the people themselves for themselves. Our Constitution has been availed of time and time again by individual citizens to assert some particular right or liberty. It enshrines in Articles 2 and 3 the clear assertion of the belief that this island should be one political unit — a belief stretching far back into history and asserted and re-asserted time and time again by the vast majority of our people North and South.

Eamon de Valera's belief in unity derived from a recognition of the simple fact that the partition of Ireland is the central problem from which many other problems have arisen and will continue to arise. In Government or in Opposition he would have fought to defeat the efforts of the present Government to give some legal validity to partition, and by doing so to abandon that aspiration to which generations of Irish men and women have dedicated themselves.

He would ask us to devote all our political strength and will to bringing the continuing tragedy in Northern Ireland to an end. I believe also that he would counsel us not to despair, pointing out that there is no political problem no matter how complex or how tragic which will not yield to the right solution when the will and the purpose to bring forward such a solution exists. He never failed to point out that as a British Government had created the evil of partition only a British Government could take the initiative required to bring it to an end.

In achieving what they did, Eamon de Valera and his comrades had at all times to fight against the remnants of that colonial mentality that still linger on in Irish life, a mentality that cannot come to terms with the concept of a separate, independent Irish Ireland. To Eamon de Valera, Ireland and the Irish people, their culture, their traditions and their qualities were the reality. He would never accept that we should not occupy our own separate, independent place in the world, achieving our own destiny in our own way and in accordance with our own traditions, developing and enjoying our own cultural life and attaining any goals we set ourselves.

As we assemble here today to honour the memory of Eamon de Valera, we can see emerging once more in modern Ireland that mentality against which de Valera had to battle all his life. Once again we are being asked to accept a jaundiced view of ourselves. Once again we are asked to look only at our faults and to believe that somewhere else things are ordered much better than they are here and there exists a superior form of society which we must imitate.

In Ennis today I want to send out a call to those in every part of Ireland who believe that our nation should not be merely a pale reflection of some other to stand up now and say so in clear and ringing tones. Let us declare that we will not apologise to anyone for being what we are, or for holding the beliefs we do, and that we angrily reject accusations of either inferiority or sectarianism.

Let us remind our accusers that, under the Constitution framed by Eamon de Valera and adopted freely and democratically by the Irish people, two out of the six people who have held the highest office in this land have been members of the Protestant faith.[1]

Let us reiterate also that, following in the tradition established by Eamon de Valera, we seek no dominance, threaten no coercion; rather do we seek a solution to the ancient historical problem which has for the last sixty years stultified normal political development in this island on the basis of a constructive partnership in which any guarantees or undertakings, which may be required, would be willingly and generously forthcoming: a partnership in which neither side would seek to absorb or change the other.

It is helpful for us at this time to contemplate what Eamon de Valera would say to us were he amongst us here today in Ennis. He set no limit to the march of the Irish nation.[2] He sought an Ireland, unified and free, which would in its constitution and its laws respect and accommodate the diverse traditions that exist in this island and he would urge us to continue to work for that objective.

He would urge us to create a just, compassionate, and tolerant society. He would glory in the fact that we have an increasing population consisting largely of a new generation of educated, talented young

1. Douglas Hyde (1860–1949) was the first President of Ireland 1937–45. Erskine Childers (1905–74) was the fourth President of Ireland (May 1973-November 1974).
2. See Charles Stewart Parnell: 'no man has a right to fix the boundary of the march of a nation.' (Volume II, p. 307)

people and he would urge us to give them the encouragement, the support and leadership they need, to achieve their full potential. He would urge us also to have a special care for the less well off and weaker sections of our community; to make their welfare our deep and abiding concern and to see that they are fully protected from the hazards of life and the harsh effects of economic forces. He would certainly talk to us in simple and compelling language about the need to cherish our own language and develop a rich and satisfying Irish culture for the whole community to enjoy.

Today we look back with pride on the life and work of Eamon de Valera and renew our resolve to continue to work for the achievement of the aims and ideals he cherished and to the pursuit of which he devoted a noble and dedicated life. I am honoured to avail of this occasion to commit the Fianna Fáil Party of today to his ideals of unity and his objectives of social and economic progress. . . .

STATEMENT ON THE ANGLO-IRISH SUMMIT, DÁIL ÉIREANN, 20 NOVEMBER 1984

[At the Chequers summit of 18–19 November 1984, between the British prime minister, Margaret Thatcher, and the Irish Taoiseach, Dr Garret FitzGerald, the three solutions outlined in the report of the New Ireland Forum were considered. Mrs Thatcher, speaking at a press conference after the meeting, said, 'The unified Ireland was one solution that is out. The second solution was a confederation of two States, that is out. A third solution was joint authority, that is out, that is a derogation from sovereignty.' This was humiliating for the Taoiseach, even though the 'third solution' may be said to be incorporated into the Anglo-Irish Agreement Mrs Thatcher signed one year later. Mr Haughey confronted the Taoiseach in Dáil Eireann on the following day.]

It is of crucial importance that we endeavour to assess the present position in regard to Northern Ireland, its status as an issue in Anglo-Irish relations, and what now, after Chequers, are the prospects for the future.

The Summit, and in particular, the British Prime Minister's press conference following the Summit, can only be seen by reasonable people as a defeat for Irish nationalism of historic dimensions.

The way the Forum Report, its analysis and conclusions have been totally and completely rejected by the British Government, is only part of the picture, only one element of a complete disaster. The language used in rejecting the combined wisdom of Irish constitutional Nationalist politicians was of a brutality far beyond anything called for by the circumstances. But much more was said and promulgated at that press conference which will go down in history as one of the black spots in Anglo-Irish relations. The Unionist position in Northern Ireland has been copper-fastened in detail in a way that has not been witnessed in modern times. Nationalist hopes and aspirations of even the most modest kind have been trampled into the ground. There was no mention of an Irish dimension to the problem of Northern Ireland, no mention of any part or role of any kind for an Irish Government in helping to find a solution.

Yesterday's Summit between the Taoiseach and the British Prime Minister was one of the most depressing and humiliating meetings between Heads of Government that I can ever recall. Yesterday the Report of the New Ireland Forum, the carefully considered view of the democratic Nationalist representatives of three-quarters of all the Irish people, was unceremoniously and aggressively rejected by the British Prime Minister, and this rejection was accepted without a whisper of remonstration from the Taoiseach. There can be no escape from the dismal fact that constitutional nationalism took a beating yesterday, and the evasiveness and incoherence of the Taoiseach in his press conference afterwards served only to accentuate that humiliating reality.

When we recall now some of the things that were fed out and canvassed before the meeting, we can begin to grasp the fraudulent nature of the Government, its propaganda and those who serve it. In an election speech on 18 November 1982 the Taoiseach proclaimed that 'a complete and radical rethinking of British policy is now needed, and needed quickly, if the situation is to be retrieved from a drift towards chaos. It must be the purpose and prime objective of the Government elected to office on 14 December next to secure from the British Government a recognition of the need for such a radical review of its policy while there is yet time to save the situation'. It is evident from the whole tone and quality of the British Prime Minister's press conference that whatever rethinking has taken place it was not directed towards political progress or a solution of the Northern problem.

The Minister for Justice claimed at Béal na Bláth[1] on 26 August 1984: 'The present indications are that London has come to share our sense of urgency about this problem and that this sense of urgency must be transformed into a major Anglo-Irish initiative.' A sense of urgency? A major Anglo-Irish initiative? What we were told by the British Prime Minister was that the situation was not new, that it had lasted for generations and centuries and that it would drag on. Béal na Bláth is clearly a long way from Chequers.

The Minister for Foreign Affairs[2] on 23 July claimed: 'Britain is now more interested in solving the Northern Ireland problem than at any time in the past ten years'. At the press conference yesterday such interest was no more in evidence than was the Minister himself.

The Taoiseach in an interview with *Newsweek* on 24 September stated: 'We have identified the problem as the alienation of the minority in Northern Ireland', and he claimed that 'for the first time' the British now recognised the alienation of the minority, so that 'we are now approaching the problem from the same perspective'.

But Mrs Thatcher explicitly rejected any such concept. She stated, and I quote: 'Well, this word alienation has come in somehow in the last year, and I'm bound to say that as far as my information is concerned one could not find alienation . . . somehow this word alienation has crept into the vocabulary — I don't think it's a very good one'. Indeed, as late as 20 October in an interview with the *Irish Times* the Taoiseach was claiming the British and Irish Governments have a similar analysis of what the problem is. It is now quite obvious that there is no basis for that claim. It was fraudulent. The alienation of the Nationalist community, which was perhaps the basic premise of the Forum Report, has been rejected totally.

Worst of all, the Taoiseach and the Minister for Foreign Affairs had claimed that there could be some dramatic breakthrough at the Summit. The Minister at the British-Irish Association on 15 September 1984 claimed that: 'One way or the other, our relations are about to be transformed'. Transformed they have been, but to the clear disadvantage of all the people of this country.

Nor did the British Prime Minister hesitate to castigate those who had roused expectations about the British response to the Forum Report. All those media manipulators around the Taoiseach have discovered the hard way that floating stories in the domestic media can be counter-productive. The fostering of illusions about British interest, about British goodwill and about British receptiveness, about twenty-year treaties, about personal preferences, where did it all lead — to a cold, calculated reprimand for both master and servants.

The rebuff to the Government is one thing. But let us now take a close look at the rebuff to the Forum. Yesterday the British Prime Minister rejected not merely the conclusion of the report and the other constitutional models outlined, but also every single thesis of consequence contained in the Forum Report. She also threw out the realities and the requirements, so emphasised by the Taoiseach.

A central thesis of the New Ireland Forum Report was a rejection of British Government thinking hitherto: 'that the risks of doing something to tackle the fundamental issues are greater than the risks of doing nothing'. The Prime Minister refuses to accept this. She stated that the situation had gone on for a long time, and that a solution could not be imposed from Westminster.

The Forum Report adverted to the obstructive nature of the constitutional guarantee. It stated in Chapter 4.1. 'In practice, however, this has been extended from consent to change in the constitutional status of the North within the United Kingdom into an effective Unionist veto on any political change affecting the exercise of Nationalist rights and on the form of government for Northern Ireland.' The British Prime Minister repeatedly emphasised that any proposals would have to have the agreement of both the majority and the minority. In fact, she yesterday very clearly and explicitly expanded the constitutional guarantee in precisely the manner the Forum complained of. This, of course, as stated last night, completely precluded any prospect of political progress.

Another fundamental thesis in the Forum Report was that 'a settlement which recognises the legitimate rights of Nationalists and Unionists must

1. Michael Noonan in an address at the place in County Cork, between Macroom and Bandon, where Michael Collins was murdered in August 1922.
2. Peter Barry held this post in the coalition government 1982–87.

transcend the context of Northern Ireland'. The Taoiseach in an RTE interview on 6 May 1984 agreed that an internal solution on its own was not on, and he said: 'I think at this stage the degree of alienation amongst the minority is such that it's difficult to see their coming back into the consensus and being willing to accept political structures and security structures if they're to be solely within the existing Northern Ireland area as part of the United Kingdom'. This too has now been clearly rejected by the British Prime Minister, who made it clear yesterday that her only interest is in the internal situation of Northern Ireland with no all-Ireland dimension of any kind. The communiqué, which the Taoiseach has subscribed to, effectively underwrites Mrs Thatcher's position, when it states: 'the identities of both the majority and the minority communities *in Northern Ireland* should be recognised and respected, and reflected in the structures and processes *of Northern Ireland* in ways acceptable to both communities'.

The Taoiseach has therefore subscribed on the dotted line to a renewed attempt by the British Government to achieve nothing more than internal improvement without any reference to any Irish dimension. Nor is there any reference either to power-sharing, which has been regarded by the Taoiseach in the past as a minimum requirement of any internal solution. As the *Irish Times* cogently pointed out this morning, the communiqué does not say that the identities of both majority and minority communities *will or shall* be respected and reflected. It is a mere aspiration, not a binding political commitment.

When the British Prime Minister was asked whether the right of the majority and minority should be recognised as equal, she replied clearly and deliberately: 'That's not what we said — we said "recognised and respected" '.

This passage in the communiqué about identities does not reflect, as is alleged, the thinking of the Forum Report which stated: 'The validity of both the Nationalist and Unionist identities in Ireland and the democratic rights of every citizen on this island must be accepted; both of these identities must have equally satisfactory, secure and durable, political, administrative and symbolic expression and protection.'

It is a tragic betrayal of the position of all the Nationalist parties in the Forum that the Taoiseach should now have agreed to underwrite the vain search for another internal political solution. He knows that it offends against the first two realities in the Forum Report, that 'existing structures and practices in Northern Ireland have failed to secure either peace, stability or reconciliation', and secondly, that because 'the conflict of Nationalist and Unionist identities has been concentrated within the narrow ground of Northern Ireland, this has prevented constructive interaction between the two traditions'.

The Forum Report also had important things to say about security 'as an acute symptom of the crisis in Northern Ireland', and that the Nationalist community would not accept the security forces without a change of 'political context'. All parties have insisted that a new political framework is required, that existing security policies simply amount to crisis management and contribute nothing towards a solution. Yet in paragraph four of the communiqué the only role envisaged for the Irish Government is one of security. It states: 'Co-operation between their two Governments in matters of security should be maintained and where possible improved.' This apparently is the only role an Irish Government is to be permitted to have. Once again the communiqué reflects an abject capitulation to a new British intransigence and craven desertion of the principles of the Forum Report.

There has been no acceptance by the British Government in any significant number of either the realities or the requirements laid out in the Forum Report. They have not been accepted as a basis of discussion or negotiation. I invite the Members of this House to go through the ten realities and the eleven requirements, and to say in the light of the communiqué and of the comments of the British Prime Minister whether there has been any significant acceptance of them. In my view, they have been simply brushed aside and ignored. I was alarmed to hear the Taoiseach suggest last night that the four points in the communiqué will now be substituted for the realities and the requirements contained in the Forum Report as a basis for further discussion. This is an inexplicable departure from the carefully constructed, reasonable Nationalist Forum position.

In my view the British Prime Minister's statements yesterday constitute a flat and comprehensive rejection of the entire Report of the New Ireland

Forum. It is no use the Taoiseach deluding himself by saying: 'We had a considered reaction, but by no means a complete considered reaction.'

No one is taken in by the suggestion that there is something more of significance to come. After all, what is left of the Forum Report, when every proposal, conclusion, argument or idea of any consequence in it has been rejected? The new Secretary of State, Mr Hurd, spelled out the British view when he said that no amount of Summit meetings would solve the problems facing the parties in the North.

Where do we stand now? 2,500 people in Northern Ireland have been killed since 1969. No agreement on political structures within Northern Ireland is even remotely likely. Yet now the British Prime Minister has announced a policy of attrition, of trying to wear down the communities in Northern Ireland until they agree on something within the present British context. The people of Northern Ireland are being callously condemned to more bloodshed, more violence, more misery indefinitely. The Northern economy, as we know, is in a state of decline and stagnation with the highest unemployment and some of the worst social conditions existing there. There is no hope of a recovery in investment without peace and stability. No hope of any kind is offered, except to continue in the same old rut till the cows come home.

Constitutional nationalism, the democratic voice of three-quarters of the Irish people, as presented in the Report of the New Ireland Forum, has been rejected by the British Prime Minister, and that rejection has been acquiesced in by the Taoiseach. This could have the gravest consequences on the ground in Northern Ireland.

The Taoiseach was pathetic in his unconvincing talk about new frameworks and processes. Giving a complete veto to the majority has effectively ruled these out. But what is the point of another Summit, if the Taoiseach is going to be walked all over once again? Is there any point in summit meetings if we cannot be reasonably confident of constructive results? Why should the Taoiseach pretend that there is Anglo-Irish harmony and agreement, when all can see that it does not exist? This Government cannot force us to live a lie.

One appalling aspect of yesterday's proceedings was that the general public could clearly see that one or other of the two principal actors was trying to mislead them. While the Taoiseach claimed 'We have got down to discussions in earnest, to brass tacks', the British Prime Minister stated that yesterday they were only discussing generalities.

When he was asked about alienation, the Taoiseach again endeavoured to mislead. He conveyed the impression that the British Prime Minister was discussing with him some security arrangements which would help to alleviate or reduce alienation. Everybody, however, looking at the televised press conference, knew that there was no doubt that the Prime Minister had totally rejected any idea of alienation.

The *Irish Independent* of this morning purports to give an account of an interview by reporters with the Taoiseach. According to that report, the Taoiseach was asked whether Mrs Thatcher had ruled out completely the three options spelled out in the Forum document. He replied: 'We had a considered reaction, but by no means a complete considered reaction'. I do not know what that means, but I do know that it is a blatant attempt to mislead the general public. Mrs Thatcher, in language which must be regarded as unique on an occasion of this kind, made it clear that a united Ireland was out, a confederal State was out and a joint authority was out.

Some people, for different motives, have sought to find some encouragement in paragraph 2 of the communiqué. Let me quote paragraph 2:

> The identities of both the majority and the minority communities in Northern Ireland should be recognised and respected, and reflected in the structures and processes of Northern Ireland in ways acceptable to both communities.

Of course, the key words in that paragraph are: 'in ways acceptable to both communities'. In other words, insofar as the minority is concerned, there can be no recognition or respect or reflections, unless they are accepted by the majority. That particular paragraph is of no benefit or significance whatever, insofar as Nationalists in Northern Ireland are concerned, because it means the recognition of their identity totally depends on the consent of the majority.

The official voice of Nationalist Ireland was so muffled yesterday as to be inaudible. The British Prime Minister was direct, intransigent and brutally frank. Let me also be direct and frank. We who represent Nationalist Ireland do not accept the rejection of the New Ireland Forum Report and with it all the hopes and aspirations of the majority of the Irish people. We will continue to fight at home and abroad for the only solution that will bring lasting peace and justice to this land of ours.

On a previous occasion in this House, I sought to warn the present Taoiseach about the danger inherent in his approach and attitude to Anglo-Irish relations, both in its personal and its official aspects.

My warning had no effect, and the Taoiseach continued along his foolish way till it brought him finally to yesterday's humiliation.

The timing of the two press conferences in London yesterday and their content must surely, by now, have taught this Taoiseach the most bitter lesson of his political life. For many months, he engaged in an exercise of accommodation, undertaking a series of steps designed to inculcate an atmosphere of personal friendliness, helpfulness and acceptability. Events have shown this behaviour to have been damaging and detrimental to a deadly extent. International relations, international discussions, international negotiations are not kindergarten matters, nor are they conducted as if they were some kind of amicable parlour game. . . .

JOHN HUME

(1937–)

THE IRISH QUESTION: A BRITISH PROBLEM (1980)

[John Hume has long argued that the British government guarantee to the unionists has frozen the possibility of meaningful negotiations in Northern Ireland. The collapse of the Sunningdale Agreement in May 1974 seemed to put an end to constitutional experiment and to reveal an appalling lack of will on the part of the British government to sustain the impetus of reform and change. The consequence, in Hume's view, is that the failure of constitutional politics leaves the field open to militarist violence — that of the Provisional IRA and of the protestant paramilitaries. Since then he has become a leading advocate in Europe and in the USA for government-led constitutional enterprise. His efforts culminated in the New Ireland Forum of 1983 and in the Anglo-Irish Agreement of 1985.

The article was published in *Foreign Affairs*, Winter 1979/80.]

The current cycle of conflict in Northern Ireland began over 11 years ago. As a practicing politician in Northern Ireland throughout that period, I have taken a particular interest while travelling abroad in following the world media coverage of the problem. For the most part, this has been a chronicle of atrocities reported spasmodically from London or by 'firemen' visiting from London. It has struck me that, for the outside observer, it must have been difficult during these years to avoid the impression that Northern Ireland was hopelessly sunk in incoherence and its people the victims of a particularly opaque political pathology. There have, it is true, been a few brief interludes when some measure of clarity seemed to take hold, only to be swept away in the inevitable swirling clouds of violence, intransigence and misery — in other words, the normal political climate.

The people of Northern Ireland, however divided, share a keen awareness of the bewilderment of outsiders, which occasionally finds expression in the mock-heroic couplets of the street: 'To Hell with the future and long live the past/May God in His mercy look down on Belfast.'[1]

The cynicism and dismissiveness of the Irish style (Churchill's Dunkirk exhortation, 'The situation is serious but not desperate,' is said to have evoked the somewhat bleary comment from an Irish listener, 'Over here the situation is always desperate but never serious') often conceal, as the readers of Swift and Joyce know well, a quite serious desperation. Nevertheless, in its superficial manifestation the

1. Maurice Craig, 'Ballad to a Traditional Refrain', although, correctly, the poem's final couplet is:
It's to hell with the future and let's live on the past,
May the Lord in His mercy be kind to Belfast.

hopeless wit of the people proved congenial to those who are currently responsible for the affairs of Northern Ireland, and who, of all 'outside' observers, often seem the most puzzled and wearied by its problem, i.e., the British political establishment. This is nothing new. It was, in fact, Churchill, speaking in the House of Commons in 1922, who most eloquently caught this feeling of his colleagues, then and since:

> Then came the Great War. . . . Every institution, almost, in the world was strained. Great empires have been overturned. The whole map of Europe has been changed. . . . The mode of thought of men, the whole outlook on affairs, the grouping of parties, all have encountered violent and tremendous changes in the deluge of the world, but as the deluge subsides and the waters fall, we see the dreary steeples of Fermanagh and Tyrone emerging once again. The integrity of their quarrel is one of the few institutions that have been unaltered in the cataclysm which has swept the world.[2]

Other cataclysms have since supervened, and are themselves now forgotten, but 'their quarrel' endures, now in a more grisly form than ever. Politically motivated violence is on the increase. Northern Ireland (population 1.5 million) has two new prisons and a third under construction. The skilled and the professionally trained emigrate while the economy stagnates, and the semiskilled and unskilled swell the unemployment lines as well as the ranks of the paramilitary organizations.

Some weeks ago, to coordinate its security efforts in Northern Ireland, the British government recalled from his retirement the man who reputedly furnished the model for George Smiley in John Le Carré's entertaining spy novels.[3] This may be symptomatic of a long-standing British inability to take the Irish seriously (it should be admitted that the reverse tradition also exists). However, events recently unleashed a chilling shower, drenching Irish and British alike, from which the flippant, patronizing and slightly amused attitudes of the past afforded no refuge whatever. It is beyond high time the British and the Irish took each other — and our common crisis — seriously. There is, I believe, urgent need for the friends of Britain and Ireland to do likewise, and there is heartening evidence in fact that some of them have begun to do so.

It is my strong conviction, as well as that of my party, the Social Democratic and Labour Party of Northern Ireland, that the politics of Northern Ireland are not hopelessly irrational. They do have a meaning and a structure. The protagonists do act in the light of their interests as they perceive them, though their perceptions are sometimes mistaken. Events are, in fact, predictable — often, it must be admitted, depressingly so.

My conviction that there exist structure and meaning, and therefore hope, is not based simply on Henry Kissinger's moral injunction to statesmen that they must at all costs believe in the possibility of solutions to the most intractable impasses. I believe, as the title of this paper suggests, that the perennial British view of the problem as 'their quarrel' and not 'ours' is fundamentally wrong: Britain is, in fact, included in the quarrel as a central protagonist, and must be centrally involved in the solution. It is for the acceptance of this principle that I and my party worked for years. There have, as I have implied, been moments when we seemed to have achieved as breakthrough. This does not seem to be such a moment, alas. All the more reason for putting the case again.

II

The problem, as I know from years of talking to foreign visitors, is at first sight a mass of contradictions. Some of the contradictions are real. London, for its part, exercises a reluctant sovereignty in Northern Ireland, while Dublin maintains a somewhat reluctant claim to that sovereignty. The 'loyalists' are those proponents of the union with Britain who, while they are avowedly the most patriotic of all Her Majesty's subjects, put up the most stubborn resistance to her government's designs. The Provisional wing of the Irish Republican Army believes Irish unity will be secured by waging war against a British establishment which clearly has no fundamental opposition to unity, while they ignore (and, in their campaign against Britain, further incite) those who most adamantly resist the imposition of

2. See *The World Crisis: The Aftermath* (London: Butterworth, 1939).
3. Maurice Oldfield, head of MI5, was sent to Belfast to review security in 1978. He was said to be the model for George Smiley.

unity, the one million Protestant majority. Does this mean things are hopeless? No, but it further underlines the necessity, reinforced by horrific events, that all major parties to this crisis should rigorously reexamine their own roles, responsibilities and room for manoeuvre.

The basis of British policy is concealed under layers of good intentions, ingenious initiatives, commissions of enquiry, attempted reforms, financial aid and a good deal of genial bewilderment. I do not use the word 'concealed' maliciously. Many sincere and concerned British politicians and observers have the impression that they have tried everything possible to get the Irish to agree together: that is a measure of the extent to which the basic assumption of their policy has become imperceptible to the British themselves.

The ground of their policy is the reiterated guarantee that Northern Ireland shall remain a part of the United Kingdom so long as a majority of the electorate of Northern Ireland so desire. That would seem, at first reading, to be an eminently democratic and responsible undertaking. The fact is, however, that it has not worked. It has not produced peace or stable government in Northern Ireland. Moreover, it has provided the basis for a half century of injustice, discrimination and repressive law, a situation in which the minority community (the one-third Catholics) have been the persistent losers and victims.

Northern Ireland is a divided community, divided not by theological differences but by conflicting nationalist aspirations. The Unionist majority historically favour maintenance of the union with Britain, while the one-third Catholic nationalist minority by and large favour a united Ireland. In 1921, when the overwhelming Catholic nationalist Free State was established in the south, the area of Northern Ireland was excluded from the arrangement because of British hesitancy (which proved to be an enduring feature of British policy) in the face of militant Protestant Unionist resistance.

'The British guarantee,' as it is called, proved to be a guarantee of permanent exclusive power to one side, the Unionists, and a guarantee of permanent exclusion from power to the other, the Catholic minority. Its existence undermined any hope of political negotiation between the two sides in Northern Ireland. It guaranteed the integrity of 'their' quarrel. While this guarantee exists, there is no incentive for Unionists to enter into genuine dialogue with those with whom they share the island of Ireland. The suffering and frustration of the people of Northern Ireland overwhelmingly attest to the fact that the guarantee was, to put it very bluntly, a tragic mistake. The price has been paid too long, and in too many lives.

The many attempts at reform, in which so much British as well as Irish energy was invested, all failed. The one initiative that almost succeeded was the Sunningdale Arrangement of 1973 between the British and Irish governments and the principal parties in Northern Ireland.[4] This established a power-sharing government containing representatives of both sections of the community in Northern Ireland and accepted the principle of a Council of Ireland, which would provide a forum for north-south cooperation as well as a means of expression for the Irish nationalist aspiration, while Northern Ireland would continue to be a part of the United Kingdom. The establishment of power-sharing was a tribute to the political courage and imagination of the last Conservative government in Britain. Unfortunately, the Labour administration, which succeeded it early in 1974, showed no similar courage, and in May of that year, in what was one of the most squalid examples of government irresponsibility in our times, surrendered its policy in the face of a political strike organized by a paramilitary minority on the Unionist side. As a result, the guarantee was not alone seen to be restored, it was seen to be reinforced: extreme Unionism or loyalism was encouraged in its belief that it could henceforth resist and jettison any British policy for Northern Ireland which involved conceding power to the minority.

The politics of Northern Ireland have not yet recovered from that setback, and, because of it, the problem for the British is even greater today than it was in 1973. Will the new Conservative government find the considerable courage it needs to face this compounded challenge? My hope is that Prime Minister Thatcher, in coming to grips with the

4. The Sunningdale Agreement of December 1973 established a power-sharing executive in Northern Ireland and an Anglo-Irish Law Commission. The Irish government accepted that no change in the status of Northern Ireland could come about until a majority of the people there so wished. The agreement collapsed five months later because of the pusillanimity of the British Labour government of Harold Wilson in the face of a loyalist strike.

problem, will commit all her vaunted capacity to reversing the blind momentum of British public policy, all her vaunted steadiness of nerve in the face of contrary pressure to secure and maintain a success. Failure, however, be it the failure to attempt a serious initiative or the failure to sustain an initiative under pressure, will only reinforce the difficulty, and the measure of failure will again be in the spreading field of white crosses in front of city hall in Belfast commemorating those who have died at the hand of political violence.

III

The Unionists of Northern Ireland are justly proud of their heritage and their contribution to the world. As many as eleven American presidents came of their stock. They number field marshals, captains of industry and colonial governors among their great men. They see themselves as a pragmatic, hard-headed, sceptical, robust people, and there is much in their history to justify their view. They have shown a corresponding tendency to regard their nationalist Catholic neighbours throughout the island as a more fanciful and less realistic race, and indeed there may be much in the history of the dispossession and enforced illiteracy of the Catholic community to give colour to that view.

History has changed the face and condition of Ireland, and these opinions have been overtaken by events. The south started from a platform of no industry and relatively primitive agriculture in 1921, while the north was the only part of Ireland seriously affected at that time by the Industrial Revolution. Now the south has caught up with and will shortly overtake the north economically. Northern industry is in decline and is for the most part owned by outsiders. The North has no sovereign voice in the world, nor, significantly, in the European Community. Unionists watch with envy tinged with resentment as Dublin, for the second time, exercises the presidency of the Council of the European Community during these months. Unionists are, furthermore, dismayed at the decline of Britain's greatness to a point where, most galling of all, London must now treat Dublin as an equal in the councils of Europe. A hardheaded people should logically draw the conclusion that an arrangement with the south is in its best interest. I have no doubt that they would do so now were the problem of Northern Ireland purely economic. Of course, it is not.

The Unionists are a majority in Northern Ireland, but their political behaviour there can only be understood if they are seen, as they feel themselves to be, as a threatened minority on the island of Ireland. Theirs are the politics of the besieged. Hence their stubborn refusal to share power with the minority in Northern Ireland, whom they fear as the Trojan horse of the 'real' majority in Ireland, the Catholics. Hence, the similarity between their attitudes and those of the whites of southern Africa.

Can this attitude be unfrozen? There are some grounds for believing that it can. I have mentioned the Sunningdale experiment, the most promising attempt so far to solve the problem. The main Unionist political group at that time, and particularly its leader, the late Mr Brian Faulkner, showed courage and political agility, and the response of most Unionists to the experiment was by and large benign. The pusillanimity of the Labour government in London, in failing to resist the predictable destructiveness of the demagogues and paramilitaries on the extremes of Unionism, set back the situation almost irremediably; Unionist opinion, it must be admitted, shifted further to the Right as a result, as evidenced by the growing electoral strength of Ian Paisley. Nevertheless, the reality of power-sharing did exist, however tenuously. Unionists, given the right leadership, were seen to be capable of magnanimity. The problem now is to create the conditions where magnanimity can again take hold, this time more securely.

I am also encouraged by what I take to be a resurfacing of traditional Unionist realism. There is a growing suspicion among Unionists that their dependence on the British guarantee as the sole foundation of their political survival may in the long run be a risky and unprofitable enterprise. No leader of present mainline Unionist opinion has yet found the courage to put this squarely to his people, but several have expressed concern about the trustworthiness of the British.

Now is, as I have suggested, the moment when political leaders in Northern Ireland, in the Republic, and in Britain must radically reexamine their own fundamental assumptions. As I see it, the two greatest problems in Northern Ireland are the British guarantee, which inhibits such reexamination, and the Unionist dependence on it. Given economic developments in the Republic and the growing suspicion about Britain's long-term intentions on the part of many Unionists, this would seem a propitious juncture at which to take a serious initiative. Only Britain can create the conditions in which Unionists can perceive and pursue their true interests.

I believe that the true interest of Unionists depends precisely on the exercise of their traditional gifts of self-confidence and self-reliance. The time has come for them to believe in themselves as their own best guarantors in a future shared with the other people of the island of Ireland.

IV

As it is now, Unionists see themselves as a threatened minority on the island of Ireland. If you ask a Unionist how real the threat is, he or she will tell you of friends or relatives who have been murdered or injured by the Provisional IRA. What threat could be more real? That, however, is only a vivid and chilling expression of an even deeper sense of intimidation. Unionists fear that they would be culturally and racially overwhelmed by the Catholic nationalist majority if they were to join with the rest of the island. Would they? This is the challenge to Irish nationalism, to Dublin, to the nationalist minority in Northern Ireland, and to the friends of Irish nationalism around the world.

The campaign of violence of the Provisional IRA has, more than any recent development, set back and distorted the cause of Irish nationalism in the eyes of Unionists, and of British and world opinion. It is clear that a majority of the people in Ireland as a whole, including a majority of Catholics in Northern Ireland, both favour Irish unity as a solution and reject violence as a means of promoting that solution.

The Provisionals have been relatively impervious to the universal rejection of their methods for a number of reasons. First, they are sustained by an extremely simple view of the Irish problem, and in this simplicity they find strength and purpose. For the Provisionals, the Irish problem consists of the British presence in Ireland — nothing more; remove that presence, they claim, and the problem will quickly be solved by the establishment of a unified, independent Irish state. This analysis of things not only affords a simple view of a highly complex situation, but it also provides the inspiration for violent action aimed at inducing British withdrawal. The Provisional reading of the problem also gains from its clear affinities with the vision of the partially successful, and widely revered, insurgents of the 1916–22 period, who, in their determination to secure freedom for the greater part of the Irish people, were understandably distracted from the peculiar circumstances which obtained in the six northeastern counties.

A second factor in Provisional endurance has been the encouragement which they — like the loyalist extremists — have been able to draw from British weakness and prevarication. That weakness has so shown itself not alone in the fact of loyalist intransigence but also in the intermittent British dalliance with Provisional 'political spokesmen,' whose credentials have been forged by bombs and bullets.

Third, I believe that the case for Irish nationalism has not been clearly enough expounded by Irish nationalist leaders. The Provisionals have not hesitated to exploit the ambiguities of policy and the innuendoes of the public debate to seek to claim support of, or justification for, their actions.

Fourth, unjustifiable excesses by British security forces, condemned by the European Court of Human Rights as inhuman and degrading treatment,[5] created an implacable hostility to Britain in the minds of many who were subjected to them. These excesses, together with the introduction of internment without trial in 1971 (it has since been abandoned), did more to gain recruits for the Provisionals than any exhortations to 'blood sacrifice' from the patriarchs of the movement.

Fifth, the absence of political activity from the life of Northern Ireland has provided both an opportunity and an argument to the men of violence: they can with some credibility play upon the frustrations of the minority in the absence of political hope, and they can well ask, in the face of British immobilism: Who but we are doing anything about Northern Ireland?

5. A fourteen-volume report of the European Commission of Human Rights in September 1976 found British troops guilty of torture during the interrogation of suspects during and after internment in 1971.

Finally, it can be seen that the Provisionals have hardened into a ruthless terrorist force which can compensate in terms of experience and technique for what it has lost in political support. It is a long time now since commentators invoked Mao[6] and predicted that, as the water of popular approval dried up, the guerrilla fish would have to abandon the struggle to survive. We can now see that the fish need less water than we had thought. The Provisionals have for several years received only insignificant support from the population of either Northern Ireland or the Republic; yet they retain the ability to disrupt and terrorize.

Indeed, their activities have descended to a level of savagery which has all but numbed the capacity of the public to respond with horror to even their inhuman atrocities. Life has become cheap — and the entire community to some extent dehumanized. 'Is there a life before death?' asks a piece of anonymous graffiti on a Belfast wall, with some reason. The writer might also have asked whether there is any childhood left for the battle-scarred children of the ghettos of that city, and of the rest of Northern Ireland.

Aside from the immorality of its actions, the Provisional IRA campaign has no hope of success. It is, I suppose, conceivable that it might eventually frighten a feeble British government out of Northern Ireland before any process could begin. What would undoubtedly follow would be a serious risk of a bloodbath. This would quickly spread to the south, and, after thousands of deaths, would finally resolve itself by the division of the island into two bristling, homogeneous sectarian states, neither stable, both sunk in the obscurantism of their most extreme supporters. No military victory followed by a political settlement is possible in Northern Ireland. That is true not for the Provisionals alone but for the loyalists and the British government as well.

The Irish government and most nationalists in Ireland have repeatedly given convincing evidence of their repudiation of the violence of the Provisionals — the public by its consistent rejection at the polls of those who support violence, and the Irish government by its active pursuit of the men of violence, its commitment of additional police and army units to the border areas, and the introduction of draconian legal measures to secure convictions in the courts. Dublin and Irish opinion generally clearly intend no threat to Unionists; on the contrary, the leaders of Irish-American opinion, which was generally seen by Unionists to be hostile to their interests and indeed supportive of violence, have in recent years repeatedly condemned support for violence from the United States. This has had the double effect of reducing material assistance for the Provisional IRA from the United States and of going some way toward assuaging one source of Unionist anxiety.

Despite these positive elements, there is an important sense in which the principal source of Irish nationalist sentiment, i.e., Dublin, has not yet fully clarified its intentions. Unionists will not be able to bring themselves to entertain seriously the notion of Irish unity unless Dublin unambiguously spells out what it understands by unity and gives clear evidence of its commitments.

The southern state is seen by many Unionists (in varying degrees by the majority) as a lay expression of sectarian Catholic values. As such, it is unacceptable to them. The reality, as I encounter it, is that the Republic is a modern state struggling to develop its economy and society within a European framework. The partition of Ireland, 50 years ago, created a state in the south with an overwhelmingly Catholic population. Inevitably, Catholic values were enshrined in some areas of law, particularly family law, although the state is in other respects one of the least confessional in Europe, with no official church. Unionists have a right to be convinced that the south is serious when it declares its intention to embody pluralist values in the law of the United Ireland to which it aspires. So far, the evidence for these intentions is inadequate.

Even more seriously, those who avow a nationalist solution must clarify how they would implement this. Statements which contain hints of irredentism, of conquest, of compulsion, do not promote a policy of unity; moreover, they give comfort to the men of violence. The Irish government repudiates violence and by its action is seen to do so. It should, nevertheless, in claiming the ground of nationalism, clarify, if necessary ad nauseam, its commitment to unity by agreement, only by agreement, and through reconciliation.

6. Mao Tse-tung (1893–1976), Chinese Marxist theoretician and statesman.

V

One of the difficulties about Northern Ireland which existed until recently was that the problem seemed to matter little, if at all. It mattered very little to the British. It seemed incapable of sustaining the attention of any but the most committed fanatics. Governments and serious observers, if they looked at it, had a feeling of impatience with its complexities, its anthill of competing eccentricities. There was a feeling that it ought to be like the pieces of a jigsaw, needing only to be placed in a certain arrangement for tranquillity to ensue. Unfortunately, the pieces did not seem to fit, and the puzzle quickly lost its interest.

The time has come for a positive and decisive initiative. It must be taken by both Dublin and London acting together. They should first make it clear that there are no longer any unconditional guarantees for any section of the northern community. There is only a commitment to achieving a situation in which there are guarantees for all.

Second, they should make it clear that there is in fact no pat solution as such, but only a process that will lead to a solution. They should declare themselves committed to such a process, a process designed to lead to an agreed Ireland with positive roles for all. They should invite all parties to participate in this process, the process of building a new Ireland. Some groups will undoubtedly react with an initial refusal, but the process should continue without them, leaving the door always open for their participation at any stage.

Indeed, on embarking on this process we ought to be encouraged by the example of both the United States and the European Community. In the United States, in spite of deep differences of origin and background, they have formed a constitution which is able to harness great differences for the common good. Yet the Italians remain Italian, the blacks are still black, and the Irish still parade on St. Patrick's Day. They have created a unity in diversity.

Europe itself has suffered centuries of bloody conflict. In this century alone, the peoples of Europe have been locked in the savagery of two world wars with a bitterness and slaughter that goes far beyond anything that we have experienced on this island. Yet 34 years after the Second World War, as a result of an agreed process, they have been able to create one parliament to represent them, one community — and the Germans are still Germans, the French are still French. They, too, have a unity in diversity.

Is it too much to ask that we on this small island do precisely the same thing? Is it too much to ask that these two responsible governments begin to declare themselves now in favour of such a process? Can we too build a unity in diversity?

VI

One of the few developments which has cheered those who believe that moderation and reason must prevail in Northern Ireland has been a growing interest in the problem on the part of responsible political leaders outside of Ireland and Britain. This is particularly true of the United States, and, to a significant extent, of the European Community.

I believe that the friends of Britain have been dismayed at evidence in recent years of a British retreat from a world view. Many have felt that this contraction of vision has been accompanied by, if it is not symptomatic of, a weakening of Britain's political psyche. That in itself, if true, should concern those who hope for a solution to Northern Ireland's problems which, as I have argued, will require considerable political courage on Britain's part.

Mrs. Thatcher, in recent speeches and indeed in her post-election approach to the Zimbabwe-Rhodesia problem, has shown some willingness to reverse the decline. All the more reason why she should be serious about the problem of Northern Ireland, a strategically placed area in the Atlantic approaches to northwest Europe, potentially ripe for subversion if political neglect continues. The growing serious unrest of American and European leaders reflects, I believe, an awareness of this threat. Several responsible American leaders have implicitly questioned Britain's capacity to meet the political challenge and, on Britain's record so far in Northern Ireland, they are right to have this concern.

VII

The interest of the West in the problem is not only strategic. History has made of Ireland one of the most 'internationalized' communities in the world. The foundation of her relations with the two wings of the Western world lies in the emigration of the past centuries: in the seventeenth and eighteenth centuries to France and Spain; in the eighteenth, nineteenth and twentieth centuries to America; and again, most recently, to Britain. The basis is people, the Irish diaspora.

The situation today is intriguing: the earlier links with the continent have been renewed but now rest on the solid foundation of the treaties of the European Community. The links with America are founded on the old connections of blood, friendship and heritage between the four and a half million people on the island today and upwards of 16 million people in the United States. The relationship has deepened and matured as the Republic has developed politically and economically, and as the Irish in America have prospered and built on their extraordinary political achievements of the past hundred years.

These two global relationships have played major roles in the fortunes of Ireland in recent years. From America came much of the industrial investment which created the impressive economic development of the Republic in recent years. From Europe have come the economic benefits of membership in the Community which have transformed life, particularly in the Republic, and also created a sense of political dignity and statehood, again in the Republic, which, prior to membership, had been stifled by a claustrophobic bilateral relationship with the neighbouring island.

Since the great tides of Irish emigration began to flow to America in the nineteenth century, the Irish in America tried without success to interest Washington administrations in the 'Irish question.' Great names such as John Devoy, editor of *The Gaelic-American*, and Eamon de Valera were energetically involved in this endeavour, but in vain. This is not to fault these men: it was a function of the nature of Irish political power in America during these generations, which was confined to the leadership of some of the great cities and states. It remained largely excluded from Washington. That situation changed dramatically in 1960 with the Kennedy presidency.

VIII

In recent years the influence of powerful American leaders of Irish extraction in Washington, notably Senator Edward Kennedy and House Speaker Thomas P. O'Neill, has brought the issue to a point where the Carter Administration[7] has taken a position on Northern Ireland. As a result, the support for violence from the United States has been contained and has in fact dropped. That this should have been maintained during the past years of political vacuum in Northern Ireland is an extraordinary achievement. There are many men, women and children in Northern Ireland who are alive today, I am convinced, because of the political courage and concern of these men.

President Carter has committed himself to providing economic aid in the event that a solution acceptable to both sides in Northern Ireland, and to the British and Irish governments, can be found. That was a generous, humane and unprovocative commitment. It was welcomed by the Irish and British governments as a major incentive to reconciliation, and they were both consulted about it. The Irish question has become a legitimate and serious issue in the Atlantic relationship between London and Washington.

The responsible interest of American leaders is welcome. Less welcome is the exploitation of the issue by a few less distinguished politicians. Violent men in Ireland invoke their names as certifying their own respectability and as an indication of support for their cause. The votes of Americans should not be purchased at the expense of Irish lives.

The European Community, because of its name, because of its primary historic commitment to reconciling the enmities of generations of Europeans and averting the recurrence of armed conflict, could not stand aside from the conflict between two of its own peoples. Several European leaders have expressed concern and interest. It is my hope that the European parliament will soon hold a full-scale debate on the issue, and that the Community will match America's generous incentive to peace.

The interest of the United States and of the European Community in Northern Ireland is historically inevitable and perfectly legitimate. This need not involve direct intervention or support for particular partisan policies. It should be taken as an encouragement by London, by Dublin and by parties in Northern Ireland to have the courage to resolve this old quarrel that involves them all.

7. Jimmy Carter (born 1924) was president of the United States 1977–80.

RECONCILIATION OF THE IRRECONCILABLE (1983)

[This is the text of John Hume's speech at the opening of the New Ireland Forum on 30 May 1983.]

Tradition has it that the throne in this Castle[1] was presented by William of Orange. This throne was the ultimate symbol of power and dominion in our island for the following two hundred years. Today, although carefully preserved, it is empty. For some it is a cherished symbol of a struggle honestly fought to defend, uphold and impose the principles of the Protestant tradition of liberty. For the majority in Ireland today, its importance lies in its emptiness: the empty throne symbolises the success of a long bitter struggle to defend, uphold and impose the nationalist principle of liberty.

How can we reconcile the profound contradictions of Dublin Castle on this day? To the tradition gathered in this room, Dublin Castle spells *our* historic triumph: we finally reduced and took this bastion of oppression, this seat of an alien, arbitrary and cruel power. To Unionists, it is a souvenir of an older and more congenial order, a Mecca now tragically appropriated by infidels, a fortress whose very loss to the enemy has for sixty unhappy years been the cause of uncertainty and the source of a harsh and seemingly necessary intransigence. Yet it is our declared task here today to reconcile these contradictions — somehow.

I suggest that we begin by humbly admitting that no more difficult task ever confronted the Irish people. I suggest that we also understand clearly *why* we are attempting it — not because it would be gratifying to succeed, not because it would be interesting to attempt, not because it would be to our political advantage — only because it would be dangerously irresponsible not to do this now. We are condemned to try and to succeed because each one of us, if we fail or if we shirk this challenge, will be condemned by this and future generations of Irish men, women and children as uncaring, unworthy and selfish politicians. Unworthy, not just of Ireland but of the human cause itself.

Strong words perhaps. Yet no words can sufficiently emphasise the danger for everyone on this island now of further neglect of the North. No image can conjure up adequately the dark consequences which will flow uncontrollably and overwhelmingly from inaction. You have seen on your television screens the efforts of Italian engineers to steer the course of Etna's volcanic lava away from the threatened villages of Italy. The North is a much vaster volcano whose brimstone we have hitherto only superficially contained. Unless we in common find the necessary commitment — the determination to move mountains — we will all be engulfed in a furious torrent of hatred, violence and despair. Everyone in this room knows this. I paint a black picture knowing that we have in the heart and the sinews of *our* heritage, the heritage of our own political tradition, the courage and the generosity to accomplish our extremely difficult task.

On behalf of the SDLP I commit myself and my party now to the principle that we shall not place the short-term or the long-term political interest of the SDLP above the common goal. And I ask the Taoiseach and the Tanaiste and the Leader of the Opposition[2] to commit their parties with us to this exacting principle. There is no room, there is no time for opportunism or righteousness or indeed for what is normally understood as 'politics'. Only thus will those who doubt our good intentions — the Unionists of the North — and those who for centuries have found the pretext for their inexcusable neglect of this island in our divisions — the British — take us seriously and start to take their own responsibilities seriously.

The common goal of which I speak is — and has to be — reconciliation. The reconciliation of the seemingly irreconcilable problems of this island. Let reconciliation start today in this room — between us.

Goodwill alone — and I know we have with us today the goodwill of most of the people of Ireland — goodwill alone will not suffice. We must apply all the resources of our collective intelligence, imagination, generosity and determination to this great enterprise and be seen to do so. We must mean business and the world must see that we desperately mean business.

I believe that the very fact that we are gathered in

1. Dublin Castle.

2. Respectively, Dr Garret FitzGerald, Dick Spring, leader of the Labour Party and second-in-command (Tánaiste) in the coalition government, and Charles Haughey, leader of Fianna Fáil.

this room — that the Taoiseach and the Tanaiste suspend for the purposes of this Forum their unique prerogatives to propose and to implement, that the Leader of the Opposition suspends his natural role of critic of Government — I believe that the fact that my three colleagues have been prepared to make these unprecedented political sacrifices in a common effort is a tribute to their seriousness and their generosity and an encouraging augury of success. The vast majority of the people of the North — those whose hopes are fervently with us, and even those who now doubt our intentions, will not fail to see this occasion for the remarkable, indeed unique political event that it is.

There are a minority in Northern Ireland and a minority even in this State who furiously abhor the work of reconciliation. Theirs is the way of violence. Their message is hatred, their medium murder, their achievement division and destruction. This common effort of ours to understand, to build a new Ireland, to reconcile, is anathema to them. Why? Because they suspect and they fear that we might succeed. And they can only prevail if our enterprise fails. They can achieve their stated aim of armed political domination in this land only if the forces of despair win out, only if the volcano of cruelty that they remorselessly stoke overwhelms us all. Eighty percent of the people of the island are represented in this historic Forum today and their clarion message to the men and women of violence is: 'Reconciliation Yes, Destruction No, Democracy Yes, Your Fascism Never.'

The world is looking at this Forum today, but there are two particular audiences to which we must address ourselves: The Unionists of the North and the British people and Government. They must fully understand both the seriousness of our commitment and the nature of our effort.

This Forum is not a nationalist conspiracy. Neither is it a nationalist revival mission. It is nothing less than a major effort — an effort unique in our history and I believe unexampled in divided societies anywhere in the world — to understand the encounter between our own ethos and the ethos of those who live with us on this island but who refuse to share it with us. This is no academic theoretical experiment but an honest effort to confront the real chilling circumstance of today's Ireland in the full context of the real relationship between Ireland and Britain today. This is the most serious effort that has ever been made by Irish political leaders to face reality and the Unionists and the British are entitled — indeed they are invited — to judge our work by that measure. But they are not entitled to ignore it, as it would be seriously against their own interest to do so.

The heart of this crisis in Ireland is the conviction — the profound and seemingly irreducible conviction — of the majority of Protestants in the North that their ethos simply would not survive in an Irish political settlement. This conviction, older than King Billy's throne, encrusted and gnarled with generations of embattled struggle, is rejected by the rest of us in Ireland, equally convinced by our dark past that we could never impose dominance on others, we who have known better than most the misery and sterility of oppression. The British for their part remain, if not fully convinced by these fears of the Unionists, at least not persuaded by our claims to the contrary. Hence the paralysis of politics, hence the stagnation and the conflict. There are many other important and complex dimensions to the Irish problem but there, to my mind, is its core — the belief by the Protestant tradition in this island that its ethos cannot survive in Irish political structures. This should remain the focal point of our deliberations in this Forum and the central target of those who wish to join with us in our important task.

The Protestant ethos I am talking about is not merely theological — although it contains principles such as freedom of conscience which are central to that theological heritage. It contains also and perhaps more importantly a strong expression of political allegiance to Britain which we cannot ignore and which we cannot wish away any more than Unionists could wish away our deep commitment to Irish unity. This intractable difficulty we must squarely face in this Forum. It will not be easy for us to do so. How do we accommodate in a new definition of Irishness these uncomfortable realities? How would we propose to give to Unionists an adequate sense of security — physical, religious, political, economic and cultural security — in a new Ireland? Are we, the Nationalists of Ireland, prepared to pay the painful political and economic price that this will involve? Do we have any idea of what that price will be? I fear that many of us either do not or would prefer not to. The work of this Forum will forever deprive us of the excuse of ignorance or distraction. Let the commitment and the seriousness and the nature of the New Ireland Forum be judged by our harshest critics precisely in terms of the capacity *we* demonstrate to face these painful questions in all their brutal reality and the measure of our readiness to take the consequences. It is, even at this moment, tragically clear that we have hitherto failed — we have hitherto failed because we have not attempted this task together, with the joint commitment that we now make to put this common goal above party and even above some of our most cherished assumptions. Our respect for the past, and for our heroes of the past has perhaps paralysed our attitude to the future. For we may all have different heroes. The result has been division. Division inevitably breeds opportunism and failure and meanwhile the minority in the North continue to suffer and the majority to maintain their frightened intransigence, and the British feel they can afford to continue not taking any of us seriously. This Forum must put an end, once and for all, to all this hopelessness.

It can only do so by achieving consensus. Let no one underestimate the power and strength of democratic consensus in this Forum. Let no one doubt its impact on British and International opinion. The price that our different parties may have to pay for consensus will be minimal compared to the rewards for the Irish people of a common approach to our deepest and most intractable problem.

As for the Unionists, it seems to be in their intelligent interest that we be confronted directly by their objections to an Irish political arrangement for this island, without reservation or apology, in private or in public (as they wish) by members of that tradition. Let me say to Unionists: 'We commit ourselves to take you and your convictions with deep seriousness in our effort to understand the crisis that confronts us all, our aim is neither conquest or coercion, it is primarily to understand each other so that we can solve this crisis with your agreement and your support.' We seek a solution. We do not seek victory.

There has been in the depressing and bewildering history of Anglo-Irish relations so much suffering, so much corruption, so much distortion, that all we can now usefully do is to start as it were from scratch. 'Forget the past, but take the present and the future seriously': that must be the message to come from this Forum to the British. We call on Britain to give their attention as fully as we now do to this awful tragedy and to learn with us and from us as we try honestly to devise a realistic and adequate solution.

I have not in the last heartbreaking decade personally felt that there was a more important opportunity than that which we now face. During those years, I have repeatedly longed for such a moment as this. Now that it has arrived I sense that we have come to a final crossroads. In one direction we see the old hopelessness, the old squalor, the endless bitter conflict so painfully described by Louis MacNeice, that great honest voice of the North:

> Why should I want to go back
> To you, Ireland, my Ireland?
> The blots on the page are so black
> That they cannot be covered with shamrock.
> I hate your grandiose airs,
> Your sob-stuff, your laugh and your swagger,
> Your assumption that everyone cares
> Who is the king of your castle.
> Castles are out of date,
> The tide flows round the children's sandy fancy;
> Put up what flag you like, it is too late
> To save your soul with bunting.[3]

Flag Waving will no longer do.

In the other direction beckons a more realistic hope and a more painful effort than I can recall. It seems that we must invert so many of the symbols, confound so many of the paradoxes, resist so many collective urges. I am reminded of the fact that the flag that flies over this castle, a castle that will today cease to be 'out of date', the tricolour of which we in this room are so proud, was, when it was launched as a symbol of Ireland by the Young Irelanders, the inverse of what it is today — orange, white and green. William Smith O'Brien said of it on the 29th April 1848:

> I am proud to address you under such a banner as this which floats above me tonight, and I hail it as a happy omen that you have thus united those emblems which formerly were the insignia of faction in this country — the orange and the green. Henceforth, that flag will be the Irish tricolour, as a sign that the Protestants of the

3. Louis MacNeice, *Autumn Journal* (1938), Section XVI.

North and the Catholics of the South will unite in demanding the rights of their country.[4]

The white band of this flag, uniting the orange and the green, symbolised peace, harmony and reconciliation. How is it that this flag has come today to be used as a party political symbol in the hands of a violent minority, and to be seen as such and as a symbol of terror by their Unionist victims? Our purpose must be to invert this among many other blasphemous distortions. This flag belongs as much to the orange as to the green. It does not belong to those who viciously oppose what it stands for and whose real level of respect for it is epitomised by painting its colours on kerbstones and on gable walls. It is *our* great task and opportunity to make this symbol gain for the first time its full symbolic meaning of brotherhood in this island between Catholic, Protestant and Dissenter.

And as for King Billy's throne, let this Forum give a new meaning to its emptiness today nearly three hundred years after the Battle of the Boyne. Let that throne stand today not for a nostalgic order now gone forever, not for its triumphant removal by the new order in this State: let that vacant seat continue unoccupied and become a powerful symbol to both of our traditions — that neither will conquer the other, but that both will be preserved and revered and cherished in the new Ireland that we set out to build today.

4. William Smith O'Brien (1803–64) made this remark at a meeting of the Irish Confederation in April 1848 when Thomas Francis Meagher returned to Ireland with a present of the tricolour from the citizens of France.

SEÁN MACBRIDE

(1904–88)

from: A MESSAGE TO THE IRISH PEOPLE (1985)

[This text is based on an address given to the American Irish Unity Committee on 22 July 1981: by that date six men had died on hunger-strike in the Long Kesh prison in Northern Ireland in their effort to win status as political prisoners. The text has been updated, because by 20 August 1981 the tenth man had died. The hunger strike began on 1 March; the first to die was Bobby Sands, by then an abstentionist Westminster MP, on 5 May. Of all the hunger-strikes and refusals to wear prison clothes in the attempt to assert political status, this was by far the most traumatic and prolonged. A century before, Wilfrid Scawen Blunt had refused to wear prison garb. The British government had, throughout the period, insisted on the 'criminalizing' process in order to deny that there was any political basis to the actions for which the various prisoners had been sentenced.

Seán MacBride, formerly of the IRA and a cabinet minister in the inter-party government of John A. Costello, widely known and honoured for his work with Amnesty International, gives here a traditional republican view of the hunger-strikes and of the Northern Irish crisis.]

CHAPTER 6

BRITAIN'S ROLE IN IRELAND THE HUNGER-STRIKE

Since I ceased to take an active part in politics in Ireland, I have systematically refrained from dealing publicly with Irish affairs when speaking outside the country. I considered that this was the responsibility of those who were actively engaged in politics in Ireland. Furthermore, I did not wish anything that I might say to be construed as an encouragement to those who are engaged in a campaign of violence against the British in Northern Ireland. I had hoped that persuasion and common sense would ultimately persuade the British to withdraw gracefully from Ireland without inflicting more suffering on any section of Ireland or further damaging Britain's reputation.

This apparently was an erroneous judgment on my part. I should have known from previous experience that when it comes to dealing with Ireland, the

British government and establishment lose all common sense and all sense of justice.

Before dealing with the hunger-strike situation, I should outline briefly the history of Anglo-Irish relationships for those who may not be familiar with it.

For over seven centuries Britain has sought to conquer Ireland and to treat it as a colony. Famines, amounting to genocide, confiscation of lands, executions, jails and bribery were the methods used to colonise Ireland. Because of her overwhelming strength, military and economic, Britain was able to hold on to the whole of the island of Ireland until 1921. The repression which followed the 1916 Rising unified the Irish people behind the Irish Republic. By 1921 the Irish national liberation movement, known as the Irish Republican Army, was able to bring about a situation in which the British government agreed to a truce and to enter into negotiations for an Anglo-Irish Treaty that would recognise the right to Irish self-determination.

The Truce was signed on 11 July 1921 and negotiations for an Anglo-Irish Treaty began in London on 11 October 1921. By December 1921, the British delegation in the Anglo-Irish negotiations had succeeded in dividing the Irish delegation and, on 6 December 1921, the British Prime Minister, David Lloyd George, dramatically issued an ultimatum that unless the Irish delegation signed a draft treaty, which had been prepared, there would be 'immediate and terrible war'. This Treaty and the circumstances under which it had been signed led to a deep division among the Irish people. In turn this division led to the Civil War in Ireland which began on 25 June 1922. The British government, having succeeded in splitting the Irish Republican Movement, pressed their advantage home by urging the then provisional government to assert its authority over the Irish Republican Army. Mr de Valera and the Republican forces, who refused to accept the Anglo-Irish Treaty, were finally defeated after a bitter civil war which ended nominally in May 1923, but which continued sporadically for some years to follow.

Three main issues divided the country and led to the Civil War. Firstly, the insistence of the British government that all the elected representatives of the Irish people should swear an Oath of Allegiance to the British Crown, and that provisions to this effect should be embodied in the Irish Constitution. This requirement was embodied in the first Irish Constitution of 1922.

Secondly, provisions for the partition of Ireland into two separate states: one in the north-eastern part of the island to be known as 'Northern Ireland,' would remain under British jurisdiction: the other which would include twenty-six of the thirty-two counties of Ireland would form part of the British Commonwealth and be styled 'The Irish Free State'.

Thirdly, under the Treaty imposed by Britain, Ireland was to become and remain a Member-State of the British Commonwealth owing allegiance to the British Crown. Britain was also to retain some military bases in the Irish Free State.

These provisions had been accepted by a war-weary Ireland under the threat of 'immediate and terrible war', but in reality they were unacceptable to the Irish people. Michael Collins, who had signed the Treaty and led the Provisional Government of the Irish Free State did so on the basis that it was to be a 'stepping stone' to achieve an independent Irish Republic for the nation.

After the Civil War, Mr de Valera set up a political party and became Prime Minister of the Irish Free State consisting of twenty-six of the thirty-two counties of Ireland. He promptly did away with the Oath of Allegiance to the British Crown and enacted a new Constitution on 1 July 1937, which received the overwhelming support of the Irish people. In this Constitution he rejected the concept of a partitioned Ireland and provided by Article 1 of the Constitution that: 'The National territory consists of the whole island of Ireland, its islands and the territorial seas.'

Later, another Irish government in 1949 declared the state to be the Republic of Ireland, thus terminating such links as had continued to subsist with the British Crown and the British Commonwealth.

Reluctantly, Britain had to accept the constitutional changes that had been brought about by Mr de Valera's and Mr Costello's governments. It did so with bad grace and each time announced its determination to maintain control over the six north-eastern counties known as Northern Ireland.

The British argument was that the six north-eastern counties now formed a separate state entitled to the exercise of self-determination. The Irish argument was that the right of national self-determination applied to the island of Ireland as a whole and not to twenty-six out of the thirty-two counties of Ireland.

In Northern Ireland itself, the ordinary laws were abrogated and a police-state regime was installed. Because the British authorities and those who supported British rule in Northern Ireland feared that the nationalist population, which were then a minority, would increase more rapidly than the pro-British population, which was generally Protestant, a regime of wholesale discrimination was installed. The reason for installing a draconian system of discrimination, based on religious beliefs, was that by preventing Catholics from obtaining employment or housing, their numbers could be kept down. They would not be able to get married and they would not be able to obtain employment. This would force them to leave the area, thus ensuring that the Catholic population would decrease.

Because the discrimination exercised by the British authorities in Northern Ireland was based on the religion of the population, the impression was created that the conflict in Northern Ireland was a religious conflict and not a political one. While there is some foundation for these allegations, it is a foundation that is based upon the history of the British occupation of Ireland. Until the nineteenth century, British policy had been to eradicate the Catholic religion from Ireland and to dispossess all Catholics of their property. To this end, vast tracts of land and property had been confiscated and given to 'planters' or colonists brought over to Ireland by the British who were invariably Protestant. Thus, up to Catholic emancipation at the beginning of the nineteenth century Catholics were the deprived and impoverished segment of the population. While after 1829 the Catholics were allowed to own property, the Planters nevertheless continued to exercise an official ascendancy over the ordinary Irish people insofar as employment, housing and privileges were concerned. It is by reason of these historic events that the present-day divisions between Catholics and Protestants have survived until now.

The situation is best described by no less a person than the well-known Anglican theologian, John Austin Baker (now Bishop of Salisbury), who was the Chaplain to the Speaker of the British House of Commons, and who in a sermon preached in Westminster Abbey (1 December 1980) pointed out:

> No British government ought ever to forget that this perilous moment, like many before it, is the outworking of a history for which our country is primarily responsible. England seized Ireland for its own military benefit; it planted Protestant settlers there to make it strategically secure; it humiliated and penalised the native Irish and their Catholic religion. And then, when it could no longer hold on to the whole island, kept back part to be a home for the settlers' descendants, a non-viable solution from which Protestants have suffered as much as anyone.
>
> Our injustice created the situation; and by constantly repeating that we will maintain it so long as the majority wish it, we actively inhibit Protestant and Catholic from working out a new future together. That is the root of violence, and the reason why the protesters think of themselves as political offenders.

The political parties, North and South, while not accepting the situation, did nothing about it. A new generation of young people however, resented the discrimination that was being implemented to their detriment. They could get neither employment nor housing. All employment and promotion within all services were strictly reserved to non-Catholics. Notices were displayed outside factories proclaiming: 'No Catholics employed here'.

Gradually, as was inevitable, the rising generation of young people resented a situation in which they were treated as third class citizens and were precluded from obtaining employment or housing. They became dissatisfied and disillusioned with existing political parties in the North as well as in the South, and they started a perfectly legal and constitutional civil rights campaign demanding an end to the discrimination which prevailed and insisting on their civil and political rights. They obtained the support of the majority of the nationalist population in the North, and indeed, the active support and sympathy of the population in the rest of the country. Bernadette Devlin McAliskey[1] became one of their leaders and swept aside the existing, more moderate politicians. The rise of this new Civil Rights Movement was met with violent repression by the British forces and police. Their members

1. Bernadette Devlin McAliskey (born in 1947), a prominent member of the Northern Ireland Civil Rights Association and of the People's Democracy movement. She was elected MP for Mid-Ulster in 1969, the youngest woman ever elected to Westminster. She was seriously wounded in a gun attack on her home by protestant paramilitaries in January 1981.

were arrested, interned and subjected to systematic police harassment. Their meetings were broken up by the police. This culminated in the killing of thirteen civilians at a perfectly legal public demonstration in Derry City by British soldiers on 30 January 1972, now known as Bloody Sunday.

These acts of oppression by the British forces had two results. In the first place they solidified and increased the support for the Civil Rights Movement, and on the other hand, they influenced the young people to turn more and more towards the IRA and physical force. The IRA availed of this situation to become the defenders of the Catholic population against the attacks of the police and the British military forces. The methods used by the British forces became more and more indefensible. Prisoners were systematically tortured by means of sophisticated methods imported from England. This was fully exposed and condemned in the course of legal proceedings brought by the Irish government before the European Commission of Human Rights in Strasbourg, and assurances were given by the British government that these methods would be discontinued. It is claimed by the IRA that these methods have not been discontinued, but are now being applied more secretly.

As the extent and nature of the oppression grew, so did the IRA reaction to it, and we have had a constant escalation in what is now a full-blown guerrilla war, in the course of which some 628 members of the British forces have been killed and 7,496 wounded in the period 1969-June 1981. In the same period, 1,496 civilians were killed and 16,402 wounded. The total number of persons killed in this small area over the last ten years is 2,124, and the number wounded is 23,898. There were in Northern Ireland 1,244 Republican prisoners in 1981. These are variously described by the British authorities as terrorists or criminals; by the nationalist population they are regarded as political, or Republican prisoners.

Lest the account I have given be regarded as biased because of my natural sympathy with the aspirations of the Irish people for reunification of Ireland, I should like to quote from the editorial of a well-known English Catholic Monthly magazine, *The New Blackfriars*:

> The squalid pretence that the problems of Ulster flow from the flaring up of mysterious sectarian differences and not from the misery, anger and frustration produced by the sorry mess of 50 years of British rule, and white-washing of the massacre of Bloody Sunday of January 1972, the arbitrariness and brutality concomitant with internment without trial, the hypocritical shunning of the Strasbourg Report of 1976, which found Britain guilty of the crime of torture and inhuman treatment in Northern Ireland, the method used to extract 'confessions' for the political Diplock trials, the killing of civilians by rubber and plastic bullets and speeding ferret cars: all these and many more are equally if not more responsible for the deaths of the hunger-strikers and all the violence and misery that followed.
>
> So long as these beams in the English eye remain, so long does the English condemnation of hunger-strikers lack moral credibility, even when it is made by those 'speaking as English Catholics'. We have to pause and reflect on the possibility that Cardinal Ó Fiaich and the other Northern Ireland bishops may be able to see more clearly and certainly with more compassion the complexities and subtleties of the sorry problem.

As a result of the situation described, there were on 11 June 1981, 1,244 male prisoners serving sentences in British prisons in Northern Ireland for what the British describe as terrorist type offences. In addition, there were on the same date approximately 50 women prisoners also serving sentences. It must be borne in mind that none of these prisoners were convicted after trial in due process of law. They were tried by single-judge courts without any juries. These courts are known as 'Diplock Courts'. These are courts which follow procedures that do not conform with those applicable to normal trials under the rule of law. Of the some 1,300 prisoners serving sentences in British jails in Northern Ireland, 328 have been receiving what the prison authorities describe as 'special status treatment'. The balance of some 966 have been denied this 'special status treatment' because they were convicted on a date subsequent to the withdrawal by the British authorities of the 'special status treatment'. In effect, what the hunger-strikers in the H-Blocks at Long Kesh demanded was that they should receive the special status treatment. This was spelled out by the hunger-strikers and the other prisoners in five specific demands concerning:

1. The right to wear their own clothes at all times.
2. The prisoners requested that they should not be required to do menial prison work; they were prepared to do all the work required for the maintenance and cleaning of the portions of the prison occupied by them. They also asked that study time should be taken into account in determining the amount of work which they were required to do.
3. They requested the right to associate freely at recreation time with other political prisoners.
4. They requested the right to a weekly visit, letter or parcel, as well as the right to organise their own educational and recreational pursuits in the prison.
5. The right of remission of sentences as is normally provided for all other prisoners.

The prisoners believed that the refusal of the British authorities to grant them the 'special category status' which obtained in regard to other prisoners was a political decision taken in order to criminalise their status. Several hundred of them went on what was called 'the blanket protest' from September 1976. This protest consisted of refusing to wear prison clothes and on wearing a blanket instead. As from March 1978 they escalated their protest to a 'no-wash protest'. A number of them went on hunger-strike in October 1980 and the hunger-strike ended on 18 December 1980 on the basis of an agreement put forward by Cardinal Tomás Ó Fiaich and Bishop Daly.[2] In the course of the negotiations, which took place with Cardinal Ó Fiaich and Bishop Daly, the British government had agreed substantially to the demands made by the prisoners provided that they were not described 'as acceptance of political status'. This proviso was accepted by the prisoners. However, the British government failed to implement the recommendations made by Cardinal Ó Fiaich and accepted by the British government. This caused considerable bitterness and distrust among the prisoners. They considered that they had been tricked into giving up the hunger-strike by subterfuge in which the British government availed of the good offices of Cardinal Ó Fiaich but then reneged on the agreement they had made with him.

Cardinal Ó Fiaich and Bishop Daly also considered that they had been misled by the British government. It is in this atmosphere that the later hunger-strike was started on 1 March 1981. However, on this occasion, the prisoners started the hunger-strike with the preconceived determination that they were not going to allow the British government to trick them again, or to use intermediaries; they insisted that they would continue the hunger-strike until death, in relays, until such time as the British government gave categorical assurances to them concerning the future treatment of prisoners, and the granting of the five requirements which they had specified.

In the meanwhile, a succession of well-intentioned intermediaries including a number of members of the Irish Parliament, representatives of the European Commission on Human Rights, representatives of the Irish Commission on Justice and Peace and representatives of the International Committee of the Red Cross sought to mediate, but the attitude of the British government throughout had been:

> We cannot accept that mediation between the government and convicted prisoners, even by international bodies of the highest standing, is the right course.

They also refused to negotiate directly with the prisoners. In reality, the attitude of the British government had been to avail of all the intermediaries in an effort to break the determination of the prisoners and to avoid negotiating with the prisoners thus binding themselves to alterations in the prison rules. The prisoners accused them of playing a cynical game of brinkmanship, waiting for one prisoner after the other to reach the dying point, hoping that this would break the morale of the other prisoners. Indeed, in the course of a press interview given by Mr Michael Alison, British Minister of State for Northern Ireland in the British Embassy at Washington, he made the startling but candid admission that negotiations about the hunger-strike was like:

> the efforts of authorities to keep plane hijackers occupied while plans are developed to subdue them. (*Irish Times*, 13 July 1981)

2. Cardinal Tomás Ó Fiaich (1923–90), catholic primate of All Ireland 1979–90, and Bishop Edward Daly, bishop of Derry, had negotiated with the hunger strikers and the British government in 1980 during the hunger-strikes of that year. The first hunger-strike was called off in December 1980 without any concessions being made.

In the course of this protest ten hunger strikers died. They were: Bobby Sands MP, Francis Hughes, Raymond McCreesh, Patsy O'Hara, Joe McDonnell, Martin Hurson, Kevin Lynch, Kieran Doherty TD, Thomas McElwee and Michael Devine.

I have sought to outline as objectively as I can the elements of the drama which unfurled itself in the British prison known as H-Block in Northern Ireland.

I do not agree with the violence used by the IRA and have refused to countenance their policies. Likewise, I have refused to allow myself to be used for propaganda purposes by the H-Block Committee in Ireland. Having said this, I understand fully the reasons which prompted the H-Block prisoners to undertake this ultimate form of protest; furthermore I cannot remain silent in the face of the duplicity and methods used by the British in their dealings with Ireland and with the hunger-striking prisoners.

Britain's attempts to maintain dominion over the six north-eastern counties has caused misery and suffering to the whole of Ireland for over half a century. It has been the cause of a civil war in Ireland; it has divided Irishmen all over the world; it has been responsible for thousands of deaths and untold sufferings, it has prevented the economic and political development of Ireland. In brief, as our last Taoiseach (Prime Minister) Charles Haughey, put it, it has cast long dark shadows into every aspect of Ireland's life for over half a century. Successive Irish governments, opposed as they are to partition, have been put into the impossible position of having to jail and oppress their own young people in order to protect British rule in the north-east corner of our island. A stage has now been reached where this is no longer acceptable to the Irish people.

In their own country and in countries which they do not seek to dominate, the British are reasonable, fair-minded, and even lovable! It is otherwise in areas which they regard as their preserve. In regard to Ireland, the British government and establishment are just incapable of being objective, fair-minded or just. A typical illustration of this was provided some time ago.

The British forces in Northern Ireland have been using for the last three years rubber or plastic bullets indiscriminately. They have argued that they are harmless. Over fifty people — mostly children — have been killed or permanently maimed in Northern Ireland by these plastic or rubber bullets. This was denied by the British who maintained that they were harmless. When extensive riots broke out recently in Britain, the possibility arose of using rubber or plastic bullets for crowd control. An alarmed Conservative British Home Secretary[3] said immediately that he would oppose their use 'in mainland Britain because they are lethal!' (*Irish Times*, 11 July 1981.) It is all right to use them in Ireland and to kill women and children there — but not 'on mainland Britain!'

The British government likes to portray itself in the role of the 'honest broker' who is in Northern Ireland against its will 'merely in order to protect the Protestant population'. There would be absolutely no persecution of Protestants in Ireland; the Irish government has a good record in this sphere and would willingly agree to international supervision in this area if it was thought necessary. The Convention of Human Rights would provide the necessary safeguards.

Impoverished Britain spends fourteen hundred million pounds to subsidise and occupy Northern Ireland. This is equal to approximately double the amount in U.S. dollars, $2,800,000,000. Britain has systematically used, and continues to use, its vast military and financial resources to encourage a segment of the population of the North-East to support British rule there. With such an expenditure and army of occupation it would be possible to disrupt any country. We have had examples of this external intervention all over the world.

Britain has no right or mandate to be in any part of Ireland. The overwhelming majority of the Irish people want a united Ireland and want the British out of Ireland. It is as simple as that.

By agreeing to withdraw from Ireland and by agreeing to a united Ireland, Britain could begin to establish a normal, friendly relationship with Ireland. She could only improve her international image and put an end to a shameful part of her colonial past.

In the early stages of the last decade, Paul Johnson, one of Great Britain's most distinguished journalists, editor of the *Spectator*, and one of Prime Minister Margaret Thatcher's most ardent supporters, wrote in *The New Statesman*:

3. William Whitelaw.

In Ireland over the centuries, we have tried every possible formula; direct rule, indirect rule, genocide, apartheid, puppet parliaments, real parliaments, martial law, civil law, colonisation, land reform, partition. Nothing has worked. The only solution we have not tried is absolute and unconditional withdrawal.

Why not try it now? It will happen in any event!

GERRY ADAMS

(1948–)

from: THE POLITICS OF IRISH FREEDOM (1986)

[President of Sinn Féin and Westminster MP for West Belfast, Gerry Adams was twenty years old when the so-called Troubles began. Since then, he has been a prominent and ultimately a dominant figure in the Republican movement in Northern Ireland. He gives here an account of some of the key moments in the development of the crisis, including the Peace People movement which became so celebrated and was ultimately so ineffective.]

THE IRA/ÓGLAIGH NA HÉIREANN[1]

Irishmen and Irishwomen: In the name of God and of the dead generations from which she receives her old tradition of nationhood, Ireland, through us, summons her children to the [*sic*] flag and strikes for her freedom.

1916 Proclamation

The classic period of republican struggle, the period which is impressed upon one's mind as the definitive image of the IRA, is the Tan War, with its flying columns taking on the Black and Tans. At its height it was a military campaign with a background of incipient forms of alternative government apparatus functioning through the republican courts in certain parts of the country. The flying columns moved about as fairly self-contained units; they were fed and accommodated in sympathetic households or sometimes they commandeered Unionist houses and lived off the occupants.

In the 1930s and 1940s the IRA enjoyed no such background in the country, and their military actions took place in England in the 26 counties and only in one or two places in the 6 counties. The 1950s campaign was restricted to the border counties — there was literally no activity in Belfast — and a lot of the IRA people involved came from the 26 counties and presumably worked around the border counties or maintained small flying columns based in Fermanagh, Tyrone and South Armagh. By the end this campaign like those before it consisted of just five or six active republicans skipping between five or six houses.

The current phase of armed struggle is different from any other, apart perhaps from a resemblance to the situation in the Black and Tan War in those areas that enjoyed some kind of governmental status. In the 1970s the struggle developed into a broad political and armed campaign, but even the military aspect developed its own politics of physical force.

What particularly characterises this phase is that the IRA/Óglaigh na hÉireann fights within the occupied area and exists cheek by jowl with the British forces, which have at their command a massive array of technological resources. The IRA today is one of the few guerrilla forces in the world which operates in and from within the occupied area, and despite the long duration of this phase of struggle, the IRA continues to enjoy unsurpassed community support.

I wish that physical force had never been part of the political struggle in my lifetime in Ireland. But a statelet which was born in violence has maintained itself throughout its more than sixty years of exist-

1. Irish for the 'Youth of Ireland'.

ence by violence and has been supported in so doing by the British army and government. The conflict which has resulted in the deaths of over 2,500 people began in 1966 with the UVF campaign of assassinations of Catholics; it continued in its early stages with attacks by loyalists and RUC on civil rights marchers and graduated to the joint loyalist/RUC attacks on Catholic streets in Derry and Belfast, and the first member of the RUC to be killed at this time was shot by loyalists on the Shankill Road.[2]

The IRA's armed struggle in this period originated as a defensive response to the combined attacks of the RUC, loyalists and the British army, and it has always been massively outgunned. There are in the 6 counties today something like 123,000 legally held guns, and these are not in the possession of the IRA. There are approximately 30,000 members of the British forces, between British soldiers, the UDR, the RUC and the RUC Reserve. They are armed with sophisticated weapons, with armoured cars, a massive battery of electronic surveillance equipment, with cameras trained on many streets of West Belfast and Derry, and they are backed by the law which, in Brigadier Frank Kitson's phrase, is 'just another weapon in the government's arsenal . . . little more than a propaganda cover for the disposal of unwanted members of the public.'[3]

From defensive origins the IRA campaign developed into an offensive against the state, and there is no denying the fact that innocent bystanders were killed and injured as a consequence of IRA actions.[4] Death by violence is always a sickening tragedy and no talk of 'the inevitable casualties of guerrilla warfare' can do anything to alter the fact. I deeply regret all the deaths and injuries which occur in the course of this struggle and although I have never tried to justify civilian casualties or fatalities of IRA actions I am challenged constantly by some journalists and television interviewers, imitating the attitudes of their political masters, with having placed myself and the whole republican movement outside the bounds of political debate by refusing to condemn the IRA and the IRA is commented upon in an unreal way as if its motivation were the pursuit of violence for its own sake. It is commented upon in a way which ignores and diverts attention away from the circumstances which account both for its origins and for the continuation of its armed activity.

Óglaigh na hÉireann today takes its historical and organisational origins from the forces which engaged in the Easter Rising of 1916, though one can trace its ancestry much further back if one wishes. But the circumstances which shaped the support for the IRA of today are above all the experience of the barricade days from 1969–72. These days are of continuing importance not just in terms of the IRA but because they saw the development of tremendous community solidarity, more than a memory of which remains today.

In response to joint RUC and loyalist attacks nationalist Derry was barricaded from August 1969 until July 1972; in Belfast for a much shorter period there were barricades in up to 26 Catholic enclaves, with the major concentration in West Belfast. Massive shifts in population caused by the loyalist pogroms — the biggest forced movement of population in Europe since the Second World War — led people to open up their homes behind the barricades to refugees. Everyone had to develop self-reliance and mutual solidarity in order to cope with the situation. Working people took control of aspects of their own lives, organised their own districts, in a way which deeply antagonised and traumatised the Catholic middle class and particularly the Catholic church hierarchy. It was an experience of community oneness, of unselfishness at every hand. And, when more than barricades were required for defence from the armed forces of the RUC, loyalists and, soon, the British army, this generation of the IRA emerged.

The IRA was, in August 1969, disorganised, almost completely unarmed, and unable to play the role it had played in previous pogroms in the 1920s and 30s of defending the areas under attack. In one or two instances firearms were produced by individual republicans in attempts to hold off attacks, but the IRA was in no shape to offer any organised response. Yet by March 1972 the IRA had not only created a defensive force of unprecedented effectiveness, they had also carried out a massive offensive which had succeeded in its aim of bringing

2. Constable Arbuckle, shot dead in 1970 by loyalists during a riot in the Shankill Road in Belfast. UVF is the Ulster Volunteer Force; RUC is the Royal Ulster Constabulary; UDR is the Ulster Defence Regiment.
3. Brigadier Frank Kitson, British army strategist and an officer in the Special Armed Services (SAS). The quotation is from his book *Low Intensity Operations* (London: Faber and Faber, 1971).
4. Irish Database reckoned that, by 1989, the IRA had killed 378 innocent civilians.

down the Stormont government.

In the days, weeks and months after the August 1969 pogroms republicans worked with frantic energy to raise money, to procure arms and to reorganise the IRA to meet the demands of a situation of armed siege. In a remarkably short time a people's army took shape; closely knit with the nationalist community, it was made up of the sons and daughters of ordinary people, its members indistinguishable to any outside observer from the rest of the community. Whether people in the nationalist areas agreed or disagreed with the IRA and all its actions they recognised it as their army, knew for the most part which of their neighbours were members, and referred to it simply as the 'ra'.

Street, houses, people and even churches were under attack and IRA volunteers — most of whom were very young — put their lives on the line to protect them. At first sticks and stones, petrol bombs and unsophisticated guns were used against the forces of the state, which were equipped with the most up-to-date weaponry. And in the midst of days of rioting and skirmishes the IRA was screening, training and attempting to instil discipline in large numbers of new recruits. Much had to be done under intense pressure and at breakneck speed but before long the IRA had adopted clear structures for its operations and had acquired explosives and guns that stood a chance of generating an effective counter to the firepower being directed against the nationalist areas.

When the barricades were up there was a great sense of euphoria; this was perhaps naive but it was nonetheless real. When the IRA campaign began the civil rights campaign was still going on, albeit on a smaller scale than previously, and the honeymoon period immediately after the arrival of the British troops was over. For the first time in the 6 counties one had the combination of armed struggle and mass, popular struggle. Most of the Catholics had withdrawn from the institutions of state and when internment came they all withdrew. The armed struggle began to be waged with great intensity and with major support and tolerance. There was also the feeling that things were happening in Dublin, as reflected in the Arms Trial crisis in Fianna Fáil,[5] and that tended to give Northern Catholics succour.

When Prime Minister Faulkner said things like 'We have them on the run' and the IRA came back the next day with a devastating series of operations, the effect that had in lifting people's morale was enormous. The free run for republicans in the barricaded areas meant that the areas were almost entirely free of petty crime, and this had more to do with an identification with the struggle than with any policing methods of republicans.

The ambassadors for the British government on a daily basis were the British soldiers. They were 'welcomed' initially because they were seen as relieving a siege, whether in the Falls Road or in Derry, but it was an uneasy welcome. They got tea in only a few households. People did not know whether to cheer or what to do. Even in the past when Catholics had joined the British army for lack of available jobs their families had been inclined to feel a bit guilty about it. At the very least there was a consciousness that these were British soldiers and that in one sense or another we were Irish. Another factor which came quickly into play was the racist attitude of many British army regiments. They antagonised whole communities by their behaviour and especially by their attitude to womenfolk. So, while there were initially mixed feelings about the British army, once it became apparent what their role was, then all ambiguity went out of the window. Within a very short space of time people were shouting insults at the soldiers — things like 'Dunkirk harriers', which I didn't even understand at the time and which was the most polite kind of comment; and people were suddenly talking about memories of the Black and Tans.

Bombay Street, and two months later Coates Street, were burned down by loyalist gangs and the RUC after the British troops had arrived and after the larger scale burnings had already taken place. Whole streets of houses were burned out, people were killed and about a hundred injured during the two-day attack on this Catholic area in the Lower Falls. The fact that the British army did not intervene taught nationalists an important lesson.

The Falls Road curfew in July 1970 made popular

5. In May 1970, Charles Haughey and Neil Blaney, both cabinet ministers, were asked to resign by the Taoiseach, Jack Lynch. Later they were arrested for a conspiracy to import arms and ammunition for use by the IRA in Northern Ireland. Blaney was discharged in July and Haughey was acquitted in October. The Arms Trial had enduring consequences for the Fianna Fáil party.

opposition to the British army absolute in Belfast. Three thousand British troops invaded the Falls Road and from helicopters voices over PA systems announced that the area was under a curfew: anyone on the streets was liable to be shot. Five civilians were killed, more were injured, and three hundred were arrested. The invasion and curfew lasted for two days, during which 1,600 cannisters of CS gas were fired. Troops smashed down the doors of houses, pulled up floors, wrecked people's homes. The siege was broken, at great risk to themselves, by hundreds of women who massed together and simply marched past all the squaddies,[6] who did not know how to cope with this direct expression of popular feeling. After that recruitment to the IRA was massive. IRA organisation and capability increased so dramatically that by June and July of 1971 they were able to carry out as many as 125 bombings in those two months — an average of more than two per day. The Stormont government and the British army were not succeeding in their attempts to crush the resistance.

The shooting dead in Derry of Seamus Cusack and Desmond Beattie marked a critical turning point. Prime Minister Faulkner had in May given the British army carte blanche to fire on anyone acting 'suspiciously'; on 8 July 1971 they obliged and two unarmed Catholics were killed. The struggle for civil rights had continued despite the RUC beating people to death, despite loyalist attacks, despite the Battle of the Bogside, the upheavals of August, the shootings of people in the Falls Road. But the shootings of Cusack and Beattie marked a change and this change was cemented by the use of the British army forces as the implement of repression. Before that it had been primarily a battle between beleagured [*sic*] nationalists and the Stormont administration for equal rights; then it became a battle between beleagured [*sic*] nationalists and the British establishment.

The British government could have defused the situation, could have prevented it reaching the stage of open armed conflict. If they had understood and taken note of what the Campaign for Social Justice was saying in 1965 they could have moved then to introduce the norms of democracy at a time when republicanism was virtually dead. In such circumstances it would have been impossible for the IRA to survive. If in London the will had existed to make even limited changes the long-sighted agitators would have pointed out how small the changes were and how unsatisfactory, but the British government would have succeeded in undercutting support for republicanism.

Instead of defusing the situation the British government copper-fastened popular support for the IRA. In Ballymurphy in West Belfast, for example, there were six semi-active republicans and ten supporters in 1969; today in West Belfast Sinn Féin draws its biggest vote from that area. The crucial transformation came about when a British army regiment came into Ballymurphy and attempted to beat its people into submission. If they had come in with kid gloves they would still have been unwelcome but they would not have generated the same phenomenon of implacable republican resistance.

Internment, introduced on 9 August 1971, had a major effect in making people conscious participants in the struggle. Those who were already politicised were not surprised by the introduction of internment, but there were many Catholics who did not believe that such a thing could happen, and to them internment came as a crucial indication that the road to reform was blocked off. Brutal confirmation came with the shooting dead of unarmed demonstrators in Derry on Bloody Sunday, 30 January 1972. Óglaigh na hÉireann was inundated with new recruits.

When Stormont fell in March 1972[7] it was a time of complete and utter jubilation. I remember talking to a middle-aged man in Ballymurphy in the midst of a colossal gun battle. (Although many people might not realise this, a lot of those big gun battles fought to defend an area from attack — in this case attack by the British army — had as many as two hundred people standing and watching what was happening.) This man, who had lived through the imposition of partition and the setting up of Stormont, kept saying, almost as if he was drunk, 'Jesus, you'd never think you'd see the day!' He represented a feeling that so quickly after the events of 1968/69 something that was hated, something that was symbolic of all that was wrong in the state had been

6. British soldiers.

7. After Brian Faulkner, the Northern Irish premier, and his cabinet had refused to accept the transfer of security to Whitehall, the British prime minister, Edward Heath, prorogued Stormont for a year and appointed William Whitelaw as secretary of state for Northern Ireland.

removed. And probably most people who were anti-Unionist felt quite rightly that they had played a part in the removal of Stormont. The IRA was clearly seen as acting on their behalf.

The fall of Stormont was very decidedly a watershed. The feeling was that 'we'll never go back to that again'. Today there is a section of the population, represented by the SDLP, who will be prepared to go back. And there is a section who will never again accept partitionist rule. The respective strengths of those two tendencies remain to be seen.

The impact of the fall of Stormont on the Unionists, as well as the disarming and disbanding of the 'B' Specials, must obviously have been catastrophic. Having said that, the actual impact may have been exaggerated by commentators. Just after the fall of Stormont I found myself committed to the Maidstone prison ship, which was anchored in Belfast Lough in the hinterland of loyalist East Belfast and we felt very vulnerable to attack by an Orange mob enraged at the abolition of their Protestant parliament. The Vanguard Party was in its heyday, with its parades and rallies featuring fascist salutes.[8] Unionist leaders were making threatening noises, and if there was going to be a real Orange backlash that was the moment at which it should have occurred. But it didn't; and in assessing the dangers of a loyalist backlash one must take this into account. They said they would not accept the fall of Stormont, but they did; they said they would fight to the last man, but they didn't.

What loyalist response there was came in a form which has been seen on many other occasions since. Although their fight over the proroguing of Stormont was with the British they engaged in a spiralling campaign of killings of Catholics. There was not the major backlash that had been threatened but there were the phenomena of mutilated bodies and 'romper room' torture and it was a very frightening period for many Catholics, marked also by the growth to quite massive numbers of the UDA, which paraded in paramilitary gear and masks. There was also a major confrontation between the UDA and the British army in Woodvale in Belfast. The British army climbed down.

Unionism had depended for so long on its leadership that when that leadership failed to deliver Unionism was for a period lost — not only because its leadership had proved inadequate but also because the British government on whom it depended, to which it pledged allegiance, to which it felt bound and of which it was a subject took away Stormont. Their disarray became exacerbated when the British under direct rule took more and more of the everyday decisions and there was no real role for Unionist politicians. They had no power.

On the nationalist side Óglaigh na hÉireann enjoyed credibility and popular support but the republican movement failed to intervene politically and effectively handed over the role of political representatives of the nationalist people to the SDLP. Many Catholics adopted a pragmatic attitude then of support for the IRA's military struggle and voting for the SDLP. Some elements claiming to be 'republican' or 'nationalist' made attacks on Protestants. These attacks were quite wrong and, like 'feuding' between republican and other groups, did not serve any anti-Unionist interest.

Support for the IRA amongst the nationalist population of the 6 countries has been, as the tacticians of guerrilla warfare such as Mao and Che[9] put it, the sea in which the people's army has swum and, like the sea, it has its tides, its ebbs and flows, but it is always there. The nationalist people had withdrawn their consent to being governed by Stormont; they and the IRA had brought Stormont down and proceeded in succeeding years to make the 6 counties ungovernable even in an environment of British military saturation of nationalist areas. However, a situation of deadlock in which Óglaigh na hÉireann were able to block the imposition of a British solution but were unable to force the British to withdraw produced a sense of war-weariness. The IRA had succeeded in bring down [*sic*] Stormont and they had promised victory in the form of British withdrawal. But victory had not come and the troops were still on the streets, still kicking down doors in the night, wrecking nationalists' houses, dragging people off for interrogation, torture and internment.

8. Vanguard was an Ulster unionist organization founded by William Craig, former minister for home affairs in the Northern Irish cabinet. It first emerged in February 1972. Craig made bloodthirsty speeches at rallies and was escorted by motor-cycle escorts of young men in leather outfits. The Ulster Defence Association, the largest of the protestant paramilitary groups, operated for a time under the Vanguard umbrella.

9. Mao Tse-tung (1893–1976), Chinese communist leader; Ché Guevara (1928–67), South American revolutionary.

British army patrols were sometimes truculent, sometimes terrified, but they were always there; whether you were going shopping or to work, to the pub or just round the corner to a relative or friend, they were always there. And that operated in many ways: it made people determined to resist, and it made people weary. British soldiers harassed children leaving schools; mothers went down to the schools to bring their children home and prevent them responding to the provocations of the soldiers with stones; mothers saw sons graduating from stones to petrol bombs to membership of the IRA, to Long Kesh internment camp. Hardly a family was untouched by death, internment or imprisonment. Heroically they kept their households going, often holding down a job while husband and perhaps a son as well were inside, coping on the barest level of subsistence, visiting Long Kesh regularly. Some became political activists in the Relatives Action Committee or in Sinn Féin; they marched and demonstrated and came to be the heart and soul of popular resistance.

In the face of the suffering of the war of resistance in the nationalist ghettoes it was inevitable that a war-weary opposition to the IRA would surface on occasions. It may well be, as other observers and authors have suggested, that some of these movements of opposition received encouragement and finance from British government, including British army sources. However, there is no doubt that on occasions genuine war-weariness did surface, and it is very understandable that it should, but because it occasionally attacked the IRA did not mean that it was pro-British. The appalling disruption of everyday life, the incessant assault on nerves by the tension of wondering whether a son, daughter, wife, husband, brother or sister was going to be lifted, beaten up in interrogation, interned or killed, the frequent dangers of loyalist assassination campaigns — all the strains of the situation inevitably raised the question in people's minds as to whether it was all worth it. No one wanted to go back to the 'normality' of rule by Stormont, but with no immediate prospect of a British withdrawal support for the struggle of the IRA was bound to waver. In particular, the British government exploited every opportunity to increase the sense of war-weariness; and especially when Óglaigh na hÉireann killed or injured civilians the British were always, in classical counter-insurgency fashion, cynically prepared to exploit these mistakes or to create the conditions in which they might occur.

There always has been and there always will be a yearning for peace among Irish people. The so-called 'Peace People' are the best-known example of an organised movement against the IRA campaign, but there have been other organisations through the years such as 'Women Together' and 'Protestant and Catholic Encounter', and there have been occasions when people in nationalist areas have protested against IRA actions without actually forming any organisation. But whenever this understandable and undoubtedly genuine desire for peace manifests itself it is open to exploitation for one political purpose or another. It is easy to suggest that peace is somehow not political and that peace marches are not political, and then sincere people can be swept along behind a vague and emotional demand.

I have very strong personal feelings about the 'Peace People' campaign of 1976. The IRA man, Danny Lennon, who was shot dead in the incident which gave rise to the campaign, had been a particular friend of mine since we had met at Cage 11 in Long Kesh. It was tragic enough that he and the Maguire children had been killed, but when the British lie about his death was picked up by the media and gained general acceptance I found it a great deal more difficult to deal with.

The facts of the incident were that Danny Lennon was shot dead at the wheel of the car he was driving by British soldiers firing from an armour-plated landrover and the car ploughed into the Maguire family at the side of the road. Mrs Maguire was seriously injured and three of her children, the oldest of whom was eight years and the youngest only six weeks, were killed. It was never clear whether they were killed by the car or by bullets fired by British soldiers; unusually, the results of the autopsies and inquest were never published.

No attention was focussed on the fact that the British troops had opened fire on a car without regard for the lives of civilians on the street. Instead, the headlines shouted their message that an IRA car had killed three children. And on BBC TV News that night Mrs Maguire's sister, Mairead Corrigan, broke down crying and understandably affected millions of viewers deeply.[10]

10. The Peace Movement was founded by Mairead Corrigan and Betty Williams in August 1976, after the death of the three Maguire children

Danny Lennon had been shot dead, yet he was being held solely responsible for the deaths of the Maguire children. It was bad enough that innocent children had been killed. That was awful. But Danny Lennon, now dead and unable to defend himself, was being blamed. That concern may appear ridiculous to people who have an image of IRA volunteers as terrorists, but the reality is that members of Óglaigh na hÉireann are just ordinary citizens who are forced through difficult circumstances into resistance, and Danny Lennon was an ordinary nationalist youth, a member of a large family in Andersonstown, who had become involved in resistance. The tragedy of the deaths of the children rankled; in particular, the way the British escaped any responsibility at all; the exploitation of the childrens' deaths; the cynical way in which the incident was manipulated.

The 'Peace People' lost credibility in nationalist areas very quickly. In fact, what credibility it had consisted basically of sympathy for the Maguires and, indeed, for the Lennons. Only four days after the deaths of the Maguire children a 12 year-old girl, Majella O'Hare, was shot and killed by British soldiers in South Armagh; the 'Peace People' offered no criticism of the British army. Two months later 14 year-old Brian Stewart was shot dead by British soldiers in West Belfast; again the 'Peace People' were silent, and when they went to a meeting in Turf Lodge they had to be escorted from the hall because of the fury of local people at the one-sidedness of their condemnation of violence. If that was not enough to seal their fate in Catholic areas they put the cap on it when they characterised the RUC, UDR and British army as 'the only legitimate upholders of the rule of law' and played down what they called 'the occasional instances when members of the security forces may have stepped beyond the rule of law'.

The movement showed that there is always a hope among people that there can be peace, an element of war-weariness that grabs at straws. The people who marched and prayed and engaged in rallies were expressing perfectly reasonable emotions, but these emotions were exploited. The 'Peace People' were not even calling for real and general peace: what they were calling for was an end to the armed struggle of the IRA. And that was at best a partial kind of peace, in both meanings of partial — prejudiced against only one element in a violent conflict and incomplete in that it did not base itself on the elements of social justice without which peace simply cannot grow. It was an attempt to move people away from republican physical force politics and it failed because it did not even seek to remedy the reasons why people felt compelled to have recourse to physical force.

As soon as they tried to examine what peace was and how it could be attained the leadership of the 'Peace People' began to collapse. The media, perhaps because of their nature, represent the failure as lying in the falling out between Mairead Corrigan, Betty Williams and Ciaran McKeown as they disputed who should get what money. But the real reason was far larger than this merely symptomatic disintegration. Peace rallies and prayer may give succour to people but they cannot of their own volition bring peace. Peace is a political question and cannot be successfully approached without a commitment to political change.

For a short period the 'Peace People' succeeded in diverting public — and particularly international — attention from the real problem of the political situation in the 6 counties. In the end it brought into question the credibility not only of its own leaders but also of the Nobel Peace Prize, Joan Baez, and others who associated themselves with it.

The episode — for that is what it was — of the 'Peace People' deserves to be regarded as a particularly sad one, because it represented a perversion of what is a very important demand. In practice, people have been demanding peace since long before the IRA became active. In my own area of Ballymurphy community groups have long demanded employment, decent housing, play centres, facilities for the aged, the handicapped and the young. They have sought freedom from heavy rents on homes they will never own, freedom from the dole queues and freedom from the Assistance Office. At the time of the 'Peace People' the facilities of the area were a public house, a row of shops, a bookmaker's office. One hundred of the six hundred families had more than ten people living in cramped, ill-repaired, misplanned, jerrybuilt houses. Forty-seven per cent of the residents were unemployed. Sixty per cent of the population were children and teenagers faced with a future which offered them nothing. Those demands for the kind of peace which is based on justice and equality were made year after year, and

in West Belfast. They were joined by Ciaran McKeown, a journalist. They won the Nobel Prize for Peace in 1976.

year after year they were refused.

We cannot have justice and peace in Ireland because we do not have a society capable of upholding them. Instead we have a system based on coercion, violence, sectarianism and exploitation. By its very nature British rule cannot be just or peaceful and, while this is so, revolutionary struggle will continue to strive to overthrow it in pursuit of true justice, peace and happiness. Violence in Ireland has its roots in the conquest of Ireland by Britain. This conquest has lasted through several stages for many centuries and, whether economic, political, territorial or cultural, it has used violence, coercion, sectarianism and terrorism as its methods and has had power as its objective.

ANGLO-IRISH AGREEMENT

(1985)

BETWEEN THE GOVERNMENT OF IRELAND AND THE GOVERNMENT OF THE UNITED KINGDOM

Signed at Hillsborough on 15 November 1985

Entered into force on 29 November 1985

Presented to Dáil Éireann by the Minister for Foreign Affairs

The Government of Ireland and the Government of the United Kingdom:

Wishing further to develop the unique relationship between their peoples and the close co-operation between their countries as friendly neighbours and as partners in the European Community;

Recognising the major interest of both their countries and, above all, of the people of Northern Ireland in diminishing the divisions there and achieving lasting peace and stability;

Recognising the need for continuing efforts to reconcile and to acknowledge the rights of the two major traditions that exist in Ireland, represented on the one hand by those who wish for no change in the present status of Northern Ireland and on the other hand by those who aspire to a sovereign united Ireland achieved by peaceful means and through agreement;

Reaffirming their total rejection of any attempt to promote political objectives by violence or the threat of violence and their determination to work together to ensure that those who adopt or support such methods do not succeed;

Recognising that a condition of genuine reconciliation and dialogue between unionists and nationalists is mutual recognition and acceptance of each other's rights;

Recognising and respecting the identities of the two communities in Northern Ireland, and the right of each to pursue its aspirations by peaceful and constitutional means;

Reaffirming their commitment to a society in Northern Ireland in which all may live in peace, free from discrimination and intolerance, and with the opportunity for both communities to participate fully in the structures and processes of government;

Have accordingly agreed as follows:

A

STATUS OF NORTHERN IRELAND

ARTICLE 1

The two Governments

(a) affirm that any change in the status of Northern Ireland would only come about with the consent of a majority of the people of Northern Ireland;
(b) recognise that the present wish of a majority of the people of Northern Ireland is for no change in the status of Northern Ireland;
(c) declare that, if in the future a majority of the people of Northern Ireland clearly wish for and formally consent to the establishment of a united Ireland, they will introduce and support in the respective Parliaments legislation to give effect to that wish.

B

THE INTERGOVERNMENTAL CONFERENCE

ARTICLE 2

(a) There is hereby established, within the framework of the Anglo-Irish Intergovernmental Council set up after the meeting between the two Heads of Government on 6 November 1981, an Intergovernmental Conference (hereinafter referred to as 'the Conference'), concerned with Northern Ireland and with relations between the two parts of the island of Ireland, to deal, as set out in this Agreement, on a regular basis with
(i) political matters;
(ii) security and related matters;
(iii) legal matters, including the administration of justice;
(iv) the promotion of cross-border co-operation
(b) The United Kingdom Government accept that the Irish Government will put forward views and proposals on matters relating to Northern Ireland within the field of activity of the Conference in so far as those matters are not the responsibility of a devolved administration in Northern Ireland. In the interest of promoting peace and stability, determined efforts shall be made through the Conference to resolve any differences. The Conference will be mainly concerned with Northern Ireland; but some of the matters under consideration will involve co-operative action in both parts of the island of Ireland, and possibly also in Great Britain. Some of the proposals considered in respect of Northern Ireland may also be found to have application by the Irish Government. There is no derogation from the sovereignty of either the Irish Government or the United Kingdom Government, and each retains responsibility for the decisions and administrations of government within its own jurisdiction.

ARTICLE 3

The Conference shall meet at Ministerial or official level, as required. The business of the Conference will thus receive attention at the highest level. Regular and frequent Ministerial meetings shall be held; and in particular special meetings shall be convened at the request of either side. Officials may meet in subordinate groups. Membership of the Conference and of sub-groups shall be small and flexible. When the Conference meets at Ministerial level an Irish Minister designated as the Permanent Irish Ministerial Representative and the Secretary of State for Northern Ireland shall be joint Chairmen. Within the framework of the Conference other Irish and British Ministers may hold or attend meetings as appropriate: when legal matters are under consideration the Attorneys General may attend. Ministers may be accompanied by their officials and their professional advisers: for example, when questions of security policy or security co-operation are being discussed, they may be accompanied by the Commissioner of the Garda Síochána and the Chief Constable of the Royal Ulster Constabulary; or when questions of economic or social policy or co-operation are being discussed, they may be accompanied by officials of the relevant Departments. A Secretariat shall be established by the two Governments to service the Conference on a continuing basis in the discharge of its functions as set out in this Agreement.

ARTICLE 4

(a) In relation to matters coming within its field of activity, the Conference shall be a framework within which the Irish Government and the United Kingdom Government work together
(i) for the accommodation of the rights and identities of the two traditions which exist in Northern Ireland; and
(ii) for peace, stability and prosperity throughout the island of Ireland by promoting reconciliation, respect for human rights, co-operation against terrorism and the development of economic, social and cultural co-operation.

(b) It is the declared policy of the United Kingdom Government that responsibility in respect of certain matters within the powers of the Secretary of State for Northern Ireland should be devolved within Northern Ireland on a basis which would secure widespread acceptance throughout the community. The Irish Government support that policy.

(c) Both Governments recognise that devolution can be achieved only with the co-operation of constitutional representatives within Northern Ireland of both traditions there. The Conference shall be a framework within which the Irish Government may put forward views and proposals on the modalities of bringing about devolution in Northern Ireland, in so far as they relate to the interests of the minority community.

C

POLITICAL MATTERS

ARTICLE 5

(a) The Conference shall concern itself with measures to recognise and accommodate the rights and identities of the two traditions in Northern Ireland, to protect human rights and to prevent discrimination. Matters to be considered in this area include measures to foster the cultural heritage of both traditions, changes in electoral arrangements, the use of flags and emblems, the avoidance of economic and social discrimination and the advantages and disadvantages of a Bill of Rights in some form in Northern Ireland.

(b) The discussion of these matters shall be mainly concerned with Northern Ireland, but the possible application of any measures pursuant to this Article by the Irish Government in their jurisdiction shall not be excluded.

(c) If it should prove impossible to achieve and sustain devolution on a basis which secures widespread acceptance in Northern Ireland, the Conference shall be a framework within which the Irish Government may, where the interests of the minority community are significantly or especially affected, put forward views on proposals for major legislation and on major policy issues, which are within the purview of the Northern Ireland Departments and which remain the responsibility of the Secretary of State for Northern Ireland.

ARTICLE 6

The Conference shall be a framework within which the Irish Government may put forward views and proposals on the role and composition of bodies appointed by the Secretary of State for Northern Ireland or by Departments subject to his direction and control including

the Standing Advisory Commission on Human Rights;
the Fair Employment Agency;
the Equal Opportunities Commission;
the Police Authority for Northern Ireland;
the Police Complaints Board.

D

SECURITY AND RELATED MATTERS

ARTICLE 7

(a) The Conference shall consider
(i) security policy;
(ii) relations between the security forces and the community;
(iii) prisons policy.

(b) The Conference shall consider the security situation at its regular meetings and thus provide an opportunity to address policy issues, serious incidents and forthcoming events.

(c) The two Governments agree that there is a need for a programme of special measures in Northern Ireland to improve relations between the security forces and the community, with the object in particular of making the security forces more readily accepted by the nationalist community. Such a programme shall be developed, for the Conference's consideration, and may include the establishment of local consultative machinery, training in community relations, crime prevention schemes involving the community, improvements in arrangements for handling complaints, and action to increase the proportion of members of the minority in the Royal Ulster Constabulary. Elements of the programme may be considered by the Irish Government suitable for application within their jurisdiction.

(d) The Conference may consider policy issues relating to prisons. Individual cases may be raised as appropriate, so that information can be provided or inquiries instituted.

E

LEGAL MATTERS, INCLUDING THE ADMINISTRATION OF JUSTICE

ARTICLE 8

(a) The Conference shall deal with issues of concern to both countries relating to the enforcement of the criminal law. In particular it shall consider whether there are areas of the criminal law applying in the North and in the South respectively which might with benefit be harmonised. The two Governments agree on the importance of public confidence in the administration of justice. The Conference shall seek, with the help of advice from experts as appropriate, measures which would give substantial expression to this aim, considering *inter alia* the possibility of mixed courts in both jurisdictions for the trial of certain offences. The Conference shall also be concerned with policy aspects of extradition and extra-territorial jurisdiction as between North and South.

F

CROSS-BORDER CO-OPERATION ON SECURITY, ECONOMIC AND CULTURAL MATTERS

ARTICLE 9

(a) With a view to enhancing cross-border co-operation on security matters, the Conference shall set in hand a programme of work to be undertaken by the Commissioner of the Garda Síochána and the Chief Constable of the Royal Ulster Constabulary and, where appropriate, groups of officials, in such areas as threat assessments, exchange of information, liaison structures, technical co-operation, training of personnel, and operational resources.

(b) The Conference shall have no operational responsibilities; responsibility for police operations shall remain with the heads of the respective police forces, the Commissioner of the Garda Síochána maintaining his links with the Minister for Justice and the Chief Constable of the Royal Ulster Constabulary his links with the Secretary of State for Northern Ireland.

ARTICLE 10

(a) The two Governments shall co-operate to promote the economic and social development of those areas of both parts of Ireland which have suffered most severely from the consequences of the instability of recent years, and shall consider the possibility of securing international support for this work.

(b) If it should prove impossible to achieve and sustain devolution on a basis which secures widespread acceptance in Northern Ireland, the Conference shall be a framework for the promotion of co-operation between the two parts of Ireland concerning cross-border aspects of economic, social and cultural matters in relation to which the Secretary of State for Northern Ireland continues to exercise authority.

(c) If responsibility is devolved in respect of certain matters in the economic, social or cultural areas currently within the responsibility of the Secretary of State for Northern Ireland, machinery will need to be established by the responsible authorities in the North and South for practical co-operation in respect of cross-border aspects of these issues.

G

ARRANGEMENTS FOR REVIEW

ARTICLE 11

At the end of three years from signature of this Agreement, or earlier if requested by either Government, the working of the Conference shall be reviewed by the two Governments to see whether any changes in the scope and nature of its activities are desirable.

H

INTERPARLIAMENTARY RELATIONS

ARTICLE 12

It will be for Parliamentary decision in Dublin and in Westminster whether to establish an Anglo-Irish Parliamentary body of the kind adumbrated in the Anglo-Irish Studies Report of November 1981. The two Governments agree that they would give support as appropriate to such a body, if it were to be established.

I

FINAL CLAUSES

ARTICLE 13

This Agreement shall enter into force on the date on which the two Governments exchange notifications of their acceptance of this Agreement.

In witness whereof the undersigned, being duly authorised thereto by their respective Governments, have signed this Agreement.

Done in two originals at Hillsborough on the 15th day of November 1985.

For the Government of Ireland — Gearóid Mac Gearailt[1]

For the Government of the United Kingdom — Margaret Thatcher

1. Garret FitzGerald.

Biographies/Bibliographies

These select bibliographies, chronologically arranged, are meant to supplement the individual bibliographies that follow.

Ireland 1900–1990
F. Hackett, *Ireland: A Study in Nationalism* (New York: B. W. Huebsch Inc., 1920); T. D. Williams (ed.), *The Irish Struggle 1916–26* (London: Routledge & Kegan Paul, 1966); T. D. Williams and K. B. Nowlan (eds), *Ireland in the War Years and After 1939–1951* (Dublin: Gill and Macmillan, 1969); D. Harkness, *The Restless Dominion: The Irish Free State and the British Commonwealth of Nations 1921–1931* (Dublin: Gill and Macmillan, 1969); F. S. L. Lyons, *Ireland Since the Famine* (London: Weidenfeld and Nicolson, 1971); D. George Boyce, *English Men and Irish Troubles: British Public Opinion and the Making of Irish*

Policy (London: Jonathan Cape, 1972); J. Lee, *The Modernisation of Irish Society 1848–1918* (Dublin: Gill and Macmillan, 1973); J. T. Carroll, *Ireland in the War Years 1939–45* (Newton Abbot: David and Charles; New York: Crane, Russak, 1975); J. Murphy, *Ireland in the Twentieth Century* (Dublin: Gill and Macmillan, 1975); C. Townshend, *The British Campaign in Ireland 1919–21: The Development of Political and Military Policies* (London: Oxford University Press, 1975); O. MacDonagh, *Ireland. The Union and its Aftermath* (London: Allen and Unwin, 1977); E. Rumpf and A. C. Hepburn, *Nationalism and Socialism in Twentieth Century Ireland* (Liverpool: Liverpool University Press, 1977); D. Fitzpatrick, *Politics and Irish Life 1913–1921: Provincial Experience of War and Revolution* (Dublin: Gill and Macmillan, 1977); F. S. L. Lyons, *Culture and Anarchy in Ireland 1890–1939* (Oxford, Clarendon Press, 1978); J. M. Curran, *The Birth of the Irish Free State 1921–1923* (Alabama: University of Alabama Press, 1980); T. Garvin, *The Evolution of Irish Nationalist Politics* (Dublin: Gill and Macmillan, 1981); T. Brown, *Ireland: A Social and Cultural History 1922–79* (London: Fontana, 1981); P. Bew and H. Patterson, *Sean Lemass and the Making of Modern Ireland 1954–66* (Dublin: Gill and Macmillan, 1982); M. Laffan, *The Partition of Ireland 1911–25* (Dundalk: Dundalgan Press, 1983); C. Townshend, *Political Violence in Ireland: Government and Resistance since 1848* (Oxford: Clarendon Press, 1983); D. McMahon, *Republicans and Imperialists: Anglo-Irish Relations in the 1930s* (New Haven: Yale University Press, 1984); R. Fanning, *Independent Ireland* (Dublin: Helicon, 1986); D. Fitzpatrick (ed.), *Ireland and the First World War* (Trinity History Workshop, Dublin: Lilliput Press, 1986); W. F. Mandle, *The Gaelic Athletic Association and Irish Nationalist Politics 1884–1924* (London: Macmillan; Dublin: Gill and Macmillan, 1987); E. O'Halpin, *The Decline of the Union: British Government in Ireland 1892–1920* (Dublin: Gill and Macmillan; Syracuse: Syracuse University Press, 1987); C. O'Halloran, *Partition and the Limits of Irish Nationalism: An Ideology Under Stress* (Dublin: Gill and Macmillan, 1987); B. Farrell (ed.), *De Valera's Constitution and Ours* (Dublin: Gill and Macmillan; Totowa, New Jersey: Barnes and Noble, 1988); M. Hopkinson, *Green Against Green: The Irish Civil War* (Dublin: Gill and Macmillan, 1988); R. F. Foster, *Modern Ireland 1600–1972* (London: Viking Press, 1988); K. T. Hoppen, *Ireland Since 1800: Conflict and Conformity* (London: Longman, 1989); J. Lee, *Ireland 1912–1985. Politics and Society* (Cambridge: Cambridge University Press, 1989); R. Breen, D. F. Hannan, D. B. Rottman, C. T. Whelan, *Understanding Contemporary Ireland: State, Class and Development in the Republic of Ireland* (Dublin: Gill and Macmillan, 1990).

Northern Ireland
R. Rose, *Governing Without Consensus: An Irish Perspective* (London: Faber and Faber, 1971); P. Bew and H. Patterson, *The State in Northern Ireland 1921–72: Political Forces and Social Classes* (Manchester: Manchester University Press, 1971); R. Harris, *Prejudice and Tolerance in Northern Ireland: A Study of Neighbours and 'Strangers' in a Border Community* (Manchester: Manchester University Press; Totowa, New Jersey: Rowman and Littlefield, 1972); P. Buckland, *Irish Unionism. Vol. 1: The Anglo-Irish and the New Ireland 1885–1922. Irish Unionism. Vol II: Ulster Unionism and the Origins of Northern Ireland 1886–1922* (Dublin: Gill and Macmillan, 1973); M. Farrell, *Northern Ireland: The Orange State* (London: Pluto Press, 1976); D. Miller, *Queen's Rebels: Ulster Loyalism in Historical Perspective* (Dublin: Gill and Macmillan; New York: Barnes and Noble, 1978); P. Buckland, *The Factory of Grievances: Devolved Government in Northern Ireland: The Ulster Question in British Politics to 1914* (Brighton: Harvester Press, 1980); P. Arthur, *Politics and Government in Northern Ireland* (London: Longmans, 1980); D. W. Harkness, *Northern Ireland since 1920* (Dublin: Helicon, 1983); M. Farrell, *Arming the Protestants* (London: Pluto Press, 1983); J. Downey, *Them and Us: Britain, Ireland and the Northern Question 1969–1982* (Dublin: Ward River Press, 1983); R. Fisk, *In Time of War: Ireland, Ulster and the Price of Neutrality 1939–45* (London: Deutsch, 1983; reprinted Paladin, Grafton Books, 1985); F. Wright, *Northern Ireland. A Comparative Analysis* (Dublin: Gill and Macmillan; Totowa, New Jersey: Barnes and Noble, 1987); A. Guelke, *Northern Ireland and the International Perspective* (Dublin: Gill and Macmillan; New York: St Martin's Press, 1988); C. Townshend (ed.), *Consensus in Ireland: Approaches and Recessions* (Oxford: Clarendon Press, 1989).

Horace Plunkett

LIFE. Born in Gloucestershire, England in 1854, Plunkett was educated at Eton and Oxford. He spent ten years as a rancher in Wyoming to improve his health, with annual visits to the family home in Dunsany, Co. Meath. He returned to Ireland in 1888 to manage the family estate and soon after began the Co-operative Movement with the help of the 4th Lord Dunraven and Father Thomas Finlay. As a member of the Congested Districts Board, he gained first-hand knowledge of the problems and inefficiencies of small farming and became convinced that co-operation and the elimination of the middle-man were the solutions to the country's agricultural problems. The first branch of the Co-operative Movement was founded in 1890 and thereafter it spread so quickly that a co-ordinating body, the Irish Agricultural Organization Society, was formed in 1894. Plunkett brought his friend George Russell (AE) into the movement; Russell became a full-time organizer and editor of the movement's newspaper, *The Irish Homestead*. Plunkett organized the Recess Committee which secured a government department, the Department of Agriculture and Technical Instruction, as part of the political structure. Although he had been returned as unionist MP for Dublin in 1892, Plunkett became a convert to Home Rule after 1908. He was chairman of the Irish Convention 1917–18 and was bitterly disappointed by its failure. In 1919 he founded the Irish Dominion League to seek self-government for Ireland within the British Empire. But events had already bypassed him. He became a senator of the new state in 1922 but left Ireland for good the following year when his home, Kilteragh, in Foxrock, Co. Dublin was burned by republicans during the Civil War. He died unmarried at Weybridge, Surrey, in 1932.

CHIEF WRITINGS. *Ireland in the New Century* (Dublin: Maunsel, 1904; reprinted with foreword by Trevor West, Dublin: Irish Academic Press, 1983); *Noblesse Oblige: An Irish Rendering* (Dublin: Maunsel, 1908: 2nd ed. Maunsel; London: Simpkin, Marshall & Co. Ltd, 1908); *The Unsettlement of the Irish Land Question* (Dublin: E. Ponsonby; London: Simpkin, Marshall, Hamilton, Kent, and Co. Ltd, 1909); *Plain Talks to Irish Farmers* (Dublin: Eason & Co. Ltd, 1910); *A Better Way: An Appeal to Ulster not to Desert Ireland* (Dublin: Hodges Figgis & Co. Ltd; London: Simpkin, Marshall & Co. Ltd, 1914); *A Defence of the Convention* (Dublin: Maunsel & Co. Ltd, 1917); *Home Rule and Conscription* (Dublin: The Talbot Press; London: T. Fisher Unwin, 1918); *Irish Chaos: The British Cause and the Irish Cure* (Dublin: Irish Dominion League, 1920).

BIOGRAPHY AND CRITICISM. E. MacLysaght, *Sir Horace Plunkett and his Place in the Irish Nation* (Dublin: Maunsel, 1916); R. A. Anderson, *With Horace Plunkett in Ireland* (London: Macmillan, 1935); retitled *With Plunkett in Ireland: The Co-op Organiser's Story* (Dublin: Irish Academic Press, 1983).

Michael O'Riordan

LIFE. Born in Limerick city in 1857, O'Riordan was educated locally before departing for Rome where he trained for the priesthood, attending in succession the Irish College, Propaganda, and the Gregorian University. He was ordained in 1883 and served in the diocese of Westminster and in his native diocese of Limerick. Most of his adult career was spent in Rome, where he was appointed rector of the Irish College in 1905, a post he held for fourteen years. He contributed frequently to the *Catholic Bulletin*, *Irish Ecclesiastical Record* and *New Ireland Review*. He died in Rome in 1919.

CHIEF WRITINGS. *Draper's 'Conflict between Religion and Science': A Lecture* (London: Catholic Truth Society, 1898); *A Reply to Dr. Starkie's Attack on the Managers of the National Schools* (Dublin: Ponsonby, 1903); *Catholicity and Progress in Ireland* (London: Kegan Paul, 1905); *La Lotte per La Libertà in Irlanda e in Inghilterra* (Rome: n.p., 1906); *The Mission of St. Patrick, a Witness to the Supernatural: A Sermon* (Dublin: Gill, 1909).

Frederick Ryan

For biography and bibliography, see Volume II, p. 1,019.

James Larkin

LIFE. Born in Liverpool of Irish parents in 1876, Larkin spent the years from 1881 to 1885 with his grandparents in Newry, Co. Down. He worked as a labourer, a seaman and a dock foreman in Liverpool before he was fired for striking in sympathy with the men he was supervising. In 1907 the National Union of Dock Labourers (NUDL) sent him to Belfast where he organized a series of strikes across the sectarian divide. The NUDL sent him to Dublin in 1908 and he began to organize the casual and unskilled workers and called three strikes within a year. Disowned by the NUDL, he founded his own union, the Irish Transport and General Workers' Union in 1908–09. He alienated the Irish Congress of Trade Unions by his confrontational tactics, was expelled in 1909, imprisoned in 1910 on a charge of misappropriating funds, released five months later and thereafter concentrated his fire on the Dublin employers in his newspaper *The Irish Worker*. In 1911 and 1912 he led a series of strikes which culminated in the organized resistance of the employers, led by William Martin Murphy, against the unionisation of the workers. This led to the Lock-out of 1913. Despite Larkin's attempts to organize aid from Britain and the USA and the support of James Connolly, by 1914 the workers were defeated. *The Irish Worker* was suppressed by Dublin Castle and Larkin left for the USA on a fund-raising tour. He stayed nine years, during which he involved himself with the syndicalist International Workers of the World. He was imprisoned for his activities and was not released until 1923. On his return, the changed situation in Ireland and the resistance of William O'Brien and Thomas Johnson of the ITGWU and the Labour Party respectively made it impossible for him to regain control of the union he had founded. He formed a new one, The Workers' Union of Ireland, gained recognition from the Communist International in 1924 and visited the Soviet Union as a representative of the Comintern. He rejoined the Labour Party in 1945 and won a seat for the party in Dáil Éireann. This led to bitter faction fighting, which ended with the ITGWU disaffiliating from Congress and to a split in the Labour Party. Larkin died in Dublin in 1947.

CHIEF WRITINGS. *Larkin's Scathing Indictment of Dublin Sweaters* (Manchester and London: The National Labour Press Ltd, n.d. (1920?); *A Common Loyalty — The Bridge to Unity* (Dublin: Irish Congress of Trade Unions, 1949).

BIOGRAPHY AND CRITICISM. E. Larkin, *James Larkin: Irish Labour Leader 1876–1947* (London: Routledge & Kegan Paul, 1961); A. Mitchell, *Labour in Irish Politics 1890–1930* (Dublin: Irish University Press, 1974); *Saothar* (Journal of the Irish Labour Movement), James Larkin Special Number, no. 4. 1978; H. Patterson, *Class Conflict and Sectarianism: The Protestant Working Class and the Belfast Labour Movement 1868–1920* (Belfast: Blackstaff Press, 1980); J. Gray, *City in Revolt: James Larkin and the Belfast Dock Strike of 1907* (Belfast: Blackstaff Press, 1985).

Francis Sheehy-Skeffington

LIFE. Born Francis Skeffington in Bailieborough, Co. Cavan in 1878. He was educated locally and at University College, Dublin where his friends included Tom Kettle and James Joyce. He became the first auditor of the Literary and Historical Society in 1897 and registrar of University College 1902–04. He resigned this position after a dispute over the rights of women to academic status. When he married Hanna Sheehy in 1903, he adopted her name to show that marriage was no barrier to equality between the sexes. He worked for a number of radical causes and wrote for several newspapers and journals. His campaign against conscription led to his arrest and, on being sentenced to jail, he went on a hunger-strike which helped to force his release. He supported Home Rule, disapproved of the Easter Rising and, while attempting to prevent looting during the insurrection in 1916, was arrested and subsequently murdered by Captain J. C. Bowen-Colthurst, a British officer of Anglo-Irish extraction and of an evangelical frame of mind.

CHIEF WRITINGS. *Two Essays* ('A forgotten aspect of the university question' and 'James Joyce's "The day of the rabblement" ') (Dublin: Gerrard Bros, 1901); *Michael Davitt, Revolutionary, Agitator and Labour Leader* (London: Fisher Unwin, 1908); *War and Feminism* (Dublin: n.p., 1914); *Speech from the Dock* (Dublin: Liberty Hall, 1915); *In Dark and Evil Days* (novel) (Dublin: James Duffy, 1916).

BIOGRAPHY AND CRITICISM. L. Levenson, *With Wooden Sword: A Portrait of Francis Sheehy-Skeffington, Militant Pacifist* (Boston: Northeastern University Press; Dublin: Gill and Macmillan, 1983).

James Connolly

LIFE. Born in Edinburgh in 1868, Connolly was self-educated and quickly won a reputation as a socialist theorist. He joined the British army to escape from poverty and served some time in Ireland. In 1889 he deserted, returned to Edinburgh, married, and worked at various jobs for the next seven years. Prompted by the Scottish socialist, John Leslie, he came to Dublin in 1896 and founded the Irish Socialist Republican Party and the newspaper, *The Workers' Republic*. In 1903 he emigrated to the United States and became deeply involved in American socialist movements. In 1910 he returned to Dublin, became Belfast organizer of the Irish Transport and General Workers' Union and, in 1912, co-founder of the Labour Party. He returned to Dublin to help James Larkin in the Dublin Lockout of 1913 and became a leading figure in the workers' defence force, the Irish Citizen Army. He led the Labour movement after Larkin's departure for the USA in 1914. His newspaper, *The Irish Worker*, was suppressed in 1914; he revived *The Workers' Republic* and attacked the inactivity of the Irish Volunteers. On Easter Monday 1916, he led his Citizen Army alongside Pearse's Irish Volunteers in the rebellion. He was commandant in the General Post Office and was badly wounded in the fighting. On 9 May, after being sentenced by a military tribunal, he was executed in Kilmainham Jail while propped in a chair.

CHIEF WRITINGS. *Labour, Nationality and Religion* (Dublin: Harp Library, 1910); *Labour in Ireland* (Dublin: Maunsel, 1917); D. Ryan (ed.), *Socialism and Nationalism: A Selection from the Writings of James Connolly* (Dublin: Sign of the Three Candles, 1948); *The Workers' Republic: A Selection from the Writings of James Connolly* (Dublin: Sign of the Three Candles, 1951); P. MacAonghusa and L. O'Reagain (eds), *The Best of Connolly* (Cork: Mercier Press, 1967); P. Berresford Ellis (ed.), *James Connolly: Selected Writings* (Harmondsworth: Penguin; New York: New Monthly Press, 1973); O. D. Edwards and B. Ransom (eds), *James Connolly: Selected Political Writings* (London: Cape, 1973); P. Berresford Ellis, *James Connolly: Selected Writings* (London: Pluto Press, 1990).

BIOGRAPHY AND CRITICISM. D. Ryan, *James Connolly: His Work and Writings* (Dublin: The Talbot Press, 1924); C. D. Greaves, *The Life and Times of James Connolly* (London: Lawrence and Wishart, 1961); D. Nevin, *Connolly Bibliography* (Dublin: Irish Congress of Trade Unions, 1968); O. D. Edwards, *The Mind of an Activist: James Connolly* (Dublin: Gill and Macmillan, 1970); S. Levenson, *James Connolly: A Biography* (London: Martin, Brian and O'Keeffe, 1973); S. Cronin, *Young Connolly* (Dublin: Repsol, 1978); P. Mac an Bheatha, *James Connolly and the Workers' Republic* (Baile Átha Cliath: Foilseacháin Naisiúnta Teoranta, 1978); B. Ransom, *Connolly's Marxism* (London: Pluto Press, 1980); R. D. Edwards, *James Connolly* (Dublin: Gill and Macmillan, 1981); D. Howell, *A Lost Left: Three Studies in Socialism and Nationalism* (Manchester: Manchester University Press, 1986); P. Metscher, *Republicanism and Socialism in Ireland: A Study in the Relationship of Politics and Ideology from the United Irishmen to James Connolly* (Frankfurt: Lang, 1986); A. Morgan, *James Connolly: A Political Biography* (Manchester: Manchester University Press, 1988); K. Allen, *The Politics of James Connolly* (London: Pluto Press, 1990).

Michael Collins

LIFE. Born in Woodfield, Clonakilty, Co. Cork in 1890, Collins was educated at the local national schools. He went to London in 1906 and took a job as a clerk. He joined the Gaelic Athletic Association and later, on his return to Ireland in 1915, the Irish Republican Brotherhood. He fought in the General Post Office during the Easter Rising of 1916 as aide-de-camp to Joseph Mary Plunkett, one of the leaders who was later executed. Collins was interned after the Rising. On his release in December 1916, he became adjutant-general of the provisional executive of the Irish Volunteers. He resigned his position on the executive to work with Harry Boland in the formation of an intelligence system. He became Minister for Home Affairs in the first Dáil Éireann and later Minister of Finance. He was President of the Supreme Council of the IRA and was the most powerful and admired leader during the War of Independence against the British. His personal staff, known as 'the Squad', made a series of attacks on British intelligence, culminating in the slaughter of Bloody Sunday on 21 November 1920. When the war ended, Collins reluctantly accepted the duty of going as a plenipotentiary to London for the Treaty negotiations, although he defended the Treaty on his return. He became chairman of the Provisional Government, and met with Sir James Craig in early 1922 to try to bring the unrest in the north of Ireland to an end. He also had talks with Eamon de Valera to try to heal the split which culminated in the Civil War. Collins became commander-in-chief of the National Army during the War. He was killed in an ambush at Beal na mBlath, Co. Cork on 20 August 1922.

CHIEF WRITINGS. *Arguments for the Treaty* (Dublin: M. Lester Ltd, 1922); *The Path to Freedom* (Dublin: The Talbot Press; London: T. Fisher Unwin, 1922).

BIOGRAPHY AND CRITICISM. P. Beaslai, *Michael Collins and the Making of a New Ireland* (Dublin: The Phoenix Publishing Co. Ltd, 1926); F. O'Connor, *The Big Fellow: A Life of Michael Collins* (London: Hutchinson, 1937; revised edition 1965; retitled *The Big Fellow: Michael Collins and the Irish Revolution* (Swords, Co. Dublin: Poolbeg Press, 1979); R. Taylor, *Michael Collins* (London: Hutchinson, 1958; Four Square Books, 1961); E. Neeson, *The Life and Death of Michael Collins* (Cork: Mercier Press, 1968); M. Forester, *Michael Collins: The Lost Leader* (London: Sidgwick and Jackson, 1971); C. Younger, *A State of Disunion: Arthur Griffith, Michael Collins, James Craig, Eamon de Valera* (London: Muller, 1972); P. Joannon, *Michael Collins, La Naissance de L'I.R.A.* (Paris: La Table Ronde, 1978); R. Faligot, *James Connolly et le mouvement révolutionnaire irlandais* (Paris: F. Maspéro, 1978); L. O Broin, *Michael Collins* (Dublin: Gill and Macmillan, 1980); T. Ryle Dwyer, *Michael Collins and the Treaty: His Differences with de Valera* (Cork: Mercier Press, 1981); J. M. Feehan, *The Shooting of Michael Collins: Murder or Accident?* (Dublin and Cork: Mercier Press, 1981); L. O Broin (ed.), *In Great Haste. The Letters of Michael Collins and Kitty Kiernan* (Dublin: Gill and Macmillan, 1983); P. O'Braon, *Miceál Ó Coileáin* (Mainistir na Corann: Eigse na Mainistreach, 1985); T. Ryle Dwyer, *Michael Collins: The Man Who Won the War* (Cork: Mercier Press, 1990); Padraic O'Farrell, *Break the Green Bough* (Dublin: Glendale Press, 1990).

Eamon de Valera

LIFE. Born in New York in 1882, de Valera was reared in Bruree, Co. Limerick and educated at Charleville Christian Brothers School, Co. Cork, Blackrock College, Dublin and University College, Dublin. He taught mathematics at Rockwell, Belvedere and Carysfort Colleges and lectured at the Royal University. In 1908 he joined the Gaelic League, where he met his future wife, Sinéad Ní Fhlanagáin. de Valera fought in the 1916 Rising as commandant of the Irish Volunteers at Boland's Mills. His death-sentence was commuted to life imprisonment; he was released in 1917 and was elected Sinn Féin MP for East Clare, a seat he held until 1959. He was president of Sinn Féin 1917–26 and president of the Volunteers 1917–22. de Valera drafted the anti-conscription pledge of 1918, was arrested on 17 May of that year but escaped from Lincoln Prison in February 1919. He was elected President of the first Dáil Éireann in April 1919 and later that year went to the USA to secure recognition of the Republic and to float the Dáil Éireann external loan. While in the USA he became involved in a complicated dispute with some of the Irish-American leaders. He returned to Ireland in 1921 and, after fruitless negotiations with James Craig and Lloyd George, won the support of his cabinet for his demand for a form of external association with Britain rather than the dominion status that was on offer. After the Treaty negotiations of 1921, he refused to accept what the negotiators in London had brought home, offering instead in Document no. 2 his version of external association. When the Dail approved the Treaty, he resigned the Presidency and was narrowly defeated by Arthur Griffith in a new election for that position. He formed a new political party, Clann na Poblachta, and refused to recognize the authority of the Provisional Government. The Civil War followed. After the ceasefire on 27 May 1923, de Valera was arrested by Free State troops and was held until July 1924. After his release he entered Northern Ireland and was arrested and held in solitary confinement for a month. In 1926 he founded Fianna Fáil, of which he was president 1926–59. In the general election of 1927, Fianna Fáil increased its strength, found a way of dismissing the oath of allegiance as an empty formula and eventually gained power in 1932. In 1933, another election gave Fianna Fáil the added strength to move against the fascist Blueshirt party: de Valera was supported in this by the IRA. But in 1936 he outlawed the IRA. He was President of the Council of the League of Nations in 1932, favoured non-intervention in the Spanish Civil War of 1936–39, supported Chamberlain's appeasement policy towards Hitler, and produced a new Constitution in 1937. In 1938, the Economic War with Britain came to an end and the Treaty ports were returned to Ireland. Despite severe pressures from the allied powers, de Valera successfully pursued a policy of neutrality during World War II. In 1948 his party was defeated in the general election; de Valera returned to power in 1951, lost the election of 1954 and returned to power in 1957 for the last time. He retired from the office of Taoiseach in 1959 and won the Presidential election in that year. He was again elected President in 1966 and retired from office in 1973. He died in Dublin in 1975.

CHIEF WRITINGS. M. Moynihan (ed.) *Speeches and Statements of Eamon de Valera 1917–73* (Dublin: Gill and Macmillan, 1980).

BIOGRAPHY AND CRITICISM. S. O'Faoláin, *The Life Story of Eamon de Valera* (Dublin: The Talbot Press, 1953); F. A. Pakenham, the Earl of Longford, and T. P. O'Neill, *Eamon de Valera* (Dublin: Gill and Macmillan, 1970); B. Severn, *Irish Statesman and Rebel: The Two Lives of Eamon de Valera* (Folkestone: Bailey Bros and Swinfen, 1971); S. Cronin (ed.), *The McGarrity Papers: Revelations of the Irish Revolutionary Movement in Ireland and America 1900–1940* (Tralee: Brandon Books, 1972); T. R. Dwyer, *Eamon de Valera* (Dublin: Gill and Macmillan, 1980); *De Valera's Darkest Hour: In Search of National Independence, 1919–1932*, *De Valera's Finest Hour: In Search of National Independence 1932–1959* (Dublin and Cork: Mercier Press, 1982); J. Lee and G. O. Tuathaigh (eds), *The Age of de Valera* (Dublin: Ward River Press, in association with RTE, 1982); J. Bowman, *De Valera and the Ulster Question 1917–73* (Oxford: Clarendon Press, 1982); J. P. O'Carroll and J. A. Murphy (eds), *De Valera and his Times: Political Development in the Republic of Ireland* (Cork: Cork University Press, 1983).

Frank Ryan

LIFE. Born near Elton, Co. Limerick in 1902, Ryan was educated at University College, Dublin and interrupted his studies there to fight on the republican side in the Civil War. In 1925 he graduated in Celtic Studies and worked as a teacher and for the Irish Tourist Association. He became a member of the IRA executive and editor of the movement's newspaper, *An Phoblacht*. He was arrested for his activities. In 1931 he helped found and organize Saor Éire, a left-wing movement within the IRA, and in 1934 broke with the IRA in an effort to build a united front against fascism. In 1936 Ryan led 200 Irishmen to fight in Spain in the International Brigade. He reached the rank of major, was wounded at the battle of Jarama, returned home to convalesce, stood, unsuccessfully, as a republican candidate in the general election of 1937, and returned to Spain to become brigade-adjutant to General Maija, the commander of the Spanish Republican Army. Ryan edited the history of the brigade. In 1938, he was captured by Italian forces and sentenced to death. de Valera appealed to General Franco for clemency and a nationwide campaign was launched on his behalf. After 13 months in prison under sentence of death, the judgment was commuted to 30 years. One year later, as a result of an arrangement between the Irish, Spanish and German governments, Ryan was released and taken to Berlin. There, in 1940, he met Seán Russell, chief-of-staff of the IRA, and left for Ireland with him in a German submarine. Russell died suddenly on the journey, Ryan returned to Berlin where he was treated by German intelligence as a non-party neutral. He died in a sanatorium in Dresden in 1944.

CHIEF WRITINGS. *The Book of the XV Brigade: Records of British, Canadian and Irish Volunteers in the XV International Brigade in Spain 1936–1938* (Madrid: Commissariat of War, 1938; reprinted Newcastle-upon-Tyne: Graham, 1975).

BIOGRAPHY AND CRITICISM. S. Cronin, *Frank Ryan: The Search for the Republic* (Dublin: Repsol, 1980).

George Gilmore

LIFE. Born in Belfast in 1898, Gilmore was educated locally and in Dublin, where he spent most of his life. He opposed the Treaty after the War of Independence and was secretary to Seán Lemass during the Civil War. As a member of the army council of the IRA, he founded the left-wing splinter group, Saor Éire, along with Peadar O'Donnell and Frank Ryan. He tried to come to an arrangement with the Soviet Union for the training of IRA officers, was imprisoned several times for his activities by Free State forces, led a raid on Mountjoy jail in Dublin in 1926 and rescued nineteen republican prisoners. He was jailed for five years in 1931 and began a campaign for political status. In 1932 he was released when de Valera's Fianna Fáil party came into office and later that year was wounded in a gun battle with police in County Clare. He and Frank Ryan split with the IRA and organized a short-lived Citizens' Army. Gilmore was the leading member of the Irish Republican Congress (1933–34) and remained all his life an outright opponent of fascism and all forms of colonial and sectarian oppression. He died in Dublin in 1985.

CHIEF WRITINGS. *The Irish Republican Congress* (New York: Socialist League, 1935; reprinted Cork: Cork Workers Club, 1974); *Labour and the Republican Movement* (Dublin: Republican Publications, 1966).

Michael Tierney

LIFE. Born in Ballymacward, Co. Galway in 1894, Tierney won a travelling studentship at University College, Dublin and studied classics at the Sorbonne, Athens and Berlin. In 1915 he joined the department of classics at University College, Dublin and became professor of Greek there in 1923. He was elected TD for North Mayo in 1925 as a member of Cumann na nGaedheal and was TD for the National University of Ireland from 1927 to 1932. He was elected to the reconstituted Senate in 1938 and was vice-chairman of the Senate 1939–44. In 1947 he was elected president of University College, Dublin, a position he held until his retirement in 1964. During his presidency he made the decision to move the university from its city centre location to Belfield, four miles away. He died in Dublin in 1975.

CHIEF WRITINGS. (ed.) *A Tribute to Newman: Essays on Aspects of his Life and Thought* (Dublin: Browne and Nolan, 1945); *Daniel O'Connell: Nine Centenary Essays* (Dublin: Browne and Nolan, 1949); (with others) *Newman's Doctrine of University Education* (Dublin: University College, Dublin, 1952); *Struggle With Fortune: A Miscellany for the Centenary of the Catholic University of Ireland 1854–1954* (Dublin: Browne and Nolan, 1954); F. X. Martin (ed.), *Eoin MacNeill: Scholar and Man of Action 1867–1945* (Oxford: Clarendon Press, 1980).

John A. Costello

LIFE. Born in Dublin in 1891, Costello was educated at University College, Dublin and at King's Inns. Called to the Bar in 1914, he became Attorney General in 1926, a position he held for six years. In

1933 he was elected to the Dáil for County Dublin. In February 1948, he became Taoiseach of the inter-party government and in September of that year, while on a state visit to Canada, issued the Declaration of the Republic, thus repealing the External Relations Act with Britain. The Republic was formally inaugurated on Easter Monday 1949. The government was split over the Mother and Child scheme, introducd by Dr Noel Browne. Soon after Browne resigned, a general election was called in June 1951. Fianna Fáil returned to power, but in the election of May 1954, the coalition government regained power and Costello became Taoiseach again. In 1957, Fianna Fáil, under de Valera, won the general election. Costello returned to his bar practice. He had been made a member of the Royal Irish Academy in 1948 and in 1975 was made a Freeman of the City of Dublin. He died in Dublin in 1976.

Garret FitzGerald

LIFE. Born in Dublin in 1926, FitzGerald was educated at University College, Dublin and King's Inns. He worked for the national airline, Aer Lingus, as research and schedules manager before becoming a lecturer in the department of political economy at University College, Dublin (1959–73). He was economic affairs correspondent for the BBC and various London journals and newspapers. He was managing director of the Economist Intelligence Unit of Ireland (1961–67), a Senator (1965–69), and became Fine Gael TD for Dublin South-East in 1969. In 1973 he became Minister for Foreign Affairs in the coalition government and was President of the EC Council of Ministers, January-June 1975. In 1971 he became leader of Fine Gael and was Taoiseach June 1981-March 1982 and again December 1982-March 1987. He launched his 'constitutional crusade' in 1981 and was one of the leading figures in the New Ireland Forum of 1983. He and Margaret Thatcher were co-signatories to the Anglo-Irish Agreement in November 1985.

He is a son of Desmond FitzGerald, Minister for External Affairs in the Provisional Government; Minister for External Affairs and later Minister for Defence in the Executive Councils up to 1932.

CHIEF WRITINGS. *State-Sponsored Bodies* (Dublin: Institute of Public Administration, 1959); *Planning in Ireland* (Dublin: Institute of Public Administration; London: Political and Economic Planning, 1968); *Towards A New Ireland* (London: Charles Knight & Co; Dublin: Torc Books, 1972).; *Unequal Partners* (UNCTAD, 1979).

BIOGRAPHY AND CRITICISM. R. Smith, *Garret: The Enigma. Dr Garret FitzGerald* (Dublin: Aherlow Publishers, 1985); J. Dooge (ed.), *Ireland in the Contemporary World. Essays in Honour of Garret FitzGerald* (Dublin: Gill and Macmillan, 1986); S. O'Byrne, *Hiding behind a Face: Fine Gael under Garret FitzGerald* (Dublin: Gill and Macmillan, 1986).

Charles J. Haughey

LIFE. Born in Castlebar, Co. Mayo in 1925, Haughey was educated at University College, Dublin and at King's Inns. He was a founder of the accountancy firm Haughey and Boland (1950). In 1951 he married Maureen Lemass, daughter of Seán Lemass. He was elected as Fianna Fail TD for Dublin North-East in 1957, becoming Minister for Justice (1961–64), Minister for Agriculture and Fisheries (1964–66), Minister for Finance (1966–70). In 1969 he introduced tax exemption on the literary earnings of creative writers. In 1970 he was arrested on charges of conspiring to import arms. Acquitted, he began a long rehabilitation in the Fianna Fáil party, becoming Minister for Health and Social Welfare (1977–79). He was Taoiseach December 1979-June 1981, March-December 1982, March 1987-June 1989, and again in July 1989.

CHIEF WRITINGS. M. Mansergh (ed.), *The Spirit of the Nation. The Speeches and Statements of C. J. Haughey 1957–1986* (Cork and Dublin: Mercier Press, 1986).

BIOGRAPHY AND CRITICISM. R. Smith, *Charles J. Haughey: The Survivor* (Dublin: Aherlow Publishers, 1983); J. Joyce and P. Murtagh, *The Boss: Charles J. Haughey in Government* (Swords, Co. Dublin: Poolbeg Pres, 1983); J. M. Feehan, *The Statesman: A Study of the Role of Charles J. Haughey in the Ireland of Tomorrow* (Cork: Mercier Press, 1985); R. Smith, *Haughey and O'Malley: The Quest for Power* (Dublin: Aherlow Publishers, 1986); T. Ryle Dwyer, *Charlie. The Political Biography of Charles J. Haughey* (Dublin: Gill and Macmillan, 1987).

John Hume

LIFE. Born in Derry City in 1937, John Hume was educated at St Columb's College, St Patrick's College, Maynooth and at Queen's University, Belfast. He taught for some years in Derry, engaged in business, founded a housing association and a credit union in Derry, and was president of the Credit Union League of Ireland 1964–68. He became a member of the Northern Ireland Civil Rights Association and vice-chairman of the Derry Citizens' Action Committee 1968–69. He was elected MP for Foyle at Stormont, 1969–73, was a founder-member and deputy chairman of the Social Democratic Labour Party (SDLP) 1970, was elected to the power-sharing Assembly of Northern Ireland (1973–74) and became Minister of Commerce in the power-sharing Executive (January-May 1974). He held his seat in the election to the Convention to draft a constitution (1975–76). He took up a position in the Commission of the European Community and in June 1979 was elected to represent Northern Ireland in the first directly elected European Parliament. He was elected leader of the SDLP in 1979, MP for Foyle at Westminster in 1983 and was one of the architects of the New Ireland Forum in 1983. He has been one of the most influential defenders of the Anglo-Irish Agreement of 1985.

BIOGRAPHY AND CRITICISM. B. White, *John Hume: Statesman of the Troubles* (Belfast: Blackstaff Press, 1984).

Seán MacBride

LIFE. Born in Paris in 1904, the son of Maud Gonne, the beloved of Yeats, and of Major John MacBride, executed in 1916. He was educated in Paris and Dublin and at University College, Dublin. He opposed the Treaty, fought in the Irish Civil War on the republican side, helped organize the first Saor Éire convention and was chief of staff of the IRA 1936–38. After the Constitution of 1937 was passed, he severed his connection with the IRA, protesting against the bombing campaign in England in 1939. In 1937 he was called to the bar and defended many republicans charged under the emergency legislation acts of the period. In 1946 he founded a political party, Clann na Poblachta, and joined with Fine Gael and others to form the first inter-party government, in which he was Minister for External Affairs (1948–51). When MacBride demanded the resignation of Dr Noel Browne over the Mother and Child Scheme, the government fell soon afterwards. In 1956 he proposed a 'no confidence' vote in the second inter-party government because of the emergency measures it introduced that year to deal with the IRA campaign in the North. With Fianna Fáil's support, the government was brought down. He was secretary-general of the International Commission of Jurists 1963–70, and a founder-member and sometime chairman of Amnesty International. He won the Nobel Peace Prize in 1976 and the Lenin Peace Prize in 1977. He drew up the 'MacBride Principles' that were designed to prevent firms in the United States from investing in sectarianized firms in Northern Ireland. He died in Dublin in 1988.

CHIEF WRITINGS. *Civil Liberty* (Dublin: Irish Co-operative Society, 1947); *Our People — Our Money* (Dublin: Browne and Nolan, 1949); *A Message to the Irish People* (Cork: Mercier Press, 1985).

Gerry Adams

LIFE. Born in Belfast of republican stock in 1948, Adams was educated locally. He became actively involved in Sinn Féin in the mid–1960s, in the newly formed Republican Clubs in 1965 and in the Wolfe Tone Societies, the West Belfast Housing Action Committee and the Northern Ireland Civil Rights Association. He was imprisoned on the *Maidstone* prison ship in Belfast in 1972. Later, after the split with the Official IRA, he became president of Provisional Sinn Féin. He has been Westminster MP for West Belfast since 1987.

CHIEF WRITINGS. *Falls Memories* (Dingle: Brandon Books, 1982); *The Politics of Irish Freedom* (Dingle: Brandon Books, 1986); *Cage Eleven* (Dingle: Brandon Books, 1990).

EOGHAN Ó hANLUAIN, *Editor*

Irish Writing: Prose Fiction and Poetry 1900-1988

At the end of the nineteenth century there seemed little likelihood of a revitalization of literary activity in Irish. The language had continued to decline from the middle of the century: from 1851 to 1891 the number of Irish speakers had dropped from 1,500,000 to about 680,000. The Famine and its aftermath had been calamitous for the Irish language and the literary tradition. That a vital literature should emerge at this time was quite against the tide of social, political and economic circumstances. Since the late eighteenth century, however, there had been among the cultured members of the ascendancy an increasing interest in Irish antiquities and in early Irish history and literature in particular. Various societies throughout the early nineteenth century had fostered a study of Ireland's past and with it an interest in the language that was the key to that past. Among these were the Gaelic Society (1806), the Iberno-Celtic Society (1818) and the Ossianic Society (1853); they were antiquarian in outlook and focussed on Ireland's past and its earlier literature. However, towards the end of the century the increasing awareness of national identity and the movement to national self-assertion were accompanied by a resurgent concern for the living language. With the foundation of the Society for the Preservation of the Irish Language in 1876, attention was firmly focussed on the spoken language and on the need to preserve and cultivate it. The publication of *Irisleabhar na Gaedhilge* (*The Gaelic Journal*) in 1882 was a milestone and is generally recognized as signalling the renewal of literary activity in Irish. It announced itself as 'exclusively devoted to the preservation and cultivation of the Irish language' and as a platform for those 'anxious to work for the production of a modern Gaelic literature'. The Gaelic League, founded in 1893, reiterated these ideals and became a widespread popular movement, sending large numbers on a pilgrimage of rediscovery of Irish music, customs, traditions, history and, above all, of the spoken Irish language. This reawakened interest created a demand for reading matter and, so, when it had appeared that the language and its literary tradition were about to disappear, writing in Irish was taken up again with enthusiasm. This was greatly encouraged in 1897 by the initiation of the Oireachtas, a cultural festival that offered literary prizes and provided a focal point for all kinds of literary endeavour.

In the pages of *The Gaelic Journal* and later in *An Claidheamh Soluis* (*The Sword of Light*), first published in 1899, the initial steps were taken that would facilitate the development of the new writing: problems of spelling, grammar and style were addressed that would take years and much controversy to resolve. But with *The Gaelic Journal* had begun what Douglas Hyde (1860-1949), a founder of the Gaelic League, called 'the revival and cultivation of the modern language'.

The notion of literary composition no longer existed in the Irish-speaking areas, although the tradition of storytelling still flourished; and so the first attempts at creating a literature fell to those who were acquainted with the written literature of English and other languages. The first and most influential writer with regard to style and subject matter was Canon Peter O'Leary (1839-1920), a native speaker from west Cork who late in life was attracted by the Gaelic League. His novel, *Séadna*, an extended retelling of the folktale of the man who sells his soul to the devil, began serialization in *The Gaelic Journal* in 1894 and came out in book form in 1904. It immediately captivated the new readers of Irish with its vivid descriptions of rural life and racy dialogue, but, besides, it resolved a problem that had arisen as soon as the language began to be written again. Since there were three dominant dialects still spoken, in Munster, Connacht and Ulster, it had been argued that prose writers should revive the classical literary language exemplified by the seventeenth-century historian Geoffrey Keating (Seathrún Céitinn) (*c.*1580-*c.*1644). *Séadna*, however, determined that the spoken language, no matter which dialect, should prevail.

It was fortunate for the emergent literature that two other writers were now at hand who, besides being dedicated practitioners, also had a keen literary sense, namely Patrick Pearse (1879-1916) and Pádraic Ó Conaire (1882-1928). Pearse, who at the time was editing the Gaelic League weekly *An Claidheamh Soluis*, had welcomed *Séadna* enthusiastically: 'The appearance of *Séadna* marks an epoch, for with it Ireland has once again become creative.' But he, along with Ó Conaire, knew that the idealized rural culture that O'Leary had celebrated in *Séadna* was too limiting a concept for contemporary taste. Pearse wrote what amounted to a manifesto for writers of his time: 'We lay down the proposition that a living modern literature cannot be built up on the folktale. The folktale is an echo of old mythologies, an unconscious stringing together of old memories and fancies: literature is a deliberate criticism of life . . . we would have our literature modern not only in the sense of freely borrowing every modern form which it does not possess and which it is capable of assimilating, but also in texture, tone and outlook. This is the twentieth century and no literature can take root in the twentieth century which is not of the twentieth century.' (*An Claidheamh Soluis*, 26 May 1906)

Pádraic Ó Conaire re-echoed these propositions two years later: 'The world of that ancient literature is long gone. It delights us to read it and always will but it will not blossom again. It reflected the world of its time. But we live in a more complex world and new methods and a new metaphysic are needed to explore and express it.' (*An Claidheamh Soluis*, 12 December 1908)

While Pearse's literary intelligence pointed the direction for a contemporary literature untrammelled by a pedantic concern with traditional form, his own stories, though finely crafted, are mostly confined to a simple and idealistic depiction of the people of Ros Muc in Conamara whom he had come to know and hold in deep affection. In the essay quoted above, he had exhorted Irish writers to deal with the problems of the day — 'the loves and hates and desires of modern man and woman . . . the drink evil, the increase of lunacy, the loveless marriage'. However, we find none of this in his stories, whereas these problems are the constant themes of Ó Conaire, who admitted his debt to Pearse's example in matters of form and technique. Both writers perceived how suitable the short story was to a literature finding its feet again, which was confined mainly to periodicals and whose readers were mostly learners of the language. The impetus given to the short story by Pearse and Ó Conaire has been maintained and it remains the form most consistently exploited by writers of fiction in Irish.[1]

The short stories in Irish of Liam Ó Flaithearta (1896-1984) are collected in one volume, *Dúil* (1953). The poet Seán Ó Ríordáin wrote of it in his journal: 'I have read some stories by Liam Ó Flaithearta and sensed that some living thing had been caught between the covers. If you held a robin and felt it quiver in your hands you would know what I felt when reading Liam Ó Flaithearta's Irish' (translation). In *An Chulaith Nua* (The New Suit) Ó Flaithearta describes through the amazed eyes of a young boy the rituals of shearing, bleaching, teasing, carding, spinning, weaving and tailoring. He focuses on a sequence of everyday events that conveys a whole way of life. While the reader is entertained by the lively dialogue of the characters in the foreground, he is aware of a tapestry of immemorial conventions being unfolded.

The five volumes of stories by Máirtín Ó Cadhain (1906-70) give substance to the tradition of the short story in Irish. *An Bhearna Mhíl* (The Harelip) is exemplary of much of his fiction, in that it combines the telling of a simple story of young love blighted by ineluctable social convention with his passionate concern to explore and exploit the

1. For an account of the short story, see Aisling Ní Dhonnchadha, *An Gearrscéal sa Ghaeilge 1890-1940* (Baile Átha Cliath: An Clóchomhar, 1982); Pádraig Breatnach, 'An Gearrscéal sa Ghaeilge le Blianta Beaga Anuas', *Comhar*, Lúnasa 1984.

resources of the Irish language. Liam Ó Flaithearta had advised him to prune his writing mercilessly, but Ó Cadhain's purpose to remould the language and the natural convolutions of his imagination determined his distinctive style.

Seosamh Mac Grianna (1901-90) is one of two writer brothers — Séamus Ó Grianna (1891-1969) is the other — who came from a family of traditional storytellers in the Irish-speaking area of Ranafast in west Donegal. While Séamus was the more prolific, Seosamh was more imaginative and experimental and he excels in his descriptions of characters in their native landscape, rooted in a community yet distinctly individual. The harrowing *Ar an Trá Fhoilimh* (On the Barren Shore) is an evocative reshaping of an incident of the Great Famine 1845-49.

The development of the short story in contemporary writing is best exemplified by Seán Mac Mathúna (born 1936) and Alan Titley (born 1947). Each has an extraordinary mastery of language and an original viewpoint. Although Mac Mathúna is an accomplished realist in many of his stories, there is a lyric impulse in his writing that is given its head in *Gadaithe* (Thieves) which explores the profound sense of loss involved in the death of a language. Alan Titley in *An Sísceál de réir Eoin* (The Gobspiel according to John) characteristically presents a mischievous and subversive view of language and literary conventions and writes from deep within what he has called 'the Irish word hoard.' His exuberance of language sets off a darkly comic perception of things.

The novel in modern Irish was established by O'Leary's *Séadna* and taken in an entirely new and exciting direction by Ó Conaire in his *Deoraíocht* (Exile) (1910), a tale of alienation and despair set in London, a world away from the cosy fireside setting of O'Leary. However, in the novel there is no comparable tradition to that of the short story, each writer making a new beginning in style and subject. The pre-eminent achievement here has been *Cré na Cille* (The Clay of the Churchyard) (1949) by Máirtín Ó Cadhain, a long work composed entirely in dialogue spoken by the 'residents' of a graveyard in Conamara. There has, however, been a considerable experimental working of the form in the last twenty years by such as Eoghan Ó Tuairisc (1919-82), Breandán Ó Doibhlin (born 1931), Diarmaid Ó Súilleabháin (1932-85), Alan Titley, Séamus Mac Annaidh (born 1964), and Breandán Ó hEithir (born 1930).[2]

The increasing interest in the Irish language in the early years of this century brought learners and scholars to those regions where the language still flourished. One lasting result of this cultural intercourse was that native speakers were encouraged to write accounts of their lives and of their communities. Two remarkable examples of this are the autobiographies of two natives of the Great Blasket Island off the west Kerry coast: *An tOileánach* (*The Islandman*) (1929) by Tomás Ó Crohan (1855-1937) and *Fiche Blian ag Fás* (*Twenty Years A-Growing*) (1933) by Maurice O'Sullivan (1904-50). Each has left a graphic and moving account of a way of life now vanished forever, and *An tOileánach* in particular, in its unique fusion of subject and style, is an abiding presence in the Irish literary imagination.

We must return to Patrick Pearse to see the beginnings of modern poetry in Irish. Thomas MacDonagh (1878-1916) wrote of Pearse's *Suantraidhe agus Goltraidhe* (1914): 'The production of this is already a success for the new literature'.[3] He may have been over-optimistic in his assessment of Pearse's poetry, but Pearse was the first competent poet of the Revival to speak with a contemporary voice and MacDonagh recognized this. This slight volume of poems reflected Pearse's critical precept that distinguished between traditional and folk literature, on the one hand, and the new approach necessary for the creation of a modern literature. Pearse's lyrics stand alone as the only significant work in poetry up to the early 1940s. Many applied themselves to the craft of poetry during the intervening period, but all seem in retrospect to have been waiting for the emergence of original talent.

The early 1940s saw a quickening of literary activity that can be attributed to some extent to external factors, such as the teaching of Irish and Irish literature in the schools and the consequent emergence of a generation who took literature in

2. For the development of the novel in Irish, see Seán Ó Tuama, 'The Other Tradition: Some Highlights of Modern Fiction in Irish' in Patrick Rafroídí and Maurice Harmon (eds), *The Irish Novel in Our Time* (Lille, 1976); Aisling Ní Dhonnchadha, 'Urscéalaíocht na Gaeilge 1974-1984', *Comhar*, Lúnasa 1984; Breandán Ó Doibhlin, 'Smaointe ar chúrsaí na próslitríochta', *Comhar*, Lúnasa 1984; Tadhg Ó Dúshláine, 'An Coimpléasc priompallánach', *Comhar*, Nollaig 1987.
3. *Literature in Ireland* (Dublin: The Talbot Press, 1916), p. 145.

Irish for granted, the re-establishment of the Oireachtas literary competitions in 1939 and the founding of the magazine *Comhar* in 1942, and of the new Gaelic League journal *Feasta* in 1948. What marked those years as a new beginning in poetry, however, was the fact that Máirtín Ó Direáin, Seán Ó Ríordáin and Máire Mhac an tSaoi began, opportunely, to write almost simultaneously. While each of these wrote in an individual vein, their writings taken together realized the desire for an authentic modern voice in Irish poetry.

Máirtín Ó Direáin (1910-88) has been the most productive poet in Irish during the past fifty years. His work shows a progression from nostalgic recollections of life on the Aran Islands to the use of the uncompromising landscape of his youth to explore the urban environment of later years and to affirm his commitment to poetry.

With Seán Ó Ríordáin (1916-77) one is aware of being at a frontier both of language and sensibility. The interaction of these has produced poems, at times elusive and obscure, but his extension of both language and sensibility marks one of the finer achievements in Irish writing.

One wishes that Máire Mhac an tSaoi (born 1922) had written more. The scope of her early work is confined, but her common themes of friendship, love and sexual relations are treated in her best poems with a passionate intensity. Her collected poems, *An Cion Go Dtí Seo* (1987), reveals a wider range of concern and a sustained fluency of style.

Nuabhéarsaíocht (1950) is the best introduction to the verse of the 1940s. This anthology, edited by Seán Ó Tuama (born 1926), indicated the new vitality in Irish poetry. Since the publication of *Nuabhéarsaíocht*, Ó Tuama as lecturer and critic has had a pervasive influence on writing in Irish, and his own verse, elegiac, celebratory and ironic in turn, is always elegantly made.

Eoghan Ó Tuairisc, prose writer, dramatist and poet both in English and Irish, is one of the great exemplary craftsmen of modern Irish writing. In his '*Aifreann na Marbh*' (Mass for the Dead), in memory of the dead of Hiroshima, he brings to bear a modernist temperament and a creative responsiveness to the Irish literary tradition.

Brendan Behan (1923-64) and Pearse Hutchinson (born 1927) are better known in English, but both found in Irish the medium for some of their most passionate expressions.

Michael Hartnett (born 1941) since 1975 has brought a new excitement to poetry in Irish and his imaginative resourcefulness in his 'resumed' language is remarkable.

The younger poets represented below had been introduced to the earlier 'moderns', such as Ó Ríordáin and Ó Direáin, at school and had read them later at college. They have assimilated them and now speak in their individual voices. Since the early 1970s the main forum for poetry in Irish has been the journal *Innti* which began as a broadsheet in University College, Cork in 1970. It is in the pages of *Innti*, under the discerning editorship of its founding editor, Michael Davitt (born 1950), that the course of modern poetry in Irish in recent years can be most clearly observed.

PEADAR UA LAOGHAIRE (CANON PETER O'LEARY)

(1839-1920)

from: SÉADNA (1904)

[*Séadna* is a retelling of the folktale of the man who sells his soul to the devil. O'Leary had heard a version of the story as a child and elaborated it in serialized form between 1894 and 1903. It is remarkable for its vivid descriptions of rural life in the mid-nineteenth century. The following excerpt, Chapter 28, tells of the origin of the fairy music played at a wedding feast. The translation, authorized by O'Leary, but not attributed, is from *Séadna* (Dublin: Irish Book Company, 1916).]

CAIBIDEAL A hOCHT IS FICHE

Sara raibh an lá glan i gceart bhí an chuideachta scaipithe agus na daoine imithe abhaile ach amháin an tincéir mór agus fear an cheoil sí agus Micil agus a mháthair. Bhí an ceathrar san ar a ndícheall ag glanadh an tí agus ag cur gach ní ina áit féin. Bhí an ceol sí ag déanamh buartha do Mhicil. Bhí ana-dhúil aige a dhéanamh amach conas a fuair an píobaire sin an ceol sí. D'fhair sé go bhfuair sé lom air agus chuir sé an cheist chuige.

'Cogar, a Sheáin,' ar seisean. 'Is iúntach an ceol é sin a sheinnis aréir dúinn. Níor airíos a leithéid riamh. Ní dóigh liom go bhfuil fear eile in Éirinn d'fhéadfadh an ceol san do sheinnt.'

Níor lig Seán air gur airigh sé é.

'Is dócha,' arsa Micil, 'nach é gach aoinne a fhéadfadh ceol mar é dh'fháil in aon chor. Conas a fuairis-se an ceol san, a Sheáin?'

'Dein t'iarraidh thort, a Mhicil!' arsa Seán.

Níor chuir sin Micil ón scéal. D'fhan sé go dtí go raibh Seán imithe agus ansan dúirt sé leis an dtincéir mór: 'Stad, a Phádraig,' ar seisean, 'go n-ithir rud éigin, tar éis na hoíche.'

Níor mheas Pádraig go ndéanfadh san aon cheataí dhó, agus d'fhan sé.

Ar ball, nuair a bhí rud ite ag Pádraig agus braon eile fiona ólta aige, dúirt Micil, 'e mhaoil an bháige dhó féin, mar dhea: 'A Phádraig,' ar seisean, 'nárbh uafásach an ceol é siúd a bhí aréir againn! Níor airíos a leithéid riamh, agus is minic d'airíos ceol breá. Mara mbeadh mo dhá shúil a bheith ag féachaint air agus mo dhá chluais a bheith ag éisteacht leis ní chreidfinn go bhféadfadh aon duine saolta a leithéid de cheol a bhaint a píb.'

'Agus ní fhéadfadh leis, mara bhfaigheadh sé cúnamh chuige,' arsa Pádraig. 'Nár thugais fé ndeara an tsí gaoithe! Agus nár airís na glórtha daonna, agus an gol, agus an gáirí, agus an liacharnach? Ní túisce a thosnaigh an ceol ná a bhíodar ag bailiú isteach chughainn. Geallaim dhuit gur dóigh liom gur mó go mór a bhí ann díobh, ag rince leis an gceol, ná mar a bhí ann againn féin. Thosnaíodar ar imeacht nuair a bhí glaoch an choiligh ag druidim leo. Agus féach mar a stad an píobaire díreach sarar ghlaoigh an coileach. Is mór an iúnadh liom ná beirid siad leo an píobaire. Dá mbeinn ina chás ní sheinnfinn an ceol san pé tathant a déanfaí orm chuige. B'fhearra dhó go mór ciall a bheith aige. "Ní thagann an crúiscín slán ón dtobar i gcónaí."'

'Ní fheadar 'en tsaol conas a fuair sé an ceol san, nó conas a tháinig sé suas leis,' arsa Micil.

'Is minic an cheist sin dá chur chuige,' arsa Pádraig, 'agus ní faightar d'fhreagra uaidh choíche uirthi ach "dein t'iarraidh thort".'

'Im briathar mhóide,' arsa Micil, 'gur chuireas-sa chuige ó chianaibh í agus gurb shin é díreach an freagra a thug sé orm. 'Dein t'iarraidh thort, a Mhicil,' ar seisean liom.'

'D'airíos-sa,' arsa Pádraig, 'gurb amhlaidh a bhí sé ag teacht abhaile ó Chorcaigh oíche agus píb nua ceannaithe aige, agus gur cuireadh amú é, bíodh go raibh togha na haithne aige ar an áit. Ag déanamh i leith ar Dhroichead na dTruip Sí is ea a chuaigh sé amú. Tháinig an meascán mearaí air agus d'fhéach sé ina thimpall, agus is amhlaidh a fuair sé é féin ná ar bhruach abhann, in áit nár luigh a shúil riamh air! D'iniúch sé an talamh féna chosaibh, agus scairt a bhí ina aice ann, agus pluais charraige a bhí ann, féachaint an aithneodh sé iad, agus níor aithin. Lena linn sin d'airigh sé, ar an dtaobh eile den abhainn, an ceol ba bhreátha dár airigh sé riamh. Cad deirir leis nár ghléas suas an phíb nua agus nár chrom ar an gceol gcéanna do sheinnt, in éineacht leis an gceolaí thall! Bhí an scairt láidir riamh aige. Ní chuirfeadh a bhfuil de shíofraíbh in Éirinn eagla air. Ar leagadh na súl bhí an inse ar bruach na habhann lán de dhaoine agus iad ag gluaiseacht anonn is anall i measc a chéile, fé mar a bheadh saghas éigin rince ar siúl acu. Ba ghearr gur hathraíodh an ceol thall. Má deineadh, do chuaigh an fear abhus ar an athrú gan stad gan barrthuisle, gan buille a chailliúint. Do casadh an ceol thall an tarna huair. Ba mhaith an mhaise ag an bhfear abhus é, bhí sé istigh ar an gcasadh an túisce ina raibh an casadh déanta.

'In aghaidh gach casadh agus athrú dá dtéadh ar an gceol théadh a chothrom d'athrú ar ghluaiseacht na ndaoine, nó ar an rince, má ba rince é. Do lean an scéal mar sin eatarthu, ar dhá thaobh na habhann, go dtí tráth éigin amach san oíche. Ní cuimhin leis conas do scar sé leo, ach nuair a tháinig an lá is amhlaidh a dhúisigh sé as a chodladh agus é istigh i súil tiníleach a bhí ar thaobh an bhóthair ann, agus an phíb nua ina aice. Ní túisce a bhí sé ina lándúiseacht ná a ghaibh sé air an phíb agus a chrom sé ar an gceol do sheinnt arís, díreach fé mar a sheinn sé san oíche é. Do sheinn sé ó thosach go deireadh é, arís agus arís, agus chuir sé isteach go cruinn ann gach casadh agus iompáil agus athrú, fé mar a cuireadh ann iad san oíche dhó nuair a bhíothas á sheinnt ar an dtaobh thall den abhainn, go dtí go raibh sé ar eolas aige de ghlanmheabhair agus nár bhaol dó aon chuid de do dhearmhad go deo. Nuair a bhí a aigne sásta aige air d'éirigh sé ina shuí agus tháinig sé amach a súil na tiníleach agus d'fhéach sé ina thimpall. Bhí an bóthar agus na claitheacha lán de dhaoinibh mórthimpall na tiníleach. Bhíodair ag bailiú ann an fhaid a bhí an ceol aige dá sheinnt chun taithí a dhéanamh de. Fé mar a thagadh duine nó beirt do stadaidís ag éisteacht leis an gceol go dtí go raibh an áit lán díobh. Bhí iúnadh agus alltacht orthu, mar bhí a fhios acu go n-airítí an ceol céanna go minic san áit chéanna, san oícht, ach b'shin é an chéad uair riamh a hairíodh sa lá é. Nuair a chonacadar Seán Aerach ag teacht amach a súil na tiníleach agus nuair a thuigeadar ina n-aigne gurbh é a bhí ag déanamh an cheoil aeraigh, chroitheadar a gcinn agus dúradar eatarthu féin ná rithfeadh leis i bhfad gan é a bhreith chun siúil. Do bheannaigh sé dhóibh agus bheannaíodar dó, ach níor fhiafraigh aoinne acu dhe cad fé ndeara dhó an ceol san do sheinnt. Bhí sord scáth acu roimis.

'Tháinig sé abhaile agus níorbh fhada gur buaileadh breoite é. Níor cheap aoinne go n-éireodh sé choíche ón mbreoiteacht san. Dúradh gurbh iad an mhuintir nar sheinn sé an ceol dóibh a bhí á bhreith leo i dtreo go mbeadh píobaire acu féin chomh maith leis an bpíobaire a bhí ag an muintir a bhí ar an dtaobh eile den abhainn, nó b'fhéidir níos fhearr. Ach pé scéal é do theip orthu é a bhreith leo an uair sin. Tháinig sé chuige féin dá n-ainneoin agus tá an ceol aige. Agus sin é anois agat, fé mar a airíos-sa féin é, conas mar a fuair Seán Aerach an ceol sí. Ní sheinneann sé ach go hannamh é, agus is róbheag an iúnadh san. Má thagaid siad ina thimpall i gcónaí mar a thánadar aréir ní foláir nó is mór an dúil atá acu sa cheol a sheinneann sé, agus má tá an dúil sin acu sa cheol béarfaid siad leo an ceolaí luath nó mall. Ní ceart dó bheith ag seinnt an cheoil sin in aon chor. Is minic a tugadh comhairle dhó gan bheith á sheinnt. Thugas-sa féin an chomhairle sin dó ach ní raibh aon mhaith dhom ann. Ní déarfadh sé, "déanfad", ná "ní dhéanfad". Ní fhéadfá a dhéanamh amach cad a bheadh ina aigne aige. Ní miste "Seán Aerach" a thabhairt air. Ní dóigh liom go bhfuil blúire eagla aige rompu.'

'B'fhéidir, a Phádraig,' arsa Micil, 'go bhfuil a fhios aige féin nach gá dhó aon eagla a bheith aige rompu. B'fhéidir go bhfuil cairde maithe aige eatarthu agus nach baol dó.'

'B'fhéidir é,' arsa Pádraig. 'Ach b'fhearr liom mé féin do thabhairt suas do Dhia agus gan aon bhaint in aon chor a bheith agam leo ná acu liom. Bhíos tamall aréir, nuair a bhí an toirneach agus an chaismirt mhór ar siúl, agus geallaim dhuit nárbh fhearr liom áit ina mbeinn ná sa bhaile. Thugas féachaint san aghaidh ar an gceolaí, agus is beag ná gur mheasas nárbh é féin a bhí in aon chor ann. Bhí solas éigin ina shúilibh agus ina ghnúis agus timpall a bhéil, i dtreo gur dhóigh leat go raibh sé ag féachaint orthu agus gur aithin sé iad!'

'B'fhéidir go raibh leis,' arsa Micil.

'B'fhéidir é,' arsa Pádraig. 'Ach tá aon ní amháin deimhnitheach; tá Seán Aerach ró-aerach domhsa.'

WHENCE THE FAIRY MUSIC CAME

Before the day had fully dawned the company had dispersed and the people had all gone home except the big tinker and the man of the fairy music and Michael and his mother. Those four were doing their best to tidy up the house and put everything back into its own place. The fairy music was troubling Michael's mind. He wanted very much to find out how that piper had got hold of it. He watched until he found an opportunity, and then he asked him the question.

'Listen, John,' said he. 'That was wonderful music that you played for us last night. I never heard the like of it. I don't believe there is another man in Ireland who could play such music.'

John pretended not to hear him.

'I suppose,' said Michael, 'it isn't everybody that could acquire music of that kind at all. How did *you* manage to get it, John?'

'Ask something else, Michael,' said John.

That did not put Michael off the subject. He waited until John had gone, and then he said to the big tinker, 'Stop a bit, Patrick, and have something to eat, after the night's work.'

Patrick did not think that would be in any way inconvenient to him, and he stayed.

By-and-by, when Patrick had eaten something, and when he had drunk another drop of wine, Michael said, in a careless sort of way, 'Patrick, was not that music we heard last night wonderful! I never heard the like of it, and I have often heard beautiful music. If I hadn't been looking at him with my own eyes, and listening to him with my own ears, I would not believe that any mortal man could bring such music out of pipes.'

'And he couldn't, either, unless he got help to it,'

said Patrick. 'Didn't you notice the whirlwind? And didn't you hear the human voices, and the crying, and the laughing, and the shrieking? No sooner did the music begin than *they* gathered into the house to us. I tell you I believe there were far more of *them* there, dancing to the music, than there were of ourselves. *They* began to go away when the time of cockcrow was drawing near to them. And see how the piper stopped exactly before the cock crew! It is a wonder to me that they do not carry the piper off with them. If I were in his place I would not play that music, however much I might be pressed to do it. It would be far better for him to have sense. "The jar does not always come unbroken from the well."'

'I wonder where in the world he learnt that music, or how he got hold of it,' said Michael.

'That question is often put to him,' said Patrick, 'and he never makes any answer but, "Ask something else."'

'I declare on my honour,' said Michael, 'that I asked him that question a while ago, and that that is exactly the answer he made me. "Ask something else," said he to me.'

'I heard,' said Patrick, 'that the way of it was that he was coming home from Cork one night with a new set of pipes which he had bought, and that he went astray, although he knew the place perfectly. Coming on toward Dripsey Bridge was where he went astray. A bewilderment came upon him, and he found himself on the bank of a river, in a place his eye had never rested on! He examined the ground under his feet, and a hedge that was near him, and a cave that was in a rock there, to see if he knew them, and he did not know them. At that moment he heard, at the other side of the river, the most beautiful music he had ever heard. What do you say to him if he didn't[1] fit up the new pipes and begin to play the same music, along with the musician at the other side! He always had great nerve. All the fairies in Ireland would not frighten him. In the twinkling of an eye the whole inch[2] on the bank of the river was filled with people moving over and hither among each other as if it were some sort of dance they were going on with. Soon the music at the other side changed. When it did, the man at this side took up the change without stop or stumble, and without missing a beat. The music at the other side was changed a second time. Well became the man[3] at this side, he took up the change the instant it was made.

'For every turn and change that took place in the music, a corresponding change took place in the movement of the people, or in the dancing, if it was dancing. Things went on in that way between them, at both sides of the river, until some time well on in the night. He does not remember how he parted with them, but when the daylight came he woke out of his sleep inside the eye[4] of a lime-kiln which was there at the roadside, with the new pipes beside him. No sooner was he fully awake than he fixed the pipes on him and began to play the music again, exactly as he had played it during the night. He played it from beginning to end, again and again, and he put into it correctly every twist and turn and change, as *they* put them in it during the night for him when *they* they were playing it on the other side of the river, until he knew it by heart and there was no fear of his ever forgetting any part of it. When he had satisfied his mind upon that, he stood up and came out of the lime-kiln and looked about him. The road and the fences were full of people all round the lime-kiln. They had been collecting there while he was playing the music so as to master it. According as one or two would come, they would stop to listen to the music, until the place was crowded with them. They were full of wonder and amazement, because they knew that people used to hear that same music often in the same place, at night; but that was the first time it had ever been heard during the day. When they saw "Eerie John" coming out of the eye of the lime-kiln, and when they realised that it was he that had been playing the weird music, they shook their heads and said among themselves that he would not escape long without being carried off. He saluted them, and they saluted him, but none of them asked him what made him play that music. They were half afraid of him.

'He came home, and it was not long until he fell sick. No one expected that he would ever rise from that sickness. People said it was *those* for whom he had played the music that were taking him with them in order that they themselves should have a piper as good as the piper whom those at the other side of the river had, or perhaps better. But what-

1. What did he do but . . .
2. meadow.
3. i.e. the man was equal to the occasion.
4. opening.

ever was the reason, they failed to carry him off that time. He recovered in spite of them, and he has the music. And there you have the story just as I myself heard it, of how Eerie John got the fairy music. He only plays it very seldom, and that is very little wonder. If *they* come around him always as they came around him last night, it must be that they take great delight in the music he plays, and if *they* have that delight in the music, *they* will carry the musician off home with them sooner or later. It is not right for him to be playing that music at all. He has been often advised not to play it. I have given him that advice myself, but it was no use for me to give it. He would not say "I will," or "I won't." You could not make out what he intended to do. It is no harm to call him "Eerie John." I don't think he has a bit of fear of *them*.'

'Perhaps, Patrick,' said Michael, 'that he knows himself that he need have no fear of *them*. Perhaps he has good friends among them, and that he is not in danger.'

'Perhaps so,' said Patrick, 'But I would rather give myself up to God than that I should have anything at all to do with *them* or *they* with me. There was a time last night, when all the thunder and commotion was going on, when I promise you there was no place I wished so much to be in as at home. I took a look at the face of the musician and I almost thought it was not himself that was there at all. There was a kind of light in his eyes and in his face and round his mouth, that would make you think he was looking at *them* and that he recognised *them*!'

'Perhaps he was too,' said Michael.

'Perhaps so,' said Patrick. 'But there's one thing certain; Eerie John is too eerie for *me*.'

PATRICK PEARSE

(1879-1916)

from:
AN MHÁTHAIR AGUS SGÉALTA EILE (The Mother and Other Stories) (1916)

[The text below is found in Cathal Ó Háinle (ed.), *Gearrscéalta an Phiarsaigh* (Dublin: Helicon, 1979). The translation, by Joseph Campbell, is from the *Collected Works of Pearse*, published in 1917.]

AN DEARGADAOL

Fear siúil as Dúthaigh Sheoighe a tháinig isteach i dteach m'athar a d'inis an scéal seo dúinn cois teallaigh oíche gharbh gheimhridh. Bhí an ghaoth ag caoineadh thart timpeall an tí, ar nós mná ag caoineadh marbh, le linn labhartha dó, agus níodh sé a ghlór a ardú nó a ísliú de réir mar a d'ardaíodh nó mar a d'íslíodh glór na gaoithe. Fear ard a bhí ann, súile fiáine aige, agus a chuid éadaigh beagnach ina mbalcaisí. Bhí saghas eagla orm roimhe nuair a tháinig sé isteach, agus níor lúide m'eagla a scéal.

'Na trí feithidí is beannaithe ar an domhan,' arsa an fear siúil, 'an chadóg, an spideoigín agus bó Dé. Agus na trí feithidí is mallaithe ar an domhan, an nathair nimhe, an dreoilín agus an deargadaol. Agus 'sé an deargadaol an fheithide is mallaithe acu. Is agamsa atá a fhios sin. Dá maródh fear do mhac, a bhean an tí, ná tabhair deargadaol mar ainm air. Dá dtiocfadh bean idir thú féin agus do chéile leapan, ná cuir i gcomórtas leis an deargadaol í.'

'Go sábhála Dia sinn,' a deir mo mháthair.

'Áiméan, a Thiarna,' arsa an fear siúil.

Níor labhair sé arís go ceann scaithimh. D'éisteamar ar fad, mar bhí a fhios againn to raibh sé chun scéal a insint. Ba ghearr gur thosaigh sé.

'Nuair a bhí mise i mo scorach,' arsa an fear siúil, 'bhí bean ar an bpobal se'againne a raibh faitíos ar 'chuile dhuine roimpi. I mbothán uaigneach i mám sléibhe a bhí cónaí uirthi. Ní ghabhadh aon duine i bhfoisceacht dá teach. Ní thagadh sí féin i ngar do theach duine ar bith eile. Ní labhraítí léi nuair a chastaí do dhuine ar an mbóthar í. Ní chuireadh sise focal ná fáirnéis ar dhuine ar bith. Ba thrua leat an créatúr a fheiceáil agus í ag gabháil an bhóthair ina haonar.

'"Cé hí siúd," a deirinnse le mo mháthair, "nó 'tuige nach labhraítear léi?"

'"Éist, a ghiolla," a deireadh mo mháthair liom. "Sin í an Deargadaol. Is bean mhallaithe í."

'"Céard a rinne sí, nó cé a chuir an mhallacht uirthi?" a deirinnse.

'"Sagart Dé a chuir an mhallacht uirthi," a deireadh mo mháthair. "Níl a fhios ag duine ar bith céard a rinne sí."

'Agus sin a bhfuaireas d'eolas ina taobh go rabhas i mo stócach fásta. Agus go deimhin daoibh, a chomharsana, níor chuala mé ina taobh riamh ach go ndearna sí peaca náireach eicínt i dtús a saoil agus gur chuir an sagart a mhallacht uirthi os comhair an phobail i ngeall ar an bpeaca sin. Domhnach amháin dá raibh an pobal cruinn ag an Aifreann, d'iontaigh an sagart thart orthu, agus ar seisean:

'"Tá bean anseo," ar seisean, "a thuillfeas damnú síoraí di féin agus do 'chuile dhuine a dhéanfas caidreamh léi. Agus adeirimse leis an mbean sin," ar seisean, "gur bean mhallaithe í, agus adeirimse libhse gan caidreamh ná comharsanacht a bheith agaibh leis an mbean sin ach an oiread is a bheadh le deargadaol. Éirigh romhat anois, a Dheargadaoil," ar seisean, "agus seachain comhluadar dea-dhaoine feasta."

'D'éirigh an bhean bhocht agus thug sí doras an tséipéil amach uirthi féin. Ní raibh d'ainm uirthi ó shin ach an Deargadaol. Ligeadh a hainm is a sloinne féin as cuimhne. Deirtí go raibh súil fhiata aici. Dá mbreathnaíodh sí ar ghamhain nó ar chaora nár léi, gheobhadh an beithíoch bás. Bhí faitíos ar na mná a gcuid páistí a ligean amach ar an tsráid dá mbeadh an Deargadaol ag siúl an bhealaigh.

'Phós mise cailín dóighiúil nuair a bhí mé in aois mo bhliana is fiche. Bhí gasúr beag de ghearrchaile againn agus súil againn le leanbh eile. Lá amháin dá raibh mé ag baint mhóna sa bportach, bhí mo bhean ag beathú na héanlaithe ar an tsráid nuair a chonaic sí — Dia idir sinn agus an anachain — an Deargadaol ag déanamh uirthi aníos an bóithrín agus an pataire beag ina hucht aici. Bhí lámh na girsí timpeall muineáil na mná, agus a seálsa á folach. Níor fhan caint ag mo bheansa.

'Leag an Deargadaol an cailín beag in ucht a máthar. Thug mo bheansa faoi deara go raibh a cuid éadaigh fliuch.

'"Céard a d'éirigh don leanbh?" ar sise.

'"Titim isteach i Lochán na Luachra a rinne sí," a deir an Deargadaol. "Ar thóir bileogaí báite a bhí sí. Bhí mé ag dul thart ar an mbóthar agus chuala mé a scread. Isteach thar claí liom. Ní raibh ann ach gur rug mé uirthi ar éigean."

'"Go gcúití Dia thú," arsa mo bhean. D'imigh an bhean eile sula raibh am aici níos mó a rá. Thug mo bhean an ruidín beag isteach, thriomaigh sí í, agus chuir a chodladh í. Nuair a tháinig mé féin isteach ón bportach d'inis sí an scéal dom. Thug an bheirt againn ár mbeannacht don Deargadaol an oíche sin.

'Lá arna mhárach thosaigh an cailín beag ag caint ar an mbean a shábháil í. "Bhí an t-uisce isteach i mo bhéal agus i mo shúile agus i mo chluasa," ar sise; "chonaic mé tintreacha geala agus chuala mé torann mór; bhí mé ag sleamhnú, ag sleamhnú," ar sise; "agus ansin," ar sise, "mhothaigh mé an lámh timpeall orm, agus thóg sí ina hucht mé, agus phóg sí mé. Cheap mé go raibh mé sa mbaile nuair a bhí mé ar a hucht agus a seál timpeall orm," ar sise.

'Cúpla lá ina dhiaidh sin d'airigh mo bhean an cailín beag uaithi. Bhí sí ar iarraidh ar feadh cúpla uair. Nuair a tháinig sí abhaile d'inis sí dhúinn go raibh sí tar éis cuairt a thabhairt ar an mbean a shábháil í. "Rinne sí cáca dhom," ar sise. "Níl duine ar bith sa teach aici ach í féin, agus dúirt mé léi go ngabhfainn ar cuairt aici 'chuile thráthnóna."

'Níor fhéad mise ná mo bhean focal a rá ina aghaidh. Bhí an Deargadaol tar éis anam ár ngirsí a shábháil, agus ní bheadh sé nádúrtha a chrosadh ar an leanbh dul isteach ina teach. Ón lá sin amach théadh an cailín beag suas an cnoc chuici gach re lá.

'Dúirt na comharsana linn nach raibh sé ceart. Bhí sórt amhrais orainn féin nach raibh sé ceart, ach cén neart a bhí againn air?

'An gcreidfeadh sibh mé, a dhaoine? Ón lá ar leag an Deargadaol súil ar an gcailín beag thosaigh sí ag imeacht as, ag imeacht as, mar a d'imeodh tine nach ndeasófaí. Chaill sí a goile agus a lúth. Tar éis ráithe ní raibh ann ach a scáil. Tar éis míosa eile bhí sí sa gcill.

'Tháinig an Deargadaol anuas an sliabh an lá ar cuireadh í. Ní ligfí isteach sa reilig í. D'imigh sí a bealach suas an sliabh arís go huaigneach. Bhí trua agam don chréatúr, mar bhí a fhios agam nár mhó ár mbrón-na ná a brónsa. Chuaigh mé féin suas an cnoc maidin lá arna mhárach. Bhí fúm a rá léi nach raibh aon mhilleán agamsa ná ag mo bhean uirthi. Bhuail mé ar an doras. Ní bhfuair mé aon fhreagra. Chuaigh mé isteach sa teach. Bhí an ghríosach dearg ar an teallach. Ní raibh duine ar bith le feiceáil. Thug mé leaba faoi deara sa gcúinne.

Chuaigh mé anonn go dtí an leaba. Bhí an Deargadaol ina luí ansin agus í fuar marbh.

'Ní raibh aon rath ormsa ná ar mo chomhluadar ón lá sin amach. Cailleadh mo bhean mí ina dhiaidh sin agus í ag breith a linbh. Níor mhair an leanbh. Tháinig galar ar mo bheithígh an geimhreadh dár gcionn. Chuir an tiarna amach as mo sheilbh mé. Tá mé i m'fhear siúil, agus bóithre Chonnachta romham, ó shin i leith.'

THE DEARGADAOL[1]

A walking-man, it was, come into my father's house out of the Joyce Country,[2] that told us this story by the fireside one wild winter's night. The wind was wailing round the house, like women keening the dead, while he spoke, and he would make his voice rise or fall according as the wind's voice would rise or fall. A tall man he was, with wild eyes, and his share of clothes almost in tatters. There was a sort of fear on me of him when he came in, and his story didn't lessen my fear.

The three most blessed beasts in the world, says the walking-man, are the haddock, the robin redbreast, and God's cow. And the three most cursed beasts in the world are the viper, the wren, and the *deargadaol* ('black chafer'). And it's the *deargadaol* is the most cursed of them. 'Tis I that know that. Woman of the house, if a man would murder his son, don't call him the *deargadaol*. If a woman would come between yourself and the husband of your bed, don't put her in comparison with the *deargadaol*.

'God save us,' says my mother.

'Amen, Lord,' says the walking-man.

He didn't speak again for a spell. We all listened, for we knew he was going to tell a story. It wasn't long before he began.

When I was a lad, says the walking-man, there was a woman of our people that everybody was afraid of. In a little, lonely cabin in a gap of a mountain, it was, she lived. No one would go near her house. She, herself, wouldn't come next or near any other body's house. Nobody would speak to her when they met her on the road. She wouldn't put word nor wisdom on anybody at all. You'd think a pity to see the creature and she going the road alone.

'Who is she,' I would say to my mother, 'or why wouldn't they speak to her?'

'Whisht, boy,' my mother would say to me. 'That's the *Deargadaol*. 'Tis a cursed woman she is.'

'What did she do, or who put the curse on her?' I would say.

'A priest of God that put the curse on her,' my mother would say. 'No one in life knew what she did.'

And that's all the knowledge I got of her until I was a grown chap. And indeed to you, neighbours, I never heard anything about her but that she committed some dreadful sin at the start of her life, and that the priest put his curse on her before the people on account of that sin. One Sunday, when the people were gathered at Mass, the priest turned round on them, and says he:

'There is a woman here,' says he, 'that will merit eternal damnation for herself and for every person that makes familiar with her. And I say to that woman,' says he, 'that she is a cursed woman, and I say to you, let you not have intercourse or neighbourliness with that woman but as much as you'd have with a *deargadaol*. Rise up now, *Deargadaol*,' says he, 'and avoid the company of decent people henceforth.'

The poor woman got up, and went out the chapel door. There was no name on her from that out but the *Deargadaol*. Her own name and surname were put out of mind. 'Twas said that she had the evil eye. If she'd look on a calf or a sheep that wasn't her own, the animal would die. The women were afraid to let their children out on the street if the *Deargadaol* was going the road.

I married a comely girl when I was of the age of one-and-twenty. We had a little slip of a girl, and we had hopes of another child. One day when I was cutting turf in the bog, my wife was feeding the fowl on the street, when she saw — God between us and harm — the *Deargadaol* making on her up the bohereen,[3] and she with the little, soft *pataire*[4] of a child in her arms. An arm of the child was about the woman's neck, and her shawl covering her. Speech left my wife.

The *Deargadaol* laid the little girl in her mother's breast. My woman took notice that her clothes were wet.

'What happened the child?' says she.

'Falling into Lochán na Luachra (the Pool of the

1. Pronounced 'Darrugadale'.
2. North Conamara in County Galway.
3. A narrow bye-road or lane.
4. A chubby child.

Rushes), she did it,' says the *Deargadaol*. 'Looking for water-lilies she was. I was crossing the road, and I heard her scream. In over the dyke with me. It was only by dint of trouble I caught her.'

'May God reward you,' says my wife. The other woman went off before she had time to say more. My wife fetched the little wee thing inside, she dried her, and put her to sleep. When I came in from the bog she told me the story. The two of us prayed our blessing on the *Deargadaol* that night.

The day after, the little girl began prattling about the woman that saved her. 'The water was in my mouth, and in my eyes, and in my ears,' says she. 'I saw shining sparks, and I heard a great noise; I was slipping and slipping,' says she; 'and then,' says she, 'I felt a hand about me, and she lifted me up and she kissed me. I thought it was at home, I was, when I was in her arms and her shawl about me,' says she.

A couple of days after that my wife noticed the little thing away from her. We sought her for the length of two hours. When she came home she told us that she was after paying a visit to the woman that saved her. 'She made a cake for me,' says she. 'She has ne'er a one in the house at all but herself, and she said to me I should go visiting her every evening.'

Neither I nor my wife was able to say a word against her. The *Deargadaol* was after saving our girl's life, and it wouldn't be natural to hinder the child going into her house. From that day out the little girl would go up the hill to her every day.

The neighbours said to us that it wasn't right. There was a sort of suspicion on ourselves that it wasn't right, but how could we help it?

Would you believe me, people? From the day the *Deargadaol* laid eyes on the little girl, she began dwindling and dwindling, like a fire that wouldn't be mended. She lost her appetite and her activity. After a quarter she was only a shadow. After another month she was in the churchyard.

The *Deargadaol* came down the mountain the day she was buried. She wouldn't be let into the graveyard. She went her road up the mountain again alone. My heart bled for the creature, for I knew that our trouble was no heavier than her trouble. I myself went up the hill the morning of the next day. I meant to say to her that neither my wife nor myself had any upbraiding for her. I knocked at the door. I didn't get any answer. I went into the house. The ashes were red on the hearth. There was no one at all to be seen. I noticed a bed in the corner. I went over to the bed. The *Deargadaol* was lying there, and she cold dead.

There wasn't any luck on me or on my household from that day out. My wife died a month after that, and she in childbirth. The child didn't live. There fell a murrain[5] on my cattle the winter following. I am a walking man, and the roads of Connacht before me, from that day to this.

5. A plaguelike disease in cattle.

PÁDRAIC Ó CONAIRE

(1882-1928)

from: DEORAÍOCHT (1910)

[*Deoraíocht* (Exile) describes the deranged and alienated life of a mentally and physically maimed emigrant in London. The translation is by Eoghan Ó hAnluain.]

CHAPTER 4

Tá tús an Aibreáin ann, ach má tá féin, níl an geimhreadh thart fós. Seachtain ó shin cheapas go raibh an aimsir bhreá ar fáil. Bhí dul amú orm. Nuair a dhearcas amach tríd an bhfuinneog ar maidin inniu, ar dhúiseacht dom, céard a bhí le feiceáil agam ach an sneachta!

Níor éiríos. Go deimhin féin duit, táim sa leaba fós. Tá páipéar agus peann luaidhe i ngreim agam. Tá an chos adhmaid ar chathaoir le mo thaobh. Tá ocras ag teacht orm. Le dhá lá ní mórán a d'itheas. Ruainne aráin — b'in an méid, mar bhí leisce orm mo leathshabhran deireanach a bhriseadh.

Beirim air anois agus tosaím á chaitheamh ó

láimh go láimh. Caithim suas san aer é. Beirim air ag teacht anuas dó. Cuirim i mo bheál é. Ceapaim greim a bhaint as. Nach é atá crua? Cuirim faoin leaba é, agus ligim orm féin nach bhfuil agam ach an phingin atá i mo phóca.

Pingin! Aon phingin rua amháin a bhí idir mé agus an bás! An fada go bhfaigheadh duine bás leis an ocras? Bhíos trí lá gan aon bhlas a ithe uair, agus an tríú lá níor airíos aon ocras orm ar chor ar bith. Is ag laghdú a bheadh pianta an ocrais de réir mar a bheadh an bás ag teannadh leat go dtí to dtiocfadh meisce an ocrais, buile an ocrais ort. Agus cén chaoi a dtiocfadh an bás féin? Ina ghadaí gránna agus a dhroim le claí, an ea? Dá bhféadainn fanacht go ciúin anseo sa leaba go mbeadh sé buailte liom ... ach na trí lá úd, ba mheasa iad sin ná an bás féin. Bheifeá chomh folamh taobh istigh de do ghoile i dtosach an chéad lae; ansin thiocfadh an tart millteach agus nuair a d'ólfá bolgam uisce leis an tart uafásach a shásamh, thiocfadh múisc ort ... agus cheapfá ina dhiaidh sin go raibh na mílte míle biorán te do do phiocadh ...

Éirím de gheit. Cuirim an leathshabhran i mo phóca agus téim síos an staighre go mall righin réidh agus fear óg eile ag cuidiú liom.

Faighim luach pingine aráin agus tosaím á choigilt os comhair na tine.

Bás leis an ocras! Ba mhillteach an focal é dá dtuigfí i gceart é. Ní fhéadfainn a fhulaingt ... Ach tá agam anois. A ghabháil ar lorg na déirce — sin é a dheánfaidh mé. D'fhéadfainn a dhéanamh go tofa mura mbeadh an mhórchúis. Ach nach gcaithfinn a dhéanamh sa deireadh thiar? Agus nárbh fhearr dom tosú air anois, fad is bhí an leathshabhran agam? Nár mhó an misneach a bheadh agam chuige? Arbh fhiú dom a dhéanamh? Céard eile a d'fhéadfainn a dhéanamh? Gadaíocht? Sea; bheadh sé níos fearr — ach níor chleachtaíos riamh é, agus ní bheifeá i bhfad go mbéarfaí ort agus gan cleachtadh agat ar an gceird. Cén dóchas a bheadh ansin? A ghabháil sa charcair, an ea? Is iomaí fear maith a cuireadh ann. Bheadh greim mo bhéil agam ann. Éagórach? Cé a dúirt sin? Cé a cheap an ceart agus an mícheart ach lucht na mbolg lán? Dlí Dé? Nuair atá ocras ar dhuine ní bhaineann aon dlí dó. Sea, gadaíocht a bheidh mar cheird agam feasta. B'fhearr í mar cheird ná éileamh na déirce, agus ní fada go mbeidh cleachtadh agam uirthi. An rud nach n-éireodh liom a bhaint amach le gliceas d'fhéadfainn é a fháil le láimh láidir, dá gcastaí an duine lag orm. D'fhéadfainn togha fir a leagadh le mo mhaide croise. Cén mí-ádh a bhí orm gur cheapas bás a fháil leis an ocras agus a bhfuil de shaibhreas sa chathair iontach seo! ....

Ach tá sé an-fhuar agus tá an phian ghránna sin i mo ghoile arís. Coiglím an chuid eile den arán. Tá an crústa chomh crua le cloch, ach is amhlaidh is fearr liom é, agus a laghad de atá agam. Is mór an sásamh dom na fiacla geala géara a shá isteach ann. Fáiscim an cóta i mo thimpeall, agus greadaim liom go bhfuil allas liom, go bhfuilim beagnach ag titim ón tuirse, go bhfuil an leathchos ag tabhairt uaithi, go bhfuil m'ascaill tinn scólta ón maide croise, go bhfuil orm mo scíth a ligean in áit éigin. Suím ar shuíochán mór cois na habhann ... táim róthuirseach rólag leis an abhainn mhór dhubh atá ag sleamhnú tharam mar ollphéist fhuafar a thabhairt faoi deara. Ní fheicim an ollphéist úd a bhfuil na mílte míle solas, na mílte míle súil, na mílte míle cloch luachmhar ag dealramh ina chraiceann. Ní dheánaim iontas ar bith di. Ní dhéanaim iontas ach díom féin.

Bhí breacadh an lae ann nuair a dhúisíos. Ní raibh a fhios agam céard a dhúisigh mé, ach cheapas gur sháigh duine éigin saighead i mo bholg. Ní raibh mé cinnte nach rabhas sáite gur osclaíos mo chóta agus mo léine. Ní raibh fuil ar bith le feiceáil. Bhí sé tamall maith gur ligeas orm féin gur ocras a bhí ag gabháil dom, agus gurb é an constábla a bhí ag gabháil thart a dhúisigh mé.

D'éiríos agus chuas ag spaisteoireacht, ag ceapadh go n-éireodh liom cuimhneamh ar bheart éigin. I mbailte móra eile, nuair atá duine i gcruachás, nuair atá náire agus ceann faoi agus umhlaíocht air, feictear dó nach bhfuil na rudaí atá ina thimpeall — na tithe, na ballaí, an tsráid féin, ag iarraidh aon cheo a dhéanamh air, ach i Londain ceapann duine den saghas sin go gcuirfeadh na tithe móra gruama dá chois é — go dtitfeadh siad air, lena bhrú síos sa talamh — dá mb'fhiú leo an trioblóid sin a chur orthu féin i ngeall ar shuarachán mar é.

Tithe móra aíochta a bhí i mo thimpeall anois. An bruscar a fágadh taobh amuigh de gach teach i gcannaí móra millteacha, bhí daoine á chartadh. Seandaoine, idir fhir agus mhná, a bhformhór, agus nuair a thiocfadh cuid acu ar ruainne aráin nó feola d'fheicfeá iad ag breith air lena méara caola tanaí, agus ag glanadh an tsalachair den bhia brocach sin lena gcuid ingne. Ag cromadh os cionn na soitheach stáin úd dóibh, i mbreacsholas na maidine, agus na tithe mór aíochta ag féachaint anuas orthu go scigiúil, ba gheall le scata éan mór uafásach ocrasach allta iad a bheadh ag piocadh cnámha duine lena mór chrobha garbhchnámhacha i bhfásach. Ag dearcadh dom orthu, tháinig croitheadh ball orm, mar a thiocfadh ort agus tú ag éisteach le duine ag scríobadh gloine.

TRANSLATION

It is early April but even so winter is not over yet. A week ago I thought the good weather had come. I was wrong. When I woke this morning and looked out of the window, what should I see but snow.

I didn't get up. To tell the truth I'm still in bed. I take my pencil and paper. My wooden leg is on the chair beside me. I feel hungry. For two days I have eaten little. A scrap of bread, that's all. I was reluctant to change my last half sovereign.

I pick it up now and toss it from hand to hand. I toss it in the air and catch it again. I put it in my mouth and bite on it. How hard it is. I put it beneath my bed and pretend that all I have is the penny in my pocket.

A penny! One penny between me and death! How long does it take to die of hunger? Once I went three days without eating and the third day felt no hunger at all. The hunger pangs would decrease as death approached, until the mad intoxication of hunger took over. And how would death itself come? A repulsive thief loitering in a ditch? If I could wait passively here in bed until he came ... but those three days were worse than death.

So empty in the stomach on that first day and then a fierce thirst which turned to nausea when I drank a mouthful of water to slake it ... and then a thousand hot pins stabbing.

I start up, put the half sovereign in my pocket and make my way slowly down the stairs, helped by another young man.

I buy a pennyworth of bread and eat it sparingly in front of the fire. To die of hunger. A terrifying thought if one could bear it. I couldn't. I know what I'll do. I'll beg. I could do it easily if it weren't for my pride, but I'll have to resort to it in the long run. And better to start now while I still have my half sovereign. That should encourage me. But is it worth it? Have I a choice? Theft. Yes, that could be better. But I have never tried it and it wouldn't be long until I was caught for want of practice. What hope is there? To go to prison? Many a good man went before me. I'd have a bite to eat. But is it wrong? Who says so! Who decided right and wrong but the well-fed? The law of God? There is no law for the hungry. Yes, I'll take to the thieves' trade from now on. A better trade than begging and it won't be long until I learn it. What I can't get by cunning I'll take by violence if I meet a vulnerable person. I could even knock out an able-bodied man with my crutch!

Whatever made me think of dying of hunger while there is such wealth in this wonderful city! ....

It's very cold and that horrible pain is in my stomach again. I nibble the rest of the bread. The crust is like stone but it's just as well since I have so little. It gratifies me to sink my keen bright teeth in it. I wrap my coat round me and hurry along until I roll with sweat and stagger with tiredness, my good leg failing, my armpit scalded by the crutch. I must take a rest somewhere. I sit on a big riverside bench .... I'm too exhausted to observe the vast black river gliding past, a dreadful serpent with a million lights, a million eyes, a million gems glittering on its back. It doesn't amaze me. Nothing amazes me but myself.

It was daybreak when I woke. I don't know what woke me but I felt as if I had been knifed in my belly. I wasn't sure until I opened my coat and shirt. There was no blood. It was a while before I admitted I was starving and that it was a policeman on his beat who had disturbed me.

I got up and walked up and down awhile, hoping some plan might dawn on me. In other great cities when a man is distressed, ashamed, humiliated, he is not intimidated by his surroundings — houses, walls, streets — but in London such an unfortunate senses that the great sombre buildings might destroy him, fall on him and crush him — as if they could be bothered by such a wretch. Vast lodging houses surrounded me. Persons rummaged the garbage left out in great bins. Mostly old men and women. They find a scrap of bread or meat and take it in their emaciated fingers and clean the filthy food with their nails. As they crouch over those tin containers in the bleary morning light, those vast houses rearing above them scornfully, they seem like a terrible flock of savage, ravenous desert birds picking human bones with great raw-boned claws. As I watch, I shudder as if hearing glass being scraped.

from: SCOTHSCÉALTA (1956)

[This story was first published in *An Claidheamh Soluis* in 1913. Tom MacIntyre's translation is from *The Finest Stories of Pádraic Ó Conaire* (Swords, Co. Dublin; Poolbeg Press, 1982).]

AN BHEAN AR LEAG DIA LÁMH UIRTHI

Bád níos gleoite ná *An Cailín Beag Donn* ní raibh le feiceáil ar Chuan na Gaillimhe, agus ó bhí sí le díol ag an gceannaí siopa ar leis í, cheap Pádraig Ó Nia go mba mhaith an spré ag a inín an bád dá bhféadadh sé í fháil réasúnta saor. Ach dúirt Antaine Ó Máille, an fear óg bhí ar tí an ógbhean a phósadh, go mba chóir dhóibh triail a bhaint as an mbád sul a gceannófaí í, ag féachaint an raibh sí i ngar do bheith chomh maith lena cáil. Cheap an seanfhear go mba mhaith an chomhairle í agus chuaigh sé féin agus Séamas, a mhac, agus an Máilleach amach le oíche a chaitheamh ar an bhfarraige ag iascaireacht go bhfeicfidís cén mhaith bhí leis an mbád.

Chuaigh Cáit, an iníon bhí le pósadh, go dtí an chéibh lena muintir go bhfeicfeadh sí ag imeacht iad agus d'fhan sí tamall maith ar an tulchán ag féachaint ar an gcabhlach bád iascaireachta ag dul siar an cuan faoi chóir gaoithe. Ar fhilleadh abhaile dhi bhí sé ina ardtráthnóna agus bhí béile na hoíche ullamh ag a máthair. Bhí an bord faoi réir aici agus císte á fhuaradh ar leic na fuinneoige, agus ceol taitneamhach á dhéanamh ag an túlán. Shuigh an bheirt bhan ag an mbord agus d'fhéachaidís amach thríd an bhfuinneoig ó am go ham ar na báid, bhí an-chosúil le dream ban rialta bheadh ag glacadh an aeir dóibh féin ar mhachaire a gclochair.

Bhí sé ag éirí an-chiúin. Na héanlaith bhí go ceolmhar agus go bríomhar uair roimhe sin bhíodar ag éirí an-mharbhánta. Shílfeá go mb'é an chaoi a raibh sluaite an aeir ag éirí tuirseach den chantaireacht agus nach gcleachtóidís arís choíche é. Bhí codladh ag teacht ar éanlaith agus ar bheithígh, ach d'fhan an bhean óg ag an bhfuinneoig go raibh na báid ag dul ó léargas uirthi sa doircheacht, go raibh réaltóg bhreá a raibh loinnir drochghealaí inti le feiceáil sa spéir thiar.

Lig an tseanbhean bhí ag an tine osna aisti.

'Céard tá ort a mháthair?' arsa Cáit, ag éirí agus ag dul chuici.

'Bead an-uaigneach gan tú, a chuid.'

'Nach mbeidh m'athair agat, gan trácht ar Shéamas?'

'Ní fada fhanfas Séamas linn. Ní bhíonn ó na daoine óga atá ann anois ach imeacht leo.'

'Ach nach minic chuir tú féin gáirí orainn, a mháthair, ag inseacht dúinn cé mar d'éalaigh tú le m'athair in ainneoin do mhuintire,' arsa Cáit, le croí a chur ina máthair.

'Agus féach an saol a bhí agam ó shin!'

Níor mhinic dá máthair gearán a dhéanamh, agus chuir sé as don ógbhean gur ar rudaí den sórt sin bhí sí ag smaoineamh. Bhí fhios aici go maith gur chuir muintir a máthar chomh mór sin in aghaidh a pósta is nár labhraíodar léi ó shin. Bhí tabhairt suas agus foghlaim ar a máthair ach ghlac sí leis an saol d'éirigh lena fear thabhairt di.

'Ach ní ag éalú uait atáimse,' arsa Cáit, 'feicfidh tú go minic mé. Ar ndóigh ní bheidh mé thar fiche míle uait.'

'Tá fhios agam, a stór,' arsa an mháthair, 'ach le scathamh bím ag ceapadh gur lean an mhallacht chuir m'athair orm mé. Féach mar d'imíodar uile to léir uaim — agus thú féin anois. Feictear dhom go mb'é an fáth gur imíodar uaim go mbím roinnt bheag aisteach féin scaití . . . nach ndeirtear 'go dtí an seachtú glún'?

Rug Cáit ar láimh ar a máthair agus bhí á cuimilt go ceanúil. Bhí fhios aici go maith céard bhí i gceist ag an tseanbhean. Bhí fhios aici gur beag glún de mhuintir a máthar nach raibh duine éigin air bhí 'roinnt bheag aisteach,' agus go raibh cuid díobh bhí chomh haisteach is go mb'éigean iad a chur faoi ghlas. Ach ní raibh a fhios sin ag muintir na háite; b'as condae eile an mháthair agus má bhí corrdhuine ann chuala an scéal ní raibh a chruthú ag aon neach.

'Ní ceart duit é sin a rá,' arsa Cáit go himníoch.

'Ach tá an fhírinne ann, a Cháit,' arsa an tseanbhean.

Thit an oíche. Las Cáit an lampa. Chuir sí dallóg ar an bhfuinneoig. Tháinig triúr isteach ar cuairt, triúr nach bhfeictear ach go hannamh le chéile. An Imní, an tUamhan agus an Dóchas b'ainmneacha dhóibh. Ba léir don tseanbhean bhí ag an tine iad, agus chuireadh sí ionadh ar a hinín nuair chuireadh sí féin focal beag isteach ina gcuid cainte. Ba dhóigh le Cáit go raibh a máthair ag éirí níos aistí ó ló go ló.

'Tá an ghaoith ag éirí, tá sé an-chontúirteach ar an bhfarraige anocht,' deireadh an tseanbhean agus í ag déanamh aithris ar ghlór Imní.

Bhain an iníon an dallóg den fhuinneoig. Bhí gealach sa spéir agus an fharraige an-chiúin. Ní cheapfá go mbáithfí aon duine inti arís choíche.

'Féach amach, a mháthair. Níl smeathamh ann. Codladh atá ag teacht ort.'

Ní raibh súil leis an mbád go héirí an lae.

'Fanfaidh mise anseo go maidin,' arsa an tseanbhean agus í go smaointeach, 'nach mór an lear daoine báitheadh ar an mbaile seo le mo chónaí ann? Báitheadh Pádraic Pheait agus a mhuintir anuraidh, oíche spéirghealaí mar í seo freisin; agus báitheadh Micilín Pheig Bheag agus a dheirfiúr athrú anuraidh, agus . . . an athrú anuraidh nó trí bliana ó shin báitheadh muintir an Oileáin?'

Bhí an mháthair ag cur di ag an tine ach níor chuir a cuid cainte aon imní ar Cháit. Beirt bhádóirí ab fhearr ná a hathair agus an Máilleach ní raibh le fáil sa gcuan.

'Gabh i leith anseo chugam,' arsa an tseanbhean go tobann.

Chuaigh. Rug an tseanbhean ar dhá láimh uirthi agus d'fhéach isteach ina súile.

'A Cháit, inis an fhírinne dhom,' ar sise, 'má tá duine nó beirt de chomhlucht an bháid le báitheadh anocht, cé acu ab fhearr leatsa a shábhálfaí?'

'Ar son Dé, a mháthair, agus ná bí ag caint mar sin liom,' arsa Cáit go cráite, agus scaoil sí an greim docht bhí ag a máthair uirthi agus shuigh an bheirt acu, duine ar gach aon taobh den tine. Thit néal codlata ar an tseanbhean agus thit néal ar Cháit.

Bhí sé ina mhaidneachan nuair dúisíodh an bheirt acu go tobann. Buaileadh rud trom éigin in aghaidh an dorais dúnta. D'fhéach an bheirt bhan ar a chéile.

'Oscail an doras,' arsa an tseanbhean go ciúin, 'go bhfeicfimid cé acu tháinig slán.'

Ach b'éigean di féin é dhéanamh, bhí an oiread sin uafáis ar Cháit, agus cé thitfeadh isteach ina chnap ar an urlár chucu ach an Máilleach, é fliuch báite agus sceoin ina dhá shúil . . . .

Níor fríothadh corp an mhic riamh. Cuartaíodh an cladach ó Cheann Léime isteach go Gaillimh ach níor facthas in aon áite é. Bhí tórramh acu ar an athair ach níor ghoil a bhean deor.

Scaití d'fheictí i gcúinne éigin í agus bean comharsan ag labhairt léi, agus dá mbeadh cluas ort chluinfeá a caint:

'Cuid den tseanmhallacht an báitheadh seo,' deireadh sí, 'cén chaoi bhféadfainn gol a dhéanamh? Nach bhfuil mo chroí rólán? Bhí fhios agam i gcónaí go mbáithfí lá éigin é.'

Théadh sí go seomra an choirp agus tráth mbíodh an seomra fúithí féin bhíodh sí ag caint lena fear.

'Is minic nítheá gáirí faoin mallacht, a Phádraic,' deireadh sí leis an gcorp, 'ach má tá sibh le chéile anois abair le m'athair an mhallacht a scaoileadh dhíom. Nach n-abróidh anois, a Phádraic? Bhíos ceanúil ort riamh, ón gcéad lá leagas súil ort — ar do cheann dóighiúil agus ar t'aghaidh shoineanta . . . .'

Chuireadh sí cosc léi féin nuair a thagadh comharsa isteach sa seomra, agus nuair thosaíodh an chomharsa ag déanamh trua léi ní abraíodh sí ach —

'Éist do bhéal anois. Cuid de mhallacht m'athar an báitheadh seo. Bhí sé i ndán dúinn ó thús. Tá Cáit ag imeacht freisin. Ní fada go mbead chomh haonraic is bhí i dtosach.'

B'éigean í chur a chodladh roimh lá . . . .

Tar éis a fear bheith curtha d'éirigh sí níos aistí ná riamh. D'éiríodh sí i ngan fhios do Cháit san oíche agus d'éalaíodh amach agus bhíodh sí ag imeacht ar fud na gcladach ar thóir a mic. D'fheictí go minic í de shiúl oíche ar an gcladach, a gruaig le gaoith agus gan uirthi ach culaith oíche agus í ag gluaiseacht léi ina haonar ag cuartú gach poill dá raibh ann agus ag bualadh a cos in aghaidh na gcloch géar. Baothchaint is mó cluintí uaithi ach ar uaire bhíodh rannta á gcanadh aici. Bhíodh ceann aici nár cluineadh ach uaithi féin. Deireadh sí —

Bím ag siúl de oíche
Faoi fhearthainn 'gus faoi ghaoith
Ag cuartú mo mhic is mo stóir.
Cá bhfuil tú uaim, a Shéamais?

Ansin thagadh smaoineamh eile chuici agus deireadh sí —

Ach nuair bhí an leanbh Íosa
Ina luí ag bun na Croise
Bhí tusa ann, a Mhuire,
Agus Eisean ar do ghlúin.

Agus deireadh sí go mba mhó go mór a buairt agus a doilíos féin ná doilíos Mhuire, mar nár tugadh corp a mic siúd ar ais di thar éis an Chéasta?

'Cá bhfuil tú uaim, a Shéamais? Cén fáth nach bhfuilir ar mo ghlúin?' deireadh sí.

Daoine chluineadh í agus an chaint sin ar siúl aici, shílidís í mhealladh abhaile. Uaireanta d'éiríodh leo. Uaireanta eile ní éiríodh, agus bhíodh ar Cháit dhul amach ar a tóir.

Chleachtaigh sí an tóraíocht agus an siúl oíche go raibh ar Cháit codladh dhéanamh in aon leaba léi.

Mar sin féin, is minic dhúisíodh sí san oíche agus bhíodh an mháthair imithe uaithi agus bhíodh uirthi dhul amach á cuartú.

Agus is ag dul i ndonacht bhí sí in aghaidh an lae.

D'imigh an chuimhne uaithi. Rud ar bith tharla ó phós sí deich mbliana fichead roimhe sin, ní raibh aon chuimhne aici air de ghnáth. Dá labhartá léi ar a fear déarfadh sí leat nach raibh aon fhear aici ach nach fada go mbeadh, in ainneoin a muintire. Dá n-abraíteá tada léi faoin muirín, déarfadh sí leat nach raibh aon mhuirín uirthi, cén chaoi a mbeadh nuair nár phós sí go fóill? Ach d'fhéadfadh sí inseacht duit go cruinn faoi gach ar tharla dhi le linn a hóige. Bhíodh sí ag cur síos air le Cáit agus ag ceapadh go mb'í a deirfiúr í — an deirfiúr óg ab ansa léi fadó — agus bhíodh ar Cháit bhocht éisteacht léi agus caint a choinneáil léi go mbíodh sé i bhfad san oíche agus an croí á bhriseadh ina lár . . . .

Ar a hathair is minice bhíodh sí ag cur síos. D'insíodh sí dá 'deirfiúr' céard deireadh sé léi faoin bhfear dá dtug sí searc; d'insíodh sí dhí cé mar casadh le chéile ar an aonach iad, agus an masla thug sé don fhear óg agus an buille fuair sé uaidh.

'Agus nach raibh iomlán an chirt aige?' deireadh sí leis an 'deirfiúr.' 'Nár thug sé "bacach lofa" air? Ach tiocfaidh sé dom iarraidh fós agus éalódsa leis in ainneoin a bhfuil ann acu, agus cuideoidh tusa liom, a Mhairéad, nach gcuideoidh anois?'

Ní fhéadfá gan trua bheith agat do Cháit agus í ag éisteacht lena máthair ag cur síos go bríomhar agus go fileata ar a hathair a báitheadh, agus an tseanbhean ag ceapadh go raibh sí óg fós agus go raibh sí ar tí é phósadh!

Ach ní bhuaileadh an drochthaom í go han-mhinic. Cúpla uair sa ráithe, b'fhéidir.

Nuair thagadh an drochthaom uirthi agus gan Cáit bheith ina haice, chuireadh sí uirthi an seanghúna pósta bhí i dtaisce sa gcomhra agus ghléasadh sí í féin i bhfaisean na mban bhí óg deich mbliana ar fhichid roimhe sin.

Dá gcastaí duine léi deireadh sí leis gur éirigh léi éalú óna hathair, go raibh sí gléasta feistithe i gcomhair an fhir dá dtug sí gean agus grá, agus go mbeidís le chéile roimh éirí na gréine.

B'aisteach agus ba thruamhéileach an feic í an tseanbhean sin ar leag Dia lámh uirthi, agus í ag imeacht ar fud na mbóithre agus a cuid ribíní geala agus lásaí áille ag imeacht leis an ngaoith; ach ba thruamhéilí go mór an bhean óg fheiceáil ar a lorg agus í ag cur a tuairisce go himníoch.

Ach ní raibh aon urchóid sa tseanbhean sin ar ar leag Dia lámh. Bhí sí lách le gach n-aon.

Bhí trua ag na comharsana don bheirt. Bhí an tseanbhean 'roinnt aisteach' inti féin chuile lá riamh ó tháinig sí san áit. Níor ceapadh go raibh a meabhair agus a héirim aigne caillte aici go deo, níor ceapadh go raibh an t-éagruas céanna bhuail a lán dá muintir ag gabháil di. Ní fhéadfadh muintir na háite é cheapadh agus a laghad eolais bhí acu ar an muintir dar dhíobh í, agus má bhí sí níos aistí ná riamh, nár bheag an t-ionadh é agus ar fhulaing sí, an créatúr?

Ach d'aithnigh Cáit an galar agus cheil sí a heolas ar an saol.

Níor inis sí don Mháilleach féin é agus is gearr go raibh aiféala uirthi nár inis. I dtosach ní raibh aon fhonn uirthi é cheilt air ach lá dá rabhdar ag caint d'fhiafraigh sé dhi ar cheap sí gurbh é an galar sin bhí ag gabháil don mháthair agus dúirt sise nár cheap. Níor cheap an uair sin ach oiread. Ach nuair d'aithnight sí an galar níor labhair sí, mar bheadh uirthi an scéal iomlán nochtadh dhó. Bheadh uirthi faisnéis thabhairt ar a muintir uile, ar an mbeirt dhearthár lena máthair bhí i dteach na ngealt agus ar an deirfiúr nár fhág an teach le fiche bliain gan comhluadar. Is minic rinne sí féin caint lena máthair faoin gceist agus is minice ná sin rinne sí machnamh air agus shíl sí go mbeadh an t-eolas céanna ag an bhfear óg ar an ngalar bhí aici féin. Céard déarfadh sé léi ansin? Is é an chaoi a mbrisfí an cleamhnas . . . agus an gean bhí aici air! Agus cárbh fhios di cén t-athrú thiocfadh sa saol? Nuair bheidís pósta d'inseodh sí an scéal ina iomlán dó ach níor mhór dhi é inseacht i leaba a chéile. Bheadh taithí aige ar nósa na mná sin ar ar leag Dia lámh, agus bheadh trua aige dhi agus dá muintir nuair thuigfeadh sé an scéal.

Ar chaoi ar bith cheap sí go mb'fhearr an admháil chur ar cairde.

Faoin am seo dúirt Cáit léi féin go ndéanfadh sé leas mór don othar dá bhféadfadh sí cuairt fhada thabhairt ar áit éigin i bhfad ón bhfarraige. Ar charraig ag béal na céibhe báitheadh an bád ar a hathair agus nuair bhíodh an fharraige tráite bhíodh an charraig seo leis agus d'fhéadfadh a máthair í fheiceáil ón teach féin: nár mhór an gar dá mbeadh cónaí uirthi in áit éigin i bhfad ón gcarraig mhallaithe sin?

Thíos i gCondae Mhuigheo, amuigh faoin achréidh, bhí an deirfiúr ba shine léi pósta agus cheap an bhéan óg nárbh fhearr dhí rud a dhéanfadh sí ná cuairt thabhairt uirthi. Ní rabhdar chomh muinteartha le chéile is ba chóir do bheirt dheirfiúr bheith, agus nuair bhuail Cáit isteach chuici tar éis an aistir fhada ní fáilte mhór fearadh roimpi.

Teach ósta bhí ag an deirfiúr agus ag a fear, agus ó bhí bealach níos fearr acu sa saol ná ag an muintir sa mbaile, cheap sí gur ag éileamh cabhrach orthu tháinig Cáit, rud ab éigean di dhéanamh cheana. Ní thiocfadh sí chomh fada sin gan cuireadh murach gurbh ea.

Bhí fear an tí ag freastal ar an siopa agus fágadh an bheirt deirfiúr leo féin; ach ó bhí fuinneog bheag idir an seomra ina rabhdar agus an siopa d'fhéadfaidís glórtha na bhfear bhí ag ól a chlos go soiléir.

'Sea, a Cháit, cé chaoi bhfuil Maim?' arsa bean an tí.

'Go dona, a Mháire, go han-dona.'

Bhí an bhean phósta ag cniotáil ach thógadh sí na súile den obair ó am go ham agus ansin d'fheicteá an bháidh agus an tsaint ag déanamh iomaíocht ina dhá súil.

'Bhfuil sí níos measa?'

'Tá, i bhfad níos measa.'

'An ndearna sí aon rud aisteach le scathamh, a Cháit?'

'Déanann sí rud aisteach gach uile lá sa mbliain, a Mháire.'

Níor labhair ceachtar acu go ceann tamaill bhig. Cluineadh fear óg bhí ar bogmheisce ag gabháil fhoinn sa siopa.

'Chuile lá dá n-éiríonn orm bíonn eagla an domhain orm go ndéanfaidh sí rud uafásach éigin,' arsa Cáit. 'Ní aithníonn sí mise anois ach corruair. Ceapann sí gur mise a deirfiúr, gur mise Bríd Ní Dhónaill.'

'Go sábhála Dia sinn! Agus ní fhaca sí Bríd le dhá bhliain déag is fiche, ó phós sí Deaid!'

Cluineadh fear an tí ag labhairt go borb.

'Agus tá Bríd agus a fear ag éirí an-mhór linn,' arsa bean an tí go smaointeach, 'bhíodar anseo athrú inné agus d'óladar tae linn go deas muinteartha, agus dúirt an Caiptín nár ól sé a leithéid de tae riamh ach aon uair amháin sna hIndiacha . . . .'

'Drochrath ar Bhríd agus ar an gCaiptín freisin,' arsa Cáit go mífhoighdeach, 'ní le caint dhéanamh leat fúthusan thugas an turas seo.'

Deirfiúr lena máthair bhí pósta ag caiptín airm san áit bhí i gceist acu. Níor thugadar aint ná uncail ar mhuintir na máthar riamh. Daoine móra bhí iontu, dá mb'fhíor dóibh féin, agus ní bhíodh aon bhaint acu lena muintir. Ní raibh duine acu ar an tsochraid féin.

'Nach tú atá mífhoighdeach!' arsa bean an tí. 'Ach an mbíonn sí go dona chuile lá?'

'Ní bhíonn. Uaireanta bíonn a ciall agus a meabhair cheart aici, ach is mó an trua bheith ag féachaint uirthi agus an chiall aici ná aon uair eile.'

D'éirigh Cáit ina seasamh. Tháinig borradh agus fuinneamh ina glór.

'A Mháire,' ar sise, 'tá an croí á bhriseadh i mo lár. Níl fhios ach ag Dia mór céard d'fhulaing mé le bliain anuas. Bím ansin sa gcistinigh léi, agus ise ina suí ag an bhfuinneoig ag féachaint amach ar an bhfarraige agus doilíos nach bhfaca tusa riamh ina héadan. Bíonn fonn uirthi imeacht ach nach bhféadann sí. Bíonn na súile greamaithe aici san áit a bhfuil an charraig mhallaithe sin ag béal na céibhe. Agus nuair bhíos sé ag trá, fanann sí ansin sa gcathaoir ag an bhfuinneoig go mbíonn an charraig leis; nuair fheiceann sí an charraig ag éirí aníos as an bhfarraige de réir mar bhíos sé ag trá bíonn sí ag baothchaint léi féin go dtí go mbíonn a meabhair agus a cuimhne caillte aici . . . Ba mhór an bheannacht ó Dhia é dá bhféadfadh sí imeacht ón áit mhallaithe sin ar feadh i bhfad . . . . Táim cinnte, a Mháire, go mbeadh sí sásta cuairt fhada thabhairt ortsa anseo . . . .'

D'éis sí a béal go gcluinfeadh sí céard bhí le rá ag an deirfiúr.

'Seacht is sé pingne,' arsa fear an tí. 'Glac é nó fág é!'

Níor labhair bean an tí go ceann i bhfad. Bhí an stoca bhí á chniotáil aici ar an mbord os a comhair amach agus na spéacláirí leagtha lena thaobh. Faoi dheireadh thosaigh sí ag inseacht do Cháit cén fáth nach bhféadfadh sí glacadh le cúram na máthar. Bhí an teach cúng orthu cheana féin; ní raibh aon tseomra acu lena haghaidh; bheadh orthu bean fhreastail fháil di, agus bhí an t-airgead an-ghann orthu agus a raibh d'fhiacha amuigh orthu; agus an mhuirín mhór bhí orthu, agus ag súil le ceann eile go gairid; chaithfidís Tomás a chur ar scoil in áit éigin agus nárbh shin tríocha punt eile sa mbliain orthu.

Agus mar sin di. Bhí olc ag teacht ar Cháit.

'Agus ár ndóigh, a Mháire, ba mhór an náire ort a leithéid bheith sa teach agat,' arsa Cáit go nimhneach, 'nach mbeadh fhios ag an saol . . . .'

D'éirigh an bhean eile agus cochall uirthi.

'Bheadh fhios ag an saol anseo é b'fhéidir,' ar sise,

'ach ní bheadh fhios ag an Máilleach sin atá le do phósadh é. Lena cheilt air cheap tú do mháthair bhocht a dhíbirt . . . .'

'Ní hea.'

'Sea, a deirim; ar fhaitíos nach bpósfadh sé thú dá mbeadh fhios aige cén galar uafásach bhain lenár muintir.'

'Thug tú t'éitheach.'

'Agus thug tusa do dheargéitheach is a rá gur ar leas do mháthar tá tú.'

Chuaigh na focail throma chrua ó bhéal go béal eatarthu mar sceana géara nimhneacha, gur loiteadh an bheirt go mór, gur imigh Cáit léi as an teach agus fonn díoltais ina croí.

D'imigh Cáit léi agus fuath aici don deirfiúr. Ar phort na traenach thug sí aghaidh, ach ó bhí an traen dheiridh imithe uirthi b'éigean di fanacht ar an mbaile go maidin. I dteach ósta in aice leis an mbóthar iarainn chaith sí an oíche agus bhí cuimhne aici ar an teach ósta sin agus ar an oíche chaith sí ann lena beo.

Ní dhearna sí aon chodladh ach í sa leaba gan snáth a bhaint di. Ar leas na máthar thug sí an t-aistear, nó cheap sí ar fhágáil an bhaile di gurbh ea. Ach ag déanamh na smaointe dhi, i gcaitheamh na hoíche, bhí aimhreas uirthi go mb'fhéidir go raibh roinnt bheag den cheart ag a deirfiúr; an gcuimhneodh sí ar an máthair chur chun bealaigh ar chor ar bith murach go raibh an Máilleach le teacht ar an mbaile agus tréimhse a chaitheamh ann leis an iasc? Nach mbeadh sé isteach agus amach acu gach uair sa ló? Nach dtiúrfadh sé faoi deara gan rómhoill céard bhí ag gabháil don mháthair? Agus nuair chluinfeadh sé uaithi cén bhail bhí ar chuid de mhuintir a máthar céard déarfadh sé agus an chaoi ar cheil sí an scéal air ó thosach? Nach mbeadh fuath agus gráin aige uirthi? Agus an chaoi a n-inseodh sé féin gach ní dhi! Cheap an bhean chráite go mb'iad siúd na smaointe ba siocair lena turas ó bhí an croí chomh trom inti. Bha dhóigh léi go gcaithfeadh drochbhraon bheith inti; ní dhéanfadh aon bhean eile dá raibh ar aithne aici a leithéid de ghníomh. An mháthair bhocht a rug í a dhíbirt uaithi mar gheall ar fhear!

Ar theacht na maidne ní raibh aon chuimhne aici ar an gcarraig ar ar báitheadh a gaolta, ná ar an bhfarraige mhóir ar a mbíodh an mháthair ag síorfhéachaint, ná ar an doilíos millteach bhíodh i súile na máthar sin agus biseach uirthi, ná ar an trua bhíodh aici féin di, ná ar an gcion bhí acu ar a chéile.

An focal trom sin adúradh léi d'fhan sé ina croí. Bean níos measa ná í níor rugadh riamh, cheap sí.

Ach an té níos aithrí ina dhrochghníomh tá maithiúnas le fáil aige ó Dhia agus ó dhuine. Dhéanfadh sí aithrí. Ní phósfadh sí choíche. D'fhanfadh sí sa mbaile ag tabhairt aire dá máthair agus ag freastal uirthi go lá a báis. Amárach nuair d'fheicfeadh sí an Máilleach d'inseodh sí an scéal dhó ina iomlán. Bheadh gráin aige uirthi ar ndóigh, ach i gceann roinnt aimsire b'fhéidir go maithfeadh sé dhi gur mheall sí é, agus in ndiaidh cúpla bliain nó trí nach n-éireodh sé muinteartha léi arís ar bhealach eile? . . .

Croí luaidhe bhí sa gcailín óg dathúil bhí ina suí léi féin i gcúinne de charráiste nuair d'fhág an traen an stáisiún, agus thuig sí an lá sin cén fáth go dtugtar gleann na ndeor ar an saol aoibhinn seo sa bpaidir.

Ar shroichint an bhaile dhi chonaic sí plód beag daoine taobh amuigh de theach Sheáin Uí Néill, an giúistís. Bhí carr ar an tsráid ann agus síothmhaor i ngreim sa gcapall. Ag dul thar an teach dhi thug sí faoi deara go raibh a raibh ann ag féachaint uirthi go géar agus go raibh fonn ar chuid acu labhairt léi ach go raibh cineál leisce orthu.

Ní dheachaigh sí i bhfad gur glaodh uirthi, agus chuaigh sí isteach.

Bhí a máthair istigh roimpi, an seanghúna pósta uirthi ach é fliuch salach, ribíní agus lásaí bhí geal tráth ag sileadh léi agus í ina suí ar chathaoir ag gabháil amhráin ghrá.

Bhí an Máilleach sa láthair agus mhínigh sé an scéal do Cháit. Dúirt sé gur gabhthas an mháthair ar maidin, gur éalaigh sí ón tseanbhean bhí á faire, agus gur ghortaigh sí bean comharsan bhí ar tí í thabhairt abhaile. Bhíothas lena cur isteach i dteach na ngealt.

Labhair Cáit léi ach níor aithnigh sí í. Ag baothchaint bhí sí agus ag rá go raibh sí an-bhuíoch de na daoine uaisle seo — na síothmhaoir bhí i gceist aici — go raibh sí an-bhuíoch díobh go rabhdar ar tí í thabhairt chuig an bhfear dá dtug sí cion.

Ach d'aithnigh sí Cáit nuair chuaigh sí ar an gcarr, nó shíl sí gurbh í a deirfiúr féin í.

'Bhí iontaoibh agam asatsa,' ar sí, 'ach shíl tú mé choinneáil uaidh ar nós cách. Ach níor éirigh leat. Tháinig na fir uaisle seo le cuidiú liom. Eisean chuir chugam iad . . .'

A ógánaigh na súl nglas
Dá dtug mo chroí gean,

na focail deireannacha chuala Cáit uaithi agus an carr ag dul soir an bóthar.

Chuaigh Cáit agus an Máilleach siar an bóthar chuig an teach. Bhí dhá mhíle go leith de shlí orthu agus níor labhraíodh focal ar feadh an achair, go rabhdar ag an gcéibh beagnach. Bhí sé ina thráthnóna breá aoibhinn agus na héanlaith ag ceiliúr go meidhreach sna crainn. Bhí an cabhlach bád iascaireachta ag dul siar an cuan faoi lán tseoil. Má tá doilíos agus briseadh croí sa saol cheapfá tráthnóna mar é seo nach é toil Dé é, ach toil na ndaoine.

Bhí fonn ar an Máilleach focal éigin a rá leis an gcailín óg dá dtug sé grá ach céard d'fhéadfadh sé a rá?

Sa deireadh b'éigean dó labhairt.

'Bíodh croí agat, a Cháit, a chuid,' ar seisean.

'Beidh.'

'Leag Dia lámh throm uirthi,' ar seisean.

'Ach is troime go mór an lámh leag Sé ar an muintir d'fhág sí ina diaidh,' ar sise, 'ach toil Dé go nglacaimis leis.'

Tá cloch in aice na céibhe ar a dtugtar 'an chathaoir mhór,' agus ag dul thar an gcloich seo dhóibh dúirt sise:

'Suímis anseo go fóill beag, a Antaine,' ar sise.

Shuigh. Bhí seisean i ngreim láimhe inti agus í ag féachaint amach uaithi ar an bhfarraige go smaointeach.

'Is minic a shíleas le dhá bhliain,' ar sise, agus ba dhóigh leat uirthi gur ag caint léi féin bhí sí, 'is minic a cheapas nuair bhíodh an drochthaom tagtha uirthi go mba mhiste an duine an mheabhair agus an tuiscint, agus go mb'fhearrde an duine an éigiall. Tá croí meidhreach aici anocht agus tá mo chroíse chomh dubh le gual agus chomh trom le luaidhe . . . .'

Níor thuig an fear óg i gceart í.

'An mheabhair mhill an saol orainn,' ar sise.

'Ach éist liom, a Cháit, a stór,' ar seisean, 'níor milleadh an saol orainne. Tá saol aoibhinn i ndán dúinn fós le chabhair Dé i bhfochair a chéile . . . .'

'Níl. Ní phósfaidh mé choíche.'

'Ní phósfaidh tú choíche! Cén fáth?'

'Mheallas thú, a Antaine. Níor insíos duit cén galar bhí ag gabháil do mo mháthair . . . .'

'Ach bhí fhios agam féin é. Ní déantar caint faoi rud mar sin,' arsa an fear óg agus ionadh air.

'Agus cheileas ort cén bhail bhí ar mhuintir mo mháthar; níor dhúras leat riamh go raibh beirt dhearthár léi i dteach na ngealt agus deirfiúr léi nach bhfuil i bhfad níos fearr ná iad . . . .'

'Cén mí-ádh tá ort, a Cháit,' ar seisean, 'nach raibh fhios agam é sin le blianta?' Bhí iontas ar an gcailín ach níor chuir sí aon cheist air. Bhris an gol uirthi . . . .

Bhí an ghrian ag dul faoi sa bhfarraige nuair scaradar le chéile.

'Ní haon mhaith dhuit bheith ag caint liom, ní phósfaidh mé choíche,' an focal deiridh dúirt sí leis an oíche sin.

Agus níor phós. Tháinig an Máilleach á hiarraidh go minic ach ní ghéillfeadh sí dhó. Tá sí ina cónaí sa teach beag in aice na céibhe fós, agus is minic d'fheicfeá ag an bhfuinneoig bhig í agus í ag féachaint amach ar an bhfarraige, agus ar an gcarraig mar ar báitheadh a muintir, agus súil aici leis an lá a mbeadh sí lena máthair sna Flaithis — nó i dteach na ngealt.

THE WOMAN ON WHOM GOD LAID HIS HAND[1]

A finer boat than the Cailin Beag Donn you wouldn't see in Galway Bay, and, as the shopkeeper who owned her was about to sell her, Padraig O'Nea thought she would make a good dowry for his daughter — if he could get her reasonably cheap. Anthony O'Malley, however, the young woman's intended, said that they'd be well advised to test the boat before buying, to discover if she came up to her reputation. The old man thought this good advice, and he and his son Seamus and O'Malley went out for a night's fishing to see what the boat was made of.

Kate, the engaged daughter, went to the quay with her people to see them off, and stayed a good while on the rise watching the fishing fleet go down the bay before the wind. It was late evening as she returned home, and her mother had supper prepared. The table was set and a cake cooling on the window-sill and the kettle was singing pleasantly. The two women sat at the table, gazing from time to time through the window at the boats which strongly resembled a flock of nuns taking the air in their convent garden.

1. The phrase means 'The woman whom God afflicted'.

It was growing very quiet. The birds — all lively music an hour before — were turning listless. It seemed that they'd tired of song and would never sing again. Birds and beasts were yielding to sleep but the young woman stayed at the window until the boats vanished from her in the darkness and a bright star showed fitful in the western sky.

The old woman by the fire sighed.

'What's wrong, mother? Kate asked, rising and going to her.

'I'll be very lonely without you, dear.'

'Won't you have my father, not to speak of Seamus?'

'Seamus won't stay long with us. There's nothing with the young people today only leaving.'

'But how often you yourself made us laugh telling how you eloped with my father in spite of your people,' Kate spoke encouragingly.

'And look at the life I've had since.'

Her mother wasn't a complainer and the young woman was put out to find her thinking that way. She was well aware that her mother's people had been so opposed to her marriage that they hadn't spoken to her since. Her mother had a good upbringing and education but she'd gone with the life her husband had been able to give.

'But I'm not flying away from you,' Kate said. 'You'll see me often. I won't be more than twenty miles away.'

'I know that, love,' the mother replied, 'but I've been thinking this while that my father's curse has followed me. Look how they've all left me — and now you. It seems to me they've left because I'm a little bit strange in myself now and again — isn't it said, "to the seventh generation"?'[2]

Kate took her mother's hand and caressed it. She knew well what was troubling her. She knew that there were few generations of her mother's people without one 'a little bit strange', and that some of them had been disturbed enough to require restraint. The local people weren't aware of that; her mother was from another county, and, if there was the odd one who'd heard the story, that wasn't pinning it down.

'You shouldn't talk like that,' she said anxiously.

'But it's the truth, Kate,' the old woman answered.

Night fell. Kate lit the lamp and drew the blind. Three visitors came, three not often seen together — Anxiety, Terror, and Hope. They were evident to the old woman by the fire, and she surprised her daughter when she threw the odd word into the talk of the visitors. To Kate, her mother was getting stranger by the day.

'The wind is rising, it's very dangerous on the sea tonight,' the old woman remarked, her voice that of Anxiety.

The daughter let up the blind. There was a moon and the sea was altogether calm. It would never drown anyone again, it pronounced.

'Look, mother. Not a ripple. You're dozing.'

The boat wasn't expected until daybreak.

'I'll stay here until morning,' said the old woman, brooding. 'Haven't a lot of people been drowned here in my time? Pat's Paddy and his people were drowned last year on a moonlit night just like this; and little Peg's Michael and his sister were drowned the year before last, and . . . was it two or three years ago the people of The Island were drowned?'

The mother was going on by the fire but her talk didn't worry Kate. Two better boatsmen than her father and O'Malley weren't to be had in the bay.

'Come here to me,' the old woman said abruptly.

Kate went to her. The old woman took both her hands and gazed into her eyes.

'Kate, tell me the truth,' she spoke. 'If one — or two — from the boat were to be drowned tonight, whom would you wish to be saved?'

'For God's sake, mother, don't be talking like that,' Kate answered, fearful, and she broke from her mother's grasp. The two sat by the fire, one each side. The old woman fell asleep and so did Kate. It was dawn when both were roused suddenly. Something heavy struck the closed door.

'Open the door,' said the old woman calmly, 'and we'll see which of them has come safe.'

She had to open it herself — Kate sat there numb — and it was O'Malley who fell in a heap onto the floor, soaked wet, and terror in his eyes.

He was just able to tell the women his story. The boat had been wrecked at Carraganiolar. He had managed to get the old man ashore but the life was gone out of him. The young lad had an oar but there was no knowing what had happened there.

'Let us look for the bodies,' said the old woman, going out.

The son's body was never found. The shore was

2. Said of a persistent hereditary affliction.

searched from Loop Head[3] to Galway but there was no sign of him. The father was waked but his wife never shed a tear.

Betimes she would be seen in some corner talking to a neighbour woman, and if you listened carefully you'd hear her words.

'This drowning is part of the old curse,' she would say. 'What's the point of tears? Isn't my heart too full for that? I always knew he'd be drowned one day.'

She would go to the room where the body lay and — when alone there — speak to her husband.

'You often laughed about the curse, Patrick,' she said to the corpse, 'but, if the two of you are together now, tell my father to free me of it. Would you not tell him now, Patrick? I was always fond of you — from the first day I saw you — of your handsome head and your bright face.'

She restrained herself when a neighbour came into the room, and, when the neighbour began to sympathise, she said only, 'Stay quiet now. This drowning has to do with my father's curse. It was destined from the start. Kate is going too. In no time I'll be lonely as I was at the beginning.'

She had to be sent off to rest before dawn.

After her husband's burial she turned stranger than ever. She would rise by night unknown to Kate and slip out and roam the shore searching for her son. She was often seen walking the shore by night, hair loose on the wind, wearing only her nightdress, keeping at it quite alone, searching every hole there was and striking her feet against the sharp stones. She spoke nonsense mostly but at times she sang verses. She had one never heard except from her.

It went —

I walk about at night
In rain and wind
Searching for my son, my treasure
Where are you from me, Seamus?

Then another thought would surface, and she'd say —

But when The Infant Jesus
Lay at the foot of The Cross
You were there, Mary
And He on your knee.

And she would say that her grief and hardship were far greater than Mary's because her son's body had not been returned to her after The Crucifixion.

'Where have you gone to, Seamus? Why aren't you on my knee?'

People who heard her going on like that would think of coaxing her home. Sometimes they succeeded. Sometimes they didn't and Kate would have the job of finding her.

She kept up the search and the night-walking until Kate had to sleep in the same bed with her. Even so, she awoke quite often to find the mother gone and the job there of going out to find her.

She was getting worse by the day. She lost her memory. Everything that had happened from her marriage thirty years ago was gone from her. If you mentioned her husband, she would reply that she had no husband but would shortly — in spite of her people. If anything was said of her family, she would reply that she had none: how could she since she had never married? She could, however, tell you precisely concerning all the events of her youth. She was in the habit of describing those days to Kate, imagining Kate to be her sister — the young sister dearest to her long ago. And Kate, heart-broken, had to listen to her and keep talk with her far into the night.

She went on most of all about her father. She would tell her 'sister' what he had said about the man she loved, how the two met at the fair, how he had abused the young man, and how the young man had struck him.

'And wasn't he wholly in the right?' she would say. 'Hadn't he called him "a rotten tramp"? But he'll come asking for me yet, and I'll elope with him in spite of them all, and you'll help me, Brigid, won't you now?'

You'd pity Kate listening to her mother describing vividly the father who'd been drowned, the mother imagining she was still young and about to marry him.

She didn't suffer a bad attack very often, however — perhaps a couple of times a month. When that happened, and Kate wasn't around, she would put on her wedding dress which she had laid by in a trunk and dress herself up in the fashion of the young women of thirty years back. If anyone met her, she would say that she had run away from her father, that she was dressed up for the man she loved, and that they would be together before the break of day.

3. A headland in County Clare, south of Galway Bay.

It was a strange, grievous sight to see this old woman on whom God had laid His hand wandering the roads with her bright ribbons and her beautiful lace flowing in the breeze, and a sight more grievous again was the young woman on her trail, anxiously enquiring after her.

There was no evil, however, in the old woman on whom God had laid His hand. She was gentle towards all.

The neighbours pitied them both. The old woman had been 'a little strange' from the first day she'd come to the place. It wasn't thought that she'd quite lost her mind, that the same malady as had afflicted many of her people was now taking her. The neighbours didn't know enough about her background to arrive at that conclusion. If she was stranger than before, that was not surprising in the light of what she'd been through, the creature.

Kate, nevertheless, recognised the disease but kept her knowledge from the world. She didn't even tell it to O'Malley and it wasn't long before she regretted not having told him. At the start she had no desire to conceal it from him but, one day they were talking, he asked her if she thought it was that disease her mother had, and she answered that she didn't. And, at the time, that was true. But when she recognised the affliction she said nothing because that would have meant telling the whole story. She would have to tell him all about her people, of her two uncles in the asylum, and of her aunt who hadn't left the house on her own for twenty years. She often spoke to her mother about the matter, and still more often considered it — until it seemed to her that the young man knew every bit as much about it as she herself did. What would he say to her? The match would be broken off — and how dearly she loved him — how did she know what might happen? When they were married she would tell him the whole story bit by bit. He would become accustomed to the ways of the woman on whom God had laid His hand, he would have compassion for her and her people when he understood the story. All things considered, it seemed better to postpone telling him.

About this time it occurred to Kate that it would help the patient greatly if she were able to make a long visit somewhere a distance from the sea. The boat had been wrecked on a rock not far from the quay: that rock was visible at low-tide, visible to the mother from the very house: wouldn't it be much to her advantage if she were to live somewhere well removed from that cursed sight?

Her elder married sister lived off in Mayo and the young woman decided she couldn't do better than pay her a visit. The sisters weren't as close as they might have been, and, when Kate presented herself after the long journey, the welcome wasn't particularly warm.

The sister and her husband kept a public house, and, since they'd done better in the world than the people at home, she concluded that Kate had come looking for help — something she'd had to do before. She wouldn't have come the journey without invitation unless that was the reason.

The husband was serving in the shop, and the sisters were left to themselves. Through a small window between the room they were in and the shop, they could hear plainly the voices of the men drinking.

'Well, Kate, and how's mother?' asked the sister.

'She's bad, Mary, very bad.'

The sister was knitting but, from time to time she lifted her gaze from the work, and affection and meanness could be seen struggling in her eyes.

'She's worse?'

'Yes, much worse.'

'Did she do anything strange lately?'

'She does something strange every day of the year.'

Neither of them spoke for a little while. A young man, slightly drunk, could be heard singing in the shop.

'Every day that comes I'm in dread she'll do something terrible,' Kate offered. 'She only knows me the odd time now. She thinks I'm her sister, that I'm Brigid O'Donnell.'

'God save us. And she hasn't seen Brigid in twenty-two years — since she married Dad.'

The husband could be heard talking loudly.

'And Brigid and her husband are becoming very friendly to us,' the sister continued after some reflection. 'They were here the day before yesterday, they had tea with us very agreeably, and the captain said that he'd never — except once in India — tasted such tea.'

'Bad luck to Brigid and the captain,' Kate came back impatiently. 'It isn't to talk about them that I made this journey.'

An aunt married to an army captain was the topic. They never used the word 'aunt' or 'uncle' of the mother's people. They were important persons, in their own estimation, and would have nothing to do with the 'lesser' family. Neither of them had come to the funeral.

'Aren't you very impatient?' said the married sister. 'But is she really bad every day?'

'No. Sometimes she has her right mind — but it's more pitiful to see her then than any other time.'

Kate rose. Her voice turned bitter.

'Mary,' she said, 'my heart is breaking. Only God knows what I've been through this past year. I'm there in the kitchen with her, she sitting by the window, looking out at the sea, and such grief in her face as you never saw. She wants to go away but she can't. Her eyes are stuck to the place where that cursed rock is at the mouth of the quay. Come the ebb tide, she sits there in her chair by the window until the rock is visible. When she sees the rock rising from the sea as the tide ebbs, she talks nonsense to herself until mind and memory desert her.... It'd be a great blessing if she could leave that awful place for a long spell. I'm sure, Mary, she'd be happy to come to you here for a space.'

She fell silent to hear what her sister would say.

'Seven-and-sixpence,' the husband spoke in the shop. 'Take it or leave it.'

The sister said nothing for a long time. The stocking she was knitting was on the table before her and her spectacles beside it. Finally, she began to explain to Kate why she couldn't take on the care of the mother. As it was, the house was too small for them. There was no room for her. They'd have to get her an attendant, and money was scarce — a lot was owing to them. They had a large family, and another child on the way. Thomas had to be sent off to school somewhere, and that was thirty pounds more a year ....

And so on. Listening, Kate sickened.

'And besides, Mary,' she spoke venomously, 'the shame of having the likes of her under your roof — wouldn't the whole world know?'

The other woman rose in anger.

'People here would know of it, yes,' she answered, 'but O'Malley who's going to marry you wouldn't. To keep it from him you thought of getting rid of your poor mother.'

'No.'

'Yes, I tell you. Afraid he won't marry you if he knew the terrible disease our people carry.'

'You lie.'

'And you're a worse liar to claim you're here for your mother's good.'

The hard words flashed between them like poison-tipped knives, they were both wounded, and Kate left the house with vengeance in her heart.

Hatred for the sister filled Kate as she departed. She made for the railway station but, since the last train was gone, she had to stay over in the town. She spent the night in an hotel by the railway and, long as she lived, she remembered that hotel and the night she passed there.

Lying on the bed fully-clothed, she got no sleep. She'd made the journey for the mother's good or so she'd thought leaving home. Thinking it over, however, through the night, she began to feel that maybe the sister wasn't altogether wrong; would she have come up with the plan at all were it not for the fact that O'Malley was coming to their village for the fishing season? Wouldn't he be in and out every hour of the day? Wouldn't he soon notice what was bothering her mother? And when he heard from her the story of her mother's people, what would he say — given the way she'd concealed it from the start? Wouldn't he detest her? And the way in which he was completely open with her?

The unhappy woman — in her burdened state — imagined that she'd come on the essential motive of her journey. She must have bad blood in her, no woman she'd ever known would do such a thing — to give her poor mother the road on account of a man.

Morning came, and she no longer remembered the rock on which her relatives were wrecked, nor the sea on which her mother's eyes dwelt on her better days, nor the terrible grief in those eyes, nor her own pity, nor the love between them. The hard word spoken was lodged in her heart. She felt herself the worst woman ever born.

But God and man grant forgiveness to the sinner who repents. She would repent. She'd never marry. She would stay at home looking after her mother and waiting on her till she died. Tomorrow when she'd meet O'Malley, she'd tell him the whole story. He'd hate her, doubtless, but perhaps, with the passing of time, he'd forgive her the deception, and in two or three years would he not be her friend again some other way?

The beautiful young woman sitting alone in a corner of the carriage was leaden-hearted as the train left the station. She understood that day why the prayer terms this lovely world a vale of tears.

Reaching her own town, she saw a scatter of people outside the house of John O'Neill, the magistrate. There was a car[4] in the street, and a policeman holding the horse. Going by the house, she noticed that those present were looking keenly at her and that some wanted to speak to her but hesitated to make the move.

She hadn't gone far before she was called back, and she entered the house. There was her mother, the old wedding-gown on her but sodden and dirty, the once-bright ribbons and lace trailing about her as she sat on a chair singing a love-song.

O'Malley was present, and he explained the story to Kate. He said the mother had been taken bad that morning, escaped from the old woman in charge of her, and injured a neighbour-woman about to take her home. Now they were going to commit her.

Kate spoke to her but got no sign of recognition. She was rambling, saying that she was very grateful to these good people — meaning the police — who were about to take her to the man she loved.

She recognised Kate, however, when she boarded the car — took Kate, rather, to be her own sister.

'I always trusted you,' she said, 'but you thought to keep me from him like everybody else. You failed. These good men came to my help. He sent them to me . . .

Oh, youth of the grey eyes
To whom I gave heart's love . . . .

those were the last words Kate heard from her as the car went over the road.

Kate and O'Malley went back to the house. They had two-and-a-half miles to go but not a word was spoken until they were almost at the quay. It was a fine pleasant evening and the birds were singing buoyantly in the trees. The fishing-fleet was going down the bay in full sail. If there's hardship and heartbreak in the world, you would think on such an evening that it's man's doing and not the will of God.

O'Malley wished to say something to the girl he loved but what could he say? In the end he had to speak.

4. cart.

'Have courage, Kate, love.'

'I will.'

'God laid a heavy hand on her.'

'And a much heavier hand on those she left after her — but it's the will of God that we accept it.'

There's a rock near the quay known as 'The Big Chair': as they were going past it, she said, 'Let's sit here a moment, Anthony.'

They sat there. He held her hand while she gazed at the sea, pondering.

'For two years I've often thought,' she said — and it seemed to her she was speaking to herself, 'often thought when she was having a bad turn that reason and understanding are no advantage — that loss of reason is preferable. She's easy tonight but my heart is black as coal and heavy as lead . . . .'

The young man didn't rightly understand her.

'It's reason that has destroyed us,' she said.

'But listen, Kate dear,' he said. 'Our lives haven't been destroyed. There's a grand life together before us with the help of God.'

'No. I'll never marry.'

'Never marry — why?'

'I deceived you, Anthony. I didn't tell you of the disease my mother had.'

'But I knew myself. You don't talk of the like of that,' said the young man, wonderingly.

'And I kept from you the condition of my mother's people, I never told you that she had two brothers in the asylum and a sister not much better than them . . . .'

'What's wrong with you, Kate?' he asked. 'Haven't I known that for years?'

She was surprised but she didn't question him. She burst into tears.

The sun was setting when they separated.

'No good in your talking to me — I'll never marry,' was her last word that evening.

Nor did she marry. O'Malley came asking often but she wouldn't consent. She's still living in the cottage near the quay, often to be seen in the little window looking out on the sea and on the rock where her people were wrecked, waiting for the day when she'll be with her mother in heaven or in the asylum.

LIAM Ó FLAITHEARTA (LIAM O'FLAHERTY)

(1896-1984)

from: DÚIL (1953)

[The English version, by O'Flaherty himself, is from *The Wave and Other Stories* (London: Longman, 1980).]

AN CHULAITH NUA

D'fhág na Dioláin an tseanmháthair sa mbaile chun aire a thabhairt don teach agus chuadar amach ag bearradh caorach. Shiúil an bheirt ba sine den chlann, Máire agus Tomás, in éineacht leis an athair agus an mháthair. Bhí Máire hocht mbliana déag agus bhí Tomás sé bliana déag. Dá bhrí sin bhíodar ar nós daoine fásta cheana féin. Ní raibh sa mbearradh dóibh ach obair mar obair ar bith eile. Go deimhin, is ar bhainis a bhí Máire ag caint agus í ag siúl le taobh a máthar, fad bhí Tomás ag cur síos ar an gcur lena athair.

Maidir leis an gceithre pháiste eile, ritheadar ar a ndícheall ón tsráid soir an bóthar ard nó gur shroicheadar róidín na gcrag. Chasadar isteach sa róidín agus ansin b'éigean dóibh ligean go réidh dóibh féin, mar gheall ar an gcosán bheith róchúng clochach le rith a dhéanamh tríd. Bhíodar ag sioscadh agus ag gabháil fhoinn, chomh hard agus bhí ina gceann, ag dul tríd an róidín. B'éigean dóibh bheith ag léimneach ó chloch go cloch agus a gcloigne beaga ag éirí os cionn na gclaíocha.

Cailíní beaga triúr acu, bibeanna geala orthu agus ribíní daite ina ngruaig fhionn. B'é Séamaisín beag an ceathrú duine. Bhí seisean anois ina sheachtú bliain.

Rith an buachaillín beag seo amach chun tosaigh ar gach uile dhuine eile. Sheas sé anois agus arís le impí a dhéanamh orthu deifriú. Bhí a éadan beag cruinn chomh gruama sin agus nach mbeadh fios agat an áthas nó brón a bhí air. Go deimhin ní raibh an fios sin barrainneach aige féin. Gealladh culaith nua dó as olann na bliana seo. Gealladh dhó i bhfad ó shoin an chulaith, faoin Nollaig seo caite. Gheall a athair agus a mháthair dhó go minic ó shoin an rud céanna. Anois nuair a bhí lá an bhearrtha tagtha faoi dheireadh agus obair an bhréidín le tosú, ba deacair leis an ngasúr bocht a chuid foighde a choinneáil faoi smacht. Aie! Ba chosúil le drochphian an dúil a bhí aige sa gculaith nua.

Go dtí seo, ní bhfuair sé riamh ach giota de chulaith anois agus giota eile arís. Aon bhliain amháin gheobhadh sé an treabhsar, agus an seaicéad an bhliain dar gcionn. Bheadh paistí ar an treabhsar sula gcuirfí an seaicéad ina theannta agus bheadh an seaicéad giobalach sula dtiocfadh treabhsar nua eile ag triall air as an olann. I gcruthúnas duit gur dheacair don ghasúr creideamh sa gculaith nua mhíorúilteach seo bhí geallta dhó. Dar fia! Bhí rún aige súil ghrinn a choinneáil leagtha ar an olann, gach uile orlach den bhealach ó dhroim na caorach go seol an fhíodóra agus snáthad an táilliúra. Mar sin ní fhéadfaí feall a dhéanamh air.

Bhí na caoirigh i ngleann fada caol. Bhí claí ard timpeall ar an ngleann. Bhíodar ina seasamh le taobh a chéile agus tóin le claí acu nuair a tháinig Séamaisín. Cé nach raibh mórán den lá caite fós, bhí teas mór cheana féin sa ngrian agus bhí na hainmhithe ag soláthar foscaidh uaidh. Ba doiligh leo a n-olann trom faoi theas an tsamhraidh. Bhí rith-tharraingt anála acu agus a gcinn fúthu.

'Seamhain! Seamhain!' d'fhógair Séamaisín ar theacht in amharc dhó. 'Is gearr anois go mbeidh sibh in bhur gcraiceann. Foighid libh.'

D'ardaigh na caoirigh a gcinn agus bhreathnaíodar ar an ngasúr.

'Ma-a,' adúradar.

Theannadar le chéile ansin agus a n-aghaidh go faiteach ar an mbuachaill beag, ag ceapadh go raibh gadhar ina dhiaidh aniar. Bhí sé cinn acu bán agus mór, droim orthu chomh cothrom le clár mar gheall ar an ualach mór olla. Caoirigh sléibhe na cúig cinn eile. Bhíodar beag agus dorcha. Ní raibh aon téagar ina gcuid olla agus bhí sí catach. Bhí cúig uan de chuid na bliana sin leis an tréad. Bhí trí cinn de na huain seo leathfhásta agus bhí na heireabaill gearrtha díobh. Coinníodh iad le reitheadh. Bhí an péire eile fós ag cnáfairt.

Bhí na caoirigh ar fad curtha i gcúinne ag

Séamaisín agus an triúr cailín beag nuair a tháinig an dream eile. Ansin do caitheadh ceithre cinn de na caoirigh bhána ar a ndroim agus thosaigh an bearradh. Choinnigh Séamaisín greim cinn ar an gcaora a bhí a mháthair a bhearradh.

Ar dtús bhí an chaora seo ag iarraidh éirí nuair d'airigh sí an deimheas ag teangabháil lena craiceann.

'Cheapfá nach maith léi a cuid olla a chailleadh,' adeir Séamaisín, 'an chaoi tá sí ag corraí.'

'Tá eagla uirthi,' adeir an mháthair. 'Sin é an fáth atá sí ag iarraidh éirí.'

'An gceapann sí go bhfuil tú ag braith í mharú?'

'B'fhéidir go gceapann.'

'Ach deir tú liom gur rud beannaithe caora. Deir tú gur thug Dia olann di, caoi go mbeadh ábhar eadaí againn.'

'Fíor dhuit. Rud beannaithe í. Ní mar an gabhar, nach bhfuil ruainne olla ar a dhroim.'

'Tá an gabhar olc? Tá peaca air?'

'Tá, a stór. Is drochrud é an gabhar. Is gadaí é.'

'Má tá sí seo beannaithe, cé an fáth go bhfuil eagla uirthi? Nár inis Dia di cé an fáth bhfuil olann aici? Nár innis Sé di go bhfuil iallach uirthi an olann a thabhairt dúinn?'

'Dún do bhéal agus coinnigh greim maith uirthi. Sin nó gearrfad leis an deimheas í.'

'Ó! A Thiarna! Ná gearr í. Bheadh peaca déanta agat dá ngearrfá rud naofa. Ó! A Thiarna! Chuirfeá mí-ádh ar mo chulaith nua.'

'Déanfaidh sin. Coinníodh tusa í agus ní ghearrfaidh mise í.'

'D'fhan an chaora socair nuair bhí a muineál bearrtha. Bhí an deimheas anois ag gluaiseacht go tapaidh siar an droim agus sraith olla ag titim ina dhiaidh. Bhí fréamha na holla chomh mín le síoda. Bhíodar ag scairteadh sa ngrian mar gheall ar an méid olla bhí iontu.

'Ar inis Dia do na daoine le éadach a dhéanamh?' adeir Séamaisín.

'D'inis,' adeir an mháthair.

'As olann chaorach?'

'Sea.'

'Cé dó ar inis Sé é?'

'Do naomh.'

'Ar inis Sé dhó uile é san am céanna? Bearradh agus sníomh agus fíochán agus táilliúireacht?'

'D'inis.'

'Cé an t-ainm bhí ar an naomh?'

'Níl fhios agam.'

'Mór an trua. Ba mhaith liom paidir rá leis an naomh sin. D'iarrfainn air Neidí, an táilliúir, a choinneáil ón ól nuair bheidh sé ag déanamh mo chulaith. Ach ní féidir liom paidir rá leis agus gan fios agam ar a ainm. Is aisteach nach bhfuil ainm ar naomh tréan mar é. Caitheann sé gurb é an naomh is tréine bhí riamh é, má mhúin sé do na daoine le éadach a dhéanamh. Marach é, chaillfí na daoine sa ngeimhreadh.'

'Má bhíonn tú i do bhuachaill maith nó go dtiocfaidh Neidí le do chulaith a dhéanamh, ní ligfidh Dia do Neidí bheith súgach. Ansin ní dhéanfaidh sé ciseach de; an chaoi dhéanann sé le culaith nuair atá ól déanta aige. Ar a mhalairt sin beidh sé ar meisce agus beidh do chulaith chomh gránna agus nach ligfeadh an náire dhuit í chur ort. Déanfaidh sin anois thú. Ná cuir níos mó ceisteanna orm faoin naomh seo agus an naomh siúd bhí fadó ann.'

'Déanfad gach uile rud déarfaidh tú liom, a mháthair. Ó! A Thiarnín! Is cuma liom cé an t-ainm bhí ar an naomh tréan siúd.'

Choinníodar orthu ag bearradh nó go raibh na caoirigh ar fad chomh lom le naíonáin. Tar éis mar nochtaíodh gach caora, chraith sí í féin agus thosaigh sí ag ithe go hamplach. Anois agus arís d'ardódh sí a ceann agus dhéanfadh sí méileach bheag áthais, mar gheall ar an olann bheith bainte di.

Bailíodh an olann. Cuireadh i málaí í agus tugadh abhaile í. Ansin chuaigh na mná ag plé léi, á fáil faoi réir don fhíodóir. Chuidigh Séamaisín leo. Nuair bhí an olann nite agus í scartha amach ar tuar i mbuaile, bhí bród air mar gur ligeadh dó fanacht ansin ag tabhairt aire dhi ar feadh an lae . . . Nuair bhí sí spíonta agus cardáilte agus rollaí breátha ramhra déanta di, ligeadh dó cuidiú leis an sníomh. Choinníodh sé an fhearsad fad bhí a dheirfiúr ag tarraingt an tsnáith de agus á chasadh ar an gceirtlín. Cuireadh an snáth bán ar cheirtlín amháin agus an snáth dorcha ar cheirtlín eile. Ba mhíllteach an méid bhí sa gceirtlín bhán nuair bhí an olann ar fad sníofa.

Chuaigh Séamaisín go teach an fhíodóra in éineacht lena mháthair. Bhí trí mhíle bealaigh le siúl acu go dtí é. Chuir an mháthair uirthi an t-éadach ab fhearr a bhí aici le haghaidh an aistir. Chuir a threabhsar giobalach náire ar Sheámaisín agus é ar sodar le taobh a mháthar, ach níor mhian leis casadh abhaile ina dhiaidh sin. Bhí eagla air go n-éireodh rud éigin uafásach don olann dá ligfeadh sé as amharc í. Ba mhaith leis, freisin, fiafraí den fhíodóir ainm an naoimh siúd a fuair amach cé an chaoi le éadach a dhéanamh.

Chaill sé misneach, ámh, nuair a shroich sé an teach. Sheas sé taobh istigh den doras agus a bhéal oscailte, ag breathnú ar an seol. Ba rud iontach ar fad é an seol, facthas don ghasúr. Agus é ag dearcadh ar an spól á chaitheamh anonn agus anall agus ar an éadach ag fás ar an snáth i mbealach míorúilteach éigin, thuig sé gur rud diaganta é an fíochán.

Is gearr gur thug an fíodóir faoi deara iontas an ghasúir.

'Sea anois,' adeir sé. 'An dúil atá agat fíodóireacht a fhoghlaim?'

'Gabh anall anseo, a Shéamaisín,' adeir a mháthair, a bhí ina suí cois na tine. 'Ná bí sa mbealach ar an obair.'

'Lig don ghasúr,' adeir an fíodóir. 'Fág san áit a bhfuil sé an duine bocht.'

Fear beag é an fíodóir. Bhí gruaig dhubh air agus bhí a chraiceann buí. Bhí súile an-ghealgháireach aige. Sin é an fáth nach raibh aon eagla ar Shéamaisín roimhe. Labhair sé leis an bhfear beag buí.

'Bhfuil ainm an naoimh agat?' adeir sé.

'Ná tabhair aird air,' adeir an mháthair.

Ach tháinig an fíodóir anall go dtí an gasúr agus dúirt sé:

'Cé an naomh é seo, a stór?'

'An naomh d'inis do na daoine le éadach a dhéanamh' adeir Séamaisín. 'An bhfuil sé agat?'

'Ó! Tuigim,' adeir an fíodóir. 'Muise, sin scéal fada ach inseod duit é. Is scéal brónach é, freisin, mar níl ainm an naoimh sin ag aon duine beo. Níl go deimhin. Tá sé caillte agam, díreach mar chaill muid ainm an fhir a mhúin treabhadh dhúinn agus é siúd eile a thaispeáin dúinn le tithe a dhéanamh.'

'Ó! A Thiarna!' adeir Séamaisín. 'Nach mór an feall é sin. Níl fhios ag aon duine? Ag an sagart féin?'

'Níl a fhios,' adeir an fíodóir.

'Tá dearmad déanta ag gach uile dhuine ar ainmneacha na naomh sin. Is págánaigh iad formhór na ndaoine. Níl ach corr-dhea-dhuine ina measc. Tá na págánaigh olc agus peacach. Níl ómós acu ach dóibh seo atá olc agus peacach mar iad féin, tíoránaigh agus lucht cogaidh agus lucht gaimbíne a ghoideann ó na bochtáin agus a leithéidí. Muise, is é an chaoi a chuireann siad na naoimh chun báis, i leaba ómóis bheith acu dóibh.'

'Ó! A Thiarna,' adeir Séamaisín, 'nach uafásach an scéal é féin.'

'Is fíor dhuit, a mhaicín,' adeir an fíodóir, ag dul sall go dtí an seol arís. 'Is uafásach an mac é an saol.'

Bhí scanradh ar an malrach an oíche sin tar éis dhul a chodladh, mar gheall ar an droch-chuntas a thug an fíodóir dhó ar an gcine daonna. Cheap sé go n-éireodh timpist uafásach éigin don bhréidín sula bhféadfaí a chulaith nua a dhéanamh. Ach d'éirigh a chroí arís nuair a tháinig an t-éadach as teach an fhíodóra. Ansin bhí tuilleadh oibre le déanamh.

Leagadh anuas dabhach an ramhracháin sa gcistin. Cíléar fada tanaí a bhí ann, gach ceann de caol agus é roinnt níos leithne ag a lár. Bhí áit suite ag gach ceann. Chuaigh an mháthair agus Máire isteach ann agus iad cosa nochtaithe. Shuíodar ar aghaidh a chéile. Líonadh isteach chucu cúpla slat den bhréidín i lár na daibhche. Doirteadh steall maith de bhréanuisce air agus thosaigh na mná á shuathadh lena gcosa. Nuair bhí an méid sin ramhar, cuireadh amach an taobh é agus líonadh cúpla slat eile isteach ina áit, nó go raibh sé uile go léir cóirithe.

Faoi dheireadh tháinig an lá mór. Bhí an t-éadach réidh le haghaidh an táilliúra. D'éirigh Séamaisín leis an maidneachan, nuair bhí a dhearthair Tomás ag imeacht leis an gcarr i gcoinne Neidí. Níorbh fhéidir lena mháthair iallach chur air a bhricfeasta ithe. Ní raibh sé in ann suaimhneas a dhéanamh ach ag rith amach agus isteach, airdeall ar an mbóthar aige.

'Céard tá ort anois?' adeir a mháthair faoi dheireadh. 'Eagla ort nach bhfaighir do chulaith, an ea?'

'Ní hea, a mháthair,' adeir Séamaisín. 'Eagla atá orm go raibh Neidí ag ól agus go ndéanfaidh sé ciseach de. Ní raibh mé in ann ainm an naoimh fháil amach. Mar sin de, níor dhúirt mé aon phaidir leis, ag impí air Neidí choinneáil ón ól.'

'Ná bac leis sin,' adeir an mháthair. 'Is gearr go mbeidh a fhios againn ar ól sé aréir nó nár ól.'

'Cé an chaoi mbeidh a fhios againn?' adeir Séamaisín.

'Furasta go leor,' adeir an mháthair. 'Nuair thiocfas sé isteach tairgfear cupán tae dhó. Má dhiúltaíonn sé don tae agus má iarann sé deoch bhainne ghéir, bhí sé ag ól aréir. Ach má ghlacann sé an tae agus má thagann allas leis tar éis é ól, níor ól sé deor aréir agus déanfaidh sé culaith mhaith dhuit.'

'Ó! A Thiarna!' adeir Séamaisín leis féin.

Bhí sé cinnte anois go raibh an táilliúir tar éis

meisce agus go raibh póit ar an duine gránna. Nuair a sheas an carr ar an tsráid thug Tomás gléas an táilliúra isteach sa teach. D'fhan an táilliúir é féin tamall beag suite ar a ghogaide, ag breathnú uaidh go buartha sul má thuirling sé.

'Ó! A Thiarna!' adeir an gasúr bocht. 'Tá mé réidh. Beidh mo chulaith millte.'

Ar deireadh, tháinig an táilliúir anuas den charr agus shiúil sé isteach sa teach. Bhí sé bacach. Feairín beag caite é agus cnámh scornaí cumasach mór aige. Bhí ceannaghaidh an-bháiníneach aige. Ar an ábhar sin bhreathnaigh a shúile gorma bheith an-olc. Bhí plúchadh ar an bhfear bocht. Ba deacair leis an anál a tharraingt. Rinne sé torann mar bheadh ciotal ag braith ar fiuchadh, gach uile uair tharraingíodh sé í. D'éiríodh cnámh a mhuiníl suas chomh mór le fata le gach anál.

'Céad míle fáilte romhat a tháilliúir,' adeir an mháthair. 'Suigh síos agus bíodh cupán tae agat.'

Chuir Séamaisín a mhéar ina bhéal agus é ag faire ar fhreagra an tailliúra.

'Go raibh maith agat,' adeir an táilliúir. 'Beidh cupán agam, muise, mara gcuirfeadh sin iomarca trioblóide ort, a bhean an tí.'

'Ní trioblóid ar bith, a thailliúir,' adeir Séamaisín. 'Tá sé réidh cheana againn. Bhí eagla orainn go mb'fhearr leat bainne géar.'

D'aimsigh an mháthair an tlú agus thug sí ruathar faoin ngasúr. Chuaigh Séamaisín i bhfolach faoin mbord, uafás air mar gheall ar an rud bhí ráite aige. Ach is é an chaoi a scáirt an táilliúir amach ag gáirí.

'Dar lán an leabhair!' adeir sé, nuair a bhí a dhóthain gáire déanta aige. 'Déanfad an chulaith is fearr a rinne mé riamh, mar gheall ar gur bhain tú gáire asam. Aon ghasúr atá in ann gáire a bhaint asam, is fiú culaith mhaith é. M'anam gur fiú.'

Choinnigh sé a gheallúint freisin. Mar níor facthas riamh sna bólaí sin culaith níos deise ná an chulaith a rinne sé do Sheamaisín.

An Domhnach dar gcionn bhí buachaillí beaga na háite ag déanamh iontais den chulaith ag gabháil chun an Aifrinn agus a gcuid súile ag éirí as a gceann le tnúthán.

THE NEW SUIT

Leaving the grandmother at home to look after the house, the Dillon family set forth to shear the sheep. The two oldest children, Mary and Thomas, walked with their parents. Mary was eighteen and Thomas was sixteen, so they had already assumed the dignified manner of grown-up people to whom such an event was no longer an exciting adventure. In fact, Mary was whispering about a coming wedding in a neighbouring village as she walked with her mother, while Thomas brought up the rear with his father and talked in a loud voice about the condition of the crops with the pompous arrogance of adolescence.

The other four children, however, bolted from the yard and ran at full speed until they entered the narrow lane that led to the uplands east of the village. Three of them were girls, all wearing white pinafores and with coloured ribbons tied to the ends of their plaited hair. They chattered and sang little snatches of song in chorus as they hopped along the smooth stones of the lane on their bare feet.

The youngest child was a boy called Jimmy, now in his seventh year. He ran far in front of all the others, pausing once in a while to look back and urge the laggards to make more haste. His round face looked so solemn that it was hard to say whether he felt happy or miserable. The fact was that he had been promised a new suit from this year's wool. The promise had been made as early as last Christmas and it had been repeated several times since then by both his father and mother on his ardent insistence. Yet he still could not quite believe that he would really get the suit, and the torture of waiting was almost equal to the ecstatic pleasure of anticipation.

Hitherto he had received his clothes in fragments. One year he would get a pair of trousers and the next year he would get a jacket. So he never had the pleasure of wearing a full suit, with all the garments of the same age. The trousers would be patched by the time he got a new jacket. Then, again, the jacket would be faded and threadbare before he got a new pair of trousers. The thought of wearing a whole new suit for the first time in his life was too good to be true, in spite of all the promises. For that reason, he was determined to keep a close eye on the wool, from the moment it was cut from the sheep's back until it was cloth in the hands of the tailor.

The sheep were in a long, narrow glen, which had a tall fence all around it. They stood in a row beneath the fence when Jimmy arrived. Although the morning was not far advanced, the sun was already hot and the animals were seeking shelter from it. Now that it was summer, their heavy wool irked them. They panted with exhaustion as they pressed close to the fence with their heads lowered.

'Chown, chown,' Jimmy called to them. 'You'll soon be running around in your naked pelts.'

The sheep raised their heads eagerly and looked at the boy.

'Maà,' they said expectantly.

Then they all gathered together in a group and stared at him furtively, fearing that he was accompanied by his dog, which loved to worry them. Six of them were large and white, wearing such a heavy coat of wool that their backs were quite flat. The other five were little mountain sheep with dark wool that grew short and curly. There were five lambs of that year's increase with the flock. Three of the lambs were already half-grown and they had their tails cut. They had been held over from the sale for breeding. The other two lambs were very young. They kept trying to suckle their mother.

Jimmy and his three little sisters had the sheep all herded into a corner when the others arrived. Then four of the white sheep were thrown on their backs and the shearing began. Jimmy held down the head of the animal his mother was shearing. At first the sheep kept making attempts to rise when she felt the shears against her pelt.

'You'd think she doesn't want to lose her wool,' Jimmy said, 'the way she keeps moving around.'

'She's afraid,' his mother said. 'That's why she keeps trying to get up.'

'Does she think we're going to kill her?' Jimmy said.

'Maybe she does,' said his mother.

'But you told me a sheep is a blessed animal,' Jimmy said. 'You said that God gave her wool so that we could have new clothes.'

'That's true,' his mother said. 'She is a blessed animal, not like a wicked goat that has no wool and is a thief into the bargain.'

'Then why would she be afraid we're going to kill her?' Jimmy said. 'God must have told her about her wool and why she has it, if she is blessed.'

'You hold her head and stop talking,' his mother said. 'Otherwise I might cut her with the shears.'

'You mustn't cut her, Mother,' Jimmy said. 'It would be a sin to cut a blessed animal. It might put bad luck on my new suit.'

'All right, then,' the mother said. 'You hold her and I won't cut her.'

The sheep lay quite still when all the wool had been cut from around her neck and shoulders. Now the shears were cutting deep swaths in the thick wool along her back. The thin hairs, packed closely together, were as delicate as silk near the roots. They were moist with oil and they shone brightly in the sunlight.

'Did God tell people how to make clothes of sheep's wool?' Jimmy said.

'He did,' said the mother.

'Who did He tell about it?' said Jimmy.

'He told a saint,' said the mother.

'Did He tell him everything all at once?' said Jimmy. 'How to shear and spin and weave and be a tailor, too?'

'He did,' said the mother.

'What was the saint's name?' said Jimmy.

'I don't know,' said the mother.

'That's a pity,' Jimmy said. 'I'd like to say a prayer to him and ask him to keep Neddy the tailor from drinking when he is making my new suit. But I can't say a prayer to him if I don't know his name. It's queer, though, that you wouldn't know the name of a great saint like that. He should be the most famous of all saints, if he taught people how to make clothes out of wool. Only for him[1] the people would die of cold in winter.'

'If you're a good boy,' his mother said, 'until Neddy the tailor comes to make your suit, then God will keep Neddy sober. So he won't make a botch, same as he does with clothes when he is drinking. Otherwise he'll get drunk and your suit will be so terrible that you'll be ashamed to wear it. You mustn't ask me any more questions about this saint and that saint. You must be a good boy and not ask foolish questions.'

'Oh! I will, Mother,' Jimmy said. 'I'll do everything you tell me, and I don't care who the saint was.'

The shearing continued until all the sheep were stripped of their wool. According as each sheep was released, she shook herself and began to graze with great energy, pausing now and again to murmur with satisfaction at her relief. The mother of the youngest lambs, however, had great difficulty in getting her offspring to recognise her nakedness. They were startled when they saw her approach, stripped of her wool. So they ran away from her and paid no need to her frantic bleating. Finally, they

1. If it wasn't for him . . .

had to be caught and put to her udder. Then they recognised her and suckled.

The wool was all gathered up, put into bags, and brought home. Then the womenfolk took it in hand, to prepare it for the weaver. Jimmy did his best to help with every operation. When it was washed and spread out on a field to bleach, he felt very important because he was allowed to stand guard over it all day. Then it was teased and carded into rolls for spinning. He also helped with the spinning. As the rolls of thread came off the spindle, he held them while his sister Mary wound them on to a ball. The white thread was made into one ball and the grey thread into another one. When all the wool was spun, the ball of white thread was of enormous size.

Jimmy accompanied his mother to the weaver's house with the thread. It was in another village nearly three miles distant. She put on her best clothes for the occasion and Jimmy felt terribly ashamed of his patched trousers as he trotted along beside her. Yet he would not stay at home on any account, for fear something dreadful might happen to the precious thread in his absence. Furthermore, he wanted to ask the weaver the name of that famous saint to whom God had given the secret of cloth making. Then he could ask the saint in prayer every night to keep Neddy the tailor sober.

When he arrived at the weaver's house, however, he lost courage. He stood within the kitchen door and gaped in silent wonder at the loom. It was placed in a sunken room that had no partition on the side facing the kitchen, so that he could see the whole process of weaving from where he stood. The intricate movements of the shuttles and the miraculous way the thread was changed into cloth convinced the little boy that this was a mystery similar to what happened on the altar during Mass. It pertained to God and it was just as well not to pry into it for fear of making God angry. Even so, the mysterious process acted on him as a magnet. Little by little, he crept along the wall of the kitchen until he was close to the weaver.

'Well, young man,' said the weaver, 'do you want to learn how cloth is made?'

'Come over here, Jimmy,' said his mother, who was seated by the fireplace. 'Don't interfere with the work.'

'He's not doing any harm,' the weaver said. 'Let him stay where he is.'

The weaver was a small man, with black hair and very sallow skin. He had such merry eyes that Jimmy was not the least afraid of him. So the child suddenly got courage and determined to seize the opportunity.

'Do you know the name of the saint?' he said to the weaver.

'Pay no attention to him,' the mother said, addressing the weaver apologetically. 'He asks such strange questions.'

The weaver bent close to the little boy and said: 'What saint is that, comrade?'

'The saint that told people how to make clothes out of wool,' said Jimmy.

'Oh, I see,' said the weaver, looking very solemn all of a sudden. 'Well. Now that's a long story, but I'll tell you about it. It's a sad story, as well as being a long one. For the truth is that we don't know the name of the saint that taught the people how to make clothes out of wool, no more than we know the name of the saint that taught people how to plough, or to make houses.'

'Oh, that's a great pity,' said Jimmy despondently. 'Does nobody know, not even the priest?'

'No,' said the weaver solemnly. 'Not even the priest. Everybody has forgotten the names of these great saints. That's because people were pagans in the past and there were only a few good people among them. The good people were the saints. All the others were sinful and contrary. They only remembered the names of people that were wicked like themselves, kings and tyrants and landlords and generals that made war, usurers that robbed the poor and notorious criminals of every kind. And not only did they forget the names of the saints that were their benefactors, but they even persecuted them and sometimes put them to death.'

'That's terrible,' Jimmy said. 'I thought surely you'd know the name of the saint that told people how to make cloth out of wool. I have a reason for wanting to know.'

'Will you be quiet now?' Jimmy's mother said. 'You have said enough.'

She took Jimmy away before he could ask the weaver any more questions. The little boy wept that night in bed, terrified by the weaver's melancholy description of humanity and convinced that some disaster would happen at the last moment to ruin his chance of getting a new suit.

Then again his hopes rose to a new height when the finished cloth came from the weaver. The thickening-trough was brought into the kitchen. His mother and his sister Mary sat at the ends of the long wooden trough in their bare feet. The cloth was laid in the centre of the trough, a few yards at a time. Sour water was poured on it, to soften it for the thickening. Then the women kicked at it rhythmically, until it had reached the required thickness.

The great moment had at last arrived. The cloth was ready for the tailor. Jimmy was awake at dawn on the morning his brother Thomas was going in the cart to fetch that important personage. The little boy was in such an excited state that his mother had great difficulty in getting him to eat his breakfast. After his brother had left, his agitation increased. His mother could not move a yard around the house without having him at her apron strings. Finally, she took him to task.

'What ails you now?' she said. 'Are you still afraid you won't get your suit?'

'No, Mother,' Jimmy said. 'I'm afraid that Neddy has been drinking last night and that he'll make a botch of it. I couldn't find out the name of the saint, so I couldn't pray and ask him to keep Neddy from drinking.'

'Never mind,' said his mother. 'We'll soon know whether he has been drinking last night or not. We'll know as soon as he puts foot in the house.'

'How will we know?' said Jimmy.

'That's easy,' said his mother. 'As soon as he comes into the house I'm going to offer him a cup of tea. If he refuses the tea and asks for a drink of sour milk instead of it, he has been drinking. But if he drinks the tea and if sweat begins to pour from his face after he drinks it, then he has been sober last night and he'll make good clothes.'

When at last the heavy cart came rumbling up the road towards the village, Jimmy ran down to the yard gate to meet it. There was the tailor sitting on the bottom of the cart, with his legs curled up under him and his head bent in a gloomy attitude. The boy completely lost all hope. The tailor's posture convinced him that the man had been exceptionally wicked on the previous evening. Then the cart halted in the yard. Thomas jumped down and took the tailor's gear into the house. The tailor himself, after looking about him for almost a minute in gloomy silence, also descended and limped indoors.

He was a very thin man, with a club foot and an enormous Adam's apple. His face was deadly pale and he had heavy grey eyebrows that gave his blue eyes a fierce expression. He suffered from asthma and he kept drawing in deep breaths with a hissing sound. Every time he took a deep breath, his Adam's apple rose up as large as a small potato in his throat, paused and then retreated.

'A hundred thousand welcomes to you, tailor,' said Jimmy's mother. 'Sit down and have a cup of tea.'

Jimmy put his forefinger between his front teeth and waited for the tailor's reply.

'Thank you, ma'am,' said the tailor. 'I'll have a cup of tea if it's not too much trouble.'

'Oh, it's not trouble at all,' Jimmy said, unable to keep silent owing to the happiness that suddenly overwhelmed him. 'We have it all ready to see would you drink it. We were afraid you would rather have sour milk.'

The mother picked up the tongs from the fireplace and threatened Jimmy with it. The boy blushed to the roots of his hair and retired into a corner, horrified by his mistake. The tailor, however, looked at the boy seriously for a few moments and then burst out laughing.

'Tare an' ouns,'[2] he said after he had laughed his fill. 'I'll make the best suit I ever made in my life, just because you made me laugh. Any boy that makes me laugh deserves the best suit that was ever made. A good laugh is worth a good suit any day. Get ready now till I measure you.'

So Jimmy became happy again. The tailor's gear was laid out on a big table and when the tailor had drunk his tea Jimmy was measured. Then the tailor set to work with furious energy, pausing now and again to burst out into a peal of hearty laughter.

'Tare an' ouns,' he repeated after each laugh. 'That deserves a good suit if anything ever did.'

He kept his promise, too, for the little suit fitted perfectly and on the following Sunday Jimmy was the envy of all the other village boys as he went to church.

2. A corruption of 'By Christ's bloody tears and wounds' — an expletive.

SEOSAMH MAC GRIANNA

(1901-90)

from: AN GRÁDH AGUS AN GHRUAIM (1929)

[This story is based on an incident during the Great Famine (1845-49). The translation by Séamus Ó Néill was published in Sean J. White (ed.), *Irish Writing 33* (1955)].

AR AN TRÁ FHOILIMH

Bhí sé fuar ar an Droim Dheileoir, nó bhí sé fá thrí seachtainí de Shamhain. Bhí an t-aer fuar, agus na creagacha liatha, agus an cuibhreann preátaí sin a bhí in ascaill an chnocáin. Agus bhí bhí Cathal Ó Canainn fuar, agus é ar shiúl ar fud an chuibhrinn ag tochailt thall agus abhus. Fuar, ocrach, bratógach — sean éadach ina phoill agus in phaistí, crochta ina chlupaidí ar chnámha móra loma a raibh an fheoil ar shiúl díobh. Seilg dhúthrachtach a bhí sé a dhéanamh, seilg fhiáin chraosach mar dheánfadh ainmhí, agus ina dhiaidh sin bhí sé spadánta i ngach bogadh dá ndéanadh sé. Fada buan a chaith sé ar shiúl ó iomaire to hiomaire sular mheas sé go raibh a iarraidh aige. Ní raibh a iarraidh mór, más ní é go raibh sé sásta leis an dosaen sceallán a bhí ina bhearad leis, agus gan aon cheann acu baol ar chomh mór le hubh chirce.

Soir leis go dtína theach — teach íseal ceanntuí a raibh lustan ag fás air, agus na ballaí glas tais daite ag an aimsir. D'aithneodh duine ar dheilbh an tí, ar na loitheáin a bhí fá leacacha an dorais, ina luí i suan miodamais agus caileannógach throm orthu, gur imigh an lá a raibh teaghlach greannmhar gealgháireach fá na ballaí sin. Chuaigh Cathal isteach, ag umhlú síos faoin fhardoras, isteach i ndoiléireacht, nó ní raibh ar an teach ach fuinneog amháin, nach mó ná go dtiocfadh le cloigeann a dhul amach uirthi. An leaba a bhí sa choirnéal agus an dorchadas ní ba dhlúithe uirthi, siocair í bheith druidte os a cionn le cláraí, agus cláraí ar na taobhanna aici, d'amharcódh súil aineolach uirthi athuair sula dtugadh sí fá dear go raibh duine ina luí inti, colainn lom faoi sheanchuilt dhearg, agus ceann liath giobach idir ghruaig is fhéasóg ina luí ar an cheannadhairt gan mhothú.

Chuaigh Cathal suas os cionn an fhir a bhí ina luí. 'A Airt!'

Níor labhair Art, agus nuair a leag Cathal a lámh air fuair sé amach go raibh an smaointiú sin, an eagla a fuair greim fán chroí air, go raibh sin ceart. Bhí Art chomh fuar le creig.

Chuaigh Cathal anonn agus dhúbail sé síos ar an stól a bhí faoin fhuinneog. Chuir sé a uilleanna ar a ghlúine, agus a bhos lena leiceann, agus shuigh sé ag amharc anonn ar an chorp. Ní tháinig deor leis, ní tháinig tocht air fán scornaigh. Mhothaigh sé é féin beagán níb fhuaire, beagán níb fhollmha ná bhí sé roimhe sin, agus a chroí rud beag ní ba nimhní ina chliabh. Má chaith sé féin agus an fear a bhí ina luí go híseal aon seal riamh go sámh i gcuideachta a chéile, bhí dearmad déanta aige de. Níor smaointigh sé ar dhóigh ar bith a bhí leis an tseanduine, ar a gháire, ar ghlór a chinn, ar chaint ar bith a dúirt sé ná ar ghníomh ar bith ar rinne sé, arb ansa le cara smaointiú orthu — cuimneacháin bheaga a chuireas cumha ar an té atá fágtha. Níor smaointigh sé ar urnaí a chur leis an anam a bhí i ndiaidh é féin a strócadh amach as an cholainn chaite sin tríd phianaigh. Bhí dearmad déanta de Dhia aige, nó chonachtas dó go raibh dearmad déanta ag Dia de le fada riamh — bhí ó tháinig an chéad mheath ar bharr na bpreátaí, ó tháinig tús an 'drochshaoil'. Shuigh sé ansin i bpianpháis bhrúite. Bhí a anam istigh ann mar a bheadh loitheán dorcha nach mbeadh sruthán ag sileadh ann nó amach as, ach é ina luí i gciúnas mharfach, faoi choirt dhona chaileannógaí. Rinneadh tormán ar an tseantábla a bhí i dtaobh an tí. Chlis sé suas agus chonaic sé gogán a raibh lorg bracháin bhuí air ina luí ar an urlár ar a thaobh. D'éirigh leis amharc fháil ar mhada ag teitheadh trasna an tí — ainmhí giobach ciar, agus a dhá thaobh buailte ar a chéile.

Tháinig an t-uaigneas anois air a thig ar an té a bhfuil corp sa teach aige, an t-aithleá fuaicht a thig ón bhás agus a bheir ar dhaoine cruinniú agus an marbhánach a fhaire i gcuideachta a chéile. Ach fairíor! Chuaigh am fairí thart. Do réir mar a bhí an saol ag éirí crua, bhí na daoine ag déanamh coimhthís lena chéile. In am sonais agus pléisiúir bíonn daoine dúilmhear ar a gcomharsain. In am cruatain coinníonn siad leo fein, ag cruinniú iomlán a gcuid urraidh a throid leis an tsaol. Ar na mallaibh bhí daoine ag imeacht ina gcéadta, ag leá ar shiúl leis an ocras, dá gcloí leis an fhiabhras. Cuid a bhí ag fáil adhlacadh Críostúil, cuid a bhí ina luí i gcréafóig gan choisreacadh ina mollta. D'amharc Cathal anonn ar an ardán ghlas a bhí taobh thall den abhainn. Bhí mullóg ina lár agus an féar ag toiseacht a theacht. Cuireadh síos ansin an triúr deireanach a fuair bás ar an bhaile sin, clann Mhichil Bháin. Tháinig daoine anoir ón Ard Mhór a chaith síos ansin iad fá dheifre. Ní raibh mórán trua ag an talamh chadránta sin dóibh — an talamh seasc gan sú nár dhual dó barr a bhaint arís as go leasófaí é ar fud na hÉireann le feoil agus fuil daoine. Fuair Cathal giota de rópa, agus thóg sé an corp ón leaba, agus chuir dhá iris ann mar bheadh cliabh ann. Nuair a bhí sé ag dul trasna an tí leis thoisigh urchuil uaigneach a sheinm i bplochóig dhorcha éigin i bhfad siar sa bhalla fá thaobh an bhaic. Bíonn oibrí fir meánaosta trom fán chroí agus fán chois faoi ualach. Bhí Cathal meánaosta, bhí sé ocrach agus bhí a chinniúint féin ar a dhroim leis, ag dul suas an t-ard breac éagothrom dó ag tarraingt ar an tseanbhealach mhór. An cosán a bhí aige le dul, bhí páirt de ina shlodáin agus páirt ina chreagacha; idir bhonn fhliuch agus choiscéim chorrach bhain sé an bealach mór amach. Seanbhóthar cam agus an gruaimhín go hard os cionn na bpáirceanna. Istigh faoin ghruaimhín bhí gasúr bratógach, agus loirgneacha fada loma air, ag clamhairt go haimirneach ar phreáta fuar. Nuair a chonaic sé Cathal ag tarraingt air faoin ualach d'imigh sé ina rith fá sheanteach a bhunaidh. Lig Cathal a dhroim le gruaimhín an bhealaigh mhóir agus rinne sé a scíste. Siar uaidh bhí an Droim Deileoir, rite leis an ghaoth aniar aduaidh, blár caoráin ar a chúl ina luí trasna go bun na spéire. Fada buan d'fhanódh sé ag amharc ar an talamh sin agus ar an spéir, ach gur mhúscail obair a bhí le déanamh é.

Níor casadh duine dó gur chuir sé leathmhíle talamh de, agus gur chor sé soir bealach na hAilte Móire. Istigh ansin bhí fear agus asal leis a raibh péire feadhnóg uirthi, agus d'amharc siad araon air. Níor labhair fear na hasaile. D'imigh Cathal soir uaidh go spadánta ag éirí beag ar an bhealach mhór — agus manrán beag fágtha ag an tsruthán a bhí idir iad féin agus deireadh a n-astair.

Chuir Cathal an chéad mhíle de. Ag éirí ar bharr an aird bhric do nocht ros fada fuar os a choinne, breacaithe le tithe beaga bocht a dheas dó, gan teach ná cónaí thíos ar a cheann, ach cladach íseal agus faithim do chúr gheal thart leis. Bhí aige le dul go bruach an chladaigh sin. Fhad is bhí sé san ailt bhí foscadh aige, ach nuair a d'éirigh sé ar an airdeacht, tháinig séideán fuar air. Mhothaigh sé ina thuile é istigh ar a chraiceann faoina chuid bratóg. Bhí scíste eile riachtanach nuair a bhí an mala tógtha aige. Thug sé a chúl sa ghaoith agus lig sé a thaca le cloich, agus an corpán fuar mar chumhdach aige ón aimsir.

Ag an chroisbhealach thiontaigh sé ar thaobh a láimhe deise. Ba é an bealach ab fhaide é, ach bhí anraith á thabhairt amach ag an Charnán. Bheofadh braon an t-anam ann go cionn lae eile. Bhí sé ag éirí lag, deora allais ag teacht amach ar an chraiceann agus é á mhothachtáil féin fíorfholamh istigh. Ach chonaic sé gogán anraith, gal folláin agus boladh as a chuir tuile pléisiúir tríd a cholainn. Ghéaraigh sé a choiscéim.

Bhí scaifte mór fan Charnán. Ag taobh an tí mhóir ansin bhí coire, agus lucht freastail i ndiaidh an t-anraith a dhéanamh réidh. Bhí scaifte cruinn fan choire, óg agus aosta, daoine loma ocracha agus iad ag streachailt agus ag brú, ag tarraingt isteach ar an bhia. D'imigh an trua a bhíodh ag an lag ón láidir. Bhí fir ag brú ban agus páistí as an chosán.

Chuaigh Cathal isteach ina measc agus an corp ar a dhroim leis. Níor chuir aon duine sonrú ann. Bhí trí nó ceathair de dhroimeanna ag lúbarnaigh idir é féin agus an coire. Chonaic sé cúig nó sé de lámha ag gabháil trasna ar a chéile, taobh istigh de bhéal an choire, soithigh á mbualadh ar a chéile agus iad á ndortadh. Chaill bean dhubh lom a raibh súile tinrí aici, chaill sí a sáspan san anraith.

'Mo sheacht mallacht ort, a Chaitríona na gadaíochta.' Thug sí iarraidh anall a strócadh na mná eile. Chuaigh Cathal isteach ina háit, agus chuir sé gogán a bhí leis isteach thar bhéal an choire. Leis sin beireadh greim taobh thiar ar an chorp a bhí ar a dhroim agus tarraingeadh amach ón choire go garbh é. Chuaigh sé cúig nó sé de chois-céimeanna amach agus thit sé.

Chruinnigh sé é féin suas agus d'amharc sé ar an té a chuir an truilleán leis. Fear mór toirteach agus aghaidh bhrúidúil air.

'Goidé tá tusa a dhéanamh anseo?' ar seisean. 'Mura bhfana tú amach, cuirfidh mé an corpán síos sa choire.'

'Na bac leat, a Chonchubhair,' arsa Cathal agus d'imigh sé.

Níos brúite, níos nimhní, níos laige, d'imigh sé leis. Bhí an domhan ní ba dorcha ná bhí riamh. Bhí an fuacht ní ba nimhní. Tharraing sé síos ar an ghob agus nuair a bhí sé ag an teach dheireanach, chuaigh sé isteach.

'Coisreacadh Dé orainn,' arsa guth fann sa leaba.

'Tusa 'do luí fosta, a Mhichil,' arsa Cathal.

'A Chathail Uí Chanainn, an tú atá ansin? Tá ualach bocht leat, a rún, ualach bocht.'

'Tá, tá. Tháinig mé isteach a iarraidh spáide.'

'Gheobhaidh tú ag an bhinn í, a rún. Ualach bocht, ualach bocht!'

Chuaigh Cathal síos go dtí an reilig a bhí ar léana an ghainimh. Seanreilig a raibh cnámha dheich nglún inti, ina luí ansin, rite le doininn. Ní raibh mórán tombaí inti; crosa adhmaid a ba mhó a bhí inti, an mhórchuid acu briste. Agus bhí mórán mullóg inti nach raibh crosa ar bith orthu, an áit ar caitheadh síos fá dheifre na daoine a fuair bás ó tháinig an drochshaol. Chuartaigh Cathal an coirnéal a raibh cros a athar ann — í leathbhriste agus a cloigeann sa ghaineamh. Thoisigh sé agus thochail sé slat ar doimhne. Ní raibh croí aige dul níos faide síos. Rug sé ar an chorp a bhí mar a bheadh giota de mhaide ann agus d'fhág sé ina luí ansin é. Bhí sé iontach doiligh spád ghainimh a chaitheamh ar chorp nochtaithe. Ba doiligh an úir a chur os cionn na haighdhe sin, isteach i bpoll an tsróna, tríd an fhéasóig. Bhí sé cosúil le marú duine. Do réir a chéile chuaigh an cholainn as a amharc. Ar feadh tamaill fhada bhí an dá ghlúin, a bhí rud beag crupaithe, os cionn an ghainimh agus an fhéasóg ag gobadh aníos. Chuaigh sí i bhfolach, líonadh an uaigh go dtí go raibh sí ina mullóig cosúil leis na huaigheanna eile a bhí thart uirthi.

Chaith Cathal uaidh an spád agus chaith sé é féin síos ar an uaigh, a dhá láimh crupaithe fána cheann, agus é fuaite den talamh ina phianaigh.

Tháinig faoileog gheal thart ar eiteogaí os a chionn, agus í ag screadaigh, ag screadaigh go léanmhar. Tháinig an ghrian amach as cúl néill, agus spréigh solas fann báiteach a bhí mar bheadh spiorad na tine agus spiorad an tsiocáin measctha le chéile, leath ar leath. Spréigh sé thart ar dhídean na gcorpán, ar pháirceanna preátaí gan tiontó, ar bhóithre a bhí uaigneach, ar thithe a raibh suaimhneas fána ballaí acu.

ON THE EMPTY SHORE

It was cold on the barren ridge, for it was within three weeks of All-Hallowtide.[1] The air was cold, and the grey crags and the potato field under the lee of the hill were cold. And Cathal O Canann was cold as he traversed the field, hoking here and there. Cold, hungry, ragged, his old clothes torn and patched, hung in tatters around his big bare bones. It was an avid search he was making, like the wild ravenous search of an animal, and in spite of that, his every movement was sluggish. A long long time he spent from ridge to ridge, before he reckoned that he had what he needed, and that was not much, if he was satisfied with the dozen small potatoes that he had gathered in his cap, not one of which was as big as a hen's egg.

He went over to the house, a low cabin with weeds shooting from the thatch, and the walls green and damp from time. You would have known from the appearance of the house, and from the scum on the pools sleeping around the threshold that the day had departed when those walls had sheltered a joyous laughter-filled family. Bending down under the lintel Cathal went in — into the gloom, for there was only one window in the house, scarcely big enough to allow a human head to protrude from it. There was a bed in the corner, and the darkness thicker on it, because it was closed in with boards at the top and sides, and an unpractised eye would have looked at it twice before noticing that it held someone. A lank body lay under a red quilt, and a grey unkempt head and beard rested motionless on the pillow. Cathal stood over the figure in the bed.

'Art,' said he.

Art did not speak, and when Cathal laid his hand on him, he found out that the thought, the fear which had gripped his heart, was realised. Art was as cold as a rock.

Cathal went over, and hunkered down on a stool beneath the window. He put his elbows on his knees, his palm to his chin, and he sat there looking at the body. No tear came from him, no sob to his throat. He felt himself a little colder, a little emptier than before, and his heart a little sorer in his breast. If he and the man that was gone had ever spent a while happily in each other's company, he had forgotten it. He did not recall any of the old man's peculiar ways, his laugh, or the sound of his voice, or any word he had said, or any deed he had done,

1. All-Hallowtide, more usually known as All Saints' Day, is celebrated on 1 November.

such as a friend would like to recall, the little remembrances which sadden the one that is left. He did not think of saying a prayer for the soul which had just torn itself painfully out of that wasted body. He had forgotten God, for it seemed that God had forgotten him a long time ago, ever since the blight came on the potatoes, since the beginning of the bad times. He sat there bruised in sorrow. His soul inside him was like a dark pool, which no stream entered or left, but lay there in a numbing stillness, under a sour coat of slime.

A noise was made on the old table by the wall. He started up, and he saw a noggin that had a trace of yellow stirabout in it lying on its side on the floor. He just got a glimpse of a dog fleeing across the house, a shaggy tawny animal, with its two sides hanging together.

Loneliness came on him now, the loneliness that comes on one who has a corpse in the house, the shiver of cold that comes from death, and makes people gather to wake the departed. But the time for wakes was no more. For as life was hardening, people were becoming distant with one another. In happy times people rejoice in their neighbours. In evil times they keep to themselves, and huckster up[2] all their strength to fight the world. And of late people were dying in hundreds, melting away with hunger, falling to the fever. Some of them were getting Christian burial, some of them were lying in heaps in unhallowed clay. Cathal looked over at the green hillock on the far side of the river. There was a mound in the middle of it, and grass beginning to sprout from it. There the last three who had died in the place had been buried, White Michael's family. People had come west from the Great Height, and had thrown them down in a hurry. The cruel earth had no pity for them, that sterile, barren earth that was fated not to yield another crop until it had been manured throughout Ireland with human flesh and blood.

Cathal got a piece of rope, raised the corpse from the bed, and attached two loops to it, like the suspenders on a creel. When he was crossing the floor a lonesome cricket began to sing in some dark crevice, far back in the wall by the side of the hob.

Middle-aged labourers are heavy of heart, and heavy of step under a burden. Cathal was middle-aged, he was hungry, and he was carrying his own fate on his back, as he went up the speckled uneven rise that led to the old highway. Stagnant pools and boulders lay in his path, and it was with wet feet that he staggered to the road. It was an old twisted road with its banks rising high over the fields. In the ditch a ragged spindle-shanked boy was devouring a potato. When he saw Cathal approaching he made off in the direction of his parents' cabin. Cathal rested his back against the bank of the road, and paused. Away from him stretched the Barren Ridge, exposed to the north west wind, and lying behind it as far as the eye could see was a bleak moor. A long time he might have remained gazing at the land and the horizon, but that the work he had to do roused him.

He met no one for half a mile, until he turned down the road of the Big Hollow. In the hollow there was a man with a donkey carrying panniers, and they both gazed at him. The man with the donkey did not speak. Cathal trudged on slowly, growing smaller on the road, and the murmur of the stream that was between him and the end of his journey growing clearer.

He covered the first mile. As he came to the top of the Speckled Rise, a long cold headland extended before him, dotted with mean cabins near to him, but with no human habitation down on its point, there only the low shore, and a hem of white foam around it. He had to go the margin of that shore. Whilst he was in the hollow, he was sheltered from the wind, but when he mounted the height a cold blast blew on him. He felt it in a flood on his skin under his rags. Another rest was necessary when he had gained the top of the hill. He gave his back to the wind, and leaned against a rock, the cold corpse serving him for a shield against the sky.

At the crossroads he turned at the right hand. It was the longer way, but soup was being distributed at the Cairn. A drop would keep the life in him for another day. He was getting weak. Beads of sweat were breaking out on his skin, and he was feeling very empty inside. But he saw a vessel of soup, and a healthy steam and smell rising out of it that sent a flow of pleasure through his whole body. He quickened his step.

There was a throng of people at the Cairn. There was a cauldron at the side of the big house, and the attendants had just prepared the soup. A crowd had gathered around the cauldron, both young and old, spare hungry people, struggling and jostling, making for the food. The pity the strong once had

2. gather.

for the weak had vanished. Men were brushing aside women and children.

Cathal went in among them, with the corpse on his back. No one took any notice of him. There were three or four backs swaying beween him and the cauldron. He saw five or six hands crossing one another inside its mouth, vessels being struck against one another, and being spilt. A gaunt dark woman with fiery eyes lost her saucepan in the soup.

'My seven curses on you, thieving Caitriona!'

She made a lunge at the other woman. Cathal moved into her place, and reached his noggin in over the rim of the cauldron. Just then someone caught hold of the corpse on his back, and he was pulled out roughly from the crowd. He reeled five or six steps, and fell. He gathered himself up, and looked at the man that had jerked him out. He was a big heavy man with a brutish face. 'If you don't stay out, I'll stuff that corpse down into the cauldron,' he said.

'Take care your own turn doesn't come, Connor,' replied Cathal, and he went off.

More deeply crushed, more painful, weaker, he walked on. The world was blacker than ever. The cold was keener. He made for the point of the headland, and when he reached the last house, he went in.

'The blessing of God on us,' said a weak voice from the bed.

'Are you down too Michael?' asked Cathal.

'Cathal O Canann, is it you that is there? You have a sorrowful burden with you, man, a sorrowful burden!'

'Yes, indeed! I came in for the loan of a spade.'

'You'll find it at the gable, friend. A sorrowful burden — a sorrowful burden!'

Cathal went down to the graveyard on the sandy lawn. It was an old graveyard with the bones of ten generations lying in it, raked by the tempest. Tombstones in it were few, but there were many wooden crosses in it, most of them broken. And there were many mounds in it, that had no crosses at all, where the people who had died since the famine came had been thrown down in a hurry. Cathal searched for the corner where his father's cross stood, half-broken, with its head in the sand. He set to work, and dug a yard deep. He had not the courage to go down further. He took up the corpse that was like a bit of a stick, and laid it in the grave. It was very hard to throw a spadeful of sand on an uncovered corpse. It was hard to put the clay over that face, into the nostrils, through the beard. It was like killing someone. Slowly the trunk went out of sight. For a long time the knees, which were drawn up a little, were visible above the sand, and the beard kept sticking up. It disappeared. The grave was filled, until it was a little mound like the other graves around it.

Cathal cast the spade from him, and flung himself down on the grave, with his two arms bent under his face, his body fixed to the ground in his agony.

A white seagull sailed on its wings above his head, crying and crying piteously. The sun came out from behind a cloud, and spread a weak watery light, that was like the spirit of fire and the spirit of frost commingled. It spread around over the covering of the dead, over fields of undug potatoes, over roads that were lonely, over houses where silence reigned.

MÁIRTÍN Ó CADHAIN

(1906-70)

from:
AN BRAON BROGHACH (1948)

[Eoghan Ó Tuairisc's translation appeared in *The Road to Bright City* (Swords, Co. Dublin: Poolbeg Press, 1981), a collection of short stories by Máirtín Ó Cadhain].

AN BHEARNA MHÍL

Chaith Nóra Liam Bhid oíche fearacht mar chaith sí an oíche aréir roimhe sin, ag réiteach tae do lucht na bainise. Ach anoise bhí bánsoilse smúitiúil an lae tús Faoillte ag smúracht isteach sa bparlús leathbhánaithe, agus ó bhí an glantachán déanta tar éis an tae dheireanaigh, agus Nóra ar scor, thosaigh an coimhthíos ag spochadh léi arís. Coimhthíos leis an bpósadh, leis an malairt, leis an Achréidh strainséarach: an daol céanna nár scar léi an oíche údan, tá mí ó shin, ar tháinig a hathair abhaile ó Aonach na Gaillimhe agus a ndeachaigh sé ag inseacht dá máthair go cúlráideach 'go raibh ceithearnach Achréidh déanta amach aige do Nóra'. Níor chlaochlú ar bith ar an gcoimhthíos sin di a fear agus a chuid deirfiúracha a fheiceáil den chéad uair ar an gcleamhnas an tseachtain roimhe sin. Ar nós eochrasaí a chuibhreofaí i gcaológ chalcaithe mhúnlaigh i dtosach a scríbe, agus nach mbeadh i ndán di ligean a fháil choíchin ar áthanna glana síolraithe uachtar na habhann, a chuaigh Nóra faoi chuing an phósta i séipéal an Aird, ard-tráthnóna inné. Agus anois, ó nár shólás ar bith di tláthchaint a máthar, bladar póitiúil a hathar, sáimhe shochma a fir, ná sioscadh a cuid banchliamhaineacha a raibh an spleáchas ina orlaí trína gcuid láíochta, thug sí an chisteanach síos uirthi féin chuig an gcóisir chomharsan a tháinig ón Aird leis an mbainis.

Bhí scioból an damhsa taobh amuigh bánaithe le scaitheamh agus an chistineach anois plódaithe le daoine ar bhuail tost iad ar a theacht di i láthair. Ba gheall le céadfaí corpartha an toist na hanálacha séideánacha leanna, na dlaíóga deataigh tobac agus na mionphúireanna gainimh sprusaigh den urlár stroighne a tháthaigh le chéile ina gcuisne cheo, agus a rinne uirthi mar bheadh taise ann ag féachaint an mbainfeadh sé an chaint aisti a d'fhuasclódh pioraíocha a anama. An tráth sin de mhaidin bainise a bhí ann a bhféadfadh duine a dhul ag ullmhú scléipe agus fios aige nach bhfaigheadh sé fear a bhactha. Bhí an splanc imithe as na glórtha póitiúla agus an ghile as an ngáire. Dar le Nóra go mba le mífhonn a chuaigh an t-aos óg ag damhsa an phoirt, leisce deis a thabhairt do na lánúineacha pósta agus don 'tseanmhuintir' an tost a bhí ag gabháil binne ar an teach a thapú agus a rá go raibh sé in am scortha. Má ba iad aos óg an Aird féin iad a raibh fíor ragairne agus síoraíocht sclábhaíochta iontu, ní raibh duine acu anois nach raibh an oiread támáilteachta ina ghlór agus ina leagan súl is a bhí ina chuid cos. An t-aon duine sa teach a raibh a chosa ina dtine chreasa agus a ghrua ina splanc ghealáin fós ba é Beairtlín, buachaill aimsire a hathar, é.

Bhuail Nóra a ceann fúithi, agus lig sí aithinne den tine chreasa trína hintinn agus ga den ghealán trína hanam, nó go raibh sí neamhairdiúil ar an tost agus ar an gcoimhthíos. Chuimhnigh sí ar a liachtaí uair a ndearna sí suirí gan ghoimh leis agus í ag sciobadh creathnaigh uaidh sa samhradh, nó sa bhfómhar agus iad beirt ar leac na sráide ag briseadh na gcnónna a thugadh sé chuici ó Ghorán Leasa, nó oícheanta airneáin chois na tine tar éis don seanchúpla a dhul a chodladh agus ise ag fanacht go dtagadh a dearthháir Pádraig ó chuairt. Ba mhinic cailíní óga an Aird a bhí ar an mbainis anocht á saighdeadh, ag samhailt Bheairtlín léi. Ach tar éis go mba anocht an t-aon oíche nach samhlódh ceachtar acu léi é, ba anocht an t-aon oíche nach gcuirfeadh sé a dhath mosáin uirthi. Nathaíocht Bheairtlín a bhaineadh an lionndubh dá gáire gach uile uair dá mbíodh a hathair agus a máthair ag tionscailt cleamhnais di. Cneasú thar ghoimh fós féin a bhí in aiféala Nóra de bharr a mhéad is a bhí cúl a cainte léi agus a laghad suime agus a bhí aici a dhul ag lochtú gnaithe Dé an lá údan ar dhúirt Beairtlín léi 'go raibh an seanbhuachaill ag déanamh cleamhnais di arís, agus nach mbeadh comhaireamh na sop le fáil ag aon duine nach mbeadh ina cheannaí siopa nó ina bhoicín Achréidh'. Níor le holc do Bheairtlín as ucht ar dhúirt sé a fuair sí caidéis dá bhearna mhíl an lá sin. Ina leaba sin, is éard a bhí fúithi a rá 'go n-imeodh sí bog te leis ar áit na mbonn'. Ach ar theacht don chrú ar an tairne, níor dá chruth seang deilfe, ná dá shúile glasa spéiriúla, ná dá ghrua ar dheirge 'an mhéirín' a ghéill a súile, a croí ná a béal, ach don éalang cholúil bhroinne nár fhéach sé a chlúdú le croiméal féin. Mura mbeadh a mhinice agus a chuaigh ag a col ar a rún níor chailimhineog liath chaillte a bheadh i ngréasán a saoil óig inniu. Anois féin ba í an bhearna mhíl sin a chonaic sí ag déanamh chuici mar bheadh péist an dá shúil déag ann trí lochán glas mara; agus ainneoin ar lig Beairtlín amach dá mhosán go raibh 'an teach faoina mullóg féin ag muintir an Achréidh i gcaitheamh na hoíche lena gcuid "reel sets" ', níor fhéad sí cluas ar bith a thabhairt dó go rabhadar beirt ar lom an urláir ag damhsa 'plain set' an bhaile.

'Tá an chuingir ort faoi dheireadh,' arsa seisean, mar a bheadh fonn nathaíochta air tar éis an mhosáin.

'Dia á réiteach,' arsa Nóra. Daingníodh ina ceann den chéad uair rud nár fhéad cleamhnas, pósadh, ná an bhainis féin gus nuige seo a chur i dtuiscint di mar is ceart.

'Ná bíodh cumha ar bith ort. Is maith an mhalairt agat fuíoll na bhfuíoll agus do chomhairle féin anseo ar chlár an Achréidh thar is carracáin agus sclábhaíocht an Aird Bhig ... ní áirím aireachas an tseanbhuachalla. Cuirfimid corrlastas creathnaí agus corrbhuidéal poitín aniar chugat, agus maingín chnónna sa bhfómhar.'

Scioch rud eicínt faoi chroí Nóra. Níor chuimhnigh sí go dtí sin nach raibh creathnach, cnónna ná poitín anseo.

'Chaith mé an oíche aréir fré chéile ag iarraidh thú a fheicéail, a Bheairtlín, go n-abrófá *Doire an Fhéidh Chasla* dom, ach ní raibh amharc in áit ar bith ort trí na daoine. Déarfaidh tú é th'éis an damhsa ... Déan ... Is fada go gcloise mé arís é.'

Ach ní maith a bhí a sceadamán réitithe ag Beairtlín san am ar tháinig a máthair agus deirfiúir a fir agus ar ardaigh siad siar sa bparlús arís í.

'Tá sé thar am baile againne,' arsa an mháthair. 'Sin é ina lá geal é agus Máirtín anseo ar neamhchodladh ó arú aréir. Tá sibhse sa mbaile, bail ó Dhia oraibh, ach féach an t-aistear atá romhainne.'

'Aon mhíle dhéag go Gaillimh,' arsa Máirtín Ó Riain, fear Nóra, de glór righin téachta ar chuir canúint Ghaeilge an Achréidh barr coimhthís ann. 'Cúig mhíle dhéag as sin siar, nach ea? Sin é a deireadh spailpín a bhí agam anseo, bliain, ón Aird.'

Ainneoin na mílte fada a lua agus an t-anbhá a bhí ann ag fáil cótaí agus seálta, níor lig Nóra lena hais go raibh a muintir agus a comharsana á fágáil. Níor lig sí sin lena hais gur tháinig gearrchailí an Aird chuici gur phóg siad í agus gur dhúirt siad léi 'gan aon chumha a bheith uirthi, go sciorrfaidís aniar ar cuairt corruair.' D'aithin Nóra gach uile ghlao dá raibh ó ógánaigh an Aird agus iad sna feiriglinnte ar na rothair siar bóthar na Gaillimhe, agus chuir sin tuilleadh coimhthís uirthi le muintir an Achréidh a bhí ag fágáil sláin aici i ngeamhsholas na maidine ceobránaí, agus na driúillíní fuaicht agus scátha ag snámh ina cuisleacha lena bhlasta is a bhí 'Mrs. Ryan' ar bharr a ghoib ag gach uile dhuine díobh. Na gluaisteáin a tháinig le cuid de mhuintir an Aird, bhí siad ag dordsantacht ar an mbóthar agus na haraí ag an stiúir ag séideadh na mbonnán. Ar nós mar rinne sí a liachtaí uair cheana i ndeireadh bainise agus í ag dul abhaile, chuir Nóra a cóta uirthi féin agus shiúil sí amach ar an mbóthar. Ba é Beairtlín an duine deireanach a coiglíodh isteach i gcúl an ghluaisteáin a bhí ag a muintir.

'Dia á réiteach, a Bheairtlín,' arsa sise. 'Coinnigh glac chreathnaí dom.'

Ainneoin an mheatha a raibh sí bhraith Nora meacan sa gcaint a tháinig de bhrúisc amach trí inbhear na bearna míl, de bharr a dheasaithe lena bhéal agus a bhí beanna cába a chóta báistí ag Beairtlín.

'Ná bíodh faitíos ort. Tabharfaidh mé maingín chnónna agat freisin, sa bhfómhar.'

'Tá an cuimse cna sna creigeanna anseo,' arsa a fear lena gualainn.

D'fhan Nóra ina staic ag an ngeata ag breathnú i ndiaidh an ghluaisteáin nó gur bhailigh sé siar Airdín an Chrosbhóthair, ach níor lig sí uirthi féin gur chuala sí buille scoir a máthar ag cur aithne uirthi 'gan aon chumha a bheith uirthi, gur ghearr go bhfeiceadh sí arís iad.'

Cumha! An cumha an gruiféad dobhriste a choinníos an t-anam deorata ar ancaire i gCaladh an Dúchais? Ní cumha a bhí uirthi. Ag bocáil i mbarr toinne faoi thoiliúna Dé a bhí sí, i ndiaidh téad ancaire a hanama a scor, agus gan an oiread is an t-aon sine lena dúchas a bheith fágtha ó d'imigh Beairtlín. I ndiaidh a cinn roimpi, ar nós na loinge den eolas, chuaigh sí go dtí Airdín an Chrosbhóthair. Ainneoin nach raibh Nóra riamh ní ba ghaire don cheantar seo ná Gaillimh, agus ainneoin go raibh sé ina oíche ó Ghaillimh aniar ar chóisir na bainise aréir, ní le hamharc a fháil ar an tír faoi gcuairt a tháinig sí go dtí círín an tortáin seo. Ní raibh de smaointe in intinn Nóra ach círín ar bith ba thúisce aici a ardú sula bplúchtaí í idir dhá thonn na haimsire caite agus na haimsire fáistiní. An pointe sin níorbh fheasach di an ar a deasóg nó ar a ciotóg a bhí Máirtín Ó Riain, ná níor chuir sí cronaí ar bith i gcois a phíopa ag guairdeall timpeall na n-airde; agus is é a ndearna na hainmeacha aisteacha anaithnide a bhí ag tionlacan chos an phíopa cur i gceann a coimhthís agus a bearráin. Ná níor airigh sí an Rianach ag imeacht uaithi ar ais don teach.

Bhí an ceo á chornadh féin suas agus na cornaí á mionú arís agus á bhfuadach amach ina strácaí liatha caillte go ciumhais na má leis an mbeochan gaoithe. Ar feadh a hamhairc ní fhaca sí ach páirceanna móra mine gan chloch gan charracán agus gan troigh dá gcuid fál nach raibh chomh díreach le dorú, cé is moite den áit a raibh na fálta báite ag fuarlach an turlaigh. Bhí doire coille anseo, garrán ansiúd agus corrgheadán creige síos amach uaithi, mar bheadh altanna an adhmaid trí chlár déile tar éis é a thuaradh agus a sciúradh. Ach ba é an áit a raibh sí ina seasamh an cnocán ab aeraí ar an achréidh méith marbh seo. Ní raibh na tithe ina gcaidhlíní anseo: b'facthas di go raibh an brionglán suaite deataí ba ghaire di míle ó láthair. Ba mhar a chéile na tithe ar fad. An déanamh céanna. Na háirgí céanna ina dtimpeall. Agus an fhoireann chéanna crann ag déanamh foscaidh do chlaíocha na n-iothlann. Níor thug Nóra de shamhail dóibh ach ollteach a scáinfeadh in imeacht na hoíche agus ndealódh a chuideanna chomh fada ó chéile is d'fhéad siad le teann doichill. Bhreathnaigh sí ar theach a fir. Níor neamhchosúil é ina dhreach agus ina dhéanamh le teach ceann slinne dhá stór a hathar, cé is moite go raibh gotha ní b'úire ar theach a hathar, go raibh an fharraige ina fhianaise, na maolchnoic ar a chúl, agus gan ann féin ach mar a shnoífí alt eibhir den tír charrach chreagánach i riocht is go mbeadh gallán suaitheantais eicínt i lár an chnuasaigh tithe ceann tuí a dtugtaí an Aird Bhig air. Ach ba é an méid sin an chuid ab fhánaí den idirdhealú. Bhí an dá theach thairis sin chomh neamhchosúil le chéile is atá uisce agus bainne leamhnachta. Fearacht na tíre faoi gcuairt, bhí sotal sónta eicínt i ngotha a hárais nua a mheabhródh di an meangadh sámh a dhéanas ceannaí siopa ar fhéachaint ar a leabhar bainc. Is éard a bhí gotha an tí sin a iomardú lena béal nár fhás aon oíche é — ach cuid den bhuaine féin. B'fheasach do Nóra go mba theach 'te' é. B'fheasach di mura mbeadh gurbh ea nach gcuirfeadh a hathair 'ann' í, tar éis a liachtaí boicín a d'eitigh sé fúithi, agus an spré a bhí aici. Chuaigh driog fuaicht tríthi ar chuimhniú di nach mbeadh inti feasta ach ball acara de bhaill acara an tí sin. Anseo ní raibh réim sléibhe agus farraige mar bhuairín ar an gcois luaithneach ná mar dhaoradh reatha d'aisling na hintinne fálróidí. Ní raibh ann ach an clár mín aonghnéitheach le tnúthán agus tréathra éagsúla daoine a shlogadh agus a dheilbhiú in aon uige fhuar aon snáithe, mar dheilbhíos an fharraige gach uile bhraon uisce riamh ar a haon ghné ghlas dhiamhair féin, bíodh sé ar a rogha dath nó dúchas sula mbeireann a broinn air. Arís choíchin dá laghad caidreamh dar dhóigh di a bheith aici leis 'an mbaile', ní bheadh inti sa gcaidreamh sin féin ach snáithín caol den uige dhlúth seo.

Bhí fuacht nárbh fhíorfhuacht — macasamhail láíochta a cuid deirfiúr céile — sa maidin, agus chuaigh sí isteach. Mhothaigh sí nach raibh dada dá thais ag an áit istigh. Tar éis an phléaráca ar fad ní raibh an chisteanach sách mór as a riocht le go bhféadfaí a rá go raibh sí 'tíriúil', ní áirím 'gaelach'. Ba mhinic cisteanach a dtí féin sa mbaile ina cíor thuathail i bhfad ní ba mheasa i ndiaidh cúpla uair de dhamhsa airneáin. Cé is moite den dá bhord a bhí as fad a chéile fós sa bparlús, d'fhág an lucht freastail sular imigh siad gach uile shórt ar a chóir féin, gan bun cleite amach ná barr cleite isteach a mheabhródh go ndeachaigh eang sa ngabhail, agus gur snaidhmeadh dhá anam le cuing spioradálta is colannda an aontís agus an chéileachais i riocht is go mbuanófaí foinse beatha an tí. Na cúrsaí ba mhó a bhain le cinniúint an duine, ní raibh iontu ach sciot ar uisce méaróige ar dhromchla sámh mór na tíre seo.

Shuigh sí síos agus thug súil thart faoin gcisteanach, rud nach bhfuair sí ionú a dhéanamh ó tháinig sí don teach. Bhí séala daingean an tíobhais — bean choimhdeachta na buaine — ar gach uile mhíle ball, ó na sáspain ghlana sciúrtha go dtí an dá 'phress' mhóra a raibh finne fómhair ina gcuid adhmaid. Níor dhóigh beirthe é ná go gcuimhneodh sí ar an bhfoireann a chuirtí sna hárais anlacain agus nach ndéantaí a gcorraí ná a gcaitheamh nó go rodaíodh an aimsir iad; ach, ó nach raibh eolas ar bith ag Nóra ar sheandalaíocht, ag cuimhniú a bhí sí cén chaoi ar fhéad an Rianach, agus é taobh leis féin, a theach a choinneáil chomh piocúil ornáilte agus a bhí sé. Ní raibh uireasa lámh mná ar an teach seo! Ach an rud ba choimhthí ar fad le Nóra gan teallach gan tine a fheiceáil, ach an sornán dalba doicheallach a raibh an dé tar éis múchadh in áit eicínt istigh ina bhroinn.

'Cá'il an mhóin, ní mé?' arsa sise léi féin ag éirí, arae le hoighear an choimhthís a chlaochlú chun scaláin an teanntáis níor mhór léi cladach tine a chur síos a dhéanfadh caor dhearg de chruach an tsornáin agus a chruthódh di go mba chumasaí tine agus teas ná an t-iarann fuar daingean.

'Gual ar fad a bhíonns agamsa,' arsa a fear. 'Nach mb'fhearr duit gan bacadh le tine ach spuaic a bhaint amach ar an leaba.'

Scanraigh sí. Níor chuimhnigh sí amháin ar an leaba go dtí sin. D'airigh sí ugach teanntáis an ghlóir mheathchodlataigh sin ag cur rabharta coil faoin gcuisle aici, ach thuig sí go raibh an glór ró-údarásach lena shéanadh dá mb'áil leis an scéal a chur go spriog.

'Níl aon chodladh orm,' arsa sise, faoi dheireadh agus faoi dheoidh, ach bhí a fear imithe amach i gcoinne an ghuail. Ba ghearr go raibh sé ar ais arís agus gur theilg sé sluaisteog de isteach i gcab an tsornáin. Chuir na sáití den phócar a bhí sé a thabhairt do ghríosach na tine núis ar Nóra Ba gheall le hanam a bheadh ar mheá an chathaithe ag an diabhal agus é ar a mhine ghéire ag féachaint le é féin a shlánú, coscairt dhriopásach na gríosaí ag iarraidh lasta. Thabharfadh Nóra Éire anois dá mbeadh athair céile, máthair chéile, duine de dheirfiúracha béalráiteacha a céile, nó balbhán féin chois an teallaigh. Bhí deatach phíopa an Rianaigh ag gluaiseacht go dtí an t-áiléar ina phúir chuimseartha gan mhairg gan mhúisiam. Strácaí catacha coilgneacha a sílfí orthu go raibh siad ag coraíocht le rud eicínt san aer a dhéanadh gaileanna Bheairtle agus a hathar. Ní raibh aon riasc fiáin — aon cheo de choirce scéin a ceantair féin — i gcaint a fir. Ba ar a chruachúis dó a bheith chomh cruinn barainneach murach go mba chlár mín gan ísleán gan ardán a intinn fré chéile ... Ón gcorrgheábh grinn a rinne sé, agus ón meangadh a mhaíodh i lúibinn rite a shróine lena linn sin, mheabhraigh sé do Nóra Dia na críonnachta ag iarraidh a dhul uairín le haer an tsaoil. De réir mar a bhí sí ag taithiú le leagan logánta na cainte, b'amhlaidh ba mhó a bhí a brí ag dul chun coimhthís di. Thit an driull ar an dreall uirthi. B'fhada léi go dtagadh clanna eicínt nach mbeadh d'aon uige: malairt duine, malairt lae, malairt aimsire, an oíche arís, nó dodaí ina ghlór, i leaba an doird mhairbh sháimh nach ndearna thar thoilliúint ina cluais anois.

D'éirigh sí agus chuaigh sí amach i mbéal an dorais ar an bhfionnuartas. Ainneoin nach raibh siad ach tar éis cead scoir a fháil, ba bheag an súnás a bhí ar na páineanna cearc ach ag scríobadh leo sna láithreacha bláth ar gach aon ghiall den chis stroighne taobh istigh de chéimeanna gheaitín an bhóthair. An corrbhláth a bhí tar éis goineachan trí thalamh, taltaíodh aréir é. Ba dhiacht di gan lorg coise Bheairtlín a aithneachtáil agus a liachtaí uair ar chronaigh sí cheana í ar mhóin, ar ithir agus ar ghaineamh. Ag grinneadh cumraíocht na bróige a bhí sí san am ar tháinig fear tromchosach faoina hata bog tuataigh agus a bhríste 'cord' thart an bóthar. Bhí cuimhne ag Nóra go mba chomharsa áirid dá fear é, i ngeall go bhfaca sí comaoin ar leith á cur air sa bparlús aréir. Gan claochlú ar a choiscéim agus gan a cheann a shníomh thar dhubh na fríde chuici, bheannaigh sé di chomh drogallach beagfhoclach is dá mba phingin sa gcíos gach uile shiolla den chaint. Bhí an ceo ina chochall broghach anuas faoi dhroim an chláir an athuair, agus gan tríd ach corrdhing de léargas. Ach mar sin féin níor mhóide do Nóra a dhul isteach chomh tobann, murach an taghd a bhuail í leis an gcearc otraithe a raibh cumraíocht na coise scríobtha lena crág mhístuama aici den chréafóg bhog shodhealfa ...

Shuigh Nóra ar an gcathaoir chéanna arís chois an tsornáin. De bharr teas na tine agus an tuirse bhí a fear ina shrann chodlata — srann mharbh thomhaiste, gan mhúisiam gan mhairg, mar bhréidín lách farraige loime le duirling ar théigle shamhraidh. Den chéad uair chuaigh sí ar ghrinndearcadh a fir, fearacht is dá mbeadh sí á fhágáil go deireadh mar bhall suarach dá saol nua. Fear géagánach corrghuailleach. Séala na gcéadta bliain de ghrian, de dhoineann, d'ithir agus de chrácamas ar an gcolainn urrúnta, ar an muineál féitheach agus ar an gceannaghaidh garbh bláthbhuí. Gruaig dhubh a raibh ciumhaiseog liathachain mar fhíor an nirt léi. Súile marbha malla nach ndearna Nóra faoilte an gháire, lasadh na feirge ná boige seirce a shamhailt leo. Polláirí fonsacha séidte nach bhféadfadh a bheith an-éisealach faoi bholadh. Croiméal cróndubh a bhfachtas di ón gcupla smearamharc a thug sí uirthi cheana gur ghéar a theastaigh a díogáil uaithi. Agus go háirid ó thug sí faoi deara go barainneach anois nach raibh na dosáin thiubha róine ag clúdú aon bhearna mhíl ...

THE HARE-LIP

Nora Liam Bhid spent the night as she had spent the previous one making tea for the wedding party. But now the light of an early February morning, fogged and white, was seeping into the halfdeserted parlour, and since she had cleared up after yesterday and was now free, again the strangeness of it came nagging at her. The strangeness of being married, the change, the outlandish Plain: that same flicker of unease astir in her ever since the night her father came home from the Galway Fair and began telling her mother in private that he had 'fixed up a strong farmer on the Plain for Nora'. And it had been no cure for that cut-off feeling to see the man himself and his sisters for the first time last week at the matchmaking. Like a female salmon locked in a choked up sidechannel and destined never to reach the breeding beds in the clear shallows upriver. Nora had undertaken the marriage bond in the chapel of Ard late last evening. And now, finding no comfort in her mother's mild words, her father's boozy cajolery, her husband's bland imperturbability, or in the chatter of her female in-laws friendly and sly, she went down into the kitchen to the group of her old neighbours who had come from Ard with the wedding party.

The dancing-barn outside had been for some time deserted and the kitchen was now thronged with people who fell silent when she appeared. Wheezing beerladen breaths, trails of tobacco smoke, specks of sand from the concrete floor floating in a frostfog — all this made the silence a palpable thing confronting her, a phantom, to try and drag from her the words that would express the anguish of its being. It was that time of a wedding morning when a man might go about starting a row and find none to hinder him. The fire had gone out of the drunken voices, the laughter was lifeless. The young folk, it seemed to her, got up without much heart to dance the jig, afraid that the married couples and oldtimers might take advantage of the quiet that was beginning to close in about the house and say it was time to go. Even the young folk from Ard, hardened to revelling and constant labour, every one of them by now was bleary of voice, weary of foot. The only one in the house left with some flinty fire in his footwork and the flush of life in his cheek was Beairtlin, her father's servant-boy.

Nora dropped her head and let that flintspark penetrate her mind, that flush invade her being, till the silence and the unhomely thing receded. She remembered the many spells of innocent courting with him, snatching dulse[1] from him in summer, or in the autumn the two of them on the flags of the dooryard cracking the nuts he had brought her from the hazelgrove of Liss, and nights of fireside chat together when the old couple were gone to bed and she was waiting up for Padraig her brother to come home from a visit. The girls of Ard, who were at the wedding tonight, had often given her a sly dig suggesting Beairtlin for her. Tonight was the one night none of them would think of him for her, but it was the one night she wouldn't have minded. Beairtlin's witty remarks, that's what used take the bitter edge off her laughter whenever her father and mother were settling a match for her. A pain of regret, dulled not healed. That she had been so quick to speak her mind to him that day, so willing to find fault with Providence, when Beairtlin told her that 'the old fellow was making a match for her again, and no one would be given a wisp of consideration except a shopkeeper or a boss-man of the Plain'.

It wasn't because she had been vexed with Beairtlin for what he said that she passed remarks that day about his hare-lip. Instead, she had intended to say that she'd go off warm and willing with him there and then. For when all is said and done, it wasn't his slim and shapely person, his sky-grey eye, his cheek red as foxglove, no, it was the hare-lip, that disfigurement he was marked with from the womb — he didn't even try to hide it with a moustache — that attracted her eyes and her passionate lips. It attracted and repelled her, often her disgust got the upper hand, too often, that's what left the web of her young life a heap of grey dust today. Even now it was the hare-lip she saw coming at her like a bloodsucking lamprey through a grey sea-lough. Beairtlin grumbled that 'the Plainers had taken over the house all night with their reel sets',[2] but she couldn't attend to him till the pair of them were out on the middle of the floor dancing the plain set of home.

—So you're spancelled[3] at last? he said humorously, appearing to hide his vexation.

—God help us, she answered. She realised fully for the first time what neither match, marriage nor the wedding itself had given her clearly to understand.

—Have no regrets. You've made a good swap, lashings and leavings and being your own mistress here on the level Plain, in place of the rocks and the slave-labour — and not to mention the vigilant eye of your old fellow — out at Ardbeg. We'll send you an odd cargo of dulse, an odd bottle of poteen, and a bundle of nuts in the autumn.

Nora's heart missed a beat. She had forgotten until now that there was no dulse, no nuts, no poteen here.

—I spent last night looking for you, Beairtlin, to sing *The Deer's Wood by Casla* for me, but there wasn't a sight of you in the crowd. You'll sing it after this dance. Do. It'll be a long time till I hear it again ....

But Beairtlin had hardly cleared his throat for the song when her mother and her husband's sister came and carried her off again to the parlour.

—Time for us to be home, said the mother. Look, it's broad daylight, and your husband Martin here without sleep since the night before last. You two are at home, God bless you, but look at the journey we have before us.

—Eleven miles to Galway, said Martin Ryan, the

1. Edible seaweed.

2. A kind of square-dancing.

3. tied down, hobbled (usually of a horse or cow).

new husband. He had a slow congealed kind of a voice and the unhomely accent of the Plain. —And fifteen miles farther west again, isn't that it? That's what he used to tell me, a labouring man I had here one year from Ard.

Despite their talk of the long miles and the scurry there was for coats and shawls, Nora wouldn't admit that her family and friends were leaving her. She was made realise it when the Ardbeg girls came kissing her and saying 'not to be homesick, they'd slip over an odd time on a visit'. She recognised every individual shout of the Ardbeg boys going wildly on their bikes back down the Galway road, and that left the Plainsfolk more alien than ever as they took leave of her in the misty morning light. And all with their 'Missus Ryan' so pat on the tongue causing her cold shivers of fear. The cars that had brought the Ardbeg people were humming out on the road, the drivers hooting the horns. As she had done so many times before at the end of a wedding Nora put on her overcoat and walked out to the road. Beairtlin was the last one to crush into the car that held her family.

—God help us, Beairtlin, she said. Keep me a handful of dulse.

Beairtlin had fixed the cape-ends of his raincoat across his mouth. Though her senses swam she caught the meaning in his words which came squeezed out through the hare-lip opening. —Don't worry. And I'll bring you a bag of nuts too. In the autumn.

—There's plenty of nuts in the cregs[4] hereabouts, said her husband standing alongside her.

She stood unmoving at the gate looking after the car until it had passed Crossroads rise, pretending not to have heard her mother's parting words, 'not to be homesick, she'd see them soon again'.

Homesick? That anchor, keeping the spirit though in exile fixed in its native harbour? No, she wasn't homesick. Tossed on a wave's crest at the caprice of God, having cut her life's cable, not a single link left with her natural element since Beairtlin went, she drove on straight ahead like a boat that has lost its bearings to the Crossways rise. She had never been nearer than Galway to this district and it had been dark during the wedding-drive last night, still it wasn't to view the country that she walked to the crest of this hill. Her only idea was to climb the first rise that came her way and get out of this smothering trough between the two waves of past and present. At that moment she couldn't tell whether Martin Ryan was to the left or right of her, she took no interest in the stem of his pipe circling the prominent points while he himself stabbed the queer uncouth names in the face of her illwill and detestation. She didn't notice Ryan leaving her and going back to the house.

The fog was being rolled and thinned out and dragged by a freshening wind in grey diminishing strips to the edge of the Plain. As far as her eye could see, nothing but immense flat fields, no stones, no rock-heaps, and every foot of fencing as straight as a fishing-line except where they were submerged in winter flooding. Here and there a stand of trees, a thicket, down below her a few outcrops of bedrock like knots in a deal table that had been bleached and scoured. The spot where she stood was the most airy hill of all the dull rich expanse. The houses were not strung together here, the nearest wavering thread of smoke seemed to her a mile away. All the houses alike. And the same set of trees sheltering the walls of the haggards. It appeared to her fancy that one immense house had split in the night and all its parts had separated as far as they might out of sheer unneighbourliness. She looked back at her husband's house. Not too unlike her father's house in make and appearance, two-storey, slated. But her father's house had looked newer, with a view of the sea, bare hills at the back of it, the house itself seeming a section of granite sliced out of the rock country to be set up as some tall symbolic stone in the middle of the group of thatched houses called Ardbeg. But there was a greater difference still. The two houses were as different as chalk from cheese. Like all the surrounding countryside her new house had a certain stupid arrogance, it reminded her of the smug smile of a shopkeeper examining his bank-book. Boasting to her face that it was no mushroom growth but a part of the everlasting. She knew it was a 'warm' house. She knew her father wouldn't have set her there if it wasn't, in view of her dowry and all the well-heeled upstarts he had refused on her behalf. She shivered to think that from now on she would be simply one of the conveniences among the conveniences of this house.

Here there was no barrier of mountain and sea to restrain a rambling foot or limit a wandering imagination. Nothing but the smooth monotonous Plain to absorb one's yearnings and privacies and weave

4. stony ground.

them into the one drab undifferentiated fabric, as each individual drop, whatever its shade, whatever its nature before being engulfed in the womb of it, the ocean transmutes into its own grey phantom face. From now on whatever contact she'd have with home would be only a thin thread in this close-knit stuff.

There was a chilliness in the morning, not a genuine cold — rather like the friendliness of her sisters-in-law. She went in. She noticed there was nothing out of place within. After all the merry-making the kitchen wasn't disordered enough to be called homely, not to say Irish. Their own kitchen at home had often been more of a shambles after a couple of hours dancing during a neighbourly visit. Apart from the two tables set end to end in the parlour, the attendants had set everything to rights before they went, and there wasn't the slightest thing crooked to mark that an event had taken place, that two lives had been spiritually and bodily woven together in the tie of intercourse under the one roof to ensure the spring of life in that house. The prime events of a man's destiny skimmed across the wide placid surface of this countryside as lightly as a finger-stone is flicked across water.

Sitting she looked about the kitchen, it was the first chance she had got of examining it since she came to the house. There were signs of careful housekeeping, nursing things to last long, on every single item from the saucepans cleaned and scoured to the two tall presses[5] blond and mellow. A burial chamber, the image might have occurred, vessels and furniture set in it never to be moved until time should undo them; but, ignorant of the antiquities, what she did ask herself was how Ryan all on his own had kept the place so spick and span. This house needed no woman's hand. Strangest of all, neither hearth nor fire to be seen. Instead there was a metal range, dull and unwelcoming, the last spark had died somewhere within its womb.

—I wonder where's the turf? she said to herself getting up. In order to change this alien cold into a warm intimacy she must heap up a fire that would make the iron range red hot and prove to herself that a warm fire was more than a match for the rigid iron.

—I use nothing but coal, he said. Wouldn't it be better not bother with a fire and take a lie-down on the bed?

She took fright. Till now she hadn't thought of the bed. That drowsy voice, assured, self-assertive, set up waves of repulsion in her, yet she recognised it as the voice of authority, not to be denied if he felt like bringing the thing to a head.

—I'm not sleepy, she said at last. But her husband had gone out for the coal. He soon returned and shot a shovelful of it into the maw of the range. His jabs with the poker at the embers got on Nora's nerves. Like a soul gripped by the demon on the edge of desire, the embers were quickly breaking apart and trying to flame. She'd give anything if her husband's father, mother, any of his prating sisters or even a silent one, were here at the hearth.

The smoke of Ryan's pipe was rising up to the loft in measured puffs, unruffled, unconcerned. The smoke of her father's pipe, or Beairtlín's, always made twists and angles as if they were wrestling with something in the air. There were none of the unfenced regions of her homeland in her husband's conversation, none of the wild oats of speech. Prosy and precise, he could hardly be otherwise, for his mind was a smooth plain without the slightest up or down from end to end.... With his rare attempts at a joke, a smile crinkling the stiff crease of his nose, he reminded her of the god of wisdom trying to be merry a minute. The more she grew accustomed to the local accent the more alien she felt it. She longed for a new twist in the tune — a change of person, change of day, change of time, that it might be night again, or that his voice might be angry, anything but that gentle deadly drone that did nothing now but linger in her ears.

She got up and stood in the doorway in the fresh air. Plump hens just let out were already scrabbling in the flowerbeds on each side of the concrete path that led from the steps at the front gate. What scant flowers had already poked up through the earth had been trampled last night. There was Beairtlín's footprint — how could she mistake it, the many times it had caught her eye, on the bog, in the earth, on the seasand. She was examining the shape of the boot when a heavyfoot[ed] man with the soft hat of the region and a cord breeches passed on the road. Nora remembered he was some neighbour of her husband's, he had been given special treatment in the parlour last night. Without slowing his step and with only the slightest turn of his head her way he greeted her briefly. Sparing his words as if every syllable was worth another penny towards the rent.

5. cupboards.

The fog had come down again in a drab shawl over the Plain with only odd slits of visibility. Still she wouldn't have gone back in so quickly if a filthy hen hadn't angered her by scratching away the footprint with a mindless claw from the soft impressionable earth. . . .

She sat again in the same chair by the range. With the heat of the fire and the weariness her husband was asleep and snoring — a dull measured snore peaceful and passionless. The gentle ripple of a languid sea on the shingle in a summer calm. She studied him for the first time as she might some insignificant item of her new life. Long limbs, angular shoulders. Centuries of sun and shower, soil and drudgery, had shaped and marked that robust body, the sinewy neck, the sallow features. A black head of hair edged with grey, sign of strength. Lids shut on those slow dull eyes in which she could imagine neither smile of pleasure nor flash of anger nor the soft haze of desire. Flaring nostrils that wouldn't be too squeamish of smells. A sootblack moustache — she had caught it out of the corner of her eye a few times previously and felt it needed badly to be cut. And now particularly, realising that those thick bristles weren't hiding a hare-lip.

from:
CRÉ NA CILLE (1949)

[*Cré na Cille* (The Clay of the Churchyard) tells the story of Caitríona and her relationship with the remote rural community in which she has lived and recently died. The course of the novel takes place beneath the clay of the graveyard where the conflicts of life above ground are protracted in interminable rancorous dialogue. In this opening sequence Caitríona 'revives' in her grave, broods on her death and burial and renews her animosity towards her sister Nell, her inveterate enemy in love and everything else.

The translation is by Eibhlín Ní Allmhuráin and Maitín Ó Néill.]

CHAPTER I

Ní mé an ar Áit an Phúint nó na Cúig Déag atá mé curtha? D'imigh an diabhal orthu dhá mba in Áit na Leathghine a chaithfidís mé, th'éis ar chuir mé d'fhainceachaí orthu! Maidin an lae ar bhásaigh mé ghlaoigh mé aníos ón gcisteanach ar Phádraig: 'Achainí agam ort a Phádraig a leanbh,' adeirimse. 'Cuir ar Áit an Phúint mé. Ar Áit an Phúint. Tá cuid againn curtha ar Áit na Leathghine, ach má tá fhéin. . . .'

Dúirt mé leo an chónra ab fhearr tigh Thaidhg a fháil. Cónra mhaith dharaí í ar chaoi ar bith . . . . Tá brat na scaball orm. Agus an bhraillín bharróige. Bhí siad sin faoi réir agam fhéin . . . . Tá spota ar an scaoilteoig seo. Is geall le práib shuí é. Ní hea. Lorg méire. Bean mo mhic go siúráilte. Is cosúil len a cuid pruislíocht é. Má chonaic Neil é! Is dóigh go raibh sí ann. Ní bheadh dar fia dhá mbeadh aon neart agamsa air . . . .

Is místuama a ghearr Cáit bheag na gairéadaí. Dúirt mé ariamh fhéin nár cheart aon deor len ól a thabhairt di féin ná do Bhid Shorcha nó go mbeadh an corp dealaithe den tsráid. Chuir mé fainic ar Phádraig dhá mbeadh ól déanta acu gan ligean dóibh na gairéadaí a ghearradh. Ach ní féidir Cáit Bheag a choinneál ó choirp. Ba é a buaic chuile lá ariamh marbhán a bheith in áit ar bith ar an dá bhaile. Dhá mbeadh na seacht sraith ar an iomaire d'fhanfaidís ar an iomaire, ach í ag fáil bonn coirp . . . .

Tá an chrois ar mo chliabhrach, an ceann a cheannaigh mé fhéin ag an misean . . . . Ach cáil an chrois dhubh a thug bean Thomáisín beannaithe chugam as an gCnoc an t-am sin a mb'éigin Tomáisín a cheangal go deireanach. Dúirt mé leo an chrois sin a chur orm freisin. Is cuidsúlaí go mór í ná an ceann seo. Ó a thit an chrois seo ó ghasúir Phádraig, tá cor cam sa Slánaíodóir uirthi. an Slánaíodóir atá ar an gceann dubh is mór an áilleacht é. Céard sin orm? Nach mé atá dearmadach i gcónaí. Sin í faoi mo cheann í. Nach mairg nach hí a chuir siad ar mo chliabhrach . . . .

Bhí acu snaidhm ní b'fhearr a chur ar an bpaidrín ar mo mhéarachaí. Neil fhéin, go siúráilte, a rinne é sin. Bheadh sásamh aici dhá dtiteadh sé ar an talamh san am a raibh siad do mo chur i gcónra. A Thiarna Thiarna, b'fhada amach uaimse a d'fhanfadh sí sin . . . .

Tá súil agam gur las siad na hocht gcoinneal as cionn mo chónra sa séipéal. D'fhág mé faoi réir acu iad, i gcúinne an chomhra faoi pháipéir an chíosa. Sin rud nach raibh ariamh ar chorp sa séipéal sin: ocht gcoinneal. Ní raibh ar an gCurraoineach ach cheithre cinn. Sé cinn ar Liam Thomáis Táilliúr, ach tá iníon leis sin sna mná rialta i Meiriceá . . . .

Trí leathbhairille pórtair adúirt mé a chur orm, agus gheall Éamonn na Tamhnaí dhom fhéin dhá mbeadh deoir ar bith faoi shliabh go dtiocfadh sé leis gan cuireadh gan iarraidh. Níorbh fholáir sin agus a mbeadh d'altóir ann. Ceathair déag nó cúig déag de phunta ar a laghad ar bith. Chuaigh duine nó scilling uaim i gcuid mhaith áiteachaí nach raibh sochraide ar bith dlite dhom iontu, le cúig nó sé de bhlianta ó a d'airigh mé mé fhéin ag tabhairt uaim. Is dóigh gur tháinig lucht an tsléibhe uilig. Ba bhocht dóibh nach dtiocfadh. Bhíomar acu. Sin cúnamh maith de phunt ar an gcéad iarraidh. Agus muintir Dhoire Locha leanfaidís sin na cliamhaineachaí. Sin cúnamh maith de phunt eile. Agus bhí sochraide dlite ag Gleann na Buaile as éadan dom .... Ní bheadh iontas orm mara dteagadh Stiofán Bán. Bhíomar ag chuile shochraide ariamh aige. Ach déarfadh sé nar chuala sé é, nó go raibh mé curtha. Agus an ghalamaisíocht a bheadh ansin air: 'Go deimhin dhuit a Phádraig Uí Loideáin, dhá mbeadh féith de mo chroí air, bheinn ag an tsochraide. Níor chomaoin domsa gan a theacht ar shochraide Chaitríona Pháidín dhá mba ar go ghlúine a ghabhfainn ann. Ach dheamhan smid a chuala mé faoi go dtí an oíche ar cuireadh í. Scurach le ....' An sclaibéara ós é Stiofán Bán é! ...

Dheamhan a fhios agam ar caoineadh go maith mé. Gan bhréig gan mhagadh tá racht breá bogúrach ag bid Shorcha mara raibh sí ró-óltach. Tá mé siúráilte go raibh Neil ag imeacht ag diúgaireacht ann freisin. Neil ag caoineadh agus gan deoir len a grua, an smuitín! A dúshlán sin an teach a thaobhachtáil agus mise beo ....

Tá sí sásta anois. Shíl mé go mairfinn cupla bliain eile, agus go gcuirfinn rómham an raicleach. Thug sí anuas go mór ó d'eirigh an gortú dhá mac. Bhíodh sí ag dul coitianta go leor ag an dochtúr le scaitheamh roimhe sin fhéin. Ach ní brí a bhfuil uirthi. Scoilteachaí. Ní thabharfaidh siad sin aon bhás di go ceann fada. Tá sí an-phrámhaí uirthi fhéin. Sin caoi nach raibh mise. Anois atá a fhios agam é. Mharaigh mé mé fhéin le obair agus luainn ... Dhá dtapaínn an phian sin shul a ndeachaigh sí in ainsil orm. Ach ó a bhuailfeas sé sna duánaí duine tá a chaiscín meilte ....

Bhí dhá bhliain agam ar Neil, ar aon chor ... Baba. Ansin mise agus Neil. Bliain go Féil Míchil seo caite a fuair mé an pinsean. Ach fuair mé roimh an am é. Tá Baba suas agus anuas le trí déag agus ceithre fichid. Is gearr an bás uaithi anois, th'éis a díchill. Ní raibh an mhuintir se'againne saolach. Ach a bhfaighe sí scéal mo bháis-se, beidh a fhios aici gur beag é a seal fhéin, agus déanfaidh sí a huachta go cinnte ... Ag Neil a fhágfas sí chuile chianóg ag gabháil léi. Tá sásamh maith ag an smuitín orm ina dhiaidh sin. Tá Baba blite suas aici. Ach dhá bhfaighinnse saol nó go ndéanfadh Baba uachta déarfainn go dtabharfadh sí leath an airgid dom de bhuíochas Neil. Duine sách luathintinneach í Baba. Chugamsa is mó a bhí sí ag scríobh le trí bliana anois ó d'athraigh sí ó mhuintir Bhriain Mhóir, i Norwood, go Boston. Is maith an cúnamh í a bheith dealaithe ón gcuasnóig ghangaideach sin ar aon nós ....

Ach níor mhaith sí ariamh do Phádraig é gur phós sé an agóid sin as an nGort Ribeach, agus gur fhága sé Meaig Bhriain Mhóir ina dhiaidh. Ní thaobódh sí tigh Neile beag ná mór, an uair sin a raibh sí sa mbaile as Meiriceá marach gurb é mac Neile a phós Meaig Bhriain Mhóir. Tuige a dtaobhódh .... Pruchóigín de theach. Pruchóigín bhrocach de theach freisin. Ní teach do Phuncán a bhí ann ar aon nós. Níl a fhios agam cén chaoi ar bhain sí ceart ar bith dhó i ndiaidh a bheith sa teach se'againne agus i dtithe móra Mheiriceá. Ach ba ghearr an cónaí a rinne sí ann, gur ghread sí anonn in athuair ...

Ní thiocfaidh sí go hÉirinn lena ló arís. Tá sí réidh leis. Ach cá bhfios cén mheanma a bhuailfeadh í th'éis an chogaidh seo, má bhíonn sí sa gcomhaireamh ceann. Mheallfadh Neil sin an mhil ón gcuasnóig. Tá sí sách spleách, sách aigeanta lena dhéanamh. Léanscrios uirthi mar chailleach! Th'éis gur dhealaigh sí ó Chlann Bhriain Mhóir i Norwood, tá an-ghnaoi aici ar Mheaig Bhriain Mhóir i gcónaí .... Nárbh é mo Phádraig an pleoitín nach ndéanfadh a comhairle, agus iníon an scóllacháin ghránna a phósadh. 'Níl aon mhaith dhaoibh liom,' adeir an pleoitín. 'Ní phósfainn Meaig Bhriain Mhóir dhá mba taobh léi a bheadh Éire.' D'imigh Baba suas chuig Neil mar a bhuailfí ar an gcluais í, agus níor thaobhaigh sí an teach againne ní ba mhó ach seasamh ar an urlár ar éigin an lá a raibh sí ag dul ar ais go Meiriceá.

—— ... Mo ghrá é Hitler. Sin é an buachaill acu ....

—— Má buailtear Sasana, beidh an tír in ainriocht. Tá an margadh caillte cheana againn ....

—— ... A Chineál Tháilliúr na Leathchluaise, is tú a d'fhága anseo mé leathchéad bliain roimh an am. Bhí an buille feille ariamh fhéin i gcineál na Leathchluaise. Sceanna, clocha, agus buidéil. Ní throidfeá mar a throidfeadh fear ach mé a shá ....

—— ... Cead cainte dhom. Cead cainte ....

—— Crois Críosta choisreacan Dé orainn! — an

beo nó marbh atá mé? An beo nó marbh atá siad seo? Tá siad uilig ag cur díobh chomh treán céanna agus a bhí as cionn talúna! Shíl mé ó chuirfí i gcill mé agus nach mbeadh cruóg oibre, ná imní tí, ná faitíos síne ná eile orm go mbéadh suaimhneas i ndán dom ... ach cén chiall an chathaíocht seo i gcré na cille ....

TRANSLATION

Now I wonder is it in the pound plot or in the fifteen shilling plot they have me buried. They went to the devil entirely if it's in the ten shilling place they threw me after all the warnings I gave them. The morning of the day I died I called Padraig up from the kitchen. 'Will you do me a favour, Padraig, asthore',[1] says I. 'Bury me in the pound plot. The pound plot. Some of us are laid in the ten shilling part, but if they are itself ....'

I told them to get the best coffin there was in Tadhg's shop. It's a fine oak coffin in any case .... The brown habit is on me. And the winding sheet .... I had these ready myself .... There's a spot on this sheet. It's like a plaster of soot. No, it isn't. The mark of a finger. My son's wife for sure. It's like her handiwork. If Nell saw it! I suppose she was there. By gor, she wouldn't be there if I could help it ....

Kateen did a clumsy job of the binding strips. I always said neither herself nor Bid Sorcha should get a drop of drink until the corpse would be left the street. I warned Padraig not to let them cut the binding strips if they had drink taken. But you couldn't keep that Kateen away from a corpse. She was never happy unless there was a corpse somewhere in the neighbourhood. The place could be on fire for all she cared once she got the smell of a corpse ....

The crucifix is on my chest. The one I bought at the mission ....[2] But where's the black crucifix Tomasheen's wife brought me blessed from Knock[3] that last time Tomasheen had to be tied.[4] I told them to put that crucifix on me too. It was much more stylish than this one. The Saviour on this one is crooked since one of Padraig's kids let it fall. The Saviour on the black one is gorgeous. What's wrong with me? I'm as forgetful as ever. There it is under my head. Isn't it a pity it's not that one they put on my chest ....

They might have put a better knot in the beads on my fingers. 'Twas Nell did this for sure. It would please her greatly if it fell on the ground and they putting me in the coffin. Sweet Lord, that one would keep well clear of me if ....

I hope they lit the eight candles over my coffin in the chapel. I left them ready for them under the rent form in the corner of the chest. That's something was never on a corpse in that chapel before: eight candles. On Curran there was only four. Six on Liam Thomas the Tailor, but he has a daughter a nun in America.

Three half barrels of porter I told them to have for the wake, and Éamonn from Tahmney promised myself if there was a drop of the mountainy stuff[5] to be had he'd bring it without come or call. It would all be needed with an offering[6] of that size. Fourteen or fifteen pound at the very least. Many's the place I sent someone or paid a shilling, even where I didn't owe any funeral at all, this past five or six years since I felt myself failing. I suppose all the people from the mountain came. Poor show if they wouldn't. We were at theirs. That would be the best part of a pound. And the Derrylough people, they'd follow the in-laws. That's the best part of another pound. And all the crowd in Glenabooley owed me a funeral .... I wouldn't be surprised if Stephen Bawn didn't turn up. We were at every funeral he ever had. But he'd say he didn't hear about it til I was buried. And all the blather he'd have then. 'By my soul, Padraig Lydon, if I'd got wind of the word I'd have been at the funeral. No thanks to me to go to Caitríona Paudeen's funeral if it was on my knees I'd have to go. But devil the word I heard about it til the night she was buried! A young fellow of ....' He'd talk himself out of hell, that Stephen Bawn ....

I wonder now did they keen[7] me right. To be sure Bid Shorcha has a fine doleful wail, if she was not too fluthered.[8] No doubt Nell was bumming

1. Dear one.
2. A session of intense catholic religious devotions during which religious objects may be bought and blessed.
3. A village in County Mayo where it is believed an apparition of the Blessed Virgin occurred in 1879. An Irish 'Lourdes'.
4. i.e. straitjacketed in an asylum.
5. Poteen — illegally distilled whiskey.
6. Donations to the priest on the occasion of a funeral. The amount donated was a measure of a family's esteem.
7. A formal lamentation for the dead.
8. i.e. drunk.

around there too. Nell keening and not a tear on her cheek, the get.[9] I'd like to see her coming near the house and me alive ....

She's satisfied now. I thought I'd have lived another few years and buried that rip first. She was failing badly especially since her son got that hurt. Even before that she used to go to the doctor fairly regular. But devil a much was wrong with her. Rheumatics. That would take long enough to kill her. She was very fussy about herself. That's more than I was. It's now I know it. I murdered myself with working and slaving. If I'd looked after that pain before it got a grip on me. But when it hits you in the kidneys you're done for.

Anyway, I'd be two years older than Nell .... Baba. Then me and Nell. Last Michaelmas twelvemonth I got the pension. But I got it before my time. Baba would be around about ninety-three. She can't last much longer, whether she likes it or not. Our people weren't long livers. When she hears of my death she'll know her own time is short, and she'll surely make her will.... It's to Nell she'll leave every red penny. The faggot[10] has the last laugh on me all the same. She has Baba well buttered up. But if I'd lived till Baba made her will, I'd say she'd have given me half the money in spite of Nell. Baba was as like to change her mind as not. It's to me she used to write this three years back since she left Brian More's people in Norwood and went to Boston. It's a good job she got away from that spiteful crowd anyway ....

But she never forgave Padraig for passing over Brian More's daughter Mag and marrying that little vomit from Gort Ribeach. She wouldn't go next or near Nell's that time she was home from America only for it was Nell's son that married Mag. And why would she? ... Their little hovel of a house. A stinking little hovel at that. No house for a Yank at any rate. I don't know how she put up with it at all after being in our house and in the big houses in America. Anyway her stay there was a short one til she took off to America the second time ....

She'll not come back to Ireland again as long as she lives. She's finished with it. Still you'd never know what notion she'd take after the war, if she's among the survivors. That Nell would coax the honey from the bee. She's crafty enough and cunning enough to do it. Bad cess[11] to her, the hag! Even though she left Brian More's people in Norwood, she still has a great smack for Mag. Wasn't my Padraig the fool that wouldn't be said by her[12] and marry the dirty old scald's daughter. 'Ye might as well be idle' says the little fool. 'I wouldn't marry Mag Brian More if she was the only woman in Ireland.' Away with Baba like a scalded cat up to Nell, and she never darkened our door after that except to look in the day she was going back to America.

—— ... Me life on ye, Hitler. That's the boy for them ....

—— If England's beaten the country will be ruined. We've lost the market already ....

—— ... Breed of the One-Eared Tailor, it's you that put me here fifty years before my time. The treacherous drop was ever in the One-Eared breed. Knives, stones, bottles. You couldn't fight like a man, you had to knife me ....

—— ... Let me speak. Let me ....

—— The cross of Christ be about us! — is it alive or dead I am? Is it alive or dead these others are? They're all giving off as much as they were up above! I thought when I was in my grave with no more slaving or working or household worries, and no need to fear wind or weather or anything else, that I would get a little peace ... but what's the meaning of all this squabbling in the graveyard ground.

9. A common term of abuse.
10. A common term of abuse: a meddlesome, worthless person.
11. Bad luck.
12. i.e. that would not take her advice.

SEÁN MAC MATHÚNA

(1936-)

from:
THE BRIDGE/
AN DROICHEAD (1987)

[This story was first published in the Fall 1987 issue of the Irish-American journal, with the author's own translation.]

GADAITHE

'Éirigh, a thaisce mo chroí, is dtín t-úllord siar cuir díot, mar a bhfuil an ghrian ag díbirt an earraigh de thorthaí, is Maimeo ina suí faoi leithead an lae. Is más oscailte dá radharc ar ghealas an tsaoil, abairse léi 'anocht sa spéir beidh bearna mar a mbíodh an réalt úd ar sceanadh tráth'. Ach más trom a hanáil i dtaibhreamh a seanógh, fan leat go bhfille sí ar an úlldomhan.'

Don úllord ghabhas, is d'éist le taibhreamh spéirghealaí Mhaimeo, is leis na feithidí ag tochras na gclog sa bhféar tur. Seanasal as faoin *lilac* d'fhair sinn, is b'ionadh liom daonscing a shúl, is a eireaball ag clipeadh na scáth de ghéagaibh. Gach snapadh ag gadhar ar bheacha curtha dá dtreoir ag ilmhilseacht úllord. Gríos-silíní d'itheas, pluma is dhá shú craobh, is as barr an chrainn scaoil an chéirseach a rann:

> A ghrís gach úill is a úill gach grís,
> scaipeas bhur mos ar aer,
> Ar an domhan mall cruinn 'sea lingfidh
> sibh, mar den domhan mall cruinn gach caor,
> Díreach, cam is cruinn anuas, úll is crann
> is duine,
> Mar a gcomórfaid bás i bhfuath-anás siar go
> go heirbeall linne.

D'éalaigh scáth na ngéag gur thit ar aghaidh Mhaimeo, gur dhúisigh sí is gur chuala sí go raibh réalt i ndiaidh titim. 'Barra réalt chonac á dtreascairt, is a dtitim ag bochtú na spéire. Cá miste dhom ceann breise?' ar sise á díriú féin. 'Seo, fágaimis goimh na gréine ag na torthaí atá ina gá, is bainimis amach fionnuaire an dóláis.'

Rug sí ar lámh orm is sheol go doras an tí mé mar ar uraigh a scáth an chistin. Bhuail sí isteach. D'éirigh a raibh istigh, is tháinig m'athair chuici is chuir caint uirthi, 'An gleann tréigthe ag croí eile, a mháithrín ó.'

Labhair Donncha Breac Mac Gearailt, gaol gairid, léi. 'A Mháire Mhuiris Thaidhg, d'fhuil uasal na gCarrthach Samhna, gura fada buan don gcroí úd ag bualadh ina dhruma laistiar den ré.'

D'fhreagair Maimeo. 'Níl poll ann, dá mhéid, do chroí dá leithéid, ach bánta allta na síoraíochta. Féach an tréan ar lár! Mar sin atá sé scríofa. Croí eile ar lár, beirimis urraim do na mairbh.' D'éist a raibh sa teach, is roinn gach tic ón gclog an tost — scair ghlan an duine againn. Ghluais sí trasna an urláir, gur sháigh sí méar cham trí laitís an chloig, gur cheap sí an tormán práis i lár toca. De phreib bhí an tost teite, agus b'í fuaim a chualathas ná fuaim tuirnín ina stailc. Ansin síos léi chun an tseomra. Níor labhair éinne mar sa ghleann seo 'gainne is lenár gciúnas a ghéilltear urraim do bhéal ina bhuanstailc. D'fhill sí is chuir caint ar lucht na cistine. 'Nach feasach daoibh conas ómós a thabhairt do na mairbh? Nach feasach daoibh go bhfuil a shúile gan iamh ar náire an tsaoil seo? Iatar anuas go brách na mogaill ar a dhomhan rosc-dhéanta. Tugtar boinn dom atá trom; beirtear onóir dá shúile le seanairgead.'

Chuathas ina nduine is ina nduine de réir gaoil chun slán a fhágáil ag Daideo: a mhuintir féin, muintir mo mháthar, comharsana, cairde. Agus ansin na rudaí beaga. 'Téirse go dtí do Dhaideo,' arsa Maimeo, 'is póg an cloigeann a thug gean duit thar chách. Mar istoíche chaintíodh sibh an teas as an tine, is do líon sé do mheabhair le heolas chomh sean leis na goirt.'

Ba gheal liom a dtost in onóir dom is mé ag dul faoi dhéin an tseomra. Faoi chuilt phaistí a bhí sé. Bhí eolas pearsanta agam ar chuid mhaith de na paistí céanna ina mbeatha dóibh: corda an rí liath-dhonn óm sheanchasóg, muislín dearg ó bhlús, ceaileacó uaine ó chuirtín, poiplín gorm ó léine, bréidin liath ó veist, síoda bándearg ó chóta-leath-istigh, línéadach odhar ó éadach boird, sról bán ó ghúna pósta, veilbhit oráiste ó adhairtín, olann donn ó scairf, carbhat órga breac, faoina dhá dhorn. Marmar fuar ón teampall a aghaidh, gruaig is féasóg in aimhréidh liath. Agus mar a raibh a dhá shúil, dhá bhonn d'airgead geal, ceann acu agus stail air agus na focail 'leathchoróin'; 'Éire, 1947' ar an gceann eile. Solas na fuinneoige ag fústráil timpeall a chloiginn.

Go tobann sciorr an stail a leiceann anuas, is léim de ghliogar trasna an urláir; ghreamaigh an ghrian de shúil dhonn a chuir béimghríos siar go cúl mo chinn. Fuar-rosc ón alltar ba ea é. Screadas is rásaíos suas chun an tinteáin. D'fhógraíos nárbh é Daideo a bhí ann ach duine eile. Cá raibh Daideo? Leanas den mbéiceach gur fháisc mo mháthair lena croí mé. 'Éist!' ar sise, 'níor imigh seoid de bharr ort, agus féach gur Daideo atá ann mar tá sé marbh.' Ansin a thuigeas. D'fhéachas im thimpeall agus scard orm. 'Sea, ní bheadh sé romham cois tine anocht. Nó aon oíche eile. D'fhás an eagla ionam, agus d'fhaireas na haghaidheanna im thimpeall sa chistin. Ní raibh féachaint Daideo ar éinne acu. Cé a dhéanfadh mé a chosaint anois? Ghabh freang tríom.

Seo ar ais Maimeo agus í an-ghearánach orainn. 'Nach feasach daoibh gur mór an náire gan mogaill na marbh a iamh anuas! Chonac náire tráth i dteach tórraimh mar a raibh fear ar thug tarbh adharc dó agus é tar éis dhá uair an chloig a thabhairt ag stánadh ar splinc na spéire sara bhfuair siad é. Thug sé oíche an tórraimh ag caitheamh pinginí san aer. Mór an náire, mór an náire! Nach feasach daoibh gurb iad mogaill na súl tearmann deiridh an anama ghlic agus gur le miotal fuar amháin a bhogtar chun siúil é.'

D'imigh na fir ag ól sa déirí. M'athair go dtí na ba. Ní raibh fágtha ach mná. Sciurd siad de thapaigean chun gnótha mar a dhéanfadh mná. Tógadh amach scuaibeanna, mapanna, sciomarthóirí, ceirteacha, buicéid uisce, gallúnach charbólach. Crochadh cuirtíní ar an bhfuinneog. Caitheadh cuiginn, buicéad sciodair, málaí mine agus madraí amach an doras iata. Isteach doras a' tí tháinig na comharsana agus iasachtaí árais tí acu dúinn. Hainí na hEisce Ní Shé agus mias *willow* mhór gheal aici. Cuireadh ar a faobhar ar an driosúr é. 'Beannacht leis an té a cheannaigh é is leis an mbean a thug léi é,' arsa mo mháthair. Spúnóga d'airgead geal ó Neil N'fheadar Ní Laoire. Síle na Duimhche Ní Shúilleabháin agus línéadach bán don mbord aici; Nóiní Brothall Ní Mhurchú le mias d'airgead geal ar a raibh cloigeann Uachtarán éigin Mheiriceá; cuireadh le mórtas i lár an bhoird í. Trí phunt tae, coinnleoir práis agus trí smuta dearg den Nollaig fós iontu ó Ghobnait an Choinicéir Ní Fhoghlú; ach nuair a tháinig Eibhlín Genitive Case Ní Mhuineacháin (clann an mháistir) leis na gloiní póirt scoir gach éinne dá ghnó chun féachaint orthu. Ba de chriostal iad agus glioscarnach ghloine bhriste á cur uathu. Coinneal reo fhada chaol gach cos. D'fhéach mo mháthair chomh tnúthánach sin orthu gur thuigeas go malartódh sí mé ar dhosaen acu. 'Nach triopallach atáid!' arsa bean díobh, 'ach an seasóidh siad an deoch?'

Ghabh trucail isteach san iothlann agus arán, subh, soithigh phórtair, uisce beatha, tobac, agus pórt do na mná is na páistí ar bord ann. Leath Seáiní na gCreach Ó Ceallaigh urlár coille de raithneach ar fud na gcarn aoiligh, gur dhein farraige chumhra ghlas díobh.

Bhíogas de phreib. An Gadaí Rua! Bhí Daideo, seanchaí, tar éis é a fhágáil i mbarr crainn aréir sarar thit a chodladh air cois tine. Bhí cait mhóra ag bun an chrainn. Bhíodar fíochmhar. 'Cad a tharla don nGadaí Rua?' arsa mise. Toradh ní bhfuaireas. Ní mór béic a ligint ar mhná is iad i mbun gnótha, thógfadh fear a cheann ar an gcéad shiolla. 'Cad a tharla don nGadaí Rua?' arsa mise de bhéic.

D'inis mé dóibh. 'Níl ann ach scéal,' arsa mo mháthair, is ghéaraigh sí ar an sciomradh. D'impíos orthu é a insint dom, mar gadaí maith ba ea é a dhein mé a mhealladh lena chuid gaisce is draíochta oíche as a chéile. Ach thug Maimeo aghaidh orm. 'Níl ach gadaí amháin sa teach seo anocht is tiocfaidh sé orainn amach anseo is ardóidh sé leis an snas as aŕ súil, duine ar dhuine.'

I gceann tamaill d'fhiafraíos díobh an mbéarfadh na cait mhóra air. I ngéire a chuaigh an sciomradh, deora allais óm mháthair ar an urlár anuas. Ansin stad sí is labhair sí leis na mná. 'A mhná uaisle, ní hé seo an t-ionú chuige agus Daideo ag dul i bhfad is i bhfuaire uainn, ach is amhlaidh a líon sé meabhair an gharsúin sin le seafóid is scéalta ón seanshaol. É ar fad sa Ghaeilge. Níl focal Béarla ina phluic aige. Cad a dhéanfaimid leis in aon chor agus teanga an Bhéarla ag gabháil stealladh ar an ngleann, is gach cnag aige ar an doras mar a bheadh seirbheálaí barántais. Cheana féin tá Súilleabhánaigh Crón na Scríne tite leis. Is níl le clos anois le hais a dtinteáin ach an teanga ghallda. An bhfuilimidne Carrthaigh le bheith in eireaball an fhaisin? Is bocht is is crua an scéal é ach sin mar atá.'

D'fhreagair Cáit Casúr Ní Chinnéide. 'Sea, chomh siúráilte is a ghluaiseann ceo de dhroim an tsléibhe anuas, seo aníos chugainn níos ciúine fós an Béarla. I gcuntas Dé na Glóire ach is glórai solas na gealaí is a scáth ná an Béarla ag svíomhsnámh, de shíor mar uibheacha i sciléad.' Lean mo mháthair den sciomradh is den ngearán, 'agus scéalta agus seanráite agus rannta na seanlaoch, iad ar fad sa

Ghaeilge!' Bhain sí na timpill as an scuaibín sciomartha agus b'é an snas a bhris tríd an urlár sa deireadh ná snas an Bhéarla.

Chuas go dtí na fir sa déirí, d'inseodh siadsan dom é, fearaibh iad na fearaibh. Bhíodar suite ar árais tí bainne i bhfáinne, ga gréine ag tuirlingt orthu, deatach snadhmach ag corraí tríd. I measc na soithí scimeála ar an mbord bhí buidéil uisce beatha. Chaith gach fear a eagna ar an mbord chun eagna a chomórtais nó a sháraithe a fháil, agus ba ghnách go leanfadh eagna an buidéal.

'Cad a tharla don Ghadaí Rua?' Bhí a súile ar aon drithle le rince ómra a ngloiní. 'Mhuise, cé hé an Gadaí Rua?' D'inis mé dóibh. 'Á, is tú mac Sheáin Mhuiris Thaidhg, gan aon agó, is do mheabhair líonta le hiontaisí na Gaeilge.'

'Sea, go díreach, chreach sé taisce an tseanduine agus mise á rá leat nach mór a d'fhág sé do na muca.'

Labhair Muirisín Sioc Ó Cróinín agus faobhar ar a ghuth. 'Do thréigh na tréin sinn is d'fhágadar fann ár ngleann-na, agus gliúcann an Béarla thar an leathdhoras isteach orainn mar mhadra bradach; ach is treise draíocht an tseanchaí ná méar-imsparán an Bhéarla. Scaoil amach bua gach amhráin is scéil is suíodh a dhíoltas féin ar ghualainn gach éinne!'

'Ólaimis sláinte na nGael,' arsa Muirisín, 'seasaimis i mbéal a' ghleanna, is abraimis le béarlagar seo na nGíománach orlach amháin eile is sín anam!'

'Moladh go deo leat is nár laga Dia do ghlór!' arsa siad d'aon ghuth le mórtas a seanaigne, is cuireadh an buidéal sa timpeall. Ach bhuail Séamas na hInse Ó Raghallaigh a cheann faoi is dúirt, 'A bhfuil ann d'iontaisí na nGael, dá laochra is dá scéalta, is thíos ar thaobh an teampaill atáid sínte; is ní ruaigfeadh a bhfuil de neart acu an scáth de chros a n-uaigheanna. Seasaigí i mbéal an ghleanna is bígí ag spóladh an aeir. Is cuma nó Dall na Scéal sinn a thug slán faoin ngaoth le claíomh ar an gcnoc sin thall. An Béarla a throid, muis! Tá chomh maith againn Dé Máirt a throid. Is mairg don nGael bocht nach bhfuair de dhuais as an saol seo ach briseadh gach catha air; is dá raghadh an bua féin trasna na sráide chuige ag croitheadh láimh' leis ní aithneodh sé é.'

Cúngaíodh an seomra, fairsingíodh ball iasachta den domhan. Bhí an buidéal dulta i ndísc.

'Cad a tharla don Ghadaí Rua?'

'D'itheadar é,' arsa duine acu.

'Stracadar na súile as,' arsa duine eile.

'Ach gadaí maith ab ea é,' arsa mise.

'Gach gadaí níos measa ná a chéile. Croch a bhfuil ann acu ar gach géag idir seo agus Leaba na Bó.'

'Ach dúirt Daideo—'

'Tá Seán Mhuiris Thaidhg i measc na bhfear. Thug sé leis do ghadaíse. Fág na mairbh ina suan. Seo leat, a theallaire, bí ag súgradh led choileán, is fág againn ár rámhaille.'

'Abair é,' ar siad.

Rug Diarmaid, deartháir m'athar, ar lámh orm is sheol siar go dtí an scioból mé mar ar ghearr sé féar den bhinse le scian. Ba dheas an fhuaim é spóladh tur na milliún sop féir. Sheas sé is ghlan sé an t-allas dá éadan. 'Tuairisc ar do ghadaí níl agam. Chuiris uaisleacht na bhfear as a riocht, is chuiris mairg orthu. Tá réiteach do cheiste thíos cois an teampaill sínte agus is ann a bheidh sé go séide Gabriel, aingeal, a thrumpa is go séidfear na scéalta ina mbeatha agus beidh do Ghadaí Rua ina phrionsa ar ár nósna go léir.'

'Do Lá Philib a' Chleite a thagrann tú,' arsa mise.

'Sea, go díreach, is ní miste dúinn a thúisce. Tagadh sé ar maidin is stopadh sé síol sin an oilc i mbun bradaíochta. Creachann cách sinn. Ní beag sin a deirim. Seo leat, a Ghabriel, séid leat do thrumpa anois nó fill chugat go deo é.'

'Tá beatha uaim,' arsa mise.

'É sin is eagal liom. Cad chuige? Chun dul, freisin, go dtí an teampall? In áit éigin anois ar an sliabh úd thall tá cloch agus ár sloinnte greanta air. 'Dé chúis fuireach?'

Bhí m'athair ag tabhairt féir do na ba. Sheas sé taobh le riabhach mhaol darbh ainmn Bainbhín, á slíocadh. Ansin d'fhéach sé orm, 'trí ní nach mór a fhaire, "crúb capaill, adharc bó, gáire an tSasanaigh".'

Seo isteach i gcró na mbó mo mháthair agus coinnleoir tórraimh á shnasadh aici. 'Tá an saol athraithe ó anocht. Amárach caithfidh an garsún seo an Béarla a labhairt.' Thug m'athair a dhrom léi. 'Níl puinn den teanga sin againn,' ar seisean. Thóg mo mháthair coiscéim níos goire. 'Tá an t-aer ramhar le focail Bhéarla. Dein iad a bhaint mar a bhainfí soip as an ngaoth.'

Ghlan m'athair síolta féir de mhuin an tairbh. 'An airíonn sibh mé?' ar sise, nuair a bhraith sí ár neamhshuim.

'Iad a bhaint!' arsa m'athair, 'mar a chéile focail Bhéarla a bhaint is sméara dubha a bhaint. Silfear fuil is is bocht do bhuíochas.'

Níor thug sí aon toradh air ach labhair sí liomsa. 'A thaisce gheal mo chroí, seo mo chéad fholáireamh duit sa teanga ghallda: *from on the morning out d'Inglis tongue only vill you spik — spik alvays d'Inglis*. Ar airís m'fholáireamh?'

Chroitheas mo cheann uirthi. Níor thuigeas cad dúirt sí ach bhraitheas gurbh é an teanga a sciomair sí den urlár é. 'Tá's agam nach bhfuil sé curtha rómhaith agam mar tá mo chuid focal gallda chomh gann le silíní Nollag,' ar sise. D'fhéach sí orm ag iarraidh mé a léamh. 'Is bocht an scéal é, a lao, ach cad is féidir a dhéanamh?' Rith na deora léi, is dheineas miongháire is chroitheas mo cheann uirthi. D'fhéach sí ar an bhfear le hais an tairbh, 'ar airís cad dúirt mé, a Dhaid?'

Chuir sé gigleas faoi chluasa an tairbh, is labhair leis an bhfalla. 'Tráth dá raibh bhí muintir sa ghleann seo is thriomódh a gcuid gáire éadaí duit.'

'Ní beag sin de thráth dá raibh, tá aghaidh an gharsúin seo ar fharraige mhór an Bhéarla — an ligfeá amach é i mbáidín briste?'

'Seanríthe sinn thuilleas fuath as ár seanfhocail.' B'in a dúirt sé.

'Ní beag sin de ríthe! Táimid bocht is níl againn ach féar sé bó. Saol na ngailseach faoi chlocha againn.'

Shlíoc m'athair muin an tairbh. Bhí maidhm an chochaill á thachtadh ach ní leomhfadh sé aghaidh bhéil a thabhairt ar Mham im fhianaise. Shníomh sé a chuid focal, 'Mustar na gCaisleán orainn tráth do bhí, ach dhein gráinní gainimh gan chomhaireamh de; is cá ngabhfaidh ár dteanga? Gabhfaidh sé san áit go ngabhann ceol, go gairdín geanmnaí na spéire, is ina huaigneas di ansin éileamh ní bheidh uirthi. Ach is ann a scríobhfar a draíocht in ogham gintlí na réalt go docht i ngreim ré-eolais na síoraíochta.'

Chaolaigh ar ghuth mo mháthar, 'nimheoidh do bhaothchaint a mheabhair orainn is a shlánú i mbéal na maidine roimis amach. Ní beag sin de shean-seo is sean-siúd, seanaiteann, seanríthe, seanrannta. Táim torrach de sheandacht is de laochra. Is deise liom unsa den lá inniu ná tonna den mbliain seo caite.' Dhruid sí im leith is rug ar lámh orm. 'Tógfaidh mo mhacsa a cheann chomh hard le duine fós.'

D'iompaigh sé uirthi don chéad uair, ní lena ghuth ach lena shúile. 'Is rí mo mhacsa is is airde a cheann ná các, airde na gCarrthach Samhna de mhóráil air.'

'Chomh hard sin? Is sna scamaill a bheidh a cheann agat mar sin. Faireadh sé na beanna fuara, más ea!' agus d'oscail sí doras cró na mbó. D'fhan sí nóiméad gan corraí, an coinnleoir airgid ina lámh go bagrach. 'Ón gcéad amhscarthanach de sholas maidin an lae amárach an teanga ghallda amháin. Siolla amháin as reilig na nGael agus beidh sé ina chogadh mórthimpeall oraibh. Is buafaidh mise. Mar tá sé scríofa gurb í an lámh a dhéanann an choigilt a chuirfidh údarás ar an teaghlach.' Shiúil sí amach ach chas ar ais láithreach. 'Ar inis tú dod mhac canathaobh gur tugadh Carrthaigh Samhna oraibh?' Thug sí agahaid orm is labhair go fuar, 'briseadh orthu Samhain 1599 ag na Niallaigh.'

Sháraigh an brú ar an bhfoighne m'athair is seo chuici de sheáp é. Ach faiteadh súile níor ghéill sí dhó. D'fhéach sé orm chun nach dtachtfadh sé í. 'Sea,' ar seisean, 'ár gcaisleáin leagtha is iad trí thine ach níor briseadh orainn. Féach isteach im shúile, a thaisce dhílis, an bhfeiceann tú ann an briseadh?' D'fhéachas ar an bhfear seo a bhí dhá scór d'aois, ar an gcabhail a bhí rómhór dá éadaí, ar an éadach a bhí róbheag do na paistí. Ar na súile. Is ní fhaca aon bhriseadh, ach tairne i mbeo a sheanmhórála.

'Huth!' arsa Mam, 'caisleáin na gCarrthach ag titim, cairn aoiligh na gCarrthach ag éirí.'

D'fhéach sé ar feadh tamaill ar an talamh, ansin dhírigh sé é féin, is dúirt, 'dá mb'fhear thú mharófaí ar an tuí thú as ár bhfuil a mhaslú. Bíonn mórtas ar an gCarrthach pé acu ar aoileach nó ar chaisleán a bhíonn sé. Thugas i leith anseo thú ó Fhearann Giolcach Thoir, áit ná fásann crann ann. Is mairg an talamh ná fásfaidh crann mar ná géillfidh sé suas an uaisleacht ach chomh beag,' agus ghlan sé leis amach ar an tsráid. Dhruid mo mháthair liom is rug barróg orm, is dúirt, 'chuas thar fóir, cad is féidir liom a dhéanamh. Is geal leosan tú ach is mise a chaithfidh féachaint id dhiaidh. Tá an saol ar tuathal,' is d'fháisc sí léi mé níos mó; agus mheasas nach mise a bhí á fháscadh aici ach rud a taibhríodh di, nó eachtra, malairt bheatha, b'fhéidir, nach bhfáiscfeadh sí léi go deo sa saol seo. D'éalaigh sí léi is d'iaigh an doras go bog ina diaidh.

D'fhill m'athair, gur sheas i measc na mbó. Bhí impí sa bhféachaint a thug sé orm. Chas sé uaim is d'fhéach ina thimpeall. Nuair a labhair sé bhearr a smacht colg na bhfocal. Thit siad ar an talamh. 'Tóg uaim mo chuid focal is cuirfidh mé mallacht ar mhuintir an domhain. Bundún teanga ó Dhia go raibh orthu go léir amárach agus caithfidh mé an tsíoraíocht go buíoch i dtinte ifrinn.' Suas is anuas an cró leis. 'An mhuintir thar béal an ghleanna seo amach a thug a ndrom lena bhfuil féin, chomh fada thuaidh le Droichidín an Fhústair is as san soir go Magh Ealla, níl iontu ach priompalláin. Ar airís riamh teacht thar an tseanrá 'dá airde a éiríonn an priompallán sa chac a thiteann sé.' Lig sé osna. 'Is mairg don bheagán cloigeann a iompraíonn ríocht na nGael leo mar sna laethanta gránna seo is ar éigean is fiú cloch coirce cloigeann.'

Chuir a ndúirt sé buairt orm agus dheineas tathant air bheith sámh. 'Lig dom gríos-silíní a thabhairt chugat ón úllord.'

Dhein sé machnamh air seo go ceann tamaill, ansin d'athraigh sé ar fad is theann sé liom isteach, 'a smóilín gheal mo chroí, fáinne óir ort go deo, mar is mar a chéile sinn go léir ag ithe silíní. Déithe, ríthe, amadáin, iad go léir ar aon chéim ag blas silíní úra.' Shuigh sé ar stóilín is chuir sé mé ar a ghlúin. 'An bhfuil fhios agat gur ós na nithe beaga cruinne mar silíní a thagann iontaisí an tsaoil seo. Ar inis mé riamh duit Cúig Iontas Cruinn na gCúig Céadfaí Cruinn?' Dhein sé iad a ríomhadh le flosc, 'boladh na n-úll, blas póige, teas scillinge id dhorn, cara a fheiscint ar bharr cnoic, súgradh na gcoileán a chlos.'

Thit tost ar an gcró. Bainne mífhoighneach ag sileadh de na húthanna ar an tuí. Búirtheach toll ón tarbh a chuir an doras ag canrán. In áit éigin bhí an ghrian ag dul faoi agus na simnéithe ag sá a scáth-anna trí raithneach na gcarn aoiligh. Shiúlas chomh fada leis an tarbh is chuireas mo cheist. Dhein sé a cheann a thochas agus dúirt nár chuala sé faoin a leithéid riamh. 'Nach ait an péire sinn, duine ag déanamh cumha an Ghadaí Rua is duine an Ghadaí Dhuibh.'

'Cé hé an Gadaí Dubh?' arsa mise. D'éirigh sé is d'imigh sé go béal an dorais is chuir a ghuala le hursain.

'Nach bhfuil fhios agat gurb é an seanchaí an Gadaí Dubh? Mar tagann sé i measc na ndaoine i rith dúluachair na bliana is goideann sé uathu duibhe a gcroí le draíocht a chuid scéalta. Ar ball brostófar an Gadaí Dubh deiridh ar chosa laga an portach trasna go dtí an teampall dorcha. Agus anois tuirlingíonn an oíche fhada ar an nGaeltacht, is go deo deo arís ní fhillfidh an Gadaí Dubh chun í a ardú leis. Ní ghealfaidh lá.' Chas sé uaim is ghluais sé síos tríd an iothlann, trí bhéal an gheata amach, suas ar an móinteán, ball fiáin go leor d'anam ar bith.

Chuas go dtí an t-úllord. Grian eile ag dul faoi laistiar de Shliabh Cam — anois ba lú a bheadh ann den tsíoraíocht. Sheasas faoin gcrann silíní agus d'fhéachas suas ar na géaga ab airde. D'fhógraíos don Ghadaí Rua fuireach a dhéanamh i mbarr a chrainn go deo in onóir do scéalta maithe nárbh ann dóibh a thuilleadh. Agus d'fhéachas timpeall ar chros-chrochadh na dtorthaí is an duilliúir, is labhair mé, 'a Ghadaí Dubh, go dtéir slán is pé áit ina gcasfaidh do chinniúint tú go leana an ceol tú. Póg duitse, a Ghadaí Dubh!' Agus bhaineas silín den chrann agus phógas é agus raideas uaim suas san aer é thar an *lilac* amach agus lean mo shúil é agus é ag casadh is ag imchasadh go gríosúil ar an domhan mall cruinn gur thuirling in áit ná feadar.

THIEVES

'Son, treasure house of my heart, go you unto the orchard where the sun spoils the Spring off the fruit and where Grandmother sits in the width of the day. And if her gaze is open to the light of the world say to her "tonight a gap in the sky will be where once a star shone forth". But if her breath is heavy with grey maiden dreams await her return to the apple world.'

I went to the orchard and listened to Grand-mother dream nightfalls of old stars. I heard the insects wind their dry watches in the grass; an old donkey from beneath the lilac tree gazed at us and I marvelled at the human mildness of his eyes, while his tail flicked shadows off the branches. A sheep-dog snapped at bees maddened by the scent-mis-cellany of an orchard. Flushed cherries I ate, two plums, one raspberry, while a thrush upon a tree sang this song to me:

Apples, apples, that redly peer, that redly
    peer at me,
To the slow round earth must each one fall,
    for of slow round earth are ye,
Crooked round and straight will fall, apple,
    man, and tree,
Where ye shall toast death's
    withering ghost in eternal savagery.

The shadows of the bough crept, and fell on Grandmother's face, she awoke and heard that a star had fallen.

'Crops of stars have I seen reaped, impoverishing the sky with their fall. What to me is one more?' she said arising, 'come, let us leave the wickedness of the sun to the fruit that has need of it and seek out the coolness of grief.'

She took my hand and brought us to the door of the house where her shadow darkened the kitchen. She entered. All stood. My father came forward and addressed Grandmother.

'A heart has left the valley, little mother, oh.'

Donncha of the Speckled Fitzgeralds, a close relative, also addressed her. 'Mary, daughter of Morris, son of Tadhg, proud blood of the November McCarthys, may the heart beat out forever like a drum behind the moon.'

Grandmother spoke. 'There is no hole big enough for such a heart only the wide fields of eternity. How are the mighty fallen! So it is written. A heart is laid low, let us honour the dead.' All were silent in the house and only the tick of the clock sliced the hush into equal shares for all. She moved across the floor and poked a twisted finger through the lattice of the clock and checked the brass pendulum half way through a tock. Suddenly the silence had gone and the sound that was heard was the sound of a spinning wheel that had stopped. Then she went to the room. Nobody spoke, for in our valley silence is our way of honouring a voice that had struck for ever. She came back and addressed the kitchen.

'Know ye not how to honour the dead? Know ye not that his eyes are open to the shame of this world? Let his lids be rolled down for ever on this eye-shaped earth. Let me have coins that are heavy: with old silver let his eyes be honoured.'

One by one each went in the order of blood preccedence to say farewell to Grandfather: his family, mother's family, friends, neighbours. And then the young. 'Go you to your Grandfather,' she said to me, 'and kiss the head that loved you more than any of us. For at night ye talked the heat out of the fire, and he filled your head with knowledge as old as the fields.'

I went in with great joy to the room, honoured by their silence. The patchwork quilt covered him. Most of the patches I had personally known in their former life, fawn corduroy from my old coat, red muslin blouse, green calico curtain, navy poplin shirt, grey tweed waistcoat, pink silk slip, cream linen tablecloth, white satin wedding-dress, orange velvet cushion, brown woollen scarf, gold polka-dot cravat at his joined fingers. Cold marble from a church his face, beard and hair grizzled and dishevelled. And where his eyes were two silver orbs, one with a stallion and beneath it the word *'leath-choróin'* (half-crown) the other a harp saying *'Éire, 1947.'* Light from the window framed his head on the pillow.

Suddenly the stallion slipped down his cheek and rolled across the floor and the evening sun bounced off a brown eye that peered into the back of my head. It was an eye from another world. I screamed and ran to the fire. I shouted that it wasn't Grandfather, that it was someone else. Where was Grandfather? I sobbed until my mother clutched at me and said, 'hush, it is but a little thing, and that is Grandfather for he is dead.' Then I knew. I looked about me in fear. Then he would not be joining me at the fire that night. Nor any other night. I grew frightened, and I looked about me in the kitchen — at their faces. None had the eyes of Grandfather. Who would protect me now? I shivered.

Grandmother came back and scolded us all. 'Don't ye know that it is a shameful thing not to weigh down the lids of the dead. I have witnessed the shame of a wakehouse once where a man gored by a bull gazed at the sky for two hours before they found him. All night those lids tossed pennies in the air. Great the shame, great the shame. Don't you know the eyelids are the last refuge of the reluctant soul and only cold metal will send it on its way.'

The men went to drink in the dairy, father to the cows. Only the women were left. Suddenly without a word they moved like women who decided to move. Brushes, mops, brooms, scrubbers, rags, buckets of water, carbolic soap, were pulled from places; curtains appeared on the window; three times I was thrown out of my chair; churns, buckets of sour milk, bags of meal, dogs, were thrown out of the back door; in the front door came neighbours bearing loans of goods; Hannah of the Swamp O'Sheas brought a large shining willow dish. It was placed standing on the dresser. 'Blessed is the man that bought it and the woman that brought it,' said my mother. Silver spoons from Nell of the Don't Know O'Learys. Julia of the Sand Hill O'Sullivans brought a white linen tablecloth, Nonie Hot Weather Murphy a silver dish with the head of some American President on it; it was placed proudly in the centre of the table. Gobnait of the Rabbit Warren Foleys three pounds of tea, a brass candlestick with three red stubs of Christmas candles; but when Ellen Genitive Case Moynihan (schoolmaster's family) brought the port glasses, everybody dropped whatever they were doing to look at them. They were crystal and had the lustre of broken glass. Tall slender icicles the stems. My mother beheld them so covetously that I knew she would have sold me for a dozen of them. 'They are delicate,' said someone, 'but will they withstand the weight of drink?'

A cart wheeled into the yard bearing bread, jam, barrels of porter, whiskey, tobacco and port for the women and children. John of the Southern Plunder O'Kellys spread a forest floor of ferns on all the dunghills, turning them into a sea of fragrant green.

Suddenly I started. The Red Thief! Grandfather, storyteller, had left him on a treetop last night before he fell asleep by the fire. There were big cats at the bottom of the tree. 'What happened The Red Thief?' I asked. Nobody listened. One has to shout at women at work, a man will raise his head gladly at the first syllable. 'What happened The Red Thief?' I roared.

'What ails the child?' someone asked.

I told them. ''Tis but a story,' said Mother, and she scrubbed the floor all the more furiously. I begged them to tell me. He had been a good thief who entranced me night after night with his daring and magic. But Grandmother scolded me.

'There is but one thief in this house tonight, and in time he will come for us all one by one to steal the shine out of our eye.'

After a while I asked would the big cats get him. My mother worked harder, sweat dripping on the floor. Then she stopped and addressed the room. 'Gentle ladies, this is not the time to say it while Grandfather grows colder and farther from us, but he did stuff that boy's head with stories and nonsense from the past. All in the Irish. The child has not a tittle of English in his head. What shall we do with him when the English tongue invades our valley, and raps on every door like a summons server. Already the Swarthy O'Sullivans of the Shrine have fallen, and now only the foreign tongue is heard by their fireside. Are we, the McCarthys, to be in the tail of fashion? It is sad, it is hard, but it is thus.'

Kate of the Sledgehammer Kennedys said 'Yes, as sure as the fog sweeps down our mountain, English sweeps up more quietly. Great Heavenly God, but moonlight and its shadow would make more noise than English creeping, always creeping, across our lands. Soon we shall be surrounded like eggs in a skillet pot.' My mother continued to scrub. 'And tales and proverbs and poems and dead heroes, all in the Irish Tongue!' Round and round went her scrubbing brush and the shine that broke through the floor was the shine of English.

I went to the men in the dairy, they would tell me, men were men. They sat on milk churns in a circle, a little sunbeam poking through their group through which tobacco smoke tumbled. On the table some bottles of whiskey amid pewter skimming pans. Each man tossed his wisdom on the table to be matched or trumped, and wisdom usually followed the bottle.

'What happened The Red Thief?' Their eyes outglistened the dancing amber in their glasses. 'Who is The Red Thief?' they asked. I told them.

'You are the son of John Morris Tadhg, indeed and your head full of all the wonders of Irish.'

'Yes, he plundered the treasurehouse of the old man, and I warrant 'twas little enough he left for the pigs.'

Then Little Morris of the Frost Cronins spoke up with fire on his breath. 'This Glen is weak, the strong have deserted us, English peers over our halfdoors like a thieving dog; but the triumph of the storyteller is louder than the pickpocket rustle of English. Let out the might of song and story and let each man's vengeance sit on his own shoulder!'

'Hear! Hear!' said all together.

'Let us drink the health of the Gael,' said Morris, 'let us stand in the mouth of the glen and say to that Yeoman's prattle "one more inch and yield up thy ghost!"'

'Praise be to God on high to you and may your voice never strike!' said they all in ancient jubilation, and the bottle was sent upon its round. But James of the Waterlogged Callows O'Reilly hung his head and said 'All the wonders of the Gael, all their heroes and their stories sleep in the Churchyard dark; and all their collected power wouldn't hunt the shadows off their tombstones. Stand in the mouth of the Glen and fight the air? We are like Blind, the Great one, who challenged the wind on yonder hill with his sword. Fight English? Ye might as well fight Tuesday! Woe to the Gael who never got as share from this life but the breaking of every battle on him, and were victory itself to cross the street to him and shake his hand, he would know it not.'

The room got smaller, an alien part of the world got bigger. The bottle had run dry.

'What happened The Red Thief?'

'They ate him,' spat one.

'They tore his eyes out,' said another.

But I cried out that he was a good thief. 'No thief is good. Hang them on every tree from here to Bed of the Cow.'

'But Grandfather said. . . .'

'Old John is no more. He has taken your thief with him. Let the dead sleep in peace. Young fellow go play with a pup and leave us to our dreams.'

'Aye!' said they.

Diarmuid, Father's brother, took my hand and led me to the hayshed where he cut hay off the bench with the hayknife. It was a pleasing sound, the dry slicing of millions of hay stems. He stood and wiped the sweat from off his brow. 'I have no tidings of your thief. You have troubled the men and set their grandeur astray. The answer you seek is stretched in the graveyard and there it will remain till Gabriel, Angel, blows his trumpet, and all the stories will burst to life and The Red Thief will be a prince like us all.'

'You speak of Judgement Day,' I said.

'Aye! Sweet Christ, send it in the morning and halt that robbers' seed in their wild rapine. All plunder us. I say enough! Come Gabriel, blow your trumpet now or still for ever your bugling.'

'Life I seek,' said I.

'So I fear. For what? To go, also, to the churchyard? Somewhere now on the mountains yonder is a stone with our names upon it. For what do we wait?'

Father was feeding the cows. He stood beside a small polly Kerry, called Little Bonham, and patted her. Then he looked at me, 'three things must you avoid, the horn of a cow, the hoof of a horse, the laugh of an Englishman.'

My mother came into the cowhouse polishing a mortuary candlestick. 'The world has changed tonight. Tomorrow this boy must speak the English tongue.' Father turned his back to her. 'We have none of that tongue,' he said. Mother took a step closer. 'The air is strewn with English words, pick them like straws from the wind.'

'Pick!' said Father, 'picking English words is like picking blackberries. One spills more blood than one gets of berries.'

She disregarded him and addressed me. 'Son, darling son, this now is my first command to you in the foreign tongue: *from on the morning out d'Inglis tongue only vill you spik — spik alvays d'Inglis*. Did you hear my command?'

I nodded. I knew not what she spoke but I felt it was the tongue she had scraped off the floor. 'I know it's not well said, for my foreign words are as rare as winter cherries.' She looked at me to guess my feeling. 'It is cruel, little calf, but what can I do?' Her eyes began to fill. I hastened to nod quickly with a smile. She turned to the man by the bull, 'you have heard my words, Father?'

He tickled the ears of the bull, and addressed the wall. 'Once there were people in this valley and their laughter would dry clothes for you.'

'Enough of long ago, this child is faced into the sea of English — would you send him forth in a leaky boat?'

'Old kings are we, despised for our words,' was all he said.

'Enough about kings! We are poor and have only the grass of six cows. We live like earwigs under stones.'

Father rubbed the back of the bull. Deep down he was seething but daren't round on Mother in my presence. He choked out words, 'proud as castles were we once, now turned into an infinity of dust. And whither goes our tongue? It goes where music goes, into the chaste garden of the sky; there in her solitude she will not be sought, but her magic alphabet will wink forth forever in starry gleam.'

Mother's voice rose, 'You will poison the mind of our heir against his own salvation if you speak like that. Enough of old this and that, old furze, old kings, old verses. We weary of oldness and heroes. Sweeter to me is an ounce of today than a ton of yesteryear.' She moved towards me and squeezed my hand, 'my son will carry his head as high as any man yet.'

He rounded on her for the first time, not with his tone but with his eyes. 'My son is a king and his head is higher than any in the land — the height of a November McCarthy.'

'Yes, so high you would have it in the clouds. Let him beware of cold peaks, then,' and she opened the cowhouse door. She stood there for a minute, the silver candlestick like a weapon. 'From the first gleam of dawn tomorrow — only the foreign tongue. Not a syllable from the graveyard of the Gael. If there is there will be war and I shall be the victor. For it is written that the hand that stokes the fire shall rule the house.' She went out but returned immediately. 'Have you told your son why you are called a November McCarthy.' She turned to me and said with great scorn. 'They were defeated in

November 1599 by the Lord O'Neill.'[1]

It was too much for Father. He rushed at her but she yielded not the flicker of an eyelash. He turned to me as if to stop himself choking her. 'Yes,' he roared, 'our castles did he knock and burn. But defeated, no. Look into my eyes, darling son, do you see defeat?' I looked at this man of two score years, at the body too large for the clothes, at the clothes too small for the patches. At the eyes. And I saw not defeat but a thorn in the flesh of his ancient pride. 'Huh,' said Mother, 'McCarthys' castles falling, McCarthys' dunghills rising!'

He looked for a time at the ground, then drew himself to his full height and said. 'If you were a man you would die on this straw for insulting our blood. A McCarthy is proud whether on dunghill or battlement. I brought you to this place from Land of Reeds East, where no tree grows. Beware the land that will not support a tree for neither will it support nobility,' and he strode out to the haggard. Mother came to me and hugged me and said, 'Beyond the beyond have my words pushed me. What can I do? They love you but I must look after you. The world is wrong,' and she sobbed and as she did she hugged me tighter than ever before; and I felt it was not me she hugged but some dream, some tale, another way, which would never be hugged by her in this world. She left, closing the cowhouse door ever so quietly.

Father came back and stood in the middle of the byre. He looked at me appealingly. Then he turned away and looked about him. When he spoke control had sapped the force out of his words. They fell at his feet. 'Take my words from me and I wish the world ill. God strike them all dumb tomorrow and I will gladly burn for all eternity.' He walked up and down the byre. 'The people beyond this valley who have denied their own, as far north as Little Bridge of Fusspot River, as far east as The Plains of Swans are nothing short of dung beetles. Did you ever hear the old saying "no matter how high the dung beetles fly, they always land on shit".' He sighed. 'Woe to the few heads remaining, mine and yours, that carry the kingdom of the Gael about, for a head in these rotten days isn't worth much more than a stone of oats.'....

1. An event of the Nine Years' War when Hugh O'Neill (1547-1616), earl of Tyrone, asserted his authority over the south of Ireland.

His tone and what he said disturbed me, and I begged him to be happy. 'Please let me bring you bright cherries from the orchard.'

He considered my offer then changed suddenly. He came over to me and hugged me. 'Little thrush of my heart, a kiss for you, gold rings on your fingers for ever, for cherries are the same to all. Gods, kings and fools are equal made by the taste of cherries.' He sat on a milking stool and I sat on his knee. 'Do you know,' he said, 'that the great wonders of this earth come from simple free things as round as a cherry. Did I ever tell you the Five Round Wonders of the Five Round Senses?' He sang them out happily. 'The smell of apples, the taste of a kiss, the feel of a warm shilling in your fist, the sight of a friend on a hilltop, the hearing of young puppies at play.'

A hush fell on all the cowhouse. Impatient milk dripped from all the udders on the straw. The bull lowed deep and made the door rattle. Somewhere a sun was going down and the chimneys pushed their shadows through the ferny dunghills. I walked as far as the bull and from there asked my question. He scratched his head and after a while said he had never heard of such a one. Finally he smiled and said, 'what an odd pair are we, one grieves for a red thief, the other for a black.'

'Who is the Black Thief?' I asked. He got up and walked to the doorway and leaned against the jamb.

'Don't you know that the Black Thief is the story teller, the stealer of black, who comes among the people during the long winter nights to steal away the darkness from their hearts with the magic of his tales. Soon on stumbling feet we hurry the last of the Black Thieves across the bogs to the churchyard dark. And now the long night descends upon our Gaeltacht,[2] and never, never, again will the Black Thief come to steal it away. There shall be no dawn.' He turned away from me and moved through the haggard, through the gate, out onto a moor, wild enough for any soul.

I went to the orchard. Another sunset behind Crooked Mountain — now there would be less eternity. I stood beneath the cherry tree and gazed up at its topmost branches. I told the Red Thief to remain on his treetop high for ever, as an honour to all good tales that were no more. And then I looked around the orchard at the tumble of fruit and leaf,

2. Irish-speaking district.

and I said, 'Black Thief, for you good bye, and wherever you go may music be always at your feet. A kiss for you, Black Thief.' And I picked a cherry from the tree, and I kissed it and tossed it out, high and beyond the lilac tree and gazed upon it tumbling, tumbling crimsonly towards the slow round earth to land I know not where.

ALAN TITLEY

(1947-)

from: EIRICEACHTAÍ AGUS SCÉALTA EILE (1987)

[The English translation is by the author and has been published in *Translation: The Journal of Literary Translation*, Vol. XX (Fall 1989).]

AN SÍSCÉAL DE RÉIR EOIN

Déan é seo; déan é siúd; éirigh i do shuí; dúisigh aníos; cuir ort do bhríste is do stoca; oscail an doras; seachain an strainséara; tabhair dom do phláta; ith suas do dhinnéar; caith siar an bainne; croch suas do chóta; cóirigh do leaba, bí ar ais ag a sé; abair amhrán; inis an fhírinne; déan d'obair bhaile; nigh na gréithre; cuir slacht ar do sheomra; ceartaigh na botúin; líon isteach na bearnaí; fainic an t-uisce; múch an teilifiseán; faigh an salann; cuir amach an cat; scuab an t-urlár; glan amach an gluaisteán; gléas do dheirfiúr; íoc do dheasca; dún do chlab; fan siar ón mbóthar; meas an luach; éiligh do chearta; cuimhnigh ort féin; eachtraigh leat; oscail do shúile; nigh d'fhiacla; féach ar dheis agus ar chlé; éist do bhéal; bain an féar; fuaraigh do chuid; giollaigh an dall; bailigh glaneolas go cruinn; las solas san doircheacht; cuir do chos cheart chun tosaigh; tapaidh an deis; caomhnaigh do neart; tóg na cúilíní; buail an t-iarann te; lean leat; coinnibh ort; foghlaim do bhéasa; cuir isteach an bhróg; déan do dhualgas; faigh an craiceann is a luach; imir an cluiche; bailigh leat; bí liom; pós anuraidh; feic a bhfeicir; foc do leithscéalta tá mo chuid airgid uaim; abair do phaidreacha; ná bac leis siúd; ná bris an dlí; ná salaigh do bhéal; ná mungail do chuid cainte; ná satail ar na bláthanna; ná bris an fhuinneog; ná hardaigh an leanbh; ná héist le comhairle an amadáin; ná glac le masla; ná santaigh ráite baoise; ná labhair fad is atá do bhéal lán; ná cuimil an smuga ar do mhuinchille; ná téir in airde sa lochta; ná téir síos an gairdín; ná tit anuas den chrann; ná téir ró-chóngarach don uisce; ná habair nach ndúirt mé leat é; ná hinis bréag; ná hob troid; ná himir go fealltach; ná caill an cluiche; ná déan muc díot féin; ná múch do choinneall; ná fliuchaigh do bhríste; ná bí mar sin; ná cas an citeal leis an gcorcán; ná cuir do mhéar sa phióg mhícheart; ná cuir do shúil thar do chuid; ná luigh ar chneá do chara; ná rothaigh rothar gan solas; ná féach sa treo eile; ná tuirling go stada an bus; ná scríobh ar dhá thaobh an leathanaigh; ná srac an t-éadach; ná bac le mac an bhacaigh; ná caoin tú féin; ná heitigh aon ní ach billí Dé Luain; ná raibh maith agat; ná bí meata le mannar na mórtach; ná tar isteach anseo ar meisce riamh; ná téir ró-fhada in achrann; ná bí in aon amhras ar chor ar bith in aon chor faoi; ná cuir guma coganta ar chnaiste na leapa; ná déan feall ar aon taobh; ná bí thíos leis; ná déan é sin arís nó cuirfidh mé do chuid fiacla siar trí do thóin; na hadhraigh déithe bréige.

Ní fhéadfainn a rá ach go raibh sé ag dul dó an bastard bhí sé tuillte aige ón gcéad nóiméad ar leag sé an strapa ar mo láimh cé go raibh marsbars agus i.q. ciontach san fhrog a thabhairt isteach sa seomra leis mar sin féin leag sé an milleán go léir ormsa an conús agus ba dhóbair dó an craiceann a bhaint de mo lámha ach níorbh é sin ba mheasa ar chor ar bith ach an straois a bhí air ó chluais go cluais faoi mar a bheadh sé ag baint pléisiúir as tar éis dó é a bhualadh isteach inár gcloigne nár cheart dúinne pléisiúr a bhaint as míle rud agus nár cheart dúinn ach go háirithe dul isteach sa bhothán ar an tslí abhaile mar go raibh na buachaillí móra ón séú bliain istigh ansin agus nach rabhadar iontrust le buachaillí beaga agus bhíodh straois de shaghas eile air á rá ach go háirithe nuair a d'fheicimis na fiacla buí agus an chlais a bhíodh ag dul síos trí lár a theanga ar nós scoiltghleann mór an mhapa a dtugadh sé léasadh dúinn ina thaobh mura bhféadfaimis é a aithint ach bhí marsbars agus i.q. breá sásta nuair a chuala siad an díoltas a bhí beartaithe agam dó an t-am seo an focar murab ionann agus an uair roimhe sin nuair a chuireamar an t-ispín caca isteach sa bhosca agus é a fheistiú le páipéar bronntanais agus le ribín buí agus é a chur chuige tríd an bpost ionas go bhfaigheadh sé lena bhricfeasta é ó nár mhór go léir an spórt a bhí againn an mhaidin sin agus an aghaidh mhílítheach a bhí air ag iarraidh na briathra laidine a mhúineadh dúinn agus nuair ba dhóbair do mharsbars turdo turdas turdat a rá in ionad cibé rud a hiarradh air ach an t-am seo bhí sé i gceist againn dul thar fóir ar fad lena thaispeáint dó nach bhféadfadh sé cibé olc a bhí air a ídiú orainne an ceann caca mar bhraitheamar go raibh sé de dhualgas naofa sacrálta orainn gan ligean le múinteoirí ná le tuismitheoirí an ceann is fearr a fháil orainn ar son ár ndínitne féin agus níl aon amhras ná gurb é an bás an dul thar fóir is géire ar fad agus dá bhféadfaimis é a mharú gur dócha go mbainfeadh sin an mhóráil de ar feadh tamaill chuir sé iontas orainn a shimplí is a bhí sé toisc guth láidir toll a bheith ag i.q. agus é a bheith ina aisteoir maith freisin a d'fhéadfadh aithris a dhéanamh ar ghuthanna chomh maith le peannaireacht b'eisean an té a d'fhaighimis chun nótaí ár dtuismitheoirí a scríobh agus dá bhrí sin ní raibh aon amhras ar chailín an nuachtáin nuair a mhínigh sé di idir snaganna goil go raibh a athair tar éis séalú gur éag gur tharraing sé an scríd gur thit an t-anam tur te as gan choinne gur imigh an tséideog dheiridh as amuigh ar mhachaire an ghailf gur sclog sé ar an tríú faiche déag agus a chlub á luascadh aige agus gurbh é sin a bhuille scoir agus go mba mhéala mór do chách ach go háirithe a bhean is a pháistí agus go bhfágfadh an tsochraid eaglais Pheadair is Phóil an tráthnóna dár gcionn ag a cúig a chlog agus go bhféadfaí an bille a chur chucu a theaghlach brónach féin ag an seoladh a thug sé dóibh an smugasmoirt agus ní dóigh liom gur thuig sé riamh an fáth a raibh aoibh an gháire ar ár n-aghaidh fiú nuair a bhí sé ag lascadh an leathair linn ina dhiaidh sin ach níor thada é sin i gcomórtas le haoibh an gháire a bhí ar ár dtóin óir thuigeamar gurbh fhiú é mar nach bhfuil díoltas ar bith chomh milis le díoltas an bháis ach b'é an t-aon aiféala amháin a bhí orainn nach bhfacamar a aghaidh ná aghaidh a mhná nuair a chuala siad go raibh fógra a bháis ar an nuachtán an sciodarbhuinneach buí ba sinne na buachaillí dó mise á rá leat bhí sé ag dul dó an cuntanós caca.

Cloistear ceol mall rómánsúil. Focail mhilse chrónánacha ag teacht ó amhránaí nach bhfuil le feiceáil. Soilse fanna. Scata ban óg ar thaobh na láimhe clé. Iad ag féachaint ar a chéile, ar a n-ingne, a gcosa, ar a bhfeisteas. Iad ag tnúth le rud éigin. Gluaiseann fear óg amach ina dtreo ón gcliathán ar dheis.

EOIN: *(go béasach)* Ar mhiste leat dá mbeadh an chéad rince eile agam leat?

CAILÍN ARD: *(ag féachaint le drochmheas air ó bhaitheas go bonn)* Hmrlf! *(Iompaíonn sí uaidh agus imíonn as i measc an tslua)*

EOIN: *(de ghuth ard)* Tá brón orm, ní raibh fhios agam go raibh tú ag iompar! *(Triaileann sé duine eile)* Ar mhaith leat damhsa?

CAILÍN DONN: Leatsa? *(ionadh uirthi)* An dóigh leat go bhfuilim as mo mheabhair?

EOIN: Tá brón orm, ní raibh fhios agam gur leisbiach tú! *(Siúlann tamall siar sa scuaine.)* Ar mhaith leat an t-urlár a ghreadadh liom?

CAILÍN DATHÚIL: *(go tur)* Nílim ag rince.

EOIN: Tá brón orm, ní raibh fhios agam go raibh bí ó agat! *(Triaileann duine eile fós)* Céard fútsa, hah? 'Bhfuil tú ag teacht? *(ní deireann sí tada ach tagann amach ar an urlár ina theannta)*

CAILÍN FIONN: (ar nós cuma liom) An maith leat Nimh Chruthanta?

EOIN: Tá siad ceart go leor. Ní shílim go bhfuil siad chomh maith le Seacht Norlach, áfach.

CAILÍN FIONN: Áfach tú féin leis. Níl éinne chomh maith le Nimh Chruthanta.

EOIN: Tá siad ró-leictreach.

CAILÍN FIONN: Is maith liomsa leictreachas. Tá cic ann ar a laghad. *(Ní deireann siad tada go ceann tamaill ach fáisceann Eoin isteach uirthi de réir mar a théann an ceol i mboige)*

EOIN: (isteach ina cluais) 'Bhfuil árasán agat nó ar tháinig tú le cara?

CAILÍN FIONN: *(isteach ina chluais siúd ar ais)* An raibh cabáiste agatsa i gcomhair do dhinnéir?

EOIN: *(roc ar a éadan)* Ní raibh, go bhfios dom. Cén fáth ar fhiafraigh tú díom é?

CAILÍN FIONN: Cheap mé gur mhothaigh mé an stumpa.

Agus an séú lá bhí cluiche le himirt acu sa Pháirc agus bhí Eoin ann. Agus bhí cuireadh faighte ag na buachaillí eile, leis, chun an chluiche. Agus bhí an bainisteoir ann os a gcomhair amach agus fearg air. Agus dúirt sé leo: Cad é sin daoibhse nó domsa é má dhéantar calaois ar dhuine daichead slat amach. Is é adeirim libh gur fearr cúilín ar an gclár ná cúl sa líontán. Agus d'ordaigh sé dóibh go dian éisteacht go géar lena raibh á rá aige óir bhí siad mar a bheadh caora gan aoire agus chrom sé ar a lán nithe a theagasc dóibh. Óir chonaic sé an mheatacht a bhí iontu agus dúirt sé leo: An té a bhfuil camán aige, tá tua aige agus an té a bhfuil tua aige is féidir leis crann fíge an fhreasúra a leagadh. Óir cad é an tairbhe do dhuine na liathróidí go léir a bhuachan má chailleann sé an cluiche féin. Agus dhein sé osna ina spiorad mar thuig sé ina chroí istigh nach raibh aon mhaitheas iontu. Agus tháinig na sluaite ag triall orthu ón dá pharóiste agus leath a lán de na daoine a mbratacha anuas ar an bhféar agus d'oscail a thuilleadh acu a scátha fearthainne óir b'shin é an saghas lae a bhí ann agus an mhuintir a bhí ar tosach agus ar deireadh agus ar an dá thaobh bhí siad ag liúirigh agus ag béicigh agus ag déanamh hósannanaí. Agus nuair a tháinig leath-am bhí sé fós ar fiuchadh agus bhí an deirg in a phluca agus cheistigh sé iad agus dúirt sé: Ó, a shliocht gan chiall, cad é an fad a bheidh mé eadraibh? Cad é an fad a fhulaingeoidh mé libh? Má tá cluasa chun éisteachta agaibh, éisteadh sibh. Agus labhair sé an chaint go soiléir ionas go dtuigfeadh siad: Ní beag é. Tá an uair tagtha. Go deimhin adeirim libh nach n-aithníonn sibh agus nach dtuigeann sibh fós? An bhfuil bhur gcroí dall fós? Bíodh an salann ionaibh. Bíodh an fhaghairt agus an miotal ionaibh. Óir an té a bhfuil aige tabharfar tuilleadh dó agus an té nach bhfuil aige bainfear den pháirc é. D'inis mé na nithe seo daoibh ionas nach nglacfadh sibh scannal. Agus tá na nithe seo inste agam daoibh i dtreo, nuair a thiocfaidh an t-am dóibh, go gcuimhneoidh sibh ar mé á n-insint daoibh. An té atá le leagadh, leagaigí é agus an té atá le scoilteadh scoiltigí é agus an té nach bhfuil libh tá sé in bhur gcoinne. Agus tá mórán nithe eile agam le rá libh, ach ní féidir daoibh iad a bhreith libh anois. Agus thug sé foláireamh dóibh gan a insint d'éinne i dtaobh na comhairle a thug sé dóibh. Agus thuig Eoin go maith an bheart a bhí le déanamh aige agus d'fhéach sé orthu agus dúirt sé leo: Lean mise. Agus nuair a bhain sé na cosa dá chéile comhraic an tríú huair ghlaoigh an réiteoir anonn air agus dúirt sé: Nach bhfuil fhios agat go bhfuil sé scríofa nach bhfuil cead agat do chéile comhraic a phleancadh? Agus shéan seisean agus dúirt: Níl fios ná eolas agam ar cad deir tú. Agus chrom sé ar eascainí agus ar a dhearbhú: Níl aon aithne agam ar an duine sin adeir tú. Níor leag mé cos ná camán air. Agus chuir an réiteoir den pháirc é ag lua an leabhair agus na rialacha. Agus níor thuig sé brí na cainte sin, agus bhí an bhrí i bhfolach uaidh, agus níor lig eagla dó é a cheistiú i dtaobh na cainte sin. Agus nuair a shuigh na seanóirí síos chun a chás a phlé thug siad fionraíocht sé mhí dó agus ghabh sé amach ina aonar ar an gcnoc chun urlacain.

Tá an oíche dorcha mar sin, tá an t-aer dubh, tá gíoscán san adhmad, tá na sciatháin leathair amuigh ag seilg na duibhré, tá na mairnéalaigh ag ól, tá an cat ag cogaint a cuid clúimh, tá an capall sa ghort ag méanfach go meafarach, tá púdar agus bean laistigh de ag siúl na sráide, tá an gadaí ag feitheamh, tá an iupaí ag iupáil sa chlub oíche, tá an sagart ag cuimhneamh ar pheacaí na mblianta fadó, tá na tonntracha ag beannú don ghaoth, tá an sceimhlitheoir idirnáisiúnta ag cur buama síos gan scíth is á fhaire go géar, tá an múinteoir calctha, tá an striapach stromptha, tá na gluaisteáin ag caitheamh tobac, tá an mheirg ag cogarnach le seanbhróiste ar bhrollach na mná, tá eireaball na muice ag casadh siar air féin, tá an t-uisce truaillithe ina luí sna píobáin, tá dallóg na fuinneoige ag slogadh na scáthanna, tá na toir spíonán ag cur a dteanga amach sa ghairdín, tá an t-uan ag múineadh méilí dá mháthair, tá an staighre ag dul in airde, tá an rón ag caitheamh smugairlí ar an trá, tá na scamaill ag déanamh bolg le cnoic, tá na splancacha céille ag dul as in intinn na ndaoine, tá guthanna na bpáistí ina dtost faoi dheoidh, tá na cosáin ag dúiseacht, tá an ghaois ag bailiú sna cloigne folmha, tá na crainn ag iomrascáil leis na réalta, tá duine éigin ag fáil bháis amuigh ansin, tá duine éigin ag cniotáil ionar an uafáis, tá duine éigin ag déanamh cloichshneachta dá charr, tá duine éigin ag pógadh cuaille na sráide, tá duine éigin ag scaipeadh ceo ar an drúcht, tá duine éigin ag casadh coinnle san doircheacht, tá duine éigin ag cumadh ceapairí i gcomhair na maidine, tá duine éigin ag iarraidh Freud a léamh, tá duine éigin ag cur salainn sa leamhnacht, tá duine éigin ag marú an cheoil, tá an fear óg seo ag aoireacht a choirp, tá an fear óg seo ag bulladh a bháisín, tá an fear óg seo ag iompó an bhioráin, tá an fear óg seo ag damhsa an gheataire, tá an fear óg seo ag caitheamh a dhíslí, tá an fear óg seo ag déanamh cleas a ghaile, tá an fear óg seo ag bogadh a dhúraim, tá an fear óg seo ag stocadh a bhróicéara, tá an fear óg seo ag ribeadh a rabúin, tá an fear óg seo ag loisceadh a loine, tá an fear óg seo ag greadadh a ghríbhe, tá an fear óg seo ag longadúdal a líreacáin, tá an fear óg seo ag tochas a phéiste, tá an fear óg seo ag pléireacht a phéitseoige, tá an fear óg seo ag feádóireacht a fheimín, tá an fear óg seo ag teacht in inmhe, tá an fear óg seo ag fás suas, tá an fear óg seo ag dul a chodladh.

Fear óg saibhir a bhí ann, agus d'imigh sé ag tuilleamh a bheatha dó féin mar ba ghnách leis. Bhí sé ag cur de riamh is choíche, agus ní raibh aon aimsir aige á fháil chun gur casadh isteach go club uaigneach é tráthnóna déanach. Ní raibh puinn daoine sa chlub seo, dar leis. Chuaigh sé isteach go seomra a bhí ann, agus is é a bhí istigh roimhe scata ban óg. D'fhiafraigh sé díobh an bhfaigheadh sé tamall spóirt ina dteannta nó an bhfaigheadh sé lóistín na hoíche go lá. Dúirt siad leis nach bhfaigheadh, bheith sa tsiúl dó féin, agus áit éigin eile a dhéanamh amach, agus daoine eile a chrá. Bhí sé tamall ón gclub, agus an oíche ag déanamh air. Bhuail bean leis ar an tsráid.

'Nach déanach atá tú ag máirseáil?' adúirt sé leis an mbean. 'An raibh tú sa chlub sin thíos istigh?' adúirt sé.

'Bhíos', ar sise.

'Cé bhí istigh romhat?'

Bhí scata fear', ar sise.

'Agus ní thabharfadh siad lóistín na hoíche duit?' ar seisean.

'Ní thabharfadh', arsa an bhean.

'Ná domsa', adúirt sé, ar seisean.

'Is olc an fear nach bhfanfadh isteach in ainneoin scata daoine díomhaoine! Téanam ort', adúirt sí, 'agus b'fhé go bhfaighfeá lóistín na hoíche fós!'

Bhí siad ag imeacht leo i gcaitheamh na hoíche, ag siúl rompu, go dtí gur casadh go háit iad a raibh teach breá slinne ar thaobh an bhóthair. Voil, chuaigh siad isteach ar aon chuma agus bhuail sí síos corcán breá feola ag beiriú, agus corcán breá prátaí.

'Ó, suigh síos', adúirt an bhean, 'agus caith díot do chóta!'

'Tá sé luath fós', adúirt sé, 'chun stad!'

'Ó, níl aon fhear de do shórtsa a ghabhann chugainn mar seo ná go gcoinním é i gcomhair na hoíche', arsa an bhean.

Sea! Chaith sé de a chóta go háirithe. Bhí tine bhreá ar lasadh istigh aici agus tharraing sí chuici paca cártaí.

'An imireofá breith?' adúirt sí.

'Imreoidh mé', adúirt an fear.

D'imríodar, agus bhuaigh sí an bhreith ar an bhfear.

'Cuirim de cheist, de bhreith, agus de mhórualach ort', adúirt sí, 'gan dhá bhéile bia a ithe ar aon bhord ná dhá oíche a chodladh ar aon leaba chun go ndéanfaidh tú an bheart liom!' adúirt sí.

Sea! Ghléas sé suas é féin agus d'ardaigh sé a peatachótaí bogóideacha bándearga i mbarr na gcos comhfhada, comhdhíreach mar a mbíodh slurpadáin, slapadáin, féilte móra, gréisc is lóiste, silíní éigiallda na n-arraingeacha ag teacht ar buis agus ar bais agus ar shlais mhaidí rámha ag déanamh ceoil, spóirt agus imiris. Dhein siad ardán den ísleán, agus ísleán den ardán agus tharraing siad toibreacha fíoruisc aníos tríd an screadam cloch. Bhí siad ag gabháil dá chéile nó go raibh drúcht agus deireanaí agus meirígín cheo ag teacht, an láir bhán ag dul ar scáth na cupóige, an chupóg ag teitheadh uaithe, aghaidh na ngluaisteán ar an mbaile, aghaidh na gcat ar an luaith, madraí an bhaile ag amhastraigh san áit go mbíonn siad agus san áit nach mbíonn siad ní labhrann siad focal! Sa deireadh bhain Eoin aon fháisceadh amháin aisti. Thit sí siar ar an urlár agus í breá sásta léi féin.

'Hu! Hu! Tá sin déanta agat, a fhir in airde!' ar sise. 'Caithfidh tú mé a phósadh anois', adúirt sí, 'sin é dlí na tíre. Bhfuil tú sásta?' ar sise.

Bhí go maith is ní raibh go holc agus d'fhéach sé síos uirthi.

'Mhuise', ar seisean, 'an é sin an scéal agat é? Voil', adúirt sé, an fear óg, 'tá sin go maith ceart go leor, by dad. An ní is toil leatsa, is é is toil liomsa chomh minic agus atá méara agus ladhra orm'.

'Seo', adúirt sí, d'aon ghnó, 'bíodh sé sin agat go fóill beag', ag caitheamh a bhríste chuige. 'Dé bheathasa a ghrá ghil', ar sise, 'bímis ag cur dínn go maith i dteannta a chéile'.

Deirtí gur mar sin a phós Eoin a bhean rua agus gur mhinic fheictí ag rith i measc na gcocaí iad, ag rancás is ag pléisiúr dóibh féin.

Sin scéal gan aon bhréag, bíodh fhios agat!

CAD A D'FHOGHLAIM SÉ I GCAITHEAMH A SHAOIL?

D'fhoghlaim sé nárbh aon dóichín é féin, gurbh fhearr an phraiseach ó aréir ná an phraiseach ar fud na mias, go raibh an lámh go dtí an béal agus ar ais aige, go raibh cead oilc is mhaitheasa aige, go raibh úll an aineolais chomh blasta le húll na slogaide, gur milis an rud é an tallann, gurbh ionann a dó is a dó agus a ceathair cuid éigin den am, gurbh fhearr bó i lár an tsiopa ghloine ná a bheith gan aon bhó go deo, go mbíonn duine ina leanbh míle uair, gurbh fhearr buinneach mhaith ná a bheith gan seasamh, nach raibh an scríbhneoireacht ar an mballa soiléir ar chor ar bith, go raibh nead seangán ina chroí istigh, gurbh é féin bunrúta agus barrfháth an tsaoil, nár tada é ach cú fiaigh, go raibh fiaclóirí barbartha, go raibh gamal roimhe agus gamal ina dhiaidh agus é féin ina lár ina ghamal mar chách, go raibh na hamanna ag athrú san lá a bhí i gcónaí inniu ann, gurbh é gorm dath gruaige a fhíorghrá ar maidin nuair a d'éirigh sé, go raibh mangairí guagach, nach raibh an chaithir mar a tuairisc, gur fhan an húr agus gur imigh an óinseach, go raibh an ghrís chloigíneach ar dhaoine eile seachas é féin, nárbh fhurasta oisirí a shlogadh gan chóiriú, go raibh gliú roisíneach uiscedhíonach agus teasdíonach, nár ghá ach mantissae logartamaí slánuimhreacha a tháibhliú, go raibh máilín neachtair ag bun gach piotail, go raibh páirceanna leibhéalta agus cnocánach, go raibh deora goirt agus deora áthais ann, go raibh londubh mór os cionn a gháire, gurbh fhiú mámh a chur ina chás féin, gur phraiseach an peata é an scéal, nárbh fholáir dul ó theach an domhain go teach an díola, go raibh an freagra ag séideadh sa ghaoth, go raibh a ghunna ar cíos mura mbeadh ann ach a bheith ag rince san doircheacht, go raibh fáthanna maithe gan tada a dhéanamh agus a mhalairt, go raibh an t-amadán ar an gcnoc ag faire orthu go léir, gurbh fhusa éirí ná fanacht thuas, gur mhair na bréaga tamall fada, gur tuar míámharach bean rua istoíche, gurbh olc an bhroim nach séideann boladh do dhuine éigin, nach raibh sé ró-ghlan ar muin an muice, gur ró-chiúin é brúcht na carraige báine, nár réidh d'fhear na dtrí ghnó, nárbh fhada é ina luí le Louis, gur bhreá leis coiméide ard na huaire, gurbh é an bálghéim ainm an chluiche, gur labhair an mhaidhc d'aon ghruth, go raibh gach lár ina lúb, nar thaitin an Luan leis, go raibh an taobh eile mícheart, nach mbuafadh Ceatharlach Craobh na hÉireann riamh, nárbh fhéidir an líomóin a fháisceadh as líomanáid, gur chuma nó cac fear gan speilp, go raibh umar na haimiléise neamhdheas, go raibh an saol is a mháthair mídhlistineach, gur shlán iad leacacha an tí mhóir, go raibh uasal seachas íseal thuas seal agus suas seal, nárbh aon mhaith cara sa chúirt má bhí airgead ag an duine eile, nach mbíonn aon smacht mar a mbíonn an tslat, go raibh an pictiúr mór as fócas agus an fophictiúr cam, nach raibh aon riail go hainriail, gur chuma sa bhfoc leis faoi dhuine ná daonnaí, go raibh a anam clúdaithe le craiceann, go raibh colún leathair síos trína lár agus go raibh gach aon ní ina chacstaí ar an nós.

Is dhein rudaí eile fós a chuir an croí ag léim ann
Nach bhfuil léamh ná insint scéil i mball ar bith
orthu
Ach gur fusa trácht anseo ar fhuadar spride buile
Seachas gnóthaí ardphoiblí arbh iad a gcúram
suite
Teacht taobh na gaoithe aniar ar an speach ba
dhual
Is an gnó caoch balbh a chur in uachtar
Aghaidh an eagarfhocail laethúil a chaitheamh
gan fhidil
Is oifig chruinn a dhéanamh den teampall íon
éagruthach.
A aghaidh a iompó ar mhuir na hintleachta uile
Is tumadh go domhain faoi pholl i lathaigh fhéithe
Tionóil a mheas go fuar thar chraos a gcéille
Is magadh ard a mhaíomh de charúl na séite.
'Ardaigí libh bíoma mór na bhfrathacha, a
shiúinéirí!
Is cuir na fothaí síos go sdriog, a chonsailéirí!
Seo duit do phas i lár na cuilithe i dtír na sceirde!'
Ha! Tá an léarscáil sractha le broid is slad na
raidhse
Gan fíon ná treo ach oiread is bláth nó taibhse,
Mise an sprioc, is mo shlí féin chun na sprice,
Linne an phéacáil, a chroí istigh, is mairfidh fad a
mhaireann.
An cóta mór a chaitheamh in éadan na cinniúna
Is pócaí do chruinne féin a fhágáil lomascúite
Nár ghamalach an ghaois a cheannódh muc i mála
Is a d'fhulaingeodh an reacht lasmuigh de
sheamanna ládálta?
Tar éis na treise fada ó stáir go stáir go fiata
Bhí haiste úd na heagna chomh docht is bhí riamh
iata.
Ach cad é sin don té sin a mbíonn a bholg sásta?
Is 'sé do bheatha a dhuine tusa atá lán de ghrásta!

Seo duit do mhaidí croise, seo duit do chathaoir shúgáin, seo duit do chupán tae, seo duit do spúnóg siúcra, seo duit do phiollaí suain, seo duit do mhuga bainne, seo duit do bhráillín glúine, seo duit do shlipéirí boga, seo duit do chlár teilifíse, seo duit do ghloine uisce, seo duit do phláta leitean, seo duit do chrúiscín leapa, seo duit do phota Pádraig, seo duit do chipín is do mheanaithí, seo duit do thicéad dubh, seo duit do phingin rua, seo duit do chúpla unsa tobac, do phíopa is d'úll, seo duit do mhadra dílis, seo duit do spéaclaí láidre, seo duit do sheanphort ceoil, seo duit d'unga álainn, seo duit do chiarsúr corcra, seo duit d'fhiacla bréige, seo duit do mhaicíní is do mhuicíní, seo duit d'albam grianghraf, seo duit do ghunna folamh, seo duit do chuimilt guailne, seo duit do shúisín bán, seo duit do chóta fionnaidh, seo duit do sheáiní fada, seo duit do ghoradh uaire, seo duit do chasadh timpeall, seo é an staighre in airde, seo é an doras oscailte, seo é an leaba ullamh, seo í an adhairt bhrionglóideach, seo é an dochtúir saibhir, seo é an buidéal draíochta, seo é luí na laoithe, seo é an codladh gairid, seo í pian na dúiseachta, seo é an scáth sa seomra, sin í an ghrian lasmuigh, sin iad na páistí ag súgradh, sin iad na ba ar an mbóthar ó thuaidh, sin é an seordán i do chluasa, sin í an chuimhne ag cabaireacht, sin é an fabhra ag dúnadh, sin í an lámh ag sileadh, sin é an bíogadh tamall, ach seo í bitseach an bháis, agus seo iad do chaidhp is do chónra.

THE GOBSPIEL ACCORDING TO JOHN

Do this; do that; get up; shake yourself; stir your carcass; shift your ass; put on your trousers; pull up your socks; open the door; mind the stranger; give me your plate; eat your dinner; drink your milk; don't eat with your mouth full; hang up your coat; make your bed; be home before dark; sing a song; tell the truth; do your homework; wash the dishes; tidy your room; correct the mistakes; fill in the boxes; watch the water; turn off the television; get the salt; put out the cat; sweep the floor; clean out the car; dress your sister; pay your debts; shut your face; cop on; stay back from the road; reckon the cost; demand your rights; don't forget yourself; keep talking; open your eyes; scrub your teeth; look left and right; keep your mouth closed; cut the grass; hold your piece; help the poor; learn what you can; put it all down to experience; light a candle in the dark; put your right foot forward; take your chance; don't waste your energy; strike the iron when it's hot; keep going; watch your manners; put in the boot; do your duty; squeeze the last ounce; play the game; get stuffed; see what you see; whatever you say, say nothing; don't get caught; there will be jam tomorrow; shape up; shake down; get on with it; bugger off; tune up, turn back, drop dead; move right on; fuck your excuses I want my money; say your prayers; it's my party and I'll cry if I want to; if you call me pretty I'll hit you; thou shalt not have strange yobs before me; don't mind him; don't break the law; don't dirty your mouth; don't mumble; don't walk on the flowers; don't lift the child; don't suffer fools gladly; don't take insults lying down; don't wipe your snot on your sleeve; don't go up into the attic; don't go down the garden; don't fall off the tree; don't keep your hands to yourself; don't put your paws in the till; don't say I didn't tell you; don't tell lies; don't funk a fight; don't play dirty; don't lose the match; don't make a pig of yourself; don't quench the candle; don't be like that; don't put your finger in the dyke; don't put the cat in the microwave; don't jump the gun; don't wet your pants; don't ride a bike without a light; don't go without one of them things in your pocket; don't look the other way; don't disembark until the bus stops; don't write on the two sides of the page; don't have it off when you should have it on; don't put your trust in ponces; don't let woebegones be woebegones; don't let them get you; don't get off the bandwagon until the music stops; don't come in here drunk; don't let your meat loaf; don't be in any doubt about it whatsoever; don't put chewing gum on the bedpost overnight; don't forget your contribution on the way out; don't throw your granny off the bus; don't hit the nail with your head; don't do that again or I'll put your teeth out through your arse; don't worship false gods.

Well I have to say that he had it coming the bastard he deserved it from the moment he laid the strap on my hand the weak-faced wimp even though it was marsbars and i.q. who brought the frog into the class he blamed me completely who does he think he is the poop or something and he nearly took the skin from my hands the nerd but that wasn't the worst of it o no it wasn't but the leer he had from ear to ear the craphead as if he was getting pleasure from it the born-again asshole after he telling us we shouldn't get pleasure from anything and that we shouldn't go behind the shed with the big boys on the way home the whore's git and he'd have another kind of a leer on his snout as he told us and we'd see his tobacco-stained teeth the dickhead and the big gash down the middle of his tongue like the riftvalley he beat us to know so he did herr haemorrhoid but marsbars and i.q. were over the moon when they heard of the revenge I had planned this time the fucker not like the last time when we wrapped up the lumpa shit in the pretty box and festooned it with christmas ribbons the coprophagous cunt and sent it to him by registered post so that he would get it with his breakfast of greasy sausages and hairy bacon the pedagogic pisspot and we were the ones grinning from our elbe to our euphrates that morning as he tried to the rectal rambo think of the latin verbs turdo turdas turdat he was one page ahead of us in the book but this time we were determined to go the whole hog the zapped-out zeroid just to show that low-life forms like him or like he couldn't get away with it the bumbo because we knew it was our duty not to let teachers or parents ride roughshod over us on account of our dignity like and as killing is the ultimate organism we said why not as with i.q.'s deep voice and he being a good actor and all as well as being a good forger we used to get him to write our parents' notes that we were sick or visiting the dentist or that our aunt down the country died and so the girl in the newspaper office didn't suspect anything when he told her between sobs that his father had snuffed it had kicked the slopbucket had pissed away had gone to his beloved sleep had shipped it quietly had gone to his eternal sward had put out the flame was now as good as the door-nails he hammered and that he was dearly beloved of and much regretted by his dear wife and children and that the remains would leave The Church of Perpetual Suckers at five o clock and they could send the bill to him as the eldest son the fartfaggot and I don't think he ever understood the grin on our faces even when the leather was hopping off our hands because it was nothing compared with the leer on our backsides because we knew in our heart of hearts and from our history lessons and from the tv that there was no revenge as sweet as death the bedmesser but we only regretted we didn't see his face or his wife's when they read of his death the vindictive vasectomised vamper for we were the boys for him and his prolapsed pile I'm telling you the old shitfaced bollocky bastard.

Slow romantic music in the background. Sugary-sweet singing coming from a singer off-stage. Dim lights. Young ladies in their teens on the left. They are examining themselves and one another with some expectation. A young man enters from the right and approaches them.

JOHN: (*Good manneredly*) May I have the pleasure of the next dance with you, please?

TALL GIRL: (*Looking at him disdainfully*) Hmrlfx! (*She turns away and retreats into the crowd*)

JOHN: (*Out loud*) Sorry, I didn't know you were pregnant! (*Trying another one*) Would you care to dance?

BRUNETTE: With you? (*Nose up, chin out, baring her teeth*) Do you think I'm nuts or something?

JOHN: Sorry, I didn't know you were gay! (*Walks down the line of girls*) Shake the floor, will we?

REDHEAD: (*Stiffly*) I'm not dancing.

JOHN: Sorry, I didn't know you had B.O.! (*Tries another*) What about you, hah? Are you coming?

She says nothing but follows him out onto the floor centre-stage

BLONDE: (*Chewing gum*) Are you into Genghis Can?

JOHN: They're ok. But they're not as good as Time Flies, I think.

BLONDE: I wouldn't call that thinking. Nobody's as good as Genghis Can. At least they live up to their reputation.

JOHN: And you should know?

BLONDE: (*Emphatically*) I know everything.

They don't say anything for a while but JOHN *snuggles in closely to her as the music gets softer and slower*

JOHN: (*Speaking into her ear*) Do you have an apartment or did you come with a friend?

BLONDE: (*Into his ear also*) Did you have cabbage for your dinner?

JOHN: (*Puzzled*) Not as far as I know. Why do you ask?

BLONDE: I just thought I felt the stump.

And on the sixth day it came to pass that there was a game in the Field and John was there. And the other boys were invited also unto the game. And the manager was there before them with anger on his countenance. And he said unto them: What is it to thee or to me if you foul forty yards out from the goal. For I say unto you that a point on the score-board is better than a goal in your net. And he ordained them to listen carefully unto him because they were like sheep without a shepherd and he began to instruct them that what was highly esteemed among men was an abomination in his sight. But he saw the cowardice in them and he said: whosoever amongst you hath a hurley also hath a hatchet, and he who hath a hatchet is able to cut down the fig tree of the enemy. For what doth it profit a man to win all the balls and to lose the game itself. And he sighed inwardly in his spirit for he knew that they were no bloody good. And the multitudes came from the two parishes unto them and they laid their cloaks upon the grass and some amongst them even did open their umbrellas as that was the kind of day it was and those who were first and those who were last and those who were on both sides were shouting and roaring and making whoopee and hosannas. And when half-time came he was still angry and the red was in his cheeks and he lifted up his eyes and he charged them saying: O, you brutes of vipers, give an account of your stewardship. For how long will I have to suffer thus? He who hath ears to hear let him hear. And he spoke to them in plain bad language so that they might understand. Take heed to yourselves. Gird your lines for the winning of all is within you. Remember your wives' lot for even thus shall it be on the day of reckoning. It is impossible but that offences will come; but woe unto him through whom they come. Between us and them there is a great gulf fixed so that they who pass to them are guilty of the abomination of execration. For verily I say unto you, this kind can be driven forth by nothing but by flailing and hacking. For he who has much more will be given unto him and he who has nothing will be taken off the field. These things I have told you so that you would not be scandalised. He who is to be floored, floor him, and he who is to be split, split him and he who is not with you is against you. And I have many more things to tell you which I cannot say now. But he sent them away and charged them straight way not to disclose any part of the advice he had given them. But John knew well what had to be done and he looked at them and said: Follow me. And when he had taken the legs from under his opponent the third time and had smote him upon the right ear the referee called unto him and said: Dost thou not know that it is written that thou shalt not bear false violence against thine opposing player? And he denied it and said: I know not what thou sayest. But he began to curse and to swear, saying, I know not this man of whom you speak. Why askest thou me? I laid neither leg nor stick on him. But the referee sent him forth from the field so that the strictures would be fulfilled that a bone of them should not be broken. But he understood not what had been said and the meaning was hidden from him. And when the chief cheese and the elders sat down to discuss his case they suspended him for six months and he went off alone unto the mountain to throw his guts up.

So then the night is dark and the air is black and the wood is creaking, the bats are abroad hunting the blue moon, the sailors are drinking, the cat is chewing its fur, the horse is in the field yawning metaphorically, powder with a woman inside it is stalking the streets, the thief is waiting her chance, the yuppie is yuppieing in the night club, the priest is thinking of the great sins of the past, the waves are saying farewell to the wind, the international terrorist is tending his bomb, the teacher is tetchy, the painted lady is pounding the pavement, the cars are smoking their pipes, the rust is doing its worst on the brooches of breasts, the pig's tail is curling its wee, the contaminated water is waiting in the taps for the morning, the window-blind is swallowing the shadows, the gooseberry bushes are sticking out their tongues at the garden, the child is teaching wisdom to the psychologist, the lamb is lying down with the lion but is keeping his options open, the stairs is on the way up, the train is setting the night on fire, the seal is blowing his nose on the beach, the clouds are bustle pinching the mountains, the flashes of inspiration are leaving people's heads, the children have at last shut up, the sidewalks are beginning to stir, wisdom is gathering in the brains of fools, trees are wrestling with the stars, cats are howling on their beat, whorls of sleep are coming in on the west wind, somebody out there is dying, somebody out there is knitting the garment of horror, somebody out there is smashing his car, somebody out there is kissing a lamp-post, somebody out there is spreading dew on the grass, somebody out there is turning candles in the dark, somebody out there is making sandwiches for the morning, somebody out there is trying to read Freud, somebody out there is putting salt in the buttermilk, somebody out there frankly doesn't give a damn, somebody out there is murdering the musak, this young man knows what he's made of, this young man has the right stuff, this young man is acting the mick, this young man is doodling the dandy, this young man is hugging the mugger, this young man is kneading the dough, this young man is plucking the fig, this young man is tapping the column, this young man is stirring the stew, this young man is flaking the flint, this young man is venting the venison, this young man is besting the beaver, this young man is hauling the ashes, this young man is dunking the pumpkin, this young man is honking the donkey, this young man is tooting the rootie, this young man is happening the stance, this young man is wobbling the colly, this young man is jollying the roger, this young man is humouring the hubris, this young man is porking the beans, this young man is burning the bush, this young man is abrogating the absolute, this young man is reintegrating himself with the basic stuff of the universe, this young man has the poof of the pudding, this young man has had enough, this young man is going asleep.

A fine young man he was, so he was, and he went off to earn his keep as I will tell you now. He was going off now and always and was getting no good of it at all until he came to this club as the dark twilight of night was coming down. It was the last of the day then and there was neither soul nor sinner in the club, so he thought. And so he betook himself into the back room and who should he meet there but three fine women on whom he pitched his fancy. He asked them was there any chance of a bit of sport or what or could he stop the night until the morrow. They told him that there was not indeed to be sure and to be off with himself and to make out somewhere else and to be annoying other bodies. He was a distance from the club and the black of night upon him when he met another woman.

'Isn't it late you're out gallivanting?' he said to the woman. 'Were you in that club down there below?' he said.

'I was,' she said.

'Who was before you within?' he said.

'There were some men,' she said.

'And they wouldn't give you lodgings for the night?' he said.

'They would not,' she said.

'Nor me neither,' says he, he said.

'Success and benison to you for you're one after my own art,' she said. 'Come along you blasted man and maybe you'll get lodgings for the night yet.'

Well and good. They rose and bestirred themselves and went on their way. And when they were a while going along the road there was nobody for them to see and nothing for them to notice only fine tall mansions with big gardens and fancy cars which would gladden your heart. They did not stop nor shorten the journey until they came to a neat cottage beside the road. Anyway they went in and she put down a big pot of stew and a big pot of potatoes to boil.

'Ah well, upon my soul,' said the woman, 'sit down or do something useful.'

'It's early days yet,' he said, 'to be stopping the night.'

'There is no man the likes of you who passes this way that I do not keep for the duration of the whole night,' she said.

Well then! He took off his coat anyway. She had a big fire blazing and she produced a pack of cards.

'Will you play a game with me?' she said.

'I will why not,' he said.

They started to play, herself and himself, and when they did she won the game against him at the very first go.

'A ha,' she said, 'I put as a judgement and binding spells on you, and under the great displeasure of the year not to eat two meals at the same table nor to sleep twice on one bed until you do the job with me!' she said.

Well then this was bad news for him but it is as well for me to shorten the story. Well he rose up with a leap and they went at it hammer and tongues, sally and forth, blazes and boiling, curry and fervour, cods and wallop, box and cox, derry and down, nonny and know, lute and nail, snatch and berry, milk and cunny, rump and stake, peak and boo, rod and sinker, smullet and stern, rattle and roll, storm and drang, hokey and pokey, gammon and baking, what and knot, jimmy and joys, willie and sing, whoops and daisy, dick and cavet, jackall and hide, fan and winkle, hock and pintle, whole and shebang, needle and anchor, frankly and further, knead and gnashing, hairs and aces, yin and yang, excal and burr, gung and ho, yank and oodle, cannon and ball, bracket and hinge, amoor and priap, mills and boon, jiggery poker crackling baloney tickula tickulorum for ovur and ovum onan.

'Well that's over now anyhow, my man above,' she said. 'You must marry me now,' she said, 'that's the law of the land. Are you willing?' she said.

Well and good and not otherwise and he gave her a long look.

'Wisha, is that the way it is?' he said, rubbing a palm to his eyes, to his forelock, to his brows. 'Well,' he said, the young man said, 'that's not bad at all, by dad. What I want is what you want as long as the day rises on the morrow and the sap rises in the marrow.'

And it is what she said, 'Here,' she said, 'take that for now', throwing him his clothes. 'Great stuff and

God's greeting to you,' she said, 'we'll be knocking good times out of the hard times for many times to come.'

It is reported that that is how John married the red woman and it was said that they were often seen abroad among the cocks of hay making their sport for themselves in joy and happiness.

And that's a true story without any lie, you know!

WHAT DID HE LEARN IN THE COURSE OF HIS LIFE?

He learned that he was nobody's fool, that money opened all doors, that speech is the mother of troubles, that the house of bondage had many whips, that a small still voice is never heard, that out of the mouths of babes and sucklings comes forth dribble, that two and two made four sometimes, that the writing on the wall was never clear, that there was not much beyond wit's end, that he that spareth the rod had no sons, that the philosophic pill gilded nothing, that between the candy store on the corner and the chapel on the hill there was a lot of corn, that blue was the colour of his true love's hair in the morning, that there were many good reasons for doing nothing, that the long finger was better than a thumb, that the sheiks shall inherit the earth, that those who go down to the sea in ships are usually sailors, that the whores of wood had drawers of water, that one should give a lie for a lie and a truth for a truth, that whereof one cannot speak one is obliged to bullshit, that the only way out was back, that the answer was blowing in the wind, that it was always dirty on the pig's back, that the ball was the name of the game, that a radical chic goes to the root of things, that the delta of venus demanded a lot of tributes, that the fool on the hill watches over all, that he didn't like Mondays, that coke was the real thing, that a friend indeed was a friend with speed, that the ogres of thought were not as effective as the curses of obstruction, that raw data tastes best when cooked, that most pottery is a heinous sham, that going to the wall doesn't mean you have to wail about it, that now is sooner than then, that the Great Architect never got a degree, that it was difficult to swing on the roundabouts, that the tooth doesn't always out, that to be or not to be isn't even a question, that he who dares sins, that every tom and dick is hairy, that smart cookies don't crumble, that a wild goose chase sometimes caught a white elephant, that it was easier to fly than to stay up, that hush puppies rarely bark, that forked fingers were more feared than forked tongues, that screw ball was a kind of cock tail, that a bird in the hand meant none in the bush, that walking the plank meant you made a big splash, that farce was better than force, that the brobdingnag wasn't half as bad as the bob-tailed nag, that insultants should earn more than consultants, that you couldn't squeeze the lemon out of lemonade, that his gun was for hire even if he was only dancing in the dark, that lust we are and unto lust we always turn, that hard cheese was a tough titty, that the flighty are often callen, that crabbed sages and truth don't always go together, that life was a hard slut to crack, that there was no rule like misrule, that nobody mattered diddly-squat and that everything was a long way up the creek and past turning.

Other things he did also which made his spirit
leap,
The flight of owls whom he feared from within
the deep
Where all the ladders start in the old tack and
toe slop of his parts; these he exorcised and got
A new cheap toy lamp that gave little light
But loved the signs, the embranglement that tried
To dismember the dully sober from the wildly fue
And showed this from that betimes in our
antediluvial zoo.
So hoyted he upfront downmarket between the
shots
While others wavered between the profit and the
loss
That his soul purpled itself on carls of turd
While others lived the beefy breathing of the
herds,
And scobberlotchery became a kind of loam
Wherein the calm empire of a happy soul
Was thrunged with sense and hate and love and
howls and peace
That the unpurged images of day were forced to
recede
Before the cobbled force of all those and them
and that
The monstrous regiment of Being and All This
Crap and Fact.
'So raise the roof beams high, you team of
carpenters
And forget the fears of ancient harbingers!'
The cry is me, and mine, and member and même
chose

And ourselves and us and all we have is ours,
For in and out, about, above and below
It is always the same old stupid asshole show,
And for all the priests and goodmen and sages say
Their nutritious images only choke the simple
  way
From hand to mouth and the other orifices given
Whose ordures we must, our luck, just do their
  bidding.
So that's it then, have fun, be good, what's new?
I'm me myself, but for fuck's sake, who are you?

Here then are your crutches, here then is your rocking chair, here is your cup of tea, here is your sugar daddy, here are your sleeping tablets, here is your mug of milk, here is your knee blanket, here are your soft slippers, here is your television programme, here is your glass of water, here is your plate of porridge, here is your bed pot, here is your scrambled egg, here is your wedge and thin edge, here is your black ticket, here is your red penny, here is your woolly fold, here is your pipe and tobacco, here is your jolly grog, here is your faithful old dog, here are your strong glasses, here is your same old tune, here is your purple hankie, here are your false teeth, here are your muffs and your miffs, here is your photo album, here is your empty gun, here is your fur coat, here is your buttwipe, here is your longjohn, here are your heavy boots, here is the pale horse, here is the bottom line, here is the endgame, here is the candle to light you to bed, this is the stairs up, this is the open door, this is the beddy ready, this is the pillow of dreams, this is the rich doctor, this is the magic bottle, this is the lay of lays, no that is not an angel, this is your parting shot, this is your big jump, this is the final curtain, that is only a shadow, this is the man with the scythe, do you hear the plug being pulled, that is a buzz in your ears, that is the memory muttering, that is your droopy drawing, that is the hand that slipped, that is the beautiful memory, that is the way of all trash, that is your bier and casket, that's about it.

TOMÁS Ó CRIOMHTHAINN (TOMÁS Ó CROHAN)

(1855-1937)

from: AN tOILEÁNACH (The Islandman) (1929)

[O'Crohan tells of an encounter with the island poet. The translation is by Robin Flower (1881-1946).]

. . . Theastaigh uaim dul ag baint dorn móna, lá, mar bhí an lá an-bhreá agus gan mórán den tseanmhóin ar ár láimh san am céanna. Phreabas liom an doras amach agus ramhann néata agam i bhfearas agus i bhfaobhar, agus cé ná rabhas i bpearsain cosúil le haoinne d'Fhianna Éireann ní rabhas le cáineadh i mo cháilíocht féin. Bhíos mear, tapaidh, dea-eolais.

Chuireas chun bóthair i gcoinne an chnoic gan luas anáile, gan crampa i gcois, gan freanga i láimh, gan tinneas i gcroí, nó gur shroicheas lantán dar liom a raibh mianach maith ann, agus oiread i mo thimpeall di agus a dhéanfadh mo ghnó. Bhí faobhar chun gnótha orm agus chun saothar a dhéanamh.

Toisc ná raibh aon ghadsádaí a bhéarfadh mo dhinnéar chugam sa tigh agam ach an bheirt aosta, bhuaileas féin chugam canta maith aráin, arán cruaidh buí go maith de mhin gharbh, ach go raibh sé geal lasmuigh le plúr ar nós mar a bheadh aol faoi thigh, buidéal pint bainne ó chois na bó agus tuairim gearrphráta maith d'ailp ime, agus cé ná fuil na nithe seo le moladh anois acu chun bídh ba shásta a bhíos-sa leo an uair úd, mar bhí muileann béil chun a meilte agam.

Ach b'fhada ón bhfuadar chun obair a chur chun cinn an lá san mé. Níor rófhada a bhíos i dtosach mo ghreise agus faobhar chun gnótha orm an t-am ar bhuail an file Seán Ó Duinnshléibhe chugam agus ramhann faoina ascaill aige chun cos mhóna a bhaint é féin agus cuid mhaith eile a ghluais mar é chun portaigh, mar bhí an lá go haoibhinn agus gan mórán den tseanmhóin ann an uair sin acu gan a bheith dóite.

Ní dóigh liom go raibh file riamh le moladh chun aon obair shaothrach eile a chur chun cinn ach an fhilíocht amháin agus dob in ionua ag Seán é. Tá sórt deimhniú agam ar an méid sin mar gach uair dá dtugaim féin faoi ranna a chur le chéile, ós minic déanta agam é, níor mhaith ar bhuíon ná ar mhachaire mé an fhaid a bheidís idir lámha agam.

'Sea,' arsa an file liom, á chaitheamh féin ar an turtóg, nach mór an obair duit a bheith ag baint mhóna a leithéid de lá chomh te leis'. 'Suigh, tamall,' ar seisean, 'tá an lá seo fada agus beidh fionnuar tráthnóna ann.'

Ní rabhas róbhuíoch dá chomhrá ach gur bhuail náire mé gan suí ina theannta. Rud eile, thuigeas mura mbeadh an file buíoch díom go ndéanfadh sé aor orm ná beadh ar fónamh agus mé i mbéal mo thugtha amach san am san. Shuíos ina theannta.

'Sea,' arsa an file, 'an chéad amhrán a dheineas riamh, b'fhéidir ná fuil sé agat. Is í an 'Chaora Odhar' an chéad cheann a cheapas riamh, agus fáth maith agam lena dhéanamh maidir le holc.'

Cad deire leis ná gur thosnaigh le gach focal a rá di agus é sínte siar ar shlat a dhroma. Turtóg de mhínfhraoch thíos faoi agus teas agus brothall ó lonradh na gréine ag teacht anuas ón spéir fhíoghorm ghlan a bhí os ár gcionn ag tabhairt teasaíochta don taobh a bhí os a chionn den fhile.

Do mholas an t-amhrán go crannaibh na gréine cé go raibh sé am ghriogadh go nimhneach ar shlí eile, am choimeád ón ngnó tábhachtach a chuireas romham ar maidin a bheith déanta agam. Do bhí cosc curtha ag samsaireacht an fhile leis.

'Beidh an t-amhrán ar lár,' ar seisean, 'mura bprioctar suas é. An bhfuil aon rud i do phóca agat go scríobhfá síos e?'

An té ná bíonn an t-ádh ina bhóthar ar maidin agus Dia leis, níl sé i gcumas an pheacaigh bhoicht féin mórán á dhéanamh. Dhá ualach seanasail de mhóin níor thit le Tomás bocht an lá san a raibh an saothar mór beartaithe aige le déanamh; agus bhí an lá úd ar na chéad laethanta riamh ar bhraitheas an saol ag teacht i mo choinne, mar is ea a bhí lá liom agus chúig lá i mo choinne as san amach.

Níorbh ar mhaithe leis an bhfile a fuaireas mo pheann luaidhe agus páipéar éigin a bhí i mo phóca ach ar eagla go dtabharfadh sé aghaidh a gharbh-bhéil orm féin, agus chromas ar bhreacadh síos mar a ligeadh seisean as a bhéal. Ní sa teanga seo a bhíos ag scríobh mar ná rabhas oilte uirthi san am san.

Ní raibh puinn suilt ag baint liom lena linn sin. Níorbh iontas sin, fear a raibh gnó fuaimintiúil ar siúl ar maidin aige agus anois é curtha i leataobh ag gnó gan aird. Ar oscailt a bhéil don fhile bhí sleabhac ar a bhéal ag ligean na gutha amach. Bhreacas síos mar fhéadas ar shlí a thug sruthmheabhair dom ar an amhrán agus rud eile, má raghadh focal ar iarraidh féin uaim ní raibh an ceannródaí rófhada uaim agus eisean go héasca chun smut dá shaol a chaitheamh á chur i dtuiscint dom dá mbeadh an tseisreach sa bhfód aige féin.

San am a raibh an bheirt againn réidh le chéile bhí an ghrian ag maolú thar cnoc agus ba dhícheall do Thomás aon splanc céille a bheith aige san am sin. Tar éis an fhile scarúint uaim is é an chéad rud a dheineas dul go dtí an turtóg a raibh mo dhinnéar le hais léi ach b'é an dinnéar gan aird é. An canta d'arán buí a bhí ann ní dhéanfadh capall é a mheilt, agus mo chuid bainne ina chloch sa bhuidéal!

THE ISLANDMAN

. . . One day I wanted to go and cut some turf, for it was a very fine day, and we hadn't much of the old turf left to hand at that time. I went off through the door with a first-rate turf spade all ready and sharp. And though, as far as looks went, I was no match for the Fenians[1] of old, nobody could say a word against me for what I was — I was quick and deft, and knew what was what.

Off I started up the hill, and my breath never came short, my foot had no cramp, my hand didn't shake, there was no pain in my heart till I came to a place where, thought I, there was good turf, and enough of it round me to do my business. I was wild to get to work and do my job. As I had no young folk in the house to bring me my dinner, only the two old people, I took a good hunk of bread with me in the morning — bread of coarse meal, very hard and yellow, only whitened outside with flour, like whitewash on a house wall; a pint bottle of milk from the cow, and a lump of butter about the size of a small potato. And, though no one has a word to say in favour of that sort of food nowadays, I was pleased enough with it then, for I had a mill in my mouth to grind it.

But I had little chance to turn my keenness for

1. Ancient Irish heroes.

work to profit that day. I hadn't long begun on the job, working hard, when the poet Dunlevy came up with a spade under his oxter,[2] to cut a bit of turf for himself; and there were a lot of others with him who had come out to the bog as he had, for it was a lovely day, and at that time there was very little of last year's turf that hadn't been burnt.

I fancy that no poet has ever been much good at carrying through any job that had any work in it except only poetry, and that was the way with Shane, too. I can produce some sort of evidence for this statement, for, whenever I take it in hand to compose quatrains (and I often do) I shouldn't be much use in a gang of workers or in the field so long as I was engaged upon them.

'Well,' says the poet, throwing himself down on a tussock, 'isn't it a pity for you to be cutting turf on such a hot day. Sit down a bit, the day is long and it'll be cool in the afternoon.'

I didn't care much for what he had to say, but I was rather shy of refusing to sit down with him. Besides, I knew that if the poet had anything against me, he would make a satire on me that would be very unpleasant, especially as I was just about coming out in the world. So I sat down beside him.

'Now,' says the poet, 'perhaps you haven't got the first poem ever I made. "The Black-faced Sheep", that was my first, and I had good reason for making it as far as provocation goes.'

Would you believe it — he started to recite every word of it, lying there stretched out on the flat of his back! There was a hummock of soft heather under him, and the scorching heat of the sun was flaming down from the cloudless, deep blue sky over our head, toasting the side of the poet that was uppermost.

I praised the poem to the skies, though it was vexing me sorely from another point of view — keeping me back from the profitable work that I had promised myself that morning should be done. The poet had put a stop to that with his babbling.

'The poem will be lost,' says he, 'if somebody doesn't pick it up. Have you anything in your pocket that you could write it down with?'

If a man isn't in luck's way in the morning and God's favour with him, the poor wretch can't hope to do much. The hapless Tom didn't cut as much turf as would make two loads for an old ass that day that he planned to do so much. And that was one of the first days that I felt the world going against me, for the fact is, for one day that went well with me, five would go wrong for me from that day out.

It wasn't to oblige the poet that I fished out my pencil and some paper I had in my pocket, but for fear he would turn the rough side of his tongue to me. I set about scribbling down the words as they came out of his mouth. It wasn't in the usual spelling that I wrote them, for I hadn't enough practice in it in those days.

I wasn't too happy then; and no wonder: a man who had a sensible bit of work on hand in the morning, and now it was laid aside for a pointless job! When once he'd opened his mouth, the poet had a jut on his jaw to send his voice out. I scribbled away at the words as best I could after a fashion that kept the poem more or less in my memory, and, besides, if a word should drop out here and there, the guide wasn't far from me, ready and willing to waste a bit of his life explaining it to me, even if the plough-team were waiting for him in the furrow.

When the pair of us had done with one another, the sun was sinking over the hill, and it was as much as Tom could do to keep his wits together by that time. When the poet had left me, the very first thing I did was to go to the tussock at the side of which my dinner was, and the dinner was utterly ruined: a horse couldn't have champed the hunk of yellow bread, and my milk had turned to stone in the bottle!

2. armpit.

MUIRIS Ó SÚILLEABHÁIN (MAURICE O'SULLIVAN)

(1904-50)

from: FICHE BLIAN AG FÁS (Twenty Years A-Growing) (1933)

[Maurice O'Sullivan's grandfather tells him of the poet and chieftain Pierce Ferriter (Piaras Feirtéar +1653). Ferriter, a leader of Irish forces in the war of 1641, was captured and hanged in Killarney in 1653. He became a prominent figure in the folklore of west Kerry. The translation, *Twenty Years A-Growing*, is by Moya Llewelyn Davis and George Thomson and was first published in 1933.]

SCAIRT PHIARAIS

Lá breá gréine i mí Iúil 1912, bhíos féin agus m'athair críonna sínte in airde ar Mhullach an Dúna. Bhí an ghrian ag scoltadh na gcloch le racht brothaill agus an féar dóite go dtí an bpréamh dá dheascaibh. Cím uaim ó dheas Uíbh Ráthach, gach aon tsaghas dathanna breacaithe anso is ansúd ann ag an ngréin, agus as san uaim siar ó dheas bhí na Sceilgí agus scáilghlioscarnach orthu ag an ngréin mar an gcéanna agus an fharraige ina dtimpeall breacaithe ag báid iascaigh ó Shasana. — Nach breá folláin an saol atá acu san, a dhaideo, arsa mise.

Ní bhfuaireas aon fhreagra uaidh. D'iontaíos tharm, agus cad a bheadh ach an seanduine ina shámhchodladh. Lena linn sin do mhachnaíos agus níor labhras focal ach ag féachaint air. Do bhís-se lá fé bhláth na hóige, arsa mise i m'aigne féin, ach mo léan géar, is casta atá an craiceann inniu ar t'éadan agus is liath atá do ghruaig, gan lúth id bhallaibh agus gan spéis agat sa radharc bhreá atá ó mhullach an chnoic seo fé láthair; ach faríor, má mhairim, bead lá mar thú.

Bhí teas thar barr anois ann, agus dá bhrí sin chuimhníos ar é mhúscailt le heagla go maródh an ghrian é. Bheireas ar mheigeall liath air agus bhaineas stothadh as. D'oscail sé a shúile agus d'fhéach ina thimpeall. — Ó a Mhuirisín, ar seisean, thiteas im chodladh, nó an bhfuilim i bhfad ann? — Ní fada a bhís, arsa mise, ach cheapas go mb'fhearr thú dhúiseacht do dheascaibh na gréine. — An-cheart, ar seisean. — An bhfeiceann tú na tráiléirí sin in íor na spéire? arsa mise; is é an rud a bhí agam á rá gur breá folláin an saol atá acu. — Mhuise mo chroí thú, arsa m'athair críonna, ní raibh saol maith riamh ag fear farraige agus ní bheidh go deo, mar is agamsa atá a fhios a chaith mo shaol uirthi, agus tá a oiread contúrthaí fachta agam uirthi agus tá ribí liatha im cheann, agus mise á rá leatsa, pé áit go seolfaidh Dia thú, fan ón bhfarraige. — Mhuise, arsa mise, tuigtear dom ná fuil fear ar domhan comh suáilceach le fear na farraige.

D'fhéachas uaim soir ó dheas ar Chruacha Mhic Giolla Choda a bhí dar liom ag scríobadh na spéire. — Mhuise, nach ard na cnoic iad san soir ó dheas, arsa mise. — Tá siad san ard go maith, ar seisean, dá mbeifeá thíos féna mbun. — Is dócha é, arsa mise, agus lena linn sin tagann beach mhór timpeall ag crónán di féin. Seo le m'athair críonna ag iarraidh í chur uainn lena hata, agus nuair a bhailíonn sí léi, labhrann sé arís. — Níl aon áit fé luí na gréine, arsa m'athair críonna ag síneadh a mhéire i dtreo Chuan Uíbh Ráthaigh, is breátha ná an áit sin. Thógfadh sé mairbh as uaigh, gan aon bhréag, nuair a gheofá isteach ann maidean bhreá shamhraidh. Bheadh Oileán Dairire ar do láimh dheis agus Beiginis ar t'aghaidh isteach. — Is dócha gurb áit an-chiúin é, arsa mise. Ó, leamhach ar fad, ar seisean; tá an góilín sin ag rith trí mhíle suas tríd an dtalamh go dtí an Chathair. Agus an bhfeiceann tú, ar an dtaobh thoir don ngóilín, tá cuan eile le feiscint, sin é Cuan Una; agus soir arís tá Cuas Cromtha, agus soir uaidh sin arís, glaonn siad na Ródanna air. — Féachann an scéal go bhfuil an-eolas agatsa ar na háiteanna san, a dhaideo, arsa mise. — Ó mo léir, ar seisean, is minic a chaitheas smut maith dom shaol ansan.

Lena linn sin, cuireann sé lámh ina phóca ag tarrac a sheandhúid amach agus á deargadh. Éiríonn ina sheasamh. — Téanam anois, ar seisean, agus tabharfaidh mé isteach go dtí Scairt Phiarais Fheirtéar thú, an áit go dtéadh sé i bhfolach nuair a bhíodh saighdiúirí Shasana ar a thóir. — Ó, th'anam 'on diucs, tá an ceart agat, arsa mise.

Seo linn síos Claiseacha an Ghairdín, speatháin mhóra craoibhe ag dul go cluasa orm agus raithneach go leor. — Féach anois, ar seisean ag síneadh a mhéire síos, a bhfeiceann tú an leac san thíos? — Feicim, arsa mise. — Sin í anois, ar seisean, Scairt Phiarais. — Nár mhór an obair dó dul comh fada san síos, arsa mise. — Ó, sin é an áit a bhí uaidh, a bhuachaill, ar seisean, an áit gur féidir leis saighdiúirí Shasana do dhísc. — Conas? arsa mise. — Ná feiceann tú an leac? Díreach ar scéimh na faille atá an dul isteach. Bhíodh sé féin ar an dtaobh istigh agus maide mór aige. Ansan, an chéad saighdiúir a théadh go dtí béal an phoill, ní dhéanfadh Piaras ach sonc don maide a chur ann agus é chaitheamh síos leis an bhfaill. — Nárbh iontach an duine é, arsa mise. — Ó, nár dhein sé léirscrios ar na Sasanaigh an uair úd, ar seisean.

Bhíomair thíos ag an Scairt anois. Isteach le m'athair críonna romhamsa ag lamhncán agus mise ina dhiaidh, mar ní raibh sa doras ag dul isteach ach cúpla troigh. Ansan, nuair a chuamair isteach, bhí neart againn seasamh suas go breá, os cionn seacht dtroithe go maith ar aoirde ann. D'fhéachas timpeall ar an Scairt. — Mhuise, a dhaideo, nach compordach an áit a bhí aige. Ach is dócha, arsa mise arís, ná fágadh sé amach in aon chor é. Ambriathar féin go bhfágadh, nuair a bhíodh na saighdiúirí imithe ón Oileán. — Agus conas a bhíodh a fhios san aige? — Dhera a dhuine, ná bíodh na daoine anso ag friotháil air nuair a dh'fhaighidís an uain chuige? — Ó, is fíor dhuit, arsa mise. — Féach anois an leac san, arsa m'athair críonna, sin í an adhart a bhíodh féna cheann. — Ba chruaidh í, arsa mise. — Níl dabht air, ar seisean. Is dócha nár chualaís riamh an rann a dhein sé oíche, nuair a bhí sé tuirseach don áit seo, agus bhí an oíche chéanna fuar garbh go maith. — Níor chuala riamh mhuis, arsa mise, an mbeadh sí agat? — Tá, ar seisean, ach níl inti ach cúpla focal, ag suí síos ar chloich.

Tógann a hata dá cheann agus cuireann lámh féna smeigín. — Éist go haireach anois, ar seisean:

A Dhia atá thuas, an trua leat mise mar táim,
Im chaonnaí uaigneach nach mór go bhfeicim an lá,
An braon atá thuas in uachtar lice go hard
Ag titeam im chluais agus fuaim na toinne lem sháil.

Agus le linn dó an focal déanach a bheith ráite aige, do thit na frasa deor leis an seanfhear agus do bhuail a cheann fé ar feadh tamaill.

— Mhuise, a dhaideo, arsa mise, nach uaigneach deas an cheathrú é sin, agus rud eile atá sa scéal, is mó fear breá léannta dh'fhág na Sasanaigh ar lár san am chéanna. — Á, Mhuire, is fíor dhuit é, arsa m'athair críonna ag tarrac a sheáilín póca aníos agus ag tiormú a shúl. Deirim leat, a Mhuiris, gur fhuilig Piaras anso é má fhuilig aon fhear bán riamh é. An bhfuil an cheathrú anois agat? ar seisean. — Is dóigh liom go bhfuil, arsa mise, mar chuaigh sí im chroí. Éist liom anois, féach an bhfuil sí ceart agam. — Lean leat, ar seisean.

A Dhia atá thuas, an trua leat mise mar táim,
Im chaonnaí uaigneach nach mór go bhfeicim an lá,
An braon atá thuas in uachtar leice go hard
Ag titeam im chluais agus fuaim na tuinne lem sháil.

— Tá gach focal agat dó, ar seisean. — Nach iontach, arsa mise, mar choimeádfá aon ní id cheann go gcuirfeá spéis ann? — Tá san go han-cheart, ar seisean, mar nuair a bhíos-sa óg ar do chumasa, níl aon rud a chloisinn ag m'athair á rá, beannacht Dé lena anam, ná go bhfuil istigh im cheann fós go daingean. — Tá gan dabht, arsa mise. — Tá mhuis ambriathar, ar seisean ag éirí ina sheasamh. — Tá sé chomh maith againn bheith ag baint an tí amach anois in ainm Dé, ar seisean. — Tá comh maith, arsa mise ag bailiú linn amach.

D'fhéachas féin suas i gcoinne na faille agus as san uaim síos mar a raibh na tonnta ag briseadh go feargach. — Níl aon bhaol, a dhaideo, arsa mise, ná go raibh fuaim na toinne go maith lena shálaibh.

Bhí an ghrian ag maolú siar anois agus í comh buí leis an ór, na héanlaithe ag canadh ceoil ar bharra na gcraobh, coiníní ina gcéadta amuigh ar na rabháin, cuid acu ag rith nuair a chonaiceadar sinne agus a n-eireabaill bheaga bhána cocálta san aer acu, cuid eile acu agus a gcluasa ina seasamh in airde díreach ag breithniú orainn. — Fan anois, arsa m'athair críonna ag lúbadh síos agus ag tógaint cloiche, go bhfeicfidh tú ag scaipeadh iad ar an nóimint. Do chaith sé an chloch ach níor chorraíodar. — Ambriathar ach go bhfuil siad go dána, ar seisean arís. Lena linn sin chuir sé glam as, agus tuigeadh dom féin gur fhreagair cúigear in aonacht é leis an macalla a bhain sé amach as na cuaiseanna féna bhun thíos; agus ansan do chonac na coiníní ag rith ar bhás agus ar dhícheall, a gcluasa scúite siar díreach acu agus a n-eireabaill ina seasamh in airde, agus ar thic an chloig ní raibh le feiscint ach aon cheann amháin a bhí comh liath le broc.

— Nach mór an obair nár chorraigh an ceann liath san, arsa mise. — Ó a bhuachaill, arsa m'athair críonna, sean-shaighdiúir é sin go bhfuil a shaol caite aige agus eolas maith aige ar an nglamaíl sin. — Ní fheadar 'on domhan, a dhaideo, cad é an saol atá ceapaithe dhóibh? — Níl ach trí bliana, ar seisean, agus deirim leat go n-oibríonn siad na trí bliana san comh cruaidh leis an bpeacach chun a mbeatha do thuilleamh.

— Dara fia, táimid sa bhaile, arsa m'athair críonna ñuair a thánamair ar radharc na dtithe, agus deirim leat, a Mhuiris, gur mó coiscéim atá ann aniar ó Scairt Phiarais. — Ach tánn tusa an-mhaith, arsa mise, chun an tslí do chiorrú. — Ambriathar féin, a Mhuirisín, go mbeinn níos fear dá mbeinn suite isteach ar chairt chapaill, ach is deacair le seanfhear bheith ag caint agus ag siúl.

PIERCE'S CAVE

My grandfather and I were lying on the Castle[1] Summit. It was a fine sunny day in July. The sun was splitting the stones with its heat and the grass burnt to the roots. I could see, far away to the south, Iveragh painted in many colours by the sun. South-west were the Skelligs[2] glistening white and the sea around them dotted with fishing-boats from England.

'Isn't it a fine healthy life those fishermen have, daddo?'[3] said I.

I got no answer. Turning round I saw the old man was asleep. I looked at him, thinking. You were one day in the flower of youth, said I in my own mind, but, my sorrow, the skin of your brow is wrinkled now and the hair on your head is grey. You are without suppleness in your limbs and without pleasure in the grand view to be seen from this hill. But, alas, if I live, some day I will be as you are now.

The heat was very great, and so I thought of waking him for fear the sun would kill him. I caught him by his grey beard and gave it a pull. He opened his eyes and looked round.

'Oh, Mirrisheen,'[4] said he, 'I fell asleep. Am I long in it?'

'Not long,' said I, 'but I thought I had better wake you on account of the sun. Do you see those trawlers out on the horizon? I was just saying 'tis a fine healthy life they have.'

'Musha, my heart,' said my grandfather, 'a man of the sea never had a good life and never will, as I know well, having spent my days on it, and I have gone through as many perils on it as there are grey hairs in my head, and I am telling you now, wherever God may guide you, keep away from the sea.'

'Musha, it seems to me there is no man on earth so contented as a seaman.'

I looked south-east to the Macgillicuddy Reeks.[5] They seemed as if they were touching the sky.

'Musha, aren't those high mountains?'

'They are indeed, if you were down at their foot.'

At that moment a big bee came around murmuring to itself. My grandfather started to drive it away with his hat. 'There is no place under the sun is finer than that,' said he, stretching his finger south towards the harbour of Iveragh. 'When you would be entering that harbour you would have the Isle of Oaks[6] on your right hand and Beg-Inish[7] out before your face.'

'I dare say the water is very still there.'

'A dead calm. The creek runs three miles up through the land to Cahirciveen. And do you see, on the east of the creek, there is another harbour? That is Cuan Una. And east again is Cuas Cromha, and east again the place they call the Ródana.'

'It seems you know those places well, daddo.'

'Ah, my sorrow, it is many a day I spent in them.'

He put his hand in his pocket and drew out his pipe. When he had it lighted, he got up. 'Come now and I will take you into Pierce Ferriter's Cave.'

We moved down through the Furrows of the Garden, up to our ears in fern and dry heather.

'Look now,' said he, pointing down, 'do you see that ledge of rock? That's the Cave.'

'Isn't it a great wonder he went down so far?'

'Sure that's the place he wanted, my boy, where

1. A high point on the Great Blasket Island, Co. Kerry.
2. Rocky islands off the Kerry coast.
3. grandfather.
4. Little Maurice.
5. A mountain range in County Kerry.
6. Valentia Island.
7. An island north of Valentia Island.

he could cut down the soldiers of England.'

'How?'

'Don't you see the ledge? The entrance is under the overhanging cliff. He used to be inside with a big stick. Then the first soldier who would come down to the mouth of the cave, Pierce would just give him a thrust with the stick and send him over the cliff.'

'Wasn't he a wonderful man?'

'Oh, he did great destruction on the English at that time.'

We were down at the Cave now. My grandfather crept in on all fours and I behind him, for the entrance was not more than two feet high. Once inside, there was room to stand up, for it was above seven feet. I looked around: 'Musha, isn't it a comfortable place he had, but I dare say he used never to leave it.'

'Indeed he did, whenever the soldiers left the Island.'

'And how would he know that?'

'The people here used to be coming to attend on him whenever they got the chance. Look at that stone. That's where he used to lay his head.'

'It was a hard pillow.'

'No doubt. Did you ever hear the verse he composed here when he was tired of the place, on a wild and stormy night? It is only a couple of words.'

He sat down on the stone and, taking off his hat, he recited:

'O God above, look down on my lonely bed,
Where no light falls from dawn to dusk, and no
Sound but the rain dripping beside my head
On the stony pillow, and the roar of the waves
below.'

As he spoke the last words, the tears fell from the old man.

'Musha, daddo, isn't it a nice lonesome verse? And another thing, it is many the fine learned man the English laid low at that time.'

'Ah, Mary, it is true. I tell you, Maurice, Pierce suffered here if ever a man did. Have you the verse now?' said he.

'I think I have, for it went to my heart.' And I repeated it to him.

'You have every word of it.'

'Isn't it wonderful the way you would keep in your head anything you would take an interest in?'

'That is very true, for when I was young like yourself there is not a word I would hear my father saying, dear God bless his soul, but it would stay in my memory. It is time for us to be making for the house now in the name of God.'

I looked up at the cliff and then down where the waves were breaking angrily. 'There's no doubt, daddo,' said I, 'but he had the roar of the waves below.'

The sun was fading in the west, yellow as gold, the birds singing in the heather, hundreds of rabbits out on the clumps of thrift, some of them, when they saw us, running off with their white tails cocked in the air, others with their ears up looking hard at us.

'Wait now, till you see them scatter in a moment,' said my grandfather, picking up a stone. He threw it, but they did not stir. 'Upon my word but they are bold,' said he and gave a shout, and it seemed five voices answered him with the echo in the coves below. Then I saw the rabbits running, tails up and ears back, and in a moment there was not one to be seen save an old one as grey as a badger.

'Isn't it strange the grey one didn't stir?'

'Ah, my boy, that's an old soldier at the end of his life, and he is well used to that shouting.'

'I wonder what length of life is appointed for them?'

'Only three years, and I assure you they work those three years for a livelihood, as hard as any sinner. But here we are home again,' said he as we came in sight of the village.

'You are very good at shortening the road.'

'Upon my word, Mirrisheen, I would be better still if I were seated up on a horse-cart, for it is hard for an old man to be talking and walking together.'

PATRICK PEARSE

from: SUANTRAIDHE AGUS GOLTRAIDHE (1914)

[The translation by Thomas MacDonagh was published in *Literature in Ireland* (Dublin: The Talbot Press, 1916).]

Fornocht do Chonac Thú

Fornocht do chonac thú,
a áille na háille,
is do dhallas mo shúil
ar eagla go stánfainn.

Do chualas do cheol,
a bhinne na binne,
is do dhúnas mo chluas
ar eagla go gclisfinn.

Do bhlaiseas do bhéal
a mhilse na milse,
is do chruas mo chroí
ar eagla mo mhillte.

Do dhallas mo shúil,
is mo chluas do dhúnas;
do chruas mo chroí,
is mo mhian do mhúchas.

Do thugas mo chúl
ar an aisling do chumas,
is ar an ród so romham
m'aghaidh do thugas.

Do thugas mo ghnúis
ar an ród so romham,
ar an ngníomh do-chím,
is ar an mbás do gheobhad.

Ideal

Naked I saw thee,
O beauty of beauty!
And I blinded my eyes
For fear I should flinch.

I heard thy music,
O melody of melody!
And I shut my ears
For fear I should fail.

I kissed thy lips,
O sweetness of sweetness!
And I hardened my heart
For fear of my ruin.

I blinded my eyes,
And my ears I shut,
I hardened my heart
And my love I quenched.

I turned my back
On the dream I had shaped,
And to this road before me
My face I turned.

I set my face
To the road here before me,
To the work that I see,
To the death that I shall get.

MÁIRTÍN Ó DIREÁIN

(1910-88)

from:
DÁNTA 1939-1979 (1980)

[The translations of these poems of Ó Direáin are from Douglas Sealy, Tomás Mac Síomóin, *Máirtín Ó Direáin: Selected Poems/Tacar Dánta* (Newbridge: Goldsmith Press, 1984).]

Dínit an Bhróin

Nochtaíodh domsa tráth
Dínit mhór an bhróin,
Ar fheiceáil dom beirt bhan
Ag siúl amach ó shlua
I bhfeisteas caointe dubh
Gan focal astu beirt:
D'imigh an dínit leo
Ón slua callánach mór.

Bhí freastalán istigh
Ó línéar ar an ród,
Fuadar faoi gach n-aon,
Gleo ann is caint ard;
Ach an bheirt a bhí ina dtost,
A shiúil amach leo féin
I bhfeisteas caointe dubh,
D'imigh an dínit leo.

Grief's Dignity

I once had a glimpse
Of grief's great dignity
When I saw two women
Emerge from a crowd
In dark funereal garb
Neither uttering a word:
Dignity departed with them
From the large and noisy crowd.

A tender was in
From a liner in the roadstead,
Everyone was scurrying around,
Hubbub and loud chatter;
But the silent couple
Who emerged on their own
In dark funereal garb
Dignity departed with them.

Cuimhní Cinn

Maireann a gcuimhne fós i m'aigne:
Báiníní bána is léinte geala,
Léinte gorma is veistí glasa,
Treabhsair is dráir de bhréidín baile
Bhíodh ar fheara cásacha aosta
Ag triall ar an Aifreann maidin Domhnaigh
De shiúl cos ar aistear fhada,
A mhúsclaíodh i m'óige smaointe ionamsa
Ar ghlaine, ar úire, is fós ar bheannaíocht.

Maireann a gcuimhne fós i m'aigne:
Cótaí cóirithe fada dearga,
Cótaí gorma le plúirín daite,
Seálta troma aníos as Gaillimh,
Bhíodh ar mhná pioctha néata
Ag triall ar an Aifreann mar an gcéanna;
Is cé go bhfuilid ag imeacht as faisean,
Maireann a gcuimhne fós i m'aigne
Is mairfidh cinnte go dté mé i dtalamh.

Memories

Their memory lives on in my mind:
White bawneen[1] coats and gleaming shirts,
Blue shirts and grey waistcoats,
Trousers and drawers of homespun tweed
That old and honoured men used to wear
As they went to Mass on Sunday morning
Making the long journey by foot,
When I was young they turned my thoughts
To purity, freshness, and also to piety.

Their memory lives on in my mind:
Long stately skirts coloured crimson,
Blue skirts that were dyed with indigo,
Heavy shawls down from Galway,
That neat and well-dressed women used to wear
As they went to Mass in the selfsame manner;
And though they're rapidly going out of fashion
Their memory lives on in my mind
And will still live on till I go to the graveyard.

1. White homespun cloth.

Rún na mBan

Tráthnóna Domhnaigh ab ionduala
Ansiúd iad cois tine,
Na mná agus na seálta
Casta ar a gcloigne,
Bhíodh tae ann i gcónaí
Ar ócáid den chineál,
Is braon ag dul thart de
Ó dhuine go duine.

Thosaíodh an chaint
An broideadh is an sioscadh,
Uille ar ghlúin ag cur leis na focla;
D'ordaítí mise amach ar na bóithre,
Gan a bheith istigh ag slogadh gach focail,
Go mba folláine amuigh mé
Ar nós mo leithéid eile.

D'imínn sa deireadh,
M'aghaidh lasta is mé gonta
Ach is mairg nach bhfanainn:
Nuair a smaoiním anois air
Cá bhfios cén rúndiamhair
Nach eol d'aon fhear beirthe
A phiocfainn ó mhná
Scartha thart ar thine,
Iad ag ól tae
Is seálta ar a gcloigne?

The Women's Secret

Nearly every Sunday evening
There they were by the fire,
The women with their shawls
Wrapped about their heads.
There was always tea
On such occasions,
And they passed a sup around
From one to another.

The talk started,
The nudge and the whisper,
Elbow on knee emphasizing the words;
I used to be ordered out on the roads,
Not to be inside wolfing each word,
I'd be healthier out in the air
Like the rest of the lads.

I left in the end,
Blushing and hurt
But I wish I had stayed:
When I think of it now
Who knows what secret lore
Unknown to any man alive
I'd have snatched from the women
Ranged round a fire,
Drinking tea
With their shawls on their heads?

An tEarrach Thiar

Fear ag glanadh cré
De ghimseán spáide
Sa gciúnas séimh
I mbrothall lae:
  Binn an fhuaim
  San Earrach thiar.

Fear ag caitheamh
Cliabh dá dhroim,
Is an fheamainn dhearg
Ag lonrú
I dtaitneamh gréine
Ar dhuirling bhán:
  Niamhrach an radharc
  San Earrach thiar.

Mná i locháin
In íochtar díthrá,
A gcótaí craptha,
Scáilí thíos fúthu:
  Támhradharc sítheach
  San Earrach thiar.

Tollbhuillí fanna
Ag maidí rámha,
Currach lán éisc
Ag teacht chun cladaigh
Ar órmhuir mhall
I ndeireadh lae:
  San Earrach thiar.

Spring in the West

A man scraping clay
From the tread of a spade
In the serene calm
On a warm day:
  The sound is sweet
  During Spring in the west.

A man throwing
A creel[1] off his back,
And the red seaweed
Glittering
In the sunshine
On a white stone beach:
    A vivid sight
    During Spring in the west.

Women in the shallows
At furthest ebb
With their skirts tucked up
And reflections beneath them:
    A tranquil sight
    During Spring in the west.

Faint hollow strokes
Of oars,
A currach[2] full of fish
Approaching the shore
On a slow gold sea
At day's end:
    During Spring in the west.

1. A basket for carrying turf or seaweed.
2. A canvas-bottomed boat.

Árainn 1947

Feadaíl san oíche
Mar dhion ar uaigneas,
Mar fhál idir croí is aigne
Ar bhuairt seal,
Ag giorrú an bhealaigh
Abhaile ó chuartaíocht,
An tráth seo thiar
    Níor chualas.

Amhrán aerach,
Scaradh oíche is lae,
Ó ghroífhear súgach,
gaisce ard is goití dúshláin
Is gach uaill mhaíte
Ag scoilteadh clár an chiúnais,
Tráth a mbíodh gníomha gaile a shinsear
Á n-aithris do dhúile an uaignis,
An tráth seo thiar
    Níor chualas.

Liú áthais ná aitis
Ó chroí na hóige
Ag caitheamh 'cloch neart'
Mar ba dhual tráthnóna Domhnaigh,
Nó ag cur liathróid san aer
Le fuinneamh an bhuailte,
An tráth seo thiar
    Níor chualas.

Ní don óige feasta
An sceirdoileán cúng úd.

Aran 1947

Whistling at night
As a defence against the eeriness,
A barrier between heart and brain
In a time of disquiet,
Shortening the road
Home from late visiting,
This time in the West
    I heard not.

A lively song,
When day left night behind,
From a tipsy stalwart,
Loud boasts and defiant gestures
And many an arrogant yell
Splitting the length of the silence
While the brave deeds of their forefathers
Were named to the spirits of solitude,
This time in the West
    I heard not.

A shout of joy or pleasure
From the heart of the young
As they tossed the great stone,
Their Sunday evening custom,
Or shot a ball in the air
With force behind the stroke,
This time in the West
    I heard not.

Not for the young any more,
That narrow windswept island.

Stoite

Ár n-aithreacha bhíodh,
Is a n-aithreacha siúd,
In achrann leis an saol
Ag coraíocht leis an gcarraig loim.

Aiteas orthu bhíodh
Tráth ab eol dóibh
Féile chaoin na húire,
Is díocas orthu bhíodh
Ag baint ceart
De neart na ndúl.

Thóg an fear seo teach
Is an fear úd
Claí nó fál
A mhair ina dhiaidh
Is a choinnigh a chuimhne buan.

Sinne a gclann,
Is clann a gclainne,
Dúinn is éigean
Cónaí a dhéanamh
In árais ó dhaoine
A leagfadh cíos
Ar an mbraon anuas.

Beidh cuimhne orainn go fóill:
Beidh carnán trodán
Faoi ualach deannaigh
Inár ndiaidh in Oifig Stáit.

Uprooted

Our fathers
And their fathers before them
Were at grips with life
And wrestled with the naked rock.

They were happy
When the seasons revealed to them
Earth's kindly abundance
And they were eager
To hold their own
Against the force of the elements.

One man built a house
And another
A dyke or a wall
Which outlived him
And kept his name alive.

We, their children,
And their children's children,
Are compelled
To make our homes
In apartments whose owners
Would levy rent
On the drip from the ceiling.

We will be remembered yet:
A stack of files
Weighed down with dust
Will survive in a government office.

Ó Mórna

A ródaí fáin as tír isteach
A dhearcann tuama thuas ar aill,
A dhearcann armas is mana,
A dhearcann scríbhinn is leac,
Ná fág an reilig cois cuain
Gan tuairisc an fhir a bheith leat.

Cathal Mór Mac Rónáin an fear,
Mhic Choinn Mhic Chonáin Uí Mhórna,
Ná bí i dtaobh le comhrá cáich,
Ná le fíor na croise á ghearradh
Ar bhaithis chaillí mar theist an fhir
A chuaigh in uaigh sa gcill sin.

Ná daor an marbh d'éis cogar
  ban,
D'éis lide a thit idir uille
Is glúin ar theallach na sean,
Gan a phór is a chró do mheas,
A chéim, a réim, an t-am do mhair,
Is guais a shóirt ar an uaigneas.

Meas fós dúchas an mhairbh féin
D'eascair ó Mhórna mór na n-éacht,
Meabhraigh a gcuala, a bhfaca sé,
Ar a chuairt nuair a d'éist go géar,
Meabhraigh fós nár ceileadh duais air,
Ach gur ghabh chuige gach ní de cheart.

Chonaic níochán is ramhrú dá éis,
Chonaic mná ag úradh bréidín,
Gach cos nocht ó ghlúin go sáil
Ina slis ag tuargain an éadaigh,
Bean ar aghaidh mná eile thall
Ina suí suas san umar bréige.

Chonaic is bhreathnaigh gach slis ghléigeal,
Chonaic na hógmhná dá fhéachaint
Dá mheas, dá mheá, dá chrá in éineacht,
D'fhreagair fuil an fhireannaigh thréitheach,

Shiúil sí a chorp, las a éadan,
Bhrostaigh é go mear chun éilimh.

'Teann isteach leo mar a dhéanfadh fear,
Geallaimse dhuit go dteannfar leat,
Feasach iad cheana ar aon nós,
Nach cadar falamh gan géim tú,
Ach fear ded' chéim, ded' réim cheart.'
Pádhraicín báille a chan an méid sin.
Briolla gan rath! mairg a ghéill dó.

Iar ndul in éag don triath ceart
Rónán Mac Choinn Mhic Chonáin,
Ghabh Cathal chuige a chleacht,
A thriúcha is a chumhachta,
A mhaoir, a bháillí go dleathach,
A theideal do ghabh, is a ghlac.

An t-eolas a fuair sna botháin
Nuair a thaithigh iad roimh theacht i seilbh,
Mheabhraigh gach blúire riamh de,
Choigil is choinnigh é go beacht,
Chuaigh chun tairbhe dó ina dhiaidh sin
Nuair a leag ar na daoine a reacht.

Mheabhraigh sé an té bhí uallach,
Nach ngéillfeadh go réidh dá bheart,
Mheabhraigh sé an té bhí cachtúil,
An té shléachtfadh dó go ceart,
Mheabhraigh fós gach duais inionda
Dár shantaigh a mhian ainsrianta.

Mhair ár dtriath ag cian dá thuargain,
Ba fánach é ar oileán uaigneach,
Cara cáis thar achar mara
B'annamh a thagadh dá fhuascailt,
Is théadh ag fiach ar na craga
Ag tnúth le foras is fuaradh.

Comhairlíodh dó an pósadh a dhéanamh
Le bean a bhéarfadh dó mar oidhre
Fireannach dlisteanach céimeach
Ar phór Uí Mhórna na haibhse,
Seach bheith dá lua le Nuala an Leanna,
Peig na hAirde is Cáit an Ghleanna.

An bhean nuair a fuair Ó Mórna í
Níor rug aon mhac, aon oidhre ceart;
Níor luigh Ó Mórna léi ach seal,
Ba fuar leis í mar nuachair;
Ina cuilt shuain ní bhfuair a cheart,
É pósta is céasta go beacht.

Imionn Ó Mórna arís le fuadar,
Thar chríocha dleathacha ag ruathradh,
Ag cartadh báin, ag cartadh loirg,
Ag treabhadh faoi dheabhadh le fórsa,
Ag réabadh comhlan na hóghachta,
Ag dul thar teorainn an phósta.

Ag réabadh móide is focail
Ag réabadh aithne is mionna,
A shúil thar a chuid gan chuibheas,
Ag éisteacht cogar na tola
A mhéadaigh fothram na fola,
Ina rabharta borb gan foras.

Ceasach mar mheasadh den chré lábúrtha
Leanadh Ó Mórna cleacht a dhúchais,
Thógadh paor thar chríocha aithnid,
Go críocha méithe, go críocha fairsing,
Dhéanadh lá saoire don subhachas
Dhéanadh lá saoire don rúpacht.

Maoir is báillí dó ag fónamh
Ag riaradh a thriúcha thar a cheann,
Ag comhalladh a gcumhachta níor shéimh,
Ag agairt danaide ar a lán,
An t-úll go léir acu dóibh féin
Is an cadhal ag gach truán.

Sloinnte na maor a bheirim díbh,
Wiggins, Robinson, Thomson, agus Ede,
Ceathrar cluanach nár choigil an mhísc,
A thóg an cíos, a dhíbir daoine,
A chuir an dílleacht as cró ar fán,
A d'fhág na táinte gan talamh gan trá.

Níor thúisce Ó Mórna ar ais
Ar an talamh dúchais tamall
Ná chleacht go mear gach beart
Dár tharraing míchlú cheana air:
Threabhadh arís an chré lábúrtha,
Bheireadh dúshlán cléir is tuata.

Tháinig lá ar mhuin a chapaill
Ar meisce faoi ualach óil,
Stad in aice trá Chill Cholmáin
Gur scaip ladhar den ór le spórt,
Truáin ag sciobadh gach sabhrain
Dár scaoil an triath ina dtreo.

Do gháir Ó Mórna is do bhéic,
Mairbh a fhualais sa reilig thuas
Ní foláir nó chuala an bhéic;
Dhearbhaigh fós le draothadh aithise
Go gcuirfeadh sabhran gan mhairg
In aghaidh gach míol ina n-ascaill.

Labhair an sagart air Dé Domhnaigh,
Bhagair is d'agair na cumhachta,
D'agair réabadh na hóghachta air,
Scannal a thréada d'agair le fórsa,
Ach ghluais Ó Mórna ina chóiste
De shodar sotail thar cill.

D'agair gach aon a dhíth is a fhoghail air,
D'agair an ógbhean díth a hóghachta air,
D'agair an mháthair fán a háil air,
D'agair an t-athair talamh is trá air,
D'agair an t-ógfhear éigean a ghrá air,
D'agair an fear éigean a mhná air.

Bhí gach lá ag tabhairt a lae leis,
Gach bliain ag tabhairt a leithéid féin léi,
Ó Mórna ag tarraingt chun boilg chun léithe
Chun cantail is seirbhe trína mheisce,
Ag roinnt an tsotail ar na maoir
Ach an chruimh ina chom níor chloígh.

Nuair a rug na blianta ar Ó Mórna,
Tháinig na pianta ar áit na mianta:
Luigh sé seal i dteach Chill Cholmáin,
Teach a shean i lár na coille,
Teach nár scairt na grásta air,
Teach go mb'annamh gáire ann.

Trí fichid do bhí is bliain le cois,
Nuair a cuireadh síos é i gCill na Manach
D'éis ola aithrí, paidir is Aifreann;
I measc a shean i gCill na Manach
I dteannta líon a fhualais,
Ar an tuama armas is mana.

An chruimh a chreim istigh san uaigh tú,
A Uí Mhórna mhóir, a thriath Chill Cholmáin,
Níorbh í cruimh do chumais ná cruimh d'uabhair
Ach cruimh gur cuma léi íseal ná uasal.
Go mba sámh do shuan sa tuama anocht
A Chathail Mhic Rónáin Mhic Choinn.

Ó Mórna[1]

Traveller straying in from the mainland,
You who gaze at a tomb on a cliff-top,
Who gaze at a coat of arms and a slogan,
Who gaze at inscription and flagstone,
Do not leave the graveyard by the bay
Before you know the dead man's story.

The man was Cathal Mór the son of Rónán,
Son of Conn son of Conán Ó Mórna,
But don't rely on common hearsay
Nor crone signing the cross on her forehead
To give you a true report of the man
Who entered the grave in that churchyard.

Don't condemn the dead man because of women's
 whispers
Following a hint let fall between elbow
And knee by the old people's hearth,
Before you consider his blood and lineage,
His station, his power, the age he lived in,
And the snares that loneliness sets for his sort.

Consider also the dead man's heredity,
How he sprang from the line of great Ó Mórna,
Think of all he heard, all he saw,
As he went around he listened intently,
Remember also no prize was denied him
But all that he took was taken by right.

He saw the washing and then the thickening,
Saw the women scouring frieze,
Each naked leg from knee to heel
Like a wash-staff pounding the cloth,
Woman sitting opposite woman
Along the sides of the makeshift trough,

Saw and noted each white wash-staff,
Saw the young women gazing at him,
Sizing him up and tantalizing him.
The blood of the robust male responded,
Traversed his body, suffused his face
And urged him on to swift demand.

1. The name Ó Morna derives from Goll Mac Morna, a legendary warrior of early Irish literature. Ó Direáin uses it here to conceal the real subject of his poem, James O'Flaherty, a land-steward who imposed a notorious tyranny on the people of Aran in the mid-19th century.

'Press in there close to them like a man,
I warrant you'll feel an answering pressure,
Sure they know already
You're no empty spunkless cod
But a man of your rank and direct ancestry.'
Pádhraicín the bailiff spoke those words.
A worthless rascal! You should have ignored him.

After the death of the titular lord,
Ronán the son of Conn the son of Conán,
The young Cathal took over his prerogative,
His lands and his jurisdictions,
His stewards and bailiffs as the law appointed,
He took his title and his power.

The knowledge gained in the cabins
Frequented before his accession,
He'd remembered every least bit of it,
Saved it up and treasured each detail;
He used it later for his own advantage
When he laid his law on the people.

He thought of the one who'd been stiffnecked,
Who wouldn't readily comply with his schemes,
He thought of the one who'd been obsequious,
The one who'd truly grovel before him,
He thought long of each virginal prize
For which he hankered with unbridled passion.

Our chief lived prey to melancholy's assaults,
Odd man out on a remote island,
An understanding friend from across the sound
Seldom came to his rescue
And he hunted on across the crags
Yearning for ease and alleviation.

He was advised to take in marriage
A woman who would bear him as heir
A legitimate and noble male-child
To continue the line of mighty Ó Mórna,
Instead of consorting with Alehouse Nuala,
Peg of Ard and Kate of Glen.

The wife, after Ó Mórna found her,
Bore him no son, no proper heir;
Ó Mórna lay with her only a while,
His newfound bride made a frigid mate;
In her drowsy bed his right was denied,
His marriage was nothing but torture.

Ó Mórna departs once more in haste,
Rampaging beyond the legal limits,
Digging the fallow land, digging the furrowed,
Ploughing with headlong violence,
Forcing the gate of virginity,
Crossing the bounds of marriage.

Breaking pledge and word,
Breaking commandment and vow,
Prompted by his greed's excess,
Listening to the whisper of desire
Increasing the clamour of his blood
In its rich and restless springtide.

Sated, they said, of base-born flesh,
Ó Mórna followed the ways of his forebears,
Used to take jaunts from known domains
To lush domains, to vast domains,
Abandoning all for the sake of pleasure,
Abandoning all for the harlot's embrace.

Stewards and bailiffs were at his disposal,
Administering his territories on his behalf,
Cruelly carrying out his instructions,
Causing grievous loss to many;
They had the whole of the apple to themselves,
Each starveling had the peel.

I give you the names of the stewards,
Wiggins, Robinson, Thomson and Edge,
Four crafty men who shunned no evil,
Who collected rents, who evicted tenants,
Who drove the orphan away from his hovel,
Who left hundreds without field or strand.

No sooner had Ó Mórna been back
On his native ground for a while
Than he quickly got up to the same tricks
Which had already gained him disrepute;
He ploughed again the base-born flesh
In open defiance of priest and layman.

One day he came on horseback,
Laden to the gills with drink,
Stopped beside the strand of Kilcolman
To scatter a handful of gold for sport;
The starvelings snatched at each sovereign
The lord tossed at their feet.

Ó Mórna roared and gave a shout,
The dead of his kin in the graveyard above

Must have heard that shout;
He declared as well with a sneer of contempt
That he could easily put up a sovereign
To match each louse in their arm-pits.

The priest named him on Sunday,
Threatened to use the powers against him,
Denounced him for profaning virginity,
Vehemently denounced the scandal to his flock,
But Ó Mórna set off in his coach
At an arrogant trot past the church.

Denounced by all for raiding and rapine,
Denounced by the girl for taking her maidenhead,
Denounced by the mother for her family scattered,
Denounced by the father for field and strand,
Denounced by the youth for raping his sweetheart,
Denounced by the husband for raping his wife.

Each day that passed meant one day less,
Each year that passed meant another gone,
Ó Mórna was falling to flesh and greyness,
More sour and petulant in his drunken bouts,
Venting his spleen on the stewards
But the worm in his flesh he could not defeat.

When the years caught up with Ó Mórna
The aches of desire were replaced by pain,
He lay for a while in the house of Kilcolman,
His ancestral house in the heart of the wood,
A house that grace had never shone on,
A house where laughter seldom sounded.

Threescore he was and a year besides
When he was buried in Cill na Manach
After Unction, Penance, prayer and Mass:
Among his ancestors in Cill na Manach
Along with the tally of his kin,
On the tomb a coat of arms and a slogan.

The worm that gnawed you in the grave,
Great Ó Mórna, lord of Kilcolman,
Was not the worm of your vigour nor of your hauteur
But a worm that heeds not birth nor blood.
Calm be your slumber in the tomb tonight,
Cathal, son of Ronán son of Conn.

Ómós do John Millington Synge

An toisc a thug tú chun mo dhaoine
Ón gcéin mhéith don charraig gharbh
Ba chéile léi an chré bheo
Is an leid a scéith as léan is danaid.

Níor éistis scéal na gcloch,
Bhí éacht i scéal an teallaigh,
Níor spéis leat leac ná cill,
Ní thig éamh as an gcré mharbh.

Do dhuinigh Deirdre romhat sa ród
Is curach Naoise do chas Ceann Gainimh,
D'imigh Deirdre is Naoise leo
Is chaith Peigín le Seáinín aithis.

An leabhar ba ghnáth i do dhóid
As ar chuiris bréithre ar marthain;
Ghabh Deirdre, Naoise is Peigín cló
Is thug léim ghaisce de na leathanaigh.

Tá cleacht mo dhaoine ag meath,
Ní cabhair feasta an tonn mar fhalla,
Ach go dtaga Coill Chuain go hInis Meáin
Beidh na bréithre a chnuasaís tráth
Ar marthain fós i dteanga eachtrann.

Homage to John Millington Synge

The impulse that brought you to my people
From the distant pasture to the harsh rock
Was partnered by the living clay
And the intimations of loss and sorrow.

You didn't listen to the tale of the stones,
Greatness lived in the tale of the hearth,
You paid no heed to tombstone or graveyard,
No whimper escapes the lifeless dust.

Deirdre[1] appeared before you on the road
And Naoise's currach weathered Ceann Gainimh;[2]
Deirdre and Naoise went to their death
And Pegeen flung abuse at Shawneen.[3]

The book was always in your hand —
You brought the words in it to life;
Deirdre, Naoise and Pegeen took form
And leaped like heroes from the pages.

1. Deirdre and Naoise are legendary lovers of early Irish literature.
2. Pronounced 'k'awn gon uv', a sandy headland on Inishmaan (Inis Meáin), one of the Aran Islands.
3. Pegeen and Shawneen are characters in Synge's 'The Playboy of the Western World'.

The ways of my people decay.
The sea no longer serves as a wall.
But till Coill Chuain[4] comes to Inis Meáin
The words you gathered then
Will live on in an alien tongue.

4. In Scotland where Deirdre eloped with Naoise. Since Coill Chuain (pron. Kyle Coon) can never move to the Aran Islands, the line suggests that Synge's writings will survive forever.

Leigheas na hEagla

An cuimhin libhse an malrach
A ghoin sibh go deacrach,
Tráth ar chuir sibh thart scéal
Is nath ó duine go duine
Is m'athair ag fanacht
Lena chónra chláir uaibh?

Murar cuimhin fós, a fheara,
Ní thógaim oraibh feasta é,
Is gur fadó a dáileadh
Libh féin an chré dhubh,
Is go dtuigim le sealad
Nach bhfuil leigheas ar an eagla
Ach scéal, is nath, is gáire.

Salve for Fear

Do you remember the youth
You wounded to the quick
When you passed tale
And quip from man to man
And my father waiting
For his coffin from your hands?

Even if you don't remember, men,
I no longer blame you
For long ago you were committed
To the dark earth
And I have known for some time now
That the only salve for fear
Is story, quip and laughter.

Cranna Foirtil

Coinnigh do thalamh a anam liom,
Coigil chugat gach tamhanrud,
Is ná bí mar ghiolla gan chaithir
I ndiaidh na gcarad nár fhóin duit.

Minic a dhearcais ladhrán trá
Ar charraig fhliuch go huaigneach;
Mura bhfuair éadáil ón toinn
Ní bhfuair guth ina héagmais.

Níor thugais ó do ríocht dhorcha
Caipín an tsonais ar do cheann,
Ach cuireadh cranna cosanta
Go teann thar do chliabhán cláir.

Cranna caillte a cuireadh tharat;
Tlú iarainn os do chionn,
Ball éadaigh d'athar taobh leat
Is bior sa tine thíos.

Luigh ar do chranna foirtil
I gcoinne mallmhuir is díthrá,
Coigil aithinne d'aislinge,
Scaradh léi is éag duit.

Stout Oars

Stand your ground, my soul;
Cleave to every rooted stock;
Don't behave like a callow youth
When your false friends depart.

You've often seen a redshank
Alone on a wet rock;
Though he drew no wealth from the wave
His lapse incurred no censure.

From your dark realm you brought
No lucky caul around your head
But the ritual wands were placed
To protect you in your cradle.

Useless sticks were placed around you;
An iron tongs above,
Beside you a piece of your father's clothing,
A poker placed in the fire.

Lean on your own stout oars
Against neap-tide and ebb,
Keep alight the coal of your vision;
To part with that is death.

Mar Chaitheamar an Choinneal

Cheapamar tráth go mbeadh an lá linn
An bua ar fáil, an t-athaoibhneas ag teacht,

Is chaitheamar an choinneal de ráig
Ag fónamh dár gcleacht;
Ní náir linn os comhair cáich
Ár gcloichín ar charn na sean,
Cé gur eagal linn le seal
Go bhfuilimid ag cur gainimh i ngad,
Murar i gCionn tSáile an léin
A cuireadh ár gcleacht ó rath,
Arbh iad na cinnirí críonna
Nó cléirigh an tréis a d'fheall?
Ach mar chuaigh an choinneal go dtí seo,
Téadh an t-orlach ina bhfuil romhainn amach.

How We Wasted the Candle

Once we thought the day would be ours,
The victory gained, the old joy returning,
And we burned the candle prodigally
In the service of our cause.
We are not ashamed before any one
Of our pebble on the ancestral cairn,
Though I fear that of late
Our rope binds only sand;
If it was not in Kinsale of the sorrow
That our civilisation was ruined,[1]
Was it the cautious leaders
Or the treacherous clerks that reneged?
But as the candle has wasted till now
Let the last inch waste in the time to come.

1. The battle of Kinsale (1601) marked the end of the old Gaelic order.

SEÁN Ó RÍORDÁIN

(1916-77)

from: EIREABALL SPIDEOIGE (1952) and BROSNA (1964)

[The translations are by Seán Dunn and appear in *Poets of Munster* (Dingle, Co. Kerry: Brandon Press, 1985).]

Adhlacadh Mo Mháthar

Grian an Mheithimh in úllghort,
  Is siosarnach i síoda an tráthnóna,
Beach mhallaithe ag portaireacht
  Mar screadstracadh ar an nóinbhrat.

Seanalitir shalaithe á léamh agam,
  Le gach focaldeoch dar ólas
Pian bhinibeach ag dealgadh mo chléibhse,
  Do bhrúigh amach gach focal díobh a dheoir féin.

Do chuimhníos ar an láimh a dhein an scríbhinn,
  Lámh a bhí inaitheanta mar aghaidh,
Lámh a thál riamh cneastacht seana-Bhíobla,
  Lámh a bhí mar bhalsam is tú tinn.

Agus thit an Meitheamh siar isteach sa Gheimhreadh,
  Den úllghort deineadh reilig bhán cois abhann,
Is i lár na balbh-bháine i mo thimpeall
  Do liúigh os ard sa tsneachta an dúpholl.

Gile gearrachaile lá a céad chomaoine,
  Gile abhlainne Dé Domhnaigh ar altóir,
Gile bainne ag sreangtheitheadh as na cíochaibh,
  Nuair a chuireadar mo mháthair, gile an fhóid.

Bhí m'aigne á sciúirseadh féin ag iarraidh
  An t-adhlacadh a bhlaiseadh go hiomlán,
Nuair a d'eitil tríd an gciúnas bán go míonla
  Spideog a bhí gan mhearbhall gan scáth:

Agus d'fhan os cionn na huaighe fé mar go mb'eol di
  Go raibh an toisc a thug í ceilte ar chách
Ach an té a bhí ag feitheamh ins an gcomhrainn,
  Is do rinneas éad fén gcaidreamh neamhghnách.

Do thuirling aer na bhFlaitheas ar an uaigh sin,
  Bhí meidhir uafásach naofa ar an éan,
Bhíos deighilte amach ón diamhairghnó im thuata,
  Is an uaigh sin os mo chomhair in imigéin.

Le cumhracht bróin do folcadh m'anam drúiseach,
  Thit sneachta geanmnaíochta ar mo chroí,
Anois adhlacfad sa chroí a deineadh ionraic
  Cuimhne na mná a d'iompair mé trí ráithe
    ina broinn.

Tháinig na scológa le borbthorann sluasad,
  Is do scuabadar le fuinneamh an chré isteach
    san uaigh,
D'fhéachas-sa treo eile, bhí comharsa ag glanadh a
    ghlúine,
  D'fhéachas ar an sagart is bhí saoltacht ina ghnúis.

Grian an Mheithimh in úllghort,
  Is siosarnach i síoda an tráthnóna,
Beach mhallaithe ag portaireacht
  Mar screadstracadh ar an nóinbhrat.

Ranna beaga bacacha á scríobh agam,
  Ba mhaith liom breith ar eireaball spideoige,
Ba mhaith liom sprid lucht glanta glún a dhíbirt,
  Ba mhaith liom triall go deireadh an lae go brónach.

My Mother's Burial

June sun in an orchard, a rustle in the silk of evening, an ill-tempered bee droning like a scream renting the evening-cloth.

Reading an old soiled letter, and with every word-drink I sip, a sharp pain pierces my side, each word pressing out its own tear.

I remembered the hand that made the writing, a hand distinguishable as a face, a hand which bestowed old Bible kindness, a hand that was balsam when you were ill.

And June fell back into winter, the orchard became a white cemetery by a river and in the middle of the dumb whiteness around me the black hole shouted out loud in the snow.

The brightness of a young girl on her first communion day, the brightness of the host on a Sunday altar, the brightness of milk squirting, escaping from the paps. When they buried my mother, brightness of the sod.

My mind was scourging itself trying to fully taste the burial, when, gently through the white silence, a robin flew without confusion or fear.

And she stayed above the grave as if she knew the reason that brought her was hidden from all but the person waiting in the coffin, and I was jealous of the extraordinary intimacy.

The air of Heaven descended on that grave, there was a terrible saintly gaiety about the bird. A layman, I was kept apart from the mysterious business; the grave before me in the distance.

My lustful soul was bathed with the fragrance of sorrow, a snow of chastity fell on my heart. Now I will bury in the heart made upright the memory of the woman who carried me nine months in her womb.

The gravediggers came with the violent noise of shovels and they vigorously swept the earth into the grave. I looked the other way, a neighbour was wiping his knee. I looked at the priest, there was worldliness in his face.

June sun in an orchard, a rustle in the silk of evening, an ill-tempered bee droning like a scream renting the evening-cloth.

I'm writing small halting verses, I'd like to catch hold of a robin's tail, I'd like to banish the spirit of knee-wipers. I'd like to journey sadly to the end of day.

Cúl an Tí

Tá Tír na nÓg ar chúl an tí,
  Tír álainn trína chéile,
Lucht ceithre chos ag siúl na slí
  Gan bróga orthu ná léine,
  Gan Béarla acu ná Gaeilge.

Ach fásann clóca ar gach droim
  Sa tír seo trína chéile,
Is labhartar teanga ar chúl an tí
  Nár thuig aon fhear ach Aesop,
  Is tá sé siúd sa chré anois.

Tá cearca ann is ál sicín,
  Is lacha righin mhothaolach,
Is gadhar mór dubh mar namhaid sa tír
  Ag drannadh le gach éinne,
  Is cat ag crú na gréine.

Sa chúinne thiar tá banc dramhaíl'
  Is iontaisí an tsaoil ann,
Coinnleoir, búclaí, seanhata tuí,
  Is trúmpa balbh néata,
  Is citeal bán mar ghé ann.

Is ann a thagann tincéirí
  Go naofa, trína chéile,
Tá gaol acu le cúl an tí,
  Is bíd ag iarraidh déirce
  Ar chúl gach tí in Éirinn.

Ba mhaith liom bheith ar chúl an tí
Sa doircheacht go déanach
Go bhfeicinn ann ar chuairt gealaí
An t-ollaimhín sin Aesop
Is é ina phúca léannta.

Behind the House

The Land of Youth's behind the house, a beautiful mixed-up land, four-footed ones walking the way without shoe or shirt, without English or Irish.

But in this higgledy-piggledy land a cloak grows on every back, and a language is spoken behind the house that no one understood but Aesop,[1] and he is under the clay now.

There are hens there and a clutch of chickens; a steady clueless duck and a big black hound like an enemy in the land snarling at everyone, and a cat milking the sun.

In the far corner there's a rubbish heap with the wonders of the world there: candlesticks, buckles, an old straw hat; a neat dumb Jew's harp and a white kettle like a goose there.

It's there tinkers come, saintly, pell-mell. They are related to the back of the house and they beg behind every house in Ireland.

I'd like to be behind the house late in the darkness to see little Professor Aesop on a moonlight visit, and he a learned pooka.[2]

1. Aesop (*c.* 620-564 B.C.), a Greek teller of animal fables.
2. Hobgoblin, puck.

Cnoc Mellerí

Sranntarnach na stoirme i Mellerí aréir
Is laethanta an pheaca bhoig mar bhreoiteacht
ar mo chuimhne,
Laethanta ba leapacha de shonaschlúmh an tsaoil
Is dreancaidí na drúise iontu ag preabarnaigh ina
mílte.

D'éirigh san oíche sidhe gaoithe coiscéim,
Manaigh ag triall ar an Aifreann,
Meidhir, casadh timpeall is rince san aer,
Bróga na manach ag cantaireacht.

Bráthair sa phroinnteach ag riaradh suipéir,
Tost bog ba bhalsam don intinn,
Ainnise naofa in oscailt a bhéil,
Iompar mothaolach Críostaí mhaith.

Do doirteadh steall anchruthach gréine go mall
Trí mhúnla cruiceogach fuinneoige,
Do ghaibh sí cruth manaigh ó bhaitheas go bonn
Is do thosnaigh an ghrian ag léitheoireacht.

Leabhar ag an manach bán namhdach á léamh,
Go hobann casachtach an chloig,
Do múchadh an manach bhí déanta de ghréin
Is do scoilteadh an focal 'na phloic.

Buaileadh clog Complin is bhrostaigh gach aoi
Maolchluasach i dtreo an tséipéil;
Bhí beatha na naomh seo chomh bán le braitlín
Is sinne chomh dubh leis an daol.

Allas ar phaidrín brúite im láimh,
Mo bhríste dlúth-tháite lem ghlúin,
Ghluais sochraid chochallach manach thar bráid,
Ba shuarach leat féachaint a thabhairt.

Ach d'fhéachas go fiosrach gan taise gan trua
Mar fhéachadar Giúdaigh fadó
Ar Lazarus cúthail ag triall as an uaigh
Is géire na súl thart á dhó.

Do thiteadar tharainn 'na nduine is 'na nduine,
Reilig ag síorphaidreoireacht,
Is do thuirling tiubhscamall de chlúimh liath na cille
Go brónach ar ghrua an tráthnóna.

'Tá an bás ag cur seaca ar bheatha anseo,
Aige tá na manaigh ar aimsir,
Eisean an tAb ar a ndeineann siad rud,
Ar a shon deinid troscadh is tréanas.

'Buachaill mar sheanduine meirtneach ag siúl,
Masla ar choimirce Dé,
An té 'dhéanfadh éagóir dá leithéid ar gharsún
Do chuirfeadh sé cochall ar ghréin;

'Do scaipfeadh an oíche ar fud an mheán lae,
Do bhainfeadh an teanga den abhainn,
Do chuirfeadh coir drúise in intinn na n-éan
Is do líonfadh le náire an domhan.

'Tá an buachaill seo dall ar an aigne fhiáin
A thoirchíonn smaointe éagsúla,
Gan bacadh le hAb ná le clog ná le riail
Ach luí síos le smaoineamh a dhúile.

'Ní bhlaisfidh sé choíche tréanmheisce mná
A chorraíonn mar chreideamh na sléibhte,
'Thug léargas do Dante ar Fhlaitheas Dé tráth,
Nuair a thuirling na haingil i riocht véarsaí,'

Sin é dúirt an ego bhí uaibhreach easumhal,
Is é dallta le feirg an tsaoil,
Ach do smaoiníos ar ball, is an ceol os ar gcionn,
Gur mó ná an duine an tréad.

D'fhéachas laistiar díom ar fhásach mo shaoil,
Is an paidrín brúite im dhóid,
Peaca, díomhaointeas is caiteachas claon,
Blianta urghránna neantóg.

D'fhéachas ar bheatha na manach anonn,
D'aithníos dán ar an dtoirt,
Meadaracht, glaine, doimhinbhrí is comhfuaim,
Bhí m'aigne cromtha le ceist.

Do bhlaiseas mórfhuascailt na faoistine ar maidin,
Aiseag is ualach ar ceal,
Scaoileadh an t-ancaire, rinceas sa Laidin,
Ba dhóbair dom tuirling ar Neamh.

Ach do bhlaiseas, uair eile, iontaoibh asam féin,
Mo chuid fola ar fiuchadh le neart,
Do shamhlaíos gur lonnaigh im intinn Spiorad
Naomh
Is gur thiteadar m'fhocail ó Neamh.

Buarach ar m'aigne Eaglais Dé,
Ar shagart do ghlaofainn coillteán,
Béalchráifeacht an Creideamh, ól gloine gan léan,
Mairfeam go dtiocfaidh an bás!

Manaigh mar bheachaibh ag fuaimint im cheann,
M'aigne cromtha le ceist,
Nótaí ag rothaíocht anonn is anall,
Deireadh le Complin de gheit.

Sranntarnach na stoirme i Mellerí aréir
Is laethanta an pheaca bhoig mar bhreoiteacht ar
mo chuimhne
Is na laethanta a leanfaidh iad fá cheilt i ndorn Dé,
Ach greim fhir bháite ar Mhellerí an súgán seo
filíochta.

Mount Melleray[1]

The snoring of the storm in Melleray last night, and days of soft sin like sickness on my memory, days that were beds of life's downy contentment where the fleas of lust leaped by the thousands.

A fairy-wind of footsteps rose in the night, monks on their way to Mass, merriment, twirling and dancing in the air, the monks' shoes chanting.

A brother in the refectory preparing supper, soft silence was balsam for the mind, a saintly misery in the opening of his mouth, the guileless conduct of a good Christian.

A formless splash of sunlight was spilt slowly through the lancet window, it took the shape of a monk from head to foot and the sun began to read.

A book being read by the white, hostile monk. Suddenly, the coughing of the bell, the monk made of sunlight was extinguished and the words in his cheeks were split.

The bell rang for Compline[2] and all the guests hurried sheepishly towards the chapel, these saints' lives were white as a sheet and ourselves as black as a beetle.

Sweat on the rosary pressed in my hand, my trousers firmly stuck to my knee, a cowled procession of monks moved past, you'd think to look at them would be mean.

But I looked enquiringly without pity or compassion, as the Jews looked long ago on shy Lazarus coming from the grave, the sharpness of the eyes around burning him.

They went past one by one, a graveyard incessantly praying, and a dense cloud of the church's green mould fell sadly on the evening's cheek.

'Death puts a frost over life here, the monks are his servants, he is the abbot they serve, on whose behalf they fast and abstain.

'A boy walking like a weary old man, an insult to God's protection, whoever would do such injustice to a boy would put a cowl over the sun.

'Would spread night over midday, would take the tongue from the river, would place a crime of lust in the birds' minds and fill the world with shame.

'This boy is blind to the lively mind that fertilises various thoughts, without care for abbot or bell or rule but to lie down mulling over its desire.

1. A Cistercian monastery in County Waterford. A place of retreat.
2. The last religious service of the day in the Roman catholic liturgy.

'He will never taste the strong headiness of woman that moves mountains like faith, that once gave Dante a vision of Paradise when angels descended in the form of verses.'[3]

So spoke the ego, haughty and proud, blind with life's anger. But I thought later on, when the music was hanging over us, the flock is greater than the person.

I looked back at the desert of my life, the rosary squeezed in my hand, sin, sloth, misspent energy, hateful nettle-years.

I looked at the life of the monk over there, I immediately grasped a poem, metre, clarity, depth of meaning, alliteration, my mind was bent with anxiety.

I tasted the great release of confession this morning, restoration, a weight laid aside. The anchor was released, I danced in Latin, I almost landed in Heaven.

But once more I tasted trust in myself, my blood boiling with strength, I imagined the Holy Spirit settled in my mind and my words falling from heaven.

God's church was a spancel[4] on my mind, I would call the priest a eunuch, the faith hypocrisy; drink a glass without grief, let's live until death comes!

Monks like bees murmuring in my head, my mind bowed with anxiety, notes wheeling hither and thither, Compline suddenly over.

The snoring of the storm in Melleray last night, and days of soft sin like sickness on my memory, and the days that will follow them hidden in God's fist, but this straw-rope of poetry is a drowning man's grip on Melleray.

3. Dante, *La Vita Nuova*.
4. A rope used to tie a cow at milking time.

Reo

Maidin sheaca ghabhas amach
Is bhí seál póca romham ar sceach,
Rugas air le cur im phóca
Ach sciorr sé uaim mar bhí sé reoite:
Ní héadach beo a léim óm ghlaic
Ach rud fuair bás aréir ar sceach:
Is siúd ag taighde mé fé m'intinn
Go bhfuaireas macasamhail an ní seo —
  Lá dar phógas bean dem mhuintir
  Is í ina cónra reoite, sínte.

Freeze

One frosty morning I roved out and a handkerchief was before me on a bush. I took it to put in my pocket but it slipped from me because it was frozen. It wasn't a living cloth that slipped from my grasp but a thing that died last night on a bush. And there I went searching in my mind until I found an equivalent for this event — a day I kissed a woman of my people when she lay in her coffin frozen.

Fiabhras

Tá sléibhte na leapa mós ard,
Tá breoiteacht 'na brothall 'na lár,
Is fada an t-aistear urlár,
  Is na mílte is na mílte i gcéin
  Tá suí agus seasamh sa saol.

Atáimid i gceantar bráillín,
Ar éigean más cuimhin linn cathaoir,
Ach bhí tráth sar ba mhachaire sinn,
  In aimsir choisíochta fadó,
  Go mbímis chomh hard le fuinneog.

Tá pictiúr ar an bhfalla ag at,
Tá an fráma imithe ina lacht,
Ceal creidimh ní féidir é bhac,
  Tá nithe ag druidim fém dhéin,
  Is braithim ag titim an saol.

Tá ceantar ag taisteal ón spéir,
Tá comharsanacht suite ar mo mhéar,
Dob fhuirist dom breith ar shéipéal,
  Tá ba ar an mbóthar ó thuaidh,
  Is níl ba na síoraíochta chomh ciúin.

Fever

The mountains of the bed are rather high and sickness a heat in there, the floor a long journey, and miles, miles away, life's sittings and standings go on.

We are in a place of sheets, we barely remember a chair. There was a time before we were a plain, in walking-times long ago, that we were tall as a window.

A picture swells on the wall, the frame has turned into liquid. Lacking faith we cannot stop it, things are moving towards me and I feel the world falling.

A place is travelling from the sky, a neighbourhood is settled on my finger, I could easily catch hold of a church. There are cows on the road to the North and the cows of eternity aren't as quiet.

Na Leamhain

Fuaim ag leamhan leochaileach, iompó leathnaigh,
Bascadh mionsciathán,
Oíche fhómhair i seomra na leapa, tá
Rud leochaileach á chrá.

Oíche eile i dtaibhreamh bhraitheas-sa
Peidhre leamhan-sciathán,
Mar sciatháin aingil iad le fairsingeacht
Is bhíodar leochaileach mar mhná.

Dob é mo chúram lámh a leagadh orthu
Is gan ligean leo chun fáin,
Ach iad a shealbhú gan sárú tearmainn
Is iad a thabhairt chun aoibhnis iomlán.

Ach dhoirteas-sa an púdar beannaithe
'Bhí spréite ar gach sciathán,
Is tuigeadh dom go rabhas gan uimhreacha,
Gan uimhreacha na fearúlachta go brách.

Is shiúil na deich n-uimhreacha as an mearbhall
Is ba mhó ná riamh a n-údarás,
Is ba chlos ciníocha ag plé le huimhreacha,
Is cách ba chlos ach mise amháin.

Fuaim ag leamhan leochaileach, iompó leathanaigh,
Creachadh leamhan-scannán,
Oíche fhómhair is na leamhain ag eiteallaigh
Mór mo bheann ar a mion-rírá.

The Moths

Sound of a fragile moth, turning of a page, bruising of small wings, an autumn night in the bedroom, a fragile thing is being tormented.

Another night in a dream I felt a pair of moth-wings. They were ample as an angel's wings, fragile as women.

It was my duty to touch them and not to let them go away, but to possess them without violating sanctuary and to bring them to full delight.

But I spilt the blessed powder that was spread on every wing and I realised I was without numbers, without the numbers of virility forever.

The ten numbers walked out of the confusion and their authority was greater than ever. And races were heard considering numbers and everyone was heard but me alone.

Sound of a fragile moth, turning of a page, ruining of the moth-film. Autumn night and the moths fluttering, I'm preoccupied with their minor uproar.

Claustrophobia

In aice an fhíona
Tá coinneal is sceon,
Tá dealbh mo Thiarna
D'réir dealraimh gan chumhacht,
Tá a dtiocfaidh den oíche
Mar shluaite sa chlós,
Tá rialtas na hoíche
Lasmuigh den bhfuinneoig;
Má mhúchann mo choinneal
Ar ball de m'ainneoin
Léimfidh an oíche
Isteach im scámhóig,
Sárófar m'intinn
Is ceapfar dom sceon,
Déanfar díom oíche,
Bead im dhoircheacht bheo:
  Ach má mhaireann mo choinneal
  Aon oíche amháin
  Bead im phoblacht solais
  Go dtiocfaidh an lá.

Claustrophobia

Beside the wine there's a candle and terror, the statue of my Lord appears to be powerless. What will come of the night is like a crowd in the yard, the government of night is outside the window. If my candle is quenched later in spite of me, the night will leap into my lung; my mind will be taken over and terror will be made for me. A night will be made of me, I will be a living darkness. But if my candle survives one night, I will be a republic of light until day comes.

EOGHAN Ó TUAIRISC

(1919-82)

from: LUX AETERNA (1964)

[These two sections from 'Aifreann na Marbh' (Mass for the Dead) are translated by Eoghan Ó hAnluain.]

Aifreann na Marbh

fuair bás ag Hiroshima Dé Luain, 6ú Lúnasa, 1945

I. *Introitus*
Músclaíonn an mhaidin ár míshuaimhneas síoraí.
Breathnaím trí phána gloine
Clogthithe na hÁdhamhchlainne
Ár gcuid slinn, ár gCré, ár gcúirteanna
Ar snámh san fhionnuaire.
Nochtann as an rosamh chugam
An ghlanchathair mhaighdeanúil
Ag fearadh a haiséirí:
Músclaíonn an mhaidin ár míshuaimhneas síoraí.

Broinneann an ceatal binnuaigneach i mo chroí
Ar fheiscint dom a háilleachta,
Géagshíneadh a gealsráideanna
Le hais na habhann, na coillte,
Líne na gcnoc pinnsilteach
Á háitiú ina céad riocht —
Mo chailín cathrach fornocht
Ina codladh ag áth na gcliath:
Músclaíonn an mhaidin ár míshuaimhneas síoraí.

Tagann an aisling rinnuaibhreach anoir,
Scaipeann rós is airgead
Trí smúit a calafoirt
Ina lá léaspairte, súnas
Ag éigniú a maighdeanais
Nó go bhfágtar gach creat
Gach simléar, gach seolchrann
Ina chnámh dhubh, ina ghrianghraf
Ag léiriú inmhíniú mo laoi:
Músclaíonn an mhaidin ár míshuaimhneas síoraí.

Mass for the Dead

who died at Hiroshima Monday, 6 August, 1945

I. *Introitus*
Morning awakens our eternal unrest.
I observe through a glass pane
The steeples of humankind
Our slated roofs, our creed, our courts
Floating in the cool air.
From out the morning haze the pure virgin city
Is revealed to me
Performing her resurrection
Morning awakens our eternal unrest.

A poignant music swells my heart
As I observe her loveliness
Stretching her limbs in sunlit streets
Along the river — the woods
And outlined hills
Give her her pristine place,
My naked girl of a city
Asleep by the ford of the hurdles.

The arrogant vision comes from the east
Dispensing its rose and silver hue
Through her murky seaport
The day's flashing lust
Violates her maidenhood
Leaving every chimney stack and sailing mast
A blackened bone, a sungraph,
Revealing the hidden burden of my poem:
Morning awakens our eternal unrest.

Graduale

Ná tóg orm a Chríost
Go ndearnas an ghadaíocht
Is foirm do cheatail ghlinn
A dhealbhú dom aisling.

Buairt m'anama nach beag
I mo sheasamh ar chéimeanna
Na cathrach céasta, ceannocht,
Is cúis dom an ghadaíocht.

Sinne na mairbh fuair bás
In Áth Cliath is in antráth
Lá gréine na blaisféime
Shéideamar Hiroshima.

Ní Gaeil sinn a thuilleadh de shloinneadh Ír is
Éibhir,
Ní hoidhe linn an spéirling a fuineadh do bhláth
Dhéirdre,
An tráth seo chois Life an loingis i gcríon mo laetha
Is léir dom ár ngin is ár ngoineadh, síol Éabha.

Graduale[1]

Don't blame me, oh Christ
For this misappropriation
Stealing the form of your vivid symphony
To frame my own vision,

But my deeply anguished soul
As I stand uncovered on the steps

1. An antiphon sung between the Epistle and Gospel at the steps of the altar during the Eucharist.

Of the crucified city
Has urged this violation.

We are the dead who died
Here in Dublin, untimely
On this bright day of blasphemy
We blasted Hiroshima

No longer the mere Irish named for Ír and
Éibhear,[2]
The storm of violence that Deirdre's[3] beauty stirred
seems little now,
Here at this time on Liffeyside, in my withered days
I see our true begetting, and our hurt — children of
Eve.

2. Pronounced 'Eer' and 'Ayver.' Pseudo-historical ancestors of the Irish.
3. A heroine of early Irish saga, whose beauty caused tragic death.

MÁIRE MHAC AN tSAOI

(1922-)

from:
AN CION GO DTÍ SEO (1987)

[The translations are by Máire Mhac an tSaoi herself, except for 'Mary Hogan's Quatrains', which is by James Gleasure. This was first published in *Poetry Australia* 63 (May 1977).]

Inquisitio 1584

Sa bhliain sin d'aois Ár dTiarna
Chúig chéad déag cheithre fichid,
Nó blianta beaga ina dhiaidh sin,
Seán mac Éamoinn mhic Uilig
Lámh le Sionainn do crochadh —

Lámh le Sionainn na scuainte
I Luimnigh, cathair na staire,
Seán mac Éamoinn mhic Uilig
Aniar ó pharóiste Mhárthain,
Ba thaoiseach ar Bhaile an Fhianaigh.

Tréas an choir, is a thailte
Do tugadh ar láimh strainséara;
Is anois fé bhun Chruach Mhárthain
Níl cuimhne féin ar a ainm,
Fiú cérbha díobh ní feasach ann . . . .

Nára corrach do shuan,
A Sheáin mhic Éamoinn mhic Uilig,
Ar bhruach na Sionainne móire
Nuair shéideann gaoth ón bhfarraige
aniar ód cheantar dúchais.

Inquisitio[1] 1584

In that year of the age of Our Lord
Fifteen hundred and eighty
Or some few short years after
Sean MacEdmund MacUlick
Hard by Shannon was hanged.

1. A court of inquiry into the ownership of land.

Hard by the shoals of Shannon
In Limerick, history's city,
Sean MacEdmund MacUlick
Come west from the parish of Marrhan
Who was chieftain of Balleneenig.[2]

Treason his crime, his lands
Were given in hand of the stranger
And now around Mount Marrhan
His name is not even remembered
Nor is his kindred known there.

Undisturbed be your sleep
Sean MacEdmund MacUlick
On the banks of the mighty Shannon
When the wind blows in from the sea
From the west and from your own country.

2. Marrhan and Balleneenig are in west Kerry.

Finit

Le seans a chuala uathu scéala an chleamhnais
Is b'ait liom srian le héadroime na gaoithe —
Do bhís chomh hanamúil léi, chomh domheabhartha,
Chomh fiáin léi, is chomh haonraic, mar ba
 chuimhin liom.

Féach feasta go bhfuil dála cáich i ndán duit,
Cruatan is coitinne, séasúr go céile,
Ag éalú i ndearúd le hiompú ráithe
Gur dabht arbh ann duit riamh, ná dod leithéidse...

Ach go mbeidh poirt anois ná cloisfead choíche
Gan tú bheith os mo chomhair arís sa chúinne
Ag feitheamh, ceol ar láimh leat, roimh an rince
Is diamhaireacht na hoíche amuigh id shúile.

Finit

By chance I learned from them the marriage-contract
And wondered at this check on the wind's lightness;
You were so unpredictable, spontaneous,
Untamed like it, and lonely, I remember.

Know now the lot of all is yours henceforward,
Hardship and commonplace each following season,
Slipping from memory as turns the quarter —
We doubt you or your like ever existed.

But that there will be tunes I'll not hear ever
Without your being again there in the corner,
Waiting, music to hand, before the dancing,
Your eyes the mystery of the night outside.

Do Shíle

Cuimhním ar sheomra ó thaobh na farraige,
Aniar is aneas do bheireadh scríb air,
Is báisteach ar fhuinneoig ina clagarnaigh,
Gan sánas air ó thitim oíche,
Is is cuimhin liom go rabhais ann, a Shíle,
Suite go híseal cois na tine
Is an fáinne óir ar do mhéir linbh.

Do thugais dúinn amhrán croíbhuartha,
Is ba cheol na fliúite le clos do ghlór ann,
Comharthaí grá ón bhFrainc ar cuairt chughainn —
Bhí gile do chinn mar an t-airgead luachra
Fé sholas an lampa leagtha ar bord ann.

Nach cuma feasta, a naí bhig, eadrainn
Deighilt na mblianta nó fuatha an charadais?
Dob é mo dhán an tráth san t'aithne.

For Sheila

I remember a room on the seaward side —
The squall caught it from the south-west —
And the rain a tattoo on the window
Unslackening since the fall of night,
And I remember that you were there, Sheila,
Sitting low by the fire,
The gold ring on your childlike finger.

You gave us a heartbroken song,
And your voice was the music of flutes,
Love's catalogue brought here from France —
The fairness of your head was like the meadowsweet
Under the light of the lamp set on the table ....

What do they matter more, little dear one, between us,
Separation of years and aversions bred of friendship?
It was my lot to know you at that time.

Gníomhartha Corportha na Trócaire

Chuas ar thuairisc na seanamhná san óspaidéal —
Bhí an t-éadach caite anuas den leabaidh aici,
Bhí a léine oíche éalaithe in airde fána coim,
Truamhéil a bléine liaite, scáinte —

Samlaíodh sicín ag dul dó 'on oigheann dom —
'A 'níon ó,' ar sise, 'tá an iomarca plaincéadaí
anuas orm!

Bhí an bheirt leanbh crapaithe ar chlár an droichid
Gorm ón bhfuacht —
Gomh in oíche na cathrach —
Thugas mo mhiasam uaim is dúrt,
'Bailígh libh anois abhaile as so!'
Ní ligfeadh dóibh eagla —
'Fios ar na gardaí' ars' an fear ag gabháil tharam —
Bhíodar glanta as mo radharc mar thit an sneachta
ar an adharta!

Bím i gcónaí ag teitheadh roimpi,
I bpoll tarathair más gá san —
Ba gheall le déirc fanúint léi
D'fhonn babhta comhráidh léi —
Ach ó d'imigh an gluaisteán san thar a maicín mánla
Níl ach an t-aon ábhar cainte amháin aici —
Is bíonn imshníomh orm go gcoireoidh sí mo
bheirtse
I mbarr a sláinte.

Bhíodh fáilte isteach roimh chlann na gcomharsan —
Tá sneá anois i gceann Phádraig is caithfear a
bhearradh!

The Corporal Works of Mercy

I went to visit the old woman in the hospital — she had thrown the bed clothes down off the bed; her nightdress had slipped up round her waist; the pathos of her loins was grey and scant; I thought of a chicken ready to go in the oven — 'Daughter dear,' she said, 'I have too many blankets on top of me!'

The two children were crouched on the flat of the bridge, blue with cold; the city night was venomous. I gave my New Year token and said, 'Clear off home now out of this'; they could not for fear. 'Send for the Guards',[1] said the man passing by; they were clean out of sight as if snow had fallen on a hearthstone!

I am always fleeing before her; up an auger hole if necessary. It would be like a charity to wait for her for a spell of conversation, but, ever since the motor car went over her mild little son, she has only one subject to talk about — and I am uneasy lest she should ill-wish my pair in the height of their health!

The neighbours' children were always welcome; now there are nits in Patrick's head and we will have to cut his hair!

1. Garda Síochána (police).

Cré na Mná Tí

Coinnibh an teaghlach geal
Agus an chlann fé smacht,
Nigh agus sciúr agus glan,
Cóirigh proinn agus lacht,
Iompaigh tochta, leag brat,
Ach, ar nós Sheicheiriseáide,
Ní mór duit an fhilíocht chomh maith!

The Housewife's Credo

Keep the dwelling bright and the children in order; wash and scour and clean; prepare meal and beverage; turn mattress — spread cloth — but, like Scheherazade,[1] you will need to write poetry also!

1. In the *Arabian Nights*, Scheherazade kept her husband, Schariar, legendary king of Samarkand, from killing her by telling the tales over 1,001 nights, until he relented.

Ceathrúintí Mháire Ní Ógáin

I

Ach a mbead gafa as an líon so —
Is nár lige Dia gur fada san —
Béidir go bhfónfaidh cuimhneamh
Ar a bhfuaireas de shuaimhneas id bhaclainn.

Nuair a bheidh ar mo chumas guíochtaint,
Comaoine is éisteacht Aifrinn,
Cé déarfaidh ansan nach cuí dhom
Ar 'shonsa is ar mo shon féin achaine?

Ach comhairle idir dhá linn duit,
Ná téir ródhílis in achrann,
Mar go bhfuilimse meáite ar scaoileadh
Pé cuibhrinn a snaidhmfear eadrainn.

II

Beagbheann ar amhras daoine,
Beagbheann ar chros na sagart,
Ar gach ní ach a bheith sínte
Idir tú agus falla —

Neamhshuím liom fuacht na hoíche,
Neamhshuím liom scríb is fearthainn,
Sa domhan cúng rúin teolaí seo
Ná téann thar fhaobhar na leapan —

Ar a bhfuil romhainn ní smaoinfeam,
Ar a bhfuil déanta cheana,
Linne an uain, a chroí istigh,
Is mairfidh sí go maidin.

III

Achar bliana atáim
Ag luí farat id chlúid,
Deacair anois a rá
Cad leis a raibh mo shúil!

Ghabhais de chosaibh i gcion
A tugadh go fial ar dtúis,
Gan aithint féin féd throigh
Fulaing na feola a bhrúigh!

Is fós tá an creat umhal
Ar mhaithe le seanagheallúint,
Ach ó thost cantain an chroí
Tránn áthas an phléisiúir.

IV

Tá naí an éada ag deol mo chí'se,
Is mé ag tál air de ló is d'oíche;
An gárlach gránna ag cur na bhfiacal,
Is de nimh a ghreama mo chuisle líonta.

A ghrá, ná maireadh an trú beag eadrainn,
Is a fholláine, shláine a bhí ár n-aithne;
Barántas cnis a chloígh lem chneas airsin,
Is séala láimhe a raibh gach cead aici.

Féach nach meáite mé ar chion a shéanadh,
Cé gur sháigh an t-amhras go doimhin a phréa'cha;
Ar láir dhea-tharraic ná déan éigean,
Is díolfaidh sí an comhar leat ina shéasúr féinig.

V

Is éachtach an rud í an phian,
Mar chaitheann an cliabh,
Is ná tugann foiseamh ná spás
Ná sánas de ló ná d'oích' —

An té atá i bpéin mar táim
Ní raibh uaigneach ná ina aonar riamh,
Ach ag iompar cuileachtan de shíor
Mar bhean gin féna coim.

VI

'Ní chodlaím ist oíche' —
Beag an rá, ach an bhfionnfar choíche
Ar shúile oscailte
Ualach na hoíche?

VII

Fada liom anocht!
Do bhí ann oíche
Nárbh fhada faratsa —
Dá leomhfainn cuimhneamh.

Go deimhin níor dheacair san,
An ród a d'fhillfinn —
Dá mba cheadaithe
Tar éis aithrí ann.

Luí chun suilt
Is éirí chun aoibhnis
Siúd ba chleachtadh dhúinn —
Dá bhfaighinn dul siar air.

Mary Hogan's[1] Quatrains

I

O to be disentangled from this net —
And may God not let that be long —
Perhaps the memory will help
Of all the pleasure I had in your arms.

When I shall have the ability to pray,
Take communion and hear Mass,
Who will say then that it is not seemly
To intercede on his and on my own behalf?

But meanwhile my advice to you,
Don't get too firmly enmeshed,
For I am determined to be let loose
Whatever bond between us is tied.

1. Máire Ní Ógáin is the proverbial 'fool' of the female variety. There is a tradition that the poet/schoolmaster Donnchadh Ruadh MacConmara (Red Denis MacNamara), 1715-1810, had a mistress called Máire Ní Ógáin. (J. Gleasure)

II

I care little for people's suspicions,
I care little for priests' prohibitions,
For anything save to lie stretched
Between you and the wall —

I am indifferent to the night's cold,
I am indifferent to the squall or rain,
When in this warm narrow secret world
Which does not go beyond the edge of the bed —

We shall not contemplate what lies before us,
What has already been done,
Time is on our side, my dearest,
And it will last till morning.

III

For the space of a year I have been
Lying with you in your embrace,
Hard to say now
What I was hoping for!

You fell headlong in love,
A love which was freely given at first,
While you yourself were unaware
Of the suffering of the flesh you crushed under foot.

And yet the flesh is willing
For the sake of an old familiar pledge,
But since the heart's singing has ceased
The joy of pleasure ebbs.

IV

The child of envy is sucking my breast,
While I yield to it day and night;
The ugly brat is cutting teeth,
My veins throb with the venom of its bite.

My love, may the little wretch not remain between us,
Seeing how healthy and full was our knowledge of
each other;
It was a skin warranty that kept us together,
And a seal of hand that knew no bounds.

See how I am not determined to avoid love,
Though doubt has plunged its roots deep;
Do not force a willing mare,
And she will recompense you in her own season.

V

Pain is a powerful thing,
How it consumes the breast,
It gives no respite day or night,
It gives no peace or rest —

Any who feel pain like me,
Have never been lonely or alone,
But are ever bearing company
Like a pregnant woman, in her womb.

VI

'I do not sleep at night' —
Of no account, but will we ever know
With open eyes
The burden of the night?

VII

Tonight seems never-ending!
There was once a night
Which with you was not long —
Dare I call to mind.

That would not be hard, for sure,
The road on which I would return —
If it were permitted
After repentance.

Lying down for enjoyment
And rising for pleasure
That is what we practised —
If only I could return to it.

BREANDÁN Ó BEACHÁIN (BRENDAN BEHAN)

(1923-64)

from: POEMS AND A PLAY IN IRISH (1981)

[Brendan Behan's first published work was in the Irish language and appeared in the journals *Comhar*, *Feasta* and *Envoy*. He was a contributor to *Nuabhéarsaíocht* (ed. Seán O Tuama, 1950), the seminal anthology of modern poetry in Irish. His play *An Giall* (later *The Hostage*) was staged first in Irish in 1958.

The translations are by Valentin Iremonger and are taken from *Horan's Field* (1972).]

Jackeen ag Caoineadh na mBlascaod

Do Sheán Ó Briain as Baile an Fheirtéaraigh

Beidh an fharraige mhór faoi luí na gréine mar ghloine,
Gan bád faoi sheol ná comhartha beo ó dhuine
Ach an t-iolar órga deireanach thuas ar imeall
An domhain, thar an mBlascaod uaigneach luite . . .

An ghrian ina luí is scáth na hoíche á scaipeadh
Ar ardú ré is í ag taitneamh i bhfuacht trí scamaill,
A méara loma sínte síos ar thalamh
Ar thithe scriosta briste, truamhar folamh . . .

Faoi thost ach cleití na n-éan ag cuimilt thar tonna
Buíoch as a bheith fillte, ceann i mbrollach faoi shonas,
Séideadh na gaoithe ag luascadh go bog leathdhorais
Is an teallach fuar fliuch, gan tine, gan teas, gan chosaint.

Mountjoy, Lúnasa 1948

A Jackeen[1] Laments the Blaskets

To Seán Ó Briain from Ballyferriter[2]

The great sea under the sun will lie like a mirror,
Not a boat sailing, not a living sign from a sinner,
The golden eagle aloft in the distance, the last
Vestige of life by the ruined abandoned Blaskets.

The sun will be gone, the shadow of night spreading
As the moon, rising, through a cloud coldly stretches
Its ghostly fingers over the silent earth
Where, wracked, the shells of the houses stand deserted

— Silent save for the birds all homeward flying
Glad to be back, their heads on their breasts lying,
And the wind soughing, softly a half-door swinging
By cold wet hearths, their fires forever extinguished.

Mountjoy,[3] *August 1948*

1. A Jackeen is a Dublin man.
2. Seán Ó Briain was a fellow republican prisoner who taught Behan Irish.
3. Mountjoy Jail, Dublin.

Do Sheán Ó Súilleabháin

Oscar Wilde, Poéte et Dramaturge, né à Dublin le 15 Octobre, 1856, est mort dans cette maison le 30 Novembre, 1900.

Tar éis gach gleo
a chuir sé as beo
le teann anfa,
seo sínte sa chlapsholas
corpán na beochta
balbh sa dorchadas.

Faoi thost, ach coinnle
an tórraimh ina lasracha.

A cholainn sheang
is a shúil go daingean iata
i seomra fuar lom,
is an *concierge* spídiúil
faoin iomarca freastail
ar phótaire iasachta
a d'imigh gan *service*
an deich faoin gcéad íoctha.

Aistrithe ón *Flore*
go fásach na naofachta,

ógphrionsa na bpeacach
ina shearbhán aosta,
seoid órga na drúise
ina dhiaidh aige fágtha
gan *pernod* ina chabhair aige
ach uisce na cráifeachta;
ógrí na háilleachta
ina Narcissus briste
ach réalta na glan-Mhaighdine
ina ga ar an uisce.

Ceangal

Dá aoibhne bealach an pheacaigh
is mairg bás gan bheannacht;
mo ghraidhin thú, a Oscair,
bhí sé agat gach bealach!

Quartier Latin, 1949

Oscar

To Seán Ó Súilleabháin[1]

After all the strife
That, alive, he caused,
Ravaged with fear,
In the half-light stretched,
The gay spark's body
Lies dumb in the dark,

1. Seán Ó Súilleabháin (1906-64), painter.

Silent, the funereal
Candles guttering,
The graceful body,
The firm gaze, spent
In a cold bare room
With a concierge spiteful
From too much attendance
On a foreign tippler
Who left without paying
The ten per cent service.
Exiled from the Flore
To a saintly desert
The young prince of sin
A withered churl
The gold jewel of lust
Left far behind him.
No pernod to brace him
Only holy water
— The young king of Beauty,
A ravished narcissus
As the star of the pure Virgin
Glows on the water.

Envoi

Delightful the path of sin
But a holy death's a habit.
Good man yourself there, Oscar:
Every way you had it.

SEÁN Ó TUAMA

(1926-)

from:
SAOL FÓ THOINN (1978) and AN BÁS I dTÍR NA nÓG (1988)

[The translations are by the author.]

Rousseau na Gaeltachta

Lig di, adúirt an file,
is ná smachtaigh í,
níl inti seo ach gearrchaile
is is breoiteacht é an t-eagla
a chrapann an nádúr.

Lig di, adúirt an file,
is ná smachtaigh í,
lig di fás gan bac ar bith
go dtína haoirde cheapaithe,
tá an t-aer fós bog os a cionn.

A Gaeltacht[1] Rousseau

Let her be, said the poet;
do not chastise her,
she is still a stripling
and fear is a sickness
that stunts all human growth.

Let her be, said the poet;
do not chastise her,
let her grow unimpeded
to whatever height she is meant for:
the air is still soft above her head.

1. Irish-speaking district.

Cá siúlfam?

Cá siúlfam? Tá na cosáin reoite,
carnáin chalcaithe de shneachta cruaite
ar bhlaincéadaí an bhóthair mar a mbíodh ár siúl.
'S tá an ghaoth ag aimsiú ioscada na nglún
chomh géar chomh glic le fuip....
Ní shiúlfad leat. Tá an corp ina chloch.

Tiomáinfeam? Racham ar an aifreann déanach
Ag éisteacht le *Hosanna in Excelsis*
á ghreadadh amach go buach caithréimeach,
is bainfeam sásamh as an at gan éifeacht
a thagann ar an gcroí....
Chauffeur mé, lá seaca, ar dheabhóidí.

Ar deireadh: ní chorródsa amach inniu,
tá fuil i gcúl mo bhéil le mí ón sioc,
is ó inchinn go talamh síos
tá bánú déanta ar gach artaire
a dhéanann duine den daonaí....
Fanfam féach an bhfillfidh teas arís.

Where shall we walk?

Where shall we walk? The paths are all iced over,
On the grassy blankets of the roads we've known
Calcified mounds of slush and snow,
The wind stings the hollows of the knees
As slyly and as sharply as a whip....
I shall not walk with you. The flesh is stone.

We shall drive then, go to Mass,
Listen to *Hosanna in Excelsis*
Being ground out triumphally,
And feed upon the silly satisfaction
Of music swelling up the heart....
On a frosty day I act as chauffeur to the mysteries.

No, just no: I will not move today;
The chill has bloodied up my throat this long month
And every artery that makes a human burn
From brain down to the ground
Has been whitened to debility....
We'll wait and see if heat returns.

Ise Seachtó hOcht, Eisean Ochtó Ceathair

Nuair pósadh iad adúramar
'Coinneoidh siad teas le chéile'
(ise caoga hocht, eisean seasca ceathair);
nuair cailleadh eisean, bhlaiseamar
an domlas 'nár mbéalaibh.

Ar dhéirc an stáit 'sea mhaireadar,
an tseanchaíocht a sólaist —
ach bhí aghaidh seanrí ársa anois
ar chorp a fir sa tseomra.

Liúigh sí le fíoch, do chuardaigh é
le méireanna págánta,
is sinne go críostaí ag guí
go gcoiscfí an sruth bolcánach.

Is ba bhaintreach ise ó oirthear domhain,
seál dubh is beol féasógach,
an taon bhean riamh lem mharthainse
a thit i ngrá le prionsa
(ise seachtó hocht, eisean ochtó ceathair).

She being 78, He being 84

When they got married, we said
'They'll help to heat each other'
(she being 58, he being 64).
When he passed away we felt
bile rising in our mouths.

They had lived on dole and grants,
gossip their one solace —
but the dead face in the room now
was of an old king from the past.

She shrieked with rage, and combed him
with pagan fingerings
while we sound Christians prayed
that the lava-flow would stop.

She looked a widow of the Eastern world,
black shawl and moustached mouth,
the only woman in my lifetime
to have loved a prince
(she being 78, he being 84).

'Besides, who knows before the end what light may shine'

Maidin ghorm ins an Ghréig
(an leathchéad scoite agam)
faoi bhíomaí buí is giolcaigh fhite —
mo chorp ar teitheadh ón ngréin.

Liszt go glinn im chluais ag cumasc
le lapaíl shámh na dtonn,
táim síoraí anseo sa bhfuarthan
idir fallaí bána an tí.

An túisce stopann an pianó
tránn an mhuir fém chroí,
is cuimhním ar dhaoine age baile
a bhí mór im chathair tráth.

Ceathrar fear im chathairse
a éiríonn romham sa tost,
an luisne ard do mhúscail siad
do dheineas cimilt léi.

An saoi a chrith le gile an tsolais
i gceártain seanfhilí,
an draoi scaoil caisí ceoil thar chora —
is a bháigh é féin sa tsruth.

An file cráite a mhúnlaigh nua -
scamhóga Gaeilge dúinn,
an dealbhadóir chuir clocha ag rince
lena sheanchaíocht.

File, ceoltóir, dealbhadóir,
is rompu an máistir-saoi,
ina measc siúd do tharlaíos-sa;
ní tharlóidh sé arís.

Maidin ghorm ins an Ghréig
(an leathchéad scoite agam),
ag cuimhneamh ar an luisne a bhí —
is cúrsa é roimh bás.

Anois an t-am don rince aonair
ar ghainimh bheo na trá —
na cosa a chaitheamh go háiféiseach
is leá d'aonghnó sa teas.

'Besides, who knows before the end what light may shine'

A blue mid-morning here in Greece
(my fiftieth year passed by),
under mottled beams and woven reeds —
body flees from sun.

Liszt, lucid in my ears, is merging
with the soft lap of the waves,
I'm immortal in this coolness,
enclosed between white walls.

As soon as the piano ceases
the sea ebbs from my heart
and I think of people home in my city
who, not long ago, stood high.

Four men from my native city
rise before me now,
the glow of mind which they created
I rubbed against a while —

a sage[1] who trembled at the brightness
in the forge of ancient poets,
a druid[2] who released our dammed-up music
and perished in the flood,

a tortured poet[3] who fashioned for us
new Irish-language lungs,
a sculptor[4] who set headstones dancing
with his carefree lore.

Musician, poet and sculptor,
and before them master-sage,
I happened to occur amongst them,
it will not occur again.

A blue mid-morning here in Greece
(my fiftieth year passed by)
thinking of the glow that was —
that's matter for the dying.

Better rise up now, a solo-dancer,
on the hot sands of the beach,
throw out both legs, at random,
and melt down in the sun.

1. Daniel Corkery (1878-1964), author, critic.
2. Seán Ó Riada (1930-71), composer.
3. Seán Ó Ríordáin (1916-77), poet.
4. Seamus Murphy (1907-75), sculptor and stone-carver.

PEARSE HUTCHINSON

(1927-)

from: FAOISTÍN BHACACH (1968)

[The translation of 'Maitheamh' is by James Liddy and is from his collection *In a Blue Smoke* (1964).]

Maitheamh

Ní iarrfad maitheamh
go humhal ar shagart
i mbosca dorcha
tromdonn docht
a rinne fá ghrásta
fear éigin cráite.

Ní gheobhad faoiseamh
ach oiread uaibhse,
a lucht síormhaoite
na leapan folaimhe;
ná ní chuirfead i bhfolach
mo náire ghonta
fád chlúmhsa, a dhuine
nár chaill riamh suirí.

Ar mo chomharsain, ar mo dhéithe,
ar chumhacht na gréine,
ar na daoine a ghoineas-sa,
ar na pianta a cuireadh orm,
ar an bhfear sa sagart,
ar mo scáthán briste,
iarrfadh maitheamh.

Forgiveness

I will not ask forgiveness
humbly from a priest
in a dark box,
in a narrow brown box
that was made under grace
by some tormented man.

I will not get release
from you either,
people that always boast
of empty beds,
nor will I hide my
wounded shame under your
trappings, man who got
your way at every love-making.

Of my neighbours, of my gods,
of the power of the sun,
of the people I have hurt,
of the pain inflicted on me,
of the man in the priest,
of my broken mirror:
I will ask forgiveness.

TOMÁS MAC SÍOMÓIN

(1938-)

from: CODARSNAÍ (1981) AND CRE AGUS CLÁIRSEACH (1983)

[The translation of 'Eadartheangachadh' is by the author and that of 'Níl in aon fhear ach a fhocal' is by Eoghan Ó hAnluain.]

Eadartheangachadh

As cláirseach gan sreang
atá ceol an fhómhair
ag siosarnach anuas

siollaí bhalbh-ionadh
ag cruinneáil ag na crosairí

is tádar ar a dtáirm anocht
'donn' agus 'buí' á rá acu
de chogar
na cainteoirí dúchais seo
gan fiacla

ach ní thuigir a dhath
ná bac
is gearr eile a mhairfidh siad

agus tá feadóg gan pholl agam
ar a gcasfaidh mé
(duitse ach go h-áirithe)

an port
ceanann
céanna.

TRANSLATION

From a stringless harp/autumn music/buzzes down/syllables in dumb surprise/gather at the crossroads/they're doing their best tonight/these native-speakers/sans teeth/'yellow' and 'brown'/ they whisper/and you understand nothing/no matter/their days are numbered/these days/I carry a chanter without stops/on which I shall play/(for you especially)/that/selfsame/tune.

Níl in aon fhear ach a fhocal *(seanfhocal)*

Is mé ar mo mharana ag faire,
Leabhar Uí Chriomthainn im láimh,
Ar rince Mhanannáin ilsúiligh
Um chríocha an oileáin —

Tír ghorm ghainéad is ghuairdeall
Go faillte Uíbh Ráthaigh ag síneadh
Is An Cnoc Mór mar chloch chinn
Ar phaidrín mo bhalla críche ...

'A nae seisean nochtóidh nóimead ar bith'
Bhí an Tomás seo ag machnamh,
'Is fillfidh an Tomás eile aneas
Ar a róda goirte ón gCathair.'

Ach má gháireann cuan faoi aoibh na gréine,
Ceann Sreatha is Binn Dhiarmada,
Tá fothrach sramach taobh thíos ag feo
Is níl gáir i gcoileach na muintire;

Tá Tost ina Rí ar gach maoileann abhus
Is tá ceol na ndaoine go follas ar iarraidh;
An gadaí gan ghéim, nár fhan, mo léan,
Ina pholl taobh thiar den Tiaracht,

A réab gan taise thar chuan isteach,
A shealbhaigh gort an bhaile seo,
A strap anuas trí shúil gach dín
Gur shuigh isteach cois teallaigh ....

Tá sé ag fuireach abhus ó shin;
Chím a scáth faoi scáth gach balla,
Is an chloch á baint ón gcloch aige,
An fhuaim ó gach macalla ...

Ach má taoi ag déanamh cré sa chill,
A Chriomhthannaigh an oileáin,
Gad do ghinealaigh fós níor bhris
Ó chuiris cor id dhán.

Ó d'íocais deachú an fhocail led nós,
Ó bhreacais caint do dhaoine ar phár,
Strapann do nae fós fál na toinne
Idir Muir na mBeo is Muir na Scál ...

Tá mise fós ar mo mharana ag faire
Is ó bhuanaigh do dhán a ndáil
Tá sluaite na marbh ag siúl go socair
Ar bhealaí an oileáin.

Is cluintear gáire mná le gaoth
Ag bearnú thost an bháis
Is cluintear gáir an choiligh arís
Ag baint macallaí as an ard.

'A man is only as good as his word' *(proverb)*

While I reflect here, watching, O'Crohan's[1] book in my hand, the dance of sparkling Manannán[2] around the margins of the island —

1. Tomás Ó Crohan (1855-1937), author of *The Islandman*.
2. Son of the sea-god Lir.

A region of gannets and petrels stretching as far as the cliffs of Iveragh[3] with Knockmore[4] as the largest bead on the rosary of my boundary wall . . . .

'His boat will appear at any moment' this Thomas reflected and that other Thomas will return from Caher[5] to his salty moorings.

But even if the bay smiles beneath the sun's smile Ceann Sreatha and Binn Dhiarmada,[6] a damp ruin disintegrates below and no cock crows in this community.

Silence is king on every summit here and the music of the people is so obviously absent: that spiritless thief who did not stay, alas, in his lair beyond Teeraght,[7]

3. A peninsula in west Kerry, south of the Blasket Islands.
4. A mountain in west Kerry.
5. Cahirciveen, a town on the Iveragh peninsula where Blasket Islanders sometimes sold their fish catches.
6. K'aun Sraha/Been Yeermuda. Two significant landmarks on the Dingle peninsula.
7. One of the Blasket Island group, on which there is a lighthouse.

Who broke his way mercilessly into this harbour, and possessed the fields of this community, who climbed down each chimney and sat in beside the hearth.

He has remained ever since; I see his shade beneath each wall's shadow, taking stone from stone, the sound from every echo . . . .

But if you, O'Crohan, islandman, are turning to clay, your lineage has not failed since you intervened in your destiny.

Since you paid the tithe of words to your way of life and wrote down the language of your people, your boat still climbs the wave's wall between the sea of life and the sea of ghosts . . . .

I am still here, reflecting, watching, and since your craft has perpetuated their way of life, the faithful departed calmly walk the island roads,

And a woman's laugh is heard in the wind breaking the silence of death, and the cock's crow is heard again re-echoing from the heights.

MICHAEL HARTNETT

(1941-)

from: ADHARCA BROIC (1978), DO NUALA: FOIGHNE CRAINN (1984), AN LIA NOCHT (1984)

[The translations by the author appear in *A Necklace of Wrens* (Dublin: The Gallery Press, 1987).]

An Dobharchú Ghonta

Dobharchú ghonta
ar charraig lom
ga ina taobh,
í ag cuimilt a féasóige
ag cuimilt scamaill a cos.

Chuala sí uair
óna sinsir
go raibh abhainn ann,
abhainn chriostail,
gan uisce inti.

Chuala fós go raibh breac ann
chomh ramhar le stoc crainn,
go raibh cruidín ann
mar gha geal gorm;
chuala fós go raibh fear ann
gan luaith ina bhróga,
go raibh fear ann
gan chúnna ar chordaí.

D'éag an domhan,
d'éag an ghrian i ngan fhios di
mar bhí sí cheana

ag snámh go sámh
in abhainn dhraíochta an chriostail.

The Wounded Otter

A wounded otter
on a bare rock
a bolt in her side,
stroking her whiskers
stroking her webbed feet.

Her ancestors
told her once
that there was a river,
a crystal river,
a waterless bed.

They also said
there were trout there
fat as tree-trunks
and kingfishers
bright as blue spears —
men there without cinders
in their boots,
men without dogs
on leashes.

She did not notice
the world die
nor the sun expire.
She was already
swimming at ease
in the magic crystal river.

Fís Dheireanach Eoghan Rua Uí Shúilleabháin

Do thál bó na maidine
ceo bainne ar gach gleann
is tháinig glór cos anall
ó shleasa bána na mbeann.
Chonaic mé, mar scáileanna,
mo spailpíní fánacha,
is in ionad sleán nó rámhainn acu
bhí rós ar ghualainn chách.

The Last Vision of Eoghan Rua Ó Súilleabháin[1]

The cow of morning spurted
milk-mist on each glen
and the noise of feet came
from the hills' white sides.
I saw like phantoms
my fellow-workers
and instead of spades and shovels
they had roses on their shoulders.

1. Owen Roe O'Sullivan (*c.* 1748-84), a Gaelic poet from County Kerry, who worked as a 'spalpeen' or travelling labourer.

Gné na Gaeltachta

i.m. C.M.

Sea, iad so na carraigeacha,
is iad so na botháin bhacacha —
tá seantaithí agam ar an áit seo:
feamainn ar na clocha
mar chróch báite,
linnte lán de mhíolta corcra,
éan ann chomh dubh le hocras.
Sea, is iad so na seansléibhte
atá anois déanta de bhréidín
(seantaithí agam ar an nGaeltacht —
duine mé de na stróinséirí).
Sea, is iad so na haighthe
d'eibhear déanta,
aighthe Atlantacha, creimthe le mórtas:
tá seantaithí agam ar na haighthe —
lán de shotal is d'éadóchas.
Sliabh, carraig is aghaidh — an buan iad?
Leathnaíonn criostal an tsalainn iontu
's pléasctar gach scoilt go smúit —
an salann, is sioc é gan séasúr,
an salann, tá sé buan.
Má mhaireann an charraig
go deireadh an domhain seo
mairfidh aghaidh áirithe
liom go lá mo mhúchta.
Na réalta bheith dall, an ghaoth bheith balbh,
raghaidh an ghné sin liom sa talamh
is eibhear a scéimhe millte le salann.

The Gaeltacht[1] Face

i.m. C.M.[2]

Yes, these are the rocks,
these the crooked cottages.
I knew this place well,

1. An Irish-speaking district.
2. Caitlín Maude (1941-82), poet and traditional singer from Ros Muc, an Irish-speaking district in Conamara, Co. Galway.

kelp on the stones, oh yes —
like drowned crocuses:
pools full of purple creatures,
a bird as black as hunger is.
Yes, these, the old hills,
now made of Irish tweed:
I know this Gaeltacht well,
I, a stranger here.
Yes, these are the faces
with their granite glance
Atlantic faces, pride-eroded:
I know these faces well
full of despair and arrogance.
Hills, faces, rocks upthrust.
In them the salt expands,
each crack explodes in dust
from salt, an everlasting frost,
this salt endures, and must.
Whether rock endures
until the world ends
a certain face will live with me
until my life is quenched.
Though stars not see, though wind not sound,
this face will follow me underground,
the granite of its beauty all salt-devoured.

Uch a athair, fan go fóill . . .

Sliocht as an dán fada 'An Lia Nocht'

Uch, a athair, fan go fóill,
fan liom beo go ndéanfar glan
gúna na cruinne bhíodh uair
chomh húr le croí an cháil.
An cuimhin leatsa bainne na mban
mar bhainne colm chothaíonn an t-ál?
Tálfar arís é — a athair, fan.

Do chonaic mé aréir é,
sa spéir ó thuaidh uaim
níos báine ná aon fhuil
ag sileadh ó chíoch na ré
is d'oscail fód spallta gach uaighe
is rinneadh as cré is bainne taos
as a fuineadh arán bheidh úr go buan.

Éist, a athair, éist go cruinn:
cé bodhrán é díon an domhain
is geocach sleamhain ag damhsa air,
tá siansa eile thar a ghlór.
Ná bíodh deifir ort, tóg mall é:
tá deoch an dearmaid romhat sa ród
is malairt cheoil ón bhfeadaire thall.

An bhfaca tú aréir iad,
nóiníní oíche go geal
go gleoite sa bhféar dubh
is caisearbháin go tiubh leo,
sabhrain greanta ar shról bhí seal
ar ghuaillí na ndéithe nach bhfuil beo
ach marbh ó d'imigh draíocht na sean?

An cuimhin leat réim an tsíl,
ríocht na míolta, cumhacht an aeir
(ina aonar ní raibh sé,
an duine daonna is a thíos),
an t-eas glasbhán ó chrann troim do léim —
cúr le cúr mar chlúmh-bhrat ar linn?
An cuimhin leat smúit gach dias féir?

Ná bí díomách: an fiú deoir
raic na staire, pór an oilc?
Na clocha bhí i gcónaí fuar,
túr gan díon is úllord na leac?
Éist, tá corcrán coille ar a thoil
ar inneoin ceárta go binn beacht —
is stair shíoraí siansa sáil a ghoib.

Is a athair, fan go fóill:
níl aon cheol tar éis an bháis,
níl rian daonna ná tuar ann
ach titim domhan sa ghréin.
Beidh an chruinne ina brídeach bhán,
muince réalta ar a gúna glé —
le hais gach crosaire beidh ardán
is feadóg stáin ag spalpadh ceoil —
go réidh a athair, is fan don spórt!

Ach níor fhan.
Obit. 3/10/84

Listen, father, wait a while —

from the long poem 'The Naked Surgeon'

. . . Listen, father, wait a while —
stay live with me till clean again
the universe's gown
once fresh as a cabbage-heart.
Do you remember mothers' milk
like pigeons' milk that feeds the flock?
It will pour again — wait on.

I saw it last night
in the northern sky
whiter than any blood
dripped from the moon's pap
and every parched grave opened up
and the dough of milk and earth
made a bread forever fresh.

Listen, father, listen close —
though the sky's a tambourine
danced on by an iron fool
there's harmony beyond his noise.
Take time and slow your pace —
the dark drink waits for you
and strange music out in space.

Did you see them last night,
night's-eyes brilliant bright
in the black grass
and dandelions *en masse*,
guineas on velvet once
an old god's shoulders
dead since the ancient magic passed?

Remember the age of the seed,
kingdom of creatures, power of air?
(Man was not alone,
man and his household).
Waterfall tumbling from elder-tree,
foam on pools like feather-capes?
Remember pollen from grasses' ears?

Listen, father, cry no tear
for evil seed, for history's debris,
for the cold eternal stones,
ruined towers, groves of graves.
Listen: a bullfinch sings sweetly
(musical anvil in forge)
his harmony's all history.

So, my father, wait a while.
There's no music after dying,
no inkling of a human sigh —
just worlds falling into suns.
Earth will be the brightest bride,
star-necklets on her gown —
tinwhistles cracking tunes,
platform dances in each town.
Easy, father, wait a while.

But he did not wait.
Obit. 3/10/84

MICHAEL DAVITT

(1950-)

from: SELECTED POEMS/ ROGHDA DÁNTA 1968-1984 (1987)

[The translations, published in the same volume, are by Gabriel Rosenstock, Michael Hartnett, Paul Muldoon and Philip Casey.]

Meirg agus Lios Luachra

do Mháire

gur imigh an t-am
mar seo mar siúd
sall timpeall
faoi
gurbh é an t-am a d'imigh
an t-am a bhí romhainn
sa todhchaí
is go rabhamar
tráthnóna síoraí samhraidh
i reilig seanghluaisteáin
ar fán
i measc fothraigh
na *model t's*
go raibh meirg ar do lámha
ar do ghúna fada bán
go rabhamar cosnocht
beo bocht
griandóite go cnámh
go rabhthas ag sméideadh orainn
trí fhuinneog traenach
a bhí ag filleadh

ó chraobh na héireann
i naoi déag tríocha ceathair
gur leanamar í tamall
feadh an iarnróid
gur fhilleamar abhaile
ar an gcoill rúnghlas
thíos ar ghrinneal locha
mar a raibh ár lios luachra
go raibh ceol mileoidin in uachtar
mediums pórtair á n-ól
arán tí ar bord
go raibh pearsana anaithnid
ina scáileanna ar snámh
idir sinn agus dán
go raibh bearnaí mistéireacha le dathú
agus véarsaí le cur lenár ngrá
sara mbeadh an pictiúr
iomlán.

Rust and Rampart of Rushes

for Máire

that time weaved
this way that way
over around
under
so that time past
was time before us
in the future
and that we were
one eternal summer evening
in a graveyard of old cars
wandering
among the ruins
of model t's
that there was rust on your hands
rust on your long white dress
that we were barefoot
penniless
sunburnt to the bone
that we were waved to
from the window of a train
returning from
the all-ireland final
in nineteen thirty four
that we followed it awhile
along the line
home
to our green and secret wood
down in the lake's bed
where our rampart of rushes stood
that it was all melodeon music
porter by the medium[1]
home-made bread on the table
that unknown persons
were shadows floating
between us and fate
that there were gaps of mystery to be painted
and verses to be added to our love
before the picture be
complete

translated by Gabriel Rosenstock and Michael Hartnett

1. A half-pint measure drawn from the barrel.

An Scáthán

i gcuimhne m'athar

I

Níorbh é m'athair níos mó é
ach ba mise a mhacsan;
paradacsa fuar a d'fháisceas,
dealbh i gculaith Dhomhnaigh
a cuireadh an lá dár gcionn.

Dhein sé an-lá deora, seirí
fuiscí, ceapairí feola is tae.
Bhí seanchara leis ag eachtraí
faoi sciurd lae a thugadar
ar Eochaill sna tríochaidí
is gurbh é a chéad pháirtí é
i seirbhís Chorcaí/An Sciobairín
amach sna daicheadaí.
Bhí dornán cártaí Aifrinn
ar mhatal an tseomra suí
ina gcorrán thart ar vás gloine,
a bhronntanas scoir ó C.I.E.

II

Níorbh eol dom go ceann dhá lá
gurbh é an scáthán a mharaigh é . . .

An seanscáthán ollmhór Victeoiriach
leis an bhfráma ornáideach bréagórga
a bhí romhainn sa tigh trí stór
nuair a bhogamar isteach ón tuath.

Bhínn scanraithe roimhe: go sciorrfadh
anuas den bhfalla is go slogfadh mé
d'aon tromanáil i lár na hoíche . . .

Ag maisiú an tseomra chodlata dó
d'ardaigh sé an scáthán anuas
gan lámh chúnta a iarraidh;
ar ball d'iompaigh dath na cré air,
an oíche sin phléasc a chroí.

III

Mar a chuirfí de gheasa orm
thugas faoin jab a chríochnú:
an folús macallach a pháipéarú,
an fhuinneog ard a phéinteáil,
an doras marbhlainne
a scríobadh. Nuair a rugas ar an scáthán
sceimhlíos. Bhraitheas é ag análú tríd.
Chuala é ag rá i gcogar téiglí:
I'll give you a hand, here.

Is d'ardaíomar an scáthán thar n-ais in airde
os cionn an tinteáin,
m'athair á choinneáil
fad a dheineas-sa é a dhaingniú
le dhá thairne.

The Mirror

in memory of my father

I

He was no longer my father
but I was still his son;
I would get to grips with that cold paradox,
the remote figure in his Sunday best
who was buried the next day.

A great day for tears, snifters of sherry,
whiskey, beef sandwiches, tea.
An old mate of his was recounting
their day excursion
to Youghal in the Thirties,
how he was his first partner
on the Cork/Skibbereen route
in the late Forties.
There was a splay of Mass cards
on the sitting-room mantelpiece
which formed a crescent round a glass vase,
his retirement present from C.I.E.[1]

II

I didn't realise till two days later
it was the mirror took his breath away.

The monstrous old Victorian mirror
with the ornate gilt frame
we had found in the three-storey house
when we moved in from the country.
I was afraid that it would sneak
down from the wall and swallow me up
in one gulp in the middle of the night . . .

While he was decorating the bedroom
he had taken down the mirror
without asking for help;
soon he turned the colour of terracotta
and his heart broke that night.

III

There was nothing for it
but to set about finishing the job,
papering over the cracks,
painting the high window,
stripping the door, like the door of a crypt.
When I took hold of the mirror
I had a fright. I imagined him breathing through it.
I heard him say in a reassuring whisper:
I'll give you a hand, here.

And we lifted the mirror back in position
above the fireplace,
my father holding it steady
while I drove home
the two nails.

translated by Paul Muldoon

1. Córas Iompair Éireann, the Irish transport system.

Ó Mo Bheirt Phailistíneach

— 18/19/82, iar bhfeiscint dom tuairisc theilifíse ar shlad na bPailistíneach i nBeirut

Bhrúigh mé an doras
oiread a ligfeadh solas cheann an staighre
orthu isteach:

na héadaí leapa caite díobh acu
iad ina luí sceabhach
mar ar thiteadar:

a gúna oíche caite aníos thar a mása
fuil ar a brístín lása,
as scailp i gcúl a cinn

a hinchinn sicín ag aiseag ar an bpiliúr,
putóg ag úscadh as a bholgsan
mar fheamainn ar charraig,

ae ar bhraillín,
leathlámh fhuilthéachta in airde.
Ó mo bheirt Phailistíneach ag lobhadh sa teas lárnach.

O My Two Palestinians

— having watched a television report on the Palestinian massacre in Beirut, 18/9/82

I pushed open the door
enough to let light from the landing
on them:

blankets kicked off
they lay askew
as they had fallen:

her nightgown tossed above her buttocks
blood on her lace knickers
from a gap in the back of her head

her chicken brain retched on the pillow,
intestines slithered from his belly
like seaweed off a rock,

liver-soiled sheets,
one raised bloodsmeared hand.
O my two Palestinians rotting in the central heat.

translated by Philip Casey

I gCuimhne ar Lís Ceárnaighe, Blascaodach (†1974)

Tráth bhíodh cártaí ar bord,
Coróin is mugaí tae faoi choinneal
Cois tine ar caorthainn;
Asal amuigh san oíche,
Madraí tamall gan bhia
Is seanbhean dom mharú le Gaolainn.

Tráth bhíodh an chaint tar éis Aifrinn
Is nárbh í a dhamnaigh faisean
Stróinséirí in aon fhéachaint shearbhasach amháin
Is nár chuir sí Laethanta Breátha
Ó Ollscoil Chorcaí ina n-áit:
'An tuairgín', 'an coca féir', 'an fuaisceán.'

Tráth prátaí is maicréal
Le linn na nuachta i lár an lae
Ba mhinic a fiafraí
Mar nár fhlúirseach a cuid Béarla
Is déarfainn dhera go rabhadar ag marú a chéile
I dtuaisceart na hÉireann.

Tráth bhíodh sí ina dealbh
Ag fuinneog bharr an staighre
Ar strae siar amach thar ché
Abhaile chun an oileáin i dtaibhreamh
Is dá dtiocfainn suas de phreib taobh thiar di:
'Ó mhuise fán fad' ort, a chladhaire.'

In Memory of Elizabeth Kearney, Blasketislander[1] (†1974)

Once it was cards on the table,
Rosary and mugs of tea in candlelight
Beside a blazing fire;
Outside, a donkey in the night,
Dogs denied their diet
And an old woman destroying me with Irish.

Once, there was the after-Mass chatting,
And she would trim the sails
Of strangers with one caustic look of her eye
Putting the College Trippers[2]
Firmly in their places
With 'pestles' and 'hencrabs' and 'haycocks'!

Once, at mackerel and potatoes
During the news at noon-time
She'd ask for a translation

1. The last Blasket islanders left to live on the mainland of County Kerry in 1953.
2. Students who had come to the district to learn Irish.

Because her English was lacking
And I'd say: 'Yera, they're killing each other
In the North of Ireland.'

Once, she was like a statue
At the top-stairs window
Wandering west from the quayside
Home in a dream to her island
And if I suddenly came up behind her
She'd say: 'Oh, you thief, may you long be
homeless!'

Dán do Sheosamh Ó hÉanaí

(†Lá Bealtaine 1984)

Ba chomaoin ar an teach tú a theacht.
Comharthaí sóirt an tseanfhóid
a thugais leat thar lear
bhíodar leat arís abhaile
thar tairseach isteach:
an iall bróige a cheangail do chás cnagaosta
is an gáire gáirisiúil sin, gáire an fhir
nár scag na blianta an buachaill as
is nach bhfuair a bhéasa *foyer* an lámh in uachtar
ar a bhéasa tinteáin
(thaispeánfá ar ball
go raibh do bhéasa stáitse gan cháim.)

Mhaireamar mí ar an sean-nós.
Tharchéimnigh do mhóinghlór
leamhas leathscartha an bhruachbhaile:
do shúile uaigneacha teallach-oscailte
do scéalta faoin seansaol i gCárna
do thóir laethúil ar ronnachaí úra
i margaí sráide na seanchathrach
do mhallachtaí ar phúdarthae na málaí
dá dhuibhe — níor mhór duitse
fianaise láidir duilleog i dtóin gach muga.
Chuiris deilín ar dheilín i mbéal na leanaí
is chuiris na fataí ag ceiliúradh
is ag brú a mbolg amach
sa bhfastaím.

Nuair a dhúntá do shúile istoíche
théimis ag siúl leat
siar na bóithríní
cosnochtaithe
ag portaireacht
ag cruinniú aislingí ar an Trá Bháin.

Poem to Joe Heaney[1]

(†Mayday 1984)

Your coming was a communion in our house.
Odd symbols of the old sod
you brought with you abroad
returned home with you
over the threshold:
the shoelace that tied your travel-worn suitcase
and that dirty grin, the grin of a man
from whom the years had not sifted the boy
and whose foyer manner had not got the better
of his fireside manner
(soon you would show us
your stage manner was faultless).

We lived for a month in the old style.
Your turf voice transcended
the semidetachedness of the suburb:
your lonely open-hearth eyes
your stories of the old life in Carna
your daily hunt for fresh mackerel
through street markets of the old city
your curses on the teabag powder no matter
how black we brewed it, you needed
strong proof of leaves at the bottom of every mug.
You handed on rigmarole and rhyme to the children
and made the potatoes celebrate
pushing out their bellies
for the fun of it.

When you closed your eyes at night
we would walk with you
down the backroads
barefoot
lilting
gathering *aislingí* [2] in Trá Bháin.

1. A master of Irish traditional singing from Carna, Conamara, Co. Galway.
2. visions, dreams.

LIAM Ó MUIRTHILE

(1950-)

from: TINE CHNÁMH (1984), INNTI II (1988)

[The translations, from *The Bright Wave/An Tonn Geala: Poetry in Irish Now* (Dublin: Raven Arts Press, 1986), are by Ciaran Carson, Dermot Bolger, Con Daly and Philip Casey. Translations of 'Tobhar' and 'Sa Daingean' are by Caoimhín Mac Giolla Léith.]

Portráid Óige I

do Annie Bowen/Julia Brien

Bhraitheas i mo stumpa de thornapa scúite
Tar éis duit mo chloigeann a lomadh
Sa chathaoir i lár an bhóthair.
'Tabharfaidh mé *clip* duit,' a dúraís,
Is b'ait liom an focal sin
Mar go rabhas i mo bhuachaill.
Bhís oilte ar chorpáin a réiteach amach
Is cé nach bhfaca riamh tú
Ag gabháil den cheird sin,
Shamhlaíos nach bhféadfadh éinne
A bheith marbh i gceart
Idir neart na gcnámh i do ghéagasa.
Ní raibh ann ach reo sealadach,
Is d'fhuinfeá an t-anam ar ais arís ann
Dá mba mhaith leat é.
Ach nuair a deineadh Dan Brien a thórramh
Comhrá moltach, tobac is deoch
Ag imeacht go flúirseach, dúraís-se:
'Dhera, bhí sé chomh craiceáilte
Le láir faoi eachmairt
Gach lá riamh dár mhair sé.'
Tráthnóna tar éis an cnoc a chur díot,
Lán an mhála chnáibe ar an rothar
D'earraí siopa ó Chaipín,
Sheasaís, scarais do dhá chois is dúirt:
'Caithfead mé féin a dhraenáil,'
Is dhein chomh mináireach le bó i bpáirc.
Cloisim fós do ghlór garbh,
Feicim casóg, bairéad, bróga d'fhir chéile ort,
Is santaím an spás leathan sin
A bhíodh eadrainn ag tús comhrá,
Tusa stadta i lár an bhóthair
Mise ag druidim de réir a chéile
Le garbhchríocha do dhaonnachta.

Portrait of Youth I

for Annie Bowen/Julia Brien

I felt like the stump of a scaldy turnip
When you had finished shearing me
In a chair planked down on the roadway.
'I'll give you a *clip*,' you said.
I was only a boy; the strange word stuck.
You had a knack of laying out a corpse.
Though I never saw you at the trade
It seemed that no-one could be rightly dead
When touched by your bony strength.
That stiffness could not last—
I thought that at your whim
Your hands could knead the soul back in.
But at Dan Brien's wake
When praise, tobacco, drink
Were brimming over, you came out with
'Sure every day of his life
Was a horse-fair;
He was as cracked as a mare in season.'
Mounting the hill one afternoon
With a full string bag
Dangling from your bike
You got off, spread your legs out wide
And said, 'I have to give the drains a go'—
And so you did;
You pissed as shamelessly as any cow.
I can still hear your gruff voice,
See your cassock, cap and man's boots.
I want it again, that easy space
That yawned between us as we yarned,
Your halting halfway on the road
As I drew in, bit by bit,
To the rough skirts of your humanity.

translated by Ciaran Carson

An Ceoltóir Jazz

Níl sa ghealach amuigh anocht
Ach spotsholas eile
A aimsíonn tine dhraíochta
Ina fheadóg mhór;
Scinneann lasracha
Óna gha airgid

Anois le fuadar stoirme
Éist! ní féidir breith air.
Ní lena chroí amháin
A sheinneann sé
Ach lena chorp iomlán,
Féach! tá taoide rabharta
Ag líonadh a chromáin,
Is nuair a thránn sé
Chím iasc ciúin
In íochtar an aigéin
Agus loinnir an cheoil
Ina shúil.

The Jazz Musician

Tonight the moon becomes
Just another spotlight
Igniting the magic spark
Within his jazz flute:
Flames spurt out
From the bewitched dart
With the force of a tempest,
Listen: he can't be caught.
Music surges
Not only from his heart
But through his whole body.
Look: a swirling spring tide
Floods between his hips,
And when it recedes
I see a swamped fish
Nestling on the ocean bed
With the glint of music
In its eye.

translated by Dermot Bolger

Do Chara Liom

Bhí d'fhéasóg riamh ciardhubh trom;
Maidin in óstán I nGaillimh chomhairlís dom
An fás saonta ar m'aghaidh féin
A bhogadh amach ar dtúis le huisce
Sula raghainn á bhearradh le lann.
Tá tú anois briste, ar bhinse i ndump daonna
Mar sheantreabhsar caite i gcúinne i ndearmad,
Is é do dhoircheacht is túisce a thagann chun mo chuimhne
San ospidéal, tráthnóna rothaíochta ar cuairt;
Is náiríonn mo bheith chomh mór le chéile mé i do láthair,
Tá na hothair ag imirt leadóg bhoird le do smionagar cinn
Tá pána amháin ar iarraidh sa bhfuinneog choirceogach
Is cuireann othar ina dhrárs gach cúpla nóiméad a lámh amach tríd.
Is deireann tú féin go mbraitheann tú uait Beethoven,
Ní ligfidh siad amach ag siúl sinn sa ghairdín—
Tá eagla orthu go n-éireoidh na bláthanna scitsifréineach
Is go mbéicfidh siad ar Wordsworth in ard a gcinn—
Is náirím arís nuair a deireann tú go fírinneach
Gur mhaith leat go bhfaighinn pianó duit i dtigh na ngealt
Chun go bhféadfá do laethanta a thabhairt ag méirínteacht
Ar na nótaí ciúine uafáis in *soledad*.

For My Friend

Your beard was always sable and thick;
In a Galway hotel one morning you counselled
To first soften the downy growth
On my own face with water
Before shaving it with a blade.
Now you are broken, on a bench in a human dump
Like a discarded pair of trousers forgotten in a corner,
And it's your state of darkness that strikes me first
In the hospital, cycling there one evening on a visit;
And I'm embarrassed by my bonhomie in your presence,
The patients are playing ping-pong with your shattered psyche,
There is a pane missing from the conical window
And every few minutes a patient in drawers sticks his hand through.
And you yourself say you sense Beethoven's absence,
They won't let us out to walk in the garden—
Afraid the flowers will become schizophrenic
And yell Wordsworth at the top of their heads—
And again I'm embarrassed when you truthfully say

You would like me to bring you a piano to the house of the mad
So you could spend your days fingering
On the quiet awful notes in *soledad*.[1]

translated by Con Daly and Philip Casey

1. (Spanish) solitude.

Tobar

Fé mar a ghearrfaí glan le lann líofa
ceann d'fhéitheacha reatha na beatha
scéitheann as an éasc sa chloch ghréine
cuisle uisce trí na criostail gan staonadh.
Líonann de réir a chúrsa lodartha an tobar modartha
is sníonn thar maoil go habhainn trí'n draein fholaithe.
Téim go hioscaid na nglún sa phluda ar an imeall
is taoscaim lem láimh athuair an draoib ón ngrinneall.

Braithim go hobann mo mhéireanta ar maos i gcorp duine
i mbun máinliacht chun foinse sruth fola a thaighde.
Coimeádfad leis ag fuilaistriú go nglanfaidh sé uaidh féin
ní foláir an beo a thabhairt slán gan géilleadh don aol.

Daingním na clocha rabhanálta a roghnaigh an té a bhí romham
is á dhíonadh le leacacha dom is ea 'tharlaím ar a mheon.
Táim fé dhraíocht aige bainim slat ghlas den bhfuinseoig
is deirim ortha na fola os a chionn im chaomhnóir.

I Reifidím i bhFásach Sín a thug Maois le hómós
Masá agus Miríbeá ar an áit gur steall an charraig le n-ól.
Athbhaistimse mo pholl in Achadh 'Mhíl le hais Abhainn na Seangán
'Tobar an Mhonabhair' a thug croí nua dhom agus taoscán den síocháin.

A Well

As if a keen-edged knife
had sliced clean through one of life's
rich arteries the water pulses out
from the quartz-stone's crystal wound.

It winds its muddy way to fill the turbid well
and spills over into the river through the hidden drain.
I plunge to my knees in mire at the well's edge
and try again to dredge its clotted bowl by hand.

My hand are suddenly a surgeon's hands
awash in crimson depths, fingering for a source.
I must maintain this steady transfusion, let it run its course.
Life must be preserved despite the lime's demands.

I carefully replace the round stones chosen long since
by another and chance upon the rhythm of his mind.
Entranced, I cut a green ash wand
and recite the charm for bleeding as if at his insistence.

In Rephidim, in the wilderness of Sin, Moses humbly named
the rocks from which the precious water was released
Massah and Meribah. I rename my well at Aughaveel.
here by the Shangaun's banks, *Tobar an Mhonabhair*.[1]
It has given me new heart and a cooling draught of peace.

translated by Caoimhín Mac Giolla Léith

1. 'The murmuring well'.

Sa Daingean

Tráthnóna sa Daingean,
Dearmadaim cad as mé leathshoicind—
Is a bhfuil d'eachtrannaigh líofa ag siúl an bhaile seo
Gléasta go cuí don bháisteach;
Folmhaíonn siad amach
As a mbusanna steireafónacha:

Na Herranna, na Fraunna, na Monsieuranna,
Na Madameanna, na Signoreanna, na
Signorinanna,
Gogalach choitianta na hEorpa i gCorca
Dhuibhne;
Agus sa Daingean tagann na bliúnna orm
Mar a chiúnaíonn an ceo anuas ar Cheann Sléibhe,
Tá an dúthaigh seo lán de thíosanna agus
thuasanna
Agus mise im chuairteoir aimnéiseach aonlae.
Is cuimhním ar an té a scríobh i dtarra
Ar an bhfalla ag barr an chalaidh i nDún Chaoin:
Rith síos má tá ceamara agat — íoróin in aisce
I mionteanga Eorpach nach dtuigeann puinn.
Is searraim díom na bliúnna ar Ché an Daingin,
Tá leaba na hoíche thiar i nGleann Fán
Ar díthreabh i mbungaló i measc na gcloichtheach
Agus cheal áit ar bith eile raghad ann.

In Dingle[1]

An afternoon in Dingle,
For one split second I forget where I am from —
Surrounded by polished foreigners who stroll about
Precision-dressed for rain.
They empty out
Of their stereophonic buses;
The Herrs and Fraus, Messieurs
and Madames, Signors and Signorinas,
A gaggle of common Europeans 'doing' Corca
Dhuibhne,[2]
And in Dingle the blues catch me napping
Like a mist sneaking up on Slea Head;[3]
This place is full of ups and downs
And I, an amnesiac daytripper, suddenly recall
The hand that wrote in tar on the Dunquin harbour
wall
Rith síos má tá ceamara agat[4] — an irony lost
In a minor European tongue obscure to most,
And I shake off the blues at Dingle quay,
Back in Gleann Fán there is a bed for me, I know,
Cloistered in a bungalow among the beehive huts;
I'll spend the night there — there's nowhere else
to go.

translated by Caoimhín Mac Giolla Léith

1. A town on the Dingle peninsula in County Kerry.
2. Historical name for the Dingle peninsula.
3. Prominent headland on the Dingle peninsula.
4. 'Run down here if you have a camera'.

NUALA NÍ DHOMHNAILL

(1952-)

from:
AN DEALG DROIGHIN (1981), FÉAR SUAITHINSEACH (1984)

[The translations of 'Leaba Shíoda' and 'I mBaile an tSléibhe' are by the author. The other versions are by Michael Hartnett. All are from *Selected Poems* (1986).]

Leaba Shíoda

Do chóireoinn leaba duit
i Leaba Shíoda
sa bhféar ard
faoi iomrascáil na gcrann
is bheadh do chraiceann ann
mar shíoda ar shíoda
sa doircheacht
am lonnaithe na leamhan.

Craiceann a shníonn
go gléineach thar do ghéaga
mar bhainne á dháil as crúiscíní
am lóin
is tréad gabhar ag gabháil thar chnocáin
do chuid gruaige
cnocáin ar a bhfuil faillte arda
is dhá ghleann atá domhain.

Is bheadh do bheola taise
ar mhilseacht shiúcra
tráthnóna is sinn ag spaisteoireacht
cois abhann

is na gaotha meala
ag séideadh thar an Sionna
is na fiúisí ag beannú duit
ceann ar cheann.

Na fiúisí ag ísliú
a gceann maorga
ag umhlú síos don áilleacht
os a gcomhair
is do phriocfainn péire acu
mar shiogairlíní
is do mhaiseoinn do chluasa
mar bhrídeog.

Ó, chóireoinn leaba duit
i Leaba Shíoda
le hamhascarnach an lae
i ndeireadh thall
is ba mhór an pléisiúr dúinn
bheith géaga ar ghéaga
ag iomrascáil
am lonnaithe na leamhan.

Labasheedy (The Silken Bed)

I'd make a bed for you
in Labasheedy[1]
in the tall grass
under the wrestling trees
where your skin
would be silk upon silk
in the darkness
when the moths are coming down.

Skin which glistens
shining over your limbs
like milk being poured
from jugs at dinnertime;
your hair is a herd of goats
moving over rolling hills,
hills that have high cliffs
and two ravines.

And your damp lips
would be as sweet as sugar
at evening and we walking
by the riverside

1. See the excerpt from *The Islandman* by Tomás Ó Crohan, pp. 880-82.

with honeyed breezes
blowing over the Shannon
and the fuchsias bowing down to you
one by one.

The fuchsias bending low
their solemn heads
in obeisance to the beauty
in front of them
I would pick a pair of flowers
as pendant earrings
to adorn you
like a bride in shining clothes.

O I'd make a bed for you
in Labasheedy,
in the twilight hour
with evening falling slow
and what a pleasure it would be
to have our limbs entwine
wrestling
while the moths are coming down.

I mBaile an tSléibhe

I mBaile an tSléibhe
tá Cathair Léith
is laistíos dó
tigh mhuintir Dhuinnshléibhe;
as san chuaigh an file Seán
'on Oileán
is uaidh sin tháinig an ghruaig rua
is bua na filíochta
anuas chugam
trí cheithre ghlún.

Ar thaobh an bhóthair
tá seidhleán
folaithe ag crainn fiúise,
is an feileastram
buí
ó dheireadh mhí Aibreáin
go lár an Mheithimh,
is sa chlós tá boladh
lus anainne nó camán meall
mar a thugtar air sa dúiche
timpeall,
i gCill Uru is i gCom an Liaigh
i mBaile an Chóta is i gCathair Boilg.

Is lá
i gCathair Léith
do léim breac geal
ón abhainn
isteach sa bhuicéad
ar bhean
a chuaigh le ba
chun uisce ann,
an tráth
gur sheoil trí árthach
isteach sa chuan,
gur neadaigh an fiolar
i mbarr an chnoic
is go raibh laincisí síoda
faoi chaoire na Cathrach.

In Baile an tSléibhe

In Baile an tSléibhe
is Cathair Léith
and below it
the house of the Dunleavies;
from here the poet Seán
went into the Great Blasket[1]
and from here the red hair
and gift of poetry came down to me
through four generations.

Beside the road
there is a stream
covered over with fuchsias
and the wild flag
yellow
from the end of April
to mid-June,
and in the yard there is a scent
of pineapple mayweed or camomile
as it is commonly known in the surrounding countryside,
in Cill Uru and in Coumaleague
in Ballincota and in Caherbullig.

And one day
in Cathair Léith
a white trout leapt
out of the river
and into the bucket
of a woman
who had led her cows
to water there;
a time
when three ships came sailing
into the bay
the eagle was still nesting
on the top of the hill
and the sheep of Cathair
had spancels of silk.

1. See the excerpt from *The Islandman* by Tomás Ó Crohan pp. 880-82.

An bhábóg bhriste

A bhábóigín bhriste ins an tobar,
caite isteach ag leanbh ar bhogshodar
anuas le fánaidh, isteach faoi chótaí a mháthar.
Ghlac sé preab in uaigneas an chlapsolais
nuair a léim caipíní na bpúcaí peidhl chun a bhéil,
nuair a chrom na méaracáin a gceannaibh ina threo
is nuair a chuala sé uaill chiúin ón gceann cait ins an dair.
Ba dhóbair nó go dtitfeadh an t-anam beag as nuair a ghaibh
easóg thar bráid is pataire coinín aici ina béal,
na putóga ar sileadh leis ar fuaid an bhaill
is nuair a dh'eitil an sciathán leathair ins an spéir.

Theith sé go glórach is riamh ó shin
tánn tú mar fhinné síoraí ar an ghoin
ón tsaighead a bhuail a chluais; báite sa láib
t'fhiarshúil phlaisteach oscailte de ló
is d'oíche, chíonn tú an madra rua is a hál
ag teacht go bruach na féithe raithní taobh lena bpluais
is iad ag ól a sá; tagann an broc chomh maith ann
is níonn a lapaí; sánn sé a shoc san uisce is lá
an phátrúin tagann na daoine is casann siad seacht n-uaire
ar deiseal; le gach casadh caitheann siad cloch san uisce.

Titeann na clocha beaga seo anuas ort.
Titeann, leis, na cnónna ón gcrann coill atá ar dheis
an tobair is éireoir ramhar is feasach mar bhreac
beannaithe sa draoib. Tiocfaidh an spideog bhroinndearg
de mhuintir Shúilleabháin is lena heireaballín
déanfaidh sí leacht meala d'uiscí uachtair an tobair
is leacht fola den íochtar, fós ní bheidh corraí asat.
Taoi teanntaithe go síoraí ins an láib, do mhuineál tachtaithe

le sreanganna 'lobelia'. Chím do mhílí ag stánadh orm
gan tlás as gach poll snámha, as gach lochán, Ophelia.

The Broken Doll

Oh small doll in the well, broken,
thrown by a child easily ambling
downhill, to his mother's skirts.
He got a fright in the lonesome dusk
when toadstool caps jumped to his mouth
when the foxgloves nodded towards him
when he heard an owl hoot in an oaktree.
His small soul nearly left him when
a stoat passed, a fat rabbit in her teeth
(its guts spilling out around the place)
and the bat flew through the air.

He ran crying and ever since
you are eternal witness to the wound
the arrow gave his ear: drowned in mud
your ever-open plastic squint
sees the vixen and her brood
come to the tangled bracken by their swampy den
and drink their fill: the badger also comes,
licks its paws and in the water shoves his snout
and people on pattern day[1] make seven circuits sunwise
with every turn throw pebbles in the well.

The small stones fall on you
and hazelnuts from the hazel to the right
of the well and you grow fat and wise
a sacred trout in the mire. The red robin
of the Sullivans will come and with its tail
will make liquid honey of the surface water
and liquid blood of the depths. You will not move
stuck forever in the mud
strangled by tendrils of lobelia,
I see you pallor stare at me
ungently from every swimming place and pool
Ophelia.

1. i.e. patron day, when people visit and pray at a well dedicated to the local or patron saint.

Dán do Mhelissa

Mo Pháistín Fionn ag rince i gcroí na duimhche,
ribín i do cheann is fáinní óir ar do mhéaranta,
duitse nach bhfuil fós ach a cúig nó a sé do bhlianta
tíolacaim gach a bhfuil sa domhan mín mín.

An gearrcach éin ag léimt as tóin na nide
an feileastram ag péacadh sa díog
an portán glas ag siúl fiarsceabhach go néata
is leatsa iad le tabhairt faoi ndeara, a iníon.

Bheadh an damh ag súgradh leis an madra allta
an naíonán ag gléachas leis an nathair nimhe,
luífeadh an leon leis an uan caorach
sa domhan úrnua a bhronnfainn ort mín mín.

Bheadh geataí an ghairdín ar leathadh go moch is go déanach,
ní bheadh claimhte lasrach á fhearadh ag Ceiribín,
níor ghá dhuit duilliúr fige mar naprún íochtair
sa domhan úrnua a bhronnfainn ort mín mín.

A iníon bhán, seo dearbhú ó do mháithrín
go mbeirim ar láimh duit an ghealach is an ghrian
is go seasfainn le mo chorp idir dhá bhró an mhuilinn
i muilte Dé chun nach meilfí tú mín mín.

Poem for Melissa

My fair-haired child dancing in the dunes
hair be-ribboned, gold rings on your fingers
to you, yet only five or six years old,
I grant you all on this delicate earth.

The fledgling bird out of the nest
the iris seeding in the drain
the green crab walking neatly sideways:
they are yours to see, my daughter.

The ox would gambol with the wolf
the child would play with the serpent
the lion would lie down with the lamb
in the pasture world I would delicately grant.

The garden gates forever wide open
no flaming swords in hands of Cherubin
no need for a fig-leaf apron here
in the pristine world I would delicately give.

Oh white daughter here's your mother's word:
I will put in your hand the sun and the moon
I will stand my body between the millstones
in God's mills so you are not totally ground.

Breith Anabaí Thar Lear

Luaimnigh do shíol i mo bhroinn,
d'fháiltíos roimh do bhreith.
Dúrt go dtógfainn go cáiréiseach thú
de réir gnása mo nuamhuintire.

An leabhar beannaithe faoi do philiúr
arán is snáthaid i do chliabhán,
léine t'athar anuas ort
is ag do cheann an scuab urláir.

Bhí mo shonas
ag cur thar maoil
go dtí sa deireadh
gur bhris na bainc
is sceith
frog deich seachtainí;
ní mar a shíltear a bhí.

Is anois le teacht na Márta
is an bhreith a bhí
le bheith i ndán duit
cuireann ribíní bána na taoide
do bhindealáin i gcuimhne dom,
tointe fada na hóinsí.

Is ní raghad
ag féachaint linbh
nuabheirthe mo dhlúthcharad
ar eagla mo shúil mhillteach
do luí air le formad.

Miscarriage Abroad

You, embryo, moved in me —
I welcomed your emerging
I said I'd rear you carefully
in the manner of my new people —

under your pillow the holy book,
in your cot, bread and a needle:
your father's shirt as an eiderdown
at your head a brush for sweeping.

I was brimming
with happiness
until the dykes broke
and out was swept
a ten-weeks frog —
'the best-laid schemes . . .'

and now it's March
your birthday that never was —
and white ribbons of tide
remind me of baby-clothes,
an imbecile's tangled threads.

And I will not go to see
my best friend's new born child
because of the jealousy
that stares from my evil eye.[1]

1. Traditionally an envious or begrudging look, which can inflict harm.

Gaineamh shúraic

A chroí, ná lig dom is mé ag dul a chodladh
titim isteach sa phluais dhorcha.
Tá eagla orm roimh an ngaineamh shúraic,
roimh na cuasa scamhaite amach ag uisce,
áiteanna ina luíonn móin faoin dtalamh.

Thíos ann tá giúis is bogdéil ársa;
tá cnámha na bhFiann 'na luí go sámh ann
a gclaimhte gan mheirg — is cailín báite,
rópa cnáibe ar a muinéal tairrice.

Tá sé anois ina lag trá rabharta,
tá gealach lán is trá mhór ann,
is anocht nuair a chaithfead mo shúile a dhúnadh
bíodh talamh slán, bíodh gaineamh chruaidh
romham.

Quicksand

My love, don't let me, going to sleep
fall into the dark cave.
I fear the sucking sand
I fear the eager hollows in the water,
places with bogholes underground.

Down there there's ancient wood and bogdeal:[1]
the Fianna's[2] bones are there at rest
with rustless swords — and a drowned girl,
a noose around her neck.

1. Deal wood found buried in bogs.
2. Ancient Irish warriors.

Now there is an ebb-tide:
the moon is full, the sea will leave the land
and tonight when I close my eyes
let there be terra firma, let there be hard sand.

Masculus Giganticus Hibernicus

Trodaire na dtriúch, fear beartaithe na miodóige,
is cuma más i *jeans* nó i do dhiabhal nóin
piocaithe feistithe i do chulaith *pinstripe*
a bhíonn tú,
is í an bheart chéanna agat í i gcónaí.

Iarsma contúirteach ón Aois Iarainn,
suíonn tú i bpubanna is beartaíonn
plean gníomhaíochta an fhill
ná filleann,
ruathar díoltais ar an bhfearann baineann.

Toisc nach leomhfaidh tú go bhféadfadh eascar
rós damascach cróndearg i gcroí do mháthar
caithfidh tú a gairdín a iompó
ina chosair easair
á phasáilt is á loit faoi do dhá spág crúb.

Is tánn tú ceáfrach, buacach, beannach;
Tá do bhuilín déanta.
Thiocfá suas ar aiteann
nó ar an bhfraoch a fhásann
ar leirgí grianmhara mná óige.

Masculus Giganticus Hibernicus

Country lout, knife thrower (dagger-wielder)
whether in jeans or a devil at noon
all dolled up in your pinstriped suit
you're always after the one thing.

Dangerous relic from the Iron Age
you sit in pubs and devise
the treacherous plan
that does not recoil on you —
a vengeful incursion to female land.

because you will not dare to halt the growth
of the dark-red damask rose in your mother's heart
you will have to turn the garden
to a trampled mess
pounded and ruined by your two broad hooves.

And you're frisky, prancing, antlered —
your bread is baked.
You'd live off the furze
or the heather that grows
on a young girl's sunny slopes.

CATHAL Ó SEARCAIGH

(1956-)

from:
SUIBHNE (1987)

[The translation, by Sarah Berkeley, is from Dermot Bolger (ed.) *The Bright Wave* (Dublin: Raven Arts Press, 1986).]

Súile Shuibhne

Tá mé ag tarraingt ar bharr na Bealtaine
go dúchroíoch i ndorchacht na hoíche
ag ardú malacha i m'aistear is i m'aigne
ag cur in aghaidh bristeacha borba gaoithe.

B'ise mo mhaoinín, b'ise mo Ghort a'Choirce
mise a thug a cuid fiántais chun míntíreachais
ach tá a claonta dúchais ag teacht ar ais arís
anocht bhí súile buí i ngort na seirce.

Tchím Véineas ansiúd os cionn Dhún Lúiche
ag caochadh anuas lena súile striapaí
agus ar ucht na Mucaise siúd cíoch na gealaí
ag gobadh as gúna dubh na hoíche.

Idir dólas agus dóchas, dhá thine Bhealtaine,
caolaím d'aon rúid bhuile mar leathdhuine.
Tá soilse an Ghleanna ag crith os mo choinne —
faoi mhalaí na gcnoc sin iad súile Shuibhne.

Sweeney's[1] Eyes

I am making for the summit of Bealtaine[2]
My heart heavy in the black of night
Scaling the rockface of mind and matter
Defending myself in the wind's harsh fight.

She was my wealth, she my harvest.
Her wild country made fertile by my hand
But the natural barrenness creeps back once more
Tonight there were weeds choking the land.

I see Venus over Dún Lúiche
Staring down with her whoring eyes
And the streak of the moon in Mucaise's lap
Rents the black dress of night's disguise.

Between horror and hope, two flames of Bealtaine[3]
I swing in one movement as madmen will
The lights in the valley tremble before me
And Sweeney's eyes are below the hill.

1. Poet-king in early Irish literature, who under a curse lived as a wild outcast from society.
2. A hill in County Donegal.
3. Here 'Bealtaine' is the Irish for the month of May. The phrase means 'in a dilemma' from 'the practise of driving cattle between two fires with a view to their preservation'. (Rev. Patrick S. Dineen (ed.), *Irish-English Dictionary* (1927)).

Biographies/Bibliographies

Peadar Ua Laoghaire (Canon Peter O'Leary)

LIFE. Born at Liscarrigane, near Macroom, Co. Cork in 1839, Peadar Ua Laoghaire was reared bilingually. He was educated at home by his mother until he was thirteen. After spending two years in St Colman's College, Fermoy, he went to the catholic seminary of St Patrick's, Maynooth in 1861, where he was ordained in 1867. It appears that he learned to read and write Irish at Maynooth. He ministered as chaplain in various parts of County Cork and was appointed parish priest of Castlelyons in 1891. He became active in the Gaelic League and his novel *Séadna* was serialized in *Irisleabhar na Gaedhilge* (*The Gaelic Journal*) between 1894 and 1897. *Séadna* was published in book form in 1904 and had a profound effect on the teaching and writing of modern Irish. It was his prolific output, about forty published books, which to a great extent established the living language, rather than the classical literary style, as the norm for contemporary writers. His pre-eminence in his time is indicated by his being awarded the freedom of the cities of Cork and Dublin in 1912 and a doctorate of the National University of Ireland in 1919. An t-Athair Peadar, as he was popularly known, died in Castlelyons in 1920.

CHIEF WRITINGS. *Séadna* (Baile Átha Cliath: Irish Book Company, 1904); new edition: Liam Mac Mathúna (ed.) (Baile Átha Cliath: Carbad, 1987).

BIOGRAPHY AND CRITICISM. Peadar Ua Laoghaire, *Mo Sgéal Féin* (autobiography) (Baile Átha Cliath: Irish Book Company, 1915); Sheila O'Sullivan, *My Own Story* (translation of *Mo Sgéal Féin*) (Dublin: Gill and Macmillan, 1973); Shán Ó Cuív, 'Materials for a Bibliography of the Reverend Peter Canon O'Leary 1839-1920', *Celtica* 11 (Part 2) 1954; 'Maol Muire' (Sister Mary Vincent), *An tAthair Peadar Ó Laoghaire agus a Shaothar* (Dublin: Brún agus Ó Nualláin, 1939); Pádraig A. Breatnach, 'Séadna: Saothar Ealaíne', *Studia Hibernica* 9; *Feasta*, Bealtaine 1989.

Patrick Pearse

LIFE. Born in Dublin in 1879, Pearse was educated by the Christian Brothers at Westland Row, Dublin, at University College, Dublin and at King's Inns, where he took a BA and BL respectively in 1901. In 1903 he was appointed editor of the Gaelic League's newspaper *An Claidheamh Soluis* (*The Sword of Light*). During his editorship (1903-09) his ideas on literary theory and practice and his incisive criticism had a crucial influence on the development of a modern literature in Irish. His two collections of stories, *Iosagán agus Sgéalta Eile* (1907) and *An Mháthair agus Sgéalta Eile* (1916), and his one collection of poems, *Suantraidhe agus Goltraidhe* (1914), established the short story and the individual lyric voice. In 1908 he founded a school in Dublin, St Enda's, in which he put into effect his progressive ideas on education. Through his involvement with the Gaelic League, the Irish Volunteers and the Irish Republican Brotherhood, Pearse made a profound contribution to the cultural and national revival which for him culminated in the Easter Rising and his execution on 3 May 1916.

CHIEF WRITINGS. *Collected Works of P.H. Pearse. Plays, Stories, Poems* (Dublin: Maunsel, 1917); Séamus Ó Buachalla (ed.), *The Literary Writings of Patrick Pearse* (Dublin: Mercier Press, 1979); Cathal Ó Háinle (ed.), *Gearrscéalta an Phiarsaigh* (Baile Átha Cliath: Helicon, 1979); Ciarán Ó Coigligh (ed.), *Filíocht Ghaeilge Phádraig Mhic Phiarais* (Baile Átha Cliath: An Clóchomhar, 1981).

BIOGRAPHY AND CRITICISM. Ruth Dudley Edwards, *Patrick Pearse: The Triumph of Failure* (London: Gollancz, 1977); Raymond J. Porter, *P.H. Pearse* (New York: Twayne, 1973).

Pádraic Ó Conaire

LIFE. Born in Galway city in 1882, Ó Conaire was orphaned by the age of eleven and went to live with relatives in Ros Muc, an Irish-speaking district in Conamara, Co. Galway. He attended Blackrock College, Co. Dublin and in 1889 entered the British civil service in London. He joined the Gaelic League there and met many of those involved in the Irish literary and national revival movements and found the encouragement to write in Irish. He read widely in modern European literature which left its mark on his writings. Although Pearse had pioneered the idea of a contemporary literature in Irish, it was Ó Conaire who gave that idea real effect in the best of his stories. He returned to Ireland in 1914 and earned his living as a contributor to newspapers and journals until his untimely death in Dublin in 1928.

CHIEF WRITINGS. *Nóra Mharcuis Bhig* (Baile Átha Cliath: Clódhanna Teo., 1909); *Deoraidheacht* (a novel) (Baile Átha Cliath: Clódhanna Teo., 1910) new edition: *Deoraíocht* (Baile Átha Cliath: Cló Talbot, 1973); *An Chéad Chloch* (Baile Átha Cliath: Clódhanna Teo., 1914) new edition: Pádraigín Riggs (ed.), (Baile Átha Cliath agus Corcaigh: Cló Mercier, 1978); *Seacht mBuaidh an Éirighe Amach* (Baile Átha Cliath: Maunsel, 1918) new edition: Tomás De Bhaldraithe (ed.), (Baile Atha Cliath: Sáirséal & Dill, 1967); *Síol Éabha* (Baile Átha Cliath: Martin Lester, 1922); *Scothscéalta* (selected stories), Tomás De Bhaldraithe (ed.), (Baile Átha Cliath: Sáirséal & Dill, 1956); *The Finest Stories of Pádraic Ó Conaire* (Swords, Co. Dublin: Poolbeg Press, 1982).

BIOGRAPHY AND CRITICISM. Áine Ní Chnáimhín, *Pádraic Ó Conaire* (Baile Átha Cliath: Oifig an tSoláthair, 1947); Seosamh Mac Grianna, *Pádraic Ó Conaire agus Aistí eile* (Baile Átha Cliath: An Gúm, 1963); Gearóid Denvir, *Aistí Phádraic Uí Chonaire* (Indreabhán: Cló

Chonamara, 1978); Cathal Ó Háinle, *Promhadh Pim* (Maigh Nuad: An Sagart, 1978); Tomás De Bhaldraithe, *Pádraic Ó Conaire: Clocha ar a Charn* (Baile Átha Cliath: An Clóchomhar, 1982); Proinsias MacAonghusa, 'Pádraic Ó Conaire: Notaí beaga faisneise', *Feasta*, Feabhra 1982; Gearoid Denvir (ed.), *Léachtaí Cuimhneacháin* (Indreabhán, Co. na Gaillimhe: Cló Chonamara, 1983).

Liam Ó Flaithearta (Liam O'Flaherty)

LIFE. Born in 1896 on Inishmore, Aran Islands, Ó Flaithearta was educated at Rockwell College, Co. Tipperary, Blackrock College, Co. Dublin and University College, Dublin. He joined the Irish Guards in 1915 and was invalided out of the army in 1917. He moved to London, where his first novel, *Thy Neighbour's Wife*, was published in 1922. He was a founder member of the Irish Academy of Letters. His short stories in Irish were written at two distinct periods — the early 1920s and during the late 1940s and early 1950s. Liam Ó Flaithearta died in Dublin in 1984.

CHIEF WRITINGS (in Irish). *Dúil* (Baile Átha Cliath: Sáirséal & Dill, 1953).

BIOGRAPHY AND CRITICISM. Breandán Ó hEithir, 'Liam Ó Flaithearta agus a dhúchas', in *Comhar*, Lúnasa 1976; Paul Doyle, *Liam O'Flaherty* (New York: Twayne, 19); Tomás De Bhaldraithe, 'Liam O'Flaherty — Translator?', in *Éire-Ireland*, Summer 1968; Seán Ó Faoláin, 'Dúil' in John Jordan (ed.), *The Pleasures of Gaelic Literature* (Dublin and Cork: Mercier Press in collaboration with Radio Telefís Éireann, 1977); William Daniels, 'Introduction to the Present State of Criticism of Liam O'Flaherty's Collection of Short Stories: *Dúil*, in *Éire-Ireland*, Vol. 23, 1988.

Seosamh Mac Grianna

LIFE. Born in the Irish-speaking area of Ranafast, Co. Donegal in 1901, Mac Grianna was educated at St Eunan's College, Letterkenny, St Columb's College, Derry and at St Patrick's College, Drumcondra in Dublin where he qualified as a primary schoolteacher in 1921. Imprisoned as a Republican during the Civil War, he eventually abandoned teaching and lived precariously as a writer until 1940 when he ceased writing altogether. Much of his energy was given to translating English novels under a Department of Education scheme to provide reading matter in the Irish language. He lived in and around Dublin during the 1940s and 1950s and returned to Donegal in 1957. Mac Grianna received belated recognition in 1969 when he was awarded the Irish-American Cultural Institute Award for his novel *An Druma Mór*, which had been written in the 1930s. He died in Donegal in 1990.

CHIEF WRITINGS. *Dochartach Dhuibhlionna agus Scéaltaí Eile* (Baile Átha Cliath, 1925); *An Grádh agus an Ghruaim* (Baile Átha Cliath: Oifig an tSoláthair, 1929); *Eoghan Ruadh Ó Néill* (Baile Átha Cliath: Oifig an tSoláthair, 1931); *Pádraic Ó Conaire agus Aistí eile* (Baile Átha Cliath: Oifig an tSoláthair, 1936) (new edition, 1969); *Mo Bhealach Féin* (Baile Átha Cliath: Oifig an tSoláthair, 1940) (new edition, 1965); *An Druma Mór* (Baile Átha Cliath: Oifig an tSoláthair, 1969).

BIOGRAPHY AND CRITICISM. Riobard Ó Faracháin, 'Seosamh Mac Grianna', *The Bell*, Vol. I, No. 2 (November 1940); Breandán Ó Doibhlin, 'Fear agus Finscéal', *Irisleabhar Mhá Nuad*, 1969; Proinsias Mac an Bheatha, *Seosamh Mac Grianna agus Cúrsaí Eile* (Baile Átha Cliath: Foilseacháin Náisiúnta Teo., 1970); Proinsias Mac Cana, 'An Druma Mór', *Comhar*, Bealtaine 1971; Oilibhéar Ó Croiligh, *Bealach Mhic Ghrianna* (Corcaigh agus Baile Átha Cliath: Cló Mercier, 1972); Declan Kiberd, 'Idir dhá thraidisiún' in Seán Ó Mórdha (ed.), *Scríobh* 5 (Baile Átha Cliath: An Clóchomhar, 1981); Liam Ó Dochartaigh, 'Mo Bhealach Féin: Saothar Nualitríochta' in Seán Ó Mórdha (ed.), *Scríobh* 5 (Baile Átha Cliath: An Clóchomhar, 1981); Donnchadh Ó Baoill, 'Druma Mór na Filíochta' in *Nua-Aois* (An Cumann Liteartha, Coláiste na hOllscoile, Baile Átha Cliath, 1986); Seamus Deane, 'Mo Bhealach Féin' in John Jordan (ed.), *The Pleasures of Gaelic Literature* (Dublin and Cork: Mercier Press, in collaboration with Radio Telefís Éireann, 1977); Nollaig Mac Conghail, 'Foinsí béaloidis i ngearrscéalta Sheosaimh Mhic Ghrianna', *Comhar*, Feabhra 1978.

Máirtín Ó Cadhain

LIFE. Born in the Irish-speaking area west of Spiddal in Conamara, Co. Galway in 1906, Ó Cadhain was educated locally and at St Patrick's College, Drumcondra in Dublin, where he qualified as a primary teacher in 1926. He lost his job as a teacher as a result of his involvement in the Irish Republican Army, and was held in the internment camp at the Curragh, Co. Kildare from 1940 to 1944. In 1949 he joined the Translation Department of Dáil Éireann (Irish Parliament). He was appointed lecturer in modern Irish in Trinity College, Dublin in 1956 and professor of Irish in 1969. In 1967 he was awarded the Irish-American Cultural Institute Award. He died in Dublin in 1970, leaving several unpublished manuscripts.

CHIEF WRITINGS. *Idir Shúgradh agus Dáiríre* (Baile Átha Cliath: Oifig an tSoláthair, 1939) (new edition, 1975); *An Braon Broghach* (Baile Átha Cliath: Oifig an tSoláthair, 1948) (new edition, 1968); *Cois Caolaire* (Baile Átha Cliath: Sáirséal & Dill, 1953); *An tSráith ar Lár* (Baile Átha Cliath: Sáirséal & Dill, 1967); *An tSraith Dhá Tógáil* (Baile Átha Cliath: Sáirséal & Dill, 1970); *An tSraith Tógtha* (Baile Átha Cliath: Sáirséal & Dill, 1970); *Cré na Cille* (novel) (Baile Átha Cliath: Sáirséal & Dill, 1949); *Páipéir Bhána agus Páipéir Bhreaca* (an essay on his own development as a writer) (Baile Átha Cliath: An Clóchomhar, 1969).

BIOGRAPHY AND CRITICISM. An tSr. Bosco Costigan, Seán Ó Curraoin, *De Ghlaschloich an Oileáin* Beatha agus Saothair Mháirtín Uí Chadhain (Gaillimh: Cló Iarchonnacht, 1987); Gearóid Denvir, *Cadhain Aonair: Saothair Eiteartha Mháirtín Uí Chadhain* (Baile Átha Cliath: An Clóchomhar, 1975); Alan Titley, *Máirtín Ó Cadhain: Clár Saothair* (Baile Átha Cliath: An Clóchomhar, 1975) — these three books contain extensive bibliographies; 'Máirtín Ó Cadhain 1906-1970', *Comhar* (special edition, Deireadh Fómhair, 1980).

Seán Mac Mathúna

LIFE. Born in Tralee, Co. Kerry in 1936, Mac Mathúna was educated at St Brendan's College, Killarney and at University College, Cork and worked for many years as a teacher. He writes in Irish and in English and has been director of the National Writers' Workshop. He lives in Dublin.

CHIEF WRITINGS. *Ding agus Scéalta eile* (Dublin: Helicon, 1982); *The Atheist and Other Stories* (Dublin: Wolfhound Press, 1987).

BIOGRAPHY AND CRITICISM. Agallamh le Siobhán Ní Fhoghlú in *The Bridge/An Droichead*, New York and Dublin, Fall 1987; Siobhán Ní Fhoghlú, 'Ding thú!', in *Comhar*, Nollaig 1987; Agallamh: Liam Ó Muirthile ag caint le Seán Mac Mathúna, *Comhar*, Deireadh Fómhair, 1989.

Alan Titley

LIFE. Born in Cork city in 1947, Titley was educated at Coláiste Críost Rí, Cork, at St Patrick's College in Drumcondra, Dublin and at University College, Dublin. He taught in West Africa for several years and is now head of the Irish Department in St Patrick's College. In 1988 he received the Irish-American Cultural Institute Award. He has written a play, *Tagann Godot*, for the Peacock Theatre.

CHIEF WRITINGS. *Méirscrí na Treibhe* (novel) (Baile Átha Cliath: An Clóchomhar, 1978); *Stiall Fhial Feola* (novel) (Baile Átha Cliath: An Clóchomhar, 1980); *Máirtín Ó Cadhain: Clár Saothair* (Baile Átha Cliath:

An Clóchomhar, 1975); *Eiriceachtaí agus Scéalta Eile* (Baile Átha Cliath: An Clóchomhar, 1987).

BIOGRAPHY AND CRITICISM. Seán Ó Tuama, 'An Domhan a chruthaigh Titley', *Comhar*, Nollaig 1987.

Tomás Ó Criomhthainn (Tomás Ó Crohan)

LIFE. Born in 1855 on the Great Blasket Island, Ó Criomhthainn lived there all his life. He married in 1878 and had ten children. He was a skilled stone mason and fisherman and learned to read and write English at school. He was well over forty when he learned to read and write in Irish. The increasing intrest in the Irish language at the turn of the century brought learners and scholars to the island and Tomás Ó Criomhthainn became a teacher to the Norwegian scholar Carl Marstrander (1881-1965) and the Englishman Robin Flower (1881-1946). The latter wrote an account of island life, *The Western Island* (Oxford, 1944), and made a collection of stories and poems from Ó Criomhthainn, later published as *Seanchas ón Oileáin Tiar* (Dublin, 1956). In 1917 Brian Ó Ceallaigh (1889-1936), a native of Killarney and a graduate of Trinity College, Dubin, came to the island to learn Irish and struck up a close friendship with Ó Criomhthainn. It was he who encouraged Ó Criomhthainn to write an account of daily life on the island and eventually an account of his own life. On Ó Ceallaig's departure for Europe (he died in Yugoslavia in 1936), he left the Ó Criomhthainn material with Pádraig Ó Siochfhradha (1883-1964), the Irish teacher and scholar who had first sent him to the Blasket and it was he who prepared the two books for publication. *Allagar na hInise* (Island Cross-Talk) was published in 1928 and the celebrated autobiography, *An tOileánach* (The Islandman), in 1929. Tomás Ó Criomhthainn died in 1937.

CHIEF WRITINGS. *Allagar na hInise* ('An Seabhac', .i. Pádraig Ó Siochfhradha (ed.), Baile Átha Cliath: C.S. O Fallúin i gcomhar le hOifig an tSoláthair, 1928) 2nd edition, Pádraig Ua Maoileon (Baile Átha Cliath: Oifig an tSoláthair, 1977); *An tOileánach* ('An Seabhac', .i. Pádraig Ó Siochfhradha (ed.), Baile Átha Cliath: C.S. Ó Fallúin i gcomhar le hOifig an tSoláthair, 1929) 2nd edition, Pádraig Ua Maoileoin (ed.) (Baile Átha Cliath: Cló Talbot, 1973); *The Islandman*, Tomás O'Crohan (translation of *An tOileánach*) Robin Flower (Dublin: The Talbot Press; London: Chatto and Windus, 1937; Oxford: Oxford University Press, 1951); *Island Cross-Talk*, a translation of *Allagar na hInise* by Tim Enright (Oxford: Oxford University Press, 1986).

BIOGRAPHY AND CRITICISM. Muiris Mac Conghail, *A Blasket Island Library* (Dublin: Country House, 1987). This is the best introduction to the writings of Tomás Ó Criomhthainn and other Blasket Island writers. It contains an extensive bibliography.

Muiris Ó Súilleabháin (Maurice O'Sullivan)

LIFE. Born on the Great Blasket Island in 1904, Ó Súilleabháin, on the death of his mother, was sent to an orphanage on the mainland, where he grew up speaking English. On his return to the island at six years of age, he learned Irish and in this respect was greatly influenced by his grandfather, who was a storyteller and *seanchaí* (versed in local lore). The English classical scholar George Thomson (1903-87), who came to the Blasket in 1923, encouraged him to stay in Ireland and join the Garda Síochana (Civic Guard). Ó Súilleabháin was posted to Conamara, and there, further encouraged by Thomson, wrote his autobiography, *Fiche Blian ag Fás*, which along with its English translation, *Twenty Years A-Growing*, was published in 1933. German and French translations followed. Ó Súilleabháin left the Gardaí to take up writing full-time, but his second volume of autobiography, *Fiche Blian faoi Bhláth* (*Twenty Years A-Flowering*), was never published. He rejoined the Gardaí in 1950 and drowned while swimming that same year.

CHIEF WRITINGS. *Fiche Blian ag Fás* (Baile Átha Cliath: Clólucht an Talbóidigh, 1933) (2nd and 3rd editions, Má Nuad: An Sagart, 1976, 1981); *Twenty Years A-Growing*, Maurice O'Sullivan (translation by Moya Llewelyn Davis and George Thomson) (London: Chatto and Windus, 1933; Oxford: Oxford University Press, 1953).

BIOGRAPHY AND CRITICISM. Muiris Mac Conghail, *A Blasket Island Library* (Dublin: Country House, 1987).

Máirtín Ó Direáin

LIFE. Born in Inishmore, Aran Islands in 1910, Ó Direáin was educated locally and in 1928 left Aran to work in the Post Office in Galway city. Here he became involved in the Irish-language movement and acted in Taibhdhearc na Gaillimhe (Irish language theatre). He moved to Dublin in 1938, in which year he began to write poems. At his own expense he published two collections, *Coinnle Geala* in 1942 and *Dánta Aniar* in 1943. His *Rogha Dánta* in 1949 and *Ó Mórna agus Dánta Eile* in 1957 established him as a significant poet with a distinctive voice. He received the Irish-American Cultural Institute Award in 1967. In 1977 the National University of Ireland conferred on him an honorary D.Litt. and in the same year the FVS Foundation Hamburg awarded him its *Ossian-Preis*. He remained in the civil service until his retirement in 1975. He died in 1988.

CHIEF WRITINGS. *Coinnle Geala* (Baile Átha Cliath: Brún agus Ó Nualláin, 1942); *Dánta Aniar* (Baile Átha Cliath, 1943); *Rogha Dánta* (Baile Átha Cliath: Sáirséal & Dill, 1949); *Ó Mórna agus Dánta Eile* (Baile Átha Cliath: Cló Morainn, 1957); *Ár Ré Dhearóil* (Baile Átha Cliath: An Clóchomhar, 1963); *Cloch Choirnéil* (Baile Átha Cliath: An Clóchomhar, 1966); *Crainn is Cairde* (Baile Átha Cliath: An Clóchomhar, 1970); *Ceacht an Éin* (Baile Átha Cliath: An Clóchomhar, 1979); *Dánta 1939-1979* (Baile Átha Cliath: An Clóchomhar, 1980); *Béasa an Túir* (Baile Átha Cliath: An Clóchomhar, 1984); Douglas Sealy, Tomás Mac Siomóin, *Máirtín O Direáin: Selected Poems/Tacar Dánta* (Newbridge: Goldsmith Press, 1984); Prose: *Feamainn Bhealtaine* (Baile Átha Cliath: An Clóchomhar, 1961) (contains valuable autobiographical material).

BIOGRAPHY AND CRITICISM. Muiris Mac Conghail, 'Dia agus Diabhail' in *Comhar*, Deireadh Fómhair, 1984; 'Comhrá le Máirtín Ó Direáin' in *Innti* 6; Frank O'Brien, *Filíocht Ghaeilge na Linne Seo* (Baile Átha Cliath: An Clóchomhar, 1968), pp. 203-99; Mícheál Mac Craith, 'Filíocht Mháirtin Uí Dhireáin' in *Comhar* (Eanáir-Meitheamh, 1981); Mícheál Ó hUanacháin, 'Máirtín Ó Direáin' in Seán Mac Réamoinn (ed.), *The Pleasures of Gaelic Poetry* (London: Allen Lane, Penguin Books, 1982); Liam Prút, *Máirtín Ó Direáin: File Tréadúil* (Maigh Nuad: An Sagart, 1982); Maureen Murphy, 'Elegy for Aran: The Poetry of Máirtín Ó Direáin in James D. Brophy and Raymond J. Porter (eds), *Contemporary Writing in Irish* (New York: Iona College Press, 1972), pp. 143-56; Breandán Ó Doibhlin, 'Máirtín Ó Direáin agus an tOilean Rúin', *Irisleabhar Mhá Nuad*, 1966; Tomás Ó Floinn, 'An áit atá ag saothar Mháirtin Uí Dhireáin i dtraidisiún na filíochta Gaeilge', *Comhar*, Deireadh Fómhair, 1984; Eoghan Ó hAnluain, 'Nóta faoi Blianta an Chogaidh le Máirtín Ó Direáin', *Scríobh* 2; Seán Ó Mórdha (ed.), (Baile Átha Cliath: An Clóchomhar, 1975); 'An Choinneal agus an tOrlach', *Scriobh* 3; Seán Ó Mórdha (ed.), (Baile Átha Cliath: An Clóchomhar, 1978); 'Fearann Coimirce m'Aislinge', *Comhar*, Deireadh Fómhair, 1984.

Seán Ó Ríordáin

LIFE. Born in 1916 into the bilingual community of Ballyvourney, Co. Cork, Ó Ríordáin was educated locally and by the Christian Brothers at the North Monastery in Cork city. From his teens he suffered the life-long effects of tuberculosis and spent long periods in sanatoria. After taking the leaving certificate in 1936, he went to work in the motor taxation department of Cork Corporation and remained there until his early retirement in 1965. His poems began to appear in the magazine *Comhar* (founded in 1942) and the originality of his voice was soon recognized. His first collection, *Eireaball Spideoige* (1952), aroused controversial critical interest. In 1967 he began a remarkable column in *The Irish Times* which he wrote weekly until 1975. His unique prose style had been cultivated over the years in diaries which he had kept since 1940. The honorary degree D.Litt. was conferred on him by the National University of Ireland in 1976. He died in Cork in 1977.

CHIEF WRITINGS. *Eireaball Spideoige* (Baile Átha Cliath: Sáirséal & Dill, 1952); *Brosna* (Baile Átha Cliath: Sáirséal & Dill, 1964); *Línte Liombó* (Baile Átha Cliath: Sáirséal & Dill, 1967); *Tar éis mo Bháis* (Baile Átha Cliath: Sáirséal & Dill, 1967); *Rí na nUile* (modern versions from early Irish in collaboration with Seán S. Ó Conghaile) (Baile Átha Cliath: Sáirséal & Dill, 1964).

BIOGRAPHY AND CRITICISM. Seán Ó Coileáin, *Seán Ó Ríordáin: Beatha agus Saothar* (Baile Átha Cliath: An Clóchomhar, 1982); Seán Ó Tuama, *Filí faoi Sceimhle* (Baile Átha Cliath: Oifig an tSoláthair, 1978); Sean Ó Tuama, 'Seán Ó Ríordáin' in Seán Mac Réamoinn (ed.), *The Pleasures of Gaelic Literature* (London: Penguin Books, 1982); Frank O'Brien, *Filíocht Ghaeilge na Linne Seo* (Baile Átha Cliath: An Clóchomhar, 1968), pp. 301-35; Breandán Ó Doibhlin, 'Seán Ó Ríordáin agus an Spiorad Barocach' in *Irisleabhar Mhá Nuad*, 1967; Tadhg Ó Dúshláine, 'Seán Ó Ríordáin: Homo Ludens' in *The Maynooth Review*, Vol. 4, No. 1 (May 1978), pp. 53-62; *Comhar* (special Seán Ó Ríordáin edition) Bealtaine 1977; Máire Mhac an tSaoi, 'Fireann ar an Uaigneas' in Seán Ó Mórdha (ed.), *Scríobh* 1 (Baile Átha Cliath: An Clóchomhar, 1974); John Jordan, 'Seán Ó Ríordáin: After His Death', *Cyphers* 11 (Winter 1978), 45-49.

Eoghan Ó Tuairisc

LIFE. Born in Ballinasloe, Co. Galway in 1919 and christened Eugene Rutherford Louis Watters, Ó Tuairisc was educated at St Joseph's College, Garbally, St Patrick's College, Drumcondra (where he qualified as a primary teacher in 1939) and at University College, Dublin, where he took an MA in English literature in 1947. He was commissioned in the army in 1939 and served during the war years. He taught at Finglas, Co. Dublin until, following the publication of two novels, *A Murder in Three Moves* and *L'Attaque* (a novel in Irish on the theme of the French landing at Killala in 1798), he resigned from teaching to become a full-time writer, and edited the Gaelic League journal *Feasta*. In 1964 he published two volumes of poetry, *The Weekend of Dermot and Grace* and *Lux Aeterna*; the second contained 'Aifreann na Marbh', his sombre requiem for those who 'died at Hiroshima' and one of the high points of modern poetry in Irish. He published two more novels, both innovative in style, *Dé Luain* (1966) and *An Lomnochtán* (1977). In 1972 he married the writer Rita E. Kelly and went to live in Mageney, near Carlow town and began a new phase of literary activity. He became a member of Aosdána on its inauguration. His second volume of poems, *Dialann sa Díseart* (1981), was written in collaboration with his wife. He died at Caim, Co. Wexford in 1982.

CHIEF WRITINGS. (In Irish) *L'Attaque* (novel) (Baile Átha Cliath: Allen Figgis, 1960); *Lux Aeterna* (poems) (Baile Átha Cliath: Allen Figgis, 1964); *Dé Luain* (novel) (Baile Átha Cliath: Allen Figgis, 1966); *An Lomnochtán* (novel) (Baile Átha Cliath agus Corcaigh: Cló Mercier, 1977); *Lá Fhéile Mhíchíl* (play) (Baile Átha Cliath: Clodhanna Teo., 1967); *Aisling Mhic Artáin* (play) (Baile Átha Cliath: Clodhanna Teo., Folens, 1978); *Fornocht do Chonac* (play) (Baile Átha Cliath: Foilseacháin an Rialtais, 1981); *Dialann sa Díseart* (poems, with Rita E. Kelly) (Baile Átha Cliath: Coiscéim, 1981); *Religio Poetae' agus Aistí eile* (essays, Máirín Nic Eoin (ed.)) (Baile Átha Cliath: An Clóchomhar, 1987).

BIOGRAPHY AND CRITICISM. Máirín Nic Eoin, *Eoghan Ó Tuairisc: Beatha agus Saothar* (Baile Átha Cliath: An Clóchomhar 1988); *Poetry Ireland Review*, Special Eugene Watters Issue, Conleth Ellis, Rita E. Kelly (eds), No. 13, Spring 1985 (contains biographical notes, critial essays and bibliography); 'Comhrá le hEoghan Ó Tuairisc', *Innti* 6, 1981; *Comhar*, 'Eoghan Ó Tuairisc 1919-1982', Deireadh Fómhair, 1985.

Máire Mhac an tSaoi

LIFE. Born in Dublin in 1922, Máire Mhac an tSaoi spent much of her childhood in Dún Chaoin in the west Kerry Gaeltacht. She was educated at University College, Dublin and was awarded a travelling studentship. Máire Mhac an tSaoi was a scholar in the School of Celtic Studies in the Dublin Institute for Advanced Studies and served in the Department of Foreign Affairs. She married Conor Cruise O'Brien in 1962 and has lived in Ghana and New York. She now lives in Howth, Co. Dublin.

CHIEF WRITINGS. *Margadh na Saoire* (Baile Átha Cliath: Sáirséal & Dill, 1956); *Codladh an Ghaiscígh* (Baile Átha Cliath: Sáirséal & Dill, 1973); *An Galar Dubhach* (Baile Átha Cliath: Sáirséal & Dill, 1980); *An Cion Go Dtí Seo* (Baile Átha Cliath: Sáirséal & Ó Marcaigh, 1987); *A Heart Full of Thought*, translations from the Irish (Dublin: Dolmen Press, 1959).

BIOGRAPHY AND CRITICISM. 'Comhrá le Máire Mhac an tSaoi', *Innti* 8, 1984; Siobhán Ní Fhoghlú, Interview with Máire Mhac an tSaoi, *The Bridge/An Droichead*, Summer 1989; Seán Mac Réamoinn, 'Filíocht Mhaire Mhac an tSaoi', *Comhar*, Aibreán 1957; Seán Mac Réamoinn, 'An Traidisiún Athnuaite', *Comhar*, Eanáir 1989; Máire Ní Annracháin, 'Ait Liom Bean a Bheith ina File', *Léachtaí Cholm Cille XII* (Maigh Nuad: An Sagart, 1982); Bríona Nic Dhiarmada, 'Bláthú an Traidisiún', *Comhar*, Bealtaine 1987; Frank O'Brien, *Filíocht Ghaeilge na Linne Seo* (Baile Átha Cliath: An Clóchomhar, 1968), pp. 163-201.

Breandán Ó Beacháin (Brendan Behan)

For biography and bibliography, see p. 232.

Seán Ó Tuama

LIFE. Born in 1926 in Cork city, Seán Ó Tuama was educated at University College, Cork where he is now professor of modern Irish literature. He has been visiting professor at Harvard University and Jesus College, Oxford and has lectured extensively in American, English and French universities. His anthology *Nuabhéarsaíocht, 1939-1949* (Baile Átha Cliath: Sairséal & Dill, 1950) first focussed attention on the achievement of contemporary poets in Irish, and his influence as writer, critic, teacher and mentor has been pervasive in modern writing in Irish.

CHIEF WRITINGS. His three collections of poems are *Faoileán na Beatha* (Baile Átha Cliath: An Clóchomhar, 1962); *Saol fó thoinn* (Baile Átha Cliath: An Clóchomhar, 1978); *An Bás i dTír na nÓg* (Baile Átha Cliath: Coiscéim, 1988). *Gunna Cam agus Slabhra Óir* (play) (Baile Átha Cliath: Sáirséal & Dill, 1967); *Molony agus Drámaí Eile* (plays) (Baile Átha Cliath: An Clóchomhar, 1966).

Other writings: *An Grá in Amhráin na nDaoine* (a study of the relationship between Irish folksong and medieval French verse) (Baile Átha Cliath: An Clóchomhar, 1960); *Caoineadh Airt Uí Laoghaire* (ed.) (Baile Átha Cliath: An Clóchomhar, 1961); *The Gaelic League Idea* (ed.) (Dublin and Cork: Mercier Press, 1972); *Filí faoi Sceimhle* (critical essays on Seán Ó Ríordáin and Aogán Ó Rathaille) (Baile Átha Cliath: Oifig an tSoláthair, 1978); *An Duanaire: Poems of the Dispossessed, 1600-1900* (a bilingual anthology in collaboration with Thomas Kinsella) (Dublin: Dolmen Press, 1981); *An Grá i bhFilíocht na nUasal* (Baile Átha Cliath: An Clóchomhar, 1988).

BIOGRAPHY AND CRITICISM. 'Comhrá le Seán Ó Tuama', *Innti* 9, 1985.

Pearse Hutchinson

LIFE. Born in Glasgow in 1927 of Irish parents, Hutchinson was educated by the Christian Brothers at Synge Street, Dublin, where he learned Irish, and at University College, Dublin, where he learned Castilian. His first poems in English were published in *The Bell* in 1945 and his first poems in Irish in *Comhar* in 1951. He has spent long periods in Spain; here he learned Catalan and he has translated extensively from that language. His first collection of poems, *Tongue without Hands* (Dolmen Press) was published in 1963.

CHIEF WRITINGS. (In Irish) *Faoistín Bhacach* (Baile Átha Cliath: An Clóchomhar, 1968); *Le Cead na Gréine* (Baile Átha Cliath: An Clóchomhar, 1989).

BIOGRAPHY AND CRITICISM. '"Rus in urbe", comhrá le Pearse Hutchinson', *Innti* 11, 1988.

Tomás Mac Síomóin

LIFE. Born in 1938 in Dublin, Tomás Mac Síomóin was educated at the Christian Brothers School, Westland Row, Dublin and at University College, Dublin, where he studied biology. Following postgraduate studies in Holland and the United States, he took his doctorate at Cornell University in 1974. His first poems in Irish were published in *Comhar* in 1967 and his first collection, *Damhna agus Dánta Eile* (1974), won an Arts Council award. He has lectured in biology at the Kevin Street College of Technology in Dublin and has edited the Irish language journal *Comhar*. He lives in Dublin.

CHIEF WRITINGS. *Damhna agus Dánta Eile* (Baile Átha Cliath: Sairséal & Dill, 1974); *Codarsnaí* (Baile Átha Cliath: Clodhanna, 1981); *Cré agus Cláirseach* (Baile Átha Cliath: Sairséal agus Ó Marcaigh, 1983); *Scian* (Baile Átha Cliath: Sairséal agus Ó Marcaigh, 1989).

BIOGRAPHY AND CRITICISM. Agallamh. Tomás Mac Síomóin ag caint le Proinsias Ní Dhorchaí agus le Gabriel Rosenstock, *Innti* 5, 1980; 'Tomás Mac Síomóin — File Trialach', Declan Kiberd, *Comhar*, Lúnasa 1984; '*1845*', mionchritic, Ciarán Ó Coigligh, *Comhar*, Feabhra 1986.

Michael Hartnett

For biography and bibliography, see p. 1434.

Michael Davitt

LIFE. Michael Davitt was born in Cork in 1950. While a student at University College, Cork, he founded the poetry journal *Innti*, which subsequently became the main forum for poetry in Irish. He has taught Irish at all levels and has managed the national youth festival *Slógadh*. He has worked as reporter/presenter and is now a television producer/director with Radio Telefís Éireann.

CHIEF WRITINGS. *Innti* (1970-) Journal of Contemporary Poetry in Irish (ed.); *Gleann ar Ghleann* (Baile Átha Cliath: Sairséal agus Ó Marcaigh, 1982); *Bligeárd Sráide* (Baile Átha Cliath: Coiscéim, 1983); *Selected Poems/Rogha Dánta 1968-1984* (Dublin: Raven Arts Press, 1987).

BIOGRAPHY AND CRITICISM. Liam Prút, 'Céard tá "Innti"?', *Irisleabhar Mhá Nuad*, 1984; Seán Ó Tuama, 'Michael Davitt: File Séimh Foréigneach', *Innti* 12, 1989.

Liam Ó Muirthile

LIFE. Born in 1950 in Cork, Ó Muirthile was educated at Coláiste Críost Rí and University College, Cork. While at college he was associated with the poetry broadsheet, *Innti*, which later become a journal. In 1984 he received the Irish-American Cultural Institute Award. He works as a journalist with Radio Telefís Éireann, and writes a weekly column in *The Irish Times*.

CHIEF WRITINGS. *Tine Chnámh* (Baile Átha Cliath: Sáirséal agus Ó Marcaigh, 1984).

BIOGRAPHY AND CRITICISM. 'Liam Ó Muirthile "The Gaeilgeoir: modern style"', *The Irish Times*, 21 April 1977; Gearóid Denvir, 'Aidhe í, Aidhe ó! Mairimid Beo', alt léirmheasa ar *Tine Chnámh*, *Comhar*, Bealtaine 1984; Máire Mhac an tSaoi, Náisiún na mBailte Fearann' (alt léirmheasa ar *Tine Chnámh*), *Comhar*, Lúnasa 1984.

Nuala Ní Dhomhnaill

LIFE. Born in 1952 in Lancashire, Nuala Ní Dhomhnaill grew up in the west Kerry Gaeltacht. She was educated at University College, Cork and has lived in Holland and Turkey. She now lives in Dublin.

CHIEF WRITINGS. *An Dealg Droighin* (Baile Átha Cliath agus Corcaigh: Cló Mercier, 1981); *Féar Suaithinseach* (Maigh Nuad: An Sagart, 1984); *Selected Poems/Rogha Dánta*, translated by Michael Hartnett with introduction by Máire Mhac an tSaoi (Dublin: Raven Arts Press, 1986).

BIOGRAPHY AND CRITICISM. Fiachra Ó Marcaigh, 'Ag caint le Nuala Ní Dhomhnaill', *Comhar*, Eanáir 1982; Máirín Nic Eoin, 'Agallamh le Nuala Rua', *The Bridge/An Droichead*, Vol. 2, 1985; Tomás Ó Floinn, 'Sappho a thuirling ag geataí na glóire' (léirmheas ar *An Dealg Droighin*) *Comhar*, Samhain 1981; Louis De Paor, 'Feár Suaithinseach' (review) *Comhar*, Nollaig 1984; Seán Ó Tuama, 'Filíocht Nuala Ní Dhomhnaill', *Léachtaí Cholm Cille XVII* (Maigh Nuad: An Sagart, 1986); Bróna Nic Dhiarmada, 'Bláthú an Traidisiún', *Comhar*, Bealtaine 1987;'Translations', Nuala Ní Dhomhnaill talking to Ciaran Carty, *Sunday Tribune*, 27 July 1986; 'Ó Liombó go dti Sráid Grafton', an interview with Nuala Ní Dhomhnaill, *Innti* 12 (1989).

Cathal Ó Searcaigh

LIFE. Born in 1956, Ó Searcaigh is a native speaker of Irish from Meenala, Co. Donegal. He was educated locally and studied French, Russian and Irish at the National Institute for Higher Education, Limerick. He has worked in Radio Telefís Éireann and now lives on a mountain farm in County Donegal.

CHIEF WRITINGS. *Miontraigéide Cathrach* (Baile Átha Cliath: Cló Uí Chuirreáin, 1975); *Tuirlingt* (with Gabriel Rosenstock) (Baile Átha Cliath: Carbad, 1979); *Súile Shuibhne* (Baile Átha Cliath: Coiscéim, 1983); *Suibhne* (Baile Átha Cliath: Coiscéim, 1987).

BIOGRAPHY AND CRITICISM. Liam Mac Cóil, 'Sainchomhartha na nádúrthachta' (review of *Súile Shuibhne*), *Comhar*, Márta 1984.

JOHN WILSON FOSTER, *Editor*

Irish Fiction 1965–1990

Irish fiction of the last quarter century has been ornamented with several international reputations — those of William Trevor, Brian Moore, Edna O'Brien and, of course, Samuel Beckett — but would still amount to a considerable body of work without them. Although no revolutionary genius like Joyce or Beckett has emerged, it is necessary to go back to the heyday of the Irish Revival to find as copious an output of good fiction as the last twenty-five years have produced. A selection of this fiction that, unfortunately, cannot spare room for the fine work of Bryan MacMahon, Molly Keane and John Broderick (among others) is clearly embarrassed by riches. Indeed, recent Irish fiction presents a problem of characterization, due to its volume, its diversity of competing modes — romanticism, realism and post modernism — and its peculiar ancestry, which we might see as originating in the Revival period.

The Irish Revival itself encouraged poetry, drama and folklore at the expense of the traditional novel and short story in English, which were apparently regarded as inappropriate vehicles for a romantic national revival in literature. This romanticism of the Revival, like the political ruptures and social upheavals with which it became implicated, has proven an enduring influence, but a difficult one for novelists and short-story writers. There were, of course, more familiar narratives written during the years of the Revival that are best seen in a British context — novels by Forrest Reid, Canon Sheehan, St John Ervine and Shan Bullock. Far more importantly for Irish writers who came after them, there was also the 'Irish' fiction of George Moore and the fiction of the young Joyce, Daniel Corkery and Brinsley MacNamara, which tended towards realism and consciously opposed the romantic euphoria of the Revival. If these writers have been deeply influential, as realists, as individualists and as dissidents, their novels and stories nevertheless have sponsored the idea that realism in Ireland is a rearguard and tricky manoeuvre, and idle, perhaps impossible, to repeat once accomplished. (Moore and Joyce followed their realism with other modes.)

In 1947 Seán O'Faoláin saw the difficulty as antedating the Revival: he claimed that a bare dozen realistic Irish novels (by which he meant good Irish novels) had been written between *Castle Rackrent* (1800) and Elizabeth Bowen's *The Last September* (1929). The romanticism of the Revival did not interrupt an Irish realist fiction of any substance, but it did promote both a literary sensibility and a social outlook that made it difficult to achieve. We may recall O'Faoláin's opinion because as a writer he has been active well into the 1980s, and because he was diagnosing in the 1940s a condition in Irish fiction that has continued to this day, even if it has improved.

Exception has been taken to O'Faoláin's view of the matter and also to Frank O'Connor's related opinion that, whereas Ireland could produce interesting short-story writers, it could not produce interesting novelists — an opinion, commented Benedict Kiely in 1968, that pleasantly ignored the existence of Kate O'Brien, Samuel Beckett, Brinsley MacNamara, Francis MacManus, Flann O'Brien, Francis Stuart, Peadar O'Donnell, Mervyn Wall and Forrest Reid. Yet it would be folly to dismiss outright the views of two of the most influential writers of prose fiction between the Revival and mid-century. This is especially the case since the hazardous pursuit of realism and regret for the failure of the sensitive individual to connect with his native society became the preoccupation of so many Irish novels and stories after Moore and the young Joyce. Such fictions lament the absence not only of a literary but also of a social tradition; yet, paradoxically, they constitute their own tradition in doing so, a tradition still alive at the close of the 1980s.

Certainly there was a turning away from social reality by many Revival writers, some of whom produced interesting fiction, but this would qualify without refuting O'Faoláin's proposition that the lack of Irish realism (and of good novels) was due, at least up until 1947 when he made the statement, to a lack of intellectual discrimination, due in turn to the overwhelmingly moral nature of Ireland (he was thinking of the South of Ireland, not Northern Ireland) in which, even in Dublin, an Anouilh, a Sartre or a de Montherlant would have been unthinkable.

Other features of Irish society over the years might also be adduced, but tentatively, to explain the oddity and fitfulness of the novel tradition in Ireland: the relative smallness of its bourgeoisie, the island-wide instability of political life in the years leading up to independence (and its wearying repetitiveness after partition), its unstimulating provincialism, and the peculiar and uneasy relationship many Irish writers have had with the English language (and English literature), a language in an ancestral or racial sense not their own. All these may be characterized as colonial and post-colonial insecurities and discontinuities, from the Parnellite division that so affected Joyce, through the insurrection of 1916, the War of Independence and World War I, the Civil War, the reactionary exploitation of independence by de Valera, to the present Troubles in Northern Ireland. This absence of normal political and cultural life reinforced the large role that legend, fantasy, anecdote, folktale and romance have played in Ireland (associated with the peasantry and with the gentry, at first native, then Anglo-Irish). It may have militated against the creation of a fictional tradition comparable to those of England or France. What took its place may have been a kind of Irish realism (cousin to Latin American 'magic realism'), but it has not been 'classical' realism.

Through some law of the excluded middle, from Moore and Joyce onwards, a perilous subjectivity has been for the discriminating Irish imagination the reaction both to the surrenders required by myth and nationalism and to the unacceptability of their society's structure society. The excluded middle is realism, with its consolatory marriages of self and community, individual and history. If subjectivity was a necessary evil, it could also subvert the Revival philosophy of self-transcendence. The realistic presentation of locality could likewise subvert the romantic glorification of the West. Joyce countered the latter with his depiction of lower middle-class Dublin, Brinsley MacNamara with his depiction of the Midlands, home to the 'clayey villainies of earth'. Beginning with MacNamara and continuing (between the 1930s and 1970s) with Patrick Kavanagh, Francis MacManus, Mervyn Wall and John Broderick, the literary image of the provinces has been a caustic reply to the extravagant Revival love of Ireland. Since Kavanagh, it has been unnecessary for the Irish writer to establish explicitly the falsity of earlier depictions of Irish society; the diagnosis of a flawed culture is embedded in the fiction of many modern authors — Brian Moore, John McGahern, Eugene McCabe and Bernard MacLaverty, for instance. Yet as recently as 1972, in her novel *Night*, Edna O'Brien makes her heroine, Mary Hooligan, an ironic hybrid of the Virgin Mary and Kathleen Ní Houlihan and has her undermine with obscenity the false poeticism her native place conjures up for her in England: 'Oh Connemara, oh sweet mauve hills, where will I go, where will I not go, no? Fucking nowhere.' And Julia O'Faoláin's use of a Yeats quotation as a title for her more recent story, 'Why Should Not Old Men Be Mad?' allows her swingeing social criticism to expose the ironies of Irish history since the Revival.

In the light of the work by Moore, Joyce, Gerald O'Donovan and MacNamara, it is inaccurate to locate the source of the problem for twentieth-century Irish fiction writers in the 1930s, as in that same decade did O'Faoláin, who saw himself as a victim of the problem in a very direct way. Certainly on the social front, after the disappointments of Parnell's fall, of the Revival, of independence, things got bad in a different way in de Valera's Ireland (which exacerbated matters in Northern Ireland), and the symptoms of social and cultural malaise between the 1920s and the 1960s have been familiarly catalogued: a brutal civil war, a narrow and aggressive Catholic church, a chauvinistic and isolationist government, censorship, uncultivated bourgeois and petty bourgeois classes. Instead of finding this adversity enlivening and challenging, the writers, by their own testimony, found it deadening and alienating: at least those like Frank O'Connor, O'Faoláin and Kavanagh, who stayed in Ireland. Others, such as Beckett and Francis Stuart (both still alive and publishing in the late 1980s as if to prove the wisdom of their position) left and prospered artistically; Flann O'Brien stayed and prospered through aliases and protective artifice. There are imponderables here, but what is certain is that Moore, Joyce, O'Donovan and MacNamara had encountered a version of the problem a generation earlier.

Nevertheless, Seán O'Faoláin pronounced the problem native to the 1930s and after. 'The whole social picture is upside down', he wrote in 1935, 'and we do not know where we are or what is real or unreal.' Realism is therefore impossible, and the Irish writer must turn inward, 'for there alone in his own dark cave of self can he hope to find certainty or reality.' O'Connor in 1942 thought too that 'the forces that had made for natural dignity, that had united Catholic and Protestant, aristocrats like Constance Markiewicz, labour revolutionists like Connolly and writers like AE, began to disintegrate rapidly, and Ireland became more than ever sectarian, utilitarian (the two nearly always go together), vulgar and provincial.' O'Connor was surely overestimating the social harmony that obtained during Revival times. What disintegrated rapidly was a starkly stratified society in which vertical harmony worked only in those wheels of social life that had the Big House at their hub. (Jennifer Johnston, like such predecessors as Elizabeth Bowen and Kathleen Coyle, has given us an urbane, lyrical and elegiac depiction of this disintegration.) Although O'Faoláin and O'Connor are regarded as critics of the Revival, their desire at this period for wholeness, and their belief that the novel requires a pre-existent social harmony, is romantic idealism and reads like envy of the movement that preceded them. It promotes in their work the nostalgia that was part and parcel of the Revival and that has persevered in more recent fiction, for example in Benedict Kiely, John McGahern and Jennifer Johnston, distanced (but there nevertheless) in Julia O'Faoláin's 'Why Should Not Old Men Be Mad?', William Trevor's 'Beyond the Pale', Ita Daly's 'The Lady with the Red Shoes' and Michael J. Murphy's 'Return of the Boy'.

In such an unshaped society as he perceived Ireland to be in the 1930s and 1940s, Seán O'Faoláin maintained (in 1949) that 'there are many subjects for little pieces, that is for the short story writer; the novelist or the dramatist loses himself in the general amorphism, unthinkingness, brainlessness, egalitarianism and general unsophistication.' This is a vulnerable thesis on several counts, including his own diagnosis in 1947 of the longstanding failure of realism in Ireland. Elizabeth Bowen, Kathleen Coyle and Kate O'Brien wrote fine novels between the 1920s and 1940s without losing themselves: indeed, a common characteristic is their narrative and linguistic poise. Still, O'Faoláin's thesis would have to be given consideration in any explanation of the eminence of the short story in twentieth-century Irish literature. The relative scarcity of good novels is less significant, in any case, than the fact that so many Irish writers, whether or not they have written successful novels, have produced volumes of fine stories. Since 1965, a quarter century after O'Faoláin's remarks, these have come from Bryan MacMahon, Patrick Boyle, Benedict Kiely, William Trevor, Edna O'Brien, Julia O'Faoláin, John McGahern, Neil Jordan, Clare Boylan and Aidan Higgins. I mention only the more eminent short-story writers who have also published novels.

A fuller explanation would include the persistence among Irish people of the gift of anecdote, of idiomatic flair, of the comic tradition, and of the real-life 'characters' (an endangered species today) who offer themselves ready-made for portraiture in the economical short form. Patrick Boyle, Benedict Kiely and John Morrow still exploit this declining combination in their stories and so too (with the comedy subordinated to a serious purpose) do Michael J. Murphy and Eugene McCabe in the selections below. All this work has that strong oral element that Frank O'Connor recommended in the short story. These writers are 'good storytellers' in the most fundamental, yarn-spinning sense. It requires the talent of a Flann O'Brien to maintain the combination over the distance of the novel, or the talent of a Patrick McGinley, O'Brienesque author of several recent and remarkable novels.

O'Faoláin thought the short story suitable for the enforced, unwanted but accepted subjectivity of the Irish writer, a more interesting notion if we remember that it was Moore and Joyce who invented the short story as a vehicle for what

O'Connor called 'the lonely voice'. Moreover, we must also remember that Kathleen Coyle and Kate O'Brien chose to write novels that dealt with love, the feminine version, it seems, of male subjectivity. Sexual love is on the whole handled badly, when at all, by Irish male writers. It is odd, though, that Irish male writers have hardly considered it worth exploring love and sex as avenues of escape from history and politics (Bernard MacLaverty's *Cal* is an uncommon exception and exhibits the difficulties), even if they are subsequently rejected. Among current women writers, Edna O'Brien has most notably continued to explore the theme of love, but male critics show reluctance to engage her fiction, possibly for this reason.

Meanwhile Frank O'Connor's lonely voice can be heard not only in short stories but also in those novels that are governed by the lonely sensitivity of an alienated hero or narrator, figuratively 'an only child', to borrow the title of O'Connor's autobiography. *Cal* (1983) is a vivid recent example. Among those earlier, numerous *Bildungsromane*, mostly stories of growth (or deformation) in adversity, are: O'Faoláin's *Bird Alone* (1936), Kavanagh's *The Green Fool* (1938) and *Tarry Flynn* (1948), O'Connor's *Dutch Interior* (1940), Antony C. West's *The Ferret Fancier* (1963), McGahern's *The Dark* (1965), Brian Moore's *The Emperor of Ice-Cream* (1965), Maurice Leitch's *The Liberty Lad* (1965) and Edna O'Brien' *A Pagan Place* (1970).

It was *Dubliners* and *A Portrait of the Artist*, at once works of realism and of intense self-consciousness, that inspired O'Faoláin and later writers. Nineteenth-century European realists, of course, had portrayed sensitive and artistic young people, such as Stephen Dedalus, struggling against middle-class philistinism. Joyce extended the range of that struggle by his bitter canvassing of the notion that Ireland itself, not just a specific class, compels a false consciousness among its idealistic and imaginative inhabitants. Irish realism is a subjective realism, the depiction of the objective hostile forces that force a retreat into unhealthy privacies of space. The more objective one is about these forces, the more subjective one is compelled to be. So aware of this bind were the writers of the 1930s and 1940s (like Joyce and MacNamara before them) that we might call their fiction 'critical realism', the representation of what prevents their own realisation as 'classical' realism.

We are speaking of a kind of exile. It is implied in *Bird Alone* that until Ireland 'deserves' to see one's true self, then one should maintain an inner exile. Many Irish writers of course opted for outer, not just inner exile. The natural flight from provincialism to London of Shaw, Wilde and Moore in the late nineteenth-century was followed by the more painful and thought-out exile of Joyce, O'Donovan and Moore (second time around, in 1911). Later still was the small exodus when Eimar O'Duffy, Seán O'Casey, James Stephens and AE left, all finding post-revolutionary Ireland unacceptable. The yet later case of Francis Stuart is more difficult, since he was born in Australia, spent schooldays in England, and travelled in Europe before choosing, in the most vivid way, to turn his back on both Ireland and England in 1940. He spent the war years and after in Germany (later yet in France and England) and did not return to Ireland until 1958. In his remarkable two-stage career (reminiscent of that of Molly Keane) Stuart has been a writer of the 1930s and 1940s (commemorating events experienced at first-hand before the War of Independence) and a writer of the 1970s and 1980s (dealing with the Troubles in Northern Ireland), as long lived and productive as his contemporary, Seán O'Faoláin. Like that of Keane, O'Faoláin and Beckett, Stuart's work crosses the entire period from pre-war to the present. The second stage was inaugurated by *Black List, Section H* in 1971. It is, in subtext, a justification of his war-time activities in Berlin. Whether or not we accept Stuart's fictional justification depends on whether or not we find his hero, H, sympathetic. He may be the more so since he fits the mould of the Stuart hero, a mould made long before World War II, as early as *Women and God* (1931). His Nazi activities are meant to be less important than the sense of alienation from all respectable causes they permit H to achieve and which he deems essential to his status as an artist.

Francis Stuart is a counter-Revival writer, with O'Connor, O'Faoláin and Kavanagh. Like them, he shares features of the Revival philosophy; in his case, pursuit of the apocalyptic. He may have rejected W.B. Yeats and Maud Gonne (characters in *Black List, Section H*), but Yeats's work is peopled by artists of the kind Stuart has imagined himself to be — wayward, disaffected, self-destructive, thirsty for accusation. At the same time his heroes inhabit the real world of car-racing, horse-racing, gambling, food, women: the world of O'Connor and O'Faoláin, as well as of Yeats and AE.

If exile is commonly practised by Irish writers, there are varieties of exile. The departures of Joyce and Stuart were a principled part of an aesthetic agenda. In contrast, the later departures of Edna O'Brien, Aidan Higgins, Clare Boylan, Julia O'Faoláin, William Trevor and Maurice Leitch seem less like aesthetic compulsion than the simple search for a bigger pond to swim in; in some instances, the attraction of a livelier publishing market and a potentially larger readership. 'Exile' is an increasingly outmoded word to use, given the social and professional reality of jet-flights, long holidays, second homes, and invitations to overseas universities.

Yet 'exile' was surely appropriate in the case of John McGahern in 1965. The Irish Customs seized the incoming copies of *The Dark*, published by Faber and Faber in London, and the novel was subsequently banned in the Republic of Ireland for its sexual realism. *The Dark* explores McGahern's cave of self with a vengeance. McGahern's contract as a teacher was not renewed and he left for London, unable to work at his chosen profession in his own country. (He later returned to Ireland.) Ironically, McGahern's plight was relayed to the United States (in the pages of the *Chicago Review*) by Augustine Martin. In the same year (1965), Martin took Irish writers to task in *Studies* for continuing to peddle an outworn 'antecedent dissent', inspired by Joyce, that had hardened into derivative stereotype, and for aligning themselves with the 'forces of rejection' rather than the 'forces of affirmation'.

The new Ireland was being ignored by writers, an Ireland of industrialization, foreign investment, an enlightened priesthood and advanced education, and into this Ireland a writer could fit, if he or she wished, and cease imagining himself an outcast or subjective troglodyte. A further irony was that Martin was accusing the post-Joycean dissidents of turning away from the reality of Irish society, as previous dissidents accused the Revivalists of doing. Around the same time, another critic, Maurice Harmon, announced the imminent demise of what he called 'the era of inhibitions', which he dated from 1920 to 1960. In 1964, John Montague, the poet (and author of a notable collection of stories, *Death of a Chieftain*, returned to Ireland and quipped, parodying Yeats: 'Puritan Ireland's dead and gone,/A myth of O'Connor and O'Faoláin').

It is too easy to find these obituaries, like Martin's strictures, premature, using the McGahern case as evidence. For Martin's accusation had a measure of justification and it was not shoneenism that stimulated him to contrast the contemporaneity in 1965 of British writers like Angus Wilson, Graham Greene, C.P. Snow, John Wain, Kingsley Amis and Muriel Spark with the inward look of their Irish peers. (O'Connor had already drawn the contrast, citing C.P. Snow as an example.) The repetitive subjectivity of Irish fiction needed in the 1960s to be qualifed or balanced by a larger social canvas, a more normative viewpoint, a greater objectivity. Moreover, there is no doubt that the social landscape of Ireland changed markedly in that same decade, when the country, under the leadership of Seán Lemass, entered the international economic and political order. (Northern Ireland was not dragged, screaming, into that same order until the Troubles got under way in the 1970s.) Nor is there any doubt that Irish writers were slow to register this in their fiction. The otherwise different narratives of John Broderick and John Montague were fairly exceptional.

But it was easy, apparently, to overestimate the changes and to be too optimistic about their projection into the future. The ironic ambivalence of Julia O'Faoláin in 'Why Should Not Old Men Be Mad?' in charting some of those changes from 1958 to the 1970s seems, in hindsight, a balanced stance.

Such changes as have occurred, though they might throw doubt on the viability of early Joycean dissent in its particular literary form, did not make dissent unearned or outmoded. If anything, Ireland in the 1960s required new kinds of dissent, as well as affirmation, if only because the state and the society it had helped create had not delivered a sufficiency of human freedoms and personal opportunities. Certainly it seemed timely for Irish writers to explore Irish life 'with an objectivity never hitherto applied to it'. These words were written by Seán O'Faoláin in 1962, and were quoted approvingly by Martin, words that signal O'Faoláin's reinstatement of 'classical realism' and an exit from the cave of self, but as possibility not actuality. It was after these words that Edna O'Brien published *Night*, McGahern published *The Dark* and Bernard MacLaverty published *Cal*. And in the 1980s the forces of conservatism and reaction won important political victories.

As often as not, social change is seen in Irish fiction as threatening a rural way of life (the selections below by Murphy and McGahern are vivid examples), lending to the social realism an elegiac and nostalgic quality deriving from an older Irish romanticism. The change that has exercised that otherwise celebrative writer, Benedict Kiely, is the IRA terrorism in Ulster since 1970; in his novella *Proxopera* (1977), he attacks militant republicanism for despoiling an almost pastoral order of things. The degeneration of republicanism from idealism to mindlessness (alleged in Val Mulkerns's *Antiquities* as well) represents that lack of harmony that has been a theme in Irish fiction since Yeats. Another significant work among the many (and usually inferior) 'Troubles' novels, often aimed ingenuously at the popular market, MacLaverty's *Cal* transposes Kiely's loss of Eden into Cal's orphanhood, lapse from faith and growth into disillusioned manhood.

Elegiac lament, pastoral fantasy, thwarted optimism (things did not have to be this way), and the denial of history (life was once gold, now it is brass) — romantic responses — are compatible with the realism of the depicted degeneration. In much modern fiction, however, realism accompanies acceptance of the burden of Irish history on the individual. Despite *Night*, *The Dark*, and *Cal*, most recent Irish writers have emerged from the dark cave of self to ponder history. It is astonishing how much history has been packed into such small fictions; witness the selections below of James Plunkett, Michael J. Murphy, Kiely, Robert Harbinson, Trevor, Morrow, McCabe, O'Faoláin and McGahern (Plunkett in 1969 went the whole hog and published his ambitious and bestselling historical novel, *Strumpet City*.)

If this is change, the implication nevertheless has been that any social changes are belied by the persistence of past occurrences. Irish history has been repetition; this implication of a total determinism is its own denial of history and re-admits the familiar romanticism behind the apparent objectivity. The past is inescapable but two-dimensional. Plunkett's Marty, Moore's Judith Hearne, Morrow's Lonely Heart, Julia O'Faoláin's Edward, McGahern's narrator all are victims of history. Harbinson's Miss Skelly and Stuart's heroes are among the few to defeat or evade history, the former through an undaunted missionary zeal, the latter through Nietzschean fantasy.

Other recent writers have decided as creators to share the burden of the threat of history with their heroes. Taking history as their subject, Stuart in (*Black List*), Aidan Higgins, John Banville and Ronan Sheehan have attempted to subdue that history within their own self-conscious rewriting of it. It is possible to derive their self-reflexive kind of fiction from the modernism of Joyce and the later modernism of Beckett and Flann O'Brien, writers for whom the author's quest for aesthetic victory supersedes (or parodies) the hero's quest for moral or spiritual or epistemological victory. It would be dangerous, though, to divide Irish fiction simply into traditional and post modernist, because of the reflective nature of 'critical realism' and of the role in Joycean modernism of the Irish comic tradition, the medieval mind, and ancient narrative structures. Joyce, Beckett, Flann O'Brien, and Patrick McGinley constitute a particularly Irish modernism in their recycling of Irish modes and material. The recycling can solve the problem we have been examining.. If history can be rewritten (or reimagined), it was perhaps written (or imagined) in the first place; and if it is an imaginative construct anyway, then the romantic-realist contest can be conjured out of existence: making and remaking is freedom, and one does not have to live inside or outside the cave of self, nor permit history to enslave or tyrannize one. A corollary is that literature (itself history) can also be productively rewritten: hence the element of pastiche and travesty in modernism and post-modernism (Jordan in 'Nights in Tunisia' rewrites a trite episode from some *Bildungsroman*), and the obtrusive density of prose of the sort we meet in Higgins, Banville and Dermot Healy.

Rewriting suggests a kind of revision, and there is in the post-modernists a critical acumen, once felt by Seán O'Faoláin to be missing in Ireland, that happens to have gathered force at the same time that a discriminating native literary criticism and revisionist historiography appeared in the 1970s. One does not wish to put Ronan Sheehan's recent narratives into precisely this context. In addition, we meet a new, almost gothic, realism in the work of Patrick McGinley that sits strangely with the designedly flat candour of Dermot Bolger. There is also a growing Europeanness and Americanness of setting (cf. Aidan Mathews), a cultural plurality rather self-conscious (as befits post-modernism), less like the urbane Europeanness of Kate O'Brien, Edna O'Brien and Julia O'Faoláin, and more like the obtrusive Europeanness of Francis Stuart. This has accompanied as cause or effect the increasing internationalism of the writers' market, its publication outlets and readership, and an expansion into film, radio and television. (Unfortunately, this has made the health of native Irish literary magazines slightly less important.) One can only predict a continuing broadening of setting, cast and theme in Irish fiction as the writers themselves inhabit an increasingly international milieu, and as Irish fiction shares the fate and career of fiction in the English-speaking world.

FRANCIS STUART

(1902-)

from: REDEMPTION (1949)

[This is an extract from two consecutive chapters in Stuart's novel *Redemption*. A group of victims, survivors and moral outsiders consort in an Irish provincial town after World War II and establish by the novel's end a rudimentary commune. The connecting force is the somewhat mysterious Ezra Arrigho, who, like Stuart himself, has returned to Ireland after surviving the war in Berlin. This detester and flouter of idealism, provincialism and morality is a familiar Stuart hero, courting catastrophe and revelation. Whereas the novel as a whole seems rather overheated, there is an authentic and proportionate energy in Ezra's memories of Berlin during the last days of the Third Reich and the entry into the city of the Russians. The Allied bombing and the Russian soldiers violate the street in which Ezra has taken refuge, but for Ezra violation of the conventional self (of which the street is site and symbol) is necessary if a new vision and a new world are to come to pass. The old walls must collapse, and they include the bonds of marriage and the family. Even violence must be contemplated (Kavanagh, the Dublin fishmonger, commits a murder that endears him in the logic of the novel to Ezra) if redemption for twentieth-century man is to be possible.]

CHAPTER 2

'When I walk down the main street of this town,' Ezra said, 'past the small busy shops and the pubs with Guard Higgins on point duty at the corner and Father Mellowes coming down the steps from the church after hearing confessions, for a moment I too breathe a breath of sweetness. I am tempted to believe that this is peace and righteousness and that they're justified in protecting it. But it's no good. Because I know where this street leads and where all streets lead. Your sergeant and the others can't see beyond the end of their street. The words that they speak in this street would be meaningless in the other street, in the street in which I was.'

'What street was that?' asked Kavanagh, fondling Annie with one hand while he held his glass of Guinness in the other.

'The street of a great city. It had been a street like the others, with tailors' dummies draped in the newest fashions in the shop-windows and restaurants with table lamps on the white cloths and a big, ugly church on the square at one end and hotels where they changed the towels in your bedroom every morning, and if a child fell and cut its knee on the pavement there was a great to-do and its mummy brought out her hanky and dabbed away the blood.'

'Ha!' said Kavanagh blankly. He did not know what Ezra was getting at.

'As long as there were clean handkerchiefs to dab at scratched knees and glass in the shop-windows,' Ezra went on, 'the same sermons were being preached in the church at the corner as Father Mellowes preaches here.

'I knew that street as I know this street. I had been into each restaurant along it at one time or other. I had sat in the summer nights on the terraces of the cafés and seen the lights shining on to the leaves of the lime trees planted along it when it was still secure and sheltered between its shops and houses, leading to all the other streets of the world.

But slowly there was a change along it. Not only that I was now alone in it, or that the bombs had ground down many of the houses to piles of rubble. A street between walls of rubble is still a street and the shape of the ruins becomes as familiar and homely as the shape of the houses were. But now I began to know where it led.

'The street had its own air, its own atmosphere. Even when the houses collapsed they lay in their own dust, in their own light. Everything moves or stands in its own light or shadow, I suppose, a tree, a street, a rock, and the earth itself, and the final violation is the stripping from a thing of its own air. That is what happens to you when you're arrested; the little protective sanctum around you is violated — strange hands feel in your pockets, strange voices strip away the protective layer of space around you.

'I knew this first when the shells began to fall into the street. Shells are different from bombs. Shells are the first touch of the *others*, the sign of their presence; shells begin to strip away the familiar air and bring the first breath of the unknown darkness with them.

'It was the growing strangeness of the street that is what I remember of those days. I felt it turning into something different. Along part of it a column of tanks and heavy guns had been abandoned — for want of petrol, I suppose. I came on them there one evening, grey hulks of steel, like strange monsters washed up on a shore during a night of storm. I wasn't allowed in the streets because I was a foreigner, but I came out at night to look around. I came up out of the cellar where we were waiting, and each evening there was a new darkness in the street. It wasn't the same darkness through which the lights from the shops had shone and the buses rattled or even the darkness in which the houses had burnt after the raids. The street was being stripped of its own light and its own darkness and it lay there like the dead lie, without the halo of their own beings around them any more, exposed.

'I didn't know what was coming. There were no more newspapers and no wireless. There were only rumours, words in the darkness, names. But there were no names for the unknown shape; when they had spoken the strange names of Russian generals and Russian armies, there was still something that had not been given a name, the thing that would appear in the street at a certain coming hour of the day or of the night. There was another name being spoken like an incantation against the unknown horror: the army Wenck.[1] In the cellars under the street and along the street at night there was this name spoken, in a question, an assertion or in irony. The army Wenck. That was the name of all that was familiar, the known, the past, fighting its way back to the city and the street. The army Wenck was the name of all that was known and familiar, the familiar pain, the familiar ruins and the familiar hunger and the small familiar joys and securities still left amid the ruins and the hunger. And the other names were the names of death, of the angel of death, of Astoreth,[2] and they had the sound of the last trumpet. The horribly strange sound of something announcing the unknown doom.

'And in the street at night there were always new signs and new portents. No one knew what they meant, except that they meant the end coming nearer. There were the German lieutenant and sergeant hanging under the bridge of the elevated railway with a placard with words on it that confirmed the hopelessness of those who read it furtively as they passed. "Found without arms in face of the enemy."

'In face of the enemy. Those too were words that were mysterious and horrible. The street was now in face of the enemy! The street that had led to a bridge across the railway and beyond that to a leafy avenue that in its turn went out to a suburb now led only into the jaws of the enemy.

'I as a neutral might not have any enemy, but I had lived for five years in the street; through the war I had lived there and its smells and its ruins were familiar to me and I too was touched by the passing of that world. For a street is a world, with its air and its shape and its order. And it is a great shock, no matter how detached one may be, to see the actual hour in which order passes away and chaos appears. It is a shock in the depth of the heart. The heart cannot absorb the shapelessness of chaos, it is shocked, it is like a great scandal to it.'

'That was what he said to Annie,' Kavanagh interrupted. 'That we were causing a scandal in this town.'

'There were a couple of days and nights when I didn't leave the cellar,' Ezra went on, 'because we

1. General Walther Wenck commanded the hastily mustered German Twelfth Army; it became Germany's last hope as the Allies closed on Berlin in the spring of 1945.
2. The Palestinian moon goddess; the Israelites brought retribution on themselves by worshipping her (Judges 10.6); the Emperor Constantine (*c*.280-337) destroyed a sanctuary of the Phoenician version of Astoreth (Astarte).

heard that foreign workers had been shot for being out in the street. All the people of the house were living in the cellars, Germans and foreigners together. The cellar had become a thoroughfare; holes had been broken through into the cellars of the next-door houses and it was possible to go from street to street through the cellars. I stayed two or three days in the cellar with the others from the house, sometimes in the dark and sometimes with a bit of candle burning. There in the cellar there were no more pretences; I had a glimpse of how a tribe must live in their huts in the depth of an African forest. All the escapes, the cinemas and radios and books, were gone and privacy was gone; no one lived any more in the little civilised isolation of his own room and his own possessions. There was no more dressing up or washing. If we stank, we stank. At least it was the stench of life and not the other stench that was beginning to drift through the streets.

'We were a little tribe in the midst of the forest on the edge of death. There were no more differences between us except what could be seen or felt. We were not Germans or Poles or Irish or railway officials or dressmakers or schoolteachers, but we were still men and women because the man and woman difference is a thing of shape and sensation and shape and sensation were left. Indeed, there was only shape and sensation. The shape of the shadows in the dark cellar, the new shape of time, flowing slower and slower, like a river at its mouth beginning to meet the pressure of the sea, and the shape of our own cramped bodies. The underground darkness was full of sensation as the day or the night up above in the world seldom is. The two dry slices of black bread which we would eat once every twelve hours were a sensation, they were sweeter than manna, and the quivering of the darkness from the bombs and the shower of shells that they called Stalin organs was a sensation in the spine and in the guts, like a tree whose roots are shaken by a storm. And when we prayed it was a different praying to most of the church praying; it was a turning of our dirty, pale faces to the face of darkness beyond the cellar-darkness; it was the feeling in the trembling of the cellar and the falling of the plaster, the passing of the angel of death and the angel of the end. And if a man took the hand of the girl huddled next to him it was another touch from the old touching, the old mechanical caressing.

'But even down there we could sense the progress of the battle.

'Soldiers came through, passing down the street through the cellars, their dull-painted, steel helmets like dark hoods over their faces in the shine of their electric torches. And they were questioned, questioned. And the same blank look in reply, tinged with impatience, and then the long, empty, noisy hours again with no one coming through, with whispers and only the minute break of going out into the passage to make water.

'It was about the third night that I went up and out into the street again. Now it had changed again. In two days there was a change that normally would have taken centuries. There were corpses lying in the street and no one paying any attention to them. Even two days before, when someone was killed they were picked up and carried away. Death had still been an accident, a part of disorder to be quickly tidied up. Now there was only disorder; chaos and death were beginning to be in the street, not as something accidental, but as part of the street. There were women with basins and buckets and a few men with knives cutting up a dead horse in the middle of the street. I went back to the cellar and got a basin and a knife and hacked away between the white bones, filling the basin with slabs of dark flesh. That was the treasure of those nights, the dark slabs of flesh, and it was lusted after more than the flesh of women. There were many living women and girls in the streets and only a few horses. There was a crowd round the horses with buckets and basins, and those who had not basins took the wet chunks of meat in their arms, hugging them to their breasts. In the morning the dead were still lying in the street in the full light of day and I stood and looked at a group of four or five bodies in their dusty sleep, a child and young woman and an old woman, drinking in this new shape, the shape of death that was strange and shocking and fascinating at first, as the shape of a woman's naked body at a window had been to me long ago as a boy. But as I walked down the street I had learnt this new shape, death-in-the-street, the dead sharing the street with the living and making again something different out of the street, signing it with their dusty, still and huddled sign.

'We feasted on the meat in the candle-lit cellar and the girl next me kissed my hands and pressed them to her breast in rapture at satiating her hunger.

'That night I was out in the street again. There were a lot of shells falling, and while I was sheltering under the remains of the bridge of the elevated railway I got a piece of shrapnel through my shoulder. There was a dressing-station further up the street and although it was a military station I went there with a sergeant who had been wounded in the leg and, as I was helping him, they let us both in. They couldn't do much for us; there were no bandages, no antiseptics, only the candle-lit rooms with the shadowy, blanket-covered forms. There was only one sister, and as she was washing the sergeant's leg wound he talked to her. He was a small, thick-set little fellow of forty-five and he had a way with him, an air of knowing a great deal of what was going on.

'"What are they holding out for? Do you really expect the army Wenck to break through from the West?" the sister asked. She could hardly hold the basin of water for tiredness.

'The sergeant shrugged his shoulders and smiled his weary, knowing smile.

'"We heard the capitulation would come tonight," said the nurse. "They are said to be discussing terms."

'"Terms!" said the little sergeant with his thin smile. "All I know is they have thrown in the Norwegian S.S. Division, all big, young fellows of twenty or so. I saw some of them in the Friedrichstrasse area."

'"There's no sense in it; no sense," said the girl, slopping water from the basin to the floor in her weariness.

'Afterwards the sergeant and I sat in the hall. The outer door was ajar and the street was just beyond, and we were both drawn towards it, not wanting to be far from it. We sat in the hall and through the door came the night air from the street with the smoky tang that had been in it for weeks. And there was a faint smell of excrement; it had been there, too, for days, like the scent of savoury, slightly rotten cooking, and I did not know whether it was only a memory in my nose lingering from the cellar or whether here, too, there was no sanitation. Now and then the sergeant asked me to go to the door and have a look out; he couldn't move so easily because of his leg wound.

'It was a clear night with a waning moon and I could see along the street. The smooth black surface of the wide street gleamed and it seemed very quiet. There was always the background of noise, but that we were used to and there were no new noises and no shells. Only the street lying empty with its dark, traffic-polished surface leading away into the night. Such a moment of quiet there had not been in these weeks, and I stood there alone and came to myself as I had not in all that time. In the long hours in the cellar I had only been capable of waiting with the others, dreaming of food, of a bed, waiting for the hour of eating the two slices of bread or the two cold potatoes, drinking in every scrap of rumour. But now in the street outside the dressing-station I felt a change in myself. I had strength again, and not drifting here and there with each pang of hunger, each wave of sleepnessness, each new whispered announcement. It was as if I had got strength at the last minute. But so it is with me; all happens to me at the last minute.

'When I came back the sergeant had got hold of an old civilian suit and was putting it on, slowly drawing the trousers on over his stiff leg.

'"How's it look?" he asked.

'"Worn. But that doesn't matter if it fits."

'"Not the suit, man, the street."

'"It's quiet," I said. "It's quieter than it's been for a long time."

'He was taking papers and things out of the pocket of his uniform, tearing them up, tearing up his soldier's *soldbuch*,[3] and laying a few things aside, a comb and some money and a small tattered New Testament. There was an envelope stuck in it as a marker and he opened it and said to me: "Do you know that all this was prophesied in the Bible. Listen." He held the small book close to the hurricane lamp on the table and began to read: "Then he said unto them: Nation shall rise against nation and kingdom against kingdom and great earthquakes shall be in divers places, and famines and pestilences; and fearful sights and great signs shall there be from heaven.... For these be the days of vengeance, that all things which are written may be fulfilled...."[4]

'And these words were themselves a sign to me,' Ezra went on, 'coming in and hearing these words I knew what it was that I had seen in the street.'

'What was it?' Kavanagh asked. Annie, too, was listening with her big, freckled face against Kavanagh's shoulder.

'I had seen how these things must be if we were

3. Army paybook.
4. Luke 21. 10-11.

not to go on swimming round our duck-pond. We dare not be given too much security. As soon as we have a little security, we settle down by our duck-ponds, and it doesn't matter whether it's a religious duck-pond, a cultural duck-pond or an economic duck-pond. It's all the same old mud. The little duck-pond writers, the duck-pond reformers, and the little white duck-pond God with its neat crown of thorns. That's our great genius: to tame! We have our tame God and our tame art, and it is only when the days of vengeance come that there's a flutter around the pond.'

'A flutter around the pond!' repeated Kavanagh with a cackle. Ezra looked at the big, slightly bemused face with a momentary dislike. He, knowing nothing of the price paid in horror, in starving and sweating and bleeding, had no call to use the words that Ezra might use without offence.

'After the days of vengeance there comes a new breath. Here and there, among those who have survived, comes a new vision, further than the duck-pond vision. That's the only hope for us now: a new vision and a new god. That's what I saw that last hour before the end, with the wide, empty street waiting under the moon. It was a strange moon, the colour of flesh bled bluish-white. And then I went back to the dressing-station and the little sergeant was reading those words out of the book he had come across emptying out his uniform pockets: "And there shall be signs in the sun and in the moon ... and upon the earth distress of nations, with perplexity, the sea and waves roaring."'[5]

5. Luke 21.25.

CHAPTER 3

Ezra stopped speaking to take a swill of the black stout. By now Kavanagh was slightly drunk. Not really drunk, though, because what Ezra was saying kept him from drifting down on the dark tide of Guinness in his blood.

'At midnight the sergeant and I were still sitting in the hall of the flat that had been turned into a hospital,' Ezra was saying. 'I was thinking of going back to the cellar. "Hold on a bit," the sergeant would say. "You've got all night, haven't you?" But I had seen the sign in the moon and I wanted to be back in my own corner——'

'What sign was that?' asked Kavanagh.

'That's only a way of speaking. It was a sign in myself,' Ezra said; 'the sign that I was ripe for what was coming. And the moment you are ripe for what is coming, it comes. Death, pain, love, whatever it may be.'

'That's a queer word,' said Kavanagh. 'What about all the others who weren't ripe, as you call it?'

'I don't know. There are two faces to reality, and I have seen them both. There was the bloody face of the sister as I saw her a little later, one of all the faces of the raped, the dying, the horror-stricken and the other face, the face of "Not a sparrow falls without the Father —"[1] and whoever has seen these two faces as one is finally delivered and at peace. But I haven't. And now I never shall.

'I wanted to go but I kept staying on to keep the sergeant company. We had been talking and we stopped talking. There was a new sound from the street, a soft, even sound after all the loud and intermittent sounds of the time before. I peered out from behind the door. I saw dimly a column of men pass down the other side of the street.

'"What is it?" asked the sergeant. I didn't know, and yet I knew. I did not want to give it a name. To name the hour for which all had been waiting in fear and trembling.

'"Well, what is it, man?"

'"The Russians," I said.

'We were speaking lower. "Did you see them?" he asked. I thought that in spite of all his air of knowingness even he had still a hope about the army Wenck. We heard more of them passing and then the door was pushed open and some of them came in, in their baggy, belted uniforms. They had come. The Apocalyptic rider on the pale horse had dismounted and come through the door into the hall and gone on into the wards. There was a sentry at the door, and the sergeant and I went back into the ward, where a Russian colonel was standing talking in German to the chief orderly and a soldier with a tommy-gun[2] stood just behind him. Then the officer went into the small room where we had had our wounds dressed by the sister, and the soldier stood outside the closed door. In a few minutes they came out again and the colonel went upstairs with his bodyguard and the sister went about her duties, silent. I was spoken to by a big,

1. cf. Matthew 10.29.
2. A .45 calibre Thompson sub-machine gun.

slouching fellow in German and I showed my passport which, being printed in English, French and Gaelic, he could not read. But he did not want to read it. That was the first thing I learnt about these Apocalyptic hordes. They had not yet come to the complete faith in documents and documentation that the Germans and Americans and English have. He looked at me out of his small, peasant eyes and repeated after me, 'Irländer,' and seemed to think it over and think me over. He handed me back my papers and slouched off down the room, the gun dangling from his big hand, stooping over a mattress now and then as the fancy took him and demanding the papers of the man lying on it, but then hardly looking at them, dangling the gun and kicking the straw of the mattress with his big boot.

'The colonel's orderly came down and went back upstairs with the sister. All the time I wanted to get back to the cellar. My few belongings were there. I felt that the end had come and caught me far from home.

'"Wait a bit," the sergeant told me. "Wait an hour or two and let things settle down." I would have been still waiting if I'd waited for that,' Ezra went on.

'An hour or two,' repeated Kavanagh in his own slow way, wiping his mouth. 'An hour or two, ha!'

'The little sergeant and I went back and sat in the hall. "This is the best place to be, in a hospital," he said.

'The long, long waiting was over; the end had come. The sergeant had heard that the city had capitulated. No more bombs would fall, no more shells; the rocking of the earth that loosened the roots of the heart in your breast was over; the earth was still. I could see out into the street past the sentry lounging at the half-open door and it was still. But it was not the beginning of peace. "There was silence in heaven and on earth for the space of half an hour."[3]

'The sister came downstairs. Her face was scratched and bitten and bloody. I went to the door and stood outside it, looking up and down the street. I did not want to seem to be in a hurry. I must move like these men moved, easily, slouching without haste. There were two of them outside the door talking and I stood beside them. I felt the breath of violence in which we stood and moved and had our being. The former, explosive violence had passed away and there was this new, quieter, more intimate violence in the air of the street. All these years we had moved in and breathed the air of hatred, of violence and the threat of violence. Not only the explosive violence, the violence that came down out of heaven, but the other soft-footed, official violence. I knew much about the shape of violence and I could sniff it around me, in all its different shapes and forms. If you have a kind of quietness and suppleness in you you can often slip through under the very jaws of violence, but if you haven't, if you're nervous and excitable and if your movements of body and of soul are too quick or too set in one direction, then you're lost from the start. I had lived with it, in a city where all the offices in all the official buildings were ante-rooms of violence, and, waiting outside them, waiting for one's turn, however quiet you tried to be, your armpits got damp. That was the mechanical, statistical violence, and you couldn't escape it if, because of your papers, you came into one of the doomed categories. That was the violence of order, the terrible statistical violence of the great machine of order and it had its lair in every street, in dusty corridors and offices and its threat was in every ring of the bell, in every strange voice.

'In the street as long as I had lived there had always been the unseen presence and pressure of violence like an invisible hand laid on the heart. Even in my room it was there, the slight pressure always there, subtly altering the shape of everything, squeezing everything a little bit smaller. Just as long before I had sometimes been in another great city and I had lived in the pressure of another hand laid on me, the hand of sex. Sex was then the great mystery for me; it was in the belly, in the house and in the streets. And later in this other city and in this other street it was violence.

'I thought about this as I stood at the door of the dressing-station and tried to sense the new violence that had come to replace the old. And I felt that this new violence was not so statistical, and you might escape it not so much by having the right papers, the right signatures, but by the way you moved and looked, by keeping a small centre of quiet in you.

'As I say, I know all about violence and its different shapes. I have sat waiting in corridors with violence hidden on the other side of a door and known it there, known in my stomach that it was there, unseen, and waited, gone dead and numb

3. cf. Revelation 8.1.

between chest and belly with the touch of its invisible hand in my guts. You get so that you can sniff it from far away, when it's hidden away behind doors and walls. You can walk down a street full of shops and traffic and the sun shining and the old women calling the latest editions of the papers, and you can know in a slight sensation below the ribs that behind all this, like a boy who has wound up his train and sits back watching it go, there is violence. I got so that I could sense it in the very stone of the houses, in the reflection of the windows. And I hadn't completely escaped it, either. For some months I had been locked away with the others, though later I had been let out again to walk in the street or sit in the cafés and restaurants, moving in the pseudo-freedom of a world in which everyone is numbered and registered and summoned from time to time into one of the ante-rooms of the great machine. I had lived all this time in this order of brooding, hidden violence that was broken through from time to time by the other violence, the open violence of destruction. It had a different face, but from its mouth came the same breath of the pit, and when the cellar rocked you knew it was the same hand that rocked it as the cold hand that grabbed you in the guts as you waited for your turn outside one of the closed doors in the big building down the street.

'And tonight the hand of violence had another grip. So far I had only caught a glimpse of it in the night air and in the marks of its claws on the face of the nurse, which was no more than a touch in passing. I leant up against the door lintel and smoked my cigarette to the end, and as I threw the butt down I moved off into the street, trying to make my movements quiet and familiar as I think I would try to move in a lion's cage. The two soldiers stopped talking together. I did not look back, but strolled on very slowly, and I heard them talking again and at that moment I had a kind of love for them, because they had left me alone.

'I walked down the street. It had changed since I had walked up it with the little sergeant limping on my arm some hours before. There had been that silence, as for the space of half an hour, and in that space the last wall had fallen that had surrounded it, that had made it, in spite of all, still a street in a city with still some faint air of being sheltered, as towns and cities were once shelters. But now it was a space open to all the winds that blew.'

PATRICK BOYLE

(1905-82)

from:
AT NIGHT ALL CATS ARE GREY (1966)

[Boyle once jokingly described the writer as someone with 'the morals of a tom-cat, the tenderness of Jack the Ripper, the respect for private property of a racecourse pickpocket.' These traits Boyle often passes on to his characters, who are appropriately conveyed by the raw colloquialism of their Irish-English, for which the author has an ear as keen as Joyce's or Flann O'Brien's. Yet Boyle's work is essentially moral, satirizing as much the vulgarity it affects as the prudery that disowns the vulgarity. 'Myko', from Boyle's first collection of stories (he became a writer late in life), was at one stage in its career rejected by Radio Éireann (Irish Radio) on the grounds that it was too macabre for most listeners. Like other Boyle stories, it highlights small rather than large injustices, and the author, like the narrator, clearly relishes the ironic reversal suffered by hypocritical respectability.]

MYKO

You'd get people to say that a barman couldn't put a foot wrong. That all he has to do is stick to the old reliable two-for-myself-and-one-for-the-boss system and he'll have a business of his own in no time. Well, God grant them better sense. It's well seen they don't know the Boss. If ever there was a skinflint born, bred and come to maturity — it's Myko Connors. You'd have a poor chance of ringing up a double on the cash register with him prowling around, breathing down the back of your neck like a jealous husband.

He runs a funeral undertaking business as a side line but believe you me, he has as little regard for a coffined Christian as he has for the relatives walking overground. And of all mankind, alive or dead, the class he has least time for are travelling gentry. He wouldn't serve a drink to a tinker, not if the seat of his trousers was patched with ten pound notes.

So you can imagine my feelings when the first person to darken the door on a Monday morning turns out to be the Cracker, son of old Maggot Feeney, the head bombardier of a notorious band of tinkers who camp out every winter a couple of miles outside the village.

'You'll get no drink here,' says I, giving him no time to open his mouth. 'So about turn and on your way.'

'I want to see the Boss,' says he, as cheeky as you like.

'It's a matter of business,' he says.

'Is it the measures you want to check? Or are you collecting for the Foreign Missions?' says I.

'It's a coffin I want,' he says. 'Me ould fellah's after dying.'

'Why the hell didn't you say that when you came in?' I says, when I got my second wind. 'I'll get the Boss for you now.'

'I'm sorry for your trouble,' I says, making for the door.

You should have seen Myko's face when I told him that the Maggot Feeney was dead and looking [for] burial.

'Is it that bloody little ruffian?' he says. 'Why didn't he die at the Galway races? Or in his ancestral home in Granard where every tinker from hell to Bedlam was spawned? It'll give that Feeney menagerie a foot in the door if he's buried beyond in the graveyard.'

'Did you leave that young marauder on his tod[1] in the bar?' he says. 'Get down to hell at once or he'll have the shelves stripped.'

When I got down to the bar I slipped young Cracker a right dart of whiskey for decency's sake.

'Drink it up before the Boss comes down,' I says. 'Poor ould Maggot wasn't the worst of them.'

The young buck was still licking his chops when Myko comes into the bar and tears into him.

'What's this I hear about you wanting a coffin?' he says, as if it was a criminal offence to die.

'Much use a coffin would be when you've no place to bury it. Are you going to put it standing in a corner of the caravan like a grandfather clock?'

'Or maybe,' he says, and you could nearly taste the vinegar on his tongue, 'Maybe you've a plot taken, beyond in the cemetery?'

'Me brother's away up to the Parochial House to fix up that end of it,' says Cracker, without turning a hair.

'What's that?' says Myko and you could have snared his two eyes with a hay rope. 'A plot in the graveyard. It's late in the day for your father to be thinking of settling down.'

'It was me ould fellah's last wish. He picked the spot himself a while back. And put aside enough to pay for it.'

Myko changed his tack.

'Funerals are an expensive item these days,' he says. 'D'you know you couldn't put a man under the clay for less than twenty pounds. And that would be little better than a pauper's funeral. Coffin, hearse and a single mourning car.'

'You'd be better,' says he, 'to phone your uncle in Galway. He was very devoted to your poor father, they tell me. I'm certain sure he'd rather the body was brought to Galway. From what they say, he can well afford the funeral expenses.'

'It's the coffin I want,' says Cracker. 'No hearse. No car.'

'And how d'you propose transporting the remains to the church? Are you going to hoist the coffin on your back like a creel[2] of turf?'

'We can take him in the spring-cart. The coffin's all we want.'

'Aren't you the callous young brute! You'd expose your poor dead father to the wind and the weather and the jeers of the populace.'

'Never mind that. How much for the coffin? The cheapest you've got?'

'Ten pounds for a job in spruce. Including breast-plate, handles and the rest of the gear. To be padded, trimmed and caulked before delivery—'

Myko was going into his sales talk when Feeney pulled him to a halt.

'How much for the bare boards, put together and varnished?' says he.

1. on his own.

2. basket.

'Cash down,' he added.

Myko's frown came apart at the seams and he started rubbing his hands together like a courting cricket.

'Eight pounds,' says he. 'That's the best I can do. And I'd be losing money at that figure.'

The Cracker bid him four and they chewed the fat till the differ was split at five pounds ten.

The young fellow paid up like a man. Myko told me to go out to the store and help get the coffin on to the spring-cart. Only when we pulled the coffin out from under the heap of lumber where it had lain since Adam was a pup, could you see the full extent of the robbery the Boss was after committing. You wouldn't put a brute beast in it let alone a Christian. It was warped and twisted and knotted and there were cracks gaping open that did away with the privacy a person's entitled to — dead or alive. If there came rain the deceased would be afloat before he reached the graveyard.

'There's nothing here that a lick of a paint-brush won't cure,' says I, to cheer up the bereaved.

'Of course,' I says, 'it's maybe a bit on the large size,' (It could have housed Finn McCool[3] let alone a wee runt like Maggot Feeney) 'but some padding here and there'll do the job for you. You can't have him rattling about like a pea in a whistle.'

As we were hoisting the wooden monster on to the cart Feeney says:

'I'm not holding this against you, chum. I know you're only the ha'penny boy around here.'

'So's your sister,' was all the answer I could rake up.

I went back to the Monday morning work, but all the time I was dusting shelves and replacing bottles, polishing the bar mirrors, serving the odd drink, with my ears deeved[4] by the bloody drivel that the first pint of the day provokes in a craw-sick customer, I was debating in my own mind the case of *Feeney v Connors* and I felt sure there would be an appeal lodged.

I was right. Around five o'clock, with the bar packed and the Boss and myself going like a pair of red-shanks[5] who should come sloping in but the Cracker and slinking in after him his young brother Merley — a shifty-eyed jackal, if ever there was one. They pushed their way up the crowded bar to where Myko was serving. Cracker leans over and says:

'Are ye busy, Mr Connors? Could I speak to ye a minute?'

Myko looked up from filling a pint. When he saw who was in it[6] he ducked under the counter again.

'I did what you told me, Boss,' says Cracker. 'I phoned the Uncle and they're sending down a coffin and hearse. We're taking the remains to Galway the night.'

Myko pushed the pint over to the waiting customer, got him his change and turned to Cracker.

'What's that to do with me?' he says, acting it out real cagey.

'We'll not be wanting the coffin now,' says Cracker. 'It's outside on the spring-cart. Will we leave it in the shed?'

By this time all hands were earwigging.[7] Drinks were sitting untouched on the counter: conversation had dried up.

Myko took the ball on the hop. He says:

'It's all one to me what you do.'

'You'll refund the money, of course,' says Cracker.

Myko ignored him. He turns to me.

'Go out to the shed,' he says, 'and see what damage the coffin has suffered since it left the premises.'

I finished serving a round of drinks and when I got out to the shed the Feeneys had brought in the coffin. I got them to help me throw the lumber back on it, till it was decently hidden.

'To tell you nothing but the truth, men,' says I, when we had the wretched thing shrouded with broken boards, crushed cardboard boxes and empty ten-glass bottles, 'I'm just as glad you returned this bloody horse-box. No one but a hungry cleg[8] would have let it out of here in the first place.'

'Amen,' says Merley, the impudent whelp.

'Will that ould miser cough up the dough?' says Cracker. 'He's liable to get a belt of a porter bottle if he tries to renegue.'

'Don't be getting your dander up over nothing,' I says. 'The Boss may be a hard man but he's always straight in his dealings.'

3. A legendary Irish warrior and giant.
4. deafened.
5. Birds — sandpipers — with long, slender legs.
6. i.e. there: an Irish idiom.
7. i.e. everyone was eavesdropping.
8. A stinging fly (Northern Ireland dialect).

'He'd better be,' says Cracker.

When the two Feeney boys came in by the street door, the crowd at Myko's end of the bar pushed back to let them in to the counter. Leaving them room to swing a bottle, I figured.

It was the Boss who went into the attack first.

'What's it like?' he calls down to me. 'Is it badly scratched? How many dents in the timber?'

It would make you doubt the existence of God when a man can come out with the like of that without being struck dead.

'Nothing that I could see,' I says, and I couldn't resist adding, 'it's in no worse shape than it was leaving the storehouse.'

Myko never let on to feel that kick in the fork. He goes to the till and takes out a sheaf of notes.

'Well,' says he, for the benefit of the congregation. 'In that case I must fulfil my obligations.'

He starts slapping the notes down on the counter under Cracker's nose.

'One ... two ... three ... four ... five ...' he counts. 'Now the ship's on an even keel again.'

So help me loving Jasus, I nearly foaled a fiddler.

Cracker made no move to lift the notes. He eyed Myko thoughtfully, as if trying to decide what part of the bald skull he'd split open with the first crack of the bottle.

'There's another ten bob,' he says. 'You were paid five, ten.'

'I'm well aware of that,' Myko says, taking it nice and cool.

'You can divvy up[9] so,' says Cracker.

Myko puts his thumbs into the arm-holes of his waistcoat and starts playing four finger exercises on his chest.

'Listen here, young Feeney,' he says. 'We'd better get this matter straightened out. You didn't get that coffin out on appro.[10] You bought it from me for five pounds, ten. Right? Then I buy a coffin from you for five pounds. Right? If you don't like the price you can take it home to the caravan and use it for a settle-bed.'

I won't deny I was proud of Myko at that moment. With a wig and gown he'd have passed for the attorney general himself.

Cracker was shaken, but there was fight left in him still.

'The bloody coffin was bought and brought back the same day. How [the] hell d'you make that out two separate deals?' he says.

Myko blew out his chest and addressed the bar customers as though they were a bench of jurymen.

'D'you mind the Harvest Fair a year back? D'you mind a jack donkey changing hands that day? The Feeneys sold it to Charlie Ruadh[11] from the back of the mountain. And him too drunk to know whether he was buying an ass or an African elephant. Sure everyone at the Fair thought it was only a bit of a joke. But when Charlie sobered up and searched out the Feeneys at the tail-end of the Fair, how did they treat the poor old fellow? Did they refund him his money? They did in my arse. He bloody near had to go on his benders to get them to take it back for three pounds less than he paid for it. No use in Charlie saying he was only returning something he had bought that day but didn't want. He'd never have showed up at a Fair again if he had renegued on a deal like that.'

It was a masterly performance. Daniel O'Connell himself couldn't have bettered it. It was more like that cold lantern-jawed Northerner, Carson,[13] larding into some poor quaking sinner for breaking laws that he himself meant to break before nightfall.

The steam was taken out of young Cracker. He hadn't a word to say. It was Merley came to the rescue.

'That was different, Mr Connors,' he says. He had the real tinker's voice, half-whine, half-bluster. 'That was different. It was the ould fellah sold the donk. This deal's between yourself and himself here. And leave the ould fellah out of it. If he was here to speak up for himself, there'd be no chawing the fat about the price of coffins.' He finishes up with a sneering kind of a laugh.

Cracker gives a gulp, as if he'd been kicked in the stomach. 'Who the hell asked you to butt in?' he says. I could see him getting set to play welt[14] at Merley. 'You keep out of this or I'll plaster you to the wall.'

Myko chipped in at once.

'Now, now, boys!' he says. 'No fighting in the bar.'

9. pay up (from dividend, a bonus paid out by a co-operative society).
10. on approval.
11. Red-haired Charlie.
12. bended knees.
13. Daniel O'Connell (1775-1847) was the great leader of the catholic nation from 1810 to 1845. Edward, later Lord, Carson (1854-1935) was in fact a Dubliner who took up the cause of the anti-Home Rule northern unionists.
14. i.e. deliver a blow (welt).

'Here you,' he calls down to me. 'Draw a couple of pints for the two lads.'

When the tumblers were in front of them he says:

'Drink up now, lads, and no hard feelings. You've the sympathy of all here in your sad bereavement.'

'And don't be leaving the money lying on the counter,' he says.

Could you beat it? The soft word and the kindly advice. Like a ministering angel. It wouldn't have surprised me if he had poked his head under one wing and started picking out fluff.

Cracker takes up the notes and the two play-boys start negotiating their pints.

I have always held that you could tell the form a man is in by the way he deals with his drink. Well, if you'd heard the clatter of the two Adam's apples glugging up and down as the Feeneys laid into the porter, gulching it back as if they couldn't get finished and away quick enough, you'd have known they were a beaten and a sorry pair.

When they put down their empty glasses, Myko says:

'Let you be on your way now. It's a long distance to Galway and you wouldn't know how the weather would turn.'

It wasn't the bum's rush, I'll grant you, but if he'd kicked them out with his stocking feet, it would have been much the same thing.

It was just a week afterwards to the day, that the smell started. The kind of smell that would put you wrinkling your nose wondering should you change your socks. The Boss was snoking[15] around the yard all morning trying to trace the broken sewer-pipe. There was a shelf of stout to be labelled. I was taking it easy, with a bottle in one hand and the racing page of the *Press* in the other trying to pick out a likely double for Hurst Park when Myko burst in from the yard with a face the colour of putty. I was so startled I put the bottle under the counter instead of the paper.

'What's wrong, Boss?' I says.

'I'm ruined,' he says. 'I'm destroyed completely.'

'I'll never live this down till the day I die,' he says.

'What's eating you?' I says.

'Come out to the shed,' he says, 'and you'll soon see what's eating me.'

'And stir your stumps,' he shouts back at me from the yard.

When I got out to the shed, it was to find the five-ten job in spruce cleared of litter and the Boss standing over it horror-stricken. And no wonder. There was a cuckoo in the nest. A bloody coffin-dweller, no less. Not the usual one — to be coffined, conveyed, and dumped underground before there was time, so to speak, for your-man to warm the timbers. Oh, no! This was a real old residenter, long enough on the premises to claim squatter's rights. There was no need to unscrew the coffin-lid to put a name on the tenant. Myko might as well slap a breast-plate worded: *James* (*Maggot*) *Feeney* on the lid and be done with it.

It dawned on me that Myko's obligations wouldn't end there.

'Boss,' says I. 'You'll have to bury the little weasel. The Health Inspector'll be around if he stays here much longer.'

Myko was muttering away to himself. It sounded like:

'Oh, the dirty tinkerous tribesman and his treacherous gets!'[16]

'Hadn't he a grave-plot bespoke?'

At the thought of that disreputable tomtit — never a creature of fixed abode — coiled up, in an odour of respectability, in a corner of the graveyard, with maybe a granite headstone over him erected by his sorrowing relatives, I could do nothing else, God forgive me, but laugh. I tried to gasp out an explanation:

'The Feeney clan'll be doing a pilgrimage ... to ould Maggot's grave every year ... and tinkers from every art and part ... will be lined along the bar counter ... drinking and fighting and smashing bottles and glasses ... to do honour to the decent man that buried the Maggot Feeney.'

15. searching furtively (Northern Ireland dialect, possibly a combination of poking, snooping and sneaking).

16. brats, but closer to the pejorative, non-legalistic 'bastards' (Northern Ireland dialect, from the verb 'to beget').

JANET McNEILL

(1907-)

from:
TALK TO ME (1965)

[Janet McNeill's adult fiction is not Irish in any hand-me-down or obvious fashion, but as a 1967 novel, *The Small Widow*, set mainly in England, showed, she abandons the fading gentilities of post-Victorian, middle-class Belfast at some risk. In *The Maiden Dinosaur* (1964), one of the best novels to have come out of Northern Ireland, that suburban milieu is captured with drollery and finely judged pathos. However, the decline of the Victorian middle class is but a metaphor for the recurring human predicament of her novels: her middle-aged characters' fear of both intimacy and isolation, and their uneasy occupation of the defensive middle ground of fantasy and ritual. In *Talk to Me* (1965), lack of intimacy and the difficulty of communication are made more evident with Alice's blindness, but the predicament is the same. The author's forte is the conveyance of barely controlled anguish and resentment, with only occasional lapses into sentimentality.]

CHAPTER 3

She came down the hall towards him, with her hands held out in front of her, anticipating their meeting. They would not have met until she had touched him. He was coming into harbour. While he stood waiting he made that candid examination of her which was only possibly before her fingers, breath, warmth, had reached him. This was something he always did, needed to do; he could only do it now, during this moment of rebellion against their necessity for each other, before he had allowed himself to be swallowed up by her. It made him feel lonelier than ever, so that in the end he was ready to go to her running.

In appearance now she reminded him of a ship's figurehead. Her hair was cropped short and brushed back, as if it were blown by a constant wind — this was the most practical way for her to wear it — and she rose, moved, talked with her head raised, chin tilted, so that every stimulus was received directly on her face. Her expression was sensitive and wholly unprotected, and it never varied very much, as if her face was altogether occupied in absorbing, and through its ignorance of itself had forgotten that it was necessary to register any response. It received him, and at the same time shut him out. It was scaldingly artless and yet wholly critical. It was unfair of her to be able to look like that.

Her features had thickened a little and grown more defined. She had always had a strong face for a woman, one was more aware of her bones than her flesh. Not really his type, he'd told himself, even at the beginning. Not that he had ever been very selective. They'd had oval faces, heart-shaped faces, fragile faces, pretty-pretty faces, some of them had been the faces of what he supposed nowadays were called cool chicks. They formed an album in his memory, and his imagination had coloured them in picture-postcard colours, and slipped a few extra ones into the collection — girls he'd seen across the room at a party, girls half-way down the aisle in church with that silky Sunday blessing on them, raising their eyes from the hymnbook while their mouths, disciplined to a note, softened suddenly when they saw he was watching, girls in pubs looking up at the moment when the liquid reached their lips, girls in other men's offices, pert and deliciously brisk behind their typewriters; the common factor in them all was that they returned to him something of himself, that they had a quality of receptiveness and recognition, like a mirror.

She never had it. Alice Campbell, Dr. Campbell's daughter. Alice Campbell, the clever one. Alice Campbell, who hadn't been known to go around with anyone. Alice Campbell, the unassessed female quantity. Alice Campbell whose voice was cool and smooth, so that he found himself listening to his native roughness. Alice Campbell who so startlingly became warm and tender, and who married him.

Alice Garland, blind, fifty-one, claiming him now with her hands on his breast and her fingers fanning out over his lapels.

'Give me your coat. Raining, is it? I didn't know it was raining. Is it your hip or your back that's troubling you? I know by the way you were walking it must be one or the other. I knew when you were half-way up the path. Which is it, Aubrey — the hip?'

'Neither,' he said, a little hopelessly. 'I had a

tedious day in the shop and the streets were crowded coming home, and I am a little tired, that's all.'

'Tired, poor Aubrey. Have you seen the cat? Did he come in with you?'

'Only myself. No cat.'

'Your face is cold. Poor face.' She laid her cheek against his, their skins clung. Alice was tall. This also had been unexpected. One didn't readily love a woman whose face was level with your own and whose breasts identified themselves against your chest when you stood close to her. This proves again, how uniquely I loved her. She is the reality, the fact, the essence; the others are little dolls that I keep at the back of the drawer. They are all caricatures of Alice.

'Did you forget your scarf this morning?'

'No. I am wearing it.'

Her fingers plucked and found it. 'There it is. Which one is it, Aubrey? The warm one? The one with the stripes?'

'That's right. The striped one.'

'And your hands, they are cold. Why weren't you wearing your gloves?'

Other men's wives discover whether they look tired or cheerful when they come home in the evening. I have come home to her through terror, and she lays her face on mine and decides whether I feel warm or cold. With difficulty he said, 'I took off my gloves when I opened the gate. The leaves have been coming down fast, and it was jammed.'

'Your hat, where is your hat?'

'On the chair. I set it down.'

'Wet, was it?'

'No. There was no rain to speak of.'

Soon I shall be analysed, appraised, classified and finally arrived home.

'I wish I knew where the cat was. He's not been near me all day.'

'Don't worry. The cat comes and goes as he pleases, you know that.'

He glanced in the hall mirror to gain reassurance from his reflection. She waited. He knew she knew that he was looking at himself, and this robbed him of privacy, so that there was no satisfaction in what he saw. He tried to reduce life to the scale in which she lived it.

'Was the bus full?'

'No more than usual.'

'Were you busy in the shop?'

'Slack — pretty slack today.'

'And Doris — how is Doris?'

'Doris is blooming.'

'And the other girl — Ellie?'

'Ellie is well.'

This is what I needed, wasn't it? The sharing, the trade in words, the answer to the bogyman, the rout of the cardboard. What am I complaining about?

'Ellie was crying today,' he said, giving her a bonus.

'Ellie? Crying? Poor child. What was the matter?'

'Doris says it was one of the travellers. He often makes her cry.'

'Poor Ellie. You must do something about it, Aubrey. It isn't right.'

Irritably he said, 'What do you suppose I can do?'

'Speak to the man.'

'The man is simply doing his job. There is no reason why the girl should cry.'

'What is his line?'

'Paper handkerchiefs, mostly.'

She clutched him and began to laugh. Alice always laughed suddenly and unpredictably, and too loudly in proportion to the joke. He tried to be glad that he had said something that amused her. 'Paper handkerchiefs! And Ellie crying!' Her features shook and coloured. He wished she would stop.

She put her fingers to her eyes. Her finger-nails, he noticed, were grey. He tried not to condemn her, it was a fault in him to notice it. Middle-aged women, even those who could see, sometimes went that way. But he suspected there was an unnecessary bravado in her carelessness, that she enjoyed the excuse for it. She had never had much confidence in her appearance or been one for make-up. She'd stared at him, laughed, when he told her she was beautiful. Her face hardened with laughter where the faces of other women grew soft. And now, if it was easier for her to be careless than to try, he mustn't blame her.

Even before she became blind his own preoccupation with personal cleanliness had amused her. 'I know it's part of your trade, Aubrey dear, but isn't it a bit lower-class? Nobody needs to be all that clean. You wouldn't have a guilt-complex, would you?'

Maybe she was right, he didn't know about these things, the suggestion made him uneasy. So he had become secretive about his toilet, bathing quietly, sucking lozenges on the sly, gargling *sotto voce* in the morning, scrubbing his body shyly, and taking care that she hadn't an opportunity to count how many shirts he took to the launderette every week.

He followed her into the kitchen. While the kettle warmed again to its climax they returned to the usual routine.

'Who came in today?'

'Robert Harris and that dog of his —'

'That poor animal —'

'And Mrs. Hutchinson —'

'Talking as much as ever, I suppose?'

'And wearing a green hat.'

'Green? Was she?'

'An absurd kind of hat.'

'Tell me about it.' She waited with a kind of fierce eagerness to be entertained by his account of Mrs. Hutchinson's green hat.

'Like long grass growing out of her head.'

'Grass?' She sounded puzzled.

'One of those Cossack affairs — they're all wearing them this year — fur — only green.'

'I didn't know they were wearing fur hats.'

Mrs Hutchinson's hat was a dead loss. 'Never mind, Aubrey,' she consoled, 'it doesn't matter. Who else was in?'

'The tall, round-shouldered young man from the bank —'

'The one who coughs?'

'The other one. It's the cashier who coughs.'

'They both cough. Did they give you a good lunch today?'

He skipped the next question and reported, 'Steak and kidney pie and stewed prunes.'

She reached for the basket. 'Did you bring all the messages?'

'Yes. They're all there.'

Her fingers made an inventory. 'Fish — where has that cat got to? And biscuits — did you remember to ask if they were fresh?'

'I asked. They said they were.'

'And my wool. Your newspaper — here it is, take it. The sweets — good. My pension book. You always put it down at the bottom, don't you?'

'It's the safest place.'

'I expect you are ashamed of my pension book, are you, Aubrey?'

He looked at her face, but there was nothing there to help him.

'If I didn't it could fall out.'

'Not when it's at the bottom.'

'That's why I put it there,' he said, and scored a small unwanted victory.

She made no come-back. Sometimes this was the way it went. By common consent they rested after the sour little engagement. This is the way we are. Duty or irritation, there's nothing in between them except pity, and we can't live on pity, can we? On guilt then? Oh my darling, I am sorry.

He stood watching her while she completed the preparations for the meal, trying not to see how slow and careful she was. He asked what she had been doing this afternoon and heard about Mr. Eakins and the siren from the fire-station and the ice-cream van, and how some of the children coming home from school had rattled at the gate. And that Mary Kelso had been washing sheets.

He always made it his business to insist that Alice and Mary were friends. 'What news had Mary?'

'Nothing much; you know the way she goes on.'

'No impending patter of little feet?' he asked bleakly. The remark was as fruitless as Mary. Alice said, 'Not this month,' and maybe she smiled.

He returned to the hall and took something out of the pocket of his coat. 'I've got something here for you.'

Her hands were wet and she shook them and wiped them down the sides of her skirt. 'Aubrey! A present?' Her face became bright, like a child's. 'Why didn't you tell me? What is it?'

He said it was nothing much, really. He was afraid she was going to make a thing out of it. 'It's only a trifle.'

'Presents! Something for each of us? If I have a present then you must have one as well.' She always snatched at every little excuse for gaiety. 'Something for you as well, Aubrey?'

He tore off the tissue paper. 'That's right, one each. This is yours. Here — take it.'

She made a pleased noise as he put it into her hands. 'Careful, don't let it drop.'

'What is it?'

'Well — you tell me.' She liked to play the guessing game.

'A pear!' she decided. 'Is it a pear?'

'Two pears. One for me — one for you. The biggest one for you.'

'But that's not fair!'

'Of course it is.'

'What a monster!' She nursed it in her palms, as if it were something very precious. 'Where did you buy it?'

'From a man at the park gate.'

'You didn't tell me you'd been in the park.'

'On my way back from lunch. It was sunny, almost warm.'

'Did you see the little girl today?'

'Yes. She was there.'

'You didn't tell me you'd seen the little girl.'

'And the man was at the gate, selling pears. They looked rather splendid, I thought.'

'They are, they are! Here — feel it against your cheek! Feel!' She pressed it to his face.

'I thought you'd be pleased.'

'And smell it, Aubrey — how sweet!' He sniffed obediently. 'Tight with juice,' she cried.

He said he would peel it for her after they had eaten. 'Now let me put it in a dish.'

But her fingers tightened on the fruit and she said, 'Let me feel your pear now.'

'Give me yours then. I'll set it in a safe place.'

'No. Give me yours first. Let me hold it. I want to feel it in my hand.'

'They're both the same, no difference except that yours is the biggest. The best pear for Alice.'

'Give it to me. No — I'll keep my own. I want yours to hold, Aubrey.'

He stood feeling hopeless and defeated, smoothing the paper out between his fingers. At last she said, 'There's only one pear.'

Children were playing in the opposite garden, crying to each other in clear bird cries.

'You only brought one pear, Aubrey.'

The taut paper ripped. 'The man had only one good one left when I got there. It was for you. The others weren't worth buying.'

'You said there were two pears.'

'One pear or two, what does it matter?'

'It wasn't true.'

He tried to keep his voice light and easy. 'If there had been two good pears I would have bought two. But there was only one. I knew you liked pears, so I bought it.'

'And told me there were two.'

'Listen — I simply didn't care whether I had a pear or not. It's you who likes pears.'

'All right — so why tell me there were two?'

'I wanted you to enjoy it, that was why.'

'And what were you going to do while I was enjoying it? Made appropriate noises and told me how sweet your pear was?'

'I only wanted to please you.'

He wanted to shout or yell or weep. He wanted to walk out of the house and have sky above his head. He simply wanted to stop trying. It should be possible to stop. It was a kind of blasphemy to feel so deeply about something as trivial as this, couldn't she see it?

'To please you,' he said.

She caught his sleeve. 'Poor Aubrey, you try so hard to be good to me.'

'I am good to you.'

'Good and patient and kind.'

'I try to be kind.'

She released the sleeve with a little flick of scorn and said, 'I try to endure kindness.'

He was filled with pity for himself. If she could see me, if only she could look at my face. He shouted, 'Why do you say things like that? Twisting words and making them sound clever.'

She folded her arms across her body and stood rocking from heel to toe, very close to him so that he felt her breath. 'My function in life, Aubrey — to provide a stage for kindness. Something for people to exercise their charity on.'

'People like to do what they can, you shouldn't blame them for it.'

'I suppose I am a means of grace — is that what you'd call me?'

'You shouldn't say things like that.'

'Why not? I was always a size too big for you, wasn't I? Well — wasn't I? Too bright? Too loud? And brighter and louder since I stopped seeing you. A blind woman ought to be quiet and humble. Aubrey, don't you agree a blind woman should be humble?'

He was very tired, as if all the words had been used up.

'Say something, Aubrey.'

'What do you want me to say?'

'Talk to me.'

'If you tell me what you want me to say I'll say it.'

She turned her head away, as if on this rare occasion she knew he was looking at her. 'It doesn't matter.'

'How do I know if you won't tell me? You ought to be able to tell me what to say.'

'I said it didn't matter.'

Across garden hedges children were bidden indoors to bed. They came, protesting and doors were closed and gardens silent.

She took his hands, made a cup out of them and set the pear into it. 'Put it somewhere for me, Aubrey.' Her fingers were unsteady. The skin of the fruit was still warm from them.

'Where shall I put it?'

'Into the bowl with the other fruit.'

He did as she told him. 'There,' he reported, 'I've put it with the other fruit.'

They moved gratefully into an easier pattern.

'That's right, Aubrey. So that I can find it when I want it.'

'That's right.'

She made the coffee. He felt tense until it was over, and the hot liquid safely in the pot.

'All ready now,' she said.

'We'll go through then, shall we?'

He picked up the tray and they went along the hall. Thank God for the occupation of eating and drinking, the easy things, the common domestic tune.

'Here we are,' she said.

It was impossible to tell her now that the light was not lit and that she had not drawn the curtains.

'Splendid, dear.'

They sat down. 'You're hungry, Aubrey?'

'Ready for it, I must say.'

'After a tiresome day you're bound to be hungry.'

'That's right.'

'Shall I pour your coffee right away?'

'Yes, pour it.'

'Hot and strong, what you need.'

'Yes.'

'You won't be so tired when you've had your coffee.'

'That's right.'

He munched an almost invisible salad, feeling grateful that he had come safely into harbour at last.

MICHAEL J. MURPHY

(1913-)

from: THE DUBLIN MAGAZINE (1973)

[Michael J. Murphy's expertise as a folklorist lends authenticity in this story to his depiction of a vanishing rural Ireland, one of rich sayings, half-doors, hiring-fairs, forges, indeed of the folk mind itself, in which the past lived in intimate association with the present. The cautious nostalgia that is the narrator's and, in the end, Felim's, is balanced by the bigotry and inequality that were part and parcel of the vanishing countryside, in which catholics were hewers of wood and drawers of water. Murphy's contempt for inherited sectarian bigotry is not on the grounds of its perverse justification of inequality but of its awful power to prevent love and understanding. Felim A'Heer is a striking creation — cantankerous, repressed, pious, heart-scalded; he is torn between nostalgia and remembered injury. Like the narrator, he learns how the bitter past, when revisited, can disarm us by having in the interim become the pathos of the present through both the agency of morality and the ironic misinterpretations that underlay and fed at least some of the original bitterness.

The story first appeared in *The Dublin Magazine* (Winter-Spring 1973), Vol. 10, No. 1. It was included in Benedict Kiely (ed.), *The Penguin Book of Irish Stories* (Harmondsworth: Penguin Books, 1987).]

RETURN OF THE BOY

I wonder was I wise in letting old Felim go back to that pub: for my own peace of mind more than his. It won't bother him any more; but I'll neither know nor be satisfied until I've completed the venture as I promised. Because, platitudinous or not, few of us know ourselves as adequately as we think — or should.

One of my weak spots I know to be a nagging, obstinate, obsessional quirk of conscience. And knowing it I should never have promised Felim I would go back some day. Now I'll have to go back to that pub in the lonely hills of Co. Down, one side of Banbridge in the North of Ireland, 'The Bann' to us in South Armagh: back to make an outrageous toast, loud and declamatory, as Felim would have made it.

The pub, mercifully, may now be closed. More than likely it's a jazzed-up chromium 'Inn' with a sign in garish illumination at night; with barmen wearing crested jackets and epaulettes; or with satiny American sleeve-waistcoats and arm-bands. Even if they don't throw me out it would be almost blasphemy to make the toast Felim requested against a background of perpetual Pop from in-built loud-speakers.

Unless of course the bar-room remains as it was: stone-flagged floor, open fire and long wooden stools, and pints of stout served in thick fluted glasses, so that thirsty locals with a first drink 'drive the stout below the chapel windows': the sort of bar-room, against carpeted lounges, that locals have come to title in sardonic, resentful guffaws as 'The Eejits' Ward'.

They had a folk saying in our part of South Armagh about going back — or not going back; I can't remember which. But maybe a man has to go back if only to find out why he shouldn't have gone — or why he should: as old Felim certainly found out that time we went back to The Bann where he'd been a hired servant as a barefooted boy of ten years of age. Or did he find out?

I wish I could recall that vernacular saying; but idiomatic sayings and half-doors and the custom of the Hiring Fairs all seem to have gone out together. Few in our parish at Slieve Gullion remember the old sayings; certainly not the saying they made about Felim himself.

It was a bitter saying better forgotten. If people wanted to spike an impulsive promise, or belittle any emotional threat, they'd say with sarcasm: 'Suppin' scaldin' broth with the point of an awl — the way Felim A'Heer went back to The Bann.'

They said it even after he had gone back; for no one except his daughter-in-law and myself ever knew he had — not even his son Joe. Like myself, Felim must have remembered his threat mouthed through porter at the dances held to celebrate the return of hired servants from their six months' terms down around The Bann: dances held on kitchen floors; himself with the old men around the fireside recalling their own gruelling days as servants in the same Black North among Orange Protestant Masters. At every dance Felim would make his threat. He would go back: back to The Bann some fine November day when the crop had been happed[1] and saved; when he had a decent stitch to his back; one shilling not having to break its neck overtaking the other in his pocket; back down to the place he'd been hired in at ten years of age; back to hammer the Orange soul-case out of the Protestant hide of the gett[2] who had been his master, a proper old rip by the name of William Andrew McAlecson. . . .

He had been saying that every May and November for years, but had never ventured further than the town of Newry in Co. Down to sell a beast or make a market. And so they had inevitably tagged that saying about scalding broth on the point of an awl to his name when the occasion of emotional threat or promise called for it.

Only for his son Joe he might never have gone back. Joe was an only child and at the time doing well as a navvy-ganger with an excavation company in England; Joe's wife and two young children remained at home with Felim on the ten acres of moory mountain land; as well of course as Felim's wife, who was bed-fast. When she died I knew Joe meant to change things and had been biding his time. He planned to close the house, let the land and bring the whole family including Felim to England.

But after the funeral Felim was stunned. For three days he sat at the fan-bellows idly turning the wheel and watching the fire, always wearing his long, old, heavy overcoat. He continually smoked his cutty clay with its notched tin lid. He spoke to no one, not even the children he worshipped. Felim was tall and gaunt with deep-sunk grey eyes in a narrow head, and he seemed to shrink. On the third day, Joe announced that he was leaving for England and would return in a month to bring the whole family, including Felim, back to England.

Felim roused like a scalded wolfhound that had been dozing. Go to England among the strangers, was it? What would happen the likes of him at his time o' day in a mad country like England? — What would happen the land?

Land . . . Land? Joe had countered; land that wouldn't physic a snipe: half the fields no different than graveyards except that the stones had no names cut on them: land of that sort could go to hell as far as he was concerned. . . .

I tried to intervene; so did Joe's wife, a stranger to South Armagh. Felim growled like a beagle; and before we could stop Joe, he had said it:

'You'll neither lead nor drive an' never have. Never would. You'll go nowhere. "Suppin' scaldin' broth with the point of an awl—"'

'Joe—?'

'"The way Felim A'Heer went back to The Bann. . . ."'

Felim couldn't have heard the saying until then; but he knew what it meant and how it had been

1. covered for protection.
2. See Patrick Boyle's 'Myko', note 16 (p. 953).

coined. He seemed to stagger up to the room to his bed.

Joe regretted his outburst and told me so as we left that evening from Newry railway station (gone now too). I was with him as far as Portadown; here I changed for Omagh on my way to the Sperrin Mountains in Co. Tyrone where I was collecting folklore at the time; he went on to Belfast on his way to England. About noon the next day I had a wire from Joe's wife: Felim was missing and would I return. I did so at once. We searched everywhere and in every pub for miles around; he had been in a few but had left. Towards midnight of the second day police found him one side of Camlough Lough half-immersed in a disused flax-dam beside an old road, trapped by a net of briars over the water and weeds. The briars probably saved his life, but he was horribly torn around the face. The police said he appeared to be somewhat delirious, saying something about going back somewhere....

We got him home and attended to. I heard nothing more until the day before a November market in Newry. Could I, his daughter-in-law wrote, be in Newry when the banks opened? Felim was determined to pay the rent himself and insisted on going alone. He was, she said, much drawn in on himself of late, speaking little. She even wondered if it might be a wise turn to bring him back to The Bann and set his mind at rest. It might settle and satisfy him. Rather than leave him alone she had refused to join Joe in England. The children doted on him. She'd never do a day's good if anything else happened to him....

I went to Newry. The morning broke calmly out of a November fog, and by the time I got there the worn November sun was fingering scrolls of ear-plug cloud out of the folds of the hills around the town. Opposite a bank I saw Felim. He was along with a few men dressed in sober country clothes like himself. They all seemed to be fascinated by the great brass knob on the door of the bank, watching it even when they exchanged a few words among one another.

When the bank door opened they crossed the street in fits and starts like men going apprehensively to a court-house or gaol. I watched Felim go in; watched him come out. In the doorway of the bank he lit his cutty clay pipe. He blew out a great cloud of smoke. I knew the other men would do the same: a votive incense to a deep-rooted notion of land freedom still haunted by fugitive memories of landlords, bailiffs and eviction.

When I bumped into him at a corner, as if by accident, his grey eyes stirred and then glared into mine. He didn't offer to shake hands and at once I got uneasy.

Before I could make a mock exclamation he says: 'Thon[3] daughter-in-law of mine? She wrote somethin'?'

I denied it black and blue, aware that the shrewd eyes were fixed on me. I swore I had heard of an old folk storyteller somewhere near The Bann and was on my way to hunt for him. I even invented a name for the man; said I would have to inquire for him in pubs along the way. Certainly in the pubs since forges were closing then for good.

'You'll never make a good liar,' he says, and added: 'but before you make a bigger liar of yourself, the wisest thing for us to do is to go in somewhere ourselves.' And he set off ahead of me, his long coat flapping to his swinging gait.

In the bar over the second half-one of whiskey, his morose mood began to break up. He muttered laments for his dead wife. Next he berated the world, then his son Joe. No nature in the young people any more. But he rhapsodized over his two grandchildren — healthy as trouts — his hand was on my shoulder by then — he'd give his heart's blood for any of them. And the daughter-in-law was as good as gold — and then he began to roar for the barman to fill up our drinks. I protested but he slapped the counter and cried:

'Hell roast me skin, aren't we out? An' when a fella's out let him *be* out!'

A little plump man on a stool beside us may have thought we were getting rowdy, for he slid off. Just then Felim whirled from the bar calling for the bowsey[4] of a barman and bumped into the little man, who excused himself and stepped round Felim. Felim grabbed him, apologized himself and asked him to wait for a drink. The little man thanked him and said he couldn't; he had to catch a bus to Banbridge. And he trundled off.

Felim stood staring at the door for a moment. Then he whirled to me. The barman had meanwhile appeared and was waiting.

'When a fella's out,' Felim cried, 'let a fella be out. Are you game?'

3. Yon (short for 'yonder') meaning 'that'.
4. Irish slang for 'a rude fellow'.

'Game ball,'[5] I cried, hoping to match his humour.

'No sooner said than done. Come on.'

I caught a glimpse of the barman twitching up nostrils and shoulders in the same movement as we left. The bus for Banbridge stood with engine running just along the main street.

Beside me in the side-seat of the Banbridge bus he was in great form.

'Did I ever tell you,' he began, pawing the clay pipe from under his huge moustache, 'how I come walkin' out of The Bann after me hirin' term in borrowed boots?' He had, but I didn't say so. A few heads tentatively half-turned towards us. The little plump man sat in the seat immediately in front, his back to us. 'Me father,' says Felim — and he touched his cap in respect — 'I hope the man's happy in Heaven — me father walked the whole road down one Sunday to The Bann where I was hired with an old half-done pair of boots for me. An ould pair of elastic-sided woman's boots borrowed off a neighbour at home. But at a penny a week, mind you. An old hag of a woman they called Sadie the Cailleach — "Cailleach" means "hag". Isn't that right?'

I assured him he was right; up the bus the heads turned sufficiently to enable me to see smirks being exchanged. Felim hadn't noticed.

'Sadie the Cailleach,' he goes on. 'She's dead an' rotten this years on top of years above in Dromintee graveyard — may Heaven be all their bed.' And again touched his cap.

He was going to continue when the conductor moved to take our fares. Felim stayed my hand and hauled out a fistful of silver. Then he was stumped: he didn't know where we were going. Neither did I. Suddenly he remembered and, once more, heads turned and faces smirked, for he shouted the name like a slogan of freedom or triumph:

'The road to McAlecson's shop an' pub! This side of the forge!'

At that the conductor was stumped and looked for assistance to me. But the little man in the seat before us half-turned and said over his shoulder knowingly that it was a 'wheen[6] o' years since there was a forge there'. He told the conductor where he thought we wanted to get off. I hadn't a chance to note how the others passengers accepted this event.

Felim paid, and then leaned towards the plump little man and asked him if he knew McAlecson's.

'Only the old doll in the pub,' he replied, without turning full to face Felim. 'You might say I didn't.'

'You missed nothin'.' And Felim was already jabbing the little man's shoulder with the stem of his pipe. 'That old doll would be the stuck-up damsel used to help in the pub, I'd say. I'll say this for her though — she used to sneak out the bottle of stout for me to carry to the fella of McAlecson's who was in bad health — with the weakness you understand — consumption. What they call TB the day.'[7]

The little man was trying to whistle.

'He was put sleepin' on the loft with me — for company. Coughin' his heart's blood out many a night. An' him heart-afeared of the rats,' Felim guffawed. The little man was chewing his lip. The heads turned again but the smirks had frozen. 'I used to chase the rats for him with Sadie the Cailleach's bleddy ould elastic-sided boots — fire them at the rats. As for William Andrew McAlecson himself I hope he's in hell — a thief with as much nature in his Orange heart as a stickin' bull, as black as the. . . .'

Felim's voice switched off like the fading drone of a siren. The little man had begun to whistle loudly, looking up at one side of the roof of the bus, then the other, in uneasy disassociation. Felim himself hadn't noticed, but had at least realized that he wasn't at an old-time Hiring Dance fireside, saying his piece as he had always done. He fidgeted. I couldn't think of anything to say. He began to ransack his pockets. I asked him what he was looking for.

'The flamin' pipe,' he whispered, as morosely as ever.

I told him the pipe was in his mouth.

Houses flashed by, aloof, spaced, lonely; a lake with a cranog island;[8] guttery straw-strewn yards with moping cattle. Felim growled: 'A lonely ould sort of a country like I thought it was. But changed. This is a fool's errand we're on. I'm surprised you let me.'

The landscape was lonelier still when we left the bus, although cars sped up and down the main

5. Very willing and ready.
6. i.e. a good few. A rural colloquialism in Northern Ireland.
7. i.e. today.
8. Irish, *crannóg*: an island with a dwelling on it.

highway and stirred the fallen leaves. Somewhere among the hillocks of land a threshing-mill was at work; the drum of the mill moaned and soughed as it gulped sheaves of oats; it might have been making its own lament for the dying year. The only soul in sight was a road surfaceman shovelling a drain along a road to our right.

Felim turned up the road. Screened by tall hawthorns red with haw we found the pub. It looked as if a high wind had rattled it. The door was closed and every window but one and a kitchen window was shuttered and all had iron bars. There was a signboard, but the blubberings of ancient paint had spat away the name.

As I knocked on the door I heard Felim groan like an ailing animal. I knocked again and heard him swear; but it was his son Joe he was cursing. He was muttering something about getting to hell away from the place when surprisingly the door opened slowly and a little woman with hair as white as fine teased new rope let us in. She closed the door on our heels as if to keep out the whimper of the leaves drifting in hosts like lost hungry elves over the cobbles. The woman led us to a room; it was the room with the unshuttered window. A fire had been set in a huge open grate but not lighted.

I ordered whiskey and she left us silently, not having said a word. Felim was moaning again. To lift his mind I asked him if the room had been a shop or a bar-room, for great hooks coated in whitewash hung from ceiling beams. But he didn't seem to care or want to talk; just glared at me and up at the ceiling, then down at the stone-flagged floor.

The woman came back as silently as she had left. We took the drinks from her hands. I had the correct sum in coins ready and these she dropped casually into some pocket in her dress. Still without speaking she crossed to the window and stood looking out. Looking at her, Felim let a groan which echoed as if the room were a vault. It was as cold as a vault too.

I didn't know what to say. The woman stood at the window as vague as a cobweb against the wan light outside. She was dressed entirely in black, right to the neck where a ruffle-like collar pushed against her hair. I wondered if she was listening, hoping we would speak. Or was she looking at something?

But there was nothing to see, only the road, the leaves, silently now, drifting, a bare hedge shivering in the winds, and beyond it a field of potatoes yet to be dug, the drills of dead stalks bleached and as withered as her own hair. Once, an amber light fondled the stalks, then withdrew — snail-horn quick — as if from a touch as cold as death.

I pretended to study the old hooks in the ceiling; to study an old faded print of a calendar; to finger the notches in the stools along the wall stained and smoothed by generations of trouser-seats in hard corduroy. Behind me I heard Felim burst a sigh in his groaning way, like a saturated cow. He said as if speaking thought aloud:

'Well man aye elastics . . .'

'You mean Sadie the Cailleach's elastics?' I said.

'An' if I did?'

'Shouldn't we see the loft you slept in? Where you fired Sadie's elastics at the rats?'

He swirled his drink and prepared to let it down. 'We better,' he said resignedly, 'be makin' our road short back home be Newry.'

'But you always said —'

'Never mind what the hell I said. I can mind thon loft too bleddy well — especially the night thon fella died on me — choked in his own blood.'

There was a movement at the window — a cobweb stirring in a draught — and the woman was suddenly gone. His graphic memory was perhaps too vivid for her. Yet at the door she appeared to pause, then went on, silent as ever in her sandals. Felim had been watching her too.

'We can't leave now without orderin' another round. When you get it, lower it quick till we get to hell outa here. We should never have come.' There was something I should say but couldn't think of it. He went on gratingly, watching the window: 'A black, cold lonely country an' always was. Not a bleddy mountain in sight. No houses. Ask them for a drink in my time an' they handed you a tin an' pointed to a pump. Wouldn't give you the black of their nail. . . .'

The woman returned almost unnoticed: she was carrying two full glasses of whiskey. She gave one to me because I was nearest, the other to Felim. He gaped at the drink, then at the woman.

'I was goin' to order a half-one, mam, not a full glass, but seein' as it's here . . .' And he took the glass in one hand and with the other reached into his pocket.

She held his hand in the pocket through the cloth. The amber light was back outside, and against the window I couldn't see her face. But I heard her voice, low and trembling.

'Keep your money in your pocket. That drink's on me. For Sadie the Cailleach's elastic boots.'

Without another word she turned and went back to the window, again looking out.

A passing car blasted sound like blasphemy into the room. It faded in a drone. The leaves stirred and whirled in concert, silently. Felim seemed to wait for the woman to speak. She remained silent. He said huskily:

'How — do you mean, mam?'

'Don't think it ill-bred of me,' she replied, the words spoken to the window, 'but you have an up-the-country tongue: where the hired servant boys came from. You would be the boy with Sadie the Cailleach's elastic-sided boots.'

Felim didn't answer; but I watched his glass tilt until the whiskey began to drip, then spill. With her back to us the woman went on:

'Your master William Andrew was my uncle. He lived beyond his hundredth year and had a clear mind almost to the last.' She spoke as if saying something she had to say so that she could forget it for ever. 'He had scores of boys he could never remember. But he never forgot the boy with Sadie the Cailleach's elastics.'

'You mean he — minded[9] me a boy here?'

'Because of the elastics. It amused him.' You felt she was trying desperately to smile. Then she said: '"Cailleach" is your old Gaelic word for hag, I believe.'

'Old woman,' I put in gently, quickly.

'Hag I was told.' Edged with sharp authority she dismissed me; I took the hint and stayed quiet. Felim was gaping at her back. Her voice softened as she said: 'That young man you saw die on the loft — he was my brother.'

'Lord rest him,' Felim whispered, instinctively, instantly raising his hand to his cap in the traditional touch of respect, but suddenly cutting short the gesture: as if he had been about to raise his cap to a strange Catholic Chapel only to be told it was a Protestant Church.

'He never forgot you — my uncle I mean.' She seemed actually to chuckle. 'Never. Neither did I, but — we won't go in to that now.' And this time she chuckled outright and turned to face us though remaining at the window. 'I'm the last of the McAlecsons — the name I mean. I have a cousin who runs the place — she's in The Bann on business or she'd — we should have the fire lit, I know. But we rarely have anyone until night-time now.'

'An' I mind the rows of carts outside there —'

She cut him off abruptly: 'All gone now.' Maybe she was wise not to want to remember. 'All gone. All changed.'

'The world's changed.' Felim's voice boomed in the room. 'An' the people changed with them.'

'Drink that up,' she said quickly. 'Then you must have tea with me.'

We both protested; Felim was gesturing as well. Too much bother. Hadn't we whiskey? More than good enough. Anyway he wanted to see the old loft up the road. Was it there? She nodded, merely blinking at him, but shrewdly. He would call on his way back — Felim swore he would call. In between he was gulping the whiskey. I thought I knew what was in his mind and said nothing; for I was watching the woman, believing I knew what went on in her mind as well. She was watching him now intently. She watched him finish his drink — gulp, cough, splutter — then look for a place except the stool to set down his glass. She seemed as if about to step forward to take it from him, then held back, folded one hand over the other and blinked again. Her eyes were close and red-rimmed. And then she slowly turned back to look out the window.

Suddenly, silently as ever, she turned to go. Felim almost loped after her. She opened the door and let us out. Once outside she closed the door on the whimpering scurry of the inrushing leaves.

From the doorstep Felim strode out ahead of me, back down the road towards the main highway. I let him go. Suddenly he yanked off his cap. The wind tweaked at his scant hair and I saw his shoulders shake; the cap he held to his face. He roughly drew it on again, striding ahead until he came abreast of the surfaceman shovelling in the roadside drain. Again he whipped off his cap, stopped, wheeled about, seemed to see me for the first time, and turned back to the surfaceman. He took out half-a-crown and speech rushed from him as he said to the man:

'I want you to give a message to the old woman back in the pub there.'

The man, crouched over his shovel, knew we had just left, and though he barely paused in his work the halt revealed his justifiable suspicion. He said at length:

9. remembered.

'Is it old Sadie you mean?'

I repeated her name. I'm sure Felim kept repeating it in his mind too; for now his own face was as stunned-looking as the surfaceman's was stiff with suspicion. Under his breath he said to the man:

'Aye, then . . . to old Sadie. Tell her the boy with Sadie the Cailleach's elastics hadn't —'

'Sowl an' I'll not,' the man cut in. He went on working with pointed determination. 'An old uncle, if you must know, put that nickname on Sadie ages ago an' she never took well till[10] it. She took law of a man once over that nickname . . .'

'Do you tell me that? Felim said, as if a deep secret of existence had been revealed to him for the first time. He straightened. Then he burst into great guffaws of laughter which startled me as well as the surfaceman who, with shovel-shaft resting on a knee, was staring up at him. He went on laughing into the wind. The leaves seemed to caper to his mood. I mused on the delicate, fragile, even madly ironic supports that can sustain the memory of a human relationship over the decades: the image of a pair of old boots forming such a link was at once farcical and frightening. That's why Felim's laughter had startled me.

I saw him press the coin into the surfaceman's hand.

'Never mind about Sadie the Cailleach, then.' He paused. 'Just tell old Sadie that . . . McAlecson's up-the-country boy with the ould boots hadn't the heart to go back. Can you mind to tell her that?'

'Wi' pleasure man,' said the surfaceman, spitting on the coin before he put it in his waistcoat pocket.

We had twenty minutes to wait on a bus back to Newry, but Felim didn't speak; indeed he stood apart with his back to me as if to stall any intention to talk. He almost flung himself into the bus. But once seated, we both turned as if moved by the same thought and looked back through the window.

Haws on the roadside hedges made crimson blurs. Leaves swirled in our wake like outsize burnished chaff. I remembered the sound of that threshing-mill . . . and saw a road running back imponderably into Time, powered by the endless irony of living that reminded me of the endless pulley-belt on that threshing-mill, linking engine to mill, memory to man and woman; the sound of that drum lamenting for man and land and blighted love and inherited bigotry and beliefs; and yet that sound at the same time fulfilling the promise of Harvest! Of life.

In Newry Felim refused to take a drink. He even insisted on seeing me to the railway station on my way back to The Sperrins in Co. Tyrone; he had time on his hands. He was tongue-tied. His eyes were misty. Not once did he refer to my mythical storyteller, a lie I'd forgotten about by then myself. When the train pulled in, he took my hand in both his own and squeezed hard. His eyes were now moist. I knew it wasn't altogether because he was parting with me.

'If we had our lives to live over again — Ah, but sure, what's the good of talkin'?' He stared with his moist eyes unashamedly for a long time into mine. 'I want you to promise' — he was finding difficulty in speaking — 'Promise you'll go back one day. It looked mean the way I run out. But I had to. I had to.'

I said I believed the old woman would have understood.

'Just the same,' he went on, 'I want you to promise. You'll be near the place — you're all over the country. Your hand an' word to God?' I promised. 'I want you to go in an' drink a health to her — we clean forgot to drink her health. Tell her why. Above all, anyway, go back: go back even if she's not there an' drink my health an' your own to Sadie the Cailleach. When I think that an ould pair of elastic-sided boots . . . Ah, what's the use o' talkin'? What's a man to say?'

The train came in then and drowned whatever else he had hoped to say. And quickly he squeezed a pound note into my fist and was away before I could protest. Without gesture of any kind he staggered through passengers joining the train and was gone.

I next heard about him from his daughter-in-law; she was in England by then with her family and Joe — and Felim. I wrote to him but he didn't reply. I wasn't too disappointed — he was never much of a hand with the pen; but I believed he had other reasons for keeping silent.

Last week his own granddaughter wrote to tell me about his death and burial in an English grave in the Midlands. The young hand had the impersonal tone of the modern young blood and seemed to be awfully amused in writing an awfully funny thing: that before his death the old man raved for two whole days about an old pair of elastic-sided boots! Exclamation mark and all.

10. to.

I replied, but ignored her remarks on the boots.

Now I suppose I will have to go back to that pub near The Bann. I want to go back anyway. One should go back sometimes, as I think tradition told us. The old woman will be dead of course. Some relation will have taken the place over — perhaps that young cousin she mentioned. Married now no doubt. If there is an 'Eejits' Ward' of a bar — and even if there isn't — it tempts some odd quirk of humour or cussedness to imagine the reaction when — aloud of course — I give my toast to 'Sadie the Cailleach's ould elastic-sided boots'.

Someone in the pub may have heard of the nickname, perhaps from the old woman, or from someone in the area; they may even resent it as the woman had, except to ourselves. And they may not have heard: total recall is no longer a necessity for the folk mind. They may indulgently think me funny, or mad, or unsuitably bucolic for the trendy drinkers of today entrenched in new patterns of suspect belief more ignorant in superstition than the old.

I won't be content with delivering the toast; I may even declaim it tauntingly. Then I'll go on to propound the ludicrous supports which tenuously sustain and preserve a human relationship arrested in memory where none was thought to exist. I'll talk of the implied denunciation of partisan emotions. At that they will become convinced I'm about to talk sectarian politics and will certainly throw me out.

I've been thrown out of pubs for less worthy reasons. The very thought of it makes me more than a little drunk already. What the hell: when a fella's out — let him *be* out!

BENEDICT KIELY

(1919-)

from: A BALL OF MALT AND MADAME BUTTERLY (1973)

[Novelist, memoirist, critic, raconteur — Benedict Kiely may well come to be remembered chiefly as a short-story writer of considerable stature. Owing to their affable recounting, the genial complicity of their narration, their demotic imprinting by the mundane, their humour and threat of sentimentality, it is tempting for the critic to underestimate Kiely's stories. In fact, his is a highly cultivated and personal style. His narratives are typically stream-like, lazily meandering, but really broadening in significance as they gather in their motion apparent debris (but really motifs, images, layers of meaning) to the end of making a generous and fertilizing exit. If Kiely occasionally lapses into ballad metres in his phrasing (as well as quoting Irish ballads), this apparent incongruity is appropriate, since the author is something of a balladeer in prose, whose worldview is akin to that of the old ballads, in which life is fraught with trouble but relieved by sporadic joys, a give-and-take world that in the end must be accepted in its essentials since it will not be bullied into changing.

'A Great God's Angel Standing', from the second of Kiely's volumes of stories, is characteristically deceptive. The attentive recreation of a time and place (rural west Ulster during World War II) might distract us from the story's theological parable with its varieties of hell and heaven and a confusion between the two as strange as the friendship between the rake and the priest.]

A GREAT GOD'S ANGEL STANDING

Pascal Stakelum, the notorious rural rake, and Father Paul, the ageing Catholic curate of Lislap, met the two soldiers from Devon by the bridge over the Camowen River and right beside the lunatic asylum. It was a day of splitting sunshine in the year of the Battle of Dunkirk.[1] Pascal and the priest were going to visit the lunatic asylum, Father Paul to hear confessions, Pascal to bear him company and to sit at a sealed distance while the inmates cudgelled what wits they had and told their sins.

1. 1940.

The two soldiers, in battledress and with heavy packs on their backs, were on their way home from Dunkirk, not home to Devon exactly but to Sixmilecross, to the house of two sisters they had married in a hurry before they set off for France. It was, as you may have guessed, six miles from our garrison town of Lislap to the crossroads village where the two sisters lived, and it was a very warm day. So every one of the four, two in thick khaki, two in dull black, was glad to stop and stand at ease and look at the smooth gliding of the cool Camowen.

The bridge they rested on was of a brownish grey stone, three full sweeping arches and, to the sides, two tiny niggardly arches. In a blue sky a few white clouds idled before a light wind, and beyond a wood at an upstream bend of the river a two-horse mowing-machine ripped and rattled in meadow grass. The stone of the bridge was cut from the same quarry as the stone in the high long wall that circled the lunatic asylum and went for a good half-mile parallel with the right bank of the river.

—In France it was hot, said the first soldier.

—He means the weather was hot, said the second soldier.

The four men, priest and rake and soldiers two, laughed at that: not, Pascal says, much of a laugh, not sincere, no heartiness in it.

—Hot as hell, said the second soldier. Even the rivers was hot.

—Boiling, said the first soldier. That canal at Lille was as hot as a hot bath.

—Ruddy mix-up, said the second soldier. The Guards, they fired at the Fusiliers, and the Fusiliers, they fired at the Guards. Nobody knew who was what. Ruddy mix-up.

They took the cigarettes Pascal offered.

—Boiling hot and thirsty, said the second soldier. Never knew such thirst.

Father Paul said: You could have done with some Devon cider.

—Zider, said the first soldier. There were zomething.

—Zomerzet you are, said the second soldier.

They all laughed again. This time it was a real laugh.

The Camowen water where it widened over gravel to go under the five stone arches was clear and cool as a mountain rockspring. Upstream, trout rings came as regularly as the ticks of a clock.

The two soldiers accepted two more cigarettes. They tucked them into the breast-pockets of their battledress. They hitched their packs, shook hands several times and knelt on the motorless roadway for Father Paul's blessing. They were not themselves Arcees,[2] they said, but in camp in Aldershot in England they had been matey with an Arcee padre, and they knew the drill. Blessed after battle, they stood up, dusted their knees as carefully as if they'd never heard of mud or blood and, turning often to wave back, walked on towards the two sisters of Sixmilecross.

—Virginia, Father Paul said, was the best place I ever saw for cider.

Just to annoy him, Pascal said: Virginia, County Cavan, Ireland.

They were walking together on a narrow foot-walk in the shadow of the asylum wall.

—Virginia, U.S.A., Paul said. The Old Dominion. Very well you know what Virginia I mean. They had great apple orchards there, and fine cider presses, around a little town called Fincastle under the shadow of the Blue Ridge Mountains. That was great country, and pleasant people and fine horses, when I was a young man on the American mission.

It was a period out of his lost youth that Paul frequently talked about.

In those days of his strange friendship with Pascal he was thin and long-faced and stoop-shouldered with the straining indignant stoop that is forced on tall people when the years challenge the power to hold the head so high. That day the sun had sucked a little moisture out of his pale cheeks. He had taken off his heavy black hat to give the light breeze a chance to ruffle and cool his thin grey hair, but the red line the hat rim had made was still to be seen and, above the red line, a sullen concentration of drops of sweat. He was though, as Pascal so often said, the remains of a mighty handsome man and with such dignity, too, and stern faith and such an eloquent way in the pulpit that it was a mystery to all of us what the bishop of the diocese had against him that he had never given him the honour, glory and profit of a parish of his own.

—In the mood those two boyos are in, Pascal said, it will take them no time at all walking to the sisters at Sixmilecross.

That was the way Pascal, in accordance with his

2. i.e. RCs — Roman Catholics.

animal nature, thought; and Sixmilecross was a village in which, as in every other village in our parts, Pascal had had some of the rural adventures that got him his dubious reputation, and that made us all marvel when we'd see a character like him walking in the company of a priest. In Burma, I once heard an old sweat say, adulterers kill a pig to atone for their crime, so it was only apt and proper, and even meet and just, that Pascal should be a pork butcher. When he went a-wooing in country places he'd never walk too far from his rattly old Morris Cowley without bringing with him a tyre lever or starting handle, for country girls were hell for having truculent brothers and if they didn't have brothers they had worse and far and away worse, male cousins, and neither brothers nor male cousins, least of all the male cousins, had any fancy for Pascal rooting and snorting about on the fringes of the family. That's Pascal, for you. But at the moment, Paul is speaking.

—A man hungers to get home, he said. The men from Devon won't count the time or the number of paces. Time, what's time? They've come a long walk from the dreadful gates of eternity. Once I told you, Pascal boy, you were such a rake and run-the-roads you'd have to live to be ninety, to expiate here on this earth and so dodge the devil.

Complacently Pascal said: The good die young.

—Ninety's a long time, Father Paul said. But what's time? Here in this part of my parish. . . .

They were walking in at the wide gateway. He waved his black wide-brimmed hat in a circle comprehending the whole place, as big almost as the garrison town itself, for all the crazy people of two counties, or those of them that had been detected and diagnosed, were housed there.

—This part of my parish, he said. As much happiness or unhappiness as in any other part of the parish. But one thing that doesn't matter here is time. As far as most of them know, time and eternity are the same thing.

They walked along a serpentine avenue, up sloping lawns to the main door. The stone in the walls of the high building was cut from the same quarry as the stone that bridged the river, as the stone in the encircling wall. The stone floor in the long cool corridor rang under their feet. They followed a porter along that corridor to a wide bright hospital ward. Unshaven men in grey shirts sat up in bed and looked at them with quick bright questioning eyes. The shining nervous curiosity of the ones who sat up disturbed Pascal. He preferred to look at the others who lay quietly in bed and stared steadily at points on the ceiling or on the opposite wall, stared steadily but seemed to see neither the ceiling nor the opposite wall, and sometimes mumbled to nobody words that had no meaning. A few men in grey suits moved aimlessly about the floor or sat to talk with some of the bright curious men in the beds. Beside the doorway a keeper in blue uniform dotted with brass buttons sat and smoked and read a newspaper, raised his head and nodded to the priest, then returned to his pipe and his newspaper.

Father Paul moved from bed to bed, his purple stole about his neck. The murmur of his voice, particularly when he was at the Latin, was distinctly audible. His raised hand sawed the air in absolution and blessing. Once in a while he said something in English in a louder voice and then the man he was with would laugh, and the priest would laugh, and the man in the next bed, if he was a bright-eyed man, would laugh, and another bright-eyed man several beds away would start laughing and be unable to stop, and a ripple of laughter would run around the room touching everybody except the staring mumbling men and the keeper who sat by the door.

Pascal sat beside an empty bed and read a paper-backed book about a doctor in Germany who was, or said he thought he was, two men, and had murdered his wife, who had been a showgirl, by bathing her beautiful body in nitric acid. That sinful crazy waste of good material swamped Pascal in an absorbing melancholy so that he didn't for a few moments even notice the thin hand gripping his thigh. There, kneeling at his feet, was a man in grey clothes, misled into thinking Pascal was a priest because Pascal wore, as did the gay young men of that place and period, a black suit with, though, extremely wide and unclerical trousers. Pascal studied, with recognition, the inmate's grey jacket, the scarce grey hair, the spotted dirty scalp. The kneeling man said: Bless me, father, for I have sinned.

—Get up to hell Jock Sharkey, Pascal said. I'm no priest. You're crazy.

He was, he says, crimson in the face with embarrassment. The keeper was peeking over his newspaper, laughing, saying Jock sure was crazy and that, in fact, was why he was where he was. The keeper also blew smoke-rings from thick laughing lips, an irritating fellow. He said: Fire away, Pascal. It'll keep him quiet. I hear him two or three times a week.

—It wouldn't be right, Pascal said.

He had theological scruples, the only kind he could afford.

Only once in my life, he was to say afterwards, did a man ever ask me to listen to him confessing his sins and, fair enough, the place should be a lunatic asylum and the man, poor Jock Sharkey, that was put away for chasing women, not that he ever over-took them or did anybody any harm. They walked quick, he walked quick. They walked slow, he walked slow. He was just simply fascinated, the poor gormless bastard, by the sound of their feet, the hobbled trot, the high heels, you know, clickety-click, thigh brushing thigh. Poor Jock.

—What he'll tell you, said the keeper, is neither right nor wrong. Who'd anyway be better judge than yourself, Pascal? Even Father Paul doesn't know one half of what you know. You, now, would know about things Paul never heard tell of.

The man on his knees said: I suppose you'll put me out of the confession box, father. I'm a terrible sinner. I wasn't at mass or meeting since the last mission.

—Why was that? said Pascal the priest.

—The place I'm working in, they won't let me go to mass.

—Then it's not your fault, said Pascal. No sin. Grievous matter, perfect knowledge, full consent.[3]

He did, he said afterwards, remember from his schooldays that impressive fragment of the penny catechism of Christian doctrine: the stud-book, the form-book, the rules for the big race from here to eternity.

—But when I go to confession, father, I've a bad memory for my sins. Will you curse me, father, if I forget some of them?

—By no means, Jock. Just recite what you remember.

The keeper, more offensive as his enjoyment increased, said that Pascal wouldn't know how to curse, that he didn't know the language. The head of the kneeling man nodded backwards and forwards while he mumbled the rhythmical words of some prayer or prayers of his childhood. Now and again the names of saints came clearly out of the confused unintelligible mumble, like bubbles rising from a marshy bottom to the surface of a slow stream. Then he repeated carefully, like a child reciting, these words from an old rebel song: I cursed three times since last Easter Day. At mass-time once I went to play.[4]

Pascal was seldom given to visions except in one particular direction, yet he says that at that moment he did see, from his memory of school historical pageants, the rebel Irish boy, kneeling in all innocence or ignorance at the feet of the brutal red-coated captain whose red coat was, for the occasion, covered by the soutane of the murdered rebel priest.

The keeper said: You should sing that, Jock.

—I passed the churchyard one day in haste, Jock said, and forgot to pray for my mother's rest.

—You're sure of heaven, said the keeper, if that's the sum total of your sins. The Reverend Stakelum himself, or even Father Paul, won't get off so easy.

The penitent looked up at Pascal and Pascal looked down at stubbly chin, hollow jaws, sorrowful brown eyes. Poor Jock, Pascal thought, they put you away just for doing what I spend all my spare time, and more besides, at: to wit, chasing the girls. Only you never even seemed to want to catch up with them.

For poor Jock was never more than what we called a sort of a mystery man, terrifying the girls, or so they claimed, by his nightly wanderings along dark roads, his sudden sprints that ended as sharply and pointlessly as they began, his shouted meaning-less words provoked perhaps by a whiff of perfume in his nostrils or by that provocative tap-tippity-tap of high hard heels on the metalled surface of the road. A child might awaken in the night and cry that there was a man's face at the window. A girl might run home breathless and say that Jock had followed her for half a mile, suiting his pace to hers, like a ghost or a madman. He couldn't be a ghost, although he was as thin and as harmless as any ghost. So we put him away for a madman.

He stared long and hard at Pascal. His thin right hand tightly grasped Pascal's knee.

—David Stakelum's son, he said. I'd know you anywhere on your father. Thank God to see you in the black clothes. Your father was a decent man and

3. In catholic theology, the conditions necessary for the commission of mortal sin.

4. Two lines from the Irish ballad 'The Croppy Boy'.

you'll give me the blessing of a decent man's son.

He bowed his head and joined his hands. Behind the newspaper the keeper was gurgling. Pascal said afterwards that his father wouldn't be too pleased to think that his hell's own special hell-raker of a son bore him such a resemblance that even a crazy man could see it. But if his blessing would help to make Jock content then Jock was welcome to it. So he cut the sign of the cross over the old crazy dirty head. He touched with the tips of the fingers of both hands the bald patch on the dome. He held out those fingers to be kissed. The most fervent young priest fresh from the holy oil couldn't have done a better job. Pascal had so often studied the simple style of Father Paul. The keeper was so impressed that he folded the newspaper and sat serious and quiet.

Father Paul walked slowly towards them, along the narrow passage between the two rows of beds. Walking with him came a fat red-faced grey-headed inmate. The fat inmate talked solemnly, gestured stiffly with his right hand. The priest listened, or pretended to listen, turning his head sideways, stretching his neck, emphasising the stoop in his shoulders. He said: Mr. Simon, you haven't met my young friend, Pascal.

The fat man smiled benevolently at Pascal but went on talking to the priest. As you know, sir, I am not of the Roman Catholic persuasion, yet I have always been intrigued by the theory and practice of auricular confession. The soul of man, being walled around and shut in as it is, demands some outlet for the thoughts and desires that accumulate therein.

He had, Pascal says, a fruity pansy voice.

—The child, he said, runs to its mother with its little tale of sorrow. Friend seeks out friend. In silence and secrecy souls are interchanged.

It was exactly, Pascal was to say, as if the sentences had been written on the air in the loops and lines of copper-plate. You could not only hear but see the man's talk: A Wesleyan I was born, sir, and so remain. But always have I envied you Roman Catholics the benefits of the confessional, the ease that open confession brings to the soul. What is the Latin phrase, sir?

Paul said: Ad quietam conscientiam.[5]

—Ad quietam conscientiam, Simon repeated. There is peace in every single syllable. There is much wisdom in your creed, sir. Wesley knew that. You have observed the spiritual similarity between Wesley and Ignatius of Loyola.[6]

The keeper said: Simon, Doctor Murdy's looking for you. Where in hell were you?

—He asks me where I have been, sir. Where in hell.

Father Paul said: He means no harm, Simon. Just his manner of speaking.

Simon was still smiling. From elbow to bent wrist and dangling hand, his right arm was up like a question mark. He said to Father Paul: Surveillance, sir, is a stupid thing. It can accomplish nothing, discover nothing. If I were to tell this fellow where I had been, how could he understand? On this earth I have been, and beyond this earth.

He shook hands with the priest but not with Pascal nor the keeper nor Jock Sharkey. He walked with dignity past the keeper and back down the ward.

—There goes a travelled man, Pascal said.

Father Paul was folding his purple stole. He said: There are times when religion can be a straitjacket.

—It's not Simon's time yet for the straitjacket, the keeper said. When the fit takes him he'll brain the nearest neighbour with the first handy weapon.

At the far end of the ward where Simon had paused for a moment, there was a sudden noise and a scuffling. The keeper said: Too much learning is the divil.

He thumped down the passage between the beds.

—Now for the ladies, Father Paul said. You'll be at home there, Pascal. They say all over the town that no man living has an easier way with the ladies.

Pascal was to report to myself and a few others that if Paul had wanted to preach him a sermon to make his blood run cold and to put him off the women for the rest of his life, he couldn't have gone about it in a better way.

Is it true that, as the poet said, you never knew a holy man but had a wicked man for his comrade and heart's darling?[7] Was it part of Paul's plan to pick Pascal as his escort and so to make an honest boy out

5. To appease, to give peace to, the conscience.

6. John Wesley (1703-91), English preacher and founder of methodism. Ignatius of Loyola (1491-1556), the Spanish ecclesiastic who, in 1534, founded the Society of Jesus.

7. The poet is W.B. Yeats, and a blind beggar makes the claim in his play *The Cat and the Moon* (1924).

of him or, at least, to cut in on the time that he would otherwise spend rummaging and ruining the girls of town and country? The thing about Pascal was that, away from the companionship of Paul, he thought of nothing but women when, of course, he wasn't butchering pork, and perhaps he thought of women even then. Like many another who is that way afflicted he wasn't big, violent, handsome, red-faced or blustering. No, he went about his business in a quiet way. His hair was sparse, of a nondescript colour, flatly combed and showing specks of dandruff. He wore horn-rimmed spectacles. He was one of those white-faced fellows who would, softly and secretly and saying nothing about it to their best friends, take advantage of their own grandmothers. The women were mad about him. They must have been. He kept himself in fettle and trim for his chosen vocation. When the two soldiers and Paul were, in the sunshine on the Camowen Bridge, talking of Devon cider, Pascal was thinking, he says, of sherry and raw eggs, and oysters, porter and paprika pepper.

On the day of Paul's funeral he said to me: A decent man and I liked him. But, my God, he had a deplorable set against the women or anybody that fancied the women.

—Except myself, he said. For some reason or other he put up with me.

—That day at the female ward, he said, at the geriatrics you call 'em, I cheated him, right under his nose, God forgive me. And may Paul himself forgive me, since he knows it all now.

Pascal stood at the threshold of this female ward while Father Paul, purple stole again around his neck, moved, listening and forgiving with God's forgiveness, from bed to bed. Pascal wasn't much of a theologian, yet looking at the females in that female ward he reckoned that it was God, not the females, who needed forgiveness. They were all old females, very old females, and as such didn't interest Pascal. He had nothing, though, against old age as long as it left him alone. His father's mother was an attractive, chubby, silver-haired female, sweet as an apple forgotten and left behind on a rack in a pantry, wrinkled, going dry, yet still sweet beyond description. But these sad old females, a whole wardful of them, were also mad and misshapen, some babbling like raucous birds, some silently slavering.

He couldn't make up his mind whether to enter the ward and sit down or to walk up and down the cool echoing corridor. He always felt a fool when walking up and down like a sentry, but then he also felt a fool when standing or sitting still. He was just a little afraid of those caricatures of women. This was the first time he had ever been afraid of women, and afraid to admit to himself that these creatures were made in exactly the same way as women he had known. He was afraid that if he went into the ward and sat down he would see them in even greater detail than he now did from the threshold. He was young. Outside the sun was shining, the Camowen sparkling under the sun, the meadow grass falling like green silk to make beds for country lovers. But here all flesh was grass and favour was deceitful and beauty was vain. It was bad enough looking at the men. To think what the mind could do to the body. But it was hell upon earth looking at the women. Jock Sharkey, like a million lovers and a thousand poets, had gone mad for beauty. This, in the ward before him, was what could happen to beauty.

He stepped, shuddering, back into the corridor and collided with a tall nurse. He apologised. He smelled freshly-ironed, starched linen and disinfectant, a provoking smell. A quick flurried glance showed him a strong handsome face, rather boyish, brick-red hair bursting out over the forehead where the nurse's veil had failed to restrain it. He apologised. He was still rattled by his vision in the ward. Contrary to his opportunist instinct he was even about to step out of the way. But the nurse didn't pass. She said: It is you, Pascal Stakelum, isn't it? Did they lock you up at last? A hundred thousand welcomes.

He had to do some rapid thinking before he remembered. There were so many faces in his memory and he was still confused, still a little frightened, by those faces in the ward. She didn't try to help. She stood, feet apart and solidly planted, and grinned at him, too boyish for a young woman but still fetching. She was, if anything, taller than he was. Her brother, then he remembered, had gone to school with us, a big fellow, as dark as she was red, very clever but capricious, making a mockery of things that he alone, perhaps, of all of us could understand and, in the end, throwing the whole thing up and running away and joining the Royal Air Force. So the first thing Pascal said, to show that he knew who she was, was to ask about the brother, and when would he be coming home. She said: He won't be coming home.

—Why for not?

She said he had been killed at Dunkirk.

Coming right after the prospect of the mad old women, that was a bit of a blow in the face, but at least, he told himself, clean death in battle was not madness, deformity, decay; and the moment gave Pascal the chance to sympathise, to get closer to her. He held her hands. He said he was sorry. He said he had always liked her brother. He had, too. They had, indeed, been quite friendly.

She said: It's war. He would always do things his own way.

She seemed proud of her brother, or just proud of having a brother dead at Dunkirk.

—This is no place to talk Pascal said. And I'm with Father Paul. Meet me this evening at the Crevenagh Bridge.

That was the old humpy seventeenth-century bridge on the way to a leafy network of lovers' lanes and deep secret bushy ditches.

—Not this evening, she said. I'm on duty. But tomorrow.

—Eight o'clock on the dot, said Pascal.

That was his usual time during the summer months and the long warm evenings. And he was very punctual.

She walked away from him and towards Father Paul. He looked after her, no longer seeing the rest of the ward. She was a tall strong girl, stepping with decision and a great swing. Jock Sharkey would have followed her to the moon.

Father Paul, the shriving done, was again folding his stole. He joked with a group of old ladies. He told one of them that on his next visit he would bring her a skipping rope. He told another one he would bring her a powderpuff. He distributed handfuls of caramels to the whole crew. They cackled with merriment. They loved him. That was one bond between Pascal and himself. The women loved them both.

—But if he meant to preach to me that time, Pascal said to us, by bringing me to that chamber of horrors, I had the laugh on him.

In the sunshine on the lawn outside, the superintending doctor stood with his wife and his dogs, three Irish setters, one male, two female. The doctor and his wife, stood, that is, and the setters ran round and round in erratic widening circles.

Those smart-stepping Devon men were by now approaching Sixmilecross, and the two sisters, and rest after battle and port after stormy seas.

The doctor was a handsome cheery fellow, even if he was bald. He wore bright yellow, hand-made shoes, Harris tweed trousers and a high-necked Aran sweater. The wife was small and dainty and crisp as a nut, and a new wife; and the two of them, not to speak of the three setters, were as happy as children. They talked — the doctor, the woman, Paul and Pascal — about the war, and about the two soldiers from Devon and their two women in Sixmilecross. Then Father Paul wished the doctor and his wife many happy days, and he and Pascal stepped off towards the town. At the gateway they met a group of thirty or forty uniformed inmates returning, under supervision, from a country walk. One of them was gnawing a raw turnip with which, ceasing to gnaw, he took aim at Pascal and let fly. Pascal fielded the missile expertly — in his schooldays he had been a sound midfield man — and restored it to the inmate who was still chewing and looking quite amazed at his own deed. All this, to the great amusement of the whole party, inmates and three keepers. But, oddly enough, Paul didn't join in the merriment. He stood, silent and abstracted, on the grass at the side of the driveway. He looked at the sky. His lips moved as though he were praying, or talking to himself.

Pascal gave away what cigarettes he had left to the hiking party and he and the priest walked on, Paul very silent, over the Camowen. When they were halfways to the town, Paul said: Some men can't live long without a woman.

Pascal said nothing. He remembered that there was a story that Paul had once beaten a loving couple out of the hedge with a blackthorn stick. He remembered that Paul came from a stern mountainy part of the country where there had been a priest in every generation in every family for three hundred years. He thought of the red nurse and the hedge ahead of her. So he said nothing.

—That new wife of his, Paul said, was American. Did you notice?

—She dressed American, Pascal said. But she had no accent.

—She comes from a part of the States and from a class in society where they don't much have an accent, Paul said. At least not what you in your ignorance would call an American accent.

Pascal said: The Old Dominion.

—You're learning fast, Paul said.

The town was before them.

—Three wives he had, Paul said. One dead. Irish. One divorced. English. And now a brand new one from Virginia. Some men can't go without.

Pascal made no comment. He contented himself with envying the bald doctor his international experience. He resolved to travel.

—Most men, said Paul, aren't happy unless they're tangled up with a woman. The impure touch. But the French are the worst. Their blood boiling with wine. From childhood. How could they keep pure?

Pascal hadn't the remotest idea. So he made no comment. He didn't know much about the French but he reckoned that just at that moment in history they had enough and to spare on their plates without also having to worry about purity.

—But pleasures are like poppies spread, Paul said.

He was a great man always to quote the more moralising portions of Robert Burns. Pascal heard him out: You seize the flower, its bloom is shed. Or like the snow falls in the river — a moment white, then melts forever. Or like the borealis race, that flit ere you can point their place. Or like the rainbow's lovely form, evanishing amid the storm.[8]

—Burns, said Father Paul, well knew what he was talking about. Those, Pascal, are the words of wisdom gained through sad and sordid experience.

Pascal agreed. He was remembering the nurse's dead brother who had been a genius at poetry. He could write parodies on anything that any poet had ever written.

When Pascal met the nurse at the Crevenagh Bridge on the following evening she was, of course, in mourning. But the black cloth went very well with that brilliant red hair. Or like the rainbow's lovely form. There was something about it, too, that was odd and exciting, like being out, he said, with a young nun. Yet, apart from the colour of her clothes, she was no nun. Although, come to think of it, who except God knows what nuns are really like?

Pascal, as we know, was also in black but he had no reason to be in mourning. It had rained, just enough to wet the pitch. Otherwise the evening went according to Operation Pascal. When he had first attacked with the knee for the warming-up process he then withdrew the knee and substituted the hand, lowering it through the band of her skirt, allowing it to linger for a playful moment at the bunker of the belly button. Thereafter he seemed to be hours, like fishermen hauling a net, pulling a silky slip out of the way before the rummaging hand, now living a life of its own, could negotiate the passage into her warm drawers. Pascal didn't know why he hadn't made the easier and more orthodox approach by laying the girl low to begin with and then raising skirt and slip, except it was that they were standing up at the time, leaning against a sycamore tree. The rain had passed but the ground was wet, and to begin his wooing by spreading his trenchcoat (many's the fine rump, he boasted, that trenchcoat had kept dry, even when the snow was on the ground) on the grass, seemed much too formal. Pascal Stakelum's days, or evenings or nights, were complex with such problems.

Later came the formal ceremonious spreading of the trenchcoat on a protective mattress of old newspapers, and the assuming by both parties, of the horizontal. By that time the big red girl was so lively that he swore she'd have shaken Gordon Richards,[9] the King of them All, out of the saddle. She kept laughing and talking, too, so as to be audible, he reckoned, thirty yards away but fortunately he had chosen for the grand manoeuvre a secluded corner of the network of lanes and ditches. He had a veteran's knowledge of the terrain and he was nothing if not discreet.

He was not unmindful of the brother dead in faraway France. But then the brother had been such an odd fellow that even in Pascal's tussling with his strong red sister he might have found matter for amusement and mockery. As Pascal bounced on top of her, gradually subduing her wildness to the rhythmic control of bridle and straddle and, in the end, to the britchen[10] of his hands under her buttocks, he could hear her brother's voice beginning the schoolboy mockery of Shelly's soaring skylark: Hell to thee, blithe spirit. Pascal and the splendid panting red girl moved together to the poet's metre.

That was one brother Pascal did not have to guard against with starting handle or tyre lever. Working like a galley slave under the dripping sycamore he was in no fear of ambush.

8. Robert Burns, 'Tam o' Shanter'. The third line should read 'Or like the snowfall in the river'.

9. A famous champion English jockey.

10. breeching.

Paul got his parish in the end, the reward of a well-spent life, he said wryly. He died suddenly in it before he was there for six months. That parish was sixty miles away from Lislap, in sleepy grass-meadow country where the slow River Bann drifts northwards out of the great lake. Pascal missed Paul's constant companionship more than he or anybody else would have believed possible and began, particularly after Paul's sudden death, to drink more than he had ever done before, and went less with the girls, which puzzled him as much as it did us. It worried him, too: for in the house of parliament or public house that we specially favoured, he asked me one day was he growing old before his time because he was growing fonder of drink and could now pass a strange woman on the street without wondering who and what she was.

—You're better off, Pascal, I said. What were you ever doing anyway but breaking them in for other men? You never stayed long enough with any one woman to be able in the long run to tell her apart from any other woman.

He was more hurt than I had imagined he would be. But he sadly agreed with me, and said that some day he hoped to find one real true woman with whom he could settle down.

—Like with poor Paul that's gone, he said. Some one woman that a man could remember to the last moment of his life.

—No, I'm not crazy, he said. Two days before his death I was with Paul in his parish, as you know. We went walking this evening after rain, by the banks of a small river in that heavy-grass country. That was the last walk we had together. The boreen[11] we were on went parallel with the river bank. We met an old man, an old bewhiskered codger, hobbling on a stick. So Paul introduced us and said to Methusalah: What now do you think of my young friend from the big garrison town of Lislap?

—The old fellow, said Pascal, looked me up and looked me down. Real cunning country eyes. Daresay he could see through me as I was a sheet of thin cellophane. But he lied. He said: Your reverence, he looks to me like a fine clean young man.

—That was an accurate description of me, Pascal Stakelum, known far and wide.

Pascal brooded. He said: A fine clean young man.

—Then that evening, he said, we sat for ages after dinner, before we knelt down to say the holy rosary with those two dry sticks of female cousins that did the housekeeping for him. One quick look at either of them would put you off women for time and eternity. There's an unnerving silence in the houses that priests live in: the little altar on the landing, you know, where they keep the sacrament for sick calls at night. Imagine, if you can, the likes of me on my bended knees before it, wondering would I ever remember the words when it came my turn to lead the prayers. But I staggered it. Closed my eyes, you might say, and took a run and jump at it, and landed on the other side word perfect. It would have been embarrassing for Paul if I hadn't been able to remember the words of the Paterandave[12] in the presence of those two stern cousins. One evening one of them sat down opposite me in a low armchair and crossed her legs, poor thing, and before I could look elsewhere I had a view of a pair of long bloomers, passion-killers, that were a holy fright. You wouldn't see the equal of them in the chamber of horrors. Six feet long and coloured grey and elastic below the knee. But when the two cousins were off to bed, and good luck to them, we sat and talked until all hours, and out came the bottle of Jameson,[13] and Paul's tongue loosened. It could be that he said more than he meant to say: oh, mostly about Virginia and the Blue Ridge Mountains and the lovely people who always asked the departing stranger to come back again. Cider presses near Fincastle. Apple orchards. Dogwood trees in blossom. He went on like that for a long time. Then he got up, rooted among his books, came back with this one book covered in a sort of soft brown velvet with gold lettering and designs on the cover and, inside, coloured pictures and the fanciest printing you ever saw, in red and in black. He said to me: Here's a book, Pascal, you might keep as a memory of me when I'm gone.

—So I laughed at him, making light of his gloomy face, trying to jolly him up, you know. I said: Where, now, would you be thinking of going?

—Where all men go sooner or later, he said.

—That was the end of my laughing. That's no way for a man to talk, even if he has a premonition.

—Keep the book as a token, Paul said to me. You

11. lane.

12. The words of the rosary: fifteen decades of Aves (Hail Marys), each decade being preceded by a Paternoster (Our Father).

13. A brand of Irish whiskey.

were never much for the poetry, I know. But your wife when you find her might be, or, perhaps, some of your children. You've a long road ahead of you yet, Pascal, all the way to ninety, and poetry can lighten the burden. That book was given to me long ago by the dearest friend I ever had. Until I met yourself, he said. Long ago in a distant country and the wench is dead.[14]

—Those were the last words I ever heard Paul speak, excepting the Latin of the mass next morning, for my bus passed the church gate before the mass was rightly over, and I had to run for it. But bloody odd words they were to come from Paul.

—Common enough words, I said. Anybody could have said them.

—But you didn't see the book, Pascal said. I'll show it to you.

He did, too, a week later. It was an exquisite little edition, lost on Pascal, I thought with some jealousy, both as to the perfection of the book-maker's art and as to the text, which was William Morris telling us, there in a public house in Lislap, how Queen Guenevere had defended herself against the lies of Sir Gauwaine, and a charge of unchastity.[15] Fondling the book, I was not above thinking how much more suitable than Pascal I would have been as a companion for old Paul. So that I felt more than a little ashamed when Pascal displayed to me with what care he had read the poem, underlining here and there in red ink to match the rubric of the capitals and the running titles on the tops of the pages. It was, almost certainly, the only poem to which he had ever paid any particular attention, with the possible exception of that bouncing parody on Shelley's skylark.

—It's like a miniature mass book, he said. Red and black. Only it was by no means intended for using at the mass. See here.

He read and pointed with his finger as he read: She threw here wet hair backward from her brow, her hand close to her mouth touching her cheek.

—Coming from the swimming-pool, Pascal said, when the dogwoods were in blossom. You never knew that Paul was a champion swimmer in his youth. Swimming's like tennis. Brings out the woman in a woman. Arms wide, flung-out, breasts up. Oh, there were a lot of aspects to Paul. And listen to this: Yet felt her cheek burned so, she must a little touch it. Like one lame she walked away from Gauwaine.

—Time and again, Pascal said, he had heard it said that lame women had the name for being hot. Once he had seen on the quays of Dublin a one-legged prostitute. The thought had ever afterwards filled him with curiosity, although at the time he wouldn't have risked touching her for all the diamonds in Kimberley.

—And her great eyes began again to fill, he read, though still she stood right up.

That red nurse, he remembered, had had great blue eyes, looking up at him like headlamps seen through mist.

—But the queen in this poem, he said, was a queen and no mistake. And in the summer it says that she grew white with flame, white like the dogwood blossoms and all for this Launcelot fellow, lucky Launcelot, and such a pansy name. One day, she says, she was half-mad with beauty and went without her ladies all alone in a quiet garden walled round every way, just like the looney bin where I met that nurse. And both their mouths, it says, went wandering in one way and, aching sorely, met among the leaves, Warm, boy, warm. Then there's odd stuff here about a great God's angel standing at the foot of the bed, his wings dyed with colours not known on earth, and asking the guy or girl in the bed, the angel has two cloths, you see, one blue, one red, asking them, or him or her, to guess which cloth is heaven and which is hell. The blue one turns out to be hell. That puzzles me.

It puzzled both of us.

—But you must admit, said Pascal, that it was a rare book for a young one to be giving a young priest, and writing on it, look here, for Paul with a heart's love, by the Peaks of Otter in Virginia, on a day of sunshine never to be forgotten, from Elsie Cameron. Usually the women give breviaries to the priests, or chalices, or amices, or albs, or black pullovers. She must have been a rare one, Elsie Cameron. Would you say now that she might have had a slight limp? It's a Scottish name. Paul was forever talking about what he called the Scots Irish in Virginia and the fine people they were. All I know is that Socttish women are reputed to be very hot. They're all Protestants and don't have to go to confession.

Pascal had known a man who worked in

14. cf. a speech by Barabas in Christopher Marlowe's *The Jew of Malta*, Act IV, Scene 1.
15. William Morris's *The Defence of Guinevere* (1858).

Edinburgh who said that all you had to do to set a Scotswoman off was to show her the Forth Bridge, the wide open legs of it. That man had said that the Forth Bridge had never failed him.

When I said to Pascal that all this about Paul could have been as innocent as a rose, he said he was well aware of that: he wasn't claiming that Paul had done the dirty on the girl and left her to mourn out her life by the banks of the James River. But that it may all have been innocent for Paul and Elsie only made it the more mournful for Pascal. Fond memories and memories, and all about something that never happened.

—Any day henceforth, Pascal said, I'll go on a journey just to see for myself those Blue Ridge Mountains. Were they ever as blue as Paul thought they were? Cider's the same lousy drink the world over. What better could the orchards or women have been in Virginia than in Armagh? You see he was an imaginative man was old Paul, a touch of the poet, and soft as putty and sentimental away behind that granite mountainy face. Things hurt him, too. He told me once that one day walking he met that mad Maguire one from Cranny, the one with the seven children and no husband, and tried to talk reason to her, and she used language to him the like of which he had never heard, and he turned away with tears in his eyes. He said he saw all women degraded and the Mother of God sorrowful in Nancy Maguire who was as bad as she was mad. An odd thought. He should have taken the stick to her the way I once heard he did to a loving couple he found under the hedge.

But pleasures are like poppies spread,[16] as Paul would say, walking the roads with Pascal ad quietam conscientiam, looking at mad Nancy and listening to her oaths, seeing Elsie Cameron under the apple trees under the Blue Mountains in faraway Virginia. Once I wrote a story about him and it was printed in a small little-known and now defunct magazine. That story was all about the nobility of him and the way he used to chant the words of Burns; and then about how he died.

He came home to his parochial house that morning after reading the mass and sat down, one of the cousins said, at the breakfast table, and sat there for a long time silent, looking straight ahead. That wasn't like him. She asked him was he well. He didn't answer. She left the room to consult her sister who was fussing about in the kitchen. When she came back he had rested his head down on the table and was dead.

Looking straight ahead to Fincastle, Virginia, and seeing a woman white with flame when the dogwood blossomed, seeing the tall angel whose wings were the rainbow and who held heaven, a red cloth, in one hand, and hell, a blue cloth, in the other.

There was no place in that story of mine for Pascal Stakelum, the rural rake.

16. Robert Burns, 'Tam o' Shanter', line 59.

JAMES PLUNKETT

(1920-)

from: THE TRUSTING AND THE MAIMED AND OTHER IRISH STORIES (1955)

[In this story, Marty Callaghan, one of the maimed, still rehearses in his shell-shocked mind the horrors of the Great War in which he fought as a Dublin Fusilier. (In their distinguished history, the Royal Dublin Fusiliers fought in the Crimean War, the Indian Mutiny, the Boer War, and the Easter Rising.) Marty is assailed by the reproving ghosts of patriotic ancestors of his republican family whose tradition he violated by enlisting, like many otherwise patriotic Irishmen, in the British army. He enlisted 'for the sake of a slip of a girl' and for the same sake Faust, according to the pavior, sold his soul to the devil. That Marty had been a 1913 striker furthers the theme of betrayal in the story. Yet Marty both recalls the wrongs done to Ireland during its troubled history and queries some Irish responses to those wrongs. Victim rather than victimizer, he might even stand for post-independent Ireland in a surprisingly rich story informed by Plunkett's characteristic and occasionally risky sympathy for the maimed and the trusting, usually of the Irish working class.]

DUBLIN FUSILIER

Marty came swinging across town. Beneath the tall lamps and the broad white-faced clocks, by picture houses and odorous restaurant gratings, under the pillar where what was left of Nelson[1] posed proudly against the sky, came what was left of Marty. The General Post Office pushed out its ponderous chest, and Marty did likewise. In the darkness white faces passed him, warm scents assailed him, shoulders brushed his shoulder. A newsboy bawled in his ear, '*Herald* or *Mail*, sir?' But Marty walked his own path in his own city, the present like a soft mist trailing past him. For Marty and Nelson were aloof. Nelson on his pillar stuck his head a little higher up into the dark arch of the night, and his stony fingers were curled irrevocably on his sword. And beneath him marched Marty with his satchel of grenades. Both bore arms always.

Marty with his pale foxy face, the nose of a snipe, the chest of a pigeon, the gait of a halty mongrel, walked his own lonely inaccessible way. There was a drop on the end of his nose, which he removed from time to time by wiping with the back of his hand.

Tramp, tramp, tramp, came Marty the Dublin Fusilier. Pride in me heart, said Marty, and porter in me belly. Tramp, tramp, tramp, thunderously across the city came Marty.

'Tell me, me dear Lord Roberts,'[2] says Queen Victoria, 'whose them?'

'Them, ma'am,' says Lord Roberts, 'is the Black Watch.'

'Hmm,' says the Queen.

Tramp, tramp, tramp.

'And who,' says the Queen, 'is them?'

'Them, ma'am,' says Lord Roberts, 'is the Coldstream Guards.'[3]

'Hmm,' says the Queen.

Tramp, tramp, tramp.

'Quick,' says the Queen, plucking at his arm, 'whose them?'

'Them, ma'am,' says Lord Roberts, 'is the Dublin Fusiliers.'

'Jasus,' says the Queen, 'them's Troops!'

Marty began to sing 'Tipperary'.

'It's a long way, to Tipperary, it's a long way to go.'

'Are you going far?' asked the voice. It was dark on the bridge and hard to see. Marty squinted from his height of five foot seven at a silver button and a big helmet. He halted. 'Attenshun,' he bawled. So the policeman grinned broadly at the thin sick face under the peaky cap, and the sharp nose with its pendulent drop.

'So that's the way it is,' he said.

That was on the wide bridge over the river. People passed and twisted to look closer, but did not stand because the breeze blew coldly from the river. Trams with lighted windows clanged past, with here half a man reading a paper or smoking, and there a girl staring straight ahead of her or perhaps patting her hair with deft fingers.

So the policeman grinned again and putting his fingers in his belt, turned and walked away.

Marty swung his grenades. Was he not Marty, an Irishman and a Dublin Fusilier? Son of no carey[4] nor scab, but now and then the son of a seacook, and sometimes a son of a bitch, and always an oul' son of a gun. No sugarin' policeman would lay a hand on Marty. No dirty Jerry, nor snooping Boer, nor bloody Black and Tan. He'd banjax the whole issue, Marty would, all on his Barney Malone.[5] But in the meanwhile, would you manage a pint, Marty? Would a duck swim, wha'? Willy is a bad fella. Right you are, oul' son, off we go for a loaf of Bolands.[6]

Marty, letting out a shout, began to take his pint. A young man sat at the bar with his back to a partition, his raincoat unbuttoned, his hat on the back

1. A statue of the British admiral, Lord Nelson, who lost an eye and an arm in battle, stood on top of a pillar in Dublin's O'Connell Street. In 1966, an explosion, set off by Irish republicans, irreparably damaged both pillar and statue. Nothing of them now remains.
2. Lord Roberts (1832-1914), popularly known as 'Bobs', was born in India of Anglo-Irish stock. He became a hero of Victorian England during the Afghan War (1879-80).
3. The Black Watch and the Coldstream Guards are regiments of the British army.
4. James Carey was a member of a group of terrorists calling themselves the Invincibles, who assassinated the chief secretary for Ireland and the permanent undersecretary in 1882. Carey turned crown witness, earning himself the epithet 'prince of informers'. (In *Ulysses*, Carey enters Leopold Bloom's mind several times in the course of his day.)
5. 'Banjax' is Irish, especially Dublin, slang, meaning to ruin or scuttle, here in the sense of 'violently resolve'. Barney Malone is Cockney rhyming slang for 'alone'.
6. Circumlocution for 'a drink'. Bolands is a large Dublin bakery.

of his head. He had been talking to two men about music.

'I've been rehearsing for three solid hours,' he said. 'Bloody *Faust*. I've a thirst that a parish priest would sell his soul for.'

'All the same,' said the pavior, '*Faust* is a lovely opera.'

'It's lovely,' said the young man, 'because it gives you a lovely thirst after rehearsing it for three solid hours.'

'Mick and me,' said the pavior, 'used to play in the Trade Union band. We were thrown out for hocking[7] the instruments when we were short for a few pints. We used to play selections from *Faust*.'

'Rehearsing *Faust*,' said Mick, 'used to give us a lovely thirst too.'

'What band was that?'

'Tell him what they called us, Tommy.'

'They used to call us The Sufferin' Ducks,' said the pavior reminiscently.

'It was very insultin' . . . .' added Mick sadly.

Marty gave another yell out of him.

'That's Marty,' the pavior said, 'a harmless poor divil.' He put a finger to his temple and twisted it significantly. His left eye winked.

'That was a terrible man once,' said Mick, 'that was a holy terror.'

'Poor Marty,' said the pavior.

'I remember the band during the big strike.[8] We were marching down to a meeting at the docks. But when we got to Butt Bridge every bloody policeman in the country was there waiting for us.'

'Drawn in a cordon across the street,' put in Mick, 'standing about ten deep with their batons in their hands and murder in their hearts.'

'Your man Marty was the Bandmaster,' the pavior continued, 'and he gave us the order to halt. "Where do you think you're going?" the Inspector came up and asked him. "Down to a meeting," said Marty. "My men are drawn across there in front of you," said the Inspector, "and if you try to pass them they'll leave the lot of you for dead." "Will they?" said Marty, and the Inspector walked away. So Marty turned round to us. "Strike it up, boys," he shouted, "and forward on the double tap." He waves his stick. "Close your eyes, boys," he says, "and you won't feel the pain."'

'It was slaughter, right enough,' Mick commented.

'The police didn't like music,' said the young man.

'They didn't like *our* music,' Mick said sadly. 'Marty had us playing "The Peeler and the Goat".'[9]

'That was Marty for you,' concluded the pavior, turning to consult his pint.

Marty crouched staring in his corner, his head at an angle. The curate,[10] who knew Marty of an old date, nodded his head towards him and then winked at the pavior.

'We're off,' said the pavior, 'pension on Wednesday and pop goes the thinking cabinet.'

'We're over the top all right,' said Mick. 'Next stop Blighty.'[11]

'What's wrong with him?' asked the young man, upset because Marty was staring at him with violence and hatred in his eyes.

'Shellshock,' the pavior said. 'I soldiered with Marty in France.' Then he said loudly, 'How's tricks, Marty oul' son?'

Marty continued to stare.

'He doesn't know you,' Mick said. 'Maybe he'll come round later.'

Marty lived in the same house as the pavior, and a married sister who lived there looked after him. The pavior said Marty was a fine Soccer player once. He played for St. Patricks when they won the Leinster Senior Cup. That was against Sligo. They had a dinner after it in a hotel and then drove out to the Strawberry Beds on hacks[12] and played melodeons and drank a lot of porter. But that was in Oul' God's time. In those days you could get a pint for twopence and any amount of cheese and biscuits for nothing. They were on the counter. You wouldn't see the like of that today.

'Them days is done,' Mick declared. 'You'd see white blackbirds before you'd see that again.'

The pavior spat into the sawdust, and then scrubbed his heavy boot over it so that it made a trundling noise on the floor. The young man regarded Marty with curiosity. Marty, however, was watching the fellow with the machine-gun. In

7. pawning, putting the instruments in hock.
8. Dublin suffered an intense labour dispute in 1913, resulting in unemployment, starvation and violence.
9. An early nineteenth-century rebel song satirizing the police force, which had been introduced into Ireland by Sir Robert Peel.
10. A peculiarly Irish word for a (usually assistant) barman.
11. Soldiers' name for England.
12. A once well-frequented place of recreation in Dublin, west of the Phoenix Park; 'hacks' are hackney cabs.

France Marty had been going forward with his eye on that machine-gun when the explosion blew him off his feet. He woke up blind, with a buzzing in his head. The blindness went away after a while but the buzzing remained intermittently. When it became bad Marty crouched and watched. Sometimes he would throw himself flat with a sudden wild movement, a loud obscenity. If he did this where there was concrete, Mrs. White, his married sister, had to get the enamel basin and bathe away the blood. Quite often he did it where there was concrete.

Marty took a grenade from the satchel, bit out the pin and swung his arm in a slow loop. When the flame and smoke subsided he saw in front of him the three shiny handles, like rifle nozzles protruding above three shoulders, which were used for pulling pints, and beyond them the glass mirror with its gilt advertisement for DWD potstill whiskey, the yellow pear of the electric bulb with its white shade, hanging plumb and without movement from the ceiling, and the pavior's broad back. He heard also the hum of conversation and cars blowing horns now and then in the street. He found his pint almost finished. Would you have another, Marty? He would because a bird never flew on one wing. He fetched out a bright silver shilling from his pocket.

O Brian you've been drinking Brian O
I know it by your winking Brian O . . .
I took the Saxon shillin' for to do their dirty killin'
The oul' sergeant found me willin'
Molly O[13]

So Marty gave his bright silver shilling to the curate and in return he received his pint and a few pence in change.

'All the same,' the pavior said, '*Faust* is a fine opera.'

'I remember it well,' Mick said. 'The Devil has a bit to do with it.'

'Too much,' agreed the young man.

'He sells his soul to the Devil,' continued the pavior thoughtfully, 'for the sake of a slip of a girl.'

'Shockin',' Mick said, 'a bloody poor bargain.'

'Many a man sold his soul for less, for a pint of porter or a piece of silver.'

'That's the truth,' Mick said.

'Yiz sold yer sowls for penny rolls and a cut of streaky bacon,' quoted the pavior.

13. The Saxon shilling referred to in this street ballad was the 'King's shilling' given to the newly enlisted man by a recruiting officer.

'No doubt about it,' said Mick.

'Marty sold his soul for a shillin',' said the pavior with a finality which caused Mick, who did not quite follow, to shake his head in solemn agreement.

Marty gave his shilling. In the good days when he was young he would think himself well off with a shilling in his pocket of a Sunday morning.

One bright Sunday morning he left his mother's house in Patrick Street, his cap set gallantly, his shirt clean, his boots shining. Marty, young and vigorous, cocked an eye at the light cloud and the sun high up over the spire of the Cathedral. The clamouring bells shook the street, St. Audeon's, St. Patrick's, John's Lane and Christ Church, shouting and singing above the rattling cabs and the slaty cobbles. 'Come and worship all ye true followers of Christ.' He was going to Mass but he was thinking of other things. The bells he had grown up with made his head spin.

'Come and worship, Marty oul' son,' said John's Lane. 'Don't be dallying there with the sun warming your back and your eye giving the beck to the young girls with the feathers and the flowers in their hats.'

'And them on their way to holy Mass too,' said St. Audeon's. 'Don't be hanging about there looking at the artificial sprays in the artificial ponds, and the dirty little urchins sailing paper boats in the close of St. Patrick's, the little desecrators of the Blessed Sabbath.'

'He's dreaming about the medal he'll wear in his chain when they knock the stuffin' out of Sligo,' said St. Patrick's. 'He's thinking he might give it to Annie.'

'Taking her out to the hollow in the park or maybe down the Shellybanks, God forgive him, that's what's occupying him.'

As he walked, the hand which was in his pocket holding the shilling sweated so that he felt a moist circle in his palm.

'Come in, Marty,' said John's Lane, 'and pray a while for your soul. It could do with it. And pray for the souls of them that's gone — a summer's day is a long day.'

Everybody harped at him.

'Marty Callaghan,' his mother had said to him previously, 'are you going to Mass at all?' He said he was ready, he had lashings of time. 'It's on your knees in the church you should be now, not polishing your boots. If it was a football match you'd be in time, never fear.' Marty whistled and winked at his young sister.

He stepped out of the sunlight into the porch of John's Lane, and taking off his cap and dipping his warm brown fingers in the holy water font, he crossed himself and sprinkled some at the door for the pour souls in purgatory. A large dim church cluttered with poor people. A warm place, the air shimmering with the tapering flame of candles and sour with the smell of devout bodies. He was in time for the gospel and came out after the last, leaving the women to light their lamps to Saint Anne, patron of childing mothers, and the old men with rosary beads and yellow faces to keep watch against the thief who came by night. In the afternoon he walked with Annie through the Pigeon House fort where the soldiers practised firing, to the Shelly-banks with their rough grasses which were sweet to lie in. They paddled in the shallow water and ate oranges, and Annie wore her blue dress. He asked her to marry him. Not immediately, he said, but soon. She said she didn't know really, she always thought she'd have liked a soldier. Dinny Andrews was a soldier and she thought it was a brave thing that, to be a soldier. He said he always thought she cared for him more than Dinny Andrews, and she said she did too, honest. Her eyes were blue and she laughed when she saw that he was moodily plucking at the grass. The grass cut his finger. She became very concerned, and made him bathe it in the salt water. After that she thought she might marry him. He went down to the men's place to swim, his heart singing, his lithe body pulsing with a new excitement. When he came back they bought oranges and sweets from the peddling women and ate them lying in the sandy grasses, watching the boats and the people who passed, laughing at the antics of little children and making love to one another.

In the evening he left her home, and that night he sat for a long time dreaming at the kitchen window, until it was midnight, and the bells of St. Patrick's, having struck the hour, began as they always did at that hour to play a little tune, which stole quietly to him over streets and roof-tops.

Some nights later he told his father. He didn't know what to say to his mother. His father told her.

'Ellen,' he said, 'Marty's took the shillin'.' He was sitting in a high armchair with his feet on the hob.

'I'm going to France, Mother,' Marty said, twiddling his cap in his hands. 'I'm a soldier.'

That was in the kitchen where the picture of Parnell hung between two bronze horses with warriors tilting at one another across the mantel-piece, and the speech of Robert Emmet stood framed on age-spotted parchment. 'Let no man write my epitaph; for as no man who knows my motives dares now vindicate them, let not prejudice nor ignorance asperse them.' Lovely round phrases which rolled in splendour from the mouth of his grandfather when he had a few jars in him.

One for the road and a bit of a song, Marty. Why not? It was a long time waiting for the war to be over. What would it be? Make it something Irish, was what they used to say to him.

Marty closed his eyes and turned his white face upwards. The sunken mouth opened and yellow molars stood up like cartridges. He sang 'Danny Boy'. His voice was cracked and wobbly, like his broken body. His voice was a thing sewn and stitched together, wrapped like a ragged bandage about his song.

'*There's* a bit of a tune now for you,' said Mick. Marty had his eyes fixed on the ceiling, displaying a scrawny neck where his Adam's apple ran to and fro between two deep ridges when he paused for breath after each line. The three of them turned to stare.

'He's putting his heart into it,' said the pavior. They laughed.

O Danny Boy, the pipes the pipes is callin'
From glen to glen and down the mountain side,
The summer's gone and all the flowers is dying
'Tis you must go, and so 'tis I must bide...

Two big tears rolled from Marty's eyes and lay on his cheeks on either side of his nose, matching the drop which now hung unmolested. The lower lids of both eyes, which sagged slightly outwards, were blood rimmed.

It was a sad song. Often his father had sung it at parties in their house in Patrick Street, because of course it was his father's song. It used to make his mother cry. It was always sad to think of the brave soldier marching off to the wars, leaving his father and his poor mother and the good kind people he loved. And his sweetheart too, who would wait for him until he came back.

In sunshine or in shadow,
And I will stand, still waiting there for you.

But as like as not, he never came back.

A very sad, beautiful song, just like all the old songs. 'When the fields are white with daisies I'll return' had been his mother's song. Marty had a face which made the barman exchange another nod and a wink with the three, who looked on happily, and a heart which was broken for love of poor dead days and their poor dead people, a spirit which groped back, always back with tearing and torture to his mother, God bless her, and his good father who drank come-day-go-day God-send-pay-day may the sod rest light on him, to Mick his brother who'd give the shirt off his back and Little One his sister who said give us a penny Marty there's a darlin' Marty for to buy seedy cake and he always gave it to her, and to other poor souls dead and gone this many a long day, may perpetual light shine upon them, may they rest in peace. Amen.

Marty stared at the ceiling. His mouth remained open. He found he was walking down by Dublin Castle and the clock striking midnight. A moon stared down at him from the cloud-racked sky. His grandfather stepped out from the shadows.

'Remember your oul' grandfather,' said the voice, 'I cobbled boots for fifty years in Nash's Court. You used to laugh at me when my mouth was full of nails. You were only a dawny chisler[14] then, Marty.' He laughed again heartily at his grandfather, remembering the green baize apron and the cock of his hawky face over the boot. 'An oul' cod,' said Marty. He swung down the steep cobbles of Lord Edward Street.[15]

'What about me,' said a Callaghan with a greasy cloak, 'that carried the keg of dynamite to the castle gate the time they pulled Kilwarden[16] from his coach. They stuck twenty pitchforks in him to make sure he wouldn't remember who done it. Emmet was bloody annoyed, I can tell you.'

'That was a wrong thing to do,' Marty said, 'even though he was only a Protestant.' His boots rang on the cobbles. Under a guttering lamp another joined him. He was long and broad-shouldered, but he had the hawky face.

'Did I ever tell you about 1534, Marty? I was keeping an eye on things after piling a bit of hay and me and Silken Thomas[17] was having a drink together. "Well, Fitzgerald," says I, "how's tricks?" "Bad, Callaghan," says he. "They're after murdering the poor father. Do you see me sword of office?" "I do," I says. "Well," says he, "as soon as I finish this mouthful I'm going straight over to the Abbey, and do you know what I'll do then?"

'"I don't."

'"I'm going to take it off and throw it at the bloody Archbishop."

'"You'd be a foolish young man to do that," I says.

'"Foolish or not," says he, "that's the programme; and what's more, I hope it takes the bloody head off him, mitre an' all."'

Marty yelled out loud at the idea of it. But a vague figure was following, whining and pulling at his sleeve. It had a death's head of a face, and a scrawny neck. 'Fine talk,' it said, 'and fine men. But my potatoes withered in the ground and my youngest died with the green ooze of grass on his lips.'

'They broke the house about my head,' said another, 'and the bailiff stood watching them and laughing.'

'What odds; didn't you tie him to a gate afterwards and roast him over a fire?'

'We did — and when he died with God's mercy he went on roasting. I declared to God his carcase turned black as his heart.'

Said the Inspector to him, 'My men are drawn across in front of you, Marty, and if you try to pass them they'll leave the lot of you for dead.'

But that was poor Erin for you, the tear and the smile in her eye.

He would meet Annie on some cool summer's evening out at the Strawberry Beds. In the distance someone would play a melodeon. Or once again perhaps in Phoenix Park on a day when the fields were white with daisies and golden with buttercups he'd return and the sky would be wide and blue above them, and the river a silver girdle far below. But it was a long time waiting for the war to be over.

The glass he was holding was flung violently to the ground. Mick and the barman jumped. 'My Christ,

14. A little or slight child (Dublin slang.)

15. A street named for Lord Edward Fitzgerald, an enthusiast for Irish insurrection, who died during his arrest amid the unsuccessful 1798 Rebellion.

16. In 1803, a mob of Dubliners attacked Dublin Castle, on their way dragging the lord chief justice of Ireland, Lord Kilwarden, from his coach and murdering him. Robert Emmet was captured and hanged.

17. Silken Thomas, Lord Offaly, rose against Henry VIII in 1534-35 and was executed at Tyburn in 1537.

Marty,' said the barman, rushing out, 'what the hell do you think you're doing?'

Marty swung both arms out wide.

'Atten-shun,' he bawled.

'Attenshun nothing,' said the barman, 'that bloody glass cost eightpence.' Marty screwed up his face and glared.

'Forward,' he commanded. 'At the double,' he bawled.

'Leave him alone,' said the pavior, 'you might as well talk to the wall.'

'He's over the top,' averred Mick sadly.

'Breaking glasses is a new one. What the hell am I to do if everyone that has a pint can smash hell out of me glasses without an after you or by your leave? It's all bloody fine.'

'He couldn't help it, Joe,' said the pavior soothingly.

'*Non compass mensit*,'[18] explained Mick.

Marty, brushing aside the commotion, drew himself up and with dignity demanded a pint.

'There you are,' the barman complained bitterly. 'Now he has the bloody neck to ask me for a pint.'

'Give it to him,' they said, 'he's all right now.' Marty got his pint. He was talking to himself. They heard him arguing and swearing. Then he swung his grenades into position and marched out.

Tramp, tramp, tramp, went Marty the Dublin Fusilier. Pride in his heart and porter in his belly. The night hung mildly over the city, the streets were quiet, the dark houses stood up like tall sentries. Some taxi men, who were waiting for the theatres to close, stood smoking at the great gate of Stephen's Green. A faint scent of flowers hung in the air. Marty stood still at the corner. He stared ahead of him. Then he motioned with his arm. Then he stood still again. Then he howled an obscenity and began to lope forward. Now and then his arm swung in a wide loop. The noise of battle was about him. Once more in front of him was the fellow with the machine-gun. His cheeks were grey and streaky with sweat and dust but his bared teeth were blinding white. Marty shouted out Tipperary, flung grenades, ran and stopped. But the machine-gun continued to swing to and fro. When its black unwinking eye cocked itself wickedly in the centre of his regimental belt, Marty shouted and flung himself violently to the ground. His head struck on stone steps.

They said it was disgraceful that a man should get into such a condition. It was hard to know who was more to blame, the man himself or the publican who served him. A small knot had gathered when the pavior came along with Mick and the young man. The pavior knelt down and lifted him up. The pavior was the slightest bit tipsy.

'Marty oul' son,' he said. Marty stirred.

'Come on, Marty, never say die. Old soldiers like you and me never die, Marty, we only fade away.'

Marty murmured, 'Attenshun.'

'That's the spirit, Marty oul' son, that's the stuff to give the troops.' He said to Mick, 'For the love of God, will you take one side of him and don't stand there like a bloody statue.'

Some money fell from his pocket as they lifted him, which Mick and the young man searched for while the pavior wiped blood from his face with his cap. There were traces of foam on Marty's mouth which he removed gently. 'Have you his few ha'pence?' asked the pavior.

Mick, after peering around helplessly two or three times, said he didn't see any more. They helped him home. The spot where Marty had fallen was marked a little with blood, and in a corner by the iron railings where a little mound of dust had gathered winked a silver shilling. It lay waiting to be found by some passer-by with sharper eyesight than Mick. They took Marty up the broad carpetless stairs, their boots kicking each step and echoing as they struggled with their burden. Mrs. White, his sister, was in tears. 'His poor face,' she said when she saw him, 'me poor Marty, what did they do to you?' And she got her green enamel basin and washed his face, and with her husband they put him to bed. Then she said there was tea waiting on the hob and they might as well have a cup.

'You're a good neighbour, God bless you,' she said to the pavior. So they sat round drinking tea and saying Marty would be right as rain again tomorrow morning. But she kept saying, 'What am I to do with him at all, at all? I can't be managing him for ever.' And again she said, looking at her husband, 'Wouldn't it be an unnatural thing to have him put away?' They talked until midnight in that way.

Marty lay in the little room. The window was open and let in the night noises, and the curtain stirred now and then faintly. The muscles of his

18. Mick's imperfect rendering of the Latin phrase *non compos mentis* (of unsound mind).

hawky face twitched nervously, his mouth moved unceasingly. Sometimes his hands groped out for his satchel of grenades. St. Patrick's sounded midnight and the room reverberated. The bells died away. It was quiet and peaceful once more, with only the murmur of voices from the next room to break the silence. Marty slept. Then the bells of St. Patrick's, with their time-mellowed tongues, began to play a little tune.

BRIAN MOORE

(1921-)

from: THE LONELY PASSION OF JUDITH HEARNE (1955)

[Moore's novel is one of the finest to come out of twentieth-century Ulster, indeed Ireland. Its precision, unity and polish of writing would flatter a good short story, yet it also has the deep texture of attentive realism. The following extract, the novel's second chapter, is in several ways a scale-model of the entire book. It begins with the hallucinatory optimism of Judith Hearne's morning (her first in her new boarding-house) and closes after a downward spiral of spirit with the quiet despair and isolation of her evening. The passage contains deft descriptions of the provincial and claustrophobic mind that still bedevils certain levels of Irish society, a life-denying mentality that receives its appropriate imagery in the chapter's closing vision of dark rain in Belfast Lough. The city of Belfast has never been captured with such deadly but apparently incidental care as in this novel.]

CHAPTER 2

Her eyes, opening, saw the ceiling, the frozen light of what day? Sight, preceding comprehension, mercifully recorded familiar objects in the strangeness of the whole. Led the blind mind to memory; to this awakening.

She sat up, her hair falling around her shoulders, feeling a gelid draught through the flannel stuff of her nightgown. Her thighs and calves, warmed in the moist snuggle of sheets, were still lax, weary, asleep. The gilded face of her little travelling clock said ten past seven. She lay back, pulling the yellow blankets up to her chin, and looked at the room.

A chair, broadbeamed, straightbacked, sat in the alcove by the bay window, an old pensioner staring out at the street. Near the bed, a dressing table, made familiar by her bottle of cologne, her combs and brushes, and her little round box of rouge. Across the worn carpet was a wardrobe of brown varnished wood with a long panel mirror set in its door. She looked in the mirror and saw the end of her bed, the small commotion of her feet ruffling the smooth tucked blankets. The wardrobe was ornamented with whorls and loops and on either side of the door mirror was a circle of light-coloured wood. The circles seemed to her like eyes, mournful wooden eyes on either side of the reflecting mirror nose. She looked away from those eyes to the white marble mantelpiece, cracked down one support, with its brass fender of Arabic design. Her Aunt D'Arcy said good day in silver and sepia-toned arrogance from the exact centre of this arrangement, while beside the gas fire a sagging, green-covered armchair awaited its human burden. The carpet below the mantelpiece was worn to brown fibre threads. She hurried on, passing over the small wash basin, the bed table with its green lamp, to reach the reassurance of her two big trunks, black-topped, brassbound, ready to travel.

She twisted around and unhooked the heavy wool dressing gown from the bedpost. Put it on her shoulders and slid her feet out of bed into blue, fleecy slippers. Cold, a cold room. She went quickly to the gas fire and turned it on, hearing its startled plop as the match poked it into life. She spread her underthings to warm; then fled back across the worn carpet to bed. Fifteen minutes, she said, it will take fifteen minutes to heat the place at all.

There was no hurry. Friday, a dull day, a day with nothing at all to do. Although it would be interesting at breakfast to see what sort of food Mrs Henry Rice gave and who the others were. She lay abed twenty minutes, then washed in cold water and went shivering to the mean heat of the stove. She slipped on her underthings under the concealing envelope of her nightgown, a habit picked up at the Sacred Heart convent in Armagh and retained, although keeping warm had long supplanted the original motive of modesty, which occasioned the fumblings, the exertions and the slowness of the manoeuvre. When she finally pulled the nightgown over her head, she was fully dressed, except for the dress itself. It was time for her morning hair-brushing exercise. She set great store by it: it kept one's hair dark, she said, and if you did not wash the hair, ever, it kept its sheen and colour. Her hair, visible proof, was dark brown with a fine thickness and smooth lustre.

So each morning it was her custom to sit conscientiously at the mirror, her head bent to one side, tugging the brush along the thick rope of her hair, counting the strokes, thinking of nothing except the act of doing the exercise, her head jerking slightly with each long, strong stroke of the brush.

But this morning, hair brushing actually had to be hurried because it would never do to be late one's first morning in a new place. Especially when there were other boarders to meet. She had said three, Mrs Henry Rice. Were they men or women? Maybe, most likely, men, and what if one were charming?

Her angular face smiled softly at its glassy image. Her gaze, deceiving, transforming her to her imaginings, changed the contour of her sallow-skinned face, skilfully refashioning her long pointed nose on which a small chilly tear had gathered. Her dark eyes, eyes which skittered constantly in imagined fright, became wide, soft, luminous. Her frame, plain as a cheap clothes rack, filled now with soft curves, developing a delicate line to the bosom.

She watched the glass, a plain woman, changing all to the delightful illusion of beauty. There was still time: for her ugliness was destined to bloom late, hidden first by the unformed gawkiness of youth, budding to plainness in young womanhood and now flowering to slow maturity in her early forties, it still awaited the subtle garishness which only decay could bring to fruition: a garishness which, when arrived at, would preclude all efforts at the mirror game.

So she played. Woman, she saw her womanish glass image. Pulled her thick hair sideways, framing her imagined face with tresses. Gipsy, she thought fondly, like a gipsy girl on a chocolate box.

But the little clock chittering through the seconds said eight-fifteen and Oh, what silly thoughts she was having. Gipsy indeed! She rose, sweeping her hair up, the hairpins in her mouth coming out one by one and up, up to disappear in her crowning glory. There (pat) much better. A little more (pat) so. Good. Now, what to wear? A touch of crimson, my special *cachet*. But which? Reds are so fickle. Still, red is my colour. Vermilion. Yes. The black dress with the vermilion touch at collar and cuffs. Besides, it hasn't been crushed by the moving.

She opened the wardrobe, breaking the unity of its imagined face. Her dressing-gown fell like a dismantled tent at her feet as she shrugged her angular body into the tight waist seams of the dress. Then, her garnets and the small ruby on her right hand. She rummaged in the jewel box, deciding that the pink and white cameo would be a little too much. But she wore her watch, the little gold wristlet watch that Aunt D'Arcy had given her on her twenty-first birthday. It didn't really work well any more. The movement was wearing out. But it was a good watch, and very becoming. And goodness knows, she thought, first impressions are often last impressions, as old Herr Rauh used to say.

Then back to the dressing table to tidy the strands of hair which her dress had ruffled. A teeny touch of rouge, well rubbed in, a dab of powder and a good sharp biting of her lips to make the colour come out. There, much better. She smiled fondly at her fondly smiling image, her nervous dark eyes searching the searching glass. Satisfied, she nodded to the nodding, satisfied face. Yes. On to breakfast.

The dining room of Mrs Henry Rice's Camden Street residence was furnished with pieces bought by her late husband's father. A solid mahogany sideboard bulged from one wall, blossoming fruit bowls and empty whisky decanters on its marble top. The table, a large oval of the same wood, islanded itself in the centre of the room, making passage difficult on either side. Around the table eight tall chairs rode like ships at anchor. Daylight fought its way down to the room past grey buildings and black backyards, filtering through faded gauze curtains which half hid two narrow windows. Over the sideboard this light discerned a gilt-framed oil painting in which a hunter raised his gun to fire at the misty outline of a stag. Beside the door, like an old blind dog, a grandfather clock wagged away the hours.

Around the table the guests sat in semi-gloom, silent except for the tiny crash of teacups and the tearing of hard toast. Cups and saucers moved up and down the table like items on an assembly belt, entering the little fortress where, ringed around by teapot, hot water jugs, tea cosies, milk jug, sugar bowl, plates, cutlery, and a little bell, Mrs Henry Rice dispensed stimulants. Matutinal in a flowered housecoat, her hair sticking out from her head like a forkful of wet hay, she smiled a welcome to Miss Hearne and gestured her to a seat at the opposite end of the room.

'This is Miss Hearne, our new boarder, everybody. I'll do the rounds so that you can all get to know her. Now, first this is Miss Friel. Miss Friel. Miss Hearne.'

Miss Friel bit on her toast and laid the crust reluctantly on her plate. She looked to Miss Hearne and nodded. Light blue dress, grey lisle stockings, short clipped whitish hair, like a fox terrier. A Pioneer Total Abstinence Pin[1] rode her shelving bosom. Hard chapped hands and a red roughness about the wrists. There was a book in front of her, propped up against the jampot.

'Mr Lenehan.'

Mr Lenehan rose, his head turned sideways, his thin mouth curving into a sickled smile. His clothes were clerical black and a battery of cheap fountain pens raised their silver and gold nozzles like a row of decorations across his chest. His collar was white, waxy, uncomfortable, imprisoning a dark green tie, loosely knotted around a brass collar stud.

'Vary pleased to meet you, I'm sure,' Mr Lenehan intoned.

Miss Hearne nodded, smiled, her eyes going on to the next, the most interesting.

'And this is my brother James. Mr Madden. Miss Hearne.'

He was a big man. He alone had risen when she entered. He held his linen napkin like a waiter, waiting to seat her. She looked at his well-fed, rough-red face. His smile showed white false teeth. He was neat, but loudly dressed. A yellow tie with white golf balls on it, a suit of some brown silky stuff like shantung.[2] Her brother, Mrs Henry Rice had said, but surely he was an American. Who else but an American would wear that big bluestone ring on his finger?

'Glad to know you, Miss Hearne.'

I guessed right. An American for sure, by the sound of him. She smiled, waited for his male movement, the turning away, the rejection. But he winked at her with a merry blue eye and, bending down, he drew her chair out from the table. He did not turn away.

They sat down, formally. Mrs Henry Rice asked her preference in matters of sugar and milk. The assembly line was set in motion and from the American's blue-ringed hand a cup of tea was given into Miss Hearne's possession. She said her thanks. Mrs Henry Rice smacked the little bell. Jing-jing-jing it cried.

Mary, young and flustered, put her face around the edge of the door.

'Yes, 'm.'

'Did you bring Mr Bernard up his tray?'

'Yes, 'm.'

'Well, bring some hot toast then, for Miss Hearne. And see if the *Irish News*[3] is here.'

Miss Hearne stirred genteelly. Miss Friel turned a page in her book and noisily bit off another mouthful of toast. Mr Lenehan took out a silver watch, consulted it, snapped the case shut. He slurped his tea and wiped his mouth with a napkin.

'I'm late,' he told the company. Nobody said anything. Miss Hearne, trying to be polite, looked at him in inquiry. He saw his audience. 'Time and tide wait for no man, alas. Isn't that a fact, Miss Hearne?'

'Indeed it is, Mr Lenehan.'

'Well, vary nice to have met you,' Mr Lenehan said, pushing his chair back from the table. He looked at the others. 'So long, all.'

The American waved his hand. Miss Friel did not look up. Mrs Henry Rice nodded absent-mindedly.

'So long,' Lenehan said again. And hurried out on his match-thin legs. Good riddance, Miss Hearne thought, to bad rubbish. Why did I dislike him so much? Oh, well, maybe he's not so bad after all. Old before his time. And something about him. Unpleasant.

She looked at the other. Mr Madden. And saw that he was looking at her. Embarrassed, she turned to Mrs Henry Rice.

'I see a family resemblance. You and your

1. A catholic temperance and devotional society.
2. A heavy silk fabric with a knobbly surface.
3. A Belfast daily newspaper read mainly by the nationalist community.

brother. Yes, there's a family resemblance, all right.'

'James spent most of his life in the United States,' Mrs Henry Rice told Miss Hearne. 'Some see the likeness between us, but it escapes me. Still, I suppose it's always that way with brothers and sisters.'

Mr Madden seemed pleased to be included in the conversation. 'May's younger than me,' he offered.

'But the likeness is there,' Miss Hearne said. 'Oh, it's there, all right. Are you just over for a holiday, Mr Madden?'

Mr Madden carefully buttered a slice of toast and spread it thick with jam. 'Lived thirty years in the States,' he said. 'New York City. I came back here four months ago.'

'Oh! To stay?'

He did not answer. He ate toast. Quickly, she hurried over her *gaffe*, feeling her face grow hot at his silent snub. 'I've always wanted to visit America,' she said.

He did not look up. She hurried on: 'I'm sure you must find Belfast dull, after New York. My goodness, after all that excitement. It's so up-to-date and everything, New York, I mean.'

Mr Madden arrested his teacup in midair, put it back on his saucer. 'You can say that again. Greatest city in the world.' His eyes focused, found her, and he smiled as though they had mutually agreed on something which had escaped the others. Her awkwardness was forgotten. For once, she had found the key.

'What part of Ireland you come from?' he said.

'Oh, I'm from Ballymena originally. But I've spent most of my time here in Belfast.'

'That so?' He produced a package of cigarettes. 'Mind if I smoke?'

'Oh, no. I don't smoke myself but smoking never bothers me.'

'That's good.' He laughed without laughter, watching Miss Hearne.

He wants to talk, she thought, he's lonely. And she returned his look. Then she helped him, made it easy for him to tell what he wanted to tell: America.

'Oh, Belfast's not like New York, I suppose. You must get lots of snow and sunshine there.'

'All kinds of weather. I've seen it go up to a hundred and ten in the shade, in summer. And in winter, down to ten below zero. I've seen it so hot you'd have to change your shirt twice in one morning.' He stopped, vaguely conscious of indelicacy. But she put him at ease.

'Well, there must be an awful lot of laundry to do then. It must be exhausting. In summer, I mean.'

'We've got air conditioning, and central heating in winter. They never heard of that over here.'

Miss Friel closed her book with a snap and stared at the grandfather clock. She got up and went out without a good-bye. Mrs Henry Rice, informative, drooped her huge bosom over the table like a bag of washing. 'She's a schoolteacher,' she said. 'Public elementary.'

'Oh?'

Mary came in with toast and the *Irish News*. Miss Hearne took toast, noticed that there were four slices, no sign of an egg, or anything.

'Butter?' Mr Madden offered butter and she saw that he was admiring the little gold wristlet watch on her wrist. She was glad she'd worn it. She looked at Mrs Henry Rice but Mrs Henry Rice had opened the *Irish News* and was reading births, marriages, and deaths.

'And how do you find Ireland, Mr Madden, now that you've come home?'

'Been a lot of changes.' He stared at the teacup. 'It's different.'

'So you prefer New York then?'

Mr Madden inhaled. Cigarette smoke spewed from his large nostrils. 'New York's a rat race,' he said.

She didn't know what to answer. Really, what could he mean, a rat race? They certainly had queer expressions, these Yankees.

Mrs Henry Rice put the paper down. 'You'll excuse me now, Miss Hearne, but I must go up and say good morning to Bernard. Just ring for Mary if you want more tea.'

As Mrs Henry Rice moved toward the door, Miss Hearne's nervousness increased. She had been forward, no two ways about it, asking all those questions, leading him on. And now she was to be left alone with him. Alone. The dining room with its cold morning light, its heavy furniture, its dirty teacups and plates, became quiet as a church. Alone with this lonely stranger, she waited for his fumbled excuses, his departure. For now that the others had gone, it would be as it had always been. He would see her shyness, her stiffness. And it would frighten him, he would remember that he was alone with her. He would listen politely to whatever inanity she would manage to get out and then he would see the hysteria in her eyes, the hateful hot flush in her cheeks. And he would go as all men had gone before him.

And as she waited, with her hands pressed hard against the edge of the table, she felt the blushes start, the hateful redness and fire creep up her neck. She set her features in a stiff, silly smile and scuffed her feet under the table. She turned to him, still smiling, and a mechanical silly voice leaped out of her mouth, shocking her with the forward thing it said:

'Oh, you must tell me more about America, Mr Madden. I'd love to go there.'

'Well,' he said. 'I could talk all day and never finish. What did you have in mind?'

In mind. Something, something had to be said. 'Well, is it true that the men over there put their wives on a pedestal, so to speak?'

He laughed, a big heavy laugh. He didn't seem at all put out by her blushes, by her silly voice.

'Yes, that's correct, more's the pity. That's what's wrong with the system, if you want to know. Guys beating their brains out to keep their wives in mink. It's the women's fault. No good. You should see some of the girls that walk on Broadway or Fifth. All dressed up with a dollar sign for a heart. Walking cash registers. Me, I wouldn't have nothing to do with them.'

Wouldn't have nothing, well, he certainly wasn't very well educated, whatever else he was. So he didn't get married. 'Oh, that's not like Ireland, Mr Madden. Why, the men are gods here, I honestly do believe.'

'And right too. Head of the house. That's the teaching of the Church. What the man says goes. Now, in the States, the women want it both ways. They do no work and they want to be boss as well. And dumb, well, you wouldn't believe how dumb some of those dames are.'

He was so big, so male as he said it that she felt the blushes start up again. His big hand thumped the table.

'Well,' she said. 'Irishmen certainly wouldn't stand for that, would they?'

'Every man's a sucker for a good shape. I know. In my business, you see some funny things.'

Dangerous waters. Discussing women's figures, well, who but an American would have the vulgarity? Change the subject. 'And what is your business, Mr Madden?'

'Hotel business. I was in the hotel business right on Times Square. You've heard of Times Square?'

'Oh, yes, of course. I've seen it on the newsreels. When the war was over and it showed all the people cheering. And all those huge advertisements. Oh, it must be an exciting place to live.'

He smiled: 'Times Square. Watch the world go by. The things I've seen in fifteen years on Broadway. It's an education. Why, I couldn't even begin to. . . .'

'Well, don't begin then,' Mrs Henry Rice said. She stood at the opened door, monumental, stern. 'I'm sorry, Miss Hearne, but I must let Mary tidy up. Jim would sit here all day boring the life out of you with his talk about New York.'

'Oh, but it isn't boring, Mrs Rice. On the contrary, I think it's most exciting.'

Mr Madden stood up, indignant. He pointed at Miss Hearne. 'This lady is interested in what goes on in the world. Not like you and Bernie.'

Mrs Rice did not seem to hear. 'There's such a lot of work to be done. You know what maids are like, Miss Hearne. You have to be after them all the time. That's why I like to have the dining room done by ten.'

'Of course.'

Mr Madden went to the door. 'Glad to have met you, Miss Hearne. We must have another talk real soon.'

'Yes, indeed we must.' Said with her gayest smile to show him she liked him.

Then Mrs Henry Rice offered her the *Irish News* to read and she took it and went upstairs to her room to finish unpacking. No need to hurry. Going over her linens, her packages of letters, and her collection of picture postcards, laying each thing away carefully in tissue paper, all of it could take a long time if you did it methodically. A long time.

But when the big trunks were opened and their trays were laid on the bed, Miss Hearne knelt in silence on the floor, abstracted, her hand idle, her mind filled with what had happened that morning. He had been so glad to talk to her. And he had looked so big and stern and manly, hammering his fist on the table while he laid down the law to her. A big handsome man with that strange American voice.

He came into the room, late at night, tired after a day at work in his hotel. He took off his jacket and hung it up. He put his dressing gown on and sat down in his armchair and she went to him prettily, sat on his knee while he told her how things had gone that day. And he kissed her. Or, enraged about some silly thing she had done, he struck out with his great fist and sent her reeling, the brute. But, contrite afterward, he sank to his knees and begged forgiveness.

Judy Hearne, she said, you've got to stop right this minute. Imagine romancing about every man that comes along.

Her busy hands flew, unpacking the linen sheets, putting them away in the dresser drawer. But she paused in the centre of the room. He noticed me. He was attracted. The first in ages. Well, that's only because I've been keeping myself to myself too much. Go out and meet new people and you'll see, she told her mirror face. And the face in the mirror told it back to her, agreeing.

Why did he come home to Ireland? A visit maybe, to see his family. But he doesn't seem on very good terms with his sister. He'll go back to New York, of course, back to his hotel. Mr and Mrs James Madden, of New York, sailed from Southampton yesterday in the *Queen Mary*. Mr Madden is a prominent New York hotelier and his bride is the former Judith Hearne, only daughter of the late Mr and Mrs Charles B. Hearne, of Ballymena. The honeymoon? Niagara Falls, isn't that the place Americans go? Or perhaps Paris, before we sail.

But the mirror face grew stern and cross. You hardly know him, it said. And he's common, really he is, with that ring and that bright flashy tie. Oh, no he's not, she said. Don't be provincial. Americans dress differently, that's all.

A church bell tolled far away and she prayed. The library book would be due Wednesday, wasn't it? Do you know, I'm awfully uninformed about America, when I come to think of it. Outside, the grey morning light held, the rain still threatened. I could go down to the Carnegie library and read up on it. Especially New York. And then tomorrow at breakfast, I'd have questions to ask.

Maybe, she said, hurrying toward the wardrobe to pick out her red raincoat, maybe he'll be in the hall and I'll meet him and we might walk downtown together. I must hurry because if he's going out, it should be soon.

But the hall was a dark, damp place with no sign of anyone in it. Mary had cleared the dining room, restoring the chairs to their original anchorage around the table. The curtained door to Mrs Henry Rice's kitchen was shut and the house was silent, a house in midmorning when all the world is out at work.

She went out, dejected, and walked along Camden Street with her head full of black thoughts. Why had she bothered to come out at all? The library and looking up America was only nonsense, when all was said and done. Besides, going out only made you peckish and it was such a temptation to have a regular restaurant lunch. Well, you won't. You'll fast, that's what you'll do.

At the library on Royal Avenue the man wasn't helpful. But she made him climb the ladder twice to get her three books, one a picture book of New York and two books on America in general. She carried them to one of the slanting reading tables and sat down, slipping her neutral coloured glasses from her bag. Then amid the old men and students in the muted noises induced by 'Silence' signs, she read about America, Land of the Free, the New Colossus. All very heavy going, economic tables and business articles. She turned to the picture book and there was a picture of Times Square, and (gracious!) the hotels were immense, five times as big as the Grand Central, the Royal Avenue, or even the Gresham, in Dublin. Oh, he couldn't own one of those. And what was his job? There were so many jobs in a hotel. Maybe an assistant manager. Surely in the administration somewhere. Otherwise, he would have said a cook, or a waiter, or whatever. Oh certainly nothing like that.

She read and read because she could feel the little crab of hunger nipping away at her insides. She tried to forget him, the expensive little rascal, but he just nipped harder. Finally, when the clock on the wall said three, she decided that just this once she'd have to give in to him, despite her resolution. So she gave the books back and went to a milk bar at Castle Junction and treated herself to a glass of milk and a raspberry tart. Afterward, she looked at the shop windows for a while. But they hadn't changed since last week, so this was dull sport.

As she was looking in the window at Robb's, a little boy came running out, dragging his school satchel, his grey wool stockings down about his heels.

Tommy Mullen! She hurried over to him, forcing him to stop. His mother was a friend of the Breens, before the Breens moved to Dublin. Tommy had taken piano lessons last year. She saw the keyboard, his rather dirty hands, his wandering inattention, his fits of sulks and rages. No talent. His mother had stopped the lessons.

'Well, if it isn't little Tommy Mullen. And how are we getting along?'

'Lo, Miss Hearne,' he said, turning his cold-cheeked little face away from her kiss.

'Well, and how's my boy? My, we're getting big. Too big to kiss, I suppose. I'm sure we've forgotten all our piano lessons now.'

He looked indignant. 'No. I've got a new teacher. A man. Mr Harrington is his name.'

'Oh, is that so?' she said bleakly. 'Well, isn't that nice. I hope you are practising hard, eh, Tommy?'

'Yes, Miss Hearne.' He looked around, inattentive. 'There's the bus,' he yelled. 'Bye, bye.' And ran off in the direction of the Albert Memorial.[4]

A man. Another teacher. She walked down Cornmarket slowly, feeling the shaking start inside of her. No wonder his mother was so cool, nodding from the other side of the street when I saw her. Well, it wasn't because I charged too much, goodness knows. Could I have said anything that time I stayed for tea? No, of course not. I never said he had no talent. Oh, anyway.

Still, one less pupil, that's what it amounts to. Or two less. Because she didn't want Tommy to keep on but she said she'd get in touch with me about the little girl. She won't now. Harrington, who's he? Well, the nerve of some people. After all the time I slaved away with that boy. After all the extra half-hours without any additional charge. I don't know what's happened to my lucky star these past months. What's happened to me, anyway? You'd think I had the plague, or something. That's four pupils gone in the last six months. Only little Meg Brannon now and goodness knows how long that will last. As much ear for music as a heathen chinee.

The clock in Cornmarket said four. She walked down Ann Street with its jumble of cheap shops, its old shawled women, and its loud crying fruit vendors. I wonder will the Technical School take me on for the embroidery class next term? Mr Heron said he hoped he would be able. But nobody does embroidery any more, that's the truth of it. They have to have enough to make a class. And you can't sell it. Ruin your eyes at piece rates.

4. A Belfast landmark; a tower built in memory of Queen Victoria's consort, Prince Albert.

She came out near the docks and turned hastily back toward the centre of the city. The docks were no place for a woman to be wandering about, in among all those rough pubs and the Salvation Army. At Castle Junction the clock said half-past four. Go home. She walked back toward Camden Street. It began to drizzle, but she was thinking about money, so she paid it no heed.

Her Aunt D'Arcy had never discussed money. A lady does not discuss her private affairs, she used to say. And the D'Arcys never had to look where their next penny was coming from. There had been the house on the Lisburn Road. She had thought that it would fetch quite a bit. And then her aunt had said that Judy wouldn't have to worry, there would be plenty until the right man came along and even if he didn't. That was a long time ago, she said that. Ten years. More, thirteen, if I'm to be honest about it, Miss Hearne thought. First, there was the mortgage on the house. And then money we owed Dan Breen. And the annuity she left me, it was small then and nobody in the whole length and breadth of Ireland could live on a hundred pounds a year nowadays.

Oh, I should have kept up my shorthand and typing, no matter what. The piano lessons, yes, I tried to make a go of it. And fair's fair, I was doing quite well until Mrs Strain spread that story about Edie and me all over town. You might know, being a Protestant, she wouldn't have one ounce of Christian charity in her. Bad enough for me, but poor Edie, lying up there in that home, couldn't raise a hand to help herself. I should go and see her. But the last time, all those bars on the windows and the old women in dressing gowns. Depressing. Mrs Strain, what did she know anyway, going off half-cocked like that? Amanda, her little girl's name. What a silly name.

No charity, isn't it the truth. People have none. And the Technical School, you'd think they could keep the embroidery class going just for old times' sake. After all, there might be a revival of interest. Still, two girls dropped out last term, that leaves only four, not enough unless they can find new students.

She stopped at Bradbury Place. The rain was quite heavy now. She went into a shop and bought a quarter-pound of Kraft cheese and a bag of thick white biscuits. I have enough cocoa, she said, two cups. An apple, I must buy, to get the goodness of some fruit.

It was half-past five when she walked up Camden Street, wet with the rain in her shoes and her hair tossed by the blustery rainy wind. She let herself in as quietly as possible, hoping Mrs Henry Rice would think she had come home later, after having dinner out somewhere. She took her shoes off as she went up the creaky stairs.

The bed-sitting room was cold and musty. She lit the gas fire and the lamps and drew the grey curtains across the bay window. Her wet raincoat she put over a chair with a part of the *Irish News* underneath to catch the drops. Then she took off her wet stockings and hung her dress up. In her old wool dressing gown she felt warmer, more comfortable. She put her rings away in the jewel box and set a little kettle of water on the gas ring. It boiled quickly and she found only enough cocoa for one cup.

The rain began to patter again on the windows, growing heavier, soft persistent Irish rain, coming up Belfast Lough, caught in the shadow of Cave Hill. It settled on the city, a night blanket of wetness. Miss Hearne ate her biscuits, cheese, and apple, found her spectacles and opened a library book by Mazo de la Roche.[5] She toasted her bare toes at the gas fire and leaned back in the armchair, waiting like a prisoner for the long night hours.

5. Mazo de la Roche (1879-1961), a prolific Canadian writer of popular romantic novels.

VAL MULKERNS

(1925-)

from: ANTIQUITIES: A SEQUENCE OF SHORT STORIES (1978)

[At the centre of this story is the narrator's gentle nostalgia for a vanished girlhood and a vanished and generous countryside around Dublin in which that girlhood's most vivid moments were spent. But if it is skirted by some indignation at the contemporary wilderness of concrete, it is also flecked by intimations of cruelty, feeble-mindedness, and retribution, and the narrator's barely acknowledged impression of having been in some sense an interloper in her own past.

Antiquities is a volume of linked stories that subtly uncover the relationships between members of a family through three generations. The chief character is the middle-aged Emily, the narrator of 'A Bitch and a Dog Hanging', whose perspective dominates the book. Her professional and suburban family's experience from the Easter Rising to the present constitutes a profile of the Irish twentieth century, especially of the degeneration of idealistic republicanism into the mindless life-taking of the contemporary Irish Republican Army.]

A BITCH AND A DOG HANGING

The nearest I ever came to a country childhood was at Sheeran's place. Practically every girl I knew at school had at some time or another spent long holidays in the west or south, with grandparents, uncles or aunts. My relations all lived within a stone's throw of the city and when one went to stay with them it was just like at home except that there were more treats, less food and no discipline at all. It was, in short, very agreeable, but years later when I first went to the west of Ireland and learned about people who live according to the natural rhythm of the seasons I knew I had come across their lives before, at Sheeran's place.

One Sunday when I'd been married four or five years and when the restrictions of new motherhood began to irk me more than usual, I picked a quarrel with Denis (which was difficult) and drove, not into the mountains for a long walk as was my usual habit, but across the mutilated city from the Victorian south suburb where I live. I didn't try to find the house where I grew up among a desolation of similar small houses with no trees in sight except the sycamore which my father gradually allowed to take over the garden. I never wanted to see that house again, but what I would have loved to know I could find was Sheeran's place, whitewashed among its green fields, with a sloping thatched roof that was cross-patched with straw of varying colours. Behind it used to be the byre, the piggery, the kitchen garden and the strange evil-smelling dry lavatory with rose bushes flourishing around it. Sheltering the farmhouse were lines of beeches, some of them very old, but not so old as the single chestnut tree that stood in the middle of the fields. It was like a cathedral, like a world of its own when you were small and stood staring up into its living green twilight. Magpies lived there and smaller birds of every kind and a colony of rooks. I remembered their circling about the farmhouse in the smoky pink sky before bedtime every evening; I remember their raucous yet friendly voices. In the loft where I slept in an old settle I could hear them before I dropped asleep, drunk with fresh air and the multiple pleasures of a world I hadn't known existed.

Mick Sheeran (always referred to by his wife as 'Sheeran') had made a swing for my brother and me there and I remembered him trying for a long time to loop a thick rope high enough up in the branches. I remembered how patiently he went on trying although he cursed aloud sometimes when it kept falling down and I remember his bellow of triumph when at last he had a swing actually operating for us. He fetched an old brown horse blanket from the house and made a seat softer than the rope for us and then (putting my brother gently aside with the reproof, 'Ladies first, if you please, young sir,') he lifted me onto the cushion and sent me soaring up into the very body of the tree, part of its gloom, part of its mystery, free as the birds that flitted constantly to and fro among its intricate green leaves backlit by the sun. On the up stroke I was higher than the house; I could look over the thatch at the tops of the trees behind, at the blue mountains on the other side of the city. When I swung down again my stomach fell first in a sickening heave and sometimes I shouted to Mick not to push me any higher while at the same time half-hoping he would. Once I looked right into the face of a startled wood pigeon and once the toes of my sandals cracked off a small dead twig left over from the winter gales. The branch on which the swing depended often creaked and shook, but Mick Sheeran said it would never break. Even years ago, when his own children were small, it had held them. It held them still when they were big fellows finished with school.

Below me where I swung happy as a queen my brother restlessly paced, tugging at Mick's sleeve to know if it was his turn, shouting in a way he knew was futile at me to come down. Up there in the green drunken gloom a kind of madness would take hold of me. Fair play meant nothing to me any more. I shouted to be given five minutes longer, two minutes, and then my brother would begin to blubber and Mick's sense of equity would be touched. He would grab me as I swung past him and it would be over, the sense of power and freedom, of belonging where one had no right to be, not being a bird.

It's hard to believe now that it didn't go on all summer. It went on for precisely two weeks and when we went sadly home again to the narrow streets it was to a usurper in the house. My mother had her second and last son to look after, an unbelievably small ugly creature called Fergus who cried most of the day and all night and created a completely different house for us to live in. Only Mrs Sheeran whom we called Nanny was the same. She was not, of course, a children's nurse, merely a large-hearted charlady who came to us three days a week and happened to have been known to everybody always as Nanny although her name was Anne. She was not a farmer's wife either, which is why she went out to work for another family as well as ourselves. Sheeran was a herdsman for a landowner called Ffrench whose grandfather had built the Sheeran house for another herdsman. The Big House which Mick Sheeran sometimes spoke about was all of two miles away across the fields, and we had never even seen it. Mr Ffrench paid poor wages, my father said, but a large family of Sheerans was reared on the pickings. No fresh meat or vegetables or milk ever had to be bought, no flour or bacon or potatoes. I often wonder now what sort of 'arrangement' was made for our keep during those two weeks when my mother was in the nursing home. Could such princely entertainment as we were given be bought for money? Was Nanny paid double or treble wages for those weeks or was she paid just the usual weekly sum which she earned in a different way — by keeping us children rather than cleaning our house? Who at this stage knows? It is more than likely she refused indignantly to take an extra penny — wasn't she only doing what she'd do for any neighbour in the same circumstances? Maybe my mother gave her a big tin of biscuits when she got back home and maybe my father sent Sheeran a bottle of whiskey. At the time such questions never occurred to me.

Nanny was my contact with the green fields

which I'd been told had once rolled up nearly to the edge of Dublin Castle. In the classroom, on the wireless, in a book, I would come across the magic word 'country' and it was Sheeran's place I would see, the black pig that for some unknown reason preferred to eat sweet pea in Nanny's flower garden than nourishing swill in the piggery; the hen which would lay nowhere but in a certain bush near the oak tree where we could find the eggs and carry them carefully back to the kitchen; the red calf we had seen being dropped the very day before we went home. The mystery and excitement of that stupendous event is forever mixed up in my mind with the monotony of my young brother and the sense of shock that both my parents were pleased about him.

That the winter which followed was not much different from the others was entirely because of Nanny Sheeran. Our Saturdays, in particular, were exactly the same. Always on Saturday my parents went out together, usually to a matinee performance at the Abbey Theatre, and then Nanny would feed and change the baby and hush him to sleep by some magic of her own, not to waken again until my mother's voice sounded in the hall. Once his nagging cry had stopped, the old peace and sense of fun descended on the little kitchen again. By this time the housework would be finished apart from the ironing, and the Sheerans' Sunday joint would be sizzling away in our oven. There was a proper gas oven out in the scullery but Nanny preferred the old kitchen range which twice a week she black-leaded to make it shine. She didn't open up the little door on Saturdays (as we always did to watch the glowing coals inside the bars) because that would be diverting heat away from the oven, but it was always warm in the kitchen anyway and dusky even in summer because of the sycamore. Sometimes when Nanny did the ironing the heat was overpowering but we never complained as we might to our mother. Heat and half-darkness and for long periods silence were part of those magic afternoons. Nanny for a lot of the time was probably very tired. She sighed often and pushed back wisps of hair from the small lined face that had weak red-rimmed eyes: in winter her eyes were often watering. But her smile was something to remember. She had no teeth but didn't show the bare gums. Her mouth turned up mostly at the corners and crinkled like the small old eyes. I never before or since saw anybody's hands so seamed and shrunken yet so clean. Had rubber gloves not been invented then? If so, Nanny Sheeran never heard of them. Her hands were constantly in and out of hot water and carbolic soap, washing floors, cleaning out fires, blackening ranges and polishing brasses. On the days of the week when she didn't work for us she worked even harder for the wife of a government minister whose living-in help wouldn't touch rough work of any kind. Nanny complained sometimes and other times laughed about the heap of old newspapers the minister's lady commanded to be left in the corner of the kitchen. They had to be lifted out of the way when the floor was being scrubbed and put back again when the job was finished. Some day, she told Nanny, some day she would sit down and read all her husband's speeches in Dáil Éireann[1] and then the big bundle could be thrown out. 'That'll be the day,' Nanny used to chuckle to my mother. 'That'll be the day, ma'am, when pigs will take wing and fly.'

Sometimes on Saturdays there would be a spitting explosion from the oven and then Nanny would go over and open the door to emit a blast of succulent heat. The big roasting dish would be lifted out with a damp towel and the meat basted, and if the bones were done they would be picked up with a long fork and left to cool in a dish on the scrubbed deal table. They were the bones removed by the butcher before he rolled the beef and they were never taken to Nanny's home. If there were only two, one went to me and the other to Barry, but if there were three Nanny had one too and we would all pull up our chairs to the range and bite blissfully into the shreds of crispy meat. Nanny having no teeth just sucked away at hers and sometimes this was the story-telling stage. Occasionally she would tell us a conventional fairytale we knew already, but more often it would be a long rigmarole about, perhaps, a fox hunt and the various efforts of the fox to outwit his pursuers.

The details of these stories have, alas, all vanished from my mind and so have the fragments of rhyme with which Nanny enlivened the narrative. One line only remains: 'A bitch and a dog hanging.' Disembodied as the smile of the Cheshire Cat, it haunted me for years after we let Nanny go and finally lost track of her. I told it once to Aunt Harry and she was shocked. 'Just as well,' she told my mother, 'that Mrs Sheeran had to give up work if that

1. The lower house (parliament) of the Republic of Ireland.

was the sort of language she taught Barry and Emily.'

What sort of language? It had been the exciting culmination of a good story about a mean man who tried to cut his sons out of his will — was that it? Anyway, to open the door of his outhouse one day and find a bitch and a dog hanging from a pair of ropes (horrible grins on their dead faces) had been a sign of ill luck for that miserly man. A bitch and a dog hanging . . . they hung still, after all these years, grinning in the cobwebs of the outhouse. Sometimes Nanny's stories were grim like this, and certainly they had none of the cosiness of Beatrix Potter or anything like that, but you never had bad dreams because of them. They were all part of stripping delicious crispy meat off warm bones by the fireside, of lashing rain outside maybe and the boundless comfort of Nanny within. She knew what to do for toothache and earache and how to stop soap from stinging your eyes: she just breathed on a soft corner of the towel and laid it at once against the aching eye which instantly felt better. She knew how to evade telling the truth to enquiring parents who came home one day when Barry and I had been obstinate and rowdy and Nanny had refused to tell any stories. She never on this or any other occasion made complaints. On the contrary, if she came in to work on a day when we were already in trouble she would smooth things over and miraculously make peace. 'Sure weren't we young once like them ourselves ma'am, God be with the days we'll never see again.'

Nobody we knew, except my grandfather, owned a car, certainly not my parents. But when they would come home from the theatre in the rain, happy and full of chat, my father would add an extra layer of heavy brown paper to the parcelled meat and insist on carrying it for Nanny to the bus stop half a mile away. Sometimes, as we all knew, Nanny would be met at the other end by P.J., her eldest son, carrying a bicycle lamp. That would be on P.J.'s good days. Sometimes he had bad days when he would fall foaming on the floor of the farmhouse and Nanny would have to rush to get a spoon between his teeth. I found it hard to associate this damaged stranger with the quiet red-faced fellow in a cloth cap that I knew well and was a little afraid of. Sometimes during that unforgotten summer holiday he would come up soundlessly behind the swing his father had made and push me far away into the highest branches, which smelt of evening even in the middle of the day. I would swing down and twist my head to see P.J. grinning under his cap before he ran to send me up again out of reach. He hardly ever spoke and he hadn't attended school since the age of ten when one of the Christian Brothers had hit him with a pointer on the side of the head and he had fallen to strike the other temple against the desk opposite.

One day I strolled into the farmhouse kitchen to find P.J. a huddle on the stone flags in front of the fire covered by a dark blanket like the one on our swing, and hovered over by Nanny who hunted me away sharply for the one and only time I ever remember. When I saw P.J. again he was just as usual, vaguely smiling and quiet and red-faced, feeding the hens in the yard for his mother. He didn't mind doing women's work. Some of his brothers laughed at him for it. It was over P.J. that I saw Nanny angry with my mother for the first and only time, and the sad thing was that she was coming towards the end of her work for us anyway. Why?

Forcing my memory, I am sure that some time around the beginning of the '39 war my father's job became even more precarious because the gas ovens and other equipment couldn't be imported any more. My school kept me on at reduced fees and the Saturday visits to the theatre (which as we grew older we sometimes shared) stopped. Barry and I were big enough now to look after ourselves. Fergus was ten and my mother was learning of necessity to do her own housework. There came the embarrassed day when Nanny Sheeran had to be told that we couldn't afford to keep her on any longer, though my mother hoped she would drop in for tea as often as she was near the house. Wouldn't she? Nanny's already watery eyes filled up with tears and she said of course she would and the childer (the old plural is known to me only because of her) would surely run in and out to her place now that they were bigger and had bicycles? But before she left us my mother — who always had to be meddlesome if she felt it was for somebody else's good — had a word with Nanny about P.J. I was supposed to be doing my homework at the kitchen table and I heard it all.

My mother said she knew how fond Nanny was of P.J. and what a good fellow he was. But surely she should let him go to the specialist place that was willing to take him, now that they all knew he would never be better but certainly worse as time went on. Hadn't the doctor warned her he might at some future date be dangerous, even to Nanny herself?

'If he did itself, ma'am, God spoke before him,' Nanny said coldly. 'Sheeran and me will never part with our own flesh and blood to strangers, no matter what happens.'

What had become of them all? Christmas cards were exchanged for a while and we heard that the old house fell to a raw new corporation housing estate at the end of the war. The corporation built a new bungalow for the Sheerans in compensation, but how could you compensate for the way of life they had lost for ever? I vaguely remember the bungalow, modern and garish and full of ghastly new furniture to replace the settle by the fire and the wooden benches and the scrubbed deal table on which Nanny used to roll dough which she baked on the griddle over the open fire.

I could have found my way blindfold to the old farmhouse, but the exact whereabouts of the bungalow I had forgotten. Anyhow the housing estate which filled the fields I had known was now a quite elderly suburb, with beyond it new and even uglier acres of housing. You could drive five miles from where Mick Sheeran had put up the swing for us and not see a field or a tree anywhere. Somewhere in this wilderness of concrete, however, great-grandchildren of Nanny's and Mick Sheeran's were probably playing and there was nothing to tell me which children. I left the car and went wandering through the little streets, each called by the name of an Irish clan. A group of lounging boys in high boots consulted silently together when I asked them if they knew of a bungalow tucked away somewher here among the houses. It was a small child several groups later however who pointed up a laneway between the houses before running away with her skipping rope. I fancied she crinkled up her small eyes the way Nanny used to do.

And she was right about the bungalow. There it was where I should have remembered it, standing forlornly in a small vacant lot that was surrounded by the untidy back gardens of the other houses. Its own garden was bosky and overgrown; it was a long time since the front had seen any paint.

Something about the large pale middle-aged woman who opened the door reminded me of the Sheerans' youngest daughter whom I had known as a slender giggling girl working in a jam factory. Rosaleen? When I announced my own name she let me in. Rosaleen it was. Her husband was at Croke Park[2] and her children were all out — she had been just going to lie down for a while. When I asked for her mother she looked a little defensive.

'Alive and well thank God, ma'am, and living in St Kevin's — I wasn't strong enough to look after her now that her eyes are so bad.'

'And your father?' I said.

'Dead and buried this twenty years,' the large woman said. 'He never did a day's good after we left the old house.'

'I can hardly believe he's dead. He used to swing me up to the birds long ago. Not as high as P.J. did, though. How is P.J.?'

'Not a bother on him. Easier than any of us. He got too much for us all and we had to sign him in one day when she wasn't here herself. She never knew it till she came home from Tommy's place and found him gone. He's better off where he is, that's what we all say, but of course she broke her heart over him. . . .'

'Of course. Could I call to see your mother some time?'

I wanted to show Nanny our daughter Sarah. I wanted to watch her pondering resemblances between the small wilful golden creature and my dead parents.

'Visiting between two and four Sundays and Wednesdays,' Rosaleen said. 'I'd be much obliged to you for visiting her, ma'am, because it's a long trek over from here. I try to go every second Sunday if I'm not too tired.'

I refused the cup of tea that she offered me with all the courtesy of Nanny herself and let her go to her rest. Some day I might visit St Kevin's. But not today, although it was Sunday. Some day I might say to her: 'Tell me how you and Sheeran lived happily together all those years of endless work for other people. Tell me how you reared six or seven children and still had grace to spare on less money per week than Sarah has now for pocket money. Tell me.'

Before I reached the city centre I knew I wasn't confident enough or generous enough or brave enough ever to see Nanny again. If she couldn't tell me it was all true, if she could no longer charm away the pain from my eyes how could I live and bear it?

2. The celebrated Gaelic sports stadium in Dublin.

AIDAN HIGGINS
(1927-)

from:
SCENES FROM A RECEDING PAST (1977)

[Aidan Higgins's celebrated novel, *Langrishe, Go Down* (1966), and his early stories in *Felo de Se* (1960) are remarkable and, in the Irish context, ambitious artistic contrivances, dense narratives that threaten to fall victim to portentousness, but instead manage to achieve the distinctiveness of artistry. *Scenes from a Receding Past* is a novel of sorts that is experimental in a less demanding way. The narrative, like an album, comprises disparate items of recollection (including the score-sheet of a 1938 cricket Test match) fitfully connected by the narrator, Dan Ruttle. 'The Institution' is one of the more conventional scenes in a riskily conceived book, but is on its own a poignant commemoration.]

THE INSTITUTION

Wally and I were sitting before the fire, not speaking. Nothing unusual in that, for now we never spoke to each other. One day he closed up and after that you could get nothing out of him but grunts.

He was sitting forward in his easy-chair, staring into a heaped-up fire of slack that burned in the grate. Behind him, on the table, cartridge paper had been tacked down and drawn on in one of his coldly perfect designs. T-squares and set squares, ruler and eraser, callipers and Indian ink, mapping pens and sharply pointed pencils cut down to a third, all meticulously set out. A pot of tea and buttered toast stood warming at his feet. He worked every evening after a day in the quantity surveyor's office; worked steadily and neatly for final examination, not tolerating in himself anything short of perfection, and flying into a great rage if his papers were shifted or disturbed in any way. Indications of displeasure were conveyed through his mother, who cooked for him, saw to his washing, mended his socks. His life was arranged in a set pattern from which any deviation would not be tolerated; life without order was intolerable to him. At home he spoke only to utter heartfelt curses, sucking the dear Redeemer's name out of the impalpable air . . .*'Jesus Christ!'*

Our father was a passive, evasive man who only wanted to agree with people, at least to their faces and mother deferred to him, in company at least; from where did this Corsican fury emanate?

On this particular evening he was not working, but sitting before the fire in his weekend pullover and carpet slippers, looking into the fire, sighing at intervals, looking at his hands. The fire spluttered, sending out licks of blue flame. The thin smoke was drawn up the chimney, released into the darkness and blown away. A sudden green jet of gas spat out at right angles, aimed at Wally's ankles. Wally sat crouched as close as he could get, the pot of tea at his feet, the jar of home-made jam, the wireless knob within easy reach. He liked to work to subdued music: Sinatra singing 'Moonlight in Vermont'. Hoagy Carmichael's 'Stardust'. 'Begin the Beguine'. His favourite programme was 'Hi, Gang! Ben Lyons (a fatly unctuous voice) and Bebe Daniels, Vic Oliver, serenading the Marshall Plan in close harmony:

Gee, Mr Roozy-Felt, it's swell of you,
Thewayyou'rehelpingustowin-the-war!

Perhaps Wally was secretly in love with Bebe Daniels? Next to 'Hi, Gang!' he liked AFN[1] broadcasts of American news and entertainment programmes, cross-talk between Jack Benny and Bob Hope, sports coverage of baseball and American football, ice-hockey. The fast wit sometimes drew a snigger from Wally. The wide-open vowels of the newscasters must have pleased him, assertively open: 'Nö-WOW' they said for now. 'OW-ër' for hour. From six until midnight he sat by the wireless, turned the dials; on wet weekends he monopolised the set. My father was disinterested [*sic*], immersed in newspapers. My mother listened only to *Mrs Dale's Diary*.[2]

But on this particular evening he neither worked nor tuned in to AFN to hear Sinatra singing about Vermont; other matters occupied his mind. Some uneasiness troubled him.

I had enjoyed a little of his confidence while we

1. American Forces Network, a radio network for American servicemen in Europe.
2. A long-running BBC radio serial; Mrs Dale was the wife of a doctor.

were in boarding school and later at college, but towards the end of his time there Wally had begun to withdraw into himself, to close up. He had no friends; he confided only to a small pocket diary, meticulous records of day-to-day activities, his sharp judgements on people. Never in his life had he used my Christian name; it was 'you', or *him*, or *that fellow*. Once it had been 'The Brat' (the bite under the table, the ill-judged snowball); never Dan. And to his father the same unwillingness to call him 'Da' or Father; the same foghorn voice mooing in the distance. Keep your distance. Stand off.

Wally was mean to my mother, even cruel, like a lover. Smirking, looking at his well-cared-for nails, having his own way, even sharing jokes.

'He has a lovely smile,' my mother liked to say. 'When he chooses to use it.'

It was a rare smile. When Wally brought it out, his brown eyes twinkled, his head wobbled, his lips curved and, shaking all over, Wally went 'Hehehe, hehehehe!'

'Piece of cake,' Wally said through compressed lips. Cole Porter's 'Night and Day'. Gershwin. The continuing war.

Now that he wanted to speak, he found it was too late; he could not. It was years since we had spoken to each other. Living in the same house, eating at the same table. We had accepted this as quite natural, if that was what he wanted; we would have accepted anything he did, no matter how unnatural. Wally growing corpulent, taking short womanly strides, that secrecy of his, the rare soprano giggle.

'Hear that?'

I looked over at him; had I heard aright, had he addressed me? He was fixed rigid on the edge of his chair, wringing his hands. His profile told me nothing. He looked as poised as the jumper on the high parapet. He would not look at me. Wally all his life, his adult life at least, had avoided exchanging eye-glances, hand-clasps. I strained my ears, waiting until he spoke again. He sat there rigid, his tea untouched. There was something in the air between us; faint as the singing of telegraph wires in the county, in the winter, far removed from human habitations. Some alarming or tragic message hummed in the wires, over frozen ditches; somewhere a hand, hesitating, reached out, lifted a receiver; an ear heard. I did not speak, leaning forward in the same pose as my brother. He would not look directly at me, only that oblique look he had for others. His attention appeared to be directed at a violet cone of coal gas that curled through the bars turning a vivid green as it emerged, fiercely ejecting a funnel of brilliant white smoke. It spat gas.

'Hear it?'

Silence, but for the gas. It fanned out, withdrew itself behind the bars again, subsided. Unconsumed slag, dry now, eaten with fire from within, fell into the heart of the fire. It was too hot. Our faces glowed.

'Hear what?' I asked.

Wally made an indistinct sound in his throat, heaved himself out of his chair as he pushed it back, hurried in an awkward way out of the room. He had taken the red-hot poker with him. I heard him scuffling out, heavy on his feet, the sound of the wooden bar being dragged from the back door; came a gust of cold air, and Wally vanished into the night.

I stayed where I was. After some time I heard the door being bolted. He came in and sat down again, replacing the poker. He was breathing hard, white in the face, sweating. I looked into the fire where the jet of gas had retreated back into the flames.

Then the pale hands were extended once more to the flames, to the toast, the knobs, to 'Moonlight in Vermont'.

One damp afternoon I visited Wally at the mental institution known as Hazelwood House at Ballina,[3] taking the bus across in the rain to that low town. The prevailing wind was blowing in dirty weather from Killala Bay, the streets deserted save for a few miserable curs and cyclists. Ballina was awash in cowshit. Passing an open doorway through which came the odour of roast beef, I made my way to the institution and asked for my brother. I was informed that he was waiting for me in his room. He had a bad cold.

'Oh, hullo,' the faint voice said as though we were at home. He seemed pleased to see me, and did not appear to be demented or altered in any obvious way; not until he spoke.

Wally spoke!

That was an event in itself. He had filled out; certainly they were not starving him. He looked quite bloated, and spoke in that far-away wind-voice he used so sparingly at home, asking for this and that at table, before subjecting what was placed before him to that microscopic study with which we had

3. A town in County Mayo.

grown familiar, the long chewing process that followed. He spoke a lot, for Wally. Electroshock had changed him, had loosened his tongue. It was much like being back in prep school with him, all his hopes intact, going down the 360 steps to the sunken Pleasure Gardens, so-called, the swimming pool silted up with dead leaves. Madame Patrick Claire walking with her pets hand-in-hand.

My drenched raincoat was steaming on the radiator, the exposed rubber lining gave off an unpleasant odour. The room stank of Institution; it was like boarding school on the first day of term, the place full of new faces; only this was worse. I draped my sodden raincoat over the end of the bed.

'What do you know about snow?' Wally asked, nodding his head, half-smiling.

I was taken aback; what did this signify? Once I had thrown a snowball that had struck him about the knee, filling the turn-ups of his trousers. I stood in the ditch below; Wally looked down at me, a coldly dismissive stare. 'Take that out!' was all he said; and I had obeyed.

'It falls in winter,' I said lamely now, 'From the sky.'

'No.'

'No?' I said.

Wally made a canonical gesture with his hands.

'It comes up out of the ground.'

I looked at his pale hands, marked by hard manual work, those unused hands of his. Work on the land he must, the doctor had said, in order to be well again in his head; and we had believed him. We would have believed anything. Had the shock treatment addled his brains?

'Oh?' I said, watching a puddle form on the floor under my raincoat.

Wally pressed his hands together between his knees. He opened them to reveal discoloured bruises, calluses that had split.

'You find the work hard?'

'Yes,' Wally said, staring at his marked hands. 'It is. I do.'

For years now we had not spoken or exchanged confidences, avoiding each other's eyes. It was possible to be in the same room and yet not acknowledge the presence of another. Wally now was even looking towards me with that humid brown eye. He did not seek to catch mine, but looked off to one side; it was close. He regarded me from the side of his musing eye.

Feeling ill at ease, I searched for subjects in my head, but could only think of the Hurley brothers, who lived in Ballina. What had become of the Hurley brothers? One had been in Wally's year, one in mine, both bettering themselves before entering their father's grocery trade; both had distinguished themselves at mathematics, my worst subject; one was known for his prurient ways, his filthy limericks. Two great oafs, scummy-lipped champions of the ruck, the brawl. They had come and gone.

'Where are the Hurley brothers now?'

'Here,' Wally said, his head wobbling. 'Both here. Poets.'

I looked out the window where a pack of grey clouds were being driven before the wind. A cold damp day at the end of a wet week in the latter end of a wet year. It was Sunday, visiting day; it felt like it. In college days, our father had called in a closed car; we drank Bulmer's cider, handled the clippings he had cut from newspapers, miscellaneous information, a pilot decapitated in Japan, Panzer divisions and pincer movements, maps of the war in Europe. Somewhere in the sodden town a dog barked, a church bell rang. What did I personally know of the ways of the world?

Snow, smelling like roast beef, rose up from the ground, the Hurley brothers putting their heads together, and farting loudly, wrote metrical poetry. Crocuses bloomed in cowdung in the depths of winter.

'No!' I cried.

'They spend the whole day admiring themselves in front of mirrors,' Wally said. 'They never go out.'

A dog was barking, a church bell ringing. My brother sat on the edge of his bed with shoulders bowed, pressing the palms of his hands together. At college he had fainted when about to receive 'pandies' (the leaded leather strap), had been excused punishment by Father Minister, wrote 'lines' instead, spending much of his time in the infirmary, well muffled up. Quick to pick up a virus; a model boy in all respects, no one bullied him. Others put on the gloves, wrestled on the mat, not Wally.

'Here in Hazelwood . . . Is that permitted?'

The Hurley brothers, scalped like convicts, gravely examining their faces all day in mirrors, opening wide their eyes, writing lines of poetry on small pads supplied by the Institution. Surely not.

'Yes,' Wally said with all solemnity. 'Here . . . downstairs.'

'Go to God!'

A knock on the door. Wally opened it. 'Tay,' a female voice said, and in came a slattern with a tray of tea and buttered bread. She set it down on a table by the window. A country-bred, convent-trained girl, often on her knees, close to subservience, smelling of Carbolic. There were two cups. The girl looked at the widening puddle from my raincoat, then at me, and went out. I poured. It was powerful tea. I handed a cup to Wally.

'You could trot mice on this,' I said. One of father's hoary witticisms.

I felt stupid; my thoughts were heavy and slothful. We spoke of relatives we had in common, a subject which did not interest me greatly; but Wally had always cultivated his relatives, an aunt in Adelaide, an uncle in the Argentine, Cissy Maxwell and the rest, all blood relations, unspeakable bores.

College friends too he mentioned, Wally who had no friends; he liked to keep in touch with the old Alma Mater, read the school annual, familiarising himself with the comings and goings and present whereabouts of former class-mates and teachers — Mike Clarson (maths), The General, Horney Ward (Science), Father Gerald O'Byrne (Ancient Greek). College is not a time I myself look back upon with any pleasure.

Wally assured me that he knew of this one and that and old so-and-so; all were known to him personally and were, furthermore, all downstairs, even the dead. Others too. All below. Cousin McAllister killed under a tram.

I heard blurred voices calling in the corridor, heavy feet passing by the door. I thought of Wally working in the fields, going back passively with the others as daylight left the land, sitting at supper. Retiring early, too tired to think. Hazelwood House, the nut house. In the seventeenth century, the hazel had represented Stupidity. What did it represent today? Wally looking forward to visiting day.

I heard doors banging in the corridor and the sound of visitors leaving. Time was up. I gave Wally the parcel from his mother, knitted socks and a spare shirt, cake and newspapers. Somewhere a handbell was ringing. Wally saw me down, offering no comment. The place was teeming with patients and visitors in heavy overcoats, crowding at the entrance. At the foot of the stairs I took my leave, saying I would be over soon again. He handed me a slip of paper. 'Get me this' he said. At the door I looked back. He was going back to his room, gripping the bannisters, head down.

Outside, everything looked wet under a watery sun. The rain had blown over. I saw a bathtub piled with laundry. Two fellows in brown boiler suits and Wellington boots stood resting, inmates or staff. They gaped after me, perhaps envious, for was I not passing out through the institution gates.

In a bar in Ballina I examined Wally's slip of paper. He wanted Stendhal's '*Le Rouge et le Noir*' in English. His small precise hand had not changed since boarding-school days.

ROBERT HARBINSON

(1928-)

from: TATTOO LILY, AND OTHER ULSTER STORIES (1961)

[The unfairly overlooked author of a four-volume autobiography and of numerous travel books (over his real name, Robert Bryans), Robert Harbinson is also an accomplished storyteller. He is a muscular, droll and humane writer, and the nostalgia in his autobiographies is never cloying because it is balanced by a recognition of man's essential helplessness amid the accidents of life — despite the buoyant determination of his autobiographical persona.

The theme of 'Benedicite' is also nostalgic, but Miss Skelly subverts the feeling in herself by interpreting everything, with determination, as the will of the Lord. The story explores the perversity of nostalgia and the psychology of exile, but more specifically the forms these take for the zealous Christian mind in all its crusading, life-suspicion and self-excoriation. Finally the story is a tribute of sorts to the triumphalism of that mind, and the missionary zeal of the evangelicalism that once dominated Northern Irish society. The story charts the secularization of Ulster in the twentieth century, but along the way recreates not only Belfast (once 'the city of ships and Protestant zeal') but also the County Antrim countryside, and India before it too changed forever with partition and the end of the British Empire — a provocative parallel to Miss Skelly's partitioned homeland, and indeed to Miss Skelly's partitioned soul. (The title of the story is the first word of the canticle in the Book of Common Prayer that is an alternative to the Te Deum at Morning Prayer.)]

BENEDICITE

For forty years Miss Skelly had dreamed of a cottage in the Antrim glens. Even during her maiden voyage to India as a young missionary, the dream of a whitewashed cottage amongst her native hills had torn her heart to shreds. For one dreadful moment before the ship's gangway was taken away from Ulster soil she had been tempted to fly down it leaving luggage and all behind. But she recalled the bitter remorse suffered by St. Peter when he denied his Lord, so she had manned the rail and watched the coastline drop below the horizon. Miss Skelly was a woman with inexhaustible powers of dedication called to minister to India's millions, to their bodies and souls, and from the outset she determined not to allow homesickness to interfere with her work. When your hand is on the plough, she always told herself, you don't look back. But the very mention of the word 'plough' brought to her mind scenes of rich turned earth, soft skies, and the noble profile of Antrim.

At first she had tried complete denial and lived in the mission compound like an ascetic. The resultant torture, however, proved to be more of a stumbling block than the occasional bouts of homesickness which her pictures might bring. So she got them out of the trunks and hung them about her rooms. There were views of Antrim valleys and Antrim hills and sad watercolours of lonely coasts. In each a cottage could be seen, white against a background of blue distance. A painting showing the soup-plate hump of Slemish[1] held the principal place in this private collection. It gave Miss Skelly at once her proudest and tenderest memories. On this mountain where St. Patrick had herded Milchu's swine and filled his young soul with missionary vision, Miss Skelly had given her life to the Muslims of India. Sitting amongst the mountain's heather she had studied her first Urdu characters. Compared with some, her missionary society had been generous in the amount of furlough, and when returning from each leave she took more and more bric-à-brac back to the subcontinent. They were tiny links in the chain that bound her to home. She had even made a miniature stack of turves, bringing a few peats each time from the beloved moors. But they were not for fires because sinister dust-devils often besieged the mission, tall columns of soil and sand that raced across the burning plains like tiny tornadoes. The heat had been a greater enemy to Miss Skelly than any temptations from the Evil One.

For the past ten years, however, Miss Skelly had not seen Ulster. The war made furlough impossible. When that was over there were the upheavals of partition into India and Pakistan, and the consequent uncertainty as to whether the mission would be allowed to stay at all. Naturally in such times as these you stuck to your post of duty. And then, it seemed in no time at all Miss Skelly was crossing vast parched wastes of the Sindi desert and was sailing from Karachi for the last time. Such an air of finality settled on this journey, as dry dust settled in the railway carriage. Miss Skelly knew that she was leaving India and the new Pakistan for ever. At least she could feel happy that her beloved people had achieved Iqbal's vision of the 'pure land'[2] even though the Lord had not converted them. Their bright future would blush, as it were, unseen in the desert, for Miss Skelly would not be there. She was old and ailing, and her life's work was done. But at last (was it possible?) she was going to the dream cottage. The simple life which seemed the Lord's reward for all the selfless years of service in His vineyard would soon be hers. There would be no more New Testaments in Pushtu[3] to pack for the Khyber traveller, no more escaping to the hill stations nor conventions at Murree.[4]

Within a month Miss Skelly's trunks and cases were landed at Belfast and she walked down the gangway as forty years previously she had walked up it. Where had the forty years gone? Now that they

1. A small mountain in County Antrim.

2. Muhammad Iqbal (1873-1938), poet, politician, philosopher, has been called the spiritual founder of Pakistan. Above all, he came to champion the creation of a Muslim state inside and outside India.

3. The language of the Afghans.

4. A town in Pakistan near the northwest frontier of India.

were over they seemed only like a few months. Miss Skelly certainly could not believe that a whole decade had slipped by since her last visit to the city of ships and Protestant zeal. At first sight she could see no changes in the welcome skyline of roofs and turrets and domes, except perhaps in the shipyards where the gantries seemed denser than she remembered. But Queen's Bridge was still there with busy people hurrying across it like lemmings. When she emerged from the Customs Shed, Miss Skelly noticed that there were no trams any more. Fear and disappointment laid a finger on her heart.

All the way from Karachi, through the swelter of the Red Sea, over the ethereal blue of the Mediterranean, under the shadow of the Rock, up through the muddy Bay of Biscay, Miss Skelly had played a game with herself. It consisted of enjoying in anticipation the thrill to be experienced on getting her first tram. She specially arranged her luggage so that there was nothing to carry except a valise filled with last minute purchases from the trading boys at Port Said who had swarmed the liner. With this bag she had proposed climbing on to the top of the tram and seeing the sights before going to the station. Miss Skelly knew the number of the trams she must get and the amount of the fare. The tram smell and the hissing of wheels on rails filled her imagination. Several times on board ship she had gone up the gangway between one deck and another, pretending that it was the tram stairs. She had muttered to an imaginary conductor at the bottom that if he wished she would pay her fare now and save him at least *one* journey. 'I've just come back from the East you know,' she had planned to whisper confidentially in his ear as the tram lurched forward. Some passengers on board ship had caught her at this game and came to the conclusion that the old lady was definitely gaga, running up and down like that, talking to herself. But Miss Skelly had merely smiled sweetly at them, after all *they* had no idea what lay behind her behaviour. And now there were no trams.

The Albert[5] struck the hour and Miss Skelly tried to get a taxi. Even her beloved Ulster was becoming modernized, not excluding the Belfast people's manners. The way some of them jumped the queue and bundled in the taxis that drew up, because they were younger and quicker than Miss Skelly, was quite outrageous. She found it most unworthy too of such a Christian capital as Belfast. To conceal from herself a growing apprehension as to what other losses and changes she was to discover, Miss Skelly allowed herself a little righteous anger which burst from her as 'Really!' and, 'Excuse me, but I was. . . .' In the end she let out a breath, half sigh, half sob. For a moment the crowd of loving faces that had seen her off in Pakistan had come unbidden into her mind. How different their warmth was from the hostility of her own people, where not a soul had come to welcome her home. When a taxi-driver did take notice of her he grumbled about the small amount she tipped him. How could this coarse man, she thought, understand that those living on faith in the mission field even nowadays received no more than a hundred pounds in the year? Everything was awkward, difficult, frustrating, expensive. The city had become foreign to her. Luggage difficulties repeated themselves at the station and once again Miss Skelly's thoughts flew back to Sammy, the mission's camel with oily black sides like old *Lederhosen*,[6] who had pulled the boxes to the station with such dignified steps.

Once in the train and well away from unpleasant experiences in the horrid capital Miss Skelly recovered. She asked forgiveness for her indulgence in self-pity, a sin she regarded as practically unforgiveable. During a long life in the East she had witnessed so much suffering, seen so many people die of hunger and disease that she had vowed never to complain about anything that might happen to her. With thankful heart Miss Skelly knew she was going towards rest and peace in the glens of her childhood, the moorland home of her questing spirit, and the rugged shores of the sandy-pickers.[7] With infinite joy she saw the well-loved landscape forming round the train. Her heart leapt as landmarks she had forgotten came into view — a hill shoulder there, a farm by a river, and wayside stations whose names were poetry. So with a great deal of fussing and hissing the train pulled into the market town. And there to crown the wanderer's return was a splendid sight which reduced Miss Skelly to tears. By pressing against the glass she had seen what they had all done to welcome her back

5. The clock on the Albert Memorial tower in Belfast.

6. Leather shorts with H-shaped braces, worn by men in Bavaria and Austria.

7. Ringed plovers.

from a life's labour in the Lord's service. On the platform stood a grand welcoming committee, and behind them Miss Skelly caught a glimpse of the town's brass band. The eyes that looked into the mirror were moist, and Miss Skelly found it difficult to make sure that her grey locks were firmly caged under the elastic of her straw hat. In case they asked her to make a speech when she stepped from the train, Miss Skelly slipped a pocket Testament into the coat she was wearing, so that an appropriate word of scripture might be to hand.

Although the train crept into the station at a pace no faster than a snail's, it stopped with an almighty jolt which threw Miss Skelly off balance. It also interrupted her thoughts as to how she would address the committee. Should it be 'Dear Brethren in the Lord' or simply 'Friends'? Being not entirely without a sense of drama Miss Skelly considered the greatest impact would be made if she sat on and let them burst into the compartment. This would have the added advantage that they could then manage her luggage too. By now the engine noise had subsided to whisper of escaping steam. The blissful strains of 'Home Sweet Home' as rendered by the band seemed to Miss Skelly as the most beautiful music she had ever heard. And it was not until she had wiped her glasses for the second time that Miss Skelly realized that the music was retreating down the platform and out into the station yard. The banging of carriage doors told her that the train was about to move on. She shouted from the window, and the guard stopped the train in time. Apart from him the platform was empty. Confused and upset Miss Skelly got her boxes out. Eyes brimming and lip quivering the old lady then noticed four of her old friends at the barrier. She was so pleased that she failed to notice how much older, more lined and sadder they all looked. Miss Skelly tried to be brave when they told her that the welcoming committee and band had not been for her at all, but for a young Satanite who had been to some international sports abroad and won a silver medal in hop, step and jump.

In their sincere expression of joy for her safe return from foreign parts, however, her friends more than compensated the disappointment. Miss Skelly realized she had been vain and proud and full of self-pity again. Her skill in diagnosing particular forms of the Evil One's attacks was one quality not diminished by advancing years. Any canker within herself was dealt with immediately. But what could she do about the wickedness without? Miss Skelly observed that it invaded even her own home-town. Her friends drove her in an old motor-car home to tea, and she could see many changes. When she voiced her disapproval, the friends said that worse than the things which could be seen, were those that could not. For instance, the rector allowed dancing at the church-hall socials, and the squire had divorced his poor arthritic wife to marry a painted Jezebel from the city, and she, of all things, was said to have once been an actress. Then the car turned into the High Street and Miss Skelly got the biggest shock of all. There was the fine Georgian house that used to be her Uncle Willie's home. Now it stood desecrated for all to see, transformed into a sinner's nest. Godless women sat brazenly in the front parlour windows reading magazines while their permanently-waved hair dried under plastic beehives. Now Miss Skelly did give way to her tears. What hours of prayer and praise had echoed through the High Street from that very room, a place that had been sacred for many generations, ever since John Wesley had preached in it while on his farmhouse mission to Ulster.

Miss Skelly's first night back in Ireland was to be spent with the local prayer-secretary of her missionary society. This woman was also deaconess at a church in the town. Though growing older like her missionary friend the deaconess was still giving fine witness on the new housing estate. Miss Skelly, however, was too excited to take in all the soul-winning news and excused herself for bed. But she could not sleep and lay staring at the square of window waiting for it to lighten with the dawn, and herald her last lap to the cottage.

One of the things for which she felt most grateful was that a cottage had been got for her already, and indeed its new paint was still wet. It could boast of nothing and had been a humble shepherd's affair. When the ancient man died Miss Skelly had wired the first and only cable in her life, arranging with a friend to make an offer for the cottage. Soon she would be living out on the moors along with God's own creatures and the pure winds of the wide oceans. What a wonderful end to her days, where she could close her door on the world, snug inside the thick walls, that under their guardian elms were the true Hebron[8] of her dreams. Indeed, the excite-

8. A city on the west bank of the Jordan, sacred to Moslems and Jews.

ment of achieving her heart's desire made Miss Skelly think of the young bride Achsah[9] being offered the upper and nether springs of Hebron. Miss Skelly felt certain that her cottage was a place of fellowship with God, the land of living water and streams of spiritual refreshment flowing through the unspoilt pastures of Antrim. Nothing could be plainer than that this was the Lord's reward to her for those long years in the wilderness.

As early in the morning as was decently possible she left the town and made her way to the country. A tractor had already taken the luggage. Miss Skelly tactfully avoided the help of friends who wanted to go with her and assist in arranging the furniture that had laid in store since her mother's death. To be entirely alone at her long dreamt-of home-coming was essential to Miss Skelly, now that it was actually happening. Forty years of anticipation could not be spoilt by others' chatter, however well-meaning. Even as a little girl she had left her brothers and sisters to climb hedges and hills, so that she could play at keeping house by herself in a disused corbelled pigsty.

She got a carter to take her up to the cottage which proved to be more beautiful than ever she had expected or remembered. The excitement flustered her so that she dropped things and could not find others that were right under her nose. At last she took control of herself and determined to tackle one problem at a time. She hummed a Gospel chorus that had been a favourite with her Punjabi people and plied her needle to the adjustment of some curtains. The material was rough and woven with a pattern of red and green stripes on a white background, typical in fact of the material woven by Punjabi women within the confines of purdah. These particular lengths of the material reminded her of the old carpet-seller who had sat every day by the mission gates, shaving his legs and armpits until a customer came along. The lengths of curtain had been bought from him years ago and packed away against this very day. And they were still as good as new, perhaps better than she remembered now they were actually in the Antrim light. And what glorious, heavenly light of a bright September morning it was, shining and serene. Miss Skelly rejoiced and looked from her tiny windows on to the splendid landscape around her, pure, mellow, haunted by plovers, enriched with bilberries.

The interior decoration could not be completed at once because the paint on the walls had still to dry. Their colour was the palest of greys and this was lucky for on the sitting-room walls she intended to hang her Turkoman tent-bag and her prayer-rug from Bokhara. The light grey would show up the lustrous sheen, the ancient but soft pile, the diapason of dyes and textures, the stately gardens and streams of eternity that wreathed richly on her carpet hangings. Miss Skelly had brought enough oriental rugs and camel-bags besides *durris*[10] woven by the mission women from their own sheep, back to Ireland to cover every wall and floor in the whole cottage. But whether she would do this or only have a few up at a time and change them periodically would be something to think about during the coming weeks. All her life Miss Skelly had been a hard worker, never resting until a job was complete. She neglected food, neglected letters to her friends, except for one of great length to the mission, telling with praise of all her journeying mercies. Miss Skelly slaved until the cottage was 'shipshape and true' as she liked to describe a task well done. When she sat back and surveyed her handiwork, the trim neatness of it all, she knew that her happiness was replete.

Now she could turn her eyes unto the hills,[11] especially the hill which towered above the cottage and which was all hers except for a handful of silent ewes. One afternoon in the second week Miss Skelly locked the cottage and dropped the key into her new leather shoulder-bag bought at Port Said and tooled with a view of camels passing the pyramids of Gizah. Miss Skelly also carried her lunch of home-griddled scones and cheese for she planned to conquer the highest peak. On top of the lunch packets rested her pocket Testament where a hand could easily reach it. Not since she had gone to the hill station at Nathiagali at the feet of the Himalayas four years previously had Miss Skelly done so much climbing. Shortly she was out of breath and wondered if she would ever make the top. By resting and lightening her shoulder-bag by eating, she came gradually to the heights and finally

9. Achsah was the daughter of Caleb (see Joshua 15. 16-19; Judges 1. 10-15).

10. Colourful pieces of cotton carpet (Hindi, *dhurrie*).

11. cf. the opening of Psalm 121.

to the cloud-dappled panorama of Antrim. Not far away, shining like silver filigree, was the sea. But Miss Skelly turned her back on that. It was still painful to her to think that the sea ran unbroken all the way to Karachi. So she studied the noble landscape instead.

Elevated places in which to sit had always excited her. She gave vent to her feelings of exultation by means of the *Benedicite*. Whenever she contemplated the wonders of creation seen in concert together the canticle came to her lips. But it seldom corresponded liturgically to that *Benedicite* which can be found in the order for Morning Prayer. Miss Skelly's canticle was not in fact to be found in *any* book. She took her cue from Bishop Taylor Smith whom she had once heard in the big tent at the Keswick convention.[12] He explained how once he had walked in the gardens at Oxford and addressed the flowers, *'O all ye delphiniums, bless ye the Lord: praise him, and magnify him for ever.'* Since that day Miss Skelly had never hesitated to improvise upon the theme wherever she might be, whether walking through the pine woods at Murree towards Lawrence College, or breathing the crisp air among the alpine splendours of Nathiagali. But wherever her *Benedicite* had been uttered she always remembered Ulster, *'O all ye orange lilies and thundering Lambeggers, bless ye the Lord: praise him and magnify him for ever.'*[13]

Gratefully, joyfully, Miss Skelly sank into the soft bed of heather on the mountain's flank. When a little strength returned she straightened her back and began to sing. All the same, it did not seem odd that her *Benedicite* was not of Ulster and its beauties, not of the green land that had haunted all her years in the heat of the Punjab plains, but of those very plains themselves. Her tone rang clear and strong so that she failed to detect in it a marked nostalgia.

'O ye spreading pipal trees, bless ye the Lord: praise him, and magnify him for ever.

'O ye bobbed-haired dancing boys, bless ye the Lord: praise him, and magnify him for ever.

'O ye Tajiks and Persian traders of the sharbet booths, bless ye the Lord: praise him, and magnify him for ever.

'O ye tribal lads and hairy Sikhs, bless ye the Lord: praise him, and magnify him for ever.

'O let Pakistan bless the Lord: praise him, and magnify him for ever.'

When Miss Skelly finished she was surprised not only to find herself standing up, but also that her eyes were wet, and that it was the first time she had actually allowed herself to weep for the life she had left behind. Miss Skelly did not consciously torture herself by dwelling on the past. But she could not help thinking of the East and all the loving, friendly people from whose bosoms she had been torn. Even the birds which sang around her cottage recalled her favourite walk through the Street of Partridge Lovers in Peshawar, the narrow way hung with colourful doves and parrots, *mainas* and *bulbuls*.[14]

However, Miss Skelly did not intend to forget *The glamour of thy footsteps in the north* and on the very next night had planned her house-warming. All remaining friends and relatives had been invited out from the town. Miss Skelly was going to surprise and please them with an Eastern repast. That night she went early to bed, heavily but pleasantly tired with her climbing, and was up early in the morning to prepare her feast. But the feast had taken years to prepare, years of patient learning from her Punjabi women. Miss Skelly's arms ached beyond endurance by the time she had finished beating the silver sheet to a diaphragm hardly more substantial than breath in frosty air. When laid and folded gently over the pudding this precious flake of silver looked as lavish and extravagant as she hoped her guests would expect of oriental food. The silver coating was supposed to strengthen the heart and she would tell them so — though she was not trying to charm the heart of the old Army Scripture Reader as the Queen of Sheba had presumably done when serving her sweetmeats in silver to Solomon.

Miss Skelly worked so hard preparing the feast that she barely had time to dress herself before the first guests arrived. Apart from the transformation their hostess had effected on the cottage, giving it quite an oriental flavour with rugs and carpets,

12. An annual gathering of evangelical Christians in Keswick, England. Miss Skelly might have heard Bishop J. Taylor-Smith in 1913 when he addressed the convention on 'The Blessed Life'.
13. Miss Skelly's own canticle is a peculiarly Ulster one: orange lilies are flowers dear to Ulster protestants, while Lambeggers are beaters of the Lambeg drum, an instrument close to the hearts of Northern protestants.
14. *Miana* is the Hindi for the mynah bird. The *bulbul* is a songbird, often taken to be the nightingale.

there was the table. She had put a whole month's allowance into the meal. The stiff table linen was crowded with dishes and graced by the slender-necked *aftabas* full of spring water. Everyone agreed that these silver ewers gave the final touch of Eastern splendour. Beaming, Miss Skelly bade her guests sit down. When they began to eat the strange concoctions their pleasure visibly wilted. For soup there was a sumptuous *kalla paincha*, but on stirring hers and seeing a sheep's eye looking up at her, the prayer-secretary nearly fainted. This created a stir from which the party never recovered. Out of sheer kind politeness, the others toyed with odd pieces, but Miss Skelly's sharp eye observed that apart from nibbling at the comparatively harmless *chappatis*, hardly a thing was eaten. Things barely brightened when the evening finished with green tea. But after chatting and singing a few choruses to the accompaniment of the small collapsible harmonium Miss Skelly had used at the mission, they all began with one consent to make excuse, and by ten o'clock had gone.

A curious thought then came to Miss Skelly. Looking back afterwards she recognized that the beginning of the end, as it were, could be dated from it. After closing the gate behind the last departed visitor she went inside the house again and surveyed the room and the remains. How odd, how very odd, she said aloud several times. For what she had once done to her rooms in the mission compound, she had now been doing to her dream cottage, only in reverse. Forty years ago she had done everything possible to make the mission like a little bit of Antrim. In the bazaar she could never reckon except in pounds and shillings. But now, here she was doing her best to make the cottage as Pakistani as she could, even in the way she entertained her friends. Only outside did the house resemble the white cottage in the hills that had lured her and helped her through an arduous life in the field. In fact, on recalling her dream of the delectable mountains and the white cottage, Miss Skelly realized that she had always thought of it from the outside. In her imaginary future life, in the wanderings and walks she had planned, she had always been approaching the cottage, or walking away from it, or gazing down at it from an Antrim hilltop. But apart from sitting snugly by the turf fire with roaring gales outside, she had never conceived of herself being in it. And she had not, in fact, had the idea of hanging her rugs and camel-bags and the placing of her fine Peshawari metal work until the last few days on the voyage. While putting them up, while preparing her feast Miss Skelly knew that uppermost in her mind was not the home-coming to Antrim, but the far-away mission and her smiling Pakistanis. They were constantly in her mind. Everyday she stopped to look at her watch and say, 'Now if I were *there* I should be opening the dispensary.' Most peculiar of all was that she calculated her monthly allowance and the price of groceries out from the town in rupees and annas.

Depressed, Miss Skelly sat by the fire. The pile of plates and cutlery waiting to be washed seemed malevolent. And there was not enough water left in the house to wash them. She could not push open a wire fly-screen door and call a water-carrier nor call even the meanest of sweeper-boys to come and tidy the room. She would have to do it herself, and in the morning she would have to make yet another journey to the well. For nearly half a century Miss Skelly had been waited on hand and foot, was served by her own bearer and received all the other attentions that befitted a white woman under the shadow of the Union Jack. Miss Skelly did not think that to do such tasks in her cottage would be to demean herself, for she believed and taught that the Lord could be glorified in the humblest of duties. Yet it was hard to change a whole way of life just when peace and stillness and rest had appeared to be just within reach. But beyond reach were the ordinary blessings of life, even a bath. Miss Skelly would have fled from the cottage. But there was no refuge where the patter of the bearers' bare feet over the tiles could be heard as the men filled the old mission bath-tub, and where she could see the fat yellow lizards clinging to the ceiling to catch flies. Taking an oil lamp Miss Skelly went into the bedroom knowing she would never have a proper bath at the cottage. Then she cried herself to sleep.

But fresh and salty Antrim mornings are medicine for any ills of the heart. Miss Skelly woke late with the sun bright and clear. She set to at once, fetched her water and long before midday had removed every sign of the feast from both the cottage and her own mind. A wariness possessed her now, however, and she was cautious in her love for the cottage. When she looked from the windows at the hills she checked the flow of poetic thoughts that had rushed unfailing through her mind before. From those hills would come the winds and the storms that would double the work of keeping warm, and the long dreary days of rain that would mean a soaking to the skin every time she went to the well. And so, of course, it came to be. Summer died slowly, but Miss Skelly noted with misgiving how the sun's heat grew uncertain and how it set earlier and more angrily. Mornings were tart with autumn and long trails of mist hung eerily about hollows in the valleys. Her friends no longer came so frequently to see her and sit on the bit of lawn by the roses to gossip and drink tea. Instead they sent short notes saying how difficult the mountain roads were in the rain but of course dear Miss Skelly was always more than welcome whenever she went into the town.

This isolation wounded Miss Skelly, for though it had been part of her dream, she had always imagined that her retirement would be filled with loving fellowship just whenever she wished. But now the difficult winter days locked her in a windy prison. Bitter cold set in by January and Miss Skelly kept the fire in day and night. She had forgotten the old skill of banking up the turf fire to make it last through the night, so she was often up stoking and stacking. She had never known such cold before, not even up at Nathiagali where Himalayan winds brought snow and frosts to the pine-clad slopes. She supposed that the tropics had thinned her blood. With the same courage that had sent her to the mission field Miss Skelly faced the winter's onslaught. For ten days she was snowed in and not a human soul came near. When the thaw came the roof began to leak in a dozen places so that she had to set buckets and jars to catch the falling stalactites of water. The drip, drip, drip sounded like whispering voices and played on her nerves. As soon as the roads were clear Miss Skelly went into town and bought a dog. Living so far away from help Miss Skelly had decided that a dog was necessary to warn of approaching strangers, though being strong in the fear of the Lord she was no coward.

Again she was snowed in and although the patter of the dog's feet at night was a comfort, Miss Skelly faced the days ahead until the thaw with dread. In the midst of the fever of life and work in the mission she had often paused to think wistfully and longingly of such a situation. When the fiercest Indian summer sun and hot dry winds had scorched the very air she breathed, snow and snow-covered hills and a crackling fire, and hot tea and toast had meant more to her than Paradise itself. After Partition the mission compound was filled with hopeless, homeless refugees who squatted in hundreds about the place, waiting patiently like animals to be fed, clothed and housed. As Miss Skelly walked out of her house they followed her with their eyes dumbly begging for things she could not give them. Compassion filled her, pity ruled her heart. But there had been times when Miss Skelly cried to the Lord to give her rest and relief if only for a week or so — no *Benedicites* then, only the psalmist's longing for the wings of a dove. In Antrim now her prayer was answered with a vengeance, for not even the deaf postman came near the place. Not since girlhood when she played alone in the old pigsty had Miss Skelly been so alone.

Memories of girlhood showed Miss Skelly all too clearly that she had not faced so many fundamental probings of her soul since the day she had wrestled with the Lord on Slemish and finally surrendered to His call. As she sat in the silent cottage watching the dog worrying her precious Kirman saddle-cover to shreds, Miss Skelly peered deep into her innermost being. Could it be that the Lord was using this as a testing time and that greater things than ever before lay yet in store? Then she would be filled with remorse for such dour ungratefulness. Such were the fancies of the lonely woman who could not hide from herself the fact that what she had wanted for so long, and on first achieving had loved, was now bitter and hateful. She began to neglect the cottage, and let dust collect on the fringes of her hanging carpets, and did not polish the metalware, so that it grew dull and lifeless. The cold seemed to be in her bones and she stayed in bed nearly all day in the worst weather.

But Miss Skelly was not idle. In her blue fingers she held the pocket Testament, and as always when distressed she searched its pages for comfort and strength. At that time her daily portion of scripture was taken from the Pentateuch which had always been her favourite books. Her thoughts lingered over Pharaoh's dreams. The ill favoured and lean-fleshed kine coming out of the river to devour the well favoured and fat-fleshed kine seemed so like her own life. The years on the hot plains and by the North-West Frontier had swallowed her youth and womanhood whole, leaving her quite incapable of settling in the bracing winds of Antrim. She had always been too busy to stop and think about herself too much and to observe how every hour on the sub-continent was changing her and making the dream life of retirement an impossibility. When winter began to ebb, and the last snows disappeared and tiny swellings that would become buds were seen on twigs once more, Miss Skelly's mind was made up. Quite definitely the cottage was not the Lord's will. In the practical way that she always treated God, Miss Skelly left the next move to Him.

As soon as spring was well in, she set out for Slemish to rededicate herself, and beg forgiveness for the self-centredness that had led her from the true path of duty. Lord deliver me, she cried, but recognizing at the same time that this was rather a tall order, for as far as she could tell, she was quite unable to do anything but stay put at the cottage. All her savings had gone into buying the little place and nothing could be done on her minute allowance. Nevertheless, she had faith and by the end of the week she had a token of the Lord's forgiveness.

The deaf postman handed her a letter with a London postmark. The spidery handwriting was familiar yet she could not place it exactly. From the importance letters played in the old days in India (she was always calling them old days) Miss Skelly had devised a means of making the pleasure of their arrival last longer. This was to postpone slitting the envelopes until she guessed the sender's identity from the handwriting. For this reason she had deplored the introduction of typewriters and had always asked her friends not to use them. Miss Skelly shouted thanks at the postman, which he did not hear, and took the letter to the fireside. She tapped it on her knee, held it up to the light but could not guess. The writing was not by any of the few lady friends she had who lived in London. Strangely, she would have expected that sort of writing from pupils at her mission school. Defeated but delighted she inserted the point of a paper-knife and opened the envelope. No longer able to bear the suspense she turned the sheet of notepaper over and read the signature. There were two — Abdul and Khalid.

A flush of pleasure reddened her face. Of course, how stupid of her to have forgotten those two delightful boys on the ship who shared much of her journey home! Miss Skelly had spent a lot of time with them trying to improve their English as they were going to London to study engineering. When younger, the boys had been pupils at the mission school. There had been times when they were so lively and full of untrammelled energy that they threatened to wreck the mission's quiet discipline. But Miss Skelly had always been specially fond of them. Had she ever got children of her own she would have wanted two boys exactly like the mischievous Abdul and Khalid.

Miss Skelly was excited because the boys had not forgotten her, and she read the letter through without taking in a single thing it said. Then she made a cup of tea and settled down. It was difficult to read, of course, because the boys' English grammar was bad and their spelling worse. But then it always had been. Gradually it dawned on Miss Skelly that the boys were asking if they might come to Ireland and visit her. Their winter too had been bad both with studies and health. Abdul particularly had been ill with a cough and now both of them wanted to stay in the green Irish countryside during the Easter vacation to recuperate. When she digested it all Miss Skelly immediately sat at her desk and replied, bidding the brothers come at once. Then she sang choruses in Urdu and dashed about the cottage cleaning and brightening, and had the Punjabi curtains washed and flying in the wind like flags. On board ship when she had given the young students her address, Miss Skelly had not believed they would ever bother about her. The boys had gone through the mission school and yet had not come out on the Lord's side, and even now were still devout Muslims. Nevertheless Miss Skelly felt sure that the Lord's hand was in this thing and that wonderful works were prepared for her to do.

Easter came bringing Abdul and Khalid. Miss Skelly went to meet them at the station and they embraced, she with tears. As they rocked up the rutted roads the boys skylarked and sang and frightened the horse, and when they saw the cottage said that it was just like home which, of course, with all its Indian bric-à-brac, it was. Miss Skelly's happiness overflowed now that she once more had someone to appreciate her curries and *chappatis*, carry her water, sing to her in subtle quarter-tones, and wear the gleaming white *shalwars*[15] to bring back the lost years. In her letter she had insisted that they bring their baggy cotton trousers and behave just as they would in Pakistan. Abdul and Khalid needed no encouragement and the silent cottage was noisy and full of laughter. Even the dog

15. A garment, resembling trousers, worn by Indian women.

stopped biting the carpets. It went for such long walks over the hills with the boys that in the evenings it just lay exhausted by the fire, following every move with soulful eyes and occasional throbs at the end of a straggly tail.

And then the four blissful weeks were over and they were all down at the station again, the boys in staid suits and Miss Skelly with another flow of tears. The only twinge of conscience felt by Abdul and Khalid was that they had done no studying, and by Miss Skelly that she had not helped them by speaking Urdu instead of English.

The future, however, was far from gloomy, for in eight weeks they promised to return and stay with their old missionary teacher during the long summer vacation. Miss Skelly's days now were filled with radiant life. The winter rigours lay forgotten as the beauty of Antrim blossomed again. Birds came back to their familiar haunts and in every crevice surprising, nameless wild flowers sprang up. Miss Skelly pondered on the turn of events. Had the Lord brought these two young men all the way from the East in order that she might be instrumental in saving their Muslim souls? It seemed most likely, although she never discussed religion for she was afraid that a broadside attack would scare them away.

By June Miss Skelly was busy making her jams and pickles in preparation for a more cheerful winter. Then came another letter from London. Abdul and Khalid had fared badly with their studies and could not sit the examinations, so they were working in restaurants. Unfortunately they would not be able to come over to Ireland as planned. No more picnics up on the moors, they wrote with bland cheerfulness.

This so upset Miss Skelly that she put the letter down unfinished and wept bitterly. When the paroxysm passed she read on and found sorrow turned to joy. If only they could lay their heads on a few hundred pounds the boys had a wonderful chance of opening an Indian restaurant of their own, though, wrote Khalid in his engaging frankness this could only be a success if they had someone really experienced like Miss Skelly to cook for them. No doubt remained in Miss Skelly's mind as to where the Lord was leading. Even at the end of her life, He had given her work for Him, even given her the special skills required for its doing, since she knew at least a hundred dishes which would make the London business a flourishing success. The sale of the old, damp cottage would easily fetch the necessary capital and what a setting her carpets and camel-bags would provide. Naturally, the restaurant being both Muslim and Christian would not be licensed, and a prayer would go out with every plate of curry.

Miss Skelly's farewells with her friends in the town were brief. The prayer-secretary thought she was mad and said so. But then the prayer-secretary did not know how delicious a properly cooked sheep's eye can be, or how refreshing the fragrant green tea of the sharbet booths really is.

Praise flowed from Miss Skelly during the whole journey. London loomed before her a visionary city, and yet the greatest vineyard that needed dressing. Crossing the water, and on the long train journey she sang a new canticle, the finest *Benedicite* she had ever sung.

'O ye smogs and chilly evenings, bless ye the Lord: praise him, and magnify him for ever.

'O ye green parks and flowing Thames, bless ye the Lord: praise him, and magnify him for ever.

'O let Piccadilly and Leicester Square bless the Lord: praise him, and magnify him for ever.'

WILLIAM TREVOR

(1928-)

from: BEYOND THE PALE AND OTHER STORIES (1981)

[Among William Trevor's many well-turned, acute and wide-ranging short stories is 'Beyond the Pale' (the title story of his 1981 volume), one of the most powerful responses in story form to the current Troubles in Northern Ireland where, in the green perfection of County Antrim, the action takes place. The story is a masterly exercise in sustained and deepening irony. Glencorn Lodge is an illusion of home counties tranquillity in Ulster, a museum of complacent Anglo-Irish privilege. By the story's end, the illusion is shattered and the museum abandoned (at least by one set of visitors). Subversively within Milly's waspish (and in the end naive) narration is the greater perceptiveness of the ill-fitting Cynthia's despised but disabused analysis of the affair (political and sexual), an analysis closer, one assumes, to the author's own opinion of the Irish situation now and in the past. Not only Cynthia's saga but the entire action of the story is perhaps an allegory of the original English colony in Ireland (the Pale), British hypocrisy about and ignorance of Ireland from then until the present, and the likelihood of British withdrawal after a crisis and a British awakening to the reality of the island.]

BEYOND THE PALE

We always went to Ireland in June.

Ever since the four of us began to go on holidays together, in 1965 it must have been, we had spent the first fortnight of the month at Glencorn Lodge in Co. Antrim. Perfection, as Dekko put it once, and none of us disagreed. It's a Georgian house by the sea, not far from the village of Ardbeag. It's quite majestic in its rather elegant way, a garden running to the very edge of a cliff, its long rhododendron drive — or avenue, as they say in Ireland. The English couple who bought the house in the early sixties, the Malseeds, have had to build on quite a bit but it's all been discreetly done, the Georgian style preserved throughout. Figs grow in the sheltered gardens, and apricots, and peaches in the greenhouses which old Mr Saxton presides over. He's Mrs Malseed's father actually. They brought him with them from Surrey, and their Dalmatians, Charger and Snooze.

It was Strafe who found Glencorn for us. He'd come across an advertisement in the *Lady* in the days when the Malseeds still felt the need to advertise. 'How about this?' he said one evening at the end of the second rubber, and then read out the details. We had gone away together the summer before, to a hotel that had been recommended on the Costa del Sol, but it hadn't been a success because the food was so appalling. 'We could try this Irish one,' Dekko suggested cautiously, which is what eventually we did.

The four of us have been playing bridge together for ages, Dekko, Strafe, Cynthia and myself. They call me Milly, though strictly speaking my name is Dorothy Milson. Dekko picked up his nickname at school, Dekko Deakin sounding rather good, I dare say. He and Strafe were in fact at school together, which must be why we all call Strafe by his surname: Major R. B. Strafe he is, the initials standing for Robert Buchanan. We're of an age, the four of us, all in the early fifties: the prime of life, so Dekko insists. We live quite close to Leatherhead, where the Malseeds were before they decided to make the change from Surrey to Co. Antrim. Quite a coincidence, we always think.

'How *very* nice,' Mrs Malseed said, smiling her welcome again this year. Some instinct seems to tell her when guests are about to arrive, for she's rarely not waiting in the large low-ceilinged hall that always smells of flowers. She dresses beautifully, differently every day, and changing of course in the evening. Her blouse on this occasion was scarlet and silver, in stripes, her skirt black. This choice gave her a brisk look, which was fitting because being so busy she often has to be a little on the brisk side. She has smooth grey hair which she once told me she entirely looks after herself, and she almost always wears a black velvet band in it. Her face is well made up, and for one who arranges so many vases of flowers and otherwise has to use her hands she manages to keep them marvellously in condition. Her fingernails are varnished a soft pink, and a small gold bangle always adorns her right wrist, a wedding present from her husband.

'Arthur, take the party's luggage,' she commanded the old porter, who doubles as odd-job man. 'Rose, Geranium, Hydrangea, Fuchsia.' She referred to the titles of the rooms reserved for us: in winter, when no one much comes to Glencorn Lodge, pleasant little details like that are seen to. Mrs Malseed herself painted the flower-plaques that are attached to the doors of the hotel instead of numbers; her husband sees to redecoration and repairs.

'Well, well, well,' Mr Malseed said now, entering the hall through the door that leads to the kitchen regions. 'A hundred thousand welcomes,' he greeted us in the Irish manner. He's rather shorter than Mrs Malseed, who's handsomely tall. He wears Donegal tweed suits and is brown as a berry, including his head, which is bald. His dark brown eyes twinkle at you, making you feel rather more than just another hotel guest. They run the place like a country house, really.

'Good trip?' Mr Malseed enquired.

'Super,' Dekko said. 'Not a worry all the way.'

'Splendid.'

'The wretched boat sailed an hour early one day last week,' Mrs Malseed said. 'Quite a little band were left stranded at Stranraer.'

Strafe laughed. Typical of that steamship company, he said. 'Catching the tide, I dare say?'

'They caught a rocket from me,' Mrs Malseed replied good-humouredly. 'A couple of old dears were due with us on Tuesday and had to spend the night in some awful Scottish lodging-house. It nearly finished them.'

Everyone laughed, and I could feel the others thinking that our holiday had truly begun. Nothing had changed at Glencorn Lodge, all was well with its Irish world. Kitty from the dining-room came out to greet us, spotless in her uniform. 'Ach, you're looking younger,' she said, paying the compliment to all four of us, causing everyone in the hall to laugh again. Kitty's a bit of a card.

Arthur led the way to the rooms called Rose, Geranium, Hydrangea and Fuchsia, carrying as much of our luggage as he could manage and returning for the remainder. Arthur has a beaten, fisherman's face and short grey hair. He wears a green baize apron, and a white shirt with an imitation-silk scarf tucked into it at the neck. The scarf, in different swirling greens which blend nicely with the green of his apron, is an idea of Mrs Malseed's and one appreciates the effort, if not at a uniform, at least at tidiness.

'Thank you very much,' I said to Arthur in my room, smiling and finding him a coin.

We played a couple of rubbers after dinner as usual, but not of course going on for as long as we might have because we were still quite tired after the journey. In the lounge there was a French family, two girls and their parents, and a honeymoon couple — or so we had speculated during dinner — and a man on his own. There had been other people at dinner of course, because in June Glencorn Lodge is always full: from where we sat in the window we could see some of them strolling about the lawns, a few taking the cliff path down to the seashore. In the morning we'd do the same: we'd walk along the sands to Ardbeag and have coffee in the hotel there, back in time for lunch. In the afternoon we'd drive somewhere.

I knew all that because over the years this kind of pattern had developed. We had our walks and our drives, tweed to buy in Cushendall, Strafe's and Dekko's fishing day when Cynthia and I just sat on the beach, our visit to the Giant's Causeway[1] and one to Donegal perhaps, though that meant an early start and taking pot-luck for dinner somewhere. We'd come to adore Co. Antrim, its glens and coastline, Rathlin Island and Tievebulliagh. Since first we got to know it, in 1965, we'd all four fallen hopelessly in love with every variation of this remarkable landscape. People in England thought us mad of course: they see so much of the troubles on television that it's naturally difficult for them to realise that most places are just as they've always been. Yet coming as we did, taking the road along the coast, dawdling through Ballygally, it was impossible to believe that somewhere else the unpleasantness was going on. We'd never seen a thing, nor even heard people talking about incidents that might have taken place. It's true that after a particularly nasty carry-on a few winters ago we did consider finding somewhere else, in Scotland perhaps, or Wales. But as Strafe put it at the time, we felt we owed a certain loyalty to the Malseeds and indeed to everyone we'd come to know round about, people who'd always been glad to welcome us back. It seemed silly to lose our

1. A spectacular rock formation on the coast of County Antrim, favoured by tourists.

heads, and when we returned the following summer we knew immediately we'd been right. Dekko said that nothing could be further away from all the violence than Glencorn Lodge, and though his remark could hardly be taken literally I think we all knew what he meant.

'Cynthia's tired,' I said because she'd been stifling yawns. 'I think we should call it a day.'

'Oh, not at all,' Cynthia protested. 'No, please.'

But Dekko agreed with me that she was tired, and Strafe said he didn't mind stopping now. He suggested a nightcap, as he always does, and as we always do also, Cynthia and I declined. Dekko said he'd like a Cointreau.

The conversation drifted about. Dekko told us an Irish joke about a drunk who couldn't find his way out of a telephone box, and then Strafe remembered an incident at school concerning his and Dekko's housemaster, A.D. Cowley-Stubbs, and the house wag, Thrive Major. A. D. Cowley-Stubbs had been known as Cows and often featured in our after-bridge reminiscing. So did Thrive Major.

'Perhaps I *am* sleepy,' Cynthia said. 'I don't think I closed my eyes once last night.'

She never does on a sea crossing. Personally I'm out like a light the moment my head touches the pillow; I often think it must be the salt in the air because normally I'm an uneasy sleeper at the best of times.

'You run along, old girl,' Strafe advised.

'Brekky at nine,' Dekko said.

Cynthia said good-night and went, and we didn't remark on her tiredness because as a kind of unwritten rule we never comment on one another. We're four people who play bridge. The companionship it offers, and the holidays we have together, are all part of that. We share everything: the cost of petrol, the cups of coffee or drinks we have; we even each make a contribution towards the use of Strafe's car because it's always his we go on holiday in, a Rover it was on this occasion.

'Funny, being here on your own,' Strafe said, glancing across what the Malseeds call the After-Dinner Lounge at the man who didn't have a companion. He was a red-haired man of about thirty, not wearing a tie, his collar open at the neck and folded back over the jacket of his blue serge suit. He was uncouth-looking, though it's a hard thing to say, not at all the kind of person one usually sees at Glencorn Lodge. He sat in the After-Dinner Lounge as he had in the dining-room, lost in some concentration of his own, as if calculating sums in his mind. There had been a folded newspaper on his table in the dining-room. It now reposed tidily on the arm of his chair, still unopened.

'Commercial gent,' Dekko said. 'Fertilisers.'

'Good heavens, never. You wouldn't get a rep in here.'

I took no part in the argument. The lone man didn't much interest me, but I felt that Strafe was probably right: if there was anything dubious about the man's credentials he might have found it difficult to secure a room. In the hall of Glencorn Lodge there's a notice which reads: *We prefer not to feature in hotel guides, and we would be grateful to our guests if they did not seek to include Glencorn Lodge in the Good Food Guide, the Good Hotel Guide, the Michelin, Egon Ronay or any others. We have not advertised Glencorn since our early days, and prefer our recommendations to be by word of mouth.*

'Ah, thank you,' Strafe said when Kitty brought his whisky and Dekko's Cointreau. 'Sure you won't have something?' he said to me, although he knew I never did.

Strafe is on the stout side, I suppose you could say, with a gingery moustache and gingery hair, hardly touched at all by grey. He left the Army years ago, I suppose because of me in a sense, because he didn't want to be posted abroad again. He's in the Ministry of Defence now.

I'm still quite pretty in my way, though nothing like as striking as Mrs Malseed, for I've never been that kind of woman. I've put on weight, and wouldn't have allowed myself to do so if Strafe hadn't kept saying he can't stand a bag of bones. I'm careful about my hair and, unlike Mrs Malseed, I have it very regularly seen to because if I don't it gets a salt and pepper look, which I hate. My husband, Ralph, who died of food-poisoning when we were still quite young, used to say I wouldn't lose a single look in middle age, and to some extent that's true. We were still putting off having children when he died, which is why I haven't any. Then I met Strafe, which meant I didn't marry again.

Strafe is married himself, to Cynthia. She's small and ineffectual, I suppose you'd say without being untruthful or unkind. Not that Cynthia and I don't get on or anything like that, in fact we get on extremely well. It's Strafe and Cynthia who don't seem quite to hit it off, and I often think how much happier all round it would have been if Cynthia had married someone completely different, someone like Dekko in a way, except that that mightn't quite have worked out either. The Strafes have two sons, both very like their father, both of them in the Army. And the very sad thing is they think nothing of poor Cynthia.

'Who's that chap?' Dekko asked Mr Malseed, who'd come over to wish us good-night.

'Awfully sorry about that, Mr Deakin. My fault entirely, a booking that came over the phone.'

'Good heavens, not at all,' Strafe protested, and Dekko looked horrified in case it should be thought he was objecting to the locals. 'Splendid-looking fellow,' he said, overdoing it.

Mr Malseed murmured that the man had only booked in for a single night, and I smiled the whole thing away, reassuring him with a nod. It's one of the pleasantest of the traditions at Glencorn Lodge that every evening Mr Malseed makes the rounds of his guests just to say good-night. It's because of little touches like that that I, too, wished Dekko hadn't questioned Mr Malseed about the man because it's the kind of thing one doesn't do at Glencorn Lodge. But Dekko is a law unto himself, very tall and gangling, always immaculately suited, a beaky face beneath mousy hair in which flecks of grey add a certain distinction. Dekko has money of his own and though he takes out girls who are half his age he has never managed to get around to marriage. The uncharitable might say he has a rather gormless laugh; certainly it's sometimes on the loud side.

We watched while Mr Malseed bade the lone man good-night. The man didn't respond, but just sat gazing. It was ill-mannered, but this lack of courtesy didn't appear to be intentional: the man was clearly in a mood of some kind, miles away.

'Well, I'll go up,' I said. 'Good-night, you two.'

'Cheery-bye, Milly,' Dekko said. 'Brekky at nine, remember.'

'Good-night, Milly,' Strafe said.

The Strafes always occupy different rooms on holidays, and at home also. This time he was in Geranium and she in Fuchsia. I was in Rose, and in a little while Strafe would come to see me. He stays with her out of kindness, because he fears for her on her own. He's a sentimental, good-hearted man, easily moved to tears: he simply cannot bear the thought of Cynthia with no one to talk to in the evenings, with no one to make her life around. 'And besides,' he often says when he's being jocular, 'it would break up our bridge four.' Naturally we never discuss her shortcomings or in any way analyse the marriage. The unwritten rule that exists among the four of us seems to extend as far as that.

He slipped into my room after he'd had another drink or two, and I was waiting for him as he likes me to wait, in bed but not quite undressed. He has never said so, but I know that that is something Cynthia would not understand in him, or even attempt to comply with. Ralph, of course, would not have understood either; poor old Ralph would have been shocked. Actually it's all rather sweet, Strafe and his little ways.

'I love you, dear,' I whispered to him in the darkness, but just then he didn't wish to speak of love and referred instead to my body.

If Cynthia hadn't decided to remain in the hotel the next morning instead of accompanying us on our walk to Ardbeag everything might have been different. As it happened, when she said at breakfast she thought she'd just potter about the garden and sit with her book out of the wind somewhere, I can't say I was displeased. For a moment I hoped Dekko might say he'd stay with her, allowing Strafe and myself to go off on our own, but Dekko — who doesn't go in for saying what you want him to say — didn't. 'Poor old sausage,' he said instead, examining Cynthia with a solicitude that suggested she was close to the grave, rather than just a little lowered by the change of life or whatever it was.

'I'll be perfectly all right,' Cynthia assured him. 'Honestly.'

'Cynthia likes to mooch, you know,' Strafe pointed out, which of course is only the truth. She reads too much, I always think. You often see her putting down a book with the most melancholy look in her eyes, which can't be good for her. She's an imaginative woman, I suppose you would say, and of course her habit of reading so much is often useful on our holidays: over the years she has read her way through dozens of Irish guide-books. 'That's where the garrison pushed the natives over the cliffs,' she once remarked on a drive. 'Those rocks are known as the Maidens,' she remarked on another occasion. She has led us to places of interest which we had no idea existed: Garron Tower on Garron Point, the mausoleum at Bonamargy, the Devil's Backbone. As well as which, Cynthia is extremely knowledgeable about all matters relating to Irish history. Again she has read endlessly: biographies and autobiographies, long accounts of the centuries of battling and politics there've been. There's hardly a town or village we ever pass through that hasn't some significance for Cynthia, although I'm afraid her impressive fund of information doesn't always receive the attention it deserves. Not that Cynthia ever minds; it doesn't seem to worry her when no one listens. My own opinion is that she'd have made a much better job of her relationship with Strafe and her sons if she could have somehow developed a bit more character.

We left her in the garden and proceeded down the cliff path to the shingle beneath. I was wearing slacks and a blouse, with the arms of a cardigan looped round my neck in case it turned chilly: the outfit was new, specially bought for the holiday, in shades of tangerine. Strafe never cares how he dresses and of course she doesn't keep him up to the mark: that morning, as far as I remember, he wore rather shapeless corduroy trousers, the kind men sometimes garden in, and a navy-blue fisherman's jersey. Dekko as usual was a fashion plate: a pale green linen suit with pleated jacket pockets, a maroon shirt open at the neck, revealing a medallion on a fine gold chain. We didn't converse as we crossed the rather difficult shingle, but when we reached the sand Dekko began to talk about some girl or other, someone called Juliet who had apparently proposed marriage to him just before we'd left Surrey. He'd told her, so he said, that he'd think about it while on holiday and he wondered now about dispatching a telegram from Ardbeag saying, *Still thinking*. Strafe, who has a simple sense of humour, considered this hugely funny and spent most of the walk persuading Dekko that the telegram must certainly be sent, and other telegrams later on, all with the same message. Dekko kept laughing, throwing his head back in a way that always reminds me of an Australian bird I once saw in a nature film on television. I could see this was going to become one of those jokes that would accompany us all through the holiday, a man's thing really, but of course I didn't mind. The girl called Juliet was nearly thirty years younger than Dekko. I supposed she knew what she was doing.

Since the subject of telegrams had come up, Strafe recalled the occasion when Thrive Major had sent one to A.D. Cowley-Stubbs: *Darling regret three months gone love Rowena*. Carefully timed, it had arrived during one of the Cows' Thursday evening coffee sessions. Rowena was a maid, known as the Bicycle, who had been sacked the previous term, and old Cows had something of a reputation as a misogynist. When he read the message he apparently went white and collapsed into an armchair. Warrington P. J. managed to read it too, and after that the fat was in the fire. The consequences went on rather, but I never minded listening when Strafe and Dekko drifted back to their schooldays. I just wish I'd known Strafe then, before either of us had gone and got married.

We had our coffee at Ardbeag, the telegram was sent off, and then Strafe and Dekko wanted to see a man called Henry O'Reilly whom we'd met on previous holidays, who organises mackerel-fishing trips. I waited on my own, picking out postcards in the village shop that sells almost everything, and then I wandered down towards the shore. I knew that they would be having a drink with the boatman because a year had passed since they'd seen him last. They joined me after about twenty minutes, Dekko apologising but Strafe not seeming to be aware that I'd had to wait because Strafe is not a man who notices little things. It was almost one o'clock when we reached Glencorn Lodge and were told by Mr Malseed that Cynthia needed looking after.

The hotel, in fact, was in turmoil. I have never seen anyone as ashen-faced as Mr Malseed; his wife, in a forget-me-not dress, was limp. It wasn't explained to us immediately what had happened, because in the middle of telling us that Cynthia needed looking after Mr Malseed was summoned to the telephone. I could see through the half-open door of their little office a glass of whisky or brandy on the desk and Mrs Malseed's bangled arm reaching out for it. Not for ages did we realise that it all had do to with the lone man whom we'd speculated about the night before.

'He just wanted to talk to me,' Cynthia kept repeating hysterically in the hall. 'He sat with me by the magnolias.'

I made her lie down. Strafe and I stood on either side of her bed as she lay there with her shoes off, her rather unattractively cut plain pink dress crumpled and actually damp from her tears. I wanted to make her take it off and to slip under the bed-clothes in her petticoat but somehow it seemed all wrong, in the circumstances, for Strafe's wife to do anything so intimate in my presence.

'I couldn't stop him,' Cynthia said, the rims of her eyes crimson by now, her nose beginning to run again. 'From half past ten till well after twelve. He had to talk to someone, he said.'

I could sense that Strafe was thinking precisely the same as I was: that the red-haired man had insinuated himself into Cynthia's company by talking about himself and had then put a hand on her knee. Instead of simply standing up and going away Cynthia would have stayed where she was, embarrassed or tongue-tied, at any rate unable to cope. And when the moment came she would have turned hysterical. I could picture her screaming in the garden, running across the lawn to the hotel, and then the pandemonium in the hall. I could sense Strafe picturing that also.

'My God, it's terrible,' Cynthia said.

'I think she should sleep,' I said quietly to Strafe. 'Try to sleep, dear,' I said to her, but she shook her head, tossing her jumble of hair about on the pillow.

'Milly's right,' Strafe urged. 'You'll feel much better after a little rest. We'll bring you a cup of tea later on.'

'My God!' she cried again. 'My God, how could I sleep?'

I went away to borrow a couple of mild sleeping pills from Dekko, who is never without them, relying on the things too much in my opinion. He was tidying himself in his room, but found the pills immediately. Strangely enough, Dekko's always sound in a crisis.

I gave them to her with water and she took them without asking what they were. She was in a kind of daze, one moment making a fuss and weeping, the next just peering ahead of her, as if frightened. In a way she was like someone who'd just had a bad nightmare and hadn't yet completely returned to reality. I remarked as much to Strafe while we made our way down to lunch, and he said he quite agreed.

'Poor old Cynth!' Dekko said when we'd all ordered lobster bisque and entrecôte béarnaise. 'Poor old sausage.'

You could see that the little waitress, a new girl this year, was bubbling over with excitement; but Kitty, serving the other half of the dining-room, was grim, which was most unusual. Everyone was talking in hushed tones and when Dekko said, 'Poor old Cynth!' a couple of heads were turned in our direction because he can never keep his voice down. The little vases of roses with which Mrs Malseed must have decorated each table before the fracas had occurred seemed strangely out of place in the atmosphere which had developed.

The waitress had just taken away our soup-plates when Mr Malseed hurried into the dining-room and came straight to our table. The lobster bisque surprisingly hadn't been quite up to scratch, and in passing I couldn't help wondering if the fuss had caused the kitchen to go to pieces also.

'I wonder if I might have a word, Major Strafe,' Mr Malseed said, and Strafe rose at once and accompanied him from the dining-room. A total silence had fallen, everyone in the dining-room pretending to be intent on eating. I had an odd feeling that we had perhaps got it all wrong, that because we'd been out for our walk when it had happened all the other guests knew more of the details than Strafe and Dekko and I did. I began to wonder if poor Cynthia had been raped.

Afterwards Strafe told us what occurred in the Malseeds' office, how Mrs Malseed had been sitting there, slumped, as he put it, and how two policemen had questioned him. 'Look, what on earth's all this about?' he had demanded rather sharply.

'It concerns this incident that's taken place, sir,' one of the policeman explained in an unhurried voice. 'On account of your wife —'

'My wife's lying down. She must not be questioned or in any way disturbed.'

'Ach, we'd never do that, sir.'

Strafe does a good Co. Antrim brogue and in relating all this to us he couldn't resist making full use of it. The two policemen were in uniform and their natural slowness of intellect was rendered more noticeable by the lugubrious air the tragedy had inspired in the hotel. For tragedy was what it was: after talking to Cynthia for nearly two hours the lone man had walked down to the rocks and been drowned.

When Strafe finished speaking I placed my knife and fork together on my plate, unable to eat another mouthful. The facts appeared to be that the man, having left Cynthia by the magnolias, had clambered down the cliff to a place no one ever went to, on the other side of the hotel from the sands we had walked along to Ardbeag. No one had seen him except Cynthia, who from the cliff-top had apparently witnessed his battering by the treacherous waves. The tide had been coming in, but by the time old Arthur and Mr Malseed reached the rocks it had begun to turn, leaving behind it the fully dressed corpse. Mr Malseed's impression was that the man had lost his footing on the seaweed and accidentally stumbled into the depths, for the rocks were so slippery it was difficult to carry the corpse more than a matter of yards. But at least it had been placed out of view, while Mr Malseed hurried back to the hotel to telephone for assistance. He told Strafe that Cynthia had been most confused, insisting that the man had walked out among the rocks and then into the sea, knowing what he was doing.

Listening to it all, I no longer felt sorry for Cynthia. It was typical of her that she should so sillily have involved us in all this. Why on earth had she sat in the garden with a man of that kind instead of standing up and making a fuss the moment he'd begun to paw her? If she'd acted intelligently the whole unfortunate episode could clearly have been avoided. Since it hadn't, there was no point whatsoever in insisting that the man had committed suicide when at that distance no one could possibly be sure.

'It really does astonish me,' I said at the lunch table, unable to prevent myself from breaking our unwritten rule. 'Whatever came over her?'

'It can't be good for the hotel,' Dekko commented, and I was glad to see Strafe giving him a little glance of irritation.

'It's hardly the point,' I said coolly.

'What I meant was, hotels occasionally hush things like this up.'

'Well, they haven't this time.' It seemed an age since I had waited for them in Ardbeag, since we had been so happily laughing over the effect of Dekko's telegram. He'd included his address in it so that the girl could send a message back, and as we'd returned to the hotel along the seashore there'd been much speculation between the two men about the form this would take.

'I suppose what Cynthia's thinking,' Strafe said, 'is that after he'd tried something on with her he became depressed.'

'Oh, but he could just as easily have lost his footing. He'd have been on edge anyway, worried in case she reported him.'

'Dreadful kind of death,' Dekko said. His tone suggested that that was that, that the subject should now be closed, and so it was.

After lunch we went to our rooms, as we always do at Glencorn Lodge, to rest for an hour. I took my slacks and blouse off, hoping that Strafe would knock on my door, but he didn't and of course that was understandable. Oddly enough I found myself thinking of Dekko, picturing his long form stretched out in the room called Hydrangea, his beaky face in profile on his pillow. The precise nature of Dekko's relationship with these girls he picks up has always privately intrigued me: was it really possible that somewhere in London there was a girl called Juliet who was prepared to marry him for his not inconsiderable money?

I slept and briefly dreamed. Thrive Major and Warrington P. J. were running the post office in Ardbeag, sending telegrams to everyone they could think of, including Dekko's friend Juliet. Cynthia had been found dead beside the magnolias and people were waiting for Hercule Poirot to arrive. 'Promise me you didn't do it,' I whispered to Strafe, but when Strafe replied it was to say that Cynthia's body reminded him of a bag of old chicken bones.

Strafe and Dekko and I met for tea in the tea-lounge. Strafe had looked in to see if Cynthia had woken, but apparently she hadn't. The police officers had left the hotel, Dekko said, because he'd noticed their car wasn't parked at the front any more. None of the three of us said, but I think we presumed, that the man's body had been removed from the rocks during the quietness of the afternoon. From where we sat I caught a glimpse of Mrs Malseed passing quite briskly through the hall, seeming almost herself again. Certainly our holiday would be affected, but it might not be totally ruined. All that remained to hope for was Cynthia's recovery, and then everyone could set about forgetting the unpleasantness. The nicest thing would be if a jolly young couple turned up and occupied the man's room, exorcising the incident, as newcomers would.

The family from France — the two little girls and their parents — were chattering away in the tea-lounge, and an elderly trio who'd arrived that morning were speaking in American accents. The honeymoon couple appeared, looking rather shy, and began to whisper and giggle in a corner. People who occupied the table next to ours in the dining-room, a Wing-Commander Orfell and his wife, from Guildford, nodded and smiled as they passed. Everyone was making an effort, and I knew it would help matters further if Cynthia felt up to a rubber or two before dinner. That life should continue as normally as possible was essential for Glencorn Lodge, the example already set by Mrs Malseed.

Because of our interrupted lunch I felt quite hungry, and the Malseeds pride themselves on their teas. The chef, Mr McBride, whom of course we've met, has the lightest touch I know with sponge cakes and little curranty scones. I was, in fact, buttering a scone when Strafe said:

'Here she is.'

And there indeed she was. By the look of her she had simply pushed herself off her bed and come straight down. Her pink dress was even more crumpled than it had been. She hadn't so much as run a comb through her hair, her face was puffy and unpowdered. For a moment I really thought she was walking in her sleep.

Strafe and Dekko stood up. 'Feeling better, dear?' Strafe said, but she didn't answer.

'Sit down, Cynth,' Dekko urged, pushing back a chair to make room for her.

'He told me a story I can never forget. I've dreamed about it all over again.' Cynthia swayed in front of us, not even attempting to sit down. To tell the truth, she sounded inane.

'Story, dear?' Strafe enquired, humouring her.

She said it was the story of two children who had apparently ridden bicycles through the streets of Belfast, out into Co. Antrim. The bicycles were dilapidated, she said; she didn't know if they were stolen or not. She didn't know about the children's homes because the man hadn't spoken of them, but she claimed to know instinctively that they had ridden away from poverty and unhappiness. 'From the clatter and the quarrelling,' Cynthia said. 'Two children who later fell in love.'

'Horrid old dream,' Strafe said. 'Horrid for you, dear.'

She shook her head, and then sat down. I poured another cup of tea. 'I had the oddest dream myself,' I said. 'Thrive Major was running the post office in Ardbeag.'

Strafe smiled and Dekko gave his laugh, but Cynthia didn't in any way acknowledge what I'd said.

'A fragile thing the girl was, with depths of mystery in her wide brown eyes. Red-haired of course he was himself, thin as a rake in those days. Glencorn Lodge was derelict then.'

'You've had a bit of a shock, old thing,' Dekko said.

Strafe agreed, kindly adding, 'Look, dear, if the chap actually interfered with you —'

'Why on earth should he do that?' Her voice was shrill in the tea-lounge, edged with a note of hysteria. I glanced at Strafe, who was frowning into his tea-cup. Dekko began to say something, but broke off before his meaning emerged. Rather more calmly Cynthia said:

'It was summer when they came here. Honeysuckle he described. And mother of thyme. He didn't know the name of either.'

No one attempted any kind of reply, not that it was necessary, for Cynthia just continued.

'At school there were the facts of geography and arithmetic. And the legends of scholars and of heroes, of Queen Maeve and Finn MacCool. There was the coming of St Patrick to a heathen people. History was full of kings and high-kings, and Silken Thomas and Wolfe Tone, the Flight of the Earls, the Siege of Limerick.'

When Cynthia said that, it was impossible not to believe that the unfortunate events of the morning had touched her with some kind of madness. It seemed astonishing that she had walked into the tea-lounge without having combed her hair, and that she'd stood there swaying before sitting down, that out of the blue she had started on about two children. None of it made an iota of sense, and surely she could see that the nasty experience she'd suffered should not be dwelt upon? I offered her the plate of scones, hoping that if she began to eat she would stop talking, but she took no notice of my gesture.

'Look, dear,' Strafe said, 'there's not one of us who knows what you're talking about.'

'I'm talking about a children's story, I'm talking about a girl and a boy who visited this place we visit also. He hadn't been here for years, but he returned last night, making one final effort to understand. And then he walked out into the sea.'

She had taken a piece of her dress and was agitatedly crumpling it between the finger and thumb of her left hand. It was dreadful really, having her so grubby-looking. For some odd reason I suddenly thought of her cooking, how she wasn't in the least interested in it or in anything about the house. She certainly hadn't succeeded in making a home for Strafe.

'They rode those worn-out bicycles through a

hot afternoon. Can you feel all that? A newly surfaced road, the snap of chippings beneath their tyres, the smell of tar? Dust from a passing car, the city they left behind?'

'Cynthia dear,' I said, 'drink your tea, and why not have a scone?'

'They swam and sunbathed on the beach you walked along today. They went to a spring for water. There were no magnolias then. There was no garden, no neat little cliff paths to the beach. Surely you can see it clearly?'

'No,' Strafe said. 'No, we really cannot, dear.'

'This place that is an idyll for us was an idyll for them too: the trees, the ferns, the wild roses near the water spring, the very sea and sun they shared. There was a cottage lost in the middle of the woods: they sometimes looked for that. They played a game, a kind of hide and seek. People in a white farmhouse gave them milk.'

For the second time I offered Cynthia the plate of scones and for the second time she pointedly ignored me. Her cup of tea hadn't been touched. Dekko took a scone and cheerfully said:

'All's well that's over.'

But Cynthia appeared to have drifted back into a daze, and I wondered again if it could really be possible that the experience had unhinged her. Unable to help myself, I saw her being led away from the hotel, helped into the back of a blue van, something like an ambulance. She was talking about the children again, how they had planned to marry and keep a sweetshop.

'Take it easy, dear,' Strafe said, which I followed up by suggesting for the second time that she should make an effort to drink her tea.

'Has it to do with the streets they came from? Or the history they learnt, he from his Christian Brothers,[2] she from her nuns? History is unfinished in this island; long since it has come to a stop in Surrey.'

Dekko said, and I really had to hand it to him: 'Cynth, we have to put it behind us.'

It didn't do any good. Cynthia just went rambling on, speaking again of the girl being taught by nuns, and the boy by Christian Brothers. She began to recite the history they might have learnt, the way she sometimes did when we were driving through an area that had historical connections. 'Can you imagine,' she embarrassingly asked, 'our very favourite places bitter with disaffection, with plotting and revenge? Can you imagine the treacherous murder of Shane O'Neill the Proud?[3]

Dekko made a little sideways gesture of his head, politely marvelling. Strafe seemed about to say something, but changed his mind. Confusion ran through Irish history, Cynthia said, like convolvulus in a hedgerow. On May 24th, 1487, a boy of ten called Lambert Simnel, brought to Dublin by a priest from Oxford, was declared Edward VI of all England and Ireland, crowned with a golden circlet taken from a statue of the Virgin Mary. On May 24th, 1798, here in Antrim, Presbyterian farmers fought for a common cause with their Catholic labourers. She paused and looked at Strafe. Chaos and contradiction, she informed him, were hidden everywhere beneath nice-sounding names. 'The Battle of the Yellow Ford,' she suddenly chanted in a sing-song way that sounded thoroughly peculiar, 'the Statutes of Kilkenny. The Battle of Glenmama, the Convention of Drumceat. The Act of Settlement, the Renunciation Act. The Act of Union, the Toleration Act.[4] Just so much history it sounds like now, yet people starved or died while other people watched. A language was lost, a faith forbidden. Famine followed revolt, plantation followed that. But it was people who were struck into the soil of other people's land, not forests of new trees; and it was greed and treachery that spread as a disease among them all. No wonder unease clings to these shreds of history and shots ring out in answer to the mockery of drums. No wonder the air is nervy with suspicion.'

2. A Roman catholic congregation of male religious, founded in 1802, principally for the Christian education of the sons of the poor and the working class.

3. An uncompromising opponent of English rule in Ireland, specifically of English law in Ulster. He was murdered in 1567 by the Scots of Antrim, to whom he had fled for protection, having been defeated by the O'Donnells.

4. At the battle of the Yellow Ford in 1598, the Irish defeated the English. The Statutes of Kilkenny (1366) bound the island of Ireland to English law. In 999 Brian Boru, king of Munster, defeated the Norse at the battle of Glenmama. In 575 at the Convention of Drumceat (County Derry), a national council of kings and abbots, Columba (later St Columba) settled disputes between Scotland and Ireland. There were two Acts of Settlement: by the first (1652), Oliver Cromwell sought by punitive laws of confiscation and resettlement to subdue Ireland, while by the second (1660), the restored monarchy lessened the harshness of the first. In the Renunciation Act (1783), Britain renounced her right to bind Ireland by British acts of parliament. In 1801, by the Act of Union, the parliaments of Britain and Ireland were united. The Toleration Act of 1719 restored freedom of worship to protestant Dissenters (most of whom were northerners).

There was an extremely awkward silence when she ceased to speak. Dekko nodded, doing his best to be companionable. Strafe nodded also. I simply examined the pattern of roses on our tea-time china, not knowing what else to do. Eventually Dekko said:

'What an awful lot you know, Cynth!'

'Cynthia's always been interested,' Strafe said. 'Always had a first-rate memory.'

'Those children of the streets are part of the battles and the Acts,' she went on, seeming quite unaware that her talk was literally almost crazy. 'They're part of the blood that flowed around those nice-sounding names.' She paused, and for a moment seemed disinclined to continue. Then she said:

'The second time they came here the house was being rebuilt. There were concrete-mixers, and lorries drawn up on the grass, noise and scaffolding everywhere. They watched all through another afternoon and then they went their different ways: their childhood was over, lost with their idyll. He became a dockyard clerk. She went to London, to work in a betting shop.'

'My dear,' Strafe said very gently, 'it's interesting, everything you say, but it really hardly concerns us.'

'No, of course not.' Quite emphatically Cynthia shook her head, appearing wholly to agree. 'They were degenerate, awful creatures. They must have been.'

'No one's saying that, my dear.'

'Their story should have ended there, he in the docklands of Belfast, she recording bets. Their complicated childhood love should just have dissipated, as such love often does. But somehow nothing was as neat as that.'

Dekko, in an effort to lighten the conversation, mentioned a boy called Gollsol who'd been at school with Strafe and himself, who'd formed a romantic attachment for the daughter of one of the groundsmen and had later actually married her. There was a silence for a moment, then Cynthia, without emotion, said:

'You none of you care. You sit there not caring that two people are dead.'

'Two people, Cynthia?' I said.

'For God's sake, I'm telling you!' she cried. 'That girl was murdered in a room in Maida Vale.'[5]

5. A district in central London.

Although there is something between Strafe and myself, I do try my best to be at peace about it. I go to church and take communion, and I know Strafe occasionally does too, though not as often as perhaps he might. Cynthia has no interest in that side of life, and it rankled with me now to hear her blaspheming so casually, and so casually speaking about death in Maida Vale on top of all this stuff about history and children. Strafe was shaking his head, clearly believing that Cynthia didn't know what she was talking about.

'Cynthia dear,' I began, 'are you sure you're not muddling something up here? You've been upset, you've had a nightmare: don't you think your imagination, or something you've been reading —'

'Bombs don't go off on their own. Death doesn't just happen to occur in Derry and Belfast, in London and Amsterdam and Dublin, in Berlin and Jerusalem. There are people who are murderers: that is what this children's story is about.'

A silence fell, no one knowing what to say. It didn't matter of course because without any prompting Cynthia continued.

'We drink our gin with Angostura bitters, there's lamb or chicken Kiev. Old Kitty's kind to us in the dining-room and old Arthur in the hall. Flowers are everywhere, we have our special table.'

'Please let us take you to your room now,' Strafe begged, and as he spoke I reached out a hand in friendship and placed it on her arm. 'Come on, old thing,' Dekko said.

'The limbless are left on the streets, blood spatters the car-parks. *Brits Out* it says on a rock-face, but we know it doesn't mean us.'

I spoke quietly then, measuring my words, measuring the pause between each so that its effect might be registered. I felt the statement had to be made, whether it was my place to make it or not. I said:

'You are very confused, Cynthia.'

The French family left the tea-lounge. The two Dalmatians, Charger and Snooze, ambled in and sniffed and went away again. Kitty came to clear the French family's tea things. I could hear her speaking to the honeymoon couple, saying the weather forecast was good.

'Cynthia,' Strafe said, standing up, 'we've been very patient with you but this is now becoming silly.'

I nodded just a little. 'I really think,' I softly said, but Cynthia didn't permit me to go on.

'Someone told him about her. Someone mentioned her name, and he couldn't believe it. She sat alone in Maida Vale, putting together the mechanisms of her bombs: this girl who had laughed on the seashore, whom he had loved.'

'Cynthia,' Strafe began, but he wasn't permitted to continue either. Hopelessly, he just sat down again.

'Whenever he heard of bombs exploding he thought of her, and couldn't understand. He wept when he said that; her violence haunted him, he said. He couldn't work, he couldn't sleep at night. His mind filled up with images of her, their awkward childhood kisses, her fingers working neatly now. He saw her with a carrier-bag, hurrying it through a crowd, leaving it where it could cause most death. In front of the mouldering old house that had once been Glencorn Lodge they'd made a fire and cooked their food. They'd lain for ages on the grass. They'd cycled home to their city streets.'

It suddenly dawned on me that Cynthia was knitting this whole fantasy out of nothing. It all worked backwards from the moment when she'd had the misfortune to witness the man's death in the sea. A few minutes before he'd been chatting quite normally to her, he'd probably even mentioned a holiday in his childhood and some girl there'd been: all of it would have been natural in the circumstances, possibly even the holiday had taken place at Glencorn. He'd said good-bye and then unfortunately he'd had his accident. Watching from the cliff edge, something had cracked in poor Cynthia's brain, she having always been a prey to melancholy. I suppose it must be hard having two sons who don't think much of you, and a marriage not offering you a great deal, bridge and holidays probably the best part of it. For some odd reason of her own she'd created her fantasy about a child turning into a terrorist. The violence of the man's death had clearly filled her imagination with Irish violence, so regularly seen on television. If we'd been on holiday in Suffolk I wondered how it would have seemed to the poor creature.

I could feel Strafe and Dekko beginning to put all that together also, beginning to realise that the whole story of the red-haired man and the girl was clearly Cynthia's invention. 'Poor creature,' I wanted to say, but did not do so.

'For months he searched for her, pushing his way among the people of London, the people who were her victims. When he found her she just looked at him, as if the past hadn't even existed. She didn't smile, as if incapable of smiling. He wanted to take her away, back to where they came from, but she didn't reply when he suggested that. Bitterness was like a disease in her, and when he left her he felt the bitterness in himself.'

Again Strafe and Dekko nodded, and I could feel Strafe thinking that there really was no point in protesting further. All we could hope for was that the end of the saga was in sight.

'He remained in London, working on the railways. But in the same way as before he was haunted by the person she'd become, and the haunting was more awful now. He bought a gun from a man he'd been told about and kept it hidden in a shoe-box in his rented room. Now and again he took it out and looked at it, then put it back. He hated the violence that possessed her, yet he was full of it himself: he knew he couldn't betray her with anything but death. Humanity had left both of them when he visited her again in Maida Vale.'

To my enormous relief and, I could feel, to Strafe's and Dekko's too, Mr and Mrs Malseed appeared beside us. Like his wife, Mr Malseed had considerably recovered. He spoke in an even voice, clearly wishing to dispose of the matter. It was just the diversion we needed.

'I must apologise, Mrs Strafe,' he said. 'I cannot say how sorry we are that you were bothered by that man.'

'My wife is still a little dicky,'[6] Strafe explained, 'but after a decent night's rest I think we can say she'll be as right as rain again.'

'I only wish, Mrs Strafe, you had made contact with my wife or myself when he first approached you.' There was a spark of irritation in Mr Malseed's eyes, but his voice was still controlled. 'I mean, the unpleasantness you suffered might just have been averted.'

'Nothing would have been averted, Mr Malseed, and certainly not the horror we are left with. Can you see her as the girl she became, seated at a chipped white table, her wires and fuses spread around her? What were her thoughts in that room, Mr Malseed? What happens in the mind of anyone who wishes to destroy? In a back street he bought his gun for too much money. When did it first occur to him to kill her?'

'We really are a bit at sea,' Mr Malseed replied

6. shaky, unsteady (British slang).

without the slightest hesitation. He humoured Cynthia by displaying no surprise, by speaking very quietly.

'All I am saying, Mr Malseed, is that we should root our heads out of the sand and wonder about two people who are beyond the pale.'

'My dear,' Strafe said, 'Mr Malseed is a busy man.'

Still quietly, still perfectly in control of every intonation, without a single glance around the tea-lounge to ascertain where his guests' attention was, Mr Malseed said:

'There is unrest here, Mrs Strafe, but we do our best to live with it.'

'All I am saying is that perhaps there can be regret when two children end like this.'

Mr Malseed did not reply. His wife did her best to smile away the awkwardness. Strafe murmured privately to Cynthia, no doubt beseeching her to come to her senses. Again I imagined a blue van drawn up in front of Glencorn Lodge, for it was quite understandable now that an imaginative woman should go mad, affected by the ugliness of death. The garbled speculation about the man and the girl, the jumble in the poor thing's mind — a children's story as she called it — all somehow hung together when you realised they didn't have to make any sense whatsoever.

'Murderers are beyond the pale, Mr Malseed, and England has always had its pales. The one in Ireland began in 1395.'

'Dear,' I said, 'what has happened has nothing whatsoever to do with calling people murderers and placing them beyond some pale or other. You witnessed a most unpleasant accident, dear, and it's only to be expected that you've become just a little lost. The man had a chat with you when you were sitting by the magnolias and then the shock of seeing him slip on the seaweed —'

'He didn't slip on the seaweed,' she suddenly screamed. 'My God, he didn't slip on the seaweed.'

Strafe closed his eyes. The other guests in the tea-lounge had fallen silent ages ago, openly listening. Arthur was standing near the door and was listening also. Kitty was waiting to clear away our tea things, but didn't like to because of what was happening.

'I must request you to take Mrs Strafe to her room, Major,' Mr Malseed said. 'And I must make it clear that we cannot tolerate further upset in Glencorn Lodge.'

Strafe reached for her arm, but Cynthia took no notice.

'An Irish joke,' she said, and then she stared at Mr and Mrs Malseed, her eyes passing over each feature of their faces. She stared at Dekko and Strafe, and last of all at me. She said eventually:

'An Irish joke, an unbecoming tale: of course it can't be true. Ridiculous, that a man returned here. Ridiculous, that he walked again by the seashore and through the woods, hoping to understand where a woman's cruelty had come from.'

'This talk is most offensive,' Mr Malseed protested, his calmness slipping just a little. The ashen look that had earlier been in his face returned. I could see he was beside himself with rage. 'You are trying to bring something to our doorstep which most certainly does not belong there.'

'On your doorstep they talked about a sweetshop: Cadbury's bars and different-flavoured creams, nut-milk toffee, Aero and Crunchie.'

'For God's sake pull yourself together,' I clearly heard Strafe whispering, and Mrs Malseed attempted to smile. 'Come along now, Mrs Strafe,' she said, making a gesture. 'Just to please us, dear. Kitty wants to clear away the dishes. Kitty!' she called out, endeavouring to bring matters down to earth.

Kitty crossed the lounge with her tray and gathered up the cups and saucers. The Malseeds, naturally still anxious, hovered. No one was surprised when Cynthia began all over again, by crazily asking Kitty what she thought of us.

'I think, dear,' Mrs Malseed began, 'Kitty's quite busy really.'

'Stop this at once,' Strafe quietly ordered.

'For fourteen years, Kitty, you've served us with food and cleared away the tea-cups we've drunk from. For fourteen years we've played our bridge and walked about the garden. We've gone for drives, we've bought our tweed, we've bathed as those children did.'

'Stop it,' Strafe said again, a little louder. Bewildered and getting red in the face, Kitty hastily bundled china on to her tray. I made a sign at Strafe because for some reason I felt that the end was really in sight. I wanted him to retain his patience, but what Cynthia said next was almost unbelievable.

'In Surrey we while away the time, we clip our hedges. On a bridge night there's coffee at nine o'clock, with macaroons or *petits fours*. Last thing of all we watch the late-night News, packing away our cards and scoring-pads, our sharpened pencils. There's been an incident in Armagh, one soldier's had his head shot off, another's run amok. Our lovely Glens of Antrim, we all four think, our coastal drives: we hope that nothing disturbs the peace. We think of Mr Malseed, still busy in Glencorn Lodge, and Mrs Malseed finishing her flower-plaques for the rooms of the completed annexe.'

'Will you for God's sake shut up?' Strafe suddenly shouted. I could see him struggling with himself, but it didn't do any good. He called Cynthia a bloody spectacle, sitting there talking rubbish. I don't believe she even heard him.

'Through honey-tinted glasses we love you and we love your island, Kitty. We love the lilt of your racy history, we love your earls and heroes. Yet we made a sensible pale here once, as civilised people create a garden, pretty as a picture.'

Strafe's outburst had been quite noisy and I could sense him being ashamed of it. He muttered that he was sorry, but Cynthia simply took advantage of his generosity, continuing about a pale.

'Beyond it lie the bleak untouchables, best kept as dots on the horizon, too terrible to contemplate. How can we be blamed if we make neither head nor tail of anything, Kitty, your past and your present, those battles and Acts of Parliament? We people of Surrey: how can we know? Yet I stupidly thought, you see, that the tragedy of two children could at least be understood. He didn't discover where her cruelty had come from because perhaps you never can: evil breeds evil in a mysterious way. That's the story the red-haired stranger passed on to me, the story you huddle away from.'

Poor Strafe was pulling at Cynthia, pleading with her, still saying he was sorry.

'Mrs Strafe,' Mr Malseed tried to say, but got no further. To my horror Cynthia abruptly pointed at me.

'That woman,' she said, 'is my husband's mistress, a fact I am supposed to be unaware of, Kitty.'

'My God!' Strafe said.

'My husband is perverted in his sexual desires. His friend, who shared his schooldays, has never quite recovered from that time. I myself am a pathetic creature who has closed her eyes to a husband's infidelity and his mistress's viciousness. I am dragged into the days of Thrive Major and A. D. Cowley-Stubbs: mechanically I smile. I hardly exist, Kitty.'

There was a most unpleasant silence, and then Strafe said:

'None of that's true. For God's sake, Cynthia,' he suddenly shouted, 'go and rest yourself.'

Cynthia shook her head and continued to address the waitress. She'd had a rest, she told her. 'But it didn't do any good, Kitty, because hell has invaded the paradise of Glencorn, as so often it has invaded your island. And we, who have so often brought it, pretend it isn't there. Who cares about children made into murderers?'

Strafe shouted again. 'You fleshless ugly bitch!' he cried. 'You bloody old fool!' He was on his feet, trying to get her on to hers. The blood was thumping in his bronzed face, his eyes had a fury in them I'd never seen before. 'Fleshless!' he shouted at her, not caring that so many people were listening. He closed his eyes in misery and in shame again, and I wanted to reach out and take his hand but of course I could not. You could see the Malseeds didn't blame him, you could see them thinking that everything was ruined for us. I wanted to shout at Cynthia too, to batter the silliness out of her, but of course I could not do that. I could feel the tears behind my eyes, and I couldn't help noticing that Dekko's hands were shaking. He's quite sensitive behind his joky manner, and had quite obviously taken to heart her statement that he had never recovered from his schooldays. Nor had it been pleasant, hearing myself described as vicious.

'No one cares,' Cynthia said in the same unbalanced way, as if she hadn't just been called ugly and a bitch. 'No one cares, and on our journey home we shall all four be silent. Yet is the truth about ourselves at least a beginning? Will we wonder in the end about the hell that frightens us?'

Strafe still looked wretched, his face deliberately turned away from us. Mrs Malseed gave a little sigh and raised the fingers of her left hand to her cheek, as if something tickled it. Her husband breathed heavily. Dekko seemed on the point of tears.

Cynthia stumbled off, leaving a silence behind her. Before it was broken I knew she was right when she said we would just go home, away from this country we had come to love. And I knew as well that neither here nor at home would she be led to a blue van that was not quite an ambulance. Strafe would stay with her because Strafe is made like that, honourable in his own particular way. I felt a pain where perhaps my heart is, and again I wanted to cry. Why couldn't it have been she who had gone down to the rocks and slipped on the seaweed or just walked into the sea, it didn't matter which? Her awful rigmarole hung about us as the last of the tea things were gathered up — the earls who'd fled, the famine and the people planted. The children were there too, grown up into murdering riff-raff.

LELAND BARDWELL

(1928-)

from: DIFFERENT KINDS OF LOVE (1987)

[This story appears in the first collection of stories by a writer who is chiefly a novelist and poet. Like the other stories in the volume, 'The Hairdresser' is a fierce narrative, written in a peremptory prose that pushes realism towards surrealism. It is Bardwell's nightmarish vision of Dublin's imminent future, a city of hopeless housing estates peopled by abandoned and victimized women and plagued by unemployment, poverty, vigilantism, civil disorder, criminality, gangs, even cannibalism. Amidst the chaos is depicted one character's grim rage for order.]

THE HAIRDRESSER

Long ago they had painted the houses. Pale pastel shades — mauves, pinks, greys. The estate had expanded up Trevor's Hill, across the old sheep-field, curling back down like an anvil until it seemed that the mountain had grown a second crust. Attempts to divert the streams had failed and water ran freely into the residents' gardens and rotted the foundations of the houses.

Paint cracked, window frames warped; there seemed no wisdom in the continuous building of new dwellings but after the last of the city clearances, the Local Authority brought out their trucks, their cranes, their earth-movers and parked them in the road that ran directly through the estate till it could run no more and ended, T-shaped, beneath the higher slopes.

Electric wires, pylons blew down in the storms and were seldom repaired so the estate lay mostly in darkness during the winter. There were strange happenings behind those closed doors at night. Many of the middle-aged women, whose husbands had taken off or been gaoled during the nineties took in men — those who roamed the country homeless — with whom they shared their bed and welfare payments. Their sons, who were also mostly incarcerated in some institution or other, and many of their daughters, too, left them free and lonely. Occasionally a daughter would return with a new brood. This accounted for second-generation children. Those men came and went; domestic unease, lack of money, young children crowding and squabbling frequently drove them out after a few months.

The women did their best and it was not unusual to see a middle-aged woman perched on her roof, trying to pin over bits of plastic or rope up a piece of guttering.

Like many another family, Mona and her mother inhabited one of the highest buildings, therefore victim of the worst winter weather, and they spent many hours plastering, drying, mending window frames and replacing slates. But apart from this they were not run-of-the-mill, because the daughter was one of the few people — if not the only one — who attended secondary school. A rather plain girl with dry ribbed hair and a boxy[1] figure, she was something of a scholar. Her mother was a gaunt angular woman with fierce energy. Unlike the other women she attracted a certain type of man, more chaotic, more unprincipled than the average, who would enjoy her passionate responses but who wearied quickly and took his revenge with calculated cruelty.

To Mona, her mother gave the recurring excuse

1. i.e. square.

that 'they were safer with a man about'. Mere excuse, of course, because the marauding gangs 'cased' every house and in theirs there was little or nothing to steal. The video was the usual target and they had long ago sold theirs, sold almost everything in fact. The house was bare of furniture except for minimum requirements. In the kitchen, which was also the sitting room, there was a table, covered in a thin plastic cloth, a few upright chairs and in the bedrooms there were mattresses on which lay bundles of matted blankets. Only Mona's room was spotless. Her fastidious nature forbore squalor of any kind, and to this room, as soon as she had cooked the dinner, she would retire, her lesson books spread before her, a stub of a candle lighting the immediate circle on the floor and with her stiff hair tied behind her neck she would concentrate on her studies to the exclusion of all else.

For some weeks now a new man had established himself in their household. Although he combined all the complexities and evil ways of his forerunners he was as yet an unknown quantity to Mona. Her mother, forever alert, listened to his speeches — for he made speeches all day long — claiming an intellectual monopoly on all subjects under the sun. This irked Mona who had a fine mathematical brain and knew that he was often wrong in his summing up of various points of social or political argument. However, for the sake of her mother she held her peace.

Today she had decided to scrub the lino. As she scrubbed and picked between the cracks she was conscious of his saturnine gaze following her around in between bouts of exclamations at the latest atrocities committed by the latest governments; snippets of which he read from the newspaper.

Mona scrubbed. The man stared, rustled his paper, sniffed back a lozenge of water from the end of his nose. His eyes, still as glass, were his most unsettling feature. She rose in confusion eventually; there were rings of mud on the knees of her stockings.

'Why don't you kneel on a bit of newspaper?' he asked, looking down at her legs as if she were a yearling in the ring.

'Ah, shut up,' Mona for once lost her temper. 'If you'd shift your arse I'd get on more quickly.'

All this time her mother was sitting on the edge of her chair, watching him with the air of one who waits for a child to take its first few steps.

'Don't be rude,' she said, her voice rusty from smoking.

Mona went to the sink to wring out her cloth; she looked round at him, sizing him up once again. There was madness there, she felt, in his posture, his teeth grinding, the occasional bouts of pacing; he was leaning over now, elbows on knees, his stained overcoat folded back like the open page of an almanac; his hands were gyrating as though he were shuffling a pack of cards. He had strangely delicate hands: his fingers tapered into neat girlish nails, yet he had huge tense shoulders. His face was stippled and pocked from long hours spent in the open. Looking at him now left her cold and sick. Yes, this man was not simply like the others — ruthless, fighting for survival — there were qualities within him, seams of impatience and rage that were beyond his control. Her outburst had annoyed him and she wished she had controlled her temper; she had witnessed his anger once already and it had seemed to lift out of him with inhuman urgency. Yet far from antagonising her mother, his rages seemed to make her more submissive, more caressing, more loving than ever. Or perhaps she sensed the danger; Mona wasn't sure.

When they were alone she tried to warn her mother, but the latter touching her own brow with the hand of [her] lover and with her other hand taking Mona's, said, 'Don't worry, darling. It will all be over one day.'

Winter crawled; snow came and went. It was no longer possible to patch the roof, so they caught the water in buckets placed under the worst of the leaks. On a sleety February afternoon, Mona, returning wearily from her long journey back from school — it was dole[2] day and they had bought cider — found them both slightly drunk, sitting by the fire — one more kitchen chair had been burnt — and there was a glow of frivolity between them. But on her entry he addressed her rudely, finishing up by shaking his fists and saying 'You're a nasty piece of work.' Mona snapped back, 'You're a fucking creep, yourself.'

He laughed and held out his glass for more cider.

Her mother rose, picked up the flagon, and poured the cider straight into his eyes.

The kitchen exploded. He jumped to his feet and went at her, got her on the ground, his fists round

2. Unemployment benefit.

her neck, tables and chairs went flying. His delicate fingers — those lovely fingers — closing, closing on her mother's throat. With all her strength Mona kicked him from behind and he let go, roaring obscenities and trying to wipe his eyes with his sleeve. Her mother pulled herself up, screaming, apologising, begging for 'another chance.' But he was up and heading for the door, his large frame bent like a sickle, his arms stiffly held from his body, he banged out of the house. The stricken women stood face to face as though hoping for a message that would never come.

Then her mother strained after him.

Mona grasped her mother's jumper. 'No, no, Mammy, let him, let him go.'

'But I must,' her mother said, 'save him from the police.' She slipped out of her jumper like a snake shedding its skin and she too had run into the night.

The cold mountain air crept into the hall; gusts ran under the mat, up her legs, as she shouldered shut the door. She stood for a while, knowing now that her life was beyond the ken of the two people out there. Who was she now? Mona the lucky one, she used to call herself, the only member of the family to forestall the fate that had swallowed up the rest of them — one brother killed in a hit-and-run, another in and out of Mountjoy Gaol, a sister killed by an abortion in England, another sister who had quite disappeared. But long ago she had made a pact with herself: to work and work, to use her ability to study, to use her interests that lay beyond the hinterland of misery into which she had been born so that one day, one far-off day, she would take her mother and herself away from this no-man's territory where rats and dogs got a better living than they did. Another thing she'd promised herself was that she would never have anything to do with men, she would never allow her neat parts to be touched by the opposite sex, she would never succumb to the martyrdom of sexual love. In the estate children gave birth to children, women were already grandmothers in their thirties. But she, Mona, trod a different path. Or did she? Should she now just pack her bags, go, too, into the recondite night, join the packs of girls and boys, small criminals, who got by by 'doing cheques' or robbing the rich suburbs on the other side of the city?

But no. She must give it one more try.

She climbed the stairs, the re-lit candle dripping hot wax over her hand. In her room her books, her friends, all stacked neatly, were suddenly strangers, strangers like the two people who had recently fled into the unyielding night. She went on her knees taking each book and fondling it. The ones she cared for most, those on quantitative and applied mathematics, she held longingly, opening them, smoothing the pages. But it was no use; they denied the half of her that was her pride. She threw them from her, went to the window, hoping she'd see her mother returning alone. But the street was dark, the houses down the hill derelict as an unused railway station. She left the window open and sank down on the bed.

A little while later she heard them; they came into the hall. They were speaking in low tones; the fight had been patched up and Mona knew that once again she'd act as though nothing had happened. Get wearily up, shop, make the dinner, return to her room and make some sort of a fist of studying.

She went downstairs; a rat or a mouse scuttled at her feet; she was used to the rodents so she kicked out at it and threw on her coat.

In the shop she would spend the few shillings that she had — money that she earned from her better off student friends, the ones she helped with their homework. Most of her mother's dole went on cigarettes and drink and lasted for about a day. So it was up to her to keep them for the rest of the week, eking out her money on bits of food that kept them barely alive.

There was so little spending in the neighbourhood that frequently the thin girl at the cash desk wasn't at her post and Mona often edged out without paying. She prayed that it would be so, now, as she slipped into the darkness.

She skirted the heaps of rubble, piles of sand that had been there for years. There was no street lighting so she had to use her memory in order to avoid the worst puddles and even so her shoes filled up with icy water. The journey to the shop usually took about twenty minutes — it was over a mile away — and as it was nearly six Mona began to run.

The fierce cold of that day was the one thing that stuck in Mona's memory above all else. How dirty papers had flared up in front of her feet as she'd run the last few paces home; how the unending gale had pierced her chest and how she had clasped her inadequate coat collar round her chin. It had always been difficult to get the key to work properly — it had been badly cut and one had to twist it this way and that in order to slot it in, and it had seemed to take longer than usual, as her white fingers grappled with the Yale, and finally with the help of the wind the door blew in and a glass fell at the end of the passage — a glass of dead flowers — and water dripped quickly onto the floor. At first she had not seen her mother; the man had gone from the kitchen and Mona assumed they had gone upstairs to continue their moments of reparation.

So Mona had begun to unwrap the meat before she saw the blood; in fact it was when she was about to throw the plastic wrapping into the rubbish bin that her eyes lit on the dark expanding pool. And before the horror had fully struck her her first thought had been that the body contains eight pints of blood — a gallon — and that this is what will now run over the floor, sink into the cracks of the lino, make everything red and slimy. Yes, he had slit her throat with the kitchen knife and left the body curled up in a heap, half-hidden by the piece of oil cloth that dripped down over the back of the table.

But the years had now passed. That murder had just become another legend in the estate, one of the many legends of killings and rapings. The football pitch, which had once been a place of recreation, had now become a graveyard for the people who died daily of diseases brought on by malnutrition and were bundled into the ground. There were thousands of dogs who crowded the 'funerals' and who, when night came, dug up the corpses and ate them. Soon the people had ceased to care and left the bodies unburied for the scavengers. Everyone pretended they had not eaten human flesh.

And what of Mona?

After her mother's murder the madman had disappeared and was never found — no doubt he had holed up with some other lonely woman. Mona had left school and gone to work in a better off estate ten miles nearer the city, as a hairdresser's assistant. She had continued to live in the same house which was now neat and tidy, the roof well patched and the gutters straightened. She had no friends and seldom went out after dark. But as the years passed and the country fell more and more deeply into the well of poverty her job folded and for want of something to do she took over the old hardware shop and turned it into an establishment of her own. Nobody could pay, so Mona accepted anything they could offer, from watercress — which still proliferated in the hills — to bits of food stolen from the inner suburbs or raided from the shops that had managed to survive the 'starving eighties'.

People would do anything to get their hair fixed by Mona; it was the only entertainment left to them; women, men and children flocked in happy to queue for hours, their absent expressions momentarily lit by narcissistic anticipation. Yes, there was nothing for them to do; the revolution that everyone had hoped for had never evolved. The only way in which they might have expressed themselves would have been to fight the gangs of vigilantes who held the city in a grip of violence. But that would have meant a long trek into town and people were too underfed to face it. So Mona cut and dyed and permed from nine to six; the mathematician in her enjoyed the definition of a pleasant hair-do. She had grown gaunt, like her mother, and she was a strange sight behind her broken windows as she measured and sized up individual hairs. She would assess the sweep of a customer's locks with the same fixed expression in her eyes as that which her mother had used to pin down her menfriends.

The smell from the football pitch would waft in from outside while people admired their reflections in the mirror; at times the purple fissures and cracks enhanced or disguised their gaunt features, their hollow eye-sockets or their sagging skin.

Mona didn't care about all this but she cared, oh so deeply about her own expertise; if a person moved his head suddenly she'd get into a stifling rage. One day, she knew, she would kill one of her customers with the scissors, she would murder them as cold-bloodedly and as bloodily as her mother had been murdered; she'd clip them up inch by inch, first the ears, then she'd shove the scissors up their nostrils and so on and so forth.

JOHN MORROW

(1930-)

from: SECTS AND OTHER STORIES (1987)

[Much of John Morrow's fiction is characterized by humour, street energy, and brass-tack sentiment, but it runs the risk of self-congratulation and of allowing a colloquial verve to become a colloquial vision of life. Yet 'Lonely Heart' is an impressive story by anyone's standards and bears comparison with the work of Frank O'Connor. It uses the 'envelope' or 'flashback sandwich' device to great effect, establishing the irony of Tommy Woods's fatuous death during World War II, his having survived the Great War and — after an odd involvement — the Easter Rising in Dublin. The marginalized victim of the twentieth century (and therefore one of the 'submerged populations' O'Connor considered primary subjects for the short story), Lonely Heart was at the heart of recent Irish history, a fact unknown to himself and to others — as Ulster Volunteer, British soldier in France, and execution squad member after the Easter Rising. Attention to the story's chronology reveals that Tommy Woods helped the British authorities execute Easter rebel leaders on Wednesday 3 May: on that day were executed Thomas MacDonagh, Patrick Pearse and Thomas J. Clarke, the latter presumably the grey-haired man Tommy sees in his sights, first subscriber to the Proclamation of the Provisional Government of the Irish Republic.]

LONELY HEART

One blacked-out evening in January 1944 a jeep-load of drunk Yanks mounted the pavement alongside the one-and-ninepenny queue at the Ritz cinema and squashed him dead against a blind lamp-post. At the moment it happened the one-and-ninepennies began to move in, so when a joint patrol of Yank MPs and British red-caps came on the scene minutes later there were no witnesses bar the jeep's cargo, and they were paralytic.[1] When the British red-caps saw, by flashlight, that the broken heap lying at the base of the bent lamp wore a khaki greatcoat with a British lance-jack's stripe on the sleeve, they wanted to kill the cargo, or at least the driver, there and then. The Yank MPs, naturally, wouldn't hear tell of it. Angry words were exchanged, lead-loaded flashlights brandished, gun butts fondled in dark confusion. Only the arrival of a civilian policeman saved the incident from developing into something really nasty. Turning the heap over with his toe, he said: 'Och sure, it's only oul Lonely Heart. He's a busker, a shell-shock case.' And they saw then that the greatcoat was faded and threadbare, and that the right hand still clutched a battered mouth-organ. One of the red-caps, a long service man, noted that the few remaining buttons on the greatcoat bore the insignia of the Horse Artillery and remarked to himself the incongruity between this and the crossed rifles of a marksman on one sleeve: damn few of those in the horse-guns.

The legally necessary post-mortem on the remains of Thomas Woods, known as Lonely Heart to generations of cinemagoers, was held the next day. One thing brought to light was a fragment of a German dum-dum bullet which had been wandering around in his puddings for twenty-eight years. Giving evidence at the coroner's inquest, the city pathologist said that the deceased must have lived in almost continual torment. The coroner declared that it showed again just how beastly the Boche[2] were, recorded a verdict of accidental death, and the one hungover newsman present came away with the impression that Lonely Heart, writhing in agony, had fallen in front of the jeep. Those responsible for inter-allied harmony in the city heaved a sigh of relief.

People read about his death, and about the dum-dum nagging away all those years, like a grain of sand in a barren oyster, and their sadness was tinged with remorse. Lonely Heart had been a case, a character on a par with 'Andy Gump', 'Oily Boke', 'Skin-the-goat'; all tattered derelicts who prowled the city, minds turned by war, drink, love or, in the case of one who lectured pigeons on the Customs House steps, 'The Books'. They'd called him lonely Heart because he had never been known to play anything other than the mournful dirge 'I

1. MPs are Military Police; paralytic means 'very drunk'.

2. Derogatory slang for 'German soldiers'.

Wandered Today to the Hills, Maggie', his appearance at the head of a cinema queue the signal for a chorus of cheerful abuse and a barrage of small missiles. And through it all he had played his dirge, the mouth-organ in one hand and his extended cap, clinking, in the other.

His funeral column was the longest in living memory in his home district. At the cemetery the laid-out wreaths covered a dozen graves on either side of the waiting pit, most of them from people who had never known his proper name ... 'For Lonely Heart — from the girls in Murray's snuff room'.

But there was one other, a small spray placed far back and almost hidden behind a neighbouring headstone, which puzzled those few of the mourners who noticed it when, after the service, they made the traditional tour of the tributes to make sure their florist hadn't welshed.

'For Shooter,' the card on the spray said. 'Quis Separabit'.[3]

Tommy Woods had been a gunner in the Horse Artillery. Unlike most of his Belfast contemporaries in the Ulster volunteers (Carson's Army)[4] — Hostilities Only men — he was a regular and had been one of the first on French soil in 1914, retreating from Mons almost as fast as the contemptible Field Marshal French[5] himself. When the armies were bogged down in trench warfare in 1915 Tommy was unhorsed and given a rifle, and it was as an infantryman near Ypres in early 1916 that he stopped the German dum-dum with his guts. They managed to extract most of the fragments in the field hospital, after which Tommy was sent to a rest camp near Abbeville to convalesce.

He had been courting a girl called Aggie Gamble on and off since they had been half-timers at the mill school together, and they had corresponded regularly since his enlistment. They had talked of marriage, but always as a post-war happening — until the wound. Aggie's letters suddenly became very torrid and peremptory: all her friends were getting married; she was nearly twenty — she'd be left on the shelf; she'd heard of 'Blighty wounds' — surely Tommy's was one; an Easter wedding would be nice ... Tommy applied for leave in February, it was granted on the first week in March and Aggie set in train arrangements for them to be married on the Thursday of Easter week.

And so, in the early morning of Tuesday the 25th of April, 1916, Tommy Woods stood in a crowd of other happy 'Blighty Ones' at the rail of the Holyhead-Kingstown[6] ferry as the gangplank thumped onto Irish cobbles. He could see the Belfast train lying just up the wharf, steaming on the leash, welcoming doors gaping. He also noticed a hobnailed scurry of military activity on and around the wharf — but being wartime, that was only to be expected. One of the returning warriors made a joke about 'Fireside Fusiliers' and Tommy, full of beery euphoria, was still laughing as he clattered down the gangplank ... his last laugh ever. He had one foot on the cobbles when a hand fell on his shoulder. Its owner was a middleaged Sergeant of the Dublin Fusiliers, very white-faced and nervous. 'Thanks be to Christ, an artilleryman!' he cried, thumping Tommy's shoulder. 'Tell us, do you know anything about eighteen-pounders?'

'Aye, but what ...' Tommy stuttered.

'Never mind,' said the Sergeant. 'Come with me.'

He started to drag Tommy by the arm across the wharf in the direction of some army lorries. The Belfast train made shunting noises, its doors banging impatiently. Tommy found his tongue. 'Here ... hi ... that's my train,' he fairly yelled, wrenching free from the Sergeant and hoking[7] in his tunic pocket for paybook and leave pass. 'I'm getting married the day after —'

The Sergeant took hold of Tommy by the webbing with one hand and half-drew a revolver from its holster on his belt with the other. 'She'll have to wait,' he said through his teeth, close to Tommy's face. 'Everything'll have to wait. If Christ himself walked up that harbour this minute and knew one end of an eighteen-pounder from the other he'd be up on that wagon double quick or I'd blow his fuckin' head off. Jump!'

3. Who Shall Separate? The Latin words are the motto of the Royal Irish Rifles.
4. The Ulster Volunteer Force, Northern unionists who organized themselves to resist Home Rule, became part of the British army when hostilities broke out in Europe in 1914. Sir Edward Carson (1854-1935) was the leader of the unionist cause.
5. John Denton Pinkstone French (1852-1925) commanded the British expeditionary force in France and Belgium 1914-15.
6. Kingstown was renamed Dun Laoghaire on Irish independence. 'Blighty ones' were troops sent home to England (Blighty) because of a slight wound.
7. Searching with a burrowing action (Northern Ireland dialect).

Tommy jumped. He had seen men like the Sergeant at that stage of hysteria before and he knew it was either jump or be crippled. The authority of such men rested on sincere presentation of stark choices.

For part of the way along the Dublin road the lorry ran abreast of the Belfast train. Then road and line parted company and Tommy felt as though his stomach was about to fall out. 'Cheer up,' said the Sergeant, shoving a lit Woodbine[8] between Tommy's lips. 'The day after tomorrow, is it? Sure you could be on the evening train. They brought up four eighteen-pounders from Athlone[9] this morning. They'll soon winkle the bastards out.'

He took it for granted that Tommy had heard of the Sinn Fein rising, which he hadn't. It wasn't until long after the event that its true nature dawned on him, and then only as part of the long dream sequence his past life had become, a brief illumination in the fog behind him, quickly snuffed.

As the lorry clattered through deserted suburban streets and the familiar boom of eighteen-pounders and the fitful sparkle of small arms grew louder, Tommy barely noticed. He was thinking of Aggie. She'd be leaving work today. The girls in the mill would truss her up with hanks of flax, daub her face with loom grease and wheel her around the streets in a trolley, chanting:

Here comes the bride
Forty inches wide
See how she wobbles
Her big backside ...

The lorry stopped close to the roar of guns. The Sergeant screamed: 'Out!' and they dropped off the tailboard and ran crouching behind a wall beside a river. Two eighteen-pounders at either flank of a wide bridge ... black-faced gunners training and laying. As Tommy and the Sergeant reached the nearest gun it fired. Tommy swivelled to look and saw a wide street of tall buildings with, in the centre, tallest of all, a thin pillar, masonry crumbling. 'Close, fuck yis,' howled a Bombardier. 'Mind what the General said, knock the one-eyed matelot down an' yis are all on a fizzer!'[10]

The Sergeant thrust Tommy forward and shouted into the Bombardier's ear. The Bombardier glared at Tommy's cap badge and growled: 'Christ! The galloping peashooters, that's all I needed. Come on, King Billy[11] — at least you'll be no worse than the huer[12] on the breech. I've been waitin' for his sporran an' bollocks to go scatterin' up Sackville Street.' A private of the Black Watch staggered to the rear and Tommy took his place. 'Prime ... load ... brush ... fire!' And so began the waking nightmare of Tommy's life.

For two days he stoked the gun, with brief respites for bully and char[13] and, once, champagne and cold chicken from the kitchen of a wrecked hotel. The air was still and the smoke and fumes hung around them, growing thicker by the hour, turning day into night and night into a small room containing the gun and themselves, lit spasmodically by muzzle flame.

Once, during a lull whilst ammunition was brought up, Tommy wandered out of the stour[14] and over to the parapet of the river bank. It was night time. Across the stretch of flame-tinted water the big street burned. A four-storied shell glowed like a Hallowe'en turnip and then, as he watched, collapsed like an old gas-mantle. But the one-eyed matelot still posed on his pillar, and that was all the Bombardier cared about. 'Come away ar' that, King Billy, and lave that river alone.'

The rest spells became more frequent throughout Wednesday, and at dusk the word came to stand down — they'd run out of ammo. Most of the crews dropped where they stood, asleep before they hit the ground. The Bombardier came across Tommy sitting on a shell box, curled up in a knot, heaving silently, holding what had been a khaki handkerchief over his mouth; it was now sopping red. 'Jasus! Is it the lung rot ye have?' asked the Bombardier, slapping his back. 'You should have spoke up. That cordite's a bastard.'

Tommy managed to explain that the blood was from his stomach, not his lungs; they'd told him this might happen, and not to worry. The Bombardier went away and came back with two thick horse blankets. He wrapped Tommy from head to toe like a cigar and, lifting him bodily, carried him to one of

8. A brand of cigarette, popular with the working class.
9. A town in the centre of Ireland.
10. The 'one-eyed matelot' is Horatio Nelson atop a pillar in Dublin's Sackville (now O'Connell) Street; 'on a fizzer' means 'in serious trouble'.
11. That is, 'you protestant Ulsterman' (after King William of Orange).
12. Pejorative Irish term: colloquial for 'whore'.
13. Canned corned beef and tea.
14. Commotion, turmoil (Scottish dialect).

the waiting lorries. Stretched in the back, blanket-cowled head on his pack, Tommy didn't hear the engine start up or feel one jolt of the cobbled journey.

He awoke in familiar surroundings. He lay on a low camp-cot between two high hospital beds, all around him the muted hubbub of an early morning ward: a steady base of groaning and coughing overlaid by the clanking of utensils, the scurry and squeak of orderlies' feet, the raised voices of nurses. An RAMC[15] stretcher party picked its way through rows of cots down the centre of the ward. For a dazed moment Tommy thought he was back in Abbeville; then everything came back to him ... Aggie.

'How are ye now, Rip Van Winkle?'

A Belfast voice, issuing from a hairy face with Woodbine attached, framed in bandages, glaring over the edge of the bed to his right.

'What time is it?' asked Tommy.

'Eight o'clock or thereabouts. The way you've been snorin' you should be askin' the day, not the time.'

Tommy thought back frantically, heart in mouth. 'It's Thursday,' he said.

The man wheezed joyfully. 'There y'are! ... Rip Van Winkle. They gave you a quare dose of somethin' when they carted you in. You've slep the clock roun' an' then some. It's bloody Friday mornin', an' if you don't believe me, just take a whiff ... bloody fish! They start boilin' it at the scrake[16] of dawn so's all the good'll be out of it by dinner hour. Fenian bastards! Here, where are you off to?'

Tommy was pulling on his trousers. Luckily they had piled his clothes and pack, army fashion, beside the cot. 'Home,' he replied, 'as soon as I can get a train.'

'They'll niver let ye.'

'They'll never notice, if I know anything about these places.'

Neither they did, all their attention being taken up at that moment with an intake of wounded from the field stations. Tommy pushed his way through a jam of bearers and stretchers and cadged a lift in an ambulance that left him off not far from Amiens Street station.

The city lay under a haze of smoke from the fires of Sackville Street. From there still arose an incessant rattle of machine-gun and rifle fire. But the vicinity of Amiens Street was quiet enough as Tommy hurried towards the station. In the almost deserted entrance hall he asked a railwayman about trains for Belfast. 'No civvies or leave men,' was the reply, 'only goods and troops-in-transit.'

Nevertheless, Tommy ran towards the platforms — and into the Dubliner Sergeant, who now wore the red armband of an RTO[17] ... 'King Billy! I heard you were in hospital. When's that weddin' of yours?'

'Yesterday,' said Tommy. 'And I want home as soon as I can get. They say it's all troops-in-transit.'

The Sergeant, suddenly grim-faced, again laid hold of Tommy by the webbing and started running him towards a train that was making its first jerky shunts out of platform one. He shouted in Tommy's ear: 'Say you're attached to the Sherwoods. Give my name ... McKenna.'

Sergeant McKenna wrenched open the door of the last carriage and heaved Tommy in and across the legs of twelve tired Sherwood Foresters. They cursed, but none queried him and he settled on the floor for the long journey home. He tried to think. Aggie, the whole thing a bloody shambles. What'll her people say? But no matter how hard he tried he couldn't grasp the fragments, and the harder he tried the worse his guts ached; like ducking for apples in a bucket; wits gun-scrambled. He'd seen it too often in others.

It was late afternoon when Tommy marched up Railway Street to his own house. The train had crawled all the way because of the danger of derailment by the rebels. In the hallway of the house he met two of Aggie's six brothers coming, one a sailor on leave, the other a shipyardman. Without speaking they launched themselves at Tommy, knocking him back through the front door. The neighbours, who had been watching from behind curtains, swarmed into the street and managed to drag the berserk brothers off him, but not before the sailor had cracked the toe of his boot on Tommy's ear and the shipyardman had planted his clog, several times, in his gut.

His father and brother carried Tommy into the

15. Royal Army Medical Corps.
16. crack (Northern Ireland dialect).
17. Railway Transport Officer.

house while the neighbours saw off the still belligerent Gambles. Tommy's guts were on fire and the blood started coming again. The doctor was sent for, and being ex-army himself and knowing something of the ways of wandering foreign bodies he prescribed coagulant and a sleeping draught. In the meantime Tommy had been told that Aggie, ashamed to face her mates at the mill, had left on the Liverpool boat the previous night. Mercifully, the draught combined with the residue of that given to him in Dublin knocked him out almost immediately.

On Saturday Tommy awoke as the person he was to be for the rest of his days. The family were puzzled. He talked to them quite cogently, about France, about his wound — but never a mention of Aggie, or of the happenings in Dublin. Still, he seemed to be well enough physically considering, and very placid in himself, so they thought it a 'wee kink' that would pass.

Tommy stayed in bed, sleeping most of the time, until Tuesday morning. Then he got up, washed, shaved and polished his boots. His ten-day pass included travelling time, so his return warrant was made out for the five-thirty train to Dublin that day (though there would be no connecting boat from Kingstown until Wednesday morning). At two o'clock his father and brother accompanied him to the Crown bar opposite the station, and between then and train time all three made fair inroads on Tommy's wedding money — so much so that when train time came the Da, footless and maudlin, was unable to cross the road to see Tommy off, and the brother wasn't far behind him. Tommy had matched them drink for drink, but he marched to the train stone sober. Throughout the drunken garrulity of the afternoon no mention had been made of Aggie or the wedding. Afterwards, the brother said that Tommy had been so strangely calm he had been afraid to say or do anything that might draw blood.

Before the train drew to a halt in Amiens Street Tommy saw Sergeant McKenna on the platform. He appeared to be on the look-out for someone, scanning faces at the window of each carriage as it passed. He spotted Tommy. 'How's me oul son? Come on down an' have a cuppa char. You've plenty of time, there's no boat the night.'

Tommy followed the sergeant to an RTO hut at the end of the platform. They had the place to themselves. The sergeant put a kettle on a coke stove and said: 'I've been wondering how you got on. What about the weddin'?'

At this point he had his back to Tommy, poking the stove to get a flame. When no reply came he turned and faced him. At first Tommy looked puzzled, then his eyes closed tightly and he moved his head slowly from side to side. He held his big square hands clasped to front, the thumbs circling one another frantically, clockwise then counter clockwise. They reminded the sergeant of mice on a treadmill.

The tea when it came was twenty-five per cent Power's whiskey, causing Tommy's guts to burn pleasurably. 'Rest easy, lad,' said the sergeant. 'I've a billet for you the night and we'll get you down to Kingstown in good time for the morning boat.'

After the tea they went to a nearby pub and the sergeant ordered hot whiskies. The place was packed with troops, a rag-tag-and-bobtail of all the units in Ireland plus a few press-gang jobs like Tommy. Tommy sat at the bar while the sergeant circulated, quartering the company with an appraising eye. When he rejoined Tommy there were two men with him, one an elderly corporal of the South Staffords and the other a youthful private in the Irish Rifles who hailed from Cullybackey, a raw looking ganch.[18]

More hot whiskies, which the Cullybackey man threw into the flat remains of his pint. The sergeant went off on another tour, and after they'd been talking for a while Tommy noticed that both men wore crossed rifles on the sleeves of their tunics, the insignia of a marksman. When he commented on this, the Stafford corporal said: 'That's why we're drinking whiskey instead of beer, mate.'

'Aye mon, we're the boys for the job!' cried the ganch, spitting on his hands and slapping them together.

'What's the job?' asked Tommy.

The ganch started to reply, but the corporal caught him by the arm and said authoritatively: 'If the sergeant wants him to know he'll tell him soon enough.' The ganch winked conspiratorially.

When the sergeant returned again he had another man in tow, a Cameronian. Tommy looked at his sleeve . . . crossed rifles. He waited until the three marksmen were engaged in a separate conversation and then broached the subject.

18. An uncouth fellow (Northern Ireland dialect).

'What's the job?'

McKenna hesitated for a moment, pondering. Then he said: 'I was going to tell you. That's why I kept a look-out at the train. But then. . . .'

Tommy sensed what he meant, though even now Amiens Street and the RTO hut seemed years behind him. Now was a clear circle in the fog that closed rapidly at his back and swirled impenetrably a yard in front of his face.

'I'm all right now,' he said.

'You're not, not near it,' growled the sergeant. 'But then who in the name of Christ is. I'll tell you, but under your hat, mind.'

He told Tommy, briefly, the nature of the job.

'How many?' asked Tommy.

'Thirty ... three tens ... one apiece,' sighed McKenna. 'And hard enough to scrape up when the huer-in-charge wants them all crossed rifle wallahs.'[19]

'How many do you need still?'

'Three.'

'What about me? I'll do it for you.'

The sergeant doffed his cap and took something from the inside band. He laid it on the bar between them, a khaki patch embroidered with crossed rifles. 'There's not many of them in the Horse Guns, but the bastard'll never notice. Are you sure now?'

'I'm your man,' said Tommy, and pocketed the patch.

They visited two other pubs that night and Sergeant McKenna got rid of the last two patches from his cap band. He also had a needle and thread in the cap band, and in the packed lorry on the way to the billet he affixed the patches to the appropriate sleeves by the light of a carbide lamp. Tommy stood and looked out over the cab of the lorry as they ran in under a lighted archway to the billet. He saw a name carved in the stone above the archway but couldn't make it out in the dark.

Almost the next thing he remembered was a hand on his shoulder and McKenna's voice saying: 'Stand to. Up you get, oul son.'

It was still dark. In the dim gaslight, only two small mantles at either end of the long barrack hut, hungover men struggled into cold-stiff uniforms. On the bed next to Tommy's the Cullybackey ganch spewed noisily into an enamel bucket. Sergeant McKenna and two corporals roved around like sheep-dogs, snapping at the heels of each man until he was ready and on his way to the square outside. At the door each was handed a rifle from a rack of thirty.

In the square they formed up and dressed off in a single line. After being inspected by the 'huer-in-charge', a young captain, they formed twos and then wheeled into six lines of fives. The paired lines were designated squads one, two and three; Tommy was in number two, rear rank. By this time one side of the sky was beginning to lighten.

'Number one squad, stand fast! Number two and three squads, dismiss!'

The corporals shepherded the dismissed men to a hut in the corner of the square in which there was a tea urn and a tray of wads.[20] Tommy drew himself a mug of tea, but didn't feel hungry. He noticed that very few touched the wads. From the hut window he watched number one squad being inspected again by the captain; a rifle was found wanting and another fetched; the bamboo cane flicked a piece of maladjusted webbing and Sergeant McKenna adjusted it; the encroaching light erased the last weak stars from the patch of sky bounded by the high roofs of the prison blocks. The sergeant's commands to move out were subdued. The squad marched off and disappeared around the corner of the main block.

'Any minute now. They don't keep you waiting,' whispered a man beside Tommy. It was so quiet inside and out that Tommy could hear the first chirruping of sparrows. The two corporals stood on either side of the hut door, facing inwards, scanning the company and drawing nervously on cupped fags. It was full daylight now.

The crash of the volley cannoned wildly in the square, sending hordes of sparrows hurling skywards from the high eaves. Tommy saw the fag drop from a corporal's hand as he crossed himself. From down the hut came the thud and rattle of a body, rifle and tea-mug hitting the earthen floor: the ganch had fainted.

There was a lot of noise after that. The corporals pounced on the prostrate ganch and hauled him onto a bench. Everyone crowded around and everyone seemed to be shouting. The Catholic corporal

19. Wallahs are fellows engaged in some capacity. The word is Anglo-Indian.

20. Buns or small cakes sold in forces' canteens.

kept slapping the ganch's face and screaming, 'Wake up, you thick bastard!' Then Sergeant McKenna was amongst them, pushing, using his fists, bellowing. The men fell back and shut up — all except the corporal, who still screeched and lashed at the horizontal ganch. McKenna signalled to the other corporal and then took an arm apiece and ran him out of the hut. Some of the men managed to get the ganch sitting upright and poured tea down his throat. He awoke choking and immediately went into a bout of violent sobbing. When McKenna and the corporal returned, McKenna lifted the ganch's rifle off the floor, handed it to the corporal and shouted: 'Number two squad — fall in.'

'Just my bloody luck,' growled the corporal, opening the breech to check the barrel for dust.

The sergeant stood at the door of the hut and patted each man on the shoulder as he passed. Tommy looked at him as the hand fell, but it was as if the sergeant didn't see him, his lips forming the word 'seven'.

The captain was tall, thin and droop-moustached; a young Kitchener.[21] He was the first officer Tommy had seen wearing a sword. Everything was to his liking until he came to the corporal, who had taken the ganch's place beside Tommy in the rear rank. He tapped the corporal's right sleeve with his cane and said: 'This man is not a marksman, sergeant.'

'Sah. We had a bit —'

'Report to me at stand down, sergeant. Carry on.'

'Squad . . . left turn. By the left, quick march.'

They rounded the corner of the main block and entered a narrow tunnel, the crash of hobnails deafening. Emerging into daylight, they were halted almost at once, the front two men close to a high wall.

'Left turn. Order arms.'

Tommy could see that they were drawn up at one end of a narrow yard, cramped between high walls, but not much else because of the tall fellow in front.

'Front rank — one pace forward. Front rank — kneel.'

He saw, at twenty paces, a sand-bagged wall and a black-painted post. Just then the captain emerged from a door on the left of the yard, followed by two sergeant-majors with silver-knobbed canes clamped under their oxters,[22] marching on either side of a small man in dark trousers and a white shirt.

'Rear rank — port arms.'

When the little procession reached the black post, one of the S-Ms pulled the man's arms around the back of it and the other knelt in front. Tommy saw that there were straps on the post, one to circle his body, the other his legs. As they were doing this the captain stood facing the man and appeared to be reading something to him from a piece of paper. Their job done, the S-Ms marched back through the door. The captain finished his reading and fell back to take up position beside the squad.

Tommy could see the man clearly now. He had long grey hair that fell down over his ears. His eyes were closed and his lips were moving. Tommy could hear the drone of his voice in the drum of the killing alley, but indistinctly, as though very far away. . . .

The captain's sword slid from its scabbard. He gave the orders now.

'Squad — load.'

Working the rifle bolt, Tommy kept his eyes on the man. His lips were still moving and his eyes were open now.

'Squad — present.'

It was the heaviest weapon he had ever hefted. His left arm started to tremble and he had difficulty centring on the white shirt . . . steady the Buffs[23] . . . what the hell was keeping him? Tommy raised his eye from the sighting line to the man's face. He was still talking.

'Fire!'

Most of the white shirt vanished; the head slumped, grey hair spilling forward. The corporal beside Tommy dropped his rifle and clasped his ears, face twisted in agony. Tommy didn't hear it fall because he was stone deaf: the noise in the enclosed space had been shattering. McKenna moved to the front of the squad and made gestures as he shouted the commands to retire. The return march through the tunnel was a shambles. As he left the yard, out of the corner of his eye Tommy saw the captain remove plugs from his ears before

21. Earl Kitchener (British war minister 1914-16) featured in a famous World War I recruiting poster.

22. armpits.

23. A once popular quotation from Rudyard Kipling's 'The Story of the Gadsbys' (1888) and uttered by Kipling's captain hero as a self-exhortation and warning. (The Buffs were the East Kent Regiment.)

moving towards the post, unholstering his pistol as he went. And he wondered if the talking man had known that the captain's ears were plugged.

For the twenty minutes or so it took number three squad to do its work, Tommy sat in the back of a lorry with the nine members of number two squad. Number one squad was sealed in a lorry alongside, another awaited number three. Their kits had already been loaded; all were for the boat, whether they wanted to or not. Curiously, no one talked or even smoked until the muffled crash of the third volley; then matches flared and voices were raised in obscene complaint about being shipped out without as much as a by-your-leave, and without as much as a decent breakfast. Presently number three squad marched out and the convoy set off for Kingstown, Sergeant McKenna riding with number two squad.

At Kingstown the sergeant stood at the bottom of the gangplank and counted-off the men as they embarked. When his hand fell on Tommy's shoulder, Tommy paused and turned to face him.

'What was that fella talking about, sergeant?' he asked.

'Damn all of interest to the likes of you or me,' McKenna replied testily. 'An' for Christ's sake remember to take that patch off your sleeve before you report to depot. Damn few of them in the Horse Guns.'

But Tommy never did remember; and nobody noticed until one blacked-out evening twenty-eight years later, when a jeep-load of drunk Yanks mounted the pavement alongside the one-and-ninepennies at the Ritz.

JENNIFER JOHNSTON

(1930-)

from: THE CAPTAINS AND THE KINGS (1972)

[In this passage from the opening chapter of the novel, we see the beginning of the tender relationship between the young catholic boy from the village and the widowed Charles Prendergast, a rather enfeebled member of the old ascendancy class. The decay of his house and of his life and the squalid village environment and mentality conspire together to make the relationship impossible. Nevertheless, it develops, it struggles into existence and not even its extinction can deny its truth. As usual with Jennifer Johnston, the class lines are sharply drawn. A faded culture stares at the grocers' republic that has replaced it. This is one of the many novels of contemporary Ireland in which the Big House theme, dating from the nineteenth century, resumes an unexpected and anomalous life.]

CHAPTER ONE

... It was late May. The few remaining daffodils that fringed the avenue were turning brown and papery. The leaves were curling at the top. The early rose bushes in Clare's formal beds were covered in buds, which would begin to open with another couple of days' sun.

Since Nellie's death almost six months before, Mr. Prendergast had taken to living more or less completely in the study. Books on the tables (where his father used to display his adequate collection of duelling pistols), on some chairs even and also in piles on the faded Chinese carpet. The piano sat in the middle of the room and in one corner there was a divan that he and Sean had carried from upstairs, in case of some unmentionable need. The two long windows faced south-west across the terrace at the wooded hills, and behind them the gaunt blue mountains constantly changed from one elusive colour to another. As the evening thickened, he would sit in his chair by the window and watch the green quivering lights spring up across the valley as people lit their lamps, and the moving fingers of light from cars on the main road below. It was almost his only pleasurable connection with the world. He would drink his first evening glass of whiskey as he watched and then, when he rose and crossed the room to switch on his own lights, he would refill his glass and settle down to read for the rest of the evening.

During the last few months of Clare's illness he had formed the habit of driving down to the church to play the organ. As the house became enclosed by the half light each evening, he had become obsessed by her eyes. For four months she had lain, propped up by pillows, in her bed, one side of her face pulled down into a sour little grin, her right arm useless, a cashmere shawl covering her thin shoulders. He would arrive in her room each afternoon as the clock on her mantelpiece chimed three and, picking up whatever book happened to be at hand, he would sit in the wing chair and read to her for an hour. The book was then closed and put away. He would move to the end of the bed and force himself to smile down at her.

'Anything you want, my dear?'

One eye stared coldly up at him, the other drooped as if in sleep.

'You're looking a little better today. Quite distinctly better. Have you up and about soon. Come the summer and you'll be out enjoying the garden again.'

He would bow and leave the room. He found it all most disconcerting, almost disagreeable. The memory of her eyes stayed with him until he left the house and drowned such thoughts in the vast chords of Bach.

He played the organ more often in the daytime now, as he found his eyes were giving him trouble in electric light. It was time he took himself to the oculist for new glasses but he preferred to live without them than make the journey to Dublin and back. From the moment of his marriage to Clare until his mother's death, his life had been spent in continuous movement. He had never stopped anywhere long enough to become accustomed to its rhythm. The moment a feeling of familiarity began to creep over him, or a new acquaintance seemed to have the audacity to be becoming a friend, then the trunks were packed, servants dismissed, tickets booked. They would move on. Clare's only pregnancy had been an irritating hiatus in his life. They had returned to sit it out with her family in North Oxford.

The atmosphere had affronted him. The roads upon roads of red brick, high-gabled houses, the smell of newly cut grass, the politesse over tea cups, the indestructible goodwill of the English middle-class. After several weeks he had gone upstairs one afternoon and packed a suitcase.

'What are you doing?'

Clare had arrived home early from her daily walk.

'It should be obvious.'

'Are you going away?'

'Yes.'

He was embarrassed by the situation.

'I, ah, feel I'm wasting my time here. I thought I'd have a look at Sicily. Perhaps get in a few music festivals round the place.'

'You could go up to concerts in London from here.'

Her eyes dazzled with tears. He looked away from her, continued to pile neatly folded shirts one upon the other. 'I'm sorry, Clare. I can't stay here.'

'What will I say to mother? She'll think it's all most peculiar.'

'Say anything you like.'

Silently she watched him fasten his suitcase.

'You would have gone before I came home?'

He nodded.

'It would have been easier.'

'For you perhaps.'

'Quite.'

He picked up his case and leant forward to kiss her formally. 'Well, goodbye, my dear.'

She moved her head out of his reach. 'I don't understand.'

He ignored this. 'You'll be perfectly all right. After all, what could I do?'

After their daughter's birth they moved on again, leaving the child in the care of both her grandmothers. Neither lady had anything in common, apart from Sarah. Even this, they felt, wasn't a strong enough reason for them to become involved in the exhausting processes of communication, so the child shuttled between them, in the care of a good, old-fashioned nanny who knew her place and stood no nonsense, either from children or interfering adults.

Her parents made it their business to visit Sarah at least once a year. They made responsible decisions about her education. They followed her scholastic career with interest and a certain amount of pride. She was a clever child. They sent her presents, not extravagant, for they were not flamboyant people, but interesting, sometimes beautiful, objects from every corner of the earth.

The war caught them in Mexico, where they stayed for a couple of years and then moved on to the United States. There they continued their nomadic life until the war was over. In 1946 they came cautiously back to Europe to find tired people desperately trying to build a new world. It seemed, at that time, as if it might be going to be a world in which there would be very little place for people like the Prendergasts.

One evening, as they sat in North Oxford surrounded by bleak post-war people and problems, ration books and a scarcity of domestics, a telegram arrived to say that the old lady was dead. She was being driven to dine with some friends by her man, Sean. Snow lay thinly on the higher hills and the roads between the black hedges sparkled with frost. Sean, exhilarated by a drop too much before setting out, drove just too fast on to an icy patch and the car went into a skid. They went off the left-hand side of the road into the ditch and hit a telegraph pole. Sean was unhurt but the old lady was dead. Her ringed hands were clasped, as usual, in her lap but her neck was broken. There was no sound anywhere but the humming of the telegraph wires and the drop of snow falling from the branches of the trees.

Surprisingly, they settled down. They didn't mix much; in fact, withdrew gently but firmly from the social ramifications created by the past. Clare and Sean had taken at once to each other and had thrown themselves, for their own different reasons, into the re-shaping of the old lady's garden. Mr. Prendergast took to reading. He wandered through books as he had wandered through the world, never quite grasping what it really was that he was looking for. He never read one at a time, always a pile were tumbled by his chair or bed. He roamed from author to author, century to century, prose, poetry, biography, essays, philosophy, history. He read, with fluency, books in French and struggled through German ones. Parcels arrived regularly from London and Dublin and he would tear the paper off like a impatient child and then carry the books into the study, where he would pick one of them at random, almost throw himself into a chair and start reading.

For pleasure, he played the piano. As a young man he had had reasonable talent but through the travelling years he had played little and his fingers had stiffened, and he played now with more than average skill but with caution.

Sarah intruded seldom. When her grandmother died she had been in her last term at school. Her hair lay in two plaits on her grey uniform coat. Her face was like marble, white and still.

'So, you're off.'

Clare seemed to flutter in the hall behind him, like a moth in a cobweb.

'We haven't had much time for conversation. You've never told us why you've picked on Cambridge.'

'I thought it was time for a change of scene.' She wasted no words.

'We, ah, your mother and I have decided to stay on here for a while. At any rate. Straighten things up. We actually thought we might settle down here.'

'Oh.'

'You wouldn't think of . . .?'

She shook her head. 'No. I think not.'

'Your mother, perhaps. . . .'

Sarah looked briefly across his shoulder in her mother's direction. 'I think we'll all manage all right.' They kissed each other's cheeks. She went down the steps and got into the waiting taxi. The way she moved reminded him of his mother.

In order to keep the house alive old Mrs. Prendergast had sold the land, hills, fields, bogland and wood to men who had been her husband's tenants and labourers. She watched with ironic eyes the golden and purple weed flowers creeping up through the corn as the years passed and barbed wire filling the gaps in walls. To keep himself and Clare alive, Mr. Prendergast had closed the house room by room, floor by floor. Rows of unused keys hung on the wall by the kitchen door, under the coiled and silent bell springs. Only Nellie remained, indoors, and Sean, in the garden. After several years the book parcels dwindled and finally stopped altogether. Now he was alone and, it seemed to him, the way that he had always wanted to be.

Approaching nine o'clock and after his third glass of whiskey, the old man found his eyes sore and heavy and he threw his book down on the floor by his chair. He watched, for a moment, a furious fly beating himself against the window, bewildered by what seemed to be the sudden solidification of the air. He pushed himself out of the chair with a certain amount of trouble and went over to the piano. He sat pulling at his fingers, cracking the knuckles, trying to press the stiffness and swellings out of the joints. His head nodded as the fingers pressed. There was no point in looking for music. He would have to play what was in his head. He could hear it there, played to a perfection that he could never reach, or have reached, even before his fingers became so tired. The bell rang, a great jumping clatter of sound. He could see in his mind's eye the tarnished bell jumping on the end of its spring. Number one, the left-hand bell of the long, numbered line, high up on the damp wall below. Number two was the drawing room, three, the dining room, four, this room, father's study. There were only two things father had rung his bell for — turf and his boots. He had always refused to burn coal in this room and from September to May each morning the ashes were raked through and a neat pyramid built in the hearth. He could remember the fascination of watching the dry turves catch and the timid first flames crawling up the inside of the structure.

The bell clattered again and, whoever the unexpected guest might be, he was banging now with the huge iron knocker. The old man got up slowly and crossed the room. Sometimes, now, in the evenings, if he moved too fast or incautiously, cramp knotted the muscles in his calves so inextricably that he had to sit, motionless, in his chair for up to half-an-hour. 'Coming, coming,' he muttered irritably in reply to the hammering. 'Coming.'

He opened the door and found a boy on the step. As far as the old man was concerned he could have been any age between a large seven and an under-nourished, under-privileged seventeen. Tight coiled springs of orange hair covered his head.

'No need to batter the door down.'

The eyes that peered up at him were honey-coloured, secretive. The face pale, already fatigued by living.

'Who might you be?'

The boy didn't answer. He pulled a white envelope out of his pocket and offered it.

'Hey?' Mr. Prendergast ignored the letter. 'Can't you speak?'

The boy stared down at his black shoes, which looked as if they had been contorted into their particularly alarming shape by a hundred pairs of feet.

'For heaven's sake, boy, I'm not going to eat you! Hey? I don't often eat boys. Never Celts. They're stringy.' He looked down at the outstretched hand, the bitten nails, the envelope. 'I joke,' he muttered to the air.

It was almost dark and he knew that the last rays of the sun now painted the chimney stacks away above their heads. The air was sweet and moist.

'Look at me, hey, boy.' The boy looked up. 'You know my name?' The boy nodded. 'What is it, then? Let me hear you say it.'

'Mr. Prendergast, sir.'

'Splendid. That's the first hurdle over. At least I know you're not a deaf mute. Now, tell me your name.'

'Diarmid, sir.'

'A splendid name.' The boy's mouth stretched slightly in a smile. 'An historical name. Tell me, Diarmid, what do you know about the Diarmids that have gone before? If anything, hey?'

'I don't know, sir.'

'You don't know what?'

'I don't suppose I know anything much.'

'That's honest, anyway. There's many a man goes to the grave without admitting as much.'

'I'm not too keen on school, like. I don't go much . . . I mean . . . you wouldn't let on?'

'I wouldn't. What do you do when you're not at school?'

For the first time the boy really smiled. 'I keep out of the way, sir.'

'A wise precaution.'

They both looked at each other, weighing up carefully what they saw.

'Come in,' ordered the old man. 'There's a rising mist.' He stood back and let the boy pass him. Then he closed the remaining light out. The hall was large and very dark now, like a cave. 'Straight across. I presume you have another name.'

'No, just Diarmid.'

'A tribal name, at least. You must belong to someone.'

They came into the study and the old man groped on the wall for the light switch. Illuminated, he stood, his head shaking slightly, looking at the boy with a mixture of interest and embarrassment, wondering why he had invited him in. 'Diarmid . . .?' he asked.

The boy was staring round the room. Outside, a gold pencil line divided the black sky from the black earth. In a moment that, too, would disappear.

'Oh, Toorish. It's like a shop in here. Are all these things yours?'

'Mine? Yes, yes, they're mine all right. I take it you're connected with my late housekeeper in some way. Miss Nellie Toorish.'

'Yes,' said the boy vaguely, still trying to come to grips with the room. Suddenly he remembered the letter and held it out once more towards the old man. 'This,' he said.

'Ah, yes. Thank you.'

Mr. Prendergast took the letter and inspected the writing on the envelope, leaving the boy free to edge round the room touching things, picking up a book, a dusty Meissen[1] figure, a photograph, examining them with fingers and eyes. It was only when he came to the piano and touched the bottom note that the old man reacted.

'Ah, no,' he said. 'The hands must be clean. Otherwise the notes become grimy, unpleasant to touch. Come.' The boy stood by the piano, listening to the fading growl of A. 'Diarmid Toorish. This way.'

He spoke sharply. The boy followed him out of the room and down the passage to the kitchen. The old man filled the sink with hot water, placed the Sunlight soap to hand and fetched a towel from behind the door.

'There.' He pointed to the sink and then to the boy's hands, just in case any mistake might be made. 'Wash.'

Mr. Prendergast opened the letter while Diarmid washed his hands and then dried them on the towel, leaving long grey streaks as he rubbed. The old man waved the half-read letter in his direction. 'So Nellie was your aunt.'

The boy nodded and began edging towards the door.

'I'm surprised she never taught you the importance of clean hands.' He hung the towel up on the back of the door again, looped over a printed overall that had been Nellie's and a greasy Burberry that had been there for ever, unworn, unclaimed. This had been the flower room before circumstances had made it necessary to close up the basement. A glass door led out on to the flight of stone steps that arched over the area and down on to a sanded path.

'I never seen much of her. She didn't get along with Mam.'

'She had a strong personality.'

The boy wasn't interested. He held his hands up in front of the old man's face and perked his head in the direction of the other room. 'May I ...?'

'Run along.'

1. Meissen, a German town, is famous for its porcelain (Dresden china).

The words were neatly placed on grey lines, each loop meticulous, each bar neither too long nor too short.

Dear Sir,

begging your pardon for troubling you. My husband, J. Toorish Groceries ltd, is the brother of the late Miss Nellie Toorish, RIP, as you will know, and we wondered if you would have a place for the boy in the garden, as he must leave school come June, being then almost fifteen. He can read and write, but much more for him I cannot say as he hasn't spent much time on his studies. He has no great wish to go into the shop, but I'm sure he'd learn the gardening easily. One thing to be said for him is he's honest.

yours truly
Kathleen Toorish (Mrs.)

In the study the boy was touching the piano notes, singly at first, then in discordant combinations.

'Ah,' said the old man with irritation. He folded the letter and put it into his pocket. As he entered the room, the boy looked up and smiled.

'No, no, no, boy. You go and sit down. Anywhere. I'll play something for you. It must please the ear. Make yourself at home. Just a minute.' He went over to the window and picked up the whiskey bottle from beside his chair. He looked vaguely round for glasses. 'In the kitchen, by the sink.'

They both stood looking at each other.

'Well, jump to it.'

'But what, sir?'

'Glasses, for heaven's sake, boy. Upside down, draining. And some water.'

Diarmid moved.

'A jug. . . .'

'I'll find something, sir.'

'For God's sake stop calling me sir,' muttered the old man, unscrewing the top of the bottle. The need for a drink suddenly became so great that he quickly took a short, guilty swallow. The boy came back, balancing three glasses, one filled with water.

'I couldn't see a jug handy.'

'Splendid. A fellow of initiative. Here, just a little for you. Fill it up with water. When I was your age I was a veteran drinker. My father believed in teaching a man to hold his drink.'

'My father's a pioneer.'[2]

'Poor, misguided fellow . . . . The trouble with us, as I see it — Celts in general, I mean — is that we tend to exaggerate. We exaggerate the limits of both liberality and frugality. Other examples spring to mind.' He looked at the boy's blank face and waved him to a chair. 'Sit down, boy, whatsit. I'll play you something. Then we'll discuss your mother's letter. I suppose.'

He shut his eyes to play and visualised the notes of a Nocturne rising and falling on the empty page of his mind. The boy sat in the chair by the window holding carefully in his hands, as if it were alive, the faded, brown silk tassel on one end of the silk rope that tied the curtain back.

'Frederic Chopin,' said the old man, turning round from the piano, 'born in 1810. He was a Pole. Poland is a country with a history not unlike our own. Tragic and violent. I don't know when he died but it's immaterial. He was comparatively young. How do you like your drink?'

'I don't mind it.'

'And the music?'

'I didn't mind that either.'

'Well.' He got up slowly. Every joint ached if treated roughly. 'To business. I suppose you know what is in your mother's letter.' He took it out of his pocket and waved it round in the air for a moment.

'No.'

'Your mother thinks it would be a good idea if you came and worked in my garden.'

Diarmid looked up at him, totally surprised. 'Garden?'

'Mmmm. I suppose they think that Sean can teach you something. Misguided. Sean is . . . well . . . .'

'Barking'.[3]

'Well, I suppose you could put it like that. Only when the spirit moves him. Spirits, I should say. That's beside the point. I haven't the money to pay another hand.'

'I don't want to be a gardener.'

'Well, that seems to sort out that problem.' He poured himself another drink.

'I always thought I'd like to be a soldier. I suppose they wouldn't take me yet a while.'

'I think you're possibly a little young.'

'I thought the British army.'

The old man was suddenly tired of the whole thing. 'I think it's time you went home. High time you were in bed.'

Reluctantly the boy got up. He swallowed the last drains of the coloured water and looked around the room, trying to find some reasonable excuse for staying. A glass-topped table caught his eye. He moved towards it.

'Are those medals?'

'They are. Let me see now . . . .' He felt in his pocket and found a two-shilling piece. 'Here. I'll write a note to your mother in the morning. Don't feel up to it now. You come up sometime tomorrow and collect it.'

The boy paid no attention to the coin. 'Yes. I'll do that. You can tell me about the medals then. O.K.?'

'I suppose so.' He put the money back into his pocket and brought the boy to the hall door. . . .

2. The Pioneer Total Abstinence Association is a catholic organization, founded to combat heavy drinking.

3. Barking mad.

EUGENE McCABE

(1930-)

from: HERITAGE AND OTHER STORIES (1978)

[This story crosses some of the same terrain as Michael J. Murphy's 'Return of the Boy' — the relationship between rural protestant and catholic in Ulster: neighbourly and tolerant in normality, venomous and frightened in crisis. McCabe's fictional territory, which he knows intimately, is the troubled countryside bordering the Republic of Ireland and in which inherited bigotry and hatred for the other side are, for McCabe, a kind of cancer, apparently inoperable and terminal: when the story was written, civil war in Ulster seemed likely. The uniformed farmers in the pub near Lisnaskea are part-time members of the Ulster Defence Regiment, a regiment of the British army raised to localize the war against the IRA. The IRA atrocity in the story actually occurred, as did, to square the historical account, the expulsion of the great family McMahon from Monaghan by the Cromwellians.]

CANCER

Today there was an old Anglia[1] and five bicycles outside the cottage. Boyle parked near the bridge. As he locked the car Dinny came through a gap in the ditch: 'Busy?'

'From the back of Carn Rock and beyont: it's like a wake inside.'

For a living corpse Boyle thought.

'How is he?'

'Never better.'

'No pain?'

'Not a twitch ... ates rings round me and snores the night long.' Boyle imagined Joady on the low stool by the hearth in the hot, crowded kitchen, his face like turf ash. Everyone knew he was dying. Women from townlands about had offered to cook and wash. Both brothers had refused. 'Odd wee men,' the women said. 'Course they'd have no sheets, and the blankets must be black.' 'And why not,' another said, 'no woman body ever stood in aither room this forty years.' At which another giggled and said, 'or lay'. And they all laughed because Dinny and Joady were under-sized. And then they were ashamed of laughing and said 'poor Joady cratur' and 'poor Dinny he'll be left: that's worse'. And people kept bringing things: bacon and chicken, whiskey and stout, seed cake, fresh-laid eggs, wholemeal bread; Christmas in February.

In all his years Joady had never slept away from the cottage so that when people called now he talked about the hospital, the operation, the men who died in the ward. In particular he talked about the shattered bodies brought to the hospital morgue from the explosion near Trillick. When he went on about this Protestant neighbours kept silent. Joady noticed and said: 'A bad doin', Albert, surely, there could be no luck after thon.'[2] To Catholic neighbours he said: 'Done it their selves to throw blame on us' and spat in the fire.

It was growing dark at the bridge, crows winging over from Annahullion to roost in the fibrous trees about the disused Spade Mill.

'A week to the day we went up to Enniskillen,' Dinny said.

'That long.'

'A week to the day, you might say to the hour. Do you mind the helicopter?' He pointed up. 'It near sat on that tree.'

Boyle remembered very clearly. It had seemed to come from a quarry of whins[3] dropping as it crossed Gawley's flat. Like today he had driven across this Border bridge and stopped at McMahon's iron-roofed cootage. Without looking up, he could sense the machine chopping its way up fom the Spade Mill. He left the car engine running. Dinny came out clutching a bottle of something. The helicopter hung directly over a dead alder in a scrub of egg bushes between the cottage and the river. Dinny turned and flourished the bottle upwards shouting above the noise: 'I hope to Jasus yis are blown to shit.' He grinned and waved the bottle again. Boyle looked up. Behind the curved, bullet-proof shield two pale urban faces stared down, impassive.

'Come on, Dinny, get in.'

He waved again: a bottle of Lucozade.[4]

Boyle put the car in gear and drove North. They could hear the machine overhead. Dinny kept twisting about in the front seat trying to see up.

'The whores,' he screeched, 'they're trackin' us.'

On a long stretch of road the helicopter swooped ahead and dropped to within a yard of the road. It turned slowly and moved towards them, a gigantic insect with revolving swords. Five yards from the car it stopped. The two faces were now very clear: guns, uniform, apparatus, one man had ear-phones. He seemed to be reading in a notebook. He looked at the registration number of Boyle's car and said something. The helicopter tilted sharply and rose clapping its way towards Armagh across the sour divide of fields and crooked ditches. Boyle remained parked in the middle of the road, until he could hear nothing. His heart was pumping strongly: 'What the hell was all that?'

1. An English car made by Ford.
2. = you: the demonstrative pronoun and adjective. The sense here is 'that'.
3. gorse.
4. The brand name of a glucosic soft drink favoured by the ailing.

'They could see we had Catholic faces,' Dinny said and winked. There was a twist in his left eye. 'The mouth' McMahon neighbours called him, pike lips set in a bulbous face, a cap glued to his skull. Boyle opened a window. The fumes of porter were just stronger than the hum of turf smoke and a strong personal pong.

'It's on account of Trillick,' Boyle said, 'they'll be very active for a day or two.'

'You'll get the news now.'

Boyle switched on the car radio and a voice was saying: 'Five men in a Land Rover on a track leading to a television transmitter station on Brougher Mountain near Trillick between Enniskillen and Omagh. Two B.B.C. officials and three workers lost their lives. An Army spokesman said that the booby trap blew a six-foot deep crater in the mountainside and lifted the Land Rover twenty yards into a bog. The bodies of the five men were scattered over an area of 400 square yards. The area has been sealed off.'

Boyle switched off the radio and said: 'Dear God.'

They passed a barn-like church set in four acres of graveyard. Dinny tipped his cap to the dead; McCaffreys, Boyles, Grues, Gunns, McMahons, Courtneys, Mulligans; names and bones from a hundred townlands.

'I cut a bit out of the *Anglo-Celt*[5] once,' Dinny said, 'about our crowd, the McMahons.'

'Yes?'

'Kings about Monaghan for near a thousand years, butchered, and driv' north to these bitter hills, that's what it said, and the scholar that wrote it up maintained you'll get better bred men in the cabins of Fermanagh than you'll find in many's a big house.'

Boyle thumbed up at the graveyard: 'One thing we're sure of, Dinny, we'll add our bit.'

'Blood tells,' Dinny said, 'it tells in the end.'

A few miles on they passed a waterworks. There was a soldier pacing the floodlit jetty.

'Wouldn't care for his job, he'll go up with it some night.'

'Unless there's changes,' Boyle said.

'Changes! What changes. Look in your neighbour's face; damn little change you'll see there. I wrought four days with Gilbert Wilson before Christmas, baggin' turf beyont Doon, and when the job was done we dropped into Corranny pub, and talked land, and benty turf, and the forestry takin' over and the way people are leavin' for factories, the pension scheme for hill farmers and a dose of things: no side in any of it, not one word of politics or religion, and then all of a shot he leans over to me and says: "Fact is, Dinny, the time I like you best, I could cut your throat." A quare slap in the mouth, but I didn't rise to it; I just said: "I'd as lief[6] not hear the like, Gilbert." "You," says he, "and all your kind, it must be said." "It's a mistake, Gilbert, to say the like, or think it." "Truth," he said, "and you mind it, Dinny".

He looked at Boyle: 'What do you think of that for a spake?'[7]

They came to the main road and Moorlough: 'Are them geese or swans,' Dinny was pointing. He wound down his window and stared out. On the Loughside field there seemed to be fifty or sixty swans, very white against the black water. Boyle slowed for the trunk road, put on his headlights.

'Hard to say.'

'Swans,' Dinny said.

'You're sure?'

'Certain sure.'

'So far from water?'

'I seen it before on this very lake in the twenties, bad sign.'

'Of what?'

'Trouble.'

The lake was half a mile long and at the far end of it there was a military checkpoint. An officer came over with a boy soldier and said 'Out, please.' Two other soldiers began searching the car.

'Name?'

'Boyle, James.'

'Occupation?'

'Teacher.'

'Address?'

'Tiernahinch, Kilrooskey, Fermanagh.'

'And this gentleman?'

Boyle looked away. Dinny said nothing. The officer said again: 'Name?'

'Denis McMahon, Gawley's Bridge, Fermanagh.'

'Occupation?'

5. A newspaper published in Cavan.

6. rather.

7. speech.

'I'm on the national health.'

The boy beside the officer was writing in a notebook. A cold wind blowing from the lake chopped at the water, churning up angry flecks. The officer had no expression in his face. His voice seemed bored and flat.

'Going where?'

'Enniskillen,' Boyle said.

'Purpose?'

'To visit this man's brother, he's had an operation.'

'He's lying under a surgeont,' Dinny said.

The officer nodded.

'And your brother's name?'

'Joady, Joseph, I'm next-of-kin.'

The boy with the notebook went over to a radio jeep. The officer walked away a few paces. They watched. Boyle thought he should say aloud what they were all thinking, then decided not to; then heard himself say: 'Awful business at Trillick.'

The officer turned, looked at him steadily for a moment and nodded. There was another silence until Dinny said: 'Trillick is claner nor a man kicked to death by savages fornenst his childer.'[8]

The officer did not look round. The boy soldier came back from the jeep and said everything was correct, Sir. The officer nodded again, walked away and stood looking at the lake.

Dinny dryspat towards the military back as they drove off. '"And this gentleman!" Smart bugger, see the way he looked at me like I was sprung from a cage.'

'His job, Dinny!'

'To make you feel like an animal! "Occupation" is right!'

Near Lisnaskea Dinny said: 'Cancer, that's what we're all afeerd of, one touch of it and you're a dead man. My auld fella died from a rare breed of it. If he went out in the light, the skin would rot from his face and hands, so he put in the latter end of his life in a dark room, or walkin' about the roads at night. In the end it killed him. He hadn't seen the sun for year.'

He lit a cigarette butt.

'A doctor tould me once it could be in the blood fifty years, and then all of a shot it boils up and you're a gonner.'

'For miles after this they said nothing, then Dinny said: 'Lisbellaw for wappin'[9] straw,/ Maguiresbridge for brandy./Lisnaskea for drinkin' tay,/But Clones town is dandy/... that's a quare auld one?'

He winked with his good eye.

'You want a jigger, Dinny?'

'I'll not say no.'

Smoke, coughing, the reek of a diesel stove and porter met them with silence and watching. Dinny whispered: 'U.D.R.,[10] wrong shop.'

Twenty or more, a clutch of uniformed farmers, faces hardened by wind, rutted from bog, rock and rain, all staring, invincible, suspicious.

'Wrong shop,' Dinny whispered again.

'I know,' Boyle said, 'we can't leave now.'

Near a partition there was a space beside a big man. As Boyle moved towards it a woman bartender said: 'Yes?'

'Two halfs, please.'

'What kind?'

'Irish.'

'What kind of Irish?'

'Any kind.'

Big enough to pull a bullock from a shuck[11] on his own Boyle thought as the big man spat at the doosy[12] floor and turned away. Dinny nudged Boyle and winked up at a notice pinned to a pillar. Boyle read:

Lisnaskea and District Development Association
Extermination of Vermin
1/- for each magpie killed.
2/- for each grey crow killed.
10/- for each grey squirrel killed.
£1 for each fox killed.

Underneath someone had printed with a biro:

For every Fenian Fucker: one old penny.

As the woman measured the whiskies a glass smashed in the snug at the counter end. A voice jumped the frosted glass: 'Wilson was a fly boy, and this Heath man's a bum boy, all them Tories is tricky whores, dale with Micks and Papes and lave

8. Dinny is being heavily ironic, relying on the officer's not understanding his use of dialect (claner: cleaner; nor: than; fornenst: in front of; childer: children).

9. weaving, for straw used in thatching.

10. Ulster Defence Regiment, an almost exclusively protestant regiment, notorious for its anti-catholic behaviour.

11. ditch; also spelled 'sheugh'.

12. sprinkled with sawdust.

us here to rot.[13] Well, by Christ, they'll come no Pope to the townland of Invercloon, I'll not be blown up or burned out, I'll fight to the last ditch.'

All listening in the outer bar, faces, secret and serious, uncomfortable now as other voices joined: 'You're right, George.'

'Sit down, man, you'll toss the table.'

'Let him say out what's in his head.'

'They'll not blow me across no bog; if it's blood they want then, by Jasus, they'll get it, all they want, gallons of it, wagons, shiploads.'

'Now you're talking, George.'

The big man looked at the woman. She went to the hatch, pushed it and said something into the snug. The loudness stopped. A red-axe face stared out, no focus in the eyes. Someone snapped the hatch shut. Silence. The big man spat again and Dinny said: 'I'd as lief drink with pigs.'

He held his glass of whiskey across the counter, poured it into the bar sink and walked out. Boyle finished his whiskey and followed.

In the car again the words came jerking from Dinny's mouth: 'Choke and gut their own childer. Feed them to rats.'

He held up a black-rimmed nail to the windscreen.

'Before they'd give us *that*!'

'It's very sad,' Boyle said, 'I see no answer.'

'I know the answer, cut the bastards down, every last one of them and it'll come to that, them or us. They got it with guns, kep' it with guns, and guns'll put them from it.'

'Blood's not the way,' Boyle said.

'There's no other.'

At Enniskillen they went by the low end of the town, passed armoured cars, and the shattered Crown buildings. Outside the hospital there were four rows of cars, two police cars and a military lorry. Joady's ward was on the ground floor. He was in a corner near a window facing an old man with bad colour and a caved-in mouth. In over thirty years Boyle had never see Joady without his cap. Sitting up now in bed like an old woman, with a white domed head and drained face, he looked like Dinny's ghost shaved and shrunk in regulation pyjamas. He shook hands with Boyle and pointed at Dinny's bottle: 'What's in that?'

'Lucozade,' Dinny said.

'Poison.'

'It's recommended for a sick body.'

'Rots the insides; you can drop it out the windy.'[14]

'I'll keep it,' Dinny said, 'I can use it.'

Boyle could see that Dinny was offended, and remembered his aunt's anger one Christmas long ago. She had knit a pair of wool socks for Joady and asked him about them.

'Bad wool, Miss,' he said, 'out through the heel in a week, I dropped them in the fire.'

She was near tears as she told his mother: 'Ungrateful, lazy, spiteful little men, small wonder Protestants despise them and us, and the smell in that house . . . you'd think with nothing else to do but draw the dole and sit by the fire the least they could do is wash themselves: as for religion, no Mass, no altar, nothing ever, they'll burn, they really will, and someone should tell them. God knows you don't want thanks, but to have it flung back in your teeth like that it's . . . .'

'It's very trying, Annie,' his mother said.

And Boyle wanted to say to his aunt: 'No light, no water, no work, no money, nothing all their days, but the dole, fire poking, neighbour baiting, and the odd skite[15] on porter, retched off that night in a ditch.'

'Communists,' his aunt mocked Joady, 'I know what real Communists would do with those boyos, what Hitler did with the Jews.'

'Annie, that's an awful thing to say.'

There was a silence and then his aunt said: 'God forgive me, it is, but . . .' and then she wept.

'Because she never married, and the age she's at,' his mother said afterwards.

Joady was pointing across a square of winter lawn to the hospital entrance: 'Fornenst them cars,' he said, 'the morgue.' His eyes swivelled round the ward, 'I heard nurses talk about it in the corridor, brought them here in plastic bags from Trillick, laid them out on slabs in a go of sawdust on account of the blood. That's what they're at now, Army doctors tryin' to put the bits together, so's their people can recognise them, and box them proper.'

The old man opposite groaned and shifted.

13. Harold Wilson and Edward Heath, successive British prime ministers, were both distrusted in the 1970s by Ulster protestants, who suspected them of being soft on Irish republicans. 'Micks', 'Papes' and 'Fenians' are pejorative synonyms for catholics (therefore, in protestant eyes, nationalists, overt or closet).

14. window.

15. Brief carousal.

Joady's voice dropped still lower: 'They say one man's head couldn't be got high or low, they're still tramping the mountain with searchlights.'

'Dear God,' Boyle said.

'A fox could nip off with a man's head handy enough.'

'If it came down from a height it could bury itself in that auld spongy heather and they'd never find it or less[16] they tripped over it.'

'Bloodhound dogs could smell it out.'

'They wouldn't use bloodhound dogs on a job like that, wouldn't be proper.'

'Better nor lavin' it to rot in a bog, course they'd use dogs, they'd have to.'

'Stop!'

Across the ward the old man was trying to elbow himself up. The air was wheezing in and out of his lungs, he seemed to be choking: 'Stop! Oh God, God, please, I must go ... I must ...'

Boyle stood up and pressed the bell near Joady's bed. Visitors round other beds stopped talking. The wheezing got louder, more irregular, and a voice said: 'Someone do something.'

Another said: 'Get a doctor.'

Boyle said: 'I've rung.'

A male nurse came and pulled a curtain round the bed. When a doctor came the man was dead. He was pushed away on a trolley covered with a white sheet. Gradually people round other beds began to talk. A young girl looking sick was led out by a woman.

'That's the third carted off since I come down here.'

'Who was he?' Boyle asked.

'John Willie Foster, a bread server from beyont Five-mile town, started in to wet the bed like a child over a year back, they couldn't care for him at home, so they put him to "Silver Springs", the auld people's home, but he got worse there so they packed him off here.'

'Age,' Dinny said, 'the heart gave up.'

'The heart broke,' Joady said, 'no one come to see him, bar one neighbour man. He was towld he could get home for a day or two at Christmas, no one come, he wouldn't spake with no one, couldn't quit' cryin'; the man's heart was broke.'

'Them Probsbyterians is a hard bunch, cauld,[17] no nature.'

There was a silence.

'Did he say what about you Joady? ... the surgeont?'

'No.'

'You asked?'

'"A deep operation," he said, "very deep, an obstruction," so I said "Is there somethin' rotten, Sir, I want to know, I want to be ready?" "Ready for what," says he and smiles, but you can't tell what's at the back of a smile like that. '"Just ready," I said.

'"You could live longer nor me," says he.

'He hasn't come next nor near me since I've come down here to the ground ... did he tell yous anythin?'

'Dam' to the thing,' Dinny said.

And Boyle noticed that Joady's eyes were glassy.

There was a newspaper open on the bed. It showed the Duke of Kent beside an armoured car at a shattered customs post. On the top of the photograph the name of the post read 'Kilclean', Boyle picked up the newspaper, opened it and saw headlines: 'Significance of bank raids'; 'Arms for Bogsiders';[18] 'Failure to track murderer'; 'Arms role of I.R.A.'

He read, skipping half, half listening to the brothers.

'In so far as ordinary secret service work is concerned, could be relied on and trusted ... under the control of certain Ministers. Reliable personnel ... co-operation between Army intelligence and civilian intelligence ... no question of collusion.'

'Lies,' Joady said to Dinny, 'you don't know who to believe.' His voice was odd and his hand was trembling on the bedspread. Boyle didn't want to look at his face and thought, probably has it and knows. Dinny was looking at the floor.

'Lies,' Joady said again. And this time his voice sounded better. Boyle put down the paper and said: 'I hear you got blood, Joady.'

'Who towld you that?'

'One of my past pupils, a nurse here.'

'Three pints,' Joady said.

Boyle winked and said: 'Black blood, she told me you got Paisley's[19] blood.'

Joady began shaking, his mouth opened and he seemed to be dry-retching. The laughter when it

16. unless.
17. cold.

18. Inhabitants of the catholic area of Derry city known as the Bogside.
19. Ian Paisley (born 1926), a leading protestant loyalist politician, the epitome of the 'black' (bigoted) protestant.

came was pitched and hoarse. He put a hand on his stitches and stopped, his breathing shallow, his head going like a picaninny on a mission box.

'Paisley's blood, she said that?'

'She did.'

'That's tarror,'[20] he said, but was careful not to laugh again. Boyle stood up and squeezed his arm: 'We'll have to go, Joady, next time can we bring you something you need?'

'Nothin',' Joady said, 'I need nothin'.'

Walking the glass-walled, rubber corridor Boyle said: 'I'll wait in the car, Dinny.'

Dinny stopped and looked at the bottle of Lucozade: 'We could see him together.'

'If you want.'

The surgeon detached a sheet of paper from a file, he faced them across a steel-framed table: 'In your brother's case,' he was saying to Dinny, 'it's late, much, much, too late.' He paused, no one said anything and then the surgeon said: 'I'm afraid so.'

'Dying?'

'It's terminal.'

'He's not in pain,' Boyle said.

'And may have none for quite a while, when the stitches come out he'll be much better at home.'

'He doesn't know,' Dinny said.

'No, I didn't tell him yet.'

'He wants to know.'

The surgeon nodded and made a note on a sheet of paper. Dinny asked: 'How long has he got, Sir?'

The surgeon looked at the sheet of paper as though the death date were inscribed: 'Sometime this year . . . yes, I'm afraid so.'

The Anglia and bicycles were gone now. It had grown dark about the bridge and along the river. Boyle was cold sitting on the wall. Dinny had been talking for half an hour: 'He was never sick a day, and five times I've been opened, lay a full year with a bad lung above at Killadeas; he doesn't know what it is to be sick.'

20. terrible (terribly funny).

Raucous crow noise carried up from the trees around the Spade Mill, cawing, cawing, cawing, blindflapping in the dark. They looked down, listening, waiting, it ceased. 'He knows about dying,' Boyle said.

'That's what I'm comin' at, he's dyin' and sleeps twelve hours of the twenty-four, ates, smokes, walks, and for a man used never talk much, he talks the hind leg off a pot now, make your head light to hear him.'

He took out a glass phial: 'I take two of them sleeping caps every night since he come home, and never close an eye. I can't keep nothin' on my stomach, and my skin itches all over; I sweat night and day. I'll tell you what I think: livin's worse nor dyin', and that's a fact.'

'It's upsetting, Dinny.'

It was dark in the kitchen: Joady gave Boyle a stool, accepted a cigarette, and lit it from the paraffin lamp, his face sharp and withered: a frosted crab.

'Where's the other fella gone?'

'I'm not sure,' Boyle said, 'he went down the river somewhere.'

Joady sucked on the cigarette: 'McCaffreys, he's gone to McCaffreys, very neighbourly these times, he'll be there until twelve or after.'

He thrust at a blazing sod with a one-pronged pitch fork: 'Same every night since I come home, away from the house every chance he gets.'

'All the visitors you have, Joady, and he's worried.'

'Dam' the worry, whingin' and whinin', to every slob that passes the road about *me* snorin' the night long, didn't I hear him with my own ears . . . .'

He spat, his eyes twisting: 'It's *him* that snores not *me,* him: it's *me* that's dyin', *me,* not him . . . Christ's sake . . . couldn't he take a back sate until I'm buried.'

He got up and looked out the small back window at the night, at nothing: 'What would you call it, when your own brother goes contrary, and the ground hungry for you . . . eh! Rotten, that's what I'd call it, rotten.'

EDNA O'BRIEN

(1932-)

from: MRS REINHARDT AND OTHER STORIES (1978)

[Edna O'Brien's early reputation was as a novelist of rural and provincial Ireland. The affecting naivety of her central characters threatened to suggest a naivety of artifice in the work that contained them. But she has since become a writer of 'international' fiction (metropolitan settings, an upper middle class or professional cast) of the sort sponsored by the *New Yorker*. This has dispelled the suspicion of naivety, for the later fictions have appropriately more urbane voices. But O'Brien's chief interest remains love, and she rings enviable changes on what ought to be a somewhat limiting theme. 'Number Ten' can be adduced as evidence. The story explores the survival tactics employed by the psyche of an anxious woman in a crisis of ageing and marriage.]

NUMBER TEN

Everything began to be better for Mrs Reinhardt from the moment she started to sleepwalk. Every night her journey yielded a fresh surprise. First it was that she saw sheep — not sheep as one sees them in life, a bit sooty and bleating away, but sheep as one sees them in a dream. She saw myriads of white fleece on a hilltop, surrounded by little lambs frisking and suckling to their hearts' content.

Then she saw pictures such as she had not seen in life. Her husband owned an art gallery and Mrs Reinhardt had the opportunity to see many pictures, yet the ones she saw at night were much more satisfying. For one thing she was inside them. She was not an outsider looking in, making idiotic remarks, she was part of the picture: an arm or a lily or the grey mane of a horse. She did not have to compete, did not have to say anything. All her movements were preordained. She was simply aware of her own breath, a soft steady, sustaining breath.

In the mornings her husband would say she looked a bit frayed or a bit intense, and she would say, 'Nonsense,' because in fifteen years of marriage she had never felt better. Her sleeping life suited her and, of course, she never knew what to expect.

Her daily life had a pattern to it. Weekday mornings she spent at home, helping or supervising Fatima, the Spanish maid. She gave two afternoons a week to teaching autistic children, two afternoons were devoted to an exercise class, and on Fridays she shopped in Harrods[1] and got all the groceries for the weekend. Mr Reinhardt had bought a farm two years before, and weekends they spent in the country, in their newly renovated cottage. In the country she did not sleepwalk, and Mrs Reinhardt wondered if it might be that she was inhibited by the barbed-wire fence that skirted their garden. But there are gates, she thought, and I should open them. She was a little vexed with herself for not being more venturesome.

Then one May night, in her house in London, she had an incredible dream. She walked over a field with her youngest son — in real life he was at university — and all of a sudden, and in unison, the two of them knelt down and began scraping the earth up with their bare hands. It was a rich red earth and easy to crumble. They were so eager because they knew that treasure was about to be theirs. Sure enough, they found bits of gold, tiny specks of it, which they put in a handkerchief, and then to crown her happiness Mrs Reinhardt found the loveliest little gold key, and held it up to the light while her son laughed and in a baby voice said, 'Mama.'

Soon after this dream Mrs Reinhardt embarked on a bit of spring cleaning. Curtains and carpets for the dry cleaners, drawers depleted of all the old useless odds and ends that had been piling up. Her husband's clothing, too, she must put in order. A little rift had sprung up between them and was widening day by day. He was moody. He got home later than usual and, though he did not say so, she knew that he had stopped at the corner and had a few drinks. Once of late he had pulled her down beside him on the living-room sofa and stroked her thighs and started to undress her within hearing distance of Fatima, who was in the kitchen chopping and singing. Always chopping and singing or humming. For the most part, though,

1. An expensive London store.

Mr Reinhardt went straight to the liquor cabinet and gave them both a gin, pouring himself a bigger one because, as he said, all her bloody fasting made Mrs Reinhardt lightheaded.

She was sorting Mr Reinhardt's shirts — tee shirts, summer sweaters, thick crew-neck sweaters — and putting them each in a neat pile, when out of his seersucker jacket there stumbled a little gold key that caused her to let out a cry. The first thing she felt was a jet of fear. Then she bent down and picked it up. It was exactly like the one in her sleepwalk. She held it in her hand, promising herself never to let it go. What fools we are to pursue in daylight what we should leave for night-time.

Her next sleepwalking brought Mrs Reinhardt out of her house into a waiting taxi and, some distance away, to a mews house. Outside the mews house was a black and white tub filled with pretty flowers. She simply put her hand under a bit of foliage and there was the latchkey. Inside was a little nest. The wallpaper in the hall was the very one she had always wanted for their house, a pale gold with the tiniest white flowers — mere suggestions of flowers, like those of the wild strawberry. The kitchen was immaculate. On the landing upstairs was a little fretwork bench. The cushions in the sitting room were stiff and stately, and so was the upholstery, but the bedroom — ah, the bedroom.

It was everything she had ever wanted their own to be. In fact, the bedroom *was* the very room she had envisaged over and over again and had described to her husband down to the last detail. Here it was — a brass bed with a little lace canopy above it, the entire opposite wall a dark metallic mirror in which dark shadows seemed to swim around; a light-blue velvet chaise longue, a hanging plant with shining leaves and a floor lamp with a brown-fringed shade that gave off the softest of light.

She sat on the edge of the bed, marvelling, and saw the other things that she had always wanted. She saw, for instance, the photo of a little girl in First Communion attire; she saw the paperweight that when shaken yielded a miniature snowstorm; she saw the mother-of-pearl tray with the two champagne glasses — and all of a sudden she began to cry because her happiness was so immense. Perhaps, she thought, he will come to me here, he will visit, and it will be like the old days and he won't be irritable and he won't be tapping with his fingers or fiddling with the lever of his fountain pen. He will smother me with hugs and kisses and we will tumble about on the big foamy bed.

She sat there in the bedroom and she touched nothing, not even the two white irises in the tall glass vase. The little key was in her hand and she knew it was for the wardrobe and that she had only to open it to find there a nightdress with a pleated top, a voile dance dress, a silver fox cape, and a pair of sling-back shoes. But she did not open it. She wanted to leave something a secret. She crept away and was home in her own bed without her husband being aware of her absence. He had complained on other occasions about her cold feet as she got back into bed, and asked in Christ's name what was she doing — making tea or what? That morning her happiness was so great that she leaned over, unknotted his pyjamas, and made love to him very sweetly, very slowly and to his apparent delight. Yet when he wakened he was angry, as if a wrong had been done him.

Naturally, Mrs Reinhardt now went to the mews house night after night, and her heart would light up as she saw the pillar of the house with its number, ten, lettered in gold edged with black. The nought was a little slanted. Sometimes she got into the brass bed and she knew it was only a question of time before Mr Reinhardt followed her there.

One night as she lay in the bed, a little breathless, he came in very softly, closed the door, removed his dressing gown, and took possession of her with such a force that afterward she suspected she had a broken rib. They used words that they had not used for years. She was wild and young. A lovely fever took hold of her. She was saucy while he kept imploring her to please marry him, to please give up her independence, to please be his — adding that even if she said no he was going to whisk her off. Then to prove his point he took possession of her again. She almost died, so deep and so thorough was her pleasure, and each time as she came back to her senses she saw some little object or trinket that was intended to add to her pleasure — once it was a mobile in which silver horses chased one another around, once it was a sound as of a running stream. He gave her some champagne and they drank in utter silence.

But when she wakened from this idyll she was in fact in her own bed and so was he. She felt mortified. Had she cried out in her sleep? Had she moaned? There was no rib broken. She reached for the hand mirror and saw no sign of wantonness on her face, no tossed hair, and the buttons of her nightdress were neatly done up to the throat.

He was a solid mass of sleep. He opened his eyes. She said something to him, something anxious, but he did not reply. She got out of bed and went down to the sitting room to think. Where would it all lead to? Should she tell him? She thought not. All morning she tried the key in different locks, but it was too small. In fact, once she nearly lost it because it slipped into a lock and she had to tease it out with the prong of a fork. Of course she did not let Fatima, the maid, see what she was doing.

It was Friday, their day to go to the country, and she was feeling reluctant about it. She knew that when they arrived they would rush around their garden and look at their plants to see if they'd grown a bit, and look at the rose leaves to make sure there were no greenfly. Then, staring out across the fields to where the crows were, they would tell each other how lucky they were to have such a nice place, and how clever. The magnolia flowers would be fully out and she would stand and stare at the tree as if by staring at it she could imbue her body with something of its whiteness.

The magnolia was out when they arrived — like little white china eggcups, each bloom with its leaves lifted to the heavens. Two of the elms definitely had the blight, Mr Reinhardt said, as the leaves were withering away. The elms would have to be chopped, and Mr Reinhardt estimated that there would be enough firewood for two winters. He would speak to the farm manager, who lived down the road, about this. They carried in the shopping, raised the blinds, and switched on the central heating. The little kitchen was just as they had left it, except that the primroses in the jar had faded and were like bits of yellow skin. She unpacked the food they had brought, put some things in the fridge, and began to peel the carrots and potatoes for the evening meal. Mr Reinhardt hammered four picture hooks into the wall for the new prints that he had brought down. From time to time he would call her to ask what order he should put them in, and she would go in, her hands covered with flour and rather absently suggest a grouping.

She had the little key with her in her purse and would open the purse from time to time to make sure that it was there. Then she would blush.

At dusk she went out to get a branch of apple wood for the fire, in order to engender a lovely smell. A bird chirped from a tree. It was more sound than song. She could not tell what bird it was. The magnolia tree was a mass of white in the surrounding darkness. The dew was falling and she bent for a moment to touch the wet grass. She wished it were Sunday, so that they could be going home. In London the evenings seemed to pass more quickly and they each had more chores to do. She felt in some way she was deceiving him.

They drank some red wine as they sat by the fire. Mr Reinhardt was fidgety but at the very same time accused her of being fidgety. He was being adamant about the Common Market. Why did he expound on the logistics of it when she was not even contradicting him? He got carried away, made gestures, said he loved England, loved it passionately, that England was going to the dogs. When she got up to push in a log that had fallen from the grate, he asked her for God's sake to pay attention.

She sat down at once, and hoped that there was not going to be one of those terrible, unexpected, meaningless rows. But blessedly they were distracted. She heard him say, 'Crikey!' and then she looked up and saw what he had just seen. There was a herd of cattle staring in at them. She jumped up. Mr Reinhardt rushed to the phone to call the farm manager, since he himself knew nothing about country life, certainly not how to drive away cattle.

She grabbed a walking stick and went outside to prevent the cows from falling in the swimming pool. It was cold out of doors and the wind rustled in all the trees. The cows looked at her, suspicious. Their ears pricked. She made tentative movements with the stick, and at that moment four of them leaped over the barbed wire and back into the adjoining field. The remaining cow began to race around. From the field the four cows began to bawl. The fifth cow was butting against the paling. Mrs Reinhardt thought, I know what you are feeling — you are feeling lost and muddled and you have gone astray.

Her husband came out in a frenzy because when he rang the farm manager no one was there.

'Bloody never there!' he said. His loud voice so frightened the fifth cow that she made a leap for it and got stuck in the barbed wire. Mrs Reinhardt could see the barb in her huge udder and thought what a place for it to have landed. They must rescue her. Very cautiously they both approached the animal, and the intention was that Mr Reinhardt would hold the cow while Mrs Reinhardt freed the flesh. She tried to be gentle. The cow's smell was milky, and soft compared with her roar, which was beseeching, Mr Reinhardt caught hold of the hindquarters and told his wife to hurry up. The cow was obstreperous. As Mrs Reinhardt lifted the bleeding flesh away, the cow took a huge jump and was over the fence and down the field, where she hurried to the river to drink.

The others followed her and suddenly the whole meadow was the scene of bawling and mad commotion. Mr Reinhardt rubbed his hands and let out a sigh of relief. He suggested that they open a bottle of champagne. Mrs Reinhardt was delighted. Of late he had become very thrifty and did not permit her any extravagances. In fact he had been saying that they would soon have to give up wine because of the state of the country. As they went indoors he put an arm around her. And back in the room she sat and felt like a mistress as she drank the champagne, smiled at him and felt the stuff coursing through her body. The champagne put them in a nice mood and they linked as they went up the narrow stairs to bed. Nevertheless, Mrs Reinhardt did not feel like any intimacy; she wanted it reserved for the hidden room.

They returned to London on Sunday evening, and that night Mrs Reinhardt did not sleep. Consequently she walked nowhere in her dreams. In the morning she felt fidgety. She looked in the mirror. She was getting old. After breakfast, as Mr Reinhardt was hurrying out of the house, she held up the little key.

'What is it?' she said.

'How would I know,' he said. He looked livid.

She called and made an appointment at the hairdresser's. She looked in the mirror. She must not get old. Later, when her hair was set she would surprise him — she would drop in at his gallery and ask him to take her to a nice pub. On the way she would buy a new scarf and knot it at the neck and she would be youthful.

When she got to the gallery, Mr Reinhardt was not there. Hans, his assistant, was busy with a client from the Middle East. She said she would wait. The new secretary went off to make some tea. Mrs Reinhardt sat at her husband's desk brooding, and then idly she began to flick through his desk diary, just to pass the time. Lunch with this one and that one. A reminder to buy her a present for their anniversary — which he had done. He had brought her a beautiful ring with a sphinx on it.

Then she saw it — the address that she went to night after night. Number ten. The digits danced before her eyes as they had danced when she drove up in the taxi the very first time. All her movements became hurried and mechanical. She gulped her tea, she gave a distracted handshake to the Arab gentleman, she ate the ginger biscuit and gnashed her teeth, so violently did she chew. She paced the floor, she went back to the diary. The same address — three, four, or five times a week. She flicked back to see how long it had been going on. It was no use. She simply had to go there.

At the mews, she found the key in the flower tub. In the kitchen were eggshells and a pan in which an omelette had been cooked. There were two brown eggshells and one white. She dipped her finger in the fat; it was still warm. Her heart went ahead of her up the stairs. It was like a pellet in her body. She had her hand on the doorknob, when all of a sudden she stopped in her tracks and became motionless. She crept away from the door and went back to the landing seat.

She would not intrude, no. It was perfectly clear why Mr Reinhardt went there. He went by day to keep his tryst with her, be unfaithful with her, just as she went by night. One day or one night, if they were very lucky, they might meet and share their secret, but until then Mrs Reinhardt was content to leave everything just as it was. She tiptoed down the stairs and was pleased that she had not acted rashly, that she had not lost her head.

JULIA O'FAOLÁIN

(1932-)

from: DAUGHTERS OF PASSION (1982)

[This story borrows its title from a poem by Yeats which itself recalls *King Lear*. In place of Yeats's adduced reasons for madness in later life, O'Faoláin offers others — a repressive, church-ridden Irish Republic of the 1940s and 1950s, the machinations of the clergy and the darkness of Vatican politics, and the contempt of the young for the old. The ironies of their respective careers and their lifelong acquaintance do not diminish for the two main characters (the rake and the priest) the repression and unfulfilment they come to feel. Indeed, it deepens them, adding bitterness to unhappy minds. O'Faoláin's fictions cut a wide social swathe, as this story exemplifies, and are emboldened by a various social conscience.]

WHY SHOULD NOT OLD MEN BE MAD?

It was a ridiculous occasion. The beginning of the row did nobody credit, and Edward could not for the life of him remember its end. Over the years, his memories of the thing were to curdle, growing spotty and sulphurous, until they put him in mind of the reflections one sees in mirrors which have hung in damp, haughty, old houses and perpetuate their gloom.

The evening got off to a bad start. Jammet's, for decades Dublin's smartest restaurant, had, towards the end, accumulated a stable of rickety old waiters with hamburger faces who that night — here memory sharpened to a knife-edge — snubbed the party's host.

Jim Farrel, a student fresh from the country and unused to restaurants, had chosen to spend half a term's allowance on dinner for four men he didn't know. The guests were Edward, who had just been elected to the Senate, Monsignor Macateer, later to become Bishop of Oglish, a German theologian, and an English Catholic MP who was in Dublin for a conference. The four knew of each other but did not know Farrel, who had led each to suppose that one of the others had asked him to arrange the gathering. His white lies were exposed when he came to pay the bill, and his guests overcome by awkwardness, mirth and doubt as to whether he could possibly have found their conversation worth the expenditure. Had they, they covertly asked each other, sung sufficiently well for their supper? They must, Edward privately supposed, be feeling like an inexperienced young girl who has been treated too sumptuously by a suitor. What, she as they must wonder, would now be expected?

Perhaps it was to bridge the ticklish moment that the German offered a round of brandies and that Edward, feeling light-hearted, resolved to consult Mikey Macateer about his marital problems. Discreetly, man to man — he had known Mikey since school — he brought up the matter of an annulment. Two annulments. Both Jennifer and he were married. The year was 1958. Was there, he asked Mikey, any chance?

The Monsignor rounded on him like a snake.

Possibly, he had found the evening a strain? The German, an ascetic with advanced ideas, was not the sort of man with whom Mikey felt at ease, and he must have been on pins and needles lest Edward, a Civil-Liberties supporter, let the country down in front of the English MP. Annulments were the last straw.

Mikey's lips had quivered like the cardiogram of a wildly pumping heart. Between them his tongue wavered forth, as he asked in a hiss of enraged and spittly Gaelic whether Edward was deliberately giving scandal to foreigners. Trying for annulments was an erosion of the system, said Mikey. It was a factor for disorder, a time-bomb placed at the heart of Mother Church who, whether Edward knew it or not, was going through risks and trials unknown since the days of Martin Luther.

Tics sucked Mikey's cheeks inwards as though it were being pierced by sewing-pins. Edward, he said, was a fornicator and he a man who called a spade a spade.

'Spayed is what you are,' Edward had answered in English. 'Hiding,' he had shouted, 'behind your dog collar.' The Irish clergy, said Edward, reaching for old invective, were living in the Dark Ages, leaving no choice to the laity but between total abstinence and having six children.

'Sex,' wondered the German doubtfully, 'children?'

'Six,' Edward corrected him.

After that, the level of discourse sank. Appearances ceased to be kept up. Scandal was given, but memory drew a veil. Edward's recollection of the end of the business was a blank. Luckily, he had no further occasion to meet anyone who had been present that evening and his host, Jim Farrel, faded utterly from his ken.

News did, however, continue to reach him of Mikey Macateer's rise. Over the years, the fellow was made a bishop, called to Rome, given a place in the Curia and there alleged to be a man of influence. It stuck particularly in Edward's craw to hear that, after Vatican Two,[1] Macateer became a big progressive, famed for his fight to ditch the cult of abnegation and find the human face of Catholicism. He was hot for reform, it seemed, and instrumental in making annulments easy to get — too late, of course, for Edward and for Jennifer, who was by then so seized up with arthritis that she had had to go and live in Palm Springs.

'Fuck,' mourned Edward when he thought of this.

It was eighteen years after the Jammet's row that someone in Edward's hearing mentioned Macateer as possibly *papabile*[2] — at any rate, a Power in the Vatican, a dexterous string-puller and an *Eminence Verte*. This was at the Irish Embassy in Rome, so Edward allowed for exaggeration. Still, no smoke without fire. There must be some flicker of truth to it. Edward felt green-eyed — well, why wouldn't he? There *he* was, having to turn his mind to retirement and hobbies while that ecclesiastical turncoat slithered upwards in his pride and power. To be sure, churchmen paid a price for their long span of active life: no sex, no kids, loneliness — *what* loneliness? There'd be precious little loneliness for chaps who had made a go of it. Peaking late, they had the best of both worlds in the end. There was Mikey surrounded — Edward supposed he was surrounded — by priestly boot-lickers, pious catamites, a court, and snowed under by invitations.

Edward refused to attend a lunch where the ambassador — a busybody — had hoped to bring the estranged friends together. Having pretended that he had to press on to Venice, he was then obliged to leave the Eternal City earlier than planned. This too stuck in his craw. It wasn't that foolish old business at Jammet's which made him refuse to see Mikey. That was water under the bridge. After eighteen years you buried — or drowned — hatchets. No, no, but, oh, somehow, the invitation had found him in low fettle. He'd been feeling his age. Rome mocked him with memories of old adulteries — it had been a favourite venue for them and, maddeningly, the props were still there: mimosa, *carrozze*,[3] that piss-poor wine that in the old days had not tasted pissy at all. He remembered saying to Jennifer that it was like drinking bottled sunlight.

So, 'No,' he told the embassy chap who rang. 'Sorry.'

It seemed unfair; it seemed *wrong* that Macateer should be reaping what he hadn't sown: esteem, good fellowship and the company of youth, when Edward, who had given so much of himself to so many, was alone.

Two years went by. Then came a letter from Macateer, apparently back in Ireland. It was a summons to visit, and Edward disregarded it. The twit was clearly puffed up with self-esteem. Celibates got that way. Proponents of a married clergy should make use of the point. Hammer it home. Edward thought of saying this in a card to Mikey since *he* was now such a reformer. Instead, he forgot about him.

Weeks later, casting about for gossip with which to enliven a letter to a favourite cousin, he remembered him. Susan was the last attractive female in Edward's entourage and he cherished her with a sad ironic gaiety. Like himself, she suffered from withdrawal symptoms. It wasn't that she or he were withdrawing from anything. No, things were withdrawing from *them* and at such a clip that this time Edward could think of no news to tell her. He fell back on working Mikey's summons into an anecdote and, having done so, began to believe that maybe there *was* more to it than met the eye. Jaundiced spectacles? Perhaps.

'His Grace the Bishop of Oglish,' wrote Edward,

1. An ecumenical council convoked in 1959 by Pope John XXIII and in which he attempted to render the church's doctrine more understandable, its constitution simpler, its forms better adapted to current needs. Vatican II was widely regarded as a liberalizing of Roman catholicism.
2. Italian, meaning 'capable of becoming pope'.
3. Horse-drawn carriage.

'writes from an ecclesiastical loony-bin somewhere near Athlone, i.e. in the soggy middle of the country, saying he would like a visit. Princely command? Cry for help? What is His Grace doing in a bin in the bog? A Beckettian fix — unless he's running it. But even then what a comedown from the corridors of the Curia where, they say, he was *un très Grand Manitou.*[4] His nicknames tell much: Macchiatelly, because of being smooth on the box, Macateer the Racketeer, inevitably, Mac the Knife. Has someone got their knife into Mikey? I shall go, see and report. Hope I whet your appetite for further bulletins?'

It was all fantasy, including the nicknames — or was it?

Elation at having managed to make something out of nothing led to a doubt that there might be something where he had at first seen nothing. Edward, a virtuoso barrister, had in his prime been able to convince juries of anything he chose. Now, cut off from the medicinal cynicism of day-to-day reality, he found that he could all too easily convince himself.

Satan fodder finds for idle minds — or so Mikey and he had been told in kindergarten.

He wished — God, how he wished — that he was still racked by intimate doubts and choices. For years his letters to Susan had been mined with anguished questions: Should he leave his wife, who would pine incapably if he did, and take off with Mil? Leave Mil for Jennifer? Sell up this house and follow Jennifer to Palm Springs? Return to his pining wife before she died? No alternatives left now. Susan held his hand in a desert awful with the lack of them. Oh shit, oh *shit*! Well, *there* was one function left to him still and quite satisfactory, thanks.

'Life,' he wrote and probed an ear with his pen while wondering what to write next, 'here is as calm as a gold-fish tank with one half-animate inmate: me. A silvered one. My hair pales and drops, as I soon shall myself. Contemporaries drop like flies and my address-book turns into a graveyard guide. I have to keep pencilling out names for fear of gaffes like the one I made with poor Martin Clancy last month at the Yacht Club. "How's Mil?" I asked. He looked at me in shock: "Mil's been dead three years." Had I known? Suppressed and blinked away knowledge? Perhaps. Like black tennis-balls smashed at you across a net, like objects dark against the sun, news like that darkens the mind and sets up a refusal. Silly Milly Clancy — you won't remember, but thirty years ago her beauty was breathtaking — Mil dead? Mil laid down in Glasnevin and rendered to a compost fit to blow half Dublin sky-high. Or just gone? Whoo, like a puff of air. Whee, like the intervocalic Latin *t* that became a *d*, then disappeared: *vita, vida, vie. La vida es un sueño*,[5] so why, as Willy Yeats rightly if rhetorically demanded, should not old men be mad?'

Edward supposed he was being literary, but what the hell? He felt weepy, too, and to yield to *that* would be worse. In one corner of his eye, Milly Clancy lurked in luminous tennis-dress and a rainbow casing of teardrop: like Snow White awaiting a kiss in her glass coffin. Get away, Mil! What else was I — ah, yes, madness and the Case of Mikey Macateer.

Old grudges had dissolved into a ferocious solidarity with Mikey, a possible victim of Vatican foul play. Could he have been nudged from his Curial niche? He could. He could. Priestly machinations were infamous and ditto the ruthlessness of today's youth. Edward was in a position to know, having been edged out of his own firm by his own sons — well, he'd *let* himself be edged out. The three were too dim to make a living on their own, and perhaps he was trying to repay their dead mother by being soft with her sons? Blood was thicker than water, though *they* didn't strike him as having a drop in their veins. Put the three through a mangle and he'd be surprised if anything came out: blood, juice or jism. Plastic men. Their passions were for crosswords, beagling and messing with small intricate boats. Small, mark, nothing on a scale to accommodate the lurch and sway of sea-borne loves. No, tinkering with stalled engines was what they liked. They rarely left the harbour.

To be fair — fairness had been Edward's loadstone — *they* found him trying. His flourish embarrassed them. He knew. He saw. Freesias in his lapel, the length of his cuffs. Even his concern with human rights struck them as spiritual social-

4. A very great force. For the Algonquian Indians, a *manitou* was a deified spirit.

5. Spanish: Life is a dream. The phrase is the title of a play (1635) by Pedro Calderón de la Barca.

climbing. 'Pragmatic' was their favourite word. Economics, they instructed, was what mattered now. No, *not* in the Marxist sense. Forget words like 'left' and 'right'. Ireland had never had it so good. In the convex diminishing-mirrors of their eyes, he saw himself as a sentimental old codger fighting the fights of long ago.

An Americanized generation, they admitted to boredom when not working. Yet all three had married and were, as they were quick to point out, nicer to their wives than Edward had ever been to their mother. So alien were they that if she'd had it in her to take a lover he'd have thought them bastards. She hadn't. Maybe they'd been sired by gamma rays on evenings when she'd been sitting back, legs apart, watching re-runs of *Peyton Place*?[6]

Edward was seized by an urge to see old Mikey Mac who, in another era, used to climb on his shoulders to sneak back in over the seminary wall after the two had stayed out till dawn dancing at a Ceilidh.[7]

Wet furry fields lay like the stomachs of soft animals bared to the sky. The train, with Edward in it, tore masterfully through the flat lands of middle Ireland. He felt zesty and wondered whether Mikey needed help. Edward was still President of Civil Liberties. Had some Lilliputian bureaucrats pinned Mikey down? Ah, look out there for the old war-horse twitch. Edward. Delusions of grandeur! Watch it, do! It was a typical daydream to fancy that you were needed by the powerful. Since Aesop's mouse, God help us, all mice must dream of saving lions. And what worse dreamer than the mouse emeritus?

He took a taxi from the station, arrived unannounced and gave his card to the porter: Senator Edward O'Hourraghan, President of Civil Liberties, hon. sec. of this, that and the other. He was in the honoraries these days, thought of the condition as akin to the DTs: shivery syllables, a ghostly status. He wanted, he told the flunkey, to see the Bishop. The man was a bit ghostly himself: cobweb hair, dandruff powderings, a silhouette from eighteenth-century farce. Which bishop? he asked. How many had they got, then? Edward briskly inquired. 'Oglish,' he bullied, 'Bishop Michael Macateer.' He knew how to inject authority into his voice.

Twenty minutes later he was in an institutional parlour — all angles, vacancy and reflecting surfaces — facing a silver-haired Mikey dressed in velvet pants and the sort of purple poloneck you might expect to find in a Jermyn Street shop.[8] Failing to determine Mikey's status, Edward wondered whether this was trendy wear in the Vatican.

'Are you here for long?' he probed.

Mikey's palms were like powder-puffs and his eyes had the bloom of sloes. How good of Edward to have come, he marvelled, and held Edward's hands between his own as though they were infinitely precious. 'At our age one should hasten to repair bridges, don't you think?' He gazed intently and in a rather Latin way at Edward. 'What'll you have?' he asked. 'Wet your whistle?'

Edward chose whiskey and, when Mikey opted for tea, wondered might the Bishop have come here to dry out discreetly.

A man in a white coat hovered, summoned the porter to bring a trolley with refreshments, then took himself off to a window-seat. Mikey made some inadequate introduction which Edward failed to catch and the man kept looking out of the window in a way which made it unclear whether he was to be included in the conversation. At one point he turned and disconcerted Edward by the energy of his stare. It was targeted on the teacup which Mikey had raised to his lips. Edward, following it, expected to see a palsied quiver, but Mikey's hand was steady. His complexion did, perhaps, suggest drink? Priests, being denied one outlet, turned traditionally to the other. The surrogate, accepted in Ireland, might shock in Rome. Bloody Eyeties,[9] thought Edward, high on sympathy for Macateer, whose stamina should not — any more than Edward's own — be put in doubt over a matter of tippling. The man in the white coat was about the same age as Edward's sons. What was he? Doctor? Minder? Terrible for old Macateer to be under scrutiny. Edward, on a surge of brotherly feeling, slapped his old sparring partner on the back before the cup was safely returned to its saucer. Drops slopped onto Mikey's trousers and Edward's sleeve. Slow reflexes there, Edward acknowledged. Mikey

6. An American soap-opera of the 1960s, considered sensational because of its sexual content.
7. A lively night's dancing and entertainment.
8. A London street of fashionable shops and boutiques.
9. Derogatory slang for 'Italians'.

was getting slow. His own mind was a bit murky suddenly. Was the minder watching *him*? he wondered, but was embarrassed to check.

'Well,' he mustered heartiness. 'It's grand to see you.'

Mikey confessed that he had been hurt that time when Edward had avoided him in Rome. He'd put the ambassador up to issuing the invitation, so the refusal had been something of a slap in the face. 'One needs old friends,' he said sadly. New ones tended not to be disinterested.

Edward couldn't have agreed more. Feeling emotional, he dredged up the old lie about how he couldn't have stayed in Rome that time. Wanted to. Couldn't. Believing himself, he swore that the thing had been out of his hands.

'Oh, I never held it against you,' said Mikey. 'It goes back to that night in Jammet's when I was so bloody-minded. I've often wanted to apologize for that. Times change, eh? New criteria. Besides there were things on my mind. You wouldn't know this, but the lady in question. . . .'

'Jennifer.' Edward was annoyed by Mikey's terminology. It came straight from police files. It was a tongs for picking up dirt. 'Jennifer Dooley,' he said firmly.

'Her sons,' said the Bishop, 'were pupils of mine at Gonzaga.'[10]

'I never knew that.'

'They were. Nice boys. Vulnerable. Still, I suppose I was a bit straitlaced. Fighting doubts of my own. The toughest hour comes before the breakthrough, and I took it out on you. I've always regretted that.' Macateer's forthright look seemed a touch too good to be true. 'How is she now?' he asked.

Edward, hardened rather than softened, found himself testing Mikey's apology, mentally fingering it for flaws.

'A nice woman,' said Mikey. Jennifer had never been that. 'How did you say she was?'

Edward hadn't and wasn't going to. There was a sinister symmetry to poor Jennifer's condition. Arthritis sounded like an old penance for making too free with your limbs. She, who frolicked in alien beds and meadows — for a moment he smelled flattened grass — she, whose bum once flashed like milk or mushrooms, shall be confined to a wheelchair in a desert city in the circle of the Californicators. He imagined rows of raddled, leathery, legless old things. Or was Palm Springs in Nevada? Surely not? That name suggested snow. Niveous belly. Snowy thighs. Once smooth as egg-shells — were they scrambled now?

Edward's distress brimmed for Mikey too, who had his own afflictions. Anguished, he found he'd finished the whiskey which he'd been planning to nurse. He hoped drinking in Mikey's presence didn't upset him. Trying to slide the glass out of sight, he found that he'd only succeeded in attracting the attention of the doctor or minder who asked would Edward like a refill.

'No, no.' Edward repudiated excess. 'Thanks, though,' he conciliated and was shocked to receive a wink. The man in the white coat stared with a poker face at Edward then, for a second time, coolly and deliberately winked at him. Edward shifted his gaze hurriedly to Mikey who, sitting with his back to the doctor, was discoursing on how happiness was the goal of marriage, the fleshly bond a holy one and the day fast approaching when the Church would admit a dead marriage to be dead. 'Or so,' he wound up, 'I fervently hope. *I've* been fighting hard for that. Too hard for my own good.'

Edward looked at the whiskey-bottle and saw spots in the amber. Black, like flies congealed, they moved when he shifted his gaze. This new weakness appalled him. Had that man winked or hadn't he? The laity, he heard Macateer state, were far more backward than the clergy. Women, especially, were frightened of divorce.

'Think of farmers' wives in a place like this.' Macateer waved out at lush pasturage beyond the Institution lawn. A cow stared in at Edward, its mouth moving from right to left and back. 'What does divorce mean to *them*? That some young strap could catch their man's fancy and take their place on the farm. Have them put off the land. Evicted. Turned into landless vagrants.' The racial and sexual terrors there, said Macateer, ran deep. The Church had to consider the needs of the bulk of the people, the more traditional as well as those impatient for change.

The maggoty things in the whiskey leaped like letters on a screen. 'Impatient,' Edward heard and decided that Macateer thought that he, Edward, had been impatient because he'd known he'd soon be past it, now *was* past it and could look forward to no new embraces. Macateer mentioned the hare

10. A Jesuit school in Dublin.

and the tortoise. A judicious clergy would not, said Macateer, and *should* not try to keep up with the wilder elements, the hares . . . .

'By the time the tortoise reached the goal,' Edward remarked, 'the hare had probably either left in disgust or gone mad with impatience. You can't please *everyone*.' No sooner was the word 'mad' out of his mouth than he saw his gaffe. You didn't say that word in a madhouse any more than you said 'rope' in the house of a hanged man. Nervously, his eye met the minder's and in confusion he stretched out his glass and accepted the refill he didn't want. Change, said Macateer's imperturbable voice, *would* come. There was no *doctrinal* objection to divorce . . . . Edward stopped listening. Could the man really imagine that he wanted to hear all this? That he would find solace in being told *now* that he might as well have left his wife and run off with Jennifer? Could he? In Edward's prime it had been professional suicide in Dublin for a man to defy the Church, and Edward had had no choice but to knuckle under. His needs, it seemed, had been subordinated to those of the wives of randy farmers. To avoid a quarrel he tried to change the subject. 'Tell me about Rome,' he said. 'What's the state of play there? No,' he amended, 'I mean in the Vatican.'

Rome, sweet Rome, was something else; at least for Edward it was. A cruel fleshy town. Mentioning it had brought its crusty flavours to his tongue: meat cooked till it fell off the bone, rosemary twigs tied to the legs of lambs slaughtered when they were no bigger than a cat, spitted skylarks. Jennifer had once confessed to feeling guilt over her greed for these birds so unsportingly netted on their migration southwards. A blithe but not spiritual pleasure, she'd admitted, while wiping flecks of charred songbird from her nose and chin. Shame, she'd reminded shrewdly, gave eating that extra tingle usually peculiar to sex, and she and he, in all that enormous Roman *rosticceria*,[11] would be alone in feeling it: a bond. He had kissed her sucked and greasy fingers.

'Keats isn't our tradition really,' he'd argued.

Open fires, turning spits and flushed faces gave the place a look of old-time visions of hell.

'Eat the carcases,' a waiter had shouted at them, laughing in sensual empathy. 'They're the tastiest part. Hold them by the beak and chew the heads.'

Edward's mouth was dry with memory and tears pricked at his eyes. In places like that, Jennifer and he found bliss tuned to perfervid pitch by their nervous adulterers' yearnings. It had been on a Roman weekend that they had admitted to each other that they would never make the break.

'So what's the news from the Vatican?' he asked again.

Raising his eyes, he saw that behind Mikey's head the man in the white coat was vigorously shaking his own.

'The news' — Macateer tilted his broad boxer's chin — 'is that I'm giving you a chance to return good for evil.' The chin jutted. It always had. Mikey led with it, but its aggression now was subverted by tremors. 'I take it you're still head of Civil Liberties?'

The man in the white coat could have been directing a tangle of traffic. Stop, menaced his gestures: careful. Or was it deaf-and-dumb language? Maybe *he* was the inmate and Macateer in charge?

'Are you?'

'Yes.'

'In the past, you and I have differed over definitions and indeed over the desirability of freedom, but today,' said the Bishop lucidly, 'I am asking you to help me to regain my own in its basic, physical form.' The word seemed to set off a reflex. 'Fizzz-z-z . . .' he faltered in a spurt of hilarity. 'Physical.' Mirth drained from his face as quickly as it had come. 'I want you,' he ended quietly, 'to get me out of here.'

Edward feared that a laugh would be inappropriate. One had, however, got half-way up his throat.

'You may question my right to ask,' said Macateer. 'It is the right of the helpless.' He jabbed a finger at Edward.

As though reading subtitles, Edward peered to where the man behind seemed now to be exhorting patience. With whom? Was Macateer bonkers, then? And, if he was, then why was he allowed to write *and post* imperious letters? It was an outrage that a man of Edward's age and station should be dragged half-way across the country at a madman's whim. Embarrassing, too.

Yet Macateer was the picture of sanity. He smiled at Edward then, reproaching himself, shook his head. 'I've sprung it on you. Tss.'

11. rotisserie.

The chap in the coat was familiar from somewhere. Where? The puzzle kept popping into the foreground of Edward's mind, distracting him. He wished the chap would leave the room, or else that Mikey would. They he could ask one about the other.

Mikey, anxious lest Edward be harbouring grudges, was launched on a history of his own doctrinal waverings. Where he had ended up, he told Edward, was in the same boat as himself, with the other side out to get him.

Get whom?

'Me.' Macateer added that, though Edward might think him a Johnny-come-lately to the cause of liberalism, this was far from true. There was a tide in such movements and to anticipate it could only be counter-productive, self-indulgent and, in a sense, yes, mad. Was Edward being called mad now? It seemed he was. Mikey's face had grown supercilious. It reminded Edward of some portrait of a doge. Was it in the Wallace Collection?[12] he wondered, but thought not. His attention kept dodging and scampering. It was the intensity of Mikey's onslaught. Made one back off. 'Voltairian rationalism,' he heard Mikey sneer, was all liberalism could be in the context of the forties and fifties when Edward was a liberal. Later, on the other hand .... Bullying rhythms drummed. Mikey's fingers formed a knot as taut as a cricket-ball ready to lunge out and bash the bails off all obstacles to Mikey's will. Edward, inevitably reminded of the dogmatic old Mikey, saw that the memory showed, for, perceptibly, the tones softened and gave way to ingratiating ones so wrong for Mikey that Edward, teeth on edge, felt a panicked urge to plead: 'Stop, don't do this to us. Don't humiliate yourself.' Maybe, in fairness, he *should* do this? But wouldn't it be *more* humiliating for Macateer if he did? As a compromise, he tried to catch his eye, but its beam was wavering evasively over Edward's shoulder.

'You don't like me,' said Macateer surprisingly. 'Isn't that a good reason why you *should* help me?' Now his eye did catch Edward's in an iron-blue clench. 'Isn't that the liberal ethic?' he challenged. 'I have served an institution,' said Macateer. 'You fight the tyranny of institutions. What about taking on this one?' He gestured at the walls of the room. He had always admired Edward's gutsiness, he said, which was why he was appealing to him now. In the past Edward had stood up and been counted, defending sacked schoolteachers and other radicals and, at the risk of damaging his practice, held out against a domineering Church.

The bathos made Edward wonder if he was being mocked. 'Are you,' he checked, 'making fun of me?'

'Fun?'

'We achieved so little.'

'You kept the idea of liberty alive.'

The man's face puffed with assurance. What did he believe? Now the man in the white coat was listening with interest. Edward's struggles, said Macateer, reminded him of the dissidents in the Soviet Union.

'You embarrass me,' said Edward. 'We have no Siberia in Ireland.' He laughed at the ridiculousness of this.

'No, but people can,' said Macateer, 'get committed to asylums! Not that the agency which committed *me* was Irish.'

There was a silence. A sweaty gleam, hovering, halo-like, about the Bishop, could come from strain or the stimulus of drugs. The white-coated man guffawed with sudden violence.

'Ah, now, yer Grace, yet not comparing the Vatican to the Kremlin, I hope?' He winked at Edward, who again was shocked.

Macateer ignored him. 'Would Civil Liberties,' he asked Edward, 'take on the Vatican? Just to the extent of opening an inquiry? It would not, you understand, be limited to my case?'

'You've turned against the Church?'

'A certain church.'

'You mean,' Edward pressed incredulously, 'that you would take legal action against ... some agency ... in the Vatican?' The man was deranged, he decided with relief and a feeling of let-down. His fighting spirit, roused like an old horse taken too briefly from its paddock, was all a-tremble. He looked at Mikey, an awful old man, the spirit of smug Irish Catholicism personified, and saw no reason why freedom-lovers should fight for him. Mad or sane now, he had in his day been as repressive as he had had the power to be and was unrepentant. Mikey's mind was tidy, his commitment extreme. Once, it had been expedient for the Church to be traditionalist and tough. Now Mikey

12. A collection of French eighteenth-century paintings and some Dutch masters, housed in a London Georgian mansion.

saw it as wise to move the other way. 'Wise' meant politic.

'I am no defector.' Mikey's eyes were blazing, his cheeks concave. Fragility reached a taut climax in him as in a windblown candle. Edward was responsive to this passion of the flesh as he had not been to Mikey's words. These, however, came grating and panting out in a gravelly torrent. A man loyal to his institution, said Mikey, arguing with the fluency of habit, did not refrain from criticizing it when necessary. Neither did he leave it. He laboured to change it from within. Went *into* labour to produce a new version of it. To leave was easy — and ineffective. Defectors became enemies. 'To stay and struggle,' said Mikey, his eyes bulging painfully, 'is the test of loyalty.' Here Mikey's discourse grew obscure, black, thought Edward, like the tip of a smoking candle-flame. He had been persecuted, it appeared, had roused unworthy passion, courted isolation, trouble, personal animosities which — well, all communities harboured such. Edward must understand. Edward didn't. Conspiracies were hinted at. Mikey smoked and fumed.

Suddenly, the man in the white coat had taken a glass of water from the trolley and, walking over to the quivering Macateer, handed him a coloured pill. 'Mustn't excite yourself,' he admonished. 'He gets worked up,' he told Edward. 'Dangerous at his age, don't you know. Here,' he harried Macateer. 'Remember our agreement?'

Macateer snatched the pill and swallowed it with a gulp of water. 'Sycophant!' he shouted.

The minder went back to his window-seat.

Macateer tilted the back of his head at him. 'Bet you don't know who *he* is? Our genial host: Jim Farrel. Name mean nothing to you?' Macateer's angry eyes stabbed at Edward. 'Had us all to dinner,' he prompted. 'Twenty years ago? Remember? Poured champagne, buttered us up and footed the bill. Throwing a sprat to catch a salmon, mm? He's the original Platonic pragmatist and parasite.' Macateer paused. When he spoke again it was with diminished energy. 'If you help me,' he told Edward, 'Jim'll play ball. He likes to be on a winning team. If you don't....' He pointed his thumb downwards.

Farrel winked. 'A joke,' he said. 'His Grace likes to —'

'Toady!' Like a schoolyard insult, the word pebbled over Macateer's shoulder. To Edward he spoke quietly. 'Jim's mum had a hardware shop down the country. A tidy little concern. He has the sensitivity of cast-iron *and* its toughness. *I* found that useful, mind. I took him to Rome with me — aha, you didn't know that? Yes, yes, he was my minion there for years. My catspaw. Forgive the quaint diction. He's a quaint creature. Turned his coat. In the end he helped my enemies certify me. Why not? From his and their point of view, a man who ceases to know his own interest is mad, and I, feeling my time run out, ceased to bide it. Thus they could think that I would be best off in my native island with my old slavery enslaving me. Italian journalists are inquisitive; it was best to get me out of reach. He's tapping his forehead, isn't he?' Macateer, without looking round to where Farrel was indeed making this gesture, mimicked it perfectly. The hand tapping his high papery forehead was covered with raised brown moles. Macateer seemed older and more overgrown by the moment. A loser? 'My crime,' he told Edward, 'was your own failing: intemperateness. Also,' Mikey smiled without gaiety, 'love. Love of my family, which is and was the Church.'

Edward's brain buzzed. His stomach was making itself felt. Drink and excitement were lethal at his age. He should get out of here. But a quick withdrawal could look heartless. Antagonistic forces tugged. Emotionally, he could have been being quartered by wild horses. Sectioned. Minced. Eagerness pulsed in him: that lethal itch to live. Poor bloody Mikey! *Mon semblable, mon frère!*[13] Yes? No? Issues which Edward had long thought settled and jelled beneath the veneer of age's mellowness had begun to toss, jumbled like notions in an adolescent's brain. The sensation was nostalgic and disagreeable.

'Don't excite yerself, now,' said Jim Farrel, perhaps speaking to both old men.

Proscrastinating, Edward decided not to catch the train tonight. He'd stay in a local hotel he'd seen touted by the gastronomic guides.

'You're not going?' Mikey was aghast.

'Must.' Edward tapped his watch. 'Only to Ballylea House. I'll come again tomorrow.' This was a false promise. He'd have to see. When he

13. 'My double, my brother!' From the prefatory poem to *Les fleurs du mal* (1857) by Charles Baudelaire (1821-67), expressing both the speaker's distaste for his reader and his kinship to him.

pressed Mikey's hand, it felt like spaghetti: a mess of veins. Mikey's eyes looked at him with equally soft appeal and unearned comradeliness. Not many of us left, Edward. Who's 'us', Mikey?

Farrell took Edward to the front door, then through a portcullis of rain to canvass the car-park for lifts. He dashed back with news that a Dr Ryan would be dining at Ballylea House and could take Edward there.

'Was it you posted his letter to me?' Edward managed to ask as he was being settled into the car.

'It was, yes. He has high hopes of you, Senator.' Farrel's face was a blur magnified by the wet window and his tone a concerned nanny's. Edward wondered would he be mad to involve Civil Liberties in this intricate sub-world. 'Phone if you're coming tomorrow,' Farrel shouted as the car drove off. 'Ask for me, Senator: Jim Farrel.'

Dr Ryan accepted a drink in the hotel bar. He was a fresh-faced gossipy psychiatrist and revealed that Farrel wasn't. Wasn't a psychiatrist? Not even a doctor? Edward, remembering Jammet's, and Farrel's weakness for slipping a rung or so above his station, asked, 'A male nurse, then?'

His guest conciliated. 'You could say that. More of an inmate, actually. *You* wouldn't know, to be sure, but in places like this . . . .' The lines, it seemed, were fluid, the outfit run by priests, not doctors. 'Oh, ours is definitely a subsidiary capacity.' He mused. 'Odd customers wash up on Irish shores. Gulf Arab girls come here to study nursing. Our reliable chastity is why. Equally, our pious discretion brings anonymous prelates to the Institution. Enough said,' said Ryan, lowering a lid. Farrel, he admitted, *was* an inmate, though of a special sort. 'Mind, it's not my department. All hearsay. But it seems they came together from Rome: Master and Man.'

'Surely both can't be mad?' And what, Edward wondered, about the white coat? The pill?

'Farrel's good with patients.' The doctor tee-heed. 'Listen, he was a medical student in his youth. We lay man-traps for men like that. You can't imagine how short-handed we are. So, he's humoured, let have the coat and the parlour. Staff in places like this is impossible to get. I married a local girl myself or I'd never have stayed. Then I like the horses. I'm a country type. But I'm unusual.'

'Is anyone in the Institution clinically mad?'

The doctor made the most of this cue. Was Edward a Laingian? He discoursed on madness, quoted Foucault.[14] On wet nights, it seemed, he read. Sure, wasn't it all relative? A matter of being out of step with your immediate community? And hadn't some societies seen madness as divine? Mind you, Pope's[15] crack about great wits being near to madness had especial relevance in the context of the Church. With abstract men subjected to great pressure — especially now, my God, with all the controversy — you'd *expect* breakdowns, wouldn't you? Moments of uncertainty. The Institution specialized in distinguished key thinkers who came here to recuperate. *Sub rosa.*[16] Much could hinge on their emotional health.

'Not mental?'

'Mental, emotional — some may just need a rest.'

'Or to be kept out of the way?'

The doctor — now on his third whiskey — whispered, 'Ah, now, Senator, mum's the word!'

Could he be a semi-inmate himself? Or was Edward succumbing to an insidious folly: believing himself alone in his sanity in a world of lunatics? Ryan, face fat with alcohol, continued his chat. Important with innuendo, he grew big on it, amplifying gestures, grinning, nudging ribs.

'Ah, but silence is golden, eh, Senator, what?' Edward's title seemed all of a sudden to set off a train of thought, for the face shuttered itself at speed. Ryan's mouth twisted, like a key in a lock, as he revealed that he was anxious about his dinner and had better phone his wife pronto. She was late and the table booked for half an hour since. Sorry, Senator, must be off. Great privilege to meet you. Thanks for the drink.

Later, Edward saw him dodge across the lobby under the wing of a woman. Not acknowledging Edward's wave, he scuttled into the dining-room.

Alone in the bar's dimness, Edward was assailed by memories of the decades — his middle ones — when Dubliners had scuttled from him in droves. The town, when he was not yet a senator but

14. A Laingian is a disciple of the radical Scottish psychiatrist, R. D. Laing (1927-89), whose work, especially *The Divided Self*, was popular in the 1960s. Michel Foucault is a French intellectual and author of *Madness and Civilization* (1961).
15. It was in fact Dryden who wrote in *Absalom and Achitophel*, lines 164-65: 'Great wits are sure to madness near alli'ed,/And thin partitions do their bounds divide.'
16. In privacy, out of the public eye.

already active in Civil Liberties, had been populated with citizens made in the mould of glove-puppets, each equipped with dissimilar sides to his face. The side for public viewing was pious and non-committal. The private side, a glitter of keyed-up bravery, peered, in the shadow of raised collar and lowered hat, like a rabbit from his hole. 'Keep up the good work, Eddy,' these secret fans hissed furtively. 'We'd back ye all the way if it wasn't for the aul' job, don't ye know, the wife, the kids, the pension. Sure you know what it's like yourself. Cross the priests in this country and you're a goner. But we're with you in spirit. You're doing Trojan work!'

He remembered the public ostracism with a cold shudder which he had never let himself feel at the time. In the heat of the fight, pugnacity kept you going. And his swagger had appealed to women. He had enjoyed, even exploited, being odd man out. Now he would get nothing from it. An old man needed approval, needed the goodwill of acquaintances to tether him to a receding world.

What *right* had Mikey to come whining to him? Let him take his come-uppance. According to his own reckoning, the man who played against the odds was a fool.

And what about Edward's reckoning? Wasn't abandoning a principle a way of letting death steal a pass on you? Was it? It was. You became less yourself. Ah, to hell, Mikey wasn't worth fighting for, and it would be a terrible fight. It could bring Civil Liberties into disrepute and stir up untold scandal. A caper like that could lead to not one but two old men being thought demented.

Edward's bladder was bothering him, and he set off for the gents. Passing the dining-room, he saw Ryan's face duck behind a menu in pretence of non-recognition. The light in the men's room was dusty neon, cold as a twilit sea. In a tidal mirror, the face floating towards Edward was fearful, peppered with the marks of doubt, clenched, shifty, explosive and — it struck him with a slow surge of pleasure — vehemently alive. As he came closer, a pink flush began to give it a healthier glow; the lips parted in amusement and a fist lunged ahead of it, pronging two fingers aloft and erect in a waggling V-sign.

He decided to have a bottle of Château Haut Brion 1970 with dinner. It was good neither for his liver nor for his wallet, but seize the moment, seize the day. He'd drink in it to his own and Mikey's intemperate future.

Next morning he was up early. Nowadays, he scarcely slept anyway, and dreams sparked off by his day's doings were best suppressed. He was aware of them slithering back now beneath a mud of oblivion.

The breakfast-room was a splatter of neon. Tables were ice-floes where guests who last night had stayed too long at the bar flipped open napkins and lowered dispirited walrus faces towards their kippers. Edward, however, was brisk. Purpose enlivened him, and his grapefruit was a zesty pleasure. He chatted with the waiter, deciding to walk to the Institution which, the man assured, was no more than a mile off as the crow flew.

It proved a bracing stroll, and he was breathing pastoral air with relish when, half-way up the Institutional avenue, Jim Farrel emerged from the ambush of a rhododendron.

'I had an idea you mightn't phone,' he reproached. 'Listen, Senator, I need a word with you.'

He needed many, it turned out, for Edward would have to be put in the picture if he was to be of any use to Macateer.

'For his sake,' Farrel appealed, 'you should hear both sides.'

Edward, the old lawyer, had to agree that, if there were indeed sides, he'd better take a look at both. He let himself be led through foliage towards a rustic tea-house. The estate had once belonged to members of the old ruling class and bits of pretty pomp subsisted. A lake, visible from where they sat, was fenced off by wire netting.

What Edward must know, said Farrel, was that the Bishop's folly was not personal. 'Madness' — Farrel's face streamed with excited sweat — 'has the whole bloody Vatican in its grip. It's an infection, Senator: a disease. You'd have to know the place to understand. It's very closed off. Patronage and slavery are rampant. You heard our friend call me a hanger-on and worse. Well, that's what I was, and the place is full of men like me: men who carry other men's briefcases for a decade or so, open car-doors for them, dust down their rosaries, live on hope. Hope is the disease, hope and impatience, and the top men are not immune. *They* hope for something else maybe: the Kingdom of Heaven on earth with freedeom to love and live carnally extended to all. A new reformed God comforting His creatures with apples of all knowledge and licence.' Through Farrel's tones came a flicker of quotation marks. Clearly, this was parody of something or anyway an echo.

'Macateer?' wondered Edward.

'Aye. You heard what he said: he used to fight it and then he succumbed to it. That's not uncommon, Senator. Look how the old witch-hunters grew fascinated by the thing they were suppressing. There's scholars will tell you that they invented it, that all we know of witches comes from the witch-hunters' reports and that maybe there were no witches at all.' Farrel grinned shyly. 'You pick up queer lore. Well, to come back to the present, the dream that's haunting the place now is old, too: an old heresy. This time, though, it's biting right into the heart of the Church. Right to the *sanctum sanctorum*[17] — and when that happens who's to condemn it?' Farrel's grin grew wolfish and his eyes glittered with an appetite for scandal. 'They say,' he whispered, 'that in the last couple of years *two* popes had to be knocked off. One for sure was done in. Eliminated for the greater good. Can you credit that, Senator?' Cunning pause. Insinuating smile. How far will you go with me? asked Farrel's long streamer of a face. Flecked with dimples of darkness, it flowed whitely in Edward's troubled vision — the tea-house was dusky, and Farrel's presence had an unsettling effect on him. The chap was actually swaying like a cobra in his excitement, and this impeded Edward's apprehension of what he was saying.

'Men like me,' confided Farrel, 'get to know things that the red hats[18] themselves don't know, let alone the bishops. In a sense, we run the place. Why else would we put up with the sort of shit you saw me take from Macateer? We know our worth and that it depends on not being known. Eh, Senator, can you believe that it was men like myself who arranged for those two popes' disposal — men that I maybe know? Doing someone's bidding, to be sure — but tell me this: what's a head without a hand to do its bidding? It's not much, is it? Listen' — he gripped Edward's arm — 'how do you imagine he was got out? Our friend? Mm? Brought over here? By whom? Why? I'll tell you: it was I did it and for his own good. For his safety. Better a spell in the bin than what *can* happen, mm? To be sure, he's in no state to appreciate this.' Farrel paused, waited, but Edward had nothing to say to him. 'You'll have guessed,' the fellow went on, 'that there are factions. What you mightn't guess is how ruthless the fight has to be. No holds barred. The dreamers *have* to be stopped. He — our friend — is the one who taught me that. He was an institution man himself. Trained me up to think like him. Well, it's common sense: when you're afloat in a boat you don't drive a hole in its bottom and you don't let anyone else do it, either. Right? But then he joined the dreamers: started wanting the fruits of eternity in the here and now. Like those popes I mentioned. No need to name names. Impatience, Senator, is a hazard of the profession. Listen, sit down, it's only fair to hear me out. I want to make sure you have things clear. Then you can judge. Sit down, sit down. Have you understood, Senator, that the man in there,' Farrel gestured in the direction of the Institution, hidden behind trees, 'that the Macateer in there is a changeling?'

'I've got to go.'

'I'm speaking metaphorically.'

'Let me pass.'

'In a moment, a wee moment, there's plenty of time.'

'I have a tight schedule.' Edward waved his wrist and watch.

'What's madness, you may ask?' Farrel thrust his face into Edward's, barring his exit from the tea-house. 'Maybe its worst strain is altruism?'

'Let's discuss this later. I want to see Macateer now.'

'You're suspicious of me?' An urchin's humour twiddled at the corners of Farrel's mouth. 'These things are hard to take in.' The cobra sway of Farrel's head made Edward's spin. Right, left, right swayed Farrel, like a goalie guarding his goal. He was in fact guarding the door. 'What have I to gain by hurting you?'

'Is that a threat?'

'Senator!' Farrel was every inch the reproachful nurse — nanny or nursery-school teacher. 'It is because of my deep respect for you,' he spoke with formality, 'that I'm appealing to you on his behalf. He had to be made to see sense first, *then* restored to his former position.'

'So that he'll restore you to yours?' But Edward was not interested in this dialogue. Its premises were absurd. On the other hand, he hesitated to push past the man, fearing to let things get physical. He wondered would anyone hear him if he were to

17. Holy of holies.
18. i.e. cardinals.

shout. No, probably not. 'I need,' he improvised, 'to go to the bathroom.'

'Take a leak in the bushes.'

'That's not what I need.'

'OK then, OK.' Farrel, a policeman's grip on Edward's elbow, walked him in custody back towards the avenue. 'First we must talk sense to him,' he explained, while pushing foliage out of Edward's path, 'then help him legally. He has a strong case, but must be persuaded to behave with prudence. Otherwise, things will just start up again the same way. We'll be back to square one. The Progressives are just not going to be let wreck the Church. I wish I had more time to make this clear to you, Senator. I know you find it hard to believe. The new is strange and the strange seems mad — but ours is a time of polarities. You, an old liberal and a man of the middle, owe it to us to hold the ring.' In his excitement, Farrel was backing Edward into brambles and had made him lose his balance. 'Oh, Jesus, I'm sorry,' he shouted and caught the lurching Edward in his arms. 'Steady now, Senator. You don't think *I'd* hurt you, now do you, surely? Me?'

'Why not you? Who are you anyway?'

'I'm your spiritual son. I picked you out twenty years ago.'

'What rubbish.'

'Not rubbish. You remember the dinner at Jammet's? You must. You do. The Bishop mentioned it yesterday. Well, why do you think I gave it? I'd picked you out: you and him. You represented the two sides of my tradition: the Irish heritage. I wanted to apprentice myself. I was looking for a mentor. My father died early, you know. Anyway, he was a limited man. I had ambitions. I wanted short cuts: an adoptive father. One adopted by me who could instruct me, give me a leg up. I planned to get to know you and the Monsignor, as he then was, both. That's why I gave the dinner. The two foreigners were bait. I knew you'd want to meet them — well, I hardly hoped you'd want to meet *me*. But, normally, you should have extended some hospitality after accepting mine. I counted on that. If it hadn't been for the fight you had with Macateer — you'll remember that? — it would have worked. As it was, I had to choose between the two of you right off. I could have brought you home in a taxi — drunk as you were. But your wife would have been there. She wouldn't have let me stay. So I plumped for him, stayed on, flattered him, became his factotum. Secretary. Well, you know all that. But I've often wondered what it would have been like if you'd been my patron. Here we are. You said you needed a bathroom.'

They had reached the door of the Institution.

'I want a taxi,' said Edward. 'I'm leaving.' He couldn't bear to see Macateer now, or indeed anyone else. The fumes of Farrel's unbalanced eagerness made him feel unbalanced himself. It was like getting drunk off another man's breath. He had to be alone for a while.

'He's expecting you. He'll be disappointed. At least say "hello".'

'I'm too old for all this.'

'Too old to turn away from it. The young don't need you. Do your sons need you?'

Edward was astounded at the chap's knowing insolence. Had he been ferreting our information? Gossip? Into that madhouse he was resolved not to put foot.

'I'm going.' He turned, stepped down some steps, hastened, as he heard Farrel come after him and, losing his footing, fell and rolled down the rest of the flight. Feeling the fellow try to pick him up — his leg ached where he had perhaps pulled a muscle — he was impelled by pain and fury to lunge for the bloody ass's face. His knuckles hit something hard — teeth perhaps? — and he felt blood on his fist. Was it his own? He could have wept with exasperation. Feeling himself being further manhandled, he lunged again and realized that he had managed to break his own glasses. Splinters ran into his palm and he could see nothing but blur. Voices reached him confusingly.

'What's up? What's it now? What's the matter?'

'... gone berserk. Here, give me a hand.'

'Who is it?'

'A visitor. I know him. Gently now.'

'Who did you say?'

'Drunk?'

'... do himself an injury — or us. A friend of Farrel's, is he?'

'What set him off? Here, Pat, Joe, we need help. Those buggers are never there when you need them.'

'Quiet now, Senator ... need to give him a shot of something. Tough old bastard, isn't he? Music in the old bones yet, what?'

'A damn sight too much. What was it you said ...?'

'Off his head — doting.' That was Farrel's voice. 'A shot of something. Someone call Dr Ryan.'

Struggling and captive like a newborn infant, Edward felt himself carried in the door.

JOHN McGAHERN

(1934-)

from: NIGHTLINES (1970)

[The power of economy that we associate with the short story is fully demonstrated in 'Korea' from *Nightlines* (1970). The story tangles the last of the narrator's youth and the last of his family's way of life. The imminent end of that life causes the narrator's father to wish to reverse the ill-gains (as he sees them) of one war (the Irish War of Independence) by exploiting the ill-gains of another war. Korea is a grim variation on the perennial theme of Irish emigration to the United States.

McGahern's economy is not merely structural; his telling observations and circumstantialities have a quick poetic precision that helps establish the characteristic bitter-sweetness of his vision.]

KOREA

'You saw an execution then too, didn't you?' I asked my father, and he started to tell as he rowed. He'd been captured in an ambush in late 1919, and they were shooting prisoners in Mountjoy as reprisals at that time.[1] He thought it was he who'd be next, for after a few days they moved him to the cell next to the prison yard. He could see out through the bars. But no rap to prepare himself came to the door that night, and at daybreak he saw the two prisoners they'd decided to shoot being marched out: a man in his early thirties, and what was little more than a boy, sixteen or seventeen, and he was weeping. They blindfolded the boy, but the man refused the blindfold. When the officer shouted, the boy clicked to attention, but the man stayed as he was, chewing very slowly. He had his hands in his pockets.

'Take your hands out of your pockets,' the officer shouted again; there was irritation in the voice.

The man slowly shook his head.

'It's a bit too late now in the day for that,' he said.

The officer then ordered them to fire, and as the volley rang, the boy tore at his tunic over the heart, as if to pluck out the bullets, and the buttons of the tunic began to fly into the air before he pitched forward on his face.

The other heeled quietly over on his back; it must have been because of the hands in the pockets.

The officer dispatched the boy with one shot from the revolver as he lay face downward, but he pumped five bullets in rapid succession into the man, as if to pay him back for not coming to attention.

'When I was on my honeymoon years after, it was May, and we took the tram up the hill of Howth from Sutton Cross.[2] We sat on top in the open on the wooden seats with the rail around that made it like a small ship. The sea was below, and smell of the sea and furze bloom all about, and then I looked down and saw the furze pods bursting, and the way they burst in all directions seemed shocking like the buttons when he started to tear at his tunic; I couldn't get it out of my mind all day; it destroyed the day,' he said.

'It's a wonder their hands weren't tied?' I asked him as he rowed between the black navigation pan and the red where the river flowed into Oakport.

'I suppose it was because they were considered soldiers.'

'Do you think the boy stood to attention because he felt that he might still get off if he obeyed the rules?'

'Sounds a bit highfalutin to me. Comes from going to school too long,' he said aggressively, and I was silent. It was new to me to hear him talk about

1. During the War of Independence (1919-21), the British executed prisoners in reprisal for attacks on their forces. Mountjoy is a prison in Dublin.

2. Howth is a hilly promontory on the north shore of Dublin Bay. Sutton Cross is on the neck of the peninsula.

his own life at all. Before, if I asked him about the war, he'd draw fingers across his eyes as if to tear a spider web away, but it was my last summer with him on the river, and it seemed to make him want to talk, to give of himself before it ended.

Hand over hand I drew in the line that throbbed with fish; there were two miles of line, a hook on a lead line every three yards. The license allowed us a thousand hooks, but we used more. We were the last to fish this freshwater for a living.

As the eels came in over the side I cut them loose with a knife into a wire cage, where they slid over each other in their own oil, the twisted eel hook in their mouths. The other fish — pike choked on hooked perch they'd tried to swallow, bream, roach — I slid up the floorboards towards the bow of the boat. We'd sell them in the village or give them away. The hooks that hadn't been taken I cleaned and stuck in rows round the side of the wooden box. I let the line fall in its centre. After a mile he took my place in the stern and I rowed. People hadn't woken yet, and the early morning cold and mist were on the river. Outside of the slow ripple of the oars and the threshing of the fish on the line beaded with running drops of water as it came in, the river was dead silent, except for the occasional lowing of cattle on the banks.

'Have you any idea what you'll do after this summer?' he asked.

'No. I'll wait and see what comes up,' I answered.

'How do you mean *what comes up*?'

'Whatever result I get in the exam. If the result is good, I'll have choices. If it's not, there won't be choices. I'll have to take what I can get.'

'How good do you think they'll be?'

'I think they'll be all right, but there's no use counting chickens, is there?'

'No,' he said, but there was something calculating in the face; it made me watchful of him as I rowed the last stretch of the line. The day had come, the distant noises of the farms and the first flies on the river, by the time we'd lifted the large wire cage out of the bulrushes, emptied in the morning's catch of eels, and sunk it again.

'We'll have enough for a consignment tomorrow,' he said.

Each week we sent the eels live to Billingsgate[3] in London.

3. London's biggest fish market.

'But say, say even if you do well, you wouldn't think of throwing this country up altogether and going to America?' he said, the words fumbled for as I pushed the boat, using the oar as a pole, out of the bulrushes after sinking the cage of eels, the mud rising a dirty yellow between the stems.

'Why America?'

'Well, it's the land of opportunity, isn't it, a big, expanding country; there's no room for ambition in this poky place. All there's room for is to make holes in pints of porter.'

I was wary of the big words, they were not in his voice or any person's voice.

'Who'd pay the fare?' I asked.

'We'd manage that. We'd scrape it together somehow.'

'Why should you scrape for me to go to America if I can get a job here?'

'I feel I'd be giving you a chance I never got. I fought for this country. And now they want to take away even the license to fish. Will you think about it anyhow?'

'I'll think about it,' I answered.

Through the day he trimmed the brows of ridges in the potato field while I replaced hooks on the line and dug worms, pain of doing things for the last time as well as the boredom the knowledge brings that soon there'll be no need to do them, that they could be discarded almost now. The guilt of leaving came: I was discarding his life to assume my own, a man to row the boat would eat into the decreasing profits of the fishing, and it was even not certain he'd get renewal of his license. The tourist board had opposed the last application. They said we impoverished the coarse fishing for tourists — the tourists who came every summer from Liverpool and Birmingham in increasing numbers to sit in aluminium deck chairs on the riverbank and fish with rods. The fields we had would be a bare living without the fishing, and it'd be vinegar for him to turn what he called boarding-house zookeeper.

I saw him stretch across the wall in conversation with the cattle-dealer Farrell as I came round to put the worms where we stored them in clay in the darkness of the lavatory. Farrell leaned on the bar of his bicycle on the road. I passed into the lavatory thinking they talked about the price of cattle, but as I emptied the worms into the box, the word *Moran* came, and I carefully opened the door to listen. It was my father's voice; it was excited.

'I know. I heard the exact sum. They got ten

thousand dollars when Luke was killed. Every American soldier's life is insured to the tune of ten thousand dollars.'

'I heard they get two hundred and fifty dollars a month each for Michael and Sam while they're serving,' he went on.

'They're buying cattle leftandright,' Farrell's voice came as I closed the door and stood in the darkness, in the smell of shit and piss and the warm fleshy smell of worms crawling in too little clay.

The shock I felt was the shock I was to feel later when I made some social blunder, the splintering of a self-esteem, and the need to crawl into some lavatory and think.

Luke Moran's body had come from Korea in a leaden casket, had crossed the stone bridge to the slow funeral bell with the big cars from the embassy behind, the coffin draped in the Stars and Stripes. Shots had been fired above the grave before they threw in the clay. There were photos of his decorations being presented to his family by a military attaché.

He'd scrape the fare, I'd be conscripted there, each month he'd get so many dollars while I served, and he'd get ten thousand if I was killed.

In the darkness of the lavatory between the boxes of crawling worms before we set the night line for the eels I knew my youth had ended.

I rowed as he let out the night line, his fingers baiting each twisted hook so beautifully that it seemed a single movement. The dark was closing from the shadow of Oakport to Nutley's boathouse, bats made ugly whirls overhead, the wings of ducks shirred as they curved down into the bay.

'Have you thought about what I said about going to America?' he asked, without lifting his eyes from the hooks and the box of worms.

'I have.'

The oars dipped in the water without splash, the hole whorling wider in the calm as it slipped past him on the stern seat.

'Have you decided to take the chance then?'

'No. I'm not going.'

'You won't be able to say I didn't give you the chance when you come to nothing in this fool of a country. It'll be your own funeral.'

'It'll be my own funeral,' I answered, and asked after a long silence, 'As you grow older, do you find your own days in the war and jails coming much back to you?'

'I do. And I don't want to talk about them. Talking about the execution disturbed me no end, those cursed buttons bursting into the air. And the most I think is that if I'd conducted my own wars, and let the fool of a country fend for itself, I'd be much better off today. And I don't want to talk about it.'

I knew this silence was fixed forever as I rowed in silence till he asked, 'Do you think, will it be much good tonight?'

'It's too calm,' I answered.

'Unless the night wind gets up,' he said anxiously.

'Unless a night wind,' I repeated.

As the boat moved through the calm water and the line slipped through his fingers over the side I'd never felt so close to him before, not even when he'd carried me on his shoulders above the laughing crowd to the Final. Each move he made I watched as closely as if I too had to prepare myself to murder.

PATRICK McGINLEY

(1937-)

from: BOGMAIL (1978)

[McGinley's work is macabre and vivid. He seems to have combined features of the Irish folk-tale with the practices of the contemporary novel. His native County Donegal is the setting for his fiction. The period in this case seems to be Ireland in the nineteen fifties. Roarty's murder of Eales, recounted here in the third chapter of the novel, brings after it a trail of blackmail, destruction and misconception.]

THREE

It was Saturday evening, the pub was crowded, and Roarty was at his most landlordly. After pouring himself the sixth double since dinnertime he had gone with no perceptible outward change through what he called the well-being barrier. It was always like that. The first double had no effect and neither had the second; the third thawed him; the fourth warmed him; and the fifth lit a taper in his mind that shone on the surrounding dark, colouring it like a winter moon bursting through low cloud. The self-destructive edge vanished from his thoughts, words flowed as bright as spring water, and laughter came easily and without overt reason. Between the fifth and the twelfth double he lived on a plateau of unconsidered pleasure which he tried to prolong until after closing time. The twelfth double was followed by a period of deterioration during which the commonest words seemed like tongue-twisters, and thoughts came slowly like the last drops from a squeezed lemon. That was regrettable, and it was a stage which he usually avoided. He liked to arrange matters so that he was on his twelfth double at closing time. Then, after he and Eales had washed up, he would scorn the optic and pour himself what Potter called 'a domestic double' straight from the bottle. This he would take to his bedroom and sip as he read his 'office' for the day, an outmoded article on some aspect of science from the scholar's *Britannica*.

Pulling a pint of stout for a long-haired tourist, Roarty listened with enjoyment to the catechetical conversation between Crubog, Cor Mogaill, Rory Rua, Gimp Gillespie and the Englishman Potter who, though new to the glen, was learning fast.

'Why do seagulls no longer follow the plough?' asked Crubog.

'Because of the lack of earthworms in the sod,' said Rory Rua who had heard this conversation before.

'And why are earthworms as scarce as sovereigns?' Crubog demanded to know.

'Because of the artificial manure,' Cor Mogaill sniggered.

'When we used to put nothing on the land but wrack and cow dung,' said Crubog, 'the sod was alive with earthworms, big fat red ones, wriggling like elvers as the spade or the coulter sliced them. And the air would be thick with a *gliobach*[1] of gulls on a spring day, there would be so many of them. But now you could plough from June to January without even attracting the notice of a robin. The fertiliser has killed the goodness in the soil so that not even an earthworm can live in it. How can you grow good oats in dead earth? Answer me that, Cor Mogaill.'

'What we need is humus,' said Gimp Gillespie, the local journalist. 'Science has upset the natural cycle. Render to the earth the things that are the earth's and to the laboratory the manufactures of science.'

'Hear, hear,' said Potter.

'How many tons of earth does your average earthworm turn over in a year?' Crubog asked darkly. 'Answer me that, Cor Mogaill. And you can consult your personal library if you like.'

Cor Mogaill, a youth of no more than twenty, regarded himself as the village intellectual. He never came to the pub without his knapsack in which he kept his bicycle pump, certain back copies of *The Irish Times* and *A History of Ireland* by Eleanor Hull.[2] He would then spend the evening trying to start an argument that would provide him with an opportunity of consulting what he called his

1. Irish for 'multitude', 'flock'.
2. Eleanor Hull (1860-1935), noted Celtic scholar, wrote a *History of Ireland* in two volumes, published in 1926 and 1931.

personal library. Now he looked menacingly at Crubog but the knapsack remained on his back.

'What do you know about the physiology of earthworms?' he asked Crubog.

'I've had it on good authority, the best there is. Forty tons, not an ounce less. Now a Bachelor of Agricultural Science could put out the spool of his arse without achieving that.'

'Who told you?' Cor Mogaill demanded.

'Sir Valentine Matlock told my father, and my father told me.'

'With his dying breath,' suggested Cor Mogaill sarcastically.

'They were two good men, may God be good to them, and now they're doing more to improve the quality of the soil than you've ever done, Cor Mogaill. There are some men who wouldn't even make good humus,' Crubog laughed on his way to the outside lavatory.

It was an evening of energetic conversation. Crubog was at his most entertaining, full of trenchant anecdotes and antique lore, and Cor Mogaill and Gimp Gillespie drew him out with unobtrusive skill to the evident delight of the Englishman Potter who presided over the conversation with the intellectual discrimination which he saw as befitting a man of scientific background. Their talk took colour from the obscurity of the topics and the need of the speakers to make up for their relative ignorance by embroidering their thoughts with humorous whimsy. First, they considered whether a doe hare drops all her litter in one form or if she places each leveret in a separate nest for safety's sake. When they had failed to find an answer, they turned to the trapping of mountain foxes. Here Rory Rua proved the most knowledgeable or at least the most confident in his opinion. He impressed everyone by saying that he would bet his shirt that a dead cat, preferably in an advanced state of decomposition, was the best bait because a fox could wind it even on a windless night. But Crubog was not to be bested. He demanded to know how curlews, when they are feeding inland, can tell that the tide has begun to ebb and that it is time to make for the shore. And he posed the question with such an air of dark omniscience that Potter said that it was as well they did not have an ornithologist in the company, that his specialist knowledge would kill all conversation.

Now and again they tried to draw Roarty into their circle but he told them that their talk was too abstruse for a mere publican. He felt remote from those on the other side of the bar, the distance between himself and them increasing with each double. Besides he could not banish last night's dream from his thoughts.

He was a boy of twelve chasing his ten-year-old sister Maureen in a field full of daisies when suddenly she stopped and said:

'Bring me that butterfly.'

'Why?' he asked, sensing that his will was not free.

'Because I want to pull its wings apart,' she laughed.

It seemed such a natural desire that he ran after the butterfly at once, dizzy with its rise and fall in the sunlight and the whiteness of its wings like the whiteness of the daisies in the grass.

Suddenly he stopped on the shore of a lake. The butterfly had escaped him, fluttered over the unruffled surface of the water and rested on a solitary lough lily in the centre.

'You can walk on the water — if you don't look down at your feet,' his sister explained from behind.

Reluctantly he dipped his toe, and the water retreated before him. He stepped off the bank, the water still retreating, exposing the soft, peaty mud that cooled the soles of his feet and oozed between his toes. The earth swallowed the water with a sucking and a gurgling until the entire bottom of the lake was bare and the water lily, lacking the support of its natural element, lay besmirched and bedraggled on the black mud. He examined the stem and how it grew out of the darkness of the mud, and finally the round hole in the delicate heart of the flower. He held it tenderly between his fingers, and an ugly green caterpillar poked its head through the hole and crawled over the leaf with odious contractions.

'You've pursued evil to its lair,' Maureen called from the shore.

'And I've found it at the heart of beauty,' he replied.

The tenderness he experienced as he held the lily between his fingers and his horror at the ravishment of the flower merged in dark vexation, and he lost count of the number of drinks in a round.

'Roarty will have the answer,' said Crubog. 'After all he's the second best snipe shot in the county.'

'What's that?' Roarty asked, measuring a double Scotch for Potter.

'How does the snipe beat his tattoo in the spring?' Crubog asked.

'Tattoo?'

'How does he drum?' Potter rephrased.

'With his outer tail feathers,' Roarty replied. 'He holds them out stiffly at right angles as he swoops.'

'Wrong,' said Eales. 'Every one of you is wrong.'

'Enlighten us,' said Roarty, reddening beneath his beard.

'With his syrinx, of course,' said Eales.

'Fair play to you, Eamonn,' said Cor Mogaill.

'With his syringe?' asked Crubog, who was rather deaf.

'Syrinx,' Eales shouted. 'That's how most birds make sounds.'

'But the snipe's drumming is a different kettle of fish,' said Roarty.

'I'll bet a double whiskey I'm right,' said Eales.

'And I'll bet a bottle,' said Roarty, who did not take kindly to being challenged by his barman.

'I'll keep the bets,' laughed Crubog.

'Can you prove you're right?' asked Eales.

'Not this minute. I'll look it up after closing.'

It was half-past eleven by the clock, and they would expect twenty minutes to drink up. He put two towels over the dispensers and went out the back for a breath of cool air. He was disappointed, however. It was a humid night with a faintly touching land breeze that died away every now and then, leaving him becalmed by the back door with a constriction in his throat and made breathing difficult. The eastern sky was a mass of inky cloud, a low roof that pressed on the tops of the hills and obliterated the moon and stars. These rain clouds had come up since dinnertime, and it surprised him that no one in the pub had mentioned them. He listened to the hum of conversation from the bar, and thought that a pub at that hour of the evening was the most unreal place on earth.

'Where is your proof?' asked Eales self-confidently when they had washed up and the last customer had gone.

'In my encyclopedia. I'll go fetch it.'

He went up to his bedroom and scanned the article on 'Snipe', too distraught to take much pleasure in being right.

The house was quiet now; the last few stragglers had taken the country roads home. Sadness and impossible longings choked him as he remembered summer evenings with Cecily on holiday sitting at the piano in her room, the whole house flowing with liquid music. 'On Wings of Song', 'Für Elise', 'Jesu Joy of Man's Desiring': all the old favourites. The purity of those evenings brought a tear to his eye. The purity of those evenings gone for ever.

After he had found the letter to Eales in the waste-paper basket, he wrote to Maureen asking her to invite Cecily to London for the summer. It was not what he wanted but he did not have a choice. If she came home, it would be to the lust finger;[3] and if he sacked Eales without good reason, Cecily would never forgive him. Even if he did sack him, he felt certain that he would not leave the glen. He would find another job in the neighbourhood so that he could continue to defile Cecily. And now all Roarty's precautions had come to naught because Eales was planning to go to London in a week's time. He didn't say whom he was going to see; he didn't have to. Roarty's hands shook with rage and frustration. Eales was evil. Eales must be destroyed.

He found himself half-way down the stairs, clutching the twenty-fifth volume of *Britannica* in his right hand, the fingers opening and closing involuntarily on the spine.

Eales was behind the bar, bent over a barrel, examining a length of plastic tube.

'Have you found it?' he asked without looking up.

Roarty raised the book in both hands and brought it down with all his might on the back of Eales's head. The breath went out of him with a reedy murmur and his face struck the edge of the barrel. He put both hands on the barrel in an attempt to get up. The barrel moved. Roarty raised the book again but Eales sank on his haunches and fell back on the floor without as much as a whimper.

Roarty shuddered in horror. His act had been involuntary, and being involuntary was unwise. What if someone had been passing and Eales had called out in his agony? But he had been lucky. He had not cracked the skull. There was no blood, and that was a good thing because blood told irrefutable tales. But perhaps Eales was just stunned. He put the evening paper under his head, got a hand mirror from the kitchen and put it to his mouth and nose but there was no condensation that he could see. Difficult though it was to credit, he must have died instantaneously from the severity of the shock. The

3. Roarty had discovered an advertisement for a 'lust finger' in a sex magazine in Eales's room.

mirror test, he had heard McGing say, was not foolproof. The surest indication of death was the temperature of the rectum falling to 70°F or below; but, though he had a thermometer in the bedroom, there was a limit to what he was prepared to do in the interest of science. Anyhow, the body was still warm. It might take an hour or more for the temperature of the rectum to fall to that extent. As an afterthought, he felt Eales's pulse but there was no perceptible stir in the blood stream. He noticed that the upper lip had blood on it where he had come against the rim of the barrel, and he got a plastic bag and put it over the head and tied a piece of string round the neck.

He took the stairs two steps at a time and reached the toilet not a moment too soon. His bowel movement was the most violent he had experienced since his mother gave him an overdose of Glauber salts at the age of eleven. Homicide, he was interested to discover, was as good as a physic.

He was sweating profusely, a cold, clammy sweat that drenched his shirt under the arms and made tickling rivulets down his forehead and into his eyebrows. He came downstairs again, weak at the knees and very thirsty. He reached for the Bushmills but as he unscrewed the top of the bottle he remembered the immensity of the next problem — how on earth to get rid of the body — and he put the bottle back on the shelf and filled a tumbler of water from the tap. Though he felt uncomfortably sober, he could not risk taking another drink. If he was to make this a perfect murder, if he was to survive undetected, he would have to act with foresight and intelligence; but when he tried to think of the next step, he found that coherent thought was beyond him. His mind was a sieve; no thought would remain long enough in focus to connect logically with another. To encourage concentration he went into the kitchen and sat at the deal table with an open notebook in front of him. Thought came slowly, and when it did he wrote down seven words:

Fire

Water { sea
lough

Earth { garden
bog

Burning was impracticable; he had only a range, and roasting flesh and bone would raise an unearthly smell. That left him with immersion and burial, and of these he favoured the first because it involved less work. He could drive west to the sea cliffs and heave the body over the brink into the water. Or he could tie a weight to the body, row out into the bay and cast it overboard. But when he began to imagine the details of the actions, he realised that there were snags. He was reluctant to take out his boat in the dark because he did not know the positions of submerged rocks well enough to be entirely confident. There were houses along the shore and it was just possible that he might meet someone. Besides, the body might be washed ashore. There would be an autopsy, the forensic pathologist would discover that there was no salt water in the lungs and that therefore death was not the result of drowning. There would be an investigation into the cause of death, and questions, searching questions, would have to be answered. Of course he could dump the body in one of the mountain loughs but, as they were a long distance from the road, he would have to carry an eleven-stone burden for well over a mile. Not an inviting prospect on a dark night and over rough ground. That left him with the third possibility: disposal by burial. The easiest course would be to bury him in the garden but if there was an investigation it would be the first place the police would look. He would have to choose a less obvious grave, the bog for example. He would drive out the Garron road for two miles, take the right-hand bog road, and bury the body in the centre of the moor, away from the areas where turf was now being cut. The bog road was a lonely spot, there was not a house within three miles, and the likelihood of being seen was remote. The only danger was the possibility of meeting another car on the main road, returning perhaps from a dance in Garron. He hastily looked in the *Dispatch* but there were no advertisements for dances in any of the local towns. Nevertheless, you never knew what late-night straggler you might meet on a country road, and his car was known to everyone in the glen. He would need an excuse, and what conceivable excuse could he have for driving towards Garron at two o'clock on Sunday morning? A sudden gripe, a severe stomach pain, that made an urgent visit to Dr McGarrigle unavoidable. If he were seen, he could say that the pain had abated when he was half-way there and that he had come home without seeing the doctor. It was not the best of excuses but it would have to do.

He went to the back door to look at the night sky. The clouds in the east seemed blacker and closer, and the air was still and heavy, hanging like an invisible net over his head, laden with the scent of snuff-dry hay. Though it was nearly one o'clock, there was light in several of the cottages on the south mountain; he would have to wait at least until two before venturing out. He sighed sorely under the weight of the night air and the unbearable burden of his thoughts.

Ploddingly he went upstairs and opened a volume of *Britannica*. He lay on his side on the bed, sipped an orange juice and looked up the article on 'Murder' only to be directed with simple brevity to 'Homicide'. It was a disappointing article, probably written by some verbose solicitor or criminologist rather than a scholar with first-hand experience. It occurred to him that some newspaper editor might welcome the type of account he himself could now write — a story that would tell of the murderer's grim sense of inevitability as he looks on the sprawled body of his victim. From youth he has been conditioned by novels, stories, plays and films that imply at the very least that crime does not pay, that it is the criminal himself who pays; and he cannot help but wonder if he will be one of the rare exceptions. He looks at the cooling body which in death is a more formidable opponent than it ever was in life, aided by all the arcane resources of forensic science. After months perhaps of obsession with his victim, he is truly alone, facing the instinctive revulsion of every decent citizen, the impersonal tenacity of the police and the relentless treadmill of the courts; and all he has to ensure his survival is his cunning and intelligence. Roarty could not help wondering if he were intelligent enough.

There might be so many possibilities which he had not considered, so many things he may have overlooked, when on this night of all nights he needed to anticipate every contingency. He had not thought of the moon, for example. It was only two days before the full, and if the sky should clear he would have to bury Eales in ghostly but too revealing light. Obviously he would have to be careful, dig with one eye on the night sky. Another indication of his incapable abstraction was the way he had looked up the *Donegal Dispatch* when even the most rudimentary presence of mind would have told him that there was never a dance in Garron on Saturday.

He had written down seven options, and now the intimation of an eighth tantalised him beyond endurance, his freedom of action constrained by his inability to extend through imagination his gamut of choice. The man who is most free is the man who is most aware of possibilities, and in the past he had prided himself on being such a man. But now the effective possibilities in his life had shrunk from seven to one, and that one not particularly attractive. For a moment the eighth possibility illumined the internal dark; he would smash the front window, break open the till, hide the money, and pretend that Eales had been struck down by a burglar. It had the advantage that he could stay put, go to bed and get up in the morning at the usual time, and after a black coffee and a hot toddy 'discover' Eales and ring the police. However, that would lead to questions, and murder was better concealed than advertised. His eighth possibility had disintegrated like gossamer, leaving him tantalisingly with just the one. But having thought of the eighth, he was now harassed by the possibility that there might be a ninth. He went downstairs and stared stonily at his note of seven choices but, try as he might, they refused to multiply. He had always regarded himself as intelligent, at least a deal cleverer than most of those he met, and now when intelligence most mattered he was faltering. Many people, he thought, were reasonably intelligent; they had the kind of brightness that is related primarily to memory, that relies on noting how things are done and on an unthinking ability to imitate accurately. The truly intelligent were a race apart, as distinct from the rest of humanity as a salmon in season from a kelt.[4] Their incisiveness went straight to the core of every crux and their capacity for dispassionate reasoning carried them far beyond the bourne of past experience. They possessed the logic of a computer with the intuition and mental agility of a man. This ability could be described in one word — analysis. And that was his present failure: an inability to analyse a situation.

He put a match to the incriminating note of options and ground the ashes into powder with the poker. He changed into an old pair of trousers which he used for painting, a dark shirt which would not show conspicuously in moonlight, and a pair of wellingtons that would keep out the bog

4. A young salmon, after spawning.

water. He went upstairs again, took Eales's hold-all from the wardrobe and stuffed into it the glossy sex magazine, the puce pyjamas, Eales's toothbrush, toothpaste, razor and shaving lather, a spare shirt and three bottles of deodorant. This latter, he thought a brilliant stroke because Eales would not have gone to the door without his deodorant. Not quite analysis that, he decided, but rather good nevertheless. Premature self-congratulation was to be avoided though. The time for hubris, if there was one, was tomorrow morning or perhaps even in three years when Eales would be as remote in time as a fossilised pterodactyl. He would not fossilise, however. Bogs were noted for their powers of preservation. In five hundred years some slow-thinking turfcutter would unearth him with his slane,[5] a time capsule preserved by tannin, the date of the magazine in the hold-all providing a perplexing *terminus a quo*[6] for the rural constabulary.

When he came downstairs again, it was two by the clock, time to make a move now that the glen was abed. He quietly opened the back door of the garage, lifting it slightly so that it did not drag on the concrete floor, and put the hold-all and Eales in the boot of his car. The body had hardly cooled. Rigor mortis had not yet set in though the skin had begun to lose its elasticity. It was difficult to believe that this limp deadweight, this inedible carcass, this uneconomic commodity, had been the man who had threatened the peace and sweetness of his mind for the last four months. Somehow it did not seem possible, and he half-expected him to open one eye and recite once more his favourite piece of verse:

> If ever I marry a wife,
> I'll marry a landlord's daughter,
> For then I may sit in the bar
> And drink cold brandy and water.

With a sudden chill of the spine he remembered that the battery of his car was almost flat. If he used the self-starter, the whole village would realise as they turned in their beds whose car was giving trouble. He opened the off-side window and pushed the car into the road, facing it down the hill that ran out of the west end of the village. He would have to start it on the run when he was clear of the houses, double back along the North Circular as they called it, and take the Garron road without re-entering the village. He was about to move off when he remembered that he had forgotten the spade. Brilliant! He went back to the garage and took both a slane and a spade as well as a torch in case he should need it for the car. He put the car in second gear and with his foot on the clutch pedal moved off down the slope. When he was almost half-way down and had begun to gather speed, he let in the clutch. The engine fired at once and he was off with a song of minor achievement in his heart.

The Garron road climbed steeply out of the glen for the first mile. He drove in third with the accelerator to the floor, enjoying the cool rush of the night air coming through the open window. He looked down at the glen on his left; there was not one light along the whole length of the north mountain. Even the ever-vigilant McGing with his arse to his wife was dreaming of suggilation, saponification and a score of other forensic arcana which to his chagrin mattered little in booking men for poteen-making and other rural offences which, he complained, were somewhat beneath his consideration.[7] If only he knew of the opportunity he was missing.

Soon he was driving straight into the black clouds in the east, the heathered hills stretching darkly on either side. Once he had to change down to second because of two foolhardy wethers in the centre of the road, and then suddenly after a sharp bend he had reached the flat plateau of bogland that separated the twin parishes of Glenkeel and Glenroe. He took the narrow bog road, little better than a dirt track, the rushes along the selvage brushing the wings and doors. The swinging rays of headlamps came over the crest of the hill to his left. He stopped and switched off his own lights, and waited for the car to pass down the main road into the glen. He had got off the Garron road just in time.

He parked the car at the end of the road where the tractors usually turned and switched off the lights and the engine, the blackness of the night rushing up simultaneously to his very eyeballs. The night was uncannily quiet, the sky low and opaque

5. A spade for cutting turf.
6. Latin: end from which; a point of departure.
7. McGing is the local policeman; saponification is the conversion of fat into soap; suggilation is bruising, discoloration caused by beating.

and the air heavy with humidity. He listened with strained ears but not a bird, animal or insect stirred. The whole bog was asleep. He alone was abroad.

He took the body from the boot, slung it over one shoulder so that the arms dangled at his back, gripped the legs and hold-all in his right hand, and the spade and slane in the other. Standing on the verge of the road, he groped with the spade for the narrow drain which he knew to run alongside. Then he stepped gingerly over it and set off across the bog, treading slowly in the thick dark in case he should trip on a stump of bog fir or fall into a hole or drain. It was so dark that he could not see the turf stacks until he was right beside them, but soon he was on the open bog which stretched flat and unbroken for two miles. He would bury Eales in the centre, in an out-of-the-way spot untrodden by human foot except perhaps that of a sheep farmer in search of a straying ewe or wether. He jumped involuntarily as a flushed snipe rose with a loud 'scrape'. It was a hard summer on the poor buggers. They favoured damp or marshy ground but even the bogs were now quite dry.

When he had walked for fifteen minutes, he tested the ground with his boot and put down the body with a sense of well-deserved relief. After urinating at some length he began to pare the top sod from a patch six feet by three, just wide enough to allow comfort in the digging. The entangled roots of the mountain grass were so tough that he had to put all his strength behind each drive of the spade, and soon the sweat was making runnels down his forehead and into his beard but he worked like a man possessed until he had dug two spits and could turn to the slane which he preferred to the spade. In spite of four months of dry weather, there was a surprising amount of water in the lower layers of the bog, and before long his trousers and shirt were filthy from rubbing against the sides of the grave. When his shoulder was level with the brink, he stopped digging. He put Eales lying on his back on the bottom, clutching the hold-all over his chest, the plastic bag still over his head. He filled the grave quickly with the spade and made sure that he had cleared all the turf before putting the top sods back in place. When he had finished, he tamped the sods with his boot and stood for a moment in the centre, savouring the spring of the ground. In next to no time, he thought, Eales would be shooting up the most picturesque of bog cotton.

What he now wanted most was to get home without mishap and pour himself a quadruple whiskey. An overwhelming tiredness had begun to creep up his legs and arms, but he walked back doggedly to the car, the slane and spade on his right shoulder. As he neared the road, a ragged splotch of ghostly light appeared in the southern sky. The moon momentarily showed a veiled face before vanishing behind an enormous swag of cloud, but in that moment something caught his eye, a movement perhaps at the end of a turf stack. His grip on the spade tightened and he stole across to the stack and leaned against the end, listening for the faintest stir in the dark. He must have imagined it. There was no one there. Who could be there? Not at this hour of the night — except perhaps someone planning to steal a neighbour's turf. But that was unlikely, and with an effort he put the disquieting thought from his mind. When he reached the car, he took off his wellingtons, trousers and shirt, stowed them in the boot and put on clean clothes and shoes.

It was almost four o'clock when he got home. As he closed the garage door a great raindrop stung the back of his neck. He took no notice, however, but went straight to the bar and poured himself half a tumbler of whiskey. There were several things he should do. He should wash the floor where Eales had fallen, have a bath, and burn the trousers and shirt he had worn because in the event of an investigation he would find it difficult to explain how they had become so turf-caked. But he decided to put off until tomorrow what he need not do that night. He would get up in time for eleven o'clock Mass and open the pub as usual at twelve. Then in the holy hours between two and four, when all good Catholics were at lunch, he would attend to what was necessary.

He wanted above all to sleep and forget, but his mind was still too active, racing madly, dwelling on minutiae, now that the action of the night was over. He put Schumann's cello concerto on the gramophone and lay over the bed clothes, sipping the whiskey and listening to the recurring sadness of the first movement. He needed ambiguous music, sound that would bring glimpses of heaven while hinting at the depth of the darkness in the well of life, and Schumann in this respect was the composer par excellence, particularly the Schumann of the cello concerto. Never was the struggle between light and dark, between conscious and unconscious, keener than in Schumann, and yet it was not expressed as a struggle but as a fusion of opposites, weighing the very air with mystery, leaving it laden with an uneasy sense of other, less imperfect, musical possibilities. Listening to him was like looking into a well after a pebble had disturbed the water: a precise reflection threatened to form but the water continued to tilt and sway, distorting the image, teasing the mind in search of facile symmetry. And yet as you looked, it was possible to gain an indistinct idea of the reflection. Though the image was broken, it was recognisable as something remote yet deeply personal.

With a gratifying awareness of rhythmic abridgement he closed his eyes while his fingers clasped the tumbler on the bedside table. He opened his eyes again, aware of nothing but the searing pain in his rectum, a keenly stinging pain that made salty tears run into his mouth. He realised that he must have slept. The record had finished and he could not remember having heard the end of the last movement. He ground his teeth and pressed hard as if pressing would expel the pain. Was this to be his punishment, a summary visitation, cancer of the rectum followed by total colostomy to prolong a life no longer worth prolonging? God! As a punishment it was more appropriate to buggery than homicide. Bent in two he groped his way to the toilet in the dark and sat hunched on the naked bowl, too absorbed in his pain to remember the wooden seat. What he now desired was an elephantine defecation, to discharge in one blistering avalanche the ache in his arse, but, though he pressed, the pain continued to cut like a twisting knife and nothing came. Was this, not cancer, to be his punishment: a phantom crap to plague and trouble till the end of his time? He pressed again, the blood rising to his face until a fart, fierce as a shot from a gun barrel, ripped through his rear, dispelling in a moment all but the memory of the pain. What relief! It was as if he had been reprieved at the point of death. The absence of pain was pure pleasure. Tears came to his eyes as he remembered how he had inflicted the ultimate pain on a fellow creature and yet could not himself stand the agony of a recalcitrant fart.

He was about to go to bed when he realised that he was at the centre of a rushing river. A clap of thunder, a cracking, splintering sound, reminded him of his tree, and he went to the open window and pulled back the heavy curtains. They were stiff to saturation and the carpet was wet under his feet. The rain was falling out of the sky, not in drops but in a continuous, splashing stream that came through the window and poured down his face and neck. The night was shaken by horrendous thunder, the sky torn by fleeing light that seemed to have neither pattern nor purpose, neither beginning nor end.

He put on his slippers and went downstairs and out into the garden. It was within half-an-hour of dawn, and he could see before him the dark pyramidal outline of the stricken tree. In a moment he was soaking from head to foot as if someone had emptied a keeler of water on his head. He stood under the conifer as the rain made rivulets down his face and chest, imagining the heavenly water being absorbed by the tinder-dry leaves, into the sapwood, into the very heartwood. The sky was a mass of flame, and he saw the darkness over the bog being rent by bluish light and the water flooding in streams where there had never been a stream before, expunging footprints, swelling the surface of the sod, burying his secret deeper, making a fathom unfathomable. It all ended as quickly as it had presumably begun. The streaming and splashing became a flurry of droplets and he became aware of the dripping of the tree like the susurration of blood in his ears.

As the storm receded into the north-west he went inside, towelled himself with luxurious care, and went to bed in his pelt. He woke in daylight, refreshed by a sleep without dreams. After a copious breakfast of black pudding, bacon, eggs and tomatoes, he went into the garden again to savour the freshest, most intoxicating smell in the world, the smell of the earth after rain. Under the warmth of the forenoon sun the flowers, grass and leaves, after a long parching, gave off a subtle odour that cleansed his mind of the remaining shades of agitation. It was as if he had never heard of Eales. Suddenly he was strong and full of purpose. It seemed to him that there was nothing he could not do.

BERNARD MACLAVERTY

(1942-)

from:
A TIME TO DANCE (1982)

[Bernard MacLaverty has written searchingly and with integrity novels and stories about Irish victims and loners, but he is represented here by a story with a much lighter and funnier touch. The story has as butt a hypochondriac philosopher whose lockjaw is a comic refutation of the primacy of language in which he professes — as a philosopher of the linguistic school of British empiricism — to believe; his domestic and marital life is a comic refutation of the more vivid empiricism of D. H. Lawrence's philosophy. The title good-humouredly mocks A.J. Ayer's *Language, Truth and Logic*, a seminal text in British empiricism.]

LANGUAGE, TRUTH AND LOCKJAW

Norman sat in the dentist's waiting room. Outside, the rain needled down from a grey sky. The wet shining roofs descended like steps to the sea. Because he was an emergency he had to wait for over an hour while people with appointments filed past him.

Then the dentist's bespectacled head appeared round the door and said,

'Mr Noyes?'

There were two dentists on the island and it was immediately obvious to Norman that he had picked the wrong one. As he called out his secret codes to his assistant he breathed halitosis. He dug into the molar that was causing the trouble and Norman yelled, his voice breaking embarrassingly.

'That seems to be the one,' said the dentist. 'I don't think we can save it. It's a whited sepulchre.'

He went to the window and filled a large syringe. Before he approached the chair he considerately hid it behind his back.

'Open up,' he said. 'That should go dead in a minute. On holiday?'

'Yes.'

'The weather has been poor.'

'You can say that again.'

He had known from the minute the trip had been proposed that everything would go wrong. Patricia said that he had helped in no small measure to *make* it go wrong by his bloody-minded attitude. When *she* was a child on holiday her father, when it rained, had dressed them up in bathing suits and wellies and Pakamacs[1] and taken them for riotous walks along the beach. He had litten — her own word — blue smoke fires with damp driftwood. But now when it rained he, Norman, retreated to the bedroom with his books. His defence was that he had work to do and that he had agreed to the trip only on condition that he could finish his paper on Ryle.[2]

'What do you do?' asked the dentist.

'I teach. Lecturing at the University.'

'Oh. What in?'

'Philosophy.'

'That's nice.'

Things were beginning to happen in his jaw like pins and needles.

'Where are you staying?'

'We have a bungalow up at Ard-na-something.'

'Oh yes. Beside the old Mansion House. Interesting neighbours.'

Norman supposed he was referring to the mentally handicapped men he had seen staring at him over the wall. They stood for hours in the rain, immobile as sentries, watching the house. At night he heard hooting laughter and yelps and howls which previously he had only associated with a zoo.

'Open wide.' He hung a suction device like a walking stick in Norman's mouth. 'Relax now. Sometimes I think it would be better to hook that thing down the front of your trousers. Some patients sweat more than they salivate.'

The assistant smiled. She was plain but from where he lay Norman could see that the middle button of her white coat was undone and he could just see the underslope of her breast in a lacy bra.

The dentist leaned on Norman's bottom jaw and began working inside his mouth. There was a cracking sound and the dentist tut-tutted and went to a cupboard behind the chair. He's broken it, thought Norman.

'How long are you here for?' asked the dentist.

1. Easily folded plastic raincoats.
2. Gilbert Ryle (1900-76), British philosopher.

'A ort igh.'

'That's nice.'

'I cank cose i jaw.'

'What?'

Norman pointed to his lower jaw making foolish noises.

'Oh,' said the dentist. He manipulated the jaw and clicked it back into place. 'The muscle must be weak.'

'Is it broken — the tooth?'

'No, it's out.'

Norman was astonished. He had felt nothing.

Patricia shouted out from the kitchen.

'Well, love, how did it go?'

Norman had to step over the children, who were playing with a brightly coloured beach-ball on the carpet of the hallway. Although it was five o'clock on a summer's afternoon the light had to be switched on.

'O.K. He pulled it.' Norman produced a Kleenex with its soggy red spot and offered it to his wife. She refused to look at it, telling him to throw it in the bin. She asked,

'Did you expect something from the fairies for it?'

'I just thought you might be interested, that's all.'

'Aww you poor thing,' she said, kissing him lightly on the cheek. 'Did you feel that? Perhaps I should kiss you on the side that's not numb.' She had a levity and a patronising approach to him in sickness which he did not like.

'I think I'll lie down for a while. One *ought* to after an extraction.'

'Whatever you say. Will you want something to eat?'

'What are you making?'

'Spaghetti.'

'We'll see.'

In the bedroom he kicked off his shoes and stood at the rain-spotted window. They were there again, standing amongst the trees at the wall. Their heads were just visible, hair plastered wet and flat. After enquiring at the shop they had found out that the Mansion House was a holiday home for the region and that a party of mentally retarded men was staying there. A mixture of mongols and cretins and God knows what. When they saw Norman appear at the window they faded back into the trees.

He lay down on the bed and got beneath the coverlet. The room smelled damp. It had probably been empty over the summer months as well as the winter. Who in their right mind would want to stay beside a madhouse? He closed his eyes and his left ear began to whine like a high-pitched siren in the distance. He wondered if this was normal. With relief he heard the noise fade as his ear tingled back to ordinary sensation. He knew he was a hypochondriac. At night when he couldn't sleep, usually after working on a lecture or a paper, he would become aware of his heart-thud and lie awake waiting for it to miss. A discomfort in his arm, in time, would become a definite pain and a symptom of an impending heart attack. A discomfort anywhere else in his body would lead to thoughts of cancer. Laziness could be mistaken for debility, which would become a sure sign of leukaemia. This laziness could last for days and gave him much to worry about.

Although he did not say these things out loud somehow Patricia knew his nature and treated him in an off-hand way like a child. Before he married her she had been a primary school teacher and there was always a hint of it in the way she talked to him when he was ill or said he was feeling unwell. She had spotted the medical dictionary he had slipped in among his other books to be taken on holiday but he had made an excuse, saying that in remote places, like an island off the Scottish coast, anything could happen to her or the kids. She had pointed out to him that there was an air-ambulance service straight to the nearest fully equipped hospital on the mainland at any time of the day or night. At his insistance she had checked with the tourist board by phone that this was so.

Without articulating it they both knew that they had reached a stale point in their nine-year-old marriage. They no longer talked or argued as they once did and sarcasm coloured most of the things they said to one another.

Each year they went to the same place for a month's holiday along with other families they knew. In March Norman had been sitting reading the paper when Patricia said,

'I think we should go away for a holiday just by ourselves.'

'What about the children?'

'Oh, we would take *them*.'

'How can we be by ourselves if the children are there?'

'It would get us away from the same old faces.

The same old interminable conversations. Get away somewhere isolated. We would be by ourselves at night.'

'But I have this paper to finish . . . .'

'You're at the sports page already,' she squawked and fell about laughing. It was something which had endeared her to him when they first met, but now after ten years of knowing her it was something he couldn't understand — how something she considered funny seemed to take over her whole body and flop it about. One night at a party someone had told her a joke and she had slid down the wall, convulsing and spilling her drink in jerking slops on the floor. In the morning when he asked her she couldn't remember what the joke was about.

His tendency was to smile, a humour of the mind, something witty rather than funny affected him. There were times when the company about him were in fits of laughter and he couldn't see the joke.

The children in the hallway began to fight, then one of them broke into a howl of tears. Norman turned his good ear to the pillow. Children, especially of their age, were totally irrational. The younger was Becky, a gap-toothed six-year-old who refused to eat anything which was good for her and insisted on everything which was sweet and bad. John was two years older and had his mother's loud sense of humour. At least he ate cauliflower. He must have fallen asleep because the children wakened him with whispers, creeping round the bed.

'Mum says tea,' they shouted, seeing him awake.

Norman got up. His mouth tasted awful and he washed what remained of his teeth ruefully with peppermint toothpaste, thinking about old age. He sucked some spaghetti into the unaffected side of his mouth and crushed it carefully with his tongue against the roof of his mouth.

'How do you feel now, dear?' asked Patricia.

'So-so,' he said. 'I think the dentist must have served his time in an abattoir. My jaw is sore.'

'Look, Mum, there they are again,' said Becky.

'Who, dear?'

'The loonies.'

'So they are, God love them,' said Patricia.

Norman looked over his shoulder out of the dining room window. They were standing at the wall again, six of them. They had moved from the bedroom to the dining room. When they saw Norman turn his head they ducked down, then slowly came up again. The one who stood with his mouth hanging open shouted something unintelligible and the others laughed.

'You shouldn't call them loonies,' said Norman.

'Spacers, then,' said John.

'You shouldn't call them that either.'

'That's what they are, isn't it?'

Norman looked at his wife.

'I suppose it didn't mention this fact in the brochure for the house?'

'No, dear, it didn't. Four minutes from the beach was enough for me. Shall I pull the blind for you?'

'No, but it's something animal in me. I don't like to be watched while I'm eating.'

'It's good to know there's some animal in you.'

Norman gave her a look then switched his gaze to his son.

'John, is that the way to hold your fork?'

The rest of the evening the children spent watching the black and white television set which they had scorned when they first arrived. Norman went to the bedroom to do some work. He was writing a paper sparked off by Ryle's distinction between pleasure and pain — that they were not elements on the same spectrum, that positive quantities of one did not lead to minus quantities of the other. He had become involved in tortuous arguments about sadism and masochism. He had shown his draughts to the Prof who had said, after some consideration, that the paper was tending more to the physiological than the philosophic. He had added, looking over his glasses, that he much preferred a wank. 'Marriage is all right,' he had said, 'but there's nothing like the real thing.'

Norman never knew how to take him, never knew when he was serious. The man could be guilty of the most infantile jokes. He repeatedly accused Norman of talking a lot of hot Ayer and of being easily Ryled. What could you say to a man like that? He was always goosing and patting his young secretary — and she didn't seem to mind. He was a woolly existentialist who spoke about metaphysical concepts that could not be defined. He said that, with its pernickety approach to language, British philosophy was disappearing up its own arse while the world around it was in chaos. Also that British philosophy — including Norman — was like a butcher sharpening his knives. Eventually the knives would wear away but the meat would still be there to be cut. Norman thought, what more could you expect from the son of a County Derry farmer?

Norman had just written the first sentence of the severe rewriting the Prof had suggested when Patricia came into the room.

'Norman, the rain's gone off. Let's go for a walk.'

'But the writing is just beginning to go well.'

She put her arms around his neck.

'Don't be so solemn. It has stopped piddling for the first time since we arrived. There is even some blue in the sky. Come for a walk to the pier with us.'

Outside, the light had an eerie translucent quality. It was about ten o'clock and the low white sun had come through the cloud out over the Atlantic and was highlighting the gable ends of houses. The road was still wet and shining. The children in anoraks ran on ahead, leaving Norman and Patricia walking together.

'How's the toofy-peg?' Patricia asked.

'How is its absence, you mean.'

'Well, if you insist.'

'Not too bad now.'

'As night approaches.'

'You could put it that way.' He smiled. 'What do you think?'

'Yes. Holidays I feel like it more often.'

'Tomorrow this socket will begin to heal — usually that's bad news. Isn't it funny how you can never smell your own breath?'

He reached out and took her by the hand. Her face showed mock surprise but she responded by squeezing his fingers.

'Of course we don't have to kiss,' he said, smiling.

'Like an egg without salt. A total perversion.'

She leaned over and kissed him as they walked. They stopped in the middle of the road and kissed mouth to mouth lightly, friendly. John whistled *wheet-weeo* at them from a distance and they laughed. Norman was much taller than she and it was easy for him to put his arm around her shoulder as they walked.

At eleven Patricia turned on the ancient electric blanket at its highest — it had gears, almost, instead of settings — to try to get rid of the damp smell. Norman was reading a journal by the fire. She sat opposite him, her hands empty. A grandfather clock ticked loudly in the corner.

'One of the ideas of this holiday was that we should talk,' she said.

'Uh-huh.' He turned the page.

'You don't talk to me any more.'

'I'm sorry, what's that?'

'We don't talk any more.'

He closed the journal with a smile but kept his place with a finger.

'O.K. What would you like to talk about?'

'Anything.'

The grandfather clock worked itself up to a long whirr before striking a quarter past.

'The more I think of it,' began Norman, 'the more I am convinced that there might be something in what the Prof says — that British philosophy is trying to commit hara-kiri. And I'm not sure that that is such a good thing. I would hate to end up believing the same things as that man.'

'I would like to talk about us. What we think, what we feel.'

'Hard words, Trish. "Think" and "feel". It's difficult to know what we mean by them. It's essential that we get our concepts straight.'

'Bollocks, Norman. Let's talk about something else.'

'Why? You said we could talk about anything.'

'O.K.' She thought for a moment, then said. 'Those people who stare over the wall. Do you think because they are less intelligent they have less vivid emotions?'

'What are "vivid" emotions?'

'You know what I mean.'

'Seriously I don't.'

'The kind of thing you find in Lawrence.'

'That man is a fog of urges. He's groping all the time — making up words. Blood consciousness; the dark forest of the human soul. Patricia, if you can't put a thing into language, it doesn't exist.'

'Norman, what utter . . . .'

'To answer your question. It's a problem for physiologists or neurologists or somebody like that. I don't know what loonies feel.'

'It's no wonder we don't talk any more.'

'Why's that?'

'Because you talk such utter balls. That someone should dismiss Lawrence with a wave of . . . .'

'Trish.'

'What?'

'Trish. Let's have a cup of tea and go to bed. Arguing will put us off. You can't make love when you're seething. Besides this tooth of mine is beginning to hurt.'

'Absence of tooth.'

'O.K. If we sit up much longer you'll go sleepy on me.'

Patricia sighed and made a cup of tea while Norman finished reading the article in his journal.

'It's a good question,' he said, softening his biscuit in his tea and sucking it into the good side of his mouth, 'but I honestly don't know the answer to it. Taken logically it would mean that the most intelligent men have the — as you call them — the most vivid emotional responses. That is obviously not true.'

'Not in your case anyway.' She smiled or sneered at him, he couldn't tell which because he only caught the end of it.

'But I thought we weren't going to argue.'

On holidays they had agreed to do equal shares of the housework. It was Norman's turn to wash the cups, which he did even though he had had a tooth out. While he was in the kitchen Patricia took a burning peat from the fire with a pair of tongs and incensed the bedroom.

'I love that smell,' she said. 'Do you want to come to bed now?'

'I'll just wait till the smoke clears.'

As he slowly dried the cups and tidied up, his tongue sought out the jellied cavity and he touched and tasted its coppery acidity. There was no pain in it now. Perhaps he was a better dentist than he gave him credit for. Just in case he took three Disprin dissolved in water before he locked up and turned out the lights.

In the bedroom Patricia lay reading with her bare arms outside the counterpane. Her hair was undone. A strange ululating cry came from the direction of the Mansion House. Norman looked out between the drawn curtains, half expecting to see six heads lined up at the windowsill to watch, but the Mansion House was in darkness. The sound, like a child's version of a long Red Indian war cry, came again, chilling him.

'Woolawoolawoolawoolawoolawoolwoola.'

'He undressed and slipped in naked beside her nakedness. She was still a beautiful woman and, although he had come to know her body, he never ceased to be awed by it in total nakedness. She told him how aroused she was. A simple thing like holding hands earlier in the evening had been the start of it. Her voice was hushed. Her arousal touched him and they made love. Because of his condition he suggested that she did not put her tongue in his mouth. Nevertheless, Norman got the feeling that this was good sex in this strange, lightly creaking bed. When they came together he made an involuntary animal noise far back in his throat and his mouth fell wide open.

'Agggghrrrrr,' he said.

The noise he made was followed by an audible click. Patricia, with her eyes closed, was listening to her own breathing subside and touching his shoulders with her fingertips. She opened her eyes and looked at him. His mouth was open and his eyes were staring wide in fright.

'i aws gust,' said Norman.

'What?'

'i aw. It's gust.'

Patricia began to laugh, shaking and cupping her ear to him as if she couldn't hear properly.

'What are you saying?'

Norman pointed to his yawning mouth and said as clearly as he was able,

'ock jaw.'

'I thought you were having a heart attack.'

Now that she understood she advised him with amused concern that the best thing he could do in the circumstances would be to get off her. Norman struggled into a pair of pyjama bottoms and regarded himself in the mirror. He kept trying to close his mouth but nothing happened. Somewhere in his jaw the circuits had fused again. Over his shoulder he saw his wife's reflection sitting up in bed heaving in suppressed bare-breasted laughter. When he turned to face her with his mouth agape her laughter became sound. Loud, whinnying and vulgar.

'Oh Norman, you look so *stupid*. You're like one of the loonies,' she managed to say between wheezes. 'Are you kidding me?'

He turned away from her and tried to remember what the dentist had done. He took his lower jaw in his left hand and pushed. Nothing happened. He tried to push upwards and sideways and sideways and downwards but with no effect.

Patricia had put on her nightdress and was now standing looking at him in the mirror. She turned him and looked into his mouth.

'You look like the man in the moon,' she said, giggling. She tried to put it back into place. He had to bend his knees to let her reach up and he had his arms hanging loose by his sides. Patricia stepped back and looked at him, then subsided into peals of laughter again. 'Better still. One of those monkey moneyboxes.' She clapped her hands. 'You put a penny in his hand and he went — gulp.' She demonstrated. 'We had one with its jaw broken.' Norman turned away from her and scrabbled about in the cardboard box of his philosophy books until he found his medical dictionary. He wondered what heading would be the most helpful to read. With his jaw locked open he couldn't swallow his saliva and it drooled over his bottom lip on to the page. He pored over the book.

'anky.'

Patricia gave him a handkerchief from the open case on the dresser and he staunched his dribbles.

'I'm getting to interpret your grunts quite well,' she said. Norman could find nothing which related to his case except under tetanus which he was fairly sure he didn't have. He thought of going to the square and phoning from a callbox for the ambulance plane, until he remembered that he couldn't even speak and they would think he was drunk. Patricia would have to do it. He imagined arriving alone in the infirmary at Glasgow or somewhere in his pyjama bottoms and trying with gestures and groans to explain the complexities of what had happened. With great difficulty he told his wife the thought.

'If you're going out,' she said wiping the tears from her cheeks, 'we'll have to put a coffee-tin lid in your mouth to keep the draught out.' She fell on the bed and rolled about. 'You're agog,' she shrieked. 'Agog describes you perfectly. Norman, you're the perfection of agogness.'

'or ucks ake Trish,' he said, 'ee serious.'

The noise from the Mansion House came again, ridiculing him.

'Woolawoolawoolawoolawoolawoola.'

Patricia was by now as inarticulate as he was. She was becoming almost hysterical and Norman, even in the midst of his trouble, wondered if he should slap her face to bring her out of it. It was obviously a nervous reaction to what had happened. As if he didn't have enough to cope with.

He went to the bathroom to see if a change of mirror would help. Sexual pleasure had reduced him to a slavering moron. He thought of D. H. Lawrence and Patricia's admiration for him. He pulled and pushed and wiggled at his bottom jaw. He looked and felt like the mental defectives who had peered at him over the wall. To be like this for ever. In the distance the grandfather clock tolled midnight. He had been like this for the best part of half an hour. He would *have* to go to hospital. There was the dentist but he didn't know where he lived. He didn't even know his name. Then suddenly he remembered that the Prof's wife had been a practising dentist at one time. He could phone him long distance and ask her advice. Again he remembered that he couldn't speak. It would only give the Prof another chance to say, 'Noyes, you're full of sound and fury signifying nothing.' The bastard.

All Patricia's squawking and hooting had wakened John and he came, puffy-faced with sleep, to the bathroom. He peed, forgot to flush it and walked past his father as he stared in the mirror.

'Hunggh,' said Norman. The boy turned. Norman pointed to the lavatory.

'What?'

'uh it.'

The child stood not understanding, holding up his pyjama trousers by the loose waist. Norman took him by the shoulders and led him back to the lavatory. A little saliva spilled on to John's head and Norman rubbed it.

'uh it.'

'Daddy, what's wrong?'

Norman lifted the child's hand and rested it on the handle — then pressed both hand and handle. The lavatory flush noisily and the child staggered sleepily back to his bedroom.

'What's wrong with Daddy?' Norman heard him ask in the hallway.

'He's having a long yawn, dear. Now go back to bed.'

Patricia came in with the medical dictionary opened at a page.

'Look, this is it,' she said pointing to a diagram, 'down and out and *then* up. Here, let me try.'

She set the book on the Vanitory unit, stood on tip-toe, still consulting it over her shoulder, and took his jaw firmly in her hands. She pulled downwards and towards herself. Norman agghed and she pushed hard. There was a gristle-snapping sound and his mouth closed. He tried it tentatively, partially opening and closing it, like a goldfish.

'You've done it,' he said. He wiggled it laterally just to make sure. 'I was imagining all kinds of terrible things.' He laughed nervously.

'But you looked *so* funny, Norman. I'm sorry for laughing.' Her shoulders were still shaking.

'You have a strange sense of humour.' He wiped the shine off his chin with the handkerchief. 'The next time I get my foreskin caught in my zip I'll let you know and we can have a night's entertainment.'

Back in the bedroom, Patricia imitated a chimpanzee with her mouth open and arms dangling and said,

'Poor Norm.'

When they were settled in bed he sighed.

'I thought I was a goner. The dentist says I must have a weak muscle.'

'There's nothing wrong with your muscle, darling,' she said and snuggled in to his side. The fine rain had begun again and he heard it hiss off the roof and the surrounding trees. He would never understand this crazy woman he was married to. It was hurtful to be laughed *at*. But he was grateful to her for putting his jaw back and, in a kind of thanksgiving, he resolved to take the whole family for a walk along the beach the next day to light bonfires, whether it rained or not.

He turned out the light. The yelling from the Mansion House seemed to have stopped but he couldn't be sure it would not begin again. In the dark, as they were drifting off to sleep, Patricia shook the bed with giggles in the same way as shudders remain after a long bout of crying.

ITA DALY

(1944–)

from: THE LADY WITH THE RED SHOES (1980)

[The title story of Ita Daly's collection bears certain resemblances to William Trevor's 'Beyond the Pale'. Both stories have privileged narrators recreating in a similar location their apparently intact and secure world. Both, however, write an epitaph for their world when they recount an apparently isolated incident that symbolically brings their world to a close and ushers in a new dispensation. Whereas Trevor treats of Irish history, politics and social class, Daly settles for social class. Her narrator is also more likeable than Trevor's because he confesses his snobbery so readily. In his condemnation of the modern world (compare Edward's in Julia O'Faoláin's story) and his nostalgia for a vanishing order, he nevertheless leaves room for the possibility that change will right injustice. Privilege and poverty in Ireland were, after all, of the same world — one supporting the other — and that (so the narrator has it) is passing.]

THE LADY WITH THE RED SHOES

The West of Ireland, as every schoolboy knows, is that part of the country to which Cromwell banished the heretical natives after he had successfully brought the nation to heel. Today, it is as impoverished and barren as ever it was, bleak and lonesome and cowering from the savagery of the Atlantic which batters its coastline with all the fury that it has gathered in over three thousand miles. But the West of Ireland can also be heartbreakingly beautiful; and on a fine April morning with the smell of gorse and clover filling the air and the bees showing the only evidence of industry in a landscape that is peopleless as far as the eye can see — on such a morning in the West of Ireland you can get a whiff of Paradise.

It is an irony which pleases me mightily that we as a family have such a strong attachment to the West. Our ancestors, you see, came over with Cromwell, foot soldiers who fought bravely and were rewarded generously and have never looked back since. And every Easter we leave Dublin and set out westwards where we spend a fortnight in McAndrews Hotel in North Mayo. It is a family tradition, started by my grandfather, and by now it has achieved a certain sacredness. Nothing is allowed to interfere with the ritual, and so when I married Judith one April day, some twenty-five years ago, it seemed quite natural that we should spend our honeymoon there. We have gone there every Easter since and if Judith has found it somewhat dull on occasion, she accepts gracefully a period of boredom in the knowledge that it gives me so much pleasure, while I in turn have been known to accompany her to Juan-les-Pins.[1] An experience which, however, I have not been foolish enough to repeat.

McAndrews is one of the puzzles of the world. Built on the outskirts of Kilgory, looking down on the hamlet and on the sea, it dates back to the late nineteenth century. A large, square house, red-bricked and turreted, it is a reminder of the worst excesses of the Gothic revival, and every time I see its monstrous outline, lonely on the hill, my heart bounds and my pulse quickens. Nobody knows whether it was there before Kilgory and the village grew up around it or whether Kilgory was there first. But certainly it seems an odd place to have built a hotel, miles from a town, or a church, or even a beach. It is situated on a headland overlooking the Atlantic, but the cliffs are so steep and the sea so treacherous here that there is neither boating nor swimming available. Strange to build a hotel in such a place, stranger still that there have been enough eccentrics around to keep it in business for almost a century. My father, as a boy, used to arrive by train. The main line ran from Dublin to Westport and from there a branch line went to the hotel — not to Kilgory mark you, but to the actual hotel grounds. 'Any guests for McAndrews?' the porters used to shout as one disembarked at Westport and was ushered onto a toy train with its three or four first-class carriages, to be shunted along the fifteen miles and deposited a stone's throw from the grand front door of McAndrews with its noble stone balustrade.

The toy station is still there, although nowadays the guests arrive by motor. I am always glad when I see my Daimler disappearing into the cavernous garages, and most of the other guests seem to experience a similar sense of relief, for though they arrive in motor-cars, they continue thereafter on foot and the grounds and environs are delightfully free of petrol fumes. We are of a kind, McAndrews clientele, old-fashioned, odd perhaps; some would say snobbish. Well, if it is snobbish to exercise one's taste, then I admit that I am a snob. I do not like the bad manners, the insolence of shop assistants and taxi-drivers which passes for egalitarianism in this present age; I resent chummy overtures from waiters who sometimes appear to restrain themselves with difficulty from slapping one on the back. I am irritated by cocktail bars and at a loss in the midst of all that bright and fatuous chatter. I like peace and quiet and reserve in my fellow-man — decent reserve, which appears to be the *raison d'être* of McAndrews. I know most of my fellow-guests' names — like me they have been coming here since they were children — yet I can rest assured that when I meet any of them again in any part of the hotel, I shall be spared all social intercourse apart from a civil word of greeting. Such respect for dignity and personal privacy is hard to come by in commercial establishments these days.

This year, Judith was ill and did not accompany me. To say that she was ill is something of an exaggeration, for if she had been, I would certainly not have left her. But she was somewhat under the weather, and as her sister was in Dublin from London, she decided to stay there with her while I went to Mayo alone. In truth, I was somewhat relieved, for I am only too aware of how difficult it must be for Judith, gay and outgoing, to be married to a dry stick like myself all these years. I am glad when she gets an opportunity to enjoy herself and I had no doubt that Eleanor and she would be much happier without my inhibiting presence. Still, I was going to miss her, for like many solitary people I am very dependent on the company of those few whom I love.

But the magic of McAndrews began to re-assert itself as soon as I got down to breakfast the first morning and found Murphy, with his accustomed air of calm and dignity, presiding over the dining-room. Murphy has been head waiter here for over thirty years now, although I always see him more as a butler, a loyal family retainer, rather than as a smart *maître d'hôtel*. His concern for each guest is personal and his old face is suffused with genuine pleasure when he sees you again each year. He came forward to greet me now. 'Good morning, sir.'

'Good morning, Murphy. Nice to see you again.'

'And you, sir, always such a pleasure. I'm sorry Mrs Montgomery will not be with us this year, sir.'

'Afraid not.'

'Nevertheless, I hope you will have a pleasant stay. May I recommend the kippers this morning, sir? They are particularly good.'

Such exchanges would be the extent of my intercourse with the world for the next fortnight — formal, impersonal, remote, and totally predictable. I have always found it a healing process, part of the total McAndrews experience, helping one to relax,

1. A smart resort on the French Riviera.

unbend, find one's soul again.

I quickly re-established my routine, falling into it with the ease and gratitude one feels on putting on again an old and much-worn jacket. Breakfasts were latish but hearty, then a walk as far as the village and back. Afterwards an hour or two spent in the library in the delightful company of Boswell,[2] a man to be enjoyed only in leisured circumstances — I never read him in Dublin. Lunch and an afternoon in a deck-chair in the gardens, looking out to sea, dozing, dreaming, idling. After dinner another walk, this time more strenuous, perhaps two miles along the coast road and then back to McAndrews for a final glass of port followed by early bed with a good detective novel. The bliss of those days is hard to convey, particularly the afternoons, when it never seemed to rain. I would take my deck-chair and place it in a sheltered spot and sit, hour upon hour, and watch the Atlantic at its ceaseless labours. I'd watch as the light changed — from blue to green and from green to grey — until an occasional sea-gull would cut across my line of vision and I would raise my eyes and follow its soaring flight to the great vault of heaven. A couple of afternoons like that and things were back in perspective. The consciousness of one's encroaching age, the knowledge that one is regarded as a has-been, became less painful, and there, on the edge of the Atlantic, a peace began to make itself felt.

But then I have always been out of step with the world and even as a young man McAndrews was a retreat, a haven for me. However as I grow older and my unease increases, McAndrews becomes more precious. Here I can escape from all those aggressive young men with their extraordinary self-confidence and their scarlet-nailed women and their endless easy chatter. My son, Edward, who is married to a beautician — a profession which, I am assured, has some standing in this modern world — this son of mine tells me that my only problem is that I am a nasty old snob. This apparently puts me completely beyond the pale, and he views me as a pariah, almost as someone who should be put down. But we are all snobs of one variety or other, and what he really means is that my particular brand of snobbery has gone out of fashion. He has working-class friends and black friends, but no stupid friends; he would not dream of spending his holidays in such a bastion of privilege as McAndrews, but then neither would he think of going to the Costa Brava; he drinks pints of Guinness but abhors sweet wine. And he tells me that the difference between us is that he has discernment and that I am a snob.

The generation gap is what any modern sociologist would inelegantly and erroneously call it, for, as I have said, there has always been as big a gap between me and most of my own generation as there is between me and Edward's. It is a painful sensation, constantly feeling that the time is out of joint, although as I sit sipping sherry in McAndrews, in the pleasant expectation of a good dinner, I can laugh at my own foolishness and that of my son, and indeed, at the general idiocy of the human animal. This is what makes McAndrews so dear to me, but it is also what makes each leave-taking so difficult. I grow increasingly apprehensive before every return to the world, and as this holiday drew to a close and I finally sat waiting for dinner on the last evening, I was aware of my mounting nervousness and depression. I decided to console myself with that nectar of so many ageing men — a bottle of vintage claret. Now as I sought Murphy's advice, I ignored, with unaccustomed recklessness, both the price and the knowledge that if I drank the whole bottle, I would undoubtedly spend a sleepless night. There were worse things than insomnia.

By dinner-time the light had changed outside and a soft blue opacity was flooding in from the Atlantic through the great windows of the dining-room. This is the Irish twilight, most beautiful of times and that part of the day I missed most during those few years I spent in West Africa as a young man. It is a time that induces a half-wilful melancholia — helped no doubt by the glass in one's hand — and in McAndrews they respect this mood, for the curtains are never drawn nor the lights switched on until darkness finally descends. As I moved through the flickering pools of yellow light — for there were many diners already present and many candles lit — I was struck again by the solemnity of the room. Years and years of ritual have given it a churchlike quiet, a hint of the ceremony and seriousness with which eating is invested by both guests and staff. I took my usual seat against the wall, facing out towards sea, and as Murphy murmured, priest-like, over the wine, we were both startled by a raised and discordant voice. 'Waiter, come here please.'

2. James Boswell (1740-95), the Scottish writer noted for his *Life of Samuel Johnson* (1791).

Together we turned towards the voice, both acutely conscious of the solecism that had been committed in referring to Murphy as 'Waiter'. The offender was sitting about six feet away at a small table in the middle of the room. It was an unpopular table, unprotected, marooned under the main chandelier, seldom occupied except when the hotel was very busy. I guessed now that some underling, flustered by the novelty of the situation, had forgotten himself to such an extent as to usher this person to it without first consulting Murphy. And the arrival of this new diner *was* a novelty. She was not a resident, which was odd in itself, for McAndrews has never been the sort of place to seek out a casual trade; then she was alone, unescorted, a sight which was not only odd, but simply not done: ladies, one feels, do not dine alone in public. But the most striking thing of all about our newcomer was her appearance. She was in her fifties, maybe sixty, with hair and dress matching, both of an indeterminate pink. She wore spectacles which were decorated with some kind of stones along the wings. These shone and sparkled as she moved her head, but no more brightly than her teeth, which were of an amazing and American brightness. She flashed them up at Murphy now, and as he shied away from their brilliance, I could see that for once he was discomposed. But Murphy is a gentleman and within seconds he had himself again in hand. Stiffening his back, he bowed slightly in the direction of the teeth. 'Madam?' he enquired, with dignity.

'Could I have a double Scotch on the rocks, and I'd like a look at the menu.' Her voice had that familiarity which so many aspects of American life have for Europeans who have never even crossed the Atlantic. I don't think I have ever met an American, but I have a great fondness for their television thrillers, and I immediately identified the voice as a New York voice, tough New York, like so many of my favourite villains. Proud of my detective work, I sat back to listen.

The whiskey had appeared with that speed to which we McAndrews guests are accustomed, and if Murphy disapproved of this solitary diner, his training was too perfect to even suggest it. He hovered beside her now, solicitously, as she studied the menu, and as she turned it over and turned it back again I noticed her face grow tight and apprehensive. I should say here that McAndrews does not have a menu in the usual commercial sense of that word. Mrs Byrne, who has been cooking there for the past thirty years, is an artist, and it would offend her artistic sensibility, and indeed equally displease the guests, if she were asked to produce the commonplace, vast à la carte vulgarity that one finds in so many dining places today. For festive occasions she will prepare a classic dish in the French tradition, and otherwise she keeps us all happy cooking simple but superb dishes using the local fish and meat and the vegetables which grow a couple of hundred yards away. She is a wonder certainly, but I can perfectly understand that one used to the meaningless internationalism of the modern menu might find Mrs Byrne's handwritten and modest proposals something of a puzzle. One would look in vain for the tired Entrecôte Chasseur or the ubiquitous Sole Bonne Femme in this dining-room and be somewhat at a loss when faced with the humble, boiled silverside of beef followed by stewed damsons with ginger.

I could see that this was precisely the position in which our lady diner now found herself. She toyed with the piece of paper and looked up helplessly at Murphy. Murphy coughed encouragingly behind a genteel hand and began, 'Perhaps Madam, I could recommend tonight the —'. But she gathered her shoulders together and threw back her head. 'No, you could not, waiter. I know exactly what I want.' Her voice had taken on an added stridency. 'I want a filet mignon with a green salad. Surely a place like this can produce that — huh?'

'It is not on the menu, Madam, but certainly if that is what you require, we can arrange it.' I though I noticed a hint of disapproval in Murphy's silky tones.

'Yeah, that's what I want. Nothing to start and I want the steak medium-rare, and I mean medium-rare. All you Irish overcook meat.'

I thought for a moment that Murphy was going to lose control, that years of training and polish would at last begin to give way before this latest onslaught of rudeness, but again he recovered himself. For a second he paused over his order and then looked up again and said, still politely, 'And to drink Madam, would you like something?' The lady looked at him, genuinely puzzled as she held up her whiskey glass. 'I've gotten it already — remember?' It was now Murphy's turn to look puzzled and I could see him struggling mentally before the implication of her remark became clear to him. This extraordinary person intended to drink whiskey with her filet mignon!

As I watched my fellow-diner I wondered how on earth she had ever found her way to McAndrews. It was not a fashionable spot, not the sort of place that attracted tourists. There was a hideous motel only ten miles away, much smarter than McAndrews, flashing neon lights, full of Americans, supplying what they called an ensemble for the gratification of their guests. Surely this woman would have been much more at home in such a place? But as I studied her, I began to realize that this strange creature was actually impressed by McAndrews. I was sure now that she hadn't accidentally happened upon it as I had at first surmised, but that for some unknown reason she had chosen it deliberately. And I saw too that her apparent rudeness was no more than awkwardness, an effort to hide her awe and inexperience in such surroundings. My daughter-in-law — the beautician — when she visited me here once gave a display of genuine rudeness, authentic because it was based on contempt, for Murphy, for me, for our kind of world. She shouted at Murphy because she saw him as an inefficient old fogey. But he didn't impinge at all on her world and was only a nuisance to her because he did not mix her cocktail in the correct proportions. This woman however was different, although I saw that Murphy didn't think so — indeed whereas he was prepared to make excuses for Helen, as one of the family, I could tell that he had put up with as much as he was going to from an outsider. As the waiter placed the steak in front of her, Murphy approached, disapproval in every line of his stately person. 'Medium rare, as you required,' he said, and even I, sitting some distance away, drew back from the sting of his contempt.

Other guests were taking notice now, attracted perhaps by Murphy's slightly raised voice, a unique occurrence in this dining-room. I could feel a current of mild disapproval beginning to circulate and I saw that the lady was noticing something too. She was looking discomfited but bravely she took up her knife and fork and tucked in her chin. I was beginning to admire her pluck.

Decency demanded that I leave her some privacy to eat so reluctantly I looked away. Soon, I was glad to see, the other guests lost interest in her, and when after a safe interval I glanced back at her table, she had finished her meal and was wiping her mouth with an air of well-being and relaxation. It must have been a satisfactory filet mignon. When Murphy brought the menu again, she actually smiled at him. 'No, no,' she said waving it away, 'nothing more for me. We women have to watch our figures — eh?' And as she glanced at him archly, I thought for an awful moment that she was going to dig him in the ribs. Murphy looked at her coldly, making no effort to return her smile. 'Very well, Madam.' The words hung between them and as she sensed his unfriendliness, indeed hostility, the smile, still awkward upon her lips, became transfixed in an ugly grimace. 'I guess you'd better bring me another Scotch.' Defeat was now beginning to edge out defiance in her voice. She grasped her drink when it arrived, and gulped it, as a drowning man gulps air. This seemed to steady her somewhat and taking another, slower sip, she drew out a cigarette from her bag and lit it. It was then that she discovered, just as Murphy was passing on his way towards my table, that there was no ashtray. 'Excuse me,' she sounded embarrassed, 'could you bring me an ashtray please?' Murphy turned slowly in his tracks. He looked at her in silence for fully five seconds. 'I am sorry, Madam,' — and it seemed to me now that the whole dining-room was listening to his even, slightly heightened tones — 'I am sorry, but our guests do not smoke in the dining-room.' In essence this is true, it being accepted among the guests that tobacco is not used in here — a measure of their consideration for each other as smoke fumes might lessen someone's enjoyment of an excellent meal. I thoroughly approve of this unwritten rule — it seems to me to be eminently civilized — but I know well that on occasion, people, newcomers for example, have smoked in McAndrews dining-room, and Murphy, though perhaps disapproving, has never demurred. I looked at him now in amazement and maybe he caught my expression of surprise, for he added, 'Coffee is served in the blue sitting-room, Madam, there are ashtrays there. However, if you'd prefer it, I can —' The woman stood up abruptly, almost colliding with Murphy. Her face and neck were flooded with an ugly red colour and she seemed to be trying to push him away. 'No, not at all, I'll have the coffee,' and she blundered blindly towards the door. It seemed a long, long journey.

I finished my cheese and followed her thoughtfully into the sitting-room. All evening something had been niggling me, something about that voice. I have a very sensitive ear I believe — I am rather proud of it — and although, as I had noticed, this woman spoke with an American accent, there was some underlying non-American quality about it. Something familiar but different about those vowels and th's. Now as I sat and lit my cigar, I realized what it was — it was so obvious that I had missed it until now. Her voice, of course, was a local voice, a North Mayo voice with that thick and doughy consistency that I was hearing around me since I had come down. It had become Americanized, almost completely so, but to my ear its origins were clear. I could swear that that woman had been born within ten miles of this very hotel.

We both sipped our coffee, the tinkle of coffee-spoons falling between us. I watched her as she sat alone, isolated and tiny in the deep recess of the bay window, looking out at the darkening gardens. Beyond, there were still some streaks of light coming from the sea, and I knew that down below on the rocks the village children would be gathering their final bundles of seaweed before heading off home to bed. The seaweed is sold to the local factory where it is turned into fertilizer of some kind and the people here collect it assiduously, sometimes whole families working together, barefooted, for the salt water rots shoe-leather. Even the little ones often have hard and calloused feet, sometimes with ugly cuts. Life is still hard in the West of Ireland. I looked across at my lady — *her* feet were encased in red high-heeled shoes with large platform soles. Her face, as she gazed out unseeing, was sad now, sad and crumpled-looking. I recalled again her voice, and as we sat there, drinking our coffee, I suddenly knew without any shadow of doubt what she was doing there. I knew *her* intimately — her life was spread out in front of me. I could see her as a little girl, living nearby in some miserable cottage. Maybe, when I was out walking as a child with my Mama, I had even passed her, not noticing the tattered little girl who stood in wonder, staring at us. McAndrews must have been a symbol to her, a world of wealth and comfort, right there on the doorstep of her own poverty-stricken existence. Perhaps she had even worked in the hotel as a maid, waiting to save her fare to America, land of opportunity. And in America, had she been lonely, frightened by that alien place, so different from her own Mayo? Had she wept herself to sleep many nights, sick for a breath of home? But she had got on, sent money back, and always, all those years, she had kept her dream intact: one day she would return home to Kilgory, a rich American lady, and she would go into McAndrews Hotel, not as a maid this time but as a guest. She would order a fine dinner and impress everyone with her clothes and her accent and her wealth.

She sat now, a rejected doll in her pink dress and red shoes, for tonight she had seen that dream disintegrate like candy-floss. I wanted to go to her, to tell her, explain to her that it didn't matter any more — the world itself was disintegrating. She should realize that places like McAndrews weren't important any longer, people only laughed at them now. She had no need to be saddened, for she, and all those other little Irish girls who had spent their days washing other people's floors and cooking other people's meals, they would inherit the earth. The wheel had come round full circle.

Of course I didn't approach her. I finished my coffee and went straight to bed thinking how the world is changing, my world, her world. Soon McAndrews itself will be gone. But for me, this landscape has been caught forever — caught and defined by its heroine, the lady with the red shoes. Of course, you, on reading this, are going to see me as a sentimental old codger, making up romantic stories about strangers, because I am lonely and have nothing better to do. But I know what I know.

JOHN BANVILLE

(1945-)

from: LONG LANKIN (1970, 1984)

['De Rerum Natura' was added to the 1984 revised version of *Long Lankin* (1970), while a novella and a second story were omitted, the effect being to make *Long Lankin* read less like a novel and more like a volume of short stories. 'De Rerum Natura' concocts a characteristically odd Banvillean world, a suggestively Anglo-Irish one, revelling in decline and assuming for the writer a gothic atmosphere: overgrowth ('Life everywhere') as the ironic manifestation of decline. Nature's overstatement is answered by the old man's crazy schemes, themselves portions of Banville's own exotic imaginings, here and elsewhere. For the nature of things is Banville's invention, and Banville, after the early stories in *Long Lankin*, became a writer whose subject is the nature of fiction, fiction meaning not only storytelling but all making, all perceiving, even all interpreting.

The influence of Lucretius's poem on Banville's story, from the title onwards, is worth pondering. Lucretian man has an absolute trust in the senses; he regards pleasure as the greatest good; he believes Nature paramount in the universal scheme of things and experiences awe in the midst of it; he feels free of the fear of death while in it; ideally, he withdraws from public commerce with his fellows and is independent. A morbid strain, even a streak of madness, has been detected in the Latin writer. Why then should not Banville's old man, quoting Lear, be mad?]

DE RERUM NATURA

The old man was hosing the garden when the acrobats appeared. They were unexpected, to say the least. Elves, now, would not have surprised him, or goblins. But acrobats! Still, he got used to them, and in the last weeks came to value them above all else the world could offer. Glorious weeks, the best of the year, sweltering dog days drenched with sun and the singing of skylarks. He spent them in the garden, thrashing about in the waist-high grass, delirious with the heat and a suffocating sense of the countless lives throbbing all around him, the swarming ants, the birds in the trees, glittering bright blue flies, the lizards and spiders, his beloved bees, not to mention the things called inanimate, the earth itself, all these, breeding and bursting and killing. Sometimes it all became too much, and then he would take the hose and saturate the garden, howling in a rapture of mad glee and disgust. It was at the end of one of these galas that he first saw the acrobats.

George and Lucy hardly recognised him. If they had met him in the garden they might have taken him for a tree, burned mahogany as he was, with that long beard like grizzled ivy. He had stopped using the cutthroat for fear that it would live up to its name some morning, and he had no intention of giving them by accident an excuse for an orgy of mourning. Anyway, at that time it looked as if he would soon starve to death. Then he discovered that the garden was rich with food, cabbages and rhubarb, potatoes, raspberries, all manner of things flourishing under the weeds. There were even roses, heavy bloodred blooms, unsettling. His fits of fury with the hose helped all this growth. What a silence there was after the deluge, and in the silence the stealthy drip of water slipping from leaf to limb to root, into the parched earth.

The acrobats appeared through a mist of sparkling light, a troupe of short stout fellows in black striped leotards, with furred bandy legs and leather straps on their arms and incongruously dainty black dancing pumps. An hallucination, he said, sure that in a moment they would vanish, leaving nothing behind but a faintly reverberating *ping*! But he was wrong. They set up their trampoline and parallel bars in the clearing at the bottom of the orchard and began to leap and prance about, clapping their hands and urging each other on with enthusiastic squeaks and cries. Allez up! There was one woman only, fat, with hot dark eyes, who managed to be the undisputed centre of the show even though she did nothing more than pose, and toss her hair, and flash those brimming eyes. The first performance was brief, and they went away puffing and sweating.

Next day they were back. He was tending the hives when he saw through the trees a figure sailing up and down with leisurely grace on the trampoline. Already he detected a distinct improvement in their act. They rounded it off with a human pyramid, a wobbly edifice fraught with unacknowledged hilarity. He sat in the shade of an apple tree and watched them bouncing and tumbling, wondering if he was expected to applaud. To the third show he brought along a saucepan and a pair of forks, with which he produced a tattoo as of a snare drum during those moments of stillness and suspense before the last daring splendour of a stunt was attempted. The woman waddled forward, smiling haughtily, and swept him a low bow.

He poured rapturous accounts of their antics into crazed messianic letters which he stuffed stampless in the postbox in the village at dead of night, laughing in the dark at the thought of the storm and panic they would precipitate on the breakfast tables of his family and friends. No replies came, which surprised and annoyed him, until he realised that all to whom he had written were dead, save his son and daughter-in-law, who arrived in the heart of the country one burning noon and laid siege to his sanctuary.

—He must be really bad this time, said George.

—No stamp, said Lucy. Typical.

The house was silent, the windows blind, the doors barricaded against them. They hammered on it with their fists, and heard within the sound of muffled laughter. They called to him, pleaded, and were turning away when suddenly there erupted a plangent discord of piano music, followed by a shriek of castors rolling on stone. The door collapsed slowly into the hall, and there was the old man grinning at them from behind the piano, his little blue eyes glinting in the gloom. His clothes were in tatters, his feet bare and crusted with grime. He looked more than anything like a baby, the bald dome and bandy legs, the eyes, the gums, an ancient mischievous baby.

—My god, Lucy murmured, appalled.

—That's right! that's me! the old man cried. He executed a brief dance on the flagstones, capering and gesticulating, then stopped and glared at them.

—What do you want?

George stepped forward, stumbled over the fallen door, and blushed.

—Hello there! he yelled. How are you . . .?

The heartiness fell sickeningly flat, and he blanched. Although well into middle age, George had the air of a gawky, overgrown schoolboy. His long thin frame gave an impression first of all of paleness, pale eyes and hands, pale dusty hair. When he smiled, the tip of a startlingly red tongue appeared between his teeth. There was an eggstain like a bilious sunburst on his tie. The old man eyed him unenthusiastically and said with heavy sarcasm:

—Rakish as ever, eh Georgie? Well come on, get in here, get in.

Lucy did not stir, rooted by her fury to the spot. How dare this decrepit madman order her George about! A hot flush blossomed on her forehead. The old man smiled at her mockingly, and led his son away down the hall.

He conducted them on a tour of his kingdom as though they were strangers. The house was a shambles. There were pigeons in the bedrooms, rats in the kitchen. That was fine with him, he said. Life everywhere. He told them how he locked himself out one day and broke the door off its hinges to get in again, then had to jam the piano against it to hold it up. The old woman from the farms in the hills who took care of him fled after that episode. He lived in the drawing-room, in a lair of old blankets and newspapers and cobwebs, yet he felt that his presence penetrated every nook and corner of the house like a sustained note of music. Even the mice in the attic were aware of him, he knew it.

In a corridor upstairs Lucy grabbed her husband's arm and whispered fiercely:

—How long are we going to stay fooling around here?

George ducked his head as though avoiding a blow. He glanced nervously at the old man shambling ahead of them and muttered:

—It's all right now, don't fuss, we've plenty of time.

Lucy sighed wearily, and closed her eyes. She was a plump woman, still pretty, with large expressive breasts which trembled when she was angry. There was a damp sheen on her nose and chin, and she exuded a faint whiff of sweat. Summer did not agree with her.

—Tell him we're taking him away, she said. Tell him about the home.

—Lucy, he's my *father*.

He turned his face resolutely away from her and quickened his step. Once again he noticed how odd this house was, with its turrets and towers and pink and white timbering, like an enormous birthday cake set down in the midst of the fields. Only his father had felt at home here, while the rest of the family dreamt vague fitful dreams of escape into a world free of his malevolent, insidious gaiety.

George remembered, with a shudder, his childhood, the genteel penury, the mockery of the village, the friends in whose homes he sat with his hands pressed between his bony knees, inwardly wailing in envy of the simple, dull normalcy of lives where fathers in suits and ties returned at evening, scowling and tired, to newspapers and slippers and huge fried teas. A door at the end of the corridor led into one of the turrets, a tiny eyrie of glass and white wood, capped by an unexpectedly graceful little spire. Here, suspended and insulated in this bubble of light, the old man had spent his days working out with meticulous logic the details of his crazy schemes, oblivious of his wife's slow dying, the children's despair. George felt stirring within him the first tendrils of confused rage, and he retreated into the corridor. His father came trotting after him.

—Wait there, I want to show you my plans for the distillery.

George halted.

—Distillery . . .?

—Aye. With potatoes. The place is full of them out there.

Lucy, behind them, let fall a shrill gulp of laughter.

They had lunch in the ruined dining-room, raw carrots, beans, mounds of raspberries, honey. Lucy found knives and forks and three cracked plates, but the old man would have none of these niceties.

—Do animals use forks? he asked, leaning across the table, his eyes wide. He had put in his dentures. They lent his face an odd look, both comical and savage.

—Well, do they?

—We're not animals, she said sullenly.

He grinned. That was the answer he had wanted.

—O yes we are, my girl, yes we are, poor forked animals.

Lucy's chest began to surge, and her forehead darkened, and George, his legs twisted under the table in a knot of anxiety, searched frantically for a way to head off the argument he could see approaching.

—Well listen, why, why don't you tell us about these fellows in the garden that you see, these acrobats?

The old man's eyes grew shifty, and he munched on a carrot and mumbled to himself. Then he sat upright suddenly.

—They dance, you know. They have this little dance when they're flying in that tells the ones coming out where the source is, how far, what direction, precisely. You don't believe me? I'll show you. O aye, they dance all right.

Lucy looked blankly from the old man to George and back again, and in her bafflement forgot herself and ate a handful of beans off the bare boards.

—Who? she asked.

The old man glared.

—Who what? Bees, of course. Haven't I just told you? Snails too.

—Snails! George cried, trying desperately to sound astounded and intrigued, and fired off a nervous laugh like a rapid volley of hiccups.

—*Yuck*, Lucy grunted in disgust.

The old man was offended.

—What's wrong? Snails, what's wrong with snails? They dance. Everything dances.

He picked up the honeycomb. The thick amber syrup dripped unnoticed into his lap. His lips moved mutely for a moment, striving painfully to find the words. Grime gathered at the corners of his mouth.

—It takes six hundred bees to gather a pound of honey. Six hundred, you'll say, that's not bad, but do you know how much flying it takes? Twenty-five thousand miles. Did you know that, did you?

They shook their heads slowly, gazing at him with open mouths. He was trembling, and all at once tears started from his eyes.

—Think of all that work, thousands of miles, on the flowers, that labour, the queen getting fat, the eggs hatching, then the frost, thousands dead, another world. Another world! You'll say it's blind instinct, cruel, like a machine, nature's slaves, and you're right, you're right, but listen to me, what is it at the centre, how do they keep it all going? *They dance.*

Suddenly he leaped from his chair and began to zoom about the room, bowing and gliding, crooning and laughing, the tears flowing, waving the comb aloft and scattering honey on the chairs, the table, until at last he tripped on the fender and fell into the fireplace in a storm of dust and soot and cobwebs, out of which his voice rose like the tolling of a bell.

—Poor forked animals, and they dance.

Days passed. Lucy and George cleared the spiders and the mousedirt out of the big front bedroom, and there they spent the hot nights, waking up at all hours to engage in one-sided arguments. George dithered, lapsed into a kind of moral catatonia, smiled a chilling smile, giggled sometimes inexplicably. Once he interrupted her in full flight by saying dreamily:

—Did you know that whales sing? O yes, in the depths of the oceans, songs. So he says.

—George! Get a grip of yourself.

—Yes, yes. But still ....

After the first day the old man ceased to acknowledge their presence, and went back to his life in the garden. Often they saw the water cascading in the orchard, and heard his howls. When he met them in the house he would glance at them furtively and smile to himself, like a man recognising familiar, harmless phantoms. Lucy's rage turned into despair. She confronted her husband with final, unavoidable decisions, which somehow he always managed to avoid. The weather held, sun all day, breathless nights. She became obsessed with herself, her sweat, damp hair, scalding flesh. The taps in the bathroom did not work. She smelled, she was sure of it. This could not go on.

—George, it's him or me, I mean it, make your choice.

His head sank between his shoulders, and he cracked his knuckles. That noise made her want to scream. He said:

—What do you mean, you or him? I don't understand.

—You do!

—Do I? Well, I don't know about that.

She looked at him closely. Was he making fun of her? His pale eyes slid away from her gaze. She changed course.

—George, please, I can't stand it here. Can you not see that? I'll go mad, I'll be like him, worse.

He looked at her directly then, for the first time, it seemed, since they had arrived, and she saw in his face the realisation dawning that she was indeed in pain. She smiled, and touched his hand. The door burst open and the old man came bounding in, waving his arms.

—They're swarming, they're swarming! Come on!

She held George's arm. He smirked at her in a travesty of appeasement, and wriggled out of her grasp. The old man disappeared from the doorway. George raced after him. When he reached the garden it was empty. The air throbbed with a deep, malevolent hum. He stumbled through the briars and the tangled grass, into the orchard, ducking under the branches. The old man lay on his back among the hives, eyes wide, the hose clutched in his hands, the water rising straight up and splashing back on his face. George knelt by his side, under the spray. The orchard quivered around him. Under the sun all was gloom and growth, green things, stalks, lichen, rot and wrack. He stared into thorns and sodden mould, drenched leaves, the purple hearts of roses. His flesh crawled. Then he saw the snails. They were everywhere in the wet, on the leaves, the trees, glued along slender stalks of grass, gleaming silver and black brutes straining out of their shells as though in ecstasy, their moist horns erect and weaving. It was a dance. The snails were dancing. A black cloud of bees rose from the hives and spun away into the sky, thrumming. The old man was dead.

George stood in the bedroom.

—I had better stay here for a day or two, he said. Clear things up. You know.

She nodded absently, wandering about the room, picking up things, a newspaper, clothes, a tube of lipstick. She seemed hardly to notice him, and avoided meeting his eyes. He stood in the drawing-room and watched her clatter away down the drive, stumbling in her high heels, and then he went down and pushed the piano against the door.

Glorious weather, days drenched with sun and the singing of larks, a lavender haze over the sweltering meadows, the silence trembling on the upper airs of evening, and then the nights, the glossy black and the pale radiance, Sirius ascending, a smokewhite breeze at dawn. He spent his time in the garden, tending the roses, the vegetables, the hives. Sometimes he took the hose and sprayed the parched plants, the trees, the earth, and then sat for hours studying the surging life around him, the spiders, the birds and flies, his beloved bees. A swarm of them settled in a corner of the drawing room, under the ceiling. That was fine with him. Life everywhere.

from:
MEFISTO (1986)

[This excerpt comprises the second and third 'chapters' of Part I of *Mefisto*; Part I is called 'Marionettes' and Part II 'Angels'. *Mefisto* is the final novel in Banville's tetralogy (*Doctor Copernicus* (1976), *Kepler* (1981), *The*

Newton Letter (1982)) and is concerned, as were the preceding works, with one of the men whom Banville has called 'those high cold heroes' who believe or try to believe in a fundamental, elegant and mathematical order that underlies the world of chaotic experience and impression. The hero, Gabriel Swan, is a child prodigy who finds in numbers a system that can confront, but not ultimately overwhelm, the irrational.]

I don't know when it was that I first heard of the existence, if that's the word, of my dead brother. From the start I knew I was the survivor of some small catastrophe, the shock-waves were still reverberating faintly inside me. The mysterious phenomenon that produced us is the result, the textbooks tell me, of a minor arrest in the early development of a single egg, so that the embryonic streak begins dividing by binary fission. I prefer to picture something like a scene from a naughty seaside postcard, the fat lady, apple cheeks, big bubs and mighty buttocks, cloven clean in two by her driven little consort. However, the cause is no matter, only the effect. The perils we had missed were many. We might have been siamese. One of us might have exsanguinated into the other's circulation. Or we might simply have strangled one another. All this we escaped, and surfaced at last, gasping. I came first. My brother was a poor second. Spent swimmer, he drowned in air. My father, when Jack Kay fetched him home at last, looked in dull wonderment at the scene: the infant mewling in its mother's arms, and that lifeless replica of it laid out on the sheet.

My mother feared I too would die. Jack Kay reminded her how his brothers, her homuncles, had succumbed after a day. She nursed me with a kind of vehemence, willing me to live. She would not let me out of her sight. She made a nest for me in the big drawer of the wardrobe in her bedroom. I see myself lying there, unnaturally silent, slowly flexing my bandy arms and legs, like a tortoise stranded on its back. When she leans over me I look at her gropingly and frown. My vague, bleached gaze is that of a traveller come back from somewhere immensely far and strange. At night she lay awake and listened to the furtive noises this new life made, the shufflings and soft sighs, and now and then what sounded like a muffled exclamation of impatience. Later on, when I had learned to walk, and could get away by myself, I developed a private language, a rapid, aquatic burbling, which made people uneasy. It sounded as if I were conversing with someone. Hearing me, my mother would pause outside my door, on the stairs, and I in turn, hearing her, would immediately fall silent. Thus we would remain, the two of us, for a long time, alert, motionless, listening to our own inexplicably palpitant heartbeats. Jack Kay, moustache twitching, wondered aloud if maybe I was wrong in the head.

I feel a tender, retrospective concern, mixed with a trace of contempt, it's true, for this baffled little boy who moves through my memories of those first years in watchful solitude, warily. I clung to the house. My bedroom looked down through two tiny windows into the square, it was like hiding inside a head. I seemed to myself not whole, nor wholly real. Fairytales fascinated me, there was something dismayingly familiar in them, the mad logic, the discontinuities, the random cruelty of fate. I was brought to a circus, I remember it, the noise, the flashing lights, the brass farts of the band, the incongruous scent of crushed grass coming up between the seats. There were tumbling midgets, and a woman with a snake, and a brilliantined contortionist, thin as a blade, who sat down on his coccyx and assembled a series of agonized tableaux with the stony detachment of a pornographer displaying his wares. It was the clowns, though, that really unnerved me, with their pointy heads and rubber feet and oddly diffused yells, the way they kept tormenting each other, the way the short one would stand bawling in frustration and seeming pain and then whirl round suddenly and smash his lanky companion full in the face with terrible, steely insouciance. I sat without a stir throughout the show, gazing down into the lighted ring with wistful avidity, like that boy in the story who longed to learn how to shudder.

My mother took me for walks, first in a pram, then tottering ahead of her on a sort of reins, then dawdling farther and farther behind her along the hedgerows. Sometimes we went as far as Ashburn and wandered through the unkempt grounds. She showed me the cottage where she was born, behind the stables. Ashburn would be for her always an idyll. The life of the big house, at the far fringes of which she had hovered longingly, she remembered as a languorous mime to the music of tick-tocking tennis balls across green lawns and the far-off bleat of the huntsman's horn on frosty mornings, a scene small and distant, yet perfectly, preciously detailed, atinkle with tiny laughter, like a picture glimpsed of eighteenth-century aristocrats at play in a dappled glade. In the midst of this pretty pastoral stood the cottage, where the frog king Jack Kay had reigned. Here her memories were more precise, of whitewash, and rats in the thatch, the tin bath in front of the fire on Saturday nights, a speckled hen standing on one leg in a patch of sun in the kitchen doorway. And the endless squabbles, of course, the shouting, the boxed ears. Now the stables were falling, the forge where Jack Kay had worked was silent. One day, on an overgrown path, under a huge tree, we met Miss Kitty, the last of the Ashburns of Ashburn Park, a distracted and not very clean maiden lady with a great beaked nose and tangled hair, who talked to us calmly enough for a bit, then turned abruptly and ordered us off the estate, waving her arms and shouting.

There were other spectacles, other frights. I have only a single recollection of Grandfather Swan, a big effigy sitting up in bed laughing in the little house in Queen Street. It was Easter morning, and I was five years old. The sick-room smelled of pipe tobacco and piss. There was a window open beside the bed. The sunlight outside glittered after a recent shower. Grandfather Swan had been shaving, the bowl and cut-throat and bit of looking-glass were still beside him, and there was a fleck of fresh blood on the collar of his nightshirt. His hands trembled, apart from that he seemed quite hale. But he was dying. I was conscious of the solemnity of the occasion. Hard fingers prodded me between the shoulder-blades, and I stepped forward, gazing in awe at the old man's taut white brow and big moustache, the agate nails, the swept-back spikes of iron-grey hair that made it seem as if some force were dragging the head away and up, to the window, to the shining roofs, to the spring sky itself, pale blue and chill like his eyes. He must have talked to me, but I remember only his laugh, not so much a sound as something that surrounded him, like an aura, and not at all benign. For a long time death was to seem a sort of disembodied, sinister merriment sitting in wait for me in that fetid little room.

And yet, I wonder. Is this really a picture of Grandfather Swan, or did I in my imagination that Easter morn wishfully substitute another, tougher old man for this one who was doomed? I mean Jack Kay. The laugh, the alarming fingernails, the wirebrush moustache stained yellow in the middle, all these are his, surely? Jack Kay. To me he was always eighty. He wore his years like a badge of tenacity, grimly, with a kind of truculence. But let me have done with him. He lived at Ashburn, and worked the forge. He was an intermittent drunkard. He married Martha somebody, I forget the name, a scullery maid at the big house. They had children. They were unhappy.

Or at least Martha was. I do not see her clearly. She and Granny Swan died about the same time. They blur into each other, two put-upon old women, somehow not quite life-sized, dropsical, dressed in black, always unwell, always complaining. Their voices are a faint, background murmur, like the twittering of mice behind a wainscot. They must have had some effect, must have contributed a gene or two, yet there remains almost nothing of them. In the matter of heredity they were no match for their menfolk. All the same, there is a memory, which, though neither woman is really in it, is their inspiration. One of those windy damp days of early autumn, with a sky of low, dove-grey cloud, the shining pavements plastered with leaves, and an empty dustbin rolling on its side in the middle of the road. Someone had told me my granny was dead. The news, far from being sad, was strangely exhilarating, and there on that street suddenly I was filled with a snug excitement, which I could not explain, but which was somehow to do with life, with the future. I was not thinking of the living woman, she had been of scant significance to me. In death, however, she had become one with those secret touchstones the thought of which comforted and mysteriously sustained me: small lost animals, the picturesque poor, warnings of gales at sea, the naked feet of Franciscans.

I don't know which of the two women it was that had died. Let the image of that silvery light on that rainy road be a memorial, however paltry, to them both.

My father in these early memories is a remote, enigmatic and yet peculiarly vivid figure. He worked as a tallyman for a grain merchant. He smelled of chaff, dust, jute, all dry things. He had asthma, and a bad leg. His silences, into which a remark about the weather or a threat of death would drop alike without trace, were a force in our house, like a dull drumming that has gone on for so long it has ceased to be heard but is still vaguely, disturbingly felt. His presence, diffident and fleeting, lent a mysterious weight to the most trivial occasion. He took me to the Fort mountain one day on the bar of his bicycle. It was September, clear and still. The heather was in bloom. We sat on a ditch eating sandwiches, and drinking tepid milk out of lemonade bottles that my mother had filled for us and corked with twists of paper. The sanatorium was high up behind us, hidden among pines except for the steep-pitched roof and a tall cluster of chimneys, closed, silent, alluring. I toyed dreamily with the thought of myself reclining in a timeless swoon on the veranda up there, swaddled in blankets, with the dazzling white building at my back and the sun slowly falling down the sky in front of me, and a wireless somewhere quietly playing danceband music. My father wore a flat cap and a heavy, square-cut overcoat, a size too big for him, that smelled of mothballs. He pointed out a hawk wheeling in the zenith.

— Take the eye out of you, he said, one of them lads.

He was a short man, with long arms and bowed legs. His head was small, which made his trunk seem weightier than it was. With those limbs, that sharp face, the close-set dark eyes, he had something of those stunted little warriors, the dark-haired ones, Pict or Firbolg,[1] I don't know, who stalk the far borders of history. I can see him, in pelts and pointed shoon, limping at twilight through the bracken. A small man, whom the vengeful gods have overlooked. A survivor.

Sometimes I catch myself dreaming that dream in which childhood is an endless festival, with bands of blond children sweeping through the streets in sunlight, laughing. I can almost see the tunics, the sandalled feet, the white-robed elders watching indulgently from the olive tree's shade. Something must have fed this Attic fantasy, a game of tag, perhaps, on a Sunday evening in summer, the houses open to the tender air, and mothers on the doorsteps, talking, and someone's sister, in her first lipstick, leaning at gaze out of an upstairs window.

The town was twelve thousand souls, three churches and a Methodist hall, a narrow main street, a disused anthracite mine, a river and a silted harbour. Fragments of the past stuck up through the present, rocks in the stream of time: a Viking burial mound, a Norman tower, a stump of immemorial wall like a broken molar. History was rich there. Giraldus Cambrensis[2] knew that shore. The Templars had kept a hospice on the Spike peninsula.[3] The region had played its part in more than one failed uprising. By now the splendour had faded. There was too, I almost forgot, the great war against the Jehovah's Witnesses, I had watched the final rout: a priest punching in the belly a skinny young man in a mac, the crowd shouting, the bundles of *The Watchtower*[4] flying in the air. And there was a celebrated murder, never solved, an old woman battered to death one dark night in her sweetshop down a lane. It was the stuff of nightmares, the body behind the counter, the bottled sweets, the blood.

A picture of the town hangs in my mind, like one of those priceless yet not much prized medieval miniatures, its provenance uncertain, its symbols no longer quite explicable, the translucency of its faded colours lending it a quaint, accidental charm. Can it really all be so long ago, so different, or is this antique tawny patina only the varnish which memory applies even to a recent past? It's true, there is a lacquered quality to the light of those remembered days. The grey of a wet afternoon in winter would be the aptest shade, yet I think of a grocer's brass scales standing in a beam of dusty sunlight, a bit of smooth blue china — they were called chaynies — found in the garden and kept for years, and there blooms before my inward gaze the glow of pale gold wings in a pellucid, Limbourg-blue sky.

Along with the tower and the broken wall there were the human antiquities, the maimed and the mad, the hunchbacks, the frantic old crones in their bonnets and black coats, and the mongols, with their little eyes and bad feet and sweet smiles, gambolling at the heels of touchingly middle-aged mothers. They were all of them a sort of brotherhood, in which I was a mere acolyte. It had its high priests too. There was the little man who came one summer to stay with relatives on the other side of our square. He wore blue suits and shiny shoes, pearl cufflinks, a ruby ring. He had a large hand-

1. Early inhabitants of Ireland.

2. Giraldus Cambrensis (*c.* 1146-1223) visited Ireland twice: in 1183 and in 1185.

3. Spike Island, near Cork, once had a hospice kept by the Order of Knights Templars.

4. The name of the magazine published by the Jehovah's Witnesses.

some head and a barrel chest. His hair was a masterpiece, black and smooth as shellac, as if a gramophone record had been moulded to his skull. He rode an outsize tricycle. Astride this machine he held court under the trees of the square, surrounded by a mesmerized crowd of children, his arms folded and one gleaming toecap touching the ground with balletic delicacy. He was in a way the ideal adult, bejewelled, primped and pomaded, magisterially self-possessed, and just four feet tall. His manners were exquisite. Such tact! In his presence I felt hardly different from ordinary children.

I went to the convent school. Corridors painted a light shade of sick, tall windows with sash cords taut as a noose, and nuns, a species of large black raptor,[5] swooping through the classrooms, their rosaries clacking like jesses. I feared my classmates, and despised them too. I can see them still, their gargoyle faces, the kiss curls, the snot. My name for some reason they found funny. They would bring their brothers or their big sisters to confront me in the playground.

— There he is, ask him.

— You, what's your name?

— Nobody.

— Come on, say it!

And they would get me by the scruff.

— Gabriel ... ow! ... Gabriel Swan.

It sent them into fits, it never failed.

In my class there was another pair of, yes, of identical twins, listless little fellows with pale eyes and knobbly, defenceless knees. I was fascinated. They were so calm, so unconcerned, as if being alike were a trick they had mastered long ago, and thought nothing of any more. They could have had such a time, playing pranks, switching places, fooling everybody. That was what fascinated me, the thought of being able to escape effortlessly, as if by magic, into another name, another self — that, and the ease too with which they could assert their separate identities, simply by walking away from each other. Apart, each twin was himself. Only together were they a freak.

But I, I had something always beside me. It was not a presence, but a momentous absence. From it there was no escape. A connecting cord remained, which parturition and even death had not broken, along which by subtle tugs and thrums I sensed what was not there. No living double could have been so tenacious as this dead one. Emptiness weighed on me. It seemed to me I was not all my own, that I was being shared. If I fell, say, and cut my knee, I would be aware immediately of an echo, a kind of chime, as of a wine-glass shattering somewhere out of sight, and I would feel a soft shock like that when the dreamer on the brink of blackness puts a foot on a step which is not there. Perhaps the pain was lessened — how would I have known?

Sometimes this sense of being burdened, of being somehow imposed upon, gave way to a vague and seemingly objectless yearning. One wet afternoon, at the home of a friend of my mother's who was a midwife, I got my hands on a manual of obstetrics which I pored over hotly for five tingling minutes, quaking in excitement and fear at all this amazing new knowledge. It was not, however, the gynaecological surprises that held me, slack-jawed and softly panting, as if I had stumbled on the most entrancing erotica, but that section of glossy, rubensesque colour plates depicting some of mother nature's more lavish mistakes, the scrambled blastomeres, the androgynes welded at hip or breast, the bicipitous monsters with tiny webbed hands and cloven spines, all those queer, inseverable things among which I and my phantom brother might have been one more.

It seems out of all this somehow that my gift for numbers grew. From the beginning, I suppose, I was obsessed with the mystery of the unit, and everything else followed. Even yet I cannot see a one and a zero juxtaposed without feeling deep within me the vibration of a dark, answering note. Before I could talk I had been able to count, laying out my building blocks in ranked squares, screaming if anyone dared to disturb them. I remember a toy abacus that I treasured for years, with multicoloured wooden beads, and a wooden frame, and little carved feet for it to stand on. My party piece was to add up large numbers instantly in my head, frowning, a hand to my brow, my eyes downcast. It was not the manipulation of things that pleased me, the mere facility, but the sense of order I felt, of harmony, of symmetry and completeness.

St Stephen's School stood on a hill in the middle of the town, a tall, narrow, red-brick building with a

5 A bird of prey. 'Jesses' are short leather straps attached to the legs of falcons and hawks.

black slate roof and a tin weathercock. I think of damp flagstones and the crash of boots, rain in the yard, and the smell of drains, and something else, a sense of enclosure, of faces averted from the world in holy fright. On my first day there I sat with the other new boys in solemn silence while a red-haired master reached into an immensely deep pocket and brought out lovingly a leather strap.

— Say hello, he said, to teacher's pet.

The thing lolled in his hand like a parched and blackened tongue. Each boy could hear his neighbour swallow. Suddenly all of life up to this seemed a heedless, half-drunk frolic. Outside the window there was a stricken tree, then a field, then firs, then the hurt blue of a bare September sky.

I sat at the front of the class, appalled and fascinated. Each master, even the mildest, seemed mad in his own way. All were convinced that plots were being hatched behind their backs. They would whirl round on a heel from the blackboard, chalk suspended, and fix one boy or another wordlessly with a stare of smouldering suspicion. Without warning they would fly into terrible rages, diving among the desks after a miscreant and raining down blows on him as on some blunt obstruction against which they had barked their shins. Afterwards they were all shamefaced bluster, while the rest of the class averted its gaze from the victim slumped at his desk, hiccuping softly and knuckling his eyes.

At first I tried placating these distraught, violent men, offering up to them my skill at sums, tentatively, like a little gift. They were strangely unimpressed, indignant even, as if they thought it was all a trick, a form of conjuring, gaudy and shallow. I puzzled them, I suppose. I could do all sorts of mental calculations, yet the simplest things baffled me. Dates I found especially slippery. I was never sure what age I was, not knowing exactly what to subtract from what, since my first birthday had fallen not in the year in which I was born, but in the following year, and since, halfway through the present year, when another birthday arrived, I would find myself suddenly a year older, with half a year still to run on the calendar. It all had too much of actuality sticking to it. I felt at ease only with pure numbers, if a sum had solid things in it I balked, like a hamfisted juggler, bobbing and ducking frantically as half-crowns and cabbages, dominoes and sixpences, whizzed out of control around my head. And then there were those exemplars, those faceless men, measuring out the miles from A to B and from B to C, each at his own unwavering pace, I saw them in my mind, solitary, driven, labouring along white roads, in vast, white light. These things, these whizzing objects and tireless striding figures, plucked thus out of humble obscurity, had about them an air of startlement and gathering alarm with which I sympathized. They had never expected to be so intensely noticed.

— Well, Swan, how many apples does that make, eh?

A ripe red shape, with a sunburst trembling on its polished cheek, swelled and swelled in my brain, forcing out everything else.

— You are a dolt, my man. What are you?

— A dolt, sir.

— Precisely! Now put our your hand.

I would not cry, no matter how hard they hit me. I would sit with teeth clenched, my humming palms pressed between my knees and the blood slowly draining out of my face, and sometimes then, gratifyingly, it would seem the master, not I, who had suffered the worse humiliation.

Yet I did well, despite everything. I came top of the class. Every year I won the school prize for mental arithmetic. At home I kept such things dark. On the last day of every summer term, I would stop at the sluice gate behind the malt store on my way home, and tear up my report card and scatter the pieces on the surge.

Then without warning I was summoned one day to the headmaster's office. My mother was there, in hat and Sunday coat, with her bag on her knees and her hands on her bag, motionless, looking at the carpet. The room was cramped and dim. On a pedestal on the wall a statue of a consumptive Virgin stood with heart transpierced, her little hands held out in a lugubrious gesture. It was a spring day outside, windy and bright. Father Barker's big feet stuck out from under his desk, shod in lace-up black boots with thickly mended soles, and uppers worn to the texture of black crape paper. He was a large unhappy man with a moon face, blue-jowled and ponderous of gait. His nickname was Hound. This is a bit-part. He rose, delving under the skirts of his soutane, and brought out a grubby packet of cigarettes. He smoked with a kind of violence, grimly, as if performing an irksome but unavoidable duty. He had been saying, he said, what a fine scholar I was. He came from behind the desk and paced to and fro, his soutane swinging. At each turn he swerved heavily, like a horseman hauling an awkward mount. Grey worms of ash tumbled down the shiny black slope of his belly. He had high hopes, he said. He stopped, and loomed at my mother earnestly.

— High hopes, ma'am!

She lifted her gaze to me at last, reproachful, mute, a minor conspirator who has just found out the enormity of the plot. I looked away from her, to the window and the bright, blown day. Far trees heaved in silence, hugely labouring. I said nothing. Father Barker, lighting up again, was swallowed in a swirl of smoke and flying sparks.

Later, when I came home, a terrible silence reigned in the house. My mother stalked about the kitchen, still wearing her hat, buffeted by a storm of emotions, anger and pride, vague dread, a baffled resentment.

— Like a fool, I was, she cried. Like a fool, sitting there!

She had a horror of being singled out.

In the senior school our mathematics master was a man called Pender. He was English, and a layman. How he had come to St Stephen's no one seemed to know. Elderly, thin, with a narrow, wedge-shaped head and long, curved limbs, he moved with the slow stealth of some tree-climbing creature. His suits, of good broadcloth greased with age, had the loose, crumpled look of a skin about to be sloughed. His taste was for the byways and blind alleys of his subject, for paradoxes and puzzles and mathematical games. He introduced into his lessons the most outlandish things, curved geometries and strange algebras, and strange ways of numbering. I can still recite a litany of the queer names I first heard in his class: Minkowski and Euler, Peano and Heaviside, Infelt, Sperner, Tarski and Olbers.[1] He liked to bewilder his pupils, it was a form of tyranny. He would circle the room at a slow prance, his long arms intricately folded, surveying with a sardonic grin the rows of faces lifted up to him in attentive blankness. Common words when he spoke them — set, system, transformation, braid — took on an almost religious significance. He had a liturgical aspect himself, when he stood by the window, his profile lifted to the day's pale light, a halo of white hair aglow on his gleaming pate, and spoke in his thin, piping voice of the binomial theorem, or boolean algebra, or of the mysterious affinity between the numbers of a fibonacci sequence[2] and the spiral pattern of seeds on the face of a sunflower.

He was delighted with me, of course, but wary too, as if he suspected a trap. He tiptoed around me with nervous jocularity, swooping down on me suddenly as if to grab me, the wattles of his scrawny neck wobbling, and then quickly drawing back again, with a hissing laugh, darting a grey tongue-tip through a gap in his teeth where an eye-tooth was missing. By now I knew differential calculus, could solve the most delicate problems in trigonometry.

— Amazing, Mr Pender would sigh, chafing his papery hands. Quite amazing!

And he would laugh, his thin lips curling in a kind of snarl and the tip of his tongue darting out.

The class began to call me Pender's pet. But I did not welcome this cloying and somehow perilous connection. The beatings that I used to get were less embarrassing, less difficult to manage, than Mr Pender's furtive patronage. I tried retreating from him, made deliberate mistakes, pretended bafflement, but he saw through me, and smiled, with pursed mouth and cocked eyebrow, and pinched the back of my neck, and passed on blandly to other things.

Then one afternoon he appeared unannounced at our house. He sported a louche felt hat and carried a cane. Away from school he had the raffish, edgy air of an out-of-work actor.

— Mrs Swan? I was passing, and . . .

He smiled. She backed away from him, wiping her hands on her apron. Our square, she knew, was not a part of town Mr Pender would find himself in by chance. Sudden strangers worried her. She put him in the parlour and gave him a glass of sherry, bearing the thimble of tawny syrup from the sideboard with tremulous care.

— Ah, so kind.

She stood as in a trance, her hands clasped, not looking at him directly, but absorbing him in bits,

1. Hermann Minkowski (1864-1909), Russian mathematician. Leonhard Euler (1707-83), Swiss mathematician. Giuseppe Peano (1858-1932), Italian mathematician. Oliver Heaviside (1850-1925), British physicist. Leopold Infeld (1898-1968), Polish physicist. Emanuel Sperner (1905-80), German mathematician. Alfred Tarski (1902-83), Polish-American mathematician. Wilhelm Olbers (1758-1840), German astronomer and physician.

2. Named after the Italian mathematician, Leonardo Fibonacci (1170-1240).

his hat, his slender fingers, the limp bow-tie. He spoke quietly, with intensity, his eyes fixed on the table. She hardly listened, captivated by his delicate, attenuated presence. She had an urge to touch him. He sat, one narrow knee crossed on the other, fingering the stem of his glass. He had the faintly sinister self-possession of a priceless piece among fakes. Around him the familiar succumbed to a dispiriting magic. The flowered carpet, the wrought-iron firescreen, the plaster ducks ascending the wall, these things would never be the same again.

— An extraordinary phenomenon, Mrs Swan. Such a brilliant gift. A miracle, really. What can I say? One feels privileged.

An eager light glowed in his glaucous eye, and flecks of serum gathered at the corners of his mouth. She noticed the jumbled wreckage of his teeth. He stopped, and watched her, spreading the silence before her as a salesman would a sample of some wonderful costly stuff. She listened to him holding his breath. There was a wickerwork darn on the heel of his sock. She had a fleeting vision of what his rooms would be, the dust, the worn patch in the carpet, the tired light motionless in the corners. She roused herself.

— Yes, she said, smoothing her apron on her knee. Yes I see.

I sat on the sofa, looking at Mr Pender in silent amaze. His presence was an enormous and somehow daring violation. He smiled nervously when he glanced in my direction, and raised his voice and spoke rapidly, as if to hold something at bay. My mother looked at me as at an exotic, bright-plumed bird that had alighted suddenly in her parlour. First there was Father Barker and his high hopes, and now this. She felt a familiar, angry bafflement. The things he was saying, these plans, these propositions, she did not like them, she was frightened of them. They were incongruous here, like that expensive hat on the table, the cane he was twisting in his chalk-white hands. At last he rose. She showed him to the door.

— So glad, so glad to have met you, Mrs Swan.

She was suddenly tired of him and his precious manner, his smile, his gestures, the way he said her name, pressing it softly upon her like a blandishment. Outside the door he hesitated, eyeing the tender trees in the square. He should try once more, he knew, to impress this dim little woman, to wring a promise from her, but she looked so fearsome, with her arms folded and her mouth set, and he did not relish the prospect of a scene. But oh, did she realize, did she, what an extraordinary — what an amazing —? Anger and frustration reared up in him like a wave and broke, leaving a wash of sadness in their wake. How do I know these things? I just do. I am omniscient, sometimes. He smiled bleakly and turned away, lifting a finger from the knob of his cane in melancholy farewell.

When he was gone a hectic gaiety flourished briefly, as if the house like a frail vessel had brushed against disaster and survived. Then a thoughtful silence descended.

Uncle Ambrose called. He hesitated inside the door, sniffing at the strained atmosphere. He was a larger version of my father. His body was too big for the small head perched on it. He had close-set eyes and crinkly hair, and a raw, protuberant chin, deeply cleft and mercilessly shaved, like a tiny pair of smarting buttocks. He treated his ugliness with jealous attention, dressing it richly, pampering and petting it, as a mother with a defective child. Still his suits were always a shade too tight, his shoes a little too shiny. Silence came off him in wafts, like an intimation of pain. He seemed always on the point of blurting out some terrible, anguished confession. His reticence, his air of pained preoccupation, lent him a certain authority in our house. His opinion was respected. My mother told him of the teacher's visit, flaring her nostrils and almost shouting, as if she were recounting an insult. *Put him in my hands*, Mr Pender had urged her, smiling his tense, toothed smile. Uncle Ambrose nodded seriously.

— Is that so? he said with care.

She waited. Uncle Ambrose continued to avoid her eye. She turned angrily to the stove, taking down a frying pan from a nail on the wall. My father had risen quietly and was making for the door. *Bang* went the pan. He stopped in the doorway and looked back at her over his glasses. He was in shirt-sleeves and braces, with the weekly paper in one hand and the doorknob in the other. He sighed.

— What? he said dully. What is it?

— Nothing! she cried, without turning, and laughed grimly. Not a thing!

She slapped a string of sausages on the pan, and a whoosh of smoke and flying fat shot up. My father stood breathing. Their squabbles were like that, a glitter in air, over in a flash, like a knife-throwing act.

Jack Kay, dozing by the range, started awake with a grunt. He cast a covert glance about him, licking his lips. He despised old age, its hapless infirmities. He drew himself upright, muttering. He had not liked the sound of Mr Pender at all.

My father returned from the door and sat down heavily, cracking the newspaper like a whip. Uncle Ambrose cleared his throat and considered the carious rim of the sink.

— New people out at Ashburn, he said mildly to no one in particular. Queer crowd.

Uncle Ambrose knew the comings and goings of the town. He drove a hackney motor car, and sat behind the wheel outside the railway station all day waiting for the trains.

My mother would not be diverted. She swept the room with a withering glance and laughed again harshly.

— *Put him in my hands*, indeed! she said.

No one responded. She stood irresolute a moment, flushed and angry, then turned back abruptly to the seething pan. There was another uneasy silence. Uncle Ambrose drummed his fingers on the table, whistling soundlessly. Jack Kay gazed upwards out of a vacant, milky eye, his mouth ajar. My father, moving his lips, scanned the newspaper intently. They seemed ill at ease, trying to suppress something, as if a ghost had walked through their midst and they were pretending they had seen nothing. I looked about at them with interest. Why should they be alarmed? It was at me the spectre had pointed its pale, implacable hand.

DERMOT HEALY

(1947-)

from: BANISHED MISFORTUNE AND OTHER STORIES (1982)

[Healy writes in surprisingly different registers, even within the confines of a single story. His prose is sometimes lordly and ironic, at other times lyrical and precise. County Cavan provides the background and the imaginative landscape for much of his fiction. In this story, a family travels from the border county of Fermanagh in Northern Ireland to Galway. The journey through history and geography is a form of meditation on Ireland's violent present and broken past.]

BANISHED MISFORTUNE

The house that Saul lived in.

While the children slept there, outside it rained. The whole night long. Though it was warm and brown among the damp shiny chestnuts, the weather had opened under the shadows of the rambling trees. Everything was falling. The thump of chestnuts on the soft floor of the night. And the insects thrived down there in the caves of leaves. Eileen slept facing east, young child limbs learning to fly and the people of Belfast looking up in wonder. The duchess hopped along the stairs, past the dusty quiet of McFarland's door where the mother turned often in her sleep down an empty and alien past, and the cat sat up beside the small steamy window with the lead stripes to catch her breath, where the magpies had chewed the new putty. Listening to the water swirling over the stones and the loose gate banging in the lower meadow. And when little Tom coaxed her down onto the bed, she put her washing away and jumped like a little deer.

'Here, puss,' he said and she stretched out one long paw.

For whatever reason the house might fall, the sleeping McFarland would build again with a sense of adventure anywhere north of the lakes and in good time, son of Saul, master builder of Fermanagh country but by pneumonia put away while tended by his wife Olive, Glan woman and descendant of J. O'Reilly who danced once with flax in his trousers, and though nominally Christian died in foreign and pagan lands fighting an unjust war, but McFarland sensing the lie of the land grew away from a sense of guilt or desire for power and prayed that the haphazard world would not destroy his family so well grounded among the moralities of chance and nature, if one could remain loyal to the nature of a people and not the people themselves, for whatever reason the house might fall.

The door opened onto the fields.

All round, that silence and damp air of expectancy after the eerie rasp of the storm had blown over.

Judy, his wife, cooked over a single gas jet in the leafy half-light, for the electricity black-out was at its worst and it seemed to McFarland like one of those early mornings years ago when he had risen in the cold to feed the cattle and heard the groan of the house and Saul's asthmatic breathing overhead. Still the echo of the sessions that had gone on through the night when he was a child. The children put on two sets of jumpers and climbed into their boots under the stairs, and Eileen picked up a toy soldier knocked over by the foot of the father as he went round the back to examine the roof for missing slates. Soft Chinese music of the rain on glass and leaves, lightly touched cymbals, ducks crashing onto the waters, the primitive crane stretching her awkward wings in a lone high flight, the land below so cold and misty it looked as if a healing frost had settled.

Little Tom chased Eileen sideways through the mist to the end of the garden, among the penitent crumbling apple trees, in her new frock and washed hair and everywhere a silent promise that she might be well.

'The night it being dark in my favour,' the father sang fretfully to himself in the boot of the car, unconcerned about the helicopter that flew over the house and scattered the birds that a moment before had been strolling along the hedges. Humming a reel like a dream he was trying to remember, McFarland, out of an incapacity to deal with the extravagance of small details, involved his wife and children in discovering the pattern from last year for fitting in the case, instruments and bags. He scraped the fiddle bow thoughtfully under his chin and sang it backwards and forward across his ear as he went through the mathematics. Talking in a holiday voice to nuts and screws and old newspapers, while his wife reasoned with the children, losing her patience. Will Byrne, the sentinel of the hill, his brother murdered at his door, watched their activities with benign speculation as he lay against an old railing from which he propelled himself every few seconds and took a quick low whistle, escaping from the past for a few excruciating moments.

'You get in the back with your mother,' the father said and little Tom put the cat down reluctantly in the shed and dropped a chicken bone temptingly into her dish. She was sitting at a ladylike distance away, upset by the jamming of the doors and all those signs of departure. He hid another bigger bone behind the shed after whistling down the fields, watching a weasel drink water from the cup of a leaf among the chopped timber. The duchess suddenly attended to her wardrobe. The soft scuffle of leaves and harness. After they had all driven away, the dog, with pebbles hanging from his coat, came in mumbling because he had been forgotten and the cat flew up onto the rafters, while above her the rain slanted to the west.

'What'll we sing?' asked little Tom.

The father looked up to heaven, his musical children vain and happy by turns, his child wife looking steadfastly silently ahead as she always did when they journeyed together, always heading off into some fitful future, living off the excitement of leaving something intangible behind and the wheels on the road had a life of their own. Edging down the lane, the dark purple of the sloes, sour grapes, the blackberries tidily hung between the bronze leaves and yellow roots of the hedge. Lakes, a darker purple than the sloes away below the chestnut trees. A soldier's jeep was parked on the crossroads, guns cocked. 'You can learn to live with anyone,' Saul had said, 'it's imperial to me!' And McFarland, reared amongst a series of foreign and local escapades, took everywhere his copies of the Arctic and Antarctic voyages. 'Irish musicians are a crowd of drunken children,' Judy said to him once as they drank Guinness from a bedroom sill in a boarding-house. 'I suppose it wasn't what the Lord wanted,' he said eventually, away from her down to the Roscommon men strolling through the riotous, melancholy music. Still, tucked under his elbow as he sauntered through the dark deserted streets of Belfast where the men drank gin and the women drank whiskey, he always had his copy of Scott's final trip up the frozen Pole, a book he had read many many times and still felt the same harsh ecstasy the explorers must have experienced when, worn to the bone of humanity, they discovered that the Norwegians had been there before them. And the other explorers held down by the winter, frozen and breathless and singing songs under the snow.

The family drove through the clouds and Friday, the dog, chased round the farm for the scents that were fast fading.

Eileen lit the matches for her father's cigarettes, cupping her awkward hands like the men do in the yard to save the light from the wind. Like she was reading the future from the palms of her hands, stained with the juices of the early-morning leaves where so many faces were hidden. And all round strange wet farmhouses, the finely cropped trees of the north, cut like mushrooms or birds settling with wings tucked, fine cars in the driveways along the wide fields, the distinctive roadway signs, the extinct lorries. Behind the sheds like railway carriages and over the hills the grim Norse-like churches. Going over the bridges there was a great empty feeling beneath your heart as the car rose. Like a roof lifting off a house. Her mother's agitated face when their uncle threatened. If time could wait. Once Eileen's stomach turned sick, mesmerized by the sudden looseness of her limbs, her head swaying. McFarland walked her up and down a laneway off the main road with his tolerant musical strides, while overhead the trees joined branches in the mist that was blinding the islanders as they rowed ashore on the flooded Erne, adjusting to the repeated deaths beside the blue frosted lakes, at night the cool drinks, hands dextrous at cards. She hated these moments that she had no control over. But it was better to be sick and let her eyes film over with tears for a moment than arrive bleary-eyed and fatigued after dosing herself with the heavy languorous pills she took as a child that made her memory falter. Her hair was cut so short for her face that she showed pain too easily. And he was irked by Tom's cheerfulness behind her in the car, her instincts left in him.

'A big girl like you won't find the time passing,' his voice above her, afraid of any weakness that might handicap their security, humming and smoking in the mist with his hand on her shoulder, we'll be there in no time. 'We'll be there in no time,' he said.

And that's how little Tom, anxious to laugh, attracting laughter, succeeded in getting into the front seat beside his father to pull the window down and trail his hands near the low trees that flew by like the wind, too quick even for his eyes to catch, and wave at the Customs man as they crossed the last ramp and headed down the bad easy roads, the Leitrim-Cavan border where traditions had survived even the Famine itself, a roofless countryside without trees or soldiers or gunfire at night but the road through the frost-shattered mountains and stray rain-filled clouds, the bilberry bushes and cotton grass. And Sandy Byrne and Friday were leaping through hedges and streams on their way to the village after Old Byrne had cursed the skyline and chased them from his house with a broom. McFarland's eyes were fading, he grieved sometimes for them in the early morning when his vision was hazy like that shortness of breath, and now he was aware of Tom watching him squeeze his eyes, concentrate, slow down and take the centre of the road. After the humours of Ballyconnell they crossed the dry streams where the railway lines had been lifted and sold to the Congo by order of an ecumenical government, here several of his mother's people had flagged down a train and never been seen again, going away with a wisp of smoke and single words in the old Irish. Among the Chinese and gunpowder, among poets and money-grabbers his grandfather had been there for the driving of the last spike on the Great Pacific Railway[1] till he fell down a frozen thirty-foot falls, his dogs screaming in terror below him and all over the snowswept Canadian valley.

'Tisin' no wonder this is the wee county that Sean Maguire sprang from,' the father said, remembering, and thought of the boy in the gap and the lady's top dress and the day he had climbed here with Saul and had a nose-bleed on the mountain.

They left behind the pagan air of Glan, grey damp farms surrounded by cluttered rusty galvanized sheds, washing blowing in the garden, a pump on the road that nobody used, cottages with the thatch sunk in the middle. A huge aerial. The mother slept lazily, hearing Bach's Fantasy and Fugue on her husband's tape and she longed to lean out and draw someone close to her for a while, for someone, she said, tapped her on the shoulder naming various schoolchildren she had taught in Belfast, tall mousy-haired children who hardly ever talked or did in a rush and called to her house whispering angrily, and as her head bobbed against

1. The railway line from Montreal to Canada's Pacific coast was completed in 1885.

the rear seat she never saw her husband smile boyishly at her in the mirror. And Eileen copied her mother going to sleep, glancing through half-closed eyes at the blue-aproned women, sweeping, washing down their steps and the men crossing the streets with a multitude of different steps, their breath flying behind them. After the trip to Athlone the fiddle quietened, the bodhran[2] settled, trees were down everywhere after the big wind. At various times they came across groups of men standing round with saws under their arms and greatcoats hung up on the side of a ditch. The mist was lifting like the curtain in the Town Hall. They saw the first house in Connaught. They heard the musical priest. And while the sky cleared the family ate next a stone wall, sharing the air with an odd horse that had been looking at the same spot in a gorse haggard for days. Thousands of sewage pipes were piled on the footpaths, a gate opened into a new lake. 'The bit of food,' Saul had said, 'it's like the man begging, it will take you to the next door.' And the Shannon had turned the streams into wild dancing streams, sheughs[3] filled with wild water that stranded the cows who wandered about ankle-deep in the muck searching for grass. At last, when they entered the city, a Friesian calf with a white star on his forehead and white back legs stopped the car in the middle of the road and peered in with large blinking enquiring eyes. 'A white-headed calf is very hard on the beast,' he'd said, 'turn him if you can, I'm the queer quack myself.'

Peace is not necessary here, she heard that and . . . these people would rather endure. Who was it? Was it him? And again. I think it was St Patrick started this campaign. Was it drunk together on the boat to Belfast, collecting stolen timber from his brother on the docks, his fat belligerent brother who could kill, or was it on another day not in a boat but crossing the road in hot weather when traffic was heavy? My young saintly maidenly unmarried sister sleeping with a Quaker in that deserted bullet-peppered block of flats, oh my sister how sometimes I miss your crusade for there's nothing left for me but to become a victim who at the end of all resources admits nothing.

'Where are we now?' the mother said, wakening.

'Timbuktu,' the boy said.

'You so and so,' the mother said, ruffling his hair.

'I just combed that out a wee minute ago,' said Eileen and she flicked out her own short hair, the holiday at last for real, trying to create some dancing curls, and patted down her fresh autumn dress and knocked the mud of the fields from her shoes, spread out her toes to release the sweet stiffness of the journey from her body, the stifling impression of having gone nowhere till she smelt the roots of the sea, the girl in her gliding down as Ennis slowed the pipes.

Her father closing his eyes gratefully as he stopped the car.

Slates littered the streets of Galway.

Shopkeepers picked their way through the debris, gesticulating and looking up at the sky like sleepwalkers. The scene was obscenely familiar to the family from the north who felt for a moment slightly superior in their ability to deal with chaos, death, laughter at death. The family booked into a boarding house that looked out on a river that ran floundering under heavy stone bridges into the salmon sea, and the nervous landlady was filled with small talk about the storm, as a man held a ladder against the side of the building and his apprentice fought off cramp as he took a perilous path across the roof. The family listened with hidden humour to the stray southern accents, as men shouted encouragement to the climber from the street below. Little Tom mimicking. The boarding house began with a big room, advancing in smaller rooms till it ended in a tiny toilet perched over the river. They spoke self-consciously of the weather and Judy glared at the son of the house who watched Eileen with cold mischievous lust as the girl stood downstairs at the discordant piano fingering the keys in time to the waves of the sea, that same rhythm in her hands as was in her eyes when they had sat in the deserted concert halls in Belfast and she was husbandless, to listen to the orchestra practising the songs of Fauré and the tiny early piano pieces of Mozart such a long time ago.

And Friday had found the bone at the back of the shed and took it down to the edge of the stream, where he drank out of his questioning reflection in the damp mossy shadows where the hesitant rain and leaves still fell.

The slow earth.

'I'll be back early,' said McFarland when everything was settled and kisses had been handed round.

2. A hand drum, much favoured in Irish traditional music.
3. ditches.

'God, oh God man, foolish promises,' she answered him and he smilingly pursed his lips and shook his shoulders and with his fiddle case went down to a pub where the barman was a retired monk and sung songs of Napoleon and Aquinas, tapping and patting his companions down.

When first in Portaferry they crossed hands Eileen was a small delighted baby, who had to travel each day by car with her mother to school and the child never cried but lay listless for hours in the nursery, with its high windows that were not for looking through. And when he and Judy married, the child tottered quietly into the small church in autumn and laughed away brown-eyed at her mother looking so serious. For those first few weeks Judy tired easily of the endless sessions and retired early, leaving him alone among a bunch of new emptied musicianors [*sic*]. And as the constant assault of songs and music wore away with his first advances, and they learned each other's ways and the way of the child, she was no longer like a false note in a slow air returning and returning. She showed none of his cunning reticence, was eager to slip into a thousand excitable abstractions. Yet how many towns had they got so drunk in the world might end, playing squash in the early morning handball alleys to soothe a hangover, her fine excited accent a mixture of cynicism and distance. Because the city restrained people, or so he believed, it would have been customary for her sophistication to endure some rural cynicism but in this instance it was his nature gave way, slipping away into a thousand nearly familiar impressions. The complexity attracted him, the adventure of a perfume alien to his sheets, the lane to the door.

Cupping his man-root in her hand, old and awkward gamblings, and she saying slow and he for all his mock heroics learning for the first time the body's music, lightly touched cymbals that rocked them both away.

Red berries next the house, and the sycamore releasing a thousand revolving wings.

Judy brought the children for a long walk on the pier till evening caught them in an early long blue light like the sheen from a silk curtain and they strolled and ran back restlessly to the house. Not that Salthill was beautiful but ugly and plain and yet it was a necessary outing for them all although she was uncertain that any of them might feel release, know the difference in such a short time for they had burrowed down so deep in anxiety that happiness was nearly hysterical. Little Tom's cheeks were warm and Eileen's hair had blown and blown in the wind and they were tired as kings now one day had ended. Judy had grown used to being on her own. In Belfast they had worked apart, she driving out of the city each morning to Lisburn to teach and he heading off in a blue van to some new disaster area. And after the sudden move to the old house and the death of the old man they were suddenly thrown into each other's company most of the day, like young lovers, finding themselves grown strange to each other as if their previous work had sustained some missing link. But one could not but feel relieved yet cowardly after being released from the rows of terraced houses. Back in their room with the wasting wallpaper and plastic flowers, the landlady's family downstairs watching the Saturday film on television, Tom turned bad-tempered and started to argue, pulling Eileen away from the ukelele she was playing. The invisible stars that blind each other. The boy started to hammer the bed with his fists and the girl squeezed her hands against her face screaming, while below the television was lowered.

'Stop. Stop,' she screamed.

'Ya wanna see a wee bitch,' he shouted.

'Leave me alone.'

'Stop. Both of ye,' yelled Judy.

I can hardly survive any more, thought Judy. Oh nature, nature who left out my instinct for self-survival and gave me this grudging betrayal of selfishness instead. When she finally quietened them down, they sulked but with the confidence of children who know for what they are crying. 'Tomorrow is Sunday,' she said, 'and in the morning we'll all travel out to Spiddal and you'll play your whistle, Tom, for Furaisti and Pete with the bent nose will be there.' Tom was the easiest to bring back, to forgive in a slow mechanical way the world that threatened to overwhelm him. 'It will be more wonderful than any Fleadh.[4] Yes. And you have no more school for a fortnight, maybe more.' 'Will the flute player be there from England,' Tom proffered slowly, 'the one who wears the bicycle clips?' 'Yes. Aye. All your father's friends.'

'Sleep now ye pair.'

And Friday was sitting quietly in the shed beside the duchess who occasionally looked up at him and

4. An Irish musical festival.

the night was there too except there was no sound, only the sharp cries of the nightbirds from down the fields.

'That's a lovely daughter you've got there,' the landlady said when Judy opened the door to see who was tiptoeing annoyingly across the landing. Then to silk she washed herself, her first warm bath for months under the watchful eye of the awful blue staring fish and afterwards she draped herself luxuriously before a small electric fire. The glow from her flesh pleased her as did the silence and the small breaths of the sleeping. When she had left Belfast she had sworn she would never live in a city again, not for a day, but Galway she never really accepted as a city, it was more like a big drifting market town. She and her husband were changing, she knew. In Belfast they were satisfied politically, in that their bodies, like anyone else's, could stop a bullet, but living so close to the south was a totally new beginning, a loveplay, something they had forgotten as she had forgotten that in the south what appeared trivial, negative to her was a natural way of life for a people unaffected by war. But her spirit had once enlarged, as her sister's now had. Still she worried about their farmhouse in Fermanagh constantly, even when she went to the village with the kids she always searched the now familiar trees for smoke, as if in a way she needed a ritual, a gradual dismemberment.

Eileen turned in her sleep.

The wind in the wires outside reminded Judy of home, like the sound of distant geese; she rubbed her body in front of the fire as the evening drew on.

'Politics is the last thing in the world I want to hear about,' said McFarland in a pub where he was the centre of attraction as he laid his fiddle down. 'The very last thing.'

'Give us a slow air,' someone interrupted in Salthill as they went from 'Toss the Feathers' to 'The Flowers of Spring'. And the bank manager danced to the tune.

'Everybody in the north wants to get on TV or into politics,' a fisherman just in off the trawlers joked in The Largeys where an Irish soldier was playing the pipes in the backroom.

'Galway never changes.'

'*Ni bhíonn ac súil amháin ag na nGael anois,*'[5] said Furaisti softly as they sat ruminating under Conaire[6] in the square and watched a peculiar crowd spreading out from the railway station after arriving on the last train from Dublin. McFarland was restless, spending money recklessly. Saul had said, 'If I died tonight wouldn't you heel up the clothes and the money, and say didn't he hold on to it tight.' And he had left nothing but the view from the hill. McFarland remembered his own youth as warmth under a slated roof from the heavy rain, a vague wish on the side of a lake, and now returning years later to the house built like a church with its arched porch and stained-glass windows taken by bicycle from Donegal, he was learning the names for sounds he was born into, a tern fleeing from the rushes, milk churns rattling over the evening echo of the lake, a pheasant remembering the balls in her tail running over the mossy earth and perching on a fence to allow her scent bubble over the dogs, a perch bent in the scale-wet hands of his son. Oh history is a great time-saver, a repellent against honest thought. There was no release, not like the falling release of a larch breaking at last under the swing of a steady axe, the shivers showering the earth.

'You know, Furaisti, you could hardly make ceiling laths from the trees in these parts,' he said.

'Have you put down any vegetables the year?' asked Furaisti.

'No. Next year for certain,' he answered.

The dog slept by the cat in the shed and once he awoke and chased some shots off into the dark and the duchess stirred and smiled when he returned and sank beside her in the straw.

The radiators had filled the room with heavy cumbersome heat when Eileen heard the bomb open the sky in her sleep. A god filling in his time that she darted from on the verge of frightened dreams. She sank beneath the bedclothes when she awoke, silent awhile till, as her panic grew more terrible, she called to her mother in the expressionless dark. Judy came in naked from the other room and wiped the blood from her bewildered daughter's face. In this strange house, even for a day, we have to start out all over again, relearning those familiar parts of ourselves that resist even the gentlest analysis and praying for a timely scepticism. As if a child once had walked into a wet

5. 'The Irish see through only one eye now.'

6. Pádraic Ó Conaire (1883-1928) wrote more than a dozen books in Irish. His statue stands in Eyre Square, Galway.

crumbling house and felt the tang of decay, emptiness, drab sky. The scar on her own white body ran like the shadow of a man's arm from beneath her child-fallen breasts to the small warmth of her loins. I'd look fine, she thought as she comforted the child, on the inside pages of *Playboy* with my arms thrown open in tensed surprise like the cormorants we saw shading the waves from the island today. She threw open the window and pulled a deep orange robe over herself to get a drink downstairs for Eileen. The house was quiet. The boy in jeans and shirt was washing dishes in the kitchen and as he looked at her casually under his dark eyelids, she thought I'll take his mop of hair and squeeze his face between my legs so that he might scarcely breathe.

'I want to go home,' said Eileen.

'Sleep now,' the mother said and brushed Eileen's hair with her fingertips.

Judy walked through the sparse crowds, perhaps less euphoric now as they came into winter, their stale stomachs excruciated after the happy outrage of the long summer drinking, the headlights of a car brushing against the virginia creeper that nestled against the old university walls. She had hoped they might have driven out tonight to watch the wind spend itself on the drawn-grey stones of Connemara. Oh the myths the northerners love, the places where the troops will lie down! The chagrin burning on men's faces who expect answers that will confirm their own existence. In a small hostelry, up the dishevelled stairs among loud demurring students who flaunted an adopted Gaelic and what little knowledge of alcoholism they had, she drank pints of Guinness in the early flamboyant style of a girl celebrating new values and wisdom, eager for a person to steal a promise from the ennui of the drinkers. She interrupted conversations readily, her accent tending to be either American or from a corner of Kerry, unaware or scared of the laughter.

'Do you know that Will Byrne is a real old fountain-head?' she said, mimicking McFarland's accent.

'Belfast is the spiritual centre of Europe,' she told a doctor.

'Fuck ye away from that house, ye bastards,' old Byrne was shouting out of his lighted window and the dogs were barking, the duchess breaking away with raised hair through the long wet grass from the circling flames.

Meanwhile Furaisti and McFarland were rolling a stolen barrel of beer into a nurse's flat. The older man was out of breath and they had broken some strings on the fiddle. Four Connemara men in hats and coats stood drinking in the corridor with them, talking indifferently and happily among the endless traffic of people. They had a thirst like a chimney with a good draw. It took a while for McFarland to see confirmed in him and among the others a sense of other realities than being Irish, drink should let the mind wander to the present even foregoing the recent if not altogether past. And leaving in the dead of night, his arm round a friend, Saul spoke again. 'Be like a fox boy, piss on your trail and scatter the drops to puzzle the scent.' So McFarland to the air of the flogging reel took various routes home. And in the hotel the sound of his footsteps still came up the stairs to him, going from door to door searching for his room. Her clothes were scattered in a line to the bed. 'I have never known a woman like her,' he said as he lifted the sheets to Judy's chin and tucked her in next Eileen. He sat on the bed looking at them. In a word, Bach. Lord it is enough when it please Thee [to] bring my life to a close, he placed the fiddle and bow on the chair. He read a few pages of Scott's travels, but his mind wandered to the time they alighted on Portaferry strand among the sunning ladies from the seagulls' clamour all night and all day, with a single seal dipping and spreading a long straight line on the ocean and how he thought that day his eyes might never focus again.

My trouble. In a word. Never lie on the left side, boy, you'll squeeze the heart out of yourself. Tom awoke and saw the match flare up in the dark and light up his father's face who had climbed awkwardly into bed beside him.

McFarland smoked in the darkness.

'Judy, Judy,' he whispered across.

'Are you awake, Judy?'

'I heard tonight a story when Furaisti played "Banish Misfortune". It happened back in the days when death wasn't an institution. Jimmy Cummins turned to me and said, "Do you hear that? Well, there was a piper from Gurteen, a fine piper in his day who drank nothing but French wine and oddly enough just played once in a fine house. He'd mind that night if he were alive today. For there the gentry's daughter came away with him, a lightsome girl and the parents naturally enough with acres of turnips and cabbages for setting disowned her.

There was no hue or cry and the Gurteen man took her on his short travels for money and baby clothes. For the girl was expecting a piper's baby and not long after she and the baby died in this town. The coffin was put up on a cart drawn by a dray horse and no one following from the cobbles of the Spanish Arch. And the piper began a lament, not too slow or too quick on account of his losses, and the men in the fever hospital sweating from their labours counted four thousand mourners as they crossed Loch Ataile for Forthill graveyard. That's banished misfortune for you," said Jimmy Cummins.'

'Do you hear me Judy?'

She heard him in a drunken vulgar way, accessible still for all his various frailties, but she was silent for in her heart of hearts she feared he was softening, losing his sense of justice, merely protesting that erratic comedy of life. Fear was so addictive, consuming all of a body's time and she wanted so much to share this vigil with him in Fermanagh but what could you give the young if they were barricaded from the present by our lyrical, stifling past? She said nothing, knowing she shared this empty ecstasy with a thousand others who had let their laziness go on too long.

'I left home too young, that's what bothers me,' he spoke again. 'There must be a thousand stories and songs about my own place that I hardly know. But when we return, woman, we'll try.'

In a foot of land there's a square mile of learning, Saul had said, and he had learned to build from a sense of duty to the beauty of the hilly Erne.

For in April of 1910, Saul had a bad back but nevertheless he had finished building a church in Donegal town and now with Bimbo Flynn the whistler he set about kissing the air and erecting his own house. And it was a house where the best sessions of music would be held, where you could drive a tractor through the back windows. They gathered the red limestone rocks from the hills and fine washed stones from the Erne, the broached flagstones from Sliabh Buadh. Are you after work? he asked the grimy gypsies. God, you might swear mister, they said, and the gypsies carried cartloads of rocks up the hillside and sat under the chestnut tree smoking and drinking while it rained. His wife Olive came from the old house each day with tea and sandwiches for the men taking their time at their work on the edge of the woods that fell away to the lake. He'll fire everything to get back to America, the neighbours said, knowing the long travelling of the McFarlands, but as summer came he straightened up like a post in the good weather and the roof edged across the sky.

'Let it pass by.'

'Judy.'

'Piss on them, boy, piss on them.'

'Where are we for today then?'

'Men of Ireland.'

'Do him no good to be a fife player now.'

'I'd kill a man for that.'

'Look, we'll hang the door tomorrow.'

'Have done with it.'

When the burning was a long time off they put in two rows of slates as a damp course and timbered each room from the yellow larch that crashed in a fine storm, Bimbo never tiring of the saw that sang in his hands, his feet muffled in the knee-high sawdust and the briars in the hair of the gypsy children. A bird nested in the bodhran young Will Byrne, a great lad, had left in his father's barn. Boys oh boys. And in July a stray Dalmatian came whistling up through the grass to them of a Friday, his spots like squashed blackberries, jumping round himself. They adopted him for the new house. The iron shone on the range and the whistler fenced off an orchard and set forty apple trees and Olive took great care putting down their first rose bush. And folks wondered about the ornamented porch that was built out front with the stained-glass windows, and there was talk of a church but when the last stones dried and you could hear the knock-knock of a thrush breaking a snail in his new garden Saul was a proud man. Always before daylight a man thinks of his destiny, as Saul did that last morning talking with the travellers in the half-light of the chestnut hill and he was glad to see that the cream-coloured mare of the gypsies was loath to leave the fine grass now that her time had come.

NEIL JORDAN
(1951-)

NIGHT IN TUNISIA AND OTHER STORIES (1976)

[In this title story of his first book, Neil Jordan casts the familiar, even hackneyed, themes of a boy's sexual growth and his coming of age (with its familial tensions) in a new light for Irish fiction. Music, both jazz and popular, is the central character's half-articulate correlative language, appropriate in its mere suggestiveness to the melancholy of the adulthood he is soon to enter. (Music might also be a structural matter for the writer himself, the brief scenes resembling riffs. But then the scenes could be regarded with equal validity as cinematic — a temptation, given Jordan's later reputation as a major film director.) The jazz that the boy perversely refuses to improvise suggests the risks adulthood requires us to take and also, perhaps, the unacknowledged escape from venality it is necessary for the boy to make good. Despite the Americanized atmosphere of the story, the equation between the end of a son's boyhood and a father's way of life can be found as close to home as in John McGahern's 'Korea'.]

NIGHT IN TUNISIA

That year they took the green house again. She was there again, older than him and a lot more venal. He saw her on the white chairs that faced the tennis-court and again in the burrows behind the tennis-court and again still down on the fifteenth hole where the golf-course met the mouth of the Boyne.[1] It was twilight each time he saw her and the peculiar light seemed to suspend her for an infinity, a suspended infinite silence, full of years somehow. She must have been seventeen now that he was fourteen. She was fatter, something of an exhausted woman about her and still something of the girl whom adults called mindless. It was as if a cigarette between her fingers had burnt towards the tip without her noticing. He heard people talking about her even on her first day there, he learnt that underneath her frayed blouse her wrists were marked. She was a girl about whom they would talk anyway since she lived with a father who drank, who was away for long stretches in England. Since she lived in a green corrugated-iron house. Not even a house, a chalet really, like the ones the townspeople built to house summer visitors. But she lived in it all the year round.

They took a green house too that summer, also made of corrugated iron. They took it for two months this time, since his father was playing what he said would be his last stint, since there was no more place for brassmen like him in the world of three-chord showbands. And this time the two small bedrooms were divided differently, his sister taking the small one, since she had to dress on her own now, himself and his father sharing the larger one where two years ago his sister and he had slept. Every night his father took the tenor sax and left for Mosney[2] to play with sixteen others for older couples who remembered what the big bands of the forties sounded like. And he was left alone with his sister who talked less and less as her breasts grew bigger. With the alto saxophone which his father said he could learn when he forgot his fascination for three-chord ditties. With the guitar which he played a lot, as if in spite against the alto saxophone. And with the broken-keyed piano which he played occasionally.

When it rained on the iron roof the house sang and he was reminded of a green tin drum he used to hand when he was younger. It was as if he was inside it.

He wandered round the first three days, his sister formal and correct beside him. There was one road made of tarmac, running through all the corrugated houses towards the tennis-court. It was covered always with drifts of sand, which billowed while they walked. They passed her once, on the same side, like an exotic and dishevelled bird, her long yellow cardigan coming down to her knees, covering her dress, if she wore any. He stopped as she passed and turned to face her. Her feet kept billowing up the sand, her eyes didn't see him, they were puffy and covered in black pencil. He felt hurt.

1. An important river in Leinster, site of ancient tumuli and scene of the historic battle in 1690 between James II and William of Orange.

2. A holiday camp south of the Boyne estuary.

He remembered an afternoon three years ago when they had lain on the golf links, the heat, the nakedness that didn't know itself, the grass on their three backs.

'Why don't you stop her?' he asked his sister.

'Because', she answered. 'Because, because'.

He became obsessed with twilights. Between the hour after tea when his father left and the hour long after dark when his father came home he would wait for them, observe them, he would taste them as he would a sacrament. The tincture of the light fading, the blue that seemed to be sucked into a thin line beyond the sea into what the maths books called infinity, the darkness falling like a stone. He would look at the long shadows of the burrows on the strand and the long shadows of the posts that held the sagging tennis-nets on the tarmac courts. He would watch his sister walking down the road under the eyes of boys that were a little older than him. And since he hung around at twilight and well into the dark he came to stand with them, on the greens behind the clubhouse, their cigarette-tips and their laughter punctuating the dark. He played all the hits on the honky-tonk piano in the clubhouse for them and this compensated for his missing years. He played and he watched, afraid to say too much, listening to their jokes and their talk about girls, becoming most venal when it centred on her.

He laughed with them, that special thin laugh that can be stopped as soon as it's begun.

There was a raft they would swim out to on the beach. His skin was light and his arms were thin and he had no Adam's apple to speak of, no hair creeping over his togs,[3] but he would undress all the same with them and swim out. They would spend a day on it while the sun browned their backs and coaxed beads of resin from the planks. When they shifted too much splinters of wood shot through their flesh. So mostly they lay inert, on their stomachs, their occasional erections hidden beneath them, watching on the strand the parade of life.

It galled his father what he played.

'What galls me', he would say, 'is that you could be so good'.

But he felt vengeful and played them incessantly and even sang the tawdry lyrics. Some day soon, he sang, I'm going to tell the Moon about the crying game. And maybe he'll explain, he sang.

'Why don't you speak to her?' he asked his sister when they passed her again. It was seven o'clock and it was getting dark.

'Because' she said. 'Because I don't'.

But he turned. He saw her down the road, her yellow cardigan making a scallop round her fattening buttocks.

'Rita', he called. 'Rita'.

She turned. She looked at him blankly for a moment and then she smiled, her large pouting lips curving the invitation she gave to any boy that shouted at her.

He sat at the broken-keyed piano. The light was going down over the golf-links and his sister's paperback novel was turned over on the wooden table. He heard her in her room, her shoes knocking off the thin wooden partition. He heard the rustling of cotton and nylon and when the rustles stopped for a moment he got up quickly from the piano and opened the door. She gave a gasp and pulled the dress from the pile at her feet to cover herself. He asked her again did she remember and she said she didn't and her face blushed with such shame that he felt sorry and closed the door again.

The sea had the movement of cloth but the texture of glass. It flowed and undulated, but shone hard and bright. He thought of cloth and glass and how to mix them. A cloth made of glass fibre or a million woven mirrors. He saw that the light of twilight was repeated or reversed at early morning.

He decided to forget about his sister and join them, the brashness they were learning, coming over the transistors, the music that cemented it. And the odd melancholy of the adulthood they were about to straddle, to ride like a Honda down a road with one white line, pointless and inevitable.

His father on his nights off took out his Selmer,[4] old loved talisman that was even more shining than on the day he bought it. He would sit and accompany while his father stood and played — 'That Certain

3. Clothes; here swimming trunks.

4. A brand name of brass musical instruments, here a saxophone.

Feeling', 'All The Things You Are', the names that carried their age with them, the embellishments and the filled-in notes that must have been something one day but that he had played too often, that he was too old now to get out of. And to please his father he would close his eyes and play, not knowing how or what he played and his father would stop and let him play on, listening. And he would occasionally look and catch that look in his listening eyes, wry, sad and loving, his pleasure at how his son played only marred by the knowledge of how little it meant to him. And he would catch the look in his father's eyes and get annoyed and deliberately hit a bum note to spoil it. And the sadness in the eyes would outshine the wryness then and he would be sorry, but never sorry enough.

He soon learnt that they were as mistrustful of each other as he was of them and so he relaxed somewhat. He learnt to turn his silence into a pose. They listened to his playing and asked about his sister. They lay on the raft, watched women on the strand, their eyes stared so hard that the many shapes on the beach became one, indivisible. It made the sand-dunes and even the empty clubhouse redundant. Lying face down on the warm planks, the sun burning their backs with an aching languor. The blaring transistor, carried over in its plastic bag. Her on the beach, indivisible, her yellow cardigan glaring even on the hottest days. He noticed she had got fatter since he came. Under them on the warm planks the violent motions of their pricks. She who lived in the chalet all the year round.

The one bedroom and the two beds, his father's by the door, his by the window. The rippled metal walls. The moon like water on his hands, the bed beside him empty. Then the front door opening, the sound of the saxophone case laid down. His eyes closed, his father stripping in the darkness, climbing in, long underwear and vest. The body he'd known lifelong, old and somewhat loved, but not like his Selmer, shining. They get better with age, he said about instruments. His breath scraping the air now, scraping over the wash of the sea, sleeping.

The tall thin boy put his mouth to the mouth of the french letter and blew. It expanded, huge and bulbous, with a tiny bubble at the tip.

'It's getting worked up', he said.

He had dark curling hair and dark shaven cheeks and a mass of tiny pimples where he shaved. The pimples spread from his ears downwards, as if scattered from a pepper-canister. His eyes were dark too, and always a little closed.

'We'll let it float to England', he said, 'so it can find a fanny big enough for it'.

They watched it bobbing on the waves, brought back and forwards with the wash. Then a gust of wind lifted it and carried it off, falling to skim the surface and rising again, the bubble towards the sky.

He had walked up from the beach and the french letter bound for England. He had seen her yellow cardigan on the tennis-court from a long way off, above the strand. He was watching her play now, sitting on the white wrought-iron seat, his hands between his legs.

She was standing on the one spot, dead-centre of the court, hardly looking at all at her opponent. She was hitting every ball cleanly and lazily and the sound that came from her racquet each time was that taut twang that he knew only came from a good shot. He felt that even a complete stranger would have known, from her boredom, her ease, that she lived in a holiday town with a tennis-court all the year round. The only sign of effort was the beads of sweat round her lips and the tousled blonde curls round her forehead. And every now and then when the man she was playing against managed to send a shot towards the sidelines, she didn't bother to follow it at all. She let the white ball bounce impotent towards the wire mesh.

He watched the small fat man he didn't recognise lose three balls for every ball won. He relished the spectacle of a fat man in whites being beaten by a bored teenage girl in sagging high-heels. Then he saw her throw her eyes upward, throw her racquet down and walk from the court. The white ball rolled towards the wire mesh.

She sat beside him. She didn't look at him but she spoke as if she had known him those three years. 'You play him. I'm sick of it'.

He walked across the court and his body seemed to glow with the heat generated by the slight touch of hers. He picked up the racquet and the ball, placed his foot behind the white line and threw the ball up, his eye on it, white, skewered against the blue sky. Then it came down and he heard the resonant twang as his racquet hit it and it went spinning into the opposite court but there was no-one there to take it. He looked up and saw the fat man and her walking towards a small white car. The fat man gestured her in and she looked behind at him once before she entered.

As as the car sped off towards Mornington[5] he swore she waved.

The car was gone down the Mornington road. He could hear the pop-pop of the tennis-balls hitting the courts and the twang of them hitting the racquets as he walked, growing fainter. He walked along the road, past the tarmac courts and past the grass courts and past the first few holes of the golf-course which angled in a T round the tennis courts. He walked past several squares of garden until he came to his. It wasn't really a garden, a square of sand and scutch.[6] He walked through the gate and up the path where the sand had been trodden hard to the green corrugated door. He turned the handle in the door, always left open. He saw the small square room, the sand fanning across the line from the doorstep, the piano with the sheet-music perched on the keys. He thought of the midday sun outside, the car with her in the passenger seat moving through it, the shoulders of the figure in the driver's seat. The shoulders hunched and fat, expressing something venal. He thought of the court, the white tennis ball looping between her body and his. Her body relaxed, vacant and easeful, moving the racquet so the ball flew where she wished. His body worried, worrying the whole court. He felt there was something wrong, the obedient ball, the running man. What had she lost to gain that ease, he wondered. He thought of all the jokes he had heard and of the act behind the jokes that none of those who told the jokes experienced. The innuendos and the charged words like the notes his father played, like the melodies his father willed him to play. The rich full twang as the ball met her racquet at the centre.

He saw the alto saxophone on top of the piano. He took it down, placed it on the table and opened the case. He looked at the keys, remembering the first lessons his father had taught him when it was new-bought, months ago. The keys unpressed, mother-of-pearl on gold, spotted with dust. He took out the ligature and fixed the reed in the mouthpiece. He put it between his lips, settled his fingers and blew. The note came out harsh and childish, as if he'd never learnt. He heard a shifting movement in the inside room and knew that he'd woken his father.

He put the instrument back quickly and made for the tiny bathroom. He closed the door behind him quietly, imagining his father's grey vest rising from the bed to the light of the afternoon sun. He looked into the mirror that closed on the cabinet where the medicine things were kept. He saw his face in the mirror looking at him, frightened, quick glance. Then he saw his face taking courage and looking at him full-on, the brown eyes and the thin fragile jawline. And he began to look at his eyes as directly as they looked at him.

'You were playing', his father said, in the living-room, in shirtsleeves, in uncombed afternoon hair, 'the alto —'

'No', he said, going for the front door, 'you were dreaming —'.

And on the raft the fat asthmatic boy, obsessed more than any with the theatre on the strand, talking about 'it' in his lisping, mournful voice, smoking cigarettes that made his breath wheeze more. He had made classifications, rigid as calculus, meticulous as algebra. There were girls, he said, and women, and in between them what he termed lady, the lines of demarcation finely and inexorably drawn. Lady was thin and sat on towels, with high-heels and suntan-lotions, without kids. Woman was fat, with rugs and breasts that hung or bulged, with children. Then there were girls, his age, thin fat and middling, nyloned, short-stockinged —

He lay on his stomach on the warm wood and listened to the fat boy talking and saw her walking down the strand. The straggling, uncaring walk that, he decided, was none of these or all of these at once. She was wearing flat shoes that went down at the heels with no stockings and the familiar cardigan that hid what could have classified her. She walked to a spot up the beach from the raft and unrolled the bundled towel from under her arm. Then she kicked off her shoes and pulled off her cardigan and wriggled out of the skirt her cardigan

5. A town at the mouth of the Boyne.
6. Coarse patchy grass.

had hidden. She lay back on the towel in the yellow bathing suit that was too young for her, through which her body seemed to press like a butterfly already moulting in its chrysalis. She took a bottle then and shook it into her palm and began rubbing the liquid over her slack exposed body.

He listened to the fat boy talking about her — he was local too — about her father who on his stretches home came back drunk and bounced rocks off the tin roof, shouting 'Hewer'.

'What does that mean', he asked.

'Just that', said the asthmatic boy. 'Rhymes with sure'.

He looked at her again from the raft, her slack stomach bent forward, her head on her knees. He saw her head lift and turn lazily towards the raft and he stood up then, stretching his body upwards, under what he imagined was her gaze. He dived, his body imagining itself suspended in air before it hit the water. Underwater he held his breath, swam through the flux of tiny bubbles, like crotchets before his open eyes.

'What did you say she was', he asked the fat boy, swimming back to the raft.

'Hewer', said the fat boy, more loudly.

He looked towards the strand and saw her on her back, her slightly plump thighs towards the sky, her hands shielding her eyes. He swam to the side of the raft then and gripped the wood with one hand and the fat boy's ankle with the other and pulled. The fat boy came crashing into the water and went down and when his head came up, gasping for asthmatic breath, he forced it down once more, though he didn't know what whore meant.

His father was cleaning the alto when he came back.

'What does hewer mean?', he asked his father.

His father stopped screwing in the ligature and looked at him, his old sideman's[7] eyes surprised, and somewhat moral.

'A woman', he said, 'who sells her body for monetary gain'.

He stopped for a moment. He didn't understand.

'That's tautology', he said.

'What's that?' his father asked.

'It repeats', he said, and went into the toilet.

He heard the radio crackle over the sound of falling water and heard a rapid-fire succession of notes that seemed to spring from the falling water, that amazed him, so much faster than his father ever played, but slow behind it all, melancholy, like a river. He came out of the toilet and stood listening with his father. Who is that, he asked his father. Then he heard the continuity announcer say the name Charlie Parker[8] and saw his father staring at some point between the wooden table and the wooden holiday-home floor.

He played later on the piano in the clubhouse with the dud notes, all the songs, the trivial mythologies whose significance he had never questioned. It was as if he was fingering through his years and as he played he began to forget the melodies of all those goodbyes and heartaches, letting his fingers take him where they wanted to, trying to imitate that sound like a river he had just heard. It had got dark without him noticing and when finally he could just see the keys as question-marks in the dark, he stopped. He heard a noise behind him, the noise of somebody who has been listening, but who doesn't want you to know they are there. He turned and saw her looking at him, black in the square of light coming through the door. Her eyes were on his hands that were still pressing the keys and there was a harmonic hum tiny somewhere in the air. Her eyes rose to his face, unseeing and brittle to meet his hot, tense stare. He still remembered the rough feel of the tartan blanket over them, three of them, the grass under them. But her eyes didn't, so he looked everywhere but on them, on her small pinched chin, ridiculous under her large face, on the yellow linen dress that was ragged round her throat, on her legs, almost black from so much sun. The tiny hairs on them glistened with the light behind her. He looked up then and her eyes were still on his, keeping his fingers on the keys, keeping the chord from fading.

He was out on the burrows once more, he didn't know how, and he met the thin boy. The thin boy sat down with him where they couldn't be seen and took a condom from his pocket and masturbated among the bushes. He saw how the liquid was caught by the anti-septic web, how the sand clung

7. A sideman is a member of a jazz group or a dance band other than the leader.

8. Charlie Parker (1920-55), the great American jazz alto saxophonist.

to it when the thin boy threw it, like it does to spittle.

He left the thin boy and walked down the beach, empty now of its glistening bodies. He looked up at the sky, from which the light was fading, like a thin silver wire. He came to where the beach faded into the mouth of a river. There was a statue there, a Virgin with thin fingers towards the sea, her feet layered with barnacles. There were fishermen looping a net round the mouth. He could see the dim line of the net they pulled and the occasional flashes of white salmon. And as the boat pulled the net towards the shore he saw how the water grew violent with flashes, how the loose shoal of silver-and-white turned into a panting, open-gilled pile. He saw the net close then, the fishermen lifting it, the water falling from it, the salmon laid bare, glutinous, clinging, wet, a little like boiled rice.

He imagined the glistening bodies that littered the beach pulled into a net like that. He imagined her among them, slapping for space, panting for air, he heard transistors blare Da Doo Run Run, he saw suntan-lotion bottles crack and splinter as the Fisher up above pulled harder. He imagined his face like a lifeguard's, dark sidelocks round his muscular jaw, a megaphone swinging from his neck, that crackled.

He saw the thin band of light had gone, just a glow off the sea now. He felt frightened, but forced himself not to run. He walked in quick rigid steps past the barnacled Virgin then and down the strand.

'Ten bob for a touch with the clothes on. A pound without'.

They were playing pontoon on the raft. He was watching the beach, the bodies thicker than salmon. When he heard the phrase he got up and kicked the dirt-cards into the water. He saw the Queen of Hearts face upwards in the foam. As they made for him he dived and swam out a few strokes.

'Cunts', he yelled from the water. 'Cunts'.

On the beach the wind blew fine dry sand along the surface, drawing it in currents, a tide of sand.

His sister laid the cups out on the table and his father ate with long pauses between mouthfuls. His father's hand paused, the bread quivering in the air, as if he were about to say something. He looked at his sister's breasts across a bowl of apples, half-grown fruits. The apples came from monks who kept an orchard. Across the fields, behind the house. He imagined a monk's hand reaching for the unplucked fruit, white against the swinging brown habit. For monks never sunbathed.

When he had finished he got up from the table and idly pressed a few notes on the piano.

'Why do you play that', his father asked. He was still at the table, between mouthfuls.

'I don't know', he said.

'What galls me', said his father, 'is that you could be good'.

He played a bit more of the idiotic tune that he didn't know why he played.

'If you'd let me teach you', his father said, 'you'd be glad later on'.

'Then why not wait till later on and teach me then'.

'Because you're young, you're at the age. You'll never learn as well as now, if you let me teach you. You'll never feel things like you do now'.

He began to play again in defiance and then stopped.

'I'll pay you', his father said.

His father woke him coming in around four. He heard his wheezing breath and his shuffling feet. He watched the grey, metal-coloured light filling the room that last night had emptied it. He thought of his father's promise to pay him. He thought of the women who sold their bodies for monetary gain. He imagined all of them on the dawn golf-course, waking in their dew-sodden clothes. He imagined fairways full of them, their monetary bodies covered with fine drops of water. Their dawn chatter like birdsong. Where was that golf-course, he wondered. He crept out of bed and into his clothes and out of the door, very quietly. He crossed the road and clambered over the wire fence that separated the road from the golf-course. He walked through several fairways, across several greens, past several fluttering pennants with the conceit in his mind all the time of her on one green, asleep and sodden, several pound notes in her closed fist. At the fourteenth green he stopped and saw that the dull metal colour had faded into morning, true morning. He began to walk back, his feet sodden from the dew.

RONAN SHEEHAN

(1953-)

PARADISE (1991)

[This is the first publication of this story. One of the reasons for its inclusion in this anthology is its reference to Sir William Petty and the colonial past of Ireland. Petty (1623-87) came to Ireland as physician general to the army. His Down Survey of 1654 is the first scientific mapping of Ireland. His *Political Anatomy of Ireland* (1691) is his most famous political work (see Volume I, pp. 864-66). The story of Petty and Anne Green is based on fact and is transfigured here into a brilliant metaphor of Anglo-Irish relationships.

The particularity of its detail exceeds any purely metaphorical reading; yet the force of the story is in part explained by the flexibility with which it takes upon itself the weight of a painful history. 'Paradise' is a story in which imagined heavens are ironically depicted in a narrative of muted restraint. Anne Greene's paradise is that of an amnesiac; Jeffrey Reade's that of an exile. Sir William Petty's paradise is a colonized country. Ironically, the science of exploitation permits these renderings of paradise. It has its equivalent in the methodical nature of Reade's story, despite its powerful subject-matter — the strange marriage of heaven and hell.]

Two portraits of William Petty survive. The later, by an artist named Closterman, was made five years before his death. He wears a flowing wig in the French fashion begun here by Charles Stuart,[1] a full-length gown, a taffeta ruff, velvet breeches, silk stockings, silver buckled high-heeled shoes. His jowls are thick, his eyes heavy-lidded, more so the left, where Mr Vernon had thrust the pike of his cane when he assaulted Mr Petty in Bond Street. His stomach and calves are swollen by the gout which hastened his demise. Sir Peter Lely drew the earlier, which I have twice viewed. This shows how Sir William, or plain Mr Petty as he then was, appeared to us as a young man, at the time he was appointed fellow of Brasenose College, Oxford. (His remarkable skills alone qualified him for this position, which he could not however have obtained without the influence of his friends Colonel Kelsey, the Governor of the town, and Captain John Graunt, both close adherents of the Protector, who was Chancellor of the University.) His hair hangs down to his jawbones on both sides of his face in the manner used by his patrons. His nose is long and straight. His lips are set firm. His eyes appear to squint as he stares at the painter, which is an accurate detail, for Mr Petty was purblind from the studies he had made in childhood.

When first I saw this portrait the subject held a pen in his left hand. The nib rested upon a page, as though he were about to write something there. His right hand gripped the skull of a man. This detail, the skull, had been removed when next I saw the portrait, leaving Mr Petty's palm outstretched with all the fingers raised, grasping nothing but air.

No painter, I think, ever made a likeness of Anne Greene. I need no portrait to bring her image to mind, to see her as she was aged nineteen years when her father placed her upon his cart and carried her from their home in Staple Barton in Oxfordshire to my father's house, Brocket Hall. I first caught sight of her one April morning, as she stood before the stained glass window in the great hallway, her arm stretched upwards to wipe a small ruby red pane with her cloth. The light was sharp for the sky had cleared after days of downpours and thick clouds. It cast, through that pane, a rosy tinge upon her cheek. She wore her hair tied up in a bun beneath her cap. Her bodice was plain brown fustian, her apron yellow calico.

In the instant moment, I liked her.

Since then, over the years, I have often asked myself the reason why. Why do colours, shapes, attitudes, sounds, scents attract us? Why do such insubstantial matters draw us to themselves?

So, having glimpsed her, I paced out thirty steps to the office at the end of the hall where my grandfather, Sir Thomas, conducted the business of the estate. I laid my hand upon the door. An instinct bade me turn around. She was in that posture still. Perhaps she was fascinated by some aspect of the design, for she seemed fixed there, stretching upwards, gazing at the glass.

I pushed the door open and walked in.

1. Charles II, restored to the monarchy in 1660, not long after the death of Oliver Cromwell ('the Protector').

Sir Thomas was at his desk, poring over an accounts book. He pointed to an empty chair opposite him.

'Now, Master Jeffrey!' he cried. 'What are we to do about this money that is owing to us? We supplied him six cows, six sheep, six pigs, six goats, six horses, six hens, six dogs. Do you remember the terms of the contract?'

'I do indeed, grandfather,' I replied. 'The price was fixed at ten per cent less the average market rate on condition that we received payment in full on the first day of March.'

'What prompted us to agree such terms?'

'Mr Petty urgently required the carcasses for his studies. The Bursar could not release the funds to him at the time.'

'Why should we be so generous to Mr Petty?'

'He's a friend.'

'Correct. Your father's — my son's — *friend!*'

Sir Thomas twisted in his chair, so that a beam of sunlight crossed his face. I thought he was about to smile, but he did not. The lines of his forehead arranged themselves into a frown. He tilted his hat backwards on his head and pulled at the ruff around his neck, loosening it. He was perspiring and the cause was not the temperature of the room. He looked at me with an expression he reserved for this office, which was not the kindly, indulgent eye of a grandfather for his grandson, but the stern look of a master towards an apprentice.

'Now Jeffrey,' he began, in a strange low voice, 'I will tell you something you did not learn at Oxford last term, nor will you learn it next term either. There is another reason why we were ready to facilitate Mr Petty. It is because of certain of his associates. I mean the men who put the king to death. It would be a foolhardy thing to risk giving offence to these men. If they had a mind they would find some pretext to crush us. Your father, when he befriended Mr Petty, was aware of these connections. They were not his motive. He simply liked Mr Petty. The matter is complicated. We must recover what is owing to us, without jeopardizing the friendship, without affording others the opportunity to look askance at us.'

He spoke at length, patiently unravelling his strategy. The amount owing to us was not inconsiderable. We could scarcely have afforded to relinquish the debt had we desired to do so. But even then relinquishment would have been an unwise course to adopt. Some persons would have regarded our kindness as weakness and set about exploiting it. That was just one factor to be considered. It was like playing tennis in a wheelbarrow.

I left the office to find Anne Greene upon her knees in the hallway, beside Margaret Peabody. Both were scrubbing. Her head turned slowly as my steps approached her. Her back was straight as a rod, her haunches lithe. Now I was looking straight into the most enchanting eyes I ever saw before or since. They were large, brown, with flecks of green and gold scattered through the iris.

My pace never once slackened as I walked to the passage which led to the yard. But my heart was reeling.

I chose the long French cloak from the rack behind the door, the cloak with gold tassels, then strode to the stables. The temperature was not cool enough to warrant a garment of this type. I confess I was greatly attached to the item, upon which I had spent many weeks' allowance and which was everywhere admired. It flapped and fluttered in the air behind me when Lucy, my mare, broke into a canter as we passed the orchard. Tom Phillips's son, Mark, spotted it from the Broad Meadow where he and Kit Walker were ploughing. Both watched me until I was out of sight, turned west for Elliott's wood and the Oxford turnpike.

The roof of Brasenose College library was visible from Pennyfeather's rooms.

'Do you wish me to issue these proceedings, Master Reade?' Pennyfeather enquired.

'Draft them,' I replied. 'Hold them in readiness. You see, Mr Petty is my father's friend. His luck is against him at present. At such a time friendship proves its mettle or mocks its name. To proceed against him now would be treacherous, for he would discover opposition where he had expected support. But we desire that these principles, if we invoke them, be reciprocated. Let us wait and see what provision he makes to limit the damage to ourselves.'

'There is a danger,' Pennyfeather observed, 'that if you stay your hand another creditor may proceed ahead of you and recover for himself all and anything of value there is to take.'

'We have decided to take that risk for the time being.'

Pennyfeather's nose was like a duck's beak. Every minute or so he lurched suddenly across his desk. Although I anticipated this, on each several occasion I feared that this was the fatal swoop, that he was about to peck me to death. The evidence (to borrow his words) was against this fear, but the instinct was for it.

'Very well,' he drawled, in a manner that conveyed he had misgivings about my instructions, 'the papers shall be ready to proceed against your *friend* at a moment's notice. Tell me, was this the first arrangement of its kind or the last of a series? This is essential information for me. . . .'

His shoulders hunched over the desk. He cocked his ear towards me and his pen scratched a summary of the information I spoke into a notebook. The words came out of my mouth in mechanical fashion, for my consciousness followed my eyes to the window. I imagined Anne Greene there, on tiptoe, reaching up to clean the highest areas, the better to admit the light, which now fell upon her face.

I breathed farewell to Pennyfeather. He waved without looking up.

I walked to St John's church and knelt in the pew which had been in the possession of my grandmother's family since the days Duns Scotus[2] taught at the university. I prayed for guidance. I prayed for reassurance that the course we had adopted was wise. God, restore our money! Preserve our friendship with Mr Petty! . . . Doubts, fears, reservations crowded into my mind. It was of course a young man's inexperience in the main, but Sir Thomas's plans and arguments seemed hollow, his wisdom shallow, his schemes doomed to failure. We would never recover the money! All our debtors would scorn us, our creditors would move against us en masse, our property would be seized by the sheriff, our friends would fail us. We would be despised, abandoned. I should be forced to quit my studies before taking my degree. I should have to strive to earn my living at some menial task. The loafers in the street would point at me saying 'There is Jeffrey Reade, whose father made a bargain with William Petty!'

In the library I found Anne Greene, duster in hand, poring over a volume I had left open upon the escritoire. She ought to have been ashamed to be found idling and poking her nose into business which was no concern of hers. But she was not. My will to reprimand her was quite undermined by the excitement I felt at the prospect of engaging her in conversation.

'Do you read?' I enquired, affecting a tone of mild reproof.

'Your book caught my eye,' she replied, unflinching. 'My father has the very one in Staple Barton. I have read it myself.'

'And what,' said I, quite taken aback, 'is your opinion about it?'

'This author is superior when he deals with the raising of livestock, the management of crops and fisheries. But he knows little of the forest and nothing of game in particular.'

'I agree with you upon the positive point,' I said, trying to keep a straight face 'but although I am aware of them I have never read the other authors who treat of the forest, so I cannot comment upon that matter.'

'I recommend Mr Haines to you,' said Anne Greene. 'He is highly thought of.'

'I shall purchase his book when I visit Oxford next week,' I promised, now quite dumbfounded, despite myself.

So, I reflected as I sat down, this girl who dusts my books knows more of the matter they contain than I do myself. I adjusted my chair the better to take a peek at her. A bookcase concealed her. Only a pillar of dust particles, climbing upwards along a sunbeam, revealed her whereabouts.

In twenty minutes or so she passed before me on her way to the door. As I looked up to drink in the sight of her with my eyes I felt a great tumult of desire within my bowels and my soul, an emotion, a charge, a surge of feeling which has never, no not even to this day, completely ebbed. I have often dwelt upon it, for a moment, for minutes on end, without ever managing to grasp it. It was connected to the image of her before the window, which I know now I had received as an image of perfection. That image, I later decided, was redolent of purpose and movement, albeit movement suspended. And in my desire were elements of my need to *know*, my need for *purpose*. But why should that desire have become a *hunger* for her presence, her companionship, her flesh? Why could I not have been satisfied by her speech, or by the sight of her, or by learning her store of knowledge? Why did I not settle for that, since logic declared that much

2. A thirteenth-century Franciscan priest and scholastic theologian, born in Duns (Scotland), died in Cologne (Germany).

sufficient? Logic, I suppose, never had the ear of desire. A word, a glance, a movement, a breath, an image, a moment of pleasure. These may be the scents of Paradise, which call us, and will us to transform our lives.

Browsing in Mr Horton's bookshop, I found the volume by Haines to which Anne Greene had referred. Upon the vexed question of how best to turn woodlands to profit, Haines had much to offer. On matters relating to game he wrote with great authority. I perched upon a stool and was becoming quite absorbed when all of a sudden two hands gripped my arms from behind and hoisted me into the air. I twisted about to discover the face of William Petty not six inches from mine.

'My dear fellow!' he cried, or rather croaked, for his voice was hoarse, 'I have been meaning to speak to you for weeks. But I have been confined to bed. The Bursar, it seems, has defrauded us! We Fellows are conducting an investigation but we have recovered not so much as one penny!' Here he thrust a purse into my hands. 'Half of what you are owed! Balance at the end of the month if I have to starve myself to death for you. Sincerest apologies to your father and your dear grandfather!'

Bliss filled my heart, the bliss that accompanies pure and total relief. This surely was friendship! He was determined to answer, from his own slender resources, a debt which was properly the responsibility of his college. His hollow cheeks, pale lips and agitated gaze suggested that he might already have started in earnest upon the path of starvation to which he so lightly referred. I persuaded him to come with me to Fitzallen's coffee house where I fed him coffee, cake and currant bread. I marvelled at his resilience in the face of the difficulties which he outlined to me and was secretly ashamed of the fears I had entertained respecting our dealings. Perhaps something of my private thoughts and feelings were betrayed by my countenance, for soon William Petty laid a consoling hand on my wrist.

'Experience teaches,' he said, 'that the hand of Providence may be at work when the outlook seems blackest.'

He stabbed his finger through the air, over my shoulder.

'Do you see that sign? What is it?'

'It is only Fitzallen's Bill of Fare,' I replied, glancing where he pointed at the wall some fifteen feet or so behind me. 'It lists the prices of the coffee, bread, meat, biscuits and commodities he sells here.'

'I cannot read it,' he said. 'To me the sign is no more than a black blob with a scrawl upon it.'

'How very unfortunate,' I murmured, wondering what was to follow.

'No!' he cried. 'Not at all!'

As he started to tell me his story, some of which I knew already, he caught Fitzallen's eye, and ordered more coffee and biscuits, as if he had forgotten that he was the guest and I the host, not the other way around. What of it? I thought to myself. The scholar is hungry.

He had not been born to a great estate, like me, but to the house of a modest tradesman in Romsey, in Hampshire. Like Captain Graunt, his father had been a clothier. When the strife between King and parliament had upset the trade, William Petty determined to make his fortune at sea, encouraged by a little money he had made from a journey to France with some merchants. He plied the captains in the ports until he secured a ship. He was sent aloft on the very first venture, with orders to watch the coast for the spire of a certain church, for when that spire came into view the ship must alter course to avoid rocks. So up he went and kept, as he thought, a keen lookout for many hours. Some time after dawn he was startled to hear the captain roar the most frightful abuse at him, ordering him down. He obeyed and was immediately beaten. The church spire was visible to all but him. The ship was upon the rocks. No lives were lost but he, William Petty, fractured his leg in gaining shore. Captain and crew abandoned him in Caen, for they were thoroughly disgusted by him, since he might have cost them all their lives.

He increased his little store of money by teaching English to merchants in the town. As soon as he could hobble he resorted to a river which the Jesuits used for bathing and quickly won the fathers' affection with his witty Latin verses. They struck a bargain with him. He could attend their college in the town while his leg was healing, and so use the time to best advantage, in return for teaching English to their other pupils. It was a condition of the agreement that neither party would attempt to proselytize the other. Neither broke that condition. Petty profited from the arrangement which he prolonged far beyond the day his leg was pronounced mended. Besides, he was in no haste to return to a homeland ravaged by civil war. In Paris he was introduced to the circle of his countrymen then formed around the celebrated Mr Thomas Hobbes. He applied to the philosopher to study the laws of vision and later drew illustrations for Mr Hobbes's universally admired study of the matter, *Optics*, a copy of which he now produced and offered to my inspection.

'I am likely the only man here in Fitzallen's who cannot make out his bill of fare,' he observed, 'but who knows more than I of *why* I can do so, or *why* I cannot?'

'No-one,' I replied, marvelling at the cunningly crafted drawings he had made, of pupils and irises, lenses and corneae, men staring at trees in the moonlight, and whatnot.

He thanked me for my generosity, repeated his promise to pay the balance due, and left Fitzallen's. Who should come in, no more than a few seconds later, but Pennyfeather! I waved to him to come over. Then it struck me with a jolt that I, having invited him to join me, was now obliged to pay for his refreshment. All I had wanted was to inform him of this new and welcome development in our business. Before I could think of a way of extracting myself from the difficulty, Fitzallen served up a dish of bread, plover's eggs and beer, which he explained he had in readiness, for Pennyfeather always visited him at this hour and always ate the same food. Then he wrote out the sum due upon the reckoning Petty and I had already established. I am afraid I blanched when I calculated the total. If success continued in this vein, it might ultimately prove as costly as failure!

'You may jettison the proceedings,' I announced, gaily enough. 'Our friend has come good.'

'Wonderful news!' Pennyfeather exclaimed. 'For the full amount?'

'For half—balance at the end of the month if he has to starve himself to death to raise it!'

'A carcass is no use to you,' Pennyfeather observed. 'You're not an anatomist. Why not let the matter rest until the end of the month? Then we shall see if he keeps his word.'

'No. I am certain he will keep his word. I trust him and accordingly instruct you to treat the matter as closed.'

Pennyfeather's face betrayed no emotion. Even his beak — his nose rather — was motionless. Was he secretly relieved? Or frustrated?

'What are you owed, Pennyfeather?' I enquired.

'A trifle. A jot. A smithereen.'

'Attorneys' children too have mouths.'

'Do not concern yourself!' He raised a hand and allowed himself a smile, which upon his face was as rare as a parrot in Elliott's wood. 'They shall sleep more soundly in their beds knowing that matters have improved between Brocket Hall and Brasenose.'

'Very good,' said I, taking the hint. 'I'll settle with you next market day.'

'Excellent,' he said, helping himself to another egg, his fifth.

What glorious occasions they are in our lives, when the black clouds of our fears and anxieties are lifted, when harmony is restored to our hearts, vigour to our bodies! When confidence and optimism course through our spirit because our designs have been achieved, our plans realized! What, in the heady moments of success, will we not attempt? What dreams do we unleash upon our souls? The starriest horizon seems within reach. We have the aura of the Light around us and with it we set about the world.

Returning from Oxford that day I saw, from afar, a figure among the branches of the orchard's tallest tree. I knew it was Anne Greene. I went to her.

I felt she was waiting for me as I drew near, for I saw Margaret Peabody drop from a bough and walk off to the yard, carrying a bucket in either hand, while she, Anne Greene, loitered there. She was examining her cap, which must have caught in a branch, for there was a tear in it. Perhaps she had fallen — there were leaves and twigs in her hair, which was undone, as if it had been dragged through a mesh of branches. But when I looked closer it seemed these leaves had been arranged, like a garland. Immediately she caught my mood, my joy, my elation, and quickly gave them a mirror in her own. She smiled, laughed, as I unfolded my story to her. It mattered not a jot that indoors, in the Hall, I was her mistress's son, she my servant. Here in the orchard we were equals.

'Your prayer was answered,' she said, when I had finished.

'I have another prayer, Anne Greene,' I said.

I leaned forward and kissed her on the mouth. She returned my kiss. Then we stepped from one another a little. Is it possible that the *mouth* can know something? My head was startled by what I had done — my mouth knew it would kiss her again.

A river runs through our estate at Brocket Hall,

where my father had taught me to swim, and my grandfather had taught me to fish. In one part of it, not far from the house, there was a bank which the servants used to wash clothes. It was a secluded place, covered from behind by a row of hedges, in front by tall reeds which grew in a marshy bend of the river. The following day I approached this spot by water, rowing softly with the current in a skiff. I paused for a few moments when I came to the reeds. Parting them with my oar, I got a view of Anne Greene. All the clothes of the household were scattered on the grass beside her. In her left hand a nightgown, in her right a cambric shirt. I recognized both items, for they were my own. She was examining them, slowly, minutely, as if she were looking for something there. Then she lay back upon the grass, covering her face with the nightgown. Presently she rose again, rolled up her sleeves and proceeded to douse these articles in the water, to press them gently against a flat rock. Soon she spread them across a hedge to dry. Then she turned her attention to the other items there: my father's hose, my mother's shift, my grandfather's ruff et cetera. When all were scrubbed upon the rocks and laid out upon the hedges and bushes, she removed her shoes and stockings and let her feet and ankles drop into the water. The sun was very hot that day, there was not a breath of wind. Even from that distance I could see that she was perspiring from her effort.

I steered the skiff around to her.

'Come into the boat, Anne,' I said. 'The clothes will not blow away.'

Without a word she stood up and, lifting her skirt, waded a few feet through the water until she could step into the boat. I pulled away from the shore and with a few firm strokes caught the current again. I rested on the oars and we drifted away from Brocket Hall.

I could not take my eyes off her. I thrilled to every word she spoke. Her mind followed her gaze to the banks of the river and the fields. She knew the names of all the flowers we saw, and all the herbs, and the ways their juices might be combined for useful purposes. She guessed the places where the trout would hide, and the perch. She would look at a cornfield and guess how many bushels it might yield, and put a price on it. Likewise she could glance at a field of cattle, or lamb, and reckon what they were worth to the nearest guinea. I enquired how she came to know these things. Her father, it appeared, had inherited a small farm. Through a combination of skill, diligence and luck, the affairs of the family prospered. Then their fortunes declined. One by one her brothers fell to the King's enemies. Her father passed to Anne the knowledge which in the ordinary course would have gone to them, hoping that one day she might enlarge upon what he had built. Matters worsened during the months prior to her arrival at Brocket Hall. Three separate attacks were mounted on their house, at night. Her parents feared for all their lives — that is, for all that were left. Colonel Kelsey conducted enquiries in the neighbourhood — some cousins were summoned to make depositions before the authorities. They feared their father might be arrested at any time. When he was not, they were perplexed. He decided to carry through his plan anyway. This was to find secure places for all his daughters. On the basis of a service he had performed for my grandfather years before, he procured the place for her, Anne, at Brocket Hall.

A small peninsula juts into the stream one mile or so below the point where I had collected Anne Greene. There several beech trees stand, not so many as to make a wood, but enough to make a shady place. My grandfather loved to fish from there. The grass was long and the ground unspoilt by wandering animals, for he had fenced the area off. Anne Greene lay on her back in the grass and I lay on top of her. My desire for her was so intense that I was shaking. One arm she wrapped about my back, another about my neck, and grasped my hair with her fingers. I scarcely could savour or relish her kisses, so hard did I press my lips against hers, for so long. I held her so tightly with my hands that my wrists hurt. My soul swooned with pleasure. All thoughts emptied from my mind, save one, which flashed through it for an instant. How can my desire, my hunger, be satisfied by this? How can the *flesh* ease the yearning of the *heart*?

Ease it the flesh did. And more. Slowly we rocked together, she and I, as, little by little, my body entered hers. Nameless emotions swept my spirit which, from looking into her eyes, I could tell she too experienced. Pleasures beyond the pleasures language can speak of. And then thoughts, but thoughts without objects, for to know her was to know more than I could say.

We returned to the skiff. Acting upon a whim, we bathed before starting back to Brocket Hall. Watching her as she swam from the shadows cast by the beech trees to the light, and back again, put me in a state of ecstasy. Grandfather has caught many fish here, I thought, but who can count what I have found?

No sooner found than lost. Next day, together with my father and grandfather, I journeyed to Lübeck,[3] to renew the trading connections our family had among the merchants of that city, which the strife in England had all but undermined. In six months or so my companions returned to Brocket Hall. They ordered me to remain in Germany, because they held me to blame for what occurred at home while we were abroad. I was, in effect, banished. Three years elapsed before they permitted me to return. Only then could I construct a history of what had happened, from conversations with Margaret Peabody, Pennyfeather, Doctor Willis, William Petty and others.

Margaret Peabody and Anne Greene shared a bed in a room beside the kitchens. If their space was cramped, at least it was warm, for an oven or a fire was invariably lit, all the year round. In summer they slept without blankets. One night, months after our departure, Margaret was woken by Anne Greene's turning in her sleep and murmuring, which was unusual, for she had always been a still sleeper and a silent one. Margaret pressed her fingers against Anne's neck beneath the earlobe. She opened her eyes.

'Anne, what is the matter? Are you ill? Is it a nightmare?'

Anne sat up and gingerly touched her temples, shoulders and bosom, as if she expected to discover that some part of her anatomy was missing or damaged.

'I'm soaking wet!' she whispered. 'I'm perspiring. Yet I don't feel hot.'

On Margaret's advice Anne went to the kitchen to drink a cup of water. While she was gone Margaret absent-mindedly ran her hand along that part of the sheet where Anne had lain. Her fingers found a damp patch. She knew instinctively it was not perspiration. No indeed. The scent informed her it was blood. Before Anne Greene returned, Margaret pulled that sheet from the bed and replaced it with a clean one. If her companion noticed what she had done she made no comment, but promptly fell asleep. In the morning, however, she seemed pale. She said very little and often wiped her brow with a handkerchief, although the day was mild.

Margaret was afraid to imagine what might be the cause of the trouble — Anne Greene had spoken to her of the boat journey she and I had made. She was fearful in her own behalf no less than Anne Greene's, for Margaret was the senior female servant. She was answerable to the mistress for her colleagues. Their good work redounded to her credit, their errors were a liability. I therefore suspect that Margaret Peabody brought Anne Greene's illness to my grandmother's attention.

My grandmother ordered that Anne Greene should work in the barn that afternoon, screening malt. This involved using a long, heavy implement, like a spade, to toss, turn and twist the viscous matter for hours on end. Shortly after three o'clock my grandmother came to the barn — to supervise the work for a few minutes, she said. She spoke first to Anne Greene, then to Margaret Peabody. It was while she was speaking to Margaret that Anne Greene excused herself from the barn, indicating to Margaret, by pointing in the direction of the privy which the servants used, that she was going to answer a call of nature. My grandmother must have noticed the signal, for she abruptly finished the conversation and walked to the doorway of the barn. She stood there for a quarter of an hour, staring out into the yard. Then she turned to Margaret Peabody.

'Margaret,' she said, 'walk over now to the privy and see if it needs to be emptied.'

'I should think it does not, ma'am', Margaret replied. 'I ordered it emptied last week.'

'Do you refuse to carry out my instruction, Margaret?' my grandmother cried, suddenly enraged. 'Very well, then! I shall clean out the privy myself!' She strode out into the yard without another word.

Margaret, thoroughly mortified and confused, followed her. Such anger was no part of her mistress's character that she had seen. She pleaded with her to turn back, saying there was no need for it. But my grandmother would not turn back. In her haste, Margaret tripped over a stone. When eventually she reached the privy, she found my grandmother staring into the pit. Margaret did likewise. She saw an object there, a small lump of

3. A town in Schleswig-Holstein (now the largest Baltic port in Germany).

bloody flesh, about a span in length. My grandmother reached down and drew it out.

'This is a child,' she said, wrapping the object in her apron.

The constables arrested Anne Greene the next day. They put her in a cart and brought her to the gaol at Grantchester, there to await her appearance before a Justice of the Peace. No sooner had she arrived than the Justice was called to Abingdon. She was brought there after him. At Abingdon it transpired that a magistrate had been murdered and many depositions were to be sworn, business which had priority over the matter of Anne Greene. The depositions lasted two days and seemed set to occupy a third. A second Justice became available, at Avonbury. So she was fetched there and produced before this Justice without delay. Those who saw her were amazed at the calmness she displayed in the face of her predicament. She smiled to see the eyes of the Justice light up at the mention of Brocket Hall and to hear him regale the court with a tale of a day's fishing there with my grandfather when both were young men. How she felt to hear my grandmother give evidence bearing upon the discovery she had made in the privy, to hear Margaret Peabody corroborate what my grandmother had said to the Justice, I cannot say. Certainly, no-one present saw any change in her expression when all this came out.

'What do you say, Anne Greene?' the Justice demanded of her. 'I am going to charge you with concealing! And with murder! Have you a reason why I should not?'

'I did not know that I was with child,' she said. 'I was ill the day before I was arrested. I did not know what passed from me.'

The Justice said this was a question for a jury to decide. He ordered her to be imprisoned in Oxford until her trial, which he fixed for three weeks from that date.

The trial judge was no less severe with her.

'Not know that you were with child?' said he. 'This is not credible! You have heard Margaret Peabody give evidence of the admission you made to her that you had performed an act of fornication which should cause you to be with child! The same witness spoke of the issues upon your body the night before this event! You cannot be heard to say that you did not know!'

'But I did not know, my Lord.'

'Do you say that you did not know what passed from you in the privy. Do you say that you did not so much as cast a glance at that which the midwives here have described?'

'I was faint, my lord. I did not look in. I felt nothing. I saw nothing.'

'What have you to say to the evidence of the midwives?'

'What they described was scarcely a child, my Lord.'

'The jury may decide if it was a child. And whether you concealed its birth, if it was.'

The jury decided both questions against Anne Greene.

Pennyfeather (who by all private accounts had made no great effort in her defence at the trial) now declared that he would sue for a pardon. He visited the gaol to have Anne Greene put her name to a document. He found that Hunter, the gaoler, had shown some pity for her, equipping her with his longest chain, which afforded her a greater range of movement than was usual, so that she might perchance escape the attentions of the grimy, foul-mouthed, drunken wretches who were her companions. They called out to one another from the different parts of the gaol, with curses, oaths, threats. They abused Pennyfeather when they caught sight of him, as if the attorney were responsible for the punishments their crimes had earned them. He learned that one, who had the appearance of a gentleman, had given her liquor, advising that this was the best preparation for the ordeal which awaited her, but it soon became clear that this was a mere device to put her in a mind to perform with him what she had done with me, Jeffrey Reade. Anne Greene asked Pennyfeather if he could confirm what she had been told, that there were masked prisoners held in certain parts of the gaol, who were continuously moved about the building, for fear of the violence which would ensue if their identities were discovered.

Thinking the prospect of an encounter with such a creature might alarm his client, Pennyfeather denied their existence outright, which instantly proved a mistake, for just then Hunter whisked a masked prisoner by. The attorney's efforts to explain the contradiction were drowned by the shamless, brazen cries of Nance Hardcastle, a notorious strumpet of the town of Oxford, who was boasting of several crimes she had committed with impunity. Hunter shortly snuffed out her racket by pulling a sackcloth over her head and throwing her to the ground. Pennyfeather thought to employ the lull, which he knew from experience would be brief, to explain how he intended to advance the suit for pardon, but he was prevented by the sudden appearance of Anne Greene's mother in the gaol. Pennyfeather's heart had been hardened by many years at law, but even he was moved by the sight of Mistress Greene. The patches on her clothes showed clearly enough that fortune, whose favour she had enjoyed for a few short years, had abandoned her to that poverty which she had striven to overcome during the greater part of her life. Her eyes were bleary from weeping. Yet there was in her carriage a dignity which not even her daughter's circumstances could upset. They spoke quietly for a few minutes. Then Mistress Greene bade her daughter farewell, taking with her Anne's bodice, which Pennyfeather estimated to be worth five shillings, and a coat, which otherwise old Townsend would acquire next day.

Townsend showed his anger at being cheated of a prize which custom rather than law deemed his entitlement by hauling Anne Greene onto the cart in a rough manner and by attaching her manacles in a way that was designed to make it difficult to evade missiles. The chaplain, who accompanied them, pleaded her weak condition. Townsend, with typical arrogance, instructed the chaplain to look after God's affairs and leave the execution of the court's order to him.

The gaol gates opened. The mob burst through and surrounded them. The students and apprentices were to the fore, vying with one another's catcalls, shakings of the cart, jostlings of the passengers. On the streets, hawkers were offering for sale at cheap prices lavish quantities of gin, rum, wine and ale. The mob swilled it all indiscriminately. They must have begun their carousals early, for many of the whores, thieves and rogues who had emerged from their dens for the day were already drunk, although it was still only mid-morning. They abused the sheriff's officer who headed the procession, challenging him to arrest individuals in their number for whom warrants were out, saying his clothes were no better than theirs, that his horse was fit for the knacker's yard. Someone threw a dog's carcass at him, which caught him around the neck and almost unseated him. He struck out angrily with his dagger, spilling the animal's guts into the street, producing a terrible stench. A ringleader proposed wrapping the sheriff's man up in these, so that he should have the stomach for his work. The students baulked at this. So the fellow instead attempted to tear the clothes from the back of Anne Greene, but once more he was thwarted, for the chaplain did not shrink from knocking this rascal unconscious with a blow from his leaden-handled cane.

Margaret Peabody clung to the side of the cart.

'God have mercy upon you, Anne Greene!' she cried. 'To think that it should come to this!'

She wept, and struck her breasts with clenched fists, before Townsend dislodged her with his staff. Anne Greene, quite unperturbed, watched as Margaret fell on the road and was jerked to her feet by three students.

Pennyfeather stuck his head out the window as the cart passed his rooms.

'The pardon, Anne!' he shouted, trying to make himself heard above the din. 'I sent to London for it! It may yet come — these things take a little time! Don't give up hope!'

He quickly disappeared and shut the window, for brickbats were being hurled in his direction. If she heard him, Anne Greene made no rejoinder.

When the cart arrived at the foot of the scaffold, Townsend opened the manacles and hoisted Anne Greene out. He dragged her up the short flight of steps, then placed the noose around her neck as the chaplain whispered prayers into her ear. He, the chaplain, noted that she seemed quite unaware of the mob, the noose, Old Townsend or himself. As though in a waking dream, she gazed at some point far above the spire of St John's. The chaplain's prayer was cut short by a roar from the mob. A tub of liquor had fallen from its stand: those nearby scrambled to salvage what they could.

Townsend opened the trapdoor. She dropped. Someone cried 'Look! She twitches!', at which the mob let an huzza, for they delighted in the struggles of the condemned. Then she was, as it appeared, still. The mob, disappointed that their amusement was finished so soon, groaned. But in a moment she twitched again and even uttered a sound.

Her cousin Robert Greene cried out 'Despatch her, Townsend! Despatch her, for pity's sake!'

Townsend, with all his force, struck her twice upon the breasts. Robert himself, aiming to shorten the final agony of his childhood companion, rushed up the steps and delivered great strokes across her stomach and back. Whereupon she appeared to convulse. Now Margaret Peabody rushed up the steps of the scaffold. She wrapped her arms about Anne Greene's neck, as if claiming a final embrace, but actually in an effort to stop the convulsion. She leaped from the floor of the scaffold and wrapped her legs about Anne Greene's waist, promoting a tirade of obscenities from the mob. Margaret clung there, oblivious to the cries, for a minute, before dropping to the woodwork and retreating down the steps. The mob, ever fickle, warmly applauded her whom a moment before they had abused, for now they judged she had added much to their diversion.

Townsend and Robert Greene both smashed several blows upon her back and breasts and thighs and stomach. Margaret Peabody rushed the steps again, causing near hysterical laughter in the mob, to brush Townsend and Robert Greene aside. She leaped upon Anne Greene from behind, flinging her arms around her neck, perching there until the muscles in her arms grew tired. Finally Orum, who was a soldier in the militia, mounted the scaffold and struck her several times with the butt of his musket.

She was still.

Townsend cut her down. Robert Greene advanced to claim the corpse, having been charged by Anne Greene's parents to do this. Two stout beadles intervened. They produced an order from Colonel Kelsey to the effect that the corpse was the property of Mr Petty, who had paid the municipality for it. Enraged, Robert Greene wrenched a brickbat from the grip of a youth standing nearby and made to assault the beadles. But they were experienced men in this type of business and they dealt quickly enough with Robert Greene. They laid Anne Greene's body in a coffin and set off through the streets, guarded by Orum and his friend Mason, a tailor.

In seconds the mob grasped what had happened. Now thoroughly inflamed by the alcohol, they set off in pursuit of the beadles. They nearly succeeded in halting the coffin at the narrow exit from the Haymarket, where they pelted the beadles and Orum with stones, brickbats and potatoes, as they howled their protest at this injustice to the Greene family, as they saw it. Orum fired his musket over their heads — they retreated. Orum reloaded. The beadles rushed through the Haymarket and reached the maze of lanes between it and St John's church before the pursuit continued. They entered a shed adjoining premises owned by one Proudfoot, a barber. They put the coffin on a table, then sat down to catch their breath. Orum was empowered to sign a receipt for the body on Mr Petty's behalf. He gave the beadles this and they left smartly. In a little while, Mason swung open the lid of the coffin.

Anne Greene rattled in the throat.

Mason, who was a tall, heavy fellow, stamped upon her breast and stomach several times. Orum whacked her with the butt of his musket upon the neck, the back, the stomach. Despite these blows, when Mr Petty arrived with his colleague Dr Willis, her throat still rattled, ever so slightly.

A flash of that genius with which the world in time would associate his name now came to William Petty. He had paid, let us say, fifteen shillings or thereabouts for this carcass, so that he might dissect it and thereby advance his skill as an anatomist. In that instant he had a vision of something of far greater value. Dr Willis saw the gleam in his colleague's eye and did not demur from the proposal he then made, for he knew his friend.

'Friend Orum,' said Petty, 'Please stand by the door with your musket drawn. Admit no-one.'

Orum took up his position by the door.

'And you, Mr Mason, would perhaps render us all the service of lighting a fire in the grate. It's cold enough to catch your death!'

Willis laughed merrily at this.

'My dear William!' he cried, 'I have heard gallows humour often enough — but this post-scaffold sally is new to me. Careful, lest you start a fashion!'

'For shame, Willis! For shame!' said Petty, with a twinkle in his eye.

He left the premises and returned a few minutes later dragging a bed, the property of Proudfoot, and a boxful of materials from his rooms in the college, which was near.

They lifted Anne Greene from the coffin to the bed. They wrenched apart her teeth, which were tightly clamped together, so that they might force a little brandy down her throat. They were encouraged by the result of this — she seemed to cough a little. Her fingers were bent rigid and they struggled to straighten them — too much pressure could have caused them to snap. They bound her arm with a piece of cloth to bleed her and it jumped back as if in convulsion. They cut open a vein. The blood flowed so freely and so profusely that they had to staunch it, no easy matter as it transpired. They massaged her head, hands and feet.

The room was warmer now, with the fire blazing. Mason and Orum stared, as if transfixed, at Anne Greene. Seeing Willis look in his direction, Orum spoke up to him.

'Is this a woman, Dr Willis? Or a witch? She has suffered that which would settle twenty women. Can you explain it?'

'I cannot,' replied Willis, with typical frankness. 'But I think she is no witch. No witch would have been caught as she was caught.'

'It is the hand of Providence,' declared Petty.

'It's a miracle,' said Mason.

'We protestants do not speak of miracles, Mason,' said Petty, smiling, 'we speak of Providence. I did not know that you had quit us for Rome!'

'Not at all!' said Mason, blushing, 'Just an ignorant man's slip of the tongue, sir! I'm no papist, sir! Oh no, not me!'

'Do not distress yourself, Mason,' Petty returned, for he was not a man to bait a feeble wit for mischief. 'If you had been a papist, I should not have thought any the less of you.'

'He's no papist, sir', said Orum. 'I can vouch for him.'

'Enough!' cried Petty, suddenly grown impatient. 'Bring the wine, Willis.'

He scribbled a note on a piece of paper and handed it to Mason.

'Take this to Colonel Kelsey without delay and bring me his reply. Go through Proudfoot's — you may be sure the mob is still prowling.'

Willis and Petty poured strong wine down Anne Greene's throat. They rubbed her cheeks, arms, thighs, feet, ankles. They tickled her throat with a feather. Earthenware jars full of hot water were placed in the bed to warm the sheets. They bound up Anne Greene's thighs (Petty was forbearing to remark that this was shutting the stable door after the horse was bolted) and positioned her lying on her side. Petty devised a cordial of rainwater, cinnamon and sorrel, some of which they managed to pour down her throat. Where the rope had cut her neck and feet they rubbed turpentine, noticing, as they did so, that when the sides and bottom of her feet were touched she moved her lower parts.

Robert Greene caught sight of Mason making his way back from the Governor's house and followed him to Proudfoot's. He listened at the window and quickly learned that his cousin was not dead. Within the hour he, Anne Greene's parents and Margaret Peabody were upon their knees in the street outside the shed, praising the work of Providence. The remnants of the mob came to marvel at them and to jeer Townsend and the constables, who before long were knocking at the door, demanding that the anatomists cease obstructing the order of the court, namely the execution of Anne Greene.

'Open the door, Mr Petty! Dr Willis!' Townsend cried. 'I must have her back! I must have her back!'

'You shall be dismissed, Townsend!' a drunken student cried. 'You cannot even hang a girl!'

'Here!' cried another, holding up a kitten by the neck before his face. 'Why not practice upon this furry thing? Has the muse of the rope deserted you?'

William Petty, who had anticipated the position in which these officers now found themselves — especially their fear of the retribution which those in authority might visit upon them, appeared upon the roof of the shed. He called upon the constable in charge, saying he had an order from Colonel Kelsey, staying the order of execution until further notice. He invited this man to climb up upon the roof to inspect the order. Once this was done and Petty's claim confirmed, all concerned were satisfied, for they could scarcely now be charged with neglect of their duties. They duly made their way off through the streets, cuffing what students they could reach as they passed them.

Anne Greene's nostrils and temples were smeared with a mixture of mayflower and caryophylleous, her breasts with majistral.[4] An enema was inserted. This was a type of mutton broth into which ground leaves of marjoram, laurel, origan[5] and rosemary had been infused, and also bay leaves, seed of juniper, aniseed and spices.

Petty bade Orum fetch Margaret Peabody inside to him.

'You have lain with Anne Greene before, Margaret,' he said. 'Will you lie with her now?'

'Lie with *Anne Greene*, sir?' said Margaret, grown suddenly pale.

'We must keep her body warm. You will understand why I, or Mr Willis, or Orum here, or his

4. Caryophylleous is clove-pink; majistral (magistral) is a remedy for a particular case, not included in the recognized pharmacopoeia.
5. wild marjoram.

friend Mason, may not decently do this. Will you do it? You shall be well rewarded for it.'

'If it will help restore my friend, I shall do it gladly,' said Margaret, with what conviction she could muster.

'There is something else. The purpose of this, as I say, is to keep Anne Greene's body warm. To that end Dr Willis and I have been rubbing her hands, head and feet. Decency forbids *our* touching her lower parts. It would not restrain *your* doing so.'

'Very well, sir' said Margaret in a whisper. 'I understand.'

Petty, pulling the cover from Anne Greene, invited Margaret to climb in beside her. The breath stopped in Margaret's throat when she saw her friend: her thighs bound, her bosom glistening and discoloured from the potion spread across it, livid weals about her neck from the rope, the first signs of bruises where the blows had struck her, her hair tied with Townsend's string. Margaret paused for a moment on the edge of the bed, then stretched out beside Anne and pulled the cover over them. She was cold and stiff who used to warm their bed near the kitchen at Brocket Hall. Margaret drew the earthen jars close and wrapped both arms tightly about her. Then, when the men withdrew to a corner of the room, she pressed Anne Greene's lower parts with her hands as she had been instructed. Margaret quickly became terror-stricken. She had, as she thought, seen Anne Greene die upon the scaffold. What demon now possessed her body? Would it take revenge for what she had done to help Anne die quickly? Might it infuse Anne's arms with strength, cause her hands to strangle? Gradually these fears receded. There was clearly a little life stirring in Anne Greene. It was her life, which Providence alone could have preserved.

At noon Anne Greene perspired. Her face began to swell. For an instant her eyelids flickered, as if they were about to open. But they did not.

William Petty leaned over her.

'Anne Greene!' he cried. 'Anne Greene! Can you hear? Do not be afraid! You are not among the damned, but the living. Providence has spared your life. Give us a sign that you understand!'

She made no sign.

Her breathing became regular, and her pulse. In two hours the enema produced an effect. Encouraged, Petty hit upon the idea of using a candle-end as a suppository. Margaret Peabody inserted it. This also produced an effect.

'Open your eyes, girl!' William Petty said.

Slowly her eyelids opened. Yet it was not certain that she *saw*.

Petty stared into her eyes from a distance of six inches.

'Oh my America!'[6] he whispered. 'America!'

Triumph, satisfaction, relief, wonder, joy — all these feelings appeared in his countenance as he bent over her, together with something Margaret could best identify as the emotion of a man who has seen a sign from God.

Anne Greene's eyelids closed. Minutes later, she took a fit of coughing. Fearing she might catch a fever, they bled her. Then they gave a light cordial made from the alkarines plant[7] and later some water in which pressed seed of tamarind and viola was mixed. Into her mouth they put morsels of caudle.[8] She chewed these, and swallowed them.

The street outside was by now thronged with people, many of whom pressed their ears and eyes to cracks in the wall of the room where Anne Greene lay. They related what they saw and heard to the others, so that everyone was aware of the situation inside. They were moved to silence, even those who had drunk their fill of the liquors that had been on sale in the street and who had offered violence to the beadles. They too saw the work of Providence in this business and counted Mr Petty's hand at one with it. He, Petty, when he realized what the general attitude was, decided to order Orum and Mason to admit anyone who wished to enter, to satisfy their curiosity. He had another motive, too, which came out when he answered Dr Willis's objection that a stream of spectators might hinder rather than help Anne Greene's progress. Sceptics had reduced to insignificance many wonderful scientific experiments. At some time in the future such people would scoff and dismiss the evidence of a small group of people with vested interest in the proceedings. Why, they would say, unless there was something amiss, were the available impartial witnesses not afforded an opportunity to see for themselves? But no sceptic would dispute the evidence of scores of ordinary people. So, for two hours or more, while she slept, Anne

6. cf. John Donne, 'Elegie: Going to Bed', line 27.
7. A plant that yields red dye.
8. A hot spice wine drink made with gruel, and used medicinally.

Greene was viewed by small groups of students and apprentices, fishwives and journeymen, bakers and clothiers, butchers, coopers, weavers. Even the drunkards, ruffians, harlots and thieves of the town were admitted in the hope that sight of God's work might exert a benign influence upon them. Something of the effect intended was achieved. Chastened, they wandered the streets, describing what they had seen to whomever they encountered. Soon the town of Oxford was agog.

Pennyfeather turned up at a late hour. He slid a document beneath Anne Greene's pillow. Then he leaned across Margaret Peabody who, like me, was seized by a sudden irrational fear that he intended to bite her with his nose.

'Margaret,' he whispered. 'There is the answer from the Council to my suit for a pardon. It has been rejected. Please pass this information to my client, Anne Greene, should she recover consciousness.'

On his way out the door, Pennyfeather encountered William Petty and Willis, returning to the room for a final examination of Anne Greene before they retired for the night. Now there was a difficulty about which order should take priority, that of the council or that of the governor of the town. William Petty argued that Colonel Kelsey's order took priority, since it was made after the order of the council. Pennyfeather objected that the governor was subordinate to the council and that he had anyway made his order without knowledge of the council's decision. Petty enquired whether there was any obligation upon them to bring the council's order to Colonel Kelsey's attention. Pennyfeather said he didn't know. He would consult his books.

One hour after midnight Anne Greene awoke.

'Can you hear me, Anne?' Margaret asked.

'I can, Margaret', she replied. 'Have they brought you to prison also?'

'You have been brought back from the dead! This is not gaol but a place belonging to a barber, Proudfoot.'

As Margaret explained the situation, she pressed to Anne's lips the cup of julep which Petty and Willis had left for her. Anne Greene drank some of it. She offered no comment upon information Margaret gave her, save for thanking Margaret for being a true friend by lying with her. Then she fell asleep.

Petty and Willis, returning early the following morning, could scarcely contain their joy to find Anne Greene awake and speaking, but they did not forbear to suppress their instincts to celebrate in favour of their duties towards the person in their charge. She complained her throat was sore. For it they made a poultice of malva[9] and bay leaves ground down with soft bread, milk and butter. Anne Greene asked for beer. They offered instead the barley julep, which was not to her taste. Then they gave her a little warm beer. Neither was this to her taste. There was some other matter in it, she thought. Finally they gave her cold beer, which she drank with gusto.

'Sirs!' she said, in a quiet tone. 'Thank you for your kindness. I owe my life to you. But what is to prevent Townsend renewing his attempt upon it?'

'The authorities in this town share my view that the remarkable circumstances of this case afford ground for another appeal to the council,' Petty replied. 'They have stayed the order of execution, pending the outcome of it.'

'God will do his will with me.'

Willis asked what she recalled of her experiences upon the cart and upon the scaffold. She remembered nothing at all. It was as though she had fallen asleep between her meeting the chaplain and encountering Margaret Peabody in the bed beside her.

She was bathed with lotions upon her neck and breasts, ribs and thighs, for now deep black bruises were appearing where the rope had chafed and the blows had struck. Blood spots dotted her cheeks. The day following she produced her first stool, at noon. It was made with no great difficulty. The texture was somewhat loose. Next morning her monthly course flowed. She could stand to allow the sheets to be tossed, but complained of dizziness. She had pains in her breast and stomach and the tip of her tongue was numb, as if she had bitten it during her ordeal. For it Petty devised a concoction of radish, ground mummy, slate, rhubarb and castor. For her breasts an ointment of dialthea[10] and ground white of lily. For her neck, rosepetal.

Her pulse grew stronger as the days passed. The pain moved from her breast to her stomach. More of her courses came. If she held the edge of the table, she could walk. She ate chicken legs and other

9. Plant of the genus *Malvaceae* (the mallows).
10. An ointment composed of the purified essence of several plants.

such delicacies. Feeling returned to the tip of her tongue.

Some hours before her father took her home to Staple Barton, Pennyfeather paid her a visit. He advised Margaret Peabody that he had come upon important business, but it quickly became clear that curiosity, not business, had drawn him to Proudfoot's shed.

'Did you glimpse Paradise, Anne Greene?' he asked.

'I did.'

'Can you describe it?'

'There is a river there to fish in, and sail boats. Beside the river is a place where grass grows beneath tall beech trees. Here the divine light shines. Angels and other blessed creatures rest here and enjoy the sensations of celestial bliss.'

At this point Margaret Peabody hid her face in her apron and moved to the corner of the room.

'By what name,' he asked, 'were you known in Paradise?'

'They welcomed Magdalen,' she said, 'bade farewell to Lazarus.'

Petty's petition to the Privy Council argued that the child was abortive or stillborn and so malformed that it could not have been otherwise. Anne Greene probably had not known that she was with child, much less deliberately procured its death. It was excusable therefore that she had not made known the delivery as the law required. The midwives' evidence had been that the child had likely never lived. Margaret Peabody had testified that what was described as a child was in reality a lump of flesh scarcely five inches in length, not a fully formed human creature. Its sex was not discernible. The passage of blood prior to the delivery was inconsistent with life. The labour involved in screening malt was the immediate cause of the abortion.

She could have had two motives for concealing the abortion, he argued. First, to escape the shame of being pregnant. Second, to escape the responsibility of maintenance. In relation to the first, she had admitted to Margaret Peabody the nature of her relation with me, Jeffrey Reade. The shame of the child being seen would not have been greater than the shame incurred by her admission. Regarding the second, she would have known that a child, so-called, born at four months, could not survive to require maintenance. Its size was consistent with her declaration that I, Jeffrey Reade, had used her body some four to five months before the delivery. Many writers had recorded examples of miscarriages occurring, unknown, to women sitting upon the privy. Petty and Dr Willis had themselves known the like and could produce women from the town of Oxford who had had the experience. Anne Greene had borne her ordeal upon the scaffold and the deserved shame of the foul sin of fornication with patience and resolution. All good people desired that her suffering be accepted by the authorities in lieu of the punishment ordered by the court.

This petition to the Privy Council was successful. Mr Petty raised a collection among the physicians and other excellent men of Oxford to provide a dowry for Anne Greene. She married a young farmer and ultimately raised many children in the neighbourhood of Staple Barton.

William Petty profited. He quickly became celebrated throughout England as the physician who had raised from the dead. The University of Oxford made him Professor of Anatomy and then deputy-head of Brasenose College. These positions he exchanged in the following year for that of Surgeon-General to the Lord Protector's army in Ireland, a country which was, he observed, 'in the condition of Anne Greene'.

He came to acquire some two hundred and fifty thousand acres in the county of Kerry, where he founded a colony, at Kenmare.

I applied to him to join this colony, for my fortunes in England were by this time reduced to nothing. He remembered the trust I had placed in him when his own fortunes were low, and was pleased to welcome me there. It was, he said, the land of his heart's desire, and he hoped it might become mine. He assured me that, while in his public efforts on behalf of Anne Greene, he had been obliged to regard me as a fornicator, a reprobate and a criminal, he did not privately view me in so harsh a light. Besides, who in Ireland would be concerned about such matters?

And so I set out for Ireland, which already the Puritans, affecting the manner of the Israelites, called the Promised Land. I knew there were forests there, great tracts of ancient trees. My heart longed for their darkness, their silence, their twisted shapes. I bought an axe, and a copy of Haines's book.

Except Margaret Peabody, none at Brocket Hall bade me farewell. They did however grant me a little money, and allowed me to keep Lucy, my mare. To spite them, and to satisfy my own hunger, I did what they had expressly forbidden, which was to journey to Staple Barton.

I found Anne Greene milking a cow in the byre adjoining the cottage which was now her home. She turned when she heard my footsteps. Her eyes were the same as they had been the day I first saw them. When she rose from her stool and walked to meet me, I stopped. Four feet from me, she too stopped. She looked at me.

Petty had shown that her ordeal upon the scaffold had passed by her consciousness, as though she had slept all the time. She had reconstructed what had happened from the bruises upon her body, the pain she had felt, and what Margaret Peabody and others had told her. My own position was similar. I had gleaned one piece of information here, another there. I had known nothing of her ordeal as it occurred, but subsequently it became the stuff of a continuing nightmare. Once I had been unable to speak of the pleasures we had shared. Now I had no words for the suffering. I had, as I thought, planted seed in heaven. But fortune made me reap a harvest in hell.

Would my life have been better if she had abused me, dismissed me from her, blamed and condemned me for what she had endured? If she had taken a dagger, or a musket, or any other weapon, and attacked me, I should not have resisted the blows, but welcomed them.

She did not strike me. She kissed me, and took my hand, and led me out of the byre to where Lucy stood in the sunlight. And she told me to my face something and more of what Margaret Peabody had heard her tell Pennyfeather, namely what she knew of Paradise.

AIDAN MATHEWS

(1956-)

from: ADVENTURES IN A BATHYSCOPE (1988)

[The stories in Aidan Mathews's first collection, *Adventures in a Bathyscope* [*sic*] are set variously in Ireland, England, Greece, the United States and Japan. Instead of a fluid cosmopolitan style, however, the reader encounters pastiche and satire, as though Mathews were a wittily observant stylistic tourist. (Certain American writers suggest the dominant mode.) But the fiction is intent as well as versatile. In 'Fathers', the narrator learns from his father the necessity of intervention on behalf of the unjustly treated and the brutalized. The father becomes plural by the story's end and becomes indeed the continuity of justice and courage through history. The transformation is left apparently intact, despite the father's voyeuristic relationship to history and the self-requested punishment of an incorrigible schoolboy slacker.]

FATHERS

'In the lost childhood of Judas, Christ was betrayed.'

I was half-way through my homework when my father put his head round the door.

'There's a good programme starting, old man. About the Nazi death camps and the Eichmann trial.[1] I thought you might be interested.'

The night before, it had been a special report on the fate of the white rhinoceros in Zambia; and on Sunday, a documentary about the shanty towns in Rio. We'd had the television for six months, and my father still played with it like a new toy.

'I have this poem to learn the first three verses of, Bill.'

1. Adolf Eichmann (1902-62), an Austrian Nazi official, escaped to Argentina after World War II, but was captured, tried and executed in Israel as a war criminal.

'I can give you a note,' my father said. 'This programme's important. I want you to see it. Come on down.'

He took his smock off as he went downstairs, wiping clay and crayon from his hands onto the tough cloth. He could never get rid of those stains. Even on holidays in the caravan, away from work, his fingers smelled of the studio.

My mother was doing her nails in the study when we came in. She held her hands in the air like a prisoner to dry them while my father fiddled with the contrast button and the vertical hold.

'I hope it's suitable,' she said. 'I don't want him having bad dreams.'

The voice in the television began to speak up.

'Eichmann is not however a satanist or sadist. His domestic life was both modest and moral. When he was promoted from Untersturmführer to Hauptsturmführer,[2] his first action....'

'Here it is,' my father said. 'This is strong stuff, old man, but you have a right to know. The day your mother and I married, ten thousand children were gassed at Auschwitz. I went out that morning to buy flowers.'

He stood at the fire and looked into it, working the dottle from the bowl of his pipe with a pipe-cleaner. Then he came over and sat down beside me.

There was loud music. A map appeared. It was a map of Europe on which shadows were spreading like ink stains to show where the armies advanced. I glanced at my father. He was stroking his beard and nodding his head. I looked above the television, then beneath it; at the knobs; at the screen.

A boy was holding a model train in front of a soldier who struck him with the butt of his rifle so that the boy fell down and lay in the road. The voice was saying dates and places like the names in the Brothers Grimm. Heidelburg, Bucharest, Birkenau. My father put his hand on my knee.

'And you see the people standing round?' he said.

Two soldiers were dragging a man by his collar along the pavement. They passed an old man who took off his hat. Then they let go of the one they were pulling, and they kicked the old man until he kneeled down.

'Bravo. Bravo.'

My photograph was on top of the set beside the Madonna my father had made. I looked at the picture of me in my Communion suit, and at Mary taking her breast out of her blouse to give it to the baby on her lap. I did not want to see the rabbi in the snow with his face burnt.

'Would you look at that?'

'It's not fair,' said my mother's voice. 'He's too young.'

My father waved his pipe at the television. I had not seen him so upset since the programme about the baby seals.

'No man is an isthmus, Mark,' he said. 'No man. On the Last Day, it won't help to conjugate a Latin verb. Did you feed the starving? Did you visit the prisons?'

A woman walked into a yard where soldiers were smoking and lifting box cameras. She started to take off her clothes, wobbling as she pulled her dress over her head. When she opened her stockings, she fell down, and curled up like a baby with her stockings bundled around her feet.

'If not, then to Hell with you. For saying it was none of your business. For saying Pass the salt.'

My father tugged his beard like a bell.

'Are you finished?' my mother said. 'Shall I pass the plate now?'

'Mark understands,' said my father.

He went out in a bit of a huff.

My mother began to fix the cover on the couch, working it down into the edges, straightening the pattern.

'He's not content to be a father. He's not content to be a husband. He's not content to be a sculptor. He has to be a Good Man.'

My father was working with a blowtorch when I went in. He kicked the plug, and turned up his goggles.

'The soldier fought bravely before the city walls,' he said.

I thought.

'Fortiter miles ante urbis muros pugnavit.'

'Father and son went up the mountain quickly to the altar.'

That took longer.

'Pater atque filius in monte celeriter progressi sunt ad altarem.'

'Fair enough,' my father said.

He pulled his goggles down and started the torch. I sat on a box and watched the fantail from the white jet. He shouted at me over the noise.

2. Lower and higher ranks in the German SS during the Third Reich.

'What do you think?'

'It's lovely. What is it?'

'It'll keep the wolf from the door,' he shouted.

'And the roof over our heads,' I called.

The Stations[3] for the school chapel were in a pile beside me. Jesus Falls For The Third Time and Jesus Is Comforted By The Women. The parents had complained and said it was their money because Jesus was naked except for the thorns and you could see everything. My father's picture had been in the paper but it was before he had his beard. One parent had come up to me and said he respected my father and would I tell him, and I told him yes.

'Bill,' I shouted.

When he took off his goggles, there was a mark on his forehead.

'Yes, old man?'

'Just Bill,' I said.

I couldn't settle down to sleep, Whenever I closed my eyes, I saw the old rabbi and the corporal who was striking a match to set fire to his beard. Another soldier had given him a bucket of horse manure to put out the flame, but the rabbi would not do it. He kept shaking his head.

I started to look at the stain on the ceiling which was like a map of Italy, and I named the cities, the rivers, the churches. When I closed my eyes again, I smelled sulphur. I didn't breathe. I went deep in the bed. A floorboard creaked.

It was my father. He was lighting a cigarette on the landing outside, listening to hear if I was asleep; standing in the darkness.

'In the name of the Father and of the Son and of the Holy Ghost,' Fr Wilson said.

'In the name of the Father and of the Son,' I said. I was looking at the poem we had been told to learn.

Fr Wilson leaned against the blackboard, inspecting his shoes.

'Today promises well for Fr Wilson,' he said. 'Today is a fine April morning, and each member of this class knows his poetry. Isn't that so, Colin my friend?'

'Yes, Father.'

'Would you subscribe to that, Andrew?'

'Yes, Father.'

'Fine. The first three verses, Andrew. The first two verses, Andrew. We were all in bed an hour ago, and it wouldn't do to tax the mind. I know you've made a special effort not to disappoint poor Fr Wilson for the third time running.'

I knew better. Andrew Masterson had been warming his hands on the hot pipes before class, wrapping them round the bars till the tears ran down his good eye.

I was right. He got through seven lines and came to a stop.

The class was silent. I stared at my desk-lid, at the cartoon of the Nazi goosestepping on the cover of my jotter where someone had written: Sieg Heil,[4] The Sculptor's Son.

Fr Wilson parted his lips so they made a sad sound.

'Andrew falls for the third time.'

'I tried, Father.'

'Are you stupid, Andrew?'

'Yes, Father.'

'And lazy, Andrew? A lazybones?'

'Yes, Father.'

'What does that make you, Andrew?'

'A stupid lazybones, Father.'

The class laughed.

'Our Lord died on the Cross for you, Andrew. And you can't learn three verses of a poem for Him.'

Fr Wilson nodded his head up and down in patience, side to side in disbelief. He held up the note for the Dean.

'Goodbye, Andrew.'

'Goodbye, Father,' said Andrew Masterson. He walked up the aisle; and the boys tittered, moving their satchels to let him pass. When he took the slip of paper from Fr Wilson, he got down on his knees. But he was only tying his shoe.

I didn't know that I had stood up until I saw the class turning to look at me, a rush of white faces like underneath leaves when the wind blows them back. There was a shadow coming in front of me. I saw the map, and Bill's face, the rabbi knotting his bootlace, and Andrew curled on the ground with his pants at his ankles. What was an isthmus?

'You're a bully. He can't help not knowing, and you knew he wouldn't get it right. You knew.'

3. Stations of the Cross: a series of representations of the fourteen incidents of Christ's Passion displayed in catholic churches and visited successively for devotional exercises.

4. Hail to Victory: a Nazi salute, usually accompanied by the raising of the right arm.

Bill. Bill.

I felt the touch and grasp of hands pulling me down into my desk. Then the hands stopped. I saw mouths opening and moving, Fr Wilson speaking, gesturing to Andrew Masterson, and Andrew sitting down, staring at his book without moving his head; and my nails with biro[5] marks on them: a small hair, an eyelash, on the second nail.

'. . . to have an intercessor, Andrew.'

'Yes, Father.'

When I looked up, the bell had rung, Fr Wilson had left the classroom without his books, and the boys were looking at me, taking their books for the next class out of their satchels.

I waited after school until all the boys had gone. Then I walked to the bicycle shed. I was afraid I would meet Fr Wilson, and he would be ashamed. I wanted to be home so that I could tell my father everything that had happened from the beginning. He would look at me then the same way he had looked at me the night before when he had pulled down his goggles and I had said: Just Bill.

As I put my bag on the carrier. I heard the noise of twigs. Andrew Masterson came out from behind the hedge. Colin Dennis and Mick the Nose were beside him, each of them trailing a stick in the gravel.

'Hello,' Andrew Masterson said.

'Hello,' I said.

'Hello again,' he said.

'What do you mean?'

'We want to help you with your homework,' he said. 'The three of us want to.'

He flung his leg over the bike and sat on the saddle.

'I love your bike,' he said.

Dennis and Mick the Nose were marking zeros and crosses in the gravel with the sticks.

'I wish my bike was as nice as yours,' he said. He rocked it with his weight so the front wheel strained against the iron prongs in the wall.

'Go easy,' I said.

He stood on the pedals and leaned over.

'I hate to say this but I think I might have warped it.'

He pressed down on the handlebars until the front wheel buckled in the iron bracket and a spoke stuck out.

'Butterfingers,' he said.

He bent down to open the valves on the tyres.

'It'll be easier for you,' he said, 'to wheel it home.'

They were killing a pig in the yard behind the handball court. I could hear its cries peak, like a fast car braking.

I began to cry.

'I forgot what I came for,' he said. 'It was to say thanks.'

I sat down on the gravel and curled in a ball at their feet. When they saw I was ready, they started. But I felt far away. I felt I was behind the hedge, watching.

Their boots rose and fell.

'It's about the rain forests of the Amazon,' my father said. 'And the ozone layer.'

'I have to work, Bill.'

'The serious student, old man. The serious student.'

'You can tell me about it later.'

But he came back a moment later.

'I don't think I'll bother,' he said. 'I'll work for a while. Keep the old wolf from the door.'

He stood, waiting. I looked at the bits of a horse-fly on my wall.

'And the roof over our heads,' I said.

Then he was happy, and bounded down the stairs, taking them two at a time.

I put away my Latin. Below me, I heard a hanger clatter in the wardrobe as my father got his smock out; the rasp of a match on an emery board; and the dull whoosh of the torch as he pressed the foot-switch.

I had to go down.

'What did you do tonight?' he said.

'The subjunctive.'

'No less. Do you know,' he shouted, 'if you keep learning like this, I'll be more of a hindrance than a help soon.'

I watched the flame peel from the jet of the torch and drop in pellets on the floor. Quick droplets of bronze glistened.

'I might have been warned,' I said.

Monitus fu . . . monitus fuerim. Is that it?'

'I don't know,' I said.

'This is my beloved son in whom I am well pleased,'[6] he shouted.

'You do it, Bill.'

5. A ballpoint pen. Biro is a brand name.

6. Matthew 3.17.

'I've forgotten everything I knew, old man.'

He stopped the torch and slung it in its harness.

'You must be tired,' he said. 'It was hard luck about the puncture. Did you think of locking the bike?'

'It's safe.'

'Trust in God and tie up your camel,' said my father.

I lay in my bed and looked at the stain on the ceiling. I wanted to think about the churches and the squares my father said you could not see for the first time without having to cry. But when I closed my eyes, the woman fell over her stockings and lay on the gravel with her bottom showing; and I stretched out my hand to touch it.

I got up and went across the landing to my parents' bedroom. In the pitch-black, I groped along the chest of drawers until I could crouch at their door, feeling the draught on my ankles. I had to be sure that my father was all right, that he was breathing.

'Cut your nails first, Bill. It hurts.'

Bill's voice: my father's voice.

'O Jesus.'

'Honour us with a verse or two, Andrew,' Fr Wilson said. 'Unless Mark objects. Do you object, Mark?'

'No, Father.'

Masterson fought his way down twelve lines, and collapsed. I had been afraid he might finish. Before class, he had smiled at me as he doodled with a pencil, tracing a coin through tissue paper. But I had kept myself to myself.

'What do you write above your exercises, Andrew?'

'What, Father?'

'The Latin, Andrew, the Latin.'

'Ad Maiorem Dei Gloriam, Father.'

'Indeed. Translate that into modern English for the sake of the uninitiated.'

'To the Greater Glory of God.'

'A bold claim, Andrew.'

Fr Wilson inspected his shoes.

'Homework,' he said. 'is not much to write home about. It's small stuff, by and large. It's not staffing the missions or tending the sick or touring the prisons. But it pleases God that you should do it for Him. To say that you're doing it for Him, and not to do so having said so, is to do what, Andrew?'

'Father.'

'It's to commit the act of a bounder. The act of a cad.'

He held up the note.

When Masterson had left the class to go to the Dean, Fr Wilson called me. I was studying my desk-lid, not looking at anyone.

'The next verse, Mark. I'll keep time on the tin whistle.'

The class was uneasy. Everybody laughed.

'Go on,' said Fr Wilson.

The seat clanged when I stood up. I thought of the woman with the stockings. I wanted to be with her. She would take her breasts out of her blouse and set my head on them; would cover my face with her hair.

> Then out spake brave Horatius,
> The captain of the gate.
> 'To every man upon this earth,
> Death cometh soon or late;
> And how can man die better
> Then facing fearful odds,
> For the ashes of his father,
> And the temples of his gods?'[7]

From the floor below, I head the splashing of the strap. For a moment, I was sorry for Andrew Masterson, and sorry that the heating had been turned off that morning so that he had gone to the Dean without burning his hands.

'Fathers,' said Fr Wilson. 'Ashes of his fathers.'

'Fathers,' I said. 'Fathers.'

7. Stanza twenty-seven of 'Horatius', a ballad by Thomas Macaulay in *The Lays of Ancient Rome* (1842) and once popular with British schoolmasters of English.

DERMOT BOLGER

(1959-)

HIS FATHER'S SON (1988)

[This story gives a view of the lives of the Dublin workingclass, although its central focus, the relationship between father and son, is not wholly determined by those social circumstances. Nevertheless, the feelings of the young man for his father are sharpened by the sense of injustice that his father and mother have had to bear.

The story was first published in *The Irish Times* on 15 July 1988. Later it was in large part incorporated in Bolger's novel *The Journey Home.*]

At Bank[1] the elevator seemed to descend for ever, a grinding, slow motion journey into hell. The air in hell was dried up; seconds after each train passed it would be blown suddenly up the concrete steps leading down to the platform. The pubs had long closed. There were few travellers now. Uncomfortable on a row of new plastic seats, a drunk tried to sleep. A girl nonchalantly read a long advertisement, an occasional tremor betraying her fear. I got the last train to Angel;[2] the West Indian who rode the lift sighed perpetually, too bored to even take my ticket.

There was a derelict feel to parts of Islington[3] which made me feel at home. But recently the area had become fashionable. Antique shops lined the old stone arcade leading to my bedsit. A boxroom — one or six in the house — with only inches separating the bed from the window and a strip of carpet, a foot long, between the bed and the wardrobe. Yet I preferred it to the more spacious high rise blocks that towered over the Victorian street. It was tiny, the noise of other tenants woke me regularly, but it was mine. For the first time a tangible space where I could close the door on the world. The local Council paid the twenty-five pound rent, the giro[4] for thirty was mine to live on. I was rich on a Thursday and starved from Tuesday on. Brown rice and vegetables were my mainstay. I swam each afternoon and ran in the local park. On my first Sunday there I saw youths jumping high to field a ball. One broke free and soloed down the field to shoot high between two clusters of jackets. After a brief conference a point was awarded. I thought I was hallucinating until I heard the accents. Now each weekend I too climbed for the high ball and joined the arguments over the erratic scoring.[5] Some days the job centre sent me for casual labour. It paid for the unbudgeted extras, shoes, an excessive electricity bill. For now I was just happy to savour the anonymity. I trusted in fate. Whether there or in Europe, work would finally come.

Two Rastas, throwing shapes[6] on the corner, nodded. On my first morning in the house I had woken to the noise of brakes, crackling radios and voices calling 'Quickly, let's go.' This is it, I thought, a police raid. Cautiously I approached the window to see the Rastas with four others running between the houses with crates of milk while music blared from the truck. Now I slept through each morning's chart attack.[7] I returned their nod and just before I reached the front door a slight figure stepped out from the laneway beside it. For a moment I thought it was his ghost, the shape was so like his I moved forward cautiously as the figure stepped from the shadows. It was his age and his build and for a second his features, yet there was something not right about them. It was as if my father's face had been taken apart and quickly reassembled with the parts slightly out of sequence. I could see him checking me too and then I realised who he was and why he was there. Several mornings after my arrival as I lay in the B&B[8] I had found his address which my mother had given me. I had studied it again and, crumpling it into a ball,

1. Bank is a station on the London Underground.
2. Angel is another Underground station in London; like Bank, it is on the Northern Line.
3. A suburban area of London.
4. A giro cheque, operated by the British Post Office.
5. He sees men playing Gaelic football, in which both hands and feet are used and points as well as goals are scored. The arguments arise because there are no real goalposts.
6. Rastafarians, members of a Jamaican cult whose beliefs and behaviour are an exotic blend of Christianity, Voodoo and other elements. They regard Ras Tafari (the former emperor of Ethiopia, Haile Selassie) as God, and are easily distinguished by their hairstyles and dress. 'Throwing shapes' means 'looking tough and street-wise'.
7. That is, music from the pop music charts, played on the radio in the milk truck.
8. Bed and Breakfast.

packed my belongings and moved on. Now my father's brother waited for me to speak.

'It's me da, isn't it?'

'You should go home Francis,' he said. 'They've taken him into hospital.'

There was little more to say. He had visited us only once, when I was four. He knew I had his address and had ignored him. He shook hands awkwardly, walked back into the darkness.

I borrowed the money for the return ticket, knowing one half of it would be wasted. But until I reached that house I still wanted to pretend that I could return to the anonymity of that single room. There was nothing to pack. The room looked as empty leaving as when I had lived there. In Dublin I paid off the taxi at the corner of the North Road. I walked up quietly across the Metal Bridge, through the streets I had played in as a child. I had a sick feeling in my stomach as though somehow everything was starting to slip away from me. My mother sat at the table in the kitchen. She had been crying. Sean, who was twelve, sat on one of the chairs, awkward, not knowing how to console her. I sent both the boys to bed, took her hands in mine, let her tell me in her own time. For months he had been complaining about the slight pain and then a small growth had surfaced. He had kept quiet about it, scared to go to the doctor. She had only seen it the previous morning when she had walked into the bathroom where he was washing. They had rowed for two hours before he went down. The doctor sent him home to get his belongings.

'He'll be okay son, won't he?' she kept asking. 'He's an awful man, leaving it so late.'

I felt numb as I sat there lying for her sake, eventually reassuring her enough to get her to sleep. I went back downstairs and walked out into the garden. It had grown long again over that summer. I should have known all along it was something like this. My father was a country man, he would never have let that garden go to waste. I would like to think that I felt sorry for him and for her. Later on I did but that night all I could feel was the sense of being trapped. I was back again where I had left, six months before, to start a new life. Twenty hours before I had walked across a foreign city, independent, musing over the possibilities of Europe or London. And now that it was suddenly too late my heart yearned out for those autobahns that lead out across that vast continent. I closed over the door and chained it as he would have done.

The hospital was due for closure. But being rundown made it seem human and comfortable. He had never missed a day sick in his life. His illness was like a vice not to be spoken of. He fretted about whether Pascal Plunkett had been told; there was no certainty his job would be kept open. Twenty years he had worked for Plunkett, starting when that suburb was still ringed with fields. Plunkett had come home from England in '61, begun selling saucepans door to door on tick,[9] forever expanding out, furniture, lino and then loans. The garage was his first legitimate venture. My father joined him the week it opened. He was still a mechanic but now Plunkett's owned half the main street of the old village. His real money was made in farmland rezoned just after he had purchased it. In return all his premises still displayed huge posters at every election.[10] But yet he clung on to every business he had ever begun. My father was right to be worried. I told him I'd move home till he was well again. He nodded, saying the course of treatment would not take long. And then my mother came nervously in. I left them there to be by themselves to say whatever words in private their fears allowed them to.

The queues had grown longer in the employment exchange, a huge heave of bodies when the doors opened. I was shunted from hatch to hatch till all the forms were sorted out. I had grown used in London to having no money in my pocket, yet somehow what had seemed an adventure there was now a source of humiliation in my native place. An old school mate told me about the petrol station. I walked out along the carriageway to it one afternoon. The manager showed me over the pumps, the floor safe for the money, and gave me three nighttime shifts starting the next week.

When he told me the wages I knew why it was black.[11] Even doing sixty hours it would be hard to survive on it. The next Wednesday morning I put the thin wad of notes in my back pocket and stayed

9. i.e. on credit.
10. In other words, Plunkett was repaying a political favour when he displayed posters since he had received information about rezoning before he bought land. This kind of corruption was especially rife in Dublin as the new housing estates were built from the 1960s on.
11. It was part of the 'black', unofficial economy. Although he took this low-paid job, he continued to draw unemployment benefit. This is illegal but widely practiced. The unemployment benefit is too low and, in these circumstances, employers can pay scandalously low wages. The petrol companies are notorious for this form of exploitation.

up walking around town till it was time to sign on.[12]

He came home after four weeks, having finished the course of treatment. It was like his insides were burnt out was all he said about it. He felt the cold more now that it was harder to walk. He cursed the fact it might be another month before he returned to work. Christmas came and he spent the morning in bed. After dinner he fell asleep before the television like an old man. I had bought my two sisters skate boards and could hear them practising on the pavement outside. My mother and I sat on either side of him, neither of us speaking as his breath came, laboured. Whenever I looked at her she lowered her eyes. I sat there till he woke, pretending to be absorbed in the television programme.

Did he know all along? That's the question that haunted me every morning going in to see him sunken more into himself in the bed. Was he pretending he might get better for our sake or had he somehow anaesthetised himself from reality? I still don't know. There was an unreality about his plans when he had recovered. Not only did he intend to do things he had been doing before he got sick, but now to also take on larger projects that he had never dreamt of before. The whole back garden was to be dug that had been a mass of weeds for three years, a holiday home in Kerry just beside the old farm was to be purchased when every penny the family had was slowly wasting away like his flesh in this illness. Yet no matter how farcical his plans his eyes always blazed into mine as he spoke with complete conviction. I had never liked that bedroom that the sun never entered until late in the evening, filled always with the noise of pigeons and dogs from the neighbouring gardens, but now I came to dread entering it as though stepping into a crypt. If the day was warm she would light a fire in the dining-room and I would help him slowly down the stairs, one at a time, his body smelling of that room where he had lain. He would sit by the fire and she would ask him the same three or four questions. Nearer the end his answers grew more blurred and sometimes out of sequence. If either noticed neither said it.

And what of her? Did she know she was soon to be a widow? To see the father I had loved waste away was a torture, but never to be able to speak of it was much worse. Often when the younger children were at school and she was in the kitchen after turning the television on loudly so that he and I were both forced to watch the idiotic movements of cartoon figures on the screen, I would wonder, as the eldest son, as the heir, was it my duty to speak, to break this torpor the house seemed to sleep under. Yet even I was terrified to say those words, to finally take away the possibility of hope. I had the need to question him about all sorts of half understood memories, holidays in that small village in Kerry, and further back to his own childhood, the names of great uncles and grandparents. I no longer wanted to see him just as a parent, but imagine him my own age or younger, out on a hillside some dark night or taking that boat to Liverpool during the war, the ammunitions factories, the money orders sent to his new wife serving as a maid in that house in Rathgar, the weekends home when they had taken the single decker bus out to that place I called home — a warren of green fields then with its tiny village — and walking out the laneway to the field where white crosses marked the outline of the first houses to be built.

It was during his third visit to hospital for radiation treatment that my mother asked me to go with her to Plunkett for the first loan. In the garage below his office each of the mechanics came over to ask for him. They had already had two whip-arounds and sent the money up. Plunkett appeared on the stairs and beckoned her up. He eyed me for a moment before I turned away and walked out among the cars in the forecourt. Eddie, the foreman, came over. He knew, like everybody else, why she was here. It was a relief to be able to talk openly to another person.

'How's your da son?'

'Fucked.'

'Does he know it?'

I shrugged my shoulders. He shook his head and smiled as though I had made a grim joke.

'Tell him I'll be over soon.'

My mother called me and I went back in. Plunkett was standing beside her at the foot of the stairs.

'Shake hands with your daddy's boss, Francis,' she said as though addressing a child.

I nodded to Plunkett. His palm was sweaty. He gripped mine hard and seemed reluctant to let it go. Perhaps he was too used to keeping everything that came into it.

12. It is necessary to 'sign on' the unemployment register, usually twice a week, in order to retain unemployment benefit.

'He was very understanding,' my mother said, as we crossed over the carriageway. 'A hundred pounds just like that.'

'At what per cent?' I asked.

She looked hurt as though I had insulted a close relative.

'He's a generous man,' she said. 'I'm sure many people take advantage of him. He'd need to add something on just to cover himself. Anyway when your daddy's back at work we'll pay that off without blinking.'

When I turned to enter the supermarket, she scolded me. 'You couldn't expect him to have that much cash on him on a Friday morning could you? No, he gave me a note for Plunkett Stores. I can buy what I like there and use the rest as credit whenever I come down again.'

The store was only quarter the size of the supermarket, the prices a good ten per cent dearer: I wheeled the trolley for her while she chose each item carefully to sustain a family of seven for the week ahead. The cashier rang a small buzzer when my mother handed her the note and a man my own age in a suit came down from the office, looked over the note and initialled it. We filled the groceries into plastic bags. He held the door open for us. My mother thanked him repeatedly and stepped out. He grinned at me, the grin of an amused fifty-year-old handing a coin to a beggar beaming out from his eighteen-year-old face.

After ten days my father came home from hospital. There was a complication the doctors had said. He had a slight dose of pneumonia and it was wiser to discontinue the treatment until he was better. His lungs were burning after the first half of the treatment but he was so delighted to be home that he rarely complained of the pain. Even in those ten days he had become more sluggish. The old man who relieved me at seven each morning in the petrol station shook his head when I told him.

'That's it son,' he said. 'It's reached the stage where there's nothing more they can do for him now. Any excuse to get him home with the demand for beds. It will be faster now. I saw it all with my missus.'

Whatever the doctors had told him in the hospital he had twisted round into a message of hope. His story had changed now. There would be no full recovery. He would just have to live with the fact he had this and maybe once a year for the rest of his life he would have to go back for that treatment. And yet he must have known because early on that first week I arrived home to find paint and brushes in the hall. I painted the front door and the windows as I was asked, while my mother knelt, shampooing the carpet in the sittingroom still used only for visitors. They were preparing themselves for the invasion which soon began, the uncles and aunts from Kerry and Donegal arriving, the bottles of Guinness and the ham sandwiches, the talk of events forty and fifty years past. Sometimes now he would begin to nod in the chair, the untouched glass of Guinness he could not drink but which was still poured for him, going flat at his elbow and the room would grow uncomfortably silent, the relations awkward in their armchairs before he would jerk back awake and ask the same question he had asked five minutes past. The room would breathe again and the same answer be delivered eagerly.

'You will be down for the Christmas, won't you. We'll have a few glasses in Farrell's' they'd say as they shook his hand and his eyes would turn bright at the thought.

'Will we? Do you think?', he'd ask with a sense of wonder in his voice and they'd laugh and say, 'Sure we'll order them now on the way back,' and then walk out into the front garden I had neatly cut the day before, knowing they would not see him again except neatly framed in a wooden box. They were good people. I wished that they were mine but they were not. Whatever world they and my father had come from had died among the rows of new streets built here and I was cut off from that past as surely as if ten generations stood between us. I know they cried silently, driving out through the long darkness of the Irish countryside, leaving behind their brother in that alien world.

The petrol station was owned by one of the largest firms in Europe. Those of us who worked nights paid no tax, no insurance. Those who demanded such things were easily got rid of. There was no shortage of workers. Often from half eleven to half two the four pumps would be engaged at the same time with a queue of local people who climbed the hill for milk and biscuits, pressing their money into the two way hatch. Drivers had to pay in advance but there was always the danger if you were distracted that they would go on pumping after their limit. Then, from half two on the weekday nights there was almost no business. You would cradle your head in your arms sitting among the humming cables or watch the video screen switch between the six cameras positioned around the station. Sometimes a taxi driver would come in at three or four to have his car washed. There was always the danger of robbery. Some weeks before I joined, two youths had arrived with an empty can, paid in two pounds, filled it up and poured it into the hatch. They held a lighted match in the air and asked politely for the money. Often by five o'clock you would not have seen a person for over an hour. Dawn would begin to break over the tombstones in the cemetery across the carriageway and I'd think of him, lying awake in pain in that bedroom while she slept or lay awake also, holding his hand, praying to that litany of saints, believing like a child their names alone could shield him from harm. Then the old man would come, I'd unlock the door to let him in and stand out in the yellow light of the courtyard, breathing in the fresh air and climb that carriageway up by the stream to the village. She would have risen, despite my protests, to have a breakfast ready for me and, when the children had left for school, I would climb into the bed in the box room with the sheets still warm from the body of my younger brother, having arranged the blanket clumsily over the curtained window.

All my wages I gave to her except ten pounds, but twice more during the final illness I made the journey with her to Plunkett Motors, shook that sweaty hand and endured the stare that seemed to say 'I will own you too soon.'

The doctor came each morning when his surgery was over. He had been born in the village before ever the estates were built. My father had been going to him for forty years. He was a gruff man, racked by illness himself. He never lied about my father's condition, neither mentioning recovery nor bringing that note of finality into the talk. Early on when I was showing him to the door and for some reason my mother had stayed behind, he simply said, 'You know, of course.' I nodded and he drove off, a list of calls neatly written on the slip of cardboard in his breast pocket.

When the time came the hospital could not send an ambulance for him because of the shortages. The doctor himself paid for the taxi. I helped him down the stairs. He grumbled about the bother of going in when he would probably be sent back home that evening. His pneumonia was no better. It was too soon to resume the treatment. I was unable to speak. I helped him negotiate each step until we were out on the concrete path. A few neighbours called across gardens to him. He raised his hand weakly to them. On the street outside I paused in case he wished to look back a final time at the house he had spent forty years working to pay for. A green expanse of fields turning slowly under concrete. He pulled at me to get him into the taxi. I knew to look back would have been to admit he was leaving for ever. She sat beside him in the back and I sat beside the driver. He kept his head trained deliberately at the driver's neck. None of us spoke on the journey. It was too far gone for us to keep the terror out of our voices.

I had begun to think of that cancer as a human thing. Like some torturer in a prison camp saying I will not break him yet. I will give some relief today or else I will turn up the pain now and see how long he will last. In my mind I began to address it on those daily visits to the hospital where my father lay drugged with pain-killers. *Don't do this,* I would say. *Have you no mercy? Can you not wait a while?* Or else *Now please, take him while he's sleeping. Spare him any more pain.* Sometimes he woke convinced he was back at home and only gradually realised, with such intense disappointment, where he was. I questioned him now more and more about the past. Often he would stare back blankly at me as though already parts of his mind were dead. There was something I desperately needed to know now while he might still answer me and yet what it was I could not get clear in my mind.

When I arrived the last evening I knew by his breathing and his face on which the skin was stretched tight as if his bones were straining to break through that this was the end. My mother was due in in an hour, after she had finished cleaning in Plunkett Undertakers. I phoned there and asked for her. There is no phone in my house. I had never spoken to her on one before and her voice sounded so different, so scared at being called to it, that I could hardly speak. I just told her to come at once and to bring the children. Then I went back. He was still asleep but woke after a time. He called my name when he saw me, began to mutter something and then found it too much effort to continue. He was very weak but relaxed, obviously the drugs had done their work and he was in no pain. Once we had been close. I remembered that long garden being dug, him working between the rucks of potato beds while I sat on the ridge, proud to be up so late watching him. I would gather the weeds he pulled and bring them over to the unlit bonfire in the corner. And then when it was almost fully dark he would send me up for the can of paraffin. I would hold the lid when he unscrewed it and poured the liquid over the weeds and shreds of clipped hedge and hold his hand, thrilled as we watched it burn together. I think he wanted it dark for that moment, to banish the city with its terraces of houses and just have himself and his son standing among the grass and the trees in the hypnotic light that seemed to close us in and cut us off from everything.

Then those adolescence years when the world beyond that garden and terrace had begun to claim me and I was lost to him. Once it was his stories that had fascinated me. Now it was music, clothes, films he could not comprehend. He would stand in my bedroom examining a record sleeve like it had dropped from another planet. For years we had hardly spoken and now I wanted all those stories back, wanted all the years that were lost to me. We were both happy for that half an hour we spent alone while he drifted in and out of consciousness. Once he woke and looked not at me but beyond my shoulder. His eyes grew blue and for an instant vivid with recognition. I cannot swear what I heard but it seemed that he whispered the names of his parents. Then his eyes faded again but his face relaxed into a smile. I did not question him. He did not speak.

It was only when my family arrived that the horror began. While I had been there alone it was possible for us both to pretend that it was just one more visit. Now as the curtains were pulled and chairs arranged around the bed there was nowhere left for that unmentionable fear to hide. My mother said a few words and then was unable to continue. She sat stiffly, her fingers clasping the handles of her bag as though they were rosary beads. My two younger sisters fidgeted, both bewildered and frightened by this silence, still with no real idea of what was happening. One had an exercise book still in her hands. He began to pluck at the sheets, desperate now to rise from the bed. His eyes were pleading with me. When I lowered my face I could hear his hoarse whisper, 'I know I'm dying son and I don't want to.' At that moment he was a man of the country, he knew that hospital beds were for death. All he wanted was to be up, to be out in the air a last time. You could visibly see him fighting to hold on. He stopped speaking after a time and just stared back as though defying death to take him. My sisters had stopped twisting. The word death had become flesh in their nine-year-old vocabularies. They held each other's hands, crying silently. His other brother arrived from across the city and I gave him my chair. My father recognised him. When he tried to say his name it was more like a gasp for air. He was trying to tell his brother something, trying, I think, to pronounce their parent's names. I knew by my uncle's face he could not understand.

Then I had to leave. I couldn't bear to be a part of that vigil anymore. I walked out into the corridor and down the steps into the courtyard. I found a cigarette and lit it. How often had I walked out into the night air? Felt it blow about me after the heat of some room? I had never realised how precious it was before. If I was stronger I could have pulled him from that bed, down that corridor and out onto the damp grass to die beneath the clouds. Instead he was caged behind those curtains, chained to drips and meters that could not save him now and all I could do was stand here and experience the cold nocturnal breeze, the lights filtering out over the loose gravel, and inhale the rough taste of tobacco. I smoked it for him, knowing by some instinct that when its light had burnt out his life would have gone. When it had burnt down I cradled the tip between my palms till the wind had blown each loose red worm of ash away. My uncle's hand was on my shoulder. It felt for a moment like my father's. Then I realised I had no recollection of him ever touching me, except those nights years before walking up from the garden. I patted it to thank him for telling me, then walked out into the darkness and cried.

Biographies/Bibliographies

Francis Stuart

LIFE. Francis Stuart was born of Ulster parents in Townsville, Australia in 1902. Upon the death of his father the same year, his mother took him to Ireland. He spent his boyhood near Drogheda, then in Dublin. From 1912 until 1918 he attended various boarding schools in England, including Rugby. Back in Ireland, he met Maud Gonne, and her daughter, Iseult, whom he married in 1920. During the Irish Civil War he was active on the republican side and was captured by Free State forces and interned until November 1923. His first book, a volume of poems, appeared in 1924 and was praised by Yeats. In the 1930s he published eleven novels, including *Pigeon Irish* and *The Coloured Dome*. Between 1940 and 1945 he was lecturer in modern English at Berlin University; he was sympathetic to the Nazi cause and wrote propaganda talks for German radio aimed at England, some of them read by Lord Haw Haw (William Joyce). Stuart was arrested after the war by the French; after early release from prison, he lived successively in Germany (where he wrote *Redemption*), France and England. He did not return to Ireland until 1958. In 1971 his most famous novel, *Black List, Section H*, was published. This signalled a late productive phase, and in his seventies and eighties, Stuart's fictional powers were in spate.

CHIEF WRITINGS. (Novels) *Women and God* (London: Cape, 1931); *Pigeon Irish* (London: Gollancz, 1932); *The Coloured Dome* (London: Gollancz, 1932); *The Angel of Pity* (London: Grayson & Grayson, 1935); *The Pillar of Cloud* (London: Gollancz, 1948); *Redemption* (London: Gollancz, 1949); *Victors and Vanquished* (London: Gollancz, 1958; Cleveland: Pennington Press, 1959; London: Martin Brian & O'Keeffe, 1974); *Black List, Section H* (Carbondale: Southern Illinois University Press, 1971); *Memorial* (London: Martin Brian & O'Keeffe, 1973); *A Hole in the Head* (London: Martin Brian & O'Keeffe, 1977); *The High Consistory* (London: Martin Brian & O'Keeffe, 1981); *States of Mind: Selected Short Prose 1936-83* (Dublin: Raven Arts Press; London: Martin Brian & O'Keeffe, 1984); *Faillandia* (Dublin: Raven Arts Press, 1985); *A Compendium of Lovers* (Dublin: Raven Arts Press, 1990).

(Other Writings) *We Have Kept the Faith — New and Selected Poems* (Dublin: Raven Arts Press, 1982); *The Abandoned Snail Shell* (Dublin: Raven Arts Press, 1987).

BIOGRAPHY AND CRITICISM. W.J. Mc Cormack (ed.), *A Festschrift for Francis Stuart on His Seventieth Birthday* (Dublin: Dolmen Press, 1972); J.H. Natterstad, *Francis Stuart* (Lewisburg, Pennsylvania: Bucknell University Press, 1974); Patrick Rafroidi and Maurice Harmon (eds), *The Irish Novel in Our Time* (Lille: Publications de l'Université de Lille III, 1975-76), pp. 157-83; J.H. Natterstad (ed.), *The Journal of Irish Literature* (A Francis Stuart Number), 5 (January 1976); Madeleine Stuart, *Manna in the Morning: A Memoir 1940-1958* (Dublin: Raven Arts Press, 1984); Francis Molloy, 'The Life of Francis Stuart: Questions and Some Answers', *Biography* 10 (Spring 1987), 129-41; Kevin Honan, 'Refloating the Ark: Figural Motifs in the Writings of Francis Stuart', *The Irish Review* 4 (Spring 1988), 66-72; Geoffrey Elborn, *Francis Stuart — A Life* (Dublin: Raven Arts Press, 1990).

Patrick Boyle

LIFE. Patrick Boyle was born in Ballymoney, Co. Antrim in 1905. For forty-five years he worked for the Ulster Bank, in Derry, Tyrone and Donegal, and eventually became a bank manager in Wexford. He began writing in his mid-seventies but later stopped for seventeen years. Breakthrough did not come until the early 1960s when a story in *The Evergreen Review* aroused the interest of publishers. Boyle subsequently published a novel and three collections of stories. He died in Dublin in 1982.

CHIEF WRITINGS. (Novel) *Like Any Other Man* (London: MacGibbon & Kee, 1966).

(Stories) *At Night All Cats Are Grey And Other Stories* (London: MacGibbon & Kee, 1966); *All Looks Yellow to the Jaundiced Eye* (London: MacGibbon & Kee, 1969); *A View from Calvary* (London: Gollancz, 1976).

BIOGRAPHY AND CRITICISM. John Wilson Foster, *Forces and Themes in Ulster Fiction* (Dublin: Gill and Macmillan, 1974), pp. 100-11; Henri-Dominque Paratte, 'Patrick Boyle's Tragic Humanity' in Patrick Rafroidi and Terence Brown (eds), *The Irish Short Story* (Gerrards Cross, Bucks.: Colin Smythe, 1979), pp. 275-87; John G. Hynes, 'Patrick Boyle's *Like Any Other Man*: A Critical Evaluation', *Études Irlandaises* 12 (December 1987), 87-94.

Janet McNeill

LIFE. Janet McNeill was born in Dublin in 1907. She was educated in England and Scotland (receiving an MA from St Andrew's University), then worked as a journalist in Belfast until her marriage. Besides producing a quiet stream of novels, plays and children's books, she was chairwoman of the Belfast centre of the Irish branch of PEN, and served the BBC in an advisory capacity. After many years in Belfast, she moved to Bristol.

CHIEF WRITINGS. (Novels) *A Child in the House* (London: Hodder and Stoughton, 1955); *As Strangers Here* (London: Hodder and Stoughton, 1960); *The Early Harvest* (London: Geoffrey Bles, 1962); *The Maiden Dinosaur* (London: Geoffrey Bles, 1964; Belfast: Blackstaff Press; Dublin: Arlen House, 1984); *Talk to Me* (London: Geoffrey Bles, 1965); *The Small Widow* (London: Geoffrey Bles, 1967).

BIOGRAPHY AND CRITICISM. John Wilson Foster, *Forces and Themes in Ulster Fiction* (Dublin: Gill and Macmillan, 1974), pp. 228-43.

Michael J. Murphy

LIFE. Michael J. Murphy was born in Liverpool of south Armagh parents in 1913. He was taken to Armagh in 1922 where he was educated until he left school at fourteen to work for farmers. Murphy began to broadcast as a freelance with the BBC and Radio Éireann. He joined the Irish Folklore Commission in 1942, and later became a member of the Department of Irish Folklore at University College, Dublin. Murphy was a celebrated collector of folklore and published numerous volumes, as well as making broadcasts and writing articles. He also wrote plays.

CHIEF WRITINGS. *At Slieve Gullion's Foot* (Dundalk: Dundalgan Press, 1940); *Mountain Year* (Dublin: Dolmen Press; Chester Springs, Pennsylvania: Dufour Editions, 1964, 2nd edition Dundalk: Dundalgan Press, 1975); *Tyrone Folkquest* (Belfast: Blackstaff Press, 1973); *Now You're Talking: Folk Tales from the North of Ireland* (Belfast: Blackstaff Press, 1975); *Mountainy Crack* (Belfast: Blackstaff Press, 1976).

Benedict Kiely

LIFE. Benedict Kiely was born near Dromore, Co. Tyrone in 1919. He was educated by the Christian Brothers in Omagh. In 1937 he entered the Jesuit novitiate in County Laois, but during a lengthy convalescence from a tubercular spinal ailment the following year, he decided not to answer the call to clerical life. Instead he enrolled at the National University in Dublin, from which he graduated with a BA in 1943. From 1945 until 1964, Kiely was a Dublin journalist with, successively, *The Standard*, the *Irish Independent* and *The Irish Press*. Between 1964 and 1968 he was a visiting professor of creative writing at universities in Virginia, Oregon and Georgia. He returned to Dublin and lectured at University College, Dublin, and then became a full-time writer of novels, stories, newspaper features and reviews, as well as a radio and television broadcaster.

CHIEF WRITINGS. (Novels) *Land Without Stars* (London: Christopher Johnson, 1946); *In a Harbour Green* (London: Cape, 1949); *Call for a Miracle* (London: Cape, 1950); *Honey Seems Bitter* (New York: Dutton, 1952); *The Cards of the Gambler* (London: Methuen, 1953); *There Was an Ancient House* (London: Methuen, 1955); *The Captain with the Whiskers* (London: Methuen, 1960); *Dogs Enjoy the Morning* (London: Gollancz, 1968); *Proxopera* (London: Gollancz, 1977); *Nothing Happens in Carmincross* (London: Gollancz, 1985).

(Stories) *A Journey to the Seven Streams* (London: Methuen, 1963); *A Ball of Malt and Madame Butterfly* (London: Gollancz, 1973); *A Cow in the House* (London: Gollancz, 1978); *A Letter to Peachtree* (London: Gollancz, 1987).

(Non-Fiction) *Poor Scholar: A Study of the Works and Days of William Carleton* (London and New York: Sheed & Ward, 1947); *Modern Irish Fiction — A Critique* (Dublin: Golden Eagle, 1950); *All the Way to Bantry Bay — and Other Irish Journeys* (London: Gollancz, 1978); *Yeats's Ireland: An Illustrated Anthology* (London: Aurum Press, 1989).

BIOGRAPHY AND CRITICISM. Daniel J. Casey, *Benedict Kiely* (Lewisburg, Pennsylvania: Bucknell University Press, 1974); John

Wilson Foster, *Forces and Themes in Ulster Fiction* (Dublin: Gill and Macmillan, 1974), pp. 72-78, 91-100; Grace Eckley, *Benedict Kiely* (New York: Twayne, 1975); Jennifer Clarke, 'An Interview with Benedict Kiely', *Irish Literary Supplement* (Spring 1987), 10-12.

James Plunkett

LIFE. James Plunkett, pseudonym of James Plunkett Kelly, was born in Dublin in 1920. He was educated by the Christian Brothers and attended the College of Music for many years; he also played interprovincial Gaelic football. While he was a clerk in the Dublin Gas Company, he became an active trade union official, working for a short time under Jim Larkin. He visited the Soviet Union in 1955 through an invitation of *The Bell.* Plunkett joined Radio Telefís Éireann that same year, and also published his first book of stories, to acclaim by Frank O'Connor. There have been novels, plays and stories, but it was the sweeping historical novel, *Strumpet City* (1969), a novel of early twentieth-century Dublin, that brought him fame; it was successfully televised. Since retiring from RTE, Plunkett has lived in Kilmacanogue, Co. Wicklow.

CHIEF WRITINGS. (Stories) *The Trusting and the Maimed* (New York: Devin-Adair, 1955; London: Hutchinson, 1959); *Collected Short Stories* (Swords, Co. Dublin: Poolbeg Press, 1977).

(Novels) *Strumpet City* (London: Hutchinson, 1969); *Farewell Companions* (London: Hutchinson, 1977); *The Circus Animals* (London: Hutchinson, 1990).

(Play) *Big Jim* (Dublin: Martin O'Donnell, 1955).

BIOGRAPHY AND CRITICISM. Thomas MacIntyre, 'Some Notes on the Stories of James Plunkett', *Studies* XLVI (Autumn 1958), 323-37; James M. Cahalan, *Great Hatred, Little Room: The Irish Historical Novel* (Syracuse: Syracuse University Press, 1983), pp. 177-90; James M. Cahalan, 'James Plunkett: An Interview', *Irish Literary Supplement* (Spring 1986), 9-11.

Brian Moore

LIFE. Brian Moore was born in Belfast in 1921. He left Northern Ireland in 1943 when he joined the British Ministry of War Transport during World War II; he was stationed briefly in North Africa, Italy and France. In 1948 he emigrated to Canada and there took out citizenship. He spent several years as a journalist and struggling fiction writer in Montreal. In 1955 he published his first novel, *The Lonely Passion of Judith Hearne*, to critical acclaim. In 1959, a year before he won the Governor General of Canada's Award for Fiction (for *The Luck of Ginger Coffey*, a novel set in Montreal), he went to New York on a Guggenheim grant and decided to live there. Later he moved to Malibu, California, all the while maintaining a steady output of novels, well received by readers and critics alike. He has also written film scripts, including one for Alfred Hitchcock.

CHIEF WRITINGS. (Novels) *The Lonely Passion of Judith Hearne* (London: André Deutsch, 1955); *The Feast of Lupercal* (London: Deutsch, 1959); *The Luck of Ginger Coffey* (London: Deutsch, 1960); *An Answer from Limbo* (London: Deutsch, 1962); *The Emperor of Ice-Cream* (New York: Viking, 1965); *I Am Mary Dunne* (New York: Viking, 1968); *Fergus* (New York: Viking, 1971); *Catholics* (London: Cape, 1972); *The Great Victorian Collection* (London: Cape, 1975); *The Doctor's Wife* (London: Cape, 1976); *The Mangan Inheritance* (London: Cape, 1979; *The Temptation of Eileen Hughes* (London: Cape, 1981); *Cold Heaven* (New York: Holt, Rinehart and Winston, 1983); *Black Robe* (New York: Dutton, 1985); *The Colour of Blood* (Toronto: McClelland and Stewart, 1987); *Lies of Silence* (London: Bloomsbury, 1990).

BIOGRAPHY AND CRITICISM. Hallvard Dahlie, *Brian Moore* (Toronto: Copp Clark, 1969); John Wilson Foster, *Forces and Themes in Ulster Fiction* (Dublin: Gill and Macmillan, 1974), pp. 122-30, 151-85; Jeanne Flood, *Brian Moore* (Lewisburg, Pennsylvania: Bucknell University Press, 1974); Kerry McSweeney, *Four Contemporary Novelists* (Kingston, Ontario: McGill-Queen's University Press, 1983); John Wilson Foster, 'An Interview with Brian Moore', *Irish Literary Supplement* (Fall 1985), 44-45; Christopher Murray (ed.), *Irish University Review* (A Brian Moore Special Issue), 18 (Spring 1988).

Val Mulkerns

LIFE. Val Mulkerns was born in Dublin in 1925. She was educated at the Dominican College there, then worked as a civil servant between 1945 and 1949. From 1952 to 1954 she was an associate editor of *The Bell.* Among her novels, *The Summerhouse* won the Allied Irish Banks Prize for Literature in 1984. She lives in Dublin.

CHIEF WRITINGS. (Novels) *A Time Outworn* (London: Chatto & Windus, 1951); *A Peacock Cry* (London: Hodder and Stoughton, 1954); *The Summerhouse* (London: John Murray, 1984); *Very Like a Whale* (London: John Murray, 1986).

(Stories) *Antiquities* (London: André Deutsch, 1978); *An Idle Woman and Other Stories* (Swords, Co. Dublin: Poolbeg Press, 1980); *A Friend of Don Juan* (London: John Murray, 1988).

Aidan Higgins

LIFE. Aidan Higgins was born in Celbridge, Co. Kildare in 1927 and grew up in a Georgian house on a farm. He was educated at Clongowes Wood College, Joyce's alma mater. His family lived successively in Greystones, Dalkey and Dun Laoghaire. After Clongowes, Higgins worked at a variety of jobs in England and toured with a marionette company in Europe, Rhodesia and in South Africa, where he stayed for two years. Thereafter he lived in Spain, Germany, London and then Ireland (Connemara and County Cork). These various places became settings for his stories, travel books and novels. He won the James Tait Black Memorial Prize in 1961.

CHIEF WRITINGS. (Stories) *Felo de Se* (London: Calder and Boyers, 1961; reprinted as *Killachter Meadow*, New York: Grove Press, 1961); *Helsingør Station & Other Departures* (London: Secker & Warburg, 1989).

(Novels) *Langrishe, Go Down* (London: Calder and Boyars, 1966); *Balcony of Europe* (London: Calder and Boyars, 1972); *Scenes from a Receding Past* (London: Calder, 1977); *Bornholm Night-Ferry* (London: Allison & Busby, 1983).

(Travel) *Images of Africa 1956-60* (London: Calder and Boyars, 1971); *Ronda Gorge and Other Precipices* (London: Secker & Warburg, 1989).

Robert Harbinson

LIFE. Harbinson was born Robert Harbinson Bryans in Belfast in 1928. After a boyhood in working-class Belfast, he became a world traveller, publishing numerous travel guides under the pen-name Robin Bryans. The best account of his early life is to be found in his four-volume autobiography, written under a second pen-name, Robert Harbinson, as were a number of short stories. He lives in Sussex.

CHIEF WRITINGS. (Autobiographies) *No Surrender: An Ulster Childhood* (London: Faber and Faber, 1960); *Song of Erne* (London: Faber and Faber, 1960); *Up Spake the Cabin Boy* (London: Faber and Faber, 1961); *The Protégé* (London: Faber and Faber, 1963). All these books were reprinted by Blackstaff Press (Belfast) in 1988.

(Stories) *Tattoo Lily, and Other Ulster Stories* (London: Faber and Faber, 1961); *The Far World and Other Stories* (London: Faber and Faber, 1962).

William Trevor

LIFE. William Trevor was born William Trevor Cox in Mitchelstown, Co. Cork in 1928. He was educated at Trinity College, Dublin and was a sculptor before becoming a writer. His stories and novels have won many awards, including the Hawthornden Prize, the Whitbread Prize for Fiction, and the Allied Irish Banks Prize. He has written and adapted work for television. He lives in Devon.

CHIEF WRITINGS. (Novels) *The Old Boys* (London: Bodley Head, 1964); *The Boarding-House* (London: Bodley Head, 1965); *The Love Department* (London: Bodley Head, 1966); *Mrs Eckdorf in O'Neill's Hotel* (London: Bodley Head, 1969); *Miss Gomez and the Brethren* (London: Bodley Head, 1971); *Elizabeth Alone* (London: Bodley Head, 1973); *The Children of Dynmouth* (London: Bodley Head, 1976); *Other People's Worlds* (London: Bodley Head, 1980); *Fools of Fortune* (London: Bodley Head, 1983); *The Silence in the Garden* (London: Bodley Head, 1988).

(Stories) *The Day We Got Drunk on Cake* (London: Bodley Head, 1967); *The Ballroom of Romance* (London: Bodley Head, 1972); *Angels at the Ritz* (London: Bodley Head, 1975); *Lovers of Their Time* (London: Bodley Head, 1978); *Beyond the Pale and Other Stories* (London: Bodley Head, 1981); *The News from Ireland* (London: Bodley Head, 1986); *Family Sins and Other Stories* (London: Bodley Head, 1989).

BIOGRAPHY AND CRITICISM. Mark Mortimer, 'William Trevor in Dublin', *Études Irlandaises* 4 (November 1975), 77-85; John J. Stinson, 'Replicas, Foils and Revelation in William Trevor', *The Canadian Journal of Irish Studies* 12 (December 1985), 17-26; Jacqueline Stahl Aronson, 'William Trevor: An Interview', *Irish Literary Supplement* (Spring 1986), 7-8; G. A. Schirmer, *William Trevor: A Study of His Novels* (London and New York: Routledge, 1990).

Leland Bardwell

LIFE. Leland Bardwell was born in India of Irish parents in 1928. However, she grew up in Leixlip, Co. Kildare and was educated in Dublin. For a time she was a teacher in Scotland, and has lived in Paris and London. Playwright, novelist and short-story writer, she has been an editor of *Cyphers*, a Dublin literary magazine.

CHIEF WRITINGS. (Poems) *The Mad Cyclist* (Dublin: New Writers' Press, 1970); *The Fly and the Bed Bug* (Dublin: Beaver Row, 1984).

(Novels) *Girl on a Bicycle* (Dublin: Co-op Books, 1977); *The House* (Dingle, Co. Kerry: Brandon Press, 1984); *There We Have Been* (Dublin: Attic Press, 1989).

(Stories) *Different Kinds of Love* (Dublin: Attic Press, 1987).

John Morrow

LIFE. John Morrow was born in Belfast in 1930. He left school at fourteen to work in the shipyard; he served an apprenticeship in the linen trade and was also a navvy, furniture salesman and insurance agent. His short stories began to appear in literary magazines in the late 1960s. Morrow has been community arts officer with the Arts Council of Northern Ireland, and lives in Belfast.

CHIEF WRITINGS. (Novels) *The Confessions of Proinsias O'Toole* (Belfast: Blackstaff Press, 1977); *The Essex Factor* (Belfast: Blackstaff Press, 1982).

(Stories) *Northern Myths* (Belfast: Blackstaff Press, 1979); *Sects and Other Stories* (London: Black Swan, 1987).

Jennifer Johnston

LIFE. Born in Dublin in 1930 to the playwright Denis Johnston and the actress and theatre director Shelah Richards. She was educated at Trinity College, Dublin and has lived in Northern Ireland since 1951. She was forty-two when she published her first novel, but has since then produced a steady flow of novels and plays.

CHIEF WRITINGS. *The Captains and the Kings* (London: Hamish Hamilton, 1972); *The Gates* (London: Hamish Hamilton, 1973); *How Many Miles to Babylon?* (London: Hamish Hamilton, 1974); *Shadows On Our Skin* (London: Hamish Hamilton, 1977); *The Old Jest* (London: Hamish Hamilton, 1979); *The Christmas Tree* (London: Hamish Hamilton, 1981); *The Railway-Station Man* (London: Hamish Hamilton, 1984); *Fool's Sanctuary* (London: Hamish Hamilton, 1987).

BIOGRAPHY AND CRITICISM. B. Donnelly, 'The Big House in the Recent Novel', *Studies* 64 (1975), 133-42; B. O'Toole, 'Three Writers of the Big House: Elizabeth Bowen, Molly Keane, and Jennifer Johnston' in G. Dawe and E. Longley (eds), *Across A Roaring Hill: The Protestant Imagination in Modern Ireland* (Belfast: Blackstaff Press, 1985), pp. 124-38; J. M. Cahalan, *The Irish Novel: A Critical History* (Dublin: Gill and Macmillan, 1988), pp. 291-93.

Eugene McCabe

For biography and bibliography, see page 1305.

Edna O'Brien

LIFE. Edna O'Brien was born in Tuamgraney, Co. Clare in 1932. She was brought up on a farm and educated at the Convent of Mercy in Loughrea, Co. Galway, and at the Pharmaceutical College in Dublin. She moved to England in 1958 where she published her first novel, *The Country Girls*, two years later. As well as enjoying a large popular reputation as a novelist, she is also something of a celebrity. She lives in London but returns often to Ireland.

CHIEF WRITINGS. (Novels) *The Country Girls* (London: Hutchinson, 1960); *The Lonely Girl* (London: Cape, 1962); *Girls in Their Married Bliss* (London: Cape, 1964); *August is a Wicked Month* (London: Cape, 1965); *Casualties of Peace* (London: Cape, 1966); *A Pagan Place* (London: Weidenfeld & Nicolson, 1970); *Night* (London: Weidenfeld & Nicolson, 1972); *Johnny I Hardly Knew You* (London: Weidenfeld & Nicolson, 1977); *The High Road* (London: Weidenfeld & Nicolson, 1988).

(Stories) *The Love Object* (London: Cape, 1968); *A Scandalous Woman and Other Stories* (London: Weidenfeld & Nicolson, 1974); *Mrs Reinhardt and Other Stories* (London: Weidenfeld & Nicolson, 1978); *Returning: A Collection of Tales* (London: Weidenfeld & Nicolson, 1982); *A Fanatic Heart: Selected Stories* (New York: Farrar, Straus & Giroux, 1984); *Lantern Slides* (London: Weidenfeld & Nicolson; New York: Farrar, Straus & Giroux, 1990).

BIOGRAPHY AND CRITICISM. Grace Eckley, *Edna O'Brien* (Lewisburg, Pennsylvania: Bucknell University Press, 1974); Shusha Guppy, Interview with Edna O'Brien, *Paris Review* 92 (Summer 1984), 22-50; James M. Haule, 'Tough Luck: The Unfortunate Birth of Edna O'Brien', *Colby Library Quarterly* 23 (December 1987), 216-24; Peggy O'Brien, 'The Silly and the Serious: An Assessment of Edna O'Brien', *Massachusetts Review* 28 (Autumn 1987), 474-88.

Julia O'Faoláin

LIFE. Julia O'Faoláin was born in London in 1932. The daughter of Seán and Eileen O'Faoláin, she was brought up in Dublin and educated there. After graduating from University College, Dublin, she continued her education in Rome and Paris. She then lived for several years in Florence (where she married an American historian) and now commutes between London and Los Angeles. She has worked as a teacher of languages and as a translator and interpreter.

CHIEF WRITINGS. (Novels) *Godded and Codded* (London: Faber and Faber, 1970); *Women in the Wall* (London: Faber and Faber, 1975); *No*

Country for Young Men (London: Allen Lane, 1980); *The Obedient Wife* (Harmondsworth: Penguin Books, 1982); *The Irish Signorina* (New York: Viking Press, 1984).

(Stories) *We Might See Signs* (London: Faber and Faber, 1968); *Man in the Cellar* (London: Faber and Faber, 1974); *Daughters of Passion* (Harmondsworth: Penguin Books, 1982).

John McGahern

LIFE. John McGahern was born in Dublin in 1934. His father was a senior police officer. McGahern was raised in County Roscommon, and was educated in County Leitrim and at University College, Dublin. He taught in County Dublin for seven years, during which time he published his first novel. His second novel, *The Dark*, written during a leave of absence, aroused great controversy and was banned in the Republic of Ireland; McGahern's contract as a teacher was not renewed. He moved to London and has since lived in Spain, the United States, England, and County Leitrim. He has been a lecturer at various British and American universities.

CHIEF WRITINGS. (Novels) *The Barracks* (London: Faber and Faber, 1963); *The Dark* (London: Faber and Faber, 1965); *The Leavetaking* (London: Faber and Faber, 1974); *The Pornographer* (London: Faber and Faber, 1979); *Amongst Women* (London: Faber and Faber, 1990).

(Stories) *Nightlines* (London: Faber and Faber, 1970); *Getting Through* (London: Faber and Faber, 1978); *High Ground* (London: Faber and Faber, 1985).

BIOGRAPHY AND CRITICISM. Roger Garfitt, 'Constants in Contemporary Irish Fiction' in Douglas Dunn (ed.), *Two Decades of Irish Writing* (Chester Springs, Pennsylvania: Dufour Editions, 1975), pp. 207-11, 221-24; Grattan Freyer, 'Change Naturally: The Fiction of O'Flaherty, O'Faoláin, McGahern', *Éire-Ireland* 18 (Spring 1983), 138-45; Shaun O'Connell, 'Door into Light: John McGahern's Ireland', *Massachusetts Review* 25 (Summer 1984), 255-68; Karlheinz Schwartz, 'John McGahern's Point of View', *Éire-Ireland* 19 (Fall 1984), 92-110.

Patrick McGinley

LIFE. Born in Donegal in 1937 and educated at University College, Galway, Patrick McGinley taught in Ireland for four years before moving to London, where he took up a career in publishing. He now lives with his family in Kent.

CHIEF WRITINGS. *Bogmail* (London: Martin Brian & O'Keeffe, 1978; Fontana, 1986); *Goosefoot* (London: Weidenfeld & Nicolson, 1982; Fontana, 1984) retitled *The Fantasist* (London: Weidenfeld & Nicolson, 1982; Collins, Flamingo, 1987); *Foggage* (New York: St Martin's Press, 1983; London: Jonathan Cape, 1984; Fontana, 1985); *The Trick of the Ga Bolga* (London: Jonathan Cape, 1985); *The Red Men* (London: Jonathan Cape, 1987; Flamingo, 1988); *The Devil's Diary* (London: Jonathan Cape, 1988; Flamingo, 1989).

Bernard MacLaverty

LIFE. Bernard MacLaverty was born in Belfast in 1942. He was educated in Belfast and worked for ten years as a medical laboratory technician before reading English at Queen's University, Belfast, from which he graduated in 1974. He then moved to Scotland and taught for some years before resigning to become a full-time writer. He lives on the Isle of Islay.

CHIEF WRITINGS. (Novels) *Cal* (London: Cape, 1983); *Lamb* (London: Cape, 1980).

(Stories) *Secrets and Other Stories* (Belfast: Blackstaff Press, 1977); *A Time to Dance* (London: Cape, 1982); *The Great Profundo* (London: Cape, 1987).

BIOGRAPHY AND CRITICISM. Arnold Saxton, 'An Introduction to the Stories of Bernard MacLaverty', *Journal of the Short Story* 8 (Spring 1987), 113-23.

Ita Daly

LIFE. Ita Daly was born in County Leitrim in 1944. She was educated at University College, Dublin, is married to the literary editor and novelist David Marcus and lives in Dublin. She has won the Hennessy Literary Award twice and in 1975 won *The Irish Times* short story competition.

CHIEF WRITINGS. (Novels) *Ellen* (London: Cape, 1986); *A Singular Attraction* (London: Cape, 1987); *Dangerous Fictions* (London: Bloomsbury, 1989).

(Stories) *The Lady with the Red Shoes* (Swords, Co. Dublin: Poolbeg Press, 1980).

John Banville

LIFE. John Banville was born in Wexford in 1945. He was educated by the Christian Brothers and at St Peter's College in Wexford. He worked as a sub-editor on *The Irish Press* until 1984 and was appointed literary editor of *The Irish Times* in 1988. His first book was published in 1970, and later novels won the Allied Irish Banks Prize, the American-Irish Foundation Literary Award, and the James Tait Black Memorial Prize. In 1989 he was shortlisted for the Booker Prize for his novel *The Book of Evidence* and, for the same novel, won the Guinness Peat Aviation Literary Award in the same year. He is a member of the Irish Arts Council and lives in Howth, Co. Dublin.

CHIEF WRITINGS. *Long Lankin* (London: Secker and Warburg, 1970; revised edition Dublin: The Gallery Press, 1984); *Nightspawn* (London: Secker and Warburg; New York: W. W. Norton, 1971); *Birchwood* (London: Secker and Warburg, 1973; London: Panther, 1984); *Doctor Copernicus* (London: Secker and Warburg, 1976; Frogmore, St Albans: Granada, 1983; New York: W. W. Norton, 1976; Boston: Godine, 1984); *Kepler* (London: Secker and Warburg, 1981; London: Granada, 1983; Boston: Godine, 1983 and 1984); *The Newton Letter* (London: Secker and Warburg, 1982; London: Granada, 1984; Boston: Godine, 1987); *Mefisto* (London: Secker and Warburg, 1986; London: Grafton Books, 1987); *The Book of Evidence* (London: Secker and Warburg, 1989).

BIOGRAPHY AND CRITICISM. S. Deane, '"Be Assured I Am Inventing": The Fiction of John Banville' in P. Rafroidi and M. Harmon (eds), *The Irish Novel in Our Time* (Lille: Publications de l'Université de Lille, 1975-76), pp. 329-38; D. McCormick, 'John Banville: Literature As Criticism', *The Irish Review* 2 (1987), 95-99; J. McMinn, 'An Exalted Naming: The Poetical Fictions of John Banville', *The Canadian Journal of Irish Literature*, 143, I (July 1988), 17-27; R. Imhof, *John Banville. A Critical Introduction* (Dublin: Wolfhound Press, 1989); J. McMinn, *John Banville: A Critical Study* (Dublin: Gill and Macmillan, 1990).

Dermot Healy

LIFE. Dermot Healy was born in Finea, Co. Westmeath in 1947. He has lived in Cavan, Dublin and London. He won two Hennessy Literary Awards, in 1974 and 1976. For a time he edited a Cavan-based literary and local history magazine, *The Drumlin*. Healy has directed and acted in a number of plays and films. He now lives in London.

CHIEF WRITINGS. *Banished Misfortune and Other Stories* (Dingle, Co. Kerry; Brandon Books; London: Allison & Busby Ltd, 1982); *Fighting With Shadows; or Sciamachy* (Dingle: Brandon Books; London: Allison & Busby, 1984); *The Goat's Song* (London: Collins Harvill, 1990).

Neil Jordan

LIFE. Neil Jordan was born in Sligo in 1951. He worked as a labourer and teacher and began his creative career by writing short stories. In 1974 he established the Irish Writers' Co-operative. He worked with various theatre groups, travelling in Ireland, England and America, and has had plays produced. Latterly he has become a noted screenplay writer and director of well-received films, including *Angel*, *Company of Wolves* and *Mona Lisa*. He lives in Bray, Co. Wicklow.

CHIEF WRITINGS. (Novels) *The Past* (London: Cape, 1980); *The Dream of a Beast* (London: Chatto & Windus, 1983; London: Hogarth Press, 1989).

(Stories) *Night in Tunisia and Other Stories* (Dublin: Irish Writers' Co-operative, 1976; London: Hogarth Press,1989).

Ronan Sheehan

LIFE. Born in Dublin in 1953, Ronan Sheehan was educated at Gonzaga College and at University College, Dublin. After graduating, he studied at the Incorporated Law Society, Dublin 1976-80. He was a member of the Irish Writers' Co-operative 1975-80 and a member of the editorial board of *The Crane Bag* journal. In 1984 he was awarded the Rooney Prize for Literature. He lives in Dublin.

CHIEF WRITINGS. *Tennis Player* (Dublin: Co-op Books, 1977); *Boy With an Injured Eye* (Dingle, Co. Kerry: Brandon Press, 1983); *The Heart of the City* (Dingle: Brandon Press, 1988).

Aidan Mathews

For biography and bibliography, see page 1436.

Dermot Bolger

LIFE. Dermot Bolger was born in Finglas, in north Dublin in 1959. He worked as a factory hand and a library assistant and now runs the Raven Arts Press. His trilogy of Dublin life, *Night Shift*, *The Woman's Daughter*, and *The Journey Home* has received the AE Memorial Award, the Macaulay Fellowship and the *Sunday Tribune* Arts Award. His play, *The Lament for Arthur Cleary*, was one of the successes of the 1989 Dublin Theatre Festival. His most recent play is *Blinded by the Light* (1990). He is a member of the Arts Council of Ireland.

CHIEF WRITINGS. *Never A Dull Moment* (Dublin: Raven Arts Press, 1979); *The Habit of Flesh* (Dublin: Raven Arts Press, 1980); *Finglas Lilies* (Dublin: Raven Arts Press,1981); *No Waiting America* (Dublin: Raven Arts Press, 1982); *Night Shift* (Dingle, Co. Kerry: Brandon Books, 1985); (with M. O. Loughlin), *A New Primer for Irish Schools* (Dublin: Raven Arts Press, 1985); *Internal Exiles: Poems* (Mountrath, Co. Laois: Dolmen Press, 1986); (ed.), *The Bright Wave/An Tonn Gheal: Poetry in Irish Now* (Dublin: Raven Arts Press, 1986); *The Woman's Daughter: A Novel* (Dublin: Raven Arts Press, 1987); *Invisible Cities: The New Dubliners* (Dublin: Raven Arts Press, 1988); *Leinster Street Ghosts* (Dublin: Raven Arts Press, 1989); *The Journey Home* (London: Viking, 1990).

D.E.S. MAXWELL, *Editor*

Contemporary Drama 1953-1986

The original Abbey Theatre burned down in 1951. For the next fifteen years the company occupied the dilapidated Queen's Theatre, an exile widely interpreted as a fit judgment on its degeneration. Such complaint was far from new. The 1940s and 1950s, however, had been notoriously drab. The war years had provided a captive audience. Thereafter, the Abbey did not have enough popular plays to fill the Queen's large auditorium with a succession of short runs, its normal practice. Long runs of popular new plays — a diminishing number — and revivals took over. Standards of acting and production had declined. Tomás MacAnna recalls 'the grim, grey similarity of the plays that went on at the Queen's.'

In the mid-1950s Alan and Carolyn Simpson's tiny Pike Theatre presented the meteoric Behan (*The Quare Fellow* in 1954) and the absentee Beckett (*Waiting for Godot* in 1955). These plays had a largely symbolic value and instigated no sudden resurgence of Irish theatre; yet they perhaps have a place in whatever pattern of forces — or the operation of mere chance — did generate the dramatic revival of the 1960s.

Television was very probably an agent. The BBC, immune to Irish censorship, became widely available in 1953 with the construction of the Divis transmitter in the North. Radio Telefís Éireann opened in 1961. The Dublin Theatre Festival, inaugurated in 1957, had the objective of presenting international as well as new Irish plays, although it ran almost immediately into ecclesiastical opposition. It is tempting also to conjecture some common source for the artistic revival and the challenge to the assumptions and workings of the Northern state at the end of the decade.

Whatever the causes, a succession of new dramatists began to appear: Hugh Leonard (*The Big Birthday*, 1956); Brian Friel (*The Enemy Within*, 1962; *Philadelphia, Here I Come!*, 1964); Sam Thompson (*Over the Bridge*, 1960); Tom Murphy (*A Whistle in the Dark*, 1961); Eugene McCabe (*King of the Castle*, 1964); Thomas Kilroy (*The Death and Resurrection of Mr Roche*, 1968); John Boyd (*The Assassin*, 1969). Of these *Philadelphia* and the plays by McCabe, Kilroy and Boyd were first staged at the Dublin Theatre Festival.

These writers do not constitute a school or a movement. Each has his own distinctive voice. Yet they have at least their compatibilities. One locus, most firmly and diversely realized by Friel, is in fables of the fragile continuities between present and past, whether personal memory or the residues of a culture. The underlying question — how particular people in particular times and places identify 'home' — is answered only by the eloquent positing of the myriad conditions in which the question arises. The derelicts of Murphy's *The Sanctuary Lamp* (1975), for instance, look for a sanctuary in a church of bureaucratized mysteries and a secular world equally shifty. 'Home' may entail more than a snug council house or mature suburban residence.

In Michael J. Molloy's plays there is no sanctuary or home for the economically deprived and psychically disturbed inhabitants of the West of Ireland. Both in the eighteenth-century past, as in *The King of Friday's Men*, first produced in 1948, and in the mid-twentieth century, as in *The Wood of the Whispering*, first produced in 1953, Molloy's people are the victims of a political and social system that has almost destroyed them and their culture. Like Synge and George Fitzmaurice, he dramatizes the plight of a dying community by observing the behaviour of individuals under extreme pressure. Only the remains of ancient pagan and traditional Christian beliefs survive to support them. Yet, despite the imaginative potency of this maimed heritage, these people are doomed to emigration, exile and vagrancy. *The Wood of the Whispering* is a play that looks back to the peasant dramas of the early Abbey tradition and forward to the new theatre of Tom Murphy and John B. Keane. M. J. Molloy, like Synge, explores the phenomenon of the slave-mentality induced by colonialism and is also like his great predecessor in asserting that the most enduring resistance to it comes from those who are its most unfortunate and innocent victims. The country people of the West, those who filled the emigrant ships to England in the 1950s, retain an imaginative vitality that has disappeared from the suburban world of Leonard, where the present is in intermittent conference with a past that has been trivialized or erased. Molloy's characters are prototypes of Murphy's and Keane's. They are people from what we now call the Third World, the world of capitalist underdevelopment and exploitation, economic anachronisms who still insist on survival, no matter how extraordinary and painful the strategies they adopt may be.

The King of Friday's Men is Molloy's most famous play. Set in 1797, it is an elaborate presentation of the brutal system of landlord and tenant relations in eighteenth-century Ireland. Both masters and slaves are corrupted by the system, but it is Bartley Dowd, the great shillelagh fighter, who triumphs over the cynical landlord Caesar French. By killing his opponent, Bartley condemns himself to the life of a hunted man. He must also surrender the possibility of love with Oona, the young woman over whom French had wanted to exercise the *droit de seigneur*. It is in the sacrifice of Christ, the King who died on Friday, that Bartley finds a model for his own enforced surrender of a life with Oona. His Christianized resolve enables him to go off with a derelict remnant of the Gaelic culture, Rory Commons, into the hazardous world of an Ireland where folk tradition and religion, individually interpreted and lived, are the only refuge from the systematic injustice of the social and political system. In *The Wood of the Whispering*, the experience of sexuality and marriage is once more what has to be surrendered. Although there is a kind of survival for Sanbatch Daly and his fellow villagers, it has few compensations. A community that denies and is denied the opportunity to love and reproduce itself has no future. It is the recognition of this fact that gives to Sanbatch the pathos of a man driven to fantastic, almost surreal, expedients to stave off the inevitable collapse. The Druid Theatre Company's 1983 production of the play restored it to its central position in the history of the modern Irish theatre.

John B. Keane's *The Field* is in some respects a counter-statement to Molloy's play. The murder of the businessman who wants to buy the field on which 'The Bull' McCabe and his son Tadhg depend is both a squalid and rebellious act. A basic determination to survive and a contempt for all the institutional forces — police and priests — that disapprove of its violent manifestation confront the whole community with a dilemma characteristic of much Irish experience. The lack of respect for law and morality has deep historical roots; the scandalous record of government in Ireland makes it difficult, even for a native administration, to wean a community away from its instinctive readiness to refuse to co-operate with officialdom. But the destruction of Maimie Flanagan, the wife of the local auctioneer who has to sell the four-acre field, and of her son Leamy, shows the other face of this communal solidarity. It too is based on terror and fear. The community reproduces within itself the system by which it had previously been oppressed. In addition, McCabe sees no alternative. The field is his lifeline. His brutality is his response to the subsistence level of existence to which he and his family are doomed. Morality, it seems, is a luxury that can be afforded by those who are less economically exposed. Keane's play indicates that the savagery to which people can be reduced is the only primal energy that enables them to survive. McCabe is both anachronistic and repellent; yet his ferocity prevents him from becoming, like Molloy's people, ultimately disinherited.

A persistent search in modern Irish drama has been for a stage metaphor to embody this disinheritance, notably in recent years for its most intractable manifestation, the political identity enforced upon the North.

St John Ervine's *Mixed Marriage* (1911) was the

first play to portray a situation typifying the mortal outbreaks of the endemic Northern discords. The next comparable treatment of the subject is Sam Thompson's *Over the Bridge* (1960), highly controversial in its time and the harbinger of almost a genre in itself. Set in the Belfast shipyards, its action culminates, after a supposed IRA bombing, in the savage beating of a catholic worker and the solitary protestant trade union official who supports him. The instigator makes only one, chillingly controlled appearance. Sam Thompson's moral reference is to the tenets of trade unionism. Yet those are shown to be more effective as red tape than as a vision of ideal brotherhood, although some residue of reason, humdrum and finally defeated, acts in them and perhaps survives.

Thompson's dialogue closely echoes the sardonically abusive speech of Belfast. His example is evident in John Boyd's *The Flats* (1971), which works the idiom of the same factional enmities. Its playing-area — an apartment in an angular city block dominated by cramped streets and the edifices of religion, commerce and industry — images the repressions and divisions that issued in the riotous early 1970s. Protestant mobs attack the flats; a comic rag-and-bone man, not the half-wit he acts, smuggles weapons to the Donnellans. The sheer intransigence of circumstances frustrates socialist exposition, armed resistance, young love, jibing backchats, the ill-informed British army 'peace-keepers'. The play closes with a chance killing and riot unabated, a narrative of a situation confined within its present tense.

Stewart Parker envisages a drama charged by 'the instinct for play itself . . . a quintessentially ludicrous theatre.' In his own work he likes to make play with a stage full of protean levels of light, sound and spatial dissolves. In *Nightshade* (1980), the 'illusions' of Mr Quinn, an amateur magician, professionally an undertaker (American style), appropriately introduce a set that is itself something of a conjurer's cabinet of tricks. Its many dimensions unfold bizarre conjunctions of realism and fairy tale: an undertakers' strike grotesquely annotates the jargon of 'fringe benefits' and 'work-to-rule'; literal skeletons in the cupboard become metaphorical as Quinn's past unfolds its secrets into his daughter's melancholy fable of a Sleeping Beauty. Tricks of a more literary kind, stylistic parodies of Irish writers, colour Parker's interpretation in *Northern Star* (1984) of Henry Joy McCracken and the United Irishmen of 1798.

Less abstrusely, *Catchpenny Twist* (1977), subtitled 'A Charade', superimposes the songs of two aspiring pop-music composers on a backdrop of the present Northern violence. Sacked from their teaching posts after a tipsy prank, Martyn and Roy set to their song-writing, at first, for the money, ballads celebrating paramilitary martrydoms; Monagh to an unpromising singing career and an affair with a television reporter eventually shot dead in Belfast. Having inadvertently offended both factions, Martyn and Roy flee to Dublin, then London; abandon Monagh; and at an airport, after failure at a European festival, open a parcel that explodes in their faces. Those are about as many words as the play devotes to its narrative — almost an incidental concern.

The impetus of *Catchpenny Twist* is the music linking its volatile scenes: Martyn and Roy in their flat, their songs sung by Monagh, present only as a voice; the sleazy clubs, and a jail, where she performs; streets; agents' offices. The longings of the conventional love song acquire a phrasing that may allude equally to the stereotypes of political aggressions and frustrations, directly represented only in glimpses.

Commenting on his *Spokesong* (1975), Parker rejected the futility of dramatizing 'a plea' for unity between catholics and protestants. He sought instead to embody that unity in 'an artistic image' — in *Spokesong* the history of the bicycle — 'creating it as an act of the imagination, postulating it before an audience.' The latent 'artistic image' of *Catchpenny Twist* — the idiom of its music — has less to do with unity than with ambitions, betrayals, incomprehension.

Graham Reid's plays are less puckishly mounted. The image they develop is of the bystander, the 'innocent' onlooker caught up in violence. The glib Slobber in *The Closed Door* (1980) lives dangerously around the rackets of Belfast's political gangs. Beaten, stabbed, blinded, he dies slowly outside the house of a friend, too scared to help, who tries to redeem himself by lies humiliatingly exposed. In a programme note to *The Death of Humpty-Dumpty* (1979) Reid remarks upon the experience of Belfast hospitals with the victims of civil disturbances: 'There was often the question "Why me? I am innocent."'

The protagonist of *The Death of Humpty-Dumpty* is George Samson, schoolteacher, genial father, vain, cautious philanderer. Shot to prevent his bearing witness to a terrorist killing, he is paralyzed from the neck down. Mostly set in Samson's ward, with dissolves to his ruinous visits home and his former life, the play records the physical indignities of his condition, his deteriorating will, dependence on his family becoming embittered tyranny over it. One hospital friendship briefly offers hope. Gerry Doyle, also crippled, protects Samson from a ward orderly's petty sadism, defies self-pity by his harsh raillery and by his fortitude. After his discharge, he is killed in an accident. His voice opens and closes the play. Remembering it after Gerry's death, George converts its mocking sanity to his own spite; his son smothers him in his hospital bed: 'We can't take you home .... But I can't leave you here.'

The careful domesticity, shattered in these two plays by hoodlum politics, is in any case a precarious falsehood. Quite accidentally, the violence reveals pretences, weaknesses, aggressions, which it did not create. Reid's recent work, much of it for television, also explores private insecurities, always at least bordered by public upheaval. The latter does not cause the former, yet the two are associated, if only as metaphors of each other, within the personality of Reid's Belfast. It is an association commonly implied in Irish drama, and, from *The Playboy of the Western World* on, in rural as in urban settings.

In Eugene McCabe's *The King of the Castle* (1964), the Castle is the former Big House which Scober (Barney) McAdam has acquired by exploiting his land, his neighbours and himself. Publicly the King, Scober is impotent, and chooses a sexual partner for his wife, Tressa, from his workmen. Tressa romanticizes the past of her house, a discontented farmhand that of his craft. The hard-headed Scober is no more discerning. Overseeing Scober's domestic afflictions and barren successes are vanished splendours, which he scorns and cannot emulate, and the peasant ancestors of his labourers, burdened now by a modernized rapacity. The present has made nothing of its past. The lesions of the home are part of a communal estrangement. Although the play is devoid of physical violence, it is latent in the pauses of the taunting, abusive dialogue.

Frank McGuinness's *Observe the Sons of Ulster Marching Towards the Somme* (1985), which ends as the battle opens, calls for no representation of the massive slaughter of the Great War. Its horrors, their inhuman demands and mythologizing power, are presences in the minds and relationships of the eight Ulster Division soldiers whose progress the play follows. We witness the makings of legend, an interplay of history and individualities, of necessities and acceptance into available pieties — of comradeship, home, country — which makes them bearable. McGuinness's play is about legacies, here from the carnage of World War I. The battle of the Somme began on 1 July 1916, the anniversary of the battle of the Boyne in 1690. At the Somme, some 20,000 troops of the Allied armies were killed in the opening hours. It was a futile and heroic attack. Since then the two battles have joined in the Northern protestant calendar of celebration. The Somme, where the 36th (Ulster Division) suffered heavy losses, has become a latter-day symbol of sacrifices to loyalties enjoined by the Union, King, and Empire.

Stewart Parker has recommended to the Irish playwright broad, cosmopolitan issues, not the problems of Rathfarnham and Crossmaglen; adding that the two sets of issues are 'not mutually exclusive.' The parochial may allude to the universal. One can further argue that a local habitation is the necessary ground, that the Belfast and Dublin suburbs, the country life of contemporary Irish drama are recognisably of the twentieth-century emotional landscape: a dislocated world in which there is a hiatus between past and present; whose present circumstances abandon the individual to the unconvincing devices of an isolated self — whistling in the dark.

If whistling is a form of art, or of magic, the plays are a kind of superior whistling, not a distraction from the dark, but venturing to localize and sound it. This is the territory, discovered in the Dublin, Derry and Donegal, of Thomas Kilroy, Tom Murphy and Brian Friel.

In Thomas Kilroy's *The Death and Resurrection of Mr Roche* (1968) an all-male, all-night drinking party arrives at a squalid Dublin flat. Its door mysteriously opens to admit them. One of them calls it a tomb; its cellar is named the holy hole: omens of an experience beyond their more-or-less-endurable settlements with life. In the late 1960s they have jobs untouched by the 'economic miracle'; their conversation is designed to conceal failure — financial, cultural, sexual. The entry of Mr Roche, middle-aged, homosexual, Jewish, disturbs the strained camaraderie. Manhandled into the cellar, he apparently dies.

The ensuing recriminations become confessional disclosures. Mr Roche returns: mistaken diagnosis or miracle, the play leaves open. 'Resurrected', he imbues the ending with an uncertain benediction. Finally alone on stage, as he speaks into a dead telephone, he indicates to us the possibility that his tormentors will reinstate their illusions.

The flat in *Mr Roche* is basically a solid presence, Irish society of the time accurately realized in the youthful revellers. The play, however, subtly refers its events to the symbols of a religion that for the characters is at most a formal obligation: 'The Carmelites . . . I go up there regularly myself on a Sunday when it's too late to go to bed.' The epiphany of the reviled Jew disorients the purely social issues into emblems of spiritual crisis. They operate not as an ecclesiastical solace, but as a method of floating ideas of guilt and absolution in a secular world.

Talbot's Box (1977), in one view it takes of its subject, also aligns mystical and worldly perceptions. Its protagonist is Matt Talbot, a Dublin carpenter — by one account a scab in the 1913 Lockout — and Christian mystic. Born in 1856, he turned at the age of twenty-eight to a regimen of the severest physical penance. When he died in 1925 — 'myocardial degeneration', as the play reports the autopsy's dispassionate finding — a cult movement sought his canonization as 'the workers' saint'. Talbot would have been indifferent. His was a fiercely private, heretical exercise of his faith, not intended to edify by example. One sequence epitomizes that exalted egoism in a burst of blinding light and agonized cries, 'of physical discomfort to the audience'. The off-stage clamour of the Lockout leaves Talbot reciting his cryptic beatitudes, withdrawn from the contending demands on him.

Double Cross (1986) also set on a non-realistic stage, deals with comparable relationships between the private consciousness and society. It turns to an arena where personal inadequacies, in particular a paranoid mistrust of the reality outside oneself, finds a refuge of sorts in the manipulative arts of politics. Episodes in the lives of Brendan Bracken and William Joyce criss-cross, counterpoint, and reflect one another — their childhood experience, for instance, of the violent Ireland of 1919-20. They create their own concepts of the countries — Ireland, Britain, Germany — which they betray/serve. Service and betrayal, whether of the self or of the state, are motivated by psychological energies that are in the end destructive. The effect of the play is not of clinical, dispassionate analysis. The pathos of the two lives, delicately imparted, alleviates their ruthless vanities.

In Tom Murphy's first play, *A Whistle in the Dark* (1961), the despairs of an Irish immigrant family in Coventry issue in lawless brutality. The play elicits from their perverse codes of 'manliness' the inarticulate, inadmissible longings, thus evaded, for another comradeship, another acceptance. Also revealing inner lives, *A Crucial Week in the Life of a Grocer's Assistant* (1969) alters the realistic style of *A Whistle in the Dark*. Artifices of language — word-games, patter-speeches — and unearthly lighting distinguish John Joe Moran's dreams of escape from 'this corpse of a street'. Fully conscious of a village *pietas* destroyed by sanctimonious moneygrubbing, he nevertheless, in Murphy's most gently mitigating resolution, decides to stay. *The Morning After Optimism* (1971) is pure fantasy. In a modern Forest of Arden a whore and her pimp are the degraded shadows, finally the killers, of two idealized lovers.

Murphy's plays are conceiving styles of theatrical narrative to express the human faiths, rituals and fantasies that offer refuge to actualities of failure and misery — the 'whistle' commonly ineffectual in the surrounding 'dark.' In *The Sanctuary Lamp* (1975) Murphy openly turns, like Kilroy, to a Christian symbolism, discarded as a mode of belief, which persists as one way of talking about sanctuary and perdition. The play, whose 'real' duration suggests that of the Crucifixion, is following a Passion of sorts in the histories of three derelicts in a city church. Their stories incorporate a scathing account of divine power. Ultimately what emerges is a series of alternative theologies, grounded on the rare moments of comradeship and altruism in a shiftless world.

So too, but in a wholly different way, the characters in *The Gigli Concert* (1983) engage, as one of them puts it, with 'the startling thing, God had got it wrong'. Here an Irish property developer — the Man — depressed by his longing and inability to sing like the great Italian tenor, Beniamino Gigli, has five manic 'consultations' with J.P.W. King, an English practitioner of the philosophy, if so it may be called, of 'dynamatology'. In the end, JPW himself sings like Gigli; or we 'overhear' music which, after Mandrax and vodka, plays inside his head. Their relationship, convivial and savage, calls upon various therapies: drugs, confession, love, transcendental faith, psychiatry. But the dominant metaphor or therapy is that of art as illusion, or as magic, or as the agent of curative fictions.

Murphy's humour — antic, black, exultant — is a prime energy in his treatment of human despair playing with its options. It is active in *Bailegangaire* (1985), another journey through inner lives, the fables that express their truth and that may unexpectedly relieve distress. On the face of it, the situation presented here is cheerless enough: a senile old woman tended by a frustrated granddaughter and occasionally visited by another granddaughter, pregnant by someone other than her husband. The absent generation, and other losses, signify a blighted family chronicle. Out of and away from it, Mommo nightly rehearses a tale apparently destined never to end. The trio, indulging, despising, cajoling, loving each other, finally bring the tale to its conclusion and their lives possibly to new beginnings. It is a muted triumph, in which language, broken and eloquent, shaping a story, moulds divided feelings into sympathy.

Brian Friel's *Philadelphia, Here I Come!* sees Gar O'Donnell — doubly staged as a public self and as a private self unapparent to the other characters — through the eve of his emigration. In *The Loves of Cass McGuire* (1966) when Cass, back in Ireland after more than fifty years in America, disgraces herself by rowdy drinking, her brother packs her off to Eden House, where she edits her rejection into a make-believe of home. Exile, prospective and past, is a literal presence. It is also a spiritual condition caused by an incompatibility that the protagonists perceive between their actual circumstances and self-realization. Cass retreats into illusion. Gar's version of unserviceable circumstances is more significant of the inwardness to which Friel's protagonists are driven in acts of self-preservation.

Although life in Ballybeg is meanly confined, its scenes and relationships include possibly remedial moments. These remain unvalidated outside Gar's memories. Hence the brilliant public/private dialogue games. They objectify on stage the fantasies, the mockings, the estrangement and frustration which in reality are interior. Nothing to do with distance, exile is a condition of the native place, haunted in *Philadelphia* by possibilities not yet exhausted.

Gar keeps to himself the fast, diversionary spiel which is his protective role. Cass addresses her soliloquies to the theatre audience. In the later plays this commentary, which is partly an acute sizing-up of reality and partly a refuge, joins the normal dialogue, and drastically reduces any solacing glimpses in experience. In *The Gentle Island* (1971) the flippant Shane finds the Arcadian Inishkeen of his friend's fancy stripped to an anti-masque of physical and psychic mutilation.

The Freedom of the City (1973) transfers Gar's iconoclasm to Skinner's nihilistic sarcasm. Its location is Derry City, which Friel has described as 'gentle, sleepy' and 'frustrated and frustrating'. The statements are reconcilable. The gentleness was an artificial state borne by the catholic majority out of an apathy induced by heavy unemployment, a contemptuous administration, and effective disenfranchisement. Skinner's is an entirely credible response to that inheritance. Having a way with words is an attractive option in a community maintained as a political vacuum.

The Freedom conflates the Civil Rights campaign of the late 1960s with the murder of fourteen marchers by British paratroopers in Derry in 1972. The comparable deaths of Lily, Skinner and Michael, shot down by soldiers as they leave the Guildhall, are mythologized, and sanctioned by the official enquiry. All the commenting voices — judge, balladeer, television reporter — travesty the event, which has made Skinner reconsider his role. Lily reduces him to a monosyllable; his formal 'last words' admonish him, too late. In Synge, language has the last word; here, it dies in 'last words'. Yet as the three remain standing at the end, Auden's 'lie of Authority' has perhaps not finally outspoken the ruses to which it prompts the imagination.

This play inaugurated a related series: *Volunteers* (1975), *Living Quarters* (1977), *Aristocrats* (1979), *Faith Healer* (1979), *Translations* (1980), *The Communication Cord* (1982). There is a persistent strain between a group-enforcing authority and an individual urge, not wholly evasion, to disown it. In *Volunteers*, a unit of IRA prisoners works on an archaeological dig, defying the edict of their organization, which will kill them in reprisal; Keenan's flamboyant wordplay and the past that is being excavated reprehend but cannot deter their executioners. *Aristocrats* reveals the false romance of a catholic Big House; a family reunion — fact and memory, voices real and reproduced — composes an elegy for cruelty, deceit and the pathos of the house's heirs.

These plays view a disintegrating society. Their language invests the shaky covenants between self and circumstance — a vocabulary of command, military, bureaucratic, familial, interpreting and subduing — with compassion, and a vivid ameliorating humour. *Faith Healer*, a stark and startling play, comic and tragic energy astonishingly compounded, brings that artistic power into question. Its four monologues enquire into Frank Hardy's capricious, finally suicidal, healing powers, curing the deformed and crippled; and thereby into analogous acts of the imagination, imposing on its fictions a shapeliness lacking, and perhaps resisted, in reality. To brutalize a play of subtle complexity, it is in one aspect posing the question whether art makes an imprint on a world where the rhetoric of politics declares a prior claim. In so doing, it is formulating, in a definitive way, the themes of Friel's work since 1973.

In 1980 Friel and others founded the Field Day Theatre Company; like the Irish Literary Theatre, a concept, not a building. It seeks new plays canvassing the turbulence of present-day Ireland and its informing past; practically attentive, therefore, to the questions stirring in *Faith Healer*. Its first production was *Translations*, which the later *The Communication Cord* boldly parodies in a farcically 'restored' peasant cottage.

The context of *Translations* is a hedge-school in Ballybeg, where the polyglot Hugh teachers Latin and Greek through Irish, during the British army's 1833 ordnance survey, which anglicized the Irish place-names. Owen, the army's assistant, Hugh's younger son, sees his job as a technical, interpreting exercise, not the collusion with dispossessing colonialism it appears to his brother. All the Irish characters are assumed to be speaking Irish on stage. Through this superbly managed device, the love between Maire and Yolland, an English officer infatuated with exotic Ireland, becomes a symbol of the clash between a bluntly confident imperialism and the uncertainties of collaboration and resistance in a Baile Beag becoming Ballybeg. Yolland disappears. His commanding officer orders retaliation. The imperialist and parochial myths, communicating in rough translation, both ultimately doomed — like the Tyrian towers invoked in Hugh's closing speech — collide in personal tragedies that, on a larger stage, are disputes over cultural and political sovereignty. Friel's plays resume, in their tragicomic way, the dominant themes and tensions of Irish drama since the 1960s.

MICHAEL J. MOLLOY

(1917-)

THE WOOD OF THE WHISPERING (1953)

[Michael Molloy, like George Fitzmaurice, blends folk and surreal elements in his work. Inevitably, comparisons also have been made with Synge, but Molloy's world is quite different. His West of Ireland is a world integral to itself, but menaced by the threat of an extinction that seems to stimulate its most grotesque and melancholic features.

The play was first produced at the Abbey Theatre, Dublin on 26 January 1953.]

PREFACE

After the Israelites of old escaped from Egypt and long slavery, they wandered in the desert for forty years, never daring to attack the warlike tribes who occupied their Promised Land. But after forty years the old slave-born generation had died, or retired from leadership, and a bold new freeborn generation had taken over. Under new freeborn leaders the new freeborn nation crossed the Jordan, and conquered after many a fierce campaign, their Promised Land.

For forty years Ireland has been free, and for

forty years it has wandered in the desert under the leadership of men who freed their nation, but who could never free their own souls and minds from the ill-effects of having been born in slavery. To that slave-born generation it has always seemed inevitable and right that the Anglo-American plutocracies, because they are rich, should be allowed to destroy us because we are poor — destroy us root and branch through mass emigration. So for forty years we have continued to be the only dying free nation on earth, inheriting Turkey's old title of 'The Sick Man of Europe'. And for forty years our slave-born economic and financial experts have continued to assure our slave-born political leaders that the depopulation is all for the best: that big cattle ranches and big grain ranches are more economic than small farms. But neither cattle nor combine harvesters have ever fought for their country as small farmers have been known to do.

In the last war neutral Norway found itself invaded by both sides on the same day, because its position was strategically important and because its population was too small to defend its big area. And the bitter lesson of the Six Counties and of Partition, and indeed of all history, is that the worst disaster that can befall a nation is not conquest, but colonisation. And depopulation is the thing that invites colonisation and ensures its success. Ourselves and Britain lie like two vast aircraft carriers off the coast of Europe. Every year with the rise of air power our strategic position becomes more important, and every year with the fall in population our defences become weaker.

While we desert the finest farm-land in Europe, the Jews return from all over the world to the Promised Land from which they were driven nearly two thousands years ago. They set to work to make fertile and to populate land that has been desert for two thousand years, sun-scorched desert where the new grasses have to be watered four times a day. What man has done, man can do; and we could re-populate our deserted farm-lands if only we could find new freeborn leaders with minds and souls not warped or stunted by birth in slavery.

In 1910 the Great Blasket island had one hundred and fifty people and a well filled school. Forty years later the population was a handful, there was only one child, so they called their island Tir Na Sean, the Land of the Old. There are countless dying villages and townlands in rural Ireland to which the same title could be applied. The death of a village, like the death of an individual, is usually a painful business, and marked by distressing symptoms. But of this fact our suburban depopulation enthusiasts know nothing.

But country people know all about it, and they know the background of this play, the comedy of the eccentric old bachelors, and the tragedy, too. So it was no coincidence that its first amateur performances were by two tiny rural villages: Inchovea in County Clare and Killeedy in County Limerick, which between them won half a dozen drama festivals with it — before their dramatic societies were shattered by emigration. Every activity is hit by a falling population; and every activity is helped by an expanding population.

CHARACTERS

SANBATCH DALY
CON KINSELLA, *a woodsman in his middle thirties*
PADDY KING, *an old farmer*
JIMMY KING, *his brother*
STEPHEN LANIGAN, *an old farmer*
SHEILA LANIGAN, *his daughter*
MARK TRISTNAN, *a young farmer*
HOTHA BRODERICK, *a farmer in his fifties*
KITTY WALLACE, *a young girl*
SADIE TUBRIDY

THE SCENE: *A wood in the West of Ireland*
THE TIME: *1950*

ACT ONE

THE SCENE *is outside the old Main Entrance to Castle D'Arcy. An early 18th century D'Arcy did the then fashionable Grand Tour of Europe, and returned to his cramped old Norman castle full of ideas for a splendid mansion with demesne, avenues, gates and woods in the best British and Continental style. This was his Main Entrance and he made it an imposing one: a mighty wrought-iron central gate with lofty ornamental pillars and flanked on each side by smaller wooden wicket gates. But neighbouring landlords, who did the Grand Tour somewhat later, founded new market towns and cut a new main road to join them. This passed on the wrong side of the Castle, so a new avenue was made to open on it, and the old main entrance became a little-used side-entrance and woods were planted within and without. The roof of the gardener's lodge can be seen. (But if an artist is not available, a very simple set would do: a six-foot wall running across the back stage to represent the demesne wall, with a pillar at one end, as if the gates were in the wings. Some branches of trees, bushes, ivy, etc., over the top of the wall would suggest the demesne woods. When a character is supposed to hide behind a tree, he hides in the wings.*

In a little clearing, on the left-hand side of the gate, and well out from the demesne wall, lies the camp of SANBATCH DALY. *There is a fire of turf and sticks, and slanted over the fire is an iron rod with one end deeply embedded in the ground. The other end is S-shaped and from the 'S' hangs a kettle with its top half and spout broken off. Behind the fire lies a seven-foot long coffin-shaped box of rough boards, about two feet high and open at the right-hand end. Behind the middle of the box a long sheep-crook is stuck in the ground, and from the crook hangs a print of the famous old Byzantine Madonna, Our Lady of Succour, with its red Greek lettering and bright colouring. On the left of this (from the actor's point of view) stands a dung-fork or graipe, and from its handle is hung an Old Moore's Almanac and an old patched-together Rosary Beads. On the other side of the sheep-crook stands a hay-fork, and on this hangs* SANBACH's *cap.*

A huge, rusty, three-legged iron pot is on the left of the fire. The lid is on, for this pot is SANBATCH's *cupboard and toolshed and would be his wardrobe, too, if he had any clothes besides the rags on his back. A little heap of potatoes lies a yard or so away. An old battered shotgun lies against one end of the long box. An old rusty bucket stands nearby.*

SANBATCH, *the lord of all this wealth, is sitting on the long box. He is dressed in trousers, jacket and vest. He is delousing. He picks them out, and drops them into the fire. He is in the middle sixties, lanky, haggard and worn by privation and adversity, but bursting with nervous energy. He is completely un-self-conscious and serious, is a little crazy and absurd and wild, but he excites sympathy, too, for it is obvious that he has suffered more than his share. As he liquidates the lice, he chats away, addressing his remarks to someone lying in the long box.*

It is the year 1950, about sunset of a May night.

SANBATCH: 'Tis me that'd be rich, Leggy, if there was any kind of a middling price going for them at all. And to think I hadn't wan in all my life's day till I was over the sixty! Still, if we thin them middling often, we'll keep from scratching when the neighbours are around, and they'll never find out that we have them at all. And another thing: according as we're getting more starved in the blood and in the body these divils'll have less to get, till at last they might resign from us altogether.... (*Suddenly the rumble of a distant lorry is heard*) By the Blessed Iron Book! (*He grabs the gun and jumps to his feet*) That's the gang! 'Tis surely them. (*He dodges behind a tree, holding the gun at the ready*) Three warnings I'll give, then if they keep coming, the first of them'll fall. (*The lorry is heard again.* SANBATCH *is greatly relieved*) I'm thinking now that isn't them. That's more the sound of a lorry: likely a lorry with barrels for Gowlin's drink-shop. (*He comes back and leaves aside the gun*) And when they didn't come before this, they'll hardly come at all tonight, so I'll bob asleep for a few hours. (*He takes the kettle off the fire, comes round to the box and starts indignantly*) Well, more bad luck to you, as the goat said to his legs! Dozing asleep you are, and me after squandering many a fine news and tale on you, and wise advices the whole world couldn't buy from me. (*He draws out 'Leggy', a philosophical old sheep-dog, by his tether, and throws him a leg of a rabbit*) Leggy, if you lost your appetite, I wouldn't like I'd get it, because then I'd need a high income ... Now, I'll tie you to your tree, and if any strange mean-looking men come the way, start springing and roaring. (*He leads the dog off, left, is back again in a moment and puts the shotgun into the long box*) But, maybe, Leggy, they will never trace me, because I promised God, if He'd save my liberty, that I'd never grumble again no matter how poor. (*Feet first he gets into the long box and disappears from view. He pulls in his head and the dog roams around the narrow confines of his tether space*)

CON KINSELLA *comes in from the right, carrying a small window frame and boards and a little bag of tools. He is in his middle thirties, with the sturdy build and big facial bones of the work-nurtured farmer's son. He is an intelligent fellow with a quick sense of humour. He takes in the scene for a few moments, then addresses the dog, smilingly.*

CON: Where's your master gone? (*Rapping the box*) 'Tis a fine big kennel he made for you, whatever. You must have a long family.

The dog retreats into the long box, SANBATCH *pulling him by the tether.* CON *crosses to the main gate, looks through the main gate, then opens a wicket-gate and goes out. He can be seen standing with his back to the stage, surveying the scene.* SANBATCH *quickly crawls out of the box, gun in hand, and hides behind a tree.* CON *comes back, looks into the long box, then sits on it and lights a cigarette.* SANBATCH *advances stealthily and ferociously.*

SANBATCH: Put up your hands, or I'll fire. I have you marked as dead as a pointer. (CON *puts up his hands, the cigarette falling out of his mouth with surprise*) Wan minute is your time to live unless you'll swear to go back to the County Home, yourself and your ambulance, and never come again robbing Sanbatch of his liberty.

CON: I have nothing to do with the County Home. That isn't my trade at all.

SANBATCH: Evermore ye'll deny yeer trade, so as to come at the sleepy side of a poor person. But you won't fool Sanbatch. After my house fell last month, ye sent notice to say ye'd take me to the County Home if I hadn't a house got within a month. But ye'll not trap Sanbatch into the poor-house and disgrace his decent people.

CON: Cutting timber is my trade. Against the tree beyond is the boards for my hut, and on the roadside there aback is my lorry, with saws and engines of many a kind.

SANBATCH: Maybe that was the lorry I heard sounding a few minutes back?

CON: That was it.

SANBATCH *crosses and examines the boards.*

SANBATCH: The makings of a hut are in it right enough, so you are a timber-cutter. (*Throwing aside the gun*) I'll make you a dash of tea now, if we haven't to wait for the summer sun to boil the kettle. (*He hangs the kettle again, fixes fire*)

CON: 'Tisn't long since I staunched my hunger.

SANBATCH: No matter. Sure the tea is the finest weed that ever grew; though the porter gives a person better courage for working.

CON: I have bread-loaf sandwiches here, plenty and to spare. (*He takes them from his pocket*)

SANBATCH: Well, stick to them, because you'd want a wonderful great stomach and constitution to thrive on my cakes. (*He goes out left*) Leggy, I'll not be going sleeping another while, so you might have time to catch a rabbit for yourself. God is good, God bless him. (*He returns carrying the tether*)

CON: How did the house happen to fall on you?

SANBATCH: The way it was, I never was tied by priest or friar, so I had no wan to come after me, and that left me careless, and I had no wan to help me, so once the strength began to leave me both house and farm soon went to rack and ruin. I left the thatch without repairing three years, trusting to God, but He came up last month with a storm, and didn't leave a wisp in it. (*He takes an empty jam-jar out of the iron pot; rinses it in the bucket. He finds a little packet of tea and a spoon in the pot also*)

CON: (*Munching a sandwich*) How was it you could never get a wife?

SANBATCH: (*Indignantly*) Is it me? I'll have you know I was wan of the best looking men in this country, thank God, with as many curls as a prize bull, and the hardest job ever I got was to keep from getting married. The finest man's daughter I could wink at her, and she'd wink at me, and if I wouldn't put my arms around her, she'd put her arms around me.

CON: (*Amused*) I'll never meet so lucky a man till I meet yourself again.

SANBATCH: And at a dance that time, when a girl'd want to make you come home with her, she'd steal your cap. All the girls were darting like dogs to steal my cap: some of them girls that were worth hundreds of pounds. But still I never tumbled myself down to marrying any of them.

CON: Why was that?

SANBATCH: (*Solemnly*) The best man is the man that can do without them, and I was as sure as the day I was a man that could do without them.

CON: And you found out since that you couldn't?

SANBATCH: (*Putting a spoonful of tea in the jam-jar*) The night my house fell I understood at last that I wasn't a man that could do without them. For, if I had a wife, she'd keep me well fed and well scolded, and then I never would let the farm go to waste and the roof drop in. The very minute I'd have each meal finished she'd say to me: 'What in the hell are you doing in here? Go out and find some work to do.' 'Twas for our good God made them such divils with the tongue.

CON: And now you're too old to get a wife?

SANBATCH: Sure, that's the greatest treachery that's in the world. You won't know whether you can do without them till you're too old to get wan. (*He pours hot tea into the jam-jar*)

CON: You lost yourself, whatever.

SANBATCH: I did. I was full sure I could do without them. Here's a sup of tea, and the want of milk you must offer up for all that ever died.

CON: Cold water is as good. And thanks for the sup of tea. (*He cools the tea with some cold water from the bucket*)

SANBATCH: I had a little Kerry cow, and she gave

a sweet canful, but when poverty took me by the throat she had to be sold . . . While you're supping, I'll be filling this vacancy (*a hole in his trousers*) with a piece of blanket. (*Pulling the hayfork out of the ground he pokes in the long box and brings out on the prongs an old dog-eared blanket. With the sheep shears he cuts a piece from this and proceeds to patch his trousers*)

CON: 'Tis a fine mansion and demesne the D'Arcys had here.

SANBATCH: (*Proudly*) And my family were chief herds to them so long as they had a bullock or a ewe. But all their lands are sold now except the demesne and all their cattle and sheep are sold, and my sheep-crook is rusty now.

CON: I hear the last of the D'Arcys is a scholar out in Oxford.

SANBATCH: (*Nodding*) They tell me he was an M.A. but he lost it again through drink.

CON: No doubt 'twas the drink made him sell out the castle and the demesne at last.

SANBATCH: The castle and demesne sold! I wouldn't believe the first or last of that, though 'tis ten years since a Christian lived in them.

CON: Well, it's a truthful tale. Th' other day the castle was sold by young D'Arcy to Kenworthy and he has the woods sold to my boss Markey of the Sawmills.

SANBATCH: (*Excited and dismayed*) Well, cut my head off if that's so! Markey'll leave only stumps of the last fine woods in this barony, and Kenworthy'll knock the Castle and sell every slate and stick and stone, the same as he did to Browne Hall and Castle Martin.

CON: 'Tis my job to sleep hereabouts in my hut and guard the machinery. Th' other timber men'll come every morning in Markey's lorry.

SANBATCH: Sup up your tea quick. Sadie within must be told about the sale, and she won't appear if anywan[1] is here besides myself.

CON: Why so? What made her nervous?

SANBATCH: The time she was in her bloom th' oul' Depression was on, and no farmer around could afford to marry a girl that had no fortune. So she had to stop with the father and mother till they died, and then she was left alone and the lonesomeness and the darkness and the trees defeated her at last. 'Tis two years now since she spoke to anywan or went out amongst the neighbours. She spends the day and the night within there thinking and ever thinking about how she lost herself.

CON: (*Rising*) I'll be fetching another batch of boards for my hut.

SANBATCH: She'll be gone when you come back.

CON *goes out left.* SANBATCH *picks up a stone and bangs loudly on the right-hand wicket gate. Then he opens it, pokes in his head and calls out.*

SANBATCH: Sadie, I have a news for you. Come on out. The divil a wan is here only oul' Sandbatch. (*He comes back to the fire and sits on the long box with his back to the gate*)

SADIE *appears in the doorway. She is in her late forties, and poorly dressed, but not untidily — there is nothing unkempt or wild-looking about her. A good-looking girl in her day, and her eyes are out of the ordinary still. But all life and interest in life has left her: her expression is one of settled and suffering melancholy. She raises her eye-lids just sufficiently to ascertain that* SANBATCH *is alone, then her eyes return to their endless brooding.* SANBATCH *turns at last.*

SANBATCH: Sadie, step forward a small piece whatever. Let you not be afeard I'd go mocking you. How could I when myself has a middling share of craziness, too? (*Eventually she comes forward a little, but she does not look in his direction*) Castle D'Arcy is sold to Kenworthy for tearing down, and he won't leave a stone you could throw at a bird. Whether he'll turn you out of your lodge is unknown yet; if he can he will. (*He watches her for a few moments, but there is no reaction*) If he does turn you out, you'll have to go to the County Home amongst the paupers. . . . (*Still no reaction*) . . . . My reckoning is that'd be the best thing that could happen you now, for in the County Home you'd be swarmed about with paupers all day, and you'd have to alter your habits and start talking again.

This takes a few moments to sink in, but it does, and she starts and shudders and turns away.

SANBATCH: Why, wouldn't it be nicer and wholesomer to be talking to paupers itself than to be all day and every day lonesome and thinking and ever thinking about how you lost yourself?

But she turns away, much agitated, and hurries out. He goes to the gate and calls after her.

SANBATCH: Let you not go sleeping another while. I have another news for you that'll be twice better than that wan.

CON *enters, carrying more boards.*

1. anyone.

SANBATCH: I told her the good and the bad. It'll be something new for her to be thinking about, and the change might improve her.

CON: (*Sorting out boards and tools*) Myself is after passing a fellow on his way home from the drink-shop. He told me to go ahead — that he was hardly able to bring his legs after hospital and a hard operation.

SANBATCH: That's Stephen Lanigan from the village below. (*Pointing right*) The highest doctors in Galway searched his insides, and, whatever was in it, they reckon it can't be cured. A long sickness never told a lie yet, so no matter if all Ireland was trusting to him, he'll die.

CON: Sure enough, his colour is beginning to say: 'I'm going away.'

SANBATCH: He'll have a slow death, too, with leavings of praying-time, and that just suits him.

CON: Why? Was he a rake formerly?

SANBATCH: When he'd have drink in, he was as wicked as a bee for arguing and fighting and tinkering. Many a time we fought and kicked each other.

STEPHEN LANIGAN *comes in, leaning heavily on a stout stick. He makes his way to a tree stump, and sits down. He is sixty or so, not very grey, but his colour is very bad. A powerfully-built man, and in his day a lively and boisterous man, but illness and the shadow of death have begun to tame and refine him. But some of the old twinkle is still in his eye, and he is not unduly sorry for himself.*

SANBATCH: (*Solemnly*) Only last night, Stephen, I was dreaming again about your wife, and how she used to sit on my knee long ago.

STEPHEN: (*Smiling*) And she had a wish for you evermore, even after I married her.

SANBATCH: (*Hotly*) 'Tis my wife she'd be, too, only I was so sure I could do without them.

STEPHEN: (*Indicating* CON) He tells me he was in England, a pick and shovel man, for many a year.

SANBATCH: (*Eagerly, to* CON) Tell us here, would you be fond of a bit of land and money, and a wife thrown in along with it.

CON: (*Cynically*) Is she long grey?

SANBATCH: Grey? She's a blossomed flower, a fine looking girl with two big eyes like a lady's and fine features, and she has the promise of the child's breakfast, moreover.

STEPHEN: She's my daughter that lately come from England to mind me for a while after my operation. 'Twould suit me well if some wan'd coax her to marry at home and go no more to England.

SANBATCH: 'Tis a nice farm and house they have with a fine long kitchen for playing pitch-and-toss in on a wet Sunday. If some wan doesn't marry here soon, the village'll be in an awful way with no child swelling up into a man for the days when ourselves'll be without the help of hand or foot. (*Suddenly a car engine is heard*) Blood and bones! That's the ruffians coming for me, but they'll not catch Sanbatch. (*He grabs the gun and runs out left*)

STEPHEN: Sanbatch is his nickname evermore since he used be training dogs for oul' Captain Sanbatch. Sanbatch was an able and witty fellow and a lady's man, too, in his young days, but he's gone very odd these late years since he got into such poverty and bad clothes that he couldn't go to Mass or leave the woods at all hardly.

CON: You could tell from his eyes that he got a punishing from the world. (*He is working away, fitting and screwing sections together*)

STEPHEN: My daughter is finding this village too quiet and lonesome on account all the young crowd are long since gone out of it, all enticed away by the plentifulness of the money in England and America and Dublin. Maybe you'd visit our house middling often, and then she mightn't be in such a hurry racing back to London.

CON: Tomorrow night I'll draw to ye.

STEPHEN: Well, God spare you the health! I'd like she'd stop home till my trouble is over.

CON: (*Cautiously*) Till you're cured again?

STEPHEN: Yes, till my cure is landed: the only cure that never failed — death.

CON: You haven't the looks of that. Did the doctors say so?

STEPHEN: They didn't, but I'm thinking 'tis what Owen Kelly had I have.... They say the two worst times for cancer are the fall of the leaf and the budding of the leaf, so if May doesn't kill me, I might stagger out till October.

CON: 'Tisn't such a thing you have at all. Do the pains be often teasing you?

STEPHEN: (*Smiling, albeit a little ruefully*) Some days I have a pain that'd burst a sod of turf; other days I feel good but as weak as water.

CON: 'Tisn't a good thing to be living alone when a man has bad sickness.

STEPHEN: 'Tisn't good and 'tisn't safe. The worst time is the long nights when you'd be roused with the pains, and wondering would you be able to put up with them always, and wondering would the burning mountain be your sentence when you'd be taken at last. Brehoney below would never hang himself if he had anywan at all to cheer him.... (*Cheerfully*) Well, we'll have your name in the kettle tomorrow night, and a few rattles of porter on the hob for you. (*He rises*)

CON: I'll find your house out, even if I have to pull down the moon.

STEPHEN *goes right.* CON *resumes work with vigour. He is down near the footlights when* MARK *runs in from left.* MARK *is carelessly dressed in his work-a-day clothes and wears heavy nailed boots. He is about twenty-eight, is fearfully thin and pale and hollow-eyed and is highly strung and wild to the verge of madness. He runs across the stage, looks into the woods on the right, and gasps with disappointment.*

MARK: By the living! She's not here yet. (*He turns, sees* CON *and advances on him with frantic urgency*) Who are you? You must quit this place directly. 'Tis here Stephen's daughter is to meet me. In a small while we'll push ahead to the Tomb Plantation. Then you can come back here. (*Frantically*) Quick, man, before she comes!

CON: In a jiffy and a half when I have these tidied away. (*He is putting the tools together hurriedly*)

MARK: Quick, for she'll be here any minute! (*He runs right and peers into the woods again*) Neither sight nor light of her is to be seen. (*In anguish*) Maybe she never told the Post Boy she'd meet me here! He brought me false messages from girls before. He's playing that trick on me till he has old shoes made of it.

CON: If he's a joker like that, 'tis likely this girl didn't send for you either.

MARK: Sure, I know well, but what can I do but take my chance?

CON: Well, good luck! But if I was you, I'd cut home first and come back all washed and dressed.

MARK: (*Dismayed*) You have the truth! Look at my hands from the clay! She'll say I never washed them since I got them. And my hair like the tinker's wife! (*He spits on his palms and tries to make his hair lie down*) I had right to think of this before; but I amn't able to think of anything with the usage I'm suffering from the wan that's coming into my house .... Be going now. I amn't allowed to tell anywan about her.

CON: Well, good luck again. (*He goes*)

MARK *makes another of his frantic dives to the right.*

MARK: (*Despairingly*) No sign of her still! She never said she'd come! He fooled me again and that the power of his hands may leave him! (*He sits down on a tree-stump in despair; suddenly lifts his head desperately*) I will — and I must do it. (*He runs to the left*) Hi, there! Hi, there! Come back! Come back a minute.... Good man! God bless you!

CON: What did you do that she went so quick again?

MARK: She never came at all, and she won't.... Tell me first your business and how far your home is?

CON: Timber-cutting, and my home is twenty strong Irish miles from here, just outside the Lake of O'Flynn.

MARK: Good and good and very good. You'll not be long in this country, so maybe I could tell you about her. (*He takes the rosary beads from the graipe handle*) But first swear on the Cross of our Saviour that you'll not tell.

CON: (*Taking beads*) I swear I'll not tell till you give me leave.

MARK: First sit over this side for fear Stephen's daughter'd come and hear us.

CON *sits on the left end of the box. He offers a cigarette to* MARK, *but the latter waves it aside impatiently. He is hopping about behind the long box peering this way and that into the darkness. At no time during this scene does he sit down or calm down for a moment.*

MARK: 'Twas the darkest night that ever come out of the heavens; and I was within in bed with my first sleep over, and waiting for my second sleep, when, of a sudden, the darkness split up and down, and out glittered the blue elements of the sky. She stepped from the darkness into the light the same as you'd step out from behind a door. Her shawl and clothes were from the old-fashioned times, and before she opened her mouth at all, I knew 'twas Biddy Roche was in it.

CON: And who is she?

MARK: She was a servant girl in our house above a *hundred* years ago, and the people in it betrayed her hiding-place to Major D'Arcy that was landlord then and the worst bastard-maker of all the D'Arcys. She was never seen alive after, and 'twas common report that she ran down to the lake and drowned herself and put a curse on our home.

CON: What did she say to you?

MARK: 'You're the last that'll live here,' she said, 'and the sooner you quit the longer you'll live, and the longer you stop here the sooner you'll die. And,' she said, 'as soon as you're dead or gone from this house, the rats'll eat it.'

CON: What did you say, or do?

MARK: This good while back I do stop awake all night sitting between the firelight and the lamp-light. Her kind don't like the light at all, and she never come lately only two nights that I dozed off.

CON rises, comes around to where his tools and boards are, and resumes work. He is unimpressed but a little grim.

CON: Can a fellow buy bread-loafs in the shop here, or must he bake his own bread?

MARK: There's no bread-loafs selling only an odd day. A fellow must bake his own bread. And 'tis seldom the cakes come out lucky for me. Half the time the dog does refuse them.

CON: Well, there's your ghost for you. Your health got broken down with bad eating, and then you got out of your nerves at last. In this country your case is as common as grass.

MARK: (*Angrily*) If you say that, you're a fool. I tell you I seen here as plain as I see you now.

CON: You seen nightmares, and you'll see the death if you go ahead eating poison and staying awake all night.

MARK: (*Wildly*) That's why I must get a wife, no matter what kind she is. With a comrade in the house, I wouldn't be half as afeard of Biddy .... But if 'twas known I was haunted, no girl'd join me. The sweat'll be out a-through me for fear you'll tell.

CON: Sssh! (*Looking left*) There's someone stepping our way.

MARK: But that's not the side her house is. (*He looks left and starts*) Well, the divil scald them! 'Tis Jimmy King and Paddy King, two men I can't put up with at all.

CON: Why so?

MARK: They're two brothers and oul' bachelors living together near the big gate of the Castle, and lately they're going as silly as geese. They do set me fearing myself'll finish up as silly as them at last. (*He goes right, and sits on a tree-stump with his back turned on the new arrivals*)

CON: The geese may cackle away, but I can't be losing money and must go ahead with the work. (*He sets to work, screwing a window into its frame. He is sitting on the long box*)

The two brothers come meandering in in their usual formation: one six or eight yards behind the other. They are both in their seventies but are hardy and lively. PADDY is the taller and fresher of the two. In his prime he had been a fine-looking man probably, but now he is doting and imagines that he is still as young as he feels. His whole mien is complacent and jaunty; he has no doubt that he is the irresistible lady-killer of this countryside. JIMMY is smaller and much worse preserved. He is somewhat gloomy, and is very simple, and has no opinion of himself at all. PADDY comes in first singing an old ballad.

PADDY: 'My Judy, she's as fair as the flowers by the Lee,
She is neat and complete from her neck to her knee.'
Mark, did Stephen's daughter come the way?

MARK: (*Grimly*) No! Why?

PADDY: She sent word with the Postboy that she'd meet me here.

MARK: And he told me 'twas myself she wanted to meet here! He's fooling the two of us, and that he may never be the father of a family! (*He returns to his tree-trunk and to bitter reflections. During this scene he is in torment, and throws black looks at the old men from time to time*)

PADDY: 'Twas you he was fooling, not me. First she thought I was seventy-seven years, and she said 'twas too long since I was born. But the minute she heard I was only seventy-two years she said she'd wed no wan but myself. (*To* CON) How are you?

CON: All right, till the doctor sees me.

But PADDY wastes scarcely a glance upon him. He rummages in the great pot and brings up a piece of broken mirror. He takes a comb from his breast pocket, and sits down to admire and titivate his bushy grey moustache.

JIMMY: (*Who has been taking in the scene*) Is it for trapping rabbits, or for cutting trees, you're setting up a hut?

CON: Cutting trees.

JIMMY: Well, beware of that oak-tree; that's oul' Major D'Arcy's tree. In my grandfather's time some went cutting it, but th' oul' Major's voice was heard from within — 'Be off, and leave me alone or your arms'll wither.' He's within in it, a prisoner till the Judgment Day, on account he used to set five or six cradles working every year.

PADDY: (*Hotly*) Silence, there! 'Tis my turn to do the talking first.

JIMMY: (*Equally hotly*) Who said it wasn't? Say your say quick, because 'tisn't long I'll give you. (*He sits with his back turned to them, and lights his pipe. He seems completely oblivious of the following conversation*)

PADDY: (*Complacently*) Wasn't Mark the clown to think she'd prefer a rag and bone dying thing like himself that a double blanket'd smother, to me that's right in the head and strong in the back and that no girl ever got tired of looking at.

CON: How is it the years never caught up on you at all?

PADDY: I never made a day's work this many and many a year. I was the eldest and the house and farm was left to me, so I could do what I liked in it. What I liked to do was no work, and let that lad do it all. Wasn't I clever to think of that?

CON: They say there's no bread for idlers, but it wasn't so with you.

PADDY: Some must work right enough. All can't be clever. Every day I'd leave that lad working harder than any horse with his four bones, and I'd set off rambling; wan day rambling for drink, another day for kisses, and dancing and card-playing and songs and stories. I'd be wedded long ago only too many girls loved me, and my mind was always on the run from wan girl to another. (*He finds the sheep-shears in the great pot, and begins to trim his moustache and side-locks with it*)

CON: But your mind is made up now to marry this girl and finish with the rest?

PADDY: (*Nodding*) Yes. She's a good-looking piece of a dark-haired woman and a man should marry in good time before he is past his best.

CON: And you're sure she loves you?

PADDY: That was proved yesterday. I sent her sweets, and she sent them back to me straight away. So she loves me so much that she'd prefer myself to have the eating of them.

CON: When she loves you better than herself she must have a wonderful love for you.

PADDY: That's what everywan is saying.

CON: Your brother'll have to work double any more[2] on account he'll have two of ye to earn for.

PADDY: That's why he's all his life grumbling and growling against me marrying. He'll have to work double then, and she can do her share, too.

CON: 'Twill be hard on him thinking of all the sport you'll be having with her while he's miserable in his cold bed.

PADDY: Let him carry half-a-hundredweight for half-a-mile every night before he goes to bed and that'll warm him. (*Taking out paper bag of sweets*) Will you have wan of the sweets? (*He takes one himself first*)

JIMMY: (*Turning fiercely*) Now 'tis my turn to talk a while.

PADDY: (*Equally fiercely*) I didn't say it wasn't. (PADDY *turns his back upon them, and concentrates on the sweets and on romantic dreaming*)

JIMMY: Was he telling you about the clever plan he made: me to do all the work, or he'd give me the high road like the tinker gave his ass?

CON: He said a little about it all right.

JIMMY: (*Full of admiration*) No lie at all: he's as clever as the giants long ago that had three heads. Still, he doesn't understand the contrariness of the women and how many men have wives that have pains in their heads with them. And he doesn't understand the cost of anything, because 'tis me has to earn the cost of everything. (*He takes a very grubby piece of paper from his pocket*) I was reckoning up how much she'll cost me, if he marries her. First I must bring her to the town and buy the ring for her. Then another five pounds to the priest for tying them. Then the supper and dance for the neighbours'll cost within a cough of ten pounds.

CON: And she'll cost you many a sum after.

JIMMY: I'm after questioning the drapery shops all over about the cost of cladding a girl each year and, between underclothes and overclothes, I'll have to buy a score of pounds' worth for her. And we have only oul' feather-beds that she'll maybe be too swanky for. So I'll have to buy a new mattress, and put it under them.... But there's one cost I didn't find out yet: the hair-docking, what they do call the Perm.

CON: That'll be two pounds more in the year on you.

JIMMY: Two pounds for the hair-docking! Two pounds! (*He makes a note of this*) This I'll tell you: marriage is a kind of byeword, but 'tis a big undertaking.

MARK: (*Jumping up, wild-eyed*) Ye two crazy oul' fools. 'Twould give a person weak eyes and a sore heart to see ye. (*He goes out right*)

JIMMY *looks round in surprise, but* CON *distracts his attention quickly.*

CON: And she'll be coaxing your brother with bits of pleasure to make you buy her necklaces and bracelets and ribbons for decorating herself with.

JIMMY: (*Nodding*) And another thing: the women are never content till they're master in the house, and until the man has no more rights than a servant-girl in it. And if she doesn't get her own way, she'll start fighting and keep fighting. There's tally-ho

2. in future, from now on.

and Waterloo and tyrannicalism in every house ever they come into.

CON: Still, some say, 'tis better to be fighting than to be lonesome.

JIMMY: Others can't bear the fighting, and I couldn't. Sure I was a very good-looking man long ago, and could be married many a time, but I knew the fighting wouldn't suit me.

MARK: (*Entering*) Paddy, I'm after crossing her at the corner of the Pleasure Ground, and she said she couldn't meet you tonight, that her father is poorly.

PADDY: (*Rising cheerfully*) Another night'll be time enough so, and I'll go talking to the barmaid tonight.

JIMMY: (*Fiercely*) This is my turn to go first. (*He walks past* PADDY)

PADDY: (*Hotly*) I didn't say it wasn't. And it's your turn to stand the first drinks.

JIMMY: (*Shouting back angrily, from the wing*) Did I ever refuse to rap the counter when my turn came?

PADDY: And take notice of this! 'Tis my turn to enjoy the first while talking with the shop-girl. (*He follows* JIMMY *at the invariable ten yard range, and they recede roaring like bulls*)

CON: (*Looking after them*) No lie, you have some comical Irishmen in this village. Did you cross her that time?

MARK: Not me: I only wanted rid of them. They're like wasps in an ass's lug. I couldn't bear to be looking at them. Look at the case they're in though there was two of them in their house! What'll happen to me that has no wan but a bad spirit that's out to banish me?

He sits on a tree trunk near the demesne wall with his back to CON. *The latter looks at him a moment, shakes his head and comes back to his work.* SHEILA LANIGAN *comes in from right. She is tall and good-looking and aged about twenty-eight. Clothes, make-up and accent indicate that she has spent some time in England. She is serious and somewhat discontented looking. She does not see* MARK *at first.*

SHEILA: (*Forcing a smile*) Good evening!

CON: (*Turning*) Good evening to you.

MARK *jumps up enraptured. But, before attracting her attention, he attempts again to flatten his wild head of hair.*

SHEILA: My father was telling me you were in England a long while. Would you say he's learning to die?

CON: 'Twouldn't be easy for me to say on account I never saw him before. Your neighbour there'd be a better judge.

MARK: (*Shyly*) 'Tis you that's looking well, Sheila.

SHEILA: (*After a long look — doubtfully*) Are you Mark Tristnan?

MARK: Why wouldn't I [be]?

SHEILA: (*Shocked at the change in him*) Are you well?

MARK: I'm very well, Sheila. (*Eagerly*) Why?

SHEILA: You're looking very bad.

MARK: 'Tis only that I'm a little slaved out and in want of a housekeeper. That's why I was so pleased by your message.

SHEILA: What message?

MARK: To meet you here, and that you were set on making your home in Ireland.

SHEILA: (*Decisively*) That's what I'll never do while my toes are looking down. (*To* CON) How could you abide this country after England? What's in it but poverty and bad wages and slavery with no cinema within ten miles.

CON: (*Nodding*) Sure, 'twas all that kept myself from coming home years ago.

MARK *turns away, and goes back to his tree-trunk despairingly.*

SHEILA: 'Tisn't as bad here for a man. He can go drinking at night just as good as in England. But what can a girl do, or who can she talk to? There isn't a man keeping a house in this village but is part crazy.

MARK: (*Jumping up in a fury*) Isn't it you and your likes have made us crazy? Racing off to England and America after plentifulness of money and six nights dancing a week, and leaving us to do a man's work on the farm and a woman's work in the house. How can a man keep evermore working twenty hours a day? Look at how it has myself worn out and thin like a cat that'd be eating crickets. How can a man's mind stand out for ever against misery and the badness of the night?

SHEILA: Mark, I'm very sorry for your trouble, but what can I do? I'm marrying a fellow in England shortly.

MARK: (*Stunned*) Then I'm done, and she'll worry me and craze me till at last I'll be barking like a dog. (*He goes out left*)

SHEILA: Is Mark going out of his mind?

CON: The poor fellow is neglected and losing his health fast.

SHEILA: We'll talk his case over another time.

Myself and a Sligo man are friendly in London, and we're marrying as soon as we can get a flat, or room, in it. What'll I do if my father is six months dying and I'm kept here?

CON: Would he not wait for you?

SHEILA: You know how London is swarmed out with girls. If I stop in this country long, I'll surely lose him. He isn't the kind that could live long without taking out some girl.

CON: Your father'd get good treating in the County Home; but the people see great disgrace in dying there amongst all the beggars and rogues of the country.

SHEILA: If I leave him he'll stay and die at home, no matter how miserable a death he'll get.

CON: They say it isn't lucky to desert your father or mother.

SHEILA: Sadie didn't go foreign, but stopped minding her mother, smiling away there till of a sudden she saw she had lost herself. What luck had she?

CON: (*Grimly*) She lost herself over a thing that could be managed another way or done without; and that's the Irish mistake. Whatever you do, whether you'll go or stay, don't lose yourself for anywan living. For anywan can get on better without you than you can get on without yourself.

SHEILA: (*After a pause*) Come visiting a while tomorrow night, and we'll talk this out when father is gone to bed.

CON: I'll give ye a visit.

SHEILA: Good night now! (*She goes*)

CON: Good night!

He resumes work, but immediately HOTHA FLYNN *slips in from the left. He is a scraggy, somewhat stooped fellow, between fifty and fifty-five and nature has treated him very shabbily in the matter of looks. Invariably he wears a large battered hat at an outlandish angle, hence his nickname of 'Hotha'. On each arm he carries an egg-basket containing sundry grocery items. He is very quiet-spoken, but sad and obstinate and, at time, mysterious.*

HOTHA: (*Anxiously*) I didn't hear all the words ye had. Did she say Hotha courted Sadie a score of years, then curled his hair and left her and robbed her of the comfort of the world?

CON: She said no word about you, big, little or small.

HOTHA: Some have Sadie's trouble blamed black and white on me; but sure 'twas my father wouldn't allow me to wed her on account she had no fortune. And when my father died at last she was too old to have family. What good was she to me, or me to her, without a son that'd work the farm when ourselves'd be old and weak-handed at last?

CON: Did you get any younger wan since?

HOTHA: Not yet; 'tis mortal hard for a farmer. The few girls in the country are spoiled with working in shops and towns.

CON: I hear Sadie within got a nervous downfall.

HOTHA: (*Lowering his voice lest she should hear*) She did not. She was swopped.

CON: You mean the fairies took her, and left wan of their own kind in her place?

HOTHA: (*Nodding*) 'Tisn't Sadie that's in there at all, we're thinking. Sadie's dog was heard barking every night for a week keeping them back from her, but he had to sleep at last, and then they took her, and left this bad sulky thing.... But we do all we can for her, just for fear it might be Sadie. (*He leaves one basket at wicket gate*) I'll tell you the rest again. (*He goes out right*)

CON *resumes work, but in a moment or two* KITTY *runs in from left carrying a couple of newspapers under her arm. She picks up the basket, places it inside the wicket-gate, knocks on the gate, and calls out.*

KITTY: Sadie, here's yesterday's paper and last week's 'Western People' and 'Connacht Tribune'. Let you be reading them, and stop thinking, for thinking is the worst for you. (KITTY *comes in, closing the gate. She is a young pretty country girl, but not very conceited or defensive as she might be if she lived in a city, and had to stand an endless siege of admiring glances. Here her consciousness of beauty is just sufficient to increase her native good-humour and light-heartedness and coquettishness. She loves to tease*)

KITTY: Well, I'm wrong or you're a stranger.

CON: (*Suddenly cheerful and interested*) You're right and I am a stranger.

KITTY: And how are you?

CON: Faith, I'm doing well — like the people in America. (*He offers her a cigarette which she takes*)

KITTY: Thanks. Are you going building another storey on Sanbatch's house? (*Pointing to long box*)

CON: Sanbatch'll lay eyes on his house no more. Did you not meet my mates carrying him to the County Home Ambulance?

KITTY: (*Her face clouding over*) Poor Sanbatch to the County Home!

CON: He didn't like going first, but then I gave him a crack on the head with this hammer, and after that he didn't mind going.

KITTY: On the head with the hammer! (*Then, detecting a gleam in his eye, she laughs*) You divil! You're humbugging me! 'Twasn't for Sanbatch you came at all.

CON: 'Tis for cutting down every tree in all these woods, so the divil a bit of shade or shelter ye'll have left for courting.

KITTY: (*Chuckling*) The Wood of the Whispering they do call this wood on account of all the courting couples that used to be in it some years ago before all the lads and the girls went foreign.

CON: How is it you're not gone foreign yourself?

KITTY: Sure, amn't I? I'm escaped from the land and from feeding pigs at any rate. I'm behind the counter in Gowlin's drink-shop.

CON: You're badly paid there and will be for ever. All them country shops are failing fast from the depopulation.

KITTY: (*Cheerfully*) Ours is a middling strong shop still. The people around here have great belief in an old saying that 'tis unlucky to pass Gowlin's without going in for a drink.

CON: Still, you'll have to go foreign at last. And the younger you go foreign, the easier you'll settle down foreign.

KITTY: Likely enough. You have great sense in you.

CON: (*Grimly*) Like all the Irish, I got great sense at last — when 'twas too late to do me any good.

KITTY: How is that?

CON: I couldn't bring myself to settle down in England I was so lonesome for Ireland, and I couldn't bring myself to leave England and face again the poverty and bad wages of Ireland. So English landladies got my earnings and I remained a tramp navvy. Any road I go, I'm going home, because I have no home.

KITTY: Sure, you're a young fellow yet!

CON: I am not! And with the wages a man gets in this country I'll be as old as the sea and as white as bog-cotton before I'll have the price of a home.

KITTY: (*Not disposed to worry about this or about anything*) At night-time I can easy get leave from the shop on account Gowlin is always in it himself at night-time. I'll come down often and we'll have the sport of the world with Sanbatch.

CON: (*Eagerly*) Do! .... but stick to your own fellow, whoever he is. For my years for young good-looking girls are over. Any more I must be looking out for a girl with a house and land and no matter at all about what kind of age herself is.

SANBATCH *comes in whistling and calling 'Leggy!' He carries the gun and, seeing* KITTY, *is immediately in great humour*.

SANBATCH: Now, Kitty, didn't God tell me here in the night there was a fine fellow coming for you and he having a stone-weight of money after England. (*He throws aside the gun and comes round to the fire*)

MARK *comes in, following* SANBATCH.

KITTY: He's giving me strong advice to go foreign and not waste my time here.

SANBATCH: (*Jumping up in a fury*) He's sending you foreign! The last bright little face that's left in our country? (*He runs for the gun*)

MARK: (*Grappling with him*) Stop, man! Have sense, man!

SANBATCH: Out of the way till I send his heart's blood flying out of him.

KITTY: (*Grabbing hold of the gun*) Sanbatch, I'm not leaving this country, but I'll have to if there's a murder over me.

SANBATCH: (*To* MARK) Will he swear to leave the little girl alone, and not send her from us?

CON: I promise, Sanbatch! Sure, why would I want her to leave this place where I'll be staying myself?

SANBATCH: (*Grimly*) Very well, then. (*Relinquishes gun to* MARK) Kitty, leave us a while. I have words for this fellow that you shouldn't hear.

KITTY: Don't go too hard on him. (*Mischievously*) He was only trying to talk sense to me. He's fully believing he's sensible. Goodnight to ye. (*She runs out left*)

MARK and CON: Good night!

SANBATCH: (*Furious again*) D'ye hear what she said? He was talking sense to her! The rottenest action in the world wide that a man could do.

CON: What kind is she then that 'tis wrong to talk sense to her?

SANBATCH: The minute she gets sense she'll give up working for a couple of pounds a week and go to England where she'll have eight pounds a week. And if she doesn't go itself, the minute she gets sense and sees the world is hard and bad, she'll turn serious, and the last bright smile in this country'll be quenched for evermore.

CON: And d'ye think so little of her that you'd like to see her waste her time here and lose herself, the same as we're all after losing ourselves?

SANBATCH: How do you know, but 'tis God's will

her to brighten up this country a while more, and save more of us from doing what Brehoney did when he soaped a rope and hung himself? How do you know what God's will is, and, when you don't, how dare you interfere?

MARK: Don't be too hard on him! He hadn't time yet to survey this country right and understand how it is now.

SANBATCH: That is so, too. So I'll help you with your hut in the run of a few minutes when I have Leggy flocked in. Hi, Leggy! — you have me going around like the bad luck! (*He goes left*)

CON: Tell me, have you a spare bed in your house?

MARK: To be sure! My mother's bed is alive yet.

CON: I have sheets and blankets myself, but tell me honest, have you any fleas in your house?

MARK: Not yet! Sure my house is without a woman for only three years.

CON: Then I'll stop in your house tonight, and finish the hut again. (*He collects some of his things*)

MARK: Stop in my house for your term here, and God'll bless you. I won't be half as much afeard of Biddy when there's a living person in the next room to me.

CON: A lorry'll be bringing the timbermen from the town every day and they'll bring bread-loafs for you, so soon you'll coax your health back again.

They go. SANBATCH *comes in, goes to wicket gate, bangs upon it and calls out.*

SANBATCH: Sadie, come out a while. The timberman is gone sleeping at Mark's and myself only is here. (*He finds a little bag of lime in the iron pot, and takes a sheepskin down from a tree-branch. He sits on the long box sprinkling lime on the inside of the sheepskin*)

SADIE *comes out, makes sure there is no one around, and comes in a little way.*

SANBATCH: Sadie, I'm as well to camp here any more on account my house is down, and every day we can be having many a fine talk unknownt to the world. Anything is better for you than to be in there thinking always about how you lost yourself. Sit over there at your ease on my house. Don't be shy or shamed for I haven't time to look at you coming at all. (*He turns his back upon her*) The plush of my blankets is getting very bare, so to season this sheepskin I'm putting lime ticking in it.

SADIE *draws nearer, watching him fearfully out of the corner of that tragic eye, as if she was doing something criminal.*

SANBATCH: I'll keep the talk going. Sure Leggy isn't able to speak either, still we enjoy many a fine talk together.

She comes right up to the long box. Suddenly his eye falls upon his shotgun and he forgets her in his grief.

SANBATCH: Look at my poor oul' fowling gun that I must sell at last, for I'm safe no more! Tonight I very near shot a fellow that went sending away the last little bright face that was helping us to bear the world.

She sits at the opposite end of the long box. His mind is on another track now, and he has forgotten his promise not to look towards her.

SANBATCH: Oftentimes, I do be thinking poor Brehoney never would hang himself if she come to the drink-shop two months sooner. For then he'd go drinking a while every day and she'd cheer him.... God sent me in to Brehoney's that day, and there he was with a rope threw over the crossbeam and he soaping the rope. ''Tis a great sin,' I ses. 'As for sins,' he ses, 'there's bad women coming in my dreams every night at the midnight hour, and they'll not leave any night till I commit sin with them. So 'tis better for God, too, me to commit wan last sin and have done with it.' 'Twas just the week before that the sinew in my arm parted from its fellow in my shoulder, so I was very little worth that day and no match for him at all. So I made a plan, and said, 'Timmy,' I ses, 'this is the first day ever in Ireland that you hung yourself, so we'll have wan last drink to your success and happiness. I'll bring down a heel of whiskey I have in the house.' 'That'd be very lucky and very nice and decent,' he ses. But when I got help and come back he was hanging and well hung. The young priest was talking to me about it and about the unsane. 'A lot are in the asylum from leading a bad life,' he said. 'Father,' I ses, 'there's more in the asylum from the want of married life.' 'Tis easy for the priests and nuns to live straightforward; they have God every morning. But we can't go to Mass on a Sunday itself, we're gone so old, some of us, and more of us are so starved and raggedy. If only we had good learning itself. The finest thing in the world is to be a little crazy, and to have great learning. D'you remember oul' Jack the Papers and the poem he made:

Down I came for want of pence,
It grieved me sore;
Down I stayed for want of sense,
It grieved me more.

(*Putting aside pipe and tobacco*) Still there's some of

the gifts of God we didn't lose yet. I'll diddle a tune for you now that'll put the two of us in great humour. (*He folds his arms, crosses his legs, closes his eyes and lilts a lively Irish dance tune using the usual diddling words — 'Doodledum dandy, dum daree,' etc. He sings with spirit, beating time with his head and toe. But there is no change in her expression throughout this scene*). I haven't the breath for diddling now, but wan time I could keep a score of couples dancing half a night. (*Suddenly grave again*) And about the night: the greatest remark of all I'm coming to now. Always before midnight, no matter if your teeth are cracking with the fear itself, leave the fire, and creep away to your bed and quench the candle. For the oul' people had a saying: '*Leig an oidche leis fein*' (*Leave the night to itself*); and 'tis true — the night never likes any wan to interfere with it. Look at young Mark Tristnan below; he's sleeping in the day and stopping up all night with the lamp lit, and look at how the night is wasting him away and maddening him! But let you have no fear of leprechauns or fairies at all. 'Twas only last week that myself asked oul' Mickil Doogan and oul' Jimmy Walsh was there fairies out these times, and they said there was nothing out now except man. And they're two men that'd be bound to know, because they're dead thirty years.... But even the dead themselves aren't half or quarter as plentiful as they used to be in the midnight. 'Tis very near a week now since a gang of ghosts stretched their fingers at me. They were a crowd that died without christening. Now I'll diddle another tune Piper Rainey left me. (*He folds his arms, closes his eyes solemnly as before*)

Suddenly a short bark is heard from nearby. SANBATCH *jumps up roaring.*

SANBATCH: Hi, Leggy! Come back here you vagabone! (*He runs out*)

Her reactions are slow, and seconds pass before she realises that he is gone. She thinks about that a little, and then sinks back into her melancholy once more. The fire is burning low now, and the darkness closes in upon her. Suddenly she realises this, and grows frightened. She bends her head over the fire, putting her hands to her eyes in blinkers fashion to shut out the darkness. Finally she takes a rosary from her apron pocket, and blesses herself with it several times, her lips moving, her eyes full of fear. She presses the beads to her lips and to her heart, but still her fear grows. Suddenly she puts her hands over her eyes, so that she cannot see the shadows. She rises, feels her way around the end of the long box and over to the demesne wall. She misses the wicket-gate but, with one arm covering her eyes, she gropes until she finds it. With a sob she pulls it open, runs out and into her house. The door bangs shut, and there is a silence until SANBATCH *suddenly appears in the firelight with Leggy. He stands grave and erect for a moment. Then he sits on the long box and begins to tether Leggy.*

SANBATCH: You drew me away, Leggy, before I could tell her the best news: that there were prospects of a marriage in the village again. If there was only wan child in the village itself, he'd keep us smiling half a score of years more, and then he'd be hardy enough to run for the priest when we'd be suffering death. (*Suddenly gleeful and triumphant*) For we won't be always miserable, Leggy. We'll die at last. (*Chuckling cheerfully*) That much is sure. God never refused Death to any wan!

ACT TWO

THE SCENE *is the same, and the* TIME *is after nightfall at the end of September.*

SANBATCH'S *camp is as before, and the fire is burning low.* CON *comes in carrying a folded Ordnance Survey Map of Connaught. He calls out: 'Sanbatch!' a couples of times, but there is no reply. He stirs up the fire, sits on the long box, opens the map and studies it by the light of the fire, marking and ticking off various points with his pencil.* KITTY *trips in from the left. She is as youthfully lighthearted and playful as ever, but underlying this there is deep affection between herself and* CON.

KITTY: God save all here, except the dog!

CON: Did you hear today's news?

KITTY: What's the cause ye're going away so soon when ye haven't cut this wood yet, or the Tomb Plantation, or the Park of the Challenge?

CON: The Forestry Department sent word we can't cut the rest of these woods yet. No doubt some other timbermen'll get the cutting of them after a couple of years.

KITTY: And ye're off to the Castlebrowne Woods on Monday?

CON: Fifteen strong Irish miles away! Will you miss me sore, or will you miss me at all?

KITTY: (*Mischievous*) If I can't get another fellow, I'll miss you; but if I can, I won't!

CON: (*Knowing her*) Fair enough! Now, crush over here near me. I have big things to tell you tonight. But first I must humour you, or you won't listen to me right. (*He is about to kiss her*)

KITTY: Not tonight! Look! Angels are passing! (*She looks left*)

CON: Are they? (*Looks around*) The way it is, lads, if I don't throw her an odd crumb, she won't visit me at all, and then she'd have no wan to learn sense to her.... (*Listens for a moment*) And good luck to ye!

KITTY: They're gone up! Quick, while we're safe!

They kiss.

CON: I'm as serious as a ghost all hours of the day, but the minute you come I'm as hearty as a drunken fiddler. But, if we were married, would you keep light-hearted long?

KITTY: (*Slyly*) As long as you wouldn't trouble me.

CON: Faith, that wouldn't be long.... And now, look at the green patches in this map! They're the woodlands of Connacht and while they last, my job with the timbermen is safe.

KITTY: 'Tis a job for years, so! The counties are greatly sprinkled with them.

CON: There was hardly a parish, or half-parish, without its woods when this map was made forty years ago. But now they're all cut down very near, and not wan in thirty of them was ever replanted. The timbermen say the last of the woods'll keep us going for maybe three years more; after that we'll get the high road. So, before we could wed we'd spend three years waiting for a dwellingplace in some Connacht town where there'd be a thousand people too many already. Then the woods and my job'd run out, and we'd spend another three years waiting for a house in London where there's a million people too many already.

KITTY: But wouldn't we keep for that five or six years — if we salted ourselves well?

CON: You would, because you could paint yourself well. But these are my last few good years, and at the finish we might be no nearer a home, and sick and tired of each other moreover.

KITTY: (*Cheerfully incredulous*) So you'd reckon we should finish up now?

CON: (*Rising*) I'm sure of it, but I haven't the sense to do it. (*He crosses stage gloomily*) I came from England vowing I'd overlook ye young good-looking wans any more, and search the country for wan like Sheila that'd have land and a home. Instead of that I'm after squandering another five months with you! So, after thirty no man can alter his habits or improve himself any more.

KITTY: Listen! (*She looks out*) 'Tis Sanbatch coming by himself, and talking his head off the same as always.

SANBATCH *comes in left carrying some groceries in an old tattered sack, and on his left shoulder a great load of straw which prevents him from seeing the pair. He throws the straw backstage and opens the bag.*

SANBATCH: Another thing, Leggy, that ruined me; wance a man gets a bad name 'tis very hard to wash it away again. Wan year I went to a circus and a rotten liar of a circus pony picked me out as a man that was fond of kissing another man's wife. I was crying my character[1] many a month after that.... (*Seeing them*) Ye're here! (*Running left*) Mark! Mark! Come back! She's here! (*Coming over to the pair*) I know well ye two are true lovers, but 'tis no good for ye when ye have no money or a home.

CON: I drank before you there, Sanbatch. Many a time I have that told to her.

SANBATCH: (*Pulling the hayfork out of the ground*) Mark is the man for you, Kitty, on account he has a fine farm and home. And he's a wholehearted man and the finest ever you heard at saying the Rosary. You could know well he means it.

KITTY: (*Cheerfully*) Sure I know well he'd be all right for any wan that'd like him good enough.

SANBATCH: Well, if he hasn't a heated love for you, my name is Tadhg.

MARK *enters, carrying a shopping-bag. He is still a very serious-minded fellow, but in health and nerves he is now completely back to normal.*

SANBATCH: Tell the truth, Mark, wouldn't you bear snowballing with cowdung for her?

MARK: I'd bear it as long as any man in our country.

KITTY: (*Parrying this*) Sanbatch, how does a person know whether they have true love or not?

SANBATCH: (*With the fork, raking the blankets and straw out of the long box*) There's two sure signs! When you're really in love the bit you're eating doesn't be doing you much good, and you don't be learning anything new at your trade.

MARK: I'll tell you no lie at all, Kitty, I can conquer any fair meal that's put before me; and I'm up as early and as keen for the work as ever I was in my days.

SANBATCH: So you see he's back to his full health

1. I was grieving for the loss of my reputation.

and nerves again ever since Con started sleeping at his house, and cold fear was no longer waking him and shaking him in the dead hour of night.

MARK: But Con'll be gone away again after Tuesday, and the double work and the darkness'll walk away with my health and nerves again. And the timbermen'll be coming no more that were bringing me breadloaves from the town, so I'll be poisoned with my own cakes again. So, if you're to wed me at all, you must wed me now.

KITTY: Myself mightn't be wan degree a better warrant to make a cake.[2] But isn't it for Sheila your wish is?

CON *carries the fresh straw over to* SANBATCH.

MARK: That book is shut on me now. Her fellow in England is after writing to her again. (*Producing letter*)

CON: His first in two months!

SANBATCH: (*Bitterly*) 'Twould put a false face on a monkey to see it.

KITTY: Show me the letter, Mark.

MARK: Bring it to Sheila yourself. (*Hands letter*)

KITTY: That isn't his handwriting.

MARK: (*Suddenly elated*) Are you sure?

KITTY: That's from a comrade girl in London that used to write to her.

MARK: Well, if that's so, let ye tell her I'm going courting her all out tonight. And then if she won't have me, I'll ask yourself, Kitty. (*He snatches up shopping-bag, and is running off excitedly*)

SANBATCH: Wait, Mark! 'Tis Kitty you should ask and let Con marry into Sheila's farm. Then ye'll have two young families rising up in the village.

MARK: Sanbatch, if a man is to sleep forty years with a woman, the first wan he should ask is the wan he likes best. (*He goes*)

CON: (*Grimly*) Sheila won't marry him! Like myself and like all the born old maids and old bachelors, she wants to marry only some wan she can't marry, or some wan that doesn't want to marry her.

SANBATCH: If you stick to that, ye'll lose yourselves the same as our generation lost themselves.

CON: We know that well, but we can't save ourselves. The same curse is on our generation. (*He looks at his wristwatch*)

KITTY: (*Tossing her hair*) D'ye hear him, Sanbatch? He thinks he knows the depths of everything because he was in England and can tell the time by the back of his hand. Sanbatch can tell the time by the sun.

SANBATCH: (*Merrily*) I can and by the daughter.

CON: (*Rising*) And time flies, as the cobbler said when he threw the clock at his wife. (*To* KITTY) We'll be bringing her letter to Sheila. (*They set out*)

SANBATCH: (*Wistfully*) Kitty, will you leave this district when himself and the timbermen go away next week?

KITTY: (*Smiling sympathetically*) Why, Sanbatch?

SANBATCH: There's many a why, but I'll tell you only wan. To be old is to be bad, and in any village where there's no young person, there's no pleasure in the times, and even the bright summer sunshine is lonesome and sad.

KITTY: Sure, where would I go? To England where the smoke and fogs give an Irish girl T.B., or to America where wan summer leaves her as withered as a burnt leaf on a dead tree?

SANBATCH: This evening I was so afeard ye'd soon go that I went spending wild, hoping that'd cheer me. Look at all I bought! (*He empties the bag out on the ground*) A brace of socks, a bit of a decent oul' cow that saved the butcher the trouble of killing her, a glass of whiskey, an ounce of tobaccy and yesterday's paper — he said it had a lot more newses than today's. All that spending'll leave me with more dinner-times than dinners for a fortnight.

CON: But what'll you do soon at the height of winter? In that oul' coffin you'll be getting wet skin and cold every hour, and soon you'll be full of coughs and spits and diseases.

SANBATCH: (*With hayfork, tossing fresh straw into his house*) If a man'll keep himself very tidy, and dress his bed very tasty wance a fortnight, that'll keep him hardy and wholesome.

KITTY: But your farm is all lapsed back into rushes and water and bog. A snipe couldn't live on it unless he had leggings. How will you earn enough to keep life in you anymore?

SANBATCH: (*Running to the upper roots of a tree*) In here I have hid the first makings of a secret invention and, if I can finish it right, it'll make us all as rich as factory masters, and you'll have no more need to go foreign in search of a house or good pay. So, till the invention is made, let ye not go foreign.

CON: (*Sceptical*) We won't; but now we must go over the path to Sheila's.

KITTY: 'Tis easier than going under it. We'll be back soon.

2. I would be no better, you can be sure, at making a cake.

SANBATCH: Do, and God'll bless ye!

They go. He sticks the hayfork in the ground; hangs his can upon it. Suddenly he dives into the wood, and hauls back a reluctant Leggy.

SANBATCH: 'Tis noways fair, Leggy, you to be rambling evermore and leaving me without wan to talk to these days when the fear is buffeting me that the young people'll go foreign before I get time to finish the invention that'd set them up rich and happy in this village for life. (*He sits down, tethers the dog, takes out parcel of meat*) This was for myself, but I'm going dividing between us now in exactly equal parts, the same as the wren divides the worm. (*He is cutting the meat*) Some curse, Leggy, is scattering the youth from our country for evermore. Some reckon 'tis because they won't obey the Missioners, and go walking any more with their own sisters, and give up walking with other fellows' sisters. But the plentifulness of the money in England and America is drawing them, too. There'll never be sport again like long ago. A lot used to be drowned and murdered that time, and the finest of songs used to be composed about them all. You must finish it out under your own tree, because myself has to make a lump of a cake for the breakfast. (*He leads the dog off-stage and returns himself in a moment. He finds flour and soda in paper bags in the iron pot; also a big glass jam-jar. He fills the jar one-third with water, pours flour and soda on top of it, and mixes with a knife. This done he scrapes the lot into the pan, and mixes another jam-jar full. When enough has been made he sets the pan on the long box and pounds the dough with his fists and elbow. This work continues in fits and starts during the next scenes. He talks away as usual*) I wouldn't miss you, Leggy, or be lonesome at all, if I was a good Christian, and could pass the time thinking evermore about the Sacred Mysteries up there. But I'm as greedy for the world as ever I was. 'Tis only last night I was thinking of a girl I was with at Tim Crowley's wake long ago.

STEPHEN *and* HOTHA *come in from the right,* STEPHEN *leaning heavily upon his stick and upon* HOTHA. *He is very stooped and thin and sharp-featured with the strained expression of a man who has suffered much. But at the moment he is enjoying an easy spell, and the relief is so great that he is in good humour.* HOTHA *helps him to a seat on a tree-stump.*

SANBATCH: Are ye tripping far?

HOTHA: Stephen is making the last journey to Gowlin's drink-shop so he wants you to come, too.

SANBATCH: The last journey! What, man, you'll make many a trip yet, and down many a sweet glassful yet.

STEPHEN: (*Smiling*) The way it is, after each bad spell the legs are less inclined to carry me. After the next, the bed'll hold me. (*He is lighting pipe*)

SANBATCH: You're wise to go tonight, so! 'Twould be the saddest thing in the world you to go up without making the last journey. (*Washing his hands in the bucket and wiping them on blanket*) Were you vexed with me, Stephen, because I put the Blessed Candle in your hand the last night you were bad? The way it was we were full sure 'twas the death last night.

STEPHEN: I thought 'twas the death myself.

SANBATCH: You aren't vexed with me, so? I was afraid you might think we were in a hurry with you.

STEPHEN: (*Puffing resignedly*) 'Tis no loss at all to be leaving Ireland now. Anymore 'twill be a miserable bare country with all its fine mansions and woods destroyed.

SANBATCH: The springtime of the year'll lift our hearts no more. In the spring when the trees put their jackets on, they were like strangers and like giants.

HOTHA *has been setting out some papers and a pen and ink beside* STEPHEN.

HOTHA: Here you are! Sign there! Be watching this, Sanbatch.

SANBATCH: I'm watching; and Stephen you'll want to watch not to drink too much tonight. You know yourself how it makes you a rotten blackguard for fighting and the tinkers' litany and English army talk.

STEPHEN: I'll be as quiet as a stick any more.

STEPHEN *and* HOTHA *have signed.* SANBATCH *is reading the will over their shoulders, and he starts indignantly.*

SANBATCH: This will is the lowest and the saddest ever I seen. If you're leaving Sheila your house and farm you shouldn't give her power to sell them. Because she'll sell them directly you're gone, and give herself and the money away to that wastrel in London.

STEPHEN: 'Tis what she'll do, I'm afraid.

SANBATCH: Put a clause in that'll forbid her to sell it; then we might convert her to stand loyal to her own village. Which is worse, that she should have to live in her own village, and marry a farmer like her mother before her, or that us, your oul' neighbours that drank with you forty years, should be left to die on the ground, like dogs? I'll not witness such a will. (*He walks away*)

STEPHEN: If we try to tie her here, we'll only vex her, and then she'd be sure to go.

HOTHA: That's the truth. We'll put our hands in the fire altogether if we go thwarting her.

SANBATCH: All right so! I'll sign, but St. Peter'll be pulling your ears over this before you're well inside his door. (*He signs*)

HOTHA: There's as good men for her in Ireland as ever went to England. (*He pockets papers, etc., again*)

SANBATCH: You're all the year singing that tune to us. Why don't you drink half a pint of whiskey, and ask herself straight out will she marry you?

HOTHA: Tonight I'm going telling herself and Kitty about the £700 I have in the bank and my two thousand pounds' worth of land and stock. They have heads like feet if they don't understand such a man'd be better for them than young fellows that have nothing but the clothes on their backs.

SANBATCH: And when they refuse you, will you agree then to wed Sadie? 'Twould encourage the young people to see marriage stealing back into fashion again. 'Tis so long out of fashion here, the people are fearing it more than death.

HOTHA: Isn't half the country saying she never lost her mind like that so sudden: that the fairies stole Sadie and left this thing in her place, a bad thing that'd betray me to them? Didn't the village hear her dog barking at them every night for a week till he had to sleep at last, and then they took her.

SANBATCH: The same dog wouldn't be alive if he wasn't barking at some wan. Still I give in she should be challenged before 'twould be safe for anywan to marry her.

STEPHEN: (*Rising*) Are you coming to the drink-shop?

SANBATCH: In the run of a few minutes I'll be after ye.

HOTHA: Don't delay. He won't be fit to drink long.

Both help STEPHEN *out left.* SANBATCH *comes back and sits on the long box looking very troubled.*

SANBATCH: Leggy, 'tis so long since I had five pounds, if I had five pounds again, I'd sit up all night looking at it. Still I'd be better pleased than five pounds not to have to do what I have to do now — challenge poor Sadie that never took a bite out of any wan. But 'tis a thing must be done, because Hotha is the only wan that can mind and save her any more, on account that secret invention'll keep myself working far away and night and day from the Wood of the Whispering. And if I can contrive to get herself and Hotha wedded, they'd be using only wan of their two houses anymore, and then, maybe in God, Kitty and Con could marry into the idle house and bring back children to the village once more. (*He takes his rosary off the graipe handle and hangs it around his neck, under his shirt. He takes the Madonna off the sheep-crook and leaves it on the long box. The sheep-crook he places against a tree near the wicket-gate, putting it there, not to have it out of the way, but as part of his general strategy. He hangs the Madonna and Child on the graipe handle. As he does so, he addresses Them matter-of-factly and gravely*) Ye know th' oul' proverb: 'Every fool is dangerous,' so let Ye stand between me and her tonight for fear I'd go too savage. I must go middling savage, or the challenge'd be no good and unfair to Hotha. (*He opens the wicket-gate and calls out*) Sadie, Sanbatch! (*He comes back, takes off his old torn pair of socks and puts on the new ones*)

SADIE *comes in the gate, look around to make sure* SANBATCH *is alone, then comes quietly down and sits on the long box. She looks in front of her as silently as ever. Yet she seems much improved. Her reactions are quicker and more marked; she is also less fearful and ill-at-ease. He places the old torn pair of socks in front of her.*

SANBATCH: There's a needle and thread with them. If you'd sew them up for me, I'd be strongly obliged to you. (*Lacing his boots*) I bought a new brace of socks hoping they'd cheer me. The minute I heard the timbermen were leaving, God struck me that Kitty and Sheila'd soon leave this country now. If Kitty goes, the strings of my heart'll break ... (*Wildly*) ... God of Heaven, I can't stand that at all. I must do it! (*He runs to the iron pot, finds there a little brown paper packet*) Here is the last few raisins I had left since last Christmas and was keeping for this Christmas. But now I must put them in this cake, hoping they'll cheer me. (*He takes a nailing hammer from the pot, empties the raisins over the cake, and drives them in with taps of the hammer, continuing to lament the while. For the moment he has forgotten* SADIE, *who picks up the socks, and examines the holes professionally*) She's the nicest little branch that ever got her picture taken; she stirs up sport and glee wherever she goes, and her smile'd bring back the summer on Christmas Day. Just as the little children used to do when they were still in this village, she'd make you forget the world was so big and so old and so hard to understand. She's just the same as you were when you were white and rosy in your youthful days. Only your laugh had three hops. . . . (*Suddenly he pauses. He remembers the work on hand. His face darkens gradually until finally he leaps to his feet and stands over her with blazing eyes, hammer in hand*) What did ye do with our Sadie? Where did ye put her? Bring back our Sadie this minute, or I'll kill you against the ground.

She rises in terror, thinking he has gone mad, but he runs past her to the wicket-gate, and closes it. He takes the sheep-crook, and stands between her and the demesne wall.

SANBATCH: And never think you can rise in the air and fly over the wall. The sheep-crook goes with Christ, and can bring you down if ye were as high as the clouds. 'Tis only a fairy stronger than God can save you now. (*He is advancing upon her slowly and relentlessly whilst she keeps retreating around the long box and the fire*) 'Tis no good at all for you to be looking so innocent. Let ye not think at all that we didn't hear ye that night crossing the lawns with a noise like a lot of fillies that'd have no shoes, and her dog barking at the butt of her door till he bobbed asleep at last, and ye filled in and swept her with ye. . . . You're not our Sadie at all! I know for positive because there was witchery in my people, and my grandfather could put himself in the power of the divil and make thieves appear and tell me where the stolen things be. He did worse things and fearful things till at last he did what ruined Ireland, he went out into a field and cursed the weather. So here! The Earl of Hell was my god-father, and if you don't bring back our Sadie I'll open up the ground here — (*He stoops and pretends to do so*) — and in two minutes he'll be running through the streets of Hell with you in his mouth. . . . You won't? Very well then (*Raps the ground*) Open up there, and send up the worst divil ye have with horns five miles long. (*Listens*) What's delaying ye? No matter whether ye're eating or sleeping, ye're to come up this minute, or I'll set God after ye again. . . . (*He listens with ear to ground: is suddenly elated*) 'Tis shaking. 'Tis shaking and breaking, so they're coming. (*To* SADIE) Bring back our Sadie this minute and I can still save you. . . . (*Jumping up*) So ye don't care for God, man or the divil! Well, there's wan thing left that none of ye can stand, and 'tis here! (*He pulls a brand out of the fire*) Bring back our Sadie, or I'll fry the two eyes in your head!

He darts at her and she, sinking upon the long box with a gasp, pulls the Madonna picture from the graipe and squeezes it against her eyes. Immediately SANBATCH *smiles happily.*

SANBATCH: Sadie, 'tis yourself is in it for certain! If you were wan of them you wouldn't trust Our Saviour or His Mother. (*He tosses the brand back into the fire, and mops his brow*) For you and for me that was a hard hill to climb. But there's a cause for everything, and the cause of the challenge was — Hotha'd be afeard to wed you without it. (*He puts the sheep-crook back in its place, and hangs the Madonna upon it. He takes off rosary beads and hangs it on the graipe handle*) 'Tis Hotha must mind you and save you any more, and you're very near improved enough for marriage now, too. You mended greatly all the summer on account the nights were short, and, in place of thinking all day, you had many a thing to be watching: the saws cutting and the trees falling, the lorries dragging and the gangs shouting. And you had myself here spreading newses before you all hours of the day. But soon myself'll be gone, and the timbermen'll be gone, and the lonesomeness and the long winter darkness and the tree'll destroy you again. (*Coming back to her*) Will I bring Hotha and yourself together wan of the days? . . . . Nod your head so. . . . There isn't wan to see you do it only oul' Sanbatch. . . . When you'd be wedded a while the talk'd come back to you again and, if it doesn't itself, what matter? The two of ye are old enough to know what ye should do without more instructions. So let ye be hard at it, gathering up courage and sense and longing for the marriage. Stephen is gone making his last journey and I pledged my word to him. Wait till some wan comes the way for fear the cake'd burn. (*He hurries out left*)

Out of the corner of her eye she watches him go. Then she is pensive and troubled for a few moments, but shakes it off and sets to work on the socks. Suddenly she hears someone approaching from the right. She runs out through the wicket-gate bringing the socks with her. KITTY *and* SHEILA *run in from the right.*

KITTY: (*Full of mischief*) Which of them will I propose to?

SHEILA: Either of them will do.

KITTY: Poor oul' Jimmy, so, that no girl ever proposed to before.

SHEILA: That'll halt Paddy from pestering the life out of me. He has a red track worn to my house.

KITTY: That's very inconvenient for you now,

when your father is so bad. Hide, quick!

They dodge behind trees. JIMMY *comes in: sits at one end of long box.* PADDY *strolls in a little later, head and shoulders well back.*

JIMMY: (*Fiercely*) Have you the costs for a few pints?

PADDY: No.

JIMMY: You big bloater, you have all our money spent up, buying sweets for every rap in the country.

PADDY: (*Fiercely*) Have you any money yourself?

JIMMY: No.

PADDY: You bloody Daniel,[3] we'd be heavy loaded with money if only I could make you work a hard day.

JIMMY *settles down to his pipe,* PADDY *to admiring his moustache in* SANBATCH's glass. KITTY *tiptoes over to* JIMMY, *and taps him on the shoulder.*

JIMMY: (*Gloomily*) Hello, there!

KITTY: Jimmy, my aunt was out working in a field, and she left the gate open and caught a cold and is now dying. She's leaving me her public house in Curraghmore. 'Twould suit me greatly to have yourself for a husband and master over the apprentices. You wouldn't have a stroke to do only sitting on a barrel behind the counter drinking all you have room for of porter and whiskey and beer and rum and wine. So will you marry me?

JIMMY: (*Enraptured by the list of his privileges*) I will.... But no! 'Tis Paddy's turn to do the talking first.

She runs to PADDY, *who has listened to the proposal with indulgent contempt.*

KITTY: Paddy, d'ye mind if I deprive you of Jimmy, and wed him?

PADDY: (*Serenely*) Sure, how could he wed you? He has to stop on my farm and do all work for me.

JIMMY: (*Jumping up angrily*) I can wed her if I like. Any more I'll have a house of my own, and I care no more about you than the cat cares about his father.

PADDY: (*Jumping up likewise*) You hanging blackguard! How can I wed Sheila if you won't stay and work the farm for us? I don't know how to put wan stone over another to make a wall.

JIMMY: Well, 'tis time you shook hands with work, and 'tis too long I'm digging deep and splitting worms.

PADDY: So you're out to desert me! Well, take notice of this! You belong to the seventies, and you're slaved out and soon you'll be getting the invitation up or down. 'Tis a bit of a wrong age for you to be turning dishonest, but you must do it now. On account of the depopulation no shopkeeper can keep alive unless he waters the drink and sells short weight and robs both rich and poor.

JIMMY: (*Overwhelmed*) You have the truth! Girl, I can't wed you! I lived honest all my lifetime, and so long as I burned the candle down to the inch, I'm as well to finish it.

KITTY: Jimmy, we'll have no need for roguery. She's leaving me three thousand paper pounds as well.

JIMMY: (*Jumping up in delight*) Three thousand pounds! Then you're a fine plentiful girl and I will marry you.

PADDY: Take notice of this! They're all nice and sweet and wholesome till they get you bound under them, then they aren't happy any day unless they spend a while tongue-lashing and fighting. And you're a man fighting doesn't suit.

JIMMY: (*The incorrigible old bachelor in him reasserting itself*) 'Tis the truth, girl! I was evermore a very respectable man that fighting with women wouldn't suit, so I can't wed you.

KITTY: But, sure, if you aren't fighting with me in our house, you'll have to be fighting with his wife in his house.

JIMMY: That's the truth, too! And Stephen's daughter should be wan of the worst divils for fighting in the four red corners of Ireland.

PADDY: (*Spitting on his palm like a jobber at a fair*) Well, here! No woman'll ever hang up her coat in my house, if you'll come back and do all work for me the same as before.

JIMMY: (*Spitting on his palm*) 'Tis a bargain!

They shake on it.

KITTY: Stephen is gone making the last journey, so he'll stand ye black lashings of porter.

PADDY and JIMMY: (*Solemnly*) The last journey!

PADDY: 'Tis my turn to go first. (*He runs out left*)

JIMMY: Run, you divil! (*Mournfully*) Poor Stephen! As decent a man as ever got hold of a shilling. But sure the death is only the brother of sleep. (*He goes left*)

SHEILA: (*Emerging*) Good, yourself! That'll keep Paddy away from me for a few days.

MARK: (*Running in, urgently*) Kitty, could you be taking your legs out of here?

3.

KITTY: I could, and will as soon as I ask Sheila wan question — what was the best news in the letter from your comrade girl in London.

SHEILA: She sees him here and there with different girls.

KITTY: He's only a rag on every bush at that rate.

SHEILA: I well knew he was the kind that'd have to have some girl to take out. But when he's going with different wans, he's only passing the time with them.

MARK: Sure, isn't it plain he was only passing the time with you, too?

SHEILA: He was not! He'd wed me that time, only I had to come home.

KITTY: Still, he never wrote to you for very near three months, and that's as blue a look-out as any clear evening.

MARK: (*Almost fiercely*) Kitty, are you going at all?

KITTY: (*Cheerfully*) This minute, and as fast as a dog can trot. (*She runs out left*)

MARK: (*Urgently*) Sheila, Con and the timber lorry will be leaving us on Tuesday and soon my health and nerves might fail again from bad bread in the day and fear in the night. So if you won't marry me, I'm selling out both house and farm and going foreign directly.

SHEILA: 'Tis a housekeeper you want, Mark, and I'd prefer a man that'd want me.

MARK: (*Eagerly*) To be sure! You want a husband that'd have a true wish for you.

SHEILA: Marriage isn't an easy life, they say, and without true love, 'tis miserable. (*Lights a cigarette*) You're all right, Mark. You're as good as my fellow, and maybe a sight better. Still, I amn't able to alter my mind and have more wish for you.

MARK: (*Vigorously*) How can you alter your mind when you won't give me chance to court you the same as you gave him? Sure, ye should give every man a fair trial.

SHEILA: If we did that, we wouldn't get time to eat or sleep.

MARK: (*Drawing near her, urgently*) Sheila, if you'll let me court you for a while, I'll prove I can court a girl as good as him .... A few years back wasn't I as wild as any and as funny and fond of sport?

SHEILA: (*Smiling*) That time you weren't behind the door at all at courting.

MARK: I'm able still, and easy pleased. After five years any girl at all'd be Heaven to me, but your fellow'd be hard pleased. He's after skimming the cream off the finest girls in England.

KITTY: (*Entering with* CON) Are ye settled up yet?

MARK: (*Jumping up*) Con, her fellow is going with other girls as fast as he's coming up to them, and he never wrote to her in three months. But still she has every excuse for him.

CON: The reason for that is, she's a born old maid the same as I'm a born old bachelor. Unknown to ourselves, Sheila, we're afeard of marriage, and that fear won't let us want to marry any wan that could, or would, marry us.

SHEILA: That isn't so! I was well willing to marry him at a time when he was hot and warm to marry me.

CON: You thought so, but before the marriage day'd come you'd find too many faults in him, too. But what'll you do now?

SHEILA: I'll wait another while, whatever.

MARK: Well, Kitty, what will you do?

KITTY: I'll wait another while, too.

CON: 'Wait another while!' — the old maids' and old bachelors' litany. That's what Sadie used to say and Hotha and Sanbatch, when well-wishers advised them in their youthful days.

KITTY: (*Slyly*) And what'll you do yourself?

CON: I'll wait another while, too. There's no use in talking sense to us, Mark. We're fools and cowards and that's what we'll remain. Trip to England where you'll get plenty that aren't born old maids.

MARK: (*Jumping up bitterly*) Tomorrow I'm going to O'Connell the Grazier, and selling him my farm. He'll turn horses into my mother's kitchen and cattle into my father's garden. I'll blame you two women for all and I'll not wed ye after that if ye came to me on yeer two knees and ye hanging with diamonds .... Here's Stephen! We'll say no more and not go troubling his last journey. Make room for them there! (*He takes a seat in the background, and is soon lost in thought*)

The others move back and aside also. JIMMY *and* PADDY *come in first followed by* HOTHA *and* SANBATCH *who are helping* STEPHEN. SANBATCH *carries a bottle of whiskey in his jacket pocket.*

PADDY: The time Stephen and Sanbatch were playing — that was the best team of football men that ever kicked in this quarter of the country.

JIMMY: They weren't the best at football, but they were the best at tigers.

CON: Did they win all before them?

PADDY: No, mostly they were beat, but any team they played'd never be much good after. Half of them'd die the next year.

By this time STEPHEN *is seated.* SANBATCH *gets two jampots, and gives whiskey to* CON *and* MARK.

SANBATCH: That time the country was full of young, powerful men, all hair up to their throats and as wild as cross bulls. You could make many a pair of shoes out of Stephen, his hide is so tough with all the blows and kicks he got.

MARK: (*Rising*) Here's to your good health, Stephen. I'm low spirited and I must go.

SANBATCH: Did you ask the girls?

MARK: They turned me down worse than a bad shilling.

SANBATCH: And what'll you do now?

MARK: I'm skelping[4] off to England.

SANBATCH: (*Stunned*) Well, I don't know whether I'm sitting or standing! Sheila is deserting us, and the other two must go sooner or later! If you go, who'll give us a drink of water when we're dying in a few years?

MARK: If I stay, who'll give myself a sup of water when I'm dying in forty years? I'll not stop in any village where I'll be the last to die. (*He goes*)

SANBATCH: (*To the girls*) Girls, ye'll decay like snow on the mountains. Ye'll never have a day's luck for letting Mark go, that's our last chance.

HOTHA: (*Raising in anger*) Sanbatch, you know as much about marriage as my coachman that never cracked a whip, and you're after giving them girls advice that'd ruin them. They're good-looking and Mark and Con are good-looking, and 'tis the wrongest and the unluckiest thing in the world for wan good-looking person to marry another good-looking person. You should marry plain-looking persons such as me, and give our children their fair chance to be good-looking.

SHEILA: No. Hotha, we'll wed our choice, and 'tis as well for you to know it first as last.

KITTY: We'll chance our luck, and wed the first middling good-looking fellow we see.

HOTHA: All right! Marry them, and when ye die at last ye'll have more to go through than just shake hands with God Almighty!

PADDY: (*Rising gravely*) Sheila, I know the good-looking fellow you're thinking about, and I have bad tidings for you. I can't see my way to marrying you no more.

JIMMY: (*In terror*) Tell her why, quick, man! D'ye want her to sue you, and put her brand on every sheep you have?

PADDY: Right enough! Sheila and Stephen, it isn't at all that yeer blood isn't good enough. 'Tis how this lad of mine is failing fast, and he reckons he couldn't do double work and keep the two of us well fed and happy.

HOTHA: (*Angrily*) Sit down, you oul' load! She'd marry an ass before she'd marry you.

PADDY: D'ye think I'm a world's pity the same as yourself? In all your life's day you never ruined any girl but Sadie. How many girls did I send to their graves and to convents and hospitals and lunatic asylums and America?

HOTHA: That's as true as the man could hear the grass growing! Every sickness or misfortune that overtook any girl within ten miles was all over you letting her down!

PADDY: Isn't my house full of letters from them, each cursing me for destroying her?

HOTHA: How is it all the letters are in the same handwriting?

PADDY: Well, I won't curse you or damn you, but that the Lord may shorten your life!—

HOTHA: The Lord wouldn't kill a flea for your prayers.

SANBATCH: (*Stepping between them*) Well, a burning pain to each of ye with an oak wedge in it to keep it open for ever! Sit down, and don't be disturbing his last journey. (*They retreat and he comes over to* STEPHEN) Stephen, take no notice of a little word.

STEPHEN: We'll finish the whiskey at my house. Let the lot of ye be going ahead, except Sanbatch and Hotha. I must leave farewell to Sadie, if it can be managed at all.

They all set out, right.

JIMMY: Tell her we wish her well. (*Goes out right*)

PADDY: In or about a score lost themselves over me. But sure if I was the greatest man since Diarmuid of the Women,[5] I couldn't please all that loved me. (*Goes right*)

SANBATCH: (*Quickly*) Hotha, 'tis Sadie is in it for certain.

HOTHA: (*Startled*) How do you know? Did you challenge her?

SANBATCH: I brought God against her, and the

4. running off, escaping.

5. Diarmuid, the lover of Grainne, is one of the legendary lover-heroes of Irish literature and folklore.

divil, and fire at last. Then she ran for help to Our Saviour and the Blessed Virgin.

HOTHA: 'Tis Sadie is in it, so. I'll hide in the laurel bushes and see is she improved much. (*He goes right*)

STEPHEN: D'ye remember the last night when ye thought I was gone?

SANBATCH: No lie, we were full sure that was your last puff.

STEPHEN: Maybe I was dead and gone, but they kicked me back again. Maybe I won't be taken till I get Sadie's pardon for the way I used be humbugging her long ago.

SANBATCH: That could be so, and I'll tell her so. You'll want to hide first, or she won't appear. (SANBATCH *helps him to hide behind a tree. He calls her, and comes back to the fire. He looks at the cake*) 'Tis burned again, but no matter. The hunger'll eat anything. Breathe easy, let ye now. (*She comes out and takes her usual seat*) Soon Stephen'll be on his road home, and I must tell you about him. The poor fellow is suffering death greatly, and still not getting it, so there must be something else he has to do before he'll be taken. He's doubting 'tis that he must bid you farewell first. So give him chance to speak to you, or you might keep him a long time sick, sore and sorry on this earth . . . I must fetch a sup of water for the breakfast. (*He takes the bucket; goes out left. He helps* STEPHEN *in backstage, and seats him on a tree-trunk between her and the wicket-gate. Hearing something, she looks back and rises in alarm*) Never run, girl. Give him his chance to bid you farewell and die easy.

STEPHEN: (*Holding out his hand*) Sadie . . . .

She stands looking at him quite intelligently, but shyly.

SANBATCH: Sadie won't fail you. (*He leads her over, and puts her hand in* STEPHEN's) Look at that!

STEPHEN: (*Earnestly*) Some years ago I was slinging many a joke and mock at you about Hotha and yourself, and that you'd be left at last and finish as you began, weak, small and miserable in your mother's house. If any of them jests injured your mind, I'm as sorry for it as ever a man was sorry for anything. I'd never have dealt with you in such a way if it crossed my mind at all that you might ever lose yourself.

SANBATCH: (*Proudly*) Sure now she's as good as ever again, only still a little heartbroken.

STEPHEN: And, Sadie, you know how I passed my life: a bondsman to fighting and temper and drink. Be saying an odd prayer for me and 'twill cut a while off my sentence in Purgatory.

She takes a rosary beads from her apron pocket, and inclines her head a little.

STEPHEN: And I'll pray for a quick and a good ending to your own trouble.

SANBATCH: And now, Sadie, you may be going. You aren't well enough for much yet.

She goes quietly, and SANBATCH *closes the wicket-gate behind her.* HOTHA *runs in excitedly.*

HOTHA: Sanbatch, she's on the mending hand surely, and very near improved enough for marriage. But maybe she hates the living sight of me on account I let her down?

SANBATCH: The minute you have Stephen left at home, bring up your fiddle as far as Major D'Arcy's tree, and play a batch of jigs and reels for her.

HOTHA: How would music search out her view of me?

SANBATCH: That's for me to know and for you to find out!

HOTHA: Well, right! I'll run like a lamplighter. (*Runs out right*)

SHEILA: (*Entering right*) Father, come home to your bed. You're too long on the ground.

STEPHEN: I must be. I'm commencing to get dizzy again.

SANBATCH: (*Helping him out*) Faith you're heavy and hardy in your bones still.

They help him up, and out, right. SANBATCH *returns immediately and calls* SADIE.

SANBATCH: Sadie, he's gone, and I have another news for you. (*He goes to the upper roots of one of the great trees, clears away some moss and earth, and pulls out a bicycle handlebars and some pieces of piping. He is bending them and fitting them together when* SADIE *comes down to her usual place*) I up and told Hotha about the challenge, so he isn't doubting any more that 'tis yourself is in it. And d'ye know what he said in the minute? He said he'd take the fiddle down and play for you! (*She rises in alarm but he holds her*) He said he won't come into your presence till you're better improved. He'll play out there under the Major's tree. (*She sits down again*) Himself and his music is all the company you'll have soon on account myself'll be away in a secret place making an invention that's bring back riches and young marriages and children to the village. (*Showing the piping*) These are the first accoutrements of it. But, if the invention fails, a marriage between yourself and Hotha is the last chance to save the village. Wan of yeer two houses'd be idle then for Kitty and Con to wed into; and wan marriage encourages another.

HOTHA *is heard tuning his fiddle. She starts but settles down again.*

SANBATCH: 'Tis in his own interest the cat does be purring, and 'tis in his own interest Hotha is playing. He wants to make public and sure that he's sorry for leaving you and that you're again the only four bones he wants out of all the women in the world. If you don't wed him, the bad things of the long winter darkness and the thinking all day'll run down your courage and your mind again.

HOTHA *plays one lively Irish dance tune after another, and* SANBATCH *watches her stealing furtive side-glances in the direction of the music. The music changes to a slow old lullaby melody, and this gives him an idea.*

SANBATCH: The whiskey made me drowsy, so I'll nod asleep for a while. Let you be listening away. (*He slips on to the ground, settles down to sleep with his back to the long box. But his head is turned a little in her direction so that he can watch her between nearly closed eyelids*)

After some time she steals a side-glance and, finding him asleep, she becomes excited. Soon she turns round and strains her eyes long and wistfully in the direction of the music. Two or three times she looks back at SANBATCH *fearfully, as if what she was doing was the most terrible thing in the world. But on each occasion he closes his eyes just in time. So she returns to her eager gazing until suddenly the music stops. She is startled, and turns away as if fearful that* HOTHA *might come in now at any moment. But he does not, and she is sad. Suddenly her face lights up again as the music starts again. This is an exhilaratingly lively tune, and it takes her right out of herself. She smiles and with head and hands keeps time with the music. Again she peers eagerly in the direction of the music, and* SANBATCH *leans forward so as to watch her expression. Suddenly she turns, and catches him red-handed. She shrinks in confusion, and buries her face in her hands.*

SANBATCH: (*Gravely*) Let you not be shy or shamed at all. Let you be thanking God that you're coming back to yourself, and you only two years strange. Plenty never come back to themselves at all. Will I bring him in? . . . . I will! Hotha, come in! She wants to see you! Quick, man!

She jumps up looking scared and confused. Finally she runs out through the wicket-gate.

SANBATCH: Go ahead, girl, I'll send him in to you.

HOTHA: (*Entering with violin and case*) Did she ask for me surely and truly?

SANBATCH: No, but your music touched her. She was evermore twisting and turning to catch sight of you, just the same as long ago in yeer courting days when she'd be expecting you to come.

HOTHA: Good and good and very good. But she said no word good or bad?

SANBATCH: If we could only get her to say her first word! After that she'd talk the head off a minister . . . . I have it! Go in, and put your two arms around her, and squeeze her till she says 'Oh!'

HOTHA: Tonight, is it? I will not!

SANBATCH: (*Angrily*) Well, if you won't, I will! (*He sets out*)

HOTHA: (*Pulling him back equally hotly*) Sanbatch, you won't! She's mine now and you'll not go within a fist of her.

SANBATCH: D'you want to wait till the long winter darkness breaks the strings of her heart again?

HOTHA: I'll wait only wan week or two, and I'll play every night for her, and coax her by degrees like the lawyer goes to Heaven.

SANBATCH: Well, by the virtue of my oath and conscience you could be right in that . . . . (*He puts the pieces of piping back in their hiding place, and covers them with moss again*)

HOTHA: What are them for?

SANBATCH: For a secret invention that'll make many a sum for me, if it comes out right.

HOTHA: Good inventions are very hard and very costly.

SANBATCH: This invention'll drink my last shilling and, if it fails, that'll be the end of my battle against the world.

HOTHA: Keep your hands off it altogether so, and wait till we see what the next election'll do.

SANBATCH: (*Fiercely*) Isn't that what we're doing all our lives, and each gang we elected turned out to be worse than the last? Sure, they don't know how we're living at all and how could they? Wance in every five years they come down to draw our votes, halting their cars at the crossroads for five minutes, with big detectives all around them, for fear they'd see or hear us.

HOTHA: Please yourself about the invention, so; and come down to Stephen's now quick before our share of the whiskey is all drank, or spilled in the arguing and fighting.

SANBATCH: The next one that spills my glass, I'll spill his blood. (*Goes to wicket-gate*) Sadie, keep an eye to the fire for me. We're going down to Stephen's where there's an awful drink for us, a splendid drink. (*He sets out*)

HOTHA: (*Looking skywards as they go*) D'ye think will the night keep civil?

SANBATCH: 'Twill get enough to do.

They go. SADIE *comes in, sits on long box, and turns towards tethering-tree. She begins to speak anxiously and almost desperately.*

SADIE: Leggy .... Leggy .... listen a while .... I .... must .... learn .... conversation again.

ACT THREE

THE SCENE *is the same and* THE TIME *is three weeks later. The only change is that the great iron pot is missing, and its contents are scattered around.*

The wicket-gate is open and HOTHA *is seated in the gateway playing some Irish traditional airs.* PADDY *enters from right, wearing an overcoat. He looks at* HOTHA *briefly, then hurries on to* SANBATCH*'s camp where he finds the broken mirror and settles down to make minor adjustments.*

JIMMY *comes in after the usual interval. He listens to the music for a few moments, then he sits at the fire. He is wearing an old overcoat also.*

It is a sunny autumn evening.

JIMMY: (*After deep thought*) Well, I will sanction you to wed Kitty instead of me — if you'll sign over your farm to me.

PADDY: I'll do that. Why would I go dirtying my dear and fancy shoes with land when I'll have her aunt's shop and three thousand pounds?

JIMMY: I wonder who converted her to thinking you'd be better than me for her shop?

PADDY: Myself did. I ses to her: 'When your customers see behind the counter a fine, smart-looking fellow, well-fed and as honest as an egg, they'll say "This must be a well-doing, honest, up-to-date shop. Only the best'd be sold here."' But 'tis the opposite they'd say if they saw behind the counter a starved-looking, mean-looking, thievish-looking fellow such as you. Sure you're like something you'd get in a penny packet....

JIMMY: (*Impressed*) Right enough, I didn't think of that at all.... (*He crosses to* HOTHA) Had yourself and Sadie any word yet?

HOTHA: She spoke no word yet to any wan, and my good sense is telling me to wait till she has a little more improvement made. (*He rises and comes in*)

JIMMY: Let you not hurry her. Wait till she's full sure you won't desert her this time: then she'll follow you through fire and water.

HOTHA: (*Closing the gate and coming in*) But how can she keep improving when Sanbatch is for the last two days neglecting her and telling her no newses?

JIMMY: Lately he's busy as a bee in a bottle and he's still below in the Tomb Plantation with a great blazer of a fire, and he'll let no wan come near him, for fear we'd discover the invention before himself does.

HOTHA: He has the pigs' pot with him, so maybe he's seeking the invention for making beer from heather that the Danes had in Brian Boru's[1] time.

PADDY: Did you hear of the great seam of luck I struck? Kitty and her aunt's shop and money!

HOTHA: Kitty has a handsome head right enough, but when Sadie was her age, if a sixpenny bit was left on her face when she'd be going to sleep, 'twould be a half-sovereign in the morning.

SANBATCH *runs in from right, holding aloft a black bottle.*

SANBATCH: Hi for Sanbatch! that has the first blow struck against the misery of the times and the want of money and young marriages and children! Hi for Sanbatch, that has invented the only thing in the world that's before love or gold!.... I'm after succeeding in the invention for drink!

HOTHA: Is it the heather beer the ancient Danes were making long ago?

SANBATCH: Not it! 'Tis the finest of poteen whiskey. And all I want now is wan of ye to sup a share of it to make sure 'tis safe and made right. Here, Jimmy!

JIMMY: And did you not sup it yourself yet?

SANBATCH: Is it me to go supping it first? And if it wasn't altogether right and it killed me, no wan else in the village could remedy the invention. Here, Paddy, you have your fingers on eighty,[2] so, whether this poisons you or no, we'll soon be throwing clay on you.

PADDY: (*Indignantly*) Be aware of this! I'm wedding Kitty in a few days, and d'ye want to make a widow of her before she enjoyed even wan night with me?

SANBATCH: 'Twould be a mortal sin for the priest that'd marry ye. Putting funeral expenses on the

1. Brian Boru (*c.* 926-1014), high king of Ireland 1002-14.
2. i.e. you are nearly eighty years old.

girl he'd be. Here, Hotha, sup it, you!

HOTHA: (*Sniffing contents*) Who learned you the invention for drink?

SANBATCH: Wan year that I was harvesting in Lincolnshire over against the North Sea, some Connemara men were working for the masters around, and they gave me an account of the invention, but I made it better than their way. I put everything in that suited my own taste and fancy.

HOTHA: (*Handing back the bottle decisively*) Well, if you did, 'twould give us more than a red nose.

SANBATCH: (*Indignantly*) The next time you fall drunk, may it be amongst thorn bushes! Here, Jimmy, you're drinking since the olden times when whiskey was so good it wasn't a penny too dear. Smell that, and look at how clear it is!

JIMMY: It has a nice scent and 'tis as clear as spring water. If I don't sup much 'twill do no more than sicken me, and to have the invention for drink in the village'd be worth many a day's suffering. (*He puts bottle to his mouth*)

HOTHA: (*Running forward and stopping him*) Jimmy, don't even wet your lips with it. Stephen sent a bad message over since he died.

JIMMY: (*Blessing himself*) The Lord save us!

SANBATCH: (*Hotly*) And when we asked you before, you said he sent none!

HOTHA: The message was so bad that I didn't like telling ye; but now I must.

SANBATCH: How slow was his corpse in stiffening?

HOTHA: When he was a few hours dead and well cooled, I handled and tested him, but there was no stiffness in him at all. I handled him every hour after that, and he didn't begin stiffening till the black of the morning.

SANBATCH: You had no right to keep your tongue under your belt about that! When Stephen was that slow in stiffening, he must be fearful lonesome where he is, and when he's that lonesome he's sure to bring two or three of us soon from the village to keep him company. (*Taking the mirror from* PADDY) Give me a look at my oul' withered jaws till I see am I making clay.

HOTHA: 'Twas myself handled Crawley Comm after he died, and he wasn't as lonesome as Stephen; still he brought three from his village within a year.

JIMMY: With Stephen so lonesome, 'twould be safer to resign from this. (*He puts the bottle on the ground*)

SANBATCH: Look at me! I'm like a gutted herring! If I met a strange priest, he'd anoint me.

JIMMY: (*Feeling himself*) I'm afeard there's a damage in myself somewhere too. Any walking I do puts me out of puff in no time.

PADDY: (*Strolling about complacently*) 'Tis through the want of wives Stephen'll bring ye. The winter frost and ye having no wan to thaw out yeer oul' bones.

HOTHA: (*Feeling himself also*) No, 'tis some disease, or Sanbatch's whiskey.

SANBATCH: (*Rising vigorously*) 'Tis not my whiskey; 'tis the winter'll perish us. Last winter we kept ourselves all muffled up in clothes like the tinker's wife, and still we were half the time shivering and shaking worse than a miser when he'd be paying his men. (*Taking 'Old Moore's Almanac' from the graipe handle*) Old Moore has foretold that this winter's frost'll have the waterfalls tied. But if we had fine mugfulls of my whiskey every day 'twould warm us and keep our courage high till the south winds'd blow again.

JIMMY: Sanbatch, you have no word of a lie! We're in twice worse danger without your whiskey than with it.

SANBATCH: Come up, Jimmy, till I show you the invention, and you'll see 'tis as safe as the dearest Parliament whiskey that ever was. (*He sets out*)

JIMMY: (*Carried away*) Sanbatch, I'll go, and I'll sup it, too. You never were wrong yet, except a little in the head lately. (*They go*)

HOTHA: (*Calling after them*) Jimmy, if you sup that stuff you'll rue it. Remember Stephen's message!

PADDY: Sure, what harm if he's soon called up! Sure, he's not worth the water the eggs were boiled in!

HOTHA: Isn't it him that's doing all the work on your farm? And keeping you alive?

PADDY: I'm wedding Kitty, and the shop and three thousand her aunt is to leave her'll keep us going, so 'tis equal a damn about Jimmy and the farm any more.

HOTHA: Many a niece was promised shops and money, and didn't get them after. And if she doesn't and you're without Jimmy, we'll be measuring yourself for a wooden suit before St. Patrick's Day.

PADDY: (*Suddenly uneasy*) Maybe so, 'twould be safer to keep him alive another while. (*Setting out left*) I'll bring the police, and they'll arrest the invention for drink.

HOTHA: Don't do such a thing! That plan'd ruin more than 'twould cure. I'll follow them and let Jimmy sup only a thimbleful that'll not be able to sicken him bad. (*He goes out right*)

PADDY: Jimmy won't be said or led by you. He'll drink his fills of it, if 'tis any blood-cousin to whiskey at all. (*To himself gravely*) The police only can save him.

He picks up and pockets his pipe and tobacco and matches, and is about to set off, when CON *comes in, left, with* KITTY. *She immediately skips out of sight behind a tree.*

CON: Well, Paddy, how are you?

PADDY: (*Turning and immediately bridling up at him*) I'm none the better for seeing you! What brought you back to this district?

CON: The fellow that bought Mark's farm sold the timber on it to my boss, so for a few days we'll be back here slashing it down.

PADDY: Well, take notice of this! Your girl is my girl anymore[3] and I'm a very jealous-minded man, so don't let me catch you talking to her.

CON: Well, what's allotted can't be blotted, so if I do go talking to her anymore, 'twill be only about the news of the country and the twists of the world.

PADDY: (*Sternly*) Make sure you won't be guilty of praising her looks, or her figure. I'm a saint of a man only not to vex me. Wance I'm vexed I'd clear a racecourse leaving nothing but corpses lying and blood flying. If any man tried to take a girl off me, I'd bring him up to the river and jump on him.

CON: I'd be wasting my tongue and my time if I went saying more than I ought to say to her. Sure there was no man ever could coax a girl away from you.

PADDY: (*Completely mollified by this*) Since you say that, you're an honest fellow and not a moocher like some. Tell me: is there any police in the drink shop?

CON: There is a couple of them improving their health in it.

PADDY: I must be off so. I'll give you all the facts about the wedding again. (*He goes left*)

CON *sits down, unrolls his pack containing some blankets, shaving kit, drinking mug and various food parcels.* KITTY *comes from behind the tree. She wears a topcoat also, and she is as cheerful as ever.*

KITTY: Wasn't I very lonesome after you and sorely in need of cheering when I had to go teasing Paddy?

CON: (*Sorting out things*) That's as much as to say you didn't go teasing any wan younger than Paddy.

KITTY: I didn't yet.... Did you?

CON: Not yet either.

KITTY: In Castlebrowne is there any girls with land and houses and money?

CON: A few, but wan isn't as good-looking as you; and another isn't as hearty and as funny as you, and another doesn't smile and draw near the same as you. So I couldn't bring myself to bother with any of them.

KITTY: At that gait of going, you're what you said you were: a born old bachelor.

CON: I'm half a year back in this country now, and 'tis the best country in the world for learning and seeing that an oul' bachelor is seldom a good thing to be. But what about yourself?

KITTY: This place'd be too lonesome with yourself and Mark and Sheila gone; and even in the drink shop the sport is dying away and leaving.... Sheila is to search out a job for me in London.

CON: For the first while London'll seem so lonesome and sad and cruel, you'll reckon 'tis wan town God deserted and gave away to the divil.... Everywan so stern and serious and sad. After a few weeks you'll get used to that and if you reckon you could settle down in it, let me know and maybe I'll be able to cure myself out of oul' bachelor at last.

KITTY: But would you ever forgive me for parting you from the only country you ever felt contented in?

CON: I would — if you made a very good wife. And would you be able to forgive me for dragging you down to a back-street back-room with nothing in it, or around it, but dust and darkness and noise and poverty and petrol smoke?

KITTY: I would — if you made a very good husband.

CON: The two of us'll want to be very good, for we're giving up too much, maybe, and that's dangerous.

KITTY: I'm in hopes you'll bring me great luck. The divil's children do have luck, they say.

CON: And they say God likes best of all a poor person that's cheerful, so I'm in hopes you'll bring me better luck, that'll promote us out of that back-room before it withers or kills us.

MARK: (*Entering with a little bag of potatoes*) How are you, Con?

3. from now on. This phrase is used throughout the play.

CON: As you see! Here's a few loaves I brought you.

MARK: I'm very thankful to you and tell me this. You weren't in this district since the night you came back to regret the death. Would you see much change in me since?

CON: Maybe a pinch thinner....

MARK: My own cakes are fast poisoning me again, so 'tis a good thing I'll be in England in a good lodging house in a few days when the lawyers have all signed up. (*He is adding potatoes to a little heap near the fire*)

KITTY: Don't put many out, or Sanbatch'll notice, and he'll be insulted.

CON: Did you get a fat price?

MARK: (*Gloomily*) Two thousand three hundred for the land and house and seven hundred pounds for the stock.

CON: That makes you the master of three thousand pounds, and with that much you can surely get some Irish girl that has a farm, and that isn't spoiled with cities and shops like Sheila and Kitty.

MARK: (*Fiercely*) Irish women could have saved my farm and home, but they wouldn't. The last breed I want to meet is an Irishwoman. I wouldn't marry one if they were hanging over each other in hundreds. (*He crosses to the wicket-gate, and empties the remainder of the potatoes on the ground inside it*)

SHEILA *enters right. She is dressed in black, and is serious-looking as usual.*

SHEILA: How is yourself?

CON: Still tearing away at the world.... I saw your farm for sale in the papers.

KITTY: She has wan offer of £2500 got already.

CON: So between farm and stock you'll top the three thousand, too! Did you tell your fellow in London?

SHEILA: I wrote and told him all, the day after the funeral, and when he didn't answer before now he can save his ink. All is over between us.

CON: Let Mark and yourself go to the same quarter of London, and ye'll be company for each other.

SHEILA: We're two neighbour's children, and 'tis what we should do.

MARK: (*In the wicket-gate*) Who turned me down and lost me my home and farm?

CON: 'Twas this country she turned down and the want of cinemas and baths and high wages. When you taste a good thing you want a good thing, and she couldn't help that.

MARK: (*Impressed*) Well, fair play is bonny sport, and maybe she couldn't help taking a craze for England and the towns.

KITTY: Let ye tell Mark and myself about England. Is it true the English eat a boiled egg with a spoon instead of a knife?

CON: 'Tis true, but that isn't the biggest difference ye'll find. Around here the people don't think enough about this world: in England they don't think at all about the next world.

SANBATCH *runs in with the black bottle, followed by* JIMMY *who looks happy but a little unsteady, and by* HOTHA *who is still very anxious.*

SANBATCH: Sanbatch is top dog of this country any more and master of the invention of drink. Jimmy supped it well, and look at how he's still living!

JIMMY: The more I was supping the livelier I was getting and the happier. Give me another sup, and I'll show them.

SANBATCH: Give these lads a chance first. (*Offering bottle to* CON) If you drank a pint of this and, if you had a propellor, 'twould bring you as far as England.

HOTHA: Don't taste it yet till we give Jimmy another while for dying. (*He is bending over* JIMMY *who is slumped against a tree*)

CON: A taste of anything never killed anybody. (*Tastes*) By the book! 'Tis equal to the best Connemara poteen. What would you say, Mark? (*Gives him bottle*)

SANBATCH: (*To the girls*) Let ye cast out of yeer heads every notion of going foreign. Around here any more we'll be shovelling the gold the same as the D'Arcy's were long ago. Con can be selling poteen in the county above, and Mark in the county below and Hotha in the county over.

KITTY: And have you any jobs for Sheila and myself?

SANBATCH: I'll give you a queen's dowry, so you'll be able to wed your choice of the men in Ireland. And if the pair of ye'll wed two lads that whiskey puts in good humour, I'll have them as drunk as mops every day, so ye'll be the two happiest married couples in Ireland.

MARK: 'Tis dang good poteen whiskey, but more like Mayo poteen I'd say.

SANBATCH: (*Taking the bottle and setting out for the wicket-gate*) Hotha, this is the invention that'll make man and wife of yourself and Sadie. Half-a-pint of this and you'll have courage to face her, and half-a-pint in her'll loosen her tongue. Clear out, the lot of ye, for a small while.

PADDY, *looking very grave, has suddenly appeared in their midst.*

PADDY: Take notice of this! Two Civic Guards are making fast for the Tomb Plantation.

SANBATCH: Have they shotguns? Is it poaching pheasants they are?

PADDY: 'Tisn't poaching anything. I was in the drink shop and I heard wan say: 'Why are we spending good money here, when the finest of whiskey poteen is waiting for us at the Tomb Plantation?' Ses th' other blackguard: 'If we go now we might catch and arrest the gang that made it — whoever they are!' And with that, off they set at a good hand trot for the Tomb Plantation.

SANBATCH *smashes the bottle against a tree in fury and despair, and runs out right.*

PADDY: (*Shouting after him*) They'll be there before you, and you'll get yourself arrested. (*He runs after him*)

KITTY: Sanbatch, wait! Run, Con!

CON *runs after* SANBATCH.

HOTHA: (*Following*) Take body-grips on him, let ye.

JIMMY: (*Hauling the gun out of the long box*) I'll fire shots over the police and scatter them like crows. (*He is half-drunk and falls, and the gun goes off*)

MARK: (*Putting the gun away*) D'ye want to send us to Heaven without our suppers?

JIMMY: We must try some endeavour. Hard work is the only thing that can overcome misfortune.

MARK: If they lodge him in jail for the winter, wouldn't it save his life now, when he has no right fireside, and the last of his money gone?

JIMMY: Jail'd shame his mother and all belonging to him that are at God's right hand. We'll save him some ways besides jail. (*He runs out right after the others*)

SHEILA: That's the end of Sanbatch's poteen. The Guards'll be watching out twice as keen any more.

KITTY: What'll Sanbatch do now when he has no money and is too proud to take charity?

MARK: He won't surrender to the County Home either .... maybe he'll break a window the same as Dowdall did and wan or two more?

SHEILA: 'Tis a pity he doesn't know where his sisters in America are living, or whether they're living.

SANBATCH *enters, followed by* CON *and* JIMMY *and* PADDY *and* HOTHA. SANBATCH *sits on the long box staring in front of him. He is deadly pale.*

CON: The Guards are making off with the invention for drink and all the poteen.

SANBATCH: I lately got a warning that some trouble was boiling for me. I dreamt of the mother, and a mother always comes with a warning.

JIMMY: Cheer up, Sanbatch! There's wan great blessing out of this. That much poteen'll keep the Guards going for two weeks, so they won't need to be cadging drinks off us for that while.

PADDY: And the Guards can't prove who made the poteen on account 'twas found on the land of young D'Arcy that's drinking beyond in Oxford. Come down to my house, Sanbatch, for the winter.

SANBATCH: (*Rising grimly, tongs in hand*) The last of my money went on the invention, so now I must break a window. Jimmy, go for the Guards and tell them to jail me.

There is a general consternation.

HOTHA: Sanbatch, don't do it!

SHEILA: Don't, Sanbatch! 'Tis a bad place!

But he is gone through the wicket-gate.

CON: To jail he wants to go, is it?

MARK: Not it! The mental hospital at Ballinasloe. He'd prefer the asylum to the disgrace of the poorhouse.

A smashing of glass is heard.

PADDY: (*In admiration*) The same as Dowdall did. And Linehan. A clever plan, and how was it I didn't think of it?

JIMMY: I'll be hailing the Guards whatever. (*He sets out*)

CON: (*Stopping him*) Come back, Jimmy. We'll not stand for this. 'Tis crazy!

JIMMY: Why would it? For dinner every day in the asylum they get soup and fourteen wheelbarrowfuls of spuds.

SANBATCH *crosses to the fire, throws down the tongs, and loosens the tether-rope from its hook.*

SANBATCH: Mark, your farm and work is gone, and 'tis better to be knotting grass than to be idle. Sell all I have, and put in a new window for her, and buy anything else she's wanting in. (*He brings rope to a tree*) Hotha, tie me to this tree. (*Hotly*) Jimmy, may no child be at your death! What's the reason you aren't gone for the Guards yet?

CON: My hand and arm — and because this plan

is crazy. Why can't you take the loan of a few pounds from each of us all round that'll set you up again, and you can pay us in a few years when you're enjoying the Old Age Pension.

SANBATCH: (*Tying rope around his waist*) Stephen sent me a clear message tonight, and the Old Age Pension I'll never live to see. And 'tis as well. All that I drank with are dead.

MARK: Sanbatch, money is made round to go round. I have £3,000, and I'll never miss a half-score out of that.

SHEILA: I'll soon have £3,000 too, and I should pay you a score of pounds for all the nights you stayed up minding father.

SANBATCH: (*Hotly*) Ye're talking like I was a man of no account. My people were Chief Herds for the D'Arcys of Castle D'Arcy, and were every day mixing with the oldest blood in Ireland when the D'Arcys wouldn't have yeer people as dog-boys. (*He puts his back against the tree, and gives the rope to* HOTHA)

JIMMY: Don't let them fret you, Sanbatch. I'll have the Guards for you in the run of a few minutes. (*He goes out right*)

HOTHA: (*Tying* SANBATCH'*s arms and then tying the rope around the tree*) Whatever else you'll do never trust the lunatics. Never turn your back to wan of them at all, or he'll set into killing you.

SANBATCH: I'll watch well and give them no chance, no matter how innocent they look.

PADDY: The minute wan of them goes smiling at you the same as a miser'd go smiling at money, that's a sure sign he's getting ready to split you.

KITTY: (*Coming over earnestly*) But, Sanbatch, what'll we do without you? Sure, isn't it you that was keeping us all going?

SANBATCH: Leave this country, Kitty, before you lose yourself too. Soon the crows'll be flying between every two rafters in this village; then the drink-shop'll fall like a rotten egg, and you'll be flung out without a trade or riches on the waves of the world.

MARK: What'll we do with Leggy? 'Tisn't good for a dog to be too much by himself.

SANBATCH: Give him away to Tim Cawley, or to any other man that's cruel to the wife. The like do be very kind to animals.

HOTHA: (*Warmly*) Never mind the dog. What about Sadie, that you're depriving of the only wan of us she was trusting in? How can she keep improving in her reason and her memory?

SHEILA: Sanbatch, you're pleasing neither God nor man when you go deserting Sadie.

SANBATCH: (*After brief reflection*) Hotha, free me out again!

KITTY: (*Clapping her hands*) He's going to say.

MARK: (*Grimly*) Hi for Sanbatch!

HOTHA: (*Untying rope hastily*) Twelve men with white shirts will carry your coffin if you stay.

SANBATCH: Stop! Don't free my arms. (*Stepping towards the wicket-gate*) Let all of ye, except Hotha, scatter east and west till I give my last good advice to Sadie. Bring me fast warning when the Guards are drawing near. Hurry, let ye! (*Bangs loudly on wicket-gate. The others drift away except* HOTHA) Sadie, come out quick! I have news so big 'twould keep an oul' woman going for a week. (*Coming back to the tree*) Tie me to the tree again, quick! Then hide behind Major D'Arcy's tree.

HOTHA: If you see any chance at all, bring us together before they take you. (*He ties rope around tree, and hides behind the other tree*)

She comes in looking quite normal, but still shy and timid. She advances towards the fire as usual, not even looking to make sure SANBATCH *is there.*

SANBATCH: Sadie, 'tisn't at my fireside I am this time. I have promotion got to here!

She sees him, is frightened, and blesses herself.

SANBATCH: Take a last look at oul' Sanbatch . . . . The invention for drink got arrested, and my last shilling was gone, and I couldn't disgrace my decent people by going to the poorhouse. That's why I made pieces of your window, and in a few minutes when the Guards come, I'll behave foaming mad, and they'll despatch me to the asylum . . . .

She turns away in consternation, and buries her face in her hands.

SANBATCH: 'Tis no harm. I'll be as fed as a butcher in it, and there's a fine Christmas goose coming for you, too. Mark is to sell all I have and repair your window and buy a lot for you. But don't let him sell the Blessed Virgin's picture that was hung at my mother's head and my father's when they were dying. (*Suddenly alarmed*) By the Blessed Iron Book! I was nearly forgetting my rosary beads. Sadie, take it from the graipe handle and put it here in my pocket. Sadie! Stir up, you divil! Wance the Guards come I'll be roaring mad, and I couldn't ask for it then, Sadie!

She rises, takes the rosary beads from the graipe handle, puts it into his pocket.

SANBATCH: God spare you the health, girl. And may you be dead six months before the divil hears you were sick.... The beads'll be my sheep-crook and spade any more.

As she puts the beads in his pocket, she whispers something with averted face.

SANBATCH: What's that? But, sure, Sadie, *I must go*! Misfortune has defeated me the same as it can defeat any wan.... (*Listens again*).... No, I will not lose myself in it, but you'll lose yourself soon again if you don't join Hotha. Hotha! Step forward manful and face her!

HOTHA *steps out from behind his tree. She does not turn around.*

SANBATCH: Listen, now, with the ear of your heart to what Hotha has to say.

HOTHA: The way it is, Sadie, the young people are going foreign; Sanbatch is going, and this winter Stephen'll bring Jimmy and Paddy. Only ourselves two'll be left in the village and, if we don't join each other now, the lonesomeness'll destroy us both.

SANBATCH: (*To* SADIE) Thirty years you might live yet, and 'tis a fearful length to be by yourself in there between the trees. Take a last look at him, and quick! before the Guards come in. Sadie, in the honour of God....

She turns around at last, and faces HOTHA, *but she is too shy and upset to meet his gaze fully.*

HOTHA: (*After a pause*) You didn't change greatly at all, Sadie. You're a fresh-looking woman still.

SANBATCH: (*Impatiently*) What matter if ye have skins like corduroy so long as ye're company for each other. Hotha, tell her the great wish you have for her. Wouldn't you sleep on a harrow with her?

HOTHA: Sadie, I'd carry you in my two hands, I'd be that proud of you.

SANBATCH: Now, Sadie, 'tisn't two minutes since you proved there was no briar or stumbling block in your throat when you spoke to me then. Why don't you speak now to Hotha that gave you every hug you got for twenty years?

She turns around, and approaches SANBATCH*'s ear again. She seems distressed.*

SANBATCH: (*Almost despairingly*) Sadie, never mind how I'll fare, and give his answer to the only man that'll be left to pull you out of the fire in twenty years time when the age starts making you dizzy. If you saw the awful strange bad-looking smoke that was coming from oul' Mickel Kelly's the day he got roasted. I'm telling you 'tis a bad death to get roasted.

PADDY: (*Hurrying in from right*) Sanbatch, start raving! They're coming!

SANBATCH: (*Roaring out, right*) Let me out, I tell ye! Let me out till I wound ye to death with shots and fists and kicks and stones.

SADIE *runs out through the wicket-gate.*

HOTHA: She has turned me down!

SANBATCH: After her quick, before she loses herself again.

HOTHA: Is it break into her house!

SANBATCH: Don't lose her now, no matter if you have to make dust of every window and door.

HOTHA: Well.... hit or miss.... I will! (*He runs out through the wicket-gate*)

SANBATCH: (*Roaring*) Let me out, or I'll curse you, and my curses don't fall on stones. That you may choke with asthma and work into convulsions and your face turn into a monkey's backside before morning!

PADDY: (*Delighted*) Well done, Sanbatch; you're a born lunatic!

SANBATCH: My curse on Kilclooney of the night walkers and the day sleepers!

CON *and* KITTY *enter.*

CON: 'Tis too soon for you to go bawling yet!

SANBATCH: Why? Did the Guards come back again?

KITTY: Sure, they're the far side of the Tomb Plantation yet, and loaded down with poteen cans.

SANBATCH: (*Hotly*) Paddy, you're a man that'd want a great slash of a stick. Why did you tell me that they were near?

PADDY: (*Equally hotly*) Wasn't it a needful thing for you to spend a while practising?

SANBATCH: Too many months and years I'll have for practising.... Let me out now till I have a last look at the Pleasure Ground of the D'Arcys.

CON: (*Untying rope from tree*) We'll watch out for them here, and give you warning.

SANBATCH: Come with me, Paddy, holding wan end of the rope, and ye can say 'tis to break away I did.

They go out through the other wicket-gate, and turn left.

KITTY: (*Gravely coming down to fire*) Can you think of any shift at all that might save him?

CON: (*Hanging kettle on fire and getting some sandwiches and tea out of his bundle*) By hard work, in my spare time, I could make land out of Sanbatch's farm again, if he'd let us marry into it and look after him. But what can we do when there's no house or stick of furniture, or the price of either?

HOTHA: (*Running out through wicket-gate*) Sanbatch, she has more words said! Where is he?

KITTY: Taking a last look at the Pleasure Ground.

HOTHA: She declares she'll wed me, if I save Sanbatch from going to the mental hospital. I must tell him. (*He runs to the other wicket-gate*)

CON: (*Springing up*) Wait a minute! Kitty and myself are the only two that can save Sanbatch, but we can do it only with your help.

HOTHA: What way?

CON: If you wed Sadie, ye'll have two houses and ye'll want only wan. Let us wed into the other house, and we'll look after Sanbatch and his land. There'll be no charity or disgrace from him in that. He can leave us the land when he is dying.

HOTHA: Ye're welcome to my house and all that's in it, if ye can save him from going. But that plan is no good; he'd smell a charity and disgrace in it. (*He runs after* SANBATCH)

KITTY: (*Happily*) Now, haven't we friends in Heaven? There's a furnished house for us in the turn of a hand!

CON: (*Seriously*) 'Tis our first, and likely our last chance of marrying in our own country. Wance Sanbatch's land is reclaimed from the rushes and water, we'll never suffer hunger, but 'twill be the plainest of food we'll have on our table, and maybe shabby clothes on our bodies, and plenty looking down on us because we're poor. Could you be contented with that, d'ye think?

KITTY: The tinkers are raggedy and poor, too; still there's no class so happy as them.

CON: They were never worse off than they are now; but we'll be worse off than we are now, and to come down in the world is hard.

KITTY: (*Smiling*) To let Sanbatch go'd be harder still.

CON: (*Coming to her*) When you say that, you're saving Sanbatch and saving me and saving yourself, too. Like Sheila and the most of the Irish girls in England you'd soon turn English and too stern and serious and sad, and then you wouldn't be Kitty any more.

KITTY: They say a wife grows very like her husband, if she loves him greatly; so, if you'll live lighthearted, I will too....

SHEILA: (*Entering with* MARK) Where's Sanbatch?

KITTY: Taking a last look at the Pleasure Ground, but wait till ye hear! Sadie is agreeing to wed Hotha, if he can save Sanbatch from going, and we're wedding into Hotha's house and looking after Sanbatch and his land, if we can coax him from going.

CON: And ye two can help us greatly in that!

SHEILA: I'd give my right eye to save Sanbatch.

KITTY: Give Mark your ring finger, and you'll save Sanbatch. Wance he sees two young couples here and the village coming to life again, Con's lorry and ropes won't be strong enough to drag him from it.

MARK: You might be right there — but Sanbatch is so contrary....

CON: Let ye marry here for if ye marry foreign, your children will be foreign. If ye want your children to be Irish and of the same mind and knowledge and taste as yourselves, ye must marry in Ireland, and on the land of Ireland.

PADDY *comes in, breathing slaughter, and peeling off his jacket, topcoat and waistcoat.*

PADDY: (*To* CON) I hear Hotha say you're out to marry my girl! I told you before the kind of man I am — a saint, only not to vex me; and now you have me vexed enough to stick an awl in a landlord. (*He folds his jacket quickly; places it on the ground. He takes off waistcoat, folds it and leaves it on top of the jacket. He peels up his sleeves*) In wan minute, when I have stacked my drapery, I'll make bits of your bones.

KITTY: But, Paddy, I got awful bad news since. My aunt isn't dying after all. Soon she'll be as good as ever and she wants to marry you herself now. She's only thirty-two years.

PADDY: (*Furious*) Thirty-two years! I'd burn my house before I'd take such an aged woman into it!

KITTY: Please yourself about her; but she's not leaving me the shop or a penny piece now.

PADDY: (*Thoughtfully*) I see.... (*To* CON, *magnanimously*) Well, seeing as you're a man that finds it hard to get girls, I'll give her away to you. I have another girl in Tuam that's promised a butcher's shop in Chicago.

SANBATCH *comes in, followed by* HOTHA. *He goes to the tree: stands with his back to it as before.*

SANBATCH: Here, Paddy! Tie me to the tree, you!

KITTY: Sanbatch, will you not agree?

SANBATCH: My farm is only a moor of a place now. Ye couldn't live on it unless ye were fish and could live on weeds and water.

PADDY *ties rope ends around the tree.*

CON: But my job and pay'll keep us going a few years till we have land made of it again.

SANBATCH: A shorn sheep is little good to any wan, and I'd be no help to ye at all. I'd be living on your charity, and that was never the custom of my people.

KITTY: (*Coming to him*) Sure, Sanbatch, 'tis Con and myself that are asking a charity from you. We're asking you to take us in and adopt us, on account our own people have no place for us.

HOTHA: Look at that! You have a son and daughter of your own at last, and that's more than I'll ever have.

SANBATCH's *grim face suddenly begins to smile a little.*

KITTY: Your heart's wish was to save the village, and at last 'tis in your power to do it. If you'll adopt us, we can wed, and Sadie can wed Hotha, and Mark and Sheila can marry.

SANBATCH: Mark, is that so?

MARK: Well, if every wan else is marrying, I'm willing to have a run at it too.

SANBATCH: Are you willing, Sheila?

SHEILA: (*Smiling*) If you'll agree to what Kitty and Con are asking you.

SANBATCH: Two young couples in the village again! Paddy, untie the rope!

HOTHA: I'll tell Sadie. (*He runs out through the wicket-gate*)

PADDY: (*Indignantly*) I'm after making the finest double knot that ever was known, and what sense or reason is in changing your mind again?

CON: (*Whipping out knife, gaily*) 'Tis your throat, or your knot, Paddy; and I couldn't say at all which is most valuable. (*He cuts rope*)

MARK: (*Running right*) I'll tell the Guards you were only shamming mad and fooling us. (*He stops, and takes out some pound notes*) Girls, bring these to the drink-shop, and put a fire in the snug for us, and chairs and porter and whiskey and lemonade and biscuits and red-meat and the loaves there, and we'll have a night till morning. (*He runs out, right*)

KITTY: (*Counting money*) Sanbatch, tell Hotha to bring his fiddle, and we'll dance the eyes out of our heads.

SHEILA: The loaves are here. (*She is putting them together*)

CON: I'll carry them. I had a great dinner today, and it made me as strong as an elephant.

SHEILA: Let ye not be long, Sanbatch.

The three run out left. PADDY *lights his pipe.* SANBATCH *makes his way wearily as far as the fire. A reaction has set in.*

SANBATCH: This minute I'm as weak as water. When I saw I'd have to go to the mental hospital it frightened the wind in me. Linehan broke a window, too, and he didn't live two months after he went amongst them; and Keenan didn't last any length either. (*He lies down beside the fire*)

PADDY: These are decent fellows, and they'll give us three great weddings with lashings of roast goose and cold porter.

SANBATCH: Too much roast goose and cold porter killed oul' fellows at weddings before now.

PADDY: Them fellows were so done up they could hardly look against the sun. They weren't the same as me: sound and hardy as a goat's horn.

MARK: (*Running in with* JIMMY) We turned back the Guards. Come on to the drink-shop, let ye. (*He runs out left*)

JIMMY: Three great weddings and three great days at roast goose and porter! (*Hotly, to* PADDY, *who is moving off*) Stand back there! 'Tis my turn to go first! (*He runs out past him*)

PADDY: (*Hotly, after him*) Take notice of this! Four great weddings, and four great days! Tomorrow I'm off to Tuam to settle up with my girl! (*He goes off left*)

HOTHA: (*Coming out*) Sanbatch, we have all settled.... Where's the lot?

SANBATCH: Gone for a night's singing and jollying at the drink-shop. Will ye go?

HOTHA: She'd be too shy to go amongst so many yet. Wait till I bring down a batch of eatables and drinkables, and we'll have a party for ourselves and her. (*Runs to gate*) Sadie, Sanbatch only is here. (*He runs out right, and she comes in back, looking very shy and happy*)

SADIE: (*Earnestly*) Is it the truth, that you'll never go to the asylum if I wed Hotha?

SANBATCH: (*Vehemently*) If there's wan word of a lie in that, you can bury me upside down, so that when I think I'll be scratching up, I'll be scratching down. (*He imitates a man clawing his way out of the grave*)

SADIE: If I wed him, will he desert me again?

SANBATCH: Not him! Soon you'll be going out again happy amongst the neighbours, and he'll be every bit as proud of you as he used to be long ago.

SADIE: But will he be evermore fretting and blaming about our want of children?

SANBATCH: The want of a son isn't stinging him much at all any more, because myself is every day telling him that's a pure Godsend, on account himself and all his breed were so stubborn and contrary. So let ye do what ye should do as well as ye can do, and ye'll be company for each other, and so happy that ye'll think every day Christmas Day. You'll wed him?

SADIE: (*Smiling*) . . . . I will. (*She sits beside him*)

SANBATCH: In the English Army as soon as wan man is killed they enlist another; and that's God's plan, too: for each person that dies, a child to be sent into the world. But around here we reckoned we were men of brains, as good as God, and we reckoned we could do without ye, and God never said wan word only let us go ahead and ruin ourselves: and then Himself scattered all women and girls away from us to the ends of the world.... But maybe now He thinks we have enough good sense got again, and maybe soon He'll bestow children on the village again. If He does, we'll have nothing more to want or to do, only wait for the death, and then die happy because we will be leaving room for more.

SAM THOMPSON

(1916-65)

from: OVER THE BRIDGE (1960)

[Thompson wrote this play between 1955 and 1957. While in rehearsal with the Group Theatre of Belfast, it was cancelled because the directors thought it too controversial. After much public dispute and a court case, the play was finally produced in 1960 and was greeted with critical acclaim.

The setting is the Harland and Woolf shipyard in Belfast, traditionally a protestant working-class bastion and the site of pogroms against catholic workers in 1920-22 and in 1935. In this case, Peter O'Boyle is the catholic victim of the incensed workforce. Religious fundamentalism, ancient religious hatred and the difficult role of a trade union in a sectarian society dominate these scenes. Davy Mitchell is the level-headed trade union official, Rabbie White a zealous, somewhat rulebound member. The Leader is a characteristic example of the mob orator.

Over The Bridge was first presented at the Empire Theatre, Belfast, on 26 January 1960 by Ulster Bridge Productions, a company formed by Thompson and some actors from the Group Theatre.]

CHARACTERS

RABBIE WHITE
WARREN BAXTER
MR FOX
GEORGE MITCHELL
DAVY MITCHELL
ARCHIE KERR
PETER O'BOYLE
BILLY MORGAN
MOB LEADER

from PART ONE, SCENE TWO

DAVY: I'm sorry, Billy, that you see fit to resign. I hope you've given it careful thought.

BILLY: The Lord has given it careful thought for me, Davy. I'm resigning from the union.

RABBIE: Do you intend to carry on working in the shipyard at your trade?

BILLY: My trade's my only means of livelihood. I have a family to support.

RABBIE: As an ex-official of our branch you should know that you can't work as a non-union man in the shipyard.

DAVY: Billy, you have made a decision in accordance with your religious convictions. But I hope you understand that it can have serious implications?

BILLY: I understand that, Davy.

DAVY: Then you understand that if you persist in going through with your intention of working as a non-union man, it could cause a strike which would involve thousands of men?

BILLY: I'm sorry, Davy, but my mind's made up.

RABBIE: Your mind's made up. And who the hell do you think you are? We've fought all our lives against blacklegs[1] in every firm where our union is represented and we'll make no exception of you in the shipyard. You'll stay in the union, friend, or get out of your job.

BILLY: Don't you raise your voice to me, Rabbie White.

RABBIE: (*Loudly*) I'll raise the roof of hell if I feel like it.

DAVY: Now take it easy, Rabbie, keep your voice down.

RABBIE: I'll not keep my voice down, Davy. If we grant him freedom to work as a non-union man, every crackpot in the shipyard will drag the Lord in on his side to get out of the union. For years we've fought for a closed shop,[2] and he calmly walks out here and says he's going to bale out. He stays in the union, Davy, whether he likes it or not.

BILLY: I've as much right to act according to my Christian principles as you have according to your union principles. I'm leaving the union.

RABBIE: You leave the union and you'll leave your job.

BILLY: This is supposed to be a free country. But if I leave the union you're going to starve me back in again. Heth,[3] that's power for you.

RABBIE: Don't you talk to me about power. God forbid that the sect you belong to had any, for they'd do away with trade unions, cinemas, football matches, television sets, stop you from smoking and drinking and then when you die, they want to roast you in hellfire.

BILLY: (*Raising his Bible*) Agnostic, unbeliever! Damning his soul with every word that comes out of his mouth. Repent, Rabbie White! Repent before it is too late . . .

DAVY: Brother White, you can't shout your opinions down this man's throat.

RABBIE: I'm voicing the rules of this union.

DAVY: This man's entitled to a hearing, to defend his opinions.

RABBIE: No man's entitled to undermine the union.

BAXTER: Nobody's talking about undermining the union, Rabbie.

RABBIE: That's what he aims to do.

1. A blackleg is a worker who breaks a strike by staying on the job or taking the place of a striker.
2. A situation in industry in which there exists a contract between a trade union and an employer that allows only the unions' members to work.
3. A mild exclamation, 'Faith'.

DAVY: It's not an impossible situation, brother White. We had two cases like this before and they worked out all right in the end.

RABBIE: Only because the two members concerned backslid again before their membership expired.

BAXTER: Be reasonable, Rabbie, and give this man a chance to state his case.

RABBIE: Throw our union rule book away to be reasonable to him?

BAXTER: Your attitude's too aggressive. It's getting us nowhere.

RABBIE: I'll fight this form of insidious blacklegging with every ounce of strength in my body. If we grant this man permission to leave the union, every crackpot hanging on to a religious belief will want to leave too. And before we know it, Davy, our union headquarters will be turned into a mission hall.

DAVY: Have you finished yet, Rabbie?

RABBIE: No, I haven't. How do we know he'll not backslide again and make a fool out of us? Didn't it happen to Andy Jones? He saw the light when he was living with another man's wife in Liverpool. Then we had John Barr. He was dragged out of an entry in a drunken stupor, claiming his salvation. And what about Arthur Knox? He was supposed to give his heart to the Lord on a coal cart on the Newtownards Road. I only hope, Davy, that no more of the wild characters in this union of ours see the light. For by Jesus if they start to give their testimonies, they're going to put the Lord in some terrible predicaments.

DAVY: If ever a man's conduct put up a case to convince anyone why they shouldn't be in a trade union, you've certainly done that here, Rabbie.

BILLY: If that man insults me again, Davy, I'm leaving.

RABBIE: I've had my say, Davy. Now I'm anxious to hear his.

DAVY: Brother Morgan, what possible harm can it do to your beliefs to remain in the union? No-one's forcing you to take part in its activities.

BILLY: It says in the good book, Come ye out from among them. Be not of equal yoke with unbelievers.[4]

RABBIE: What does that mean?

BILLY: That any child of God cannot unite with

4. II Corinthians 6.14.

an unbeliever in a common purpose.

RABBIE: If we're unbelievers, you're uniting with us every day building boats.

BILLY: That's a different matter.

BAXTER: Next Friday we'll be getting ten bob[5] a week of a rise that was bargained for by the union ship-building confederation. As a man who now doesn't believe in unions, Billy, what will you do when you get that extra ten bob in your pay packet?

RABBIE: Will you refuse it?

BILLY: I'll decide about that when the time comes.

RABBIE: You see what I mean, brothers. He'll make a decision when the time comes, and in the meantime the whole trade union movement will have to stand by and see whether he'll be the cause of thousands of men walking the streets through strike action.

BAXTER: Don't depend on the firm standing by you, Billy. They'll have to let you go, if they want to avoid a strike.

BILLY: I know that, brother Baxter. The trade union is a murderous organisation. They'll deprive a man of his livelihood if he insists on remaining outside.

DAVY: It's the best insurance any man can have, Billy, with the cheapest premium. He gets protection. His union guards his rights under the Factories Act.[6] He's protected in every way. Employers, Billy, are only human and would take short cuts at the men's expense if they were at liberty to do so. It was the taking of such liberties that brought trade unions into existence. As an active member in the past, you should know that.

BILLY: My conscience says I must resign, Davy. I'm not altering that decision to conform to the rules of an ungodly organisation. I want my resignation sent to the district committee and confirmed.

DAVY: Very well, brother Morgan. If that's your final decision, the branch tomorrow night can forward your resignation to the next district committee meeting.

BILLY: Thanks, Davy. (*He walks to the workshop door and then stops*) I must admit you're a fair man, Davy Mitchell. A fair man. (*He leaves. There is an awkward silence*) . . .

from PART TWO, SCENE ONE

DAVY: For the sake of your wife and children, Peter, don't do or say anything to this fellow that would give the mob a green light. He controls them, Peter, but remember, he's a dangerous character. (*He goes*)

PETER *is left alone for a few moments. Then the* MOB LEADER *enters and walks to the centre of the office, while his two henchmen take up their stand at the door. He is smoking a cigarette; there is something very sinister about him. He rarely looks at* PETER *as he speaks.*

LEADER: Your name's O'Boyle — Peter O'Boyle?

PETER *slowly raises his head and looks him in the eye.*

PETER: So what?

LEADER: Did your mates not advise you to stay out today?

PETER: What if they did?

LEADER: It was good advice, friend. You should have taken it.

PETER: That's for me to decide.

LEADER: It's lucky for you I'm standing between you and that crowd out there. They wanted to tear you apart as soon as they laid eyes on you, but I stopped them and advised them to wait until ten past one to see what you intended to do. (*He pauses*) What are your intentions?

PETER: Why not wait till ten past one and find out.

LEADER: Don't try to be awkward, friend. If you're still here at ten past one, that crowd will smash your skull like a vice.

PETER: What have you got against me? I don't even know you.

LEADER: I know you are a Popehead[1] and a defiant bastard.

PETER: I'm not here to defy anyone. I have a wife and family to support.

LEADER: When there's an ultimatum sent out that Popeheads are not to come in to work, there's no exceptions. (*He pauses*) You're a Popehead.

PETER: I'm a Catholic if that's what you mean.

LEADER: (*With intensity*) And you're in work

5. ten shillings.
6. Regulations for the welfare of factory workers were consolidated in acts of 1901 and 1937. The present (1961) Factories Act was enacted after Thompson's play was written.

1. A term of abuse for a catholic.

today after what happened in that sub-station yesterday. That man died yesterday before he even reached hospital. He had a wife and kids too, but he was a good Prod,[2] friend, and that's what makes all the difference; he was a good Prod.

PETER: (*Angrily*) What that man was has nothing to do with me.

LEADER: Wasn't it your crowd caused that explosion?

PETER: I know nothing about the explosion.

LEADER: Are you sure you know nothing? (*He pauses*) There's been a lot of talk about you, friend.

PETER: What sort of talk? I'm in no illegal organisation if that's what you mean.

LEADER: We've heard different.

PETER: Well, you've heard wrong.

LEADER: Your old man was a member.

PETER: That's a dirty lie! If you've been listening to that bucketmouth Archie Kerr ...

LEADER: (*Quickly*) Come off it, friend, time's running out, you have exactly eight minutes to make up your mind.

PETER: If anybody lays a hand on me, you'll be reported to the authorities. (*He points accusingly*) I know you, mac. My friends know you and so does my foreman. If anything happens to me, you'll be responsible.

LEADER: (*Suavely*) You've got it all wrong, friend. We're only here to help you.

PETER: I wouldn't believe a word you would swear. You came after me because you're the leader of a mob of thugs who believe that three hundred men against one is a fair fight.

LEADER: Nobody leads a mob, but if you're daft enough to walk out to that bench at ten past one and lift a tool, they'll make you a target for everything they can lay their hands on — and when they make their quick move to get offside, they'll stampede all over you on their way out. So you see what I mean, friend? What chance would you have of pinning anything on anybody?

PETER: It'll be pinned on you.

LEADER: Listen, Peter, you don't seem to understand. Nobody wants to harm you. To that crowd out there you're a defiant bastard. We're only here to give you a chance. All you've got to do is to put on your coat, walk out through the gate, and on to the bus. You have a family. You've a wife and kids.

PETER: You've a mind like a sewer. You frighten me more than the mob.

LEADER: Not me, friend. Not me. It's them you should be frightened of. We're your friends.

PETER: You don't fool me, mac. I know your kind. You're as deep in this as any of those thugs out there. (*With rising hysteria*) Go on. Get out to your thugs. Tell them I'm staying at my work. Tell them that nobody chases me out of my job. Tell them that.

LEADER: You tell them. (*He pauses*) You're very foolish.

PETER: (*Losing control*) Get out! Get out or I'll kill you, you lousy skitter! (*He springs at the* MOB LEADER *but the two henchmen pull him back and thrust him into the chair where he breaks down into sobbing*)

LEADER: (*Quietly*) Now I want you to know that as soon as we get out of this office, we're walking straight through that gate out there. We came in here to help you, but from now on you're on your own, friend. That crowd is your pigeon.[3]

PETER: (*Screaming*) Get out! Do you hear, get out! (*He grabs a hammer and flings it at the* MOB LEADER. *It crashes through a fanlight. The babble of the crowd, stirred up by the sound of the struggle, rises to a crescendo, and the two henchmen put their shoulders against the door.* FOX, RABBIE, BAXTER, GEORGE, DAVY *and* ARCHIE *rush in through the side door*)

FOX: What's going on here? What's the matter?

LEADER: Nothing's the matter. Our friend here just lost the head for a minute and fired a hammer. This fellow's a troublemaker.

FOX: Who are you? What's your trade?

LEADER: (*Hurriedly*) We're only here to try and help for this fellow's own good.

FOX: If anything happens to this man, I'll hold you responsible.

HENCHMAN: (*Anxiously*) Come on, mate, let's get to hell out of here.

LEADER: You'll not hold us responsible. We're getting back to our job. (*He looks at his watch*) It's only a few minutes to the blow.[4] (*He leaves, closely followed by his henchmen*)

FOX: What did he say, Peter?

2. protestant.

3. your concern or responsibility.

4. The siren that announces the end of one shift and the beginning of another.

PETER: He told me things that weren't true, and that mob out there believes them. Stories about me that has been peddled around the shipyard by that waster there (*he points at* ARCHIE). He's the man who put them on my track; he's the one who told them I was in work today!

RABBIE: Get a grip on yourself, Peter, we want no trouble, we might get a bellyful of it before we get you out of here.

DAVY: It's no time for accusations. Everybody in this office is here to help you.

FOX: Including Archie, Peter. After all he was good enough to come all the way from the boat to warn you.

BAXTER: This is the sort of thing comes out of gossip, anyway. It's all very harmless and good fun until something like this happens. Then everybody dissects everybody else's statements until we get what we have out there — a mob piecing it together again to suit their own way of thinking.

DAVY: What did that fellow say, Peter? We must know, for we haven't much time.

PETER: He told me to get out at ten past one.

RABBIE: What in heaven's name made you come in anyway?

PETER: (*Quietly*) My wife didn't want me to come in. She said it would all blow over in a day or two, and my job would still be here for me.

FOX: Of course it would, Peter. You should have known that.

PETER: But why do they want to put me out of my job, boss? I've done nobody any harm.

FOX: We know that, Peter, but that mob can do *you* harm if you don't leave. Do as that thug says and go now, nobody here wants to see you get hurt.

PETER: I wouldn't believe a word them swine would say.

GEORGE: O'Boyle's right. That mob didn't come all this way to let him walk through the gate unmolested.

The sound of breaking glass is heard again.

MAN'S VOICE: Send out that fenian[5] bastard!

The crowd noise rises.

SECOND VOICE: You've five minutes, O'Boyle. When the horn stops blowing, we're coming for you.

5. Although the Irish revolutionary organization petered out in the last century, the term 'fenian' is still used to refer to those nationalists who are willing to fight for a united Ireland.

Again the noise increases.

FOX: Everybody do exactly as that ruffian asks and stay in this office. I'm advising you for the last time, Peter, to go.

BAXTER: What about it, Peter?

PETER *doesn't answer.*

BAXTER: (*Angrily*) You have more than yourself to think about. What about your wife and kids? — and you're not making things any easier for us by being stubborn.

PETER: (*Shouting*) You leave my wife and kids out of this. You have a bloody nerve telling me I'm stubborn. I'm standing by my rights and I refuse to be chased out of my employment because I'm a Catholic.

BAXTER: It'll only be a day or two until things blow over, and if it's the loss of a couple of days' wages you're thinking about, we'll make that up for you.

PETER: I don't care if this tension lasts two days or two weeks. I'm not goin' to be forced out of here to crawl back again when it suits the whims of a mob. When that horn blows, I'm goin' out of this office all right, but it'll be to my bench to start work.

There is a momentary stunned silence.

FOX: You're being very foolish, Peter.

BAXTER: Let him walk out there and get his skull smashed if he wants it that way. I've had a bellyful of this pleading and arguing, trying to protect him. It's about time we thought of ourselves and got out of here before that mob goes into action.

RABBIE: Is that your final answer, Peter?

PETER: You heard what I said.

RABBIE: Then it's time we were going, fellows.

FOX: You heard me say that everybody was to stay in this office.

RABBIE: I did, boss, but Peter has changed all that. If he's not prepared to walk out through that gate, I am. I'm not goin' to be witness to a scene where a man is stupid enough to offer himself as a sacrifice. In fact, there's no point in any of us staying here.

They all begin to move towards the side door except FOX, PETER *and* DAVY *who stand their ground.*

RABBIE: Are you coming, Davy?

DAVY: Where do you want me to go?

RABBIE: With us. There's nothing more we can do in here. If Peter's mad enough to think he can defy a mob, we'd be worse than him for trying to help him.

BAXTER: For Pete's sake, Davy, let's get going.

That horn will blow any second now.

RABBIE: (*Walking over to* DAVY) If you're not going with us, ould hand, just where exactly *do* you think you're going?

DAVY: To my bench out there when the horn blows — to start work.

They all look at him with shocked amazement.

BAXTER: But you can't do that, Davy, they'll tear you apart.

DAVY: Peter's my mate at that bench. If he lifts a tool to start work, I'm duty bound as a fellow trade unionist to work with him.

RABBIE: What are you trying to prove, Davy? If Peter or you lift one tool at that bench, it'll be your last.

GEORGE: Davy, I'm your brother, and I haven't agreed with you about a lot of things, but I don't want to see you getting kicked to death at that bench. I'm appealing to you to get out of this office, right now.

FOX: As your head foreman, I forbid either of you to work out there. I'm concerned for your safety.

DAVY: All my life I've fought for the principles of my union and Peter here fought for them too. Would you want me to refuse to work with him, because he upholds what is his right, to work without intimidation?

RABBIE: We all uphold that, Davy, but this is a mob we're dealing with. Mobs don't reason.

BAXTER: I don't care what happens to O'Boyle, he's had his chance. But I do care what happens to you, Davy. When the horn blows only one man is going out to that bench and it's not going to be you, for by Christ we'll stop you no matter what you do.

DAVY: Just one of you try it and see what happens. (*He lifts a hammer from the plan bench*) If I refuse to go out there and stand alongside my mate at that bench, everything I have ever fought for or believed in has been nothing.

The horn blows. It sets in motion the banging of hammers and angry voices of the mob. PETER *and* DAVY *walk to the office door. The horn stops and the hammering and angry voices continue for a few moments until* DAVY *and* PETER *are out of the office.*

Then there is a great silence.

FOX: See what's happening, Baxter.

WARREN *takes up his position on the plan bench.*

RABBIE: What's Peter and Davy doing?

BAXTER: They're at their bench, working. They're not even lifting their heads to see what's going on around them. (*With feeling*) They're working as if nothing was going to happen.

RABBIE: What's the mob doing?

BAXTER: (*After a pause*) They're closing in . . . oh God. Oh my God. Davy. (*A scream*) *Davy!*

There is a terrifying din of hammers and voices. WARREN *covers his face with his hands and slumps down on the bench, sobbing hysterically. He makes a sudden lunge towards the door, but the others hold him back. After about a minute, the din dies away.*

FOX: Are they gone?

RABBIE *goes to the door and opens it wide.*

RABBIE: They're gone all right; there's not one of them murdering bastards in the vicinity. (*He hurries out into the shop, followed by* GEORGE *and* ARCHIE)

FOX: (*Settling* BAXTER *into a chair*) Try and control yourself, Warren.

BAXTER: They hadn't a chance, boss. My God, they hadn't a chance.

FOX: I understand, son.

RABBIE *returns looking very shaken.*

RABBIE: They're in a bad way, boss. We'll have to get word through for an ambulance.

FOX: There's not time for that, Rabbie. Here's the keys of my car; get them into it and Warren here can drive you to the main ambulance room and go with them to the hospital, Rabbie.

RABBIE: Right, boss. (*He leaves, half dragging* WARREN *along beside him*)

ARCHIE: (*Coming in*) I locked away Peter's and Davy's tools, boss. There's the keys.

FOX: I'll look after them, Archie. I'm going to the main office now. I'll want you to stay here and take a note of any plans that go out.

ARCHIE: I'll do that, boss.

FOX: (*Thoughtfully*) It could have been any of us out there — if we'd worked in the wrong place.

He leaves. ARCHIE *is left alone. In the distance the sound of riveting and caulking machines can be heard coming from the slipways. It gets very loud as the curtain slowly closes.*

EUGENE McCABE

(1930-)

from:
KING OF THE CASTLE (1964)

[Although part of his hostility to Scober, Maguire's account of times past does, with Tressa's, evoke a kind of idyllic pastoral, unmechanized, aristocratic. These ideals, cynically or wistfully asserted, his marital failure, the ambiguous encounter between Tressa and Lynch, all come together to undermine the certainties that Scober so vehemently proclaims.

The play was first produced on 2 September 1964 at The Gate Theatre, Dublin.]

CHARACTERS

SCOBER (BARNEY) McADAM, *the King*
TRESSA, *his wife*
JEREMY MAGUIRE, *a small farmer*
MATT LYNCH, *a travelling thresherman*
JOADY CONLON, *a smaller farmer*

PLACE: *A Leitrim farm, Clonhaggard*
TIME: *The late 1950s*

from ACT I

[*Inside the McAdam house*]

MAGUIRE: (*Grins at her*) Does Scober give you the hand (*Pause*) I seen you — one night . . . (*he grins and winks, pointing at the mirror nodding*) Yeah . . . (*he cups his hands against his chest*) Am I right? Eh! We know somethin' . . . don't we, daughter — me and you — am I right? . . . me an' Scober, we were cubs together: that's right — you're startin' hard — lek a woman not too happy at her work — eh. (*Pause; moving away*) Line up fifty women, and Jemmy knows — this one has a man, this one has a knuck[1] — this one has a money-makin' rig. Ever ass[2] yourself — what a woman's for? — Scrape plates, twig floors — look at rocks and heather, eat, cook, sleep, drink, empty pots, feed men — and hens, talk with a hired girl, confess on Saturday, pray of a Sunday, and think of sin all day Monday? That what she's for? Keepin' her belly full and the pots empty? (*He has moved a little closer; intensely:*) No! What so?

TRESSA *has backed away, fascinated and disgusted.*

To drain a man — make a chile — and rear a man. (*Pause*) 'Less she does that — she's fat — good for nothing, but walkin' about, chewin' her cud, — empty — a loss . . .

TRESSA: (*Quietly*) Get out . . .

MAGUIRE: (*Casually*) Takes a smart man to live in kip houses — and keep his money, his health and his woman happy . . .

(*Pause*)

TRESSA: (*Alert*) What man?

MAGUIRE: Any man.

TRESSA: Barney?

MAGUIRE: Scober's one man . . . (*Pause*) Ever remark him when the crack's[3] high — he'll smile and stare, and when it's dull he'll laugh — at nothin'. Poor sign of a man that — no nature . . .

TRESSA *stares unlistening.*

TRESSA: What kip houses — where?

MAGUIRE: Big towns anywhere — he travelled a lot — still does . . .

TRESSA: (*Quietly*) You're a liar.

MAGUIRE: I seen him.

TRESSA: (*Mimicking*) *You . . . seen?*

MAGUIRE: That's right.

TRESSA: Where? When?

MAGUIRE: Years back . . .

TRESSA: (*Quietly*) With a woman?

MAGUIRE: There was a woman there — but he was like always — in a corner, smilin' — at the glass of whiskey — not the woman. (*He taps his head*) Same then as now — greed — and the fixed notion — it burns a man up — till he's good for nothin' . . .

TRESSA *thumbs towards the door.* MAGUIRE *ignores her.*

MAGUIRE: Am I right?

TRESSA: You're smaller than he says.

MAGUIRE: My son's bigger than he can stomach.

TRESSA: (*Louder*) Get out . . . Out . . .

MAGUIRE *moves towards the door still looking at* TRESSA *with cunning insolence.*

1. A thief, especially a pickpocket.
2. ask.
3. convivial talk.

MAGUIRE: Empty — a loss — but that's up to you — if he's away — and you want service with profit — Jemmy can oblige anytime — with pleasure.

MAGUIRE *goes:* TRESSA *goes to the bedroom . . . and changes for bed, opens a drawer and takes out knitting, grows impatient with it: gets a magazine and leafs tensely through it, waiting for* SCOBER. *When he comes in he glances at her; she does not look up and he goes to a small table with a lamp on it and begins rooting in his pockets. He takes out a wad of notes, removes an elastic band and counts the notes intently. He replaces the elastic band and returns the wad to his pocket. He then counts coins which he roots out of other pockets.*

* * *

TRESSA: Barney?

SCOBER: Yes.

TRESSA: Nothing.

SCOBER: Go on, daughter[4] . . . go on.

TRESSA: Are you happy?

SCOBER: Am I happy?

TRESSA: Yes?

SCOBER: Well? Yes . . . most ways . . . tethered a bit maybe . . . times I'd as lief[5] have less . . . milk a cow or two . . . up early to dig or gather the day long . . . bone tired at duskus . . . eat and drink like a horse . . . sleep sound . . . it's never that way: Rain when you wake . . . a toothache maybe or a cold . . . or your head's light from whiskey or you've been vexed from half-dark with cares . . . or up half the night at figures . . . coming or going; docks, marts; money to make: the day never comes when you do the things you'd as leif do . . . it's most times things you'd as leif not do . . . (*Pause*) . . . but . . . happy? Happy I'd say as any man . . . why?

TRESSA: Just.

SCOBER: Just what?

TRESSA: Do you love me, Barney? Please look at me . . . do you?

SCOBER: You jump things on me, woman . . . Am I happy? Do I love you? . . . Words, respect is better.

TRESSA: I say them.

SCOBER: Respect is better.

TRESSA: You don't understand . . .

SCOBER: Too well.

(*Long pause*)

TRESSA: He doesn't respect you.

SCOBER: Who?

TRESSA: Maguire.

SCOBER: He's jealous — that's respect . . . jealous, 'cause I've worked — used my head — put lorries on the road — got this place and others, bought out most of the mountain — planted timber, built barns, roofed yards — I employ men — I have a young wife . . . (*Pause, pointing up*) Electric . . . (*Longish pause*) I was in rags at school with all of them — but you've got to stay that way — raggy, stupid and poor — 'Ah! sure it's a hard life' and 'How can a man live where snipes starve?' 'But won't we get our reward afterwards?' — slobber!! (*Pointing out*) There's ton of barley to the acre from three inches of soil out there — stones, a lot of it — and there's men in Meath on the fattest land in Ireland'd lie happy with a yield like that, and still the fools'd starve before they'd ask 'How's it done?' 'Can I do it?' — Spite! Ignorance! Envy. Let 'em starve — let 'em live on spite and take the boat[6] — rotten thatch with lumps of grass — all sunk away from the chimneys — windows that leave it dusk inside of a summer's day — the dung heap and the bony cow — the messy yard and the few mousey sheep — I was born to it — know every hour of it — the waste, the crownshawning[7] by the fire in winter — Everything to blame but themselves and 'cause they don't do anything — like Maguire, they've time to watch — every turf you save and lamb you mark — the lorries that come and go — they count and question and what they don't know they guess, and if man improves — they say: 'No man bests the mountain less he's a thief like Bull Haggard'. But if you work and deal and best the mountain — you've made *dirt* of them — and that's what they hate — order — yields — business, the power to buy . . .

TRESSA: (*Remotely*) For what?

SCOBER: Eh?!

TRESSA: I said for what?

SCOBER: How do you mean? —

TRESSA: All this buying — what's it for?

(*Pause*)

SCOBER: Us. (*Pause while* SCOBER *reflects*)

4. Used with affectionate irony to address any woman.
5. willingly.
6. i.e. emigrate.
7. moaning, complaining.

Hundreds of years — we've scraped those rocks — the graveyards full of McAdams — Tobins — Mullarkeys — lived and died — lek[8] scarcecrows. When I was a cub I could see this place — these windows lit up like a ship. Now I look out of them ...

TRESSA: At neighbours ... you've bought out — at nothings. I'm listening now three years — you go on and on and on, Barney — talking to yourself — power — the mountain — spite and the neighbours — soon we'll have no neighbours — we don't even fit it right ...

SCOBER: We can afford it ...

TRESSA: Not enough ...

SCOBER: If you pay for a thing — you fit it.

TRESSA: (*Unlistening*) Those people last week ...

SCOBER: To hell with them.

(*Pause*)

TRESSA: What I didn't say was what she said when I opened the door. (*Pause*) I'd an apron on — she asked — very nicely: was there *anybody* at home ... (SCOBER *reacts with annoyance*) So I said now ... what could I say when they thought I worked here. They wanted to see round the place, the house and garden — she had spent holidays here with her aunts — did I think the present owners would mind? 'No,' I said, 'it's all right' and I went back to the kitchen.

SCOBER: This means what?

TRESSA: We don't fit it ...

SCOBER: An empty barracks with no roof when I got it — laurel branches through that window there — now look ...

TRESSA *looks up without interest.*

TRESSA: (*Pause*) It doesn't leak — it's wrong every other way ...

SCOBER *stares.*

SCOBER: We've spent money on it but — it's wrong — it should be different — how?!

TRESSA: Don't shout, Barney ... (*Pause*) Take our dump room off the hall, it used to be a library — the shelving's still there ... My first week here I counted how many books went round the walls (*Pause*) ... Guess ... (SCOBER *shrugs with annoyance*) Five thousand.

SCOBER: I'd prefer bank notes — you can buy bread with them ...

TRESSA: That's why we've none.

SCOBER: So! ...

8 like.

TRESSA: So — it's different now — we keep worm doses, cod liver oil, farming papers, syringes, pig powders — and twenty years of Old Moore's Almanac, where there used to be five thousand books — women in long dresses — candle light — wine — a big log fire.

SCOBER: 'S not so long since we were growled at by gun dogs — and handed gruel in workhouses, those with no pride — the rest stayed hungry — or left in coffin ships, and died — by the million ... If I've a sick pig — I want a pig powder, a syringe and farming papers, not some book about some knucks who don't matter any more. Anyway they're dyin' — all over the country — places like this ... It's starin' at them — a slate here and there — a few acres now and then — pressure — change — thirty — fifty years — that's all they've got — and men who understand how to buy and sell — who understand land and stock — move in — not for mouldy books, log fires — or wine ...

TRESSA: (*Muttered*) To squeeze out 'their own' ...

SCOBER: For work!

TRESSA: For nothing ...

SCOBER: (*Ironically*) Must have been the way you were reared — this taste for the old style ...

TRESSA: 'Living', Barney — living ...

* * *

from ACT 2

[*The threshing yard*]

MAGUIRE: We've a long day ahead of us. In the auld days it was the flail across a plank ... the winter long and plenty of talk ... now it's this thing howlin' chaff and dust ... combines, groups and co-ops ... All for Scober and the go go men, and we're the corn they'll fatten on, we're the chaff they'll blow to Birmingham, for good if they get their way. There'll be nothin' here soon but Scobers, tinkers and tourists.

LYNCH *comes from behind bales preoccupied, walking towards the threshing mill:* MAGUIRE *goes to him.*

MAGUIRE: How's the form, Matt?

LYNCH: Alright ... (LYNCH *nods to the other men and immediately begins flicking through defective bags: holding out the good ones*)

MAGUIRE: You're like a man didn't sleep much.

LYNCH: Rain?

MAGUIRE: Rain?

LYNCH: That's right.

MAGUIRE: What rain?

CONLON: Last night . . .

MAGUIRE: Journeymen get wise too young — eh, Lynch? Live on whiskey and other men's dreams. Low land, mountain land, winter, summer, bed down in barns, lofts, and bars, see so many faces, hear so many stories, get so many offers — of one sort an' another — they get a sickner[1] and quit the country. That it?

LYNCH: (*Ignoring him, stands up with an armful of bags*) We'll make these do . . .

MAGUIRE: What?

LYNCH: That's three dozen.

MAGUIRE: You're terrible busy, son.

LYNCH: We've a lot to do . . . Get this off — you, Tommy — tie this back — we'll have to make a start.

The two men slide off the threshing mill and begin pulling the tarpaulin off: LYNCH *bends and gathers up the driving belt and shoves it at one of the men.*

LYNCH: Line this . . .

The man puts the belt round the driving pulley of the mill and goes off stage.

LYNCH: (*Calling*) Is she on? (*Pause*) Well?

(*Off*) Dead on.

(*Pause*)

Sound of the engine starting offstage, and the mill pulley spins the drum slowly: The idea now is to suggest a day's work by lighting . . . fade right down to twilight . . . LYNCH, *now tending the bags, does not see* SCOBER *until he feels the tug at his jacket.* SCOBER *nods him away from the hum of the threshing mill.* LYNCH *takes his time finishing tying a bag, fixes a fresh one round the seed spout. He motions another man to take his job, and walks over to where* SCOBER *is waiting. The hum of the mill fades.*

SCOBER: (*Looking at the thresher and pile of bags*) . . . You done well.

(*Pause*)

LYNCH *has an oilcloth and during this brief exchange, he keeps wiping at his fingers.*

LYNCH: That's the end of it . . .

SCOBER: No bother?

LYNCH: (*Shakes his head*) No.

(*Pause*)

1. sickening amount.

SCOBER: You saw her?

LYNCH: I saw her.

SCOBER: Well?

LYNCH: Well what?

SCOBER: The story . . .

(*Pause*)

LYNCH: What story?

SCOBER: Don't mouse[2] me . . . son.

(*Pause*)

LYNCH: She'll tell it . . .

SCOBER: You first.

LYNCH: She's your wife.

SCOBER: You tell me.

Some of the men look over.

LYNCH: (*Quietly*) You hired me to thresh corn — it's done.

SCOBER: I owe you.

LYNCH: Not me, the Co-Op . . . Pay now or later . . .

(*Pause: they stare at each other*)

SCOBER: I drove away.

LYNCH: You saw me walk away.

SCOBER: There was light — I watched it from the rock . . . All night I watched.

LYNCH: You owe fifteen quid.

(*Pause;* TRESSA *comes on*)

SCOBER: She must've said somethin'.

LYNCH: (*Moving away*) She's your woman — ask her.

During this exchange the men about the threshing mill are putting the tools together in a bunch and putting on their coats. They push the bales and the bags of seed off stage. It is now almost dark. LYNCH *and* TRESSA *exchange looks.* LYNCH *goes.*

TRESSA: How did it go, Barney . . .?

SCOBER: It's finished.

TRESSA: Good as last year?

SCOBER: Better.

TRESSA: So we're set for the winter — tons and tons, let the criers cry outside the gates. We could shut ours and live well from the garden — barrels of bitter apples down there — but it's a dark time winter — lonely — 'course we can dig a little on the short bright days, only the garden's like a graveyard . . . (*Pause*) And you hate graveyards and gravestones — 'Who was this man McIntyre, McInerney, McAlvanney, McElvinney, who are they; all these buried men?' (*Pause*) (*Screams*) Why?!

2. i.e. Don't play cat and mouse with me.

SCOBER: You lit fires round me night and day . . .

TRESSA: To think I'd sweat in bed with any slob you'd pick, and have a bastard with your name tagged on, and you to watch me grow, and know and not pretend, and when the cub was in the cot, stick out your chest proud as a bicycle pump!

SCOBER: I meant it for you, woman.

TRESSA: For Christ's sake, man . . .

SCOBER: Why not!? Tinkers in a ditch . . . dogs . . . bats and sewer rats . . . everything that runs, swims and flies can throw a likeness but us . . .

TRESSA: You've never loved . . . stay or go . . . me or you . . . it doesn't matter now . . . all night I thought of this . . . so I did it.

SCOBER: Did what?

TRESSA: What you wanted . . . with Lynch . . .

SCOBER: You're lying . . .

TRESSA: No . . . that's right . . . stare 'till your eyes burn out . . . you're blind anyway . . . (*beginning to break*) Don't you know why? . . . To reach you . . . not fool you . . . God I . . . can you not see . . . know . . . feel . . . how I loved you . . . yes, . . . loved you (*she breaks*).

SCOBER: I meant it for you, woman.

TRESSA: For yourself, man . . . For respect . . . To shut Maguire and a gaggle of mockers . . . that's the truth and you know it, and I know it . . . (*Pause: faint mocking laughter offstage*) and *they* know it . . .

SCOBER: (*Almost incoherently*) . . . Dig out the badger . . . blind him with lime . . . jeer and cudgel . . . split his belly . . . spike him to a tree, or any man that cuts his way up from what *they* are to what *I* am . . . That's their religion . . . Well by Christ I'll not be fed to scaldcrows . . . I'll bury every last man of them . . . I'll out-buy . . . out-crop . . . out-credit . . .

TRESSA: Barney! You've lost . . . it's over. (*Long pause*) We're not yesterday people . . . we're alone.

END

JOHN B. KEANE

(1928-)

from:
THE FIELD (1965)

[John B. Keane's work, particularly *The Field* and *Big Maggie* (1969), has seemed to many to offer an account of rural life in Ireland that is more savage, comic and squalid than the usual stereotypes permit. Certainly each time either of these plays is produced at the Abbey Theatre, the response is enthusiastic. In this play the leasing of the field to an outsider leads to a killing and to the consolidation of the community against the police and the priest. It is a potent account of the inwardness and of the nut-tight bonding of a local Irish community.

The Field was first staged by Gemini Productions at the Olympia Theatre, Dublin on 1 November 1965.]

CHARACTERS

LEAMY FLANAGAN
'THE BIRD' O'DONNELL
MICK FLANAGAN
MAGGIE BUTLER
MAIMIE FLANAGAN
'THE BULL' McCABE
TADHG McCABE
SERGEANT TOM LEAHY

The action takes place in Carraigthomond, a small village in the southwest of Ireland
TIME: *The present*

ACT ONE

Action takes place in the bar of a public-house in Carraigthomond, a small village in the southwest of Ireland.

TIME: *The present – noon.*

LEAMY FLANAGAN *sweeping.*
Enter 'THE BIRD' O'DONNELL.

BIRD: Give us a half of whiskey for God's sake, Leamy, to know would anything put a bit of heat in me.

LEAMY: 'Tis freezing!

BIRD: 'Tis weather for snow-men and Eskimos. Where's your father?

LEAMY: He's gone down to O'Connor's for the paper.... That'll be half-a-dollar.[1]

BIRD: Take your time, will you? Why aren't you at school?

LEAMY: Still on my Easter holidays. How's trade?

BIRD: Same as it always is.... lousy!

Enter MICK FLANAGAN.

MICK: I thought I told you to sweep out the shop!

LEAMY: It's nearly finished.

MICK: You've been long enough about it. Good morning, Bird.

BIRD: How're you, Mick?

MICK: Did you clean out the store?

LEAMY: I've done the half of it.

MICK: The half of it! — I told you to do the whole of it.

LEAMY: I had to look after the kids while my mother was feeding the baby.

MICK: 'Tis too fond you are of hanging about with women and children. 'Tis a daughter you should have been, not a son. Go and ask your mother will the dinner be ready soon.

LEAMY: Yes, Da.

MICK: And finish off that store or you'll hear all about it from me.

Exit LEAMY. BIRD *whistles.*

MICK: In the name of goodness, will you cut out that bloody whistling! One would swear you were a canary.

The whistler, whose name is 'BIRD' O'DONNELL, *looks at* MICK *in surprise.*

BIRD: (*Throwing rings at a ring-board*) I thought you liked whistling?

MICK: Whistling, yes. I like whistling. But that bloody noise you're making isn't whistling.

BIRD *comes to counter. He has thrown two rings and leaves the other four on the counter.*

BIRD: Give me another half-one. It might improve my pipes.

MICK: Have you the price of it?

BIRD *draws some change from his pocket and places it on the counter.*

MICK: (*Counts money first, gets off stool, fills whiskey*) Who did you take down now?

BIRD: Take down! That's illegal, that is! I could get you put in jail for that. A pity I hadn't a witness. 'Twould pay me better than calf-buying.

MICK *places whiskey on counter and takes price of it which he deposits in cash register.* BIRD *scoops up the rest of the money.*

MICK: There must be great money in calf-buying.

BIRD: Not as much as there is in auctioneering.

MICK: (*Goes to stove, to poke and put fuel on fire*) Very funny! Very funny! Don't forget I have to use my head all the time.

BIRD: (*Leftish along counter*) Not half as much as I do. Did you ever try to take down a small farmer?

BIRD *sits in angle of bar watching what is going on. Enter a small dumpy woman wearing a black-coloured coat. She is piled with parcels. She is* MAGGIE BUTLER, *a widow.*

MICK: Good morning, ma'am. Ah! is it Mrs. Butler? I didn't see you in a dog's age.

MAGGIE: Good morning to you, Mr. Flanagan. I'm afraid I don't be in the village very often.

MICK: What will I get for you?

MAGGIE: (*Laughs at the idea*) 'Tisn't drink I'm looking for, Mr. Flanagan. 'Tis other business entirely that brought me. I've been thinkin' of payin' you a call with [*sic*] some time.

MICK: You wouldn't be selling property now, by any chance? The bit of land or the house or maybe both?

MAGGIE: No, not the house! Lord save us, do you want me on the side of the road or stuck in a room in some back lane in Carraigthomond? 'Tis the field I came to see you about. I'm a poor widow woman and I want the best price I can get. They say you're an honest man to get the last halfpenny for a person.

MICK: (*Suddenly expansive, comes from behind counter*) Sit down here, Maggie girl. I can guarantee you, you won't be wronged in this house. You came to the right spot. Am I right, Bird?

BIRD: No better man. As straight as a telephone pole.

MICK: I suppose you know The Bird O'Donnell?

MAGGIE: Only to see. How do you do, sir.

MICK *seats* MAGGIE *at a table.*

MICK: How would you like a little drop of something before we get down to business? Something to put a stir in the heart.

MAGGIE: Oh, Lord save us, no! I never touches

1. A colloquialism for half-a-crown.

it. Since the day my poor husband died, I never put a drop of drink to my lips. We used often to take a bottle of stout together. (*Sadly*) But that was once upon a time. The Lord have mercy on the dead.

MICK & BIRD: The Lord have mercy on the dead!

MICK: 'Tis easy to see you're a moral woman. 'Twould be a brighter world if there was more like you.

BIRD: That's true, God knows. (*He picks up rings and returns to throwing position*)

MICK: (*To* BIRD) 'Tis nothing these days but young married women guzzling gin and up till all hours playing Bingo or Jingo or whatever they call it. (*To* MAGGIE) You're a fine moral woman, ma'am. There's no one can deny that.

As MICK *turns,* BIRD *throws a ring and nearly hits* MICK.

MICK: For God's sake, mind what you're doing .... I'll get my jotter now for the details. (*He goes behind counter and locates a large pad. He extracts spectacles from convenient case and rejoins* MAGGIE *at the table. His manner is now more efficient and business-like*) What kind of property do you wish to sell, Missus?

MAGGIE: 'Tis the four-acre field; the one you mentioned.

MICK: There's great demand for land these days. The country is full of upstarts, on the make for grazing. No shortage of buyers. (*Has poured himself a drink. Puts jotter on counter*) Now, ma'am, your full name and address. (*He readies his jotter and pencil*)

MAGGIE: Maggie Butler.

MICK: (*Writes laboriously*) Mrs. Margaret Butler. And the address?

BIRD *throws rings at board.*

MAGGIE: Inchabawn, Carraigthomond.

MICK: (*Writing*) Inchabawn, Carraigthomond. I know that field well. The one over the river.

MAGGIE: That's the one .... the only one.

BIRD *is now watching.*

MICK: A handsome parcel of land. Fine inchy[2] grazing and dry as a carpet. How do you hold it?

MAGGIE: What?

MICK: Your title? I mean, where's your title? (MICK *comes from behind counter, glancing at* BIRD *as he passes. Sits right of* MAGGIE) (*Kindly*) In other words, who gave you the right to sell it?

MAGGIE: Well, now, wait till I think. 'Twas willed to me by my husband five years ago. 'Twas purchased under the Land Act by my husband's father, Patsy Butler. He willed it to my husband and my husband willed it to me. I'm the registered owner of the field.

MICK: That's fair enough for anything.

BIRD: (*Closing in a bit*) I know that field. You let the grazing to the Bull McCabe.

MAGGIE: That's right. He has the grazing but only till the end of the month.

MICK: I fancy the Bull won't want to see it bought by an outsider. 'Tis bordering his own land.

MAGGIE: 'Tis all the one to me. Whoever pays the most gets the field.

Look between BIRD *and* MICK. BIRD *goes back to throw last ring or two.*

MICK: And proper order, too. Well now, the acreage?

MAGGIE: Three acres one rood and thirty two perches, bordering the river, with a passage to water and a passage to the main Carraigthomond Road. 'Tis well fenced and there's a concrete stall in one corner near the river. There's two five-bar iron gates .... and there's its Folio .... 668420.

BIRD *finishes throwing rings, goes and gathers them together and hangs them on board. Then back to bar for rest of his drink.*

MICK: And the valuation?

MAGGIE: Three pounds three shillings, Poor Law.

MICK: Under Fee Simple, I take it?

MAGGIE: Fee simple.

MICK: Who's the solicitor, ma'am?

MAGGIE: Alfie Nesbitt.

MICK: No better man!

BIRD: (*Who has been whistling sotto voce*) The Bull McCabe won't like this!

MICK: You're telling me!

MAGGIE: The highest bidder will get the field.

MICK: Of that you may be sure. But the Bull is sure to be the highest bidder. He needs that field. Well, Mrs. Butler ... Maggie ... I'll stick a notice in the paper this evening and I'll have thirty six bills printed and ready the day after tomorrow.

MAGGIE: (*Gathering herself together and rising*) May God bless you, Mr. Flanagan.

MICK: It's my job, ma'am, it's my job. I suppose you'll have a reserve?

MAGGIE: You'll put a reserve of £800 on it, Mr. Flanagan.

2. thick and rich.

MICK: That's more than two hundred an acre!

MAGGIE: It's worth every penny of it. It's good land and it's well situated.

MICK: True for you! True for you! You'll get the last brown copper for it. I'll make sure of that.

MAGGIE: 'Tis all I have apart from my widow's pension and I can't live on that. God will reward you if you get a good price. (*She rises*) Is there money going to you?

MICK: No! No! That will come from the purchaser.

MAGGIE: I'll see you then, on the first of April, please God.

MICK: Please God is right and God is good, ma'am. God is good. (MICK *sees her to door*)

MAGGIE: My husband always said you were an honest man; that I was to come to you if I was ever forced to sell. The Lord have mercy on him, he was a good innocent man.

MICK: He was, to be sure. A good kindly innocent man. Good day to you, ma'am.

Exit MAGGIE BUTLER.

BIRD: You've a nice tricky job facing you now.

MICK: (*Back for jotter*) Don't I know it, but business is business, Bird, and business comes first with me.

BIRD: The Bull won't like it.

MICK: What the Bull likes and don't like is nothing to me. I have my job to do.

Enter MAIMIE, MICK'S *wife, who has come downstairs.*

MAIMIE: Your dinner is ready.

MICK: Good! . . . . I'll go right up. Will you type out a couple of copies of this for me? (*He hands her pages from jotter*)

MAIMIE: How many do you want?

MICK: Make it three. Three should do. The Bird will carry one up to the printers when you're done.

MAIMIE: All right . . . . Don't be too long . . . . I'll be going to the hairdressers when you come down.

MICK: Oh! What's on? (*Stops*)

MAIMIE: (*Goes for typewriter behind bar*) Nothing's on only that it's six weeks since I had my hair done.

MICK: Why didn't you go and get it done before this. I don't like rushing my dinner. No one ever stopped you from getting your hair done.

MAIMIE: No one . . . . only nine children. (MICK *glowers*) The baby's asleep, so you needn't turn on the wireless. If he wakes, that's the end of my hair-do.

MICK: Cripes Almighty, woman, I want to hear the news.

MAIMIE: Well, you can miss the news for one day.

MICK: (*Turns again*) What's for dinner?

MAIMIE: Corned beef and cabbage.

MICK: Again?

MAIMIE: What do you expect — turkey and ham?

MICK: No, but God damn it, if I ate any more cabbage I'll have to put up a second lavatory.

Exit MICK.

MAIMIE: (*Bringing typewriter to table d.r. and settling up to type — sitting*) No matter what you do, they aren't happy. What's for dinner, he asks. Ask him in the morning what he'd like for his dinner and he'll tell you 'tis too soon after his breakfast.

BIRD: Put a half whiskey in that, will you?

MAIMIE: Have you the price of it?

BIRD: No . . . . but I'm selling two calves this evening.

MAIMIE: Cash on the line only. (*She inserts paper into typewriter*)

BIRD: (*Rises and crosses with glass, drink not finished*) By God, you're an amazin' woman the way you keep up your appearance. I mean, after nine children, you're still the best-lookin' bird in Carraigthomond.

MAIMIE: Come off it!

BIRD: 'Twasn't me said that now: 'twas somebody else I'm only quotin'. There was a bunch of us at the corner the other night and young Nesbitt started off about you. The way these young fellows talk about married women.

MAIMIE: The solicitor's son?

BIRD: The very man! Just after you passed, he said: 'There goes the finest-lookin' woman in the village.' (*Finishes drink*)

MAIMIE: Well, when I dress I'm not bad . . . . if I had the time, that is. There's other good-looking women in Carraigthomond, you know.

BIRD: Sure, there are . . . . but it was you young Nesbitt picked out. He ought to know and he almost a doctor. (*Puts empty glass in front of her*)

MAIMIE: I don't know why I listen to you. (*She takes his glass behind bar and pours half whiskey into it*) Not a word about this and make sure you pay me when you have it.

BIRD: (*Follows to bar*) Trust me, trust me!

MAIMIE: He's not a bad-looking chap.

BIRD: Who?

MAIMIE: Young Nesbitt.

BIRD: Handsome, handsome.

MAIMIE: What had he to say for himself?

BIRD: He never stopped talking for ten minutes. Couldn't figure out why you married your man.

MAIMIE: I hadn't much sense at nineteen. Nine kids in a dump where you wouldn't get a chance to see yourself in a mirror. The drapers don't even put panties in the windows here — the hypocrites. (*She starts to type*)

BIRD: I don't know how you manage to look so good, with all you have to do.

MAIMIE: (*As if she hadn't heard*) If you get your hair done different, they whisper about you. Dress up in a bit of style and they stare at you. You'd want an armoured car if you wore a pair of slacks. They know the month you start expecting.... Do you know how long since he had a bath? A year! Imagine, a whole year. You'd think he'd comb his hair now and then and put on a drop of oil. He changes his shirt every Sunday and sleeps in it for the rest of the week. (*Typing*)

BIRD: Amazing! Amazing!

MAIMIE: The last time he wore a pair of pyjamas was 15 years ago.... the night of our honeymoon. 'Tisn't right to be talking this way but, God knows, I've a lot to put up with.

BIRD: How you stick it, I don't know.

MAIMIE *continues to type. She reads a sentence.*

MAIMIE: '... an unfailing water supply with .... (*She cannot make out the word at first*) access to the river....' Spell access?

BIRD: A... X... I... S.

Enter 'THE BULL' McCABE *followed by his son* TADHG. BULL *wears a hat and overcoat, carries ashplant.* TADHG, *his son, is well-built and dour. He is in his twenties and wears a cap.*

BULL: Was oul' Maggie Butler in here?

MAIMIE: She's only just left.

BIRD: How's the Bull?

BULL: Who gave you the right to call me Bull, you pratey-snappin' son-of-a-bitch?

BIRD: Sorry Bull, sorry. (*Retreats to head of counter*)

BULL: (*To* MAIMIE) Where's Mick? (*Peering at what she is typing*)

MAIMIE: Upstairs, having dinner. (*She covers typing, picks up the lot and goes behind counter*)

BULL: Two bottles o' stout and sixpence worth o' them round biscuits.

MAIMIE *goes for order.*

TADHG: (*To* BIRD) Hump it!

BIRD: Sure, Tadhg, sure. (*Swallows whiskey and is about to depart*)

BULL: Wait a minute! Sit down here. (*Indicates table*) Have a drink?

BIRD: (*Nervously*) A half whiskey.

BULL: Three bottles o' stout, Maimie. (*To* TADHG) What do you suppose?

TADHG: I'd say he knows all. Wouldn't you know by the cut of him?

BULL: I'd say so, too. (*To* BIRD) She was puttin' up the field, wasn't she, Bird?

BIRD: That's right! First of April is the day, by public auction.

BULL: You have a good ear, Bird.

BIRD: She made no secret of it.

TADHG: You'd think she might have told us.

BULL *grunts, rises and fetches the three bottles of stout from bar to table, also the bag of biscuits. He pays and leaves his ashplant on stage r. of counter.*

BULL: (*To* MAIMIE) Will he be long?

MAIMIE: He shouldn't be too long.

BULL: I've important business to discuss with him.

BULL *returns to seat. He takes a sip of stout and eats a biscuit, as also does* TADHG.

BULL: (*To* BIRD) The first of April, you say?

BIRD: That's it! I was here.

BULL: Did she put a price on it?

BIRD: Eight hundred pounds.

BULL: She's out of her mind!

TADHG: A head case!

MAIMIE *types and finishes, pulls out paper from machine. Then sits behind counter and reads paper.*

BIRD: 'Tis a good bit of land though. Bull. You'll have to admit that.

BULL: Oh, I'll admit it all right but 'twas the manure of my heifers that made it good. Five years of the best cowdung in Carraigthomond and forty pounds a year for grazing. That's two hundred pounds I paid her, not counting the cost of the cowdung and the thistles we cut year in year out. To me that field isn't worth a penny over four hundred pounds. Now I've paid her two hundred in rent. I reckon if she got two hundred more from me she'd be well paid. Wouldn't you say so, Tadhg?.... Bird, wouldn't you say so?

BIRD: You're a fair man, Bull.

BULL: She'd be well paid indeed, if I was to fork out two hundred pounds. (BULL *takes a drink*)

BIRD: Very well paid... but suppose there's other bidders, Bull?

BULL: (*Surprise*) There won't be any other bidders! I'll see to that. Half this village is related to me and them that isn't is related to my wife.

BIRD: There's bound to be outsiders bidding. There's a craze for land everywhere.

BULL *points at his ashplant, which is on counter, seizes it and strikes the floor with force. He brings drink with him and leans on counter.*

BULL: That's what I care about outsiders. Accursed friggers[3] with nothing in their heads only to own the ground we're walking on. We had their likes long enough, hadn't we. Land is all that matters. Own your own land. (*Sits on stool r. end of bar*)

BIRD: You're right too, Bull. Dead right.... Well, the wife'll be wonderin' what's keepin' me. She'll have the dinner on the table by now. (*He rises to go*) I'll be seein' you. So long, Tadhg.

BULL: You never ate a full dinner in your life and neither did your wife, you caffler,[4] you! Whiskey is your dinner, supper and tea. How long since you ate an egg, you little rat, you, or a pound o' beef?

BIRD: (*Coming back*) Ah, now, she'll be worryin', Bull, an you know what women are?

BULL: Why wouldn't I? Haven't I one of my own, God bless her? (*Shouts*) Sit down (*Shouts to* MAIMIE) What's he eatin' up there? (BIRD *sits*) A cow, is it?

MAIMIE: He shouldn't be very long more.

BULL: I suppose he's beginning his custard and jelly. That's good, Tadhg... custard and jelly.

TADHG: (*Rises and goes to* BULL. *Has bag of biscuits. Finishes drink*) Da!

BULL: (*Genuine affection*) Yes, Tadhg!

TADHG: We'll have to get this field.

BULL: (*Squeezing* TADHG'*s arm, taking bag of biscuits*) An' we'll get it: we'll get it, oul' stock. By all rights 'tis our property an' we're not men to be cheated out of our property.

TADHG *seizes a few biscuits.* BULL *downs his stout and examines his pocket-watch.*

BULL: One o'clock! Dinner-time! God, how I could frighten a feed of bacon and cabbage now. I guarantee you that. (*Shouts to* MAIMIE) Will he be long more?

MAIMIE: I'll give him a call. (*She comes from behind counter and goes to stairway*)

BULL: (*To* TADHG *and* BIRD) There's nothing like a bull to move a heifer, hah!

MAIMIE: Hurry on down, Mick. Mr. McCabe wants to see you.

There is a muffled reply from MICK.

BULL: What did he say?

MAIMIE: He's finishing his tea.

BULL: His tea! Is it his supper or his dinner he's havin'? Tell him to bring his tea down with him and drink it here.

MAIMIE: (*Calls upstairs*) Bring your tea down with you. Mr.McCabe is in a hurry.

BULL: Tell him myself had no dinner yet nor had Tadhg.

TADHG *gobbles a few more biscuits.*

MAIMIE: He says he'll be down in a minute. (*Make this line almost a gibe*) He has to go to the toilet. (*She sits behind bar*)

BULL: O, Merciful Father! He can't eat his dinner without going to the Laverty!

BIRD: I'll slip away.... I'll come back if you want me for anything.

BULL: (*Peevishly*) Can't you sit still? 'Tis no wonder they call you after a bird. You're worse than a bloody sparrow!

TADHG: He's here!

Enter MICK.

MICK: How're the men? How's Bull, how are you? And Tadhg, how're you?

BULL: We hadn't our dinner yet and the two of us fasting since morning.

MICK: What can I do for you?

BULL: (*Indicates* MAIMIE) 'Tis private.

MICK: (*To* MAIMIE) Are you goin' to the hairdressers?

MAIMIE *operates cash register and extracts a note. She exits without a word. As she is going off* BULL *blows up the biscuit bag and bursts it.*

MICK: Well, now, what's the problem?

BULL: The Bird here tells me you have a field for sale.

MICK: That's right!

BULL: You're aware of the fact that me and Tadhg (*referring to* TADHG) has had the grazing of this field for the past five years and has the grazin' of it now?

MICK: Yes, I am. Of course I am.

BULL: Five times forty pounds is two hundred pounds. A lot of money!

MICK: 'Tis a lot.

BULL: I'll grant you 'tis a lot. A lot of countin' in

3. nuisances.

4. A quarrelsome, disagreeable person.

hard-earned single pound notes. (BIRD *looks at* BULL. *Knowing what's coming*) Two hundred pounds in grazing alone. Who'd pay it but myself?

MICK: Five forties is a fair sum.

BULL: 'Twould give me as much claim to the field as the woman who has it for sale.

MICK *doesn't answer.*

TADHG: There wouldn't be a stitch of grass in it only for the manure of the heifers... our heifers!

BULL: And the bullocks! Don't forget the bullocks, Tadhg. Our bullocks is more fat and content than women with husbands in England.

TADHG: 'Twas us kept the donkeys out of it.

BULL: If there's one thing that addles me, it's wandering donkeys. I can't sleep at night over them. I swear to you I get into bed happy and there I'd be just settlin' down when I'd think of the long-eared thievin' pirates. No sleep for me that night. I keep thinking of the grass they eat on me, and the clover... the fine young clover.

TADHG: A hungry ass would eat as much as two cows.

BULL: If he's an ass he's after grass — someone else's grass. I often come across a lonesome ass in April when you'd see no growth anywhere an' you'd be sparin' the young fields for hungry heifers. Do you remember the black stallion donkey with the single ear and the eyes like a saint.

TADHG: Do I?

BULL: The first time I met that stallion was a Stephen's Day[5] and he staring through one of the gates of the field we're buying now. You'd think butter wouldn't melt in his mouth. To look at his face you'd think grass was the last thing in his head. He gave me a look and he trotted off. That night he broke the gate. Three months we watched him until we cornered him. Tadhg there beat him to death. He was a solid hour flaking him with his fists and me with a blackthorn.... An' do you mean to tell me I have no claim to this field? That any outside stranger can make his open bid and do us out of what's ours, after we huntin' every connivin' jackass from the countryside?

MICK: Ah, now, Bull, be fair! She's entitled to the best price she can get. The field is legally hers.

BULL: An' she'll get a fair price. I'll hand you over two hundred pounds here an' now an' you'll give me a receipt.

MICK: Two hundred pounds! Ah, you'll have to do better than that. Anyway, 'tis for public auction on these premises, the first day of April. 'Tis out of my hands, Bull.... Sorry!

BULL: Is the bills out yet for it?

MICK: No, not yet.

BULL: Did you notify the papers?

MICK: I'm just on the point of doin' it. (*Lifting* MAIMIE'S *typing*)

BULL: On the point of it, but 'tisn't done (*Pointing at typing*)

TADHG: If it goes to the papers, you'll have twenty bidding for it.

BULL: We can't have that (... *Pause*... *hand on typing*...) And we won't have that.

MICK: (*Detaches papers from* BULL'S *hand*) The auction will have to be held.

BULL: And let it be held! There will be no one here but ourselves.

MICK: Ah, now, you know well there will be more than you interested. That's a good bit of land.

BULL: If it don't go to the papers an' if there's no bills who's goin' to know except what's here?

MICK: You can't do that!

BULL: 'Twas done before. You did it yourself.

MICK: This is different. Old Nesbitt, the solicitor, knows about this.

BULL: He's an old crook and, if you ask me, he won't be here the day of the auction.

MICK: What are you going to do? Kidnap him?

BULL: There's a few old grand-uncles of mine with wills to be made. One of 'em could be dyin' that day, couldn't he? Oul' Nesbitt wouldn't want to fall out with our clan.

MICK: Hold it! Hold it! I can't be party to this. There's a reserve of eight hundred pounds and the old woman needs the money. Apart from that, it's illegal.

BULL: (*Laughs*) Illegal! That's a good one! (*Nudges his companions*) Did you hear that... illegal?

MICK: There's my commission. Five per cent of eight hundred pounds is forty pounds. I'm not going to lose forty quid because you need a cheap field.

BULL: (*Threateningly*) I need that field! I have nineteen acres and no passage to water. I have to get a passage. I'll pay you the forty pounds the day of the auction, provided my bid is accepted.

MICK: I'd like to see that in writing.

BULL: Writing?.... De you want me to be hanged? I'll sign nothing. Look! You needn't sign

5. 26 December.

over the field till I plank the forty in the palm of your hand.

TADHG: That's fair enough for anything, isn't it, Bird?

BIRD: 'Tis reasonable.

BULL: There will be something for Bird, too. We won't forget the Bird.

MICK: You don't seem to understand that this is highway robbery.

BULL: 'Tis worse robbery the other way. Do you want some hangblasted shagger of a stranger to get it?

MICK: What about Maggie Butler? 'Tis her field and no one else's.

BULL: 'Tis as much mine! Look here, Flanagan, there's nothing to prevent a boycott of your shop.

MICK: What... what do you mean?

BULL: There's a hundred relations of mine in this village and around it. Not one of them will ever set foot in this pub again if I say so.

MICK: Give me the forty pounds now and I'll do my best.

BULL *laughs and* TADHG *moves to his left shoulder.*

BULL: I'll give you half of it. I'll give you twenty now and twenty more the day of the sale. Fair enough?

MICK: Fair enough! The Bird'd better keep his trap shut.

BULL: The Bird don't like to get his feathers wet. Do you, Bird? There's many a deep hole in the river below and who's to say how a man might lose his footing?

BIRD: My lips are sealed.

BULL *draws a wallet from his pocket and extracts two tenners.*

BULL: (*To* MICK) Here's two ten pound notes. The Bird here will act as a witness. Put your hand here Bird (*He places* BIRD's *hand over* MICK's) and say after me (*Authoritative tone*)... As God is my judge....

BIRD: As God is my judge....

BULL: I swear by my solemn oath....

BIRD: I swear by my solemn oath....

BULL: That I witness the receipt of twenty pounds by Mick Flanagan....

BIRD: That I witness the receipt of twenty pounds by Mick Flanagan....

BULL: Of the first part....

BIRD: Of the first part....

BULL: From the person of Thady McCabe of the second part....

BIRD: From the person of Thady McCabe of the second part....

BULL: (*Proudly with grim humour*) Hereinafter affectionately known as the Bull.... I'm no fool when it comes to law, boys.

TADHG: Hear! Hear!

BULL: I'm as big a rogue as any solicitor.

MICK: I'll have to get the bills printed, but I'll get the lot burned when they come from the printers.

BULL: Solid thinking... very solid! Now, here's what we'll do. The morning of the auction the Bird here opens the bidding with a hundred pounds and I rise him ten. (*Increasing a tempo*) The Bird goes up to a hundred and twenty and again I rise him ten. The Bird soars up to One hundred and fifty and again I rise him ten. The Bird flies higher to One hundred and ninety but I'm there with the final bid of two hundred quid. All straight and fair and above board. Two down, as the man said, and carry one. What about the printer? Is he trustable?

MICK: Safer than a confession.

BIRD: What about me, Bull?

BULL: What about you?

BIRD: You promised me something.

BULL: What would you say to a fiver?

BIRD: I'll take it.

BULL: The minute the land changes hands, 'tis yours.

BIRD: What about a pound on deposit?

BULL: (*Wounded*) Is it how you don't trust me?

BIRD: No... No... Good God, no!

BULL: You won't be forgot, Bird. You have my guarantees on that.

BIRD: Stand us a half-one before you go.

BULL: Give him a half-one, Mick.

BULL *throws coin on counter and* MICK *goes to fetch whiskey.*

BULL: (*Leaning on bar, in an ecstasy of accomplishment*) I watched this field for forty years and my father before me watched it for forty more. I know every rib of grass and every thistle and every whitethorn bush that bounds it. (*To* BIRD) There's shamrock in the southwest corner. Shamrock, imagine! The north part is bound by forty sloe bushes. Some fool planted them once, but they're a good hedge. This is a sweet little field, this... an independent little field that wants eatin'.

BIRD: Well, you'll have it soon (*Accepts whiskey from* MICK) with the help of God.

BULL *looks at him suspiciously for a moment but goes on.*

BULL: When oul' Maggie's husband died five years ago, I knew he was dying. One look at the writin' under his eyes and I knew. I knew the wife was feelin' the pinch lately. I knew by the writin'. 'Twas wrote as plain as a process across her forehead and in the wrinkles of her cheeks. She was feelin' the pinch of hunger. (*Suddenly, to* BIRD, *who becomes transfixed*) Bird, I swear to you that I could tell what a man be thinkin' by the writin' on his face.

BIRD: Have no fear o' me!

BULL: (*Affable*) I won't, oul' stock, for I know you're to be trusted above any man I know.

TADHG: Da, what about the dinner?

BULL: (*Proudly*) There's your healthy man! When he isn't hungry for women, he's hungry for meat. Tadhg, my son, marry no woman if she hasn't land.

Enter a youngish SERGEANT *of Civic Guards in full uniform.*

SERGEANT: Good afternoon, men!

MICK: Ah, good afternoon to you, Sergeant Leahy. Will you have something on the house?

SERGEANT: Thank you, no, Mick.

MICK: Suit yourself.

BULL: (*To* TADHG) Come on away or our dinner will be perished.

SERGEANT: I didn't call to see you, Mick. I came to have a word with Mr. McCabe here.

BULL: Well, you'll have to postpone it because I'm going to my dinner.

SERGEANT: This won't take long. I'm here investigating the death of a donkey.

Laughter from all.

BULL: Investigatin' the death of an ass! You wouldn't hear it in a play! By Gor! 'tis the same law the whole time. The same dirty English law. No change at all.

SERGEANT: Maybe not, but I have to ask your son and yourself a few questions.

BULL: You're out of your mind, Sergeant. Come on away home, Tadhg. God, have ye anything else to do? What about all the murders and the robberies? 'Twould be more in your line to be solvin' them. Come on, Tadhg. This fellow is like all the rest of 'em. His brains are in the arse of his trousers.

SERGEANT: (*Sharply*) That's enough of that! Sit down and answer my questions... sit down or come to the Barracks!

BULL: Sit down, Tadhg.... Sit down. Sit down. (*Smugly*) There's more thought of donkeys in this world than there is of Christians.

SERGEANT: Where were you the night before last?

BULL: What night was that?

SERGEANT: (*To* TADHG) Where were you ere last night?

TADHG: Where's that we were again, Da?

BULL: We were at home playin' cards.

SERGEANT: Until what time?

BULL: Till morning.

SERGEANT: And did you leave the house during that time?

BULL: We were in the back-yard a few times, or is that ag'in the law, too?

SERGEANT: Can you prove that you didn't visit Mrs. Butler's field over the river on that night?

BULL: On my solemn oath and conscience, if we left the house for more than two minutes.

SERGEANT: You have that field taken for grazing, haven't you?

BULL: Everyone knows that.

SERGEANT: Well, can you prove you weren't there?

BULL: The Bird, there, was playin' cards with us till two o'clock in the mornin'.

SERGEANT: Is that the truth, Bird?

BIRD: The Gospel.

SERGEANT: Well, the donkey was killed around midnight. His cries were heard by a couple walking along the river. They reported to the S.P.C.A.[6] and the S.P.C.A. reported it to the Barrack Orderly. The donkey was poisoned around midnight.

TADHG: He wasn't poisoned!

SERGEANT: How do you know he wasn't poisoned?

TADHG: Well.....

BULL: Because there's no poison on our lands. That's how he knows an' don't be doin' the smart man with your tricky questions. What is he but an innocent boy that never told a lie in his whole life. You don't give a damn, do you, so long as you can get a conviction. Tell me, where do you disappear when there's tinkers fightin', an' law-abidin' men gettin' stabbed to death in the streets?

SERGEANT: Bird, you say you were at this man's house that night and I say — you're a liar!

BIRD: Ye all heard it! Ye all heard what he said! You called me a liar, Sergeant, and no man does that to the Bird O'Donnell. No man — uniform or

6. Society for the Prevention of Cruelty to Animals.

no uniform. As my mother is in the grave, no man will call me a liar to my face.

SERGEANT: All right! All right! I take it back. I apologise for calling you a liar.

BIRD: (*Somewhat mollified*) You better not do it again!

SERGEANT: I'm wasting my time! There's nothing in your heads but pigs and cows and pitiful patches of land. You laugh when you hear that an old jackass was beaten to death, but a man might be beaten to death here for all you'd give a damn.

Exit SERGEANT LEAHY.

BULL: And a Sergeant might get his face split open of night and all the Guards in Ireland wouldn't find out who did it . . . . not if they searched till Kingdom Come!

CURTAIN

JOHN BOYD

(1912-)

from:
THE FLATS (1971)

[Boyd's characters voice a range of political attitudes to events in the troubled Belfast of the early 1970s. These events and the responses to them invite judgment less than they identify and concentrate dormant tensions in the Donnellan family: Joe and Kathy, the father and mother; and Brid and Gerard, their children.

The play was first produced at the Lyric Players Theatre, Belfast in March 1971.]

CHARACTERS

JOE DONNELLAN. *In his mid-fifties. Still lithe. A thin muscular frame. A man whose swift intelligence has not been fully developed*

GERARD. *His son of twenty-two. Taller than his father. Careless of his appearance. Has a restless manner*

KATHLEEN. *His wife. Burly figure. Tries to take care of her appearance, but takes more care of her house, of which she is very proud*

SEAN CULLEN. *Brid's boyfriend. Twenty-five. A dark-faced young man. His accent is slightly English*

MONICA MOORE. *Aged twenty-two. A wisp of a girl. A beautiful face but somehow unawakened*

MALACHI MURRAY. *In his late forties. A thin wiry figure. A natural working-class leader*

PHIL. *A young English soldier*

CAPTAIN NEWMAN. *An English officer*

ADAM. *A street dealer. About sixty*

from ACT II

ADAM: (*Unsure*): AH . . . R . . . R . . .

GERARD: His name's Arthur . . . ARTHUR . . .

CAPTAIN: Oh Arthur . . . Arthur Adam . . . Are you a dealer? Are you in business?

ADAM: Yis . . . yis . . . that's right. . . . I dale . . .[1]

CAPTAIN: Is it a local firm?

ADAM: Yis . . . yis . . . myself. . . .

CAPTAIN: Are you from Belfast?

ADAM: Yis . . . yis . . . But I've travelled . . .

CAPTAIN: Where have you travelled?

ADAM: All round the world . . . And other places too . . .

CAPTAIN: (*To* PHIL) Is this chap a half wit? What d'you think?

PHIL: Dunno, sir, 'bout that . . .

CAPTAIN: What have you in there?

ADAM *makes a gesture. And grins.*

CAPTAIN: (*To* PHIL) Let's see . . .

PHIL *begins to throw out the contents of the pram. Rags. Then knickers. A pair of large bloomers, then briefs. Then tights.*

CAPTAIN: Sex maniac, eh?

ADAM *grins and nods agreement. The others look worried, as* PHIL *continues with the search.*

PHIL: Some bottles, sir. . . .

PHIL *places some bottles on the floor:* ADAM *notices some dregs in whisky bottle. He drinks them.*

CAPTAIN: Was that whisky?

ADAM *smacks his lips.*

1. deal.

CAPTAIN: (*To* PHIL) Probably a rummy.[2] (*Smells bottle: hands it to* PHIL)

PHIL: Meths,[3] sir . . .

PHIL *goes rummaging again. Produces a union jack.*[4]

CAPTAIN: This belong to you?

ADAM: (*Grinning*) Yis . . .

PHIL *produces a tricolour.*[5]

CAPTAIN: This too?

ADAM *grins.*

CAPTAIN: A maniac. Wasting my time . . . You may go . . .

ADAM *nods approval and folds up the flags. He kisses the union jack as he puts it away. With his little shuffle he makes off. Once outside he goes to the far end of the courtyard. He sits down. Produces butts. Peels them. Makes a cigarette. Begins smoking.*

CAPTAIN: (*To* PHIL) Anything else?

PHIL: Naow, sir . . .

CAPTAIN: (*To the others*) That's all. For the time being. I've put you in the picture, I think . . . In the army we've a lot of distasteful jobs to do . . . We don't enjoy doing them. We know you Irish don't welcome the army. But don't forget we're only doing our duty. We want to be your friends. We are your friends. We want peace. We want your co-operation. We're here to restore law and order. That's our job. Understand?

MALACHI: You've got a point of view, Captain Newman, but your trouble is you can't imagine other people havin' a point of view as well. You've never understood us — and you never will. We want our freedom. That's what we're fightin' for . . .

CAPTAIN: Your freedom? Good God, man, you're every bit as free as the English, the Scots, the Welsh, or anybody else . . . I don't know what you're all beefing[6] about. . . .

MALACHI: Exactly . . .

CAPTAIN: Huh? What d'you mean?

MALACHI: What are you here for?

CAPTAIN: Here for? To stop you Irish from murdering each other! That's what we're here for!

MALACHI: Go on home, then . . . an' let's get on with it!

MONICA *comes running into the flat.*

KATH: What's the matter, child?

MONICA: M'mother, Mrs Donnellan . . . She's taken a wee turn. Can you come an' see her?

KATH: Certainly child, I'll come . . . Is she in her bed?

MONICA: She's lying down on the sofa.

KATH: She'd far better be in her bed. . . .

MONICA: Will I go for the doctor?

KATH: You might have to . . . We'll see . . . We'll see . . . (*She throws on her coat*)

A bomb goes off near at hand.

CAPTAIN: Good God!

He and PHIL *rush out.* PHIL *upsets* ADAM*'s pram.*

ADAM: (*Waving the tricolour as the others rush out*) Only the oul' income tax office . . . Only the oul' income tax office . . . Up the rebels! Up the rebels! (*Exultantly he performs a little dance, grinning and grimacing*)

2. He means that Adam is probably an alcoholic.
3. Methylated spirits, favoured by down-and-outs.
4. Britain's national flag.
5. The Irish national flag.
6. complaining.

from ACT III

Evening. GERARD *is in his shirtsleeves.*

ANNOUNCER: Radio Free Belfast . . . Radio Free Belfast . . . Earlier this evening a bomb was exploded in Belfast, in the area of the High Flats which have been the scene of frequent attacks, the most recent being only last night; no one is reported injured. A bomb was also exploded in Ardoyne[1] about half an hour ago. It had been planted in a catholic public house which had just been reopened after having been attacked last week . . . Tonight both areas of Belfast are very tense, and small groups are gathering at street-corners. Our advice is please keep off the streets at the present time unless you have vigilante duties. We particularly ask women to see that all their children are confined to their homes. We hope that our earlier advice has been taken, and that as many as possible of our womenfolk and children have been evacuated to safer areas . . . There will be another bulletin in half an hour from now. . . .

GERARD *switches off the radio.* PHIL *appears on guard. He marches in sharply and takes up his usual post.* SEAN *walks in and nods to* PHIL. *He enters the flat.* GERARD *is putting on his tie.*

GERARD: Another explosion half an hour ago.

SEAN: Where?

GERARD: Ardoyne. (*He continues adjusting his tie. His manner is cool*)

SEAN: Anybody hurt?

GERARD *shrugs his shoulders.*

1. A catholic area of Belfast.

GERARD: The night's a pup. Is that soldier[2] still guarding us? ... Bastard!

SEAN: Where's everybody? Nobody in?

GERARD: They're across the way — Brid an' the old woman (*Pause*) Was Brid expecting you?

SEAN: Aye ... I was at my sister's.

GERARD *is now ready to go out.*

GERARD: I've got to go out.

SEAN: Oh ...

GERARD: The Moore's flat is number six ... First floor ... No point the two of them bein' there.... (*Kindly*) One samaritan's enough.

SEAN: How is the woman?

GERARD: I dunno ... They couldn't get a doctor ...

SEAN: And what's been decided? Are Brid and your mother staying on?

GERARD: Nothing's been decided yet.

SEAN: They'll leave it too late ... Then they won't be able to get out of the city.

A pause. GERARD *is ready to leave but something makes him unable to.*

SEAN: Are you in a helluva hurry?

GERARD: I've got to go in a couple of minutes ...

SEAN: Well then, let's have a drink? Eh? Long time since we'd a talk together ... (GERARD *hesitates*) Get out that bottle and see if there's anything left in it ...

GERARD *gets out the almost empty bottle and* SEAN *fetches a couple of glasses.* SEAN *pours out the drinks.*

SEAN: Well, cheers!

GERARD: Slainte Maith![3]

SEAN: Well, Gerry, let's get it off our chests ... What's the matter? Come on, out with it?

GERARD: Out with what?

SEAN: You know ... Why d'you look at me as if I'd a ... as if you'd a bad smell under your nose?

GERARD: Oh, I wasn't aware of that....

SEAN: You do. That's the way you look ... What've I done to you?

GERARD: You've done nothing to me, Sean ... mebbe to yourself ... I dunno ... you're the best judge of that, aren't you?

SEAN: Judge of what? What d'you mean?

GERARD: You've been away ... out of this country ... for ... what? About six months ...

SEAN: Not very long ... is it?

GERARD: Long enough to ... to change you completely ...

SEAN: Brid doesn't think so ... Your sister doesn't agree with you....

GERARD: I'm not Brid.... I'm not goin' to marry you!

SEAN: You're goin' to be my brother-in-law.... I'm marrying into your family ... Look, Gerry, I knew you before I knew Brid ... (*Pause*) You don't want me to marry your sister? Is that it?

GERARD: I've no feelings about that ... But mebbe you should have second thoughts ...

SEAN: About what?

GERARD: About marryin' into the Donnellans.

SEAN: But why?

GERARD: You'll have to get married in church, won't you?

SEAN: I'm prepared for that.

GERARD: You mean, you still practise? You still go to mass and to confession?

SEAN: Brid knows what I think about the church ...

GERARD: That you don't believe in it any longer ...

SEAN: Your sister has doubts herself ... And for that you're more responsible than I am.

GERARD: I'm responsible only for myself. We all go our own way in this family.

SEAN: Yet you all stick together too just like any other good catholic family ...

GERARD: You still look on me as a catholic, do you?

SEAN: Look Gerry, when you come out a teacher, you'll conform ... you'll be like all the rest ...

GERARD: We'll see about that.

SEAN: You'll toe the line all right ... or else leave the country ... Oh I know .. you're involved ... You're involved up to your neck in all this ...

GERARD: You can have my bedroom. I'll hardly be back till ... God knows what time. So you're welcome to the room.

SEAN: Thanks ... But I've made my arrangements.

GERARD *switches on the radio. Music. Then* ANNOUNCER.

ANNOUNCER: Here's a newsflash ... We've just heard that a protestant parade has been organised for this evening, and is routed in the direction of the Flats ... We appeal to all the inhabitants there not to be provoked and not to be intimidated. This parade may be already on its way. Keep calm! Keep

2. A British soldier on duty at the Flats, attracted to Monica, a protestant friend of Brid's.
3. Irish for 'Good health'.

off the streets! End of newsflash.

Music. GERARD *switches off the radio.*

GERARD: If any of them asks where I am, say you don't know ...

SEAN: Well, I don't ...

GERARD: You can say I probably won't be home tonight but not to worry ... I'll be back in the morning some time....

SEAN: Your mother'll want to know where you are, Gerry.

GERARD: Tell her I'll be quite all right, quite safe. I won't be in danger ...

SEAN: You think she'll believe that?

GERARD: I've no desire to be a martyr. I want to live, not die for Ireland. I'm not as romantic as you think....

Still the Flat

KATHLEEN *comes into the flat.*

JOE: Where've you been? It's time you were packed an' away out of this!

KATH: (*Ignoring this*) What's that soldier fella doin' with them sandbags? Is he goin' to bury us?

JOE: (*Ignoring her remark*) I want to know if you've packed yet?

KATH: (*To* SEAN) Brid is over in Mrs Moore's flat. She wants to let Monica out for a breath of air ... So away you go, Sean.

SEAN: OK. I'll run over then ... I'll be back later ...

KATH: (*To* JOE) What did you say, Joe, about packin'? I'm not goin' to Frank's the night or the morra night[1] either ... So don't go on about it now! I've made up my mind, an' that's that.

GERARD: I'm away. (*To* KATH) I won't be home till the morning.

KATH: You won't what?

GERARD: You heard me, mother ... I got a job to do ... An' I'm not goin' to start arguing ... I haven't got the time ...

KATH: You're not goin' out of this till you tell me where you're goin'! ... An' you're not stayin' out all night. (*To* JOE) If you're goin' to stand for that, Joe, I'm not! (*To* GERARD) Where are you off to? Come on, come on, tell me! Tell me, tell me, else I'll lift somethin' an' brain you!

JOE: Tell her what you're doin', son ... an' away you go!

1. i.e. tonight or tomorrow night.

KATH: Oh he's got your permission, has he? You say there's goin' to be trouble, an' you want me an' Brid to pack an' go to your brother's ... D'you think I could content myself out there knowin' what's goin' on here?

JOE: (*Insistent*) You're not stayin' here the night, woman ...

KATH: I'll do what I please, Joe ...

GERARD: Do you know what's happenin'? There's a parade of protestants comin' down the Shankill[2] an' headin' for here. This is no place for you an' Brid!

KATH: Is it not? Don't you tell me what I'm to do an' what I'm not to do; where I've to go an' where I haven't to go. I've been through all this before, son. It was like this long afore you were born, an' it luks as if it'll be no different long after ye're dead. If that mob come down the road yellin' an' bawlin' like red indians an' camp in front of us there I'd pay no heed to them. An' if the British send the whole of their army, navy an' air force an' land out there on the Square, I'd give them the sight o' me backside.

JOE: (*Pointing to suitcase*) Look, I've got everythin' ready for you ...

KATH: Oh, have you now? You've everythin' ready have you?

JOE: I've yer clothes an' things in there ...

KATH: As good as a valet, are you? Packed my clothes ...

JOE: I've arranged too for a wee van to collect you ...

KATH: Oh you have, have you? An' when is it comin' to collect me?

JOE: (*To* GERARD) What time did Malachi say he'd be here at?

GERARD: (*Looking at his watch*) In about half an hour.

KATH: Oh, you've held a committee meetin' about it ... Very nice ...

JOE: Look, what's come over you? This mornin' you said you'd go to Frank's. You even went out an' bought the case.

KATH: Mebbe I did, but I never said one word about goin' to Frank's.

JOE: Then why did you buy the case?

KATH: I bought it for Brid. She's goin' back to England with Sean.

JOE: I didn't expect that ...

2. Shankill Road, a protestant district.

KATH: Your mind's on more important matters, I'm sure.

GERARD: Right! I'm away . . .

KATH: (*Calls after him*) When'll you be back?

GERARD: When you see me!

JOE: Good luck, son!

GERARD *goes out.* KATH *begins unpacking case.*

KATH: Well . . . What's the use of me talkin' . . . Whatever I say's bound to be wrong . . . I don't know what I'm talkin' about . . . That's the only answer I ever get from him . . . Oh you packed my good clothes in, very nice . . . Used a pitchfork did you? He'll get a coolin', that Gerry, one of these days . . . afore he's much older . . . Oh, he knows everythin' . . . he knows it all . . . You packed my dirty nightie on purpose! Wantin' to shame me in front of Delia . . . You're the right one, Joe Donnellan!

He gives a gesture of resignation. Her mood changes.

KATH: You'll miss Brid, won't you Joe?

JOE: We'll both miss her . . .

KATH: Dear God almighty, what's the world comin' to? (*A helicopter is heard*) If that oul' thing dropped a bomb on us, it'd only be our deservances . . . Anythin' to get away outa this!

JOE: Look Kathleen, you're worn out. Why wouldn't you do what I wanted? A couple o' days in the country would 'a done you good. You'd 'a been away outa this. (KATHLEEN *shakes her head*) Frank would 'a been glad to have you . . . Delia would 'a lukked after you . . . A change o' scenery, that's what you need . . . an' that's what you'd 'a got . . . You're overwrought, woman . . .

KATH: Ach, shut you up!

JOE: Nobody can talk to you . . . nobody!

KATH: You're never done talkin'. You've talked to me all your life, haven't you? It's you has me the way I am . . . a bundle o' nerves! I don't know what I'm doin' or what I'm sayin' . . . everythin's got on top o' me . . . it's nothin' but work, work, work about this place an' never gettin' nowhere. You'd be well rid o' me I suppose . . . nothin' I do is right! Ever!

JOE: Why don't you lie down an' rest yourself? Go into the room an' lie down an' rest . . .

KATH: No, I don't want to . . .

JOE: That's what you need, Kathy . . . that's what you need. . . . (*The use of her christian name and his tone of voice almost undermine her emotional defences*) Can I do anythin' for you?

KATH: Nothin' . . . nothin' . . .

He lights a cigarette.

KATH: Tell me where that Gerry fella's went to?

JOE: He's helpin' with the radio station, puttin' on the records an' that . . . That's why he'll be home late . . .

KATH: Why couldn't he tell me that? Does he have to keep everythin' a secret? I don't care what he does so long as he's nothin' to do wi' them oul' guns . . . No son o' mine'll have blood on his hands . . . .

JOE: You needn't worry, Gerry'll look after himself. If there's any fightin' he's the fella to keep out of it . . . Anyway, Gerry knows damn all about how to use a gun . . .

KATH: He doesn't take after his father then . . . you were brought up to use them oul' things . . .

JOE: You need a gun about a farm, don't you? To kill a lot o' rabbits an' vermin . . . that's all I ever use a gun for.

KATH: I'd like to believe you, Joe . . .

JOE: It's true . . . why should I tell you a lie?

KATH: Oh you've told me many a lie, Joe . . . I've found you out in them . . . an' I'm sure you told me many more I never found out . . .

JOE: Go on, you're in good form for talkin' . . . What else have you against me? You've just called me a liar, an' a murderer . . . What else is there? Go on . . . I drink m' buroo money[3] an' leave you wi' nothin' . . . I've never done a day's work in m' life. . . . I've done nothin' right. . . . (*Long pause. He stubs out cigarette. He attempts reconciliation*) Are yer feet hurtin' you?

KATH: I've been on them all day . . .

JOE: Come on in an' lie down . . . I'll bring you in a cup o' tea. (*He takes her by the arm*)

KATH: I don't want no tea.

JOE: A couple of aspirins? Have you a headache?

KATH: I'm all right . . . I'm all right . . . let me be.

JOE: Go in an' lie down for half an hour an' rest yourself. Get a wee sleep . . . That's what you need, Kathy . . .

KATH: You got no sleep last night either.

JOE: I can do wi' out m' sleep. You never could . . .

KATH: You lie down a wee while too . . . with me . . .

The way she says this means it is an invitation: a rare one.

3. Unemployment benefit collected at the Unemployment Bureau (buroo).

JOE: Well ...

KATH: Go on ... think of some excuse.

JOE: It's not that ... I've got to see Malachi ...

KATH: Oh I know ... I know ... once you see the back o' me you'll be outa that door like a cork out of a bottle.

JOE: But I've got to see Malachi Murray ... I'm doin' a job for him.

KATH: (*Wearily*) You should 'a married him ... you see more of him than you do of me.

JOE: (*Irritated now*) Away to yer bed, woman ...

The moment of coming together is past.

KATH: Aye ... I might as well ... I'm as well there as anywhere else.

Wearily she goes to her room. JOE *goes to the cupboard. Finds the whisky bottle, puts it up to the light. Only the dregs left. Finishes it off ....*

STEWART PARKER

(1941-88)

from: CATCHPENNY TWIST (1977)

[The following sequence of scenes embodies much of the play's basically straightforward narrative. More to the play's real point, it illustrates the interweaving of scenes whose rapid transitions set the private struggles in their enclosure of public unrest.

The first production was in the Peacock Theatre, Dublin on 25 August 1977.]

CHARACTERS

ROY FLETCHER
MARTYN TEMPLE
MONAGH CAHOON
MARIE KYLE
THE VOCAL TRIO — MAN, WOMAN, GIRL — *who between them play all the other parts*
FOUR PIECE BAND: *lead and bass guitars, keyboard, drums/percussion*

from ACT I

Flat

ROY: (*Still at the piano*) I know what Monagh's problem is now. She can't cope with being a free agent. She can't handle it. That's why she does all these lame things. So as somebody'll rush up and give her a hand. She acts the self-reliant woman but she's crying inside for somebody to run her life for her. Trouble is, it's not me. It's that television jock, Playfair. She's still hooked on that creep. She's just using me as a home help.

MARTYN: Okay, I've got a lead on the verse.

ROY: What about the chorus?

MARTYN: It's finished.

ROY: It's only started.

MARTYN: You never listen!

ROY: All I hear is you sitting there mumbling to yourself.

MARTYN: I'm only after going through[1] the whole thing.

ROY: Where is it?

MARTYN *tears a page from his notebook, plants it down on the piano and returns to his seat.*

MARTYN: It'll sweep the country, this. From the jukebox in every sleazy waterfront dive ... to the ballroom in every Fifth Avenue hotel. (*Pause*) Will Monagh like it, do you think?

ROY: She doesn't like anything much. Except that turd Playfair. He can do no wrong.

MARTYN: I thought it was over years ago.

ROY: She says he wanted a divorce. But the wife wouldn't play along. And so on and so forth. You wouldn't think a woman of her intelligence would fall for that. But she wants to badly enough. So she does. Bitch. (*He fights his distress*) What about the verse?

MARTYN: Shaping up. Spies may be all round us, jealousy may hound us.

ROY: You and your bloody spies!

1. In this usage indicating a past event: 'I've only just gone through.'

MARTYN: Watching for the signs that say we're through. Some day they may discover ... love has got our number ... and even something something can come true ... miracles! And even miracles are sometimes true. Bullseye!

ROY: Bullshit.

Television Studio

GIRL: (*Cueing*) Go.

(*Music*)

MONAGH: (*Sings*)
Spies may be all round us
Jealousy may hound us
Watching for the signs that say we're through
One day they may discover
Love has got our number
And even miracles are sometimes true ...

The GIRL *signals to stop. They wait.*

Flat

ROY, *with tears on his cheeks, gets up suddenly and heads for the door.*

MARTYN: Where're you going?

ROY: I'm going for a walk.

MARTYN: That's only the half of it. (ROY *leaves,* MARTYN *sighs, and grimaces with exasperation. Then gets engrossed again*) Making me your bride. Nothing left to hide. Live life side by side. (*Pause*) Assuming you prefer your onions fried.

Blackout on flat

Television studio

GIRL: Straight through to the end now.

(*She cues* MONAGH)

MONAGH: (*Sings*)
You've given yourself away
You've said too much that I
Can read between the lines
Your face and hands complete the picture —

Oh, small wonder,
You and I,
Meeting in the park, touching in the dark,
Call our wonder
The eighth one of the world
We can reach so high
Higher than the sky
No small wonder, you and I.

GIRL: Okay. Lunch!

Blackout on television studio.

Bookshop

MARTYN *is looking through some poetry collections.* MARIE *enters.*

MARIE: Surprise.

MARTYN: Marie!

MARIE: So this is where you've run to?

MARTYN: What are you doing here?

MARIE: Visiting friends. Selling books. What about you? Here. (*She gives him a Sinn Fein*[2] *pamphlet from her satchel*) Thirty pence, please.

MARTYN: Roy and me are getting established, with the songs. We've got a couple of records out, with Monagh. We're doing an entry for Eurovision[3] at the minute. Listen, I'm sorry about the ballad. We had to leave Belfast in a bit of a rush.

MARIE: Very wise. I'm surprised at what's become of you, Temple.

MARTYN: Me?

MARIE: Fletcher always was a wee Orange[4] pimp, under the skin.

MARTYN: Easy on, Marie.

MARIE: You're in his pocket, that's the thing. I thought you told me your grandfather carried a gun in the twenties.

MARTYN: The past is over and done with, Marie. We're in the Common Market now.[5]

MARIE: You amuse me.

MARTYN: Men have been on the moon. It's a small world.

MARIE: Don't delude yourself, you can't just turn your back on generations of the dead. Don't imagine you'll get away with it that easy.

MARTYN: I'm in favour of a united Ireland as much as the next man.

MARIE: What are you doing reproducing this pseudo-American slop, then?

MARTYN: What? What has that got to do with it?

MARIE: Everything, that's all. The whole state

2. Literally, We Ourselves, the name of the political party associated with the Irish Republican Army.
3. A televised song contest among European, and other, countries.
4. Referring to the Orange Order, the powerful unionist, protestant organization.
5. The United Kingdom and Ireland both joined the European Community in January 1973.

apparatus of this country, North and South, is designed for one function — sell-out. Selling out the resources, the heritage, the culture, the very soil itself to foreign speculators.

MARTYN: Come off it.

MARIE: You're a cog in that machine, you and your Common Market and your Eurovision Song Contest.

MARTYN: For God's sake, Marie, that's completely wired up. I mean, people enjoying songs, a harmless entertainment . . .

MARIE: Nothing that mediocre is ever harmless.

MARTYN: You've lost touch with real life.

MARIE: You've lost touch with who and what and where you are. Don't think you can escape for ever into mass-produced catchpenny idiocies.

MARTYN: Pop songs are like the folk music of our generation. There's nothing political about it.

MARIE: That's really rich, coming from you, in your position.

MARTYN: What are you talking about?

MARIE: I'm talking about why you did a flit.

MARTYN: Somebody posted bullets to us.

MARIE: You're damn lucky they didn't arrive at a higher velocity.

MARTYN: Why do you say that?

MARIE: Considering what you were mixed up in.

MARTYN: Us? We'd no involvement in politics whatsoever as you know.

MARIE: Don't act all innocent. You took to the wing the minute it appeared in print.

MARTYN: Whatever you're on about, Marie . . . I think maybe I'd rather not know.

MARIE: You're not bluffing, are you — you really don't know what you've got yourself into. There was an article in a Protestant paper. Naming you two. It said you'd both been supplying entertainment to their drinking clubs. As a means of gaining information about them. On behalf of the British Army. The proof was that you were also doing work for the IRA. You're in dead trouble, Martyn.

MARTYN: But none of it's true!

MARIE: Oh? You did not work for the Protestants, then?

MARTYN: We wrote a few comedy numbers for a cousin of Roy's, that's all.

MARIE: You're the original babes in the wood, aren't you?

MARTYN: What'll happen? What should we do?

MARIE: These things aren't forgotten.

MARTYN: We literally didn't know. I suppose there's no point in even trying to refute it now.

MARIE: Not much.

MARTYN: Good God, Marie, surely *you* never believed it?

MARIE: I wouldn't put anything past Fletcher, but I was sceptical all the same. Even the Brits have more gumption than to employ the likes of you.

MARTYN: I can't get over it.

MARIE: Well, the best of British luck, as they say. I hope it's got more to offer than British justice. (*She makes to leave*)

MARTYN: Don't run off — what about a drink?

MARIE: Sorry — I've another three shops to go round.

MARTYN: See that girl over there?

MARIE: What about her?

MARTYN: Just before you came in, she shouts up to the woman at the cast register — Audrey . . . where the hell's the Savage Mind?[6] I thought it would make a beautiful skit. Two assistants shouting across the heads of the customers — Where's the Female Eunuch?[7] I don't know, but there's a couple of Trollopes[8] under the counter . . . (*She smiles*) You remember the old college revues?

MARIE: Of course I do, why wouldn't I?

MARTYN: You were some stage manager.

MARIE: You were some comedian.

MARTYN: We put in a lot of happy days and nights together, Marie.

MARIE: It was half a lifetime ago.

MARTYN: Seven years, that's all.

MARIE: Some seven years.

MARTYN: It's tragic to let it just completely vanish, all the same.

MARIE: You have to grow up sometime, Martyn.

MARTYN: You've time for a quick jar,[9] come on.

MARIE: No. I'm away. Incidentally, the Irish History section's over there.

She leaves. MARTYN, *left alone, tears the pamphlet in half. Blackout.*

Prison Hall

The band plays the introduction to 'Somebody Out There'. Light up on the WOMAN, *as a prison governess.*

6. C. Lévi-Strauss, *La Pensée Sauvage.*
7. By the feminist writer, Germaine Greer.
8. A pun on the name of the English novelist Anthony Trollope (1815-82).
9. A drink, especially beer.

WOMAN: Since the proceedings are now drawing to a close, I think the time has come for me to express the appreciation of all inmates and staff to our show-business guests for coming here tonight. You've given most generously of your time and talents to bring the pleasure of good entertainment into our lives, and I can assure you on behalf of all the inmates most especially of how much this kind of thing means to them. But I think you'll find them ready to express their gratitude for themselves in the customary manner, in just a moment. We all hope to see you back with us again soon — in your professional capacities, of course. And now for the last item on the agenda (*she consults a piece of paper*) a song by Monagh, her latest one, which I'm sure we all hope will do very well.

Music. Follow spot on MONAGH *entering.*

MONAGH: (*Sings*)
Somebody out there loves you, sugar,
Somebody out there wants to know you
Give them your smile, give them the eye,
They'll run a mile to be your girl or guy
Somebody in here needs some friendship
Somebody in here wants to love you
Don't be afraid of it
You can make the grade of it
Someone in there can surely see
That the somebody out here is me!

Lights come up on ROY *and* MARTYN *in their flat, singing the song at the piano.*

Life can be hard
Times can be lean
Life can get lonely too
But don't give up
Don't be mad
Don't be had
Because there's somebody out there
Yes, there's somebody out there
Yes, there's somebody out there
Somebody out there . . .

The lights have narrowed down to two small pools, one on MONAGH'S *face, the other on* ROY *and* MARTYN'S *faces. They all three stare fearfully out into the surrounding darkness, as they sing the final repeated line.*

Blackout.

END OF ACT ONE

from ACT II

An Airport, after the Song Contest

MARTYN: After her shoe came off — I couldn't watch any more.

ROY: She mixed up the chorus and the verse. It was just like gibberish. The band didn't know what to do. They limped on behind her but she was all out of key. You couldn't describe it as singing at all. It was just a prolonged howl. I had to go and help her off at the end. (*Pause*)

MARTYN: Hey, we never opened our telegrams. (*He takes four greetings telegrams and a larger packet from his case . . . He opens the first one, glances at it*) I think we ought to change our style, you know. Get back to the roots. (*Reads*) 'Monagh my sweet may your Crybaby cry all the way to the bank. Cyril.' (*He tosses the telegram back in the case*)

ROY: What roots?

MARTYN: Something ethnic. The heritage of the past. (*He opens another telegram, glances at it*)

ROY: Cecilia Street Primary School. Rock 'n' roll. Football. The pictures. That's my roots.

MARTYN: I mean further back than that. The country's history. The old culture. The tradition. (*Throws telegram into case*)

ROY: That's got nothing to do with me. It's got nothing to do with you either.

MARTYN: I'd an uncle who was a fluent Irish speaker. I was pretty good at it at school too.

ROY: You've no more a Gaelic speaker than I am.

MARTYN: You? You've never learnt a word of it.

ROY: I picked up a few phrases once from a tourist brochure. It was in a Chinese restaurant in Cork.

MARTYN: (*Opening another telegram*) Extraordinary people, the Chinese. I've been reading them up, you know. I've been thinking them over.

ROY: They write lousy tunes.

MARTYN: A quarter of the world's people. And nobody owns anything. It's all held in common. They all work for each other. For the common good. (*Throws telegram in case*)

ROY: The Japanese are a different story, however.

MARTYN: The only thing that bothers me is — I've yet to hear of a Chinese joke. I don't mean Chinese laundry jokes — chop-chop flied lice all that stuff — I mean one of their own. A Red Chinese gag. They don't appear to have a sense of humour. The way we do. It's a serious drawback, that, in my opinion. It could very well end up endangering world peace. (*He opens another telegram*) Of course I might be mistaken. I might have it wrong. The way they see things — maybe *we're* a Chinese joke. (*He throws the telegram into the case*)

ROY: You don't even like folk songs.

MARTYN: Some. Not all.

ROY: I hate them.

MARTYN: This'll ruin us, Roy. We'll be blacklisted.

ROY: They won't blame us. The song was all right. It's the end of the line for her, though.

MARTYN: Maybe we should get her to a doctor.

ROY: She'll be all right. It'll pass off. Anyway, all the money's spent.

MARTYN: We've got a present. (*He begins to pick at the tape on the remaining package*) I feel as if we've been here for days already. Years. Maybe the whole airport's been hijacked. Maybe all the ground staff are pinned down in their offices. By terrorist guns. The control tower paralysed. All the planes flying round and round stacked up above us. Running out of fuel. Any minute now they'll start falling out of the sky like asphyxiated flies. (*Pause*) It hasn't turned out the way we though it would, Roy.

ROY: Not much.

MARTYN: It's not the way we dreamed it would be.

ROY: Not yet.

MARTYN: How long are we going to have to wait in this place?

He rips the tape off the package. Simultaneously — Blackout. Explosion. A noisy drum intro. The band strikes up. A red spot comes on. Showing MONAGH *on her feet, smiling brightly, with a hand mike.* ROY *and* MARTYN'S *seats are toppled over. In the red glow, we see them on their knees, hands and faces covered in blood, groping about blindly.*

MONAGH: (*Sings*)

Laugh and the world laughs with you,[1]
Cry and you cry alone,
If you plan to make me love you,
If you want me for your own —
Don't be a crybaby
If you wanna be my baby
For when you're smiling
You're the apple of my eye
Don't heave a sigh baby
There's no earthly reason why baby
You know that loving is something
Money can't buy
You know that loving is really something
Money can't buy!

Blackout

END

1. The opening line of the poem 'Solitude' by Ella Wheeler Wilcox (1850-1919).

GRAHAM REID

(1945-)

from: THE DEATH OF HUMPTY-DUMPTY (1979)

[The first of these scenes is set at George's home, after his release from hospital, with his wife, Heather, and Caroline, with whom he has had an affair. The second is a flashback to the hospital ward. In George's obsessive sexual innuendos to his former lover, in the humiliation inflicted by Willie, we are meant to detect some kinship with the attack that has brought George to this pass.

The play was first presented at the Peacock Theatre, Dublin on 6 September 1979.]

CHARACTERS

GEORGE SAMSON, *a schoolteacher, late forties*
HEATHER SAMSON, *his wife, middle forties*
WILLIE JOHN, *an orderly, late twenties*
GERARD (GERRY) DOYLE, *a fellow patient, early thirties*
CAROLINE WILSON, *a schoolteacher, middle thirties*

from SCENE ELEVEN

GEORGE: It's a great day for lying in the grass.

HEATHER: Yes.

GEORGE: Just stretching your body out, kicking your legs in the air.

DOYLE'S VOICE: Christ you're in great form, George.

GEORGE: You always liked getting out in the good weather, didn't you Caroline? It is Caroline, isn't it?

CAROLINE: Yes.

GEORGE: I forget names you see. There were so many of you at school.

HEATHER: Pay no attention to him Caroline, he's teasing you.

DOYLE'S VOICE: That's it Heather, put the boot in. Play fair, George. Don't promise if you can't perform.

GEORGE: Are you still performing, Caroline?

CAROLINE: What?

GEORGE: Are you still playing the piano at Assembly?

CAROLINE: Yes. But I'm still not very good at it.

GEORGE: Oh I don't know. You had a lovely touch.

HEATHER: I didn't know you played the piano, Caroline.

CAROLINE: My mother always pushed me. She always wanted me to play.

GEORGE: She must have been quite a woman, your mother.

HEATHER: I tried for a while but I was never very good at it.

GEORGE: Don't be modest, darling. I always thought you were great.

HEATHER: Really George, you say the most amazing things at times. I don't think I've played more than twice since we've been married.

GEORGE: Well, you've been busy, but Caroline has had more time to keep it up. (*Pause*) Can you play 'Abide With Me'?

CAROLINE: Yes, I think so.

GEORGE: It's a beautiful tune.

HEATHER: More tea anyone?

CAROLINE: Not for me, thanks.

GEORGE: Have you had enough, Caroline?

CAROLINE: Yes, George, I have, thank you.

DOYLE'S VOICE: That's the girl, you just hit him back.

HEATHER: Do you want some more, George?

GEORGE: Yes please, I haven't had enough.

DOYLE'S VOICE: Careful son, a wheelchair is not a licence to kill. After a while you lose your cripple's immunity.

CAROLINE: I hope to get married next year. I'm marrying Norman Stewart.

DOYLE'S VOICE: Fuck me, real Mafia tactics.

CAROLINE: You remember Norman, don't you? He's now head of the History Department;

HEATHER: That's lovely, Caroline. Congratulations.

DOYLE'S VOICE: First they take over your Empire, and then they take your woman. They deserve each other. He'll be sitting at home marking his homework, and she'll be up at the Giant's Ring, praying for the Giant's return.

(*Pause*)

HEATHER: Aren't you going to say anything, George?

GEORGE: There used to be a prostitute lived just down the Avenue. She was always boasting about the important people she knew. She knew four cabinet ministers. We called her the name dropping knicker dropper.

HEATHER: George, really ....

GEORGE: No, it's a fact, after all. Caroline's future husband's the Head of the History Department and Local History is the coming thing. (*Pointing to* CAROLINE) Do you know many more important people?

HEATHER: You'll have to excuse George's sense of humour, Caroline.

GEORGE: Heather knows all about us of course. (CAROLINE *almost jumps out of her seat*) I've told her everything.[1] How you used to get your girls to make special little buns for my break.

HEATHER: (*Smiling*) I don't remember you mentioning that.

GEORGE: Really, I thought I did. Oh yes, Caroline was always giving me a little bit of . . . this and that. Do you remember we always planned to go on a picnic? Where was it you wanted to go . . ?

CAROLINE: (*Rather uncertain*) I . . . I . . . can't quite remember.

GEORGE: Ah yes, the Giant's Ring. You always wanted to go to the Giant's Ring. What in earth was the big attraction up there, eh?

CAROLINE: Ah . . . I . . . I just thought it would be nice up there.

1. She has discovered in his diaries a record of his infidelities.

GEORGE: Oh, it is, it is. It's nice there. Girls love it up there.

CAROLINE: I think I'd better go. I've lots of work to prepare for tomorrow.

HEATHER: Oh. Are you sure?

CAROLINE: I must fly.

GEORGE: Can you do that as well?

CAROLINE: Pardon?

HEATHER: (*Laughing*) Well Caroline, I'm sorry you have to go so soon. Thank you for coming, You've really brought the best out in George. I'll leave you to the door.

CAROLINE: Goodnight, George.

GEORGE: (*Suddenly gloomy as he realises he can't hit moving targets*) It could have been.

(*They exit*)

DOYLE'S VOICE: Go on you great bollocks. Sure you know by now you can't hit moving targets. You're still stuck in the trenches, old son. But today's war is a war of movement.

(*Ladies say goodnight off stage*) . . .

from SCENE TWELVE

GEORGE's *hospital ward*

DOYLE'S VOICE: This is you, George. A voice crying alone in a side ward. You're nothing, a nobody. The only life you have is what is given you by other people. What are the lessons of the past two weeks? Without Heather and the children you are absolutely nothing.

GEORGE: Why don't you go to hell, Doyle.

DOYLE'S VOICE: I'm speaking from hell, George . . . right inside your head.

GEORGE: Leave me alone, go away, Doyle, go away.

WILLIE: (*Entering quickly*) What the hell are you shouting about? I think you're cracking up. Who are you talking to?

DOYLE'S VOICE: Tell him, George . . . tell him you're shouting at a voice inside your head. Tell him, he'll understand, he's an intelligent, sensitive man.

GEORGE: I . . . I . . . I didn't realise . . .

WILLIE: This is getting serious, George old boy. We're worried about you. I mean that old head is all you've got, and if that goes, well . . . .

GEORGE: Is Sister on yet?

WILLIE: You seem to think you own Sister. There are other patients on this ward, and she's busy with one or two of them.

GEORGE: I'd like to see her. I think she has a message for me.

WILLIE: It's difficult for me carrying messages for you, George. You see with Heather not coming up anymore, I find I'm running a bit short of cash. I mean you haven't even paid me for that last shave.

GEORGE: I will Willie, I will. You see that is what I want to see Sister about. She said she would go round and see Heather and find out what is wrong.

WILLIE: She's probably got a boyfriend, George. I mean let's be reasonable, a woman needs a little bit now and again. Especially a woman who's been used to a regular dose. Tell me, how often did you do it? (*Pause*) Don't be shy, George. (*He takes a tissue from a box on* GEORGE's *locker, crumples it up and starts to tickle* GEORGE's *face with it.* GEORGE *starts moving his head to try to counteract the effects of the tickling, but* WILLIE *grips the front of his hair*) Wouldn't it be great if you were able to lift a hand and scratch yourself, wouldn't it?

GEORGE: Stop it, please Willie, please stop.

WILLIE: Of course I'll stop, George, as soon as you've answered my question.

GEORGE: Alright, alright.

WILLIE: That's better. I like co-operative patients. I want to know how often you and your wife did it? How often did Georgie lie in the Heather?

GEORGE: Not . . . not very often.

WILLIE: Did she think you were very good, George?

GEORGE: Willie, please . . . .

WILLIE: (*Starts to tickle him again*) Answer the question George.

(*Pause*)

DOYLE'S VOICE: What a country, torture on the National Health. Tell the bastard you did it twice nightly and three times a day.

GEORGE: I'll pay you, Willie. I'll pay you double.

WILLIE: I'll tell you what, George. You're going to get a big claim. I think you can afford to pay me a little on a regular basis. What about a fiver a week, monthly in advance? Then special privileges at our usual rates. (*Pause*) Look at things from my point of view, George. You'll soon be out of here. You'll have forgotten about Willie. Your wife'll put sugar in your tea and salt on your dinner, for nothing. Your son'll shave you, for nothing. This is only a short-term arrangement. You were warned, George. You listened to that bastard Doyle. What good did it do you? Remember the day he forced me to apologise to you. The bastard almost broke my arm. I knew I'd come out on top, George, but you wouldn't listen. I'll bet his right leg twitched a bit the day the bin lorry[1] hit him. Remember, George . . . (SISTER *enters*) . . . I ah . . .

SISTER: (*Angrily*) Willie, what are you doing? I told you to bath Ferguson and McBride.

WILLIE: I'm sorry Sister, George wanted me.

SISTER: Go and get those two bathed.

WILLIE: Right, Sister. (*Looking at* GEORGE) I'll get back to see you later, George. (*Goes*) . . . .

1. A truck that collects domestic refuse.

BRIAN FRIEL

(1929-)

TRANSLATIONS (1980)

[*Translations* might be seen as a drama of frustrated loves; at one level the love of Maire and Yolland, and that of Manus for Maire. Surrounding these are loves of another kind — the bewitchment of fable, the imaginary world of classical deities, and love of place — not the abstraction of 'nation' so much as the small, known lands of parish, county. The place-names echoing through the play speak of an organic community fragmenting, of its pragmatic invaders, of the allure conveyed by 'America', 'English'.

Although *Translations* is a story of loss, its humour and the power it accords to imagination in 'the landscape of facts' assert prospects of survival. *Translations* was first presented by Field Day Theatre Company in Derry on 23 September 1980.]

CHARACTERS

MANUS
SARAH
JIMMY JACK
MAIRE
DOALTY
BRIDGET
HUGH
OWEN
CAPTAIN LANCEY
LIEUTENANT YOLLAND

The action takes place in a hedge-school in the townland of Baile Beag/Ballybeg, an Irish-speaking community in County Donegal.

ACT ONE	An afternoon in late August 1833.
ACT TWO	A few days later.
ACT THREE	The evening of the following day.

(For the convenience of readers and performers unfamiliar with the language, roman letters have been used for the Greek words and quotations in the text. The originals, together with the Latin and literal translations, appear in the Appendix, p. 1235.)

ACT ONE

The hedge-school is held in a disused barn or hay-shed or byre. Along the back wall are the remains of five or six stalls — wooden posts and chains — where cows were once milked and bedded. A double door left, large enough to allow a car to enter. A window right. A wooden stairway without a banister leads to the upstairs living-quarters (off) of the schoolmaster and his son. Around the room are broken and forgotten implements: a cart-wheel, some lobster-pots, farming tools, a battle of hay, a churn, etc. There are also the stools and bench-seats which the pupils use and a table and chair for the master. At the door a pail of water and a soiled towel. The room is comfortless and dusty and functional — there is no trace of a woman's hand.

When the play opens, MANUS *is teaching* SARAH *to speak. He kneels beside her. She is sitting on a low stool, her head down, very tense, clutching a slate on her knees. He is coaxing her gently and firmly and — as with everything he does — with a kind of zeal.*

MANUS *is in his late twenties/early thirties; the master's older son. He is pale-faced, lightly built, intense, and works as an unpaid assistant — a monitor — to his father. His clothes are shabby; and when he moves we see that he is lame.* SARAH'*s speech defect is so bad that all her life she has been considered locally to be dumb and she has accepted this: when she wishes to communicate, she grunts and makes unintelligible nasal sounds. She has a waiflike appearance and could be any age from seventeen to thirty-five.*

JIMMY JACK CASSIE *— known as the Infant Prodigy — sits by himself, contentedly reading Homer in Greek and smiling to himself. He is a bachelor in his sixties, lives alone, and comes to these evening classes partly for the company and partly for the intellectual stimulation. He is fluent in Latin and Greek but is in no way pedantic — to him it is perfectly normal to speak these tongues. He never washes. His clothes — heavy top coat, hat, mittens, which he wears now — are filthy and he lives in them summer and winter, day and night. He now reads in a quiet voice and smiles in profound satisfaction. For* JIMMY *the world of the gods and the ancient myths is as real and as immediate as everyday life in the townland of Baile Beag.*

MANUS *holds* SARAH's *hands in his and he articulates slowly and distinctly into her face.*

MANUS: We're doing very well. And we're going to try it once more — just once more. Now — relax and breathe in . . . deep . . . and out . . . in . . . and out . . .

SARAH *shakes her head vigorously and stubbornly.*

MANUS: Come on, Sarah. This is our secret.

Again vigorous and stubborn shaking of SARAH's *head.*

MANUS: Nobody's listening. Nobody hears you.

JIMMY: *'Ton d'emeibet epeita thea glaukopis Athene . . .'*

MANUS: Get your tongue and your lips working. 'My name' Come on. One more try. 'My name is —' Good girl.

SARAH: My . . .

MANUS: Great. 'My name —'

SARAH: My . . . my . . .

MANUS: Raise your head. Shout it out. Nobody's listening.

JIMMY: '. . . *alla hekelos estai en Atreidao domois* . . .'

MANUS: Jimmy, please! Once more — just once more — 'My name —' Good girl. Come on now. Head up. Mouth open.

SARAH: My . . .

MANUS: Good.

SARAH: My . . .

MANUS: Great.

SARAH: My name . . .

MANUS: Yes?

SARAH: My name is . . .

MANUS: Yes?

SARAH *pauses. Then in a rush.*

SARAH: My name is Sarah.

MANUS: Marvellous! Bloody marvellous! (MANUS *hugs* SARAH. *She smiles in shy, embarrassed pleasure*) Did you hear that, Jimmy? — 'My name is Sarah' — clear as a bell. (*To* SARAH) The Infant Prodigy doesn't know what we're at. (SARAH *laughs at this.* MANUS *hugs her again and stands up*) Now we're really started! Nothing'll stop us now! Nothing in the wide world!

JIMMY, *chuckling at his text, comes over to them.*

JIMMY: Listen to this, Manus.

MANUS: Soon you'll be telling me all the secrets that have been in that head of yours all these years. Certainly, James — what is it? (*To* SARAH) Maybe you'd set out the stools? (MANUS *runs up the stairs*)

JIMMY: Wait till you hear this, Manus.

MANUS: Go ahead. I'll be straight down.

JIMMY: *'Hos ara min phamene rabdo epemassat Athene –'* 'After Athene had said this, she touched Ulysses with her wand. She withered the fair skin of his supple limbs and destroyed the flaxen hair from off his head and about his limbs she put the skin of an old man . . .'![1] The divil! The divil!

MANUS *has emerged again with a bowl of milk and a piece of bread.*

JIMMY: And wait till you hear! She's not finished with him yet!

As MANUS *descends the stairs he toasts* SARAH *with his bowl.*

JIMMY: *'Knuzosen de oi osse —'* 'She dimmed his two eyes that were so beautiful and clothed him in a vile ragged cloak begrimed with filthy smoke . . .'! D'you see! Smoke! Smoke! D'you see! Sure look at what the same turf-smoke has done to myself! (*He rapidly removes his hat to display his bald head*) Would you call that flaxen hair?

MANUS: Of course I would.

JIMMY: 'And about him she cast the great skin of a filthy hind, stripped of the hair, and into his hand she thrust a staff and a wallet'! Ha-ha-ha! Athene did that to Ulysses! Made him into a tramp! Isn't she the tight one?

MANUS: You couldn't watch her, Jimmy.

JIMMY: You know what they call her?

MANUS: *'Glaukopis Athene.'*

JIMMY: That's it! The flashing-eyed Athene! By God, Manus, sir, if you had a woman like that about

1. Homer, *Odyssey*, XIII, 433 et seq.

the house, it's not stripping a turf-bank you'd be thinking about — eh?

MANUS: She was a goddess, Jimmy.

JIMMY: Better still. Sure isn't our own Grania a class of a goddess and —

MANUS: Who?

JIMMY: Grania — Grania — Diarmuid's Grania.

MANUS: Ah.

JIMMY: And sure she can't get her fill of men.

MANUS: Jimmy, you're impossible.

JIMMY: I was just thinking to myself last night: if you had the choosing between Athene and Artemis and Helen of Troy — all three of them Zeus's girls — imagine three powerful-looking daughters like that all in the one parish of Athens! — now, if you had the picking between them, which would you take?

MANUS: (*To* SARAH) Which should I take, Sarah?

JIMMY: No harm to Helen; and no harm to Artemis; and indeed no harm to our own Grania, Manus. But I think I've no choice but to go bull-straight for Athene. By God, sir, them flashing eyes would fair keep a man jigged up constant!

Suddenly and momentarily, as if in spasm, JIMMY *stands to attention and salutes, his face raised in pained ecstasy.* MANUS *laughs. So does* SARAH. JIMMY *goes back to his seat, and his reading.*

MANUS: You're a dangerous bloody man, Jimmy Jack.

JIMMY: 'Flashing-eyed'! Hah! Sure Homer knows it all, boy. Homer knows it all.

MANUS *goes to the window and looks out.*

MANUS: Where the hell has he got to?

SARAH *goes to* MANUS *and touches his elbow. She mimes rocking a baby.*

MANUS: Yes, I know he's at the christening; but it doesn't take them all day to put a name on a baby, does it?

SARAH *mimes pouring drinks and tossing them back quickly.*

MANUS: You may be sure. Which pub?

SARAH *indicates.*

MANUS: Gracie's?

No. Further away.

MANUS: Con Connie Tim's?

No. To the right of there.

MANUS: Anna na mBreag's?

Yes. That's it.

MANUS: Great. She'll fill him up. I suppose I may take the class then.

MANUS *begins to distribute some books, slates and chalk, texts etc. beside the seats.* SARAH *goes over to the straw and produces a bunch of flowers she has hidden there.*

During this:

JIMMY: *'Autar o ek limenos prosebe —'* 'But Ulysses went forth from the harbour and through the woodland to the place where Athene had shown him he could find the good swineherd who — *o oi biotoio malista kedeto*' — what's that, Manus?

MANUS: 'Who cared most for his substance'.

JIMMY: That's it! 'The good swineherd who cared most for his substance above all the slaves that Ulysses possessed . . .'

SARAH *presents the flowers to* MANUS.

MANUS: Those are lovely, Sarah.

But SARAH *has fled in embarrassment to her seat and has her head buried in a book.* MANUS *goes to her.*

MANUS: Flow-ers.

Pause. SARAH *does not look up.*

MANUS: Say the word: flow-ers. Come on — flow-ers.

SARAH: Flowers.

MANUS: You see? — you're off!

MANUS *leans down and kisses the top of* SARAH*'s head.*

MANUS: And they're beautiful flowers. Thank you.

MAIRE *enters, a strong-minded, strong-bodied woman in her twenties with a head of curly hair. She is carrying a small can of milk.*

MAIRE: Is this all's here? Is there no school this evening?

MANUS: If my father's not back, I'll take it.

MANUS *stands awkwardly, having been caught kissing* SARAH *and with the flowers almost formally at his chest.*

MAIRE: Well now, isn't that a pretty sight. There's your milk. How's Sarah?

SARAH *grunts a reply.*

MANUS: I saw you out at the hay.

MAIRE *ignores this and goes to* JIMMY.

MAIRE: And how's Jimmy Jack Cassie?

JIMMY: Sit down beside me, Maire.

MAIRE: Would I be safe?

JIMMY: No safer man in Donegal.

MAIRE *flops on a stool beside* JIMMY.

MAIRE: Ooooh. The best harvest in living memory, they say; but I don't want to see another like it. (*Showing* JIMMY *her hands*) Look at the blisters.

JIMMY: *Esne fatigata?*

MAIRE: *Sum fatigatissima.*

JIMMY: *Bene! Optime!*

MAIRE: That's the height of my Latin. Fit me better if I had even that much English.

JIMMY: English? I thought you had some English?

MAIRE: Three words. Wait — there was a spake I used to have off by heart. What's this it was? (*Her accent is strange because she is speaking a foreign language and because she does not understand what she is saying*) 'In Norfolk we besport ourselves around the maypoll.' What about that!

MANUS: Maypole.

Again MAIRE *ignores* MANUS.

MAIRE: God have mercy on my Aunt Mary — she taught me that when I was about four, whatever it means. Do you know what it means, Jimmy?

JIMMY: Sure you know I have only Irish like yourself.

MAIRE: And Latin. And Greek.

JIMMY: I'm telling you a lie: I know one English word.

MAIRE: What?

JIMMY: Bo-som.

MAIRE: What's a bo-som?

JIMMY: You know — (*He illustrates with his hands*) — bo-som — bo-som — you know — Diana, the huntress, she has two powerful bosom.

MAIRE: You may be sure that's the one English word you would know. (*Rises*) Is there a drop of water about?

MANUS *gives* MAIRE *his bowl of milk.*

MANUS: I'm sorry I couldn't get up last night.

MAIRE: Doesn't matter.

MANUS: Biddy Hanna sent for me to write a letter to her sister in Nova Scotia. All the gossip of the parish. 'I brought the cow to the bull three times last week but no good. There's nothing for it now but Big Ned Frank.'

MAIRE: (*Drinking*) That's better.

MANUS: And she got so engrossed in it that she forgot who she was dictating to: 'The aul drunken schoolmaster and that lame son of his are still footering about in the hedge-school, wasting people's good time and money.'

(MAIRE *has to laugh at this*)

MAIRE: She did not!

MANUS: And me taking it all down. 'Thank God one of them new national schools[2] is being built above at Poll na gCaorach.' It was after midnight by the time I got back.

MAIRE: Great to be a busy man.

MAIRE *moves away.* MANUS *follows.*

MANUS: I could hear music on my way past but I thought it was too late to call.

MAIRE: (*To* SARAH) Wasn't your father in great voice last night?

SARAH *nods and smiles.*

MAIRE: It must have been near three o'clock by the time you got home?

SARAH *holds up four fingers.*

MAIRE: Was it four? No wonder we're in pieces.

MANUS: I can give you a hand at the hay tomorrow.

MAIRE: That's the name of a hornpipe, isn't it? — 'The Scholar In The Hayfield' — or is it a reel?

MANUS: If the day's good.

MAIRE: Suit yourself. The English soldiers below in the tents, them sapper fellas, they're coming up to give us a hand. I don't know a word they're saying, nor they me; but sure that doesn't matter, does it?

MANUS: What the hell are you so crabbed[3] about?

DOALTY *and* BRIDGET *enter noisily. Both are in their twenties.* DOALTY *is brandishing a surveyor's pole. He is an open-minded, open-hearted, generous and slightly thick young man.* BRIDGET *is a plump, fresh young girl, ready to laugh, vain, and with a countrywoman's instinctive cunning.* DOALTY *enters doing his imitation of the master.*

DOALTY: Vesperal salutations to you all.

BRIDGET: He's coming down past Carraig na Ri and he's as full as a pig!

DOALTY: *Ignari, stulti, rustici* — pot-boys and peasant whelps — semi-literates and illegitimates.

BRIDGET: He's been on the batter[4] since this morning; he sent the wee ones home at eleven o'clock.

DOALTY: Three questions. Question A — Am I drunk? Question B — Am I sober? (*Into* MAIRE's face) *Responde — responde!*

2. The English Whig-Liberal government of 1831 introduced a system of national primary education, largely state-funded, based on non-denominational principles, controlled by the new Board of Education. These 'national schools' developed rapidly over the next decade. They displaced the hedge-schools, the remnant of the educational system of the old Irish culture, but failed to retain the non-denominational basis.

3. Pronounced 'krab-id': irritable.

4. on the drink.

BRIDGET: Question C, Master — When were you last sober?

MAIRE: What's the weapon, Doalty?

BRIDGET: I warned him. He'll be arrested one of these days.

DOALTY: Up in the bog with Bridget and her aul fella, and the Red Coats were just across at the foot of Cnoc na Mona, dragging them aul chains and peeping through the big machine they lug about everywhere with them — you know the name of it, Manus?

MAIRE: Theodolite.

BRIDGET: How do you know?

MAIRE: They leave it in our byre at night sometimes if it's raining.

JIMMY: Theodolite — what's the etymology of that word, Manus?

MANUS: No idea.

BRIDGET: Get on with the story.

JIMMY: *Theo — theos* — something to do with a god. Maybe *thea* — a goddess! What shape's the yoke?[5]

DOALTY: 'Shape!' Will you shut up, you aul eejit you! Anyway, every time they'd stick one of these poles into the ground and move across the bog, I'd creep up and shift it twenty or thirty paces to the side.

BRIDGET: God!

DOALTY: Then they'd come back and stare at it and look at their calculations and stare at it again and scratch their heads. And Cripes, d'you know what they ended up doing?

BRIDGET: Wait till you hear!

DOALTY: They took the bloody machine apart! (*And immediately he speaks in gibberish — an imitation of two very agitated and confused sappers[6] in rapid conversation*)

BRIDGET: That's the image of them!

MAIRE: You must be proud of yourself, Doalty.

DOALTY: What d'you mean?

MAIRE: That was a very clever piece of work.

MANUS: It was a gesture.

MAIRE: What sort of a gesture?

MANUS: Just to indicate . . . a presence.

MAIRE: Hah!

BRIDGET: I'm telling you — you'll be arrested.

When DOALTY *is embarrassed — or pleased — he reacts physically. He now grabs* BRIDGET *around the waist.*

DOALTY: What d'you make of that for an implement, Bridget? Wouldn't that make a great aul shaft for your churn?

BRIDGET: Let go of me, you dirty brute! I've a headline to do before Big Hughie comes.

MANUS: I don't think we'll wait for him. Let's get started.

Slowly, reluctantly they begin to move to their seats and specific tasks. DOALTY *goes to the bucket of water at the door and washes his hands.* BRIDGET *sets up a hand-mirror and combs her hair.*

BRIDGET: Nellie Ruadh's baby was to be christened this morning. Did any of yous hear what she called it? Did you, Sarah?

SARAH *grunts: No.*

BRIDGET: Did you, Maire?

MAIRE: No.

BRIDGET: Our Seamus says she was threatening she was going to call it after its father.

DOALTY: Who's the father?

BRIDGET: That's the point, you donkey you!

DOALTY: Ah.

BRIDGET: So there's a lot of uneasy bucks about Baile Beag this day.

DOALTY: She told me last Sunday she was going to call it Jimmy.

BRIDGET: You're a liar, Doalty.

DOALTY: Would I tell you a lie? Hi, Jimmy, Nellie Ruadh's aul fella's looking for you.

JIMMY: For me?

MAIRE: Come on, Doalty.

DOALTY: Someone told him . . .

MAIRE: Doalty!

DOALTY: He heard you know the first book of the Satires of Horace off by heart . . .

JIMMY: That's true.

DOALTY: . . . and he wants you to recite it for him.

JIMMY: I'll do that for him certainly, certainly.

DOALTY: He's busting to hear it.

JIMMY *fumbles in his pockets.*

JIMMY: I came across this last night — this'll interest you — in Book Two of Virgil's *Georgics.*

DOALTY: Be God, that's my territory alright.

BRIDGET: You clown you! (*To* SARAH) Hold this for me, would you? (*Her mirror*)

JIMMY: Listen to this, Manus. '*Nigra fere et presso pinguis sub vomere terra* . . .'

DOALTY: Steady on now — easy, boys, easy —

5. A word in common Irish use to denote any inanimate object.
6. Soldiers who work at the building and repairing of fortifications; a sapper is a standard designation for a private of the Royal Engineers.

don't rush me, boys — (*He mimes great concentration*)

JIMMY: Manus?

MANUS: 'Land that is black and rich beneath the pressure of the plough ...'

DOALTY: Give *me* a chance!

JIMMY: 'And with *cui putre* — with crumbly soil — is in the main best for corn.' There you are!

DOALTY: There you are.

JIMMY: 'From no other land will you see more wagons wending homeward behind slow bullocks.' Virgil! There!

DOALTY: 'Slow bullocks'!

JIMMY: Isn't that what I'm always telling you? Black soil for corn. *That's* what you should have in that upper field of yours — corn, not spuds.

DOALTY: Would you listen to that fella! Too lazy be Jasus to wash himself and he's lecturing me on agriculture! Would you go and take a running race at yourself, Jimmy Jack Cassie! (*Grabs* SARAH) Come away out of this with me, Sarah, and we'll plant some corn together.

MANUS: Alright — alright. Let's settle down and get some work done. I know Sean Beag isn't coming — he's at the salmon. What about the Donnelly twins? (*To* DOALTY) Are the Donnelly twins not coming any more? (DOALTY *shrugs and turns away*) Did you ask them?

DOALTY: Haven't seen them. Not about these days.

DOALTY *begins whistling through his teeth. Suddenly the atmosphere is silent and alert.*

MANUS: Aren't they at home?

DOALTY: No.

MANUS: Where are they then?

DOALTY: How would I know?

BRIDGET: Our Seamus says two of the soldiers' horses were found last night at the foot of the cliffs at Machaire Buide and ... (*She stops suddenly and begins writing with chalk on her slate*) D'you hear the whistles of this aul slate? Sure nobody could write on an aul slippery thing like that.

MANUS: What headline did my father set you?

BRIDGET: 'It's easier to stamp out learning than to recall it.'

JIMMY: Book Three, the *Agricola* of Tacitus.

BRIDGET: God but you're a dose.

MANUS: Can you do it?

BRIDGET: There. Is it bad? Will he ate me?

MANUS: It's very good. Keep your elbow in closer to your side. Doalty?

DOALTY: I'm at the seven-times table. I'm perfect, skipper.

MANUS *moves to* SARAH.

MANUS: Do you understand those sums?

SARAH *nods: Yes.* MANUS *leans down to her ear.*

MANUS: My name is Sarah.

MANUS *goes to* MAIRE. *While he is talking to her the others swop books, talk quietly, etc.*

MANUS: Can I help you? What are you at?

MAIRE: Map of America. (*Pause*) The passage money came last Friday.

MANUS: You never told me that.

MAIRE: Because I haven't seen you since, have I?

MANUS: You don't want to go. You said that yourself.

MAIRE: There's ten below me to be raised and no man in the house. What do you suggest?

MANUS: Do you want to go?

MAIRE: Did you apply for that job in the new national school?

MANUS: No.

MAIRE: You said you would.

MANUS: I said I might.

MAIRE: When it opens, this is finished: nobody's going to pay to go to a hedge-school.

MANUS: I know that and I ... (*He breaks off because he sees* SARAH, *obviously listening, at his shoulder. She moves away again*) I was thinking that maybe I could ...

MAIRE: It's £56 a year you're throwing away.

MANUS: I can't apply for it.

MAIRE: You *promised* me you would.

MANUS: My father has applied for it.

MAIRE: He has not!

MANUS: Day before yesterday.

MAIRE: For God's sake, sure you know he'd never —

MANUS: I couldn't — I can't go in against him.

MAIRE *looks at him for a second. Then.*

MAIRE: Suit yourself. (*To* BRIDGET) I saw your Seamus heading off to the Port fair early this morning.

BRIDGET: And wait till you hear this — I forgot to tell you this. He said that as soon as he crossed over the gap at Cnoc na Mona — just beyond where the soldiers are making the maps — the sweet smell was everywhere.

DOALTY: You never told me that.

BRIDGET: It went out of my head.

DOALTY: He saw the crops in Port?

BRIDGET: Some.

MANUS: How did the tops look?

BRIDGET: Fine — I think.

DOALTY: In flower?

BRIDGET: I don't know. I think so. He didn't say.

MANUS: Just the sweet smell — that's all?

BRIDGET: They say that's the way it snakes in, don't they? First the smell; and then one morning the stalks are all black and limp.

DOALTY: Are you stupid? It's the rotting stalks makes the sweet smell for God's sake. That's what the smell is — rotting stalks.

MAIRE: Sweet smell! Sweet smell! Every year at this time somebody comes back with stories of the sweet smell. Sweet God, did the potatoes ever fail in Baile Beag? Well, did they ever — ever? Never! There was never blight here. Never. Never. But we're always sniffing about for it, aren't we? — looking for disaster. The rents are going to go up again — the harvest's going to be lost — the herring have gone away for ever — there's going to be evictions. Honest to God, some of you people aren't happy unless you're miserable and you'll not be right content until you're dead!

DOALTY: Bloody right, Maire. And sure St Colmcille[7] prophesied there'd never be blight here. He said:

The spuds will bloom in Baile Beag
Till rabbits grow an extra lug.

And sure that'll never be. So we're alright. Seven threes are twenty-one; seven fours are twenty-eight; seven fives are forty-nine — Hi, Jimmy, do you fancy my chances as boss of the new national school?

JIMMY: What's that? — what's that?

DOALTY: Agh, g'way back home to Greece, son.

MAIRE: You ought to apply, Doalty.

DOALTY: D'you think so? Cripes, maybe I will. Hah!

BRIDGET: Did you know that you start at the age of six and you have to stick at it until you're twelve at least — no matter how smart you are or how much you know.

DOALTY: Who told you that yarn?

BRIDGET: And every child from every house has to go all day, every day, summer or winter. That's the law.

DOALTY: I'll tell you something — nobody's going to go near them — they're not going to take on — law or no law.

BRIDGET: And everything's free in them. You pay for nothing except the books you use; that's what our Seamus says.

DOALTY: 'Our Seamus'. Sure your Seamus wouldn't pay anyway. She's making this all up.

BRIDGET: Isn't that right, Manus?

MANUS: I think so.

BRIDGET: And from the very first day you go, you'll not hear one word of Irish spoken. You'll be taught to speak English and every subject will be taught through English and everyone'll end up as cute as the Buncrana[8] people.

SARAH *suddenly grunts and mimes a warning that the master is coming. The atmosphere changes. Sudden business. Heads down.*

DOALTY: He's here, boys. Cripes, he'll make yella meal out of me for those bloody tables.

BRIDGET: Have you any extra chalk, Manus?

MAIRE: And the atlas for me.

DOALTY *goes to* MAIRE *who is sitting on a stool at the back.*

DOALTY: Swop you seats.

MAIRE: Why?

DOALTY: There's an empty one beside the Infant Prodigy.

MAIRE: I'm fine here.

DOALTY: Please, Maire. I want to jouk[9] in the back here. (MAIRE *rises*) God love you. (*Aloud*) Anyone got a bloody table-book? Cripes, I'm wrecked. (SARAH *gives him one*) God, I'm dying about you.

In his haste to get to the back seat DOALTY *bumps into* BRIDGET *who is kneeling on the floor and writing laboriously on a slate resting on top of a bench-seat.*

BRIDGET: Watch where you're going, Doalty!

DOALTY *gooses* BRIDGET. *She squeals. Now the quiet hum of work:* JIMMY *reading Homer in a low voice;* BRIDGET *copying her headline;* MAIRE *studying the atlas;* DOALTY, *his eyes shut tight, mouthing his tables;* SARAH *doing sums. After a few seconds —*

7. The prophecies of St Columcille were part of millennial tradition in Irish folklore in which the extinction of English and/or protestant rule in Ireland was predicted. In the sharpened climate of sectarian tension in the 1820s and 1830s, manifested in the struggle for catholic emancipation (1829) and the Tithe War of the 1830s, these 'prophecies' had a renewed popularity.

8. Buncrana is a coastal town on the Inishowen peninsula of County Donegal. Its inhabitants have traditionally been accused of being crafty.

9. Hiberno-English. Used as a verb, as here, it means 'to move quickly and unobtrusively out of sight or notice'.

BRIDGET: Is this 'g' right, Manus? How do you put a tail on it?

DOALTY: Will you shut up! I can't concentrate! (*A few more seconds of work. Then* DOALTY *opens his eyes and looks around*) False alarm, boys. The bugger's not coming at all. Sure the bugger's hardly fit to walk.

And immediately HUGH *enters. A large man, with residual dignity, shabbily dressed, carrying a stick. He has, as always, a large quantity of drink taken, but he is by no means drunk. He is in his early sixties.*

HUGH: *Adsum*, Doalty, *adsum*. Perhaps not in *sobrietate perfecta* but adequately *sobrius* to overhear your quip. Vesperal salutations to you all.

Various responses.

JIMMY: *Ave*, Hugh.

HUGH: James. (*He removes his hat and coat and hands them and his stick to* MANUS, *as if to a footman*) Apologies for my late arrival: we were celebrating the baptism of Nellie Ruadh's baby.

BRIDGET: (*Innocently*) What name did she put on it, Master?

HUGH: Was it Eamon? Yes, it was Eamon.

BRIDGET: Eamon Donal from Tor! Cripes!

HUGH: And after the *caerimonia nominationis* — Maire?

MAIRE: The ritual of naming.

HUGH: Indeed — we then had a few libations to mark the occasion. Altogether very pleasant. The derivation of the word 'baptise'? — where are my Greek scholars? Doalty?

DOALTY: Would it be — ah — ah —

HUGH: Too slow. James?

JIMMY: '*Baptizein*' — to dip or immerse.

HUGH: Indeed — our friend Pliny Minor speaks of the '*baptisterium*' — the cold bath.

DOALTY: Master.

HUGH: Doalty?

DOALTY: I suppose you could talk then about baptising a sheep at sheep-dipping, could you?

Laughter. Comments.

HUGH: Indeed — the precedent is there — the day you were appropriately named Doalty — seven nines?

DOALTY: What's that, Master?

HUGH: Seven times nine?

DOALTY: Seven nines — seven nines — seven times nine — seven times nine are — Cripes, it's on the tip of my tongue, Master — I knew it for sure this morning — funny that's the only one that foxes me —

MAIRE: (*Prompt*) Sixty-three.

DOALTY: What's wrong with me: sure seven nines are fifty-three, Master.

HUGH: Sophocles from Colonus would agree with Doalty Dan Doalty from Tulach Alainn: 'To know nothing is the sweetest life.' Where's Sean Beag?

MANUS: He's at the salmon.

HUGH: And Nora Dan?

MAIRE: She says she's not coming back any more.

HUGH: Ah. Nora Dan can now write her name — Nora Dan's education is complete. And the Donnelly twins?

Brief pause. Then.

BRIDGET: They're probably at the turf. (*She goes to* HUGH) There's the one-and-eight I owe you for last quarter's arithmetic and there's my one-and-six for this quarter's writing.

HUGH: *Gratias tibi ago.* (*He sits at his table*) Before we commence our *studia* I have three items of information to impart to you — (*To* MANUS) A bowl of tea, strong tea, black — (MANUS *leaves*) Item A: on my perambulations today — Bridget? Too slow. Maire?

MAIRE: *Perambulare* — to walk about.

HUGH: Indeed — I encountered Captain Lancey of the Royal Engineers who is engaged in the ordnance survey of this area. He tells me that in the past few days two of his horses have strayed and some of his equipment seems to be mislaid. I expressed my regret and suggested he address you himself on these matters. He then explained that he does not speak Irish. Latin? I asked. None. Greek? Not a syllable. He speaks — on his own admission — only English; and to his credit he seemed suitably verecund — James?

JIMMY: *Verecundus* — humble.

HUGH: Indeed — he voiced some surprise that we did not speak his language. I explained that a few of us did, on occasion — outside the parish of course — and then usually for the purposes of commerce, a use to which his tongue seemed particularly suited — (*Shouts*) and a slice of soda bread — and I went on to propose that our own culture and the classical tongues made a happier conjugation — Doalty?

DOALTY: *Conjugo* — I join together.

DOALTY *is so pleased with himself that he prods and winks at* BRIDGET.

HUGH: Indeed — English, I suggested, couldn't really express us. And again to his credit he acquiesced to my logic. Acquiesced — Maire? (MAIRE *turns away impatiently.* HUGH *us unaware of the gesture*) Too slow. Bridget?

BRIDGET: *Acquiesco.*

HUGH: *Procede.*

BRIDGET: *Acquiesco, acquiescere, acquievi, acquietum.*

HUGH: Indeed — and Item B . . .

MAIRE: Master.

HUGH: Yes? (MAIRE *gets to her feet uneasily but determinedly. Pause*) Well, girl?

MAIRE: We should all be learning to speak English. That's what my mother says. That's what I say. That's what Dan O'Connell[10] said last month in Ennis. He said the sooner we all learn to speak English the better.

Suddenly several speak together.

JIMMY: What's she saying? What? What?

DOALTY: It's Irish he uses when he's travelling around scrounging votes.

BRIDGET: And sleeping with married women. Sure no woman's safe from that fella.

JIMMY: Who-who-who? Who's this? Who's this?

HUGH: *Silentium*! (*Pause*) Who is she talking about?

MAIRE: I'm talking about Daniel O'Connell.

HUGH: Does she mean that little Kerry politician?

MAIRE: I'm talking about the Liberator, Master, as you well know. And what he said was this: 'The old language is a barrier to modern progress.' He said that last month. And he's right. I don't want Greek. I don't want Latin. I want English. (MANUS *reappears on the platform above*) I want to be able to speak English because I'm going to America as soon as the harvest's all saved.

MAIRE *remains standing.* HUGH *puts his hand into his pocket and produces a flask of whisky. He removes the cap, pours a drink into it, tosses it back, replaces the cap, puts the flask into his pocket. Then*:

HUGH: We have been diverted — *diverto — divertere* — Where were we?

DOALTY: Three items of information, Master. You're at Item B.

10. Daniel O'Connell (1775-1847), the leader of catholic Ireland in the movements for catholic emancipation and repeal of the Union, was brought up in an Irish-speaking environment in County Kerry. He frequently urged his followers to abandon Irish for English, on the grounds that English was a more useful language in the modern world.

HUGH: Indeed — Item B — Item B — yes — On my way to the christening this morning I chanced to meet Mr George Alexander, Justice of the Peace. We discussed the new national school. Mr Alexander invited me to take charge of it when it opens. I thanked him and explained that I could do that only if I were free to run it as I have run this hedge-school for the past thirty-five years — filling what our friend Euripides calls the '*aplestos pithos*' — James?

JIMMY: 'The cask that cannot be filled'.

HUGH: Indeed — and Mr Alexander retorted courteously and emphatically that he hopes that is how it will be run. (MAIRE *now sits*) Indeed. I have had a strenuous day and I am weary of you all. (*He rises*) Manus will take care of you.

HUGH *goes towards the steps.* OWEN *enters.* OWEN *is the younger son, a handsome, attractive young man in his twenties. He is dressed smartly — a city man. His manner is easy and charming: everything he does is invested with consideration and enthusiasm. He now stands framed in the doorway, a travelling bag across his shoulder.*

OWEN: Could anybody tell me is this where Hugh Mor O'Donnell holds his hedge-school?

DOALTY: It's Owen — Owen Hugh! Look, boys — it's Owen Hugh!

OWEN *enters. As he crosses the room he touches and has a word for each person.*

OWEN: Doalty! (*Playful punch*) How are you, boy? *Jacobe, quid agis?* Are you well?

JIMMY: Fine. Fine.

OWEN: And Bridget! Give us a kiss. Aaaaaah!

BRIDGET: You're welcome, Owen.

OWEN: It's not —? Yes, it *is* Maire Chatach! God! A young woman!

MAIRE: How are you, Owen?

OWEN *is now in front of* HUGH. *He puts his two hands on his father's shoulders.*

OWNE: And how's the old man himself?

HUGH: Fair — fair.

OWEN: Fair? For God's sake you never looked better! Come here to me. (*He embraces* HUGH *warmly and genuinely*) Great to see you, Father. Great to be back.

HUGH*'s eyes are moist — partly joy, partly the drink.*

HUGH: I — I'm — I'm — pay no attention to —

OWEN: Come on — come on — come on — (*He gives* HUGH *his handkerchief*) Do you know what you and I are going to do tonight? We are going to go up to Anna na mBreag's . . .

DOALTY: Not there, Owen.

OWEN: Why not?

DOALTY: Her poteen's[11] worse than ever.

BRIDGET: They say she puts frogs in it!

OWEN: All the better. (*To* HUGH) And you and I are going to get footless drunk. That's arranged. (OWEN *sees* MANUS *coming down the steps with tea and soda bread. They meet at the bottom.*) And Manus!

MANUS: You're welcome, Owen.

OWEN: I know I am. And it's great to be here. (*He turns round, arms outstretched*) I can't believe it. I come back after six years and everything's just as it was! Nothing's changed! Not a thing! (*Sniffs*) Even that smell — that's the same smell this place always had. What is it anyway? Is it the straw?

DOALTY: Jimmy Jack's feet.

General laughter. It opens little pockets of conversation round the room.

OWEN: And Doalty Dan Doalty hasn't changed either!

DOALTY: Bloody right, Owen.

OWEN: Jimmy, are you well?

JIMMY: Dodging about.

OWEN: Any word of the big day? (*This is greeted with 'ohs' and 'ahs'*) Time enough, Jimmy. Homer's easier to live with, isn't he?

MAIRE: We heard stories that you own ten big shops in Dublin — is it true?

OWEN: Only nine.

BRIDGET: And you've twelve horses and six servants.

OWEN: Yes — that's true. God Almighty, would you listen to them — taking a hand at me![12]

MANUS: When did you arrive?

OWEN: We left Dublin yesterday morning, spent last night in Omagh and got here half an hour ago.

MANUS: You're hungry then.

HUGH: Indeed — get him food — get him a drink.

OWEN: Not now, thanks; later. Listen — am I interrupting you all?

HUGH: By no means. We're finished for the day.

OWEN: Wonderful. I'll tell you why. Two friends of mine are waiting outside the door. They'd like to meet you and I'd like you to meet them. May I bring them in?

HUGH: Certainly. You'll all eat and have . . .

11. Pronounced 'potch-een': illegally distilled spirits.

12. i.e. making (affectionate) fun of me.

OWEN: Not just yet, Father. You've seen the sappers working in this area for the past fortnight, haven't you? Well, the older man is Captain Lancey . . .

HUGH: I've met Captain Lancey.

OWEN: Great. He's the cartographer in charge of this whole area. Cartographer — James?

OWEN *begins to play this game — his father's game — partly to involve his classroom audience, partly to show he has not forgotten it, and indeed partly because he enjoys it.*

JIMMY: A maker of maps.

OWEN: Indeed — and the younger man that I travelled with from Dublin, his name is Lieutenant Yolland and he is attached to the toponymic department — Father? — *responde — responde*!

HUGH: He gives names to places.

OWEN: Indeed — although he is in fact an orthographer — Doalty? — too slow — Manus?

MANUS: The correct spelling of those names.

OWEN: Indeed — indeed! (OWEN *laughs and claps his hands. Some of the others join in*) Beautiful! Beautiful! Honest to God, it's such a delight to be back here with you all again — '*civilised*' people. Anyhow — may I bring them in?

HUGH: Your friends are our friends.

OWEN: I'll be straight back.

There is general talk as OWEN *goes towards the door. He stops beside* SARAH.

OWEN: That's a new face. Who are you?

A very brief hesitation. Then.

SARAH: My name is Sarah.

OWEN: Sarah who?

SARAH: Sarah Johnny Sally.

OWEN: Of course! From Bun na hAbhann! I'm Owen — Owen Hugh Mor. From Baile Beag. Good to see you.

During this OWEN-SARAH *exchange*:

HUGH: Come on now. Let's tidy this place up. (*He rubs the top of his table with his sleeve.*) Move, Doalty — lift those books off the floor.

DOALTY: Right, Master; certainly, Master; I'm doing my best, Master.

OWEN *stops at the door.*

OWEN: One small thing, Father.

HUGH: *Silentium*!

OWEN: I'm on their pay-roll.

SARAH, *very elated at her success, is beside* MANUS.

SARAH: I said it, Manus!

MANUS *ignores* SARAH. *He is much more interested in* OWEN *now.*

MANUS: You haven't enlisted, have you?!

SARAH *moves away.*

OWEN: Me a soldier? I'm employed as a part-time, underpaid, civilian interpreter. My job is to translate the quaint, archaic tongue you people persist in speaking into the King's good English. (*He goes out*)

HUGH: Move — move — move! Put some order on things! Come on, Sarah — hide that bucket. Whose are these slates? Somebody take these dishes away. *Festinate! Festinate!*

HUGH *pours another drink.* MANUS *goes to* MAIRE *who is busy tidying.*

MANUS: You didn't tell me you were definitely leaving.

MAIRE: Not now.

HUGH: Good girl, Bridget. That's the style.

MANUS: You might at least have told me.

HUGH: Are these your books, James?

JIMMY: Thank you.

MANUS: Fine! Fine! Go ahead! Go ahead!

MAIRE: You talk to me about getting married — with neither a roof over your head nor a sod of ground under your foot. I suggest you go for the new school; but no — 'My father's in for that.' Well now he's got it and now this is finished and now you've nothing.

MANUS: I can always ...

MAIRE: What? Teach classics to the cows? Agh —

MAIRE *moves away from* MANUS. OWEN *enters with* LANCEY *and* YOLLAND. CAPTAIN LANCEY *is middle-aged; a small, crisp officer, expert in his field as cartographer but uneasy with people — especially civilians, especially these foreign civilians. His skill is with deeds, not words.* LIEUTENANT YOLLAND *is in his late twenties/early thirties. He is tall and thin and gangling, blond hair, a shy, awkward manner. A soldier by accident.*

OWEN: Here we are. Captain Lancey — my father.

LANCEY: Good evening.

HUGH *becomes expansive, almost courtly, with his visitors.*

HUGH: You and I have already met, sir.

LANCEY: Yes.

OWEN: And Lieutenant Yolland — both Royal Engineers — my father.

HUGH: You're very welcome, gentlemen.

YOLLAND: How do you do.

HUGH: *Gaudeo vos hic adesse.*

OWEN: And I'll make no other introductions except that these are some of the people of Baile Beag and — what? — well you're among the best people in Ireland now. (*He pauses to allow* LANCEY *to speak.* LANCEY *does not*) Would you like to say a few words, Captain?

HUGH: What about a drop, sir?

LANCEY: A what?

HUGH: Perhaps a modest refreshment? A little sampling of our aqua vitae?

LANCEY: No, no.

HUGH: Later perhaps when ...

LANCEY: I'll say what I have to say, if I may, and as briefly as possible. Do they speak *any* English, Roland?

OWEN: Don't worry. I'll translate.

LANCEY: I see. (*He clears his throat. He speaks as if he were addressing children — a shade too loudly and enunciating excessively.*) You may have seen me — seen me — working in this section — section? — working. We are here — here — in this place — you understand? — to make a map — a map — a map and —

JIMMY: *Nonne Latine loquitur?*

HUGH *holds up a restraining hand.*

HUGH: James.

LANCEY: (*To* JIMMY) I do not speak Gaelic, sir. (*He looks at* OWEN)

OWEN: Carry on.

LANCEY: A map is a representation on paper — a picture — you understand picture? — a paper picture — showing, representing this country — yes? — showing your country in miniature — a scaled drawing on paper of — of — of —

Suddenly DOALTY *sniggers. Then* BRIDGET. *Then* SARAH. OWEN *leaps in quickly.*

OWEN: It might be better if you *assume* they understand you —

LANCEY: Yes?

OWEN: And I'll translate as you go along.

LANCEY: I see. Yes. Very well. Perhaps you're right. Well. What we are doing is this. (*He looks at* OWEN. OWEN *nods reassuringly*) His Majesty's government has ordered the first ever comprehensive survey of this entire country — a general triangulation which will embrace detailed hydrographic and topographic information and which will be executed to a scale of six inches to the English mile.

HUGH: (*Pouring a drink*) Excellent — excellent.

LANCEY *looks at* OWEN.

OWEN: A new map is being made of the whole country.

LANCEY *looks to* OWEN: *Is that all?* OWEN *smiles reassuringly and indicates to proceed.*

LANCEY: This enormous task has been embarked on so that the military authorities will be equipped with up-to-date and accurate information on every corner of this part of the Empire.

OWEN: This job is being done by soldiers because they are skilled in this work.

LANCEY: And also so that the entire basis of land valuation can be reassessed for purposes of more equitable taxation.

OWEN: This new map will take the place of the estate-agent's map so that from now on you will know exactly what is yours in law.

LANCEY: In conclusion I wish to quote two brief extracts from the white paper which is our governing charter: (*Reads*) 'All former surveys of Ireland originated in forfeiture and violent transfer of property; the present survey has for its object the relief which can be afforded to the proprietors and occupiers of land from unequal taxation.'

OWEN: The captain hopes that the public will cooperate with the sappers and that the new map will means that taxes are reduced.

HUGH: A worthy enterprise — *opus honestum*! And Extract B?

LANCEY: 'Ireland is privileged. No such survey is being undertaken in England. So this survey cannot but be received as proof of the disposition of this government to advance the interests of Ireland.' My sentiments, too.

OWEN: This survey demonstrates the government's interest in Ireland and the captain thanks you for listening so attentively to him.

HUGH: Our pleasure, Captain.

LANCEY: Lieutenant Yolland?

YOLLAND: I — I — I've nothing to say — really —

OWEN: The captain is the man who actually makes the new map. George's task is to see that the place-names on this map are ... correct. (*To* YOLLAND) Just a few words — they'd like to hear you. (*To class*) Don't you want to hear George, too?

MAIRE: Has he anything to say?

YOLLAND: (*To* MAIRE) Sorry — sorry?

OWEN: She says she's dying to hear you.

YOLLAND: (*To* MAIRE) Very kind of you — thank you ... (*To class*) I can only say that I feel — I feel very foolish to — to — to be working here and not to speak your language. But I intend to rectify that — with Roland's help — indeed I do.

OWEN: He wants me to teach him Irish!

HUGH: You are doubly welcome, sir.

YOLLAND: I think your countryside is — is — is very beautiful. I've fallen in love with it already. I hope we're not too — too crude an intrusion on your lives. And I know that I'm going to be happy, very happy, here.

OWEN: He is already a committed Hibernophile —

JIMMY: He loves —

OWEN: Alright, Jimmy — we know — he loves Baile Beag; and he loves you all.

HUGH: Please ... May I ...?

HUGH *is now drunk. He holds on to the edge of the table.*

OWEN: Go ahead, Father. (*Hands up for quiet*) Please — please.

HUGH: And we, gentlemen, we in turn are happy to offer you our friendship, our hospitality, and every assistance that you may require. Gentlemen — welcome!

A few desultory claps. The formalities are over. General conversation. The soldiers meet the locals. MANUS *and* OWEN *meet down stage.*

OWEN: Lancey's a bloody ramrod but George's alright. How are you anyway?

MANUS: What sort of a translation was that, Owen?

OWEN: Did I make a mess of it?

MANUS: You weren't saying what Lancey was saying!

OWEN: 'Uncertainty in meaning is incipient poetry'[13] — who said that?

MANUS: There was nothing uncertain about what Lancey said: it's a bloody military operation, Owen! And what's Yolland's function? What's 'incorrect' about the place-names we have here?

OWEN: Nothing at all. They're just going to be standardised.

MANUS: You mean changed into English?

OWEN: Where there's ambiguity, they'll be Anglicised.

MANUS: And they call you Roland! They both call you Roland!

OWEN: Shhhhh. Isn't it ridiculous? They seemed to get it wrong from the very beginning — or else

13. George Steiner, *After Babel* (London: Oxford University Press), p. 234.

they can't pronounce Owen. I was afraid some of you bastards would laugh.

MANUS: Aren't you going to tell them?

OWEN: Yes — yes — soon — soon.

MANUS: But they ...

OWEN: Easy, man, easy. Owen — Roland — what the hell. It's only a name. It's the same me, isn't it? Well, isn't it?

MANUS: Indeed it is. It's the same Owen.

OWEN: And the same Manus. And in a way we complement each other. (*He punches* MANUS *lightly, playfully and turns to join the others. As he goes*) Alright — who has met whom? Isn't this a job for the go-between?

MANUS *watches* OWEN *move confidently across the floor, taking* MAIRE *by the hand and introducing her to* YOLLAND. HUGH *is trying to negotiate the steps.* JIMMY *is lost in a text.* DOALTY *and* BRIDGET *are relieving their giggling.* SARAH *is staring at* MANUS.

ACT TWO

SCENE ONE

The sappers have already mapped most of the area. YOLLAND'S *official task, which* OWEN *is now doing, is to take each of the Gaelic names - every hill, stream, rock, even every patch of ground which possessed its own distinctive Irish name — and Anglicise it, either by changing it into its approximate English sound or by translating it into English words. For example, a Gaelic name like Cnoc Ban could become Knockban or — directly translated — Fair Hill. These new standardised names were entered into the Name-Book, and when the new maps appeared they contained all these new Anglicised names. OWEN's official function as translator is to pronounce each name in Irish and then provide the English translation.*

The hot weather continues. It is late afternoon some days later.

Stage right: an improvised clothes-line strung between the shafts of the cart and a nail in the wall; on it are some shirts and socks.

A large map — one of the new blank maps — is spread out on the floor. OWEN *is on his hands and knees, consulting it. He is totally engrossed in his task which he pursues with great energy and efficiency.*

YOLLAND'S *hesitancy has vanished — he is at home here now. He is sitting on the floor, his long legs stretched out before him, his back resting against a creel, his eyes closed. His mind is elsewhere. One of the reference books — a church registry — lies open on his lap.*

Around them are various reference books, the Name-Book, a bottle of poteen, some cups etc.

OWEN *completes an entry in the Name-Book and returns to the map on the floor.*

OWEN: Now. Where have we got to? Yes — the point where that stream enters the sea — that tiny little beach there. George!

YOLLAND: Yes. I'm listening. What do you call it? Say the Irish name again?

OWEN: Bun na hAbhann.

YOLLAND: Again.

OWEN: Bun na hAbhann.

YOLLAND: Bun na hAbhann.

OWEN: That's terrible, George.

YOLLAND: I know. I'm sorry. Say it again.

OWEN: Bun na hAbhann.

YOLLAND: Bun na hAbhann.

OWEN: That's better. Bun is the Irish word for bottom. And Abha means river. So it's literally the mouth of the river.

YOLLAND: Let's leave it alone. There's no English equivalent for a sound like that.

OWEN: What is it called in the church registry?

Only now does YOLLAND *open his eyes.*

YOLLAND: Let's see ... Banowen.

OWEN: That's wrong. (*Consults text*) The list of freeholders calls it Owenmore — that's completely wrong: Owenmore's the big river at the west end of the parish. (*Another text*) And in the grand jury lists it's called — God! — Binhone! — wherever they got that. I suppose we could Anglicize it to Bunowen; but somehow that's neither fish nor flesh.

YOLLAND *closes his eyes again.*

YOLLAND: I give up.

OWEN: (*At map*) Back to first principles. What are we trying to do?

YOLLAND: Good question.

OWEN: We are trying to denominate and at the same time describe that tiny area of soggy, rocky, sandy ground where that little stream enters the sea, an area known locally as Bun na hAbhann ... Burnfoot! What about Burnfoot?

YOLLAND: (*Indifferently*) Good, Roland. Burnfoot's good.

OWEN: George, my name isn't ...

YOLLAND: B-u-r-n-f-o-o-t?

OWEN: I suppose so. What do you think?

YOLLAND: Yes.

OWEN: Are you happy with that?

YOLLAND: Yes.

OWEN: Burnfoot it is then. (*He makes the entry into the Name-Book*) Bun na hAbhann — B-u-r-n-

YOLLAND: You're becoming very skilled at this.

OWEN: We're not moving fast enough.

YOLLAND: (*Opens eyes again*) Lancey lectured me again last night.

OWEN: When does he finish here?

YOLLAND: The sappers are pulling out at the end of the week. The trouble is, the maps they've completed can't be printed without these names. So London screams at Lancey and Lancey screams at me. But I wasn't intimidated.

MANUS *emerges from upstairs and descends.*

'I'm sorry, sir,' I said, 'But certain tasks demand their own tempo. You cannot rename a whole country overnight.' Your Irish air has made me bold. (*To* MANUS) Do you want us to leave?

MANUS: Time enough. Class won't begin for another half-hour.

YOLLAND: Sorry — sorry?

OWEN: Can't you speak English?

MANUS *gathers the things off the clothes-line.* OWEN *returns to the map.*

OWEN: We now come across that beach ...

YOLLAND: Tra — that's the Irish for beach. (*To* MANUS) I'm picking up the odd word, Manus.

MANUS: So.

OWEN: ... on past Burnfoot; and there's nothing around here that has any name that I know of until we come down here to the south end, just about here ... and there should be a ridge of rocks there ... Have the sappers marked it? They have. Look, George.

YOLLAND: Where are we?

OWEN: There.

YOLLAND: I'm lost.

OWEN: Here. And the name of that ridge is Druim Dubh. Put English on that, Lieutenant.

YOLLAND: Say it again.

OWEN: Druim Dubh.

YOLLAND: Dubh means black.

OWEN: Yes.

YOLLAND: And Druim means ... what? a fort?

OWEN: We met it yesterday in Druim Luachra.

YOLLAND: A ridge! The Black Ridge! (*To* MANUS) You see, Manus?

OWEN: We'll have you fluent at the Irish before the summer's over.

YOLLAND: Oh I wish I were. (*To* MANUS *as he crosses to go back upstairs*) We got a crate of oranges from Dublin today. I'll send some up to you.

MANUS: Thanks. (*To* OWEN) Better hide that bottle. Father's just up and he'd be better without it.

OWEN: Can't you speak English before your man?[1]

MANUS: Why?

OWEN: Out of courtesy.

MANUS: Doesn't he want to learn Irish? (*To* YOLLAND) Don't you want to learn Irish?

YOLLAND: Sorry — sorry? I — I —

MANUS: I understand the Lanceys perfectly but people like you puzzle me.

OWEN: Manus, for God's sake!

MANUS: (*Still to* YOLLAND) How's the work going?

YOLLAND: The work? — the work? Oh, it's — it's staggering along — I think — (*To* OWEN) — isn't it? But we'd be lost without Roland.

MANUS: (*Leaving*) I'm sure. But there are always the Rolands, aren't there? (*He goes upstairs and exits*)

YOLLAND: What was that he said? — something about Lancey, was it?

OWEN: He said we should hide that bottle before Father gets his hands on it.

YOLLAND: Ah.

OWEN: He's always trying to protect him.

YOLLAND: Was he lame from birth?

OWEN: An accident when he was a baby: Father fell across his cradle. That's why Manus feels so responsible for him.

YOLLAND: Why doesn't he marry?

OWEN: Can't afford to, I suppose.

YOLLAND: Hasn't he a salary?

OWEN: What salary? All he gets is the odd shilling Father throws him — and that's seldom enough. I got out in time, didn't I? (YOLLAND *is pouring a drink*) Easy with that stuff — it'll hit you suddenly.

YOLLAND: I like it.

OWEN: Let's get back to the job. Druim Dubh — what's it called in the jury lists? (*Consults texts*)

YOLLAND: Some people here resent us.

OWEN: Dramduff — wrong as usual.

YOLLAND: I was passing a little girl yesterday and she spat at me.

1. A colloquial form of reference to a third party.

OWEN: And it's Drimdoo here. What's it called in the registry?

YOLLAND: Do you know the Donnelly twins?

OWEN: Who?

YOLLAND: The Donnelly twins.

OWEN: Yes. Best fishermen about here. What about them?

YOLLAND: Lancey's looking for them.

OWEN: What for?

YOLLAND: He wants them for questioning.

OWEN: Probably stolen somebody's nets. Dramduffy! Nobody ever called it Dramduffy. Take your pick of those three.

YOLLAND: My head's addled. Let's take a rest. Do you want a drink?

OWEN: Thanks. Now, every Dubh we've come across we've changed to Duff. So if we're to be consistent, I suppose Druim Dubh has to become Dromduff. (YOLLAND *is now looking out the window*) You can see the end of the ridge from where you're standing. But D-r-u-m or D-r-o-m? (*Name-Book*) Do you remember — which did we agree on for Druim Luachra?

YOLLAND: That house immediately above where we're camped —

OWEN: Mm?

YOLLAND: The house where Maire lives.

OWEN: Maire? Oh, Maire Chatach.

YOLLAND: What does that mean?

OWEN: Curly-haired; the whole family are called the Catachs. What about it?

YOLLAND: I hear music coming from that house almost every night.

OWEN: Why don't you drop in?

YOLLAND: Could I?

OWEN: Why not? We used D-r-o-m then. So we've got to call it D-r-o-m-d-u-f-f — alright?

YOLLAND: Go back up to where the new school is being built and just say the names again for me, would you?

OWEN: That's a good idea. Poolkerry, Ballybeg —

YOLLAND: No, no; as they still are — in your own language.

OWEN: Poll na gCaorach, (YOLLAND *repeats the names silently after him*) Baile Beag, Ceann Balor, Lis Maol, Machaire Buidhe, Baile na gGall, Carraig na Ri, Mullach Dearg —

YOLLAND: Do you think I could live here?

OWEN: What are you talking about?

YOLLAND: Settle down here — live here.

OWEN: Come on, George.

YOLLAND: I mean it.

OWEN: Live on what? Potatoes? Buttermilk?

YOLLAND: It's really heavenly.

OWEN: For God's sake! The first hot summer in fifty years and you think it's Eden. Don't be such a bloody romantic. You wouldn't survive a mild winter here.

YOLLAND: Do you think not? Maybe you're right.

DOALTY *enters in a rush.*

DOALTY: Hi, boys, is Manus about?

OWEN: He's upstairs. Give him a shout.

DOALTY: Manus! The cattle's going mad in that heat — Cripes, running wild all over the place. (*To* YOLLAND) How are you doing, skipper?

MANUS *appears.*

YOLLAND: Thank you for — I — I'm very grateful to you for —

DOALTY: Wasting your time. I don't know a word you're saying. Hi, Manus, there's two bucks down the road there asking for you.

MANUS: (*Descending*) Who are they?

DOALTY: Never clapped eyes on them. They want to talk to you.

MANUS: What about?

DOALTY: They wouldn't say. Come on. The bloody beasts'll end up in Loch an Iubhair if they're not capped.[2] Good luck, boys!

DOALTY *rushes off.* MANUS *follows him.*

OWEN: Good luck! What were you thanking Doalty for?

YOLLAND: I was washing outside my tent this morning and he was passing with a scythe across his shoulder and he came up to me and pointed to the long grass and then cut a pathway round my tent and from the tent down to the road — so that my feet won't get wet with the dew. Wasn't that kind of him? And I have no words to thank him ... I suppose you're right: I suppose I couldn't live here ... Just before Doalty came up to me this morning, I was thinking that at that moment I might have been in Bombay instead of Ballybeg. You see, my father was at his wits end with me and finally he got me a job with the East India Company — some kind of a clerkship. This was ten, eleven months ago. So I set off for London. Unfortunately I — I — I missed the boat. Literally. And since I couldn't

2. caught.

face Father and hadn't enough money to hang about until the next sailing, I joined the Army. And they stuck me into the Engineers and posted me to Dublin. And Dublin sent me here. And while I was washing this morning and looking across the Tra Bhan, I was thinking how very, very lucky I am to be here and not in Bombay.

OWEN: Do you believe in fate?

YOLLAND: Lancey's so like my father. I was watching him last night. He met every group of sappers as they reported in. He checked the field kitchens. He examined the horses. He inspected every single report — even examining the texture of the paper and commenting on the neatness of the handwriting. The perfect colonial servant: not only must the job be done — it must be done with excellence. Father has that drive, too; that dedication; that indefatigable energy. He builds roads — hopping from one end of the Empire to the other. Can't sit still for five minutes. He says himself the longest time he ever sat still was the night before Waterloo when they were waiting for Wellington to make up his mind to attack.

OWEN: What age is he?

YOLLAND: Born in 1789 — the very day the Bastille fell. I've often thought maybe that gave his whole life its character. Do you think it could? He inherited a new world the day he was born — the Year One. Ancient time was at an end. The world had cast off its old skin. There were no longer any frontiers to man's potential. Possibilities were endless and exciting. He still believes that. The Apocalypse is just about to happen ... I'm afraid I'm a great disappointment to him. I've neither his energy, nor his coherence, nor his belief. Do I believe in fate? The day I arrived in Ballybeg, — no, Baile Beag — the moment you brought me here, I had a curious sensation. It's difficult to describe. It was a momentary sense of discovery; no — not quite a sense of discovery — a sense of recognition, of confirmation of something I half knew instinctively; as if I had stepped ...

OWEN: Back into ancient time?

YOLLAND: No, no. It wasn't an awareness of *direction* being changed but of experience being of a totally different order. I had moved into a consciousness that wasn't striving nor agitated. And when I heard Jimmy Jack and your father swopping stories about Apollo and Cuchulainn and Paris and Ferdia — as if they lived down the road — it was then that I thought — I knew — perhaps I could live here ... (*Now embarrassed*) Where's the pot-een?

OWEN: Poteen.

YOLLAND: Poteen — poteen — poteen. Even if I did speak Irish I'd always be an outsider here, wouldn't I? I may learn the password but the language of the tribe will always elude me, won't it? The private core will always be ... hermetic, won't it?

OWEN: You can learn to decode us.

HUGH *emerges from upstairs and descends. He is dressed for the road. Today he is physically and mentally jaunty and alert — almost self-consciously jaunty and alert. Indeed, as the scene progresses, one has the sense that he is deliberately parodying himself. The moment* HUGH *gets to the bottom of the steps* YOLLAND *leaps respectfully to his feet.*

HUGH: (*As he descends*)
Quantumvis cursum longum fessumque moratur
Sol, sacro tandem carmine vesper adest.

I dabble in verse, Lieutenant, after the style of Ovid. (*To* OWEN) A drop of that to fortify me.

YOLLAND: You'll have to translate it for me.

HUGH: Let's see —
No matter how long the sun may linger on his long and weary journey
At length evening comes with its sacred song.

YOLLAND: Very nice, sir.

HUGH: English succeeds in making it sound ... plebeian.

OWEN: Where are you off to, Father?

HUGH: An *expeditio* with three purposes. Purpose A: to acquire a testimonial from our parish priest — (*To* YOLLAND) a worthy man but barely literate; and since he'll ask me to write it myself, how in all modesty can I do myself justice? (*To* OWEN) Where did this (*Drink*) come from?

OWEN: Anna na mBreag's.

HUGH: (*To* YOLLAND) In that case address yourself to it with circumspection. (*And* HUGH *instantly tosses the drink back in one gulp and grimaces*) Aaaaaaagh! (*Holds out his glass for a refill*) Anna na mBreag means Anna of the Lies. And Purpose B: to talk to the builders of the new school about the kind of living accommodation I will require there. I have lived too long like a journeyman tailor.

YOLLAND: Some years ago we lived fairly close to a poet — well, about three miles away.

HUGH: His name?

YOLLAND: Wordsworth — William Wordsworth.

HUGH: Did he speak of me to you?

YOLLAND: Actually I never talked to him. I just saw him out walking — in the distance.

HUGH: Wordsworth? ... no. I'm afraid we're not familiar with your literature, Lieutenant. We feel closer to the warm Mediterranean. We tend to overlook your island.

YOLLAND: I'm learning to speak Irish, sir.

HUGH: Good.

YOLLAND: Roland's teaching me.

HUGH: Splendid.

YOLLAND: I mean — I feel so cut off from the people here. And I was trying to explain a few minutes ago how remarkable a community this is. To meet people like yourself and Jimmy Jack who actually converse in Greek and Latin. And your place names — what was the one we came across this morning? — Termon, from Terminus, the god of boundaries. It — it — it's really astonishing.

HUGH: We like to think we endure around truths immemorially posited.

YOLLAND: And your Gaelic literature — you're a poet yourself —

HUGH: Only in Latin, I'm afraid.

YOLLAND: I understand it's enormously rich and ornate.

HUGH: Indeed, Lieutenant. A rich language. A rich literature. You'll find, sir, that certain cultures expend on their vocabularies and syntax acquisitive energies and ostentations entirely lacking in their material lives. I suppose you could call us a spiritual people.

OWEN: (*Not unkindly; more out of embarrassment before* YOLLAND) Will you stop that nonsense, Father.

HUGH: Nonsense? What nonsense?

OWEN: Do you know where the priest lives?

HUGH: At Lis na Muc, over near ...

OWEN: No, he doesn't. Lis na Muc, the Fort of the Pigs, has become Swinefort. (*Now turning the pages of the Name-Book — a page per name*) And to get to Swinefort you pass through Greencastle and Fair Head and Strandhill and Gort and Whiteplains. And the new school isn't at Poll na gCaorach — it's at Sheepsrock. Will you be able to find your way?

HUGH *pours himself another drink. Then*:

HUGH: Yes, it is a rich language, Lieutenant, full of the mythologies of fantasy and hope and self-deception — a syntax opulent with tomorrows.[3] It is our response to mud cabins and a diet of potatoes; our only method of replying to ... inevitabilities. (*To* OWEN) Can you give me the loan of half-a-crown? I'll repay you out of the subscriptions I'm collecting for the publication of my new book. (*To* YOLLAND) It is entitled: 'The Pentaglot Preceptor or Elementary Institute of the English, Greek, Hebrew, Latin and Irish Languages; Particularly Calculated for the Instruction of Such Ladies and Gentleman as may Wish to Learn without the Help of a Master'.

YOLLAND: (*Laughs*) That's a wonderful title!

HUGH: Between ourselves — the best part of the enterprise. Nor do I, in fact, speak Hebrew. And that last phrase — 'without the Help of a Master' — that was written before the new national school was thrust upon me — do you think I ought to drop it now? After all you don't dispose of the cow just because it has produced a magnificent calf, do you?

YOLLAND: You certainly do not.

HUGH: The phrase goes. And I'm interrupting work of moment. (*He goes to the door and stops there*) To return briefly to that other matter, Lieutenant. I understand your sense of exclusion, of being cut off from a life here; and I trust you will find access to us with my son's help. But remember that words are signals, counters. They are not immortal. And it can happen — to use an image you'll understand — it can happen that a civilisation can be imprisoned in a linguistic contour which no longer matches the landscape of ... fact.[4] Gentlemen. (*He leaves*)

OWEN: 'An *expeditio* with three purposes': the children laugh at him: he always promises three points and he never gets beyond A and B.

YOLLAND: He's an astute man.

OWEN: He's bloody pompous.

YOLLAND: But so astute.

OWEN: And he drinks too much. Is it astute not to be able to adjust for survival? Enduring around truths immemorially posited — hah!

YOLLAND: He knows what's happening.

OWEN: What is happening?

YOLLAND: I'm not sure. But I'm concerned about my part in it. It's an eviction of sorts.

OWEN: We're making a six-inch map of the country. Is there something sinister in that?

YOLLAND: Not in ...

3. George Steiner, *After Babel* (London: Oxford University Press), p. 227.
4. Steiner, op. cit., p. 21.

OWEN: And we're taking place-names that are riddled with confusion and . . .

YOLLAND: Who's confused? Are the people confused?

OWEN: . . . and we're standardising those names as accurately and as sensitively as we can.

YOLLAND: Something is being eroded.

OWEN: Back to the romance again. Alright! Fine! Fine! Look where we've got to. (*He drops on his hands and knees and stabs a finger at the map*) We've come to this crossroads. Come here and look at it, man! Look at it! And we call that crossroads Tobair Vree. And why do we call it Tobair Vree? I'll tell you why. Tobair means a well. But what does Vree mean? It's a corruption of Brian — (*Gaelic pronunciation*) Brian — an erosion of Tobair Bhriain. Because a hundred-and-fifty years ago there used to be a well there, not at the crossroads, mind you — that would be too simple — but in a field close to the crossroads. And an old man called Brian, whose face was disfigured by an enormous growth, got it into his head that the water in that well was blessed; and every day for seven months he went there and bathed his faced in it. But the growth didn't go away; and one morning Brian was found drowned in that well. And ever since that crossroads is known as Tobair Vree — even though that well has long since dried up. I know the story because my grandfather told it to me. But ask Doalty — or Maire — or Bridget — even my father — even Manus — why it's called Tobair Vree; and do you think they'll know? I know they don't know. So the question I put to you, Lieutenant, is this: What do we do with a name like that? Do we scrap Tobair Vree altogether and call it — what? — The Cross? Crossroads? Or do we keep piety with a man long dead, long forgotten, his name 'eroded' beyond recognition, whose trivial little story nobody in the parish remembers?

YOLLAND: Except you.

OWEN: I've left here.

YOLLAND: You remember it.

OWEN: I'm asking you: what do we write in the Name-Book?

YOLLAND: Tobair Vree.

OWEN: Even though the well is a hundred yards from the actual crossroads — and there's no well anyway — and what the hell does Vree mean?

YOLLAND: Tobair Vree.

OWEN: That's what you want?

YOLLAND: Yes.

OWEN: You're certain?

YOLLAND: Yes.

OWEN: Fine. Fine. That's what you'll get.

YOLLAND: That's what you want, too, Roland.

Pause.

OWEN: (*Explodes*) George! For God's sake! *My name is not Roland!*

YOLLAND: What!

OWEN: (*Softly*) My name is Owen.

Pause.

YOLLAND: Not Roland?

OWEN: Owen.

YOLLAND: You mean to say —?

OWEN: Owen.

YOLLAND: But I've been —

OWEN: O-w-e-n.

YOLLAND: Where did Roland come from?

OWEN: I don't know.

YOLLAND: It was never Roland?

OWEN: Never.

YOLLAND: O my God!

Pause. They stare at one another. Then the absurdity of the situation strikes them suddenly. They explode with laughter. OWEN *pours drinks. As they roll about their lines overlap.*

YOLLAND: Why didn't you tell me?

OWEN: Do I look like a Roland?

YOLLAND: Spell Owen again.

OWEN: I was getting fond of Roland.

YOLLAND: O my God!

OWEN: O-w-e-n.

YOLLAND: What'll we write —

OWEN: — in the Name-Book?!

YOLLAND: R-o-w-e-n!

OWEN: Or what about Ol-

YOLLAND: Ol- what?

OWEN: Oland!

And again they explode. MANUS *enters. He is very elated.*

MANUS: What's the celebration?

OWEN: A christening!

YOLLAND: A baptism!

OWEN: A hundred christenings!

YOLLAND: A thousand baptisms! Welcome to Eden!

OWEN: Eden's right! We name a thing and — bang! — it leaps into existence!

YOLLAND: Each name a perfect equation with its roots.

OWEN: A perfect congruence with its reality. (*To* MANUS) Take a drink.

YOLLAND: Poteen — beautiful.

OWEN: Lying Anna's poteen.

YOLLAND: Anna na mBreag's poteen.

OWEN: Excellent, George.

YOLLAND: I'll decode you yet.

OWEN: (*Offers drink*) Manus?

MANUS: Not if that's what it does to you.

OWEN: You're right. Steady — steady — sober up — sober up.

YOLLAND: Sober as a judge, Owen.

MANUS *moves beside* OWEN.

MANUS: I've got good news! Where's Father?

OWEN: He's gone out. What's the good news?

MANUS: I've been offered a job.

OWEN: Where? (*Now aware of* YOLLAND) Come on, man — speak in English.

MANUS: For the benefit of the colonist?

OWEN: He's a decent man.

MANUS: Aren't they all at some level?

OWEN: Please. (MANUS *shrugs*) He's been offered a job.

YOLLAND: Where?

OWEN: Well — tell us!

MANUS: I've just had a meeting with two men from Inis Meadhon. They want me to go there and start a hedge-school. They're giving me a free house, free turf, and free milk; a rood of standing corn; twelve drills of potatoes; and — (*He stops*)

OWEN: And what?

MANUS: A salary of £42 a year!

OWEN: Manus, that's wonderful!

MANUS: You're talking to a man of substance.

OWEN: I'm delighted.

YOLLAND: Where's Inis Meadhon?

OWEN: An island south of here. And they came looking for you?

MANUS: Well, I mean to say ...

OWEN *punches* MANUS.

OWEN: Aaaaagh! This calls for a real celebration.

YOLLAND: Congratulations.

MANUS: Thank you.

OWEN: Where are you, Anna?

YOLLAND: When do you start?

MANUS: Next Monday.

OWEN: We'll stay with you when we're there. (*To* YOLLAND) How long will it be before we reach Inis Meadhon?

YOLLAND: How far south is it?

MANUS: About fifty miles.

YOLLAND: Could we make it by December?

OWEN: We'll have Christmas together. (*Sings*) 'Christmas Day on Inis Meadhon ...'

YOLLAND: (*Toast*) I hope you're very content there, Manus.

MANUS: Thank you.

YOLLAND *holds out his hand.* MANUS *takes it. They shake warmly.*

OWEN: (*Toast*) Manus.

MANUS: (*Toast*) To Inis Meadhon. (*He drinks quickly and turns to leave*)

OWEN: Hold on — hold on — refills coming up.

MANUS: I've got to go.

OWEN: Come on, man; this is an occasion. Where are you rushing to?

MANUS: I've got to tell Maire.

MAIRE *enters with her can of milk.*

MAIRE: You've got to tell Maire what?

OWEN: He's got a job!

MAIRE: Manus?

OWEN: He's been invited to start a hedge-school in Inis Meadhon.

MAIRE: Where?

MANUS: Inis Meadhon — the island! They're giving me £42 a year and ...

OWEN: A house, fuel, milk, potatoes, corn, pupils, what-not!

MANUS: I start on Monday.

OWEN: You'll take a drink. Isn't it great?

MANUS: I want to talk to you for ...

MAIRE: There's your milk. I need the can back.

MANUS *takes the can and runs up the steps.*

MANUS: (*As he goes*) How will you like living on an island?

OWEN: You know George, don't you?

MAIRE: We wave to each other across the fields.

YOLLAND: Sorry-sorry?

OWEN: She says you wave to each other across the fields.

YOLLAND: Yes, we do; oh yes, indeed we do.

MAIRE: What's he saying?

OWEN: He says you wave to each other across the fields.

MAIRE: That's right. So we do.

YOLLAND: What's she saying?

OWEN: Nothing — nothing — nothing. (*To* MAIRE) What's the news?

MAIRE *moves away, touching the text books with her toe.*

MAIRE: Not a thing. You're busy, the two of you.

OWEN: We think we are.

MAIRE: I hear the Fiddler O'Shea's about. There's some talk of a dance tomorrow night.

OWEN: Where will it be?

MAIRE: Maybe over the road. Maybe at Tobair Vree.

YOLLAND: Tobair Vree!

MAIRE: Yes.

YOLLAND: Tobair Vree! Tobair Vree!

MAIRE: Does he know what I'm saying?

OWEN: Not a word.

MAIRE: Tell him then.

OWEN: Tell him what?

MAIRE: About the dance.

OWEN: Maire says there may be a dance tomorrow night.

YOLLAND: (*To* OWEN) Yes? May I come? (*To* MAIRE) Would anybody object if I came?

MAIRE: (*To* OWEN) What's he saying?

OWEN: (*To* YOLLAND) Who would object?

MAIRE: (*To* OWEN) Did you tell him?

YOLLAND: (*To* MAIRE) Sorry-sorry?

OWEN: (*To* MAIRE) He says may he come?

MAIRE: (*To* YOLLAND) That's up to you.

YOLLAND: (*To* OWEN) What does she say?

OWEN: (*To* YOLLAND) She says —

YOLLAND: (*To* MAIRE) What-what?

MAIRE: (*To* OWEN) Well?

YOLLAND: (*To* OWEN) Sorry-sorry?

OWEN: (*To* YOLLAND) Will you go?

YOLLAND: (*To* MAIRE) Yes, yes, if I may.

MAIRE: (*To* OWEN) What does he say?

YOLLAND: (*To* OWEN) What is she saying?

OWEN: O for God's sake! (*To* MANUS *who is descending with the empty can*) You take on this job, Manus.

MANUS: I'll walk you up to the house. Is your mother at home? I want to talk to her.

MAIRE: What's the rush? (*To* OWEN) Didn't you offer me a drink?

OWEN: Will you risk Anna na mBreag?

MAIRE: Why not.

YOLLAND *is suddenly intoxicated. He leaps up on a stool, raises his glass and shouts.*

YOLLAND: Anna na mBreag! Baile Beag! Inis Meadhon! Bombay! Tobair Vree! Eden! And poteen — correct, Owen?

OWEN: Perfect.

YOLLAND: And bloody marvellous stuff it is, too. I love it! Bloody, bloody, bloody marvellous!

Simultaneously with his final 'bloody marvellous' bring up very loud the introductory music of the reel. Then immediately go to black. Retain the music throughout the very brief interval.

SCENE TWO

The following night.

This scene may be played in the schoolroom, but it would be preferable to lose — by lighting — as much of the schoolroom as possible, and to play the scene down front in a vaguely 'outside' area.

The music rises to a crescendo. Then in the distance we hear MAIRE *and* YOLLAND *approach — laughing and running. They run on, hand-in-hand. They have just left the dance.*

Fade the music to distant background. Then after a time it is lost and replaced by guitar music.

MAIRE *and* YOLLAND *are now down front, still holding hands and excited by their sudden and impetuous escape from the dance.*

MAIRE: O my God, that leap across the ditch nearly killed me.

YOLLAND: I could scarcely keep up with you.

MAIRE: Wait till I get my breath back.

YOLLAND: We must have looked as if we were being chased.

They now realise they are alone and holding hands — the beginnings of embarrassment. The hands disengage. They begin to drift apart. Pause.

MAIRE: Manus'll wonder where I've got to.

YOLLAND: I wonder did anyone notice us leave.

Pause. Slightly further apart.

MAIRE: The grass must be wet. My feet are soaking.

YOLLAND: Your feet must be wet. The grass is soaking.

Another pause. Another few paces apart. They are now a long distance from one another.

YOLLAND: (*Indicating himself*) George.

MAIRE *nods: Yes — yes. Then:*

MAIRE: Lieutenant George.

YOLLAND: Don't call me that. I never think of myself as Lieutenant.

MAIRE: What-what?

YOLLAND: Sorry-sorry? (*He points to himself again*) George.

MAIRE *nods:* Yes-yes. *Then points to herself.*

MAIRE: Maire.

YOLLAND: Yes, I know you're Maire. Of course I know you're Maire. I mean I've been watching you night and day for the past ...

MAIRE: (*Eagerly*) What-what?

YOLLAND: (*Points*) Maire. (*Points*) George. (*Points both*) Maire and George. (MAIRE *nods: Yes-*

yes-yes) I — I — I —

MAIRE: Say anything at all. I love the sound of your speech.

YOLLAND: (*Eagerly*) Sorry-sorry? (*In acute frustration he looks around, hoping for some inspiration that will provide him with communicative means. Now he has a thought: he tries raising his voice and articulating in a staccato style and with equal and absurd emphasis on each word*) Every-morning-I-see-you-feeding-brown-hens-and-giving-meal-to-black-calf — (*The futility of it*) — O my God.

MAIRE *smiles. She moves towards him. She will try to communicate in Latin.*

MAIRE: *Tu es centurio in — in — in exercitu Britannico —*

YOLLAND: Yes-yes? Go on — go on — say anything at all — I love the sound of your speech.

MAIRE: *— et es in castris quae — quae sunt in agro* — (*The futility of it*) — O my God. (YOLLAND *smiles. He moves towards her. Now for her English words*) George — water.

YOLLAND: 'Water'? Water! Oh yes — water — water — very good — water — good — good.

MAIRE: Fire.

YOLLAND: Fire — indeed — wonderful — fire, fire, fire — splendid — splendid!

MAIRE: Ah ... ah ...

YOLLAND: Yes? Go on.

MAIRE: Earth.

YOLLAND: 'Earth'?

MAIRE: Earth. Earth. (YOLLAND *still does not understand.* MAIRE *stoops down and picks up a handful of clay. Holding it out*) Earth.

YOLLAND: Earth! Of course — earth! Earth. Earth. Good Lord, Maire, your English is perfect!

MAIRE: (*Eagerly*) What-what?

YOLLAND: Perfect English. English perfect.

MAIRE: George —

YOLLAND: That's beautiful — oh that's really beautiful.

MAIRE: George —

YOLLAND: Say it again — say it again —

MAIRE: Shhh. (*She holds her hand up for silence — she is trying to remember her one line of English. Now she remembers it and she delivers the line as if English were her language — easily, fluidly, conversationally*) George, in Norfolk we besport ourselves around the maypoll.

YOLLAND: Good God, do you? That's where my mother comes from — Norfolk. Norwich actually. Not exactly Norwich town but a small village called Little Walsingham close beside it. But in our own village of Winfarthing we have a maypole too and every year on the first of May — (*He stops abruptly, only now realising. He stares at her. She in turn misunderstands his excitement.*)

MAIRE: (*To herself*) Mother of God, my Aunt Mary wouldn't have taught me something dirty, would she?

Pause. YOLLAND *extends his hand to* MAIRE. *She turns away from him and moves slowly across the stage.*

YOLLAND: Maire. (*She still moves away*) Maire Chatach. (*She still moves away*) Bun na hAbhann? (*He says the name softly, almost privately, very tentatively, as if he were searching for a sound she might respond to. He tries again*) Druim Dubh? (MAIRE *stops. She is listening.* YOLLAND *is encouraged*) Poll na gCaorach. Lis Maol. (MAIRE *turns towards him*) Lis na nGall.

MAIRE: Lis na nGradh.

They are now facing each other and begin moving — almost imperceptibly — towards one another.

MAIRE: Carraig an Phoill.

YOLLAND: Carraig na Ri. Loch na nEan.

MAIRE: Loch an Iubhair. Machaire Buidhe.

YOLLAND: Machaire Mor. Cnoc na Mona.

MAIRE: Cnoc na nGabhar.

YOLLAND: Mullach.

MAIRE: Port.

YOLLAND: Tor.

MAIRE: Lag. (*She holds out her hands to* YOLLAND. *He takes them. Each now speaks almost to himself/herself*)

YOLLAND: I wish to God you could understand me.

MAIRE: Soft hands; a gentleman's hands.

YOLLAND: Because if you could understand me I could tell you how I spend my days either thinking of you or gazing up at your house in the hope that you'll appear even for a second.

MAIRE: Every evening you walk by yourself along the Tra Bhan and every morning you wash yourself in front of your tent.

YOLLAND: I would tell you how beautiful you are, curly-headed Maire. I would so like to tell you how beautiful you are.

MAIRE: Your arms are long and thin and the skin on your shoulders is very white.

YOLLAND: I would tell you ...

MAIRE: Don't stop — I know what you're saying.

YOLLAND: I would tell you how I want to be here

— to live here — always — with you — always, always.

MAIRE: 'Always'? What is that word — 'always'?

YOLLAND: Yes-yes; always.

MAIRE: You're trembling.

YOLLAND: Yes, I'm trembling because of you.

MAIRE: I'm trembling, too. (*She holds his face in her hand*)

YOLLAND: I've made up my mind . . .

MAIRE: Shhhh.

YOLLAND: I'm not going to leave here . . .

MAIRE: Shhh — listen to me. I want you, too, soldier.

YOLLAND: Don't stop — I know what you're saying.

MAIRE: I want to live with you — anywhere — anywhere at all — always — always.

YOLLAND: 'Always'? What is that word — 'always'?

MAIRE: Take me away with you, George.

Pause. Suddenly they kiss. SARAH *enters. She sees them. She stands shocked, staring at them. Her mouth works. Then almost to herself.*

SARAH: Manus . . . Manus!

SARAH *runs off. Music to crescendo.*

ACT THREE

The following evening. It is raining.

SARAH *and* OWEN *alone in the schoolroom.* SARAH, *more waiflike than ever, is sitting very still on a stool, an open book across her knee. She is pretending to read but her eyes keep going up to the room upstairs.* OWEN *is working on the floor as before, surrounded by his reference books, map, Name-Book etc. But he has neither concentration nor interest; and like* SARAH *he glances up at the upstairs room.*

After a few seconds MANUS *emerges and descends, carrying a large paper bag which already contains his clothes. His movements are determined and urgent. He moves around the classroom, picking up books, examining each title carefully, and choosing about six of them which he puts into his bag. As he selects these books:*

OWEN: You know that old limekiln beyond Con Connie Tim's pub, the place we call The Murren? — do you know why it's called The Murren? (MANUS *does not answer*) I've only just discovered: it's a corruption of Saint Muranus. It seems Saint Muranus had a monastery somewhere about there at the beginning of the seventh century. And over the years the name became shortened to the Murren. Very unattractive name, isn't it? I think we should go back to the original — Saint Muranus. What do you think? The original's Saint Muranus. Don't you think we should go back to that?

No response. OWEN *begins writing the name into the Name-Book.* MANUS *is now rooting about among the forgotten implements for a piece of rope. He finds a piece. He begins to tie the mouth of the flimsy, overloaded bag — and it bursts, the contents spilling out on the floor.*

MANUS: Bloody, bloody, bloody hell!

His voice breaks in exasperation: he is about to cry. OWEN *leaps to his feet.*

OWEN: Hold on. I've a bag upstairs.

He runs upstairs. SARAH *waits until* OWEN *is off. Then*:

SARAH: Manus . . . Manus, I . . .

MANUS *hears* SARAH *but makes no acknowledgement. He gathers up his belongings.* OWEN *reappears with the bag he had on his arrival.*

OWEN: Take this one — I'm finished with it anyway. And it's supposed to keep out the rain.

MANUS *transfers his few belongings.* OWEN *drifts back to his task. The packing is now complete.*

MANUS: You'll be here for a while? For a week or two anyhow?

OWEN: Yes.

MANUS: You're not leaving with the army?

OWEN: I haven't made up my mind. Why?

MANUS: Those Inis Meadhon men will be back to see why I haven't turned up. Tell them — tell them I'll write to them as soon as I can. Tell them I still want the job but that it might be three or four months before I'm free to go.

OWEN: You're being damned stupid, Manus.

MANUS: Will you do that for me?

OWEN: Clear out now and Lancey'll think you're involved somehow.

MANUS: Will you do that for me?

OWEN: Wait a couple of days even. You know George — he's a bloody romantic — maybe he's gone out to one of the islands and he'll suddenly reappear tomorrow morning. Or maybe the search party'll find him this evening lying drunk somewhere in the sandhills. You've seen him drinking that poteen — doesn't know how to handle it. Had he drink on him last night at the dance?

MANUS: I had a stone in my hand when I went

out looking for him — I was going to fell him. The lame scholar turned violent.

OWEN: Did anybody see you?

MANUS: (*Again close to tears*) But when I saw him standing there at the side of the road — smiling — and her face buried in his shoulder — I couldn't even go close to them. I just shouted something stupid — something like, 'You're a bastard, Yolland.' If I'd even said it in English ... 'cos he kept saying 'Sorry-sorry?' The wrong gesture in the wrong language.

OWEN: And you didn't see him again?

MANUS: 'Sorry?'

OWEN: Before you leave tell Lancey that — just to clear yourself.

MANUS: What have I to say to Lancey? You'll give that message to the islandmen?

OWEN: I'm warning you: run away now and you're bound to be ...

MANUS: (*To* SARAH) Will you give that message to the Inis Meadhon men?

SARAH: I will.

MANUS *picks up an old sack and throws it across his shoulders.*

OWEN: Have you any idea where you're going?

MANUS: Mayo, maybe. I remember Mother saying she had cousins somewhere away out in the Erris Peninsula. (*He picks up his bag*) Tell father I took only the Virgil and the Caesar and the Aeschylus because they're mine anyway — I bought them with the money I got for that pet lamb I reared — do you remember that pet lamb? And tell him that Nora Dan never returned the dictionary and that she still owes him two-and-six for last quarter's reading — he always forgets those things.

OWEN: Yes.

MANUS: And his good shirt's ironed and hanging up in the press and his clean socks are in the butter-box under the bed.

OWEN: Alright.

MANUS: And tell him I'll write.

OWEN: If Maire asks where you've gone ...?

MANUS: He'll need only half the amount of milk now, won't he? Even less than half — he usually takes his tea black. (*Pause*) And when he comes in at night — you'll hear him; he makes a lot of noise — I usually come down and give him a hand up. Those stairs are dangerous without a banister. Maybe before you leave you'd get Big Ned Frank to put up some sort of a handrail. (*Pause*) And if you can bake, he's very fond of soda bread.

OWEN: I can give you money. I'm wealthy. Do you know what they pay me? Two shillings a day for this — this — this — (MANUS *rejects the offer by holding out his hand*) Goodbye, Manus.

MANUS *and* OWEN *shake hands. Then* MANUS *picks up his bag briskly and goes towards the door. He stops a few paces beyond* SARAH, *turns, comes back to her. He addresses her as he did in Act One but now without warmth or concern for her.*

MANUS: What is your name? (*Pause*) Come on. What is your name?

SARAH: My name is Sarah.

MANUS: Just Sarah? Sarah what? (*Pause*) Well?

SARAH: Sarah Johnny Sally.

MANUS: And where do you live? Come on.

SARAH: I live in Bun na hAbhann. (*She is now crying quietly*)

MANUS: Very good, Sarah Johnny Sally. There's nothing to stop you now — nothing in the wide world. (*Pause. He looks down at her*) It's alright — it's alright — you did no harm — you did no harm at all. (*He stoops over her and kisses the top of her head — as if in absolution. Then briskly to the door and off*)

OWEN: Good luck, Manus!

SARAH: (*Quietly*) I'm sorry ... I'm sorry ... I'm so sorry, Manus ...

OWEN *tries to work but cannot concentrate. He begins folding up the map. As he does.*

OWEN: Is there class this evening? (SARAH *nods: yes*) I suppose Father knows. Where is he anyhow? (SARAH *points*) Where? (SARAH *mimes rocking a baby*) I don't understand — where? (SARAH *repeats the mime and wipes away tears.* OWEN *is still puzzled*) It doesn't matter. He'll probably turn up.

BRIDGET *and* DOALTY *enter, sacks over their heads against the rain. They are self-consciously noisier, more ebullient, more garrulous than ever — brimming over with excitement and gossip and brio.*

DOALTY: You're missing the crack,[1] boys! Cripes, you're missing the crack! Fifty more soldiers arrived an hour ago!

BRIDGET: And they're spread out in a big line from Sean Neal's over to Lag and they're moving straight across the fields towards Cnoc na nGabhar!

DOALTY: Prodding every inch of the ground in front of them with their bayonets and scattering animals and hens in all directions!

BRIDGET: And tumbling everything before them

1. A singularly Irish word for convivial talk, 'a good time'.

— fences, ditches, haystacks, turf-stacks!

DOALTY: They came to Barney Petey's field of corn — straight through it be God as if it was heather!

BRIDGET: Not a blade of it left standing!

DOALTY: And Barney Petey just out of his bed and running after them in his drawers: 'You hoors[2] you! Get out of my corn, you hoors you!'

BRIDGET: First time he ever ran in his life.

DOALTY: Too lazy, the wee get,[3] to cut it when the weather was good.

SARAH *begins putting out the seats.*

BRIDGET: Tell them about Big Hughie.

DOALTY: Cripes, if you'd seen your aul fella, Owen.

BRIDGET: They were all inside in Anna na mBreag's pub — all the crowd from the wake —

DOALTY: And they hear the commotion and they all come out to the street —

BRIDGET: Your father in front; the Infant Prodigy footless behind him!

DOALTY: And your aul fella, he sees the army stretched across the countryside —

BRIDGET: O my God!

DOALTY: And Cripes he starts roaring at them!

BRIDGET: 'Visigoths! Huns! Vandals!'

DOALTY: '*Ignari! Stulti! Rustici!*'

BRIDGET: And wee Jimmy Jack jumping up and down and shouting, 'Thermopylae! Thermopylae!'

DOALTY: You never saw crack like it in your life, boys. Come away on out with me, Sarah, and you'll see it all.

BRIDGET: Big Hughie's fit to take no class. Is Manus about?

OWEN: Manus is gone.

BRIDGET: Gone where?

OWEN: He's left — gone away.

DOALTY: Where to?

OWEN: He doesn't know. Mayo, maybe.

DOALTY: What's on in Mayo?

OWEN: (*To* BRIDGET) Did you see George and Maire Chatach leave the dance last night?

BRIDGET: We did. Didn't we, Doalty?

OWEN: Did you see Manus following them out?

BRIDGET: I didn't see him going out but I saw him coming in by himself later.

OWEN: Did George and Maire come back to the dance?

BRIDGET: No.

OWEN: Did you see them again?

BRIDGET: He left her home. We passed them going up the back road — didn't we, Doalty?

OWEN: And Manus stayed till the end of the dance?

DOALTY: We know nothing. What are you asking us for?

OWEN: Because Lancey'll question me when he hears Manus's gone. (*Back to* BRIDGET) That's the way George went home? By the back road? That's where you saw him?

BRIDGET: Leave me alone, Owen. I know nothing about Yolland. If you want to know about Yolland, ask the Donnelly twins. (*Silence.* DOALTY *moves over to the window*) (*To* SARAH) He's a powerful fiddler, O'Shea, isn't he? He told our Seamus he'll come back for a night at Hallowe'en.

OWEN *goes to* DOALTY *who looks resolutely out the window.*

OWEN: What's this about the Donnellys? (*Pause*) Were they about last night?

DOALTY: Didn't see them if they were. (*Begins whistling through his teeth*)

OWEN: George is a friend of mine.

DOALTY: So.

OWEN: I want to know what's happened to him.

DOALTY: Couldn't tell you.

OWEN: What have the Donnelly twins to do with it? (*Pause*) Doalty!

DOALTY: I know nothing, Owen — nothing at all — I swear to God. All I know is this: on my way to the dance I saw their boat beached at Port. It wasn't there on my way home, after I left Bridget. And that's all I know. As God's my judge. The half-dozen times I met him I didn't know a word he said to me; but he seemed a right enough sort ... (*With sudden excessive interest in the scene outside*) Cripes, they're crawling all over the place! Cripes, there's millions of them! Cripes, they're levelling the whole land!

OWEN *moves away.* MAIRE *enters. She is bareheaded and wet from the rain; her hair in disarray. She attempts to appear normal but she is in acute distress, on the verge of being distraught. She is carrying the milk-can.*

MAIRE: Honest to God, I must be going off my head. I'm half-way here and I think to myself, 'Isn't this can very light?' and I look into it and isn't it empty.

2. Irish pronunciation of 'whores'.
3. Sometimes 'git': a contemptible person.

OWEN: It doesn't matter.

MAIRE: How will you manage for tonight?

OWEN: We have enough.

MAIRE: Are you sure?

OWEN: Plenty, thanks.

MAIRE: It'll take me no time at all to go back up for some.

OWEN: Honestly, Maire.

MAIRE: Sure it's better you have it than that black calf that's ... that ... (*She looks around*) Have you heard anything?

OWEN: Nothing.

MAIRE: What does Lancey say?

OWEN: I haven't seen him since this morning.

MAIRE: What does he *think*?

OWEN: We really didn't talk. He was here for only a few seconds.

MAIRE: He left me home, Owen. And the last thing he said to me — he tried to speak in Irish — he said, 'I'll see you yesterday' — he meant to say 'I'll see you tomorrow.' And I laughed that much he pretended to get cross and he said 'Maypoll! Maypoll!' because I said that word wrong. And off he went, laughing — laughing, Owen! Do you think he's alright? What do *you* think?

OWEN: I'm sure he'll turn up, Maire.

MAIRE: He comes from a tiny wee place called Winfarthing. (*She suddenly drops on her hands and knees on the floor — where* OWEN *had his map a few minutes ago — and with her finger traces out an outline map*) Come here till you see. Look. There's Winfarthing. And there's two other wee villages right beside it; one of them's called Barton Bendish — it's there; and the other's called Saxingham Nethergate — it's about there. And there's Little Walsingham — that's his mother's townland. Aren't they odd names? Sure they make no sense to me at all. And Winfarthing's near a big town called Norwich. And Norwich is in a county called Norfolk. And Norfolk is in the east of England. He drew a map for me on the wet strand and wrote the names on it. I have it all in my head now: Winfarthing — Barton Bendish — Saxingham Nethergate — Little Walsingham — Norwich — Norfolk. Strange sounds, aren't they? But nice sounds; like Jimmy Jack reciting his Homer. (*She gets to her feet and looks around; she is almost serene now. To* SARAH) You were looking lovely last night, Sarah. Is that the dress you got from Boston? Green suits you. (*To* OWEN) Something very bad's happened to him, Owen. I know. He wouldn't go away without telling me. Where is he, Owen? You're his friend — where is he? (*Again she looks around the room; then sits on a stool*) I didn't get a chance to do my geography last night. The master'll be angry with me. (*She rises again*) I think I'll go home now. The wee ones have to be washed and put to bed and that black calf has to be fed ... My hands are that rough; they're still blistered from the hay. I'm ashamed of them. I hope to God there's no hay to be saved in Brooklyn. (*She stops at the door*) Did you hear? Nellie Ruadh's baby died in the middle of the night. I must go up to the wake. It didn't last long, did it? (MAIRE *leaves*)

Silence. Then:

OWEN: I don't think there'll be any class. Maybe you should ...

OWEN *begins picking up his texts.* DOALTY *goes to him.*

DOALTY: Is he long gone? — Manus.

OWEN: Half an hour.

DOALTY: Stupid bloody fool.

OWEN: I told him that.

DOALTY: Do they know he's gone?

OWEN: Who?

DOALTY: The army.

OWEN: Not yet.

DOALTY: They'll be after him like bloody beagles. Bloody, bloody fool, limping along the coast. They'll overtake him before night for Christ's sake.

DOALTY *returns to the window.* LANCEY *enters — now the commanding officer.*

OWEN: Any news? Any word?

LANCEY *moves into the centre of the room, looking around as he does.*

LANCEY: I understood there was a class. Where are the others?

OWEN: There was to be a class but my father ...

LANCEY: This will suffice. I will address them and it will be their responsibility to pass on what I have to say to every family in this section. (LANCEY *indicates to* OWEN *to translate.* OWEN *hesitates, trying to assess the change in* LANCEY*'s manner and attitude*) I'm in a hurry, O'Donnell.

OWEN: The captain has an announcement to make.

LANCEY: Lieutenant Yolland is missing. We are searching for him. If we don't find him, or if we receive no information as to where he is to be found, I will pursue the following course of action. (*He indicates to* OWEN *to translate*)

OWEN: They are searching for George. If they don't find him —

LANCEY: Commencing twenty-four hours from now we will shoot all livestock in Ballybeg. (OWEN *stares at* LANCEY) At once.

OWEN: Beginning this time tomorrow they'll kill every animal in Baile Beag — unless they're told where George is.

LANCEY: If that doesn't bear results, commencing forty-eight hours from now we will embark on a series of evictions and levelling of every abode in the following selected areas —

OWEN: You're not —!

LANCEY: Do your job. Translate.

OWEN: If they still haven't found him in two days' time they'll begin evicting and levelling every house starting with these townlands.

LANCEY *reads from his list.*

LANCEY: Swinefort.

OWEN: Lis na Muc.

LANCEY: Burnfoot.

OWEN: Bun na hAbhann.

LANCEY: Dromduff.

OWEN: Druim Dubh.

LANCEY: Whiteplains.

OWEN: Machaire Ban.

LANCEY: Kings Head.

OWEN: Cnoc na Ri.

LANCEY: If by then the lieutenant hasn't be found, we will proceed until a complete clearance is made of this entire section.

OWEN: If Yolland hasn't been got by then, they will ravish the whole parish.

LANCEY: I trust they know exactly what they've got to do. (*Pointing to* BRIDGET) I know you. I know where you live. (*Pointing to* SARAH) Who are you? Name! (SARAH's *mouth opens and shuts, opens and shuts. Her face becomes contorted*) What's your name?

Again SARAH *tries frantically.*

OWEN: Go on, Sarah. You can tell him.

But SARAH *cannot. And she knows she cannot. She closes her mouth. Her head goes down.*

OWEN: Her name is Sarah Johnny Sally.

LANCEY: Where does she live?

OWEN: Bun na hAbhann.

LANCEY: Where?

OWEN: Burnfoot.

LANCEY: I want to talk to your brother — is he here?

OWEN: Not at the moment.

LANCEY: Where is he?

OWEN: He's at a wake.

LANCEY: What wake?

DOALTY, *who has been looking out the window all through* LANCEY's *announcements, now speaks — calmly, almost casually.*

DOALTY: Tell him his whole camp's on fire.

LANCEY: What's your name? (*To* OWEN) Who's that lout?

OWEN: Doalty Dan Doalty.

LANCEY: Where does he live?

OWEN: Tulach Alainn.

LANCEY: What do we call it?

OWEN: Fair Hill. He says your whole camp is on fire.

LANCEY *rushes to the window and looks out. Then he wheels on* DOALTY.

LANCEY: I'll remember you, Mr Doalty. (*To* OWEN) You carry a big responsibility in all this. (*He goes off*)

BRIDGET: Mother of God, does he mean it, Owen?

OWEN: Yes, he does.

BRIDGET: We'll have to hide the beasts somewhere — our Seamus'll know where. Maybe at the back of Lis na nGradh — or in the caves at the far end of the Tra Bhan. Come on, Doalty! Come on! Don't be standing about there! (DOALTY *does not move.* BRIDGET *runs to the door and stops suddenly. She sniffs the air. Panic*) The sweet smell! Smell it! It's the sweet smell! Jesus, it's the potato blight!

DOALTY: It's the army tents burning, Bridget.

BRIDGET: Is it? Are you sure? Is that what it is? God, I thought we were destroyed altogether. Come on! Come on! (*She runs off*)

OWEN *goes to* SARAH *who is preparing to leave.*

OWEN: How are you? Are you alright?

SARAH *nods: Yes.*

OWEN: Don't worry. It will come back to you again.

SARAH *shakes her head.*

OWEN: It will. You're upset now. He frightened you. That's all wrong.

Again SARAH *shakes her head, slowly, emphatically, and smiles at* OWEN. *Then she leaves.* OWEN *busies himself gathering his belongings.* DOALTY *leaves the window and goes to him.*

DOALTY: He'll do it, too.

OWEN: Unless Yolland's found.

DOALTY: Hah!

OWEN: Then he'll certainly do it.

DOALTY: When my grandfather was a boy they did the same thing. (*Simply, altogether without irony*) And after all the trouble you went to, mapping the place and thinking up new names for it. (OWEN *busies himself. Pause.* DOALTY *almost dreamily*) I've damned little to defend but he'll not put me out without a fight. And there'll be others who think the same as me.

OWEN: That's a matter for you.

DOALTY: If we'd all stick together. If we knew how to defend ourselves.

OWEN: Against a trained army.

DOALTY: The Donnelly twins know how.

OWEN: If they could be found.

DOALTY: If they could be found. (*He goes to the door*) Give me a shout after you've finished with Lancey. I might know something then. (*He leaves*)

OWEN *picks up the Name-Book. He looks at it momentarily, then puts it on top of the pile he is carrying. It falls to the floor. He stoops to pick it up — hesitates — leaves it. He goes upstairs. As* OWEN *ascends,* HUGH *and* JIMMY JACK *enter. Both wet and drunk.* JIMMY *is very unsteady. He is trotting behind* HUGH, *trying to break in on* HUGH's *declamation.* HUGH *is equally drunk but more experienced in drunkenness: there is a portion of his mind which retains its clarity.*

HUGH: There I was, appropriately dispositioned to proffer my condolences to the bereaved mother . . .

JIMMY: Hugh —

HUGH: . . . and about to enter the *domus lugubris* — Maire Chatach?

JIMMY: The wake house.

HUGH: Indeed — when I experience a plucking at my elbow: Mister George Alexander, Justice of the Peace. 'My tidings are infelicitous,' said he — Bridget? Too slow. Doalty?

JIMMY: *Infelix* — unhappy.

HUGH: Unhappy indeed. 'Master Bartley Timlin has been appointed to the new national school.' 'Timlin? Who is Timlin?' 'A schoolmaster from Cork. And he will be a major asset to the community: he is also a very skilled bacon-curer'!

JIMMY: Hugh —

HUGH: Ha-ha-ha-ha-ha! The Cork bacon-curer! *Barbarus hic ego sum quia non intelligor ulli* — James?

JIMMY: Ovid.

HUGH: *Procede.*

JIMMY: 'I am a barbarian in this place because I am not understood by anyone.'

HUGH: Indeed — (*Shouts*) Manus! Tea! I will compose a satire on Master Bartley Timlin, schoolmaster and bacon-curer. But it will be too easy, won't it? (*Shouts*) Strong tea! Black!

The only way JIMMY *can get* HUGH's *attention is by standing in front of him and holding his arms.*

JIMMY: Will you listen to me, Hugh!

HUGH: James. (*Shouts*) And a slice of soda bread.

JIMMY: I'm going to get married.

HUGH: Well!

JIMMY: At Christmas.

HUGH: Splendid.

JIMMY: To Athene.

HUGH: Who?

JIMMY: Pallas Athene.

HUGH: *Glaukopis Athene?*

JIMMY: Flashing-eyed, Hugh, flashing-eyed! (*He attempts the gesture he has made before: standing to attention, the momentary spasm, the salute, the face raised in pained ecstasy — but the body does not respond efficiently this time. The gesture is grotesque*)

HUGH: The lady has assented?

JIMMY: She asked *me* — *I* assented.

HUGH: Ah. When was this?

JIMMY: Last night.

HUGH: What does her mother say?

JIMMY: Metis from Hellespont? Decent people — good stock.

HUGH: And her father?

JIMMY: I'm meeting Zeus tomorrow. Hugh, will you be my best man?

HUGH: Honoured, James; profoundly honoured.

JIMMY: You know what I'm looking for, Hugh, don't you? I mean to say — you know — I — I — I joke like the rest of them — you know? — (*Again he attempts the pathetic routine but abandons it instantly*) You know yourself, Hugh — don't you? — you know all that. But what I'm really looking for, Hugh — what I really want — companionship, Hugh — at my time of life, companionship, company, someone to talk to. Away up in Beann na Gaoithe — you've no idea how lonely it is. Companionship — correct, Hugh? Correct?

HUGH: Correct.

JIMMY: And I always liked her, Hugh. Correct?

HUGH: Correct, James.

JIMMY: Some one to talk to.

HUGH: Indeed.

JIMMY: That's all, Hugh. The whole story. You know it all now, Hugh. You know it all.

As JIMMY *says those last lines he is crying, shaking his head, trying to keep his balance, and holding a finger up to his lips in absurd gestures of secrecy and intimacy. Now he staggers away, tries to sit on a stool, misses it, slides to the floor, his feet in front of him, his back against the broken cart. Almost at once he is asleep.* HUGH *watches all of this. Then he produces his flask and is about to pour a drink when he sees the Name-book on the floor. He picks it up and leafs through it, pronouncing the strange names as he does. Just as he begins,* OWEN *emerges and descends with two bowls of tea.*

HUGH: Ballybeg. Burnfoot. Kings Head. Whiteplains. Fair Hill. Dunboy. Green Bank.

OWEN *snatches the book from* HUGH.

OWEN: I'll take that. (*In apology*) It's only a catalogue of names.

HUGH: I know what it is.

OWEN: A mistake — my mistake — nothing to do with us. I hope that's strong enough. (*Tea*) (*He throws the book on the table and crosses over to* JIMMY) Jimmy. Wake up, Jimmy. Wake up, man.

JIMMY: What — what-what?

OWEN: Here. Drink this. Then go on away home. There may be trouble. Do you hear me, Jimmy? There may be trouble.

HUGH: (*Indicating Name-Book*) We must learn those new names.

OWEN: (*Searching around*) Did you see a sack lying about?

HUGH: We must learn where we live. We must learn to make them our own. We must make them our new home.

OWEN *finds a sack and throws it across his shoulders.*

OWEN: I know where I live.

HUGH: James thinks he knows, too. I look at James and three thoughts occur to me: A — that it is not the literal past, the 'facts' of history, that shape us, but images of the past embodied in language. James has ceased to make that discrimination.

OWEN: Don't lecture me, Father.

HUGH: B — we must never cease renewing those images; because once we do, we fossilise. Is there no soda bread?

OWEN: And C, Father, — one single, unalterable 'fact': if Yolland is not found, we are all going to be evicted. Lancey has issued the order.

HUGH: Ah. *Edictum imperatoris.*

OWEN: You should change out of those wet clothes. I've got to go. I've got to see Doalty Dan Doalty.

HUGH: What about?

OWEN: I'll be back soon.

As OWEN *exits.*

HUGH: Take care, Owen. To remember everything is a form of madness. (*He looks around the room, carefully, as if he were about to leave it forever. Then he looks at Jimmy, asleep again*) The road to Sligo. A spring morning. 1798. Going into battle. Do you remember, James? Two young gallants with pikes across their shoulders and the *Aeneid* in their pockets. Everything seemed to find definition that spring — a congruence, a miraculous matching of hope and past and present and possibility. Striding across the fresh, green land. The rhythms of perception heightened. The whole enterprise of consciousness accelerated. We were gods that morning, James; and I had recently married *my* goddess, Caitlin Dubh Nic Reactainn, may she rest in peace. And to leave her and my infant son in his cradle — that was heroic, too. By God, sir, we were magnificent. We marched as far as — where was it? — Glenties! All of twenty-three miles in one day. And it was there, in Phelan's pub, that we got homesick for Athens, just like Ulysses. The *desiderium nostrorum* — the need for our own. Our *pietas*, James, was for older, quieter things. And that was the longest twenty-three miles back I every made. (*Toasts* JIMMY) My friend, confusion is not an ignoble condition.

MAIRE *enters.*

MAIRE: I'm back again. I set out for somewhere but I couldn't remember where. So I came back here.

HUGH: Yes, I will teach you English, Maire Chatach.

MAIRE: Will you, Master? I must learn it. I need to learn it.

HUGH: Indeed you may well be my only pupil. (*He goes towards the steps and begins to ascend*)

MAIRE: When can we start?

HUGH: Not today. Tomorrow, perhaps. After the funeral. We'll begin tomorrow. (*Ascending*) But don't expect too much. I will provide you with the available words and the available grammar. But will that help you to interpret between privacies? I have no idea. But it's all we have. I have no idea at all. (*He is now at the top*)

MAIRE: Master, what does the English word 'always' mean?

HUGH: *Semper — per omnia saecula.* The Greeks called it '*aei*'. It's not a word I'd start with. It's a silly word, girl. (*He sits*)

JIMMY *is awake. He gets to his feet.* MAIRE *sees the Name-Book, picks it up, and sits with it on her knee.*

MAIRE: When he comes back, this is where he'll come to. He told me this is where he was happiest.

JIMMY *sits beside* MAIRE.

JIMMY: Do you know the Greek word *endogamein*? It means to marry within the tribe. And the word *exogamein* means to marry outside the tribe. And you don't cross those borders casually — both sides get very angry. Now, the problem is this: Is Athene sufficiently mortal or am I sufficiently godlike for the marriage to be acceptable to her people and to my people? You think about that.

HUGH: *Urbs antiqua fuit* — there was an ancient city which, 'tis said, Juno loved above all the lands. And it was the goddess's aim and cherished hope that here should be the capital of all nations — should the fates perchance allow that. Yet in truth she discovered that a race was springing from Trojan blood to overthrow some day these Tyrian towers — a people *late regem belloque superbum* — kings of broad realms and proud in war who would come forth for Lybia's downfall — such was — such was the course — such was the course ordained — ordained by fate[5] ... What the hell's wrong with me? Sure I know it backways. I'll begin again. *Urbs antiqua fuit* — there was an ancient city which, 'tis said, Juno loved above all the lands. (*Begin to bring down the lights*) And it was the goddess's aim and cherished hope that here should be the capital of all nations — should the fates perchance allow that. Yet in truth she discovered that a race was springing from Trojan blood to overthrow some day these Tyrian towers — a people kings of broad realms and proud in war who would come forth for Lybia's downfall ...

(*Black*)

5. (see p. 1229).

APPENDIX

Greek and Latin Used in the Text

page *Τὸν* δ' ἠμείβετ' ἔπειτα θεὰ γλαυκῶπις'
1208 *Α*θήνη· (Homer, *Odyssey*, XIII, 420)
Lit: 'But the grey-eyed goddess Athene then replied to him'

1208 ἀλλὰ ἕκηλος ἧσται ἐν *'Ατρείδαο* δόμοις (Homer, *Odyssey*, XIII, 423-4)
Lit: '. . .but he sits at ease in the halls of the Sons of Athens . . .'

1208 ''Ως ἄρα μιν φαμένη ῥάβδῳ ἐπεμάσσατ' *'Α*θήνη (Homer, *Odyssey*, XIII, 429)
Lit: 'As she spoke Athene touched him with her wand'

1208 κνύζωσεν δέ *οἱ ὄ*σσε (Homer, *Odyssey*, 433)
Lit: 'She dimmed his eyes'

1208 Γλαυκῶπις *'Α*θήνη:
Lit: flashing-eyed Athene
*Α*ὐτὰρ *ὁ* ἐκ λιμέν*ος* πρσσέβη
(Homer, *Odyssey*, XIV, 1)

1209 *Lit:* 'But he went forth from the harbour . . .'
ὅ οἱ βιότοιο μάλιστα (Homer, *Odyssey*, XIV, 3-4)

1209 *Lit:* '. . . he cared very much for his substance . . .'

1209 *Esne fatigata?:* Are you tired?

1210 *Sum fatigatissima:* I am very tired

1210 *Bene! Optime!:* Good! Excellent!

1210 *Ignari, stulti, rustici:* Ignoramuses, fools, peasants

1210 *Responde – responde!:* Answer – answer!

1211 θέος: a god

1211 θέα: a goddess

1211 *Nigra fere et presso pinguis sub vomere terra* Land that is black and rich beneath the pressure of the plough

1212 *cui putre:* crumbly soil

1214 *adsum:* I am present

1214 *sobrietate perfecta:* with complete sobriety

1214 *sobrius:* sober

1214 *Ave:* hail

1214 *caerimonia nominationis:* ceremony of naming
βαπτίζειν: to dip or immerse

1214 *baptisterium:* a cold bath, swimming-pool

1214 *Gratias tibi ago:* I thank you

1214 *studia:* studies

1214 *perambulare:* to walk through

1214 *verecundus:* shame-faced, modest

1214 *conjugo:* I join together

1215 *acquiesco, acquiescere:* to rest, to find comfort in

1215 *procede:* proceed

1215 *Silentium!:* Silence!

1215 *diverto, divertere:* to turn away

1215 *aplestos pithos:* unfillable cask

1215 *Jacobe, quid agis?:* James, how are you?

1217 *Festinate!:* Hurry!
1217 *Gaudeo vos hic adesse:* Welcome
1217 *Nonne Latine loquitur?:* Does he not speak Latin?
1218 *opus honestum:* an honourable task
1222 *Quantumvis cursum longum fessumque moratur Sol, sacro tandem carmine vesper adest.*
No matter how long the sun delays on his long weary course
At length evening comes with its sacred song.
1222 *expeditio:* an expedition
1227 *Tu es centurio in exercitu Britannico:* You are a centurion in the British Army
1227 *et es in castris quae sunt in agro*
And you are in the camp in the field
1230 *Ignari! Stulti! Rustici!:* Ignoramuses! Fools! Peasants!
1233 *domus lugubris:* house of mourning

α'εί: always

1233 *infelix:* unlucky, unhappy
1233 *Barbarus hic ego sum quia non intelligor ulli:* I am a barbarian here because I am not understood by anyone
1233 *procede:* proceed
1234 *edictum imperatoris:* the decree of the commander
1234 *desiderium nostrorum:* longing/need for our things/people
1234 *pietas:* piety
1235 *Semper – per omnia saecula:* Always – for all time
1235 *aei:* always
1235 ἐνδογαμεῖν: to marry within the tribe
1235 ἐξογαμεῖν: to marry outside the tribe
1235 *Urbs antiqua fuit:* There was an ancient city.
1235 *late regem belloque superbum:* kings of broad realms and proud in war

THOMAS MURPHY

(1935-)

BAILEGANGAIRE (1985)

[The title means 'Town without laughter'. Mommo is in the dying, but not yet vanished, tradition of the traditional storyteller, the *shanachie*. Her tales are digressive and contain a mixture of the actual and the extraordinary in a style that is, by turns, vernacular and florid. Murphy exploits the opportunities given by the conventions of the oral tradition to create for us a comic-heroic individual whose narrative finally enhances both her life and the lives of her two grand-daughters. The play was first performed by the Druid Theatre Company, Galway on 5 December 1985. Words in square brackets are clarifications provided in the original text by the author.]

CHARACTERS

MOMMO
MARY
DOLLY

TIME AND PLACE

1984. The kitchen of a thatched house. The set should be stylized to avoid cliché and to achieve best effect.

ACT ONE

Dusk is setting in. The room is a country kitchen in the old style. There are some modern conveniences: a bottle-gas cooker, a radio, electric light — a single pendant. Framed photographs on the walls; brown photographs of uncles, one of a christening party. There is a double bed in the kitchen — it is the warmest room in the house (probably the central room of the traditional three-roomed thatched house). An old woman in the bed, MOMMO, *is eating and drinking something out of a mug, occasionally rejecting pieces of food, spitting them on the floor. She interrupts her meal —*

MOMMO: Scoth caoc! Shkoth![1] (*Driving imagined hens from the house, out the back door which is open*) Dirty aul' things about the place . . . And for all they lay! (*She is senile.* MARY, *her grand-daughter, is seated on a box beside the fire; the top of the box — a painted timber butter box — upholstered.* MARY *looking at nothing, not even at the fire. She wears a wrap-around apron draped tightly about her spinster frame; bare knees over half wellington boots; hair tight, perhaps in a bun. She is forty-one. A 'private' person; an intelligent, sensitive woman; a trier, but one who is possibly near breaking point. It is lovely when she laughs. She does not react to the above.* MOMMO *has again interrupted her meal to talk to imagined children at the foot of the bed*) Let ye be settling now, my fondlings, and I'll be giving ye a nice story tonight when I finish this. For isn't it a good one? An' ye'll be goin' to sleep. (*The tips of* MARY'S *fingers to her forehead and she closes her eyes*) . . . Oh ho, but he bet [*beat*] them. He bet the best of them . . . Incestuous drunkards and bastards. (*The kettle on the gas stove is whistling.* MARY *rises mechanically to make tea, lay the table. She produces the anomaly of a silver teapot . . .* MOMMO *now watching* MARY *and* MARY'S *movements suspiciously*) . . . An' no-one will stop me! Tellin' my nice story . . . (*reverts to herself*) Yis, how the place called Bochtán[2] — and its *graund* [*grand*] inhabitants — came by its new appellation, Bailegangaire, the place without laughter. Now! . . . Jolter-headed gobshites[3] . . . (*Grandly*) Ooh! and to be sure, and I often heard it said, it had one time its portion of jollification and mirth. But, I'm thinkin', the breed they wor [*were*] 'twas venom, and the dent of it, was ever the more customary manifestation. The land there so poor — Och hona ho gus hah-haa,[4] land! — when 'twasn't bog 'twas stone, and as for the weather? 'twas credited with bein' seven times worse than elsewhere in the kingdom. And so hard they had it, to keep life itself in them, whenever Bochtán was mentioned the old people in their wisdom would add in precaution, go bhfóire Dia orainn, may God protect us.[5] What time is it?

MARY: Seven. (MARY *is now taking off her apron*)

MOMMO: Yis! — Shkoth! — an' lock them in. Och haw, but I'll out-do the fox. I'll take the head of the every one of them tomorrow. Ooh! and to be sure —

MARY: (*Quietly*) Mommo?

MOMMO: And I often heard it said —

MARY: Mommo? (*She has removed her apron and in her new image is smiling bravely against an increasing sense of loneliness and demoralisation*) I have a surprise for you.

MOMMO: Pardon?

MARY: (*Switches on the light*) Look! (*She holds up an iced cake*) We never knew your birthday but today is mine and I thought we might share the same birthday together in future.

MOMMO: (*Eyes now fixed on the pendant light bulb*) The cursèd paraffin.

MARY: Though someone said once — I may be wrong — yours was the first of May, a May child — But look! —

MOMMO: The cursèd paraffin.

MARY: And the candles. And another [*candle*] here, and you can get out of bed for a little — if you want.

MOMMO: Birthday?

MARY: Yes! We'll have a party, the two of us.

MOMMO: What's birthdays to do with us?

MARY: By candlelight. (*She lights the candle on the table*)

MOMMO: What's your business here?

MARY: (*Indicating the table*) Isn't that nice?

MOMMO: Do I know you?

MARY: Mary. (*She bows her head, momentarily deflated, then smiles invitingly at* MOMMO *again*)

MOMMO: (*And there is defiance, hatred in the sound*) Heh heh heh heh.

MARY: Mary. (*And she switches off the lights*)

MARY *picks up a book en route, switches on the radio and sits at the table to have her tea. We get the end of the news in Irish on the radio, then Tommy O'Brien's programme of light classics,* Your Choice and Mine. *The candlelight, the table neatly laid, the silver teapot, the simple line of* MARY'S *dress becomes her, the book beside her, sipping tea, the grave intelligent face, a picture of strange elegance.* MOMMO *has been continuing.*

MOMMO: Ooh! and to be sure and so as not to be putting any over-enlargement on my narrative, the creatures left in it now can still *smile*, on occasion. And to be sure, the childre, as is the wont of all childre in God's kingdom on earth, are as clever at

1. 'Get out, you blind (stupid) lot' (probably from the Irish, *scáic*, to depart, go).
2. The place-name means 'pauper', 'miser'; by extension, 'a poor place'.
3. Jolter-headed = blockheaded. A 'gobshite' is a common Irish term for a worthless fool.
4. Mommo's variation on *ochón ó agus ochó ó'* — 'woe and more woe'.
5. The English translates the preceding Irish phrase.

the laughing as they are at the crying, until they arrive at the age of reason. That is well, my dears. Now to tell my story. Here! You! Miss! Take this. Did you manage to poison me? Ha-haa — No — ho-ho.

MARY: (*Takes a cup of tea to* MOMMO *and places it on the chair beside the bed, takes the mug*) And I'll get you a nice slice of cake to go with the tea.

MOMMO: Pardon?

MARY: And isn't that nice music?

MOMMO: Cake?

MARY: Every Sunday night.

MOMMO: Music?

MARY: Yes. Listen.

MOMMO: . . . An' no-one will stop me tellin' it! MARY, *suspended in the action of about to cut the cake, now sits at the table, lights a cigarette, face impassive, exhaling smoke*.

MOMMO: (*Settles herself in the bed for her story*) Now . . . It was a bad year for the crops, a good one for mushrooms, and the contrary and adverse connection between these two is always the case. So you can be sure the people were putting their store in the poultry and the bonavs[6] [*bonhams*] and the creamery produce for the great maragadh mór [*big market*] that is held every year on the last Saturday before Christmas in Bailethuama[7] in the other county. And some sold well and some sold middlin', and one couple was in it[8] — strangers, ye understand — sold not at all. And as day's business concluded there was celebration, for some, and fitting felicitations exchanged, though not of the usual protraction, for all had an eye on the cold inclement weather that boded. So, the people were departing Bailethuama in the other county in diverse directions homewards. As were the people of the place I'm talking about. And they were only middlin' satisfied, if at all. The Bochtáns were never entirely fortunate. An' devil mend them.[9] An' scald them. No matter. What time is it? . . . Miss!

MARY: Seven. Eight. (*The tips of her fingers to her forehead*)

MOMMO: I'm waiting for someone. Supa[10] tea.

MARY: It's on the chair beside you.

MOMMO: Oh an' he *will* come yet. (*A warning to* MARY) And he has a big stick.

MARY: (*Remains seated: she knows from experience what the outcome of the conversation is going to be; she does not lift her eyes*) And time to take your pills.

MOMMO: (*Has no intention of taking them*) The yellow ones?

MARY: Yes.

MOMMO: They're good for me?

MARY: I'll give you a cigarette.

MOMMO: They'll help me sleep?

MARY: Yes.

MOMMO: Heh heh heh heh.

MARY: (*To herself*) And I'd like to read, Mommo.

MOMMO: Now there was a decent man at that market and his decent wife the same. Strangers, strangers! Sure they could have come from the south of — Galway! — for all I know. And they had sold not at all. Well, if you call the one basket of pullets' eggs valiant trade. (*She takes a sip of the tea*) Too hot. No. Their main cargo which consisted of eighteen snow-white geese still lay trussed in the floor of the cart, 'gus bhár ar an mí-ádh sin [*and to make matters worse*] the pitch on an incline of the road was proving an impossibility for the horse to surmount. But he was a decent man, and he took not belt — nor the buckle-end of it as another would — to the noble animal that is the horse. Put it down. (*The last to* MARY *who is standing by having put a little more milk into* MOMMO*'s tea*) No. But spoke only in the gentlest of terms, encouraging the poor beast to try once more against the adversary. 'Try again, Pedlar.' For that was the horse's name. Is that a step?

MARY: (*Listening*) . . . Dolly was to call last night. (*The sound they have heard — if any — does not materialise further*) Nobody. She didn't call the night before either.

MOMMO: What's this? (MARY *does not understand*) Taking down the good cup!

MARY: It tastes nicer out of a —

MOMMO: Mug, a mug! — oh leave it so now! — Put it down!

MARY: And nicer to have your pills with.

MOMMO: The yellow ones? — Try again, Pedlar, for-that-was-the-horse's name! (MARY *returns to the table*) And all the while his decent wife on the grass verge and she cráite [*crestfallen*]. And a detail which you may contemplate fondly now but was only further testimonial to the misfortunes of that

6. From Irish *banbh*, a suckling pig.
7. The Irish name means 'Tuomey's town'. It could mean 'Tombstown'.
8. From the Irish expression, *Bhí mé ann*, 'I was there', literally, 'I was in it'; here, 'There was a couple there'.
9. And may they stay that way.
10. Sup of.

unhappy couple, each time she went to draw the shawl more tightly round her frailty[11], the hand peepin' out held three sticks of rock.[12] Now! Yis, gifts for her care, three small waiting grandchildren. Like ye. Isn't it a good one? (*A sip of tea*) Cold.

MARY: (*To herself*) I can't stand it. (*But she is up again in a moment to add a little hot water and a little more sugar to the tea*)

MOMMO: And she up to the fifty mark!

MARY: (*To herself*) And that bitch Dolly.

MOMMO: Or was she maybe more?

MARY: In heat again.

MOMMO: And what was her husband? Decorous efficiency in all he cared to turn his hand to, like all small men. Sure he had topped the sixty!

MARY: Taste that and see if it's alright for you.

MOMMO: But he was unlucky. He was. He was. An' times, maybe, she was unkind to him. (*Childlike*) Was she?

MARY: No. (*Returning to the table where she sits, her head back on her shoulders looking up at the ceiling*)

MOMMO: And how many children had she bore herself?

MARY: Eight?

MOMMO: And what happened to them?

MARY: Nine? Ten?

MOMMO: Hah?

MARY: What happened us all?

MOMMO: Them [*that*] weren't drowned or died they said she drove away.

MARY: Mommo?

MOMMO: Let them say what they like.

MARY: I'm very happy here.

MOMMO: Hmmph!

MARY: I'm Mary.

MOMMO: Oh but she looked after her grandchildren.

MARY: Mommo?

MOMMO: And Tom is in Galway. He's afeared of the gander.

MARY: But I'm so . . . (*She leaves it unfinished, she can't find the word*)

MOMMO: To continue.

MARY: Please stop. (*She rises slowly*)

MOMMO: Now man and horse, though God knows they tried, could see the icy hill was not for yielding.

MARY: Because I'm so lonely. (*She puts on her apron mechanically, then sets to work. Progressively working harder: scrubbing that part of the floor* MOMMO *has spat upon, clearing away and washing up the crockery, washing clothes that have been soaking in a bucket . . . . Later in the play, working, working: sheets to be put soaking in a bucket overnight, a bucket of mash for the hens in the morning, bringing in the turf . . . .*)

MOMMO: So what was there for doing but to retrace the hard-won steps to the butt-end of the road which, as matters would have it, was a fork. One road leading up the incline whence they came, the other to Bochtán.

Now that man knew that the road to Bochtán, though of circularity, was another means home. And it looked level enough stretching out into the gathering duskness. And 'deed he knew men from his own village [*who*] had travelled it and got home safe and sound. Still he paused. Oh not through fear, for if he was a man to submit he would've threwn himself into the river years ago. No. But in gentleness, sad the searching eye on the road. And sadder still the same grey eyes were growing in handsomeness as the years went by. She had noted it. But she'd never comment on this becoming aspect of his mien for, strange, it saddened her too. It did. But the two little smiles appearing, one each side of his mouth, before taking a step anywhere. Even when only to go to the back door last thing at night an' call in the old dog to the hearth.

Mary hears the 'putt-putt' of a motorcycle approaching, stopping outside. She pauses in her work for a moment. Then:.

MARY: Right! (*Suggesting she is going to have matters out with* DOLLY)

DOLLY *comes in. Like her name, dolled-up, gaudy rural fashion. She is perhaps carrying a crash-helmet. She is thirty-nine.* MOMMO *is paused in her own thoughts and does not notice* DOLLY'S *entrance;* MARY *does not acknowledge it, she has resumed working.* DOLLY *remains with her back to the front door for some time.*

MOMMO: . . . Last thing at night . . . An' then the silence, save the tick of the clock . . . An' why didn't she break it? She knew how to use the weapon of silence, and why didn't he? A woman isn't stick or stone. The gap in the bed, concern for the morrow, how to keep the one foot in front of the other. An' when would it all stop . . . What was the dog's name? (*Childlike*) D'ye know I can't remember.

11. frail form.
12. candy sticks.

DOLLY: Mo Dhuine [*The One*].

MOMMO: Shep, was it?

DOLLY: Mo Dhuine.

MOMMO: Shep? Spot? Rover? ... Mo Dhuine! Mo Dhuine! Now! Mo Dhuine.

DOLLY: Jesus.

MOMMO: He loved Mo Dhuine — Och hona ho gus hah-haa! — An' the bother an' the care on him one time filling the eggshell with the hot ember an' leavin' it there by the door.

DOLLY: Then the root[13] in the arse.

MOMMO: Then the root in the arse to poor Mo Dhuine, the twig 'cross his back, to get along with him an' the mouth burned in him! Oh but it did, *did*, cure him of thievin' the eggs.

DOLLY *switches on the light.* MOMMO's *eyes to the light bulb.*

DOLLY: What're ye doin' workin' in the dark?

MOMMO: But they had to get home.

DOLLY: Oh, she can't have everything her own way.

MOMMO: Their inheritance, the three small waiting children, left unattended.

DOLLY: (*Rooting in her bag, producing a bottle of vodka*) How yeh.

MARY *merely nods, continues working.*

MOMMO: And night fast closing around them.

DOLLY: Stronger she's gettin'. A present.

MARY: (*Hopeful that the vodka is for her birthday*) For what?

DOLLY: Cause I couldn't come up last night.

MARY: What do I! [*want with a bottle of vodka*]

DOLLY: Yeh never know. She'll last forever.

MOMMO: Then, drawing a deep breath. (*She draws a deep breath*) Oh but didn't give vent to it, for like the man he was I'm sayin', refusing to *sigh*, or submit. An', 'On we go, Pedlar' says he, an' man, horse, cart, and the woman falling in between the two hind shafts set off on the road to Bochtán, which place did not come by its present appellation, Bailegangaire, till that very night. Now.

DOLLY: Jesus, Bailegangaire — D'yeh want a fag? — night after night, can't you stop her. A fag?

MARY: (*Declines the cigarette*) No.

DOLLY: Night after night the same old story — (*Proffering cigarettes again*) Ary[14] you might as well. (MARY *ignores her*) By Jesus I'd stop her.

MARY: I wish you'd stop using that word, Dolly. I've been trying to stop her.

DOLLY: Michaeleen is sick. The tonsils again. So I couldn't come up last night. I'm worried about them tonsils. What d'yeh think? So I can't stay long tonight either.

MARY *sighs.*

MOMMO: But to come to Bailegangaire so ye'll have it all.

MARY: Aren't you going to say hello to her?

DOLLY: What's up with yeh?

MARY: Nothing.

MOMMO: Them from that place had been to the market were 'riving back home.

DOLLY: *Home*, I'm goin'.

MOMMO: One of them, Séamus Costello by name.

MARY: Aren't you going to take off your coat?

DOLLY: What do you mean?

MOMMO: Oh a fine strappin' man.

MARY: What do you mean what do I mean!

DOLLY *turns stubbornly into the fire.*

MOMMO: Wherever he got it from. The size an' the breadth of him, you'd near have to step into the verge to give him sufficient right-of-way. 'Twould be no use him extending the civility 'cause you'd hardly get around him I'm saying. And he was liked. Rabbits he was interested in. This to his widowed mother's dismay, but that's another thing. And the kind of man that when people'd espy him approaching the gurgle'd be already startin' in their mouths — Och-haw. For he was the exception, ye understand, with humour in him as big as himself. And I'm thinkin' he was the one an' only boast they ever had in that cursèd place. What time is it?

MARY: } Eight.
DOLLY: } Nine.

They look at each other and bygones are bygones.

MARY: Quarter past eight.

MOMMO: Quarter past eight, an' sure that's not late. That's a rhyme. Now for ye! (*She takes a sip of tea*) Too sweet.

MARY *rectifying the tea situation. A cajoling tone coming into* DOLLY's *voice — there is something on her mind, and she is watching and assessing* MARY *privately.*

DOLLY: They say it's easier to do it for someone else's [*to take care of a stranger*]. (*Declining tea which* MARY *offers*) No thanks. And that old story is only upsetting her, Mary. Isn't it? (MARY *is too intelligent to be taken in by* DOLLY's *tone or tactics — but this is not at issue here: she has other things on her mind. She*

13. hard kick.
14. A verbal shrug of the shoulders — 'Ah, well'.

sits by the fire with DOLLY *and now accepts the cigarette.* MOMMO *is sipping tea)* Harping on misery. And only wearing herself out. And you. Amn't I right, Mary? And she never finishes it — Why doesn't she finish it? And have done with it. For God's sake.

MARY *considers this ('Finish it? And have done with it.'), then forgets it for the moment. She is just looking into the fire.*

MARY: I want to have a talk to you, Dolly.

DOLLY: *(Cautiously)* ... About what? ... What?

MARY: Do you remember ... *(She shakes her head: she does not know)*

DOLLY: ... What? ... I know it affects you. Like, her not reco'nisin' you ever — Why wouldn't it? But you were away a long time. (MARY *looks up: she has been only half listening)* That's the reason.

MARY: ... I've often thought .... *(Just looking at the fire again)*

DOLLY: ... What?

MARY: I may have been too — bossy, at first.

DOLLY: Well, well, there could be something in that, too.

MARY: But I wanted to ... bring about change. Comfort, civilized.

DOLLY: Yes, well, but. Though I don't know. You were away an awful long time. I was left holdin' the can. Like, when yeh think of it, you owe me a very big debt.

MARY: *(Looks up)* Hmm? A very big?

DOLLY: I mean that's why she reco'nises me.

MARY *looking at the fire again;* DOLLY *watching* MARY. *Something on* DOLLY*'s mind; she coughs in preparation to speak —.*

MARY: We had a pony and trap once. The Sunday outings. You don't remember? (DOLLY, *puzzled, shakes her head)* Ribbons. Grandad would always bring ribbons home for our hair. You don't remember.

DOLLY: ... You work too hard. (MARY *laughs to herself at the remark) (Laughs)* What? (MARY *shakes her head)* And you're too serious.

MARY: Do you remember Daddy?

DOLLY: Well, the photographs. *(They glance at the framed photographs on the wall)* Aul' brown ghosts. *(Playful, but cajoling)* Y'are, y'are, too serious.

MARY: *(Eyes back to the fire)* I suppose I am. I don't know what I'm trying to say. *(Sighs)* Home.

MOMMO: *(Has put down her cup)* And that, too, is well.

DOLLY: What?

MARY, *another slight shake of her head: she doesn't know.*

MOMMO: And now with his old jiggler of a bicycle set again' the gable, Costello was goin' in to John Mah'ny's, the one and only shop for everything for miles around.

DOLLY: *(To* MARY) What?

MOMMO: 'Cold enough for ye, ladies!' Now! Cold enough for ye, ladies. And that was the first remark he was to utter that evening. And the two women he had thus accosted set to gurgling at once and together. 'Caw och-caw, Seamusheen a wockeen.[15] God bless yeh, och-caw' says the old crone that was in it buyin' the salt. And, 'Uck-uck-uck, uck-uck hunuka huckina-caw, Costello' from the young buxom woman tendin' the shop-end of the counter, and she turnin' one of the babes in her arms so that he too could behold the hero. 'Aren't they gettin' awful big, God bless them,' then saying Costello of the two twins an' they gogglin' at him. 'Jack Frost is coming with a vengeance for ye tonight,' says he, 'or the Bogey Man maybe bejingoes'. And to the four or five others now holding tight their mother's apron, 'Well, someone is comin' anaways,'[16] says he, 'if ye all aren't good.' An' then off with him to the end where the drink was.

DOLLY: } Good man Josie!
MARY: } No!

MOMMO: } 'Good man, Josie!'
MARY: } Don't encourage her.

MOMMO: } Now!
MARY: } I'm —! [*Going out of my mind*]

MOMMO: } Good man, Josie.
MARY: } I'm trying to stop it!

MOMMO: } And that was the second greeting he uttered that night.
MARY: } Talk to her!
DOLLY: } That's what I try to do!

MOMMO: He got no reply.

DOLLY: *(Going to* MOMMO; *under her breath)* Good man Josie, Jesus!

MOMMO: Nor did he expect one.

DOLLY: *(Calling back to* MARY) And I'm going at quarter to nine! — Good man, Mommo, how's it cuttin'?[17]

15. *Seamaisín a mhaicín*, 'Little Seamus, my wee son': 'Caw och-caw' might be read as *cá ach cá*, 'where but where'.
16. anyway.
17. 'how's it going?'

MOMMO: Good man —! Pardon?

DOLLY: How's the adversary[18] treatin' yeh?

MOMMO: (*To herself*) Good man Mommo?

DOLLY: I brought yeh sweets.

MOMMO: There's nothing wrong with me.

DOLLY: I didn't say there was.

MOMMO: An' I never done nothin' wrong.

DOLLY: Sweets!

MARY: Butterscotch, isn't it, Dolly?

MOMMO: (*To herself, puzzled again*) Good man — Who?

DOLLY: Butterscotch, I've oceans of money.

MARY: Your favourites.

DOLLY: You like them ones.

MARY: Try one. You [DOLLY] give it to her.

MOMMO: Do I like them ones?

MARY: Suck it slowly.

DOLLY: Gob-stoppers I should have brought her —

MARY: Shh!

DOLLY: You're lookin' fantastic. (*Going back to the fire*) It'd be a blessing if she went.

MARY: (*Placatory*) Shh, don't say things like [*that*]. Talk to her, come on.

DOLLY: About what? — It's like an oven in here — And I don't understand a word she's sayin'.

MARY: Take off your — [*coat*].

DOLLY: I — don't — want — to — take — off — my!

MARY: Tell her about the children.

DOLLY: Seafóid,[19] nonsense talk about forty years ago —

MARY: Come on —

DOLLY: And I've enough problems of my own. Why don't you stick her in there? [*One of the other rooms*]

MARY: It's damp, and she understands — recognises you a lot of the time. (DOLLY *rolling her eyes but following* MARY *back to the bed again*) Where she can see you.

DOLLY: Well, the children are all fine, Mommo. (*A slip*) Well. Well, Michaeleen is sick, the tonsils again. I've rubber-backed lino in all the bedrooms now, the Honda is going like a bomb and the *lounge*, my dear, is carpeted. I seen the lean and lanky May Glynn, who never comes near ye or this house, in the garden when I was motoring over but she went in without a salute. I must have distemper too, or whatever. Conor, that other lean and lanky bastard, is now snaking his fence in another six inches, and my darlin' mother-in-law, old sharp-eyes-and-the-family-rosary, sends her pers'nal blessings to ye both. Now. Darlin's.

MARY: Is she babysitting for you?

DOLLY: No. She is not babysitting for me. I don't want her or any of the McGrath clan in my house. But I have someone babysittin' — since you're lookin' concerned.

MARY: I wasn't.

MOMMO: (*Sucking the sweet*) They're nice.

DOLLY: An' the cat had kittens (*To* MARY) D'yeh want a kitten? Do you, Mommo? (*A touch of sour introversion*) Does anyone? Before I drown them.

MOMMO: Tom is in Galway.

MARY: Did you hear from Stephen?

DOLLY: The 'wire'[20] again on Friday, regular as clockwork.

MARY: Did you hear, Mommo?

MOMMO: I did. But she told May Glynn not to be waitin', her own mother'd be needin' her, and that they'd be home before dark for sure.

DOLLY: Eighty-five quid a week and never a line.

MARY: He's busy.

DOLLY: (*To herself*) Fuck him. I don't know what to do with the money! (*Sudden introspection again*) Or do I? I've started saving. (*Then impetuously*) Do *you* want some? Well, do you, Mommo? To go dancin'. (MARY *is laughing at her sister's personality*) What?

MARY: Stephen will be home as usual for Christmas.

DOLLY: For his goose.

MARY: Won't he, Mommo?

MOMMO: (*To herself*) Stephen, yes, fugum.[21]

They laugh. Then, DOLLY, *grimly:*

DOLLY: Well maybe it'd be better if the bold Stephen skipped his visit this Christmas. (*Rises and turns her back on them*) Jesus, misfortunes.

MARY *now wondering, concerned, her eyes on* DOLLY's *back, the stout figure.*

MOMMO: Yes. Misfortunes.

MARY: . . . Dolly?

DOLLY: Ooh, a cake, a candle — candles! What's the occasion? (*She gives a kiss to* MOMMO) Well, I'm

18. i.e. time.
19. Rambling talk.
20. Money 'wired' home.
21. fuck him.

off now, darlin', an' God an' all his holy saints protect an' bless yeh.

MOMMO: (*Buried in her own thoughts until now*) When did you arrive?

DOLLY: What?

MOMMO: When did you arrive?

DOLLY: I arrived —

MOMMO: Sure you're welcome, when did you arrive?

DOLLY: I arrived —

MOMMO: Well did yeh?

DOLLY: I did.

MOMMO: From where?

DOLLY: From —

MOMMO: Now. And is that where y'are now?

DOLLY: The very location.

MOMMO: Now! I never knew that. Where?

DOLLY: Ahm . . . Aw Jesus, Mommo, you have us all as confused as yourself! Ballindine, Bal-lin-dine.

MOMMO: Hah? Oh yes, yeh told me. Now. Who are you?

DOLLY: Dolly. I think.

MOMMO: (*Considering this, sucking her sweet*) Now. Dolly.

DOLLY: Dolly!

MOMMO: Yes.

DOLLY: Look, I have to be — [*going*] I'm Dolly, your grand-daughter, and that's Mary, your other grand-daughter, and your grandson Tom, Tom is dead.

MARY: Shh!

DOLLY: Ar, shh! (*To* MOMMO) Now do you know?

MOMMO: I do. I'm waiting for someone.

DOLLY: Who're yeh waitin' for?

MOMMO: I'm not tellin' yeh.

DOLLY: A man, is it?

MOMMO: (*Laughing*) 'Tis.

DOLLY: Och hona ho gus hah-haa, an' what'll he have for yeh?

MOMMO: (*Laughing*) A big stick.

DOLLY: M-m-m-m-m! — Stick, the bata![22] Mmmah! (*Sexual innuendo*) Now! Try that subject on her if you want to stop her.

MOMMO: Oh but they were always after me.

DOLLY: An' did they ketch yeh?

MOMMO: The ones I wanted to.

DOLLY: An' they're still after yeh?

22. Irish: stick.

MOMMO: But I bolt the door — on some of them. (*Laughing*)

DOLLY: (*To* MARY) That's what all the aul' ones like to talk about. I think you're goin' soft in the head.

MOMMO: (*Recognising her*) Is it Dolly? Aw is it my Dolly! Well, d'yeh know I didn't rec'nise yeh. Sure you were always the joker. Aw, my Dolly, Dolly, Dolly, come 'ere to me. (DOLLY *hesitates, is reluctant, then succumbs to the embrace; indeed, after a moment she is clinging tightly to the old woman.* MARY *stands by, isolated, but watching the scene. She would love to be included. The smallest gesture of affection or recognition would help greatly*) Ah, lovee. Lovee, lovee, lovee. Sure if I knew you were comin' — (*aside to* MARY) Will you put on the kettle, will you? Standing there! — I'd've baked a cake. That's an old one. Oh, mo pheata [*my pet*]. Why didn't you send word? An' you got fat. You did! On me oath! Will you put on the kettle, Miss, will you! (*Whispering*) Who is that woman?

DOLLY: (*Tearfully, but trying to joke*) She's the sly one.

MOMMO: She is. (*Loudly, hypocritically*) Isn't she nice?

DOLLY: Watch her.

MARY *goes off to another room.*

MOMMO: Why is she interfering?

DOLLY: Shh, Mommo.

MOMMO: Be careful of that one.

DOLLY: I'm in terrible trouble.

MOMMO: Yes, watch her.

DOLLY: (*Extricating herself from the embrace, brushing away a tear*) Leave her to me. I'll deal with her. (*Calls*) Miss! Will you come out, will you, an' make a brew! An' put something in it! Sure you should know about all kinds of potions. (MARY *has returned with a suitcase. She places it somewhere*) . . . Someone going on a *voyage*?

MARY: I have to come to a decision, Dolly.

DOLLY: Again?

MARY: She's your responsibility too.

DOLLY: I know you think I inveigled you back here so that Stephen and I could escape.

MARY: No one inveigled me anywhere. You're not pulling your weight.

DOLLY: (*Shrugs*) There's always the County Home.

MARY: You —

DOLLY: Wouldn't I? Why should I stick myself again back in here?

MARY: Why should I?

DOLLY: In a place like this.

MARY: Why do I? In a place like this.

DOLLY: (*Shrugs*) That's your business. Well, I have to be going.

MARY: I'd like to go out sometimes too.

DOLLY: For a 'walk'? *Home*, I'm going.

MARY: You look it.

DOLLY: Alright: I'll tell you, so that you can go, where the man is waiting.

MARY: Man? Men! (DOLLY *shrugs, is moving off*) I need to talk to — someone!

DOLLY: (*Her back to* MARY; *quietly*) I need to talk to someone too.

MARY: (*An insinuation*) Why don't you take off your coat?

DOLLY: (*Faces* MARY; *a single solemn nod of her head; then*) Because, now, I am about to leave. I'll figure out something. I might even call back, 'cause it doesn't take long, does it? Just a few minutes: that's all it takes.

MARY: You're disgusting.

DOLLY: Am I?

MARY: (*Going to one of the other rooms*) I've *come* to a decision. (*Off*) County Home! You won't blackmail me!

DOLLY: (*To herself*) I hate this house. (*To* MOMMO) Good man Josie! (*Going out; an undertone*) Ah, fuck it all.

MOMMO: Oh yes. 'Good man, Josie!' Now! Good man Josie. And that was the second greeting Costello was to utter that evening.

MARY: (*Coming in*) I'll leave everything here for you spic and span, of course. (*She has not heard* DOLLY *go out; now she stands there looking at the door, the motorcycle outside driving away, arms outstretched, her hands clapping together some of her wardrobe (as if demonstrating the possibility that she is leaving rather than confirming it)*)

MOMMO: He got no reply. Nor did he expect one. For Josie was a Greaney and none was every right in that fambly.

MARY: (*To herself*) It's not fair.

MOMMO: An' the threadbare fashion'ry, not a top-coat to him, the shirt neck open.

MARY: (*To herself*) Not a gansey.[23]

MOMMO: Nor a gansey.

MARY: *Nor* a gansey. (*Calling after* DOLLY) Stephen called me 'dearest'!

23. jersey.

MOMMO: An' the tuthree[24] raggedy top-coats on the others.

MARY: Wanted to have a child by me!

MOMMO: An' some with extra sacking bandaging around them.

MARY: A girl, he said, so that she'd look like me.

MOMMO: Though some say he had the knack of mendin' clocks, if he had.

MARY: But you'll never know a thing about it!

MOMMO: And none ever bested him at Ride-the-Blind-Donkey.[25] (*She has a sip of tea*) What's in this? Miss!

MARY: Your husband wined and dined and bedded me! (*Realising she has been talking to the door*) I'm going soft in the head.

MOMMO: Miss!

MARY: The County Home! (*Gesturing, meaning did* MOMMO *hear what* DOLLY *said*)

MOMMO: Hot drink, decent supa tea!

MARY: (*Automatically sets about making fresh tea, then she stops*) I have *come* to a decision I said. Do you understand? So if you could wait a moment. (*She starts to discard some of the clothes, packing others; talking to herself again*) Just to see who is in earnest this time. I sit there.

MOMMO: } Me mouth is dry d'ye know.
MARY: } I just sit there. And I was doing well — I was the success! Now I'm talking to myself. And I *will* leave the place spic and span.

MOMMO: Howandever. 'How the boys!' was Costello's third greeting. This time to two old men with their heads in the chimbley,[26] each minding a pint of black porter, before Costello's coming in, were in no heed or hurry to be drinkin'. The one of them givin' out the odd old sigh, smoking his pipe with assiduity and beating the slow obsequies of a death-roll with his boot. An' the other, a Brian by name, replying in sagacity 'Oh yis,' sharing the silent mysteries of the world between them. Me mouth is [*dry*], d'ye know.

MARY: Just a moment! (*Going to another room*) Dependent on a pension and that bitch.

MOMMO: Where is she? Miss!

MARY: (*Off*) Miss! Miss is coming. (*Entering with more clothes*) Miss: as if I didn't exist. That's the thanks I get — (*Winces to herself*) It's — not —

24. two-three.
25. A game played at wakes involving a broomstick balanced between two chairs with apples on them.
26. chimney.

thanks I'm looking for. (*Absently*) What am I looking for, Mommo? I had to come home. No one inveigled me. I wanted to come home.

MOMMO: Put it down, put it down!

MARY: Why can't you be civil to me? At least tonight.

MOMMO: Put it down! (*She continues her story*)

MARY, *exasperated, comes out of her reverie, dumps the clothes and sets about making more tea.*

MARY: And you know very well who I am! You do. You do.

MOMMO: Sure it's often I'd be watchin' me own father engaged in the same practice, drawing wisdom from the fire. 'Deed, on one such occasion, an' twas maybe after a full hour's contemplation, he craned his neck, the glaze to his eyes, to accost me with the philosophy that was troublin' him. 'How much does a seagull weigh?' I held my silence to be sure, for times he'd get cross — oh he'd welt yeh with the stick — if a guess was attempted or a sound itself uttered. For he wouldn't be talkin' to you at all. The groans out of that man decipherin' the enigmal. Then, at last, when he found for himself the answer to the riddle he declared in 'sured solemnity, 'I'm thinkin' two ounces'. Now! That's who I'm waitin' for. Oh, men have their ways an' women their places an' that is God's plan, my bright ones. (*She gets out of bed.* MARY *sees her and is hurrying to her assistance*) Shthap!

MARY *is stopped by the ferocity.* MOMMO *squats, hidden behind the headboard of the bed.*

MARY: ... And to change your nightdress ... I was a nurse, Mommo ... And other offers of marriage ... Plenty of them! (*Then, quickly, she takes the opportunity of remaking the bed*) Wined and dined and bedded me. I told him to keep away from me, to stop following me, to keep away from here. (*She replaces the sheets with clean ones, removes the bed-warmer — which is a cast-iron lid of a pot in a knitted woollen cover: she puts the lid into the fire to reheat it. She appears almost happy when she is working constructively. She recites as she works*)

'There is the silence of copse or croft
When the wind sinks dumb,
And of belfry loft
When the tenor after tolling stops its hum.'[27]

And sure you have lots of poems. Lots of stories, nice stories, instead of that old one. 'Mick Delaney' — do you remember that one? We loved that one. How did it begin? Or ghost stories. People used to come *miles* to hear you tell stories. Oh! and do you remember: the gramophone. Yes, we had a gramophone too. 'The banshee[28] is out tonight go down [*on*] your knees and say your prayers — Wooooo!' Or would you like me to read you a story?

MOMMO: (*Reappearing from behind the bed*) Heh heh heh heh!

MARY: (*Now her solemn grave face*) There was happiness here too, Mommo. Harmony?

MOMMO: (*Straight back, neck craned*) You can be going now, Miss.

MARY: ... Alright. (*She takes the chamberpot from behind the headboard of the bed and goes out. We can see her outside, motionless; a little later, continuing motionless except for the movements of smoking a cigarette*)

MOMMO: She knows too much about our business entirely. (*She calls hypocritically*) And thank you! (*Giggles getting back into the bed*) Now amn't I able for them? (*Sings*) 'Once I loved with fond affection, all my thoughts they were in thee, till a dork [*dark*] haired girl deceived me —'[29]

Ye like that one. But now that Costello was in it the aspect was transforming. 'An',' says old Brian, taking his head out of the fire, 'What's the news from the Big World?' 'The Dutch has taken Holland!' says Costello with such a rumble out of him near had the whole house shook asunder and all in it in ululation so infectious was the sound. Save Josie who was heedless, but rapping with severity on the counter for more libation. And 'John!' says the young buxom woman, calling to her husband — 'John!' — to come out and tend his end of the counter, an' she now putting questions on bold Costello.

'You wor in Tuam?' says she, 'I was in Tuam,' says he. 'Yeh wor?' says she, 'I was,' says he, 'An' how was it?' says she.

'Well, not tellin' you a word of a lie now,' says he 'but 'twas deadly'.

And 'Ory!' says the crone that was in it buyin' the salt.

'Did yeh hear?' says the young buxom woman

27. The opening stanza of Thomas Hardy's poem 'Silences' in *Winter Words* (1928), although the indefinite article has been omitted before 'copse' and 'belfry-loft'.

28. Old Irish *bean sídhe*, woman of the fairies, who wails before a death.
29. Traditional song, 'Once I loved'.

to her husband. John, to be sure. He had 'rived from the kitchen an' was frownin' pullin' pints. Merchants d'ye know: good market or bad, the arithmetic in the ledger has to come out correct. An' the multifarious diversifications in matters of local commerce, the head had to be working perpetually.

'Well do yeh tell me so?' says the young buxom woman.

'I do tell yeh so,' says Costello. 'Talkin' about a Maragadh Mór?[30] — I never in all me born days seen light or likes of it!'

Now they were listening. (MARY *comes in, washes and replaces the chamberpot. She selects her 'going-away' suit from the second bundle of clothes which she brought from the other room and, trying the waist against herself, she puts the suit on a chair beside the fire to air it. She leaves her clothes to go out twice through the following and bring in two armsful of turf)*
'Firkins of butter,' says he, 'an' cheese be[31] the hundred-weight. Ducks, geese, chickens, bonavs and — Geese!' says he, 'geese! There was hundreds of them! There was hundreds upon hundreds of thousands of them! The ground I tell ye was white with them!'

And 'White with them,' says the crone.

'They went ch-cheap then?' says John, still bowed frownin' over the tricks of pullin' porter.

'Cheap then?' says Costello, 'sure yeh couldn't give them away sure. Sure the sight of so many chickens an' geese an'! Sure all the people could do was stand and stare'.

'They were puzzled,' says the crone.

'I'm tellin' yeh,' says Costello, 'Napoleon Bonaparte wouldn't have said no to all the provisions goin' a-beggin' in that town of Tuam today'.

An' 'Hah?' says John, squintin', the head-work interrupted.

'On his retreat from Moscow, sure,' says Costello.

'Or Josephine[32] — Wuw! — neither.' Now! Wuw. Them were his ways, an' he off rumblin' again: 'Oh, I'm a bold bachelor aisy an' free, both city and country is aiqual to me!'[33] having the others equivalently pursuant: 'Wo ho ho, wo ho ho!'

'But you sis-sold the rabbits, d-did yeh, Costello?' says John. An' wasn't there a gap. Oh, only for the second. 'Oh I sold them,' then sayin' Costello. 'Oh I did, did,' saying he. 'Oh on me solemn 'n dyin' oath! Every man-jack-rabbit of them.' Like a man not to be believed, his bona fides in question.

'Yeh-yeh c-codjer[34] yeh-yeh,' says John. Whatever he meant. But he was not at all yet feeling cordial.

But thus was the night faring into its progression, others 'riving back home an' how did they do an' who else was in it, did they buy e'er a thing. Costello settin' them laughin', John frownin' an' squintin', an' the thief of a Christmas they wor all goin' t'have. What're ye doin' there?
MARY *is stacking the turf near the fire. She holds up a sod of turf to show* MOMMO.
Hah? ... There's nothing here for people to be prying in corners for.
MARY *holds up the woollen cover of the bed-warmer.*
Hah? ... Bring in the brishen[35] of turf an' then you may be goin' home to your own house.

MARY: ... Alright. (*She moves as if going out back door — she opens and closes the door — then moves silently to the comparative dark of the far corner of the room where she remains motionless)*

MOMMO: You couldn't be up to them.
MARY *continues silent. She is trying a new ploy, hoping* MOMMO *will stop, will sleep.*
Isn't life a strange thing too? 'Tis. An' if we could live it again? ... Would we [*live it differently*]? In harmony? Aah, I don't know. (*She yawns*) Oh ho huneo! An' 'twas round about now the rattlin' of the horse an' cart was heard evidential abroad an' had them peepin' at the windy.[36] 'Twas the decent man an' his decent wife the same was in it. And 'Stand, Pedlar,' says the man in [*a*] class of awesome whisper. And his decent wife from the heel of the cart to his side to view the spectre[37] was now before them. The aspect silver of moon an' stars reflecting off the new impossibility. Loughran's Hill. Creature. She now clutching more tightly the sweets to her breast. Switch off that aul' thing (*the radio*), there's nothing on it. (*She yawns again: her*

30. Big market.
31. by.
32. Napoleon's wife, the Empress Josephine.
33. Untraced.
34. i.e. codger.
35. armful.
36. window.
37. spectacle.

eyes close) They were silent a while.

MARY: (*Whispers*) Sleep.

MOMMO: (*Eyes open*) Hah? (*Looking around*) *Now* what was there for doing? Which way to cast the hopeful eye. No-no, not yet, in deliberate caution, would he acknowledge the shop, John Mah'ny's, forninst[38] them. But looked behind him the road they came, forward again, but to what avail? There was only John Mah'ny's now for his deep contemplation, nature all around them serenely waiting, and didn't the two little smiles come appearing again. (*Slides a little down into the bed*)

MARY: (*Whispers*) Sleep.

MOMMO: Hah?

MARY: Sleep, sleep. Peace, peace.

MOMMO: (*Yawns*) An' the strangers, that decent man an' his decent wife the same, were rounding the gable into the merchant's yard, an' sorry the night that was the decision. What time is it? . . . She's gone. An' she can stay gone. But them are the details, c'rrect to the particular. And they can be vouched for. For there was to be many's the inquisition by c'roner, civic guard and civilian on all that transpired in John Mah'ny's that night. Wasn't that a nice story? An' we'll all be goin' to sleep now.

She is asleep. Tommy O'Brien's programme is over (or nearly over); it is followed by an announcement of what The Sunday Concert *is going to be later on: 'A Schubert Evening, Symphony No. 9, 'The Great', followed by 'Notturno' in E Flat. But now we have* Archives *presented by . . . .' etc.* MARY *continues motionless for some moments. A car passes by outside.*

MARY: (*Looking at* MOMMO) Sleep? For how long? . . . (*She switches off the radio. She switches off the lights. She goes to the table and idly starts lighting three or four of the candles on the cake, using a new match to light each successive candle*) (*To herself*) Give me my freedom, Mommo . . . . What freedom? . . . . No freedom without structure . . . . Where can I go? . . . How can I go (*looking up and around at the rafters*) with all this? (*She has tired of her idle game of lighting the candles*) . . . And it didn't work before for me, did it? . . . I came back. (*To herself, and idly at first*) Now as all do know . . . Now as all do know . . . Now as all do know the world over the custom when entering the house of another — be the house public, private with credentials or no — is to invoke our Maker's benediction on all present. (*Adds a piece of sardonic humour*) Save[39] the cat. Well, as the Bailegangaires would have it later, no mention of our Maker, or His Blessed Son, was mentioned as the strangers came 'cross that threshel [*threshold*]. But no, no, no, no, no. No now! They were wrongin' that couple. (*To the sleeping* MOMMO) Weren't they? They wor. They were. (*To* MOMMO) And when you — And when that decent woman gave the whole story to her father, what did he say? (*A touch of mimicry of* MOMMO) An' believe you me he knew all about them. That the Bailegangaires were a venomous pack of jolter-headed gobshites. Didn't he? He did. Now for yeh! An ill-bred band of amadáns[40] an' oinseachs,[41] untutored in science, philosophy or the fundamental rudimentaries of elementary husbandry itself. A low crew of illiterate plebs, drunkards and incestuous bastards, and would ever continue as such — (*holds up her finger to correct her wording*) and would ever continue as *much*, improper and despicable in their incorrigibility. Them were his words. Weren't they? They're not nice, he said. Supa tea. (*Short sardonic laugh as she pours a glass of vodka for herself*) And he was the man to give the tongue-lashin'. An' 'twas from him I got my learnin'. Wasn't it? That's who I'm waitin' for. (*She has a sip of the vodka*) Too sweet. (*She dilutes the vodka with water*) Me father. He has a big stick. That's where security lies. (*She has a drink; then, whimpering as* MOMMO *might*) I wanta go home, I wanta go home. (*New tone, her own, frustrated*) So do I, so do I. *Home* (*Anger*) Where is it, Mommo? (*Then she is sorry for her anger. She pulls herself together for a few moments. The silence now being punctuated by a car passing by outside*) A lot of activity tonight. And all weekend. (*Picks up her book but does not open it*)

'There is the silence of copse or croft

(*She starts to pace the periphery of the room restlessly*)

'When the wind sinks dumb,
And of belfry loft
When the tenor after tolling stops its hum.

'And there's the silence of a lonely pond
Where a man was drowned . . . .'

(*She stops for a moment or two looking at one of the framed photographs*)

Where a man, and his brother who went to save him

38. opposite.

39. except.

40. fools.

41. Another class of fools, usually female.

... were drowned. Bury them in pairs, it's cheaper. (*Continues pacing*)

'Nor nigh nor yond
No newt, toad, frog to make the smallest sound.

'But the silence of an empty house
Where oneself was born,
Dwelt, held carouse....' Did we? Hold carouse.
'With friends
Is of all silence most forlorn.

'It seems no power can waken it —'
(*Another car passes by.* MARY's *reaction to the car:*) Come in! 'Or rouse its rooms,
Or the past permit.
The present to stir a torpor like a tomb's.'

Bla bla bla bla bla, like a tomb's. (*To the book, and dumping it*) Is that so? Well, I don't agree with you ... What time is it? Twenty past nine ... Going crazy. (*Then, on reflection*) No I'm not. (*Then suddenly to* MOMMO) Wake up *now*, Mommo. Mommo! Because I don't want to wait till midnight, or one or two or three o'clock in the morning, for more of your — unfinished symphony. I'm ready now. (*She switches on the light*) Mommo, the cursèd paraffin! (*She switches on the radio*) What else did your father say when you gave him the story? That many's the one's son or daughter married into that place went mental after and had to be took away sullyin' and bringin' disgrace on a line that had been clean up to then, maybe both sides! What else did he say? (MOMMO *is awake*) What about the snails? What about the earwigs?

MOMMO: 'Oh never step on a snail,' he intoned.

MARY: 'Nor upon the silver trail he leaves behind.'

MOMMO: 'For your boot is unworthy.'

MARY: Now!

MOMMO: 'For the snail knows his place,' he groaned, 'and understands the constant parameters — and the need for parameters — in the case under consideration, God's prize piece, the earth. And therefore the snail is free, and all he does is in innocence'. He did.

MARY: On with the story.

MOMMO: 'D'yeh consider,' says he — the fierce eyes of that man rolling — 'that God designed all this for the likes of the gobshite Bochtáns and their antics?'

MARY: Or for the likes of ourselves?

MOMMO: Or for the likes of ourselves. He did. Them wor his words. That's who I'm waitin' for.

MARY: To continue. But that decent man and his decent wife the same did as was proper on entering.

MOMMO: Sure we weren't meant to be here at all!

MARY: The customary salutation was given.

MOMMO: That was one of God's errors.

MARY: Though silently, for they were shy people, and confused in their quandary. Mommo? And then, without fuss, the man indicated a seat in the most private corner.

MOMMO: An' they were wrongin' them there again! So they wor.

MARY: They were.

MOMMO: They wor. The whispers bein' exchanged were *not* of malevolent disposition. Yis! — to be sure! — that woman! — Maybe! — had a distracted look to her. Hadn't she reason?

MARY: The Bailegangaires gawpin'[42] at them.

MOMMO: They knew no better.

MARY: Where would they learn it.

MOMMO: Oh-ho, but he bet them — Och hona ho gus hah-haa! — he bet the best of them! ... Incestuous bastards. (*Absently asking*) Cigarette. 'An' I caught Tom playin' with the mangler[43] the other evenin', his feet dancin' in the cup.' That's what she was whisperin'. And he lookin' round. 'Not at all, not at all,' tryin' to look pleasant in the house of another. 'An' won't they have to light the lamp?' That's what she was whisperin'. 'Not at all, not at all,' still lookin' for the place to put his eyes. 'Isn't Mary a big girl now an' well able to look after them.' That's what he was whisperin'. 'An' won't May Glynn be lookin' in on them.' That's what he was whisperin'. But she'd told May Glynn that mornin' not to be waitin', her mother'd be needin' her to look after her young brothers, an' they'd be home before dark for sure. And-sure-she-was-gettin'-on-his-nerves! Till he had to go an' leave her there to a quiet spot at the counter ... Sure she should've known better. An' she's sorry now. She is. She is. (*Whimpering*) I wanta see mah father.

MARY *coming to comfort her.*

Shthap! ... (*Whimpering*) I wanta go home. (*Warning* MARY; *at the same time taking the cigarette which* MARY *is offering her*) And he has a big stick.

MARY: I'm not trying to stop you, Mommo.

42. gaping.

43. A mangle, a rolling press for wringing water out of washed clothes.

MOMMO: An' he won't try to stop me. Heh heh heh heh. (*She puffs at the cigarette and then winks wisely at the imagined children at the foot of the bed*) Men long-married to tearful women are no use to them, my bright ones. But are apt to get cross, and make matters worse, when they can't see the solution. (*She becomes aware of the cigarette*) What's this? An' who asked for this?

MARY: (*Taking cigarette from her*) I'm not stopping you. And I just had an idea.

MOMMO: Me mouth is burned.
MARY: We'll do it together.

MOMMO: Rubbishy cigarettes — spendin' money on rubbishy cigarettes —
MARY: We'll finish it. What is it but an old auld story? I'm not stopping you —

MOMMO: (*Singing: her defiance to* MARY) 'Once I loved with fond affection —'
MARY: And if we finished it, that would be something at least, wouldn't it?

MOMMO: 'All my thoughts they were in thee.'

MARY: Wouldn't it?

MOMMO: 'And no more he thought of me.' (*She lapses into silence. She grows drowsy, or feigns drowsiness*)

MARY: (*Singing*) 'Tooralloo ralloo ralladdy, tooralloo ralloo rallee, till a dark — (*corrects herself*) *dork* haired girl deceived me, and no more he thought of me' ... I'll help you, Mommo.

MOMMO: Tom is in Galway. He's afeared of the gander.

MARY: Don't go to sleep. And don't be pretending to sleep either. And what'll you be havin', says John Mahony the proprietor. But the stranger was now puzzlin' something in his brain, he taking in the laughter and Costello's great bellow dominating over all.

'A lotta noise an' little wool as the devil says shearin' the pig!' sayin' Costello. Wo ho ho! 'An what'll you be havin', Mister,' says John Mahony again. 'A little drop of whiskey an' a small port wine.' And readying the drinks up above says John, 'the frost is determined to make a night of it?' Says he.

'Behell I don't know,' says old Brian, like the nestor[44] long ago, 'comin' on duskness there was a fine roll of cloud over in the west and if you got the bit of a breeze at all I'm thinkin' you'd soon see a thaw'. And the stranger had produced his purse and was suspended-paused takin' in the forecast. But the two little smiles appearing again, the compendium of his deliberations was that such good fortune as a thaw was not to be. Then — and with a deft enough flick — he pitched the coin on the counter, like a man rejecting all fortune. Good enough.

He took the drink to his decent wife and was for sitting next to her again but wasn't her head now in and out of the corner and she startin' the cryin'.

MOMMO: She should have known better.

MARY: So what could he do but leave her there again.

MOMMO: An' the church owed him money.

MARY: Did it?

MOMMO: (*Growls*) The-church-owed-him-money. Oh, the church is slow to pay out. But if you're givin', there's nothin' like money to make them fervent! There's nothin' like money t'make the clergy devout.

MARY: Yes?

MOMMO: (*Drowsily*) And I'm thinkin', that decent man of late was given to reviewin' the transpirations since his birth ... But if he was itself, wasn't his decent wife the same? ... At the end of her tether ... They were acquainted with grief ...[45] They wor ... They wor. Switch off that aul' thing (*the radio*) ... They wor.

MARY: ... Mommo? (*She has turned the volume down a bit*) I know you're pretending. Mommo? (*The silence again*) They were acquainted with grief ... Alright, I won't just help you, I'll do it for you. (*Progressively she begins to dramatise the story more*) Now John Mahony. (*She corrects her pronunciation*) Now John Mah'ny was noticing the goings-on between the two and being the proprietor he was possessed of the licence for interrogating newses. And 'you have a distance to go, Mister?' says he. (*Corrects herself again*) 'You have a d-distance teh-teh g-go, *Mister*?' says he at the stranger. An' says Grandad. An' says the stranger, class of frownin', 'Would that big man down there,' says he, 'be a man by the name of Costello?' And, 'Th-that's who he is,' says John, 'D'yeh know him?' 'No,' says the stranger, in curious introspection. An' 'No' says he again — *still* puzzled in the head — 'But that's a fine

44. The old Greek king at the battle of Troy, noted for his wisdom and eloquence.

45. Isaiah 53.3.

laugh.' 'Oh 'tis a f-fine laugh right enough,' says John, 'Hah?' Knowin' more was comin' but hadn't yet reached the senses. And the stranger now drawin' curlicues with his glass upon the counter! Then says he, 'I heard that laugh a wintry day two years ago across the market square in Ballindine, an' I had t'ask a man who he was'. 'Yeh had,' says John. 'I had,' says the stranger, still drawin' the curlicues, an' now admiring his own artistry. An' John was in suspense. And then, of a suddenness, didn't the frown go disappearin' up the stranger's cap. He had it at last. 'Well,' says he — Oh, lookin' the merchant between the two eyes. 'Well,' says he, 'I'm a better laugher than your Costello'.

What time is it? Half-nine. *Someone* will come yet. *'Nother* supa milk. (*Short laugh to herself as she gets another glass of vodka*) Well, I'm a better laugher than your Costello. (*She swallows the drink*) Now the merchant betrayed nothing. He was well-versed in meeting company, an' all he did was nod the once — (*she nods*) and then, quick enough of him, referred the matter. And 'Sh-Sheamus!' says he, 'Sh-Sh-Sheamus!' callin' Costello to come down. (*She is now listening to the 'putt-putt' of the motorcycle approaching*) A mortal laughing competition there would be. (MARY *now into action, putting away her glass, switching off the radio, getting needle, thread, scissors and the skirt of her 'going-away' suit to take in the waist*) I knew someone would call. Dolly. Again! I wonder why. (*Cynically*) Bringing tidings of great joy.[46]

MARY *is seated by the fire.* DOLLY *comes in. She stretches herself. (She has had her sex in ditch, doorway, old shed or wherever. She takes in the packed suitcase but as usual leaves such baiting topics until it suits her)*

DOLLY: I have it all figured out.

MARY: The County Home?

DOLLY: Well, maybe nothing as drastic as that. That's a nice suit.

MARY: (*Does not lift her head from her work*) Kill her?

DOLLY: (*A sideways twist of the head — 'Kill her?' — a more feasible suggestion*) Can I have a drop of this? (*Vodka*)

MARY: You brought it.

DOLLY: (*Produces two bottles of mixers*) I forgot the mixers earlier. In my haste. (*She pours two drinks*) We might as well have a wake, an American wake for yeh.

MARY: Not for me. I had a little one, thank you.

DOLLY: You had *two* little ones. (*Puts drink beside* MARY) Vodka and white.[47] It's a long time since I seen you wearing that.

MARY: Saw.

DOLLY: What?

MARY: I wore it coming home.

DOLLY: Did you have to let out the waist?

MARY: I have to take *in* my things. (*A gesture of invitation*) You need to talk to someone.

DOLLY: Go on: cheers! Since you're off. Are yeh?

MARY: (*Does not drink, does not look up but lifts her glass and puts it down again*) Cheers!

DOLLY: And it often crossed my mind the years Stephen and I were here with herself. Kill her. And it wouldn't be none of your fancy nurses' potions either. Get them out of bed, the auld reliable, start them walkin'. Walk the heart out of them. No clues left for coroner or Dr Paddy. And that's how many's the one met their Waterloo. What's the matter? (MARY *shakes her head; just when she does not want to, she is about to break into tears*) . . . What? . . . Joking . . . I have it all figured out. (MARY *is crying*) What's the matter?

MARY: Stop it, Dolly.

DOLLY: Mary?

MARY: Leave me alone. (*To get away from* DOLLY *she goes to the radio and switches it on*) Leave me alone.

DOLLY: What's the . . . Why are you . . . (MARY *emits a few whimpers*) Mary?

MOMMO: (*Has woken up and is watching them suspiciously*) Heh heh heh heh.

DOLLY: Good man Josie! (*And immediately back to* MARY) Mary? Why are you? Don't.

MOMMO: What's the plottin' an' whisperin' for?

DOLLY: Good man Josie! (*And immediately back to* MARY *again*) What? (*Crying*) What? . . . Don't. Please. (*Her arms around* MARY)

They are all speaking at once. MARY *and* DOLLY *crying.*

MOMMO: Oh yes. 'Good man, Josie!' Now! Good man Josie. And that was the second greeting he uttered that night.

DOLLY: What? . . . Shh! . . . What?

MARY: I don't know. I don't know.

46. Luke 2.10.

47. i.e. white lemonade.

MOMMO: He got no reply. Nor did he expect one. For Josie was a Greaney an' none was ever right in that fambly.

MARY: I wanted to come home.

DOLLY: What?

MARY: I had to come home.

MOMMO: An' the threadbare fashion'ry, not a top-coat to him, the shirt neck open, nor a gansey.

DOLLY: What?

MARY: This is our home.

DOLLY: I know.

MARY: This is our home.

DOLLY: I know.

MARY: (*Pulling away from* DOLLY *to shout at* MOMMO) Finish it, finish it, that much at least —

MOMMO: Och hona ho gus hah-haa! — for isn't it a good one!

MARY: Have done with it! — that much at least!

MOMMO: Och hona ho gus hah-haa!

MARY: (*To* DOLLY *who is following her*) Why don't you take off your coat! (*To* MOMMO) What was waiting for them at dawn when they got home in the morning?

MARY'S *remark to* DOLLY *has stopped* DOLLY *for a moment, but* DOLLY *comes to* MARY *and puts her arms around her again, the two of them crying through to the end. And* MOMMO *has not given way to the above, continuing without pause.*

MOMMO: Wo ho ho! — Heh heh heh! Wo ho ho! — Heh heh heh! — An' the tuthree raggedy top-coats on the others! — The poor an' neglected, the wretched an' forlorn — 'Twas the best night ever! — the impoverished an' hungry, eyes big as saucers, howlin' their defiance at the heavens through the ceilin' — Och hona ho gus hah-haa! — inviting of what else might come or care to come! Wo ho ho — Heh heh heh . . . (*Quietening down*) Though some say he had the knack of mendin' clocks, if he had. And none ever bested him at Ride-the-Blind-Donkey. Howandever. 'How the boys!' was Costello's third greeting, this time to two old men with their heads in the chimbley . . .

The lights fading through the above and music up — 'Notturno'.

ACT TWO

'Notturno' introducing Act Two: this being superimposed by the announcement for The Sunday Concert *on the radio together with* MOMMO'S *voice continuing her story.* MOMMO *has arrived at and is repeating the last section of the story where* MARY *left off in Act One.*

A sniff from MARY, *her tears are all but finished. Both she and* DOLLY *have their 'vodkas and white' and a slice of the birthday cake on plates beside them.*

MOMMO: An' John was in suspense.

DOLLY: Happy birthday!

MARY *sniffs back her tears and nods/smiles her thanks.*

MOMMO: An' then of a suddenness didn't the frown go disappearing up the stranger's cap.

MARY: I'm sorry for [*crying*].

MOMMO: He had it at last.

DOLLY: Ar — Phhh — not at all.

MOMMO: 'Well,' says he — oh lookin' the merchant between the two eyes — 'Well,' says he, 'I'm a better laugher than your Costello.'

A car passes by outside.

DOLLY: Did yeh see the helicopter on Friday? The plant, they say, is for closure. The Chinese are over.

MARY: Japanese. (*Her attention now returning to* MOMMO)

MOMMO: Now the merchant betrayed nothing.

DOLLY: I prefer to call them Chinese. (*Watching* MARY *go to* MOMMO)

DOLLY'S *mind beginning to tick over on how to present her 'proposition' to* MARY. MARY'S *nervous energy, after the lull, setting her to work again: washing her plate, removing the bed-warmer from the fire and slipping it into the bed at* MOMMO'S *feet, wrapping up the cake in tinfoil and putting it away, stoking the fire . . . but, predominantly, her eyes, concentration, always returning to* MOMMO; *a resoluteness increasing to have* MOMMO'S *story finished.*

MOMMO: He was well-versed at meeting company. And all he did was nod the once. (*She nods solemnly*)

DOLLY: I must get you a set of decent glasses the next time I'm in town.

MOMMO: Then, quick enough of him, referred the matter.

DOLLY: And I'm sure there's rats in that thatch.

MOMMO: An' 'Sh-Sheamus!' says he.

DOLLY: I could see Halligan the contractor about slatin' it.

MOMMO: 'Sh-Sheamus!' Calling Costello to come down.

DOLLY: What d'yeh think?

MARY: Shhh!

MOMMO: A laughing competition there would be.

DOLLY: (*Puzzled by* MARY's *behaviour*) And I was thinking of getting her a doll.

MARY: (*Eyes fastened on* MOMMO) No, let's see if she'll continue.

DOLLY: What?

MARY: Good enough. Then down steps the bold Costello.

MOMMO: Pardon? (*And instead of continuing, she starts singing*) 'Once I loved with fond affection, all my thoughts they were in thee, till a dork haired gurl deceived me, and no more he thought of me'

MARY: (*Through* MOMMO's *song, returning to the fire, all the time looking at* MOMMO) Down steps the bold Costello. You have some suggestion, something figured out.

DOLLY: What?

MARY: She's going to finish it.

DOLLY: Finish it? Why?

MARY: I don't know, I can't do anything the way things are.

MOMMO: Now. Ye like that one.

DOLLY: I thought you were trying to stop her. Sit down.

MARY: She's going to finish it —

DOLLY: You're always on your feet —

MARY: *Tonight*!

DOLLY: We'll have a chat, another drink.

MARY: (*Mechanically about to pour drinks, stops*) No. A laughing competition there *will* be! (*And goes to* MOMMO) Then down steps the bold Costello.

MOMMO: Pardon?

MARY: Then down steps the bold Costello.

MOMMO: Oh yes.

DOLLY: Well, as a matter of fact, I do have a proposition.

MARY: Shhh!

MOMMO: Then down steps the bold Costello. And 'Hah?' says he, seeing the gravity on the proprietor's mien. But the proprietor — John, to be sure — referred him like that (*she nods in one direction*). An' 'Hah?' says Costello, lookin' at the stranger. But weren't the two eyes of the stranger still mildly fixed on John, an' 'Hah?' says Costello lookin' back at John. But, there was no countin' John's cuteness. He takes the two steps backwards, then the one step to the sidewards slidin' his arse along the shelf, to 'scape the stranger's line of vision an' demonstrate for all his neutrality in the matter. 'Hah!' poor Costello goin', 'Hah!' to the one, 'Hah!' to the other — 'Hah!' 'Hah!' — the head swung nearly off his neck, an' now wonderin' I'm sure what on earth he'd done wrong — 'Hah!' — an' 'twas a bailey[1] in disguise maybe was the small little stranger. Costello was a delightful poacher.

DOLLY: Mary? (*Topping up the drinks*)

MOMMO: An' no help from John. Puffing a tuneless whistle at the ceiling!

DOLLY: I have a proposition.

MOMMO: 'Phuh-phuh-phuh-phuh.' (*John's tuneless whistle*)

MARY: (*Absently accepting drink*) Phuh-phuh-phuh-phuh.

MOMMO: Then says the stranger —

DOLLY: (*To herself*) Jesus!

MOMMO: His eyes now mild, lookin' straight ahead at nothing.

DOLLY: She's (MARY) gone loopey too.

MARY: Good girl.

MOMMO: Though 'twas polite introduction — 'How d'yeh do, Mr Costello, I'm Seamus O'Toole.' Costello: 'Hah! I'm very well, thanking you!' His face was a study. An' 'Oh,' says John of Costello, 'He's a Sh-Sheamus too, phuh-phuh-phuh-phuh.' 'I know that,' says the stranger, 'but I'm a better laugher than 'm.' 'Kuhaa, uck-uck-uck-khuck, kuh-haa a haa!' In Costello's throat. In response didn't the stranger make serious chuckle. And in response to that didn't Costello roar out a laugh.

A silent 'Jesus' from DOLLY. *She decides to take off her coat and see what effect flaunting her pregnancy will have.*

MARY: } (*Silently with* MOMMO) Then loud as you please.
MOMMO: } Then loud as you please says Costello: 'He says, he says, he says,' says he, 'he's a better.' (*She claps her mouth shut*) An' that was far as he got. For in the suddenness of a discovery he found out that he was cross.

'Ara phat?'[2] says he. He was nimble. The full size of him skippin' backwards an' forwards, the dancing antics of a boxing-man. An' lookin' 'bout at his supporters, now hushed an' on their marks, 'He says, he says, he says,' says he, 'he's a better laugher than me!'

What! Sure they never heard the likes. Nor how

1. A law officer.
2. 'phat' is a common Connemara pronunciation of 'what': 'Ara phat' implies aggression — 'What the hell are you saying?'

on earth to deal with it. An' the upset on their own man's face! — Oh, they wor greatly taken 'back. They wor. Oh they wor. An' not up to disseration[3] things wor lookin' dangerous.

DOLLY: She's getting tired — the creature.

MARY: Shhh!

DOLLY: Cheers!

MARY: Cheers — Things were looking dangerous.

MOMMO: They were . . . Oh, they wor.

MARY: 'Ary give me [a] pint outa that.'

MOMMO: Costello? (MARY *nods*) Swivellin' an' near knockin' them wor behind him. But then in retraction comes wheelin' back 'round, the head like a dunkey's flung up at the ceilin', eyes near out the sockets an' the big mouth threwn open, but God bless us an' save us, all the emission was a class of a rattle'd put shame to a magpie.

MARY: (*Silently, excited*) Shame to a magpie.

MOMMO: Now he was humbled, the big head on him hangin', went back to his corner, turned his back on all present — The hump that was on him! Oh his feelin's wor hurted. (*She yawns*) Oh ho hun-neo.

MARY: Aa no.

MOMMO: Oh ho hun-neo!

MARY: Don't be pretendin', you had a little nap a while ago.

MOMMO: Put the sup of milk there for me now for the night.

MARY: I'll get the milk later. And the others. Mommo?

MOMMO: Lookin' wildly, one to the other, from their giant to the stranger, none knowin' what to do.

DOLLY: (*Getting the milk*) Let her settle down.

MARY: But they were vexed.

MOMMO: An' they knew it? (MARY *nods agreement and encouragement*) Oh they knew they were cross. An' strainin' towards the stranger like mastiffs on chains, fit to tear him asunder.

DOLLY: And I don't know if you've noticed, Mary, but the turf out there won't last the winter. (*Approaching with the milk*) Here we are! I'll see to the turf.

MARY: (*Takes milk from* DOLLY) No milk.

DOLLY: What are you at?

MARY: No milk! (*She puts it away*)

MOMMO: And even Josie! — the odd one!

DOLLY: (*To herself*) Jesus Josie!

MOMMO: That always stood aloof! Even he was infected with the venom [*that*] had entered, an' all of the floor was 'vailable round him he began to walk circles screechin' 'Hackah!' at the stranger.

DOLLY: I want to have a talk!

MARY: Later.

DOLLY: A plan, a proposition.

MARY: Later.

MOMMO: Pardon?

DOLLY: And I've a little problem of my own.

MARY: I think I've noticed. Go on, Mommo, no one is stopping you.

MOMMO: Where's the milk for the night, Miss?

MARY: Then striding to the stranger — Costello: 'Excuse me there now a minute, Mister — '

DOLLY: Mary —

MARY: No! No! 'Excuse me there now a minute now — '

MOMMO: Pardon?

MARY: 'But what did you say to me there a minute ago?' (*Waits for a beat to see if* MOMMO *will continue*) . . . 'That you're a better laugher than me, is it?' . . . 'Well, would you care to put a small bet on it?'

MOMMO: (*Suspiciously, but childlike*) How do you know that?

MARY: Oh, I was told. But I never heard all of the story.

MOMMO: Hah? . . . Ar shurrup [*shut up*] outa[4] that.

MARY: 'Well would you care to put a small bet on it?' And 'No' saying the stranger going back to his wife. 'But you're challenging me, challenging me, challenging me, y'are!'

MOMMO: 'No' saying the stranger, ''twas only a notion,' his eyes on the floor. For why? Foreseeing fatalistic danger. (MARY *nods solemnly*) Then joined the two little smiles cross the width of his mouth which he gave up to the hero as evidence sincere that he was for abnegating. Can yeh go on?

MARY: No. (*Cajoling*) Can you?

MOMMO: Well. Costello was for agreein'? An' for understandin'? But th' others wor all circlin', jostlin', an' pushin' — Josie flailin' like a thrasher — eggin' for diversion. 'He is, he is, challe'gin' yeh, he is!' 'Up Bochtán, up Bochtán, Bochtán forever!' Putting confusion in the head of Costello again. But

3. discussion.

4. out of, meaning 'come out of, stop that line of talk'.

the stranger — a cute[5] man — headin' for the door, gives [*the*] nod an' wink to Costello so he'd comprehend the better the excitation [*that*] is produced by the aberration of a notion. Then in fullness of magistrature, 'Attention!' roaring Costello, 'Attention!' roaring he to declare his verdict was dismissal, an' he decreed that 'twas all over.

MARY: Yes?

MOMMO: An' 'twas.

MARY: Aa, you have more for me?

MOMMO: (*Childlike*) Have I?

MARY *nods.* MOMMO *thinking her own thoughts, then she shakes her head.*

MARY: A laughing competition there would be.

MOMMO: (*Absently*) A what?

DOLLY: She's exhausted.

MARY: She's not.

MOMMO: Where was I? ... The jostlin' an' pushin' ... (*Then her eyes searching the floor, in half-memory lamenting trampled sweets*) The sweets.

MARY: Here they are. [*The ones that* DOLLY *brought*]

MOMMO: The sweets. (*Rejecting the sweets, her eyes still searching the floor*) In the jostlin' an' pushin' ... The sweets.

MARY: Here they are, under your pillow. Here.

MOMMO: (*Takes them absently, then becomes conscious of them; issues a warning*) An' I know how many was in it.

DOLLY: Can't you see she's —

MARY: She's not.

MOMMO: Three.

DOLLY: And you're worn out too, Mary.

MARY: But if Costello decreed 'twas all over, how did it start?

MOMMO: How did — ? The small stranger, I told yeh, goin' out to check the weather for as had been forecasted the thaw was settling in.

MARY: I see!

MOMMO: An' sure they could have got home.

MARY: Yes?

MOMMO: They could have got home. (*Brooding, growls; then*) Costello could decree. All others could decree. (*Quiet anger*) But what about the things had been vexin' *her* for years? No, a woman isn't stick or stone. The forty years an' more in the one bed together an' he to rise in the mornin', and not give her a glance. An' so long it had been he had called her by first name, she'd near forgot it herself ... Brigit ... Hah? ... An' so she thought he hated her ... An'. (*Her head comes up, eyes fierce*) 'Yis, yis-yis, he's challe'gin' ye, he is!' She gave it to the Bochtáns. And her husband returning? — maybe he would recant, but she'd renege matters no longer. 'Och hona ho gus hah-haa!' — she hated him too.

MARY *leans back: she has not heard this part of the story before.*

MARY: ... And what happened then?

MOMMO: An' what happened then. Tried to pacify her. (*Growls*) But-there-was-none-would-assuage-her. An' what happened then, an' what happened then. 'Stand up then,' says Costello. They already standin'. 'Scath siar uaim'[6] to the rest to clear back off the floor. The arena was ready.

MARY: And what happened then?

MOMMO: An' what happened then ... Tired, tired.

MARY: Mommo?

MOMMO: (*Now regarding* MARY *with suspicion*) ... Shthap! ... (*To herself*) Tired ... What's your business here? ... There are no newses here for anyone about anything. Heh heh heh heh!

DOLLY: It's ten to ten. So he'll hardly come now, so off with yeh to sleep. There's the good girl, and we'll hear your confession again tomorrow night. There, there now. (*To* MARY) That was a new bit. There, there now. She's in bye-byes.

MARY: (*Quietly*) She's not.

DOLLY: She's asleep! Mommo! ... She's asleep, it's ten to ten. Ten to ten, 1984, and I read it — how long ago was it? — that by 1984 we'd all be going on our holidays to the moon in *Woman's Own.*

MARY: She's not asleep.

DOLLY: I'm not arg'in' about it. She's — resting.

MARY: And I'm going to rouse her again in a minute. You were saying?

DOLLY: (*Stretching herself, flaunting her stomach*) And a telly would fit nicely over there.

MARY: A plan, a proposition, you have it all figured out?

DOLLY: And I'm sorry now I spent the money on the video. No one uses it. You'd make more use of it. It has a remote. (*In answer to* MARY's *query 'remote'*) Yeh know? One of them things yeh —

5. cunning.

6. Literally, 'Shadow away from me', i.e. 'Back off'.

[*hold in your hand*] — and — (*further demonstrates*) — control.

MARY: I have a video here already [*Mommo*]. What's your plan?

DOLLY: Wait'll we have a drink. She's guilty.

MARY: Guilty of what?

DOLLY: I don't know.

MARY: Then why —

DOLLY: I'm not arg'in' with yeh. (*Offering to top up* MARY'*s drink*)

MARY: Why can't you ever finish a subject or talk straight? I don't want another drink.

DOLLY: I'm talking straight.

MARY: What's on your mind, Dolly? I'm up to you.

DOLLY: There's no one up to Dolly.

MARY: Tck!

DOLLY: I'm talkin' straight! (*Another car passes by outside*) Traffic. The weekend-long meeting at the computer plant place. And all the men, busy, locked outside the fence.

MARY: (*Abrupt movement to the table*) On second thoughts. (*And pours lemonade into her glass*)

DOLLY: (*Is a bit drunk now and getting drunker*) No, wait a minute.

MARY: What-are-you-saying, Dolly?

DOLLY: An' that's why she goes on like a gramophone. Guilty.

MARY: This is nonsense.

DOLLY: And so are you.

MARY: So am I!

DOLLY: An' you owe me a debt.

MARY: What do I owe you?

DOLLY: *And* she *had* to get married.

MARY: (*To herself*) Impossible.

DOLLY: No! No! — Mary? No. Wait a minute —

MARY: (*Fingers to her forehead*) Dolly, I'm —

DOLLY: I'm talkin' straight.

MARY: Trying to get a grip of — Ahmm. I'm trying to find — ahmm. Get control of — ahmm. My life, Dolly.

DOLLY: Yes. You're trying to say, make head and tail of it all, talk straight, like myself. No, Mary, hold on. You told me one thing, I'll tell you another. D'yeh remember the pony-and-trap-Sunday-outings? I don't. But I remember — now try to contradict this — the day we buried Grandad. Now I was his favourite so I'll never forget it. And whereas — No, Mary! — whereas! She stood there over that hole in the ground like a rock — like a duck, like a duck, her chest stickin' out. Not a tear.

MARY: What good would tears have been?

DOLLY: Not a tear. And — *And!* — Tom buried in that same hole in the ground a couple of days before. Not a tear, then or since. (*Wandering to the table for another drink*) Oh I gathered a few 'newses' about our Mommo.

MARY: Maybe she's crying now.

DOLLY: *All* of them had to get married except myself and Old Sharp Eyes. Mrs McGrath the sergeant said. But she bore a bastard all the same. Her Stephen. (*Wanders to the radio and switches it off*) The hypocrite.

MARY: Leave it on.

DOLLY: I've a proposition.

MARY: It's the Sunday Concert. Switch it on.

DOLLY: (*Switches on the radio*) So what d'yeh think?

MARY: About what?

DOLLY: The slated (*gestures roof*), the other things I mentioned.

MARY: It would stop the place falling down for someone alright.

DOLLY: An' half this place is mine, I'll sign it over.

MARY: To whom?

DOLLY: To whom. To Jack-Paddy-Andy, to Kitty-the-Hare, to you. And there might be — other things — you might need.

MARY: What else could anyone need?

DOLLY *now looking a bit hopeless, pathetic, offering a cigarette to* MARY, *lighting it for* MARY.

DOLLY: An' would you like another? [*Drink*] (MARY *shakes her head*) Lemonade?

MARY: No. What are you trying to say?

DOLLY: An' the turf out there won't last the winter.

MARY: You said that.

DOLLY: And one of the children. (*She looks at* MARY *for a reaction. But all this time* MARY'*s mind, or half of it, is on* MOMMO) Yeh. Company for yeh.

MARY: I get all this if I stay.

DOLLY: Or go.

MARY: (*Becoming more alert*) ... What? ... You want me to go? With one of the children? ... *Which* one of the children?

DOLLY: (*Continues with closed eyes through the following*) Jesus, I'm tired. A brand new one. (MARY *laughs incredulously*) Would you? Would you? Would you?

MARY: What?

DOLLY: Take him. It.

MARY: With me?

DOLLY: (*Nods*) An' no one need be any the wiser.

MARY: And if I stay?

DOLLY: Say it's yours. It'll all blow over in a month.

MARY: You're crazy.

DOLLY: That makes three of us. I'm not crazy. I'm — as you can see.

MARY: Yes, I've wondered for some time, but I thought you couldn't — you couldn't! — be that stupid.

A car passes by outside.

DOLLY: More take-aways for the lads. (*She starts wearily for her coat*) My, but they're busy.

MARY: No one is asking you to leave.

DOLLY: (*Stops. Eyes closed again*) You'll be paid.

MARY: I've heard you come up with a few things before, but!

DOLLY: Stephen'll kill me.

MARY: What about me?

DOLLY: Or he'll cripple me.

MARY: Do you ever think of others!

DOLLY: Or I'll fix him.

MARY: And you'll be out — gallivanting — again tomorrow night.

DOLLY: And the night after, and the night after. And you can be sure of that.

MARY: How long are you gone?

DOLLY: Six, seven months.

MARY: Six, seven months.

DOLLY: Trying to conceal it.

MARY: Who's the father?

DOLLY: I have my suspicions.

MARY: But he's busy perhaps tonight, picketing?

DOLLY: Yes, very busy. Travelling at the sound of speed. But the Chinese'll get them. (*Opens her eyes*) Hmm?

MARY: And this is the help? This is what you've been figuring out?

DOLLY: You can return the child after, say, a year. If you want to.

MARY: I thought your figuring things out were about — ? (*She indicates* MOMMO. *Then she goes to* MOMMO) Mommo, open your eyes, time to continue.

DOLLY: After a year it'll be easy to make up a story.

MARY: *Another* story! (*She laughs*)

DOLLY: You're a nurse, you could help me if you wanted to.

MARY: Trying all my life to get out of *this* situation and now you want to present me with the muddle of your stupid life to make *sure* the saga goes on.

DOLLY: Oh the saga will go on.

MARY: Mommo!

DOLLY: I'll see to that, one way or the other.

MARY: (*To herself*) I go away with a brand new baby. Mommo! (*To* DOLLY) Where! Where do I go? (DOLLY *nods*) You have that figured out too?

DOLLY: We can discuss that. (MARY *laughs*) You're its aunt.

MARY: Its! (*She laughs*)

DOLLY: Aunt! — Aunt! — And you're a nurse! — Aunt!

MARY: Mommo! I know you're not asleep.

DOLLY: (*Shrugs*) Okay. (*Now talking to herself*) And if it's a boy you can call it Tom, and if it's a girl you can call it Tom. (*Continues talking through the following, wandering to the fire and sitting there.* DOLLY'*s speech, though to herself, dominating*)

MOMMO: Supa milk, where's the milk?

MARY: Later.

MOMMO: Miss!

MARY: We're going to finish your nice story. Now! To continue. Where had you got to? Costello clearing his throat.

MOMMO: But in the jostlin' an' pushin' (*Eyes searching the floor*) The sweets ... the sweets ....

DOLLY: (*Through the above*) But I've discussed something with someone. 'Cause if I don't get him he'll get me. But I know now how to get him and that's what got me saving, of late. I've made the preliminary enquiries. That little service of fixing someone is available — 'cause it's in demand — even round here. I've discussed that.

MOMMO: The sweets.

MARY: (*To* DOLLY) Have you finished?

DOLLY: (*Intensely*) You had it easy!

MARY: I had it easy? No one who came out of this — house — had it easy. (*To herself*) I had it easy.

DOLLY: You-had-it-easy. The bright one, top of your class!

MARY: (*To herself*) What would you know about it?

DOLLY: Top marks! — Hardly had your Leaving Cert. and you couldn't wait to be gone.

MARY: I won't deny that.

DOLLY: You can't! State Registered Nurse before you were twenty —

MARY: Twenty-one.

DOLLY: A Sister before you were twenty-five,

Assistant Matron at the age of thirty.

MARY: And a midwife.

DOLLY: Yes, S.R.N., C.M.B., D.D.T![7]

MARY: All very easy.

DOLLY: Couldn't get away fast enough.

MARY: But I came back, Dolly.

DOLLY: Aren't you great?

MARY: I failed. It all failed. I'm as big a failure as you, and that's some failure. (DOLLY *is stopped for a moment by* MARY's *admission*) You hadn't considered that?

MOMMO *has started rambling again, repeating the last section of the story which she told earler, down to 'The arena was ready'.*

MOMMO: An' sure they could have got home. An' the small stranger, her husband sure, was goin' out to check the weather, for as had been forecasted the thaw was ....

DOLLY: (*Her voice over* MOMMO's) No! No! You had it easy! — You had it — You had — I had — I had ten! — I had a lifetime! A lifetime! Here with herself, doin' her every bidding, listenin' to her seafóid [*rambling*] gettin' worse till I didn't know where I was! — Pissin' in the bed beside me — I had a lifetime! Then the great Stephen — the surprise of it! — comes coortin'! Never once felt any — real — warmth from him — what's wrong with him? — but he's my rescuer, my saviour. But then, no rhyme or reason — He could've got a job at that plant, but he couldn't wait to be gone either! Then waitin' for the hero, my rescuer, the sun shining out of his eighty-five-pounds-a-week arse, to come home at Christmas. No interest in me — oh, he used me! — or in children, or the rotten thatch or the broken window, or Conor above moving in his fence from *this* side. I'm fightin' all the battles. Still fightin' the battles. And what d'yeh think he's doin' now this minute? Sittin' by the hearth in Coventry, is he? Last Christmas an' he was hardly off the bus, Old Sharp Eyes whisperin' into his ear about me. Oooo, but he waited. Jesus, how I hate him! Jesus, how I hate them! Men! Had his fun and games with me that night, *and* first thing in the morning. Even sat down to eat the hearty breakfast I made. Me thinkin', still no warmth, but maybe it's goin' to be okay. Oooo, but I should've known from *experience* about - the - great - up - stand - in' - Steph - en - evrabody's - fav - our - ite. Because, next thing he has me by the hair of the head, fistin' me down in the mouth, Old Sharp Eyes there, noddin' her head every time he struck an' struck an' kicked an' kicked an' pulled me round the house by the hair of the head. Jesus, men! (*Indicating the outdoors where she had her sex*) You-think-I-enjoy! I-use-*them*! Jesus, hypocrisy! An' then, me left with my face like a balloon — you saw a lot of me last Christmas, didn't yeh? — my body black and blue, the street angel an' his religious mother — 'As true as Our Lady is in heaven now, darlin's' — over the road to visit you an' Mommo with a little present an' a happy an' a holy Christmas now darlin's an' blessed St.-fuckin'-Jude an' all the rest of them flyin' about for themselves up there.

MOMMO: The arena was ready. A laughing competition there would be. (*She coughs in preparation*)

DOLLY: (*At* MOMMO) Och hona ho gus hah-haa! Jesus, how I hate them! I hate her [MOMMO] — I hate this house — She hates you — I hate my own new liquorice-all-sorts-coloured house —

MARY: } (*Ashen-face, shaking her head*) No... No.
DOLLY: } She! — She! — She hates you.

MARY: No.

MOMMO: } 'Wuff a wuff! A wuha wuha wuha wuha, wock-ock och ock och och ock — Naaw.'
DOLLY: } And I hate you.

MARY: Why?

DOLLY: } Why.
MOMMO: } 'Heh heh heh heh,' proud, aisy an' gentle.

DOLLY: You don't know terror, you don't know hatred, you don't know desperation.

MOMMO: An' sure Costello's laughin' wasn't right at all.

DOLLY: No one came out of this house had it easy but you had it easy.

MOMMO: 'Quock uck-uck-uck-uck quock?' (*Unwrapping a sweet and putting it in her mouth*)

MARY: Dolly, stop it at once.

DOLLY: 'Dolly, stop it at once.' Look, go away an' stay away.

MARY: Dolly —

MOMMO: 'Heh heh heh heh heh.'

DOLLY: 'This is our home' — You'll need a few bob, I'll give it to you, and my grand plan: I'll look after things here, all fronts, including lovee lovee

7. State-Registered Nurse; Certificate of Midwifery Board. D.D.T., a well-known poison/disinfectant, is ironically linked to these qualifications.

Mommo, an' Stephen'll never raise a finger to me again.

MARY: You're —

DOLLY: Am I?

MARY: You're —

DOLLY: Am I? We'll see — Hah! — if I'm bluffing.

MARY: Have you finished ranting?

DOLLY: Ooh, ranting!

MOMMO: (*Looking at the floor*) The sweets . . . the sweets (*Whispering*)

MARY: You're spoilt, you're unhappy, you're running round in circles.

DOLLY: *I'm* running round in circles? Suitcase packed — How many times? Puttin' on airs — look at the boots, look at the lady! You're stayin', you're goin', 'I need to talk to someone' — Fuck off! 'I wanted to come home, I had to come home' — Fuck off!

MARY: Stop it this moment, I won't have it. You're frightening her.

In reply to 'frightening her', DOLLY *indicates* MOMMO *who is now sucking a sweet, lost in her own thoughts. Then* DOLLY *turns to look into the fire, her back to* MARY; *she continues in quieter tone.*

DOLLY: The countryside produced a few sensations in the last couple of years, but my grand plan: I'll show them what can happen in the dark of night in a field. I'll come to grips with my life.

Short silence. MOMMO's *eyes fixed on* MARY.

MOMMO: Miss! . . . Do I know you? (MARY *shakes her head, 'No': she is afraid to speak: if she does she will cry*) . . . Pardon?

MARY *shakes her head.*

DOLLY: (*To the fire*) I'll finish another part of this family's history in grander style than any of the others.

MARY: . . . The arena was ready.

MOMMO: 'Twas.

MARY: But Costello's laugh wasn't right at all.

MOMMO: Then ''Scuse me a minute,' says he lickin' his big mouth, puts a spit in the one hand, then one in the other, an' ponderin' the third that he sent to the floor. (*Coughs*) 'A wuff.'

DOLLY: A wuff, wuff!

MOMMO: 'A wuha wuha wuha wuha, a wuha huha huha hoo, quock-uckina na hoona ho ho, a wo ho ho ho ho ho ho!' An' twasn't bad at all. Was it? An' Costello knew it. An' by way of exper'ment, though 'twasn't his turn, had a go at it again, his ear cocked to himself.

DOLLY: Heh heh heh heh heh heh heh — We filled half that graveyard.

MOMMO: We did. But then, ''Scuse me too,' says the stranger makin' Costello stiffen, an' 'Heh heh heh, heh heh heh, heh heh heh,' chuckled he.

DOLLY: Heh heh he, heh heh heh, heh heh heh — Well, I'll fill the other half.

MARY: (*Ferociously at* DOLLY) Shthap!

DOLLY: Och hona ho gus hah-haa!

MOMMO: Pardon?

MARY: (*To* MOMMO) . . . No, you don't know me. But I was here once, and I ran away to try and blot out here. I didn't have it easy. Then I tried bad things, for a time, with someone. So I came back, thinking I'd find — something — here, or, if I didn't, I'd put everything right. Mommo? And tonight I thought I'd make a last try. Live out the — story — finish it, move on to a place where, perhaps, we could make some kind of new start. I want to help you.

DOLLY: And yourself.

MARY: And myself. Mommo?

MOMMO: Where's the milk for the night?

MARY *nods that she will get it.*

MOMMO: Tck!

MARY: (*Gently to* DOLLY) She may hate me, you may hate me. But I don't hate her. I love her for what she's been through, and she's all that I have. So she has to be my only consideration. She doesn't understand. Do you understand, Dolly? Please . . . And I'm sorry.

DOLLY: (*Drunkenly*) For what?

MARY: (*Turns away tearfully*) I'm not the saint you think I am.

DOLLY: The what? Saint? That'd be an awful thing to be. 'Wo ho ho, ho ho ho!'

MARY *puts the milk by the bed.*

MOMMO: Yis. Did yeh hear? The full style *was* returnin' — 'Wo ho ho, wo ho ho!' An' like a great archbishop turnin' on his axis, nods an' winks to his minions that he knew all along. The cheers that went up in John Mah'ny's that night!

An' now what did they start doin', the two gladiators, circlin' the floor, eyes riveted together, silent in quietude to find the advantage, save the odd whoop from Costello, his fist through the ceilin', an' the small little stranger' bate[8] the odd little dance.

8. beat out.

Now! Then. And.

'Yeh sold all your cargo?' Costello roarin' it like a master to friken[9] a scholar. The laugh from his attendants, but then so did the stranger.

'Where [*are*] yeh bound for?' — stern Costello — 'Your destination, a Mhico?'[10]

'Ballindineside, your worship.'

'Ballindineside, a Thighearna!'[11]

DOLLY: Oh ho ho, wo ho ho.

MOMMO: 'Cunn ether iss syha soory.' [*Coinn iotair is saidhthe suaraighe*]

DOLLY: Hounds of rage and bitches of wickedness![12]

MOMMO: An' the description despicable more fitting their own place.

DOLLY: (*To the fire, almost dreamily*) Why the fuck did he marry me?

It only lasts a second, but MARY *holds a glance on the now pathetic-looking* DOLLY.

MOMMO: 'A farmer?' says Costello. 'A goose one,' says the stranger. An' t'be fair to the Bochtáns they plauded the self-denigration.

DOLLY: I don't hate anyone.

MOMMO: 'An' yourself?' says the stranger. 'Oh now you're questionin' me,' says Costello. 'An' Rabbits,' screeches Josie, 'Hull-hull-hull, hull-hull-hull!'

DOLLY: (*Stands*) What did I get up for?

MARY *and* DOLLY *forget themselves and start laughing at* MOMMO'*s dramatisation of this section.*

MOMMO: An', 'Rabbits!' says the stranger. 'Rabbits! says he, 'heh heh'. 'Well, heh heh heh, heh heh he, heh heh heh, heh heh heh!' 'What's the cause of your laughter?' Costello frownin' moroya.[13] [*Mar dhea; pretending seriousness*] 'Bunny rabbits!' says the stranger — 'is *that* what you're in!' (MARY *and* DOLLY *laughing their own laughter*)

'Not at all, me little man,' says Costello, 'I've a herd of trinamanooses[14] in Clash back the road'.

'Tame ones?' says the stranger.

'Tame ones, what else, of a certainty,' says Costello, 'An' the finest breed for 'atin'[15] sure!'

'But for the Townies though for 'atin',' says the stranger most sincerely. An' not able to keep the straight face, Costello roared out a laughter an' gave beck to his attendants to plaud the stranger's cleverality. (*The three of them laughing*) Now wasn't he able for them?

DOLLY: Where's the flashlamp?

MOMMO: An' the contrariety an' venom was in it while ago!

DOLLY: I want to go out the back.

MARY: It's on top of the dresser.

MOMMO: But now they couldn't do enough for that decent man an' woman, all vying with each other — an' sure they didn't have it — to buy treats for the strangers. Tumblers of whiskey an' bumpers of port wine. A strange auld world right enough. But in some wisdom of his own he made it this way. 'Twas the nicest night ever.

DOLLY: (*Has got the flashlamp; a plea in her voice*) Mary?

MARY: 'Twas the nicest night ever.

MOMMO: But they'd yet to find the topic would keep them laughin' near forever.

DOLLY: Mary?

MOMMO: Then one'd laugh solo, the other'd return, then Costello'd go winkin' an' they'd both laugh together, a nod from the stranger [*and*] they'd stop the same moment to urge riotous chorus, give the others a chance.

DOLLY: Don't want the fuggin' flashlamp. (*She discards it. Then, as if driving cattle out of the house, she goes out the back door*) How! — How! — How! — How! — Hup! — Skelong! Bleddy[16] cows! Howa-that-how! — Hup! Hup! Hup there!

MARY: What topic did they find?

MOMMO: But there can be no gainsayin' it, Costello clear had the quality laugh. 'Who ho ho, ho ho ho' in the barrel of his chest would the great rumbles start risin', the rich rolls of round sound out of his mouth, to explode in the air an' echo back rev'berations. The next time demonstratin' the range of his skill, go flyin' aloft to the heights of registration — 'Hickle-ickle-ickle-ickle!' — like a hen runnin' demented from ardent attentions, over-persistent, of a cock in the yard after his business. Now!

MARY: What about Grandad?

MOMMO: Who?

MARY: The stranger.

9. frighten.
10. my son (jocular or condescending).
11. Your Lordship/Worship.
12. Translation of the preceding line.
13. Irish *mar dhea* — 'indeed; sez you'.
14. imaginary animals: a made-up Yorkshire word.
15. eating.
16. bloody.

MOMMO: Not much by way of big sound?

MARY: No.

MOMMO: Or rebounding modulation?

MARY: No.

MOMMO: But was that a stipulation?

MARY: No.

MOMMO: He knew the tricks of providence and was cunning of exertion. Scorn for his style betimes? (MARY *nods*) But them wor his tactics.

MARY: And he was most in control.

MOMMO: He was. (*She yawns*) Tired.

MARY: No. Mommo. It *is* a nice story. And you've nearly told it all tonight. Except for the last piece that you never tell. Hmm?

MOMMO: Who was that woman?

MARY: What woman?

MOMMO: Tck! — That woman just went out the door there. (*Mimicking* DOLLY) 'Hup-hup-howa that'?

MARY: That was Dolly ... Dolly.

MOMMO: An' does she always behave that way?

MARY: Sometimes.

MOMMO: (*Thinking about this: it does not make sense to her. Then eyes scrutinising* MARY; *in this moment she is possibly close to recognising* MARY)... Who are [*you*]?

MARY: Try a guess.

MOMMO: Here she is again!

DOLLY *comes in. She looks bloated and tired. She wolfs down the slice of cake which she deliberately resisted earlier. Then looking for her bag, her overcoat, putting on her overcoat, etc.*

DOLLY: And I've been starving myself.

MOMMO: (*Whispering*) She'd eat yeh out of house an' home ... Is there something you require, Miss, that you're rummaging for over there?

DOLLY: (*Realises she is being spoken to: then humourlessly to herself*) Your pension.

MOMMO: Oh it's time for ye both to be going — ten to ten. He doesn't like calling when there's strangers in the house.

MARY: We're off now in a minute. What was that topic again that kept them on laughing?

MOMMO: Misfortunes. (*She yawns*)

MARY: Mommo? (MOMMO's *eyes are closed*)

DOLLY: (*To herself, looking at the door*) I hate going home.

MARY: Mommo? Or if you like the bit about 'Out of the bushes more of them was comin'.'

MOMMO: Tom is in Galway. (*Opens her eyes*) I bet him with nettles. Mitchin'[17] from school. D'yeh think he remembers?

MARY: (*Gently*) No.

MOMMO: (*Closes her eyes*) Well, I don't remember ... I don't remember any more of it.

MARY: (*Tired, futile*) And out of the bushes more of them was comin'?

MOMMO: (*Drowsily*) I don't remember any more of it.

MARY: Wherever were their hovels, holes in the ground ... 'cause 'twas place of desolation.

DOLLY: (*Another plea*) Mary?

MARY: (*Eyes continue on* MOMMO *who is now asleep*) Sit down.

DOLLY *remains standing, wondering is there hope for her in* MARY's *remark.*

DOLLY: ... What were you trying to do with her?

MARY: 'Twas only a notion ... She's asleep.

DOLLY: ... Maybe she'd wake up again?

MARY: (*Slight shake of her head, 'No'*) Sit down?

DOLLY: (*Sits*) ... What're yeh goin' to do?

MARY: (*Slight shake of her head; a tremulous sigh*) Ahmm.

DOLLY: ... Back to the nursing? (*Slight shake of the head from* MARY) ... What?

MARY: No. That wasn't me at all. And no confidence now anyway. (*She collects up a few odds and ends and puts them in the suitcase*) Who's looking after the children?

DOLLY: Maisie Kelly. They're stayin' the night in her house. She knows. She said if I had to go away for a day or anything ... I don't want to go away.

MARY: (*Absently*) The nicest night ever.

DOLLY: ... What were we doin' that night?

MARY: Ahmm. The shade on that light: Do you mind if I? (*She switches off the light and lights a candle*) We let the fire go out. The cursed paraffin. (*She has collected up a silver-backed hairbrush and a clothes brush*)

DOLLY: ... But if you're not going back to the nursing.

MARY: There must be *something*, some future for me, somewhere. (*She is brushing the back of* DOLLY's *coat*) I can certainly scrub floors.

DOLLY: (*A little irritably*) What're you doin'?

MARY: Just a little — dust — here.

DOLLY: Who cares?

17. Playing truant.

MARY: It's just that people talk at the slightest.

DOLLY: Na bac na ciaróigí [*ciaróga*]. [*Don't mind the gossipers*]

MARY: When I was a nurse there was a patient, terminal, an elderly woman and we became very close.

DOLLY: Do you care what people say?

MARY: I'm afraid I do. There. (*The coat is brushed; she now brushes* DOLLY'S *hair*) I don't know why she used to watch me or why she chose to make friends with me.

DOLLY: What're you doin' now?

MARY: But one day she said, in the middle of — whatever — conversation we were having, you're going to be alright. Mary. Simple remark. But it took me by surprise. Like, as if it was a promised blessing. And why I should have — (*shrugs*) carried it and — (*shrugs*) believed in it for, oh, twenty years? until recently, I don't know. There. (DOLLY'S *hair is brushed*) She left me these (*the brushes*) and this (*the teapot*) and the book. (*She dumps the lot into the suitcase*)

DOLLY: If I sat down to write a book.

MARY: Though the book has always depressed me a bit. *Winter Words*.[18] I can't do a thing for you, Dolly. Can you lend me a hundred quid? (DOLLY *nods*) Well, that's it then.

DOLLY *is just sitting there looking into the fire;* MARY *standing, her back to the suitcase, her hands resting on it: two figures frozen in time. Then the cortège of cars approaching, passing the house (at comparatively slow speed).*

DOLLY: The funeral. The weekend-long meeting is over. Now are they travelling at the sound of speed? (MARY *laughs*) I told you the Chinese'd get them. (*They are beginning to laugh. Looking at her stomach — the bulge*) Good man Josie! (MARY *laughs.* DOLLY *joins in the laughter.* DOLLY *flaunting herself, clowning*) And you're his aunt! (*They laugh louder; the laughter getting out of hand*) (*To her stomach*) Good man Josie! . . . (*Uproariously*) Jesus, misfortunes!

Then the unexpected, MOMMO'S *voice.*

MOMMO: Scoth — caoc! (*Silence*) What time is it?

MARY: Seven! (*In a whisper, waiting, frozen*)

MOMMO: Explosions of laughter an' shouts of hurrahs!

DOLLY: (*Sits heavily on the bed*) Jesus, I'm tired.

MARY: (*Pleading with* DOLLY) Dolly!

MOMMO: For excess of joy.

DOLLY: 'S alright, 'salright, Mommo: I'm Dolly, I'm like a film star. (*To* MARY) 'S alright.

MOMMO: An' didn't he ferret out her eyes to see how she was farin', an' wasn't she titherin'[19] with the best of them an' weltin' her thighs. No heed on her now to be gettin' on home. No. But offerin' to herself her own congratulations at hearin' herself laughin'. An' then, like a girl, smiled at her husband, an' his smile back so shy like the boy he was in youth. An' the moment was for them alone. Unawares of all cares, unawares of all the others. An' how long before since their eyes had met, mar gheal dhá gréine,[20] glistenin' for each other. Not since long and long ago.

And now Costello's big hand was up for to call a recession. 'But how,' says he, 'is it to be indisputably decided who is the winner?' And a great silence followed. None was forgettin' this was a contest. An' the eyes that wor dancin', now pending the answer, glazed an' grave in dilation: 'Twas a difficult question. (*Quietly*) Och-caw. Tired of waiting male intelligence, 'He who laughs last'. Says she.

An' 'cause 'twas a woman that spoke it, I think Costello was frikened, darts class of a glance at her an' — (*She gulps*) 'That's what I thought,' says he.

But wasn't that his mistake? ever callin' the recession an' he in full flight. 'Cause now, ready himself as he would, with his coughin' an' spittin', the sound emanating from a man of his talent, so forced and ungracious, he'd stop it himself.

(*Whispering*) 'He's lost it,' says someone. Och hona ho gus hah-haa!

(*Whispering*) 'He should never have stopped.' Their faces like mice.

An' he'd 'tempt it an' 'tempt it an' 'tempt it again. Ach an fear mór as Bochtán [*But the big man from Bochtán*] in respiratory disaster is i ngreas casachtaí [*and in bouts of coughing*] (*She coughs . . .*) The contest was over.

MARY: The contest was over?

MOMMO: 'Twas.

MARY: The contest was over?

MOMMO: The contest was over. Oh the strangers'd won.

18. See Act One, note 27.

19. tittering.

20. 'like the light of two suns'.

MARY: But what about the topic?

MOMMO: Hah?

MARY: Would keep them laughing near forever.

MOMMO: (*Whispers*) Misfortunes . . . *She* supplied them with the topic. And it started up again with the subject of potatoes, the damnedable crop was in it that year.

'Wet an' wat'ry? says the stranger.

'Wet an' wat'ry,' laughing Costello.

'Heh heh heh, but not blighted?'

'No ho ho, ho ho ho, but scabby an' small.'

'Sour an' soapy — Heh heh heh.'

'Yis — ho ho,' says the hero. 'Hard to wash, ladies? Hard to boil, ladies?'

'An' the divil t'ate[21] — Heh heh heh!'

But they were only getting into their stride.

'An' the hay?' says old Brian, 'behell.'[22]

'Rotted!' says the contestants, roarin' it together.

'The bita[23] oats,' shouts young Kemple — 'Jasus!' Lodged in the field. An' the turf says another. Still in the bog, laughed the answer. An' the chickens the pip, pipes up the old crone. An' the sheep, the staggers.[24] An' the cow that just died. An' the man that was in it lost both arms to the thresher. An' the dead!

MARY: . . . And the dead, Mommo?

MOMMO: (*Whimpers*) I wanta see mah father.

MARY: Who were the dead?

MOMMO: Pardon? Skitherin'[25] an' laughin' — Hih-hih-hih — at their nearest an' dearest. Her Pat was her eldest, died of consumption, had his pick of the girls an' married the widdy[26] again' all her wishes. The decline in that fambly, an' she knew the widdy'd outlast him. She told them the story — Hih-hih-hih — an' many another. An' how Pat, when he came back for the two sheep [*that*] wor his — An' they wor — An' he was her first-born. But you'll not have them she told him. Soft Willie inside, quiet by the hearth, but she knew he'd be able, the spawgs[27] of hands he had on him. 'Is it goin' fightin' me own brother?' But she told him a brother was one thing, but she was his mother, an' them were her orders to give Pat the high road, and no sheep one, two or three was leavin' the yard. They hurted each other. An' how Pat went back empty to his strap of a widdy. An' was dead within a six months. Hih-hih-hih. (*The 'hih-hih-hih' which punctuates her story sounds more like tears trying to get out rather than a giggle*) Oh she made great contribution to the roll-call of the dead. Was she what or 'toxicated? An' for the sake of an auld ewe was stuck in the flood was how she lost two of the others, Jimmy and Michael. Great gales of laughter to follow each name of the departed. Hih-hih-hih. An' the nice wife near her time, which one of them left behind him?

MARY: Daddy.

MOMMO: Died tryin' to give birth to the fourth was to be in it. An' she herself left with the care of three small childre waitin'. All contributions receiving volleys of cheers. Nothin' was sacred an' nothing a secret. The unbaptised an' stillborn in shoeboxes planted, at the dead hour of night treading softly the Lisheen[28] to make the regulation hole — not more, not less than two feet deep — too fearful of the field, haunted by infants, to speak or to pray. They were fearful of their ankles — Hih-hih-hih. An' tryin' not to hasten, steal away again, leaving their pagan parcels in isolation forever. Hih-hih-hih. Her soft Willie was her pet went foreign after the others — An' *did* she drive them all away — never ever to be heard of, ever again? Save soft Willie, aged thirty-four, in Louisaville Kentucky, died, peritonites. Spell that. A-N-T- Yes? I-P-H- Yes? F-U-L- Yes? L-O-G- Yes? E-S-T- Yes? I-N-E- Antiphfullogestine.[29] Now! That's how I taught them all to spell. Hih-hih-hih! The nicest night they ever had, that's what I'm sayin'. The stories kept on comin' an' the volleys and cheers. All of them present, their heads threwn back abandoned in festivities of guffaws: the wretched and neglected dilapidated an' forlorn, the forgotten an' tormented, the lonely an' despairing, ragged an' dirty, impoverished, hungry, emaciated and unhealthy, eyes big as saucers ridiculing an' defying of their lot on earth below — glintin' their defiance

21. 'And nothing to eat.'
22. by hell.
23. bit of, small amount of.
24. 'Pip' and 'Staggers' are colloquialisms for common diseases of chicken and sheep.
25. skittering, darting about.
26. widow.
27. From Irish *spuaic*, meaning 'blister'; indicates large, work-stained hands.
28. Irish *lisín*, meaning a small mound, sometimes used of the burial places of unbaptized children. A common place-name.
29. peritonites = peritonitis, indicating inflammation, whereas someone who is 'antiphfullogestine' (antiphlogistene) is opposed to the 'phlogiston' theory, which once posited the principle of inflammability in certain substances.

— their defiance an' rejection, inviting of what else might come or *care* to come! — Driving bellows of refusal at the sky through the roof. Och hona ho gus hah-haa! ... The nicest night ever.

MARY: An' what else was to come?

MOMMO: Nothing.

MARY: Tom.

MOMMO: Tom is in Galway.

MARY: Grandad.

MOMMO: An' when I told me father what did he say? ''Twas a *double* insolence at heaven.' We weren't meant to be here at all! 'Making mock of God's prize piece, its structure and system.' 'Oh,' he groaned, 'I have wrestled with enigmals [*all*] my life-long years. I've combed all of creation,' that man intoned, 'and, in the wondrous handiwork of God, have found only two flaws, man an' the earwig. Of what use is man, what utility the earwig, where do they either fit in the system? They are both specimens desperate, without any control, and therefore unfree. One cocks his head,' says he, 'the other his tail. But God will not be mocked. Especially when He was so clever at creating all things else. Still, God must have said, I'll leave them there an' see what transpires'. An' says me father — (*she winks shrewdly*) 'Maybe the earwig isn't doin' too bad at all'. An' then he tied his hands.

MARY: Who did?

MOMMO: Tck! Me father. That 'twas a double insolence at heaven. But they'd soon get their answer.

MARY: Who would?

MOMMO: The Bochtáns, the Bochtáns sure! Tck! Mauleogs[30] drunk? (MARY *nods*) Them all packed together? (MARY *nods*) The foul odour that was in it, you'd hardly get your breath. The ache was in the laughter. The two contestants sweating, the big man most profusely. Sure they'd been contending the title now for five or six hours. An' Costello, openin' down his shirts an' loosenin' his buckle, was doublin' up an' staggerin' an' holdin' his sides. 'Aw Jasus, lads, ye have me killed — Hickle-ickle-ickle,' an' the laughing lines upon his mien wor more like lines of pain. An' the stranger goin' 'Heh heh heh heh, heh heh heh heh'. Aisy an' gentle. Then beholding his 'ponent from contortion to convulsion, his complexion changin' colours an' arrivin' at purple: 'Heh heh heh heh, heh heh ... heh ... heh ... heh', the frown to his brow bringin' stillness upon him an' the two little smiles to the sides of his mouth. Suddenly he shouts, 'Costello's the winner!' But sure they wouldn't have it — nor herself in the corner. 'He's nat [*not*], he's nat, he's nat, he's nat!' 'On, on-on, Bochtán forever!'

'No-no! — Heh heh — he has me bet!'

'He's nat, he's nat, he's nat, he's nat!'

The others, 'Up Bochtán! — On Bochtán! Bochtán forever!'

An Costello now all the while in upper registration — 'Hickle-ickle-ickle-ickle' — longin' to put stop to it, his own cacklin' wouldn't let him. An' 'deed, when he'd 'tempt to rise an arm — an' sure he wasn't able — in gesture of cessation, th' other mistakin' of his purpose would go thinkin' t' do for 'm [*for him*] puncturin' holes in the ceilin', batin' stomps on the floor.

An' the stranger now could only stand and watch. An' late it was herself realised the Great Adversary had entered.

'Hickle-ickle-ickle-ickle — Aw Jasus, lads, I'm dyin' — Oh not without effort. Hickle, ickle, ickle, ickle. Then slow in a swoon he went down to the floor. For the last moments were left him 'twas the stranger that held him, for there was nothing now in the world to save him, or able to save him. Now!

MARY: And what's the rest of it?

MOMMO: Pardon?

MARY: For there was nothing now in the world. Only a little bit left.

MOMMO: (*Musing*) For there was nothing now in the world ...

DOLLY *is stirring in her sleep and wakes up for a moment.*

DOLLY: Mary?

MARY: (*Regards her gravely for a moment; then*) ... You're going to be alright, Dolly. Roll in under the blanket.

DOLLY *goes back to sleep.*

MOMMO: To save him ... Or able to save him. Did I not say that? Oh yis. 'An' the rabbits, lads,' says Cost'llo, 'I didn't sell e'er the one of them, but threwn them comin' home for fun again' Patch Curran's door'. And that was the last he was to utter that night or any other.

MARY: They don't laugh there anymore.

MOMMO: Save the childre, until they arrive at the age of reason. Now! Bochtáin forever is Bailegangaire.

Through the following MARY *undresses behind the*

30. From Irish *máileog*, a little bag: little bagsful drunk.

headboard and puts on her long simple nightdress; she lets down her hair, gets the hairbrush from the case and brushes her hair. Switches off the radio. She looks remarkably beautiful: she is like a young elegant woman, her face introspective and grave.

MARY: To conclude.

MOMMO: To conclude. The thaw as was forecasted was in it, an' the strangers went home.

MARY: But didn't they hurt grandad? ... The stranger, his ribs?

MOMMO: They did. But he bet them — he bet the best of them.

MARY: And wasn't his face cut?

MOMMO: Oh they did. They did. They wor for lettin' them home. D'yeh know? Home without hinder. Till the thief, Josie, started cryin', cryin' at death, and was insistently demanding the boots be took of the stranger to affirm 'twas feet or no was in them. An' from trying to quieten his gathering excitation someone of them got hit. Then he struck back. Till they forgot what they wor doin' sure, or how it had started, but all drawin' kicks an' blows, one upon the other, till the venom went rampant. They pulled him down off the cart an' gave him the kickin'. They did. Oh they gave him such a doin', till John Mah'ny an' the curate [*that*] was called prevailed again' the Bolsheviks. (MARY *gets into bed beside* MOMMO. DOLLY *is asleep on the other side*) 'Twas dawn when they got home. Not without trepidation? But the three small childre, like ye, their care, wor safe an' sound fast asleep on the settle. Now, my fondlings, settle down an' be sayin' yere prayers. I forget what happened the three sticks of rock. Hail Holy Queen. Yes? Mother of Mercy. Yes? Hail our lives? Yes? Our sweetness and our hope.

MARY: It was a bad year for the crops, a good one for mushrooms, and the three small children were waiting for their gran and their grandad to come home. Mommo? Mary was the eldest. She was the clever one, and she was seven. Dolly, the second, was like a film-star and she was grandad's favourite. And they were in and out of the road watching for the horse and cart. Waiting for ribbons. And Tom who was the youngest, when he got excited would go pacing o'er and o'er the boundary of the yard. He had confided in Mary his expectation. They would be bringing him his dearest wish — grandad told him secretly — a mouth organ for Christmas. That was alright. But in the — excitation — of their waiting they forgot to pay attention to the fire. Then Mary and Dolly heard — 'twas like an explosion. Tom had got the paraffin and, not the way grandad did it, stholled[31] it on to the embers, and the sudden blaze came out on top of him. And when they ran in and ... saw him, Mary got ... hysterical. And Dolly following suit got the same. Then Mary sent Dolly across the fields for May Glynn. And sure May was only ... eleven? Then Mary covered ... the wounds ... from the bag of flour in the corner. She'd be better now, and quicker now, at knowing what to do. And then May Glynn's mother came and they took Tom away to Galway, where he died ... two mornings later, and he had only just put the kettle on the hook, didn't grandad, the stranger, go down too, slow in a swoon ... Mommo?

MOMMO: It got him at last.

MARY: Will you take your pills now?

MOMMO: The yellow ones.

MARY: Yes.

MOMMO: Poor Séamus.(*She takes the pills with a sup of milk*)

MARY: Is there anything else you need?

MOMMO: To thee do we cry. Yes? Poor banished children of Eve.[32]

MARY: Is there anything you have to say to me?

MOMMO: Be sayin' yere prayers now an' ye'll be goin' to sleep. To thee do we send up our sighs.[33] Yes? For yere Mammy an' Daddy an' grandad is [*who are*] in heaven.

MARY: And Tom.

MOMMO: Yes. An' he only a ladeen[34] was afeared of the gander. An' tell them ye're all good. Mourning and weeping in this valley of tears.[35] (*She is handing the cup back to* MARY, *her eyes held on* MARY) And sure a tear isn't such a bad thing, Mary, and haven't we everything we need here, the two of us. (*And she settles down to sleep*)

MARY: (*Tears of gratitude brim to her eyes; fervently*) Oh we have, Mommo. (*Her tears continue to the end but her crying is infused with a sound like the laughter of relief*) ... To conclude. It's a strange old place alright, in whatever wisdom He has to have made it this way. But in whatever wisdom there is, in the year 1984, it was decided to give that —

31. spilled, poured it directly on to.
32. A phrase from the catholic prayer, 'Hail Holy Queen'.
33. Another phrase from the same prayer.
34. A small lad.
35. The prayer 'Hail Holy Queen' has the words 'To thee do we send up our sighs, mourning and weeping in this valley of tears.'

fambly . . . of strangers another chance, and a brand new baby to gladden their home.

Schubert's 'Notturno' comes in under MARY's *final speech. The lights fade.*

FRANK McGUINNESS

(1956-)

from: OBSERVE THE SONS OF ULSTER MARCHING TOWARDS THE SOMME (1985)

[The closing sequence of the play, in a trench, just before the attack begins (1 July 1916). The dialogue at this climax, as the group 'pairs' and fuses, picks up the essentially bewildering nature of the experience, which at first seems a straightforward trial of loyalties and trust. There is belligerent affirmation here, the donning and sharing of tribal symbols. Mingled with it is resignation to death, or survival into a life that will be differently apprehended; above all, a recognition of the vulnerability of the individual, and, in and beyond that, of the gods he reveres.

The play was first performed at the Peacock Theatre, Dublin in February 1985 and subsequently at the Hampstead Theatre, London in July 1986.]

CHARACTERS

KENNETH PYPER	*as an old man*
KENNETH PYPER	*in his thirties*
DAVID CRAIG	*in his late twenties*
JOHN MILLEN	*in his thirties*
WILLIAM MOORE	*in his thirties*
CHRISTOPHER ROULSTON	*in his thirties*
MARTIN CRAWFORD	*in his thirties*
GEORGE ANDERSON	*in his thirties*
NAT McILWAINE	*in his thirties*

PART 4: BONDING

A trench, the Somme. McILWAINE, the YOUNGER PYPER *and* MILLEN *are awake. The others sleep.*

McILWAINE: You'd think they were dead, it's that quiet.

PYPER: Yes.

MILLEN: When do you think word'll come?

PYPER: When we're ready.

MILLEN: What have we to do with it?

PYPER: We do the attacking.

MILLEN: We don't do the ordering.

PYPER: You above all are not beginning to panic, Millen?

MILLEN: I've been panicking since the last leave, Pyper.

McILWAINE: There won't be much of daylight before we're going over.

MILLEN: I think this is it. I think this is going to be the end.

PYPER: Millen, for Christ's sake.

MILLEN: I can't help it. I know this time.

McILWAINE: Nobody knows nothing here.

PYPER: Any officers about?

McILWAINE: One passed twenty minutes ago. Told us to get some rest.

MILLEN: I saw him. Useless bugger. Surely to God they're not going to trust us with that piece of work. Where do they dig them out of anyway? Superior rank, is that it? Superior, my arse.

McILWAINE: Keep talking like that and it'll be a court martial you'll be facing, not —

MILLEN: Let me face it and I'll tell them straight.

PYPER: Tell them what?

MILLEN: What they're doing to us.

McILWAINE: And that will stop them? That'll stop us? Save your breath for running. It's a bit late to start crying now.

MILLEN: I'm not crying.

McILWAINE: You're damn near it. Pyper? You come from a swanky family, don't you?

PYPER: Why ask that now?

McILWAINE: I'm just beginning to wonder what you're doing down with us instead of being with them.

PYPER: And who are they?

McILWAINE: Top brass.

PYPER: I'm not top brass, McIlwaine. Maybe once. Not now. I blotted my copybook.

McILWAINE: How?

MILLEN: Should we waken the boys?

McILWAINE: Give them time to dream. How, Pyper?

PYPER: Just being the black sheep.

McILWAINE: Bit of a wild one?

PYPER: Bit.

McILWAINE: Like myself. I broke the mother's heart.

PYPER: I broke my mother's arm. More practical, more painful.

MILLEN: Pyper, how can you laugh at a time like this?

PYPER: I'm not laughing, Millen.

MILLEN: Have you contacts up above there? Ones posted to watch over you and make sure you end up in some cushy corner?[1] Is that why you can laugh?

PYPER: Get something into that thick Coleraine skull of yours, Millen. Nobody's watching over me except myself. What the hell has got into you?

MILLEN: What got into you the first time we met you. Remember? Knowing we're all going to die. Knowing we're all going . . . .

McILWAINE *grabs* MILLEN.

McILWAINE: One minute, you. Just one minute. These chaps are having a well-earned kip. Now they're not going to come to their senses listening to a squealing woman keening[2] after death. Do you hear? If you want to make traitors of them, you'll deal with me first. And if you want out, start marching now.

MILLEN: I've never run away from what I had to do. I commanded —

PYPER: We all know that. But there's more than sixteen-year-old Fenians[3] you're up against now. Will that hit you once and for all?

McILWAINE: I'm warning you.

PYPER: Let him go, McIlwaine.

MILLEN: I never thought I was a coward.

McILWAINE: You're not a coward. You've done enough to prove that.

MILLEN: But I'm a soldier.

McILWAINE: You're a man. The shit's scared out of you. Do you think you're on your own?

MILLEN: No.

McILWAINE: Well then.

ROULSTON *wakes up*.

PYPER: Rise and shine, Christopher.

ROULSTON: Jesus, my mouth feels like a rat's been there.

PYPER: It probably has.

ROULSTON: Did you put it there?

PYPER: There was a time I would have.

ROULSTON: Pleasant as ever.

PYPER: Full of laughs.

ROULSTON: Any word?

MILLEN: Nothing new.

ROULSTON: I suppose they're saying the same thing over there?

McILWAINE: In German?

PYPER: No, in Gaelic.

McILWAINE: Germans don't speak Gaelic.

PYPER: They all learn it for badness, McIlwaine.

McILWAINE: Dirty bastard. So that's what they insult you in.

PYPER: Couldn't watch them. Fenians, Gaelic speakers. They get everywhere. Even in the German army.

McILWAINE: No way. Not even the Germans would have them. Did you hear about this boy Pearse?[4] The boy who took over a post office because he was short of a few stamps.

MILLEN: He did more than take over a post office, the bastard. Shot down our men until he got what he was looking for.

McILWAINE: Let me finish. He was a Fenian, wasn't he? No soldier. He took over this big post office in Dublin, kicks all the wee girls serving behind the counter out on to the streets. When the place is empty, him and his merry men all carrying wooden rifles, land outside on the street. Your man reads the proclamation of an Irish republic. The Irish couldn't spell republic, let alone proclaim it. Then he's caught, him and all hands in gaol. He starts to cry, saying he has a widowed mother and he had led the only other brother astray. Anyway, he didn't plan to take over this post office. He

1. comfortable situation.
2. lamenting.
3. Refers to an incident reported in Part 1, in which Millen and Moore punished a sixteen-year-old catholic (Fenian) youth for painting a tricolour flag, the emblem of the Irish Republic, on the wall of an Orange lodge.

4. Patrick Pearse (1879-1916), one of the leaders of the Easter Rising in 1916.

walked in to post a letter and got carried away and thought it was Christmas. Nobody believes him. They're leading him out to be shot. He's supposed to see the widowed ma in the crowd. He looks at her and says, pray for me, mother. The ma looks back at him, looks at the Tommy, he's guarding Pearse, the old one[5] grabs the Tommy's rifle. She shoots Pearse herself. She turns to the Tommy and she says, 'That'll learn him, the cheeky pup. Going about robbing post offices. Honest to God, I'm affronted.' So you see, Fenians can't fight. Not unless they're in a post office or a bakery or a woman's clothes shop. Disgrace to their sex, the whole bastarding lot of them, I say.

PYPER: Who gave you this version of events?

McILWAINE: Christopher here.

PYPER: Roulston?

ROULSTON: He invented quite a few details of his own. The best ones.

McILWAINE: I can't help that. I'm very imaginative. I play the drums, you see. An artist like yourself, Pyper. We're a breed apart, us boys. To hell with the truth as long as it rhymes.

ROULSTON: How's Johnny?

MILLEN: All right, Roulston.

ROULSTON: You're keeping up?

MILLEN: Why shouldn't I be?

ROULSTON: That's the spirit.

MILLEN: Spirit?

McILWAINE: Thanks, I'll have a double whiskey. Bushmills, if you have it. If not, anything goes. Have one yourself. It'll liven you up.

MILLEN: Doesn't take much to liven you up.

McILWAINE: No, not much. Then again, there mightn't be many more chances to be livened up. Don't forget that.

MILLEN: I'm hardly liable —

PYPER: All right, enough. Do something with yourself, Millen. Check your stuff, do anything, just keep busy.

MILLEN: Pyper, do you think I have not tried?

McILWAINE: I've warned you before —

MILLEN: I've warned myself often enough before and I cannot —

ROULSTON: Johnny, God's good. He's looked after us up to now. He's with us. He won't desert us.

MILLEN: He deserted us when he led us here.

PYPER: We led ourselves here.

ROULSTON: Pyper, leave him. Would it help you if we prayed together, Johnny?

(*Silence*)

PYPER: You heard the man, Millen.

MILLEN: It might, I haven't prayed for a long time —

ROULSTON: Neither have I. Together?

MILLEN: What? Pray what? What kind of prayer?

ROULSTON: (*Sings*)

From depths of woe I raise to thee
The voice of lamentation.
Lord, turn a gracious ear to me
And hear my supplication.
If thou shouldst be extreme to mark
Each secret sin and misdeed dark
Oh! Who could stand before Thee!

(MILLEN *joins in the hymn*)

To wash away the crimson stain
Grace, grace alone availeth.
Our works alas are all in vain
In much the best life faileth.
No man can glory in Thy sight,
All must alike confess Thy might,
And live alone by mercy.

(McILWAINE *begins to sing*)

Therefore my trust is in the Lord
And not in my own merit
On Him my soul shall rest, His word
Upholds my fainting spirit.
His promised mercy is my fort,
My comfort and my sweet support.
I wait for it in patience.[6]

(*Silence*)

PYPER: Patience. I'm growing tired of waiting. Let it come. (CRAIG *cries out in his sleep*) David? (*Silence*) Sleep.

ROULSTON: Maybe you should get a bit of rest, Millen.

MILLEN: No point. Soon have to move.

McILWAINE: Nice tune to that one, wasn't there? I could never remember words, but I never forgot a tune in my life.

ROULSTON: You're speaking in the past tense.

McILWAINE: What?

ROULSTON: Nothing.

MILLEN: I never recall it as quiet as this.

5. i.e. Pearse's mother.

6. This hymn, a version of Psalm 130, is a translation of an old German hymn, published in Leipzig in 1539. It was set to music by Felix Mendelssohn.

MCILWAINE: The smell's different today. Has anybody noticed? Or am I imagining things?

CRAWFORD *wakes up.*

PYPER: No, there's something different in the air.

ROULSTON: Stronger.

MCILWAINE: What is it?

MILLEN: Fear.

ROULSTON: Are you awake?

CRAWFORD: Just about.

ROULSTON: Cold?

CRAWFORD: Ice. I'm still tired. Christ, I'm eaten by lice. Give us a scratch. (ROULSTON *puts his hand down* CRAWFORD's *shirt*) Good man, lovely. Down to the left a bit.

MCILWAINE: Want some powder?

CRAWFORD: Useless bloody stuff. We're still here?

MCILWAINE: No, we're on our way to Bangor[7] for a bathe.

CRAWFORD: Don't tear the face off me. I was only asking.

ROULSTON: You slept all right?

CRAWFORD: All right. Up long?

ROULSTON: A while.

CRAWFORD: That's enough. Is there time for a quick match?

MCILWAINE: You have the football with you?

PYPER: I have to hand it to your nerve, Crawford.

CRAWFORD: Have to practice, man. Any time, anywhere. I want to get into the game seriously when I'm home again. Come on. A quick game.

MILLEN: Not yet.

CRAWFORD: Liven you up.

MCILWAINE: Right. I'm your man. (CRAWFORD *starts the game.* ANDERSON *wakes up. The game continues through the following dialogue*) Would you like some breakfast, son?

ANDERSON: Fried egg, bit of bacon, sausages?

MCILWAINE: Soda faral.[8]

ANDERSON: Strong tea?

MCILWAINE: Name your poison.

ANDERSON: Aye, wouldn't mind.

MCILWAINE: Sorry, haven't got it.

ANDERSON: What have you got?

MCILWAINE: Bit of shite.

ANDERSON: Horse's?

MCILWAINE: Are you mad? Can't get horse's shite for love or money.

ANDERSON: Only human?

MCILWAINE: Aye.

ANDERSON: No thanks.

MCILWAINE: Don't turn up your nose at it. It'll soon be scarce enough.

ANDERSON: Not when your mouth's still around.

MCILWAINE: Compliments flying.

ANDERSON: So's the shite.

CRAWFORD: Yous two are pretty sharp.

MCILWAINE: Lethal, son, lethal.

ANDERSON: We practise in the dark.

CRAWFORD: Did yous ever think of taking it up full time?

ANDERSON: Good idea.

MCILWAINE: What would we do?

ANDERSON: Any suggestions?

PYPER: Something sad.

ANDERSON: Damn sadness. Something to make the blood boil.

MCILWAINE: Battle of the Boyne?

ANDERSON: How the hell can two men do the Battle of the Boyne?

MCILWAINE: They do it without much more at Scarva.[9]

ANDERSON: Very thing, Battle of Scarva.

MCILWAINE: They have horses at Scarva.

ANDERSON: We'll get the horses. To your feet, Millen. You're a horse.

MILLEN: Let me be.

ANDERSON: Get him to his feet. (MCILWAINE *hauls* MILLEN *to his feet*) Now, Pyper, you're the blondie boy. King Billy at Scarva always has a white horse. You're his horse, right? Now for King Billy. Who could Pyper carry? Crawford. You, on his shoulders. Right?

CRAWFORD: Wait a minute —

ANDERSON: Do as you're told.

ROULSTON: Come on, King Billy.

CRAWFORD *gets on* PYPER's *shoulders.* PYPER *neighs loudly.*

ANDERSON: Raring to go. King Billy and his trusty white steed. Now Millen, you're King James's horse. Who could you carry?

MILLEN: I'm having no part in this.

ANDERSON: Could you carry me?

MILLEN: Go to hell.

7. A popular seaside resort in County Down, south of Belfast.
8. i.e. farl, a flour or oatmeal cake.

9. Each July, in Scarva, Co. Antrim, the Orangemen stage a re-enactment of the battle of the Boyne (1690) between the forces of the protestant King William (Billy) of Orange and the catholic King James II.

MCILWAINE: Waken Craig.

MILLEN: Craig's like a horse himself.

MCILWAINE: Moore then.

ANDERSON: Get up, Moore.

MOORE: What's wrong?

MCILWAINE: You're King James. Get on —

MOORE: I'm what?

MCILWAINE: King James. Get on Millen's shoulders.

MILLEN: I have no part in this.

MOORE: Part in what?

ANDERSON: Battle of Scarva. Come on, get on.

ANDERSON *and* MCILWAINE *lift* MOORE *on to* MILLEN's shoulders.

MILLEN: Why do we have to be King James? He has to get beaten.

MCILWAINE: Because somebody has to be King James. And anyway, you're only his horse.

MILLEN: This is not a fair fight.

ANDERSON: What fight ever is fair? Are yous right? Let battle commence. And remember, King James, we know the result, you know the result, keep to the result. (*The Mock Battle of Scarva begins*) Music.

MCILWAINE: How can we have music? Sing a hymn?

ANDERSON: Lilt or something. Go on, lilt.

ROULSTON: Lilt?

MCILWAINE: Lilt.

They lilt.

ANDERSON: King William, Prince of Orange, on his fine white charger eyes the traitor James, James who will destroy our glorious religion should he win the battle. William moves defiantly towards the bitter enemy. His white steed sniffs the dangers but continues to carry his master to glory. James swaggers forward —

MILLEN: On his trusty steed —

ANDERSON: Will his trusty steed shut his mouth when I'm in the middle of the story? Where was I? James swaggers forward, his Papist pride on high. No one shall topple the favoured son of Rome. But look at how King William —

ROULSTON: Come on, King William.

MCILWAINE: He's going to win anyway. Just lilt.

ANDERSON: Look at how King William, brandishing his golden blade, defies the might of haughty James, minion of Rome. They pass in thick of battle. But the wily James avoids the first attack. Behold, undaunted, our King returns, the loyal steed beneath him devours the ground. This time for the traitor James there is no escape. But luck is on the devil's side. James has swerved in time. Furious and bold, King Billy will not rest. This time James will fall, and with him mighty Rome in this kingdom. They must fight and fight they will until the victor stands poised before the victim.

PYPER *trips.* CRAWFORD *crashes to the ground. Silence.* MILLEN *lets* MOORE *off his shoulders.* ROULSTON *and* MOORE *help* CRAWFORD *to rise.* PYPER *lies on the ground.*

MOORE: Can you manage?

ROULSTON: He's just a bit stunned.

ANDERSON: Get up, Pyper.

PYPER: I fell.

MCILWAINE: We saw.

MILLEN: Not the best of signs.

(*Silence*)

CRAWFORD: It was as much my fault as Pyper's. I lost control of his shoulders. That's what happened.

ROULSTON: You're all right?

CRAWFORD: I'm grand.

MILLEN: Day's breaking.

MOORE: Is everybody ready?

PYPER: Better waken Craig.

ANDERSON: Better waken yourself, Pyper. Why did you do that?

PYPER: I just fell.

ANDERSON: Did you?

CRAWFORD: It's not only his fault.

MCILWAINE: Let it rest. It was only a game.

ROULSTON: Good sport while it lasted.

ANDERSON: Great. Fair great.

MOORE: Prepare us for the real thing.

ROULSTON: Yes, it's coming. Better prepare.

CRAWFORD: Were yous talking about a smell when I woke up?

MCILWAINE: Aye, why?

CRAWFORD: I find it now. What is it?

ROULSTON: The smell's always there.

CRAWFORD: But this is like, this is like —

MILLEN: What?

CRAWFORD: I don't know.

MILLEN: I noticed how quiet it was too.

PYPER: David, get up.

MILLEN: Did anyone else?

CRAWFORD: We were making that much noise, no.

PYPER: Come on, man, rise.

CRAIG: What? Are we off?

PYPER: Nearly.

CRAIG: Orders come?

PYPER: We're waiting for it. It's almost daylight.

CRAIG: Oh God. Right.

MOORE: How did you sleep through all the din, man?

CRAIG: What din?

MOORE: You must have been dead to the world.

CRAIG: I had this dream. A very clear dream.

MOORE: A nightmare?

CRAIG: No, no. Good. Very good.

McILWAINE: What about?

CRAIG: Home.

ROULSTON: Enniskillen?

CRAIG: Yes.

MOORE: 'Fare thee well, Enniskillen.'

CRAIG: 'Fare thee well for a time.'

PYPER: (*Sings*)

And all around the borders of Erin's green isle.
And when the war is over we'll return in fine bloom
And we'll all welcome home our Enniskillen dragoons.[10]

CRAIG: 'Fare thee well, Enniskillen.'

PYPER: 'Fare thee well for a while.'

CRAIG: Lough Erne.[11]

MOORE: Good weather there at the minute.

McILWAINE: How would you know?

MOORE: Letters. Great weather all over. The Bann's fair jumping with salmon at the minute.

MILLEN: Nobody to catch them.

MOORE: Young lads might.

MILLEN: They ruin a river.

CRAIG: They never know when to stop.

MILLEN: I threw back more fish than I ever ate.

CRAIG: I didn't know you were much of a fisherman.

MOORE: Oh aye. The two of us. In the summer the banks of the Bann are a second home.

PYPER: Beautiful rivers.

MILLEN: The loveliest, and say what you like, Coleraine's at its best point.

CRAWFORD: Foyle.

CRAIG: What?

CRAWFORD: I'm just remembering the Foyle. I'd forgotten it. Reared by it. Foyle Street.

McILWAINE: Well, the Lagan isn't bad either.

MOORE: Nobody said it was.

McILWAINE: It could knock the bloody Erne into the shade any day. And as for the Bann, I wouldn't make my water into it in case it would flood.[12]

MOORE: Wait one minute. Let me tell you —

PYPER: Keep it easy. (*Silence*) Jesus, that's it. The source of the strange smell. The river.

ROULSTON: The Somme?

PYPER: The Somme.

CRAWFORD: How? It's far —

PYPER: It carries for miles. It smells like home. A river at home.

ANDERSON: All rivers smell the same.

PYPER: Not your own river.

McILWAINE: I've never smelt a river.

PYPER: You can't stop smelling a river. Anyway, do you not see why it's started to change smell?

ANDERSON: What's that man on about?

PYPER: It's bringing us home. We're not in France. We're home. We're on our own territory. We're fighting for home. This river is ours. This land's ours. We've come home. Where's Belfast, Anderson?

ANDERSON: You know as well as I do where —

PYPER: It's out there. It's waiting for you. Can you hear the shipyard, McIlwaine?

McILWAINE: Your head's cut,[13] man.

PYPER: You weren't dreaming about Lough Erne, David. You're on it. It surrounds you. Moore, the Bann is flowing outside. The Somme, it's not what we think it is. It's the Lagan, the Foyle, the Bann —

CRAIG: You're trying too hard, Pyper. It's too late to tell us what we're fighting for. We know where we are. We know what we've to do. And we know what we're doing it for. We knew before we enlisted. We joined up willingly for that reason. Everyone of us, except you. You've learned it at long last. But you can't teach us what we already know. You won't save us, you won't save yourself, imagining things. There's nothing imaginary about this, Kenneth. This is the last battle. We're going out to die.

PYPER: No, David, you —

CRAIG: Yes, yes. Whoever comes back alive, if any of us do, will have died as well. He'll never be the same. Different men after this, one way or the

10.

11. A lake in County Fermanagh.

12. The river Foyle, on which Derry stands, the river Lagan, on which Belfast stands, and the river Bann, which enters the sea at Coleraine and is the boundary between east and west Ulster, are all rivers of especial significance in Northern Ireland.

13. Colloquial — you're crazy.

other. Do you know why we'll risk going through that? Because we want to.

MILLEN: None of us want[s] to die.

CRAIG: I said even to come through this will be the same as dying.

McILWAINE: How do you know it's going to be that bad?

CRAIG: The gods told me.

ROULSTON: What did they tell?

CRAIG: The Protestant gods told me. In a dream. On Lough Erne. Get yourselves ready. Make your peace with God and man.

The men divide slowly into the pairings of part 3.[14]

ANDERSON: What's got into your man Craig?

McILWAINE: Sense.

ANDERSON: He's been hanging around too long near Pyper.

McILWAINE: Has he?

ANDERSON: Did you hear that silly chat about rivers?

McILWAINE: There's more there than you think.

ANDERSON: I know what I think. That man Pyper's a lunatic.

McILWAINE: Remember that night on the Field[15] you thought he was thinking right?

ANDERSON: No.

McILWAINE: Good.

ANDERSON: What's got into you?

McILWAINE: Maybe I've got sense as well. All right?

ANDERSON: Hi, I'm sorry.

McILWAINE: What for?

ANDERSON: I don't know what's going to happen.

McILWAINE: You do, Anderson. You do.

MOORE: Are you feeling any better?

MILLEN: Willy, I lied to you. I lied to you all my life. Was it you or me lost their nerve? Who crossed the bridge?

MOORE: We did together.

MILLEN: I couldn't have done it.[16]

MOORE: You have to save yourself today, Johnny, you can't save me. We're on our own today.

MILLEN: You think like Craig we're not coming back?

MOORE: What do you think?

MILLEN: That it's over.

MOORE: Go down fighting.

MILLEN: Take me back.

MOORE: Where?

MILLEN: Home.

MOORE: This is home.

MILLEN: Death?

MOORE: You have to look it in the face. Watch yourself.

MILLEN: I need you.

MOORE: I'm beside you.

MILLEN: Then we'll sink together.

MOORE: Or swim.

MILLEN: Or swim.

MOORE *and* MILLEN *shake hands.*

CRAWFORD: It's different to what I thought.

ROULSTON: How?

CRAWFORD: Quieter.

ROULSTON: What's done has to be done.

CRAWFORD: I thought when this day came you'd have been angrier.

ROULSTON: With you?

CRAWFORD: How with me? I meant with God.

ROULSTON: I'm not sure I can tell the difference any more. Anyway, it was always leading to this.

CRAWFORD: Don't say that.

ROULSTON: Why not?

CRAWFORD: Cowardly.

ROULSTON: Is that not what I am?

CRAWFORD: You've proved yourself before. You'll do it today as well.

ROULSTON: Proved what? That I can handle a gun? Stick a bayonet where it's needed? Am as good a man as any soldier? That proves nothing. What you said about me in the church that day was the truth. It was shown to me. You showed me. I accept it. No better and no worse than any of you. None of us are.

CRAWFORD: Do you still believe?

ROULSTON: Yes.

CRAWFORD: Would you do me a favour?

ROULSTON: What?

CRAWFORD: Pray I'll come back.

ROULSTON: No.

CRAWFORD: Why not?

ROULSTON: You can do that for yourself. Do it now.

14. In Part 3, entitled 'Pairing', the eight men, on leave, are grouped in couples: Craig and Pyper on Boa Island, Lough Erne; Roulston and Crawford in a protestant church; Millen and Moore at a rope bridge; McIlwaine and Anderson in a field used for Orange Order assemblies.

15. Finaghy Field, on the outskirts of Belfast, the meeting-place of the Orange parades on 12 July.

16. Millen in fact had encouraged Moore to walk over the precarious rope bridge.

CRAWFORD: Do it with me then.

ROULSTON: Wait till the word's given to go.[17]

CRAIG: I'm sorry.

PYPER: Why did you do that?

CRAIG: To stop the heroism.

PYPER: I wasn't —

CRAIG: You were being stupid. We could do without that, you know.

PYPER: Why are you changing?

CRAIG: Because you're going back. You'll go back to your proud family. The brave eldest son. Made a man of himself in Flanders. Damn you, after listening to that bit of rabble-rousing, I saw through you. You're wasted here with us. You're not of us, man. You're a leader. You got what you wanted. You always have, you always will. You'll come through today because you learned to want it.

PYPER: I've learned to want you.

CRAIG: No. Tell me this. What kind of life do you see for us when we're out of here? It might be many things, but it won't be together.

PYPER: What do you want from me?

CRAIG: What you want.

PYPER: I don't understand you.

CRAIG: No. You don't. For the first time, and that's good. I'm your measure. Don't forget that.

PYPER: Stop this.

CRAIG: If I'm hurting you, it's about time.

PYPER: Don't go out like this.

CRAIG: It's the way I need to go out there. Kenneth, don't die. One of us has to go on.

PYPER: David —

CRAIG: Calm.

PYPER: Home.

CRAIG: Here.

ANDERSON: Hi, Pyper?

PYPER: What do you want?

ANDERSON: We've noticed something missing from your uniform. Something important. We think you should do something about it. It might get you into trouble.

PYPER: What's missing?

ANDERSON: Your badge of honour. (ANDERSON *hands out an Orange sash*[18] *to* PYPER) Well?

PYPER: It's not mine.

ANDERSON: It is now. It's a gift. From us. Am I right, McIlwaine?

McILWAINE: Right. Very right. Damned right. Anderson gets sensible when he's right, Pyper.

(*Silence*)

ANDERSON: Will you wear it this time, like the rest of us?

PYPER: Why?

ANDERSON: So we'll recognize you as one of our own. Your own.

PYPER: We're on the same side.

ANDERSON: I'm sure we are. Here, take it. (*Silence*) I said take it. Do you want me to put it round you? (PYPER *snatches the sash*) That's the man. That's the way.

CRAWFORD: Are you ready, Roulston?

MOORE: What for?

CRAWFORD: The last prayer.

ROULSTON: Together.

ALL: *(Sing)*

I'm but a stranger here,
Heaven is my home.
Earth is but a desert drear,
Heaven is my home.
Danger and sorrow stand
Round me on every hand.
Heaven is my fatherland,
Heaven is my home.

What though the tempest rage,
Heaven is my home.
Short is my pilgrimage,
Heaven is my home.
Time's wild and wintry blast
Soon will be overpast.
I shall reach home at last.
Heaven is my home.

There at my Saviour's side —
Heaven is my home —
I shall be glorified,
Heaven is my home.
There are the good and blest,
Those I love most and best,
And there I too shall rest.
Heaven is my home.

Therefore I murmur not,
Heaven is my home.
Whate'er my earthly lot,

17. Crawford has asserted that he fights for himself, not for Christ or 'empires and kings and countries', and that Roulston, for all his professions of religious faith, is merely a man like himself. Pyper's older self, the Elder Pyper, having survived the battle, but haunted by his dead comrades, opens the play with a long, brooding soliloquy.

18. The sash worn on ceremonial occasions by Orangemen, identifying the lodge to which they belong.

Heaven is my home.
And I shall surely stand
There at the Lord's right hand.
Heaven is my fatherland,
Heaven is my home.[19]

MOORE: I can see the others gathering.

MILLEN: It's time then.

McILWAINE: All together.

CRAWFORD: Better move.

ROULSTON: Every one.

CRAIG: Right.

ANDERSON: Last stage.

With the exception of PYPER, *they each begin to put on their Orange sashes.* CRAIG *watches* PYPER, *then takes his sash off, goes to* MOORE, *hands it to him.* MOORE *hesitates, then exchanges his sash for* CRAIG's. *At this there is an exchange of sashes,* CRAWFORD's *for* ANDERSON's, MILLEN's *for* McILWAINE's. ROULSTON *goes to* PYPER, *who takes* ROULSTON's *and gives him his own.*

PYPER: It's come to this, Roulston?

ROULSTON: What's decreed passes, Pyper.

PYPER: There's no fight back?

ROULSTON: There's just the fight.

PYPER: The good fight?

ROULSTON: The everlasting fight.

PYPER: Inside us?

ROULSTON: And outside us.

PYPER: Preach.

ROULSTON: No. You preach. (*Silence. They wait*) You believe. Believe.

(*Silence*)

PYPER: God in heaven, if you hear the words of man, I speak to you this day. I do it now to ask we be spared. I do it to ask for strength. Strength for these men around me, strength for myself. If you are a just and merciful God, show your mercy this day. Save us. Save our country. Destroy our enemies at home and on this field of battle. Let this day at the Somme be as glorious in the memory of Ulster as that day at the Boyne, when you scattered our enemies. Lead us back from this exile. To Derry, to the Foyle. To Belfast and the Lagan. To Armagh. To Tyrone. To the Bann and its banks. To Erne and its islands. Protect them. Protect us. Protect me. Let us fight bravely. Let us win gloriously. Lord, look down on us. Spare us. I love —. Observe the sons of Ulster marching towards the Somme. I love their lives. I love my own life. I love my home. I love my Ulster. Ulster. Ulster. Ulster. Ulster. Ulster. Ulster. Ulster. Ulster.

As the chant of 'Ulster' commences rifles and bayonets are raised. The chant turns into a battle cry, reaching frenzy. The ELDER PYPER *appears. His* YOUNGER SELF *sees him. The chant ceases.*

YOUNGER PYPER: Ulster.

ELDER PYPER: Ulster.

YOUNGER PYPER: I have seen horror.

ELDER PYPER: Ulster.

YOUNGER PYPER: They kept their nerve, and they died.

ELDER PYPER: Ulster.

YOUNGER PYPER: There would be, and there will be, no surrender.

ELDER PYPER: Ulster.

YOUNGER PYPER: The house has grown cold, the province has grown lonely.

ELDER PYPER: Ulster.

YOUNGER PYPER: You'll always guard Ulster.

ELDER PYPER: Ulster.

YOUNGER PYPER: Save it.

ELDER PYPER: Ulster.

YOUNGER PYPER: The temple of the Lord is ransacked.

ELDER PYPER: Ulster.

PYPER *reaches towards himself.*

YOUNGER PYPER: Dance in this deserted temple of the Lord.

ELDER PYPER: Dance.

(*Darkness*)

19. The words of this hymn are by Thomas Rawson Taylor (born in 1835). It was set to music by Arthur Seymour Sullivan.

THOMAS KILROY

(1934-)

DOUBLE CROSS (1986)

[Brendan Bracken and William Joyce appear on stage in the flesh and also disembodied — a screen image, a radio voice. The suggestion is of personalities both insubstantial and compelling, fabricated for an occasion. Bracken cultivated a chameleon, superficial charm devoted to securing power and position, Joyce a crude pseudo-mysticism of race, seeking an authoritarian control of reality. The play is exploring the nature of these fabrications and their roots in self-absorbed notions of national identity, 'Irishness' and 'Englishness', which pervert any genuine individuality. *Double Cross* was first presented by Field Day Theatre Company in Derry on 13 February 1986.]

There is no evidence that Brendan Bracken and William Joyce ever met nor, indeed, that they were ever aware of one another's existence. I have yoked them together in this play so that they might inhabit the one dramatic idea. For those who would like an accurate, historical account of the two men there are two excellent biographies: *Brendan Bracken* by Charles Edward Lysaght and *Lord Haw-Haw* by J. A. Cole.

I was drawn to the stories of these two men out of an interest in doubleness or doubling, that is, the way things repeat themselves in life or attract their opposites. This, of course, is the basis of acting or role-playing. It is also behind the universal desire of people to make up and tell stories, thereby inventing a reality which may reflect everyday life but is still distinct from it. This is a play which tries to move along the lines from role-playing and fiction-making to the act of political treason. Bracken is an actor at loose in the world of English politics and what used to be called Society. Clearly it was a world susceptible to the charm of a master thespian. Joyce, in the play, is a creator of fictions, driven to this out of a deep, angry impatience with life as it really is. This is the only way in which I can comprehend the essentially suicidal energy at the root of fascism.

To surrender to a vision of doubleness is to see most human behaviour (including one's own, of course) within a field of irony. Nowhere is this more evident than in politics where human behaviour may be seen at its most crude and simplistic. Oppression disables personality. But it also profoundly diminishes the humanity of the oppressor. It creates grotesque distortions in an oppressed culture, inhibiting growth, development, change. But it effects a like rigidity in the invader, the conqueror, the would-be 'superior': that baleful, paralytic stare of racism. This play attempts to deal with one kind of mobility, one kind of action across the barriers, the restrictive codes which separate countries from one another. It is the kind of action which is usually called treason. To base one's identity, exclusively, upon a mystical sense of place rather than in personal character where it properly resides seems to me a dangerous absurdity. To dedicate one's life to the systematic betrayal of that ideal seems to me equally absurd.

This play could not have been written without Field Day. Some years ago Field Day asked me to write one of their *Pamphlets* and I completely failed to do so. It was round about that time that I decided to try and write a play for the company instead, addressing the kind of topics which Field Day has restored to serious debate in Ireland. For me, Field Day is the most important movement of its kind in Ireland since the beginning of this century. It has provided a platform for the life of the mind, of whatever persuasion, at a time when mindlessness threatens to engulf us all.

Thomas Kilroy

BRENDAN BRACKEN (1901-58)

1901 (15 Feb.): Brendan Bracken born in Templemore, Co. Tipperary. His father, Joseph Bracken, was a prosperous builder, founder member of the Gaelic Athletic Association and a strong supporter of the Republican Movement.
1904: Bracken's father dies.
1908: Family move to Dublin and Brendan sent to school run by Christian Brothers.
1915: A somewhat unruly youth, Bracken sent to a Jesuit boarding school near Limerick. Runs away at the start of the following term. According to a family friend Bracken's mother decides to send him

to friends in Australia because he has shown interest in the Irish Republican Youth Movement.
1916: Arrives in the state of Victoria.
1919: Returns to Ireland. His mother, now remarried in Navan, does not welcome him back.
1920: Bracken moves to Lancashire, where he works as a tutor. Combines this with teaching at Collegiate School, where his colleagues believe he is Australian.
(Autumn): Enrols as a pupil at Sedbergh, a public school in Cumbria. Gives his date of birth as 14 December 1904, claims to be an orphan. Leaves after a term — but with the 'old school tie'.
1920-21: Movements unclear — held various teaching posts.
1922: Secures a post on the monthly *Empire Review*, an imperialist journal run by a Tory MP.
1923: Bracken meets Winston Churchill, then in his 'wilderness years'. According to Churchill's eldest daughter, Diana, it was presumed Bracken was Churchill's son.
1924: Bracken builds up his business and publishing interests. Appointed to board of publishers Eyre and Spottiswoode.
1928: On behalf of Eyre and Spottiswoode, buys the *Financial News* (later to merge with the *Financial Times*) and *The Economist*.
1929: Adopted as Conservative candidate for North Paddington. Wins by a margin of 528 votes.
1931: Rumoured that Bracken, Churchill, Lloyd George and Sir Oswald Mosley meet to discuss a grand political alliance against the Labour Party. Joyce may also have attended this meeting.
1932: Proposes to Lady Pamela Smith, daughter of the late Earl of Birkenhead, and is turned down. His affections turn to Churchill's god-daughter, Penelope Dudley Ward. Claims he never married because she refused him as well.
1935: A report appears in the *Sunday Express* that Bracken was greatly embarrassed when he had to show his birth certificate. The proprietor, Lord Beaverbrook, sends a reporter to Ireland to investigate Bracken's background.
1939: Becomes Churchill's Parliamentary Private Secretary, at the Admiralty.
1940: Churchill appointed Prime Minister of an all-party government. Bracken becomes one of the youngest members of the Privy Council.
1941: Bracken appointed Minister of Information. Defends freedom of the Press and the independent position of the BBC.
1944: *Evening Standard* reproduces a story of 'fifty years ago' from the *Waterford News* that Bracken's father had been refused a gun licence, much to Bracken's fury.
1945: Loses parliamentary seat to Labour.
1947: Bracken stands for the Conservatives in Bournemouth and wins.
1950: Bouts of illness see Bracken cutting down on his business activities. Elected to his 'old school' board of governors at Sedbergh.
1951: Declines post of Colonial Secretary.
1952: Bracken elevated to the peerage as the Viscount Bracken of Christchurch. May have regretted acceptance, and he never took his seat in the Lords.
1958: Bracken diagnosed as having throat cancer, in January. Dies the following August, aged 57 years.

WILLIAM JOYCE (1906-46)

1906 (24 April): William Joyce born Brooklyn, New York, of an Irish father and English mother.
1909: Joyce family move to Ireland.
1909-13: Joyce's father becomes a publican in Ballinrobe, Co. Mayo.
1913-21: Joyce family move to Galway, where Michael Joyce becomes a landlord of barracks occupied by the Royal Irish Constabulary.
1918-19: Michael Joyce's property burnt out by Sinn Fein supporters.
1920: William Joyce volunteers as an informer to the RIC.
1921: Joyce arrives in England, ahead of his family. Years later he claims this was due to the fact that his 'intelligence activities' were known to the Irish Republican Army.
1922: Joyce becomes a student at Battersea Polytechnic, studying science.
1923-7: Studies English Language and Literature, and History at Birkbeck College, London University.
1923: Joins British Fascists.
1927: Aged 21, marries Hazel Kathleen Barr, and has two children.
1928: Studies for one year's post-graduate course in Philology.
1928-30: Speaks for and assists Conservative Party.
1933: Applies for British passport.
1933-7: Becomes a member of Sir Oswald Mosley's party, the British Union of Fascists.

1934: Joyce and Mosley acquitted on a charge of riotous assembly.
1936: First marriage dissolved.
1937: Marries Margaret Cairns White, whom he had met at a Fascist meeting. Splits from Mosley and forms the National Socialist League.
1938-9: Charges of assault dismissed in court.
1939: Orders disbandment of National Socialist League. Travels to Germany, with Margaret, one month before war is declared. Joins German Radio. Given the nickname 'Lord Haw Haw' by a *Daily Express* journalist.
1940: Joyce definitely identified by BBC monitors.
1942: Becomes chief commentator on German Radio for English Group. Joyce sues Margaret for divorce, on the grounds of infidelity. She counters with a charge of cruelty. Their divorce is granted. Joyce and Margaret re-marry.
1944: Awarded War Service Cross (a civilian award), by Hitler. German passport issued to William Joyce in name of 'Wilhelm Hansen'.
1945: Joyce shot in the leg and arrested by British soldiers on Danish frontier. Flown to London and charged with treason. Claims American citizenship. Convicted and sentenced to death. Appeals to House of Lords. Appeal dismissed.
1946 (3 Jan.): William Joyce was hanged at Wandsworth Prison, aged 39.

CHARACTERS

WILLIAM JOYCE, known as Lord Haw Haw
BRENDAN BRACKEN, MP, Minister of Information
A FIRE WARDEN
POPSIE, an upper class English lady
LORD CASTLEROSSE, gossip columnist
LORD BEAVERBROOK, proprietor of the *Express* newspapers
MARGARET JOYCE, wife of William Joyce
ERICH, an anglophile German and reader of W. B. Yeats
A LADY JOURNALIST
TWO NARRATORS, one male, one female

The play is written so that it may be played by two actors and an actress. Although time in the play fluctuates, the basic setting is the early 1940s.

PART ONE

THE BRACKEN PLAY: LONDON

Stage left: a living room dominated by an Adam fireplace with the Romney portrait of Edmund Burke[1] *above the mantelpiece. A window into the street. A 1940s vintage wireless.*

Upstage, flying above the scene, a hanging washing line of larger than life figures, cut-out cardboard representations of Churchill, King George V and Sir Oswald Mosley. When these are reversed for Part Two they become: Dr Goebbels, Hitler and Mosley, again.

Downstage, right, a round rostrum which becomes street/roof top/broadcasting studio.

Upstage, built into the set, so that it becomes an integral part of the set when it fades, a video/film screen. Before the lights go up there is the sound of an air raid siren in the distance and then the drone of bombers and distant explosions. The sounds are brought down. Lights up on BRACKEN *in his living room, twiddling the knobs on the wireless: static, snatches of music, voices, then the clear calling code: 'Germany calling! Germany calling! This is Radio Hamburg and here is William Joyce with a commentary on today's news.'*

JOYCE: (*Voice on radio*) Today's report from the German Supreme Command announces the collapse of France. Following the surrender of St Malo and Lorient with over two hundred thousand prisoners, two hundred and sixty aircraft, an armistice has now been signed between Germany and France. My friends, the war in the West is over. After this most mighty victory in Germany history over the opponents of the greater German Reich, there are no allies left. Only one enemy of Germany remains: England.

BRACKEN *snaps off the wireless and walks about.*

BRACKEN: That's William Joyce, you know. Known as Lord Haw Haw. Could never understand why they call him that. A jumped up little fascist from the Irish Free State. Sounds more like

1. Edmund Burke (1729-97), Irish political philosopher, regarded in the nineteenth century as the intellectual founder of English conservatism; his defence of English tradition against the doctrines of the French Revolution, in works such as *Reflections on the Revolution in France* (1790), was central to his appeal. George Romney (1734-1802), English portrait painter, completed his portrait of Burke in 1775.

backstreet Brixton or Kilburn[2] on a Saturday night, wouldn't you say? Actually, I only listen to the filthy little traitor as part of my job. As Minister of Information in His Majesty's Government I do have to listen to a lot of tommyrot, I'm afraid. (*Turns on the wireless again*)

JOYCE: — Now is the time for all loyal Britons to call upon the government to resign, at once, to prevent further, useless slaughter. To rid ourselves of the warmonger Churchill and his craven supporters, the gangster Beaverbrook and that well known poseur and parasite, Mr Brendan Bracken —

BRACKEN *turns off wireless again.*

BRACKEN: Did you ever? Did you hear that? The nerve! Not going to listen to another word. Bloody twit. Knew the fellow well, you know, before he turned traitor with the Nazis. Vulgar little shit from Connemara, full of fight, ready to take on anyone. You know the kind of Paddy. Joined Tom Mosley's blackshirts. British Union of Fascists, that is. Tom eventually had to throw him out. Constantly beating up yids in the East End. The Irish are always being thrown out of something or other, aren't they? I'm absolutely convinced he's over there in Berlin, now, simply to be in the middle of the row. Coat off, sleeves up and bejasus we're off. Dreadful chap, actually.

JOYCE *appears on the video/film screen: black shirt, tie.* BRACKEN *affects a studied indifference.*

JOYCE: My friends, let me introduce the kind of crony who hangs around Churchill. Take this specimen of outrageous masquerade, Mr Brendan Bracken, MP, Minister of Information, would you believe!

BRACKEN: I'm not listening. I'm not paying the slightest attention to any of this —

JOYCE: Who is this Brendan Bracken? Who is this creature who pretends to be a member of the English establishment? I can tell you, my friends. He's the son of a Tipperary stonemason who was also a dynamite terrorist. He arrived in England with a chequebook, wangled his way into a minor public school for one year, memorized Burke's peerage[3] and back issues of the *Empire News* so that he knew the genealogy of every decent home in the country and the name of every significant clergyman in the Church of England. In this way he name-dropped his way to the top of the heap —

BRACKEN: Of course, Mosley did attract all the oddballs.

JOYCE: And this is the kind of man who now stands beside Churchill! Is it any wonder that England is in the most troubled phase of her history?

BRACKEN: All marching about with stiff elbows and that constipated swagger of the Hun. Disgruntled grocers from Battersea, proponents of cock-fighting in Norfolk —

JOYCE: Don't be misled, my friends, by the clownish demeanour of this man!

BRACKEN: Vegetarian old lady fascists from Sussex who would skewer a comma with one of their knitting needles —

JOYCE: Remember this is the man who is [the] confidant of Churchill. This is the man who controls Fleet Street. This is the man who censors and determines the flow of information to the British people during this quite unnecessary war.

BRACKEN: The question is, though: how did this chappie Joyce end up as Dr Goebbels'[4] right-hand man on the wireless?

JOYCE: The question is, what does it say about democracy if such a trickster can rise to the top?

BRACKEN: Lord Haw Haw, I ask you!

JOYCE: Mr Brendan Bracken, Tory MP for North Paddington, of all places!

BRACKEN: The traitor!

JOYCE: The trickster!

ACTOR *and* ACTRESS *forward in anonymous coats, to either side of the stage.*

ACTOR: (*Narrator*) Ladies and gentlemen, this is the story of two men who invented themselves.

ACTRESS: (*Narrator*) When a man wipes out his past and invents his own future he may have criminal or artistic tendencies.

ACTOR: On the other hand he may be simply acting out a condition of the culture from which he is trying so desperately to escape.

ACTRESS: Both men left Ireland in the twenties.

ACTOR: At the precise time when Ireland declared its independence of England.

ACTRESS: In England they both obliterated all evidence of their Irishness. Fabricating, instead,

2. Districts of London with a large number of Irish immigrants.
3. John Burke, *A Genealogical and Heraldic History of the Peerage and Baronetage of the United Kingdom* (1826). The work has been published annually since 1847.
4. Joseph Goebbels (1897-1945), Hitler's minister of propaganda from 1933.

ultra-English identities for themselves.

ACTOR: When the bombs began to fall over Western Europe after 1939 Bracken was in London, by Churchill's side, Joyce was in Berlin, on the other side of the fence.

ACTRESS: Before he died, Bracken had created modern British financial journalism —

ACTOR: Chairman of the *Financial Times* Group —

ACTRESS: Elevated to the peerage —

ACTOR: Although he never entered the House of Lords which he insisted upon calling the geriatric clinic —

BRACKEN: (*Suddenly taking over*) Actually, I died of cancer. (*Indicating throat*) Somewhere about here. If you were to put your hand there, you would feel — Now, look here. Before there's any more nonsense I simply wanted to say that I suffered one particular libel all my life. That I was the illegitimate son of Sir Winston. By the by have you noticed how people quicken at the prospect of unexpected cash or alternatively scandal among the notabilities? The whole British newspaper industry is based upon the satisfaction of those twin appetites. As for the Churchill bastardy, why should I deny it if people were prepared to indulge such a biological-historical impossibility? Randolph[5] the cad was responsible for the innuendo. Trotting around the Savoy[6] referring loudly to me as 'my bastard brother Brendan'. Do you think it might be merely the appeal of the alliteration? I replaced him, you see. Winston was, always will be, a father to me. (*Bright change*) Actually, my father was a bishop, don't you know, on the Cape —

ACTRESS: Correction!

BRACKEN: And that's another thing. (*Indicating the figure*) This fellow Joyce. Never met the chap. I want to make that perfectly clear, because you will hear otherwise later on.

JOYCE: (*Eruption*) *Wir habt doch gesiegt!*[7]

BRACKEN: He'll go on like that for hours if he's allowed —

JOYCE: This is not defeat.

BRACKEN: He's referring to the Hitler War, you know.

JOYCE: (*Rush-power*) As I face my Lord Jesus, I am purged of all impurity. The clean eye sees beyond this imperfection of limbs, this vale of tears, this habitat of the Jew plutocrat and his lickspittle protectors in high places. My friends, keep worthy company. Leave the shallow to the shallow and the nidering[8] to the nidering. Keep thine eye on the sword in the rooftree. In death as in life I defy the Jew-boy who is responsible for this late war. I defy the Power of Darkness in the Jew-pig. I pray to Almighty God that England will be great again. May the standard of the Hakenkreutz[9] be raised from the dust! I call on the dead sons of England who have died without knowing why. I call on their seed that the future generations of England may ensure the nobility of the race! *Sieg Heil! Sieg Heil! Sieg Heil!*[10] (*Bows head*)

ACTRESS: William Joyce was hanged for high treason, January 3rd 1946, at Wandsworth Prison and his body was buried in quicklime.

ACTOR: Thirty years later still, the Joyce family brought the remains back, for interment, to Galway from where young William had fled in 1922 in the wake of the retreating British Army and the Black and Tans.[11] You might say he was always a few strides behind marching feet.

Lights out on JOYCE.

BRACKEN: Actually, he was American this chap, Joyce. That's why we had such trouble hanging him. Mustn't hang a Yank. Not in 1946, at any rate. Actually, the future is with Englishness, not England, I'm afraid. The whole world will be divided between those who speak the language and those who don't. Can't imagine what the other lot will look like. Probably slanted eyes and indifferent pigmentation, wouldn't you say. It's obscene, that's what I said to Winston, it's obscene that this creature Joyce should claim to speak for England from the scaffold. Then Winston said rather a curious thing. My dear, he said, we have always taken more captives with our dictionaries than with our regiments.

ACTRESS: When *he* died in 1958, Bracken's throat had closed over the tubes through which they had tried to feed him. At the express wish of

5. Randolph Churchill (1911-68), Winston's son.
6. A famous London hotel, then much frequented by members of the 'establishment'.
7. We have won! (grammatically colloquial).
8. More usually 'niddering', a base coward or wretch.
9. Crooked Cross, Swastika, symbol of the Nazi Party.
10. Hail to Victory! The slogan of the Nazi Party.
11. A specially recruited British army corps, notorious for its barbaric behaviour in Ireland during the War of Independence, 1919-21.

the deceased there was no funeral, no memorial service.

ACTOR: You could say that he had died of the one thing calculated to kill him. Speechlessness.

Lights out on BRACKEN.

ACTRESS: Ladies and gentlemen! We cannot vouch for the accuracy of anything that is going to follow —

ACTOR: Even of what is verifiable in the history books —

ACTRESS: It has been put together to make a point.

ACTOR: Question: What is the difference between an Irishman's need to conceal his Irishness and an Englishman's need to believe in the concealment?

ACTRESS: Question: What is the connection between the Germanic love of English literature and the success of Dr Goebbels' radio propaganda?

ACTOR: Put another way: Why does the victim always try to imitate the oppressor?

ACTRESS: Women are well aware of this condition.

ACTOR: Men only discover it when they are political underdogs.

ACTRESS: Imitate that you may be free.

ACTOR: There is also the momentum of colonialism which operates like an inverted physics.

ACTRESS: The further out on the periphery, the stronger the pull to the centre.

ACTOR: Every metropolis is thronged with provincials.

ACTRESS: Each trying to be more metropolitan than the other. And so, to play! (*Bows and exits*)

ACTOR: Let us begin then with Mr Bracken in full flight upon his favourite instrument of communication, the telephone. (*Exit*)

Sounds of frantic telephone ringing. Down to: BRACKEN, *standing, holding, in turn, a variety of telephone receivers.*

BRACKEN: (*Phone*) Hello? Hello! I wish to speak with Lady Colefax, if you please. (*Short pause*) Certainly not. I haven't the slightest interest in addressing her appointments' secretary. (*Pause*) And do be quick about it, there's a dear. (*Off phone*) Bloody cow! (*Phone*) Sybil! Darling! That was a delightful Thursday. (*Pause*) Yes, well, that woman *is* a gorgon. If I may say so, you displayed the patience of Job before her antics. (*Pause*) Absolutely. (*Pause*) Absolutely. (*Impatient pause*) Absolutely. Nothing could improve her short of major surgery. Now, *The Economist*, Sybil darling. (*Pause*) Don't you remember? *The Economist*. You did promise — I simply want to be able to tell the banker chappies that you are willing to sell your holding to me. (*Pause*) Yes, I know it's all such a perfect bore but you know how I have dedicated my life to the elimination of boredom. (*Ho-ho*) (*New phone*) Charles? That you? The old sweetheart is prepared to sell. (*Pause*) Never mind how. Make it fifty thousand, would you. (*Pause*) What? How much? (*Pause*) Seventy thousand? Who is behind this bid? (*Pause*) Oh, he is, is he? Not to worry. I'll deal with him. (*Pause*) Well, I happen to know that he happens to think that I may be advising on the Civil List. Mum's the word! (*New phone*) Reggie? You can get your knickers out of a twist, dear. We're there. We now control the *Banker*, the *Financial News* and the *Investors Chronicle*. *The Economist* will be the stone at the centre of the pendant, as it were.[12] (*Pause*) Of course it's my own phrase, you idiot. By the by, who were those gorgeous people with the Duff Coopers[13] last night? (*Pause*) Really? I'd adore meeting them anon if you can arrange it. Knew their son well at Oxford, as a matter of fact. Splendid fellow. (*Pause*) Well, Balliol,[14] as a matter of fact. (*Pause*) Well, you bloody well know now, don't you! (*Off phone*) That superannuated shit! (*New phone*) Eddie? Couldn't get back before this. Got your message at White's.[15] Glad to be of help. (*Pause*) Where exactly is your boy in the clink? (*Pause*) Ah, Marseilles! Know it well. Not to worry. No one worries about such peccadillos nowadays. I'll get the FO[16] on to it first thing in the morning. Better still, let me get the brother on to it. Terribly well connected with the Frogs, the brother. Import-export, that sort of thing. He'll know exactly what to do about a prison. By the by, you do know the Bishop of Durham,

12. Of this group of commercial and financial newspapers, *The Economist*, a weekly review, founded in 1843, was the most distinguished and influential.
13. Alfred Duff Cooper, 1st viscount Norwich (1890-1954), diplomat and author, married Lady Diana Manners in 1919. Their house at 90 Gower Street was a social centre for many powerful figures, including Beaverbrook and Churchill. Cooper stood as an independent candidate in 1931, supported by Beaverbrook and Rothermere, in protest at Baldwin's leadership of the Conservative Party. Opposed to Chamberlain's policy of appeasement, he resigned as First Lord of the Admiralty in 1938; he was ambassador to France 1944-47.
14. Balliol College, Oxford (founded in 1263) included a large number of statesmen and politicians among its distinguished members.
15. A well-known London club.
16. The Foreign Office.

don't you? Want to have a word with him, if you can set it up. (*Pause*) Well, actually, it's about the Canterbury Succession.[17] (*Pause*) My dear man, the future of the Church is as dear to me as is the Empire. Anyway, old Cosmo Lang. Swine hasn't much longer to go. Terribly important to have the right man in that particular post in these troubled times. I am, after all, the publisher of the *Book of Common Prayer*,[18] you know. Besides, my father was a — a distinguished clergyman. Didn't know that, did you, now? (*New phone: entirely different tone: hurt, vulnerable*) You didn't call. I sat by the phone. (*Pause*) All night. (*Outburst*) It is not casual to me. (*Pause*) Sorry. I do not mean it as an obligation, either. (*Pause*) Well, we do not have to call it love, do we. Yes. Very well. Good night, Popsie. (*New phone: again an entirely different tone: cold anger*) It's you, is it? You must never, never, never telephone me again, do you hear! I will pay your demands. I will continue to pay your lousy demands. I will do this not because of your threats and bullying, no, because I despise such threats, but I will pay you because of our mother, because you are my brother but never again, here or anywhere else, are you to dare to telephone me. (*Long pause. Shaken. Conscious effort at recovery. Last phone call, a call to arms*) Winston! (*Pause*) Yes, well, I did hear rumours, actually. Yes. Yes. Yes. Minister of Information. Yes. Absolutely wonderful, great honour, of course. (*Pause*) You know my feelings, Winston, from the House. This war must be conducted in public. The press is one of our strongest weapons. Especially since the Hun is incapable of calling upon the same ally. (*Pause*) Yes, well I've talked to Max. And the Berrys. And Esmond Harmsworth.[19] (*Pause*) Well, you know, if you wish to control the press you talk to owners, not editors, my dear. Yes — (*End of phones.* BRACKEN *stands to attention before a hidden authority*) The Right Honourable Minister of Information (*Testing the words*) Brendan Bracken, MP, Member for North Paddington. (*Pause: fresh start*) Viscount Bracken of ... Pretoria? No. Hobart? Viscount Bracken of Hobart? No. Christchurch. Ah! Viscount Bracken of Christchurch. (*Stiffening*) In this terrible war, I will serve my country and my king against the forces of darkness which threaten our very civilization —

To POPSIE *in a peignoir at the edge of* BRACKEN's *room.* BRACKEN *is within, fiddling with the radio so that she is able to look in at him from without.*

POPSIE: (*To audience*) I loved being with him at times like that. He gave the impression of having composed the whole thing in his head, as if he had written the book in which all the important people were characters of his imagination. But how could one possibly give oneself wholly to someone who was never there, if you see what I mean? (*She disrobes to a Boy Scout uniform beneath the peignoir*) He needed costuming to become sexually — you know. Hence my Baden-Powell[20] outfit. Windswept hair on the uplands, jolly boys in tents. That kind of thing, I suppose.

BRACKEN: Popsie! Popsie! Come here! I've got the little bugger.

POPSIE *steps into the room. Stops, hands on hips.*

POPSIE: Oh, God, Brendan, not more of that boring shit. Please.

BRACKEN: Listen!

WIRELESS: (*Up*) Germany calling! Germany calling! Here are the stations: Calais One, 514 metres. Calais Two, 301.6 metres, Köln, 456 metres, Breslau, 316 metres and the short-wave transmitter DXX, 48.86 metres. And now, with a

17. The succession to the archbishopric of Canterbury, the most important see in the Church of England. Cosmo Gordon Lang (1864-1945) was archbishop of Canterbury 1928-42.

18. The Prayer Book of the Church of England evolved in the sixteenth century and was finalized in the text of 1662. It was published by Eyre and Spottiswoode, on whose board Bracken sat.

19. William Maxwell Aitken (1879-1964), created Lord Beaverbrook in 1916, was a powerful newspaper proprietor. Canadian by birth, he commanded great influence in Britain through his ownership of such papers as the *Daily Express*, the *Sunday Express* and the *Evening Standard*. He supported Chamberlain's policy of appeasement at Munich. Later he became a vigorous prosecutor of the war effort as minister of aircraft production and as a member of the war cabinet in 1940.

James Garner Berry (1883-1968) and his brother, William Ewart Berry, created a newspaper empire based on the *Daily Sketch*, *Sunday Graphic*, *Sunday Times*, *Sunday Empire News* and *Daily Telegraph*.

Harold Sidney Harmsworth (1868-1940), 1st viscount Rothermere, owned the Amalgamated Press and Associated Newspapers. He was brother of the most powerful of press barons, Alfred C. W. H. Harmsworth (1865-1922), Viscount Northcliffe, founder of the *Daily Mail*, *Daily Mirror* and proprietor of *The Times*. He supported appeasement in 1938.

Cecil Esmonde Harmsworth (1898-1978), 2nd viscount Rothermere, third son of Harold Sidney Harmsworth, was chairman of Associated Newspapers in 1932. From 1940 he and Lord Beaverbrook were rival owners of Britain's mass-circulation press.

20. Robert S. S. Baden-Powell (1857-1941), founder of the Boy Scouts and Girl Guides. He became famous for his part in the 217-day siege of Mafeking in the Boer War. His most memorable publication was *Scouting for Boys* (1908).

commentary on the news, William Joyce —

BRACKEN: The filthy little traitor with the vulgar voice —

POPSIE: (*Caught*) Sh!

WIRELESS: (JOYCE): Tonight, the Luftwaffe will give London a taste of what is to come if this war is not brought to a swift conclusion. One hundred and forty bombers will devastate the City of London —

BRACKEN: Liar!

WIRELESS: (JOYCE): Direct reprisal for the indiscriminate bombing of German citizens by the RAF, old men, women and children under the orders of the arch-murderer, Churchill. But Mr Churchill can no longer hide behind his cigar —

BRACKEN *snaps off the wireless and stands, shaking.*

POPSIE: If you find him so utterly repulsive, why do you insist upon listening to him, night after night? Really, Brendan!

She lies on the sofa and puts her legs up. BRACKEN, *in tension, turns on the wireless again.*

WIRELESS: (JOYCE): — our fleet in the North Sea. Meanwhile, Churchill's minion, Churchill's choirboy, Churchill's ingle,[21] one Mr Brendan Bracken, fumes in Whitehall. According to the High Command, over one hundred thousand gross tonnage of shipping has been sunk in the North Atlantic by —

BRACKEN, *in a fury, switches off the wireless again.*

BRACKEN: Did you hear that?

POPSIE: How can I hear if you insist on turning it off?

BRACKEN: He referred to me!

POPSIE: Rubbish. (BRACKEN *is now back at the wireless but all that comes out is a Victor Sylvester-style waltz and, then, a whole variety of stations*) Brendan! Turn that bloody thing off! At once! Brendan! (BRACKEN *obeys, switches off the wireless, buries his head in his hands*) Brendan. Are you all right?

BRACKEN: (*Sudden alertness, sudden control*) Of course. I'm perfectly fine, thank you. I refuse to think about him any more. Here. Come sit on my knee, Popsie.

POPSIE: Like this?

BRACKEN: Forward a little. Hold it. Ah!

POPSIE: Do you think you're making love to a boy?

BRACKEN: Certainly not. How could I? What a question.

POPSIE: It's simply one of the things which might occur to a casual observer of this delicate scene.

BRACKEN: How boringly literal of you, my dear.

POPSIE: The question is: are we proceeding to the inner sanctum or is this to be prolonged dalliance in the outer chambers?

BRACKEN: Who would want anything else with the pleasure of such a — such a — composition?

POPSIE: Speak for yourself.

BRACKEN: It's the image, my dear. What might otherwise be beyond our reach. I wonder if that's what it's all about? The contrivance of what is really inaccessible?

POPSIE: What? Sex?

BRACKEN: No. Art. Well, both as a matter of fact.

POPSIE: Do you not feel anything? There?

BRACKEN: Not a thing, I'm afraid.

POPSIE: Perhaps I should change into my Highland tartan? Or my gymslip? Or my Florence Nightingale?[22] I shouldn't object in the least if you had a boy. I'd find it jolly exciting, as a matter of fact. I mean there is always a certain rub-off, isn't there, between lovers?

BRACKEN *extricates himself, firmly, and leaves her sitting on the sofa.*

POPSIE: What on earth are you doing?

BRACKEN: I'm re-arranging myself.

POPSIE: So I see.

BRACKEN: You always do it, Popsie. Ruining everything with your pedestrian specifics —

POPSIE: I have to say what is what. I can't abide unreality. It's downright immoral. I was brought up to believe what is, is and what is not, is not.

BRACKEN: How can one give oneself to a dream, an image —

POPSIE: Besides, what is really bothering you is sexual truth — you spend your life constantly evading, constantly avoiding, constantly inventing — How can one possibly live like that?

BRACKEN: You're just a common little tart!

POPSIE: And you're just a twisted little Irish puritan!

BRACKEN: Whore!

POPSIE: Oh, dear, we're beginning to sound like South Americans.

BRACKEN: I can't abide lewd talk! You know that.

POPSIE: For Heaven's sake, can you not be

21. boy, homosexual lover.

22. The English nurse (1820-1910) celebrated for her work in the Crimean War (1854-55).

yourself for once! You conceal nothing from me, Brendan, nothing, and it doesn't make the slightest difference to my feeling for you, whatever you are. Don't you see that? (*Cry*) Well, why can't you trust me, then?

BRACKEN: Tell you what, Popsie! Let's dash off to the country for the weekend!

POPSIE: (*To the world*) I give up. Truly. I give up.

BRACKEN: Give some of our friends a tinkle —

POPSIE: (a) There's a war on. (b) There's no petrol. (c) I never wish to see that appalling car of yours, that Hispano Suiza with its garish blue carriage lamps, ever again, in this lifetime.

BRACKEN: We had jolly times, didn't we?

POPSIE: No. Yes, it was fun. The problem is I no longer see myself in the situation. Perhaps one needs to distance oneself from roguery in order to enjoy it.

BRACKEN: Freedom is distance, actually. Beaverbrook once said that to me. Freedom is distance, is space, Bracken. Never forget that, Bracken. We live in the one country in the world which respects that space as a matter of its very definition as a nation, as a civilized culture. That every man should have space between him and another. That every State should have space between it and its neighbour. That's what old Max said. (*Reflectively*) Every tin-pot revolutionary from the year dot has dreamed of that space, that hiving-off of another, the Other, some tyrannical shadow, some dark father and for what? For the brief space before the space is filled again and one begins again, again and again, for freedom, over and over again before one's morning shaving-mirror.

POPSIE: I would never have thought Max Aitken capable of the perception.

BRACKEN: Oh, I have embroidered upon the relatively simple-minded headline of dear Max. *Daily Express*, y'know.

POPSIE: I am sure you have.

BRACKEN: It's odd, isn't it, that patriotism and treason may be fuelled by the same hunger for space —

POPSIE: You are quite incorrigible, Brendan.

BRACKEN: But then all things are opposites of other things as my old chum Willy Yeats would say.

POPSIE: Brendan — have you listened to even one word of what I've said?

BRACKEN: What? What do you mean?

POPSIE: Every time I try to reach you, yet another Brendan Bracken is talked into existence. Like a distracting mushroom. Very disconcerting.

BRACKEN: I happen to subscribe to the Wildean notion that one must make of one's life a work of art.[23] We're given pretty dismal material to start with. One must shape it into significance. I believe that that's what's meant by salvation.

POPSIE: For God's sake, I'm talking about ordinary, basic, human feeling! I love you, Brendan.

BRACKEN: And I love you, too.

POPSIE: I know that that is the signal for us not to see one another for a while.

BRACKEN: Yes.

POPSIE: (*Hope*) Perhaps, if you could just put that past behind you —

BRACKEN: I am an orphan!

POPSIE: Balderdash!

BRACKEN: Like every other orphan I've been travelling all my life towards some closed door. When it opens I expect someone to walk through. Someone whom I shall instantly recognize.

POPSIE: For Heaven's sake, Brendan, we all know perfectly well that you're not an orphan.

BRACKEN: I am an orphan!

POPSIE: You've had those perfectly normal, nice Irish parents of yours back in the land of the shamrock. I mean, what more does one need?

BRACKEN: Orphanhood, my dear, may be as much a condition of choice as an unhappy product of the Great Reaper.

POPSIE: Sometimes, I truly believe that you contrive subjects for conversation simply in order to match phrases which you have already formed in your head.

BRACKEN: I never leave anything to chance.

POPSIE: Obviously not.

BRACKEN: Especially not the language.

POPSIE: Well, I must say I have never known anyone to use the English language quite in the way that you do, Brendan.

BRACKEN: Why not?

POPSIE: Well, it's rather as if one were speaking to someone who was discovering the words as he went along. It's aboriginal, extremely refreshing, of course —

BRACKEN: (*He means it*) That is the most appalling thing anyone has ever said to me.

POPSIE: What's the matter?

23. cf. Oscar Wilde's famous doctrine in *Intentions: The Decay of Lying* (1891): '. . . Life imitates art far more than Art imitates life.'

BRACKEN: Insulting! Denigrating!

POPSIE: What is?

BRACKEN: Forget it. That's enough.

POPSIE: What is the matter with you? You become upset at the most trivial things.

BRACKEN: Trivial!

POPSIE: I haven't an earthly idea of what all the fuss is about.

BRACKEN: You call my use of the language trivial!

POPSIE: Of course. One opens one's mouth and words come out. Perfectly straightforward I should say.

BRACKEN: It is what makes me what I am! Without it, I am nothing!

She has considerable difficulty with this.

POPSIE: Are you in pain again with that throat of yours?[24]

BRACKEN: Of course I'm in pain. I'm in pain every time my sensibility is outraged by a gross version of reality.

POPSIE: I didn't quite mean that, Brendan. How is your throat?

BRACKEN: Most days I am reduced to semolina and porridge. Not at the same time, of course. Every human person has his flowering blight. Mine just happens to be here. That is all.

POPSIE: You shouldn't be alone.

BRACKEN: You have an extraordinary aptitude, my dear, for the essential statement.

POPSIE: Very well. If you must be swinish about it I'm going to trot along. (*No response*) I expect I had better get this ridiculous uniform off, hadn't I? Can't go out dressed like this.

BRACKEN: No. One should always be appropriately dressed for the outdoors.

BRACKEN *goes, peers through the curtains into the street. She gives up on him and turns to go.*

POPSIE: Oh, blast! I've gone and ripped these bloody shorts again! Heavens! How I've put on weight!

She goes out leaving BRACKEN *by the window. Light held on* BRACKEN *a moment and then down. Meanwhile, light on the actor as* LORD CASTLEROSSE, *in an armchair, downstage right. He is dressed in a grossly padded kaftan and a floppy tasselled Turkish fez, a heavy fat man who can scarcely breathe under his own weight.*

24. There may be a suggestion that the disease is psychosomatic.

CASTLEROSSE: (*To audience*) To understand Bracken, you see, you must go back to before the war. Actually Bracken's Irish past was never much of a mystery to the rest of us. Mentioned it meself, oodles of times, in me gossip column in *The Sunday Express*.

Mr Brendan Bracken, the flamboyant Celt, was at Sybil Colefax's last Thursday. You couldn't go to a party without bumping into him, a red-haired golliwog wearing indifferent suits. Bloody marvellous company, though. The thing about the English is that they're too damned polite to ask who you are or where you're from. So what, anyway, I say, if the feller is getting on with it. He was running five newspapers by the time he was thirty. Including the *Financial News* and *The Economist*. Don't think he knew a damned thing about business, any more than the rest of us. I once asked him what was the secret of international banking. He said: a mastery of slavic monosyllables, m'dear. What a glorious scoundrel he was, dear Brendan.

I'm supposed to tell you about Beaverbrook though. Beaverbrook wanted to know about Bracken. Beaverbrook wanted to know about everyone. Kept secret files on people. In a bloody big box. Called it his Deadman's Chest.

Any rate. There was Max on the phone. Sometime in the early thirties. I say, Castlerosse, you're Irish, you'll enjoy this. I *am* Irish, actually, meself. Earl of Kenmare, 's matter of fact. Last of the line. There you are. Got a bit of a family seat over in County Kerry.[25] Trying to turn the bloody place into a golf course at present. Bloody marvellous country for golf courses, Ireland.

Any rate. There was Max, bubbling with gossip as usual. You'll get a charge out of this, old Max said. What's that, Max, I said. Bracken's father, he said. Bracken's father was a damned fenian,[26] he said. The police in Dublin Castle had a mug-shot of the old geezer on display. Notorious felon. Blowing-up places. That kind of thing. What Max had done, you see, was sent over one of his investigator fellers from the *Daily Express* to Ireland where the whole sorry tale was laid bare by the vindictive natives.

25. Valentine Charles Brown, viscount Castlerosse, earl of Kenmare (1891-1943), a socialite, friend of Beaverbrook, and gossip columnist in the *Sunday Express*.

26. A member of the Irish revolutionary Fenian organization of the late nineteenth century.

You're Irish, Valentine, Max said, what d'you think of that? Well, Max, I said, there are Irish and there are Irish and then there are other Irish. Max didn't quite get the point. Canadian, y'see. Actually, I adored Brendan. He had that splendid Irish neck, if you see what I mean. Bit nouveau, perhaps. I mean to say there was that ludicrous business of his buying that four-poster bed. Couldn't get the thing into that bloody house in North Street. Bed abandoned, apparently.

He invited Willy Yeats, once, down for the weekend to Freddy Britton-Austin's house. Pretending the house was his own. The Britton-Austins were abroad, d'you see. He even gave Yeats a book out of the library as a memento of the visit. Yeats went off, muttering and mumbling, thrilled with the hospitality. An absolute scoundrel, Brendan, but glorious fun.

What Beaverbrook wanted to find out, you see, was where did Bracken stand in the general huffle. A bloody awful time, the thirties. The cat could have jumped either way. Everyone was having secret meetings. Winston and his lot, Beaverbrook and his Imperialists, Bracken bobbing up and down between them, Mosley[27] and his gang of unemployed clerks and county types. All yelling and shouting about the fate of England. Everyone thought at the time that the only problem with Hitler was that he was frightfully common. It was only later realized, as they say in the movies, that it was him or us. Brendan had had himself elected as a Tory MP for North Paddington,[28] of all places. What Max wanted to know, y'see, was which kind of Irishman was he, the kind who went high on the swing-boats or the kind who took potshots in the shooting gallery.

(*Shift in tone*) Of course the Irish are always trying to be something other than Irish or else they're being more Irish than you could possibly believe. Dreadful people, really. Glad to be out of the place. So was Bracken. He never talked about it, though. The only thing I ever remember him saying about Ireland was that his mother had suffered there. But I never got that particular story—

He meditates upon this as the lights come down on him. A few brass pieces play 'Hearts of Oak' and 'Rule Britannia'.[29] *A Union Jack and Tory streamers float down before the cardboard cut-out figures of Churchill, the King and Mosley.* BRACKEN *is on a high platform waving to the crowds who shout and heckle. A rehearsed chorus from somewhere: 'Bracken for Britain', 'Bracken for Britain'. Hecklers: 'What about the millions on the dole, then?' Chorus of 'Rule Britannia'.*

CHAIRMAN OF ELECTION MEETING: (*Voiceover on loudspeaker*) Ladies and gentlemen of the great borough of Paddington, may I introduce the Conservative candidate for the constituency. He comes from British-Irish stock and was born in Bedfordshire, the son of a distinguished officer in the Indian Army. He has one residence in London, one in Bedfordshire, with estates in Scotland and Northern Ireland. An old Sedbergh boy and a distinguished graduate in history from Oxford University — Mr Brendan Bracken!

Cheers, cat-calls and wild trumpet playing.

BRACKEN: (*Stilling the crowd*) May I say, that there can be little wrong with England when her sons and daughters can raise their voices in joyful unison in such good old English songs. (*Jeers*) Fellow Britons! We are here today, under the Crown and flag, to rid this city, this nation, once and for all, of the socialist menace, to expose the slobbery promises of MacDonald and Henderson[30] and all their Bolshevik tribe! (*Uproar*) Let me make one thing perfectly clear. No man has a greater respect for the English working man than I. No one knows better than I, how our great Empire is founded upon the decent English labouring classes. But we are not talking about native sons of England, my friends. We are talking about foreign poison

27. Oswald Mosley (1896-1980) became a Conservative MP in 1918, but broke with the party over its policy in Ireland and its condoning of the behaviour of the Black and Tans. He joined the Labour Party in 1924, but resigned in 1930. In 1932 he created his own party, the British Union of Facists. From 1934, anti-semitism was a central element in the BUF's policy. Mosley's fascist meetings, often violent, were most popular in the East End of London. He and his second wife, Diana Guinness, one of the famous Mitford sisters, launched a peace campaign in 1936, denouncing the oncoming war as a Jewish conspiracy. They were imprisoned in 1940 and released three years later. Mosley published his apologia in *My Answer* (1946) and *My Life* (1968).

28. A largely working-class district of London.

29. 'Hearts of Oak' properly *Heart of Oak* by David Garrick (1717-79). 'Rule Britannia', a song from Thomas Augustine Arne's (1710-78) masque, *Alfred* (1740).

30. Ramsay MacDonald (1866-1937), first Labour prime minister of Britain. He led two Labour governments (1924; 1929-31) and a coalition, which the majority of the Labour Party refused to support. Arthur Henderson (1863-1935) helped to draft the Labour Party's constitution (1918). From 1929 to 1931 he was foreign secretary.

which is seeping into our system. Do we want to be controlled by the Moscow Comintern?[31] Are we to be ruled by a gang of Russian malcontents and perverts? Do we want our government clumping around the Palace in suits rented from Moss Brothers?[32] (*Laughter. Yell: 'Why not, ya bleedin' twit?'*) If there is one thing that has always been true in this great land of ours, it is respect for our leaders. (*Yell: 'Go and march with Mosley's blackshirts, then!'*) My friend, I'm glad you said that. Thank you, my friend. Thank you for allowing me to say that I respect the rights of Englishmen to walk the streets of England behind the Union Jack. I do not hold with anti-Semitism. No. But neither do I think, my friends, that our country should be over-run by alien races, the riff-raff of Russia, the refuse of the dens of the East — (*Hands aloft to uproar of cheers and boos*)

The lights fade. A voice singing in darkness:

'I fear no foe with Thee at hand to bless.
Ills have no weight, and tears no bitterness.'

Light-up on BEAVERBROOK *behind a small desk on the rostrum. Tight, small body in a black suit, white shirt, black tie. Great, balding head, tufted eyebrows, glasses on nose.*

BEAVERBROOK: (*With papers*) 'Where is death's sting, where grave thy victory? I triumph still if thou abide with me.'[33]

SERVANT: (*Voice off*) Lord Beaverbrook! Lord Beaverbrook! Sorry to bother you, lord!

BEAVERBROOK: What is it, Arthur?

SERVANT: (*Off*) Mr Bracken, lord. He wants a word with you. Says it's urgent.

BEAVERBROOK: Always is, with Brendan. Show him up, Arthur. (*Undertone*) Better get this damn well right first go.

Door opening. Closed. BRACKEN *steps up before* BEAVERBROOK.

BRACKEN: That it should come to this, Max.

BEAVERBROOK: Use the vernacular, Brendan.

BRACKEN: You're a shit, Max.

BEAVERBROOK: Hope that makes you feel better, Brendan.

BRACKEN: I would never dream of doing such a thing to a friend.

BEAVERBROOK: Baloney!

BRACKEN: Utterly without scruple —

BEAVERBROOK: Don't give me that Holy Joe act, Brendan. It won't wash.

BRACKEN: Violating my privacy.

BEAVERBROOK: Look! It's simple. I sent a man over to Ireland. I said to him: check out Bracken. I want to know everything possible about his background. Off he went. Nearly got bogged down in Dublin *en route*. But eventually he got as far as Templemore, Co. Tipperary. And was told the full story of Brendan Bracken. It's here. Over there. In an envelope. In a drawer.

BRACKEN: I see. And what do you propose to do? With this envelope?

BEAVERBROOK: Nothing. *Rien*. Forget about it.

BRACKEN: And you ask me to believe that you —

BEAVERBROOK: I'm a journalist, Brendan. I chase stories.

BRACKEN: I would never do such a thing to you —

BEAVERBROOK: Well, it's about bloody time you did. Go on. Go get a file on me. Then we'll be quits. The basis of a perfect relationship.

BRACKEN: Relationship!

BEAVERBROOK: Certainly. Based upon reality. Based upon facts and figures and not some sentimental tosh. My dear Brendan, I dislike your nanny sensitivity. It is the least agreeable side of your make-up. Besides, it's phoney. You only pull that act when you're caught on the hop. You see, what you're ignoring in all this, what you're forgetting, my friend, is that I admire you immensely. All the more because of the contents of that envelope, I might add. We're both questors, Brendan. We've both come in from the frontier. We know what the fight is all about because we've looked into the wilderness. The jungle out there —

BRACKEN: I had nothing — absolutely nothing —

BEAVERBROOK: They don't know about such things here on the mainland, Brendan. Especially not those titled asses in the Lords.[34]

BRACKEN: I had to begin. From the very beginning.

BEAVERBROOK: When I arrived here from

31. The Moscow Comintern, the Third Communist International (first was 1864, second 1889), was founded in 1919. It was an organization designed to co-ordinate the policies of anti-colonial peoples and advocated the 'Popular Front' of communists, liberals and socialists against fascism in 1933.
32. A well-known firm of bespoke tailors that rents suits and other articles of clothing.
33. 'Abide With Me', the first words of the famous hymn *Eventide* (1847) by Henry Frances Lyte (1793-1847).
34. In the Upper House of Parliament.

Montreal thirty years ago, the first thing I did was buy a Rolls-Royce. The second thing I did was decide to buy the Rolls-Royce company. Which I did.

BRACKEN: I was unfree. Every day of my childhood I would say: tomorrow, tomorrow I'm going to be free.

BEAVERBROOK: You know why I could do all this? Sure we have a free marketplace back home. But this was different. This was free entry into the most complex civilization since the Romans. This was the sign of belonging. You talk about freedom? Think of the freedom of that. And why? Why because I am British. You're British. We believe in the Empire. We believe in the greatest compromise between democracy and élitism ever devised by human political ingenuity.

BRACKEN: You know, I used to imagine, as a little boy, that people didn't recognize me, that I appeared to everyone as a stranger. I used to pretend not to recognize my name when it was called.

BEAVERBROOK: The problem with you, Brendan, is that you think you can invent the future. You can't. You can only master it when it does happen.

BRACKEN: I want no one to see these papers, Max.

BEAVERBROOK: That's the difference between you and me, Brendan. That's the reason why you'll never make money.

BRACKEN: You've heard me, Max. I don't want anyone to read that file.

BEAVERBROOK: My dear Brendan, you're missing the whole point. People would respect you for what you've done. The Englishman always respects the man who comes in from the colonies. Always has. Always found a place for him. New blood. New energy. Men tempered by the fire at the front. Men who make the choice.

BRACKEN: I want no one else to see these papers, Max.

BEAVERBROOK: What the hell's the matter with you, man?

BRACKEN: (*Outburst*) All that is dead! I want nothing to do with what was! I cannot be what I am if I'm saddled with that!

BEAVERBROOK: You can forget it. It's past.

BRACKEN: For God's sake, that isn't enough! It must be totally suppressed.

BEAVERBROOK *slowly opens a drawer in the desk. Removes an envelope. Removes papers from the envelope. Reads.*

BEAVERBROOK: 'Date of birth: February 15th, 1901.'

BRACKEN: I was born in the British Empire.

BEAVERBROOK: Yeah. Sure. Irish Free State didn't exist then.[35]

BRACKEN: And since the place in which I was born chose to break its connection with the Crown by force, I never wish to be associated with it, ever again.

BEAVERBROOK: So? What's the problem? There is no problem. My dear boy, history has been uncommonly generous to you. You should seize upon it as a sign, a charm that few are blessed with. History allowed you to choose. How many more can you say the same of down the centuries?

BRACKEN: 'To be bred in a place of estimation, to see nothing low or sordid from one's infancy — to be habituated in the pursuit of honour and duty —'

BEAVERBROOK: Eh? What's that?

BRACKEN: Edmund Burke on the British inheritance.[36]

BEAVERBROOK: Ah. You know Gandhi[37] once quoted Edmund Burke at me. You know — the Indian. The one who wants to dismantle the Empire. Do you know Gandhi, Brendan?

BRACKEN: (*Sudden turn so that it shocks* BEAVERBROOK *and drains* BRACKEN) I don't need to know him. I know his type. That sanctimonious, ascetic face with its watery eyes, running with pious self-denial. Peasants in the fields. What an image for the world to imitate! I despise him, begging bowl in one hand, dagger concealed in the other. Determined to prove the superiority of the primitive. I would happily trample him into the ground. What do these people know of law? Of grace? Cultivated living? They would overrun us, mark you. With their foul smells. Their obscene rituals. Animalism.

BEAVERBROOK: OK, OK, OK. Calm down. Here, sit. It's OK.

35. The Irish Free State was founded in 1922.
36. Edmund Burke, *An Appeal from the New to the Old Whigs* (1791): 'To be bred in a place of estimation; to see nothing low and sordid from one's infancy; . . . these are the circumstances of men that form what I should call a *natural* aristocracy, without which there is no nation.'
37. Mohandas Karamchand Gandhi (1869-1948), the great Indian leader of the civil disobedience movements against British rule in India. He used the hunger-strike or fast as a political weapon, particularly from 1933 onwards and formulated the policy of *Satyagraha* — non-violent resistance to evil. Gandhi was assassinated in 1948.

BRACKEN: I'm sorry.

BEAVERBROOK: You want a brandy?

BRACKEN: No. No.

BEAVERBROOK: We have to soldier together, Brendan, you and I.

BRACKEN: Yes.

BEAVERBROOK: We have to save England from the bloody English, we Scots and Irish. Hah?

BRACKEN: Indeed.

BEAVERBROOK: Are you all right?

BRACKEN: Yes. I'll see myself out.

BEAVERBROOK: Brendan. (*Pause*) Your father was a remarkable man.

BRACKEN: My father had the face of a condemned people.

BEAVERBROOK: Brendan —

BRACKEN *has gone*

BEAVERBROOK: (*Over the papers*) 'Mother's name: Hannah Ryan.' Pretty name, Hannah. (*Yell*) Arthur!

ARTHUR: (*Off*) Yes, lord!

BEAVERBROOK: Got some more papers, Arthur. More papers for my Deadman's Chest.

Lights down on BEAVERBROOK. *Lights up on room.* POPSIE *stands in the middle of the room in the garb of the Women's Voluntary Service: long coat, armband, satchel over shoulder, tin-hat.*

POPSIE: (*Towards hidden* BRACKEN *who is off-stage*) That's not quite what I said. What I said was that you try too hard. That's all. It can be disconcerting to people. Can you hear me in there, Brendan? (*Almost to herself*) Very odd, really. It's rather as if something had been pushed out of shape and if one were only able to push it back into shape — Brendan!

BRACKEN: (*Off*) Yes. What is it?

POPSIE: Nothing. I simply said there is absolutely no reason why you should overstate yourself.

BRACKEN: Thank you.

POPSIE: Pig.

BRACKEN: Popsie!

POPSIE: Yes?

BRACKEN: Do you think that I am false?

She is so overwhelmed by this that she has to sit down.

BRACKEN: (*Off*) Are you there?

POPSIE: Brendan, I think you're the most generous of persons.

BRACKEN: (*Off*) But do you think I'm false?

POPSIE: (*Near to tears*) No.

BRACKEN *comes on, briskly, in an overcoat and tin-hat.*

BRACKEN: There we are!

POPSIE: Where are you going?

BRACKEN: Up on the roof of the Admiralty, actually. I want to see the Hun arriving.

POPSIE: How ghastly!

BRACKEN: I have a rendezvous up there.

POPSIE: With whom, may I ask?

BRACKEN: With my great mechanical birds. Why not come with me?

POPSIE: I'm on duty now, you know. What I shall most remember of this war is the disgusting smell of tea-urns. (*Pause*) Are you really asking me to be with you, Brendan?

BRACKEN *has moved to the window and is peeping out. As he speaks she never even turns in his direction. She closes her eyes as if in discomfort.*

BRACKEN: Come here a moment, would you. Got to be careful with the light. Look! Do you see that figure by the lamppost there? The one in the shoddy raincoat. That's him. That's my brother Peter. He will stay there until I have gone to bed. Where he sleeps I do not know. He's a criminal. Broke in here. Stole that Romney portrait of Burke from over the mantelpiece. Demanded a thousand pounds. I told him to bugger off. Look at him. Have you any conception, can you possibly understand what it is like? To be haunted by one's own brother dressed like a Soho pimp and with manners to boot. There are times, darling, when I truly fear that he may never go away from beneath the lamppost, there —

POPSIE: Stop treating me like an audience!

POPSIE *rushes out and off,* BRACKEN *calling after her. He then returns to his window. She has come downstage and across, hesitating, before she addresses the audience.*

I know you must think I've been frightful to him but really! I've been obliged to listen to stories about this brother for donkey's years. At different times this brother would appear to be high-up in the Admiralty, in charge of vast tea plantations in Ceylon while, at the same time, conducting a lucrative business in the City. He seems to dread the appearance of this brother on his doorstep. Like one of those messengers in an old play. Carrying a bundle of possessions, the swaddling clothes of a lost child. Perhaps, to keep him at bay, he is always talking about him. I will speak to the brother about it. Let me talk it over with the brother. People then smile at him. Behind his back, of course. Poor Brendan.

She pulls herself together and strides off to do her duty. BRACKEN *watches through the curtains. He then steps out of the room and on to the rostrum, facing the audience, peering out. The* ACTOR *comes forward in fire-warden gear, tin-hat, water-bucket. Stooped shoulders. As he does so, his attention, with* BRACKEN'S, *is caught by the approaching drone of heavy bombers approaching London. He makes his way on to the rostrum behind* BRACKEN *from where they both look down on London from the roof of the Admiralty.*

WARDEN: Mr Bracken! Stand back from the edge there, sir.

BRACKEN: Righto, warden. (*Blitz up*) Look at them. Here they come. From beyond the Rhine. Out of the woods. Caesar saw them first. Painted bellies. Fire. And then the hordes.

WARDEN: Nothing to shout about, if you don't mind me saying so, sir.

BRACKEN: Mustn't give in to gloom, warden.

WARDEN: Not gloom, sir. Just what's before me eyes.

BRACKEN: (*Under breath*) Oh, my God, another roundhead.[38]

WARDEN: Don't much like people up here in the bombing, sir, that's all.

BRACKEN: I am a member of the War Cabinet, warden.

WARDEN: Drinking champagne. Dancing. Not right, you know.

BRACKEN: Good God, man, I am to report to the PM and General Ismay.[39]

WARDEN: Naked women in fancy clothes. Fellows in starched shirts that ought to be in the frontline. That's what I see up here, lolling about the place.

BRACKEN: (*Patriotically*) St Paul's still stands, warden. Indomitable.

WARDEN: Not much longer it won't, at this rate.

BRACKEN: This won't do, man! Haven't you seen our posters put up by the Ministry? '*Fight on the Home Front.*' '*Don't listen to Lizzie Longface and George Grumble.*' Got to keep your chin up, warden. I'm responsible for those posters, warden.

WARDEN: Bloody waste of time, if you ask me, sir. Besides we don't want to fall into the street, do we? Stones loose thereabouts. Jerry's[40] handiwork.

BRACKEN: Although I do agree with you that we have to watch for the enemy within.

WARDEN: Only one enemy hereabouts, Mr Bracken, if you don't mind me saying so, sir.

BRACKEN: Nonsense, man.

WARDEN: Jerry up there. With the stick in his hands. Only enemy we've got, sir.

BRACKEN: (*Very heated*) You've no idea, simply no idea — City filled with them! Ninnies! Twerps! Over there in Whitehall. Would sell the King for a pension. And don't forget our Lefties. Down in their cellars. Scribbling their manifestoes. Sabotaging our factories. Enemies! By god, man! Breaking into the Savoy with their filthy flags. All those Wogs and Frogs and Whatnots from every corner of Europe. Compared to that lot, warden, your Hun, your sausage-eater up there with his shaven head and his unspeakable language, why, my dear man, he's merely a schoolboy compared to that other shower —

WARDEN: Poor blighters.

BRACKEN: Who?

WARDEN: Them down there. Doesn't matter who is who down there. You English, sir?

BRACKEN: What do you mean by that, man?

WARDEN: Just asking. No offence.

BRACKEN: England is an idea, warden. Not just fifty thousand square miles of fertility on an island with some oddball Celts occuping mountains to the West and North.

WARDEN: You're an educated man, sir.

BRACKEN: Sedbergh, warden. I'm an old Sedbergian.

WARDEN: Never heard of it. One of them public schools, is it?

He is rooting about with a contraption on the floor.

BRACKEN: What's that, warden?

WARDEN: It's only me primus,[41] sir.

BRACKEN: Primus! Primus! Lighting a primus in the middle of an air-raid! This won't do, my man.

WARDEN: Now look here, sir. You may be in charge down below. I'm in charge up here.

BRACKEN: How very celestial of you.

WARDEN: I know when Jerry's coming. When he's going. When he's gone.

Blitz sounds down.

38. An unimaginative believer in plain facts.
39. General Lionel Hastings, baron Ismay (1887-1965) was departmental secretary at the Committee of Imperial Defence (1936) and chief staff officer to Churchill during the war.
40. Colloquialism for 'the Germans'.
41. Primus Stove is a trade name for a light, portable stove that burns vaporized paraffin oil.

BRACKEN: (*Shift. Profile*) I had a bit of bad news the other day, warden.

WARDEN: Oh. What's that, then?

BRACKEN: My brother. Died in action. The RAF. Died splendidly. One of 'Stuffy' Dowding's chaps. Life and soul of the mess. Shot down over the Isle of Wight. Hadn't a chance. Took down two Messerschmitts[42] with him, though.

WARDEN: Sorry to hear that, sir.

BRACKEN: Terribly well liked at Marlborough. Rugger.[43] The usual thing. Father would have been proud. Father was an admiral, y'know.

WARDEN: Didn't know that, sir.

BRACKEN: Family traditions are terribly important, warden.

WARDEN: Funny that. My boy's in the RAF, too. What squadron did you say your brother was in, sir?

BRACKEN: This is irregular, warden, most irregular. Lighting a primus in the middle of an air-raid.

WARDEN: Who did you say your brother was with, Mr Bracken? What squadron is he in?

BRACKEN: My brother — my brother is a traitor, warden.

WARDEN: Not shot down?

BRACKEN: Not shot down.

WARDEN: Gone over to the other side, is he?

BRACKEN: You might say that.

WARDEN: Well well. Well well.

BRACKEN: Where did your father live, warden?

WARDEN: Eh?

BRACKEN: Where did he live, your father?

WARDEN: You mean me home, sir?

BRACKEN: Yes.

WARDEN: Nelson Green. Baltic Street. Back of the Lavender Dock. We all worked the docks. Rotherhithe.[44] My dad, his dad before him. Maybe his before him. Mostly casual. Not much left now, though. Wiped out. Down as far as Deptford.

A sudden, heavy explosion, all lights out and a single cry. BRACKEN *in a flickering light.*

BRACKEN: (*Deep fear*) Daddy! Please — no! Mammy, Mammy! (*At first, faltering*) My father, my father who is, my father was — (*Low, strong Tipperary accent*) Me father was wan of the lads, so he was, wan of the hillside men. He took the oath. He was out in the tenants war of eighty-nine. Bejasus I was. I knew the treason prisoners of sixty-five. They were all great friends of yer father, so they were, the men that rotted away in Pentonville and Portland but bechrist their time will come again and when it does —[45]

WARDEN: (*Voice out of the darkness*) Mr Bracken! Are you all right, sir?

BRACKEN: (*Irish accent*) Come here, Peter, me son. Come here a minnit, me little man. You'll stand up for Ireland, won't you, boy, when you grow up not like that brother of yours in the corner, Brendan-Brendy, the little scut, Mammy's pet, always whinging and bawling, four-eyes — (*English accent*) Leave me alone! Leave me alone!

WARDEN: (*With light*) You all right, sir?

BRACKEN: Is that you, warden? I cannot see. My glasses! Where are my glasses, man?

WARDEN: Here. Let me look about.

BRACKEN: I can't see. I'm blind.

WARDEN: Just the shock, sir. It'll pass in no time.

BRACKEN: For God's sake, I can't see!

WARDEN: Here's the specs.

BRACKEN: Broken, are they?

WARDEN: Right as rain, sir. Try them on.

BRACKEN: What did — what was I saying a moment ago, warden? Just now.

WARDEN: Something about your father, sir. I think. Couldn't quite get it.

BRACKEN: I never knew my father, warden.

WARDEN: No, sir.

BRACKEN: He died when I was two years of age.

WARDEN: Yes, sir.

BRACKEN: They were once walked on, my glasses. I mean I once walked on them. The sound of terror, the glass. It's still black, warden.

WARDEN: It's just the blast, sir. (*Sound of all clear*) Raid's over. You want me to help you down below, sir?

BRACKEN: What? No. No. Winston will wonder where I've been. Must go. Winston has been like a father to me, warden —

WARDEN: Yes, sir.

BRACKEN: Like a father. (*Unsteady exit*)

42. German fighter planes.
43. Marlborough College, a famous public school in Wiltshire, founded in 1843. Rugger, or rugby, is the football game that originated at Rugby, another public school, in 1823.
44. These areas were all heavily bombed during the London Blitz.
45. The year 1865 was the predicted year for Fenian insurrection, although it did not happen until 1867; 1886-89 were the years of the Land War's greatest successes; Pentonville and Portland are English prisons to which Fenians and IRB prisoners were sent.

WARDEN: (*After him*) What a lulu! Absolutely up in the bleeding belfry he is!

Light out on scene. Light up on BRACKEN *in his room, still wearing his overcoat. He fiddles with the wireless until he finds some music and sits, eyes closed. What happens is that the broadcast is interrupted by the voice of* JOYCE *calling to* BRACKEN *across the airwaves, at first the call signal: 'Germany calling! Germany calling!' Then the voice of* JOYCE, *at first spasmodically and then in full flow.* BRACKEN *is gradually alerted to it and his agitation increases with the presence of the voice. He switches off the wireless; the voice continues. He rushes off but the voice follows him so that we hear it at a distance as he stumbles about, beyond. When he comes back again the voice comes back with him and continues until he silences it.*

JOYCE: (*On the radio*). We are one. You and I are one. Why then, my friends, are we at war? The Germany that I know and the England that I know are one, two halves of the one, great, Northern European culture and civilization. England is filled with our friends. In every city, in every walk of life and every class. How then have we been divided? How have we been distracted from the common enemy, the Bolshevik, the Mongolian hordes from the East, waiting to descend upon Christendom. The King of England was dethroned, not because of an American lady[46] but because he was a firm friend of the Reich. A dummy was put in his place, a puppet manipulated by Churchill who in turn is manipulated by international Jewry — (BRACKEN *switches off the wireless and the voice continues*) I've watched you, Bracken, I've watched you for years. You're just a gadabout, Bracken, bedazzled by the finery in your master's house. I've watched you, Bracken. I was at your elbow when you lectured Von Ribbentrop[47] in Lord Londonderry's house[48] in 1936, on Limoges china.[49] Limoges china! When serious offers were being made to forge the alliance of the Teutonic peoples. I was beside you and Mosley in 1935 when he told Churchill that war with Germany would mean the destruction of England and Germany with victory to red Russia and the Jewish capitalists of America. And you, Bracken! You could only offer a quip from Noël Coward.[50] I overheard you when you backed out of going to Berlin with Lord Beaverbrook. The Olympic games gave you the pip, you said. And everyone went ho-ho. What a card! You're a clown, Bracken. They know it. They know you're just a performer. They like to see you perform, don't you know that? It satisfies their taste in comedy as a scale, a measurement, politics as entertainment, entertainment as politics. In its decadence the imperial always transposes conquest into a circus. The more clownish Irish have always been willing to step into that ring. And you're the perfect clown because you believe that life is a matter of taste. That makes you entirely innocuous. They know that, Bracken. They know you do not matter. (BRACKEN *rushes off, out, the voice pursuing him*) You're perspiring, Bracken. You're sweating. I can smell the swill in your stomach. Does it mean that, finally, the shell is cracking, Bracken? Are all the careful consonants out of control? What language will you speak now, my friend? (BRACKEN *backs out, the voice with him. After the first few lines the image of* JOYCE *appears on the video, black shirt, tie, black pants, and the voice speaks for the image*) Surely you've thought about such things? You're an intelligent man. Educated by the Jesuits, back in Eire. As I was myself, indeed. We understand one another perfectly. The trouble with you, my friend, is that you have mistaken privilege for power. Privilege has nothing to do with power. Power is always rooted in reality. Ask your pal Beaverbrook. He would never make a mistake like that. I didn't make such a mistake. I have never been impressed by images, I went, instead, to the heart. I drank its blood. That is where passion is converted to power and power converted to rule. That is why I am hated and feared by you and your ilk, Bracken. Not because of my broadcasts. No. It is because I have pushed to the limits what you and your cronies would desire but could never push to the bitter end.

BRACKEN *stands before the hanging figures of Churchill, the King and Mosley and as he does so, the*

46. Mrs Wallis Simpson, later the Duchess of Windsor, the American divorcée for whom Edward VIII abdicated the English throne.
47. Joachim von Ribbentrop (1893-1946), German ambassador in London 1936-38; German foreign minister 1938-45; hanged after his conviction for war crimes at the Nuremberg Tribunals.
48. Charles Stewart Henry (1878-1949), 7th marquess of Londonderry, and his wife, Edith Chaplin (1879-1959), entertained political leaders and royalty at Londonderry House in London. He was secretary of state for air in the National Government of 1931.
49. French porcelain; the first factory was established at Limoges in 1771.
50. Noël Coward (1899-1973), actor, dramatist and composer, whose comedies *Private Lives* (1930) and *Design for Living* had made him famous.

image and voice of JOYCE *die out. Then he turns to a desk in the room and begins to busy himself with papers. He extracts an unfinished letter and makes some notes on it.*

BRACKEN: (*Reading letter*) Dearest Mother, I have only now been able to reply to your letter. Of course I do understand the pain you feel as you reflect back upon your life. Of course I know how you suffered at the hands of that man, my father, that vicious person. I remember the scenes in Ardvullen House,[51] Mother. I remember that barbaric man. How you lay in your own blood on the kitchen floor. How he broke the few pieces of china which you had brought with you as his bride into that house. I remember all these things, how could I ever forget! But, my dear, he is dead while you are living. To constantly remind oneself of past unhappiness is to be merely self-indulgent. You must put all that behind you as if it had never happened. Above all, one must utterly reject that which diminishes one, all that betrays one's higher instincts. One's sense of what it is to be civilized is what is important to one. There is nothing else. (*A moment of reflection and, then, he leaves the room and comes down centre stage*)

The ACTOR *and* ACTRESS *in their anonymous coats of the beginning, come forward as well. The* ACTOR *reverses the portrait of Edmund Burke above the mantelpiece and flips the washing-line so that the figures of Churchill, the King, and Mosley become Goebbels, Hitler and Mosley again. The* ACTRESS, *meanwhile, is helping* BRACKEN *to disrobe to* JOYCE: *beneath the overcoat there is the fascist black shirt and tie. Spectacles removed. Wig removed to close-cropped hair. A scar is exposed the full length of the face.* JOYCE, *now ready, ascends the rostrum. Background marching sounds for street corner political meeting.* ACTOR *and* ACTRESS *form a kind of audience but are eventually darkened out so that we are left, finally, with the white face of* JOYCE *in the darkness.*

JOYCE: People of Manchester! In this year of the Lord, nineteen hundred and thirty-three there is only one question, my friends: Who is the Jew? Is he your penny ha'penny shopkeeper on the corner? Is he the Shylock moneylender, the usurer? Is he the licene[52] tailor of rainproofs with his throng of Christian women and girls at the disposal of his greasy fingers? Is he your Lord Israel and your Sir Izzy in fur coats at the opera with their fat consorts? Or is he the dark Russian in the International Club on Bury New Road preaching Bolshevism? My friends, he is all these and more. He is the common figure on our streets, he is the secret agent. He is the parasite of our British economy, the corrupter of our British heritage. He is our evil otherness, the fault in our nature which we must root out. My friends, the policy of the British Union of Fascists, under our leader, Sir Oswald Mosley, is simple, effective, humane. It is that the island of Madagascar be appropriated by the International Powers. That the island of Madagascar be appointed the resting place of all Jews. That all Jews be obliged to repair there and that boats of the International Powers be employed to patrol the waters about Madagascar that no one escapes, ever again, off that island. That, my friends, is the policy of the BUF. That is our solution. For listen to this. Attend to this. Assuredly if there be no Madagascar then there will be Armageddon.[53] The serpent of Judah is encircling the globe and that encircling serpent is seeking its own head. And when that head meets its tail then this globe will be crushed by the Anti-Christ of Judah. It is the serpent of history, my friends. It raises its head at seven points in history as outlined in the Protocols of Zion,[54] the last, its apparition in St Petersburg in 1881.[55] But the Bolshevik Jew of Russia and Capitalist Jew of Wall Street are alike in this. Each reaches out to the other. Each heralds the birth of the King born in Zion, Anti-Christ. Each is the instrument of the serpent. Each is awaiting that moment of cataclysm when the world will disintegrate, Russian Jew and American Jew, when that encircling serpent swallows its head, finally, in Jerusalem.

51. Ardvullen House, the County Tipperary home of the Bracken family.
52. A neologism for 'licentious'.

53. The site of the last decisive battle on the Day of Judgment; a final, apocalyptic war. Revelation, XIV.16.
54. In 1903, the Russian journal *The Flag* published *Programme of Conquest of the World by the Jews*, which later became known as the *Protocols of the Elders of Zion (Protocoles des Sages de Sion)*. It claimed to be a report of secret meetings of the Sages of Zion, the members of an inner Zionist Council, who had met during the first Zionist Council, held at Basle in Switzerland in 1897. The Nazis took up this sample of Tsarist anti-semitic literature and added to it by incorporating passages from the anti-semitic novel *Biarritz* (Berlin, 1868) by Sir John Recliffe, the pseudonym of the anti-semite author, Hermann Godsche. The original document was a forgery. Philip Graves exposed it as such in three articles published in *The Times* in August 1921.
55. Tsar Alexander II was assassinated by the Nihilists in St Petersburg (now Leningrad) in 1881.

PART TWO

THE JOYCE PLAY: BERLIN

Before the lights go up: air-raid sounds in the distance which die out. Then a battery of different radio stations over the air. Voices rise out of static and snatches of music. The effect should be of someone spinning a dial on the radio.

RADIO VOICES: (*Male and female*) Radio Caledonia calling, Radio Caledonia calling — And now, here is Radio Free Wales — Hello, Worker's Challenge on the air — This is the New British Broadcasting Station with transmitters in West London, East Sussex and Kent. Tonight we will interview a distinguished Knight of the Realm, who must, of course, remain anonymous on why he is emigrating, with his family, to Canada — Radio Caledonia calling, Radio Caledonia calling. This is Glasgow — This is Radio Free Wales, broadcasting from Aberystwyth: the time has come for the valleys to rise up against the Saxon foe! — And, now, here is Worker's Challenge, the voice of the British proletariat and here is Bert Jones who will discuss the condition of the working class in Britain today — Radio Caledonia calling, this is Glasgow. Today we hear from Westminster that supplies of coal and other essential goods are to be cut back from Scotland — This is the BBC Home Service and our microphone on the streets of Britain today. Excuse me, madam, could we have your views on what it is like to live on rationing today? Well, I mean to say, how can a body live on what you get on the rations? It's ever so troublesome, that's what it is. What with all this bombing and no electric again yesterday I said to my friend Mavis, I said it's not bearable, that's what it is, not bearable —

Sound down. Lights up on the image of BRACKEN *on the screen.*

BRACKEN: Good evening. As Minister of Information in His Majesty's Government, it is my solemn duty to warn all loyal Britons against listening to these broadcasts.[1] Do not be tricked by the Nazis and this chap Haw Haw. What Haw Haw is doing, you see, is sending out these broadcasts from Berlin and pretending that they're coming from inside Britain. No sensible Briton will be misled by this caddish deception. We know this gang in Berlin. We know their names. Our information and intelligence agents know this Haw Haw. He is an Irish traitor called William Joyce and well known to the police in this country. I want to make one thing perfectly clear. We in the Ministry of Information do not intend to stand idly by. We are going to get this traitor. He may go on for months more. But sooner or later the time will come and this man will have to face our British courts, our British law —

Image of BRACKEN *fades.* JOYCE *is on the rostrum in a studio of the Rundfunkhaus, the broadcasting centre in Berlin, before a microphone and wearing a head-set. Panic-shouts off, stampeding feet in the building, bombs falling outside.* JOYCE *opens a drawer, removes a bottle of liquor and a glass and begins to drink, steadily. Sounds down and he stands, glass in hand, illuminated by flashes of light from outside.* ACTOR *and* ACTRESS *come on, to either side, in their neutral, narrator outfits.*

ACTRESS: (*Narrator*) And, so, our scene shifts to Berlin —

ACTOR: (*Narrator*) To the Rundfunkhaus the radio centre of Dr Goebbels, the master propagandist of the Nazi Reich —

ACTRESS: Where our hero sits.

ACTOR: At the centre of the most extraordinary factory of voices ever assembled in the history of radio —

ACTRESS: William Joyce, with his Germanic scar, acquired in a razor fight in Brixton —

ACTOR: Our transposed Irishman, born in Brooklyn, New York City but raised in the West of Ireland —

ACTRESS: After a short period as an ultra-Englishman in England he ended up a naturalized German citizen of the Third Reich.

ACTOR: To summarize: He was American but also Irish. He wanted to be English but had to settle on being German.

ACTRESS: With his English-born wife, Margaret, known in German radio circles as Lady Haw Haw.

ACTOR: Every night he brought into existence another England over the airwaves.

ACTRESS: An England of articulate discontent—

ACTOR: Is it any wonder that alone in his studio with a bottle of schnapps[2] he could sit and feel a tremor of conquest?

1. The references to these fake radio stations appropriately makes the transition from one illusionist (Bracken) to the other (Joyce).

2. A strong German or Dutch spirit.

ACTRESS: England had once offered him a dream of supremacy. When it failed to deliver, it would have to be punished, with the punishment of an invented rebellion over the air.

ACTOR: Down the corridor from him in the Rundfunkhaus were the other broadcasting stations of Dr Goebbels. There was the Indian Broadcasting Service, with real Indians, the Arab, the Scandinavian, the Irish, the Slav, the multiplying Tower of Babel of Dr Goebbels.

ACTRESS: It was as if the whole world was about to be reinvented first, before its conquest by the Panzer divisions of the Wehrmacht.[3]

ACTOR: As if conquest were a relief from such clamorous discontent.

ACTRESS: Is it any wonder that the Minister of Information was called in by the PM and asked to do something.

ACTOR: (*Imitation Churchill*) Get Brendan Bracken on the phone. Something has to be done about this chap Haw Haw.

JOYCE: We must become the voice of alternative possibilities. Find the right trigger. The spring. Take clocks, for instance. Clocks. Have you ever noticed how people become agitated when their clocks are interfered with? Hm? (*Announcement*) Listeners in Barnstead! Your town clock is fifteen minutes slow! Which, incidentally, it was. (*Result?*) Panic! (*Announcement*) Burghers of Cambridge, I promise you that the Luftwaffe will soon take care of your new Guildhall chronometer. Who the blazes told him about the clock? Or: you in Wolverhampton, go outside, go on, out you go. And look at the city clock. What do you see? Hm? Result? The release of the most potent subversion of all: the imagination of the people.

ACTRESS: You see, a very curious thing was happening —

ACTOR: As the listeners in Britain bent over the wireless every night twiddling the knobs towards Hamburg and Bremen, each listener became infected, or if you wish, inspired by the inventiveness of Mr Joyce —

JOYCE: I said to them: to be effective propaganda has to be confirmation, at some level, of people's desires.

ACTRESS: Each morning each person seemed to have a different story of what Lord Haw Haw had said the night before.

3. The German army.

ACTOR: Two people in the same room before the same wireless would report two different versions of what had been heard —

JOYCE: What we say may be questionable. It must never be distasteful.

ACTRESS: If William Joyce were re-inventing England, England was also re-inventing William Joyce.

ACTOR: This is what is known as the Principle of Circularity.

ACTRESS: Other students of the Imagination refer to it as the Double Cross Effect.

ACTOR: It is endemic in situations of conflict between nations.

ACTRESS: It frequently breaks out between writers and their readers.

ACTOR: Who is telling whose story and to whom?

JOYCE: (*Declaration of belief*) Every man has his secret desire to betray. It is intimately related to his desire for freedom. We simply need the key to unlock it.

ACTRESS: (*Announcement*) Lord Haw Haw reveals the existence of a poker school in the back of a canteen in Ipswich!

ACTOR: (*Announcement*) Lord Haw Haw warns the girls in an office in Fulham to stop sliding down the banisters! Or else!

ACTRESS: Lord Haw Haw says he'll widen Orpington High Street and thereby stop a row on the Council.

ACTOR: No wonder Mr Bracken was concerned.

ACTRESS: As Minister of Information, that is —

ACTOR: Information being his business, as it were —

ACTRESS: And therefore misinformation as well, not to mention disinformation —

ACTOR: It was as if a Ministry of Misinformation had been set up to counteract his Ministry of Information.

ACTRESS: Absolute duplication —

ACTOR: Or rather mis-duplication —

ACTRESS: Intolerable.

ACTOR: Insupportable.

ACTRESS: Action simply had to be taken!

ACTOR: And, at once!

They go off with a flourish. BRACKEN *appears, on the screen, behind a BBC microphone.*

BRACKEN: Good evening. I regret to say that I must speak to you again tonight about Haw Haw, the Nazi broadcaster. Let us be perfectly frank about this. This is a free country. We may listen to what we like upon the wireless. This is England, not Germany, where people are put behind bars for listening to the BBC. That's not our way of doing things. We English are different. And are proud to be different. May I say this. The joke is over. It's about time to put a stop to this fellow once and for all. Above all, don't invent stories about Haw Haw just to impress your neighbours. Remember our slogan: lies cost lives. Don't listen to Tittle-tattle Tom and Rumour Rodney. Put a notice on your wireless: this set doesn't listen to Haw Haw. Or something like that. Organize yourselves in groups, in the canteen, on the shop-floors: Loyalists for Britain! Loyalists against Haw Haw! And when you do hear a Haw Haw rumour report it to me at the Ministry. I will deal with it.

Lights out on the BRACKEN *image. Lights up on* JOYCE *on the rostrum in the semi-darkness before a window, out, toasting the bombing of Berlin. He is lit by flashes but otherwise there is silence. Centre rostrum: table, microphone, broadcasting studio.*

JOYCE: 'The king who fights his people fights
himself.
And they, thy knights, who loved me once,
the stroke
That strikes them dead is as my death to me.'[4]

(*He is drinking heavily throughout*) Papa always brought me with him to the Army Barracks in Galway. It was cold in the yard. Two officers were there. Is it quiet in the town, Joyce? Yes, sir. We depend upon men like you, Joyce, to keep the peace. Yes, sir. And who have we here? This is my son, sir. What age are you, boy? Fifteen, sir. And what is your name? William Brooke Joyce. Brooke? Brooke? That, surely is not an Irish name, is it? His mother's name, sir. Her father was a medical doctor from Ulster. Ah! You are all loyalists in your house, Joyce! Yes, sir. Well, carry on, Joyce. Keep up the good work. Then the lorries came in from patrol from the Clifden Road. Oughterard. Maam Cross. Moycullen.[5] The Tans were drunk. But the officers only laughed. We shot some rabbits, one of the Tans shouted. Everyone laughed and I laughed. Then Papa went to the Paymaster's Office. Then I ran after the two officers. Just a moment, please! Yes? What is it? Ah, it is young William Joyce! Now, then, speak up. I want to serve, sir. You want to serve, do you? Yes, sir. The two officers looked at one another. And what can you do, boy? I know all the Sinn Feiners of the town, sir. The two officers looked at one another again. And, tell me, William Joyce, why do you wish to serve? I want to clean out the scum, sir. He wants to clean out the scum! Ha, ha! Well done, sir. Report to me in the morning, Joyce. Yes, sir. And the two officers saluted me. And I saluted them. And I turned away. And then. The last lorry of the patrol came into the yard. (*Sudden shift. Leaps to table, seizes microphone, puts on head-set*) Hello-hello-hello. Is there anyone listening out there? Any chance of some juice, Fritz? They're all down in the bloody bomb shelter. I want to — Lord Haw Haw speaks to the besotted idealists of the earth, you know, all the starry-eyed believers in the improvement of the masses, God save the mark, as if homo sap could be dressed-up to be what he is not. Well, my friends, I've news for you. By the way, 's not bravado that I don't go down into the cellars. No. No, I have a rendezvous here with my great mechanical birds. I feed them, you see, from my window-sill. Also, there is the question of fastidiousness. Once our German friend hits the cellar during a raid he produces his sausage. The place reeks of garlic, compacted offal and broken wind. I often think there has to be significance, I mean, so much ingenuity, so much art in this race diverted into the making of sausages. (*Rise*) But back to my quixotic friends out there labouring to raise the filthy multitude to some level of decency and grace. You poor fools, can you not see that the human race is still at a primitive level of evolution? It is only our dreams that tell us what we might be if we were able, but able we are not, tied as we are to this ramshackle bag of a body. But I was about to say, my friends. There is no perfection without fire, no quickening without the burning lime, no redemption without ash. All you earnest believers in the perfectability of man, attend! When the first great fire burned, the ice melted and the monkey stood upright in that incredible heat of the young sun. His brain expanded in its box. Words came from his mouth. Words refined the hanging jaw. And the nose melted into its human proportion. When the second great fire comes man will be burned again out of his imperfection and into the shape of his dreams. (*He grabs the microphone, raises it aloft, then bangs it on the table and throws it to the floor. Drift away*) The last lorry came in from the

4. Tennyson, *The Passing of Arthur* (1869), lines 72-74.
5. Places in County Galway.

patrol. A Crossley-Tender[6] with wire netting. Only the driver got out. He went and got a bucket of water. And threw it into the back. A great stream of blood came out. He got another bucket. And another. And another. So much blood that I thought that something was still bleeding in there.

Lights down on JOYCE. *Lights up on a drab sitting room in wartime Berlin. The photograph of Hitler above the mantelpiece. The actor as* ERICH: *plus-four tweeds, Norfolk jacket, Fair Isle pullover, good brogues.*[7] *With his note-pad and pen he is taking English lessons from* JOYCE's *wife* MARGARET. *The* ACTRESS *wears a simple, floral dress: a scrubbed, tidy, pale English girl*.

ERICH: (*Reading his essay*) 'Today is Monday. I go to my friend Jeremy in Kensington. Tomorrow will be Tuesday. I will go to shop in Fortnum and Mason's. I will buy my hamper for my picnic in the historic park of Windsor. Tomorrow and tomorrow will be Wednesday. I will go to Buckingham Palace to see the King.'

MARGARET: No, Erich. That is incorrect. The day after will be Wednesday. Not tomorrow and tomorrow.[8]

ERICH: Tomorrow and tomorrow, no?

MARGARET: No. I was quoting from Shakespeare when I used that phrase.

ERICH: Ah, Shakespeare! To be or not to be, that is the question.[9]

MARGARET: Perhaps that is enough English lessons for today?

ERICH: Please?

MARGARET: I am tired, Erich.

ERICH: I am tired, yes?

MARGARET: You are tired?

ERICH: No, no, no, no. It is good the lesson. You, Margaret. And William. You will teach me English and, then, I will speak English in England.

MARGARET: Do you mean when England is occupied?

ERICH: Certainly.

MARGARET: I see.

ERICH: The English peoples and the German peoples will join together. It is the hope of civilization. William believes it, does he not?

MARGARET: Oh, yes. William believes that.

ERICH: And you also, Margaret?

MARGARET: I did not think there would be war, Erich.

ERICH: But there is war.

MARGARET: Don't misunderstand me, Erich. I believe one must be prepared to kill for what one believes.

ERICH: Certainly.

MARGARET: Are you prepared to kill, Erich?

ERICH: (*Shrugs uncomfortably*) And William? William will kill, also?

MARGARET: I don't really know, actually. So. I am the only one, then. How curious! It all seems so perfectly simple to me. William says I have a linear mind.

ERICH: Linear? What is linear?

MARGARET: Straight line. *Gerade Linie*.

ERICH: No, no, no. Not straight. (*He demonstrates curves and circles*) *Meine geliebte*[10] Margaret is all circle. (*He kisses her passionately and she responds, then pushes him away*)

MARGARET: You're very sweet, Erich. But not now, if you don't mind.

ERICH: Sweet? Please explain.

MARGARET: Sweet, warm. Passionate. Romantic.

ERICH: Ah! Romantic. And William? William is romantic with my beloved Margaret?

MARGARET: He's quite incredibly romantic but it doesn't come out that way. (*She suddenly bursts into tears*)

ERICH: Please, Margaret. Is there something wrong? *Was habe ich dir getan?*[11] Oh, this is the end! Please, Margaret. I will say my poem. (*On one knee, declamation with gestures*)

'Sweetheart, do not love too long:
I loved long and long
And grew to be out of fashion
Like an old song.'[12]

MARGARET *laughs at this. He holds her hands, shaking them and kissing when* WILLIAM JOYCE *walks in.*

JOYCE: Am I interrupting something? Do please continue. Do not let me —

MARGARET: Our lesson has ended.

JOYCE: So I see.

6. The name of a lorry favoured by the Black and Tans.
7. Another detail in the play's various fictions. This is the garb of a caricature 'stage Englishman'.
8. *Macbeth*, 5.1.19.
9. *Hamlet*, 3.1.56.
10. My beloved.
11. What have I done to you?
12. From Yeats's poem, 'O Do Not Love Too Long'.

ERICH: Your wonderful poet, Herr Joyce. The beauty of England. Moonlight and olden dances. Avalon and Lancelot and others also of the joyous island.[13]

MARGARET: Erich —

JOYCE: To whom are you referring, nay, I ask, which poet are you extemporizing with such *élan*?

ERICH: Yeets.

JOYCE: Keats?

ERICH: No, no, no, no. Yeets. I will arise and go now and go to Inishfree.[14]

JOYCE: Ah, Yeats. W. B. Yeats.

ERICH: Certainly.

JOYCE: My dear fellow, Yeats isn't English.

ERICH: No?

JOYCE: No. Yeats is Irish. He is writing about Ireland. Different place, alas.

MARGARET: Don't listen to him, Erich.

JOYCE: So, you wish to study English literature, Erich?

ERICH: Certainly.

MARGARET: You are mocking Erich.

JOYCE: Am I mocking Erich? I'm not mocking Erich. I would never dream of mocking Erich.

ERICH: (*To* MARGARET) Forgive me, Margaret, I must go. Thank you for the wonderful lesson. Will we have a lesson next week? Thank you. Yes. (*Turning to* JOYCE *with a bow*) *Mein Herr!*

Exit ERICH.

MARGARET: Shall I prepare some food?

JOYCE: No, thank you very much.

MARGARET: I think you've been beastly to him.

JOYCE: Who? What? Hm?

MARGARET: Please, William, don't —

JOYCE: What? What? What?

MARGARET: Stop it! Stop it! I can't abide your mockery now. It's so utterly out of place, so crude, so inappropriate to Erich —

JOYCE: I'm worried, Margaret. Truly. I'm worried about your judgement. I really am. This ridiculous buffoon in his Harris tweeds —

MARGARET: Erich is a friend.

JOYCE: Erich is an ass.

MARGARET: Don't you realize — everyone, every place, everyone, finally, at some point fails to measure up in your estimation — your high standard —

JOYCE: If you wish to defend that bumbling fruit —

MARGARET: Why, William? That's what I want to know?

JOYCE: He, actually, really does believe, you know that he is in possession of the mysteries of English poetry, that clown, master of the English lyric!

MARGARET: Will you ever be satisfied, William? Ever?

JOYCE: That pumped-up, would-be *Gauleiter*[15] of the British Museum —

MARGARET: Every night I sit in this miserable room waiting for you to return while you sit drinking in the Kaiserhof with those American newspapermen. It is intolerable!

JOYCE: I am surprised at you, Margaret. You've forgotten, Margaret. Have you forgotten? All those promises, those undertakings? All those talks we've had down the years. Don't you remember? How we dreamed of working together towards the one goal?

MARGARET: Yes. Absolutely.

JOYCE: The one cause.

MARGARET: I remember that we had an understanding, William. Didn't we? That each should be free. No vulgar little middle-class inhibitions and restrictions. Your own words, William. Man and woman in absolute, natural freedom. Or have I imagined it?

JOYCE: Yes, yes. The rooting out of everything that was common and shabby and second-rate —

MARGARET: Why, Erich isn't at all like that!

JOYCE: Erich! Erich? Erich is irrelevant. It is you, Margaret, we're talking about. We're talking about you.

MARGARET: This is preposterous!

JOYCE: Maybe you'd prefer to go back to Manchester? Hm? Back to East Lancaster Fabrics? Would you? Would you, Margaret? And marry that nice GP?[16] Hm? Settle down with an Austin[17] and a terrier in Whitefield? Is that what you really want, Margaret? Perhaps you regret everything you've done with me? Do you?

MARGARET: My dear William Joyce, anything I have done I have done out of my own will, I assure

13. In the Arthurian legends, Avalon is one of the Isles of the Blest, to which King Arthur is carried after his death. Lancelot, or Launcelot, was the greatest of the knights of the Round Table.
14. 'The Lake Isle of Inisfree', the best-known and most hackneyed of Yeats's poems.
15. Under Hitler, an official in charge of a region of Germany.
16. General Practitioner, a doctor who has not specialized in one field.
17. A popular and cheap car.

you. You know you're being quite offensive. I intend to ignore it.

JOYCE: Don't you ignore it, Margaret.

MARGARET: Why are you doing this? Now? At this time?

JOYCE: I do it because I intend to shake you out of this suburban mush, this wallow of mediocrity into which you periodically sink —

MARGARET: No!

JOYCE: Yes, Margaret.

MARGARET: I don't need your bullying, thank you.

JOYCE: Oh but you do. You need constant pressure, Margaret, to remain steadfast.

MARGARET: No, I do not. I have sacrificed everything to be here. There is no going back.

JOYCE: Yes but what about the bad days, Margaret? Those days, those hours when you buckle, you wilt —

MARGARET: No!

JOYCE: Yes, Margaret. And afterwards you thank me for holding tight. Thank you for holding on, William. Then you kiss my hands. And I lift you up.

MARGARET: (*Low*) Yes.

JOYCE: You do admit to that, don't you, Margaret?

MARGARET: Yes.

JOYCE: And then I take you to me.

MARGARET: (*Very low*) Yes.

JOYCE: And we become one.

MARGARET: (*Cry*) I help you, too!

JOYCE: Of course.

MARGARET: Often —

JOYCE: I could never have survived without you.

MARGARET: When you speak of giving in —

JOYCE: Yes.

MARGARET: Your depressions —

JOYCE: I know, I know.

MARGARET: When you take the razor ready to slash yourself, it is I who stop you, William.

JOYCE: Yes.

MARGARET: When you're ready to surrender, it is I who say no. When you talk of moving on, as if, good heavens, there could be anywhere left in the world for us to move to — I say stop, stop, stop, no more, this is it, this is our chosen ground, this is where we must stand because everything has led to this like a straight line across a map.

JOYCE: Yes.

MARGARET: And your howling at night, William, when you howl like that against the waste of it all it is I who take you in my arms. (*She embraces him, holds him*)

JOYCE: I know.

MARGARET: Then why do you subject me to this?

JOYCE: We must bite into our love every day.

MARGARET: I don't need to do that, William.

JOYCE: To be alive.

MARGARET: (*Kissing him*) It's really so very much more simple than that, dear, if you would allow it to be.

JOYCE: Against all contamination.

MARGARET: Dear William, I do believe you were jealous? Were you?

JOYCE: It is our bond.

MARGARET: Were you? Were you jealous?

JOYCE: What? What?

MARGARET: Of Erich? Jealous?

JOYCE: I would never insult you by associating you with that stuffed bag of wind, that obscenity — Besides, Margaret, from now on we must contain ourselves, draw ourselves into dignity. Are you listening, Margaret?

MARGARET: Pardon?

JOYCE: Germany is defeated. It is only a matter of time. We will continue as before. But our knowledge must make us resolute. We must be circumspect. We must build our own citadel. You are not listening, Margaret!

MARGARET: Sorry, no. I mean I can't attend to one of your lectures, William, not now at any rate.

JOYCE: This is not one of my lectures!

MARGARET: Yes, well, it's extremely difficult.

JOYCE: Do you not know how we must steel ourselves?

MARGARET: I didn't intend to tell you this but you've left me little choice.

JOYCE: What? What?

MARGARET: If you must know, Erich and I have been intimate.

JOYCE: Intimate?

MARGARET: Yes, intimate.

JOYCE: You what?

MARGARET: It was simply the most natural expression of what we felt for one another. He was such a dear and I, well, I was lonely. You might say that we came together playing out some impossible but perfectly delightful romance. It was nothing more than that, really.

He slaps her so that she sinks to the floor. He

immediately goes to her in a state of guilty recriminations.

JOYCE: Oh, Margaret, I'm sorry, I'm sorry, sorry, sorry. I never meant — have I hurt you, oh, please forgive me, Margaret, please —

MARGARET: It's all right, William. Help me up, would you —

JOYCE: I'm a thug, that's all, a vicious — I love you —

MARGARET: Yes, I know.

JOYCE: I want you. I want you now, Margaret. Let us make love, Margaret, now, please make love immediately. (*He is trying to kiss her so that she has to push him away*)

MARGARET: For heaven's sake, William, do you mind!

JOYCE: What have I done? What did I do wrong? How did I fail you? You weren't happy with me. Was that it? Obviously I failed you. I can understand that. But you must say it to me .Say it now, Margaret, say how I failed you. Did I fail you? What did I do? Was it something in our lives together? Why didn't you tell me?

MARGARET: Please, William —

JOYCE: Some way that I failed? I didn't know. I cannot understand it. Explain it to me. Was it sexual? Did I fail you sexually? For you to go and — was it that? You never indicated that. You never suggested you were unhappy in that way.

MARGARET: It's absolutely nothing like that!

JOYCE: Then why, why, why, why, why —

MARGARET: It is so perfectly simple, so ordinary!

JOYCE: You're a filthy cunt, you know that? You're just a whore. How many more have there been? Answer me. Acting the madam. I see it now. A vile bitch in heat allowing that dirty kraut to put his thing into you. What else did you do with him, hm? You enjoyed it, didn't you, foul, dirty bitch. I can smell him off you, you know that —

MARGARET: There is nothing wrong! There is nothing wrong!

JOYCE: Whore!

MARGARET: Don't, William, please, don't you see how you're degrading yourself?

JOYCE: It is the betrayal, the betrayal —

MARGARET: Nonsense — How could I have betrayed you if we were both free? Both meeting as absolutely independent, mature, adult persons? For heaven's sake, William, we've put all that bourgeois rubbish behind us. I could never be promiscuous. But neither is my sexuality the property of you or anyone else. Our love transcends all that, William — How could one possibly betray something which simply doesn't control one?

JOYCE: You are no longer my Margaret.

MARGARET: William, you must simply listen to what I say.

JOYCE: I should beat the shit out of you —

MARGARET: I am going to repeat your own words to you, William —

JOYCE: Leave me alone —

MARGARET: No, William, you must listen. I insist that you recover yourself, through yourself, through your own words. We must turn our violence into energy. That's what you said. We must use that energy to master the world about us. Don't you remember? Your words, William Joyce. Personal violence is waste. Violence controlled and directed is power. Power! Power!

JOYCE: I can't go on.

MARGARET: Of course you can go on. You must go on.

JOYCE: (*Sudden turn-on*) But I must have done something. What did I do? What was it? Was it sex? Was it neglect? Of course I neglected you —

MARGARET: Stop it, William. At once —

JOYCE: I did stay out late. I needed to, you see, to relax, to come back from the broadcasts, to unwind. Don't you understand that? Not neglect: no. Failure. Did I fail? How did I fail?

MARGARET: William!

JOYCE: Perhaps if I were to — By God, I'll get that idiot. Of course. I see it plainly. You've made a fool of me. I've indulged you. If only I had — You filthy fucking bitch, wallowing in that sty with that gross fucker — (MARGARET *rushes out. He follows and his voice is heard as the lights come down*) You won't get away with this, do you hear? Answer me or by Christ I will — You can't run away, you can't escape —

Lights up: MARGARET *is sitting in the room.* JOYCE *is walking about. Both are dishevelled, wasted. He talks but it is as if he no longer needs a listener. She is utterly spent.*

JOYCE: What have I done? What did I do wrong? How did I fail you? You weren't happy with me. Was that it? Obviously I failed you. I can understand that. But you must say it to me. Say it now, Margaret. Say how I failed you. Did I fail you? What did I do?

MARGARET: (*Quietly, after endless repetition*) William, stop. Please stop. You've talked non-stop for twenty-four hours. We haven't slept. We haven't eaten. We simply cannot go on like this. You must stop talking.

JOYCE: What was it? I don't understand. Try to explain to me.

MARGARET: William! (*She rushes out. He continues to sit there, mumbling down into silence. She comes down to audience*) Finally, it stopped. That sickening spill of words. I thought I should never hear that voice stop. But it did. It was like an engine running down. There was always some gap between what he said and what he really felt. When that gap widened all that was left to him was speech. When he stopped talking there was silence for weeks. Then he said we would be divorced. I said, don't be ridiculous. But he said: we must be divorced. Very well, I said, if that is what you want. We went to court. I will never forget that room: 35A Zivilkammer.[18] (JOYCE *comes down and joins her*) I had difficulty understanding the German.

JOYCE: Do you, William Joyce, petition for divorce from Margaret Joyce, on the grounds of infidelity? (*Pause*) I do.

MARGARET: Do you, Margaret Joyce, counter-petition for divorce from William Joyce, on the grounds of cruelty and neglect? (*Pause*) I do.

JOYCE: Do you, William Joyce, contest the charges of the other party? (*Pause*) I do not.

MARGARET: Do you, Margaret Joyce, contest the charges of the other party? (*Pause*) I do not.

JOYCE: And do you, Margaret Joyce, apply for the payment of alimony?

MARGARET: I am sorry. My German is poor. I do not understand the question.

JOYCE: Explain the question to the woman.

MARGARET: No. No. I am perfectly able to support myself.

JOYCE: Then this divorce is granted with the parties to pay their own costs.

They turn and face one another for a few seconds. Then they collapse, tearfully into one another's arms, crying one another's names.

JOYCE: We will get married again.

MARGARET: Not today, if you don't mind.

JOYCE: I will never leave you.

MARGARET: I don't intend to allow you.

JOYCE: Let us go home.

MARGARET: Yes. (*They re-enter the apartment together, she tense, he in a daze*) William —

JOYCE: Yes —

MARGARET: I have to tell you.

JOYCE: Yes?

MARGARET: Erich is waiting —

JOYCE: I see.

MARGARET: To say goodbye.

JOYCE: Goodbye?

MARGARET: Yes. He is going to the Eastern Front. (JOYCE *gives a wild whoop of laughter*) Please, William, do not mock.

JOYCE: The Third Reich is in serious trouble.

MARGARET: Older men and boys have been called up.

JOYCE: I see.

ERICH *makes his entrance. The effect should be striking, not least on* JOYCE. ERICH *is in the officer's uniform of the Waffen SS.*[19] *It is as if the uniform has changed the man, his carriage, status, his power. He brings with him something of the immense armour of German militarism.*

ERICH: (*Bow*) Margaret. Herr Joyce. *Ich gehe jetzt on die Front und kampfe für Volk und Vaterland.* ['I go now to the front to fight for nation and fatherland.']

MARGARET: Oh, Erich.

ERICH: I go to fight the Bolshevik, Herr Joyce.

MARGARET: But, Erich, you are too old.

ERICH: Old? Old? What is this old? Now I must go. (*He takes* MARGARET's *hand and kisses it*) '*Ein Blick von dir, ein Wort mehr unterhalt, als alle Weisheit dieser Welt,* Margaret.' ['A glance from you, a word pleases more than all the wisdom of this world, Margaret.'] Goethe's *Faust*.[20]

JOYCE: No more English poetry, Erich? Only German poetry now?

ERICH: Certainly, Herr Joyce. No English poetry. German poetry now. (*He turns to* JOYCE, *walks towards him and gives the Nazi salute*) Heil Hitler! (ERICH's *salute should have the effect of slowly forcing* JOYCE's *arm up, as if by the pressure of power. When* ERICH's *arm drops, so does* JOYCE's. ERICH *clicks his heels and departs*)

The lights come down on the noise of bombing and war sounds which reach a crescendo and then, suddenly,

18. Civil Court Room.

19. Waffen SS (*Schutz-Staffel*, 'protective squadron'), a Nazi elite paramilitary corps. The Waffen SS ('armed SS') were full-time soldiers; there was also a part-time corps.

20. *Faust* (1808) Part One, lines 3,079-80.

silence. The image of BRACKEN *appears on the screen.*

BRACKEN: The war is over. But our work at the Ministry of Information has not ended. It must continue until the whole Nazi machine is dismantled, until Nazi propaganda is silenced for ever. There is a category of war criminal that is of special interest to our ministry and to me as Minister of Information. I refer to the traitor broadcasters and in particular to the arch traitor, William Joyce. No stone must be left unturned, no loophole left open in the pursuit of these rats, these perverts. While these renegades continue to live in freedom our British self-respect, indeed our very British identity, is threatened. They cast a shadow over our very existence. Haw Haw must be taken. The full force of British justice must be executed upon this man.

As the image fades, lights up on MARGARET *and* JOYCE *dismantling their apartment and frantically packing, flashes of explosions lighting them as they work. Bombing and approaching war sounds.* JOYCE *and* MARGARET *hurriedly assemble suitcases, bundles and put on trench-coats. They come forward.*

JOYCE: Have we got all our papers?

MARGARET: Of course we do. (*They take a rest. She sits on a suitcase*)

MARGARET: (*To audience*) I watched William all the time. He had spoken so often of how he would die that I thought — I have always had contempt for suicide.

JOYCE: (*To audience*) She was magnificent. I watched her to see if she would crack. It was essential that she did not crack. I had already written our future, you see, and it was imperative that we follow the lines to the bitter end.

MARGARET: First, we were all moved to the Dutch border. The English were only twenty-five miles away. Puffs of smoke hung over the horizon and everywhere there was a sudden, great silence. Then back to Bremen. To Hamburg.

JOYCE: In Hamburg I delivered my last broadcast.

MARGARET: It was unreal. Suddenly there was no more rationing. Everyone had food and drink. And everywhere this silence.

JOYCE: I warned England. I said that without Germany, the British Empire would disappear within a decade. I said the Russian Empire already extended from Poland to the Black Sea, from Moscow to the suburbs of Berlin. I said that England would be impoverished. Reduced to selling its treasure to Americans. Is this what this war was fought for?

MARGARET: He was incoherent. Once word came of the suicides of Hitler and Goebbels he drank, steadily, day and night. We were told to say that Hitler had died at a street barricade. I insisted upon telling everyone that he had taken his own life.

JOYCE: I wanted Margaret to be with me. I wanted so desperately that she be beside me to the end.

MARGARET: I did not want William to die.

JOYCE: (*Rise*) I said that England had been denied her place in the foundry of human progress, forging the new Adam, *Novus homo*[21] of the new millennium —

MARGARET: Then one morning as papers were burned by the Propaganda Ministry and false papers handed out — that strange collection of races all yelling out different choices of new nationalities — word came on the telephone, still miraculously working, from Berlin —

JOYCE: England was ruined by a gang. The American Jew-lover Churchill and his cronies, effete degenerates like Bracken, monied gangsters like Beaverbrook.

MARGARET: It said we were to be taken by U-boat to a spot on the west coast of Ireland.

JOYCE: I will not hear of it! I will not be condemned to a living death.

MARGARET: It was then that I realized that I, too, had given myself to death. I mean I had always thought of our love as being for the sake of life. Now I knew it was for the sake of death. And, do you know, this made absolutely no difference to my love for him.

JOYCE: I loved her so much that I had to know where she was every hour of every day.

MARGARET: We left the towns with what we could carry and joined the lines of people crossing the quiet countryside, going nowhere. When the first truckloads of English soldiers came through he started — he began his dangerous, silly game —

JOYCE: (*Yell*) You all right, mate? Anyone there from Manchester?

MARGARET: Again and again he would yell out, with that wild laugh of his, even at English soldiers standing right beside him.

JOYCE: I say, officer, when is the next bus to Berlin?

21. New man.

MARGARET: He called it his Irish roulette. And, do you know, I believe he was pretty disappointed when his voice was not recognized. Did he know what he was doing?

JOYCE: I knew exactly what I was doing. I was going to the village of Küpfermühle above Wasserleben.

MARGARET: There were times, as I watched him that I felt he had already been taken away from me.

JOYCE: And when we reached Küpfermühle it was May and the sun was shining.

MARGARET: There was this English widow living in the village since 1912. She could hardly speak English any more. She took us in.

JOYCE: Sometimes I lay on the ground for hours in the sunshine contemplating the buds on the birch trees.

MARGARET: She used to invite English soldiers on duty in the village to tea. Nice boys from Bradford and Leeds. They gave us the *Daily Mirror*. They talked about going home. They never questioned who this couple might be, who called themselves Herr and Frau Hansen.

JOYCE: Sometimes I went for walks in the woods above Wasserleben.

They stand and face one another. She fusses with his coat. They kiss.

MARGARET: Do you have your papers?

JOYCE: (*Clicking heels, bow*) Fritz Hansen, teacher of English.

MARGARET: Is it possible that I may never see you again?

JOYCE: It is possible.

MARGARET: I believe that one day it will all begin again.

JOYCE: I believe so, too.

MARGARET: I have been blessed, William, to have been loved by you.

They embrace. He steps away from her and she sits on the suitcase with her back to him.

JOYCE: (*To audience*) I walked out through Wasserleben and into the woods. I left behind the smell of insufficient food, the strained faces and that impossible hiatus between conquest and punishment. And I knew precisely what was waiting for me in that clearing in the woods. I walked, quickly, now, because all that remained was to be exemplary. The two English officers were ahead of me and walking through the clearing. I almost ran after them. Just a moment, please! Yes? What is it? Speak up. I want to serve, sir. What? I want to serve. The two officers looked at one another. They seemed to be remembering, to be reminding one another of something. You wouldn't, by any chance, you wouldn't be William Joyce, would you? I said I am — and I raised my hand towards the pocket where my forged papers were. Fritz Hansen, teacher of English. He had pulled the revolver quickly and shot all in the one movement. Because I had turned slightly the bullet entered and passed through my right thigh and entered and passed my left thigh making, in all, four wounds. The man who shot me was called Perry. But that was not his real name. All Jews serving in the British Army in Germany were advised to change their names. I had been shot by a Jew pretending to be a Briton in the woods above Wasserleben.

He removes the trench-coat. MARGARET *opens a suitcase and puts in the trench-coat, having taken out a standard, 1940s prison jacket.* JOYCE *puts on the jacket and steps on to the rostrum.* MARGARET *watches him a moment. Then she gathers the bundles and suitcases and, heavily laden, goes off. Lights on the image of* BRACKEN *on the screen.*

BRACKEN: We have finally silenced Haw Haw. Throughout his trial he scarcely spoke a word. That voice which had taunted us throughout the long nights of the war, that ridiculous accent, was gone. Perhaps he was overwhelmed by the majesty of our British law? The carved, royal standard of the courtroom? The sword of justice in its jewelled scabbard above the judge's chair? Or maybe words were only available to him when he lied and threatened us on the wireless? I saw this man once. I heard him speak at one of Mosley's meetings before the war. I heard him turn speech into a deadly weapon of hate and destruction. There were other misguided Britons before the war, Nazi-sympathizers and appeasers. But most of those people rallied to the call of Mr Churchill when the time came. This man was different. He tried to turn Britain against itself. He was as much our enemy as all the saboteurs, the spies and fifth columnists who tried to bomb our cities and factories during the war. There can be no peace while a man like this is allowed to live.

The actress as a LADY JOURNALIST *comes forward to the side of the rostrum. She addresses herself to* JOYCE *as if he were a specimen to illustrate her points She is dressed in elegant, thirties clothes with, perhaps, a hat and large feather.*

LADY JOURNALIST: I covered the treason trial of

William Joyce. I was in the Old Bailey in September 1945 when he was condemned to be hanged. Here was a man driven by an inappropriate reverence for the country he had betrayed. He had spoken, at length, and even in the act of treason itself, about his British heritage, his love of the Union Jack, of the throne, of the Empire, but to civilized people of this country his extravagance was merely vulgar. When he was a demagogue on our streets his few followers were misfits and the misled. But it is a hallmark of British civilization that it sheds coarse extravagance. Its power is in its discrimination, its grace is in its refinement of what in other cultures become crude images. William Joyce would never know anything of this. Those who saw him in the dock were struck by his under-nourishment, the product of generations of peasant breeding. He did have the cockiness of your typical Donnybrook[22] Irishman but it fitted uneasily with the acquired, clicking heels and the silly teutonic bow. William Joyce was condemned out of an inexplicable desire which could only be satisfied by his own destruction. In his trial, the judge found that he had never been a British citizen at all. He was an alien. His British passport was false. But the symbol is greater than the fact. Once he carried that passport, however spurious, William Joyce had put himself beneath the King's protection and therefore could be judged a traitor to the King. His act was at once loyal and disloyal and as such was both contradictory and repugnant. No man can decide for himself what it is to be loyal to the British Crown. It is decided for him. So, William Joyce was condemned to death. And after that it was but a matter of waiting for the white card to be pasted on the door of Wandsworth Prison. *(She sits and waits) Sound of clanging doors and footsteps on corridors.* BEAVERBROOK *steps up on the rostrum and into* JOYCE's cell. BEAVERBROOK *takes notes throughout.*

BEAVERBROOK: I am Max Aitken.

JOYCE: I know who you are. You are Lord Beaverbrook.

BEAVERBROOK: It was good of you to see me.

JOYCE: I was curious. Why should you want to see me, Lord Beaverbrook, since your newspapers howl for my blood along with the Jew-boars and Jew-sows of this condemned city?

BEAVERBROOK: I am interested in the profound fidelities produced by treason.

JOYCE: During my appeal in the Lords I sat in the becoroneted chair in the Royal Robing Room and looked out on the river and Lambeth Bridge. As Conrad said, What greatness had not floated on the ebb of that river![23] And I thought it was ironical to consider that I had more Norman blood in my veins than many of those titled duds waiting outside for the kill.

BEAVERBROOK: I have always felt that there was something screwball about this emphasis on nationality.

JOYCE: Absolutely! What does some absurd, adjectival, geographical method of denoting origin actually mean? That one was sired in this hole or that hole. I am only interested in the future of the human race.

BEAVERBROOK: I have a friend. I once nearly lost his friendship by exploring his birthplace.

JOYCE: What is his name?

BEAVERBROOK: Brendan Bracken.

JOYCE: I have never met him.

BEAVERBROOK: Do you find prison very disagreeable?

JOYCE: On the contrary. Apart from my Jesuit School in Galway, prison is the only place in which I have seen psychology applied, consistently and sensibly, in the running of an institution.

BEAVERBROOK: I interviewed Rudolf Hess, too, you know, when he landed in Scotland.[24]

JOYCE: The German's reputation for psychology is grossly over-rated. That quack Freud and his stinking mind. I believe in Gestalt.[25] I believe in the survival of electro-magnetic systems. Another medium. Beyond — Margaret —

BEAVERBROOK: And what are your fidelities now, Mr Joyce?

JOYCE: I face my Lord Jesus purged of all impurities.

BEAVERBROOK: I know one thing, for sure. Betrayal produces its own fidelities. You betray the small when you give yourself to the great. That is what is known as progress. But what really grabs me

22. Boisterous, swaggering. After Donnybrook Fair, a famous traditional and often rowdy occasion. Donnybrook is a district of Dublin.

23. From the opening of Joseph Conrad's novel, *Heart of Darkness* (1899).

24. Rudolf Hess was deputy leader of the Nazi Party. In 1941 he flew from Germany on a one-man 'peace mission' and was captured when he landed in Scotland. Sentenced to life imprisonment at the end of the war, Hess died in Spandau Prison in Berlin in 1987.

25. Freud's books were publicly burnt in Berlin. 'Gestalt', meaning 'configuration' or 'pattern', is a psychological theory which claims that we perceive and experience in wholes that constitute a pattern.

is the point at which betrayal opens the abyss, where it becomes so intolerable that the betrayer has to be hunted down and destroyed.

JOYCE: Can we not get beyond this fiddle-faddle?

BEAVERBROOK: It's as if treason creates a reflection of what is betrayed — so intolerable that it has to be destroyed — a kind of terrifying mirror or something —

JOYCE: I am British.

BEAVERBROOK: Oh, anyone can be British. Doesn't matter who you are, where you come from, what the colour of your skin is. All you need is a modest command of the language and a total commitment to a handful of symbols, some of which are pretty ludicrous. But they work. Would it surprise you, Mr Joyce, if I told you that you nearly got off?

JOYCE: What is this questioning?

BEAVERBROOK: It's true —

JOYCE: I've passed beyond concern for my fate on this earth.

BEAVERBROOK: Sure. I see that.

JOYCE: (*Fury*) Getting off! Getting off! Oh, my God. (*Pause. Cry*) Where is Margaret?

BEAVERBROOK: It's true, nevertheless. I heard it from the Lord Chancellor himself. Two lords voted for acquittal. Two for the death penalty.

JOYCE: And my Lord Chancellor decided?

BEAVERBROOK: Well, they persuaded Lord Macmillan[26] to switch his vote as a matter of fact. So there were now three lords for the death penalty, one for acquittal. Much better. Then the Lord Chancellor voted for the death penalty. Although he knew perfectly well that it was bad law.

JOYCE: I see.

BEAVERBROOK: Thought you might be interested. It's politics, I'm afraid. Politics is a very simple-minded business, Mr Joyce, at its most effective.

JOYCE: You make it sound like a trivial accident, my friend.

BEAVERBROOK: Certainly not.

JOYCE: I have given my life that men may rise above their common weakness.

BEAVERBROOK: Oh, I acknowledge that, yes.

JOYCE: I have shown them how to master nature.

BEAVERBROOK: Well — yes. I'm afraid that may be why we have to hang you, Mr Joyce.

JOYCE: What is this man talking about?

BEAVERBROOK: Any man who thinks he can master nature is a threat to British civilization. The basis of our civilization, Mr Joyce, is common sense.

JOYCE: There are times when I no longer see. When there is no light. Then I call to Margaret.

BEAVERBROOK: Mr Joyce —

JOYCE: I will not be cast off, do you hear!

BEAVERBROOK: Well, it's odd. I mean, have you ever thought, it may be some consolation to you, indeed, at this terrible time — I mean, passport or no passport, Britain has acknowledged you British by deciding to execute you for treason. Identity can be a fiction, Mr Joyce, and be no less satisfactory on that account.

JOYCE: I have helped to shape things —

BEAVERBROOK: I couldn't agree more. Indeed, that's why I'm here. I am always fascinated by the select, those to whom history has given a choice —

JOYCE: And now, God my Father, I will rest in Thee.

BEAVERBROOK: I met Hitler, too, you know. Tell me. What did you think of Hitler?

JOYCE: I never saw Hitler.

BEAVERBROOK: And Goebbels? What about Goebbels?

JOYCE: I never met Goebbels.

BEAVERBROOK: Yeah — well, that's fantastic. That's a whopper!

JOYCE: Are you copying down all of this?

BEAVERBROOK: Sure. I'm a journalist. I chase stories.

JOYCE: Like all journalists you have an exaggerated sense of the power of words.

BEAVERBROOK: My friend, I've changed the government in this country through my printed words. It depends on the ability to use words to create power.

JOYCE: Maybe, indeed.

BEAVERBROOK: So, you've found religion, have you?

JOYCE: Do not patronize me or my faith.

BEAVERBROOK: I do not patronize you. In my house, on the lawn in Stornoway House[27] there is a

26. Hugh Pattison (1873-1952), Baron MacMillan, Lord of Appeal in Ordinary 1930-39, 1941-47; Lord of Appeal 1947; presiding judge in *Joyce* v. *Director of Public Prosecutions* in 1946; minister for information 1939-40.

27. Stornoway House in St James's, London was acquired by Beaverbrook in 1922. It was his centre of operations during the war years.

life-sized crucifix. I can see it as I sit at my dining room table.

JOYCE: But you're eating your dinner at the same time are you not? (BEAVERBROOK *chuckles at this*) Oh, my Christ Jesus, there is no more time! Why did Hess fly to Scotland?

BEAVERBROOK: He told me he wished to see his friend the Duke of Hamilton. Do you think he might be nuts?

JOYCE: The fools, the fools! If they had only listened to what we said in 1936.

BEAVERBROOK: Do you mean Mosley? Or the Nazis?

JOYCE: Mosley was the creation of a group of upper-class English whores who needed leather. Why are you asking me these things? It does not matter. Do you think this war was fought for some piddling sentimentality out of Rupert Brooke?[28] This war was fought and lost on behalf of the species.

BEAVERBROOK: Hess said a peculiar bloody thing. He said he saw a vision of Armageddon from his aeroplane.

JOYCE: Perhaps he was flying into freedom before he crashed. His freedom. Freedom is just beyond what is, it is the perfection of our desires and therefore cannot be achieved in the present dimension.

BEAVERBROOK: I see you've been reading, Mr Joyce. What are you reading?

JOYCE: Thomas à Kempis.[29]

BEAVERBROOK: I see.

JOYCE: I would prefer to be alone now.

BEAVERBROOK: Yes. OK. OK by me.

JOYCE: Let *me* ask *you* some questions, Lord Beaverbrook.

BEAVERBROOK: Shoot.

JOYCE: Do you think this war has destroyed the British Empire?

BEAVERBROOK: Yes.

JOYCE: And did you know that at the beginning of the war?

BEAVERBROOK: Yes.

JOYCE: And yet you, the great imperialist, gave everything to the war effort?

BEAVERBROOK: Sure.

JOYCE: I don't understand.

BEAVERBROOK: That's why you're where you are now, Mr Joyce, and why I am somewhere else. (JOYCE *laughs at this*) I never mistake rigidity for authority, Mr Joyce.

JOYCE: And am I to appear in the *Daily Express*, Lord Beaverbrook?

BEAVERBROOK: No, no, no. Those are papers for my Deadman's Chest, Mr Joyce.

JOYCE: And what is that?

BEAVERBROOK: A kind of box, Mr Joyce. Posterity, Mr Joyce. Yeah, posterity.

BEAVERBROOK *goes off and leaves* JOYCE *alone in the light. On the video* BRACKEN *appears as if behind bars or a grille of iron. The mood is one of reverie and all the lines may be spoken by the actor on stage, with closed eyes.*

JOYCE: You should not have come here.

BRACKEN: I had to come.

JOYCE: Why?

BRACKEN: Because I am searching for my brother.

JOYCE: Your brother isn't here.

BRACKEN: I have searched everywhere else.

JOYCE: What does he look like, your brother?

BRACKEN: My brother has the face of a condemned people.

JOYCE: I have seen many faces in here that look like that.

BRACKEN: I searched the streets.

JOYCE: Have you looked in all the places of detention?

BRACKEN: I have only begun the search.

JOYCE: Well, then, why not come back again, tomorrow. (JOYCE *comes alert, with uptilted face, the face of* BRACKEN *remains behind its grille of iron.* JOYCE *stands, hands behind his back, as if manacled*) Dearest Margaret, tomorrow is the day of our severance and final union. I never asked you if you wished to receive a letter from me after my death. But now I write, knowing your wishes, if unexpressed. As I move nearer to the edge of Beyond, my confidence in the final victory increases. How it will be achieved I know not. Does it matter? As surely as I know that you and I are finally one so I know that this world will be redeemed. May Christ Jesus guard you, Margaret, on this day and until he unites us in the bosom of his father. (*Head down*) *The* LADY JOURNALIST *comes forward again. As she*

28. Rupert Brooke (1887-1915), whose *1914* sonnets, published in 1915, made him famous as an exponent of patriotic verse. He confirmed the legend created around him by dying on active service.
29. Thomas à Kempis (1380-1471), German Augustinian monk and author of the famous *The Imitation of Christ*, which describes the progress of the soul to perfection by detachment from the world and union with God.

speaks the lights finally go down on the faces of BRACKEN *and* JOYCE.

LADY JOURNALIST: What I remember most, from the trial of William Joyce, when justice was done, was not that small, slight man with his ridiculous teutonic bow to the judge, nor the palpable relief of the Londoners that he was not to escape, nor indeed the bombed, blitzed city streets outside, no. What I remember was the group of young fascists, the acolytes, the loyal ones, the young men in the gallery, those pale, blue faces, their dark, shining eyes, that look of inspired poverty, inspired promise. They were weeping. Those lilting Celtic voices in grief at the death of their christus. They put on their old raincoats, like vestments, and talked raucously of patriotism. It was as if they had taken the idea of England to some terrible logical meaning of their own which England itself could never tolerate. And before they left in the rain for some secret meeting, some illicit upper-room, the tears poured down those long, emaciated, Celtic faces. They wept for Joyce. They wept for England.

Biographies/Bibliographies

Michael J. Molloy

LIFE. M. J. Molloy was born in Co. Galway in 1917. He studied for the priesthood but illness terminated his studies. Since then he has spent most of his time on his small farm outside Milltown, Co. Galway.

CHIEF WRITINGS. *The King of Friday's Men* (Dublin: James Duffy, 1953); *The Paddy Pedlar* (Dublin: James Duffy, 1954); *The Will and the Way* (Dublin: P. J. Bourke, n.d.; Dublin: Progress House, 1961); *The Wood of the Whispering* (Dublin: Progress House, 1961); *Daughter from Over the Water* (Dublin: Progress House, 1963); *The Visiting House* in *Seven Irish Plays, 1946-1964* (Minneapolis: University of Minnesota Press, 1967); *Three Plays by M. J. Molloy (The King of Friday's Men, The Paddy Pedlar, The Wood of the Whispering)* (Newark, Delaware: Proscenium Press, 1975).

BIOGRAPHY AND CRITICISM. R. Hogan, *After the Irish Renaissance* (London: Macmillan, 1968); A. Feder and B. Schrank (eds), 'The Making of Folk Plays' in *Literature and Folk Culture: Ireland and Folk Culture* (St John's, Newfoundland: Memorial University of Newfoundland, 1977), pp. 58-80; D. E. S. Maxwell, *A Critical History of Irish Drama 1891-1980* (Cambridge: Cambridge University Press, 1984); M. Etherton, *Contemporary Irish Dramatists* (London: Macmillan, 1989), pp. 86-106.

Sam Thompson

LIFE. Born in Belfast in 1916. A painter by trade, Thompson began writing radio plays and features in the 1950s. In these he gave a graphic account of the poverty and sectarian violence of the working-class society to which he belonged. He wrote *Over the Bridge* between 1955 and 1957, but had to form his own company to have it produced in 1960, such was the opposition to its candid portrayal of bigotry and discrimination. The play is now seen as historically significant, anticipating the violence that was to break out in Northern Ireland eight years later. It was the only play Thompson published. The acclaim that had greeted *Over the Bridge* was renewed for the Dublin and Belfast productions of *The Evangelist* (1961). His television play, *Cemented With Love* (1964) was also subjected to political censorship. Thompson was a passionate trade unionist. His sudden death in 1965 deprived Northern Ireland of one of its most promising writers.

CHIEF WRITINGS. *Over the Bridge*, edited and introduced by Stewart Parker (Dublin: Gill and Macmillan, 1970).

BIOGRAPHY AND CRITICISM. R. Hogan, *After the Irish Renaissance* (Minneapolis: University of Minneapolis Press, 1967; London: Macmillan, 1968), pp. 100-02; H. Mengel, 'A Lost Heritage: Ulster Drama and the Work of Sam Thompson, *Theatre Ireland* 1 (Sept./Dec. 1982), 18-19; 2 (Jan./May 1983), 80-82; P. Devlin, 'First Bridge Too Far' *Theatre Ireland* 3 (June/Sept. 1983), 122-24; H. Mengel, *Sam Thompson and Modern Drama in Ulster* (Frankfurt am Main, Bern, New York: Verlag Peter Lang, 1986).

Eugene McCabe

LIFE. Born in Glasgow in 1930, McCabe went to secondary school in Dublin and to University College, Cork. He farmed for ten years in County Monaghan, before turning to writing in 1962. His play *King of the Castle* (1964) was a success at the Dublin Theatre Festival. This was followed by *Breakdown* (1966) and *Swift* (1969). In 1976 he wrote a trilogy of plays for television, under the title *Cancer*. One section of this was published as a short novel, *Victims* (1977). The other two, 'Cancer' and 'Heritage', appeared as short stories in *Heritage* (1978). McCabe is recognized as a highly gifted if reluctant writer. He farms the family holding in County Monaghan.

CHIEF WRITINGS. *Victims* (Cork: Mercier Press, 1976; London: Gollancz, 1977); *Heritage and Other Stories* (London: Gollancz, 1978; Dublin: O'Brien Press, 1985); *King of the Castle* (Dublin: The Gallery Press, 1978); *Pull Down a Horseman/Gale Day* (Dublin: The Gallery Press, 1979); *Roma* (Dublin: Turoe Press/RTE, 1979).

BIOGRAPHY AND CRITICISM. D. E. S. Maxwell, *A Critical History of Modern Irish Drama 1891-1980* (Cambridge: Cambridge University Press, 1984), pp. 169-70; R. Hogan, *'Since O'Casey' and Other Essays on Irish Drama* (Gerrards Cross: Colin Smythe; Totowa, New Jersey: Barnes and Noble, 1983), pp. 140-42; C. FitzSimon, *The Irish Theatre* (London: Thames and Hudson, 1983), p. 196.

John B. Keane

LIFE. Born in Listowel, Co. Kerry in 1928, John B. Keane has remained there continuously, save for a two-year period spent in England in the early 1950s. He owns a public house in Listowel and is generally regarded as one of the central figures of the literary scene in County Kerry. He has played an important role in establishing and supporting the Listowel Writers' Week. His plays, first produced in Cork, have become central to the repertoire of the Abbey Theatre.

CHIEF WRITINGS.
Plays. *Sive* (Dublin: Progress House, 1959, revised version 1986); *Sharon's Grave* (Dublin: Progress House, 1960); *The Highest House on the Mountain* (Dublin: Progress House, 1961); *Many Young Men of Twenty* (Dublin: Progress House, 1961); *The Man from Clare* (Cork: Mercier Press, 1962); *The Field* (Cork: Mercier Press, 1966); *Hut 42* (Dixon, California: Proscenium Press, 1968); *The Rain at the End of Summer* (Dublin: Progress House, 1968); *Big Maggie* (Cork: Mercier Press, 1969); *The Year of the Hiker* (Cork: Mercier Press, 1978).

Prose Writings. *Self-Portrait* (Cork: Mercier Press, 1964): *Letters of a Successful T.D.* (Cork: Mercier Press, 1968); *Letters of an Irish Parish Priest* (Cork: Mercier Press, 1972); *Death Be Not Proud* (Cork: Mercier Press, 1976); *Letters of a Civic Guard* (Cork: Mercier Press, 1976); M. Etherton, *Contemporary Irish Dramatists* (London: Macmillan, 1989), pp. 69-77.

John Boyd

LIFE. Born in Belfast in 1912, educated at Queen's University, Belfast and Trinity College, Dublin. He became a producer with the BBC in Belfast in 1947 and literary adviser to the Lyric Theatre, Belfast, as well as editor, since 1971, of its journal *Threshold*. Between 1942-1946, Boyd was editor of the important literary journal *Lagan*. A man of strong socialist views, he has tried to confront in his plays the realities and the roots of political violence in Northern Ireland. His play *The Assassin* was produced at the Gaiety Theatre during the Dublin Theatre Festival of 1969. *The Flats*, produced at the Lyric Theatre in 1971, sustains the same preoccupations — the mix of religious and political fanaticism, its tragic effects on individual lives. Boyd's later plays, *The Farm* (1972) and *The Street* (1977), were both produced at the Lyric Theatre of which he has been a stalwart supporter.

CHIEF WRITINGS. *The Flats* (Belfast: Blackstaff Press, 1974); *The Collected Plays* introd. by John Boyd, 2 vols (Vol. I, *The Flats, The Farm, Guests*; Vol. 2, *The Street, Facing North*) (Belfast: Blackstaff Press, 1981, 1982); *Out of My Class* (an autobiography) (Belfast: Blackstaff Press, 1985).

BIOGRAPHY AND CRITICISM. See autobiography cited above; D. E. S. Maxwell, *A Critical History of Modern Irish Drama 1891-1980* (Cambridge: Cambridge University Press, 1984), p. 180; E. Lehmann, 'England's Ireland: An Analysis of Some Contemporary Plays' in H. Kosok (ed.), *Studies in Anglo-Irish Literature* (Bonn: Herbert Grundmann, 1982), pp. 432-33; L. Henderson, 'The Green Shoot; Transcendence and the Imagination in Contemporary Ulster Drama' in G. Dawe and E. Longley (eds), *Across A Roaring Hill: The Protestant Imagination in Modern Ireland* (Belfast: Blackstaff Press, 1985), pp. 205-07.

Stewart Parker

LIFE. Born in Belfast in 1941, educated at Queen's University. His play *Spokesong* scored a success at the Dublin Theatre Festival in 1975 and was well received the following year in London. Parker has written extensively for radio and television. *Catchpenny Twist* (1977) and *Nightshade* (1985) display his gift for blending satire and mystery or fairy material into a dramatically effective whole. His play *Northern Star* (1985), on the protestant hero of the 1798 rebellion in the north, Henry Joy McCracken, and *Pentecost*, produced by Field Day in 1987, are perhaps his finest achievements to date. He died in 1988.

CHIEF WRITINGS. *Spokesong* (London: Samuel French, 1979); *Nightshade* (Dublin: Co-op Books, 1980); *Catchpenny Twist* (Dublin: The Gallery Press, 1980); *Three Plays for Ireland: Northern Star, Heavenly Bodies, Pentecost* (London: Oberon Books, 1989). Other scripts include *Irish in the Traffic, Ruby in the Rain* (television), *The Kamikaze Ground Staff Reunion Dinner, The Traveller, I'm a Dreamer Montreal* (all radio), and, for the stage, *Pratt's Fall.*

BIOGRAPHY AND CRITICISM. A. Parkin, 'Metaphor as Dramatic Structure in Some Plays of Stewart Parker' in M. Sekine (ed.), *Irish Writers and the Theatre* (Gerrards Cross: Colin Smythe, 1986), pp. 135-50; M. Etherton, *Contemporary Irish Dramatists* (London: Macmillan, 1989), pp. 15-25.

Graham Reid

LIFE. Born in Belfast in 1945, Reid left school at 15 but returned to full-time studies at 26, and graduated from Queen's University, Belfast in 1976. His best-known play, *The Death of Humpty-Dumpty* (1979), was successfully staged at the Abbey Theatre; his second play, *The Closed Door* (1980) is also concerned with the Belfast of the present troubles. His third play was *Dorothy* (1980). *The Hidden Curriculum* (1982) and his television plays *Billy* and *Ties of Blood* have made him an established figure. *Remembrance* was staged at the Lyric Theatre in 1984.

CHIEF WRITINGS. *The Death of Humpty-Dumpty* (Dublin: Co-op Books, 1980); *The Closed Door* (Dublin: Co-op Books, 1980); *The Plays of Graham Reid; Too Late to Talk to Billy; Dorothy; The Hidden Curriculum* (Dublin: Co-op Books, 1982); *Billy: Three Plays for Television* (London: Faber and Faber, 1984); *Remembrance* (London: Faber and Faber, 1985); *Ties of Blood* (London: Faber and Faber, 1986).

BIOGRAPHY AND CRITICISM. D. E. S. Maxwell, *A Critical History of Modern Irish Drama 1891-1980* (Cambridge: Cambridge University Press, 1984), pp. 185-86; P. Campbell, 'Graham Reid — Professional', *The Linen Hall Review*, 1.2 (Summer 1984), 4-7; E. Fitzgibbon, 'All Change: Contemporary Fashions in the Irish Theatre' in M. Sekine (ed.), *Irish Writers and the Theatre* (Gerrards Cross: Colin Smythe; Totowa, New Jersey: Barnes and Noble, 1986), pp. 35-37; M. Etherton; *Contemporary Irish Dramatists* (London: Macmillan, 1989), pp. 33-38.

Brian Friel

LIFE. Born in Omagh, Co. Tyrone, in 1929, and brought up in Derry, where he taught for ten years (1950-60). During this time he began to write short stories and radio plays. Many of the stories were published in the *New Yorker*. His first major stage success was *Philadelphia, Here I Come!* (1964). Between that and 1971, Friel established himself as the most important dramatist in Ireland. With the outbreak of the Northern troubles in 1968, his dramatic range expanded and his treatment of the themes of exile, isolation and lost illusion became increasingly complex and subtle. From *The Freedom of the City* (1973) to *Aristocrats* (1979), Friel finds ways of dramatically presenting and embodying the divorce between eloquence and political power, a preoccupation that is central to the Irish theatre in this century. This phase of his work culminated in 1979 with the production of *Faith Healer* at the Longacre Theatre in New York. In this play, Friel resumes, in the metaphor of faith-healing, all that he had meditated upon in the previous decade. In 1980, Friel and the actor Stephen Rea founded the Field Day Theatre Company. Other members of the Board were Seamus Heaney, Seamus Deane, Tom Paulin and David Hammond. It was a company rooted in Derry and pledged to annual theatrical productions which would tour the country, north and south, after opening in Derry. The first Field Day theatrical venture was Friel's *Translations* (1980), widely acclaimed as a masterpiece and as a central statement of the Field Day Company's preoccupations.

Friel supplied an antidote to *Translations* in 1982, with *The Communication Cord*, a farce that undermined and chastized the pieties which *Translations* had commemorated. Since then, Field Day has continued to produce plays and pamphlets in its attempt to find some vantage point from which the present state of Irish affairs can be effectively described and understood.

CHIEF WRITINGS. *The Saucer of Larks* (London: Gollancz, 1962) (short stories); *Philadelphia, Here I Come!* (London: Faber and Faber, 1965); *The Gold in the Sea* (London: Gollancz, 1966) (short stories); *The Loves of Cass McGuire* (London: Faber and Faber, 1967); *Lovers* (New York: Farrar, Straus & Giroux, 1968; London: Faber and Faber, 1969); *Crystal and Fox* (London: Faber and Faber, 1970); *Two Plays* (contains *Crystal and Fox* and *The Mundy Scheme*) (New York: Farrar, Straus & Giroux, 1970); *The Gentle Island* (London: Davis-Poynter, 1973); *The Freedom of the City* (London: Faber and Faber, 1974); *The Enemy Within* (written 1962, Newark, Delaware: Proscenium Press, 1975; Dublin: The Gallery Press, 1979); *Living Quarters* (London and Boston: Faber and Faber, 1978); *The Enemy Within* (Newark, Delaware: Proscenium Press 1975; Dublin: Gallery Press, 1979); *Volunteers* (London and Boston: Faber and Faber, 1979); *Aristocrats* (Dublin: The Gallery Press, 1980); *Faith Healer* (London and Boston: Faber and Faber, 1980); *Translations* (London and Boston: Faber and Faber, 1981); *Making History* (London: Faber and Faber, 1988); *Dancing at Lughnasa* (London: Faber and Faber, 1990); *The Three Sisters* by Anton Chekhov (Dublin: The Gallery Press, 1981); *The Communication Cord* (London and Boston: Faber and Faber, 1983). See also *Selected Stories*, introd. by Seamus Deane (Dublin: The Gallery Press, 1979); *Selected Plays* introd. by Seamus Deane (London: Faber and Faber, 1984; Washington D.C.: The Catholic University Press of America, 1986).

BIOGRAPHY AND CRITICISM. Brian Friel, 'Self-Portrait', *Aquarius* (1972); Brian Friel, 'Extracts from a Sporadic Diary' in A. Carpenter and P. Fallon (eds), *The Writers: A Sense of Ireland* (Dublin: O'Brien Press, 1980), pp. 39-40; 'Extracts from a Sporadic Diary' in T. P. Coogan (ed.), *Ireland and the Arts* (London: Namara Press, n.d.), pp. 56-61; R. Hogan, *After the Irish Renaissance* (Minneapolis: University of Minnesota Press, 1967; London: Macmillan, 1968); R. Hogan, *'Since O'Casey' and Other Essays on Irish Drama* (Gerrards Cross: Colin Smythe; Totowa, New Jersey: Barnes and Noble, 1983); 'Brian Friel' in D. Hickey and G. Smith (eds), *A Paler Shade of Green* (London: Leslie Frewin, 1972) (American title, *Flight from the Celtic Twilight* Indianapolis: Bobbs-Merrill, 1973); Brian Friel, 'Plays Peasant and Unpeasant, *The Times Literary Supplement*, 17 March 1972; D. E. S. Maxwell, *Brian Friel* (Lewisburg, Pennsylvania: Bucknell University Press, 1973); D.E.S. Maxwell, *A Critical History of Modern Irish Drama 1891-1980* (Cambridge University Press, 1984), pp. 200-12; Seamus Deane, 'Brian Friel: The Double Stage' in *Celtic Revivals: Essays in Modern Irish Literature* (London: Faber and Faber, 1985), pp. 166-73; U. Dantanus, *Brian Friel: The Growth of an Irish Dramatist* (London: Faber and Faber, 1988); M. Etherton, *Contemporary Irish Dramatists* (London: Macmillan, 1989), pp. 147-208; R. Pine, *Brian Friel and Ireland's Drama* (London: Routledge, 1990).

Thomas Murphy

LIFE. Born in Tuam, Co. Galway in 1935. Between 1957 and 1962 he taught at a local vocational school. For the following eight years, he lived in London as a full-time writer. His first play, *A Whistle in the Dark*, was rejected by the Abbey Theatre in 1960, but was produced by Joan Littlewood at the Theatre Royal in London in 1961. Murphy returned to Dublin in 1971 and became a director on the board of the Abbey Theatre from 1973 to 1983. *The Morning After Optimism*, produced at the Abbey in 1971, was Murphy's most startling and experimental play. This, coupled with the failure of *The White House* (1972), typified the disturbing impact of his early presence in the Irish theatre. The iconoclastic element in Murphy's work intensified with *The Sanctuary Lamp* (1975) and the more political *The Blue Macushla* (1980). But with the production of *The Gigli Concert* at the Abbey in 1983, and the Druid Company's production of *Bailegangaire* in Galway in 1985 — in which Siobhán McKenna played her last and one of her most memorable roles — Murphy's work achieved a new dimension. He is now recognized as one of the dominant, if most unpredictable, of present Irish dramatists.

CHIEF WRITINGS. *A Whistle in the Dark* (New York: Samuel French, 1970; Dublin: The Gallery Press, 1984); *The Morning After Optimism* (Cork: Mercier Press, 1973); *The Orphans* (Newark, Delaware: Proscenium Press, 1974); *The Sanctuary Lamp* (Swords, Co. Dublin: Poolbeg Press, 1976); *On the Outside/On the Inside* (Dublin: The Gallery Press, 1976); *Famine* (Dublin: The Gallery Press, 1977; Newark, Delaware: Proscenium Press, 1978); *A Crucial Week in the Life of a Grocer's Assistant* (Dublin: The Gallery Press, 1978); *The Gigli Concert* (Dublin: The Gallery Press, 1984); *Conversations on a Homecoming* (Dublin: The Gallery Press, 1986); *Bailegangaire* (Dublin: The Gallery Press, 1986).

BIOGRAPHY AND CRITICISM. C. G. Griffin, 'The Plays of Thomas Murphy' (M.A. diss. University College, Dublin, 1976); 'Produced, Praised and Hammered: The Career of Thomas Murphy', *Theatre Ireland*, 4 (Sept./Dec. 1983), 17-19; D. Hickey and G. Smith (eds), *A Paler Shade of Green* (London: Leslie Frewin, 1972), pp. 220-27, (American title, *Flight from the Celtic Twilight* Indianapolis: Bobbs-Merrill, 1973); R. Kearney, 'Tom Murphy's Long Night's Journey Into Night', *Studies* LXXII (Winter 1983), 333-38; D. E. S. Maxwell, *A Critical History of Modern Irish Drama 1891-1980* (Cambridge: Cambridge University Press, 1984), pp. 162-68; C. Murray (ed.), Thomas Murphy Issue *Irish University Review*, Vol. 17, No. 1 (Spring 1987); 'Irish Drama in Transition 1966-1978', *Etudes Irlandaises*, No. 4, n.s. (December, 1979), 287-308; F. O'Toole, *The Politics of Magic: The Work and Times of Tom Murphy* (Dublin: Raven Arts Press, 1987); M. Etherton, *Contemporary Irish Dramatists* (London: Macmillan, 1989), pp. 107-46.

Frank McGuinness

LIFE. Born in 1956 in Buncrana, Co. Donegal, educated at University College, Dublin, he now lectures in English at St Patrick's College, Maynooth. The Abbey Theatre has staged *The Factory Girls* (1982), *Baglady/Ladybag* (1985) and the award-winning *Observe the Sons of Ulster Marching Towards the Somme* (1985), later produced at the Hampstead Theatre in London. *Innocence* (1986), a play on the life of Caravaggio, was staged at the Gate Theatre in Dublin in 1986. He has been writer-in-residence with Team Theatre Company and has written a play, *Scout*, for BBC 2 television. In 1987, his translation of Lorca's *Yerma* was staged at the Abbey and of Ibsen's *Rosmersholm* at the National Theatre in London. He was written a version of *Peer Gynt* for the Gate Theatre. *Carthaginians* was first performed at the Dublin Theatre Festival in 1988. McGuinness has won several important literary awards.

CHIEF WRITINGS. *The Factory Girls* (Dublin: Nonooch Line, 1982); *Observe the Sons of Ulster Marching Towards the Somme* (London: Faber and Faber, 1986); *Innocence* (London: Faber and Faber, 1987); *Carthaginians* (London: Faber and Faber, 1988); *Mary and Lizzie* (London: Faber and Faber, 1989).

BIOGRAPHY AND CRITICISM. E. Fitzgibbon, 'All Change: Contemporary Fashions in the Irish Theatre' in M. Sekine (ed.), *Irish Writers and the Theatre* (Gerrards Cross: Colin Smythe; Totowa, New Jersey: Barnes and Noble, 1986), pp. 135-50; M. Etherton, *Contemporary Irish Dramatists* (London: Macmillan, 1989), pp. 47-50

Thomas Kilroy

LIFE. Born in Callan, Co. Kilkenny in 1934, educated at University College, Dublin. From 1962 to 1965 Kilroy taught in the USA, at Notre Dame, Indiana and at Vanderbilt, Tennessee. From 1965-73 he taught in the Department of English at University College, Dublin. In 1973 he resigned from full-time teaching to devote more of his energies to writing. From 1979 to 1989 he was professor of English at University College, Galway. His play *The Death and Resurrection of Mr Roche* was a success at the Dublin Theatre Festival of 1968 and again on its transfer to London. Kilroy's next important work was a novel, *The Big Chapel* (1971). It was shortlisted for the Booker Prize and won the Guardian Prize for Fiction. In this year Kilroy was elected a Fellow of the Royal Society for Literature and a member of the Irish Academy of Letters in 1973. *Tea & Sex & Shakespeare* was produced at the Abbey Theatre during the Dublin International Festival of 1976. *Talbot's Box* (1977), a play about the Dublin working-class 'saint', Matt Talbot, extends his preoccupation with the distortions of the individual psyche in its attempts to achieve fullness within the confines of a narrow and traumatized society. It was produced at the Peacock Theatre, Dublin and subsequently was transferred to the Royal Court in London. This theatre saw the first production of *The Seagull*, an adaptation from Chekhov, in 1981. *Double Cross*, produced by the Field Day Company in 1986, brought the themes of Kilroy's earlier plays to a culmination. It was preceded by the radio play *That Man, Bracken*, first broadcast on BBC 3 on 20 June 1986. He became a director of Field Day Theatre Company in 1988.

CHIEF WRITINGS. *The Death and Resurrection of Mr Roche* (London: Faber and Faber; New York: Grove Press, 1968); *The Big Chapel* (London: Faber and Faber, 1971; London: Pan Books, 1973; Swords, Co. Dublin: Poolbeg Press, 1982); *Talbot's Box* (Dublin: The Gallery Press, 1980); *The Seagull: a new version* introd. by R. Ritchie (London: Methuen; New York: Methuen Inc., 1981); *Double Cross* (London: Faber and Faber, 1986). See also *Sean O'Casey, A Collection of Critical Essays* (Twentieth-Century Views) edited and introduced by Thomas Kilroy (Englewood Heights, New Jersey: Prentice Hall, 1975).

BIOGRAPHY AND CRITICISM. B. Cosgrove, *'Ego Contra Mundum*: Thomas Kilroy's *The Big Chapel'* in P. Rafroidi (ed.), *The Irish Novel In Our Time* (Lille: Publications de l'université de Lille, 1975); K. Kimball, 'Thomas Kilroy' in *Ten Modern Irish Playwrights: A Bibliography* (New York and London: Garland Publishing Inc., 1979); C. Murray, 'Thomas Kilroy: Contemporary Irish Writers, 5' *Ireland Today* (Department of Foreign Affairs, Dublin, 1982); G. A. Barnett, 'Thomas Kilroy' in James Vinson (ed.), *Contemporary Dramatists* (London: Macmillan, 1982); G. Dawe, 'Thomas Kilroy', *Theatre Ireland* 3 (June/Sept. 1983), 117-19; A. Roche, 'The Fortunate Fall: Two Plays by Thomas Kilroy' in M. Harmon (ed.), *The Writer and the City* (Gerrards Cross: Colin Smythe, 1984); F. McGuinness, 'A Haunted House: The Theatre of Thomas Kilroy' in B. Hayley and W. Rix (eds), *Irish Theatre Today* (Wurtzburg: Koenigen and Neuhasen, 1985); M. Etherton, *Contemporary Irish Dramatists* (London: Macmillan, 1989), pp. 51-62.

DECLAN KIBERD, *Editor*

Contemporary Irish Poetry

Even a generation after the deaths of Yeats and Joyce, a sense of anticlimax pervaded the Irish scene. Both men had been figures of international stature, and now only a sense of emptiness remained. Worse still, the idea of Ireland as one of the vibrant centres of European culture seemed to have died with them. Samuel Beckett emigrated to the Continent in 1939 with the bleak assertion that he preferred France at war to Ireland at peace.

Ireland during the years of World War II became a provincial and introverted place, its stasis manifest not only in the political failure to join the fight against fascism, but also in the growing popular contempt for modern art. A reproduction of Manet's *Olympus* was denounced when Victor Waddington put it on display in a Dublin gallery; jazz was banned for a time on Radio Éireann; and Dublin Corporation voted to refuse a gift of Rouault's *Christ Crowned with Thorns*.

In such a claustrophobic atmosphere, Irish artists lost touch with European colleagues, critics and audiences. Many of them were degraded in the eyes of fellow-citizens to the level of eccentric aesthetes, performing the role of daft artist for an audience of jeering provincials. Some succumbed to their fate as 'gas bloody men' (Patrick Kavanagh's phrase), enacting in pubs the part of writer, rather than confronting in private the anguish of actual writing. Others, like Anthony Cronin, found in the squalor of bohemian Dublin vague intimations of the dire poverty that surrounded it, and sought uneasily for analogies in Baudelaire and the writers of the French Decadence. But most poets remained introverted and even happily provincial — unsung victims of the war.

It is more rewarding to look at the poetry of Patrick MacDonogh or Padraic Fallon because their relationship to the situation briefly described here is uneasy and complicated. Fallon is especially so, in part because he, like many of his contemporaries, although to a greater extent than any of them, found it almost impossible to gain visibility. He began to be seen only in 1974, the year of his death, although his best work belongs to the 1930s and 40s. It takes, even yet, an effort on the part of the reader to realize that this man was a contemporary of Kavanagh, Austin Clarke and others. He has been chronologically displaced, but that displacement is not merely the consequence of the misfortunes of publishing. Fallon is not in any true sense a part of the reaction against the Revival. He is the most important of the poets whose most natural relationship is with what may be described as the ecumenical aspect of the Revival, best represented by Sigerson and, a little later, by W. P. Ryan. For Padraic Fallon, the Gaelic civilization, with its characteristic poet, Raftery, the nineteenth-century writer and cult figure, and the Anglo-Irish civilization, which culminated in Yeats, are equally available. These are indeed bards of the Gael and Gall, although the intermixture of the two is more rewarding than any vain attempt to identify the distinctions between them. Fallon mobilized the vision of Sigerson, Rolleston and others in his poetry, something they had never been able to do themselves. He is the poet of the 'other' Revival, the revival of the Gael rather than the revival of the Celt, the revival that had been annexed by the political will of Patrick Pearse and glimpsed in the critical writings of Thomas MacDonagh. Unlike Colum, Higgins, Campbell and Patrick

MacDonogh, Fallon found an enabling myth and was thereby freed from the provincialism of his predecessors.

Fallon achieved what Denis Devlin hoped to achieve — a fusion in poetry of Irish religious and Irish political experience that would go beyond an exclusively nationalist narrative. He was very much of his time in that, like Devlin and Seán O'Faoláin, he wanted to extend the regional to the European horizon and in that he too recognized that catholicism provided the obvious cultural bonding with the Continent. Yet his poems dwell on a paradox that becomes central to their meditative energy. His young life in the West of Ireland provided him with two cultural parents. One was the Gaelic tradition, still alive there at that time, and best represented for him by the Irish poet Raftery (to whom Yeats also addresses himself). Raftery is a wild and fierce spirit, a still-living memory from the eighteenth century. Alongside that wildness, there is the antidote to it — the catholic religion, centred on the image of the Virgin, to whom Fallon addresses several poems.

Fallon is able to see Ireland in the light of European and ancient classical experience as one more country in which the parental, cultural and biological influences determine the religious systems. Only the poet stays free of this over-determination. He lives between the mother and the father, between the old and the contemporary Ireland, between classical deities and Irish catholic images, as a free person, essentially parentless in so far as he is a poet, but limited within the parental confines of his inheritance. So, in his later work, Fallon broods on his own parents, his childhood, the death of his poet-friends. Man creates in the face of death — children, poems, religions. But these creations, amazing as they are, do not endure:

> Much is man and not enough

There is always, in Fallon's respect, a tonic touch of the sardonic. He avoids the Yeatsian annunciations on the supremacy of the imagination and of art. His is a less histrionic gesture. It is man's destiny to be creative. He produces, but, in doing so, he does not solve, he does not possess the world:

> The virtue of heaven is simply to produce
> Anything. It's a music. Birdsong or bomb,
> it's all equal.

Although in a poem like 'Yeats's Tower at Ballylee', Fallon feels the trauma of the great poet's despair, he does not continue to concede to it. Although Yeats 'knew what opposites/War in one person', and on that account became a great poet, there is also the possibility of a serenity that outlives the war. The opposition need not be permanently fretful or tragic. In reaching that serenity, Fallon passed beyond Yeats's shadow and found a voice that was neither strident with the sense of national or personal destiny, nor resigned to the sweet pastoralisms of a regional insularity.

Patrick MacDonogh achieved no comparable accommodation of conflict within his poetry. Yet he did write a number of grave and beautiful poems on the theme that 'desire begets despair', a poetry that wanted to refuse the nostalgias to which it repeatedly succumbed. Most of his memorable poems are concerned with the aftermath of a love that did not come to fruition. In a way, it is his metaphor for poetry. It has an inexhaustible desire and a finite achievement. While the two elements are not to be reconciled, he does manage to avoid the escapism and artificially induced high temperatures of the poets of the 1890s, to whom he is otherwise indebted, and to see the conflict in an impersonal light. His volume *One Landscape Still* (1958) contains all his achieved work and is certainly one of the most notable single volumes of the 1950s.

Charles Donnelly died young, fighting on the republican side in the Spanish Civil War. He too is only now being recognized as a poet, although his work is, like that of Pearse and Francis Ledwidge, dominated by the fact of his political commitment and his death. He is truly a thirties poet, deeply influenced by Auden and struggling to invent a new idiom, in which the impersonal forces of history are understood to be, by a strange paradox, the determinants of human conscience and consciousness. When consciousness is read as conscience, there is political commitment. Donnelly is very far removed from the aestheticism of the late 1890s and of the early century. His influence is greater than his achievement. It finally re-emerges in the work of writers like Anthony Cronin, Michael O'Loughlin and, with some profound modifications, of Paul Durcan. Rather than finding its source in a country, a region, a myth of heroism, it aims, by the action of the poetry itself, to create that source as a vision of human community. It is a strange irony that Ireland, so given to the various forms of communal identification and assertion, should have managed so effectively to marginalize 'left-wing' poetry, which is itself dedicated to the idea of a restored and renovated community. The reasons for this are complex and are to be found not only in the history of the poetry of this period, but also in its political history and the story of the occlusion of left-wing politics in the vital decades between 1918 and 1950. Even today, the hottest form of communal solidarity is sectarian. In that atmosphere, a vision of the restored human community struggles to survive. Much of the poetry represented here is in dedication to a cause. What Donnelly sternly reminds us of is the price the wrong cause can exact — the price, for a poet, as for an activist, of being only an instrument, of failing at a radical level to give oneself and of being thereafter subject to caricature and stereotype: 'you give ... your services but not yourself.'

The politicians of Leinster House, with the notable exception of James Dillon, endorsed Ireland's neutral stance during World War II. Many artists were less sure. Louise MacNeice had no hesitation in condemning it:

> But then look eastward from your heart, there bulks
> A continent, close, dark, as archetypal sin,
> While to the west off your own shores the mackerel
> Are fat — on the flesh of your kin.

The same point was made by Samuel Beckett on his return, as a hero of the Resistance, from war-torn France. Privately, he complained that his family had been gorging themselves while half of Europe starved. Publicly, in a broadcast written for Radio Éireann, he noted the mutal incomprehension that he had recently observed between neutral Irish Red Cross workers and the battle-scarred French whom they treated at St Lô. Discrepant experiences had left both groups with almost no common ground on which to meet. Yet those Irish who went to France, said Beckett, 'got what they could hardly give, a vision and a sense of a time-honoured conception of humanity in ruins, and perhaps even an inkling of the terms in which our condition is to be thought again'. The radio station that censored jazz did not see fit, in the event, to broadcast Beckett's talk.

The story of Irish poetry after the 1950s is the tale of how a new generation of men and women sought once again — as Yeats had at the start of the century — to free Ireland from provincialism by an exacting criticism and a European pose. Many writers headed for European artistic capitals as soon as the routes were reopened. Brendan Behan and John Montague soon made contact with Beckett in Paris. As news of the death-camp atrocities filtered out, artists slowly came to terms with the damage, to Irish minds as well as to European bodies, of the preceding decade. Poems by Montague such as 'A Welcoming Party' and 'Back to School' elaborate the theme, as ironic updatings of Kavanagh's 'Epic'. However, it was only with Thomas Kinsella's 'Downstream' and Derek Mahon's 'A Disused Shed in Co. Wexford' that the 'Lost people of Treblinka' speak out of an experience that is as Irish as it is European.

The poetry of those postwar decades was characterized also by a growing engagement with foreign — and specifically English — authors. One way of fighting free of the awesome legacy of Yeats, after all, was to set up shop under the sign of Eliot or Auden. Hence Thomas Kinsella's

> Domestic Autumn, like an animal
> Long used to handling by those countrymen,
> Rubs her kind hide against the bedroom wall

may derive, at least in its imagery, from

> ... the yellow smoke that slides along the street
> Rubbing its back upon the window-panes;

'Baggot Street Deserta' seems unthinkable without such predecessors as 'Preludes', 'Rhapsody on a Windy Night' and 'Morning at the Window'. The metre, however, is Audenesque:

> I nonetheless inflict, endure,
> Tedium, intracordal hurt,
> The sting of memory's quick, the drear
> Uprooting, burying, prising apart ....

The influence of Auden on Mahon, Longley and Montague is at least as extensive as that of Kavanagh (through whom, incidentally, Auden was siphoned on to the younger generation of poets). And there is good reason for this. Auden was, along with Philip Larkin, the artist of post-imperial England, a land of anticlimax and antimacassars, evoked with a desperately self-deprecating suburban wit. Their tone seemed strangely suitable for those Irish poets born too late to partake in the heroic phase, either of Ireland or of modern poetry. By a brutally revealing paradox, Auden's England was the appropriate model for yet another tradition winding down into self-irony. In this, as in so much else, Ireland was disappointing all by turning into a botched version of England. As Montague observes in 'Speech for an Ideal Irish Election':

Who today asks for more
— Smoke of battle blown aside —
Then the struggle with casual
Graceless unheroic things,
The greater task of swimming
Against a slackening tide?

In much the same mode, 'Casement's Funeral' by Richard Murphy is not just a weary rebuke to those 'Rebels in silk hats now' who 'exploit the grave with an old comrade's speech', but also a self-confessed example of just such exploitation, a thin parody of 'Parnell's Funeral' by Yeats. Parody proved itself to be an appropriate mode for trapped post-Yeatsian minds, unsure if they could engage in radical acts of creation. The new Ireland seemed like a parody of the old; and so the lyrics of the 1960s, which celebrated the emergent consumerism of transistor radios and weekend sex, somehow had to be couched in Yeatsian terms:

Puritan Ireland's dead and gone,
A myth of O'Connor and O'Faolain.

Eavan Boland's 'The Woman Turns Herself into a Fish' is a clear inversion of the fish-into-girl progression in Yeats's 'The Song of Wandering Aengus'. Even the more vicious assaults on Yeats could but replicate his techniques, as in Kavanagh's sour little sonnet 'Yeats'. Like Auden's elegy, and indeed like so many Yeatsian poems from 'Easter 1916' to 'The Second Coming', the title promises a celebration and the text refuses the elegiac option, reversing all readerly expectations, with painful questions:

Yeats, it was very easy for you to be frank
With your sixty years and loves (like Robert
  Graves).
It was thin and in fact you have never put the tank
On a race. Ah cautious man whom no sin
  depraves . . .
And it won't add up at least in my mind
To what it takes in the living poetry stakes . . . .

An obsession with father-son relations — mandatory for almost every poet from Anthony Cronin to Seamus Deane — was a tell-tale sign of a society no longer sure of its bearing.

Living in the backwash of a heroic time and literature, the new generations had little choice but to question all aspects of that inheritance. The common strategy, adumbrated by Kavanagh in 'Epic', was to interrogate the mythical with the quotidian banal. Hence, also, Seamus Heaney's bog-poems, which juxtapose victims of ancient Jutland sacrificial rites with the most recent targets of communal strife in Ireland. A fundamentally similar method is to be found in Eiléan Ní Chuilleanáin's slangy Odysseus, Mahon's debased Raftery, and Kinsella's Nightwalker. Kinsella, in truth, spoke for them all in locating the origins of this strategy in Joyce's *Ulysses*, and in that author's willingness to write of the shamrock lumpenproletariat, the sub-heroic Paudeens at their greasy tills: 'His stomach, unlike Yeats's, is not turned by what he sees shaping the new Ireland. He is the first major voice to speak for Irish reality since the death of the Irish language.'

Not for nothing, therefore, has a recent study of the modern Irish tradition borne the title *Irish Poetry After Joyce*. In Heaney's long poem 'Station Island', Joyce is the commanding, authorizing presence, whose injunctions ring through the final passages of a poem which flirts with the very possibility of prose.

And yet persistent questions nag. Might not all this mingling of the mythical with the matter-of-fact have even deeper roots, in the art of Yeats and the Abbey Theatre? The latter, according to Lady Gregory, set out to forge a drama 'with a base of realism and an apex of beauty', to be found in the interplay between the heroic Cuchulain and the prose-talking Fool and Blind Man in Yeats's *On Baile's Strand*. Moreover, Lennox Robinson's description of the Abbey playwrights' reconciliation of 'poetry of speech' with 'humdrum fact' might be a kind of motto for modern Irish poetry, yet the phrases were clearly intended to refer to Synge and O'Casey.

So the underlying strategies of recent Irish poetry may derive their ultimate sanctions from a by-now rooted tradition. What has undeniably changed is the weighting accorded to the dual elements. Today a poet's love is all for the quotidian; the heroic merely echoes distantly, as an ironic reminder of what we are not, and (all things considered) had better not try to be. This, in turn, has led to an almost unanimous rejection of Yeatsian rhetoric — Kennelly, Michael Hartnett, and Montague in his public poems would be the exceptions here — and a desire to play something closer to Kavanagh's true note on a dead slack string. That chosen quietude can, of course, find many tones, from the 'clean laconic style' of Murphy to the vestigial uvula of Heaney, but, in any case, rhetoric is at last having its neck wrung.

There are good reasons for this. The Abbey Theatre's balanced combination of poetic language and a landscape of prosaic constriction is now generally seen as suspect. Irish eloquence is implicitly presented in many plays as a kind of consolation for poverty, and so O'Casey's slum-dwellers are seen to create in rolling speeches a kind of spaciousness that they can never find in their tenements. While collecting folklore in a Galway workhouse, Lady Gregory pronounced herself struck by the contrast between the destitution of the tellers and the splendour of their tales, but a more modern Irish generation has been less charmed than worried by that disjunction. Current reservations about eloquence are dramatized with much subtlety in Brian Friel's *Translations*, where the hedge-schoolmaster, Hugh, explains his native culture to the visiting Englishman Yolland: 'Indeed, Lieutenant. A rich language. A rich literature. You'll find, sir, that certain cultures expend on their vocabularies and syntax acquisitive energies and ostentations entirely lacking in their material lives. I suppose you could call us a spiritual people.' He claims that a 'syntax opulent with tomorrows' is 'our response to mud cabins and a diet of potatoes'. Crucial to this exchange is the preceding stage-direction, to the effect that Hugh, as the scene progresses, is 'deliberately parodying himself' — explaining to the Englishman just why he finds that part of Donegal and its people attractive. Hugh culminates the encounter with a Shavian warning about the danger of lapsing entirely into dreams: 'it can happen that a civilization can be imprisoned in a linguistic contour which no longer matches the landscape of ... fact.' In other words, the base of realism may have lost touch with the apex of beauty, when (as Shaw put it) the facts are all brutal and the dreams all unreal. Clearly, the younger generation of Irish poets fear that such a moment may have come again.

Friel's play, in its basic situation, is a working-through of the ideas implicit in Montague's poem 'A Lost Tradition'. The play describes how, once the Ordnance Surveyors have replaced Gaelic with anglicized names, every member of the parish starts to lose his or her way. The poem expresses a sense of severance from one's own heritage, imaged in the map of Montague's native County Tyrone. The map is studded with place-names derived from the Irish language, which has been moribund in the area for generations. In an ancient Gaelic manuscript, which no contemporary reader can understand, he finds an image of his own geography of disinheritance:

> All around, shards of a lost tradition ....
>
> The whole landscape a manuscript
> We had lost the skill to read,
> A part of our past disinherited;
> But fumbled, like a blind man,
> Along the fingertips of instinct.

This is but one of dozens of attempts by contemporary Irish poets to describe — and by describing, fill — the rift between the Gaelic and the Anglo-Irish traditions. Some younger poets, like Ciaran Carson in 'The Irish for "No"' or Paul Muldoon in 'Aisling', seem able to achieve sardonic fusions of the two traditions within a single poem; but a more reverent older generation, represented by Pearse Hutchinson in 'Achnasheen', is troubled by a rift that can be bridged only by such heavy irony. That rift has been most accurately measured by Thomas Kinsella:

> A modern English poet can reasonably feel at home in the long tradition of English poetry .... An Irish poet has access to the English poetic heritage through his use of the English language, but he is unlikely to feel at home in it. Or so I find in my own case. If he looks back over his own heritage, the line must begin, again, with Yeats. But then, for more than a hundred years, there is almost total poetic silence. I believe that silence, on the whole, is the real condition of Irish literature in the nineteenth century — certainly of poetry; there is nothing that approaches the ordinary literary achievement of an age.
>
> Beyond the nineteenth century, there is a great cultural blur: I must exchange one language for another, my native English for eighteenth-century Irish. Yet to come on eighteenth-century

Irish poetry after the dullness of the nineteenth century is to find a world suddenly full of life and voices, the voices of poets who expect to be heard and understood and memorised. Beyond them is ... the course of Irish poetry stretching back for more than a thousand years.

In all of this I recognise a great inheritance and, simultaneously, a great loss. The inheritance is certainly mine, but only at two enormous removes — across a century's silence and through an exchange of words. The greatness of the loss is measured not only by the substance of Irish literature itself, but also by the intensity with which we know it was shared; it has an air of continuity and shared history which is precisely what is missing from Irish literature, in English or Irish, in the nineteenth century and today. I recognise that I stand on one side of a great rift, and can feel the discontinuity in myself. It is a matter of people and places as well as writing — of coming from a broken and uprooted family, of being drawn to those who share my origins and finding that we cannot share our lives.

Many artists, most notably Synge, have sought to bridge that schism by injecting toxins of Gaelic syntax and imagery into their writing. In lesser writers, this can give rise to the factitious eloquence that is now so despised. A psychological mechanism of compensation, it can leave a certain type of Irish chauvinist congratulating himself on his poetic deviations from standard English, in order to console himself for his failure to create anything in the Irish language. For decades, poets like Austin Clarke or F.R. Higgins sought to create in English verse the characteristic Gaelic modes of poetry. Most recently poets have abandoned such efforts, opting instead to produce occasional translations from the Irish. Such an exercise always has some validity, but it had more in the early decades of this century, when writers such as Yeats yearned for a glimpse of the Gaelic world hidden in a language they could never hope to learn. Nowadays, however, when most Irish writers have a reading knowledge of the Irish language, these versions seem less useful. They appear, more and more, as conscience-stricken gestures by those who feel some strange sense of guilt for producing their major work in a chastely English or Anglo-Irish tradition.

The most radical way out of this quandary is, of course, to abandon English and write instead in the Irish language. This Michael Hartnett did with 'A Farewell to English', in the course of which he derided Yeats for use of token Gaelic phrases gleaned from Aogán Ó Rathaille:

> Our commis-chefs attend and learn the trade,
> bemoan the scraps of Gaelic that they know:
> add to a simple Anglo-Saxon stock
> Cuchulainn's marrow-bones to marinate,
> a dash of Ó Rathaille simmered slow,
> a glass of University hic-haec-hoc:
> sniff and stand back and proudly offer you
> the celebrated Anglo-Irish stew.

Hartnett's retreat into Gaelic poetry (in which he never quite equalled his English output) lasted almost a decade, during which he discovered that it may not be a question of a writer choosing a language, so much as a case of the language choosing to work out its characteristic genius through a writer. Hence his subsequent recourse to English, a return perhaps prophesied in 'A Visit to Croom 1745' where the longed-for Gaelic court of poetry promises much but delivers 'nothing'.

The idea of a necessary choice between two traditions may appear as excessively melodramatic in a country whose leading Irish-language poets have listed Hopkins and Eliot as major influences on their art. For such as Seán Ó Ríordáin and Máirtín Ó Díreáin, the greater challenge has been to recreate favoured modes of the English poetic in a tradition still fundamentally Gaelic. As Ó Ríordáin — an Anglo-Irish poet in the literal (rather than racial) sense of that term — once wrote of his beloved language:

> Ag súrac atáirse
> on striapach allúrach;
> is sínim chugat smaointe
> a ghoideas-sa uaithi.

> You are escaping
>   from the foreign harlot;
> But I proffer to you ideas
>   I have stolen from her.

Other poets are not so ambitious, preferring to serve both traditions simply by offering searching critiques of their own. Richard Murphy's celebration-cum-accusation of Anglo-Irish Big-House mentalities is a characteristic case in point. Nevertheless, a surprising number of elements from the Gaelic tradition may be found in modern poetry, especially that of Heaney, who has taken on an almost bardic aura, infusing tight quatrains with a remarkable variety of registers. Among the duties of the ancient bards was *dinnsheanchas*, knowledge of the lore of place; and this is a field that many Northern poets, from Montague through Heaney to Paul Muldoon, have made their own.

This, too, is a Yeatsian strategy repeated — but repeated with a subtle difference. For a turn-of-the-century writer of protestant background like Yeats, the course of Irish history constituted an embarrassing accusation against his own people, and so he chose instead to embody his growing love of country in the landscape of Sligo. The protestant imagination in that generation turned away from history — the young Yeats did not even know of Sarsfield, Red Hugh or the Yellow Ford — and sought rather to impatriate itself by geography. Hence Shaw's remark that 'the men of Ireland are mortal, but her hills are eternal'.

Such a refusal of history may be found, once again, in a new generation of poets, most of them *not* of protestant background, but anxious nonetheless to disown the atavisms unleashed by the recent hostilities in Ireland, and by what many see as propagandist distortions of history. Hence the number of poems set on the Aran Islands, or in west Kerry, or on the coast of Donegal — all written by artists who act like self-conscious tourists in their own country.

This revived fashion for poetic geography has been questioned by the stringent critic Vincent Buckley, who finds in it the old Shavian idea of a people foredoomed by landscape and climate to an ineffable melancholy: 'We should not read into the geography a sadness produced among the human family by history', he argues, finding in such interpretations 'a racist determinism'. 'Ireland', Buckley avers, 'is a living testimony to the fact that its own people have absorbed history into geography, events into climate.'

One escape from this apparent impasse has been mapped by Seamus Heaney in 'From the Republic of Conscience'. Like Seamus Deane, Hugh Maxton, Michael O'Loughlin and others, Heaney uses the history of Eastern Europe as a way of regaining access to his own. The shortest way to Monasterboice — via the 'frugal republic' of de Valera — may now be also via Moscow. A more blatantly revisionist strategy is pursued, with impressive honesty, by Brendan Kennelly in 'Cromwell', where the poet seeks to balance accounts with the demon of Irish history, portraying him as the preacher of parliamentary democracy as well as of religious persecution.

For Heaney, however, the ultimate solution is to historicize geography, to excavate each layer of the soil for progressively remoter periods, the spade striking always inward and downward:

Every layer they strip
Seems camped on before . . .

The bog, he says, preserves not just bodies but human consciousness, and with it the whole of human history. So 'Viking Dublin: Trial Pieces' begins with the Norse invader and ends with that offspring of a more recent immigration, Leopold Bloom. Heaney's sense of poetry as a dig, and of the poem as something lifted out of a boggy consciousness, casts the artist as archaeologist, reading the signatures of all things in stone and clay.

Derek Mahon's answer — even more radical — is to present the poet as anthropologist, engaged in an awestruck search for some sign of the persistence of the person. Such an approach has the merit of looking forward, as well as back, and this may explain a certain jauntiness in Mahon's rhythms:

Already in a lost hub-cap is conceived
The ideal society which will replace our own.

The strategy permits him to hold the Northern violence at a chaste remove, or at least to see it against a wider pattern of universal history, by which it can be explained, if not excused. Such attempts to confront, at a necessarily oblique angle, the tragedy of the North have been greatly welcomed, in Ireland as well as overseas. Denis Donoghue has attributed this warm reception to 'the consolation of hearing that there is a deeper, truer life going on beneath the bombings and murders and torture.'

On the other hand, in only a few poems has even Heaney managed to capture the appalling intensity of that conflict. The struggle to remain a poet in a time of political strife has consumed even the best energies. The poets, though brave enough to accuse themselves of evading the deepest issues by striking postures of 'casual pity', nevertheless opt always for a mode of even-handedness:

I am neither internee nor informer;
An inner émigré, grown long-haired
And thoughtful; a wood-kerne

Escaped from the massacre ....

To such a point had Yeats come in a time of civil war, when he turned upon the stair and wondered if he could prove his worth in something that all others understand or share. But, by then, he had written 'Easter 1916' and many other works that were both political and, for all that, poems.

While the revival of poetry in the North has attracted most attention in recent years, there have also been stirrings in the Republic. Poets born in the 1950s, even those who have Northern origins, are less consolidated into groups or schools. Their regional loyalties are less insistent. Writers like Sebastian Barry, Peter Fallon, Greg Delanty, Gerald Dawe, Harry Clifton, Dennis O'Driscoll, Matthew Sweeney and many others, not all of whom can be represented here, have appeared in anthologies that declare the emergence of a new generation. Gerald Dawe's *The Younger Irish Poets* (Belfast: Blackstaff Press, 1982) and Sebastian Barry's *The Inherited Boundaries: Younger Poets of the Republic of Ireland* (Dublin: Dolmen Press, 1986) are two notable examples of the assertion of a change in the landscape that had been established over the previous twenty years. The selections offered here are no more than indications of that change. The North may still be in travail, but Europe and 1992 impinge more and more upon a world that has begun to alter in dramatic fashion. Those changes and differently angled pressures are registered in the work of these writers, although it is still too early to say to what extent they will be able to reforge their and our sense of what has happened in Irish poetry since 1950. Perhaps their turning away from the world of public events towards more personal, more specialized and even eccentric concerns is itself of general cultural and political significance.

There has been a minor renaissance in Irish poetry in the past quarter century. It coincides, almost exactly, with the period that saw the collapse of unionist government in Northern Ireland, the waxing and waning of the Irish economy, the hunger-strikes and bombings, and an apparent drift towards ungovernability on the island. Yet, with only rare exceptions, the leading poets of the period have had remarkably little to say about these things.

In raw poems and atavistic images, Padraic Fiacc has described the sufferings of Northern nationalists; and, with an always astingent irony, Tom Paulin has valuably documented the humiliations to unionist pride from the proroguing of Stormont (1972) to the Anglo-Irish agreement (1985). But the celebration of the rituals of a domestic life, to which the 'Troubles' are a merely subordinate backdrop, is the more common strategy of the generality of poets, epitomized by Paul Muldoon and Frank Ormsby.

Meanwhile, in the south, the struggles of women against a patriarchal church and an archaic legal code are, if anything, under-represented in contemporary poetry; though Eavan Boland has, in lines of cool elegance, captured for Irish poetry the experience of women in middle-class suburbia. Her poem on Irish emigration (numbered at more than 30,000 per annum by the mid-1980s) is one of the few meditations on this pervasive social theme.

The general political reticence may be a measure of the privatization of *all* poetry, after the modernist despair of the public world. But it may also reflect the growing *rapprochement* in Ireland between artists and the state, by means of bursaries, subventions and *Aosdána*, a *rapprochement* that is all the more surprising given the fact that either or both states could soon have disappeared. It is impossible to believe that a Yeats would have been similarly reticent. Perhaps the rather opportunist form of neutrality espoused by the southern state has its counterpart in the studied impartiality of its poets. Their part in these affairs is, like the legacy of Heaney's Leonard MacNally, 'inestimable'.

PATRICK MACDONOGH

(1902-61)

from: ONE LANDSCAPE STILL (1958)

No Mean City

Though naughty flesh will multiply
Our chief delight is in division;
Whatever of Divinity
We are all Doctors of Derision.
Content to risk a far salvation
For the quick coinage of a laugh
We cut, to make wit's reputation,
Our total of two friends by half.

Be Still as You are Beautiful

Be still as you are beautiful
Be silent as the rose;
Through miles of starlit countryside
Unspoken worship flows
To reach you in your loveless room
From lonely men whom daylight gave
The blessing of your passing face
Is penetrably grave.

A white owl in the lichened wood
Is circling silently,
More secret and more silent yet
Must be your love to me.
Thus, while about my dreaming head
Your soul in ceaseless vigil goes,
Be still as you are beautiful
Be silent as the rose.

Of Late

She is grown old of late, so very still.
Her voice is fallen quiet and her hands
Have lost a little sureness. She is more sparing
Of her known smile that earns a finer strength.
Her eyes are a deep shadow and a dewy light
As though, for ever, they looked back at youth
Or saw new dawns grow bright before their time.

She Walked Unaware

Oh, she walked unaware of her own increasing beauty
That was holding men's thoughts from market or plough,
As she passed by intent on her womanly duties
And she passed without leisure to be wayward or proud;
Or if she had pride then it was not in her thinking
But thoughtless in her body like a flower of good breeding.
The first time I saw her spreading coloured linen
Beyond the green willow she gave me gentle greeting
With no more intention than the leaning willow tree.

Though she smiled without intention yet from that day forward
Her beauty filled like water the four corners of my being,
And she rested in my heart like a hare in the form
That is shaped to herself. And I that would be singing
Or whistling at all times went silently then,
Till I drew her aside among straight stems of beeches
When the blackbird was sleeping and she promised that never
The fields would be ripe but I'd gather all sweetness,
A red moon of August would rise on our wedding.

October is spreading bright flame along stripped willows,
Low fires of the dogwood burn down to grey water,—
God pity me now and all desolate sinners
Demented with beauty! I have blackened my thought
In drouths of bad longing, and all brightness goes shrouded
Since he came with his rapture of wild words that mirrored
Her beauty and made her ungentle and proud.
Tonight she will spread her brown hair on his pillow,
But I shall be hearing the harsh cries of wild fowl.

Flowering Currant

From plum-tree and cherry
White blossom froths over.
The small birds make merry
And each is a lover.

But she walks by a tree
And a spring-quickened bird
Which her eyes do not see
And her ears have not heard.

For her ears hear only
The cold voice within
That wars on her lonely
Delight, and her sin.

And her looks ever bend
To the path at her feet
Lest she see to the end
Where the combatants meet.

Delight and despair
In the bright currant blossom
His lips on her hair
His hands at her bosom,

His hands at her breast,
His lips on her hair
Saying, 'Rest you, now rest
From fasting and prayer.

My floor is not stone,
My couch is no board;
And what loss is but one
Of his brides to the Lord?'

O! Come to the Land

O! Come to the land of the saint and the scholar
Where learning and piety live without quarrel,
Where the coinage of mind outvalues the dollar
And God is the immanent shaper of thought and behaviour;
Where old ceremonious usage survives as the moral
And actual pattern of grace, where the blood of our Saviour
Is real as our sin, and replenishes spirit and brain
Till they blossom in pity and love as our fields in the rain.

No, but come to a land where the secret censor
Snouts in the dark, where authority smothers
The infant conscience and shadows a denser
Darkness on ignorant minds in their tortuous groping
For spectreless day: a land where austerity mothers
The coldly deliberate sins, where harsh masters are roping
The heels of the heavenly horse and blinding the bright
Incorruptible eye that dares open in passionless light.

O! Come to the land where man is yet master
Of tyrannous time and will pause for the pleasure
Of speech or of sport though worldly disaster
Pluck at torn sleeves; a land where soft voices
Meet answering laughter, where the business of living is leisure,
Where there's no heart so poor but it's kindly and quick and rejoices
In horse or in hound or the mettlesome boy with a ball,
Where a jibe's for the proud, but a hand's for the helpless from all.

No, but come to a land where the mediaeval
Dread of the woman mutters in corners,
Thunders from pulpits, where the only evil
Lacking forgiveness is love; a land where the spirit
Withers the flowering flesh, where whispering mourners
Crowd to the grave of romance and expect to inherit
Great scandalous wealth to lighten long evenings and bring
A venomous joy to harsh lips whose kiss is a sting.

O! Come to the land where imagination
Fashions the speech of the common people
Rich as a tenement's shattered mouldings
Where the wrong of defeat has bequeathed to a nation
Ironic traditional wit, like a polished steeple
Rising precise and clear from the huddled holdings
Of intricate minds that, in face of Eternity, know
Harsh humour and absolute faith their sole strongholds below.

No, but come to a land where the dying eagle
Is mocked by the crow and the patient vulture,
Where nobility fails and the ancient regal
Pride of inheritance yields to the last invaders,

Image and hare-brained song, the scum of an alien culture
Bubbling in village and street, where unmannerly traders
And political slaves have supplanted the gentle and brave,
Where the hero will never have honour except in the grave.

PADRAIC FALLON

(1905-74)

from:
POEMS (1974)

Assumption

Some Syrian rainmaker
Invoking a minor image of power found her
Intrude, O enormous magic, and his hands
Dissolve in showers over many lands;
Earth turned woman, or woman into earth, he
Left this wild image to Syrian sorcery.
But O how they tamed her, the Greeks, the civilizing
Mythologizing Alexandrian schoolmen
And the soft Italians with the Christian eyes
Who ferried her over the tideless Mediterranean;
The muted breasts, the quiet, and on the top
A face bright as a waterdrop.

Assumed into heaven, she,
A statue among statuary,
Consumes in her single fire the line
Of barbarous virgins who dwelt between
Trinities in their season.
Heaven and earth are in division;
The gross fertilities, the ram, the bull,
Left out-of-doors while in her shuttered parlour
When she bares the nipple
No rye rises, no wheaten flower;
Only her dreams stir
The peacock presences of air.

This mild lady
Calms the gross ambitions with a steady
Country look. No drums, no dances,
No midnight fires, no sacrifice of princes;
She takes her pail among the cows
And bolts her fowl in the fowl house;
Evoe,[1] if the sun-headed god is gone, there's still
The house to be done, white linen hung
Upon the hedge. The serene axle
Goes round and round in a crucifixion,
But earth is a pot of flowers. Foreign tongues
Commune above her in a drift of wings.

1. A wail of lament or passion associated with the bacchantes.

Yeats's Tower at Ballylee

Is every modern nation like the tower
Half dead at the top?[1]
W. B. YEATS

A pilgrimage is one slow foot
After the other, the agony of the heart
That looks to a place that will ripen like a fruit.
Yet I arrive in a Ford car
At the Tower talking of markets and wool
And corn drowned in the stook, the country around
Rain-rotten, the wet road buzzing like a spool
And trees at their year's end
Dropping the loaded sky to the ground.
I arrive talking of heifers and wool
And am confronted by the soul
Of a man in whom man cried like a great wound.

Somewhere a man will touch his image and burn
Like a candle before it. What happened here

1. The lines are from Yeats's poem 'Blood and the Moon', from his volume *The Tower* (1928). The Norman tower in which Yeats made his summer home from 1917 to 1929 is at Thoor Ballylee, near Gort, Co. Galway. Fallon's poem contains echoes from the title poem of *The Tower* and to 'Meditations in Time of Civil War' from the same book. Fallon visited Thoor Ballylee in 1950, soon after the outbreak of the Korean war.

In this ruined place of water and drowned corn
May still be here.
The oaken door hangs open, I go in
To a desolate underground that drips;
Shadows are on the stairs, the walls are weeping
A peacock paint, where a shoe slips
I clamber into a chamber like a tomb
Or a dim woodcut by William Morris[2]
And suddenly I know the tower is
A boy's dream and the background of his rhyme.

Here where country blood was spilt
Neither earth nor stone cries out, for this is a
  dream-structure;
All that the brazen Norman built
To house a score of bullies in black armour
Deflected and turned to phantasy
By the boy who brooded on book and paint
Long mornings in his father's study
As mediaeval as a saint:
This is the Tower at last, its passion spent
And wearied of its own brutality
Where a boy could dream like Gabriel Rossetti;[3]
Useless as verse and as magnificent.

I turn from the arty chimneypiece where glass
Has the pale wash of dreamy things and climb
Through a rude and navel arch, I pass
A sentry-go where no man turned a rhyme;
And the narrow stairway leads me to the place
Where he worked at the great table
Or lifted his tall height to pace
The enormous floor of his own fable;
Did he wear iron then, I wonder,
Or when the shadows stole the candle-light
Imagine himself all constellated night?
Il Penseroso in the magic chamber?

Yet nothing is here but the wind in the swinging
  windows
And the roar of the flood waters far below,
Not a house in sight, the corn in rows
Drowned and the drizzle rotting in the meadows:
The earth that cares for nothing but its seasons
Of lust and fruiting and death
Worked all about him here and gave no reasons
Why any man should waste his breath
In delicate definitions of a mild
World where man is the whole,
The individual soul
A heavenly cradle for the newborn child.

From the boy's dream to this reality
Of brutal weather and brutal stone
The Norman brought him. I come on the right day
To see for myself how earth can change a scene.
Rain and desolation, isolation
And fear in civil war can bring a man
To that harsh point in contemplation
Where soul no longer sees the sun:
In that bleak vision can man live,
Not summing up heaven and earth in measure?
Can he spend himself like a rich treasure
Where only the animal qualities survive?

Here at last he knew what opposites
War in one person. He became a man.
And the man divided into the primitive cross
Of two men in one rhythm. When the Norman
Came to the top the poet's words were blood
And what was good but a mere vision
Of arrogant foray, rape, and ride.
And then soul took its turn and with precision
Divined like an architect a house of life
Where violence had an energetic place
Only to find a holy face
Stare back serenely from the end of strife.

I climb to the wasting storey at the top.
His symbol's there where water and watery air
Soak through the plaster. The higher we clamber up
Into ourselves the greater seems the danger;
For the wider the vision then
On a desolate and more desolate world
Where the inspirations of men
Are taken by man and hurled
From shape into evil shape;
With the good and the grace gone out of them
Where indeed is there hope for men?
So every civilization tires at the top.

Around me now from this great height
Is a vision I did not seek. I have avoided it
And now I am forty-five
And wars blow up again, the east is lit,
Towns burn, villages are bombed,
With people everywhere in flight,

2. William Morris (1834-96), a leading member of the Pre-Raphaelite movement, exercised a profound influence on the young Yeats.

3. Dante Gabriel Rossetti (1828-82), a Pre-Raphaelite poet, is, like Morris, a part of Yeats's mental landscape.

Their households on a handcart, or entombed
In homes that fell about them in the night,
And dragging children homeless in the air;
A mass migration of the humble
Before some war-mad general.
O the higher we climb up the wider our despair.

This tower where the poet thought to play
Out some old romance to the end caught up
The dream and the dreamer in its brutal way
And the dream died here upon the crumbling top.
I know the terror of his vision now:
A poet dies in every poem, even
As blossom dies when fruit comes on the bough,
And world is endless time in which things happen
In endless repetition, every man
Repetitive as a pattern, no soul
But the sprawling spirit of the whole
Massing upon the careless earth like frogspawn.

Everywhere is the world. And not less here
Because the stream, dividing, moats the place.
To live a fairy tale he bought this tower
And married a woman with a pleasant face;
And built in bookshelves, cupboards, hung
His pictures up and walked around
His beehive and his acre, wrung
Some civilization from the ground:
And yet instead of rhyming country ease
As in the eighteenth century we find
Him raving like a man gone blind
At the bloody vision that usurped his eyes.

Below me in the road two countrymen
Are talking of cattle and the price of wool,
Glad of the gossip and something held in common,
That scene would have been peaceful
An hour ago, but now I stumble down
In horror, knowing that there is no way
Of protest left to poet or to clown
That will enlarge his future by one day.
I could beat a policeman, bawl in a square, do gaol
For something silly. And what avails it? I
Step into the drizzle of the sky
Despairingly, to talk of the price of wool.

Women

I

The pity of it. Not to love
All the love we lean upon;
Always to be at some remove,
Always to be drawn
Towards the overwhelming one
We must meet alone.

O loneliness. We are born to them:
As mothers they mother us;
We break the navel chord like a limb
That as lovers they may love us:
But recover us
And leave them for our loneliness.

II

Rest, says the earth. And a woman delicately
Says 'it is here, it is in my arms somewhere'
But a woman is a lie
And I have a tower to climb, the tower of me,
And a quarrel to settle with the sky
But 'rest' says the woman, 'o lean back more;
I am a wife and a mother's knee,
I am the end of every tower.'

The Poems of Love

All the poems of love are one;
All women too. The name that runs
Profanely between love and lover
Is the name repeated over
In the rosaries of nuns.
All the poems of love are one.

Solar red, masochist black,
There's precedent for each in heaven;
Whatever be a body's leaven
The rosaries of the holy nation
Thrill to some transfiguration.
Love makes up the thing we lack.

All the women Tom and Jack
Buy or bed, the slumtown tits,
Have bright otherworld habits;
A queen shares pillows with a clown,
Still nebulously wears her crown,
And is most royal on her back.

When Tom and his hedge mistress come
Drunken to the judgement seat,
The obscene measures on his tongue
Start the heavens into song;

Endlessly must Tom recite
The love he made by rule of thumb.

And brawling face and bawling gums
Fade fawnlike into some young grace;
Love lives serenely many ways;
Love lives in all that it may not lack
Its body in riots, drunks and drums
And the rosaries of nuns in black.

Johnstown Castle[1]

I

The summer woods refuse to meet
Us on the levels we know. We have evolved
Too much mind for them, and picked up feet
That solve things differently, like birds:
Trees use the old vocabulary
In all its ponderous gravity;
We with inner needs to be resolved
Have learned all the new and air-borne words.

Why intrude here, and why regret
An old root that like a rocket goes
On exploding season after season
In the same galaxy of leaf, without a reason?
All it knows
Is the old wholesome suit of clothes:
Never the new and complicated rose.

II

An ornamental water
Should be backed with mercury that the
sculptured swan
May be ideal swan forever.
Here one shiver shows the mud
And I am glad because a swan
Can turn up his end and shatter mood
And shatter mirror,
Till the woods massed in an architecture shake
Because a real swan mucks up a lake.

An old lady, slender as her wand
Of ebony, and carrying her castle still about her,
Is near me anywhere I stand;
My own creation.
I give her words to say, and a world, too,
Homelier, perhaps, than that she knew,
And take an interest in the conversation:
But as I ramble on
Creating all for her
I think how certainly she lived this view
Merely by walking over the ground
Day after day; I falter
For now my words take on another hue
And such a sound
I'm half afraid to turn around.

III

Always my own monologue
Intrudes; things work into the word
Only to be imprisoned, or kennelled like a dog;
So the tall pine describes
A straight line up to the tuft of foliage
That sits it like a bird
And is only so much language
Because I use the word;
And all the ponderous oaks and the ooze underfoot,
All the harsh nerves of an old wood
That are a rumble in the nether-gut,
Are not what one transcribes
And never any good;
The monologue intrudes, my words let me
Into a poem, not into the poetry.

And yet a man must walk
Out of his mystery, if he's to meet it
Face to face, in talk,
And guess from words omitted the major and
delicate
Evasions of his ghost
Who is the host
To every massive feeling and must live it.
Create me, says the poet, I am a body
For every word, the large word that was lost
And the word you'd throw a dog;
Transform me who travel towards infinity
In a makeshift monologue.

1. The castle stands in spacious grounds just outside Wexford town.

The Young Fenians

They looked so good;
They were the coloured lithographs
Of Murat, Bernadotte and Ney

And the little Corsican.[1]
Mars had made them from our dead
And given to each his martial head.

The cavalry and plumes would come,
No doubt about it;
Every half-acre man with a sword,
The boy with a drum;
And down the Alps of every local hill
The bannered horses ride to kill.

O'Connell helpless in the house;
The old gazebos at their talk,
All to no purpose;
Tone must rise and Emmet walk,
Edward troop out of Kildare;[2]
The time had come; the day was fair.

Flags flew from our every word;
The new names sang from litanies,
Saviours each one;
They were the eagles in the morning sun;
A country rising from its knees
To upset all the histories.

1. Napoleon Bonaparte (1769-1821), born in Ajaccio, Corsica. Joachim Murat, Bernadotte and Michel Ney all fought as Napoleon's marshals.
2. Lord Edward Fitzgerald (1763-98), MP for Kildare in 1790, became one of the leaders of the United Irishmen, as did Wolfe Tone (1763-98), the most renowned revolutionary of the period. Robert Emmet (1778-1803) led an abortive rebellion in Dublin in 1802. Daniel O'Connell (1775-1847), the great political leader, was helpless in the House of Commons when the Famine struck and when the British threatened to use force against his mass meeting at Clontarf in 1845.

Kiltartan Legend[1]

Penelope pulls home
Rogue-lord, artist, world wanderer,
Simply by sitting in a house,
Its sturdy genius;
Of all sirens the most dangerous.

She'll sit them out,
The curious wonders, the ventriloquial voices,
Spacious landfalls, the women, beds in the blue;
Her oceanography
The garden pond, her compass a knitting needle.

The arc-lamped earth, she knows,
Will burn away and she
Still potter among her flowers waiting for him;
Apollo runs before
Touching the blossoms, her unborn sons.

Knitting, unknitting at the half heard
Music of her tapestry, afraid
Of the sunburned body, the organs, the red beard
Of the unshipped mighty male
Home from the fairy tale;

Providing for him
All that's left of her she ties and knots
Threads everywhere; the luminous house
Must hold and will
Her trying warlord home.

Will she know him?
Dignity begs the question that must follow.
She bends to the web where her lord's face
Glitters but has no fellow,
And humbly, or most royally, adds her own.

1. The reference is to Lady Gregory (1852-1932), who confected a local dialect called 'Kiltartanese' and whose house at Coole Park, near Gort, Co. Galway, was a second home and refuge for W.B. Yeats.

Letter from Ballylee

Raftery, a tramp poet,
Sung for the thatches around the homespun girl
Whose name was Mary Hynes:[1]
Later, of course, the beauty was debauched
By some hard-riding nameless
Country gentleman,[2]
And died lost and wrinkled in
A bog cabin.

The girl goes always to the other fellow.
Exalt no girl, my friend;
Flesh no arrow. Witness this man who plumps anew
The old stone shell by the river.
Now he sings of God and lesser things
And studies planetary ebb and flow
Who saw Helen leave the high wall for
A quite ordinary lover.

1. Antoine Raftery (1784-1835) was from Galway and wrote in praise of a famous beauty, Mary Hynes (see Volume II, pp. 726-28). His work was rediscovered and translated by Douglas Hyde.
2. A variation of Yeats's phrase 'Hard-riding country gentlemen' from his poem 'Under Ben Bulben'.

He gets by, like
A hermit crab who blunders in from the blue
Bristle of the sea.
Waiting a new skin he hears
The old shell singing. Pitiful
The story, how an old love can discompose us.
Perhaps I should sing God too
And the partial planets, did this girl allow me
Who puts me at the disposal of the Muses.

Mater Dei

In March the seed
Fell, when the month leaned over, looking
Down into her valley.
And none but the woman knew it where she sat
In the tree of her veins and tended him
The red and ripening Adam of the year.

Her autumn was late and human.
Trees were nude, the lights were on the pole
All night when he came,
Her own man;
In the cry of a child she sat, not knowing
That this was a stranger.

Milk ran wild
Across the heavens. Imperiously He
Sipped at the delicate beakers she proffered him.
How was she to know
How huge a body she was, how she corrected
The very tilt of the earth on its new course?

Magna Mater

A dove plus an
Assenting virgin is
An odd equation; the bird of Venus, the
Shotsilk woodhaunter and
A country shawl
In congress to produce
The least erotic of the gods.

Afoot on Sunday, walking green
The little roads or high
In the spring carts, they come to Mass;
Hundreds who know man,
For whom no string was plucked
Or any heavens
Thrown open;
No dichotomy
Affects the prayer; that heaven
Should have one love, and earth another seems
Entirely natural,
What Troubadour
Built this country chapel?

And out of what
Substance? Harping on what nerves?
Mothers here
All virgin, fathers none,
The child a gift of heaven
And held in common by
Each virgin mother.

O indestructible
Country mulch the Muses tread
So delicately, into the earth you go
Breeding, tending
Where flowers are born with the names of kings
You never heard of, pagan fellows
Whose histories and business
Are open secrets in your
Sunshining faces.

Painting of my Father

I

I saw him to the last, the grey
Casting of the face,
The crabbed hands like this
Yielding to the cluster of the Rosary;

I who barbered you occasionally
And filled your pipe
Dropping into your deafness the odd item
Of family news that never
Exactly reached you,

For you were away already.

So your true going was a sort
Of mutual release. 'Lord', you whispered hanging
That day in my arms naked
As Jesus down from the cross,
'Take me away'.

Now for me this vague distress
And a guilt that grows;
What is it that one owes a father?

And cannot pay,

Liaison lost with the broad
Dialect of the child where words
Were the throbs of a countryside
Big like a sheepshearing or small
As the lark pinned high above
The water meadows where we drank our tea,
The trout waiting in the fishing river;

Eternal precincts
Of a huge present tense, as if
You were not due to be left
Abandoned like an old
Settlement;
The young being
Unscrupulous in their growing up.

So you wanted little of me towards the end,
Barbering, a light
For the old pipe,
And an ear, my ear, any ear, when you spilled over
The intolerable burden
Of being a very old man.

II

An image that wounds;
Better even
The figure of power, the
All father,
Jahwah, Helios or another; not
That I'd like you in big translations
Who were rich enough
As your own man

For you were daylight's own fellow and over
The moonsuck of the mother
All male and master under heaven;
And that's how you come into mind,
In taut middleage when you were quite
The masher,
Velvet collar, tan velour
Overcoat, plush hat and handmade boot,
In those streets round the cattlemarket where
Our evenings were a summer saunter;

Hanlon's Corner, Stoneybatter,
The Broadstone, MGWR,[1]
Where trains run no more,

And I half expect round any corner
The hastening dandy, country
Things still clinging;
Blue the gaze;
Delicate the gait, the dancer,
Angler, Fowler, Hurler, football player;

Tomorrow
Formally as a bullfighter he'll pace
The horned pens and the cattle slobber,
Face the loss or net the profit
Stonily
As befits the gambler;

And at noon lean
Recomposed on the railed wall
By the City Arms, yarning, true Ulyssean,
Over a shoe shine.

III

And now here
Above the walnut desk, the only familiar in
This strange hallucinatory land I found
Late, you stare out; again
All age, all pain, at the very end
Of your long span: not you indeed
But every man;
Just waiting.

Land's End some few miles away; the tide
Is white round the Mount;[2] a bird
Stands on the sundial on the lawn; Spring
Is hovering;
And in the tulip tree — hallucination — some
Medieval person reads a tome

(To disappear battered
By a rainshower with his
Monkshood, creature of air;
The bird stays on, real enough;
A woodpecker)

A country ironed out
Into saints and menhirs where
You never put a foot,

1. Midland and Great Western Railway. The places named are in Dublin, north of the Liffey.

2. St Michael's Mount, Cornwall. The poem was written while Padraic Fallon was living near Penzance and he could see St Michael's Mount from his window.

Where the weather camps for an hour before
It stamps the soft shires, taking over
The whole south of England at a blow.

Sunday Morning

If I make way for bells on Sunday morning,
Demure, deep in
Her Sunday hat she'll walk, tipping the tall
Flowering shrub, a lilac, at
The corner
Turning into Mespil Road.

A street new from the font, an old
Arrow of canal
Mounted, tufted by an ancient swan, is leading
Somewhere;
My bible woman hardly knows
The way she goes.

She carries the total injury of me;
In jeopardy. Almost
Rural the scene with elm and planetree, sun
At summer hoist, a wisp
Of smoke from some pedestrian;
Her penitent feet will lead her on.

She does not dally by the sluice
Or the resting barge. An odd head
Hangs on the bridge at Baggot Street;
God is dead,
His shadow what I throw far
Beyond into hurt and metaphor.

The whole world can see the lover's hands
Upon her. In the din
Of sweet bells she rises to confess
The evil bruise;
Hears another gospel start
In the regions of the heart;

What penitence can she profess?
How burn away
Back into her first
Girl-simile
The garden fallen around her, simple trees
Lovers and enemies?

from:
POEMS AND VERSIONS (1983)

A Hedge Schoolmaster

Any niche is my college.
In wayside ditch roofed by a bramble
I light the small rush candle
Of knowledge in numbskulls.

No mouth-open fledglings sit
Around this Socrates on the turf
But Pat's famished son, the lout
And his daughter, scrapings of the pot.

Thankless the task, to create
Fine manners on salt and potatoes,
To hatch out the morrow's priest
From father's old waistcoat;

Spelling out for the shockhaired
The wars of Caesar,
Hannibal in the Alps or
The Emperor Nero on the fiddle;

To construct with a slate pencil the town of
  Troy,
Thumbnailing the geography of heroes;
All history from Adam down
To hobble home on bare toes;

With profit and loss and mensuration
Goes towering Agamemnon
And Arius with his heresy
Of Three-in-one and Homousion,[1]

To be lost in little walls and ricks of turf,
Dwindle down at peasant fires,
Huge ghosts in hungry fields
Wandering without memories.

No profit in it, or credit. Boors thrive
But I eat afield with the crows;
No goose gravy for Tom Euclid;
The master feasts on the hedgerows;

1. 'Homo(o)usion' was the word used by the Council of Nicaea (325) to express the divinity of Christ in refutation of the Arian heresy that denied it. The word means 'of the same essence'.

Yet, Pallas Athene, your true legionary
In the last earthworks, the lone garrison, still
Arrays himself in the delicate dactyls to
Decline you to the barbarian.

After Horace
Solvitur Acris Hiems[1]

The first soft zephyr loosens the snowman's
grip;
Ships roll down to the sea;
Cows leave the straw, the ploughman his ingle
nook;
The new pastures gaze through melting frost;

And Venus arrives in the sailing moon, with a
wave
Of dancers, nymphs and Graces linked
To a naked beat, earth thrumming, while lame
Vulcan spells
The blazing Cyclops at the furnaces.

And it's time to mingle in the happening, sport
a twig
Of myrtle or a spring flower,
And remember Faunus[2] with a lamb or a young
kid,
Whichever he prefer:

For Death, dear Sestius,[3] is always that much
closer;
In hovel or tower a door
Will open of itself, there's no escaping, here
He stands with his phantoms waiting:

And no lucky throw will make you lord of a feast
Ever again; the dice are dead, the boy
Lycidas left to delight your enemy's eye
And all those girls at his feet.

1. *Odes* I. iv, 'The Bitter Winter Yields'.

2. A god or *numen*, associated with Pan and with the forest.
3. Publius Sestius, then consul.

CHARLES DONNELLY
(1914–37)

from: CHARLIE DONNELLY. THE LIFE AND POEMS (1987)

['The Flowering Bars' was written in prison in Dublin in January 1935. It was first published in *Goodbye Twilight* in London in 1936. Donnelly had been arrested on a picketing charge along with Cora Hughes, with whom he had had a love affair since 1934. The poem refers to her trial. Cora Hughes was also imprisoned.]

The Flowering Bars

After sharp words from the fine mind,
protest in court,
the intimate high head constrained,
strait lines of prison, empty walls,
a subtle beauty in a simple place.
There to strain thought through the tightened brain,
there weave
the slender cords of thought, in calm,
until routine in prospect bound
joy into security,
and among strictness sweetness grew,
mystery of flowering bars.

[Donnelly wrote 'The Tolerance of Crows' in London in 1936, before his departure for Spain. It was first published in *Ireland Today* in February 1937.]

The Tolerance of Crows

Death comes in quantity from solved
Problems on maps, well-ordered dispositions,
Angles of elevation and direction;

Comes innocent from tools children might
Love, retaining under pillows,
Innocently impales on any flesh.

And with flesh falls apart the mind
That trails thought from the mind that cuts
Thought clearly for a waiting purpose.

Progress of poison in the nerves and
Discipline's collapse is halted.
Body awaits the tolerance of crows.

Poem

Between rebellion as a private study and the public
Defiance, is simple action only on which will flickers
Catlike, for spring. Whether at nerve-roots is secret
Iron, there's no diviner can tell, only the moment
can show.
Simple and unclear moment, on a morning utterly
different
And under circumstances different from what
you'd expected.

Your flag is public over granite. Gulls fly above it.
Whatever the issue of the battle is, your memory
Is public, for them to pull awry with crooked hands,
Moist eyes. And village reputations will be built on
Inaccurate accounts of your campaign. You're
name for orators,
Figure stone-struck beneath damp Dublin sky.

In a delaying action, perhaps, on hillside in remote
parish,
Outposts correctly placed, retreat secured to wood,
bridge mined
Against pursuit, sniper may sight you carelessly
contoured.
Or death may follow years in strait confinement,
where diet
Is uniform as ceremony, lacking only fruit.
Or on the barrack square before the sun casts
shadow.

Name, subject of all-considered words, praise and
blame
Irrelevant, the public talk which sounds the same
on hollow
Tongue as true, you'll be with Parnell and with
Pearse.
Name aldermen will raise a cheer with, teachers
make reference
Oblique in class, and boys and women spin gum of
sentiment
On qualities attributed in error.

Man, dweller in mountain huts, possessor of
coloured mice,
Skilful in minor manual turns, patron of obscure
subjects, of
Gaelic swordsmanship and mediaeval armoury.
The technique of the public man, the masked
servilities are
Not for you. Master of military trade, you give
Like Raleigh, Lawrence, Childers,[1] your services
but not yourself.

1. Sir Walter Ralegh (*c.* 1552-1618), English adventurer and author; T.E. Lawrence (1888-1935), English soldier and writer, known as 'Lawrence of Arabia'; Robert Erskine Childers (1870-1922), author of the thriller *The Riddle of the Sands*, Irish politician and rebel, executed in 1922.

Heroic Heart

Ice of heroic heart seals plasmic soil
Where things ludicrously take root
To show in leaf kindness time had buried
And cry music under a storm of 'planes,
Making thrust head to slacken, muscle waver
And intent mouth recall old tender tricks.
Ice of heroic heart seals steel-bound brain.

There newer organs built for friendship's grappling
Waste down like wax. There only leafless plants
And earth retain disinterestedness.
Thought, magnetised to lie of the land, moves
Heartily over the map wrapped in its iron
Storm. Battering the roads, armoured columns
Break walls of stone or bone without receipt.
Jawbones find new ways with meat, loins
Raking and blind, new ways with women

VALENTIN IREMONGER
(1918-)

from:
HORAN'S FIELD AND OTHER RESERVATIONS (1972)

This Houre Her Vigill[1]

Elizabeth, frigidly stretched,
On a spring day surprised us
With her starched dignity and the quietness
Of her hands clasping a black cross.

With book and candle and holy water dish
She received us in the room with the blind down.
Her eyes were peculiarly closed and we knelt shyly
Noticing the blot of her hair on the white pillow.

We met that evening by the crumbling wall
In the field behind the house where I lived
And talked it over, but could find no reason
Why she had left us whom she had liked so much.

Death, yes, we understood: something to do
With age and decay, decrepit bodies;
But here was this vigorous one, aloof and prim,
Who would not answer our furtive whispers.

Next morning, hearing the priest call her name,
I fled outside, being full of certainty,
And cried my seven years against the church's stone
wall.
For eighteen years I did not speak her name

Until this autumn day when, in a gale,
A sapling fell outside my window, its branches
Rebelliously blotting the lawn's green. Suddenly, I
thought
Of Elizabeth, frigidly stretched.

1. The title is taken from the penultimate line in John Donne's 'A Nocturnall Upon S. Lucies Day, Being the shortest day':
'This houre her Vigill, and her Eve, since this
Both the yeares, and the dayes deep midnight is.'

Shadows

Among the tall heroes are none to understand
How the lightning terrifies and the thunder hurts,
How behind the appalling couch and the rigid high
chairs
Devils crouch, snarling, waiting for their meal.

Locked in the cupboard on the top landing
For sure there are dragons, rampant and terrible,
And what horrible gnomes, over and under the bed,
Menace the unconscious hours with their bald
shrieking.

Little boy, little boy, learn to be alone,
To grasp courage like straws and float on your fear
With the relaxed wariness of the swimmer, trained
To watch the threatening wave and the deceptive
current,

For, in the banquet-hall, at the gay reception,
Walking at night with your girl-friend or alone in
your room,
You will have terror, like days, with you all the years
of your life
And, among the tall strangers, none will understand.

Underworld

Under this stone, flat, grey, undistinguished
From any other stone in this desolate village
Among the green decay, remnant of a proud
Fall of rain, descant of spring, clear aria
Of water faltering on frond of valley, falling.

There is an urgency of movement, unexpected
Like the blunt stab of sunlight into a dark room,
And where in the sunray from darkness is seen
The world of dust, its frightening industry,
The silence and the swiftness of its menace.

So, under this familiar stone, the unguessed
movements,
The reeling zigzags, the back-and-forward dartings
Importune our understanding, our stunned
concern.

Something terrible is here we had not dreamt of,
We had not allowed for in our calculations:

The hungry importance of life is precise here
beneath
The veneer of decay, the riotousness of moss — a
tailpiece
Of truth, a scut of beauty.
Lay back the stone.
It is late for walking these savage lanes.
Something unknown is doing something
unknowable,
Building, perhaps, a better poor world for its
progeny.

Icarus

As, even today, the airman, feeling the plane sweat
Suddenly, seeing the horizon tilt up gravely, the
wings shiver,
Knows that, for once, Daedalus[1] has slipped up
badly,
Drunk on the job, perhaps, more likely dreaming,
high-flier Icarus,
Head butting down, skidding along the light-shafts
Back, over the tones of the sea-waves and the
slipstream, heard
The gravel-voiced, stuttering trumpets of his heart.

Sennet[2] among the crumbling court-yards of his
brain the mistake
Of trusting somebody else on an important affair
like this;
And, while the flat sea, approaching, buckled into
oh! avenues
Of acclamation, he saw the wrong story fan out into
history,
Truth, undefined, lost in his own neglect. On the
hills,
The summer-shackled hills, the sun spanged[3] all day;
Love and the world were young and there was no
ending:

But star-chaser, big-time-going, chancer Icarus
Like a dog on the sea lay and the girls forgot him
And Daedalus, too busy hammering another job,
Remembered him only in pubs. No bugler at all
Sobbed taps for the young fool then, reported
missing,
Presumed drowned, wing-bones and feathers on
the tide
Drifting in casually, one by one.

1. Daedalus, the father of Icarus, was the great craftsman who made the waxen wings upon which Icarus flew too close to the sun.
2. To blow a fanfare on a trumpet or cornet. In Elizabethan plays, it signalled the entrance or exit of a body of players.
3. spangled, glittered.

Hector[1]

Talking to her, he knew it was the end,
The last time he'd speed her into sleep with
kisses:
Achilles had it in for him and was fighting
mad.
The roads of his longing she again wandered,
A girl desirable as midsummer's day.

He was a marked man and he knew it,
Being no match for Achilles whom the gods
were backing.
Sadly he spoke to her for hours, his heart
Snapping like sticks, she on his shoulder
crying.
Yet, sorry only that the meaning eluded him.

He slept well all night, having caressed
Andromache like a flower, though in a dream
he saw
A body lying on the sands, huddled and
bleeding,
Near the feet a sword in bits and by the head,
An upturned, dented helmet.

1. The Trojan hero who was killed in battle by the Greek hero, Achilles. Andromache was Hector's wife.

PADRAIC FIACC

(1924-)

from: NIGHTS IN THE BAD PLACE (1977)

The British Connection[1]

In Belfast Europe, your man[2]
Met the Military come to raid
The House: 'Over my dead body
Sir,' he said, brandishing
A real-life sword from some
Old half forgotten war ...

And youths with real bows and arrows
And coppers and marbles good as bullets
And old time thrupenny bits and stones
Screws, bolts, nuts, (Belfast confetti)[3]

And kitchen knives, pokers, Guinness tins
And nail-bombs down by the Shore Road

And guns under the harbour wharf
And bullets in the docker's tea tin
And gelignite in the tool shed
And grenades in the scullery larder
And weed killer and sugar
And acid in the french letter[4]

And sodium chlorate and nitrates
In the suburban garage
In the boot of the car

And guns in the oven grill
And guns in the spinster's shift

And ammunition and more more
Guns in the broken down rusted
Merry-Go-Round in the Scrap Yard

1. An echo of a phrase of Theobald Wolfe Tone, father of Irish republicanism, who vowed to break the connection with England.
2. A familiar Irish phrase to describe a person too well-known to need naming.
3. cf. Ciaran Carson's poem, p. 1406.
4. condom, used in bomb-making by paramilitary groups in Northern Ireland.

Almost as many hard-on
Guns as there are union jacks.

Credo Credo

for Aidan and Âine

You soldiers who make for our holy
Pictures, grinding the glass with your
Rifle butts, kicking and jumping on them

With your hob-nailed boots, we
Are a richer dark[1] than the Military
Machine could impose ever.

We have the ancient, hag-ridden, long
In the tooth Mother, with her ugly
Jewish Child

Hangs in the depths of our dark
Secret being, no rifles can reach
Nor bullets, nor boots:

It was our icons not our guns
You spat on. When you found our guns
You got down on your knees to them

As if our guns were the holy thing ...
And even should you shoot the swarthy-
faced Mother with her ugly Jewish Child

Who bleeds with the people, she'll win
Because she loses all with the people,
Has lost every war for centuries with us.

1. A Yeatsian word (cf. 'The Statues': 'we Irish ... climb to our proper dark').

Soldiers

for Seamus Deane

The altar boy marches up the altar steps.
The priest marches down. 'Get up now
And be a soldier!' says the nun
To the woman after giving birth, 'Get up now
And march, march: Be a man!'

And the men are men and the women are men
And the children are men!

Mother carried a knife to work.
It was the thorn to her rose ...

They say she died with her eyes open
In the French Hospital in New York.
I remember those eyes shining in the dark

Slum hallway the day after
I left the monastery: Eyes that were
A feast of welcome that said 'yes,
I'm glad you didn't stay stuck there!'

'Would you mind if I went to prison
Rather than war?'
'No, for Ireland's men all went to prison!'

At the bottom of a canyon of brick
She cursed and swore
'You never see the sky!'

A lifetime after,
just before
I go to sleep at night, I hear
That Anna Magnani voice screaming
Me deaf 'No! No, you're not
To heed the world!' In one swift
Sentence she tells me not to yield
But to *forbear*:
'Go to prison but never
Never stop fighting. We are the poor
And the poor have to be "soldiers".

You're still a soldier, it's only that
You're losing the war

And all the wars are lost anyway!'

ANTHONY CRONIN

(1925-)

from: NEW AND SELECTED POEMS (1982)

[A man of letters in the full sense of that term, Cronin has won distinction for his long poems, penetrating critical essays, comic prose and polemical journalism, as well as playing a leading part in the institution of *Aosdána*, the scheme to honour and remunerate select Irish artists by inclusion in an elective assembly.]

Concord

Sweeter to be the master, says the master.

Sweeter to be the instrument, the instrument is
crying
In delightful apprehension as he nears.

Sweeter to be the instrument, oh sweeter far
The passionate instrument cries to the dominant
master,
As all its withinness lingers before release.

Oh but sweeter to be the releaser of this answer,
This sentience that is greater, he avers,
As his tangled self is uttered by its truth.

The instrument, the master, beguiled by the one
passion,
Become master, instrument now of the same
articulation.

Sweeter to be the master, cries the world.

Plenitude

The *nostalgie de la boue*[1]
And unholy joy went together:
According to the loose assumptions anyway
They were birds of a single feather.

A notion which the lads encouraged:
Wine, sensuality and song,

1. French: yearning for the mud. The phrase is Charles Baudelaire's in *Les fleurs du mal* (1857).

While the gutter welcomed and the bloom fell early
Unto them they belonged.

And doubtless in the gutter quarter,
Where the poor were poorer still,
You could get what you wanted in the way of
  sinfulness
At a few bob a thrill.

For poverty, as we know, is relative;
And the destitute sell what they have.
In a harsh world even some puzzled responses
Might be less than half a sov.[2]

And a half a sov be riches
In the haunts where harlots were cheap,
Necessities weren't necessary
And girls grateful even for sleep.

But however the lads might sing of it,
Nymphs and nectar and lutes,
Instead of raw absinthe, disease and squalor
And poets like other brutes,

The truth is that as a Decadence
It couldn't compare with Up West[3]
Where the rich in their shining shirt-fronts
Wanted nothing but the Best,

Where everyone's health was looked after
And the thrill could be more prolonged,
And the roses went on blooming
Though flung riotously with the throng,

Where the wine-glasses sparkled like spangles
And no one heard the lament
Of the pretty little waif who soon enough discovered
Precisely what Decadence meant.

And if the knowledge of this was somewhere
In the elegiac strain
Which ran through the hedonist verses
And spoke more of loss than of gain,

Still over the poets down in dockland
Loomed an even bigger thrill
As it dawned on the more desperate
That a life like theirs could kill.

2. A coin: half a sovereign.
3. The West End of London.

And if then, to prove that they weren't
Mere misfits, but self-condemned;
They had to go on singing of sin and pleasure
Doing them down in the end;

And had to turn the grim attritions
Which are poverty's daily news,
The neglect and the dirty infections,
To distinctions choice spirits might choose;

It was only to show the fitness
Of the fate that was in store
And épater the horrid bourgeois[4]
Just that little bit more

By pretending that their dyings
Were satiated, jaded and just;
And the emptiness of existence
A surfeited life-disgust

4. i.e. shocking the horrid middle classes.

Baudelaire in Brussels

Gas-lamps abandoned by the night burn on
Grotesquely as the daylight stirs the street,
And pain as bright as dawn behind the eyes
Is pulsing as the wings of madness beat.
The archetype prays to Poe[1] to pray to God
For time to pay his debts and die of peace:
No mind can hold too many truths at once.
All contradictions cry out for release.
All contradictions: nothing equals pride
Except our hatred of ourselves: too late
God punishes in the person of his mother
One who endured before he chose his fate.

1. Edgar Allan Poe (1809-49), American symbolist poet of decadence and writer of such gothic tales as *The Fall of the House of Usher* (1839).

For a Father

With the exact length and pace of his father's stride
The son walks,
Echoes and intonations of his father's speech
Are heard when he talks.

Once when the table was tall,
And the chair a wood,
He absorbed his father's smile and carefully copied
The way that he stood.

He grew into exile slowly,
With pride and remorse,
In some ways better than his begetters,
In others worse.

And now having chosen, with strangers,
Half glad of his choice,
He smiles with his father's hesitant smile
And speaks with his voice.

Prophet

When word came back to that small whitewashed village,
Strange rumours of his ways and of his talk,
The neighbours shook their heads and didn't wonder,
His mother was bewildered more than proud.
And coming into lamplit towns at evening,
Seeing the warm red gloom behind the blinds,
Lying awake in strange rooms above rivers,
He thought he would be like them if he could.
And when at last the courteous powers took notice
And nailed him to that awful point in time
He knew that what he meant would be forgotten
Except by some as lonely as himself.

PEARSE HUTCHINSON

(1927-)

from: TONGUE WITHOUT HANDS (1963)

Eight Frontiers Distant

for John Jordan

Eight frontiers distant
from the company and gesture of his true friends,
each man becomes less perfect in affection.
Divided by a hundred seas and lakes
from the second-rate, the tenth-rate, and the unspeakable,
each man recalls their faces and their names
with gradually less disdain.
Travel is in this matter, so,
more specious than trite death.
Till, having crossed back over two frontiers,
or ten extensive deserts of water,
confronted suddenly at a cafe-table
with choice between his own alone integrity,
with all its dangerous peepshows,
and the fourth- or fifteenth-rate with an eager face,
and a Nansen passport[1] somewhere in the background,
each man hears need, putting on the voice of duty,
re-assert itself; and into his mind again
his true friends come,
smiling and loving and mercilessly absent.

1. A passport issued to stateless persons by the League of Nations after World War I. It was named after Fridtjof Nansen (1861-1930), the Norwegian arctic explorer, who was the League's high commissioner for refugees 1920-22.

from: THE FROST IS ALL OVER (1975)

Achnasheen

for Eoghan Ó Néill

'You'd miss the Gaelic from the placenames',
you said, turning from the danger-seat to me in the back swigging Talisker[1]
driving through Wester Ross making for the Kyle of Lochalsh.[2]
And the next signpost we came to was Achnasheen.[3]

How could there be any Gaelic 'for' Achnasheen?
It isn't Gaelic any more. It could never be English.
Despite the murderous maps,
despite the bereft roadsigns,
despite the casual distortions of illiterate scribes,
the name remains beautiful. A maimed beauty.

1. A brand of Scotch whiskey.
2. A small fishing port in Ross and Cromarty, Scotland.
3. From the Gaelic *each na sí* (steed of the fairies).

Hiding behind it somewhere
its real name.

You'd almost think the conquerors thought
Gaelic was God:
its real name unnameable.

And I remembered the first-time crossing the
Border,
not the Highland Line but the one from Cavan into
'Ulster',
and missing the Gaelic placenames, the maiming
ugliness of that;
guessing the real names, failing to guess, the irk of
that,
like a horsehair down the back.

The Gaelic names beating their wings madly
behind the mad cage of English;
the new names half the time transparent, but half
the time
silent as the grave
English would bury Irish in.

Later we saw Beinn Ailleagan: the jewelled
mountain —
but not called that but keeping its true name:
Beinn Ailleagan
wearing its name like a jewel
upon its snow-white breast
like the jewel of the Gaelic tongue
that old men and young women keep shining and
singing
all over the Catholic islands and the Calvinist
islands for all the invader
and his canting quisling[4] ministers could reek.

And will the black sticks of the devil, Eoghan,
ever pipe us into heaven at last —
as one night down the torchlit streets of Áth Dara —
into a heaven of freedom to give
things back
their true names?

Like streets in Barcelona,
like Achnasheen,
Belfast

4. Named after Major Vidkun Quisling (1887-1945), the Norwegian collaborator with the Nazis in World War II, the word now describes a traitor who aids an occupying enemy force.

The Frost is All Over[1]

for Michael Hartnett

To kill a language is to kill a people.
The Aztecs knew far better: they took over
their victims' language, kept them carving
obsidian beauties, weeded their religion
of dangerous gentleness, and winged them
blood-flowers
(that's a different way to kill a people).
The Normans brought and grew, but Honor
Croome
could never make her Kerryman verse English:[2]
Traherne[3] was in the music of his tears.

We have no glint or caution who we are:
our patriots dream wolfhounds in their portraits,
our vendors pose in hunting-garb, the nightmare
forelock tugging madly at some lost leash.[4]
The Vikings never hurt us, xenophilia
means bland servility, we insult
ourselves and Europe with artificial trees,
and coins as gelt[5] of beauty now
as, from the start, of power.

Like Flemish words on horseback, tongue survives
in turns of speech the telly must correct;
our music bows and scrapes on the world's
platforms,
each cat-gut wears a rigorous bow-tie.
The frost, we tell them, is all over, and they love
our brogue so much they give us guns to kill
ourselves, our language, and all the other gooks.[6]

Bobrowski[7] would have understood, he found
some old, surviving words of a murdered language,
and told a few friends; but he knew how to mourn,
a rare talent, a need not many grant.

1. The title is also the name of a well-known jig.
2. Lady Kerry, a friend of Pierce Ferriter, poet and chieftain, a leader of Irish warriors in the war of 1641, who was captured and hanged in Killarney in 1653.
3. Thomas Traherne (1637-74), English religious poet whose best work was not discovered until the twentieth century.
4. 'To touch the forelock' was a traditional phrase to describe deference to a local landlord.
5. Two meanings: (a) gold; (b) gelded (i.e. bereft).
6. A derogatory American word for people from Far Eastern countries.
7. Johannes Bobrowski (1917-65), German poet and novelist, includes in his poetry fragments of an early Teutonic language, Pruzzian, extinct since the eighteenth century. The Pruzzians were exterminated by the Teutonic Knights.

To call a language dead before it dies
means to bury it alive; some tongues do die
from hours or days inside the coffin, and when
the tearful killers dig it up they find
the tongue, like Suarez,[8] bitten to its own bone.
Others explode in the church, and stain the bishop,
whose priest could speak no Gaelic to his 'flock'
but knew to sink a splendid tawny goblet
as deep as any master of the hunt.

Is Carleton[9] where the tenderness must hide?
Or would they have the Gaelic words, like insects,
crawl up the legs of horses, and each bite,
or startle, be proclaimed a heritage?
Are those who rule us, like their eager voters,
ghosts yearning for flesh? Ghosts are cruel,
and ghosts of suicides more cruel still.
To kill a language is to kill one's self.

Summer 1973

8. According to the author, the Jesuit theologian Francisco Suarez (1548-1617) was buried alive.

9. William Carleton (1794-1869), Irish novelist and storyteller, admired for his skill at reproducing Gaelic phrases and images in his English versions.

RICHARD MURPHY

(1927-)

from: SAILING TO AN ISLAND (1963)

[A craftsman rather than a mage, Murphy has always believed in the poet as a builder and maker of structures. His keen sense of form has led to many experiments, from the long historical sequence, *The Battle of Aughrim* (1968) to the collection of sonnets in *The Price of Stone* (1985). The vocabulary is precise, the style laconic, but the rhythms themselves are remarkably muscular, as in 'The Last Galway Hooker'. Murphy combines a strong awareness of history with a sharp insight into the etymology of words. Many of his shorter poems read like elegant entries in a dictionary, elaborating the central meanings of complex and problematical words.]

The Last Galway Hooker[1]

Where the Corrib[2] river chops through the
 Claddagh
To sink in the tide-race its rattling chain
The boatwright's hammer chipped across the water

Ribbing this hooker, while a reckless gun
Shook the limestone quay-wall, after the Treaty[3]
Had brought civil war to this fisherman's town.

That 'tasty'[4] carpenter from Connemara, Cloherty,
Helped by his daughter, had half-planked the hull
In his eightieth year, when at work he died,

And she did the fastening, and caulked her well,
The last boat complete with old Galway lines.
Several seasons at the drift-nets she paid

In those boom-years, working by night in channels
With trimmel[5] and spillet and an island crew,
Tea-stew on turf in the pipe-black forecastle,

Songs of disasters wailed on the quay
When the tilt of the water heaved the whole shore.
'She was lucky always the *Ave Maria*,'

With her brown barked sails, and her hull black tar,
Her forest of oak ribs and the larchwood planks,
The cavern-smelling hold bulked with costly gear,

1. A fishing boat using hooks and lines instead of nets. Murphy bought it to transport people and supplies from island to mainland.

2. A river flowing from Lough Corrib, through the fishermen's parish of Claddagh and into Galway Bay.

3. The Anglo-Irish Treaty of 1921, signed in London, effectively partitioning Ireland into a 26-county Free State and 6-county Northern Ireland. A Civil War ensued between Free Staters and those Republicans who were opposed to the settlement.

4. skilled, neat.

5. A net whose inner fine-meshed layer is carried by the fish through the course-meshed outer layers, enclosing it in a pocket.

Fastest in the race to the gull-marked banks,
What harbour she hived in, there she was queen
And her crew could afford to stand strangers drinks,

Till the buyers failed in nineteen twenty-nine,
When the cheapest of fish could find no market,
Were dumped overboard, the price down to
nothing;

Until to her leisure a fisher priest walked
By the hungry dockside, full of her name,
Who made a cash offer, and the owners took it.

Then like a girl given money and a home
With no work but pleasure for her man to perform
She changed into white sails, her hold made room

For hammock and kettles, the touch and perfume
Of priestly hands. So now she's a yacht
With pitch-pine spars and Italian hemp ropes,

Smooth-running ash-blocks expensively bought
From chandlers in Dublin, two men get jobs
Copper-painting her keel and linseeding her throat,

While at weekends, nephews and nieces in mobs
Go sailing on picnics to the hermit islands,
Come home flushed with health having hooked a
few dabs.[6]

Munich,[7] submarines, and the war's demands
Of workers to feed invaded that party
Like fumes of the diesel the dope of her sails,

When the Canon went east into limed sheep-lands
From the stone and reed patches of lobstermen
Having sold her to one on Cleggan[8] Quay,

Who was best of the boatsmen from Inishbofin,[9]
She his best buy. He shortened the mast, installed
A new 'Ailsa Craig,'[10] made a hold of her cabin,

Poured over the deck thick tar slightly boiled;
Every fortnight he drained the sump in the bilge
'To preserve the timbers.' All she could do, fulfilled.

The sea, good to gamblers, let him indulge
His fear when she rose winding her green shawl
And his pride when she lay calm under his pillage:

And he never married, was this hooker's lover,
Always ill-at-ease in houses or on hills,
Waiting for weather, or mending broken trawls:

Bothered by women no more than by the moon,
Not concerned with money beyond the bare need,
In this boat's bows he sheathed his life's harpoon.

A neap-tide[11] of work, then a spring of liquor
Were the tides that alternately pulled his soul,
Now on a pitching deck with nets to hand-haul,

Then passing Sunday propped against a barrel
Winding among words like a sly helmsman
Till stories gathered around him in a shoal.

She was Latin blessed, holy water shaken
From a small whiskey bottle by a surpliced priest,
Madonnas wafered on every bulkhead,

Oil-grimed by the diesel, and her luck lasted
Those twenty-one years of skill buoyed by prayers,
Strength forged by dread from his drowned
ancestors.

She made him money and again he lost it
In the fisherman's fiction of turning farmer:
The cost of timber and engine spares increased,

Till a phantom hurt him, ribs on a shore,
A hulk each tide rattles that will never fish,
Sunk back in the sand, a story finished.

We met here last summer, nineteen fifty-nine,
Far from the missiles, the moon-shots,[12] the money,
And we drank looking out on the island quay,

When his crew were in London drilling a motorway.
Old age had smoothed his barnacled will,
One calm evening he sold me the *Ave Maria.*

Then he was alone, stunned like a widower—
Relics and rowlocks pronging from the wall,
A pot of boiling garments, winter everywhere,

6. small fish.
7. The appeasement by Adolf Hitler of the British prime minister, Neville Chamberlain, at Munich in 1938 was a prelude to World War II.
8. A small port in County Galway, where Murphy lived for a time.
9. An island off the coast of Galway, reached by boat from Cleggan.
10. A make of diesel engine.
11. The lowest tide.
12. In the late 1950s, the USA and the Soviet Union began to launch satellites into space.

Especially in his bones, watching things fall,
Hooks of three-mile spillets, trammels at the foot
Of the unused double-bed—his mind threaded
with all

The marline[13] of his days twined within that boat,
His muscles' own shackles then staying the storm
Which now snap to bits like frayed thread.

So I chose to renew her, to rebuild, to prolong
For a while the spliced yards of yesterday.
Carpenters were enrolled, the ballast and the dung

Of cattle he'd carried lifted from the hold,
The engine removed, and the stale bilge scoured.
De Valera's daughter[14] hoisted the Irish flag

At her freshly adzed[15] mast this Shrove Tuesday,
Stepped while afloat between the tackle of the *Topaz*
And the *St. John*, by Bofin's[16] best boatsmen,

All old as himself. Her skilful sailmaker,
Her inherited boatwright, her dream-tacking
steersman
Picked up the tools of their interrupted work,

And in memory's hands this hooker was restored.
Old men my instructors, and with all new gear
May I handle her well down tomorrow's sea-road.

13. A small rope for winding around a larger one to prevent wearing.
14. Dr Mairin de Valera, a marine biologist at University College, Galway. Eamon de Valera (1882-1975) was at this time President of Ireland.
15. Cut by a tool with an arched blade set at right angles to the handle.
16. i.e. Inishbofin's.

from: THE BATTLE OF AUGHRIM (1968)

Casement's Funeral

After the noose, and the black diary deeds
Gossiped, his fame roots in prison lime:
The hanged bones burn, a revolution seeds.
Now Casement's skeleton is flying home.[1]

A gun salutes, the troops slow-march, our new
Nation atones for her shawled motherland
Whose welcome gaoled him when a U-boat threw
This rebel quixote soaked on Banna Strand.[2]

Soldiers in green guard the draped catafalque
With chalk remains of once ambiguous bone
Which fathered nothing till the traitor's dock
Hurt him to tower in legend like Wolfe Tone.[3]

From gaol yard to the Liberator's[4] tomb
Pillared in frost, they carry the freed ash,
Transmuted relic of a death-cell flame
Which purged for martyrdom the diarist's flesh.

On the small screen I watch the packed cortège
Pace from High Mass.[5] Rebels in silk hats now
Exploit the grave with an old comrade's speech:
White hair tossed, a black cape flecked with snow.[6]

1. Roger Casement (1864-1916), reformist British consul in the Congo, where he exposed imperialist corruption. In 1911 he was knighted for his distinguished career in the diplomatic service. In 1913 he endorsed Irish nationalism and became an organizer with the Irish Volunteers. In Germany, in 1914, he sought military assistance for an Irish Rising, but was captured on his return to Ireland in April 1916. He was tried and executed for treason on 3 August 1916. To prevent interventions on his behalf, diaries (purporting to be his) were circulated, recording homosexual acts. In 1964, the newly elected Labour government in Britain decided to allow Casement's remains to be brought to Ireland. They were flown to Dublin on 23 February 1965.
2. Casement and two companions landed at Banna Strand, Co. Kerry on Good Friday, 21 April 1916. While the others went to Tralee, Casement remained at an old rath near the strand. Here he was arrested.
3. Theobald Wolfe Tone (1763-98), leader of the United Irishmen and the 1798 Rebellion. Like Casement, he was a protestant patriot-martyr.
4. The coffin lay in state at Arbour Hill Prison. From there it was taken to Glasnevin cemetery, where the 'Liberator', Daniel O'Connell (1775-1847), is also buried.
5. In the Pro-Cathedral.
6. Eamon de Valera, then President of Ireland and eighty-two years old, delivered the graveside oration. Since he had been ill, he was advised to cover his head. 'Casement,' he replied, 'deserves better than that.'

from: HIGH ISLAND (1974)

Seals at High Island

The calamity of seals begins with jaws.
Born in caverns that reverberate
With endless malice of the sea's tongue
Clacking on shingle, they learn to bark back
In fear and sadness and celebration.

The ocean's mouth opens forty feet wide
And closes on a morsel of their rock.

Swayed by the thrust and backfall of the tide,
A dappled grey bull and a brindled[1] cow
Copulate in the green water of a cove.
I watch from a cliff-top, trying not to move.
Sometimes they sink and merge into black shoals;
Then rise for air, his muzzle on her neck,
Their winged feet intertwined as a fishtail.

She opens her fierce mouth like a scarlet flower
Full of white seeds; she holds it open long
At the sunburst in the music of their loving;
And cries a little. But I must remember
How far their feelings are from mine marooned.
If there are tears at this holy ceremony
Theirs are caused by brine and mine by breeze.

When the great bull withdraws his rod, it glows
Like a carnelian[2] candle set in jade.
The cow ripples ashore to feed her calf;
While an old rival, eyeing the deed with hate,
Swims to attack the tired triumphant god.
They rear their heads above the boiling surf,
Their terrible jaws open, jetting blood.

At nightfall they haul out, and mourn the drowned,
Playing to the sea sadly their last quartet,
An improvised requiem that ravishes
Reason, while ripping scale up like a net:
Brings pity trembling down the rocky spine
Of headlands, till the bitter ocean's tongue
Swells in their cove, and smothers their sweet song.

1. spotted, streaked.
2. translucent red.

Little Hunger

I drove to Little Hunger promontory
  Looking for pink stone
In roofless houses huddled by the sea
  To buy to build my own.

Hovels to live in, ruins to admire
  From a car cruising by,
The weathered face caught in a sunset fire,
  Hollowed with exility;[1]

1. slenderness, refinement.

Whose gradual fall my purchase would complete,
  Clearing them off the land,
The seven cabins needed to create
  The granite house I planned.

Once mine, I'd work on their dismemberment,
  Threshold, lintel, wall;
And pick a hearthstone from a rubble fragment
  To make it integral.

from: THE PRICE OF STONE (1985)

Moonshine

To think
I must be alone:
To love
We must be together.

I think I love you
When I'm alone
More than I think of you
When we're together.

I cannot think
Without loving
Or love
Without thinking.

Alone I love
To think of us together:
Together I think
I'd love to be alone.

[The next poem was published under the title 'Stone Mania'. Now the poet wishes to restore the title he first used.]

The Price of Stone

How much it hurts me to tidy up when all my
    papers are heaped on the desk in a
        three-month mess,
To regain control of this drift of days I've lost in
    my passion for building in granite,
And face the bills I must pay by leaving the house
    that has cost me too much to enlarge,

Where I passed the time too quickly preparing a
place for the future to work within soundproof
walls,
So never had a moment in the present for writing
about the moments that were passing away:
How much it hurts to see the destruction that all
good building, even the best, must cause,
Not only the hedges that had to be first cut down
before the foundations were dug,
But deeper cuts through veins in the mind that
carried the blood of memory through the
brain:
How much it hurts me to have neglected all this
summer the friends whom I might have seen,
But for my mad obsession of building more rooms
to entertain them in time to come:
Because these times are apt to elude us, we die, or
our friends drop dead before we can say
I'd love you to see and enjoy the house whose
construction has kept us entirely apart.

Wellington Testimonial[1]

Needling my native sky over Phoenix Park
I obelize[2] the victory of wit
That let my polished Anglo-Irish mark
Be made by Smirke,[3] as a colossal spit.

Properly dressed for an obsolete parade,
Devoid of mystery, no winding stair[4]
Threading my unvermiculated[5] head,
I've kept my feet, but lost my nosy flair.

My life was work: my work was taking life
To be a monument. The dead have won
Capital headlines. Look at Ireland rife
With maxims: need you ask what good I've done?

My sole point in this evergreen oak aisle
Is to maintain a clean laconic style.

1. The Wellington Monument in Dublin's Phoenix Park.
2. The verb has several meanings: to mark a spurious passage in an ancient manuscript; to make a dagger-sign for a footnote; to build a four-sided, tall and tapering pillar.
3. The obelisk was designed by Robert Smirke (1780-1867) and built with subscriptions made after the battle of Waterloo.
4. A reference to W.B. Yeats's collection of that name, published in 1933.
5. not worm-eaten.

Ice Rink[1]

Reflections of a spotlit mirror-ball,
Casting a light net over a pearl pond
In oval orbits, magnify my haul
Of small fry at a disco, coiled in sound.

On anticlockwise tracks, all shod with steel,
Initiates feel exalted; starlets glide
To cut more ice with convoluted skill
Practising tricks that lure them to backslide.

Their figure-curving feet have chased my skin
With puckish onslaught. Gloss they vitiate
For pure fun, when they joust through thick and
thin,
Vanishes under frost, a hoar-stone slate.

Midnight, my crushed face melts in a dead heat:
Old scores ironed out, tomorrow a clean sheet.

1. 'Rink' is also an Anglo-Saxon word for 'warrior'. The use of an old Dublin building as an ice rink parallels Murphy's employment of the ancient sonnet-form to tackle a modern theme.

Natural Son

Before the spectacled professor snipped
The cord, I heard your birth-cry flood the ward,
And lowered your mother's tortured head, and
wept.
The house you'd left would need to be restored.

No worse pain could be borne, to bear the joy
Of seeing you come in a slow dive from the womb,
Pushed from your fluid home, pronounced 'a boy'.
You'll never find so well equipped a room.

No house we build could hope to satisfy
Every small need, now that you've made this move
To share our loneliness, much as we try
Our vocal skill to wall you round with love.

This day you crave so little, we so much
For you to live, who need our merest[1] touch.

1. purest.

THOMAS KINSELLA

(1928-)

from:
ANOTHER SEPTEMBER (1958)

[A difficult but rewarding writer, Thomas Kinsella's work is often introspective and moody. The Irish Eliot, he offers anatomies of desolation set against disorderly city streetscapes. His is a poetry of evocative images and lucid intervals, but many of the links in the expository chain have been suppressed and must be intuited by the reader. The quiet, wry style is not lacking in intensity, but achieves its subtlest effects through intermittent moments of insight or fantasy set against a usually prosaic background.]

Another September

Dreams fled away, this country bedroom, raw
With the touch of the dawn, wrapped in a minor
peace,
Hears through an open window the garden draw
Long pitch black breaths, lay bare its apple trees,
Ripe pear trees, brambles, windfall-sweetened soil,
Exhale rough sweetness against the starry slates.
Nearer the river sleeps St. John's, all toil
Locked fast inside a dream with iron gates.

Domestic Autumn, like an animal
Long used to handling by those countrymen,
Rubs her kind hide against the bedroom wall
Sensing a fragrant child come back again
— Not this half-tolerated consciousness,
Its own cold season never done,
But that unspeaking daughter, growing less
Familiar where we fell asleep as one.

Wakeful moth-wings blunder near a chair,
Toss their light shell at the glass, and go
To inhabit the living starlight. Stranded hair
Stirs on the still linen. It is as though
The black breathing that billows her sleep, her
name,
Drugged under judgment, waned and — bearing
daggers
And balances — down the lampless darkness they
came,
Moving like women: Justice,[1] Truth, such figures.

1. Justice is classically imaged as a blindfold woman holding scales of balance aloft in her hand.

Baggot Street Deserta

Lulled, at silence, the spent attack.
The will to work is laid aside.
The breaking-cry, the strain of the rack,
Yield, are at peace. The window is wide
On a crawling arch of stars, and the night
Reacts faintly to the mathematic
Passion of a cello suite
Plotting the quiet of my attic.
A mile away the river toils
Its buttressed fathoms out to sea;
Tucked in the mountains, many miles
Away from its roaring outcome, a shy
Gasp of waters in the gorse
Is sonneting origins. Dreamers' heads
Lie mesmerised in Dublin's beds
Flashing with images, Adam's morse.

A cigarette, the moon, a sigh
Of educated boredom, greet
A curlew's lingering threadbare cry
Of common loss. Compassionate,
I add my call of exile, half-
Buried longing, half-serious
Anger and the rueful laugh.
We fly into our risk, the spurious.

Versing, like an exile, makes
A virtuoso of the heart,
Interpreting the old mistakes
And discords in a work of Art
For the One, a private masterpiece
Of doctored recollections. Truth
Concedes, before the dew, its place
In the spray of dried forgettings Youth
Collected when they were a single
Furious undissected bloom.

A voice clarifies when the tingle
Dies out of the nerves of time:
Endure and let the present punish.
Looking backward, all is lost;
The Past becomes a fairy bog
Alive with fancies, double crossed
By pad of owl and hoot of dog,
Where shaven, serious-minded men
Appear with lucid theses, after
Which they don the mists again
With trackless, cotton-silly laughter;
Secretly a swollen Burke
Assists a decomposing Hare[1]
To cart a body of good work
With midnight mutterings off somewhere;
The goddess[2] who had light for thighs
Grows feet of dung and takes to bed,
Affronting horror-stricken eyes,
The marsh bird that children dread.

I nonetheless inflict, endure,
Tedium, intracordal[3] hurt,
The sting of memory's quick, the drear
Uprooting, burying, prising apart
Of loves a strident adolescent
Spent in doubt and vanity.
All feed a single stream, impassioned
Now with obsessed honesty,
A tugging scruple that can keep
Clear eyes staring down the mile,
The thousand fathoms, into sleep.
Fingers cold against the sill
Feel, below the stress of flight,
The slow implosion of my pulse
In a wrist with poet's cramp, a tight
Beat tapping out endless calls
Into the dark, as the alien
Garrison in my own blood
Keeps constant contact with the main
Mystery, not to be understood.
Out where imagination arches
Chilly points of light transact
The business of the border-marches

1. William Burke and William Hare were noted 18th-century grave-robbers and body-snatchers.
2. That is, the goddess of poetry is transmogrified by the Burke and Hare activities of critics into something grotesque and dreaded by children.
3. within the heart.

Of the Real, and I — a fact
That may be countered or may not —
Find their privacy complete.

My quarter-inch of cigarette
Goes flaring down to Baggot Street.[4]

4. Baggot Street was a thoroughfare much frequented by Dublin artists of the 1950s.

from:
MORALITIES (1960)

Song

HANDSCLASP AT EUSTON[1]

The engine screams and Murphy,[2] isolate
— Chalk-white, comedian — in the smoky glare,
Dwindles among the churns and tenders. Weight,
Person, race, the human, dwindle there.
I bow to the cases cluttering the rack,
Their handles black with sweat of exile. Wales,
Wave and home; I close my eyes. The track
Swerves to a greener world: sea-rock, thigh-scales.

AT THE HEART

Heraldic, hatched in gold, a sacred tree
Stands absorbed, tinkering with the slight
Thrumming of birds, the flicker of energy
Thrown and caught, the blows and burdens of
  flight.
Roots deepen; disciplines proliferate
And wings more fragile are brought into play.
Timber matures, the game grows nobler, yet
Not one has sped direct as appetite.

FIRE AND ICE

Two creatures face each other, fixed in song,
Satyr and nymph, across the darkening brain.
I dream of reason and the first grows strong,
Drunk as a whirlwind on the sweating grain;
I dream of drunkenness and, free from strain,
The second murmurs like a fingered gong;
I sink beneath the dream: his words grow sane,
Her pupils glow with pleasure all night long.

1. A London railway station at which most Irish emigrants arrive and depart on the Holyhead boat-train.
2. The most common surname in Ireland; hence, the generic Irishman.

from: DOWNSTREAM (1962)

Downstream

Drifting to meet us on the darkening stage
A pattern shivered; whorling in its place
Another held us in a living cage
Then broke to its reordered phase of grace.

Again in the mirrored dusk the paddles sank.
We thrust forward, swaying both as one.
The ripples widened to the ghostly bank

Where willows, with their shadows half undone,
Hung to the water, mowing like the blind.
The current seized our skiff. We let it run

Grazing the reeds, and let the land unwind
In stealth on either hand. Dark woods: a door
Opened and shut. The clear sky fell behind,

The channel shrank. Thick slopes from shore to shore
Lowered a matted[1] arch. I thought of roots
Crawling full of pike on the river-floor

To cage us in, sensed the furred night-brutes
Halt in their trails, twitching their tiny brushes.
What plopped in the reeds and stirred between the shoots?

Then I remembered how among those bushes
A man one night fell sick and left his shell
Collapsed, half eaten, like a rotted thrush's

To frighten stumbling children. 'You could tell',
My co-shadow murmured, 'by the hands
He died in terror.' And the cold of hell,

A limb-lightness, a terror in the glands,
Pierced again as when that story first
Froze my blood: the soil of other lands[2]

Drank lives that summer with a body thirst;
Nerveless by the European pit
— Ourselves through seven hundred years[3] accurst —

We saw the barren world obscurely lit
By tall chimneys flickering in their pall,
The haunt of swinish man — each day a spit

That, turning, sweated war, each night a fall
Back to the evil dream where rodents ply,
Man-rumped, sow-headed, busy with whip and maul[4]

Among nude herds of the damned. It seemed that I,
Coming to conscience on that lip of dread,
Still dreamed, impervious to calamity,

Imagining a formal drift of the dead
Stretched calm as effigies on velvet dust,
Scattered on starlit slopes with arms outspread

And eyes of silver — when that story thrust
Pungent horror and an actual mess
Into my very face, and taste I must.

Then hungry joy and sickening distress
Fumbled together by the brimming flood,
And night consumed a hopeless loneliness.

Like mortal jaws, the alleys of the wood
Fell-to behind us. At its heart, a ghost
Glimmered briefly with my gift of blood

— Spreadeagled on a rack of leaves, almost
Remembering. It looked full at the sky,
Calmly encountering the starry host,

Meeting their silver eyes with silver eye.
An X of wavering flesh, a skull of light,
Extinguished in our wake without a sigh.

Then the current shuddered in its flight
And swerved on pliant muscle; we were sped
Through sudden peace into a pit of night:

1. Covered with tangled growths.
2. Countries engaged in the hostilities of World War II.
3. The period of the English occupation of Ireland.
4. war-club.

The Mill-Hole, whose rocky fathoms fed
On moss and pure depth and the cold fin
Turning in its heart. The river bed

Called to our flesh. Across the watery skin,
Breathless, our shell trembled. The abyss ...
We shipped our oars in dread. Now, deeper in,

Something shifted in sleep, a quiet hiss
As we slipped by. Adrift ... A milk-white breast ...
A shuffle of wings betrayed with a feathery kiss[5]

A soul of white with darkness for a nest.
The creature bore the night so tranquilly
I lifted up my eyes. There without rest

The phantoms of the overhanging sky
Occupied their stations and descended;
Another moment, to the starlit eye,

The slow, downstreaming dead, it seemed, were blended
One with those silver hordes, and briefly shared
Their order, glittering. And then impended

A barrier of rock that turned and bared
A varied barrenness as toward its base
We glided — blotting heaven as it towered —

Searching the darkness for a landing place.

5. Judas's kissing of Christ.

Mirror in February

The day dawns with scent of must and rain,
Of opened soil, dark trees, dry bedroom air.
Under the fading lamp, half dressed — my brain
Idling on some compulsive fantasy —
I towel my shaven lip and stop, and stare,
Riveted by a dark exhausted eye,
A dry downturning mouth.

It seems again that it is time to learn,
In this untiring, crumbling place of growth
To which, for the time being, I return.
Now plainly in the mirror of my soul
I read that I have looked my last on youth
And little more; for they are not made whole
That reach the age of Christ.[1]

Below my window the awakening trees,
Hacked clean[2] for better bearing, stand defaced
Suffering their brute necessities,
And how should the flesh not quail that span for span
Is mutilated more? In slow distaste
I fold my towel with what grace I can,
Not young and not renewable, but man.

1. The poet is 33 years old, the age at which Jesus died.
2. pruned.

from: WORMWOOD (1966)

Wormwood[1]

I have dreamt it again: standing suddenly still
In a thicket, among wet trees, stunned, minutely
Shuddering, hearing a wooden echo escape.

A mossy floor, almost colourless, disappears
In depths of rain among the tree shapes.
I am straining, tasting that echo a second longer.

If I can hold it ... familiar if I can hold it ...
A black tree with a double trunk — two trees[2]
Grown into one — throws up its blurred branches.

The two trunks in their infinitesimal dance of growth
Have turned completely about one another, their join
A slowly twisted scar, that I recognise ...

A quick arc flashes sidewise in the air,
A heavy blade in flight. A wooden stroke:
Iron sinks in the gasping core.

I will dream it again.

1. The star referred to in Apocalypse (8. 10-11) which, by falling to earth, changed one-third of earth's waters into wormwood, from which men grew bitter and died.
2. The image suggests how people change one another, as they grow together.

from: NOTES FROM THE LAND OF THE DEAD AND OTHER POEMS (1972)

Ancestor[1]

I was going up to say something,
and stopped. Her profile against the curtains
was old, and dark like a hunting bird's.

It was the way she perched on the high stool,
staring into herself, with one fist
gripping the side of the barrier around her desk
— or her head held by something, from inside.
And not caring for anything around her
or anyone there by the shelves.
I caught a faint smell, musky and queer.

I may have made some sound — she stopped rocking
and pressed her fist in her lap; then she stood up
and shut down the lid of the desk, and turned the key.
She shoved a small bottle under her aprons
and came toward me, darkening the passageway.

Ancestor . . . among sweet- and fruit-boxes.
Her black heart . . .
Was that a sigh?
— brushing by me in the shadows,
with her heaped aprons, through the red hangings
to the scullery, and down to the back room.

1. The poet's grandmother.

Tear

I was sent in to see her.
A fringe of jet drops
chattered at my ear
as I went in through the hangings.

I was swallowed in chambery dusk.
My heart shrank
at the smell of disused
organs and sour kidney.

The black aprons I used to
bury my face in
were folded at the foot of the bed
in the last watery light from the window

(Go in and say goodbye to her)
and I was carried off
to unfathomable depths.
I turned to look at her.

She stared at the ceiling
and puffed her cheek, distracted,
propped high in the bed
resting for the next attack.

The covers were gathered close
up to her mouth,
that the lines of ill-temper still
marked. Her grey hair

was loosened out like
a young woman's all over
the pillow, mixed with the shadows
criss-crossing her forehead

and at her mouth and eyes,
like a web of strands tying down her head
and tangling down toward the shadow
eating away the floor at my feet.

I couldn't stir at first, nor wished to,
for fear she might turn and tempt me
(my own father's mother)
with open mouth

— with some fierce wheedling whisper —
to hide myself one last time
against her, and bury my
self in her drying mud.

Was I to kiss her? As soon
kiss the damp that crept
in the flowered walls
of this pit.

Yet I had to kiss.
I knelt by the bulk of the death bed
and sank my face in the chill
and smell of her black aprons.

Snuff and musk, the folds against my eyelids,
carried me into a derelict place
smelling of ash: unseen walls and roofs
rustled like breathing.

I found myself disturbing
dead ashes for any trace
of warmth, when far off
in the vaults a single drop

splashed. And I found
what I was looking for
— not heat nor fire,
not any comfort,

but her voice, soft, talking to someone
about my father: 'God help him, he cried
big tears over there by the machine
for the poor little thing.' Bright

drops on the wooden lid for
my infant sister. My own
wail of child-animal grief
was soon done, with any early guess

at sad dullness and tedious pain
and lives bitter with hard bondage.
How I tasted it now —
her heart beating in my mouth!

She drew an uncertain breath
and pushed at the clothes
and shuddered tiredly.
I broke free

and left the room
promising myself
when she was really dead
I would really kiss.

My grandfather half looked up
from the fireplace as I came out,
and shrugged and turned back
with a deaf stare to the heat.

I fidgetted beside him for a minute
and went out to the shop.
It was still bright there
and I felt better able to breathe.

Old age can digest
anything: the commotion
at Heaven's gate — the struggle
in store for you all your life.

How long and hard it is
before you get to Heaven,
unless like little Agnes
you vanish with early tears.

Hen Woman

The noon heat in the yard
smelled of stillness and coming thunder.
A hen scratched and picked at the shore.
It stopped, its body crouched and puffed out.
The brooding silence seemed to say 'Hush ...'

The cottage door opened,
a black hole
in a whitewashed wall so bright
the eyes narrowed.
Inside, a clock murmured 'Gong ...'

(I had felt all this before ...)

She hurried out in her slippers
muttering, her face dark with anger,
and gathered the hen up jerking
languidly. Her hand fumbled.
Too late. Too late.

It fixed me with its pebble eyes
(seeing what mad blur?).
A white egg showed in the sphincter;[1]
mouth and beak opened together;
and time stood still.

Nothing moved: bird or woman,
fumbled or fumbling — locked there
(as I must have been) gaping.

*

There was a tiny movement at my feet,
tiny and mechanical; I looked down.
A beetle like a bronze leaf
was inching across the cement,

1. contracting muscle.

clasping with small tarsi[2]
a ball of dung bigger than its body.
The serrated brow pressed the ground humbly,
lifted in a short stare, bowed again;
the dung-ball advanced minutely,
losing a few fragments,
specks of staleness and freshness.

*

A mutter of thunder far off
— time not quite stopped.
I saw the egg had moved a fraction:
a tender blank brain
under torsion, a clean new world.

As I watched, the mystery completed.
The black zero of the orifice
closed to a point
and the white zero of the egg hung free,
flecked with greenish brown oils.

It slowly turned and fell.
Dreamlike, fussed by her splayed fingers,
it floated outward, moon-white,
leaving no trace in the air,
and began its drop to the shore.

*

I feed upon it still, as you see;
there is no end to that which,
not understood, may yet be noted
and hoarded in the imagination,
in the yolk of one's being, so to speak,
there to undergo its (quite animal) growth,
dividing blindly,
twitching, packed with will,
searching in its own tissue
for the structure
in which it may wake.
Something that had — clenched
in its cave — not been
now was: an egg of being.
Through what seemed a whole year it fell
— as it still falls, for me,
solid and light, the red gold beating
in its silvery womb,

2. A bird's shank-bone and instep.

alive as the yolk and white
of my eye; as it will continue
to fall, probably, until I die,
through the vast indifferent spaces
with which I am empty.

*

It smashed against the grating
and slipped down quickly out of sight.
It was over in a comical flash.
The soft mucous shell clung a little longer,
then drained down.
She stood staring, in blank anger.
Then her eyes came to life, and she laughed
and let the bird flap away.
'It's all the one.
There's plenty more where that came from!'

Hen to pan!
It was a simple world.

St. Paul's Rocks: 16 February 1832[1]

A cluster of rocks far from the trade routes
a thousand miles from any other land
they appear abruptly in the ocean,
low lying, so hidden in driving mists
they are seldom sighted, and then briefly,
white and glittering against the eternal grey.

Despite the lack of any vegetation
they have succeeded in establishing
symbiosis with the surrounding water.
Colonies of birds eat the abundant fish;
moths feed on the feathers; lice and beetles
live in the dung; countless spiders
prey on these scavengers; in the crevices
a race of crabs lives on the eggs and young.

In squalor and killing and parasitic things
life takes its first hold.
Later the noble accident: the seed, dropped
in some exhausted excrement, or bobbing
like a matted skull into an inlet.

1. This is the title of an entry in Charles Darwin's journal of his voyage of 1836 in the *Beagle*.

The Dispossessed[1]

The lake is deserted now
but the water is still clean and transparent,
the headlands covered with laurels,
the little estuaries full of shells,
with enchanting parterres where the waves
ebb and flow over masses of turf and flowers.

It was like a miracle, a long pastoral, long ago.
The intoxication of a life gliding away
in the face of heaven: Spring, a plain of flowers;
Autumn, with grape-clusters and chestnuts
formed in its depths; our warm nights
passing under starlight.
We had established peace,
having learnt to practise virtue without
expectation of recompense — that we must be virtuous
without hope. (The Law is just; observe it,
maintain it, and it will bring contentment.)

Then, by the waterside, among the tortoises
with their mild and lively eyes, with crested larks
fluttering around Him, so light
they rested on a blade of grass
without bending it, He came among us
and lifted His unmangled hand:
These beauties,
these earth-flowers growing and blowing, what are they?
The spectacle of your humiliation!
If a man choose to enter the kingdom of peace
he shall not cease from struggle until he fail,
and having failed he will be astonished,
and having been astonished will rule,
and having ruled will rest.

Our dream curdled.
We awoke, and began to thirst
for the restoration of our house.
One morning, in a slow paroxysm of rage,
we found His corpse stretched on the threshold.[2]

1. Kinsella has coedited *An Duanaire: Poems of the Dispossessed 1600-1900*. The latter word refers to those Irish Gaels who lost their lands and rights after English invasion. Many 'poems of the dispossessed' in Irish explore the ancient equation between the disinherited Gaels and the wandering children of Israel.
2. The reference here, based on Renan's *Vie de Jesus* (1863) is to the murder of John the Baptist. The shadow of violence falls across the original Christian message of peace.

from: ONE AND OTHER POEMS (1974)

His Father's Hands

I drank firmly
and set the glass down between us firmly.
You were saying.

My father.
Was saying.

His finger prodded and prodded,
marring his point. Emphas-
emphasemphasis.

I have watched
his father's hands before him

cupped, and tightening the black Plug[1]
between knife and thumb,
carving off little curlicues
to rub them in the dark of his palms,

or cutting into new leather at his bench,
levering a groove open with his thumb,
insinuating wet sprigs for the hammer.

He kept the sprigs in mouthfuls
and brought them out in silvery
units between his lips.

I took a pinch out of their hole
and knocked them one by one into the wood,
bright points among hundreds gone black,
other children's — cousins and others, grown up.

Or his bow hand scarcely moving,
scraping in the dark corner near the fire,
his plump fingers shifting on the strings.

To his deaf, inclined head
he hugged the fiddle's body,
whispering with the tune

with breaking heart
whene'er I hear
in privacy, across a blocked void,

1. A form of tobacco, cut into shreds for insertion into a pipe.

the wind that shakes the barley.[2]
The wind...
round her grave...

on my breast in blood she died...
But blood for blood without remorse
I've ta'en...

Beyond that.

*

Your family, Thomas, met with and helped
many of the Croppies[3] in hiding from the Yeos[4]
or on their way home after the defeat
in south Wexford. They sheltered the Laceys
who were later hanged on the Bridge in Ballinglen
between Tinahely and Anacorra.[5]

From hearsay, as far as I can tell
the Men Folk were either Stone Cutters
or masons or probably both.
In the 18
and late 1700s even the farmers
had some other trade to make a living.

They lived in Farnese among a Colony
of North of Ireland or Scotch settlers left there
in some of the dispersals or migrations
which occurred in this Area of Wicklow and
Wexford
and Carlow. And some years before that time
the Family came from somewhere around Tullow.

Beyond that.

*

Littered uplands. Dense grass. Rocks everywhere,
wet underneath, retaining memory of the long cold.

First, a prow of land
chosen, and webbed with tracks;
then boulders chosen
and sloped together, stabilized in menace.

I do not like this place.
I do not think the people who lived here
were ever happy. It feels evil.
Terrible things happened.
I feel afraid here when I am on my own.

*

Dispersals or migrations.
Through what evolutions or accidents
toward that peace and patience
by the fireside, that blocked gentleness...

That serene pause, with the slashing knife,
in kindly mockery,
as I busy myself with my little nails
at the rude block, his bench.

The blood advancing
— gorging vessel after vessel —
and altering in them
one by one.

Behold, that gentleness already
modulated twice, in others:
to earnestness and iteration;
to an offhandedness, repressing various impulses.

*

Extraordinary ... The big block — I found it
years afterward in a corner of the yard
in sunlight after rain
and stood it up, wet and black:
it turned under my hands, an axis
of light flashing down its length,
and the wood's soft flesh broke open,
countless little nails
squirming and dropping out of it.

from:
OUT OF IRELAND (1987)

The Furnace

Imperishable creatures
returning into God's light.
A resurrection, not a vanishing.

Intensifying, as iron
melts in the furnace
— intensified into flowing fire,

2. The title of an Irish folk-dance and its accompanying music.
3. Rebels in 1798, named for their close-cropped hairstyles.
4. i.e. yeomen, soldiers of the crown forces of occupation.
5. Parishes in County Wexford.

aching for a containing Shape.
Eriugena's[1] notion matching
my half-baked, bodily own,

who have *consigned*
my designing will stonily
to your flames

and will turn again toward the same furnace
that melted the union of our will
to ineffable zero[2]

how many times in its radiant clasp
(a cancellation
certainly speechless for a minute or two)

in token of the Union and the Light.
Until gender returned
and we were made two again

Male and Female
in punishment for Man's will
and reminded of our Fall.

In token of which
I plant this dry kiss
in your rain-wet hair.

1. Johannes Scottus (Ériugena) (*c.*810-*c.*877), Irish philosopher who was dubbed the 'first scholastic' and 'father of speculative philosophy'.
2. Ériugena believed in an androgynous godhead, in keeping with St Paul's avowal that 'after baptism there is neither male nor female'.

Entrance

Crows scoured the wet evening clean
above our heads.

Two languages interchanged.

We came to a halt
with our half-certainties:

that love is
to clasp simply,
question fiercely;

and the artistic act...
long library bodies, their pens
distinct against the sinking sun.

JOHN MONTAGUE
(1929-)

[A more rhetorical poet than Kinsella, John Montague has, at times, cast himself quite unashamedly in the bardic role of spokesperson for the tribe. The emphatic rhythms and stark images, however, are qualified by an Audenesque irony and love of the grotesque. Montague excels as a lyricist of the passing mood, but also as a more analytical poet of the postmortem. Much of his work is an attempt to live the past again, in hopes of making greater sense of the present.]

from:
FORMS OF EXILE (1958)

Speech for an Ideal Irish Election

Then the visionary lady[1]
Walked like a magician's daughter
Across green acres of Ireland;
The broad bright sword
Of the politician's word
Summoned applause in every square.

The unseen[2] inhabited
A well, a corner of a field;
Houses assumed magic light
From patriots' memory;
Assemblies knelt in awe before
The supernatural in a shaking tree.

The light that never was
Enlarged profile, gun and phrase:
Green of the grass worn
On shoulder as catalytic token;

1. An image of Ireland: Cathleen ní Houlihan, whose four green fields awaited liberation.

2. i.e. fairies.

Acrid speech of rifle and gun
Easing neurosis into definite action.

The house subsides into stillness,
Buried bombs ignore the spade.
The evening light, suitably grave,
Challenges renewed activity.
The transfigured heroes assume
Grey proportions of statuary.

Now the extraordinary hour of calm
And day of limitation.
The soft grasses stir
Where unfinished dreams
Are buried with the Fianna[3]
In that remote rock cave.

Who today asks for more
— Smoke of battle blown aside —
Than the struggle with casual
Graceless unheroic things,
The greater task of swimming
Against a slackening tide?

3. An ancient military troop of mercenaries.

The Trout

Flat on the bank I parted
Rushes to ease my hands
In the water without a ripple
And tilt them slowly downstream
To where he lay, tendril light,
In his fluid sensual dream.

Bodiless lord of creation
I hung briefly above him
Savouring my own absence
Senses expanding in the slow
Motion, the photographic calm
That grows before action.

As the curve of my hands
Swung under his body
He surged, with visible pleasure.
I was so preternaturally close
I could count every stipple
But still cast no shadow, until

The two palms crossed in a cage
Under the lightly pulsing gills.
Then (entering my own enlarged
Shape, which rode on the water)
I gripped. To this day I can
Taste his terror on my hands.

from: POISONED LANDS (1961)

[A revised edition of *Poisoned Lands* appeared in 1977. The text is of that edition. The 1961 text differed in detail. In line 15 of the first poem below, 'lonely' has replaced 'ravening'; in the third line of the last stanza 'Fomorian' was 'Formorian', and the 'Billy Eagleson' of stanza five was 'Billy Harbison'.]

Like Dolmens Round my Childhood, the Old People

Like dolmens[1] round my childhood, the old people.

Jamie MacCrystal sang to himself,
A broken song, without tune, without words;
He tipped me a penny every pension day,
Fed kindly crusts to winter birds.
When he died, his cottage was robbed,
Mattress and money box torn and searched.
Only the corpse they didn't disturb.

Maggie Owens was surrounded by animals,
A mongrel bitch and shivering pups,
Even in her bedroom a she-goat cried.
She was a well of gossip defiled,[2]
Fanged chronicler of a whole countryside:
Reputed a witch, all I could find
Was her lonely need to deride.

The Nialls lived along a mountain lane
Where heather bells bloomed, clumps of foxglove.
All were blind, with Blind Pension and Wireless,
Dead eyes serpent-flicked as one entered
To shelter from a downpour of mountain rain.
Crickets chirped under the rocking hearthstone
Until the muddy sun shone out again.

1. Prehistoric chambers of erect stones, supporting a flatter cross stone.
2. Edmund Spenser described Chaucer as 'well of English undefiled' (*The Faerie Queene*, IV, 2, stanza 32).

Mary Moore lived in a crumbling gatehouse,
Famous as Pisa for its leaning gable.
Bag-apron and boots, she tramped the fields
Driving lean cattle from a miry stable.
A by-word for fierceness, she fell asleep
Over love stories, Red Star and Red Circle,
Dreamed of gypsy love rites, by firelight sealed.

Wild Billy Eagleson married a Catholic servant girl
When all his Loyal family passed on:
We danced round him shouting 'To Hell with King
Billy,'[3]
And dodged from the arc of his flailing blackthorn.[4]
Forsaken by both creeds, he showed little concern
Until the Orange drums banged past in the summer
And bowler and sash[5] aggressively shone.

Curate and doctor trudged to attend them,
Through knee-deep snow, through summer heat,
From main road to lane to broken path,
Gulping the mountain air with painful breath.
Sometimes they were found by neighbours,
Silent keepers of a smokeless hearth,
Suddenly cast in the mould of death.

Ancient Ireland, indeed! I was reared by her
bedside,
The rune[6] and the chant, evil eye and averted head,
Fomorian[7] fierceness of family and local feud.
Gaunt figures of fear and of friendliness,
For years they trespassed on my dreams,
Until once, in a standing circle of stones,
I felt their shadows pass

Into the dark permanence of ancient forms.

3. William of Orange, victor at the battle of the Boyne (1690) and hero of Ulster protestants.
4. A walking-stick hewn from the tree of that name.
5. The uniform of marching members of the Orange Order.
6. spell, magical song.
7. A warlike tribe of prehistoric Ireland.

[In the 1961 edition, 'A Welcoming Party' was entitled 'Auschwitz, mon amour'. A stanza has been omitted between stanzas 5 and 6.]

A Welcoming Party

Wie war das möglich?[1]

That final newsreel of the war:
A welcoming party of almost shades
Met us at the cinema door
Clicking what remained of their heels.

From nests of bodies like hatching eggs
Flickered insectlike hands and legs
And rose an ululation,[2] terrible, shy;
Children conjugating the verb 'to die'.

One clamoured mutely of love
From a mouth like a burnt[3] glove;
Others upheld hands bleak as begging bowls
Claiming the small change of our souls.

Some smiled at us as protectors.
Can these bones live?[4]
Our parochial brand of innocence
Was all we had to give.

To be always at the periphery[5] of incident
Gave my childhood its Irish dimension;
Yet doves of mercy, as doves of air,
Can falter here as anywhere.

That long dead Sunday in Armagh
I learned one meaning of total war
And went home to my Christian school
To kick a football through the air.

1. How is that possible?

2. lament, wailing.
3. 'burned' in the 1961 edition.
4. cf. Ezekiel 37.3: 'Son of man, can these bones live?'
5. Ireland was neutral in World War II.

from: A CHOSEN LIGHT (1967)

All Legendary Obstacles

All legendary obstacles lay between
Us, the long imaginary plain,
The monstrous ruck of mountains
And, swinging across the night,
Flooding the Sacramento, San Joaquin,
The hissing drift of winter rain.

All day I waited, shifting
Nervously from station to bar
As I saw another train sail
By, the San Francisco Chief or

Golden Gate, water dripping
From great flanged wheels.

At midnight you came, pale
Above the negro porter's lamp.
I was too blind with rain
And doubt to speak, but
Reached from the platform
Until our chilled hands met.

You had been travelling for days
With an old lady, who marked
A neat circle on the glass
With her glove, to watch us
Move into the wet darkness
Kissing, still unable to speak.

Back to School

Halting in Dungannon[1] between trains
We often wandered outside town
To see the camp where German
Prisoners[2] were kept. A moist litter
Of woodshavings showed
Ground hastily cleared, and then —

The huge parallelogram
Of barbed wire, nakedly measured
And enclosed like a football field
With the guard towers rising, aloof
As goalposts, at either end.

Given length and breadth we knew
The surface area the prisoners paced
As one hung socks to dry outside
His Nissen hut,[3] another tried
To hum and whistle *Lili Marlene*:[4]
They seemed to us much the same

As other adults, except in their
Neutral dress, and finding it normal
To suffer our gaze, like animals,
As we squatted and pried, for an hour
Or more, about their human zoo

1. A market town in County Tyrone.
2. Northern Ireland was officially on the Allied side in World War II, and there were prisoner-of-war camps near Dungannon.
3. Corrugated steel sheet huts, named after Lieutenant Colonel Peter Nissen (1871-1930), a British mining engineer.
4. Usually spelt Lilli Marlene, a favourite song of German soldiers in World War II, as sung by Marlene Dietrich.

Before it was time for shopfronts,
Chugging train, Vincentian school.[5]
A small incident, soon submerged
In our own brisk, bell-dominated rule;
Until, years later, I saw another camp —
Rudshofen in the fragrant Vosges —[6]

Similar, but with local improvements:
The stockade where the difficult knelt,
The laboratory for minor experiments,
The crematorium for Jews and Gypsies
Under four elegant pine towers, like minarets.

This low-pitched style seeks exactness
Decided not to betray the event.
But as I write, the grid of barbed
Wire rises abruptly around me
The smell of woodshavings plugs
My nostrils, a carrion stench.

5. St Patrick's College, Armagh, run by the Vincentian fathers.
6. A department of north-eastern France, in the Lorraine region.

The Siege of Mullingar, 1963

At the Fleadh Cheoil[1] in Mullingar[2]
There were two sounds, the breaking
Of glass, and the background pulse
Of music. Young girls roamed
The streets with eager faces,
Shoving for men. Bottles in
Hand, they rowed out a song:
Puritan Ireland's dead and gone,
A myth of O'Connor and O'Faoláin.[3]

In the early morning the lovers
Lay on both sides of the canal
Listening on Sony transistors
To the agony of Pope John.[4]

1. A festival of traditional Irish music, revived in the 1960s.
2. A market town in County Westmeath, in the midlands of Ireland.
3. Frank O'Connor and Seán O'Faoláin were the realists of the post-Revival generation, noted for their searing criticisms of censorship and narrow-mindedness in the early decades of the new state. This refrain parodies the chorus of W.B. Yeats's 'September 1913:' 'Romantic Ireland's dead and gone,/It's with O'Leary in the grave.' The poem's title parodies Gaelic dance-tunes such as 'The Siege of Ennis'.
4. Pope John XXIII died slowly on the June bank holiday weekend of 1963.

Yet it didn't seem strange, or blasphemous,
This ground bass of death and
Resurrection, as we strolled along:
Puritan Ireland's dead and gone,
A myth of O'Connor and O'Faoláin.

Further on, breasting the wind
Waves of the deserted grain harbour
We saw a pair, a cob and his pen,[5]
Most nobly linked. Everything then
In our casual morning vision
Seemed to flow in one direction,
Lines simple as a song:
Puritan Ireland's dead and gone,
A myth of O'Connor and O'Faolain.

5. A male and female swan.

To Cease

for Samuel Beckett

To cease
to be human.

To be
a rock down
which rain pours,
a granite jaw
slowly discoloured.

Or a statue
sporting a giant's beard
or verdigris or rust
in some forgotten
village square.

A tree worn
by the prevailing winds
to a diagram of
tangled branches:
gnarled, sapless, alone.

To cease
to be human
and let birds soil
your skull, animals rest
in the crook of your arm.

To become
an object, honoured
or not, as the occasion demands;
while time bends you slowly
back to the ground.

from: THE ROUGH FIELD (1972)

A Lost Tradition

All around, shards of a lost tradition:
From the Rough Field I went to school
In the Glen of the Hazels. Close by
Was the bishopric of the Golden Stone;
The cairn of Carleton's[1] homesick poem.

Scattered over the hills, tribal
And placenames, uncultivated pearls.
No rock or ruin, dun[2] or dolmen
But showed memory defying cruelty
Through an image-encrusted name.

The heathery gap where the Rapparee,[3]
Shane Barnagh, saw his brother die —
On a summer's day the dying sun
Stained its colours to crimson:
So breaks the heart, Brish-mo-Cree.[4]

The whole landscape a manuscript
We had lost the skill to read,
A part of our past disinherited;
But fumbled, like a blind man,
Along the fingertips of instinct.

The last Gaelic speaker in the parish
When I stammered my school Irish
One Sunday after mass, crinkled
A rusty litany of praise:
Tá an Ghaeilge againn arís ...[5]

1. William Carleton (1794-1869), Ulster catholic writer who turned protestant on his arrival in Dublin. Author of *Traits and Stories of the Irish Peasantry* (1830-33).
2. fort.
3. An outlaw who lived under protection of the woods.
4. Irish: *bris mo chroí* (break my heart).
5. We have the Irish again.

Tír Eoghain: Land of Owen,
Province of the O'Niall;
The ghostly tread of O'Hagan's
Barefoot gallowglasses[6] marching
To merge forces in Dun Geanainn[7]

Push southward to Kinsale!
Loudly the war-cry is swallowed[8]
In swirls of black rain and fog
As Ulster's pride, Elizabeth's foemen,
Founder in a Munster bog.

6. mercenary soldiers; *gall-oglaigh* means 'foreign soldiers', since many came from Scotland.
7. The Irish name for Dungannon. The reference is to the wars of Hugh O'Neill against the Elizabethan armies of the 1590s.
8. A parody of the second line of the song 'O'Donnell Abu': 'Loudly the war-cries arise on the vale'. The defeat of the Ulster armies at Kinsale in 1601 signalled the collapse of the ancient Gaelic order in Ireland.

from:
A SLOW DANCE (1975)

Mount Eagle

I

The eagle looked at this changing world;
sighed and disappeared into the mountain.

Before he left he had a last reconnoitre:
the multi-coloured boats in the harbour

Nodded their masts, and a sandy white
crescent of strand smiled back at him.

How he liked the slight, drunk lurch
of the fishing fleet, the tide hoist-

ing them a little, at their ropes' end.
Beyond, wrack, and the jutting rocks

emerging, slowly, monsters stained
and slimed with strands of seaweed.

Ashore, beached boats and lobster
pots, settled as hens in the sand.

II

Content was life in its easiest form;
another was the sudden, growling storm

which the brooding eagle preferred
bending his huge wings into the winds'

wild buffeting, or thrusting down along
the wide sky, at an angle, slideways to

survey the boats, scurrying homewards,
tacking against the now contrary winds,

all of whom he knew by their names.
To be angry in the morning, calmed

by midday, but brooding again in
the evening was all in a day's quirk

with lengthy intervals for silence,
gliding along, like a blessing, while

the fleet toiled on earnestly beneath
him, bulging with a fine day's catch.

III

But now he had to enter the mountain.
Why? Because a cliff had asked him?
The whole world was changing, with one
language dying, and another encroaching,
bright with buckets, cries of children.
There seemed to be no end to them,
and the region needed a guardian —
so the mountain had told him. And

A different destiny lay before him:
to be the spirit of that mountain.
Everyone would stand in awe of him.
When he was wrapped in the mist's caul
they would withdraw because of him,
peer from behind blind, or curtain.
When he lifted his wide forehead
bold with light, in the morning,
they would all laugh and smile with him.
It was a greater task than an eagle's
aloofness, but sometimes, under his oilskin
of coiled mist, he sighed for lost freedom.

Dowager

I dwell in this leaky Western castle.
American matrons weave across the carpet,
Sorefooted as camels, and less useful.

Smooth Ionic columns hold up a roof.
A chandelier shines on a foxhound's coat:
The grandson of a grandmother I reared.

In the old days I read or embroidered,
But now it is enough to see the sky change,
Clouds extend or smother a mountain's shape.

Wet afternoons I ride in the Rolls;
Windshield wipers flail helpless against the rain:
I thrash through pools like smashing panes of glass.

And the light afterwards! Hedges steam,
I ride through a damp tunnel of sweetness,
The bonnet strewn with bridal hawthorn

From which a silver lady leaps, always young.
Alone, I hum with satisfaction in the sun,
An old bitch, with a warm mouthful of game.

Small Secrets

Where I work
out of doors
children come
to present me
with an acorn
a pine cone —
small secrets —

and a fat
grass snail
who uncoils
to carry his
whorled house
over the top
of my table.

With a pencil
I nudge him
back into
himself, but
fluid horns
unfurl, damp
tentacles, to

probe, test
space before
he drags his
habitation
forward again
on his single
muscular foot

rippling along
its liquid self-
creating path.
With absorbed,
animal faces
the children
watch us both

but he will
have none of
me, the static
angular world
of books, papers —
which is neither
green nor moist —

only to climb
around, over
as with rest-
less glistening
energy, he races
at full tilt
over the ledge

onto the grass.
All I am left
with is, between
pine cone & acorn
the silver smear
of his progress
which will soon

wear off, like
the silvery galaxies,
mother of pearl
motorways, woven
across the grass
each morning by
the tireless snails

of the world,
minute as grains
of rice, gross
as conch or
triton,[1] bequeath-
ing their shells
to the earth.

1. Genus of gasteropods, with shells that can be used like conches (i.e. shells that double as trumpets).

from: THE GREAT CLOAK (1978)

She Walks Alone

In the white city of Evora,[1] absence accosted me,
You were reading in bed, while I walked all night
alone.
Were you worried about me, or drifting towards
sleep?

I saw the temple of Diana, bone white in the
moonlight.
I made a private prayer to her, for strength to
continue:
Not since convent days have I prayed so earnestly.

A dog came out of the shadows, brushed against my
leg.
He followed me everywhere, pushing his nose into
my hand.
Soon the cats appeared, little scraggly bundles of
need.

There were more monuments, vivid as
hallucinations.
Suddenly, a young man stepped out of the shadows:
I was not terrified, as I might have been at home.

Besides, he was smiling & gentle as you used to be.
'A kiss' he pleads 'a kiss' in soft Portuguese.
I quickened my step, but he padded behind me.

He looked so young, my heart went out to him.
I stopped in the shadows under the Cathedral.
We kissed, and the tears poured down my face.

1. An ancient Portuguese city about seventy miles south-east of Lisbon, where there are ruins of a Roman temple (the so-called temple of Diana).

JAMES SIMMONS

(1933-)

from: ENERGY TO BURN (1971)

[Wry, humorous and populist in appeal, the lyrics of James Simmons are heard to best advantage when accompanied by his music. Although resolutely rooted in Northern Ireland, his is a 1960's sensibility that has much in common with that of the Liverpool Poets and the 'performance artists' of that decade.]

The Silent Marriage[1]

A song

With your clothes on the chair
and one white sheet above you
I have no need of words
to explain how I love you.
Every touch of delight
through the long wedding night
is defining our love.
With this kiss I thee wed.

If our luck should run out
and love withers and dies, love,
don't try out of kindness
to save me with lies, love.
You won't need to explain
that I'm single again
and the marriage is done
when your kiss says goodbye.

1. The Irish 'alternative' to divorce, whereby marriage partners, by strategies of mutual tolerance and shrewd avoidance, continue to share a house but not a life.

from: THE LONG SUMMER STILL TO COME (1973)

Didn't He Ramble

for Michael Longley

'The family wanted to make a bricklayer of him, but Ferd. was too smooth and clever a fellow. He preferred

to sit in the parlour out of the sun and play piano.'
Henry Morton[1]

There was a hardware shop in Main Street[2] sold
records as well as spades and plastic bowls.
Joe, the assistant, had a taste for jazz.
The shop being empty as it mostly was
I tried out records, then, like seeing the light,
but genuine, I heard Josh White:
I'm going to mo-o-ve you, way on the outskirts of town.
Where was my turntable to set it down!
A voice styled by experience, learning to make
music listening to Blind Willie Blake,
walking the streets of a city, avoiding cops,
toting a cheap guitar and begging box.

The campus poets used to write of saxophones
disgustedly and sneer at gramophones;
but the word of life, if such a thing existed,
was there on record among the rubbish listed
in the catalogues of Brunswick and H.M.V.,[3]
healing the split in sensibility.[4]
Tough reasonableness and lyric grace
together, in poor man's dialect.
Something that no one taught us to expect.
Profundity without the po-face[5]
of court and bourgeois modes. This I could use
to live and die with. Jazz. Blues.
I love the music and the men who made
the music, and instruments they played:
saxophone, piano, trumpet, clarinet,
Bill Broonzy, Armstrong, Basie, Hodges, Chet
Baker, Garner, Tommy Ladnier,
Jelly Roll Morton, Bessie Smith, Bechet,
and Fats Waller,[6] the scholar-clown of song
who sang *Until the Real Thing Comes Along*.
Here was the risen people,[7] their feet
dancing, not out to murder the elite:
'Pardon me, sir, may we be free?
The kitchen staff is having a jamboree.'

1. Henry S. Morton (1907-85), jazz trombonist, reminiscing about Ferdinand Joseph ('Jelly Roll') La Menthe Morton (1890-1941), the great pianist and one of the creators of New Orleans jazz.
2. The relative 'that' which is suppressed here, as often in Hiberno-English.
3. Names of record companies, HMV being 'His Master's Voice'.
4. A reference to T.S. Eliot's theory of a post-Renaissance 'dissociation of sensibility', a split between thought and feeling. See Eliot's *The Metaphysical Poets* (1921).
5. i.e. solemn face.
6. All leading jazz musicians and singers.
7. A phrase used often by Irish socialists to describe the Irish insurgents who followed Connolly and Larkin.

History records how people cleared the shelves
of record shops, discovering themselves,
making distinctions in the ordinary,
seeing what they'd been too tired to see;
but most ignored the music. Some were scared,
some greedy, some condemned what they hadn't
heard,
some sold cheap imitations, watered it down,
bribed Fats to drink too much and play the clown
instead of the piano, and failed — the man was wise,
he did both painlessly. Jazz is a compromise:
you take the first tune in your head and play
until it's saying what you want to say.
'I ain't got no diplomas,' said Satchmo,
'I look into my heart and blow.'[8]

What if some great ones took to drugs and drink
and killed themselves? Only a boy could think
the world cures easy, and want to blame
someone. I know I'll never be the same.
A mad world my masters![9] We might have known
that Wardell Gray[10] was only well spoken,
controlled and elegant on saxophone.
He appeared last in a field with his neck broken.
The jazz life did it, not the Ku Klux Klan.
Whatever made the music killed the man.

8. A parody of Sir Philip Sidney's line from *Astrophel and Stella* (1591): 'Fool!' said my muse to me, 'look in thy heart, and write.'
Satchmo (Satchelmouth) was the nickname of the American jazz trumpeter and bandleader Louis Armstrong (1900-71).
9. John Taylor (1580-1653), *Western Voyage*, line 1: 'Tis a mad world, my masters'.
10. Wardell Gray (1921-55), a famous jazz saxophonist.

from:
POEMS 1956-1986 (1986)

Ulster Says Yes[1]

One Protestant Ulsterman
wants to confess this:
we frightened you Catholics, we gerrymandered,[2]
we applied injustice.

1. When the Anglo-Irish Agreement of November 1985 offered the government of the Irish Republic a limited monitoring role in Northern Ireland affairs, unionist banners of opposition bore the legend 'Ulster Says No'.
2. Voting districts were rearranged to ensure the continuing victory of the Unionist Party.

However, we weren't Nazis or Yanks,
so measure your fuss
who never suffered like Jews or Blacks,
not here, not with us;

but, since we didn't reform ourselves,
since we had to be caught
red-handed, justice is something
we have to be taught.

DESMOND O'GRADY

(1935-)

from: THE DARK EDGE OF EUROPE (1967)

[Desmond O'Grady is in part a committed modernist with Classical and European allegiances, who has lived in Rome and on the Greek island of Paros, has worked with Ezra Pound and appeared in Fellini's *La Dolce Vita*. He is also a manifestation of the native traditions of wandering scholar and rambling bard — he has translated the Irish folk poet Antoine Raftery, and taught at the universities of Alexandria and Cairo. O'Grady has lived out the role of the poet with great glamour and panache. His poems are stylistically high-flown, inclined to grand emotional and political gestures. His romantic extremism, his appetite for epic subjects and his big rhetorical note make him something of a rarity among modern Irish poets.]

The Poet in Old Age Fishing at Evening

for Ezra Pound

Comes a time
When even the old and familiar ideas
Float out of reach of the mind's hooks,
And the soul's prime
Has slipped like a fish through the once high weirs
Of an ailing confidence. O where are the books
On this kind of death?

Upright as love
Out on the tip of a tail of rock,
The sea ravelling off from the eye,
The line like the nerve
Straining the evening back from the clock,
He merges awhile into the lie
Of his own silhouette.

from: A LIMERICK RAKE: VERSIONS FROM THE IRISH (1978)

[These translations from Antoine Raftery may be compared with those of Douglas Hyde (see Volume II pp. 723-28). The first is a version of *Cill Aodáin, nó Condae Mhuigheo* while the second is the famous praise-poem in honour of Mary Hynes, a local beauty — *Máire ní Heidhin nó An Pósae Glegheal.*]

The County Mayo

Now with the spring
the days will stretch,
then after the Feast
my feet will itch,
and I'll shuffle and shunt
till I rise and go
and plant myself down
in the County Mayo.

At first in Claremorris
I'll stay, I'm thinking,
and in Balla below it
I'll start my drinking;
from there on to Killty
for a month or more,
then the last few miles
to Ballinamore.

Well honest to God
my heart whips up —
like the wind whips up
and scatters the fog —

when I think of Carna
or Balla below,
of the Gap o' the Bushes
or the plains of Mayo.

In Killaden town
there's everything good,
rich produce and fruit
and all kinds of food;
and now if I stood
among my kin
I'd feel, not old,
but young again.

The Lass from Ballynalee

On my way to Mass
to say a prayer,
the wind was high
sowing rain,
I met a girl
with wind-wild hair
and madly fell
in love again.

I spoke with learning,
charm and pride
and, as was fitting,
answered she:
'My mind is now
well satisfied
so walk me back
to Ballynalee.'

Given the offer
I didn't delay
and breaking a laugh
with this willing young lass,
I swung with her over
the fields through the day
till shortly we reached
the rump of the house.

A table with glasses
and drink was set
and then says the lassie
turning to me:
'You're welcome Raftery,
so drink a wet
to love's demands
in Ballynalee.'

I've walked in my time
across England and France,
from Spain to Greece
and back by sea;
met many a girl
at many a dance,
but none had an airy
grace like she.

If I had the power
and the flower of youth,
I'd find her out
wherever she'd be,
I'd comb all the coasts
from Cork to Beirut
to live with this gem
from Ballynalee.

No matter her name,
she's a well-bred lass,
with the looks and grace
of the queen of a tribe;
looks two hundred scholars
en masse,
or the pick of the poets
could never describe.

Venus and Deirdre
were no more grand,
nor Helen who launched
the ships in the sea.
She's the brightest blossom
of all Ireland,
this fabulous flower
from Ballynalee.

My star of light,
my autumn sun,
my curly head,
my summer sky —
in Sunday's shadow
let's rise and run
and arrange the place
where we shall lie.

All I ask is to sing
your say each Sunday night.
with drink on the table
and you on my knee.

Dear God high in heaven
who gives and takes sight,
grant me this grace
in Ballynalee.

BRENDAN KENNELLY

(1936-)

from:
COLLECTION ONE (1966)

[One of Ireland's most prolific and accessible poets, Brendan Kennelly combines an urgent utterance with a compellingly personal voice. Never obscure, his poems are more often declamatory than quiet, and the best of them carry an almost Blakean sense of indignation or anger. Some others are more sensual and erotic in effect; but all adopt a tone of voice so insistent that it seems almost to will its audience into being. For Kennelly, art is trapped energy, dramatically disciplined; and so it is unsurprising that he has attempted to rework many poetic effects in the dramatic form, with his *Antigone*, produced in 1988 at the Peacock Theatre, Dublin.]

My Dark Fathers

My dark[1] fathers lived the intolerable day
Committed always to the night of wrong,
Stiffened at the hearthstone, the woman lay,
Perished feet nailed to her man's breastbone.[2]
Grim houses beckoned in the swelling gloom
Of Munster fields where the Atlantic night
Fettered the child within the pit of doom,
And everywhere a going down of light.

And yet upon the sandy Kerry shore
The woman once had danced at ebbing tide
Because she loved flute music — and still more
Because a lady wondered at the pride
Of one so humble. That was long before
The green plant[3] withered by an evil chance;
When winds of hunger howled at every door
She heard the music dwindle and forgot the dance.

Such mercy as the wolf receives was hers
Whose dance became a rhythm in a grave,
Achieved beneath the thorny savage furze
That yellowed fiercely in a mountain cave.
Immune to pity, she, whose crime was love,
Crouched, shivered, searched the threatening sky,
Discovered ready signs, compelled to move
Her to her innocent appalling cry.

Skeletoned in darkness, my dark fathers lay
Unknown, and could not understand
The giant grief that trampled night and day,
The awful absence[4] moping through the land.
Upon the headland, the encroaching sea
Left sand that hardened after tides of Spring,
No dancing feet disturbed its symmetry
And those who loved good music ceased to sing.

Since every moment of the clock
Accumulates to form a final name,
Since I am come of Kerry clay and rock,
I celebrate the darkness and the shame
That could compel a man to turn his face
Against the wall,[5] withdrawn from light so strong
And undeceiving, spancelled in a place
Of unapplauding hands and broken song.

1. In Irish 'dark' can also mean 'blind'.
2. An incident reported during the Great Famine; bodies of a dead couple were found in this formation.
3. The potato, a staple food of the Irish peasantry.
4. Ireland's population was halved, by death and emigration, in the decade after the Famine.
5. An incident at a wedding attended by the poet, when a blind man sang with his back to the company.

The Thatcher

He whittled scallops for a hardy thatch,
His palm and fingers hard as the bog oak.
You'd see him of an evening, crouched
Under a tree, testing a branch. If it broke
He grunted in contempt and flung it away,
But if it stood the stretch, his sunken blue
Eyes briefly smiled. Then with his long knife he
Chipped, slashed, pointed. The pile of scallops grew.

Astride a house on a promised day,
He rammed and patted scallops into place
Though wind cut his eyes till he seemed to weep.
Like a god after making a world, his face
Grave with the secret, he'd stare and say —
'Let the wind rip and the rain pelt. This'll keep.'

Yes

I love the word
And hear its long struggle with no
Even in the bird's throat
And the budging crocus.
Some winter's night
I see it flood the faces
Of my friends, ripen their laughter
And plant early flowers in
Their conversation.

You will understand when I say
It is for me a morning word
Though it is older than the sea
And hisses in a way
That may have given
An example
To the serpent itself.
It is this ageless incipience
Whose influence is found
In the first and last pages of books,
In the grim skin of the affirmative battler
And in the voices of women
That constitutes the morning quality
Of yes.

We have all
Thought what it must be like
Never to grow old,
The dreams of our elders have mythic endurance
Though their hearts are stilled
But the only agelessness
Is yes.

I am always beginning to appreciate
The agony from which it is born.
Clues from here and there
Suggest such agony is hard to bear
But is the shaping God
Of the word that we
Sometimes hear, and struggle to be.

from: CROMWELL (1983)

['Cromwell' is essentially a contrapuntal work, pitting various 'protestant' against 'catholic' stereotypes, eliciting from them Kennelly's own preoccupation with the discord between conventional forms of behaviour and the freer condition of being.]

Reading Aloud

Oliver Cromwell is a cultured man
Though he's not fond of the drama.
'Buffún'[1] he said 'I once read all *The Faerie Queene*[2]
Or, to be more precise, I tried to.
Spenser had a little estate down in Cork
And he found peace there, deep, unending,
Like his poem.But think of all the work
He put for years into these singing
Stanzas. That poem is one of England's glories.
Few Englishmen bother to read it now
Though much of it is still fresh as a berry
On a hedge in the middle of the Maharees.[3]
I plan to spend next winter reading it aloud
To myself in my little estate down in Kerry.'

1. Irish adaptation of 'buffoon', sometimes shortened in this sequence to 'Buff'.
2. Edmund Spenser's epic poem, part of which was reputedly conceived during the author's service as an imperial agent in Ireland.
3. cf. J.M. Synge: 'The best plays of Ben Jonson and Molière can no more go out of fashion than the blackberries on the hedges' (Preface to *The Tinker's Wedding*). The Maharees are islands off the coast of Kerry.

Radio

The otherness of God hits me like icy rain
Or like that babble of European
Accents dancing from wall to wall when
I'm gregarious enough to turn the radio on.

An old creamery-manager left it to me in his will.
It has a brown snout, wrinkles and black nobs
That plug you in to any studio hellhole
Of your choice. It harangues my skull, chest, ribs

Like the voice of God banging Moses what to do
When his randy band surrendered to havoc
In their sweaty groping through excessive sun.

My creamery-manager measured milk justly
Every morning. Moses, I hear, came unstuck.

The otherness of my radio bleeps me alone.

Mud

Then I saw all the bodies becoming mud
Like philosophy or my best attempts to speak and
sing
Of the generating works of God
Manifest in men, women and children becoming
Mud:
and I see this toothless man
Taking a narrow path through a cornfield
Beating a goatskin drum in the morning sun.
Dozens of concerned faces come to see
And offer food to the man who tells them they are
mud
Singing:
'Let our prime boys and beautiful girls know
They are mud in the hands of the makers of pots
and plates
And cups at their lips on wine-happy nights
And walls between neighbours to challenge the
wind
And the makers themselves are mud when the same
winds blow
Like thoughts like old coats wrapped round a
freezing mind.'
Do you blame me, then, if on certain days
I tend to see my friends as articulate lumps of mud?
At such moments, I grow intolerant of lipstick
While fashions in clothes and writing almost cause
me
To scream in the streets. How pay proper homage
To the best-dressed Mud of the Year? Yet there
have been
Distinguished lumps of mud such as Oliver and Ed
Spenser down in Cork stanzaing his Queene
Despite the afforested natives threatening to drive
him mad.
The buried fertility of mud is thrilling:
Disciplined armies are stirring underground,
Sound chroniclers, critics, advocates of the life to
come,
Scrupulous creators of new styles of killing
And a youngster, awakening to the people of his
mind,
Flexing his fingers to play a goatskin drum.

'Therefore, I Smile.'

'Under it all' Oliver said, 'The problem was
simple.
How could I make Ireland work?
The Irish hate work, not knowing what it means.
I do. Work exists. It is inevitable and stark,
A dull, fierce necessity. Later ages may consider it
Superfluous but my glimpses of this world were
true.
I looked, I saw, I considered, I did what
Was necessary. To live is to work. To be is to do.

Put a man in a field
A soldier fighting a wall
A wife in bed
A whore in a street
A king on a throne

Someone must dig a grave for the dead
And the dead must rot.

Even dead flesh works in the earth
But not the Irish. Buff, not you, not your
countrymen.
They will prattle, argue, drink, yarn, but not
Work. Someone had to teach them
Not to idle their lives away.
I taught them to do things my way.
Against their will
I gave them a style.
I tendered them the terrible gift of my name,
Knowing they would make songs about me
Echoing curses soaked in verbal bile
Twisted poems and stories
To make me an excuse for what they
Would fail to do, to be, being themselves.

I am Oliver Cromwell still.

Therefore, I smile.'

Am

When I consider what all this has made me
I marvel at the catalogue:
I am that prince of liars, Xavier O'Grady,
I am Tom Gorman, dead in the bog,
I am Luke O'Shea in Limerick prison,
I sell subversive papers at a church gate,
Men astound me, I am outside women,
I have fed myself on the bread of hate,
I am an emigrant in whose brain
Ireland bleeds and cannot cease
To bleed till I come home again
To fields that are a parody of peace.
I sing tragic songs, I am madly funny,
I'd sell my country for a fist of money
I am a big family,
I am a safe-hearted puritan
Blaming it all on the Jansenists
Who, like myself, were creatures on the run.
I am a home-made bomb, a smuggled gun.
I like to whine about identity,
I know as little of love as it is possible
To know, I bullshit about being free,
I'm a softie crying at the sound of a bell,
I have a tongue to turn snakespittle to honey,
I smile at the themes of the old poets,
Being lost in myself is the only way
I can animate my foolish wits.

Do I believe myself? I spill
My selves. Believe me, if you will.

SEAMUS HEANEY

(1939-)

from:
DEATH OF A NATURALIST
(1966)

[The most vigilant of poets, Seamus Heaney can be deceptively winsome, but his poems almost invariably engage in ethical as well as aesthetic probing. His poetry is excavatory in every sense, reaching down into the ground and back into the past. His language is self-conscious, but also self-aware; and has, over the years, grown more densely allusive. A sustained attempt is made to locate the northern violence in wider patterns of universal history. The poet has also consoled himself with sweet sounds in the face of barbarism, only to accuse himself of moral evasiveness. Recent work has seen Heaney coming to terms with such predecessors in the Irish pantheon as Carleton, Joyce, Yeats and Kavanagh.]

The Early Purges[1]

I was six when I first saw kittens drown.
Dan Taggart pitched them, 'the scraggy[2] wee shits',
Into a bucket; a frail metal sound,

Soft paws scraping like mad. But their tiny din
Was soon soused. They were slung on the snout
Of the pump and the water pumped in.

'Sure isn't it better for them now?' Dan said.
Like wet gloves they bobbed and shone till he sluiced
Them out on the dunghill, glossy and dead.

Suddenly frightened, for days I sadly hung
Round the yard, watching the three sogged remains
Turn mealy and crisp as old summer dung

Until I forgot them. But the fear came back
When Dan trapped big rats, snared rabbits, shot
 crows
Or, with a sickening tug, pulled old hens' necks.

Still, living displaces false sentiments
And now, when shrill pups are prodded to drown
I just shrug, 'Bloody pups'. It makes sense:

'Prevention of cruelty' talk cuts ice in town
Where they consider death unnatural,
But on well-run farms pests have to be kept down.

1. An ironic political echo of Stalin's purges of Russian dissidents in the 1930s.
2. scrawny.

Follower

My father worked with a horse-plough,
His shoulders globed like a full sail strung
Between the shafts and the furrow.
The horses strained at his clicking tongue.

An expert. He would set the wing
And fit the bright steel-pointed sock.[1]
The sod rolled over without breaking.
At the headrig,[2] with a single pluck

Of reins, the sweating team turned round
And back into the land. His eye
Narrowed and angled at the ground,
Mapping the furrow exactly.

I stumbled in his hob-nailed wake,
Fell sometimes on the polished sod;
Sometimes he rode me on his back
Dipping and rising to his plod.

I wanted to grow up and plough,
To close one eye, stiffen my arm.
All I ever did was follow
In his broad shadow round the farm.

I was a nuisance, tripping, falling,
Yapping always. But today
It is my father who keeps stumbling
Behind me, and will not go away.

1. ploughshare.
2. A headland in a ploughed field.

from: DOOR INTO THE DARK (1969)

Requiem for the Croppies[1]

The pockets of our great coats full of barley —
No kitchens on the run, no striking camp —
We moved quick and sudden in our own country.
The priest lay behind ditches with the tramp.

1. Rebel farmers and labourers who rose unsuccessfully with pikes and pitchforks against the British in 1798. They were so named because of their closely cropped hairstyle.

A people, hardly marching — on the hike —
We found new tactics happening each day:
We'd cut through reins and rider with the pike
And stampede cattle into infantry,
Then retreat through hedges where cavalry must be
thrown.
Until, on Vinegar Hill,[2] the fatal conclave.
Terraced thousands died, shaking scythes at
cannon.
The hillside blushed, soaked in our broken wave.
They buried us without shroud or coffin
And in August the barley grew up out of the grave.

2. The scene of a crucial final battle, by the river Slaney in County Wexford, where the rebels were crushed.

Bogland

for T. P. Flanagan

We have no prairies
To slice a big sun at evening —
Everywhere the eye concedes to
Encroaching horizon,

Is wooed into the cyclops' eye
Of a tarn.[1] Our unfenced country
Is bog that keeps crusting
Between the sights of the sun.

They've taken the skeleton
Of the Great Irish Elk[2]
Out of the peat,[3] set it up
An astounding crate full of air.

Butter sunk under
More than a hundred years
Was recovered salty and white.
The ground itself is kind, black butter

Melting and opening underfoot,
Missing its last definition
By millions of years.
They'll never dig coal here,

Only the waterlogged trunks
Of great firs, soft as pulp.

1. A small mountain lake.
2. An extinct giant deer, known only by its remains.
3. Bogland, whose chemical properties preserve objects buried there.

Our pioneers keep striking
Inwards and downwards,

Every layer they strip
Seems camped on before.
The bogholes might be Atlantic seepage.
The wet centre is bottomless.

from:
WINTERING OUT (1972)

Traditions

For Tom Flanagan

I

Our guttural muse
was bulled[1] long ago
by the alliterative tradition,
her uvula grows

vestigial, forgotten
like the coccyx
or a Brigid's Cross[2]
yellowing in some outhouse

while custom, that 'most
sovereign mistress',[3]
beds us down into
the British isles.

II

We are to be proud
of our Elizabethan English:[4]
'varsity', for example,
is grass-roots stuff with us;

we 'deem' or we 'allow'
when we suppose
and some cherished archaisms
are correct Shakespearean.

1. impregnated.
2. A crucifix woven of straw, with sides irregularly joined, often hung in cottages.
3. cf. *Othello*, I.3.223: 'opinion, a most sovereign mistress ...'.
4. Many elements of Hiberno-English are petrified forms of the language that was brought to Ireland by Elizabethan occupiers.

Not to speak of the furled
consonants of lowlanders
shuttling obstinately
between bawn and mossland.[5]

III

MacMorris, gallivanting
round the Globe,[6] whinged
to courtier and groundling
who had heard tell of us

as going very bare
of learning, as wild hares,
as anatomies of death:
'What ish my nation?'

And sensibly, though so much
later, the wandering Bloom
replied, 'Ireland,' said Bloom,
'I was born here. Ireland.'[7]

5. Words with shifting meanings for northern Scots planters and southern Gaels. For planters, 'bawn' was a walled fort; for Gaels, a place for milking cows. How complicated these matters can become is clear from the name of the parish in which Heaney grew up, Mossbawn.
6. A stage-Irishman in Shakespeare's *Henry V* who excitably protests loyalty to the crown, despite the doubts of his colleagues in the king's army. The Globe was the London theatre where many of Shakespeare's plays were first staged.
7. Leopold Bloom in the 'Cyclops' episode of James Joyce's *Ulysses*.

The Tollund Man

I

Some day I will go to Aarhus[1]
To see his peat-brown head,
The mild pods of his eye-lids,
His pointed skin cap.

In the flat country nearby
Where they dug him out,
His last gruel[2] of winter seeds
Caked in his stomach,

1. A site in Denmark, where 'bog people' dug out of the Jutland marshes are displayed, their bodies preserved by the bog's chemical properties. The Tollund Man was sacrificed to the earth-goddess in a fertility rite; Heaney found in this an image of a Mother Ireland devouring her own children.
2. A thin food made by boiling oatmeal; also a pun on 'cruel'.

Naked except for
The cap, noose and girdle,
I will stand a long time.
Bridegroom to the goddess,

She tightened her torc[3] on him
And opened her fen,[4]
Those dark juices working
Him to a saint's kept[5] body,

Trove of the turfcutters'
Honeycombed workings.
Now his stained face
Reposes at Aarhus.

II

I could risk blasphemy,[6]
Consecrate the cauldron bog
Our holy ground and pray
Him to make germinate

The scattered, ambushed
Flesh of labourers,
Stockinged corpses[7]
Laid out in the farmyards,

Tell-tale skin and teeth
Flecking[8] the sleepers
Of four young brothers, trailed
For miles along the lines.[9]

III

Something of his sad freedom
As he rode the tumbril
Should come to me, driving,
Saying the names

Tollund, Grabaulle, Nebelgard,[10]
Watching the pointing hands

3. A circular Celtic brooch, or a necklace in the form of a twisted band (like a type used to hang Tollund Man). There is also a sexual innuendo here.
4. A low marshland.
5. preserved, but also 'sexually available'.
6. i.e. by praying to a pagan god, accepting Tollund man as a saint, and reconstituting his pagan world in Christian terms.
7. Victims of violence in Northern Ireland.
8. Speckling with blood-stains, like traces of red in tweed.
9. An atrocity committed in the 1920s in Northern Ireland, when the bodies of four brothers were dragged along a railway line.
10. Names of places in Denmark where bodies were dug out. See P.V. Glob, *The Bog People* (London: Faber and Faber, 1969).

Of country people,
Not knowing their tongue.[11]

Out there in Jutland[12]
In the old man-killing parishes
I will feel lost,
Unhappy and at home.

11. Perhaps a reference to non-Irish speakers visiting the Gaeltacht.
12. The setting not just of Tollund Man's burial, but of many ferocious sea-battles in World War I.

from: NORTH (1975)

Viking Dublin: Trial Pieces

I

It could be a jaw-bone
or a rib or a portion cut
from something sturdier:
anyhow, a small outline

was incised, a cage
or trellis to conjure in.
Like a child's tongue
following the toils

of his calligraphy,
like an eel swallowed
in a basket of eels,
the line amazes itself

eluding the hand
that fed it,
a bill in flight,
a swimming nostril.

II

These are trial pieces,
the craft's mystery
improvised on bone:
foliage, bestiaries,[1]

interlacings elaborate
as the netted routes

1. Of a kind often found in Celtic art.

of ancestry and trade.[2]
That have to be

magnified on display[3]
so that the nostril
is a migrant prow
sniffing the Liffey,

swanning it up to the ford,[4]
dissembling itself
in antler combs, bone pins,
coins, weights, scale-pans.

III

Like a long sword
sheathed in its moisting
burial clays,
the keel stuck fast

in the slip of the bank,
its clinker-built[5] hull
spined and plosive
as *Dublin*.

And now we reach in
for shards of the vertebrae,
the ribs of hurdle,
the mother-wet caches —

and for this trial piece
incised by a child,
a longship,[6] a buoyant
migrant line.

IV

That enters my longhand,
turns cursive,[7] unscarfing
a zoomorphic[8] wake,
a worm of thought

I follow into the mud.
I am Hamlet the Dane,

skull-handler, parablist,
smeller of rot

in the state,[9] infused
with its poisons,
pinioned by ghosts
and affections,

murders and pieties,
coming to consciousness
by jumping in graves,
dithering, blathering.

V

Come fly with me,[10]
come sniff the wind
with the expertise
of the Vikings —

neighbourly, scoretaking
killers, haggers[11]
and hagglers, gombeen-men,[12]
hoarders of grudges and gain.

With a butcher's aplomb
they spread out your lungs
and made you warm wings
for your shoulders.

Old fathers,[13] be with us.
Old cunning assessors
of feuds and of sites
for ambush or town.

VI

'Did you ever hear tell,'
said Jimmy Farrell,
'of the skulls they have
in the city of Dublin?

White skulls and black skulls
and yellow skulls, and some

2. Dublin was the trading centre for Scandinavian invaders.
3. Like Heaney's poetic technique.
4. One of the Irish names for Dublin is 'Áth Cliath' (ford of the hurdles). The Liffey is the river that flows through Dublin.
5. Made of overlapping planks nailed down.
6. A characteristic vessel that ferried the Norse invaders.
7. A flowing style of handwriting.
8. Symbolic artistic representation in animal form.
9. cf. *Hamlet*: 'Something is rotten in the state of Denmark'.
10. A parody of a Frank Sinatra song of that title.
11. Breakers of ground, especially bogland.
12. Shopkeepers who charge extortionate prices and offer usurious loans to the rural Irish poor.
13. cf. the closing sentence of Joyce's *A Portrait of the Artist as a Young Man*: 'Old father, old artificer, stand me now and ever in good stead.'

with full teeth, and some
haven't only but one,'[14]

and compounded history
in the pan of 'an old Dane,
maybe, was drowned
in the Flood.'

My words lick around
cobbled quays, go hunting
lightly as pampooties[15]
over the skull-capped ground.

14. The quotations are from Act 3 of Synge's *The Playboy of the Western World*.
15. Light footwear, made of skins, worn by the Aran Islanders.

Punishment

I can feel the tug
of the halter[1] at the nape
of her neck, the wind
on her naked front.

It blows her nipples[2]
to amber beads,
it shakes the frail rigging
of her ribs.

I can see her drowned
body in the bog,
the weighing stone,
the floating rods and boughs.

Under which at first
she was a barked sapling[3]
that is dug up
oak-bone, brain-firkin:

her shaved head[4]
like a stubble of black corn,

1. A noose put around the neck of a female victim of an ancient Jutland punishment rite. She is paradoxically preserved by the weight of the bog that suffocates her.
2. The 'voyeur' theme resounds through the poem.
3. A covered young tree.
4. Republican militants in Northern Ireland often shaved the heads of women who fraternized with the British army, sometimes tarring and feathering them, and then fastening them to railings as a public warning.

her blindfold a soiled bandage,
her noose a ring

to store
the memories of love.
Little adulteress,
before they punished you

you were flaxen-haired,
undernourished, and your
tar-black face was beautiful.
My poor scapegoat,

I almost love you
but would have cast, I know,
the stones of silence.
I am the artful[5] voyeur

of your brain's exposed
and darkened combs,
your muscles' webbing
and all your numbered bones:

I who have stood dumb
when your betraying sisters,
cauled in tar,
wept by the railings,

who would connive
in civilized outrage[6]
yet understand the exact
and tribal, intimate revenge.

5. (i) artistic; (ii) evasive.
6. Middle-class platitudes against political violence.

Singing School

EXPOSURE[1]

It is December in Wicklow:
Alders dripping, birches
Inheriting the last light,
The ash tree cold to look at.

1. The title is ironic, self-deprecating.

A comet that was lost
Should be visible at sunset,
Those million tons of light
Like a glimmer of haws and rose-hips,

And I sometimes see a falling star.
If I could come on meteorite!
Instead I walk through damp leaves,
Husks, the spent flukes[2] of autumn,

Imagining a hero
On some muddy compound,
His gift like a slingstone
Whirled for the desperate.

How did I end up like this?
I often think of my friends'
Beautiful prismatic counselling
And the anvil brains of some who hate me

As I sit weighing and weighing
My responsible *tristia*.[3]
For what? For the ear? For the people?
For what is said behind-backs?

Rain comes down through the alders,
Its low conducive voices
Mutter about let-downs and erosions
And yet each drop recalls

The diamond absolutes.
I am neither internee[4] nor informer;
An inner émigré, grown long-haired
And thoughtful; a wood-kerne[5]

Escaped from the massacre,
Taking protective colouring
From bole and bark, feeling
Every wind that blows;

2. Breezes, or the husks and leaves piled up by the autumn winds.
3. sadness.
4. Political activists, jailed without trial, in Northern Ireland in or after August 1971.
5. A wood-dweller. In Elizabethan times 'kerne' equated with 'Irish rebel', since they attacked the occupying forces from the protective coverage of woods.

Who, blowing up these sparks
For their meagre heat, have missed
The once-in-a-lifetime portent,
The comet's pulsing rose.

from: FIELD WORK (1979)

The Skunk

Up, black, striped and damasked[1] like the chasuble[2]
At a funeral mass, the skunk's tail
Paraded the skunk. Night after night
I expected her like a visitor.

The refrigerator whinnied into silence.
My desk light softened beyond the verandah.
Small oranges loomed in the orange tree.
I began to be tense as a voyeur.

After eleven years I was composing
Love-letters again, broaching the word 'wife'
Like a stored cask, as if its slender vowel
Had mutated into the night earth and air

Of California. The beautiful, useless
Tank of eucalyptus spelt your absence.
The aftermath of a mouthful of wine
Was like inhaling you off a cold pillow.

And there she was, the intent and glamorous,
Ordinary, mysterious skunk,
Mythologized, demythologized,
Snuffing the boards five feet beyond me.

It all came back to me last night, stirred
By the sootfall of your things at bedtime,
Your head-town, tail-up hunt in a bottom drawer
For the black plunge-line nightdress.

1. Figured by weaving into material.
2. A sleeveless vestment worn over the alb by a priest while celebrating mass.

from: STATION ISLAND (1984)

[The poem below is a revised version of the poem published in 1984.]

Chekhov on Sakhalin[1]

for Derek Mahon

So, he would pay his 'debt to medicine'.
But first he drank cognac by the ocean
With his back to all he travelled there to face.
His head was swimming free as the troikas[2]

Of Tyumin, he looked down from the rail
Of his thirty years and saw a mile
Into himself as if he were clear water:
Lake Baikhal from the deckrail of the steamer.

So far away, Moscow was like lost youth.
Then should it have been an ulcer in the mouth,
That cognac the bewildered literati
Packed off with him to a penal colony —

Him, born, you may say, under the counter?[3]
At least that meant he knew its worth. No cantor[4]
In full throat by the iconostasis[5]
Got holier joy than he got from that glass

That shone and warmed like diamonds warming
On some pert young cleavage in a salon,
Inviolable and affronting.
He felt the glass go cold in the midnight sun.

When he staggered up and smashed it on the stones
It rang as clearly as the convicts' chains
That haunted him. All through the months to come
It rang on like the burden of his freedom

To try for the right tone — not tract, not thesis —
And walk away from floggings. He who thought to
  squeeze
His slave's blood out and waken the free man
Shadowed a convict guide through Sakhalin.

1. Anton Chekhov's friends presented him with a bottle of cognac on his departure for the prison island of Sakhalin in Siberia, where he spent the summer of 1890 interviewing its inmates, criminals and political prisoners.
2. Russian vehicles drawn by three horses harnessed abreast.
3. A reference to Chekhov's humble rural background.
4. The leader of the singing in a church choir.
5. A screen shutting off the sanctuary in the Russian Orthodox church, on which icons are placed.

[The second part of Heaney's long poem *Station Island* is set in a penitential place of pilgrimage in Lough Derg, Co. Donegal, where sinners walk in circles around ancient stones, praying for forgiveness. In the course of his pilgrimage, the poet meets a number of figures from the Irish literary tradition, ranging from William Carleton (in this section) to Patrick Kavanagh and James Joyce.

Recent revisions, not hitherto published, are included in this version of 'Station Island'.]

Station Island

II

I was parked on a high road, listening
to peewits and wind blowing round the car
when something came to life in the driving mirror,[1]

someone walking fast in an overcoat
and boots, bareheaded, big, determined
in his sure haste along the crown of the road

so that I felt myself the challenged one.
The car door slammed. I was suddenly out
face to face with an aggravated man

raving on about nights spent listening for
gun butts to come cracking on the door,
yeomen on the rampage, and his neighbour

among men, hammering home the shape of things.
'Round about here you overtook the women,'
I said, as the thing came clear. 'Your *Lough Derg*
  Pilgrim[2]

haunts me every time I cross this mountain —
as if I am being followed, or following.
I'm on my road there now to do the station.'[3]

'O holy Jesus Christ, does nothing change?'
His head jerked sharply side to side and up
like a diver's surfacing,

then with a look that said, *who is this cub*
anyhow, he took cognizance again
of where he was: the road, the mountain top,

1. A rear-view mirror cleverly captures the prevailing sense of this episode, that Ireland, facing into the future, is merely repeating her own past.
2. One of Carleton's literary works. Carleton, though born a catholic, turned protestant.
3. Literally, stations of the cross.

and the air, softened by a shower of rain,
worked on his anger visibly until:
'It is a road you travel on your own.

I who learned to read in the reek of flax
and smelled hanged bodies rotting on their gibbets[4]
and saw their looped slime gleaming from the sacks —

hard-mouthed Ribbonmen and Orange bigots
made me into the old fork-tongued turncoat
who mucked the byre[5] of their politics.

If times were hard, I could be hard too.
I made the traitor in me sink the knife.
And maybe there's a lesson there for you,

whoever you are, wherever you come out of,
for though there's something natural in your smile
there's something in it strikes me as defensive.'

'The angry role was never my vocation,'
I said. 'I come from County Derry,
where the last marching bands of Ribbonmen[6]

On Patrick's Day still played their hymns to Mary.
Obedient strains like theirs tuned me first
and not that harp of unforgiving iron

the Fenians strung. A lot of what you wrote
I lived again: this Lough Derg station,
flax-pullings, dances, fair days, crossroads chat

and the shaky local voice of education.
All that. And the usual Orange drums.
And your neighbours on the road at night with guns.'[7]

'I know, I know, I know, I know,' he said,
'but you have to try to make sense of what comes.
Remember everything and keep your head.'[8]

4. In 1819, travelling through County Louth, Carleton saw bodies of Ribbonmen hanged on gibbets for murdering catholic peasants who would not join their society. He described the scene in *Wildgoose Lodge* (see Volume II, p. 873). Ribbonmen were members of a secret catholic sect, active in the north-west of Ireland in the early nineteenth century.
5. cow-house.
6. A reference to the Ancient Order of Hibernians, a peaceful catholic nationalist grouping, noted for its fairly mild politics; but noisy bands marched on St Patrick's Day, as a counter to Orange marching on 12 July.
7. Protestants had (and still hold) almost all legally held guns in Northern Ireland.
8. cf. Brian Friel's *Translations*: 'It is a form of madness to remember everything.'

'The alders in the hedge,' I said, 'mushrooms,
dark-clumped grass where cows or horses dunged,
the cluck when pith-lined chestnut shells split open

in your hand, the melt of shells corrupting,
old jampots in a drain clogged up with mud —'
But now Carleton was interrupting:

'All this is like a trout kept in a spring
or maggots sown in wounds instead of ointment —
another life that cleans our element.

We are earthworms of the earth, and all that
has gone through us is what will be our trace.'
He turned on his heel when he was saying this

and headed up the road at the same hard pace.

[This final section of 'Station Island' recounts the poet's imaginary meeting with James Joyce.
It is a revised version of the published poem.]

XII

Like a convalescent, I took the hand
stretched down from the jetty, sensed again
an alien comfort as I stepped on ground

to find the helping hand still gripping mine,
fish-cold and bony, but whether to guide
or to be guided I could not be certain

for the tall man in step at my side
seemed blind, though he walked straight as a rush
upon his ash plant,[1] his eyes fixed straight ahead.

Then I knew him in the flesh
out there on the tarmac among the cars,
wintered hard and sharp as a blackthorn bush.

His voice eddying with the vowels of all rivers
came back to me, though he did not speak yet,
a voice like a prosecutor's or a singer's,

cunning, narcotic, mimic, definite
as a steel nib's downstroke, quick and clean,
and suddenly he hit a litter basket

1. Stephen Dedalus carries an ash plant in *Ulysses*.

with his stick, saying, 'Your obligation
will not be shed by fasting and bare feet.
What you do you must do on your own.

The main thing is to write
for the joy of it. Cultivate a work-lust
that imagines its haven like your hands at night

dreaming the sun in the sunspot of a breast.
Stay hungry as you are. Get dangerous.
Take off from here. And don't be so earnest,

so ready with the sackcloth and the ashes.
Let go, let fly,[2] forget.
You've listened long enough. Now strike your
  note.'

It was as if I had stepped free into space
alone with nothing that I had not known
already. Raindrops blew in my face

as I came to and heard the harangue and jeers
going on and on. 'The English
belongs to us. You are raking at dead fires,

set among my stars — that one entry
has been a sort of password in my ears,
the collect of a new epiphany,

rehearsing the old whinges at your age![3]
That subject people stuff is a cod's[4] game,
infantile, like this peasant pilgrimage.

You lose more of yourself than you redeem
doing the decent thing. Keep at a tangent.
When they make the circle wide, it's time to swim

out on your own and fill the element
with signatures on your own frequency,
echo soundings, searches, probes, allurements,

2. In *A Portrait of the Artist as a Young Man*, Stephen Dedalus resolves to 'fly' by the nets of language, nationality and religion.
3. The earlier version of these lines refers to an episode in *A Portrait*, in which Stephen uses the word 'tundish' to describe a funnel. The Englishman who is dean of studies at the university queries the meaning, remarking that he has never heard the word in his life, and implying that it is mere Hiberno-English. Later, in his diary for 13 April, Stephen writes: 'That tundish has been on my mind for a long time. I looked it up and find it English and good old blunt English too. Damn the dean of studies and his funnel! What did he come here for to teach us his own language or to learn it from us? Damn him one way or the other!'
4. fool's.

elver[5]-gleams in the dark of the whole sea.'
The shower broke in a cloudburst, the tarmac
fumed and sizzled. As he moved off quickly

the downpour loosed its screens round his straight
  walk.

5. A young eel.

The Master[1]

He dwelt in himself
like a rook in an unroofed tower.

To get close I had to maintain
a climb up deserted ramparts
and not flinch, not raise an eye
to search for an eye on the watch
from his coign[2] of seclusion.

Deliberately he would unclasp
his book of withholding
a page at a time and it was nothing
arcane, just the old rules
we all had inscribed on our slates.
Each character blocked on the parchment secure
in its volume and measure.
Each maxim given its space.

Like quarrymen's hammers and wedges proofed
by intransigent service.
Like coping stones where you rest
in the balm of the wellspring.

How flimsy I felt climbing down
the unrailed stairs on the wall,
hearing the purpose and venture
in a wingflap above me.

1. Possibly a reference to W.B. Yeats, and his tower at Ballylee, Co. Galway, although it more directly means 'schoolmaster'.
2. A vantage-point, especially if hidden.

The Old Icons[1]

Why, when it was all over, did I hold on to them?

1. A poem about Leonard MacNally (1752-1820), a barrister who defended colleagues in the United Irishmen at treason trials, but was revealed after his death to have betrayed many of them, passing on their secrets to the British government (see Volume I, pp. 934-35). MacNally was also a playwright and lyricist. Heaney's poem was

A patriot with folded arms in a shaft of light:
the barred cell window and his sentenced face
are the only bright spots in the little etching.

An oleograph of snowy hills, the outlawed priest's[2]
red vestments, with the redcoats[3] toiling closer
and the lookout coming like a fox across the gaps.

And the old committee of the sedition-mongers,[4]
so well turned out in their clasped brogues[5] and
waistcoats,
the legend of their names an informer's list

prepared by neat-cuffs, third from left, at rear,
more compelling than the rest of them,
pivoting an action that was his rack[6]

and others' ruin, the very rhythm of his name
a register of dear-bought treacheries
grown transparent now, and inestimable.[7]

---

written in the 1980s against a background of 'supergrass' trials, in the course of which many political prisoners bought their freedom by giving evidence in juryless courts against former comrades.

2. Under the Penal Laws, many priests illicitly celebrated mass in the open air at so-called Mass-rocks.
3. British soldiers.
4. revolutionaries.
5. shoes.
6. An instrument for inflicting torture.
7. That which cannot be judged, but also used in England as superlative of approbation.

from: THE HAW LANTERN (1987)

From the Republic of Conscience

I

When I landed in the republic of conscience
it was so noiseless when the engines stopped
I could hear a curlew high above the runway.

At immigration, the clerk was an old man
who produced a wallet from his homespun coat
and showed me a photograph of my grandfather.

The woman in customs asked me to declare
the words of our traditional cures and charms
to heal dumbness and avert the evil eye.

No porters. No interpreter. No taxi.
You carried your own burden and very soon
your symptoms of creeping privilege disappeared.

II

Fog is a dreaded omen there but lightning
spells universal good and parents hang
swaddled infants in trees during thunderstorms.

Salt is their precious mineral. And seashells
are held to the ear during births and funerals.
The base of all inks and pigments is seawater.

Their sacred symbol is a stylized boat.
The sail is an ear, the mast a sloping pen,
The hull a mouth-shape, the keel an open eye.

At their inauguration, public leaders
must swear to uphold unwritten law and weep
to atone for their presumption to hold office —

and to affirm their faith that all life sprang
from salt in tears which the sky-god wept
after he dreamt his solitude was endless.

III

I came back from that frugal republic[1]
with my two arms the one length, the customs
woman
having insisted my allowance was myself.

The old man rose and gazed into my face
and said that was official recognition
that I was now a dual citizen.[2]

He therefore desired me when I got home
to consider myself a representative
and to speak on their behalf in my own tongue.

Their embassies, he said, were everywhere
but operated independently
and no ambassador would ever be relieved.

---

1. A phrase sometimes used to describe Eamon de Valera's aspiration to an Ireland without great wealth or great poverty.
2. Dual citizenship was one of the 'solutions' to the Northern Ireland conflict advocated by some intellectuals from the Republic in submissions to the New Ireland Forum of the early 1980s.

[There follow two of a sequence of eight sonnets written 'in memoriam' of the poet's mother, who died in 1984.]

Clearances

6

In the first flush of the Easter holidays
The ceremonies during Holy Week
Were highpoints of our *Sons and Lovers* phase.
The midnight fire. The paschal candlestick.
Elbow to elbow, glad to be kneeling next
To each other up there near the front
Of the packed church, we would follow the text
And rubrics for the blessing of the font.
As the hind longs for the streams, so my soul ...
Dippings. Towellings. The water breathed on.
The water mixed with chrism[1] and with oil.
Cruet[2] tinkle. Formal incensation
And the psalmist's outcry taken up with pride:
Day and night my tears have been my bread.

1. Consecrated oil, unction.
2. A vessel containing water and wine, used in the catholic mass.

7

In the last minutes he said more to her
Almost than in all their life together.
'You'll be in New Row on Monday night
And I'll come up for you and you'll be glad
When I walk in the door ... Isn't that right?'
His head was bent down to her propped-up head.
She could not hear but we were overjoyed.
He called her good and girl. Then she was dead,
The searching for a pulsebeat was abandoned
And we all knew one thing by being there.
The space we stood around had been emptied
Into us to keep, it penetrated
Clearances that suddenly stood open.
High cries were felled and a pure change happened.

MICHAEL LONGLEY

(1939-)

from: AN EXPLODED VIEW (1973)

[Longley may have more in common with the semi-detached suburban muse of Philip Larkin and post-war England than with Heaney or Montague. His self-effacing courtesy, his dry good humour, and his addiction to off-key closures, all align him with British post-modernism, as is manifest in his homage to L.S. Lowry. And yet the very fact that he should apply these techniques to the Belfast of the 'Troubles' indicates also his sustained attempt to widen the traditions of modern Irish poetry. With Derek Mahon, he represents a strand of Ulster that identifies itself as British and asserts its rights to the English lyric.]

The Adulterer

I have laid my adulteries
Beneath the floorboards, then resettled
The linoleum so that
The pattern aligns exactly,

Or, when I bundled into the cupboard
Their loose limbs, their heads,
I papered over the door
And cut a hole for the handle.

There they sleep with their names,
My other women, their underwear
Disarranged a little,
Their wounds closing slowly.

I have watched in the same cracked cup
Each separate face dissolve,
Their dispositions
Cluster like tea leaves,

Folding a silence about my hands
Which infects the mangle,[1]
The hearth rug, the kitchen chair
I've been meaning to get mended.

1. A rolling-press for smoothing linen.

Wounds

Here are two pictures from my father's head —
I have kept them like secrets until now:
First, the Ulster Division at the Somme[1]
Going over the top with 'Fuck the Pope!'
'No Surrender!': a boy about to die,
Screaming 'Give 'em one for the Shankill!'[2]
'Wilder than Gurkhas'[3] were my father's words
Of admiration and bewilderment.
Next comes the London-Scottish padre
Resettling kilts with his swagger-stick,[4]
With a stylish backhand and a prayer.
Over a landscape of dead buttocks
My father followed him for fifty years.
At last, a belated casualty,
He said — lead traces flaring till they hurt —
'I am dying for King and Country, slowly.'
I touched his hand, his thin head I touched.

Now, with military honours of a kind,
With his badges, his medals like rainbows,
His spinning compass, I bury beside him
Three teenage soldiers,[5] bellies full of
Bullets and Irish beer, their flies undone.
A packet of Woodbines[6] I throw in,
A lucifer[7], the Sacred Heart of Jesus
Paralysed as heavy guns put out
The night-light in a nursery for ever;
Also a bus-conductor's uniform —
He collapsed beside his carpet-slippers
Without a murmur, shot through the head
By a shivering boy who wandered in
Before they could turn the television down
Or tidy away the supper dishes.
To the children, to a bewildered wife,
I think 'Sorry Missus' was what he said.

1. A major battle (1916) of World War I, in which many Ulstermen died.
2. The Shankill Road, epicentre of protestant Belfast.
3. Members of a Hindu people, living mainly in Nepal, who serve as a special unit in the British and Indian armies. Gurkhas are noted for their courage and ferocity.
4. A short cane carried by army officers.
5. Three British soldiers, among the first to be killed in the present phase of hostilities in Northern Ireland.
6. One of the cheapest brands of cigarette; a part of British working-class culture.
7. A match.

from: MAN LYING ON A WALL (1976)

The Lodger

The lodger is writing a novel.
We give him the run of the house
But he occupies my mind as well —
An attic, a lumber-room
For his typewriter, notebooks,
The slowly accumulating pages.

At the end of each four-fingered
Suffering line the angelus rings —
A hundred noons and sunsets
As we lie here whispering,
Careful not to curtail our lives
Or change the names he has given us.

Man Lying on a Wall

Homage to L. S. Lowry[1]

You could draw a straight line from the heels,
Through calves, buttocks and shoulderblades
To the back of the head: pressure points
That bear the enormous weight of the sky.
Should you take away the supporting structure
The result would be a miracle or
An extremely clever conjuring trick.
As it is, the man lying on the wall
Is wearing the serious expression
Of popes and kings in their final slumber,
His deportment not dissimilar to
Their stiff, reluctant exits from this world
Above the shoulders of the multitude.

It is difficult to judge whether or not
He is sleeping or merely disinclined
To arrive punctually at the office
Or to return home in time for his tea.
He is wearing a pinstripe suit, black shoes
And a bowler hat: on the pavement
Below him, like a relic or something
He is trying to forget, his briefcase
With everybody's initials on it.

1. L(awrence) S(tephen) Lowry (1887-1976), English painter, remembered for his industrial landscapes of the North of England, peopled by 'matchstick' men and women.

from:
THE ECHO GATE (1979)

Second Sight

My father's mother had the second sight.
Flanders[1] began at the kitchen window —
The mangle rusting in No Man's Land,[2] gas
Turning the antimacassars[3] yellow
When it blew the wrong way from the salient.[4]

In bandages, on crutches, reaching home
Before his letters, my father used to find
The front door on the latch, his bed airing.
'I watched my son going over the top.
He was carrying flowers out of the smoke.'

I have brought the *Pocket Guide to London*,
My *Map of the Underground*, an address —
A lover looking for somewhere to live,
A ghost among ghosts of aunts and uncles
Who crowd around me to give directions.

Where is my father's house, where my father?
If I could walk in on my grandmother
She'd see right through me and the hallway
And the miles of cloud and sky to Ireland.
'You have crossed the water to visit me.'

1. A region of Belgium overlapping parts of Holland and France, where many Ulster soldiers of the British army perished in World War I.
2. Contested unoccupied area between rival armies.
3. Coverings for the backs and arms of chairs, to prevent staining by hair-oils.
4. A projection of the forward line into enemy-held territory.

SEAMUS DEANE
(1940-)

from:
GRADUAL WARS (1972)

[Born and reared in Derry, Seamus Deane has shown in his poetry, as in his criticism, a concern with the sources and effects of violence, and with the compensating power of culture to restore some sense of the human community. Like Brian Friel, he writes much of the human memory, its capacity to distort and also to restore. His more recent work has evinced a strong sense of European history and a desire to locate the Irish experience as part of that wider pattern.]

Roots

Younger,
I felt the dead
Drag at my feet
Like roots
And at every step
I heard them
Crying
Stop.

Older,
I heard the roots
Snap. The crying
Stopped. Ever since
I have been
Dying
Slowly
From the top.

Return

The train shot through the dark.
Hedges leapt across the window-pane
Trees belled in foliage were stranded,
Inarticulate with rain.
A blur of lighted farm implied
The evacuated countryside.

I am appalled by its emptiness
Every valley glows with pain
As we run like a current through;
Then the memories darken again.
In this Irish past I dwell
Like sound implicit in a bell.

The train curves round a river,
And how tenderly its gouts of steam
Contemplate the nodding moon
The waters from the clouds redeem
Two hours from Belfast
I am snared in my past.

Crusts of light lie pulsing
Diamanté with the rain
At the track's end. Amazing!
I am in Derry once again
Once more I turn to greet
Ground that flees from my feet.

from:
HISTORY LESSONS (1983)

A World Without a Name

All the colours of paradise
Lined up in bottles behind the bar.
Golden djinns, seraphs with their hearts
Of white locked up in glass
Eyed us through the smoke
And thunder-dazzle of voices.

Back there in that distant war
Beyond where the rain hums,
The sky still scorches above
The estuary when the sun burns
In the water and the wind lifts
Masonries of waves off the rocks.

This is what you saw on leaving.
Was it not better left?
But you could remember too
Wallpaper images from a nursery,
Daffodils nudging a slow Spring,
Roses a cabbage of fire.

But for us it was always a street
Hissing with rain, a ditch running
Svelte with filth, mouths crabbed
With rancour and wrong, the smooth
Almond of speech burnt. And the
Cropped hair of children with lice,

The stench of wood logged
And simmering with maggots,
The sloth-cold of the nights.
And all those colours of paradise,
A sorcery of golds and whites.
It was a world without a name;

The world we flew from and became.

History Lessons

for Ronan Sheehan and Richard Kearney

'The proud and beautiful city of Moscow
Is no more.' So wrote Napoleon to the Czar.
It was a November morning when we came
On this. I remember the football pitches
Beyond, stretched into wrinkles by the frost.
Someone was running across them, late for school,
His clothes scattered open by the wind.

Outside Moscow we had seen
A Napoleonic, then a Hitlerian dream
Aborted. The firegold city was burning
In the Kremlin domes, a sabred Wehrmacht[1]
Lay opened to the bone, churches were ashen
Until heretics restored their colour
And their stone. Still that boy was running.

Fragrance of Christ, as in the whitethorn
Brightening through Lent, the stricken aroma
Of the Czars in ambered silence near Pavlovsk,[2]
The smoking gold of icons at Zagorsk,
And this coal-smoke in the sunlight
Stealing over frost, houses huddled up in
Droves, deep drifts of lost

People. This was history, although the State
Exam confined Ireland to Grattan[3] and allowed
Us roam from London to Moscow. I brought
Black gladioli bulbs from Samarkand
To flourish like omens in our cooler air;
Coals ripening in a light white as vodka.
Elections, hunger-strikes and shots

Greeted our return.[4] Houses broke open
In the season's heat and the bulbs

1. The armed forces of the German Third Reich 1935-45.
2. The family of Czar Nicholas II were killed here.
3. Henry Grattan (1746-1820), architect of the Irish parliament 1782-1800.
4. A reference to the spring and summer of 1981, a period of electoral instability in the South and of hunger-strikes (in which ten men died) in the North.

Burned in the ground. Men on ladders
Climbed into roselight, a roof was a swarm of
fireflies
At dusk. The city is no more. The lesson's learned.
I will remember it always as a burning
In the heart of winter and a boy running.

Breaking Wood

I was breaking wood in the shed
As dark fell. The wind gusted
And slammed the door, pitching
Me into such blackness that I
Missed my stroke and struck
A spark from the floor.

It brought back my father
Chopping wood in autumn,
And with it came the smell
Of leaf-mould, the hinted
Flights of late swallows,
The shrivelled gold

Of wasps in the notches
Of wide-spoked webs. Memories
Stilled me so long it was dark
Before I rose to gather the sticks.
A sigh of resin and I felt
The stirring of seeds of regret

As I tumbled the white wood
Into the rumbling box
And heard the wind whip
On the trees and bend into
A straight stream of lament
At the razored edge of the wall.

White fall of wood and blue-red
Leaping spark, pitch black
Blow of wind, dark inks
Of still and moving waters,
The seasonable deaths of summers,
The unseasonable deaths of fathers. . . .

Should I have struck with the axe
Near darkness, called the spark
From his deep energies of enrichment
And decay? Still, in this tangled weather
I must break sticks for warmth
And split the flinty wind

For its interior noises.
Soon the red honeycomb of fire
Will sting the poker bright
Up half its length. Soon
The fume of wood upon the air
Will take my feeling to the night.

from:
SELECTED POEMS (1988)

Reading *Paradise Lost* in Protestant Ulster 1984

Should I give in to sleep? This fire's warm,
I know the story off by heart,
Was up so late last night and all the harm
That can be done is done. Far apart
From Milton's devils is the present crew
Of zombie soldiers and their spies,
Supergrasses in whose hiss
We hear the snake and sense the mist
Rise in dreams that crowd the new
Awaking with their demobbed cries.

In the old ground of apocalypse
I saw a broken church near where
Two lines of trees came to eclipse
The summer light. Beside the stair
A grey crow from an old estate
Gripped on the book of Common Prayer,
A rope of mice hung on a strip
Of altar-cloth and a blurring date
Smeared the stone beneath the choir.

Awake again, I see the window take
An arc of rainbow and a fusing rain.
None should break the union of this State
Which God with Man conspired to ordain.
But the woe the long evening brings
To the mazy ambushes of streets
Marks us more deeply now than that bower
Of deepest Eden in our first parents' hour
Of sexual bliss and frail enamourings
Could ever do. Our 'sovran Planter'[1] beats

Upon his breast, dyadic evil rules;
A syncope that stammers in our guns,

1. Milton, *Paradise Lost*, Book IV, line 691.

That forms and then reforms itself in schools
And in our daughters' couplings and our sons'.
We feel the fire's heat, Belial's doze;
A maiden city's burning on the plain;
Rebels surround us, Lord. Ah, whence arose
This dark damnation, this hot unrainbowed rain?

DEREK MAHON

(1941-)

from: NIGHT-CROSSING (1968)

[The most underrated Irish poet of the century, Mahon is finally elusive of all categories. Like Joyce, he has flown by the obvious entrapping nets — and then disappeared into his own handiwork. His style is self-deprecatory, his ironies often astringent, and his historical sense so acute that it can lead to an almost surreal telescoping of images. Behind all this may be detected the mind of a conscience-stricken anthropologist. A post-holocaust poet, in every sense, Mahon may yet prove to be the most durable talent of his generation. He writes not just of, but for, posterities.]

Glengormley[1]

'Wonders are many and none is more wonderful than man'
Who has tamed the terrier, trimmed the hedge
And grasped the principle of the watering-can.
Clothes-pegs litter the window ledge
And the long ships lie in clover.[2] Washing lines
Shake out white linen over the chalk thanes.[3]

Now we are safe from monsters, and the giants
Who tore up sods twelve miles by six
And hurled them out to sea to become islands[4]
Can worry us no more. The sticks
And stones that once broke bones[5] will not now harm
A generation of such sense and charm.

Only words hurt us now. No saint or hero,
Landing at night from the conspiring seas,
Brings dangerous tokens to the new era —[6]
Their sad names linger in the histories.
The unreconciled,[7] in their metaphysical pain,
Dangle from lamp-posts in the dawn rain;

And much dies with them. I should rather praise
A worldly time under this worldly sky —
The terrier-taming, garden-watering days
Those heroes pictured as they struggled through
The quick noose of their finite being. By
Necessity, if not choice, I live here too.

1. A region of Belfast.
2. i.e. lie in abundance, luxury (in Belfast harbour).
3. Tenants of the crown.
4. The legend explains the origin of the Giant's Causeway off the coast of Antrim.
5. The words of the rhyme are: 'Sticks and stones may break my bones/ But names can never hurt me.'
6. In former times, Irish rebels often secured help from overseas.
7. Perhaps those tied to lamp-posts for infractions of the local community code.

In Carrowdore[1] Churchyard

at the grave of Louis MacNeice

Your ashes will not stir, even on this high ground,
However the wind tugs, the headstones shake.
This plot is consecrated, for your sake,
To what lies in the future tense. You lie
Past tension now, and spring is coming round
Igniting flowers on the peninsula.

Your ashes will not fly, however the rough winds burst
Through the wild brambles and the reticent trees.
All we may ask of you we have. The rest
Is not for publication, will not be heard.
Maguire, I believe, suggested a blackbird
And over your grave a phrase from Euripides.

1. MacNeice's ashes were buried in his mother's grave at Carrowdore, Co. Antrim.

Which suits you down to the ground, like this
churchyard
With its play of shadow, its humane perspective.
Locked in the winter's fist, these hills are hard
As nails, yet soft and feminine in their turn
When fingers open and the hedges burn.
This, you implied, is how we ought to live —

The ironical, loving crush of roses against snow,
Each fragile, solving ambiguity.[2] So
From the pneumonia of the ditch, from the ague
Of the blind poet and the bombed-out town you
bring
The all-clear to the empty holes of spring;
Rinsing the choked mud, keeping the colours new.

2. See MacNeice's poem 'Snow' (p. 158 of the present volume).

['A Portrait of the Artist' initially was entitled 'Van Gogh among the Miners', then 'Van Gogh in the Borinage']

A Portrait of the Artist

for Colin Middleton

Shivering in the darkness
Of pits, slag heaps, beetroot fields,
I gasp for light and life
Like a caged bird in springtime
Banging the bright bars.

Like a glow-worm I move among
The caged Belgian miners,
And the light on my forehead
Is the dying light of faith.
God gutters down to metaphor —

A subterranean tapping, light
Refracted in a glass of beer
As if through a church window,
Or a basin ringed with coal dust
After the evening bath.

Theo, I am discharged for being
Over-zealous, they call it,
And not dressing the part.
In time I shall go south
And paint what I have seen —

A meteor of golden light
On chairs, faces and old boots,
Setting fierce fire to the eyes
Of sunflowers and fishing boats,
Each one a miner in disguise.

[First entitled 'Recalling Aran', the poem below was retitled in *Poems 1962-1978.*]

Thinking of Inishere in Cambridge, Massachusetts

for Eamon Grennan

A dream of limestone in sea light
Where gulls have placed their perfect prints.
Reflection in that final sky
Shames vision into simple sight;
Into pure sense, experience.
Atlantic leagues away tonight,
Conceived beyond such innocence,
I clutch the memory still, and I
Have measured everything with it since.

from: LIVES (1972)

Ecclesiastes[1]

God, you could grow to love it, God-fearing, God-
chosen purist little puritan that,
for all your wiles and smiles, you are (the
dank churches, the empty streets,
the shipyard silence, the tied-up swings[2]) and
shelter your cold heart from the heat
of the world, from woman-inquisition, from the
bright eyes of children. Yes you could
wear black, drink water, nourish a fierce zeal
with locusts and wild honey, and not
feel called upon to understand and forgive
but only to speak with a bleak
afflatus, and love the January rains when they
darken the dark doors and sink hard

1. The poem imagines God as a 'black protestant' preacher.
2. Protestant-controlled town councils in Northern Ireland refused to break the Sabbath by opening children's playgrounds on Sundays.

into the Antrim hills, the bog meadows, the heaped
graves of your fathers. Bury that red
bandana and stick, that banjo; this is your
country, close one eye and be king.
Your people await you, their heavy washing
flaps for you in the housing estates —
a credulous people. God, you could do it, God
help you, stand on a corner stiff
with rhetoric, promising nothing under the sun.

['An Image from Beckett' has been altered in some words and phrases since its first publication.]

An Image from Beckett

for Doreen

In that instant
There was a sea, far off,
As bright as lettuce,

A northern landscape
And a huddle
Of houses along the shore.

Also, I think, a white
Flicker of gulls
And washing hung to dry —

The poignancy of those
Back-yards — and the gravedigger
Putting aside his forceps.

Then the hard boards
And darkness once again.
But in that instant

I was struck
By the sweetness and light,
The sweetness and light,

Imagining what grave
Cities, what lasting monuments,
Given the time.

They will have buried
My great-grandchildren, and theirs,
Beside me by now
With a subliminal batsqueak
Of reflex lamentation.
Our tiny bones

Litter the rich earth,
Changing, second by second,
To civilizations.

It was good while it lasted,
And if it only lasted
The biblical span

Required to drop six feet
Through a glitter of wintry light,
There is No one to blame.

Still, I am haunted
By that landscape,
The soft rush of its winds,

The uprightness of its
Utilities and schoolchildren —
To whom in my will,

This, I have left my will.
I hope they have time,
And light enough, to read it.

I am Raftery[1]

I am Raftery, hesitant and confused among
the cold-voiced graduate students and inter-
changeable instructors. Were it not for the
nice wives who do the talking I would have
run out of hope some time ago, and of love.
I have traded-in the 'simplistic maunderings'
that made me famous, for a wry dissimulation,
an imagery of adventitious ambiguity dredged
from God knows what polluted underground spring.
Death is near, I have come of age, I doubt if
I shall survive another East Anglian[2] winter.
Scotch please, plenty of water. I am reading
Joyce by touch and it's killing me. Is it
empty pockets I play to? Not on your life,
they ring with a bright inflationary music —

1. This is a parody of the most famous lyric by the Gaelic poet Anthony Raftery (*c.*1784-1835), which begins: 'I am Raftery the poet/Full of hope and love'. It then lists his rich artistic endeavours, but ends 'Look at me, my face to the wall/Making music for empty pockets.'
2. The University of East Anglia is famous for its 'creative writing' courses, one of which Derek Mahon gave.

two seminars a week and my own place reserved
in the record library. Look at me now,
my back to the wall, taking my cue
from an idiot disc-jockey between commercials.

from: THE SNOW PARTY (1975)

[The initial title of this first poem was *'After Nerval'*.]

The Mute Phenomena

after Nerval

Your great mistake is to disregard the satire
Bandied among the mute phenomena.
Be strong if you must, your brusque hegemony
Means fuck-all to the somnolent sunflower
Or the extinct volcano. What do you know
Of the revolutionary theories advanced
By turnips, or the sex-life of cutlery?
Everything is susceptible, Pythagoras said so.[1]

An ordinary common-or-garden brick wall, the kind
For talking to or banging your head on,
Resents your politics and bad draughtsmanship.
God is alive and lives under a stone.
Already in a lost hub-cap is conceived
The ideal society which will replace our own.

1. A parodic echo of Yeats's *The Statues*, which opens 'Pythagoras planned it' and proceeds to argue for an animation of concrete objects.

A Disused Shed in Co. Wexford

Let them not forget us, the weak souls among the asphodels. — Seferis, *Mythistorema*[1]

for J. G. Farrell

Even now there are places where a thought might
grow —
Peruvian mines, worked out and abandoned
To a slow clock of condensation,
An echo trapped for ever, and a flutter
Of wildflowers in the lift-shaft,
Indian compounds where the wind dances
And a door bangs with diminished confidence,
Lime crevices behind rippling rainbarrels,
Dog corners for bone burials;
And in a disused shed in Co. Wexford,

Deep in the grounds of a burnt-out hotel,
Among the bathtubs and the washbasins
A thousand mushrooms crowd to a keyhole.
This is the one star in their firmament
Or frames a star within a star.
What should they do there but desire?
So many days beyond the rhododendrons
With the world waltzing in its bowl of cloud,
They have learnt patience and silence
Listening to the rooks querulous in the high wood.

They have been waiting for us in a foetor[2]
Of vegetable sweat since civil war days,
Since the gravel-crunching, interminable departure
Of the expropriated mycologist.[3]
He never came back, and light since then
Is a keyhole rusting gently after rain.
Spiders have spun, flies dusted to mildew
And once a day, perhaps, they have heard
something —
A trickle of masonry, a shout from the blue
Or a lorry changing gear at the end of the lane.

There have been deaths, the pale flesh flaking
Into the earth that nourished it;
And nightmares, born of these and the grim
Dominion of stale air and rank moisture.
Those nearest to the door grow strong —
'Elbow room! Elbow room!'
The rest, dim in a twilight of crumbling
Utensils and broken pitchers, groaning
For their deliverance, have been so long
Expectant that there is left only the posture.

A half century, without visitors, in the dark —
Poor preparation for the cracking lock
And creak of hinges. Magi, moonmen,
Powdery prisoners of the old regime,

1. An asphodel plant of the lily family, associated in Greek myth with death. George Seferis (1900-71), Greek poet and diplomat, who won the Nobel Prize for Literature in 1963.

2. stink, strong smell.
3. A student of fungi.

Web-throated, stalked like triffids,[4] racked by
  drought
And insomnia, only the ghost of a scream
At the flash-bulb firing squad we wake them with
Shows there is life yet in their feverish forms.
Grown beyond nature now, soft food for worms,
They lift frail heads in gravity and good faith.

They are begging us, you see, in their wordless way,
To do something, to speak on their behalf
Or at least not to close the door again,
Lost people of Treblinka[5] and Pompeii![6]
'Save us, save us,' they seem to say,
'Let the god not abandon us
Who have come so far in darkness and in pain.
We too had our lives to live.
You with your light meter and relaxed itinerary,
Let not our naive labours have been in vain!'

4. Mechanical monsters from outer space in John Wyndham's science fiction novel *The Day of the Triffids*.
5. A Nazi concentration camp in central Poland where the Jews of the Warsaw ghetto were put to death.
6. An ancient city in south-east Italy, buried by an eruption of Vesuvius in 79 B.C.

from: POEMS 1962-1978 (1979)

The Chinese Restaurant in Portrush[1]

Before the holidaymakers comes the spring
Softening the sharp air of the coast
In time for the first 'invasion'.
Today the place is as it might have been,
Gentle and almost hospitable. A girl
Strides past the Northern Counties Hotel,
Light-footed, swinging a book-bag,
And the doors that were shut all winter
Against the north wind and the sea-mist
Lie open to the street, where one
By one the gulls go window-shopping
And an old wolfhound dozes in the sun.

While I sit with my paper and prawn chow-mein
Under a framed photograph of Hong Kong
The proprietor of the Chinese restaurant
Stands at the door as if the world were young
Watching the first yacht hoist a sail —
An ideogram on sea-cloud — and the light
Of heaven upon the mountains of Donegal;
And whistles a little tune, dreaming of home.

1. A seaside resort in County Antrim.

from: THE HUNT BY NIGHT (1982)

The Globe in North Carolina

*'There are no religions, no revelations;
  there are women.'*
— Voznesensky, *Antiworlds*

The earth spins to my finger-tips and
Pauses beneath my outstretched hand;
White water seethes against the green
Capes where the continents begin.
Warm breezes move the pines and stir
The hot dust of the piedmont where
Night glides inland from town to town.
I love to see that sun go down.

It sets in a coniferous haze
Beyond Tennessee; the Anglepoise
Rears like a moon to shed its savage
Radiance on the desolate page,
On Dvorák sleeves[1] and Audubon
Bird-prints.[2] An electronic brain
Records the concrete music of
Our hardware in the heavens above.

From Hatteras to the Blue Ridge
Night spreads like ink on the unhedged
Tobacco fields and clucking lakes,
Bringing the lights on in the rocks
And swamps, the farms and motor courts,
Substantial cities, kitsch resorts —
Until, to the mild theoptic eye,
America is its own night-sky,

Its own celestial fruit, on which
Sidereal forms appear, their rich
Clusters and vague attenuations

1. Record covers of music by Antonin Dvorák (1841-1904), Czech composer.
2. John James Audubon (1785-1851), the American naturalist and artist, is best known for his paintings of birds in *Birds of America* (1827-38).

Miming galactic dispositions.
Hesperus is a lighthouse, Mars
An air-force base; molecular cars
Arrowing the turnpikes become
Lost meteorites in search of home.

No doubt we could go on like this
For decades yet; but nemesis
Awaits our furious make-believe,
Our harsh refusal to conceive
A world so different from our own
We wouldn't know it were we shown.
Who, in its halcyon days, imagined
Carthage a ballroom for the wind?

And what will the new night be like?
Why, as before, a partial dark
Stage-lit by a mysterious glow
As in the *Night Hunt* of Uccello.[3]
Era-provincial self-regard
Finds us, as ever, unprepared
For the odd shifts of emphasis
Time regularly throws up to us.

Here, as elsewhere, I recognize
A wood invisible for its trees
Where everything must change except
The fact of change; our scepticism
And irony, grown trite, be dumb
Before the new thing that must come
Out of the scrunched Budweiser can
To make us sadder, wiser men.[4]

Out in the void and staring hard
At the dim stone where we were reared,
Great mother, now the gods have gone
We put our faith in you alone,
Inverting the procedures which
Knelt us to things beyond our reach.
Drop of the oceans, may your salt
Astringency redeem our fault!

Veined marble, if we only knew,
In practice as in theory, true
Salvation lies not in the thrust
Of action only, but the trust
We place in our peripheral
Night garden in the glory-hole
Of space, a home from home, and what
Devotion we can bring to it!

. . . You lie, an ocean to the east,
Your limbs composed, your mind at rest,
Asleep in a sunrise which will be
Your mid-day when it reaches me;
And what misgivings I might have
About the true importance of
The merely human pale before
The mere fact of your being there.

Five miles away a south-bound freight
Shrieks its euphoria to the state
And passes on; unfinished work
Awaits me in the scented dark.
The halved globe, slowly turning, hugs
Its silence, and the lightning bugs
Are quiet beneath the open window
Listening to that lonesome whistle blow. . .

3. Paolo Uccello (1397-1475), Florentine painter.
4. cf. S. T. Coleridge, 'The Ancient Mariner', VII, stanza 25.

Courtyards in Delft

— Pieter de Hooch, 1659

for Gordon Woods

Oblique light on the trite, on brick and tile —
Immaculate masonry, and everywhere that
Water tap, that broom and wooden pail
To keep it so. House-proud, the wives
Of artisans pursue their thrifty lives
Among scrubbed yards, modest but adequate.
Foliage is sparse, and clings. No breeze
Ruffles the trim composure of those trees.

No spinet-playing emblematic of
The harmonies and disharmonies of love;
No lewd fish, no fruit, no wide-eyed bird
About to fly its cage while a virgin
Listens to her seducer, mars the chaste
Precision of the thing and the thing made.
Nothing is random, nothing goes to waste:
We miss the dirty dog, the fiery gin.

That girl with her back to us who waits
For her man to come home for his tea
Will wait till the paint disintegrates

And ruined dykes admit the esurient[1] sea;
Yet this is life too, and the cracked
Out-house door a verifiable fact
As vividly mnemonic as the sunlit
Railings that front the houses opposite.

I lived there as a boy and know the coal
Glittering in its shed, late-afternoon
Lambency informing the deal table,
The ceiling cradled in a radiant spoon.
I must be lying low in a room there,
A strange child with a taste for verse,
While my hard-nosed companions dream of war
On parched veldt and fields of rain-swept gorse;

For the pale light of that provincial town
Will spread itself, like ink or oil,
Over the not yet accurate linen
Map of the world which occupies one wall
And punish nature in the name of God.
If only, now, the Maenads, as of right,
Came smashing crockery, with fire and sword,
We could sleep easier in our beds at night.

1. voracious.

Derry Morning

The mist clears and the cavities
Glow black in the rubbled city's
Broken mouth. An early crone,
Muse of a fitful revolution
Wasted by the fray, she sees
Her *aisling*[1] falter in the breeze,
Her oak-grove[2] vision hesitate
By empty wharf and city gate.

Here it began, and here at least
It fades into the finite past
Or seems to: clattering shadows whop
Mechanically over pub and shop.
A strangely pastoral silence rules
The shining roofs and murmuring schools;
For this is how the centuries work —
Two steps forward, one step back.

Hard to believe this tranquil place,
Its desolation almost peace,
Was recently a boom-town wild
With expectation, each unscheduled
Incident a measurable
Tremor on the Richter Scale
Of world events, each vibrant scene
Translated to the drizzling screen.

What of the change envisioned here,
The quantum leap from fear to fire?
Smoke from a thousand chimneys strains
One way beneath the returning rains
That shroud the bomb-sites, while the fog
Of time receives the ideologue.
A Russian freighter bound for home
Mourns to the city in its gloom.

1. A Gaelic 'vision' poem, predicting the return of the Jacobite monarch.
2. Etymologically, Derry means 'oak-grove'.

MICHAEL HARTNETT

(1941-)

from: A FAREWELL TO ENGLISH (1975)

[An anatomist of the cliché and, in consequence, a poet of the anticlimax, Hartnett can shift a single lyric through a remarkable emotional range. His love of striking images is qualified by a tendency towards abstraction, which often takes the form of moral indignation at the failure of the world to live up to its own imagery. Like Kennelly, he has a keen interest in rural crafts, and an accurate skill in the portrayal of country rituals.]

Maiden Street Wake[1]

I watched the hand
until a finger moved
and veins above the index knuckle
pulsed.
That was his last movement.
She had a band
of tan tobacco juice
upon her chin. Her few teeth buckled.
That was all the grief she showed.
In public.

Columned and black with women in shawls,
yellow and pillared with penny candles,
bright-eyed and blue-toed with children
in their summer sandals,
that was the mud house, talkative and lit.
In the bed, the breeding ground and cot,
he wore his best blouse
and would have seen
the finest teacups in his life.
But he was white
as an alabaster Christ
and cold to kiss.
We shuffled round and waited.
Our respects were paid.
And then we ate soft biscuits
and drank lemonade.

1. An Irish custom of 'watching' over the corpse of a dead person on the night after his or her decease, while gathered friends share food, drink and anecdotes.

Pigkilling

Like a knife cutting a knife
his last plea for life
echoes joyfully in Camas.[1]
An egg floats
like a navel
in the pickling-barrel:
before he sinks,
his smiling head
sees a delicate girl
up to her elbows
in a tub of blood
while the avalanche
of his offal steams
among the snapping dogs
and mud
and porksteaks
coil in basins
like bright snakes
and buckets of boiling water hiss
to soften his bristles
for the blade.
I kick his golden bladder
in the air.
It lands like a moon
among the damsons.
Like a knife cutting a knife
his last plea for life
echoes joyfully in Camas.

1. A townland five miles south of Newcastle West in County Limerick where the poet spent most of his childhood.

Dryad

Walking in our public places,
seeing the latest art
made from the latest materials
is like finding words like 'dryad'
shattered from their plinths,

statues without squares
broken marble heads of beasts:
commas of culture left
and culture lost in this city of the warehouse.

Here is a figure in metallic foil
its forty-three filaments or coils
in a perpetual tremble.
Not beautiful, not useful
but the image was the maker's own:
perhaps he heard his soul
crying outside our ramparts
or honking at a vacant by-pass.

When our neon lights drop bluely
from the warehouse windowglass
and smoky rain sneaks down the walls
the figure in metallic foil
attempts a dryad of its own
takes the time-encrusted light
as its central soul
from which the broken circles spin.

Who cannot see this vision has no love —
dryad
and her attendant ghosts
caught in the pointless barbs
of the metallic foil.

A Visit to Castletown House[1]

for Nora Graham

The avenue was green and long, and green
light pooled under the fernheads; a jade screen
could not let such liquid light in, a sea
at its greenest self could not pretend to be
so emerald. Men had made this landscape
from a mere secreting wood: knuckles bled
and bones broke to make this awning drape
a fitting silk upon its owner's head.

The house was lifted by two pillared wings
out of its bulk of solid chisellings
and flashed across the chestnut-marshalled lawn
a few lit windows on a bullock bawn.[2]
The one-way windows of the empty rooms
reflected meadows, now the haunt
of waterbirds: where hawtrees were in bloom,
and belladonna,[3] a poisonous plant.

1. A large eighteenth-century mansion in Celbridge, Co. Kildare, built by William Conolly, speaker of the House of Commons.
2. Level ground used for milking cows.
3. Deadly nightshade.

A newer gentry in their quaint attire
looked at maps depicting alien shire[4]
and city, town and fort: they were his seed,
that native who had taken coloured beads
disguised as chandeliers of vulgar glass
and made a room to suit a tasteless man
— a graceful art come to a sorry pass —
painted like some demented tinker's van.

But the music that was played in there —
that had grace, a nervous grace laid bare,
Tortelier[5] unravelling sonatas
pummelling the instrument that has
the deep luxurious sensual sound,
allowing it no richness, making stars
where moons would be, choosing to expound
music as passionate as guitars.

I went into the calmer, gentler hall
in the wineglassed, chattering interval:
there was the smell of rose and woodsmoke there.
I stepped into the gentler evening air
and saw black figures dancing on the lawn,
Eviction, Droit de Seigneur,[6] Broken Bones:
and heard the crack of ligaments being torn
and smelled the clinging blood upon the stones.

4. The English designation of a county.
5. Paul Tortelier, the French cellist, gave a recital at Castletown in the 1970s.
6. Right of the master: a sexual right over female tenants.

Mrs Halpin and the Lightning

When thunder entered like an easter priest
and draped its purple on Mullach a' Radhairc[1]
a horse took fright and broke its neck
against a pierstone:
the carshafts gave like small bones
and the tilted wheel spun.
When the blue sheets crackled
with electric starch
Mrs Halpin with a goose's wing
flailed holy water drops
like the steel tips of holy whips
to beat the demons from the room.
But they would not go away.
Their garments shook her rosary

1. Hills to the south-west of Newcastle West, Co. Limerick.

as they danced on the stone floor.
Her fear was not the simple fear of one
who does not know the source of thunder:
these were the ancient Irish gods
she had deserted for the sake of Christ.
They waited in the earth and sky
to punish and destroy
their fickle congregation.
Mrs Halpin knew the reason why.

A Visit to Croom[1] 1745

for Séamus Ó Cinnéide

The thatch dripped soot,
the sun was silver
because the sky
from ruts of mud to high blaze
was water:
white-washed walls were silver,
limeflakes opened like scissored pages
nesting moss and golds of straw
and russet pools of soot:
windows small as ratholes
shone like frost-filled hoofprints,
the door was charted
by the tracery of vermin.
Five Gaelic faces stopped their talk,
turned from the red of fire
into a cloud of rush-light fumes,
scraped their pewter mugs
across the board and talked about the king.
I had walked a long time
in the mud to hear
an avalanche of turf fall down,
fourteen miles in straw-roped overcoat
passing for Irish all along the road
now to hear a Gaelic court
talk broken English of an English king.
It was a long way
to come for nothing.

1. The Limerick meeting-place of a court of poets. See Daniel Corkery, *The Hidden Ireland* (1924).

Patience of a Tree

for Nuala

A knife awaited him in London
in a drawer, in darkness
in a pocket, in darkness.
Fooling,
tricking,
mocking —
he saw the phantom knife.

He burnt the tree of fear
and went across the sea
but a knife waited in London.
In a hand, in the darkness
in a fight, in the darkness.

The knife was waiting there
and though metal formed the blade
from a tree's revenge
the hilt was made.

EAMON GRENNAN

(1941-)

from: WHAT LIGHT THERE IS (1987)

A Closer Look

Simply that I'm sick of our wars and
the way we live, wasting everything we touch
with our hands, lips, tongues, crowding
the earth with early graves, blind
to the bright little nipples of rain
that simmer on willow twigs, amber shoots
of the stumped willow itself a burning bush
on the scalloped hem of the ice-pond. So
I'm turning to winter beasts instead, their
delicate razor's-edge economies as they
shift for themselves between dens, migrant
homebodies like the souls we used to have,
leaving behind them in the shallow snow
their signatures, the thing itself, illiterate
signs that say no more than *We were here*
and mean it: handprints, footprints, midnight-
mahogany blossoms of shit, citrus
and mustardgreen swirls of piss that brighten
the eye-numbing, one blank world. Porcupine,
possum, raccoon, skunk, fox — behold them
combing the cold land for a bite, not just
taking for granted their world as it comes
and goes. They wear the weather like a shawl
and follow their noses through a sphere
of sudden death and instant satisfactions: they
lie in the sunlit pit of sleep, or the worm
of hunger winds his luminous tail to rouse
and send them coldly forth, sniffing the wind
the way lovers browse word by word by word
first letters for what stays salted
and aromatic between the lines. It isn't
innocence I find in them, but a fathoming
depth of attention anchored in the heart, in its
whorl of blood and muscle beating round — the way
they traffic between frosted starlight and the
gleamy sphere of berries and last apples, between
storm in the big cloud-bearing boughs
and the narrow breath of earthworm and beetle
barely stirring the dead leaves; now all
quivering dash, nerves purring, now the wildfire
flash of pain that lays them, an open secret,
low. I try to make my hopeless own of this, to
sense in myself their calm unthreading
between brisk teeth or busy mycelian[1] fingers, breaking
down to our common ground, as we will, the whole story
starting over in the old language: air first, then
ooze, then the solid lie of things, then fire,
a further twist, begin again. Making do.

1. White, thread-like mass of hyphae, forming the thallus of a fungus.

Four Deer

Four deer lift up their lovely heads to me
in the dusk of the golf course I plod across
towards home. They're browsing the wet grass
the snow has left and, statued, stare at me
in deep silence and I see whatever light there is
gather to glossy pools in their eight mild,
barely curious but wary eyes. When one at a time
they bend again to feed, I can hear the crisp
moist crunch of the surviving grass between
their teeth, imagine the slow lick of a tongue
over whickering[1] lips. They've come from the unlit
winter corners of their fright to find
a fresh season, this early gift, and stand
almost easy at the edge of white snow islands
and lap the grey-green sweet depleted grass. About them
hangs an air of such domestic sense, the comfortable
hush of folk at home with one another, a familiar
something I sense in spite of the great gulf of strangeness
we must look over at each other. Tails flicker
white in thickening dusk and I feel their relief at
the touch of cold snow underfoot while their faces
nuzzle grass, as if, like birds, they had crossed
unspeakable vacant wastes with nothing but hunger
shaping their brains and driving them from leaf to
dry leaf, sour strips of bark, under a thunder of guns

1. neighing, sniggering.

and into the cold comfort of early dark. I've seen
their straight despairing lines cloven in snowfields
under storm, an Indian file of famished natives, poor
unprayed-for wanderers through blinding chill, seasoned
castaways in search of home ports, which they've found
at last, here on winter's verge between our houses and
their trees. All of a sudden, I've come too close. Moving
as one mind they spring in silent waves
over the grass, then crack snow with sharp hard
snaps, lightfooting it into the sanctuary of a pine grove
where they stand looking back at me, a deer-shaped family
of shadows against the darker arch of trees and this
rusting dusk. When silence settles over us again and
they bow down to browse, the sound of grass being lipped,
bitten, meets me across the space between us. Close
enough for comfort, they see we keep, instinctively, our
distance, sharing this air where a few last shards of day-
light glitter in little meltpools or spread a skin of
brightness on the ice, the ice stiffening towards midnight
under the clean magnesium burn of a first star.

EILÉAN NÍ CHUILLEANÁIN

(1942-)

from: ACTS AND MONUMENTS (1972)

[A difficult and often oblique writer, Ní Chuilleanáin deploys arcane lore with mundane slang in striking combinations. A pleasant conversational rhythm weaves itself in and out of her most abstract lyrics, which repeatedly strive to render everyday occurrences from the acutest of angles. This may indicate the influence of the Elizabethan poets, on whose work she wrote an Oxford dissertation.]

Acts and Monuments

In imitation of the weed
Which, out of soft enclosing mud
As from a hand that holds a lead
Leans after the escaping flood,

Or when warm summer stunts the flow
In tangled coils lies tired and fine,
Or in calm weather stands tiptoe
To peer above the waterline,

The rooted trees bend in the wind
Or twist and bow on every side;
The poplar stands up straight and slim;
But their blood cannot flower or fade

Like weeds that rot when rivers dry.
Their roots embrace the stony plain,
Their branches move as one, they try
To freeze the effects of wind and rain.

And like the waterline the sky
Lids and defines the element
Where no unformed capricious cry
Can sound without its monument.

Going Back to Oxford

Something to lose; it came in the equipment
Alongside the suicide pill and the dark blue card:
'I am a Catholic, please send for a priest'
With a space below for the next of kin.

Something to lose; and going back to Oxford,
Though not for good this time, I lose it again
As the city advances like an old relation
It's no use insulting.
Notice how she repeats her effects,

The Victorian towers after the mediaeval slum,[1]
As a yawn turns into a shiver and the air
Bites like a mould pulling me north
To the evacuated roads.
Here the eye shrinks from what it sees,
The toothmarks are showing where the sharp
spires[2] got me;
And I agree to being chewed because
All that time I was looking for a reliable experience
And here it is: I give in every time,
Repeat the original despair.
This is where I learned it.

Because pleasure is astonishing, but loss
Expected, never at a loss for words;
Tearducts built in at birth: something to lose:
The best kind of innocence, which is not to have
been afraid,
Lost according to plan; and here I am, walking
Through old streets to a familiar bed.

1. Jericho, one of the oldest and poorest areas of Oxford.
2. Oxford's famous 'dreaming spires' which adorn the sandstone buildings of the colleges.

from:
SITE OF AMBUSH (1975)

Lucina schynning in silence of the night . . .[1]

Moon shining in silence of the night
The heaven being all full of stars
I was reading my book in a ruin
By a sour candle, without roast meat or music
Strong drink or a shield from the air
Blowing in the crazed window, and I felt
Moonlight on my head, clear after three days' rain.

I washed in cold water; it was orange, channelled
down bogs
Dipped between cresses.
The bats flew through my room where I slept safely.
Sheep stared at me when I woke.

Behind me the waves of darkness lay, the plague
Of mice, plague of beetles
Crawling out of the spines of books,
Plague shadowing pale faces with clay
The disease of the moon gone astray.

In the desert I relaxed, amazed
As the mosaic beasts on the chapel floor
When Cromwell had departed[2] and they saw
The sky growing through the hole in the roof.

Sheepdogs embraced me; the grasshopper
Returned with lark and bee.
I looked down between hedges of high thorn and
saw
The hare, absorbed, sitting still
In the middle of the track; I heard
Again the chirp of the stream running.

1. The first line of a poem, 'The Birth of Antichrist', by William Dunbar (*c.* 1460-*c.* 1520), Scottish poet. Lucina personifies the moon.
2. Perhaps a reference to the sacking of catholic churches by Cromwell's forces after his arrival in Ireland in August 1649.

Darkening All the Strand

The light neglects her face
To warm the fruited stone
Walls rising against her
Across brown spiral waves
Of the wandering Boyne.[1]

What retreat, convent, group
Of Gaelic-speaking vets
Or Home for Protestant
Incurables, behind
Those pointed windows, breathes?

Somebody walked, along
The sloped geranium
Path to the damp steps where
A painted gate is shut.
New ropes hold a dark boat.

(Bright streak, brown shape.) Water —
Sodden, the near flat shore
Accumulates floated
Light weathered filterings
That shift under her feet,

The firm ground flood-riddled;
This historical shore

1. The river flows into the sea at Drogheda. Near Drogheda is the site of a decisive battle between William and James (1690), as a result of which protestant hegemony was established in Ireland.

Clings to the evening shade —
A difficult stance for
Viewing the greenhouses

(Though sunlit to the left
Between a half-grown hedge
Plainly visible is
The nuns' graveyard, the small
Ranged uniform crosses.)

The cloistered Boyne gropes on
Washing out of the land's
Interrelated roots,
Under foundations, far
Streams the nuns may recall.

The Lady's Tower

Hollow my high tower leans
Back to the cliff; my thatch
Converses with spread sky,
Heronries. The grey wall
Slices downward and meets
A sliding flooded stream
Pebble-banked, small diving
Birds. Downstairs my cellars plumb.

Behind me shifting the oblique veins
Of the hill; my kitchen is damp,
Spiders shaded under brown vats.

I hear the stream change pace, glance from the stove
To see the punt is now floating freely
Bobs square-ended, the rope dead-level.

Opening the kitchen door
The quarry brambles miss my hair
Sprung so high their fruit wastes.

And up the tall stairs my bed is made
Even with a sycamore root
At my small square window.

All night I lie sheeted, my broom chases down treads
Delighted spirals of dust: the yellow duster glides
Over shelves, around knobs: bristle stroking
flagstone
Dancing with the spiders around the kitchen in the
dark
While cats climb the tower and the river fills
A spoonful of light on the cellar walls below.

from:
THE SECOND VOYAGE
(1977, 1986)

The Second Voyage

Odysseus rested on his oar and saw
The ruffled foreheads of the waves
Crocodiling and mincing past: he rammed
The oar between their jaws and looked down
In the simmering sea where scribbles of weed
defined
Uncertain depth, and the slim fishes progressed
In fatal formation, and thought
If there was a single
Streak of decency in these waves now, they'd be
ridged
Pocked and dented with the battering they've had,
And we could name them as Adam named the
beasts,
Saluting a new one with dismay, or a notorious one
With admiration; they'd notice us passing
And rejoice at our shipwreck, but these
Have less character than sheep and need more
patience.

I know what I'll do he said;
I'll park my ship in the crook of a long pier
(And I'll take you with me he said to the oar)
I'll face the rising ground and walk away
From tidal waters, up riverbeds
Where herons parcel out the miles of stream,
Over gaps in the hills, through warm
Silent valleys, and when I meet a farmer
Bold enough to look me in the eye
With 'where are you off to with that long
Winnowing fan over your shoulder?'
There I will stand still
And I'll plant you for a gatepost or a hitching-post
And leave you as a tidemark. I can go back
And organise my house then.
But the profound
Unfenced valleys of the ocean still held him;
He had only the oar to make them keep their
distance;
The sea was still frying under the ship's side.

He considered the water-lilies, and thought about fountains
Spraying as wide as willows in empty squares,
The sugarstick of water clattering into the kettle,
The flat lakes bisecting the rushes. He remembered spiders and frogs
Housekeeping at the roadside in brown trickles floored with mud,
Horsetroughs, the black canal, pale swans at dark:
His face grew damp with tears that tasted
Like his own sweat or the insults of the sea.

EAVAN BOLAND

(1944-)

from: NEW TERRITORY (1967)

[A controlled and elegant stylist, Eavan Boland can seem at times forbiddingly cerebral; but her best poems are characterized also by palpable undercurrents of emotion, played off against the chosen form. Her language is poised, her images clear, and her tone often dry and amused. She is one of the very few Irish poets to describe with any fidelity the lives now lived by half a million people in the suburbs of Dublin.]

New Territory

Several things announced the fact to us:
The captain's Spanish tears
Falling like doubloons[1] in the headstrong light,
And then of course the fuss —
The crew jostling and interspersing cheers
With wagers. Overnight
As we went down to our cabins, nursing the last
Of the grog, talking as usual of conquest,
Land hove into sight.

Frail compasses and trenchant constellations
Brought us as far as this,
And now air and water, fire and earth
Stand at their given stations
Out there, and are ready to replace
This single desperate width
Of ocean. Why do we hesitate? Water and air
And fire and earth and therefore life are here,
And therefore death.

1. Spanish gold coins.

Out of the dark man comes to life and into it
He goes and loves and dies,
(His element being the dark and not the light of day)
So the ambitious wit
Of poets and exploring ships have been his eyes —
Riding the dark for joy —
And so Isaiah[2] of the sacred text is eagle-eyed because
By peering down the unlit centuries
He glimpsed the holy boy.

2. The Old Testament prophet who foretold Christ's birth.

from: NIGHT FEED (1982)

Night Feed

This is dawn.
Believe me
This is your season, little daughter:
The moment daisies open,
The hour mercurial rainwater
Makes a mirror for sparrows.
It's time we drowned our sorrows.

I tiptoe in.
I lift you up
Wriggling
In your rosy, zipped sleeper.
Yes this is the hour
For the early bird and me
When finder is keeper.

I crook the bottle.
How you suckle!
This is the best I can be,
Housewife
To this nursery
Where you hold on,
Dear life.

A silt of milk.
The last suck.
And now your eyes are open
Birth-coloured and offended.
Earth wakes.
You go back to sleep.
The feed is ended.

Worms turn.
Stars go in.
Even the moon is losing face.
Poplars stilt for dawn
And we begin
The long fall from grace.
I tuck you in.

Ode to Suburbia

Six o'clock: the kitchen bulbs which blister
Your dark, your housewives starting to nose
Out each other's day, the claustrophobia
Of your back gardens varicose
With shrubs make an ugly sister
Of you suburbia.

How long ago did the glass in your windows subtly
Silver into mirrors which again
And again show the same woman
Shriek at a child, which multiply
A dish, a brush, ash,
The gape of a fish

In the kitchen, the gape of a child in the cot?
You swelled so that when you tried
The silver slipper on your foot
It pinched your instep and the common
Hurt which touched you made
You human.

No creatures of your streets will feel the touch
Of a wand turning the wet sinews
Of fruit suddenly to a coach,
While this rat without leather reins
Or a whip or britches continues
Sliming your drains.

No magic here. Yet you encroach until
The shy countryside, fooled
By your plainness falls, then rises
From your bed changed, schooled
Forever by your skill,
Your compromises.

Midnight and your metamorphosis
Is now complete, although the mind
Which spinstered you might still miss
Your mystery now, might still fail
To see your powers defined
By this detail:

By this creature drowsing now in every house,
The same lion who tore stripes
Once off zebras, who now sleeps
Small beside the coals and may
On a red letter day
Catch a mouse.

The Woman Turns Herself into a Fish[1]

Unpod
the bag,
the seed.

Slap
the flanks back.
Flatten

paps.
Make finny
scaled

and chill
the slack
and dimple

of the rump.
Pout
the mouth,

brow the eyes
and now
and now

1. A reference to 'The Song of Wandering Aengus' by W.B. Yeats, in which a trout turns into 'a glimmering girl' who escapes the speaker.

eclipse
in these hips,
these loins,

the moon,
the blood
flux.

It's done:
I turn,
I flab upward

blub-lipped,
hipless
and I am

sexless
shed
of ecstasy,

a pale
swimmer
sequin-skinned,

pearling eggs
screamlessly
in seaweed.

It's what
I set my heart on.
Yet

ruddering
and muscling
in the sunless tons

of new freedoms
still
I feel

a chill pull,
a brightening,
a light, a light

and how
in my loomy cold,
my greens

still
she moons
in me.

from: THE JOURNEY AND OTHER POEMS (1987)

The Journey

for Elizabeth Ryle

Immediately cries were heard. These were the loud wailing of infant souls weeping at the very entrance-way; never had they had their share of life's sweetness for the dark day had stolen them from their mothers' breasts and plunged them to a death before their time.

— Virgil, *The Aeneid*, Book VI

And then the dark fell and 'there has never'
I said 'been a poem to an antibiotic:
never a word to compare with the odes on
the flower of the raw slow for fever

'or the devious Africa-seeking tern
or the protein treasures of the sea-bed.
Depend on it, somewhere a poet is wasting
his sweet uncluttered metres on the obvious

'emblem instead of the real thing.
Instead of sulpha we shall have hyssop dipped
in the wild blood of the unblemished lamb,
so every day the language gets less

'for the task and we are less with the language.'
I finished speaking and the anger faded
and dark fell and the book beside me
lay open at the page Aphrodite[1]

comforts Sappho in her love's duress.
The poplars shifted their music in the garden,
a child startled in a dream,
my room was a mess —

the usual hardcovers, half-finished cups,
clothes piled up on an old chair —
and I was listening out but in my head was
a loosening and sweetening heaviness,

1. Goddess of fertility and love.

not sleep, but nearly sleep, not dreaming really
but as ready to believe and still
unfevered, calm and unsurprised
when she came and stood beside me

and I would have known her anywhere
and I would have gone with her anywhere
and she came wordlessly
and without a word I went with her

down down down without so much as
ever touching down but always, always
with a sense of mulch beneath us,
the way of stairs winding down to a river

and as we went on the light went on
failing and I looked sideways to be certain
it was she, misshapen, musical —
Sappho — the scholiast's nightingale

and down we went, again down
until we came to a sudden rest
beside a river in what seemed to be
an oppressive suburb of the dawn.

My eyes got slowly used to the bad light.
At first I saw shadows, only shadows.
Then I could make out women and children
and, in the way they were, the grace of love.

'Cholera, typhus, croup, diphtheria'
she said, 'in those days they racketed
in every backstreet and alley of old Europe.
Behold the children of the plague'.

Then to my horror I could see to each
nipple some had clipped a limpet shape —
suckling darknesses — while others had their arms
weighed down, making terrible pietàs.

She took my sleeve and said to me, 'be careful.
Do not define these women by their work:
not as washerwomen trussed in dust and sweating,
muscling water into linen by the river's edge

'nor as court ladies brailled in silk
on wool and woven with an ivory unicorn
and hung, nor as laundresses tossing cotton,
brisking daylight with lavender and gossip.

'But these are women who went out like you
when dusk became a dark sweet with leaves,
recovering the day, stooping, picking up
teddy bears and rag dolls and tricycles and buckets —

'love's archaeology — and they too like you
stood boot deep in flowers once in summer
or saw winter come in with a single magpie
in a caul[2] of haws, a solo harlequin'.

I stood fixed. I could not reach or speak to them.
Between us was the melancholy river,
the dream water, the narcotic crossing
and they had passed over it, its cold persuasions.

I whispered, 'let me be
let me at least be their witness,' but she said
'what you have seen is beyond speech,
beyond song, only not beyond love;

'remember it, you will remember it'
and I heard her say but she was fading fast
as we emerged under the stars of heaven,
'there are not many of us; you are dear

'and stand beside me as my own daughter.
I have brought you here so you will know forever
the silences in which are our beginnings,
in which we have an origin like water,'

and the wind shifted and the window clasp
opened, banged and I woke up to find
the poetry books stacked higgledy piggledy,
my skirt spread out where I had laid it —

nothing was changed; nothing was more clear
but it was wet and the year was late.
The rain was grief in arrears; my children
slept the last dark out safely and I wept.

The Emigrant Irish

Like oil lamps we put them out the back,

of our houses, of our minds. We had lights
better than, newer than and then

a time came, this time and now
we need them. Their dread, makeshift example.

2. covering.

They would have thrived on our necessities.
What they survived we could not even live.
By their lights now it is time to
imagine how they stood there, what they stood with,
that their possessions may become our power.
Cardboard. Iron. Their hardships parcelled in them.
Patience. Fortitude. Long-suffering
in the bruise-coloured dusk of the New World.

And all the old songs. And nothing to lose.

PAUL DURCAN

(1944-)

from: O WESTPORT IN THE LIGHT OF ASIA MINOR (1975)

[A popular reader of his own poems, Durcan writes long Whitmanesque lines that scout the borders of prose. His lyrics are chatty, and loose to the point of garrulity, as if they were mere drafts or dress-rehearsals of a poem. Yet, for all their air of relaxation, the best of them grow in tension as the poet seeks out the desired image or final phrase to which the poem was designed to give birth.]

Dún Chaoin[1]

for Bob, Angela, and Rachel, in Nigeria

I was standing at the counter
In a bar at the world's end.
The large weathered man behind it
Was more native to the place than the place itself.
His father's fathers...[2]
A big blue man like that, I thought, could not be strange
With a stranger:
So when he did not speak
An old fear whistled through me:
I am not welcome in this place.
I kept a grip on my pint glass
And my eyes to the left of me
Gripping the bay-window and outside
The red sun at nightfall
In the same plane as the bar room
Descending the window pane.
Its going down took about as long
As it takes a boy or girl to climb down a tree.
Gone and not long after
I thought I could hear
A longlost music long lost from the earth
And as I looked up from the counter shaking my head
The big man too was shaking his, birds and tears
Falling out of the rafters of his eyes. The both of us
Laughed and he turned up the volume
Of his openly concealed battered old wireless,
Telefunken,[3]
And when we were going out he said: Good night
And may God bless you on the road.
I went out willing to sleep on mountainsides anywhere
Fearing no man or beast, machine or mist.

1. Dunquin, the most westerly parish in Ireland, at the edge of the Dingle peninsula, County Kerry, which is noted as a Gaelic-speaking area.
2. cf. W.B. Yeats, 'The Curse of Cromwell': 'His fathers served their fathers before Christ was crucified.'
3. The trade-name of a popular radio-receiver.

from: TERESA'S BAR (1986)

The Baker

After a night at the ovens
In the big city bakery
The baker walks home alone:
He stalks through the dawn
Gropingly
Like a man through a plate-glass door
(There have been many such —

Oh many such — years
And nights of it
And it has been so
Hot)
He feels fragile and eerily pure
Like a loaf new out of oven,
All heat through-and-through,
And he does not look sure
That the air is not a plate-glass door;
So gropingly he stalks
In his hob-nailed boots
Up the steep terraced street:
Like a tiny giant walking in glue:
Like a human being about to split in two.

from:
JESUS, BREAK HIS FALL (1980)

The Death by Heroin of Sid Vicious[1]

There — but for the clutch of luck — go I.

At daybreak — in the arctic fog of a February
daybreak —
Shoulderlength helmets in the watchtowers of the
concentration camp
Caught me out in the intersecting arcs of the
swirling searchlights:

There were at least a zillion of us caught out there
— Like ladybirds under a boulder —
But under the microscope each of us was unique,

Unique and we broke for cover, crazily breasting
The barbed wire and some of us made it
To the forest edge, but many of us did not

Make it, although their unborn children did —
Such as you whom the camp commandant branded
Sid Vicious of the Sex Pistols. Jesus, break his fall:

There — but for the clutch of luck — go we all.

February 1979

1. Sid Vicious was a leading member of a punk music band known as The Sex Pistols, who dressed in stark Nazi-style clothes, and made robotic movements, to emphasize the modern surrender to system.

from:
THE BERLIN WALL CAFÉ (1985)

The Marriage Contract

She is the kind of person
(The kind of person I like)
Who never reads the small print in contracts:
E.g. — where it says 'he's a xenophobic psychopath',
She took no notice, taking me at face value.

Today — our broken marriage broken —
Busybodies are quick to tell her
What a noble, handsome soul she is
And what a bowsy[1] her ex-husband was:
But she has no time for these
Soothsayers of the marriage contract,
She being an anarchist herself —
With always, at the worst of times,
Dreams of good times;
And with always, at the best of times,
Memories of bad times.
Besides, it is of no piquancy to her now
To be told that her husband
Was a retarded third-degree necrophiliac:
She remembers him as he was,
Warts and all,
The man she loved and the man she married.
The warts bloomed in swarms
Quite naturally over the years
Until there were simply too many of them.
She took a second glance at the contract,
And realised that it had run out.
Afterwards, she gave it to him as a souvenir
Knowing his passion for such memorabilia:
By the light of a TV programme he was not
watching
— A black-and-white film of *King Lear* with the
sound turned down —
He sunk it into the frontal lobes of his brain,
Like a blank cheque from God sunk into stone.

1. An Irish idiom for a callow boor.

Bewley's Oriental Café,
Westmoreland Street

When she asked me to keep an eye on her things
I told her I'd be glad to keep an eye on her things.

While she breakdanced off to the ladies' loo
I concentrated on keeping an eye on her things.
What are you doing? — a Security Guard growled,
His moustache gnawing at the beak of his peaked
cap.
When I told him that a young woman whom I did
not know
Had asked me to keep an eye on her things, he
barked:
Instead of keeping an eye on the things
Of a young woman whom you do not know,
Keep an eye on your own things.
I put my two hands on his hips and squeezed him:
Look — for me the equivalent of the Easter Rising
Is to be accosted by a woman whom I do not know
And asked by her to keep an eye on her things;
On her medieval backpack and on her spaceage
Walkman;
Calm down and cast aside your peaked cap
And take down your trousers and take off your
shoes
And I will keep an eye on your things also.
Do we not cherish all the children of the nation
equally?[1]
That woman does not know the joy she has given me
By asking me if I would keep an eye on her things;
I feel as if I am on a Dart[2] to Bray,
Keeping an eye on her things;
More radical than being on the pig's back,
Keeping an eye on nothing.
The Security Guard made a heap on the floor
Of his pants and shoes,
Sailing his peaked cap across the café like a frisbee.
His moustache sipped at a glass of milk.
It is as chivalrous as it is transcendental
To be sitting in Bewley's Oriental Café
With a naked Security Guard,
Keeping an eye on his things

1. A phrase from the Proclamation of the Irish Republic, Easter 1916.
2. Dublin Area Rapid Transit train.

FRANK ORMSBY

(1947-)

from:
A STORE OF CANDLES (1977)

Islands

The week Makarios[1] fell we moved house.
His crisis was not ours or near home.
Caught from the hall those bulletins defined
Less than heaped chairs the time's upheaval.

The Turks invaded. Half-way up a wall
With hammer, nails, my focus of concern
Was hanging pictures. Above the city
Bloomed no paratroops. The streets were empty.

And years from now when people ask how long
We've lived here, we will need no calendars.
A voice, untroubled, in the mind will tell:
We moved in the week Makarios fell.

1. Archbishop Makarios (1913-77), a patriarch who in 1960 became the first president of Cyprus. In July 1974 he was overthrown in a coup initiated by Greek officers who objected to his increasingly conciliatory line. The British refused to intervene in their old colony, the Turks invaded and successfully seized the northern half of the island. Soon afterwards Makarios was restored as president of the southern, or Greek, section of the island.

from:
A NORTHERN SPRING (1986)

McConnell's Birthday

My father died among the Guinchy brickstacks
in the First War, before I was seventeen.
Daily I stopped to read his weathered name
on the dull statue in the village square
until I forgot him.

I worked the manor farm, my children grew
in a green place at the foot of the Major's trees.
The year that Bridie left they filled my days,

riding the tractor to the stable yard.
We were closer when she returned.

I've no urge to watch how the world goes,
or cry for the century and its latest war.
At forty-four I'm fed up with the first light
to feed the Major's pheasants.
I close his gates at night.

Today there are shouts on the road, McCusker's boy
going home from the creamery, Donnelly taking his
time
on a creaky bike. Slyly he stops to roar:
'We're not getting any younger.'
In this part of the world they know it's my birthday.

Home

Once, in the Giant's Ring,[1] I closed my eyes
and thought of Ireland,
the air-wide, skin-tight, multiple meaning of here.

When I opened them I was little the wiser,
in that, perhaps, one
with the first settlers in the Lagan Valley
and the Vietnamese boat-people[2] of Portadown.

1. At the Giant's Causeway, off the Antrim coast.
2. Refugees who fled in boats from the advancing North Vietnamese communists in the mid-1970s and later settled in various parts of the world.

HUGH MAXTON
(1947-)

['Hugh Maxton' is the pseudonym of critic W.J. Mc Cormack, and the poetry reflects the critical interests — in the Irish protestant tradition, the social function of art, and, in recent years, the politics and culture of Eastern Europe. At times cryptic and cerebral, Maxton's poetry is nevertheless informed by a strong political conscience.

The poet has the following note on his translation of Josef Brodsky's 'Elegy for John Donne': 'Josef Brodsky (born 1940) is undoubtedly the best known Russian poet since Boris Pasternak — best known in the West, that is. The reasons for his acclaim are not entirely poetical in character, since he has made no secret of his opposition not only to the Soviet regime generally but also to the popular figures of Soviet literature. Now living in New York, Brodsky can be made to appear like another Solzhenitsyn — an exercise which confuses the totally different relation between politics and religion in the work of each, and the unique complexity of affinity/alienation which binds Brodsky to his homeland. The comparison to Solzhenitsyn also distorts the particular achievements of Josef Brodsky as poet.

'The Great Elegy for John Donne', his finest poem, is a comparatively early work, written in 1963 when Brodsky had just earned the approval and support of Anna Akhmatova. It was in the following year that he was sentenced to five years' exile in Arkangel — he was released in 1965. In 1972 he was effectively expelled from the Soviet Union and he has subsequently lived and worked in the United States of America.

The Russian text of the poem runs to 208 lines. The rhyme scheme is ABAB CDCD et cetera, with the first, third lines and so forth ending with a masculine (i.e. stressed syllable) rhyme, and the second, fourth lines etc. ending with a feminine (unstressed) rhyme. Generally, the 'odd' lines contain ten syllables, and the 'even' ones eleven syllables. The principal decision facing the translator into English, therefore, concerned the poetic line, but the problem was compounded by the repetitions of Brodsky's poem, repetitions which in English run the high risk of converting rich tonalities into iteration. In the end, a decision was made in favour of reducing the material of the early stages of the poem (where most of the original repetition occurs) and employing an ABBA CDDC rhyme pattern — which promised in English a more satisfactory binding than would have been the case if the Russian rhyme pattern had been taken over unaltered. The basic line employed is the iambic pentameter, used with freedom.

Brodsky owes much in this poem to the English metaphysical school of the seventeenth century; nevertheless the dialectics of the poem's different 'voices' remain difficult even to native speakers of English to whom the metaphysical poets are familiar. I have introduced into *the presentation* of the translation sectional divisions which do not appear in the Russian original. These should assist readers for whom the coming together of a Russian meditative mode and the metaphysical tradition seems overwhelmingly obscure. These divisions, however, should not be regarded as indicating structural sections — dramatic, silent breathings in the spiritual dialogue more accurately are marked by a marginal enumeration which I hope is only intrusive to a minimal degree.

Nicholas Bethell published a translation of the elegy in 1967 (*Elegy to John Donne and Other Poems*, London, Longmans): written in lines of ten and eleven syllables, it does not attempt rhyme. George L. Kline published another unrhymed version in the *Tri-Quarterly*, and this is available in *Joseph Brodsky: Selected Poems* (Harmondsworth, Penguin, 1973). Bethell's version runs to 206 lines (just two short of the original), and Kline's to 213. My own translation was begun in 1972/3 when I was living in Ulster. Neil Cornwell was then teaching in the New University of Ulster, and he supplied me with an annotated literal translation of Brodsky's text. The result was 130 lines rendered by me, and yoked to an interpolated passage based on an incident from *Walton's Life of Donne:* this collage was published under the title 'Elegies' in *Atlantis* no. 6 (winter 1973-74). When *The Noise of the Fields* was published in 1976 (Dolmen Press), the interpolated passage was removed, together with a few other adjustments; thus, the version of 1976 consisted of 124 lines. With some minor alterations, this present version expands that of 1976 by adding two twelve-line translated passages, to reach a total of 148 lines. Given the nature of the repetition at the opening of the original, I now consider this 148-line translation a full rendering of Brodsky's elegy. At every stage of the translation's evolution I have had the benefit of Neil Cornwell's advice and guidance.

The Christian symbolism of the elegy is immediately apparent. This should be seen in a Russian context shaped by a reading of Pasternak and Akhmatova rather than of Solzhenitsyn. What meaning and significance the translation has in the context of my own work is not a topic I can comment on here: some discussion of it will be found in Joseph Holt's review-article on *The Noise of the Fields* in *Studies* 1978.']

Elegy for John Donne (1983)

i

When John Donne dropped to sleep all around
him slept.
Pictures were drowsy on the wall, the floor
was deep in rugs and tables; furniture
whose certain essence was a sleep that kept
the clocks as motionless as lumber.
At rest in cupboards as in dormitories
the linen slept as though it were bodies
draped in animal slumber.
Night was not idly here and there
turning the key or coiled in locks
but paused in heat exhaling human shocks
to be at once impenetrable as air.
All slept: the window in its envelope
of snow might never have been written;
the words it might have read remained unseen
when John Donne unwakened and took his sleep.

The iron weights in the butcher's shop are prone
in care of watchdogs shrunken from the chains.
Mice are asleep and cats stiffened; the Thames
nods its way towards a salted dawn
shaking the reflected tower and arch.
Ships are anchorless by the wharf safely.
The sea lies down beside a promontory,
the land her bolster, intent and white as starch.
The walls of the gaol loosen in this rest
and prisoners lie still in their freedom
heedless of a momentary calm
before light draws its finger from the east.

The angels also sleep above the globe,
a world forgotten by the sleeping saints.
In holy shame fair paradise faints
under the waves of the Lord's deepest robe.
Gehenna sleeps and man must fail to be;
John Donne fails tonight his last disaster;
his breath and kiss and manly lines are lost.
Satan sleeps and with him all enmity.
The prophets sleep. Good rests on Evil's arm.
The paling snow completes its last full stop
as his stressed and weary syllables drop
in place, to his drift of words' alarm.
Everybody sleeps: the saints, devils, God,
friends, deceitful servants, lovers in bed
led dormant on this night John Donne is dead.
And the snow shuffles its feet on the road.

ii

In the darkness of the white snowroad
I hear a cry. I hear a frightened call
as if a man were left to carry all
the bitter climate with his own painful load.
He is weeping. Yes, somebody is there,
his voice flaking at the brink of silence
like nervous hands, thin as a needle's
eye and blind of thread. Somebody is near.
'Whose tears are these that I hear in darkness?
An angel, waiting in a cape of snow

or re-birth of my last-year's love below?
Oh, seraph, do I recognize your voice?

'I have often heard them in sombre course.
Have you absconded from my sleeping church
to troop in silence under this dark birch,
or have your vain trumpetings made you hoarse?

'Then, Paul, this silence canvasses your name,
the darkness surely being pure as glass.
And yet your voice was distinctly harsh
from straight talk, driving the pegs of Christ's claim,
Or, is our Father here, whose mighty hand
has loomed over this place time out of mind?
'Speak, Lord, thy servant heareth.' Oh I find
the impress of thy silence stuns the land.
Was I alone to keep my open eyes
when guardsmen gathered in impassive gloom?
Gabriel! announce your presence, whom
I knew to summon myriads in the skies.

iii

'No, it is I your soul, John Donne, complains;
alone on heaven's pinnacle I weep
for things my labour, even at its neap,
had set afloat, thoughts heavy as chains.
You were aloft, and from the heights you saw
a people whole. Despite your load you could
fly again through sin and passion to God;
Hell having seen, first as image, then raw.
Seeing life, your *Island* was its twin.
And soaring past your Lord, in pride fell
content with burdens in the abysmal
tide of the roaring ocean.
From then the Lord seemed but a light that gleams
and all His Radiant Country was to you
a fitful image moving to and fro —
marsh-fire, a credal squint, or just a dream.
His fields persist unbroken by the plough;
the years lie fallow and the eras;
rain dances hugely in the formal grass;
a perfect tense preserves your broken vow.
The earliest woodsman, ordering by chance
his skinny mount into thorns and fright,
will climb a tree and search and barely sight
fires in his home valley held at distance.
All's at distance: and here an unclear land.
His quiet glance glides on roofs and doors.
Here such brightness, such silence from the curs
and silent falls the bells' accustomed sound.
He'll grasp the distant nature of the earth,
will turn his mount abruptly in the gorse.
With that, his trappings and his skinny horse,
his meagre Self, decline to holy dearth.
So here I stand and weep; the road is gone.
I cannot fly with my spirit's temple
before death brings to me his ample
deductions and certainty of tone.
I languish in a passion of desire
stitching the last remnant of my spirit,
the needle passing through my soul in merit
of the empty snow so uselessly pure.

'But listen! while my weeping now disturbs
your rest, the busy snow shuttles through the dark
unmelting but sewing up our hurt.
Endlessly to and fro the needle works.
It is not I who weep but you, John Donne;
who lies alone. Your poems in presses sleep
while snow assumes your house into the deep
and snow is drifting down from darkest Heaven.'

iv

Like birds he sleeps on his nest, his pure way
and thirst for a better life assigning
once and for all to that one star defined
now in the cloud-mass of the stormy sky.
Like birds his soul is pure. But worldly quests
though sinful as must be are to him
more natural than nest of crow or raven
in vacant wooden rows of breeding-nests.
Like birds he too will waken with the day
though lying prone beneath a pallid seam;
while, stitched with pallid snow and stitched with dream,
the space between the soul and dreaming clay.

All things are sunk in sleep. The final verse
awaits its cue baring its teeth to snarl
that earthly love is just a joker's role
and heavenly love becomes a friar's flesh.
We find in life companions of such pith
that life is shared and ground to common salt;
but there's no lover under Heaven's vault
can intimate our soul and share our death.
Man's coat is tattered. And it may be torn
by all who want to tear it more.
It frays and is redeemed to soar
briefly, the wearer's shroud. Once more it's worn.
Sleep soundly, Donne, and let your soul not mope

in such dejected rags as darkness gives.
The convex sky is glowing like a sieve
and holy stars invest your world with hope.

from:
AT THE PROTESTANT MUSEUM (1986)

Mount Nebo

'luminous spots, as it were . . . to cure an eye hurt by the ghastly night.' (Nietzsche)

1

It was a throbbing summer.[1]
He trotted into Gorey[2]
his thighs locked on a half-mount
his sword pointing heavenward
long arm of the outlaw's bane.[3]

Unrestless disaffection.
Broody heads of the barley
nodded with knowledge, sullen
informed bodies between trees.
The landscape glanced askance.

In it Mount Nebo swelling
bungalow with bosomy
windows. It looked on the road
with hungry satisfaction
glutted cot of John Gowan.[4]

Men of letters are lovers
of innovation: today
I like his style Lucifer.
History is Hell's buffer
scripture of Purgatory.

2

The house bakes in mid-summer.
Its master away rumoured
to point a papish finger
at the sky. The polished sky
reflects the hard-riding boss.

The picaresque wayside inn
awaits attentively in
trappings of honeysuckle.
He tables a bowl of punch
and stirs with the accusing

finger a gift for his girls.
(Sophie fondles the trophy
erects its knuckle and tip
Bridget fidgets the digit
in her hot-cup's heady swirls.)

The hunter stalks with intent
a woman in the window
she turns from him he comes on
to pop the little plunder
in the cleft between her breasts.

3

Chaos was a bit like this —
hot sex of self-division
'violence upon the roads'.[5]
Seven borrowed syllables
threaten a mythology.

Captain John Hunter Gowan
captain in the yeomanry
hunter of men from the law
sucking his light-fingered sword
he prances to Gorey now.

His vigilant Black Mob are
a little before their time
will-power doing the duty
of the imagination[6]
this is romance in its prime.

The punch explodes with laughter.
Tomorrow he will harrow
Gorey tomorrow I will
sweat in Europe condoning
uncertainty of rumour.

1. Each line of the poem contains seven syllables.
2. A market town in County Wexford.
3. destruction i.e. enemy.
4. For an account of Gowan, see notes 1 and 2 to Myles Byrne's *Memoirs* (Volume I, p. 1095).
5. A quotation from Yeats, section VII of 'Nineteen Hundred and Nineteen'.
6. A reference to Yeats's famous criticism of over-didactic writers in whose work one finds 'the will doing the work of the imagination'.

CIARAN CARSON

(1948-)

from: THE IRISH FOR NO (1987)

[Deeply interested in traditional Irish music and rural folkways, Ciaran Carson has devoted much poetic energy to ironic investigation of the place of Gaelic culture against the predominantly unionist backdrop of Northern Ireland.]

The Irish for No[1]

Was it a vision, or a waking dream?[2] I heard her voice before I saw
What looked like the balcony scene in *Romeo and Juliet*, except Romeo
Seemed to have shinned up a pipe and was inside arguing with her. The casements
Were wide open and I could see some Japanese-style wall-hangings, the dangling
Quotation marks of a yin-yang mobile. *It's got nothing*, she was snarling, *nothing*
To do with politics, and, before the bamboo curtain came down,
That goes for you too!

It was time to turn into the dog's-leg short-cut from Chlorine Gardens
Into Cloreen Park, where you might see an *Ulster Says No* scrawled on the side
Of the power-block — which immediately reminds me of the Eglantine Inn
Just on the corner: on the missing *h* of Cloreen, you might say. We were debating,
Bacchus and the pards and me, how to render *The Ulster Bank — the Bank*
That Likes to Say Yes[3] into Irish, and whether eglantine[4] was alien to Ireland.
I cannot see what flowers are at my feet, when *yes* is the verb repeated,
Not exactly yes, but phatic[5] nods and whispers. *The Bank That Answers All*
Your Questions, maybe? That Greek portico of Mourne[6] granite, dazzling
With promises and feldspar, mirrors you in the Delphic black of its windows.

And the bruised pansies of the funeral parlour are dying in reversed gold letters,
The long sigh of the afternoon is not yet complete on the promontory where the victim,
A corporal in the UDR[7] from Lisbellaw, was last seen having driven over half
Of Ulster, a legally-held gun was found and the incidence of stress came up
On the headland which shadows Larne Harbour and the black pitch of warehouses.
There is a melancholy blast of diesel, a puff of smoke which might be black or white.
So the harbour slips away to perilous seas[8] as things remain unsolved; we listen
To the *ex cathedra* of the fog-horn, and *drink and leave the world unseen* —

What's all this to the Belfast business-man who drilled
Thirteen holes in his head with a Black & Decker? It was just a normal morning
When they came. The tennis-court shone with dew or frost, a little before dawn.
The border, it seemed, was not yet crossed: the Milky Way trailed snowy brambles,
The stars clustered thick as blackberries. They opened the door into the dark:
The murmurous haunt of flies on summer eves. Empty jam-jars.
Mish-mash. Hotch-potch. And now you rub your eyes and get acquainted with the light

1. There is no precise word in the Irish language for 'no' (or, for that matter, for 'yes'). 'Ulster Says "No"' was a common unionist slogan in protest against the Anglo-Irish Agreement of 1985.
2. The penultimate line of John Keats's 'Ode to a Nightingale'. There are echoes of this ode throughout the poem.
3. An advertising motto of 'the bank that likes to say yes' to loan applicants.
4. 'The pastoral eglantine', or sweet-briar, is referred to in Keats's ode.
5. Speech used for the purpose of initiating social interaction rather than to communicate an idea.
6. Mountains in County Down.
7. Ulster Defence Regiment, a controversial reserve army, frequently accused of abusing the nationalist population and often the victim of IRA assassinations.
8. A phrase from the last stanza of Keats's 'Ode to a Nightingale'.

A dust of something reminiscent drowses over the garage smell of creosote,
The concrete: blue clouds in porcelain, a paint-brush steeped in a chipped cup;
Staples hyphenate a wet cardboard box as the upturned can of oil still spills
And the unfed cat toys with the yin-yang of a tennis-ball, debating whether *yes* is *no*.

Belfast Confetti

Suddenly as the riot squad moved in, it was raining exclamation marks,
Nuts, bolts, nails, car-keys. A fount of broken type. And the explosion
Itself — an asterisk on the map. This hyphenated line, a burst of rapid fire . . .
I was trying to complete a sentence in my head, but it kept stuttering,
All the alleyways and side-streets blocked with stops and colons.

I know this labyrinth so well — Balaclava, Raglan, Inkerman, Odessa Street —[1]
Why can't I escape? Every move is punctuated. Crimea Street. Dead end again.
A Saracen, Kremlin-2 mesh. Makrolon face-shields. Walkie-talkies. What is
My name? Where am I coming from? Where am I going? A fusillade of question-marks.

1. Belfast street-names, derived from the British imperial experience in Eastern Europe.

Clearance

The Royal Avenue Hotel collapses under the breaker's pendulum:
Zig-zag stairwells, chimney-flues, and a 'thirties mural
Of an elegantly-dressed couple doing what seems to be the Tango, in Wedgwood
Blue and white — happy days! Suddenly more sky
Than there used to be. A breeze springs up from nowhere —

There, through a gap in the rubble, a greengrocer's shop
I'd never noticed until now. Or had I passed it yesterday? Everything —
Yellow, green and purple — is fresh as paint. Rain glistens on the aubergines
And peppers; even from this distance, the potatoes smell of earth.

TOM PAULIN

(1949-)

from: THE STRANGE MUSEUM (1980)

[Parting almost regretfully with every word expressed, Paulin produces a parsimonious Northern lyric, characterized by words that are at once accurate and surprising. His images are often mischievous and mocking, his contempt for the cultural distortions of imperialism very thinly concealed. There is, nevertheless, a certain elegiac sadness in these studies in a dying culture, as if he were also haunted by that which he condemns. A nice line in self-mockery prevents his poems from taking themselves too seriously.]

Still Century

The hard captains of industry[1]
Held the province in a firm control.

Judges, your pious tyranny
Is baked bone-dry in the old

Bricks of a hundred linen mills,
The shadows of black[2] tabernacles.

1. Belfast and its environs were more heavily industrialized than the rest of Ireland.
2. The Black Preceptory, a fundamentalist protestant group.

A crowd moves along the Shankill,[3]
And lamps shine in the dull

Streets where a fierce religion
Prays to the names of power:

Ewart and Bryson, Craig and Carson.[4]
On every wall, texts or a thick char.

Stacked in the corners of factory-yards,
The wicker carboys[5] of green acid

Hold out their bitter promise of whiteness
To the bleachgreens above the city.

The orange smoke at sunset, the gruff
Accents of a thousand foremen, speak

To the chosen, saying they are the stuff
That visions, cutlery and Belleek[6]

China are laid on. They are tied
To the shade of a bearded god,

Their dream of happiness is his smile
And his skilful way with the hardest rod.

3. The central thoroughfare of protestant Belfast.
4. Militant leaders of Ulster unionism.
5. Large glass bottles, encased in wicker, containing dangerous chemicals.
6. Prized, delicate pottery, manufactured in Belleek, Co. Cavan.

from: LIBERTY TREE (1983)

Desertmartin

At noon, in the dead centre of a faith,
Between Draperstown and Magherafelt,
This bitter village shows the flag
In a baked absolute September light.
Here the Word has withered to a few
Parched certainties, and the charred stubble
Tightens like a black belt, a crop of Bibles.

Because this is the territory of the Law
I drive across it with a powerless knowledge —
The owl of Minerva in a hired car.
A Jock squaddy[1] glances down the street
And grins, happy and expendable,
Like a brass cartridge. He is a useful thing,
Almost at home, and yet not quite, not quite.

It's a limed nest, this place. I see a plain
Presbyterian grace sour, then harden,
As a free strenuous spirit changes
To a servile defiance that whines and shrieks
For the bondage of the letter: it shouts
For the Big Man[2] to lead his wee people
To a clean white prison, their scorched tomorrow.

Masculine Islam, the rule of the Just,
Egyptian sand dunes and geometry,
A theology of rifle-butts and executions:
These are the places where the spirit dies.
And now, in Desertmartin's sandy light,
I see a culture of twigs and bird-shit
Waving a gaudy flag it loves and curses.

1. A Scottish soldier in the occupying British army.

Off the Back of a Lorry

A zippo lighter
and a quilted jacket,
two rednecks troughing
in a gleamy diner,
the flinty chipmarks
on a white enamel pail,
Paisley[1] putting pen to paper
in Crumlin jail,
a jumbo double
fried peanut butter
sandwich Elvis scoffed
during the last
diapered days —
they're more than tacky,
these pured fictions,
and like the small ads
in a country paper
they build a gritty
sort of prod[2] baroque
I must return to
like my own boke.[3]

1. Rev. Ian Paisley (born 1926), fundamentalist preacher, founder of the Free Presbyterian Church (1951) and militant leader of working-class loyalism. He was jailed in the Crumlin Road prison for staging an illegal protest march in 19
2. i.e. protestant.
3. vomit.

A Written Answer[1]

This poem by Rupert Brookeborough[2]
is all about fishing and the stout B-men[3]
(they live for always in our hearts,
their only crime was being loyal),
there is a lough in it and stacks of rivers,
also a brave wee hymn to the sten-gun.
The poet describes Gough of the Curragh[4]
and by his use of many metric arts
he designs a fictionary universe
which has its own laws and isn't quite
the same as this place that we call real.
His use of metonymy is pretty desperate
and the green symbolism's a contradiction,
but I like his image of the elm and chestnut,
for to me this author is a fly[5] man
and the critics yonder say his work is alright.

1. To a parliamentary question.
2. A conflation of Rupert Brooke (1887-1915), patriot-poet of World War I, and Viscount Basil Brookeborough (1886-1973), Fermanagh landowner and unionist prime minister of Northern Ireland 1943-63. The latter founded the B-Specials and was noted for his anti-catholic speeches.
3. Part of a special constabulary of auxiliary paramilitaries, raised in 1920 by the British administration, they were part-timers who mounted patrols and check-points at night. Wholly protestant, they were recruited from the Ulster Volunteer Force and the Orange Order.
4. General Hubert Gough, the leader of the Curragh Mutiny in March 1914. He gave his name to a notorious barracks in Armagh.
5. knowing, wide awake.

Manichean[1] Geography I

Consider a coral or guano[2] atoll[3]
Where a breezy Union Jack
Flaps above the police station.

There is a rusting mission hut
Built out of flattened tin cans
(Bully beef, beans and tomato pilchards)

Where the Reverend Bungo Buller
And his prophet, Joe Gimlet,
Preach the gospel of cargoes.[4]

They worship a white god
Of dentures and worn toothbrushes
Who will come to earth, Hallelulia,

In a reconditioned Flying Fortress[5]
Humping bales of fresh calico
And a crate of Black and Deckers.

Seeding like brisk parachutes,
The ancestral spirits will fall
From the pod of an airship,

And the chosen people will serve
Themselves with orange jube-jubes
In a brand-new discount warehouse.

1. Based on the division of all things into good and evil.
2. Dung of sea-fowl, used as manure.
3. An island, usually coral, enclosing a circular lagoon. The reference is to the Falkland/Malvinas islands, subject of a brief British-Argentinian war in 1982.
4. Cargo cult is a religious movement of the south-west Pacific; spirits are expected to return in ships or planes carrying goods that will provide for the needs of the believers.
5. Planes used by the British government to ferry supplies to Fort Stanley, the chief port of the Malvinas.

Of Difference Does it Make

During the 51-year existence of the Northern Ireland Parliament only one Bill sponsored by a non-Unionist member was ever passed.

Among the plovers and the stonechats
protected by the Wild Birds Act
of nineteen-hundred-and-thirty-one,
there is a rare stint called the notawhit[1]
that has a schisty[2] flight-call, like the chough's.
Notawhit, notawhit, notawhit
— it raps out a sharp code-sign
like a mild and patient prisoner
pecking through granite with a teaspoon.

1. A parody of the unionist slogan 'Not an inch'.
2. flinty.

A Nation, Yet Again

after Pushkin

That kitsch lumber-room is stacked
with a parnassian dialect:
'love, hope, and quiet reputation
kissed us for a short season
and the gamey letters that we swopped,
in clipped verse, soon had to stop.'
No one, then, praised either side,
though some dipped down among the shades

to find Aeneas and to file
a delicate, a tough, new style
that draws the language to the light
and purifies its tribal rites.
I'm tense now: talk of sharing power,
prophecies of civil war,
new reasons for a secular
mode of voicing the word *nation*
set us on edge, this generation,
and force the poet to play traitor
or act the half-sure legislator.
No matter; there's a classic form
that's in the blood, that makes me warm
to better, raise, build up, refine
whatever gabbles without discipline:
see, it takes me now, these hands stir
to bind the northern to the southern stars.

Argument from Design

Your glooby voice
is salt and carrageen,
a dolphin fountain
among the bay trees
in a Tuscan garden
where a dwarf on a tortoise
guards the pearly grotto;
and your quaint frizz
has this ebony wrinkle
glazed with bruised purple,
an aubergine lip,
a barbel-beard.
What a baroque smörgåsbord!
bad taste of the blond north
doing a flip
with the sugars of the deep south.

from: FIVEMILETOWN (1987)

Father of History

A state schoolroom and a master talking
in a limber voice, a spiky burr
like a landrail[1] crecking in the bracken.
Ock there he is with hair like furze,
smiling obliquely on the risen town

1. Another name for the corncrake, a bird of fields and meadows.

and building Lisburn like a warm
plain-spoken sermon on the rights of man.
A sunned Antrim face, he maybe prays
to the New Light in a relished dialect,
the eager accent of a free sept,
broken in the north, in resurrection.
Folded like bark, like cinnamon things,
I traced them to the Linen Hall[2] stacks —
Munro, Hope, Porter and McCracken;[3]
like sweet yams buried deep, these rebel minds
endure posterity without a monument,
their names a covered sheugh,[4] remnants,
some brackish signs.

2. A library in the centre of Belfast.
3. Henry Munro was killed in battle in the 1798 Rebellion in Antrim; the Reverend James Porter and Henry Joy McCracken were both hanged for their part in the uprising. Jemmy Hope (1764-1847), a poet, took part in both the 1798 Rebellion and the Emmet uprising in Dublin in 1803. All were northern protestants, radicals and leading members of the United Irishmen.
4. ditch.

An Ulster Unionist Walks the Streets of London

All that Friday[1]
there was no flag —
no Union Jack,
no tricolour —
on the governor's mansion.
I waited outside the gate-lodge,
waited like a dog
in my own province
till a policeman brought me
a signed paper.
Was I meant to beg
and be grateful?
I sat on the breakfast-shuttle[2] and I called —
I called out loud —
to the three Hebrew children
for I know at this time
there is neither prince, prophet, nor leader —
there is no power
we can call our own.
I grabbed a fast black —
ack, I caught a taxi —

1. Friday, 15 November 1985 was the day when the Anglo-Irish Agreement was signed between the Irish and British governments, over the heads of unionists, who felt an acute sense of betrayal (see p. 372 of this volume).
2. An early-morning flight from Belfast to London.

to Kentish Town,[3]
then walked the streets
like a half-foreigner
among the London Irish.
What does it feel like?
I wanted ask them —
what does it feel like
to be a child of that nation?
But I went underground
to the Strangers' House —[4]
We vouch, they swore,
We deem, they cried,
till I said, 'Out ...
I may go out that door
and walk the streets
searching my own people.'

3. A London surburb with a heavily Irish immigrant population.

4. Perhaps a bitter reference to the British House of Parliament at Westminster. 'Strangers' is a polite term in Irish poetry and Hiberno-English speech for the English in Ireland.

MEDBH McGUCKIAN

(1950-)

from: THE FLOWER MASTER (1982)

[Where other poets translate the world into a set of chosen images, Medbh McGuckian begins with the image and tries to infer from it an inkling of a distant world. Beginning with metaphor, she feels her way back to reality, as if by touch. Sometimes, her images vibrate in a language rich with implication; on other occasions, they seem utterly incommunicable. She sees the world at an angle and, as a result, finds much that other poets miss.]

Slips

The studied poverty of a moon roof,
The earthenware of dairies cooled by apple trees,
The apple tree that makes the whitest wash ...

But I forget names, remembering them wrongly
Where they touch upon another name,
A town in France like a woman's Christian name.

My childhood is preserved as a nation's history,
My favourite fairy tales the shells
Leased by the hermit crab.

I see my grandmother's death as a piece of ice,
My mother's slimness restored to her,
My own key slotted in your door —
Tricks you might guess from this unfastened button,
A pen mislaid, a word misread,
My hair coming down in the middle of a conversation.

The Flitting

'You wouldn't believe all this house has cost me —
In body-language terms, it has turned me upside down.'
I've been carried from one structure to the other
On a chair of human arms, and liked the feel
Of being weightless, that fraternity of clothes ...
Now my own life hits me in the throat, the bumps
And cuts of the walls as telling
As the poreholes in strawberries, tomato seeds.
I cover them for safety with these Dutch girls
Making lace, or leaning their almond faces
On their fingers with a mandolin, a dreamy
Chapelled ease abreast this other turquoise-turbanned,
Glancing over her shoulder with parted mouth.

She seems a garden escape in her unconscious
Solidarity with darkness, clove-scented
As an orchid taking fifteen years to bloom,
And turning clockwise as the honeysuckle.
Who knows what importance
She attaches to the hours?
Her narrative secretes its own values, as mine might
If I painted the half of me that welcomes death

In a faggoted[1] dress, in a peacock chair,
No falser biography than our casual talk
Of losing a virginity, or taking a life, and
No less poignant if dying
Should consist in more than waiting.

I postpone my immortality for my children,
Little rock-roses, cushioned
In long-flowering sea-thrift and metrics,
Lacking elemental memories:
I am well-earthed here as the digital clock,
Its numbers flicking into place like overgrown
farthings
On a bank where once a train
Ploughed like an emperor living out a myth
Through the cambered flesh of clover and wild
carrot.

1. embroidered.

from:
VENUS AND THE RAIN (1984)

The Villain

This house is the shell of a perfect marriage
Someone has dug out completely; so its mind
Is somewhere above its body, and its body
Stumbles after its voice like a man who needs
A woman for every book. When you put your
Handkerchief to your lips, and turned away from
Me, I saw in the lawn that least wished itself
Known, the reverse of green fingers, taking an
Over-long walk. Once with your velvet side you
Said you would like to beget a child to look
Out of every window with his own daytime eyes:
Somewhere there's the right colour for this my
Brownest, tethered room, the unloved villain
The younger year may locate, and take into its own.

Painter and Poet

I turned his room into a shell
With the same choosiness that was icing me
All over: I choked the crimson flock
Wallpaper with sheets of mimosa,[1]
That he might be remembered for a handful
Of love poems. Still it was
The warmest room in the house, and he would say
'The closeness of my room never injured me',
Whenever we had a thunderstorm to ourselves.

Yet some exactness about the posture
Of the chairs would make me foam
Against the beautiful moist heat that could
Bring peaches to perfection on its own,
Without so much as a hint
That their bindings were as constant
As an interregnum in the rain.

Unallegorically, I wanted his quenched eyes
To feel as well as see how the moon and we
Do not amalgamate, and so I mushroomed
The hills of his ceiling into a kind of chapter
Of hats and walking shoes. I cannot say
Precisely, 'Perdidi diem',[2] though I dined
Superficially his normal, lovely, melancholic
Wife: for that evening, he scratched out
Regiments of flowers, and went with me
Some distance from the house, perhaps
An English mile,[3] until even
The ghosts of paths were out of sight.

1. A sensitive plant flower, more commonly called acacia.

2. Latin: 'I have lost a day'.
3. 1,760 yards. An Irish mile is 2,240 yards.

Catching Geese

Dreaming is after I decline to sleep
With you, but stay in the depths
Of the bed, winding you round my arm.
If I disappear, it's only to worry you
Into getting the children on their feet,
Or putting a rosary out in the rain
To turn the house gold again, facing
The wall of a church. You're unhappy
At my fern-fisted handshake, I'm unhappy
That my fresh hunger doesn't block your throat
Like a person. Even the sun should be as different
As my soon-to-be-famous blue style from
My letter-perfect rose, a period of wood
Marbleized to promise stone — hot as the
Close of summer's complete scheme in lace-trimmed
White, which, if I wanted to write about,
All I had to do to hold the sentence still
Was paint it on the circumference of a plate,
And every sound of you crying could be heard.

PAUL MULDOON

(1951-)

from:
NEW WEATHER (1973)

[A fastidious miniaturist who uses words with a kind of quiet awe, Paul Muldoon is a profoundly descriptive poet. Many of his works are simply attempts to present, in all its appropriateness, a closing image or phrase. Obsessed with boundary states, this liminal author sees his art as a balancing act, by which extremes may meet and be aligned. Words are suspended on line-endings, indicative of their author's tentative and irresolute condition.]

Thrush

I guessed the letter
  Must be yours. I recognized
The cuttle[1] ink,
  The serif[2] on
The P. I read the postmark and the date,
  Impatience held
By a paperweight.
  I took your letter at eleven
To the garden
  With my tea.
And suddenly the yellow gum secreted
  Halfwayup
The damson bush
  Had grown a shell.
I let those scentless pages fall
  And took it
In my feckless hand. I turned it over
  On its back
To watch your mouth
  Withdraw. Making a lean, white fist
Out of my freckled hand.

1. A mollusc that ejects a black inky liquid.
2. A short crossline at the end of a stroke in a letter.

The Field Hospital[1]

Taking, giving back their lives
By the strength of our bare hands,
By the silence of our knives,
We answer to no grey South

Nor blue North.[2] Not self defence,
The lie of just wars, neither
Cold nor hot blood's difference
In their discharging of guns,

But that hillside of fresh graves.
Would this girl brought to our tents
From whose flesh we have removed
Shot that George, on his day off,

Will use to weight fishing lines,
Who died screaming for ether,
Yet protest our innocence?
George lit the lanterns, in danced

Those gigantic, yellow moths
That brushed right over her wounds,
Pinning themselves to our sleeves
Like medals given the brave.

1. Such units were set up along the Irish border during periods of disturbance in Northern Ireland in the late 1960s and 1970s.
2. The colour of the uniforms in the American Civil War.

from:
MULES (1977)

The Bearded Woman, by Ribera[1]

I've seen one in a fairground,
Swigging a quart of whiskey,
But nothing like this lady
Who squats in the foreground
To suckle the baby,
With what must be her husband
Almost out of the picture.

Might this be the Holy Family
Gone wrong?

1. Jusepe or José Ribera (*c.* 1591-1652), Spanish painter who spent most of his life in Italy.

Her face belongs to my grand-da
Except that her beard
Is so luxuriantly black.
One pap, her right, is bared
And borrowed by her child,
Who could not be less childlike.
He's ninety, too, if he's a day.

I'm taken completely
By this so unlikely Madonna.

Yet my eye is drawn once again,
Almost against its wishes,
To the figure in the shadows,
Willowy, and clean-shaven,
As if he has simply wandered in
Between mending that fuse
And washing the breakfast dishes.

from: WHY BROWNLEE LEFT (1980)

Cuba[1]

My eldest sister arrived home that morning
In her white muslin evening dress.
'Who the hell do you think you are,
Running out to dances in next to nothing?
As though we hadn't enough bother
With the world at war, if not at an end.'
My father was pounding the breakfast-table.

'Those Yankees were touch and go as it was —
If you'd heard Patton[2] in Armagh —
But this Kennedy's nearly an Irishman
So he's not much better than ourselves.
And him with only to say the word.
If you've got anything on your mind
Maybe you should make your peace with God.'

I could hear May from beyond the curtain.[3]
'Bless me, Father, for I have sinned.
I told a lie once, I was disobedient once.
And, Father, a boy touched me once.'
'Tell me, child. Was this touch immodest?
Did he touch your breast, for example?'
'He brushed against me, Father. Very gently.'

1. The Cuban Missile Crisis of 1962, when US President John Kennedy verged on a military confrontation with Soviet leader Nikita Khrushchev, until the latter ordered the removal of nuclear warheads from Cuba.
2. George Patton (1885-1945), one of the toughest American generals of World War II.
3. In the confessional box.

Anseo

When the Master was calling the roll
At the primary school in Collegelands,
You were meant to call back *Anseo*
And raise your hand
As your name occurred.
Anseo, meaning here, here and now,
All present and correct,
Was the first word of Irish I spoke.
The last name on the ledger
Belonged to Joseph Mary Plunkett Ward[1]
And was followed, as often as not,
By silence, knowing looks,
A nod and a wink, the Master's droll
'And where's our little Ward-of-court?'

I remember the first time he came back
The Master had sent him out
Along the hedges
To weigh up for himself and cut
A stick with which he would be beaten.
After a while, nothing was spoken;
He would arrive as a matter of course
With an ash-plant, a salley-rod.[2]
Or, finally, the hazel-wand
He had whittled down to a whip-lash,
Its twist of red and yellow lacquers
Sanded and polished,
And altogether so delicately wrought
That he had engraved his initials on it.

I last met Joseph Mary Plunkett Ward
In a pub just over the Irish border.[3]
He was living in the open,
In a secret camp[4]
On the other side of the mountain.
He was fighting for Ireland,

1. Obviously named after Joseph Mary Plunkett, a signatory of the 1916 Proclamation and one of the leaders of the Easter Rising.
2. A willow branch.
3. i.e. in the Irish Republic.
4. An Irish Republican Army camp, from which IRA volunteers launched attacks on the forces of the Northern state.

Making things happen.
And he told me, Joe Ward,
Of how he had risen through the ranks
To Quartermaster, Commandant:
How every morning at parade
His volunteers would call back *Anseo*
And raise their hands
As their names occurred.

Why Brownlee Left

Why Brownlee left, and where he went,
Is a mystery even now.
For if a man should have been content
It was him; two acres of barley,
One of potatoes, four bullocks,
A milker, a slated farmhouse.
He was last seen going out to plough
On a March morning, bright and early.

By noon Brownlee was famous;
They had found all abandoned, with
The last rig unbroken, his pair of black
Horses, like man and wife,
Shifting their weight from foot to
Foot, and gazing into the future.

Truce[1]

It begins with one or two soldiers
And one or two following
With hampers over their shoulders.
They might be off wildfowling

As they would another Christmas Day,
So gingerly they pick their steps.
No one seems sure of what to do.
All stop when one stops.

A fire gets lit. Some spread
Their greatcoats on the frozen ground.
Polish vodka, fruit and bread
Are broken out and passed round.

The air of an old German song,
The rules of Patience,[2] are the secrets
They'll share before long.
They draw on their last cigarettes

As Friday-night lovers, when it's over,
Might get up from their mattresses
To congratulate each other
And exchange names and addresses.

1. The famous occasion in World War I when British and German soldiers fraternized, exchanged cigarettes and played football together in honour of Christmas Day.
2. A card-game for one player only.

from: QUOOF (1983)

Trance

My mother opens the scullery door
on Christmas Eve, 1954,
to empty the dregs
of the tea-pot on the snowy flags.[1]
A wind out of Siberia
carries such voices as will carry
through to the kitchen —

Someone mutters a flame from lichen
and eats the red-and white Fly Agaric[2]
while the others hunker in the dark,
taking it in turn
to drink his mind-expanding urine.
One by one their reindeer
nuzzle in.

My mother slams the door
on her star-cluster of dregs
and packs me off to bed.
At 2 a.m. I will clamber downstairs
to glimpse the red-and-white
up the chimney, my new rocking-horse
as yet unsteady on its legs.

1. flagstones, slabs.
2. Poisonous mushroom-like fungus used to kill flies.

The Right Arm

I was three-ish
when I plunged my arm into the sweet-jar
for the last bit of clove-rock.

We kept a shop in Eglish
that sold bread, milk, butter, cheese,
bacon and eggs,

Andrews Liver Salts,
and, until now, clove-rock.

I would give my right arm to have known then
how Eglish was itself wedged between
ecclesia and *église*.[1]

The Eglish sky was its own stained-glass vault
and my right arm was sleeved in glass
that has yet to shatter.

1. i.e. caught between Latin and French.

Cherish the Ladies

In this, my last poem about my father,
there may be time enough
for him to fill their drinking-trough
and run his eye over

his three mooley[1] heifers.
Such a well-worn path,
I know, from here to the galvanized bath.
I know, too, you would rather

I saw behind the hedge to where the pride
of the herd,[2] *though not an Irish*
bull, would cherish
the ladies with his electric cattle-prod.

As it is, in my last poem about my father
he opens the stand-pipe
and the water scurries along the hose
till it's curled

in the bath. One heifer
may look up
and make a mental note, then put her nose
back to the salt-lick[3] of the world.

1. hornless.
2. The name of a Gaelic song, designating the chief bull.
3. A place to which animals resort for salt.

Aisling[1]

I was making my way home late one night
this summer, when I staggered
into a snow drift.

Her eyes spoke of a sloe-year,[2]
her mouth a year of haws.

Was she Aurora, or the goddess Flora,
Artemidora, or Venus bright,
or Anorexia,[3] who left
a lemon stain on my flannel sheet?

It's all much of a muchness.

In Belfast's Royal Victoria Hospital
a kidney machine
supports the latest hunger-striker[4]
to have called off his fast, a saline
drip into his bag of brine.

A lick and a promise. Cuckoo spittle.
I hand my sample to Doctor Maw.
She gives me back a confident *All Clear*.

1. A vision-poem in the Gaelic tradition.
2. The sloe is the fruit of the blackthorn tree.
3. A parody of the form of address to the visionary lady in Gaelic *aisling* poems.
4. A reference to the hunger-strikes of Republican prisoners at Long Kesh prison in Northern Ireland in 1981.

My Father and I and Billy Two Rivers

Our favoured wrestler, the Mohawk Indian.

We would sit in the local barber shop —
'Could he not afford a decent haircut?' —
to watch him suffer the slings and arrows[1]
of a giant Negro who fought dirty.

The Negro's breath-taking crotch-hold and slam
left all of us out for a count of ten.

The barber knew the whole thing was a sham.

Next week would see Billy back on his feet
for one of his withering Tomahawk Chops
to a Britisher's craw,

dusting him out
of the ring and into the wide-mouthed crowd
like a bale of tea at the Boston Tea Party.

1. cf. *Hamlet*, III. 1. 58.

Quoof

How often have I carried our family word
for the hot water bottle
to a strange bed,
as my father would juggle a red-hot half-brick
in an old sock
to his childhood settle.
I have taken it into so many lovely heads
or laid it between us like a sword.

An hotel room in New York City
with a girl who spoke hardly any English,
my hand on her breast
like the smouldering one-off spoor of the yeti[1]
or some other shy beast
that has yet to enter the language.

1. The Abominable Snowman.

from:
MEETING THE BRITISH
(1987)

The Wishbone

Maureen in England, Joseph in Guelph,[1]
my mother in her grave.

★

At three o'clock in the afternoon
we watch the Queen's
message to the Commonwealth
with the sound turned off.

★

He seems to favour *Camelot*
over *To Have and Have Not*.[2]

★

1. A town in Ontario, Canada.
2. A novel by Ernest Hemingway made into a film.

Yet we agree, my father and myself,
that here is more than enough
for two; a frozen chicken,
spuds, sprouts, *Paxo*[3] sage and onion.

★

The wishbone like a rowelled[4] spur
on the fibula[5] of Sir — or Sir —.

3. A brand of stuffing for serving with poultry.
4. spiked (with sharp prongs).
5. The outer of the two bones between the knee and the ankle.

Christo's

Two workmen were carrying a sheet of asbestos
down the Main Street of Dingle;
it must have been nailed, at a slight angle,
to the same-sized gap between Brandon[1]

and whichever's the next mountain.
Nine o'clock. We watched the village dogs
take turns to spritz the hotel's refuse-sacks.
I remembered Tralee's unbiodegradable flags

from the time of the hunger-strikes.[2]
We drove all day past mounds of sugar-beet,
hay-stacks, silage-pits, building-sites,
a thatched cottage even —

all of them draped in black polythene
and weighted against the north-east wind
by concrete blocks, old tyres; bags of sand
at a makeshift army post

across the border. By the time we got to Belfast
the whole of Ireland would be under wraps
like, as I said, 'one of your man's landscapes'.
'Your man's? You don't mean Christo's?'

1. The Conor Pass, in the Brandon mountains of County Kerry.
2. In the summer of 1981, ten jailed Irish republicans died on a hunger-strike for the status of political prisoner. Many black flags (some made of plastic) flew throughout the Irish countryside.

PETER FALLON
(1951-)

from: WINTER WORK (1983)

[Influenced in the 1960s by a soft 'pop' idiom, Peter Fallon has developed steadily away from the metropolitan mainstream and now situates himself at the confluence of two traditions, one Irish, one American. In committing himself to the local and the quotidian in the rural life of County Meath, where he lives as a farmer, poet and publisher, he is not only heir to Patrick Kavanagh's 'parochial' achievements but is inspired by the ecological vision of transatlantic poets like Gary Snyder and Wendell Berry.]

My Care

Sometimes we sit in Phil's
and watch a film, *Hill Street Blues*,
or something. But this is new —
we make a point of turning to the news.

A kidnap, check-points, searches,
killers on the run.
The peace-keeping force can't keep
the peace. The new law is the outlaw gun.

The government debates. Here and there
it seems the talk goes on forever.
Talk, talk, talk . . . . After a while
it could be a chimney fire, or bad weather.

Should I do more? Is it enough
to keep a weather eye and talk to friends?
I honestly don't know. All I ever wanted was
to make a safe house in the midlands.

'How's all your care?' I'm asked.
'Grand. And yours?' I don't repeat
my worry for my care, my country. When I go home
the animals are healthy, safe. There's that.

I go inside and stir the fire.
Soon I'm sitting by a riot
of kindling, the soft explosions of seasoned logs.
They have shaken the roots of that familiar quiet.

Dung

Head-bowed, headstrong; like a team
in harness, matched and hitched to other;
four of the rams are mowing a meadow.

When dung dries to the sides of cattle
they're armadilloes, awkward knights in armour,
but these, these are Rastafarians!
It hangs from them like dreadlocks.
And they are music:
when they took fright last night
and raced across the paddock, there was drumming
of feet, the click and clack of castanets.

Winter Work

Friends are unhappy; their long night
finds no day, their lane no turn. They wait
for things to change, as if history
happens to others, elsewhere. They hibernate

in dreams and fear. And Cathryn writes from Dublin:
she lies awake at night and hears
the noise of cars on Rathgar Road,
far from where her life coheres.

I warm to winter work, its rituals
and routines, and find — indoors
and out — a deal of pleasure, alone
or going out to work with neighbours,

a *meitheal*[1] still. All I approve persists,
is here, at home. I think it exquisite
to stand in the yard, my feet on the ground,
in cowshit and horseshit and sheepshit.

1. A work-team of neighbours who join together on a voluntary basis.

The Heart of Ireland

Late evening in late Spring,
I saddle myself to spray
docks and nettles, a day's work done.
I could be playing a set of pipes,

pumping bellows beneath my elbow.
Late birds add grace notes to the drone.

I work at my slow walking pace,
loving the labour, and find myself begin
— lost in a rhythm — to backpack
into memory: twenty years ago
I stumbled underneath the weight
of bluestone in a brown knapsack

when the men were resting, looking on;
and backtrack further
to the far end of those drills,
to the heart of Ireland,
a stain of blight, stench on the wind,
rotten stalks and tubers, spent chlorophylls.

We strained against an end of faith
in God, toward a field
of solid fruit and flowers,
and woke with proud relief
the day the furrows glowed
as if, overnight, showers

of snow had come to stay or flocks
of white butterflies had lit along the rows.
Late evening in late Spring I'm rounding
up the weeds for grass to grow.
The nights are bright till after ten.
I work till after dark busking

away to my heart's content, and I recall
a famine carried on the wind.
Beyond the garden wall a breeze
begins to blow. The centre strains
to hold. A half-moon tilts between
dead ash- and old apple-trees.

GERALD DAWE

(1952-)

from: THE LUNDYS LETTER (1985)

[Gerald Dawe seems at times to be writing with a self-imposed parsimony, as if he had committed himself to a doctrinaire 'northern' reticence of feeling and expression. The reward of this discipline is a cleanliness of presentation and a head-on address to the subject; the penalty, however, can be abruptness and an exclusive minimalism. Dawe's lyrics are like messages from an Ulster protestant sensibility that has decided to go it alone into what is both expected and unexpected in the life of Ireland, north and south.]

The Lundys Letter[1]

You staged the ultimate *coup de grâce*
for the Union's son turned republican.
I can see you shivering in the cold
of an East Belfast morning, outside
school, the bikes upended, the quad
blown by a dusty wind, and rows of
windows, some cellophaned, gaze
back at the encroaching estate.

Even your voice was different, haughty
we thought, the grand dismissive way
you demonstrated learning, or in *Tartuffe*[2]
worked a subtle authority over our
ragged rebelliousness that we
should sit through such performances
of high art in a secondary school!

A generation growing but no hard-hats
for us or the miserable one-step up
a slippery ladder to civil service.
I don't know where you went; we got
lost in London or tried our wings
on an amalgam of desperate love
and politics at the new university.

1. Lundy is the name of a protestant who attempted to betray Derry to the besieging catholic forces in 1689. The name is synonymous with treachery, specifically by a protestant to the enemy catholic (or nationalist or republican) cause. This poem commemorates such a person, who paid for his 'treachery' with his life.

And then the next time it was a warm
summer's day at Woolworth's when
the ground shook and a tailor's dummy
crashed through sheets of glass,
and there was hardly time to ask
how you were keeping as shoe-boxes flew
all over the place and the bomb
finished its work on down High Street.

Walking to the Dole, the clang in my ears
of sirens and trampling feet,
it was another lock[3] of years
before I saw you in a pub by chance,
barely the same, chose not to recognise —
I only bear witness now to what was,
and hear your prefect's voice of derision
shout to a smoking third-form class.

3. Northern Irish dialect for 'lot'.

The Desert Campaign

On a day-trip to Donaghadee
I am free and easy,
scanning eyes over the bay
like a real sea-captain.

There certainly are women
in floral printed skirts
and, settling through news-
papers, grandmothers with

bright blue rinses chat
about making do and watch
stretch-marked daughters
carry on the way they used to,

as the various husbands,
unaccustomed to the sun,
unbutton shirt-fronts or stand
giddily at the water's edge.

I am dive-bombing
beneath the promenade wall,
leaving in my wake
a ruined city and on

my bended knees
discover an oasis
where sultry hussies drive
shaggy beasts to drink.

The Clock on a Wall of Farringdon Gardens, August 1971[1]

I am the clock on a wall
of Farringdon Gardens. I
stopped dead at 7.30. They

tried to take me away
from the burning. I remember
the whooshing smoke.

But in the rush
I was left here
as if nothing had happened.

Part of my task is
not to get panicked.
I'm regular and reliable

and wake each morning
for work —
a bulwark of my society,

but when the fires
started and the windows
cracked like ice

I was snatched up
and out under this sky
to sit defenceless,

my springs and coils
and deep chimings stopped
at 7.30.

So if you come
across me in your reading —
a photo perhaps in some

glossy history —
remember the blackened walls
and roofless houses,

of what went on
before the three monkeys
and chipped mantelpieces,

1. Farringdon Gardens was a street of houses in Belfast, burnt to the ground in the riots of August 1971.

in the backs of
sculleries and in front
bedrooms, before

the televisions
landed in tidily grown
gardens, think

just a little
of my time watching
these different people

who left their lives
in my hands
sitting on a wall of Farringdon Gardens.

The Sleepwalker

'. . . this is not the place to deplore
the miseries of our century but to
congratulate you on the ingenious
arguments you found in proof of Truth.'
Kepler to Galileo

'I am the last man on earth
you could call on,
all my time spent moon-
gazing from an attic window,

particular about the star
formations. Like my imagination
the World is done for.
See when I turn from the great

Firmament my fate is
telescoped: dirty streets
full of louts about to blast
each other into diabolic

Eternity. But I, sublime
worshipper of alternative gods,
have seen behind the future
and found it to be wanting.'

HARRY CLIFTON

(1952-)

from: COMPARATIVE LIVES (1983)

[It can sometimes seem as if Harry Clifton's poems were written by someone who has escaped from the world of James Joyce's *Dubliners*. They embody an intensity that grows claustrophobic and a scruple that turns punitive. Intelligent, honest, self-wounding, enraged in general at the demeaned circumstances of an Ireland uniquely catholic, commercial and complaisant, Clifton is the inheritor of Austin Clarke's indigenous obsessions and costive lyricism. There is, however, a distinctive, personal fever and chill about his work.]

The Seamstress

I have a seamstress, making a shirt for me
In sultry weather, in the months we are together.
She measures my shoulders with tape, I feel on my
back
The cool of her wooden yardstick, and submit

To a temporary contract, binding me
To the new and the strange. Together we lose
ourselves

Among shades of blue, the melancholy feast
A culture of silkworms creates, as Chinese tailors

Stand and wait. For me it's the stuff of dreams,
For her a labour of love ... In her house on stilts

Where women are still slaves, she sews the collarless
Garment of pure freedom I have asked for

When I leave, keeping only for herself
Dry tailor's chalk, and the diagram of a body.

from:
THE LIBERAL CAGE (1988)

The Liberal Cage

You and I, dear wife,
Are reading only the best
That was lived through and suffered for.
Our rented rooms are a nest

Of first editions, our days
Appraising them, stifled,
Consummated, behind the double glaze
Of conscience and the good life,

Are passing, passing —
And who knows, maybe rage
Goes with them, and leaves us forever
Inside this liberal age . . . .

If a face looks in
Ignore it, it speaks through a screen.
For the point of this place
Is to see without being seen

The dark, platonic cave
Of popular night —
The winter fogs, the yellow sodium lights,
Where real people move

Beyond the security gates,
Glass eyes, electronic doors
Of a novelist's estate,
A poet's ivory tower.

Make love, cook dinner —
Salt the inversions away
Below zero, until Judgement Day.
Convert outer to inner

But listen . . . not in doubt,
Contentment, or in pure mind,
But in anger alone, will we find
The key that lets us out.

Id

What if, with my life half over,
I was to go back again
On abandoned ways, and instead of taking a lover,
Instead of taking a wife,
I shook off my status, a man among men,
And disappeared back into life —

Would they still be there
To absolve me, the professional liars
With telephones unlisted and whereabouts hid
In a maze of cities, the women on hire
The desk clerk knows, and the bellhop shows
 upstairs?
The heroines of the id,

They came to me once, when I lived alone
In African hotels —
And when we had finished, they whispered to me,
As they whisper, now, to somebody else,
Young man, by the time you are thirty
Everything will be known . . . .

And so it was, on Sandal Street,
One night in old Calcutta
Of rain and cooking fires, along roof and gutter,
And families camped under plastic sheets
Among the imperial ruins the viceroys created
And rickshaw coolies waited —

I saw myself, as I washed in the copper bowl
And let cold water, a strip of towel
Restore the world to me, by slow degrees —
The girl I was with, the room I was in,
And somewhere about me, a jangle of keys
And the voices of middlemen.

Oh, marry us, they said to me,
The girls sold into slavery
So long ago, and the wards of court
Escaping from love, in need of a foreign address,
If not for ourselves, at least for the chance of a passport
To the Europe of consciousness . . . .

And far away, under Western time,
Again I lie down, in the home from home
Of a democratic city,
Whose lights I can reconstruct from, whose
 darkness I cannot defend,
Though the woman lying beside me, now,
Is conscious, and a friend.

MATTHEW SWEENEY

(1952-)

from: A DREAM OF MAPS (1981)

[Matthew Sweeney's enigmatic narratives and cameos owe something to the laid-back modes of British poetry in the 1980s. His writing can be excessively self-conscious; it gets most purchase on the reader when it is drawing upon the energies of a suppressed personal subject or following the logic of some free-wheeling fantasy.]

Last Supper

It's time for wild cooking.
A wind skims the Atlantic
so fierce it draws the future.
Cairns & transmitters shake on hilltops.
Rain reproduces the sea.

So call the butcher on the telephone,
halve his stock. Send the child
in a thick anorak up the garden.
Set the six gas-rings on at once.
Gather the herbs and go.

Beyond the pane, slates are falling.
The mail is late. But the water
piped from the reservoir on the horizon
is flowing freely. Enough
for six pots & more.

And the guests owed for years
can arrive with wine,
abandoning cards in the yard,
hats held tight with gloves
as they ring the bell,

then enter the vacuumed corridor
to lights dimmed, candles arrayed
on tables with Christmas silver.
And the odour adrift in the air
preceding the feast.

And the sound of Brahms, say,
drowning the wind. And the topics,
between mouthfuls, kept to the past:
religion's mercy, and Mass
in those days read in Latin.

from: BLUE SHOES (1989)

Blue Shoes

I see that day's non-headlines, as he did
though they're smoky now —
a prince at playschool, a brat's betrothal.
Some days they rob the gossip entries
in lieu of disasters.
They missed his later.

The weather inch reads more like Sicily
than England. I see him
hurrying towards the train, his hand
raised to his eyes, the sunglasses at home.
I have his notes here,
the last of any consequence.

All the women, it seems, wore blue shoes
in keeping with the morning.
He played with patterns, with omens
he deciphered later. That particular day
it was blue shoes
for want of any better.

I see him with a letter and xeroxed map
leaving the station.
He is sucking mints, perhaps hungover.
At the school gates he checks his flies.
He goes in the office,
is lost from sight.

Did they know the strain of these visits?
Did the kids care?
It was a long day, but not outlandish.
In his honour they had lunch in a pub.
On another day
it would have relaxed him.

He was chauffeured to the train in the end,
an overwound watch.
He queued at a phone, his heart chugging.
A woman was speaking, a man waiting —
the woman, he wrote,
wore blue shoes.

Hard for me in this library to imagine
that home journey,
the mounting pain in his mind and chest,
the prison of that train in motion.
All I know is
he thought he was dead.

And got off at a surburban station
to ride in an ambulance
through all the jams of South London
to nurses and a narrow bed with wheels
and electric wires
on feet, wrists and heart.

I am reading over his own description
of that evening —
how later, at home, he imagined
he'd got away with it, and drank.
He got away
for the time being.

For years, even, but what does it matter —
he never forgot
that day of the interrupted train,
the only time in his life, late sun
and pretty women
wearing blue shoes.

How Witches went Invisible

They boiled a black cat alive,
boiled it till the bones loosened,
took these singly in their teeth,
then stood before a mirror
till one bone defied reflection.

With this they were grinning winds
whooshing through the alleys,
masturbating in the marketplaces,
making pigs' heads float,
heading for home with fresh roots
and black cats at their seethrough feet.

The Border

Twenty miles south is the North
where I was booked in to be born —
a nursing home in a Derry suburb,
but my mother went on playing bridge
and never made it past the border.

Fireworks, coconuts and kippers
came over later, and stones of butter
packed under the Volks's back set,
away from the confiscating urge
of the Customs man in his warm hut.

It wasn't butter the B Specials wanted
when their bullets skimmed our bumper —
we'd missed their waved red light,
so shouts interrogated us
while a torch-beam frisked the car.

These nights headlights go off
as you cross the border, and rifles
in soldiers' hands motion you to stop
outside the sandbagged checkpoint
that gave some local mason work.

DENNIS O'DRISCOLL

(1954-)

from: HIDDEN EXTRAS (1987)

[Dennis O'Driscoll's is a poetry that unrelentingly displays the skull beneath the skin. Haunted by the evil that may lurk in the golden moment, it is equally responsive to the rich potentials of quotidian suburban lives. His is a world of prospects and retrospects, and his language is appropriately elegiac, grave and reserved.]

Thurles

after Zbigniew Herbert

A childhood too boring for words
is lost without a fragment in that town.
And, so, I have held my tongue about its gutturals;
its sky slated consistently with cloud;
its mossy roofs restraining excesses of rain.

One house watches out for me, though.
I know where its cabbage colander is kept
and the special knack required to use its tin-opener
and the exact key in which the kitchen door,
scuffed by a ring-board, creaks:

things I cannot depict in dictionary terms,
through heartless words that fail to resonate.
Others are suppressed in embarrassment or pain
(all families have passed their own equivalents
to the Official Secrets Act).

Yet everything there translates into feeling:
the plates the dead have eaten from before us,
the layers of wallpaper that still pattern memory,
the hairline crack in marble that was my fault,
the rose-arched garden explored down to its last
stone.

Back in the city, I resort to standard words again.
Unable to identify possessions by their first names,
I call them only by their surnames
— by their brand names —
and will never discover their real names.

Brief Lives

I

after the house has been pilfered
the private things fingered
and a phone call poses a new threat
after your child's accident affects your sales drive
the smear test turns out positive
and your worst fears are confirmed again

how should you spend the next day, the rest of your
life
what keeps you going — cowardice, forgetfulness
or hope
what is it you are impelled towards

II

so many hurt feelings and frustrated desires
toast- and coffee-scented pleasures also
at fires grinding into muesli ash

so many seconds harnessed to just being
years and decades consolidating to experience
it takes an eternity to recover from them all

III

the calm between storms
is the silence in which
the dead are not named
until relatives are informed

IV

in the end death worries only bones

THOMAS McCARTHY

(1954-)

from:
THE SORROW GARDEN (1981)

[Thomas McCarthy is a wry, musical poet, with an eye for the radiant detail and a strong sense of local Munster tradition. At their best in registering the personal effects of political life, his poems are an eloquent reminder that for the individual a major public event is also an intensely private experience. Many of his lyrics deal with the decline of the nationalist ideal in post-independent Ireland, the growing mendacity of politicians, and the bored alienation of the young; but he is in no sense a provincial, having tackled subjects as diverse as Gide and Nabokov, Edwardian England and present-day France.]

A Meeting with Parnell[1]

That day's event began with a lady's parasol
tripping across the grey Victorian sands

1. Charles Stewart Parnell (1846-91), leader of the Irish Parliamentary Party at Westminster, and cited as co-respondent in the Captain

of Dublin and two polite female calls
for help. The passing bather lent a hand;

with an athletic zest he pursued her shade,[2]
catching it beautifully near the pebble wall
while her child and its day-nurse delayed
as their mistress practised her protocol.

'You *are* a kind man', she said, when she saw
that he was a handsome one. 'Please sit here
and take a little shade. Nobody will know:
I'm a Castle person,[3] so you need have no fear.'

'I must warn you, Madam, about who I am,'
the dark man announced, 'I'm the awful Parnell.'
Then she feigned boredom with political games;
Things like State Affairs, she said, *makes one ill.*

The sun blazed at the edge of the Century
where they spoke, and the sea came in
to wash their flirting feet. He held her baby
in his scandalous hands and it seemed

to enjoy his cheerfulness. All that afternoon
its small joy stretched across the Dublin sand,
as if it knew what foes were sharing the sun;
as if it felt a new Love seeping from the land.

O'Shea divorce petition of December 1889. Deserted by English non-conformist opinion, by the Irish catholic hierarchy and by most of his political associates, he married Katharine O'Shea in June 1891. Fourteen weeks later he died in her arms.

2. 'Shade' is a Yeatsian word, applied to Parnell in 'To a Shade'.
3. Attached to Dublin Castle, the seat of British power in Ireland.

Windows

The windows of our flat: their shutters
disperse the worst fogs of the winter
so that I can see the quays falling
into the tidal mouth of the river —[1]
since I moved as high as these windows
I've overheard the nightlife of ghosts:
British officers taking their boots off,[2]
Cork whores dropping hints and slips,
their accents putting on airs. Also,
servants in the evening (the year 1901,
maybe) when all their chores were done
tip-toeing to their bedrooms. The horses
on Wellington Road are made of glass,
their liveried coachmen are throwing
wet oats at the windows of our flat.

1. The Lee, Cork's main river.
2. Cork was a British garrison town.

from: THE NON-ALIGNED STORYTELLER (1984)

Black Flags at a Party Meeting

The black flag is a Fascist tag. My father,
we've been there too long before
in the land of anger, land of fear.

The anger that has overtaken you
has touched me too. I want to hunt
the anonymous historian. I want to chase
him into a corner and say *I'll never forget!*

I know how they left you with scars —
but there's no historian of the *might have been*
to count those who died at the precipice.
Fold that flag and let your face be seen.

An elbow on the nose, a baton in the mouth,
a blueshirt or a green pushing through a crowd:
come home to memory where these are understood.

The Non-Aligned Storyteller

Soon there would be no reason to remember
Parkers in that place. Because the present
prevails . . .

Patrick White: The Tree of Man

Everything that happened here, that could be trapped,
By light, lies abandoned in my shop:
Who would bother to look, now that my lease
Is up? I have photographic plates
Of weddings as old as any villager's memory;
A perfect plate of the first Model T[1] in town,
A file of annual Blackwater[2] floods, action shots
From the Carnival held for[3] the Abbey chapel —
All of them useless. I gave my only child
A box of unclaimed, unknown Communion

1. The first Ford cars in rural Ireland.
2. A Munster river that runs through Cork into Waterford.
3. The sense is 'held to raise money for'.

Prints, perfectly justified and guillotined;
So perfect, in fact, that the subjects couldn't pay.
The first thing I photographed in this town
Was fire, a subject dangerous and ephemeral
Brought on by politics. The new Party[4]
Had made its first great leap. That time,
The poor in celebration burned tar in barrels.
Fire made a kaleidoscope of wet streets.

I loved to stroll about in windy rain to watch
Streets training themselves to be abandoned
By then the young had begun to disappear,[5]
Leaving a melancholia like a dark pothole
That only the rains could fill. In the long
Afternoons of Sundays there would be a flood
Of black shawls and a brief sleet of children
As well as a drought of able-bodied men —
Factories overseas had claimed them, or a
    combination
Of T.B.[6] and the ever-promising vagrant sea.
The villagers never trusted me, so for years
I photographed only what they could trust and see:

Corpus Christi[7] processions, sycamore trees, local
Football teams or scullers bolting down the river.
But politics was the most awkward field. I hung
Around to collect images at the centre of its
World; dragging old men from the stifling alcoves
Of meetings. I didn't know what I was meant to see

Because I was called in at the end of events
With camera and tripod. My wife arranged
The lights above their heads. She created
An aura of strength around their tired faces,
A sort of grey metallic, a solder of wisdom.
Their chairman I remember best. He wore
A gold watch-chain to every meeting;
He had a voice as revered as a Miraculous Medal —[8]
That gold chain sparkled in my best photographs,
Though I tried to dampen it in the negative.
His secretary owned innumerable fields.
I photographed him in one perfect moment
During a 1960 snowstorm; a starched
Figure caught against a herd of yearlings.
My wife remembers them too, under our lights,
As they held resolutely to tenancies and laws.
'If only they had strength,' she used to say, when
They were building anew, shedding bloody days.

4. Fianna Fáil, the republican party, which won power for the first time in 1933, although just ten years earlier it had been on the losing side in the Civil War.
5. The waves of emigration between the 1930s and 1950s.
6. Tuberculosis, a disease of the lungs, was a major cause of death in Ireland until the 1950s, when the Minister of Health, Dr Noel Browne, launched a very successful eradication scheme.
7. Roman catholic feast-day, celebrating the body of Christ, on which the communion wafer is carried in its monstrance in ceremonial procession across the parish.
8. A sodality medal to honour the Virgin Mary.

SEBASTIAN BARRY

(1955-)

from: THE RHETORICAL TOWN (1985)

[Sebastian Barry's poetry combines a coolness of tone with an elaborately figured vocabulary. The poems take an especial delight in turning worlds into words.]

The Tree Alphabet

Each tree in this autumn script
shadows the white drawing of a letter.
It might join our gray language
and the benign trees,
our language which is the wrong one
till we reapply the oaks to it
and make English of the winter place,
Hibernian and rootable
so we can return forward
and call the circle we spin in home.
Home will be where the trees

are the drawings and still the songs
but changed. Because we can not recover
the robbed notation for the life of us
we had better bring an instinctive
and unnaming alphabet

to the wretch that hangs around us
at the present or as a present,
the soup of the English being language really.
We know how necessary it was to drink it.
It had the metamorphic letters in it,
the first unfunny alphabet soup.

The Real Snow

for Anne Tallentire

In the white dark of the dominion house
we filled the stairs, mere butts of sleep,
concealing our track from the known map,
a chart of picnics in the hall,
and the spiders flew on their boreal strings
across cow-pats and acres.

The lake was smooth enough to take
the stones of your diagrammed eyes
in the serene pigment of the frost.
And no alley to negotiate
without hawthorn and orphan green.
The starless, ambiguous moon
lingered in our hesperic morning like a kite
and the voles ran under the real water,
tugging at old floats beneath the ice.
Someone was cutting a first line on the lake,
scribbles going nowhere in his wake
translating into a white language.

The February Town

Who owns the garden sketched by rain
with housewifed cobbles, puddled flags
and fourteenth century buildings shined like new?
It chastens the street you wander in
as you descend towards the river
peering into geometric alleys,
progressing that way to please her whim.
Two roads serve the same ground
as you sway beside her to the first café
in the perfection of the pretty tram,
the sky with child and the snow on cue.
You embrace her charter by the kiosk
with raw noses and all of time
in a green light that sinks down from the roofs.
There is a threat which you employ
to give the square the distance of a dream.

AIDAN MATHEWS

(1956-)

from: WINDFALLS (1977)

An Answer[1]

The hermits have left Meru, Mr. Yeats:
No forwarding address. They are gone
Into the reality of desolation.

We did not choose this patrimony, sir,
And are dismayed by the inheritance.
The more so since you died intestate.

1. To W.B. Yeats's 'Meru', one of his 'Supernatural Songs'.

from: MINDING RUTH (1983)

Passages

Traipsing from school, I used mouth them —
Eleusinian,[1] Rubicon —[2]
Big and elaborate and lapidary,

1. Relating to Eleusis in Atrea, or to the mysteries of Demeter celebrated there.
2. A small river in central Italy, crossed symbolically by Caesar (49 B.C.) in his declaration of war against the Roman republic.

Dominions of sound. Tonight I need
A second language like the silent reading
Of place-names for a homecoming.

A meal eaten under one red candle
Which you clear away, humming and swaying
To a quick clatter of stacked plates.

Listening, I would learn by heart
Those dialects of touch and gesture
That utter you like forms of greeting,

And would give them force of law
By right of seizure on old words,
The blue, possible vowels I starve for.

But you draw down your face to become
Other and hidden, a known country
I can cross to only in silences,

Through plain water. So I say nothing,
Hunkering over the fire-guard
To tend a small coal with the brass tongs.

The Death of Irish

The tide gone out for good,
Thirty-one words for seaweed
Whiten on the foreshore.

Keeping Pacific Time

The last class over,
You are walking to your car now;

And your day winds down,
A penny spun on a table.

Gravel and crushed grass sigh
Where the night wind crosses them,

For the warm rubbish of picnics,
Toddlers held among bushes;

And the park, policed at nightfall,
Privately dreams of children

While the statues throw their arms
To a sky refusing pigeons:

Many white faces,
Longhaired in the moonlight.

On the other side of the world
Where I live, missing you,

It is early morning. Light
Collects like rain in the awnings.

Dew on the closed newsstands,
And the first bread cooling.

Soon the crows will come,
Just as they do at home

To the trellis sloped like Pisa,
For the crumbs on my window:

A scone broken in bits,
And softened under the cold tap.

MICHAEL O'LOUGHLIN

(1958-)

from: THE DIARY OF A SILENCE (1985)

The Black Piano

The language turns to mush in our mouths —
Like the brown slush flooding the streets
Beneath my window. But now it's snowing,
White flakes falling on the frozen canals.
In my room, I turn the pages of Russian books
Trying to understand, knowing
That the storm that swept them away
Is the storm that swept me here
To stand in the place where they once stood
My head ringing with their echoes.
Through the wall of my room I hear
The tuneless tentative notes
Of my neighbour's pupils,
Their fingers stumbling over the keyboard.
Coming home late at night, I like
To climb the steps and peer
Into her tiny front room,
Filled with a frozen black piano
Basted with hidden light, like a shrine.
In my room I stalk on,
Imagining listeners behind the white wall
Their ears bent to the tuneless tentative sound
Of my black boots plodding through virgin snow.

On hearing Michael Hartnett read his poetry in Irish

First, the irretrievable arrow of the military road[1]
Drawing a line across all that has gone before
Its language a handful of brutal monosyllables.

By the side of the road the buildings eased up;
The sturdy syntax of castle and barracks
The rococo flourish of a stately home

The formal perfection and grace
Of the temples of neoclassical government
The avenues describing an elegant period. Then,

The red-brick constructions of a common coin
To be minted in local stone, and beyond them
The fluent sprawl of the demotic suburbs

Tanged with the ice of its bitter nights
Where I dreamt in the shambles of imperial iambs,
Like rows of shattered Georgian houses.

I hear our history on my tongue,
The music of what has happened![2]
The shanties that huddled around the manor

The kips that cursed under Christchurch Cathedral
Rising like a madrigal into the Dublin sky
— But tonight, for the first time,

I heard the sound
Of the snow falling through moonlight
Onto the empty fields.

1. A road built across the Dublin mountains and into County Wicklow; the scene of killings during Ireland's Civil War.
2. A common Russian phrase.

GREG DELANTY

(1958-)

from: CAST IN THE FIRE (1986)

[Cool and candid at the same time, Greg Delanty's poems move at a quick pace and at an equal distance from the sentimental and the skilful. His innocent pitch of voice, which was there from the start, has been maintained and developed through his subsequent absorption of the open styles of American poetry.

The author has provided minor corrections to the published text.]

Thrust & Parry

You're sure you heard something break. Something snap.
Deep within her. Like a twig split in two
& cast in the fire. Or like the snap
of a violin string, halting all music.
And witnessing tears break in her face
you discovered the magic, the black magic,
of your words, no magic could take back.
And, loathing the terrifying maniac in you,
you shattered a vase of flowers and fled,
as if from yourself, out into the dark.
Leaving her to pick up the flowers,
restring the violin, await your next attack,
but this time of fawning words & flowers,
and her breakfast in bed for at least a week.

Out of the Ordinary

Skin-head pigeons strut in a gang
along the road's white line
& fly from under a fuming cop car.
Lazy, contented seagulls catch rides
on the conveyor belt of a river —
Others glide & hover in the slow air
of a busking tin whistle player
as if conjured from his upside-down hat.
Singing thrushes play on the fret board
of electric wires & sparrows
arrow upward, seemingly desperate
to enter heaven, not noticing heaven
has descended to the ordinary
as we saunter along Union Quay.

Interrogative

Even the flimsiest, most vulnerable creatures
are equipped with devices to outwit death:
the night moth blends into its surroundings,
lichen-coloured, it conceals itself on bark;
other creatures don the colours of a wasp,
fooling predators into believing they can sting;
but how could your father outwit death's grasp,
snatched forever & too soon, under its dark wing,
always out in the open without sting or cunning.

Leavetaking

After you board the train, you sit & wait,
to begin your first real journey alone.
You read to avoid the window's awkwardness,
knowing he's anxious to catch your eye,
loitering out in never-ending rain,
to wave, a bit shy, another final goodbye;
you are afraid of having to wave too soon.

And for a moment you think it's the train
next to you has begun, but it is yours,
and your face, pressed to the window pane,
is distorted & numbed by the icy glass,
pinning your eyes upon your father,
as he cranes to defy your disappearing train.
Both of you waving, eternally, to each other.

Bibliographical Note

Commentary on many of the poets listed below may be found in the following: T. Brown, *Northern Voices: Poets from Ulster* (Dublin: Gill and Macmillan, 1975); S. Deane, *Celtic Revivals* (London: Faber and Faber, 1985, 1986; Winston-Salem, North Carolina: Wake Forest University Press, 1987); S. Deane, *A Short History of Irish Literature* (London: Hutchinson, 1986; Notre Dame, Indiana: University of Notre Dame Press, 1987); D. Donoghue, *We Irish: Essays in Irish Literature and Society* (Brighton, Harvester Press; New York: Alfred Knopf, 1986); R. F. Garratt, *Modern Irish Poetry: Tradition and Continuity from Yeats to Heaney* (Berkeley, Los Angeles, London: University of California Press, 1986); D. Johnston, *Irish Poetry After Joyce* (Notre Dame, Indiana: University of Notre Dame Press; Dublin: Dolmen Press, 1985); E. Longley, *Poetry in the Wars* (Newcastle-upon-Tyne: Bloodaxe Books, 1986); T. Brown and N. Grene (eds), *Tradition and Influence in Anglo-Irish Poetry* (London: Macmillan, 1989).

Biographies/Bibliographies

Patrick MacDonogh

LIFE. Patrick MacDonogh was born in the North of Ireland in 1902. He was educated at Avoca school and at Trinity College, Dublin, where he distinguished himself as an athlete. He taught secondary school and then took a clerical position in a brewery. After an initial burst of creativity, he published nothing between 1929 and 1941. Thereafter, he published regularly, particularly in *The Dublin Magazine*. He died in 1961.

CHIEF WRITINGS. *Flirtation, Some Occasional Verses* (Dublin: G. F. Healy, 1927); *A Leaf in the Wind* (Belfast: Quota, 1929); *The Vestal Fire, a Poem* (Dublin: Orwell Press, 1941); *Over the Water and Other Poems* (Dublin: Orwell Press, 1943); *One Landscape Still and Other Poems* (London: Secker and Warburg, 1958).

Padraic Fallon

LIFE. Padraic Fallon was born in Athenry, Co. Galway in 1905. He worked as a customs official for forty years. Although he made a number of contributions to periodicals and wrote successful plays (*Diarmuid and Gráinne* (1950) and *The Vision of MacConglinne* (1953) and plays for the stage (*The Seventh Step* (1954) and *Sweet Love Till Morn* (1974)), his poems were not collected in his lifetime. As a consequence, he has suffered undeserved neglect. From 1930 he lived in Wexford until his retirement from the civil service in 1970. He died in Kent in 1974.

CHIEF WRITINGS. *Lighting-Up Time*, Tower Press Booklets, 3rd Series (Dublin: Orwell Press, 1938); *Poems* (Dublin: Dolmen Press, 1974); B. Fallon (ed.), *Padraic Fallon, Poems and Versions* (Manchester: Carcanet Press; Dublin: Raven Arts Press, 1983); *Collected Poems*, introduction by Seamus Heaney (Oldcastle, Co. Meath: The Gallery Press; Manchester: Carcanet Press, 1990).

BIOGRAPHY AND CRITICISM. D. Davie, 'Austin Clarke and Padraic Fallon' in D. Dunn (ed.), *Two Decades of Irish Writing* (Cheadle: Carcanet Press; Chester Springs, Pennsylvania: Dufour Editions, 1975), pp. 37-58; M. Harmon, 'The Poetry of Padraic Fallon', *Studies* (Autumn 1975), 269-81; R. F. Garratt, *Modern Irish Poetry: Tradition and Continuity from Yeats to Heaney* (Berkeley, Los Angeles, London: University of California Press, 1986), pp. 70-77.

Charles Donnelly

LIFE. Charles Donnelly was born at Killbrackey, near Dungannon, Co. Tyrone in 1914. The family moved to Dundalk and Donnelly was sent to the local Christian Brothers School. In 1929, the family moved to Dublin. In 1931, Donnelly, who had become interested in radical politics, entered University College, Dublin where he was a contemporary of Flann O'Brien, Denis Devlin, Mary Lavin, Donagh MacDonagh and others. He joined the Irish Republican Congress in 1933 and was elected a member of the national executive the following year. In 1935 he was sentenced to a month in prison for picketing a shop. On his release, he went to London, where he formed the first London branch of the Republican Congress and cooperated with Leslie Daiken in producing the magazine *Irish Front*; he wrote and lectured on left-wing politics for a variety of newspapers, journals and organizations. As a member of a committee organized by the New Fabian Research Bureau, he researched the nationalist uprisings in the Asturias and Catalonia in 1934. With the outbreak of the Civil War in Spain, Donnelly demanded that the Republican Congress send a message of support to the Republican government at Madrid. This led to a stormy meeting with Peadar O'Donnell, George Gilmore and Frank Ryan which ended with the Congress publicly committing itself to support for the Spanish government. With the formation of General Eoin O'Duffy's brigade to fight for Franco in Spain, an Irish unit of the Left was formed and Donnelly went to Spain with it in 1936. He was killed in action at the Jarama River on 27 February 1937.

CHIEF WRITINGS. J. Donnelly (ed.), *Charlie Donnelly. The Life and Poems* (Dublin: The Dedalus Press, 1987).

BIOGRAPHY AND CRITICISM. J. O'Connor, *The Life and Work of Charles Donnelly* (unpublished NUI thesis, University College, Dublin, 1986).

Valentin Iremonger

LIFE. Valentin Iremonger was born in Dublin in 1918 and was educated at Synge Street Christian Brothers School and Coláiste Mhuire. In 1945 he won the AE Memorial Prize for Literature. From 1949 to 1951, he was poetry editor of the magazine *Envoy*. His career as a diplomat in the Irish foreign service included ambassadorial positions in Sweden, Norway, Finland and India.

CHIEF WRITINGS. *Reservations* (Dublin: Envoy, 1950); Trans. *The Hard Road to Klondike* by M. MacGowan (London: Routledge & Kegan Paul, 1962); Trans. *An Irish Navvy, the Diary of an Exile* by D. MacAmhlaigh (London: Routledge & Kegan Paul, 1964); ed. with R. Greacen, *Contemporary Irish Poetry* (London: Faber, 1949); ed. *Irish Short Stories* (London: Faber and Faber, 1960); *Horan's Field and Other Reservations* (Dublin: Dolmen Press, 1972); *Sandymount, Dublin* (Dublin: The Dedalus Press, 1988).

Padraic Fiacc

LIFE. Born Joseph O'Connor in Belfast in 1924, he took the pseudonym Padraic Fiacc for his writings. His family emigrated to New York, where Fiacc was educated. He returned to Belfast in 1946, won the AE Memorial Award in 1947, and has lived in Belfast since.

CHIEF WRITINGS. *By the Black Stream* (Dublin: Dolmen Press, 1969); *Odour of Blood* (Newbridge, Co. Kildare: Goldsmith Press, 1973); *Nights in the Bad Place* (Belfast: Blackstaff Press, 1972); (ed.) *The Wearing of the Black; An Anthology of Contemporary Ulster Poetry* (Belfast: Blackstaff Press, 1974); T. Brown (introd.), *The Selected Padraic Fiacc* (Belfast: Blackstaff Press, 1979); *Missa Terribilis* (Belfast: Blackstaff Press, 1986).

Anthony Cronin

For biography and bibliography, see p. 559.

Pearse Hutchinson

LIFE. Born in Glasgow in 1927, Pearse Hutchinson was educated at University College, Dublin. From 1951 to 1953, he was translator for the International Labour Organisation in Geneva. He was drama critic for Radio Éireann 1957-61 and for Radio Telefís Éireann 1968. He won the Butler Award for Gaelic Writing in 1969 and was Gregory Fellow in Poetry at the University of Leeds 1971-73. Pearse Hutchinson has spent several years in Spain and has translated extensively from Spanish. In 1977-78 he compiled and presented the weekly radio programme *Oro Domhnaigh* on Radio Éireann. He is a co-editor of the magazine *Cyphers*.

CHIEF WRITINGS. *Tongue Without Hands* (Dublin: Dolmen Press, 1963); *Faoistín Bhacach* (Dublin: An Clochamhar, 1968); *Expansions*

(Dublin: Dolmen Press, 1969); *Watching the Morning Grow* (Dublin: Gallery Press, 1972); *The Frost is All Over* (Dublin: Gallery Press, 1975); *Selected Poems* (Dublin: Gallery Press, 1982); *Climbing the Light* (Dublin: Gallery Press, 1985).

Translations. *Josep Carner: 30 Poems* (from the Catalan) (Oxford: Dolphin Books, 1962); *Friend Songs: Medieval Love-Poems* (from Galicio-Portuguese) (Dublin: New Writers' Press, 1970); *Antica Lirica Irlandese* (with Melita Cataldi) (Torino, 1982).

Richard Murphy

LIFE. Born at Milford House, Co. Galway in 1927, Richard Murphy spent part of his childhood in Ceylon, where his father was an imperial official. Later he studied at Magdalen College, Oxford, and at the Sorbonne. A short spell as an English master in Crete (1953-54) was followed by a longer period in Connemara, where he restored two Galway hookers (fishing boats), using them in summer to ferry visitors to Inishbofin island. He has read and lectured extensively in North America, being most recently writer-in-residence at Pacific Lutheran University in Washington State (1985). He lives in Killiney, Co. Dublin and divides his time between Ireland and Sri Lanka.

CHIEF WRITINGS. *Archaeology of Love* (Dublin: Dolmen Press, 1974); *Sailing to an Island* (London: Faber and Faber, 1963); *The Battle of Aughrim* (London: Faber and Faber, 1968); *High Island* (London: Faber and Faber, 1974); *Selected Poems* (London: Faber and Faber, 1979); *High Island: New and Selected Poems* (New York: Harper and Row, 1974); *The Price of Stone* (London: Faber and Faber, 1985); *The Price of Stone and Earlier Poems* (Winston-Salem, North Carolina: Wake Forest University Press, 1985); *New Selected Poems* (London: Faber and Faber, 1989); *The Mirror Wall* (Newcastle-upon-Tyne: Bloodaxe Books; Dublin: Wolfhound Press, 1989).

BIOGRAPHY AND CRITICISM. M. Harmon, *Richard Murphy, Poet of Two Traditions* (Dublin: Wolfhound Press, 197?); (ed.) *Irish University Review*, Richard Murphy Special Issue, Vol. 7, No. 1 (Spring 1977).

Thomas Kinsella

LIFE. Born in Dublin in 1928, Thomas Kinsella attended University College, Dublin and thereafter entered the Irish civil service. In 1965 he left his position as assistant principal officer in the Department of Finance to take up a post at Southern Illinois University. In 1970 he began to teach at Temple University in Philadelphia. Kinsella was a founder-member, with Liam Miller, of the Dolmen Press and was founder of the Peppercanister Press with which imprint he publishes most of his work. He has won several awards — the Denis Devlin Memorial Award, the Guinness Poetry Award, the Irish Arts Council Triennial Book Award and two Guggenheim Fellowships. He now lives in County Wicklow.

CHIEF WRITINGS: *Poems* (Dublin: Dolmen Press, 1956); *Another September* (Dublin: Dolmen Press, 1958); *Moralities* (Dublin: Dolmen Press, 1960); *Downstream* (Dublin: Dolmen Press; London: Oxford University Press, 1962); *Wormwood* (Dublin: Dolmen Press, 1966); *Nightwalker* (Dublin: Dolmen Press, 1967); *Nightwalker and Other Poems* (Dublin: Dolmen Press, 1968); (trans.) *The Táin* (Dublin: Dolmen Press, 1969, 1985); *Davis, Mangan, Ferguson? Tradition and The Irish Writer* (Dublin: Dolmen, 1970); (trans.) *The Tain* (London and New York: Oxford University Press in association with Dolmen Press, 1970); *Notes from The Land of the Dead* (Dublin: Cuala Press, 1972); *Notes from The Land of the Dead and Other Poems* (New York: Knopf, 1973); *New Poems 1973* (Dublin: Dolmen Press, 1973); *Selected Poems 1956-1968* (Dublin: Dolmen Press, 1973; London, Oxford University Press, 1974); *One and Other Poems* (Dublin: Peppercanister Press, 1974); *Peppercanister Poems, 1972-1978* (Winston-Salem, North Carolina: Wake Forest University Press, 1979); *Poems 1956-1973* (Winston-Salem: Wake Forest University Press, 1979); *Poems 1956-1973* (Dublin: Dolmen Press in association with Wake Forest University Press, 1980); (trans.) *An Duanaire: Poetry of the Dispossessed 1600-1900* selected by Seán Ó Tuama (Dublin: Dolmen Press, 1981); *Songs of the Psyche* (Dublin: Peppercanister Press, 1985); *Her Vertical Smile* (Dublin: Peppercanister Press, 1985); (ed. with translations) *The New Oxford Book of Irish Verse* (Oxford, New York: Oxford University Press, 1986); *Out of Ireland: A Metaphysical Love Sequence* (Dublin: Peppercanister Press, 1987); *St. Catherine's Clock* (Dublin: Peppercanister Press, 1987); *Blood and Family* (Oxford: Oxford University Press, 1988); *Fifteen Poems from Centre City* (Dublin: The Dedalus Press, 1990); *Personal Places* (Dublin: The Dedalus Press, 1990).

BIOGRAPHY AND CRITICISM. M. Harmon, *The Poetry of Thomas Kinsella* (Dublin: Wolfhound Press, 1974). See also the books by Deane, Johnston and Garratt cited in the Bibliographical Note (p. 1430).

John Montague

LIFE. Born in Brooklyn, New York, of Irish parents in 1929, John Montague grew up on his aunt's farm in County Tyrone. He went to school at St Patrick's College, Armagh and afterwards was a student at University College, Dublin. He lived for many years in France, taught first at the University of California in Berkeley and later at several other universities in the USA. He returned to Ireland in 1972. Until 1988 he was senior lecturer in English at University College, Cork, from which he retired to teach again in the United States. He has won many awards for his poetry.

CHIEF WRITINGS. *Forms of Exile* (Dublin: Dolmen Press, 1958); *Poisoned Lands and Other Poems* (London: MacGibbon & Kee, 1961; Philadelphia: Dufour Editions, 1963); *Poisoned Lands* new edition (Dublin: Dolmen Press; London: Oxford University Press, 1977); *A Chosen Light* (London: MacGibbon & Kee, 1967; Chicago: Swallow Press, 1969); *Tides* (Dublin: Dolmen Press, 1970; Chicago: Swallow Press, 1971; reissued, 1978); *The Rough Field 1961-1971* (Dublin: Dolmen Press; Winston-Salem, North Carolina: Wake Forest University Press, 1972; 4th edition Dublin: Dolmen Press; Belfast: Blackstaff Press; Winston-Salem: Wake Forest University Press, 1984); *A Slow Dance* (Dublin: Dolmen Press; London: Oxford University Press; Winston-Salem: Wake Forest University Press, 1975); *The Great Cloak* (Dublin: Dolmen Press; London: Oxford University Press; Winston-Salem: Wake Forest University Press, 1978); *Selected Poems* (Toronto: Exile Editions; Winston-Salem: Wake Forest University Press; Dublin: Dolmen Press; London: Oxford University Press, 1982); *The Dead Kingdom* (Dublin: Dolmen Press; Winston-Salem: Wake Forest University Press; London: Oxford University Press; Belfast: Blackstaff Press, 1984); *Mount Eagle* (Dublin: Gallery Press, 1988; Winston-Salem, Wake Forest University Press; Newcastle-upon-Tyne; Bloodaxe Books, 1989; *New Selected Poems* (Dublin: Gallery Press, 1989); (ed.) *The Faber Book of Irish Verse* (London: Faber and Faber, 1974); published as *The Book of Irish Verse* (New York: Macmillan, 1976; revised edition 1988).

Prose. *The Death of a Chieftain and Other Stories* (London: MacGibbon & Kee, 1964; Philadelphia: Dufour Editions, 1967; Swords, Co. Dublin: Poolbeg Press, 1978); *The Lost Notebook* (Cork and Dublin: The Mercier Press, 1987); *The Figure in the Cave and Other Essays* (Dublin: The Lilliput Press, 1989).

BIOGRAPHY AND CRITICISM. F. Kersnowski, *John Montague* (Lewisburg, Pennsylvania: Bucknell University Press, 1975); *Irish University Review* Vol. 19, No. 1 (Spring 1989), Special Issue on John Montague.

James Simmons

LIFE. Born in Derry in 1933, James Simmons was educated at Foyle College and the University of Leeds. He taught in a Quaker Grammar

School in Lisburn 1958-63. From 1963 to 1966 he taught at Ahmadu Bello University, Nigeria, returned to Belfast in 1967 and founded *The Honest Ulsterman* in 1968. He was editor for two years. From 1968 to 1986 he taught at the New University of Ulster at Coleraine. Since then he has become literary editor of the journal *The Linen Hall Review* and the magazine *Fortnight*. He received the Cholmondeley Award for Poetry in 1977.

CHIEF WRITINGS: *Late but in Earnest* (London: The Bodley Head, 1967); *In the Wilderness and Other Poems* (London: The Bodley Head, 1969); *Energy to Burn* (London: The Bodley Head, 1971); *No Land is Waste, Dr Eliot* (Belfast: Keepsake Press, 1972); *The Long Summer Still to Come* (Belfast: Blackstaff Press, 1973); *West Strand Visions* (Belfast: Blackstaff Press, 1974); (ed.) *Ten Irish Poets* (Cheadle, Cheshire: Carcanet Press, 1974); *Judy Garland and the Cold War* (Belfast: Blackstaff Press, 1976); *Constantly Singing* (Belfast: Blackstaff Press, 1980); *From the Irish* (Belfast: Blackstaff Press, 1985); E. Longley (ed.), *The Selected James Simmons* (Belfast: Blackstaff Press, 1978); *Poems 1956-1986* (Dublin: Gallery Press; Newcastle-upon-Tyne: Bloodaxe Books, 1986); *Sean O'Casey* (Dublin: Gill and Macmillan, 1986).

Desmond O'Grady

LIFE. Born in Limerick in 1935, Desmond O'Grady was educated at University College, Dublin and, later, at Harvard University where he studied with Professor John Kelleher. He was for many years a close friend of Ezra Pound, by whom he was deeply influenced, most especially as a translator. He has taught in Rome and Cairo and divides his time between the Greek island of Paros and Kinsale, Co. Cork.

CHIEF WRITINGS. *Chords and Orchestrations* (Limerick: The Echo Press, 1956); *Reilly* (London: The Phoenix Press, 1961); *The Dark Edge of Europe* (London: MacGibbon and Kee, 1967); *Off Licence: translations* (Dublin: Dolmen Press, 1968); *The Dying Gaul* (London: MacGibbon and Kee, 1968); *Hellas* (Dublin: New Writers' Press, 1971); *Separations* (Dublin: The Goldsmith Press, 1973); *Stations* (Cairo: American University in Cairo Press, 1976); *Sing Me Creation* (Dublin: Gallery Press, 1977); *The Gododdin: translations* (Dublin: Dolmen Press, 1977); *A Limerick Rake: Versions from the Irish* (Dublin: Gallery Press, 1978); *The Headgear of the Tribe; New and Selected Poems* (Dublin: Gallery Press, 1978); *His Skaldcrane's Nest* (Dublin: Gallery Press, 1979).

Brendan Kennelly

LIFE. Born in Ballylongford, Co. Kerry in 1936, Brendan Kennelly was educated at St Ita's College and subsequently at Trinity College, Dublin, where he is now professor of modern literature. A novelist and playwright on occasion, he has, however, devoted most of his energies to poetry.

CHIEF WRITINGS. *Collection One: Getting Up Early* (Dublin: Allen Figgis, 1966); *Good Souls to Survive* (Dublin: Allen Figgis, 1967); *Dream of a Black Fox* (Dublin: Allen Figgis, 1968); *Selected Poems* (Dublin: Allen Figgis & Co., 1969; enlarged edition: New York: Dutton & Co., 1971); *A Drinking Cup: Poems from the Irish* (Allen Figgis & Co., 1970); *Bread* (Dublin: Tara Telephone, 1971); *Love-Cry* (Dublin: Allen Figgis & Co., 1972); *Up and At It* (Dublin: Tara Telephone, 1972); *Salvation, the Stranger* (Dublin: Tara Telephone, 1972); *Shelley in Dublin* (Dublin: Dublin Magazine Press, 1974); *A Kind of Trust* (Dublin: Gallery Press, 1975); (ed.) P. Fallon, *New and Selected Poems* (Dublin: Gallery Press, 1976); *The Boats Are Home* (Dublin: Gallery Press, 1980); *Cromwell* (Dublin: Beaver Row Press, 1983); *Selected Poems* edited by K. Byrne (Dublin: Kerrymount Publications, 1985); (ed.) *The Penguin Book of Irish Verse* (Harmondsworth: Penguin, 1970, 1986); *A Time for Voices: Selected Poems 1960-1990* (Newcastle-upon-Tyne: Bloodaxe Books, 1990).

Seamus Heaney

LIFE. Born in Mossbawn, Co. Derry in 1939, Seamus Heaney was educated at St Columb's College and Queen's University, Belfast. He lectured at St Joseph's College of Education in Belfast (1963-66) and at Queen's University, Belfast (1968-72). In 1970-71 he spent the year as guest lecturer at the University of California at Berkeley. From 1972-75 he lived in County Wicklow, writing full-time. In 1975, he became head of the English Department at Carysfort Training College, Dublin; he left this post in 1981 for Harvard University where he became Boylston professor of rhetoric. Heaney has won every major literary award in Britain and Ireland and several in the USA. He was the leading figure in the 'Northern Poets' movement of the mid-1960s. In 1980 he became a director of the Field Day Theatre Company. In 1986 he gave the T.S. Eliot Memorial Lectures at Canterbury and in 1988 inaugurated the Richard Ellmann Lectures in Modern Literature at Emory University, Atlanta, Georgia. He was elected Oxford professor of poetry in June 1989.

CHIEF WRITINGS. *Death of a Naturalist* (London: Faber and Faber; New York: Oxford University Press, 1966); *Door into the Dark* (London: Faber and Faber; New York: Oxford University Press, 1969); *Wintering Out* (London: Faber and Faber; New York: Oxford University Press, 1972); *North* (London: Faber and Faber, 1975; New York: Oxford University Press, 1976); *Field Work* (London: Faber and Faber; New York: Farrar, Straus & Giroux, 1979); *Preoccupations: Selected Prose 1968-1978* (London: Faber and Faber; New York: Farrar, Straus & Giroux, 1980); *Selected Poems 1965-1975* (London: Faber and Faber, 1980); *Poems 1965-1975* (New York: Farrar, Straus & Giroux, 1980); *Sweeney Astray* (Derry: Field Day, 1983; London: Faber and Faber, 1984; New York: Farrar, Straus & Giroux, 1985); *Station Island* (London: Faber and Faber, 1984; New York: Farrar, Straus & Giroux, 1985); *The Haw Lantern* (London: Faber and Faber; New York: Farrar, Straus & Giroux, 1987); *The Government of the Tongue; The 1986 T. S. Eliot Memorial Lectures and Other Critical Writings* (London: Faber and Faber, 1988); *The Place of Writing* (Atlanta, Georgia: Scholars Press, 1989); *New Selected Poems 1966-1987* (London: Faber and Faber, 1990).

BIOGRAPHY AND CRITICISM. R. Buttel, *Seamus Heaney* (Lewisburg, Pennsylvania: Bucknell University Press; London: Associated University Presses, 1975); B. Morrison, *Seamus Heaney* (London: Methuen, 1982); T. Curtis (ed.), *The Art of Seamus Heaney* (Bridgend: Poetry Wales Press, 1982, 1985); N. Corcoran, *Seamus Heaney* (London: Faber and Faber, 1986); H. Bloom (ed.), *Seamus Heaney* (New Haven, New York, Philadelphia: Chelsea House Publishers, 1986): E. Andrews, *Seamus Heaney: The Realms of Whisper* (London: Macmillan, 1989); Thomas C. Foster, *Seamus Heaney* (Dublin: O'Brien Press; Boston: Twayne, 1989).

Michael Longley

LIFE. Born in Belfast in 1939, Michael Longley was educated at Royal Belfast Academical Institution and at Trinity College, Dublin, from which he graduated with a degree in classics. After seven years as a schoolteacher in England and Ireland, he was assigned to the Arts Council of Northern Ireland in which he is now combined arts director. In 1965 he won an Eric Gregory Award. He is married to the critic Edna Longley.

CHIEF WRITINGS. *No Continuing City* (London: Macmillan, 1969); *An Exploded View* (London: Gollancz, 1973); *Man Lying on a Wall* (London: Gollancz, 1976); *The Echo Gate* (London: Secker and Warburg, 1979); *Selected Poems 1963-1980* (Winston-Salem, North Carolina: Wake Forest University Press, 1981); *Poems 1963-1983* (Edinburgh: The Salamander Press, 1985; Harmondsworth: Penguin Books, 1986); (ed.) *Over the Moon and Under the Stars* (Belfast: Arts Council, 1971), an anthology of children's poetry.

Seamus Deane

LIFE. Seamus Deane was born in Derry in 1940 and educated at St Columb's College, Queen's University, Belfast and Cambridge University. He was a Fulbright Lecturer and Woodrow Wilson Fellow at Reed College, Oregon and the University of California at Berkeley 1966-68. He was visiting professor at the University of Notre Dame and the University of California 1977-78; Walker Ames Professor at the University of Washington, Seattle, 1987 and Benedict Distinguished Visiting Professor at Carleton College, Minnesota 1988. He is professor of modern English and American literature at University College, Dublin, a member of the Royal Irish Academy and a director of the Field Day Theatre Company. He lives in Dublin. He has won the AE Award for Literature (1973) and the American Ireland Fund Literary Award (1989).

CHIEF WRITINGS. *Gradual Wars* (Dublin: Irish University Press, 1972); *Rumours* (Dublin: Dolmen Press, 1977); *History Lessons* (Dublin: Gallery Press, 1983); *Civilians and Barbarians* (Derry: Field Day, 1983); *Celtic Revivals: Essays in Modern Irish Literature 1880-1980* (London: Faber and Faber, 1985; Winston-Salem, North Carolina: Wake Forest University Press, 1986); *Heroic Styles: The Tradition of an Idea* (Derry: Field Day, 1985); *A Short History of Irish Literature* (London: Hutchinson, 1986; Notre Dame: University of Notre Dame Press, 1987); *The French Enlightenment and Revolution in England 1789-1832* (Cambridge, Massachusetts: Harvard University Press, 1988); *Selected Poems* (Dublin: Gallery Press, 1988); *Reading in the Dark* (London: Granta, 1990).

Derek Mahon

LIFE. Born in Belfast in 1941 to a family with a tradition in the city's shipyard engineering industry, Derek Mahon was educated at Royal Belfast Academical Institution and Trinity College, Dublin. After travels in North America, he returned to Ireland in 1967 and co-founded *Atlantis*, a literary-political magazine, with Seamus Deane. From 1970, he worked in London for magazines, literary reviews and television. His successful television adaptations include works by Jennifer Johnston, John Montague and Elizabeth Bowen. He lived in Kinsale, Co. Cork 1986-88 and began to review regularly for *The Irish Times*. In 1975 he won the Denis Devlin Award. His adaptation of Molière's *School for Husbands* for the Field Day Company in 1984 was highly praised. He was writing fellow in Trinity College, Dublin in 1986.

CHIEF WRITINGS. *Night-Crossing* (London: Oxford University Press, 1969); *Lives* (London: Oxford University Press, 1972); (ed.) *The Sphere Book of Modern Irish Poetry* (London: Sphere Books, 1972); *The Snow Party* (London: Oxford University Press, 1975); *Poems: 1962-78* (London: Oxford University Press, 1980); *Courtyards in Delft* (Dublin: Gallery Press, 1981); *The Chimeras* (after Nerval) (Dublin: Gallery Press, 1982); *The Hunt by Night* (Oxford: Oxford University Press, 1982; Winston-Salem, North Carolina: Wake Forest University Press, 1983); *High Time* (after Molière) (Dublin: Gallery Press, 1985); *Antarctica* (Dublin: Gallery Press, 1985); *The School for Wives* (Dublin: Gallery Press, 1986); *Philippe Jaccottet, Selected Poems*, selected and translated with an introduction by Derek Mahon (Harmondsworth: Penguin Books; Winston-Salem: Wake Forest University Press, 1988); ed. with P. Fallon, *The Penguin Book of Contemporary Irish Poetry* (London: Penguin Books, 1990).

Michael Hartnett

LIFE. Born in Newcastle West, Co. Limerick in 1941 and educated locally, Michael Hartnett worked for many years in the Department of Posts and Telegraphs and later as lecturer in creative writing at Thomond College, Limerick. In 1975 he announced that he would henceforth write only in Irish and persisted with this avowal until 1985, when he returned to writing in English. He lives in Dublin. He was awarded the American Ireland Fund Literary Award in 1990.

CHIEF WRITINGS. *Anatomy of a Cliché* (Dublin: Dolmen Press, 1968); *Selected Poems of Michael Hartnett* (Dublin: New Writers' Press, 1970); *Tao: A Version of the Chinese Classic of the Sixth Century* (Dublin: New Writers' Press, 1971); *Gypsy Ballads: A Version of the 'Romancero Gilato'* (Dublin: Goldsmith Press, 1973); *A Farewell to English* (Dublin: Gallery Press, 1975; enlarged edition 1978); *Poems in English* (Dublin: Dolmen Press, 1977); *Adharca Broic* (Dublin: Gallery Press, 1978); *An Phurgoid* (Dublin: Coiscéim, 1983); *Do Nuala: Foighne Crainn* (Dublin: Coiscéim, 1984); *Collected Poems in English* 2 vols (Dublin: Raven Arts Press, 1984-85); *Inchicore Haiku* (Dublin: Raven Arts Press, 1985); *Ó Bruadair: Selected Poems of Dáibhí Ó Bruadair translated and introduced by Michael Hartnett* (Dublin: Gallery Press, 1985); *A Necklace of Wrens: Selected poems in Irish with English translations by the author* (Dublin: Gallery Press, 1987); *Poems to Younger Women* (Dublin: Gallery Press, 1988).

Eamon Grennan

LIFE. Born in Dublin in 1941, Eamon Grennan was educated at University College, Dublin and Harvard University. He lives in the USA, where he teaches English at Vassar College, New York.

CHIEF WRITINGS. *Wildly for Days* (Dublin: Gallery Press, 1983); *What Light There Is* (Dublin: Gallery Press, 1987).

Eiléan Ní Chuilleanáin

LIFE. Born in Cork in 1942, daughter of novelist Eilís Dillon and of Professor Cormac Ó Cuilleanáin, Eiléan Ní Chuilleanáin was educated at University College, Cork, from where she won a travelling scholarship to Oxford University. There she took a B. Litt. degree in Renaissance English; this work deeply influenced her poetry thereafter. Since 1966, she has lectured in English at Trinity College, Dublin and for many years has edited the poetry magazine *Cyphers*. She is married to the poet Macdara Woods.

CHIEF WRITINGS. *Acts and Monuments* (Dublin: Gallery Press, 1972); *Site of Ambush* (Dublin: Gallery Press, 1975); *The Second Voyage* (Dublin: Gallery Press; Winston-Salem, North Carolina: Wake Forest University Press, 1977; 2nd edition Dublin: Gallery Press, 1986); *Cork* (Dublin: Gallery Press, 1977); *The Rose-Geranium* (Dublin: Gallery Press, 1981); (ed.) *Irish Women: Image and Achievement* (Dublin: Arlen House, 1985); *The Magdalene Sermon* (Dublin: Gallery Press, 1990).

Eavan Boland

LIFE. Born in Dublin in 1944, into a diplomatic family, Eavan Boland was educated in Dublin, London and New York before taking a degree in Trinity College, Dublin. She has lectured widely on poetry in North America, reviews regularly for *The Irish Times* and played a leading part in the development of Arlen House, a Dublin-based feminist publishing company. She is married to the novelist Kevin Casey.

CHIEF WRITINGS. *New Territory* (Dublin: Allen Figgis & Co., 1967); *The War Horse* (Dublin: Arlen House; London: Victor Gollancz, 1975); *In Her Own Image* (Dublin: Arlen House, 1980); *Introducing Eavan Boland: Poems* (Princeton, New Jersey: The Ontario Review Press, 1981); *Night Feed* (Dublin: Arlen House; London and Boston: Marion Boyars, 1982); *The Journey and Other Poems* (Dublin: Arlen House, 1986; Manchester: Carcanet Press, 1989); *Selected Poems* (Manchester: Carcanet Press, 1989); *Outside History: Poems 1980-90* (New York: Norton, 1990).

Paul Durcan

LIFE. Born in Dublin in 1944, Paul Durcan was educated at University College, Cork, where he studied history and archaeology. In 1974 he won the Patrick Kavanagh Award for poetry. He is a very popular reader and has had reading tours in North America, Yugoslavia and the USSR.

CHIEF WRITINGS. *O Westport in the Light of Asia Minor* (Dublin: Anna Livia Press, 1975); *Teresa's Bar* (Dublin: Gallery Press, 1976); *Sam's Cross* (Dublin: Profile Press, 1978); *Jesus, Break His Fall* (Dublin: Raven Arts Press, 1980); *Ark of the North* (Dublin: Raven Arts Press, 1982); *Jumping the Train Tracks with Angela* (Dublin: Raven Arts Press; Manchester: Carcanet New Press, 1983); *The Berlin Wall Café* (Belfast: Blackstaff Press, 1985); E. Longley (ed.), *The Selected Paul Durcan* (Belfast: Blackstaff Press, 1982); *Going Home to Russia* (Belfast: Blackstaff Press, 1987); *Jesus and Angela* (Belfast: Blackstaff Press; Philadelphia: Dufour Editions, 1988); *Daddy, Daddy* (Belfast: Blackstaff Press, 1990).

Frank Ormsby

LIFE. Born in Enniskillen, Co. Fermanagh in 1947, Frank Ormsby was educated at Queen's University, Belfast. He teaches English at the Royal Belfast Academical Institution and is editor of *The Honest Ulsterman*. He won a Gregory Award for poetry in 1974 and lives in Belfast.

CHIEF WRITINGS. *A Store of Candles* (Oxford, London, New York: Oxford University Press, 1977); (ed.) *Poets from the North of Ireland* (Belfast: Blackstaff Press, 1979); *A Northern Spring* (London: Secker and Warburg; Dublin: Gallery Press, 1986); (ed.) *The Long Embrace: Twentieth-Century Irish Love Poems* (Belfast: Blackstaff Press, 1987); (ed.) *Northern Windows: An Anthology of Ulster Autobiography* (Belfast: Blackstaff Press, 1987).

Hugh Maxton

LIFE. Born outside Aughrim, Co. Wicklow in 1947, Hugh Maxton (the pen-name of W.J. Mc Cormack) was educated at Trinity College, Dublin, and has taught at the New University of Ulster, the University of Leeds, the University of Antwerp, Clemson University in the USA and University College, Dublin. He has also been visiting lecturer at the University of Budapest. He lives in Dublin. He is general editor of the projected *Companion to Irish Culture* (Basil Blackwell).

CHIEF WRITINGS. *Stones* (Dublin: Dolmen Press, 1970); *The Noise of the Fields* (Dublin: Dolmen Press, 1976); *Jubilee for Renegades: Poems 1976-1980* (Dublin: Dolmen Press, 1982); *At the Protestant Museum* (Dublin: Dolmen Press, 1986); *The Puzzle Tree Ascendant* (Dublin: Dedalus Press, 1988); *Between* (translation of Agnes Nemes Nagy's poems) (Dublin: Dedalus Press; Budapest: Corvince, 1988).
As W.J. Mc Cormack:
Sheridan Le Fanu and Victorian Ireland (London: Oxford University Press, 1980); *Ascendancy and Tradition: Anglo-Irish Literary History from Burke to Yeats* (London: Oxford University Press, 1985); *The Battle of the Books* (Gigginstown, Co. Westmeath: The Lilliput Press, 1987).

Ciaran Carson

LIFE. Born in Belfast in 1948, Ciaran Carson was educated at Queen's University, Belfast. His first language is Irish. He has worked as a teacher and a civil servant and is at present the traditional arts officer of the Arts Council of Northern Ireland. He won a Gregory Award for poetry in 1976.

CHIEF WRITINGS. *The Insular Celts* (Belfast: Ulsterman Publications, 1973); *The New Estate* (Belfast: Blackstaff Press; Winston-Salem, North Carolina: Wake Forest University Press, 1976, enlarged 1988); *The Pocket Guide to Irish Traditional Music* (Belfast: Appletree Press, 1986); *The Irish for No* (Dublin: Gallery Press; Winston-Salem: Wake Forest University Press, 1987); *Belfast Confetti* (Belfast: Blackstaff Press, 1989).

Tom Paulin

LIFE. Born in Leeds in 1949, Tom Paulin was brought up in Belfast. He was educated at Belfast, and at the Universities of Hull and Oxford. In 1976 he won an Eric Gregory Major Award for poetry. In 1977 he won a Somerset Maugham Award, and in 1982 he was joint winner, with Paul Muldoon, of the Geoffrey Faber Memorial Prize. Since 1980 he has been a director of the Field Day Theatre Company, which performed his play *The Riot Act* (a version of *Antigone*) in 1985. In 1986 he was visiting professor at the University of Virginia. He is a regular reviewer for the chief English literary journals and for television and radio. He now lives in Oxford and is Reader in Poetry at the University of Nottingham.

CHIEF WRITINGS. *Thomas Hardy: The Poetry of Perception* (London: Macmillan, 1975); *A State of Justice* (London: Faber and Faber, 1977); *The Strange Museum* (London: Faber and Faber, 1980); *The Book of Juniper* (Newcastle-upon-Tyne: Bloodaxe Books, 1982); *Liberty Tree* (London: Faber and Faber, 1983); *A New Look at the Language Question* (Derry: Field Day, 1983); *Ireland and the English Crisis* (Newcastle-upon-Tyne: Bloodaxe Books, 1984); *The Riot Act* (London: Faber and Faber, 1984; (ed.) *The Faber Book of Political Verse* (London: Faber and Faber, 1986); *The Hillsborough Script: A Dramatic Satire* (London: Faber and Faber, 1986); *Fivemiletown* (London: Faber and Faber, 1987); *Seize the Fire* (A version of Aeschylus's *Prometheus Unbound* (London: Faber and Faber, 1990); (ed.) *The Faber Book of Vernacular Verse* (London: Faber and Faber, 1990).

Medbh McGuckian

LIFE. Born in Belfast in 1950, Medbh McGuckian attended Queen's University, Belfast and now works as a schoolteacher. She has won the National Poetry Competition in Britain and the Rooney Prize in Ireland. She was the first woman to be named Writer-in-Residence at Queen's University, Belfast and lives in Belfast.

CHIEF WRITINGS. *Portrait of Joanna* (Belfast: Ulsterman Publications, 1980); *The Flower Master* (Oxford, New York: Oxford University Press, 1982); *Venus and the Rain* (Oxford: Oxford University Press, 1984); *On Ballycastle Beach* (Oxford: Oxford University Press; Winston-Salem, North Carolina: Wake Forest University Press, 1988); (with Nuala Archer), *Two Women, Two Shores* (Baltimore: Chestnut Hills Press; Galway, Salmon Publishing, 1989).

Paul Muldoon

LIFE. Born near Moy in County Armagh in 1951, Paul Muldoon was educated at St Patrick's College and Queen's University, Belfast. After graduating, he worked for some years as a radio talks' producer with the BBC Northern Ireland in Belfast. He resigned in 1986 and lived for a time in the Kerry Gaeltacht before taking up a post as visiting writer at Cambridge University, England. In 1982 he was joint winner of the Geoffrey Faber Memorial Prize. He now lives and teaches in New York.

CHIEF WRITINGS. *New Weather* (London: Faber and Faber, 1973); *Mules* (London: Faber and Faber; Winston-Salem, North Carolina: Wake Forest University Press, 1977); *Why Brownlee Left* (London: Faber and Faber; Winston-Salem: Wake Forest University Press, 1980); *Quoof* (London: Faber and Faber; Winston-Salem: Wake Forest University Press, 1983); *Mules and Early Poems* (Winston-Salem: Wake Forest University Press, 1985); *Selected Poems 1968-83* (London: Faber and

Faber, 1986); (ed.) *The Faber Book of Contemporary Irish Poetry* (London: Faber and Faber, 1986); *Meeting the British* (London: Faber and Faber, 1987); *Madoc: A Mystery* (London: Faber and Faber, 1990).

Peter Fallon

LIFE. Peter Fallon was born in Germany in 1951 of Irish parents. His family moved to Ireland in 1957 and he grew up on a County Meath farm. He was educated at Trinity College, Dublin. In 1970 he founded the Gallery Press, which has become one of the most important and distinguished poetry publishers of recent times. In 1976-77 Fallon was poet-in-residence at Deerfield Academy, Massachusetts. He divides his time between farming and publishing.

CHIEF WRITINGS. *Coincidence of Flesh* (Dublin: Gallery Press, 1972); *The First Affair* (Dublin: Gallery Press, 1974); *The Speaking Stones* (Dublin: Gallery Press, 1978); ed. with S. Golden, *Soft Day: A Miscellany of Contemporary Irish Writing* (Dublin: Wolfhound Press; Notre Dame, Indiana: Notre Dame University Press, 1979); ed. with A. Carpenter, *The Writers: A Sense of Ireland* (Dublin: O'Brien Press: New York: George Braziller, 1981); *Winter Work* (Dublin: Gallery Press, 1983); *The News and Weather* (Dublin: Gallery Press, 1987); ed. with Derek Mahon, *The Penguin Book of Contemporary Irish Poetry* (London: Penguin Books, 1990).

Gerald Dawe

LIFE. Born in Belfast in 1952, Gerald Dawe was educated at the New University of Ulster and at University College, Galway. He has taught in the English Department at University College, Galway and at Trinity College, Dublin. He received a major state award for research (1974-77), an Arts Council Bursary for Poetry (1980) and won the Macaulay Fellowship in Literature in 1984 and the Hawthornden International Fellowship in 1987. In 1986 he founded the literary magazine *Krino*.

CHIEF WRITINGS. *Sheltering Places* (Belfast: Blackstaff Press, 1978); ed. *The Younger Irish Poets* (Belfast: Blackstaff Press, 1982); ed. with E. Longley, *Across a Roaring Hill: The Protestant Imagination in Modern Ireland* (Belfast: Blackstaff Press, 1985); *The Lundys Letter* (Dublin: Gallery Press, 1985); *Sunday School* (Dublin: Gallery Press, 1990).

Harry Clifton

LIFE. Born in Dublin in 1952, Harry Clifton was educated at University College, Dublin. He taught in Africa for two years and later worked for the government in the administration of aid programmes for Indo-Chinese refugees in Thailand. He won the Patrick Kavanagh Memorial Award in 1981 and Arts Council Bursaries for Literature in 1982 and 1987. In 1986 he was poet-in-residence at The Robert Frost Place, New Hampshire. He lives in Italy.

CHIEF WRITINGS. *The Walls of Carthage* (Dublin: Gallery Press, 1977); *Office of the Salt Merchant* (Dublin: Gallery Press, 1979); *Comparative Lives* (Dublin: Gallery Press, 1983); *The Liberal Cage* (Dublin: Gallery Press, 1988).

Matthew Sweeney

LIFE. Born in Donegal in 1952, Matthew Sweeney has lived abroad since 1973, in London and in southern Germany. He won the Prudence Farme Award in 1984 and a Cholmondeley Award in 1987.

CHIEF WRITINGS. *A Dream of Maps* (Dublin: Raven Arts Press, 1981); *A Round House* (Dublin: Raven Arts Press; London: Allison and Busby, 1983); *The Lame Waltzer* (Dublin: Raven Arts Press; London: Allison and Busby, 1985); *Blue Shoes* (London: Secker and Warburg, 1989).

Dennis O'Driscoll

LIFE. Born in Thurles, Co. Tipperary in 1954, Dennis O'Driscoll now works as a tax inspector. A keen student of international (and especially Eastern European) poetry, he is one of Ireland's foremost reviewers of poetry. He was awarded an Arts Council bursary in 1985.

CHIEF WRITINGS. *Kist* (Dublin: Dolmen Press, 1982); *Hidden Extras* (London: Anvil Press Poetry, 1987).

Thomas McCarthy

LIFE. Thomas McCarthy was born in Cappoquin, Co. Waterford in 1954 and educated at University College, Cork, where he founded the Poetry Workshop. He now works at the City Library, Cork. In 1977 he won the Patrick Kavanagh Award; in 1978-79 he was a fellow of the international writing programme at the University of Iowa. He has translated poems from the Irish. In 1981 he was joint winner of the Poetry Society's Alice Hunt-Barlett Award and in 1984 won the Irish-American Literary Fund Award.

CHIEF WRITINGS. *The First Convention* (Dublin: Dolmen Press, 1978); *The Sorrow-Garden* (London: Anvil Press, 1981); *The Non-Aligned Story-Teller* (London: Anvil Press, 1984); *Seven Winters in Paris* (London: Anvil Press, 1989).

Sebastian Barry

LIFE. Born in Dublin in 1955, Sebastian Barry was educated at Trinity College, Dublin. He lived abroad for several years before returning to Ireland. He has written fiction, plays and works for children, as well as poetry. In 1982 he won an Arts Council bursary.

CHIEF WRITINGS. *Macker's Garden* (Dublin: Co-op Books, 1982); *Time Out of Mind* (Dublin: Wolfhound Press, 1983); *The Water-Colourist* (Dublin: Dolmen Press, 1983); *The Rhetorical Town* (Dublin: Dolmen Press, 1985); *Elsewhere: The Adventures of Belemus* (Portlaoise: Brogan Books; Dublin: Dolmen Press, 1985); (ed.) *The Inherited Boundaries: Younger Poets of the Republic of Ireland* (Dublin: Dolmen Press, 1986); *The Engine of Owl-Light* (Manchester: Carcanet Press, 1987); *Boss Grady's Boys* (Dublin: Raven Arts Press, 1989).

Aidan Mathews

LIFE. Aidan Mathews was born in Dublin in 1956, educated at University College, Dublin and Trinity College, Dublin. He received the Patrick Kavanagh Award in 1976 and the Macaulay Fellowship in 1978. From 1981 to 1983, he held a writing fellowship at Stanford University, California and won the Ina Coolbrith Poetry Prize for his poem 'Minding Ruth'. Since his return to Ireland, he has worked as a producer for Radio Telefís Éireann. He has written three plays, *Exit/Entrance* (produced 1984, winner of the Listowel Drama Award), a version of *Antigone* (1984) and *The Diamond Body* (1985).

CHIEF WRITINGS. *Windfalls* (Dublin: Dolmen Press, 1977); *Minding Ruth* (Dublin: Dolmen Press, 1983); (ed.) *Immediate Man. Cuimhní ar Chearbhaill Ó Dálaigh* (Dublin: Dolmen Press, 1983); *Adventures in a*

Bathyscope (London: Secker and Warburg, 1988); *Muesli at Midnight* (London: Secker and Warburg, 1990).

Michael O'Loughlin

LIFE. Born in Dublin in 1958, Michael O'Loughlin has worked and travelled extensively abroad. He spent some years in Barcelona and now lives in Amsterdam.

CHIEF WRITINGS. *Stalingrad: The Street Dictionary* (Dublin: Raven Press, 1980); *Atlantic Blues* (Dublin: Raven Arts Press, 1982); *Patrick Kavanagh & The Discourse of Contemporary Irish Poetry* (Dublin: Raven Arts Press, 1985); *The Diary of a Silence* (Dublin: Raven Arts Press, 1985); *Frank Ryan: Journey to the Centre* (Dublin: Raven Arts Press, 1988).

Greg Delanty

LIFE. Born in Cork in 1958, Greg Delanty was educated at University College, Cork. He won the Patrick Kavanagh Memorial Award in 1983 and in 1986 was awarded the Alan Dowling Poetry Fellowship in the United States. He was poet-in-residence at Franconia, New Hampshire, in 1988. He now teaches at St Michael's College, Vermont.

CHIEF WRITINGS. *Cast in the Fire* (Dublin: Dolmen Press, 1986).

Select General Bibliography

The General Editor wishes to thank Dr Andrew Carpenter, Dr Gabriel Cooney, Dr Terry Dolan, Dr J. C. C. Mays, Dr James McGuire, Dr Daithí Ó hÓgáin and, above all, Dr Kevin Whelan for their assistance in the compiling of these lists.

Additional references are given at the beginning of some of the bibliographies to the individual sections.

Bibliographies

Baumgarten, R., *Bibliography of Irish Linguistics and Literature 1942-71* (Dublin: Dublin Institute of Advanced Studies, 1980).

Begley, D. F. (ed.), *Irish Genealogy. A Record Finder* (Dublin: Heraldic Artists, 1981).

Best, R. I., *Bibliography of Irish Philology and of Printed Irish Literature* (Dublin: Dublin Institute of Advanced Studies, 1913).

_________, *Bibliography of Irish Philology and Manuscript Literature: Publications 1913-1941* (Dublin: Browne and Nolan, Dublin Institute of Advanced Studies, 1942).

Brody, E. and C. Brook, *The Music Guide to Great Britain: England, Scotland, Wales, Ireland* (New York: Dodd Mead, 1975).

Brown, S. J., *A Guide to Books on Ireland* (Dublin: Hodges Figgis, 1912).

_________, *Ireland in Fiction: A Guide to Irish Novels, Tales, Romances and Folklore* (Dublin: Maunsel, 1916; 2nd edition 1919; reprinted Shannon: Irish Academic Press, 1969).

Darby, J., N. N. Dodge, A. C. Hepburn and J. Leonard, *A Register of Economic and Social Research on Northern Ireland 1980-83* (London: Social Science Research Council, 1983).

De Hae, R. and B. Ní Dhonnchadha (eds), *Clár Litridheacht na Nua-Ghaedhilge 1850-1936*, 3 vols (Baile Átha Cliath: Oifig Dhiolta Foillseacháin Rialta, 1938-40).

Eager, A., *A Guide to Irish Bibliographical Material* (London: London Library Association, 1964; enlarged 2nd edition 1980).

Edwards, R. D. and M. O'Dowd (eds), *Sources for Early Modern Irish History 1534-1641* (Cambridge: Cambridge University Press, 1985).

Finneran, R., *Anglo-Irish Literature: A Review of Research* (New York: The Modern Language Association of America, 1976).

_________, *Recent Research on Anglo-Irish Writers* (New York: The Modern Language Association of America, 1983).

Harmon, M., *Select Bibliography for the Study of Anglo-Irish Literature and Its Backgrounds: An Irish Studies Handbook* (Dublin: Wolfhound Press, 1977).

Hayes, R. J., *Manuscript Sources for the History of Irish Civilisation*, 11 vols (Boston: G. K. Hall, 1965); *First Supplement*, 3 vols (1979).

_________, *Sources for the History of Irish Civilisation: Articles in Irish Periodicals*, 9 vols (Boston: G. K. Hall, 1970).

Kamen, R. H., *British and Irish Architectural History: A Bibliography and Guide to Sources of Information* (London: Architectural Press, 1981).

Kimball, K., *Ten Modern Irish Playwrights: A Comprehensive Annotated Bibliography* (New York: Garland, 1979).

Kosok, H., 'Anthologies of Anglo-Irish Literature: 1772-1986: A Check-list', *Irish University Review*, Vol. 18, No. 2 (Autumn 1988), 251-62.

McKenna, B., *Irish Literature 1800-1875: A Guide to Information Sources* (Detroit: Gale Information Guide Library, Vol. XIII, 1978).

McParland, E., *A Bibliography of Irish Architectural History* (Dublin: reprint from *Irish Historical Studies*, Vol. XXVI, No. 102, November 1988; Jordanstown; Irish Historical Studies, 1989).

Mikhail, E. H., *A Bibliography of Modern Irish Drama 1899-1970* (London: Macmillan, 1972).

Munter, R., *A Dictionary of the Print Trade in Ireland 1550-1775* (New York: Fordham University Press, 1988).

Nolan, W., *Tracing the Past. Sources for Local Studies in the Republic of Ireland* (Dublin: Geography Publications, 1982).

Ó Danachair, C., *A Bibliography of Irish Ethnology and Folk Tradition* (Dublin and Cork: Mercier Press, 1978).

Shannon, M. O., *Modern Ireland. A Bibliography on Politics, Planning, Research and Development* (Westport; Connecticut: Greenwood Press, 1981).

_________, *Irish Republic*, World Bibliographical Series Vol. 69 (Oxford, Santa Barbara, Denver, 1986).

Takemoto, H., *A Bibliography of Irish Writers in the Seventeenth and Eighteenth Centuries* (Tokyo: Tokyo University Press, 1985).

Watson, G. (ed.), *New Cambridge Bibliography of English Literature* III (Cambridge: Cambridge University Press, 1969).

Willison, I. R. (ed.), *New Cambridge Bibliography of English Literature*, IV (Cambridge: Cambridge University Press, 1972).

Biographical Dictionaries

Boylan, H., *A Dictionary of Irish Biography* (Dublin: Gill and Macmillan, 1978; 2nd edition 1987).

Cleeve, B., *Dictionary of Irish Writers*, 3 vols (Cork: Mercier Press, 1967-71).

Crone, J. S., *Concise Dictionary of Irish Biography* (Dublin: The Talbot Press, 1928).

Hickey, D. J. and J. E. Doherty, *A Dictionary of Irish History since 1800* (Dublin: Gill and Macmillan, 1980); reprinted as *A Dictionary of Irish History 1800-1980* (Dublin: Gill and Macmillan; Totowa, New Jersey: Barnes and Noble, 1987).

Hogan, R. (ed.), *Dictionary of Irish Literature* (Dublin: Gill and Macmillan; Westport, Connecticut: Greenwood Press, 1979); published as *The Macmillan Dictionary of Irish Literature* (London: Macmillan, 1980).

Loeber, R., *A Biographical Dictionary of Architects in Ireland 1600-1720* (London: John Murray, 1981).

O'Donoghue, D. J., *The Poets of Ireland, A Biographical and Bibliographical Dictionary* (Dublin: Hodges Figgis, 1912; reprinted Detroit: Gale Information Guide Library, 1968).

Strickland, W. G., *A Dictionary of Irish Artists*, 2 vols (Dublin and London: Maunsel, 1912; reprinted Shannon: Irish University Press, 1969).

Webb, A. J., *Compendium of Irish Biography* (Dublin: M. H. Gill, 1878).

Archaeology

Barry, T., *The Archaeology of Medieval Ireland* (London: Methuen, 1987).
Bradley, J. (ed.), *Settlement and Society in Medieval Ireland* (Kilkenny: Boethius Press, 1990).
Burenhult, G., *The Archaeology of Carrowmore, Co. Sligo* (Stockholm: Institute of Archaeology, 1984).
Clarke, H. B. and M. Brennan, *Columbanus and Merovingian Monasticism* (Oxford: British Archaeological Reports, 1981).
Clarke, H. B. and A. Simms, *The Comparative History of Urban Origins in Non-Roman Europe* (Oxford: British Archaeological Reports, 1985).
Cuppage, J., *Archaeological Survey of the Dingle Peninsula* (Ballyferriter, Co. Kerry: Oidhreacht Chorca Dhuibhne, 1986).
de Paor, L. and M. de Paor, *Early Christian Ireland* (London: Thames and Hudson, 1958; reprinted 1966).
de Valera, R. and S. O Nuallain, *Survey of the Megalithic Tombs of Ireland*, 4 vols (Dublin: Stationery Office, 1961, 1964, 1971, 1982).
Eames, E. S. and T. Fanning, *Irish Medieval Tiles* (Dublin: Royal Irish Academy, 1988).
Edwards, K. J. and W. P. Warren, *The Quaternary History of Ireland* (London: Academic Press, 1985).
Eogan, G., *Hoards of the Irish Later Bronze Age* (Dublin: University College, Dublin, 1983).
__________, *Excavations at Knowth* (Dublin: Royal Irish Academy, 1984).
__________, *Knowth and the Passage Tombs of Ireland* (London: Thames and Hudson, 1986).
Filip, J., *Celtic Civilisation and Its Heritage* (Prague: Czechoslovak Academy of Sciences, 1960; 2nd edition Wellingborough, Northants: Collets; Prague: Academia, 1977).
Flanagan, E., *Ireland's Armada Legacy* (Dublin: Gill and Macmillan, 1988).
Hamlin, A. and C. Lynn, *Pieces of the Past. Archaeological Excavations by DOENI 1970-86* (Belfast: HMSO, 1988).
Harbison, P., *Guide to the National Monuments of Ireland* (Dublin: Gill and Macmillan, 1970).
__________, *Pre-Christian Ireland. From the First Settlers to the Early Celts* (London: Thames and Hudson, 1988).
Henderson, G., *From Durrow to Kells: The Insular Gospel-Books 650-800* (London: Thames and Hudson, 1987).
Herity, M., *Irish Passage Graves* (Dublin: Irish University Press, 1974).
Herity, M. and G. Eogan, *Ireland in Prehistory* (London: Routledge and Kegan Paul, 1977; 1989).
Higgins, J, *The Early Christian Cross Slabs, Pillar Stones and Related Monuments of Co. Galway, Ireland* (Oxford: British Archaeological Reports, 1987).
Killanin, Lord and M. V. Duignan, *The Shell Guide to Ireland* revised and updated by Peter Harbison (Dublin: Gill and Macmillan, 1989).
Lacy, B., *Archaeological Survey of County Donegal* (Lifford: Donegal County Council, 1983).
MacNiocaill, G. and P. Wallace (eds), *Keimelia: Studies in Medieval Archaeology and History* (Galway: Galway University Press, 1989).
McNeill, T. E., *Anglo-Norman Ulster* (Edinburgh: John Donald, 1980).
Mitchell, G. F., *Man and Environment in Valencia Island* (Dublin: Royal Irish Academy, 1989).
Movius, H. L., *The Irish Stone Age: Its Chronology, Development and Relationships* (Cambridge: Cambridge University Press, 1942).
Murray, H., *Viking and Early Medieval Buildings in Dublin* (Oxford: British Archaeological Reports, 1983).
Norman, E. R. and K. St Joseph, *The Early Development of Irish Society* (Cambridge: Cambridge University Press, 1969).
O'Corrain, D. (ed.), *Irish Antiquity* (Cork: Mercier Press, 1981).
O'Kelly, M. J., *Newgrange: Archaeology, Art and Legend* (London: Thames and Hudson, 1982).
__________, *Early Ireland. An Introduction to Irish Prehistory* (Cambridge: Cambridge University Press, 1989).
O'Riordain, S. P., *Antiquities of the Irish Countryside* (Cork: Cork University Press, 1943; London: Methuen, 1953; 4th edition 1964; 5th revised edition 1979).
Raftery, B., *La Tène in Ireland: Problems of Origin and Chronology* (Marburg: Veroffentlichung des Vorgesschichtlichen Seminars, 1984).
Raftery, J., *Prehistoric Ireland* (London: Batsford, 1951).
Reeves Smyth, T. and F. Hammond (eds), *Landscape Archaeology in Ireland* (Oxford: British Archaeological Reports, 1983).
Ryan, M. F. (ed.), *Ireland and Insular Art A.D. 500-1200* (Dublin: Royal Irish Academy, 1987).
Rynne, E. (ed.), *Figures from the Past. Studies on Figurative Art in Christian Ireland* (Dublin: Glendale Press, 1987).
Weir, A., *Early Ireland. A Field Guide* (Belfast: Blackstaff Press, 1980).
Woodman, P., *The Mesolithic in Ireland: Hunter-gatherers in an Insular Environment* (Oxford: British Archaeological Reports, 1987).

Architecture, Art, Music

This select list in part derives from and may be supplemented by Edward McParland's 'A Bibliography of Irish Architectural History', *Irish Historical Studies*, Vol. XXIV, No. 102 (1988), 161-22; reprinted Jordanstown: Irish Historical Studies, 1989. See also R. H. Kamen, *British and Irish Architectural History; A Bibliography and Guide to Sources of Information* (London: Architectural Press, 1981) and the bibliography in P. Harbison, H. Potterton and J. Sheehy, *Irish Art and Architecture from Prehistory to the Present* (London: Thames and Hudson, 1978).

Arnold, B., *A Concise History of Irish Art* (London: Thames and Hudson, 1969; revised edition 1977).
Beckett, J. C. and R. E. Glasscock (eds), *Belfast: The Origin and Growth of an Industrial City* (London: Faber and Faber, 1967).
Bieler, L., *Ireland: Harbinger of the Middle Ages* (Oxford: Oxford University Press, 1963).
Bodkin, T., *Four Irish Landscape Painters* (Dublin: The Talbot Press, 1920).
Boydell, B., *A Dublin Musical Calendar 1700-1760* (Dublin: Irish Academic Press, 1990).
Brennan, M., *The Stars and Stones: Ancient Art and Astronomy in Ireland* (London: Thames and Hudson, 1983).
Brett, C. E. B., *Buildings of Belfast 1700-1914* (London: Weidenfeld and Nicolson, 1967; revised edition Belfast: Friars Bush Press, 1985).
Butel, P. and L. M. Cullen (eds), *Cities and Merchants: French and Irish Perspectives on Urban Development 1500-1900* (Dublin: Department of Modern History, Trinity College, 1986).
Clarke, H. (ed.), *Medieval Dublin: The Living City* (Dublin: Irish Academic Press, 1990).
__________, *Medieval Dublin: The Making of a Metropolis* (Dublin: Irish Academic Press, 1990).
Craig, M. J., *Dublin 1660-1800* (London: Cresset Press, 1952; reprinted 1969; Dublin: Figgis, 1980).
__________, *Classic Irish Houses of the Middle Size* (London: Architectural Press, 1976).
__________, *The Architecture of Ireland from the Earliest Times to 1880* (London: Batsford; Dublin: Eason, 1982).
Craig, M. J. and the Knight of Glin, *Ireland Observed* (Cork: Mercier Press, 1970).
Crookshank, A., *Irish Sculpture from 1600 to the Present Day* (Dublin: Department of Foreign Affairs, 1984).
Crookshank, A. and the Knight of Glin, *The Painters of Ireland* (London: Barrie and Jenkins, 1978; 2nd edition 1979).
Danaher, K., *Ireland's Vernacular Architecture* (Cork: Mercier Press, 1975).
de Breffny, B. and R. ffolliott, *The Houses of Ireland* (London: Thames and Hudson, 1975).
de Breffny, B. and G. Mott, *The Churches and Abbeys of Ireland* (London: Thames and Hudson, 1976).
Dixon, H., *An Introduction to Ulster Architecture* (Belfast: Ulster Architectural History Society, 1975).
Evans, D., *An Introduction to Modern Ulster Architecture* (Belfast: Ulster Architectural Heritage Society, 1977).
Evans, D., and M. Patton, *The Diamond as Big as a Square: An Introduction to the Towns and Buildings of Ulster* (Belfast: Ulster Architectural Heritage Society, 1981).
Fenlon, J., N. Figgis and C. Marshall (eds), *New Perspectives: Studies in Art History in Honour of Anne Crookshank* (Dublin: Irish Academic Press, 1987).

Finlay, I., *Celtic Art: An Introduction* (London: Faber and Faber, 1973).
Flood, W. H. G., *A History of Irish Music* (Dublin: Browne and Nolan, 1905; reprinted Shannon: Irish University Press, 1970).
Gailey, A., *Rural Houses of the North of Ireland* (Edinburgh: Donald, 1984).
Gilbert, John T., *History of the City of Dublin*, 3 vols (Dublin: McGlashan, 1854-59; reprinted Shannon: Irish University Press, 1972).
Green, M., *Symbol and Image in Celtic Religious Art* (London: Routledge, 1989).
Guinness, D., *Georgian Dublin* (London: Batsford, 1979).
Guinness, D. and W. Ryan, *Irish Houses and Castles* (London: Thames and Hudson, 1971).
Guinness, D. and J. T. Sadler Jr., *The Palladian Style in England, Ireland and America* (London: Thames and Hudson, 1976).
Harbison, P., H. Potterton and J. Sheehy, *Irish Art and Architecture from Prehistory to the Present* (London: Thames and Hudson, 1978).
Harkness, D. and M. O'Dowd (eds), *The Town in Ireland* (Belfast: Appletree Press, 1981).
Harvey, J. H., *Dublin, A Study in Environment* (London: Batsford, 1949).
Henry, F., *Early Christian Irish Art* (Dublin: Three Candles, 1963).
———, *Irish Art in the Early Christian Period (to 800 A.D.)* (London: Methuen, 1940; 3rd edition 1965).
———, *Irish Art during the Viking Invasions (800-1020 A.D.)* (London: Methuen, 1967).
———, *Irish Art in the Romanesque Period (1020-1170 A.D.)* (London: Methuen, 1970).
———, *La Sculpture Irlandaise pendant les douze premiers siècles de l'Ere chrétienne*, 2 vols (Paris: Leroux, 1933).
Hogan, I. M., *Anglo-Irish Music 1780-1830* (Cork: Cork University Press, 1966).
Hurley, R. and W. Cantwell, *Contemporary Irish Church Architecture* (Dublin: Gill and Macmillan, 1985).
Jackson, R. W., *Cathedrals of the Church of Ireland* (Dublin: APCK, 1971).
Kearns, K. C., *Georgian Dublin: Ireland's Imperilled Architectural Heritage* (Newton Abbot: David and Charles, 1983).
Leask, H. G., *Irish Castles and Castellated Houses* (Dundalk: Tempest, 1941).
———, *Irish Churches and Monastic Buildings* I. *The First Phases and the Romanesque*; II. *Gothic Architecture to A.D. 1400*; III. *Medieval Gothic: The Last Phases* (Dundalk: Dundealgan Press, 1960).
Longford, C. (Countess of), *A Biography of Dublin* (London: Methuen, 1936).
Mahr, A. and J. Raftery, *Christian Art in Ancient Ireland*, 2 vols (Dublin: Stationery Office, 1932-41; New York: Hacker, 1976).
Malins, E., *Irish Gardens* (Dublin: Eason, 1977).
Malins, E. and P. Bowe, *Irish Gardens and Demesnes from 1830* (London: Barrie and Jenkins, 1980).
Malins, E. and D. FitzGerald (Knight of Glin), *Lost Demesnes: Irish Landscape Gardening 1660-1845* (London: Barrie and Jenkins, 1976).
Malton, J., *A Picturesque and Descriptive View of the City of Dublin* (London, 1792-99; reprinted Dublin: The Dolmen Press, in association with the Irish Georgian Society, 1981).
Maxwell, C., *Country and Town in Ireland under the Georges* (London: Harrap, 1940).
———, *Dublin under the Georges 1714-1830* (London: Harrap, 1936; revised edition London: 1956).
McCarthy, M., *All Graduates and Gentlemen: Marsh's Library* (Dublin: O'Brien Press, 1980).
McCullough, N., *Dublin: An Urban History* (Dublin: Anne St. Press, 1990).
McCullough, N. and V. Mulvin, *A Lost Tradition: The Nature of Architecture in Ireland* (Dublin: Gandon Editions, 1987; 1990).
McDermott, M., *Ireland's Architectural Heritage: An Outline History of Irish Architecture* (Tallaght, Co. Dublin: Folens, 1975).
McParland, E., *James Gandon, Vitruvius Hibernicus* (London: Zwemmer, 1985).
McParland, E., A. Rowan and A. M. Rowan, *The Architecture of Richard Morrison (1767-1849) and William Vitruvius Morrison (1794-1838)* (Dublin: Irish Architectural Archive, 1990).
Murray, H., *Viking and Early Medieval Buildings in Dublin* (Oxford: B. A. R., 1983).
O'Dwyer, F., *Lost Dublin* (Dublin: Gill and Macmillan, 1981).
Olbricht, K.-H. and H. M. Wegener, *Irish Houses: History, Architecture, Furnishing* (London: Thames and Hudson, 1984).
Pool, R. and J. Cash, *Views of The Most Remarkable Public Buildings, Monuments and Other Edifices in The City of Dublin* (Dublin: J. Williams, 1780; reprinted with introduction by M. Craig, Shannon: Irish University Press, 1970).
Potterton, H., *Irish Church Monuments 1570-1880* (Belfast: Ulster Architectural Heritage Society, 1974).
Richardson A. E., *Monumental Classic Architecture in Great Britain and Ireland during the Eighteenth and Nineteenth Centuries* (London: Batsford, 1914; reprinted 1982).
———, *An Introduction to Georgian Architecture* (London: Art and Technics, 1949).
Richardson, D. S., *Gothic Revival Architecture in Ireland*, 2 vols (New York and London: Garland, 1983).
Rothery, S., *Everyday Buildings of Ireland* (Dublin: College of Technology, Bolton Street, 1975).
———, *The Shops of Ireland* (Dublin: Gill and Macmillan, 1978).
Rowan, A., *The Buildings of Ireland: North-west Ulster: The Counties of Londonderry, Donegal, Fermanagh and Tyrone* (Harmondsworth: Penguin Books, 1979).
Shaffrey, P., *The Irish Town: An Approach to Survival* (Dublin: O'Brien Press, 1975).
———, *Irish Countryside Buildings: Everyday Architecture in the Rural Landscape* (Dublin: O'Brien Press, 1985).
Shaffrey, P. and M. Shaffrey, *Buildings of Irish Towns: Treasures of Everyday Architecture* (Dublin: O'Brien Press, 1983; London: Architectural Press; Springfield, Illinois: Templegate Press, 1984).
Sheehy, J., *J. J. McCarthy and the Gothic Revival in Ireland* (Belfast: Ulster Architectural Society, 1977).
———, *The Rediscovery of Ireland's Past; The Celtic Revival 1830-1930* (London: Thames and Hudson, 1980).
Stalley, R. A., *Architecture and Sculpture in Ireland 1150-1350* (Dublin: Gill and Macmillan, 1971).
———, *The Cistercian Monasteries of Ireland* (London and New Haven: Yale University Press, 1987).
Walsh, T. J., *Opera in Old Dublin 1819-1838* (Wexford: The Free Press, 1952).
———, *Opera in Dublin 1705-1797: The Social Scene* (Dublin: Allen Figgis, 1973).
Warren, P., *Irish Glass: The Age of Exuberance* (London: Faber and Faber, 1970; 2nd revised edition 1981).
Weir, H., *The Houses of Clare* (Ballinakella: Ballinakella Press, 1986).
White, H. and G. Gillen (eds), *Irish Musical Studies I* (Dublin: Irish Academic Press, 1990).
White, J., *The National Gallery of Ireland* (London: Thames and Hudson, 1968).
Wynne, M., *Irish Stained Glass* (Dublin: Eason, 1977).

Folklore and Folk Music

More detailed listings are to be found in C. Ó Danachair (Kevin Danaher), *A Bibliography of Irish Ethnology and Folk Tradition* (Dublin and Cork: Mercier Press, 1978) and in S. Ó Duilearga, *Leabhar Sheáin Í Chonaill, Scéalta agus Seanchas ó Íbh Ráthach* (Baile Átha Cliath: An Coláiste Ollscoile, Comhairle Bhéaloideas Éireann, 1977), pp. 397-413. The journal *Béaloideas* is indispensable.

Brady, J., *The Big Sycamore. Reminiscences* (Dublin: M. H. Gill and Son, 1958).
Breathnach, B., *Irish Folkmusic and Dances* (Dublin: The Talbot Press, 1967; revised edition 1977).
Bruford, A., *Gaelic Folktales and Medieval Romances* (Edinburgh: Edinburgh University Press, 1969).
Carbery, M., *The Farm by Lough Gur* (London: Longmans, Green, 1937; Cork: Mercier Press, 1973).
Christiansen, R. T., *Studies in Irish and Scandinavian Folk Tales* (Copenhagen: Rosenkilde and Bagger, 1959).

Delargy, J. H, *The Gaelic Storyteller* (London: Cumberlege, 1945).
de Vries, J. (trans. B. J. Timmer), *Heroic Songs and Heroic Legend* (London: Oxford University Press, 1963).
Evans, E. E., *Irish Folkways* (London: Routledge and Kegan Paul, 1957).
Gailey, A., *Irish Folk Drama* (Cork: Mercier Press, 1969).
Gailey, A. and D. Ó hÓgáin (eds), *Gold Under the Furze: Studies in Folk Tradition: Presented to Caoimhín Ó Danachair* (Dublin: Glendale Press, 1982).
Lysaght, P., *The Banshee: The Irish Supernatural Death-Messenger* (Dublin: Glendale Press, 1986).
MacNeill, M., *The Festival of Lughnasa* (London: Oxford University Press, 1962).
McGrath, M. (ed.), *Cinnlae Amhlaoibh Uí Shúilleabháin: The Diary of Humphrey O'Sullivan* (London: Irish Texts Society, 1936-37).
Ó Caithnia, P., *Scéal na hIomána ó thosach ama go 1884* (Baile Átha Cliath: An Clóchomhar, 1980).
Ó Catháin, S., *Irish Life and Lore* (Dublin and Cork: Mercier Press, 1982).
Ó Catháin, S. and P. O'Flanagan, *The Living Landscape; Kilgalligan, Erris, Co. Mayo* (Baile Átha Cliath: An Coláiste Ollscoile, Comhairle Béaloideas Éireann, 1975).
Ó Danachair, C., *In Ireland Long Ago* (Cork: Mercier Press, 1962; reprinted 1976).
———, *Folktales of the Irish Countryside* (Dublin and Cork: Mercier Press, 1965; reprinted 1976).
———, *Irish Country People* (Cork: Mercier Press, 1966).
———, *The Pleasant Land of Ireland* (Cork: Mercier Press, 1967).
———, *The Year in Ireland* (Dublin and Cork: Mercier Press, 1972).
O'Dowd, A., *Meitheal: A Study of Co-operative Labour in Rural Ireland* (Baile Átha Cliath: Comhairle Béaloideas Éireann, 1981).
O hEochaidh, S. (ed.), *Síscéalta ó Thír Chonaill/Fairy Legends from Donegal* (Baile Átha Cliath: Comhairle Béaloideas Éireann, 1977).
Ó hOgáin, D., *An File: Staidéar ar Osnádúrthacht na Filíochta sa Traidisiún Gaelach* (Baile Átha Cliath: Oifig an tSólathair, 1982).
———, *Fionn mac Cumhaill: Images of the Gaelic Hero* (Dublin: Gill and Macmillan, 1988).
O'Neill, F., *Irish Folk Music* (Chicago: Regan, 1910; reprinted Darby, Pennsylvania: Norwood, 1973).
———, *Irish Minstrels and Musicians* (Chicago: Regan, 1913; reprinted Darby, Pennsylvania: Norwood, 1973).
O'Neill, F., (ed.), *O'Neill's Music of Ireland* (Chicago: Ryan and Healy, 1910).
O'Neill, T., *Life and Tradition in Rural Ireland* (London: Dent, 1977).
O'Rourke, B., *Blas Meala, A Sip from the Honey-Pot: Gaelic Folksongs with English Translations* (Dublin: Irish Academic Press, 1985).
———, *Pale Rainbow: Gaelic Folksongs with English Translations* (Dublin: Irish Academic Press, 1989).
Ó Súilleabháin, S., *A Handbook of Irish Folklore* (Dublin: Educational Company, 1942; Detroit: Singing Tree Press, 1970).
———, *Folktales of Ireland* (London: Routledge and Kegan Paul, 1966).
———, *Irish Folk Custom and Belief* (Dublin: Three Candles, 1967).
———, *Irish Wake Amusements* (Cork: Mercier Press, 1967).
———, *Storytelling in Irish Tradition* (Cork: Mercier Press, 1973).
———, *The Folklore of Ireland* (London: Batsford, 1974).
——— and R. T. Christiansen, *The Types of Irish Folktale* (Helsinki: Suomalinan Tiedakatemia Academia Scientiarum Fennica, 1963).
Ó Tuama, S., *An Grá an Amhráin na nDaoine* (Baile Átha Cliath: An Clóchomhar, 1960).
Shields, H., *Narrative Songs in Ireland: Lays, Ballads and Come-all Yes* (Dublin: Irish Academic Press, 1990).
Thompson, S., *The Folk Tale* (New York: Dryden, 1946; reprinted New York: AMS, 1979).

Historical Geography

Aalen, F. H., *Man and the Landscape in Ireland* (London: Academic Press, 1978; New York: Academic Press Inc, 1978).
Andrews, J. H., *A Paper Landscape: The Ordnance Survey in Ireland* (Oxford: Clarendon Press, 1975).
———, *Irish Maps* (Dublin: Eason, 1978).
———, *Plantation Acres. An Historical Study of the Irish Land Surveyors* (Belfast: Ulster Historical Foundation, 1985).
Atlas of Ireland (Dublin: Irish National Committee for Geography, Royal Irish Academy, 1979).
Buchanan, R. H., E. Jones and D. F. McCourt (ed.), *Man and his Habitat; Essays presented to E. E. Evans* (London: Routledge and Kegan Paul, 1971).
Camblin, G., *The Town in Ulster* (Belfast: Mullan, 1951).
Davies, G. L. Herries (ed.), *The Geographical Society of Ireland. Golden Jubilee 1934-1984* (Dublin: Irish Geographical Society, 1984).
Davies, G. L. Herries and N. Stephens, *Ireland, A Geomorphology* (London: Methuen, 1978).
Evans, E., *The Personality of Ireland: Habitat, Heritage and History* (Cambridge: Cambridge University Press, 1973).
Feehan, J., *The Landscape of Slieve Bloom* (Dublin: Blackwater Press, 1979).
Flatrès, P., *Geographie Rurale de Quatre Contrées Celtiques, Irlande, Galles, Cornwall et Man* (Rennes: Librairie Universitaire Philon, 1957).
Freeman, T. W., *Pre-Famine Ireland: A Study in Historical Geography* (Manchester: Manchester University Press, 1957).
———, *Ireland: Its Physical, Historical, Social and Economic Geography* (London: Methuen, 1956; revised edition 1960).
Graham, B. J., *Anglo-Norman Settlement in Ireland* (Dublin: Group for the Study of Irish Historic Settlement, 1985).
Hayes-McCoy, G. A., *Ulster and Other Irish Maps c. 1600* (Dublin: Stationery Office, 1964).
Jones, E., *A Social Geography of Belfast* (London: Oxford University Press,1960).
Kearney, H., *The British Isles. A History of Four Nations* (Cambridge: Cambridge University Press, 1989).
Lee, J. (ed.), *Ireland: Towards a Sense of Place* (Cork: Cork University Press, 1985).
Leister, I., *Peasant Openfield Farming and Its Territorial Organisation in County Tipperary* (Marburg: Marburger Geographische Schriften, 1976).
Mannion, J., *Irish Settlement in Eastern Canada: A Study of Cultural Transfer and Adaptation* (Toronto: University of Toronto Press, 1974).
Mitchell, G. F., *The Irish Landscape* (London: Collins, 1976).
———, *The Shell Guide to Reading the Irish Landscape* (incorporating *The Irish Landscape*) (Dublin: Country House, 1986).
Mould, D. D. C. Pochin, *Ireland from the Air* (Newton Abbot: David and Charles, 1972).
Nolan, W., *Fassadinin: Land Settlement and Society in South-east Ireland 1600-1850* (Dublin: Geography Publications, 1979).
———, *Tracing the Past: Sources for Local Studies in the Republic of Ireland* (Dublin: Geography Publications, 1982).
Nolan, W. (ed.), *Tipperary: History and Society* (Dublin: Geography Publications, 1985).
———, *The Shaping of Ireland: The Geographical Perspective* (Dublin and Cork: Mercier Press, 1986).
Nolan, W. and K. Whelan (eds), *Kilkenny: History and Society* (Dublin: Geography Publications, 1990).
O'Connor, P. J., *Exploring Limerick's Past: An Historical Geography of Urban Development in County and City* (Newcastle West, Co. Limerick: Oireacht na Mumhan Books, 1987).
O' Flanagan, P., P. Ferguson and K. Whelan (eds), *Rural Ireland 1600-1900. Modernisation and Change* (Cork: Cork University Press, 1987).
Orme, A. R., *The World's Landscapes — Ireland* (London: Longman, 1970).
Praeger, R. L., *The Way that I Went* (Dublin: Allen Figgis; London: Methuen, 1937; reprinted 1969, 1980).
Robinson, P. S., *The Plantation of Ulster: British Settlement in an Irish Landscape* (Dublin: Gill and Macmillan; New York: St Martin's Press, 1984).
Smyth, A. P., *Celtic Leinster. Towards a Historical Geography of Early Irish Civilisation A.D. 500-1600* (Dublin: Irish Academic Press, 1982).
Smyth, W. J. and K. Whelan (eds), *Common Ground. Essays on the Historical Geography of Ireland* (Cork: Cork University Press, 1988).
Stephens, N. and R. E. Glasscock (eds), *Irish Geographical Studies in Honour of E. Estyn Evans* (Belfast: Department of Geography, Queen's University, Belfast, 1970).

Thomas, C. (ed.), *Rural Landscapes and Communities* (Dublin: Irish Academic Press, 1987).
Whelan, K. (ed.), *Wexford: History and Society* (Dublin: Geography Publications, 1987).

History

The annual lists of *Writings on Irish History* in *Irish Historical Studies* (1936-1978; 1986-) should be consulted. For the intervening years, see *Writings on Irish History 1979 to 1983* (microfiche), published by the Irish Committee of Historical Sciences, and J. R. Hill (ed.), *Writings on Irish History 1984, Incorporating Addenda from 1973-83* (Dublin: Irish Committee of Historical Sciences, 1986) and C. Cullen (ed.), *Writings on Irish History 1985* (Dublin: Irish Committee of Historical Sciences, 1987).

Akenson, D. H., *The Irish Education Experiment: The National System of Education in the Nineteenth Century* (London: Routledge and Kegan Paul, 1970).
Andrews, K. R., N. Canny and P. E. H. Hair (eds), *The Westward Enterprise: English Activities in Ireland, The Atlantic and America 1480-1650* (Liverpool: Liverpool University Press, 1978).
Bagwell, R., *Ireland Under the Tudors*, 3 vols (London: Longmans Green, 1885-90).
——, *Ireland Under the Stuarts*, 3 vols (London: Longmans Green, 1909-16).
Barnard, T. C., *Cromwellian Ireland: English Government and Reform in Ireland 1649-60* (London: Oxford University Press, 1975).
Bartlett, T. and D. Hayton (eds), *Penal Era and Golden Age: Essays in Irish History 1690-1800* (Belfast: Ulster Historical Foundation, 1979).
Beckett, J. C., *Protestant Dissent in Ireland 1687-1780* (London: Faber and Faber, 1948).
——, *The Making of Modern Ireland 1603-1923* (London: Faber and Faber, 1966).
——, *Confrontations: Studies in Irish History* (London: Faber and Faber, 1972).
——, *The Anglo-Irish Tradition* (London: Faber and Faber, 1976).
Bell, J. B., *The Secret Army: A History of the IRA 1916-70* (London: Blond, 1970; Dublin: Academy Press, 1979).
Bew, P., *Land and the National Question in Ireland 1858-82* (Dublin: Gill and Macmillan, 1978).
——, *Conflict and Conciliation in Ireland 1890-1910: Parnellites and Radical Agrarians* (Oxford: Clarendon Press, 1987).
Bew, P., P. Gibbon and H. Patterson, *The State in Northern Ireland 1921-72: Political Forces and Social Classes* (Manchester: Manchester University Press, 1979).
Black, R. D. C., *Economic Thought and the Irish Question 1817-70* (Cambridge: Cambridge University Press, 1960).
Bowen, D., *The Protestant Crusade in Ireland 1800-1870: A Study of Protestant-Catholic Relations* (Dublin: Gill and Macmillan, 1978).
——, *Protestants in a Catholic State: Ireland's Privileged Minority* (Montreal and Kingston: McGill-Queen's University Press; Dublin: Gill and Macmillan, 1983).
Bowman, J., *De Valera and the Ulster Question 1917-73* (Oxford: Clarendon Press, 1982).
Boyce, D. G., *The Dissolution of the Religious Orders in Ireland under Henry VIII* (Cambridge: Cambridge University Press, 1974).
——, *Nationalism in Ireland* (London: Croom Helm, 1982).
Bradshaw, B., *The Irish Constitutional Revolution of the Sixteenth Century* (Cambridge: Cambridge University Press, 1979).
Brady, C. and R. Gillespie (eds), *Natives and Newcomers: Essays on the Making of Irish Colonial Society 1534-1641* (Dublin: Irish Academic Press, 1986).
Brooke, P., *Ulster Presbyterianism: The Historical Perspective 1610-1970* (New York: St Martin's Press, 1987).
Buckland, P., *Irish Unionism:* Vol I. *The Anglo-Irish and the New Ireland 1885-1922* (Dublin: Gill and Macmillan, 1972); Vol. II. *Ulster Unionism and the Origins of Northern Ireland 1886-1922* (Dublin: Gill and Macmillan; New York: Barnes and Noble, 1973).
——, *The Factory of Grievances: Devolved Government in Northern Ireland 1921-39* (Dublin: Gill and Macmillan, 1979).
Byrne, F. J., *Irish Kings and High Kings* (London: Oxford University Press, 1973).
Canny, N. P., *The Elizabethan Conquest of Ireland: A Pattern Established 1565-76* (Hassocks, Sussex: Harvester Press, 1976).
——, *From Reformation to Restoration: Ireland 1534-1660* (Dublin: Helicon, 1987).
——, *Kingdom and Colony: Ireland in the Atlantic World 1560-1800* (Baltimore: Johns Hopkins University Press, 1988).
Canny, N. P. and A. Pagden (eds), *Colonial Identity in the Atlantic World 1500-1800* (Princeton: Princeton University Press, 1987).
Chadwick, N. K., *The Age of the Saints in the Early Christian Church* (London: Oxford University Press, 1961).
Chubb, B., *The Government and Politics of Ireland* (London: Oxford University Press, 1970).
Clark, S., *Social Origins of the Irish Land War* (Princeton: Princeton University Press, 1979).
Clark, S. and J. Donnelly (eds), *Irish Peasants: Violence and Political Unrest 1780-1914* (Manchester: Manchester University Press, 1983).
Clarke, A., *The Old English in Ireland 1625-42* (London: MacGibbon and Kee, 1966).
Comerford, R. V., *The Fenians in Context: Irish Politics and Society 1848-82* (Dublin: Wolfhound Press; Atlantic Highlands, New Jersey: Humanities Press, 1985).
Connell, K. H., *The Population of Ireland 1750-1845* (Oxford: Clarendon Press, 1950).
Corish, P. J., *The Catholic Community in the Seventeenth and Eighteenth Centuries* (Dublin: Helicon, 1981).
——, *The Irish Catholic Experience: A Historical Survey* (Dublin: Gill and Macmillan, 1985).
Coughlan, P. (ed.), *Spenser and Ireland: An Interdisciplinary Perspective* (Cork: Cork University Press, 1990).
Crotty, R., *Irish Agricultural Production: Its Volume and Structure* (Cork: Cork University Press, 1966).
——, *Ireland in Crisis: A Study in Capitalist Colonial Underdevelopment* (Dingle, Co. Kerry: Brandon Press, 1986).
Cullen, L., *An Economic History of Ireland Since 1660* (London: Batsford, 1972; 2nd edition 1988).
——, *The Emergence of Modern Ireland 1600-1900* (London: Batsford, 1981).
——, *The Hidden Ireland: Reassessment of a Concept* (Mullingar, Co. Westmeath: The Lilliput Press, 1988).
Curtis, E., *History of Ireland* (London: Methuen, 1936; reprinted 1937, 1950, 1968).
——, *History of Medieval Ireland from 1086 to 1513* (Dublin: Maunsel and Roberts, 1923; 2nd revised and enlarged edition London: Methuen, 1938).
Curtis, L. P., *Coercion and Conciliation in Ireland 1880-92: A Study in Constructive Unionism* (Princeton: Princeton University Press; London: Oxford University Press, 1963).
——, *Anglo-Saxon and Celts: A Study of Anti-Irish Prejudice in Victorian England* (Bridgeport, Connecticut: Conference on British Studies, 1968).
Daly, M., *Dublin, The Deposed Capital: A Social and Economic History 1860-1914* (Cork: Cork University Press, 1985).
Davis, R., *The Young Ireland Movement* (Dublin: Gill and Macmillan, 1987).
de Paor, L., *Divided Ulster* (Harmondsworth: Penguin Books, 1970).
——, *The Peoples of Ireland: From Prehistory to Modern Times* (London: Hutchinson, 1986).
——, *Unfinished Business* (London: Hutchinson Radius, 1990).
Dickson, D., *New Foundations: Ireland 1660-1800* (Dublin: Helicon, 1987).
Dickson, D. (ed.), *The Gorgeous Mask, Dublin 1700-1850* (Dublin: Trinity History Workshop, 1987).
Dickson, R. H., *Ulster Emigration to Colonial America 1718-85* (Belfast: Blackstaff Press, 1966).
Donnelly, J. S., *The Land and the People of Nineteenth-Century Cork* (London and Boston: Routledge and Kegan Paul, 1975).
Doyle, D. N., *Ireland, Irishmen and Revolutionary America 1760-1820* (Cork: Mercier Press, 1981).

Edwards, R. Dudley, *Church and State in Tudor Ireland* (Dublin and Cork: The Talbot Press, 1935).
Edwards, Ruth Dudley, *An Atlas of Irish History*, 2nd edition (London: Methuen, 1981).
Elliott, M., *Partners in Revolution: The United Irishmen and France* (London and New Haven: Yale University Press, 1978).
__________, *Wolfe Tone. Prophet of Irish Independence* (London and New Haven: Yale University Press, 1989).
Ellis, S. G., *Tudor Ireland: Crown, Community and the Conflict of Cultures* (London: Longman, 1985).
Farrell, M., *Northern Ireland: The Orange State* (London: Pluto Press, 1980).
__________, *Arming the Protestants: The Formation of the Ulster Special Constabulary and the Royal Ulster Constabulary 1920-72* (London: Pluto Press; Dingle, Co. Kerry: Brandon Press, 1983).
Fisk, R., *Ireland, Ulster and the Price of Neutrality 1939-45* (Dingle, Co. Kerry: Brandon Press; London: André Deutsch, 1983).
Fitzpatrick, D., *Politics and Irish Life 1913-1921: Provincial Experience of War and Revolution* (Dublin: Gill and Macmillan, 1977).
__________, *Irish Emigration 1801-1920* (Dundalk: Dundealgan Press, 1984).
Foster, R. F., *Modern Ireland 1600-1972* (London: Penguin Books, 1988).
Foster, R. F., (ed.), *The Oxford Illustrated History of Modern Ireland* (London: Oxford University Press, 1989).
Gailey, A., *Ireland and the Death of Kindness: The Experience of Constructive Unionism 1890-1905* (Cork: Cork University Press, 1987).
Garvin, T., *The Evolution of Irish Nationalist Politics* (Dublin: Gill and Macmillan, 1981).
__________, *Nationalist Revolutionaries in Ireland 1858-1928* (Oxford: Clarendon Press, 1987).
Gillespie, R., *Colonial Ulster: The Settlement of East Ulster 1600-1641* (Cork: Cork University Press, 1985).
Goldstrom, J. A. and L. A. Clarkson (eds), *Irish Population, Economy and Society. Essays in Honour of the Late K. H. Connell* (Oxford: Clarendon Press, 1981).
Gough, H. and D. Dickson (eds), *Ireland and the French Revolution* (Dublin: Irish Academic Press, 1990).
Harkness, D., *The Restless Dominion: The Irish Free State in the British Commonwealth of Nations 1921-31* (Dublin and London: Gill and Macmillan, 1969).
__________, *Northern Ireland since 1920* (Dublin: Helicon, 1983).
Hopkinson, M., *Green Against Green: The Irish Civil War* (Dublin: Gill and Macmillan, 1988).
Hoppen, K. T., *Elections, Politics and Society in Ireland 1832-85* (Oxford: Oxford University Press, 1985).
Hughes, K., *The Church in Early Irish History* (London: Methuen, 1966).
James, F. G., *Ireland in the Empire 1688-1770* (Cambridge, Massachusetts: Harvard University Press, 1973).
Kee, R., *The Green Flag: A History of Irish Nationalism* (London: Weidenfeld and Nicolson, 1972).
Kelly, F., *A Guide to Early Irish Law* (Dublin: Institute for Advanced Studies, 1988).
Kendle, J., *Ireland and the Federal Solution: The Debate over the United Kingdom Constitution 1870-1920* (Montreal and Kingston: McGill-Queen's University Press, 1989).
Laffan, M., *The Partition of Ireland 1911-25* (Dundalk: Dundealgan Press, 1983).
Larkin, E., *The Making of the Roman Catholic Church in Ireland 1850-1860* (Chapel Hill: University of North Carolina Press, 1980).
__________, *The Historical Dimension of Irish Catholicism* (New York: Catholic University Press, 1984).
__________, *The Consolidation of the Roman Catholic Church in Ireland 1860-1870* (Chapel Hill: University of North Carolina Press, 1987).
Lebow, R. N., *White Britain and Black Ireland: The Influence of Stereotypes on Colonial Policy* (Philadelphia: Institute for the Study of Human Issues, 1976).
Lee, J., *The Modernisation of Modern Irish Society 1848-1918* (Dublin: Gill and Macmillan, 1973).
__________, *Ireland 1912-1985. Politics and Society* (Cambridge: Cambridge University Press, 1989).
Lydon, J. F., *Ireland in the Later Middle Ages* (Dublin: Gill and Macmillan, 1973).
Lyons, F. S. L., *Ireland Since the Famine* (London: Fontana, 1971).
__________, *Culture and Anarchy in Ireland 1890-1939* (Oxford: Oxford University Press, 1979).
MacArdle, D., *The Irish Republic: A Documented Chronicle of the Anglo-Irish Conflict* (London: Gollancz, 1937; reprinted 1968, 1977).
MacCurtain, M., *Tudor and Stuart Ireland* (Dublin: Gill and Macmillan, 1972).
MacDonagh, O., *Ireland* (Englewood Cliffs, New Jersey: Prentice Hall Inc., 1968), retitled *Ireland: The Union and its Aftermath* (London: Allen and Unwin, 1977).
__________, *States of Mind: A Study of Anglo-Irish Conflict 1780-1980* (London: Allen and Unwin, 1983).
Malcolmson, A. P. W., *John Foster, The Politics of the Anglo-Irish Ascendancy* (Oxford: Oxford University Press, 1978).
Mansergh, N., *The Irish Question 1840-1921* (London: Allen and Unwin, 1965; 2nd edition 1968; 3rd revised edition 1975).
McCarthy-Morrogh, M., *The Munster Plantation* (Oxford: Clarendon Press, 1986).
McCartney, D., *The Dawning of Democracy: Ireland 1800-1870* (Dublin: Helicon, 1987).
McDowell, R. B., *Irish Public Opinion 1750-1800* (London: Faber and Faber, 1944).
Meenan, J., *The Irish Economy since 1922* (Liverpool: Liverpool University Press, 1970).
Miller, D., *Queen's Rebels: Ulster Loyalism in Historical Perspective* (Dublin: Gill and Macmillan; New York: Barnes and Noble, 1978).
Miller, K., *Emigrants and Exiles* (Cambridge: Cambridge University Press, 1987).
Mokyr, J., *Why Ireland Starved: A Quantitative and Analytical History of the Irish Economy 1800-1845* (London: Allen and Unwin, 1985).
Moody, T. W. (ed.), *The Fenian Movement* (Cork and Dublin: Mercier Press, 1968).
Moody, T. W. and F. X. Martin (eds), *The Course of Irish History* (Cork: Mercier Press, 1967).
Moody, T. W., F. X. Martin, F. J. Byrne (eds), *A New History of Ireland*, Vol. II. *Medieval Ireland*; Vol. III. *Early Modern Ireland 1534-1691*; Vol. IV. *Eighteenth-century Ireland 1691-1800*; Vol. V. *Ireland under the Union 1801-1900*; Vol. VIII. *Chronology of Irish History to 1976*; Vol. IX. *Maps, Genealogies, Lists. A Companion to Irish History, Part II* (Oxford: Clarendon Press, 1976-90).
Munter, R. L., *The History of the Irish Newspaper 1685-1760* (Cambridge: Cambridge University Press, 1967).
Murphy, J. A., *Ireland in the Twentieth Century* (Dublin: Gill and Macmillan, 1975; 1989).
Nicholls, K., *Gaelic and Gaelicised Ireland in the Middle Ages* (Dublin: Gill and Macmillan, 1972).
O'Brien, C. C., *States of Ireland* (London: Hutchinson, 1972).
O'Brien, C. C. (ed.), *The Shaping of Modern Ireland* (London: Routledge and Kegan Paul, 1960).
O'Farrell, P., *England's Irish Question: Anglo-Irish Relations 1534-1970* (London: Batsford, 1971).
O Grada, C., *Ireland Before and After the Famine. Explorations in Economic History 1800-1925* (Manchester: Manchester University Press, 1988).
O Raifeartaigh, T. (ed.), *The Royal Irish Academy: A Bicentennial History 1785-1985* (Dublin: Royal Irish Academy, 1985).
Orpen, G. H., *Ireland Under the Normans 1169-1333*, 4 vols (Oxford: Oxford University Press, 1911-20).
O Tuathaigh, G., *Ireland Before the Famine* (Dublin: Gill and Macmillan, 1972; reissued 1990).
Otway Ruthven, A. J., *A History of Medieval Ireland* (London: Ernest Benn; New York: Barnes and Noble, 1968).
Pakenham, T., *The Year of Liberty* (London: Hodder and Stoughton, 1969).
Patterson, H., *Class Conflict and Sectarianism: The Protestant Working Class and the Belfast Labour Movement 1868-1920* (Belfast: Blackstaff Press, 1980).
Pawlisch, H. S., *Sir John Davies and the Conquest of Ireland: A Study in Legal Imperialism* (Cambridge: Cambridge University Press, 1985).

Philpin, C. H. E. (ed.), *Nationalism and Popular Protest in Ireland* (Cambridge: Cambridge University Press, 1987).

Pollard, M., *Dublin's Trade in Books 1550-1800* (Oxford: Oxford University Press, 1990).

Power, T. P. and K. Whelan (eds), *Endurance and Emergence: Catholics in Ireland in the Eighteenth Century* (Dublin: Irish Academic Press, 1990).

Quinn, D. B., *The Elizabethans and the Irish* (Ithaca, New York: Cornell University Press, 1966).

Richter, M., *Medieval Ireland: The Enduring Tradition* (London: St Martin's Press, 1988).

Roebuck, P. (ed.), *Plantation to Partition: Essays in Ulster History, in Honour of J. L. McCracken* (Belfast: Blackstaff Press, 1981).

Rumpf, E. and A. C. Hepburn, *Nationalism and Socialism in Twentieth-Century Ireland* (Liverpool: Liverpool University Press, 1977).

Simms, J. G., *The Williamite Confiscation in Ireland 1690-1703* (London: Faber and Faber, 1958).

_________, *Jacobite Ireland 1685-91* (London: Routledge and Kegan Paul, 1969).

Solow, B., *The Land Question and the Irish Economy 1870-1903* (Cambridge, Massachusetts: Harvard University Press, 1971).

Stewart, A. T. Q., *The Narrow Ground: Aspects of Ulster 1609-1969* (London: Faber and Faber, 1977; 1989).

Swift, R. and S. Gilley (eds), *The Irish in Britain 1815-1939* (London: Pinter, 1989).

Townsend, C., *Political Violence in Ireland: Government and Resistance since 1848* (Oxford: Oxford University Press, 1983).

Truxes, T., *Irish-American Trade 1660-1783* (Cambridge: Cambridge University Press, 1988).

Vaughan, W. E., *Landlords and Tenants in Ireland 1848-1904*, Studies in Irish Economic and Social History, No. 2 (Dundalk: Dundealgan Press, 1984).

Wall, M., *Catholic Ireland in the Eighteenth Century: Collected Essays of Maureen Wall*, edited by G. O'Brien (Dublin: Geography Publications, 1989).

Whyte, J., *Church and State in Modern Ireland 1923-79* (Dublin: Gill and Macmillan, 1971; 2nd edition 1980).

Literature and Language

The *Irish University Review* publishes regular bibliographical listings.

Alspach, R. K., *Irish Poetry from the Invasion to 1798* (Philadelphia: University of Pennsylvania Press, 1943; 2nd edition 1960).

An Coiste Comhairleach Pleanála, *The Irish Language in a Changing Society* (Dublin: Bord na Gaeilge, 1988).

Bartley, J. O., *Teague, Shenkin and Sawney: Being an Historical Study of the Earliest Irish, Welsh and Scottish Characters in English Plays* (Cork: Cork University Press, 1954).

Bell, S. Hanna, *The Theatre in Ulster* (Dublin: Gill and Macmillan, 1972).

Bliss, A., *Spoken English in Ireland 1600-1740* (Dublin: Cadenus Press, 1979; The Dolmen Press, 1979).

Boyd, E. A., *Ireland's Literary Renaissance* (Dublin and London: Maunsel, 1916; revised edition New York: Knopf, 1922; reprinted New York: Barnes and Noble, 1968).

Brown, M., *The Politics of Irish Literature: From Thomas Davis to W. B. Yeats* (Seattle: University of Washington Press; London: Allen and Unwin, 1972).

Brown, T., *Ireland: A Social and Cultural History 1922-1985* (London: Fontana, 1985).

_________, *Ireland's Literature: Selected Essays* (Mullingar, Co. Westmeath: The Lilliput Press; Totowa, New Jersey: Barnes and Noble, 1988).

Cahalan, J., *Great Hatred, Little Room. The Irish Historical Novel* (Syracuse, New York: Syracuse University Press, 1983).

_________, *The Irish Novel: A Critical History* (Dublin: Gill and Macmillan, 1988).

Cairns, D., and S. Richards, *Writing Ireland: Colonialism, Nationalism and Culture* (Manchester: Manchester University Press; New York: St Martin's Press, 1988).

Carney, J. (ed.), *Early Irish Poetry* (Cork: Mercier Press, 1965).

_________, *Early Irish Literature* (New York: Barnes and Noble, 1966).

Carpenter, A. (ed.), *Place, Personality and the Irish Writer* (Gerrards Cross: Colin Smythe, 1977).

Clarke, W. S., *The Early Irish Stage. The Beginnings to 1720* (Oxford: Clarendon Press, 1955).

_________, *The Irish Stage in Country Towns 1720-1860* (Oxford: Clarendon Press, 1965).

Corkery, D., *The Hidden Ireland: A Study of Gaelic Munster in the Eighteenth Century* (Dublin: Gill, 1925; reprinted Gill and Macmillan, 1979).

_________, *Synge and Anglo-Irish Literature* (Cork: Cork University Press, 1931).

Cronin, A., *Heritage Now: Irish Literature in the English Language* (Dingle, Co. Kerry: Brandon Press; New York: St Martin's Press, 1982).

Cronin, J., *The Anglo-Irish Novel*, Vol. I. *The Nineteenth Century* (Belfast: Appletree Press, 1980).

Dawe, G. and E. Longley (eds), *Across a Roaring Hill; The Protestant Imagination in Modern Ireland* (Belfast: Blackstaff Press, 1985).

Deane, S., *Celtic Revivals: Essays in Modern Irish Literature 1880-1980* (London: Faber and Faber, 1985; Winston-Salem, North Carolina: Wake Forest University Press, 1986).

_________, *A Short History of Irish Literature* (London: Hutchinson; Notre Dame: University of Notre Dame Press, 1986).

Deane, S. (ed.), *Nationalism, Colonialism and Literature* (Minneapolis: Field Day Company and University of Minnesota Press, 1990).

de Blacam, A., *Gaelic Literature Surveyed*, revised edition (Dublin: The Talbot Press, 1974).

de Fréine, S., *The Great Silence*, 2nd edition (Dublin and Cork: Mercier Press, 1978).

Dillon, M., *The Cycles of Kings* (London: Oxford University Press, 1946).

_________, *Early Irish Literature* (Chicago: University of Chicago Press, 1948).

_________, *Early Irish Society* (Dublin: Sign of the Three Candles, 1954).

Dillon, M. (ed.), *Irish Sagas* (Cork: Mercier Press, 1968).

Dillon, M. with N. Chadwick, *The Celtic Realms* (London: Weidenfeld and Nicolson, 1967).

Dolan, T. P. (ed.), 'The English of the Irish', *Irish University Review*, Vol. 20, No. 1 (Spring 1990).

Donoghue, D., *We Irish: Essays on Irish Literature and Society* (Brighton: Harvester Press, 1986; New York: Knopf, 1987).

Duggan, G. C., *The Stage Irishman: A History of the Irish Play and Stage Characters from the Earliest Times* (Dublin and Cork: The Talbot Press, 1937).

Dunn, D. (ed.), *Two Decades of Irish Writing* (Cheadle Hulme, Cheshire: Carcanet Press, 1975).

Dunne, T. J. (ed.), *The Writer as Witness: Literature as Historical Evidence* (Cork: Irish Historical Studies, 1987).

Edwards, P., *Threshold of a Nation: A Study in English and Irish Drama* (Cambridge: Cambridge University Press, 1979).

Ellis-Fermor, U., *The Irish Dramatic Movement* (London: Methuen, 1939; revised edition 1954).

Fallis, R., *The Irish Renaissance* (Syracuse, New York: Syracuse University Press, 1977).

Field Day Theatre Company, *Ireland's Field Day* (London: Hutchinson, 1985; Notre Dame: University of Notre Dame Press, 1986).

Flanagan, T., *The Irish Novelists 1800-1850* (New York: Columbia University Press, 1959).

Flower, R., *The Irish Tradition* (Oxford: Clarendon Press, 1947).

Foster, J. W., *Forces and Themes in Ulster Fiction* (Dublin: Gill and Macmillan; Totowa, New Jersey: Rowman and Littlefield, 1974).

_________, *Fictions of the Irish Revival* (Dublin: Gill and Macmillan, 1988).

Ganz, J. (transl.), *Early Irish Myths and Sagas* (Harmondsworth: Penguin Books, 1981).

Garratt, R., *Modern Irish Poetry: Tradition and Continuity from Yeats to Heaney* (Berkeley: University of California Press, 1986).
Greene, D., *The Irish Language* (Dublin: Three Candles, 1966).
Hall, W. E., *Shadowy Heroes: Irish Literature of the 1890s* (Syracuse, New York: Syracuse University Press, 1980).
Harmon, M. (ed.), *Image and Illusion: Anglo-Irish Literature and its Contexts* (Dublin: Wolfhound Press, 1979).
_________, *The Irish Writer and the City* (Gerrards Cross: Colin Smythe; Totowa, New Jersey: Barnes and Noble, 1984).
Heaney, S., *Preoccupations: Selected Prose 1968-1978* (London: Faber and Faber, 1980).
_________, *The Government of the Tongue* (London: Faber and Faber, 1988).
Hederman, M. P. and R. Kearney (eds), *The Crane Bag Book of Irish Studies 1977-1981* (Dublin: Blackwater Press, 1982).
_________, *The Crane Bag Book of Irish Studies 1982-1985* (Dublin: Blackwater Press, 1986).
Howarth, H., *The Irish Writers 1880-1940* (London: Rockliff, 1958).
Hull, E., *A Text Book of Irish Literature*, 2 vols (Dublin: M. H. Gill and Son: London: David Nutt, 1906).
Hunt, H., *The Abbey, Ireland's National Theatre 1904-1979* (Dublin: Gill and Macmillan, 1979).
Hutchinson, J., *The Dynamics of Cultural Nationalism: The Gaelic Revival and the Creation of the Irish Nation State* (London: Allen and Unwin, 1987).
Hyde, D., *A Literary History of Ireland* (London: T. Fisher Unwin, 1899; revised editions London: Ernest Benn, 1967, 1980).
Jackson, K. H., *Studies in Celtic Nature Poetry* (Cambridge: Cambridge University Press, 1935).
_________, *The Oldest Irish Tradition: A Window on the Iron Age* (Cambridge: Cambridge University Press, 1964).
_________, *A Celtic Miscellany: Translations from the Celtic Literatures* (London: Routledge and Kegan Paul, 1951; Harmondsworth: Penguin Books, 1971).
Jeffares, A. N., *Anglo-Irish Literature* (London: Macmillan, 1982).
Johnston, D., *Irish Poetry After Joyce* (Notre Dame: Notre Dame University Press; Dublin: The Dolmen Press, 1985).
Joyce, P. W., *English As We Speak It In Ireland* (London: Longmans, 1910; reprinted Dublin: Wolfhound Press, 1979, 1988).
Kiely, B., *Modern Irish Fiction: A Critique* (Dublin: Golden Eagle Books, 1950).
Knott, E., *Irish Classical Poetry* (Dublin: Sign of the Three Candles, 1957).
Leersen, J. T., *Mere Irish and Fior-Ghael* (Amsterdam and Philadelphia: John Benjamins, 1986).
Loftus, R., *Nationalism in Modern Anglo-Irish Poetry* (Madison and Milwaukee: University of Wisconsin Press, 1964).
Longley, E., *Poetry in the Wars* (Newcastle-upon-Tyne: Bloodaxe Books, 1986).
Lubbers, K., *Geschichte der irischen Erzählprosa, Bd.1: Von den Anfängen bis zum ansgehenden 19. Jahrhundert* (Munich: Fink, 1985).
MacCana, P., *Celtic Mythology* (London: Hamlyn, 1970).
MacGiolla, C., *Díolaim Próis 1450-1850* (Baile Átha Cliath: Foilseacháin Náisiúnta Teo, 1971).
Mac Réamoinn, S. (ed.), *The Pleasures of Gaelic Poetry* (London: Allen Lane, 1982).
Malone, A. E., *The Irish Drama 1896-1928* (London: Constable, 1929).
Martin, A. (ed.), *The Genius of Irish Prose* (Dublin and Cork: Mercier Press, 1984).
Maxwell, D. E. S., *Modern Irish Drama 1891-1980* (Cambridge: Cambridge University Press, 1985).
McCone, K., *Pagan Past and Christian Present in Early Irish Literature* (Maynooth: An Sagart, 1990).
McCormack, W. J., *Ascendancy and Tradition in Anglo-Irish Literature 1789-1939* (Oxford: Oxford University Press, 1985).
McHugh, R. and M. Harmon, *Short History of Anglo-Irish Literature: From its Origin to the Present Day* (Dublin: Wolfhound Press; New York: Barnes and Noble, 1982).
Mercier, V., *The Irish Comic Tradition* (Oxford: Clarendon Press, 1962).
M'Gee, T. D'Arcy, *The Irish Writers of the Seventeenth Century* (Dublin: Duffy, 1846; reprinted New York: Lemma, 1974).
Montague, J., *The Figure in the Cave and Other Essays* (Dublin: The Lilliput Press, 1989).
Murphy, G., *Saga and Myth in Ancient Ireland* (Dublin: Sign of the Three Candles, 1955; reprinted 1971).
_________, *Early Irish Lyrics: Eighth to Twelfth Century* (Oxford: Clarendon Press, 1956).
Nic Eoin, M., *An Litríocht Réigiúnach* (Baile Átha Cliath: An Clóchomhar, 1982).
O'Brien, F., *Filíocht Ghaeilge na linne seo: staidéar criticúil* (Baile Átha Cliath: An Clóchomhar, 1968).
Ó Buachalla, B., *I mBéal Feirste Cois Cuan* (Baile Átha Cliath: An Clóchomhar, 1968).
Ó Conchuir, B., *Scríobháithe Chorcaí 1700-1850* (Baile Átha Cliath: An Clóchomhar, 1982).
Ó Conghaile, M., *Conamara agus Árainn 1880-1980: Gnéithe den Stair Shóisialta* (Gaillimh: Cló Iar-Chonnachta, 1988).
O'Connor, F., *The Backward Look. A Survey of Irish Literature* (London: Macmillan, 1967); retitled *A Short History of Irish Literature* (New York: Putnam, 1967).
Ó Cúiv, B. (ed.), *Léann na Gaeilge in Eirinn; Seven Centuries of Irish Learning 1000-1700* (Dublin: Oifig an tSoláthair, 1961).
_________, *A View of the Irish Language* (Dublin: Stationery Office, 1969).
Ó Doibhlin, B., *Aistí critice agus cultúir* (Má Nuad: An Sagart, 1975).
Ó Fiannachta, P., *Léas Eile ar ár Litríocht* (Má Nuad: An Sagart, 1982).
Ó Hainle, C., *Éigse lár na hÉireann* (Má Nuad: An Sagart, 1975).
_________, *Promhadh Pinn* (Má Nuad: An Sagart, 1978).
O'Muirithe, D. (ed.), *The English Language in Ireland* (Dublin and Cork: Mercier Press, 1977).
Orel, H. (ed.), *Irish History and Culture: Aspects of a People's Heritage* (Lawrence: University Press of Kansas, 1976; reprinted Dublin: Wolfhound Press, 1979).
O'Rourke Murphy, M. and J. MacKillop (eds), *Irish Literature. A Reader* (Syracuse, New York: Syracuse University Press, 1987).
Ó Tuama, S., *An Grá in Amhráin na nDaoine: leiriú tearmúil* (Baile Átha Cliath: An Clóchomhar, 1978).
Paulin, T., *Ireland and the English Crisis* (Newcastle-upon-Tyne: Bloodaxe Books, 1984).
Porter, R. and J. D. Brophy (eds), *Modern Irish Literature: Essays in Honour of William York Tindall* (New York: Iona College Press, 1972).
Power, P., *The Story of Anglo-Irish Poetry* (Cork: Mercier Press, 1967).
_________, *A Literary History of Ireland* (Cork: Mercier Press, 1969).
Rafroidi, P., *Irish Literature in English: The Romantic Period*, 2 vols (Gerrards Cross: Colin Smythe, 1980).
Ronsley, J. (ed.), *Myth and Reality in Irish Literature* (Waterloo, Ontario: Wilfrid Laurier University Press, 1977).
Seymour, St J. D., *Anglo-Irish Literature 1200-1582* (Cambridge: Cambridge University Press, 1929).
Sloan, B., *The Pioneers of Anglo-Irish Fiction 1800-1850* (Gerrards Cross: Colin Smythe; Totowa, New Jersey: Barnes and Noble, 1984).
Stanford, W. B., *Ireland and the Classical Tradition* (Dublin: Allen Figgis, 1976).
Stockwell, La Tourette, *Dublin Theatres and Theatre Customs 1637-1820* (Kingsport, Tennessee: Kingsport Press; New York: Benjamin Blom, 1968).
Taniguchi, J., *A Grammatical Analysis of Artistic Representation of Irish English with a brief discussion of sounds and spelling* (Tokyo: Shinozaki Shorin, 1971).
Todd, L., *The Language of Irish Literature* (Basingstoke: Macmillan, 1989).
Tovey, H., D. Hannon and H. Abramson, *Cad Chuige An Ghaeilge? Teanga agus Feiniúlacht in Eirinn ar Linne/Why Irish? Irish Identity and the Irish Language* (Dublin: Bord na Gaeilge, 1989).
Truninger, A., *Paddy and the Paycock: A Study of the Stage Irishman from Shakespeare to O'Casey* (Berne: Francke, 1976).
Vance, N., *Irish Literature: A Social History* (Oxford: Blackwell, 1990).
Walsh, P., *Irishmen of Learning* (Dublin: Sign of the Three Candles, 1947).
Watson, G. J., *Irish Identity and the Literary Revival* (London: Croom Helm, 1979).

Welch, R., *Irish Poetry from Moore to Yeats* (Gerrards Cross: Colin Smythe, 1980).
________, *A History of Verse Translation from the Irish* (Gerrards Cross: Colin Smythe, 1989).
Williams, J. E. Caerwyn, agus M. Ní Mhuíriosa, *Traidisiún Literartha Na nGael* (Baile Átha Cliath: An Clóchomhar, 1979).
Worth, K., *The Irish Drama of Europe from Yeats to Beckett* (London: Athlone Press; Atlantic Highlands, New Jersey: Humanities Press, 1978).
Zach, W. and H. Kosok (eds), *Literary Interrelations: Ireland, England and the World*, 3 vols (Tübingen: Gunter Narr, 1987).

Social Anthropology

Aalen, F. H. A., *Gola. The Life and Last Days of an Island Community* (Cork: Mercier Press, 1969).
Arensberg, C. M., *The Irish Countryman, An Anthropological Study* (London: Macmillan, 1937; reprinted 1959).
Arensberg, C. M. and S. T. Kimball, *Family and Community in Ireland* (Cambridge, Massachusetts: Harvard University Press, 1968).
Breen, R., D. F. Hannon, D. B. Rottman, C. T. Whelan, *Understanding Contemporary Ireland: State, Class and Development in the Republic of Ireland* (Dublin: Gill and Macmillan, 1990).
Brody, H., *Inishkillane. Change and Decline in the West of Ireland* (London: Allen Lane, 1973).
Cresswell, R., *Une Communauté Rurale de l'Irlande* (Paris: Musée de l'homme, Institut d'ethnologie, 1969).
Fox, R, *The Tory Islanders. A People of the Celtic Fringe* (Cambridge: Cambridge University Press, 1978).
Glassie, H., *Passing the Time: Culture and History of an Ulster Community* (Dublin: O'Brien Press; Philadelphia: University of Pennsylvania Press, 1982).
Harris, R., *Prejudice and Tolerance in Ulster: A Study of Neighbours and Strangers in a Border Community* (Manchester: Manchester University Press; Totowa, New Jersey: Rowman and Littlefield, 1972).
Messenger, J. C. *Inis Beag: Isle of Ireland* (New York: Holt, Rinehart and Winston, 1969).
Mogey, J., *Rural Life in Northern Ireland* (London: Oxford University Press, 1947).
Peillon, M., *Contemporary Irish Society: An Introduction* (Dublin: Gill and Macmillan, 1982).

Essential Journals

This short list gives the titles, place of origin and initial date of publication of each journal.

Analecta Hibernica (Dublin: 1930).
Archaeology Ireland (Dublin: 1987).
Archivium Hibernicum (Maynooth, Co. Kildare: 1912).
Béaloideas (Dublin: 1927).
Collectanea Hibernica (Dublin: 1958).
Eighteenth-Century Ireland/Iris an Dá Cultúr (Dublin: 1986).
Eigse (Dublin: 1940).
Éigse Cheoil Tire (Irish Folk Music Studies) (Dublin: 1972).
Ériu (Dublin: 1904).
Hermathena (Dublin: 1873).
Irish Economic and Social History (Belfast: 1974).
Irish Geography (Dublin: 1944).
Irish Historical Studies (Dublin: 1938).
Irish Literary Supplement (New York: 1982).
Irish Review (Cork: 1986).
Irish University Review (Dublin: 1970).
Linen Hall Review (Belfast: 1984).
Peritia (Cork: 1982).
Scríobh (Dublin: 1978).
Studia Hibernica (Dublin: 1961).
Theatre Ireland (Belfast: 1987).

PERMISSIONS ACKNOWLEDGMENTS

Volumes I, II & III

While the publisher has made every effort to acquire all permissions needed, some may have been inadvertently omitted. Field Day would be glad to hear from any permissions holders who have not been included.

For permission to reprint copyright material the General Editor and publisher gratefully acknowledge the following:

Anvil Books Limited for extracts from *On Another Man's Wound* by Ernie O'Malley (Anvil Books, 1979); *Ireland Yesterday and Tomorrow* by Bulmer Hobson (Anvil Books, 1968)

Anvil Press Poetry Ltd. for 'A Meeting With Parnell' and 'Windows' by Thomas McCarthy from *The Sorrow Garden* (Anvil Press Poetry, 1981; 'Black Flags at a Party Meeting' and 'The Non-Aligned Storyteller' from *The Non-Aligned Storyteller* (Anvil Press Poetry, 1984)

Attic Press, for 'The Hairdresser' by Leland Bardwell from *Different Kinds of Love* (Attic Press, 1987)

Eve Bieler for 'The Confession of St. Patrick' from *The Works of St. Patrick* edited by Ludwig Bieler

The Blackstaff Press for excerpts from chapters 2, 8, 18, 19 of *Voices and the Sound of Drums: An Irish Autobiography* by Patrick Shea (Blackstaff Press, 1981); excerpts from Acts II and III of *The Flats* by John Boyd (Blackstaff Press, 1971); 'The Boys of Sandy Row' from *No Surrender: An Ulster Childhood* by Robert Harbinson (Blackstaff Press, 1960); 'The Marriage Contract', 'Bewley's Oriental Cafe, Westmoreland Street' from *The Berlin Wall Cafe* by Paul Durcan (Blackstaff Press, 1985); 'The British Connection', 'Credo, Credo', 'Soldiers', from *Nights in the Bad Place* by Padraic Fiacc (Blackstaff Press, 1977)

Bloodaxe Books for excerpt from *Poetry in the Wars* by Edna Longley (Bloodaxe Books, 1986)

The Bodley Head for extracts from *Ulysses* by James Joyce (Bodley Head, 1961)

The Estate of Patrick Boyle for 'Myko' by Patrick Boyle from *At Night All Cats Are Grey* (McGibbon & Kee, 1966)

Brandon Books, for 'The IRA/Oglaigh Na hEireann' from *The Politics of Irish Freedom* by Gerry Adams (Brandon Book Publishers Ltd., 1987)

Calder, John (Publishers) Ltd. for 'Dante and the Lobster' from *More Pricks than Kicks* copyright © Samuel Beckett 1934; 'Gnome', 'Echo's Bones', 'Saint Lo', 'Dieppe', 'my way is in the sand flowing', 'je suis ce cours de sable qui glisse', 'I would like my love to die', and 'Je voudrais que mon amour meur' from *Collected Poems 1930–1978* copyright © Samuel Beckett 1934, 1935, 1937, 1946, 1948, 1986; Chapters 1, 6, 13 of *Murphy* copyright © Samuel Beckett 1938, 1963, 1977; *Come and Go* copyright © Samuel Beckett 1967; 'Enough' from *Collected Shorter Prose 1945–1980* copyright © Samuel Beckett 1966. Translation copyright © Samuel Beckett 1967, 1984; 'Ping' from *Collected Shorter Prose 1945–1980* copyright © Samuel Beckett 1967, 1975, 1986; 'Lessness' from *Collected Shorter Prose 1945–1980* copyright © Les Editions de Minuit, translation copyright © Samuel Beckett 1970, 1986; *Company* copyright © Samuel Beckett 1979, 1980, now in *Nohow On* copyright © Samuel Beckett 1989 for 'The Institution' from *Scenes from a Receding Past* by Aidan Higgins (John Calder, 1977)

Caliban Books Ltd. for extracts from *The Rat-Pit* by Patrick McGill (Caliban Books, 1983)

Jonathan Cape Ltd. for 'Language, Truth and Lockjaw' from *A Time to Dance* by Bernard Mac Laverty (Jonathan Cape, 1982); to the author and Jonathan Cape Ltd. for 'Number Ten' from *Mrs. Reinhardt and Other Stories* (Jonathan Cape, 1978) by Edna O'Brien; for 'Araby' and 'Ivy Day in the Committee Room' by James Joyce from *Dubliners* edited by Robert Scholes (Cape, 1967); for extracts from *A Portrait of the Artist as a Young Man* by James Joyce edited by Chester B. Anderson (Cape, 1964); for extract from *Stephen Hero* by James Joyce edited Theodore Spencer, rev. John J. Slocum and Herbert Cahoon (Cape, 1969)

Carcanet Press Limited for 'The Journey', 'The Emigrant Irish' from *The Journey and Other Poems* by Eavan Boland (Carcanet Press, 1987)

Coiscéim for 'Súile Suibhne' by Cathal Ó Searcaigh from *Suibhne* (Coiscéim, 1987); for 'An Scáthán', 'Ó Mo Bheirt Phailistíneach' by Michael Davitt from *Bligeárd Sráide* (Coiscéim, 1983)

Dardis Clarke for 'The Lost Heifer' from *The Cattledrive in Connaught* (Allen & Unwin, 1925); 'Pilgrimage', 'The Scholar' from *Pilgrimage and Other Poems* (Allen & Unwin, 1929); 'Tenebrae' from *Night and Morning* (Orwell, 1938); 'Ancient Lights' from *Ancient Lights* (Bridge, 1955); 'The Last Republicans', 'Martha Blake at Fifty-One', 'Eighteenth-Century Harp Songs' from *Flight To Africa* (Dolmen, 1963); excerpt from *Mnemosyne Lay in Dust*

(Dolmen, 1966); 'The Healing of Mis' from *Orphide and Other Poems* (Bridge, 1970); for excerpt from *A Penny in the Clouds* (Routledge, 1968); for excerpt from *The Bright Temptation* (Allen & Unwin, 1932)

An Clóchomhar for 'Dínit an Bhroin', 'Cuimhní Cinn', 'Rón na mBan', 'An tEarrach Thiar', 'Árainn 1947', 'Stoite', 'Ó Mórna', 'Ómós do John Millington Synge', 'Leigheas na hEagla', 'Cranna Foirtil', 'Mar Chaitheamar an Choinneal' by Máirtín Ó Direáin from *Dánta 1939–1979* (An Clóchomhar, 1980); for 'An Sísceál de Réir Eoin' by Alan Titley from *Eiriceachtaí agus Scéalta Eile* (An Clóchomhar, 1987)

Lucy Rodgers Cohen for 'White Christmas' from *Awake and Other Poems* copyright © W. R. Rodgers 1941

Constable Publishers for 'A Visit to the Cemetery', 'In the Middle of the Fields' from *Collected Stories* by Mary Lavin (Constable, 1985); 'Intercession against Plague', 'Easter Sunday' from *Medieval Latin Lyrics* by Helen Waddell (Constable, 1933); for 'Midsummer Night's Madness' by Sean O'Faolain (Constable, 1932)

The Crane Bag for excerpts from 'Ireland's Identities' (*The Crane Bag*, vol 3, no.1, 1979) by Liam de Paor; for excerpts from 'Going West', (*The Crane Bag*, vol. 9, no. 2, 1985) by Fintan O'Toole: for excerpts from 'Post-Traditional English Literature' (*The Crane Bag* vol. 3, no. 2, 1979) by Sean Golden

Curtis Brown Associates for 'Midsummer Night's Madness' from *Midsummer Night's Madness* by Sean O'Faolain (Constable, 1932); for 'A Great God's Angel Standing' by Ben Kiely from *A Ball of Malt and Madame Butterfly: A Dozen Stories* (Gollancz, 1973); for extract from *Vive Moi!* by Sean O'Faolain (Little, Brown, 1964); for extract from *Seven Winters* by Elizabeth Bowen (Knopf, 1962)

Curtis Brown Ltd. for extract from *The Last September* by Elizabeth Bowen (Constable, 1931); and for extract from *Seven Winters* by Elizabeth Bowen (Longmans, Green, 1943)

Ita Daly for 'The Lady with the Red Shoes' from *The Lady with the Red Shoes* by Ita Daly, copyright © Ita Daly, 1980 (Poolbeg Press, 1980)

R.G. Davis-Poynter for chapters 1 and 5 from *Dead As Doornails* by Anthony Cronin (Dolmen Press and Oxford University Press, 1975)

Dedalus Press and the Devlin family for 'Lough Derg', 'The Colours of Love', 'Encounter', 'The Tomb of Michael Collins' from *Collected Poems* by Denis Devlin, edited by J.C.C. Mays (Dedalus Press, 1990)

The author for 'Thrust and Parry', 'Out of the Ordinary', 'Interrogative', 'Leavetaking' by Greg Delanty from *Cast in the Fire* (Dolmen, 1986) copyright © Greg Delanty 1989

Department of Irish Folklore, University College, Dublin for excerpts from MS1074, 1068, 'Memories of the Famine', © Department of Irish Folklore, University College, Dublin

Andre Deutsch Ltd. for chapter 2 from *The Lonely Passion of Judith Hearne* by Brian Moore (Deutsch, 1955); for extract from *The Price of My Soul* by Bernadette Devlin (Deutsch, 1969)

Joseph Donnelly for 'The Flowering Bars', 'The Tolerance of Crows', 'Poem', 'Heroic Heart' from *Charlie Donnelly: the Life and Poems* ed. Joseph Donnelly (Dedalus, 1987)

The Dublin Institute of Advanced Studies for excerpts from *Táin Bo Cuailone, Recension I* by Cecile O'Reilly (ed.) (Institute of Advanced Studies, 1976); 'The Poet on his dead wife' from O. Bergin (ed.), *Irish Bardic Poetry* (Institute of Advanced Studies, 1970); 'Onward my Barque', 'Three Dwelling Places of the Soul', 'An Invocation by the writer of this Book, 'Bishop Patrick' from A. Gwynn (ed.), *Scriptores Latini Hiberniae* vol. I (Institute of Advanced Studies, 1955); 'Instructio VIII; Regulae VIII, IX, X' from G.S.M. Walker (ed.), *Scriptores Latini Hiberniae* vol. II (1957); 'Concerning the Site of Jerusalem', 'Concerning a Church of Round Shape', 'Concerning the Image of the Holy Mary' from D. Meehan (ed.), *Scriptores Latini Hiberniae* vol. III (Institute of Advanced Studies, 1958); 'Letter to the Soldiers of Coroticus' from L. Bieler (ed.), *Scriptores Latini Hiberniae* vol. V (Institute of Advanced Studies, 1963); 'Introduction', sections VI and VII from J. J. Tierney (ed.), *Scriptores Latini Hiberniae* vol. VI (Institute of Advanced Studies, 1965); 'Liber Angeli', 'Collectanea Concerning St. Patrick', 'Vita Sancti Patricii' from L. Bieler (ed.), *Scriptores Latini Hiberniae* vol. X (Institute for Advanced Studies, 1979); 'Concerning the Science of Numbers' from I. P. Sheldon-Williams (ed.), *Johannis Scotti Eriugenae Periphyseon* (Institute of Advanced Studies, 1970)

Gerald Duckworth and Company Ltd. for extracts 'Dionysius the Areopagite', 'My Poetry, My Times', 'A Plea for Patronage', 'My Patron's House and Mine', 'Mock Epyllion on A Gelded Ram / Epitaph'. 'My Life' from Peter Godman (ed.), *Poetry of the Carolingian Renaissance* (Duckworth, 1985)

Council of the Early English Text Society for 'The Pride of Life' from *Non-Cycle Plays and Fragments* (Early English Text Society, 1975)

Estate of Joyce Cary for excerpts from *A House of Children* (Michael Joseph, 1941)

Faber and Faber for 'Korea' by John McGahern from *Nightlines* (Faber, 1970); for extract from *Observe the Sons of Ulster Marching Towards the Somme* by Frank McGuinness (Faber, 1986); for *Translations* by Brian Friel (Faber, 1980); for *Double Cross* by Thomas Kilroy (Faber, 1986); for 'Belfast', 'Snow', 'Bagpipe Music', 'Meeting Point', 'The Strand', 'House on A Cliff', 'Charon', 'Autumn Journal XVI' by Louis MacNeice from *Collected Poems* (Faber, 1966); for extract from *The Strings Are False* by Louis MacNeice (Faber, 1965); for 'The Last Galway Hooker' by Richard Murphy from *Sailing To An Island* (1963); for 'Casement's Funeral' by Richard Murphy from *The Battle of Aughrim* (Faber, 1968); for 'Seals At High Island', 'Little Hunger' by Richard Murphy from *High Island* (Faber, 1974); for 'Moonshine', 'The Price of Stone', 'Wellington Testimonial', 'Ice Rink', 'Natural Son' by Richard Murphy from *The Price of Stone* (Faber, 1985); for 'Still Century' by Tom Paulin from *The Strange Museum* (Faber, 1980); for 'Desertmartin', 'Off the Back of a Lorry', 'A Written Answer', 'Manichean Geography I', 'Of Difference Does it Make', 'A Nation, Yet Again', 'Argument from Design' by Tom Paulin from *Liberty Tree* (Faber, 1983); for 'Father of History', 'An Ulster Unionist Walks the Streets of London' by Tom Paulin from *Fivemiletown* (Faber, 1987); for 'The Early Purges', 'Follower' by Seamus Heaney from *Death of a Naturalist* (Faber, 1966); for 'Requiem for the Croppies', 'Bogland' by Seamus Heaney from *Door Into the Dark* (Faber, 1969); for 'Traditions', 'The Tollund Man' by Seamus Heaney from *Wintering Out* (Faber, 1972); for 'Viking Dublin: Trial Pieces', 'Punishment', 'Singing School: Exposure' by Seamus Heaney from *North* (Faber, 1975); for 'The Skunk' by Seamus Heaney from *Field Work* (Faber, 1979); for Chekhov on Sakhalin', 'Station Island: II, XII', 'The Master', 'The Old Icons' by Seamus Heaney from *Station Island* (Faber, 1984); for 'From the Republic of Conscience', 'Clearances' by Seamus Heaney from *The Haw Lantern* (Faber, 1987); for 'Thrush', 'The Field Hospital' by Paul Muldoon from *New Weather* (Faber, 1973); for 'The Bearded Woman, by Ribera' by Paul Muldoon from *Mules* (Faber, 1977); from 'Cuba', Anseo', 'Why Brownlee Left', 'Truce' by Paul Muldoon from *Why Brownlee Left* (Faber, 1980); for 'Truce', 'The Right Arm', 'Cherish the Ladies', 'Aisling', 'My Father and I and Billy Two Rivers' by Paul Muldoon from *Quoof* (Faber, 1983); for 'The Wishbone', 'Christo's' by Paul Muldoon from *Meeting the British* (Faber, 1987); for extract from *Celtic Revivals* by Seamus Deane (Faber, 1985); for extract from *No Surrender: An Ulster Childhood* by Robert Harbinson (Faber, 1960); for extracts from *Critical Writings* by James Joyce edited by Ellsworth Mason and Richard Ellmann (Faber, 1959)

Brian Fallon for 'Assumption', 'Yeats's Tower at Ballylee', 'Women', 'The Poems of Love', 'Johnstown Castle', 'The Young Fenians', 'Kiltartan Legend', 'Letter from Ballylee', 'Mater Dei', 'Magna Mater', 'Painting of my Father', 'Sunday Morning' from Padraic Fallon, *Poems* (Dolmen, 1974); 'A Hedge Schoolmaster', 'After Horace. Solvitur Acris Hiems' from Padraic Fallon, *Poems and Versions* (Dedalus, 1983)

Farrar, Straus & Giroux Inc., for 'Number Ten' from *Mrs. Reinhardt and Other Stories* by Edna O'Brien (Farrar, Straus & Giroux, 1979); for 'Follower', 'Requiem for the Croppies', 'Bogland' 'The Tollund Man', 'Viking Dublin: Trial Pieces', 'Punishment', 'Singing School: Exposure', 'The Skunk', 'Chekhov on Sakhalin', 'Station Island: II, XII', 'The Master', 'From the Republic of Conscience', 'Clearances' by Seamus Heaney from *Selected Poems 1966–1987* (Farrar, Straus & Giroux, 1990)

The author and Open Air for 'Against Revisionism' by Desmond Fennell from *The Revision of Irish Nationalism* (Open Air, 1988)

Field Day and the author for excerpt from Declan Kiberd, *Anglo-Irish Attitudes* (Field Day, 1984)

The author for Chapter 9 from *Towards A New Ireland* (Charles Knight & Co.; Torc Books, 1972) copyright © Garret FitzGerald

Gallery Press for 'Id' and 'Seamstress' from *The Liberal Cage* by Harry Clifton (Gallery Press, 1988); for 'The Lundys Letter', 'The Desert Campaign', 'The Clock on the Wall of Farringdon Gardens, 1971' and 'The Sleepwalker' by Gerald Dawe, *The Lundys Letter* (Gallery Press, 1985); for 'Winter Work', 'The Heart of Ireland' from *Winter Work* by Peter Fallon, (Gallery Press, 1983); for 'My Care' and 'Dung' from *The News and Weather* by Peter Fallon (Gallery Press, 1987); for 'Islands' from *A Store of Candles* by Frank Ormsby (Gallery Press, 1977, 1986); for 'McConnell's Birthday' and 'Home' from *A Northern Spring* by Frank Ormsby (Gallery Press, 1986); for 'The Silent Marriage', 'Didn't He Ramble' and 'Ulster Says Yes' from *Poems 1956–1986* by James Simmons (Gallery Press, 1986); for 'Roots', 'Return', 'A World Without A Name', 'History Lessons', 'Breaking Wood' and 'Reading Paradise Lost in Protestant Ulster 1984' from *Selected Poems* by Seamus Deane (Gallery Press, 1988); for 'A Closer Look' and 'Four Deer' from *What Light There Is* by Eamon Grennan (Gallery Press, 1987); for 'The Irish for No', 'Belfast Confetti' and 'Clearance' from *The Irish for No* by Ciaran Carson (Gallery Press, 1987 and Wake Forest University Press, 1988); for 'Acts and Monuments', 'Going Back to Oxford', from *Acts and Monuments* (Gallery Press, 1972); for 'Lucina Schynning in Silence of the Nicht', 'Darkening All the Strand', 'The Lady's Tower' from *Site of Ambush* by Eiléan Ní Chuilleanáin (Gallery Press, 1975) and 'The Second Voyage' from *The Second Voyage* by Eiléan Ní Chuilleanáin (Gallery Press, 1977 and Wake Forest University Press, 1986); for 'Maiden Street Awake', 'Pigkilling', 'Dryad', 'A Visit to Castletown House', 'Mrs. Halpin and the Lightning' and 'A Visit to Croom' from *A Farewell to English* by Michael Hartnett (Gallery Press, 1975, 1978); for 'Patience of a Tree', 'An Dobharchu Gota / The Wounded Otter', 'Fís Deireannach Eoghain Rua Uí Shuilleabháin / The Last Vision of Eoghain Rua O Suilleabháin', 'Gné na Gaeltachta / The Gaeltacht Face, and 'An Lia Nocht / The Naked Surgeon' from *A Necklace of Wrens* by Michael Hartnett (Gallery Press, 1987); for 'Eight Frontiers Distant' from *Selected Poems* by Pearse Hutchinson (Gallery Press, 1980); for 'Acnasheen' and 'The Frost is all Over' from *The Frost Is All Over* by Pearse Hutchinson, (Gallery Press, 1975) and *Selected Poems;* for 'The Trout', 'Like Dolmens Round my Childhood the Old People', 'All Legendary Obstacles', 'The Siege of Mullingar' and 'Dowager' from *New Selected Poems* by John Montague (Gallery Press and Wake Forest University Press, 1989); for 'A Lost Tradition' from *The Rough Field* by John Montague (Dolmen and Oxford University Press, 1972; Gallery Press, 1989); for 'Mount Eagle' from *Mount Eagle* by John Montague (Gallery Press, 1988); for 'Passages', 'The Death of Irish' and 'Keeping Pacific Time' from *Minding Ruth* by Aidan Mathews (Gallery Press, 1983); for 'De Rerum Natura' from *Long Lankin* by John Banville (1970, Gallery Press, 1984); for excerpts from *The King of the Castle* by Eugene McCabe (Gallery Press, 1978); for excerpts from *Catchpenny Twist* by Stewart Parker (Gallery Press, 1981); for *Bailegangaire* by Thomas Murphy (Gallery, 1985)

Gill and Macmillan for extracts from *Over the Bridge* (Gill and Macmillan, 1960) by Sam Thompson; for extract from *Synge and Anglo-Irish Literature* by Daniel Corkery (Gill and Macmillan, 1931); for 'Gaudeant caeli, mare, cuncta, terra . . .' of Sedulius Scottus by James Carney from Robert McNally S.J. (ed.), *Old Ireland* (Gill and Macmillan, 1947); for extract from *Against the Tide* by Noel Browne (Gill and Macmillan, 1982)

The Goldsmith Press for translations from *Tacar Dánta/Selected Poems* translated by Tomás Mac Síomóin and Douglas Sealy (The Goldsmith Press Limited, Newbridge, Co. Kildare, 1984)

Victor Gollancz Ltd. for 'Cancer' from *Heritage And Other Stories* by Eugene McCabe (Gollancz, 1978)

Grove Press for 'Dante and the Lobster' from *More Pricks than Kicks* copyright © Samuel Beckett 1934; 'Gnome', 'Echo's Bones', 'Saint Lo', 'Dieppe', 'my way is in the sand flowing', 'je suis ce cours de sable qui glisse', 'I would like my love to die', and 'Je voudrais que mon amour meur' from *Collected Poems 1930–1978* copyright © Samuel Beckett 1934, 1935, 1937, 1946, 1948, 1986; Chapters 1, 6, 13 of *Murphy* copyright © Samuel Beckett 1938, 1963, 1977; *Come and Go* copyright © Samuel Beckett 1967; 'Enough' from *Collected Shorter Prose 1945–1980* copyright © Samuel Beckett 1966. Translation copyright © Samuel Beckett 1967, 1984; 'Ping' from *Collected Shorter Prose 1945–1980* copyright © Samuel Beckett 1967, 1975, 1986; 'Lessness' from *Collected Shorter Prose 1945–1980* copyright © Les Editions de Minuit, translation copyright © Samuel Beckett 1970, 1986; *Company* copyright © Samuel Beckett 1979, 1980, now in *Nohow On* copyright © Samuel Beckett 1989.

An Gum for 'An Bhearna Mhil' from *An Braon Broghach* (An Gum, 1968) by Máirtín Ó Cadhain

Hamish Hamilton for extract from *The Captains and the Kings* by Jennifer Johnston (Hamish Hamilton, 1972)

Paul Hamlyn for *The Quare Fellow* by Brendan Behan (Eyre Methuen, 1978)

Harvester Press for extract from *We Irish* by Denis Donoghue (Harvester, 1986)

William Heinemann Ltd. for extract from *The Ante-Room* by Kate O'Brien (Heinemann, 1937)

Hermathena for 'Irish History and Irish Mythology' (*Hermathena*, CXXIV, Summer, 1978) by T.W. Moody

David Higham Associates for extract from *The Ante-Room* (Heinemann, 1934) by Kate O'Brien

Houghton Mifflin for 'A Visit to the Cemetery', 'In The Middle of the Fields' from *Collected Stories* by Mary Lavin (Houghton Mifflin, 1971)

The author for 'This Houre her Vigill', 'Hector', 'Shadows', 'Underworld', 'Icarus' by Valentin Iremonger from *Horan's Field and Other Reservations* (Dolmen, 1972) copyright © Valentin Iremonger

The Editors of *The Irish Review* for 'We Are All Revisionists Now' by Roy Foster (*Irish Review*, 1986); for the extract from 'The Colonial Subject' by David Lloyd (*The Irish Review*, 1988)

The author for 'Night in Tunisia' by Neil Jordan from *Night in Tunisia and Other Stories* (Co-op Books, 1976)

The author for 'Another September' and 'Baggot Street Deserta' from *Another September* (Dolmen, 1958); for 'Song' from *Moralities* (Dolmen, 1960); for 'Downstream' and 'Mirror in February' from

Downstream (Dolmen, 1962); for 'Wormwood' from *Wormwood* (Dolmen, 1966); for 'Ancestor', 'Tear', 'Hen Woman', 'St. Paul's Rocks: 16 February 1832' and 'The Dispossessed' from *Notes from the Land of the Dead and Other Poems* (Cuala, 1972); for 'His Father's Hands' from *One and Other Poems* (Peppercanister Press, 1974); for excerpt from *The Irish Writer* (Dolmen, 1966) by Thomas Kinsella; for translations from *An Duanaire 1600–1900: Poems of the Dispossessed* (Dolmen, 1981) by Thomas Kinsella and Sean O' Tuama

Alfred A. Knopf Ltd. for 'Guests of the Nation' by Frank O'Connor from *The Stories of Frank O'Connor* (Knopf, 1952); for extract from *An Only Child* by Frank O'Connor (Knopf, 1961)

Lilliput Press for excerpt from 'The Whole Protestant Community' in *Ireland's Literature* (Lilliput Press, 1989) by Terence Brown; for excerpt from *Escape from the Anthill* (Lilliput Press, 1985) by Hubert Butler; for excerpt from *The Village of Longing* (Lilliput Press, 1987) by George O'Brien

Little, Brown and Company for 'Midsummer Night's Madness' from *The Collected Stories of Sean O'Faolain* © 1932 by Sean O'Faolain

Macmillan for 'Song for the Clatter-Bones', 'Chinese Winter' from *The Gap of Brightness* (Macmillan, 1940) by Frederick Robert Higgins; for extracts from *Father Ralph* by Gerald O'Donovan (Macmillan, 1913); for *The Shadow of A Gunman* (Macmillan, 1923) and Act 2 of *The Plough and the Stars* (Macmillan, 1926) by Sean O'Casey. Copyright © Sean O'Casey 1923 (and) © Sean O'Casey 1926, published by Macmillan, London and Basingstoke; for extract from *Drama At Inish* by Lennox Robinson (Macmillan, 1933); for extract from *An Only Child* by Frank O'Connor (Macmillan, 1962); for 'Guests of the Nation' by Frank O'Connor from *Guests of the Nation* (Macmillan, 1931)

Martin, Brian and O'Keefe for 'At Lisnaskea', 'Derry', 'The Sad Queen', 'A Dream' by Francis Ledwidge from *The Complete Poems of Francis Ledwidge* ed. Alice Curtayne (Martin, Brian and O'Keefe, 1974)

Martin, Secker & Warburg for 'Blue Shoes', 'How Witches Went Invisible', 'The Border' from *Blue Shoes* (Martin, Secker & Warburg, 1989) by Matthew Sweeney

Mercier Press and the editor for excerpts from M. Mansergh (ed.), *The Spirit of the Nation: The Speeches and Statements of C.J. Haughey 1957–1986* (Mercier, 1986); for an excerpt from *A Message to the Irish People* (Mercier, 1985) by Sean MacBride; for an extract from *The Field* by John B. Keane (Mercier, 1966)

The author for 'Speech for An Ideal Irish Election', 'The Trout' by John Montague from *Forms of Exile* (Dolmen, 1958); 'Like Dolmens Round My Childhood', 'The Old People', 'A Welcoming Party' by John Montague from *Poisoned Lands and Other Poems* (MacGibbon & Kee, 1961; Dolmen, 1977); 'All Legendary Obstacles', 'Back to School', 'The Siege of Mullingar', 'To Cease' by John Montague from *A Chosen Light* (MacGibbon & Kee, 1967); 'A Lost Tradition' by John Montague from *The Rough Field* (Dolmen and Oxford University Press, 1972); 'Mount Eagle', 'Dowager', 'Small Secrets' by John Montague from *A Slow Dance* (Dolmen, 1975); 'She Walks Alone' by John Montague from *The Great Cloak* (Dolmen, 1978)

Michael J. Murphy for 'Return of the Boy' from *The Penguin Book of Irish Stories* ed. B. Kiely (Penguin, 1981)

Cathal Ó Hainle for 'An Deargadaol' by P. H. Pearse from *Gearrscéalta an Phiarsaigh* (Helicon, 1979)

Oxford University Press for 'Slips' and 'The Flitting' from *The Flower Master* (1982) by Medbh McGuckian; 'The Villain', 'Painter and Poet' and 'Catching Geese' from *Venus in the Rain* by Medbh McGuckian; for 'Glengormley', 'Ecclesiastes', 'The Mute Phenomena', 'A Disused Shed in County Wexford' and 'The Chinese Restaurant in Portrush' from *Poems 1962–1978* by Derek Mahon; 'Courtyards in Delft', 'Derry Morning' and 'The Globe in North Carolina' from *The Hunt By Night* by Derek Mahon. Reprinted by permission of Oxford University Press; extracts from *Ascendancy and Tradition in Anglo-Irish Literature* (1985) by W. J. McCormack, reprinted by permission of Clarendon Press, Oxford; 'Abroad', 'In Dream' and 'In A Dream' © Oxford University Press 1962. Reprinted from John Millington Synge: *Collected Works vol. 1* edited by Robin Skelton by permission of Oxford University Press; 'The Land of Cockayne' from *Early Middle English Verse and Prose* edited by J. A. W. Bennett and G. V. Smithers (2nd. ed. 1968); extracts from *The Irish Tradition* by Robin Flower (1947); *Adamnan's Life of Columba* edited and translated by A. O. and M. O. Anderson (Nelson Medieval Texts, 1961): *Early Irish Lyrics* edited and translated by Gerard Murphy (1956), reprinted by permission of Oxford University Press; for extract from *My Story* by T. O'Céirin (Oxford University Press, 1965), reprinted by permission of Oxford University Press; for extract from *Twenty Years A-Growing* by Maurice O'Sullivan, translated by Moya Llewelyn Davis and George Thomson (Oxford University Press, 1953); for extract from *The Islandman* by Tomás Ó Crohan translated by Robin Flower (Oxford University

Press, 1951), reprinted by permission of Oxford University Press

The author for 'Gospel Power' from *Paisley. The Man and His Message* (Martyrs Memorial Publications, 1976); 'What Think Ye of Christ?' from *An Exposition of the Epistle to the Romans* by Ian Paisley (Marchall, Morgan and Scott, 1968)

Penguin Books Ltd. for extract from *War In An Irish Town* by Eamon McCann (Penguin, 1974)

Penguin USA for 'Araby', 'Ivy Day in the Committee Room' from *Dubliners* by James Joyce edited by Robert Scholes and A. Walton Litz (Viking, 1969); for extracts from *Portrait of the Artist as a Young Man* by James Joyce edited by Chester G. Anderson (Viking, 1968); for II, III, XXXIV, XXXV by James Joyce from *Chamber Music* edited by William York Tindall (Columbia, 1954); for 'Tilly', 'A Flower Given To My Daughter', 'She Weeps Over Rahoon' by James Joyce from *Pomes Penyeach*, for 'Flood!', 'Nightpiece' by James Joyce from *Collected Poems* in *The Portable James Joyce* edited Harry Levin (Viking, 1947); for extract from *Finnegans Wake* by James Joyce (Viking, 1939)

Peters Fraser and Dunlop for 'A Bitch and a Dog Hanging' by Val Mulkerns from *Antiquities: A Sequence of Short Stories* (Deutsch, 1978); for 'Dublin Jubilee' by James Plunkett from *The Trusting and the Maimed* (Hutchinson, 1955); for 'Beyond the Pale' by William Trevor from *Beyond The Pale* (Bodley Head, 1981); 'The New Suit' by Liam O'Flaherty from *Two Lovely Beasts And Other Stories* (Gollancz, 1973), 'The Lodger', 'Man Lying On A Wall' by Michael Longley from *Man Lying On A Wall* (Gollancz, 1976); 'Second Sight' by Michael Longley from *The Echo Gate* (Secker and Warburg, 1979). Copyright © Michael Longley 1973, 1976, 1979, 1985 Poolbeg Press for 'The Harelip' by Eoghan O Tuairisc from *The Road to Bright City* (Poolbeg, 1973); for 'The Game Cock' by Michael McLaverty from *Collected Stories* (Poolbeg, 1978)

Proscenium Press and the author for *The Wood of the Whispering* by M. J. Molloy from *Three Plays by M. J. Molloy* (Proscenium, 1975)

Random Century Group and the Estate of Elizabeth Bowen for 'The Happy Autumn Fields' from *The Demon Lover And Other Stories* (Jonathan Cape, 1945)

Random House for extracts from *Ulysses* by James Joyce (Random House, 1961)

Raven Arts Press for 'Leaba Shíoda', 'Labasheedy (The Silken Bed)', I mBaile an tSléibhe', 'In Baile an tSléibhe', 'An Bhábóg bhriste', 'The Broken Doll', 'Dán Do Mhelissa', 'Poem for Melissa', 'Breith Anabaí Thar Lear', 'Miscarriage Abroad', 'Gaineamh Shúraic', 'Quicksand', 'Masculus Giganticus Hibernicus' by Nuala Ní Dhomhnaill from *Selected Poems* (Raven Arts Press, 1986); for 'Concord', 'Plenitude', 'Baudelaire in Brussels', 'For A Father', 'Prophet' by Anthony Cronin from *New And Selected Poems* (Raven Arts, 1982); for 'Last Supper' from *A Dream of Maps* by Matthew Sweeney (Raven Arts, 1981)

An Sagart and the author for 'An Bhábóg bhriste', 'Dán do Mhelissa', 'Breith Anabaí Thar Lear', 'Gaineamh shúraic', 'Masculus Giganticus Hibernicus' by Nuala Ní Dhomhnaill from *Fear Suaithinseach* (An Sagart, 1984)

Sáirséal Ó Marcaigh for 'An Bhean ar Leag Dia Lámh Uirthi' by Pádraic Ó Conaire from *Scothscéalta* edited by Tomás de Bhaldraithe (Sáirséal & Dill, 1956); for 'An Chulaith Nua' by Liam Ó Flaithheartha from *Dúil* (Sáirséal & Dill, 1953); for 'Adhlacadh Mo Mháthar', 'Cul An Tí', 'Cnoc Mellerí' by Seán Ó Ríordáin from *Eireaball Spideoige* (Sáirséal & Dill, 1952); for 'Reo', 'Fiabhras', 'Na Leamhain', 'Claustrophobia' from *Brosna* (Sáirséal & Dill, 1964); for 'Inquisitio 1584', 'Finit', 'Do Shile', 'Gníomhartha na Trócaire', 'Cré na Mná Tí', 'Ceathrúintí Mháire Ní Ógáin' by Máire Mac an tSaoi from *An Cion Go Dtí Seo* (Sáirséal & Ó Marcaigh, 1987); from 'Níl in aon fhear ach a fhocal' by Tomás Mac Síomóin from *Cláirseach* (Sáirséal Ó Marcaigh, 1983); for 'Portráid Oige I', 'An Ceoltóir Jazz', 'Do Chara Liom', 'Tobar', by Laim Ó Muirthile from *Tine Chnámh* (Sáirséal & Ó Marcaigh, 1984); for 'Meirg agus Lios Luachra' and 'I gCuimhne ar Lis Ceárnaighe, Blascaodach' (1974) from *Gleann ar Ghleann* by Michael Davitt (Sáirséal & Ó Marcaigh, 1988)

Anthony Sheil Associates Ltd. for extract from *Mefisto* by John Banville (Martin Secker & Warburg, 1986; Grafton Books, 1987)

Colin Smythe Limited for extract from *The Old Lady Says 'No!'* by Denis Johnston from *Collected Plays* (Colin Smythe, 1977)

The Society of Authors as the literary representative of the Estate of James Joyce for extracts from *Stephen Hero* (Jonathan Cape/New Directions, 1944) and from *Finnegans Wake* (Faber and Faber/Viking, 1939) and from *Ulysses* (Bodley Head/Random House, 1961) and for extracts from *Critical Writings* edited by Ellswoth Mason and Richard Ellmann (Faber/Viking, 1959) and for extracts from *Portrait of the Artist as a Young Man* edited by Chester G. Anderson (Cape, 1964/Viking, 1968); and for 'Gas from a

Burner', 'The Holy Office', 'Ecce Puer', poems II, III, XXIV, XXV from *Chamber Music*, 'Tilly', 'A Flower Given To My Daughter', 'She Weeps Over Rahoon' from *Pomes Penyeach*, 'Flood!', 'Nightpiece' from *Collected Poems* in *The Portable James Joyce* ed. Harry Levin (Viking, 1947)

The Society of Authors as the literary representative of the George Bernard Shaw estate for *John Bull's Other Island* (Penguin, 1978); for *John Bull's Other Island: Preface for Politicians*, for *O'Flaherty V.C.*, for 'The Protestants of Ireland', 'A Note on Aggressive Nationalism', for extracts from *Immaturity*, 'How To Settle the Irish Question' and 'War Issues for Irishmen' from *The Bodley Head Bernard Shaw. Collected Plays with Their Prefaces* (Max Reinhardt, 1970–74)

The Society of Authors as the literary representative of the estate of James Stephans for extract from *The Crock of Gold* (Macmillan, 1912) and 'Hunger' from *Reincarnations* (Macmillan, 1918) and 'Light O'Love' from *The Hill of Vision* (Macmillan, 1912), 'The Ancient Elf' from *Songs from the Clay* (Macmillan, 1915), 'The Snare', 'A Glass of Beer' and 'I Am Writer' from *Collected Poems* (Macmillan, 1926; 2nd. ed., 1954)

Studies, editors Brian Lennon S.J. and Noel Barber S.J. for extract from 'Ireland and the Corporate State' by Michael Tierney (*Studies*, 1933) and for extract from 'The Canon of Irish History' by Frank Shaw (*Studies*, 1972)

Transworld Publishers Limited for 'Lonely Heart' by John Morrow from *Sects and Other Stories* (Corgi, 1987), © John Morrow. All rights reserved.

Unwin Hyman Limited for extracts from *States of Mind* by Oliver MacDonagh (Unwin Hyman, 1983)

A.P. Watt Limited for 'A Great God's Angel Standing' by Benedict Kiely from *A Ball of Malt and Madama Butterfly: A Dozen Stories* (Gollancz, 1973); for extract from *The Lonely Passion of Judith Hearne* by Brain Moore (Deutsch, 1955)

Weidenfeld & Nicolson Ltd. for extract from 'Ireland: The Shirt of Nessus' by Conor Cruise O'Brien from *Passion and Cunning: Essays* (Weidenfeld and Nicolson, 1988); for 'Number Ten' by Edna O'Brien from *Mrs Reinhardt and Other Stories* (Weidenfeld and Nicolson, 1978)

Wolfhound Press for extract from *Transitions: Narratives in Modern Irish Culture* (Wolfhound Press, 1987) by Richard Kearney

INDEX OF FIRST LINES OF POEMS

VOLUME III

First lines of excerpts are marked by an ellipsis.

GENERAL INDEX

VOLUME III

This index includes only those names that have particular importance for the texts in this volume. Names that occur only in annotations and in fleeting references have been excluded.

Bold numerals indicate text selections; italic numerals indicate biographical and bibliographical listings; roman numerals indicate other references.